Plymouth	1672	Ulster	1750	**ZAMBIA**	
Portsmouth	1677	Wales	1753	Copperbelt	1820
Queen Margaret C., Edinburgh	1682	U. of Wales, Aberystwyth	1754	U. of Zambia	1821
Queen's U. of Belfast	1683	U. of Wales, Bangor	1757		
Reading	1690	U. of Wales, Cardiff	1761		
Robert Gordon	1695	U. of Wales Swansea	1766		
Royal C. of Art	1696	U. of Wales, Lampeter	1770	**ZIMBABWE**	
St Andrews	1696	U. of Wales C. of Med.	1771	Africa U.	1824
Salford	1700	U. of Wales Institute, Cardiff	1774	National U.S.T., Bulawayo	1824
Sheffield	1704	U. of Wales C., Newport	1777	Solusi	1825
Sheffield Hallam	1714	Warwick	1779	U. of Zimbabwe	1826
South Bank	1720	West of England, Bristol	1784		
Southampton	1723	Westminster	1789		
Staffordshire	1730	Wolverhampton	1793	**APPENDIX 1**	
Stirling	1730	York	1798	ACU Members of Former Commonwealth	
Strathclyde	1733			Countries	
Sunderland	1738			People's Republic of China/Hong Kong	
Surrey	1740	**WEST INDIES**		Chinese U. of Hong Kong	1831
Surrey I. of Art and Design	1745	U. of the West Indies	1811	U. of Hong Kong	1836
Sussex	1745	Cave Hill Campus	1813	Hong Kong Polytech. U.	1845
Teesside	1748	Mona Campus	1814	Open U. of Hong Kong	1848
Thames Valley	1749	St Augustine Campus	1816		

Principal features of the ACU Yearbook

University profiles: facts and figures

Essential general information normally covers:
- foundation date, history and location
- library holdings
- academic year: term/semester dates
- statistics: staff/student figures
- recurrent income levels

Courses and student enrolment

Detailed entries in the institutional profiles typically include:
- entry to first degree courses: application procedures and basic education requirements
- first and higher degrees: titles, course lengths and general admission requirements
- language of instruction
- tuition fees: home/international
- academic awards: scholarships, bursaries, etc.

Degree guides

Specially compiled subject directories identify study opportunities available in many countries. The directories list a number of broad subject areas and indicate which universities offer facilities for study and/or research at undergraduate, postgraduate and doctoral level. These detailed tables appear at the end of the larger country sections: Australia, Bangladesh, Canada, Ghana, Hong Kong, India, Malaysia, New Zealand, Nigeria, Pakistan, South Africa, Sri Lanka and the United Kingdom.

National introductions

A series of national introductory texts preface many of the country sections into which the book is divided and provide background information on the education systems in these larger countries. Reference is normally made to: the university system, academic year, language of instruction, pre-university education, admission to first degree courses, method of application, university finance, student finance, staff and student numbers. In countries where there are considerable numbers of universities, **maps** pinpoint the location of institutions.

Staff lists: 150,000 senior academics and administrators

The staff lists form the most comprehensive source available for locating academics in the Commonwealth. Full entries include:
- principal officers listed by name in order of seniority
- deans and secretaries of faculties/schools
- alphabetical listing by department of all senior teaching and research staff
- directors of research and other centres
- administrative contact officers
- heads of campuses/constituent colleges
- degree qualifications with awarding institutions for all staff
- phone and fax numbers for faculties, departments and special centres

Research strengths

Summaries of the general areas of research currently undertaken by academic units and special centres complement the detailed staff lists. Entries, where supplied by the university, normally include brief descriptions of five separate fields of research and follow the departmental staff entries.

Contact officers

Commonwealth-wide listings of key contact officers identify up to 45 areas of special administrative responsibility in each university and name the officer in charge. These areas include: academic affairs, accommodation, admissions, alumni, careers, computing services, conferences/corporate hospitality, distance education, estates and buildings, finance, industrial liaison, language training for international students, public relations, quality assurance and accreditation, sport and recreation, student welfare *et al.*

Affiliated colleges

In Bangladesh, India, Pakistan and Sri Lanka, where teaching takes place in colleges affiliated to a university, the colleges are listed alphabetically by location.

Four substantial indexes complete the scope of the Yearbook:

- to the 2,500 university institutions, their constituent colleges and selected centres, and the location of affiliated colleges
- to the World Wide Web addresses of those universities with Internet access
- to the titles of the 25,000 academic departments and special/research centres
- to the 150,000 academic and administrative staff listed in the university chapters.

COMMONWEALTH UNIVERSITIES YEARBOOK 1999

A Directory to the
Universities of the Commonwealth
and the Handbook of their Association

Volume 2

Association of Commonwealth Universities
John Foster House, 36 Gordon Square, London WC1H 0PF
Tel: +44(0) 171-387 8572 Fax: +44(0) 171 387 2655 E-mail: info@acu.ac.uk
WWW: http://www.acu.ac.uk

HAVE A HIGHER OPINION
FOR A LOWER CONSIDERATION

Subscribe today and save 30% on the normal cover price

The world of higher education never stands still. This is why so many academics, researchers and lecturers find The Times Higher Education Supplement compulsory reading. The THES comprehensively details the latest developments in higher education, highlighting common problems and concerns and provides a central reference point in this truly global 'industry'. Easy to locate articles and sections are combined with 'at a glance' graphics and information summaries and our correspondence and opinion pages offer a forum for lively debate. As well as educational matters, the THES features book reviews covering topics as diverse as women & gender studies, literature, engineering and art & music.

Subscribe now to guarantee delivery of your copy every week and save 30% on the normal price. Simply fill in the form below or call the subscriptions hotline on +44 (0)1858 438 805 (for US & Canada subscriptions call 1–800–370–9040).

Subscription rates for one year (52 issues)

UK £40	Europe £58	USA $69	Canada $95	ROW (Air Mail) £72

Name _____

Address _____ Postcode _____

☐ Please invoice me. ☐ I enclose a cheque for _____ made payable to, **The Times Higher Educational Supplement**

Please charge my Visa ☐ Mastercard ☐ Amex ☐ Card No. ☐☐☐☐☐☐☐☐☐☐☐☐☐☐☐☐

Expiry Date _____ Signature _____ Date _____

Please send to: The Times Supplement Ltd, Tower House, Sovereign Park, Market Harborough LE87 4JJ, UK.

☐ Please tick if you do not wish to receive mailings from companies whose products and services we feel may be of interest.

4390

TAKE MORE THAN AN ACADEMIC INTEREST
http://www.thesis.co.uk

"Colleges and universities as we know them are obsolete" *Forbes Magazine*

● Change is the only certainty in the new global network economy – colleges and universities must cope with the international spread of new funding structures, new management policies and new information technologies.

● More people than ever before will be accessing higher education in the coming years, bringing greater student diversity, greater teaching challenges and greater economic opportunities.

● More people than ever before will be taking an interest in the design, delivery and validation of higher education courses.

One organisation is perfectly positioned to provide an overview of the global situation – the **Association of Commonwealth Universities**. With over 480 members, the ACU stands at the centre of a world-class network of outstanding human and scientific resources.

The ACU Bulletin, **abcd**, is now available on subscription after nearly thirty years of controlled circulation. With a wealth of experience behind it, and a determination to be at the forefront of developments in higher education and research, **abcd** represents a unique conduit for information, knowledge and ideas from the Commonwealth and beyond.

Subscribe now

Institutional UK£40/US$70 ☐

Individual UK£35/US$60 ☐

ACU member institution staff/student UK£20/US$35 ☐

Name _____

Address_____

_____

_____

_____

> Get *your* message across to the key players in higher education by advertising in **abcd**.
> For details, contact
> **Siobhan O'Shea**,
> Marot & Co.
> Tel: +44(0) 171 278 3686
> Fax: +44(0) 171 837 2764

Please make cheques payable to the **Association of Commonwealth Universities (Dept. 50)** and send to
ABCD
John Foster House
36 Gordon Square
London WC1H 0PF
UK.

Or please give details of your Master/Visa/Delta card (delete as appropriate), and fax this form to
+44 (0) 171 387 2655

Cardholder name _____   Expiry date (mm/yy) ____ /____

Card number _____

CONTENTS

CONTENTS

Volume 2

Full university listings with page references appear on the inside front cover

Appendices

Indexes

PAKISTAN

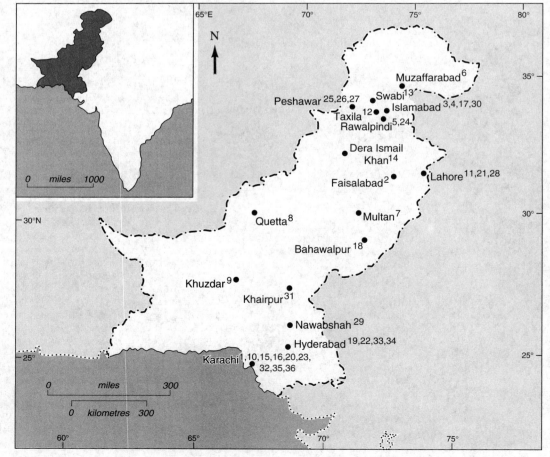

The places named are the seats of the university institutions numbered above

THE UNIVERSITIES OF PAKISTAN

Information compiled by the Vice-Chancellors' Committee of Pakistan as at July 1998

The University System

Universities in Pakistan may be broadly categorised as either general or professional. The professional category includes 11 engineering institutions, four each in agricultural, medical, and management sciences and one in distance learning. The general universities, with the exception of Quaid-I-Azam which is a teaching (unitary) type, are both teaching and affiliating institutions. Thus there are at present 28 public sector universities/degree-awarding institutions and 13 privately established universities/institutions. Though fully autonomous, the universities' affairs are subject to a certain amount of governmental control, due to provisions in their acts of incoporation relating to the appointment of vice-chancellors and pro-vice-chancellors by the chancellor, the president of Pakistan or the provincial governors as ex-officio chancellors, and nominations by the government to university senates and syndicates. The University Grants Commission (UGC) acts as a co-ordinating agency between government and the universities.

The internal authorities of the universities are generally the senate, syndicate, academic council, board of faculties and studies, selection boards, advanced studies and research board, finance and planning committtee, affiliation committee, and the discipline committee. The vice-chancellor is the principal executive and academic head of the university.

A new national education policy declared in March 1998 recognises the contributory role of higher education in economic development and proposes new initiatives to increase its efficiency, strengthen existing graduate study programmes, improve delivery, expand the capabilities of the universities to create new knowledge, and enhance the universities' entrepreneurial role. The policy acknowledges that higher education needs both structural and functional changes. Structural changes relate to private provision of higher education, autonomy for a greater number of institutions, decentralisation, cost-effectiveness, responsiveness, public accountability, liaison with industry, and a system of accreditation. Functional aspects include faculty development, revision of curricula, academic audit, a corruption-free system of examination, selectivity of higher education, and diversity of higher education institutions.

The policy calls for access to higher education to expand over the next 12 years to cover 7% of the age group compared to the current level of 2.6%. This expansion will demand the establishment of 21 new universities, 500 new degree-awarding colleges and 250 professional colleges. The policy aims eventually to establish a 50:50 balance between arts and science subjects to produce the manpower needed in science, technology, business and industry. Curricula for science, engineering, medicine and other technological disciplines will be revised to make them compatible with international standards.

Academic Year

The academic year generally begins in early September and ends in June. In most universities the academic year consists of three terms, though some institutions follow a two-semester system.

Pre-University Education

Pre-university education comprises three stages; primary, secondary and higher secondary. The primary stage (grades 1–5) extends over five years (age 5+ to 10+). Secondary education consists of two well-defined stages: middle school (grades 6–8) and high school (grades 9–10). Higher secondary schools (grades 11–12) are also known as intermediate colleges. Secondary and higher secondary education together last seven years and cover the 11–18 age group. There is a matriculation or secondary school certificate examination at the end of the tenth class. Beyond the secondary school stage the two years of college study at higher secondary level lead to the intermediate examination or higher secondary certificate, which is a prerequisite for university entrance.

Admission to First Degree Courses

The basic entrance requirement is the intermediate or higher secondary certificate, or its equivalent. Admission to professional colleges and universities is based on performance in the public examinations at higher secondary level conducted by the boards of intermediate and secondary education. Entry tests are also being progressively introduced. Places are not available to all who qualify and desire to enter. There is a high demand for professional courses in medicine, dentistry, engineering and business, etc, as a result of which admission to these courses is much more difficult than admission to general university education. Competition for admission to the general universities is not as keen since the wide network of affiliated colleges enables a large portion of students to gain admission. There is also a quota system under which a number of seats are reserved for students from minorities and underdeveloped areas and for foreign students.

Method of application. Usually direct to the university.

Finance

The public universities are funded mainly by the government, and federal grants constitute 65% of university income. Eleven universities depend on government for between 70% and 85% of their income and five for less than 70%. Universities' income from their own sources in general now represents 35%. The heavy dependence on federal grants in Pakistan has historically left the universities under-funded. Since 1979, universities have received less than they have requested and the total expenditure on higher education has consistently fallen. To counteract the lack of funding, some universities now admit students on a self-financing basis. Under the scheme, a certain number of seats are 'sold' (for the full cost of tuition fees) in demand-oriented subjects, such as business and management sciences, computer sciences and engineering. Encouraged by the success of this scheme, some public sector universities have launched programmes on a full-cost basis and are also enhancing their service charges and the rate of tuition fee. By the year 2010, the government expects that the ratio of government funding to universities will be reduced to 50%.

Student finance. Tuition fees have remained frozen for decades. On average, a university student pays between Rs60 and Rs100 per month and a professional college/university student between Rs100 and Rs300. Foreign students pay (per annum) Rs38,000 for general and US$10,000 for professional courses in some institutions (from Rs150,000 to Rs300,000 in others), though in the case of a number of students from the Middle East and Africa fee concessions are liberally given.

Staff and Student Numbers

The total number of teaching staff in the universities is 6033, in professional colleges 6173, and in colleges 20,907. Only 26% of university teachers and 2% of college teachers hold a research degree. A majority of teachers have been trained in the United States, the United Kingdom, Canada and Australia, and a minority in the former USSR and other Eastern European countries.

University student enrolments are distributed among first degree students, master's level and post-master's level in the ratio of 40:20:1. The professional single-discipline colleges and general degree colleges enroll three times as many students at the first degree level as the professional and general universities. The total number of students in public universities is a little over 100,000, and there are 7152 in private universities. The total number of students in professional colleges is 160,969 and total college enrolment is around 1,000,000.

Staff:student ratios vary across types, levels of educational institutions and course programmes, ranging from 1:5 to 1:85.

Teacher:student ratios in degree colleges range between 1:11 and 1:85; in general universities between 1:5 and 1:20; and in professional universities between 1:6 and 1:46.

Further Information

Government of Pakistan. Eighth five-year plan 1993–98. Islamabad, Planning Commission, 1994.

Ministry of Education. Pakistan education statistics 1985–87. Islamabad, Central Bureau of Education, 1989.

——————————. The Development of education in Pakistan 1996. Country report for the 45th session of International Conference on Education, Islamabad, 1996.

——————————. National Education Policy, 1998–2010. Islamabad, 1998.

The World Bank. Higher education and scientific research: strategy for development and reform. Islamic Republic of Pakistan. Population and Human Resources Division, Country Department 1II, South Asia Region, 1992.

AGA KHAN UNIVERSITY

Founded 1983

Member of the Association of Commonwealth Universities

Postal Address: Stadium Road, PO Box 3500, Karachi 74800, Sindh, Pakistan
Telephone: (021) 493 0051 **Fax**: (021) 493 4294, 493 2095 **E-mail**: cvellani@akuc.edu **Cables**: Akaproject
Telex: 29667 AKHMC PK **WWW**: http://www.aku.edu **E-mail formula**: username@akuc.edu

CHANCELLOR—Aga Khan, His Highness The
CHAIRMAN, BOARD OF TRUSTEES—Khan, Sahabzada Y.
CHIEF ACADEMIC OFFICER AND RECTOR*—Vellani, Camer W., MB BCh *Wales*, MD *Wales*, FRCP
PRESIDENT‡—Lakha, Shamsh K., MBA

GENERAL INFORMATION

History. The university was established in 1983 as the first private university in Pakistan. It comprises a school of nursing, a medical college, and Institute for Educational Development (IED). The Aga Khan University hospital is located on campus.

Admission to first degree courses (see also Pakistan Introduction). Information on admission to specific courses can be obtained from the student affairs department (student.affairs@aku.edu).

First Degrees (see also Pakistan Directory to Subjects of Study). BScN (2 years post-registration or 4 years), MB BS (5 years).

Higher Degrees (see also Pakistan Directory to Subjects of Study). MEd, MSc (both courses last 2 years).

Libraries. 22,000 volumes and monographs; approximately 500 journals subscribed to; large collection of audio-visual material.

Academic Year begins first week of October.

FACULTIES/SCHOOLS

Health Sciences
Dean: Sutton, Prof. Roger A. L., DM Oxf., FRCP, FRCPCan
Secretary: Mirza, Elly

ACADEMIC UNITS

Anaesthesiology
Chohan, Ursula, MB BS *Karachi*, FFARCS Assoc. Prof.
Hooda, M. Qamarul, MB BS *Karachi*, FFARCS Asst. Prof.
Kamal, Rehana S., MB BS *Punjab*, FFARCS, FFARCSI Prof.; Head*
Khan, F. H., MB BS *Karachi* Asst. Prof.
Khan, Fauzia A., MB BS *Punjab*, FRCA, FFARCS Prof.
Naqvi, Hamid A., MB BS *Punjab*, FFARCSI, FRCA Asst. Prof.
Zubair, Naeem A., MB BS *Karachi*, DSc Assoc. Prof.

Anatomy
Khan, K. M., MSc *Karachi*, MS *Col.*, PhD *N.Y.* Prof.
Shoro, A. A., MB BS *Sindh*, MPhil *Karachi*, PhD *Lond.* Jaffarali Lalji Prof.; Head*

Biochemistry
Ashfaq, M. K., DVM *Punjab*, PhD *Cornell* Asst. Prof.
Iqbal, M. P., MS *N.Y.*, PhD *N.Y.* Prof.
Javed, M. H., MSc *Karachi*, MPhil *Quaid-i-Azam*, PhD *Middle East Tech.* Assoc. Prof.
Rahman, Abdur, MSc *Pesh.*, PhD *Cornell* Asst. Prof.
Siddiqui, A. A., MPhil *Quaid-i-Azam*, PhD *Belf.* Assoc. Prof.
Waqar, M. A., PhD *Flin.*, FIBiol Akbar Ali H. Bandeali Prof.; Head*

Community Health Sciences
Akhtar, Syed, MSc *Karachi*, MS *Calif.*, PhD *Calif.* Asst. Prof.
Ali, Badar S., MB BS *Punjab* Asst. Prof.
Bryant, John H., MD *Col.* Prof. Emer.
Fikree, Fariyal, MD *Shiraz*, MPH *Johns H.* Asst. Prof.
Husain, Mumtaz, MB BS *Punjab* Prof.; Acting Head*
Karim, M. S., MS *Chic.*, PhD *Cornell* Assoc. Prof.
Khan, Kausar S., MA *Karachi*, MA *McM.* Asst. Prof.
Luby, Stephen P., MD *Texas* Asst. Prof.
Qureshi, Asma F., MB BS *Karachi* Prof.
Qureshi, Riaz, MB BS *Karachi*, FRCGP Assoc. Prof.
Rahbar, M., BS *Shiraz*, MS *Shiraz*, PhD *Mich.* Prof.
Zuberi, Rukhsana, MB BS *Punjab* Assoc. Prof.

Dentistry, see Surg.

Educational Development
within Faculty of Health Sciences
Talati, Jamsheer, MB BS *Karachi*, FRCSEd Habiba Subjali Prof.; Head*

English Language Unit
Husain, P. F., BA *Minn.*, MAEd *Beirut* Sr. Instr.; Acting Head*

Islamic and Pakistan Studies
Jafri, H. M., MA *Lucknow*, PhD *Lond.* Prof.†

Medicine
Abdulla, A., MD, FRCPCan, FACP Prof.
Ahmed, Aasim, MB BS *Karachi* Asst. Prof.
Ahmed, Akhter, MB BS *Karachi*, FRCPEd Hon. Prof.
Akhter, J., MB BS *Newcastle(UK)* Asst. Prof.
Badruddin, Salma, PhD *Tor.* Assoc. Prof.
Baig, S., MB BS *Punjab*, MD *Karolinska*, PhD *Karolinska* Assoc. Prof.
Basir, M. N., MB BS *Pesh.* Asst. Prof.
Hameed, K., MB BS *Karachi* Asst. Prof.
Hamid, S., MB BS *Karachi* Asst. Prof.
Hussain, S. Fayyaz, MB BS *Karachi*, FRCPEd Asst. Prof.
Hyder, S. S., MB BS *Karachi* Asst. Prof.
Islam, N., MB BS *Karachi* Asst. Prof.
Jabbar, A., MB BS *Karachi* Asst. Prof.
Jafri, S. M. W., MB BS *Karachi*, FRCP, FRCPEd, FACP Assoc. Prof.
Kazmi, K. A., MB BS *Punjab* Asst. Prof.
Khan, A. J., MB BS *Karachi*, FRCPEd Assoc. Prof.
Khan, H., MB BS *Lucknow*, FRCPCan Prof.
Khan, M. A., MB BS *Sindh*, FRCP, FACP Karim Jiwa Prof.
Pathan, Asad, MB BS *Karachi* Asst. Prof.
Rab, S. M., MB BS *Karachi*, FRCPEd, FRCPGlas Hon. Prof.
Rasmussen, Z. A., MD *Harv.*, MPH *Johns H.* Asst. Prof.
Sarwari, Arif R., MB BS *Aga Khan* Asst. Prof.
Shah, H., MB BS *Punjab* Asst. Prof.
Siddiqui, T., MB BS *Karachi*, FRCPCan Assoc. Prof.

Sutton, Roger A. L., DM *Oxf.*, FRCP, FRCPCan Prof.; Head*
Vellani, C. W., MB BCh *Wales*, MD *Wales*, FRCP Ibn-e-Sina Prof.

Microbiology
Farooqui, B. J., MB BS *Sindh*, MSc *Lond.*, PhD *Karachi* Asst. Prof.
Hasan, Rumina, MB BS *Lond.*, PhD *Lond.* Asst. Prof.
Hussain, Rabia, MSc *Karachi*, PhD *W.Ont.*, FRCPath Ghulamali Hirji Prof.
Zaman, V., MB BS *Karachi*, PhD *Edin.*, DSc *Sing.*, FRCPath Prof.; Head*

Nursing, School of
Amarsi, Yasmin, BScN *McM.*, MSN *Arizona* Asst. Prof.; Dir.*
Miller, Grace, BSc(N) *McG.*, MA *C'dia.*, PhD *Wales* Assoc. Prof.

Development of Women Health Professionals Programme
Tel: (021) 453 8308, 453 6829, 453 6831
Fax: (021) 453 8149
Aziz, Anwar, BScN *Punjab*, MSc *Sheff.* Co-Executive Dir.*
Fisher, Anita L., BA *Windsor*, MHScMcM. Co-Executive Dir.*

Nursing—Bachelor's Programme
Bryant, Nancy, BSN *Col.*, MPH *Col.* Acting Dir.*
Gulzar, Laila, BScN *Aga Khan*, MSN *Boston* Asst. Prof. (on leave)

Nursing—Diploma Programme
Kanji, Zeenat K., MSc *Ill.*, BScN Hon. Asst. Prof.; Head*

Obstetrics and Gynaecology
Chaudry, Nasreen, MB BS *Karachi*, FRCOG Assoc. Prof.
Khan, Zeenat E., MB BS *Karachi* Asst. Prof.
Naru, Tahira Y., MD *Düsseldorf* Asst. Prof.
Pal, Jahan A., MB BS *Karachi*, FRCOG Prof.; Head*
Qureshi, Rahat N., MB BS *Karachi* Assoc. Prof.
Rizvi, Javed, MB BS *Karachi*, FACS, FRCOG Prof.†
Wasti, Shahnaz, MB BS *Punjab*, FRCOG Asst. Prof.

Paediatrics
Ahmed, I., MB BS *Calc.*, FRCPEd Prof.†
Atiq, Mehnaz, MB BS *Marath.* Asst. Prof.
Bhutta, Z. A., MB BS *Pesh.*, PhD *Karolinska*, FRCPEd Prof.
Ibrahim, Shahnaz H., MB BS *Karachi* Asst. Prof.
Khan, I. A., MB BS *Pesh.* Assoc. Prof.
Lindblad, Bo S., MD *Karolinska*, PhD *Karolinska* Kamruddin M. Jessani Prof.; Head*
Nizami, S. Q., MB BS *Pesh.* Assoc. Prof.
Yusuf, Kamran, MB BS *Punjab* Asst. Prof.

Pathology
Ghani, F., MB BS *Karachi*, PhD *Boston* Asst. Prof.

Hasan, Sheema H., MB BS *Punjab*,
FRCPath   Assoc. Prof.
Hussainy, A. S., MB BS *Sindh*   Asst. Prof.
Kayani, Naila, MB BS *Punjab*   Asst. Prof.
Khurshid, M., MB BS *Karachi*, FRCPath   Prof.;
Head*
Moatter, Tariq, MPhil *Karachi*, PhD   Asst. Prof.
Pervez, S., MB BS *Baloch.*, PhD *Lond.*,
FRCPath   Assoc. Prof.
Soomro, I. N., MB BS *Sindh*, PhD *Lond.*   Asst.
Prof.

Pharmacology and Physiology

Afzal, M. Nasir, MB BS PhD, FRCP   Asst. Prof.
Ahmad, H. R., MD *Bochum*, PhD *Bochum*   Prof.
Gilani, A. H., MSc *Faisalabad*, PhD *Syd.*   Prof.
Herzig, Joachim W., MSc *Bochum*, PhD
Heidel.   Prof.; Head*
Khan, Akhlaque N., MB BS *Punjab*, MPhil
Karachi, PhD *Indiana*, FRCPEd   Prof.†
Saeed, S. A., MSc *Newcastle(UK)*, PhD
Newcastle(UK), FIBiol   Prof.
Saeed, S. A., MSc *Quaid-i-Azam.*, MPhil *Quaid-i-
Azam.*, PhD *Aberd.*   Asst. Prof.
Shah, B. H., MSc *Faisalabad*, PhD *Boston*   Assoc.
Prof.
Siddiqui, A., MSc *Karachi*, PhD *Glas.*   Asst. Prof.
Suria, A., MSc *Karachi*, PhD   *Vanderbilt* Prof.†

Postgraduate Medical Education

Moazam, F., MD, FACS   Quaid-e-Azam Prof.;
Head*

Psychiatry

Faizi, A., MB BS *Pesh.*   Assoc. Prof.; Head*
Naliyawala, Abdul H., MB BS *Karachi*   Asst.
Prof.
Syed, Ehtesham H., MB BS *Karachi*   Asst. Prof.
Zaman, Riffat M., MA *Karachi*, PhD
Mich.   Assoc. Prof.†

Radiology

Ahmed, Nadeem M., MB BS *Karachi*   Asst. Prof.
Husein, Yousuf, MB BS *Karachi*   Asst. Prof.
Naeem, Shabbir A., MB BS *Punjab*   Assoc. Prof.
Pui, Margaret, MD *Tor.*, FRCPCan   Assoc. Prof.
Rees, Jeffrey, MB ChB *Edin.*, FRCR,
FRCPCan   Prof.
Rizvi, I. H., MB BS *Sindh*, FRCR   Prof.; Head*
Sheikh, M. Y., MB BS *Dhaka*, FRCPCan   Assoc.
Prof.

Surgery

Abbas, F., MB BS *Sindh*, FRCSEd,
FRCSGlas   Asst. Prof., Urology
Ahmed, M., MB BS *Karachi*, FRCS   Hassanali
Sajan Prof., General Surgery; Head*
Ahmed, Sohail, MB BS *Karachi*, FRCS, FRCSGlas,
FRCSEdin   Assoc. Prof., Opthalmology
Ali, Azam, MB BS *Aga Khan*, FRCSEdin,
FRCSGlas   Asst. Prof., Opthalmology
Azami, R., MB BS *Karachi*   Assoc. Prof., General
Surgery
Banday, Ninette, BDS *Sindh*, MPH DDS
DMS   Asst. Prof., Dentistry
Beg, Mirza R., MB BS *Sindh*,, FRCSGlas   Assoc.
Prof., Orthopaedics
Chisti, K. N., MB BS *Karachi*, FRCSEd   Asst.
Prof., Neurosurgery

Hameed, K., MB BS *Karachi*, FRCSI   Asst. Prof.,
General Surgery
Hasan, S., MB BS *Karachi*, FRCSCan   Asst. Prof.,
Cardiothoracic Surgery
Kazi, Z. A., MB BS, FRCS   Hon. Prof.
Khan, M. Arif M., MB BS *Karachi*   Asst. Prof.,
Orthopaedics
Khan, S. H., MB BS *Pesh.*, FRCSGlas   Asst.
Prof., Orthopaedic Surgery
Khan, Shaista M., MB BS *Karachi*,
FRCSEd   Assoc. Prof., General Surgery
Khan, Tahir A. S., MB BS *Punj*, FRCSEd   Asst.
Prof., Plastic Surgery
Ladakawala, Riaz H., MB BS *Karachi*   Asst.
Prof., Orthopaedics
Memon, A., MB BS *Karachi*, FRCSEd   Assoc.
Prof., Urology
Merchant, Amyna, MB BS *Aga Khan*   Asst. Prof.,
Opthalmology
Mian, M. Yousuf, MB BS *Punjab*,
FRCSEdin   Assoc. Prof., Otolaryngology
Moazam, Farhat, MB BS *Karachi*, FACS   Quaid-
e-Azam Prof., Paediatric Surgery
Nazir, Z., MB BS *Islamia, Bahawal.*, FRCSEd,
FRCSGlas   Asst. Prof., Paediatric Surgery
Patel, Habib, MS, FACS   Prof. Emer.
Sami, Shahid A., FRCSEd   Asst. Prof.,
Cardiothoracic Surgery
Talati, J., MB BS *Karachi*, FRCSEd   Habiba
Sabjaali Jiwa Prof., Urology
Umar, M., MB BS *Punjab*, FACS, FAAOS   Assoc.
Prof., Orthopaedic Surgery
Waheed, I., MB BS *Karachi*, FRCSEd   Hon.
Prof., Orthopaedics

SPECIAL CENTRES, ETC

Educational Development, Institute for

Tel: (021) 634 7611 Fax: (021) 634 7616
Ali, M. Ahmed, MEd *Harv.*, PhD *Mich.*   Asst.
Prof.
Baker, Robert A., MEd *Tor.*, PhD *Tor.*   Prof.;
Dir.*
Farah, Iffat, PhD *Penn.*   Assoc. Prof.
Halai, Nilofer, MSc *S.Mississippi*   Asst. Prof.
Khamis, Tasmin, PhD *Lond.*   Asst. Prof.
Memon, M., PhD *Sur.*   Assoc. Prof.
Pardhan, S., MBA *Alta.*, PhD *Uppsala*   Asst.
Prof.; Assoc. Dir.*
Siddiqui, Shahid, PhD *Tor.*   Assoc. Prof.
Wheeler, A., MEd *Alta.*, PhD *Alta.*   Prof.;
Assoc. Dir.*

CONTACT OFFICERS

Academic affairs. Chief Academic Officer and
Rector: Vellani, Camer W., MB BCh *Wales*,
MD *Wales*, FRCP
Accommodation. Associate Dean, Student
Affairs: Zaidi, S. A. A., MSc *Karachi*, MPhil
Islam., PhD *Karolinska*
Admissions (first degree). Associate Dean,
Student Affairs: Zaidi, S. A. A., MSc *Karachi*,
MPhil *Islam.*, PhD *Karolinska*
Admissions (higher degree). Associate Dean,
Student Affairs: Zaidi, S. A. A., MSc *Karachi*,
MPhil *Islam.*, PhD *Karolinska*
Alumni. Director, Alumni Affairs: Shoro, A.
A., MB BS *Sindh*, MPhil *Karachi*, PhD *Lond.*

Computing services. Director, Information
Technology: Siddiqui, N. Z., BE *Karachi*, MS
Purdue
Development/fund-raising. Senior Director,
Resource Development and Public Affairs:
Fancy, Asif B., MBA
Estates and buildings/works and services.
Senior Director, Facilities and Project
Management: Sultan, M. S., BSc *Mass.*, MSc
Karachi, MSc *Mass.*
Examinations. Associate Dean, Student Affairs:
Zaidi, S. A. A., MSc *Karachi*, MPhil *Islam.*, PhD
Karolinska
Finance. Chief Financial Officer, Senior
Director: Merchant, N. A.
General enquiries. President: Lakha, Shamsh
K., MBA
General enquiries. Chief Academic Officer
and Rector: Vellani, Camer W., MB BCh
Wales, MD *Wales*, FRCP
Health services. Medical Director and
Associate Dean, Clinical Affairs: Mirza, Y. K.,
MB BS *Punjab*, FRCSEd
International office. Associate Dean, Student
Affairs: Zaidi, S. A. A., MSc *Karachi*, MPhil
Islam., PhD *Karolinska*
Library. Chief Librarian: Qureshi, A., MLS
Karachi, MLIS *Kent State*
Personnel/human resources. Personnel
Director: Surani, N., LLB *Karachi*, BCom
Karachi, MBA *Karachi*
Public relations, information and marketing.
Senior Director, Resource Development and
Public Affairs: Fancy, Asif B., MBA
Publications. Senior Director, Resource
Development and Public Affairs: Fancy, Asif
B., MBA
Purchasing. Director, Material Management:
Shahabuddin, Sulaiman, MBA *Karachi*
Safety. Manager, Safety, Security and
Administration: Salim-ur-Rahman, BSc *Pesh.*
Scholarships, awards, loans. Associate Dean,
Student Affairs: Zaidi, S. A. A., MSc *Karachi*,
MPhil *Islam.*, PhD *Karolinska*
Schools liaison. Associate Dean, Student
Affairs: Zaidi, S. A. A., MSc *Karachi*, MPhil
Islam., PhD *Karolinska*
Security. Manager, Safety, Security and
Administration: Salim-ur-Rahman, BSc *Pesh.*
Sport and recreation. Associate Dean, Student
Affairs: Zaidi, S. A. A., MSc *Karachi*, MPhil
Islam., PhD *Karolinska*
Staff development and training. Personnel
Director: Surani, N., LLB *Karachi*, BCom
Karachi, MBA *Karachi*
Student welfare/counselling. Associate Dean,
Student Affairs: Zaidi, S. A. A., MSc *Karachi*,
MPhil *Islam.*, PhD *Karolinska*
Students from other countries. Associate
Dean, Student Affairs: Zaidi, S. A. A., MSc
Karachi, MPhil *Islam.*, PhD *Karolinska*
Students with disabilities. Associate Dean,
Student Affairs: Zaidi, S. A. A., MSc *Karachi*,
MPhil *Islam.*, PhD *Karolinska*

[*Information supplied by the institution as at 25 July
1998, and edited by the ACU*]

UNIVERSITY OF AGRICULTURE, FAISALABAD

Founded 1961; previously established as Punjab Agricultural College and Research Institute, 1909

Member of the Association of Commonwealth Universities

Postal Address: Faisalabad 38040, Punjab, Pakistan
Telephone: (041) 30281-89 **Fax**: (041) 647846 **E-mail**: agf@paknet1.ptc.pk **Cables**: Agrivarsity, Faisalabad

CHANCELLOR—The Governor of the Punjab (*ex officio*)
PRO-CHANCELLOR—The Minister for Agriculture, Punjab (*ex officio*)
VICE-CHANCELLOR*—Sheri, Ahmad N., BSc *Punjab*, MSc *Punjab*, PhD
Wat.
REGISTRAR—Akram, Sheikh Muhammad, MES *N.Carolina*
TREASURER—Jamil, Muhammad, BA
CONTROLLER OF EXAMINATIONS—Haleem, Anwar, MSc *Faisalabad*
LIBRARIAN—......

GENERAL INFORMATION

History. The university was established in 1961 from the former Punjab Agricultural College Research Institute.

Admission (see also Pakistan Introduction). Applicants living in Punjab Province: intermediate science exam with 45% marks (60% for BSc in agricultural engineering). Applicants from other provinces must be nominated by the relevant body in their province. International applicants must be nominated by Pakistan's ministry of education and must hold qualifications equivalent to those listed above.

First Degrees (see also Pakistan Directory to Subjects of Study) (* = honours only). BScAgri*, BScAgriEngg, BScAH*, BScHomeEconomics, DVM.
All courses are full-time and most last 4 years. BScHomeEconomics: 2 years.

Higher Degrees (see also Pakistan Directory to Subjects of Study). MSc, MPhil, PhD.
Candidates for admission to master's degree courses must normally hold a relevant first degree. MPhil, PhD: relevant master's degree.

Libraries. 175,100 volumes; 15 periodicals subscribed to.

Fees. Home students (per semester): undergraduate, Rs150; MSc/MPhil, Rs350; PhD, Rs400. International students (annual): undergraduate, Rs45,000; postgraduate, Rs50,000.

Academic Awards (1995–96). Approximately 2000 awards ranging in value from Rs50 to Rs1200 per student per month.

Academic Year. Two semesters of 19 weeks each, beginning in late Sepember/early October and early February.

Income. Total, Rs210,088,000.

Statistics. Students (undergraduate): full-time 2852 (2599 men, 253 women); international 30 (all men).

FACULTIES/SCHOOLS

Agricultural Economics and Rural Sociology

Dean: Aslam, Prof. Muhammad C., MSc *Faisalabad*, PhD *Faisalabad*

Agricultural Engineering and Technology

Dean: Chaudhry, Prof. Allah D., BScEngg *W.Pak.Eng.*, MSc *Newcastle(UK)*, PhD *Massey*

Agriculture

Dean: Alam, Prof. Khurshid, MScAgri *Punjab*, PhD *Faisalabad*

Animal Husbandry

Dean: Sial, Prof. Munawar A., MSc *Faisalabad*, PhD *Faisalabad*

Sciences

Dean: Baig, Prof. Mirza A., MSc *Alig.*PhD

Veterinary Science

Dean: Chaudhry, Prof. Shaukat A., BSc(AH) *Punjab*, PhD *R.Vet.& Agric., Denmark*

ACADEMIC UNITS

Agricultural Economics

Ahmad, Munir, MSc *Faisalabad*, PhD   Asst. Prof.
Chaudry, M. Aslam, MScAgri *Punjab*   Assoc. Prof.
Hussain, Zakir, PhD   Prof.
Javed, M. Siddique, MSc *Faisalabad*, PhD   Asst. Prof.
Shah, Nazar M., MSc *Faisalabad*   Asst. Prof.

Agricultural Education

Akbar, M. Jamil, MSc MEd   Assoc. Prof.
Khan, Saeed A., PhD *Moscow*, MSc   Prof.
Malik, Niaz H., MSc   Assoc. Prof.

Agricultural Entomology

Akbar, Shamshad, MSc *Faisalabad*, PhD *Faisalabad*   Prof.
Hassan, Mansoorul, MSc *Faisalabad*   Asst. Prof.
Pervez, Muhammad A., MSc *Faisalabad*, PhD *Faisalabad*   Asst. Prof.
Rana, M. Ashfaq, MSc *Faisalabad*, PhD *Faisalabad*   Prof.
Sabri, Muhammad A., MSc *Faisalabad*   Asst. Prof.
Shah, Aftab H., MSc *Faisalabad*, PhD   Asst. Prof.
Shah, Syed H. A., MSc   Assoc. Prof.
Sohail, Anjum, MSc *Faisalabad*, PhD *Faisalabad*   Asst. Prof.
Wahala, Mahmood A., MScAgri *Punjab*, PhD   Prof.
Yousaf, Muhammad, MSc *Faisalabad*, PhD *Faisalabad*   Prof.
Other Staff: 1 Lectr.

Agricultural Extension

Ali, Tanwir, MSc *Faisalabad*, PhD   Asst. Prof.
Muhammad, Sher, MSc *Faisalabad*, PhD   Asst. Prof.
Zia, Muhammad A., MSc   Asst. Prof. (on deputation)

Agricultural Marketing

Din, Qamar M., MS *Hawaii*, MSc   Assoc. Prof.
Mustafa, Khalid, MSc *Faisalabad*, PhD   Asst. Prof.
Raoof, Abdul, MSc   Assoc. Prof.
Wahla, Mukhtar A., MSc *Faisalabad*   Asst. Prof.

Agricultural Meteorology

No staff at present

Agronomy

Ahmad, Riaz, MSc *Faisalabad*, PhD *Faisalabad*   Asst. Prof.

Ahmad, Saeed, MScAgri *Punjab*, PhD *Wales*   Prof.
Akhtar, Mehboob, PhD *Faisalabad*, MSc   Assoc. Prof.
Ali, Asghar, MSc *Faisalabad*, PhD *Wales*   Assoc. Prof.
Amanullah, MSc *Faisalabad*, PhD   Assoc. Prof.
Ayub, Muhammad, MSc *Faisalabad*   Assoc. Prof.
Chaudhry, Fateh M., MSc *Faisalabad*, PhD *Nagoya*   Prof.
Cheema, Zahid A., MSc *Faisalabad*, MS PhD   Assoc. Prof.
Hussain, Abid, PhD *NZ*   Assoc. Prof.
Iqbal, Muhammad, MSc *Faisalabad*, PhD   Asst. Prof.
Malik, Muhammad A., MSc *Faisalabad*, PhD *Faisalabad*   Assoc. Prof.
Mehmood, Tariq, MSc *Faisalabad*, PhD *Faisalabad*   Asst. Prof.
Sabir, Muhammad R., MSc *Faisalabad*   Asst. Prof.
Saeed, Muhammad, MSc *Faisalabad*, PhD   Assoc. Prof.
Shah, Shamshad H., MSc *Faisalabad*, MEd *Faisalabad*, PhD *Wales*   Prof.
Sharar, M. Siddique, MSc *Faisalabad*   Assoc. Prof.

Animal Breeding and Genetics

Ahmad, Zaheer, BSc(AH) *Punjab*, PhD *Faisalabad*, MSc   Prof.
Khan, M. Aftab, MSc *Faisalabad*, PhD *Faisalabad*   Assoc. Prof.
Khan, Muhammad S., MSc PhD   Asst. Prof.
Tahir, Muhammad, BSc(AH) *Punjab*, MSc   Assoc. Prof.

Animal Nutrition

Abid, Abdur R., BSc(AH) *Punjab*, MSc *Faisalabad*, MSc *Lond.*   Assoc. Prof.
Alam, Zafar, MSc   Assoc. Prof.
Asad, Muhammad A., MSc *Faisalabad*   Asst. Prof. (on leave)
Barq, Altafur R., BSc(AH) *Punjab*, MSc *Faisalabad*, PhD *Faisalabad*   Prof.
Gilani, Abrar H., MSc *Faisalabad*, PhD *Faisalabad*   Prof.
Hashmi, Abu S., BSc *Punjab*, MSc *Faisalabad*, PhD *Faisalabad*   Assoc. Prof.
Khan, M. Laiq, MSc *Faisalabad*, PhD *Faisalabad*   Assoc. Prof.
Rasul, Shahid, MSc *Faisalabad*, PhD *Faisalabad*   Asst. Prof.
Sarwar, Muhammad, PhD   Asst. Prof.
Sial, Munawar A., MSc *Faisalabad*, PhD *Faisalabad*   Prof.
Sultan, Javed I., DVM MSc PhD   Assoc. Prof.

Animal Reproduction

Ahmad, Khalid M., MSc *Faisalabad*   Asst. Prof.
Ahmad, Maqbool, MSc *Faisalabad*, PhD   Asst. Prof.
Ahmad, Nazir, MSc *Faisalabad*, PhD   Asst. Prof.
Lodhi, Laeeq A., MSc *Minn.*, PhD *Minn.*   Assoc. Prof.
Najeeb-ur-Rehman, MSc *Faisalabad*, PhD   Asst. Prof.

Qureshi, Zafar I., MSc *Faisalabad*, PhD
  Faisalabad Asst. Prof.
Samad, Hafiz A., MSc *Faisalabad*, PhD
  Faisalabad Assoc. Prof.

Biochemistry, see Chem. and Biochem.

Botany

Ahmad, Abid N., MSc *Punjab* Assoc. Prof.
Akbar, Muhammad, MSc MPhil Assoc. Prof.
Qureshi, Muzammil S., MPhil Assoc. Prof.
Rasool, Ijaz, MSc *Punjab*, PhD Prof.
Sadiq, Muhammad, MSc *Sindh*, MPhil Assoc.
  Prof.

Chemistry and Biochemistry

Ahmad, Sarfraz, MSc *Faisalabad* Asst. Prof.
Ahmed, Riaz, MSc *Punjab*, PhD *Lond.* Prof.
Chughtai, Fiyyaz A., MSc *Punjab*, PhD
  Moscow Assoc. Prof.
Khan, Khalid M., PhD *Edin.* Prof. (on
  deputation)
Nawaz, Rakhshanda, MPhil *Quaid-i-*
  Azam Assoc. Prof.
Parveen, Zahida, MSc *Faisalabad*, MPhil *Faisalabad*,
  PhD Asst. Prof. (on deputation)
Perveen, Najma, MSc *Faisalabad*, MPhil
  Faisalabad Asst. Prof. (on deputation)
Saleem, Bushra, MSc *Faisalabad* Asst. Prof.
Sheikh, Munir A., MSc *Faisalabad*, MPhil
  Faisalabad, PhD Assoc. Prof.
Yaqoob, Muhammad, MSc *Punjab*, PhD
  Oklahoma Prof.

Co-operation and Credit

Bajwa, Muhammad A., MSc Assoc. Prof.
Gill, Zulfiqar A., MSc *Faisalabad*, PhD Assoc.
  Prof.
Kausar, M. Bashir, BSc *Punjab*, MSc Assoc.
  Prof.

Crop Physiology

Ahmad, Nazir, BScAgri *Punjab*, PhD *Wales*,
  MS Prof.
Ahmad, Rashid, MSc PhD Asst. Prof.
Arif, Humayun, PhD *Wales* Asst. Prof. (on
  leave)

Data Processing Unit

No staff at present

Engineering, Basic

Chaudhry, M. Aamanat A., BScEngg *W.Pak.Eng.*,
  MSc *Lond.*, PhD *Leeds* Prof.
Rana, M. Asghar, MEng *Asian*
  I.T.,Bangkok Assoc. Prof.
Shafi, Ahmad, BScEng *Punjab*, MSc
  Faisalabad Asst. Prof.
Sial, Jahangir K., MS *Iowa State*, PhD *Iowa*
  State Prof.

Farm Machinery and Power

Ahmad, Mumtaz, MSc *Faisalabad* Asst. Prof.
Chaudhry, Allah D., BScEngg *W.Pak.Eng.*, MSc
  Newcastle(UK), PhD *Massey* Prof.
Hussain, Kh. Altaf, MSc *Faisalabad* Asst. Prof.
Iqbal, Muhammad, MEng *Asian I.T.,Bangkok*,
  BSc Asst. Prof.
Sabir, M. Shafi, PhD *Sask.*, MSc Assoc. Prof.
Tahir, Abdul R., MSc *Manit.*, BSc PhD Prof.

Farm Management

Ahmad, Bashir, MSc PhD Prof.

Fibre Technology

Jamil, Nisar A., MSc Assoc. Prof.
Nawaz, Muhammad, MSc Assoc. Prof.
Shad, Shahid S., MSc *Faisalabad* Asst. Prof.

Fisheries, see Zool. and Fisheries

Food Technology

Ali, Amjad, BScAgri *Punjab*, PhD *Leeds*,
  MSc Prof.
Anjum, Faqir M., PhD Assoc. Prof.
Awan, Javed A., MSc PhD Assoc. Prof.
Hashmi, Abdul M., MSc *Faisalabad* Asst. Prof.
Mohyuddin, Ghulam, MSc PhD Assoc. Prof.
Rasul, Ghulam, MSc *Faisalabad* Asst. Prof.
Riaz, Riaz A., PhD Assoc. Prof.

Saleem-ur-Rehman, MSc *Faisalabad*, PhD Asst.
  Prof.
Shah, Syed T. H., MSc *Reading*, MSc
  Faisalabad Assoc. Prof.
Siddique, M. Ismail, MSc *Faisalabad*, PhD
  Faisalabad Assoc. Prof.

**Forestry, Range Management and
Wildlife**

Khan, Rashid A., MSc *Faisalabad*, PhD Asst.
  Prof. (on leave)
Khan, Sarwar G., MSc *Faisalabad*, PhD Assoc.
  Prof.
Qureshi, Masood A. A., PhD *Ill.* Prof.
Yaqub, Shahid, MSc *Faisalabad* Asst. Prof.

Genetics, see Animal Breeding and Genetics,
  and Plant Breeding and Genetics

Home Economics, see Rural Home Econ.

Horticulture

Amjad, Muhammad, MSc *Faisalabad*, PhD Asst.
  Prof.
Asi, Abdur R., MSc Assoc. Prof.
Ibrahim, Muhammad, PhD *Faisalabad*,
  MS Assoc. Prof.
Khan, Iqrar A., PhD *Calif.*, MSc Assoc. Prof.
  (on leave)
Khan, M. Aslam, PhD *Wales*, MSc Prof.
Khan, M. Mumtaz, MSc *Faisalabad* Asst. Prof.
Malik, Mahmood N., MSc *W.Pak.Ag.*, PhD
  Calif. Prof.
Maqbool, Muhammad, MSc *Faisalabad*, MSc
  Mich., PhD Assoc. Prof.
Pervez, Muhammad A., MSc *Faisalabad*,
  PhD Asst. Prof.
Siddique, Muhammad, MSc *Faisalabad* Assoc.
  Prof.

Human Environmental Cell

No staff at present

Humanities, see Soc. Scis. and Humanities

Irrigation and Drainage

Ahmad, Niaz, MSc *Faisalabad*, PhD Asst. Prof.
  (on leave)
Awan, Qurban A., MEng *Asian I.T.*, *Bangkok*,
  MSc Assoc. Prof.
Chaudhry, M. Rafiq, MEng *Asian I.T.*, *Bangkok*,
  PhD *Col.* Assoc. Prof.
Iqbal, Muhammad, MEng *Asian I.T.*, *Bangkok*,
  MSc PhD Asst. Prof.

Islamic Studies

Aleem, Khalil A., MA *Punjab* Asst. Prof.
Iqbal, Qari M., MA *Punjab*, MPhil *A.Iqbal*
  Open Asst. Prof.

Livestock Management

Abdullah, Muhammad, MSc PhD Asst. Prof.
Gill, Raza A., PhD *Wis.*, MSc Prof.
Gondal, Khalid Z., PhD *Newcastle(UK)*,
  MSc Assoc. Prof.
Tufail, Muhammad, MSc Assoc. Prof.
Younas, Muhammad, MSc *Faisalabad*,
  PhD Assoc. Prof.

Mathematics and Statistics

Ahmad, M. Idrees, MA *Punjab*, PhD Assoc.
  Prof. (on leave)
Ahmad, Nazir, MA *Punjab* Assoc. Prof.
Ashfaq, Muhammad, MA *Punjab* Assoc. Prof.
Latif, Abdul, MA Assoc. Prof.
Muhammad, Faqir, PhD *Glas.*, MSc Assoc.
  Prof. (on deputation)
Sabir, Abdul A., MA *Punjab* Assoc. Prof.

Physics

Anwar, Muhammad, MSc *Punjab*, PhD *Durh.*,
  BEd Assoc. Prof.
Hussain, M. Yousaf, MSc Asst. Prof.
Niaz, Javed, MSc Asst. Prof.

Plant Breeding and Genetics

Alam, Khurshid, MScAgri *Punjab*, PhD
  Faisalabad Prof.
Aslam, Muhammad, MSc *Faisalabad*, PhD
  Wales Assoc. Prof.

Azhar, Faqir M., MSc *Faisalabad*, PhD
  Liv. Assoc. Prof.
Gilani, Mohsin M., MScAgri *Punjab*, PhD
  Wales Prof.
Hussain, Medhat K., MSc *Faisalabad*, MAg
  Colorado, PhD *Faisalabad* Prof.
Khan, Iftikhar A., MSc *Faisalabad*, PhD
  Faisalabad Prof.
Khan, Muhammad A., PhD Prof.
Medhi, Sadaqat, MSc *Faisalabad*, PhD
  S.Dakota Assoc. Prof.
Salam, Abdus, MSc *Faisalabad*, PhD Assoc. Prof.
Saleem, Muhammad, MSc *Faisalabad*, PhD
  Wales Assoc. Prof.

Plant Pathology

Chohan, Riaz A., BSc *Reading*, MSc Assoc. Prof.
Ilyass, M. Bashir, PhD *Ill.*, MSc Prof.
Khan, Sultan M., MSc *Faisalabad*, PhD
  Faisalabad Prof.
Nasir, Masood A., MSc *Faisalabad* Assoc. Prof.
Randhawa, M. Ashraf, MSc *Faisalabad*, PhD
  Faisalabad Assoc. Prof.

Poultry Husbandry

Ahmad, Husnat, PhD *Salonika*, MSc Assoc.
  Prof.
Ahmad, Nazir, MSc *Faisalabad*, PhD
  Faisalabad Prof.
Haq, Ahsanul, MSc *Faisalabad*, PhD
  Faisalabad Asst. Prof.
Mahmood, Sultan, MSc PhD Asst. Prof.
Shah, Tassawar H., MSc *Faisalabad*, PhD
  Faisalabad Assoc. Prof.

Range Management, see Forestry, Range
  Management and Wildlife

Rural Home Economics

Abbas, Naheed, MSc *Faisalabad* Asst. Prof.
Almas, Kausar, PhD *Lond.*, MSc Assoc. Prof.
Bhatti, Nighat, MSc *Faisalabad* Asst. Prof.

Rural Sociology

Ahmad, Ashfaq, MA PhD Asst. Prof.
Cheema, Asghar M., MSc *Faisalabad*,
  PhD Assoc. Prof. (on leave)
Ijaz, Kishwar, MA *Punjab*, MSc Assoc. Prof.
Zafar, Muhammad I., MSc *Faisalabad*,
  PhD Assoc. Prof.

Short Courses

Bajwa, Munir A., MSc Assoc. Prof.
Khan, Muhammad Y., MSc Assoc. Prof.
Siddiqui, M. Zubair, PhD *Faisalabad* Prof.

Social Sciences and Humanities

No staff at present

Soil Science

Arshad, Muhammad, MSc *Faisalabad*, PhD Asst.
  Prof.
Aslam, Muhammad, MSc *Faisalabad*, PhD
  Faisalabad Assoc. Prof.
Ghafoor, Abdul, MSc *Faisalabad*, PhD
  Faisalabad Assoc. Prof.
Gill, Maqsood A., MSc *Faisalabad*, PhD Assoc.
  Prof.
Hassan, Anwarul, PhD *Calif.*, MSc Assoc. Prof.
Hussain, Tahir, MSc *Faisalabad*, PhD
  Philippines Prof.
Qureshi, Riaz H., MSc *Faisalabad*, PhD Prof.
Ranjha, Atta M., MSc *Faisalabad*, PhD
  Faisalabad Assoc. Prof.
Razzaq, Abdul, MSc PhD Asst. Prof.
Shahid, Shabbir A., PhD *Wales*, MSc Assoc.
  Prof.

Statistics, see Maths. and Stats.

Veterinary Anatomy

Hur, Ghulam, BSc(AH) *Punjab*, MSc Assoc.
  Prof.
Sarwar, Anas, MSc *Faisalabad*, PhD Asst. Prof.

Veterinary Clinical Medicine and Surgery

Amin, Muhammad K., MSc   Assoc. Prof.
Choudhry, Nusrat I., BSc(AH) Punjab, MS Wash.State   Prof.
Khan, Mumtaz A., MSc PhD   Asst. Prof.
Muhammad, Ghulam, MSc PhD   Asst. Prof.

Veterinary Microbiology

Afzal, Hameed, MSc Faisalabad, PhD   Assoc. Prof.
Arshad, Muhammad, MSc Faisalabad   Asst. Prof.
Ashfaq, Muhammad, MSc   Assoc. Prof.
Hussain, Iftikhar, MSc Faisalabad, PhD   Asst. Prof.
Siddique, Muhammad, MSc PhD   Assoc. Prof.

Veterinary Parasitology

Anwar, Anwarul H., MS Ill., MSc   Assoc. Prof.
Hayat, Birjees, MSc Punjab, PhD Faisalabad   Assoc. Prof.
Hayat, Sikandar, PhD Oklahoma, MSc   Prof.
Iqbal, Zafar, MSc Faisalabad, PhD Faisalabad   Asst. Prof.

Veterinary Pathology

Ahmad, Abrar, MSc Faisalabad, PhD Faisalabad   Asst. Prof. (on leave)
Ahmad, Ahrar, MSc Faisalabad, PhD Faisalabad   Asst. Prof.
Anjum, Ahmad D., PhD Lond., MSc   Assoc. Prof.
Khan, M. Zargham, MSc Faisalabad, PhD   Asst. Prof.
Sabri, M. Alam, MSc   Assoc. Prof.

Veterinary Physiology and Pharmacology

Akhtar, M. Shoaib, MPhil Karachi, PhD Munich   Prof.
Chaudhry, Shaukat A., BSc(AH) Punjab, PhD R.Vet.& Agric., Denmark   Prof.
Hassan, Ijaz J., MSc Faisalabad   Asst. Prof.
Khaliq, Tanwir, MSc Faisalabad   Asst. Prof.
Khan, Faqir H., MSc Faisalabad, PhD Faisalabad   Asst. Prof.
Nawaz, Muhammad, PhD R.Vet.& Agric., Denmark   Prof.
Zia-ur-Rehman, MSc Faisalabad, PhD   Assoc. Prof. (on deputation)

Wildlife, see Forestry, Range Management and Wildlife

Zoology and Fisheries

Ahmad, Iftikhar, MSc Faisalabad, PhD Faisalabad   Asst. Prof.
Baig, Mirza A., MSc Alig., PhD   Prof.
Chaudhry, Haji Muhammad A., MSc   Assoc. Prof.
Javed, Muhammad, MSc Faisalabad, PhD Faisalabad   Asst. Prof.
Khalid, Shakila, PhD Karachi, MSc   Asst. Prof.
Khan, Akbar A., MSc Faisalabad, PhD Faisalabad   Prof.
Qureshi, Junaid I., MSc Faisalabad., PhD Faisalabad   Prof.

Rana, Shahnaz A., MSc Faisalabad, PhD Faisalabad   Asst. Prof.
Sheri, Ahmad N., MSc Punjab, PhD Wat.   Prof.

SPECIAL CENTRES, ETC

Advanced Studies, Directorate of

Aslam, Haji M., MSc   Dir.*

Research, Directorate of

Ibrar Hussain Gilani, PhD   Dir.*

COLLEGE OF VETERINARY SCIENCE, LAHORE

Constituent College

Afzal, Muhammad, BSc(AH) MSc   Assoc. Prof.
Ahmad, Ashfaq, MSc Faisalabad   Asst. Prof.
Ahmad, Iftikhar G., MSc Faisalabad   Asst. Prof.
Ahmad, Ijaz, MSc Faisalabad, PhD Minn.   Assoc. Prof.
Ahmad, Nisar, MSc PhD   Prof.
Ahmed, Manzoor, MSc Faisalabad   Asst. Prof.
Ahmed, Masood, MSc   Assoc. Prof.
Asghar, M. Nawaz, MSc   Assoc. Prof.
Ashraf, Muhammad, PhD Minn., MSc   Assoc. Prof.
Bhatti, M. Aleem, MSc Faisalabad, PhD   Asst. Prof.
Bhatti, M. Aslam, MSc Manit., PhD Manit.   Prof.
Chaudhry, Rashid A., MSc Faisalabad   Prof.
Chaudhry, Zafar I., MSc   Assoc. Prof. (on leave)
Hashmi, Haji Ahmad, PhD Camb., MSc   Assoc. Prof.
Iqbal, Mazhar, MSc   Assoc. Prof.
Jaffari, Saghir A., MSc   Prof.
Khan, Imtiaz H., MSc   Assoc. Prof.
Khan, M. Athar, PhD Minn., MSc   Assoc. Prof.
Khan, Muhammad A., MSc Faisalabad   Asst. Prof.
Khan, Muhammad S., DVM Faisalabad, MSc Faisalabad   Asst. Prof.
Khan, Naeem U., DVM Faisalabad, MSc Faisalabad   Asst. Prof. (on leave)
Khan, Shakil A., MSc Faisalabad, PhD   Asst. Prof.
Muhammad, Khushi, MSc Faisalabad, PhD   Asst. Prof.
Munir, M. Akram, PhD Minn., MSc   Assoc. Prof.
Naeem, Muhammad, MSc   Assoc. Prof.
Pasha, Talat N., MSc PhD   Assoc. Prof.
Pervez, Khalid, MSc PhD   Assoc. Prof.
Qureshi, Javed A., MSc   Asst. Prof.
Rabbani, Asif, BSc(AH) MSc   Assoc. Prof.
Rashid, Javed, MSc Faisalabad   Asst. Prof.
Rizvi, Ataur R., MSc PhD   Prof.
Sabir, Muhammad, PhD Leeds, MSc   Assoc. Prof.
Saga, Faqir H., BSc(AH) MSc   Assoc. Prof.
Saleem, Muhammad, MSc   Assoc. Prof.
Sheikh, M. Amin, PhD Punjab, MSc   Assoc. Prof.

Younas, Muhammad, MSc   Assoc. Prof.

CONTACT OFFICERS

Academic affairs. Registrar: Akram, Sheikh Muhammad, MES N.Carolina
Accommodation. Hall Warden: Ahmad, Nazir, PhD Faisalabad
Admissions (first degree). Deputy Registrar: Ch. Muhammad Hussain
Admissions (higher degree). Director, Advanced Studies: Aslam, Haji M., MSc
Adult/continuing education. Director, Division of Education and Extension: Khan, Prof. Saeed A.
Archives. Director, Division of Education and Extension: Khan, Prof. Saeed A.
Careers. Director, Division of Education and Extension: Khan, Prof. Saeed A.
Computing services. (Contact the Department of Mathematics and Statistics)
Development/fund-raising. Registrar: Akram, Sheikh Muhammad, MES N.Carolina
Distance education. Director, Division of Education and Extension: Khan, Prof. Saeed A.
Estates and buildings/works and services. Registrar: Akram, Sheikh Muhammad, MES N.Carolina
Examinations. Controller of Examinations: Haleem, Anwar, MSc Faisalabad
Finance. Treasurer: Jamil, Muhammad, BA
General enquiries. Registrar: Akram, Sheikh Muhammad, MES N.Carolina
Health services. Senior Medical Officer: Hafeez, Abdul, MB BS Punjab
International office. Librarian: ......
Library (chief librarian). Librarian: ......
Ombudsperson. University Auditor: ......
Publications. Chairman, Publications Committee: Sial, Prof. Munawar A., MSc Faisalabad, PhD Faisalabad
Purchasing. Store Officer: Ali, Ferzand
Research. Director, Research: Ibrar Hussain Gilani, Prof. , PhD
Safety. Security Officer: Hameed, Abdul
Scholarships, awards, loans. Deputy Registrar: Ch. Muhammad Hussain
Security. Security Officer: Hameed, Abdul
Sport and recreation. Chairman, Sports Board: Gillani, Dr. Mansoor M.
Staff development and training. Assistant Registrar (Est.): Javaid, Mahboob A.
Student welfare/counselling. Director, Students' Affairs: Rauf, Abdul, MSc
University press. Deputy Registrar (Planning and Development): Javed, M.

CONSTITUENT COLLEGE HEADS

College of Veterinary Science, Lahore. Principal: Chaudhry, Rashid A., MSc Faisalabad

[Information supplied by the institution as at 28 February 1998, and edited by the ACU]

AL-KHAIR UNIVERSITY AJK

Established 1994

Postal Address: Camp Office, House No 324, Street 66, Sector I-8/3, Islamabad, Pakistan
Street Address: Mirpur, Azad Kashmir, Pakistan
Telephone: (051) 449727-9 **Fax**: (051) 443712

RECTOR AND VICE-CHANCELLOR*—Khattak, Prof. G. J. Pareshan, MA
Pesh., DLit Gomal
REGISTRAR‡—Hussain, S. Akhtar, BA Punjab

ALLAMA IQBAL OPEN UNIVERSITY

Founded 1974

Member of the Association of Commonwealth Universities

Postal Address: Sector H-8, Islamabad, Pakistan
Telephone: (051) 264880-7, 264891-6, 252577 **Fax**: (051) 264319, 252510 **Cables**: Openvarsity, Islamabad

CHANCELLOR—H.E. The President of the Islamic Republic of Pakistan (ex
officio)
PRO-CHANCELLOR—H.E. The Federal Minister for Education (ex officio)
VICE-CHANCELLOR*—Siddiqui, Anwar H., BA Sindh, MPA Karachi, PhD
S.Calif.
REGISTRAR‡—Saeed, Ch. Ahmed, MEd Punjab, MSc Punjab
ACTING TREASURER—Jafri, A. J., BCom Punjab
LIBRARIAN—Mahmud, Zamurad, MA Pesh., MA Karachi

GENERAL INFORMATION

History. The university was established in 1974. It is located in Islamabad.

First Degrees. BA, BBA, BCom, BCS, BLIS.

Higher Degrees. MA, MBA, MEd, MSc, MPhil.

Language of Instruction. English and Urdu.

Fees (per full credit course). BA: Rs335; BA (computer studies), BBA, BCom: Rs385; BEd: Rs510; BEd (practical): Rs760; MA, MEd, MSc: Rs760; MBA: Rs910; MPhil: Rs1510.

Academic Year. Two semesters.

Income. Rs264,654,000.

Statistics. Students: 262,310.

FACULTIES/SCHOOLS

Basic and Applied Sciences
Dean: Liaqat, Prof. Perveen, MSc Punjab, PhD
Reading
Secretary: Muhammad, Sheikh Y., BE NED Eng.

Education
Dean: Rashid, Prof. Muhammad, LLB Punjab,
MA Punjab, MPhil Quaid-i-Azam, PhD Wales

ACADEMIC UNITS

Agriculture Sciences
Tel: (051) 857128
Nowshad Khan, MSc Pesh., MSc Reading   Asst.
Prof. (on leave)
Shabbir, Ahmed, MSc Faisalabad, PhD
Bucharest   Asst. Prof.
Other Staff: 2 Lectrs.

Arabic
Tel: (051) 850224
Asjad, Shehnaz, MA Quaid-i-Azam   Asst. Prof.
Hashmi, M. T., MA Punjab, PhD Punjab   Prof.;
Head*
Muhammad, Yasin, MA Sindh, MA Khart.   Asst.
Prof.

Basic Sciences
Tel: (051) 857138
Abdul, Ghafoor, MSc Punjab, MSc Salf., PhD
Manc.   Prof. (on leave)
Masood, Amin, MSc Punjab   Asst. Prof.
Naeem, Shahida, MSc Punjab, MPhil Quaid-i-
Azam, PhD Quaid-i-Azam   Assoc. Prof.; Head*
Other Staff: 1 Lectr.

Commerce
1 Instr./Lectr.

Computer Sciences, see Maths., Stats. and
Computer Scis.

Economics
Naeem, A. R., MSc Leningrad, PhD Glas.   Asst.
Prof.; Head*
Other Staff: 1 Lectr.

**Education, Distance, Non-Formal and
Continuing**, see also Mass Educn.
Tel: (051) 858221
Iqbal, M. J., MA Punjab, MPhil A.Iqbal
Open   Asst. Prof.
Shahid, S. M., MA Punjab   Asst. Prof.
Other Staff: 1 Lectr.

Education, Science
Tel: (051) 857129
Riffat, Qudsia, MSc Pesh., PhD Keele   Assoc.
Prof.; Head*
Other Staff: 3 Lectrs.

Education, Special
Tel: (051) 859473
Awan, M. H., MA Sindh, MEd Sindh   Asst. Prof.;
Head*
Other Staff: 1 Lectr.

Education Studies
Saghir, A. R., LLB Punjab, MA Punjab, MEd
Punjab, PhD Punjab   Assoc. Prof.; Head*

Education, Teacher
Tel: (051) 253614, 263175
Anwar, Mussarrat, MA Pesh., MEd Pesh., MS
Indiana, PhD Indiana   Assoc. Prof.; Head*
Muhammad, G. R., MA Punjab, MEd Karachi,
MPhil A.Iqbal Open   Asst. Prof.
Raja, Sabir H., MA Punjab, MEd Punjab, PhD
Glas.   Asst. Prof.
Waqar, Salma, BEd Gomal, MEd Gomal, MA
Pesh.   Asst. Prof.
Other Staff: 2 Lectrs.

Education, Technical and Vocational
Tel: (051) 850391
Asghar, M. Aslam, MA Punjab, MEd Punjab, MEd
Missouri, PhD Missouri   Prof.; Head*

Education, Women's
Tel: (051) 280598
Hyder, Nuzhat, MSc Punjab   Asst. Prof.
Liaqat, Perveen, MSc Punjab, PhD Reading   Prof.;
Head*
Other Staff: 4 Lectrs.

Educational Planning and Management
Tel: (051) 853121, 853292
Akbar, Aisha, MA Punjab, MAEPM A.Iqbal
Open   Asst. Prof.
Pervez, Rashida, MEd Punjab, MA Punjab, MA
Lond.   Asst. Prof.
Rashid, Muhammad, LLB Punjab, MA Punjab,
MPhil Quaid-i-Azam, PhD Wales   Prof.; Head*

Saghir, Allaha R., LLB *Punjab*, MA *Punjab*, MEd *Punjab*, PhD *Punjab* Assoc. Prof.
Zulkaif, Ahmed, MA *Punjab*, MEd *Punjab*, PhD *Punjab* Assoc. Prof.
Other Staff: 1 Lectr.

English
Tel: (051) 856033

Abbas, Shemeem, MA *Punjab*, MA *Leeds*, PhD *Texas* Prof.
Abdul, Hafeez, MA *Pesh.*, MA *Manc.* Asst. Prof.; Head*
Siddiqui, S. K., MA *Punjab*, MA *Manc.*, PhD *Tor.* Assoc. Prof. (on leave)
Siraj, Shagufta, MA *Punjab*, MA *Manc.* Asst. Prof.
Ursani, Farzana, MA *Sindh* Asst. Prof.
Waseem, Raazia, MA *Punjab*, MA *Essex* Assoc. Prof.
Other Staff: 1 Lectr.

Iqbaliyat
Tel: (051) 856031

Kamran, S. I., MA *Punjab*, MPhil *A.Iqbal Open* Asst. Prof.
Other Staff: 1 Lectr.

Islamic Studies
Tel: (051) 856032

Charan, Jan M., MLIS
Hashmi, M. T., MA *Punjab*, PhD *Punjab* Prof.; Head*
Hashmi, S. M., MA *Pesh.* Asst. Prof.
Yaseen, Muhammad, MA Asst. Prof.
Other Staff: 1 Lectr.

Languages of Pakistan
Tel: (051) 856034

Kamran, Norina, MA *Karachi* Asst. Prof.
Qureshi, N. A., MA *Punjab*, PhD *Punjab* Assoc. Prof. (on leave)
Saifi, M. B., MA *Punjab*, PhD *Punjab* Asst. Prof.
Shaheen, R. B., MA *Punjab*, PhD *Sindh* Assoc. Prof.; Head*
Other Staff: 2 Lectrs.

Library and Information Sciences
Bhatti, N. H., MA *Karachi* Asst. Prof.; Head*
Other Staff: 1 Lectr.

Management Sciences
Tel: (051) 253898

Aziz, Nisar A., MPA *Punjab* Assoc. Prof.
Sheikh, Ayub M. M., MBA
Zulkaif, Ahmed, MA *Punjab*, MEd *Punjab*, PhD *Punjab* Assoc. Prof.; Head*
Other Staff: 4 Lectrs.

Mass Communication
Siraj, S. A., MA *Gomal* Asst. Prof.; Head*
Other Staff: 1 Lectr.

Mass Education
Tel: (051) 856042

Farooq, Nighat, MA *Pesh.* Material Co-ordinator
Haq, Riffat, MSc *Quaid-i-Azam*, MPhil *Quaid-i-Azam* Project Manager
Saif, Lubna, MSc *Quaid-i-Azam* Assoc. Prof.; Head*
Shahid, Farzana, MSc RE Co-ordinator
Zaman, Rehana, MA *Punjab* Field Co-ordinator
Other Staff: 2 Designers; 2 Res. Assocs.

Mathematics, Statistics and Computer Sciences
Tel: (051) 251860

Arshad, Mehmood, MSc *Quaid-i-Azam*, PhD *Shanghai* Asst. Prof.
Awan, M. D., BEd *Karachi*, MA *Karachi*, CandMag *Oslo*, CandPol *Oslo*, PhD *Oslo* Prof.; Head*
Other Staff: 5 Lectrs.

Pakistan Studies
Memon, Aman U., MA *Sindh* Asst. Prof.; Head*
Other Staff: 1 Lectr.

Population Studies
Masood, Rukhsana, MSc *Faisalabad*, PhD *Essex* Asst. Prof.; Head*
Other Staff: 1 Res. Assoc.; 1 Lectr.

Social Sciences
Tel: (051) 853316

Solangi, M. F., MA *Sindh*, MA *Penn.* Assoc. Prof.; Head*

Statistics, see Maths., Stats. and Computer Scis.

SPECIAL CENTRES, ETC

Academic Planning and Course Production, Bureau of
Amjad, Falak N., MA *Sindh* Course Production Co-ordinator
Muhammad, Amjad A., MA *Punjab* Course Production Co-ordinator
Sulman, Arifa, MSc *Quaid-i-Azam* Sr. Course Production Co-ordinator

Computer Centre
Tel: (051) 854204

Liaqat, Hussain, BA *Punjab* System Devel. Manager*

Educational Technology, Institute of (IET)
Tel: (051) 854212

Azeem, Sh. F. Sr. Photographer
Hussain, Ashique Sr. Calligraphist
Other Staff: 1 Designer

Graphic/Design Unit
Tel: (051) 852865

Haroon, Muhammad Chief Designer
Qureshi, Mehmood A. Sr. Designer
Sheikh, M. H. Sr. Designer*
Other Staff: 3 Designers; 1 Lectr.

Production and Management Unit
Tel: (051) 857127

Ali, M. Mehmood Sr. Engineer
Bhurgari, Ghulam H., MA *Sindh* Dep. Dir.
Javed, Mahmood, MA *Punjab* Dep. Dir.*
Khan, S. Muhammad B., MA Material Co-ordinator
Khawaja, Abid H., MA *Baloch.*, MA *Punjab* Dep. Dir.
Talpur, Mukhtar H., MA *Sindh* Sr. Producer
Other Staff: 3 TV Engineers; 1 Producer

Research and Evaluation Centre
Saghir, Allaha R., LLB *Punjab*, MA *Punjab*, MEd *Punjab*, PhD *Punjab* Dir.*
Other Staff: 1 Sr. Res. Officer; 3 Res. Assocs.

South Asia Distance Education Resource Centre (SADERC)
Tel: (051) 854306

Bukhari, A. H., MA *Islamia, Bahawal.* Asst. Librarian; Head*

CONTACT OFFICERS

Academic affairs. Dean of Basic and Applied Sciences: Liaqat, Prof. Perveen, MSc *Punjab*, PhD *Reading*
Academic affairs. Dean of Education: Rashid, Prof. Muhammad, LLB *Punjab*, MEd *Punjab*, MPhil *Quaid-i-Azam*, PhD *Wales*
Accommodation. Project Director: Abdul, Jalil, BE *Pesh.*
Admissions (first degree). Controller: Muhammad, Khurshid, MA *Pesh.*, MEd *Pesh.*
Admissions (higher degree). Controller: Muhammad, Khurshid, MA *Pesh.*, MEd *Pesh.*
Adult/continuing education. Muhammad, Prof. Rashid, LLB *Punjab*, MA *Punjab*, MPhil *Quaid-i-Azam*, PhD *Wales*
Alumni. Director: Haroon, Shagufta, MA *Pesh.*
Archives. Librarian: Mahmud, Zamurad, MA *Pesh.*, MA *Karachi*

Archives. Deputy Director: Javed, Mahmood, MA *Punjab*
Careers. Director: Haroon, Shagufta, MA *Pesh.*
Computing services. System Development Manager: Liaqat, Hussain, BA *Punjab*
Consultancy services. Registrar: Saeed, Ch. Ahmed, MEd *Punjab*, MSc *Punjab*
Credit transfer. Controller: Muhammad, Khurshid, MA *Pesh.*, MEd *Pesh.*
Development/fund-raising. Acting Treasurer: Jafri, A. J., BCom *Punjab*
Development/fund-raising. Planning and Development Officer: Muhammad, Rafiq, MA *Punjab*
Distance education. Muhammad, Prof. Rashid, LLB *Punjab*, MA *Punjab*, MPhil *Quaid-i-Azam*, PhD *Wales*
Equal opportunities. Registrar: Saeed, Ch. Ahmed, MEd *Punjab*, MSc *Punjab*
Estates and buildings/works and services. Project Director: Abdul, Jalil, BE *Pesh.*
Examinations. Controller: Muhammad, Khurshid, MA *Pesh.*, MEd *Pesh.*
Finance. Acting Treasurer: Jafri, A. J., BCom *Punjab*
General enquiries. Registrar: Saeed, Ch. Ahmed, MEd *Punjab*, MSc *Punjab*
Health services. Registrar: Saeed, Ch. Ahmed, MEd *Punjab*, MSc *Punjab*
Industrial liaison. Zulkaif, Ahmed, MA *Punjab*, MEd *Punjab*, PhD *Punjab*
Library (chief librarian). Librarian: Mahmud, Zamurad, MA *Pesh.*, MA *Karachi*
Minorities/disadvantaged groups. Registrar: Saeed, Ch. Ahmed, MEd *Punjab*, MSc *Punjab*
Ombudsperson. Registrar: Saeed, Ch. Ahmed, MEd *Punjab*, MSc *Punjab*
Ombudsperson. Controller: Muhammad, Khurshid, MA *Pesh.*, MEd *Pesh.*
Personnel/human resources. Registrar: Saeed, Ch. Ahmed, MEd *Punjab*, MSc *Punjab*
Public relations, information and marketing. Mumtaz, Abaidullah, BA
Publications. Senior Printer: Shahab ud din Shahab, MA *Punjab*
Purchasing. Acting Treasurer: Jafri, A. J., BCom *Punjab*
Quality assurance and accreditation. Vice-Chancellor: Siddiqui, Anwar H., BA *Sindh*, MPA *Karachi*, PhD *S.Calif.*
Research. Senior Research Officer: Chaudhary, Masooda, MA *Punjab*
Safety. Project Director: Abdul, Jalil, BE *Pesh.*
Scholarships, awards, loans. Registrar: Saeed, Ch. Ahmed, MEd *Punjab*, MSc *Punjab*
Schools liaison. Director, Regional Services: Asghar, Aslam, MSc *Punjab*, MEd *Punjab*
Security. Project Director: Abdul, Jalil, BE *Pesh.*
Sport and recreation. Director, Regional Services: Asghar, Aslam, MSc *Punjab*, MEd *Punjab*
Staff development and training. Registrar: Saeed, Ch. Ahmed, MEd *Punjab*, MSc *Punjab*
Staff development and training. Muhammad, Prof. Rashid, LLB *Punjab*, MA *Punjab*, MPhil *Quaid-i-Azam*, PhD *Wales*
Student union. Director, Regional Services: Asghar, Aslam, MSc *Punjab*, MEd *Punjab*
Student welfare/counselling. Director: Haroon, Shagufta, MA *Pesh.*
Students from other countries. Controller: Muhammad, Khurshid, MA *Pesh.*, MEd *Pesh.*
Students with disabilities. Controller: Muhammad, Khurshid, MA *Pesh.*, MEd *Pesh.*
University press. Senior Printer: Shahab ud din Shahab, MA *Punjab*
Women. Liaqat, Prof. Perveen, MSc *Punjab*, PhD *Reading*
Women. Saif, Lubna, MSc *Quaid-i-Azam*

CONSTITUENT COLLEGE HEADS

Abbottabad Regional Services, House No. K-217, Kunj Jadeed, near Fawara Chowk, G. T. Road, Abbottabad, North-West Frontier Province, Pakistan. (Tel: (0598) 2296.) Assistant Regional Director: Jilani, S. A., MSc *Pesh.*

Abu Dhabi Regional Services, c/o Islamia English School, PO Box 2157, Abu Dhabi, United Arab Emirates. .) Regional Co-ordinator: Ali, Prof. Hamid

Bahawalpur Regional Services, House No 85-B, Model Town B, Bahawalpur, Punjab, Pakistan. (Tel: (0621) 5831.) Deputy Regional Director: Hussain, K. S., MA *Punjab*

Chitral Regional Services, near Polo Ground, Chitral, North-West Frontier Province, Pakistan. (Tel: (0533) 2891.) Assistant Regional Director: Elahi, Maqbool, MA *Pesh.*

Dera Ghazi Khan Regional Services, House No 237, Block A, Housing Scheme No 1, Khayaban-e-Sarwar, Dera Ghazi Khan, Punjab, Pakistan. (Tel: (064) 2373.) Assistant Regional Director: Jahangir Akhtar, MA *Punjab*

Dera Ismail Khan Regional Services, Kuokab Colony, West Circular Road, Dera Ismail Khan, North-West Frontier Province, Pakistan. (Tel: (0529) 3230.) Assistant Regional Director: Shaukatullah, MA *Gomal*

Faisalabad Regional Services, 82, A Officer Colony, Susan Road, 213/RB Madina Town, Faisalabad, Punjab, Pakistan. (Tel: (0411) 41411.) Deputy Regional Director: Pervez, Shaheena, MSc *Punjab*

Gilgit Regional Services, VVIP Road, near Fateh Bagh, Gilgit, Pakistan. (Tel: (0572) 2973.) Assistant Regional Director: Ahmed, Bashir, BA *A.Iqbal Open*

Gujranwala Regional Services, House No 4, Delta Road, Satellite Town, Gujranwala, Punjab, Pakistan. (Tel: (0431) 82672.) Deputy Regional Director: Qureshi, Mazhar ul Haq, BEd *Punjab*, MA *Punjab*

Hyderabad Regional Services, House No 48, Unit-1, G. O. R. Colony, Hyderabad, Sindh, Pakistan. (Tel: (0221) 782981.) Assistant Regional Director: Khawaja, P. A., MA *Sindh*

Islamabad Regional Services, Services Block H-8, Allama Iqbal Open University, Islamabad, Pakistan. (Tel: (051) 854313.) Regional Director: Qureshi, S. A., MA *Punjab*

Jacobabad Regional Services, c/o Government High School, Jacobabad, Sindh, Pakistan. Regional Co-ordinator: Khattu, N. A.

Karachi Regional Services, House No C-252, Block No 6, F. B. Area, Karachi, Sindh, Pakistan. (Tel: (021) 675298.) Regional

Director: Kamrani, Nazar, MA *Sindh*, PhD *Sindh*

Lahore Regional Services, 346 Raza Block, Allama Iqbal Town, Lahore 18, Punjab, Pakistan. (Tel: (042) 431205.) Deputy Regional Director: Saleemi, T. B.

Larkana Regional Services, Bungalow No A/39, New Housing Colony, Wagan Road, Larkana, Pakistan. Regional Co-ordinator: Punwar, N. H., BCom *Sindh*

Mianwali Regional Services, 392/A Ballo Khel Road, Mianwali, Punjab, Pakistan. Assistant Regional Director: Khan, M. S., MA *Punjab*

Mingora Regional Services, New Road, Mingora, North-West Frontier Province, Pakistan. (Tel: (0536) 5964.) Assistant Regional Director: Khan, M. A., MA *Pesh.*

Mirpur Regional Services, House No 35, Sector B-4, Mirpur, Azad Kashmir, Pakistan. (Tel: (054) 3236.) Regional Director: Muhammad Bashir, Ch., MA *Karachi*, MPhil *Quaid-i-Azam*

Mithi Regional Services, Muslim Colony, Mithi, Sindh, Pakistan. (Tel: Mithi 111.) Regional Co-ordinator: Arisar, M. H., LLB *Sindh*, MA *Sindh*

Multan Regional Services, House No 337-338/B, Gulgasht, Multan, Punjab, Pakistan. (Tel: (061) 5228000.) Regional Director: Malik, A. H., BEd *B.Zak.*, MA *Punjab*, PhD *Pesh.*, BEd

Muslim Bagh Regional Services, c/o Government High School, Muslim Bagh, Balochistan, Pakistan. Regional Co-ordinator: Umar, Muhammad, BA

Muzaffarabad Regional Services, Lower Plate, Neelam Road, opposite House Building Finance Corporation, Muzaffarabad, Azad Kashmir, Pakistan. (Tel: (058) 2956.) Assistant Regional Director: Khan, M. R., BA *A.Iqbal Open*, MA *Punjab*

Peshawar Regional Services, Sikandarpura, G. T. Road, House No 59, Nishtarabad, Peshawar City, North-West Frontier Province, Pakistan. (Tel: (0521) 215398.) Assistant Regional Director: Hidayat Ullah, MA *Pesh.*, MAEPM *A.Iqbal Open*

Quetta Regional Services, House No B-20/127, Meconghy Road, Quetta, Balochistan, Pakistan. (Tel: (081) 73049.) Deputy Regional Director: Tareen, S. S., LLB *Baloch.*, MA *Baloch.*

Rawalpindi Regional Services, 2-A Satellite Town, Rawalpindi, Islamabad, Pakistan. (Tel: (051) 844750.) Regional Director: Khan, A. H., MA *Punjab*

Regional Services (Central Office). Director, Regional Services: Asghar, Aslam, MSc *Punjab*, MEd *Punjab*

Sahiwal Regional Services, House No 33, East Block, Scheme No 2, Farid Town, Sahiwal, Punjab, Pakistan. (Tel: (0441) 76500.) Assistant Regional Director: Mohammad, Tayyab, BEd *Punjab*, MA *Baloch.*

Sargodha Regional Services, House No 18-X, New Satellite Town, near Passport Office, Sargodha, Punjab, Pakistan. (Tel: (045) 66428.) Assistant Regional Director: Rana, S. N., MA *Punjab*

Sehwan Sharif Regional Services, House No 105 Khosa Mohallah, Opposite Golden Gate, Sehwan Sharif, District Dadu, Sindh, Pakistan. (Tel: (02292) 402.) Assistant Regional Director: Channa, A. K., MA *Sindh*

Sharjah Regional Services, c/o Pakistan Islamia Higher Secondary School, PO Box 1493, Sharjah, United Arab Emirates. (Tel: (051) 854313.) Regional Co-ordinator: Khan, Maqbool N.

Sibi Regional Services, c/o Government Model High School, Sibi, Balochistan, Pakistan. Regional Co-ordinator: Rehmatullah, BA

Skardu Regional Services, Link Road, Sukamaidan, Skardu, Pakistan. (Tel: (0575) 2586.) Assistant Regional Director: Yousaf, Muhammad, MA *Punjab*

Sujjawal Regional Services, near HBL Doctor Gali Sujjawal, Sindh, Pakistan. (Tel: Sujjawal 195.) Assistant Regional Director: Memon, M. A., MA *Sindh*

Sukkar Regional Services, House No C-120/1-A Jeelani Road, Sukkar, Sindh, Pakistan. (Tel: (071) 22230.) Assistant Regional Director: Maka, G. A., MA *Sindh*

Umarkot Regional Services, c/o Government High School No 2, Umarkot, Sindh, Pakistan. Regional Co-ordinator: Lonomal Kushnami

[*Information supplied by the institution as at 12 August 1998, and edited by the ACU*]

UNIVERSITY OF ARID AGRICULTURE, RAWALPINDI

Established 1994; previously Barani Agricultural College, Rawalpindi 1979

Postal Address: Murree Road, Shamsabad, Rawalpindi 46300, Pakistan
Telephone: (051) 843882, 847695-7 **Fax**: (051) 429586 **Cables**: AGRICOL

VICE-CHANCELLOR*—Azam Khan, Muhammad, LLB *Punjab*, MSc *Beirut*, MS *Mass.*, PhD *Mass.*
REGISTRAR‡—Mahmood, Shaukat, MSc *Faisalabad*, PhD *Montana State*

AZAD JAMMU AND KASHMIR UNIVERSITY

Established 1980

Member of the Association of Commonwealth Universities

Postal Address: Muzaffarabad, Azad Kashmir, Pakistan
Telephone: (058) 2060, 3328, 2366, 3306, 4444 **Cables**: University Muzaffarabad **Telex**: 4717

CHANCELLOR—The President of Azad Jammu and Kashmir (ex officio)
VICE-CHANCELLOR*—Abbasi, M. Sarwar, MA Punjab, PhD Punjab
REGISTRAR—Khan, Raja M. A., MA Punjab, MPhil Quaid-i-Azam
DIRECTOR OF FINANCE—Khan, Raja A. K., MBA Punjab, MS Drexel
CHIEF LIBRARIAN—Yaqoob, Ch. Muhammad, MLS Karachi

FACULTIES/SCHOOLS

Administrative Sciences, University College of
Dean: Shaikh, Saeed A., MAS Karachi

Agriculture, University College of
Dean: Choudhry, M. B., MSc Faisalabad, PhD Reading

Arts
Dean: Rauf, Dr. Abdul

Engineering, University College of
Dean: Mirza, Abdul G., MPhil Pesh.

Home Economics, University College of
Dean: Shah, Saeeda J. A., MA Punjab, MEd Manc.

Sciences
Dean: Khan, Abdul R., MSc Punjab, PhD Ankara

Textile Designing
Dean: Atta, Saleema, MA Punjab

ACADEMIC UNITS

Agriculture
Tel: (058) 2688 Fax: (058) 2826
Abbasi, M. K., MSc Faisalabad Asst. Prof. (on leave)
Ali, C. Y., MSc Faisalabad, PhD Zhejiang Ag. Assoc. Prof.
Anjum, M. S., MSc Faisalabad Asst. Prof. (on leave)
Awan, M. S., MSc Faisalabad Asst. Prof.
Choudhry, M. B., MSc Faisalabad, PhD Reading Assoc. Prof.
Hamid, A., MSc Faisalabad Asst. Prof.
Hussain, M., MSc Faisalabad Asst. Prof. (on leave)
Ilyas, M., MSc Faisalabad, PhD Utah State Assoc. Prof.
Iqbal, M., MSc Faisalabad Asst. Prof.
Javed, A., BSc Faisalabad Asst. Prof.
Khaliq, A., MSc Faisalabad, PhD Faisalabad Assoc. Prof.
Khan, M. F., MSc Pesh., PhD Halle Asst. Prof. (on leave)
Khan, M. R., MSc Karachi, PhD Newcastle(UK) Asst. Prof.
Khan, S. A. R., MA Karachi, MPhil Karachi Assoc. Prof.
Khan, S. Ali, MScAgric Pesh. Asst. Prof.
Khan, S. M. N., MSc Pesh., MPhil Assoc. Prof.
Majeed, A., MSc Punjab Asst. Prof.
Qureshi, M. A., MSc Faisalabad Asst. Prof. (on leave)
Shabbir, S. M., MSc Faisalabad, PhD Prof.
Shah, D. N. A., PhD Wales Asst. Prof.
Shah, S. R., MSc Faisalabad Asst. Prof.
Sher, M., MScAgric Pesh. Asst. Prof.
Zafar, S. M. A., MA Punjab Asst. Prof.

Arabic
Hussain, B., MA Punjab Assoc. Prof.
Rajorvee, M. S., MA Punjab Assoc. Prof.
Rashid, I., MA Punjab Asst. Prof.

Botany
Tel: (058) 4131
Akhtar, T., MSc Punjab, MPhil Quaid-i-Azam Asst. Prof.
Aslam, K. M., MSc Punjab, PhD Leeds Prof.
Choudhry, A. H., MSc Punjab, MPhil Sheff. Asst. Prof.
Gorsi, M. S., MSc Karachi, MPhil Asst. Prof.
Hussain, T., MSc Pesh. Asst. Prof.
Khattak, T. M., MSc Karachi, MPhil Karachi Asst. Prof.
Malik, Z. H., MPhil Pesh. Asst. Prof.
Rehman, S., MSc Punjab Asst. Prof.

Business
Tel: (058) 2972
Arashad, M., MSc Faisalabad, MPhil Faisalabad Asst. Prof.
Chaudhary, M. A., MPA Gomal Asst. Prof.
Chaudhary, M. S., MBA Gomal Asst. Prof.
Ghous, G., MSc Multan Asst. Prof.
Hussain, S., MSc Karachi Asst. Prof.
Khan, M. A., MBA Pesh. Asst. Prof.
Malik, A. D., MA Punjab Assoc. Prof.
Malik, M. A., MA Manc., MLitt Assoc. Prof.
Sheikh, S. A., MAS Karachi Assoc. Prof.

Chemistry
Tel: (058) 2301
Aziz, K. A., MSc Punjab Asst. Prof.
Khan, M. H., MSc Punjab, PhD Punjab Asst. Prof.
Rehman, H., MSc Karachi, PhD Karachi Assoc. Prof.
Tahir, M. K., PhD Stockholm Prof.
Tahir, M. M. K., MSc Queb. Asst. Prof.

Computer Centre
Tel: (058) 4107
Khan, M. W., MSc Asst. Prof.

Economics
Tel: (058) 4983
Ali, Khadija, MA Punjab, MS Northeastern Asst. Prof. (on leave)
Altaf, N., MA Queb., MPhil Asst. Prof.
Bhatti, R. H., MA Gomal, PhD Asst. Prof.
Choudhary, M. K., MA Punjab, PhD Salf. Prof. (on deputation)
Khan, M. A., MA Punjab Assoc. Prof.
Qureshi, E., MA Punjab Asst. Prof.

Education, see Teachers' Training and Res., Inst. of (ITTR)

Engineering
Tel: (058) 2612
Ahmad, M. S., PhD Cracow Asst. Prof.
Ahmed, M., MA Punjab Asst. Prof.
Chaudhary, I. A., MSc Punjab Assoc. Prof.
Chaudhary, M. B., MA MPhil Asst. Prof. (on deputation)
Chaudhary, N., BE Newcastle(NSW) Asst. Prof.
Ghous, M., BSc Asst. Prof.
Hussain, Manzoor Asst. Prof.
Hussain, N., BSc Newcastle(UK) Asst. Prof.
Islam, M. K., BSc Azad J&K Asst. Prof.
Khalid, M., MSc Brun. Asst. Prof.

Khalid, M., MSc Faisalabad Asst. Prof.
Mirza, A. G., MSc Punjab Assoc. Prof.
Moghal, M. R., MSc Wayne State Asst. Prof.
Nasrullah, M., MSc Punjab Assoc. Prof.
Qureshi, A. J., BSc Lahore UET Asst. Prof.
Qureshi, M. A., BSc Pesh. Asst. Prof.
Riaz, M., BSc Lahore UET Asst. Prof.
Shabbir, M., BSc Azad J&K Asst. Prof.
Yasmin, Z., MSc Pesh. Asst. Prof.
Zaman, S., BSc Pesh. Asst. Prof. (on leave)

English
Tel: (058) 2523
Akhtar, R. N., MLitt Strath. Asst. Prof. (on leave)
Chaudhary, M. A., MA Punjab Assoc. Prof. (on deputation)
Chaudhary, S. K., MEd Prof. (on deputation)
Gilani, S. I., MA Punjab, MPhil Glas. Assoc. Prof.

Geology
Tel: (058) 3119
Andrabi, B., MSc Asst. Prof.
Ashraf, M., MSc Punjab, PhD Punjab Prof.
Awan, A., MS Purdue, PhD Purdue Assoc. Prof.
Baig, M. S., MSc Punjab, PhD Oregon Asst. Prof.
Jaral, A. W., MSc Punjab Asst. Prof.
Khan, M. A., MSc Karachi, PhD Karachi Asst. Prof.
Khan, M. K., MSc Punjab Asst. Prof.
Khan, M. R., MSc Punjab Asst. Prof.
Khan, M. S., MSc Pesh. Asst. Prof.
Munir, M., MSc Punjab Asst. Prof.
Qureshi, M. A., MSc Punjab Asst. Prof.
Qureshi, Z., MSc Punjab Asst. Prof.
Saeed, Z., MSc Punjab Asst. Prof.
Saleem, M., MSc Punjab Asst. Prof.
Saraf, T. M. Asst. Prof.
Sidiqi, I., MSc Punjab Asst. Prof.

Home Economics
Tel: (058) 3681
Bakshi, R. A., MA Punjab Asst. Prof.
Fatima, K., MSc Quaid-i-Azam Asst. Prof.
Fatima, N., MA Punjab Assoc. Prof.
Jabeen, M., MA Punjab Asst. Prof.
Khanum, R., MSc Quaid-i-Azam Asst. Prof.
Khanum, S., MSc Asst. Prof. (on deputation)
Mehmooda, T., MA MPhil Asst. Prof.
Nayyar, S., MA Punjab Assoc. Prof.
Pervaiz, S., MSc Punjab Asst. Prof. (on deputation)
Rafique, N., MSc Punjab Asst. Prof.
Shah, Saeeda J. A., MA Punjab, MEd Manc. Assoc. Prof.
Yousaf, S., MA Punjab Asst. Prof.

Islamic Studies
Anjum, N., MA Punjab Asst. Prof.
Khaliq, A., PhD Punjab Asst. Prof.
Mehmood, K. M., PhD Punjab Asst. Prof.
Peerzada, H. A., MA Punjab, PhD Leeds Asst. Prof.
Rajorvi, M. S., MA Punjab Assoc. Prof.
Sarfaraz, F., MA Punjab Assoc. Prof.

Kashmir Studies

Tel: (058) 3963

Dar, S., MA Punjab Assoc. Prof.
Gilani, S. T., MA Punjab Assoc. Prof.
Mirza, K. Z., MA Punjab, MPhil Quaid-i-
Azam Prof.

Mathematics

Tel: (058) 3623

Baig, M. S., PhD Ankara Asst. Prof.
Chaudhary, H. A., MSc Punjab Assoc. Prof.
Khalid, H. M., MSc Punjab, MPhil Multan Asst.
Prof.
Khan, A. R., MSc Punjab, PhD Ankara Prof.
Khan Aman Ullah, PhD Kiev Assoc. Prof.
Khan, M. S., MA Quaid-i-Azam Asst. Prof.
Lodhi, T. M., MPhil PhD Asst. Prof.
Qureshi, M. N., MSc Punjab Asst. Prof. (on
leave)
Siddique, M., MSc Punjab, MPhil Assoc. Prof.

Physics

Tel: (058) 2513

Abbasi, G. A., MSc Punjab, MPhil Punjab, PhD
Brun. Asst. Prof.
Habib, S., MSc Punjab Asst. Prof.
Iqbal, A., MSc Pesh., PhD Nott. Assoc. Prof.
Majid, A., MSc Pesh. Asst. Prof.
Rathore, B. A., MSc Punjab, PhD Belgrade Prof.
Satti, J. A., PhD Wayne State Asst. Prof.

Teachers' Training and Research, Institute of (ITTR)

Tel: (058) 162

Jaffari, M. H., MA Punjab Asst. Prof.
Khan, M. S., PhD Karachi Asst. Prof. (on
leave)
Malik, M. A., PhD Pesh. Asst. Prof.

Textile Designing

Tel: (058) 2748

Ali, S. R., MA Pesh. Asst. Prof.
Atta, Saleema, MA Punjab Assoc. Prof.
Khawaja, Z., MA Punjab Asst. Prof.
Kousar, R., MSc Punjab Asst. Prof.
Naqvi, F., MA Punjab Asst. Prof.
Riaz, N., MA Punjab Asst. Prof.
Shazadi, F., MA Punjab Asst. Prof.

Zoology

Tel: (058) 4505

Anwar, K. K., MSc Punjab Asst. Prof.
Chaudhary, B. A., MSc Punjab Asst. Prof.
Khan, K. H., MSc Pesh. Assoc. Prof.
Khan, M. N., MSc Quaid-i-Azam, MPhil Quaid-i-
Azam Asst. Prof.
Malik, M. A., MSc Asst. Prof. (on leave)

Nayyar, A. Q., MSc Punjab Asst. Prof.
Ratyal, A. H., MSc MPhil Asst. Prof. (on
leave)

SPECIAL CENTRES, ETC

Development Studies, Kashmir Institute of

Tel: (058) 4983

Chaudhary, Prof. M. K., PhD Salf. Dir.* (on
deputation)

Geology, Institute of

Tel: (058) 3119

Ashraf, Prof. M., MSc Punjab, PhD Punjab Dir.*

Islamic Studies, Institute of

Mehmood, Prof. K. M., PhD Punjab Dir.*

Kashmir Studies, Institute of

Tel: (058) 3963

Mirza, Prof. Khan Z., MA Punjab, MPhil Quaid-i-
Azam Dir.*

CONTACT OFFICERS

Academic affairs. Assistant Registrar,
Academic: Ahmed, Mushtaq
Academic affairs. Deputy Registrar: Abbasi,
Shabbir A.
Accommodation. Project Director: Durrani,
Muhammad R., BSc NUST(P'stan.)
Accommodation. Provost, Hostels: Khattak,
Taj M., MPhil Pesh.
Admissions (first degree). Deputy Registrar:
Tahir, Abdul Q., MPA Punjab
Admissions (higher degree). Deputy Registrar:
Tahir, Abdul Q., MPA Punjab
Careers. Registrar: Khan, Raja M. A., MA
Punjab, MPhil Quaid-i-Azam
Computing services. Assistant Professor,
Computer Centre: Khan, Muhammad W.,
MSc
Consultancy services. Project Director:
Durrani, Muhammad R., BSc NUST(P'stan.)
Development/fund-raising. Project Director:
Durrani, Muhammad R., BSc NUST(P'stan.)
Equal opportunities. Registrar: Khan, Raja M.
A., MA Punjab, MPhil Quaid-i-Azam
Estates and buildings/works and services.
Project Director: Durrani, Muhammad R.,
BSc NUST(P'stan.)
Estates and buildings/works and services.
Estate Officer: Naqvi, Zawar H., MA Karachi
Examinations. Controller of Examinations:
Khan, Sardar K. H.

Finance. Director of Finance: Khan, Raja A. K.,
MBA Punjab, MS Drexel
General enquiries. Registrar: Khan, Raja M.
A., MA Punjab, MPhil Quaid-i-Azam
Health services. Medical Officer: Haider,
Waqar, MB BS
International office. Deputy Registrar: Tahir,
Abdul Q., MPA Punjab
Library (chief librarian). Chief Librarian:
Yaqoob, Ch. Muhammad, MLS Karachi
Minorities/disadvantaged groups. Registrar:
Khan, Raja M. A., MA Punjab, MPhil Quaid-i-
Azam
Ombudsperson. Deputy Registrar: Tahir,
Abdul Q., MPA Punjab
Personnel/human resources. Registrar: Khan,
Raja M. A., MA Punjab, MPhil Quaid-i-Azam
Public relations, information and marketing.
Deputy Registrar: Tahir, Abdul Q., MPA
Punjab
Publications. Deputy Registrar: Tahir, Abdul
Q., MPA Punjab
Purchasing. Director of Finance: Khan, Raja A.
K., MBA Punjab, MS Drexel
Quality assurance and accreditation. Registrar:
Khan, Raja M. A., MA Punjab, MPhil Quaid-i-
Azam
Research. Director, Institute of Kashmir
Studies: Mirza, Prof. Khan Z., MA Punjab,
MPhil Quaid-i-Azam
Safety. Project Director: Durrani, Muhammad
R., BSc NUST(P'stan.)
Scholarships, awards, loans. Registrar: Khan,
Raja M. A., MA Punjab, MPhil Quaid-i-Azam
Security. Estate Officer: Naqvi, Zawar H., MA
Karachi
Sport and recreation. Director, Sports:
Minhas, Mushtaq A., MSc Gomal
Staff development and training. Registrar:
Khan, Raja M. A., MA Punjab, MPhil Quaid-i-
Azam
Student union. Director, Students' Affairs:
Qureshi, Zaheer-Ud-Din, MA Punjab
Student welfare/counselling. Director,
Students' Affairs: Qureshi, Zaheer-Ud-Din,
MA Punjab
Students from other countries. Deputy
Registrar: Tahir, Abdul Q., MPA Punjab
Students with disabilities. Deputy Registrar:
Tahir, Abdul Q., MPA Punjab
Students with disabilities. Director, Students'
Affairs: Qureshi, Zaheer-Ud-Din, MA Punjab
Women. Registrar: Khan, Raja M. A., MA
Punjab, MPhil Quaid-i-Azam

[Information supplied by the institution as at 13 January
1996, and edited by the ACU]

BAHAUDDIN ZAKARIYA UNIVERSITY

Founded 1975 as University of Multan; present name adopted 1979

Member of the Association of Commonwealth Universities

Postal Address: Multan, Punjab, Pakistan 60800
Telephone: (061) 224371-4 **Fax**: (061) 220091, 520303 **E-mail**: registrar@zakuniv.bzu.nahe.unet
Cables: Univzakariya Multan

CHANCELLOR—The Governor of the Punjab (*ex officio*)
PRO-CHANCELLOR—Dhillon, Brig. (Retd.) Zulifiqar A.
VICE-CHANCELLOR*—Durrani, Prof. Ashiq M. K., MA *Punjab*, PhD
B.Zak.
REGISTRAR—Malik, Zain A., LLB *Punjab*, MA *Punjab*
TREASURER—Abbas, Tahir, PhD

GENERAL INFORMATION

History. The university was established in 1975 as the University of Multan; the present name was adopted in 1979. It has 72 affiliated colleges.

The university campus is located about 9km from the centre of the city of Multan.

First Degrees. BA, BSc.

Higher Degrees. LLB, MA, MBA, MCom, MSc, MPhil, PhD.

Language of Instruction. English and Urdu.

Libraries. 100,000 volumes.

Fees (1997–98). Day programmes: Rs2960 (MA part I); Rs2995 (LLB part I); Rs3435 (MSc part II); Rs3570 (MSc in computer science, first semester); Rs805 (MSc in computer science, second semester); Rs5225 (MBA). Evening programmes: Rs13,445 (MCom, first semester); Rs10,580 (MCom, second semester); Rs15,875 (MA part I); Rs16,175 (MA in education part I).

Income (1997–98). Total, Rs81,313,599.

Statistics (1997–98). Students: 4212 (2833 men, 1379 women).

FACULTIES/SCHOOLS

Arts and Social Sciences
Dean: Chaudhry, Prof. Ghulam M., LLB *Punjab*, MA *Punjab*, PhD *S.Carolina*

Commerce, Law and Business Administration
Dean: Awan, Prof. Hayat M., MSc *Kerala*, MBA *Edin.*, PhD *Tor.*

Islamic Studies and Languages
Dean: Chaudhry, Prof. Abdul H., MA *Punjab*, PhD *Berlin*

Medicine and Dentistry
Dean: Nasir, Prof. Shabbir A., MB BS *Punjab*, FRCPEd

Pharmacy
Dean: Khan, Prof. Muhammad Afzal, MSc *Brun.*, PhD *Brun.*

Science, Engineering and Agriculture
Dean: Rauf, Prof. Abdur, MSc *Birm.*, PhD *Birm.*

ACADEMIC UNITS

Agriculture, see University College of Agriculture

Arabic
Tel: (061) 220096
Chaudhry, Muhammad A., PhD *Glas.*, MA Prof.
Shah, Muhammad H., PhD Assoc. Prof.
Sialivi, Muhammad S., MA PhD Assoc. Prof.; Chairman*

Ullah, Muhammad S., MA PhD Asst. Prof.
Other Staff: 3 Lectrs.

Biology, Pure and Applied, see Special Centres, etc

Business Administration
Tel: (061) 220139
Ali, Mujahid, MBA *Punjab* Assoc. Prof.
Awan, Hayat M., MSc *Kerala*, MBA *Edin.*, PhD *Tor.* Prof.
Bodla, Mahmood A., MBA *Wayne State*, PhD *Wayne State* Asst. Prof.
Muhammad, Ghulam, MBA *Gomal* Asst. Prof.
Qureshi, Muhammad A., MBA Asst. Prof.
Zafarullah, Muhammad, PhD *Strath.*, MBA Prof.; Chairman*
Other Staff: 12 Lectrs.

Chemistry
Tel: (061) 220088
Arif, Muhammad, MSc *Lond.*, PhD *Lond.* Assoc. Prof.
Hafeez, Samia, MSc Asst. Prof.
Ikram, Naheed, MSc *Punjab* Asst. Prof.
Iqbal, Muhammad, PhD Prof.
Khokhar, Muhammad Y., MPhil *Quaid-i-Azam*, MSc PhD Assoc. Prof.
Malana, Muhammad A., PhD *Lond.* MSc Assoc. Prof.
Niazi, Shahida B., MSc *Lond.*, PhD *Lond.* Prof.
Perveen, Riffat, MSc *Lond.*, PhD *Lond.* Assoc. Prof.
Pervez, Humayun, MSc *Strath.*, PhD *Strath.* Prof.
Rauf, Abdur, MSc *Birm.*, PhD *Birm.* Prof.; Chairman*
Shad, Muhammad A., MSc Asst. Prof.
Other Staff: 4 Lectrs.

Commerce
Tel: (061) 220170
Awan, Hayat M., MSc *Kerala*, MBA *Edin.*, PhD *Tor.* Prof.
Malik, Ghulam M., MBA Asst. Prof.; Teacher-in-Charge*

Computer Science
Tel: (061) 220170
Akhter, M. Aziz, MSc Asst. Prof.
Khan, Aman U., MSc PhD Assoc. Prof.; Chairman*
Other Staff: 4 Lectrs.

Economics
Tel: (061) 220135
Ahmed, Mushtaq, MA *Wales*, PhD *Wales* Assoc. Prof.
Ali, Karamat, MA *Vanderbilt*, PhD *Vanderbilt* Prof.
Azid, Toseef, MA *Quaid-i-Azam*, PhD Assoc. Prof.
Chaudhry, Abdul H., MA *Punjab*, PhD *Berlin* Prof.; Chairman*
Hussain, Syed A., MA *Punjab*, MA *Manc.*, PhD Asst. Prof.
Malik, Shah N., MSc *Hull*, DPhil Assoc. Prof.
Other Staff: 5 Lectrs.

Education
Tel: (061) 220146
Malik, Ali A., MA *New Mexico*, PhD *New Mexico* Asst. Prof.
Perveen, Mumtaz, MA Asst. Prof.
Shah, Ahmad F., PhD Assoc. Prof.; Chairman*
Shah, Jamil H., MSc *Quaid-i-Azam*, MPhil *Quaid-i-Azam*, MEd *Karachi* Asst. Prof.
Tariq, Riaz-ul-Haq, MSc *E.Anglia*, PhD *E.Anglia* Assoc. Prof.
Yousaf, Muhammad, PhD Asst. Prof.
Other Staff: 2 Lectrs.

English
Tel: (061) 220143
Asif, Saiqa I., MA MSc Asst. Prof.
Iqbal, Zafar, PhD Assoc. Prof.; Chairman*
Qadir, Samina A., MA *Wales*, PhD Asst. Prof.
Tallat, Mubina, MA *Nott.*, MPhil *Nott.* Asst. Prof.
Yousaf, Farida, MA *Punjab* Asst. Prof.
Zubair, Shirin, MA *Wales*, MSc Asst. Prof.
Other Staff: 2 Lectrs.

History
Tel: (061) 220098
Asghar, Azra, PhD Asst. Prof.
Dasti, Humaira F., MA PhD Asst. Prof.
Khan, Abdul R., MA *Lond.*, PhD *Lond.* Assoc. Prof.; Chairman*
Qadir, Khurram, MA PhD Assoc. Prof.
Qalb-i-Abid, S., MA *Leeds*, PhD *Leeds* Assoc. Prof.

Islamic Studies
Tel: (061) 220096
Jami, Noor-ud-Din, LLB MA PhD Assoc. Prof.; Chairman*
Khan, Muhammad B., PhD Asst. Prof.
Rana, Muhammad A., PhD *St And.*, MA Asst. Prof.
Saeed-ur-Rehman, MA PhD Asst. Prof.
Saleemi, Ali A., MA *Islamia, Bahawal.*, LLB Asst. Prof.
Other Staff: 2 Lectrs.

Mass Communication
Tel: (061) 220092
Khalid, Muhammad, MA *Berlin*, PhD *Berlin* Asst. Prof.
Malik, Karim, MA PhD Asst. Prof.; Teacher-in-Charge*
Other Staff: 2 Lectrs.

Materials Science
Tel: (061) 220087
Abbas, Tahir, MSc *Moscow*, PhD *Moscow* Prof.; Chairman*
Ansari, M. Iqbal, MSc PhD Prof.
Rana, Mazhar-ud-Din, MSc *Wayne State*, MSEE Asst. Prof.
Other Staff: 2 Lectrs.

Mathematics, Pure and Applied, see
Special Centres, etc

Pakistan Studies

Tel: (061) 220098

Sohail, Musarrat, PhD   Assoc. Prof.;
Chairperson*
Other Staff: 3 Lectrs.

Pharmacy

Tel: (061) 220157

Ahmad, Bashir, PhD   Assoc. Prof.
Ahmad, Maqsood, PhD   Asst. Prof.
Ansari, M. Tayyab, MSc *Hangzhou*, PhD
Hangzhou   Asst. Prof.
Farzana, Kalsoom, MPharmacy *Punjab*,
MPhil   Asst. Prof.
Ijaz, Abdul S., MSc PhD   Assoc. Prof.
Iqbal, Muhammad, MPharmacy *Punjab*,
MPhil   Asst. Prof.
Jafri, Syed H. A., BPharm *Karachi*, MSc
Karachi   Asst. Prof.
Janbaz, Khalid H., PhD   Asst. Prof.
Khan, Muhammad Afzal, MSc *Brun.*, PhD
Brun.   Prof.
Mahboob-e-Rabbani, MPharm *Lond.*, PhD
Lond.   Assoc. Prof.; Chairman*
Razi, Muhammad T., MSc *Lond.*, PhD
Lond.   Assoc. Prof.
Zabta, Muhammad, PhD   Assoc. Prof.
Other Staff: 3 Lectrs.

Physics

Tel: (061) 220092

Ahmad, Ejaz, PhD   Asst. Prof.
Ahmad, Ishtiaq, PhD   Asst. Prof.
Arif, M. Zakariya, MSc *Wales*, PhD *Wales*   Prof.
Bhatti, Muhammad T., MSc PhD   Asst. Prof.
Chaudhry, Muhammad A., MSc PhD   Prof.
Nadeem, Muhammad Y., MSc *Lond.*, PhD
Lond.   Assoc. Prof.
Saleh, Muhammad, MSc *Lond.*, PhD
Lond.   Prof.; Chairman*
Sheikh, Zahoor A., MSc *Punjab*, PhD   Assoc.
Prof.
Other Staff: 3 Lectrs.

Political Science and International Affairs

Tel: (061) 220094

Akhtar, Shahnaz, MA   Asst. Prof.
Chaudhry, Ghulam M., LLB *Punjab*, MA *Punjab*,
PhD *S.Carolina*   Prof.
Chaudhry, Ishtiaq A., PhD   Assoc. Prof.;
Chairman*
Hussain, Fayyaz A., MA *Lond.*, MPhil
Lond.   Asst. Prof.
Hussain, S. Ahmad-ud-Din, MA *Karachi*, MPhil
Karachi, PhD   Asst. Prof.
Rana, Ayyaz M., MA *Punjab*   Asst. Prof.
Other Staff: 2 Lectrs.

Statistics

Tel: (061) 220131

Akram, Muhammad, MSc   Asst. Prof.
Iqbal, Ejaz, MSc *Kent*, PhD *Kent*   Assoc. Prof.
Mahmud, Zafar, MSc *Wales*, PhD *Wales*   Assoc.
Prof.
Pasha, Ghulam R., MSc *Warw.*, PhD
Warw.   Chairman*
Wajid, Rana A., MSc *S'ton.*, PhD   Asst. Prof.
Other Staff: 4 Lectrs.

Urdu

Tel: (061) 220136

Ahmad, Anwar, MA PhD   Prof.
Bukhari, Alamdar H., MA   Asst. Prof.
Kausar, Abdul R., PhD   Prof.
Najeeb-ud-Din, MA PhD   Assoc. Prof.
Tareen, Rubina, MA PhD   Assoc. Prof.;
Chairperson*
Other Staff: 3 Lectrs.

SPECIAL CENTRES, ETC

Pure and Applied Biology, Institute of

Botany

Tel: (061) 220134

Ashraf, Muhammad, MSc *Liv.*, PhD *Liv.*   Assoc.
Prof.
Malik, Saeed A., MSc *Punjab*, PhD *Punjab*   Assoc.
Prof.
Mirza, Javed I., MSc *Aberd.*, PhD *Aberd.*   Assoc.
Prof.
Rana, Saeed A., MSc *Lond.*, PhD *Lond.*   Assoc.
Prof.
Other Staff: 2 Lectrs.

Zoology

Tel: (061) 220134

Khan, Tasawar H., MSc *Punjab*   Asst. Prof.
Mian, Afsar, MSc *Punjab*, PhD   Assoc. Prof.
Salam, Abdus, MSc *Nott.*, PhD *Nott.*   Assoc.
Prof.; Dir.*
Other Staff: 4 Lectrs.

Pure and Applied Mathematics, Centre for Advanced Studies in

Tel: (061) 220164

Ahmad, Bashir, DSc *Ghent*, MSc   Prof.; Dir.*
Akram, Zahida, PhD   Asst. Prof.
Butt, Rizwan A., MSc *Leeds*, PhD *Leeds*   Asst.
Prof.
Chaudhry, Muhammad A., DSc *Kyushu*,
MSc   Prof.
Kamal, Muhammad A., MSc *W.Ont.*, PhD
W.Ont.   Prof.
Khan, Abdul R., MSc *Wales*, PhD *Wales*   Prof.
Khan, Khizar H., PhD   Asst. Prof.
Mir, Nazir A., MSc *Hamburg*, PhD
Hamburg   Prof.
Siddique, Akhlaq A., PhD   Asst. Prof.
Sultana, Nazra, MSc *Wales*, PhD *Wales*   Asst.
Prof.
Yasmin, Nusrat, PhD   Asst. Prof.
Other Staff: 4 Lectrs.

UNIVERSITY COLLEGE OF AGRICULTURE

Constituent College

Abid, Muhammad, MSc   Asst. Prof.
Ali, Asghar, MSc DPhil   Prof.; Principal*
Anjum, Muhammad A., PhD   Asst. Prof.
Aslam, Muhammad, MSc *Faisalabad*, PhD
Beirut   Assoc. Prof.
Daud, Rana K., MSc   Asst. Prof.
Khan, Muhammad B., MSc *Faisalabad*   Asst.
Prof.
Mahmood, Abid, PhD   Asst. Prof.
Other Staff: 13 Lectrs.

UNIVERSITY COLLEGE OF ENGINEERING AND TECHNOLOGY

Constituent College

Tel: (061) 220089

Civil Engineering

Jillani, Ghulam, BSc   Asst. Prof.
Malik, Akhtar A., MSc PhD   Asst. Prof.;
Teacher-in-Charge*
Other Staff: 6 Lectrs.

Electrical Engineering

2 Lectrs.

Mechanical Engineering

1 Lectr.

UNIVERSITY GILLANI LAW COLLEGE

Constituent College

Tel: (061) 75692

Hanif, Ch. Muhammad, LLB *Baloch.*, MA
LLM   Asst. Prof.
Qureshi, Inam B., LLB *Karachi*, BA   Asst. Prof.
Rashid, Abdur, PhD   Prof.; Principal*
Sheikh, Muhammad S., BA LLB   Asst. Prof.
Other Staff: 3 Lectrs.

CONTACT OFFICERS

Academic affairs. Registrar: Malik, Zain A.,
LLB *Punjab*, MA *Punjab*
Accommodation. In-Charge, Guest House:
Iqbal, Ejaz, MSc PhD
Accommodation. Warden, Girls' Hostel: Ejaz,
Abdul S.
Accommodation. Warden, Boys' Hostel:
Kamal, Prof. Muhammad A., MSc PhD
Admissions (first degree). Registrar: Malik,
Zain A., LLB *Punjab*, MA *Punjab*
Admissions (first degree). Chairman,
Admissions Committee: Rauf, Prof. Abdul,
MSc *Punjab*, PhD *Birm.*
Admissions (higher degree). Registrar: Malik,
Zain A., LLB *Punjab*, MA *Punjab*
Admissions (higher degree). Chairman,
Admissions Committee: Rauf, Prof. Abdul,
MSc *Punjab*, PhD *Birm.*
Computing services. Chairman, Department of
Computer Science: Khan, Aman U., MSc
PhD
Consultancy services. Director, Student Affairs:
Sheikh, Zahoor A., MSc PhD
Estates and buildings/works and services.
Project Director: Ahmad, Mian A., BScEngg
Estates and buildings/works and services.
University Engineer: Sahu, Aftab A.
Examinations. Controller of Examinations:
Shafique, Chaudhry M., BA
Finance. Treasurer: Abbas, Tahir, PhD
General enquiries. Registrar: Malik, Zain A.,
LLB *Punjab*, MA *Punjab*
Health services. Medical Officer: Warraich,
Aftab S., MB BS
Health services. Medical Officer (Women):
Wasim, Samina, MB BS
Library (chief librarian). Librarian: Ahmad,
C. Maqbool, MA LLB
Public relations, information and marketing.
In-Charge, Public Relations and Publications:
Malik, Karim, MA PhD
Publications. In-Charge, Public Relations and
Publications: Malik, Karim, MA PhD
Purchasing. Treasurer: Abbas, Tahir, PhD
Research. Chairman, Research Planners' Group:
Kamal, Prof. Muhammad A., MSc PhD
Safety. Resident Officer: Hussain, Malik M.
Scholarships, awards, loans. Treasurer: Abbas,
Tahir, PhD
Security. Security Officer: Gill, Muhammad Y.
Sport and recreation. Director (acting), Sports:
Khan, Zafar M., MA
Sport and recreation. Assistant Directress,
Sports: Masood, Salma, MA
Students from other countries. In-Charge,
Foreign Students: Sheikh, Zahoor A., MSc
PhD

CONSTITUENT COLLEGE HEADS

University College of Agriculture. Principal:
Ali, Prof. Asghar, MSc DPhil
**University College of Engineering and
Technology**. (Tel: (061) 220089.) Teacher-
in-Charge: Malik, Akhtar A., MSc PhD
University Gillani Law College. Principal:
Rashid, Prof. Abdur, PhD

AFFILIATED COLLEGES

[Institutions listed by location below provide
courses leading to degrees, etc. of the
university]

Abdul Hakim. Government College
Alipur. Government College

Arifwala. Government College; Government College for Women

Burewala. Government College; Government College for Women

Chichwatani. Government College; Government College for Women

Dera Ghazi Khan. Citi College of Commerce; Government College; Government College for Women; Government College of Commerce; Government College of Education; Indus Law College

Jampur. Government College; Government College for Women

Kabirwala. Government College for Women

Karoor. Government College; Government College for Women

Khenawal. Government College for Women; Government Islamia College

Kot Adu. Government College; Government College for Women

Layyah. Government College; Government College for Women

Lodhran. Government Degree College; Government Degree College for Women

Malsi. Government College; Government College for Women

Mian Channu. Government College; Government College for Women; Islamia Girls' College

Multan. Allama Iqbal College of Commerce; Central Degree College; Central Law College; Government Alamdar Hussain Islamia College; Government College (Bosan Road); Government College (Civil Lines); Government College for Women; Government College of Commerce; Government College of Education; Government College of Science; Government W. H. Islamia College; International College of Commerce; Multan College of Commerce; Multan Law College; Musa Pak Shaheed Law College; N. F. C. College of Engineering; National College; Nishtar Medical College; Petromen Degree College

Multan Cantt.. F. G. College for Women

Mumtazabad. Government College for Women

Muzaffar Garh. Government College; Government College for Women

New Multan. Zakariya College of Commerce

Pakpattan. Government College for Women; Government Farida College

Rajan Pur. Government College; Government College for Women

Sahiwal. College of Advanced Science and Technology; Government College; Government College for Women; Government College of Commerce; Government Imamia College; Hi-Career College of Commerce; Multan Law College

Shujabad. Government College

Tounsa. Government College; Government College for Women

Vehari. Government College; Government College for Women

[Information supplied by the institution as at 11 September 1998, and edited by the ACU]

UNIVERSITY OF BALOCHISTAN

Founded 1970

Member of the Association of Commonwealth Universities

Postal Address: Sariab Road, Quetta, Balochistan, Pakistan
Telephone: (081) 440431 **Cables**: Balochistan University Quetta

CHANCELLOR—The Governor of the Province of Balochistan (ex officio)
VICE-CHANCELLOR*—Riaz Baloch, D. K., MB BS
REGISTRAR—Bugti, Muhammad K.
TREASURER—Khan, Attaullah
DIRECTOR GENERAL (PLANNING)—Kasi, Amir M. K.
LIBRARIAN—Shahwani, Ghulam M.

FACULTIES/SCHOOLS

Science
Dean: Hassan, Prof. Naeem M., MSc Sindh, PhD Lond.

ACADEMIC UNITS

Administrative Science
Ali, Barkat, MBA Karachi   Asst. Prof.

Biochemistry Institute
Azam, Mohammad   Asst. Prof.
Khan, Abbas H., MSc Punjab, PhD Hull   Prof.
Malghani, M. A. K., MSc Baloch., PhD   Asst. Prof.; Head*
Masoom, Mohammad, MSc Baloch., PhD Hull   Prof.
Mehmood, Zahid, MSc Baloch.   Asst. Prof.
Nasir-ud-Din, PhD Edin.   Dir.
Sultana, Fouzia, MSc Baloch.   Asst. Prof.

Botany
Asghar, Rehana, MSc Baloch.   Asst. Prof.
Asrar, Mudasir, MSc Karachi, MPhil Baloch.   Assoc. Prof.
Bakhsh, Rasool, MSc Karachi, MPhil Baloch.   Assoc. Prof.
Jan, Mufakhara, MSc Baloch., MPhil Baloch.   Asst. Prof.
Kayani, Safdar A., MSc Punjab, PhD Punjab   Prof.; Chairman*
Khan, Abdul K., MSc Baloch.   Asst. Prof.
Saeed-ur-Rehan, MSc Baloch.   Museum Curator

Chemistry
Akbar, Sher, MSc Punjab, PhD Brad.   Prof.
Anwar, Mohammad, MSc Baloch.   Asst. Prof.
Hamid-ul-Qadir, M., MSc Agra, PhD Birm.   Prof.
Hassan, Naeem M., MSc Sindh, PhD Edin..   Prof.; Chairman*
Hussain, Syed A., MSc Sindh, PhD Lond.   Prof. (on deputation)
Khan, Abdullah, MSc Baloch., PhD St And.   Assoc. Prof.
Khatoon, Sabia, MSc Baloch.   Asst. Prof.
Nabi, Abdul, MSc Baloch., PhD Hull   Assoc. Prof.
Qureshi, Mohammad H., MSc Baloch.   Asst. Prof.
Rashid, Rehana, MSc Baloch., PhD Wittenberg   Assoc. Prof.
Siddiqui, Hamid L., MSc Baloch., PhD   Asst. Prof.
Zamir, Talat, MSc Baloch.   Asst. Prof.

Commerce
Jamil, Mohammad, MCom Karachi   Asst. Prof.; Chairman*
Lateef, Abdul, MSc Baloch.   Asst. Prof.
Rashid, Abdul, MA Baloch.   Asst. Prof.
Zafar, Qamar, MA Baloch.   Assoc. Prof.

Computer Science
Nasir, Sher M.   Asst. Prof.; Chairman*

Economics
Akhtar, Tousif, MA Karachi, MSc Karachi   Asst. Prof.
Arif, Syed M., MA Baloch., MSc   Assoc. Prof. (on deputation)
Jamil, Mohammad, MA Baloch., PhD Dund.   Asst. Prof.; Chairman*
Khan, Badrul I., MA Baloch.   Asst. Prof.
Khan, Fazal M., MA Baloch.   Asst. Prof.

Education
Ahmed, Ejaz, MEd Punjab   Asst. Prof.
Bakhsh, Rasool, MEd Baloch., PhD   Asst. Prof. (on leave)
Khawaja, Iftikhar-ud-Din, MScE Livingston, EdD Virginia   Prof.; Chairman*
Mujahid, Abdul S., MEd Punjab   Asst. Prof.
Qaisrani, Naseem, MEd Punjab, PhD   Assoc. Prof.

English
Ali, Liaquat, MA Baloch.   Asst. Prof.
Aurangzab, Farkhanda, MA Punjab   Asst. Prof.
Khan, Abdullah, MA Karachi, MA   Asst. Prof.; Chairman*

English Language Centre
Jaffar, Salma M., MA Baloch.   Asst. Prof.

Fine Arts
Dost, Mohammad A.   Lectr.; Chairman*

Geography
Ahmed, Qazi S., MA Chic., PhD Chic.   Prof.; Chairman* (on contract)

Nawaz, Mohammad, MSc *Pesh.*   Asst. Prof.

Geology

Jan, Mohammad R., MSc *Baloch.*   Museum Curator
Khan, Hassan, MSc *Baloch.*   Asst. Prof.
Mohammad, Akhtar, MSc *Baloch.*, PhD *St And.*   Prof.
Nabi, Ghulam, MSc *Baloch.*   Asst. Prof.; Chairman*
Niamatullah, MSc *Baloch.*, PhD *Keele*   Assoc. Prof.
Salam, Abdul, MSc *Baloch.*   Asst. Prof.
Siddiqui, Shameem A., MSc *Karachi*   Asst. Prof. (on leave)

History

Balochistan, Munir A., MA *Karachi*, PhD   Asst. Prof.; Chairman*
Shah, S. Abdul W., MA *Sindh*   Asst. Prof.

International Relations

Chughtai, Zulfiqar A.   Asst. Prof.
Salahuddin Ahmed, S., MA *Karachi*, PhD *Nigeria*   Prof.; Chairman*

Islamic Studies

Dishteri, Ghulam H., MA *Karachi*   Asst. Prof.
Jaffar, Ghulam M., MA *Baloch.*, PhD   Asst. Prof.
Rehman, Moulana A., MA *Karachi*   Asst. Prof.; Chairman*
Shahin, Mohammad A., MA *Baloch.*   Asst. Prof.

Languages

Abid, Syed A. S.   Assoc. Prof.
Kakar, Wali M. S.   Assoc. Prof.
Khan, Mir A.   Assoc. Prof.
Panezai, Nazar M.   Asst. Prof.
Qambrani, Nadir   Assoc. Prof.
Sabir, Abdul R.   Asst. Prof.
Sana, Zeenat   Asst. Prof.

Library Science

Akhtar, Kurshid, MLS *Punjab*   Asst. Prof.
Jamali, Mir H., MLS *Karachi*   Assoc. Prof.; Chairman*

Mass Communication

Raja, Suleman, MA   Asst. Prof.
Tahir, Seemi N., MA *Karachi*   Asst. Prof.; Chairperson*

Mathematics

Akram, Mohammad, MSc *Islam.*   Asst. Prof.
Hussain, Imdad, MSc *Punjab*, PhD *Dund.*   Prof.; Chairman*
Kamal, Lala R., MSc *Islam.*, PhD   Asst. Prof.

Pharmacy

Bukhari, Syeda I., MPharm *Karachi*   Asst. Prof.
Hussain, Izhar, MSc *Baloch.*, PhD   Asst. Prof.; Chairman*
Kausar, Perveen, MSc *Karachi*   Asst. Prof.
Malik, Bushra, MSc *Punjab*   Asst. Prof.

Philosophy

Khan, Hamid H., MA *Karachi*   Asst. Prof.; Chairman*

Physics

Ahmed, Ashfaq, MSc *Baloch.*, PhD *Lond.*   Assoc. Prof.
Asghar, Mohammad, MSc *Punjab*   Asst. Prof.
Farooqi, Naeem, MSc *Baloch.*   Assoc. Prof.
Fazal-ur-Rehman, MSc *Karachi*, MPhil *Islam.*   Asst. Prof.
Illyas, Zafar   Asst. Prof.
Mohsin Raza, S., MSc *Baloch.*, PhD *Brun.*   Prof.; Chairman*
Nasir, Sher M., MSc *Baloch.*   Asst. Prof.
Usmani, Sabir H., MSc *Punjab*, PhD   Assoc. Prof.

Political Science

Bakht, Nadir, MA *Punjab*   Assoc. Prof.
Iqbal, Naheed, MA *Punjab*   Asst. Prof.
Kandi, Mansoor A., MA *Pesh.*   Assoc. Prof.; Chairman*
Shah, Mehmood A., LLB *Karachi*, MA *Karachi*, PhD *Karachi*   Prof.

Psychology

Firdus, Neelam, MSc *Punjab*   Lectr.; Chairperson*

Social Work

Hussain, Atiq, MA *Sindh*   Asst. Prof.
Rizvi, Maqsood H., MA *Dacca*   Assoc. Prof.; Chairman*
Siddiqui, Ghias-ud-Din, MA *Karachi*   Asst. Prof.

Sociology

Achakzai, Ghulam N., MA *Karachi*, MPhil *Baloch.*   Prof.; Chairman*

Jahangir, Arbab M., MA *Karachi*, PhD *Karachi*   Asst. Prof.
Raza, Mah G., MA *Baloch.*   Asst. Prof.
Sharani, Saif-ur-Rehman, MA *Punjab*, PhD *Kent*   Asst. Prof.

Statistics

Ahmed, Zahoor, MSc *Baloch.*   Asst. Prof.
Iqbal, Mohammad, MSc *Baloch.*   Asst. Prof.
Sajjed, Mohammed N., MSc *Karachi*   Asst. Prof.; Chairman*
Zohra, Yasmeen, MSc *Baloch.*   Asst. Prof.

Urdu

Ahmed, Farooq, MA *Baloch.*   Assoc. Prof.
Khaliq, Abdul, MA *Baloch.*, MPhil *Baloch.*   Asst. Prof.
Nasir, Agha M., MSc *Baloch.*   Asst. Prof.
Qazi, Firdus A., MA *Karachi*, PhD *Baloch.*   Prof.; Chairperson*

Zoology

Ahmed, Zahoor   Museum Curator
Bano, Shaher, MSc *Karachi*, MPhil *Baloch.*   Asst. Prof.
Mushtaq, Rehana, MSc *Islam.*   Asst. Prof.
Nawaz, Mohammad, MSc *Pesh.*   Prof.; Chairman*
Nawaz, Yasmin, MSc *Karachi*, MPhil *Baloch.*   Asst. Prof.

UNIVERSITY LAW COLLEGE, QUETTA

Constituent College

3 Lectrs.

CONTACT OFFICERS

General enquiries. Registrar: Bugti, Muhammad K.

CAMPUS/COLLEGE HEADS

University Law College, Quetta. Principal: Aurangzaib, Mir

[Information supplied by the institution as at 17 December 1995, and edited by the ACU]

BALOCHISTAN UNIVERSITY OF ENGINEERING AND TECHNOLOGY

Founded 1994

Postal Address: Khuzdar, Balochistan, Pakistan
Telephone: (0871) 412524

VICE-CHANCELLOR*—Anwar-ul-Haq, Col. (Retd.) Mirza
REGISTRAR‡—......

BAQAI MEDICAL UNIVERSITY

Founded 1996

Postal Address: 51 Deh Tor, Gadap Road, Super Highway, PO Box 2407, Karachi 74600, Pakistan
Telephone: (021) 75319 **Fax**: (021) 661 7968

VICE-CHANCELLOR*—Ahmad, Lt.-Gen. (Retd.) Prof. Syed A.
REGISTRAR‡—Sabir Ali, Prof. Syed

UNIVERSITY OF ENGINEERING AND TECHNOLOGY, LAHORE

Established 1961

Member of the Association of Commonwealth Universities

Postal Address: Grand Trunk Road, Lahore 54890, Pakistan
Telephone: (042) 682 2012, 339205 **Fax**: (042) 682 2566 **Cables**: Univengtech, Lahore 31

CHANCELLOR—The Governor of Punjab (*ex officio*)
VICE-CHANCELLOR*—Khan, Lt.-Gen. (Retd.) Muhammad A., MSc
PRO-VICE-CHANCELLOR—Akhtar, Prof. Shaheen, PhD *Manc.*, MScEngg
REGISTRAR—Shah, Zulfiqar A., BA *Punjab*
TREASURER—Aslam, M., MA *Punjab*
LIBRARIAN—Ahmad, Muzaffar, MA *Punjab*

FACULTIES/SCHOOLS

Architecture and Planning
Tel: (042) 339250
Dean: Mahmood, Prof. S., MSc *H.-W.*, PhD *Edin.*

Chemical, Mineral and Metallurgical Engineering
Tel: (042) 339230
Dean: Khan, Prof. A. G., MScEngg

Civil Engineering
Tel: (042) 339222
Dean: Sheikh, Prof. A. S., BSEngg *Asian I.T.,Bangkok*, MEngg *Asian I.T.,Bangkok*

Electrical Engineering
Tel: (042) 339234
Dean: Durrani, Prof. K. E., MScEngg, PhD

Mechanical Engineering
Tel: (042) 339221
Dean: Zuberi, Prof. M. U. H., MScEngg

Natural Sciences, Humanities and Islamic Studies
Dean: Amjad, Prof. M., MSc *Punjab*, PhD, FRSChem

ACADEMIC UNITS

Architecture
Tel: (042) 339223
Ahmad, T., BArch   Asst. Prof.
Akbar, S., BArch PhD   Assoc. Prof.
Arshad, M., BArch   Asst. Prof.
Awan, M. Y., BArch   Assoc. Prof.
Butt, A. Q., MSc *Asian I.T.,Bangkok*, PhD *Lond.*, BSc BArch   Asst. Prof.
Gelani, I. A. S., MSc *Asian I.T., Bangkok*, BArch   Prof.
Hussain, Mahmood, BArch *Lahore UET*, PhD *Sheff.*   Prof.; Chairman*

Jamal, S., BArch   Asst. Prof.
Mahmood, S., MSc *H.-W.*, PhD *Edin.*   Prof.
Malik, R. A., PhD *Sheff.*, BArch   Assoc. Prof.
Mir, N., BArch   Assoc. Prof.
Naz, Neelum, BArch, PhD   Asst. Prof.
Qureshi, Ali I.   Asst. Prof.
Rashid, Wasim, BArch *Lahore UET*, MSc *Strath.*   Asst. Prof.
Rehman, A., PhD   Assoc. Prof. (on leave)
Sheikh, Waqar A., MA *Punjab*   Asst. Prof.

Chemistry
Tel: (042) 339239
Ahmad, M., MSc *Punjab*   Assoc. Prof.
Amjad, M., MSc *Punjab*, PhD, FRSChem   Prof.
Ansari, Zamir A., MSc *Punjab*   Asst. Prof.
Haq, I., MSc *Punjab*, PhD   Assoc. Prof.
Iqbal, Q., BEd *Punjab*, MSc *Punjab*, PhD *Nott.*   Prof.; Chairman*
Tahira, Fazeelat, MSc *Punjab*, PhD *Curtin*   Assoc. Prof.

City and Regional Planning
Tel: (042) 339203
Abbas, G., BSc   Asst. Prof. (on leave)
Bajwa, E. U., PhD *Glas.*, BSc MPhil   Prof.
Farooqi, N. H., BSc   Asst. Prof.
Malik, T. H., PhD *C.England*, BSc   Asst. Prof.
Qamar-ul-Islam, MPhil *Edin.*, MSc, PhD   Prof.
Shabih-ul-Hassan Zaidi, S., MSc *Asian I.T., Bangkok*, PhD   Prof.; Chairman*

Computer Science
Tel: (042) 339260
Ahmad, Malik A., LLB *Punjab*, MSc *Punjab*, MPhil *Punjab*, BSc PhD   Prof.
Akhtar, Y. A., MA *Punjab*, PhD *Belf.*, BSc   Prof.
Asim, M. R., MSc *Punjab*   Asst. Prof. (on leave)
Butt, S., MSc *Punjab*, PhD   Assoc. Prof. (on leave)
Raja, A. K., MA *Punjab*, PhD *Belf.*   Prof.; Chairman*
Samdani, M. Y., MSc *Punjab*   Assoc. Prof.

Engineering, Chemical
Tel: (042) 339288
Ahmad, M. M., PhD *Wales*, BScEngg   Prof.
Aqil, M. R. K., BScEngg *Punjab*, MSc *Punjab*   Assoc. Prof.
Bashir, S., MScEng *Akron*, PhD *Akron*, BScEngg   Asst. Prof.
Feroze, N., MScEngg   Asst. Prof. (on leave)
Hakim, J., MSc *Sheff.*, PhD *Sheff.*   Prof.; Chairman*
Hussain, M., MScEngg   Asst. Prof.
Khan, J. R., MScEngg PhD   Prof.
Mamoor, G. M., BScEngg PhD   Prof.
Mir, M., BScEngg MBA   Asst. Prof. (on leave)
Naqvi, S. H. J., BScEngg   Asst. Prof.
Naveed, S., MScEngg PhD   Assoc. Prof.
Noon, M. Z., PhD *Leeds*, BScEngg   Asst. Prof.
Rasool, S., BScEngg PhD   Assoc. Prof.
Salarya, A. K., MSc *Wales*, PhD *Wales*   Prof.
Saleemi, A. R., PhD   Prof.
Shah Muhammad, BScEngg   Asst. Prof.

Engineering, Civil
Tel: (042) 339202
Ahmad, I., BScEngg   Assoc. Prof.
Akhtar, M. N., BScEngg   Asst. Prof.
Akhtar, S., PhD *Manc.*, MScEngg   Prof.
Akram, M., BScEngg   Asst. Prof.
Ali, M., PhD *Moscow*   Prof.
Ali, M. M., BScEngg MSc   Asst. Prof.
Ali, Z., BScEngg   Asst. Prof. (on leave)
Amer, M., MScEng *Rice*, BSc   Asst. Prof.
Ashraf, M., MSc *Sur.*, PhD *Sur.*   Prof.
Chaudhry, M. Y., MSc   Prof.
Chishti, F. A., BScEngg *Asian I.T., Bangkok*, MEngg *Asian I.T., Bangkok*   Prof.; Chairman*
Chishti, S., BScEngg   Asst. Prof.
Ilyas, M., BScEngg PhD   Assoc. Prof.
Javed, M. A., BScEngg MSc   Assoc. Prof.
Khalifa, W., MSc *Tor.*, BScEngg PhD   Assoc. Prof.
Khan, S. B., BScEngg   Assoc. Prof. (on leave)
Mian, Z., MSc *Sur.*, MSc *Lahore UET*   Prof.

Qayyum, T. I., BScEngg MSc Asst. Prof. (on leave)
Qureshi, M. S., MScEngg Prof.
Rahman, Habib, MScEngg
Rasul, J., BSc Assoc. Prof.
Rehman, A., MSc Assoc. Prof.
Rizwan, S. A., MSc Sur. Prof.
Saleem, Imran, MScEngg
Shaheen, A. G., BSc Asst. Prof. (on leave)
Shakir, A. S., BScEngg PhD Assoc. Prof.
Shami, H. I., BScEngg Asst. Prof. (on leave)
Sheikh, A. S., BScEngg Asian I.T., Bangkok, MEngg Asian I.T., Bangkok Prof.
Siddiqi, Jamal ur Rehman, MScEngg Lahore UET Asst. Prof.
Siddiqui, Z. A., BScEngg Asst. Prof.
Tahir, M. A., BScEngg MSc Assoc. Prof. (on leave)

Engineering, Electrical

Tel: (042) 339229

Ahmad, M., MScEngg Texas, BScEngg Asst. Prof.
Ahmed, H. N., MScEngg Lahore UET, BScEngg Asst. Prof.
Ali, H., MScEngg Lahore UET, BScEngg Asst. Prof.
Aslam, F., MScEngg Lahore UET, BScEngg Asst. Prof.
Ayyaz, M. N., MScEngg Asst. Prof. (on leave)
Bokhari, S. H., PhD Mass. Prof.
Chughtai, M. A., MSc Manc., PhD Manc. Prof. (on leave)
Durrani, K. E., MScEngg PhD Prof.
Goraya, I. A., BScEngg N.E.D. Eng., MScEngg Lahore UET Asst. Prof.
Hameed, A., MScEngg Prof.
Hassan, H. T., MSc Assoc. Prof.
Hussain, A., MScEngg Assoc. Prof.
Iqbal, J., MSc Assoc. Prof.
Iqbal, A., PhD Lahore UET, MScEngg Prof.
Izhar, T., MScEngg Lahore UET, BScEngg Asst. Prof. (on leave)
Khan, A. B., MScEngg Keio, BScEngg Assoc. Prof.
Khan, M. A., PhD Assoc. Prof.
Khan, M. A. H. Asst. Prof. (on leave)
Khan, M. Zubair A., MScEng Manc., PhD Manc. Prof.
Khan, W. M., MScEngg Asst. Prof.
Mahmood ul Hassan, K., BScEngg Asst. Prof. (on leave)
Qureshi, S. A., MSc Manc., PhD Manc., BScEngg Assoc. Prof.
Saeed, M., BScEngg MSc Assoc. Prof.
Saleem, M., BScEngg MSc Prof.
Shah, A. H., MScEngg Prof.
Shami, S. H., MScEngg Lahore UET, BScEngg Asst. Prof.
Shami, T. A., PhD Manc. Prof.
Sheikh, N. M., PhD Prof.; Chairman*
Suleman, M., MScEngg Assoc. Prof.
Yasin, M., MScEngg Assoc. Prof.
Yousaf, M., MScEngg Lahore UET, BScEngg Asst. Prof.

Engineering, Mechanical

Tel: (042) 339208

Abbas, A., MSc Asst. Prof.
Ahmad, M., BScEngg Asst. Prof.
Ali, S., MSc Prof.
Aman ul Haq,, MScEngg Asst. Prof. (on leave)
Aslam, A., MScEngg Asst. Prof.
Chaudhry, I. A., MScEngg Asian I.T., Bangkok, PhD Asst. Prof.
Cheema, J. M. I., BSc MScEngg Assoc. Prof. (on leave)
Cheema, S. N., BSc MScEngg Asst. Prof. (on leave)
Hussain, Dilshad, BScEngg Lahore UET, MSc Manc. Prof.
Hussain, M. I., BSc MScEng PhD Prof.; Chairman*
Jamal, Y., MScEngg Asian I.T., Bangkok, BScEngg PhD Assoc. Prof.
Kaleem, A., BScEngg Asst. Prof.

Mahmood, T., PhD Lond., MSc Assoc. Prof. (on leave)
Mirza, A. R., MSc Assoc. Prof.
Mirza, M. R., MSc Manc., PhD Newcastle, BSc Assoc. Prof.
Mughal, Hameed U., MScEngg PhD Prof.
Piracha, J. L., BScEngg Assoc. Prof.
Qureshi, A. H., PhD Prof.
Qureshi, N. A., BScEngg MSc Assoc. Prof.
Rauf, Abdul, MScEngg
Rehman, F., BScEngg Asst. Prof.
Rehman Sheikh, M. A., MScEngg PhD Prof.
Shah, F. H., PhD Assoc. Prof.
Shahid, Ijaz M., MScEngg
Shaikh, A. A., MScEngg Asst. Prof.
Siddique, Z., BScEngg Asst. Prof.
Tabassum, S. A., BScEngg PhD Assoc. Prof.
Waheed, A., BScEngg Asst. Prof.
Zuberi, M. U. H., MScEngg Prof.

Engineering, Metallurgical, and Material Science

Tel: (042) 339207

Ahmad, A., PhD Birm., MScEngg Asst. Prof.
Ajmal, M., MSc Manc., PhD Manc. Assoc. Prof.
Anwar, M. Y., MScEngg PhD Asst. Prof.
Ashraf, M., MSc Assoc. Prof.
Bajwa, S. A., MScEngg Asst. Prof.
Ghauri, K. M., PhD Strath., MScEngg Asst. Prof.
Hasan, F., PhD Manc., BScEngg Prof.
Iqbal, J., MSc Manc., PhD Manc. Assoc. Prof.
Munsha, M., MSc PhD Prof.
Shuja, M. S., MScTech PhD Prof.; Chairman*
Zaidi, S. Q. H., MSc Prof.

Engineering, Mining

Ahmad, B., MSc BScEngg Prof.
Butt, N. A., MScEngg PhD Prof.; Chairman*
Chattha, N. H., BSc MScEngg Prof.
Chaudhry, M. A., BSc PhD Prof.
Cheema, S. N., BScEngg Asst. Prof. (on leave)
Gillani, S. T. A., BScEngg PhD Assoc. Prof.
Hussain, S. A., MScEngg MPhil PhD Prof.
Khan, A. G., MScEngg Prof.
Khan, R. M. T., MSc Prof.
Khokhar, A. A., MSc Prof.
Kirmani, F. A., BScEngg PhD Prof.
Tariq, S. M., BScEngg Asst. Prof.
Yaqub, BScEngg PhD Asst. Prof.

Engineering, Petroleum

Tel: (042) 339271

Afzal, J., BScEngg Assoc. Prof.
Ali, A., BScEngg MSc Assoc. Prof.
Ali, M., BScEngg Assoc. Prof.
Inamullah, M., BScEngg Asst. Prof.
Khan, A. S., MScEngg Prof.; Chairman*
Malik, S. A., MScEngg Asst. Prof.

Humanities and Social Sciences

Tel: (042) 339291

Zaidi, S. M. H., MA Punjab, MSc Asst. Prof.; Chairman*

Islamic Studies

Tel: (042) 339246

Ayub, H. M., MA Punjab Assoc. Prof.; Chairman*
Farooqi, H. M. I., MA Punjab Asst. Prof.
Saeed, H. M., MA Punjab Asst. Prof.
Shahbaz, M. Z. I., MA Islamic(B'desh). Asst. Prof.
Yahya, M., MA Punjab Asst. Prof.

Material Science, see Engin., Metall., and Material Sci.

Mathematics

Tel: (042) 339210

Ahmad, O., MSc Islam., MPhil Islam., PhD Asst. Prof.
Ahmad, S., MSc Punjab Assoc. Prof.
Bashir Sadiq, M., MA Punjab, PhD Lond. Prof.
Chaudhry, M. A., MSc Punjab Asst. Prof.
Chaudhry, M. Nasir, MA Punjab, MSc Tor., PhD Windsor Prof.; Chairman*

Chaudhry, Muhammad N., MSc Punjab Asst. Prof.
Gul, M. N., MSc Punjab, MPhil Lahore UET Asst. Prof. (on leave)
Saleemi, A. H., BSc Punjab, MA Punjab, MSc Brun. Assoc. Prof.
Shah, N. A., BEd Punjab, MSc Punjab, PhD Prof.
Shahid, N. A., MSc Punjab Asst. Prof.

Physics

Tel: (042) 339204

Iqbal, C. Mohammad, MSc Punjab, CandReal Bergen Assoc. Prof.
Jafari, Z. H., MSc Punjab, MSc Lahore UET, PhD Sur. Asst. Prof.
Kayani, S. A., MSc Punjab, PhD Manc. Prof.
Khaleeq ur Rehman, MSc Punjab, PhD Manc. Assoc. Prof.
Latif, A., MSc Punjab Asst. Prof.
Shafiq, M., MSc Punjab, PhD Lond. Prof.; Chairman*

Social Sciences, see Humanities and Soc. Scis.

SPECIAL CENTRES, ETC

Environmental Engineering and Research, Institute of

Tel: (042) 339248

Ahmad, K., BSc Punjab, PhD Punjab Prof.
Ali, S. M. R., MSc Punjab Assoc. Prof.
Ali, W., BScEngg MS PhD Prof.
Aziz, J. A., MEng Bangkok, PhD Birm., BScEngg Prof.; Dir.*
Bari, A. J., MEngg Asian I.T., Bangkok, BScEngg Assoc. Prof.
Hayat, S., MScEngg Prof.
Qureshi, T. A., MSEng PhD Assoc. Prof. (on leave)
Rashim, Atif, MSc Asst. Prof.
Ziai, K. H., BScEngg MS Prof.

CONTACT OFFICERS

Academic affairs. Director, Student Affairs: Anwar, M. Y., PhD
Accommodation. Resident Officer: Qureshi, S. A., PhD
Admissions (first degree). Deputy Registrar (Students Section): Mohyuddin, Ghulam, BA Punjab
Admissions (higher degree). (Contact chairman of department concerned)
Alumni. Resident Officer: Qureshi, S. A., PhD
Careers. Chairman, Placement Bureau: Salarya, Prof. A. K., MSc Wales, PhD Wales
Computing services. Chairman, Computer Science Department: Raja, Prof. A. K., MA Punjab, PhD Belf.
Development/fund-raising. Deputy Registrar (Planning and Development): Aslam, M., MA Punjab
Estates and buildings/works and services. Project Director: Hussain, K., MScEngg
Examinations. Controller: Amjad, Prof. M., MSc Punjab, PhD, FRSChem
Finance. Treasurer: Aslam, M., MA Punjab
General enquiries. Registrar: Shah, Zulfiqar A., BA Punjab
Health services. Chief Medical Officer: Amin, Muhammad, MB BS Punjab
Industrial liaison. Director, Research: Durrani, K. E., MSc PhD
International office. Deputy Registrar (Students Section): Mohyuddin, Ghulam, BA Punjab
Library (chief librarian). Librarian: Ahmad, Muzaffar, MA Punjab
Personnel/human resources. Registrar: Shah, Zulfiqar A., BA Punjab
Public relations, information and marketing. Public Relations Officer: Shah, Zulfiqar A., BA Punjab
Publications. Head, Publications: Shah, Zulfiqar A., BA Punjab
Purchasing. Treasurer: Aslam, M., MA Punjab

Research. Director, Research: Durrani, K. E., MSc PhD

Safety. Resident Officer: Qureshi, S. A., PhD

Scholarships, awards, loans. Chairman, Placement Bureau: Salarya, Prof. A. K., MSc *Wales*, PhD *Wales*

Security. Resident Officer: Qureshi, S. A., PhD

Sport and recreation. Director, Physical Education: Qureshi, F. M.

Staff development and training. Registrar: Shah, Zulfiqar A., BA *Punjab*

Student welfare/counselling. Director, Student Affairs: Anwar, M. Y., PhD

Students from other countries. Director, Student Affairs: Anwar, M. Y., PhD

Students with disabilities. Director, Student Affairs: Anwar, M. Y., PhD

AFFILIATED COLLEGES

[Institutions listed by location below provide courses leading to degrees, etc. of the university]

Bahawalpur. Government College of Technology, Bahawalpur

Faisalabad. Government College of Technology, Faisalabad; Institute of Engineering and Fertilizer Research; National College of Textile Engineering

Lahore. Government College of Technology, Lahore

Multan. Government College of Technology, Multan

Rasul. Government College of Technology, Rasul

[*Information supplied by the institution as at 8 June 1998, and edited by the ACU*]

UNIVERSITY OF ENGINEERING AND TECHNOLOGY, TAXILA

Founded 1993; previously established as University College of Engineering, Taxila 1975

Postal Address: Taxila 47050, Pakistan
Telephone: (0596) 2482, 2202, 2496 **Fax**: (0596) 2821 **E-mail**: uett!root%nahe@uunet.uu.net
E-mail formula: uett!name%nahe@uunet.uu.net

VICE-CHANCELLOR*—Bhatti, Muhammad S., BScEngg *Lahore UET*, PhD *Lond.*
REGISTRAR‡—Rashid, Abdul, BSc *Punjab*, MSc *Pesh.*, MAEPM *A.Iqbal Open*, MEdAdmn *Penn. State*

GHULAM ISHAQ KHAN INSTITUTE OF ENGINEERING SCIENCES AND TECHNOLOGY

Founded 1992

Postal Address: Topi 23460, District Swabi, North-West Frontier Province, Pakistan
Telephone: (0938) 71858-61, 71875, 71897 **Fax**: (0938) 71862, 71864 **E-mail**: rector@giki.sdnpk.undp.org
WWW: http://giki.edu.pk

RECTOR/VICE-CHANCELLOR*—Raouf, Prof. Abdul, MS *Toledo(Ohio)*, PhD *Windsor*, FPAS
REGISTRAR‡—......

GOMAL UNIVERSITY

Founded 1974

Postal Address: Dera Ismail Khan, North-West Frontier Province, Pakistan
Telephone: (0961) 750279, 750239, 750266 **Fax**: (0961) 750266 **Cables**: University Campus, D.I. Khan

VICE-CHANCELLOR*—Khan, Prof. Abdul W.
REGISTRAR‡—Khan, Nawabzada U. D., MA

HAMDARD UNIVERSITY

Founded 1991

Postal Address: Madina-tal-Hikmat, Muhammad Bin Qasim Avenue, Karachi 74700, Pakistan
Telephone: (021) 690 0000, 699 6001-2 **Fax**: (021) 664 1766 **Cables**: HAMDARD **Telex**: 24529 HAMD PK

VICE-CHANCELLOR*—Qazi, Mahmood H.
REGISTRAR/PROJECTS CO-ORDINATOR—Saeed Ghaus, S. M.

INSTITUTE OF BUSINESS ADMINISTRATION

Founded 1955; university status conferred 1994

Postal Address: Karachi University Campus, Karachi 75270, Pakistan
E-mail: ibakhi@biruni.erum.com.pk

DIRECTOR*—Wahab, Prof. Abdul
REGISTRAR‡—......

INTERNATIONAL ISLAMIC UNIVERSITY

Founded 1980 as Islamic University; reconstituted with present name, 1985

Member of the Association of Commonwealth Universities

Postal Address: PO Box 1243, Islamabad 44000, Pakistan
Telephone: (051) 850751 (5 lines), 857741 **Fax**: (051) 853360 **Cables**: Aljamia **Telex**: 54068 IIU Pk

CHANCELLOR—The President of the Islamic Republic of Pakistan (ex officio)
PRO-CHANCELLOR—Mohsin, Al-Turki A., PhD
RECTOR—Maraj Khalid, BA LLB
PRESIDENT*—Hassan, Hussain H., LLB Cairo, LLB Al-Azhar, MCJ N.Y., PhD
VICE-PRESIDENT (RESOURCE DEVELOPMENT)—Al-Assal, A., PhD Al-Azhar
VICE-PRESIDENT (ACADEMICS)/DIRECTOR GENERAL, SHARIAH ACADEMY—Ghazi, M. A., PhD Punjab
VICE-PRESIDENT (PLANNING)/DIRECTOR GENERAL, INTERNATIONAL INSTITUTE OF ISLAMIC ECONOMICS—
Siddiqui, Anwar H., PhD Calif.
DIRECTOR (ACADEMICS)‡—Khwaja, Gulzar A., MSc A.Bello
DIRECTOR (FINANCE AND ADMINISTRATION)—Dar, M. A., MBA

FACULTIES/SCHOOLS

Arabic
Dean: Gabr, Prof. Ragaa A. M., MA *Paris*, PhD *Paris*

Economics, School of
Director: Akhter, Prof. Muhammad R., MA *Punjab*, PhD *Boston*

Languages, Institute of
Director: Abdul Azeez, M. Kamal, PhD

Shariah and Law
Dean: Sulyman, Prof. Ahmed Y., MA *Cairo*, PhD *Cairo*

Usuluddin
Dean: Tawwab, Muhammad A., MA *Al-Azhar*, PhD *Al-Azhar*

ACADEMIC UNITS

Aqidah, see Compar. Religion, Faith (Aqidah), Human Thought and Dawah

Arabic
Tel: (051) 850167
Abdul Aziz, M. Kamal, PhD   Dir.*
El-Din, Mahmood S., MA *Al-Azhar*, PhD *Al-Azhar*   Prof.
Rehman, Habibur, MA   Asst. Prof.
Sahibzada, S. A., PhD   Asst. Prof. (on leave)

Business Administration
Tel: (051) 212942 Fax: (051) 853360
Farooqi, M. N., PhD   Assoc. Prof.
Hijazi, Tahir, PhD   Asst. Prof.
Khan, Amanullah, MBA   Prof.; Head*
Mehdi, Haider R.   Assoc. Prof.

Comparative Religion, Faith (Aqidah), Human Thought and Dawah
Tel: (051) 851178
Afifi Talat, M., PhD   Asst. Prof.
Ahmed, Anis, PhD   Prof.
Idrees, M.-Jala'a, PhD   Assoc. Prof.; Head*
Idrees, Muhammad J., PhD   Assoc. Prof.
Mohammad, M. M. D., PhD   Asst. Prof.
Omer, Shauki A., PhD   Asst. Prof.
Qutub, Q. A. H., MA PhD   Asst. Prof.

Computer Science
Tel: (051) 212942
Ali, Shahid A., PhD   Asst. Prof.
Khalid Rashid, MSc *Punjab*, PhD *Nagoya*   Prof.; Head*

Economics, School of
Tel: (051) 851046
Akhter, Muhammad R., MA *Punjab*, PhD *Boston*   Prof.; Dir.*
Atiquzzafar, MSc   Asst. Prof.
Hijazi, Tahir, MPhil   Asst. Prof.
Hussain Muhammad, PhD   Prof. (on leave)
Iqbal, Nuzhat, MA   Asst. Prof.
Maqlid, R., PhD   Asst. Prof.
Rehman, Q. N., MSc PhD   Asst. Prof.
Sherazi, N. S., MA PhD   Assoc. Prof.
Tahir, Rizwan, MSc PhD   Asst. Prof. (on leave)
Tahir, Sayyid, PhD   Prof.

English
Tel: (051) 850167
Gillani, Syeda S., MA   Asst. Prof.
Iqbal, M. M., MA   Asst. Prof.
Kazim, Anwar, MA   Asst. Prof.
Rauf, S. M. A., MA   Assoc. Prof.; Head*
Rehman Ahsanur, MA   Asst. Prof.
Sheikh, Mehnaz, MA   Asst. Prof.

Fiqh
(Islamic Jurisprudence)
Tel: (051) 854370
Awad, A. A., PhD   Assoc. Prof.; Head*
Shahata, A. Q., PhD   Asst. Prof.

Sulyman, Ahmed Y., MA *Cairo*, PhD *Cairo*   Prof.

Hadith, see Tafseer and Hadith

Law
Tel: (051) 854370
Dar, M. S., LLM   Asst. Prof.; Head*
Nyazee, Imran A., LLM   Asst. Prof.

Linguistics
Tel: (051) 850167
Akrat, Adil M., PhD   Asst. Prof.
Al-Qasim, Abu, PhD   Asst. Prof.
Daim, Abdul A., PhD   Asst. Prof.
El-Sharfdin, Mahmoud, PhD   Prof.
Jalil, Abdul J., PhD   Asst. Prof.
Marsi, Shaban M., PhD   Asst. Prof.

Literature
Tel: (051) 850167
Gabr, Ragaa A. M., MA *Paris*, PhD *Paris*   Prof.; Head*
Rehman, Khalilur, PhD   Assoc. Prof.

Pakistan Studies
Tel: (051) 851178
Akhtar, Safeer, PhD   Asst. Prof.; Head* (on leave)

Religion, see Compar. Religion, Faith (Aqidah), Human Thought and Dawah

Tafseer and Hadith
(Quran and Hadith Sciences)
Tel: (051) 851178
Hashmi, Farhat N., PhD   Asst. Prof.
Hussain Al-Jaboori, PhD   Asst. Prof.
Kakakhel, Abdullah, MA   Asst. Prof.
Khalil, Al-Ajammi D., PhD   Prof.; Head*
Mohsin, Ahmed A., PhD   Assoc. Prof.
Mukhtar Marzooq, PhD   Assoc. Prof.
Razziq, M. Abdul, PhD   Assoc. Prof.
Rehman, Q. A., MA   Asst. Prof.
Tajuddin Al-Azhari, MA   Asst. Prof.
Tawwab, Muhammad A., PhD   Head*
Zubair, Idris, PhD   Asst. Prof.

Technical Education, Centre for
Tel: (051) 256056
Iqbal, Javed, BSc *W.Pak.Eng.*   Principal*
Mahmood, Sajid, MSc *Quaid-i-Azam*   Course Coordinator

Usul-ul-Fiqh
(Principles of Islamic Jurisprudence)
Tel: (051) 854370
Faizullah, Attaullah, PhD   Asst. Prof.
Jabali, M. A. S., PhD   Asst. Prof.
Jabali, Sa'ad-al, PhD   Asst. Prof.
Jawad, D. A., PhD   Prof.; Head*
Kazim, Yousaf, MA   Asst. Prof.
Makki, M. A., PhD   Asst. Prof.
Rehman, Fazlur, PhD   Asst. Prof.

SPECIAL CENTRES, ETC

Dawah Academy
Tel: (051) 858640
Ahmed, Anis, PhD   Dir.-Gen.*
Chishti, A. A., MA PhD   Asst. Prof.
Mehr, Maulana A., MA   Asst. Prof.

Dawah Study Centre
Staff of the Dawah Academy also belong to the Centre
Tel: (051) 280305
Shah, Safdar A., MA *Pesh.*   Principal*

Islamic Economics, International Institute of
Staff of the School of Economics also belong to the Institute
Tel: (051) 856572

Siddiqui, Anwar H., PhD *Calif.*   Dir.-Gen.*

Islamic Research Institute
Tel: (051) 851303
Ansari, Z. I., PhD   Prof.; Dir.-Gen.*
Azad, G. M., MA   Asst. Prof.
Ghazali, M. A., PhD   Assoc. Prof.
Hussan Sohail, MA   Asst. Prof. (on leave)
Massod, Khalid, PhD   Prof.
Rehman, Sajadur, MA PhD   Asst. Prof.
Siddiqui, M. Mian, PhD   Asst. Prof.
Tufail, Muhammad, PhD   Asst. Prof.

Shariah Academy
Tel: (051) 851113, 856219 Fax: (051) 851113
Ghazi, M. A., PhD *Punjab*   Dir.-Gen.*

CONTACT OFFICERS

Academic affairs. Director (Academics): Khwaja, Gulzar A., MSc *A.Bello*
Accommodation. Provost: Habib-ur-Rehman, MA *Punjab*
Admissions (first degree). Director (Academics): Khwaja, Gulzar A., MSc *A.Bello*
Computing services. Head, Department of Computer Sciences: Khalid Rashid, MSc *Punjab*, PhD *Nagoya*
Credit transfer. Director (Academics): Khwaja, Gulzar A., MSc *A.Bello*
Development/fund-raising. Vice-President (Resource Development): Al-Assal, A., PhD *Al-Azhar*
Distance education. Director (Academics): Khwaja, Gulzar A., MSc *A.Bello*
Distance education. Course Co-ordinator, Dawah Academy: Chishti, A. A., PhD *Punjab*
Distance education. Course Co-ordinator, Shariah Academy: Sham, S. I., LLB *IIU(P'stan.)*
Estates and buildings/works and services. Director (Planning and Projects): Mushtaq Ali, MA *Punjab*
Examinations. Deputy Director: Rehman, M. Ur, MPA
Finance. Deputy Director (Finance): Muhammad Iqbal, MCom *Punjab*
General enquiries. Director (Academics): Khwaja, Gulzar A., MSc *A.Bello*
Health services. Incharge Medical Centre: Shabir Ahmed, MB BS *Punjab*
International office. Director (Academics): Khwaja, Gulzar A., MSc *A.Bello*
Library (chief librarian). Librarian: Mohamad Rafiq
Library (enquiries). Assistant Librarian: Mohammad Afzal, MLS
Personnel/human resources. Director (Personnel and Administration): Khan, Amanullah, MBA *Karachi*
Public relations, information and marketing. Deputy Director (Protocol): Khurshid Ahmed, MA *Punjab*
Publications. Deputy Director (Publications), Islamic Research Institute: Mumtaz Liaqat, BA *Punjab*
Publications. Deputy Director (Publications), Dawah Academy: Farooqi, Mahmood A., MA *Karachi*
Purchasing. Deputy Director (P&S): Khan, S. B., BA *Punjab*
Research. Director General, Shariah Academy: Ghazi, M. A., PhD *Punjab*
Research. Director General, Dawah Academy: Ahmed, Anis, PhD *Penn.*
Research. Director General, Islamic Research Institute: Ansari, Zafar I., PhD *McG.*
Research. Director General, International Institute of Islamic Economics: Siddiqui, Anwar H., PhD *Calif.*
Scholarships, awards, loans. Director (Academics): Khwaja, Gulzar A., MSc *A.Bello*
Schools liaison. Director (Academics): Khwaja, Gulzar A., MSc *A.Bello*
Security. Director (Finance and Administration): Dar, M. A., MBA
Sport and recreation. In-Charge, Sports: Shah, Manzoor H., BA *Punjab*
Student welfare/counselling. Student Adviser: Azzam, A. A., PhD *Al-Azhar*

Students from other countries. Director (Academics): Khwaja, Gulzar A., MSc *A.Bello*
Students with disabilities. Director (Academics): Khwaja, Gulzar A., MSc *A.Bello*

University press. Press Manager, Islamic Research Institute: Zafar Ali
Women. In-Charge, Women's Section: Begum Zaitoon, PhD *Punjab*

[Information supplied by the institution as at 20 November 1996, and edited by the ACU]

ISLAMIA UNIVERSITY, BAHAWALPUR

Founded 1975

Member of the Association of Commonwealth Universities

Postal Address: Bahawalpur, Pakistan
Telephone: (0621) 80331, 80372 **Fax**: (0621) 80372 **Cables**: Islamia University, Bahawalpur

CHANCELLOR—The Governor of the Punjab
VICE-CHANCELLOR*—Khan, Prof. M. Shafiq, BSc *Punjab*, MSc *Punjab*, PhD *Lond.*
REGISTRAR—Arshad, Rana M., MA *Punjab*, MAEPM *A.Iqbal Open*
TREASURER—Dahir, Ghulam H., MA

GENERAL INFORMATION

History. The university was originally established in 1925 as Jamia Abbasia, an institution for higher education in religious science. It was renamed Jamia Islamia in 1963 and became a university under its present name in 1975.

First Degrees (see also Pakistan Directory to Subjects of Study). BA, BSc.

Higher Degrees (see also Pakistan Directory to Subjects of Study). MA, MSc, PhD.

Language of Instruction. English and Urdu.

Libraries. 112,776 volumes; 169 periodicals subscribed to.

Fees. MA students: Rs790; MSc students: Rs1320.

Academic Year. September–August.

Income. Rs26,544,450.

Statistics. Staff: 539 (305 academic, 234 administrative). Students: 3082.

FACULTIES/SCHOOLS
Arts
Dean: ......

Islamic Learning
Dean: Farooqi, Prof. M. Y., Fazil Dars-e-Nizami Punjab, MA *Punjab*, PhD *Exe.*

Science
Dean: ......

ACADEMIC UNITS
Arabic
Dar, Surrya, MA *Punjab*, PhD *Punjab*   Assoc. Prof.; Head*
Hafiz, M. A., MA *Punjab*, Fazil Dars-e-Nizami Punjab, MOL *Punj.*, PhD *Islamia, Bahawal.*   Asst. Prof.
Khan, S. T., MA *Punjab*, PhD *Punjab*   Assoc. Prof.
Rabbani, Muhammad A., MA *B.Zak.*, PhD *Glas.*   Assoc. Prof.

Business Administration
Haider, I., MBA *B.Zak.*   Asst. Prof.; Head*

Chemistry
Abdul Jabbar, MSc *Punjab*, PhD *Aberd.*   Assoc. Prof.
Aminud Din, MSc *Lond.*, MSc *Dacca*, PhD *Lough.*   Assoc. Prof.
Ashraf, M., MSc *Islamia, Bahawal.*, PhD *Manc.*   Asst. Prof.
Chohan, Z., MSc *Karachi*, MSc *Glas.*, PhD *Aberd.*   Asst. Prof.
Ghouri, M. S., MSc *Punjab*, PhD *Wales*   Asst. Prof.
Iqbal, J., MSc *Punjab*, PhD *Glas.*   Assoc. Prof.
Khan, Z. F., MSc *Punjab*, PhD *Glas.*   Assoc. Prof.
Majeed, A., MA *Punjab*, MSc *Punjab*, PhD *Sindh*   Prof.
Mehmood, K., MSc *Punjab*, PhD *Punjab*   Asst. Prof.
Mirza, M. L., MSc *Islam.*, PhD *Glas.*   Prof.
Moazzam, M., MSc *Punjab*, PhD *Brun.*   Prof.; Head*
Nasim, Faizul H., MSc *Islamia, Bahawal.*, PhD *Brown*   Assoc. Prof.
Sheikh, Q. I., MSc *Faisalabad*   Asst. Prof. (on leave)
Syed, A. T., MSc *Islam.*, PhD *Brown*   Asst. Prof.

Computer Science
Taqveem, A., MSc *B.Zak.*   Lectr.; Head*

Desert Studies, Cholistan Institute of,
see Special Centres, etc

Economics
Ashraf, M., MA *Punjab*, PhD *Manc.*   Assoc. Prof.; Head*
Basit, Amir B., MA *Islamia, Bahawal.*, MPhil *Quaid-i-Azam*   Asst. Prof.
Kausar, Tasnim, MA *Punjab*   Asst. Prof.
Khan, Naheed Z., MA *Punjab*, PhD   Asst. Prof.
Qureshi, Z. A., LLB *Karachi*, MA *Punjab*   Asst. Prof.
Syed, N. H., MA *Sindh*   Asst. Prof.

Education
Adeeb, M. A., MA *B.Zak.*, PhD *Brad.*   Prof.; Head*

English
Khattak, Zahir J., MA *Karachi*, PhD *Tufts*   Prof.; Head*
Salahuddin, Shahnaz, MA *Islamia, Bahawal.*   Asst. Prof.

Geography
Abdul Sattar, MSc *Punjab*   Asst. Prof.
Khan, Asad A., MSc *Punjab*   Asst. Prof.

Malik, M. K., MSc *Punjab*, PhD *Lond.*   Assoc. Prof.; Head*

History and Pakistan Studies
Ahmad, Muhammad S., MA *Calif.*, MA *Karachi*, PhD *Lond.*   Prof.; Head*
Bhatti, Abdul J., MA *Punjab*   Asst. Prof.
Khurshid, M., LLB *Punjab*, MA *Punjab*, PhD   Assoc. Prof.
Rizvi, M. A., MA PhD   Assoc. Prof.
Shahid, Abdul R., MA *Islamia, Bahawal.*, MPhil *Quaid-i-Azam*   Asst. Prof.

Iqbaliyat, see Urdu and Iqbaliyat

Islamic Studies
Ahmed, M., MA   Asst. Prof.
Cheema, Shahza K., MA *Punjab*, PhD *B.Zak.*   Assoc. Prof.
Farooqi, M. Y., Fazil Dars-e-Nizami Punjab, MA *Punjab*, PhD *Exe.*   Prof.
Khan, M. G., MA *Islamia, Bahawal.*, PhD *Islamia, Bahawal.*   Assoc. Prof.
Khan, S. B., MA *Karachi*, LLB *Karachi*   Asst. Prof. (on leave)
Lodhi, Muhammad I., MA *B.Zak.*   Asst. Prof.
Mohiuddin, Abrar, MA *Islamia, Bahawal.*   Asst. Prof.
Rehmat, A. R., MA *Punjab*, PhD *Lond.*   Prof.; Head*
Syed, I. H., MA   Asst. Prof.
Zafar, A. R., PhD *Glas.*, MA   Prof.

Law
Bukhari, A. H., LLB   Asst. Prof. (on leave)
Butt, M. N., LLB *Punjab*, MCL *Emory*   Asst. Prof. (on leave)
Sial, A. Q., LLB *Islamia, Bahawal.*   Asst. Prof.; Head*

Library and Information Science
Abbas, G., MLS *Karachi*   Asst. Prof.
Hashmi, Fouzia, MLS *Sindh*   Asst. Prof.
Khalid, H. M., MLS *Karachi*, PhD *Manc.Met.*   Asst. Prof.
Khan, M. F., MA *Punjab*, MLS *Karachi*, PhD *Islamia, Bahawal.*   Assoc. Prof.; Head*

Mass Communication
Ahmed, S., MA *Gomal*   Asst. Prof.
Shamsuddin, Muhammad, MA *Karachi*, PhD *Lond.*   Head*
Zulqarnain, M., MA *Punjab*   Asst. Prof. (on leave)

Mathematics

Abbasi, G. Q., MSc Punjab, PhD Moscow Assoc. Prof.; Head*

Akhtar, K. P., MSc Punjab, PhD Manc. Asst. Prof.

Hafiz, A. M., MSc Punjab, MPhil Islam. Asst. Prof.

Mahmood, T., MSc Punjab, PhD Manc. Assoc. Prof.

Pakistan Studies, see Hist. and Pakistan Studies

Persian

Ahmad, M., MA MPhil Asst. Prof.; Head*

Pharmacy

Ahmed, Mehmood, PhD Punjab Assoc. Prof.

Nisar-ur-Rehman, MPhil Punjab, MSc Asst. Prof.

Shafique, M. K., MSc Punjab, PhD Lond. Prof.; Head*

Physics

Ahmad, K., MSc Islam., MPhil Islam., PhD Asst. Prof.

Asghar, M., MPhil Quaid-i-Azam, PhD Quaid-i-Azam, MSc Asst. Prof.

Chaudhry, M. A., MSc Punjab, PhD Sur. Assoc. Prof.

Faridi, B. A. S., MSc Punjab, PhD Sur. Assoc. Prof.; Head*

Khan, M. Afzal, MSc Punjab Asst. Prof. (on leave)

Muhammad, J., MSc Punjab, PhD Sur. Asst. Prof.

Naveed, S., MSc Asst. Prof.

Shaheen, M. H., MSc B.Zak., PhD Manc. Asst. Prof.

Sheikh, A. A., MSc Punjab, PhD Sur. Assoc. Prof.

Sukhera, Muhammad B., PhD Paris (on deputation)

Political Science

Abbasi, Hina Q., MA Karachi, PhD Moscow Assoc. Prof.; Head*

Khan, A. H., MA Punjab, LLB Karachi, PhD Islamia, Bahawal. Asst. Prof.

Musarrat, Razia, PhD Islamia, Bahawal., MA Asst. Prof.

Syed, K. A., MA Kent, PhD Kent, MSc Islam. Asst. Prof.

Saraki

Chandio, J. H., MA Islamia, Bahawal. Lectr.; Head*

Statistics

Akhtar, M., MSc Punjab, PhD S'ton. Prof.; Head*

Aleem, M., MSc Asst. Prof.

Malik, M. A., MSc Punjab, MA Punjab, PhD Prof.

Rasool, M., MSc Punjab, PhD Sur. Assoc. Prof.

Shah, A. M., MSc Asst. Prof.

Shah, M. A. A., MSc Asst. Prof.

Urdu and Iqbaliyat

Ahmad, S., MA Punjab, PhD Punjab Assoc. Prof.; Head*

Malik, M. S., MA Karachi, PhD Karachi Asst. Prof.

Najeeb-Ud-Din Jamal, PhD Karachi Prof. (on leave)

Rao, Roshan A., BEd Punjab, MA Punjab, PhD Punjab Asst. Prof.

Shaheen, Aqeela, MA B.Zak., PhD Karachi Asst. Prof.

SPECIAL CENTRES, ETC

Desert Studies, Cholistan Institute of

Rao, Altaf ur Rehman, PhD Wales Dir.*

Pakistan Gallery

No staff at present

CONTACT OFFICERS

Examinations. Controller of Examinations: Safique, Muhammad, MA

Finance. Treasurer: Dahir, Ghulam H., MA

General enquiries. Registrar: Arshad, Rana M., MA Punjab, MAEPM A.Iqbal Open

Health services. Senior Medical Officer: Bashir-ud-Din Hashmi, Muhammad

Library (chief librarian). Acting Librarian: Rashid, Abdul

Public relations, information and marketing. Deputy Registrar (Public Relations): Abbasi, Rahim Y., MA Punjab, PhD Islamia, Bahawal.

Purchasing. Administrative Officer, Store and Purchase: Muhammad, Ghulam

Scholarships, awards, loans. Planning and Development Officer: Sadiq, Muhammad C.

Sport and recreation. Director, Physical Education: Akhtar, Muhammad A.

Student welfare/counselling. Director, Student Office: Arshad, Muhammad, MSc Punjab, PhD Sur.

[Information supplied by the institution as at 18 July 1998, and edited by the ACU]

ISRA UNIVERSITY

Postal Address: Hala Road, PO Box 313, Hyderabad, Sindh, Pakistan
Telephone: (0221) 620185, 620187 **Fax**: (0221) 456 0461 **E-mail**: isra@hyd.compol.com
WWW: http://www.isra.edu.pk

PRESIDENT*—Kazi, Asadullah, MSc Lond., PhD Lond.
REGISTRAR‡—Memon, Prof. M. Saleh, MB BS Sindh, MPhil Karachi

UNIVERSITY OF KARACHI

Established 1951

Member of the Association of Commonwealth Universities

Postal Address: University Road, Karachi 75270, Sindh, Pakistan
Telephone: (021) 479001-7 **Fax**: (021) 496 9277 **Cables**: Karachi University

CHANCELLOR—The Governor of Sindh (*ex officio*)
PRO-CHANCELLOR—The Minister of Education of Sindh (*ex officio*)
VICE-CHANCELLOR*—Zaidi, Prof. Zafar H., BSc *Sindh*, MSc *Sindh*, PhD *Leeds*, DSc *Leeds*
PRO-VICE-CHANCELLOR—......
REGISTRAR—Mahmud, Tariq, MSc *Karachi*
DIRECTOR OF FINANCE—Khan, Younus A., MBA
CONTROLLER OF EXAMINATIONS—......
LIBRARIAN—Sherwani, Malahat K., MLS *Karachi*

GENERAL INFORMATION

Higher Degrees. MPhil, PhD.

Language of Instruction. English and Urdu.

Academic Year. January–December.

FACULTIES/SCHOOLS

Arts
Tel: (021) 474595

Dean: Siddiqui, Prof. Tahira, MA *Karachi*, PhD *Teheran*

Education
Tel: (021) 450 3076

Dean: Qureshi, Prof. Khushnuma, BEd *Karachi*, MEd *Karachi*, MA *Karachi*

Islamic Studies
Tel: (021) 498 5662

Dean: Akhtar Saeed Siddiqi, Prof. M., MA *Punjab*, MA *Karachi*, PhD *Edin*.

Law
Tel: (021) 773 1824

Dean: Farooq Khan, Prof. Umer, BSc *Karachi*, MA *Karachi*, LLB *Karachi*

Medicine
Tel: (021) 920 1300

Dean: Waheed, Irshad, MB BS, FRCS, FACS

Pharmacy
Tel: (021) 474694

Dean: Saify, Prof. Zafar S., MSc *Karachi*, PhD *Lond.*

Science
Tel: (021) 474690

Dean: Ahmed, Prof. Viqaruddin, MSc *Alld.*, PhD *Karachi*, DrRerNat *Bonn*, DSc *Karachi*

ACADEMIC UNITS

Arabic
Haq Ihsanul, MA *Karachi*, PhD *Karachi*   Prof.; Chairman*
Ishaque, Muhammad, MA *Karachi*   Asst. Prof.
Khalil Arab, Atiya, MA *Karachi*, PhD *Karachi*   Prof.
Shaheed, Abdul, MA *Karachi*, PhD *Karachi*   Prof.

Bengali
Mohiuddin Chaudhri, A. B., MA *Dacca*   Asst. Prof.

Biochemistry
Aftab, Najma, MSc *Karachi*, MPhil *Karachi*   Prof.
Akhtar, Naheed, MSc *Karachi*, MPhil *Karachi*, PhD *Karachi*   Assoc. Prof.
Ali Athar, Hafiz S., MSc *Karachi*, MPhil *Karachi*   Prof.; Chairman*
Azhar, Abid, MSc *Karachi*, PhD *Canberra*   Prof.
Bano, Samina   Asst. Prof.

Haider, Saida   Asst. Prof.
Haleem, Darakshan J., MSc *Karachi*, MPhil *Karachi*, PhD *Lond.*   Prof.
Haleem, M. A., MSc *Karachi*, PhD *Leeds*   Prof.
Hasani, Saleha, MSc *Karachi*, MSc *Dund.*, PhD *Karachi*   Prof.
Ishaq, Muhammad, MSc *Karachi*, MPhil *Penn.*, PhD *Penn.*   Prof.
Jahangir, Shakila, MSc *Karachi*, PhD *Warw.*   Prof.
Khanam, Aziza, MSc *Karachi*, MPhil *Karachi*, PhD *Karachi*   Prof.
Mahboob, Tabassum, MSc *Karachi*, MPhil *Karachi*, PhD *Karachi*   Asst. Prof.
Nazrul Hasnain, Syed, MSc *Karachi*, MPhil *Karachi*, DrRerNat *Bonn*   Prof.
Parveen, Tahira   Asst. Prof.
Qasim, Rashida, MSc *Karachi*, PhD *Karachi*   Prof.
Qidwai, Iqbal M., MSc *Karachi*   Prof.
Siddiqi, Nikhat S., MSc *Karachi*, PhD *Sur.*   Prof.
Sultana, Vaqar, MSc *Karachi*, PhD *Karachi*   Assoc. Prof.
Zarina, Shamshad   Asst. Prof.

Botany
Ahmed, Soaleha, MSc *Karachi*, PhD *Exe.*   Prof.
Ajmal Khan, M., MSc *Karachi*, PhD *Ohio*   Prof.
Azhar Ali, Hajra, MSc *Karachi*, MPhil *Karachi*   Prof.
Aziz, Khadija, MSc *Karachi*, PhD *Auck.*   Asst. Prof.
Begum Zahid, Phool, MSc *Karachi*, PhD *Prague*   Prof.; Chairman*
Hashmi, Masoodul H., MSc *Montr.*, MSc *Karachi*, PhD *Karachi*   Prof.
Iqbal, Zafar, MSc *Karachi*, PhD *Lanc.*   Prof.
Ishaq Khan, M., MSc *Karachi*, PhD *Sheff.*   Prof.
Ismail, Shoaib   Asst. Prof.
Khatoon, Khalida, MSc *Karachi*, PhD *Bath*   Prof.
Khatoon, Surayya, MSc *Karachi*, PhD *Karachi*   Asst. Prof.
Mehdi, Fatima, MSc *Karachi*, MPhil *Lond.*   Prof.
Qaisar, Muhammad, MSc *Karachi*, PhD *Karachi*   Prof.
Saifullah, S. M., MSc *Karachi*, PhD *McG.*   Prof.
Shameel Qadri, Mustafa, MSc *Karachi*, PhD *Karachi*   Prof.
Shaukat, Shahid, MSc *Wales*, MSc *Karachi*, PhD *W.Ont.*   Prof.
Usman, Mubina, MSc *Karachi*, PhD *Auck.*   Prof.

Chemistry, see also Special Centres, etc
Ali, Kazim   Asst. Prof.
Ali, Syed A., MSc *Karachi*, MPhil *Quaid-i-Azam*   Asst. Prof.
Arayne, M. Saeed, MSc *Karachi*, MPhil *Karachi*   Prof.
Arif Kazmi, S., MSc *Karachi*, PhD *Kent State*   Prof.
Begum, Saeedan, MSc *Karachi*, MPhil *Quaid-i-Azam*, DrRerNat *Bonn*   Prof.
Fahimuddin, MSc *Karachi*, PhD *Karachi*   Prof.
Firdous, Saddiqa, MSc *Karachi*, PhD *Karachi*   Assoc. Prof.
Ifzal, Rehana, MSc *Karachi*, MPhil *Karachi*   Assoc. Prof.

Jabeen, Shaisla   Asst. Prof.
Khalid, Zahida   Asst. Prof.
Khan, Bushra, MSc *Karachi*, MPhil *Karachi*   Assoc. Prof.
Khan, Mohsin A., MSc *Sindh*, PhD *Lond.*   Prof.
Khan, Muhammad A., MSc *Karachi*, PhD *Karachi*   Prof.
Khan, Nasiruddin   Asst. Prof.
Malik, S. Abdul, MSc *Karachi*, PhD *St And.*   Prof.
Maqsood, Zahida, MSc *Karachi*, PhD *Karachi*   Prof.
Mumtaz, Majid   Asst. Prof.
Naqvi, Iftikhar I., MSc *Karachi*, PhD *Leeds*   Prof.
Nizami, Sh. Sirajuddin, MSc *Karachi*, MPhil *Karachi*, PhD *Aberd.*   Asst. Prof.
Noor, Fatima, MSc *Sindh*, PhD *Lond.*   Prof.
Quadri, Masooda   Asst. Prof.
Qureshi, Abu M., MSc *Karachi*, PhD *Camb.*   Prof.
Raunaq Raza Naqvi, S., MSc *Karachi*, PhD *Camb.*   Prof.; Chairman*
Rehman, Mutiur   Asst. Prof.
Sami, M. A., MSc *Rajsh.*, PhD *Leeds*   Prof.
Saqib Qureshi, M., MSc *Karachi*, PhD *Karachi*   Asst. Prof.
Siddiqui, Zaheeruddin, MSc *Karachi*, PhD *Karachi*   Prof.
Usmani, Abu A., MSc *Karachi*, PhD *Lond.*   Prof.
Viqar, Dilshad   Asst. Prof.

Chemistry, Applied
Abbas, Syed P., MSc *Karachi*, PhD *Salf.*   Asst. Prof.
Ahmed, Akhlaq, MSc *Karachi*, PhD *Exe.*, FRSChem   Prof.; Chairman*
Ali, Syed I., MSc *Karachi*, PhD *Strath.*   Prof.
Hameed, Saira, MSc *Alig.*, PhD *Karachi*   Prof.
Khan, Fasihullah, MSc *Karachi*, PhD *Bath*   Prof.
Niaz, G. R., MSc *Karachi*, PhD *Camb.*   Prof.
Rashid, Abdul, MSc *Karachi*   Asst. Prof.
Sadiq Rizvi, M., MSc *Lucknow*, PhD *Birm.*   Assoc. Prof.
Shaista, A. R., MSc *Karachi*   Asst. Prof.
Shams, Najma, MSc *Dacca*, PhD *Sheff.*   Prof.
Siddiqui, Iqbal, MSc *Karachi*, DrRerNat *Mün.*   Assoc. Prof.
Zaidi, Syed, A. H.   Prof.

Commerce
Khalid, M. Ibrahim   Asst. Prof.
Qadir Ahmed, Syed, MCom *Sindh*, PhD *Karachi*   Prof.
Sajidin, M., MA *Vanderbilt*, MA *Karachi*, MPhil *Karachi*   Prof.; Chairman*
Zafar, Dilshad, MCom   Asst. Prof.
Zaki, Abdul R.   Asst. Prof.

Computer Science
Aquil Burney, S. M., MSc *Karachi*, MPhil *Karachi*, PhD *Strath.*   Prof.; Chairman*
Ezamuddin, M. M., MSc *T.U.Berlin*, MSc *Karachi*   Asst. Prof.
Naqvi, Syed A., MSc *Karachi*, MA *Chic.*   Asst. Prof.
Sami, Badar   Asst. Prof.

Zaidi, S. Abbas K., MSc *Virginia*, PhD
Virginia Asst. Prof.

Economics

Arshad, Rabia, MA *Brist.*, MA *Karachi* Asst.
Prof.
Hussain, S. M. Ahsan, MSc *Karachi*, MA *Karachi*,
MA *Vanderbilt* Assoc. Prof.; Chairman*
Irfan, Misbahul, MA *Wat.* Asst. Prof.
Safdar, Rubina, MA *Karachi* Asst. Prof.
Shafiq-ur-Rehman, MA *Wat.*, MA
Karachi Assoc. Prof.

Education

Abbasi, Pervez, MEd *Sindh* Asst. Prof.
Hamid, Malka Asst. Prof.
Memon, Ghulam R., MEd *Karachi* Asst. Prof.
Razi, Fatima, MA *Karachi*, MEd *Karachi*, PhD
Karachi Assoc. Prof.; Chairman*

English

Ali, Masood A., MA *Karachi* Prof.
Ali, Naghmana, MA *Karachi* Asst. Prof.
Bano, Dilshat, MA *Karachi* Asst. Prof.
Karim, Rafat, MA *Punjab* Prof.; Chairman*
Kazi, Amberina M., MA *Karachi* Asst. Prof.
Khan, M. Kalim R., MA *Karachi*, MA *Lanc.* Asst.
Prof.
Moosvi, Noushaba, MA *Karachi* Asst. Prof.
Sayeed-ur-Rehman, Syed, MA *Patna* Prof.
Shameem, Fauzia, MA *Karachi*, PhD
Leeds Assoc. Prof.
Wasti, S. Munir, MA *Karachi*, MPhil
Karachi Assoc. Prof.

Food Science and Technology

Abid Hasnain, M., MSc *Karachi*, MPhil
Karachi Asst. Prof.
Asad Sayeed, S., MSc *Karachi* Asst. Prof.
Ifzal, S. M., MSc *Karachi*, PhD *Wales* Prof.;
Chairman*

Genetics

Ahmad, Nuzhat, MSc *Karachi*, PhD *Lond.* Prof.
Ansari, Maqsood A., MSc *Karachi*, MS
Calif. Asst. Prof.
Farooqi, Shakeelur R., MSc *Karachi*, PhD *Kansas
State* Asst. Prof.
Haider, Talat, MSc *Karachi*, MPhil
Karachi Assoc. Prof.
Nasir, Farzana, MSc *Karachi*, MPhil
Karachi Assoc. Prof.; Chairman*
Vehidy, Ahsan A., MSc *Karachi*, PhD
Hawaii Prof.

Geography

Ali, Syed S., MSc Asst. Prof.
Burke, Farkhanda, MA *Karachi*, MPhil *Karachi*,
PhD *Alig.* Asst. Prof.
Talat, Birjis, MA *Karachi* Asst. Prof.
Zainab, Khalida, MA *Karachi* Asst. Prof.

Geology

Azmatullah, MSc *And.*, PhD *Moscow* Prof.
Farooqi, M. Aquil, MSc *Karachi* Prof.
Hamid, Gulraiz Asst. Prof.
Khan, Nadeem A. Asst. Prof.
Malick, Khalil A., MSc *Sindh*, MSc *McG.*, PhD
Karachi Prof.; Chairman*
Mohsin, Syed I., MSc *Karachi*, PhD *Prague* Prof.
Naseem, Shahid, MSc *Karachi* Asst. Prof.
Qadri, Majeedullah, MSc *Karachi*, PhD
Karachi Assoc. Prof.
Shaikh, Shamim A., MSc *Karachi* Assoc. Prof.

History, General

Afroz Murad, Mehr, MA *McG.*, MA
Karachi Prof.
Aftab, Tahira, MA *Lucknow*, PhD *Karachi* Prof.
Afzal, Nasreen, MA *Karachi* Asst. Prof.
Habeeb, Shama, MA *Karachi* Asst. Prof.
Hussain, Javaid, MA *Pesh.*, PhD *Camb.* Prof.;
Chairman*
Rasheed, Nargis, MA *Karachi* Asst. Prof.
Siddiqui, Israr A., MA *Karachi* Asst. Prof.

History, Islamic

Ahmad, Nisar, MA *Karachi*, PhD *Karachi* Prof.
Mujahid, Sanaullah, MA *Karachi*, MPhil
Karachi Asst. Prof.

Sajjid Zaheer, Nigar, MA *Karachi* Asst. Prof.
Shakeel Siddiqui, M., MA *Karachi* Asst. Prof.
Sultana, Zakia, MA *Karachi*, PhD *Karachi* Assoc.
Prof.; Chairman*

International Relations

Ahmer, Monis, MSc *Islam.*, MPhil *Karachi*, PhD
Karachi Assoc. Prof.
Ghous, Khalida, MA *Karachi*, PhD
Karachi Assoc. Prof.
Mahmood, Khalid, MA *Ill.*, MA *Karachi* Assoc.
Prof.
Mehdi, S. Sikander, MA *Dacca* Prof.
Wizarat, Talat A., MA *S.Carolina*, MA
Karachi Prof.; Chairman*

Islamic Learning, see also Hist., Islamic

Ahmed, Moulvi F., MA *Karachi*, PhD
Karachi Asst. Prof.
Akhtar Saeed Siddiqi, M., MA *Punjab*, MA
Karachi, PhD *Edin.* Prof.
Auj, M. Shakeel Asst. Prof.
Firdous, Rehana, MA PhD Asst. Prof.
Hisamuddin, MA Asst. Prof.
Mehdi, Ghulam, MA *Karachi* Assoc. Prof.;
Chairman*
Noori, Jalaluddin, MA *Punjab*, PhD
Karachi Asst. Prof.
Rashid, Abdul, MA *Karachi*, PhD *Karachi* Prof.

Library and Information Science

Fatima, Nasim, MLS *Karachi*, MA *Karachi*, PhD
Karachi Prof.
Haider, S. Jalaluddin, MLS *Rutgers*, MA
Karachi Prof.; Chairman*
Khan, Anwar S., MLS *Karachi* Asst. Prof.
Qureshi, Naimuddin, LLB *Karachi*, MA *Karachi*,
MLS *Pitt.*, PhD *Pitt.* Prof.
Sherwani, Malahat K., MLS *Karachi* Prof.
Siddiq, Muhammad, MLS *Karachi* Asst. Prof.

Marine Science, see also Special Centres, etc

Mehr, Fatima, MSc *Karachi* Asst. Prof.

Mass Communications

Bari Jafri, M. Inam, MA *Karachi* Asst. Prof.
Ghaznavi, Mahmood, MA *Karachi* Asst. Prof.
Masood, Tahir, MA *Karachi*, PhD *Karachi* Asst.
Prof.
Murteza, Matinur R., MA *Karachi* Prof.
Naseem, Sarwar Asst. Prof.
Qazi Mirza, Shahida, MA *Karachi* Assoc. Prof.
Taj, Rafia Asst. Prof.
Zubiri, Nisar A., MA *Karachi*, PhD
Karachi Prof.; Chairman*

Mathematics

Ali, Syed S., MSc *Karachi*, MPhil *Karachi* Asst.
Prof.
Anwar Ali, S., MSc *Karachi*, MPhil *Karachi* Asst.
Prof.
Fahim, Rashida, MSc*Islam.*, MPhil *Islam.* Asst.
Prof.
Hussain, S. Izhar, MA *Punjab*, MSc *Stras.* Asst.
Prof.
Islamuddin, MSc *Karachi* Assoc. Prof.;
Chairman*
Jahan Abbasi, Sarwar, MA *Karachi*, PhD
Edin. Asst. Prof.
Jahan, Akhtar, MSc *Karachi* Asst. Prof.
Jamil, Anwar A., MA *Karachi*, MPhil
Karachi Asst. Prof.
Jamil, M., MSc *Karachi*, MS *W.Illinois* Asst. Prof.
Kamal, S. Arif, MSc *Karachi*, MS *Indiana*, MA *Johns
H.*, PhD *Karachi* Assoc. Prof.
Khan, Nasiruddin, MSc *Bucharest*, MSc *Karachi*,
PhD *Karachi* Prof.
Naeem, Rana K., MSc *Windsor*, MSc *Karachi*, PhD
Windsor Prof.
Paracha, Ali Asst. Prof.
Qamar, Jawaid, MA *Karachi*, MPhil *Karachi*, PhD
Islam. Prof.
Qamar, Naweda, MSc *Karachi*, MPhil
Karachi Asst. Prof.
Qureshi, Muhammad S., MSc *Karachi*, MPhil
Karachi Asst. Prof.
Qureshi, Shuja M., MSc *Karachi*, MPhil
Karachi Asst. Prof.

Shakeel, Rehana, MSc *Karachi*, MPhil
Karachi Asst. Prof.
Syed, Ansaruddin, MSc *Karachi*, PhD *Lond.* Prof.
Tauhid, Nasir, MA *Calif.*, MS *Calif.*, MSc
Karachi Assoc. Prof.
Zaidi, Shaista, MA *Edin.*, MA *Karachi* Asst. Prof.

Microbiology

Ahmed, Aqil, MSc *Karachi*, PhD *Karachi* Assoc.
Prof.
Ali, Anisa M., MSc *Karachi* Asst. Prof.
Ali, Tasneem A. Assoc. Prof.
Altaf Khan, Muhammad, MSc *Karachi*, PhD
Nott. Prof.
Ansari, Fasihuddin A., MSc *Karachi*, MPhil
Karachi, PhD *Lond.* Asst. Prof.
Jamil, Nusrat, MSc *Karachi*, PhD *Lond.* Prof.
Kazmi, Shahana U., MSc *Karachi*, PhD
Maryland Prof.
Khalid, S. M. Assoc. Prof.
Khan, Abdul F., MSc *Karachi* Prof.
Khatoon, Hajra, MSc *Karachi*, PhD *Ott.* Prof.
Rafi Shaikh, Muhammad, MSc *Karachi*, PhD
Glas. Prof.
Rasool, Shaikh A., MSc *Karachi*, PhD
Moscow Prof.; Chairman*
Razzaki, Tashmeem F., MSc *Purdue*, MSc *Karachi*,
PhD *Karachi* Prof.
Shakeel Ahmed Khan, M., MSc *Karachi* Asst.
Prof.
Siddiqui, Ruquayya, MSc *Karachi*, PhD
Lond. Assoc. Prof.
Siddiqui, Shamim A., MSc *Karachi* Asst. Prof.
Tariq, Perveen, MSc *Karachi*, MPhil
Karachi Assoc. Prof.
Vahidy, Prof. Rehana, MSc *Hawaii*, MSc
Karachi Prof.

Pakistan Study Centre, see Special Centres,
etc

Persian

Afsar, Rehana, MA *Karachi* Asst. Prof.
Siddiqui, Tahira, MA *Karachi*, PhD *Teheran* Prof.
Tafhimi, Sajidullah, MA *Karachi*, PhD
Karachi Prof.; Chairman*

Pharmaceutical Chemistry

Ahmed, Iqbal, MSc *Karachi*, PhD *Lond.* Prof.
Ahmed, Tauqir, MSc *Brad.*, MSc *Karachi*, PhD
Karachi Prof.; Chairman*
Alam, Mumtaz, MSc *Karachi*, PhD *Lond.* Assoc.
Prof.
Ali, Qazi N. M., MSc *Karachi*, PhD *Moscow* Prof.
Arif, Muhammad, MSc *Karachi*, PhD
Karachi Assoc. Prof.
Chishti, Kamran A. Asst. Prof.
Hussain, Waqar, MPharm *Karachi*, PhD
Exe. Prof.
Saify, Zafar S., MSc *Karachi*, PhD *Lond.* Prof.
Siddiqui, Hanifa S. Asst. Prof.
Sultana, Najma, MSc *Karachi*, PhD *Karachi* Prof.

Pharmaceutics

Ahmed, Mirza A., MPharm *Karachi* Assoc.
Prof.; Chairman*
Ahmed, Tasneem, MPharm *Karachi*, PhD
Karachi Assoc. Prof.
Ayub Ali, S., BPharm *Punjab*, PhD *Lond.* Prof.
Baqir Shyum Naqvi, S., MSc *Karachi*, PhD
Karachi Assoc. Prof.
Beg, Anwar E., MSc *Karachi*, MPhil *Karachi*, PhD
Bath Prof.
Hasan, Fauzia, MPharm *Karachi*, MPhil
Karachi Asst. Prof.
Rizvi, Nighat, MPharm *Karachi*, MPhil *Karachi*,
PhD *Karachi* Asst. Prof.
Shaikh, Dilnawaz, MSc *Karachi*, PhD
Karachi Prof.

Pharmacognosy

Ahmed, Mansoor, MSc *Karachi*, PhD *E.T.H.
Zürich* Assoc. Prof.; Chairman*
Ahmed, Waseemuddin S., MPharm *Karachi*, PhD
Karachi Asst. Prof.
Khan, Usman G., MSc *Karachi*, MPharm *Osaka*,
PhD *Karachi* Prof.
Rizwani, Ghazala H., BPharm *Karachi*, MPharm
Karachi, PhD *Karachi* Assoc. Prof.

Siddiqui, Shahida, MSc Sindh, PhD Sindh   Assoc.
Prof.

Pharmacology

Ahmed, Shahida P., MSc Karachi, MPhil Karachi,
PhD Karachi   Prof.
Rashid, Shahid, MSc Alig., PhD Brad.   Prof.
Rehman, Asif B., MSc Karachi, MPhil Karachi,
MD   Asst. Prof.; Chairman*
Sheikh, Khairun-Nisa   Asst. Prof.

Philosophy

Farid, Arifa, MA Hawaii, MA Karachi, PhD
Arkansas   Prof.
Tayyab, Basharat, MA Karachi, PhD
Karachi   Assoc. Prof.; Chairman*

Physics

Ahmed, Feroz, MSc ANU, MSc Karachi, PhD
Karachi   Prof.
Akhtar, S. Kaab, MSc Karachi, MSc Laur., PhD
Sing.   Assoc. Prof.
Akhter, Wasim, MSc Karachi, MPhil Karachi, PhD
Wales   Assoc. Prof.
Anis, Khalid, MSc CNAA, MSc Karachi, PhD
CNAA   Assoc. Prof.
Bano, Naquiba, MSc Karachi, MPhil Karachi, PhD
Lond.   Assoc. Prof.
Ghani, Abdul, MSc Karachi, PhD Lond.   Assoc.
Prof.
Jamila, Sajida, MSc Karachi, PhD Nott.   Asst.
Prof.
Khan, Hameedullah, MSc Karachi   Asst. Prof.
Khan, Iqbal A., MSc Karachi, PhD Kent
State   Assoc. Prof.
Nafis, Birjees, MSc Karachi, PhDLond.   Asst. Prof.
Naqvi, S. Munir M. R., MSc Durh., MSc Karachi,
PhD Moscow   Prof.; Chairman*
Naseeruddin, MSc Karachi, MPhil Karachi   Asst.
Prof.
Qidwai, Ansar A., MSc Karachi, MPhil Karachi,
PhD Durh.   Prof.
Rahim, Tahseen, PhD Lond.   Asst. Prof.
Raof, M. A., MSc Karachi, MSc Birm., PhD
Lond.   Prof.
Razi Husain, M., MSc Lond., MSc Karachi, PhD
Lond.   Assoc. Prof.
Rizvi, Dabir H., MSc Karachi   Assoc. Prof.
Siddiqui, Khurshid A., MSc Karachi, PhD
Nott.   Prof.

Physics, Applied

Ansari, Azhar A., MSc Manc., MSc Karachi, PhD
Lond.   Prof.
Ayub Khan Yousufzai, M., MSc Laur., MSc
Karachi   Asst. Prof.
Qadeer, Abdul, MSc Karachi, MSc Laur., PhD
Hull   Prof.
Siddiqui, Najeeb, MSc Karachi, PhD Lond.   Asst.
Prof.
Zaidi, Shahid H., MSc Karachi, PhD Lond.   Prof.;
Chairman*

Physiology

Ameer, Shahla, MSc Karachi, PhD Exe.   Asst.
Prof.
Arshad, Ruqayya, MSc Karachi   Assoc. Prof.
Azeem, Muhammad A., MSc Karachi, PhD
Karachi   Assoc. Prof.
Hasan, Ruqiya, MSc Karachi   Asst. Prof.
Javaid, Aisha, MSc Karachi   Asst. Prof.
Khan, Kalimur R., MSc Karachi, PhD
Innsbruck   Prof.
Naim, Tazeen, MSc Karachi   Asst. Prof.
Qureshi, Masood A., MSc Punjab, PhD
Aston   Prof.; Chairman*
Qureshi, Nasreen M., MSc Karachi, PhD
Karachi   Prof.
Rafi, Farkhunda, MSc Punjab, PhD
Newcastle(UK)   Prof.
Siddiqui, Pirzada Q. R., MSc Karachi, PhD
Newcastle(UK)   Prof.
Siddiqui, Ubaida, MSc Karachi   Asst. Prof.
Zafar, Farhat, MSc Karachi   Asst. Prof.

Political Science

Ali, Mehrunnisa, MA Alta., MA Karachi   Prof.
Azhar Ali, S., MA Dacca, PhD Karachi   Prof.
Khalid, Tanweer, MA Karachi   Prof.

Qadri, Hafiz M. A., MA Karachi, PhD
Karachi   Asst. Prof.
Qadri, Muhammad A., MA Karachi, MPhil
Karachi, PhD Karachi   Asst. Prof.
Rizvi, Nihal H., MA Wash., MA Karachi   Prof.;
Chairman*

Psychology

Ara, Anjum, MA Patna, PhD Patna   Asst. Prof.
Hashmi, Muhammad S., MA Karachi   Prof.
Ismail, Zeenat, MA Karachi, PhD Karachi   Prof.;
Chairman*
Raees, Sohaila, MA Karachi, PhD Karachi   Asst.
Prof.
Razzak, Rubina, MA Karachi   Asst. Prof.
Rizvi, Haider A., MSc Karachi   Asst. Prof.
Sultana, Anwar, MA Karachi   Asst. Prof.
Talat Hussain, Rukhshinda, MA Karachi   Asst.
Prof.

Public Administration

Baloch, Akhtar   Asst. Prof.
Humayun, Syed, MA Karachi, PhD Karachi   Prof.
Wajidi, M. Abuzar, MA Karachi, PhD
Karachi   Prof.; Chairman*

Sindhi

Abbasi, Khurshid, MA Karachi   Asst. Prof.
Hussain, Fahmida, MA Sindh, PhD Karachi   Prof.
Memon, Muhammad S., MA Karachi   Prof.;
Chairman*

Social Work

Ara Shafi, Husna, MA Karachi   Asst. Prof.
Ayub, Nasreen   Asst. Prof.
Aziz, Shama   Asst. Prof.
Farman, Najma, MA Karachi   Asst. Prof.
Hussain, Anzar, MA Karachi   Asst. Prof.
Jafri, S. K. H., MA Lucknow   Prof.; Chairman*
Kazi, Kulsoom, MA Karachi   Asst. Prof.
Shabid, M   Asst. Prof.
Shah, M. Aslam, MA Punjab, MA Calif.   Prof.

Sociology

Faridi, Farhat, MA Karachi   Asst. Prof.
Iqbal, Musarat, LLB Karachi, MA Karachi   Asst.
Prof.
Muhammad, Fateh, MA Karachi   Asst. Prof.
Qizibash, Ansar H., MA Karachi, PhD
Karachi   Prof.; Chairman*
Rehman, Khalida, MA Karachi   Prof.
Saba, Rana   Asst. Prof.

Statistics

Ahmed, Ejaz, MSc Karachi, PhD Strath.   Prof.
Ahmed, S. Afrozuddin, MSc Karachi   Assoc.
Prof.
Ali, Tasneem, MSc Karachi   Asst. Prof.
Aslam, Muhammad   Asst. Prof.
Haq, Masoodul, MA Hawaii, MSc Karachi   Prof.;
Chairman*
Hussain, Ehtesham   Asst. Prof.
Hussain, Ghulam, MSc Karachi   Asst. Prof.
Khurshid, Anwar, MSc Karachi   Asst. Prof.
Mahmood, Zahid, MA Punjab   Prof.
Siddiqui, Asim J., MSc McG., MSc Karachi   Prof.
Siddiqui, Junaid S., MSc Karachi, PhD
Exe.   Prof.

Urdu

Ansari, Anwar M. S., MA Karachi   Prof.;
Chairman*
Aqeel, Moinuddin, MA Karachi, PhD
Karachi   Assoc. Prof.
Arman, Siddiqa, MA Karachi, PhD
Karachi   Assoc. Prof.; Chairman*
Iqbal, Zafar, MA Sindh, PhD Sindh   Assoc. Prof.
Khan, Jamil A., MA Karachi   Prof.
Zaidi, Mehjabeen, MA Karachi, PhD
Karachi   Asst. Prof.

Zoology

Afzal Kazmi, M., MSc Alig., PhD Karachi   Prof.;
Chairman*
Ahmed, Imtiaz, MSc Karachi, PhD Lond., DSc
Lond.   Prof.
Arshad, M., MSc Karachi, MPhil Karachi, PhD
Karachi   Asst. Prof.

Barkati, Sohail, MSc Karachi, PhD Karachi   Assoc.
Prof.
Begum, Farida, MSc Karachi, PhD Karachi   Asst.
Prof.
Hasan, Habibul, MSc Karachi, PhD
Karachi   Assoc. Prof.
Haseen, Fatima,   Asst. Prof.
Iqbal, Muhammad   Prof.
Jawaid, Waqar, MSc Alig., PhD Karachi   Asst. Prof.
Kazmi, Quddusi B., MSc Karachi, PhD
Karachi   Prof.
Khan, Jafar A., MSc Karachi, PhD Kiel   Prof.
Malik, Kulsum F., MSc   Prof.
Muhammad, Fatima A., MSc Karachi, PhD
Karachi   Asst. Prof.
Qureshi, Wali M., MSc Vikram   Asst. Prof.
Rehana Farooq, Yasmeen   Asst. Prof.
Rizvi, Sayida N., MSc Karachi, PhD
Karachi   Prof.
Saqib, Tasneem   Asst. Prof.
Siddiqui, Nikhat Y., MSc Karachi, PhD
Karachi   Prof.
Siddiqui, Pervez A., MSc Karachi   Prof.
Zaidi, Raees H., MSc Karachi, PhD Karachi   Asst.
Prof.

SPECIAL CENTRES, ETC

Applied Economics Research Centre
Ahmad, Nuzhat   Dir.*

Biological Research and Flora of West Pakistan Centre
Ali, Prof. S. I., MSc Alld., PhD Lond., DSc
Lond.   Dir.*

Chemistry, H. E. J. Research Institute of
Tel: (021) 498 3591 Fax: (021) 496 3373,
496 3124
Abbasi, Atiya, MSc Karachi, PhD Karachi   Assoc.
Prof.
Ahmed, Viqaruddin, MSc Alld., PhD Karachi,
DrRerNatBonn, DSc Karachi   Prof.
Ali, Shaiq, MSc Karachi, PhD Karachi   Asst. Prof.
Ateeq, Humayun S., PhD St. Louis   Asst. Prof.
Begum, Sabira, MSc Karachi, PhD Karachi   Asst.
Prof.
Dar, Ahsan, MSc Karachi, MPhil Karachi, MS
St.Louis, PhD Karachi   Asst. Prof.
Darakshanda, Shehnaz, MSc Karachi, MSc Strath.,
PhD Strath.   Asst. Prof.
Ejaz, M. Saleh, MSc Karachi, MPhil Islam., PhD
Karachi   Asst. Prof.
Faizi, Shaheen, MSc Karachi, PhD Karachi   Assoc.
Prof.
Iqbal, Chaudhary M, MSc Karachi, PhD
Karachi   Assoc. Prof.
Khan, Khalid M.   Asst. Prof.
Malik, Abdul, MSc Karachi, PhD Karachi   Prof.
Rahman, Attaur, MSc Karachi, PhD Camb., ScD
Camb.   Prof.; Dir.*
Shekhani, M. Saleh, MSc Karachi, PhD
N.Y.   Assoc. Prof.
Siddiqui, Bina S., MSc Karachi, MPhil Karachi,
PhD Karachi   Prof.
Zaidi, Zafar H., MSc Sindh, PhD Leeds, DSc
Leeds   Prof.

Environmental Studies, Institute of
Tel: (021) 474843
Khan, M. Altaf   Prof.; Dir.*

Europe, Area Study Centre for
Tahir, Navid A., MA   Dir.*

M. A. H. Qadri Biological Research Centre
Vahidy, Prof. A. A., MSc Karachi, PhD
Hawaii   Dir.*

Marine Biology, Centre of Excellence in
Tel: (021) 470572
Ahmed, Muzamil, PhD Wash., MSc   Prof.;
Dir.*

Marine Reference Collection and Resource Centre

Kazmi, Quddusi B., MSc *Karachi*, PhD *Karachi* Prof.; Dir.*

Marine Science, Institute of

Qadri, Prof. Mustafa S., MSc *Karachi*, PhD *Karachi* Dir.*

National Nematological Research Centre

Tel: (021) 496 9019

Maqbool, M. A., MScAgri PhD Dir.*

Pakistan Study Centre

Tel: (021) 496 2497

Jafri, Prof. S. H. M., MA *Lucknow*, PhD *Lucknow*, PhD *Lond.* Dir.*

Pure and Applied Physics, Institute of

Vacant Posts: Dir.*

Shaikh Zayed Islamic Research Centre

Shaheed, Prof. Abdul, MA *Karachi*, PhD *Karachi* Dir.*

Women's Studies, Centre of Excellence for

Farid, Asifa, MA *Hawaii*, MA *Karachi*, PhD *Arkansas* Prof.

CONTACT OFFICERS

Examinations. Controller of Examinations: ......
Finance. Director of Finance: Khan, Younus A., MBA
General enquiries. Registrar: Mahmud, Tariq, MSc *Karachi*
Library (chief librarian). Librarian: Sherwani, Malahat K., MLS *Karachi*
Public relations, information and marketing. Public Relations Officer: ......

[*Information supplied by the institution as at 21 April 1998, and edited by the ACU*]

LAHORE UNIVERSITY OF MANAGEMENT SCIENCES

Founded 1985

Member of the Association of Commonwealth Universities

Postal Address: Opposite Sector U, Lahore Cantonment Co-operative Housing Society, Lahore 54792, Pakistan
Telephone: (042) 572 2670-9 **Fax**: (042) 572 2591 **Cables**: Legsba, LHR **Telex**: 44866 PKGS PK
WWW: http://www.lums.edu.pk

CHANCELLOR—The President of Pakistan (*ex officio*)
PRO-CHANCELLOR—Babar, Ali S.
RECTOR*—Razak Dawood, Abdul, BSc *Newcastle(UK)*, MBA *Col.*
DEAN—Azhar, Prof. Wasim, MSc *Penn.*, MSc *Lahore UET*, MBA *Wake Forest*, PhD *Penn.*
GENERAL MANAGER (FINANCE AND ADMINISTRATION)—Ashraf, Mohammad, MCom

GENERAL INFORMATION

History. The university was established in 1985. It is located 8km south east of Lahore airport.

Admission to first degree courses (see also Pakistan Introduction). General Certificate of Education (GCE) A level or equivalent.

First Degrees (see also Pakistan Directory to Subjects of Study). BSc (honours): 4 years full-time.

Higher Degrees (see also Pakistan Directory to Subjects of Study). MBA, MS.
Applicants for admission to MBA must hold a first degree from an institution recognised by this university.
MS: 1 year full-time; MBA: 2 years full-time.

Libraries. Over 17,000 volumes; 200 periodicals; 1500 government publications.

Fees (annual). BSc: about Rs150,000; MBA: about Rs230,000.

Academic Year (1997–98). BSc course: four quarters (25 August–7 November; 17 November–23 January; 9 February–2 May; 11 May–June). MBA course: three quarters (8 September–28 November; 15 December–6 March; 24 March–June).

Income (1996–97). Total, about Rs136,000,000.

Statistics. Staff: 270 (including 54 research and teaching staff). Students, total 485.

ACADEMIC STAFF

Ali, Anjum, MSc *Pet.& Min.*, *Saudi Arabia*, PhD *Alabama* Asst. Prof.
Ali, Imran, MSc *Lahore UET*, MS *N.Y.State*, MBA *Ohio State*, PhD *ANU* Prof.
Amir, Irfan, MBA *Punjab*, PhD *Manc.* Asst. Prof.
Aslam, Sohail, MS *Kansas*, MS *Colorado*, PhD *Ill.* Assoc. Prof.
Azhar, Wasim, MSc *Penn.*, MSc *Lahore UET*, MBA *Wake Forest*, PhD *Penn.* Prof.
Ghani, Jawaid, SB *M.I.T.*, PhD *Penn.* Prof.
Haque, Ehsan Ul, BSc *Lahore UET*, MBA *Penn.*, PhD *Texas* Assoc. Prof.
Hasan, Naveed, MBA *Punjab*, PhD *Lond.* Asst. Prof.
Hassan, S. Zahoor, MS *Stan.*, MSEM *Stan.*, PhD *Stan.* Prof.
Ikram, Shahid, MS *Syr.*, PhD *Syr.* Asst. Prof.
Ilahi, Nadeem, MS *Calif.*, PhD *Calif.* Asst. Prof.
Khan, Bashir A., BSc *Lond.*, MBA *Penn.State*, MSc *Oxf.*, DPhil *Oxf.* Asst. Prof.
Khan, Jamshed H., BSME *Texas*, MBA *Texas*, MSIE *Texas*, PhD *Texas* Assoc. Prof.
Khan, Wasif M., BSc *Lahore UET*, MSc *Oregon State*, MPPM *Yale* Assoc. Prof.
Khurshid, Anwar, MSc *Lahore UET*, MS *N.Y.State*, MBA *Ohio State*, PhD *Mich.State* Prof.
Mubashir Ali, S., PhD *Manc.* Asst. Prof.
Nasim, Anjum, BSc *Lond.*, MA *Essex*, PhD *Essex* Prof.
Qureshi, Zafar I., MBA *Beirut*, PhD *Pitt.* Prof.
Rana, Arif I., MS *Purdue*, PhD *Rensselaer* Asst. Prof.
Shah, Syed I. A., MSc *Ott.*, PhD *Col.* Asst. Prof.
Sherazi, Saima N., MA *Punjab* Asst. Prof.
Sipra, Naim, MBA *Texas*, PhD *Texas* Prof.
Zafar, Ansa, BA *Camb.*, MA *Liv.* Asst. Prof.
Zaman, Arif, MA *Claremont*, PhD *Stan.* Prof.
Zia, Farrukh, MSc *Syr.*, PhD *Syr.* Asst. Prof.

CONTACT OFFICERS

Academic affairs. Associate Dean (MBA): Qureshi, Prof. Zafar I., MBA *Beirut*, PhD *Pitt.*; *Associate Dean (BSc)*: Hassan, Prof. S. Zahoor, MS *Stan.*, MSEM *Stan.*, PhD *Stan.*
Accommodation. Manager, Administration: Ramzan, Col. M., BSc
Admissions (first degree). Manager, Student Affairs: Malik, Shazi, MBusEd
Admissions (higher degree). Manager, Student Affairs: Malik, Shazi, MBusEd
Alumni. Associate Editor: Hyat, Humaira, MBA *Lahore MS*
Archives. Chief Librarian: Riaz, Bushra, MLS
Careers. Senior Manager, Programme Development: Khan, Mohammad A., MS *Ill.*
Computing services. Manager, Computer Resources: Yazdani, Saeed, MSc *Maryland*
Consultancy services. Dean: Azhar, Prof. Wasim, MSc *Penn.*, MSc *Lahore UET*, MBA *Wake Forest*, PhD *Penn.*
Development/fund-raising. Senior Manager, Programme Development: Khan, Mohammad A., MS *Ill.*
Equal opportunities. Manager, Human Resources: Malik, Shazi, MBusEd
Estates and buildings/works and services. Senior Manager, Maintenance: Khan, Azmatullah, BSc BE
Examinations. (Contact the faculty concerned)
Finance. General Manager (Finance and Administration): Ashraf, Mohammad, MCom
General enquiries. General Manager (Finance and Administration): Ashraf, Mohammad, MCom
International office. Manager, Student Affairs: Malik, Shazi, MBusEd
Library (chief librarian). Chief Librarian: Riaz, Bushra, MLS

Personnel/human resources. General Manager (Finance and Administration): Ashraf, Mohammad, MCom

Public relations, information and marketing. Senior Manager, Programme Development: Khan, Mohammad A., MS *Ill.*

Publications. Associate Editor: Hyat, Humaira, MBA *Lahore* MS

Purchasing. Purchase Officer: Zahoor, Tariq, MAdSc

Quality assurance and accreditation. General Manager (Finance and Administration): Ashraf, Mohammad, MCom

Research. Sipra, Naim, MBA *Texas*, PhD *Texas*;

Associate Dean: Ghani, Prof. Jawaid, SB M.I.T., PhD Penn.

Safety. General Manager (Finance and Administration): Ashraf, Mohammad, MCom

Scholarships, awards, loans. Manager, Student Affairs/Manager, Human Resources: Malik, Shazi, MBusEd

Schools liaison. Manager, Programme Co-ordination: Riaz, Aaliya, MBA

Security. Manager, Administration: Ramzan, Col. M., BSc

Sport and recreation. Manager, Administration: Ramzan, Col. M., BSc

Staff development and training. General Manager (Finance and Administration): Ashraf, Mohammad, MCom

Student welfare/counselling. Associate Dean (MBA): Qureshi, Prof. Zafar I., MBA *Beirut*, PhD *Pitt.*; Associate Dean (BSc): Hassan, Prof. S. Zahoor, MS *Stan.*, MSEM *Stan.*, PhD *Stan.*

Students from other countries. Manager, Student Affairs: Malik, Shazi, MBusEd

[*Information supplied by the institution as at 13 February 1998, and edited by the ACU*]

MEHRAN UNIVERSITY OF ENGINEERING AND TECHNOLOGY

Founded 1963 as Sindh University Engineering College; present status, 1977

Member of the Association of Commonwealth Universities

Postal Address: Jamshoro 76062, Sindh, Pakistan
Telephone: (0221) 771197 **Fax**: (0221) 771382 **Cables**: MUET JAM

CHANCELLOR—H.E. The Governor of Sindh (*ex officio*)
VICE-CHANCELLOR*—Memon, Prof. Abdul R., MSc *Bath*, PhD *City(UK)*
REGISTRAR—Qureshi, Muhammad N., LLB *Sindh*, MA *Sindh*
DIRECTOR, FINANCE—Narejo, Muhammad M., BCom *Sindh*
DIRECTOR, PLANNING AND DEVELOPMENT—Memon, Muhammad S., LLB *Sindh*, MA *Sindh*, MEd *Sindh*

GENERAL INFORMATION

History. The university was founded in 1963 as Sindh University Engineering College, a constituent college of the University of Sindh. In March 1977 it achieved university status and was renamed Mehran University of Engineering and Technology.

Admission to first degree courses (see also Pakistan Introduction). International applicants, nominated by the Ministry of Finance and Economic Affairs, may be admitted under a cultural exchange programme.

First Degrees. BEngg (4 years).

Higher Degrees. MEngg, MPhil, PhD.

Libraries. Central library: about 90,000 volumes; about 75 periodicals subscribed to.

Fees. Undergraduate, (annual): Rs6360. Postgraduate: (Pakistani students) Rs16,800 (MEngg), Rs16,050 (MPhil), Rs20,650 (PhD); (international students) Rs28,950 (MEngg), Rs27,300 (MPhil), Rs32,000 (PhD).

Academic Year. Two terms.

Income. Total, Rs90,867,000.

Statistics. Staff: 886 (247 academic, 639 administrative). Students: 3893.

FACULTIES/SCHOOLS
Architecture
Tel: (0221) 771638
Dean: Khowaja, Dost A., BE *Mehran*, PhD *Strath.*

Engineering
Tel: (0221) 771352
Dean: Memon, Prof. Haji Mehmood, BE *Karachi*, PhD *Lond.*

ACADEMIC UNITS

Architecture, see also City and Regional Planning
Tel: (0221) 771638
Halephota, A. R., BArch *Mehran*, MA *Sindh* Asst. Prof.
Irfan, N., BArch *NED Eng.* Asst. Prof.
Jokhio, M. H., BArch *Mehran* Asst. Prof.
Khan, Nadeemullah, BArch *Lahore UET* Asst. Prof.; Chairman-in-Charge*
Mahesar, Saeed Y., BArch *Mehran* Asst. Prof.
Pathan, Moazim A., BArch *Mehran* Asst. Prof.
Shar, B. K., BArch *Mehran* Asst. Prof. (on leave)
Soomro, A. R., BArch *Mehran*, MA Asst. Prof. (on leave)

Basic Sciences and Related Studies
Tel: (0221) 771409
Abro, Saifullah, MSc *Sindh* Asst. Prof.
Baloch, Ahsanullah, BSc *Sindh*, MSc *Sindh*, PhD *Wales* Prof.
Chajro, K. M., MSc *Sindh* Asst. Prof.
Ghanghro, Abdul R., MA *Sindh*, PhD *Sindh* Asst. Prof.
Hashmi, Ibne H., BSc *Sindh*, MSc *Sindh* Prof.
Jamali, Yasmin, MA *Sindh* Asst. Prof.
Memon, Nasrullah, MSc *Sindh* Asst. Prof.
Pahore, A. H., MSc *Sindh* Asst. Prof.
Pathan, A. N., MSc *Sindh* Asst. Prof.
Rathi, K. L., MSc *Sindh* Asst. Prof. (on leave)
Shaikh, M. U., MSc *Cran.* Prof.; Chairman*

City and Regional Planning
Tel: (0221) 771638
Dahri, M. A., BE *Mehran* Assoc. Prof.
Khowaja, Dost A., BE *Mehran*, PhD *Strath.* Prof.; Chairman*
Memon, Noor M., BE *NED Eng.*, MCP Visiting Prof.

Engineering, Chemical
Tel: (0221) 771642
Ansari, A. K., BE *Sindh*, MSc *Wales*, PhD *Wales* Prof.
Memon, Hidayatullah, MSc *Sindh*, MPhil *Sheff.* Prof.
Memon, Munawar A., BE *Sindh*, MSc *Sheff.* Prof.; Chairman*
Pathan, M. I., BE *Sindh*, MSc *Salf.*, PhD *Salf.* Prof.
Pirzada, A. H., BE Asst. Prof.
Rajput, A. A., BE *Sindh*, LLB *Sindh* Asst. Prof.
Shaikh, Naeem A., BE *NED Eng.* Asst. Prof.
Soomro, Suhail A., BE *Mehran*, MSc *Brad.* Asst. Prof.
Syed, Farman A. S., BE *Mehran* Asst. Prof.
Talpur, A. N., BE *Sindh*, LLB *Sindh* Assoc. Prof.
Talpur, Abdul K., MSc *Sindh*, PhD *Sindh* Assoc. Prof.

Engineering, Civil
Tel: (0221) 771269
Abro, A. A., BE *Sindh*, MSc *Lond.*, PhD *S'ton.* Prof.
Ansari, Javed K., BE *Mehran* Asst. Prof.
Balouch, A. A., BE *Mehran* Asst. Prof.
Channa, A. B., BE *Sindh*, ME *Mehran* Prof.; Chairman*
Gugarman, M. M., BE *Mehran*, PhD Assoc. Prof.
Khaskheli, G. B., MEng *Sheff.*, PhD *Glas.* Prof.
Khatri, M. S., BE *Sindh*, MSc *Glas.* Prof.

Kumbhar, M. Y., BE(Agri) *Sindh*, ME
  Mehran Assoc. Prof.
Lashari, Abdul N., BE NED Eng., MS *King
  Fahd* Asst. Prof.
Leghari, M. M., BE *Sindh*, MPhil *Brad.* Assoc.
  Prof.
Mahesar, Ghulam H., MSc *Sindh* Asst. Prof.
Memon, Abdul R., BE NED Eng. Asst. Prof.
Memon, Ali A., BE *Sindh*, MPhil *Brad.* Prof.
Memon, Allah B., BE *Roor.*, ME *Roor.* Assoc.
  Prof
Memon, Ashfaque A., BE *Mehran*, ME
  Mehran Asst. Prof.
Memon, G. H., BE *Sindh*, MSc *Glas.* Prof.
Memon, Hizbullah, BE *Mehran* Asst. Prof.
Memon, Muhammad S., BE *Sindh*, ME Assoc.
  Prof
Memon, Mumtaz A., BE *Sindh*, ME *Asian I.T.*,
  Bangkok Prof.
Oad, M. C., BE *Sindh*, MSc *Iowa* Assoc. Prof.
  (on lien)
Phul, A. M., BE Asst. Prof.
Shaikh, Pervez A., BE Asst. Prof.
Shaikh, Rafique A., BE *Sindh* Asst. Prof.

Engineering, Computer Systems
Tel: (0221) 771206

Hafiz, T., BE *Mehran* Asst. Prof.
Halepota, Muhammad M. A. A., BE
  Mehran Asst. Prof. (on leave)
Jaffery, Naveed A., BE *Mehran* Asst. Prof.
Lakhani, Azim, BE *Mehran*, MSc Asst. Prof.
Rajput, Abdul Q. K., BE *Sindh*, MSc *Leeds*, PhD
  Pitt. Prof.; Chairman*
Shaikh, Muhammad Z., BE *Mehran* Asst. Prof.
Thebo, L. A., BE *Mehran* Asst. Prof.
Unar, M. H., BE MSc Assoc. Prof.

Engineering, Electrical
Tel: (0221) 771531

Abro, M. R., BE *Sindh*, PhD *Sheff.* Prof.
Baloch, B. H., BE *Sindh*, ME Assoc. Prof.
Burdi, M. K., BE *Sindh*, MSc *Lough.*, PhD
  Bath Prof.; Chairman*
Chang, A. Q., BE *Sindh* Prof.
Memon, A. S., BE *Sindh* Asst. Prof.
Memon, Anwar A., BE *Sindh* Asst. Prof.
Memon, F. I., BSc *Ankara* Asst. Prof.
Memon, Shabir A., BE *Sindh*, MEng *Manc.* Prof.
Mirani, M. A., BE *Sindh*, MA *Sindh* Assoc. Prof.
Pathan, A. Z., BE *Sindh*, MSc *T.H.Dresden* Prof.
Shaikh, Abdul R., BE *Sindh*, MPhil *Brad.* Prof.
Uqaili, M. A., BE NED Eng., MA *Sindh*, PhD
  Leeds Assoc. Prof.

Engineering, Electronics
Tel: (0221) 771334

Aboo, Farzana R., BE NED Eng. Asst. Prof.
Ansari, Abdul S., BE NED Eng. Asst. Prof.
Baloch, A. K., BE *Sindh*, MPhil *S'ton*, PhD
  Brad. Prof.
Chowdhry, B. S., BE *Mehran*, PhD *S'ton.* Prof.;
  Chairman*
Memon, Abdul R., MSc *Bath*, PhD
  City(UK) Prof.
Memon, Aftab A., BE *Mehran*, MSc
  Louisiana Asst. Prof.
Unar, M. A., BE Asst. Prof. (on leave)
Wasan, I. A., BE NED Eng. Asst. Prof.
Waseer, Turfail A., BE *Mehran* Asst. Prof.

Engineering, Industrial
Tel: (0221) 771197

Abbasi, Aitbar A., BE *Mehran* Asst. Prof.
Abbasi, S. A., BE *Mehran* Asst. Prof.
Maree, H. B., BE Asst. Prof. (on leave)
Nebhwani, M., BE Assoc. Prof.; Chairman*
Qureshi, Najamul H., BSc *Lahore UET*, ME
  Arizona Asst. Prof.
Shah, Aijaz A., LLB *Sindh*, MA *Sindh* Asst. Prof.
Shaikh, Ghulam Y., BE *Mehran*, MBA Asst.
  Prof.
Sohag, R. A., BE *Sindh*, PhD Prof.
Soomro, G. M., BE *Sindh* Assoc. Prof. (on
  leave)
Tanwari, A., BE *Mehran* Asst. Prof. (on leave)

Engineering, Mechanical
Tel: (0221) 771205

Brohi, K. M., BE *Mehran*, MA *Sindh* Asst. Prof.
Dewani, M. L., BE *Sindh*, LLB *Sindh*, ME
  Mehran Prof.; Chairman*
Durani, H. A., BE *Mehran* Asst. Prof. (on lien)
Junejo, A. A., PhD *Wales* Prof. (on lien)
Khaliqdino, J. H., BE *Mehran* Asst. Prof.
Khowaja, N., BE *Mehran* Assoc. Prof.
Memon, Abdul S., BE *Mehran* Asst. Prof.
Memon, Abu B., BE *Sindh* Assoc. Prof.
Memon, Ashfaque A., BE *Sindh* Assoc. Prof.
Memon, Mujeebuddin, BE *Mehran*, DPhil
  Sus. Assoc. Prof.
Memon, Mushtaque A., ME Assoc. Prof.
Memon, Saeed A., BE *Mehran* Asst. Prof.
Memon, Shoukat A., BE *Mehran* Asst. Prof.
Nizamani, R. A., BE *Mehran* Asst. Prof.
Panhwar, M. I., BE *Sindh*, PhD *Sheff.* Prof.
Shah, Pir R., BE *Mehran*, MSc *Nott.*, PhD
  Nott. Assoc. Prof.
Shaikh, Nazimuddin, BE *Sindh*, MEng
  Sheff. Prof.

Engineering, Metallurgical

Abbasi, Faizullah, BE *Sindh*, PhD *Sheff.* Prof.
  (on lien)
Abbasi, Khursheed A., BE *Sindh* Asst. Prof.
Ansari, Baqar A., BE *Mehran* Asst. Prof.
Essani, Ashfaque A., BE *Mehran* Asst. Prof.
Jokhio, M. H., BE NED Eng., ME *Mehran* Asst.
  Prof.
Mallah, A. H., BE *Sindh*, MMet *Sheff.*, PhD
  Sheff. Prof.; Chairman*
Memon, Ali N., BE *Mehran* Asst. Prof.
Memon, Riaz A., BE *Mehran* Asst. Prof.
Memon, Sikandar A., BE *Mehran* Asst. Prof.
Memon, Sultan A., BE *Mehran* Asst. Prof.
Sabayo, M. R., BE *Sindh*, MSc *Manc.*, PhD
  Manc. Prof.

Engineering, Mining
Tel: (0221) 771167

Channa, N. R., BE *Mehran* Asst. Prof.
Halepota, G. R., BE *Sindh*, MPhil *Nott.* Prof.
Memon, Ahsan A., BE *Mehran* Asst. Prof.
Pathan, A. G., BE *Mehran*, PhD *Nott.* Prof.;
  Chairman*
Pathan, Pervez A., MSc *Sindh* Assoc. Prof.
Rind, Muhammad H., BE *Mehran* Asst. Prof.
Sahito, Wasayo, BE *Mehran* Asst. Prof.
Shah, Mohammad A., BEng *Nott.*, LLB *Nott.*,
  PhD *Nott.* Assoc. Prof.
Sherazi, M. A., BE *Mehran* Asst. Prof.

Engineering, Textile, see Special Centres,
  etc (Technol., Inst. of)

Petroleum and Natural Gas Engineering, Institute of

Arbani, S. A., BE *Mehran*, MSc Prof.; Director*
Memon, H. R., BEng *Leeds*, PhD *Leeds* Assoc.
  Prof.
Qazi, Rafique A., BEng *Salf.*, PhD *Salf.* Prof.
Qureshi, Nafeesa, BE *Mehran* Asst. Prof. (on
  leave)
Sahito, M. H., BE *Mehran* Asst. Prof.
Soomro, M. Y., BE *Sindh*, MSc *Salf.*, PhD
  Salf. Prof.
Soomro, Zulekha, MSc *Sindh* Assoc. Prof.

Planning, see City and Regional Planning

SPECIAL CENTRES, ETC

English Language Centre
Tel: (0221) 771286
Bodlo, M. H., MA *Sindh*, MA *Edin.* Prof.; Dir.*

Environmental Engineering and Management, Institute of
Tel: (0221) 771282
Ansari, A. K., BE *Sindh*, MSc *Wales*, PhD
  Wales Prof.; Dir.*

Irrigation and Drainage Engineering, Institute of
Tel: (0221) 771226

Babar, M. M., BE ME Asst. Prof. (on leave)
Chandio, S. N., BE *Sindh*, ME *S'ton* Prof.; Dir.*
Kori, Shafi M., BE *Mehran*, ME *Mehran* Asst.
  Prof.
Lashari, B. K., BE(Agri) *Sindh Ag.*, ME*Mehran*,
  PhD Prof.
Memon, Haji Mehmood, BE *Karachi*, PhD
  Lond. Prof.
Qureshi, A. L., BE *Mehran*, ME *Mehran* Asst.
  Prof.

Technology, Institute of
Textile Engineering
Tel: (0221) 771197

Khiani, Raj K., BSc *Faisalabad* Asst. Prof.
Memon, A. R., MSc *Bath*, PhD *City(UK)* Dir.*
Samo, A. R., MSc *Sindh*, MSc *Leeds* Prof.;
  Chairman*

CONTACT OFFICERS

Academic affairs. Dean, Engineering: Memon,
  Prof. Haji Mehmood, BE *Karachi*, PhD *Lond.*
Accommodation. Project Director: Kandhar, G.
  S., BE *Sindh*, ME
Admissions (higher degree). Registrar:
  Qureshi, Muhammad N., LLB *Sindh*, MA *Sindh*
Admissions (higher degree). Agha, Prof.
  Zafarullah K. P., BE *Sindh*, MSc
Adult/continuing education. : ......
Computing services. Siddiqui, S., MSc *Sindh*,
  MS *N.Y.*
Consultancy services. Memon, A. A., BE *Sindh*,
  MPhil *Brad.*
Development/fund-raising (development).
  Project Director: Kandhar, G. S., BE *Sindh*,
  ME
Development/fund-raising (fund-raising).
  Director, Finance: Narejo, Muhammad M.,
  BCom *Sindh*
Distance education. Registrar: Qureshi,
  Muhammad N., LLB *Sindh*, MA *Sindh*
Estates and buildings/works and services.
  Project Director: Kandhar, G. S., BE *Sindh*,
  ME
Examinations. Controller of Examinations:
  Rajput, Abdul A., BE *Sindh*, LLB *Sindh*
Finance. Director, Finance: Narejo,
  Muhammad M., BCom *Sindh*
General enquiries. Registrar: Qureshi,
  Muhammad N., LLB *Sindh*, MA *Sindh*
Health services. Registrar: Qureshi,
  Muhammad N., LLB *Sindh*, MA *Sindh*
Industrial Liaison. Director: Baloch, Abdul K.,
  BE *Sindh*, MPhil *S'ton.*, PhD *S'ton.*
International office. Registrar: Qureshi,
  Muhammad N., LLB *Sindh*, MA *Sindh*
Library (enquiries). Munshey, Mumtaz I., MA
  Sindh, MSc *Hawaii*
Ombudsperson. Vice-Chancellor: Memon,
  Prof. Abdul R., MSc *Bath*, PhD *City(UK)*
Public relations, information and marketing.
  Assistant Registrar (Public Relations): Baloch,
  Mushtaque A., MA *Sindh*
Publications. Director: Rajput, Abdul Q.K., BE
  Sindh, MSc *Leeds*, PhD *Pitt.*
Purchasing. Director, Finance: Narejo,
  Muhammad M., BCom *Sindh*
Research. Director: Rajput, Abdul Q. K., BE
  Sindh, MSc *Leeds*, PhD *Pitt.*
Safety. Registrar: Qureshi, Muhammad N., LLB
  Sindh, MA *Sindh*
Sport and recreation. Deputy Director:
  Lashari, Abdul A. (on leave)
Staff development and training. Director,
  Planning and Development: Memon,
  Muhammad S., LLB *Sindh*, MA *Sindh*, MEd
  Sindh
Student welfare/counselling. Abro, A. A., BE
  Sindh, MSc *Lond.*, PhD *S'ton.*
Students from other countries. Abro, A. A.,
  BE *Sindh*, MSc *Lond.*, PhD *S'ton.*
Students with disabilities. Abro, A. A., BE
  Sindh, MSc *Lond.*, PhD *S'ton.*

AFFILIATED COLLEGES

[Institutions listed by location below provide courses leading to degrees, etc. of the university]

Hyderabad. Government College of Technology

[Information supplied by the institution as at 23 February 1998, and edited by the ACU]

N. E. D. UNIVERSITY OF ENGINEERING AND TECHNOLOGY

Founded 1977; previously established as Prince of Wales Engineering College, 1922; renamed as N.E.D. Government Engineering College, 1947

Member of the Association of Commonwealth Universities

Postal Address: Karachi 75270, Pakistan
Telephone: (021) 496 9262-8 **Fax**: (021) 496 1934 **E-mail**: ned@paknet3.ptc.pk
Cables: NED University of Engineering & Technology, Karachi

CHANCELLOR—The Governor of Sindh (*ex officio*)
VICE-CHANCELLOR*—Kalam, Abul, BSc *Madr.*, MA *Madr.*, FIEE, FIMechE
REGISTRAR—Shah, Syed G. K., BSc LLB MA
DIRECTOR OF FINANCE—Warsi, S. A., BCom MA(Econ)
CHIEF LIBRARIAN—Mehar, Yasmin, BA DLS MLS

GENERAL INFORMATION

History. The university was established in 1977. It is situated about 12km east of Karachi.

Admission to first degree courses (see also Pakistan Introduction). Higher Secondary Certificate (HSC) of the Board of Intermediate Examination or equivalent qualification, such as USA 12th grade exam or General Certificate of Education (GCE) A levels in chemistry, mathematics and physics.

First Degrees (see also Pakistan Directory to Subjects of Study). BE.

Higher Degrees (see also Pakistan Directory to Subjects of Study). MSc.

Libraries. 95,243 volumes; 1460 periodicals subscribed to.

Fees. BE (annual): home students, Rs3600; international students, Rs12,000. MSc (per semester): Rs500–1000.

Academic Year. January–December.

Income (1997–98). Total, Rs23,755,000.

Statistics. Staff: 825 (166 academic, 659 administrative).

FACULTIES/SCHOOLS

Architecture and Planning

Tel: (021)498 6342
Dean: Ahmad, Prof. K. B., MArch

Engineering

Dean: Fahim Ahsan, Prof. P., BSc(Engg) *Alig.*, MSc *Leeds*

Science and Technology

Dean: Quidwai, Prof. M. A., MSc *Karachi*, MA *Wayne State*

ACADEMIC UNITS

Engineering, Civil

Ahmad, S. F., BE MS   Assoc. Prof. (on leave)
Ahmed, Z., PhD *Purdue*, BE   Prof.
Ali, M. M., BE MS   Assoc. Prof.
Ali, M. S., BE MS   Asst. Prof. (on leave)
Alvi, A. Q., BE *Hawaii*, MS *Hawaii*, PhD *Nott.*   Prof.
Fahim Ahsan, P., BSc(Engg) *Alig.*, MSc *Leeds*   Prof.
Hussain, S. N.   Asst. Prof.
Iqbal, S. M., BE MS   Asst. Prof.
Ismail, M. S., BSc *Asian I.T., Bangkok*, ME *Asian I.T., Bangkok*   Assoc. Prof.
Kalim, ur Rehman   Asst. Prof. (on leave)
Kazim, M. S. Jaffri   Asst. Prof.
Khan, A. S., PhD *S'ton.*, BE MS   Prof.; Chairman*
Khan, Javed A., ME *Asian I.T., Bangkok*   Asst. Prof.
Khan, M. J., MEng *McG.*, BE   Asst. Prof.
Khan, S. A., BE *Calif.*, MS *Calif.*   Assoc. Prof.
Lodhi, S. H., BE MS   Asst. Prof. (on leave)
Makhdumi, S. M., MSc *Manc.*, PhD *Nott.*, BE   Prof.
Mohiuddin, Aliya, ME *Asian I.T., Bangkok*   Assoc. Prof. (on leave)
Naqvi, Y. M., BE   Asst. Prof.
Qadr, S. A., BSc BE MSc   Assoc. Prof.
Qazi, M. A., BE MS   Asst. Prof. (on leave)
Razzaque, Z., BE   Asst. Prof.
Shafiq, N., BE MEng   Asst. Prof. (on leave)
Shah, S. J., BE MS   Assoc. Prof.
Talat, M. M.   Asst. Prof.

Engineering, Computer System

Khan, A. A., BE MS   Asst. Prof.
Khan, M. A., BE MS   Asst. Prof.
Mirza, S. H., BSc BE MS PhD   Prof.; Chairman*
Siddiqi, A. A., BE   Prof.
Siddiqui, Fahimuddin, BE   Asst. Prof.

Engineering, Electrical

Altaf, T., BE *Alig.*, MSc *Alig.*   Prof.; Chairman*
Haider, T., BE   Asst. Prof.
Hussain, S. G., MSc *Nott.*, BE   Prof.
Ibrahim, M., BE   Asst. Prof. (on leave)

Ismail, Aquila, BE   Assoc. Prof.
Muhammad, A., BE   Asst. Prof.
Nauman, M., BE MSEE   Assoc. Prof.
Qadir, A., BE   Asst. Prof.
Qazi, Abdul Q., BE NED *Eng.*, MSc *Zagreb*, PhD *Oklahoma State*   Prof. (on deputation)
Qureshi, M. I. A., BE   Assoc. Prof.
Shaikh, N., BE MSEE   Prof.
Sheikh, M. S., BE   Asst. Prof.
Siddiqui, A. A., BE MSEE   Assoc. Prof.
Other Staff: 2 Instrs.

Engineering, Mechanical

Abass, Z. A.   Asst. Prof.
Ahmad, Aijaz, BE MS   Assoc. Prof.
Ahmad, Jameel, BE DrIng PhD   Prof.
Ahmad, M. S., BE   Asst. Prof. (on leave)
Ahmed, Aftab, BE   Asst. Prof.
Ahmed, Afzal, BE PhD   Prof.
Ahmed, M., BSc BE   Asst. Prof.
Akhlaque, A., BE   Asst. Prof.
Aqil, M. H.   Asst. Prof.
Haider, R., BE   Asst. Prof.
Haque, M. A., BE PhD   Prof. (on deputation)
Iqbal, M. A., BSc   Asst. Prof.
Kamal, M. P., BE MS   Asst. Prof.
Khalid, A., BE   Asst. Prof.
Khan, K. A., BSc *Alig.*, MS   Assoc. Prof. (on leave)
Khan, M. K., BSc BE   Assoc. Prof.
Mahmood, K., BE MSc PhD   Assoc. Prof.
Mahmood, M., BE MSc PhD   Prof.; Chairman*
Muhammed, Mukhtiar, BSc   Asst. Prof.
Qureshi, M. A., BE MS   Assoc. Prof.
Shoaib, Muhammad   Asst. Prof.
Siddiqui, Z. A., BE   Asst. Prof. (on leave)
Soomro, A. G., BE MSc MPhil   Prof.
Sultan, M. S., BE   Asst. Prof.
Other Staff: 6 Instrs.

Engineering, Textile

Mahmood, M., BE MSc PhD   Prof.; Chairman*
Soomro, Noorullah, BE   Asst. Prof.

Humanities

Ahsan, Nasreen M., MA *Dacca*   Asst. Prof.
Azhar, Afifa Z., MA *Karachi*   Asst. Prof.
Jalil, Sima Z., MA *Karachi*   Asst. Prof.

Seljuq, A., MA *Karachi*, PhD *Teheran* Assoc. Prof.; Chairman*
Usmani, S. F., LLB *Karachi*, MA *Karachi* Asst. Prof.

Mathematics and Sciences

Ahmed, Afaq, MSc Asst. Prof.
Fatemi, Masooma, MSc *Karachi* Asst. Prof.
Haque, Shamsul, MSc *Karachi*, MPhil *Karachi*, PhD Assoc. Prof.; Chairman
Hussain, Ather, MSc *Karachi* Asst. Prof.
Khan, A. A., MA *Karachi*, DPhil *York(UK)* Prof.
Khan, Jawaid A., MSc *Karachi* Asst. Prof.
Khan, Sohail A., BSc MSc MPhil PhD Assoc. Prof.
Master, Neelofur, MSc *Tennessee State* Asst. Prof.
Mujeeb-ur-Rehman, MSc Asst. Prof. (on leave)
Nauman, S. K., PhD *Penn.State*, MSc MPhil Assoc. Prof. (on leave)
Nizami, S. T., MSc *Karachi* Asst. Prof.
Noaman, S. M., MSc *Karachi* Asst. Prof.
Pervez, Tahira, MSc *Karachi* Asst. Prof.
Quidwai, M. A., MSc *Karachi*, MA *Wayne State* Prof.
Rafiq, M., MSc *Sindh*, MPhil *S'ton*. Asst. Prof.

CONTACT OFFICERS

Academic affairs. Deputy Registrar (Academic): ......
Accommodation. Provost: ......
Admissions (first degree). Chairman, Admissions Committee: ......
Admissions (higher degree). (Contact the chairman of the relevant department)
Alumni. Deputy Registrar (Academic): ......
Archives. Director, Planning and Development: ......
Careers. Director, Student Affairs: ......
Computing services. Director, Planning and Development: ......
Consultancy services. Director, Planning and Development: ......
Credit transfer. Dean, Engineering: Fahim Ahsan, Prof. P., BSc(Engg) *Alig.*, MSc *Leeds*
Development/fund-raising. Director of Finance: Warsi, S. A., BCom MA(Econ)
Estates and buildings/works and services. Estate Officer: ......
Examinations. Controller of Examinations: ......
Finance. Director of Finance: Warsi, S. A., BCom MA(Econ)
General enquiries. Registrar: Shah, Syed G. K., BSc LLB MA
Health services. Senior Medical Officer: ......
Industrial liaison. Director: Kamal, Wahid
Library (chief librarian). Chief Librarian: Mehar, Yasmin, BA MLS
Minorities/disadvantaged groups. Director, Student Affairs: ......
Ombudsperson. Vice-Chancellor: Kalam, Abul, BSc *Madr.*, MA *Madr.*, FIEE, FIMechE
Personnel/human resources. Registrar: Shah, Syed G. K., BSc LLB MA
Public relations, information and marketing. Public Relations Officer: ......
Publications. Public Relations Officer: ......
Purchasing. Purchase Officer: ......
Safety. Campus Engineer: ......
Scholarships, awards, loans. Deputy Registrar (Academic): ......
Schools liaison. Registrar: Shah, Syed G. K., BSc LLB MA
Security. Superintendent, Watch and Ward: ......
Sport and recreation. Advisor, Sports/ Director, Physical Education: ......
Staff development and training. Registrar: Shah, Syed G. K., BSc LLB MA
Student union. Director, Student Affairs: ......
Student welfare/counselling. Director, Student Affairs: ......
Students from other countries. Registrar: Shah, Syed G. K., BSc LLB MA
Students with disabilities. Senior Medical Officer: ......

[Information supplied by the institution as at 19 February 1998, and edited by the ACU]

NATIONAL UNIVERSITY OF SCIENCES AND TECHNOLOGY

Founded 1992

Postal Address: Tamiz Ud Din Road, Cantonment Rawalpindi, Pakistan
Telephone: (051) 585826 **Fax**: (051) 580030

RECTOR*—Hussain, S. Shujaat
DIRECTOR (EXAMINATIONS AND ACADEMICS)‡—Tasleem, Muhammad

NORTH-WEST FRONTIER PROVINCE AGRICULTURAL UNIVERSITY

Founded 1981

Postal Address: PO Pakistan Forest Institute, Peshawar, North-West Frontier Province, Pakistan
Telephone: (0521) 40230-9 **Fax**: (0521) 840147 **E-mail**: vc@vcnwfp.psw.erum.com.pk
Cables: Agriculture University Peshawar

VICE-CHANCELLOR*—Khan, Yar M., BScAgric
REGISTRAR‡—Malik, Dr. Arshad S.

NORTH-WEST FRONTIER PROVINCE UNIVERSITY OF ENGINEERING AND TECHNOLOGY

Founded 1980

Member of the Association of Commonwealth Universities

Postal Address: POB 814, Peshawar, North-West Frontier Province, Pakistan
Telephone: (091) 40573, 40382, 41297, 40386, 44253 **Fax**: (091) 841758
Cables: NWFP University of Engineering & Technology, Peshawar (Pakistan) **Telex**: 52477 ENGUP (PK)

CHANCELLOR—The Governor of North-West Frontier Province (ex officio)
VICE-CHANCELLOR*—Humayun Zia, Prof., BSc Lahore UET
REGISTRAR—Ruhullah, Prof. Ghulam, BSc(Engg)
DIRECTOR OF FINANCE—Khan, Mohammad S., MCom

GENERAL INFORMATION

History. Originally established in 1952 as the faculty of engineering, University of Peshawar, the university achieved independent status in 1980.

It is temporarily based on the campus of the University of Peshawar, which is located 8km west of Peshawar.

Admission to first degree courses (see also Pakistan Introduction). Intermediate (pre-engineering) exam, from a Board of Intermediate and Secondary Education in Pakistan (or other recognised equivalent qualification); or BTech(pass) degree; or 3-year post-matriculation diploma in engineering. A minimum 60% pass mark is required in all cases. All applicants must take the university's entry test.

First Degrees. BScEngg.

Higher Degrees. MScEngg.

Libraries. Central library: 85,000 volumes.

Fees (monthly). Pakistani students: Rs80; international students: Rs250.

Academic Year. 1 December–30 September.

Statistics (1997–98). Students: 1556.

FACULTIES/SCHOOLS

Engineering
Dean: Mussarat Shah, Prof. S., BE Pesh., MS Calif.State

ACADEMIC UNITS

Basic Sciences and Islamiat
Tel: (0521) 41953
Ali, Sadar, MSc Pesh., MPhil Quaid-i-Azam Assoc. Prof.
Asadullah, Mir, MSc Pesh., PhD Essex Prof.
Atiq, Mohammad T., MSc Pesh., MPhil Quaid-i-Azam Asst. Prof.
Fakhruddin, MSc Pesh. Assoc. Prof.
Gul, Khair, MSc Pesh. Assoc. Prof.
Jawaid, Mohammad, MSc Pesh., PhD R.I.T.Stockholm, DSc R.I.T.Stockholm Prof.
Jehan, Shah, MSc Pesh., MPhil Quaid-i-Azam Assoc. Prof.
Kamal, Mohammad M., BEd Pesh., MSc Pesh. Asst. Prof.
Khadim-ul-Faqir, MSc Pesh. Prof.; Chairman*
Khan, Misal, MSc Pesh. MPhil Pesh. Asst. Prof.
Khan, Mumtaz, MSc Pesh., MPhil Assoc. Prof.
Khurshid-ul-Wahab, MSc Pesh., MPhil Quaid-i-Azam Assoc. Prof.
Kifayatullah, MSc Quaid-i-Azam Asst. Prof.
Mohmaud, Adam K., MSc Pesh., MSc Prof.
Nawaz, Mir, MSc Pesh. Prof.
Pervez, Khalid, MSc Pesh., MPhil Strath. Assoc. Prof.
Qasim, Ghulam, MSc Gomal, PhD Assoc. Prof.
Raza-ur-Rehman, Qazi, MSc Pesh. Asst. Prof.
Rehman, Saeedur, MSc Pesh., MPhil Pesh. Assoc. Prof.
Salahuddin, MSc Pesh. Assoc. Prof.
Shah, Wahid A., BEd Pesh., MA Asst. Prof.
Waliullah, MA Pesh., MPhil Pesh. Prof.

Engineering, Agricultural
Tel: (0521) 41223
Abrar, Sayyedul, BScEngg Pesh., MS Utah, MPhil Assoc. Prof.
Alamgir, Muhammad, BScEngg Pesh., MS Assoc. Prof.

Ashraf, Saadat, BScEngg Pesh., MSc Pesh., MSc Asst. Prof.
Aslam, Novid, BScEngg Pesh., MS Nebraska Asst. Prof. (on leave)
Aziz, Arsaid, BE Pesh., MS Calif.State, MSc Prof.; Chairman*
Badruddin, BE Pesh., MS Prof.
Din, Mirajud, BScEngg Pesh., MSc Assoc. Prof.
Ibrahim, Muhammad, BScEngg Pesh., MSc Pesh. Asst. Prof.
Khan, Daulat, BScEngg Pesh., MSc Asst. Prof. (on leave)
Mahmood, Zahid, BScEngg Pesh., MS Philippines, PhD Prof.

Engineering, Chemical
Tel: (0521) 84273
Arshad, Muhammad, BScEngg Punjab Asst. Prof.
Jawaid, Muhammad, MSc Pesh., PhD R.I.T.Stockholm, DSc R.I.T.Stockholm Prof.
Mussarat Shah, S., BE Pesh., MS Calif.State Prof.; Chairman*

Engineering, Civil
Tel: (0521) 41946
Ahmad, Navid, BScEngg Pesh.,MSc Asst. Prof. (on leave)
Ali, Amjad, BScEngg Pesh., MS MPhil Assoc. Prof.
Durrani, Altaf A., BScEngg Pesh., MSc Asst. Prof. (on leave)
Durrani, Muhammad A. Q. J., BScEngg Pesh., MSc Punjab, PhD Assoc. Prof.
Gul, Rahat, BE Pesh., MS Assoc. Prof.
Jabbar, Abdul, BE Pesh., MS N.Y. Prof.; Chairman*
Khaliq, Fazal, BE Pesh., MSc Punjab Prof.
Khan, Akhtar N., BSc Pesh., MScEngg Pesh., PhD Assoc. Prof.

Khan, Muhammad F., BE Pesh., MSc
Punjab Prof.
Khan, Sher A., BScEngg Pesh., MS N.Carolina
State, PhD Assoc. Prof.
Mussarat Shah, S., BE Pesh., MS Calif.State Prof.
Qazi, Mehmood K., BE Pesh., MS
Calif.State Prof.
Salim, Shahid, BScEngg Pesh., MS Asst. Prof.
(on leave)
Shah, Imtiaz A., BSc Pesh., MSc Pesh. Asst.
Prof. (on leave)
Ullah, Mian I., BScEngg Pesh. Asst. Prof.

Engineering, Electrical and Electronic

Tel: (0521) 40371

Akhtar, Javed, BSc Pesh., MS Asst. Prof.
Arbab, Muhammad N., BScEngg Pesh., MSc
PhD Prof. (on leave)
Asar, Azzamul, BScEngg Pesh., MSc PhD Prof.
Jadoon, Tariq M., BScEngg Pesh., MSc
PhD Asst. Prof.
Khalil, Abdul Q., BE Pesh., MSc Brad. Prof.;
Chairman*
Khan, Muhammad Z., BE Karachi, MSc
Strath. Assoc. Prof.
Khan, Sheroz, BScEngg Pesh., MSc Strath.,
PhD Assoc. Prof. (on leave)
Khattak, Shahid, BScEngg Pesh. Asst. Prof. (on
leave)
Mutlib, Abdul, BE Pesh., MSc Strath. Assoc.
Prof.
Noor, Sahibzada F., BE Pesh., BScEngg Pesh. MSc
Pesh., MEd Oregon, PhD Assoc. Prof. (on
leave)
Qayyum, Fazli, BE Pesh., MS Calif.State,
PhD Prof.
Qureshi, Abdul Q., BE Pesh., MSc Punjab Assoc.
Prof.
Saleem, Zahid, BScEngg Pesh., MS PhD Assoc.
Prof.
Shah, Syed L., BE Pesh., MSc Pesh. Assoc. Prof.
Tariq, Muhammad, BScEngg Pesh., MS Asst.
Prof.
Ullah, Amjad, BScEngg Pesh. Asst. Prof.
Yahya, Khawaja M., BScEngg Pesh., MS
Mich. Asst. Prof.
Zaman, Haider, BE Pesh., MSc Pesh. Prof.

Engineering, Mechanical

Tel: (0521) 40375

Ahmad, Iftikhar, BScEngg Pesh., MSc
Punjab Assoc. Prof.
Ahmad, Muhammad N., BScEngg Pesh. Assoc.
Prof.
Arif, Muhammad A., BScEngg Pesh., MS Asst.
Prof. (on leave)
Baseer, Muhammad A., BScEngg Pesh., MSc
Shiraz, PhD Bath Prof.
Hadi, Abdul, BScEngg Pesh., MS Asst. Prof.
Hakeem, Imtiaz, BScEngg Pesh., MSc Punjab,
PhD Prof.
Hussain, Iftikhar, BScEngg Pesh., MSc
Punjab Asst. Prof. (on leave)

Irfan, Muhammad, BSc Pesh., MSc Pesh. Asst.
Prof. (on leave)
Irfan, Muhammad A. A., BScEngg Pesh., MSc
Punjab Asst. Prof. (on leave)
Khan, Jehanzeb, BScEngg Pesh., MS PhD Prof.
Khan, Muhammad N., BScEngg Pesh.,
MSc Asst. Prof.
Parvez, Muhammad, BScEngg Pesh., MSc
Punjab Prof.
Shah, S. Munawwar, BScEngg Pesh., MSc Asst.
Prof.
Shah, Sayed R. A., BSc Pesh., MS Asst. Prof.
(on leave)
Tajik, Saeed J., BScEngg Pesh., MPhil
City(UK) Prof.
Ullah, Irfan, BScEngg Pesh., MS PhD Prof.;
Chairman*
Waheed, Abdul, BScEngg Pesh., MSc Asst.
Prof. (on leave)

Engineering, Mining

Tel: (0521) 41160

Afridi, Abdul J., BScEngg Pesh., MSc S.Dakota
State Asst. Prof.
Akbar, Saddique, BScEngg Pesh. Assoc. Prof.
Amanul-Mulk, BScEngg Pesh., MSc Pesh. Asst.
Prof. (on leave)
Aziz-ur-Rehman, BScEngg Pesh., MSc
PhD Assoc. Prof.
Jadoon, Khan G., BScEngg Pesh., PhD Assoc.
Prof.
Khan, Ehtishamullah, BScEngg Pesh.,
MScEngg Asst. Prof.
Khan, Muhammad M., BSc Punjab, PhD Prof.;
Chairman*
Mohammad, Noor, BScEngg Pesh., MSc Assoc.
Prof. (on leave)
Naseem, Tariq, BScEngg Pesh., MPhil
Nott. Assoc. Prof.

Islamiat, see Basic Scis. and Islamiat

SPECIAL CENTRES, ETC

Workshops

Tel: (0521) 44034

Khan, Aasar, BScEngg Pesh., MSc Punjab Asst.
Prof. (on leave)

CONTACT OFFICERS

Academic affairs. Dean, Faculty of
Engineering: Mussarat Shah, Prof. S., BE
Pesh., MS Calif.State
Academic affairs. Vice-Chancellor: Humayun
Zia, Prof., BSc Lahore UET
Accommodation. Provost: Fazl-e-Qayyum,
Prof.
Admissions (first degree). Dean, Faculty of
Engineering: Mussarat Shah, Prof. S., BE
Pesh., MS Calif.State
Admissions (higher degree). Director,
Postgraduate Studies: Qazi, Prof. Khalid M.

Adult/continuing education. Registrar:
Ruhullah, Prof. Ghulam, BSc(Engg)
Alumni. Vice-Chancellor: Humayun Zia, Prof.,
BSc Lahore UET
Consultancy services. (Contact the chairman
of the relevant department)
Development/fund-raising. Director of
Finance: Khan, Mohammad S., MCom
Distance education. Secretary, Board of
Advanced Studies and Research: Aziz, Prof.
Arshad, BE Pesh., MS Calif.State
Estates and buildings/works and services.
Director of Works: Faz-le-Khaliq, Prof., BE
Pesh., MSc Punjab
Examinations. Controller of Examinations:
Nisar, Mohammad
Finance. Director of Finance: Khan,
Mohammad S., MCom
General enquiries. Registrar: Ruhullah, Prof.
Ghulam, BSc(Engg)
Health services. Medical Officer, Islamia
College, Peshawar: Ayaz, Mohammad
Industrial liaison. Registrar: Ruhullah, Prof.
Ghulam, BSc(Engg)
International office. (Contact the Academic
Section)
Library (chief librarian). Librarian: Rashid,
Abdul
Minorities/disadvantaged groups. Registrar:
Ruhullah, Prof. Ghulam, BSc(Engg)
Ombudsperson. Registrar: Ruhullah, Prof.
Ghulam, BSc(Engg)
Publications. Chief Editor: Razvi, Prof. M. A.
Purchasing. Director of Finance: Khan,
Mohammad S., MCom
Research. Secretary, Board of Advanced Studies
and Research: Razvi, Prof. M. A.
Safety. Administrative Officer: Khan, Alam
Scholarships, awards, loans. Registrar:
Ruhullah, Prof. Ghulam, BSc(Engg)
Schools liaison. Director of Finance: Khan,
Mohammad S., MCom
Security. Administrative Officer: Khan, Alam
Sport and recreation. Director of Sports:
Awan, Abdul H.
Staff development and training. Registrar:
Ruhullah, Prof. Ghulam, BSc(Engg)
Student union. Registrar: Ruhullah, Prof.
Ghulam, BSc(Engg)
Student welfare/counselling. Provost: Fazl-e-
Qayyum, Prof.
Students from other countries. Foreign
Students' Advisor: Badruddin, Prof., BE Pesh.
Students with disabilities. Dean, Faculty of
Engineering: Mussarat Shah, Prof. S., BE
Pesh., MS Calif.State
University press. Registrar: Ruhullah, Prof.
Ghulam, BSc(Engg)

[Information supplied by the institution as at 20 August
1998, and edited by the ACU]

UNIVERSITY OF PESHAWAR

Founded 1950

Postal Address: Peshawar, North-West Frontier Province, Pakistan
Telephone: (0521) 41001 Fax: (0521) 41979 E-mail: registrar%pulib@pwr.sdnpk.undp.org
Cables: Peshawar University

VICE-CHANCELLOR*—Jan, M., MS Oregon, PhD Lond.
REGISTRAR‡—Hamid, Fazli, MA Pesh., MA Lond.

UNIVERSITY OF THE PUNJAB, LAHORE

Founded 1882

Member of the Association of Commonwealth Universities

Postal Address: Punjab, Lahore, Pakistan
Telephone: (042) 735 4428 Fax: (042) 583 0752 Cables: Punjab University, Lahore

CHANCELLOR—The Governor of Punjab (ex officio)
PRO-CHANCELLOR—Dhaloo, Brig. Zulfiqar A.
VICE-CHANCELLOR*—Sheikh, Prof. Khalid H., MSc Punjab, PhD Lond.
PRO-VICE-CHANCELLOR—......
REGISTRAR—Saad-ud-Din, Muhammad, BA Punjab, LLB Punjab
TREASURER—Khan, Abrar M., MCom Punjab

FACULTIES/SCHOOLS

Arts
Tel: (042) 586 3997, 583 9725
Dean: Chaudhry, Prof. A. R.
Secretary: Razzaq, Abdul

Commerce
Tel: (042) 586 6839, 586 3917, 586 3937
Dean: Ahmad, Prof. M. A. I., MCom
Secretary: Ishaq, Muhammad

Education
Tel: (042) 586 4468, 588 0644, 586 4004
Dean: Mirza, Prof. Munawar S.
Secretary: Ahmad, Bashir

Engineering and Technology
Tel: (042) 586 4946, 586 4918
Dean: ......
Secretary: Bhatti, Muhammad S.

Islamic and Oriental Learning
Tel: (042) 735 5541, 731 1496
Dean: Shaukat, Prof. Jamila, PhD Camb., MA
Secretary: Masood, Khalid

Law
Tel: (042) 586 3993, 583 4163
Dean: Malik, Dil M., PhD Punjab
Secretary: Zaheer-ud-Din

Medicine and Dentistry
Dean: ......
Secretary: ......

Pharmacy
Tel: (042) 735 5003, 735 5259
Dean: Afzal Sheikh, Prof. M., PhD Lond., MSc
Secretary: ......

Science
Tel: (042) 586 8369, 586 8375
Dean: Iqbal, Prof. Muhammad Z.

Secretary: Riaz, Muhammad

ACADEMIC UNITS

Administrative Science
Tel: (042) 586 4515
Jabeen, Nasira, MA Punjab   Asst. Prof.
Jadoon, M. Z. I., MPA   Assoc. Prof.
Jafri, S. A. R., MPA Calif., PhD Calif., MA   Prof.; Chairman*
Khalid, Mubeen, MCom Punjab   Asst. Prof.

Arabic, see University Oriental College, below

Biochemistry and Biotechnology, Institute of
Tel: (042) 583 1512, 583 8533 Fax: (042) 583 1512
Akhtar, M. Waheed, PhD Strath., MSc   Prof.; Dir.*

Botany
Tel: (042) 586 8367
Bajwa, Rukhsana, PhD Sheff., MSc   Assoc. Prof.
Firdaus-e-Bareen, MSc   Asst. Prof.
Hasnain, Shahida, PhD Birm., MSc   Assoc. Prof.
Iqbal, Javed, MSc PhD   Prof.; Chairman*
Khan, R. M., MSc   Assoc. Prof.
Nasim, Ghazala, MSc   Asst. Prof.
Razzaq, Najma, MSc Punjab, PhD Punjab   Asst. Prof.
Shamsi, S. R. A., PhD Lond., MSc   Prof.
Sheikh, K. H., PhD Lond., MSc   Prof.

Business Administration, Institute of
Tel: (042) 586 3917
Ahmad, M. A. I., MCom   Prof.; Dir.*
Ajmal, M. N. A., MCom   Assoc. Prof.
Bhatti, M. A., MBA MSc   Asst. Prof.
Butt, Z. A., MCom   Assoc. Prof.
Khalid, Zaheer, MBA Punjab, PhD   Asst. Prof.
Mahmood, Wasiq, MBA Karachi   Asst. Prof.
Mushtaq-ur-Rahim, MBA Punjab   Asst. Prof.

Chemical Engineering and Technology, Institute of
Tel: (042) 586 4116, 586 7115
Aamir, Ijaz, BSc PhD   Asst. Prof.
Abdus, Salam, BSc(Engg) PhD   Asst. Prof.
Ahmad, Akhtar N., BSc(Engg) PhD   Asst. Prof.
Ali, Muhammad, BSc(Engg)   Assoc. Prof.
Butt, M. A., DEng Nagoya, MSc   Prof.
Butt, M. A. A., DPhil Sus., MSc(Tech)   Prof.
Butt, T. Z., BSc(Engg)   Assoc. Prof.
Chughtai, M. A., MSc Quaid-i-Azam   Assoc. Prof.
Dilawari, A. H., PhD Lond., MSc   Prof.
Jamil, Arif, BSc(Engg)   Asst. Prof.
Javed, Ahmad, BSc(Engg) PhD   Assoc. Prof.
Khan, Durrani A., BSc(Engg) MSc   Asst. Prof.
Mahmood, Liaqat, MSc Birm., MSc Punjab   Asst. Prof.
Naushahi, M. K., PhD Wales, MSc   Assoc. Prof.
Nawaz, Shafqat, PhD Leeds, MSc   Prof.
Qureshi, M. M., PhD Prague, MSc   Prof.
Rafiq, Ahmad, BSc(Engg) PhD   Asst. Prof.
Rashid, Zafar, PhD Essex, MSc   Assoc. Prof.
Rauf, Abdul, BSc(Engg) PhD   Asst. Prof.
Rehman, Abdul, BSc(Engg)   Asst. Prof.
Rizvi, Z. H., MEng Brad., BSc(Engg)   Assoc. Prof.
Sheikh, M. Z. U., PhD Prague, MSc   Prof.; Dir.*

Chemistry, Institute of
Tel: (042) 586 8369, 586 8375
Ahmad, Ashafaq, PhD Pardubice C.C.T., MSc   Assoc. Prof.
Anwar, Jamil, PhD Aberd., MSc   Assoc. Prof.
Hussain, Ghulam, MSc   Asst. Prof.
Hussain, Ishtiaq, PhD St And., MSc   Assoc. Prof.
Hussain, Kazim, MSc   Assoc. Prof.
Kausar, A. R., MSc Karachi, PhD   Assoc. Prof.
Khokhar, Irshad, MSc PhD   Assoc. Prof.
Mahmood Tariq, MSc MPhil   Asst. Prof.
Mahmood, Zaid, MSc Punjab, PhD   Asst. Prof.
Malik, N. N., MSc PhD   Assoc. Prof.

Nagra, S. A., MSc *Quaid-i-Azam*, PhD   Assoc.
  Prof.
Nasir, B. A., MSc PhD   Prof.
Rahman, Abdul, PhD *Brown*, MA MSc   Assoc.
  Prof.
Shahid, Gulerana, MSc MPhil   Assoc. Prof.
Ullah, Habib, PhD *Lond.*, MSc   Assoc. Prof.
Younas, Muhammad, PhD *Camb.*, MSc   Prof.
Zafar, Iqbal M.   Prof.; Dir.*

Commerce, see Hailey College of
  Commerce, below

Economics
Tel: (042) 586 3997, 586 9725
Ahmad, Khalil, MA *Punjab*   Asst. Prof.
Butt, A. R., MSc *Idaho*, PhD *Wash.*, MA   Prof.
Chaudhry, Amatul R., MA PhD   Chairperson*
Hafeez-ur-Rahman, BEd MA   Asst. Prof. (on
  leave)
Hamid, Naveed, BA *Camb.*, MA *Stan.*, PhD
  Stan.   Assoc. Prof. (on leave)
Shaheen, Shaheen R., MA *Punjab*, MA   Asst.
  Prof.

Education and Research, Institute of
Tel: (042) 586 4004, 586 4468, 588 0644
Ghafoor, Ch. Abdul   Asst. Prof.
Iqbal, Hafiz M.   Asst. Prof.
Khalid, M. I., MA PhD   Assoc. Prof.
Khan, Shahbaz   Assoc. Prof.
Khan, Z. A., MA MEd PhD   Prof.
Mahmood, Tehseen, MA   Asst. Prof.
Mirza, M. S., MEd   Assoc. Prof.
Mirza, Munawar S.   Prof.; Dir.*
Nawaz, M. M., MEd   Asst. Prof.
Rahim, Nighat, MSc MEd   Asst. Prof.
Sadiq, M. I., MA   Assoc. Prof.
Shah, V. A., MEd   Asst. Prof.
Siddiqui, Mushtaq-ur-Rehman, MA PhD   Prof.
Zaidi, N. R., MEd   Assoc. Prof.

English Language and Literature
Tel: (042) 588 2337
Imrana, Iqbal, MA *Punjab*, PhD   Asst. Prof.
Sannu, Shaista, MA *Camb.*, MLitt *Oxf.*   Prof.;
  Chairperson*
Tehmina, Alvi, MA *Punjab*, MEd *Punjab*   Asst.
  Prof.

Fine Arts
Tel: (042) 735 3795
Ahmad, Najma W., MA   Asst. Prof.
Amjad, Pervez, MFA *Punjab*   Asst. Prof.
Azami, Agha M., MFA *Punjab*   Asst. Prof.
Butt, K. S., MFA   Asst. Prof.
Farooq, Safia, MFA   Asst. Prof.
Haider, Zulqarnain, MFA *Paris*, MA   Assoc.
  Prof.
Masud, Rahat N., MA   Asst. Prof. (on leave)
Sayed, T. R., MFA   Asst. Prof.
Sohail, Wali   Asst. Prof.
Ullah, M. Z., MFA   Asst. Prof.
Zaidi, H. S., MFA   Assoc. Prof.; Chairman*

French
Tel: (042) 735 8309
Khan, Raana, MA *Punjab*   Asst. Prof.

Geography
Tel: (042) 586 4013
Gulzar, Farhat, MA PhD   Prof.
Kausar, Tasneem, MSc   Asst. Prof.
Mian, M. A., PhD *Lond.*, MA   Prof.; Chairman*

Geology, Institute of
Tel: (042) 586 6809
Ahmad, Nazir, MSc PhD   Asst. Prof.
Ahmad, S. A., MSc   Asst. Prof.
Ahmad, Sarfraz, MSc PhD   Assoc. Prof.
Ahmad, Shafiq, MSc PhD   Prof.
Ahmad, Zulfiqar, PhD *Lond.*   Prof.
Baloch, I. H., MSc PhD   Asst. Prof.
Butt, A. A., PhD   Prof.
Farooq, Saeed M., MSc   Asst. Prof.
Farooq, Umar, MSc *Lond.*, MSc *Punjab*   Assoc.
  Prof.

Ghazanfar, Munir, MSc *Sheff.*, MSc *Punjab*,
  MA(Econ) PhD   Assoc. Prof.
Hafeez, Muhammad, MSc   Asst. Prof. (on
  leave)
Khan, Z. K., PhD *Punjab*, MSc   Assoc. Prof.
Mahmood, Aftab, MSc   Assoc. Prof.
Malik, M. H., MSc PhD   Assoc. Prof.
Nawaz, M., PhD *Lond.*, MSc   Prof.; Dir.*
Saleemi, A. A., MSc PhD   Asst. Prof.
Sheikh, R. A., MSc PhD   Asst. Prof.

History
Tel: (042) 586 3983
Gil, S. A., MA *Karachi*, MA *Punjab*, MPhil *Kansas*,
  PhD *Kansas*   Prof.; Chairman*
Habib, Tahira, MA   Asst. Prof.
Malik, I. A., BA *Lond.*, MA   Prof.
Muhamad, Iqbal, MSc *Punjab*   Asst. Prof.
Shah, Raza-ul-Haq, DLit *Ankara*, MA   Asst.
  Prof.
Syed, Q. A., MA   Assoc. Prof.

Islamic Studies
Tel: (042) 586 7993
Alvi, M. S. K., PhD *Edin.*, MA   Seerat Prof.
Fatima, Samar, MA *Karachi*, PhD *Durh.*   Prof.
Hafiz, M. A., MA   Assoc. Prof.
Mansoori, S. A., MA *Karachi*, MA *Punjab*   Assoc.
  Prof.
Saad, Siddiqui M., MA *Punjab*, PhD *Punjab*   Asst.
  Prof.
Salik, M. A., MA *Islamia, Bahawal.*, MA
  Punjab   Asst. Prof.
Shaukat, Jamila, PhD *Camb.*, MA   Prof.;
  Chairperson*
Tahira, Basharat, MA *Punjab*, PhD *Punjab*   Asst.
  Prof.
Ullah, Hamid, PhD *Punjab*, MA   Asst. Prof.

Kashmiriyat, see University Oriental College,
  below

Law, see University Law College, below

Library Science
Tel: (042) 586 3764
Ghani, Imran, MA   Asst. Prof.
Khan, Tanweer J., MA   Asst. Prof.
Qarshi, A. H., MA   Asst. Prof.; In-Charge*
Shah, Umera, MA   Asst. Prof.

Mass Communication
Tel: (042) 586 4021
Ali, Afirah H., MA PhD   Asst. Prof.
Jullandhry, M. S., MA PhD   Assoc. Prof.;
  Chairman*
Khalid, A. R., LLB MCom MA PhD   Assoc.
  Prof.
Mansoori, M. A., MA   Asst. Prof.
Mughees-ud-Din, MA PhD   Asst. Prof.

Mathematics
Tel: (042) 586 4184
Bhatti, S. A., MPhil *Islam.*, MBA MSc   Asst.
  Prof.
Habibullah, Ghulam M., PhD   Prof.
Husnaine, Muhammad, PhD   Asst. Prof.
Iqbal, Muhammad, MSc *Dund.*, PhD *Wales*,
  MA   Assoc. Prof. (on leave)
Jafri, S. H., MSc *Dund.*, MSc *Punjab*   Asst. Prof.
Mir, K. L., MSc *Durh.*, PhD *Manc.*, BSc
  MA   Prof.; Chairman*
Saeed, Siddiqi S., MSc *Punjab*, PhD   Asst. Prof.
Sarfraz, Muhammad, MSc PhD   Asst. Prof. (on
  leave)
Sharif, Muhammad, PhD   Asst. Prof.
Shoaib-ud-Din, MSc *Wales*, MSc *Punjab*, PhD
  Wales   Assoc. Prof.

Molecular Biology, Advanced, see Special
  Centres, etc

Pakistan Studies, see Special Centres, etc

Persian, see University Oriental College,
  below

Pharmacy
Tel: (042) 735 5003, 735 5259
Afzal Sheikh, M., PhD *Lond.*, MSc   Prof.;
  Chairman*
Ahmad, Ahmad M., PhD   Asst. Prof.
Ahmad, Bashir, MPharmacy PhD   Assoc. Prof.
Alam, Mahboob, PhD *Wales*, MSc   Prof.
Ali, Haider, DSc   Prof.
Haider, Haider K. H., PhD   Asst. Prof.
Jamshaid, Muhammad, PhD *Wales*,
  MPharmacy   Assoc. Prof.
Javed, Khan M. T., PhD *Punjab*   Asst. Prof.
Khan, F. Z., PhD *Wales*, MSc   Assoc. Prof.
Khan, K. I., MSc *Karachi*, PhD   Assoc. Prof.
Khan, N. H., MPharmacy   Assoc. Prof.
Rasheed, Azmat, MPharmacy MPhil
  PhD   Assoc. Prof.
Riaz, Muhammad, PhD *Lond.*, MSc   Assoc.
  Prof.
Saeed, Asif, MSc PhD   Asst. Prof.

Philosophy
Tel: (042) 586 3984
Ahmad, Absar, MA *Karachi*, MPhil *Reading*, PhD
  Lond.   Assoc. Prof.
Ahmad, Naeem, MA PhD   Assoc. Prof.;
  Chairman*
Ali, Sajid, MA PhD   Asst. Prof.
Irfan, Ghazala, MA PhD   Asst. Prof.

Physics, see also Special Centres, etc

Tel: (042) 588 1012
Akram, Muhammad, PhD *Moscow*, MSc   Assoc.
  Prof.
Alam, M. A., PhD *Durh.*, MSc   Prof.
Ali, Shaukat, PhD *Tübingen*, MSc   Prof.
Azhar, Iqbal M., PhD   Asst. Prof.
Hussain, Manzoor, MPhil *Quaid-i-Azam*, MSc
  PhD   Asst. Prof.
Kamran, Majahid, MSc PhD   Prof.; Chairman*
Mughal, S. A., PhD *St And.*, MSc   Assoc. Prof.
Saleem, Bhatti A., PhD   Asst. Prof.
Zaheer, M. Y., PhD *Penn.*, MSc   Assoc. Prof.

Political Science
Tel: (042) 586 3982
Fateh Naseeb Chaudhry, MA   Asst. Prof.
Naseer, Sajjad, MA   Assoc. Prof.; Chairman*
Rashid Ahmad Khan, MA PhD   Assoc. Prof.
Rizvi, H. A., MPhil *Leeds*, MA *Penn.*, MA *Punjab*,
  PhD *Penn.*   Prof.
Sohail, Mahmood, MA PhD   Asst. Prof.
Syed, F. H., MA *Wash.*, MA *Punjab*, MCJ *Howard*,
  LLB PhD   Assoc. Prof.

Psychology, Applied
Tel: (042) 586 4289
Ahmad, Aftab, LLB MSc MA   Asst. Prof.
Alam, Seemeen, DPhil *Sus.*, MSc   Assoc. Prof.
Farooqi, Yasmin N., MSc PhD   Assoc. Prof.
Khalid, Ruhi, PhD *Glas.*, MSc   Prof.
Najam, Najma, MSc MA PhD   Prof.;
  Chairman* (on leave)
Rukhsana, Kausar, PhD   Asst. Prof.
Sheikh, M. H., PhD *Syd.*, MSc   Prof.

Psychology, Clinical, see Special Centres, etc

Punjabi, see University Oriental College,
  below

Social Work
Tel: (042) 724 4341
Chaudhry, M. A., MPH *Hawaii*, MA   Prof.;
  Chairman*
Chaudhry, T. R., MA   Asst. Prof.
Hussain, Nazir, MA   Asst. Prof.
Jafary, S. M., MA   Asst. Prof. (on leave)

Sociology
Tel: (042) 583 5038, 586 3981
Hafeez, Muhammad, MA   Asst. Prof.
Naeem, Muhammad, MA *W. Ont.*, MSc
  Hawaii   Assoc. Prof.

Sulma, Ahmad, MA *Punjab* Asst. Prof.
Usmani, M. S. A., MA Assoc. Prof.;
  Chairman*

South Asian Studies, see Special Centres,
  etc

Space Science
Tel: (042) 583 9660, 583 9823
Ali, Muhammad, MSc PhD Assoc. Prof.
Chaudhry Rahim, Abdul, PhD *Salf.*, MSc Prof.;
  Chairman*

Statistics, Institute of
Tel: (042) 586 4008, 586 6981
Ahmad, Muhammad, MSc Asst. Prof.
Akhtar, A. S., PhD *Essex*, MSc Assoc. Prof.;
  Dir.*
Chaudhry, M. Ashraf, MSc *Islamia, Bahawal.*, MSc
  S'ton., PhD Asst. Prof. (on leave)
Chaudhry, M. I., MA Asst. Prof.
Gilani, Ghausia M., MSc Asst. Prof.
Khan, K. D., MSc PhD Asst. Prof.
Shahid, Kamal, MSc *Punjab*, PhD Asst. Prof.

Urdu, see Special Centres, etc, and University
  Oriental College, below

Zoology
Tel: (042) 586 4028, 586 8376
Akhtar, M. S., MSc PhD Assoc. Prof.;
  Chairman*
Akhtar, Muhammad, PhD *Punjab*, MSc Asst.
  Prof.
Akhtar, Tanveer, PhD *Punjab*, MSc Asst. Prof.
Ali, Firdausia A., PhD *Lond.*, MSc Prof.
Ali, S. S., PhD *Punjab*, MSc Asst. Prof.
Cheema, A. M., PhD *Aston*, MSc Assoc. Prof.
Lone, K. P., PhD *Aston*, MSc Prof.
Riaz ul Haq, MSc *Punjab*, PhD *Punjab*, PhD *Troy*,
  PhD *N.Y.* Asst. Prof.
Sarwar, Muhammad, MSc PhD Assoc. Prof.
Shakoori, A. R., DSc *Hohenheim*, MSc Prof.

SPECIAL CENTRES, ETC

Advanced Molecular Biology Centre
Tel: (042) 522 1235
Afroze, Talat, PhD Asst. Prof.
Ahmad, Zahoor, PhD Asst. Prof.
Amjad, Muhammad, PhD Asst. Prof.
Athar, Amin, PhD Asst. Prof.
Husnain, Tayyab, PhD Asst. Prof.
Riaz-ud-Din, Sheikh, PhD *Reading*, MSc Prof.;
  Dir.*
Sohail, Anjum, PhD Asst. Prof.

Clinical Psychology Centre
Tel: (042) 586 3992
Najam, Najma, MSc MA PhD Prof.; Dir.*
Rehman, Nosheen K., MSc PhD Assoc. Prof.

High Energy Physics Centre
Tel: (042) 586 3932
Ali, Ali S., PhD *Punjab*, MSc Asst. Prof.
Fazal-e-Aleem, MSc *Quaid-i-Azam*, MPhil *Quaid-i-*
  Azam, PhD Assoc. Prof.; Dir.*
Khawaja Haris Rashid, MSc PhD Assoc. Prof.
Masud, Masud B., MSc PhD Asst. Prof.

Iqbaliyat
Zaidi, Nadira, PhD *Punjab* Research Officer-in-
  Charge*

Islam, Urdu Encyclopaedia of
Tel: (042) 735 3353
Amin, Muhammad, PhD Sr. Ed.
Mahmood-ul-Hasan Arif, H., MA PhD Sr.
  Ed.; Chairman*

Pakistan, Research Society of
Tel: (042) 732 2542
Ahsan, A. S., MA *Alig.*, LLB *Alig.*, PhD Dir.*

Pakistan Study Centre
Ahmad, Rafiq, MA *Manc.*, MA *Punjab*, DPhil
  Oxf. Prof.; Dir.*

Social Sciences Research Centre
Tel: (042) 586 3968 Fax: (042) 586 4534
Anwer, Muhammad, MA PhD Acting Dir.*

Solid State Physics Centre
Tel: (042) 586 4185
Abdullah, Tariq, MSc *Lond.* Assoc. Prof.
Durrani, I. R., MSc PhD Asst. Prof.
Hussain, Khadim, PhD *Manc.*, MSc Prof.
Ikram, Nazma, MPhil *Quaid-i-Azam*, PhD *Camb.*,
  MSc Prof.
Naeem, Shahid, PhD *Lond.*, MSc Asst. Prof.
Nazar, F. M., PhD *Lond.*, MSc Prof.
Salah-ud-Din, PhD *Lond.*, MSc Assoc. Prof.
Shah, H.A., PhD *Quaid-i-Azam*, MSc Asst. Prof.
Siddiqui, S. A., MSc *Newcastle*, MSc *Punjab*, PhD
  Newcastle Assoc. Prof.
Suleman, Muhammad, PhD *Reading*, MSc Prof.;
  Dir.*

**South Asian Studies, Area Study Centre
for**
Tel: (042) 586 4014
Ahmad, Rafiq, MA *Manc.*, MA *Punjab*, DPhil
  Oxf. Prof.; Dir.*

Urdu Development Committee
Tel: (042) 731 2911
Khan, S. A., MA PhD Convenor*

HAILEY COLLEGE OF COMMERCE
Constituent College
Tel: (042) 586 3937, 586 8909
Abdul, Jabbar, MCom *Punjab* Asst. Prof.
Ahmad, Ejaz, MCom Assoc. Prof.
Ahmad, Nazir, MCom Assoc. Prof.; Acting
  Principal*
Ali, Liaqat, MCom Asst. Prof. (on leave)
Chaudhry, A. R., MSc *Quaid-i-Azam* Assoc.
  Prof.
Ehsan, Muhammad, MCom Asst. Prof. (on
  leave)
Gulzar, M. Tayyab, MA *Punjab* Asst. Prof.
Mahmood, Khalid, MCom LLB Asst. Prof.
Mobeen, Alam H., MCom *Punjab* Asst. Prof.
Moghal, M. M., MCom Asst. Prof.
Naeem, Muhammad, MCom Asst. Prof.
Rahim, Abdul, MCom Assoc. Prof.
Sohail, Akhtar, MCom Asst. Prof.

UNIVERSITY LAW COLLEGE
Constituent College
Tel: (042) 586 3970, 586 4215, 586 4756
Ahmad, S. Z., BCom LLB MA Assoc. Prof.
Ahmad, Zulfiqar, LLB *Punjab* Assoc. Prof.
Akhtar, Javed, LLB *IIU(P'stan.)* Asst. Prof.

Amin, Muhammad, LLM *Virginia*, LLB
  MA Assoc. Prof.
Chaudhry, M. H., LLB *Karachi*, MA *Karachi*,
  MPhil *Lond.*, PhD *Lond.* Prof.; Principal*
Dogar, Nawaz, LLB Asst. Prof.
Khan, A. A., LLB MA Asst. Prof.
Muhammad, Dil, LLM *Louisiana State*, LLB
  PhD Prof.
Naeem, Muhammad, ML *Emory*, LLB
  PhD Assoc. Prof.
Ozair, Samee, LLM *IIU(P'stan.)* Asst. Prof.
Qureshi, Shazia N., LLB *Camb.*, LLM
  Camb. Asst. Prof.
Zafar, S. U., LLM *Lond.*, LLB Assoc. Prof. (on
  leave)

UNIVERSITY ORIENTAL COLLEGE
Constituent College
Tel: (042) 731 1496, 735 5541

Arabic
Tel: (042) 735 2573
Akram, M., PhD Prof.; Chairman*
Dad, Khaliq, MA PhD Asst. Prof.
Malik, M. M., MA PhD Assoc. Prof.
Moeen, Mazhar, MA PhD Assoc. Prof.
Shakir, Dost M., PhD Asst. Prof.
Syed, M. K. A. M., MA Assoc. Prof.
Syed, Q. A., MA PhD Asst. Prof.

Kashmiriyat
Tel: (042) 732 2057
Syed, M. Y. B., MA PhD Assoc. Prof.;
  Chairman*

Persian
Tel: (042) 735 4212
Asghar, Aftab, PhD *Teheran*, MA Prof.;
  Chairman*
Irshad, Nasreen, PhD *Teheran*, MA Assoc. Prof.

Punjabi
Tel: (042) 735 4973
Humayun, Khalid, MA *Quaid-i-Azam*, MA
  Punjab Asst. Prof.
Zahid, I. U., MA PhD Asst. Prof.; In-Charge*

Urdu
Tel: (042) 731 2911, 735 7116
Firaqi, M. A. T., MA PhD Assoc. Prof.
Hashmi, Rafi-Ud-Din Assoc. Prof.
Khan, S. A., MA PhD Prof.; Chairman*
Khawaja, M. Z., MA PhD Prof. (on leave)
Noori, Fakhr-ul-Haq, MA Asst. Prof.
Tahir, Marghoob, MA Asst. Prof.

CONTACT OFFICERS
General enquiries. Registrar: Saad-ud-Din,
  Muhammad, BA *Punjab*, LLB *Punjab*

CONSTITUENT COLLEGE HEADS
Hailey College of Commerce. (Tel: (042) 586
  3937, 586 8909.) Principal: Ahmad, Nazir,
  MCom
University Law College. (Tel: (042) 586
  3970, 586 4215, 586 4756.) Principal:
  Chaudhry, Prof. M. H., LLB *Karachi*, MA
  Karachi, MPhil *Lond.*, PhD *Lond.*
University Oriental College. (Tel: (042) 731
  1496, 735 5541.) Principal: Khan, Sohail
  A., MA PhD

*[Information supplied by the institution as at 20 June
1998, and edited by the ACU]*

QUAID-I-AWAM UNIVERSITY OF ENGINEERING AND TECHNOLOGY

Postal Address: Nawabshah, Pakistan
Telephone: (0241) 62405 **Fax**: (0241) 60523

VICE-CHANCELLOR*—Qazi, A. Q.
REGISTRAR‡—......

QUAID-I-AZAM UNIVERSITY

Founded 1965 as University of Islamabad; incorporated 1967; name changed 1976

Member of the Association of Commonwealth Universities

Postal Address: PO Box 1090, Islamabad, Pakistan
Telephone: (051) 214801, 827259 **Fax**: (051) 821397 **Cables**: Quaid-i-Azam University, Islamabad

CHANCELLOR—The President of the Islamic Republic of Pakistan (ex officio)
VICE-CHANCELLOR*—Siddiqui, M. Tariq, BA Punjab, MSc Punjab, MPA Syr., PhD Syr.
REGISTRAR—Ikram-ul-Haq, MA Punjab
ACTING TREASURER—Pirzada, Qamaruz Z.
LIBRARIAN—Shaikh, M. Hanif

FACULTIES/SCHOOLS

Medicine
Dean: Khan, Lt. Gen. M. Ayub

Natural Sciences
Dean: Murtaza, Prof. G., MSc Punjab, PhD Lond.

Social Sciences
Dean: Qureshi, Prof. M. A., MSc S.Calif., PhD Rensselaer

ACADEMIC UNITS

Administrative Sciences
Ahmad, M. I., MA Punjab, MBA Wis.   Asst. Prof.
Hafeez, M. A., MBA Anna Maria, MS Mass., MA   Asst. Prof.
Kaleem, M. Y., MBA Karachi   Asst. Prof.
Mahmood, N., MBA Karachi   Asst. Prof.
Nauman, H., MA Pesh., MPA Quaid-i-Azam   Asst. Prof.
Niazi, G. S. K., MA Lanc., MSc Quaid-i-Azam   Asst. Prof.
Qureshi, M. A., MSc S.Calif., PhD Rensselaer   Prof.; Head*

Anthropology
Chaudhary, M. A., PhD Heidel.   Asst. Prof.
Haq, H., MPhil Wash., PhD Wash.   Asst. Prof.
Rahat, N., MSc Quaid-i-Azam, DPhil Sus., MS PhD   Assoc. Prof.; Head*
Rehman, H., MSc Quaid-i-Azam   Asst. Prof.

Biology
Ahmad, M., MSc Punjab, PhD Wales   Prof.
Ahmad, M. M., MSc Punjab, PhD Aston   Prof.
Ahmad, T., MSc Punjab, PhD Nancy   Assoc. Prof.
Ashraf, M., PhD Lond.   Asst. Prof.
Ayub, N., MSc Punjab, PhD Aberd.   Asst. Prof.
Bano, A., MSc Dacca, PhD Glas.   Asst. Prof.
Bari, A., MSc W.Pak.Ag., MPhil Quaid-i-Azam, PhD Quaid-i-Azam   Asst. Prof.

Chaudhry, M. F., MSc Punjab, MPhil Quaid-i-Azam, PhD Brad.   Assoc. Prof.
Dar, M. I., MSc Punjab, MSc Reading   Asst. Prof.
Fatima, N., MSc Sind, MPhil Quaid-i-Azam, PhD Quaid-i-Azam   Asst. Prof.
Hafeez, M. A., MSc Alig., MSc Br. Col., PhD Calif.   Prof.; Head*
Hameed, A., MS Bucharest, MPhil Bucharest, PhD Bucharest   Asst. Prof.
Jalali, S., MSc Punjab, MPhil Quaid-i-Azam, PhD Bonn   Assoc. Prof.
Khan, M. A., PhD Leic.   Asst. Prof.
Malik, S. A., MSc Glas., PhD Glas.   Asst. Prof.
Pal, R. A., MSc Sindh, PhD E.Anglia   Prof.
Qureshi, A. S., PhD Sindh   Prof.
Shahab, M., PhD   Asst. Prof.
Shami, S. A., MSc Punjab, PhD Wales   Assoc. Prof.
Sultana, K., MSc Punjab, MPhil Quaid-i-Azam, DPhil Sus.   Asst. Prof.
Zaheer, K., PhD Belf.   Asst. Prof.

Chemistry
Ahmad, J., MSc Punjab, PhD F.U.Berlin   Prof.
Ahmad, N., MSc Pesh., PhD Wayne State   Prof.
Ahmad, Roshan, MSc Punjab, PhD Munich   Prof.
Ahmad, Z., MSc Punjab, PhD Pesh., PhD Manc.   Assoc. Prof.
Ali, S., MSc Pesh., PhD Torun   Asst. Prof.
Ansari, M. S., MSc Quaid-i-Azam, MPhil Quaid-i-Azam, PhD Quaid-i-Azam   Assoc. Prof.
Butt, P. K., MSc Punjab, PhD Lond.   Prof.
Hasan, A., MSc Pesh., MPhil Lyons I, PhD Lyons I   Asst. Prof.
Hasan, M., PhD Fran.   Prof.
Ikram, M., MSc Punjab, PhD Lond.   Assoc. Prof.
Iqbal, M. J., MSc Punjab, PhD Brad.   Asst. Prof.
Iqbal, R., MSc Pesh., PhD Lond.   Prof.
Jaffar, M., MSc Punjab, MPhil Quaid-i-Azam, PhD Quaid-i-Azam   Prof.
Khan, A. Y., MSc Karachi, PhD S'ton.   Prof.
Khan, N., MSc Pesh., PhD Lond.   Assoc. Prof.
Mazhar, M., PhD Bud.   Assoc. Prof.
Muhammad, M., MSc Karachi, PhD N.Y.   Prof.

Munir, C., MSc Pesh., PhD Wayne State   Assoc. Prof.
Rama, N. H., MSc Karachi, PhD Lond.   Assoc. Prof.
Rauf, M. A., MSc Texas Woman's, MPhil Texas Woman's, PhD Texas Woman's   Asst. Prof.
Saleem, M., MSc Punjab, PhD Edin.   Prof.; Head*
Shah, S. S., MSc Pesh., PhD Marburg   Assoc. Prof.
Subhani, M. S., MSc Karachi, PhD Leeds   Assoc. Prof.
Yousaf, S. M., MPhil Quaid-i-Azam, PhD Akron   Asst. Prof.
Zulfiqar, S., MSc Punjab, MSc Glas., PhD Glas.   Assoc. Prof.

Computer Sciences
Afzal, M., PhD Kent   Asst. Prof.
Bhatti, N. A., MSc A.Bello, MS New Haven   Asst. Prof.
Bhatti, S. A., MA Punjab, MSc Brad., PhD A.Bello   Assoc. Prof.
Gul, E. A., MSc Quaid-i-Azam, MS Pitt.   Asst. Prof.
Malik, M. A., MA Punjab, PhD Belf.   Prof.; Head*
Mirza, M. D., MSc Manc., MSc Quaid-i-Azam, PhD Manc.   Asst. Prof.
Saifuddin, A. B., PhD   Asst. Prof.

Defence and Strategic Studies
Cheema, M. Z. I., MA Punjab, PhD Lond.   Prof.
Hussain, N., MSc Quaid-i-Azam   Asst. Prof.
Khalid, M. R., MSc Quaid-i-Azam, MPhil Quaid-i-Azam   Asst. Prof.
Naseem, M. A., MSc Quaid-i-Azam, MPhil Quaid-i-Azam   Asst. Prof.
Raza, M. J., MSc Quaid-i-Azam, MPhil Quaid-i-Azam   Asst. Prof.

Earth Sciences
Ahmad, Z., MSc Lond., PhD Kentucky   Asst. Prof.
Ali, K. A., MSc Pesh., PhD Tas.   Prof.; Head*
Ali, M., MSc Punjab, PhD Glas.   Assoc. Prof.

Ghazi, G. R., MSc Punjab Asst. Prof.
Jadoon, I. A. K., MSc Pesh., PhD Oregon State Asst. Prof.
Qureshi, S. N., MS Hamburg, PhD Hamburg Asst. Prof.

Economics
Ahmad, E., PhD Assoc. Prof.
Azim, P., PhD Texas A.&M. Asst. Prof.
Burkie, A. A., PhD Kansas State Asst. Prof.
Chaudhry, M. Ali, MSc W.Pak.Ag., PhD Hawaii Prof.
Chaudhry, M. Aslam, PhD Assoc. Prof.; Head*
Javed, M. T., MSc S.Fraser, MSc Quaid-i-Azam Asst. Prof.
Javed, M. T., PhD Nebraska Asst. Prof.
Khan, A. H., PhD Glas. Asst. Prof.
Malik, N. S., MSc McM. Asst. Prof.

Electronics
Bhatti, G. S., MSc Punjab, PhD Lanc. Assoc. Prof.
Chohan, M. S., MSc Strath., PhD Strath. Assoc. Prof.
Naqvi, A. A., BSc W.Pak.Eng., PhD Lond. Asst. Prof.
Qureshi, I. M., MS Middle East Tech., PhD Tor. Asst. Prof.
Rizvi, A. A., BE Shiraz, PhD Cal.Tech. Asst. Prof.
Zubairy, M. S., MSc Roch., PhD Roch. Prof.; Head*

History
Afzal, M. M. Rafique, MA Punjab, PhD Tor. Prof.
Ahmad, A., MA Punjab, MPhil Quaid-i-Azam Asst. Prof.
Ahmad, R., MA Punjab, MPhil Quaid-i-Azam, PhD Quaid-i-Azam Assoc. Prof.
Akhtar, M., MPhil Quaid-i-Azam Asst. Prof.
Hayat, S., MA Pesh., MPhil Col., PhD Quaid-i-Azam Assoc. Prof.
Saiyid, D. H., MPhil Lond., PhD Col. Asst. Prof.
Shah, W. A., MA Pesh., MPhil Pesh. Asst. Prof.
Syed, J. H., MA Punjab, MPhil Quaid-i-Azam Asst. Prof.
Syed, M. A., PhD Col. Prof.

International Relations
Ali, L. A., MSc Quaid-i-Azam Asst. Prof.
Amin, T., MA Car., MA Quaid-i-Azam, PhD M.I.T. Assoc. Prof.

Aziz, R. I., MA Karachi, MPhil Col. Asst. Prof.
Butt, Mahmudul H., MPhil Quaid-i-Azam Asst. Prof.
Cheema, P. I., MA Punjab, MA Oslo, PhD Quaid-i-Azam Prof.
Hussain, I., PhD Nice Prof.
Hussain, S. R., MA Denver, MSc Quaid-i-Azam, PhD Denver Asst. Prof.
Khawaja, A., MA Punjab, MA Calif. Asst. Prof.
Siddiqui, R., MA Drew, PhD Penn. Assoc. Prof.; Head*
Waseem, M., MA Punjab, PhD Lond. Assoc. Prof.

Mathematics
Ahmad, N., MSc Punjab, MPhil Quaid-i-Azam, PhD Quaid-i-Azam Asst. Prof.
Ahmed, F., MSc Punjab, PhD Manc. Assoc. Prof.
Asghar, S., MSc Punjab, MPhil Quaid-i-Azam, PhD Quaid-i-Azam Prof.; Head*
Aslam, M., MSc Punjab, PhD Asst. Prof.
Ayub, M., PhD Quaid-i-Azam Asst. Prof.
Azad, H., MSc Punjab, MS Notre Dame, PhD Notre Dame Prof.
Beg, I., MSc Punjab, PhD Bucharest Assoc. Prof.
Bokhari, A. H., MSc Punjab, MPhil Quaid-i-Azam, PhD Quaid-i-Azam Assoc. Prof.
Farid, M., MSc Quaid-i-Azam, MPhil Quaid-i-Azam, PhD Glas. Asst. Prof.
Iqbal, Q., PhD Quaid-i-Azam Asst. Prof.
Khan, L. A., MSc Punjab, PhD Wales Assoc. Prof.
Muhammad, N., MSc Moscow, PhD Moscow Assoc. Prof.
Mushtaq, Q., DPhil Oxf. Assoc. Prof.
Nasir, M. Y., MSc Punjab, PhD Bucharest Assoc. Prof.
Qadir, A., BSc Lond., PhD Lond. Prof.
Siddiqui, A. W., MSc Brun., MSc Quaid-i-Azam, MPhil Quaid-i-Azam Asst. Prof.
Yab, M. Z., MSc Punjab, MSc Liv., PhD Liv. Assoc. Prof.
Ziad, M., PhD Quaid-i-Azam Asst. Prof.

Physics
Ahmad, K., MSc Punjab, PhD Lond. Prof.; Head*
Ashraf, I., PhD Quaid-i-Azam Asst. Prof.
Baig, M. A., MSc Karachi, MPhil Karachi, PhD Lond. Prof.
Hasanain, K. S., MSc Karachi, PhD Boston Assoc. Prof.
Hoodbhoy, P. A., PhD M.I.T. Prof.

Iqbal, M. Z., PhD Camb. Prof.
Khan, M. K., PhD Quaid-i-Azam Asst. Prof.
Khawaja, F. A., MSc Moscow, PhD Moscow Prof.
Mahmood, S., PhD Quaid-i-Azam Asst. Prof.
Maqsood, A., MSc Oxf., PhD Gothenburg Prof.
Mirza, A. M., MPhil Quaid-i-Azam, PhD Quaid-i-Azam Asst. Prof.
Murtaza, G., MSc Punjab, PhD Lond. Prof.
Nayyar, A. H., MSc Karachi, MPhil Lond., PhD Lond. Assoc. Prof.
Saifuddin, MSc Punjab, MSc McG., PhD McG. Prof.
Saleem, S., MPhil Quaid-i-Azam, PhD Quaid-i-Azam Asst. Prof.
Zafar, N., MSc Punjab, PhD Camb. Assoc. Prof.
Zakaullah, M., MPhil Quaid-i-Azam, PhD Quaid-i-Azam Asst. Prof.

Strategic Studies, see Defence and Strategic Studies

CONTACT OFFICERS
Academic affairs. Registrar: Ikram-ul-Haq, MA Punjab
Computing services. Director, Computer Centre: Mohammad, Ghulam, BSc W.Pak.Eng., MSc Belf., PhD Belf.
Estates and buildings/works and services. Project Director: Khan, Major (R) M. Ilyas, BSc(Engg)
Estates and buildings/works and services. Assistant Registrar (Estate): Rehman, A.
Examinations. Controller of Examinations: Raoof, M. A., MA Punjab
General enquiries. Registrar: Ikram-ul-Haq, MA Punjab
Health services. Senior Resident Medical Officer: Abbas, Hasan, MB BS MPhil
Library (chief librarian). Librarian: Shaikh, M. Hanif
Purchasing. Purchase and Store Officer: Sabir, M. Sharif
Scholarships, awards, loans. Registrar: Ikram-ul-Haq, MA Punjab
Security. Security Officer: Satti, Mushtaq A.
Sport and recreation. Director of Sports: Rafiq, Mohammad
Student welfare/counselling. In-Charge, Students Affairs: Yab, M. Z., MSc Punjab

[Information supplied by the institution as at 9 December 1996, and edited by the ACU]

SHAH ABDUL LATIF UNIVERSITY

Established 1987

Member of the Association of Commonwealth Universities

Postal Address: Khairpur, Sindh, Pakistan
Telephone: (0792) 551719, 551914 **Fax**: (0792) 551795 **Cables**: Saluni

CHANCELLOR—H.E. The Governor of Sindh (ex officio)
VICE-CHANCELLOR*—Shah, Prof. Rashid A., BSc Karachi, MA Beirut, PhD N.Y.
REGISTRAR‡—Malik, Noorullah G., LLB MA
DIRECTOR OF FINANCE—Khawaja, Hidyatullah, MCom
LIBRARIAN—Bhatti, Mohammad S., LLB MLS

FACULTIES/SCHOOLS
Arts
Dean: Shaikh, Prof. Rasool B., MCom

Law
Dean: Memon, Prof. Qadir B., LLB MA

Science
Dean: Memon, Prof. Abdul G., MSc

ACADEMIC UNITS
Anthropology
1 Lectr.

Archaeology

Kazi, Mohammad M., MSc   Prof.; Chairman*
Mangi, Altaf H., MSc *Sindh*   Asst. Prof.
Shaikh, Nilofer, PhD *Sindh*   Prof.
Shar, Ghulam M., MSc *Sindh*   Asst. Prof.

Botany

Bhatti, Ghulam R., MSc PhD   Asst. Prof.
Bhatti, Noor M., MSc   Prof.; Chairman*
Ismaili, Noor J., MSc MPhil   Asst. Prof.
Mahar, Abdul R., MSc MPhil   Asst. Prof.
Malik, Abdul R., PhD   Prof.
Markhand, Ghulam S., MSc MPhil   Asst. Prof.
Soomro, Rashida, MSc MPhil   Assoc. Prof.

Business Administration

Luhrani, Shah M., MCom MBA   Assoc. Prof.;
   Chairman*

Chemistry

Brohi, Athar N., MSc   Asst. Prof.
Kumar, Vinod, MSc   Asst. Prof.
Mal, Lakhu, MSc   Asst. Prof.
Memon, Ishfaque A., MSc   Asst. Prof.
Memon, Qurban A., MSc   Asst. Prof.
Noomrio, Mohammad H., MSc   Asst. Prof.
Pathan, Agha S., PhD   Prof.
Phulpoto, Manzoor H., MSc   Asst. Prof.
Qureshi, Mumtaz A., PhD   Prof.; Chairman*
Rajput, Musrat, MPhil   Asst. Prof.
Ujjan, Karimdad D., MSc   Asst. Prof.

Commerce

Jalbani, Amanat A., MCom PhD   Assoc. Prof.;
   Chairman*
Jamali, Mohammad B., MCom   Asst. Prof.
Maitlo, Ghulam M., MCom MPhil   Asst. Prof.
Memon, Mohammad A., MCom   Asst. Prof.
Phulpoto, Lutuf A., MCom   Asst. Prof.
Shah, Qasim A., MCom   Asst. Prof.

Economics

Ansari, Altaf H., MA   Asst. Prof.
Chand, Mohammad N., MA   Assoc. Prof.

Chand, Rukhsana N., MA MPhil   Asst. Prof.
Manwani, Asandas, PhD   Prof.; Chairman*
Memon, Abdul L., MA   Assoc. Prof.
Memon, Musrat, MA   Asst. Prof.
Soomro, Abdul S., MA MPhil   Asst. Prof.

Education

1 Advisor

English

Samma, Liaquat A., MA   Asst. Prof.;
   Chairman*
Shah, Farzand A., MA   Asst. Prof.

Geography

1 Lectr.

History, see Muslim Hist.

International Relations

Bhatti, Amanullah, MA   Assoc. Prof.
Chandio, Abdul M., MA PhD   Asst. Prof.
Isran, Manzoor A., MA   Asst. Prof.
Phulpoto, Abdullah, MA   Assoc. Prof.
Shah, Ahmed H., MA   Assoc. Prof.;
   Chairman*
Shaikh, Moonis A., MA   Asst. Prof.

Islamic Culture

Kalhoro, Israr A., MA   Asst. Prof.

Mathematics

Bhatti, Fakir M., PhD   Assoc. Prof.
Chand, Lal, MSc   Asst. Prof.
Soomro, Khuda D., PhD   Prof.; Chairman*

Microbiology

Badar, Yasmeen, PhD   Asst. Prof.
Budhani, Rajkumar, MSc   Asst. Prof.
Memon, Badaruddin, PhD   Asst. Prof.
Zardari, Miandad D., PhD   Prof.; Chairman*

Muslim History

1 Lectr.

Pakistan Studies

Sahito, Imdad H., MA MPhil   Asst. Prof.

Physics

Bhatti, Qurban A., MSc   Asst. Prof.
Ismail, Mohammad, MSc   Asst. Prof.

Political Science

Jalbani, Mahmooda, MA   Asst. Prof.

Sindhi

Malik, Abdul R., MA   Assoc. Prof.; Chairman*

Sociology

1 Lectr.

Statistics

Kalwar, Abdul H., MSc   Prof.; Chairman*
Nizamani, Ghulam Q., MSc   Asst. Prof.
Phulpoto, Ghulam Q., MSc   Asst. Prof.

Urdu

Rahat, Marghoob, MA   Asst. Prof.; Chairman*

CONTACT OFFICERS

Examinations. Controller of Examinations:
   Shaikh, Abdul K., LLB MA
Finance. Director of Finance: Khawaja,
   Hidyatullah, MCom
General enquiries. Registrar: Malik, Noorullah
   G., LLB MA
Library. Librarian: Bhatti, Mohammad S., MLS
Purchasing. Assistant Purchase and Store
   Officer: Dogar, Noor N., MA
Security. Security Officer: Khaskhelli,
   Mustaque A., MA

[Information supplied by the institution as at 22 April 1996, and edited by the ACU]

SHAHEED ZULFIKAR ALI BHUTTO INSTITUTE OF SCIENCE AND TECHNOLOGY

Founded 1995

Additional Member of the Association of Commonwealth Universities

Postal Address: 90 Clifton, Karachi, Pakistan
Telephone: (021) 583 0447-8 **Fax**: (021) 583 0446 **E-mail**: info@szabist.edu.pk
WWW: http://www.szabist.edu.pk **E-mail formula**: surname@szabist.edu.pk

CHANCELLOR—Bhutto, Benazir
ACTING PRESIDENT AND PROJECT DIRECTOR*—Laghari, Javaid R., BE *Sindh*, MS *Middle East Tech.*, PhD
   N.Y.State
ADMINISTRATIVE CONTROLLER‡—Azeem, Mohammad, MPA *Karachi*
FINANCIAL CONTROLLER—Hanif, Mohammad, BCom *Karachi*
PUBLIC RELATIONS OFFICER—Haq, Anwar Ul, BSc *Karachi*
LIBRARIAN—Ruqayia, Khatoon, MLib&InfSc *Karachi*

GENERAL INFORMATION

History. The institute was established by an
act of the Sindh Assembly in 1995. It is
located in Karachi, the provincial capital of
Sindh.

Admission to first degree courses (see also
Pakistan Introduction). Pakistani applicants:
Higher School Certificate (HSC). International

applicants: certificates/diplomas satisfying
matriculation requirements in country of
origin are generally accepted. All candidates
must demonstrate ability in English (eg by
TOEFL/IELTS scores).

First Degrees (see also Pakistan Directory to
Subjects of Study). BBA, BCS.
   All courses are full-time and normally last 3
years.

Higher Degrees (see also Pakistan Directory
to Subjects of Study). MBA, MCS, MS, PhD.
   MS: 1 year; MCS: 2 years full-time; MBA: 2
years full-time or 3 years part-time; PhD: 3
years.

Libraries. Over 4000 volumes; 45 periodicals
subscribed to; CD collection.

Fees (1998–99). Undergraduate: first year: Rs98,600; second and third years: Rs83,600. Postgraduate: first year: Rs81,000 (full-time); Rs54,600 (part-time); second year: Rs66,000 (full-time); Rs46,200 (part-time).

Academic Year (1998–99). Three terms: 3 August–28 November; 4 January–1 May; 1 June–31 July.

Income (1997–98). Rs14,700,000.

Statistics. Staff: 80 (70 academic, 10 administrative). Students: full-time 160 (141 men, 19 women); part-time 128 (123 men, 5 women); total 288.

ACADEMIC UNITS

Accounting
Aslam, Javed M., MBA Lond.
Ayubi, Sharique, MBA Inst.Bus.Ad.(P'stan.)
Azeem, Salman
Choudhry, Humayun Z.
Mehar, Ayub, MPhil Karachi
Siddiqui, S. A., MBA Inst.Bus.Ad.(P'stan.)
Siddiqui, Ziaullah

Computer Science
Abbasi, Hafeez, MSc Quaid-i-Azam
Ahmed, Feroz, MLS W.Ont.
Akhter, Nadeem, MS W.Chester
Barni, Obbia, MS Bhutto IST
Daudpota, Nadeem, PhD Beijing
Hanif, Mohammad, MS C.U.N.Y.
Hashmi, Qutubuddin, MSc Karachi
Kazi, Asif, MSc Sindh
Khalid, Syed Mohammad, MSc Karachi
Khan, Wajeehuddin
Quraishi, Shuja Mohammad, MPhil Karachi
Shah, Mubarak Ali, PhD Wayne State
Siddiqui, M. Irfan, MSc Newcastle(UK)
Yousuf, Syed, MSc Karachi

Economics
Ejaz, Muhammad, MBA Inst.Bus.Ad.(P'stan.)
Hussain, Syed Asad, MA C.U.N.Y.
Memon, Naheed, MSc Lond.

Finance
Fazli, Fakhre Alam, MBA Inst.Bus.Ad.(P'stan.)
Jilani, M. Khalid
Kherati, G. M.
Mustaqim, Asif, MBA Inst.Bus.Ad.(P'stan.)
Samad, Imran, MBA Pesh.
Siddiqui, Kamran, MBA Inst.Bus.Ad.(P'stan.)
Waheed, Amjad, PhD S.Illinois
Zia-ur-Rahman, MBA Inst.Bus.Ad.(P'stan.)

Management
Alam, Faisal, MBA Inst.Bus.Ad.(P'stan.)
Ismail, Muneer, MBA Inst.Bus.Ad.(P'stan.)
Kamal, Ahsan, MBA Inst.Bus.Ad.(P'stan.)
Kazi, Aftab, PhD Pitt.
Murad, Hasnain, MBA Liv.
Panwher, Iqbal, PhD Sindh Ag.
Shah, Masood Anwar, MPA Punjab

Marketing
Abedin, Salman, MBA Inst.Bus.Ad.(P'stan.)
Effendi, Qashif, MBA Inst.Bus.Ad.(P'stan.)
Jalees, Tariq, MBA La Verne
Khan, Mansoor Ali, MBA Inst.Bus.Ad.(P'stan.)
Mapara, Shakeel, MBA Quaid-i-Azam
Naqvi, Asad Mujtaba, MBA Inst.Bus.Ad.(P'stan.)
Noor, Ayesha Fazal, MBA Inst.Bus.Ad.(P'stan.)

Mathematics and Statistics
Asif, Zaheeruddin, MBA Inst.Bus.Ad.(P'stan.)
Hanfi, Wajid, MBA Inst.Bus.Ad.(P'stan.)
Ismail, Abbas, MBA Inst.Bus.Ad.(P'stan.)
Kamal, Syed Arif, PhD Karachi
Khan, M. Sohail, MBA Inst.Bus.Ad.(P'stan.)
Khan, M. Tariq, MBA Inst.Bus.Ad.(P'stan.)
Nadeem-ud-din, M., MBA Inst.Bus.Ad.(P'stan.)

Software Engineering
Ahmed, Munira, MES Syd.
Aijazuddin, MSc Karachi

Ansar, Muqtadir, MS Bhutto IST
Karamat, Perwaiz, MBA W.Coast
Khan, Rao Adnan M., BE NED Eng.
Rauf, Abdur, MSc Birm.
Sangi, A. Aziz, MSc Ill.
Shaikh, Zubair A., PhD N.Y.Polytech.
Tunio, Salma, MSc Sindh

Statistics, see Maths. and Stats.

Other Appointments
Abbasy, Hafsa, MBA Inst.Bus.Ad.(P'stan.) BBA Co-ordinator
Maqsood, Azra, MBA Inst.Bus.Ad.(P'stan.) MBA Co-ordinator
Sangi, Nazir A., PhD Liv. MCS Co-ordinator

CONTACT OFFICERS

Academic affairs. Administrative Controller: Azeem, Mohammad, MPA Karachi
Admissions (first degree). Administrative Controller: Azeem, Mohammad, MPA Karachi
Admissions (higher degree). Administrative Controller: Azeem, Mohammad, MPA Karachi
Alumni. Public Relations Officer: Haq, Anwar Ul, BSc Karachi
Computing services. System Administrator: Kazi, Asif, MSc Sindh
Consultancy services. Maqsood, Azra, MBA Inst.Bus.Ad.(P'stan.)
General enquiries. Administrative Controller: Azeem, Mohammad, MPA Karachi
International office. Public Relations Officer: Haq, Anwar Ul, BSc Karachi
Public relations, information and marketing. Public Relations Officer: Haq, Anwar Ul, BSc Karachi
Research. Maqsood, Azra, MBA Inst.Bus.Ad.(P'stan.)
Students from other countries. Public Relations Officer: Haq, Anwar Ul, BSc Karachi

[Information supplied by the institution as at 20 May 1998, and edited by the ACU]

UNIVERSITY OF SINDH

Founded and incorporated 1947

Member of the Association of Commonwealth Universities

Postal Address: Jamshoro, Sindh, Pakistan
Telephone: (0221) 771363, 771193 **Fax:** (0221) 771376, 771372 **Cables:** Unisindh

CHANCELLOR—H.E. The Governor of Sindh, Karachi (ex officio)
PRO-CHANCELLOR—Minister of Education, Government of Sindh
VICE-CHANCELLOR*—Mughal, Prof. Nazir A., LLB Sindh, MA Sindh, PhD S.Illinois
REGISTRAR—Rajar, Muhammad S.

FACULTIES/SCHOOLS

Arts
Dean: Larik, Prof. K. M., MA Sindh, MPhil Sindh, PhD Sindh

Commerce and Business Administration
Dean: Kazi, Prof. Ferozuddin, MCom

Education and Social Sciences
Acting Dean: Mughal, Prof. Nazir A., LLB Sindh, MA Sindh

Islamic Studies
Dean: Bhutto, Prof. Mumtaz, MA Sindh, PhD Sindh

Law
Dean: Zubedi, Prof. Muhammad J.

Medicine and Health Sciences
Dean-in-Charge: Memon, Prof. Jan M.

Natural Sciences
Dean: Kazi, Prof. Gul H., MSc Sindh, PhD Lond.

ACADEMIC UNITS

Arabic, see Langs., Inst. of

Botany
Abro, Hidayatullah, MSc Sindh, PhD Sindh Prof.
Afsari, Sharif, MSc Sindh, PhD Sindh Prof. (on deputation)
Arain, Basir A., MSc Sindh, MPhil Sindh, PhD Sindh Assoc. Prof.
Arain, Ch. Rehmatullah, MSc Sindh, MPhil Sindh, PhD Moscow Prof.
Arain, Shamsa Y., MSc Sindh, MPhil Sindh, PhD Sheff. Prof.
Channar, Bashir A., MSc Strath., MSc Sindh Assoc. Prof.

Hassany, Syeda S., MSc Sindh, MSc Syd., PhD Sindh Assoc. Prof.
Khoja, Ashraf B., MSc Sindh Asst. Prof.
Khushk, Muhammad T., MSc Sindh, MPhil Lond. Assoc. Prof.
Mangrio, Shahazdi, MSc Sindh Asst. Prof.
Memon, Abdul H., MSc Sindh Assoc. Prof.
Memon, Haroon R., MSc Sindh, MPhil Sindh, PhD Syd. Prof.
Memon, Mah-Jabeen, MSc Sindh, MPhil Sindh Asst. Prof.
Nizamani, Zafar A., MSc Sindh, PhD Sindh Prof.
Porgar, Abdul S., MSc Sindh Asst. Prof.
Rajput, Muhammad T., MSc Sindh, MPhil Sindh, PhD Syd. Prof. (on lien)
Sahito, Mushtaque A., MSc Sindh, MPhil Sindh, PhD Sindh Assoc. Prof.
Shah, Syed A. G., MSc Sindh, MPhil Sindh Assoc. Prof.
Shahani, Pirsumal H., MSc Sindh Asst. Prof.
Shaikh, Wazir, MSc Sindh, PhD Karachi Assoc. Prof.
Soomro, Abdul Q., MSc Sindh, PhD Moscow Prof.; Chairman*
Soomro, Shamshad, MSc Sindh, MPhil Sindh Assoc. Prof.
Syed, Ahmed A., MSc Karachi, PhD Prague Prof.
Tirmizi, S. A. Saeeduddin, MSc Sindh, MPhil Sindh, PhD Sindh Assoc. Prof.
Other Staff: 1 Lectr.; 1 Res. Assoc.

Business Studies, Institute of

Gopang, Nazir A., MBA Sindh Asst. Prof.
Larik, Ghulam S. Asst. Prof. (on leave)
Memon, Zarina, MA Sindh, PhD Assoc. Prof. (on lien)
Mughal, Muhammad H., BE Sindh, LLB Sindh, MBA Sindh Asst. Prof.
Pandhiani, Ali A., LLB Sindh, MBA Sindh, MA Webster Asst. Prof.
Pathan, Muhammad A., MBA Sindh Asst. Prof.
Shah, Syed A. A., LLB Sindh, MCom Sindh, MBA Leeds, PhD Wales Prof. (on deputation)
Zardari, Khair M., LLB Sindh, MCom Sindh, MBA Leeds Assoc. Prof.; Dir.*
Other Staff: 11 Lectrs.; 3 Res. Assocs.

Chemistry, Institute of

Abbasi, Ubedullah, MSc Sindh, PhD Manc. Prof., Analytical Chemistry
Arain, Muhammad R., MSc Sindh, PhD Moscow Prof., Analytical Chemistry
Baloch, Mushtaque A., MSc Sindh, PhD Sur. Assoc. Prof., Inorganic Chemistry
Bhatti, Abdul G., MSc Sindh, PhD Sindh Asst. Prof.
Bozdar, Rasool B., MSc Sindh, PhD Sindh Assoc. Prof., Inorganic Chemistry
Bughio, Muhammad N., MSc Sindh, MPhil Sindh Asst. Prof., Inorganic Chemistry
Burdi, Dadu K., MSc Sindh, PhD Quaid-i-Azam Asst. Prof., Organic Chemistry
Dahot, Muhammad U., MSc Sindh, PhD Sindh Asst. Prof., Biochemistry
Hashmi, Iqbal H., MSc Sindh, PhD Exe. Prof., Inorganic Chemistry
Kazi, Fayyaz A., MSc Sindh Asst. Prof., Physical Chemistry
Kazi, Gul H., MSc Sindh, PhD Lond. Prof., Analytical Chemistry
Khand, Fatehuddin, MSc Sindh, PhD Sindh Assoc. Prof., Biochemistry
Khaskhelly, Ghulam K., MSc Sindh, PhD Sindh Asst. Prof., Organic Chemistry
Khuhawar, Muhammad Y., MSc Sindh, PhD Birm. Prof., Analytical Chemistry
Mahesar, Muhammad A., MSc Sindh, PhD Sur. Asst. Prof. (on deputation)
Mangrio, Niaz A., MSc Sindh, PhD Assoc. Prof.
Memon, Allah N., MSc Sindh, PhD Sindh Assoc. Prof., Biochemistry
Memon, Muhammad A., MSc Sindh, MPhil Assoc. Prof., Organic Chemistry
Memon, Muhammad H., MSc Sindh, PhD Hull Assoc. Prof., Analytical Chemistry
Memon, Saifullah, MSc Sindh, PhD Moscow Prof., Physical Chemistry

Memon, Sikandar A., MSc Sindh, PhD Lond. Assoc. Prof., Analytical Chemistry
Memon, Zahida P., MSc Sindh, PhD Sindh Assoc. Prof., Organic Chemistry
Qureshi, Abdul S., MSc Sindh, PhD Leip. Assoc. Prof., Inorganic Chemistry
Qureshi, Attaur R., MSc Sindh, PhD Sindh Prof., Organic Chemistry
Qureshi, Muneer A., MSc Sindh, PhD Sur. Prof., Organic Chemistry; Dir.*
Shah, Zahoor H., MSc Sindh, PhD Sindh Assoc. Prof., Physical Chemistry
Shaikh, Muhammad S., MSc Sindh, PhD Moscow Assoc. Prof., Physical Chemistry
Tanwari, Zafarullah, MSc Sindh Assoc. Prof., Organic Chemistry
Valhary, Muhammad U., MSc Sindh, MPhil Lough. Assoc. Prof., Organic Chemistry
Vasandani, Abdul G., MSc Sindh, PhD Sindh Asst. Prof., Physical Chemistry
Other Staff: 7 Lectrs.; 1 Chem. Analyst

Commerce

Agha, Riaz H., MCom Sindh Assoc. Prof.
Jamali, Ghulam R., LLB Sindh, MCom Sindh Asst. Prof.
Jamali, Noor M., MCom Sindh Asst. Prof.
Kanasro, Hakim A., MCom Sindh Asst. Prof. (on lien)
Kazi, Ferozuddin, MCom Prof.
Shaikh, Khalid H., MCom Sindh Asst. Prof.; Chairperson*
Shaikh, Manzoor A., MCom Sindh Assoc. Prof.
Shaikh, Muhammad A., MCom Sindh Asst. Prof.
Soomro, Muneeruddin, LLB Sindh, MCom Sindh Asst. Prof.
Other Staff: 4 Lectrs.

Comparative Religion and Islamic Culture

Memon, Abdul R., MA Sindh Prof.
Memon, Zarina B., MA Sindh Assoc. Prof.
Pathan, Kulsoom, MA Sindh Assoc. Prof.; Chairperson*
Turk, Muhammad I., MA Sindh Prof.
Usman, Najama, MA Sindh Asst. Prof.
Other Staff: 3 Lectrs.

Computer Science, see Maths. and Computer Sci., Inst. of

Economics

Jamali, Khalida, MA Sindh Prof.
Jamali, Sobho K., MA Sindh Asst. Prof.
Kazi, I. H., LLB Sindh, MA Sindh Prof.
Khaskhelly, Ghulam H., LLB Sindh, MA Sindh, MSc Strath. Prof.
Mangi, Roshan A., MA Sindh Asst. Prof. (on lien)
Panhwar, Murad K., MA Sindh Prof.
Pirzada, Imtiaz A., MSc Quaid-i-Azam Asst. Prof.
Qasmi, Merhab, MA Sindh Assoc. Prof.
Rajar, Wasayo, LLB Sindh, MA Sindh Prof.; Chairman*
Shah, Parveen, MA Sindh, MPhil Sindh Prof.
Shallawani, Shabnam, MA N.Y., MA Sindh Assoc. Prof.
Thebo, Naseem, MA Sindh Asst. Prof.
Umrani, Anwar H., MA Sindh Assoc. Prof.
Other Staff: 4 Lectrs.; 3 Res. Assocs.

Education, Technical, see Sci. and Tech. Educn.

Educational Administration and Instructional Technology

Bukhari, Syed S. H., MA Sindh, MEd Sindh Asst. Prof.
Channa, Din M., MA Sindh, MEd Sindh Asst. Prof.
Leghari, Mian B., MA Sindh, MEd Sindh Assoc. Prof.
Siddiqui, Abdul R., MA Sindh, MEd Sindh Prof.; Chairman*
Other Staff: 3 Lectrs.

English

Abbasi, Shehla, MA Sindh Asst. Prof.
Ansari, Arifa, MA Sindh Assoc. Prof.
Baloch, Ghulam H., MA Sindh Asst. Prof.
Farida, Yasmeen, MA Sindh Asst. Prof.
Larik, K. M., MA Sindh, MPhil Sindh, PhD Sindh Prof.
Memon, Rafique A., MA Sindh Asst. Prof.
Mughal, Najma, MA Sindh, MA Edinboro State Asst. Prof. (on lien)
Otho, Nargis R., MA Sindh Asst. Prof.
Palli, Abdul A., MA Sindh Asst. Prof.
Panhwar, Muhammad M., MA Sindh Asst. Prof.
Shah, Syed Q. B., BEd Sindh, MA Sindh Prof.; Chairman*
Shah, Syed S. A., MA Sindh Asst. Prof.
Shaikh, Abdul G., MA Sindh Prof.
Suhag, Asif A., MA Sindh Assoc. Prof.
Other Staff: 6 Lectrs.

Fine Arts

Abro, Mansoor A., MA Sindh Asst. Prof.
Arbani, Ashique H., MA Sindh Asst. Prof.
Bhatti, Muhammad A., MA Punjab, MFA Edinboro State Assoc. Prof.; Chairman*
Mirza, Mussarat, MA Punjab Assoc. Prof.
Pirzada, Anjum J., MA Punjab Asst. Prof.
Other Staff: 2 Lectrs.

Fisheries, see Freshwater Biol. and Fisheries

Foundation of Education and Curriculum Development

Choudhry, Muhammad A., MA Sindh, MEd Sindh, PhD Sindh Prof.; Chairman*
Shah, Syed G. A., BEd Sindh, MA Sindh, MEd Sindh Asst. Prof.
Other Staff: 1 Lectr.

Freshwater Biology and Fisheries

Abbasi, Abdul R., MSc Sindh, PhD Wales Assoc. Prof.
Daudpota, Naeemuddin, MSc Sindh Asst. Prof.
Jaffary, Syed I. H., MSc Karachi, PhD Liv. Prof.; Chairman*
Leghari, Sultan M., MSc Sindh, PhD Sindh Prof.
Sahito, Gulshan A., MSc Sindh, PhD Sindh Assoc. Prof.
Other Staff: 2 Lectrs.

Geography

Dhanani, Muhammad R., MSc Karachi, MSc Asian I.T., Bangkok Assoc. Prof.; Chairman*
Kazi, Shahnaz, MSc Sindh Asst. Prof.
Panhwar, Mehrunnisa, MSc Sindh, MPhil Manc. Assoc. Prof.
Pathan, Mushtaque A., MSc Asst. Prof.
Siddiqui, Imdadullah, MSc Asst. Prof.
Other Staff: 3 Lectrs.

Geology

Abro, Abdul R., MSc Sindh, PhD Moscow Prof.
Ansari, Qudsia, MSc Sindh Asst. Prof.
Bablani, Saeed A., MSc Quaid-i-Azam, MPhil Trondheim Asst. Prof.
Baig, M. Atique A., MSc Karachi, PhD S'ton. Asst. Prof.
Baryar, Muhammad A., MSc Sindh, PhD Sindh Prof.
Bozdar, Lal B., MSc Sindh, PhD Leeds Prof.; Chairman*
Brohi, Imdad A., MSc Sindh, PhD Hiroshima Asst. Prof.
Gemnani, Srichand, MSc Sindh Asst. Prof.
Kazi, Mansoor A., MSc Sindh, PhD Leeds Prof.
Memon, Ahmed A., MSc Sindh, MSc Lond. Assoc. Prof.
Memon, Allah D., MSc Lond., MSc Sindh, PhD Bucharest Prof.
Solangi, Sarfraz H., MSc Sindh, PhD Wales Asst. Prof.
Soomro, Saeed A., MSc Sindh, PhD Wales Prof.
Usmani, Parveen A., MSc Sindh, MPhil Sindh, PhD Sindh Prof.
Other Staff: 2 Lectrs.

History, General

Lakho, Ghulam M., MA Sindh   Asst. Prof.
Soomro, Allah D., MA Sindh, PhD Sindh   Prof.;
  Chairman*
Soomro, Muhammad Q., MA Sindh, MPhil
  Quaid-i-Azam   Assoc. Prof.
Other Staff: 1 Lectr.; 1 Res. Assoc.

History, Muslim

Ansari, Abdul S., MA Sindh, MPhil Sindh, PhD
  Sindh   Prof.
Bhutto, Mumtaz, MA Sindh, PhD Sindh   Prof.;
  Chairman*
Bughio, Mir M., MA Sindh   Assoc. Prof.
Other Staff: 1 Lectr.; 1 Res. Assoc.

Information Technology, Institute of

Abbasi, Haji K., MSc Sindh   Asst. Prof.
Ansari, Abdul W., MSc Sindh, PhD   Assoc.
  Prof. (on deputation)
Bukhari, Abdul H. S., MSc Sindh, PhD
  Moscow   Prof.; Dir.*
Ismaili, Imdad A., MSc Sindh, PhD Lond.   Assoc.
  Prof.
Pathan, Amir H., MSc Sindh, PhD   Asst. Prof.
  (on lien)
Seehar, Lubna M., MSc Sindh   Asst. Prof.
Shaikh, Asad A., MSc Clarkson, MSc   Assoc.
  Prof.
Soomro, Haji K., MSc Sindh, PhD   Prof.
Other Staff: 10 Lectrs.; 2 Res. Assocs.

Instructional Technology, see Educnl.
  Admin. and Instrucnl. Technol.

International Relations

Afridi, Parveen, MA Sindh   Assoc. Prof.
Chachar, Abdul K., LLB Sindh, MA Sindh, MSc
  Quaid-i-Azam   Assoc. Prof.
Kandhar, Azra, LLB Sindh, MA Sindh   Asst. Prof.
Lakho, Abdul H., LLB Sindh, MA Sindh   Asst.
  Prof.
Mangi, Lutufullah, MA Sindh, MA Wat., PhD
  Lond.   Assoc. Prof.
Mangrio, Naghma, MA Sindh   Asst. Prof.
Mirza, Parvez H., LLB Sindh, MA Sindh   Assoc.
  Prof.; Chairman*
Shah, Mehtab A., MA Sindh, MA Warw., PhD
  Lond.   Prof.
Tunio, Abdul L., MA Sindh   Asst. Prof.
Other Staff: 1 Lectr.

Islamic Culture, see Compar. Religion and
  Islamic Culture

Languages, Institute of

Jalbani, Attaullah, MA Sindh   Asst. Prof., Arabic
Leghari, Abdul Q., MA Sindh   Asst. Prof.,
  Arabic
Shaikh, Hafiz A. G., LLB Sindh, MA Sindh, PhD
  Sindh   Asst. Prof., Arabic; Dir.-in-Charge*
Other Staff: 1 Lectr.

Library and Information Science

Ansari, Khadija, MA Sindh, MLIS Sindh   Asst.
  Prof.
Butt, Allah R., MLIS Sindh, MPhil Sindh, PhD
  Wales   Prof.
Gangani, Gurdino, BEd Sindh, LLB Sindh, MLIS
  Sindh   Assoc. Prof.
Shaikh, Rafia A., MA Sindh, MA Lough., PhD
  Lond.   Prof.; Chairperson*
Soomro, Sheerin G., MA Sindh, MLIS
  Sindh   Asst. Prof.
Other Staff: 4 Lectrs.

Mass Communication

Agha, Rafique A., MA Sindh   Asst. Prof.
Chang, Rizwana, MA Sindh   Asst. Prof.
Jaffery, Fouzia R., MA Karachi, PhD Sindh   Prof.;
  Chairperson*
Makhijani, Har B., LLB Sindh, MA Sindh   Asst.
  Prof.
Panhwar, Khan M., MA Karachi, MPhil Sindh,
  PhD Sindh   Asst. Prof.
Rashdi, Ibadullah, MA Sindh   Assoc. Prof.
Soomro, Badaruddin, MA Sindh   Asst. Prof.
Other Staff: 1 Lectr.; 1 Res. Assoc.

Mathematics and Computer Science,
  Institute of

Brohi, Abdul W., MSc Sindh   Asst. Prof.
Brohi, Muhammad N., MSc Quaid-i-Azam, PhD
  Shenyang   Asst. Prof.
Chandio, Muhammad S., MSc Sindh   Asst. Prof.
Jalbani, Shamsuddin, MSc Sindh   Asst. Prof.
Kazi, Asif A. G., MSc Karachi, MPhil Leeds   Prof.
Khan, Muhammad Z., MSc Sindh, MPhil Quaid-i-
  Azam, PhD Sindh   Prof.
Kundnani, Doulat R., MSc Sindh   Asst. Prof.
Memon, Ali A., MSc Sindh   Asst. Prof.
Memon, Kamaluddin, MSc Sindh   Asst. Prof.
Memon, Manzoor A., MSc Sindh, MPhil Islamia,
  Bahawal.   Assoc. Prof.
Memon, Muhammad A., MSc Sindh, MPhil
  Quaid-i-Azam   Assoc. Prof.
Memon, Riaz A., MSc Sindh, PhD
  Shanghai   Assoc. Prof.
Memon, Sirajuddin, MSc Sindh   Assoc. Prof.
Shaikh, Noor A., MSc Sindh, MPhil Quaid-i-Azam,
  PhD Sindh   Assoc. Prof.
Shaikh, Noor M., MSc Sindh, PhD S'ton.   Prof.;
  Dir.*
Soomro, Abdul S., MSc Sindh, PhD   Asst. Prof.
Other Staff: 11 Lectrs.

Pharmacy

Ansari, Ahmed F., MSc Karachi, PhD Glas.   Prof.
Memon, Muhammad A., MSc Sindh, PhD
  Xiamen   Asst. Prof.
Memon, Muhammad S., MSc Sindh, PhD
  Moscow   Prof.
Memon, Muhammad U., MSc Sindh, PhD
  Kobe   Prof.; Chairman*
Mughal, Najmunnisa   Asst. Prof. (on lien)
Ozra, Ahsan, BPharm Dhaka, MPharm
  Dhaka   Assoc. Prof.
Other Staff: 12 Lectrs.

Philosophy

Bhutto, Javaid A., MSc   Asst. Prof.; Chairman-
  in-Charge*
Other Staff: 1 Lectr.

Physics

Ansari, Ghulam M., MSc Sindh   Prof.
Baloch, Gulzar A., MSc Sindh   Assoc. Prof.
Kalhoro, Muhammad S., MSc Sindh   Asst. Prof.
  (on leave)
Keerio, Muhammad U., MSc Sindh   Asst. Prof.
Khushk, Muhammad M., MSc Sindh   Prof.
Memon, Muhammad K., MSc Sindh, MPhil
  Reading   Prof.; Chairman*
Mughal, Aftab A., MSc Sindh   Asst. Prof.
Mughal, Akhtar H., MSc Sindh, PhD
  Brun.   Assoc. Prof.
Shah, Syed G. S., MSc Sindh   Asst. Prof.
Shah, Syed I., MSc Sindh, MSc Lond., PhD
  Lond.   Assoc. Prof.
Shaikh, Altaf A., MSc Sindh, PhD Gött.   Prof.
Ujjan, Anwaruddin, LLB Sindh, MSc
  Sindh   Assoc. Prof.
Other Staff: 2 Lectrs.

Physiology

Ansari, Abdul Q., MSc Sindh, PhD S'ton.   Prof.
  (on lien)
Bhatti, Rashida, MSc Sindh   Asst. Prof.
Chughatai, Latafat A., MSc Sindh   Asst. Prof.
Jokhio, Rukhsana, MSc Sindh   Asst. Prof.
Mahasar, Hidayatullah, MSc Sindh   Asst. Prof.
Memon, Fehmida, MSc Sindh   Asst. Prof.
Seehar, Ghulam M., MSc Sindh, PhD
  Glas.   Prof.; Chairman*
Shaikh, Bilquees B., MSc Sindh, MPhil Quaid-i-
  Azam   Assoc. Prof.
Shaikh, Jiando, MSc Sindh   Asst. Prof.
Shaikh, Muhammad A., MSc Sindh   Asst. Prof.
Other Staff: 1 Lectr.; 1 Res. Assoc.

Political Science

Abbasi, Saifullah, LLB Sindh, MA Sindh   Asst.
  Prof.
Ansari, Abdul R., LLB Sindh, MA Sindh   Prof.;
  Chairman*
Bukhari, Syed M. S., LLB Sindh, MA
  Sindh   Assoc. Prof.
Jalbani, Din M., MA Sindh   Assoc. Prof.
Mehranvi, Abdul A., LLB Sindh, MA
  Sindh   Assoc. Prof.
Memon, Aslam P., LLB Sindh, MA Sindh   Asst.
  Prof.
Pardasi, Yasmeen Y., LLB Sindh, MA Sindh   Asst.
  Prof.
Phul, Gul M., MA Sindh   Prof.
Qureshi, Iqbal A., LLB Sindh, MA Sindh   Prof.
Rashdi, Razia S., MA Sindh   Assoc. Prof.
Shaikh, Bashir A., LLB Sindh, MA Sindh   Assoc.
  Prof.
Shaikh, Munawar S., LLB Sindh, MA Sindh   Asst.
  Prof.
Other Staff: 2 Lectrs.

Psychological Testing, Guidance and
  Research

Arain, Manzoor-ul-Haq, MA Sindh, MEd Sindh,
  PhD Sindh   Prof.; Liaison Officer*
Jafri, Syed I. H., MSc Sindh   Asst. Prof.
Solangi, Ghulam M., MEd Sindh   Asst. Prof.
Other Staff: 2 Lectrs.

Psychology

Khowaja, Laila B., MA PhD   Asst. Prof.
Shah, Irfana, MA Sindh   Asst. Prof.;
  Chairperson-in-Charge*
Shaikh, Ahmed M., MA Sindh   Asst. Prof.
Thaheem, Nagina P., MA Sindh   Asst. Prof.
Other Staff: 3 Lectrs.; 1 Res. Assoc.

Public Administration

Lalani, Farah, MPA Sindh   Asst. Prof.
Pardasi, Muhammad Y., MA Sindh, MA Edinboro
  State, MPA Penn.State   Prof.; Chairman*
Shaikh, Ghulam S., MPA Quaid-i-Azam   Asst.
  Prof.
Siddiqui, Siraj J., MA Edinboro State, MA
  Sindh   Assoc. Prof.
Other Staff: 6 Lectrs.; 2 Res. Assocs.

Science and Technical Education

Askari, Syed H., MSc Sindh, MEd Sindh   Asst.
  Prof.
Kamboh, Mohammad A., MA Sindh, MEd
  Sindh   Asst. Prof.
Memon, Abdul S., MSc Sindh, MEd Sindh   Asst.
  Prof.; Chairman*
Munshi, Parveen, MA Sindh, MEd Sindh   Asst.
  Prof.; Co-ordinator, BEd Off-Campus
  Programme
Musarrat, Bano, MSc Karachi   Asst. Prof.
Siyal, Nabi B., MSc Sindh, MEd Sindh   Asst.
  Prof.
Solangi, Sultana, MA MEd   Asst. Prof.
Other Staff: 1 Lectr.; 3 Res. Assocs.

Sindhi

Akhund, Hidayatullah, MA Sindh, PhD
  Sindh   Assoc. Prof.
Bughio, Muhammad Q., LLB Sindh, MA Sindh,
  PhD Essex   Prof.
Kazi, Khadim H., LLB Sindh, MA Sindh, PhD
  Sindh   Prof.; Chairman*
Khuwaja, Noor A., MA Sindh   Prof.
Mirza, Qamar J., MA Sindh, PhD Sindh   Assoc.
  Prof.
Mufti, Tehmina, MA Sindh, PhD Sindh   Asst.
  Prof.
Sahar, Imdad, MA Sindh   Assoc. Prof.
Other Staff: 1 Lectr.

Social Work

Baloch, Ghulam H., MA Sindh   Asst. Prof. (on
  lien)
Dahri, Ghulam R., MA Sindh   Asst. Prof.
Khokhar, Ghulam M., MA Sindh   Assoc. Prof.
Mastoi, Gul M., MA Sindh   Asst. Prof. (on lien)
Mughal, Nazir A., LLB Sindh, MA Sindh   Prof.
Nizamani, Muhammad Z., LLB Sindh, MA
  Sindh   Assoc. Prof.
Shah, Ghulam R., LLB Sindh, MA Sindh   Prof.;
  Chairman*
Shah, Zaibunissa, MA Sindh   Assoc. Prof.
Other Staff: 1 Lectr.

Sociology

Junejo, Tanvir S., MA *Sindh* Assoc. Prof.
Khowaja, Izzat K., LLB *Sindh*, MA *Sindh*, MEd
 Sindh, MA *Keele* Prof.
Shaikh, Khalida, MA *Sindh* Prof.; Chairperson*
Shaikh, Naseem B., BEd *Sindh*, MA *Sindh* Prof.
Talpur, Fakhrunnisa, BEd *Sindh*, MA
 Sindh Assoc. Prof.
Other Staff: 3 Lectrs.; 1 Res. Assoc.

Statistics

Fazlani, Abdullah, MSc *Sindh* Assoc. Prof.
Khuwaja, Jawaid H., MSc *Sindh* Asst. Prof.
Memon, Azizullah, MSc *Sindh* Assoc. Prof.
Mirza, Anis A., MSc *Sindh* Assoc. Prof.
Rajput, Muhammad I., LLB *Sindh*, MSc
 Sindh Assoc. Prof.
Sabhayo, Rahim B., MSc *Sindh* Assoc. Prof.
Shah, Syed A. N., MSc *Sindh* Asst. Prof.
Shah, Syed M. A., MSc *Sindh*, PhD
 Bucharest Prof.; Chairman*
Talpur, Ghulam H., MSc *Sindh*, PhD *Shanghai*
 U.S.T. Asst. Prof.
Other Staff: 5 Lectrs.; 1 Res. Assoc.

Urdu

Jilani, Atiq A., MA *Sindh* Asst. Prof.
Mirza, Saleem B., MA *Sindh* Asst. Prof.
Sartaj, Naseem A., MA *Sindh*, PhD *Sindh* Prof.;
 Chairperson*
Shaikh, Fahmida, BEd *Sindh*, MA *Sindh* Assoc.
 Prof.
Syed, Javed I., MA *Sindh*, MPhil *Sindh* Asst.
 Prof.
Other Staff: 2 Lectrs.

Zoology

Ashok, Kumar, MSc *Sindh*, MPhil *Sindh* Assoc.
 Prof.
Awan, Muhammad S., MSc *Sindh*, PhD
 Adel. Prof. (on lien)
Dharejo, Ali M., MSc *Sindh* Prof.
Gachal, Ghulam S., MSc *Sindh* Asst. Prof.
Kehar, Aijaz A., MSc *Sindh* Asst. Prof.

Khan, Muhammad M., MSc *Sindh*, PhD
 Sing. Prof.
Khan, Rizwana M., MSc *Sindh* Assoc. Prof.
Memon, Nasreen, MSc *Sindh* Asst. Prof.
Mughal, Mufarrah, MSc *Sindh* Assoc. Prof.
Pitafi, Karim D., MSc *Sindh*, PhD *Nott.* Prof.
Shah, Syed A. A., MSc *Sindh* Asst. Prof.
Shaikh, Azra A., MSc *Tuskegee*, MSc
 Sindh Assoc. Prof.
Shaikh, Ghulam S., MSc *Sindh* Asst. Prof.
Shaikh, Muhammad Y., MSc *Sindh*, PhD
 Bucharest Prof.; Chairman*
Shaikh, Shamsuddin A., MSc *Sindh*, PhD *Quaid-i-*
 Azam Prof.
Soomro, Mahmoodul H., MSc *Sindh* Asst.
 Prof.
Soomro, Naheed S., MSc *Sindh* Asst. Prof.
Wagan, Muhammad S., MSc *Sindh*, PhD
 Sindh Prof.
Other Staff: 3 Lectrs.; 1 Res. Assoc.

SPECIAL CENTRES, ETC

Analytical Chemistry, National Centre of Excellence in

Ansari, Iqbal A., MSc *Sindh*, PhD *Strath.* Prof.;
 Dir.*
Bhangar, Muhammad I., MSc *Sindh*, PhD
 Lond. Prof.
Kazi, Tasneem G., MSc *Sindh*, PhD *Sindh* Prof.
Khanzada, Abdul W. K., MSc *Sindh*, PhD
 Br.Col. Prof.
Other Staff: 1 Sr. Res. Assoc.

Far East and South East Asia Study Centre

Firdous, Nilofer, LLB *Sindh*, MA *Sindh* Assoc.
 Prof.
Ghaloo, Raza H., MA *Sindh* Assoc. Prof.
Jarwar, Jamila, MA *Sindh* Asst. Prof.
Khushk, Muhammad I., LLB *Sindh*, MA
 Sindh Assoc. Prof.
Shah, Deedar H., MA *Sindh*, PhD *Moscow* Prof.

Soomro, Hidayat A., MA *Sindh* Asst. Prof.;
 Dir.*
Other Staff: 1 Res. Assoc.

Health and Physical Education, Centre for

Qureshi, Yasmeen I., MA MHPEd Assoc.
 Prof.; Dir.-in-Charge*
Shah, Akhtar A., MB BS *Sindh* Asst. Prof.
Other Staff: 2 Lectrs.

Pakistan Study Centre

Chand, Bibi S., LLB *Sindh*, MA *Sindh*, MA *Pesh.*,
 MA Assoc. Prof.; Dir.*
Jiskani, Lal B., MA *Sindh* Assoc. Prof.
Sahar, Ghulam N., MA *Sindh* Asst. Prof.
Other Staff: 1 Lectr.; 1 Res. Fellow

Sindh Development Studies Centre

Kazi, Aftab A., MA *Sindh*, MA PhD Ad Hoc
 Prof.
Panhwar, Iqbal A., MA *Sindh*, MSc *Sindh*, MA
 Windsor, PhD *Sindh Ag.* Prof. (on lien)
Pathan, Parvez A., MBA *Sindh*, MSc *Lond.* Asst.
 Prof.
Taherani, Abida, MA *Sindh*, MA *Lond.*, PhD
 Colorado State Prof.; Dir.*
Other Staff: 5 Lectrs.; 1 Res. Assoc.

CONTACT OFFICERS

Admissions (first degree). Director,
 Undergraduate Admissions: Qureshi,
 Mushtaque A.
Examinations. Controller of Examinations:
 Palijo, Ali N.
Finance. Director of Finance: Shaikh, Niaz M.
General enquiries. Registrar: Rajar,
 Muhammad S.

[*Information supplied by the institution as at 10 October
1998, and edited by the ACU*]

SINDH AGRICULTURE UNIVERSITY

Founded 1977

Postal Address: Tandojam, District Hyderabad, Sindh, Pakistan
Telephone: (02233) 5869 **Fax**: (02233) 5300 **Cables**: Sauni

VICE-CHANCELLOR*—Memon, Rajab A., MSc *Sindh*, PhD *Iowa*
 State
REGISTRAR—Rajper, Mir M., MSc *Sindh*, PhD *Agric.Coll.Norway*

SIR SYED UNIVERSITY OF ENGINEERING AND TECHNOLOGY

Founded 1993

Member of the Association of Commonwealth Universities

Postal Address: Gulshan-e-Iqbal University Road, Karachi 75300, Pakistan
Telephone: (021) 498 8000-2 **Fax**: (021) 498 2393 **E-mail**: zafar@ssuet.edu.pk **WWW**: http://www.ssuet.edu.pk
E-mail formula: user@sirsyed.ssuet.edu.pk

PATRON—Haider, Lt. Gen. Moinuddin, Governor of Sindh
CHANCELLOR—Nizami, Z. A.
VICE-CHANCELLOR*—Ahmad, Prof. Saiyid N., BSc(Engg) *Alig.*, PhD *Lond.*
REGISTRAR—Naim, Prof. Zafar, PhD *Alig.*, MSc
CONTROLLER OF EXAMINATIONS—Faruqi, Prof. A. R., MA
DIRECTOR, FINANCE—Alam, Nisar
DIRECTOR, PLANNING AND DEVELOPMENT—Khan, Abdul J., BSc *Alig.*
LIBRARIAN—Parveen, Riffat, MLib&InfSc *Karachi*

GENERAL INFORMATION

History. The university, sponsored by Aligarh Muslim University Old Boys' Association of Pakistan, was established in 1993 by a provincial government ordinance.

Fees (annual). Home students: Rs48,000; international students: US$5500 (first year), $1800 (subsequent years).

Academic Year. Two semesters, starting January and July.

Income (1997–98). Total (approximate), Rs48,000,000.

Statistics. Staff: 269 (60 academic, 209 other).

FACULTIES/SCHOOLS

Basic and Applied Sciences
Dean: Tirmizi, Prof. S. M. A., MSc *Alig.*, DPhil *Oxf.*, FIP, FRS

Engineering
Dean: Haq, Prof. Syed E., BSc *Cornell*, MS *Cornell*, PhD *Brad.*

ACADEMIC UNITS

Engineering, Biomedical
Haque, Enamul Prof.; Chairman*
Hassan Janjua, Naeemul, BE *NED Eng.*, MSc In-Charge

Engineering, Civil
Ghani, Ekramul, PhD *Birm.* Prof.; Chairman*

Engineering, Computer
Haque, Enamul Prof.; Chairman*
Mehboob, Ather, BSEE MSEE In-Charge

Engineering, Electronic
Haque, Enamul Prof.; Chairman*
Karim, Abid, BE *NED Eng.*, MSc PhD In-Charge

Mathematics, Applied
Alam Khan, Khursheed, BA *Karachi*, MA *Karachi*, MA *Karachi*, MSc *Alta.*, PhD *Lond.* Prof.in-Charge

Physics, Applied
Tirmizi, S. M. A., MSc *Alig.*, DPhil *Oxf.*, FPS Prof.-in-Charge

CONTACT OFFICERS

Academic affairs. Dean, Engineering: Haq, Prof. Syed E., BSc *Cornell*, MS *Cornell*, PhD *Brad.*
Accommodation. Director, Students' Affairs: Durrani, Abdul N. K.
Admissions (first degree). Registrar: Naim, Prof. Zafar, PhD *Alig.*, MSc
Admissions (higher degree). Dean, Engineering: Haq, Prof. Syed E., BSc *Cornell*, MS *Cornell*, PhD *Brad.*
Adult/continuing education. Associate Professor, Electronic Engineering: Karim, Abid
Alumni. Secretary General, Aligarh Muslim Old Boys' Association: Khan, Zakir A.
Careers. Associate Professor, Electronic Engineering: Karim, Abid
Computing services. Mehboob, Ather
Conferences/corporate hospitality. Registrar: Naim, Prof. Zafar, PhD *Alig.*, MSc
Consultancy services. Dean, Engineering: Haq, Prof. Syed E., BSc *Cornell*, MS *Cornell*, PhD *Brad.*
Credit transfer. Dean, Engineering: Haq, Prof. Syed E., BSc *Cornell*, MS *Cornell*, PhD *Brad.*
Development/fund-raising. Director, Finance: Alam, Nisar
Development/fund-raising. Honorary Treasurer: Munif, M. Afzal
Distance education. Dean, Engineering: Haq, Prof. Syed E., BSc *Cornell*, MS *Cornell*, PhD *Brad.*
Estates and buildings/works and services. Director, Planning and Development: Khan, Abdul J., BSc *Alig.*
Examinations. Controller of Examinations: Faruqi, Prof. A. R., MA
Finance. Director, Finance: Alam, Nisar
General enquiries. Assistant Registrar: Aziz, Nasreen
Health services. Lecturer, Biomedical Engineering: Shahnaz, Syeda
Industrial liaison. Bhatti, Iqbal
International office. Deputy Secretary to the Chancellor: Zaman, Mubarak

Language training for international students. Dean, Basic and Applied Sciences: Tirmizi, Prof. S. M. A., MSc *Alig.*, DPhil *Oxf.*, FIP, FPS
Library (chief librarian). Librarian: Parveen, Riffat, MLib&InfSc *Karachi*
Library (enquiries). Cataloguer: Bano, Shamim
Minorities/disadvantaged groups. Director, Students' Affairs: Durrani, Abdul N. K.
Personnel/human resources. Registrar: Naim, Prof. Zafar, PhD *Alig.*, MSc
Public relations, information and marketing. Deputy Secretary to the Chancellor: Zaman, Mubarak
Publications. Deputy Secretary to the Chancellor: Zaman, Mubarak
Purchasing. Purchase Office: Siddiqui, Ajaz M.
Quality assurance and accreditation. Dean, Engineering: Haq, Prof. Syed E., BSc *Cornell*, MS *Cornell*, PhD *Brad.*
Research. Dean, Engineering: Haq, Prof. Syed E., BSc *Cornell*, MS *Cornell*, PhD *Brad.*
Safety. Chief Security Officer: Ibrahim, Tariq B.
Scholarships, awards, loans. Secretary General, Aligarh Muslim Old Boys' Association: Khan, Zakir A.
Security. Chief Security Officer: Ibrahim, Tariq B.
Sport and recreation. Sports Officer: Hussain, Qazi M.
Sport and recreation. Honorary Sports Adviser: Miandad, Javed
Staff development and training. Vice-Chancellor: Ahmad, Prof. Saiyid N., BSc(Engg) *Alig.*, PhD *Lond.*
Student welfare/counselling. Director, Students' Affairs: Durrani, Abdul N. K.
Students from other countries. Director, Students' Affairs: Durrani, Abdul N. K.
Students with disabilities. Associate Professor, Biomedical Engineering: Janjua, Naeemul H., BE *NED Eng*, MSc
University press. Sir Syed University Press: Hassan, Khawaja Q.

[*Information supplied by the institution as at 25 July 1998, and edited by the ACU*]

ZIAUDDIN MEDICAL UNIVERSITY

Founded 1995

Postal Address: St-4/B, Block-6, Clifton, Karachi 75600, Pakistan
Telephone: (021) 586 2937-9 **Fax**: (021) 586 2940 **E-mail**: zmu@khi.compol.com **Telex**: 29321 ZIA PK

VICE-CHANCELLOR*—Jafarey, Prof. Naeem A., MB BS *Punjab*
REGISTRAR‡—Aziz, Jawed, MB BS *Alig.*, MD *Alig.*

PAKISTAN : DIRECTORY

The table below shows which of the institutions indicated provide facilities for study and/or research in the subjects named. The table covers *broad subject areas* only: ie the individual subjects of specialisation in certain professional fields such as education, law, medicine or veterinary science, are not included. In the case of related subject areas which have been grouped together (eg Agronomy/Soil Science), it should be borne in mind that one or more of the subjects may be offered by the institution concerned.

	Aga Khan	Agric., Faisalabad	Eng. & Technol., Lahore	Islamia, Bahawalpur	Lahore U. of Management Scis.	Mehran U.E.T.	N.E.D. Univ. of Eng. & Technol.	Shaheed Zulfikar Ali Bhutto I.S.T.	Sir Syed U.E.T.
Agriculture/Agricultural Science		X			UM				
Agronomy/Soil Science		X							
Animal Husbandry/Science		X							
Arabic				X					
Architecture			UM		U	U			
Biochemistry		X		X					
Biology		U		U					
Botany/Plant Science		X			UM				
Business/Commerce		UM			UM	M		X	
Chemistry		X	M	X					
Computer Science		UM	M	M	UM			X	U
Economics		UM		X	UM				
Education	M			X					
Engineering									
Agricultural		X							
Chemical			UM				X	U	
Civil			UM				X	M	U
Computer		UM	M				U	M	U
Electrical/Electronic			X				X	M	U
Mechanical			X				X	M	
Metallurgical/Materials			UM				U	M	
Mining/Petroleum			UM				U		
English		U			UM	U			
Fisheries Technology		UM							
Food Science/Nutrition		X							
Forestry		X							
Geography					UM				
History				X	UM				
Horticulture		X							

TO SUBJECTS OF STUDY

For further information about the individual subjects taught at each institution, please refer to the *Index to Department Names* at the end of the Yearbook, but for full details about subjects/courses offered at universities in the Commonwealth each institution's own official publications must be consulted. U = may be studied for first degree course; M = may be studied for master's degree course; D = research facilities to doctoral level; X = all three levels (UMD). **Note**—the table only includes information provided by institutions currently in membership of the Association of Commonwealth Universities, submitted for this edition of the Yearbook.

	Aga Khan	Agric., Faisalabad	Eng. & Technol., Lahore	Islamia, Bahawalpur	Lahore U. of Management Scis.	Mehran U.E.T.	N.E.D. Univ. of Eng. & Technol.	Shaheed Zulfikar Ali Bhutto I.S.T.	Sir Syed U.E.T.
International Relations					U				
Islamic Studies		X		X	UM				
Law				U	M				
Library/Information Science				M					
Management/Administration					M				
Mathematics		UM	M	X	U				
Medicine/Surgery	UM	UM							U
Microbiology		UM							
Nursing	U								
Pakistan Studies		U		U	UM				
Persian				UM					
Pharmacy/Pharmaceutical Science				X					
Pharmacology/Pharmacognosy		UM		X					
Philosophy					U				
Physics		M		X	U				
Planning, Urban and Regional		UM	UM			U			
Politics/Political Science				X	U				
Psychology					U				
Punjabi				U					
Religion/Theology				U					
Social Work		UM							
Sociology		UM			U				
Statistics		UM		X	UM				
Teacher Training				UM					
Textiles/Fibre Science			U			U	U		
Urdu				X					
Veterinary Science		X							
Zoology		UM		U					

PAPUA NEW GUINEA

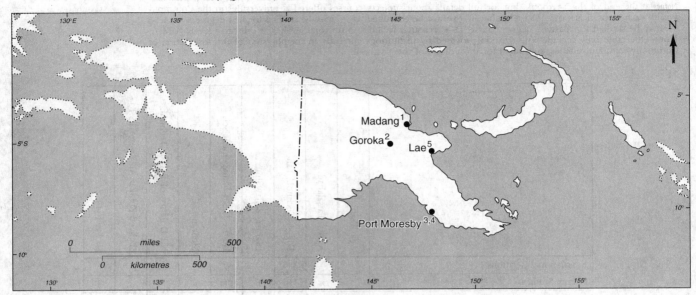

The places named are the seats of the university institutions numbered above

DIVINE WORD UNIVERSITY

Founded 1980

Postal Address: PO Box 483, Madang, Papua New Guinea
Telephone: 852 2937, 852 3572 **Fax**: 852 2812 **E-mail**: jjczuba@global.net.pg

PRESIDENT*—Czuba, Fr. Jan
REGISTRAR‡—Gesch, Fr. Patrick

UNIVERSITY OF GOROKA

Founded 1997; previously established as a college of the University of Papua New Guinea, 1975

Member of the Association of Commonwealth Universities

Postal Address: PO Box 1078, Goroka, Eastern Highlands Province, Papua New Guinea
Telephone: 731 1700 **Fax**: 732 2620

ACTING VICE-CHANCELLOR*—Solon, Mark, BEd PNG, MEdAdmin NE, PhD Alta.
ACTING PRO-VICE-CHANCELLOR (ADMINISTRATION)‡—Yakopya, Frederick, BEd PNG, MEdAdmin Flin.

PACIFIC ADVENTIST UNIVERSITY

Postal Address: Private Mail Bag, Boroko, NCD, Papua New Guinea
Telephone: 328 0251 **Fax**: 328 1257

PRINCIPAL*—Hughes, Owen, PhD *Newcastle(NSW)*
DEPUTY VICE-CHANCELLOR‡—Whitson, Drian, PhD *Newcastle(NSW)*

UNIVERSITY OF PAPUA NEW GUINEA

Founded 1965

Member of the Association of Commonwealth Universities

Postal Address: PO Box 320, University, Papua New Guinea
Telephone: 326 7200 **Fax**: 326 7187 **Cables**: University, Port Moresby **Telex**: NE22366 **WWW**: http://upng.ac.pg

CHANCELLOR—Kekedo, Rosemary, DBE, BA *N.Colorado*, Hon. DTech *PNG Tech.*, Hon. DEd
PRO-CHANCELLOR—Kidu, Carol
VICE-CHANCELLOR*—Hills, Rodney C., BA *Brist.*, PhD *Brist.*
PRO-VICE-CHANCELLOR (ACADEMIC AFFAIRS)—Luluaki, J., LLM *Warw.*, PhD *Camb.*, LLB
PRO-VICE-CHANCELLOR (PLANNING AND DEVELOPMENT)—Nembou, Cecilia, BSc *PNG*, MSc *Sus.*, PhD *NSW*
PRO-VICE-CHANCELLOR (TAURAMA CAMPUS)—Igo, J. D., FRCPA
REGISTRAR‡—Malaibe, V., MSc *Auck.*, MSc *Arizona*, BSc
BURSAR—Tafawa, Weusi A.

FACULTIES/SCHOOLS

Arts (Waigani Campus)
Dean: Yeates, D. B., BA *W.Ont.*, MA PhD

Creative Arts (Waigani Campus)
Dean: Umayan, D. V., BSIE *T.U.Philippines*, BSArch *Quezon*, MA *Quezon*

Health Sciences (Taurama Campus)
Dean: Burger, C. H., MSc *Qld.*, PhD *Qld.*

Law (Waigani Campus)
Dean: Linge, G. T., LLM *American(D.C.)*, LLB

Medicine (Taurama Campus)
Dean: Amevo, B., PhD *Newcastle(NSW)*, MB BS

Science (Waigani Campus)
Dean: Agyeman, K., BSc *Ghana*, SM *M.I.T.*, PhD *M.I.T.*

ACADEMIC UNITS

Administrative Studies, see Pol. and Admin. Studies

Anthropology and Sociology
Tel: 326 7164
O'Collins, E. Maev, BA *Melb.*, MSSW *Col.*, DSW *Col.* Prof. Emer.
Warakai, V. S., MA *Sus.*, BA(SW) Lectr.; Acting Head*
Yeates, D. B., BA *W.Ont.*, MA PhD Sr. Lectr.
Vacant Posts: 1 Prof.

Biology
Tel: 326 7210 Fax: 326 0369
Hill, L., BSc *Syd.*, PhD *Syd.* Prof.; Head*
Hyslop, E. J., BSc *Aberd.*, PhD *Open(UK)* Sr. Lectr.
Kumar, R., BSc *Agra*, MSc *Agra*, PhD *Raj.*, PhD *Qld.* Sr. Lectr.

Menzies, J. I., BSc *Lond.*, MSc *Lond.* Assoc. Prof.
Saulei, S., MSc *Wat.*, PhD *Aberd.*, BSc Sr. Lectr.

Chemistry
Tel: 326 7230 Fax: 326 0369
Singh, K., BSc *Delhi*, MSc *Delhi*, MACS *Wash.*, PhD *Delhi*, FRSChem Prof.
Tamate, J., MChem *NSW*, MSc *ANU*, PhD *Otago*, BSc Sr. Lectr.; Head*

Commerce
Tel: 326 7590
Moshi, H. S., MBA *Curtin* Sr. Lectr.
Oliga, J. C., MA *Sheff.*, PhD *Sheff.*, FCIS Prof.; Head*
Onedo, A. E. O., BCom *Mak.*, MBA *Nair.* Assoc. Prof.
Pok, F., MEc *NE*, PhD *NE*, BA(Com) Sr. Lectr. (on leave)

Communication and Information in Development, South Pacific Centre for (SPCENCIID)
Tel: 326 7472 Fax: 326 7175
Evans, J. A., BSc *Leic.*, MSc *Sheff.*, PhD *Leic.* Sr. Lectr.
Kaima, S. T., MA *Hawaii*, BEd BA Sr. Lectr. (on leave)
Obi, Margaret J., MLS *Hawaii*, BA Sr. Lectr. (on leave)
Robie, D., MA *Technol.Syd.* Lectr., Print Media; Acting Head*

Economics
Tel: 326 7443
Mannur, H. G., MA *Karn.*, MA *Indiana*, PhD *Indiana* Assoc. Prof.
Tautea, L., MEc *NE*, BEc Lectr.; Acting Head*
Vacant Posts: 1 Prof.

Environmental Science
Tel: 326 7392 Fax: 326 0369
Mowbray, D. L., BSc *Syd.*, PhD *Syd.* Assoc. Prof.

Geography
Tel: 326 7120
Hayes, G. R., BA *Br.Col.*, MA *Tor.*, PhD *Br.Col.* Assoc. Prof.
Miskaram, N., MSc *Lond.*, PhD *James Cook*, BA Sr. Lectr.
Ranasinghe, P. C. Hema, BA *Ceyl.*, PhD *Camb.* Assoc. Prof.; Acting Head*

Geology
Tel: 326 7395 Fax: 326 0369
Davies, H., MSc *W.Aust.*, PhD *Stan.* Prof.
Winn, R., BSc *Oregon State*, MS *Lehigh*, PhD *Wis.* Lectr.; Head*

History
Tel: 326 7455
Huch, R. K., BA *Thiel*, MA *Penn.State*, PhD *Mich.* Prof.; Head*
Kituai, A. K., MA *Flin.*, PhD *ANU*, BA Sr. Lectr.

Information Studies, see Communicn. and Information in Devel., South Pacific Centre for

Language and Literature
Tel: 326 7288
Faraclas, N., BA *New Orleans*, MA *Calif.*, PhD *Calif.* Sr. Lectr.
Ford, K., BA *Acad.*, PhD *Ghana* Assoc. Prof.
Nekitel, O. M., MA *Hawaii*, PhD *ANU*, BEd BA Prof.
Peni, Garua, MA *Syd.*, BEd BA Lectr.; Head*
Richardson, I., BA *Camb.*, PhD *OFS* Sr. Lectr.
Vacant Posts: 1 Lectr. (French)

Law

Tel: 326 7646 Fax: 326 0714

James, R. W., LLM *Lond.*, PhD *Lond.* Prof.
Luluaki, J., LLM *Warw.*, PhD *Camb.*, LLB Sr. Lectr.
Mawa, P. N., LLM *Harv.*, LLB Lectr.; Acting Head*

Legal and Clinical Programmes

Tel: 326 7644 Fax: 326 0714

Nonggorr, J., LLM *Lond.*, PhD *Syd.*, LLB Prof.; Head*
Russell, C. J., BA *Syd.*, LLB *Syd.*, LLM *Lond.* Sr. Lectr.

Literature, see Lang. and Lit.

Mathematics

Tel: 326 7414

Arganbright, D., BS *Bowling Green*, BSEd *Bowling Green*, MA *Wash.*, PhD *Wash.* Prof.; Head*
Hvorecky, J., BSc *Bratislava*, PhD Sr. Lectr.
Nembou, Cecilia, BSc *PNG*, MSc *Sus.*, PhD *NSW* Sr. Lectr.
Plaskacz, S., MSc *Wroclaw*, PhD *Toruń* Sr. Lectr.
Renaud, J.-C., BSc *NE*, MSc PhD Assoc. Prof.
Salvadori, A., BSc *N.U.I.*, MSc *N.U.I.*, PhD *McM.* Sr. Lectr.
Sekkappan, R., BA *Annam.*, MSc *Annam.*, MMath *Wat.*, PhD *Wat.* Assoc. Prof.
Vacant Posts: 3 Sr. Tutors

Medicine, see Taurama Campus

Motupore Island Research Department

Tel: 326 7181; (Island) 325 4725 Fax: 326 0369

Rewald, J. A. Head*

Performing Arts

Tel: 326 0900

Crowdy, D., MusB *W.Aust.* Sr. Tutor; Head*
Vacant Posts: 1 Prof.

Physics

Tel: 326 7220 Fax: 326 0369

Agyeman, K., BSc *Ghana*, SM *M.I.T.*, PhD *M.I.T.* Assoc. Prof.
Lawrence, S. A., MSc *Madr.*, PhD *Meerut* Sr. Lectr.
Srivastava, R. N., BSc *Delhi*, MSc *Delhi*, MS *Georgia*, PhD *Alaska* Sr. Lectr.; Head*
Yeboah-Amankwah, D. K., BSc *Lond.*, SM *M.I.T.*, PhD *M.I.T.* Prof.

Political and Administrative Studies

Tel: 326 7190

Anere, R. L., MA *ANU*, PhD *Claremont*, BA Sr. Lectr.; Head*
Saffu, Y. O., BA *Ghana*, DPhil *Oxf.* Prof.

Psychology

Tel: 326 7481

2 Lectrs. (on leave); 1 Tutor; 2 Sr. Tutors†; 1 Tutor†
Vacant Posts: Head*

Sociology, see Anthropol. and Sociol.

Visual Arts

Tel: 326 0900

Ajokpaezi, O., BA *Nigeria*, MFA *Benin* Lectr.; Head*
Browne, R. J. Sr. Lectr.
Umayan, D. V., BSIE *T.U.Philippines*, BSArch *Quezon*, MA *Quezon* Sr. Lectr.

SPECIAL CENTRES, ETC

Distance and Continuing Education, Institute of

Tel: 326 7450 Fax: 326 2365

Harding, B., BA *Syd.* Lectr.; Acting Dir., Univ. Centre, Madang

Kepo, A., BSc Sr. Tutor; Dir., Univ. Centre, Manus
Lera, J., BEd *Macq.*, BEd *PNG* Lectr.; Dir., Univ. Centre, North Solomons
Mark, G., MA *Syd.*, BEd Lectr.; Dir., Univ. Centre, Enga
Markowitz, Prof. Harold, BA *Flor.*, MA *Flor.*, EdD *Col.* Dir.*
Minol, B., MA *Indiana*, PhD *Qld.* Sr. Lectr.; Dir., Univ. Centre, New Ireland
Ole, S., BA Lectr.; Dir., Univ. Centre, Fly River
Pamanani, J., BEd Sr. Tutor; Dir., Univ. Centre, W. New Britain
Pita, A., MEd *Pitt.*, BEd Lectr.; Dir., Univ. Centre, E. New Britain
Pumuye, H., BASW Lectr.; Dir., Univ. Centre, Southern Highlands
Rere, S., BAgric MEd Lectr.; Dir., Univ. Centre, Eastern Highlands
Sakei, F., BEd Sr. Tutor; Acting Dir., Univ. Centre, Sandaun
Seinau, I., BEd Lectr.; Dir., Univ. Centre, Sandaun
Topa, C., BEd Lectr.; Dir., Univ. Centre, Western Highlands
Vacant Posts: Lectr/Dir., Univ. Centre, E. Sepik

TAURAMA CAMPUS

HEALTH SCIENCES

Basic Health Sciences

Tel: 323 2682 Fax: 323 2679

Fadri, Nory, BSc *Philippine Union* Sr. Tutor; Head*

Dental Auxiliary Sciences

Tel: 323 2682 Fax: 323 2679

Perera, S. L., BDS *Ceyl.* Lectr.; Head*
Vacant Posts: 1 Lectr.

Medical Laboratory Sciences

Tel: 324 3847 Fax: 323 2679

Ballinger, M., BEd *Darwin I.T.* Lectr.; Head*

Medical Radiography

Tel: 323 2682, 324 3843 Fax: 323 2679

Sikot Jurgens, R. Sr. Tutor; Head*

Pharmacy

Tel: 323 2682 Fax: 323 2679

Kigodi, P. G. K., BSc *Dar.*, PhD *Aston* Sr. Lectr.
Lauwo, J. A. K., MSc *Semmelweis*, PhD *Semmelweis* Sr. Lectr.; Head*
Rai, P. P., BSc MSc PhD Sr. Lectr.
Vacant Posts: 1 Sr. Lectr.

MEDICINE

Basic Medical Sciences

Tel: 324 3801 Fax: 325 0809

Amevo, B., PhD *Newcastle(NSW)*, MB BS Sr. Lectr.
Ezeilo, G. C., MB BS *Lond.*, MSc *Roch.*, MD *Lond.*, FRCPGlas, FRCPEd Sr. Lectr.; Head*
Gambhir, S. S., MB BS *Agra*, MD *Agra*, PhD *Ban.* Sr. Lectr.
Harding, J. G. O., MSc *Lond.*, PhD *Wales* Sr. Lectr.
Matainaho, T., PhD *Qld.*, BSc Sr. Lectr.
Mazumdar, S., MB BS *Calc.*, MD *Ban.* Assoc. Prof.
Vacant Posts: 1 Prof.

Clinical Sciences

Tel: 324 3801 Fax: 325 0809

Johnson, F. A., MB ChB *Brist.*, MPhil *Lond.* Assoc. Prof.
Kevau, I. H., CBE, MM *Syd.*, PhD *Syd.*, MB BS, FRACP Prof.
Mola, G., MB BS *Melb.*, FRACOG Assoc. Prof.
Naraqi, S., MD *Teheran*, FACP, FRACP Prof.
Saweri, A. Lectr.; Head*
Tefuarani, N., MB BS MMed Sr. Lectr. (on leave)

Vince, J., MB ChB *Dund.*, FRCPEd Prof.
Watters, D. A. K., BA *Camb.*, MB ChB *Edin.*, ChM *Edin.*, FRCSEd Prof.

Community Medicine

Tel: 324 3801 Fax: 324 3859

Han, A. M., MB BS *Yangon Med.*, MSc *Lond.* Sr. Lectr.
Taufa, T., MPH *Harv.*, MMed Sr. Lectr.
Vacant Posts: Head*

Pathology

Tel: 324 3801 Fax: 325 0809

Fagbami, A. H., PhD *Lond.*, FRCPath Sr. Lectr.
Igo, J. D., FRCPA Prof.
Murthy, D. P., MB BS *S.Venkat.*, MD *S.Venkat.*, FRCPA Assoc. Prof.; Head*
Ogunbanjo, B. O., MB BS *Ib.* Sr. Lectr.
Vacant Posts: Teaching Fellows

CONTACT OFFICERS

Academic affairs. Deputy Registrar (Academic): Naing, Benjamin B., MEdAd *Mass.*, BA
Accommodation (staff). Housing Officer: Dambe, J.
Accommodation (students). Director, Student Services: Maip, Simon, BEd
Admissions (first degree). Senior Assistant Registrar (Enrolment): Auma, Edina, BSc
Admissions (higher degree). Senior Assistant Registrar (Academic): ......
Adult/continuing education. Director, Institute of Distance and Continuing Education: Markowitz, Prof. Harold, BA *Flor.*, MA *Flor.*, EdD *Col.*
Alumni. Development Manager, Unisearch PNG Pty Ltd and Director, Planning and Implementation Unit: Mannan, Mohammad A., MA *Chitt.*
Archives. New Guinea Collection Librarian: Naguwean, Joseph, BA
Careers. (Contact the Dean of the appropriate faculty)
Computing services. Director, Computer Services: Nicol, Brian
Consultancy services. Acting Director, Unisearch PNG Pty Ltd: Evans, John A., BSc *Leic.*, MSc *Sheff.*, PhD *Leic.*
Development/fund-raising. Development Manager, Unisearch PNG Pty Ltd and Director, Planning and Implementation Unit: Mannan, Mohammad A., MA *Chitt.*
Distance education. Director, Institute of Distance and Continuing Education: Markowitz, Prof. Harold, BA *Flor.*, MA *Flor.*, EdD *Col.*
Estates and buildings/works and services. Head, Buildings and Estates: Kawage, W., BEng *PNG Tech.*
Examinations. Senior Assistant Registrar (Examinations and Graduations): Ire, Mathias G., BA
Finance. Bursar: Tafawa, Weusi A.
General enquiries. Registrar: Malaibe, V., MSc *Auck.*, MSc *Arizona*, BSc
Health services. Director, Health Services: Moiya, N., MB BS
Industrial liaison. Project Manager, Unisearch PNG Pty Ltd: ......
Library (chief librarian). University Librarian: Griffin, Florence J., BA
Ombudsperson. Nonggorr, Prof. J., LLM *Lond.*, PhD *Syd.*, LLB
Personnel/human resources. Deputy Registrar (Staffing): Linge, Christine, BA
Public relations, information and marketing. Development Manager, Unisearch PNG Pty Ltd and Director, Planning and Implementation Unit: Mannan, Mohammad A., MA *Chitt.*
Publications. Acting Co-ordinator, Information and Publications Unit: Vari, Falesoa
Purchasing. Bursar: Tafawa, Weusi A.
Research. Chairman, University Research and Publications Committee: Winn, R., BSc *Oregon State*, MSc *Lehigh*, PhD *Wis.*
Security. Acting Chief of Security: Alu, Mark

Sport and recreation. Sports and Recreation Office Executive Officer: Tamean, Lapule

Staff development and training. Acting Director, Staff Development Unit: Kote, Nakanat, BSc

Student welfare/counselling. Student Counsellor: Kila, Rai

Student welfare/counselling. Student Counsellor: Dep, Walter, BA

Students with disabilities. Yeates, D. B., BA W.Ont., MA PhD

University press. Acting Director, Unisearch PNG Pty Ltd: Evans, John A., BSc Leic., MSc Sheff., PhD Leic.

CAMPUS/COLLEGE HEADS

Taurama Campus, PO Box 5623, Boroko National Capital District, Papua New Guinea. (Tel: 248100; Fax: 217658.) Pro-Vice-Chancellor (Taurama Campus): Igo, J. D., FRCPA

[Information supplied by the institution as at January 1997, and edited by the ACU]

PAPUA NEW GUINEA UNIVERSITY OF TECHNOLOGY

Founded 1973; previously established as Papua New Guinea Institute of Higher Technical Education 1965

Member of the Association of Commonwealth Universities

Postal Address: Private Mail Bag, Lae, Morobe Province, Papua New Guinea
Telephone: 434999 **Fax**: 457667 **Cables**: Utech, Lae

CHANCELLOR—Tololo, Sir Alkan, KBE, Hon. LLD PNG, Hon. DTech
PRO-CHANCELLOR—Togolo, Mel, BEc PNG, MA Hawaii
VICE-CHANCELLOR*—Kaiulo, James V., BAg PNG, MSc Hawaii, PhD Macq.
PRO-VICE-CHANCELLOR (ACADEMIC)—Siaguru, P., MSc Edin., PhD Aberd., PhD Camb., BSc
PRO-VICE-CHANCELLOR (ADMINISTRATION)—Tovirika, Wilson, BSc PNG, MEd Philippines
PRO-VICE-CHANCELLOR (PLANNING AND DEVELOPMENT)—......
REGISTRAR—Chan, Tess, BTech
BURSAR—Aniong, Mesengi, BTech
UNIVERSITY LIBRARIAN—Reu, Polycarp, BA PNG, MLib NSW

GENERAL INFORMATION

History. The university was first established in 1965 as Papua New Guinea Institute of Higher Technical Education. Its name was changed to Papua New Guinea Institute of Technology in 1970, and in 1973 it became a university under its present name.

It is located about 9km from the centre of Lae.

First Degrees. BArch, BBld, BCart, BCom, BCommBusEcon, BComSc, BEng, BInfoSyst, BLS, BSc, BScAgr, BScApPh (applied physics), BScApSc, BScFdTechnol, BScFor, BScForMan, BScHumNut, BSurv, BTechnol.

All courses are full-time and normally last 4 years.

The following subjects may be studied at first degree level: accountancy, agriculture, applied physics, applied science, architecture, building, cartography, commerce, communications for development, computer science, electronics and instrumentation, engineering (civil, electrical, mechanical, mineral processing, mining), food technology, forest management, forestry, human nutrition, information systems, land studies, management, surveying, technology.

Higher Degrees. MPhil, PhD.

MPhil: 2 years full-time or 4 years part-time; PhD: 5 years full-time or 8 years part-time.

Libraries. 103,000 volumes; 100 periodicals subscribed to. Special collection: rare Papua New Guinea books.

Fees (1998). Undergraduate: (home students) K3000 full-time, K500 part-time; (international students) K6580 full-time, K1280 part-time.

Academic Awards. Awards range in value from K50 to K500.

Academic Year. Two semesters.

Income (1998). K24,000,000.

Statistics. Staff: 565 (191 academic, 374 administrative and technical). Students: full-time 1795 (1368 men, 427 women); part-time 28 (26 men, 2 women); international 101 (89 men, 12 women).

ACADEMIC UNITS

Agriculture

Fax: 475 7373

Bindir, U., BSc Cran.IT, MSc Cran.IT, PhD Cran.IT Sr. Lectr.
Grant, I. B., MVSc Melb. Sr. Lectr.
Onwueme, I. C., BSc Calif., PhD Calif. Prof.; Head*
Wagih, M., MSc Alexandria, PhD Qld. Sr. Lectr.
Other Staff: 5 Lectrs.; 1 Asst. Lectr.
Vacant Posts: 1 Sr. Lectr.
Research: crop improvement through biotechnology; efficient small-scale farming systems; improving animal husbandry/ animal health in Papua New Guinea; sustainable root-crop production in Papua New Guinea

Architecture and Building

Fax: 475 7633

Costigan, K., BArch Melb. Sr. Lectr.
Gonduan, C. K., MSc Stuttgart, BArchBldg Sr. Lectr.
Milani, R. B., BEnvDes Minn., MArch Minn. Prof.; Head*
Other Staff: 2 Principal Tech. Instrs.; 6 Lectrs.; 1 Asst. Lectr.; 1 Temp. Prof.
Research: adobe for housing construction in Papua New Guinea; computer-aided design; conservation of architectural heritage; local natural resources/traditional building materials; traditional colonial and contemporary indigenous architecture

Business Studies

Tel: 434999

Afosa, K., MBA Ghana Sr. Lectr.
Agyei, A. K., MBA Ghana Assoc. Prof.
Diallo, A., MSc Warw., PhD Warw. Sr. Lectr.
Dixit, N., BSc Ud., MA McM., PhD N.Y.State Sr. Lectr.
Flemming, S., BEng Strath., PhD H.-W., PhD Utah State Sr. Lectr.
Gipe, G., BA PNG, MCom W'gong. Acting Head*
Greenland, L., BA Utah, MEd Utah, PhD Utah Sr. Lectr.
Mionzing, T. S. W., LLB PNG, LLM Warw. Sr. Lectr.
Thomas, K., BA Melb.
Torres, Lawrence K., BTech BComm Sr. Lectr.
Other Staff: 11 Lectrs.; 2 Sr. Tech. Instrs.; 2 Asst. Lectrs.; 7 Temp. Lectrs.
Vacant Posts: 2 Lectrs.
Research: critical success factors for small business in the South Pacific; managerial competencies and skills of small-business owners in Papua New Guinea; regional income distribution in Papua New Guinea; strategies for managing organisational change in Papua New Guinea; use of Mundell-Fleming model in analysis of the kina

Communication Studies, see Lang. and Communicn. Studies

Computer Science, see Maths. and Computer Sci.

Engineering, Civil

Fax: 475 7215

Aggarwal, A. K., BTech IIT Delhi, MEng Car., PhD Assoc. Prof.
Puvanachandran, V. M., MSc Brad., PhD Warw. Assoc. Prof.

Venkataramana, J., MTech IIT *Kanpur*, PhD IIT *Kanpur* Sr. Lectr.
Young, B. W., BSc *Lond.*, PhD *Camb.* Prof.; Head*
Other Staff: 1 Principal Tech. Instr.; 7 Lectrs.; 1 Asst. Lectr.; 1 Sr. Tech. Instr.; 1 Tech. Instr.
Vacant Posts: 2 Lectrs.
Research: analysis and design of rain pumps; beam/column connections in earthquakes; investigating ways to reduce road traffic; management of pedestrian and vehicular traffic; optimisation of water distribution

Engineering, Electrical and Communication
Fax: 475 7209

Al-Dabbagh, M., MSc *Manc.*, PhD *UMIST* Prof.; Head*
Hazra, S. N., BSc *Edin.*, PhD IIT *Delhi* Visiting Prof.
Indulkar, C., BSc *Agra*, BTech *Kharagpur*, MScTech *Manc.*, PhD *Manc.* Sr. Lectr.
Khadumazad, K., MSc *N.Y.* Sr. Lectr.
Korzeniowski, K., MSc *T.U.Lodz*, PhD *T.U.Lodz* Assoc. Prof.
Kostecki, W., MSc *T.U.Lodz*, PhD *T.U.Lodz* Sr. Lectr.
Popov, A., PhD *Russian Acad.Sc.* Sr. Lectr.
Other Staff: 1 Principal Tech. Instr.; 3 Lectrs.; 3 Asst. Lectrs.; 5 Sr. Tech. Instrs.; 3 Temp. Lectrs.
Vacant Posts: 1 Assoc. Prof.; 3 Lectrs.; 2 Sr. Tech. Instrs.
Research: electrical railways linking coastal areas with highlands; engineering role of yagi antenna as television antenna; new technologies for energy systems; radiometric rainfall measurement; small satellite beam steering antennae

Engineering, Mechanical
Fax: 475 7017

Benson, W. M., BE *Syd.*, ME *W'gong.* Sr. Lectr.
Luo, Z. C., BSc *Qinghua*, MSc *Huazhong U.S.T.*, PhD *Huazhong U.S.T.* Sr. Lectr.
Satter, M. A., BTech *Lough.*, PhD *Lough.* Prof.; Head*
Seddigh, F., BEng *Teheran*, PhD *Oregon* Sr. Lectr.
Other Staff: 7 Lectrs.; 2 Asst. Lectrs.; 1 Sr. Tech. Instr.
Vacant Posts: 1 Assoc. Prof.
Research: flammability limits and related phenomena; fluidised bed combustion for coffee husks; increasing productivity in Papua New Guinea industries; performance of heat pipe solar collectors under local conditions; robust design of industrial gears against wear

Engineering, Mining
Fax: 475 7534

Afenya, P. M., BSc *Ghana*, MSc *Lond.*, PhD *Lond.* Assoc. Prof.
Bordia, S. K., BSc *Ban.*, PhD *Ostrava* Prof.; Head*
Subasinghe, G. K. N. S., BSc *S.Lanka*, MMinTech *Otago*, PhD *Auck.* Sr. Lectr.
Other Staff: 4 Lectrs.; 2 Asst. Lectrs.; 2 Temp. Lectrs.
Vacant Posts: 1 Sr. Lectr.
Research: computer applications in mineral processing; engineering education (survey of continuing education facilities in South East Asia and the Pacific); extent of copper liberation in Ok Tedi copper ore; stability of cuttings in mudstones in the Pogera area; taxation systems for mining and petroleum

Forestry
Fax: 475 7622

Mulung, K., MSc *Wales* Lectr.; Acting Head*

Other Staff: 6 Lectrs.; 2 Asst. Lectrs.; 1 Temp. Lectr.
Vacant Posts: 1 Prof.; 1 Assoc. Prof.
Research: issues of sustainable land management in Papua New Guinea; land tenure arrangements and forest-based development in Papua New Guinea; primary industry education; use of small portable sawmills in forest management; utilisation of forests in harmony with conservation

Land Studies, see Surv. and Land Studies

Language and Communication Studies
Tel: 434999

Buschenhofen, P. F., BA *Adel.*, MSc *Syd.*, PhD *Syd.* Sr. Lectr.
Kila, A., MA *PNG* Sr. Lectr.
Yarapea, A., BA *PNG*, MA *Syd.*, MPhil *Syd.* Sr. Lectr.
Other Staff: 8 Lectrs.; 3 Asst. Lectrs.; 4 Temp. Lectrs.
Vacant Posts: 1 Prof.; 2 Sr. Lectrs.; 1 Lectr.
Research: communication for national development; learning literacy in Papua New Guinea; logic, experience and reality in communication; microcommunication in development

Mathematics and Computer Science
Fax: 475 7458

Majewski, M. L., PhD *Torún* Sr. Lectr.
Nyondo, A. C., BA(Educn) *Zambia*, MSc *Lond.* Sr. Lectr.
Phythian, J. E., BA *Manc.*, MSc Prof.; Head*
Sukthanker, N., MA *Bom.*, PhD *Bom.* Sr. Lectr.
Wilkins, C. W., BSc *Adel.*, PhD *Adel.* Sr. Lectr.
Other Staff: 1 Principal Tech. Instr.; 7 Lectrs.; 1 Sr. Tech. Instr.; 1 Asst. Lectr.; 4 Temp. Lectrs.
Vacant Posts: 1 Sr. Lectr.; 1 Lectr.
Research: computer graphics; distributed/timetable databases; gender in mathematics; ray tracing; structurally regular semigroups

Physics, Applied
Fax: 475 7005

Boeha, B., BEd *PNG*, BSc *PNG*, MEd *Monash*, PhD *Monash* Sr. Lectr.
Drake, W. K., MSc *Wales*, PhD *S'ton.* Sr. Lectr.
Kachirski, I., MSc *Irkutsk*, PhD *Irkutsk* Assoc. Prof.
Nonie, S. E., PhD *S.Leone*, BSc MSc Sr. Lectr.
Other Staff: 5 Lectrs.; 1 Sr. Tech. Instr.; 1 Tech. Instr.; 1 Asst. Lectr.
Vacant Posts: 1 Prof.
Research: instrumentation design for environmental measurements; materials studies using X-ray fluorescence and diffraction; preparation and evaluation of polymer solar cell materials; spatial distribution of seismicity; users of micro-controllers in physics

Sciences, Applied
Fax: 475 7505

Amoa, B., BSc *Ghana*, PhD *Leeds* Sr. Lectr.
Carrick, M. T., BSc *Qld.*, PhD *Qld.* Sr. Lectr.
Khan, M. R., BSc *Pesh.*, MSc *Pesh.*, MTech *Brun.*, PhD *C.N.A.A.* Prof.; Head*
Leach, M., BSc *Lough.*, PhD *Salf.* Sr. Lectr.
Rumney, T. G., BSc *Sur.*, PhD *Sur.* Sr. Lectr.
Sopade, P., MSc *Reading*, PhD *Reading* Sr. Lectr.
Other Staff: 6 Lectrs.; 1 Sr. Tech. Instr.; 1 Asst. Lectr.; 6 Temp. Lectrs.
Vacant Posts: 2 Assoc. Profs.; 1 Sr. Lectr.
Research: environment; herbal medicine; nutrition; traditional foods

Surveying and Land Studies
Fax: 475 7483

Armitage, L., MEnvPlan *Macq.* Assoc. Prof.
Bannerman, S., BAppSc *S.Aust.I.T.* Sr. Lectr.

Little, R. P., BAppSc *RMIT*, MSurv *Qld.*, MAppSc *Qld.* Prof.; Head*
Other Staff: 2 Principal Tech. Instrs.; 4 Lectrs.; 4 Sr. Tech. Instrs.; 1 Tech. Instr.; 1 Asst. Lectr.
Research: attenuation anomalies in GPS signals in heavy rainfall; crustal motion studies; GPS data transmission using high-frequency radio; rapid mapping using geographic information systems and GPS; volcanic deformation studies

CONTACT OFFICERS

Academic affairs. Registrar: Chan, Tess, BTech
Accommodation. Pro-Vice-Chancellor (Administration): Tovirika, Wilson, BSc *PNG*, MEd *Philippines*
Admissions (first degree). Registrar: Chan, Tess, BTech
Admissions (higher degree). Registrar: Chan, Tess, BTech
Adult/continuing education. Acting Head of Open and Distance Learning: Koigiri, A.
Alumni. Registrar: Chan, Tess, BTech
Careers. Career Development Officer: Vuira-Kama, Mathias
Computing services. Computer and Electronic Services Unit Manager: Johnson, R.
Consultancy services. Executive Manager, University Development Company: Warvi, E.
Development/fund-raising. Executive Manager, University Development Company: Warvi, E.
Distance education. Acting Head of Open and Distance Learning: Koigiri, A.
Estates and buildings/works and services. Head of Buildings and Grounds: Tzilu, B.
Examinations. Senior Assistant Registrar (Academic): Aruai, Goodnius
Finance. Bursar: Aniong, Mesengi, BTech
General enquiries. Registrar: Chan, Tess, BTech
Health services. Medical Officer: Uppal, Z.
Industrial liaison. Executive Manager, University Development Company: Warvi, E.
International office. Director, Student Services: Sako, Allan
Library (chief librarian). University Librarian: Reu, Polycarp, BA *PNG*, MLib *NSW*
Ombudsperson. Registrar: Chan, Tess, BTech
Personnel/human resources. Deputy Registrar (Administration): Fainame, John
Publications. Information Officer: Lahies, Corney
Purchasing. Stores and Transport Manager: Micah, Danny
Research. Registrar: Chan, Tess, BTech
Safety. Director, Security Service: Pisae, Eka
Scholarships, awards, loans. Scholarships Officer: Fugre, Leo
Schools liaison. Admissions Officer: Rapi, Yawi
Security. Director, Security Service: Pisae, Eka
Sport and recreation. Student Representative Council Executive Officer: Lavatu, Philip
Staff development and training. Career Development Officer: Vuira-Kama, Mathias
Student welfare/counselling. Director, Student Services: Sako, Allan
Students from other countries. Director, Student Services: Sako, Allan
Students with disabilities. Director, Student Services: Sako, Allan
University press. Registrar: Chan, Tess, BTech

CAMPUS/COLLEGE HEADS

Vudal University College, Private Mail Bag, Rabaul, East New Britain, Papua New Guinea. Principal: Quartermain, A. R., BAgr *Massey*, MAgrSc *Massey*, PhD *Iowa*

[*Information supplied by the institution as at 20 June 1998, and edited by the ACU*]

SIERRA LEONE

UNIVERSITY OF SIERRA LEONE

Founded 1967

Member of the Association of Commonwealth Universities

Postal Address: Private Mail Bag, Freetown, Sierra Leone
Telephone: (022) 226859, 224921, 223989 **Cables**: Unisal, Freetown

CHANCELLOR—Head of State (*ex officio*)
PRO-CHANCELLOR—Porter, Prof. A. T., MRSL, JP, BA *Durh.*, MA *Camb.*, PhD *Boston*, Hon. LHD *Boston*, Hon. LLD *Malta*, Hon. DLitt *S.Leone*
VICE-CHANCELLOR*—Wright, Prof. Ernest H., BSc *Hull*, PhD *Hull*, FRSChem
PRO-VICE-CHANCELLOR—Taqi, Prof. A. M., MMEd *Mak.*, MD *Moscow*
UNIVERSITY SECRETARY AND REGISTRAR—Thomas, J. A. G., MEd *Manc.*, BA

GENERAL INFORMATION

History. The university was established by the University of Sierra Leone Act, 1967. The university is made up of three constituent colleges: Fourah Bay College, Njala University College, and the College of Medicine and Allied Health Sciences.

Admission. See separate college entries.

First Degrees. (* = also available with honours; † = only available with honours).
BA*, BAEd, BChD, BEng†, BSc†, BSc joint honours (health sciences), BScAgric, BScAgricEd, BSc(Econ)†, BScEd, BScEnv†, BScHomeEcon, BScHomeEconEd, LLB†, MB ChB.

Higher Degrees. MA, MAEd , MEd, MEng, MPhilEnv, MSc, MSc(Econ), MScAgric, MScEd, MScEnv, PhD.

Fees. See separate college entries.

Academic Year (1998–99). Three terms: October–December; January–March; April–June.

ACADEMIC UNITS

Education, Institute of
Tel: (022) 226874
Jonah, Melisa F., BSc *Lond.*   Acting Dir.*

In-Service Division
Lappia, A., BS *Huntingdon*, MA *Wis.*, MEd *Massey*   Co-ordinator
Vacant Posts: Head of Div.

Library Studies, Institute of
Tel: (022) 240290
Sheriff, Gladys M. O., BA *Durh.*, MS *Col.*, FLA   Dir.*

Public Administration and Management, Institute of
Tel: (022) 224801
May-Parker, I. I., BSc(Agric) *Reading*, BPhil *Glas.*   Dir.*

Accountancy and Finance
Tel: (022) 224477
Amosun, Joya, BSc *S.Leone*   Sr. Teaching Fellow; Head*
Vacant Posts: 1 Sr. Lectr.; 1 Lectr.

Administration and Management
Tel: (022) 224477
Rogers-Wright, L. B., BA *Durh.*, MEd *Brist.*   Lectr.; Head*
Vacant Posts: 1 Sr. Lectr.; 2 Lectrs.

Business Studies and Entrepreneurial Development
Tel: (022) 224477
Parker, S. A., BA *CNAA*   Lectr.; Head*
Vacant Posts: 1 Sr. Lectr.

Computer Studies
Tel: (022) 224477
Chaytor, D. T., BEng MSc   Lectr.; Head*
Vacant Posts: 1 Sr. Lectr.

Women's Unit

SPECIAL CENTRES, ETC

University Research and Development Services Bureau
Palmer, Isaac F., MSc *Cracow*, PhD *Cracow*, BSc   Acting Dir.*

CONTACT OFFICERS

Academic affairs. Assistant Registrar (Academic Affairs): Bongay, F. P., BA
Accommodation. (Contact the Warden of the relevant college)
Admissions (first degree). (Contact the Deputy Registrar of the relevant college)
Admissions (higher degree). Dean, Postgraduate Studies: Williams, Prof. Modupe, BA *Trinity(Dub.)*, PhD *Glas.*
Adult/continuing education. Director, Institute of Adult Education and Extra Mural Studies: Turay, E. D. A., BA *Birm.*, MA *Birm.*, MEd *Glas.*
Alumni. (Contact the Deputy Registrar of the relevant college)
Archives. University Librarian: Jusu-Sheriff, Gladys M., BA *Durh.*, MS *Col.*, FLA

Consultancy services. Acting Director, University Research and Development Service Bureau: Palmer, Isaac F., MSc *Cracow*, PhD *Cracow*, BSc
Development/fund-raising. Public Relations Officer: Cole, Bernadette P., BA *Durh.*, MA *Wales*
Estates and buildings/works and services. University Architect: Lisk, E. J. O.
Examinations. (Contact the Deputy Registrar of the relevant college)
Finance. Acting Finance Officer: Thomas, Leslie R. M., BSc *S.Leone*
General enquiries. University Secretary and Registrar: Thomas, J. A. G., MEd *Manc.*, BA
Health services. (Contact the Deputy Registrar of the relevant college)
Library (chief librarian). University Librarian: Jusu-Sheriff, Gladys M., BA *Durh.*, MS *Col.*, FLA
Personnel/human resources. Senior Assistant Registrar (Personnel): Carter, Arthur G., BA *Durh.*
Public relations, information and marketing. Public Relations Officer: Cole, Bernadette P., BA *Durh.*, MA *Wales*
Publications. Chairman, University Press Committee: Wright, Prof. E. H., BSc *Hull*, PhD *Hull*, FRSChem
Purchasing. Acting Finance Officer: Thomas, Leslie R. M., BSc *S.Leone*
Research. Acting Director, University Research and Development Service Bureau: Palmer, Isaac F., MSc *Cracow*, PhD *Cracow*, BSc
Sport and recreation. Assistant Registrar (General): Sawyerr, Edward F., BA
Staff development and training. Staff Development and Training Officer: Beckley, Josie A., BA MEd
Student union. (Contact the Deputy Registrar of the relevant college)
Student welfare/counselling. (Contact the Warden of the relevant college)
University press. Chairman, University Press Committee: Wright, Prof. E. H., BSc *Hull*, PhD *Hull*, FRSChem
Women. Chair, Task Force: Dworzak, Juliette A., MA *Col.*, MEd *Lond.*, BA

[Information supplied by the institution as at 8 April 1998, and edited by the ACU]

COLLEGE OF MEDICINE AND ALLIED HEALTH SCIENCES

Established 1988

Postal Address: Private Mail Bag, Freetown, Sierra Leone
Telephone: (022) 240884, 240583 **Cables**: COMAHS, Freetown

PRINCIPAL*—Taqi, Prof. A. M., MMed Mak., MD Moscow
DEPUTY REGISTRAR—Campbell, M. A., MA Reading, FCIS
ESTATE OFFICER (ACTING)—Davies, F. C. O.

GENERAL INFORMATION

History. The college was established and became a constituent college of the University of Sierra Leone in 1988. The college campus is located in Kossoh Town, about 18km from Freetown.

Admission to first degree courses. General Certificate of Education (GCE) with 5 O level passes in approved subjects, plus 3 approved A level subjects (2 approved A level subjects for BSc).

First Degrees (of University of Sierra Leone). BChD, MB ChB.

Fees (1996–97, annual). Le29,000. International students: US$5000.

Academic Year (1998–99). Three terms: October–December; January–March; April–June.

Statistics. Staff: 85 (67 academic, 18 administrative). Students: full-time 299 (211 men, 88 women).

FACULTIES/SCHOOLS

Basic Medical Sciences
Dean: George, J. K., MA Kiev, MD Kiev PhD Kiev

Clinical Sciences
Dean: Gordon-Harris, L. G. O., MD

Pharmaceutical Sciences
Dean: Ayitey-Smith, Prof. E., BPharm Kumasi, MSc McG., PhD Ott.

ACADEMIC UNITS

Anatomy
George, J. K., MA Kiev, MD Kiev, PhD Kiev Sr. Lectr.; Head*

Biochemistry
Mansaray, Y. K. C., BScEd Wis., MSc Wis., PhD S'ton. Lectr.; Head* (on leave)

Community Health Care
Alghali, S. T. O., BSc Wales, MSc Lond., PhD Glas., FLS Sr. Lectr.; Head*
Gage, G. N., MD Tübingen, MSc Assoc. Prof.

Dentistry

Haematology
Gevao, S. M., MB BS Lagos Lectr.; Head*

Histopathology
Williams, A. C., MD Berl. Head*

Mathematics

Medicine
Lisk, D. R., MB BS Lond., FRCS Assoc. Prof.; Head*

Microbiology
Morgan, H. G., BSc Durh., MSc Liv., PhD Prof.

Obstetrics and Gynaecology
Frazer, G. B., MB ChB Aberd., FRCOG Sr. Lectr.; Head*
Kargbo, T. K., MB ChB Leeds Sr. Lectr. (on leave)

Paediatrics
Taqi, A. M., MMEd Mak., MD Moscow Prof.; Head*

Pharmacognosy
Cole, M. L., PhD
Jonsyn, F. E. D., BSc Kalamazoo, PhD Kalamazoo, MSc Lectr.; Head*

Pharmacology
Ayitey-Smith, E., BPharm Kumasi, MSc McG., PhD Ott. Prof.; Head*

Physiology
Odonkor, P. O., BSc Ib., MB ChB Ghana, PhD McG. Teaching Fellow; Head*

Surgery
Cole, W. B., MB ChB Birm., FRCSEd Sr. Teaching Fellow; Head*
Gordon-Harris, L. G. O., MD Sr. Lectr.
Wright, A. D. O., MD Kiel, MSc Lond., PhD Glas., FRCSEd Sr. Lectr.

[Information supplied by the institution as at 14 April 1998, and edited by the ACU]

FOURAH BAY COLLEGE

Established as Fourah Bay College, 1827; incorporated by Royal Charter as University College of Sierra Leone, 1960 and became a constituent college of the University of Sierra Leone, 1966

Postal Address: PO Box 87, Freetown, Sierra Leone
Telephone: (022) 27260 **Cables**: Fourahbay

VISITOR—Head of State (ex officio)
PRINCIPAL*—Strasser-King, Prof. V. E., BSc Durh., PhD Manc.
DEPUTY REGISTRAR—Dumbuya, S. N., MEd Manc., BA
ESTATE OFFICER—Thomas, C. J.
LIBRARIAN—Thomas, D. E., BA Durh., MSc Ill., MA

GENERAL INFORMATION

History. The college was founded by the Church Missionary Society in 1827. It became affiliated to the University of Durham in 1876, and in 1966, a constituent college of the University of Sierra Leone.

It is located on Mt. Auzeol, on the outskirts of Freetown.

Admission to first degree courses. General Certificate of Education (GCE) with O level passes (minimum grade 6 in not more than 2 sittings) in 5 approved subjects including English language.

First Degrees (of University of Sierra Leone). (* = also available with honours; † = only available with honours). BA*, BEng†, BSc†, BSc(Econ)†, LLB†.

Higher Degrees (of University of Sierra Leone). MA, MEng, MSc, MSc(Econ).

Fees (1996–97, annual). Undergraduate: Le26,500. International students: US$1800.

Academic Year (1998-99). Three terms: October–December; January–March; April–June.

Statistics. Staff: 248 (202 academic, 46 administrative). Students: full-time 2100 (1650 men, 450 women).

FACULTIES/SCHOOLS

Arts

Dean: Shyllon, Rev. L. E. T., MTh St.And., PhD Aberd., LDiv

Economic and Social Studies

Dean: Abraham, A. A., PhD Birm., BA MA

Engineering

Dean: Davidson, Prof. O. R., MSc Manc., PhD Salf., BEng

Law

Dean: Smart, Prof. Joko H. M., BA Durh., LLM Sheff., PhD Lond.

Pure and Applied Science

Dean: Godwin, V. E., BSc Durh., MScOregon, PhD Missouri

ACADEMIC UNITS

Accounting

Doherty, A. M., BA MA   Sr. Teaching Fellow; Head*
Vacant Posts: 1 Prof.; 1 Asst. Lectr.

African Studies, Institute of, see Special Centres, etc

Botany

Cole, Norman H. A., BSc Leic., MSc Lond., PhD Calif.   Prof.; Head*

Chemistry

Faulkner, D. F., BSc Durh., MS Georgetown, PhD Strath.   Sr. Lectr.
Kormoh, M. K., PhD Lond., MSc   Sr. Lectr.
Pratt, Nana C., BSc Durh., PhD Strath., MSc   Sr. Lectr.
Wright, E. H., BSc Hull, PhD Hull, FRSChem   Prof.; Head*
Wurie, A., PhD Brun., BSc   Sr. Lectr. (on leave)
Yormah, T. B. R., PhD Birm., MSc   Sr. Lectr.
Vacant Posts: 1 Asst. Lectr.

Classics, see Philos. and Classics

Economics

Cole, J. K. E., BA Lond., MA Penn.   Sr. Teaching Fellow; Head*
Vacant Posts: 1 Prof.; 1 Sr. Lectr.

Education

Eleady-Cole, Nathalie K., MA Edin., MA Lond., PhD Wis.   Lectr.; Head*

Labor, A. F., BSc Birm., MSc Lond., PhD Alta.   Assoc. Prof.
Vacant Posts: 1 Prof.

Engineering, Civil

Gilpin, Arthur E. O., BSc Lond., MS Pitt., PhD Pitt.   Sr. Lectr.
Ibrahim, B. B., BSc(Eng) Lond., MSc Lond., MS Ill.   Assoc. Prof. (on leave)
Lisk, W. E. A., BSc(Eng) Lond., MSc Lond., PhD Lond.   Sr. Lectr.; Head*
Vacant Posts: 1 Prof.

Engineering, Electrical

Redwood-Sawyerr, J. A. S., MSc(Eng) Lond., PhD Essex, BEng   Sr. Lectr.; Head*
Vacant Posts: 1 Prof.

Engineering, Maintenance

Cole, R. C. A., BSc(Eng) Lond., MSc Strath.   Lectr.; Head*
Vacant Posts: 1 Prof.

Engineering, Mechanical

Davidson, O. R., MSc Manc., PhD Salf., BEng   Prof.; Head*
Massaquoi, J. G. M., MSc Wales, PhD W.Virginia   Assoc. Prof. (on leave)
Vacant Posts: 1 Sr. Lectr.

English

Sesay, Kadiatu A., MA Sheff., PhD Lond., BA   Sr. Lectr. (on leave)
Spencer, J. S., MA Ib., PhD Ib., BAEd   Sr. Lectr. (on leave)

Geography

Johnson, R. G., MSc Odessa, PhD Odessa   Lectr.; Acting Head*
Vacant Posts: 1 Prof.

Geology

Fode, D. V. A., DrenSc Louvain, MSc   Lectr.; Head*
Vacant Posts: 1 Prof.; 1 Sr. Lectr.; 1 Lectr.

History

Wyse, Akintola J. G., BA Durh., PhD Aberd.   Prof.; Head*

Law

Smart, Joko H. M., BA Durh., LLM Sheff., PhD Lond.   Prof.; Head*
Vacant Posts: 1 Sr. Lectr.

Linguistics

Coker, E. A. M., BA Durh., MA Montpellier, PhD Montpellier   Lectr.; Acting Head*
Vacant Posts: 1 Sr. Lectr.; 1 Asst. Lectr.

Marine Biology and Oceanography, Institute of, see Special Centres, etc

Mathematics

Bockarie, A., PhD Mich., BScEd MSc   Sr. Lectr.
Jonah, D. A., BSc Canberra, PhD Birm.   Assoc. Prof.; Head*
Other Staff: 1 Sr. Teaching Fellow

Vacant Posts: 1 Prof.; 2 Lectrs.

Modern Languages

Fofana, S. R., MA Penn.   Teaching Fellow; Acting Head*
Vacant Posts: 1 Prof.; 1 Sr. Lectr.

Philosophy and Classics

Labor, A. B. C., BA Louvain, MA Indiana, PhD Duquesne   Lectr.; Acting Head*
Other Staff: 1 Teaching Fellow
Vacant Posts: 1 Assoc. Prof.; 1 Sr. Lectr.; 1 Lectr.

Physics

Awunor-Renner, E. R. T., BSc Hull, MSc Lond., PhD Uppsala   Prof.; Head*
Godwin, V. E., BSc Durh., MSc Oregon, PhD Missouri   Assoc. Prof.
Vacant Posts: 1 Sr. Lectr.; 2 Lectrs.

Political Science

Dumbuya, Ahmed R., BA Durh., MA Wash., PhD Wash.   Sr. Lectr. (on leave)
Kabba, M. R. A., BA Br.Col., MA McM., DrRerSoc Bielefeld   Lectr.; Acting Head*
Vacant Posts: 1 Prof.; 1 Sr. Lectr.

Population Studies, Institute of, see Special Centres, etc

Sociology

Kabba, M. R. A., BA Br.Col., MA McM., DrRerSoc Bielefeld   Lectr.; Acting Head*
Vacant Posts: 1 Prof.; 1 Sr. Lectr.

Theology

Shyllon, Rev. L. E. T., MTh St And., PhD Aberd., LDiv   Sr. Lectr.; Head*
Vacant Posts: 1 Prof.

Zoology

Williams, M. O., MA Trinity(Dub.), PhD Glas.   Prof.; Head*

SPECIAL CENTRES, ETC

Adult Education and Extra-Mural Studies, Institute of

Turay, E. D. A., MA Birm., MEd S'ton.   Dir.*

African Studies, Institute of

Abraham, A. A., PhD Birm., BA MA   Dir.*

Marine Biology and Oceanography, Institute of

Findlay, I. W. O., BA Keele, PhD Durh.   Sr. Res. Fellow; Dir.*
Vacant Posts: 1 Sr. Res. Fellow

Population Studies, Institute of

Thomas, A. C., BA Durh., MA Ghana, PhD Lond.   Dir.*

[Information supplied by the institution as at 14 April 1998, and edited by the ACU]

NJALA UNIVERSITY COLLEGE

Incorporated 1964

Postal Address: Private Mail Bag, Freetown, Sierra Leone
Telephone: Njala 4 **Cables**: Njalun

PRINCIPAL*—Turay, Prof. H. M., BA *Durh.*, MA *Ott.*, PhD *Durh.*
DEPUTY REGISTRAR—Gorvie, M. H., MA *Indiana*, MA *Warw.*
ESTATE OFFICER—Manyeh, A. B. J., BSc *Reading*
LIBRARIAN—Deen, A. N. T., MS *Pitt.*, BScAgric

GENERAL INFORMATION

History. The college was incorporated in 1964 and became a constituent college of the University of Sierra Leone in 1966. It is located about 200km east of Freetown.

Admission to first degree courses. General Certificate of Education (GCE) with O level passes (minimum grade 6 in not more than 2 sittings) in 5 approved subjects including English language.

First Degrees(of University of Sierra Leone). BAEd, BScAgric, BScAgricEd, BScEd, BScHomeEcon, BScHomeEconEd.

Higher Degrees(of University of Sierra Leone). MAEd, MEd, MScEd.

Fees (1996–97, annual). Undergraduate: Le26,500. International students: US$1800.

Academic Year(1998-99). Three terms: October–December; January–March; April–June.

Statistics. Staff: 125 (104 academic, 21 administrative). Students: full-time 1600 (1250 men, 350 women).

FACULTIES/SCHOOLS

Agriculture
Dean: Alghali, A. M., MSc *Ib.*, PhD *Ib.*, BSc

Education
Dean: Saidu, P. K., BA *Durh.*, MEd *Wales*

Environmental Sciences
Dean: Tucker, B. J., PhD *Sur.*, BSc

ACADEMIC UNITS

Agricultural Economics and Extension
Josiah, B. P., PhD *Reading*, BA   Lectr.; Head*
Vacant Posts: 1 Prof.; 1 Sr. Lectr.

Agricultural Education
Bangura, K. M.   Sr. Lectr.; Head*
Vacant Posts: 1 Prof.

Agricultural Engineering
Noah, A. R., MSc *Reading*, BScAgric   Lectr.; Acting Head*
Vacant Posts: 1 Sr. Lectr.

Animal Science
Matturi, A. S., PhD *W.Aust.*, BScAgric   Lectr.; Head*
Vacant Posts: 1 Prof.; 2 Sr. Lectrs.; 1 Lectr.

Biological Sciences
Gbakima, A. A., BSc *Elon*, MSPH *N.Carolina*, PhD *N.Carolina*   Assoc. Prof. (on leave)
Sesay, Abu, BScEd *Iowa*, MSc *Iowa*, PhD *Iowa*   Assoc. Prof. (on leave)
Tucker, E. S., PhD   Lectr.; Acting Head*
Vacant Posts: 1 Prof.

Chemistry
Tucker, B. J., PhD *Sur.*, BSc   Sr. Lectr.; Head*
Vacant Posts: 1 Sr. Lectr.; 2 Lectrs.

Crop Protection
Alghali, A. M., MSc *Ib.*, PhD *Ib.*, BSc   Assoc. Prof.; Head*

Crop Science
Dahniya, M. T., MS *Ill.*, PhD *Ib.*, BScAgric   Prof.
George, J. B., MSc *WI*, PhD *Lond.*, BScAgric   Prof.; Head*
Vacant Posts: 2 Sr. Lectrs.; 1 Lectr.

Geography and Rural Development
Bomah, A. K., MA *Clark*, PhD *Clark*, BA   Lectr.; Head*
Kamara, S. I., MSc *Sheff.*, BAEd   Sr. Lectr. (on leave)
Kandeh, H. B. S., MA *Penn.*, PhD *Penn.*, BA   Assoc. Prof. (on leave)
Vacant Posts: 1 Lectr.

Home Economics
Dahniya, Florence N., MS *Howard*, BScHomeEconEd   Sr. Lectr.; Head*
Vacant Posts: 1 Prof., 1 Lectr.

Language Education
Davies, Amy Z., BA *Durh.*, MA *Newcastle(UK)*, MEd *Exe.*, PhD *Exe.*   Sr. Lectr.
Manyeh, M. K., PhD *Leeds*, BAEd   Lectr.; Head*

Pemagbi, J. R., MPhil *Leeds*, BAEd   Assoc. Prof. (on leave)
Vacant Posts: 2 Lectrs.

Mathematics
Briggs, Kamara M., MA *Lond.*   Head*
Other Staff: 1 Lectr.
Vacant Posts: 1 Prof.; 1 Sr. Lectr.

Physical Education
Johnson, S. W.   Co-ordinator
Thomas, S., BEd *Sus.*   Lectr.; Head*
Vacant Posts: 1 Prof.

Physics
Lavaly, A. K., BSc *Durh.*, MSc *Keele*, PhD *Keele*   Lectr.; Head*
Vacant Posts: 1 Prof.

Rural Development, see Geog. and Rural Devel.

Soil Science
Amara, Dennis S., MS *Ill.*, PhD *Ohio*, BScAgric   Sr. Lectr.; Head*
Rhodes, E. R., PhD *Aberd.*, BSc   Prof.

Teacher Education
Vacant Posts: 1 Prof.; 1 Sr. Lectr.; 1 Lectr.

SPECIAL CENTRES, ETC

Certificate Training Centre
Lakoh, A. K., MPhil *Ife*, PhD *Cornell*, BScAgric   Dir.*

Educational Services Centre
Saidu, P. K., BA *Durh.*, MEd *Wales*   Dir.*

Science Curriculum Development Centre
Amara, Juliana, MS *Ill.*, MEd *Col.*, BScEd   Sr. Lectr. (on leave)
Cole, M. J. A., BSc *Durh.*, MS *Ill.*, PhD *Ill.*   Assoc. Prof.; Acting Dir.*
Kamanda, D. M. S., MS *Ill.*, PhD *Ill.*, BScEd   Sr. Lectr.

[*Information supplied by the institution as at 14 April 1998, and edited by the ACU*]

SINGAPORE

Nanyang Technological University (p. 1135)   National University of Singapore (p. 1145)

NANYANG TECHNOLOGICAL UNIVERSITY

Founded 1991, originally established as Nanyang Technological Institute, 1981

Member of the Association of Commonwealth Universities

Postal Address: Nanyang Avenue, Singapore 639798, Republic of Singapore
Telephone: 791 1744 **Fax**: 791 1604 **Cables**: SINNTU **WWW**: http://www.ntu.edu.sg
E-mail formula: username@ntuvax.ntu.edu.sg

CHANCELLOR—Ong Teng Cheong, BArch *Adel.*, MCD *Liv.*
PRO-CHANCELLOR—Vijiaratnam, A., PPA, DLitt *Sing.*, FICE, FIStructE
PRO-CHANCELLOR—Hochstadt, Herman R., PPA, BA *Malaya*
PRO-CHANCELLOR—Owyang, Hsuan, PJG, BS *Dubuque*, MBA *Harv.*
PRO-CHANCELLOR—Tang I-Fang, DUBC, BSc *Natnl.Central(Nanking)*, MBA *Harv.*
CHAIRMAN OF COUNCIL—Koh Boon Hwee, BSc *Lond.*, MBA *Harv.*, BBM
PRESIDENT*—Cham Tao Soon, PPA, BE *Malaya*, BSc *Lond.*, PhD *Camb.*, Hon. DU *Strath.*, Hon. DUniv *Sur.*, Hon. DTech *Lough.*, Hon. DUniv *Soka*
DEPUTY PRESIDENT—Chen Charng-Ning, Prof., PPA, BS *Cheng Kung*, MS *Iowa State*, PhD *Georgia I.T.*
DEPUTY PRESIDENT—Lim Mong King, Prof., BEng *Sing.*, MSc *Maine(France)*, DrSc *Maine(France)*
DIRECTOR, NATIONAL INSTITUTE OF EDUCATION—Tan Wee Hin, Prof. Leo, BSc *Sing.*, PhD *Sing.*
REGISTRAR—Teo Hwee Choo, BSc *Sing.*
BURSAR—Tan En Lin, FCIS
DIRECTOR OF PERSONNEL (YUNNAN GARDEN CAMPUS)—Lun Chor Yee, BSc *Sing.*, MBA *City(UK)*
LIBRARIAN (YUNNAN GARDEN CAMPUS)—Foo Kok Pheow, BSc *Nan.*, MA *Mich.*

GENERAL INFORMATION

History. The university was founded in 1991, having been originally established as Nanyang Technological Institute in 1981.

Admission to first degree courses. Singapore applicants: General Certificate of Education (GCE) with: passes in at least 2 subjects at A level; a pass in the general paper (waived in special cases); minimum grade D7 in a second language; and minimum grade C6 in English as a first language at GCE O level. For certain courses special entry requirements must also be fulfilled. Candidates with relevant diplomas from a polytechnic in Singapore may also apply, but for admission to related courses only. The annual admission process is conducted jointly by the university and the National University of Singapore; only one application is required for both universities.

International applicants: qualifications considered include: Sijil Tinggi Persekolahan Malaysia (STPM), Certificate of Unified Examination for Independent Chinese Secondary Schools in Malaysia (UEC), International Baccalaureate, GCE A levels of UK examining boards.

First Degrees (* = also available with honours). BA (with DipEd), BAcc, BASc(CompEng)*, BASc(MatlEng)*, BBus, BCommStudies (honours only), BEng, BSc(with DipEd).

BAcc, BASc(CompEng), BASc(MatlEng) and BBus last 3 years; BA (with DipEd), BEng, BSc (with DipEd) and honours degrees last 4 years.

Higher Degrees. MA, MA(ApplLing), MA(ApplPsy), MA(EdMgt), MAcc, MASc, MBA(Acc), MBA(B&F), MBA(BusLaw), MBA(HTM) (hospitality and tourism management), MBA(IB), MBA(MgtofIT),

MBA(MOT) (management of technology), MBA(StratMgt), MBus, MCommStudies, MEd, MEng, MMassComm, MSc, MSc(CIM), MSc(Comm&NetworkSyst), MSc(CompContr&Autom), MSc(ConsElec) (consumer electronics), MSc(GeotechEng), MSc(InfoStudies), MSc(IntlConstrMgt), MSc(Log), MSc(ManagerialEcons), MSc(Mech&ProcofMatl), MSc(PrecEng), MSc(SPD) (small product design), MSc(StrategicStudies), MSc(TptEng), PhD, PhD(Bus).

Applicants for admission to master's degrees by coursework must normally hold an appropriate first degree and, for some courses, have relevant work experience. Master's degrees by research (MA, MAcc, MASc, MBus, MCommStudies, MEng, MSc): a first degree with at least second class honours and the ability to pursue research in the proposed field. PhD: a master's degree and the ability to pursue research in the proposed field.

Master's degrees by research last 1–3 years full-time or part-time; MSc(ManagerialEcons): 1–2 years full-time; MSc(StrategicStudies): 1–3 years full-time; MSc(TptEng): 1–3 years full-time or 1½–4 years part-time; MSc(Comm&NetworkSyst): 1–3 years full-time or 2–4 years part-time; MMassComm: 1–4 years full-time or part-time; MBA degrees: 1.3–2 years full-time or 2–4 years part-time; MSc(IntlConstrMgt): 1.3–4 years part-time; MSc(CIM), MSc(CompContr&Autom), MSc(ConsElec), MSc(GeotechEng), MSc(InfoStudies), MSc(Log), MSc(Mech&ProcofMatl), MSc(PrecEng), MSc(SPD): 2–4 years part-time; PhD: 2–5 years full-time or part-time; PhD(Bus): 2–5 years full-time or 3–6 years part-time.

Libraries. 565,000 volumes; 3100 periodicals subscribed to. Special collections include: CAD/CAM; education.

Fees (1998–99). Singaporeans and Singapore permanent residents: S$5500(full-time undergraduate); S$1500–6000 (part-time postgraduate coursework programmes); S$9000 (full-time postgraduate coursework programmes, non-laboratory-based); S$3000–8000 (full-time postgraduate coursework programmes, laboratory-based); S$1650 (research programmes, non-laboratory-based); S$1800 (research programmes, laboratory-based). International students: S$6050 (full-time undergraduate); S$1650–6000 (part-time postgraduate coursework programmes); S$9000 (full-time postgraduate coursework programmes, non-laboratory-based); S$3300–8000 (full-time postgraduate coursework programmes, laboratory-based); S$2100 (research programmes, non-laboratory-based); S$2250 (research programmes, laboratory-based).

Academic Awards (1997–98). 69 awards ranging in value from S$3000 to S$12,000.

Academic Year (1998–99). Two semesters: 13 July–31 October; 11 January–1 May. Three trimesters: 6 July–10 October; 19 October–6 December and 4 January–20 February; 8 March–12 June.

Income (1996–97). Total, S$260,156,000.

Statistics. Staff: 2105 (Yunnan Garden Campus). Students: total 16,690 (9961 men, 6729 women).

FACULTIES/SCHOOLS

Accountancy and Business, School of

Dean: Neo Boon Siong, BAcc NU *Singapore*, MBA *Pitt.*, PhD *Pitt.*
Secretary: Ang-Choong, Michele

Applied Science, School of

Dean: Singh, Prof. Harcharan, BSc Punjab, MSc Belf., PhD NU Singapore

Secretary: Wong, Serene

Arts, School of

Tel: 460 5115 Fax: 469 8433

Dean (Bukit Timah Campus): Koh Tai Ann, BA Sing., PhD Sing.

Secretary: ......

Civil and Structural Engineering, School of

Dean: Cheong Hee Kiat, BE Adel., MSc Lond., PhD Lond.

Secretary: Chim, Janet

Communication Studies, School of

Dean: Kuo, Prof. Eddie C.-Y., BA Natnl.Chengchi, MA Hawaii, PhD Minn.

Secretary: Chan, Daphne

Education, School of

Tel: 460 5057 Fax: 469 9007

Dean (Bukit Timah Campus): Saravanan, Gopinathan, BA Sing., MEd Sing., PhD N.Y.State

Secretary: Tan Bin Eng, Cecilia

Electrical and Electronic Engineering, School of

Dean: Er Meng Hwa, Prof., BEng NU Singapore, PhD Newcastle(NSW)

Secretary: Tan, Elaine

Mechanical and Production Engineering, School of

Dean: Lim Mong King, Prof., BEng Sing., MSc Maine(France), DrSc Maine(France)

Secretary: Lim, Jesamine

Physical Education, School of

Tel: 460 5351 Fax: 468 7506

Dean (Bukit Timah Campus): Quek, Jin Jong, BS Oregon, MS Oregon, PhD Qld.

Secretary: Murugiah, Mala

Science, School of

Tel: 460 5185 Fax: 469 8952

Dean (Bukit Timah Campus): Tan Wee Hin, Prof. Leo, BSc Sing., PhD Sing.

Secretary: Pereira, Mary S.

ACADEMIC UNITS

Arranged by Schools

Accountancy and Business

Tel: 799 5683-4 Fax: 791 3697

Neo Boon Siong, BAcc NU Singapore, MBA Pitt., PhD Pitt. Assoc. Prof.

Other Staff: 3 Adjunct Profs.; 2 Adjunct Assoc. Profs.; 10 Adjunct Sr. Lectrs.

Actuarial Science and Insurance

Tel: 799 5005 Fax: 792 4694

Koh, Hian Chye, BAcc NU Singapore, PhD Virginia Polytech. Assoc. Prof.

Lian, Robert K. H., BA Sing., MS Northeastern Sr. Lectr.

Loi, Soh Loi, BSc Nan., MSc Lough., PhD Cant. Sr. Lectr.

Low, Chan Kee, BEc Monash, PhD Monash Sr. Lectr.; Head*

Tan, Khye Chong, BSc Cant., MSocSc Sci.U.Malaysia, PhD Lond. Sr. Lectr.

Tan, Lee Lee, BSc Malaya, MS Northeastern Sr. Lectr.

Wong, YokeWai, BSc City HK, MBA City HK Sr. Lectr.

Yee, Wah Chin, BBA Sing., MBA Strath., FCIS Sr. Lectr.

Other Staff: 1 Sr. Fellow; 4 Lectrs.; 1 Sr. Tutor

Research: captive insurance and reinsurance; life and disability underwriting; medical statistics; mortality studies; motor vehicles rating

Applied Economics

Tel: 799 4761 Fax: 793 0523

Chen, Kang, BS Xiamen, MS Ohio PhD Maryland Sr. Lectr.

Chew, Soon Beng, BCom Nan., MSocSci Sing., PhD W.Ont. Assoc. Prof.; Head*

Das-Gupta, Arindam, MA BITS, MA Cinc., PhD Cornell Sr. Lectr.

Lall, Ashish, BA Delhi, MA Car., MA Delhi, PhD Car. Sr. Lectr.

Leu, Mike G.-J., BS Natnl.Taiwan, MA Calif., MS Nebraska, PhD Calif. Sr. Lectr.

Lim, Chong Yah, BBM, PJG, BA Malaya, MA Malaya, DPhil Oxf. Prof.

Maung Shein, BA Rangoon, BSc(Econ) Lond., PhD Camb. Visiting Prof.

Ng, Beoy Kui, BEc Malaya, MSc Lond. Sr. Lectr.

Sakellariou, Christos, BA Athens Sch.Econ., MA Windsor, PhD Ott. Sr. Lectr.

Soon, Lee Ying, BA Malaya, MEc Malaya, PhD Penn. Sr. Lectr.

Tan, Khee Giap, BA CNAA, MA E.Anglia, PhD E.Anglia Sr. Lectr.

Tan, Kim Heng, BE Adel., MCom NSW, PhD Syd. Sr. Lectr.

Other Staff: 13 Lectrs.

Research: industrial relations and trade unions in Asia; macroeconomic performance of the Chinese economy; macroeconomic performance of the Singapore economy

Auditing and Taxation

Tel: 799 4754 Fax: 792 4535

Ambanpola, E. M. K. B., BSc(Econ) Lond., FCA Sr. Lectr.

Choo, Teck Min, BAcc NU Singapore, PhD Pitt. Sr. Lectr.

Foo, See Liang, BCom NSW, PhD Hull, FCA Sr. Lectr.

Goodwin, Jennifer D., BBS Massey, MEc Adel., PhD Lincoln(NZ) Sr. Lectr.

Pang, Yang Hoong, BAcc Sing., MEc Monash, PhD Qu. Assoc. Prof.; Head*

Seah-Teo Chai Lian, BAcc Sing. Sr. Lectr.

Tan, Angela P. N., BAcc Sing., MBA NU Singapore Sr. Lectr.

Tan, Hung Tong, BAcc NU Singapore, MA Mich., PhD Minn. Sr. Lectr.

Tan, Khoon Eng, BAcc Sing., MBA Indiana Sr. Lectr.

Tan, Pearl H. N., BAcc Sing., MSc Lond. Sr. Lectr. (on leave)

Tay, Joanne S. W., BA Liv., PhD Exe. Sr. Lectr.

Other Staff: 5 Lectrs.; 1 Sr. Tutor

Research: accounting earnings and equity valuation; accounting for financial instruments; determinants of expertise and identification of decision biases of managers; executive compensation issues; informativeness of financial statement numbers

Banking and Finance

Tel: 799 5622 Fax: 791 3697

Cheng, Philip Y. K., BA Macq., MBus Technol.Syd. Sr. Lectr.

Fock Siew Tiong, BA NU Singapore, BSocSci NU Singapore, MSc NU Singapore Sr. Lectr.

Gerrard, Philip, BSc Birm., PhD Birm. Sr. Lectr.

Ho, Kim Wai, BSc Lond., MFin RMIT, FCA Sr. Lectr.

Lee, Andrew T. K., BAcc NU Singapore, MS Roch., PhD N.Y. Sr. Lectr.

Los, Cornelis A., Cand Gron., MPhil Col., Drs Gron., PhD Col. Assoc. Prof.

Low, Buen Sin, BAcc NU Singapore, MBA Tor. Sr. Lectr.

Shrestha, Keshab M., BS Tribhuvan, MA Tribhuvan, MA N.Y.State, MS N.Y.State, PhD N.Y.State Sr. Lectr.

Srinivasan, Bobby S., BSc Madr., MSc Madr., MS Case W.Reserve, PhD Case W.Reserve Sr. Lectr.

Sun, Qian, BS(Econ) Beijing, MBA Wm.Paterson, PhD Arizona State Sr. Lectr.

Tan, Kok Hui, BA Minn., PhD Arizona State Sr. Lectr.

Tsang, Eric W.-K., BSocSc HK, LLB Beijing, MBA Chinese HK, PhD Camb. Sr. Lectr.

Vong, John H. C., BA CNAA, MBA Brad., PhD Brad. Sr. Lectr.

Yam Wee Lee, BAcc Sing., SM M.I.T. Sr. Lectr.

Yeo, Gillian H. H., BAcc Sing., MS Ill., PhD Ill. Sr. Lectr.; Head*

Other Staff: 1 Sr. Fellow, 5 Lectrs.; 1 Sr. Tutor

Research: bond markets and analysis; corporate financial policies and practices; mergers and acquisitions; risk management

Business Law

Tel: 799 5657 Fax: 793 5189

Ang, Steven B. W., LLB NU Singapore, LLM Lond. Sr. Lectr.

Goh-Low, Erin S. Y., LLB NU Singapore, LLM Lond. Sr. Lectr.

Leow Chye Sian, LLB NU Singapore, LLM Camb. Sr. Lectr.

Low, Kee Yang, LLB NU Singapore, LLM Lond., PhD Lond. Sr. Lectr.; Head*

Ong, Dennis C. S., LLB Lond., LLM Lond. Sr. Lectr.

Ong, Patricia G. S., LLB NU Singapore, LLM Lond. Sr. Lectr.

Pulle, Austin I., LLB S.Lanka, LLM Harv., SJD Harv. Sr. Lectr.

Shenoy, George T. L., BCom Madr., LLB Bom., LLM Bom., PhD Lond. Sr. Lectr.

Tabalujan, Benny S., BEc Monash, LLB Monash, LLM Melb. Sr. Lectr. (on leave)

Tan Lay Hong, LLB NU Singapore, LLM Lond. Sr. Lectr.

Toh, See Kiat, LLB NU Singapore, LLM Harv., PhD Lond. Sr. Lectr. (on leave)

Other Staff: 11 Lectrs.; 1 Sr. Tutor

Entrepreneurship Development Centre (ENDEC)

Tel: 799 5690 Fax: 791 4538

Tan Wee Liang, LLB NU Singapore, LLM Camb., SM M.I.T., FCIS Dir.*

Research: corporate venturing: factors motivating, process and innovation; entrepreneurship environment: cross-country comparison, socio-cultural influence; family business: succession, growth models and impact of professionalisation; information technology and performance: implementation process and performance, cross-country comparison; venture capital: strategic management styles, investment strategy and performance

Financial and Management Accounting

Tel: 799 5692 Fax: 792 4535

Ang, Kong Beng, BCom Nan., MBA Br.Col. Sr. Lectr.

Chan Sow Lin, BAcc Sing., MSc Aston Sr. Lectr.

Chan, Yoke Kai, BAcc Sing., MCom NSW Sr. Lectr.

Chung Lai Hong, BAcc NU Singapore, PhD Pitt. Sr. Lectr.

Debreceny, Roger S., BCom Auck., MCom Auck., MPP Well., FCPA Sr. Lectr.

Foo, Wendy T. S., BSc(Econ) Lond., MBA NU Singapore, FCA Sr. Lectr.

Gan, Tin Hua, FCA Assoc. Prof.

Goh, Chye Tee, BCom Nan., MCom NSW Sr. Lectr.

Goodwin, David R., BBS Massey, MBA Otago, PhD Adel., FCPA Sr. Lectr.

Hwang Soo Chiat, BAcc Sing., MEc Monash, PhD Macq. Sr. Lectr.

Khoo, Teng Aun, BAcc Sing., MEc Macq. Sr. Lectr.

Kung Gek Neo, BAcc Sing., MCom NSW Sr. Lectr.

Kwok, Branson C. H., BCom W.Aust., MBA W.Aust. Sr. Lectr.

Lee, Lip Nyean, BEc Malaya, MBA Strath. Sr. Lectr.

Lee, Marina F. T., BCom Nan., MBA Melb., FCPA Sr. Lectr.

Leong, Kwong Sin, BAcc Sing., MCom Cant., SE M.I.T. Assoc. Prof.; Head*

Low, Richard S. S., BCom Cant., MCom Cant. Sr. Lectr.

Ng, Eng Juan, BEc Malaya, MBA S.Calif. Sr. Lectr.

Ong Poh Wah, BAcc Sing., MSc Lond. Assoc. Prof.

Rahman, Asheq R., BCom Dacca, MBA Dacca, MBA E.Illinois, PhD Syd. Sr. Lectr.

Seaman, Alfred E., BBA New Br., PhD Qu. Sr. Lectr.

Tan, Clement K. G., BAcc NU Singapore, MSc(Econ) Lond. Sr. Lectr.

Tan, Patricia M. S., BAcc NU Singapore, PhD Br.Col. Sr. Lectr.

Teo, Susan P. P., BAcc NU Singapore, MAcc Wis., MBA Wis., PhD Wis. Sr. Lectr.

Teoh, Hai Yap, BA Malaya, MBA Br.Col. Assoc. Prof.

Williams, John J., BComm Alta., MBA Alta., PhD Penn.State Assoc. Prof.

Other Staff: 3 Lectrs.; 5 Sr. Tutors; 1 Adjunct Prof.; 1 Adjunct Sr. Lectr.

Research: information content of corporate reports; productivity and management accounting practices

Human Resource and Quality Management

Tel: 799 4717 Fax: 791 3697

Ang Soon, BAcc NU Singapore, MCom NSW, PhD Minn. Sr. Lectr.; Head*

Beck, John E., BA Sheff., MA Leeds, PhD Manc. Assoc. Prof.

Chew, Irene K. H., BA Sing., MA Leeds, PhD NSW Sr. Lectr.

Chew, Rosalind S. L., BSocSci Sing., MA W.Ont., PhD NU Singapore Sr. Lectr.

Ho Mian Lian, BA Sing., MA Monash, PhD Monash Sr. Lectr.

Justus, Helen L., MA Edin., PhD Edin. Sr. Lectr.

Lim, Boon Chye, BE Newcastle(NSW), BCom Newcastle(NSW), MBA NU Singapore Sr. Lectr.

Osman-Gani, Ahad A. M., BSc Chitt., MBA Dhaka, MA Ohio State, PhD Ohio State Sr. Lectr.

Quazi, Hesan A., BSc(Engin) B'desh.Engin., MSc(Engin) B'desh.Engin., MBA Indiana, DPhil Sus. Sr. Lectr.

Tay, Cheryl S. L., BAcc Sing., MBA NU Singapore Sr. Lectr.

Walker, John, MSc Cran.IT, PhD Cran.IT Sr. Lectr.

Wong, Irene F. H., BA Malaya, MA Malaya, PhD Alta. Sr. Lectr.

Wright, Roger E., BEng RMC, MBA Qu., PhD Qu. Sr. Lectr.

Other Staff: 17 Lectrs.; 1 Sr. Tutor; 1 Adjunct Sr. Lectr.

Research: bench-marking of plant practices; cross-cultural research in human resource management; global practices in TQM; managing high technology professionals; supply chain management

Marketing and Tourism Management

Tel: 799 5682 Fax: 791 3697

Blanch, Gregory F., BA Ohio State, MA Calif.State, PhD Claremont Sr. Lectr.

Dana, Leo-Paul, BA McG., MBA McG., PhD E.H.E.C., Paris Sr. Lectr.

Erramilli, Murali K., BSc Poona, MSc Poona, MBA Poona, PhD Arkansas Sr. Lectr.

Ghosh, Bibhas C., BCom Calc., MPhil Lough. Assoc. Prof.

Hooi, Den Huan, BSc Brad., PhD Manc. Sr. Lectr.; Head*

Leong, Choon Chiang, BBA Hawaii, MS Wash. Sr. Lectr.

Leung, Roberta, BA Hawaii, BBA Hawaii, MBA San Francisco State Sr. Lectr.

Litvin, Stephen W., BSc Bentley, MBA Babson Sr. Lectr.

Low, Sion Siam, BBus Curtin, BCom W.Aust., MCom W.Aust.

MacLaurin, Donald J., BS Florida Internat., MS Nevada, PhD Kansas State Sr. Lectr.

MacLaurin, Tanya L., BS Kansas State, MS Kansas State, PhD Kansas State Sr. Lectr.

Marshall, Roger, BCom Auck., MCom Auck., PhD W.Aust. Sr. Lectr.

McGovern, Ian, BA Manc., MBA City(UK), PhD Manc. Sr. Lectr.

Mummalaneni, Venkatapparao, BSc Samb., PhD Penn.State Sr. Lectr.

Murthy, Bvsan, BSc And., MSc And., PhD Virginia Polytech. Sr. Lectr.

Noble, Peter M., BS Calif., BFT Amer.Inst.Foreign Trade, MBA Iowa, PhD Iowa Sr. Lectr.

Piron, Francis M., BSc S.W.Louisiana, MIM Amer.Grad.Sch.Internat.Mgt., PhD S.Carolina Sr. Lectr.

Sadi, Muhammad A., BA Punjab, MA Punjab, MBA Indiana Central, PhD Virginia Polytech. Sr. Lectr.

Smith, Russell A., BArch Qld., MArch Qld., DDes Harv., FRAIA Sr. Lectr.

Tan, Wee Liang, LLB NU Singapore, LLM Camb., SM M.I.T., FCIS Sr. Lectr.

Toh, Thian Ser, BSocSci Sing., MBA NU Singapore Assoc. Prof.

Tran-Kiem, Luu, MBA George Washington, DBA George Washington Sr. Lectr.

Zafar Uddin Ahmed, BCom Alig. Muslim, MCom lAlig. Muslim, PhD Alig. Muslim, PhD Utah State

Other Staff: 5 Lectrs.; 4 Sr. Tutors

Research: cross-cultural consumer behaviour; international business strategies in Asia; service quality measurement and control; tourism strategy

Strategy and Information Systems

Tel: 799 5697 Fax: 792 2313

Chiang Hsiang-Li, BS Natnl.Chiao Tung, MS Roch., MS Mich.State, PhD Roch. Sr. Lectr.

Gilbert, Arthur L., BA Denver, MA Oregon, PhD Northeastern Sr. Lectr.

Lee, Kenny K. F., BSc Lond., MSc Lond. Sr. Lectr.

Neo, Boon Siong, BAcc NU Singapore, MBA Pitt., PhD Pitt. Assoc. Prof.

Sethi, Vijay, BTech IIT Delhi, MBA Ohio, PhD Pitt. Sr. Lectr.

Soh, Christina W. L., BAcc NU Singapore, PhD Calif. Sr. Lectr.; Head*

Tung Lai Lai, BAcc NU Singapore, MBA Indiana, PhD Indiana Sr. Lectr.

Wan, Chew Yoong, MBA Lausanne Sr. Lectr.

Webster, John F., BS Indiana, MBA Penn.State, PhD Pitt. Assoc. Prof.

Wong Soke Yin, BAcc NU Singapore, MBA Tor. Sr. Lectr.

Zutshi, Ravinder K., BTech IIT Delhi, MS Flor., PhD Pitt. Sr. Lectr.

Other Staff: 8 Lectrs.; 2 Sr. Tutors

Research: business process re-engineering; corporate governance; data and knowledge management; outsourcing and HR issues in IT; strategic alliances

Applied Science

Tel: 799 5788 Fax: 791 9414

Khong, Chooi Peng, BA Malaya, MA Birm., MEd Pitt., PhD Malaya Sr. Lectr.

Singh, Harcharan, BSc Punjab, MSc Belf., PhD NU Singapore Prof.; Head*

Other Staff: 3 Lectrs.; 1 Adjunct Assoc. Prof.

Advanced Materials Research Centre

Fax: 792 6559

Fong Hock Sun, BSc Sing., PhD Birm., FIM Dir.*

Other Staff: 1 Res. Fellow; 1 Postdoctoral Fellow

Research: ceramics for microelectronic packaging and IR sensors; diamond, DLC, CN and magnetic coatings; joining of aerospace materials; polymer composite, LCP and conducting polymers; thermal spray coatings for implant

Computing Systems

Tel: 799 5788 Fax: 791 9414

Abdul Wahab Bin Abdul Rahman, BSc Essex, MSc(ElectEng) NU Singapore Sr. Lectr.

Abut, Huseyin, BSEE Robert(Istanbul), MSEE N.Carolina State, PhD N.Carolina State, Dr Visiting Prof.

Annamalai, Benjamin P., BE IISc., BSc B'lore., MS N.Dakota State, PhD Idaho Sr. Lectr.

Chan, Tony K. Y., BE NSW, PhD NSW Sr. Lectr.

Chong, Man Nang, BEng Strath., PhD Strath. Sr. Lectr.

Goh, Wooi Boon, BSc Birm., MPhil Warw. Sr. Lectr.

Gul, Nawaz K., BSc Punjab, BSc Lahore UET, MS Syr., PhD Lond. Sr. Lectr.

Gupta, Anil K., BE Roor., ME Roor., PhD Ott. Sr. Lectr.

Lau, Chiew Tong, BEng Lake., MASc Br.Col., PhD Br.Col. Sr. Lectr.

Lee, Bu Sung, BSc Lough., PhD Lough. Sr. Lectr.

Lee, Keok Kee, BEng NU Singapore, MEE Rice Sr. Lectr.

Leedham, Charles G., BSc Leeds, MSc S'ton., PhD S'ton. Sr. Lectr.

Loh, Peter K. K., BEng NU Singapore, MSc(ElectEng) NU Singapore, MSc Manc. Sr. Lectr.

Radhakrishnan, Damodaran, BSc(Eng) Kerala, MTech IIT Kanpur, PhD Idaho Sr. Lectr.

Sagar, Vijay K., BSc Essex, PhD Essex Sr. Lectr.

Seah, Hock Soon, BEng NU Singapore, MSc Lond. Sr. Lectr.

Singh, Harcharan, BSc Punjab, MSc Belf., PhD NU Singapore Prof.; Head*

Sluzek, Andrzej, MSc Warsaw U.T., PhD Warsaw U.T., DSc Warsaw U.T. Sr. Lectr.

Srikanthan, Thambipillai, BSc CNAA, PhD CNAA Sr. Lectr.

Sriskanthan, Nadarajah, BSc(Eng) Lond., MSc Cran.IT Sr. Lectr.

Vun, Nicholas C. H., BE Monash, MEngSc Monash Sr. Lectr.

Wong, Kin Keong, BEng Monash, MEngSc Monash Sr. Lectr.

Yeo, Chai Kiat, BEng NU Singapore, MSc(ElectEng) NU Singapore Sr. Lectr.

Other Staff: 8 Lectrs.; 3 Postdoctoral Fellows

Research: computer architecture and digital systems; computer communications and network technology; computer graphics and computer vision; intelligent systems and automation technology; parallel processing

Information Studies

Tel: 799 1393 Fax: 792 6559

Cave, Roderick G. J. M., MA Lough., PhD Lough., FLA Assoc. Prof.

Chaudhry, Abdus S., BA Punjab, MA Punjab, MS Hawaii, PhD Ill. Sr. Lectr.

Chowdhury, Gobinda G., BSc Burd., BLISc Burd., MLISc Burd., PhD Jad., PhD Sheff. Sr. Lectr.

Foo, Schubert S. B., BSc Strath., MBA Strath., PhD Strath. Sr. Lectr.; Head*

Hepworth, Mark, BA Lond., MSc Sheff. Sr. Lectr.

Other Staff: 2 Lectrs.

Research: collection, organisation and dissemination of information; human-computer interaction and user interfaces; information literacy; information retrieval and digital libraries; information services and systems

Materials Engineering

Tel: 799 4904 Fax: 792 6559

Chandel, Roop S., BE Nag., PhD Birm., FIM Sr. Lectr.

Cheang, Philip H. N., BE Monash, PhD Monash Sr. Lectr.

Fong, Hock Sun, BSc Sing., PhD Birm., FIM Prof.; Head*

Heng, Keng Wah, BSc Malaya, MSc Brist. Sr. Lectr.

Hing, Peter, BSc Baroda, DPhil Oxf., FIM Assoc. Prof.

Hu Xiao, BE Tsing Hua, MSc Manc., PhD UMIST Sr. Lectr.

Liang, Meng Heng, BEng Liv., PhD Liv., FIM Sr. Lectr.

Manoharan, Mohan, BTech IIT Madras, MS Ohio State, PhD Ohio State Sr. Lectr.

Mridha, Shahjahan, BSc(Engin) B'desh.Engin., MSc(Engin) B'desh.Engin., PhD Leeds Sr. Lectr.

Oh, Joo Tien, BSc(Eng) Lond., MEng NU Singapore, MMet Sheff. Sr. Lectr.

Qiu Jianhai, BE Beijing Iron & Steel, PhD Sur. Sr. Lectr.

Sarkar, Gautam, BE Calc., MTech IIT Kanpur, PhD Marquette Sr. Lectr.

Seow, Hong Pheow, BE Qld., MEngSc Qld. Sr. Lectr.

Sritharan, Thirumany, BScEngin Peradeniya, PhD Sheff., DMet Sheff. Sr. Lectr.

Other Staff: 2 Lectrs.; 2 Sr. Programme Fellows; 1 Res. Fellow; 1 Postdoctoral Fellow

Research: ceramics: inter-relationship between processing, properties, performance and micro-structure; materials evaluation: fracture mechanics, corrosion, non-destructive testing; metal processing: welding, aerospace alloys brazing; microelectronics materials and processing: wafer fabrication, IC packaging, thin films; polymer technology: advanced polymers and composites including biomaterials

Software Systems

Tel: 799 4929 Fax: 792 6559

Cai, Wentong, BS Nankai, MS Nankai, PhD Exe. Sr. Lectr.

Erdogan, Sevki S., BS Middle East Tech., MSc Manc., PhD Manc. Sr. Lectr.

Goh, Angela E. S., BSc Manc., MSc Manc., PhD Manc. Assoc. Prof.; Head*

Heng, Alfred C. K., BEng Sing., MSc Manc. Sr. Lectr.

Hsu, Wen Jing, BS Natnl.Chiao Tung(Taiwan), MS Natnl.Chiao Tung(Taiwan), PhD Natnl.Chiao Tung(Taiwan) Sr. Lectr.

Huang Shell Ying, BSc(Eng) Lond., PhD Lond. Sr. Lectr.

Hui, Siu Cheung, BSc Sus., DPhil Sus. Sr. Lectr.

Hura, Gurdeep S., BE Jab., ME Roor., PhD Roor. Sr. Lectr.

Leong, Peng Chor, BSc Essex, MS Calif. Sr. Lectr.

Ng, Geok See, BMath Wat., MASc Wat. Sr. Lectr.

Quek, Hiok Chai, BSc H.-W., PhD H.-W. Sr. Lectr.

Shaw, Venson M. H., BS Natnl.Chiao Tung(Taiwan), MBA Phoenix, MBA Golden Gate, MSEE Johns H., PhD Johns H. Sr. Lectr.

Sourin, Alexei I., MSc Moscow Phys.& Engin.Inst., PhD Moscow Phys.& Engin.Inst. Sr. Lectr.

Tan, Eng Chong, BSc Nan., MSc Auck., PhD Melb. Sr. Lectr.

Yap, Ma Tit, BSc City(UK), MPhil Lanc. Sr. Lectr.

Other Staff: 8 Lectrs.; 1 Postdoctoral Fellow

Research: database and knowledge engineering: data warehousing, CAD/CAM databases, semi-structured databases, database integration; digital libraries: advanced digital library applications, information retrieval; intelligent systems: handwriting recognition, intelligent multimedia tutoring, intelligent training system; simulation and decision support: support tools for large-scale complex decision problems; web technologies: advanced web applications, web query processing, web computing, electronic commerce

Business, see Accty. and Business

Civil and Structural Engineering

Tel: 799 5265 Fax: 791 0676

Cheung, Dorothy S. L., BPhil(Ed) Birm., MA Birm. Sr. Lectr.

Other Staff: 3 Lectrs.; 1 Teaching Fellow; 2 Adjunct Assoc. Profs.

Advanced Construction Studies, Centre for

Tel: 799 4916 Fax: 791 6697

Yip Woon Kwong, BEng Sing., MSc NU Singapore, PhD NU Singapore Dir.*

Research: construction project cost estimating and modelling; construction project financing and risk management; effects of

design on buildability; precast concrete technology; productivity management at construction work sites

Geotechnical Research Centre

Tel: 799 6455 Fax: 791 0676

Harianto, Rahardjo, MSc Sask., PhD Sask. Dir.*

Research: foundations of high-rise buildings; tropical soils engineering; underground space development

Geotechnics and Surveying

Tel: 799 5307 Fax: 791 0676

Chang Ming-Fang, BS Natnl.Taiwan, MEng Asian I.T., Bangkok, PhD Purdue Assoc. Prof.

Goh, Anthony T. C., BEng Monash, PhD Monash Sr. Lectr.

Goh Pong Chai, BSurv NSW, MSurv NSW Sr. Lectr.

Harianto, Rahardjo, MSc Sask., PhD Sask. Sr. Lectr.

Koo Tsai Kee, BSurv NSW, MSc Lond., MPhil Lond. Sr. Lectr. (on leave)

Leong Eng Choon, BEng NU Singapore, MEng NU Singapore, PhD W.Aust. Sr. Lectr.

Low Bak Kong, BS M.I.T., MS M.I.T., PhD Calif. Sr. Lectr.

Teh Cee Ing, BE Malaya, DPhil Oxf. Sr. Lectr.; Head*

Tor Yam Khoon, BSurv NSW, MSurv NSW Sr. Lectr.

Wong Kai Sin, BSCE Ill., MS Calif., PhD Calif. Assoc. Prof.

Zhao Jian, BSc Leeds, PhD Lond., FGS Sr. Lectr.

Other Staff: 2 Lectrs.; 3 Res. Fellows; 2 Postdoctoral Fellows

Research: applications of GIS and GPS technology; geotechnics of reclaimed land

Structures and Construction

Tel: 799 5306 Fax: 791 0676

Alum, Jahidul A. K. M., BSc Rajsh., BSc(Engin) Dacca, DrIng T.H.Karlsruhe Assoc. Prof.

Ang Chee Keong, BS Natnl.Taiwan, MS N.Y. Sr. Lectr.

Ang, Paul T. C., BEng Sing., MSc NU Singapore Sr. Lectr.

Brownjohn, James M. W., BSc Brist., PhD Brist. Sr. Lectr.

Chan Kin Seng, MEng Asian I.T., Bangkok, DEng Asian I.T., Bangkok Sr. Lectr.

Cheong Hee Kiat, BE Adel., MSc Lond., PhD Lond. Assoc. Prof.

Chew, David A. S., BEng Sing., MASc Wat., MBA Oklahoma City Sr. Lectr.

Chiew Sing Ping, BSc Wales, MSc Wales, PhD NU Singapore Sr. Lectr.

Choi, Edmund C. C., BSc(Eng) HK, PhD HK Assoc. Prof.

Chuang Poon-Hwei, BEng Sing., MSc S'ton., PhD Lond. Sr. Lectr.

Fan Sau Cheong, BSc(Eng) HK, PhD HK Assoc. Prof.

Fung Tat Ching, BSc(Eng) HK, PhD HK Sr. Lectr.

Guan Lingwei, BE N.Jiaotong, ME N.Jiaotong, MS Rutgers, PhD Rutgers Sr. Lectr.

Hao Hong, BS Tianjin, MS Calif., PhD Calif. Sr. Lectr.

Hartono, Wibisono, MEng Asian I.T., Bangkok, DEng Tokyo Sr. Lectr.

Lam Yow Thim, BEng Sing., MSc Sing., PhD Lough. Sr. Lectr.

Lee Sai Cheng, BEng Sing., MSc Lond. Sr. Lectr.

Lie Seng Tjhen, BSc(Eng) Lond., MSc Lond., PhD UMIST Sr. Lectr.

Lim Ewe Chye, BSc(Eng) Lond., MSc Lond., PhD Lough. Sr. Lectr.

Lok Tat Seng, BSc Aston, PhD Warw. Sr. Lectr.

Pan Tso-Chien, BS Cheng Kung, MS Calif., PhD Calif. Assoc. Prof.

Poh, Paul S. H., BSc Edin., MBA Dund., PhD Edin. Sr. Lectr.

Soh Chee Kiong, BEng C'dia., SM M.I.T., PhD Wales Assoc. Prof.; Head*

Tan Kang Hai, BSc Manc., PhD Manc. Sr. Lectr.

Tan Teng Hooi, BEng Sing., MSc NU Singapore Sr. Lectr.

Teng, Susanto, BSCE Iowa, MSCE Iowa, PhD Iowa Sr. Lectr.

Ting Seng Kiong, BE Monash, MEng NU Singapore, MS M.I.T., SD M.I.T. Sr. Lectr.

Tiong, Robert L. K., BSc Glas., ME Calif., PhD Nan.Tech. Sr. Lectr.

Wong Wai Fan, BEng Sing., MSc Sing., MBA Oklahoma City Sr. Lectr.

Yap Sook Foong, BEng Sing., MSc NU Singapore Sr. Lectr.

Yip Woon Kwong, BEng Sing., MSc NU Singapore, PhD NU Singapore Assoc. Prof.

Zhao, Zhiye, BS Tsing Hua, MSc Lond., PhD CNAA Sr. Lectr.

Other Staff: 4 Lectrs.; 1 Teaching Fellow; 3 Postdoctoral Fellows; 1 Adjunct Prof.

Research: computational mechanics; construction technology and management; effects of seismic and dynamic loading; structural connections; wind engineering and building envelopes

Transportation Studies, Centre for

Tel: 799 5328

Fan, Henry S. L., BS Natnl.Taiwan, MS Idaho, PhD Calif. Dir.*

Research: applications of advanced technology in transportation; congestion management and traffic control; pavement materials and technology; transport planning and modelling

Water Resources and Transportation

Tel: 799 5308 Fax: 791 0676

Appan, Adhityan, BSc Madr., BE Karn., MSc Lond., PhD Sing., FICE Assoc. Prof.

Chen Charng-Ning, PPA, BS Cheng Kung, MS Iowa State, PhD Georgia I.T. Prof.

Chiew Yee Meng, BE Auck., PhD Auck. Sr. Lectr.

Chin Chen Onn, BE Auck., ME Auck., PhD Auck. Sr. Lectr.

Chui Peng Cheong, BEng NU Singapore, MSc NU Singapore Sr. Lectr.

Fan, Henry S. L., BS Natnl.Taiwan, MS Idaho, PhD Calif. Prof.

Jeyaseelan, S., BSc(Eng) Ceyl., MEng Asian I.T., Bangkok, DEng Tokyo Sr. Lectr.

Lee, Jin, BSc Manc., MEng Asian I.T., Bangkok, DEng Tokyo Sr. Lectr.

Lim Siow Yong, BEng Liv., PhD Liv. Sr. Lectr.

Lo, Edmond Y.-M., BSc Cal.Tech., MSc Cal.Tech., PhD M.I.T. Sr. Lectr.

Luk, James Y. K., BSc Chinese HK, MEngSc NSW, PhD La Trobe, FIEAust Assoc. Prof.

Lum Kit Meng, BEng NU Singapore, MSc NU Singapore, MSE Texas Sr. Lectr.

Olszewski, Piotr S., MgrInz T.U.Warsaw, DrInz T.U.Warsaw Sr. Lectr.

Shuy Eng Ban, BE W.Aust., MSc Sing., PhD Qld. Sr. Lectr.

Tan Soon Keat, BE Auck., ME Auck., PhD Auck. Sr. Lectr.

Tan Yan Weng, BE Monash, MEngSc Monash Sr. Lectr.

Tay Joo Hwa, BS Natnl.Taiwan, MS Cinc., PhD Tor. Prof.; Head*

Wilson, Francis, BSc Liv., PhD Liv. Sr. Lectr.

Wong, Tommy S. W., BSc Leeds, MSc Birm., PhD NU Singapore, FGS Sr. Lectr.

Wong Yiik Diew, BE Cant., PhD Cant. Sr. Lectr.

Other Staff: 1 Lectr.; 2 Res. Fellows; 1 Postdoctoral Fellow; 1 Adjunct Assoc. Prof.

Research: biotechnological application on wastewater treatment; coastal management and sediment transport; urban stormwater management; waste recycling and reuse

Communication Studies

Tel: 799 1333 Fax: 791 3082

Communication Research

Tel: 799 6108 Fax: 792 4329

Choi, Alfred S. K., BA York(Can.), MA York(Can.), PhD York(Can.) Sr. Lectr.

Holaday, Duncan A., BA Wesleyan, MA Cornell, PhD Penn. Assoc. Prof.; Head*

Kuo, Eddie C.-Y., BA Natnl.Chengchi, MA Hawaii, PhD Minn. Prof.

Levy, Mark R., BA Johns H., MA Rutgers, MPhil Col. Visiting Prof.

Other Staff: 2 Sr. Fellows; 2 Lectrs.

Research: communication and national integration in China; cultivating unity: media and social reality; cultural identity in global communication; media and agenda management; strategies for refusal: culture and communication

Electronic and Broadcast Media

Tel: 799 6113 Fax: 792 7526

Chua Siew Keng, BA Sing., MA Auck., PhD Auck. Assoc. Prof.; Head*

Hukill, Mark A., BA Wis., MA Hawaii, PhD Hawaii Sr. Lectr.

Liu, Sharon M. K., BA Nan., MA Hull Sr. Lectr.

Other Staff: 2 Sr. Fellows; 2 Lectrs.

Research: broadcasting policies in Asia; film studies; multimedia and worldwide web; telecommunication policies in Asia

Journalism and Publishing

Tel: 799 6109 Fax: 792 4329

Ang Peng Hwa, LLB NU Singapore, MA S.Calif, PhD Mich.State Sr. Lectr.; Head*

Hao Xiaoming, BA Beijing Teachers', MA Chinese Acad.Soc.Sc., MA Missouri, PhD Missouri Sr. Lectr.

Richstad, Jim A., BA Wash., PhD Minn. Visiting Prof.

Other Staff: 6 Lectrs.; 1 Adjunct Sr. Lectr.

Research: media law and ethics; newswork reform movement of civic journalism; online journalism and news story sourcing; political and social use of news in Asia; press freedom indicators

Public and Promotional Communication

Tel: 799 6108 Fax: 792 4329

Firth, Katherine T., BS Chestnut Hill, MEd Mass., EdD Mass.

Other Staff: 5 Lectrs.; 1 Teaching Assoc.; 1 Adjunct Assoc. Prof.

Research: advertising campaign processes; application of integrated marketing communication; interactive multimedia instruction software development; internet marketing possibilities; public relations activities in non-profit enterprises

Education, National Institute of, see

Special Centres, etc

Information Communication Institute of Singapore Siew, David C. K., BEng Sing., MSc Lond., PhD Lond. Sr. Lectr.

Electrical and Electronic Engineering

Tel: 799 5402 Fax: 791 2687

Er Meng Hwa, BEng NU Singapore, PhD Newcastle(NSW) Prof.

Heng, Michael S. H., BA Sing., BSocSc Sing., MSc Lond. Sr. Lectr.

Lai, Phooi Ching, BA Wellesley, EdM Harv., EdD Hawaii Sr. Lectr.

Ng-Lim, Jessica J. P., BA Sing., LLB Lond., LLM Lond. Sr. Lectr.

Tan, Ooi Kiang, BEng NU Singapore, MSc Edin. Sr. Lectr.

Other Staff: 5 Lectrs.; 1 Adjunct Assoc. Prof.; 3 Adjunct Sr. Lectrs.

Circuits and Systems

Tel: 799 5439 Fax: 791 2687

Birlasekaran, Sivaswamy, BE Madr., ME IISc., PhD Qld. Sr. Lectr.

Chang, Joseph S., BEng Monash, PhD Melb. Sr. Lectr.

Chin, Edward H. L., BS Chiao Tung, MSEE Carnegie Tech. Sr. Lectr.

Chua, Hong Chuck alias Hong Chuek, BS Natnl.Taiwan, MSc Lond. Sr. Lectr.

Do, Manh Anh, BSc Saigon, BE Cant., PhD Cant., FIEE Assoc. Prof.; Head*

Jong, Ching Chuen, BSc(Eng) Lond., PhD Lond. Sr. Lectr.

Koh, Liang Mong, BSc Salf., PhD UMIST Sr. Lectr.

Lam, Yvonne Y. H., BSc Aston, MSc S'ton. Sr. Lectr.

Lau, Kim Teen, BSEE Cornell, MEng Cornell Sr. Lectr.

Lim, Meng Hiot, BS S.Carolina, MS S.Carolina, PhD S.Carolina Sr. Lectr.

Liu, Po-Ching, BSEE Natnl.Taiwan, MSEE Rice, PhD Rice Assoc. Prof.

Ng, Lian Soon, BEng NU Singapore, MSc S'ton. Sr. Lectr.

Ong, Vincent K. S., BEng NU Singapore, MEng NU Singapore, PhD NU Singapore Sr. Lectr.

Ooi, Tian Hock, BS Natnl.Taiwan, MS Natnl.Taiwan Assoc. Prof.

Rofail, Samir S., BSEE Cairo, BS Ain Shams, MASc Wat., PhD Wat. Sr. Lectr.

Siek, L. alias Hsueh L., BASc Ott., MEngSc NSW Sr. Lectr.

Tan, Han Ngee, SB M.I.T., SM M.I.T., PhD M.I.T. Sr. Lectr.

Tang, Hung Kei, BSc(Eng) Qu., MSc Lond. Sr. Lectr.

Tong, Yit Chow, BE Melb., PhD Melb. Assoc. Prof.

Wong, Eddie M. C., BSc Manc., MSc Manc., PhD UMIST Sr. Lectr.

Wong-Ho, Duan Juat, BEng Sing., MSEE N.Y.State Sr. Lectr.

Other Staff: 4 Lectrs.; 1 Postdoctoral Fellow; 2 Adjunct Sr. Lectrs.

Research: IC CAD tools and automation; IC design; system applications

Communication Engineering

Tel: 799 5429 Fax: 791 2687

Arichandran, Kandiah, BSc Lond., BE Malaya, PhD Malaya Assoc. Prof.

Bialkowski, Marek E., MEngSc Warsaw U.T., PhD Warsaw U.T. Assoc. Prof.

Cheng Tee Hiang, BEng Strath., PhD Strath. Sr. Lectr.

Chin, Leonard, BEE C.U.N.Y., MEE C.U.N.Y., MS N.Y. Polytech., PhD N.Y.State Assoc. Prof.

Dubey, Vimal K., BSc Raj., BE IISc., ME IISc., PhD McM. Sr. Lectr.

Fu, Jeffrey S., BS Chung Cheng I.T., MS Chung Cheng I.T., PhD Cornell Sr. Lectr.

Gosling, Ian G., BA Camb., MA Camb., PhD Camb. Sr. Lectr.

Gunawan, Erry, BSc Leeds, MBA Brad., PhD Brad. Sr. Lectr.

Gupta, Surender K., BTech Kharagpur, MS Penn., MA Redlands, MS Wash., DS Wash., FIEE Assoc. Prof.

Hook, Paul R. P., BSc CNAA, MSc Oxf., DPhil Oxf. Sr. Lectr.

Ke Youan, BS Beijing I.T., MS Beijing I.T. Prof. Fellow

Koh, Soo Ngee, BEng Sing., BSc Lond., MSc Lough., PhD Lough. Assoc. Prof.; Head*

Law, Choi Look, BSc(Eng) Lond., PhD Lond. Sr. Lectr.

Li Kwok Hung, BSc Chinese HK, MS Calif., PhD Calif. Sr. Lectr.

Lu Chao, BS Tsing Hua, MSc Manc., PhD UMIST Sr. Lectr.

Lu Yilong, BE Harbin, ME Tsing Hua, PhD Sur. Sr. Lectr.

Ng, Chee Hock, BEng NU Singapore, MS(CompEng) S.Calif. Sr. Lectr.

Oh, Soon Huat, BEng Sing., MSc Lond. Sr. Lectr.

Ong, Jin Teong, BSc(Eng) Lond., MSc Lond., PhD Lond. Assoc. Prof.

Rao, Mukkamala K., BSc Ravi., MSc IIT Bombay, PhD IIT Bombay Sr. Lectr.

Ser, Wee, BSc Lough., PhD Lough. Assoc. Prof.

Siew, David C. K., BEng Sing., MSc Lond. Sr. Lectr.

Sivaprakasapillai, Pratab, BSc(Eng) Ceyl., PhD Lond., FIEE, FIE(SL) Sr. Lectr.

Soong Boon Hee, BE Auck., PhD Newcastle(NSW) Sr. Lectr.

Subramanian, Krishnappa R., BE Madr., MSc Alta. Assoc. Prof.

Tan, Chee Heng, BEng Sing., MSc(IndEng) Sing., MEng NU Singapore Sr. Lectr.

Tan, Soon Hie, BE Auck., PhD Auck. Sr. Lectr.

Yu, Lee Wu, BE Auck., ME Auck. Sr. Lectr.

Zhang, Liren, BE Shandong U.T., MEng S.Aust.I.T., PhD Adel. Sr. Lectr.

Other Staff: 5 Lectrs.; 2 Res. Fellows; 4 Postdoctoral Fellows

Research: microwave circuits, antennas and propagation; modulation, coding and signal processing; personal communication networks; satellite communications

Control and Instrumentation Engineering

Tel: 799 5423 Fax: 791 2687

Chan, John C. Y., BE Cant., ME Cant., PhD Cant. Sr. Lectr.

Chan, Sai Piu, BS Ill., MS Calif., PhD Calif. Sr. Lectr.

Chin, Teck Chai, BSc Strath., MSc(IndEng) NU Singapore, MEng Sheff. Sr. Lectr.

Choo, Fook Hoong, BSc Leeds, MSc Manc. Sr. Lectr.

Chutatape, Opas, BE Chulalongkorn, MSc Alta., PhD Qu. Sr. Lectr.

Devanathan, Rajagopalan, BSc Madr., BE IISc., ME IISc., MSc(Eng) Qu., PhD Qu. Assoc. Prof.

Er, Meng Joo, BEng NU Singapore, MEng NU Singapore, PhD ANU Sr. Lectr.

Ho, Yeong Khing, BSc Strath., MSc Lond. Sr. Lectr.

Krishnan, Shankar M., BE Bom., ME Bom., PhD Rhode I. Sr. Lectr.

Lee Peng Hin, BEng NU Singapore, MSEE S.Calif., MSc(IndEng) NU Singapore Sr. Lectr.

Li Ziqing, BS Hunan, MS Natnl.U.Defence Technol.(China), PhD Sur. Sr. Lectr.

Mahmoud, Magdi S., BSEE Cairo, MSEE Cairo, PhD Cairo, FIEE Visiting Prof.

Saratchandran, Paramasivan, BSc(Eng) Kerala, MTech Kharagpur, MSc City(UK), DPhil Oxf. Assoc. Prof.

Sim, Siong Leng, MSc Lond. Sr. Lectr.

Soh, Cheong Boon, BE Monash, PhD Monash Sr. Lectr.

Soh, William Y. C., BE Cant., PhD Newcastle(NSW) Assoc. Prof.; Head*

Song, Qing, BS Harbin Shipbldg.Engin., MS Dalian Maritime, PhD Strath. Sr. Lectr.

Sundararajan, Narasimhan, BE Madr., MTech IIT Madras, PhD Ill. Assoc. Prof.

Sung, Eric, BEng Sing., MSEE Wis. Sr. Lectr.

Tan, Yoke Lin, BEng NU Singapore, MSc Lond. Sr. Lectr.

Teoh, Eam Khwang, BE Auck., ME Auck., PhD Newcastle(NSW) Assoc. Prof.

Wang, Dan Wei, BE S.China Tech., MSE Mich., PhD Mich. Sr. Lectr.

Wang, Han, BE N.E.Heavy Machinery Inst., Qiqihaer, PhD Leeds Sr. Lectr.

Wang, Jianliang, BE Beijing I.T., MS Johns H., PhD Johns H. Sr. Lectr.

Wen, Changyun, BE Xi'an Jiaotong, PhD Newcastle(NSW) Sr. Lectr.

Xie Lihua, BE E.China Inst.Eng., ME E.China Inst.Technol., PhD Newcastle(NSW) Sr. Lectr.

Yan Wei-Yong, BS Nankai, MS Chinese Acad.Sc., PhD ANU Sr. Lectr.

Zribi, Mohamed, BSEE Houston, MSEE Purdue, PhD Purdue Sr. Lectr.

Other Staff: 6 Lectrs.; 2 Res. Fellows; 2 Postdoctoral Fellows

Research: computer vision and machine intelligence; control theory and applications; intelligent instrumentation systems; robotics and automation

Information Communication Institute of Singapore

Ang, Yew Hock, BSc Strath., PhD Strath. Sr. Lectr.

Siew, David C. K., BEng Sing., MSc Lond. Dir.*

Sng, Hock San, BEng NU Singapore, MSc(ElectEng) NU Singapore Sr. Lectr.

Other Staff: 6 Lectrs.

Research: multimedia ATM communication; software technology

Information Engineering

Tel: 799 5399 Fax: 791 2687

Babri, Haroon A., BSc *Lahore UET*, MSEE *Penn.*, PhD *Penn.* Sr. Lectr.

Bi, Guoan, BS *Dalian I.T.*, MSc *Essex*, PhD *Essex* Sr. Lectr.

Chan, Chee Keong, BEng *NU Singapore*, MSc *Lond.* Sr. Lectr.

Chan, Choong Wah, BSc *CNAA*, MSc *Manc.*, PhD *UMIST* Sr. Lectr.

Chiam, Tee Chye, BSc *Monash*, PhD *Monash* Sr. Lectr.

Chua Hock Guan, BEng *NU Singapore*, MSc *Purdue* Sr. Lectr.

Er Meng Hwa, BEng *NU Singapore*, PhD *Newcastle(NSW)* Prof.

Falkowski, Bogdan J., MgrInz *T.U.Warsaw*, PhD *Portland State* Sr. Lectr.

Gan, Woon Seng, BEng *Strath.*, PhD *Strath.* Sr. Lectr.

Goh, Wee Leng, BEng *Sing.*, MSEE *Wis.* Assoc. Prof.

Kong, Hinny P. H., BS *Nebraska*, MS *Mass.* Sr. Lectr.

Kot, Alex C. C., BSEE *Roch.*, MBA *Roch.*, MS *Rhode I.*, PhD *Rhode I.* Sr. Lectr.; Head*

Liu, Jun, BS *Xi'an Jiaotong*, MS *Xi'an Jiaotong*, PhD *Oakland* Sr. Lectr.

Ma Kai Kuang, BE *Chung Yuan*, MSEE *Duke*, PhD *N.Carolina State* Sr. Lectr.

Mital, Dinesh P., BTech *IIT Kanpur*, MS *N.Y.State*, PhD *N.Y.State*, FIEE Assoc. Prof.

Ong, Patrick K. S., BSc *S'ton.*, MSc *Lond.* Sr. Lectr.

Tan, Boon Tiong, BEng *NU Singapore*, MSEE *Wis.* Sr. Lectr.

Tan, Daniel T. H., BSc *Aston*, PhD *UMIST* Sr. Lectr.

Toh, Guan Nge, BEng *NU Singapore*, MSc *Manc.* Sr. Lectr.

Other Staff: 14 Lectrs.; 3 Postdoctoral Fellows

Research: information systems engineering; neural networks and applications

Microelectronics

Tel: 799 5637 Fax: 791 2687

Ahn, Jaeshin, BS *Seoul*, MSc *Alta.*, PhD *Alta.* Sr. Lectr.

Au Yeung Tin Cheung, BSc *HK*, MPhil *HK*, PhD *HK* Sr. Lectr.

Choo, Seok Cheow, PPA, BSc(Eng) *Lond.*, PhD *Lond.* Prof.

Ho, Anthony T. S., BSc *CNAA*, MSc *Lond.*, PhD *Lond.*, FIEE Sr. Lectr.

Kam, Chan Hin, BEng *Sing.*, MSc *Nan.*, MSEE *S.Calif.*, PhD *NU Singapore* Sr. Lectr.

Lam, Yee Loy, BEng *NU Singapore*, MSc(IndEng) *NU Singapore*, MSE *Mich.*, PhD *Mich.* Sr. Lectr.

Lim, Tuan Kay, BSc *Nan.*, MASc *Wat.*, PhD *McM.* Sr. Lectr.

Ng Geok Ing, BSE *Mich.*, MSE *Mich.*, PhD *Mich.* Sr. Lectr.

Prasad, Krishnamachar, BE *B'lore.*, MTech *IIT Madras*, PhD *W.Aust.* Sr. Lectr.

Shi, Xu, BS *Tongji*, PhD *Reading* Sr. Lectr.

Swaminathan, Sundaram, BSc *Calc.*, BTech *Calc.*, MTech *Calc.*, PhD *Warw.* Sr. Lectr.

Tam, S. C., BSc(Eng) *HK*, MSc *Lond.*, PhD *Lond.*, FIP Assoc. Prof.

Tan, Hong Siang, BSc(Eng) *Lond.*, MSEE *M.I.T.*, PhD *McG.*, FIEE Prof.; Head*

Tan, Ooi Kiang, BEng *NU Singapore*, MSc *Edin.* Sr. Lectr.

Tay Beng Kang, MSc(ElectEng) *NU Singapore* Sr. Lectr.

Tjin, Swee Chuan, BSc *New Eng.(U.S.A.)*, PhD *Tas.* Sr. Lectr.

Tse, Man Siu, BSc *HK*, MPhil *Chinese HK* Sr. Lectr.

Yoon, Soon Fatt, BEng *Wales*, PhD *Wales* Assoc. Prof.

Zhang, Dao Hua, BS *Shandong*, MS *Shandong*, PhD *NSW* Sr. Lectr.

Zhou Yan, BS *Changsha I.T.*, ME *Changsha I.T.*, PhD *Glas.* Sr. Lectr.

Zhu, Weiguang, BS *Shanghai Jiaotong*, MS *Shanghai Jiaotong*, PhD *Purdue* Sr. Lectr.

Other Staff: 10 Lectrs.

Research: III-V compound semiconductor materials and devices; diamond and diamond-like carbon; photonics; sensors and actuators; silicon process and devices

Power Engineering

Tel: 799 5406 Fax: 791 2687

Chan, David T. W., BS *Natnl.Taiwan*, MSc *Manc.* Sr. Lectr.

Choi, San Shing, BE *Cant.*, PhD *Cant.* Assoc. Prof.; Head*

Duggal, Bal Raj, BE *Delhi*, MScTech *Manc.*, PhD *UMIST* Sr. Lectr.

Foo, Chek Fok, BSc *Manc.*, MSc *Manc.*, PhD *UMIST* Sr. Lectr.

Goel, Lalit Kumar, BSc *Delhi*, BTech *Kakatiya*, MSc *Sask.*, PhD *Sask.* Sr. Lectr.

Gooi, Hoay Beng, BS *Natnl.Taiwan*, MScE *New Br.*, PhD *Ohio State* Sr. Lectr.

Lee, Tat Man, BSc(Econ) *Lond.*, MSc *Lond.*, BSc(Eng) *HK* Sr. Lectr.

Lie Tek Tjing, BS *Oklahoma State*, MS *Mich.State*, PhD *Mich.State* Sr. Lectr.

Luo, Fang Lin, BS *Sichuan*, PhD *Camb.* Sr. Lectr.

Maswood, Ali I., BEng *Moscow Power Inst.*, MEng *Moscow Power Inst.*, PhD *C'dia.* Sr. Lectr.

Shrestha, Govinda B., BEE *Jad.*, MBA *Hawaii*, MS *Rensselaer*, PhD *Virginia Polytech.* Sr. Lectr.

Sng, Yeow Hong, BSc *Strath.*, MSc *Manc.* Sr. Lectr.

Teo, Cheng Yu, BS *Natnl.Taiwan*, MSc *Lond.*, FIEE Assoc. Prof.

Wang, Youyi, BE *Beijing U.S.T.*, MS *Tsing Hua*, PhD *Newcastle(NSW)* Sr. Lectr.

Zhou, Rujing, BS *Huazhong U.S.T.*, MS *Huazhong U.S.T.*, PhD *Syd.* Sr. Lectr.

Other Staff: 3 Lectrs.; 6 Res. Fellows; 5 Postdoctoral Fellows

Research: power electronics and drives systems; power system control and operations

Signal Processing, Centre for

Ser, Wee, Bsc *Lough.*, PhD *Lough.* Dir.*

Other Staff: 8 Res. Fellows

Research: adaptive signal processing; audio processing; DSP hardware and implementation; image and video processing; speech processing

Manufacturing Technology, Gintic Institute of, see Special Centres, etc

Mechanical and Production Engineering

Tel: 799 5487 Fax: 791 1859

1 Adjunct Prof.; 1 Adjunct Assoc. Prof.

Research: advanced materials and modelling processes; bio materials; biomedical engineering; electronics packaging; intelligent manufacturing systems; intelligent machines and robotics; micro-electromechanical systems; precision engineering; product design and realisation; sensors and actuators; virtual reality and soft computing; vision and control

Biomedical Engineering Research Centre

Tel: 799 6420

Krishnan, Shankar M., BE *Bom.*, ME *Bom.*, PhD *Rhode I.* Dir.*

Engineering Mechanics

Tel: 799 5521 Fax: 792 4062

Ang Hock Eng, BSc *Wales*, MSc *Lond.* Sr. Lectr.

Asundi, Anand K., BTech *IIT Bombay*, MTech *IIT Bombay*, PhD *N.Y.State* Assoc. Prof.

Chai Gin Boay, BSc *Strath.*, PhD *Strath.* Sr. Lectr.

Chan Yiu Wing, BSc *Leeds*, MSc *Manc.* Sr. Lectr.

Chen Guang, BE *Tsing Hua*, MS *Tsing Hua*, PhD *Georgia I.T.* Sr. Lectr.

Cheung, John S. T., BSc(Eng) *HK*, PhD *Lond.* Assoc. Prof.

Chou Siaw Meng, BEng *Strath.*, PhD *Strath.* Sr. Lectr.

Cotterell, Brian, BSc(Eng) *Lond.*, PhD *Camb.* Visiting Prof.

Du, Hejun, BE *Nanjing Aeron.Inst.*, ME *Nanjing Aeron.Inst.*, PhD *Lond.* Sr. Lectr.

Fan Hui, BS *Tsing Hua*, MS *Tsing Hua*, PhD *Ill.* Sr. Lectr.

Fok Wing Chau, BSc *Strath.*, PhD *Strath.*, FIMechE Assoc. Prof.

Hoon Kay Hiang, BSc *Strath.*, PhD *Strath.* Sr. Lectr.

Khong Poh Wah, BSc *Strath.*, PhD *Strath.* Sr. Lectr.

Liew Kim Meow, BS *Mich.Tech.*, MEng *NU Singapore*, PhD *NU Singapore* Sr. Lectr.

Lim Geok Hian, BSc(Eng) *Lond.*, MSc *Lond.* Sr. Lectr.

Lim Tau Meng, BSc *Strath.*, PhD *Strath.* Sr. Lectr.

Lin Rongming, BS *Zhejiang*, PhD *Lond.* Sr. Lectr.

Ling Shih Fu, BS *Cheng Kung*, MSME *Purdue*, PhD *Purdue* Assoc. Prof.; Head*

Low Kin Huat, BS *Cheng Kung*, MASc *Wat.*, PhD *Wat.* Sr. Lectr.

Ng Heong Wah, BEng *Liv.*, PhD *Liv.* Sr. Lectr.

Ong Jor Huat, BSc *Nott.*, PhD *Nott.* Sr. Lectr.

Ong Lin Seng, BSc *Strath.*, PhD *Strath.* Sr. Lectr.

Pang, John H. L., BSc *Strath.*, PhD *Strath.* Sr. Lectr.

Quek Meng Yin, BSc *Strath.*, SM *M.I.T.* Sr. Lectr.

Seah Leong Keey, BSc *Strath.*, PhD *Strath.* Sr. Lectr.

Senanayake, Rohana S. K., BSc(Eng) *Ceyl.*, MSc *Aston* Sr. Lectr.

Shu Dongwei, BS *Peking*, MS *Peking*, PhD *Camb.* Sr. Lectr.

Tan Soon Huat, BEng *Strath.*, PhD *Strath.* Sr. Lectr.

Teo Ee Chon, BSc *Nott.*, MSc *Nott.*, PhD *Strath.* Sr. Lectr.

Wu Qunli, BS *Beijing*, MS *Chinese Acad.Sc.*, PhD *Syd.* Sr. Lectr.

Xiao, Zhongmin, BS *China U.S.T.*, MS *Chinese Acad.Sc.*, MS *Rutgers*, PhD *Rutgers* Sr. Lectr.

Yeo, Song Huat, BSc *Birm.*, PhD *Birm.* Sr. Lectr.

Yi, Sung, BS *Hanyang*, MS *Wash.*, PhD *Ill.* Sr. Lectr.

Other Staff: 7 Lectrs.; 1 Teaching Fellow; 10 Res. Fellows; 8 Postdoctoral Fellows

Research: kinematics and dynamics of machinery: design and analysis of compact mechanical system; mechanics of structures: analysis of structural problems; structural dynamics and acoustics: machine monitoring, vibration and noise pollution control

Manufacturing Engineering

Tel: 799 1219 Fax: 792 4062

Batchelor, Andrew W., BSc(Eng) *Lond.*, PhD *Lond.* Sr. Lectr.

Boey, Freddy Y. C., BE *Monash*, PhD *NU Singapore* Assoc. Prof.

Chian, Kerm Sin, BSc *Manc.*, PhD *UMIST.* Sr. Lectr.

Chua Chee Kai, BEng *NU Singapore*, MSc *NU Singapore*, PhD *Nan.Tech.* Sr. Lectr.

Gan, Jacob G. K., BEng *Sing.*, MSE *Mich.*, PhD *Mich.* Sr. Lectr.

Hsu Jong-Ping, BS *Cheng Kung*, MS *Houston*, PhD *Purdue* Visiting Prof.

Jana, Sukumar, BE *Calc.*, MS *Ill.*, PhD *Ill.*, FIM Assoc. Prof.

Khoo Li Pheng, BEng *Tokyo*, MSc *NU Singapore*, PhD *Wales* Assoc. Prof.

Khor Khiam Aik, BSc *Monash*, PhD *Monash* Sr. Lectr.

Lam Yee Cheong, BE *Melb.*, PhD *Melb.* Assoc. Prof.

Lee, Stephen S. G., BEng *Sing.*, MSc *Manc.*, PhD *Nan.Tech.* Assoc. Prof.

Lee Yong Tsui, BSc *Leeds*, MS *Roch.*, PhD *Leeds* Sr. Lectr.

Leong Kah Fai, BEng *NU Singapore*, MSE *Stan.*, MSME *Stan.* Sr. Lectr.

Lim, Lennie E. N., BSc *Sur.*, PhD *Sur.* Prof.

Lim Teow Ek, BSc *Aston*, MSc *NU Singapore*, PhD *Aston* Sr. Lectr.

Loh Nee Lam, BEng Liv., PhD Liv., FIM   Assoc. Prof.

Loh Ngiap Hiang, BSc Aston, PhD Aston   Assoc. Prof.

Lye Sun Woh, BSc Bath, PhD Bath   Assoc. Prof.

Ngoi, Bryan K. A., BEng NU Singapore, PhD Cant.   Sr. Lectr.

Nguyen Phu Hung, BS Mich., MS Mich., PhD Calif.   Sr. Lectr.

Ong Nan Shing, BSc Manc., MSc NU Singapore, PhD Nan.Tech.   Sr. Lectr.

Phung, Viet, BE Qld., MEngSc Monash   Sr. Lectr.

Tam Kam Chiu, BE Monash, PhD Monash   Sr. Lectr.

Tan Ming Jen, BSc(Eng) Lond., PhD Lond.   Sr. Lectr.

Taplin, David, BSc Aston, DPhil Oxf., DSc Aston, MA, FIM, FIMechE   Visiting Prof.

Tay Meng Leong, BEng Sing., MSc Lond.   Sr. Lectr.

Teoh Lean Lee, BAppSc Melb., MSc Aston   Assoc. Prof.

Thiruvarudchelvan, Sinnathamby, BSc(Eng) Ceyl., PhD Lond.   Assoc. Prof.

Tor Shu Beng, BSc CNAA, PhD CNAA   Sr. Lectr.

Venkatesh, Vellore C., BSc Mys., PhD Paris, DSc Paris VI   Visiting Prof.

Wong, Brian S., BSc Manc., MSc Manc., PhD UMIST   Sr. Lectr.

Yang Lin Jiang, BS Cheng Kung, ME Cant., PhD NU Singapore, FIM   Assoc. Prof.

Yeo Swee Hock, BSc(Eng) Lond., MEng NU Singapore, PhD NU Singapore   Sr. Lectr.

Yeong Hin Yuen, BEng Sing., MSc Aston   Assoc. Prof.

Yue Chee Yoon, BE Monash, PhD Monash   Assoc. Prof.; Head*

Zhou, Wei, BS Tsing Hua, PhD Camb.   Sr. Lectr.

Other Staff: 2 Lectrs.; 1 Sr. Fellow; 4 Res. Fellows; 7 Postdoctoral Fellows

Research: manufacturing: laser processing, machining, metal forming, and CAD/CAM; materials: polymers and composites, metal matrix composites and engineering ceramics

Robotics Research Centre

Tel: 799 6317

Seet, Gerald G. L., BSc CNAA, MSc Dund., PhD Aston   Dir.*

Systems and Engineering Management

Tel: 799 5502 Fax: 792 4062

Britton, Graeme A., BE Cant., PhD Cant., FIMechE   Sr. Lectr.

Cheah, Diane S. L., BA Monash, MA Syd., PhD Aston   Sr. Lectr.

Chua, Chee Kai, BEng NU Singapore, MSc NU Singapore, PhD Nan.Tech.   Sr. Lectr.

Chua, Patrick S. K., BEng Liv., PhD Liv.   Sr. Lectr.

De Souza, Robert B. R., BSc CNAA, MSc Lough., PhD Lough.   Sr. Lectr.

Fok Sai Cheong, BASc Ott., PhD Monash   Sr. Lectr.

Foo Check Teck, LLB Lond., MBA City(UK), PhD St And.   Sr. Lectr.

Kam Booi Chung, BE Malaya, BSc(Econ) Lond., MBA Br.Col.   Sr. Lectr.

Koh, Christopher K. H., BEng Sing., MSE(MechEng) Mich., MSE(ElectEng) Mich., PhD Mich.   Sr. Lectr.

Lau, Michael W. S., BEng Sing., MSc NU Singapore   Sr. Lectr.

Lew Sin Chye, BE Adel., LLB Lond., MSc Lond.   Sr. Lectr.

Lim Choon Seng, BSc Strath., MSc Manc., PhD UMIST   Sr. Lectr.

Lim Kee Yong, BSc Lond., MSc Lond., PhD Lond.   Sr. Lectr.

Lim, Samuel Y. E., BSc Strath., PhD Strath.   Sr. Lectr.

Ling, Anna K. T., BA HK, MA HK, MPhil Leeds, PhD Leeds   Assoc. Prof.

Lwin, Daniel Tint, BEng Rangoon I.T., MASc Windsor   Assoc. Prof.

Ng Wan Sing, BEng NU Singapore, MEng NU Singapore, PhD Lond.   Sr. Lectr.

Seet, Gerald G. L., BSc CNAA, MSc Dund., PhD Aston   Sr. Lectr.

Sim Siang Kok, BSc Newcastle(UK), MSc Essex   Sr. Lectr.

Spedding, Trevor A., BSc CNAA, PhD CNAA   Sr. Lectr.

Teo Ming Yeong, BSc Leeds, SM M.I.T.   Sr. Lectr.

Wu Zhang, BS Huazhong U.S.T., MEng McM., PhD McM.   Sr. Lectr.

Xie Ming, BE China Textile, PhD Rennes   Sr. Lectr.

Yap Kian Tong, BEng Sing., MSc Sing., PhD Wis.   Assoc. Prof.

Yeo Khim Teck, BEng Sing., MBA Strath., MSc Manc., PhD UMIST   Assoc. Prof.; Head*

Yu Wei Shin, BE Cant., PhD Cant.   Assoc. Prof.

Other Staff: 5 Lectrs.; 4 Res. Fellows; 4 Postdoctoral Fellows

Thermal and Fluids Engineering

Tel: 799 5588 Fax: 792 4062

Ameen, Ahmadul, BSc(Engin) Dacca, MSc Strath., FIMechE   Sr. Lectr.

Bong Tet Yin, BEng Bandung I.T., MSME Kentucky, PhD Kentucky   Assoc. Prof.

Chan Siew Hwa, BS Natnl.Taiwan, MSc Birm., PhD Lond.   Sr. Lectr.

Chan Swee Kim, BSc(Eng) Lond., PhD Camb.   Sr. Lectr.

Chan Weng Kong, BEng Sing., DrIng École Nat.Sup.d'Arts & Métiers, Paris   Assoc. Prof.; Head*

Chu Hung, BSME Oklahoma, MSME Oklahoma, PhD Oklahoma   Assoc. Prof.

Chua Leok Poh, BE Newcastle(NSW), PhD Newcastle(NSW)   Sr. Lectr.

Damodaran, Murali, BTech IIT Kanpur, MS Cornell, PhD Cornell   Sr. Lectr.

Ghista, Dhanjoo N., BE Bom., MS Stan., PhD Stan.   Visiting Prof.

Gong, Thomas H., BE Wuhan Water Transportation Eng., MS Delaware, PhD Delaware   Sr. Lectr.

Ho Hiang Kwee, BSc Newcastle(UK), SM M.I.T.   Sr. Lectr.

Huang Xiaoyang, BS Nanjing, MS Chinese Acad.Sc., PhD Camb.   Sr. Lectr.

Lam Chung Yau, BSc(Eng) Lond., PhD Lond.   Sr. Lectr.

Leong Kai Choong, BEng NU Singapore, MSME Calif.   Sr. Lectr.

Liu Chang Yu, BS Chinese Naval Coll., MS Colorado State, PhD Colorado State   Prof.

Low, Jeffrey C. F., BSc Sur., MSc Newcastle(UK)   Sr. Lectr.

Low Seow Chay, BEng Sing., MSc Manc., PhD UMIST   Assoc. Prof.

Lua Aik Chong, BEng Sheff., PhD Sheff.   Sr. Lectr.

Nathan, Kamal G., BSc(Eng) Ceyl., MBA Adel., PhD Lond., FIEAust, FIMechE   Assoc. Prof.

Ng Yin Kwee, BEng Newcastle(UK), PhD Camb.   Sr. Lectr.

Ooi Kim Tiow, BEng Strath., PhD Strath.   Sr. Lectr.

Ramli b Osman, BESc W.Ont., MSc NU Singapore   Sr. Lectr.

Tan Fock Lai, BEng NU Singapore, MSME Rensselaer   Sr. Lectr.

Tay Seow Ngie, BEng Sing., MSc Manc., PhD CNAA   Sr. Lectr.

Teh Soo Lee, BAppSc W.Aust.I.T., MEngSc Newcastle(NSW), PhD NSW   Sr. Lectr.

Toh Kok Chuan, BE Auck., MSME Stan.   Sr. Lectr.

Tou, Stephen K. W., BSc(Eng) Qu., MEng C'dia., PhD City(UK)   Assoc. Prof.

Tso Chih Ping, BTech Lough., SM M.I.T., PhD Calif., FIMechE   Assoc. Prof.

Wong Teck Neng, BEng Strath., PhD Strath.   Sr. Lectr.

Wong Yew Wah, BEng Sing., MSc NU Singapore   Sr. Lectr.

Yeo Joon Hock, BSc Strath., PhD Lond.   Sr. Lectr.

Yeung, William W. H., BASc Br.Col., MASc Br.Col., PhD Br.Col.   Sr. Lectr.

Yu, Simon C. M., BEng Lond., PhD Lond.   Sr. Lectr.

Other Staff: 2 Lectrs.; 1 Res. Fellow; 6 Postdoctoral Fellows

Research: energy and environment: energy conservation, environmental impact and pollution control; flow measurement techniques: measurement techniques and instrumentation; micro thermo fluids systems: fluid mechanics and heat transfer in micro systems; thermal management of electronic packaging: design of heat sinks, thermal design and management

SPECIAL CENTRES, ETC

Chinese Language and Culture, Centre for

Tel: 799 6301 Fax: 792 2334

Chew Cheng Hai, BA Nan., MA Chinese HK, PhD NU Singapore   Assoc. Prof.; Dir.*

Lu Jianming,   Visiting Prof.

Woon Wee Lee, BA Nan., MA Nan., PhD Leeds   Sr. Lectr.

Other Staff: 4 Lectrs.; 2 Res. Fellows

Continuing Education, Centre for

Tel: 799 1279 Fax: 791 6178

Lwin, Daniel Tint, BEng Rangoon I.T., MASc Windsor   Assoc. Prof.

Environmental Technology Institute

Tel: 794 1500 Fax: 792 1291

Brouzes, Raymond, BSc Laur., MSc McG., PhD McG.   Dir.*

Research: air emission control; environmental management tools; environmental services; solid waste; water

Graphics and Imaging Technology, Centre for

Tel: 799 5443 Fax: 792 4117

Seah Hock Soon, BEng NU Singapore, MSc Lond.   Dir.*

Other Staff: 2 Res. Fellows; 3 Postdoctoral Fellows

Research: computer animation: visual realism, physically based, ease-of-use; computer vision and imaging: object recognition and tracking, document processing; geographical information system: map analysis, resource optimisation and scheduling; modelling and visualisation of shapes; multimedia: image/video retrieval and multimedia databases

Innovation Centre

Tel: 799 5533 Fax: 792 1737

Yeong Hin Yuen, BEng Sing., MSc Aston   Dir.*

Research: advanced audio processing, acoustical imaging; environmental technology, waste management, recycling; information technology, graphic imaging, virtual reality; intelligent automation, machine version technology; systems design, management information systems

Manufacturing Technology, Gintic Institute of

Tel: 793 8200 Fax: 791 2927

Carpay, F. M. A., MSc Utrecht, PhD Utrecht   Managing Dir.*

Automation Technology Division

Tel: 793 8277 Fax: 791 2927

Fong, A. M., BSc Lond., PhD Lond.   Div. Dir.*

Manufacturing Information Technology Division

Tel: 793 8280 Fax: 791 2927

Gay, R. K. L., MEng Sheff., PhD Sheff.   Dir., Grad. Programmes

Yee Hsun, BSEE MBA PhD

Process Technology Division

Tel: 793 8283 Fax: 791 2927

Lee, L. C., BE Malaya, MSc Lond., PhD Lond. Div. Dir.*

Network Technology Research Centre

Tel: 799 5418 Fax: 792 6894

Subramanian, Krishnappa R., BE Madr., MSc Alta. Dir.*

Research: broadband network design; multimedia systems and networks; network performance; network protocol development

EDUCATION, NATIONAL INSTITUTE OF

Arts

Tel: 460 5115 Fax: 469 8433

Chinese Language and Culture

Tel: 460 5101 Fax: 469 8433

Chan, Chiu Ming, BA HK, MA Wis., PhD Wis. Sr. Lectr.

Chew, Cheng Hai, BA Nan., MA Chinese HK, PhD NU Singapore Assoc. Prof.; Head*

Chia, Shih Yar, BA Nan., MA Natnl.Taiwan, PhD NU Singapore Sr. Lectr.

Leong, Weng Kee, BA Malaya, MA HK, PhD Natnl.Taiwan Sr. Lectr.

Neo, Eng Guan, BA Nan., MA Natnl.Taiwan Lectr.

Ong, Yong Peng, BA Nan., MA Natnl.Taiwan, PhD Nan.Tech. Sr. Lectr.

Woon, Wee Lee, BA Nan., MA Nan., PhD Leeds Sr. Lectr.

Other Staff: 1 Sr. Fellow; 3 Lectrs.; 1 Sr. Tutor

Research: Chinese grammar and linguistics: lexicology, phonology, etymology and semantics; Chinese literature and philosophy: literary theory and criticism, theory and practice of translation; Chinese literature, language and culture of Singapore; Southeast Asian Chinese language and dialects; Southeast Asian Chinese literature, history, folklore, customs and beliefs

English Language and Applied Linguistics

Tel: 460 5101 Fax: 469 8433

Brown, Adam A., MA Edin., PhD Edin. Sr. Lectr.

Chew Ghim Lian, P., BA Sing., MA Hawaii, PhD Macq. Sr. Lectr.

Deterding, David H., BA Durh., MPhil Camb., PhD Camb. Sr. Lectr.

Goatly, Andrew P., BA Oxf., MA Oxf., MA Lond., PhD Lond. Sr. Lectr.

Hvitfeldt, Christina G. O., BSEd N.Illinois, MA Wis., PhD Wis. Sr. Lectr.

Kramer-Dahl, Anneliese, BA Mainz, MA Mich., PhD Mich. Sr. Lectr.

Poedjosoedarmo, Gloria R., BA Penn., MA Cornell, PhD Cornell Sr. Lectr.

Saravanan, Vanithamani, BA Sing., MA Leeds, PhD Monash Sr. Lectr.

Seet Beng Hean, O., BA Malaya, MA Essex, PhD NU Singapore Sr. Lectr.

Steele-Skuja, Rita V., BA Well., MA Well., MA Birm., PhD Lond. Sr. Lectr.; Head*

Wong Yeang Lam, R., BA Sing., MEd NU Singapore, PhD Tor. Sr. Lectr. (on leave)

Yan, Victoria H., BA Sing., MEd Col., EdD Col. Sr. Lectr.

Other Staff: 1 Sr. Fellow; 17 Lectrs.; 6 Teaching Fellows

Research: research and development of the NIE computerised English language test (NIE-CELT); six-country project on language and literacy

Geography

Tel: 460 5141 Fax: 469 2427

Goh, Kim Chuan, BA Malaya, MA Malaya, PhD Leeds Assoc. Prof.; Head*

Lee, Christine, BA Sing., MA Col., MEd Col., EdD Col. Sr. Lectr.

Nichol, Janet E., BSc Lond., MA Colorado, PhD Aston Sr. Lectr.

Singh, Mohan, BA Agra, MA Agra, MPhil Panjab, PhD ANU Sr. Lectr.

Teh, Puan Loon, G., BA Malaya, MEd W.Aust.I.T., PhD Curtin Sr. Lectr.

Wong, Shuang Yann, BA Sci.U.Malaysia, MA Hiroshima, PhD Wat. Sr. Lectr.

Wong, Tai Chee, BA Paris, MA Paris, PhD ANU Sr. Lectr.

Yee, Sze Onn, BA Malaya, MA Mich.State, MA Otago Sr. Lectr.

Other Staff: 5 Lectrs.

Research: assessment of urban microclimate, air pollution and the urban heat island; classroom organisation, co-operative learning and school effectiveness; regional economic development, industry and change in the growth zones of Malaysia, Singapore and Indonesia; remote sensing of tropical forest in southeast Asia; socio-economic variables and Singapore's population : health and ageing

History

Tel: 460 5603 Fax: 463 5840

Crosswell, Daniel K. R., BA Windsor, MA W.Mich., PhD Kansas State Sr. Lectr.

Loh May Chan, G., MEd NU Singapore, BA Qld., PhD Qld. Sr. Lectr.; Head*

Wang, Zhenping, MA Prin., PhD Prin. Sr. Lectr.

Other Staff: 5 Lectrs.; 2 Teaching Assocs.; 1 Adjunct Assoc. Prof.; 1 Adjunct Sr. Lectr.

Research: Australian history; contemporary South Asian history (e.g. partition and its aftermath); relations between China and Japan in premodern times; Southeast Asian history (e.g. entrepreneurship, maritime history)

Literature and Drama

Tel: 460 5603 Fax: 463 5840

Chin, Woon Ping, BA Malaya, MA Toledo(Ohio), PhD Toledo(Ohio) Assoc. Prof.

De Souza, D., BA Sing., MA Sing., PhD NU Singapore Sr. Lectr.

Hazell, Stephen, BA Oxf., PhD Lond. Sr. Lectr.

Kirpal, Singh, BA Sing., MA Sing., PhD Adel. Assoc. Prof.; Head*

Tombrello, Drew, BFA Alabama, MFA Alabama Sr. Lectr.

Yeo Cheng Chuan, R., BA Sing., MA Lond. Sr. Lectr.

Other Staff: 1 Sr. Fellow; 3 Lectrs.; 1 Teaching Fellow; 1 Adjunct Assoc. Prof.

Research: community theatre in Australia and ASEAN; feminism and Asian-American literature; intercultural approaches to dramatic production; literature in the Singapore classroom; post-colonial approaches to Southeast Asian literature

Malay Language and Literature

Tel: 460 5603 Fax: 463 5840

Abdullah, Kamsiah, BA Lond., MEd Malaya, PhD Lond. Sr. Lectr.

Other Staff: 3 Lectrs.; 1 Teaching Assoc.

Research: development of Malay language in Singapore; language use and social support network among Malay families; Malay school education in Singapore

Music

Tel: 460 5141 Fax: 469 2427

No staff at present

Research: contemporary computer composition techniques; creative thinking in music; development of the Malay gambus; perception/aural skills development; phenomenology of music

Tamil Language and Literature

Tel: 460 5141 Fax: 469 2427

Kalimuthu, Raniah, BA Madr., MEd NU Singapore, PhD Nan.Tech. Sr. Lectr.

Thinnappan, S. P., BA Madr., MA Madr., MLitt Annam., PhD Annam. Sr. Lectr.

Other Staff: 1 Lectr.; 1 Teaching Assoc.

Visual and Performing Arts

Tel: 460 5140 Fax: 469 2427

Chia, Wei Khuan, BA Nan., BMus Ohio, MMus Cinc., DMA Cinc. Sr. Lectr.

Ho, Hwee Long, MMus Northwestern Sr. Lectr.

Howard, John S., BA Durh., PhD Durh. Assoc. Prof.; Head*

Matthews, John S., MPhil Lond., PhD Lond. Sr. Lectr.

Smith, John W., BFA Flor., MEd Flor., EdD Flor. Sr. Lectr.

Yu, Chen Chee E., MDes RCA, PhD Lond. Sr. Lectr.

Other Staff: 7 Lectrs.; 2 Teaching Fellows; 1 Teaching Assoc.

Research: art curriculum development; contemporary Southeast Asian art; development of children's use of visual media; relationships between Eastern and Western art practices

Education

Tel: 460 5057 Fax: 469 9007

Instructional Science

Tel: 460 5055 Fax: 469 9007

Chen, Ai Yen, BA Malaya, MA N.Y., PhD Indiana Sr. Lectr.; Head*

Goh, Swee Chiew, BA Sing., MEd Bath, PhD Curtin Sr. Lectr. (on leave)

Williams, Michael D., BS Minn., MA Minn., PhD Minn. Sr. Lectr.

Wong, Angela, BSc Sing., MEd Hawaii, PhD Curtin Sr. Lectr.

Wong Siew Koon, P., BSc Malaya, MS(Ed) Indiana, PhD Minn. Sr. Lectr.

Yeap, Lay Leng, BA Malaya, MSL W.Mich., MS(Ed) E.Illinois, EdD Pitt. Sr. Lectr.

Other Staff: 6 Lectrs.; 1 Teaching Fellow; 1 Adjunct Sr. Lectr.; 1 Adjunct Lectr.

Research: cognition-ethnicity connection in mathematics learning; enhancing individuals' learning capability in IT and creativity; improving cognitive strategies browsing electronic bases; reflective thinking and practices among teachers; strategic use of computers in constructing effective studies

Policy and Management Studies

Tel: 460 5206 Fax: 467 7808

Chew Oon Ai, J., BA Sing., BSocSci Sing., MSocSci Sing., PhD Monash Sr. Lectr.; Head*

Chong, Keng Choy, BSc Sing., BSc(Econ) Lond., MEd Manc., EdD George Washington Sr. Lectr.

Crawford, Lachlan E. D., BEd W.Aust., MEd W.Aust., PhD W.Aust. Sr. Lectr.

Leong, Wing Fatt, BSc Qld., MA W.Mich. Sr. Lectr.

Low, Guat Tin, BEd Adelaide C.A.E., BA Flin., BEd Flin., MEd Flin., MA Mich., EdD Mich. Sr. Lectr.

Mau, Rosalind I. P. Y., BEd Hawaii, MEd Hawaii, MA Hawaii, PhD Hawaii Sr. Lectr.

Moo, Swee Ngoh, BA Sing., MA Lond., PhD Syd. Sr. Lectr.

Sharpe, Leslie, MA Sus., DPhil Sus. Sr. Lectr.

Stott, Kenneth R., MSc CNAA, PhD Middx. Sr. Lectr.

Tan, Tan Wei, BA Sing., MA Sing., PhD NU Singapore Sr. Lectr.

Zhang, Yenming, MS S.Connecticut, MEd Harv., EdD Harv. Sr. Lectr.

Other Staff: 1 Sr. Fellow; 3 Lectrs.; 1 Adjunct Prof.; 1 Adjunct Sr. Lectr.; 2 Adjunct Lectrs.

Research: analysis of future trends from delphi panels; classroom management and discipline in normal academic classes; developing resiliency in secondary schools; diverse expectations in principalship mentoring; world religion, morality and moral education

Psychological Studies

Tel: 460 5055 Fax: 469 9007

Chang Shook Cheong, A., BSc Sing., MEd Sing., PhD Macq. Assoc. Prof.

Lam Tit Loong, P., BSc Lond., MEd NU Singapore, EdD Mass. Sr. Lectr.

Lim, Tock Keng, BSc *Lond.*, MA *Texas*, MPhil *Auck.*, PhD *Texas*   Sr. Lectr.

Lui Hah Wah, E., BSocSci *Chinese HK*, MA *Mich.State*, EdS *Mich.State*, PhD *Mich.State*   Sr. Lectr.

Poh, Sui Hoi, BSc *Malaya*, MEd *Pitt.*, PhD *Tor.*   Sr. Lectr.

Seng, Seok Hoon, BA *Sing.*, MEd *Colorado State*, PhD *Hawaii*   Sr. Lectr.

Smith, Ian D., BA *Syd.*, MA *Stan.*, PhD *Stan.*   Assoc. Prof.

Tan, Esther, BA *HK*, MSW *Tor.*, EdD *Tor.*   Assoc. Prof.; Head*

Tan, Wee Kiat, BSc *Sing.*, MA *Pitt.*, PhD *Pitt.*   Sr. Lectr.

Tay-Koay, Siew Luan, BA *Malaya*, MA *Col.*, MEd *Col.*, MEd *Philippines*, PhD *Oregon*   Sr. Lectr. (on leave)

Other Staff: 1 Sr. Fellow; 11 Lectrs.

Research: adolescent studies: coping styles of Singapore adolescents; longitudinal study of secondary school: cognitive, psychosocial development and school adjustment; pedagogical practice in primary mathematics classrooms; preschoolers' talents and skills: interaction between environment, ability and curriculum; teacher development: struggles, strategies and successes of teachers

Specialised Education

Tel: 460 5206 Fax: 467 7808

Lim Swee Eng, , A., BA *Sing.*, MA *NU Singapore*, PhD *Syr.*   Sr. Lectr.

Quah May Ling, M., MS *Wis.*, PhD *Qld.*   Sr. Lectr.; Head*

Sharpe, Pamela J., MPhil *Lond.*, PhD *Lond.*   Sr. Lectr.

Other Staff: 7 Lectrs.; 1 Teaching Fellow; 3 Sr. Tutors

Research: early intervention for preschoolers with disabilities; gifted adolescents: relationship between perception and academic achievement; parental training: effects on children's development and learning; preschool children in transition: cognitive, language and socio-emotional adjustments; preschoolers with special needs: play and language development

Educational Research, National Institute of Education Centre for

Tel: 799 5264 Fax: 468 7945

Gopinathan, Saravanan, BA *Sing.*, MEd *Sing.*, PhD *N.Y.State*   Head*

Research: classroom organisation for school effectiveness; item banking and computerised adaptive testing; language use and social support networks; philosophy for children

Media Resource Centre

Tel: 460 5201 Fax: 468 4839

Chan, Ronnie, MS *Boston*   Head*

Physical Education

Tel: 460 5355 Fax: 468 7506

Abernethy, Arthur B., BHMS(Ed) *Qld.*, PhD *Otago*   Visiting Prof.

Haslam, Ian, BEd *Keele*, MA *Alta.*, EdD *N.Y.State*   Assoc. Prof.

Horton, Peter A., BEd *Brisbane C.A.E.*, MEd *NE*, PhD *Qld.*   Sr. Lectr.

Schmidt, Gordon J., BEd *McG.*, MS *Indiana*, PhD *Indiana*   Sr. Lectr.

Smith, Daniel E., BS *Brigham Young*, MC *Brigham Young*, PhD *Ill.*   Sr. Lectr.

Teo-Koh, Sock Miang, BPE *Alta.*, MSc *Alta.*, PhD *Oregon*   Sr. Lectr.

Wright, Helen C., BEd *Lond.*, MSc *Lough.*, PhD *Leeds*   Sr. Lectr.

Wright, Steven C., BS *St.Lawrence*, MEd *Boston*, EdD *Boston*   Sr. Lectr.

Other Staff: 13 Lectrs.; 3 Sr. Tutors; 1 Adjunct Sr. Lectr.

Research: children with learning difficulties and the motor performance of school children; inter-generational coronary risk factors in school children and their families; military

experience and the teaching of secondary physical education; physical activity and physical fitness in overweight children: teaching psychological skills to school age athletes

Science

Biology

Tel: 460 5400 Fax: 469 8928

Chew, Shit Fun, BSc *NU Singapore*, PhD *NU Singapore*   Sr. Lectr. (on leave)

Chia, Tet Fatt, BSc *NU Singapore*, MSc *NU Singapore*, PhD *NU Singapore*   Sr. Lectr.

Diong, Cheong Hoong, BSc *Malaya*, MS *Hawaii*, PhD *Hawaii*   Sr. Lectr.

Gan, Yik Yuen alias Yap Y. Y., BSc *Nan.*, PhD *Aberd.*   Assoc. Prof.

He, Jie, BS *S.China Normal*, PhD *Macq.*, MS   Sr. Lectr.

Lee, Sing Kong, BHortSc *Cant.*, PhD *NU Singapore*   Assoc. Prof.; Head*

Lim Siew-Lee, S., BSc *Sing.*, MSc *NU Singapore*, PhD *W.Ont.*   Sr. Lectr.

Yeoh, Oon Chye, BSc *Malaya*, BSc *Qld.*, PhD *Stan.*   Sr. Lectr.

Other Staff: 7 Lectrs.; 1 Adjunct Prof.

Research: agrotechnology focusing on aeroponic technology; environmental science focusing on resource management; issues relating to biology education; medical biotechnology focusing on diagnostics

Chemistry

Tel: 460 5400 Fax: 469 8928

Chia, Lian Sai, BSc *Nan.*, MA *Mich.State*, MSc *Br.Col.*, PhD *Br.Col.*   Sr. Lectr.

Chin, Long Fay, BSc *W.Aust.*, PhD *Ohio State*   Sr. Lectr.

Chu, Chit Kay, BSc *Malaya*, MSc *Malaya*, PhD *Nfld.*   Sr. Lectr.

Foong, Yoke Yeen, BSc *Lond.*, MA *Lond.*, EdD *Mass.*   Sr. Lectr.

Gan, Leong Huat, BSc *Well.*, MSc *Well.*, PhD *Qu.*   Assoc. Prof.

Goh, Ngoh Khang, BSc *Nan.*, MSc *Mün.*, PhD *Mün.*   Assoc. Prof.; Head*

Khoo, Lian Ee, BSc *Malaya*, MSc *Malaya*, PhD *Georgetown*   Sr. Lectr.

Lee, Kam Wah, BSc *Nan.*, MSc *E.Anglia*, PhD *Monash*   Sr. Lectr.

Tan, Swee Ngin, BSEd *Ag.U.Malaysia*, PhD *Deakin*   Sr. Lectr.

Teo, Khay Chuan, BSc *Nan.*, PhD *W.Ont.*   Assoc. Prof.

Other Staff: 5 Lectrs.; 1 Teaching Assoc.

Research: catalysts and sensors; environmental science; organic and organometallic chemistry; polymer and surfactant chemistry; science and chemical education

Mathematics

Tel: 460 5150 Fax: 469 8952

Ahuja, Om P., BSc *Delhi*, BEd *Raj.*, MSc *Delhi*, MA *Panjab*, PhD *Khart.*   Sr. Lectr.

Cheung Yiu Lin, J., BSc *HK*, MSc *Sur.*, MEd *Exe.*   Sr. Lectr.

Chong, Tian Hoo, BSc *Malaya*, MS *W.Mich.*, MS(Ed) *E.Illinois*, PhD *Pitt.*   Sr. Lectr.

Fong, Ho Kheong, BSc *Malaya*, MEd *Brisbane C.A.E.*, PhD *Lond.*   Sr. Lectr.

Foong, Pui Yee, BSc *Sing.*, MEdSt *Monash*, PhD *Monash*   Sr. Lectr.

Lee, Cho Seng, BSc *Sing.*, MSc *Malaya*, PhD *Arizona State*   Sr. Lectr.

Lee, Peng Yee, BSc *Nan.*, MSc *Belf.*, PhD *Belf.*   Assoc. Prof.; Head*

Lim-Teo, Suat Khoh, BSc *Sing.*, MSc *Qld.*, PhD *NU Singapore*   Sr. Lectr. (on leave)

Pereira-Mendoza, Lionel, BSc *S'ton.*, MSc *S'ton.*, EdD *Br.Col.*   Assoc. Prof.

Phang, Lay Ping R., BSc *Manc.*, MSc *Manc.*, PhD *Manc.*   Sr. Lectr.

Wong, Jia Yiing P., MSc *NU Singapore*, PhD *NU Singapore*   Sr. Lectr.

Yap, Sook Fwe, BSc *Sing.*, MSc *Auck.*, PhD *Wis.*   Sr. Lectr.

Other Staff: 12 Lectrs.; 1 Teaching Assoc.

Research: analysis; mathematical modelling; mathematics education; statistics

Physics

Tel: 460 5400 Fax: 469 8952

Chia, Teck Chee, BSc *Nan.*, MSc *Dal.*, PhD *Dal.*   Sr. Lectr.

Lee, Sing, BSc *Malaya*, MSc *Malaya*, PhD *ANU*   Prof.; Head*

Springham, Stuart V., BSc *Strath.*, PhD *Edin.*   Sr. Lectr.

Toh, Kok Ann, BSc *Malaya*, MA *Stan.*, DPhil *Oxf.*   Assoc. Prof.

Xu, Shuyan, BS *Nanjing*, PhD *Flin.*   Sr. Lectr.

Yap, Kueh Chin, BSc *Malaya*, MSc *Sur.*, PhD *Georgia*   Sr. Lectr.

Other Staff: 10 Lectrs.

Research: laser-based biophysics: problem-solving and IT in education; radio-frequency plasmas for advanced materials deposition; soft X-ray source for microelectronics lithography; visualisation techniques for AI and IT

CONTACT OFFICERS

Academic affairs. Senior Assistant Registrar (Bukit Timah Campus): Koh, Sou Keaw, BSc *Nan.*, MSc *Auck.*

Academic affairs. Deputy Registrar (Yunnan Garden Campus): Chua, Poh Gek, BA *Malaya*

Accommodation. Senior Assistant Registrar (Bukit Timah Campus): Koh, Sou Keaw, BSc *Nan.*, MSc *Auck.*

Accommodation. Assistant Director (Yunnan Garden Campus): Shang, Angela L. P., BA *NU Singapore*

Admissions (first degree). Senior Assistant Registrar (Bukit Timah Campus): Koh, Sou Keaw, BSc *Nan.*, MSc *Auck.*

Admissions (first degree). Assistant Registrar (Yunnan Garden Campus): Lim, Paik Suan, BA *NU Singapore*

Admissions (higher degree). Senior Assistant Registrar (Bukit Timah Campus): Koh, Sou Keaw, BSc *Nan.*, MSc *Auck.*

Admissions (higher degree). Assistant Registrar (Yunnan Garden Campus): Grace, Leong, BCom *Dal.*

Adult/continuing education. Director, Centre for Continuing Education (Yunnan Garden Campus): Lwin, Daniel Tint, BEng *Rangoon I.T.*, MASc *Windsor*

Adult/continuing education. Head, National Institute of Education Centre for Educational Research (Bukit Timah Campus): Saravanan, Gopinathan, BA *Sing.*, MEd *Sing.*, PhD *N.Y.State*

Alumni. Senior Assistant Registrar (Bukit Timah Campus): Koh, Sou Keaw, BSc *Nan.*, MSc *Auck.*

Alumni. Assistant Director (Yunnan Garden Campus): Chua, Nam Leng, BA *Kent*, MA *Oklahoma City*

Careers. Senior Assistant Registrar (Bukit Timah Campus): Koh, Sou Keaw, BSc *Nan.*, MSc *Auck.*

Careers. Director, Office of Professional Attachments (Yunnan Garden Campus): Ng, B. H., BE *Malaya*, MSc *Sing.*

Computing services. Deputy Director, Computer Centre (Yunnan Garden Campus): Goh, T. C., BSc *Nan.*, MSc *N.Y.State*

Computing services. Deputy Director, Computer Centre (Bukit Timah Campus): Tan, H. C., BSc *Nan.*, MA *Lanc.*

Conferences/corporate hospitality. Director, Centre for Continuing Education (Yunnan Garden Campus): Lwin, Daniel Tint, BEng *Rangoon I.T.*, MASc *Windsor*

Conferences/corporate hospitality. Head, National Institute of Education Centre for Educational Research (Bukit Timah Campus): Saravanan, Gopinathan, BA *Sing.*, MEd *Sing.*, PhD *N.Y.State*

Consultancy services. Senior Assistant Director (Yunnan Garden Campus): Lu, T. S., BA *Sing.*

Consultancy services. Assistant Director (Bukit Timah Campus): Wong, W. C., BSc *Sing.*

Credit transfer. Senior Assistant Registrar (Bukit Timah Campus): Koh, Sou Keaw, BSc Nan., MSc *Auck.*

Credit transfer. Assistant Registrar (Yunnan Garden Campus): Lim, Paik Suan, BA *NU Singapore*

Development/fund-raising. Administrative Officer (Yunnan Garden Campus): Ku, Daniel, BSc *Melb.*

Estates and buildings/works and services. Deputy Director, Estate Office (Yunnan Garden Campus): Lam, H. P., BS *Cheng Kung*, MSc *NU Singapore*

Estates and buildings/works and services. Senior Estate Officer (Bukit Timah Campus): Selvaratnam, Selvarajan, BSc(Bldg) *H.-W.*

Examinations. Senior Assistant Registrar (Bukit Timah Campus): Koh, Sou Keaw, BSc Nan., MSc *Auck.*

Examinations. Senior Assistant Registrar (Yunnan Garden Campus): Lee, C. F., BA *Malaya*

Finance. Deputy Bursar (Yunnan Garden Campus): Soh, Wee Kwan, BAcc *Sing.*

Finance. Senior Assistant Bursar (Bukit Timah Campus): Choong, Michelle A. L., BAcc *Sing.*

General enquiries. Deputy Registrar (Yunnan Garden Campus): Chua, Poh Gek, BA *Malaya*

General enquiries. Deputy Registrar (Bukit Timah Campus): Sim, C. T., BA *Sing.*

Industrial liaison. Director, Office of Professional Attachments (Yunnan Garden Campus): Ng, B. H., BE *Malaya*, MSc *Sing.*

International office. Director, International Relations Office (Yunnan Garden Campus): Lee, Prof. Brian, PBM, JP, BE *NSW*, MEngSc *NSW*, FIEE, FIEAust

Language training for international students. Associate Dean of Engineering and Dean of Students (Yunnan Garden Campus): Choa, Prof. Victor, BA *Camb.*, MA *Camb.*, MSc *Birm.*, PhD *NUSingapore*

Language training for international students. Senior Lecturer (Bukit Timah Campus): Steele-Skuja, Rita, BA *Well.*, MA *Well.*, MA *Birm.*, PhD *Lond.*

Library (chief librarian). Librarian (Yunnan Garden Campus): Foo Kok Pheow, BSc Nan., MA *Mich.*

Library (enquiries). Deputy Librarian (Yunnan Garden Campus): Wong-Yip, Chin Choo, BA *Malaya*

Library (enquiries). Deputy Librarian (Bukit Timah Campus): Yeo-Tang, Isabel I.-S., BSc *Sing.*

Ombudsperson. Deputy President: Chen Charng-Ning, Prof., PPA, BS *Cheng Kung*, MS *Iowa State*, PhD *Georgia I.T.*

Personnel/human resources. Senior Assistant Director (Bukit Timah Campus): Goh-Yap, Ivy G. Y., BSocSci *Sing.*, MSc *Maryland*

Personnel/human resources. Senior Assistant Director (Yunnan Garden Campus): Chua, Lian Kee, BSocSci *Sing.*

Public relations, information and marketing. Head, Public Relations Office (Yunnan Garden Campus): Ho, Irene J. W., BCom Nan.

Public relations, information and marketing. Administrative Officer (Bukit Timah Campus): Chan, Guet Har, BA *NU Singapore*

Publications. Senior Assistant Registrar (Bukit Timah Campus): Koh, Sou Keaw, BSc Nan., MSc *Auck.*

Publications. Assistant Registrar (Yunnan Garden Campus): Woon-Ong, Ning Ning, BBA *NU Singapore*

Purchasing. Senior Assistant Bursar (Bukit Timah Campus): Choong, Michelle A. L., BAcc *Sing.*

Purchasing. Deputy Bursar (Yunnan Garden Campus): Chew, H. S., BCom Nan.

Quality assurance and accreditation. Senior Assistant Registrar (Bukit Timah Campus): Koh, Sou Keaw, BSc Nan., MSc *Auck.*

Quality assurance and accreditation. Deputy Registrar (Yunnan Garden Campus): Chua, Poh Gek, BA *Malaya*

Research. Head, National Institute of Education Centre for Educational Research (Bukit Timah Campus): Saravanan, Gopinathan, BA *Sing.*, MEd *Sing.*, PhD *N.Y.State*

Research. Director of Research (Yunnan Garden Campus): Tan, Prof. H. S., BSc(Eng) *Lond.*, MSEE *M.I.T.*, PhD *McG.*, FIEE

Safety. Senior Estate Officer (Yunnan Garden Campus): Phua, K. J., BEng *NU Singapore*

Safety. Senior Estate Officer (Bukit Timah Campus): Selvaratnam, Selvarajan, BSc *H-W*

Scholarships, awards, loans. Senior Assistant Registrar (Bukit Timah Campus): Koh, Sou Keaw, BSc Nan., MSc *Auck.*

Scholarships, awards, loans. Assistant Registrar (Yunnan Garden Campus): Cheong, William E. G., BA *NU Singapore*

Security. Assistant Director (Yunnan Garden Campus): Teo, H. K., BA Nan.

Security. Senior Estate Officer (Bukit Timah Campus): Selvaratnam, Selvarajan, BSc *H-W*

Sport and recreation. Deputy Director (Yunnan Garden Campus): Chong, P. J., BA Nan., MSS *U.S.Sports Acad.*

Sport and recreation. Dean, School of Physical Education (Bukit Timah Campus): Quek, Jin Jong, BS *Oregon*, MS *Oregon*, PhD *Qld.*

Staff development and training. Senior Assistant Director (Bukit Timah Campus): Goh-Yap, Ivy G. Y., BSocSci *Sing.*, MSc *Maryland*

Staff development and training. Administrative Officer (Yunnan Garden Campus): Khoo, Lay See, BBA *NU Singapore*

Student union. Deputy Director (Yunnan Garden Campus): Liaw, W. C., BSc Nan.

Student welfare/counselling. Senior Assistant Registrar (Bukit Timah Campus): Koh, Sou Keaw, BSc Nan., MSc *Auck.*

Student welfare/counselling. Assistant Director (Yunnan Garden Campus): Lee, Sue K. S., BA *York(Can.)*

Students from other countries. Senior Assistant Registrar (Bukit Timah Campus): Koh, Sou Keaw, BSc Nan., MSc *Auck.*

Students from other countries. Deputy Registrar (Yunnan Garden Campus): Chua, Poh Gek, BA *Malaya*

Students with disabilities. Senior Assistant Registrar (Bukit Timah Campus): Koh, Sou Keaw, BSc Nan., MSc *Auck.*

Students with disabilities. Deputy Registrar (Yunnan Garden Campus): Chua, Poh Gek, BA *Malaya*

University Press. Administrative Officer (Bukit Timah Campus): Chan, Guet Har, BA *NU Singapore*

University press. Head, Public Relations Office (Yunnan Garden Campus): Ho, Irene J. W., BCom Nan.

[Information supplied by the institution as at 26 February 1998, and edited by the ACU]

NATIONAL UNIVERSITY OF SINGAPORE

Founded 1980 through the amalgamation of the University of Singapore and Nanyang University

Member of the Association of Commonwealth Universities

Postal Address: 10 Kent Ridge Crescent, Singapore 119260, Republic of Singapore
Telephone: 775 6666 **Fax**: 778 5281 **WWW**: http://www.nus.sg
(**London Office**: c/o Contact Singapore (London),
Charles House, Lower Ground Floor, 5-11 Regent Street, London, England SW1Y 4LR **Telephone**: (0171) 976 2090
North America Office: 55 East 59th Street, New York, NY, USA 10022 **Telephone**: (212) 751 0331
Fax: (212) 751 0339)

CHANCELLOR—Ong Teng Cheong, BArch *Adel.*, MCD *Liv.*
PRO-CHANCELLOR—Baker, M., BBM, BA *Lond.*, Hon. LLD
PRO-CHANCELLOR—Lien Ying Chow, PJG, Hon. DLitt
PRO-CHANCELLOR—Ridzwan bin Haji Dzafir, PPA, BBM, BA *Malaya*
PRO-CHANCELLOR—Chew Guan Khuan, Andrew, PPA, PJG, MB BS *Malaya*, FRCP, FRCPEd
PRO-CHANCELLOR—Nathan, S. R., BBM, PPA, PJG
CHAIRMAN OF COUNCIL—Cheong Siew Keong, BSc(Eng) *HK*, Hon. DLitt
VICE-CHANCELLOR*—Lim Pin, Prof., PJG, PPA, MB BChir *Camb.*, MA *Camb.*, MD *Camb.*, FRCP, FRCPEd, FACP, Hon. FRCSGlas, Hon. FRCSEd, Hon. FRACOG
DEPUTY VICE-CHANCELLOR—Hang, Prof. C. C., BEng *Sing.*, MSc *Warw.*, PhD *Warw.*, FIEE
DEPUTY VICE-CHANCELLOR—Chong, Prof. C. T., BS *Iowa State*, PhD *Yale*
DEPUTY VICE-CHANCELLOR—Shih, Prof. Choon-Fong, MSc *Harv.*, PhD *Harv.*
REGISTRAR—Wong, Joanna, BBM, BSc *Sing.*
BURSAR—Leo Lian Lim, BA *Sing.*
LIBRARIAN—Quah, Jill, BA *Sing.*, MLS *Col.*
DIRECTOR (PERSONNEL)—Ong, Jin-Soo, BSc *Sing.*
DIRECTOR (OFFICE OF ESTATE AND DEVELOPMENT)—Yong, Kwet Yew, BEng *Sheff.*, PhD *Sheff.*
DIRECTOR (UNIVERSITY LIAISON OFFICE)—Sukumar, E., BA *Sing.*

GENERAL INFORMATION

History. The university, whose predecessor institutions include the University of Malaya (1949), was inaugurated in 1980 with the merger of the University of Singapore (1962) and Nanyang University (1955).

The main campus at Kent Ridge is located about 12km from the city centre.

Admission to first degree courses. Singapore–Cambridge General Certificate of Education (GCE) A level exam, or GCE A level/Higher School Certificate (HSC) exam (English and Malay medium, conducted by the Cambridge Local Examinations Syndicate), or HSC exam (conducted by the Malaysian Examinations Syndicate in collaboration with the Cambridge Local Examinations Syndicate), or Sijil Tinggi Persekolahan Malaysia (STPM) (conducted by the Malaysian Examinations Council).

First Degrees (* = also available with honours; † = available with honours only). BA*, BA(ArchStud), BArch, BBA*, BDS, BEng, BSc*, BSc(Bldg), BSc(Comp&InfoSci)*, BSc(EstMgt), BSc(Pharm)*, BSc(RealEst), BSocSci †, BTech, LLB, MB BS.

Higher Degrees. LLM, MA, MA(ApplLing), MA(ChineseStud), MA(EngLang), MA(EngLit), MA(EngStud), MA(SEAsianStud), MA(UrbanPlanning), MArch, MBA, MBldgSc, MCL (comparative law), MClinEmbry, MDS(Oral&MaxillofacialSurg) MDS(Orthodontics), MDS(Prosthodontics), MEd, MEng, MMed(Anaesth), MMed(DiagnosticRadiology), MMed(FamilyMed), MMed(IntMed), MMed(ObstandGynae), MMed(OM), MMed(Ophthalmology), MMed(Paed), MMed(PH), MMed(Psychiatry), MMed(Surg), MPP, MSc, MSc(Bldg), MSc(BldgSc), MSc(CivilEng), MSc(Comp&InfoSci), MSc(ElectEng), MSc(EnvEng), MSc(EstMgt), MSc(Ind&SysEng), MSc(MatSciEng), MSc(Mechatronics), MSc(MechEng), MSc(Mgt), MSc(MgtofTech), MSc(Pharm), MSc(ProjectMgt), MSc(Prop&MainMgt), MSc(RealEst), MSc(TranspSys&Mgt), MScD, MSocSci, MSocSci(ApplEcons), MSocSci(ApplSociology), MSocSci(Econs), MTech, PhD, DDS, DLitt, DSc, DSurg, LLD, MD.

Applicants for admission to coursework programmes must hold a good bachelor's degree in the relevant discipline and, in some cases, should also have a period of relevant work experience. Research programmes: a relevant bachelor's degree with at least second class honours and the ability to pursue research in the proposed field.

Libraries. 2,120,000 volumes; 20,240 current periodical titles; 340 electronic journals and indexes; 224 CD-ROM databases; 15,415 audio-visual programmes; 352,660 fiches; 48,260 reels. Special collections: Singapore/ Malaysia.

Fees (1998–99). Singaporeans and Singapore permanent residents: S$5500 (undergraduate); S$15,450 (undergraduate medicine and dentistry); S$3000 (postgraduate degrees by coursework, except MBA, medicine and dentistry); S$6300 (MBA); S$7100–9750 (postgraduate medicine and dentistry). International students: S$6050 (undergraduate); S$17,000 (undergraduate medicine and dentistry); S$3300 (postgraduate degrees by coursework except MBA, medicine and dentistry); S$6950 (MBA); S$7100–10,750 (postgraduate medicine and dentistry).

Academic Year (1998–99). Two semesters: 13 July–14 November; 4 January–30 April. Special term: 10 May 1999–3 July 1999.

Income (1996–97). Total, S$177,317,000.

Statistics. Students: total 24,141 (12,425 men, 11,716 women); international 3416.

FACULTIES/SCHOOLS

Architecture and Building
Tel: 874 3475 Fax: 777 3953

Acting Dean: Lam, Kee Poh, BArch *Nott.*, BA *Nott.*, PhD *Carnegie-Mellon*

Arts and Social Sciences
Tel: 874 3986 Fax: 777 0751

Dean: Tong, Chee Kiong, BSocSci *Sing.*, MA *Cornell*, PhD *Cornell*

Business Administration
Tel: 874 3076 Fax: 777 1296

Dean: Wee, Prof. Chow Hou, BBA *Sing.*, MBA *W.Ont.*, PhD *W.Ont.*

Dentistry
Tel: 772 4988 Fax: 778 5742

Dean: Chew, Prof. Chong Lin, BDS *Sing.*, MSD *Indiana*, MDS *Sing.*, FDSRCSEd

Engineering
Tel: 874 2142 Fax: 777 3847

Dean: Nee, Prof. A. Y. C., MSc *Manc.*, PhD *Manc.*

Law
Tel: 874 3631 Fax: 779 0979

Dean: Chin, Tet Yung, LLB *Lond.*, BCL *Oxf.*

Medicine
Tel: 874 3296 Fax: 778 5743

Dean: Tan, Chorh Chuan, MB BS *NU Singapore*, MMed *NU Singapore*, PhD *NU Singpaore*, FRCPEd

Science
Tel: 874 2774 Fax: 777 4279

Dean: Lee, Prof. Soo Ying, BSc *Malaya*, PhD *Chic.*

ACADEMIC UNITS

Accounting, see Finance and Acctg.

Anatomy, see Medicine

Architecture, School of
Tel: 874 3402 Fax: 779 3078

Chan, Yew Lih, MA *York(UK)* Sr. Lectr.
Chew Weng Kong Sr. Lectr.
Chou Shiuh Lin, David, BA *Brist.*, MSc *Lond.*, PhD *Camb.* Sr. Lectr.
Foo, Ah Fong, MArch *NU Singapore*, PhD *Lond.* Assoc. Prof.
Gerondelis, Ann I., BSc *Georgia I.T.*, MArch *Georgia I.T.* Sr. Lectr.

Harrison, James D., BArch Sheff. Sr. Lectr.
Heng, Chye Kiang, PhD Calif. Sr. Lectr.
Indorf, Pinna Lee, BArch Texas, PhD NU Singapore Sr. Lectr.
Kong, Shee Chong, BArch Houston, MArch Cornell Sr. Lectr.
Lam, Kee Poh, BA Nott., BArch Nott., PhD Carnegie-Mellon Sr. Lectr.
Lim, Guan Tiong, BSc CNAA, PhD Lanc. Sr. Lectr.
Lim, Joseph E. M., BArch NU Singapore, MSc Strath., PhD H.-W. Sr. Lectr.
Ng Yan Yung, Edward, BArch Manc., BA Nott., PhD Camb. Sr. Lectr.
Ong, Boon Lay, BArch Auck., MArch Auck., PhD Camb. Sr. Lectr.
Parker, Kenneth J., BSc Bath, MSc Lond. Sr. Lectr.
Rao, S. P., BE B'lore., ME IISc. Sr. Lectr.
Sabapathy, T. K., BA Sing., MA Calif. Sr. Lectr.
Tan, Milton, BA Nott., BArch Nott., PhD Harv. Assoc. Prof.; Head*
Teh, Kem Jin, BSc Belf., MSc Belf. Sr. Lectr.
Tse, Swee Ling Sr. Lectr.
Waller, Edward, MLA Penn. Sr. Lectr.
Wong Chong Thai, Bobby, MDesSt Harv. Sr. Lectr.

Biochemistry, see Medicine

Biological Sciences, School of

Tel: 874 2692 Fax: 779 2486

Chan, W. K., BSc NU Singapore, PhD NU Singapore Sr. Lectr.
Chou, L. M., BSc Sing., PhD Sing. Assoc. Prof.; AB Co-ordinator
Ding, Jeak Ling, BSc Wales, PhD Lond. Assoc. Prof.; CMB Co-ordinator
Goh, C. J., BSc Sing., PhD Newcastle(UK) Prof.
Hew, C. S., BSc Nan., MSc Qu., PhD Qu. Prof.
Ho, K. K., BA N.Y.State, MA N.Y.State, PhD Purdue Assoc. Prof.
Ho, Shuit Hung, BSc Malaya, PhD Lond. Assoc. Prof.
Ip, Y. K., BSc Minn., MA Rice, PhD Rice Assoc. Prof.
Kara, Anna U., MSc Marburg, DrRerNat Marburg Sr. Lectr.
Khoo, H. W., BSc Sing., MSc Sing., PhD Br.Col. Assoc. Prof.
Kumar, P. P., BSc Mys., MSc Madr., PhD Calg. Sr. Lectr.
Lam, T. J., BSc Br.Col., PhD Br.Col. Prof.; Dir.*
Lane, D. J. W., BSc Lond., MSc Wales, PhD Wales Sr. Lectr.
Lee, Y. H., BSc Nan., MSc W.Ont., PhD Manit. Sr. Lectr.
Leong, K. Y., BSA Sask., MSc Sask., PhD Guelph Sr. Lectr.
Lim, T. M., BSc NU Singapore, PhD Camb. Sr. Lectr.
Loh, C. S., BSc Nan., MSc Sing., PhD Camb. Assoc. Prof.
Munro, A. D., BSc St And., PhD Wales Sr. Lectr.
Ng, P. K. L., BSc NU Singapore, PhD NU Singapore Sr. Lectr.
Ong, Bee Lian, BSc Sing., MSc NU Singapore, DrRerNat T.H.Darmstadt Sr. Lectr.
Phang, Violet, BSc Sing., PhD Massey Assoc. Prof.
Pua, E. C., BSc Natnl.Taiwan, MSc McG., PhD McG. Sr. Lectr.
Shim, K. F., BSc Nan., PhD Lond. Assoc. Prof.
Sin, Y. M., BSc Nan., MSc W.Ont., PhD W.Ont. Assoc. Prof.
Tan, Benito C., BSc Far Eastern, MSc Philippines, PhD Br.Col. Sr. Lectr.
Tan, C. H., BSc Malaya, PhD Hull Assoc. Prof.
Tan, H. T. W., BSc Sing., PhD NU Singapore Sr. Lectr.
Tan, T. K., BSc Sing., PhD NU Singapore Assoc. Prof.
Wong, S. M., BSc Nan., MS Virginia, PhD Cornell Sr. Lectr.
Wong, V. W. T., BSc Lond., PhD Lond. Sr. Lectr.

Yeoh, H. H., BSc Malaya, MSc Malaya, PhD ANU Assoc. Prof.; PB Co-ordinator
Other Staff: 7 Lectrs.; 1 Prof. Fellow; 2 Fellows; 1 Res. Officer; 1 Sci. Officer; 1 Adjunct Prof.; 2 Hon. Sr. Fellows
Research: biodiversity, systematics and ecology; fish/marine biology, biotechnology and aquaculture; orchid biology and horticulture; pathogenesis and disease/pest management; plant molecular biology and tissue culture

Building and Real Estate, School of

Tel: 874 3414 Fax: 775 5502

Addae-Dapaah, Kwame, BSc(LandEconomy) Kumasi, MSc Reading, PhD Strath. Sr. Lectr.
Briffett, Clive, MSc Lond., MSc Oxf.Brookes, FRICS Sr. Lectr.
Chew, Michael Y. L., BBldg NSW, MEngSc Syd., PhD NSW Sr. Lectr.
Chin, Lawrence K. H., BSc(EstateManagement) Sing., PhD Georgia Sr. Lectr.
Christudason, Alice, LLB Sing., LLM Lond., PhD Lond. Sr. Lectr.
Foo, Tuan Seik, BSc Sci.U.Malaysia, MSc Asian I.T., Bangkok, DTechSc Asian I.T., Bangkok Sr. Lectr.
Gan, Cheong Eng, BSc Sing., MBM Asian Inst.Management, MEd Sheff., PhD NU Singapore Sr. Lectr.
Haque, Mohammed A., BSc Rajsh., MSc Lond. Sr. Lectr.
Khor, Amy L. S., BSc(EstateManagement) Sing., MBA San Jose, PhD Reading Sr. Lectr.
Lee, Siew Eang, BSc H.-W., MSc H.-W., PhD H.-W. Sr. Lectr.
Leong, Christopher H. Y., BSc Sing., MSc Lough., PhD Lond. Sr. Lectr.
Leong, Tuck Wah, BSc Natnl.Taiwan, ME Auck., PhD NSW Assoc. Prof.
Lim, Chong Nam, BBldg Melb., MSc Sing. Sr. Lectr.
Lim, Lan Yuan, BSc(EstateManagement) Sing., BSc Lond., LLB Lond., MBA NU Singapore, MSc Bath, FRICS Assoc. Prof.; Head*
Liow, Kim Hiang, BSc(EstateManagement) NU Singapore, MSc(Prop&MainMgt) NU Singapore, PhD Manc. Sr. Lectr.
Low, Sui Pheng, BSc(Bldg) NU Singapore, MSc Birm., PhD Lond. Sr. Lectr.
Malone-Lee, Lai Choo, BSc(EstateManagement) Sing., MTCP Syd., PhD Tokyo I.T. Sr. Lectr.
Mathur, Krishan S., BTech IIT Kanpur, MTech IIT Kanpur, PhD Strath. Assoc. Prof.
Ofori, George, BSc Kumasi, MSc Lond., PhD Lond. Assoc. Prof.
Rajendran, Sabaratnam, BSc(Engin) Ceyl., PhD Camb. Sr. Lectr.
Roy, Salil K., BSc Calc., MSc(Tech) Calc., DSc M.I.T. Assoc. Prof.
Sekhar, S. C., BE Raj., PhD Adel. Sr. Lectr.
Sim, Loo Lee, BA Sing., LLB Lond., MSc Lond., PhD N.U.S'pore. Assoc. Prof.
Tan, Willie C. K., BSurv Newcastle(NSW), MSc NU Singapore, PhD Syd. Sr. Lectr.
Teo, Ho Pin, BSc NU Singapore, MSc H.-W., PhD H.-W. Sr. Lectr.
Teo, Pin, BSc Reading, FRICS Sr. Lectr.
Tham, Kwok Wai, BEng NU Singapore, MBldg Syd., PhD Syd. Sr. Lectr.
Thang, Doreen Chze Lin, BSc(EstateManagement) Sing., MBA Sing., PhD Sr. Lectr.
Ullah, Mohammad B., BSc W.Pak.Eng., MSc B'desh.Engin., PhD Manc. Assoc. Prof.
Yu, Shi Ming, MSc Reading, PhD Reading Sr. Lectr.
Yuen, Belinda K. P., BA Sing., MA Sheff., PhD Melb. Sr. Lectr.

Business Policy

Tel: 874 3105 Fax: 779 5059

Ch'ng, Hak Kee, BCom Nan., MBA Hawaii, MPhil Warw. Sr. Lectr.
Chow, Kit Boey, BS Utah State, MS Utah State Sr. Lectr.
Davis, Rachel, BA B'lore., MA J.Nehru U., MBA Ill., PhD Ill. Sr. Lectr.

Leung, Hing Man, BSc Brist., MSc Lond., PhD Lond. Sr. Lectr.
Lim, Chin, BAgrSc Malaya, MSc Br.Col., PhD Qu. Assoc. Prof.
Lim, Gaik Eng, BA Simmons, MPhil N.Y., PhD N.Y. Sr. Lectr.
Loh, Lawrence Y. K., BBA NU Singapore, PhD M.I.T. Sr. Lectr.
Low, Linda, BSocSci Sing., MSocSci Sing., PhD NU Singapore Assoc. Prof.
Ouliaris, Sam, BCom Melb., MCom Melb., MA Yale, MPhil Yale, PhD Yale Sr. Lectr.
Pang, Eng Fong, BA Sing., MA Ill., PhD Ill. Prof. (on leave)
Pant, Narayan, BTech IIT Delhi, PhD N.Y. Sr. Lectr.
Phan, Phillip, BBA Hawaii, PhD Wash. Sr. Lectr.
Rajam, Chandrasekaran, BTech Kharagpur, PhD Penn.State Sr. Lectr.
Sikorski, Douglas J., BS U.S.Military Acad., MBA Calif., PhD Brad. Sr. Lectr.
Singh, Kulwant, BBA NU Singapore, MBA NU Singapore, PhD Mich. Sr. Lectr.
Tan, Kong Yam, BA Prin., MA Stan., PhD Stan. Assoc. Prof.; Head*
Tan, Thiam Soon, BSc Sing., MBA Br.Col., PhD Lond. Sr. Lectr.
Tay, Catherine S. K., LLB Lond., LLM Lond. Sr. Lectr.
Ter, Kah Leng, LLM Brist. Assoc. Prof.
Toh, Mun Heng, BA Sing., BSocSci Sing., MSc Lond., PhD Lond. Assoc. Prof.
Wee, Chow Hou, BBA Sing., MBA W.Ont., PhD W.Ont. Prof.
Wong, Poh Kam, BSc M.I.T., BSEE M.I.T., MSc M.I.T., PhD M.I.T. Assoc. Prof.

Chemistry

Tel: 874 2658 Fax: 779 1691

Ang, H. G., BBM, PBM, BSc Malaya, MSc Malaya, MA Camb., PhD Monash, PhD Camb., DSc NU Singapore, FRSChem, FRACI Prof. Fellow
Ang, Siau Gek, BSc NU Singapore, MSc NU Singapore, PhD Camb. Sr. Lectr.
Chan, H. S. O., BSc CNAA, PhD Manc., FIM Prof.
Chew, Chwee Har, BSc Nan., PhD McG. Assoc. Prof.
Chuah, Gaik Khuan, BSc NU Singapore, MSc NU Singapore, PhD Texas A.&M. Sr. Lectr.
Gan, L. M., BSc Nan., MSc Akron, PhD Akron Prof.
Goh, S. H., BSc Nan., MSc Akron, PhD Akron, DSc NU Singapore, FIM Prof.
Harrison, L. J., BSc Glas., PhD Glas. Sr. Lectr.
Hor, A. T. S., BSc Lond., DPhil Oxf., FRSChem Assoc. Prof.
Huang, H.-H., PPA, BSc Malaya, MSc Malaya, DPhil Oxf., DSc Sing., FRAI, FRSChem Prof. Fellow
Jaenicke, S., BSc Cologne, MSc Karlsruhe, PhD Karlsruhe Sr. Lectr.
Kang, H. C., BS Yale, PhD Cal.Tech. Sr. Lectr.
Khoo, S. B., BSc Sci.U.Malaysia, PhD Alta. Sr. Lectr.
Khor, E., BSc Lake., PhD Virginia Polytech. Sr. Lectr.
Lai, Y. H., BSc Nan., PhD Vic.(BC) Assoc. Prof.
Lee, C. K., BSc Malaya, MSc Reading, PhD Reading, DSc NU Singapore, FRSChem Assoc. Prof.
Lee, H. K., BSc Cant., PhD Cant. Assoc. Prof.
Lee, Soo Ying, BSc Malaya, PhD Chic. Prof.; Head*
Lee, Swee Yong, BSc Nan., PhD Minn. Assoc. Prof.
Leung, P. H., BSc CNAA, PhD ANU Sr. Lectr.
Li, S. F. Y., BSc Lond., PhD Lond. Assoc. Prof.
Loh, T. P., BEng Tokyo I.T., MEng Tokyo I.T., MA Harv., PhD Harv. Sr. Lectr.
Mok, K. F., BSc NZ, MSc NZ, PhD Well., FRSChem, FNZIC Assoc. Prof.
Ng, S. C., BA Oxf., DPhil Oxf. Sr. Lectr.
Novak, I., BSc Zagreb, MSc Zagreb, PhD Zagreb, FIP, FRSChem Sr. Lectr.
Ranford, J. D., BSc Massey, PhD Massey Sr. Lectr.

Vittal, J. J., BSc Madr., MSc Madr., PhD IISc.   Sr. Lectr.

Wong, R. M. W., BSc Newcastle(NSW), BMath Newcastle(NSW), PhD ANU   Sr. Lectr.

Xu, G. Q., BS Fudan, MA Prin., PhD Prin.   Sr. Lectr.

Other Staff: 3 Lectrs.; 5 Res. Fellows; 2 Adjunct Profs.

Chinese Studies, see also Special Centres, etc

Tel: 874 3901 Fax: 779 4167

Kow, M. K., BA Nan., MA ANU, PhD NU Singapore   Sr. Lectr.

Lee, C. L., BA NU Singapore, MA NU Singapore, MA Ill., PhD Ill.   Sr. Lectr.

Lee, C. Y., BA HK, MPhil HK, PhD ANU   Sr. Lectr.

Li, L. D., BA Nankai   Visiting Prof.

Lim, B. C., BA Nan., MA Nan., PhD NU Singapore   Sr. Lectr.

Lim, C. T., BA Malaya, MA Malaya, PhD Sing.   Prof. Fellow

Liu, Xiaogan, MA Peking, PhD Peking   Sr. Lectr.

Luo, Z., BA Nankai   Visiting Prof.

Tan, E. C., BA Nan., MA Sing., PhD Sing.   Assoc. Prof.; Head*

Wong, Y. W., BA Natnl.Chengchi, MA Wis., PhD Wis.   Assoc. Prof.

Yeo, S. N., BA Nan., MA HK, PhD HK   Assoc. Prof.

Yuan, X. P., BA Peking   Visiting Prof.

Yung, S. S., BA HK, MPhil Prin., PhD Prin.   Sr. Lectr.

Zhan, B. H., BA Sun Yat-Sen   Visiting Prof.

Zhang, M., BA Peking, PhD Peking   Sr. Lectr.

Computational Science

Tel: 874 6864 Fax: 774 6756

Chen, K., BSc China U.S.T., PhD Ohio State   Sr. Lectr.

Lai, Choy Heng, BA Chic., MSc Chic., PhD Chic.   Assoc. Prof.; Head*

Wang, J. S., BSc Jilin, MSc Carnegie-Mellon, PhD Carnegie-Mellon   Sr. Lectr.

Computer Science, see Information Systems and Computer Sci.

Decision Sciences

Tel: 874 3003 Fax: 779 2621

Ang, James S. K., BSc Sing., MASc Wat., PhD Wat.   Sr. Lectr.

Brah, Shaukat A., BSc Lahore UET, MSc Iowa, PhD Houston   Sr. Lectr.

Chang, Zeph Yun, BS Natnl.Taiwan, PhD Liv.   Sr. Lectr.

Chou, Fee Seng, BSc Cant., PhD Cant.   Sr. Lectr.

Chu-Chun-Lin, Singfat, BSc Qu., PhD Br.Col.   Sr. Lectr.

Goh, Mark K. H., BSc Adel., MBA Deakin, PhD Adel.   Sr. Lectr.

Hui, Tak Kee, BSc Nan., MMath Wat., PhD Tor.   Sr. Lectr.

Hum, Sin Hoon, BCom Newcastle(NSW), BE Newcastle(NSW), PhD Calif.   Assoc. Prof.; Head*

Hwarng, Brian H., BS Tunghai, MS Missouri, PhD Arizona State   Sr. Lectr.

Lee, Kee Beng, BSc Nan., MSc McM., PhD McM.   Sr. Lectr.

Li, Hong Yu, BS Beijing Aeron., MS Beijing Aeron., PhD Texas   Sr. Lectr.

Li, Jingwen, BSc Nanjing, MSc Colorado State, PhD Texas   Sr. Lectr.

Liang, Thow Yick, BSc Lond., BSc Sing., MSc Sing., PhD NU Singapore   Sr. Lectr.

Ou, Jihong, BS Zhengzhou I.T., MS Chinese Acad.Sc., MS Mass., PhD M.I.T.   Sr. Lectr.

Pavri, Neville F., BEng Sing., MBA W.Ont., PhD W.Ont.   Sr. Lectr.

Quah, Siam Tee, BSc Sing., MSc Sus.   Sr. Lectr.

Quek, Ser Aik, BSc Manc., MS M.I.T., PhD Calif.   Sr. Lectr.

Sum, Chee Chuong, BEng NU Singapore, PhD Minn.   Sr. Lectr.

Sun, Jie, BS Tsing Hua, MS Chinese Acad.Sc., MS Wash., PhD Wash.   Sr. Lectr.

Ta, Huu Phuong, BSc Sing., MSc Lond., PhD Lond.   Assoc. Prof.

Tan, Boon Wan, BSc Sing., MSc Lond., PhD Lond.   Sr. Lectr.

Tan, Margaret J. Y., BCom Newcastle(NSW), MBA Adel., PhD Qld.   Sr. Lectr.

Teo, Thompson S. H., BEng NU Singapore, MSc NU Singapore, PhD Pitt.   Sr. Lectr.

Wong, Yue Kee, BASc Windsor, BA Windsor, MA Penn., PhD Mich.   Sr. Lectr.

Yang, Kum Khiong, BEng NU Singapore, MBA Indiana, PhD Indiana   Sr. Lectr.

Yeong, Wee Yong, BSc Nan., MMath Wat., PhD Wat.   Assoc. Prof.

Dentistry, see below

Economics and Statistics

Tel: 874 3955 Fax: 775 2646

Abeysinghe, T., BA Ceyl., MSc Colombo, MA Thammasat, PhD Manit.   Sr. Lectr.

Asher, M. G., BA Bom., MA Wash.State, PhD Wash.State   Assoc. Prof.

Balasooriya, U., BA S.Lanka, MA W.Ont., PhD W.Ont.   Sr. Lectr.

Bian, G., BSc Fudan, PhD Minn.   Sr. Lectr.

Chan, W. S., BBA Chinese HK, MPhil Chinese HK, MSc Temple, PhD Temple   Sr. Lectr.

Chia, Ngee Choon, BSocSc NU Singapore, MA W.Ont., PhD W.Ont.   Sr. Lectr.

Chin, A. T. H., BA CNAA, MA Leeds, PhD Macq.   Sr. Lectr.

Chng, M. K., MA Camb., PhD Camb.   Assoc. Prof.

Chow, Hwee Kwan, BSocSci NU Singapore, MSc Lond., PhD Lond.   Sr. Lectr.

Chua, T. C., BSc Nan., MSc Manit., PhD Iowa State   Sr. Lectr.

Chua, V. C. H., BSc Bath, MSocSci NU Singapore, PhD Chic.   Sr. Lectr.

Hoon, H. T., BSocSci NU Singapore, MA Col., MPhil Col., PhD Col.   Sr. Lectr.

Huang, Huei Chuen, BS Natnl.Taiwan, MS Yale, PhD Yale   Sr. Lectr.

Hui, W. T., BEc Tas., MEc ANU, PhD ANU   Sr. Lectr.

Kapur, B. K., BSocSci Sing., MA Stan., PhD Stan.   Prof.; Head*

Khan, M. H., MA Dacca, PhD NSW   Sr. Lectr.

Koh, Ai-Tee, BSocSci Sing., MA Roch., PhD Roch.   Sr. Lectr.

Lim, B. T., BSc Sing., MPhil Oxf., PhD Calif.   Sr. Lectr.

Lim, H. G. H., BS Gannon, MA Pitt., PhD Pitt.   Assoc. Prof.

Lim, Kim Leong, BSc Nan., MA Br.Col., PhD Alta.   Sr. Lectr.

Lin, T. K., MSc Malaya, MSc Iowa State, PhD NU Singapore   Sr. Lectr.

Lu, Ding, BA Fudan, MA Fudan, MA Northwestern, PhD Northwestern   Sr. Lectr.

Lu, Wang Shu, BS Wuhan, MA Texas, PhD Texas   Sr. Lectr.

Ng, Hock Guan, BEc W.Aust., MA Stan., PhD Stan.   Sr. Lectr.

Ngiam, K. J., BSocSci Sing., MA Car., PhD Car.   Sr. Lectr.

Peebles, G. S., BScEcon Wales, BPhil Liv., MLitt Glas., PhD HK   Sr. Lectr.

Phang, S. Y., BSocSci Sing., MA Harv., PhD Harv.   Sr. Lectr.

Quah, E. T. E., BA S.Fraser, MA Vic.(BC), PhD NU Singapore   Sr. Lectr.

Rao, V. V. B., MA And., PhD Sing.   Assoc. Prof.

Sadooghi-Alvandi, S., MSc Lond., PhD Camb.   Sr. Lectr.

Saw, S. L. C., BSc Monash, MA Penn., PhD Penn.   Sr. Lectr.

Shantakumar, G., MSocSci Sing., PhD Sing.   Assoc. Prof.

Soon, T. W., MSc Lond., PhD Lond.   Sr. Lectr.

Tan, A. H. H., MA Stan., MA Sing., PhD Stan.   Assoc. Prof.

Tan, Lin Yeok, BA Sing., MA Sus., DPhil Sus.   Sr. Lectr.

Tay, B. N., BCom Nan., MA Tor., PhD Hawaii   Sr. Lectr.

Tongzon, J. L., BA Manila, MA Manila, PhD Tas.   Sr. Lectr.

Tse, Y. K., BSocSc HK, MSc Lond., PhD Lond.   Assoc. Prof.

Tsui, A. K. C., BSSc Chinese HK, MS Kentucky, PhD Kentucky   Sr. Lectr.

Wilson, P. R. D., BA Exe., PhD Warw.   Sr. Lectr.

Wong, C. M., BSocSc HK, MA Chic., PhD Chic.   Sr. Lectr.

Wong, W. K., BSc Chinese HK, MSc Wis., PhD Wis.   Sr. Lectr.

Yeoh Mun See, Caroline, BA Leeds, MSc Oxf., DPhil Oxf.   Sr. Lectr.

Yu, Qiao, BA Sichuan, MA Mich.State, PhD Mich.State   Sr. Lectr.

Zhang, Zhaoyong, BA Shandong, MBA Leuven, MA Leuven, PhD Leuven   Sr. Lectr.

Engineering

Dean's Office

Tel: 874 2101 Fax: 777 3847

Eleuterio, H. S., BSc Tufts, PhD Mich.State   Visiting Prof.

CAE/CAD/CAM Centre

Dean's Office

Tel: 874 2994 Fax: 777 8691

Choo, Yoo Sang, BSc Manc., MSc Manc., PhD Manc., FIMarE

Engineering, Chemical

Tel: 874 3044 Fax: 779 1936

Chiew, Y. C., BSc Edin., PhD Penn.   Assoc. Prof.

Ching, C. B., BSc Aston, PhD Aston   Assoc. Prof.

Chiu, M. S., BSc Natnl.Taiwan, MS W.Virginia, PhD Georgia I.T.   Sr. Lectr.

Chung, N. T. S., BS Chung Yuan, MS Natnl.Taiwan, PhD N.Y.State   Assoc. Prof.

Farooq, S., BSc B'desh.Engin., MSc B'desh.Engin., PhD New Br.   Sr. Lectr.

Feng, S., BSc Peking, MSc Tsing Hua, PhD Col.   Sr. Lectr.

Garland, M. V., BSc Penn.State, MSc Northwestern, PhD E.T.H.Zürich   Sr. Lectr.

Hidajat, K., BSc Manc., PhD Camb.   Sr. Lectr.

Kang, E. T., BA Nebraska, BS Wis., MS N.Y.State, PhD N.Y.State   Assoc. Prof.

Kocherginsky, N. M., MS Moscow, PhD Russian Acad.Sc.   Sr. Lectr.

Krishnaswamy, P. R., BSc Ban., PhD New Br.   Assoc. Prof.

Lau, W. W. Y., BSc Qu., MASc Wat., PhD Wat.   Assoc. Prof.

Lee, J. Y., BSc Sing., MSc(Eng) Mich., PhD Mich.   Assoc. Prof.

Li, K., BSc Shanghai Chem.Technol., MSc Salf., PhD Salf.   Sr. Lectr.

Neoh, Koon Gee, BSc M.I.T., DSc M.I.T.   Assoc. Prof.; Head*

Pandu Rangaiah, G., BTech And., MTech IIT Kanpur, PhD Monash   Assoc. Prof.

Srinivasan, M. P., BTech Madr., PhD Calif.   Sr. Lectr.

Stanforth, R. R., BSc Heidelberg Coll., MSc Wis., PhD Wis.   Sr. Lectr.

Tan, R. B. H., BSc Lond., MEng NU Singapore, PhD Camb.   Sr. Lectr.

Tan, T. C., BE Otago, PhD Manc.   Assoc. Prof.

Teo, W. K., BSc Natnl.Taiwan, MASc Wat., PhD Wat.   Assoc. Prof.

Ti, H. C., BSc Natnl.Cheng Kung, PhD Leeds   Sr. Lectr.

Tien, Chi, BSc Natnl.Taiwan, MS Kansas State, PhD Northwestern   Visiting Prof.

Ting, Y. P., BSc Manc., MSc Manc., PhD Monash   Sr. Lectr.

Uddin, M. S., BSc B'desh.Engin., MSc Manc., PhD Manc.   Sr. Lectr.

Viswanathan, S., BTech Madr., MASc Windsor, PhD Windsor   Sr. Lectr.

Yap, Miranda G. S., BSc Sing., MSc Lond., PhD Tor.   Assoc. Prof. (on leave)

Zeng, H. C., BSc Xiamen, PhD Br.Col.   Sr. Lectr.

Engineering, Civil

Tel: 874 2149 Fax: 779 1635

Alwis, W. A. M., BSc(Eng) Ceyl., MEng Asian I.T Bangkok, PhD Monash   Assoc. Prof.; Dir., Computer-Based Learning Centre

Ang, K. K., BEng Sing., MEng NU Singapore, PhD NSW   Sr. Lectr.

Balendra, T., BSc S.Lanka, MEng Asian I.T., Bangkok, PhD Northwestern   Assoc. Prof.; Dir., Centre for Wind-Resistant Structures

Chan, E. S., BEng Sing., MEng NU Singapore, ScD M.I.T.   Assoc. Prof.; Head, Phys. Oceanog. Res. Lab.

Chan, W. T., BEng Sing., MEng NU Singapore, MSc Stan., PhD Stan.   Sr. Lectr.

Cheong, H. F., BEng Sing., MS Cinc., PhD Colorado State   Prof.

Chin, H. C., BEng Sing., MEng NU Singapore, PhD S'ton.   Sr. Lectr.

Chow, Y. K., BSc Manc., MSc Manc., PhD Manc.   Assoc. Prof.

Chua, D. K. H., BE Adel., MEng NU Singapore, MSc Calif., PhD Calif.   Sr. Lectr.

Fwa, T. F., BEng Sing., MASc Wat., PhD Purdue   Assoc. Prof.; Dir., Centre for Transportation Res.

Karunaratne, G. P., BSc(Eng) Ceyl., PhD Manc., FGS   Visiting Assoc. Prof.

Koe, L. C. C., BEng Sing., MSc Sing., PhD Qld.   Assoc. Prof.

Koh, C. G., BEng Sing., MEng NU Singapore, MS Calif., PhD Calif.   Sr. Lectr.

Lee, F. H., BEng Monash, MEng NU Singapore, MPhil Camb., PhD Camb.   Assoc. Prof.

Lee, S. L., BSCE Mapua I.T., Manila, MSE Mich., PhD Calif.   Emer. Prof.

Leung, C. F., BEng Liv., PhD Liv.   Assoc. Prof.

Liaw, C. Y., BSc Natnl.Taiwan, MASc Wat., PhD Calif.   Assoc. Prof.

Liew, R. J. Y., BEng NU Singapore, MEng NU Singapore, PhD Purdue   Sr. Lectr.

Liong, S. Y., PhD Iowa   Assoc. Prof.

Lo, K. W., BSc Lond., MSc Lond., PhD Lond.   Sr. Lectr.

Loo, Y. H., BEng Sing., PhD Melb.   Sr. Lectr.

Mansur, M. A., BSc(Engin) B'desh.Engin., MSc(Engin) B'desh. Engin., PhD NSW   Assoc. Prof.

Ng, W. J., BSc Lond., MSc Birm., PhD Birm.   Assoc. Prof.; Dir., Environmental Engin. Specialisation Programme

Ong, G. K. C., BEng Sing., PhD Dund.   Assoc. Prof.

Ong, S. L., BEng Sing., MESc W.Ont., PhD Tor.   Assoc. Prof.

Paramasivam, P., BE Madr., MSc Madr., PhD IIT Kanpur   Prof.; Dir., Centre for Construcn. Materials and Technol.; Head, Struct. and Construcn. Engin. Div.

Quek, S. T., BEng Monash, MEng NU Singapore, MS Ill., PhD Ill.   Sr. Lectr.

Shankar, N. J., BE Mys., MTech IIT Madras, PhD Texas   Prof.; Head, Hydraulic and Environmental Engin. Div.

Shanmugam, N. E., BE Madr., MSc(Engg) Madr., PhD Wales   Assoc. Prof.

Swaddiwudhipong, S., BEng Chulalongkorn, MEng Asian I.T., Bangkok, PhD HK   Assoc. Prof.

Tan, K. H., BEng Tokyo I.T., MEng NU Singapore, DrEng Tokyo   Sr. Lectr.

Tan, S. A., BEng Auck., MEng NU Singapore, MSc Calif., PhD Calif.   Sr. Lectr.

Tan, T. S., BE Cant., MSc Cal.Tech., PhD Cal.Tech.   Assoc. Prof.; Dir., Centre for Soft Ground Engin.

Thevendran, V., BSc(Eng) Ceyl., PhD Camb.   Sr. Lectr.

Wang, C. M., BEng Monash, MEng Monash, PhD Monash   Assoc. Prof.

Wee, T. H., BEng Tokyo I.T., MEng NU Singapore, DrEng Tokyo I.T.   Sr. Lectr.

Yong, K. Y., BEng Sheff., PhD Sheff.   Assoc. Prof.; Head*

Yu, C. H., BEng Sing., MSc Wis., PhD Wis.   Sr. Lectr.

Other Staff: 4 Lectrs.; 1 Sr. Tutor; 4 Postdoctoral Fellows; 5 Res. Fellows; 2 Res. Engineers; 1 Adjunct Assoc. Prof.

Engineering, Electrical

Tel: 874 2109 Fax: 779 1103, 777 3117

Ashraf, A. Kassim, BEng NU Singapore, MEng NU Singapore, PhD Carnegie-Mellon   Sr. Lectr.

Chan, D. S. H., BSc Manc., MSc Manc., PhD Salf.   Prof.; Head*

Chang, C. S., MSc Manc., PhD Manc.   Assoc. Prof.

Chen, Benmei, BS Xiamen, MS Gonzaga, PhD Wash.   Sr. Lectr.

Chim, W. K., BEng NU Singapore, PhD NU Singapore   Sr. Lectr.

Cho, B. J., PhD Korea A.I.S.T.   Sr. Lectr.

Choi, W. K., BSc Edin., MBA Edin., PhD Edin.   Sr. Lectr.

Chong, T. C., BEng Tokyo I.T., MEng NU Singapore, ScD M.I.T.   Sr. Lectr.

Chor, Eng Fong, BEng Sing., MEng NU Singapore, PhD S'ton.   Sr. Lectr.

Chua, K. C., BEng Auck., MEng NU Singapore, PhD Auck.   Sr. Lectr.

Chua, S. J., BEng Sing., PhD Wales   Assoc. Prof.

Devotta, J. B. X., BSc S.Lanka, PhD Lond.   Sr. Lectr.

Eccleston, K. W., BSc Beijing Aeron.& Astron., PhD Qld.   Sr. Lectr.

Elangovan, S., BE Annam., MSc(Engg) Annam., PhD IIT Madras   Assoc. Prof.

Farhang-Boroujeni, B., BSc Teheran, MEng Wales, PhD Lond.   Sr. Lectr.

Foo, S. W., BEng Newcastle(UK), MSc Sing., PhD Lond.   Assoc. Prof.

Garg, H. K., BTech IIT Madras, MEng C'dia., PhD C'dia.   Sr. Lectr.

Haldar, M. K., BE Jad., ME IISc., PhD Camb.   Sr. Lectr.

Hang, C. C., BEng Sing., MSc Warw., PhD Warw.   Prof.

Ho, W. K., BEng NU Singapore, PhD NU Singapore   Sr. Lectr.

Jabbar, M. A., BSc(Engin) Dhaka, PhD S'ton.   Assoc. Prof.

Kam, P. Y., BS M.I.T., MS M.I.T., PhD M.I.T.   Assoc. Prof.

Karunasiri, Gamani, BSc Colombo, MS Pitt., PhD Pitt.   Sr. Lectr.

Khursheed, A., BSc Edin., PhD Edin.   Sr. Lectr.

Ko, C. C., BSc Lough., PhD Lough.   Assoc. Prof.

Kooi, P. S., BSc Natnl.Taiwan, MSc Manc., DPhil Oxf.   Prof.

Lee, T. H., BA Camb., MEng NU Singapore, MSc Yale, PhD Yale   Assoc. Prof.

Leong, M. S., BSc(Eng) Lond., PhD Lond.   Prof.

Li, M. F.   Prof.

Liang, Y. C., MEng Natnl.Tsing Hua, PhD Syd.   Sr. Lectr.

Lie, T. J., BSc(Eng) Lond., PhD Lond.   Sr. Lectr.

Liew, A. C., BE Qld., PhD Qld.   Prof.

Lim, Y. C., BSc Lond., PhD Lond.   Assoc. Prof.

Ling, C. H., BSc Lond., PhD Lond.   Assoc. Prof.

Loh, Ai Poh, BEng Malaya, DPhil Oxf.   Sr. Lectr.

Low, T. S., BSc S'ton., PhD S'ton.   Prof.

Lu, Y. F., BEng Tsing Hua, MEng Osaka, PhD Osaka   Sr. Lectr.

Lye, K. M., BSc Alta., MEng Sing., PhD Hawaii   Assoc. Prof.

Mendis, F. V. C., BSc(Eng) Ceyl., MSc(Eng) Birm., PhD Birm.   Assoc. Prof.

Ng, C. S., BEng Sing., MEng NU Singapore, PhD Wis.   Sr. Lectr.

Ng, S. S., BSc Birm., PhD Birm.   Sr. Lectr.

Ong, K. K. W., BSc Leeds, PhD Camb.   Assoc. Prof.

Ong, S. H., BE W.Aust., PhD Syd.   Sr. Lectr.

Oruganti, R., BTech IIT Madras, MTech IIT Madras, PhD Virginia Polytech.   Sr. Lectr.

Phang, J. C. H., BA Camb., MA Camb., PhD Camb.   Prof.

Ranganath, S., BTech IIT Kanpur, ME IISc., PhD Calif.   Sr. Lectr.

Samudra, G. S., BSc Nag., MSc IIT Bombay, MS Purdue, PhD Purdue   Sr. Lectr.

Tan, B. T., BSc Leeds, MEng NU Singapore, PhD Camb.   Sr. Lectr. (on leave)

Tan, L. S., BEng Sing., MEng NU Singapore, PhD Hawaii   Sr. Lectr.

Tay, T. T., BEng NU Singapore, PhD ANU   Sr. Lectr.

Thong, J. T. L., BA Camb., MA Camb., PhD Camb.   Sr. Lectr.

Tjhung, T. T., BEng Car., MEng Car., PhD Qu.   Prof.

Uysal, S., BEng E.Mediterranean, MSc Lond., PhD Lond.   Sr. Lectr.

Wang, Q. G., BEng Zhejiang, MEng Zhejiang, PhD Zhejiang   Sr. Lectr.

Wong, L. W. C., BSc Lough., PhD Lough.   Assoc. Prof.

Wu, Y. H., BSc Shaanxi Normal, MEng Shizouka, PhD Kyoto   Sr. Lectr.

Xu, J. X., BSc Zhejiang, MEng Tokyo, PhD Tokyo   Sr. Lectr.

Ye, Q. Z., BSSc Shanghai, Lic Linköping, PhD Linköping   Sr. Lectr.

Yeo, S. P., BA Camb., MA Camb., MEng NU Singapore, PhD Lond.   Assoc. Prof.

Yeo, T. S., BEng Sing., MEng NU Singapore, PhD Cant.   Assoc. Prof.

Engineering, Industrial and Systems

Tel: 874 2249 Fax: 777 1434

Ang, B. W., BSc Nan., PhD Camb.   Assoc. Prof.

Chew, E. P., BEng NU Singapore, MEng NU Singapore, MS Georgia I.T., PhD Georgia I.T.   Sr. Lectr.

Goh, T. N., BE Sask., PhD Wis.   Prof.; Head*

Ibrahim, Y., BEng Sing., MSc N.U.Singapore, PhD Stan.   Sr. Lectr.

Ong, H. L., BSc Nan., MSc Lake., MSc McM., PhD Wat.   Assoc. Prof.

Poh, K. L., BEng NU Singapore, MEng NU Singapore, MS   Sr. Lectr.

Tan, K. C., BS Mass., MS Mass., PhD Virginia Polytech.   Sr. Lectr.

Tang, L. C., BEng NU Singapore, MEng NU Singapore, MSc Cornell, PhD Cornell   Sr. Lectr.

Xie, M., MSc R.I.T.Stockholm, PhD Linköping   Sr. Lectr.

Yap, C. M., BEng NU Singapore, MS Pitt.   Sr. Lectr.

Engineering, Mechanical and Production

Tel: 874 2212 Fax: 779 1459

Ang, M. H., BS De La Salle, MS Hawaii, MS Roch., PhD Roch.   Sr. Lectr.

Chau, F. S., BSc Nott., PhD Nott.   Assoc. Prof.

Cheng, L., MS Tsing Hua, PhD Tsing Hua   Sr. Lectr.

Chew, C. H., BEng Sing., MS(ME) Georgia I.T., PhD Georgia I.T.   Sr. Lectr.

Chew, T. C., BE Monash, MEng NU Singapore, PhD Camb.   Sr. Lectr. (on leave)

Chew, Y. T., BE W.Aust., MEngSc W.Aust., PhD Camb.   Prof.

Chou, S. K., BEng Sing., DrIng École Nat.Sup.d'Arts & Métiers, Paris   Assoc. Prof.

Fuh, J. Y. H., BSc Natnl.Chiao Tung, MBA Natnl.Taiwan, MSc Calif., PhD Calif.   Sr. Lectr.

Gupta, M., BE Nag., ME IISc., PhD Calif.   Sr. Lectr.

Hawlader, M. N. A., BSc(Engin) Dhaka, MSc Strath., PhD Strath.   Assoc. Prof.

Ho, J. C., BSc Lond., MS Wis., PhD Wis.   Assoc. Prof.

Hong, G. S., BEng Sheff., PhD Sheff.   Sr. Lectr.

Khoo, B. C., BA Camb., MEng NU Singapore, PhD M.I.T.   Sr. Lectr.

Krishnan, H., BE Anna, MASc Wat., PhD Mich.   Sr. Lectr.

Lai, M. O., BE Auck., ME Auck., PhD Auck.   Assoc. Prof.

Lam, K. Y., BSc Lond., MSc M.I.T., PhD M.I.T.   Assoc. Prof.

Lee, H. P., BA Camb., MA Camb., MEng NU Singapore, MS Stan., PhD Stan.   Sr. Lectr.

Lee, K. H., BSc Lond., PhD Lond.   Assoc. Prof.

Lee, K. S., BSc Manc., MSc Manc., PhD Manc.   Assoc. Prof.

Lee, T. S., BE NSW, PhD NSW   Assoc. Prof.

Leng, G. S. B., BS Ill., MS Ill., PhD Ill.   Sr. Lectr.

Li, X. P., BEng Guangxi, MEng Guangxi, PhD NSW   Sr. Lectr.

Lim, K. B., BEng Sing., DrIng École Centrale des A.&M. Sr. Lectr.

Lim, L. C., BSc Nan., MSc Leeds, PhD Cornell Assoc. Prof.

Lim, S. C., BA Oxf., MA Oxf., MEng NU Singapore, PhD Camb. Assoc. Prof.

Lim, S. P., BSc Sing., MSc S'ton., PhD S'ton. Sr. Lectr.

Lim, T. T., BE Melb., PhD Melb. Sr. Lectr.

Liu, G. R., BEng Hunan, MEng Beijing Aeron.& Astron., PhD Tohoku Sr. Lectr.

Loh, H. T., BE Adel., MEng NU Singapore, MSc Mich., PhD Mich. Sr. Lectr.

Low, H. T., BEng Sheff., MEng McG., PhD McG. Sr. Lectr.

Lu Li, BEng Qinghua, MEng Qinghua, PhD Leuven Sr. Lectr.

Luo, S. C., BE Melb., MEng NU Singapore, PhD Lond. Sr. Lectr.

Mannan, M. A., MSc P.F.U., Moscow, PhD R.I.T.Stockholm Sr. Lectr.

Nee, A. Y. C., MSc Manc., PhD Manc. Prof.

Ng, K. C., BSc Strath., PhD Strath. Assoc. Prof.

Ong, C. J., BEng NU Singapore, MEng NU Singapore, MSE Mich., PhD Mich. Sr. Lectr.

Poo, A. N., PPA, BEng Sing., MSc Wis., PhD Wis. Assoc. Prof.

Rahman, M., BSc(Engin) Dhaka, MEng Tokyo I.T., DrEng Tokyo I.T. Assoc. Prof.

Seah, W. K. H., BSc S'ton., MSc Qu., PhD Qu. Assoc. Prof.

Seeram, R., BE And., MTech IIT Madras, PhD Camb. Sr. Lectr.

Shah, D. A., BSc Baroda, BTech IIT Madras, ME IISc., PhD Newcastle(NSW) Sr. Lectr.

Shang, H. M., BEng Sing., MSc Aston, PhD Aston Prof.; Head*

Shim, V. P. W., BE Auck., MEng NU Singapore, PhD Camb. Assoc. Prof.

Shu Chang, BEng Nanjing Aeron.& Astron., MEng Nanjing Aeron.& Astron., PhD Glas. Sr. Lectr.

Tay, A. A. O., BE NSW, PhD NSW Assoc. Prof.

Tay, C. J., BSc Strath., PhD Strath. Assoc. Prof.

Tay, T. E., BE Melb., PhD Melb. Sr. Lectr.

Teo, C. L., BEng Sing., MEng NU Singapore, PhD Calif. Sr. Lectr.

Teoh, S. H., BEng Monash, PhD Monash Assoc. Prof.

Toh, S. L., BSc Strath., PhD Strath. Assoc. Prof.

Wijeysundera, N. E., BSc S.Lanka, MSc Birm., PhD Birm. Assoc. Prof.

Winoto, S. H., BSc Lond., MSc Lond., PhD Lond. Sr. Lectr.

Wong, Y. S., BEng Sing., MEng NU Singapore, PhD Manc. Assoc. Prof.

Yap, C. R., BESc W.Ont., MEng NU Singapore, PhD Manc. Sr. Lectr.

Yeo, K. S., BE Auck., MEng NU Singapore, PhD Camb. Assoc. Prof.

Zhang, Y. F., BSc Shanghai Jiaotong, PhD Bath Sr. Lectr.

Engineering, Postgraduate, School of

Tel: 874 6510 Fax: 777 2264

Poo, A. N., PPA, BEng Sing., MSc Wis., PhD Wis. Dir.*

English Language and Literature, see also Special Centres, etc

Tel: 874 3914 Fax: 732 2981

Allison, D., BA Sus., MèsL Dijon, PhD Reading Sr. Lectr.

Ban, K. C., BA Sing., PhD Sing. Assoc. Prof.; Head*

Bao, Zhiming, PhD M.I.T. Sr. Lectr.

Dawson, T. R., BA E.Anglia, PhD E.Anglia Sr. Lectr.

Foley, J. A., BA Trinity(Dub.), PhD Lond. Assoc. Prof.

Lee, Tzu-Pheng, BA Sing., PhD Sing. Assoc. Prof.

Leong, Liew-Geok, BA La Trobe, MA Leic., PhD George Washington Sr. Lectr.

Lindley, A. D. L., BA Calif., MA Col., PhD Rutgers Sr. Lectr.

Mohanan, K. P., BSc Kerala, MA Meerut, MS M.I.T., PhD M.I.T. Assoc. Prof.

Mohanan, Tara W., BA Kerala, MA Calicut, MLitt CIE&F Langs., PhD Stan. Sr. Lectr.

Pakir, Anne, BA Sing., MA Calif., PhD Hawaii Sr. Lectr.

Pan, Daphne, BA Sing., MSc Sur., MA York(Can.), PhD York(Can.) Sr. Lectr.

Patke, R. S., BA Poona, MA Poona, DPhil Oxf. Sr. Lectr.

Rubdy, R. S., BA Shiv., MA Shiv., MLitt CIE&F Langs., PhD CIE&F Langs. Sr. Lectr.

Seet, K. K., MA Tor., PhD Exe. Sr. Lectr.

Talib, I. S., BA Sing., MA NU Singapore, PhD E.Anglia Sr. Lectr.

Tan, P. K. W., BA Malaya, PhD Edin. Sr. Lectr.

Thompson, L. A., BPhil(Ed) Birm., MA Birm., PhD Durh. Sr. Lectr.

Thumboo, E., BBM, BA Malaya, PhD Sing. Prof. Fellow

Turner, B. E., BA Br.Col., MA E.Anglia, PhD Oregon Sr. Lectr.

White, T. R., BA Oakland, MA Wis., PhD Wis. Sr. Lectr.

Yong, L. L., BA Oxf., PhD Lond. Sr. Lectr.

European Studies Programme

Dean's Office, Faculty of Arts and Social Sciences

Tel: 874 6346 Fax: 775 9104

Gilberg, T., BA Wis., MA Wis., PhD Wis. Assoc. Prof.

Finance and Accounting

Tel: 874 3003 Fax: 779 2083

Chang, Shih Kang Jack, BS Natnl.Taiwan, ME Tor., MBA Houston, PhD Houston Sr. Lectr.

Chong, Sebastian Y. S., BAcc Sing., MEc Syd. Sr. Lectr.

Fong, Wai Mun, BSocSci NU Singapore, PhD Manc. Sr. Lectr.

Hameed, Allaudeen, BBA NU Singapore, PhD N.Carolina Sr. Lectr.

Koh, Annie, BA Sing., BSocSci Sing., MPhil N.Y., PhD N.Y. Sr. Lectr.

Koh, Seng Kee, BBA NU Singapore, PhD Penn. Sr. Lectr.

Lam, Swee-Sum, BAcc Sing., PhD Wash. Sr. Lectr.

Lim, Joseph Y. S., BBA Sing., MBA Col., MPhil N.Y., PhD N.Y. Sr. Lectr.

Lim, Kian Guan, BSc Manc., MS Stan., MA Stan., PhD Stan. Assoc. Prof.

Loh, Alfred L. C., BAcc Sing., MCom NSW, PhD W.Aust. Sr. Lectr.

Mak Yuen Teen, BCom Otago, PhD Well. Sr. Lectr.

Mao, Jennifer M. H., BBA Natnl.Taiwan, MCom Natnl.Chengchi, PhD Br.Col. Sr. Lectr.

Muthuswamy, Jayaram, BSc Lond., MBA Penn., MS Stan., PhD Chic. Sr. Lectr.

Ng, Edward H. K., BBA NU Singapore, PhD Ohio State Sr. Lectr.

Shih, Sheng-Hua Michael, BS Natnl.Taiwan, MS Akron, PhD Minn. Sr. Lectr.

Tan, Ruth S.-K., BAcc NU Singapore, MSc Penn.State, PhD Wash. Sr. Lectr.

Tsui, Kai Chong, BA CNAA, MPhil N.Y., PhD N.Y. Sr. Lectr.

Wilkins, Trevor A., MCom NSW, BCom Qld., PhD Qld. Assoc. Prof.

Wong, Kie Ann, BCom Chinese HK, MCom Chinese HK, PhD Liv. Assoc. Prof.; Head*

Wu, Chuang C.-Y. C., BA Natnl.Taiwan, BS Minn., MS Calif.State, PhD Calif. Sr. Lectr.

Zubaidah Bte Ismail, BAcc Sing., MCom NSW, PhD NSW Sr. Lectr.

Geography

Tel: 874 3853 Fax: 777 3091

Cheng, L. K., BA Nan., MA Well., PhD Lond. Sr. Lectr.

Chia, L. S., BA Syd., MSc McG., PhD Sing. Assoc. Prof.

Greer, Anthony, BA Lond., PhD Lond. Sr. Lectr.

Grundy-Warr, Carl, BA Leic., MA Durh., PhD Durh. Sr. Lectr.

Gupta, A., MA Calc., PhD Johns H. Assoc. Prof.

Huang, Shirlena S. L., BA Sing., MA NU Singapore., PhD Tor. Sr. Lectr.

Kong, Lily L. L., BA NU Singapore, MA NU Singapore, PhD Lond. Sr. Lectr.

Perry, Martin, BSc H.-W., PhD CNAA, MRTP Sr. Lectr.

Raguraman, K., BA NU Singapore, MA NU Singapore, PhD Wash. Sr. Lectr.

Rahman, A., BSc Karachi, MSc Karachi, MSc Hawaii, PhD Hawaii Assoc. Prof.

Savage, V. R., BA Sing., MA Calif., PhD Calif. Assoc. Prof.

Taylor, David, BSc Leeds, DPhil Ulster Sr. Lectr.

Teo Cheok Chin, Peggy, BA Sing., MA NU Singapore, MS Penn.State, PhD Penn.State Sr. Lectr.

Teo, Siew Eng, BA Syd., MA ANU, PhD Sing. Assoc. Prof.; Head*

Wong, P. P., BA Sing., MA Sing., PhD McG. Assoc. Prof.

Yeoh, Brenda S. A., BA Camb., MA Camb., DPhil Oxf. Sr. Lectr.

History

Tel: 874 3839 Fax: 774 2528

Borschberg, Peter, BA Kent, PhD Camb. Sr. Lectr.

Chew, E. C. T., PBM, MA Sing., PhD Camb. Assoc. Prof.

Hashmi, T. I., MA Dacca, PhD W.Aust. Sr. Lectr.

Hong, Lysa, BA Sing., PhD Syd. Sr. Lectr.

Huang, Jianli, BA NU Singapore, PhD ANU Sr. Lectr.

Kratoska, P., BSc Iowa State, MA Chic., PhD Chic. Sr. Lectr.

Kwan, Siu Hing, BA HK, PhD Lond. Sr. Lectr.

Lau, A. K. H., BA NU Singapore, PhD Lond. Sr. Lectr.

Lee, E. S. C., BA Sing., MA Cornell, PhD Assoc. Prof.; Head*

Major, A. J., MA Cant., PhD ANU Sr. Lectr.

Murfett, M. H., BA Leeds, DPhil Oxf. Assoc. Prof.

Ng, C. K., BA Nan., MA Wis., PhD ANU Assoc. Prof.

Tan, Tai Yong, BA NU Singapore, MA NU Singapore, PhD Camb. Sr. Lectr.

Yeo, K. W., MA Sing., PhD ANU Assoc. Prof.

Yong, M. C., BA Sing., MA Yale, PhD Assoc. Prof.

Information Systems and Computer Science

Tel: 874 2726 Fax: 779 4580

Ananda, A. L., BE B'lore., MTech IIT Kanpur, MSc Manc., PhD Manc. Assoc. Prof.

Ang, C. H., BSc Nan., MSc Nan., PhD Maryland Sr. Lectr.

Aravind, Srinivasan, BTech IIT Madr., MS Cornell, PhD Cornell Sr. Lectr.

Chan, H. C., BA Camb., MA Camb., PhD Br.Col. Sr. Lectr.

Chee, Y. S., BSc(Econ) Lond., PhD Qld. Sr. Lectr.

Chi Chi-Hung, BSc Wis., PhD Purdue Sr. Lectr.

Chin, Wei Ngan, BSc Manc., MSc Manc., PhD Lond. Sr. Lectr.

Chionh, E. W., BSc Nan., MMath Wat., PhD Wat. Sr. Lectr.

Chong, C. T., BS Iowa State, PhD Yale Prof.; Head*

Chua, T. S., BSc Leeds, PhD Leeds Assoc. Prof.

Heng, A. K., BSc Nan., MSc Nantes, PhD Toulouse Sr. Lectr.

Ho, Y. S., BSc Natnl.Taiwan, MSc Tor., PhD Wat. Sr. Lectr.

Hui Chi Kwong, Lucas, BSc HK, MPhil HK, MSc Calif., PhD Calif. Sr. Lectr.

Jaffar, Joxan, BSc Melb., MSc Melb., PhD Monash Prof.

Jain, Sanjay, BTech Kharagpur, MSc Roch., PhD Roch. Sr. Lectr.

Jarzabek, S., BSc Warsaw, MSc Warsaw, PhD Warsaw Sr. Lectr.

Khoo, Siau Cheng, BSc NU Singapore, MSc NU Singapore, PhD Yale Sr. Lectr.

Kiong, D. B. K., BSc Manc., PhD Qld. Sr. Lectr.

Lam, K. Y., BSc Lond., PhD Camb. Sr. Lectr.

Leong, H. W., BSc Malaya, MSc Ill., PhD Ill. Sr. Lectr.

Lim Leong Chye, Andrew, BCompSci Minn., MS Minn., PhD Minn. Sr. Lectr.

Ling, T. W., BSc Nan., MMath Wat., PhD Wat. Assoc. Prof.

Liu, B., BEng N.W.Inst.of Light Industry, PhD Edin. Sr. Lectr.

Liu, Huan, BEng Shanghai Jiaotong, MSc S.Calif., PhD S.Calif. Sr. Lectr.

Loe, K. F., BSc Nan., MSc Nan., DrSc Tokyo Sr. Lectr.

Loh, W. L., BSc Cheng Kung, PhD Reading Sr. Lectr.

Lu, H. J., BSc Tsing Hua, MSc Wis., PhD Wis. Assoc. Prof.

Lua, K. T., BSc Sing., PhD NU Singapore Assoc. Prof.

McCallum, J. C., BSc W.Ont., PhD York(Can.) Sr. Lectr.

Ong, G. H., BSc Nan., MSc Nan., MSc Lond., PhD Lough. Sr. Lectr.

Ooi, B. C., BSc Monash, PhD Monash Sr. Lectr.

Phua, P. K. H., PBM, BSc Nan., MSc Vic.(BC), PhD Tor. Assoc. Prof.

Png, P. L. I., BA Camb., PhD Stan. Prof.

Poo, C. C., BSc Manc., MSc Manc., PhD Manc. Sr. Lectr.

Poo, G. S., BSc Sing., MSc Lond., PhD Leeds Assoc. Prof.

Pung, H. K., BSc Kent, PhD Kent Sr. Lectr.

Setiono, R., BSc E.Mich., MSc Wis., PhD Wis. Sr. Lectr.

Sung, S. Y., BSc Natnl.Taiwan, MSc Minn., PhD Minn. Sr. Lectr.

Tan, S. T., BSc Nan., MSc Essex, PhD Essex Sr. Lectr.

Tan, Tiow Seng, BSc NU Singapore, MSc NU Singapore, PhD Ill. Sr. Lectr.

Teo, Y. M., BTech Brad., MSc Manc., PhD Manc. Sr. Lectr.

Wang Ke, BSc Chongqing, MSc Georgia I.T., PhD Georgia I.T. Sr. Lectr.

Wei, K. K., BSc Nan., DPhil York(UK) Assoc. Prof.

Wong, Weng Fai, BSc NU Singapore, MSc NU Singapore, DrEngSc Tsukuba Sr. Lectr.

Yap, C. S., BEng Lond., PhD Camb. Sr. Lectr.

Yeo, G. K., BSc Sing., MMath Wat., MASc Wat., PhD Wat. Sr. Lectr.

Yuen, C. K., BSc Alta., MSc Tor., PhD Syd. Prof.

Other Staff: 1 Adjunct Prof.; 1 Adjunct Sr. Lectr.

Japanese Studies
Tel: 874 3728 Fax: 776 1409

Teow, See Heng, BA NU Singapore, PhD Harv. Sr. Lectr.; Head*

Tsu, Timothy Yun Hui, BA Internat.Christian(Tokyo), MA Prin., PhD Prin. Sr. Lectr.

Law
Tel: 874 3604 Fax: 779 0979

Beckman, Robert C., BBA Wis., JD Wis., LLM Harv. Assoc. Prof.

Chan, Helena H. M., LLB NU Singapore, LLM Harv. Sr. Lectr.

Chin, Tet Yung, LLB Lond., BCL Oxf. Assoc. Prof.; Head*

Chong, David G. S., LLB NU Singapore, LLM Lond. Assoc. Prof. (on leave)

Crown, Barry C., LLB Jerusalem, LLM Lond., MLitt Oxf. Sr. Lectr.

Ellinger, E. P., MJur Jerusalem, DPhil Oxf. Prof.

Ho, Peng Kee, LLB Sing., LLM Harv. Assoc. Prof. (on leave)

Hor, Michael Y. M., BCL Oxf., LLB NU Singapore Sr. Lectr.

Hsu, Locknie, LLB NU Singapore, LLM Harv. Sr. Lectr.

Iyer, T. K. K., BSc Madr., BL Madr., LLM Lond., PhD Lond. Sr. Lectr.

Jayakumar, S., BBM, LLB Sing., LLM Yale Prof. (on leave)

Kaan, Terry S. H., LLB NU Singapore, LLM Harv. Sr. Lectr.

Koh, Kheng-Lian, LLB Malaya, LLM Sing., PhD Sing. Prof.

Koh, Tommy T. B., PJG, BBM, DUBC, LLB Malaya, LLM Harv., LLD Yale Prof. (on leave)

Leong Wai Kum, LLB Malaya, LLM Harv. Assoc. Prof.

Li, Mei Qin, LLM Col., LLB Peking Sr. Lectr.

Lye, Irene L. H., LLB Sing., LLM Lond., LLM Harv. Assoc. Prof.

Neo, Dora S. S., BA Oxf., MA Oxf., LLM Harv. Sr. Lectr.

Ng, Siew Kuan, LLB Lond., LLM Camb. Sr. Lectr.

Penna, L. R., BCom Osm., LLB Osm., LLM Osm., LLM Stan. Assoc. Prof.

Phang, Andrew B. L., LLB NU Singapore, LLM Harv., SJD Harv. Assoc. Prof.

Phua Lye Huat, Stephen, LLB NU Singapore, LLM Lond. Sr. Lectr.

Pinsler, Jeffrey D., LLB Liv., LLM Camb. Assoc. Prof.

Poh, Chu Chai, LLB Sing., LLM Lond., LLD Lond. Assoc. Prof.

Soh, Kee Bun, LLB NU Singapore, BCL Oxf. Sr. Lectr.

Sornarajah, M., LLB Ceyl., LLM Lond., LLM Yale, PhD Lond., LLD Lond. Prof.

Tan Cheng Han, LLB NU Singapore, LLM Camb. Sr. Lectr.

Tan, Keng Feng, LLB Camb., LLB Sing., MBA Geneva Assoc. Prof.

Tan, Kevin Y. L., LLB NU Singapore, LLM Yale, JSD Yale Sr. Lectr.

Tan, Sook-Yee, BA Trinity(Dub.), LLB Trinity(Dub.) Assoc. Prof.

Tan, Yock Lin, BSc Lond., BA Oxf., BCL Oxf. Assoc. Prof.

Tay, S. C. Simon, LLB NU Singapore, LLM Harv. Sr. Lectr.

Teo, Keang Sood, LLB Malaya, LLM Malaya, LLM Harv. Sr. Lectr.

Tijo, Hans, BA Camb., LLM Harv. Sr. Lectr.

Wei, George S. S., LLM Lond. Assoc. Prof.

Winslow, V. S., LLB Camb., MA Camb. Assoc. Prof.

Woon, Walter C. M., LLB NU Singapore, LLM Camb. Assoc. Prof. (on leave)

Yeo, Hwee Ying, LLB Sing., LLM Lond. Sr. Lectr.

Yeo Tiong Min, LLB NU Singapore, LLM Lond. Sr. Lectr.

Malay Studies
Tel: 874 2635 Fax: 773 2980

Shaharuddin, M., BSocSc Sci.U.Malaysia, MA PhD Sr. Lectr.; Head*

Teoh, Boon Seong, BA Malaya, MA Ill., PhD Ill. Sr. Lectr.

Tham, S. C., BA Malaya, PhD Sing. Prof. Fellow

Marketing
Tel: 874 3003 Fax: 776 3604

Abdur Razzaque, M., BSc B'desh.Engin., MBA Indiana, PhD NSW Sr. Lectr.

Ang, Swee Hoon, BBA NU Singapore, PhD Br.Col. Sr. Lectr.

Kau, Ah Keng, BEc Malaya, MA Lanc., PhD Lond. Assoc. Prof.; Head*

Lau, Geok Theng, BBA NU Singapore, PhD W.Ont. Sr. Lectr.

Leong, Siew Meng, BBA NU Singapore, MBA Wis., PhD Wis. Assoc. Prof.

Shamdasani, Prem, BBA NU Singapore, PhD S.Calif. Sr. Lectr.

Tan, Chin Tiong, BBA Sing., MBA W.Illinois, PhD Penn.State Prof.

Materials Science
Tel: 874 2610 Fax: 777 6126

Blackwood, D. J., BSc S'ton., PhD S'ton. Sr. Lectr.

Bourdillon, Antony J., BA Oxf., DPhil Oxf. Visiting Prof.

Chan, H. S. O., BSc South Bank, PhD Manc. Prof.; Head*

Ding, J., DrRerNat Bochum Sr. Lectr.

Gong, Hao, BSc Yunnan, MSc Yunnan, PhD T.H.Delft Sr. Lectr.

Li, Yi, BSc Huazhong U.S.T., PhD Sheff. Sr. Lectr.

Ng, S. C., BSc Nan., MSc Dal., PhD McM. Prof.

Wang, J., PhD Leeds, BSc Sr. Lectr.

Xu, G., MSc Pitt., PhD Pitt., DES Col. Assoc. Prof.

Mathematics
Tel: 874 2737 Fax: 779 5452

Agarwal, R. P., MSc Agra, PhD IIT Madras Assoc. Prof.

Aslaksen, H., CandMag Oslo, PhD Calif. Sr. Lectr.

Berrick, A. J., BSc Syd., DPhil Oxf. Prof.

Chan, G. H., BSc Nan., PhD Br.Col. Assoc. Prof.

Chan, Onn, BSc NU Singapore, PhD Johns H. Sr. Lectr.

Chan, S. P., BA Camb., MA Camb., PhD Camb. Sr. Lectr.

Chan, Y. M., BA HK, MSc Tor., PhD Tor. Sr. Lectr.

Chen, C. C., BSc Nan., MSc Qu., PhD Qu. Assoc. Prof.

Chen, L. H.-Y., BSc Sing., MS Stan., PhD Stan. Prof.; Head*

Chen, Z. H., BSc Wuhan, MSc Iowa, PhD Wis. Sr. Lectr.

Cheng, Kai Nah, BSc Sing., MSc Sing., PhD Mainz Sr. Lectr.

Chew, T. S., BSc Nan., MSc Nan., PhD NU Singapore Sr. Lectr.

Choi, K. P., BSc HK, MSc Ill., PhD Ill. Sr. Lectr.

Chong, C. T., BS Iowa State, PhD Yale Prof.

Chow, Shui Nee, BSc Sing., PhD Maryland Prof.

Chua, Seng Kee, BSc NU Singapore, MSc NU Singapore, PhD Rutgers Sr. Lectr.

Feng, Qi, BS Harbin, MA Penn.State, PhD Penn.State Sr. Lectr.

Gan, F. F., BSc Malaya, MSc Iowa State, PhD Iowa State Sr. Lectr.

Gupta, R. C., MSc Agra, PhD IIT Kanpur Assoc. Prof.

Hsing, T., BSc Natnl.Taiwan, MSc N.Carolina, PhD N.Carolina Assoc. Prof.

Hu, K. Y., BA HK, MA Calif., PhD Calif. Sr. Lectr.

Jesudason, Judith, BA Wesleyan, MA Wesleyan, PhD Harv. Assoc. Prof.

Kan, C. H., BA HK, PhD McG. Sr. Lectr.

Koh, K. M., BSc Nan., MSc Manit., PhD Manit. Prof.

Koh, Liang Khoon, BSc NU Singapore, PhD Calif. Sr. Lectr.

Kwek, Keng Huat, BSc NU Singapore, MSc NU Singapore, PhD Georgia I.T. Sr. Lectr.

Lang, M. L., BSc Natnl.Central, PhD Ohio State Sr. Lectr.

Lawton, Wayne M., BA Wesleyan, PhD Wesleyan Res. Assoc. Prof.

Lee, S. L., BSc Malaya, MSc Malaya, PhD Alta. Prof.

Lee, Soo Teck, BSc NU Singapore, PhD Yale Sr. Lectr.

Leong, Y. K., BSc Sing., PhD ANU Sr. Lectr.

Leung, D. H. H., BS Illinois State, PhD Ill. Sr. Lectr.

Leung, F. P. F., BA HK, MA York(Can.), MSc Notre Dame(Ind.), PhD Notre Dame(Ind.) Sr. Lectr.

Leung, K. H., BSc HK, PhD Calif. Sr. Lectr.

Leung, Man Chun, BSc HK, MSc Mich., PhD Mich. Sr. Lectr.

Lim, C. H., BSc NU Singapore, MA Calif., PhD Calif. Sr. Lectr.

Lim, C. S., BSc Sing., PhD Leeds, FIMA Prof.

Lim, K. S., BSc Nan., MSc Manc., PhD Manc. Sr. Lectr.

Ling, K. D., BSc Nan., MA W.Ont., PhD W.Ont. Sr. Lectr.

Ling, San, BA Camb., MA Camb., PhD Calif. Sr. Lectr.

Loh, W. L., BSc Sing., MSc NU Singapore, MS Stan., PhD Stan. Sr. Lectr.

Loo, B. K. O., BA Hanover, MA N.Y.State, PhD N.Y.State Sr. Lectr.

Lou, J. H., BSc Natnl.Taiwan, PhD Cornell Sr. Lectr.

Ma, L. S. L., BSc HK, PhD HK Sr. Lectr.

Man, Shing Hing, BSc Lond., PhD Lond. Sr. Lectr.

McInnes, B. T., BSc Qld., MSc Syd., PhD Syd. Sr. Lectr.

Ng, T. B., BSc Warw., MSc Br.Col., PhD Warw. Sr. Lectr.

Pang, P. Y. H., BSc Tor., PhD Ill. Sr. Lectr.

Peng, Tsu Ann, BSc Sing., PhD Lond. Prof. Fellow

Poh, R. K. S., BSc Nan., MSc Nan., PhD NU Singapore Sr. Lectr.

Qu, Ruibin, BSc Xi'an Jiaotong, MSc Xi'an Jiaotong, PhD Brunel Sr. Lectr.

Quek, T. S., BSc Sing., MSc Sing., PhD Sing. Assoc. Prof.

Shen, Zuowei, BSc Hehai, MSc Alta., PhD Alta. Sr. Lectr.

Sun, Y. N., BS China U.S.T., MS Ill., PhD Ill. Sr. Lectr.

Tan, E. C., BSc NU Singapore, MSc Yale, PhD Yale Sr. Lectr.

Tan, H. H., BSc Adel., PhD Adel. Sr. Lectr.

Tan, Kok Choon, BSc NU Singapore, PhD M.I.T. Sr. Lectr.

Tan, R. C. E., BAppSci RMIT, BSc La Trobe, PhD La Trobe Sr. Lectr.

Tan, S. K., BSc Nan., MPhil Lond., PhD Nan. Sr. Lectr.

Tan, S. P., BA Oxf., MA Calif., PhD Calif. Sr. Lectr.

Tang, W. S., BSc HK, MSc Tor., PhD Tor. Sr. Lectr.

Tay, T. S., BSc Malaya, MMath Wat., PhD Wat. Sr. Lectr.

Tay, Y. C., BSc Sing., MS Harv., PhD Harv. Sr. Lectr.

To, W. K., BSc HK, MA Col., PhD Col. Sr. Lectr.

Wan, F. S., BSc Malaya, MSc Sing., PhD ANU Sr. Lectr.

Wang, H. Y., BSc Nanjing, MA Nanjing, PhD Peking Sr. Lectr.

Wilson, S. J., BSc Ceyl., MSc Sing., PhD Sing. Prof.

Wong, Y. L., BSc HK, MPhil HK, PhD Calif. Sr. Lectr.

Xu, Kai, BSc Peking, MSc Peking, PhD Aberd. Sr. Lectr.

Xu, X. W., BSc Nanjing, MSc Nanjing, PhD Conn. Sr. Lectr.

Yap, H. P., BSc Sing., MSc Sing., PhD Sing. Assoc. Prof.

Yap, L. Y. H., MS Wash., PhD Wash. Prof. Fellow

Zhang, D. Q., BSc E.China Normal, MSc Osaka, PhD Osaka Sr. Lectr.

Zhu, Chengbo, BSc Zhejiang, MSc Yale, PhD Yale Sr. Lectr.

Medicine, see below

Organisational Behaviour

Tel: 874 3004 Fax: 775 5571

Campbell, Donald J., BA N.Y., MS Purdue, PhD Purdue Assoc. Prof.

Campbell, Kathleen M., BA Fordham, MA C.U.N.Y., PhD Purdue Sr. Lectr.

Chan, Audrey H. H., MA S.Dakota, PhD Texas A.&M. Sr. Lectr.

Chay, Yue Wah, BSc Wales, DPhil Oxf. Sr. Lectr.

Koh, William L. K., BBA NU Singapore, PhD Oregon Sr. Lectr.

Lee, Jean S. K., BA NU Singapore, MEd Mass., PhD Mass. Sr. Lectr.

Tan, Chwee Huat, BAcc Sing., MBA Wis., MSc Wis., PhD Wis. Prof.

Teo, Albert C. Y., BSocSci NU Singapore, MS Calif., PhD Calif. Sr. Lectr.

Tseng, Anthony T. P., BS Natnl.Taiwan, MA Utah, PhD Utah Sr. Lectr.

Wan, David T. W., BCom W.Aust., PhD Manc. Sr. Lectr.

Yuen, Edith C. C., BA Internat.Christian(Tokyo), PhD Syd. Assoc. Prof.; Head*

Pharmacy

Tel: 874 2647 Fax: 779 1554

Chan, E. W. Y., BPharm China Med.Coll., PhD Manc. Sr. Lectr.

Chan Lai Wah, BSc(Pharm) NU Singapore, PhD NU Singapore Sr. Lectr.

Chui, Wai Keung, BSc(Pharm) NU Singapore, PhD Aston Sr. Lectr.

Go, Mei Lin, BSc(Pharm) Sing., PhD NU Singapore Assoc. Prof.; Acting Head*

Heng, P. W. S., BSc(Pharm) Sing., PhD NU Singapore Sr. Lectr.

Ho Chi Lui, Paul, BPharm Qld., PhD Qld. Sr. Lectr.

Kurup, T. R. R., BPharm Raj., MPharm BITS, MSc Lond., PhD Lond. Sr. Lectr.

Lim, Lee Yong, BSc(Pharm) NU Singapore, PhD Manc. Sr. Lectr.

Ngiam, T. L., BPharm Sing., MPharm Sing., PhD Lond. Assoc. Prof.

Philosophy

Tel: 874 3896 Fax: 777 9514

Balasubramaniam, Arunasalam, BSc Sing., MSc Sing., MSc Sus., PhD W.Ont. Sr. Lectr.

Chan Kam Leung, Alan, BA Winn., MA Manit., PhD Tor. Sr. Lectr.

Chong, Kim Chong, BA Sing., PhD Lond. Sr. Lectr.; Head*

Ho, Hua Chew, BA Sing., MA Sing., MA Wash., PhD Wash. Sr. Lectr.

Patterson, Wayne A., BA Tor., MA Tor., PhD Melb. Sr. Lectr.

Physics

Tel: 874 2603 Fax: 777 6126

Baaquie, B. E., BS Cal.Tech., PhD Cornell Assoc. Prof.

Chia, T. T., BSc Sing., MSc Dal., PhD Qu. Assoc. Prof.

Chowdari, B. V. R., BSc And., MSc Baroda, PhD IIT Kanpur Assoc. Prof.

Feng, Y. P., BSc Lanzhou, PhD Illinois Tech.Inst. Sr. Lectr.

Hsu, T. S., BSc Nan., DrIng Inst.Natnl.Poly., Toulouse Sr. Lectr.

Huan, A. C. H., BA Oxf., MA Oxf., DPhil Oxf. Sr. Lectr.

Ji, W., BSc Fudan, MSc H.-W., PhD H.-W. Sr. Lectr.

Koh, C. J., BSc Nan., MA Boston, PhD Boston Sr. Lectr.

Kok, Wai Choo, BSc Sing., PhD Camb. Assoc. Prof.

Kuok, M. H., BSc Cant., PhD Cant. Assoc. Prof.

Lai, C. H., BA Chic., MS Chic., PhD Chic. Assoc. Prof.

Lim, H., BSc Sing., PhD Reading Assoc. Prof.

Lin, J. Y., BS Xiamen, MS Xiamen, PhD Stan. Sr. Lectr.

Ng, S. C., BSc Nan., MSc Dal., PhD McM. Prof.

Oh, C. H., BSc Otago, PhD Otago Assoc. Prof.

Ong, C. K., BSc Nan., MSc Manit., PhD Manit. Prof.

Ong, P. P. P., BSc Sing., PhD Lond. Prof.

Orlic, I., MSc Zagreb, PhD Zagreb Sr. Lectr.

Phua, K. K., BSc HK, BSc Lond., PhD Birm. Assoc. Prof.

Shen, Z. X., BSc Jilin, PhD Lond. Sr. Lectr.

Sim, H. K., BSc Nan., PhD Notre Dame(Ind.) Sr. Lectr.

Sy, H. K., BSc Sing., PhD Col. Prof.

Tan, B. T. G., PBM, PPA, BSc Sing., DPhil Oxf. Assoc. Prof.

Tan, H. S., BSc Malaya, MA Roch., PhD Roch. Sr. Lectr.

Tan, K. L., BSc Sing., DPhil Oxf. Prof.; Head*

Tang, S. H., BSc Sing., MA N.Y.State, PhD N.Y.State Prof.

Tang, S. M., BSc Indiana, MSc Indiana, MSc Newcastle(UK), PhD Indiana Prof.

Watt, F., BSc Newcastle(UK), PhD Newcastle(UK) Assoc. Prof.

Wee, A. T. S., BA Camb., MA Camb., DPhil Oxf. Sr. Lectr.

Zhang, X., BSc Fudan, MSc Shanghai Jiaotong, DPHil Oxf. Sr. Lectr.

Physiology, see Medicine

Political Science

Tel: 874 3971 Fax: 779 6815

Chan, Heng Chee, BA Sing., MA Sing., MA Cornell, PhD Sing. Prof.

Chin, Kin Wah, BSc Lond., PhD Lond. Assoc. Prof.

Cibulka, Frank, BA Penn.State, MA Penn.State, PhD Penn.State Sr. Lectr.

Ganesan, N., BA McM., MA McM., PhD N.Illinois Sr. Lectr.

Haque, Shamsul, BSS Dhaka, MA Dhaka, MPA S.Calif., PhD S.Calif. Sr. Lectr.

Ho, Khal Leong, BA NU Malaysia, MA W.Mich., PhD Ohio State Sr. Lectr.

Hossain, Ishtiaq, BA Dacca, MA Dacca, MA Car., PhD NU Singapore Sr. Lectr.

Jones, David S., BA Leic., MSc Strath., PhD Belf. Sr. Lectr.

Lee, Boon Hiok, BA Calif., MA Calif., PhD Hawaii Assoc. Prof.

Lee, Lai To, BA Chinese HK, MA Calif., PhD Calif. Assoc. Prof.

Mutalib, M. H., BSocSci Sing., MA ANU, PhD Syd. Assoc. Prof.

Quah, J. S. T., BSocSci Sing., MSocSci Sing., PhD Florida State Assoc. Prof.; Head*

Seah Chee Meow, David, BA Sing., MSocSci Sing., PhD Manc. Assoc. Prof.

Shee, Poon Kim, BA Nan., MA Indiana, PhD Indiana Sr. Lectr.

Singh, B., BSocSci NU Singapore, MA ANU, PhD ANU Sr. Lectr.

Sridharan, Kripa, BA Baroda, MA Baroda, MSc(Econ) Lond., PhD NU Singapore Sr. Lectr.

Suryadinata, Leo, BA Nan., MA Ohio, MA Monash, PhD American(D.C.) Assoc. Prof.

Public Policy Programme

Dean's Office, Faculty of Arts and Social Sciences

Tel: 874 6134 Fax: 778 1020

Asher, Mukul G., BA Bom., MA Wash., PhD Wash. Assoc. Prof.

Knetsch, Jack L., BSSc Mich.State, MSSc Mich.State, MPA Harv., PhD Harv. Visiting Prof.

Ong, Jin Hui, BSocSci Sing., MA Indiana, PhD Indiana Dir.*

Other Staff: 2 Lectrs.; 2 Adjunct Lectrs.

Research: fiscal policy; international political economy; public policies and regulations; public sector management and governance

Social Work and Psychology

Tel: 874 3812 Fax: 778 1213

Ang, John, BSocSci Sing., MSW Hawaii Sr. Lectr.

Barrett, Mark E., BS James Madison, MS Murray State, PhD Texas Sr. Lectr.

Bentelspacher, Carl E., BA Calif.State, MSc Wis., PhD S. Calif. Sr. Lectr.

Bernard-Opitz, Vera, PhD Gött. Sr. Lectr.

Bishop, George D., BA Hope, MS Yale, PhD Yale Assoc. Prof.

Chang, Anthony P. M., BSocSci Sing., MSocSci NU Singapore, PhD S.Fraser Sr. Lectr.

Chang, Wei-ning Chu, BA Natnl.Taiwan, MA Houston, PhD Houston Assoc. Prof.

Cheung, Paul P. L., BSocSci Sing., MA Hawaii, MSW Hawaii, PhD Mich. Sr. Lectr.

Chua, Fook Kee, BA Well., MA Cant., PhD Calif. Sr. Lectr.

Elliott, John M., BA Camb., MA Camb., PhD Sheff. Assoc. Prof.

Howard, Richard, BA Oxf., PhD Belf. Sr. Lectr.

Liow, Susan J., BSc Lond., PhD Lond. Sr. Lectr.

Nair, Elizabeth, BPsych W.Aust., PhD Nott. Sr. Lectr.

Ngiam, Tee Liang, BSocSci Sing., MSc Wales, PhD Calif. Sr. Lectr.

Ong, Teck Hong, BA Nan., MEd Wash., PhD Wales Sr. Lectr.

Ow, Rosaleen S. O., BSocSci Sing., MSc Wales, PhD NU Singapore Sr. Lectr.

Singh, Ramadhar, BA Bihar, MA Bihar, MSc Purdue, PhD Purdue Assoc. Prof.

Sriram, N., BTech IIT Madras, MS Oregon, PhD Oregon Sr. Lectr.

Tan, Ngoh Tiong, BA Sing., MSW Penn., PhD Minn. Sr. Lectr.

Vasoo, S., MSW HK, PhD HK Sr. Lectr.; Head*

Ward, Colleen A., BS Spring Hill, PhD Durh. Assoc. Prof.

Sociology

Tel: 874 3822 Fax: 777 9579

Alatas, Syed F., BSc Oregon, MA Johns H., PhD Johns H. Sr. Lectr.

Chan, Kwok Bun, BA Alta., MA W.Ont., PhD York(Can.) Assoc. Prof.

Chang, Han-Yin, MA Calif., PhD Calif. Sr. Lectr.

Chen, Peter S. J., BA Chinese HK, MA Wash., PhD Wash. Assoc. Prof.

Chua, Beng Huat, BSc Acad., MA York(Can.), PhD York(Can.) Assoc. Prof.

Erb, Maribeth, BA N.Y.State, MA N.Y.State, PhD N.Y.State Sr. Lectr.

Hing, Ai Yun, BSocSci Sing., MSocSci Sing., PhD Aberd. Assoc. Prof.

Ho, Kong Chong, BSocSci Sing., MSocSci NU Singapore, PhD Chic. Sr. Lectr.

Jesudason, James, BA Wesleyan, MA Harv., PhD Harv. Sr. Lectr.

Khondker, H. H., BA Dacca, MA Dacca, MA Car., MA Pitt., PhD Pitt. Sr. Lectr.

Ko, Yiu Chung, BSocSci Chinese HK, MA Calif., PhD Calif. Sr. Lectr.

Lian, Kwen Fee, BA Sing., MA Well., PhD Well. Sr. Lectr.

Mani, A., BA Malaya, MSocSci Sing., PhD Wis. Sr. Lectr.

Ong, J. H., BSocSci Sing., MA Indiana, PhD Indiana Assoc. Prof.; Head*

Quah, Stella R., BA Colombia Natnl., MSc Florida State, PhD Sing. Assoc. Prof.

Rajah, Ananda, BSocSci Sing., PhD ANU Sr. Lectr.

Shotam, Nirmala P., BSocSci Sing., MSW Tata Inst.Soc.Scis., PhD N.U.S'pore. Sr. Lectr.

Tan, Ern Ser, BSocSci Sing., MSocSci NU Singapore, PhD Cornell Sr. Lectr.

Tong, Chee Kiong, BSocSci Sing., MA Cornell, PhD Cornell Assoc. Prof.

Waterson, Roxana H., BA Camb., MA Camb., PhD Camb. Sr. Lectr.

Wong, Aline, BA HK, MA Calif., PhD Calif. Prof. (on leave)

Southeast Asian Studies Programme

Dean's Office, Faculty of Arts and Social Sciences

Tel: 874 6338 Fax: 777 6608

Miksic, John N., AB Dartmouth, MA Ohio, MA Cornell, PhD Cornell Sr. Lectr.

Master of Arts

Daquila, T. C., BS Central Luzon, MA Leuven, PhD ANU Sr. Lectr.

Yong, M. C., BA Sing., MA Yale, PhD Sing. Assoc. Prof.; Dir.*

Statistics, see Econ. and Stats.

DENTISTRY

Oral and Maxillofacial Surgery

Tel: 772 4932 Fax: 773 2600

Ho, Kee Hay, BDS Sing., FDSRCPSGlas, FDSRCSEd Assoc. Prof.

Loh, Hong Sai, BDS Sing., MDS Sing., FDSRCSEd, FDSRCPSGlas Prof.; Head*

Yeo, Jinn Fei, BDS Sing., MDS NU Singapore, MSc Lond., FDSRCSEd Assoc. Prof.

Postgraduate Dental Studies, School of

Tel: 772 4158 Fax: 779 6520

Chew, Chong Lin, BDS Sing., MSD Indiana, MDS Sing., FDSRCSEd Dir.†*

Preventive Dentistry

Tel: 772 4943 Fax: 773 2602

Lim, Lum Peng, BDS Sing., MSc Lond., PhD HK Assoc. Prof.

Lo, Geok Lam, BDS Sing., MSc Lond. Sr. Lectr.

Ong, Grace H. L., BDS Sing., MSc Lond. Sr. Lectr.

Sandham, Andrew, BDS Durh., PhD Edin., FDSRCSEd Visiting Prof.

Teo, Choo Soo, BDS Sing., MSc Lond. Assoc. Prof.; Head*

Restorative Dentistry

Tel: 772 4954 Fax: 773 2603

Chew, Chong Lin, BDS Sing., MSD Indiana, MDS Sing., FDSRCSEd Prof.; Head*

Keng, Siong Beng, BDS Sing., MSc Lond., MDS Sing., FFDRCSI Assoc. Prof.

Liu, Hao Hsing, BDS NU Singapore, MSc Northwestern Sr. Lectr.

Loh, Poey Ling, BDS Sing., MScD Indiana Sr. Lectr.

Neo, Jennifer C. L., BDS Sing., MSc Iowa Assoc. Prof.

Ow, Richard K. K., BDS Sing., MSc Lond. Assoc. Prof.

Tan, Beng Choon Keson, BDS Sing., MSD Wash. Sr. Lectr.

Thean, Pik Yen Hilary, BDS Sing., MSc Lond. Sr. Lectr.

Yap, U Jin Adrian, BDS Sing., MSc Lond. Sr. Lectr.

MEDICINE

Tel: 772 4350 Fax: 779 4112

Anaesthesia

Tel: 772 4207 Fax: 777 5702

Chen, Edward F. G., MB BS NU Singapore, MMed NU Singapore, FFARACS Sr. Lectr.

Dhara, Sasanka S., MB BS Calc., FFARCSI Assoc. Prof.

Koh, Kwong Fah, MB BS NU Singapore, MMed NU Singapore Sr. Lectr.

Lee, Tat Leang, MB BS Sing., MMed NU Singapore, FFARACS Assoc. Prof.; Head*

Anatomy

Tel: 874 3201 Fax: 778 7643

Bay, Boon Huat, MB BS NU Singapore, PhD NU Singapore Sr. Lectr.

Gopalakrishnakone, P., MB BS S.Lanka, PhD Lond. Assoc. Prof.

Kaur, Charanjit, BSc Punjab, MB BS Punjab, PhD NU Singapore Sr. Lectr.

Leong, Seng Kee, BDS Sing., PhD Malaya, FDSRCSEd Prof.; Head*

Ling, Eng Ang, BSc Natnl.Taiwan, PhD Camb., DSc NU Singapore Prof.

Ong, Wei Yi, BDS NU Singapore, PhD NU Singapore Sr. Lectr.

Rajendran, K., MB BS Sing., FRCSEd Sr. Lectr.

Singh, Gurmit, MB BS Sing., FRACS Sr. Lectr.

Sit, Kwok Hung, MB BS Sing., MD NU Singapore, PhD Lond. Prof.

Tay, Samuel S. W., BSc Sing., MSc Sing., PhD NU Singapore Sr. Lectr.

Voon, Francis C. T., MB BS Malaya, PhD Lond. Sr. Lectr.

Wong, Wai Chow, MB BS Malaya, PhD Lond. Prof. Fellow†

Other Staff: 1 Lectr.; 1 Sr. Tutor

Biochemistry

Tel: 874 3241 Fax: 779 1453

Candlish, J. K., BSc St And., LLB Lond., PhD St And. Assoc. Prof.

Chang, Chan Fong, BSc Birm., PhD Lond. Sr. Lectr.

Chua, Kim Lee, BSc NU Singapore, PhD Camb. Sr. Lectr.

Chung, Maxey C. M., BSc Well., MSc Well., PhD Well. Assoc. Prof.

Jeyaseelan, K., BSc S.Lanka, PhD Sheff. Assoc. Prof.

Khoo, Hoon Eng, BA Smith, PhD Lond. Sr. Lectr.

Kon, Oi Lian, MB BS Sing., MD NU Singapore, FRCPCan Assoc. Prof.

Li, Qiu-Tian, BSc S.China U.T., MSc Natnl.U.Defence Technol.(China), PhD Melb. Sr. Lectr.

Sit, Kim Ping, BSc Sing., MSc McG., PhD McG., DSc NU Singapore Prof.; Head*

Tan, Chee Hong, BSc Sing., MSc Tor., PhD Tor. Assoc. Prof.

Teo, Tian Seng, BSc Sing., MSc Sing., PhD Manit. Sr. Lectr.

Too, Heng Phon, BSc Lond., PhD Lond. Sr. Lectr.

Community, Occupational and Family Medicine

Tel: 874 4988 Fax: 779 1489

Chia, Kee Seng, MB BS NU Singapore, MSc NU Singapore, MD NU Singapore Assoc. Prof.

Chia, Sin Eng, MB BS NU Singapore, MSc NU Singapore, MD NU Singapore Sr. Lectr.

Foo, Swee Cheng, BSc Natnl.Cheng Kung, ME Asian I.T., Bangkok, MSc Cinc., PhD Qld. Assoc. Prof.

Goh, Lee Gan, MB BS Sing., MMed Sing. Assoc. Prof.

Hong, Ching Ye, MB BS Malaya, FRACGP Sr. Lectr.

Hughes, Kenneth, BA Oxf., BM BCh Oxf., MA Oxf., MD Oxf., MSc Lond., FRCP Assoc. Prof.

Koh, David S. Q., MB BS Sing., MSc NU Singapore, PhD Birm. Assoc. Prof.

Lee, Hin Peng, MB BS Sing., MSc(PublicHealth) Sing. Prof.; Head*

Lun, Kwok Chan, BSc Sing., MSc Lond., PhD Birm. Assoc. Prof.

Ng, Tze Pin, MB BS Sing., MD NU Singapore, MSc NU Singapore Assoc. Prof.

Ong, Choon Nam, BSc Nan., MSc Lond., PhD Manc. Prof.

Phua, Kai Hong, BA Harv., MSc Harv., PhD Lond. Sr. Lectr.

Seow, Adeline, MB BS Sing., MSc(PublicHealth) Sing. Sr. Lectr.

Wong, Mee Lian, MB BS Malaya, MPH Malaya Sr. Lectr.

Dermatology and Venereology

National Skin Centre

Tel: 253 4455 Fax: 253 3225

1 Clin. Assoc. Prof.; 4 Sr. Consultants; 4 Consultants

Diagnostic Radiology

Tel: 772 4210 Fax: 773 0190

Choo, Isobel H. F., MB BS Sing., FRCR Sr. Lectr.

Tan, Lenny K. A., MB BS Sing., FRCR, FRACR Prof.; Head*

Wong, Jill S. L., MB ChB Liv., FRCR Sr. Lectr.

Forensic Medicine

Tel: 321 4923 Fax: 225 0217

Clin. Teachers

General Practice

Community, Occupational and Family Medicine

Tel: 974 4988 Fax: 779 1489

Clin. Teachers

Medicine

Tel: 772 4350 Fax: 779 4112

Chan, Heng Leong, MB BS Sing., FRACP, FRCP, FRCPEd, FACP Prof.; Head*

Cheah, Jin Seng, MB BS Sing., MD Sing., FRACP Prof.

Chia, Boon Lock, MB BS Sing., FRACP, FACP Prof.

Ho, Khek Yu, MB BS Syd., FRACP Sr. Lectr.

Ho, King Hee, MB BS Sing. Sr. Lectr.

Kong, Hwai Loong, MB BS Sing., MMed(IntMed) NU Singapore Sr. Lectr.

Kueh, Yan-Koon, BSc Br.Col., MSc Br.Col., MD Br.Col., FRCPCan Assoc. Prof.

Lee, Evan J. C., MB BS Sing., MD NU Singapore, FRCPEd Assoc. Prof.

Lee, Kang Hoe, MB BChir Camb., BA Camb., MA Camb. Sr. Lectr.

Lee, Kok Onn, BSc Belf., MB BCh BAO Belf., MD Belf., FRCPEd, FRCP, FRCPI Assoc. Prof.

Lehnert, Manfred, MD Graz Assoc. Prof.

Lim Pin, PJG, PPA, BA Camb., MB BChir Camb., MD Camb., MA Camb., FRCP, FRACP, FRCPEd, FACP Prof.
Lim, Seng Gee, MB BS Monash, MD Monash, FRACP Sr. Lectr.
Lim, Tai Tian, MD Amst. Sr. Lectr.
Lim, Tow Keang, MB BS Malaya, MMed NU Singapore Assoc. Prof.
Lim, Yean Teng, MB BS NU Singapore, MMed NU Singapore Sr. Lectr.
Ling, Lieng Hsi, MB BS Malaya Sr. Lectr.
Lo, Su Kong, MB ChB Liv., PhD Oxf. Sr. Lectr.
Oh, Vernon M. S., BA Camb., MA Camb., MB BChir Camb., MD Camb., FACP, FRCP, FRCPEd Prof.
Ong, Benjamin K. C., MB BS NU Singapore, MMed NU Singapore Assoc. Prof.
Suri, Rajiv, MB BS Sing., MMed Sing. Assoc. Prof.
Tan, Chorh Chuan, MB BS NU Singapore, MMed NU Singapore, PhD NU Singapore, FRCPEd Assoc. Prof.
Tan, Wan Cheng, MB ChB Aberd., MD Aberd., FRCP, FRCPEd, FRACP Prof.
Thai, Ah Chuan, MB BS Sing., MMed Sing., FRCPEd Assoc. Prof.
Wong, John E. L., MB BS NU Singapore Assoc. Prof.
Wong, Soon Tee, MB BS Sing. Sr. Lectr.
Yeo, Peter P. B., MB BS Sing., MD Sing., FRACP, FRCP Prof. (on leave)
Yeoh, Khay Guan, MB BS Sing., MMed(IntMed) Sing. Sr. Lectr.

Microbiology

Tel: 874 3276 Fax: 776 6872

Chan, Soh Ha, MB BS Monash, PhD Melb., FRCPA Prof.; Head*
Chow, Vincent T. K., MB BS NU Singapore, MSc Lond., MD NU Singapore, PhD NU Singapore Sr. Lectr.
Ho, Bow, BSc Bom., PhD Wales Assoc. Prof.
Lee, Yuan Kun, BSc Nan., MSc Nan., PhD Lond. Assoc. Prof.
Ng, Mary M. L., BSc Monash, PhD Monash Assoc. Prof.
Nga, Been Hen, BSc Malaya, PhD Sheff. Assoc. Prof.
Poh, Chit Laa, BSc Monash, PhD Monash Assoc. Prof.
Ren, E. C., BSc Malaya, PhD NU Singapore Sr. Lectr.
Sim, Tiow Suan, BSc Lond., PhD Lond. Assoc. Prof.
Singh, Malkeet, BSc Sing., MSc Birm., PhD Sing. Assoc. Prof.
Tan, Hai Meng, BSc NU Singapore, MSc NU Singapore, PhD Lond. Sr. Lectr.
Yap, Eu Hian, BSc Sing., PhD Sing. Assoc. Prof.

Obstetrics and Gynaecology

Tel: 772 4260 Fax: 779 4753

Adaikan, P. Ganesan, MSc PhD Res. Assoc. Prof.
Anandakumar, Chinnaiya, MB BS Sing., MMed NU Singapore Assoc. Prof.
Arulkumaran, S., MB BS Ceyl., PhD NU Singapore, FRCSEd, FRCOG Visiting Prof.
Biswas, Arijit, MB BS Calc., MD All India IMS Sr. Lectr.
Bongso, T. A., BVSc Ceyl., MSc Guelph, PhD Guelph, DSc NU Singapore Res. Prof.
Chan, Clement L. K., MB BS HK, FACS, FRACOG Assoc. Prof.
Chew Siong Lin, Stephen, MB BS NU Singapore Sr. Lectr.
Foong, Lian Chuen, BSc Lond., MB BS Lond. Sr. Lectr.
Goh, Victor H. H., BSc Sing., PhD Sing. Res. Assoc. Prof.
Kumar, Jothi, MB BS Sing., MMed NU Singapore, PhD Monash Sr. Lectr.
Lim, Fang Kan, MB BS Malaya, MMed NU Singapore Sr. Lectr.
Loh, Foo Hoe, MB BS NU Singapore, MMed NU Singapore Sr. Lectr.
Mongelli, J. M., MD Nott., BMMS Sr. Lectr.

Ng, Soon Chye, MB BS Sing., MD NU Singapore, MMed NU Singapore, FRCOG Prof.; Head*
Prasad, R. N. V., MB BS Sing., MMed Sing., MD NU Singapore, DSc NU Singapore, FACS, FRCOG Assoc. Prof.
Ratnam, S. S., PPA, BBM, MB BS Ceyl., MD Sing., Hon. DSc S.Lanka, Hon. MD, FRCS, FRCSGlas, FRACS, FRCSEd, FRCOG, Hon. FRACOG Prof. Fellow†
Roy, Ashim C., BSc MSc PhD Res. Assoc. Prof.
Singh, Kuldip, MB BS Sing., MA Exe., MMed NU Singapore, MD NU Singapore, FRCOG Assoc. Prof.
Tamby Raja, R. L., MB BS Ceyl., PhD NU Singapore, FRCSEd, FRCOG Prof. Fellow
Tham, Kok Fun, MB BS NU Singapore, MMed NU Singapore Sr. Lectr.
Trounson, Alan O., BSc NSW, MSc NSW, PhD Syd. Visiting Prof.
Wong, Yee Chee, MB BS Sing., MMed Sing., FRCOG Assoc. Prof.
Yong, Eu Leong, MB BS Sing., MMed NU Singapore, PhD NU Singapore Sr. Lectr.

Ophthalmology

Tel: 772 5317 Fax: 777 7161

Balakrishnan, Vivian, MB BS NU Singapore, MMed NU Singapore, FRCSEd Sr. Lectr.
Chan, Tat Keong, MB BS NU Singapore, MMed NU Singapore, FRCSEd Sr. Lectr.
Chew, Paul T. K., MB BS NU Singapore, MMed NU Singapore, FRCSEd Sr. Lectr.
Chew, Sek Jin, MB BS NU Singapore, MS Louisiana State, PhD Rockefeller, FRCSEd Sr. Lectr.
Lim, Arthur S. M., BBM, MB BS Sing., FRCS, FRACS, FRCSEd Clin. Prof.; Head*

Otolaryngology

Tel: 874 5370 Fax: 775 3820

Smith, James D., MD Visiting Prof.
Tan, Henry K. K., MB BS NSW, FRCSEd Sr. Lectr.
Tan, Luke Kim Siang, MB BS Sing., FRCSEd, FRCSGlas Sr. Lectr.
Yeoh, Kian Hian, MB BS HK, FRCSEd Clin. Prof.; Head*
Other Staff: 2 Res. Scientists

Paediatrics

Tel: 772 4420 Fax: 779 7486

Joseph, Roy, MB BS Madr., MMed Sing. Assoc. Prof.
Lee, Bee Wah, MB BS Sing., MMed NU Singapore, MD NU Singapore Assoc. Prof.
Loke, Kah Yin, MB BS NU Singapore, MMed NU Singapore Sr. Lectr.
Low, Poh Sim, MB BS Sing., MMed Sing., MD NU Singapore, FRCPEd Assoc. Prof.; Head*
Murugasu, Belinda, MB BS NU Singapore, MMed NU Singapore Sr. Lectr.
Quah, Thuan Chong, MB BS Sing., MMed Sing. Assoc. Prof.
Quak, Seng Hock, MB BS Sing., MMed Sing., MD NU Singapore, FRCPGlas Assoc. Prof.
Quek, Swee Chye, MB BS NU Singapore, MMed NU Singapore Sr. Lectr.
Tan, Kim Leong, MB BS Sing., FRCPEd, FRACP Prof.
Tay, Agnes Hou-Ngee, MB BS NU Singapore, MMed NU Singapore, PhD Tor. Sr. Lectr.
Wong, Hock Boon, PJG, PPA, MB BS Malaya, FRCPEd, FRACP, FRCPGlas, FRCP Prof. Fellow†
Wong, May Ling, MB BS NU Singapore, MMed NU Singapore Sr. Lectr.
Yap, Hui Kim, MB BS Sing., MMed NU Singapore, MD NU Singapore, FRCPEd Assoc. Prof.

Pathology

Tel: 772 4319 Fax: 778 0671

Aw, Tar Choon, MB BS Malaya, MMed(IntMed) Sing., MPP NU Singapore, FRCPA Assoc. Prof.
Chong, Siew Meng, MB BS Malaya, FRCPA, FRCPath Sr. Lectr.
Koay, Evelyn S. C., BSc Malaya, MSc Lond., PhD Hawaii Sr. Lectr.

Lee, Szu Hee, BA Camb., MB BChir Camb., MA Camb., PhD CNAA, FRCPA Assoc. Prof.
Lee, Yoke Sun, MB BS Sing., MD NU Singapore, FRCPA Prof.; Head*
Raju, Gangaraju C., MB BS S.Venkat., MD S.Venkat., FRCPath Assoc. Prof.
Sethi, Sunil K., MB BS NU Singapore, MMed(IntMed) NU Singapore, PhD Sur. Sr. Lectr.
Shanmugaratnam, K., PPA, LMS Malaya, MD Malaya, PhD Lond., FRCPath, FRCPA Prof. Fellow†
Sinniah, R., BA Trinity(Dub.), MB BCh BAO Trinity(Dub.), MA Trinity(Dub.), MD Dub., PhD Belf., FRCPA, FRCPI, FRCPath Prof.
Teh, Ming, BA Yale, MD Johns H., FRCPA Sr. Lectr.
Tock, Edward P. C., PPA, MB BS Malaya, MD Sing., PhD Lond., FRCPA, FRCPath Prof.
Wee, Aileen, MB BS Sing., FRCPA Assoc. Prof.

Pharmacology

Tel: 874 3264 Fax: 773 0579

Gwee, Kok Ann, MB BS NU Singapore, MMed NU Singapore Sr. Lectr.
Gwee, Matthew C. E., BPharm Sing., PhD Sing., MHPEd NSW, FIBiol Assoc. Prof.
Lee, Edmund J. D., MB BS Sing., MMed Sing., PhD NSW Assoc. Prof.
Lee, How-Sung, BPharm Sing., MPharm Sing., PhD Sing. Assoc. Prof.; Head*
Sim, Meng Kwoon, BSc Sing., MSc Syd., PhD Syd. Assoc. Prof.
Tan, Benny K. H., MB BS Sing., PhD NU Singapore Sr. Lectr.
Tan, Chay Hoon, MB BS Sing., MMed NU Singapore Sr. Lectr.
Ti, Teow Yee, MB BS Malaya, FRCPCan Assoc. Prof.
Wong, Peter T. H., BSc Lond., PhD Lond. Assoc. Prof.

Physiology

Tel: 874 3223 Fax: 778 8161

Ho, Ting Fei, MB BS Sing., MMed Sing., MD NU Singapore Assoc. Prof.
Hooi, Shing Chuan, MB BS NU Singapore, PhD Harv. Sr. Lectr.
Hwang, Peter L. H., MB BS Sing., PhD McG., FRCPCan Prof.; Head*
Koh, Dow Roon, MB BS NU Singapore, MMed NU Singapore, PhD Tor. Sr. Lectr.
Lee, Chee Wee, BSc McG., MSc McG., PhD Alta. Sr. Lectr.
Wong, Chong Thim, BSc W.Aust., PhD W.Aust. Sr. Lectr.

Postgraduate Medical Studies, School of

Tel: 874 3300 Fax: 773 1462

Ratnam, S. S., PPA, BBM, MB BS Ceyl., MD Sing., Hon. DSc S.Lanka, Hon. MD, FRCS, FRCSGlas, FRACS, FRCSEd, FACS, FRCOG, Hon. FRACOG Dir.†*
Other Staff: 1 Postgrad. Advisor and Dep. Dir.

Psychological Medicine

Tel: 772 4514 Fax: 777 2191

Ang Wee Kiat, Anthony, MB BS NU Singapore, MMed NU Singapore Sr. Lectr.
Ko, Soo Meng, MB BS NU Singapore, MMed NU Singapore Sr. Lectr.
Kua, Ee Heok, PBM, MB BS Malaya, MD NU Singapore, FRCPsych Assoc. Prof.; Head*
Lim, Lionel C. C., MB BS Sing., PhD Lond. Sr. Lectr.
Yeo, Kah Loke Brian, MB BS NU Singapore, MMed NU Singapore Sr. Lectr.

Radiotherapy

Diagnostic Radiology

Tel: 772 4210 Fax: 773 0190

Lectrs.†

Surgery

Tel: 772 4221 Fax: 777 8427

Chan, Steven T. F., MB BS Monash, PhD Lond., FRACS, FRCSEd Assoc. Prof.

Esuvaranathan, Kesavan, MB BS, FRCSGlas, FRCSEd Sr. Lectr.

Goh, Peter M. Y., MB BS Sing., MMed NU Singapore, FRCSEd, FRCSGlas Assoc. Prof.

Isaac, John R., MB BS NU Singapore, MMed NU Singapore, FRCSEd, FRCSGlas Sr. Lectr.

Kum, Cheng Kiong, MB BS NU Singapore, FRCSEd Sr. Lectr.

Lee, Timothy K. Y., MB BS Melb., FRCSEd Assoc. Prof.

Lim, Thiam Chye, MB BS Malaya, FRCSEd Sr. Lectr.

Prabhakaran, K., MB BS Sing., MMed Sing., FRCSEd, FRCSGlas Assoc. Prof.

Sim, Eugene K. W., MB BS NU Singapore, FRCSEd, FRCSGlas Sr. Lectr.

Tan, Walter T. L., MB BS Sing., MMed Sing., FRCSEd, FRCSGlas, FRACS, FACS Assoc. Prof.; Head*

Ti, Thiow Kong, MB BS Sing., MD Malaya, FRCS, FRACS, FRCSEd Prof.

Surgery, Orthopaedic

Tel: 772 4327 Fax: 778 0720

Balasubramaniam, P., PPA, MB BS Ceyl., FRCS Prof. Fellow†

Bose, Kamal, PBM, MB BS Calc., MSc Calc., MChOrth Liv., MS All India IMS, FRCSEd, FRACS Prof.; Head*

Das De, Shamal, MB BS Calc., MChOrth Liv., MD NU Singapore, FRCSEd, FRCS Assoc. Prof.

Kour, Anam K., MB BS Sing., MMed NU Singapore, FRCSGlas Sr. Lectr.

Lee, Eng Hin, MD W.Ont., FRCSCan Assoc. Prof.

Nather, Abdul A. M., MB BS Sing., MD NU Singapore, FRCSEd, FRCSGlas Assoc. Prof.

Palaniappan, Thiagarajan, MB BS NU Singapore, MChOrth Liv., FRCS Sr. Lectr.

Pho, Robert W. H., MB BS Syd., FRCSEd Prof.

Prem Kumar, V., MB BS Sing., FRCSEd, FRCSGlas Assoc. Prof.

Satkunanantham, Kandiah, MB BS Sing., MMed Sing., FRCSEd Assoc. Prof.

Wong, Hee Kit, MB BS Sing., MChOrth Liv., MMed NU Singapore, FRCSGlas Assoc. Prof.

Venereology, see Dermatol. and Venereol.

SPECIAL CENTRES, ETC

Advanced Studies, Centre for

Tel: 874 6284 Fax: 779 1428

Lim, G. H. Hank, BSSc Gannon, MA Pitt., PhD Pitt. Acting Dir.*

Arts, Centre for the

Tel: 874 2493 Fax: 778 1956

Thumboo, E., BBM, BA Malaya, PhD Sing. Chairman/Dir.*

Bioprocessing Technology Centre

Tel: 874 6222 Fax: 775 4933

Chung, M., BSc Well., MSc Well., PhD Well. Assoc. Prof.; Consultant

Too, H. P., BSc Lond., PhD Lond. Sr. Lectr.; Consultant

Yap, M. G. S., BSc Sing., MSc Lond., PhD Tor. Dir.*

Other Staff: 1 Sr. Res. Scientist; 2 Res. Fellows

Research: animal cell and tissue culture; DNA and peptide technology; microbial fermentation; protein and gene expression

Bioscience Centre

Tel: 874 2711 Fax: 777 0052

Goh, C. J., BSc Sing., PhD Newcastle(UK) Prof.; Dir.*

Other Staff: 1 Sr. Scientist; 1 Res. Assoc.; 1 Res. Fellow

Research: screening, purification and characterisation of bioactive compounds

Chinese Language Proficiency Centre

Tel: 874 3328 Fax: 777 7736

Chen, Chung Yu, BA Natnl.Taiwan, MA Hawaii, PhD Cornell Assoc. Prof.; Dir.*

Ku, Kathy C. M., BA Natnl.Taiwan, MA Natnl.Taiwan, PhD Wis. Sr. Lectr.

Data Storage Institute

Tel: 874 6852 Fax: 776 6527

Chong, T. C., BEng Tokyo, MEng NU Singapore, ScD M.I.T. Assoc. Prof.; Dep. Dir.

Low, T. S., BSc S'ton., PhD S'ton. Assoc. Prof.; Dir.*

Other Staff: 1 Bus. Devel. Manager; 5 Res. and Devel. Managers; 3 Group Leaders; 1 Dep. Res. and Devel. Manager; 1 Asst. Res. and Devel. Manager

English Language Communication, Centre for

Tel: 874 3866 Fax: 777 9152

Ng En Tzu, Mary, BA Wis., MSc Wis., PhD Wis. Sr. Lectr.

Tan, Cheng Lim, BA Lond., BA Nan., MS(TESL) Indiana, PhD NU Singapore Sr. Lectr.

Wang, Su Chen, BA Sing., MA Lond., PhD Lond. Sr. Lectr.

Wong, Lian Aik, BA Taiwan Normal, MA Essex, PhD Indiana Sr. Lectr.; Head*

Immunology, WHO Collaborating Centre for Research and Training in

Tel: 874 3315 Fax: 777 5720

Chan, Prof. S. H., MB BS Monash, PhD Melb., FRCPA Dir.*

Microelectronics, Institute of

Tel: 779 7522 Fax: 778 0136

Chen, B. Y. S., BSc Natnl.Taiwan, MSc Georgia I.T., PhD Stan. Dir.*

Other Staff: 4 Res. and Devel. Managers

Molecular Agrobiology, Institute of

Tel: 872 3339 Fax: 774 2857

Chua, N. H., BSc Sing., AM Harv., PhD Harv. Prof.; Chairman

Kwang, Jimmy, MS Rhode I., PhD Calif. Assoc. Prof.; Sr. Scientist

Soong, T. S., BS Natnl.Chung Hsing, MS Natnl.Taiwan, PhD Ill. Assoc. Prof.

Sundaresan, Venkatesan, BSc Poona, MSc IIT Kanpur, MS Carnegie-Mellon, PhD Harv. Assoc. Prof.; Dir.*

Other Staff: 10 Sr. Scientists; 24 Res. Fellows

Research: animal pathogenesis; fish developmental biology; plant developmental biology; plant–pathogen interactions; yeast biology

Molecular and Cell Biology, Institute of

Tel: 874 3755 Fax: 779 1117

Bernard, Hans-Ulrich, BSc Gött., PhD Max-Planck Assoc. Prof.

Chia, William, BSc Cal.Tech., MSc Wis., PhD Lond. Prof.

Hong, Wan-jin, BSc Xiamen, PhD N.Y.State Prof.

Hui, Kam Man, BSc Wash.State, MSc Wash.State, PhD Northwestern Assoc. Prof.

Pallen, Catherine, BSc W.Ont., PhD Calg. Assoc. Prof.

Porter, Alan G., BSc Liv., PhD Brist. Assoc. Prof.

Ruan, Jisheng, BSc Beijing Agric., PhD Russian Acad.Sc. Visiting Prof.

Tan, Christopher Y. H., BSc Sing., PhD Manit. Prof.; Dir.*

National Supercomputing Research Centre

Tel: 778 9080 Fax: 778 0522

Boek, Peter Dir.*

National University Medical Institutes

Tel: 874 8098 Fax: 773 5461

Hwang, Peter L. H., MB BS Sing., PhD McG., FRCPCan Prof.; Dir.*

Natural Product Research, Centre for

Tel: 874 6814 Fax: 779 1117

Carte, Brad, BSc Arizona, PhD Scripps Assoc. Prof.; Dep. Head

Yap, Miranda G. S., BSc Sing., MSc Lond., PhD Tor. Assoc. Prof.; Head*

Remote Imaging, Sensing and Processing, Centre for

Tel: 874 3220 Fax: 775 7717

Lim, H., BSc Sing., PhD Reading Assoc. Prof.; Dir.*

Systems Science, Institute of

Tel: 874 2075 Fax: 778 2571

Lim, Swee Cheng, BSc Lond., MSc Lond. Dir.*

Other Staff: 1 IT Continuing Educn. Manager; 1 Postgrad. Studies Manager; 1 Consultancies Manager; 1 Telelearning Manager; 1 Res. Manager; 1 Systems Management Manager

Teaching and Learning, Centre for Development of

Tel: 772 3052 Fax: 777 0342

Pan, Daphne, BA Sing., MSc Sur., MA York(Can.), PhD York(Can.) Dir.*

Wireless Communications, Centre for

Tel: 872 9030 Fax: 779 5441

Lye, K. M., BSc Alta., MEng Sing., PhD Hawaii Dir.*

Other Staff: 5 Sr. Members of Tech. Staff; 19 Members of Tech. Staff; 36 Sr. Res. Engineers; 61 Res. Engineers

Research: digital broadcasting; mobile-aware networks; multimedia personal communications; national telecommunications research and development; radio systems

CONTACT OFFICERS

Academic affairs. Registrar: Wong, Joanna, BBM, BSc Sing.

Accommodation. Assistant Director, Office of Student Affairs: Khoo, Heng Keow, BSc Sing., MBA NU Singapore

Admissions (first degree). Registrar: Wong, Joanna, BBM, BSc Sing.

Admissions (higher degree). Deputy Registrar: Chen, Christine, BA Sing.

Adult/continuing education (continuing education). Director: Tan, Chin Tiong, BBA Sing., MBA W.Illinois, PhD Penn.State

Alumni. Director, Alumni Affairs and Development Office: Chia, Lawrence, BSc Syd., MSc Syd., PhD Syd.

Careers. Assistant Director, Office of Student Affairs: Tan, Phaik Lee, BA Adel.

Computing services. Director, Computer Centre: Thio, H. T., PPA, BSc Nan., MA Roch., PhD Roch.

Development/fund-raising. Director, Alumni Affairs and Development Office: Chia, Lawrence, BSc Syd., MSc Syd., PhD Syd.

Estates and buildings/works and services. Principal Estate Officer: Chua, Raymond, BEng Auck., MSc NU Singapore

Examinations. Deputy Registrar: Yeo, Su-Inn, LLB Sing.

Finance. Deputy Bursar: Tay, Sok-Kian, BSc Manc., FCA

General enquiries. Senior Assistant Director, University Liaison Office: Wong, Mabel, BA Sing.

Health services. Senior Health Physician, University Health Service: Chua, Catherine, MB BS NSW

Industrial liaison. Director, Industry and Technology Relations Office: Chou, S. K., BEng Sing., DrIng École Nat.Sup.d'Arts & Métiers, Paris

International office. Principal Administrative Officer, International Relations Office: Lau, Geoffrey C. F., BA *Sing.*

Library (chief librarian). Librarian: Quah, Jill, BA *Sing.*, MLS *Col.*

Personnel/human resources. Director (Personnel): Ong, Jin-Soo, BSc *Sing.*

Public relations, information and marketing. Senior Assistant Director, University Liaison Office: Wong, Mabel, BA *Sing.*

Scholarships, awards, loans. Registrar: Wong, Joanna, BBM, BSc *Sing.*

Security. Senior Estate Officer, Estate Office: Sulaiman bin Salim, BA *Sing.*

Sport and recreation. Principal Sports Officer, Office of Student Affairs: Kuok, Alec

Staff development and training. Director (Personnel): Ong, Jin-Soo, BSc *Sing.*

Student welfare/counselling. Senior Student Counsellor, Office of Student Affairs: Lowe, Josephine

Students from other countries. Assistant Director, Office of Student Affairs: Khoo, Heng Keow, BSc *Sing.*, MBA NU *Singapore*

Students with disabilities. Senior Student Counsellor, Office of Student Affairs: Lowe, Josephine

University press. Editor, Singapore University Press: Tay, Patricia, BA *Sing.*

[*Information supplied by the institution as at 6 March 1998, and edited by the ACU*]

SOUTH AFRICA

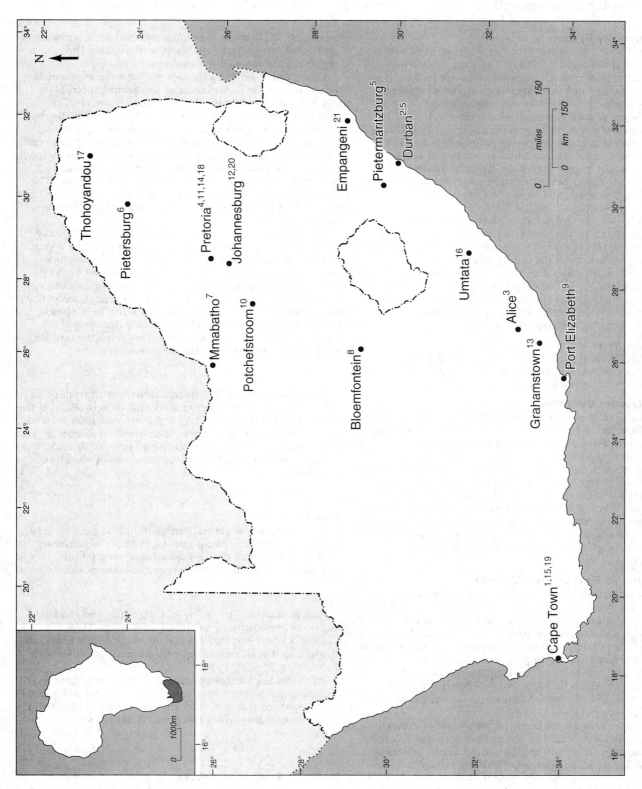

N

Thohoyandou[17]

Pietersburg[6]

Pretoria[4,11,14,18]

Johannesburg[12,20]

Mmabatho[7]

Potchefstroom[10]

Bloemfontein[8]

Empangeni[21]

Pietermaritzburg[5]

Durban[2,5]

Umtata[16]

Alice[3]

Grahamstown[13]

Port Elizabeth[9]

Cape Town[1,15,19]

The places named are the seats of the institutions numbered on the previous page

0   150
miles

0   150
km

0

1000m

THE UNIVERSITIES OF SOUTH AFRICA

Information compiled by the South African Universities' Vice-Chancellors' Association as at 13 August 1998

The University System

In terms of the 1997 Higher Education Act, higher education in South Africa is the responsibility of national government.

The control, governance and executive power of the university is vested in its council, which typically comprises senior management (at least the vice-chancellor), representatives of staff, donors, students, alumni, local government and a number of government appointees. The senate, which largely consists of full professors or heads of academic departments, is normally the guardian of academic standards. Faculty boards (which are typically standing sub-committees of senate) generally consist of academic staff of the various faculties. Senate and faculty boards will also have student representatives.

The chief executive officer of the university is the vice-chancellor, who is usually also called the rector or principal. The vice-chancellor is a council appointee for a predetermined period, after which he or she can normally be re-elected.

South African universities also have statutory institutional fora on the campuses. These bodies, which are representative of all the important stakeholders for the higher education institutions, give guidance on the transformation of the institutions in line with the new national dispensation.

Academic Year

The academic year typically starts in January and final examinations are taken in November for undergraduate and in January for postgraduate courses.

Pre-University Education

Pre-tertiary education is the responsibility of the nine provincial governments, although the national Department of Education retains responsibility for determining national policy.

The present basis of pre-university education is 12 years of schooling: seven spent in primary school and five in secondary school. In the senior secondary phase (last three years) subjects can be taken at higher grade or standard grade. At the end of the 12 years a senior certificate is obtained (to be replaced by a further education certificate). Holders of senior certificates who qualify for admission to first degree studies at university receive a 'matriculation endorsement' from the South African Certification Council.

Admission to First Degree Courses

The present requirements for a matriculation endorsement are that a person must have obtained a senior certificate for which six subjects must be presented from four of the six available groups. Five subjects must be passed satisfying a predetermined aggregate and certain grouping requirements. The requirements include pass merits in two languages of which at least one must be a local university tuition language, on the higher grade, and two additional higher grade subjects from two different groups with a 40% pass mark in the compulsory three higher grade subjects.

Revised matriculation endorsement requirements, currently under consideration, would be the equivalent of one university tuition language (at present English and Afrikaans) and three additional higher grade subjects with a 50% average in these four subjects and 40% sub-minimum in each subject. A major difference from the existing regulations is that they propose to do away eventually with the grouping of subjects and the requirement of subjects to be taken from different groups. Perhaps more importantly they do away with the requirement of more than one higher grade language as part of the senior certificate. This is likely to broaden the access basis without lowering admission standards.

Prospective students who come from a non-South African schooling system, which must be at least equivalent to the local system, can apply to the matriculation board for a certificate of conditional exemption as applicable to foreigners. The condition to be satisfied is completion of the degree.

A prospective student who does not meet the requirements for a matriculation endorsement or an exemption certificate may apply for a certificate of conditional exemption. This allows the student to proceed with his/her degree studies but the outstanding requirement, or an equivalent requirement, must in some cases be met either before proceeding to second-year level of degree study or before the degree can be awarded.

Mature age conditional exemption certificates are on a university's application issued to persons who are aged 23 or over and who have passed at least one higher grade subject and three further higher and/or standard grade subjects for the senior certificate.

The worldwide challenge to higher education to do more with less has a special meaning in South Africa where access must be opened up to a majority of people who have been educationally disadvantaged for so long. This must be done whilst maintaining standards and in the face of enormous demands on the state coffers. It means that foreign students at undergraduate level from non-Southern Africa Development Community (SADC) countries are typically discouraged to register at South African universities. This is not the case for postgraduate students, who are welcomed.

Methods of tuition. The traditional lecturer in front of his/her class is still predominant at residential universities, as is the written text as tuition material for distance education students. Video lecturing and other forms of information technology are rapidly gaining ground, however, particularly for distance education universities and removed campuses of residential universities.

Finance

University income in general derives from two main sources: government subsidies (the major single source of university funding) and student fees. Donations and income from investments form the other two important income categories.

Student finance. The setting of student fees and residential fees is the prerogative of individual universities. There is a National Student Financial Aid scheme under which financially disadvantaged students can apply for financial assistance with their studies.

State subsidies for foreign students, except those from SADC countries, will be suspended according to national policy and it can be expected that such students will become full-fee-paying at those universities where this policy is not already implemented.

Staff and Student Numbers

The rankings customarily used in academic staff appointments are: professor, assistant professor, senior lecturer, lecturer and junior lecturer. In 1997, there were 10,999 academic staff in South African universities.

In 1997, approximately 368,000 students were registered at 21 South African universities, of whom approximately 155,000 studied through distance education. A minority of the students studying at residential universities are part-time, doing evening classes.

UNIVERSITY OF CAPE TOWN

Founded 1918; previously established as South African College

Member of the Association of Commonwealth Universities

Postal Address: Private Bag, Rondebosch, 7701 South Africa
Telephone: (021) 650 2115 **Fax**: (021) 650 2138 **E-mail**: aeshta@bremner.uct.ac.za **Telex**: 522208
WWW: http://www.uct.ac.za

CHANCELLOR—......
VICE-CHANCELLOR*—Ramphele, Mamphela A., MB ChB *Natal*, BCom *S.Af.*, PhD *Cape Town*, Hon. MD *Natal*, Hon.
  DHL *Hunter*, Hon. DSocSc *Tufts*, Hon. DSc *Lond.*, Hon. LLD *Prin.*, Hon. Dr *Inst.Soc.Stud.(The Hague)*
SENIOR DEPUTY VICE-CHANCELLOR—Gevers, Prof. Wieland, MB ChB *Cape Town*, MA *Oxf.*, DPhil *Oxf.*, FRSSAf
DEPUTY VICE-CHANCELLOR—Martin, Prof. John B., BSc *Natal*, PhD *Camb.*, DSc *Natal*, Hon. DSc *Natal*
DEPUTY VICE-CHANCELLOR—West, Prof. Martin E., MA *Cape Town*, PhD *Cape Town*
DEPUTY VICE-CHANCELLOR—Ncayiyana, Prof. Daniel J. M., MD *Gron.*
REGISTRAR‡—Amoore, Hugh T., BA *Cape Town*
FINANCE DIRECTOR—Pienaar, H. J., BCompt *S.Af.*
DIRECTOR, PUBLIC AFFAIRS—Zille, Helen, BA *Witw.*
DIRECTOR, DEVELOPMENT—Sillen, Andrew, PhD *Calif.*
DIRECTOR, UNIVERSITY LIBRARIES—Rapp, Joan

GENERAL INFORMATION

History. The university was established in 1829 as the South African College, and achieved university status in 1918.

Its main campus is located at Groote Schuur, Cape Town, on the slopes of Table Mountain.

Admission to first degree courses (see also South African Introduction). Minimum requirement: senior certificate endorsed for university admission, or certificate from Matriculation Board granting exemption from this endorsement; or matriculation/exemption certificate issued by the Matriculation Board or Joint Matriculation Board. In addition, each faculty has its own minimum requirements. International applicants may be granted conditional exemption. The university's Alternative Admissions Research Project (AARP) administers its own entrance tests, which are open to all applicants on a voluntary basis.

First Degrees (see also South African Directory to Subjects of Study) (* = also available with honours; † = honours only). BA*, BA(FA) (fine art), BArch, BAS (architectural studies), BBibl†, BBusSc, BCom*, BEd, BEd(EducationalPsychology), BMus*, BSc*, BSc(CM) (construction management), BSc(Eng), BSc(GeographicalSystems)†, BSc(Log), BSc(Med)*, BSc(OccTher), BSc(Phys), BSc(Survey), BSc(QS) (quantity surveying), BSocSc*, BSocSc(SW), BTh, LLB, MB ChB.

All courses are full-time and normally last 3 or 4 years. Honours degrees last an additional year. Extended undergraduate degree programmes in medicine and engineering are 1 year longer. BBibl, BEd, BSc(GeographicalSystems), BSc(Med): 1 year; BEd(EducationalPsychology): 1 or 2 years; MB ChB: 6 years.

Higher Degrees (see also South African Directory to Subjects of Study). BALLB, ChM, LLB, LLM, MA, MA(FA) (fine art), MArch, MBA, MBibl, MBusSc, MCom, MCPUD (city planning and urban design), MCRP (city and regional planning), MD, MEd, MEngMan, MFA, MFamMed, MIndAdmin, MMed, MMus, MPubAd, MSc, MSc(ApplSc), MSc(CEM) (construction economics and management), MSc(Eng), MPhil, PhD, DArch, DEconSc, DEd, DFA (fine art), DLitt, DMus, DSc, DSc(Eng), DSc(Med), DSocSc, LLD.

Master's degrees normally last 1 year and doctorates 2 years. DArch, DEconSc, DEd, DFA, DLitt, DSc(Eng), DSc(Med), DSocSc: 1 year; ChM, MCPUD, MD, MCRP, MIndAdmin: 2 years; LLB, MFamMed, MMed: 3 years; BALLB: 5 or 6 years.

Libraries. Over 1,000,000 volumes; over 7000 journals.

Fees (1998). South African undergraduates: R9050 (BA, BA(FA), BSocSc); R10,450 (BMus); R12,425(MB ChB). Master's: R3125 (MA, MPhil); R20,700 (MBA). ChM by thesis, DMus, MD, PhD (annual): R2500. International undergraduates (other than those from South African Development Community countries): about US$5300. Semester/study abroad international students: about US$3200.

Academic Year (1998-99). Two semesters: 23 February–26 June; 20 July–11 December.

Statistics. Students: over 15,500.

FACULTIES/SCHOOLS

Arts
Dean: Atkinson, John E., BA *Durh.*, PhD *Cape Town*

Commerce
Dean: Kantor, Prof. Brian S., BA *Cape Town*, BCom *Cape Town*

Education
Dean: Ashley, Prof. Michael J., BA *Witw.*, MEd *Aberd.*

Engineering
Acting Dean: O'Connor, Prof. Cyril T., BSc *S.Af.*, BSc *Cape Town*, PhD *Cape Town*

Fine Art and Architecture
Dean: Japha, Derek A., BArch *Cape Town*

Law
Dean: Visser, Prof. Daniel P., Blur *Pret.*, LLB *Pret.*, LLD *Pret.*, DrJur *Ley.*

Medicine
Dean: Van Niekerk, Johannes P. de V., MD *Cape Town*, MMed *Cape Town*, FRCR

Music
Dean: ......

Science
Dean: Moran, Prof. Vincent C., MSc *Rhodes*, PhD *Rhodes*, FLS, FRSSAf

Social Science and Humanities
Dean: Bunting, Prof. Ian A., MA *Rhodes*, PhD *ANU*

ACADEMIC UNITS

Accounting
Tel: (021) 650 2257 Fax: (021) 689 7582
Botha, Derek, BCom *Rhodes*, BProc *S.Af.*, MCom *S.Af.*, DCom *P.Elizabeth*   Assoc. Prof.
Bourne, Peter J. M.   Assoc. Prof.
Clayton, Roderick D., MCompt *S.Af.*   Sr. Lectr.
Correia, Carlos, MCom *Cape Town*   Assoc. Prof.
Everingham, Geoffrey K., BCom *P.Elizabeth*, BCom *Cape Town*, MAS *Ill.*   Richard Sonnenberg Prof.
Graham, M., BBusSc *Cape Town*   Sr. Lectr.
Huxham, Keith T., BSc *Cape Town*, BCom *Cape Town*   Assoc. Prof.
Macdonald, D., BCompt *S.Af.*, MBA *Cape Town*   Sr. Lectr.
Minter, Marie T., BSc *Cape Town*   Assoc. Prof.
Morris, J. R. P., BCom *Witw.*   Prof.†, Taxation
Puttick, George A., BCom *Cape Town*   Sr. Lectr.
Rhoda, Herman J. C., BA *Cape Town*   Sr. Lectr.
Roeleveld, J., BCompt *S.Af.*, BCom *Cape Town*, LLM *Cape Town*   Sr. Lectr.
Smith, C. C., BSocSc(SW) *Cape Town*, BCompt *S.Af.*   Sr. Lectr.
Taylor, Josephine, BCom *Cape Town*   Sr. Lectr.
Uliana, Enrico O., MCom *Cape Town*, PhD *Stell.*   Prof.; Head*
Watson, Alexandra, BCom *Cape Town*   Assoc. Prof
Wormald, Michael P., BCom *Cape Town*   Assoc. Prof.
Other Staff: 1 Assoc. Prof.†, 7 Lectrs.
Research: auditing; financial accounting; financial management; management accounting; taxation

Adult Education and Extra Mural Studies
Tel: (021) 650 3250 Fax: (021) 650 2893
Fiske, Ingrid J., BA *Witw.*, BA *Cape Town*, MA *Qu.*   Sr. Lectr.; Dir. of Extra-Mural Studies
Millar, Clive J., BEd *Cape Town*, MA *Cape Town*, MSc *Stir.*   Prof., Adult Education
Morphet, Anthony R., BA *Natal*, BA *Lond.*, MPhil *Cape Town*   Assoc. Prof.; Head*
Prinsloo, Mastin H., BA *Natal*, MEd *Lond.*   Sr. Lectr.
Saddington, James A., BSc(Eng) *Cape Town*, MPhil *Cape Town*   Sr. Lectr.
Other Staff: 4 Lectrs.; 1 Asst. Lectr.
Research: communities in development; cultural studies; curriculum development and evaluation; national policy

African Languages and Literatures
Tel: (021) 650 2301
Gowlett, Derek F., MA *Witw.*   Sr. Lectr.
Gxilishe, D., BA *Fort Hare*, MEd *Col.*, MA *Stell.*, DLitt *Stell.*   Assoc. Prof.

Kaschula, Russell H., BA Rhodes, LLB Rhodes, PhD Rhodes   Sr. Lectr.
Satyo, Sizwe C., BA Fort Hare, MA S.Af., DLitt&Phil S.Af.   Prof.; Head*
Other Staff: 3 Lectrs.; 1 Asst. Lectr.
Research: historical linguistics; lexicography; oral literature; second language acquisition; sociolinguistics

African Studies, Centre for

Tel: (021) 650 3273 Fax: (021) 689 7560
Cooper, Brenda L., BA Cape Town, MA Birm., DPhil Sus.   Assoc. Prof.; Dir.*
Mamdaru, Mahmood, MA Fletcher, MALD Fletcher, PhD Harv.   A. C. Jordan Prof.
Research: contemporary South African art; movements for rights, justice and state reform; West African magical realism

Afrikaans and Netherlandic Studies

Tel: (021) 650 2312 Fax: (021) 650 4032
Hambidge, Joan H., BA Stell., MA Pret., PhD Rhodes   Sr. Lectr.
Snyman, Henning J., BA Stell., PhD Cape Town, DLitt Cape Town   Prof.; Head*
Van der Merwe, Chris N., BA Stell., MA Stell., LittDrs Utrecht, DLitt&Phil Rand Afrikaans   Assoc. Prof.
Van Heerden, E. R., BA Stell., LLB Stell., MA Witw., PhD Rhodes   Assoc. Prof.
Waher, Hester J., BA Cape Town, PhD Cape Town   Sr. Lectr.
Wolfswinkel, Rolf M., LittDrs Amst., PhD Cape Town   Sr. Lectr.
Other Staff: 2 Lectrs.; 4 Lectrs.†; 1 Asst. Lectr.
Research: Caribbean Dutch studies; children's literature; historical linguistics; war literature

Anatomy, see Medicine

Archaeology

Tel: (021) 650 2353 Fax: (021) 650 2352
Hall, Martin J., MA Camb., PhD Camb.   Prof., Historical Archaeology
Maggs, Timothy M. O'C., BA Cape Town, PhD Cape Town   Hon. Prof.
Parkington, John E., MA Camb., PhD Camb.   Prof.; Head*
Sealy, Judith C., MSc Cape Town, PhD Cape Town   Assoc. Prof.
Sillen, Andrew, MA Penn., PhD Penn.   Prof.
Smith, Andrew B., PhD Calif.   Assoc. Prof.
Van der Merwe, Nikolaas J., MA Yale, PhD Yale   Prof.
Other Staff: 2 Chief Sci. Officers; 1 Sr. Sci. Officer; 1 Sr. Res. Officer

Architecture and Planning, School of

Tel: (021) 650 2359 Fax: (021) 689 7564
Cooke, C. Julian, BA Witw.   Prof.
De Beer, Peter F., BArch Pret., MArch Pratt   Sr. Lectr./Studiomaster
Dewar, David, BA Cape Town, MURP Cape Town, PhD Cape Town   BP Prof., Urban and Regional Planning
Gasson, Barrie, BA Cape Town, BSc Cape Town, MURP Cape Town   Sr. Lectr./Studiomaster
Japha, Derek A., BArch Cape Town   Assoc. Prof.
Japha, Vivienne M., BArch Cape Town   Assoc. Prof.
Le Grange, Lucien P., BArch Cape Town, MArch(UD) Rice   Sr. Lectr./Studiomaster
Moyle, Johan M., BArch Cape Town   Sr. Lectr./Studiomaster
Murray, K. D., BArch Cape Town   Sr. Lectr./Studiomaster
Pike, G., BArch Cape Town   Sr. Lectr./Studiomaster
Prinsloo, I. C., BArch Witw., MSc(Tn&RegPlanning) Witw., PhD Calif., Hon. FAIA   Prof.
Righini, Paul, BArch Cape Town   Sr. Lectr./Studiomaster
Todeschini, Fabio, BArch Cape Town, MArch(UD) Penn., MCP Penn.   Assoc. Prof.; Dir.*
Uytenbogaardt, Roelof S., BArch Cape Town, MArch Penn., MCP Penn.   Prof.

Watson, Vanessa J., BA Natal, MCRP Cape Town   Assoc. Prof.
Wilkinson, Peter B., BScEng Natal, MCRP Cape Town   Sr. Lectr./Studiomaster
Research: city planning and urban design in the African context; conservation; contemporary architectural theory and practice; urbanism and housing

Art, History of, see History of Art

Astronomy

Tel: (021) 650 2391 Fax: (021) 473639
Fairall, Anthony P., BSc Cape Town, PhD Texas   RAS Assoc. Prof.
Feast, Michael W., BSc Lond., PhD Lond., FRSSAf   Hon. Prof.
Kurtz, Donald W., BA San Diego, MA Texas, PhD Texas   Assoc. Prof.
Warner, Brian B., BSc Lond., MA Oxf., PhD Lond., DSc Lond., DSc Oxf., FRSSAf   Prof.; Head*
Research: cataclysmic and degenerate stars; cepheids and RR lyrae stars; long period red variables; short period variables; theory and observation of variable stars

Biochemistry

Tel: (021) 650 2402 Fax: (021) 685 5931
Brandt, Wolf F., BSc Cape Town, PhD Cape Town   Assoc. Prof.
Illing, Nicola, MSc Cape Town, DPhil Oxf.   Assoc. Prof.; Head*
Klump, Horst H., DrRerNat Freib.   Prof.
Lindsey, George G., BSc Sus., DPhil Sus.   Assoc. Prof.
Other Staff: 1 Lectr.; 1 Principal Sci. Officer; 1 Hon. Res. Officer
Research: identification of signals that control differentiation of neurons from olfactory neuroepithelium; proteins involved in dessication tolerance in plants and yeast; stability of proteins from hyperthermophiles; structure and function of chromosomal proteins

Botany

Tel: (021) 650 2447 Fax: (021) 650 4041
Bolton, John J., BSc Liv., PhD Liv.   Assoc. Prof.
Bond, William J., BSc Exe., MSc Cape Town, PhD Calif.   Harry Bolus Prof.
Cowling, Richard M., BSc Cape Town, PhD Cape Town   Leslie Hill Prof., Plant Conservation
Dakora, Felix D., BSc Ghana, MSc Syd., PhD W.Aust.   Sr. Lectr.
Farrant, Jill, BSc Natal, PhD Natal   Sr. Lectr.
Huntley, Bryan J., BSc Natal, MSc Pret.   Hon. Prof.; Chief Dir., Natnl. Bot. Inst.
Lewis, Oliver A. M., MSc Natal, PhD Lond., FIBiol, FLS, FRSSAf   Emer. Prof.
Linder, H. Peter, BSc Cape Town, PhD Cape Town   Prof., Keeper, Bolus Herbarium
Midgley, Jeremy, BSc Cape Town, PhD Cape Town   Sr. Lectr.
Stock, William D., BSc Cape Town, PhD Cape Town   Assoc. Prof.; Head*
Other Staff: 1 Lectr.; 1 Emer. Assoc. Prof.
Research: biogeography and evolutionary biology of Cape flora; floristics; plant population, community and reproductive ecology; systematics

Business, see Grad. Sch. of Business

Chemistry

Tel: (021) 650 2446 Fax: (021) 689 7499
Auf der Heyde, T., MSc Cape Town, PhD Cape Town   Sr. Lectr.
Bull, James R., MSc Natal, DPhil Oxf., FRSChem, FRSSAf   Mally Prof., Organic Chemistry
Caira, Mino R., MSc Cape Town, PhD Cape Town   Assoc. Prof.
Hunter, Roger, BSc Lond., PhD Lond.   Assoc. Prof.
Hutton, Alan T., MSc Cape Town, PhD Cape Town   Sr. Lectr.
Irving, Ann, MA Oxf., PhD Leeds   Sr. Lectr.

Jackson, Graham E., BSc Cape Town, PhD Cape Town   Assoc. Prof.
Koch, Klaus R., BSc Cape Town, PhD Cape Town   Assoc. Prof.
Linder, P. W., MSc Natal, PhD Camb.   Emer. Prof.
Moss, John R., BSc Leeds, PhD Leeds   Jamison Prof., Inorganic Chemistry; Head*
Nassimbeni, Luigi R., MSc Rhodes, PhD Cape Town   Prof., Physical Chemistry
Rodgers, A. L., MSc Cape Town, PhD Cape Town   Assoc. Prof.
Stephen, A. M., MSc Cape Town, PhD Cape Town, DPhil Oxf.   Emer. Prof.
Thornton, D. A., BSc Cape Town, PhD Cape Town, DSc Cape Town, FRSChem, FRSSAf   Emer. Prof.
Other Staff: 6 Lectrs.; 1 Chief Sci. Officer; 4 Sr. Sci. Officers
Research: inclusion compounds, polymorphism and related solid state phenomena; synthetic studies in organic, organometallic and co-ordination chemistry

Classics

Tel: (021) 650 2607-8
Atkinson, John E., BA Durh., PhD Cape Town   Assoc. Prof.
Hewett, Margaret L., BA Cape Town, BEd Cape Town   Sr. Lectr.
Wardle, David, MA Oxf., DPhil Oxf.   Sr. Lectr.
Whitaker, Richard A., BA Witw., MA Oxf., PhD St And.   Prof.; Head*
Other Staff: 1 Lectr.
Research: ancient Greek and Roman world; key ideological phenomena in ancient history; modern reflections of and reactions to the ancient world; translation and interpretation of texts

Computer Science

Tel: (021) 650 2663 Fax: (021) 650 3726
Berman, Sonia, BSc Rhodes, MSc Cape Town, PhD Cape Town   Sr. Lectr.
Blake, Edwin H., BSc Witw., PhD Lond.   Assoc. Prof.; Head*
Hutchison, A. C. M., MSc Cape Town, PhD Zür   Sr. Lectr.
Kritzinger, Pieter S., MSc(Eng) Witw., PhD Wat.   Prof.
Linck, Michael H., MSc Cape Town, PhD Cape Town   Sr. Lectr.
MacGregor, Kenneth J., BSc Strath., MSc Glas.   Prof.
Other Staff: 2 Lectrs.
Research: collaborative visual computing; databases; data network architectures

Construction Economics and Management

Tel: (021) 650 2449 Fax: (021) 689 7564
Boaden, Bruce G., BSc(QS) Witw., MBA Br.Col., PhD Witw.   Anglo-American Prof., Building Management; Head*
Bowen, Paul, BScQS Natal, BCom Natal, MSc H-W, PhD P.Elizabeth, FRICS   Prof.
Cattell, Keith S., BSc(QS) P.Elizabeth, MPhil Cape Town   Sr. Lectr.
Hindle, Robert D., MSc Cape Town   Sr. Lectr.
Rwelamila, Pantaleo D., MSc Brun., PhD Cape Town   Sr. Lectr.
Stevens, Alan J., MSc Cape Town, PhD P.Elizabeth   Murray and Roberts Prof.
Vacant Posts: 1 Assoc. Prof
Research: computer-based education; effectiveness of building procurement systems; housing development and management; property management; training and human resource management

Criminology, Institute of

Tel: (021) 650 2988-9 Fax: (021) 650 3790
Schärf, Wilfried, BCom Witw., LLB Witw., MSocSc Cape Town   Assoc. Prof.
Van Zyl Smit, Dirk, BA Stell., LLB Stell., PhD Edin.   Prof.; Dir.*
Other Staff: 1 Lectr.
Vacant Posts: Sr. Res. Officer

Research: legal education; social justice

Dance, School of

Tel: (021) 650 2398-9

Cheesman, Dianne   Sr. Lectr.
Tomlinson, Dudley H.   Sr. Lectr.
Triegaardt, Elizabeth E., BSc *Cape Town*   Assoc. Prof.; Dir.*
Other Staff: 2 Lectrs.; 6 Lectrs.†
Research: African dance; choreography; ethnology; practical teaching; teaching methodology

Drama

Tel: (021) 480 7100, 480 7121 Fax: (021) 242355

Banning, Yvonne, BA *Natal*, MA *Witw.*   Sr. Lectr.
Haynes, David J., BA *Cape Town*, MA *Lanc.*   Prof.
Morris, Jennifer G., BA *Cape Town*, MA *Cape Town*   Sr. Lectr.; Head*
Weare, Christopher B., BA *Rhodes*   Sr. Lectr.; Dir., Little Theatre
Other Staff: 3 Lectrs.

Economics, School of

Tel: (021) 650 2727 Fax: (021) 650 2854

Abedian, Iraj, BA *Cape Town*, MA *Cape Town*, PhD *S.Fraser*   Assoc. Prof.
Abraham, Haim, MA *Tel-Aviv*, PhD *Jerusalem*   Assoc. Prof.
Archer, Sean F., BA *Cape Town*, BA *Camb.*   Assoc. Prof.
Barr, Graham D. I., BSc *Cape Town*, BA *Cape Town*, MSc *Cape Town*, PhD *Cape Town*   Assoc. Prof.
Black, Anthony H., BA *Cape Town*, BA *Sus.*, MSocSc *Natal*   Sr. Lectr.
De Klerk, Michael J., MA *Cape Town*   Sr. Lectr.
High, S. Hugh, BA *Texas Christian*, MA *Duke*, PhD *Duke*, JD *Wake Forest*   Sr. Lectr.
Kahn, S. Brian, BA *Cape Town*, MA *Cape Town*   Prof.; Dir.*
Kaplan, David E., BA *Cape Town*, BCom *Cape Town*, MA *Kent*, DPhil *Sus.*   Assoc. Prof.
Leibbrandt, Murray V., BSocSc *Rhodes*, MA *Notre Dame(Ind.)*, PhD *Notre Dame(Ind.)*   Sr. Lectr.
Leiman, Anthony, BA *Natal*, BA *S.Af.*, MA *Cape Town*   Sr. Lectr.
Nathan, Cedric D., BCom *Witw.*, MSc *Lond.*, PhD *S.Fraser*   Sr. Lectr.
Nattrass, Nicoli J., BA *Stell.*, BSocSc *Cape Town*, MA *Natal*, MSc *Oxf.*, DPhil *Oxf.*   Assoc. Prof.
Standish, J. B., BCom *Natal*, MA *Cape Town*
Wilson, Francis A. H., BSc *Cape Town*, MA *Camb.*, PhD *Camb.*   Prof.
Other Staff: 2 Lectrs.
Research: health economics; manpower and labour practices in southern Africa; science and technology policies

Education, School of, see also Adult Educn. and Extra Mural Studies

Tel: (021) 650 2771 Fax: (021) 650 3489

Ashley, Michael J., BA *Witw.*, MEd *Aberd.*   Prof.
Bakker, Nigel, BA *Cape Town*, BEd *Cape Town*, MPhil *Cape Town*   Sr. Lectr.
Baxen, J., BA *S.Af.*, MEd *Leeds*   Sr. Lectr.
Breen, Christopher J., BSc *Cape Town*, MEd *Exe.*, MPhil *Camb.*   Assoc. Prof.
De Jong, Terence A., BA *Cape Town*, BA *S.Af.*, MEd *Exe.*   Sr. Lectr.
Donald, David R., BEd *S.Af.*, MA *Natal*, MEd *Exe.*, PhD *Cape Town*   Old Mutual Prof., Educational Psychology
Ensor, Margaret P., BSocSc *Natal*, BA *Cape Town*, MSc *Lond.*   Sr. Lectr.
Esterhuyse, Johannes S., BA *Cape Town*, MA *Cape Town*   Sr. Lectr.
Gilmour, James D., BBusSc *Cape Town*, MA *Sus.*   Sr. Lectr.
Green, Lena C., BA *Cape Town*, BA *S.Af.*, MSocSc *Cape Town*   Sr. Lectr.
Jacklin, Heather J., BA *Witw.*, MEd *Witw.*   Sr. Lectr.
Meyer, J. H. F., BSc *Witw.*, MSc *Witw.*, PhD *Witw.*   Prof.

Muller, Johan P., MA *P.Elizabeth*, Dr *Ley.*   Prof.; Head*
Rochford, Kevin, BSc *Melb.*, MEd *Cape Town*, PhD *Cape Town*   Assoc. Prof.
Siebörger, Robert F., BA *Rhodes*, BEd *Rhodes*, MA *Rhodes*, MPhil *Exe.*   Sr. Lectr.
Soudien, Crain A., BA *Cape Town*, BEd *S.Af.*, MA *Cape Town*, EdM *N.Y.State*, PhD *N.Y.State*   Sr. Lectr.
Young, Douglas N., BA *Witw.*, MLitt *Edin.*   Edinburgh Old Mutual Prof., Educational Psychology
Other Staff: 2 Temp. Lectrs.
Research: knowledge development and transfer; policy evaluation and support; race, culture, identity and language studies; student learning in higher education

Engineering, Chemical

Tel: (021) 650 4036 Fax: (021) 689 7579

Deglon, D. A., BSc *Witw.*   Sr. Lectr.
Dry, Mark E., MSc *Rhodes*, PhD *Brist.*   Hon. Prof.
Fraser, Duncan McK., BSc(ChemEng) *Cape Town*, PhD *Cape Town*   Assoc. Prof.; Dir., Undergrad. Studies
Hansford, Geoffrey S., BSc(ChemEng) *Cape Town*, MSc *Cape Town*, MSE *Penn.*, PhD *Penn.*   Prof.
Harrison, Susan T. L., BSc *Cape Town*, PhD *Camb.*   Assoc. Prof.
Lewis, A. E., MSc(Eng) *Cape Town*, PhD *Cape Town*   Sr. Lectr.
O'Connor, Cyril T., BSc *S.Af.*, BSc *Cape Town*, PhD *Cape Town*   Prof.; Head*
Petrie, James G., BSc(Eng) *Cape Town*, MSc *Houston*, PhD *Cape Town*   Assoc. Prof.
Swartz, Christopher L. E., BSc(Eng) *Cape Town*, PhD *Wis.*   Assoc. Prof.
Van Steen, Eric W. J., MSc(Eng) *T.U.Eindhoven*, PhD *Karlsruhe*   Sr. Lectr.
Other Staff: 1 Hon. Assoc. Prof.
Research: bacterial leaching of ores; bioprocess engineering; catalysis; environmental process engineering; minerals processing

Engineering, Civil

Tel: (021) 650 2591 Fax: (021) 689 7471

Abbott, John, BSc(Eng) *Lond.*, MSc(Eng) *Witw.*, PhD *Witw.*   Prof., Urban Engineering
Alexander, Mark G., MSc(Eng) *Witw.*, PhD *Witw.*   Corporation Prof.; Head*
Armitage, Neil P., BScEng *Natal*, MSc(Eng) *Cape Town*   Sr. Lectr.
De Kock, Michael O., BSc(Eng) *Cape Town*   Assoc. Prof.
Ekama, George A., BSc(Eng) *Cape Town*, PhD *Cape Town*   Prof., Water Quality Engineering
Kratz, Rolf D., BSc *Br.Col.*, MASc *Br.Col.*   Assoc. Prof.
Loewenthal, Richard E., BSc(Eng) *Witw.*, MSc *Cape Town*, PhD *Cape Town*   Assoc. Prof.
Marais, G. van R., BSc(Eng) *Cape Town*, MSc(Eng) *Witw.*, DSc(Eng) *Cape Town*   Emer. Prof.
Marais, Nicholas J., BSc(Eng) *Cape Town*, PhD *Cape Town*   Sr. Lectr.
Scheele, Friedrich, DrIng *Munich*   Sr. Lectr.
Sparks, Abyn D. W., BScEng *Natal*, MSc(Eng) *Witw.*, F(SA)ICE   Assoc. Prof., Foundations and Soil Mechanics
Wentzel, M. C., BSc *Cape Town*, PhD *Cape Town*   Assoc. Prof.; Chief Res. Officer
Other Staff: 1 Lectr.; 2 Lectrs.†; 1 Emer. Assoc. Prof.; 1 Hon. Res. Assoc.
Research: concrete; geotechnics; providing engineering infrastructure to developing communities; urban engineering and urban management; water quality

Engineering, Electrical

Tel: (021) 650 2802 Fax: (021) 650 3465

Bell, Prof. J. F. W., BSc *Durh.*, PhD *Durh.*, DSc *Aston*   Hon. Prof.
Braae, Martin, MSc(Eng) *Cape Town*, PhD *Manc.*   Corporation Prof.
Braun, Robin M., BSc *Brighton*, MSc *Cape Town*, PhD *Cape Town*   Sr. Lectr.

De Jager, Gerhardus, MSc *Rhodes*, MBL *S.Af.*, PhD *Manc.*   Post Office Prof., Telecommunications and Signal Processing
Dingley, Charles E., BSc(Eng) *Witw.*, MSc *Lond.*   Sr. Lectr.
Downing, Barry J., MSc *Brad.*, PhD *Sheff.*   Prof.; Head*
Einhorn, H. D. E., DrIng *Berlin*, PhD *Cape Town*   Hon. Prof.
Gieras, Jacek F., MSc *Lodz*, PhD *Poznan*, DSc *Poznan*   Assoc. Prof.
Greene, John R., MSc(Eng) *Cape Town*   Assoc. Prof.
Hodgart, G. M., BA *Camb.*, PhD *Sur.*   Visiting Assoc. Prof.
Inggs, Michael R., BSc *Rhodes*, PhD *Lond.*   Assoc. Prof.
Malengret, Michel, BScEng *Natal*, MSc(Eng) *Cape Town*   Sr. Lectr.
Mashao, D. J., MSc(Eng) *Cape Town*, PhD *Brown*   Sr. Lectr.
McLaren, S. G., BSc *Cape Town*, PhD *Cape Town*   Emer. Prof.
Petroianu, A., DrIng *Bucharest*   Prof.; Hon. Res. Assoc.
Reineck, Karl M., PhD *Newcastle(UK)*, FIEE   Prof.
Tapson, Jonathan C., BSc(Eng) *Cape Town*   Sr. Lectr.
Tattersfield, George M., BSc(Eng) *Cape Town*, MA *Camb.*, FRAS   Sr. Lectr.
Van Nierop, Johann, BSc(Eng) *Cape Town*, MSc *Cape Town*   Sr. Lectr.
Other Staff: 2 Lectrs.; 1 Assoc. Prof.†

Engineering, Materials

Tel: (021) 650 3172-3 Fax: (021) 689 7571

Allen, Colin, BSc *Lond.*, PhD *Lond.*   Assoc. Prof.
Ball, Anthony, BSc *Birm.*, PhD *Birm.*, DEng *Birm.*, FIM, FRSSAf   Prof.; Head*
Hewitt, Jack, FIM   Hon. Prof.
Knutsen, Robert D., BSc *Cape Town*, PhD *Cape Town*   Assoc. Prof.
Lang, Candace I., BSc *Cape Town*, PhD *Cape Town*   Assoc. Prof.
Other Staff: 1 Sci. Officer; 1 Hon. Lectr.; 1 Hon. Res. Fellow
Research: choice of materials for energy-producing sectors of South Africa; development of new alloys, polymers, ceramics and hard materials; relationships between production processes, structure, properties and performance of engineering materials

Engineering, Mechanical

Incorporating the School of Engineering Management

Tel: (021) 650 3231 Fax: (021) 650 3240

Bennett, Kevin F., BSc(Eng) *Cape Town*, MSc *CNAA*, PhD *Cape Town*   Prof.
Gryzagoridis, Jasson, BSc *Lamar*, MSc *Texas A.& M.*, PhD *Cape Town*   Assoc. Prof.; Head*
Lister, Gordon, BSc(Eng) *H.-W.*, BCom *S.Af.*, MSc(Eng) *Lond.*   Sr. Lectr.
Nurick, Gerald N., MScEng *Natal*, PhD *Cape Town*, F(SA)IME   Prof.
Redelinghuys, Christian, BEng *Stell.*, MS *Stan.*, PhD *Stell.*   Sr. Lectr.
Ryan, Thomas B., BSc(Eng) *Cape Town*, MIndMan *Cape Town*   Assoc. Prof.; Dir., Sch. of Engin. Management
Sass, Andrew S., BSc(Eng) *Cape Town*   Assoc. Prof.
Sayers, Anthony T., BSc *City(UK)*, MSc *Birm.*, PhD *Cape Town*   Assoc. Prof.
Tait, Robert B., BSc *Rhodes*, BSc(Eng) *Cape Town*, MA *Oxf.*, PhD *Cape Town*   Assoc. Prof.
Vicatos, George, BSc *Newcastle(UK)*, MSc *Lond.*, PhD *Cape Town*   Sr. Lectr.
Yates, Andrew D. B., MSc(Eng) *Cape Town*, PhD *Cape Town*   Sr. Lectr.
Other Staff: 4 Lectrs.; 1 Lectr./Principal Researcher; 1 Sr. Res. Officer
Research: fluid mechanics; fracture mechanics; internal combustion engines; manufacturing systems; quality management

Engineering, Surveying and Geodetic

Tel: (021) 650 3577 Fax: (021) 650 3572

Barry, Michael B., BSc(Survey) *Cape Town*, MBA *Cape Town* Sr. Lectr.

Mason, Scott O., BSurv *Newcastle(NSW)*, MSc *Ill.*, DrScTech *Zür.* Sr. Lectr.

Merry, Charles L., BSc(Survey) *Cape Town*, PhD *New.Br.* Assoc. Prof.

Rüther, Heinz, PhD *Cape Town* Prof.; Head*

Whittal, Jennifer F., BSc(Survey) *Cape Town*, MSc(Eng) *Cape Town* Sr. Lectr.

Other Staff: 2 Lectrs.†

Research: measurement and modelling of the earth's gravity field, vertical datums and networks and satellite positioning; quality control and information gathering; Urban Modeller Project

English Language and Literature

Tel: (021) 650 2861

Bertelsen, Evelyn J., BA *Natal*, PhD *Lond.* Assoc. Prof.

Brink, Andre P., MA *Potchef.*, DLitt *Rhodes*, Hon. DLitt *Witw.* Prof.

Coetzee, John M., MA *Cape Town*, PhD *Texas*, Hon. DLitt *Strath.*, Hon. DLitt *Buffalo*, FRSL Arderne Prof.

Driver, Dorothy J., MA *Rhodes*, PhD *Rhodes* Prof.

Edgecombe, Rodney S., MA *Rhodes*, PhD *Camb.* Assoc. Prof.

Glenn, Ian E., BA *Natal*, BPhil *York(UK)*, MA *Penn.*, PhD *Penn.* Assoc. Prof.

Haresnape, Geoffrey L., BA *Cape Town*, MA *Cape Town*, PhD *Sheff.* Assoc. Prof.

Higgins, John A., MA *Camb.* Sr. Lectr.

Lee, Brian S., BA *Cape Town*, BEd *Cape Town*, BD *Lond.*, BLitt *Oxf.*, MA *Oxf.* Sr. Lectr.

Makoni, Sinfree, BA *Ghana*, MSc *Edin.*, PhD *Edin.* Assoc. Prof.

Marx, Leslie G., MA *Cape Town*, PhD *Cape Town* Sr. Lectr.; Head*

Schalkwyk, David J., BA *Stell.*, BA *S.Af.*, MA *Stell.*, MA *York(UK)*, DPhil *York(UK)* Sr. Lectr.

Sole, Kelwyn, BA *Witw.*, MA *Lond.*, PhD *Witw.* Sr. Lectr.

Visser, Nicholas W., BA *Cape Town*, BA *Rhodes*, PhD *Rhodes* Assoc. Prof.

Watson, Stephen, MA *Cape Town*, PhD *Cape Town* Assoc. Prof.

Other Staff: 5 Lectrs.; 1 Asst. Lectr.

Vacant Posts: De Beers Prof.

Environmental and Geographical Science

Tel: (021) 650 2873-4 Fax: (021) 650 3791

Davies, Ronald J., MSc *Rhodes*, PhD *Lond.* Emer. Prof.

Dewar, Neil, MA *Cape Town*, MCRP *Cape Town*, PhD *Cape Town* Sr. Lectr.

Fuggle, Richard F., BSc *Natal*, MSc *Louisiana State*, PhD *McG.* Shell Prof., Environmental Studies; Head*

Hewitson, Bruce C., BSc *Cape Town*, MSc *Penn.*, PhD *Penn.* Sr. Lectr.

Largier, John L., BSc *Cape Town*, PhD *Cape Town* Sr. Lectr.

Meadows, Michael E., BSc *Sus.*, PhD *Camb.* Assoc. Prof.

Parnell, S. M., MA *Witw.*, PhD *Witw.* Assoc. Prof.

Other Staff: 4 Lectrs.; 1 Chief Sci. Officer; 1 Hon. Res. Fellow

Research: biogeographical research; hydrodynamics and physical characteristics of estuaries; impact of development projects on biophysical and social environment; regional implications of global climate change, climate modelling, precipitation controls and satellite climatology

Fine Art, Michaelis School of

Tel: (021) 480 7100, 480 7111 Fax: (021) 242355

Arnott, Bruce M., MA(FA) *Cape Town* Assoc. Prof.

Atkinson, Kevin J., MA(FA) *Cape Town* Assoc. Prof.

Delport, Peggy M., MFA *Cape Town* Sr. Lectr.

Dubow, Neville E., BArch *Cape Town*, FRSA Prof.

Grundlingh, G. P. Sr. Lectr.

Inggs, Stephen C., MAFA *Natal* Sr. Lectr.

Jansen van Vuuren, Louis T., BA *Stell.* Sr. Lectr.

Payne, Malcolm J., MFA *Cape Town* Sr. Lectr.

Skotnes, Philippa A., MFA *Cape Town* Sr. Lectr.

Starcke, Helmut Sr. Lectr.

Younge, J. Gavin F., BA *S.Af.*, MA(FA) *Cape Town* Assoc. Prof.; Dir.*

Other Staff: 1 Lectr.

Research: changing notion of monuments; iconographic experimentation; issues of identity, the body, memory; modernist and post-modernist technologies in plastic and time-based arts; visual exegesis through display

French Language and Literature

Tel: (021) 650 2895

Cornille, Jean-Louis, Dr *Nijmegen*, LicPhilRom MenPhil Prof., Modern French Literature; Head*

Robertson, Jane, MA *Oxf.*, DPhil *Oxf.* Sr. Lectr.

Salazar, Philippe-J., MèsL *Paris IV*, MenPhil *Paris IV*, MenSciPol *Paris I*, Dr *Paris V*, Drd'Etat *Paris IV* Prof., French Language and Literature

Wynchank, Anny, LèsL *Bordeaux*, MA *Bordeaux*, PhD *Cape Town* Sr. Lectr.

Other Staff: 2 Lectrs.

Research: foreign/second language didactics and teaching strategies; francophone and African studies; gay, lesbian and women's studies and the literature of the seventeenth, nineteenth and twentieth centuries; West African cinema

Geography, see Environmental and Geog. Sci.

Geological Sciences

Tel: (021) 650 2931 Fax: (021) 650 3783

Ben-Avraham, Zvi, BSc *Jerusalem*, PhD *Mass.* Max Sonnenberg Prof., Marine Geoscience

Compton, John S., BA *Calif.*, PhD *Harv.* Sr. Lectr.

De Wit, Maarten J., BSc *Trinity(Dub.)*, PhD *Camb.* Philipson-Stow Prof., Mineralogy and Geology

Duncan, Andrew R., BSc *Cape Town*, PhD *Well.* Assoc. Prof.

Fey, Martin V., BScAgric *Natal*, PhD *Natal* Sr. Lectr.

Frimmel, Hartwig E. E., MSc *Vienna*, PhD *Vienna* Sr. Lectr.

Gurney, John J., BSc *Cape Town*, PhD *Cape Town*, FRSSAf Prof.

Harris, Christopher, BA *Oxf.*, DPhil *Oxf.* Sr. Lectr.

Hartnady, Christopher J., MSc *Cape Town*, PhD *Cape Town* Assoc. Prof.

Le Roex, Anton P., BSc *Stell.*, BSc *Cape Town*, PhD *Cape Town* Prof.; Head*

Minter, Wyatt E. L., BSc *Cape Town*, PhD *Witw.* Prof., Economic Geology

Reid, David L., MSc *Well.*, PhD *Cape Town* Assoc. Prof.

Richardson, Stephen H., BSc *Cape Town*, PhD *M.I.T.* Sr. Lectr.

Tredoux, Marian, BSc *Stell.*, BSc *Cape Town*, PhD *Witw.* Sr. Lectr.

Willis, James P., MSc *Cape Town*, PhD *Cape Town* Assoc. Prof.

Other Staff: 1 Sr. Res. Officer; 1 Principal Sci. Officer; 1 Sr. Sci. Officer; 2 Sci. Officers; 1 Hon. Sr. Lectr.

Research: geochemistry; igneous and metamorphic petrology; marine geology; sedimentology; structural geology and tectonics

German Language and Literature

Tel: (021) 650 2936-7 Fax: (021) 650 3726

Horn, Peter R. G., BA *Witw.*, PhD *Witw.* Prof.; Head*

Klingmann, Ulrich, BEd *Cape Town*, MA *Cape Town*, PhD *Cape Town* Sr. Lectr.

Noyes, John K., MA *Witw.*, PhD *Cape Town* Assoc. Prof.

Pakendorf, Gunther, MA *Witw.*, PhD *Cape Town* Sr. Lectr.

Pasche, Wolfgang E., BEd *Cape Town*, MA *Cape Town* Sr. Lectr.

Other Staff: 1 Lectr.

Research: colonial discourses; literature from 1770 to the present; theory and didactics; women's studies and psychoanalysis

Graduate School of Business

Tel: (021) 406 1345 Fax: (021) 215510

Bond, Dave, BA *Sus.*, MA *Z'bwe.*, MSocSc *Cape Town*, MA *Stell.* Sr. Lectr.

Browning, Vicky, BA *Natal*, MA *Cape Town* Sr. Lectr.

Faull, Norman H. B., BSc *Stell.*, BEng *Stell.*, MSc *Cran.*, MBA *Cape Town*, PhD *Cape Town* Prof.

Foster-Pedley, Jonathan, MBA Sr. Lectr.

Horwitz, Frank M., BA *Witw.*, MPM *Witw.*, PhD *Witw.* Prof.

Jowell, Kate, BSc *Cape Town*, MBA *Cape Town* Prof.; Dir.*

Marks, Amy S., BA *Mt.Holyoke*, PhD *Northwestern* Sr. Lectr.

Miller, Jonathan, BSc *Cape Town*, MCom *Cape Town*, PhD *Cape Town* Sr. Lectr.

Morris, Michael, MA *Wright*, PhD *Virginia Polytech.* Prof.

Nel, Deon, BCom *P.Elizabeth*, MCom *Pret.*, DCom *Pret.* Prof.

Page, Michael J., BSc(Eng) *Natal*, MBA *Cape Town*, PhD *Cape Town* Prof.

Sulcas, Paul, BA *Cape Town*, MCom *Cape Town*, DComm *Stell.* Prof.

Van Wyk, Rias J., MCom *Pret.*, MPA *Harv.*, DComm *Stell.* Prof.

Other Staff: 6 Visiting Profs.; 1 Lectr

Research: effective manufacturing worldwide; entrepreneurship; marketing and management of technology; monitoring employment equity in South Africa; social marketing of tobacco products

Hebrew and Jewish Studies

Tel: (021) 650 2945 Fax: (021) 650 3062

Gitay, Yehoshua, BA *Jerusalem*, PhD *Emory* Isidore and Theresa Cohen Prof., Hebrew Language and Literature

Shain, Milton, MA *S.Af.*, MA *Leeds*, PhD *Cape Town* Prof.; Head*

Stier, O., BA *Prin.*, PhD *Calif.* Sr. Lectr.

Other Staff: 1 Lectr.

Research: biblical literature and rhetoric; Jewish feminism; modernity and Jewish memory; South African Jewry

History

Tel: (021) 650 2741 Fax: (021) 689 7581

Adhikari, Mohammed, MA *Cape Town* Sr. Lectr.

Bickford-Smith, Vivian J., MA *Camb.*, PhD *Camb.* Sr. Lectr.

Bradford, Helen, BA *Cape Town*, BSc *Cape Town*, PhD *Witw.* Assoc. Prof.

Harries, Patrick A. L., BA *Cape Town*, PhD *Lond.* Assoc. Prof.

Mendelsohn, Richard, BA *Cape Town*, PhD *Witw.* Sr. Lectr.

Nasson, William R., BA *Hull*, MA *York(UK)*, PhD *Camb.* Prof.

Penn, Nigel G., BA *Witw.*, PhD *Cape Town* Sr. Lectr.

Phillips, Howard, BA *Cape Town*, MA *Lond.*, PhD *Cape Town* Sr. Lectr.

Phimister, Ian R., BA *Nott.*, BA *Z'bwe.*, DPhil *Z'bwe.* Prof.

Saunders, Christopher C., BA *Cape Town*, MA *Oxf.*, DPhil *Oxf.* Assoc. Prof.

Worden, Nigel A., BA S.Af., MA Camb., PhD Camb. Prof.
Other Staff: 4 Lectrs.
Vacant Posts: King George V Prof.
Research: Cape Town history; environmental history; gendered history; medical, mining, maritime and public history; Western Cape oral history

History of Art

Tel: (021) 650 2685-6 Fax: (021) 650 3726
Godby, Michael A. P., BA Trinity(Dub.), MA Birm., PhD Witw. Prof.; Head*
Klopper, Sandra, BA Witw., MA E.Anglia, PhD Witw. Sr. Lectr.
Other Staff: 1 Lectr.

Information Systems

Tel: (021) 650 2266-1 Fax: (021) 689 7582
Cloete, E., BSc Stell., MSc Natal Sr. Lectr.
Eccles, Michael G., MCom Cape Town Sr. Lectr.
Erlank, Stephen, BSc Cape Town, BCom Cape Town Sr. Lectr.
Hart, Michael L., BSc Cape Town, MSc Cape Town, PhD Cape Town Assoc. Prof.
Hoffman, A. R., MCom Cape Town Sr. Lectr.
Mattison, James H. K., BCom Cape Town Sr. Lectr.
McLeod, G., BCom Cape Town Sr. Lectr.
Smith, Derek C., BTech Brad., MCom Cape Town Prof.
Van Belle, J. P., BCom Cape Town, MBA Stell. Sr. Lectr.
Vacant Posts: 1 Lectr.; 1 Asst. Lectr.
Research: health information systems; management (technological and social aspects); personnel-related issues; systems development approaches

Italian Studies

Tel: (021) 650 3058
Saxby, Cornelia N., BA Lond., MPhil Lond., PhD Cape Town Assoc. Prof.; Head*
Other Staff: 1 Lectr.
Research: Renaissance dialogue; twentieth-century women's writing; unpublished manuscripts of the fifteenth century

Law, Commercial

Tel: (021) 650 3065-8 Fax: (021) 686 2577.
(Devel. and Labour Law Unit) 689 7567
Blackman, Michael M. S., BA Cape Town, LLB Cape Town, LLM Harv., PhD Cape Town, PhD Camb. Prof.; Head*
Davis, Dennis M., BCom Cape Town, LLB Cape Town, MPhil Camb. Prof.
Emslie, T. S., BA Witw., LLB Witw., BCom Cape Town, MBA Cape Town Assoc. Prof.
Hare, John E., BCom Cape Town, LLB Cape Town, LLM Lond. Assoc. Prof.; Dir., Shipping Law Unit
Jooste, Richard D., BA Cape Town, BCom Cape Town, LLB Cape Town, LLM Camb. Prof.
Kalula, Evance R., LLB Zambia, LLM Lond., PhD Warw. Assoc. Prof.; Dir., Devel. and Labour Law Unit
Rubin, N., BA Cape Town, LLB Cape Town Hon. Prof
Thompson, Clive R., BA Stell., LLB Cape Town Assoc. Prof.
Other Staff: 4 Lectrs.
Research: admirality law and practice; development and labour in southern Africa

Law, Criminal and Procedural, see also Criminol., Inst. of

Tel: (021) 650 2672 Fax: (021) 686 2577
De La Hunt, Virginia, BA Cape Town, LLB Cape Town Sr. Lectr.; Dir., Legal Aid Clinic
Leeman, Israel, BA Stell., LLB Stell. Prof.; Head*
Van Zyl Smit, Dirk, BA Stell., LLB Stell., PhD Edin. Prof.
Other Staff: 1 Lectr.

Law, Private

Burman, Sandra B., BA Cape Town, LLB Cape Town, MA Oxf., DPhil Oxf. Prof.

De Vos, W., BA Stell., LLB Stell., DrsJur Ley., LLD Cape Town Emer. Prof.
Fagan, A. G., BA Cape Town, LLB Cape Town, DPhil Oxf. Sr. Lectr.
Himonga, C. N., LLB Zambia, LLM Lond., PhD Lond. Sr. Lectr.
Hutchison, Dale B., BCom Cape Town, LLB Cape Town, PhD Camb. Prof.; Head*
Nhlapo, Ronald T., BA UBLS, LLB Glas., DPhil Oxf. Prof.
Van Heerden, Belinda J., BA Stell., LLB Stell., MA Oxf. Assoc. Prof.
Visser, Daniel P., BIur Pret., LLB Pret., LLD Pret., DrJur Ley. Prof.
Other Staff: 1 Lectr.

Law, Public

Tel: (021) 650 3072-8 Fax: (021) 689 8546
Bennett, Thomas W., BA Rhodes, LLB Rhodes, PhD Cape Town Prof.; Head*
Corder, Hugh M., BCom Cape Town, LLB Cape Town, LLB Camb., DPhil Oxf. Prof.; Dir., Sch. for Advanced Legal Studies
Devine, Dermott, BA N.U.I., LLB N.U.I., LLB S.Af., LLD Cape Town Prof.
Maluwa, Tiyanjana, LLB Malawi, LLM Sheff., PhD Camb. Prof.
Murray, Christina M., BA Stell., LLB Stell., LLM Mich. Prof., Constitutional and Human Rights Law; Dir., Law, Race and Gender Res. Unit
Sachs, Albie, BA Cape Town, LLB Cape Town, DPhil Sus., Hon. LLD S'ton. Hon. Prof.
Other Staff: 1 Hon. Sr. Res. Officer
Research: law of the sea

Legal History and Method

Tel: (021) 650 3082 Fax: (021) 686 2577
Du Bois, François G., BA Oxf., BA Stell., BCL Oxf., LLB Stell. Sr. Lectr.
Hofman, Julien, BL Z'bwe., LLB Z'bwe., BTheol Greg., LJC Greg., LPhil Heythrop Sr. Lectr.
Meyerson, Denise Y., BA Witw., BPhil Oxf., LLB Cape Town, DPhil Oxf. W. P. Schreiner Prof.; Head*

Librarianship, School of

Tel: (021) 650 3091 Fax: (021) 650 3489
De Jager, Karin, BA Rhodes, MA Rhodes, MBibl Cape Town, PhD Cape Town Sr. Lectr.
Nassimbeni, Mary M., BA Rhodes, PhD Cape Town Sr. Lectr.
Smith, Janette G., BSc Stell, MA Cape Town Sr. Lectr.
Underwood, Peter G., MBA Cran., FLA Prof.; Head*
Research: information literacy; information management; information needs analysis; library performance measurement and evaluation

Linguistics

Tel: (021) 650 3138 Fax: (021) 650 3726
Lass, Roger G., BA New.Sch.Soc.Res., PhD Yale Prof.
Love, Nigel L., MA Oxf., DPhil Oxf. Assoc. Prof.; Head*
Mesthrie, Rajend, BPaed Durban-W., BA Cape Town, BA S.Af., MA Texas, PhD Cape Town Assoc. Prof.
Other Staff: 1 Lectr.; 1 Visiting Res. Assoc.
Research: descriptive linguistics; historical linguistics; philosophy of language; phonology; sociolinguistics and applied sociolinguistics

Management Studies, School of

Tel: (021) 650 2311 Fax: (021) 689 7570
Birt, Martin, BA Rhodes, BA Cape Town, MBA Stell., MSc Lond., PhD Cape Town Sr. Lectr.
Dorrington, Robert E., BA S.Af., BCom Natal, BSc Cape Town, FIA Prof., Actuarial Science
Firer, C., BSc Witw., MBA Witw., PhD Cape Town Frank Robb Prof., Finance
Hipkin, I. B., BScEng Natal, BCom Cape Town, MA S.Af., MPhil Cape Town Sr. Lectr.
MacDonald, Iain L., BSc Cape Town, MSc Oxf., PhD Cape Town Assoc. Prof.

Razis, Vincent V., MA Oxf., MBA Cape Town, PhD Cape Town Sr. Lectr.
Simpson, John D., BSc Cape Town. MBA Cape Town, PhD Cape Town John Garlick Prof., Business Science; Head*
Slater, Mark E., BSc Bath, FIA Sr. Lectr.
Slattery, Garrett, MSc Witw., PhD Witw., FIA Sr. Lectr.
Sully, Preis M., BA Natal, MA Natal, PhD Rhodes Sr. Lectr.
Thomson, Trevor G., BBusSc Cape Town, MA Cape Town, PhD Stell. Assoc. Prof.
Other Staff: 4 Lectrs.
Vacant Posts: South African Assocn. of Marketeers Prof. (Marketing); 1 Prof. (orgnl. psychol. and human resource management)
Research: finance; human resource management; knowledge organisations; marketing; occupational psychology

Mathematics and Applied Mathematics, see also Stat. Scis.

Tel: (021) 650 3190 Fax: (021) 650 3159, 650 2334
Barashenkov, Igor V., MSc Moscow, PhD Jt.Inst.Nuclear Res., Dubna Sr. Lectr.
Becker, Ronald I., BSc Cape Town, PhD M.I.T. Prof.
Brink, Christoffel, MSc Rhodes, MA Rhodes, PhD Camb., DPhil Rand Afrikaans Prof.; Head*
Brümmer, Guillaume C. L., MSc Stell., DrMath Amst., PhD Cape Town Prof.
Butterworth, Douglas S., MSc Cape Town, PhD Lond. Prof.
Cherenack, Paul F., MA Penn., PhD Penn. Assoc. Prof.
Conradie, Jurie J., MSc Stell., PhD Camb. Sr. Lectr.
Cross, Ronald W., MA St And., PhD Lond. Assoc. Prof.
Ellis, George F. R., BSc Cape Town, BCom Cape Town, PhD Camb., FRAS, FIMA Prof.
Gilmour, Christopher R. A., MSc Cape Town, PhD Cape Town Assoc. Prof.
Hahn, Brian D., BSc Cape Town, PhD Camb. Assoc. Prof.
Hughes, Kenneth R., BSc Cape Town, PhD Cape Town, PhD Warw. Sr. Lectr.
Mabizela, Sizwe, MSc Fort Hare, PhD Penn.State Sr. Lectr.
Ntantu, Ibula, MSc Virginia Polytech., PhD Virginia Polytech. Sr. Lectr.
Reddy, Batmanathan D., BSc(Eng) Cape Town, PhD Camb. Prof.
Ronda, Jacek, MSc(Eng) U.T.Warsaw, MSc(Math) Warsaw, PhD Polish Acad.Sc., DSc Polish Acad.Sc. Sr. Lectr.
Rose, Henry, BSc La Trobe, PhD Vanderbilt Sr. Lectr.
Rynhoud, Alan N., MSc Cape Town Sr. Lectr.
Webb, John H., BSc Cape Town, PhD Camb. Prof.
Other Staff: 11 Lectrs.; 1 Sr. Res. Officer; 1 Sr. Sci. Officer; 1 Sci. Officer; 1 Temp. Sr. Lectr.; 1 Temp. Lectr.
Research: computational and applied mechanics; cosmology and relativity; formal aspects of computer science; marine resource management; topology and category theory

Microbiology

Tel: (021) 650 3269-70 Fax: (021) 689 7573
Rawlings, Douglas E., BSc Rhodes, PhD Rhodes Prof.
Reid, Sharon J., BSc Rhodes, PhD Rhodes Sr. Lectr.
Rybicki, Edward P., MSc Cape Town, PhD Cape Town Assoc. Prof.
Thomson, Jennifer A., BSc Cape Town, MA Camb., PhD Rhodes Prof.; Head*
Other Staff: 3 Lectrs.; 1 Res. Officer
Research: molecular biology (bacteria and viruses important in industry, agriculture, mariculture and medicine)

Music, South African College of

Tel: (021) 650 2634 Fax: (021) 650 2627

Campbell, Michael I., BMus N.Texas, MMus Cape Town   Assoc. Prof., Jazz Studies

Crowson, J. Lamar   Emer. Prof., Piano

Davids, Virginia   Sr. Lectr., Singing

Du Toit, Francois, BMus Cape Town, FTCL   Sr. Lectr., Piano

Fitch, G., MMus Manhattan Sch.   Sr. Lectr., Piano

Gie, Shirley A., BMus S.Af., FRCO   Sr. Lectr., Keyboards, Musicology

Gobbato, Angelo M. G., BSc Cape Town   Assoc. Prof.; Dir., Opera Sch.

Hansen, Deirdre D., MMus Rhodes, PhD Witw.   Sr. Lectr., Ethnomusicology

Hofmeyr, Hendrik, MMus Cape Town   Sr. Lectr., Musicology

Kierman, Sean A., BA Antioch, BMus Witw., MA P.Elizabeth, BA   Sr. Lectr., Brass

Klatzow, Peter J. L.   Assoc. Prof., Composition

Liebl, Brad L., MM Cinc., DMA Cinc.   Sr. Lectr., Singing

Lilley, Andrew C. P., BAS Cape Town   Sr. Lectr., Jazz Studies

May, James W., MMus Cape Town   Assoc. Prof., Musicology; Dir.*

Rommelaere, Paul F. M., MMus Cape Town   Sr. Lectr., Music Education

Schwietering, Jürgen   Assoc. Prof., Violin and Viola

Smith, Albert E. B., MA Rhodes, PhD Rhodes, FTCL   Assoc. Prof., Organ and Chamber Choir

Tuffin, Michael P., FTCL   Sr. Lectr., Musicology

Other Staff: 6 Lectrs.; 30 Teaching Staff†

Oceanography

Tel: (021) 650 3277-8 Fax: (021) 650 3979

Brundrit, Geoffrey B., BSc Manc., PhD Manc.   Prof., Physical Oceanography; Head*

Lutjeharms, Johann R. E., MSc Cape Town, PhD Wash., DSc Cape Town, FRSSAf   Prof., Ocean Climatology

Shannon, L. Vere, MSc Cape Town, PhD Cape Town   Hon. Prof.

Shillington, Frank A., BSc Witw., MSc Cape Town, PhD Cape Town   Assoc. Prof.

Other Staff: 1 Chief Sci. Officer

Vacant Posts: 1 Sr. Lectr.

Research: air-sea interaction; coastal meteorology; marine climatology; physical oceanography; ocean modelling; shelf dynamics

Philosophy

Tel: (021) 650 3316 Fax: (021) 650 3490

Goldstein, L., BA Liv., PhD St And.   Assoc. Prof.

Ross, D. A., MA W.Ont., PhD W.Ont.   Sr. Lectr.

Shutte, Michael F. N., BA Cape Town, MA Stell., DPhil Stell.   Sr. Lectr.

Taylor, Paul A., MA Stell., MPhil Lond., PhD Lond.   Assoc. Prof.; Head*

Other Staff: 1 Lectr.

Physics

Tel: (021) 650 3326 Fax: (021) 650 3342; (Theoret. Phys.) 650 3352

Allie, Muhammed S., MSc Cape Town   Sr. Lectr.

Aschman, David G., BSc Cape Town, DPhil Oxf.   Prof.; Head*

Ball, Donald, BSc Cape Town, PhD Monash   Sr. Lectr.

Britton, David T., MSc Lond., PhD Lond.   Sr. Lectr.

Brooks, Francis D., MSc Rhodes, DSc Rhodes   Emer. Prof.

Cleymans, Jean W. A., MSc Louvain, DèsSc Louvain, FRSSAf   Prof., Theoretical Physics

Comrie, Craig M., MSc Natal, PhD Camb.   Assoc. Prof.

Dominguez, Cesareo A., MSc Buenos Aires, PhD Buenos Aires, FRSSAf   Prof.

Driver, Harry S. T., MSc Cape Town, PhD Br.Col.   Assoc. Prof.

Fearick, Roger W., BSc Witw., PhD Witw.   Sr. Lectr.

Perez, Sandro M., BSc Witw., DPhil Oxf.   Prof.

Robertson, Gerald N. van der H., BSc Cape Town, DPhil Oxf.   Assoc. Prof.

Viollier, Raoul D., DrPhilNat Basle, FRSSAf   Prof.

Other Staff: 2 Lectrs.; 1 Lectr.†; 2 Sr. Res. Assocs.; 1 Emer. Assoc. Prof.

Research: applied optics; nuclear physics; physics education; theoretical physics

Physiology, see Medicine, below

Political Studies

Tel: (021) 650 3916 Fax: (021) 689 7574

Cameron, Robert, PhD Cape Town   Assoc. Prof.

Du Toit, Andries B., MA Stell., DPhil Stell., DrsPhil Ley.   Prof.

Giliomee, Hermann B., MA Stell., PhD Stell.   Prof.

Kuye, J., BA Manit., MPA Winn., PhD Manit.   Sr. Lectr.

MacLaughlin, Donald B., BA Yale, MSc Lond.   Sr. Lectr.

Schrire, Robert A., BCom Cape Town, MA American(D.C.), PhD Calif.   Prof.; Head*

Seegers, Annette, MA Pret., PhD Loyola(Ill.)   Prof.

Other Staff: 1 Lectr.

Research: civil-military relations; comparative politics; intellectual history and local government; political ethics; South African politics and policy analysis

Psychology

Tel: (021) 650 3430 Fax: (021) 689 7572

Dawes, Andrew R. L., BSocSc Cape Town, MSc Cape Town   Assoc. Prof.

De la Rey, C., MA Natal   Sr. Lectr.

Du Preez, Peter D., PhD Cape Town   Prof.

Finchilescu, Gillian, MSc Cape Town, DPhil Oxf.   Sr. Lectr.

Foster, Donald H., BA Stell., MSc Lond., PhD Camb.   Prof.

Louw, Johannes, MA Stell., DrsPsy Ley., PhD Amst.   Assoc. Prof.; Head*

Oxtoby, Richard M., BSc Natal, PhD Cape Town   Sr. Lectr.

Schomer, Hein H., PhD Cape Town   Sr. Lectr.

Swartz, Sally G., MA Cape Town, MSc Cape Town, PhD Cape Town   Sr. Lectr.

Tredoux, Colin G., PhD Cape Town   Sr. Lectr.

Other Staff: 1 Lectr.; 1 Asst. Lectr.

Research: child development; gender; intergroup relations; policy development; social change in southern Africa

Religious Studies

Tel: (021) 650 3452 Fax: (021) 689 7575

Chidester, David S., BA Calif.State, PhD Calif.   Prof., Comparative Religions

Cochrane, J. R., BSc Cape Town, MDiv Chic., PhD Cape Town   Prof.

Cumpsty, John S., BSc Durh., MS Carnegie-Mellon, PhD Durh.   Prof.; Head*

De Gruchy, John W., BA Rhodes, BD Rhodes, MTh Chic., DD S.Af.   Robert Selby-Taylor Prof., Christian Studies

Mazamisa, Llewellyn W., BD Theol.Sch.Kampen, ThDrs Theol.Sch.Kampen, PhD Theol.Sch.Kampen   Sr. Lectr.

Moosa, Ebrahim E., BA Kanpur, MA Cape Town, PhD Cape Town   Sr. Lectr.

Stier, O. B., BA Prin., MA Calif., PhD Calif.   Sr. Lectr.

Tayob, Abdulkader I., BA Durban-W., BA Cape Town, PhD Temple   Assoc. Prof.

Villa-Vicencio, Charles M. L., BA Rhodes, BA Natal, STM Yale, PhD Drew   Prof., Religion and Society

Wanamaker, Charles A., BA Lincoln Christian, MA Ill., MCS Regent Coll.(Br.Col.), PhD Durh.   Assoc. Prof.

Other Staff: 1 Lectr.; 2 Asst. Lectrs.

Research: contemporary religion; religious education curricula; resource development for schools

Russian Studies, Centre for

Tel: (021) 650 3059 Fax: (021) 650 3059

Davidson, Apollon B., PhD U.S.S.R.Acad.Sc., DrHist&PolSci U.S.S.R.Acad.Sc.   Prof.; Dir.*

Other Staff: 1 Lectr.

Research: archival documents on Russia and Africa, eighteenth century to 1960; Comintern and South Africa; twentieth-century South Africa-Russia relations

Social Anthropology

Tel: (021) 650 3679

Honwana, A., MA Paris, PhD Lond., BA   Sr. Lectr.

Reynolds, Pamela F., BA Cape Town, BEd Cape Town, MEd Harv., MLitt Delhi, PhD Cape Town   Prof.; Head*

Spiegel, Andrew D., MA Cape Town, PhD Cape Town   Assoc. Prof.

Other Staff: 2 Lectrs.

Research: anthropology of tourism; boundaries; children; domestic dynamics and family violence; urbanisation

Social Work, School of

Tel: (021) 650 3493

Louw, Lionel R., BA(SW) W.Cape, MSocSc Cape Town, MDiv Wilberforce, Hon. DD Wilberforce   Sr. Lectr.

Smit, Andre De V., BSocSc(SW) Cape Town, BCom Cape Town, MPubAd Cape Town   Assoc. Prof.; Dir.*

Other Staff: 4 Lectrs.; 1 Asst. Lectr.

Research: cultural diversity; gender studies; mental health; social security systems; substance abuse

Sociology

Tel: (021) 650 3501, 650 3517 Fax: (021) 689 7576

Cooper, David M., BSc(Eng) Cape Town, MSocSc Birm., PhD Birm.   Sr. Lectr.

Crankshaw, O., BSc Witw., BA Witw., PhD Witw.   Sr. Lectr.

Graaff, Johan F. D., BA Stell., LLB Stell., MSc Brist., PhD Stell.   Sr. Lectr.

Jubber, Kenneth C., MA Witw., PhD Cape Town   Assoc. Prof.; Head*

Lincoln, Merwyn D., BA Natal, MA W.Laur., PhD Cape Town   Sr. Lectr.

Maree, Johannes J., BSc Rhodes, MA Oxf., MA Sus., PhD Cape Town   Prof.

Russell, M., BSocSc(SW) Natal, MSocSc Natal, PhD E.Anglia

Seekings, Jeremy F., BA Oxf., BA Witw., DPhil Oxf.   Sr. Lectr.

Other Staff: 4 Lectrs.

Statistical Sciences, see also Maths. and Appl. Maths.

Tel: (021) 650 3219 Fax: (021) 689 7578

Barr, Graham D. I., BSc Cape Town, BA Cape Town, MSc Cape Town, PhD Cape Town   Assoc. Prof.

Bradfield, David J., MSc Cape Town, PhD Cape Town   Assoc. Prof.

Dunne, Timothy T., BA Natal, BEd Natal, PhD Cape Town   Assoc. Prof.

Guo, Renkuan G., BSc Tsing Hua, MSc Iowa State, PhD Iowa State   Sr. Lectr.

Juritz, June M., BSc S.Af., MSc Cape Town, PhD Cape Town   Assoc. Prof.

Stewart, Theodor J., BSc(ChemEng) Cape Town, MSc S.Af., PhD S.Af.   Prof.; Head*

Troskie, Casparus G., MSc Pret., PhD S.Af.   Prof.

Underhill, Leslie G., MSc Cape Town, PhD Cape Town   Prof., Avian Demography; Dir., Avian Demography Unit

Van den Honert, Robin C., MSc Cape Town, PhD Cape Town   Sr. Lectr.

Wegner, Trevor, MBusSc Cape Town, MSc Sus., PhD Cape Town   Assoc. Prof.

Other Staff: 3 Lectrs.

Research: biostatistics; decision theory; multiple-criteria decision-making; multivariate analysis; stochastic hydrology and meteoorology

Surveying, see Engin., Surveying and Geodetic

Zoology

Tel: (021) 650 3604 Fax: (021) 650 3301

Branch, George M., BSc Cape Town, PhD Cape Town, FRSSAf Prof.
Brown, Alexander C., MSc Rhodes, PhD Cape Town, DSc Cape Town Emer. Prof
Bruton, M. N., BSc Rhodes, MSc Rhodes, PhD Rhodes Hon. Prof.
Chinsamy-Turan, BSc Witw., PhD Witw. Assoc. Prof.
Cluver, M., MSc Stell., PhD Stell., FRSSAf Hon. Prof.
Cook, Peter A., BSc Wales, PhD Wales Assoc. Prof.
Crowe, Timothy M., MSc Chic., PhD Cape Town Assoc. Prof.
Davies, Bryan R., BSc Newcastle(UK), PhD CNAA Assoc. Prof.
Day, Jennifer A., BSc Cape Town, PhD Cape Town Sr. Lectr.
Du Plessis, M. A., MSc Pret., PhD Cape Town
Field, Johannes G., BSc Cape Town, PhD Cape Town, FRSSAf Prof.
Gäde, Gerd, MS Mün., PhD Mün. Prof.
Griffiths, Charles L., BSc S'ton., PhD Cape Town Assoc. Prof.; Head*
Hockey, Philip A. R., BSc Edin., PhD Cape Town Assoc. Prof.
Hoffman, John H., MSc Rhodes, PhD Rhodes Assoc. Prof.; Chief Res. Officer
Jarvis, Jennifer U. M., MSc Cape Town, PhD E.Af., FRSSAf Assoc. Prof.
Lucas, M. I., BSc Wales, PhD Wales Sr. Lectr.
Nicolson, Susan W., BSc Auck., PhD Camb. Sr. Lectr.
Other Staff: 4 Lectrs.; 1 Asst. Lectr.
Research: biochemistry; ecology; ethology; physiology

MEDICINE

Tel: (021) 406 6347, 406 6106 Fax: (021) 478955

Anaesthesia

Tel: (021) 404 9111 Fax: (021) 475206

Butt, A. R., MB ChB Cape Town Sr. Lectr.
Dyer, Robert A., BSc Stell., MB ChB Cape Town Sr. Lectr.
Falanga, Franca M., MB ChB Cape Town Sr. Lectr.
Harrison, G. G., MD Cape Town, DSc(Med) Cape Town, FFARACS, FRCA Emer. Prof.
Hayse-Gregson, Paul B., BSc(Eng) Cape Town, MSc(Eng) Cape Town, MB ChB Cape Town Sr. Lectr.
Heijke, Slvyia A. M., MB ChB Cape Town Sr. Lectr.
James, Michael F. M., MB ChB Birm., PhD Witw., FRCA Prof.; Head*
Lopez, Juliette T., MB BS Lond., FFARCS Sr. Lectr.
Macdonald, Alistair G., MB ChB Cape Town Sr. Lectr.
Misnuner, Zelik, MB ChB Cape Town Sr. Lectr.
Nieuwveld, R. W., MB BCh Witw. Sr. Lectr.
Ozinsky, J., MB ChB Cape Town, FFARCSI Assoc. Prof.
Thomas, J. M., MB ChB Cape Town Sr. Lectr.
Viljoen, John F., MB ChB Cape Town, FRCA, FFARCSI Prof.
Wells, K. F., MB ChB Cape Town, FRCPCan Sr. Lectr.
Other Staff: 1 Principal Specialist; 5 Lectrs.; 5 Lectrs.†

Anatomical Pathology

Tel: (021) 406 6160 Fax: (021) 448 1789, 404 2386

Bowen, Robert M., MB ChB Cape Town, MMedPath Cape Town Sr. Lectr.
Cruse, J. Peter, MB ChB Cape Town, PhD Lond., FRCPath Wernher and Beit Prof.; Head*

Taylor, D. A., MB ChB Z'bwe., MMedPath(Anat) Cape Town, PhD Manc., FRSChem Sr. Lectr.
Wainwright, Helen C., MB ChB Cape Town Sr. Lectr.
Other Staff: 3 Sr. Lectrs.†; 2 Lectrs.†
Research: diseases prevalent in local or national communities (tuberculosis, viral infections - HIV, EBV, CMV -and various cancers), particularly those affecting disadvantaged groups

Paediatric Pathology

Tel: (021) 658 6044, 658 5208 Fax: (021) 689 1287

Hanslo, David H., MB ChB Cape Town, MMedPath Cape Town, FRCPath Sr. Lectr.
Henderson, Howard, BSc Cape Town, PhD Cape Town Assoc. Prof.
Kaschula, Ronald O. C., MB ChB Cape Town, MMedPath Cape Town, FRCPath Assoc. Prof.; Head of Lab.
Lastovica, Albert J., BSc McM., MSc McM., PhD Natal Sr. Lectr.
Purves, L. R., MB BCh Witw., MMed(Path) Witw. Assoc. Prof.
Shuttleworth, Margaret H. G., BSc Cape Town, MB ChB Cape Town, MMedPath Cape Town Sr. Lectr.
Sinclair-Smith, C. C., MB ChB Cape Town, MMedPath Cape Town Assoc. Prof.
Other Staff: 2 Lectrs.; 1 Lectr.†

Anatomy and Cell Biology

Tel: (021) 406 6273 Fax: (021) 448 7226

Els, Willem J., MS Ill., DSc Stell. Assoc. Prof.
Kidson, Susan H., PhD Witw. Sr. Lectr.
Louw, Graham J., DVSc Pret. Sr. Lectr.
Morris, Alan G., BSc Wolv., PhD Witw. Assoc. Prof.
Omlin, François X., MSc Zür., PhD Zür. Assoc. Prof.
Rawdon, Benjamin B., BSc Nott., PhD Nott., DSc Nott. Prof.; Head*
Slater, Charles P., MB ChB Cape Town Sr. Lectr.
Warton, Christopher M. R., MB ChB Rhodesia Sr. Lectr.
Other Staff: 2 Lectrs.; 1 Asst. Lectr.
Research: biological anthropology; cell and development biology; development of innovative teaching material

Biomedical Engineering

Tel: (021) 406 6238 Fax: (021) 448 3291

Adams, Laurence P., BSc(Eng) Witw., PhD E.Af., FRICS Emer. Prof.
Boonzaier, David A., MB ChB Cape Town Sr. Lectr.; Chief Med. Officer
Bridger, Robert S., MSc Lond., PhD Cape Town Sr. Lectr.; Principal Specialist Scientist
Capper, Wayne L., BScEng Natal, MSc(Med) Cape Town, PhD Cape Town Sr. Lectr.; Principal Biomed. Engineer
Poluta, Mladen A. J., BSc(Eng) Witw. Sr. Lectr.; Principal Biomed. Engineer
Vaughan, Christopher L., BSc Rhodes, PhD Iowa Hyman Goldberg Prof.; Head*
Other Staff: 5 Hon. Lectrs.

Cardiothoracic Surgery

Tel: (021) 406 6181-3 Fax: (021) 448 1145

Brink, Johan G., MB ChB Cape Town Sr. Lectr.
De Groot, M., MD Manit., FRCSCan Assoc. Prof.
Hewitson, John P., MB ChB Cape Town Sr. Lectr.
Von Oppell, Ulrich O., MB BCh Witw., PhD Cape Town Prof.; Head*
Worthington, M., MB ChB Cape Town
Zilla, P., MD Vienna, PhD Cape Town Assoc. Prof.
Research: improving the life-span of biological heart valves; lining prosthetic materials with autologous endothelial cells; methods of myocardial protection

Chemical Pathology

Tel: (021) 406 6185 Fax: (021) 448 8150

Berman, Mervin C., BSc Cape Town, MB ChB Cape Town, MMedPath(Chem) Cape Town, PhD Cape Town Prof.
Berman, Peter A., MB ChB Cape Town, MMedPath(Chem) Cape Town Sr. Lectr.
Davidson, James S., MA Camb., MB ChB Cape Town, PhD Cape Town Assoc. Prof.; Head*
Harley, Eric, MB BS Lond., MS Lond., MSc Lond., PhD Lond. Prof.
King, Judy A., MSc Cape Town, PhD Cape Town Sr. Lectr., Medical Biochemistry
McIntosh, David B., BSc Witw., PhD Cape Town Assoc. Prof.
Millar, Robert P., BSc Rhodes, MSc Lond., PhD Liv. Prof.; Dir., UCT/MRC Unit for Molecular Reproductive Endocrinol.
Owen, Elizabeth P., BSc Lond., PhD Lond. Sr. Lectr.; Asst. Dir., Med. Nat. Scis.
Vreede, Helena, MB ChB Cape Town, MMedPath(Chem) Cape Town Sr. Lectr.
Other Staff: 1 Lectr.; 3 Med. Scientists; 3 Sr. Res. Officers; 2 Res. Officers
Research: biochemical parasitology; G protein-coupled receptor/function; haemoglobin crosslinking; inherited metabolic disorders/molecular evolution; molecular pumps and transporters/anti-malarial drug development; reproductive endocrinology

Community Health

Tel: (021) 406 6495 Fax: (021) 406 6163

Hoffman, BSc Cape Town, MB ChB Cape Town Assoc. Prof.; Dir., Women's Health Res. Unit
Kirigia, J., BEd Nair., MA Nair., MSc York, PhD York Sr. Lectr.
London, L., BSc Cape Town, MB ChB Cape Town, MMed Cape Town, MD Cape Town Assoc. Prof.
McIntyre, Diane E., BCom Cape Town, BA Cape Town, MA Cape Town Sr. Lectr.; Dir., Health Economics Unit
Myers, Jonathan, BSc Cape Town, MB ChB Cape Town, MD Cape Town Prof.; Dir., Occupnl. and Health Res. Unit; Head*
Strachan, B., MSc PhD
Other Staff: 2 Sr. Specialists; 1 Specialist Scientist; 1 Chief Res. Officer; 3 Sr. Res. Officers; 1 Assoc. Prof.†; 1 Med. Officer†; 6 Hon. Lectrs.
Research: epidemiology; health economics and policy; occupational and environmental health; primary health; women's health

Dermatology

Tel: (021) 406 3376 Fax: (021) 473282

Saxe, Norma, MB ChB Cape Town Assoc. Prof.; Head*
Todd, Gail, BScAgric Natal, MB ChB Cape Town, PhD Cape Town Assoc. Prof.
Other Staff: 8 Sr. Lectrs.†
Research: anticonvulsants; genetics of psoriasis; primary and secondary dermatological care; psychological aspects of skin diseases

Forensic Medicine and Toxicology

Tel: (021) 406 6412 Fax: (021) 448 6815

Du Toit, E., MD Cape Town Visiting Prof.
Knobel, Gideon J., MB ChB Stell., MMed Stell. Prof.; Head*
Phillips, V. M., BDS Witw., MChD Stell. Visiting Prof.
Wadee, Shabir A., BSc Wat., MB ChB Natal, MMed Natal Sr. Lectr.
Other Staff: 1 Sr. Lectr.; 1 Lectr.
Research: alcohol and unnatural deaths; community epidemiology network on drug use; public policy and health promotion; violence and injury in the Cape Town metropole

Haematology

Tel: (021) 404 3073, 406 6156 Fax: (021) 448 8607

Holland, E., MB ChB *Cape Town*, PhD *Cape Town* Sr. Lectr., Haematologist
Novitsky, Nicolas, PhD *Cape Town*, FCP(SA) Prof.; Head*
Other Staff: 2 Lectrs./3 Lectrs./Haematologists; 1 Asst. Dir./Med. Natural Scientist; 1 Principal Med. Natural Scientist; 1 Hon. Lectr.
Research: blood stem cell transplantation; Hodgkin's disease and malignant lymphomas; myeloma; the leukaemias and myelo-dysplastic syndromes

Human Genetics

Tel: (021) 406 6194 Fax: (021) 477703
Beighton, Peter H., MD *Lond.*, PhD *Witw.*, FRCP, FRCPEd, FRSSAf Prof.; Head* Dir., UCT/MRC Res. Unit for Med. Genetics
Ramesar, R., BSc *Natal*, MSc *Natal*, PhD *Cape Town* Assoc. Prof.
Viljoen, D., MB ChB *Birm.*, MD *Cape Town* Assoc. Prof.
Other Staff: 1 Hon. Assoc. Prof. ; 5 Hon. Sr. Lectrs.; 1 Hon. Lectr.
Research: childhood handicap (blindness, hearing loss, crippling and mental retardation); colonic cancer; foetal alcohol syndrome; genetic basis of manic depressive psychosis

Immunology

Tel: (021) 406 6147 Fax: (021) 448 6116
Potter, Paul C., BSc *Cape Town*, MB ChB *Cape Town*, MD *Cape Town*, FCP(SA) Assoc. Prof.
Ryffel, B., MD PhD
Wilson, Elaine L., PhD *Cape Town* Hon. Prof.
Other Staff: 9 Lectrs.; 1 Principal Med. Officer
Research: allergology; clinical immunology; infectious immunology; transplantation immunology

Logopaedics

Tel: (021) 406 6313 Fax: (021) 448 8157
Tuomi, Seppo K., MA *Turku*, PhD *Northwestern* Assoc. Prof.; Head*
Other Staff: 4 Lectrs.; 1 Asst. Lectr.; 7 Clin. Supervisors†
Vacant Posts: 1 Sr. Lectr.
Research: cleft palate; laryngectomy; swallowing; voice, stuttering and language

Medical Biochemistry

Tel: (021) 406 6335 Fax: (021) 477669
Ehlers, Mario R. H., MB ChB *Cape Town*, PhD *Cape Town* Prof.; Head*
Gevers, Wieland, MB ChB *Cape Town*, MA *Oxf.*, DPhil *Oxf.*, FRSSAf Prof.
Parker, M. Iqbal, BSc *Cape Town*, PhD *Cape Town* D. G. Murray Prof., Cancer Research
Thilo, Lutz R., MSc *Pret.*, DrRerNat *Heidel.* Assoc. Prof.
Other Staff: 1 Lectr.; 2 Hon. Sr. Lectrs.
Research: cellular and molecular biology of breast and oesophageal cancer; endocytic trafficking and characteristics of the mycobacterial phagosome; molecular basis of mycobacterium tuberculosis-host cell interaction; proteolytic processing of membrane proteins

Medical Microbiology

Tel: (021) 406 6363 Fax: (021) 448 4153
Hardie, D. R., MB ChB *Cape Town*, MMedPath *Cape Town* Sr. Lectr.
Keen, Gustav A., MMedPath *Cape Town* Sr. Lectr., Clinical Virology; Acting Head*
Oliver, Stephen P., MMedPath *Cape Town* Sr. Lectr.
Roditi, D., MMedPath *Cape Town*
Steyn, L. M., MB ChB *Stell.*, PhD *Cape Town* Assoc. Prof.
Other Staff: 1 Principal Specialist Scientist; 1 Sr. Specialist Scientist; 3 Specialist Scientists; 2 Hon. Lectrs.; 2 Sr. Lectrs.†;
Vacant Posts: Wernher and Beit Prof.; Head
Research: clinical microbiology; molecular medical microbiology; paediatric medical microbiology; virology

Medical Physics

Tel: (021) 406 6266 Fax: (021) 404 6269
Hering, E. R., MSc *Cape Town*, PhD *Cape Town* Sr. Lectr.; Acting Head*
Other Staff: 6 Lectrs.; 3 Hon. Lectrs.

Medicine

Fax: (021) 448 6815
Abbo, Abdul A., MB ChB *Cape Town*, FCP(SA) Sr. Lectr.
Ainslie, Gillian M., MB ChB *Cape Town* Sr. Lectr.
Ascott Evans, B., MB ChB *Cape Town* Sr. Lectr.
Bateman, Eric D., MB ChB *Cape Town*, MD *Cape Town*, FRCP Ad Hominem Prof., Respiratory Medicine
Benatar, Solomon R., MB ChB *Cape Town*, FRCP, Hon. FACP Prof.; Head, Centre for Bio-Ethics; Head of Dept.*
Bonnici, François, MB ChB *Cape Town*, MMed *Cape Town*, FCP(SA) Assoc. Prof.
Bryer, Alan, MB BCh *Witw.*, MMed *Cape Town*, PhD *Cape Town*, FCP(SA) Sr. Lectr.
Commerford, Patrick J., MB ChB, FCP(SA) Helen and Morris Mauerberger Prof., Cardiology
Eastman, R. W., MB ChB *Cape Town* Assoc. Prof.
Hift, Richard J., MB ChB *Cape Town*, MMed *Cape Town*, FCP(SA) Sr. Lectr.
Kalla, Asgar A., MB ChB *Cape Town*, MD *Cape Town*, FCP(SA) Assoc. Prof.
Keeton, G. Roy, MB BCh *Witw.*, FCP(SA) Emer. Prof.†
Kies, Brian M., MB ChB *Cape Town*, FCP(SA) Sr. Lectr.
Kirsch, Ralph E., MB ChB *Cape Town*, MD *Cape Town*, DSc(Med) *Cape Town*, FCP(SA) Prof.; Co-Dir., UCT/MRC Liver Res. Centre
Lee Pan, Edward B., MB ChB *Cape Town*, MMed *Stell.* Sr. Lectr.
Levitt, Naomi S., MB ChB *Cape Town*, MD *Cape Town* Assoc. Prof.
Louw, Jacob A., MB ChB *Stell.*, MMed *Stell.*, PhD *Cape Town*, FCP(SA) Prof., Gastroenterology
Louw, Stephanus J., MB ChB *Cape Town*, MD *Cape Town*, FCP(SA) William Slater Prof., Geriatrics
Maartens, Gary, MB ChB *Cape Town*, MMed *Cape Town*, FCP(SA) Assoc. Prof.
Marais, Adrian D., MB ChB *Cape Town*, FCP(SA) Assoc. Prof.
Muller, Greta M. M., BSc *Witw.*, MB BCh *Witw.*, MMed *Cape Town*, FCP(SA) Sr. Lectr.
Opie, Lionel H., BM BCh *Oxf.*, MD *Cape Town*, DPhil *Oxf.*, DSc(Med) *Cape Town*, FRCP, FRSSAf Ad Hominem Prof.; Dir., UCT/MRC Ischaemic Heart Disease Res. Unit
Pascoe, Michael, MB ChB *Cape Town*, FCP(SA) Sr. Lectr.
Raine, Richard I., MB ChB *Cape Town*, MMed *Cape Town*, FCP(SA) Sr. Lectr.
Rayner, Brian L., MB ChB *Cape Town*, FCP(SA) Sr. Lectr.
Ress, Stanley R., MB ChB *Pret.*, FCP(SA) Assoc. Prof.
Scott-Millar, Robert N., MB BCh *Witw.*, FCP(SA) Assoc. Prof.
Seggie, Janet L., BSc *Birm.*, MB ChB *Birm.*, MD *Birm.*, FRCP Assoc. Prof.
Shephard, Enid, BSc *Cape Town*, PhD *Cape Town* Assoc. Prof.
Stevens, John, MD *Lond.*, FRCP Sr. Lectr.
Swanepoel, Charles R., MB ChB *Cape Town*, FRCP Sr. Lectr.
Tooke, A., MB ChB *Cape Town* Sr. Lectr.
Van Zyl Smit, Roal, MB BCh *Witw.*, FRCP Assoc. Prof.
White, Neil W., MB ChB *Cape Town*, MD *Cape Town*, FCP(SA) Sr. Lectr.
Willcox, Paul A., BSc *Birm.*, MB ChB *Birm.* Assoc. Prof.
Wood, R., BM BCh *Oxf.* Sr. Lectr.
Yellon, J. D., PhD *Bath*, Hon. DSc
Other Staff: 8 Lectrs.; 15 Sr. Lectrs.†; 13 Lectrs./Physicians†; 7 Hon. Sr. Lectrs.

Neurosurgery

Tel: (021) 406 6213-4 Fax: (021) 406 6555
De Villiers, Jacquiz C., Hon. MD *Stell.*, Hon. DSc *W.Cape*, MD, FRCS, FRCSEd Emer. Prof.
Peter, Jonathan C., MB ChB *Cape Town*, FRCSEd Helen and Morris Mauerberger Prof.; Head*
Semple, Patrick, L., MB ChB *Cape Town*, MMed *Cape Town*, FCS(SA) Sr. Lectr.
Other Staff: 4 Lectrs.; 4 Sr. Lectrs.†; 3 Lectrs.†
Research: epilepsy; paediatric, pituitary, spinal and vascular neurosurgery

Nuclear Medicine

Tel: (021) 404 4169-70 Fax: (021) 404 3402
Benningfield, Stephen J., MB ChB *Cape Town* Prof.; Acting Head*
Fataar, A. B., MB ChB *Cape Town*, MMed *Cape Town*
Research: abnormalities of cerebral perfusion in patients with Alzheimer's disease; effects of drugs on renal function; effects of treatments on bone density; gastrointestinal tract; Tc-99m Sestamibi imaging

Nursing

Tel: (021) 406 6431 Fax: (021) 406 6497
Clow, Sheila E., BSocSc *Natal*, MSc(Nursing) *Cape Town* Sr. Lectr.
Mayers, Patricia, BANursing *Stell.*, BCur *S.Af.* Sr. Lectr.
Thompson, Rosalie A. E., BSocSc *Natal*, MPubAd *Cape Town* Helen and Morris Mauerberger Prof.; Head*
Other Staff: 2 Lectrs.; 3 Lectrs.†
Research: chronic fatigue syndrome; domestic workers' health; mature women's health; political violence and health; quality assurance

Obstetrics and Gynaecology

Tel: (021) 406 6117 Fax: (021) 448 6921
Anthony, John, MB ChB *Cape Town* Sr. Lectr.
Coetzee, Edward J., MB ChB *Cape Town*, FRCOG Sr. Lectr.
Davey, D. A., PhD *Lond.*, FRCOG Emer. Prof.†
de Jong, Peter R., MB ChB *Pret.*, MMed *Cape Town* Sr. Lectr.
Denny, L. A., MB ChB *Cape Town* Sr. Lectr.
Dommisse, Johannes, MB ChB *Cape Town*, FRCOG Emer. Prof.
Dyer, S. J., MB ChB *Munich* Sr. Lectr.
Fawcus, S. R., MB BS *Lond.*, MA *Lond.* Sr. Lectr.
Gunston, Keith D., MB ChB *Cape Town*, FRCOG Sr. Lectr.
Ncayiyana, Daniel J. M., MD *Gron.* Hon. Prof.
Nevin, J., MB BCh *Witw.*, MMed *Cape Town* Sr. Lectr.
Stewart, C. J. M., MMed *Cape Town* Sr. Lectr.
Van der Spuy, Zephne M., MB ChB *Stell.*, PhD *Lond.*, FRCOG Prof.; Head*
Wright, Michael, MB BCh *Witw.* Sr. Lectr.
Other Staff: 1 Med. Natural Scientist; 2 Lectrs.; 4 Sr. Lectrs.†; 27 Lectrs.†; 2 Emer. Assoc. Profs.; 4 Hon. Sr. Lectrs.

Occupational Therapy

Tel: (021) 406 6323 Fax: (021) 406 6323
Beeton, Hilary J., BA *S.Af.* Sr. Lectr.; Control Occupational Therapist
Bloom, Elizabeth A. Lectr.; Chief Occupational Therapist
Buchanan, Helen, BSc(OccTher) *Cape Town* Lectr.; Chief Occupational Therapist
Dewas, Susan, BSc(OccTher) *Cape Town* Lectr.; Chief Occupational Therapist
Duncan, E. Madeleine, BA *Durban-W.*, BOccupationalTherapy *OFS* Sr. Lectr.
Lorenzo, T., BSc(OccTher) *Cape Town* Lectr.; Chief Occupational Therapist
Nicholls, Lindsay E., BSc(OccTher) *Cape Town* Lectr.; Chief Occupational Therapist
Van Nierkerk, Lana, BOccupationalTherapy *OFS*, MA *OFS* Lectr.; Chief Occupational Therapist

Watson, Ruth M., BSc *Witw.*, MEd *Stell.*, PhD *Stell.* Assoc. Prof.; Head*

Other Staff: 2 Lectrs.†

Ophthalmology

Tel: (021) 406 6215-6 Fax: (021) 406 6218

Barron, Adrian J., MB ChB *Cape Town*, FRCSEd Sr. Lectr.

Grotte, R. H., MB BS *Newcastle(UK)*, FRCSEd Sr. Lectr.

Ivey, A., MB ChB *Cape Town*, FRCSEd Sr. Lectr.

Johnston, M., MB ChB *Cape Town* Sr. Lectr.

Lecuona, K., MB ChB *Cape Town* Sr. Lectr.

Murray, A. D., MB BCh *Witw.*, FRCSEd Morris Mauerberger Prof., Opthalmology; Head*

Other Staff: 11 Sr. Lectrs.†

Research: cataract surgery; corneal disease; glaucoma; paediatric opthalmology; ocular tumours

Orthopaedic Surgery

Tel: (021) 406 6157-8 Fax: (021) 472709

Hoffman, E. B., MB ChB *Stell.* Assoc. Prof.

Maraspini, Christiana, MB ChB *Cape Town* Sr. Lectr.

Walters, Johan, MB ChB *Cape Town* Pieter Moll and Nuffield Prof.; Head*

Other Staff: 3 Lectrs.; 18 Sr. Lectrs.†

Research: arthritis surgery; hand surgery; hip joint replacement surgery; paediatric surgery

Otorhinolaryngology

Tel: (021) 406 6420 Fax: (021) 448 6461

Prescott, Christopher A. J., MB ChB *St And.*, FRCS Sr. Lectr.

Sellars, Sean L., MB BChir *Camb.*, MA *Camb.*, FRCS, FACS, Hon. FRCSEd Leon Goldman Prof.; Head*

Other Staff: 1 Lectr.; 3 Sr. Lectrs.†; 5 Lectrs.†; 1 Clin. Res. Fellow

Research: alaryngeal speech; childhood cholesteatoma; percutaneous tracheostomy; profoundly deaf pre-school children; swallowing disorders

Paediatric Pathology, see under Anat. Pathol.

Paediatric Surgery

Tel: (021) 658 5012, 658 5339 Fax: (021) 689 1287

Bass, D. H., MMed *Cape Town*, FCS(SA) Sr. Lectr.

Brown, R. A., MB ChB *Cape Town*, FRCSEd, FCS(SA) Sr. Lectr.

Millar, A. J. W., MB ChB *Cape Town*, FRCS, FRCSEd, FRACS Assoc. Prof.

Morrison, C., MB ChB Sr. Lectr.

Rode, Heinz, MMed *Pret.*, FCS(SA), FRCSEd Charles F. M. Saint Prof.; Head*

Other Staff: 1 Med.Officer†; 3 Res. Social Workers

Research: burn therapy; child accident prevention; common diseases of Africa; liver transplantation; surgical care

Paediatrics and Child Health

Tel: (021) 658 5074 Fax: (021) 689 1287

Allie, A., MB ChB *Cape Town*, FCP(SA) Sr. Lectr.

Argent, A., MB BCh *Witw.*, MMed *Witw.* Sr. Lectr.

Beatty, David W., MB ChB *Cape Town* MD *Cape Town*, FCP(SA) Prof.; Head*

Bonnici, F., MB ChB *Cape Town*, MMed *Cape Town*, FCP(SA) Assoc. Prof.

Burgess, J. D., MB ChB *Cape Town*, FCP(SA) Sr. Lectr.

Daubenton, J. D., BSc *Witw.*, MB BCh *Witw.*, MD *Cape Town*, FCP(SA) Sr. Lectr.

Delport, Stephen V., MB ChB *Cape Town*, MMed *Cape Town*, FCP(SA) Assoc. Prof.

Harrison, Vincent C., MB ChB *Cape Town*, MMed *Cape Town*, MD *Cape Town* Assoc. Prof.

Hartley, P. S., MB ChB *Cape Town*, FCP(SA) Sr. Lectr.

Heese, H. De V., BSc *Stell.*, MB ChB *Cape Town*, MD *Cape Town*, FRCPEd Emer. Prof.

Henley, L. D., MSocSc *Cape Town*, PhD *Cape Town* Sr. Lectr.

Hussey, G. D., MB ChB *Cape Town*, MMed *Cape Town*, MSc *Lond.* Assoc. Prof.

Ireland, J. D., MB ChB *Cape Town*, MD *Cape Town*, FCP(SA) Sr. Lectr.

Jacobs, M. E., MB ChB *Cape Town*, FCP(SA) Stella and Paul Loevenstein Prof., Child Health

Karabus, C. D., MB ChB *Cape Town*, MMed *Cape Town*, FRCPEd Assoc. Prof.

Kibel, M. A., MB BCh *Witw.*, FRCPEd Emer. Prof.

Klein, Max, MB ChB *Cape Town*, FCP(SA) Assoc. Prof.

Leary, P. M., MB ChB *Cape Town*, MD *Cape Town*, FCP(SA) Assoc. Prof.

Mann, M. D., MB ChB *Cape Town*, MMed(Paed) *Cape Town*, MMed(NucMed) *Cape Town*, PhD *Cape Town* Assoc. Prof.

Moller G. H., MB ChB *Cape Town*, FCP(SA) Sr. Lectr.

Motala, C., MB ChB *Cape Town*, FCP(SA) Sr. Lectr.

Power, David J., MB BS *Lond.*, MD *Cape Town* Prof.

Reynolds, L. G. Von B., MB ChB *Cape Town*, FCP(SA) Sr. Lectr.

Roux, Paul, MB ChB *Cape Town*, MD *Cape Town*, FCP(SA) Sr. Lectr.

Sive, A. A., MB ChB *Cape Town*, MD *Cape Town*, FCP(SA) Sr. Lectr.

Swingler, G. H., MB ChB *Cape Town*, FCP(SA) Sr. Lectr.

Van der Elst, Clive W., MB ChB *Cape Town*, MD *Cape Town*, FCP(SA) Sr. Lectr.

Weinberg, E. G., MB ChB *Cape Town*, FCP(SA) Assoc. Prof.

Woods, David L., MB ChB *Cape Town*, MD *Cape Town*, FRCP Assoc. Prof.

Other Staff: 12 Lectrs.; 9 Sr. Lectrs.†; 23 Lectrs.†; 1 Emer. Assoc. Prof. ; 5 Hon. Sr. Lectrs.; 4 Hon. Lectrs.†

Research: immunology; infectious diseases, especially HIV and tuberculosis; nutrition-related disorders

Pharmacology

Tel: (021) 404 6286 Fax: (021) 448 6181

Barnes, K., MB ChB *Cape Town* Sr. Lectr.

Folb, Peter I., MD *Cape Town*, FCP(SA), FRCP Prof.; Head*

Robins, Ashley H., MB ChB *Cape Town*, MD *Witw.* Sr. Lectr./Sr. Specialist

Smith, Peter J., BSc *Cape Town*, PhD *Cape Town* Sr. Lectr./Specialist Scientist

Other Staff: 1 Med. Natural Scientist; 1 Hon. Sr. Lectr.

Research: adverse effects of medicines in the body; blood levels of drugs with narrow therapeutic ranges; traditional medicines; use and safety of essential medicines

Physiology

Tel: (021) 406 6241 Fax: (021) 477669

Beardwood, Cyril J., BScAgric *Natal*, BSc *Witw.*, PhD *Lond.* Sr. Lectr.

Belonje, Peter C., MMed *Pret.*, DVSc *Pret.* Prof.; Head*

Dennis, Steven G. C., BSc *Lond.*, PhD *Lond.* Assoc. Prof.

Derman, Elton W., BSc(Med) *Cape Town*, MB ChB *Pret.*, PhD *Cape Town* Sr. Lectr.

Hawley, John A., BSc *Lough.*, MA *Ball*, PhD *Cape Town* Assoc. Prof.

Lambert, Michael I., BScAgric *Natal*, BA(PhysEd) *Rhodes*, MSc *S.Carolina*, PhD *Cape Town* Sr. Lectr.

Noakes, Timothy D., MB ChB *Cape Town*, MD *Cape Town* Liberty Life Prof., Exercise and Sports Science; Dir., UCT/MRC Biogenetics of Exercise Res. Unit

Querido, David, MSc *Cape Town*, PhD *Cape Town* Sr. Lectr.

Schwellnus, Martin P., MB BCh *Witw.*, MSc *Cape Town*, MD *Cape Town* Sr. Lectr.

Other Staff: 1 Principal Sci. Officer; 3 Sr. Sci. Officers; 1 Lectr.†

Vacant Posts: 1 Lectr.

Research: electromagnetic field effects; electrophysiology; mineral metabolism; neurophysiology; postmortem changes

Physiotherapy

Tel: (021) 404 4407, 406 6401 Fax: (021) 448 8157

Bowerbank, Patricia, BA *S.Af.*, MBL Assoc. Prof.

Farquharson, Margaret Sr. Lectr.; Control Physiotherapist

Futter, Merle J., BA *S.Af.*, MSocSc *Cape Town* Sr. Lectr.; Acting Head*

Other Staff: 8 Lectrs.; 2 Clin. Lectrs.

Research: clinical supervision; ecology theory and changes in physiotherapy practice; recruitment of black scholars; role of physiotherapists in sports medicine

Plastic, Reconstructive and Maxillo-facial Surgery

Tel: (021) 406 6415, 404 3426 Fax: (021) 448 6461

Bloch, Cecil M., MB ChB *Cape Town*, FCS(SA), FRCSEd Assoc. Prof.; Head of Teaching Dept.*

Hudson, Donal A., MB ChB *Cape Town*, FCS(SA), FRCS Assoc. Prof.

Other Staff: 9 Sr. Lectrs.†

Primary Health Care

Tel: (021) 406 6510 Fax: (021) 448 6815

Baqwa, Jeffrey D., BSc *Fort Hare*, MB ChB *Saar.*, MCommH *Liv.* Prof.; Head*

Other Staff: 5 Lectrs.; 1 Lectr.†; 4 Lectrs.†(Gen. Practice)

Psychiatry

Tel: (021) 406 6566, 404 2164 Fax: (021) 448 8158

Berard, Raymond M. F., BSc *Witw.*, MB BCh *Witw.* Sr. Lectr./Sr. Specialist

Daubenton, François, MB BCh *Witw.*, BA *S.Af.* Sr. Lectr./Principal Specialist

De Jager, W., MA *P.Elizabeth* Sr. Lectr./Sr. Clin. Psychologist

Dirks, B., MB ChB *Cape Town*, MMed *Cape Town* Sr. Lectr./Sr. Specialist

Kaliski, Sean Z., BA *Witw.*, MB BCh *Witw.* Sr. Lectr./Sr. Specialist

Katz, Paul H., BSc *Cape Town*, MB ChB *Cape Town* Sr. Lectr./Sr. Specialist

Lay, Stephen J., BA *Witw.*, MA *Cape Town* Sr. Lectr./Sr. Clin. Psychologist

Malcolm, Charles, MA *Witw.*, PhD *Rhodes* Sr. Lectr./Principal Clin. Psychologist

Molteno, Christopher D., BA *S.Af.*, MB ChB *Cape Town*, MMed *Cape Town*, MD *Cape Town*, PhD *S.Af.* Vera Grover Prof., Mental Handicap

Robertson, Brian A., MD *Cape Town* Prof.; Head*

Shorthall, N., MB ChB *Cape Town* Sr. Lectr./Sr. Specialist

Soltau, H., MA *P.Elizabeth* Sr. Lectr./Sr. Clin. Psychologist

Westaway, Joan L., MB ChB *Cape Town*, MPhil *S.Af.* Sr. Lectr./Specialist

Wilson, Donald A. B., BSc *Cape Town*, MB ChB *Cape Town* Sr. Lectr./Principal Specialist

Zabow, Tuviah, MB ChB *Cape Town* Assoc. Prof./Principal Specialist

Ziervogel, Carl, MB BCh *Witw.* Sr. Lectr./Principal Specialist

Other Staff: 9 Lectrs./Specialists; 15 Lectrs./Clin. Psychologists; 5 Lectrs./Med. Officers; 7 Sr. Lectrs.†/Sr. Specialists†; 1 Sr. Lectr./Sr. Clin. Psychologist†; 9 Lectrs./Specialists†; 6 Lectrs./Psychologists†; 5 Med. Officers†; 1 Hon. Sr. Lectr./Psychiatrist; 1 Hon. Lectr.

Research: adolescent mental health in sub-Saharan Africa; epidemiological studies in children and adolescents; genetics in schizophrenia; mental health provision at primary care level; risk-taking behaviour in adolescents

Radiation Oncology

Tel: (021) 404 4265, 406 6505 Fax: (021) 404 5259

Abratt, Raymond D., MB ChB Pret., MMed Cape Town Assoc. Prof.

Blekkenhorst, G., BSc Natal, PhD Cape Town Assoc. Prof.

Geddes, Christina H. C., MB ChB Edin. Sr. Lectr.

Kranold, Dorothea, MB ChB Cape Town Sr. Lectr.

Murray, Elizabeth M., MB ChB Cape Town, MMed Cape Town Sr. Lectr.

Stannard, C., BSc Lond., MB BS Sr. Lectr.

Van Wijk, Adrian L., MB ChB Cape Town Sr. Lectr.

Werner, Isaac D., BSc Cape Town, MB ChB Cape Town, MMed Cape Town, FRCR Nellie Atkinson Prof.; Head*

Wilson, J. A. G., MB ChB Cape Town Sr. Lectr.

Other Staff: 1 Lectr.; 4 Hon. Lectrs.

Research: drug-related clinical studies; incidence of cancer and epidemiological characteristics; proton and neutron beam radiotherapy; retinoblastoma and ocular malignant melanoma; stereo-photogrammatric patient positioning

Radiology

Tel: (021) 404 4184, 406 6426 Fax: (021) 404 4185

Ball, Helen S., BSc St And., MB ChB Dund. Sr. Lectr.

Beningfield, Stephen J., MB ChB Cape Town Prof.; Head*

Fisher, R. M., MB ChB Cape Town Sr. Lectr.

Garb, Minnie, MB BCh Witw., FRCR Sr. Lectr.

Goodman, Hillel T., MB ChB Cape Town, MPraxMed Pret., FRCR Sr. Lectr.

Handler, Leonard C., MB ChB Cape Town, MMed Cape Town Assoc. Prof.

Kottler, Ronald E., MB ChB Cape Town, MMed Cape Town, FRCR Emer. Prof.†

Magnus, K., BSc Cape Town, MB ChB Cape Town, MMed Stell. Sr. Lectr.

Roman, Trevor E., MB ChB Cape Town Sr. Lectr.

Seggie, Robert McK., MB ChB Cape Town Sr. Lectr.

Wright, Michael G. E., MB BCh Witw., FRCSEd Sr. Lectr.

Young, Christopher M., MB BS, FRCSEd Sr. Lectr.

Other Staff: 7 Lectrs.; 1 Sr. Lectr.†

Research: interventive radiology; neuroradiology; abdominal, head and neck hepatobiliary, pancreatic, thoracic, trauma, urological and vascular radiology

Surgery

Tel: (021) 406 6475 Fax: (021) 448 6461

Bautz, Peter, MB BCh Witw., FCS(SA) Sr. Lectr.; Head, Trauma Unit

Bornman, Peter C., MB BCh Pret., MMed OFS, FRCSEd Prof.; Head, Surg. Gastroenterol.

Dent, David M., MB ChB Cape Town, ChM Cape Town, FCS(SA), FRCS Prof.; Head, Surg. Oncol. and Endocrinol.

Goldberg, Paul, MB ChB Cape Town, MMed Cape Town, FCS(SA) Sr. Lectr.; Head, Colorectal Unit

Immelman, Edward J., MB ChB Cape Town, FCS(SA), FRCS Prof.; Head, Vascular Surg.

Kahn, Delawir, MB ChB Birm., ChM Cape Town, FCS(SA), FRCS Assoc. Prof.; Head, Organ Transplant Unit and Surg. Labs.

Kariem, G., BChD W.Cape, MChD Stell. Dental Surgeon†; Acting Head, Oral and Dent. Surg.

Krige, Jacobus E. J., MB ChB Cape Town, FRCSEd, FCS(SA) Assoc. Prof.

Michalowski, M. D. Sr. Lectr.

Michell, W. Lance, MB ChB Cape Town Sr. Lectr.; Head, Surg. Intensive Care Unit

Terblanche, John, MB ChB Cape Town, ChM Cape Town, FCS(SA) , FRCS, FRCPGlas, FRCSGlas,

Hon. FACS, Hon. FACP, Hon. FCSEd Prof.; Co-Dir, UCT/MRC Liver Res. Centre; Head*

Other Staff: 7 Lectrs.; 22 Sr. Lectrs.†; 1 Lectr.†; 1 Sr. Med. Nat. Scientist; 2 Consultants (Maxillofacial and Oral Surg.); 5 Consultants† (Maxillofacial and Oral Surg.); 4 Hon. Sr. Lectrs.; 1 Hon. Lectr.

Research: critical care medicine; breast, colorectal, hepatobiliary, pancreatic and vascular diseases; transplantation; trauma

Urology

Tel: (021) 406 6529 Fax: (021) 406 6122

Barnes, Richard D., MB ChB Cape Town, FRCSEd Sr. Lectr.

Naude, Johannes H., MB ChB Pret. Assoc. Prof.; Head*

Pontin, Alan R., MB ChB Birm., FRCSEd Sr. Lectr.

Other Staff: 7 Sr. Lectrs.†

SPECIAL CENTRES, ETC

Academic Development Programme

Tel: (021) 650 3793 Fax: (021) 685 3793

Scott, Ian R., BA Cape Town Dir.*

Research: curriculum development; effects of educational disadvantage

African Ornithology, Percy Fitzpatrick Institute of

Tel: (021) 650 3297 Fax: (021) 650 3295

Du Plessis, M. A., MSc Pret., PhD Cape Town Dir.*

ASPECT (ASPECT)

Academic Support Programme for Engineering in Cape Town

Tel: (021) 650 3238 Fax: (021) 685 3938

Pearce, H. T., BSc(Eng) Cape Town, MS Ill., PhD Ill. Co-ordinator*

Bolus Herbarium

Tel: 021) 650 3773 Fax: (021) 650 4041

Linder, H. Peter, BSc Cape Town, PhD Cape Town Keeper

Child Guidance Clinic

Tel: (021) 650 3901, 650 3905 Fax: (021) 650 3657

Dowdall, Terence L., BA Natal, MA Cape Town Dir.*

Computational and Applied Mechanics, FRD/UCT Centre for Research in (CERECAM)

Tel: (021) 650 3787

Martin, Prof. John B., BScEng Natal, PhD Camb., Hon. DScEng Natal, F(SA)ICE, FRSSAf Dir.*

Research: development of stable and computational solution techniques; fundamental mechanical processes; mathematical modelling of complex material behaviour; simulation of deformation processes and failure of engineering components and artefacts

Energy and Development Research Centre

Tel: (021) 650 2824 Fax: (021) 650 2830

Eberhard, Anton A., BSc(Eng) Cape Town, BA S.Af., PhD Edin. Dir.*

Research: energy efficiency and environment; energy markets and governance; energy, poverty and development

Energy Research Institute

Tel: (021) 705 0120 Fax: (021) 705 6266

Dutkiewicz, Prof. Ryszard K., MSc(Eng) Witw., PhD Camb., FIMechE, F(SA)IME Dir.*

Research: commercial energy production and usage; economic effects of energy production and use; energy management; environmental aspects

Engineering Education, Centre for Research in

Tel: (021) 650 3351

Jawitz, J., BSc Cape Town, MPhil Cape Town Co-ordinator*

Gerontology, HSRC/UCT Centre for

Tel: (021) 406 6538 Fax: (021) 478714

Fereira, Monica, PhD Pret. Dir.*

Industrial Health Research Group

Tel: (021) 650 3508 Fax: (021) 685 5209

No staff at present

Research: developing educational media; education and training of workers; health care funding and medical schemes; health problems of workers; occupational medical services

International Labour Resource and Information Group (ILRIG)

Tel: (021) 476375 Fax: (021) 448 2282

Daphne, Jeremy T., MA Inst.Soc.Stud.(The Hague) Dir.*

Jewish Studies and Research, The Isaac and Jessie Kaplan Centre for

Tel: (021) 650 3062

Shain, Prof. Milton, MA S.Af., MA Leeds, PhD Cape Town Dir.*

Legal Practice, School for

Tel: (021) 650 3762, 650 3764 Fax: (021) 650 2972

Forbes, Elsie, BA Stell., LLB Stell. Dir.*

Marine Law, Institute of

Tel: (021) 650 3074-5

Devine, Prof. Dermott, BA N.U.I., LLB N.U.I., LLB S.Af., LLD Cape Town Dir.*

Other Staff: 5 Hon. Consultants

Research: coastal zone law

Marine Studies, Centre for

Tel: (021) 650 3283 Fax: (021) 650 3979

Brown, Prof. Alexander C., MSc Rhodes, PhD Cape Town, DSc Cape Town Dir.*

Plant Conservation, Institute for

Tel: (021) 650 2440 Fax: (021) 650 4046

Cowling, Prof. Richard M., BSc Cape Town, PhD Cape Town Dir.*

Professional Communication Unit

Tel: (021) 650 3409 Fax: (021) 650 3408

Borcherds, Maria M., BA Cape Town Dir.*

Socio-Legal Research, Centre for

Tel: (021) 650 2505 Fax: (021) 685 7576

Burman, Sandra B., BA Cape Town, LLB Cape Town, MA Oxf., DPhil Oxf. Dir.*

Other Staff: 3 Res. Assocs.

South African Bird Ringing Unit

Tel: (021) 650 3227 Fax: (021) 650 9111

Underhill, Prof. Leslie G., MSc Cape Town, PhD Cape Town Dir.*

Teaching and Learning Resources Centre (TLRC)

Tel: (021) 650 3276 Fax: (021) 650 3489

Versfeld, Ruth E., BA Cape Town, MPhil Cape Town Dir.*

CONTACT OFFICERS

Academic affairs. Deputy Registrar (Academic and Research): Wild, P. A. T., MSc Rhodes, PhD Manc.

Accommodation. Manager, Student Accommodation: Bunting, Sheila

Admissions (first degree). Director, Recruitment and Enrolment: ......

Admissions (higher degree). Director, Recruitment and Enrolment: ......

Adult/continuing education. Fiske, Ingrid J., BA *Witw.*, BA *Cape Town*, MA *Qu.*

Alumni. Alumni Officer: Hendricks, Patricia A.

Archives. University Archivist: Drew, John D. C., MA *Oxf.*

Careers. Director, Careers Office: Wetmore, Mervyn, BA *Rhodes*

Computing services. Director, Information Technology Services: Martin, Duncan, BSc *Natal*, MBL *S.Af.*, PhD *S.Af.*

Conferences, corporate hospitality. Co-ordinator: Smit, Judy

Consultancy services. Deputy Registrar (Academic and Research): Wild, P. A. T., MSc *Rhodes*, PhD *Manc.*

Credit transfer. Co-ordinator, Student Administration (SAS): Rich, Sigi M.

Development/fund-raising. Director, Department of Development: Sillen, Andrew, PhD *Calif.*

Equal opportunities. Equal Opportunity Officer: Molteno, Frank D., MSocSc *Cape Town*

Estates and buildings/works and services. Deputy Registrar (Buildings and Services): Roach, Malcolm G.

Examinations. Examinations Officer: Garnett, Eileen, BSc *Cape Town*, BMus *Cape Town*, MSc *Cape Town*

Finance. Director, Finance Department: Pienaar, Hek J., BCompt *S.Af.*

General enquiries. Registrar: Amoore, Hugh T., BA *Cape Town*

Health services. Director, Student Health Service: Gough, Kevin J., MB ChB *Cape Town*

Industrial liaison. Deputy Registrar (Academic and Research): Wild, P. A. T., MSc *Rhodes*, PhD *Manc.*

International office. International Officer, Academic Programmes: Shackleton, Lesley Y., BSc *Cape Town*, MSc *Cape Town*

Library (chief librarian). Director, University Libraries: Rapp, Joan

Minorities/disadvantaged groups. Equal Opportunity Officer: Molteno, Frank D., MSocSc *Cape Town*

Personnel/human resources. Deputy Registrar (Human Resource Management): Fish, Joy, BSocSc *Natal*, BCom *S.Af.*

Public relations, information and marketing. Director, Development and Public Affairs: Zille, Helen, BA *Witw.*

Purchasing. Purchasing Officer: Adams, Trevor

Quality assurance and accreditation. Senior Deputy Vice-Chancellor: Gevers, Prof. Wieland, MB ChB *Cape Town*, MA *Oxf.*, DPhil *Oxf.*, FRSSAf

Research. Deputy Registrar (Academic and Research): Wild, P. A. T., MSc *Rhodes*, PhD *Manc.*

Safety. Buildings and Services: Fire and Safety Officer: Tunstall, John

Scholarships, awards, loans. Head, Postgraduate Scholarships Office: Vranas, Linda J.

Scholarships, awards, loans. Head, Financial Aid Office: Koopman, June A.

Schools liaison. Head, Student Recruitment: Hilton, Mary

Security. Head, Campus Control: Grierson, Douglas

Sport and recreation. Head, Sports Administration: Donald, John A., BA *Rhodes*

Staff development and training. Deputy Registrar (Human Resource Management): Fish, Joy, BSocSc *Natal*, BCom *S.Af.*

Student union. Deputy Registrar (Student Affairs): Ebrahim, Moosa, BSocSc *Cape Town*

Student welfare/counselling. Deputy Registrar (Student Affairs): Ebrahim, Moosa, BSocSc *Cape Town*

Students from other countries. International Officer, Academic Programmes: Shackleton, Lesley Y., BSc *Cape Town*, MSc *Cape Town*

Students with disabilities. Head, Disability Unit: Jagoe, Kathryn, BFineArt *Rhodes*, BEd *Rhodes*, Hon. PhD *Rhodes*

University press. Publisher, UCT Press: Meny-Gilbert, Rose, BA *Cape Town*

Women. Equal Opportunity Officer: Molteno, Frank D., MSocSc *Cape Town*

[*Information supplied by the institution as at 7 March 1998, and edited by the ACU*]

UNIVERSITY OF DURBAN-WESTVILLE

Founded 1961 as University College, Durban

Member of the Association of Commonwealth Universities

Postal Address: Private Bag X54001, Durban, 4000 South Africa
Telephone: (031) 204 4111 **Fax**: (031) 204 4383 **E-mail**: knaicker@pixie.udw.ac.za **Cables**: UDWEST
Telex: 6-23338 SA

VICE-CHANCELLOR AND PRINCIPAL*—Ramashala, Prof. Mapule F., BA *Witw.*, MPH *Mass.*, EdD *Mass.*
REGISTRAR (ACADEMIC)—Brimer, Prof. Alan, BA *P.Elizabeth*, MA *P.Elizabeth*, DLitt *P.Elizabeth*
DEPUTY VICE CHANCELLOR—Kekana, N. S., BA *North(S.Af.)*, BA *S.Af.*, PhD *Rand Afrikaans*
REGISTRAR (ADMINISTRATIVE)—Stewart, M. J., BCom *Cape Town*
UNIVERSITY LIBRARIAN—Moodley, M., MA *Durban-W.*, MLS *Pitt.*, MS *Indiana*

GENERAL INFORMATION

History. The university was founded in 1961 as a university college, and achieved full university status in 1972.

The Rand campus is about 12km from central Durban.

Libraries. 208,000 volumes.

Fees. R8000–10,000, with an 8% increase each year.

Academic Year. 8 February–31 March; 12 April–11 June; 12 July–23 September; 4 October–3 December.

Statistics. Staff: 1230 (465 academic, 765 administrative). Students: 9500.

FACULTIES/SCHOOLS

Arts
Tel: (031) 204 5059 Fax: (031) 204 4160
Dean: McCracken, Prof. Donal P., BA *Ulster*, DPhil *Ulster*, FRHistS
Secretary: Joseph, Y.

Commerce and Administration
Tel: (031) 204 5046 Fax: (031) 204 4561
Dean: Pillay, Prushothman S., BCom *Natal*, BCompt *S.Af.*
Secretary: Govender, P.

Dentistry
Tel: (031) 295323 Fax: (031) 204 4872
Dean: ......
Secretary: Pillay, S.

Education
Tel: (031) 204 5064 Fax: (031) 204 4866
Dean: Kistan, Ganas, BA *Durban-W.*, BEd *S.Af.*, MEd *S.Af.*, PhD *Natal*
Secretary: Sanasy, K.

Engineering
Tel: (031) 204 5038 Fax: (031) 204 4969
Dean: Masu, Leonard M., BScEng *Nair.*, MScEng *Nair.*, PhD *Leeds*
Secretary: Sivasamy, S.

Health Sciences
Tel: (031) 204 5019 Fax: (031) 204 4872
Acting Dean: Holland, Kathy E.
Secretary: Naidoo, S.

Law
Tel: (031) 204 5036 Fax: (031) 204 4848
Dean: Mowatt, Prof. James G., BA *Natal*, LLB *Natal*, LLM *Durban-W.*
Secretary: Nagan, E.

Science
Tel: (031) 204 5066 Fax: (031) 204 4780
Dean: Ori, Prof. Ramesh G., BSc *S.Af.*, MSc *Colorado*, PhD *Colorado*
Secretary: Brijlal, V.

Theology

Tel: (031) 204 5032 Fax: (031) 204 4286

Dean: Kruger, Hennie A. J., BA Stell., BTh Stell., MTh Stell., DTh Stell.

Secretary: Subramoney, P. V.

ACADEMIC UNITS

Accountancy

Tel: (031) 204 4366 Fax: (031) 204 4429

Chambers, J. D.   Sr. Lectr.

Dawood, M. A. I. S., BCom Natal, BCompt S.Af.

De Waal, Frederick J.   Assoc. Prof.

Erwin, Geoffrey J., BEc Syd., MSc Lond.   Assoc. Prof.

Forsyth, Derek, BCom Natal   Assoc. Prof.

Garach, Dilipkumar I., BCom Durban-W.   Assoc. Prof.

Geach, Walter D., BA Cape Town, LLB Cape Town   Prof.

Naidoo, Ugandra I., BAcc Durban-W., BCom Durban-W.   Sr. Lectr.

Parekh, N. G., BCom   Sr. Lectr.

Petkova O. S., BEd Natal, MSc Pret., PhD Pret.   Sr. Lectr.

Pillay, Prushotman S., BCom Natal, BCompt S.Af.   Sr. Lectr.

Quilling, R. D., BSc Natal   Sr. Lectr.

Razak, Mahomed H. Y., BAcc Durban-W.   Sr. Lectr.; Head*

Sullivan, Phillip L., BCom Natal, LLB Natal, LLM Natal   Sr. Lectr.

Wallach, Thomas H., BCom Natal, BCom S.Af., MCom S.Af.   Sr. Lectr.

Other Staff: 1 Lectr.

Afrikaans and Nederlands

Tel: (031) 204 4546 Fax: (031) 204 4160

Doubell, Maryann, BA(Ed) P.Elizabeth, MA Natal, MA Durban-W.   Lectr.; Head*

Sienaert, Aletta M., BA Pret., MA Cape Town, PhD Natal   Assoc. Prof.

Other Staff: 3 Lectrs.

Anthropology

Tel: (031) 204 4793 Fax: (031) 204 4160

Singh, Anand, BA Durban-W., MA Cape Town, MSc Lond.   Lectr.; Head*

Other Staff: 3 Lectrs.

Applied Curriculum Studies

Tel: (031) 204 4602 Fax: (031) 204 4866

De Villiers, Michael D., BSc Stell., BEd OFS, MEd Stell., DEd Stell.   Assoc. Prof.

Kistan, Ganas, BA Durban-W., BEd S.Af., MEd S.Af., PhD Natal   Sr. Lectr.; Head*

Other Staff: 8 Lectrs.

Arabic, Urdu and Persian

Tel: (031) 204 4793 Fax: (031) 204 4160

Aziz, Ahmed K., BA Durban-W., BA S.Af., MA S.Af., DLitt&Phil S.Af.   Sr. Lectr.; Head*

Jadwat, A. Y., PhD St And., BA   Sr. Lectr.

Other Staff: 2 Lectrs.

Biblical Literature

Tel: (031) 204 4239 Fax: (031) 204 4286

Büchner, Dirk L., BA Rand Afrikaans, BTh Stell., MA Rand Afrikaans, DLitt Stell.   Sr. Lectr.

Kruger, Hendrik A. J., BA Stell., BTh Stell., LTh Stell., MTh Stell., DTh Stell.   Assoc. Prof.

Maartens, Pieter J., BA Witw., BD Pret., DD Pret.   Prof.; Head*

Other Staff: 1 Lectr.

Biochemistry

Tel: (031) 204 4271 Fax: (031) 204 4942

Ariatti, Mario, BSc Lond., DPhil Rhodesia   Prof.

Gupthar, Abinda S., BSc Durban-W., MSc Witw., PhD Witw.   Sr. Lectr.; Head*

Other Staff: 3 Lectrs.

Botany

Tel: (031) 204 4365 Fax: (031) 204 4364

Baijnath, Himansu, BSc S.Af., MSc Durban-W., PhD Reading, FLS   Assoc. Prof.

Barnabas, Alban D., BSc S.Af., MSc S.Af., DSc Durban-W.   Prof.

Naidoo, Gonasageran, BSc S.Af., MSc Durban-W., PhD Tennessee   Prof.; Head*

Other Staff: 4 Lectrs.

Business Economics

Tel: (031) 204 4431 Fax: (031) 204 4561

Dumisa, Bonke C., BCom NUL, BCom S.Af., MBA Bentley, MSc(Econ) Lond., DBA Durban-W.   Sr. Lectr.

Mutyaba, Wilson E., BCom Raj., MCom Raj., PhD Raj.   Sr. Lectr.

Perumal, Sadhasivan, BCom S.Af., MCom S.Af., DCom Durban-W.   Sr. Lectr.

Poovalingam, Kasturi, BCom Durban-W., MCom Durban-W., DCom Durban-W.   Sr. Lectr.; Head*

Other Staff: 2 Lectrs.

Business, Graduate School of

Tel: (031) 765 7062 Fax: (031) 765 6142

Bhana, Narendra, BSc S.Af., BCom S.Af., MCompt S.Af., DCom Durban-W.   Prof.

Gani, Abdool S., MSc Punjab, MBA Durban-W.   Sr. Lectr.

Kambuwa, Marvin M., BA Lanc., MA Lanc., MPA Harv.   Prof.; Head*

Mansfield, Willard R., BSc Natal, PhD Witw.   Prof.

Chemistry

Tel: (031) 204 4324 Fax: (031) 204 4780

Jonnalagadda, Sreekantha B., BSc And., MSc Vikram, PhD Vikram   Prof.

Pienaar, Daniel H., BSc Natal, MSc Natal, PhD Natal   Sr. Lectr.

Rogers, Barney C., BSc Natal, MSc Natal, PhD Natal   Assoc. Prof.

Sankar, Munessar, BSc Rhodes, BSc Natal, MSc Natal, PhD Natal   Prof.; Head*

Other Staff: 1 Lectr.

Church History and Missiology

Tel: (031) 204 4762 Fax: (031) 204 4286

Balia, Daryl M., BTheol Durban-W., MTheol Durban-W., ThM Prin., DTheol Durban-W.   Assoc. Prof.

Classical Languages

Tel: (031) 204 4343 Fax: (031) 204 4160

Botha, Allan D., BA Pret., MA Pret.   Sr. Lectr.

Matier, Kenneth O., BA Cape Town, MA Aberd., PhD Rhodes   Prof.; Head*

Other Staff: 3 Lectrs.

Computer Science

Tel: (031) 204 4136 Fax: (031) 204 4780

Baboolal, Satyanand, BSc Durban-W., MSc Dund., PhD Natal   Assoc. Prof.

Hajek, Miloslav, MSc Inst.Chem.Tech., Prague, PhD Inst.Chem.Tech., Prague   Sr. Lectr.; Head*

Laidlaw, Michael G. G., BSc St And., PhD N.Carolina   Prof.

Other Staff: 2 Lectrs.

Criminology

Tel: (031) 204 4793 Fax: (031) 204 4160

Chetty, Vanitha R., BA S.Af., MA Durban-W., DPhil Durban-W.   Lectr.; Head*

Other Staff: 1 Lectr.

Curriculum Studies

Tel: (031) 204 4604 Fax: (031) 204 4866

Jansen, Jonathan D., BSc W.Cape, BEd S.Af., MS Cornell, PhD Stan.   Prof.; Head*

Other Staff: 9 Lectrs.

Dentistry, see below

Drama

Tel: (031) 204 4626 Fax: (031) 204 4830

Govender, Subbalakshmi D., BA Durban-W., MA Durban-W.   Sr. Lectr.

Schauffer, Dennis L., BA Natal, MA Leeds, PhD Natal   Prof.

Singh, Rabindra, BA Durban-W., MA N.Y.   Sr. Lectr.; Head*

Other Staff: 2 Lectrs.

Economics

Tel: (031) 204 4431 Fax: (031) 204 4561

Brijlal, Premchund, BA Durban-W., MA Durban-W., DPhil Durban-W.   Sr. Lectr.; Head*

Contogiannis, Eleftherios, BSc Athens, MA(Econ) Manc., PhD Kent   Prof.

Other Staff: 5 Lectrs.

Education, see Appl. Curric. Studies, Curric. Studies, Foundations of Educn., Psychol. of Educn.

Engineering

Tel: (031) 204 4778 Fax: (031) 204 4755

Govender, Ramachandran, BSc Durban-W., MA Oxf., MSc Lond.   Sr. Lectr.

Quadir, Roshan, BSc W.Ont., MSc W.Ont., PhD   Sr. Lectr.

Engineering, Chemical

Tel: (031) 204 4778 Fax: (031) 204 4755

Abashar, Mohamed E. E., BSc Salf., MSc Salf., PhD Salf.   Sr. Lectr.

Carsky, Milan, PhD Prague   Assoc. Prof.; Head*

Zhelev, T., PhD Sofia   Assoc. Prof.

Other Staff: 5 Lectrs.

Engineering, Civil

Tel: (031) 204 4749 Fax: (031) 204 4755

Oloo, Simon Y., BSc Nair., MSc Lond., PhD Sask.   Sr. Lectr.

Onyejekwe, Okey O., BSc Ib., MS Calif., PhD Calif.   Prof.

Otieno, Frederick A. O., BSc Nair., MSc Newcastle(UK), PhD Newcastle(UK)   Sr. Lectr.; Head*

Teshome, Dellelegne S., BSc Addis Ababa, MSc Addis Ababa, DrEng Tokyo   Sr. Lectr.

Other Staff: 3 Lectrs.

Engineering, Electrical

Tel: (031) 204 4186 Fax: (031) 204 4755

Chitamu, P. J. J., BSc Dar., PhD S'ton., MSc   Sr. Lectr.

Eitelberg, Eduard, DrIng Karlsruhe, DrIngHabil Karlsruhe   Prof.

Ijumba, Nelson L., BSc(Eng) Dar., MSc Salf., PhD Strath.   Assoc. Prof.

Jimoh, A. A., BEng A.Bello, MEng A.Bello, PhD McM.   Sr. Lectr.

Mneney, Stanley H., BSc(Eng) Kumasi, MASc Tor., PhD Dar.   Assoc. Prof.; Head*

Other Staff: 3 Lectrs.

Engineering, Mechanical

Tel: (031) 204 4184 Fax: (031) 204 4775

Goolam, Ebrahim, BEng Durban-W., MSc Natal   Sr. Lectr.

Kaunda, M. A. E., DPhil Cape Town, BSc MSc   Sr. Lectr.

Masu, Leonard M., BScEng Nair., MScEng Nair., PhD Leeds   Assoc. Prof.

Navon, U., BSc(Eng) Haifa(Technion), MSc(Eng) Haifa(Technion), PhD(Eng) Prin.   Assoc. Prof.

Roy-Aikins, Joseph, BSc Manc., MSc Car., PhD Cran.   Sr. Lectr.; Head*

Vadasz, Peter, BSc(Eng) Haifa(Technion), MSc(Eng) Haifa(Technion), DSc Haifa(Technion), F(SA)IME   Prof.

Other Staff: 3 Lectrs.

English

Tel: (031) 204 4193 Fax: (031) 204 4160

Brimer, Alan, BA Cape Town, BA P.Elizabeth, MA P.Elizabeth, DLitt P.Elizabeth   Prof.

Coullie, Judith E., BA Natal, MA Syr., PhD Natal   Sr. Lectr.

Olivier, Theo, PhD Natal   Assoc. Prof.; Head*

Wade, Jean-Philippe, BA Natal, MA Essex, PhD Essex   Assoc. Prof.

Other Staff: 12 Lectrs.

Other Staff: 2 Lectrs.

Ethics, see Systematic Theol. and Ethics and Practical Theol.

Fine Art

Tel: (031) 204 4580 Fax: (031) 204 4197

Marshall, Sabine, Dr *Tübingen*　Sr. Lectr.

Ntuli, V. C. A., BA(FA) *Fort Hare*, MA *Lond.*　Lectr.; Head*

Thathiah, Kirendra V., BA(FA) *Durban-W.*, MA(FA) *Durban-W.*　Sr. Lectr.

Other Staff: 5 Lectrs.

Foundations of Education

Tel: (031) 204 4604 Fax: (031) 204 4866

Karodia, Yusuf M., BA *Durban-W.*, BEd *Durban-W.*, MEd *S.Af.*, PhD *Pret.*　Sr. Lectr.

Other Staff: 3 Lectrs.

Geography

Tel: (031) 204 4317 Fax: (031) 204 4934

Maharaj, Bridgemohan, BPaed *Durban-W.*, BA *Durban-W.*, MA *Durban-W.*, PhD *Natal*　Assoc. Prof.; Head*

Soni, Dhirajlal V., BA *Durban-W.*, MA *Durban-W.*, DPhil *Durban-W.*　Prof.

Watson, Helen K., BSc *Natal*, MSc *Natal*, DPhil *Durban-W.*　Assoc. Prof.

Other Staff: 1 Lectr.

Geology

Tel: (031) 204 4318 Fax: (031) 204 4650

Cooper, Michael R., BSc *Natal*, MSc *Natal*, DPhil *Oxf.*, FGS　Prof.

Dunlevey, John N., BSc *Durh.*, MSc *Stell.*, PhD *Stell.*, FGS　Assoc. Prof.

Liu, Kuiwu, BSc *Chengdu Coll.Geol.*, MSc PhD　Sr. Lectr.

McCourt, Stephen, BSc *Exe.*, PhD *Exe.*, FGS　Prof.; Head*

Mitchell, Andrew A., BSc *Rhodes*, MSc *Rhodes*, PhD *Rhodes*　Sr. Lectr.

Other Staff: 1 Lectr.

Health Sciences, see below

Hindu Studies and Indian Philosophy

Tel: (031) 204 4657 Fax: (031) 204 4160

Dewa, Harilal G., BA *Natal*, BA *Durban-W.*, MA *Durban-W.*, DPhil *Durban-W.*　Sr. Lectr.

Kumar, Penumala, PhD *Calif.*　Sr. Lectr.; Head*

Other Staff: 1 Lectr.

History

Tel: (031) 204 4145 Fax: (031) 204 4160

Filatova, Irina I., BA *Moscow*, MA *Moscow*, PhD *Moscow*　Prof.

Goedhals, Mary M., BA *Rhodes*, MA *Rhodes*, PhD *Rhodes*　Sr. Lectr.; Head*

McCracken, Donal P., BA *Ulster*, DPhil *Ulster*, FRHistS　Prof.

Pillay, Poobalan R., BA *Bom.*, MA *Bom.*, DPhil *Durban-W.*　Assoc. Prof.

White, William B., BA *Natal*, BEd *Natal*, MA *Natal*, PhD *Natal*　Sr. Lectr.

Wood, John R. T., BA *Rhodes*, PhD *Edin.*, FRHistS　Prof.

Other Staff: 1 Lectr.

Human Physiology and Physical Chemistry

Tel: (031) 204 4312 Fax: (031) 204 4192

Gathiram, Premjith, PhD *Natal*　Prof.

Somova, Liliana I., MD *Sofia*, PhD *Sofia*, DMedSc *Sofia*　Prof.; Head*

Other Staff: 3 Lectrs.; 1 Assoc. Lectr.

Indian Languages

Tel: (031) 204 4546 Fax: (031) 204 4160

Prabhakaran, Varijakski, BA *And.*, MA *And.*, DLitt *Durban-W.*, DPhil *Durban-W.*　Sr. Lectr.

Rambilass, B., BA *Durban-W.*, MA *Meerut*, PhD *Meerut*　Sr. Lectr.

Shukla, Usha D., BA *Durban-W.*, MA *Durban-W.*, DLitt *Durban-W.*　Sr. Lectr.

Sitaram, Rambhajun, BA *S.Af.*, LLB *S.Af.*, MA *Ban.*, PhD *Ban.*　Sr. Lectr.; Head*

Other Staff: 5 Lectrs.

Indian Philosophy, see Hindu Studies and Indian Philos.

Industrial Psychology

Tel: (031) 204 4431 Fax: (031) 204 4561

Louw, Everhardus J., BCom *S.Af.*, MCom *OFS*　Sr. Lectr.

Thomson, Elza, BA *Stell.*, BCom *S.Af.*, MCom *Stell.*, DCom *Rand Afrikaans*　Prof.; Head*

Other Staff: 5 Lectrs.

Islamic Studies

Tel: (031) 204 4303 Fax: (031) 204 4160

Dangar, Sulman E., BA *Durban-W.*, MA *Durban-W.*, DPhil *Durban-W.*　Assoc. Prof.

Ebrahim, Abul F. M., BA *Al-Azhar*, MA *Temple*, PhD *Temple*　Assoc. Prof.

Nadvi, Syed S., MA *Karachi*, PhD *Chic.*　Prof.; Head*

Other Staff: 1 Lectr.

Law, see Mercantile Law, Private Law, and Public Law

Mathematics and Applied Mathematics

Tel: (031) 204 4134 Fax: (031) 204 4806

Baboolal, Dharmanand, BSc *Durban-W.*, MSc *Oxf.*, DPhil *Oxf.*　Prof.; Head*

Brüning, Erwin A. K., DrRerNat *Gött.*　Prof.

Maharaj, Manoj S., BSc *Durban-W.*, MSc *Witw.*, PhD *Natal*　Sr. Lectr.

O'Hara, John, BSc *Ulster*, MSc *Belf.*, PhD *Witw.*　Sr. Lectr.

Ori, Ramesh G., BSc *S.Af.*, MSc *Colorado*, PhD *Colorado*　Prof.

Pillay, Poobhalan, BSc *Durban-W.*, MSc *Chic.*, PhD *Witw.*　Prof.

Singh, Pravin, BSc *Durban-W.*, MSc *Durban-W.*, PhD *Natal*　Sr. Lectr.

Xu, Hong-Kun, MSc *Zhejiang*, PhD *Xi'an Jiaotong*　Assoc. Prof.

Other Staff: 4 Lectrs.

Mercantile Law

Tel: (031) 204 4372 Fax: (031) 204 4848

Gering, Leonard J., BCom *Cape Town*, LLB *Cape Town*　Prof.; Head*

Leslie, Andrew B., BA *Cape Town*, LLB *Cape Town*, LLM *Rhodes*　Sr. Lectr.

Mneney, Edith, LLB *Dar.*, LLM *Dar.*　Sr. Lectr.

Mowatt, James G., BA *Natal*, LLB *Natal*, LLM *Durban-W.*　Assoc. Prof.

Vahed, Mahomed A., BProc *Durban-W.*, LLB *S.Af.*　Sr. Lectr.

Microbiology

Tel: (031) 204 4401 Fax: (031) 204 4806

Achar, Premila N., BSc *Mys.*, BEd *Mys.*, MSc *Mys.*, MPhil *Mys.*, PhD *Mys.*　Assoc. Prof.; Head*

Pillay, Balakrishna, BSc *Durban-W.*, MSc *Durban-W.*, DrRerNat *Würzburg*　Assoc. Prof.

Pillay, Dorsamy, BSc *Durban-W.*, MSc *Durban-W.*, DPhil *Durban-W.*　Sr. Lectr.

Modern European Languages

Tel: (031) 204 4793 Fax: (031) 204 4160

Greyling, Elizabeth J., BA *S.Af.*, MA *Stell.*　Lectr.; Head*

Other Staff: 1 Lectr.

Music

Tel: (031) 204 4138 Fax: (031) 204 4160

Goodall, Sallyann, BMus *Cape Town*, BMus *S.Af.*, MMus *S.Af.*, DMus *Durban-W.*　Sr. Lectr.; Head*

Jackson, Melveen B., BA *Natal*, BMus *Natal*, MMus *Natal*　Sr. Lectr.

Jacobs, Rosalie K., MMus *Pret.*, DMus *Durban-W.*　Sr. Lectr.

Other Staff: 5 Lectrs.

Persian, see Arabic, Urdu and Persian

Philosophy

Tel: (031) 204 4124 Fax: (031) 204 4340

More, Percy S. M., BA *North(S.Af.)*, MA *S.Af.*, MA *Indiana*　Sr. Lectr.; Head*

Other Staff: 1 Lectr.

Physical Chemistry, see Human Physiol. and Phys. Chem.

Physics

Tel: (031) 204 4663 Fax: (031) 204 4780

Baines, Charles G. S., BSc *Natal*, MSc *Natal*, MSc　Sr. Lectr.

Bharuth-Ram, Krishanlal, BSc *Rhodes*, BSc *Natal*, MSc *Natal*, DPhil *Oxf.*　Prof.

Engel, Dennis W., BSc *Cape Town*, MSc *Cape Town*, DrRerNat *T.U.Munich*　Prof.; Head*

Horsfield, Edgar C., BSc *Natal*, MSc *Natal*　Sr. Lectr.

Naidoo, Krishna, BSc *S.Af.*, MSc *S.Af.*, PhD *S.Af.*　Sr. Lectr.

Political Science

Tel: (031) 820 2124 Fax: (031) 820 2340

Daniel, Arthur J. C., BA *Natal*, MA *W.Mich.*, MA *N.Y.State*, PhD *N.Y.State*　Prof.

Habib, Adam M., BA *Witw.*, MA *Natal*　Sr. Lectr.

Sonkosi, Z., MA *Basle*, PhD *F.U.Berlin*　Sr. Lectr.

Suransky, Leonard S., MSc *Lond.*, PhD *Mich.*, BA　Sr. Lectr.

Venkatrathnam, S. K., BA *Natal*, BCompt *S.Af.*, MA *Col.*　Lectr.; Head*

Other Staff: 4 Lectrs.

Private Law

Tel: (031) 204 4372 Fax: (031) 204 4848

Phewa, C. A. T., BProc LLB　Sr. Lectr.

Singh, Divya, BA *Durban-W.*, LLB *Durban-W.*, LLM *Durban-W.*　Sr. Lectr.

Wood-Bodley, Michael C., BCom *Natal*, LLB *Natal*　Sr. Lectr.

Zaal, Frederick N., BA *Natal*, LLB *Natal*, LLM *Durban-W.*, LLM *Col.*　Prof.; Head*

Other Staff: 1 Lectr.

Psychology

Tel: (031) 204 4423 Fax: (031) 204 4340

Balkisson, Bernard A., BSc *Durban-W.*, MSc *Durban-W.*, DPhil *Durban-W.*　Prof.

Bhana, Arvinkumar, BA *Durban-W.*, MA *Durban-W.*, PhD *Ill.*　Sr. Lectr.; Head*

Magwaza, Adelaide S., BA *S.Af.*, MA *Durban-W.*, DPhil *Durban-W.*　Sr. Lectr.

Mahabeer, Manorunjunie, BA *Durban-W.*, MA *Durban-W.*, PhD *Natal*　Sr. Lectr.

Parekh, Angina G., BA *Durban-W.*, MA *Durban-W.*, MA *Kansas*, DPhil *Durban-W.*　Sr. Lectr.

Other Staff: 2 Lectrs.

Psychology of Education

Tel: (031) 204 4602 Fax: (031) 204 4866

Chohan, Ebrahim A., BSc *S.Af.*, MSc *Durban-W.*, DPhil *Durban-W.*　Sr. Lectr.

Other Staff: 1 Lectr.

Public Administration

Tel: (031) 204 4756 Fax: (031) 204 4848

Moodley, Sathiasiven, BA *Durban-W.*, MA *Durban-W.*, DPhil *Durban-W.*　Sr. Lectr.

Reddy, Purshottama S., BAdmin *Durban-W.*, MAdmin *Durban-W.*, DAdmin *Durban-W.*　Assoc. Prof.

Sing, Deoram, BA *S.Af.*, BAdmin *S.Af.*, MAdmin *S.Af.*, DAdmin *S.Af.*　Assoc. Prof.; Head*

Wallis, Malcolm A. H., BSc(SocSc) *S'ton.*, MA *Lond.*, PhD *Manc.*　Prof.

Public Law

Tel: (031) 204 4445 Fax: (031) 204 4848

Hulme, David H., BA *Natal*, LLB *Natal*　Sr. Lectr.

Kaburise, John B. K., LLB *Ghana*, LLM *Penn.*　Prof.

Nadasen, Sundrasagaran, BA Durban-W., LLB
Durban-W., DrJur Ley., LLD Ley.   Assoc. Prof.;
Head*
Pather, Suloshini, BA Durban-W., LLB Durban-W.,
LLM Natal   Sr. Lectr.

Science of Religion
Tel: (031) 204 4714 Fax: (031) 204 4160
Naidoo, Thillayvel, BA S.Af., MA Madr., DPhil
Durban-W.   Sr. Lectr.; Head*

Social Work
Tel: (031) 204 4430 Fax: (031) 204 4160
Kasiram, Madhubala I., BA(SW) Durban-W.,
MA(SW) Durban-W., DPhil Durban-W.   Sr.
Lectr.
Ramphal, Ritha, BA(SW) Durban-W., MA(SW)
Durban-W., DPhil Durban-W.   Prof.; Head*
Other Staff: 1 Lectr.

Sociology
Tel: (031) 204 4521 Fax: (031) 204 4160
Chetty, Thiagaraj D., BA Durban-W., MA Durban-
W., DPhil Durban-W.   Sr. Lectr.
Desai, Ashwin G., BA Rhodes, MA Rhodes, PhD
Mich.State   Sr. Lectr.
Stears, Louw H. P., BA Stell., BEd Stell., MA
Stell., DPhil Potchef.   Sr. Lectr.; Head*

Sport Science
Tel: (031) 204 4394 Fax: (031) 204 4903
Coopoo, Yoganathan, BA Durban-W., MA
Durban-W., DPhil Durban-W.   Prof.; Head*
Hudgson, Norma M., BA Natal, BEd S.Af., MEd
Durban-W., DEd Durban-W.   Sr. Lectr.
Other Staff: 2 Lectrs.

Statistics
Tel: (031) 204 4756 Fax: (031) 204 4561
Arnab, Raghunath, MSc Calc., PhD
I.Stat.I.   Assoc. Prof.; Head*
North, Delia E., MSc Natal, PhD Natal   Sr.
Lectr.
Ryan, Keven C., MSc Lond., PhD Lond.   Prof.

Systematic Theology and Ethics and Practical Theology
Tel: (031) 204 4239 Fax: (031) 204 4286
Heuer, Neville A. C., BA Natal, MA Natal, PhD
Natal   Prof.; Head*
Pitchers, Alrah L. M., BA S.Af., PhD Natal, MDiv
ThM   Sr. Lectr.

Urdu, see Arabic, Urdu and Persian

Zoology
Tel: (031) 204 4120 Fax: (031) 204 4790
Baker, Carolyn M., BSc Natal, MSc Natal, PhD
Natal   Sr. Lectr.
Biseswar, Ramlall, BSc Durban-W., MSc Durban-
W., PhD Cape Town   Assoc. Prof.
Marinier, Susan L., BSc Natal, PhD Natal   Sr.
Lectr.
Thandar, Ahmed S., BSc S.Af., MSc Durban-W.,
DPhil Durban-W.   Prof.; Head*
Vawda, Ahmed I., BSc Durban-W., MSc Durban-
W., PhD Birm.   Prof.

Zulu
Tel: (031) 204 4728 Fax: (031) 204 4106
Zungu, Phyllis J., BA Zululand, BA Natal, BEd
Natal, MA Natal, DLitt Durban-W.   Prof.;
Head*
Other Staff: 1 Lectr.

DENTISTRY
Oral Health and Dental Therapy
Tel: (031) 295323 Fax: (031) 290827
Laher, Mahomed H. E., BSc Reading, BDS Lond.,
MSc Lond.   Sr. Lectr.; Head*
Nair, Yogambal P., BA S.Af.   Sr. Lectr.

HEALTH SCIENCES
Anatomy
Tel: (031) 204 4195 Fax: (031) 204 4890
Haffajee, Mohamed R., MB ChB Natal,
FRCSEd   Prof. (Med.); Head*
Satyapal, Kapil S., MD Natal, FCS(SA)   Prof.
(Med.)

Occupational Therapy
Tel: (031) 204 4310 Fax: (031) 204 4227
Joubert, Robin W. E., BA S.Af.   Sr. Lectr.;
Head*
Van Der Reyden, Dain, BA S.Af.   Sr. Lectr.

Optometry
Tel: (031) 204 4294 Fax: (031) 204 4666
Mehta, Meena, BSc BOptom MOptom   Sr.
Lectr.
Naidoo, Kevin, BSc Durban-W., BOptom Durban-
W.   Sr. Lectr.; Head*
Randeria, D. N.   Sr. Lectr.
Rasengane, T. A., BOptom North(S.Af.),
MOptom Durban-W., PhD   Sr. Lectr.

Pharmacology
Tel: (031) 204 4767 Fax: (031) 204 4907
McFadyen, Margaret L., BSc(Pharm) Potchef.,
MSc(Med) Cape Town, DPhil Durban-
W.   Assoc. Prof.
Pillai, Goonaseelan, BPharm Durban-W.,
MPharm Durban-W., DPharm Durban-W   Sr.
Lectr.
Rambiritch, Virendra, BSc(Pharm) Durban-W.,
MMedSc   Sr. Lectr.

Pharmacy
Tel: (031) 204 4358 Fax: (031) 204 4792
Chetty, Dushendra J., BPharm Rhodes, MPharm
Durban-W.   Sr. Lectr.
Dangor, Cassim M., BSc(Pharmacy) S.Af.,
MSc(Pharm) Mississippi, DPharm Durban-
W.   Prof.; Head*
Seedat, Mahomed A., MB BS, FRCPEd,
FRCP   Sr. Lectr.
Smit, Jennifer A., BPharm Rhodes, MSc
Oregon   Sr. Lectr.
Other Staff: 1 Lectr.

Physiotherapy
Tel: (031) 360 3241
Gounden, Poobalan, MPhysiotherapy Durban-
W., PhD S.Af.Med.   Prof.; Head*
Gumede, Nokubekisisa L.   Sr. Lectr.
Puckree, Thayananthee, BSc(Physio) Durban-W.,
MEd S.Af., PhD N.Y.State   Sr. Lectr.
Other Staff: 1 Lectr.

Speech Therapy and Audiology
Tel: (031) 204 4438 Fax: (031) 204 4622
Govender, Cyril D.,
BA(Speech&HearingTherapy)Witw.,
MAudiology Durban-W.   Sr. Lectr.; Head*
Kathard, Harsha M.,
BSpeechandHearingTherapy Durban-W.,
MSpPath Durban-W.   Sr. Lectr.

SPECIAL CENTRES, ETC

Academic Development, Centre for
Tel: (031) 204 4337 Fax: (031) 204 4412
Hann, Philippa R., BA Alaska, MAT New
Mexico   Sr. Lectr.
Naidoo, Nadasen A., BA Durban-W., MA
Witw.   Sr. Lectr.

Biomedical Resource Centre
Tel: (031) 204 4671 Fax: (031) 204 4730
No staff at present

Computer Services – Academic
Tel: (031) 204 4136 Fax: (031) 204 4909
Laidlaw, Michael G. G.   Prof.

Documentation Centre
Tel: (031) 204 4350
No staff at present

Electron Microscope Unit
Tel: (031) 204 4765
No staff at present

External Research
Tel: (031) 204 4298 Fax: (031) 204 4834
Cunnan, Priscilla   Dir., Research*

Language Laboratory
Tel: (031) 204 4217

Social and Economic Research, Institute for
Tel: (031) 204 4298 Fax: (031) 204 4834
Hindson, Douglas C.   Prof.
Vaughan, Anne   Head*

University Research (Internal)
Tel: (031) 204 4298 Fax: (031) 204 4834
No staff at present

CONTACT OFFICERS

Academic affairs. Registrar (Academic):
Brimer, Prof. Alan, BA P.Elizabeth, MA
P.Elizabeth, DLitt P.Elizabeth
Accommodation. Head: ......
Alumni. Head: C. Ngidi
Archives. Head, Documentation Centre: N.
Ramdhani
Careers. Head: ......
Computing services. Head, Computer Services
(Academic): ......
Computing services. Head, Computer Services
(Administration): ......
Development/fund-raising. Head: ......
Estates and buildings/works and services.
Chief Director: ......
Finance. Chief Director (Finance):
Govindsamy, M.
General enquiries. Registrar (Academic):
Brimer, Prof. Alan, BA P.Elizabeth, MA
P.Elizabeth, DLitt P.Elizabeth
Health services. Head: Balgobind, R. P., MB
ChB S.Af.
Library (chief librarian). University Librarian:
Moodley, M., MA Durban-W., MLS Pitt., MS
Indiana
Personnel/human resources. Head: Fynn, F.
A. E.
Public relations, information and marketing.
Head: ......
Publications. Head: ......
Purchasing. Head: Asrie, P.
Research. Vice-Rector: ......
Safety. Safety Officer: Turner, R. A.
Scholarships, awards, loans. Head: Moodley,
Y., BA S.Af.
Schools liaison. Head: ......
Security. Head: ......
Sport and recreation. Chief Sports Officer:
......
Staff development and training. Vice-Rector:
......
Students from other countries. Registrar
(Academic): Brimer, Prof. Alan, BA
P.Elizabeth, MA P.Elizabeth, DLitt P.Elizabeth
Students with disabilities. Registrar
(Academic): Brimer, Prof. Alan, BA
P.Elizabeth, MA P.Elizabeth, DLitt P.Elizabeth
University press. Printing Supervisor: Haupt,
R. B.

[Information supplied by the institution as at October
1998, and edited by the ACU]

UNIVERSITY OF FORT HARE

Member of the Association of Commonwealth Universities

Postal Address: Private Bag X1314, Alice, Eastern Cape, 5700 South Africa
Telephone: (040) 22011 **Fax**: (040) 31643 **E-mail**: sheena@admin.ufh.ac.za **Cables**: Unifort

VICE-CHANCELLOR AND RECTOR*—Mzamane, Prof. Mbulelo V., BA *UBLS*, MA *UBLS*, PhD *Sheff.*
REGISTRAR (ACADEMIC)—Pityana, S. M.

MEDICAL UNIVERSITY OF SOUTHERN AFRICA

Mediese Universiteit Van Suider-Afrika

Founded 1976

Member of the Association of Commonwealth Universities

Postal Address: PO Box 197, PO Medunsa, 0204 South Africa
Telephone: (012) 521 4111 **Fax**: (012) 560 0086 **E-mail**: berndt@mcd4330.medunsa.ac.za
WWW: http://www.medunsa.ac.za/

VICE-CHANCELLOR AND PRINCIPAL*—Mokgokong, Prof. Ephraim T., BSc *Fort Hare*, MB ChB *Natal*, MD *Natal*
DEPUTY VICE-CHANCELLOR AND VICE-PRINCIPAL—Mogotlane, Prof. Ramaranka A., MB ChB *Natal*, FRCPSGlas, FRCSEd
VICE-PRINCIPAL (ADMINISTRATION)‡—Masihleho, Prof. Thabo P., MSc *North(S.Af.)*
CHAIRMAN OF COUNCIL—Marivate, C. D., BA *S.Af.*, MB ChB *Natal*, MPraxMed *S.Af.Med.*
REGISTRAR—Berndt, Carl W., BA *OFS*
UNIVERSITY LIBRARIAN—Vink, Christian M., BA *OFS*, MBibl *Pret.*

GENERAL INFORMATION

History. The university was established in 1976 to provide training in a wide range of health disciplines, including animal health.

It is located 30km north west of Pretoria.

Admission to first degree courses (see also South African Introduction). Matriculation Exemption Certificate with passes in mathematics and physical science at matriculation level. For BSc: mathematics and physical science or biology; for BCur and BOccTher: 2 passes in mathematics, physical science, or biology.

International applicants must comply with Matriculation Board requirements to obtain full or conditional exemption from the South African matriculation examinations.

First Degrees (see also South African Directory to Subjects of Study). BCur, BCur(I&A), BDentTher, BDS, BOccTher, BOralHyg, BPharm, BRad(Diagn), BSc, BSc(Diet), BSc(Physio), BVMCh, MB ChB.

Courses normally last 4 years. BCur(I&A), BDentTher, BOralHyg, BRad(Diagn), BSc: 3 years; BDS: 5½ years; BVMCh, MB ChB: 6 years.

Higher Degrees (see also South African Directory to Subjects of Study). MCur, MDent, MDS, MMed, MOccTher, MPublicHealth, MSc, PhD, DDent, DPublicHealth, DSc.

Applicants for admission must normally hold an honours degree in the subject intended for study at master's level. Doctorates: appropriate master's degree; equivalent qualifications may be accepted by senate.

Master's courses normally last a minimum of 1 year; doctorates: minimum 2 years.

Libraries. 75,013 volumes; 749 periodicals.

Fees (1998, annual). Undergraduate: health sciences: R6780–8457 (South African students), R13,560–16,914 (international students); nursing sciences: R6404–7538 (South African students), R12,808–15,076 (international students); medical sciences: R5450–12,340 (South African students), R10,900–24,680 (international students); veterinary science: R9680 (South African students), R19,360 (international students). Postgraduate: average R12,000.

Academic Awards (1997). 58 awards ranging in value from R250 to R6000.

Academic Year (1999). Two semesters: 25 January–4 June; 7 June–26 November.

Income (1996). Total, R165,138,187.

Statistics (1997). Staff: 1545 (432 academic, 1113 administrative and other). Students: full-time 3493 (2004 men, 1489 women).

FACULTIES/SCHOOLS

Basic Sciences
Tel: (012) 521 4371 Fax: (012) 521 3070
Dean: Groenewald, Prof. J. V., PhD *P.Elizabeth*
Secretary: von Wyk, S.

Dentistry
Tel: (012) 521 4800 Fax: (012) 521 4102
Dean: de Vries, Prof. J., MDent *Pret.*
Secretary: Fouché, M.

Medicine
Tel: (012) 521 4321 Fax: (012) 521 5811
Dean: Bomela, Prof. M. D., MB ChB *Natal*, MMed *S.Af.Med.*
Secretary: Chapell, M.

Public Health
Tel: (012) 521 4613
Dean: Herman, Prof. A. A., MB ChB *Natal*, PhD *Witw.*
Secretary: Mhlambi, V.

Veterinary Science
Tel: (012) 521 4453 Fax: (012) 521 4225
Dean: Terblanché, Prof. H. M., BVSc *Pret.*, MMedVet *Pret.*
Secretary: Holtzhausen, P.

ACADEMIC UNITS

Anaesthesiology
Tel: (012) 521 4088
Bomela, Mpumelelo D., MB ChB *Natal*, MMed *S.Af.Med.* Prof.†
Mthombeni, Elizabeth L., MB ChB *S.Af.Med.*, MMed *S.Af.Med.* Sr. Lectr.
Rantloane, J. L. Arthur, MB ChB *S.Af.Med.*, MMed *S.Af.Med.* Prof.; Head*
Other Staff: 1 Prof.; 1 Sr. Lectr.
Research: controlling nosocomial infection in theatre; haemodynamic monitoring: Swan-Ganz versus CUP; low-flow anaesthesia; pain of Propofol injection

Anatomy, see also Veterinary Science
Tel: (012) 521 5912 Fax: (012) 521 4512
Ackermann, Pieter C., BMedSc *OFS*, MMedSci *Pret.* Sr. Lectr.
Bosman, Marius C., BMEdSci *Pret.*, BSc *S.Af.Med.*, MSc(Med) *S.Af.Med.*, PhD *S.Af.Med.* Prof.; Head*
de Kock, Willem T., BChD *Pret.*, DSc *Pret.* Sr. Lectr.
Green, Edward D., BEd *S.Af.*, BSc *Pret.*, MSc *Pret.* Assoc. Prof.
Human, Henry H., BMedSci *Pret.*, MSc(Med) *S.Af.Med.* Sr. Lectr.

la Rose, James R., MB BS *WI*, MA *Col.*,
 MPraxMed *S.Af.Med.* Sr. Lectr.
Lebona, Gregory T., MB ChB *Mak.*, MSc(Med)
 S.Af.Med. Sr. Lectr.
Missankov, Alexander A., MSc *Sofia*, PhD
 Sofia Prof.; Res. Co-ordinator
Other Staff: 6 Lectrs.
Vacant Posts: 1 Sr. Lectr.; 1 Lectr.
Research: cartilage histology; ectoparasitology;
 functional neuroanatomy; microvascular
 surgery; neural regeneration

Biochemistry, see Chem. and Biochem.

Biology

Tel: (012) 521 4065 Fax: (012) 521 4246
Els, Daniel A., BSc *Pret.*, MSc *Ib.*, PhD
 S.Af.Med. Assoc. Prof.
King, Peter H., MSc *Ib.*, PhD *OFS* Sr. Lectr.
Oberholzer, Gouws, BSc *Potchef.*, MSc *Ib.*, DSc
 Ib. Prof.; Head*
van Heerden, Eurika, BSc *Rand Afrikaans*, MSc *Ib.*,
 PhD *Ib.* Sr. Lectr.
Other Staff: 3 Lectrs.; 1 Jr. Lectr.; 1 Sr. Nat.
 Scientist
Research: ticks (acari, metastigmata)

Cardio-Thoracic Surgery

Tel: (012) 521 4992
Mohlala, M. L., MB ChB *Natal*,
 FRCSGlas Prof.; Head*
Other Staff: 4 Lectrs.; 1 Hon. Lectr.

Cardiology

Tel: (012) 521 4627 Fax: (012) 521 5810
Hossain, M. Z., MB BS, FCP(SA)
Mntla, Pndile S., MB ChB *S.Af.Med.*,
 FCP(SA) Lectr.; Acting Head*
Research: dilated cardiomyopathy; heart failure:
 endothelium nitric oxide and potassium
 channels; rheumatic mitral valve disease

Chemistry and Biochemistry

Tel: (012) 521 4367 Fax: (012) 521 5809
Cukrowska, Ewa, PhD *Lublin* Sr. Lectr.
Mphahlele, Malose J., BSc *Fort Hare*, MSc *Pret.*,
 PhD *Rhodes* Prof.; Head*
van Wyk, J. Pieter H., BSc *OFS*, MSc *OFS*, PhD
 S.Af.Med. Sr. Lectr.; Acting Head*
Other Staff: 5 Lectrs.
Research: bio-organic chemistry; specialization
 chemistry

Clinical Psychology

Tel: (012) 521 4632 Fax: (012) 521 4632
Botha, Alida A., BA *Rand Afrikaans*, MA *Rand
 Afrikaans* Sr. Lectr.
Brown, Garfield A., BA *S.Af.*, MA(ClinPsych)
 S.Af. Sr. Lectr.
Kruger, Carine, BA *Pret.*, MA *Pret.* Sr. Lectr.
Mokhuane, Esther, M. Q., MA *Natal*, DLitt&Phil
 S.Af. Prof.; Head*
Mpumlwana, Vuyo B. N., BSc *Ib.*, MA *Manit.*,
 PhD *Manit.* Assoc. Prof.
Teunissen, Robert, BA *Amst.*, MA *Amst.* Sr.
 Lectr.
Vorster, Charl, BA *OFS*, MA(ClinPsych) *S.Af.*,
 PhD *S.Af.* Assoc. Prof.; Academic Co-
 ordinator
Other Staff: 5 Lectrs.
Research: clinical psychology and
 neuropsychology

Community Health

Tel: (012) 521 4257 Fax: (012) 521 4399
Coetzer, Pieter W. W., MD *Pret.* Prof.; Head*
Herbst, A. Jacobus, MB ChB *Pret.*, MSc(Med)
 Cape Town Sr. Lectr.
Kocks, Daan J., MMed *S.Af.Med.*, MD
 S.Af.Med. Assoc. Prof.
Matjila, Maila J., MB ChB *Natal*, MMed
 Natal Sr. Lectr.
Other Staff: 1 lectr.
Vacant Posts: 2 Sr. Lectrs.†
Research: health systems evaluation; hospital
 informatics; occupational health

Dentistry, see below

Tel: (012) 529 4111

Dermatology

Tel: (012) 521 4001 Fax: (012) 521 4126
Mahapa, Dimakatso H., BSc *North(S.Af.)*, MB
 ChB *S.Af.Med.*, MMed *S.Af.Med.* Acting Head*

Diagnostic Radiology and Imaging

Tel: (012) 521 3676
Snyman, P. J. N. H., MMed Head*
Other Staff: 1 Specialist; 2 Lectrs.

English Language

Tel: (012) 521 5683 Fax: (012) 521 4471
Morake, Rachel M., MA *Durh.* Sr. Lectr.;
 Head*
Other Staff: 2 Lectrs.

Environmental Health, see Occupnl. and
 Environmental Health

Family Medicine

Tel: (012) 521 4314 Fax: (012) 521 4172
Blok, Ferdi, MB ChB *Ley.*, MPraxMed *Ley.* Sr.
 Lectr.
Dabek, Elizabeth, MFamMed *S.Af.Med.* Sr.
 Lectr.
Fehrsen, Sam G., MB ChB *Cape Town* Emer.
 Prof.
Hugo, Jannie, M. F., MB ChB *OFS*, MFamMed
 OFS Assoc. Prof.; Head*
Mhlongo, Sam W. P., MB BS *Lond.*, MSc
 Lond. Sr. Lectr.
Ragavan, S., MFamMed *S.Af.Med.* Sr. Lectr.
Russel, L. Gordon, MB ChB *Witw.* Sr. Lectr.
Van Deventer, Claire, MFamMed *S.Af.Med.* Sr.
 Lectr.
Research: descriptive studies of health care;
 international comparison of health care;
 qualitative research in family medicine

General Surgery

Tel: (012) 521 4153 Fax: (012) 521 4467
Mageza, Ralph B., MB BCh *Natal*, MMed
 S.Af.Med. Sr. Lectr.
Modiba, Mphaiko C. M., MB ChB *Natal*, MD,
 FCS(SA) Prof.; Head*
Mtshali, Zulu, MB ChB *Natal*, FRCSGlas Assoc.
 Prof.
Ntlhe, Letlhogela M., MB ChB *Natal*,
 FCS(SA) Principal Specialist; Sr. Lectr.
Nxumalo, Jo L. M., MD *Tor.* Principal
 Specialist; Sr. Lectr.
Shelley, Artha, MD *Oklahoma*, FACS Principal
 Specialist; Sr. Lectr.
Other Staff: 4 Lectrs.; 12 Registrars; 1 Med.
 Nat. Scientist; 1 Principal Med. Tech. Officer
Research: AIDS; breast; carcinoma; rectum;
 thyroid

Hand and Microsurgery

Tel: (012) 521 4219 Fax: (012) 521 4219
Matime, Archibald M., MB ChB *Natal*, MMed
 S.Af.Med. Sr. Lectr.
Mennen, Ulrich, MB ChB *Pret.*, MMed *Pret.*, MD
 Pret., FRCSEd, FRCSGlas, FCS(SA) Prof.;
 Head*
Van der Westhuizen, Michael J., MMed
 S.Af.Med., FCS(SA)
Other Staff: 2 Lectrs.
Research: effect of surgery and rehabilitation in
 paralysed upper limbs (Efful system);
 peripheral nerve (end to nerve suture, bone
 healing and internal fixation clamp on plate
 microsurgical techniques, wound healing,
 neurovascular endplates)

Human Nutrition

Tel: (012) 521 4186 Fax: (012) 521 4776
Glatthaar, Ingrid I., PhD *S.Af.Med.* Prof.;
 Head*
Kuzwayo, Pauline, M. N., MPH *N.Carolina*,
 BSc(Diet) *S.Af.Med.* Assoc. Prof.
Nesamuuni, A. Edgar, BScDiet *Natal*, MNutr
 North(S.Af.) Sr. Lectr.
Other Staff: 4 Lectrs.; 16 PIT Lectrs.; 1 Med.
 Tech. Officer

Research: breastfeeding; coronary heart disease
 risk factors

Intensive Care

Tel: (012) 521 4351 Fax: (012) 521 5723
Mokgokong, M. S., BSc *North(S.Af.)*, MMed
 S.Af.Med., FCS(SA) Prof.; Head*

Internal Medicine

Tel: (012) 521 4584 Fax: (012) 521 4108
Ally, Mahmood M. T. M., FCP(SA) Sr. Lectr.
Bam, Willem J., MA *Witw.*, MMed *Pret.* Sr.
 Lectr.
Carrim, Abdool R. J., FCP(SA) Sr. Lectr.
Hussain, Fida, MMed *S.Af.Med.* Sr. Lectr.
Mayeza, Mildred N. T., BSc *Fort Hare*, MMed
 S.Af.Med. Sr. Lectr.
Mokhobo, K. Patrick, FCP(SA) Prof.; Head*
Moshesh, Florence M., MMed *S.Af.Med.* Sr.
 Lectr.
Mpe Matlawene, John, FCP(SA) Sr. Lectr.
Mukadan, Ashraf A., FCP(SA) Sr. Lectr.
Mzileni, M. Olga, MMed *S.Af.Med.* Sr. Lectr.
van der Merwe, Christiaan F., MSc *Pret.*, MD
 Gron. Assoc. Prof.
Other Staff: 6 Lectrs.; 1 Sr. Med. Tech. Officer

Mathematics and Statistics

Tel: (012) 521 4964 Fax: (012) 521 4809
Gopalraj, Perumal, MSc *Madr.* Sr. Lectr.
Schoeman, Hermanus S., BSc *Pret.*, MSc *Pret.*,
 DSc *Pret.* Prof.; Head*
Tönsing, Hilde M., MSc *Pret.* Sr. Lectr.
Other Staff: 4 Lectrs.
Research: applied mathematics; biostatistics; pure
 mathematics

Medical Physics

Tel: (012) 521 4390 Fax: (012) 521 4384
Daniels, Frank, MSc *W.Cape* Sr. Lectr.
Strydom, Wynand J., PhD *OFS* Prof.; Head*
van Reenen, Otto R., BSc *OFS*, MMedSc
 OFS Sr. Lectr.
White, Anthony J., MSc *Brighton* Sr. Lectr.
Other Staff: 2 Lectrs.; 1 Sr. Med. Nat. Scientist;
 1 Med. Nat. Scientist; 1 Med. Tech. Officer
Research: nuclear medicine and Monte Carlo
 techniques; radiation dosimetry;
 radiotherapy

Microsurgery, see Hand and Microsurg.

Neurology

Tel: (012) 521 4209 Fax: (012) 521 4758
Gledhill, Richard F., BSc *Lond.*, MD *Lond.* Prof.;
 Head*
Other Staff: 2 Sr. Lectrs.; 2 Lectrs.
Vacant Posts: 2 Sr. Lectrs.; 2 Lectrs.
Research: contemporary problems in clinical
 practice

Neurosurgery

Tel: (012) 521 4353 Fax: (012) 521 3510
Copley, Ian B., MB ChB *Leeds*, FRCSI Prof.;
 Head*
Other Staff: 5 Clin. Lectrs. 1 Hon. Lectr.
Research: application of omentum to the CNS;
 hydrocephalus children; treatment of
 hydatidosis of the CNS; treatment of intra-
 ventricular hydatid cists

Nuclear Medicine

Tel: (012) 521 5753
Clauss, Ralf P., MMed *S.Af.Med.*, MD
 Düsseldorf Prof.; Head*
Frankl, Alexander G., MB ChB *Jerusalem*, MD
 Jerusalem Sr. Lectr.
Other Staff: 3 Lectrs.
Research: bone tumours; lung physiology;
 neurological disease; renal function

Nursing Science

Tel: (012) 521 4664 Fax: (012) 521 4481
Kganakga, M. Constance, BA *S.Af.*, MA *Pret.*,
 MPH *Tulane* Assoc. Prof.
Mogotlane, Sophie M., BA *S.Af.*, MA *S.Af.*, PhD
 Natal Prof.; Head*

Naudé, J. Marita,, BCur *Rand Afrikaans*, MCur
Rand Afrikaans, DCur *Rand Afrikaans* Sr. Lectr.
Ringani, Rebecca C. T., BCur(I&A) *S.Af.Med.*,
MA *S.Af.* Sr. Lectr.
van Aswegen, Elsie J., BA *S.Af.*, MCur *Rand
Afrikaans*, DLitt&Phil *S.Af.* Sr. Lectr.
Zwane, Theressa B., BA *S.Af.*, MCur *Rand
Afrikaans*, DCur *Rand Afrikaans* Sr. Lectr.
Other Staff: 14 Lectrs.; 5 Lectrs.†
Research: attitudes of health workers about AIDS;
cancer research, evaluation of cancer
awareness amongst black communities

Obstetrics and Gynaecology

Tel: (012) 521 4461 *Fax*: (012) 521 5858
Kambaran, Sunder R., MB ChB *Natal*
Marivate, Martin, MB ChB *Natal* Prof.; Head*
Masihleho, Moepa, E. G., BSc *North(S.Af.)*, MB
ChB *S.Af.Med.*, MMed *S.Af.Med.* Sr. Lectr.
Mazibuko, Donald M., MB ChB *Natal* Sr.
Lectr.
Moja, Letticia V. M., MB ChB *Natal*, MMed
S.Af.Med. Sr. Lectr.
Simelela, Nono P., MB ChB *S.Af.Med.*, MMed
S.Af.Med. Sr. Lectr.
Van Bogaert, Louis-Jacques, MD *Louvain*, MMed
Louvain, PhD *Louvain*
Other Staff: 6 Lectrs.
Research: infertility; oncology (cervix and
ovarian cancer); perinatology

Occupational and Environmental Health

Tel: (012) 521 4355 *Fax*: (012) 521 4399
Kocks, Daniel J., MB ChB *Pret.*,
MMed(ComHealth) *S.Af.Med.*, MD
S.Af.Med. Prof.; Principal Specialist; Head*
Seema, Mmabonno T., BCur(I&A)
S.Af.Med. Occupnl. Health Controller
Other Staff: 5 Sr. Lectrs.†
Research: occupational and environmental health
issues in South Africa

Occupational Therapy

Tel: (012) 521 4133 *Fax*: (012) 521 5730
Holsten, A. E., BA *S.Af.* Sr. Lectr.
Shipham, Estelle, MSc *Witw.* Assoc. Prof.;
Head*
Other Staff: 6 Lectrs.; 1 Principal Med. Tech.
Officer; 1 Sr. Indust. Technician
Research: rehabilitation

Ophthalmology

Tel: (012) 521 3118 *Fax*: (012) 521 3118
Pienaar, A., MMed *S.Af.Med.* Principal
Specialist
Stegmann, R. C., MMed *Pret.* Prof.; Head*
Other Staff: 2 Lectrs.

Orthopaedics

Tel: (012) 521 4049 *Fax*: (012) 521 4029
Golele, Robert, MB ChB *Natal*, MMed
S.Af.Med. Prof.; Head*
Lukhele, Mlchululi, MB ChB *S.Af.Med.*, MMed
S.Af.Med., FCS(SA) Sr. Lectr.
Other Staff: 5 Lectrs.
Research: bone tumours; pulmonary embolism;
spine

Otorhinolaryngology

Tel: (012) 521 4234
Fidos, Michael H., BSc *Pret.*, MB ChB *Pret.*,
MMed *S.Af.Med.* Sr. Lectr.
Vorster, Willem F., BSc *Cape Town*, MB ChB *Cape
Town*, MMed *Cape Town* Prof.; Head*
Other Staff: 1 Lectr.
Research: auto-immune deafness;
electronystagmography; high frequency
audiometry; neonate deafness; sinus
carcinoma

Paediatric Surgery

Tel: (012) 521 4153 *Fax*: (012) 521 4467
Marcisz, Leczek T., MMed *S.Af.Med.*, MD,
FCS(SA) Sr. Lectr.; Acting Head*
Vacant Posts: 1 Prof.; 1 Lectr.

Paediatrics and Child Health

Tel: (012) 521 4444 *Fax*: (012) 521 3627
Boom, Maria E. J., MMed *S.Af.Med.* Sr. Lectr.;
Community Paediatrician
de Villiers, Francois P. R., BA *S.Af.*, MB ChB
Stell., MMed *Witw.*, PhD *Witw.* Prof.; Head*
Larisma, José S. D. S. R. Principal Specialist;
Sr. Lectr.
MacIntyre, Una E., MSc(Diet) *S.Af.Med.* Asst.
Dir., Medical Natural Sciences
Magongoa, Daphney I. S., MMed
S.Af. Principal Specialist; Sr. Lectr.
Mawela, M. Patience D., MMed *S.Af.Med.* Sr.
Lectr.
Owange-Iraka, John W., MMed
Mak. Principal Specialist; Sr. Lectr.
Other Staff: 4 Lectrs.; 2 Med. Tech. Officers
Vacant Posts: 2 Lectrs.
Research: clinical paediatrics; community
paediatrics; infant and child nutrition;
maternal and child health

Pathology, Anatomical

Tel: (012) 521 4414 *Fax*: (012) 521 5855
Bida, N. M., MMed *S.Af.Med.* Sr. Lectr.
Muthuphei, M. N., MMed *S.Af.Med.* Sr. Lectr.
Wichrzycka-Lancaster, E. J., PhD
Warsaw Prof.; Head*
Research: causes of perinatal death;
leyomyopathy in black children;
nephroblastoma and other childhood kidney
tumours; oesophageal resection;
telepathology

Pathology, Chemical

Tel: (012) 521 4253 *Fax*: (012) 521 4157
Bester, C. J., BSc *Pret.* Sr. Lectr.
Elias, J., MMed *S.Af.Med.* Assoc. Prof.
Joubert, Herman F., MMed *Pret.* Prof.; Head*
van der Walt, P. E., MMed *S.Af.Med.* Sr. Lectr.
Other Staff: 4 Lectrs.; 2 Med. Nat. Scientists; 2
Control Med. Technicians; 2 Principal Med.
Tech. Officers; 1 Sr. Med. Tech. Officer

Pathology, Forensic

Tel: (012) 521 4119
Dubasi, Percy M., BSc *S.Af.*, MPraxMed
S.Af.Med., MMed *S.Af.Med.* Sr. Lectr.
Fosseus, Christer G. H., MB ChB *Witw.*, MMed
Cape Town Prof.; Head*

Pathology, Haematological

Tel: (012) 521 4442 *Fax*: (012) 521 4582
Culligan, Gary A., MSc *Pret.*, MB ChB *Pret.* Sr.
Lectr.
Pool, Roger, MMed *S.Af.Med.* Sr. Lectr.
Welgemoed, David J., BSc *Pret.*, MMed(Path)
Pret. Prof.; Head*
Research: flow cytometry; haematology of
mammals; molecular biology (factor XIII
defect stroke in young people); oncology/
interferon

Pathology, Microbiological

Tel: (012) 521 5667 *Fax*: (012) 521 5727
Hoosen, Anwar A., BSc *Karachi*, MSc *Karachi*, MB
ChB *Natal*, MMed *Natal* Prof.; Head*
Pochee, Ebrahim, MSc *N.U.I* Principal Med.
Nat. Scientist
Other Staff: 3 Lectrs.; 1 Med. Nat. Scientist; 1
Chief Med. Techn.; 2 Principal Med. Tech.
Officers
Research: diarrhoeal pathogens; sexually
transmitted diseases; tuberculosis (laboratory
diagnosis and characterisation of organism)

Pharmacology and Therapeutics

Tel: (012) 521 4145 *Fax*: (012) 521 4123
du Plooy, Wim J., BScPharm *Potchef.*, PhD
S.Af.Med. Prof.; Head*
Joubert, Pieter H., MD *OFS* Hon. Prof.
Lategan, Andries, BPharm *Potchef.*, PhD
Potchef. Sr. Lectr.
Muntingh, George L., BPharm *Pret.*, MSc(Med)
S.Af.Med. Sr. Lectr.
Steyn, Mariette, MB ChB *Pret.*, MSc *Potchef.* Sr.
Lectr.

Walubo, Andrew, MB ChB *Mak.*, MPhil *HKUST*,
MD *Cape Town* Sr. Lectr.
Other Staff: 2 Lectrs.; 1 Res. Fellow
Research: cardiovascular pharmacology; clinical
trials; immuno-pharmacology;
toxicokinetics; toxicology

Pharmacy, School of

Tel: (012) 521 4312 *Fax*: (012) 521 3992
Rossiter, Dawn P., MPharm *Pret.*
Summers, R. S., PhD *Brad.* Prof.; Head*
Other Staff: 1 Lectr.; 3 Sr. Lectrs.†

Physics

Tel: (012) 521 5749 *Fax*: (012) 521 5798
Das, Arran G. M., BSc *Kerala*, MSc *Bom.*, MSc
Durh., PhD *Durh.* Sr. Lectr.
Mafokwane, Daniël, BSc *North(S.Af.)*, MSc
S.Af. Assoc. Prof.; Head*
Nolting, Volkma,, BSc *Mün.*, MSc *Mün.*, PhD
S.Af. Sr. Lectr.
Other Staff: 3 Lectrs.
Research: electronic circuits; semi-conducting
materials

Physiology, see also Veterinary Science

Tel: (012) 521 4221 *Fax*: (012) 521 5823
Apatu, Richard S. K., MB ChB *Ghana*, PhD
Camb. Sr. Lectr.
Dippenaar, Nola G., MPhil *Camb.*, PhD
S.Af.Med. Prof.
Hay, Leon, BSc *Pret.*, PhD *S.Af.Med.* Assoc.
Prof.
Schutte, Paul J., BSc *Potchef.*, PhD
S.Af.Med. Assoc. Prof.
Smith, Keith A., PhD *Salf.* Prof.; Head*
Other Staff: 5 Lectrs.
Research: cardiovascular physiology; carnitine
metabolism

Physiotherapy

Tel: (012) 521 4050 *Fax*: (012) 521 5684
Mbambo, Nonceba P., BSc(Physio)
S.Af.Med. Lectr.; Head*
Mokwena, Kebogile E., MSc *S.Af.Med.* Sr.
Lectr.
Taukobong, Nomathembo, BSc(Physio)
S.Af.Med.
Other Staff: 9 Lectrs.
Research: community physiotherapy;
involvement in international sports; student
performance in clinical education and factors
affecting the performance

Plastic and Reconstructive Surgery

Tel: (012) 521 4006 *Fax*: (012) 521 4006
Hoffman, Danie, MB ChB *S.Af.Med.*, MMed
S.Af.Med.
Scholtz, Jacobus F., MB ChB *OFS*, BSc *OFS*,
MMEd *OFS* Prof.; Head*
van Heerden, Schalk P., MB ChB *S.Af.Med.*,
MMed *S.Af.Med.* Sr. Lectr.
Other Staff: 7 Lectrs.
Research: cleft lip and palate management; cost
effectiveness in wound care; effects of COZ
laser; post-abdominoplasty and post-
liposuction embolism

Psychiatry

Tel: (012) 521 4143
Baquio, Zanele I. Z. Sr. Lectr.
Gangat, Abubaker E., MMed *Natal* Prof.;
Head*
Mashayamombe,Leonard,MMedPsych*S.Af.Med.*
Rataemane, Solly Sr. Lectr.

Psychology

Tel: (012) 521 4076 *Fax*: (012) 521 4982
Els, Nicolaas J. S., DLitt&Phil *Rand
Afrikaans* Prof.; Head*
Murray, Sean D. O., PhD *S.Af.Med.*
Pistorius, Agatha G., MA *Pret.*
Other Staff: 5 Lectrs.
Research: behavioural psychology; community
mental health; neuropsychology

Radiation Oncology

Vacant Posts: 1 Prof.

Radiography

Tel: (012) 521 4531 Fax: (012) 521 3929

Ebrahim, Nazeema Sr. Lectr.
Moalusi, Titus S. M., BEd *Witw.* Sr. Lectr.; Head*
Research: radiographic techniques

Statistics, see Maths. and Stats.

Urology

Tel: (012) 521 4236 Fax: (012) 521 3930

Segone, A. M., BSc *Rhodes*, MB ChB *Sheff.*, FRCS Prof.; Head*
Other Staff: 2 Lectrs.; 1 Chief Med. Technologist; 1 Sr. Med. Technologist

Veterinary Science, see below

Tel: (012) 529 4111

Virology

Tel: (012) 521 4227 Fax: (012) 521 5792

Geyer, Annelist, MSc *S.Af.Med.* Sr.Lectr.
Lecatsas, Gerasimos, PhD *Witw.*, DSc *Pret.* Prof.; Head*
Steele, Andrew D., PhD *S.Af.Med.* Prof.
Other Staff: 1 Lectr.; 1 Sr. Med. Nat. Scientist; 1 Control Med. Techn.; 1 Chief Med. Techn.; 1 Principal Med. Tech. Officer
Research: gastroenteritis; hepatitis; medical virology including AIDS

DENTISTRY

Community Dentistry

Tel: (012) 521 4848 Fax: (012) 521 5767

Gugushe, Tshepo S., BSc *S.Af.*, BDS *Witw.*, MDent *Witw.* Prof.; Head*
Volschenk, Henriëtte, BChD *Pret.*, MDS *S.Af.Med.* Sr. Lectr.
Other Staff: 8 Lectrs.
Research: clinical trials; epidemiology at risk; oral and dental epidemiology; oral health systems; social and behavioural research among deprived communities in South Africa

Diagnostics and Radiology

Tel: (012) 521 4903 Fax: (012) 521 5901

Maselle, Iuan, MDS Sr. Lectr.
Pretorius, Stephan, BChD *Pret.*, MChD *Stell.*, Prof.; Head*
Other Staff: 8 Lectrs.
Research: clinical epidemiology; surgical endodontics

Maxillofacial and Oral Surgery

Tel: (012) 521 4858 Fax: (012) 521 4858

Bouckaert, Michael M. R., BChD *Stell.*, MDent *S.Af.Med.*, FFDRCSI Asst. Prof.
de Lange, Ben, MB ChB *Pret.*, MMed *S.Af.Med.* Sr. Lectr.
Jacobs, Frederick J., BChD *Pret.*, MChD *Pret.* Prof.; Head*
Kemp, Jurie A., BChD *Pret.* Sr. Lectr.
Munzhelele, T. Irene, BDS *S.Af.Med.* Sr. Lectr.
Other Staff: 4 Registrars†
Research: cryosurgery for odontogenic tumours; microsurgery; nutritional status of trauma patients; teeth in fracture line

Operative Dentistry

Tel: (012) 521 4825 Fax: (012) 521 4826

Botha, Claudius T., BDS *Witw.*, MDS *S.Af.Med.* Prof.; Head*
Swanepoel, S. J. M., BChD *Pret.* Sr. Lectr.
van Os, Barry E., MDent *Pret.* Assoc. Prof.
Van Rooyen, J. J. C., BChD *Pret.*, MDS *S.Af.Med.* Sr. Lectr.
Other Staff: 5 Lectrs.; 5 Lectrs.†
Research: endodontics; operative dentistry; paedodontics

Oral Pathology and Oral Biology

Tel: (012) 521 4839 Fax: (012) 521 4838

Raubenheimer, Erich J., MChD *Pret.* Prof.; Head*
Research: oral tumours in Africa; structure and composition of dentine and ivory

Orthodontics

Tel: (012) 521 4854 Fax: (012) 521 4812

Lewis, C. D., BChD *Pret.*, MDS *S.Af.Med.* Sr. Lectr.; Acting Head*
Vacant Posts: 1 Prof./Chief Specialist

Periodontology and Oral Medicine

Tel: (012) 521 3834 Fax: (012) 521 4835

McClure, William P. J., BSc *Pret.*, BChD *Pret.*, MSc *Witw.* Sr. Lectr.
Verwayen, F. Darryll, MChD *Pret.* Prof.; Head*
Other Staff: 4 Lectrs.; 6 Lectrs.†
Vacant Posts: 1 Asst. Prof.; 2 Lectrs.; 2 Registrars
Research: epidemiological re-oral diseases; pharmacotherapeutics

Prosthodontics

Tel: (012) 521 4817 Fax: (012) 521 4826

Brummer, Dicky C., BChD *Pret.*, MChD *Stell.* Sr. Lectr.
Owen, Peter C., BDS *Lond.*, MSc(Dent) *W.Cape*, MChD *W.Cape* Prof.; Head*
Prinsloo, Pallet A. J., BDS *Rand Afrikaans* Sr. Lectr.
Other Staff: 10 Lectrs.; 1 Lectr.†
Research: clinical practice; educational practice; equipment development; materials science; patient care

Stomatological Studies

Tel: (012) 521 4870 Fax: (012) 521 4871

Blignaut, Elaine, BScAgric *OFS*, BChD *Pret.*, MSc *Pret.*, PhD *OFS* Prof.; Head*
du Plessis, Jan B., BChD *Pret.* Emer. Prof.†
du Preez, Ignatius C., BSc *OFS*, BChD *Pret.*, MSc *OFS*, MDS *S.Af.Med.*, DSc *OFS* Prof.
Grotepass, Wilhelm P., BChD *Pret.*, MChD *Pret.* Sr. Lectr.
Harris, Marcelle J. P., BChD *Stell.*, MBL *S.Af.* Sr. Lectr.
Other Staff: 4 Lectrs.
Research: dental materials; epidemiology; fluorides; oral biology (mineralized tissues, embryology); oral microbiology

VETERINARY SCIENCE

Anatomy

Tel: (012) 521 4752

Aire, Thomas A., DVM *Ib.*, PhD *Ib.* Sr. Lectr.
Booth, Kenneth K., BS *Youngstown*, MS *Iowa State*, PhD *Iowa State* Prof.; Head*
Green, Edward D., BSc *Pret.*, MSc *Pret.* Assoc. Prof.
Ohale, Levi O. C., DVM *Ib.*, PhD *Iowa State* Sr. Lectr.

Animal Health and Production

Tel: (012) 521 4741 Fax: (012) 521 4649

Abrams, L., BVSc *Pret.*, PhD *S.Af.Med.* Assoc. Prof.
Boyazoglu, P. A., BVSc *Pret.*, PhD *Minn.* Prof.; Head*
Donkin, Edward F., BScAgric *Natal*, MPhil *Lond.*, PhD *S.Af.Med.* Assoc. Prof.
Els, H. C., BSc(Agric) *Pret.*, MSc *Pret.* Sr. Lectr.
Linington, Margaret J., BSc(Agric) *Stell.*, PhD *Witw.* Sr. Lectr.; Principal Nat. Scientist
MacGregor, R. G., MScAgric *Fort Hare* Assoc. Prof.
Research: beef cattle production; dairy cattle management; disease resistance in indigenous livestock; mineral imbalances in herbivores; poultry production and medicine

Animal Hospital

Tel: (012) 521 4436 Fax: (012) 521 4270

Campbell, Mervyn C. O., MVSc *Pret.*, MBL *S.Af.* Dir.*

Companion Animal Medicine and Surgery

Tel: (012) 521 4293 Fax: (012) 521 4288

du Plessis, Cornelius J., BVSc *Pret.* Sr. Lectr.
Marais, Hendrik J., BVSc *Pret.* Sr. Lectr.
Rajput, Jyotika I., BVMCh *S.Af.Med.* Sr. Lectr.
Shulman, Martin L., BVSc *Pret.*, BSc *Witw.*, MMedVet *Pret.* Sr. Lectr.
Stadler, Pieter, BVSc *Pret.*, MMedVet *Pret.*, MBA *Pret.* Prof.; Head*
Williams, June H., BVSc *Pret.* Sr. Lectr.
Research: lactate levels in colic horses

Farm Animal Production Unit

Tel: (012) 521 4747

Schoeman, Petrus J., BSc(Agric) *Stell.* Dep. Dir.*

Herd Health and Reproduction

Tel: (012) 521 4281 Fax: (012) 521 4273

Carrington, Christopher A. P., BVSc *Pret.*, BComm *S.Af.* Sr. Lectr.
Harmse, Johan G., BVSc *Pret.* Sr. Lectr.
Pettey, Kenneth P., BSc *Witw.*, BVSc *Pret.* Assoc. Prof.; Head*
Robinson, James T. R., BVSc *Pret.*, MMedVet(Hyg) *Pret.* Sr. Lectr.
Research: comparisons in a naturally infected pig herd in South Africa (effects of in-feed medication, vaccination on lung scores, growth rate); small dairy farming

Infectious Diseases and Public Health

Tel: (012) 521 4277 Fax: (012) 521 4273

Bryson, Nigel R., BSc *Rhodes*, BVSc *Pret.* Sr. Lectr.
Crafford, Jan E., BVSc *Pret.* Sr. Lectr.
Karama, M., DVM *Lubumbashi*
Riley, Alistair E., BVSc *Pret.* Sr. Lectr.
Stewart, Colin G., BVMS *Edin.*, BVSc *Pret.*, MSc *Lond.* Prof.; Head*
Other Staff: 2 Lectrs.; 1 Sr. Vet. Technologist

Pathology

Tel: (012) 521 4300 Fax: (012) 521 4270

Bolton, Lorna A., BVSc *Pret.* Sr. Lectr.
Boomker, Jacob F. D., BVSc *Pret.*, MSc *Rand Afrikaans*, MMedVet *Pret.*, DVSc *S.Af.Med.* Prof.
Duncan, Neil M., BVSc *Pret.*, MMedVet *S.Af.Med.* Assoc. Prof.; Head*
Sigobodhla, Alice T., BSc *Z'bwe.*, BVSc *Z'bwe.* Sr. Lectr.
Verster, Ryno S., BVSc *Pret.* Sr. Lectr.
Research: helminths of game; indigenous goats and fish

Pharmacology and Toxicology

Tel: (012) 521 4433

Cotton, Colin G., BSc *Witw.*, BVSc *Pret.* Assoc. Prof.; Head*

Physiology

Tel: (012) 521 4249 Fax: (012) 521 4270

Brinders, J. M., BSc *W.Cape*, MSc *W.Cape*
Cornelius, S. T., BVMCh *S.Af.Med.*, BVSc *Pret.* Assoc. Prof.; Head*
Yeates, S. V., BVSc *Pret.* Sr. Lectr.
Other Staff: 1 Hon. Prof.

Production Animal Medicine

Tel: (012) 521 4506 Fax: (012) 521 4090

du Preez, Ebeneser R., BVSc *Pret.*, BSc(Agric) *Pret.* Sr. Lectr.
McCrindle, Cheryl M. E., BVSc *Pret.*, PhD *Pret.* Assoc. Prof.
Myburgh, Jan G., BVSc *Pret.* Sr. Lectr.
Rautenbach, Gert H., BVSc *Pret.*, MMedVet *Pret.* Prof.; Head*

SPECIAL CENTRES, ETC

Community Services, MEDUNSA Institute for
Mathebula, Matsontso P., MB ChB S.Af.Med. Dir.*

Gold Fields Nutrition Unit
Vacant Posts: Dir.*

MEDUNSA/MRC Diarrhoeal Pathogens Research Unit
Tel: (012) 521 4117 Fax: (021) 521 5794

Steel, A. Duncan, BSc Cape Town, PhD S.Af.Med. Prof.; Dir.*

Research: molecular epidemiology and molecular characterisation of microbial diarrhoeal pathogens

Bacterial Laboratory
Tel: (012) 529 4117 Fax: (012) 521 5794

1 Researcher; 1 Technologist; 1 Res. Officer

Virology Laboratory
Tel: (012) 521 4117 Fax: (012) 521 5794

2 Researchers; 1 Res. Officer

CONTACT OFFICERS

Academic affairs. Registrar: Berndt, Carl W., BA OFS

Accommodation. Director, Campus Control and Business Administration: van Rooyen, Johannes T. I., BCom S.Af.

Admissions (first degree). Administrative Control Officer: Deas, Aletta C.

Admissions (higher degree). Administrative Control Officer: Deas, Aletta C.

Adult/continuing education. Director, Academic Staff Development: MacLarty, Prof. Angus H., BA Witw., MA Oxf., MEd S.Af.

Alumni. Director, Public Relations and Development: Olwagen, Laurika L.

Archives. Deputy Director, Library: van Niekerk, John S., BA Natal, BBibl Pret.

Careers. Director, Bureau for Student Development and Advice: Ngwezi, Arthur A., BEd S.Af., MA Pret.

Computing services. Director: Maree, Hermanus A. P., BSc S.Af., MBL S.Af.

Conferences/corporate hospitality. Director, Public Relations and Development: Olwagen, Laurika L.

Consultancy services. Registrar: Berndt, Carl W., BA OFS

Credit transfer. Administrative Control Officer: Deas, Aletta C.

Development/fund-raising. Director, Development: Metz, Jacob, BA Pret.†

Distance education. Deputy Vice-Chancellor and Vice-Principal: Mogotlane, Prof. Ramaranka A., MB ChB Natal, FRCPSGlas, FRCSEd

Equal opportunities. Director, Equal Opportunities: Pahliney, Kethamonie, BEd S.Af., BA S.Af., MA Natal

Estates and buildings/works and services. Vice-Principal (Administration): Masihleho, Prof. Thabo P., MSc North(S.Af.)

Examinations. Administrative Control Officer: Potgieter, Johanna J. P., BA S.Af.

Finance. Vice-Principal (Administration): Masihleho, Prof. Thabo P., MSc North(S.Af.)

General enquiries. Registrar: Berndt, Carl W., BA OFS

Health services. Head, Health Services: Russel, L. Gordon, MB ChB Witw.†

Industrial liaison. Director, Human Resources: Molefe, G. N., BA BComm MBA

International office. Assistant Registrar: Themba, Mosia N., BA North(S.Af.), MA Portland State

Language training for international students. Morake, Rachel, MA Durh.

Library (chief librarian). Director, Library: Vink, Christian M., BA OFS, MBibl Pret.

Minorities/disadvantaged groups. Deputy Vice-Chancellor and Vice-Principal: Mogotlane, Prof. Ramaranka A., MB ChB Natal, FRCPSGlas, FRCSEd

Personnel/human resources. Director, Human Resources: Molefe, G. N., BA BComm MBA

Public relations, information and marketing. Director, Public Relations and Development: Olwagen, Laurika L.

Publications. Director, Public Relations and Development: Olwagen, Laurika L.

Purchasing. Director, Campus Control and Business Administration: van Rooyen, Johannes T. I., BCom S.Af.

Quality assurance and accreditation. Registrar: Berndt, Carl W., BA OFS

Research. Director: Aspinall, Prof. Sanet, PhD S.Af.Med.

Safety. Director, Campus Control and Business Administration: van Rooyen, Johannes T. I., BCom S.Af.

Scholarships, awards, loans. Senior Administrative Officer, Financial Aid Bureau: Hermann, Karin

Schools liaison. Schools Liaison Officer: Mtsweni, J.

Security. Director, Campus Control and Business Administration: van Rooyen, Johannes T. I., BCom S.Af.

Sport and recreation. Registrar: Berndt, Carl W., BA OFS

Staff development and training. Director, Academic Staff Development: MacLarty, Prof. Angus H., BA Witw., MA Oxf., MEd S.Af.

Student union. (Contact Student Representative Council)

Student welfare/counselling. Director, Bureau for Student Development and Advice: Ngwezi, Arthur A., BEd S.Af., MA Pret.

Students from other countries. Registrar: Berndt, Carl W., BA OFS

Students with disabilities. Head, Health Services: Russel, L. Gordon, MB ChB Witw.†

University press. Director, Public Relations and Development: Olwagen, Laurika L.

Women. Mokhuane, E. M. Q., BBibl Natal, MA Natal

[Information supplied by the institution as at June 1998, and edited by the ACU]

UNIVERSITY OF NATAL

Founded 1949; previously established as Natal University College 1909

Member of the Association of Commonwealth Universities

Postal Address: King George V Avenue, Durban, 4041 South Africa
Telephone: (031) 260 2206 **Fax**: (031) 260 2204 **E-mail**: trotter@admin.und.ac.za **Cables**: UNIVERSITY
Telex: (031) 621231 SA **WWW**: http://www.und.ac.za **E-mail formula**: surname@department.und.ac.za

CHANCELLOR—Hurley, The Most Rev. D. E., ThL Greg., STL Pontif.U.S.Th.Aq., DD, Archbishop Emeritus of Durban

VICE-CHANCELLOR AND PRINCIPAL*—Gourley, Prof. Brenda M., MBL S.Af., Hon. LLD Nott.

CHAIRMAN OF THE COUNCIL—Rogoff, Alec

SENIOR DEPUTY VICE-CHANCELLOR—Maughan Brown, Prof. David A., BA Cape Town, MA Camb., DPhil Sus.

DEPUTY VICE-CHANCELLOR (ACADEMIC)—Bawa, Prof. Ahmed C., BSc Natal, MSc Durban-W., PhD Durh.

DEPUTY VICE-CHANCELLOR (RESEARCH AND DEVELOPMENT)—Preston-Whyte, Prof. Eleanor M., BSocSc Natal, PhD Natal

DEPUTY VICE-CHANCELLOR (STUDENTS AND TRANSFORMATION)—Ngara, Prof. Emmanuel A., BA Rhodesia, MPhil Lond., PhD Lond.

REGISTRAR AND SECRETARY OF COUNCIL—Trotter, Prof. George J., BA Natal, MA Duke

PRESIDENT OF CONVOCATION—Mlisana, Zolile S., MB ChB Natal

GENERAL INFORMATION

History. The university was originally established in 1910 as Natal University College. It achieved independent status in 1949, when it was renamed University of Natal. The university has two campuses, located in Durban and Pietermaritzburg.

Admission to first degree courses (see also South African Introduction). Matriculation exemption or equivalent. International students require certificates with equivalent qualifications.

First Degrees (see also South African Directory to Subjects of Study). BA, BAcct, BAgricMgt, BBA, BCom, BCur, BMedSc, BMus, BSc, BScAgric, BSc(Arch), BSc(ConsMgt), BScDiet, BSc(Eng), BScQS, BScSur, BSocSc, BSocSc(SW), BTh, LLB, MB ChB. Courses normally last 3 years. BScAgric, BSc(Eng), LLB: 4 years. MB ChB: 6 years.

Higher Degrees (see also South African Directory to Subjects of Study). BArch(Advanced), BBibl (honours), BCur, BEd, BPrimEd, LLM, MA, MAcct, MClinPharm, MCom, MD, MFamMed, MMed, MMedSc, MMus, MRTP, MSc, MScAgric, MScDiet, MScEng, MScQS, MScSur, MSocSc, MSocSc(SW), MTh, PhD.

Libraries. 910,584 volumes; 9829 periodicals subscribed to. Special collection: Campbell (Africana).

Fees (1998, annual). Undergraduate: R8500–10,700 (humanities); R9500–10,700 (sciences); R11,500 (clinical medicine). Postgraduate: R7000–10,000 for the first year (and second year for coursework degrees); R1200 for subsequent years.

Academic Awards (1997). 203 awards with a total value of R1,720,124.

Academic Year (1998). Two semesters and a winter session. First semester, 9 February–20 June; winter session, 29 June–7 August; second semester, 11 August–28 November.

Income (1997). Total, R400,000,000.

Statistics. Staff: 2898 (960 academic, 1938 administrative/labour). Students: 17,305.

FACULTIES/SCHOOLS

Agriculture (Pietermaritzburg Campus)
Tel: (0331) 260 5450, 260 5420 Fax: (0331) 260 5072

Dean: Rijkenberg, Prof. Frits H. J., MScAgric Natal, PhD Natal
Faculty Officer: Dewing, Des

Architecture and Allied Disciplines (Durban Campus)
Tel: (031) 260 3271 Fax: (031) 260 1252

Dean: Kahn, Prof. Michael, MSc(TRP) Witw., PhD Natal
Faculty Officer: Tait, Estelle

Commerce (Pietermaritzburg Campus)
Tel: (0331) 260 5693 Fax: (0331) 260 6228

Dean: Stobie, Prof. Bruce S., BCom Natal, MAcct Natal
Faculty Officer: Willington, Jenny

Economics and Management (Durban Campus)
Fax: (031) 260 1312

Dean: Lumby, Anthony B., BCom Witw., PhD Natal
Secretary: Longano, Gail

Education (Durban Campus)
Tel: (031) 260 1169 Fax: (031) 260 2609

Dean: Chapman, Prof. Michael J. F., BA Lond., MA Natal, DLitt&Phil S.Af.
Secretary: van Wyk, J.

Education (Pietermaritzburg Campus)
Tel: (0331) 260 5248 Fax: (0331) 260 5080

Dean: Nicolson, Ronald B., BA Natal, PhD Natal
Secretary: Cumming, Sally

Engineering (Durban Campus)
Tel: (031) 260 2221 Fax: (031) 260 1233

Dean: Roberts, Lancian W., MScEng Natal, PhD Lond.
Faculty Officer: Higginson, Fiona

Humanities (Durban Campus)
Tel: (031) 260 1508 Fax: (031) 260 1507

Dean: Chapman, Prof. Michael J. F., BA Lond., MA Natal, DLitt&Phil S.Af.
Secretary: Hatcher, Norma

Humanities (Pietermaritzburg Campus)
Tel: (0331) 260 5717 Fax: (0331) 260 5715

Dean: Nicolson, Prof. Ronald B., BA Natal, PhD Natal
Faculty Officer: Molete, Amanda

Law (Durban Campus)
Tel: (031) 260 2487 Fax: (031) 260 2522

Dean: Rycroft, Prof. Alan J., BA Rhodes, LLB Natal, LLM Lond.
Secretary: Laing, Kim

Medicine (Durban Campus)
Tel: (031) 260 4267 Fax: (031) 260 4410

Dean: Van Dellen, Prof. James R., MB BCh Witw., PhD Witw., FRCSEd
Secretary: Bond, Cathi

Science (Durban Campus)
Tel: (031) 260 2350 Fax: (031) 260 1345

Dean: Hellberg, Prof. Manfred A., BSc Cape Town, PhD Camb., FRSSAf
Secretary: Farrington, Avril

Science (Pietermaritzburg Campus)
Tel: (0331) 260 5184 Fax: (0331) 260 5969

Dean: Haines, Prof. Raymond J., MSc Natal, PhD Lond., FRSSAf
Faculty Officer: Alcock, Laura

Social Science (Durban Campus)
Tel: (031) 260 2325 Fax: (031) 260 2372

Dean: Sitas, Prof. Ari, BA Witw., PhD Witw.
Secretary: Khunoethe, Halima

Social Science (Pietermaritzburg Campus)
Tel: (0331) 260 5699 Fax: (0331) 260 5799

Dean: Stopforth, Prof. Peter, BSocSc Rhodes
Secretary: Jacobsen, Beulah

ACADEMIC UNITS

DURBAN CAMPUS

Accounting and Finance
Tel: (031) 260 2650 Fax: (031) 260 3292

Blewett, Craig, BCom Natal, MCom Natal Sr. Lectr.
Crossman, Trevor D., BA Natal, MCom Witw., PhD Witw. Prof.
Fouche, Sean, BCom Natal, BComm Stell. Sr. Lectr.
Gibson, Lee K., BCom S.Af. Sr. Lectr.
Gokal, Hemraj, BSc Durban-W. Sr. Lectr.
Jackson, Robert D., BAcc Natal, MCom Rhodes Prof.
Kierby-Smith, Briditte F., BCom Natal, Sr. Lectr.
Lord, Jeremy W., MBL S.Af., PhD Natal Assoc. Prof.
Luke, James T. C., BCom Natal Sr. Lectr.
Miller, Jean A., MBL S.Af., BCom Natal Prof.
Mitchell, Lindsay D., BCom Natal Prof.; Head*
Penn, Gary S., BCom Natal Sr. Lectr.
Skea, F. Owen, MCom Rhodes, MBA Durh.
Stent, Warwick J., BCom Rhodes Sr. Lectr.
Vigario, Frisco A. A., BCom Natal Prof.
Wood, Nicholas A., BCom Sr. Lectr.
Other Staff: 5 Lectrs.
Vacant Posts: 1 Prof.; 3 Sr. Lectrs.; 2 Lectrs.; 2 Temp. Lectrs.
Research: current fiscal legislation limits; employee's demands for and understanding of financial information; provisions and regulations governing tax litigation in South Africa

Adult and Community Education
Tel: (031) 260 3086 Fax: (031) 260 1168

Hemson, Crispin M. C., BA Natal, BEd Natal Sr. Lectr.
von Kotze, Astrid E., BA Witw., PhD Witw. Sr. Lectr.
Wallis, John V., BA Birm., MA Birm., PhD Nott. Head*
Other Staff: 2 Lectrs.; 1 Tutor
Research: education and development provision for out-of-school youth; investigation of adult education in context of reconstruction and development; literacy and language; professional development in Adult Basic Education

Afrikaans en Nederlands
Tel: (031) 260 2382 Fax: (031) 260 2409

Maartens, Jeanne, MA Stell. Assoc. Prof.; Head*
Other Staff: 4 Lectrs.
Vacant Posts: 1 Prof.
Research: teaching Afrikaans to speakers of other languages

Anthropology, see Soc. Anthropol.

Architecture
Tel: (031) 260 2699 Fax: (031) 260 1252

Adebayo, Ambrose A., MArch Vienna, DrTechn Vienna Assoc. Prof.
Harber, Rodney R., BArch Natal, MScURP Assoc. Prof.
Jekot, Barbara, MScArch Silesia, PhD Wroclaw Sr. Lectr.
Peters, Walter H., BArch Natal, MSc H.-W., DrIng Hanover Prof.
Radford, Dennis J. C., BArch Cape Town, MSc H.-W., PhD Witw. Prof.; Head*
van Zyl, Douw G., BArch Cape Town Sr. Lectr.
Wang, Derek T., BSc Natal, PhD Natal Assoc. Prof.
Other Staff: 5 Lectrs.
Vacant Posts: 2 Sr. Lectrs.
Research: alternative technology in tropical housing; history of architecture and housing

Biology
Tel: (031) 260 3192 Fax: (031) 260 2029

Amory, Alan M., BSc Witw., PhD Witw. Assoc. Prof.
Appleton, Chris C., BSc Rhodes, MSc Rhodes, PhD Murd. Prof.
Berjak, Patricia, BSc Witw., MSc Natal, PhD Natal Prof.
Campbell, Glen K., BSc Natal, PhD Natal Sr. Lectr.
Cooke, John A., BSc Newcastle(UK), PhD Newcastle(UK) Prof.; Head*
de Freitas, Antonio J., MSc Witw., PhD Witw. Hon. Prof.
Forbes, Anthony T., MSc Rhodes, PhD Rhodes Assoc. Prof.
Pammenter, Norman W., MSc Natal, PhD Leeds Prof.
Watt, M. Paula, BSc Witw., PhD Witw. Sr. Lectr.
Other Staff: 5 Lectrs.; 1 Tutor; 1 Hon. Lectr.; 2 Hon. Res. Fellows
Research: cell and molecular biology; cytogenical aspects of speciation; eco-toxicology; plant physiology; terrestrial, marine and estuarine ecology

Business Administration
Tel: (031) 260 2593 Fax: (031) 260 2169

Bhowan, Kanti, BCom S.Af., MBA Witw. Sr. Lectr.
Cassim, Shahida, BCom S.Af., MCom Natal Sr. Lectr.
Coldwell, David A. L., BSc Lond., BA(Econ) S.Af., MA S.Af., DLitt&Phil S.Af. Assoc. Prof.; Acting Head*
Dancaster, Lisa, BCom Natal, LLM Natal Sr. Lectr.
K'Obonyo, Peter O., BA Mak., MBA Nair., PhD S.Carolina

MacDonald, John D., MCom *S.Af.*, DCom *S.Af.* Sr. Lectr.
Other Staff: 2 Lectrs.
Vacant Posts: 1 Prof.
Research: affirmative action; competencies of future South African managers; deceptive advertising; entrepreneurship; tertiary level management education

Chemistry and Applied Chemistry

Tel: (031) 260 3090 Fax: (031) 260 3091
Brookes, Hugh C., BSc *Cape Town*, PhD *Cape Town* Prof.
Ford, T. Anthony, BSc *Wales*, MSc *Wales*, PhD *Dal.*, FRSChem Prof.; Head*
Jeremy, J., MSc *Pret.*, PhD *Rand Afrikaans*
Laing, Michael J., MSc *Natal*, PhD *Calif.* Prof.
Letcher, Trevor M., BSc *Natal*, BEd *Natal*, MSc *Natal*, PhD *Natal*, FRSChem, FRSSAf Prof.
Martincigh, Bia S., MSc *Natal*, PhD *Natal* Sr. Lectr.
Mulholland, Dulcie A., MSc *Natal*, PhD *Natal* Assoc. Prof.
Spark, Andrew A., BSc *Lond.*, PhD *Lond.*
Other Staff: 5 Lectrs.; 1 Hon. Res. Assoc.; 1 Hon. Res. Fellow
Research: co-ordination chemistry; environmental analysis; molecular spectroscopy; natural product chemistry; thermodynamics and photochemistry of solutions

Classics

Tel: (031) 260 2312 Fax: (031) 260 2698
Dominik, William J., BA *Pacific*, MA *Texas*, PhD *Monash* Assoc. Prof.
Gosling, M. Anne, BA *Natal*, MA *Natal* Sr. Lectr.; Head*
Hilton, John L., BA *Cape Town*, BA *S.Af.*, MA *Reading* Sr. Lectr.
Jackson, Steven B., BA *Ulster*, MA *Belf.*, PhD *Trinity(Dub.)*
Mackay, E. Anne, MA *Cant.*, PhD *Well.* Prof.
Other Staff: 1 Lectr.
Research: Greek poetry; Greek pottery; Hellenistic poetry; Neronian and Flavian literature; Ovid

Computer Science

Tel: (031) 260 3018 Fax: (031) 260 6550
Goddard, Wayne, BSc *Natal*, PhD *Natal*, PhD *M.I.T.* Assoc. Prof.
Meyerowitz, Jane J., BScCompSc *Natal*, MSc *Natal* Sr. Lectr.
Murrell, Hugh C., BSc *Natal*, MSc *Rhodes*, PhD *Natal* Sr. Lectr.
Sartori-Angus, Alan G., BSc *Kent*, PhD *Kent* Prof.; Head*
Other Staff: 2 Lectrs.

Creative Arts, Centre for

Tel: (031) 260 3134 Fax: (031) 260 3074
Breytenbach, Breyten, Hon. DLitt *Natal* Visiting Prof.
Donker, Adriaan

Cultural and Media Studies, Centre for

Tel: (031) 260 2505 Fax: (031) 260 1519
Teer-Tomaselli, Ruth E., BA *Witw.*, MA *Witw.*, PhD *Natal* Sr. Lectr.
Tomaselli, Keyan G., BA *Witw.*, MA *Witw.*, PhD *Witw.* Prof.; Head*
Other Staff: 1 Lectr.
Research: African indigenous modes of communal work, communication and development; dialectics of hegemony and mythology; racial sterotyping and content in television commercials; role of the news agency

Drama and Performance Studies

Tel: (031) 260 3133 Fax: (031) 260 1410
McMurtry, Mervyn E., BA *Natal*, MA *Natal*, PhD *Natal* Prof.; Head*
Other Staff: 3 Lectrs.; 1 Tutor

Economic History

Tel: (031) 260 2628 Fax: (031) 260 1061
Freund, William M., BA *Chic.*, MPhil *Yale*, PhD *Yale* Prof.; Head*
Vacant Posts: 3 Lectrs.
Research: poverty and food security in Southern Africa; fuel use in low-income households; timber industry in Natal

Economics

Tel: (031) 260 2589 Fax: (031) 260 2811
Amin, Nick, BSc *Reading*, MSc(Econ) *Lond.* Sr. Lectr.
Hart, John S., BA *Rhodes*, MA *S.Af.*
Hofmeyr, Julian F., BA *Cape Town*, MA *Natal*, PhD *Natal* Assoc. Prof.
Holden, Merle G., BCom *Natal*, MA *Duke*, PhD *Duke* Prof.; Acting Head*
Jones, Trevor B., MA *Natal* Assoc. Prof.
Lumby, Anthony B., BCom *Witw.*, PhD *Natal* Assoc. Prof.
Meth, Charles E., MA *Natal* Sr. Lectr.
Stefanski, Bogdan, MSc *Warsaw*, MPhil *Warsaw*, PhD *Warsaw*, DSc *Warsaw* Sr. Lectr.
Tewari, Devi, BScAg&AH *GBP*, MScAg *GBP*, MSc *Sask.*, PhD *Sask.*
Whiteside, Alan W., MA *E.Anglia* Res. Prof.
Research: discounting; fighting corruption; joint forest management programmes; sustainable energy strategy for South Africa

Education, see also Adult and Community Educn.

Tel: (031) 260 2611 Fax: (031) 260 2609
Criticos, Costas, BSc *Natal*, BEd *Natal*, MS *Syr.* Sr. Lectr.
Graham-Jolly, Michael, BA *Lond.*, MEd *Zululand* Sr. Lectr.
Harber, Clive R., BA *Reading*, MA *Leic.*, PhD *Birm.* Prof.; Head*
Moletsane, Relebohile, BEd *Fort Hare*, MS *Indiana*, PhD *Indiana*, BA Sr. Lectr.
Morrell, Robert G., BJourn *Rhodes*, BA *Rhodes*, MA *Witw.*, PhD *Natal* Sr. Lectr.
Muthukrishna, Nithi, BEd *S.Af.*, MEd *Birm.*, MSc *Oregon*, PhD *Notre Dame Sem.* Sr. Lectr.
Soobrayan, Parmosivea B., BSc *Durban-W.*, MEd *Natal* Sr. Lectr.
Thurlow, Michael H. J., BA *Open(UK)*, MEd *Natal*, EdD *Calif.State* Assoc. Prof.
Other Staff: 4 Lectrs.
Research: children with disabilities in ordinary schools; development of visual literacy in second-language, pre-school learners; gender, race and class in colonial Natal; poststructural approaches to textual studies; theory, politics and change after post-modernism

Education Development Unit

Tel: (031) 260 3255 Fax: (031) 260 1340
Frame, Janet, BA(HDE) *Natal*, BEd *Natal*, MEd *Natal* Head*
Other Staff: 1 Lectr.

Engineering, Chemical

Tel: (031) 260 3115 Fax: (031) 260 1118
Brouckaert, Christopher J., BScEng *Natal* Sr. Lectr.
Buckley, Christopher A., MScEng *Natal* Assoc. Res. Prof.
Loveday, Brian K., PhD *Natal* Albert Baumann Prof.; Head*
Mulholland, Michael, PhD *Natal* Prof.
Pillay, Bavanethan, BScEng *Natal*, MSc *Calif.*, PhD *Calif.* Sr. Lectr.
Ravno, Brian D., BScEng *Witw.* Sr. Lectr.
Starzak, Maciej, MSc *Lodz*, PhD *Lodz* Sr. Lectr.
Research: industry-related research in vapour-liquid equilibrium; mineral processing; process control

Engineering, Civil

Tel: (031) 260 3058 Fax: (031) 260 1411
Dougherty, Brian K., BScEng *Natal*, MScEng *Natal*, PhD *Natal* Hon. Prof.

Everitt, Philip R., BScEng *Natal*, MScEng *Natal*, F(SA)ICE Sr. Lectr.
King, William T., BScEng *Natal* Sr. Lectr.
Little, Robert D., BSc(Eng) *Cape Town*, MSc(Eng) *Cape Town* Sr. Lectr.
Pegram, Geoffrey G. S., BScEng *Natal*, MScEng *Natal*, PhD *Lanc.* Prof.
Roebuck, Christopher S., BTech *Brad.*, MSc *Brad.*, PhD *Brad.* Prof.
Schreiner, H. Deneys, BScEng *Natal*, MScEng *Natal*, PhD *Lond.* Sr. Lectr.; Head*
Stephens, Dave J., BScEng *Leeds*, MEng Sr. Lectr.
Stretch, Derek D., BScEng *Natal*, MScEng *Natal*, PhD *Camb.* Sr. Lectr.
Sugden, Michael B., BScEng *Natal*, MScEng *Natal* Sr. Lectr.
Vacant Posts: 2 Lectrs.
Research: effect on roads of increasing maximum legal axle mass; expansiveness of clay soils; labour-intensive construction; masonry arch bridges; stochastic hydrology

Engineering, Electrical

Tel: (031) 260 2725 Fax: (031) 260 1300
Boje, Edward S., BSc(Eng) *Witw.*, MScEng *Natal*, PhD *Natal* Assoc. Prof.
Diana, Gregory, BScEng *Natal* Sr. Lectr.
Harley, Ronald G., MScEng *Pret.*, PhD *Lond.* Prof.; Head*
Hippner, Meciej, MScEng *Poznan*, PhD *Wroclaw* Sr. Lectr.
Hoch, Derek, BScEng *Witw.*, PhD *Witw.* Sr. Lectr.
Odendal, Eugene J., BScEng *Pret.*, MScEng *Natal* Assoc. Prof.
Other Staff: 1 Res. Assoc.
Vacant Posts: 1 Prof.; 1 Sr Lectr.
Research: artificial intelligence in non-linear control; design of synchronous reluctance motors; energy efficient electrical motor drives and electrical power quality; tension control in paper making

Engineering, Electronic

Tel: (031) 260 2728 Fax: (031) 260 2111
Broadhurst, Anthony D., BScEng *Cape Town*, PhD *Cape Town* Prof.; Head*
Peplow, Roger C. S., MScEng *Natal* Assoc. Prof.
Prentice, John, BScEng *Natal*, MScEng *Natal* Sr. Lectr.
Takawira, Fambirai, BSc *Manc.*, PhD *Camb.* Telkom Prof., Digital Communications
Other Staff: 3 Lectrs.
Vacant Posts: 1 Prof.
Research: artificial intelligence; digital signal processing; digital systems design; microwave antennas and measurements; optical fibre communications

Engineering, Mechanical

Tel: (031) 260 3202 Fax: (031) 260 3217
Adali, Sarp, BScEng *Cornell*, METech *Cornell*, PhD *Cornell* Sugar Millers' Prof., Design
Bindon, Jeffery P., BScEng *Pret.*, MSc(Eng) *Lond.*, PhD *Lond.* Prof.
Bodger, Robert, BScEng *Natal* Sr. Lectr.
Bright, Glen, MScEng *Natal*, PhD *Natal* Sr. Lectr.
Kaczmarczyk, Stefan, BSc *Gliwice*, MSc(Eng) *Gliwice* Sr. Lectr.
Morozov, Evgeny, MScEng *Moscow*, PhD *Moscow*, DSc *Moscow* Prof.
Roberts, Lancian W., MScEng *Natal*, PhD *Lond.* James Fulton Chair Prof.
Smith, Graham D. J., MScEng *Natal*, PhD *Camb.* Assoc. Prof.; Head*
Verijenko, Viktor E., MScEng *Kiev*, PhD *Kiev* Prof.
Other Staff: 1 Lectr.
Research: design of composites under buckling loads; dynamics and vibration of machines and structure; manufacturing technology for fabrication of prepegs; theoretical modelling of enhanced heat transfer processes

English

Tel: (031) 260 2334 Fax: (031) 260 1243

Brown, Duncan J. B., MA Natal, PhD Natal
Chapman, Michael J. F., BA Lond., MA Natal, DLitt&Phil S.Af. Prof.
Daymond, Margaret J., BA Natal, MA Camb., PhD Natal Prof.
Green, Michael M., BA Natal, MA Stan., DPhil York(UK) Assoc. Prof.
Jacobs, Johan U., BA Pret., BA S.Af., MPhil Col., PhD Col. Prof.
Joffe, Philip H., BA Natal, MA Br.Col., PhD Lond. Sr. Lectr.
Kearney, John A., BA Natal, MPhil York(UK), DPhil York(UK) Assoc. Prof.; Head*
Lenta, Margaret M., BA Manc., BA Natal, MA Natal, PhD Natal Prof.
Newmarch, David M., BA Natal, MPhil York(UK) Sr. Lectr.
Vaughan, Michael S., MA Camb. Sr. Lectr.
Other Staff: 7 Lectrs.
Research: South African literature

Foreign Languages

Tel: (031) 260 2375 Fax: (031) 260 1242

de Kadt, Elizabeth, BA Natal, DrPhil Freib. Assoc. Prof.; Head*
Lieskounig, Jürgen, DrPhil Salzburg Sr. Lectr.
Machabeis, Jacqueline M-A., Drd'Etat Paris Assoc. Prof.
Mejia, Gustavo, LicFil&Lett Los Andes, Bogotá, MA Essex, PhD Essex Sr. Lectr.
Other Staff: 5 Lectrs.; 2 Sr. Tutors; 1 Tutor
Research: inter-cultural communication; German language in South Africa; German speaking theatre; Greek words in the German language; language planning (contrasting local trends with those towards multilingualism in Spain)

Geographical and Environmental Sciences

Tel: (031) 260 2416 Fax: (031) 260 1391

Diab, Roseanne D., MSc Natal, PhD Virginia Prof.
Garland, Gerald G., BA Belf., MSc I.T.C.Enschede, PhD Natal Assoc. Prof.
Preston-Whyte, Robert A., MA Natal, PhD Natal Prof.; Head*
Research: ecology and dynamics of Okavango River; forecasting air pollution potential; open space plan for kwaZulu-Natal; ozone research; sustainable harvesting of hardwood

Geology and Applied Geology

Tel: (031) 260 2516 Fax: (031) 260 2280

Bell, Frederick G., MSc Durh., PhD Sheff., FGS Prof.; Head*
Jeremy, Colin A., BSc Wales, MSc Newcastle(UK), FGS Sr. Lectr.
Marsh, Carol A., BSc Belf., PhD Belf. Sr. Lectr.
Maud, Rodney R., BSc Natal, PhD Natal Hon. Prof.
Stacey, T. Richard, BScEng Natal, MSc Natal, DSc Pret. Hon. Prof.
Viljoen, Richard P., MSc Witw., PhD Witw. Hon. Prof.
Watkeys, Michael K., BSc Wales, PhD Witw. Assoc. Prof.
Wilson, Allan H., BSc Lond., PhD Rhodesia Prof.
Other Staff: 1 Hon. Res. Assoc.
Research: engineering geology; environmental geology; geochemistry; geodynamics; sedimentary geology

History

Tel: (031) 260 2620 Fax: (031) 260 2621

Guy, Jefferson J., BA Natal, PhD Lond. Prof.; Head*
Seleti, Yona N., BA(Educn) Zambia, MA Zambia, PhD Dal. Sr. Lectr.
Other Staff: 3 Lectrs.
Research: history and politics of mineworkers; history of Indians in South Africa; oral history of Lesotho migrants; post-colonial historiography; Zulu history

Language Learning Centre

Tel: (031) 260 2009 Fax: (031) 260 2411

Durgiah, O. Dir.*

Law, Business

Tel: (031) 260 2563 Fax: (031) 260 2837

Baqwa, Selby, BJuris Fort Hare, LLB S.Af. Hon. Prof.
Cohen, Tamara, LLB Natal, BA Sr. Lectr.
Greenbaum, Lesley A., BA Natal, LLB Natal Sr. Lectr.
Hickman, Bruce V., BSocSc Natal, BCom Natal, LLB Natal Sr. Lectr.
Konyn, Isobel E., BA Natal, LLB Natal Assoc. Prof.; Head*
McLennan, John S., BCom Rhodes, LLB Rhodes, LLM Witw. Prof.
Steyn, Lee, BA Natal, LLB Natal, LLM S.Af. Sr. Lectr.
Woker, Tanya A., BA Natal, LLB Natal Assoc. Prof.
Other Staff: 1 Lectr.
Research: advertising; company law; insurance; international insolvency issues

Campus Law Clinic

Tel: (031) 260 1562 Fax: (031) 260 1558

Ramgobin, Ayesha S., BA Durban-W., LLB Durban-W. Dir.*

Law, Maritime, Institute of

Tel: (031) 260 2556 Fax: (031) 260 1456

Staniland, Hilton, BA Natal, LLB Natal, LLM S'ton., PhD S'ton. Prof.; Dir.*
Research: maritime insurance; maritime lien act; ship arrests and the arrest convention

Law, Private

Tel: (031) 260 2551 Fax: (031) 260 2559

Glavovic, Peter D., BA Rhodes, LLB Rhodes, PhD Natal Prof.
Olmesdahl, Michael C. J., BA Natal, LLB Natal Prof.
Schembri, Christopher C., BA Natal, LLB Natal Sr. Lectr.; Head*
van Dokkum, Niel, BSocSc Rhodes, LLB Natal, LLM Natal Sr. Lectr.
Other Staff: 1 Lectr.
Research: detection and treatment of child abuse; environmental law; intellectual property; law of persons

Law, Procedural and Clinical

Tel: (031) 260 2558 Fax: (031) 260 2559

Didcott, The Hon. Mr. Justice John M., BA Cape Town, LLB Cape Town Hon. Prof.
McQuoid-Mason, David J., BCom Natal, LLB Natal, LLM Lond., PhD Natal Prof.; Head*
Palmer, Robin, BA Witw., LLB Witw., LLM Natal Sr. Lectr.
Rycroft, Alan J., BA Rhodes, LLB Natal, LLM Lond. Prof.
Research: affirmative action policies; consumer law; human rights

Law, Public

Tel: (031) 260 2488 Fax: (031) 260 2867

Boister, Neil B., BA Natal, LLB Natal, LLM Natal Sr. Lectr.
Devenish, George E., BSc Witw., LLB S.Af., LLD S.Af. Prof.
Govender, Karthigasen, LLB Lond., LLB Natal, LLM Mich. Assoc. Prof.; Head*
Louw, Ronald H., BProc S.Af., BA Cape Town, LLM Cape Town Sr. Lectr.
Pete, Stephen A., BA Natal, LLB Natal, LLM Cape Town, MPhil Camb. Sr. Lectr.
Research: constitutional law; human rights; minority group discrimination

Linguistics

Tel: (031) 260 2617 Fax: (031) 260 1253

Adendorff, Ralph D., BA Rhodes, MA Indiana Sr. Lectr.
Chick, J. Keith, BA Natal, BEd Natal, MA Lanc., PhD Natal Prof.; Head*
Dace, Roy W., BA Witw., MA Syr. Sr. Lectr.

Other Staff: 3 Lectrs.
Research: acquisition of scientific literacy; code-switching across cultures; connection between language and the language faculty; pronunciation of Natal English dialects; relationship between structures of societal institutions and discourse

Mathematical Statistics

Tel: (031) 260 3011 Fax: (031) 260 1009

Berezner, Sergie, MSc Moscow, PhD Moscow Sr. Lectr.
Dale, Andrew I., MSc Cape Town, PhD Virginia Polytech. Prof.
Matthews, Glenda B., MSc Pret., PhD Pret. Sr. Lectr.
Murray, Michael, MSc Natal, PhD Natal Sr. Lectr.
Troskie, Leon, MSc Pret., PhD Natal Prof.; Head*
Research: financial statistics; generalised linear models; probability theory; telecommunication networks

Mathematics and Applied Mathematics

Tel: (031) 260 3000 Fax: (031) 260 1017

Banasiak, Jack, MSc Lodz, PhD Glas. Sr. Lectr.
Krige, J. Dan, BSc Natal, MA Camb., MSc Newcastle(UK) Sr. Lectr.
Leach, Peter G. L., BSc Melb., MSc La Trobe, PhD La Trobe Prof.
Maharaj, Suril D., BSc Durban-W., MSc Witw., PhD Witw. Prof.
Raftery, James G., PhD Natal
Swart, Henda C., MSc Stell., DSc Stell. Prof.
Swart, John H., MSc Stell., PhD S.Af. Prof.; Head*
van den Berg, Johann J., MSc Pret. Assoc. Prof.
Winter, Paul A., BEd Natal, MEd(EdPsych) Natal, MSc Natal, PhD Natal Sr. Lectr.
Other Staff: 6 Lectrs.; 1 Tutor; 1 Hon. Res. Assoc.; 1 Hon. Res. Fellow
Research: graph theory; meta-and epistemic cognitive cues; population dynamics; symmetries of space-time manifold; univerisal algebra and algebraic logic

Medicine, see below

Music

Tel: (031) 260 3351 Fax: (031) 260 1048

Ballantine, Christopher J., BMus Witw., MLitt Camb., DMus Cape Town Prof.
Brauninger, Jurgen, MA Calif.State(San Jose) Assoc. Prof.
Brubeck, Darius D., BA Wesleyan Assoc. Prof.
Franke, Veronica, MMus Cape Town, DPhil Oxf. Sr. Lectr.
Goveia, Ruth, BMusEd OFS, MMus Cinc. Sr. Lectr.
Parker, Beverly L., BMus Boston, MA Mich., PhD Mich. Prof.; Head*
Shabalala, J. Visiting Prof., African Music
Smith, David I., BMus Cape Town, PhD Cape Town
Other Staff: 3 Lectrs.
Research: ethnomusicology; indigenous women's musical styles; intercultural education through music; romantic symphonic literature; socio-political dynamics of the Manhattan Brothers

Nursing

Tel: (031) 260 2499 Fax: (031) 260 1543

Gwele, Thandi S., MSocSc Missouri, MEd Missouri, PhD Natal Sr. Lectr.
Uys, Leana R., DSocSc(Nursing) OFS Prof.; Head*
van der Merwe, Anita S., BA OFS, MSocSc(Nursing) OFS, PhD Natal Sr. Lectr.
Research: child abuse needs assessment of health education in schools; comprehensive psychiatric care in the primary health system; psychosocial rehabilitation; vocational rehabilitation; women's organisation in community health

Philosophy
Tel: (031) 260 2292 Fax: (031) 260 1459
Gouws, Andries S., BA S.Af., DrsPhil Utrecht Sr. Lectr.
Herwitz, Daniel A., BA Brandeis, PhD Chic. Prof.; Head*
Other Staff: 1 Lectr.
Research: creativity and Kant; freedom and physicalism; Richard Rorty's epistemology and political philosophy

Physics
Tel: (031) 260 2775 Fax: (031) 260 6550
Alport, Michael J., MSc Natal, PhD Iowa Assoc. Prof.
Bedford, Donald M. M., MA Sask., PhD ANU Assoc. Prof.
Doyle, Terry B., BSc Durh., PhD Witw. Assoc. Prof.
Hellberg, Manfred A., BSc Cape Town, PhD Camb., FRSSAf Prof.
Hey, John D., BSc Cape Town, MSc Cape Town, PhD Maryland Prof.; Head*
Hughes, Arthur R. W., MA Trinity(Dub.), MSc Trinity(Dub.), PhD Sheff., FRAS Prof.
Krumm, H. Peter Sr. Lectr.
Michaelis, Max M. C., MA Oxf., DPhil Oxf. Prof.
Rash, Jonathan P. S., MSc Cape Town, PhD Rhodes Sr. Lectr.
Schuster, David G., MS Wis., PhD Witw. Assoc. Prof.
Scourfield, Malcolm W. J., BSc Keele, MSc Calg., PhD Calg.
Spalding, Dennis R., MSc Natal, PhD Camb. Sr. Lectr.
Walker, A. David M., BSc Rhodes, MSc Rhodes, PhD Camb., FRSSAf Prof.
Other Staff: 2 Lectrs.; 1 Sr. Tutor; 1 Hon. Res. Assoc.
Research: computational physics; inter-metallic alloys; physics education; space and plasma physics; superconductivity

Politics
Tel: (031) 260 2627 Fax: (031) 260 1061
de Kadt, Raphael H. J., BA Witw. Assoc. Prof.
Grest, Christopher J., BA Rhodes, MA Lond. Sr. Lectr.
Hughes, Heather, BA Witw., MA Lond., PhD Lond.
Johnston, Alexander McI., MA Aberd., MEd Aberd. Assoc. Prof.; Head*
Other Staff: 1 Lectr.
Research: politics of kwaZulu-Natal

Property Development and Construction
Tel: (031) 260 2687 Fax: (031) 260 1252
Botha, Lee G., BScQS Natal Sr. Lectr.
Dobson, H. Philip, BSc Manc. Sr. Lectr.
Martins, Rui H., BAS Cape Town, MSc Bath Sr. Lectr.
Norval, George H. M., BScQS Natal, BCom Natal Sr. Lectr.
Pearl, Robert G., MSc(QS) Cape Town Prof.; Head*
Taylor, Robert G., BScQS Natal, MSc H.-W. Prof.
White, Martin J., MBA Durban-W. Sr. Lectr.
Vacant Posts: 1 Lectr.

Psychology
Tel: (031) 260 2527 Fax: (031) 260 2618
Collings, Steven J., MSocSc Natal, PhD Natal Sr. Lectr.
Gaitskell, Ian W., BEd Natal, MA Natal Sr. Lectr.
Gillmer, Bruce T., BSocSc Rhodes, MSocSc Natal, PhD OFS Sr. Lectr.; Head*
Henzi, Peter, BA Natal, PhD Natal Prof.
Miller, Ronald, BA Witw., MA Witw., PhD Witw. Prof.
Other Staff: 8 Lectrs.
Research: academic performance and under-preparedness; sexual abuse; student needs in a multi-cultural society

Social Anthropology
Tel: (031) 260 2401 Fax: (031) 260 1459
de Haas, Mary E., BSocSc Natal, MSocSc Natal Sr. Lectr.
Jones, Sean J. W., BA Cape Town, MA Cape Town, PhD Camb.
Kiernan, James P., BA N.U.I., MA(Econ) Manc., PhD Manc. Emer. Prof.
Plaice, Evelyn, BA Oxf.Brookes, MA Nfld., PhD Manc. Sr. Lectr.
White, Caroline F., BA Natal, MA Sus., DPhil Sus. Prof.; Head*
Other Staff: 1 Res. Assoc.
Research: adolescent pregnancy in South Africa; social construction of Zulu culture; South African human rights; traditional herbal medicine; Zulu interpretations of AIDS

Social Work
Tel: (031) 260 2390 Fax: (031) 260 2700
Gray, Mel M. A., BSocSc Natal, MSocSc Natal, PhD Natal Prof.; Head*
Wint, Eleanor, BSc WI, MSW Boston Coll., PhD WI
Other Staff: 4 Lectrs.; 4 Academic Supervisors
Research: definitions of youth; development training; environmental awareness; social work students and termination of pregnancy; support groups for HIV+ mothers

Socio-Legal Studies, Centre for
Tel: (031) 260 1291 Fax: (031) 260 1540
No staff at present
Vacant Posts: Dir.*

Sociology
Tel: (031) 260 2302 Fax: (031) 260 2347
Crothers, Charles H. G., BA Waik., BA Well., PhD Well. Prof.; Head*
Ginsburg, David B., BA Witw., MA Sus. Sr. Lectr.
Mar, P. Gerhard, BA Natal, BA Witw., MA Witw., PhD Natal Assoc. Prof.
Waters, Geoffrey H., BA Natal, MA(Econ) Manc. Sr. Lectr.
Other Staff: 6 Lectrs.

Surveying and Mapping
Tel: (031) 260 3148 Fax: (031) 260 2376
Forbes, Angus M., BScSur Natal, MScSur Natal Sr. Lectr.
Fourie, Clarissa D., BA Natal, PhD Rhodes Sr. Lectr.
Hepburn, Robert M., BScSur Natal, MScSurEng New Br. Assoc. Prof.; Acting Head*
Jackson, Jonathan, BScEng Witw., MScSur Cape Town, MILS W.Cape Sr. Lectr.
Vacant Posts: 1 Prof; 1 Sr. Lectr.; 1 Lectr.
Research: alternative forms of cadastral surveying; land management; precise geodetic uses of global positioning system

Tertiary Education, Division of
Tel: (031) 260 3255 Fax: (031) 260 1340
Mbali, V. Charlotte, MA Oxf., MPhil Oxf., PhD Lond. Head*

Town and Regional Planning
Tel: (031) 260 2689 Fax: (031) 260 1252
Harrison, Philip, BSc Natal, MTRP Natal Sr. Lectr.
Kahn, Michael, MSc(TRP) Witw., PhD Natal Prof.
Robinson, Peter S., MA Natal, MSc Reading, PhD Natal Prof.; Head*
Todes, Alison E., BSc Cape Town, MCRP Cape Town Sr. Lectr.
Vacant Posts: 1 Sr. Lectr.
Research: environmental management and conservation through planning procedures; land tenure and housing development; restructuring migration and regional planning

Zulu
Tel: (031) 260 2510 Fax: (031) 260 3362
Canonici, Noverino N., BA Natal, BA S.Af., MA Natal, PhD Natal Emer. Prof.
Muller, Beverley K. B., BA Natal, MA Natal Sr. Lectr.
Ngubane, Sehawu, BA Zululand, MA Natal Lectr.; Acting Head*
Other Staff: 4 Lectrs.
Vacant Posts: 1 Prof.
Research: materials for teaching Zulu as a second language; social significance of Zulu names; terminology for modern technology; traditional literature; Zulu children's poetry

MEDICINE

Anaesthetics
Tel: (031) 260 4262 Fax: (031) 260 4527
Bösenberg, Adrien T., MB ChB Cape Town Assoc. Prof.
Burrows, Richard C., BA Trinity(Dub.), MB BCh BAO Trinity(Dub.) Sr. Lectr.
Daniel, Clive, MB ChB Cape Town, MMed Stell. Sr. Lectr.
Rocke, David A., MB BCh Wales, FRCPEd Prof.; Head*
Rout, Chris C., MB BS Lond., FFARCS
Rubin, Joseph, BSc Cape Town, MB ChB Cape Town, MD Boston, FFARCS Sr. Lectr.
Williamson, Ronald, BSc Brist., MB ChB Brist., FFARCS Sr. Lectr.
Other Staff: 7 Lectrs.
Research: epidural analgesia; HIV+ children and intensive care units; obstetrics and anaesthesia; paediatric anaesthesia

Cardiology, see under Medicine

Cardiothoracic Surgery
Tel: (031) 484311 Fax: (031) 461 1724
Blyth, David F., MB ChB Cape Town, FRCSEd Lectr.; Acting Head*
Other Staff: 5 Lectrs.; 3 Hon Lectrs.
Research: efficacy of plasma preparation; major surgery on HIV+ patients; stentless mitral valves

Chemical Pathology
Tel: (031) 260 4309 Fax: (031) 260 4517
Akanji, Abayomi O., MB BS Ib., MSc Ib., DPhil Oxf. Prof.; Head*
Deppe, Walter M., MScAgric Natal Sr. Lectr.
Joubert, Septi M., MSc Stell., MB ChB Edin., FRCPath Emer. Prof
Ojwang, Peter J., MB ChB Nair., FRCPath Sr. Lectr.
Other Staff: 2 Lectrs.; 1 Sr. Res. Fellow; 1 Hon. Res. Assoc.; 1 Hon. Tutor
Research: atomic absorption spectrometry; tumour suppressor in cervical and breast cancers

Community Health
Tel: (031) 260 4383 Fax: (031) 260 4211
Jinabhai, Champaklal C., BSc Durban-W., MB ChB Cape Town, MMed Natal Prof.; Head*
Naidoo, Kala, MB ChB Natal, MMed Natal Sr. Lectr.
Spencer, Ian W. F., MD Witw. Emer. Prof.
Other Staff: 1 Hon. Lectr.
Research: environmental pollutants (especially lead); health promotion and behavioural changes for control of parasitic diseases and STDs among primary school children; policy and planning for health management; primary school nutrition programmes

Dermatology, see under Med.

Experimental and Clinical Pharmacology
Tel: (031) 260 4334 Fax: (031) 260 4415
Bhoola, Kanti D., MB BCh BAO N.U.I., BSc N.U.I., MD N.U.I., PhD Lond. Res. Prof.
Botha, Julia H., BPharm Rhodes, PhD Rhodes Prof.; Head*

Maharaj, Breminand, MB ChB Natal, MD Natal, FCP(SA) Assoc. Prof.
Other Staff: 2 Lectrs.
Research: bioregulation of kinins; clinical pharmokinetics; evaluation of cardiovascular and renal drugs

Family Medicine

Tel: (031) 260 4485 Fax: (031) 260 4410
Cassimjee, H. Mahomed, BMedSc Durban-W., MPraxMed Natal Sr. Lectr.; Acting Head*
Other Staff: 14 Hon. Lectrs.
Research: generic prescribing

Forensic Medicine

Tel: (031) 215141 Fax: (031) 216258
Dada, Mohammed A., MB ChB Natal, MMed Natal, MMed Stell. Prof.; Head*
Other Staff: 1 Lectr.; 1 Lectr.†
Vacant Posts: 2 Lectrs.
Research: forensic anthropology; human rights and torture medicine; pathology of diffuse brain injury; tumour oncogenesis

General Surgery

Tel: (031) 260 4219 Fax: (031) 260 4389
Baker, Lin W., MB BCh Witw., MSc McG., FRCSEdin, FRCPSGlas
Barker, Edward M., MB ChB Witw., FRCS Sr. Lectr.
Haffejee, Aref A., MB ChB Natal, FRCSEd Prof.
Madiba, T. Enos, MB ChB Natal, MMed Natal, FCS(SA)
Muckart, David J. J., MB ChB Dund., FRCSGlas Sr. Lectr.
Robbs, John V., MB ChB Cape Town, ChM Cape Town, FRCSEd Prof.; Head*
Singh, Bhugwan, MB ChB Natal, FCS(SA) Sr. Lectr.
Thomson, Sandie R., MB ChB Aberd., ChM Aberd., FRCS Assoc. Prof.
Other Staff: 3 Lectrs.; 2 Hon. Lectrs.
Research: AIDS-related vasculopathies; biliary anatomy variations in Africans; oesophageal cancer; surgical nutrition; wound healing

Haematology

Tel: (031) 260 4283 Fax: (031) 260 4410
Jogessar, Vinod B., MB ChB Natal, MMed Natal Sr. Lectr.; Acting Head*
Kenoyer, D. Gayle Sr. Lectr.
Other Staff: 1 Lectr.
Research: adaptive immune reponse in neonates; HIV; inflammatory central nervous system disease; oncology; sickle cell anaemia

Histology, see under Physiol.

Human Anatomy

Tel: (031) 260 4270 Fax: (031) 260 4410
Goldner, Frits H., DrMed F.U.Berlin, MD Monash Prof.; Head*
Vawda, G. Hoosen M., BSc Durban-W., MB ChB Natal, PhD Witw. Assoc. Prof.
Other Staff: 3 Lectrs.

Medical Microbiology

Tel: (031) 260 4395 Fax: (031) 260 4431
Bhamjee, Ahmed, FRCPath Sr. Lectr.
Coovadia, Yacoob M., MB ChB Cape Town Sr. Lectr.
Sturm, A. Willem, MB BS Amst., PhD Amst., MD Amst. Prof.; Head*
Other Staff: 4 Lectrs.; 1 Hon. Sr. Lectr.
Research: bacterial vaginosis; chancroid Haemophilus ducreyi; M.tuberculosis

Medicine

Tel: (031) 260 4216 Fax: (031) 260 4420
Gathiram, Vinod, MB ChB Natal, MD Natal, FCP(SA) Prof., Infectious Diseases
Lalloo, Umesh G., MB ChB Natal, MD Natal, FCP(SA) Prof.; Head*
Mody, Girish M., MB ChB Natal, MD Cape Town, FCP(SA), FRCP Aaron Beare Family Prof., Rheumatology
Motala, Ayesha A., MB ChB Natal, MD Natal, FCP(SA), FRCP Prof.

Naicker, Sarela, MB ChB Natal Sr. Lectr.
Naidoo, Datshana P., MB ChB Natal, FCP(SA) Sr. Lectr.
Naiker, Indiran P., MB ChB Cape Town Sr. Lectr.
Pudifin, Dennis J., MB ChB Cape Town, FRCP, FCP(SA) Prof.
Rajput, Mangoo C., MB ChB Natal, FCP(SA) Sr. Lectr.
Seedat, Yacoob K., MD N.U.I., Hon. PhD Durban-W., FRCP, FRCPI, FACP, FCP(SA) Res. Prof.
Simjee, Ahmed E., MB ChB Natal, FRCP Assoc. Prof.
Soni, Pierre N., MB ChB Natal, MMed Natal, FCP(SA) Sr. Lectr.
Other Staff: 10 Lectrs; 1 Hon. Assoc. Prof.; 3 Hon. Sr. Lectrs.; 2 Hon. Lectrs.
Research: auto-antibody patterns in collagen-vascular diseases; endocrine dysfunction in South African Zulus; genetic factors in premature coronary artery disease; kinins and cytokines in rheumatic arthritis; non-insulin-dependent diabetes mellitus in South African Indians

Cardiology

Tel: (031) 484311 Fax: (031) 487334
Mitha, Abdul S., FRCP, FRCPI Prof.; Head*
Patel, Jai B., MB BCh Witw., FCP(SA) Sr. Lectr.
Other Staff: 4 Lectrs.
Research: pre-menopausal females and coronary artery disease; valvular heart disease; ventricular arrhythmias

Dermatology

Tel: (031) 360 3772 Fax: (031) 360 3549
Aboobaker, Jamila, MB ChB Natal Sr. Lectr.; Head*
Other Staff: 1 Lectr.
Research: common skin diseases in kwaZulu-Natal; erythoderma; HTLV-1 in skin manifestations; kinins in psoriasis

Neurology

Fax: (031) 489654
Bhigjee, Ahmed I., MB ChB Natal, MMed Cape Town, FCP(SA), FRCP Prof.
Bill, Pierre L. A., MB BCh Witw., FRCP, FCP(SA) Prof.; Head*
Other Staff: 2 Hon. Lectrs.
Research: central nervous system and tuberculous meningitis; gene deletions in Duchenne muscular dystrophy; HTLV-1 myelopathy

Neurosurgery

Tel: (031) 484311 Fax: (031) 461 2897
Nadvi, Sameer S., MB ChB Natal, FCS(SA) Sr. Lectr.; Acting Head*
Other Staff: 3 Lectrs.
Vacant Posts: 1 Prof; 1 Sr. Lectr.
Research: automatic nerve preservation and cyclic guanosine monophosphate and kinin measurement in hydro-cephalus; cerebral blood flow in subdural empyema; HIV+ mass lesions

Obstetrics and Gynaecology

Tel: (031) 260 4390 Fax: (031) 260 4427
Green-Thompson, Ronald W., MB ChB Natal, FRCOG Hon. Prof.
Massel, Peter, MB BCh Witw. Sr. Lectr.
Moodley, Jodasa (Jack), MD Natal, FRCOG Prof.; Head*
Pitsoe, Samuel B., MB ChB Natal Sr. Lectr.
Ross, Samuel M., MB BS Lond., FRCOG Emer. Prof.
Other Staff: 10 Lectrs.
Research: antiretroviral drugs and transmission of HIV; doppler and prediction of pre-eclampsia; HIV infection in carcinoma of the cervix; hypertensive disorders in pregnancy

Ophthalmology

Tel: (031) 260 4341 Fax: (031) 260 4221
Peters, Anne L., MB ChB Cape Town, MMed Natal Prof.; Head*

Other Staff: 2 Lectrs.; 1 Hon Lectr.
Research: external eye disease and vitamin A status in children; herpes zoster opthalmics in the HIV+ patient

Orthopaedic Surgery

Tel: (031) 260 4374 Fax: (031) 260 4418
Goga, Ismail E., FRCS, FCS(SA) Sr. Lectr.
Govender, S. (Teddy), MB BS Bom., FRCSGlas Prof.; Head*
Naidoo, Krishnasamy S., MB BS Patna, FRCSEd
Other Staff: 5 Lectrs.
Research: adolescent idiopathic scoliosis; fractures of the thoracolumbar spine; hand surgery

Otorhinolaryngology

Tel: (031) 260 4292 Fax: (031) 260 4480
Singh, Barath, MB ChB MMed Sr. Lectr.; Head*
Other Staff: 1 Lectr.
Research: management of allergic rhinitis; management of epistaxis; metastatic carcinoma in the neck

Paediatric Surgery

Tel: (031) 260 4227 Fax: (031) 260 4410
Hadley, G. (Larry) P., MB ChB St And., FRCSEd Prof.; Head*
Mickel, Robert E., MB BCh Witw., FRCSEd Emer. Prof.
Wiersma, Rinus, BSc(Zoo) Natal, MB ChB Rhodesia, FRCSGlas Sr. Lectr.
Vacant Posts: 1 Lectr.
Research: Wilm's tumour; wound healing

Paediatrics and Child Health

Tel: (031) 260 4345 Fax: (031) 260 4388
Adhikari, Miriam, MB ChB Cape Town, MD Natal, FCP(SA) Prof.
Coovadia, Hoosen M., MB BS Bom., MSc Birm., MD Natal, FCP(SA) Prof.; Head*
Loening, Walter E.K., MB ChB Cape Town, FCP(SA) Emer. Prof.
Smythe, P. C., MD Camb., FRCP
Solarsh, Geoffrey, MB BCh Witw., FCP(SA) Stella and Paul Lowenstein Prof., Maternal and Child Health
Other Staff: 12 Lectrs.; 3 Hon. Lectrs.
Research: breastfeeding choices for HIV+ mothers; childhood cancers; nephrotic syndrome; tubercular meningitis and encephalopathy; vitamin A and transmission of HIV from mother to baby

Pathology, see also Chem. Pathol.

Tel: (031) 260 4228 Fax: (031) 252711
Chetty, Runjan, MB ChB Natal, DPhil Oxf., FRCPA Prof.; Head*
Chrystal, Vivien, BA S.Af., MB BCh Witw., FRCPath Sr. Lectr.
Other Staff: 4 Lectrs.; 3 Hon. Tutors
Vacant Posts: 1 Sr. Lectr.
Research: nephroblastomas; paediatric oncology; penile cancers

Physiology

Tel: (031) 260 4218 Fax: (031) 260 4455
Dutton, Michael F., BSc Salf., PhD Salf. Prof.; Head*
Mars, Maurice, MB ChB Cape Town Assoc. Prof.
Raidoo, Des M., BSC Durban-W., MB ChB Natal Sr. Lectr.
Other Staff: 3 Lectrs.
Research: aflatoxins; bradykinin receptors and human brain neurons; maize storage and health implications; mycotoxins; sports injuries and treatments

Biochemistry

Chuturgoon, Anil A., BSc Natal, MSc Natal, Sr. Lectr.
Other Staff: 1 Lectr.
Research: chemical herbicides and their effects on parasites; chemotherapeutic drugs and Wilm's tumours

Histology

McLean, Michelle, BSc *Natal*, PhD *Natal* Sr. Lectr.
Other Staff: 1 Lectr.
Vacant Posts: 1 Sr. Lectr.
Research: phytotoxic fungal metabolites

Plastic and Reconstructive Surgery

Tel: (031) 484311 Fax: (031) 461 3049
Madaree, Anil, MB ChB *Natal*, MMed *Natal*, FCS(SA) Prof.; Head*
Other Staff: 1 Lectr.; 2 Hon Lectrs.
Research: basal cell carcinomas; cleft lip nose deformities; skin graft donor dressings; transcranical doppler studies in craniosynostosis; wound healing

Psychiatry

Tel: (031) 260 4321 Fax: (031) 260 4322
Dunn, John A., MSc *Witw.*, MB BCh *Witw.*, MMed(Path) *Witw.*, MMed *Natal* Sr. Lectr.
Lasich, Angelo J., MB BCh *Witw.* Assoc. Prof.; Acting Head*
Nair, Margaret G., MB ChB *Natal*, MMed *Natal* Sr. Lectr.
Wessels, Wessel H. C., MB ChB *Pret.*, DM OFS Emer. Prof.
Other Staff: 8 Lectrs.; 5 Hon. Lectrs.
Vacant Posts: 1 Prof.
Research: Alzheimer's disease; cancer and psychiatric morbidity; marital rape

Medically Applied Psychology

Tel: (031) 260 4324 Fax: (031) 260 4325
Pillay, Anthony L., BA *Durban-W.*, MA *Durban-W.*, MSc *Natal* Sr. Lectr.
Pillay, Basil J., BA *Durban-W.*, MA *Durban-W.*, PhD *Natal* Sr. Lectr.
Schlebusch, Lourens, BA *S.Af.*, MA *Natal*, MMedSc *Natal*, PhD *Natal* Prof.; Head*
Other Staff: 14 Lectrs.; 2 Hon. Lectrs.; 1 Hon. Tutor
Research: cross-cultural health beliefs and primary health care; multiple personality disorder; psychological aspects of cancer; stress management; suicidal behaviour

Radiology

Tel: (031) 260 4301 Fax: (031) 260 4408
Corr, Peter D., MB ChB *Z'bwe.*, MMed *Cape Town* Prof.; Head*
Engelbrecht, Hercules E., MB ChB *Cape Town* Emer. Prof.
Gosling, Athol R., MB BCh *Witw.* Sr. Lectr.
Movson, Issy J., MB ChB *Pret.* Sr. Lectr.
Patel, Ahmed, MB ChB *Natal* Sr. Lectr.
Rubin, David L., MB BCh *Witw.* Sr. Lectr.
Other Staff: 9 Lectrs.; 3 Hon. Sr. Lectrs.; 1 Hon. Lectr.
Research: cerebrovascular diseases and AIDS; interventional radiology; musculoskeletal disease; ultrasound and contrast agents; vascular diseases

Radiotherapy and Oncology

Tel: (031) 322111 Fax: (031) 372962
Jordaan, Johann P., MB ChB *Stell.*, MMed *Stell.* Prof.; Head*
Other Staff: 1 Lectr.
Research: drug trials

Urology

Tel: (031) 260 4312 Fax: (031) 260 4410
Bereczky, Zoltan B., MB ChB *Cologne*, MMed *Cologne*, MMed *Witw.* Sr. Lectr.; Head*
Marszalek, Wlodzimierz W., MB ChB *Wroclaw*, MD Emer. Prof.
Other Staff: 1 Lectr.
Research: bladder cancer in various population groups; calculi; cancer of the prostate

Virology

Tel: (031) 260 4403 Fax: (031) 260 4441
Smith, Alan N., MB BCh *Witw.*, MSc *Sur.*, MMed *Witw.* Prof.; Head*
York, Denis F., BSc *Natal*, MSc *Natal*, PhD *Natal* Sr. Lectr.

Research: contagious lung cancer in sheep; HIV and AIDS; maedi visna virus; polymerase chain reaction testing of infants; retroviruses

SPECIAL CENTRES, ETC

Built Environment Support Group

Tel: (031) 260 2267 Fax: (031) 260 1236
Marx, Colin, BSocSc *Natal*, MTRP *Natal* Dir.*

Campbell Collections

Tel: (031) 207 3711 Fax: (031) 291622
Edwards, Iain, BA *Natal*, PhD *Natal* Prof.; Dir.*
Research: effect of climate on storage of archive materials

Economic Research Unit

Tel: (031) 260 2588 Fax: (031) 260 2587
Whiteside, Alan W., MA *E.Anglia* Assoc. Res. Prof.; Acting Dir.*
Other Staff: 1 Res. Fellow; 1 Res. Fellow
Research: impact of HIV/AIDS on developing countries; South Africa-EU free trade agreement and its impact on other countries of Southern African Customs Union; small business development

Environment, School for the

Tel: (031) 260 2416 Fax: (031) 260 1391
Garland, Gerald G., BA *Belf.*, MSc *I.T.C.Enschede*, PhD *Natal* Dir.*

Housing Programme

Tel: (031) 260 3271 Fax: (031) 260 1252
Adebayo, Ambrose A., MArch *Vienna*, DrTechn *Vienna* Dir.*
Other Staff: 1 Lectr.

Immunology, Natal Institute of

Tel: (031) 784311 Fax: (031) 708 5739
Bubb, Martin O., MSc(Agric) *Natal*, PhD *Natal* Dir., Immunochemistry
Conradie, Jan D., MSc *Pret.*, PhD *Natal* Dir., Natal Blood Transfusion Service
Fernandes-Costa, Francisco J. T. D., MB ChB *Witw.*, PhD *Witw.* Dir.*
Hammond, Michael G., BSc *S.Af.*, PhD *Natal* Dir., Transplantation

Industrial and Organisational Labour Studies, Centre for

Tel: (031) 260 1097 Fax: (031) 260 2347
Maré, P. Gerard, BA *Natal*, BA *Witw.*, PhD *Natal* Dir.*

Jazz and Popular Music, Centre for

Tel: (031) 260 3385 Fax: (031) 260 2085
Brubeck, Darius, BA *Wesleyan* Assoc. Prof.; Dir.*
Other Staff: 1 Lectr.

Medical Research Council (MRC)

Tel: (031) 251481 Fax: (031) 258840
Abdool-Karim, Salim S., MSc *Col.*, MMed *Natal* Dir.*
Jackson, Terry F. H. G., PhD *Natal* Hon. Prof.
Sharp, Brian L., PhD *Natal* Programme Leader
Research: amoebiaisis; community health; malaria; TB; trauma

Oceanographic Research Institute

Tel: (031) 373536 Fax: (031) 372132
de Freitas, Antonio J., MSc *Witw.*, PhD *Witw.* Dir.*
Research: coral reefs; environmental consultancies; fisheries (fish and invertebrates or bait organisms); fisheries catch statistics

Oral Studies, Centre for

Tel: (031) 260 3043 Fax: (031) 260 3033
Sienaert, Edgard R., MA *Ghent*, PhD *Witw.* Prof.; Dir.*
Research: English among non-mother tongue tertiary students; influence of oral culture;

spoken, written and gestural expression of learners

Plasma Physics Research Institute

Tel: (031) 261 2775 Fax: (031) 261 6550
Hellberg, Manfred A., BSc *Cape Town*, PhD *Camb.*, FRSSAf Prof.; Dir.*

Social and Development Studies, Centre for

Tel: (031) 260 2360 Fax: (031) 260 2359
Morris, Michael L., BA *Cape Town*, DPhil *Sus.* Assoc. Prof.; Dir.*
Padayachee, Vishnu, MCom *Durban-W.*, PhD *Natal* Res. Prof.
Research: capacity building in kwaZulu-Natal rural livelihoods; reconstruction and development issues in South Africa; violence and sustainable development; women and survival

Sugar Milling Research Institute

Tel: (031) 261 6882 Fax: (031) 261 6886
Purchase, Brian S., BScAgric *Natal*, PhD *Lond.* Dir.*
Research: climbing film evaporators; colour transfer during crystallisation; measurement of soil levels in sugarcane; molasses clarification; nutsch filtration

---

PIETERMARITZBURG CAMPUS

Accountancy

Tel: (0331) 260 5392 Fax: (0331) 260 5347
Cassimjee, Mohammed E., BCom *S.Af.* Sr. Lectr.
Lane, Walter T. F., BA *Natal*, BEd *Natal* Sr. Lectr.
Latiff, Omar A., BCom *Durban-W.*, BCompt *S.Af.* Sr. Lectr.
Stainbank, Lesley J., BA *Natal*, BCom *Natal*, MCom *Natal* Prof.; Head*
Stegen, Philip K., BCom *Natal* Sr. Lectr.
Stobie, Bruce S., BCom *Natal*, MAcct *Natal* Prof.
Vally, Imtiaz A. S., BAcc *Natal* Sr. Lectr.
Well, Michael J., BCom *Natal* Sr. Lectr.
Other Staff: 1 Lectr.
Vacant Posts: 1 Prof.
Research: cash value added statements; domestic pricing policy of listed South African industrial companies; employee reporting; transfer pricing theory

Adult Education, Centre for

Tel: (0331) 260 5070 Fax: (0331) 260 5756
Aitchison, John J. W., BA *Natal*, MA *Natal* Dir.*

Afrikaans en Nederlands

Tel: (0331) 260 5562 Fax: (0331) 260 5575
Jonckheere, Wilfrid F., LicFil *Ghent*, PhD *Rhodes* Prof.
van der Berg, Dietloff Z., BA *Stell.*, MA *Rhodes*, PhD *Natal* Assoc. Prof.; Acting Head*
Other Staff: 1 Lectr.

Agricultural Economics

Tel: (0331) 260 5493 Fax: (0331) 260 5970
Darroch, Mark A. G., BScAgric *Natal*, MScAgric *Natal* Sr. Lectr.
Lyne, Michael C., BScAgric *Natal*, MScAgric *Natal*, PhD *Natal* Assoc. Prof.
Nieuwoudt, W. Lieb, BSc(Agric) *Stell.*, MScAgric *Pret.*, MEcon *N.Carolina*, PhD *Natal* Prof.; Head*
Ortmann, Gerald F., BScAgric *Natal*, MScAgric *Natal*, PhD *Natal* Assoc. Prof.
Research: policy issues relating to commercial farming and rural development

Agricultural Engineering

Tel: (0331) 260 5490 Fax: (0331) 260 5818
Hansen, Alan C., MScEng *Natal*, PhD *Natal* Prof.

Lyne, Peter W. L., MScEng Natal, PhD
Natal Prof.; Head*
Schulze, Roland E., MSc Natal, PhD Natal Prof.
Other Staff: 1 Lectr.; 6 Res. Fellows
Vacant Posts: 1 Sr. Lectr.; 1 Lectr.
Research: ground water recession; haulage
vehicle simulation; hydrological impacts of
sugarcane; multi-media based tools for
engineering; optimisation of environment of
intensive animal housing

Agronomy

Tel: (0331) 260 5510 Fax: (0331) 260 5426
Cairns, Andrew L. P., BScAgric Stell., MScAgric
Stell., PhD Stell. South African Sugar Assocn.
Prof., Crop Science
Greenfield, Peter L., BScAgric Natal, MSc Wis.,
PhD Wis. Assoc. Prof.
Haynes, Richard J., BSc Cant., PhD Cant. Prof.,
Soil Science
Hughes, Jeffrey C., BSc Reading, MSc Qu., PhD
Reading Assoc. Prof.
Johnston, Michael A., BScAgric Natal, MScAgric
Natal, PhD Natal Sr. Lectr.
Savage, Michael J., BSc Natal, PhD Natal Prof.,
Agrometeorology; Head*
Other Staff: 2 Lectrs.; 1 Hon. Res. Assoc.
Research: environmental soil science;
hydrological catchment research; soil/plant/
atmosphere energy and water

Animal Science and Poultry Science

Tel: (0331) 260 5476 Fax: (0331) 260 5067
Ferguson, Neil S., MScAgric Sr. Lectr.
Gous, Robert M., BScAgric Natal, MScAgric
Natal, PhD Natal Prof.; Head*
Nsahlai, Ignatius, BSc Yaounde I, Maîrise Yaounde
, PhD Reading Sr. Lectr.
Other Staff: 2 Lectrs.
Research: effect of diet and temperature on
performance of broiler chickens; food intake
and laying performance in poultry

Applied Language Studies

Tel: (0331) 260 5498 Fax: (0331) 260 5575
Clarence-Fincham, Jennifer A., BA Natal Sr.
Lectr.
Wildsmith-Cromarty, Rosemary, MA Witw.,
PhD Lond. Prof.; Head*
Other Staff: 4 Lectrs.
Research: coherent writing at tertiary level;
effective communication for teaching and
learning

Biochemistry

Tel: (0331) 260 5467 Fax: (0331) 260 5462
Anderson, Trevor R., MScAgric Natal, PhD
Natal Sr. Lectr.
Coetzer, Theresa H. T., BSc Stell., MSc Stell.,
PhD Natal Sr. Lectr.
Dennison, Clive, BScAgric Natal, MScAgric
Natal, PhD Natal Prof.; Head*
Goldring, Dean, BSc Dund., DPhil Z'bwe.
Other Staff: 1 Lectr.
Vacant Posts: 1 Lectr.
Research: immunoglobulins; infectious bursal
disease virus; poultry pathogens; proteinases
and cancer; trypanosomal proteinases

Botany

Tel: (0331) 260 5130 Fax: (0331) 260 5897
Beckett, Richard P., PhD Brist. Sr. Lectr.
Cress, William A., PhD New Mexico State Sr.
Lectr.
Finnie, Jeff F., PhD Natal
Granger, J. Edward, PhD Natal Sr. Lectr.
Johnson, Steven D., PhD Cape Town
Smith, Michael T., PhD Natal Sr. Lectr.
van Staden, Hannes, MSc Stell., PhD Natal,
FRSSAf Prof.; Head*
Other Staff: 1 Lectr., 1 Hon. Lectr.
Research: indigenous plants in small-scale
farming; medicinal plants; plant molecular
biology; science management

Business Administration

Tel: (0331) 260 5390 Fax: (0331) 260 5219
Bbenkele, Edwin C., BA Zambia, PhD
Stir. Assoc. Prof.
de Waal, Duncan P., BA Rhodes, MBL S.Af. Sr.
Lectr.
McEwan, Thomas, BA S.Af., MBA Cran., PhD
Cran. Prof.; Head*
Ndu, Chiaku N., BSc Nigeria, MBA Nigeria, PhD
Nigeria Assoc. Prof.
Poulter, Michael, BCom Natal, BSc Natal, MSc
Natal Sr. Lectr.
van Uytrecht, Paul M., BIur S.Af., MBA Witw.,
LLM Natal
Other Staff: 1 Lectr.
Vacant Posts: 2 Sr. Lectrs.
Research: financing small business in developing
countries; managing the resources of local
governments in Africa

Chemistry and Chemical Technology

Tel: (0331) 260 5326 Fax: (0331) 260 5009
Field, John S., MSc Natal, PhD Camb. Prof.;
Head*
Haines, Raymond J., MSc Natal, PhD Lond.,
FRSSAf Prof., Inorganic Chemistry
Other Staff: 7 Lectrs.
Vacant Posts: 1 Prof.; 1 Lectr.; 1 Tutor
Research: carbamates and the chelating silicon
atom; chemical properties of tea;
coordination compounds; 'muti' plants
extraction; synthetic organic chemistry

Classics

Tel: (0331) 260 5557 Fax: (0331) 260 5575
Lambert, Michael, BA Natal, MA Natal Sr.
Lectr.
Packman, Zola M., BA Wash., PhD Yale Prof.
Pike, David L., BA Lond., BA Brist., MPhil
Lond. Assoc. Prof.; Head*
Tennant, Peter M. W., BA Natal, MA Natal Sr.
Lectr.
Research: early Roman religion and foundation
legends of the Roman state; Greek
mythology; Greek papyrology; Greek
religion and ritual; New Testament Greek

Computer Science and Information Systems

Tel: (0331) 260 5646 Fax: (0331) 260 5966
Clarke, Matthew C., BMath Newcastle(NSW),
MCogSc NSWUT, MSc Natal Sr. Lectr.
Dempster, Robert M., BSc Natal, BSc S.Af. Sr.
Lectr.
Petkov, Doncho, MSc Brno, PhD Sofia Sr. Lectr.
Ram, Vevek, BSc Durban-W., BEd Durban-W.,
MBA Durban-W., PhD Natal Assoc. Prof.
Velinov, Yiuriy, MSc Sofia, PhD Sofia Assoc.
Prof.
Warren, Peter R., BSc Natal, MSc Cape Town,
PhD Camb. Prof.; Head*
Other Staff: 1 Lectr.; 2 Tutors
Research: category theory; intelligent scheduling;
making logic; multi-criteria decision
making; systems thinking

Dietetics and Community Resources

Tel: (0331) 260 5428 Fax: (0331) 260 6270
Green, J. Mary-Ann, BScHomeEc Stell.,
BScHomeEcon Natal, PhD Oklahoma State Sr.
Lectr.
Maunder, Eleni M. W., BSc Lond., PhD
Lond. Prof.; Head*
Other Staff: 5 Lectrs.
Research: determinants of stunting; entry criteria
on training courses for women from low-
income families; household expenditure on
food; nutrition of schoolchildren; training in
housing in South Africa and community
needs for housing education

Drama Studies

Tel: (0331) 260 5550 Fax: (0331) 260 5593
Barnes, Hazel S., BA Natal, MA Lanc. Assoc.
Prof.
Kendall, Kathryn M., BA New Orleans, MA New
Orleans, PhD Texas Prof.; Head*

Other Staff: 3 Lectrs.
Research: folk culture and ceremony as drama

Economics

Tel: (0331) 260 5296 Fax: (0331) 260 5599
Banach, John A., MCom Rhodes Sr. Lectr.
Bromberger, Norman, BSc Cape Town, BA Cape
Town, BA Oxf., MA Essex Assoc. Prof.
Hickson, Michael M., BA Natal, BA S.Af., MA
Leeds Sr. Lectr.
Kusi, Newman K., BA Ghana, MSc Ghana,
PhD Assoc. Prof.
Mainardi, Stefan, MA Bocconi, MPhil
Inst.Soc.Stud.(The Hague), PhD Natal Assoc.
Prof.
McGrath, Michael D., BCom Natal, PhD
Natal Prof.; Head*
Oldham, George W., BCom Natal, MSc
Stir. Sr. Lectr.
Other Staff: 4 Lectrs.
Research: exchange rate reform; food security in
developing countries; public finance; role of
the economy in modernisation in South
Africa; taxes and government expenditure

Education, School of

Tel: (0331) 260 5248 Fax: (0331) 260 5080
Harley, Ken L., BEd Natal, MEd Natal, PhD
Natal Prof.
Kaabwe, M. E. Stella, BA(Educn) Zambia, MEd
Regina, EdD N.Y.State Sr. Lectr.
Knox, David A., BSc St And., MSc Durh., MEd
Lond. Sr. Lectr.
Ndhlovu, D. Themba, BA Fort Hare, BEd Natal,
MEd Natal
Parker, Ben P., BA Rhodes, MA Rhodes, PhD
Natal Prof.; Acting Head*
Other Staff: 3 Lectrs.; 1 Sr. Tutor
Research: distance education; leadership and
gender: the experience of women principals;
models of whole school development;
school management; social relations and
identity in secondary schools

Educational Psychology

Tel: (0331) 260 5360 Fax: (0331) 260 5363
Adams, Harvey B., BEd Lond., MEd Lond. Prof.;
Head*
Farman, Robin H., BPhil Birm., MEd Birm. Sr.
Lectr.
Schoeman, Rose, BA Natal, MA Natal, PhD
OFS Sr. Lectr.; Dir., Child and Family
Centre
Other Staff: 3 Lectrs.
Research: adult children of alcoholics; attitudes
of nurses towards AIDS and patient care;
family support systems and AIDS; secondary
traumatisation and coping mechanisms
among trauma counsellors

English

Tel: (0331) 260 5300 Fax: (0331) 260 6213
Attwell, David I. D., BA Natal, MA Cape Town,
PhD Texas Prof.
Beale, Donald A., BA Durh., PhD Natal Assoc.
Prof.
Bizley, William H., BA Natal, MPhil York(UK),
PhD Natal Sr. Lectr.
Gunner, Elizabeth, BA Natal, MA Kent, PhD
Lond. Prof.
Hugo, Francois J., BA Natal, PhD Natal Sr.
Lectr.
van der Hoven, Anton, BA Natal, BA Cape Town,
PhD Northwestern Sr. Lectr.; Head*
Research: South African literature, particularly J.
M. Coetzee

Entomology, see Zool. and Entomol.

Fine Art and History of Art

Tel: (0331) 260 5170 Fax: (0331) 260 5599
Armstrong, Juliet, BAFA Natal, MAFA Natal Sr.
Lectr.
Calder, Ian M. S., BAFA Natal, MAFA Natal Sr.
Lectr.
Davies, Roger H. D., BAFA Natal Sr. Lectr.
King, Terence H., BAFA Witw., MAFA
Witw. Prof.; Head*

Other Staff: 3 Lectrs.
Research: art of kwaZulu-Natal; kwaZulu-Natal artists and craftspeople; Mary Stainbank's sculpture; production and reception of photography in South Africa; revival of the use of isishweshwe (indigo dried cloth)

French

Tel: (0331) 260 5541 Fax: (0331) 260 5575

Beckett, Carole M., BEd Natal, MA Natal   Sr. Lectr.
Ménager, Serge D., MA Clermont-Ferrand, PhD Natal   Prof.; Acting Head*
Other Staff: 1 Lectr.
Research: Maghrebin French Literature; poetry of the Commores; translations

Genetics

Tel: (0331) 260 5435 Fax: (0331) 260 5435

Gevers, Hans O., BScAgric Natal, MScAgric Stell., PhD Natal   Hon. Prof.
Hastings, John W., BSc Witw., MSc Pret., PhD Alta.   Prof.; Head*
Hohls, Trevor, BScAgric Natal, PhD Natal
Meyer, Edvard H. H., MSc(Agric) Pret., DSc(Agric) Pret.   Prof.
Shanahan, Paul E., BScAgric Natal, PhD Natal
Research: diagnostic DNC typing of DUMPS carriers in Holstein-Freisian cattle; genetic origin and control of bacteriocins from Leuconostos; quantitative inheritance of eldana borer resistance in sugarcane; quantitative genetics

Geography

Tel: (0331) 260 5341 Fax: (0331) 260 5344

Beckedahl, Heinz R., MSc Witw., PhD Natal   Sr. Lectr.
McGee, Owen S., BSc Natal, MSc Wis., PhD Natal   Assoc. Prof.; Acting Head*
Slade, D. Graeme B., BSc Cape Town, PhD Liv.   Assoc. Prof.
Other Staff: 2 Lectrs.
Research: air pollution; community based nutrition surveillance; debris deposits in the high Drakensberg; geographical information systems; waterfront developments

Geology

Tel: (0331) 260 5667 Fax: (0331) 260 5599

von Brunn, Victor, BA Natal, BSc Cape Town, MSc Cape Town, PhD Cape Town   Assoc. Prof.
Other Staff: 1 Lectr.
Research: sedimentology with particular emphasis on ancient glaciation in kwaZulu-Natal

German

Tel: (0331) 260 5548 Fax: (0331) 260 5575

Fourie, Regine B. J., BA Natal, MA Natal, PhD Witw.   Sr. Lectr.
Lyttle, Gerlind, MA Natal   Lectr.; Acting Head*
Sandner, Karl, MA Vienna, DrPhil Vienna   Sr. Lectr.
Research: ethnic and religious conflicts; pragmatist theory and its application in literary teaching and feminism; translation and equivalence principles

Historical Studies

Tel: (0331) 260 5290 Fax: (0331) 260 5012

Benyon, John A., BA Rhodes, MA Oxf., DPhil Oxf., DLitt&Phil S.Af.   Prof.
Edgecombe, D. Ruth, MA Rhodes, PhD Camb.   Assoc. Prof.
Gravil, Roger, BA Nott., MSc Lond., PhD CNAA   Prof.
Guest, William R., MA Natal, PhD Natal   Prof.
Laband, John P. C., MA Camb., MA Natal, PhD Natal   Prof.; Head*
Nuttall, Timothy A., BA Natal, DPhil Oxf.   Sr. Lectr.
Thompson, Paul S., BA Virginia, MA Virginia, PhD Virginia   Assoc. Prof.
Wright, John B., MA Natal, PhD Witw.   Assoc. Prof.

Research: black urban politics; kwaZulu/Natal history: wars, politics and rediscovering the oral history of the Zulu people

Horticultural Science

Tel: (0331) 260 5444 Fax: (0331) 260 5073

Cowan, A. Keith, BSc Rhodes, PhD Rhodes   Prof.
Wolstenholme, B. Nigel, BScAgric Natal, PhD Natal   Prof.; Head*
Other Staff: 1 Lectr.; 1 Hon. Res. Assoc.
Vacant Posts: 1 Lectr.
Research: crops of sub-tropical environment; post-harvest physiology

Information Studies

Tel: (0331) 260 5007 Fax: (0331) 260 5092

Kaniki, Andrew M., BA(LibStudies) Zambia, MS Ill., PhD Pitt.   Prof.; Head*
Radebe, Thuli, BBibl Zululand, BBibl Natal, MIS Natal   Sr. Lectr.
Stilwell, Christine, BA Natal, MIS Natal, PhD Natal   Sr. Lectr.
Other Staff: 2 Lectrs.
Research: development of school libraries in kwaZulu-Natal; relevance of popular English fiction to black adult readers

Law, School of

Tel: (0331) 260 5778 Fax: (0331) 260 5014

Burchell, Jonathan M., BA Natal, LLB Natal, LLM Camb., PhD Witw.   Prof.
Cowling, Michael G., BA Rhodes, LLB Natal, LLM Camb., MPhil Camb.   Assoc. Prof.
Grant, Brenda, BA Natal, LLB Natal, LLM Natal   Sr. Lectr.
Jagwanth, Saras, BA Natal, LLB Natal, LLM Natal   Sr. Lectr.
Kidd, Michael A., BCom Natal, LLB Natal   Sr. Lectr.
Lund, James R., BA Natal, LLB Natal   Prof.
Lupton, Michael L., BA OFS, LLB OFS, PhD Natal   Prof.
Milton, John R. L., BA Natal, LLM Natal, PhD Natal   James Scott Wylie Prof.; Dir.*
Mitchell, Kevin I., BCom Natal, BCom Cape Town   Hon. Prof.
Schwikkard, Pamela J., BA Witw., LLB Natal   Sr. Lectr.
Sharrock, Robert D., BA Natal, LLB Natal   Prof.
Williams, Robert C., BA Cape Town, LLB Cape Town, LLM Lond., PhD Macq.   Assoc. Prof.
Other Staff: 3 Lectrs.
Research: contract law; criminal law and criminal justice; environmental law; gender law; genetics/medical law

Legal Advice Centre

Tel: (0331) 260 5690 Fax: (0331) 260 5014

Pennefather, Rob C., BA Rhodes, BCom Rhodes, LLB Natal   Dir.*

Mathematics and Applied Mathematics

Tel: (0331) 260 5647 Fax: (0331) 260 5648

Hearne, John W., BSc Cape Town, MSc Pret., DSc Pret.   Assoc. Prof.
Henning, Michael A., BSc Natal, PhD Natal   Assoc. Prof.
Moori, Jamshid, BSc Meshed, MSc Birm., PhD Birm.   Prof.; Head*
Ng, Siu-Ah, BA Wis., MA Wis., PhD Wis.   Sr. Lectr.
Swart, Johan, BSc Witw., MSc Witw., PhD S.Af.   Prof.
Uys, Pieter W., PhD Natal   Sr. Lectr.
van den Berg, John E., MSc Natal, PhD Natal   Sr. Lectr.
Zaverdinos, Constantin, BA Natal, BSc Rhodes, BSc Witw., MSc Natal, PhD Natal   Sr. Lectr.
Other Staff: 1 Lectr.; 5 Tutors
Research: combinatorics; ecological modelling; evolutionary game theory; finite groups and finite geometrics; general topology

Microbiology and Plant Pathology

Tel: (0331) 260 5525 Fax: (0331) 260 5919

da Graca, John V., MScAgric Natal, PhD Natal   Assoc. Prof.
Howgrave-Graham, Alan R., MSc Pret., PhD Natal   Sr. Lectr.

Laing, Mark D., BSc Natal, PhD Natal
Rijkenberg, Frits H. J., MScAgric Natal, PhD Natal   Prof.
Senior, Eric, BSc Liv., PhD Kent   Prof.
Wallis, F. Michael, MScAgric Natal, PhD Natal   Prof.; Head*
Research: cabbage chocolate spot disease; characterising citrus viruses; co-disposal of toxic substances in landfill sites; EM of plant/rust fungus interaction; microbiological aspects of environmental problems such as bioremediation of oil and creosote contaminated soil

Philosophy

Tel: (0331) 260 5582 Fax: (0331) 260 5575

Beck, Simon M., BA Rhodes, MA Rhodes, PhD Cape Town   Sr. Lectr.; Acting Head*
Other Staff: 2 Lectrs.
Vacant Posts: 1 Prof.

Physics

Tel: (0331) 260 5329 Fax: (0331) 260 5876

Chetty, Nithayanathan, BSc Natal, MS Ill., PhD Ill.   Sr. Lectr.
de Lange, Owen L., BSc Witw., MSc Witw., PhD Clarkson   Prof.
Graham, Clive, BSc Natal, MSc Natal, PhD Natal, PhD Camb.   Prof.; Head*
Ilchev, Assen S., BSc Sofia, MSc Sofia, PhD Sofia   Sr. Lectr.
Pierrus, John, BSc Natal, MSc Witw., PhD Natal   Sr. Lectr.
Raab, Roger E., BSc Natal, DPhil Oxf.   Prof.
Other Staff: 1 Lectr.; 2 Tutors
Vacant Posts: 1 Lectr.
Research: diffusion of oxygen in high-Tc superconductors; lattice gauge theories; operator methods in quantum mechanics; optical physics; oscillations in confined gases

Political Studies

Tel: (0331) 260 5007 Fax: (0331) 260 5599

Lawrence, Ralph B., BA Natal, MA Cape Town, MPhil Lond.   Prof.; Head*
Uzodiki, Nwabufo I., BA Wake Forest, MA S.Carolina, PhD N.Carolina   Sr. Lectr.
Other Staff: 2 Lectrs.
Research: censorship in South Africa; educating adolescents about AIDS; elites and democracy; ethical responsibilities of management

Psychology

Tel: (0331) 260 5853 Fax: (0331) 260 5809

Basson, Clive J., BEd S.Af., MA Natal   Assoc. Prof.
Griessel, Raoul D., BA S.Af., MA Natal, PhD Witw.   Assoc. Prof.
Killian, Beverly J., BSc Cape Town, MSc Cape Town   Sr. Lectr.
Lachenicht, Lance G., BA Cape Town, BSc Cape Town, BSc Witw., PhD Witw.   Assoc. Prof.
Lindegger, Graham C., BA S.Af., BA MA PhD   Assoc. Prof.
Richter, Linda, PhD Natal   Prof.; Head*
Wassenaar, Douglas R., BA Natal, MA Natal   Sr. Lectr.
Research: child molestation; chronic fatigue syndrome; cross-cultural attitudes to food and eating; sexual harassment

Range and Forage Resources

Tel: (0331) 260 5505 Fax: (0331) 260 5708

Klug, John R., MScAgric Natal   Sr. Lectr.
O'Connor, Tim G., MSc Z'bwe., PhD Witw.   Prof.; Head*
Zacharias, Peter J. K., MScAgric Natal, DSc Fort Hare   Prof.
Other Staff: 1 Lectr.; 1 Hon. Lectr.; 1 Hon. Res. Assoc.
Vacant Posts: 1 Lectr.
Research: management of planted pastures; rehabilitation of degraded rangeland; sustainable and efficient utilisation of southern African rangeland by domestic and indigenous herbivores; wildlife conservation

Religious Studies

Tel: (0331) 260 5573 Fax: (0331) 260 5575

Maxwell, Patrick S., BA Natal, MA Oxf.   Sr. Lectr.; Acting Head*

Nicolson, Ronald B., BA Natal, PhD Natal   Prof.

Prozesky, Martin H., BA Rhodes, MA Oxf., DPhil Rhodesia   Prof.

Research: conceptual creativity; constitutional place of religion in South Africa; religious resources (particularly Buddhism) in information networking; the church and AIDS

Sociology

Tel: (0331) 260 5320 Fax: (0331) 260 5972

Burton, Simon I. R., BSocSc Cape Town, BA Cape Town, MSocSc Natal   Sr. Lectr.; Head*

Marcus, Tessa S., BSc(Econ) Lond., MSocSc Lodz, PhD Lodz   Assoc. Prof.

Stopforth, Peter, BSocSc Rhodes   Prof.

Other Staff: 1 Lectr.; 1 Tutor

Research: communication and development issues; land and agricultural issues; population and demography

Statistics and Biometry

Tel: (0331) 260 5608 Fax: (0331) 260 5648

Clarke, G. Peter, BScAgric Natal, PhD Lond.   Prof.; Head*

Dicks, Harvey M., BScAgric Natal   Sr. Lectr.

Haines, Linda M., BSc Natal, MA Camb., MPhil Lond., PhD S.Af.   Assoc. Prof.

Other Staff: 1 Lectr.; 1 Tutor

Vacant Posts: 2 Lectrs.

Research: design of malaria drug trials; image processing in medicine; neural networks; quantitative genetics

Theology, School of

Tel: (0331) 260 5540 Fax: (0331) 260 5858

Denis, Philippe M. B. R., LicHist Liège, DLitt&Phil Liège   Assoc. Prof.

Draper, Jonathan A., BA Durh., BD Rhodes, PhD Camb.   Prof.

Nurnberger, Klaus B., BScAgric Pret., DrTheol Marburg, DTh S.Af.   Prof.

Richardson, R. Neville, BA Natal, BD Rhodes, MPhil Oxf., PhD Natal   Assoc. Prof.; Head*

West, Gerald O., BA Natal, BD Rhodes, MA Sheff., PhD Sheff.   Assoc. Prof.

Wittenberg, Gunther, BA Natal, CandTheol Kiel, CandMin Hanover, PhD Natal, DTh Tübingen   Emer. Prof.

Other Staff: 5 Lectrs.

Research: contextual theology; memories of the growth of the indigenous church in Southern Africa; oral historiography

Zoology and Entomology

Tel: (0331) 260 5104 Fax: (0331) 260 5105

Akhurst, E. G. John, BSc Natal, BEd Natal, PhD Natal   Assoc. Prof.; Acting Head*

Brothers, Denis J., BSc Rhodes, PhD Kansas   Prof.

Hart, Robert C., BSc Natal, PhD Rhodes, DSc Natal   Prof.

Lawes, Michael J., BSc Natal, PhD Natal   Sr. Lectr.

Lovegrove, Barry G., BSc Cape Town, PhD Cape Town   Sr. Lectr.

Miller, Ray M., BSc Ohio, MA Ohio, PhD Iowa   Sr. Lectr.

Perrin, Michael R., BSc Lond., PhD, FLS   Prof.

Piper, Steven E., BSc Natal, MSc Witw., PhD Natal

Samways, Michael J., BSc Nott., PhD Lond.   Prof.

Other Staff: 3 Lectrs.; 1 Tutor; 1 Hon. Lectr.

Research: African parrot conservation; invertebrate conservation; nectar-feeding in birds; physiology of small mammals; population dynamics of plankton

Zulu

Tel: (0331) 260 5539 Fax: (0331) 260 5575

Davey, Antony S., BA Witw., MA S.Af., MLitt Edin., DLitt&Phil S.Af.   Prof.

Hlengwa, Msawakhe A., BA Zululand, BEd Zululand, BA Natal   Sr. Lectr.; Head*

Koopman, Adrian, BA Natal, MA Natal   Assoc. Prof.

Other Staff: 1 Lectr.; 1 Tutor

Research: modern trends in language change; onomastics; tone; Zulu medicinal terms

SPECIAL CENTRES, ETC

Commercial Forestry Research, Institute for

Tel: (0331) 62314 Fax: (0331) 68905

Roberts, Peter J. T., MSc Rhodes, PhD Rhodes   Dir.*

Research: aerial spraying of insecticides; flowering and pollination studies; fungal disease of pines

Natural Resources, Institute of

Tel: (0331) 460796 Fax: (0331) 460895

Breen, Charles M., MSc Rhodes, PhD Rhodes   Dir.*

Erskine, John M., BSc Liv., PhD Lond.   Assoc. Prof.

Rugege, Denis, BSc NUL   Res. Fellow; Dir.*

Research: integrated development processes; natural resource management; rural enterprise development; rural settlement planning; small-scale farmer training and sustainable agriculture

Rural Community Development, School of

Tel: (0331) 260 5585 Fax: (0331) 260 5495

Vacant Posts: Dir.*

Water Research, Computing Centre for

Tel: (0331) 260 5178 Fax: (0331) 61896

Dent, Mark C., BScEng Natal, MScEng Natal, PhD Natal   Dir.*

Research: integrated catchment management: equity and sustainability

CONTACT OFFICERS

Academic affairs. Acting Director, Student Academic Affairs (Durban Campus): Machi, Sisana, BAdmin Zululand, BAdmin S.Af.

Academic affairs. Director, Student Academic Affairs (Pietermaritzburg Campus): Winterbach, L. J. Vic., BA S.Af.

Accommodation. Director, Student Accommodation (Durban Campus): Jansen, Douglas, BA W.Cape

Admissions (first degree). Acting Director, Student Academic Affairs (Durban Campus): Machi, Sisana, BAdmin Zululand, BAdmin S.Af.

Admissions (first degree). Director, Student Academic Affairs (Pietermaritzburg Campus): Winterbach, L. J. Vic., BA S.Af.

Admissions (higher degree). Acting Director, Student Academic Affairs (Durban Campus): Machi, Sisana, BAdmin Zululand, BAdmin S.Af.

Admissions (higher degree). Director, Student Academic Affairs (Pietermaritzburg Campus): Winterbach, L. J. Vic., BA S.Af.

Adult/continuing education. Director, Adult Education (Durban Campus): von Kotze, A. Erika, BA Witw., PhD Witw.

Adult/continuing education. Director, Adult Education (Pietermaritzburg Campus): Aitchison, John J. W.

Alumni. Alumni Officer: Eathorne, Claire

Alumni. Alumni Officer: Wheatley, Robynne

Archives. University Archivist (Pietermaritzburg Campus): ......

Careers. Director, Student Counselling (Durban Campus): Rajab, Devi R., BA S.Af., MSc Kansas, PhD Missouri

Careers. Director, Student Counselling (Pietermaritzburg Campus): Braine, Julia D., BA Natal, MEd Natal

Computing services. Director (Durban Campus): Gibbon, Rodney W., BSc S.Af.

Computing services. Director (Pietermaritzburg Campus): Wallis, David L., BScAgric Natal, BSc S.Af.

Consultancy services. Acting Director, University of Natal Education and Innovation Foundation (Durban Campus): Senior, Eric, BSc Liv., PhD Kent

Credit transfer. Director, Student Academic Affairs (Pietermaritzburg Campus): Winterbach, L. J. Vic., BA S.Af.

Credit transfer. Acting Director, Student Academic Affairs (Durban Campus): Machi, Sisana, BAdmin Zululand, BAdmin S.Af.

Development/fund-raising. Director, Communication and Publicity: Saunderson-Meyer, William J., MSc Oxf.

Distance education. Bulman, Fiona, MEd Natal

Equal opportunities. Ngara, Prof. Emmanuel A., BA Rhodesia, MPhil Lond., PhD Lond.

Estates and buildings/works and services. Director, Administration (Durban Campus): Fraser, Graham, MBL S.Af.

Estates and buildings/works and services. Director, Administration (Pietermaritzburg Campus): Critien, John

Examinations. Examinations Officer (Durban Campus): Parker-Weekes, Barbara

Examinations. Examinations Officer (Pietermaritzburg Campus): Naidoo, Sandra

Finance. Finance Officer: Leonard, Anthony

General enquiries. Registrar and Secretary of Council: Trotter, Prof. George J., BA Natal, MA Duke

Health services. Director, Student Counselling (Durban Campus): Rajab, Devi R., BA S.Af., MSc Kansas, PhD Missouri

Health services. Director, Student Counselling (Pietermaritzburg Campus): Braine, Julia D., BA Natal, MEd Natal

Industrial liaison. Industrial Relations and Labour Law Adviser (Durban Campus): Finden, Paul F., BSocSc Natal, LLB Natal

International office. Deputy Registrar (Academic): Kishun, Roshen, BA Durban-W., MA Durban-W., PhD S.Calif.

Library (chief librarian). University Librarian (Durban Campus): Haffajee, G. H., BBibl S.Af., BBibl Durban-W., MBibl Natal

Library (chief librarian). University Librarian (Pietermaritzburg Campus): Merrett, Christopher E., BA Oxf., MALib Sheff., MA Natal

Library (enquiries). University Librarian (Pietermaritzburg Campus): Merrett, Christopher E., BA Oxf., MALib Sheff., MA Natal

Library (enquiries). Deputy University Librarian (Durban Campus): Buchanan, Nora, BA Natal, BBibl Natal

Minorities/disadvantaged groups. Director, Student Counselling (Durban Campus): Rajab, Devi R., BA S.Af., MSc Kansas, PhD Missouri

Personnel/human resources. Director, Human Resources (Durban Campus): De Klerk, Willem A.

Personnel/human resources. Director, Human Resources (Pietermaritzburg Campus): Binnendyk, Case J., BA Cape Town

Public relations, information and marketing. Director, Communication and Publicity: Saunderson-Meyer, William J., MSc Oxf.

Publications. Publisher (Durban Campus): ......

Purchasing. Chief Buying Officer (Durban Campus): Lamprecht, Nelis

Purchasing. Principal Buying Officer (Pietermaritzburg Campus): Eglington, Graham R.

Quality assurance and accreditation. Maughan Brown, Prof. David A., BA Cape Town, MA Camb., DPhil Sus.

Research. Deputy Vice-Chancellor (Research and Development): Preston-Whyte, Prof. Eleanor M., BSocSc Natal, PhD Natal

Safety. Director, Campus Affairs (Durban Campus): Trinder, James, BA Natal

Safety. Director, Administration (Pietermaritzburg Campus): Beaven, David M., FCIS

Scholarships, awards, loans. Bursary Officer (Financial Aid): Morrison, Richard C., BA Natal, BA S.Af.

Schools liaison. Director, Student Counselling (Pietermaritzburg Campus): Braine, Julia D., BA Natal, MEd Natal

Schools liaison (Durban Campus). Dumsford, Julie

Security. Director, Campus Affairs (Durban Campus): Trinder, James, BA Natal

Security. Director, Administration (Pietermaritzburg Campus): Critien, John

Sport and recreation. Head, Sports Administration (Durban Campus): Holm, C. R. Poenie, BA Stell.

Sport and recreation. Head, Sports Administration (Pietermaritzburg Campus): Edmondson, David C., BA Natal

Staff development and training. Co-ordinator, Staff Training and Development (Durban Campus): Tyrrell, Ralph W., BSocSc Natal, BA Natal

Staff development and training. Manager, Staff Training and Development (Pietermaritzburg Campus): Price, Lil, BA Natal

Student union. Pro Vice-Principal (Students): Zulu, Prof. Paulus M., BA Natal, PhD Natal

Student welfare/counselling. Acting Dean of Student Services (Durban Campus): Rajab, Devi R., BA S.Af., MSc Kansas, PhD Missouri

Student welfare/counselling. Dean of Student Services (Pietermaritzburg Campus): Wills, Trevor, BA Natal, MA Natal

Students from other countries. Deputy Registrar (Academic) and Director, International Office: Kishun, Roshen, BA Durban-W., MA Durban-W., PhD S.Calif.

Students with disabilities. Student Counselling (Durban Campus): Nursoo, Navin, BA Durban-W., MEd Natal

Students with disabilities. Director, Student Counselling (Pietermaritzburg Campus): Braine, Julia D., BA Natal, MEd Natal

University press. Publisher (Durban Campus): ......

Women. Co-ordinator of Gender Studies: Posel, Ros, PhD Natal

[Information supplied by the institution as at 16 March 1998, and edited by the ACU]

UNIVERSITY OF THE NORTH

Established 1959

Member of the Association of Commonwealth Universities

Postal Address: Private Bag X1106, Sovenga, 0727 South Africa
Telephone: (015) 268 2121, 268 9111 **Fax**: (015) 267 0154, 267 0485

CHANCELLOR—The President of the Republic of South Africa
VICE-CHANCELLOR AND PRINCIPAL*—......
DEPUTY VICE-CHANCELLOR (TEACHING AND RESEARCH)—Mashego, Prof. S. N.
CHAIRPERSON OF COUNCIL—Phaswana, Rev. N. P.
UNIVERSITY REGISTRAR (ACTING)—Malgas, M. P.
UNIVERSITY LIBRARIAN—Tsebe, J. K.

GENERAL INFORMATION

History. University College of the North was established in 1959 under the academic trusteeship of the University of South Africa. In 1970 it gained university status and became known under its present name.

Admission to first degree courses (see also South African Introduction). South African Matriculation Certificate or a certificate of exemption.

First Degrees. (* = also available with honours). BA*, BA(SW)*, BA(Th), BAdmin*, BAgric*, BAgric(Ed), BBibl*, BBibl(Ed), BCom*, BCom(Ed), BCurIA, BIur, BNutr, BOptom, BPharm, BProc, BR, BSc*, BSc(Agric)*, BSc(Ed), BSc(MS).
Most courses last 4 years. BA, BAdmin, BAgric, BA(TH), BCom, BCurIA, BIur, BSc,: 3 years; honours degree: 1 year after pass degree.

Higher Degrees. BD, BEd, LLB.
Applicants should hold a relevant honours degree or equivalent.
BEd: 1 year; LLB: 2 years; BD: 3 years.

Academic Year. 25 January–31 March; 7 April–2 July; 26 July–3 December.

FACULTIES/SCHOOLS

Agriculture
Tel: (015) 268 2371 Fax: (015) 268 2892
Dean: Machethe, C. L.
Secretary: Burger, V.

Arts
Tel: (015) 268 2613 Fax: (015) 268 2868
Acting Dean: Mashamaite, K. J.
Secretary: Mabotja, C.

Education
Tel: (015) 268 2415 Fax: (015) 268 2965
Dean: Rampedi, M. A.
Secretary: Jansen, R.

Health Sciences
Tel: (015) 268 2352 Fax: (015) 268 2865
Dean: Sheni, Prof. D. D.
Secretary: Oelofse, J.

Law
Tel: (015) 268 2686 Fax: (015) 268 2897
Dean: Breed, Prof. P. F.
Secretary: Letsoalo, M. M.

Management Sciences
Tel: (015) 268 2685 Fax: (015) 268 3511
Dean: Franks, Prof. P. E.
Secretary: Choma, C.

Mathematics and Natural Sciences
Tel: (015) 268 2142 Fax: (015) 268 2893
Dean: Sibara, Prof. M. M.
Secretary: Mogano, L.

Theology
Tel: (015) 268 2683 Fax: (015) 268 2866
Dean: Dolamo, Prof. R. T. H.
Secretary: Herholt, B.

ACADEMIC UNITS

Accounting and Auditing
Tel: (015) 268 2630 Fax: (015) 236 3511
van Schalkwyk, Prof. N. J.   Head*

African Law
Tel: (015) 268 2912 Fax: (015) 268 2897
Cloete, Prof. P. H.   Head*

Afrikaans
Tel: (015) 268 2244 Fax: (015) 268 2868
Terblanche, Prof. C. J. J.   Head*

Agricultural Economics
Tel: (015) 268 2373 Fax: (015) 268 2892
Hedden-Dankhorst, B.   Head*

Agricultural Extension
Tel: (015) 268 2192 Fax: (015) 268 2892
Molau, Prof. N. M.   Head*

Animal Production
Tel: (015) 268 2376 Fax: (015) 268 2892
Pretorius, M.   Head*

Anthropology
Tel: (015) 268 2181 Fax: (015) 268 2868
Malan, Prof. J. S.   Acting Head*

Applied Mathematics
Tel: (015) 268 2459 Fax: (015) 268 2893
Malaza, Prof. E. D.   Head*

Aquaculture Research Unit
Tel: (015) 268 2151 Fax: (015) 268 2893
Prinsloo, Prof. J. F.   Head*

Biblical Science
Tel: (015) 268 2229 Fax: (015) 268 2866
Ramashapa, Rev. J. M.   Head*

Biochemistry
Tel: (015) 268 2313 Fax: (015) 268 2893
Abotsi, E. K.   Acting Head*

Biology, see Zool. and Biol.

Botany
Tel: (015) 268 2933 Fax: (015) 268 2893
Wessels, Prof. D. C. J.   Acting Head*

Business Management
Tel: (015) 268 2646 Fax: (015) 268 3511
van Niekerk, Prof. J. T.   Head*

Chemistry, see also Pharmaceut. Chem.
Tel: (015) 268 2194 Fax: (015) 268 2893
Darkwa, Prof. J.   Head*

Classical Languages
Tel: (015) 268 2582 Fax: (015) 268 2868
Saayman, Prof. F.   Head*

Comparative Education
Tel: (015) 268 2934 Fax: (015) 268 2965
Mocke, Prof. E. J.   Head*

Computer Science
Tel: (015) 268 2627 Fax: (015) 268 2893
Oosthuizen, Prof. H. J.   Head*

Criminal Law and Procedure
Tel: (015) 268 2811 Fax: (015) 268 2897
Thoka, A. T.   Head*

Criminology
Tel: (015) 268 3348 Fax: (015) 268 2868
Moolman, Prof. C. J.   Head*

Development Studies
Tel: (015) 268 2424 Fax: (015) 268 3511
de Villiers, Prof. A.   Head*

Didactics
Tel: (015) 268 2928 Fax: (015) 268 2965
Temane, M.   Acting Head*

Economics, see also Agric. Econ.
Tel: (015) 268 2643 Fax: (015) 268 3511
Meyer, W. N.   Acting Head*

Education, see Compar. Educn., Educnl.
Practice, Hist. of Educn., Philos. of Educn.,
and Psychol. of Educn.

Educational Practice
Tel: (015) 268 2967 Fax: (015) 268 2965
Mosimege, Prof. M. D.   Head*

English
Tel: (015) 268 2573 Fax: (015) 268 2868
Roscoe, Prof. A. A.   Head*

French
Tel: (015) 268 2257 Fax: (015) 268 2868
Mathebula, P. N.   Head*

General Linguistics and Literary Studies
Tel: (015) 268 3083 Fax: (015) 268 2868
Mmusi, S. O.   Acting Head*

Geography
Tel: (015) 268 2323 Fax: (015) 268 2868
Olivier, Prof. J.   Acting Head*

German
Tel: (015) 268 2750 Fax: (015) 268 2868
Gottwald, Prof. J. G.   Acting Head*

History
Tel: (015) 268 2250 Fax: (015) 268 2868
Pretorius, Prof. J. G.   Head*

History of Education
Tel: (015) 268 2961 Fax: (015) 268 2965
Mminele, Prof. S. P. P.   Head*

Industrial Psychology
Tel: (015) 268 2709 Fax: (015) 268 3511
Tladi, W. S.   Head*

Information Studies
Tel: (015) 268 3194 Fax: (015) 268 2868
Ralebipi, Prof. M. D.   Head*

Jurisprudence
Tel: (015) 268 2904 Fax: (015) 268 2897
Rossouw, D. H.   Head*

Kinesiology and Physical Education
Tel: (015) 268 2392 Fax: (015) 268 2965
Britz, S.   Head*

Language Methodology
Tel: (015) 268 2349 Fax: (015) 268 2965
Maibelo, J. K.   Head*

Law, see African Law, Criminal Law and
Procedure, Jurisprudence, Mercantile Law,
Private Law, and Public Law

Library and Information Science, see also
Information Studies
Ralebipi, Prof. R. D.   Head*

Linguistics, see Gen. Linguistics and Literary
Studies

Literary Studies, see Gen. Linguistics and
Literary Studies

Mathematical Statistics
Tel: (015) 268 2787 Fax: (015) 268 2893
Mashike, Prof. S. R.   Head*

Mathematics, see also Appl. Maths.
Tel: (015) 268 2787 Fax: (015) 268 2893
Mashike, Prof. S. P.   Head*

Medical Sciences
Tel: (015) 268 2277 Fax: (015) 268 2865
Venter, Prof. P. A.   Head*

Mercantile Law
Tel: (015) 268 2901 Fax: (015) 268 2897
Letsoalo, R.   Head*

Microbiology
Tel: (015) 268 2862 Fax: (015) 268 2893
Myburgh, J.   Head*

Missiology, see Religion, Sci. of, and Missiol.

Nursing
Tel: (015) 268 3114 Fax: (015) 268 2865
Mekwa, Prof. J. N.   Head*

Nutrition
Tel: (015) 268 2871 Fax: (015) 268 2865
Ladzani, R.   Head*

Optometry
Tel: (015) 268 3143 Fax: (015) 268 2865
Oduntan, Prof. O. A.   Acting Head*

Pharmaceutical Chemistry
Tel: (015) 268 2938 Fax: (015) 268 2865
Jali, Prof. V. L. M.   Head*

Pharmaceutics
Tel: (015) 268 2347 Fax: (015) 268 2865
Lombard, Prof. R. H.   Head*

Pharmacology
Tel: (015) 268 2353 Fax: (015) 268 2865
Lombard, Prof. J. C.   Head*

Philosophy
Tel: (015) 268 3158 Fax: (015) 268 2868
Duvenhage, Prof. P. N. J.   Acting Head*

Philosophy of Education
Tel: (015) 268 2418 Fax: (015) 268 2965
Kgorane, Prof. P. M.   Head*

Physical Education, see Kinesiol. and Phys.
Educn.

Physics
Tel: (015) 268 2271 Fax: (015) 268 2893
de Neijs, Prof. E. O.   Head*

Physiology
Tel: (015) 268 2267 Fax: (015) 268 2893
Smit, Prof. G. L.   Head*

Plant Production
Tel: (015) 268 2190 Fax: (015) 268 2892
Ayisi, K. K.   Head*

Political Science
Tel: (015) 268 2253 Fax: (015) 268 2868
Herholdt, Prof. A. N. J.   Head*

Private Law
Tel: (015) 268 2906 Fax: (015) 268 2897
Songca, R.   Head*

Psychology, see also Indust. Psychol.
Tel: (015) 268 2316 Fax: (015) 268 2316
Peltzer, Prof. K. F.   Head*

Psychology of Education
Tel: (015) 268 2751 Fax: (015) 268 2751
Cherian, Prof. V. L.   Head*

Public Administration
Tel: (015) 268 2710 Fax: (015) 268 3511
Wamala, A. S.   Acting Head*

Public Law
Tel: (015) 268 2903 Fax: (015) 268 2897
Letsoalo, Prof. J. L. H.   Head*

Religion, Science of, and Missiology
Tel: (015) 268 2711 Fax: (015) 268 2866
Rathete, Rev. B. M.   Head*

Semitic Languages
Tel: (015) 268 2571 Fax: (015) 268 2868
Chabane, J. S.   Acting Head*

Sesotho
Tel: (015) 268 2284 Fax: (015) 268 2868
Ramone, P. M.   Acting Head*

Setswana
Tel: (015) 268 2285 Fax: (015) 268 2868
Thubisi, M. C.   Head*

Social Work
Tel: (015) 268 2239 Fax: (015) 268 2868
Malaka, Prof. D. W.   Head*

Sociology
Tel: (015) 268 2585 Fax: (015) 268 2868
Nindi, Prof. B.   Head*

Soil Science
Tel: (015) 268 2377 Fax: (015) 268 2892
Rosanov, A.   Head*

Sotho, Northern
Tel: (015) 268 2281 Fax: (015) 268 2868
Sekhukhune, P. D.   Head*

Statistics and Operations Research, see
also Mathl. Stats.
Tel: (015) 268 2787 Fax: (015) 268 2893
Mashike, Prof. S. P.   Head*

Systematic Theology, Ethics and Practical Theology

Tel: (015) 268 2228 Fax: (015) 268 2866

Zupa, Rev. M. A.   Head*

UNIFY

Tel: (015) 268 3058 Fax: (015) 268 2893

Cantrell, Prof. M. A.   Head*

Venda

Tel: (015) 268 2283 Fax: (015) 268 2868

Milubi, Prof. N. A.   Head*

Xitsonga

Tel: (015) 268 2744 Fax: (015) 268 2868

Nxumalo, N. E.   Head*

Zoology and Biology

Tel: (015) 268 2303 Fax: (015) 268 2893

Jooste, Prof. A.   Acting Head*

CONTACT OFFICERS

General enquiries. University Registrar (Acting): Malgas, M. P.

[Information supplied by the institution as at 20 October 1998, and edited by the ACU]

UNIVERSITY OF NORTH-WEST

Established as University of Bophuthatswana 1980; renamed 1996

Member of the Association of Commonwealth Universities

Postal Address: Private Bag X2046, Mmabatho, North-West Province, 2735 South Africa
Telephone: (0140) 892111 **Fax**: (0140) 25775 **Cables**: Unibo Mmabatho **Telex**: (0140) 3072 BP

VICE-CHANCELLOR*—Melamu, Prof. M. John, BA Rhodes, MA S.Af., DPhil Sus.
ACTING DEPUTY VICE-CHANCELLOR (ACADEMIC)—Mofokeng, Prof. T. A., ThM Prin., DrsTh Theol.Sch.Kampen
REGISTRAR‡—Banda, John R., BA Lond.
FINANCIAL CONTROLLER—Thurarairajah, S., BSc S.Lanka

FACULTIES/SCHOOLS

Commerce and Administration
Dean: Simbo, Prof. Emeric I., BSc Lond., PhD S'ton.

Agriculture
Dean: Funnah, Prof. Samuel M., BScAgric S.Leone, MSc Flor., PhD Malaya

Education
Dean: Humphrey, Godfred L., BSc Salf., MSc Salf., PhD Manc.

Human Sciences
Dean: Mabetoa, Phineas J., BA S.Af., BA Leeds, MA Keele, MPhil Brad.

Law
Dean: Manda, Peter J., BJuris Fort Hare, LLB Witw., LLM Georgetown

Social Sciences
Dean: ......

Science and Technology
Dean: ......

ACADEMIC UNITS

Accounting
Tel: (0140) 892066
Ayaya, O. O.   Sr. Lectr.
Claassens, M.   Sr. Lectr.
Manda, D. C.   Sr. Lectr.
Meko, Kate M., BCom North(S.Af.), MBA Col.   Sr. Lectr.
Mokua, R. S.   Sr. Lectr.
Other Staff: 2 Lectrs.
Vacant Posts: 1 Prof.

Afrikaans
Tel: (0140) 892181
Buscop, Jan, BA S.Af., BA Pret., MA Pret., PhD Bophut.   Sr. Lectr.
Devey, L., BA S.Af.   Lectr.; Head*
Gouws, Thomas, BA Potchef., MEd Potchef., MA Potchef., DLitt Potchef.   Prof.
Other Staff: 1 Lectr.

Vacant Posts: 2 Lectrs.

Agricultural Economics and Extension
Tel: (0140) 861322-6 Fax: (0140) 862686
Yeboah-Asuamah, Kofi, BSc(Agr) McG., MSc Guelph   Sr. Lectr.
Vacant Posts: 1 Prof.

Animal Health
Tel: (0140) 861322-6 Fax: (0140) 862686
Bakunzi, Francis R., BVM Mak., MSc Guelph   Sr. Lectr.
Beighle, Dale E., MS Kentucky, PhD S.Af.Med., DVM Auburn   Prof.
Molefe, Mphane S., BVMCh S.Af.Med.   Sr. Lectr.
Ntshabele, Boitshoko R., BVMCh S.Af.Med.   Sr. Lectr.
Other Staff: 1 Lectr.
Vacant Posts: 1 Prof.

Animal Production
Tel: (0140) 861322-6 Fax: (0140) 862686
Benyi, K., BSc(Agric) MSc(Agric) PhD   Sr. Lectr.
Syed, Hafiz U. H., BScAgric Pesh., MScAgric Pesh., MScAgric Beirut   Sr. Lectr.
Other Staff: 2 Lectrs.
Vacant Posts: 1 Prof.; 1 Assoc. Prof.

Biological Sciences
Tel: (0140) 892290
Phalatse, S. David, BSc North(S.Af.), MSc North(S.Af.)   Sr. Lectr.
Simpson, B. K., BSc Kumasi, PhD Nfld.   Prof.
Thahane, L., BSc UBLS, MSc Sheff.   Sr. Lectr.; Head*
Other Staff: 5 Lectrs.

Chemistry
Tel: (0140) 892344
Humphrey, Godfred L., BSc Salf., MSc Salf., PhD Manc.   Sr. Lectr.
Isabirye, David A., BSc Mak., PhD HK   Sr. Lectr.
Selvaratnam, Mailoo, BSc Ceyl., PhD Lond., FRSChem   Prof.; Head*
Other Staff: 4 Lectrs.

Communication
Tel: (0140) 892417
Forbes, Derek G., BA CNAA, MA Lond.   Sr. Lectr.; Head*
Other Staff: 3 Lectrs.
Vacant Posts: 1 Prof.

Development Studies
Tel: (0140) 892517
Chikulo, Bornwell C., BA Zambia, MA(Econ) Manc., PhD Manc.   Assoc. Prof.
Other Staff: 3 Lectrs.

Economics
Tel: (0140) 892066
Abbott, John G., BSc Aberd., MSc Brad.   Sr. Lectr.
Anand, V. K.   Prof.
Other Staff: 2 Lectrs.

Education, see Foundations of Educn., and Teaching and Curric.

Educational Planning and Administration
Tel: (0140) 892081
Legoibo, M. W., BA S.Af., BEd Bophut., MEd Bophut., PhD Potchef.   Sr. Lectr.; Head*
Motshabi, Eunice V. N., MEd Fort Hare, PhD Potchef., BA   Sr. Lectr.
Vacant Posts: 1 Prof.

English, see also Special Engl.
Tel: (0140) 892016
Butler, I., BA Rhodes, MA Rhodes   Sr. Lectr.
Dunton, Chris, MA Oxf., DPhil Oxf.   Prof.
Hlatawayo, A., BA Swazi., BA S.Af., MEd Manc.   Sr. Lectr.; Head*
Mosieleng, Percival, BA North(S.Af.), MLitt Aberd.   Sr. Lectr.
Segatlhe, David, BA S.Af., BA North(S.Af.), BA Rhodes, MA Mich.State   Sr. Lectr.
Other Staff: 2 Lectrs.
Vacant Posts: 1 Prof.

Environmental Studies, see Geog. and Environmental Studies

Fine Arts

Tel: (0140) 892181

Marais, Estelle, BA *Rhodes*, BA(FA) *Rhodes*, MA(FA) *Rhodes*   Prof.; Head*
McLean, D. L., BA(FA) *Rhodes*, MA(FA) *Rhodes*   Sr. Lectr.
Other Staff: 3 Lectrs.
Vacant Posts: 1 Sr. Lectr.

Foundations of Education

Tel: (0140) 892081

Maqsud, Mohammad, BA *Punjab*, BEd *Punjab*, MA *Lond.*, PhD *Lond.*   Prof.; Head*
Other Staff: 3 Lectrs.

Geography and Environmental Studies

Tel: (0140) 892303

Bootsman, Cornelis S., BSc *V.U.Amst.*, MSc *V.U.Amst.*   Sr. Lectr.
Cowley, Jonathan W., BA *Durh.*, MSc(Ed) *S'ton.*   Assoc. Prof.; Head*
Wagner, Michael J., BS *Wis.*, MA *Tor.*, MEd *Manit.*, PhD *McG.*   Sr. Lectr.
Other Staff: 1 Lectr.

History

Tel: (0140) 892191

Bottomley, John, BA *Natal*, MA *Natal*, PhD *Qu.*   Sr. Lectr.
Manson, Andrew H., BA *Natal*, MA *Natal*, PhD *Cape Town*   Prof.
Mbanga, B. K., BA(Educn) *Zambia*, MA *York*, PhD *S.Af.*   Sr. Lectr.
Olynick, T., BA *Cape Town*, BA *Witw.*, MA *Witw.*, PhD *Qu.*   Sr. Lectr.; Head*
Other Staff: 2 Lectrs.

Industrial Psychology

Tel: (0140) 892066

Louw, E. J., BCom *S.Af.*, MCom *OFS*, DPhil *OFS*   Assoc. Prof.
Other Staff: 2 Lectrs.
Vacant Posts: 1 Sr. Lectr.

Information Systems

Tel: (0140) 892066

Eyono-Obono, S., BSc *Nancy*, PhD *Rouen*   Sr. Lectr.
Gosebo, Ntjatji, BSc *St.Peter's*, MSc *New Jersey I.T.*   Sr. Lectr.
Simbo, Emeric J., BSc *Lond.*, PhD *S'ton.*   Prof.

Law, Criminal and Procedural

Tel: (0140) 892060

Cassim, Yusuf, BA *Durban-W.*, BProc *S.Af.*, LLB *S.Af.*, LLM *S.Af.*, MA *Leic.*   Prof.
Manda, Peter J., BJuris *Fort Hare*, LLB *Witw.*, LLM *Georgetown*   Sr. Lectr.
Mocwaladi, O. I., BCrimJustice *N-W(S.Af.)*, LLB *N-W(S.Af.)*, LLM *S.Af.*   Sr. Lectr.
Monareng, P. B., LLB *N-W(S.Af.)*   Sr. Lectr.
Other Staff: 4 Lectrs.
Vacant Posts: 1 Assoc. Prof.

Law, Mercantile

Tel: (0140) 892060

Tayob, A. O., BA LLB LLM   Sr. Lectr.
Vacant Posts: 1 Prof.; 1 Assoc. Prof.; 1 Sr. Lectr.; 1 Lectr.

Law, Private and Customary

Tel: (0140) 892060

Kakula, Liyoka, LLB *Zambia*, LLM *Zambia*, LLM *Wis.*, SJD *Wis.*   Prof.
Kettles, Robert L., BA *Cape Town*, LLB *Cape Town*, LLM *Edin.*   Sr. Lectr.
Other Staff: 1 Lectr.
Vacant Posts: 1 Prof.

Law, Public, and Legal Philosophy

Tel: (0140) 892060

Balatseng, Debora G., BJur *Bophut.*, LLB *Bophut.*, LLM *Georgetown*   Sr. Lectr.

Mbao, Melvin L. M., LLB *Zambia*, LLM *Zambia*, MPhil *Camb.*, PhD *Camb.*   Assoc. Prof.
Other Staff: 1 Lectr.
Vacant Posts: 1 Prof.

Management

Tel: (0140) 892066

Godji, Lovelace J. K., BA *Cape Coast*, MBA *Ghana*   Sr. Lectr.
Pelsner, Andries S., BCom *Potchef.*, MCom *Venda*   Sr. Lectr.
van Rensburg, Jansen W. P., BCom *OFS*, BCom *S.Af.*, MCom *S.Af.*, DCom *S.Af.*   Prof.
Other Staff: 1 Lectr.
Vacant Posts: 1 Assoc. Prof.

Mathematical Sciences

Tel: (0140) 892319

Ibragimov, N. H., DSc *Novosibirsk*   Prof.
Kambule, Matthew T., BSc *S.Af.*, BSc *North(S.Af.)*, MSc *S.Af.*, PhD *Mass.*   Sr. Lectr.
Khalique, Chaudry M., BSc *Punj.*, MSc *Islam.*, MPhil *Islam.*, MSc *Dund.*, PhD *Dund.*   Assoc. Prof.; Head*
Pooe, Charlemagne A., BSc *Fort Hare*, BSc *Cape Town*, MSc *Witw.*, MSc *Potchef.*   Sr. Lectr.
Other Staff: 4 Lectrs.

Nursing Science

Tel: (0140) 892236

Masipa, Asnatha L., BACur *S.Af.*, MA *Col.*, MEd *Col.*   Sr. Lectr.
Modungwa, N. M., BN *Bophut.*, MCur *Rand Afrikaans*, BSocSc   Lectr.; Head*
Mokoene, B. A., BACur   Sr. Lectr.
Other Staff: 3 Lectrs.
Vacant Posts: 1 Prof.; 1 Lectr.

Physics

Tel: (0140) 892344

Gadinabokao, Wilson L., BSc *S.Af.*, MSc *Witw.*, MSc(Eng) *Pret.*   Assoc. Prof.
Kgwadi, N. D., BScEd *Bophut.*, MSc *Ball State*   Lectr.; Head*
Perera, Ambalangoda K., BSc *Ceyl.*, PhD *Birm.*   Sr. Lectr.
Taole, Simeon H., MSc *Wales*, PhD *Ott.*   Prof.
Other Staff: 1 Lectr.

Plant Production

Tel: (0140) 861322-6 Fax: (0140) 862686

Funnah, Samuel M., BScAgric *S.Leone*, MSc *Flor.*, PhD *Malaya*   Prof.
Kasirivu, John B. K., BSc(Agric) *Mak.*, MSc(AgricBio) *Ib.*   Sr. Lectr.
Materachara, S. A., BSc(Agric) *Malawi*, MSc *McG.*, PhD *S.Aust.*   Assoc. Prof.
Vacant Posts: 2 Lectrs.

Political Studies

Tel: (0140) 892066

Makgetianang, S., BA *Clark Coll.*, MPA *Atlanta*, PhD *Atlanta*   Sr. Lectr.
Matheba, G. A., BA *North(S.Af.)*, MA *Monterey*, MPhil *Bophut.*   Sr. Lectr.

Psychology, see also Indust. Psychol.

Tel: (0140) 892532

Mabetoa, Phineas J., BA *S.Af.*, BA *Leeds*, MA *Keele*, MPhil *Brad.*   Assoc. Prof.
Mwaba, Kelvin, BA *Zambia*, MA *Syr.*, PhD *Syr.*   Sr. Lectr.
Temane, Michael Q., BA *North(S.Af.)*, MSocSc *Bophut.*   Sr. Lectr.
Other Staff: 2 Lectrs.
Vacant Posts: 2 Sr. Lectrs.; 1 Lectr.

Public Administration

Tel: (0140) 892066

Kawadia, L. M., BA *NUL*, MPA *Car.*   Sr. Lectr.
Setsetse, G. D., BAdmin *North(S.Af.)*   Sr. Lectr.
Other Staff: 2 Lectrs.
Vacant Posts: 1 Prof.

Setswana

Tel: (0140) 892369

Malope, M. Racias, BA *S.Af.*, BEd *S.Af.*, BA *North(S.Af.)*, MA *North(S.Af.)*   Prof.
Mashike, Jeremiah W., BA *North(S.Af.)*, MA *Potchef.*   Sr. Lectr.; Head*
Rapoo, Elizabeth E., BA(Ed) *Bophut.*, BA *Bophut.*, MA *Potchef.*   Sr. Lectr.
Other Staff: 2 Lectrs.
Vacant Posts: 1 Prof.

Social Work

Tel: (0140) 892193

Anderson, William W., BA(SW) *Pret.*, BA *Pret.*, MA *Pret.*, DPhil *Pret.*   Prof.
de Chevennes-Vrugt, M. M., MA *Pret.*   Sr. Lectr.
Ratefane, Tumelo A., BASocWk *Bophut.*, MSocSc *Cape Town*   Sr. Lectr.
Thekigho, G. N., BA(SW) *North(S.Af.)*, BA(SW) *Fort Hare*, MSocSc *Rhodes*, MWD *Inst.Soc.Stud.(The Hague)*   Sr. Lectr.
Other Staff: 4 Lectrs.
Vacant Posts: 1 Sr. Lectr.

Sociology

Tel: (0140) 892264

Kaya, H. O., BA *Dar.*, MA *Dar.*, PhD *F.U.Berlin*   Assoc. Prof.
Milazi, Dominic B. T., BA *North(S.Af.)*, MA *C.U.A.*, PhD *F.U.Berlin*   Prof.
Other Staff: 3 Lectrs.
Vacant Posts: 1 Sr. Lectr.

Special English

Tel: (0140) 892016

7 Lectrs.

Statistics

Tel: (0140) 892066

Sinha, S. K.   Prof.
Other Staff: 3 Lectrs.

Teaching and Curriculum

Tel: (0140) 892081

Awudetsey, Samuel A., BA *Ghana*, MA *Col.*, EdD *Col.*   Assoc. Prof.; Head*
Mokoena, M. Amelia, BAPaed *North(S.Af.)*, BEd *North(S.Af.)*, MEd *Witw.*, EdM *Boston*   Sr. Lectr.
Nyakutse, A. C., BEd *Wales*, MEd *Wales*   Sr. Lectr.
Other Staff: 1 Lectr.
Vacant Posts: 1 Sr. Lectr.; 2 Lectrs.

SPECIAL CENTRES, ETC

Academic Development Centre

Tel: (0140) 892107

Rakubutu, M. C., MEd *Mass.*   Acting Dir.*

Business and Management Development, Centre for

Tel: (0140) 892073

Bootha, Ishmael, BCom *S.Af.*   Dir.*

Development Research, Institute of

Tel: (0140) 892180

Maaga, Modise P., BA *S.Af.*, MA *Howard*, PhD *Howard*   Acting Dir.*

Education, Institute of

Tel: (0140) 892230

Mahape, M. I., BA *S.Af.*, BEd *North(S.Af.)*, MA *Minn.*   Dir.*

Guidance and Counselling Centre

Tel: (0140) 892077

Malefo, E. V., BA *Cape Town*   Dir.*

Unibo Law Clinic

Tel: (0140) 892314

Stander, John S., BL *Z'bwe.*, LLB *Z'bwe.*, LLB *S.Af.*   Dir.*

CONTACT OFFICERS

Academic affairs. Deputy Registrar (Academic): Dire, M. D., BPA *Bophut.*
Accommodation. Deputy Registrar (Administration): Paadi, R. D., BJuris *Bophut.*, LLB *Bophut.*
Admissions (first degree). Admissions Officer: Paadi, R. A., BSocSc *Bophut.*
Admissions (higher degree). Admissions Officer: Paadi, R. A., BSocSc *Bophut.*
Alumni.......
Computing services. Director: Deslande, Gerald G., BSc *Paris*
Development/fund-raising. Director of Public Relations: ......
Estates and buildings/works and services. Director: ......

Examinations. Examinations Officer: Modiga, Bogadi R., BPA *Bophut.*
Finance. Financial Controller: Thurarairajah, S., BSc *S.Lanka*
General enquiries. Registrar: Banda, John R., BA *Lond.*
Health services. Nursing Sister: Mokgoro, Teresa B., BN *Bophut.*, BSocSc *Bophut.*
Library (chief librarian). University Librarian: Malefo, P., BA *North(S.Af.)*, BPA *Bophut.*
Library (enquiries). Kambule, Addis N., BBibl *Zululand*, BBibl *S.Af.*, MEd *Mass.*, MSc *Simmons*
Personnel/human resources. Deputy Registrar: ......
Public relations, information and marketing. Acting Director of Public Relations: Hammond, N., MDP
Publications. Chairperson: Manson, Andy, BA *Natal*, MA *Natal*, PhD *Cape Town*

Purchasing. Purchasing Officer: ......
Research. Chairperson: Manson, Andy, BA *Natal*, MA *Natal*, PhD *Cape Town*
Scholarships, awards, loans. Administrative Officer: Tlatsana, T. D.
Security. Tredoux, A.
Sport and recreation. Sports Officer: Van Rooyen, F., BA *OFS*
Staff development and training. Deputy Registrar: ......
Student welfare/counselling. Malefo, E. V., BA *Cape Town*
University press. Molete, R.

[*Information supplied by the institution as at 9 October 1998, and edited by the ACU*]

UNIVERSITY OF THE ORANGE FREE STATE

Established 1908 as Grey University College; present name adopted 1950

Member of the Association of Commonwealth Universities

Postal Address: PO Box 339, Bloemfontein, 9300 South Africa
Telephone: (051) 401 2123 **Fax**: (051) 401 2117 **E-mail**: ardp@rs.uovs.ac.za

RECTOR AND VICE-CHANCELLOR*—Coetzee, Prof. Stefanus F., BA *Stell.*, MA *Stell.*, DPhil *OFS*
VICE-RECTOR: ACADEMIC—Small, Prof. J. G. C., DSc(Agric)
VICE-RECTOR: ACADEMIC SUPPORT—Khotseng, Prof. B. M., DPhil
GENERAL MANAGER: FINANCE AND INFORMATION—Schoonwinkel, Prof. A. J., DCom

GENERAL INFORMATION

History. The university was established in 1908 as Grey University College. The present name was adopted in 1950.

Admission to first degree courses (see also South African Introduction). South African applicants: a certificate of full exemption as issued by the South African Certification Council. International applicants: compliance with requirements set by South African Matriculation Board.

First Degrees (see also South African Directory to Subjects of Study) (* = also available with honours; † = honours only).
BA†, BA(CommunicationScience)*, BA(DramaandTheatreArts)*, BA(Ed), BA(FineArts), BA(General), BA(Languages)*, BA(Music), BA(Musicology)†, BA(PhysEduc)†, BALibraryScience†, BAdmin*, BAgric*, BAgric(Ed), BArchStud, BBibl† (library science), BCom*, BCom(Ed), BCompt*, BEcon*, BEcon(Ed), BEd, BMedSc†, BMus*, BMus(Ed), BOccupationalTherapy, BPL* (personnel leadership), BPrimEd, BRad†, BSc*, BSc(ConstructionManagement), BSc(Dietetics), BSc(DomesticScience)†, BSc(Ed), BSc(Physiotherapy), BSc(QS), BScAgric*, BSecEd, BSocSc*, BSocSc(Nursing)*, BSocSc(SocialWork)*, BTh, LLB, MB ChB.

Higher Degrees (see also South African Directory to Subjects of Study). LLM, MA, MA(ClinicalPsychology), MA(CommunicationScience), MA(CounsellingPsychology), MA(DramaandTheatre), MA(FineArts), MA(Languages), MA(Musicology), MA(PhysEduc), MABib, MAdmin, MAgric,

MArch, MBibl, MCom, MCompt, MD, MEcon, MEdMSc, MEnvironmentalManagement, MFamMed, MMed, MMed(CH), MMed(MA), MMedSc, MMus, MOccupationalTherapy, MPA, MPL (personnel leadership), MRad, MSc(BuildingManagement), MSc(ClinicalPsychology), MSc(ConstructionManagement), MSc(CounsellingPsychology), MSc(Dietetics), MSc(DomesticScience), MSc(Physiotherapy), MSc(QS), MScAgric, MSocSc, MSocSc(ClinicalPsychology), MSocSc(CounsellingPsychology), MSocSc(Nursing), MSocSc(SocialWork), MTh, PhD, DAdmin, DArch, DBibl, DCom, DCompt, DEcon, DEd, DLitt, DMedSc, DMus, DPhil, DPhil(FineArts), DPhil(Musicology), DPL, DSc, DSocSc, DSocSc(SocialWork), DTh, LLD.

Language of Instruction. English and Afrikaans.

Libraries. 455,043 volumes; 64,476 audio-visual materials. Special collections: Africana, including Anglo-Boer War.

Fees (1998–99) (annual). South African students: £500–1125 (undergraduate); £875–1200 (postgraduate). International students: additional service fee of £150.

Academic Awards (1997–98). 685 senior undergraduate awards ranging in value from £25 to £1100.

Academic Year. Two semesters: February–June; July–December.

Income. Total, £53,000,000.

Statistics. Students: total 10,459 (5024 men, 5435 women); international 310.

FACULTIES/SCHOOLS

Agriculture
Tel: (051) 401 2535
Dean: Wilke, Prof. P. I., PhD
Secretary: ......

Arts
Tel: (051) 401 2240
Dean: ......
Secretary: Peyper, J. H.

Economic and Management Sciences
Tel: (051) 401 2310
Dean: Fourie, Prof. F. C. v. N., PhD *Harv.*
Faculty Manager: du Preez, E. S.

Education
Tel: (051) 401 2238
Dean: ......
Secretary: van Tonder, A. J.

Law
Tel: (051) 401 2319
Dean: Henning, Prof. J. J., LLD
Secretary: Kleynhans, A. J.

Medicine
Tel: (051) 405 3911
Dean: Nel, Prof. C. J. C., MB ChB MMed(Chur)
Secretary: Naude, C.

Science
Tel: (051) 401 2322
Dean: Van Wyk, Prof. G. N., PhD
Secretary: Havemann, C.

Social Sciences
Tel: (051) 401 2247
Dean: ......
Secretary: Knoetze, H. E.

Theology
Tel: (051) 401 2667
Dean: Potgieter, Prof. P. C., DTh
Secretary: Nel, H. C.

ACADEMIC UNITS

Accounting, see Special Centres, etc

African Languages
Duyvene de Wit, H. E., PhD *Vista* Assoc. Prof.
Moleleki, M. A., MA Assoc. Prof.

Afrikaans and Nederlands
Jenkinson, A. G., DLitt Sr. Lectr.
Van Coller, H. P., DLitt Prof.; Head*
Van Zuydam, S. W., PhD Assoc. Prof.
Venter, L. S., DLitt Prof.

Agricultural Economics
Oosthuizen, L. K., PhD Prof.
Van Schalkwyk, H. D., PhD Assoc. Prof.; Head*
Viljoen, M. F., PhD Prof.

Agricultural Engineering
Van Staden, J. J., BEng Sr. Lectr.; Head*

Agrometeorology
Walker, S., PhD Prof.; Head*

Agronomy/Horticulture
Pretorius, J. C., PhD Prof.; Head*
Pretorius, J. P., PhD Assoc. Prof.; Researcher

Animal Science
Du Toit, J. E. J., PhD Assoc. Prof.
Erasmus, G. J., PhD Prof.
Greyling, J. P. C., PhD Assoc. Prof.; Head*
Groenewald, I. B., PhD Sr. Lectr.
Neser, F. W. C., PhD Sr. Lectr.
Van Der Merwe, H. J., PhD Prof.
Van Wyk, J. B., PhD Assoc. Prof.

Anthropology
Erasmus, P. A., DPhil Assoc. Prof.

Applied Mathematics
Bargenda, H. W., PhD Sr. Lectr.
Cloot, A. H. J., PhD Assoc. Prof.
Meyer, J. H., PhD Assoc. Prof.
Murray, D. M., PhD Prof.
Raubenheimer, H., DSc Prof.
Schoombie, S. W., PhD Prof.
Viljoen, G., PhD Prof.; Head*

Architecture
Britz, B. J., DArch Prof.; Head*
Joubert, P. G., BArch Sr. Lectr.
Kotze, C. P., MArch Prof.
Roodt, A. J., MURP Sr. Lectr.
Smit, J. D., MArch Sr. Lectr.
Smit, P., MArch Sr. Lectr.

Art, see Fine Arts, and Hist. of Art

Banking, see Money and Banking

Biblical and Religious Studies, see also New Testament, and Old Testament
No staff at present

Biochemistry, see Microbiol. and Biochem.

Biostatistics
No staff at present

Botany and Genetics
Du Preez, P. J., PhD Sr. Lectr.
Grobbelaar, J. U., DSc Prof.; Head*
Roos, J. C., PhD Sr. Lectr.
Scott, L., PhD Prof.
Spies, J. J., PhD Prof.
Van Der Westhuizen, A. J., PhD Assoc. Prof.
Van Wyk, P. W. J., PhD Sr. Lectr.

Venter, H. J. T., DSc Prof.
Verhoeven, R. L., PhD Assoc. Prof.

Business Management
Crous, M. J., DCom Prof.; Head*
Du Plessis, I. P., PhD Sr. Lectr.
Lazenby, J. A. A., PhD Sr. Lectr.
Smit, A. V. A., DCom Assoc. Prof.
Van Der Merwe, W. J. C., DCom Prof.

Chemistry
Basson, S. S., DSc Prof.; Head*
Brandt, E. V., PhD Prof.
Ferreira, D., DSc Prof.
Lamprecht, G. J., PhD Prof.
Purcell, W., PhD Assoc. Prof.
Roodt, A., PhD Prof.
Steenkamp, J. A., PhD Assoc. Prof.
Swarts, J. C., PhD Sr. Lectr.

Communication Science
Breytenbach, H. J., DPhil Sr. Lectr.
Terblanche, F. H., DPhil Prof.; Head*

Comparative Education and Educational Management
Brazelle, R. R., DEd Assoc. Prof.
De Wet, N. C., DEd Sr. Lectr.
Heyns, M. G., BA Assoc. Prof.
Niemann, G. S., DEd Prof.; Head*
Niemann, S. M., PhD Sr. Lectr.
Van Staden, J. G., PhD Prof.

Computer Science and Informatics
McDonald, T., PhD Prof.
Messerschmidt, H. J., PhD Prof.; Head*
Tolmie, C. J., PhD Prof.

Criminology
Calitz, A. W., MA Sr. Lectr.; Head*

Didactics
Du Toit, G. F., PhD Prof.; Head*
Korff, W. P., BA Sr. Lectr.
Kotze, G. S., PhD Sr. Lectr.
Le Roux, P. J., DEd Assoc. Prof.
Louw, L. P., PhD Sr. Lectr.
Messerschmidt, J. J. E., DLitt Sr. Lectr.

Drama and Theatre
Luwes, N. J., MA Sr. Lectr.
Welman, A. C. F., MA Sr. Lectr.

Economics, see also Agric. Econ.
Lourens, J. J., DCom Prof.; Head*
Smit, M. R., PhD Sr. Lectr.
Van Zyl, J. S., MCom Sr. Lectr.
Strauss, J. P., DEd Prof.; Researcher

Educational Management, see Compar. Educn. and Educnl. Management

English
Greyling, W. J., DLitt Assoc. Prof.
Muller, F. R., DLitt Prof.; Head*
Raftery, M. M., MTh Sr. Lectr.
Ullyatt, A. G., DLitt Prof.

Entomology, see Zool. and Entomol.

Fine Arts
No staff at present

Food Science
Botha, W. C., PhD Assoc. Prof.
Jooste, P. J., PhD Prof.; Head*
Osthoff, G., PhD Assoc. Prof.
Viljoen, B. C., PhD Assoc. Prof.

French
Visagie, E. M., DLitt Sr. Lectr.

Genetics, see Bot. and Genetics

Geography
De Villiers, G. D. V. T., PhD Prof.; Head*
Krige, D. S., PhD Sr. Lectr.

Geology
Beukes, G. J., DSc Assoc. Prof.
Colliston, W. P., PhD Sr. Lectr.
De Bruiyn, H., PhD Sr. Lectr.; Researcher
Loock, J. C., MSc Sr. Lectr.
Van Der Westhuizen, W. A., PhD Sr. Lectr.; Researcher
Visser, J. N. J., DSc Prof.; Head*

German
Saayman, E. C. C., MA Head*

Grassland Sciences
Smit, G. N., PhD Assoc. Prof.
Snyman, H. A., PhD Prof.; Head*

Greek
Cronje, J. V. W., DLitt Prof.; Head*
Le Roux, L. V., DLitt Sr. Lectr.

History
Barnard, S. L., DPhil Prof.; Head*
Combrink, N. L., MA Sr. Lectr.
Wessels, A., DPhil Assoc. Prof.

History of Art
Kuijers, A., MA Sr. Lectr.
Van den Berg, D. J., DLitt Prof.; Head*

Home Economics
Steyn, H. J. H., PhD Assoc. Prof.; Head*

Horticulture, see Agron./Hort.

Human Movement Science
Bloemhoff, H. J, DPhil Sr. Lectr.
Coetzee, F. F., DPhil Sr. Lectr.
Coetzee, N. A. J., DEd Prof.; Head*
Jansen Van Ryssen, J. C., DSc Sr. Lectr.

Human Nutrition
Badenhorst, A. M., PhD Assoc. Prof.
Dannhauser, A., PhD Assoc. Prof.; Head*

Industrial Arts and Graphics
Combrinck, G. P., PhD Prof.; Head*

Industrial Psychology, see also Psychol.
Bester, C. L., DPhil Prof.; Head*
Kotze, M., DPhil Sr. Lectr.
Van Zyl, E. S., DPhil Assoc. Prof.

Latin
Cilliers, L., DLitt Prof.; Head*

Law, Constitutional, and Philosophy of Law
Pretorius, J. L., LLD Prof.; Head*
Raath, A. W. G., DPhil Prof.
Strydom, H. A., LLD Prof.

Law, Criminal and Medical
Oosthuizen, H., LLD Sr. Lectr.
Verschoor, T., LLD Prof.; Head*

Law, Mercantile
Dednam, M. J., LLB Assoc. Prof.
Du Plessis, J. V., LLD Prof.; Head*
Ellis, A. J., LLB Sr. Lectr.
Kelling, A. S., LLD Prof.
Viljoen, D. J., MCom Prof.

Law, Private
Claassen, N. J. B., LLM Sr. Lectr.
Fick, C. P. v. D. M., LLD Prof.
Grobler, N. J., DSc Assoc. Prof.
Jansen, R., BIur Sr. Lectr.
Van Schalkwyk, J. H., LLD Prof.; Head*

Law, Roman, History of Law and Comparative Law
Alberts, R. W., LLM Sr. Lectr.

Linguistics, General
Broekman, H. W., DLitt Sr. Lectr.
Du Plessis, L. T., DLitt Sr. Lectr.
Nel, P. J., DLitt Prof.; Head*

Mathematics, see also Appl. Maths., and
Stats., Mathl. Stats.
No staff at present

Medicine, see below

Microbiology and Biochemistry
Botha, A., PhD   Sr. Lectr.
Du Plessis, C. A., MSc   Sr. Lectr.
Du Preez, J. C., PhD   Prof.
Killian, S. G., PhD   Assoc. Prof.
Kock, J. L. F., PhD   Prof.
Litthauer, D., PhD   Assoc. Prof.
Patterton, H. G., PhD   Sr. Lectr.
Prior, B. A., PhD   Prof.; Head*
Riedel, K. H. J., MSc   Sr. Lectr.
Smit, M. S., PhD   Sr. Lectr.
Van Biljon, P. L., PhD   Sr. Lectr.
Van Tonder, A., PhD   Sr. Lectr.

Money and Banking
Van Zyl, H., DCom   Assoc. Prof.
Wessels, G. M., DCom   Prof.; Head*

Music
Heunis, G. J. L., DPhil   Sr. Lectr.
Kloppers, L., BA   Sr. Lectr.
Lamprecht, G. P., DPhil   Prof.; Head*
Viljoen, N. G. J., DPhil   Sr. Lectr.

Near-Eastern Studies
Naude, J. A., DLitt   Sr. Lectr.
Nel, P. J., DLitt   Prof.; Head*

New Testament
Tolmie, D. F., BTh   Sr. Lectr.
Van Zyl, H. C., DTh   Prof.; Head*

Nursing, School for
Van Rhyn, W. J. C., DSocSc   Sr. Lectr.
Viljoen, M. J., DSocSc   Prof.; Head*

Old Testament
Snyman, S. D., BTh   Prof.; Head*

Philosophy
Smit, J. H., DPhil   Prof.
Strauss, D. F. M., DPhil   Prof.†
Visagie, P. J., DPhil   Assoc. Prof.

Philosophy and History of Education
Coetzee, D., PhD   Sr. Lectr.; Head*

Physics
Berning, G. P. L., PhD   Prof.; Head*
Du Plessis, J., PhD   Prof.
Maritz, M. F., PhD   Sr. Lectr.
Meintjies, P. J., PhD   Sr. Lectr.
Roos, W. D., MSc   Sr. Lectr.
Swart, H. C., PhD   Assoc. Prof.
Viljoen, E. C., PhD   Sr. Lectr.

Plant Breeding
Labuschagne, M. T., PhD   Assoc. Prof.
Van Deventer, C. S., PhD   Prof.; Head*

Plant Pathology
Kloppers, F. J., PhD   Sr. Lectr.
Pretorius, Z. A., PhD   Prof.; Head*
Swart, W. J., PhD   Assoc. Prof.

Political Science
Duvenhage, A., PhD   Sr. Lectr.
Luyt, N., DPhil   Sr. Lectr.
Wessels, D. P., PhD DAdmin   Prof.; Head*

Practical Theology
Janse Van Rensburg, J., DTh   Sr. Lectr.

Psycho-Education
Du Plooy, J., DEd   Assoc. Prof.
Kotze, C. J., PhD   Assoc. Prof.; Head*

Psychology, see also Indust. Psychol.
Beukes, R. B. I., DPhil   Sr. Lectr.
Esterhuyse, K. G. F., MA   Sr. Lectr.
Fourie, M. C., DEd   Sr. Lectr.
Grobler, J. J., DLitt&Phil   Assoc. Prof.
Herbst, I., DSocSc   Sr. Lectr.
Heyns, P. M., DPhil   Prof.; Head*

Huysamen, G. K., PhD   Prof.
Le Roux, A., DPhil   Sr. Lectr.
Louw, D. A., DPhil   Prof.
Rossouw, P. J., MA   Prof.
Swartz, J. F., MA   Sr. Lectr.

Public Administration
Bekker, J. C. O., DAdmin   Prof.; Head*
Geldenhuys, A. J., DAdmin   Prof.
Van Straaten, F. P., DCom   Sr. Lectr.

**Quantity Surveying and Construction
Management**
Border, M., BA   Sr. Lectr.
Verster, J. J. P., PhD   Prof.; Head*

Religious Studies, see Bibl. and Religious
Studies

Science of Literature
Strydom, L., DPhil   Prof.; Head*

Social Work
De Jager, H. J., MA   Sr. Lectr.
Mouton, G. E., DSocSc   Assoc. Prof.

Sociology
Botes, L. J. S., MSocSc   Sr. Lectr.
De Klerk, G. W., DPhil   Prof.; Head*
Groenewald, D. C., DLitt   Prof.
Pelser, A. J., PhD   Assoc. Prof.
Pretorius, E., DPhil   Assoc. Prof.

Soil Science
Du Preez, C. C., PhD   Prof.; Head*

Statistics, Mathematical Statistics
De Waal, D. J., PhD   Prof.; Head*
Groenewald, P. C. N., PhD   Prof.
Steyn, P. W., PhD   Sr. Lectr.
Van Der Merwe, A. J., PhD   Prof.
Van Zyl, J. M., PhD   Sr. Lectr.; Researcher

Systematic Theology
Strauss, S. A., BTh   Prof.; Head*

Theatre, see Drama and Theatre

Theology, see Practical Theol., and Systematic
Theol.

Urban and Regional Planning
Botha, W. J. V. H., PhD   Prof.; Head*
Steyn, J. J., PhD   Sr. Lectr.

Zoology and Entomology
Basson, L., PhD   Assoc. Prof.
Du Preez, L. H., PhD   Sr. Lectr.
Fourie, L. J., PhD   Assoc. Prof.
Kok, D. J., DSc   Prof.
Kok, O. B., PhD   Prof.
Louw, S. V. D. M., DSc   Assoc. Prof.
Van As, J. G., PhD   Prof.; Head*
Van Der Linde, T. C. D. K., PhD   Sr. Lectr.
Van Der Westhuizen, M. C., PhD   Sr. Lectr.

MEDICINE

Anaesthesiology
Boshoff, T. L., MMed   Sr. Lectr.; Sr. Specialist
Diedricks, B. J. S., MMed   Prof.; Chief
Specialist; Head*
Kachelhoffer, A. M., MMed   Sr. Lectr.;
Principal Specialist
Koning, W. P., MMed   Sr. Lectr.; Principal
Specialist
Louw, L. S., MB ChB   Sr. Lectr.; Specialist
Myburgh, A. M., MMed   Sr. Lectr.; Sr.
Specialist
Odendaal, C. L., MMed   Prof.; Second Chief
Specialist
Reyneke, J. J., MMed   Sr. Lectr.; Sr. Specialist

Anatomical Pathology
Beukes, C. A., MD   Assoc. Prof.
Middlecote, B. D., MMed   Prof.; Chief
Specialist; Head*
Roussouw, J., MMed   Sr. Lectr.; Sr. Specialist

Anatomy and Cell Morphology
De Bruyn, L., MB ChB   Sr. Lectr.; Principal
Med. Officer
De Jager, L., PhD   Sr. Lectr.
Geyer, H. J., PhD   Sr. Lectr.
Gous, A. E. F., DSc   Sr. Lectr.
Louw, L. D. E. K., PhD   Prof.
Nel, P. P. C., PhD   Prof.; Chief Specialist*

Biophysics
Duvenhage, J., PhD   Sr. Lectr.; Control Med.
Physicist
Herbst, C. P., PhD   Assoc. Prof.; Principal
Specialist
Lotter, M. G., PhD   Prof.; Chief Dir.*
Van Aswegen, A., PhD   Prof.; Dir.; Med.
Physicist
Willemse, C. A., PhD   Sr. Lectr.; Dir.; Med.
Physicist

Cardiology
Jacobs, J. J. P., MMed   Sr. Lectr.; Sr. Specialist
Jordaan, P. J., MMed   Principal Specialist; Sr.
Lectr.
Marx, J. D., MD   Prof.; Chief Specialist; Head*
Theron, H. D. T., MMed   Principal Specialist;
Sr. Lectr.

Cardiothoracic Surgery
De Vries, W. J., MMed   Principal Specialist;
Sr. Lectr.
Hough, J., MMed   Prof.; Chief Specialist;
Head*
Long, M. A., MMed   Sr. Lectr.
Swart, M. J., MMed   Sr. Lectr.; Sr. Specialist

Chemical Pathology
Kriegl, J. M., MMed   Prof.

Community Health
Liebenberg, S. J., MMed   Prof.; Chief
Specialist; Head*

Critical Care
De Vaal, J. B., MMed   Prof.; Chief Specialist;
Head*
Spruyt, M. G. L., MMed   Sr. Lectr.; Sr.
Specialist
Van Der Berg, P. S., MMed   Sr. Lectr.; Sr.
Specialist

Dermatology
Venter, I. J., MMed

Diagnostic Radiology
Bruna, J., PhD   Sr. Lectr.; Sr. Specialist
De Villiers, J. F. K., MRad   Prof.; Chief
Specialist; Head*
Markgraaff, C., MRad   Sr. Lectr.; Sr. Specialist
Stassen, L. W., MMed   Principal Specialist; Sr.
Lectr.

Family Practice
Hiemstra, L. A., MFamMed   Sr. Lectr.;
Principal Family Practitioner
Kleynhans, T. L., MFamMed   Sr. Lectr.;
Principal Family Practitioner
Myburgh, J., MFamMed   Sr. Lectr.; Sr. Family
Practitioner
Pistorius, G. J., MD   Prof.; Chief Family
Practitioner; Head*
Rabie, W. J., MFamMed   Sr. Lectr.; Sr. Family
Practitioner
Stander, D. C. H., MFamMed   Sr. Lectr.;
Principal Family Practitioner
Van Rooyen, J. P., MFamMed   Sr. Lectr.; Sr.
Family Practitioner
Van Vuuren, M. V. J., MMed   Assoc. Prof.;
Principal Specialist

Forensic Medicine
Book, R. G., MMed   Sr. Lectr.; Sr. Specialist
Botha, J. B. C., MMed   Prof.; Chief Specialist;
Head*
Wagner, L., MMed   Sr. Lectr.; Principal
Specialist

Haematology

Badenhorst, P. N., MMed   Prof.; Chief
  Specialist; Head*
Cloete, F., MSc   Sr. Lectr.
Coetzee, M. J., MMedSc   Sr. Lectr.; Sr.
  Specialist
Kotze, H. F., PhD   Assoc. Prof.
Pieters, H., PhD   Sr. Lectr.; Sr. Specialist
Pretorius, G. H. J., DSc   Assoc. Prof.

Internal Medicine

Bouwer, D. J., MMed   Sr. Lectr.; Sr. Specialist
Grundling, H. D. E. K., MMed   Assoc. Prof.;
  Principal Specialist
Jansen Van Rensburg, B. W., MMed   Assoc.
  Prof.; Principal Specialist
Mollentze, W. F.   Prof.; Chief Specialist
Otto, W. S. J., MB ChB   Sr. Lectr.; Sr.
  Specialist
Pansegrouw, D. F., MMed   Principal Specialist;
  Sr. Lectr.
Pauw, F. H.   Sr. Lectr.; Sr. Specialist
Prins, M., MMed   Sr. Lectr.; Sr. Specialist
Van Zyl, J. H., MMed   Principal Specialist; Sr.
  Lectr.
Weich, D. J. V., MMed   Prof.; Chief Specialist;
  Head*
Other Staff: 1 Sr. Researcher

Medical Microbiology

Chalkley, L. J., PhD   Sr. Lectr.; Specialist
Janse Van Rensburg, M. N., MMed   Sr. Lectr.;
  Principal Specialist
Van der Ryst, E., MMed   Sr. Lectr.; Sr.
  Specialist

Medical Physiology

Botha, H. K., PhD   Sr. Lectr.
Crous, A., PhD   Assoc. Prof.
De Wet, E. H., MD   Prof.; Chief Specialist
Muller, F. A., PhD   Sr. Lectr.
Nel, W. E., MFamMed   Sr. Lectr.; Principal
  Family Practitioner
Oosthuizen, J. M. C., MD   Prof.; Head*
Van Der Spuy, H. J., DEd   Sr. Lectr.
Van Der Westhuizen, L. L., MB ChB   Lectr.;
  Chief Med. Officer

Neurology

Duvenage, A., MMed   Sr. Lectr.; Sr. Specialist
Henderson, B. D., MMed   Sr. Lectr.; Sr.
  Specialist
Janse Van Rensburg, F. P., MMed   Principal
  Specialist; Sr. Lectr.
Kruger, A. J., MMed   Prof.; Chief Specialist;
  Head*

Neurosurgery

Albertyn, J., MMed   Prof.; Chief Specialist;
  Head*
Aldrich, C. G., MMed   Principal Specialist; Sr.
  Lectr.

Nuclear Medicine

Otto, A. C., MMed   Prof.; Chief Specialist;
  Head*

Obstetrics and Gynaecology

Cooreman, B. F., MMed   Principal Specialist;
  Sr. Lectr.
Cronje, H. S., MD   Prof.; Chief Specialist;
  Head*
Nel, J. T., MMedSc   Assoc. Prof.; Principal
  Specialist
Nortje, J. D., MMedSc   Sr. Lectr.; Sr. Specialist
Schoon, M. G., MMed   Sr. Lectr.; Specialist
Wessels, P. H., MD   Prof.; Chief Specialist

Occupational Therapy

Murray, A. J.   Sr. Lectr.; Head*
Pretorius, J., MOccupationalTherapy   Sr. Lectr.

Oncotherapy

Bester, A. C., MMed   Sr. Lectr.; Sr. Specialist
Goedhals, L., MMed   Prof.; Chief Specialist

Van Huyssteen, G. J., MSc   Sr. Lectr.;
  Specialist

Ophthalmology

Stulting, A. A., MMed   Prof.; Chief Specialist;
  Head*

Orthopaedics

Joubert, C. J., MMed   Sr. Lectr.; Sr. Specialist
Shipley, J. A., MMed   Assoc. Prof.; Principal
  Specialist
Smit, J. P. J., MB ChB   Sr. Lectr.; Sr. Specialist
Snowdowne, R. B., MMed   Prof.; Chief
  Specialist; Head*
Visser, E. M., MMed   Sr. Lectr.; Sr. Specialist

Otorhinolaryngology

Claassen, A. J., MMed   Prof.; Chief Specialist;
  Head*
De Jager, L. P., MMed   Sr. Lectr.; Sr. Specialist

Paediatrics and Child Care

Brown, S. C., MMed   Sr. Lectr.; Sr. Specialist
Bruwer, A. D., MMed   Sr. Lectr.; Principal
  Specialist
Grobler, J. M., PhD   Sr. Lectr.; Sr. Specialist
Hoek, B. B., MMed   Prof.; Second Chief
  Specialist
Kriel, J., MMed   Sr. Lectr.; Sr. Specialist
Schoeman, C. J., MMed   Assoc. Prof.;
  Principal Specialist
Stones, D. K., MMed   Sr. Lectr.; Specialist
Van der Vyfer, A. E., MB ChB   Sr. Lectr.; Sr.
  Specialist
Venter, A., MMed   Prof.; Chief Specialist,
  Head*

Pharmacology

Steyn, J. M., DSc   Sr. Lectr.
Venter, K. F., MFamMed   Sr. Lectr.

Physiotherapy

Krause, M. W., MSc   Prof.; Head*

Plastic Surgery

Smith, A. W.   Sr. Lectr.; Sr. Specialist

Psychiatry

Calitz, F. J. W., DPhil   Sr. Lectr.
Gagiano, C. A., MMed   Prof.; Chief Specialist;
  Head*
Janse Van Rensburg, P. H. J., MMed   Prof.;
  Chief Specialist
Le Roux, J. F., MA   Sr. Lectr.
Van der Merwe, L. M., DPhil   Sr. Lectr.;
  Specialist

Surgery

Du Toit, R. S., MMed   Prof.; Chief Specialist;
  Head*
Fichardt, J. B., MMed   Principal Specialist; Sr.
  Lectr.
Smit, S. M., MMed   Sr. Lectr.; Sr. Specialist

Urology

Viljoen, I. M., MMed   Prof.; Chief Specialist;
  Head*

Vascular Surgery, Unit for

Barry, R., MMed   Prof.; Chief Specialist

SPECIAL CENTRES, ETC

Accounting, Centre for

Becker, A. I., BCompt   Sr. Lectr.
Blair, J. H., BCom   Sr. Lectr.
Lindemann, E. R.   Sr. Lectr.
Lubbe, D. S., DCom   Prof.; Head*
Raubenheimer, E. J.   Sr. Lectr.
Swanepoel, J., BCom BCompt   Sr. Lectr.
Van Wyk, H. A., MCom   Prof.; Head*
Van Zyl, J. B., MCom   Sr. Lectr.

Agriculture Management, Centre for

Nel, W. T.   Head*

Construction Management, Centre for

Van Vuuren, BSc(QS)   Head*

Contemporary History, Institute for

Coetzer, P. W., DPhil   Prof.; Researcher
Van Der Westhuizen, L. J., DPhil   Sr. Lectr.;
  Researcher

Education Planning, Research Institute
for

Strauss, J. P., DEd   Prof.; Researcher
Van der Linde, H. J., DEd   Prof.; Head*

FARMOVS Research Unit

Groenewoud, G., PhD   Exec. Dir.*
Hundt, H. K. L., PhD   Exec. Dir.*
Van Niekerk, N., MB ChB   Exec. Dir.*

Groundwater Studies, Institute for

Van Tonder, G. J., PhD   Assoc. Prof.

Health Systems Research, Centre for

Vans Rensburg, H. C. J., DPhil   Prof.; Head*

Hoechst Research Unit

Medicine

Meyer, B. H., PhD   Exec. Dir.*
Scholtz, H. E., MMed   Dir., Clin. Services

Mangaung University Free State
Community Partnership Programme

Wessels, S. J., PhD   Dir.*

CONTACT OFFICERS

Admissions (first degree). Faculty Officer:
  Burger, J., BSocSc
Admissions (higher degree). Assistant
  Director: Venter, N. T.
Alumni. Assistant Director: Meader, C. J., BA
Archives. Librarian: Steyn, M. E., MBibl
Careers. Director: Venter, Prof. J. A., DPhil
  DEd
Computing services. Director: Altona, E. T.,
  BMedSc
Credit transfer. Deputy Director: Potgieter, G.
  D.
Estates and buildings/works and services.
  Director: Barkhuysen, W. J., MAdmin
Examinations. Nel, D., BA BSocSc
Finance. Director: Van der Bijl, A., BCom
General enquiries. Registrar: Malherbe, W. S.,
  MA MTRP
Health services. Director: Holtzhausen, L. J.,
  MB ChB
International office. Administrative Assistant:
  Du Preez, E. S., BCivJuris
Library (chief librarian). Director: Dippenaar,
  A. M., BBibl
Personnel/human resources. Director: Uys,
  D., MA
Publications. Public Co-ordinator: Swanepoel,
  A. P.
Purchasing. Deputy Director: Bezuidenhout, I.
  S.
Research. Assistant Director: Benson, N. J.,
  BA(Com) BSocSc
Safety. Assistant Director: Hansen, I. P. T.
Scholarships, awards, loans. Deputy Director:
  Buytendag, B., MAdmin
Security. Head: Du Plooy, L. J., BA
Sport and recreation. Director: Strydom, S.,
  BA BEd
Staff development and training. Senior
  Personnel Practitioner: Van Niekerk, M. M.,
  BA
Student union. (Contact the Student Council)
Student welfare/counselling. Social Worker:
  Kotze, H. M. C., BSocSc
University press. Manager: Engelbrecht, E. H.
  F.

[Information supplied by the institution as at 24 February
1998, and edited by the ACU]

UNIVERSITY OF PORT ELIZABETH

Founded 1964

Member of the Association of Commonwealth Universities

Postal Address: PO Box 1600, Port Elizabeth, 6000 South Africa
Telephone: (041) 504 2111 **Fax**: (041) 504 2574 **E-mail**: topnyw@upe.ac.za **WWW**: http://www.upe.ac.za
E-mail formula: contact postmaster@upe.ac.za to request individual e-mail addresses

CHANCELLOR—Eksteen, Johannes P. G., QC, BA *Cape Town*, LLB *Cape Town*
VICE-CHANCELLOR AND PRINCIPAL*—Kirsten, Prof. Johannes M., MA *Stell.*, DLitt&Phil *Rand*
Afrikaans
REGISTRAR‡—Coetzee, Johannes, BA *Pret.*
DIRECTOR, FINANCE—Katzke, Dawid, BCom *S.Af.*
UNIVERSITY LIBRARIAN—Fokker, Dirk W., BA *Potchef.*, MSc *Sheff.*

GENERAL INFORMATION

History. The university was founded in 1964. Located on the south-eastern coast, the university is situated in the city of Port Elizabeth in the Eastern Cape province.

Admission to first degree courses (see also South African Introduction). Matriculation certificate issued by the Matriculation Board, or exemption certificate. International applicants: exemption certificate issued by the Matriculation Board.

First Degrees (see also South African Directory to Subjects of Study) (* = also available with honours; † = honours only). BA*, BA(HumanMovementScience)†, BA(SW)*, BBdgA(Arch), BBdgA(ConstrMan), BCom*, BCom(Ed), BCom(Rationum), BCur*, BCur(IetA), BMus, BMus(Ed), BPharm, BPrimEd, BPsych, BSc*, BSc(QS), LLB.
Courses normally last 3 years full-time or 5 years part-time. BA(SW), BCom(Ed), BCom(Rationum), BCur, BMus, BPharm, BPrimEd, BSc(QS), LLB: 4 years full-time. Honours degree courses last 1 additional year full-time, 2 additional years part-time.

Higher Degrees (see also South African Directory to Subjects of Study). BArch, BEd, BSc(ConstrMan), LLM, MA, MA(ClinPsych), MA(CounsPsych), MA(SW), MArch, MCom, MCom(Tax), MCur, MEd, MEd(EdPsych), MMus, MPA, MPharm, MPhil, MSc, MSc(ConstrMan), MSc(QS), PhD, DArch, DCom, DCur, DEd, DLitt, DMus, DPhil, DSc, LLD.
Applicants for admission to BArch, BEd, BSc(ConstrMan) must normally hold an appropriate first degree; master's: appropriate first degree with honours; doctorates: appropriate master's degree.
BArch, BEd, BSc(ConstrMan) last 1 year full-time or 2 years part-time; master's: minimum 1 year, or minimum 2 years for a coursework programme; doctorates: at least 2 consecutive years.

Language of Instruction. English and Afrikaans, with duplication of classes where numbers warrant it. A policy of multilingualism (English, Afrikaans and Xhosa) is currently being phased in.

Libraries. 385,000 volumes and other holdings; 1271 periodicals subscribed to. Special collections: Steyn (Roman-Dutch Law).

Fees (1998). Undergraduate (annual): R5500–8800 (arts/humanities); R5700–9200 (sciences, including economic/management sciences); R1040–3545 (extra year of honours degrees, per course). Postgraduate: R1040–3545 (taught master's degrees, per course); R2950–3720 (master's degrees by dissertation); R2950–3670 (doctorates).

Academic Awards (1998). 34 awards ranging in value from R500 to R6000.

Academic Year (1999). Two semesters: 10 February–1 April and 12 April–24 June; 19 July–17 September and 27 September–25 November.

Income (1998). Total, R111,000,000.

Statistics. Staff: 1180. Students: full-time 4339 (1997 men, 2342 women); part-time 1624 (679 men, 945 women); international 250; total 5963.

FACULTIES/SCHOOLS

Arts
Tel: (041) 504 2187 Fax: (041) 504 2827
Dean: Naude, Prof. Petrus J., LTh *Stell.*, MA *Stell.*, DTh *Stell.*
Secretary: Slabber, Zelda, BA *P.Elizabeth*

Economic Sciences
Tel: (041) 504 2205 Fax: (041) 504 2755
Dean: Wait, Prof. Charles V. R., BComm *Stell.*, MComm *Stell.*, DPhil *P.Elizabeth*, DComm *Stell.*
Secretary: Zwiegelaar, Tersia, BA *P.Elizabeth*

Education
Tel: (041) 504 2371 Fax: (041) 504 2822
Dean: Van der Westhuizen, Prof. Conrad P., BA *Stell.*, BEd *Stell.*, BA *Cape Town*, DEd *P.Elizabeth*
Secretary: Van Rensburg, Susan

Health Sciences
Tel: (041) 504 2815 Fax: (041) 583 5324
Dean: Fullard, Prof. Josua P. P., BA *Stell.*, MA *P.Elizabeth*, DrsPhil *V.U.Amst.*, DPhil *P.Elizabeth*
Secretary: Ehbel, Gail

Law
Tel: (041) 504 2190 Fax: (041) 504 2818
Dean: Van Loggerenberg, Prof. Christo, BJuris *P.Elizabeth*, LLB *P.Elizabeth*, DJur *Ley.*
Secretary: Fourie, Marieta

Science
Tel: (041) 504 2873 Fax: (041) 504 2369
Dean: Ball, Prof. Conrad A. B., MSc *Pret.*, PhD *S.Af.*
Secretary: Barclay, Olivia

ACADEMIC UNITS

Accounting
Tel: (041) 504 2176 Fax: (041) 504 2755
Black, Margery J. G., BCom *Rhodes* Sr. Lectr.
Brettenny, Alexander J. N., BCom *Cape Town* Assoc. Prof.
De Villiers, David J., BSc(Eng) *Cape Town* Sr. Lectr.
Gardner, John B., BCom *Cape Town*, MEd *Cape Town* Prof.
Jones, Tracy, BCom *Rhodes* Sr. Lectr.
Prinslon, Frans E., BCom *P.Elizabeth* Sr. Lectr.
Prinsloo, Keith S., MCom *Rhodes* Prof.; Head*
Ramsay-Slogrove, Sean D., BCom *Cape Town* Prof.

Rowlands, Jeffrey E., BCom *Natal*, BEd *Rhodes*, MCom *Rhodes* Prof.
Singleton, Amanda, BCompt *P.Elizbeth* Sr. Lectr.
Other Staff: 1 Lectr.; 2 Sr. Tutors
Research: accounting education; accounting for goodwill, brands and trademarks; accounting for mergers and management buyouts; corporate and group financial reporting; equity method of accounting

African Languages
Tel: (041) 504 2871
Britz, Rudolph M. J., DLitt *P.Elizabeth* Sr. Lectr.
Thipa, Henry M., BEd *Fort Hare*, PhD *Natal* Prof.; Head*
Other Staff: 1 Lectr.; 1 Contract Lectr.
Research: African linguistics; Xhosa computer programming; Xhosa grammar; Xhosa language teaching; Xhosa literature (including oral)

Afrikaans and Dutch
Tel: (041) 504 2871
Janse van Vuuren, Hermina E., MA *Stell.*, LittDrs *Utrecht*, DLitt *Stell.* Prof.
Jordaan, Daniel J., BA(Ed) *P.Elizabeth*, MA *P.Elizabeth*, DLitt *P.Elizabeth* Sr. Lectr.
Kotzé, Ernst F., MA *Witw.*, PhD *Witw.* Prof.; Head*
Other Staff: 1 Lectr.
Research: Afrikaans poetry and prose; intercultural interaction in South African literature; lexicography; linguistics (historical, socio-, and linguistic nationalism); translation

Anthropology
Tel: (041) 504 2188
Booyens, Johan H., MA *Potchef.*, DPhil *Potchef.* Sr. Lectr.
Pauw, Hendrik C., BA *Pret.*, DPhil *P.Elizabeth* Assoc. Prof.; Head*
Research: archaeology; culture (kinship, marriage, health/religious/political/economic/legal systems); diversity management; indigenous law; physical anthropology

Architectural Subjects
Tel: (041) 504 2552 Fax: (041) 504 2345
Herholdt, Albrecht D., BArch *OFS* Sr. Lectr.
Lear, Stephen C., BBuild *P.Elizabeth*, BArch *P.Elizabeth* Sr. Lectr.
McLachlan, Gavin, BBuild *P.Elizabeth*, BArch *P.Elizabeth*, MScT&RP *Pret.* Sr. Lectr.
Theron, Jacobus D., BArch *Cape Town*, MArch *Penn.*, MCP *Manit.* Prof.; Head*
Other Staff: 1 Lectr.; 3 Contract Lectrs.
Research: architectural computing and CAD programming; architectural conservation; design; technical aspects of construction; town planning and town design

Biblical and Religion Studies
Tel: (041) 504 2152
Mouton, Aletta E. J., BA *Stell.*, MA *P.Elizabeth*, DTh *W.Cape* Sr. Lectr.

Oosthuizen, Marthinus J., LTh Stell., BA Stell., MTh Stell., DTh S.Af.   Prof.; Head*
Van Huyssteen, Jacobus W. F., BTh Stell., MA Stell., DTh V.U.Amst.   Hon. Prof.
Other Staff: 1 Lectr.
Research: contextual theology; interreligious dialogue; narratology; Old Testament legal texts; rhetoric and ethics

Biochemistry and Microbiology

Tel: (041) 504 2441 Fax: (041) 504 2814

Naude, Ryno J., MSc P.Elizabeth , PhD P.Elizabeth   Assoc. Prof.
Oelofsen, Willem, MScAgric Pret., PhD Calif.   Prof.; Head*
Other Staff: 4 Lectrs
Vacant Posts: 1 Sr. Lectr.
Research: biochemistry of fat tissue; biochemistry of the ostrich; bioseparation technology; cleaning and sanitation in food industry; molecular genetics

Botany

Tel: (041) 504 2397 Fax: (041) 532317

Bate, Guy C., BScAgric Natal, MSc Qu., PhD Qu.   Prof.
Robertson, Bruce L., MScAgric Pret., PhD P.Elizabeth   Prof.; Head*
Other Staff: 3 Lectrs.
Research: estuarine ecology and environmental management; management of commercial seaweed resources; mariculture and phycology; plant physiology and biochemistry; recreational patterns, utilisation of coastal zone

Business Management

Tel: (041) 504 2201

Bosch, Johan K., BCom Stell., DBA Stell.   Prof.; Head*
Boshoff, Hendrik C., DCom Pret.   Prof.
Tait, M., DCom P.Elizabeth   Sr. Lectr.
Other Staff: 3 Lectrs.; 1 Contract Jr. Lectr.
Research: entrepreneurship, small and micro-businesses; finance and investments (corporate); general and strategic management; marketing management; purchases management

Chemistry

Tel: (041) 504 2437

Du Preez, Jan G. H., DSc Stell.   Extraordinary Prof., Inorganic Chemistry
Gerber, Thomas I. A., BSc P.Elizabeth, MSc OFS, PhD S.Af.   Sr. Lectr.
McCleland, Cedric W., MSc P.Elizabeth, PhD P.Elizabeth   Prof., Organic Chemistry; Head*
McGill, William J., BSc Witw., PhD Witw.   Prof., Physical Chemistry; Gentyre Prof., Polymer Chemistry
Rohwer, Hans E., MSc Stell., PhD P.Elizabeth   Prof., Analytical Chemistry
Taljaard, Benjamin, MSc P.Elizabeth, PhD P.Elizabeth   Sr. Lectr.
Van Brecht, Bernardus J. A. M., MSc P.Elizabeth, PhD P.Elizabeth   Sr. Lectr.
Other Staff: 3 Lectrs.
Research: metal ion separation; new materials; nuclear medicine and radiopharmaceuticals; organic, inorganic and analytical chemistry; vulcanisation

Computer Science and Information Systems

Tel: (041) 504 2322 Fax: (041) 504 2323

Calitz, André P., BCom P.Elizabeth, MSc P.Elizabeth, PhD P.Elizabeth   Prof.
Cowley, Niel L. O., BEd P.Elizabeth , MSc P.Elizabeth   Sr. Lectr.
De Kock, Gideon de V., MSc Stell.   Prof.; Head*
Nicholls, Leon E., MSc P.Elizabeth   Sr. Lectr.
Wesson, Janet L., MCom P.Elizabeth, PhD P.Elizabeth   Prof.
Other Staff: 2 Lectrs.
Research: computer-aided learning; genealogical information systems; internet technology;

multi-media computing and development; user interface design

Construction Management

Tel: (041) 504 2790 Fax: (041) 504 2345

Eksteen, Brian, BScBdgMan Pret., MBA Pret.   Mars-White Prof.; Head*
Malherbe, André C., BScEng Witw.   Sr. Lectr., Building Science
Smallwood, John J., MSc(ConstrMgt) P.Elizabeth   Sr. Lectr.
Steenkamp, Ivan L., BSc Stell., BIng Stell., BCom P.Elizabeth, MArch P.Elizabeth   Assoc. Prof., Building Science
Research: construction dispute resolution; construction health, safety, productivity and quality; construction tendering; functional behaviour and performance of buildings; timber structures

Didactics

Tel: (041) 504 2371 Fax: (041) 504 2822

Holderness, William L.,, BA Rhodes., BEd Rhodes., PhD Lond.   Prof.
Other Staff: 1 Lectr.
Research: community development; curriculum development; educational management and school improvement; in-service teacher education; teaching methods

Dutch, see Afrikaans and Dutch

Economics and Economic History

Tel: (041) 504 2205

Hosking, Stephen G., MCom Rhodes, PhD Rhodes   Assoc. Prof.
Müller, André L., MA Stell., DPhil Stell.   Prof.; Head*
Other Staff: 1 Lectr.; 1 Contract Lectr.
Research: drug-related crime; economics of education; inflation; microeconomics; unemployment

Educational Psychology

Tel: (041) 504 2371 Fax: (041) 504 2822

Badenhorst, Hendrik J., BCom Potchef., MEd Pret., DEd P.Elizabeth   Assoc. Prof.; Head*
Olivier, Matilda A. J., BA P.Elizabeth, DEd P.Elizabeth   Sr. Lectr.
Other Staff: 1 Lectr.
Research: behaviour and emotional problems in children and adults; child development; hypnosis, hypnotherapy, hypnodiagnosis; learning, learning styles, brain dominance; school readiness and pre-primary education

English

Tel: (041) 504 2229

Bowker, Veronica J., BA P.Elizabeth, MA P.Elizabeth, DLitt P.Elizabeth   Sr. Lectr.
Fugard, Athol, Hon. DLitt P.Elizabeth   Hon. Prof.
Jeffery, Christopher D., BCom Cape Town, BA Cape Town, BA Lond., MA Trinity(Dub.), PhD Lond.   Prof.
McDermott, John B. S., MA P.Elizabeth   Sr. Lectr.
Other Staff: 1 Lectr.
Research: literary theory; metafiction, the post-modernist novel; modern drama; South African English; South African literature

French and German

Tel: (041) 504 2245

Thomas, Hilda M. B., MA P.Elizabeth, DLitt P.Elizabeth   Sr. Lectr., French; Head*
Wozniak, Janina, BA Pret., MA Cape Town, PhD Cape Town   Sr. Lectr., German
Research: language teaching (French, Italian, Spanish); literary criticism; literature of 16th to 20th centuries; teaching of German as a foreign language; translation

Geography

Tel: (041) 504 2355 Fax: (041) 504 2498

Christopher, Anthony J., BA Lond., MA Natal, PhD Natal   Prof.; Head*

Rootman, Petrus J., MA Stell., DPhil P.Elizabeth   Sr. Lectr.
Other Staff: 2 Lectrs.
Research: biogeography; development studies; geographic information systems; historical and political geography; land policy

Geology

Tel: (041) 504 2325

Booth, Peter W. K., MSc Rhodes, PhD Cape Town   Sr. Lectr.
Schumann, Eckart H., MSc S.Af., MSc Camb., PhD Natal   Sr. Lectr.
Shone, Russell W., BSc Rhodes, PhD P.Elizabeth   Assoc. Prof.; Head*
Research: East Cape coastal geology; economic minerals; fossils; groundwater; oceanography

German, see French and German

History

Tel: (041) 504 2210

Appel, André, MA Stell., DPhil P.Elizabeth   Sr. Lectr.
Rautenbach, Theodorus C., BEd P.Elizabeth, MA S.Af., DPhil P.Elizabeth   Sr. Lectr.; Head*
Terblanche, Hendrik O., BA Stell., MA P.Elizabeth, DPhil P.Elizabeth   Sr. Lectr.
Research: African history; Afrikaner history; apartheid; distance learning of history; Voortrekker history

Human Movement Science

Tel: (041) 504 2497 Fax: (041) 504 2770

Buys, Frederick J., MSc Potchef., DSc Potchef.   Prof.; Head*
Du Randt, Rosa, BSc Stell., MPhysEd Stell., PhD Stell.   Prof.
Du Toit, D. Etienne, MA P.Elizabeth, DPhil P.Elizabeth   Sr. Lectr.
Other Staff: 2 Lectrs.
Research: exercise physiology; exercise prescription and rehabilitation; kinesiology; movement education; sport/exercise science and psychology

Industrial and Organisational Psychology

Tel: (041) 504 2360

Rousseau, Gabriel G., MA P.Elizabeth, DPhil P.Elizabeth   Prof.; Head*
Snelgar, Robin J., MA Rhodes, PhD Rhodes   Sr. Lectr.
Van der Merwe, Roelof P., MA Stell., DPhil Stell.   Sr. Lectr.
Research: alcohol and drug abuse; assessment of human potential; compensation and job evaluation; consumer affairs (rights, education, complaints, behaviour); selection testing

Labour Relations and Human Resources Unit

Tel: (041) 504 2363 Fax: (041) 504 2825

Anstey, Mark, MA Witw., DPhil P.Elizabeth   Prof.; Dir.*
Cunningham, Peter W., DPhil P.Elizabeth   Assoc. Prof.
Finnemore, Martheanne, BA Rhodes, MA P.Elizabeth   Prof.
Van Der Walt, Jan A., BA P.Elizabeth, BJuris P.Elizabeth, LLB S.AF.   Sr. Lectr.

Law

Tel: (041) 504 2190 Fax: (041) 504 2818

Badenhorst, Petrus J., BLC Pret., LLM Witw., LLM Yale, LLD Pret.   Prof.
Carnelley, Marita, BA Stell., LLB Stell., LLM S.Af.   Sr. Lectr.
Delport, Hendrik J., BA Pret., LLD Pret.   Prof.
Hoctor, Shannon V., BA Cape Town, LLM Cape Town, DJur Ley.   Sr. Lectr.
Knoetze, Elmarie, BJuris P.Elizabeth, LLM P.Elizabeth   Sr. Lectr.
Le Roux, Lindi, BJuris P.Elizabeth, LLB P.Elizabeth   Sr. Lectr.
Marx, Frans E., BCom Stell., BJuris P.Elizabeth, LLD P.Elizabeth   Assoc. Prof.

Schwellnus, Teresa, BA P.Elizabeth, LLM Potchef., DJur Ley. Assoc. Prof.
Van der Berg, Eugene, BJuris P.Elizabeth, LLB P.Elizabeth Sr. Lectr.
Van der Walt, Jan A., BA P.Elizabeth, BJuris P.Elizabeth, LLB S.Af. Assoc. Prof.
Van Loggerenberg, Christo, BJuris P.Elizabeth, LLB P.Elizabeth, DJur Ley. Prof.; Dean*
Vrancken, Patrick H. G., LLD Cape Town Assoc. Prof.
Other Staff: 3 Lectrs.
Research: commercial and property law; human rights; international law; labour law; mineral rights

Management, see Public Admin. and Management

Mathematical Statistics

Tel: (041) 504 2310 Fax: (041) 504 2730
Hilliard-Lomas, Julia L., MSc P.Elizabeth Sr. Lectr.
Litvine, Igor, MSc Kiev, PhD Kiev Prof.; Head*
Mels, Gerhard, BSc P.Elizabeth, MSc S.Af. Sr. Lectr.
Other Staff: 3 Lectrs.
Research: correlation structures, covariance structures; statistical computing and programming, stochastic systems; statistical modelling; statistical theory of paired comparisons

Mathematics and Applied Mathematics

Tel: (041) 504 2300
Glover, Owen H., BEd P.Elizabeth, MSc P.Elizabeth Prof.
Gonsalves, John W., PhD P.Elizabeth Assoc. Prof.
Groenewald, Nicolas J., MSc P.Elizabeth, PhD Rhodes Prof.; Head*
Hall, Peter R., MSc S.Af., PhD Ill. Prof.
Olivier, Werner A., MSc P.Elizabeth, PhD P.Elizabeth Assoc. Prof.
Snyders, Andries J. M., BSc Rand Afrikaans, MSc S.Af., PhD P.Elizabeth Assoc. Prof.
Stirling, Desmond R., BSc Witw., MSc P.Elizabeth Sr. Lectr.
Veldsman, Stefan, PhD P.Elizabeth Prof.
Other Staff: 4 Lectrs.
Research: algebra; analysis; education, professional development of mathematics teachers; mechanics (Newtonian, quantum, water waves); numerical methods

Microbiology, see Biochem. and Microbiol.

Music

Tel: (041) 504 2253
Albertyn, Erik, MMus P.Elizabeth Sr. Lectr.; Head, Kodupe Music Centre
Bezuidenhout, Morne P., BMus P.Elizabeth, DMus S.Af. Sr. Lectr.
Bruno, Eugenia D. Sr. Lectr.
Du Plooy, David, BMus Witw., MMus Pret. Sr. Lectr.
Troskie, Albertus J. J., BMus Cape Town, MMus P.Elizabeth, DMus S.Af. Prof.; Head*
Other Staff: 5 Lectrs.
Research: brass, piano, choral/singing, percussion, violin; chamber music; music technology; musicology and composition; organ and organ building

Nursing Science

Tel: (041) 504 2122
Kotzé, Wilhelmina J., BA(Nursing) Pret., MCur Pret., DCur Pret. Prof.; Head*
Strümpher, Johanita, BCur Pret., MCur P.Elizabeth, DCur P.Elizabeth Sr. Lectr.
Wannenburg, Iona, BCur Pret., MCur Pret., DCur P.Elizabeth Assoc. Prof.
Other Staff: 5 Lectrs.
Research: clinical teaching and evaluation; crisis intervention, care of the dying; critical care nursing; nursing ethics, regulation, education; primary health care

Pharmacy

Tel: (041) 504 2128 Fax: (041) 504 2744
Boschmans, Shirley-Anne I., MSc P.Elizabeth Sr. Lectr.
Milne, Petrus J., BPharm Potchef., MSc Potchef., DSc Potchef. Sr. Lectr.
Naidoo, Nadasen T., BScPharm Rhodes, MSc Rhodes, PhD Rhodes Assoc. Prof.
Perkin, Michael F., MPharm W.Cape Sr. Lectr.
Van Oudtshoorn, M. C. B., DScPharm Potchef. Prof. Extraordinary
Wiseman, Ian C., MScPharm Rhodes, DSc Potchef. Prof.; Head*
Other Staff: 5 Lectrs.; 1 Contract Lectr.
Research: alternative medicine; cardiovascular pharmacology; cosmeticology; drug utilisation; pharmaceutical chemistry and drug design

Philosophy

Tel: (041) 504 2237
Olivier, Gysbert, MA P.Elizabeth, DPhil Pret. Prof.
Van Heerden, Christiaan F., BA Rand Afrikaans, BD Pret., MA P.Elizabeth, DPhil P.Elizabeth Sr. Lectr.; Head*
Research: communicative ethics and action (Habermas, Benhabib); critical theory; modernism and post-modernism; philosophy of art, architecture, film, culture; political theory

Philosophy of Education

Tel: (041) 504 2382 Fax: (041) 504 2822
Van Rensburg, Susan E., BA P.Elizabeth, BEd P.Elizabeth, DEd P.Elizabeth Sr. Lectr.
Other Staff: 1 Lectr.
Vacant Posts: 1 Prof./Head*
Research: comparative education; history of education

Physics

Tel: (041) 504 2143 Fax: (041) 504 2573
Engelbrecht, Jacobus A. A., MSc P.Elizabeth, PhD P.Elizabeth Prof.; Head*
Leitch, Andrew W. R., MSc P.Elizabeth, PhD P.Elizabeth Assoc. Prof.
Neethling, Johannes H., PhD P.Elizabeth Assoc. Prof.
Other Staff: 2 Lectrs.; 1 Contract Lectr.
Research: crystal growth; electron microscopy; photovoltaics/solar energy; semiconductors (electrical, optical and structural characterisation)

Political Studies

Tel: (041) 504 2175 Fax: (041) 504 2848
Booysen, Susan, BA Rand Afrikaans, MA Rand Afrikaans, PhD Rand Afrikaans Prof.; Head*
Bradshaw, Gavin J., BA P.Elizabeth, MA Hull Sr. Lectr.
Other Staff: 1 Lectr.
Research: conflict resolution; development politics; elections and voter education; South African government and policies; South African political parties and opposition politics

Psychology

Tel: (041) 504 2354 Fax: (041) 583 5324
Foxcroft, Cheryl D., MA P.Elizabeth, DPhil P.Elizabeth Prof.
Luiz, Delores M., MA P.Elizabeth, DPhil P.Elizabeth Prof.; Head*
Watson, Mark B., MA P.Elizabeth, DPhil P.Elizabeth Prof.
Other Staff: 2 Lectrs.; 1 Contract Lectr.
Research: marital and family functioning; problems in career development and choice; psychological effects of violence and trauma; psychological factors relating to health; standardisation and validation of psychological measuring instruments

Public Administration and Management

Tel: (041) 504 2123
Kroukamp, Hendrik J., BA Stell., MA P.Elizabeth, DPhil P.Elizabeth Sr. Lectr.
Meiring, Michael H., BA S.Af., DPhil P.Elizabeth Assoc. Prof.; Acting Head*
Thornhill, Christopher, MA Pret., DPhil Pret. Hon. Prof.
Other Staff: 1 Lectr.
Research: administration for developing areas; environment/institutional framework; municipal and regional government and administration; policy and organisational processes; public sector financial administration and budgets

Quantity Surveying

Tel: (041) 504 2385 Fax: (041) 532276
Buys, Nicolaas S., BBdgA P.Elizabeth, MSc P.Elizabeth Sr. Lectr.
Le Roux, Gaye K. Prof.; Head*
Other Staff: 1 Lectr.
Research: building economics; computer-assisted learning in quantity surveying; information technology in quantity surveying; mechanical and electrical installation; property economics and property development

Social Work

Tel: (041) 504 2353
Potgieter, Michiel C., MA Stell., DPhil Stell. Prof.
Tshiwula, Juliet L., MA P.Elizabeth, DPhil P.Elizabeth Lectr.; Head*
Other Staff: 3 Lectrs.
Research: community education and development; counselling (family, premarital, marital, divorce); management of not-for-profit organisations; substance abuse; the aged

Sociology

Tel: (041) 504 2146
Bezuidenhout, Frans J., BA Pret., BA(SW) P.Elizabeth, DPhil P.Elizabeth Sr. Lectr.
Cunningham, Peter W., DPhil P.Elizabeth Assoc. Prof.
Haines, Richard J., MA Natal, PhD Lond. Prof.; Head*
Other Staff: 3 Contract Lectrs.
Research: development studies; economic and industrial policy; media and communications; sociology of business and of work; sociology of health and socio-medical issues

Teacher Education

Tel: (041) 504 2387 Fax: (041) 504 2822
Bean, Patrick, BComEd P.Elizabeth, BEd P.Elizabeth, MEd Rhodes Sr. Lectr.
Lemmer, André N., BA Rhodes, BEd Rhodes, MEd Exe. Sr. Lectr.
Van der Westhuizen, Conrad P., BA Cape Town, BA Stell., BEd Stell., DEd P.Elizabeth Prof.; Head*
Other Staff: 4 Lectrs.
Research: computers in education; curriculum development; education for the gifted; music education; remedial teaching

Textile Science

Hunter, Lawrance, BSc Cape Town, MSc P.Elizabeth, PhD P.Elizabeth Phillip Frame Prof., Textile Technol.; Prof. Extraordinary; Head*
Other Staff: 2 Lectrs.
Research: chemical textile processes and products; high-tech fibres and applications; physical textile processes and properties

University Education

Tel: (041) 504 2572
Havenga, André J., BJur P.Elizabeth, DEd P.Elizabeth Prof.; Head*

Zoology

Tel: (041) 504 2341 Fax: (041) 504 2317

Baird, Daniel, BSc Pret., MSc Stell., PhD Stell. Prof.; Head*

Kerley, Graham I. H., MSc Pret., PhD P.Elizabeth Sr. Lectr.

Rossouw, Gideon J., MSc Stell., PhD P.Elizabeth Sr. Lectr.

Webb, Paul, MSc P.Elizabeth Assoc. Prof.

Winter, Paul E. D., PhD P.Elizabeth Sr. Lectr.

Wooldridge, Tristram H., BSc Rhodes, PhD P.Elizabeth Assoc. Prof.

Other Staff: 1 Lectr.; 4 Accredited Lectrs.

Research: crustaceans, amphibians, reptiles, mammals, birds, elasmobranchs; environmental physiology; estuaries; reproduction; skeletons

SPECIAL CENTRES, ETC

Accounting, School of

Tel: (041) 504 2176 Fax: (041) 504 2755

Prinsloo, Keith S., MCom Rhodes Prof.; Dir.*

All lecturers in the Department of Accounting are members of the School

Advanced Studies, School for

Tel: (041) 504 2218

Olivier, Gysbert, MA P.Elizabeth, DPhil Pret. Prof.; Co-ordinator*

Applied Business Management, Centre for

Tel: (041) 504 2176

Boshoff, Hendrik C., DCom Pret. Prof.; Dir.*

Coastal Resources, SAB Institute for

Tel: (041) 504 2396 Fax: (041) 532317

Bate, Guy C., BScAgric Natal, MSc Qu., PhD Qu. Prof.; Dir.*

Wooldridge, Tristram H., BSc Rhodes, PhD P.Elizabeth Assoc. Prof.

Research: botany: estuaries, mariculture, dunes, surf zone; geography: demographics, geographic information systems, mapping; geology: sedimentology, dunes, estuarine hydrodynamics, weather profiles, coastal geology; microbiology: water pollution; zoology: fisheries, estuarine macrobenthos, birds, water chemistry

Conflict, Institute for the Study and Resolution of

Tel: (041) 504 2376

Bradshaw, Gavin J., BA P.Elizabeth, MA Hull Dir.*

Research: causes and dynamics of conflict; conflict management mechanisms and techniques

Continuing Education, Centre for

Tel: (041) 585 8718 Fax: (041) 586 5419

Burkett, Beverley L., BA P.Elizabeth, BA Rhodes Project Leader, Language Education

Glover, Owen H., BEd P.Elizabeth, MSc P.Elizabeth Project Leader, Mathematics Education

Lamont, A. J. Programme Dir., Southern Cape Learning Resource Unit

Shelver, Shelagh A., BA S.Af. Project Leader, Community Development Unit

Venter, Adolph Z. Manager, Small Business Unit

Webb, Paul, BSc Rhodes, MEd Rhodes, MSc P.Elizabeth Project Leader, Science Education

Research: community development, training for NGOs; education and training of English and second language teachers; education and training of mathematics teachers; education and training of science teachers; small business development, entrepreneurship, management development

Development Planning and Research, Institute for

Tel: (041) 504 2336 Fax: (041) 531769

Pretorius, Deon, BA S.Af., MA P.Elizabeth, PhD Warw. Dir.*

Other Staff: 5 Researchers

Research: education and training: capacity building/development planning; institutional-organisational development and transformation; local economic development; socio-economic development studies; urban and rural community development

Eastern Cape Studies, Centre for

Tel: (041) 504 2236

Jeffery, Christopher D., BCom Cape Town, BA Cape Town, BA Lond., MA Trinity(Dub.), PhD Lond. Prof.; Dir.*

Research: Eastern Cape anthropology, architecture, environmental issues, geography, history, literature, politics

Economic Processes, Unit for the Study of

Tel: (041) 504 2205

Müller, André L., MA Stell., DPhil Stell. Prof.; Dir.*

Legal Clinic

Tel: (041) 573388 Fax: (041) 573335

Coetzee, Rudolf D. J., BJuris P.Elizabeth, LLB P.Elizabeth Dir.*

Mercantile Law, Bureau for

Tel: (041) 504 2191 Fax: (041) 504 2818

Delport, Hendrik J., BA Pret., LLD Pret. Prof.; Dir.*

Metal Ion Separation, Research Unit for

Tel: (041) 504 2286

Du Preez, Jan G. H., DSc Stell. Extraordinary Prof.; Dir.*

Gerber, Thomas I. A., BSc P.Elizabeth, MSc OFS, PhD S.Af. Sr. Lectr.

Rohwer, Hans E., MSc Stell., PhD P.Elizabeth Prof.

Van Brecht, Bernardus J. A. M., MSc P.Elizabeth, PhD P.Elizabeth Sr. Lectr.

Public Administration and Management, School for

Tel: (041) 504 2123

De Villiers, Pieter F. A., MA Pret., DPhil P.Elizabeth Prof.; Dir.*

Science and Mathematics Education, Institute for

Tel: (041) 504 2301

Kriel, Dawid J., BSc Pret., MSc Potchef., DEd P.Elizabeth Dir.*

Statistical Consultation and Methodology, Institute for

Tel: (041) 504 2392

Venter, Danie J. L., BSc P.Elizabeth Dir.*

All staff of the Department of Mathematical Statistics are members of the Institute

Research: operational research and decision-making; research data analysis and statistical inference; statistical methodology; statistical modelling and simulation analysis; statistical software

University Clinic

Tel: (041) 504 2330 Fax: (041) 583 5324

Elkonin, D. Dir.*

CONTACT OFFICERS

Academic affairs. Assistant Registrar (Academic): Bishop, Jennifer M., BSocSc Rhodes

Accommodation. Director, Residences: Mkwanazi, Thandiwe N., BA Lond.

Admissions (first degree). Head Admissions Officer: Hosten, Luc W., BA P.Elizabeth

Admissions (higher degree). Head Admissions Officer: Hosten, Luc W., BA P.Elizabeth

Adult/continuing education. Acting Director, Centre for Continuing Education: Wait, Prof. Charles V. R., BComm Stell., MComm Stell., DPhil P.Elizabeth, DComm Stell.

Alumni. Administrator: Van Loggerenberg, Susan L.

Archives. Fokker, Margaretha I., BA Potchef.

Careers. Head, Unit for Student Counselling: De Jager, André C., BA Pret., MA S.Af., MA(Ed) S'ton., DPhil P.Elizabeth

Careers. Graduate and Student Placement Office: Pratt, Lorna I.

Computing services. Director, Computing Centre: Nel, Christiaan J., BSc P.Elizabeth

Conferences/corporate hospitality. Functions Co-ordinator: Moodley, Suriya

Development/fund-raising. Director, Communication and Marketing Services: Smit, Susan S. W.

Distance education. Head, University Education: Havenga, André J., BJur P.Elizabeth, DEd P.Elizabeth

Equal opportunities. Director, Human Resources: Zide, Gordon N., MA Fort Hare

Estates and buildings/works and services. Director, Support Services: Horne, Charles W. D., BScEng Natal, MScEng Natal

Examinations. Examinations Officer: Voges, Jacoba M.

Finance. Director, Finance: Katzke, Dawid, BCom S.Af.

General enquiries. Registrar: Coetzee, Johannes, BA Pret.

Health services. Registered Nurse and Midwife: Goosen, Antoinette P., BCur P.Elizabeth

Industrial liaison. Director, Communication and Marketing Services: Smit, Susan S. W.

International office. Director, International Office: Havenga, André J., BJur P.Elizabeth, DEd P.Elizabeth

Library (chief librarian). University Librarian: Fokker, Dirk W., BA Potchef., MSc Sheff.

Ombudsperson. Secretary to Transformation Forum: Hattle, Janette J.

Personnel/human resources. Director, Human Resources: Zide, Gordon N., MA Fort Hare

Public relations, information and marketing. Director, Communication and Marketing Services: Smit, Susan S. W.

Publications. Senior Librarian: Gerber, Samuel J., BA Stell.

Purchasing. Chief, Buying and Stores: Rathbone, Aubrey

Quality assurance and accreditation. Head, University Education: Havenga, André J., BJur P.Elizabeth, DEd P.Elizabeth

Research. Administrative Officer, Research: Ncwadi, Mcebisi R., BA Vista

Safety. Safety, Health and Environment Manager: Lovemore, Annette T., BSc Cape Town

Scholarships, awards, loans. Head, Financial Aid: Dennis, Frederick P.

Schools liaison. Marketing Manager: Geswindt, Paul G. G., BCom(Ed) P.Elizabeth

Security. Head, Protection Services: Coetzer, André L.

Sport and recreation. Director, Sports Bureau: Van der Walt, Jacobus S., BA Potchef.

Staff development and training (academic staff). Director, Organisational and Academic Development: Havenga, André J., BJur P.Elizabeth, DEd P.Elizabeth

Staff development and training (other staff). Manager, HR Systems Development and Training: Botha, Le Breton F., BA Cape Town, LLB Cape Town

Student union. Administrative Officer, Student Representative Council: Knoetze, Felicity E.

Student welfare/counselling. Director, Student Services: Matiso, Khaya G., BA Vista

Students from other countries. Director, International Office: Havenga, André J., BJur P.Elizabeth, DEd P.Elizabeth

Students with disabilities. Director, Student Services: Matiso, Khaya G., BA *Vista*

University press. Senior Librarian: Gerber, Samuel J., BA *Stell*.

[*Information supplied by the institution as at 9 July 1998, and edited by the ACU*]

POTCHEFSTROOM UNIVERSITY FOR CHRISTIAN HIGHER EDUCATION

Potchefstroomse Universiteit vir Christelike Hoër Onderwys

Founded 1869; university status conferred 1951

Member of the Association of Commonwealth Universities

Postal Address: Private Bag X6001, Potchefstroom, 2520 South Africa
Telephone: (018) 299 1111 **Fax**: (018) 299 2799 **E-mail**: username@puknet.puk.ac.za
Cables: PUK, Potchefstroom **Telex**: 346-019 S.Af.

CHANCELLOR—......
VICE-CHANCELLOR AND PRINCIPAL*—Reinecke, Prof. Carolus J., BSc *Potchef.*, MSc *Potchef.*, DSc *Ley.*, Hon. DTh *Kosin*
VICE-PRINCIPAL—Viljoen, Prof. A. J., MABibl *Potchef.*, DPhil *Potchef.*
VICE-PRINCIPAL (ACADEMIC)—Scott, Prof. W. E., BComm *Potchef.*, LLD *Potchef.*
VICE-PRINCIPAL (DEVELOPMENT)—Zibi, M. S., BCom *Fort Hare*, MA *Bochum*
VICE-PRINCIPAL (VAAL TRIANGLE CAMPUS)—Prinsloo, Prof. P. J. J., DLitt *Potchef.*
REGISTRAR—Van der Walt, Prof. C. F. C., BJur&Art *Potchef.*, LLB *Rand Afrikaans*, LLD *S.Af.*
REGISTRAR, FINANCE—Rost, Prof. I. J., MComm *Potchef.*

GENERAL INFORMATION

History. The university was originally founded in 1869 as a theological seminary for Christian teaching. In 1919 it became a university college and in 1951 achieved independent university status. In 1966 a satellite campus in the Vaal Triangle was established.

The university is located in Hoffman Street, Potchefstroom.

Admission to first degree courses (see also South African Introduction). Applicants must have full matriculation exemption and also comply with the specific requirements set out by individual faculties.

First Degrees (see also South African Directory to Subjects of Study) (* = also available with honours; † = honours only). BA*, BA(MW)† (social work), BArtetScien(Planning), BA(SocialWork), BA(Theology)*, BBA(Telematic), BBC, BBibl*, BCom*, BCom(BusinessCommunication), BCur, BDS†, BEd, BEng, BMus*, BMus(Ed), BPharm, BPrimEd, BSc*, BSc(Dietetics), BScPharm†, LLB.

Higher Degrees (see also South African Directory to Subjects of Study). ThB, LLM, MA, MA(MW) (social work), MArtetScien(Planning), MBA, MBA(Telematic), MBibl, MCom, MDS, MEd, MEng, MMus, MPharm, MSc, ThM, PhD, DBA, DCom, DEd, DEng, DLitt, DMus, DPharm, DPhil, DSc, LLD, ThD.

Language of Instruction. Afrikaans (Potchefstroom campus). Other languages may be used for instruction when necessary. Students may obtain permission to write tests/exams in English. Vaal Triangle Campus: the circumstances of each class determine language of instruction used, thus parallel courses are offered in Afrikaans and English. The Telematic Learning Campus at present conducts courses in English only.

Libraries. 512,047 volumes; 115,466 journal volumes; 131,248 other materials.

Fees (annual). Average: R7315.

Academic Year (1998–99). Four semesters: 3 February–1 April; 15 April–8 July; 20 July–26 September; 5 October–8 December.

Income (1997–98). Total, R133,207,784.

Statistics. Staff: 2131 (654 academic, 1477 administrative). Students: full-time 6660 (3019 men, 3641 women); part-time 3785 (2262 men, 1523 women); international 92 (67 men, 25 women); total 10,445.

FACULTIES/SCHOOLS

Arts
Dean: Van der Elst, Prof. J., BA *Potchef.*, BA *Rhodes*, MA *Pret.*, DrsLitt *Utrecht*, PhD *Natal*
Secretary: Barnard, S. J. J.

Economics and Management Science
Dean: Havenga, Prof. J. J. D., MComm *Potchef.*, DEcon *V.U.Amst.*
Secretary: Jones, W. J. F.

Education
Dean: Van der Walt, Prof. J. L., DEd *Potchef.*, DPhil *Potchef.*
Secretary: Labuschagne, F. J. C.

Engineering
Dean: Greyvenstein, Prof. G. P., MBL *S.Af.*, DEng *Pret.*
Secretary: Pretorius, V.

Interfaculty Academic Board
Tel: (016) 807 3111 Fax: (016) 807 3116
Dean: Malan, Prof. D. J., DPhil *Stell.*
Secretary: Minnaar, S.

Law
Dean: Vorster, Prof. I., BA *Potchef.*, LLB *Potchef.*
Secretary: de Beer, H.

Natural Science
Dean: Geertsema, Prof. J. C., MSc *Pret.*, PhD *Calif.*
Secretary: Venter, H.

Pharmacy
Dean: Koeleman, Prof. H. A., DSc(Pharm) *Potchef.*, DSc *Potchef.*
Secretary: Venter, E. M. E.

Theology
Dean: Du Plooy, Prof. A. le R., BA *Potchef.*, ThD *Potchef.*
Secretary: Postma, C.

ACADEMIC UNITS

Accountancy, Statistics and Mathematics, School of
Grobler, J. J., MSc *Potchef.*, DSc *Ley.* Prof.; Head*

Accountant Training, Chartered
Ducharme, G. E., BR *Potchef.* Dir.*

Accountant Training, Financial
Stoop, A. A., BR *Potchef.*, MCom *Potchef.* Dir.*

Accountant Training, Management
Visser, S. S., DCom *OFS* Prof.; Dir.*

Accounting Science, School for
Eloff, T., BPhil *Potchef.*, DCom *Potchef.* Prof.; Head*

African Languages
Vermeulen, G. J. G., DLitt *Potchef.* Head*

Afrikaans and Dutch
Carstens, W. A. M., MA *Stell.*, DLitt *Stell.* Prof.; Head*

Afrikaanse Taal-en Kultuurvereniging Creative Writing School
Du Plessis, H. G. W., BA *Potchef.*, MA *Rand Afrikaans*, MIJ *Baylor*, DPhil *Potchef.* Prof.; Head*

Basic Management Training, Institute for

Coetzee, W. N., LLB Potchef., HBA Potchef., LLD Pret. Prof.; Head*

Biochemistry

Pretorius, P. J., DSc Potchef. Prof.; Head*

Biokinetics, Institute for

Strydom, G. L., DPhil Potchef. Prof.; Dir.*

Business and Personnel Management

Barnard, A. L., BComm Stell., DCom OFS Prof.; Head*

Business Management

De Klerk, G. J., BSc(Econ) Potchef., DComm Potchef. Prof.; Head*

Business Mathematics and Informatics

Erasmus, C. M., BSc Rand Afrikaans, MSc Rand Afrikans, MCom Pret., PhD S.Af. Prof.

Chemistry

Steyn, P. S., MSc Stell., PhD S.Af. Prof.; Head*

Classics and Semitics

Kroeze, J. H., ThB Potchef., PhD Potchef. Head*

Communication Research, Institute for

De Beer, A. S., BA Potchef., MA Rand Afrikaans, MIJ Baylor, DPhil Potchef. Prof.; Head*

Computer Science and Information Systems

Hattingh, J. M., DSc Potchef. Prof.; Head*

Diaconiology and Missiology

Venter, C. J. H., BA Potchef., ThD Potchef. Prof.; Head*

Dogmatology and Ecclesiology

Du Plooy, A. le R., BA Potchef., ThD Potchef. Prof.; Head*

Education, Postgraduate School of

Van der Westhuizen, P. C., BA Potchef., DEd Potchef., DEd S.Af. Prof.; Dir.*

Engineering, Chemical and Mineral

Everson, R. C., BSc Witw., MSc Natal, PhD Natal Prof.; Dir.*

Engineering, Electrical and Electronic

Hoffman, A. J., BSc Pret., BEng Pret., MEng Pret., PhD Pret. Prof.; Head*

Engineering, Mechanical and Metallurgical

Greyvenstein, G. P., MBL S.Af., DEng Pret. Prof.; Head*

English Language and Literature

Combrink, A. L., DLitt Potchef. Prof.; Head*

Geography and Environmental Studies

De Villiers, A. B., MSc Potchef., PhD OFS Prof.; Head*

History

Du Pisani, J. A., DPhil OFS Prof.; Head*

Human Movement Science

Strydom, G. L., DPhil Potchef. Prof.; Head*

Industrial and Personnel Psychology, School for

Scholtz, P. E., DPhil Potchef. Prof.; Dir.*

Industrial Pharmacy, Institute for

Dekker, T. G., DSc Potchef. Prof.; Head*

Information Studies

Lessing, C. J. H., DBibl Potchef. Prof.; Head*

Labour Science, School for

Van den Berg, J. H., BA Pret., BA Potchef., DPhil Potchef. Prof.; Dir.*

Law, Mercantile

Stander, A. L., LLB Potchef., LLM S.Af., LLD Potchef. Prof.; Head*

Law, Private

Pienaar, G. J., BJur&Comm Potchef., LLD Potchef. Prof.; Head*

Law, Public, and Legal Philosophy

Venter, F., BJur&Comm Potchef., LLD Potchef. Prof.; Head*

Legal Pluralism and Legal History

Du Plessis, W., BJuris Potchef., LLD Potchef. Prof.; Head*

Legal Studies, Applied

Coetzee, T. J., BJur&Art Potchef., LLD Potchef. Prof.; Head*

Life Sciences

Van Hamburg, H., DSc Pret. Prof.; Head*

Mathematics and Applied Mathematics

Van Wyk, D. J., DSc Potchef. Prof.; Head*

Music

Jooste, S. J., BMus S.Af., DMus Potchef. Prof.; Head*

Non-formal Education Programmes, School for

Mentz, P. J., BA Pret., BEd Pret., MEd Rand Afrikaans, DEd Potchef. Prof.; Dir.*

Nursing Science

Greeff, M., DCur Rand Afrikaans Prof.; Head*

Nutrition and Human Ecology

Venter, C. S., BSc Pret., BSc Potchef., DSc Potchef. Prof.; Head*

Old and New Testament

Van Rooy, H. F., ThB Potchef. Prof.; Head*

Pharmaceutical Chemistry

Bergh, J. J., BSc Stell., BSc(Pharm) Potchef., BSc(IndPharm) Potchef., DSc Potchef. Prof.; Head*

Pharmaceutics

Van der Watt, J. G., MSc(IndChem) Potchef., DSc Potchef. Prof.; Head*

Pharmacology

Venter, D. P., DSc Potchef. Prof.; Head*

Pharmacy Practice

Gerber, J. J., BSc Potchef., DSc Potchef. Head*

Philosophy

Venter, J. J., DrsPhil V.U.Amst., DPhil Potchef. Prof.; Head*

Physics

Moraal, H., DSc Potchef. Prof.; Head*

Physiology

Malan, N. T., MSc OFS, DSc Potchef. Prof.; Head*

Plant and Soil Sciences

Pieterse, A. J. H., MSc Potchef., PhD Wash. Prof.; Head*

Political Science

Wyk, W. J., BAdmin OFS, MAdmin OFS, DAdmin S.Af. Prof.; Head*

Psychology

Wissing, M. P., DrsClinPsych V.U.Amst., DPhil Potchef. Prof.; Head*

Recreation and Tourism

Meyer, C. D. P., MA Potchef. Head*

Social Work

Kotze, G. J., DPhil Stell. Prof.; Head*

Sociology

Moller, P. H., DPhil OFS Prof.; Head*

Statistics and Operational Research

Venter, J. H., MSc Potchef., PhD Chic. Prof.; Head*

Teacher Training, School for

Steyn, H. J., BA Potchef., DEd Potchef. Prof.; Dir.*

Tourism and Leisure Studies, Institute for

Saayman, M., MA Pret., DPhil Pret. Dir.*

Town and Regional Planning

Nieuwoudt, A., MA Stell., DPhil Potchef. Prof.; Head*

Zoology

Loots, G. C., MSc Rand Afrikaans, DSc Potchef. Prof.; Head*

SPECIAL CENTRES, ETC

Bank, Asset and Liability Management, Unit for

Styger, P., MCom OFS, DCom Potchef. Prof.; Dir.*

Community Law, Centre for

Meyer, S. W. J., BJur Potchef. Dir.*

Development Economy, Unit for

Naude, W. A., MSc Warw., PhD Potchef., MCom Prof.; Dir.*

Economy, Money and Banking, Centre for

Naude, W. A., MSc Warw., MCom Potchef., PhD Potchef. Prof.; Dir.*

Education and Traffic Safety, Centre for (CENETS)

Venter, P. R., BA S.Af., BEd Potchef., MEd Potchef. Dir.*

Human Resource Development, Centre for

Barnard, A. L., BCom Stell., DCom OFS Prof.; Head*

Phonetics and Phonology, Research Unit for

Wissing, D. P., MA Potchef., DrsLitt V.U.Amst., DLitt Utrecht Prof.; Dir.*

Physics and Chemistry, Unit for Advancement of

Smit, J. J. A., DSc Potchef. Prof.; Dir.*

Psychotherapy and Counselling, Institute for

Du Plessis, W. F., MA Potchef., DPhil Potchef. Prof.; Dir.*

Quality Assurance and Medicine, Centre for (CENQAM)

Bonseschans, B., BSc(Pharm) Potchef., DSc Potchef. Prof.; Head*

Reclamation Ecology, Research Institute for

Booysen, J., MScAgric OFS, PhD Nebraska Prof.; Dir.*

Reformational Studies, Institute for

Van der Walt, B. J., ThB Potchef., DPhil Potchef. Prof.; Dir.*

Separation Technology, Sasol Centre for

Steyn, P. S., MSc Stell., PhD S.Af., FRSSAf Prof.; Dir.*

Small Business Advisory Bureau (SBAB)

Moolman, P. L., BCom OFS, DCom Potchef. Prof.; Dir.*

Sport Science and Development, Institute for

Malan, D. D. J., DSc Potchef.　Prof.; Head*

Training of Trainers, Centre for

Jacobsz, J. M., BEd Rand Afrikaans, MEd Rand Afrikaans　Dir.*

VAAL TRIANGLE CAMPUS

Accountancy and Audit

Tel: (016) 807 3111 Fax: (016) 807 3116
Lucouw, P., MCom Potchef.　Prof.; Head*

Arts, Faculty of

Tel: (016) 807 3111 Fax: (016) 807 3116
Malan, D. J., DPhil Stell.　Prof.; Head*

Biblical Studies and Philosophy

Tel: (016) 807 3111 Fax: (016) 807 3116
Rabali, T. C., BA S.Af., ThM Potchef., DTh S.Af.　Prof.; Head*

Business and Personnel Management

Tel: (016) 807 3111 Fax: (016) 807 3116
Stander, M. W., MComm Potchef.　Head*

Business Management

Tel: (016) 807 3111 Fax: (016) 807 3116
Pretorius, J. B., MBL S.Af., DBA Potchef.　Prof.; Head*

Computer Science and Information Systems

Tel: (016) 807 3111 Fax: (016) 807 3116
Venter, L. M., PhD Potchef.　Prof.; Head*

Cost and Management Accounting

Tel: (016) 807 3111 Fax: (016) 807 3116
Van den Berg, N. J. B., DComm Potchef.　Head*

Economics

Tel: (016) 807 3111 Fax: (016) 807 3116
Van der Westhuizen, G., BCom OFS, DComm Potchef.　Prof.; Head*

Economics and Management Science

Tel: (016) 807 3111 Fax: (016) 807 3116
Lucouw, P., MComm Potchef.　Prof.; Head*

Educational Sciences

Tel: (016) 807 3111 Fax: (016) 807 3116
Theron, A. M. C., BA OFS, MEd OFS, DEd S.Af.　Prof.; Head*

History and Public Administration

Tel: (016) 807 3111 Fax: (016) 807 3116
De Klerk, P., DLitt Potchef., DEd Potchef.　Prof.; Head*

Industrial Sociology

Tel: (016) 807 3111 Fax: (016) 807 3116
Van Wyk, C. de W., DComm Potchef.　Prof.; Head*

Languages

Tel: (016) 807 3111 Fax: (016) 807 3116
Willies, W. H., BA Cape Town, BEd Cape Town, DLitt Cape Town　Prof.; Head*

Mathematics and Applied Mathematics

Tel: (016) 807 3111 Fax: (016) 807 3116
Laurie, D. P., MSc Stell., PhD Dund.　Prof.; Head*

Psychology

Tel: (016) 807 3111 Fax: (016) 807 3116
Malan, D. J., DPhil Stell.　Prof.; Head*

Sociology

Tel: (016) 807 3111 Fax: (016) 807 3116
Bester, C. W., DPhil Potchef.　Prof.; Head*

Statistics and Operational Research

Tel: (016) 807 3111 Fax: (016) 807 3116
De Wet, A. G., MSc Potchef., SM Chic., PhD Chic.　Prof.; Head*

CONTACT OFFICERS

Academic affairs. Registrar: Van der Walt, Prof. C. F. C., BJur&Art Potchef., LLB Rand Afrikaans, LLD S.Af.

Accommodation. Director: De Klerk, W.

Admissions (first degree). Director: Pienaar, W. J., BA Potchef.

Admissions (higher degree). Director: Pienaar, W. J., BA Potchef.

Adult/continuing education. Vice-Principal (Development): Zibi, M. S., BCom Fort Hare, MA Bochum

Alumni. Director, Public Relations: Cloete, T. T., BA Potchef.

Archives. Archivist: Van der Schyff, Prof. P. F., DLitt Potchef.

Careers. Head: Kotzé, H. N., MSc Potchef., DPhil Potchef.

Computing services. Director: Van der Walt, A. J., DSc Potchef.

Development/fund-raising. Director, Public Relations: Cloete, T. T., BA Potchef.

Distance education. Chief Director, Telematic Learning Systems: Van Wyk, Prof. L. A., MA Harv., DComm Potchef.

Estates and buildings/works and services. Director: Van der Ryst, L. G.

Examinations. Director: Pienaar, W. J., BA Potchef.

Finance. Registrar, Finance: Rost, Prof. I. J., MComm Potchef.

General enquiries. Registrar: Van der Walt, Prof. C. F. C., BJur&Art Potchef., LLB Rand Afrikaans, LLD S.Af.

International office. Director, Public Relations: Kruger, A. J., BA Potchef., MBA Potchef.

Library (chief librarian). Director, Library Services: Lessing, Prof. C. J. H., DBibl Potchef.

Personnel/human resources. Chief Director: Van der Watt, Prof. C. J., DSc Potchef.

Public relations, information and marketing. Director, Public Relations: Cloete, T. T., BA Potchef.

Publications. Director, Public Relations: Cloete, T. T., BA Potchef.

Purchasing. Senior Accountant: Scott, N. J. de W., BCom Potchef.

Safety. Director: Van der Ryst, L. G.

Scholarships, awards, loans. Director: Van der Walt, P. J.

Schools liaison. Head, Unit for Educational Services: Gibbs, M. G., BA Potchef.

Security. Director: Engels, A. S., BA Potchef.

Sport and recreation. Head: Hugo, J. J., BA Pret., BEd S.Af., MEd P.Elizabeth, MA Lanc., DEd Potchef.

Staff development and training. Chief Director: Van der Watt, Prof. C. J., DSc Potchef.

Student union. Chairman: Horn, G.

Student welfare/counselling. Students Dean: Potgieter, Prof. P. J. J. S., DPhil Potchef.

University press. Manager: Badenhorst, E. E., BA Potchef.

CAMPUS/COLLEGE HEADS

Vaal Triangle Campus, PO Box 1174, Vanderbijlpark, 1900 South Africa. (Tel: (016) 807 3111; Fax: (016) 807 3114.) Vice-Principal: Prinsloo, Prof. P. J. J., DLitt Potchef.

[Information supplied by the institution as at 2 March 1998, and edited by the ACU]

UNIVERSITY OF PRETORIA

Founded 1930; previously established as Transvaal University College 1910

Member of the Association of Commonwealth Universities

Postal Address: Pretoria, 0002 South Africa
Telephone: (012) 420 4111 **Fax**: (012) 362 5168, 362 5190 **Cables**: Puniv **Telex**: 3-22 723
WWW: http://www.up.ac.za

CHANCELLOR—Stals, C. L., MCom Pret., DCom Pret.
VICE-CHANCELLOR AND PRINCIPAL*—Van Zyl, Prof. Johan, BSc(Agric) Pret., MSc(Agric) Pret., PhD Vista, DSc(Agric) Pret., Hon. FRSSAf
VICE-PRINCIPAL—De Beer, Prof. C. R., BJur&Art Potchef., LLB Potchef., LLM Rand Afrikaans, LLM W.Cape, DrsJuris Ley., LLD Ley.
VICE-PRINCIPAL—Erasmus, Prof. T., MSc(Agric) Pret., DSc(Agric) Pret.
VICE-PRINCIPAL—Marx, Prof. S., BCom Pret., MCom Pret., MBA Pret., DCom Pret.
ACTING REGISTRAR‡—Marais, D. D., MA Pret., DPhil Pret.
UNIVERSITY LIBRARIAN—Gerryts, Prof. E. D., BA S.Af., MA(Lib) Pret., DLitt&Phil S.Af.
EXECUTIVE DIRECTOR—Sinclair, Prof. J. D., BA Witw., LLB Witw., LLD Witw.

FACULTIES/SCHOOLS

Arts
Tel: (012) 420 2318 Fax: (012) 420 2698
Dean: Van Wyk, Prof. Wouter C., MA Pret., DD Pret.
Secretary: Potgieter, Ann S.

Biological and Agricultural Sciences
Tel: (021) 420 2478 Fax: (021) 362 5189
Dean: Crewe, Prof. Robin M., MScAgric Natal, PhD Georgia
Secretary: Scheepers, Alta

Dentistry
Tel: (021) 319 2225 Fax: (021) 323 7616
Dean: Ligthelm, Prof. Attie J., MChD Stell., PhD Stell.
Secretary: Odendaal, Marie A.

Economic and Management Sciences
Tel: (021) 420 2425 Fax: (021) 362 5194
Dean: Thornhill, Prof. Christopher, MA Pret., PhD Pret.
Secretary: Van den Berg, Irene

Education
Tel: (021) 420 3513 Fax: (021) 362 5122
Dean: Bondesio, Prof. Michael J., BA Pret., MEd Pret.
Secretary: Steyn, Orgina J. C.

Engineering
Tel: (012) 420 2440 Fax: (012 362 5173
Dean: Malherbe, Prof. Johannes A. G., BSc Stell., BEng Stell., PhD Stell., DEng Pret.
Secretary: Schoeman, Margaret E.

Law
Tel: (012) 420 2412 Fax: (012) 362 5184
Dean: Olivier, Prof. Nicolaas J. J., LLB Pret., MA Pret., DPhil Pret., LLD Pret., DrsJuris Ley., LLD Ley.
Secretary: Rosslee, Anna M.

Medicine
Tel: (012) 354 2386 Fax: (012) 329 1351
Dean: Du Plessis, Prof. Dionisius J., MMed Pret.
Secretary: Hibbert, Marietjie S.

Science
Tel: (012) 420 2574 Fax: (012) 362 5084
Dean: Sauer, Prof. Niko, MSc Pret., PhD S.Af.
Secretary: Smith, Eurina

Theology (Dutch Reformed Church)
Tel: (012) 420 2322 Fax: (012) 420 4016
Dean: Wethmar, Prof. Conrad J., BA Stell., BTh Stell., MA Stell., ThD Amst.
Secretary: Aucamp, Carla

Theology (Dutch Reformed Church of Africa)
Tel: (012) 420 2348 Fax: (012) 420 2887
Dean: Koekemoer, Prof. Johannes H., BA Pret., BD Pret., DD Pret.
Secretary: Pretorius, Johanna C.

Veterinary Science
Tel: (012) 529 8000 Fax: (012) 529 8313
Dean: Coubrough, Prof. Rhoderick I., BVSc Pret., MVSc Tor.
Secretary: Prinsloo, Linda

ACADEMIC UNITS

Accountancy
Tel: (012) 420 2422 Fax: (012) 342 2757
Buys, Willem J. Prof.
Cronje, Christo J. Sr. Lectr.
De Villiers, Charl J. Prof.
Du Plessis, Daniel E. Extraordinary Prof.
Du Plessis, Leana Sr. Lectr.
Gouws, Daniel G. Prof.
Greyling, Annemie Sr. Lectr.
Koornhof, Carolina Prof.
Loots, Jacobus A. J. Extraordinary Prof.
Myburgh, Jean E. Sr. Lectr.
Pistorius, Carl W. I. Extraordinary Prof.
Ramano, M. Hon. Prof.
Skosana, Israel B. Extraordinary Prof.
Stiglingh, Madeleine Sr. Lectr.
Van der Merwe, Johannes G. Sr. Lectr.
Van Niekerk, Marita C. Assoc. Prof.
Van Zyl Smit, Jacobus Extraordinary Prof.
Venter, Jan M. P. Sr. Lectr.
Vermaak, Frans N. S. Sr. Lectr.
Vorster, Quintus, BCom OFS, MCom Stell., PhD Stell. Prof.; Head*
Other Staff: 6 Lectrs.

Accountancy, School of
Tel: (012) 420 2701 Fax: (012) 342 2450
Botha, Willem J. J. Sr. Lectr.
Butler, Rika Sr. Lectr.
De Beer, Linda Sr. Lectr.
De Jager, Hermanus, BEd Pret., MEd Potchef., MCom Pret., DCom Pret. Prof.; Dir.*
Fourie, Karen Sr. Lectr.
Gloeck, Juergen D. Prof.
Koen, Marius Prof.
Kriel, Angela L. Sr. Lectr.
Leith, Karin B. Sr. Lectr.
Lombard, Pieter E. Sr. Lectr.
Loots, Jacobus A. J. Extraordinary Prof.
Nieuwoudt, Margaretha J. Sr. Lectr.
Oberholster, Johan G. I. Sr. Lectr.
Oosthuizen, Rudi Sr. Lectr.
Pienaar, Abraham J. Sr. Lectr.
Plant, Gregory J. Sr. Lectr.
Prinsloo, Isabel Sr. Lectr.
Roode, Monica Sr. Lectr.
Schumann, Eckhard F. Sr. Lectr.
Shotter, Magdalena Assoc. Prof.

Steyn, Maxi Sr. Lectr.
Other Staff: 2 Lectrs.

Actuarial Science, see Insurance and Actuarial Sci.

African Languages
Tel: (012) 420 2492 Fax: (012) 420 3163
Gauton, Rachelle Sr. Lectr.
Goslin, Benjamin du P. Sr. Lectr.
Groenewald, Pieter S., MA Pret., DLitt Pret. Prof.; Head*
Malimabe, Refilwe M. Sr. Lectr.
Maphumulo, Abednego M. Sr. Lectr.
Marggraff, Margaret M. Sr. Lectr.
Mojalefa, Mawatle J. Sr. Lectr.
Prinsloo, Daniel J. Prof.
Sekeleko, Daniel M. G. Sr. Lectr.
Skhosana, Philemon B. Sr. Lectr.
Taljard, Elizabeth Sr. Lectr.
Wilkes, Arnett Prof.
Other Staff: 1 Lectr.; 1 Res. Fellow

Afrikaans
Tel: (012) 420 2349 Fax: (012) 420 2349
Carstens, Adelia Prof.
De Wet, Karen Sr. Lectr.
Dlamini, Nombuso S. Sr. Lectr.
Janse van Rensburg, Marthinus C., MA Pret., DLitt Pret. Prof.; Head*
Malan, Charles Extraordinary Prof.
Marais, Rene Sr. Lectr.
Nolte, Katie E. Prof.
Ohlhoff, Carl H. F. Prof.
Roodt, Pieter H. Prof.
Snyman, Martha E. Sr. Lectr.
Webb, Victor N. Prof.

Agricultural Economics, Extension and Rural Development
Tel: (012) 420 3250 Fax: (012) 342 2713
Botha, Cornelius A. J. Assoc. Prof.
Duvel, Gustav H. Prof.
Hassan, Rashid M. Prof.
Kirsten, Johann F., MSc(Agric) Pret., PhD Pret. Prof.; Head*
Nyampfene, Kingston Extraordinary Prof.
Thirtle, Colin G. Extraordinary Prof.
Other Staff: 4 Lectrs.; 1 Res. Fellow

Ancient Languages
Tel: (012) 420 2350 Fax: (012) 420 4008
Barkhuizen, Jan H. Prof.
Botha, Philippus J. Assoc. Prof.
Da Silva, Andrew A. Assoc. Prof.
Mans, Marthinus J. Prof.
Martin, Magretha E. B. Sr. Lectr.
Potgieter, Johan H., BA Potchef., MA Pret., BD Pret., DD Pret. Prof.; Head*
Prinsloo, Gert T. M. Assoc. Prof.
Stander, Hendrik F. Prof.
Swart, Gerhardus J. Assoc. Prof.
Other Staff: 1 Lectr.

Animal and Wildlife Sciences

Tel: (012) 420 2539 Fax: (012) 432 2713
Bothma, Jacobus du P. Prof.
Casey, Norman H., MSc(Agric) Natal,
  DSc(Agric) Pret. Prof.; Head*
Cronje, Pierre B. Assoc. Prof.
Jansen van Ryssen, Jannes B. Prof.
Prinsloo, Jacobus F. Extraordinary Prof.
Smith, Gerhard A. Prof.
Van Hoven, Wouter Assoc. Prof.
Van Niekerk, Willem A. Sr. Lectr.
Vermeulen, Gysbert T. J. Sr. Lectr.
Webb, Edward C. Sr. Lectr.
Other Staff: 1 Lectr.; 2 Res. Officers

Anthropology and Archaeology

Tel: (012) 420 2595 Fax: (012) 420 2698
Boonzaaier, Carl C. Sr. Lectr.
Els, Herman Sr. Lectr.
Hartman, Jan B., MA Pret., DPhil Pret. Prof.;
  Head*
Kriel, Johannes D. Assoc. Prof.
Meyer, Andrie Assoc. Prof.
Pistorius, Julius C. C. Sr. Lectr.
Other Staff: 2 Lectrs.

Architecture, see also Landscape Archit.

Tel: (012) 420 2550 Fax: (012) 420 2552
Bakker, Karel A. Sr. Lectr.
De Villiers, Adriaan J. Assoc. Prof.
Fisher, Roger C. Sr. Lectr.
Holm, Dietrich, MArch Pret., DArch
  Pret. Prof.; Head*
Kemp, Johannes T. Assoc. Prof.
Wegelin, Hans W. Sr. Lectr.
Other Staff: 5 Lectrs.

Biblical Studies

Tel: (012) 420 3155 Fax: (012) 420 4016
Bezuidenhout, Louis C., MA Pret., BD Pret., DD
  Pret. Prof.; Head*
Geyser, Petrus A. Sr. Lectr.
Human, Dirk J. Assoc. Prof.
Joubert, Stephanus J., BA Pret., BD Pret., DD
  Pret. Prof.
Other Staff: 1 Lectr.

Biochemistry

Tel: (012) 420 2906 Fax: (012) 432 2713
Apostolides, Zeno Sr. Lectr.
Gaspar, Anabella R. M. Sr. Lectr.
Louw, Abraham I. Prof.
Neitz, Albert W. H., MSc(Agric) Pret.,
  DSc(Agric) Pret. Prof.; Head*
Verschoor, Jan A. Prof.
Visser, Leon, MSc(Agric) Pret., PhD Harv. Prof.
Other Staff: 1 Lectr.

Biological and Agricultural Sciences (General)

Tel: (012) 420 2478 Fax: (012) 342 2713
Annandajayasekeram, Ponniah Extraordinary
  Prof.
Coutinho, Teresa A. Sr. Lectr.
Oberholster, Anna-Maria Assoc. Prof.
Van Rooyen, Cornelius J. Prof.
Wingfield, Michael J. Prof.

Botany

Tel: (012) 420 2487 Fax: (012) 432184
Aveling, Theresa A. S. Sr. Lectr.
Bredenkamp, George J. Prof.
Coetzer, Lourens A. Sr. Lectr.
Eicker, Albert, MSc Potchef., DSc Potchef. Prof.;
  Head*
Meyer, Jacobus J. M. Assoc. Prof.
Smith, Gideon F. Extraordinary Prof.
Van de Venter, Hendrik A. Prof.
Van Greuning, Johannes V. Sr. Lectr.
Van Rooyen, Noel Prof.
Van Wyk, Abraham E. Prof.
Von Teichman Undlogischen, Irmgard Sr.
  Lectr.
Other Staff: 1 Lectr.; 1 Res. Officer; 2 Res.
  Fellows

Business Management

Tel: (012) 420 2411 Fax: (012) 342 1457
De Villiers, Jacques A. Prof.
De Wit, Pieter W. C. Prof.
Janse van Vuuren, Johannes J. Sr. Lectr.
Maasdorp, Edward F. de V. Prof.
Marx, Andrew E. Prof.
Nieman, Gideon H. Sr. Lectr.
Oost, Ebo J. Prof.
Van Rooyen, Dirk C., BCom Pret., MBA Pret.,
  DBA Pret. Prof.; Head*
Visser, Johannes H. Extraordinary Prof.
Other Staff: 8 Lectrs.

Chemistry

Tel: (012) 420 2512 Fax: (012) 432863
Bauermeister, Sieglinde Sr. Lectr.
De Waal, Danita Sr. Lectr.
Lotz, Simon Prof.
Modro, Agnieszka M. Assoc. Prof.
Modro, Tomasz A., MSc Lodz, PhD Polish
  Acad.Sc., DSc Lodz Prof.; Head*
Rademeyer, Cornelius J. Prof.
Rohwer, Egmont R. Prof.
Roos, Hester M. Sr. Lectr.
Schoeman, Wentzel J. Assoc. Prof.
Strydom, Christiena A. Assoc. Prof.
Van Dyk, Martha M. Sr. Lectr.
Van Rooyen, Petrus H. Prof.
Van Staden, Jacobus F. Prof.
Venter, Elise M. M. Sr. Lectr.
Vleggaar, Robert Prof.
Wessels, Philippus L. Prof.
Other Staff: 2 Lectrs.; 3 Res. Fellows

Church History and Church Policy (Dutch Reformed Church)

Tel: (012) 420 2669 Fax: (012) 420 4016
Hofmeyr, Johannes W., BA Pret., BD Pret., ThD
  Theol.Sch.Kampen Prof.; Head*

Communication Pathology

Tel: (012) 420 2357 Fax: (012) 420 3517
Alant, Erna Prof.
Hugo, Susanna R., MA(Log) Pret., DPhil
  Pret. Prof.; Head*
Louw, Brenda Prof.
Ras, Nicholaas M. Sr. Lectr.
Tesner, Hermanus E. C. Sr. Lectr.
Uys, Isabella C., BA(Log) Witw., MA(Log) Pret.,
  DPhil Pret. Prof.
Van der Merwe, Anita Assoc. Prof.
Other Staff: 5 Lectrs.; 3 Sr. Clin. Lectrs.; 6
  Clin. Lectrs.

Computer Science

Tel: (012) 420 2361 Fax: (012) 436454
Bishop, Judith M. Prof.
Kourie, Derrick G., MSc Pret., MSc S.Af., PhD
  Lanc. Prof.; Head*
Oosthuizen, Gerhard D. Assoc. Prof.
Roos, Johannes D. Prof.
Watson, Bruce W. Assoc. Prof.
Other Staff: 4 Lectrs.

Construction Management

Tel: (012) 420 2576 Fax: (012) 420 3598
Cloete, Christiaan E. Prof.
Hauptfleisch, Andries C., BSc Pret., MBA Pret.,
  PhD Pret. Prof.; Head*
Other Staff: 1 Lectr.

Criminology

Tel: (012) 420 2030 Fax: (012) 420 2698
Pretorius, Ronelle, MA Pret., DPhil Pret. Prof.;
  Head*
Theron, Aubrey Prof.
Other Staff: 5 Lectrs.

Dentistry, see below

Didactics

Tel: (0120 420 2966 Fax: (012) 420 3003
Bagwandeen, Dowlat R. Extraordinary Prof.
Basson, Nicolaas J. S. Prof.
Cronje, Johannes C. Assoc. Prof.
De Kock, Dorothea M. Sr. Lectr.

Du Toit, Pieter H. Sr. Lectr.
Fraser, William J., BSc Potchef., DEd S.Af. Prof.;
  Head*
Hodgkinson, Cheryl A. Sr. Lectr.
Knoetze, Jan G. Assoc. Prof.
Kotze, Annemarie Sr. Lectr.
Kuhn, Marthinus J. Assoc. Prof.
Le Roux, Susanna S. Sr. Lectr.
Slabbert, Johannes A. Sr. Lectr.
Spengler, Josephus J. Sr. Lectr.
Van Staden, Marthinus J. Hon. Prof.

Dogmatics and Christian Ethics (Dutch Reformed Church)

Tel: (012) 420 2818 Fax: (012) 420 4016
De Villiers, Dawid E. Prof.
Wethmar, Conrad J., BA Stell., BTh Stell., MA
  Stell., ThD Amst. Prof.; Head*

Dogmatics and Christian Ethics (Dutch Reformed Church of Africa)

Tel: (012) 420 2348 Fax: (012) 420 2887
Koekemoer, Johannes H., BA Pret., BD Pret., DD
  Pret. Prof.; Head*

Drama

Tel: (012) 420 2558 Fax: (012) 433283
Odendaal, Louwrens B., MA Pret., DLitt
  Pret. Prof.; Head*
Trichardt, Carolus G. Sr. Lectr.
Other Staff: 4 Lectrs.

Economics

Tel: (012) 420 2413 Fax: (012) 433362
Asante, S. K. B. Extraordinary Prof.
Blignaut, James N. Sr. Lectr.
Brink, Sansia M. Sr. Lectr.
Du Toit, Charlotte B. Sr. Lectr.
Harmse, Christoffel Prof.
Jordaan, Andre C. Sr. Lectr.
Koekemoer, Renee Sr. Lectr.
Maasdorp, Gavin G. Extraordinary Prof.
Mollentze, Sandra L. Sr. Lectr.
Parsons, Raymond W. K. Extraordinary Prof.
Schoeman, Nicolaas J. Prof.
Scholtz, Frederik J. Sr. Lectr.
Stals, Christian L. Extraordinary Prof.
Steyn, Frederick G. Prof.
Truu, Mihkel L. Prof.
Van Heerden, Jan H., BCom Pret., MCom Rand
  Afrikaans, MA Rice, PhD Rice Prof.; Head*
Other Staff: 5 Lectrs.

Education Management

Tel: (012) 420 2902 Fax: (012) 420 3723
Beckmann, Johannes L. Prof.
Berkhout, Susara J. Prof.
Calitz, Louis P., BSc Pret., BEd Pret., MEd Pret.,
  DEd Rand Afrikaans Prof.; Head*
Conradie, Johan J. Sr. Lectr.
Van der Bank, Anna J. Assoc. Prof.

Engineering, Aeronautical, see Engin., Mech. and Aeron.

Engineering, Agricultural and Food

Tel: (012) 420 2177 Fax: (012) 432816
Du Plessis, Hendrik L. M., MSc(Eng) Pret., PhD
  Pret. Prof.; Head*
Eckard, John H. Sr. Lectr.
Smit, Cornelius J. Sr. Lectr.
Other Staff: 2 Lectrs.

Engineering and Technology Management

Tel: (012) 420 3530 Fax: (012) 436218
Barnard, Willem J. Extraordinary Prof.
De Klerk, Antonie M., MSc(Eng) Pret., MS Stan.,
  PhD Stan. Prof.; Head*
Lombaard, Jan M. Extraordinary Prof.
Steyn, Hermanus De V. Prof.
Visser, Jacobus K. Prof.
Winzker, Dietmar H. Extraordinary Prof.
Other Staff: 1 Lectr.

Engineering, Chemical

Tel: (012) 420 2475 Fax: (012) 432816

De Vaal, Philip L. Prof.
De Villiers, Gideon H. Sr. Lectr.
Focke, Walter W. Extraordinary Prof.
Grimsehl, Uys H. J., BEng Pret., DEng
 Pret. Prof.; Head*
Heydenrych, Mike D. Sr. Lectr.
Kornelius, Gerrit Sr. Lectr.
Mandersloot, Willem G. B. Extraordinary
 Prof.
Pretorius, William A. Prof.
Schutte, Christiaan F. Assoc. Prof.
Skinner, William Extraordinary Prof.
Tolmay, Andries T. Sr. Lectr.
Other Staff: 3 Lectrs.

Engineering, Civil

Tel: (012) 420 2978 Fax: (012) 433589

Basson, Gerrit R. Assoc. Prof.
Burdzik, Walter M. G. Prof.
Dehlen, George L. Extraordinary Prof.
Dekker, Nicolaas W. Prof.
Del Mistro, Romano F. Prof.
Ebersohn, Willem Prof.
Heymann, Gerhard Sr. Lectr.
Janse van Rensburg, Barend W. Prof.
Kearsley, Elizabeth P. Sr. Lectr.
Maree, Leon Prof.
Marshall, Vernon Prof.
Michael, Ronald Sr. Lectr.
Robberts, Johannes M. Sr. Lectr.
Rohde, Archibald W., BSc OFS, BSc(Eng) Natal,
 BEng Pret., MEng Pret. Prof.; Head*
Roodt, Louis De V. Sr. Lectr.
Rust, Ebenhaezer Sr. Lectr.
Smit, Johannes E. Sr. Lectr.
Smith, Raymond A. F. Extraordinary Prof.
Van As, Sebastiaan C. Extraordinary Prof.
Van der Walt, Adriaan Assoc. Prof.
Van Harmelen, Tiana Sr. Lectr.
Van Heerden, Johan Prof.
Van Vuuren, Stefanus J. Prof.
Vermeulen, Nicolaas J. Sr. Lectr.
Visser, Alex T. Prof.
Other Staff: 5 Lectrs.

Engineering, Electrical and Electronic

Tel: (012) 420 2164 Fax: (012) 433254

Baker, Duncan C. Prof.
Botha, Elizabeth C. Prof.
Cilliers, Petrus J. Prof.
Coetzee, Jacob C. Assoc. Prof.
Craig, Ian K. Prof.
Delport, Gabriel J. Assoc. Prof.
Du Plessis, Monuko Prof.
Ehlers, Gavin W. Sr. Lectr.
Frangos, Constantine Assoc. Prof.
Gitau, Michael Sr. Lectr.
Hancke, Gerhardus P. Prof.
Hanekom, Johannes J. Sr. Lectr.
Holm, Johann E. W. Sr. Lectr.
Joubert, Johan Prof.
Joubert, Trudi-Heleen Assoc. Prof.
Leuschner, Friedrich W., MEng Pret., DEng
 Pret. Prof.; Head*
Linde, Louis P. Prof.
Malan, Willie R. Sr. Lectr.
Nieuwoudt, Christoph Sr. Lectr.
Odendaal, Johann W. Prof.
Pauw, Christoff K. Prof.
Seevinck, Evert Prof.
Smith, Edwin D. Assoc. Prof.
Snyman, Lukas W. Assoc. Prof.
Taute, Willem J. Extraordinary Prof.
Van Alphen, Johannes C. Extraordinary Prof.
Van Niekerk, Hendrik R. Assoc. Prof.
Van Rooyen, Pieter G. W. Assoc. Prof.
Van Schalkwyk, Johannes J. D. Prof.
Vermaak, Jaco Sr. Lectr.
Xia, Xiaohua Assoc. Prof.
Yavin, Yaakov Prof.
Other Staff: 3 Lectrs.

Engineering, General

Fax: (012) 362 5173

No staff at present

Engineering, Industrial and Systems

Tel: (012) 420 2433 Fax: (012) 342 2508

Claasen, Schalk J., BScEng Pret., MBA Pret.,
 MScEng Arizona, PhD Pret. Prof.; Head*
Conradie, Pieter J. Sr. Lectr.
Janse van Rensburg, Antonie C. Sr. Lectr.
Kruger, Paul S., MBA Pret., MSc(Eng) Pret.,
 DSc(Eng) Pret. Prof.
Lubbe, Andries J. Assoc. Prof.
Pretorius, Petrus J. Sr. Lectr.
Rottier, Johannes Sr. Lectr.
Van Schoor, Christiaan de W. Sr. Lectr.
Warren, Graeme M. H. Sr. Lectr.

Engineering, Mechanical and Aeronautical

Tel: (012) 420 2452 Fax: (012) 342 1379

Burger, Nicolaas D. L. Sr. Lectr.
Coetzee, Jasper L. Sr. Lectr.
Craig, Kenneth J. Assoc. Prof.
Crosby, Charles P. Sr. Lectr.
De Wet, Philippus R. Sr. Lectr.
Dreyer, Hector N. Extraordinary Prof.
Fourie, Eugene Prof.
Grobbelaar, Barry Sr. Lectr.
Groenwold, Albert A. Sr. Lectr.
Heyns, Michiel Assoc. Prof.
Heyns, Philippus S. Prof.
Lombard, Christoffel Sr. Lectr.
Mathews, Edward H. Prof.
Naude, Alwyn F. Sr. Lectr.
Snyman, Johannes A. Prof.
Steyn, Jasper L., MSc(Eng) Pret., DEng
 Pret. Prof.; Head*
Ungerer, Cornelius P. Assoc. Prof.
Van Graan, Frederik J. Sr. Lectr.
Van Heerden, Eugene Sr. Lectr.
Van Niekerk, Johannes L. Prof.
Van Schoor, Marthinus C. Extraordinary Prof.
Van Waveren, Cornelis C. Sr. Lectr.
Van Wyk, Adriaan J. Sr. Lectr.
Van Wyk, Waldo Sr. Lectr.
Visser, Jan A. Prof.
Von Wielligh, Adam J. Sr. Lectr.
Wannenburg, Johann Sr. Lectr.
Other Staff: 1 Lectr.

Engineering, Metallurgical, see Material
Sci. and Metall. Engin.

Engineering, Mining

Tel: (012) 420 2443 Fax: (012) 432816

Esterhuizen, Gabriel S. Sr. Lectr.
Fourie, Gert A., BSc(Eng) Pret., MSc(Eng)
 Witw., PhD Pret. Prof.; Head*
Jansen van Vuuren, Petrus J. Sr. Lectr.
Moolman, Coenraad J. Sr. Lectr.
Thompson, Roger J. Assoc. Prof.
Webber, Ronald C. W. Sr. Lectr.

Engineering, Systems, see Engin., Indust.
and Systems

English

Tel: (012) 420 2421 Fax: (012) 420 2698

Brown, Molly A. Sr. Lectr.
Dreyer, Christian L. Sr. Lectr.
Finn, Stephen M. Prof.
Gray, Rosemary A. Prof.
Lenahan, Patrick C. Sr. Lectr.
Marx, Petronella J. M. Sr. Lectr.
McKay, Walter Sr. Lectr.
Titlestad, Peter J. H., BA Cape Town, BEd Cape
 Town, MA Cant., DLitt Pret. Prof.; Head*
Wessels, Johan A. Sr. Lectr.
Other Staff: 5 Lectrs.

Entomology, see Zool. and Entomol.

Food Science

Tel: (012) 420 3211 Fax: 012) 342 2752

Bester, Bernardus H. Assoc. Prof.
Minaar, Amanda Sr. Lectr.
Taylor, John R. N., BSc CNAA, PhD
 Nott.Trent Prof.; Head*
Other Staff: 1 Lectr.

Genetics

Tel: (012) 420 3258 Fax: (012) 342 4058

Fossey, Annabel Assoc. Prof.
Hofmeyr, Jan H. Hon. Prof.
Huismans, Hendrik, MSc Stell., DSc Pret. Prof.;
 Head*
Liebenberg, Heinrich Assoc. Prof.
Roux, Carl Z. Prof.
Van Staden, Vida Sr. Lectr.
Wingfield, Brenda D. Prof.
Other Staff: 2 Lectrs.

Geography

Tel: (012) 420 2489 Fax: (012) 420 3284

Fairhurst, Unita J. Assoc. Prof.
Hattingh, Phillippus S., BA Witw., MA Witw.,
 DLitt&Phil S.Af. Prof.; Head*
Hugo, Marthinus L. Prof.
Meiklejohn, Keith I. Sr. Lectr.
Wilson, Gideon D. H. Sr. Lectr.
Other Staff: 2 Lectrs.

Geology

Tel: (012) 420 2454 Fax: (012) 433430

Botha, Willem J. Prof.
De Waal, Sybrand A., MSc Pret., DSc
 Pret. Prof.; Head*
Eriksson, Patrick G. Prof.
Fortsch, Erich B. Prof.
Grantham, Geoffrey H. Assoc. Prof.
Hattingh, Pierre J. Assoc. Prof.
Merkle, Rolland K. W. Assoc. Prof.
Snyman, Carel P. Prof.
Van Rooy, Jan L. Sr. Lectr.
Van Schalkwyk, Alfonso Prof.
Other Staff: 6 Lectrs.

History and Cultural History

Tel: (012) 420 2323 Fax: (012) 420 2656

Bergh, Johannes S., BA Stell., MA S.Af., DPhil
 Stell. Prof.; Head*
Ferreira, Ockert J. O. Prof.
Grobler, John E. H. Sr. Lectr.
Pretorius, Fransjohan Prof.
Other Staff: 4 Lectrs.

History of Art, see Visual Arts and Hist. of
Art

History of Christianity (Dutch Reformed Church of Africa)

Tel: (012) 420 2738 Fax: (012) 420 2887

Botha, Schalk J., BA Pret., BD Pret., DD
 Pret. Prof.; Head*

Home Economics

Tel: (012) 420 2575 Fax: (012) 436867

Blignaut, Anita S. Sr. Lectr.
Boshoff, Elizabeth, BSc Stell., MSc Iowa State,
 PhD Stell. Prof.; Head*
Botha, Priscilla Prof.
De Klerk, Helena M. Assoc. Prof.
Erasmus, Aletta C. Sr. Lectr.
Reynders, Hendrik J. Sr. Lectr.
Trollip, Anna M. Assoc. Prof.

Human Movement Science

Tel: (43) 420 7711 Fax: (012) 362 0463

Goslin, Anna E. Assoc. Prof.
Knobel, Daniel P. Hon. Prof.
Kruger, Pieter E. Assoc. Prof.
Steyn, Barend J. M. Sr. Lectr.
Van Heerden, Hendrik J. Sr. Lectr.
Van Wyk, Gerrit J., BA OFS, MA Pret., DPhil
 Pret. Prof.; Head*
Other Staff: 3 Lectrs.

Human Resources Management

Tel: (012) 420 3074 Fax: (012) 420 3574

Basson, Johan S. Prof.
Brand, Heinrich E. Prof.
Buys, Michiel A. Sr. Lectr.
De Beer, Johannes J. Sr. Lectr.
De Villiers, David Assoc. Prof.
Schaap, Pieter Sr. Lectr.
Steyn, Gideon J. Sr. Lectr.
Theron, Schalk W. Assoc. Prof.

Van Tonder, Jan A. Extraordinary Prof.
Vermeulen, Leopold P., MA Pret., DPhil
Pret. Prof.; Head*
Other Staff: 1 Lectr.

Informatics

Tel: (012) 420 3085 Fax: (012) 434501

Burger, A. P. Extraordinary Prof.
De Villiers, Carina Assoc. Prof.
Du Plooy, Nicolaas F. Prof.
Heymann, Werner Sr. Lectr.
Introna, Lucas D. Extraordinary Prof.
Leonard, Abraham C. Sr. Lectr.
Phahlamohlaka, Letlibe J. Sr. Lectr.
Pistorius, Carl W. I. Extraordinary Prof.
Roode, Johannes D., BSc Potchef., MSc Potchef.,
PhD Ley. Prof.; Acting Head*
Scheepers, Helana Sr. Lectr.
Smith, Abraham J. Extraordinary Prof.
Viktor, Herna L. Sr. Lectr.
Other Staff: 3 Lectrs.

Information Science

Tel: (012) 420 2961 Fax: (012) 342 2012

Boon, Johannes A. Extraordinary Prof.
Bothma, Theodorus J. D., BA Pret., MA S.Af.,
DLitt&Phil S.Af. Prof.; Head*
Britz, Johannes J. Assoc. Prof.
De Bruin, Hendrik Extraordinary Prof.
Fouché, Benjamin Extraordinary Prof.
Snyman, Maria M. M. Sr. Lectr.
Other Staff: 2 Lectrs.

Insurance and Actuarial Science

Tel: (012) 420 3469 Fax: (012) 432567

Fourie, I. J. v H. Extraordinary Prof.
Marx, George L., BSc(Econ) Potchef. Prof.;
Head*
Other Staff: 1 Lectr.

Landscape Architecture

Tel: (012) 420 2582 Fax: (012) 420 2582

Le Roux, Schalk W. Prof.
McMillan, Gwen Sr. Lectr.
Vosloo, Pieter T. Sr. Lectr.
Young, Graham A. Sr. Lectr.
Other Staff: 1 Lectr.

Law, Criminal

Tel: (012) 420 2417 Fax: (012) 342 1886

Van Oosten, Ferdinand F. W. Prof.
Van Rooyen, Jacobus C. W., BA Pret., LLB Pret.,
LLD Pret. Prof.; Head*

Law, Indigenous

Tel: (012) 420 2415 Fax: (012) 342 2638

Labuschagne, Johan M. T., MA Potchef., DPhil
Potchef., LLD Potchef. Prof.; Head*
Van Heerden, Frederick J. Assoc. Prof.

Law, Mercantile and Labour

Tel: (012) 420 2363 Fax: (012) 420 4010

Boraine, Andre Assoc. Prof.
Damons, Juanito M. Sr. Lectr.
De Villiers, Willem P. Sr. Lectr.
Delport, Petrus A. Prof.
Düvel, Ludwig H. Sr. Lectr.
Fourie, Joël D. Extraordinary Prof.
Jacobs, Linthi Sr. Lectr.
Katz, Michael M. Extraordinary Prof.
Klopper, Hendrik B. Prof.
Kruger, Corlia Sr. Lectr.
Lotz, Dirk J. Prof.
Nagel, Christoffel J. Prof.
Prozesky, Birgit Sr. Lectr.
Roestoff, Melanie Sr. Lectr.
Swart, J. D. M. Extraordinary Prof.
Van Eck, Bruno P. S. Prof.
Van Jaarsveld, Stephannes R., BA Pret., LLB Pret.,
LLD Pret. Prof.; Head*
Other Staff: 3 Lectrs.

Law, Private

Tel: (012) 420 2307 Fax: (012) 342 2638

Davel, Catharina J. Prof.
De Gama, Juaquim J. Sr. Lectr.
Grove, Nicolaas J. Prof.
Schoeman, Magdalena C. Prof.

Scott, Tobias J., BA Pret., LLB Pret., LLD
Ley. Prof.; Head*
Van der Linde, Anton Sr. Lectr.
Van der Spuy, Pieter de W. Sr. Lectr.
Van Schalkwyk, Llewelyn N. Prof.
Visser, Petrus J. Prof.
Other Staff: 1 Lectr.

Law, Public

Tel: (012) 420 2415 Fax: (012) 342 2638

Bekink, Bernard Sr. Lectr.
Viljoen, Henning P. Prof.
Vorster, Marthinus P., BA Pret., LLB Pret., DrsJur
Ley. Prof.; Head*

Legal Law, Comparative Law and Philosophy of Law

Tel: (012) 420 2374 Fax: (012) 434021

Heyns, Christoffel H. Prof.
Kleyn, Duard G. Prof.
Le Roux, Jolandi Sr. Lectr.
Rwelamira, Medard R. K. Prof.
Thomas, Philippus J., LLD S.Af. Prof.; Head*
Van der Westhuizen, Johann V. Prof.
Viljoen, Frans J. Sr. Lectr.

Management, Graduate School of

Tel: (012) 420 3366 Fax: (012) 437223

Alberts, Nicolaas F., MA Pret., DPhil Pret., MBL
S.Af. Prof.; Head*
Boshoff, Adre B. Prof.
Brummer, Leon M. Prof.
Cilliers, Willem W. Sr. Lectr.
De la Rey, Jacobus H. Prof.
De Villiers, Willem A. Sr. Lectr.
De Wet, Johannes M. Prof.
Dekker, Gerhardus M. Prof.
Erwee, Ronel Prof.
Lambrechts, Hugo A. Prof.
Nel, Pieter S. Prof.
Roodt, Gert K. A. Assoc. Prof.
Steyn, Pieter G. Prof.
Wolmarans, Hendrik P. Sr. Lectr.
Other Staff: 1 Res. Officer

Marketing and Communications Management

Tel: (012) 420 3395 Fax: (012) 342 3632

Dreyer, Willem W. Sr. Lectr.
Jordaan, Yolanda Sr. Lectr.
North, Ernest J. Sr. Lectr.
Puth, Gustav Prof.
Schreuder, Andries N., BCom Pret., MCom Pret.,
DCom Rand Afrikaans Prof.; Head*
Ströh, Ursula M. Sr. Lectr.
Van Heerden, Cornelius H. Sr. Lectr.
Other Staff: 6 Lectrs.

Material Science and Metallurgical Engineering

Tel: (012) 420 3182 Fax: (012) 342 6812

Bader, Fritz K. Sr. Lectr.
Du Toit, Madeleine Sr. Lectr.
Geldenhuis, Jacobus M. A. Prof.
Havemann, Paul C. W. Sr. Lectr.
Jansen van Vuuren, Cornelius P. Assoc. Prof.
Pienaar, Gert Prof.
Pistorius, Petrus C. Prof.
Pistorius, Pieter G. H. Prof.
Sandenbergh, Roelof F., MEng Pret., DEng
Pret. Prof.; Head*
Other Staff: 1 Res. Fellow

Mathematics and Applied Mathematics

Tel: (012) 420 2520 Fax: (012) 434853

Diestel, Joseph Hon. Prof.
Engelbrecht, Johannes C. Prof.
Fouche, Willem L. Prof.
Grabe, Petrus J. Prof.
Greybe, Willem G. Sr. Lectr.
Griffiths, Anna-Marie Sr. Lectr.
Janse van Rensburg, Nicolaas F. Sr. Lectr.
Labuschagne, Louis E. Assoc. Prof.
Meiring, Anna F. Sr. Lectr.
Moller, Magrieta P. Sr. Lectr.
Penning, Frans D. Prof.
Potgieter, Petrus H. Sr. Lectr.

Pretorius, Lourens M. Prof.
Rosinger, Elemer E. Prof.
Schoeman, Marius J. Prof.
Stroh, Anton Assoc. Prof.
Swart, Barbara Sr. Lectr.
Swart, Johan, BSc Potchef., MSc Potchef., DrPhil
Zür. Prof.; Head*
Theron, Frieda Sr. Lectr.
Van der Merwe, Aletta J. Sr. Lectr.
Van Niekerk, Frederik D. Prof.
Other Staff: 8 Lectrs.

Medicine, see below

Microbiology and Plant Pathology

Tel: (012) 420 3265 Fax: (012) 420 3266

Brozel, Volker S. Assoc. Prof.
Cloete, Thomas E., MSc OFS, DSc Pret. Prof.;
Head*
Korsten, Liza Assoc. Prof.
Labuschagne, Nico Sr. Lectr.
Nel, Louis H. Prof.
Qhobela, Molapo Sr. Lectr.
Steyn, Pieter L. Extraordinary Prof.
Wehner, Friedrich C. Prof.
Other Staff: 2 Lectrs.

Modern European Languages

Tel: (012) 420 2031 Fax: (012) 420 2698

Holmshaw, Lorraine B. Sr. Lectr.
Peeters, Leopold F. H. M. C., LèsL Ghent, PhD
Witw. Prof.; Head*
Tesmer, Gertrud Sr. Lectr.
Other Staff: 5 Lectrs.

Music

Tel: (012) 420 2316 Fax: (012) 420 2248

Devroop, Chatradari Sr. Lectr.
Fourie, Ella Assoc. Prof.
Grové, Stefans Extraordinary Prof.
Hinch, John de C. Sr. Lectr.
Olivier, Gerrit C. Assoc. Prof.
Solomon, Allan Assoc. Prof.
Stanford, Hendrik J. Prof.
Temmingh, Hendrik, BMus Potchef., MMus
Potchef., DMus Pret. Prof.; Head*
Van der Mescht, Heinrich H. Assoc. Prof.
Van Niekerk, Caroline Prof.
Van Wyk, Wessel Sr. Lectr.
Viljoen, Willem D. Assoc. Prof.
Other Staff: 3 Lectrs.

New Testament (Dutch Reformed Church)

Tel: (012) 420 2384 Fax: (012) 420 4016

Breytenbach, Jan C. Extraordinary Prof.
Van der Watt, Jan G., BA P.Elizabeth, BD Pret.,
MA Pret., DD Pret. Prof.; Head*

New Testament (Dutch Reformed Church of Africa)

Tel: (012) 420 2399 Fax: (012) 420 2887

Pelser, Gerhardus M. M. Prof.
Van Aarde, Andries G., MA Pret., DD
Pret. Prof.; Head*
Other Staff: 1 Res. Fellow

Old Testament (Dutch Reformed Church)

Tel: (012) 420 2892 Fax: (012) 420 4016

Le Roux, Jurie H. Prof.

Old Testament (Dutch Reformed Church of Africa)

Tel: (012) 420 2074 Fax: (012) 420 2887

Breytenbach, Andries, BA Pret., DD Pret. Prof.;
Head*
Venter, Pieter M. Prof.

Orthopedagogics

Tel: (012) 420 2894 Fax: (012) 342 2914

Bouwer, Anna C. Prof.
Derbyshire, Elizabeth J. Assoc. Prof.
Du Toit, Petrusa Sr. Lectr.
Ferreira, Gerhard V., MEd Pret., DEd
Pret. Prof.; Head*
Prinsloo, Heila M. Sr. Lectr.

Viljoen, Johan   Assoc. Prof.
Other Staff: 2 Lectrs.

Philosophy

Tel: (012) 420 2326 Fax: (012) 420 4008

Antonites, Alexander J.   Prof.
Du Toit, Andrew P., BA Pret., BA Rhodes, MA
  Pret., DPhil Pret.   Prof.; Head*
Gericke, John D.   Assoc. Prof.
Schoeman, Marinus J.   Sr. Lectr.
Visage, Johannes H. N.   Sr. Lectr.

Philosophy of Religion and Missions (Dutch Reformed Church)

Tel: (012) 420 2890 Fax: (012) 420 4016

Meiring, Pieter G. J., BA Pret., DrsTheol
  V.U.Amst., DD Pret.   Prof.; Head*

Philosophy of Religion and Missions (Dutch Reformed Church of Africa)

Tel: (012) 420 2777 Fax: (012) 420 2887

Van der Merwe, Pieter J., BA Pret., BD Pret., DD
  Pret.   Prof.; Head*

Physics

Tel: (012) 420 2455 Fax: (012) 342 4143

Alberts, Hendrik W.   Prof.
Auret, Francois D.   Prof.
Bredell, Louis J.   Assoc. Prof.
Brink, Daniel J.   Prof.
Carter, Rachel M.   Assoc. Prof.
Davidson, Neil J.   Sr. Lectr.
Friedland, Erich K. H., MSc Pret., DSc
  Pret.   Prof.; Head*
Gaigher, Horace L.   Prof.
Goodman, Stewart A.   Assoc. Prof.
Hayes, Michael   Sr. Lectr.
Kok, Frederik J.   Sr. Lectr.
Kunert, Herbert W.   Sr. Lectr.
Malherbe, Johan B.   Prof.
Miller, Henry G.   Prof.
Myburg, Gerrit   Assoc. Prof.
Scheffler, Theophilus B.   Sr. Lectr.
Van der Berg, Nicolaas G.   Sr. Lectr.
Other Staff: 1 Lectr.; 2 Res. Fellows

Plant Production and Soil Science

Tel: (012) 420 3224 Fax: (012) 342 2713

Annandale, John G.   Sr. Lectr.
Barnard, Robin O.   Prof.
Claassens, Andries S.   Sr. Lectr.
Hammes, Pieter S., MSc(Agric) Pret.,
  DSc(Agric) Pret.   Prof.; Head*
Laker, Michael C.   Prof.
Pieterse, Pieter A.   Sr. Lectr.
Reinhardt, Carl F.   Prof.
Rethman, Norman F. G.   Prof.
Other Staff: 5 Lectrs.

Political Science

Tel: (012) 420 2464 Fax: (012) 420 2464

Bekker, Johannes T.   Sr. Lectr.
Du Plessis, Anton   Prof.
Hough, Michael   Prof.
Maphai, Vincent   Extraordinary Prof.
Muller, Marie E., DLitt Rand Afrikaans   Prof.;
  Head*
Other Staff: 2 Lectrs.

Practical Theology (Dutch Reformed Church)

Tel: (012) 420 2669 Fax: (012) 420 4016

Muller, Julian C.   Prof.
Vos, Casparus J. A., BA Pret., DD Pret.   Prof.;
  Head*

Practical Theology (Dutch Reformed Church of Africa)

Tel: (012) 420 2399 Fax: (012) 420 2887

Dreyer, Theunis F. J., BA Pret., BD Pret., DTheol
  Utrecht   Prof.; Head*

Procedure and Evidence

Tel: (012) 420 3198 Fax: (012) 420 3119

Cloete, Rian   Sr. Lectr.
Horn, Jan G. G.   Prof.
Jamneck, Daniel B.   Sr. Lectr.

Kotze, Dirk J. L.   Prof.
Van der Merwe, Frans E., Blur S.Af., LLB S.Af.,
  LLD Pret.   Prof.; Head*

Psycho-and Socio-Pedagogics

Tel: (012) 420 2570 Fax: (012) 342 2914

Bender, Cornelia J. G.   Sr. Lectr.
Hartell, Cycil G.   Sr. Lectr.
Le Roux, Johann   Prof.
Moller, Theodore   Assoc. Prof.
Pretorius, Jacobus W. M., MEd Pret., DEd Pret.,
  PhD Pret.   Prof.; Head*
Van Rooyen, Linda   Prof.

Psychology

Tel: (012) 420 3430 Fax: (012) 420 2404

Aronstam, Maurice   Sr. Lectr.
Beyers, Dave, BTh Stell., MA S.Af., DPhil
  OFS   Prof.; Head*
Botha, Ailka   Sr. Lectr.
Botha, Petrus A.   Sr. Lectr.
De la Rey, Ruben P.   Prof.
Fiedeldey, Andre C.   Assoc. Prof.
Fiedeldey-Van Dijk, Catharina   Sr. Lectr.
Gildenhuys, Andries A.   Sr. Lectr.
Langley, Petronella R.   Prof.
Marchetti-Mercer, Maria C.   Sr. Lectr.
Moleko, Anne-Gloria S.   Sr. Lectr.
Schoeman, Johannes B.   Prof.
Uys, Jacobus S.   Extraordinary Prof.
Van Vuuren, Rex J.   Prof.
Other Staff: 4 Lectrs.

Public Management and Administration, School for

Tel: (012) 420 3342 Fax: (012) 342 4964

Brynard, Petrus A.   Prof.
Fourie, David J.   Sr. Lectr.
Katz, M. M.   Hon. Prof.
Roux, Nicolaas L.   Assoc. Prof.
Vil-Nkomo, Sibusiso, BA Lincoln, MA Delaware,
  PhD Delaware   Prof.; Head*
Other Staff: 3 Lectrs.

Quantity Surveying

Tel: (012) 420 2551 Fax: (012) 420 3598

Botha, Pieter C.   Prof.
Brummer, Diederick G.   Sr. Lectr.
Klopper, Carl H.   Prof.
Maritz, Marthinus J.   Sr. Lectr.
Siglé, Hendrik M., PhD Pret.   Prof.; Head*
Visser, Roelof N.   Sr. Lectr.

Rural Development, see Agric. Econ., Extension and Rural Devel.

School Guidance

Tel: (012) 420 2878 Fax: (012) 342 2914

Malan, Francine   Sr. Lectr.
Maree, Jacobus G.   Prof.
Other Staff: 1 Lectr.

Science (General)

Tel: (012) 420 2574 Fax: (012) 362 5084

Carr, Benjamin A.   Sr. Lectr.
De Lange, Adriaan M.   Sr. Lectr.
Rogan, John M.   Assoc. Prof.
Van Staden, Johan C.   Assoc. Prof.
Other Staff: 1 Lectr.

Social Work

Tel: (012) 420 2325 Fax: (012) 420 2093

Carbonatto, Charlene L.   Sr. Lectr.
Du Preez, Maria S. E., MA(Soc) Pret., DPhil
  Pret.   Prof.; Head*
Lombard, Antoinette   Assoc. Prof.
Schoeman, Johanna P.   Sr. Lectr.
Terblanche, Lourens S.   Assoc. Prof.
Van der Westhuizen, Catherina H. J.   Sr.
  Lectr.
Van Staden, Susara M.   Sr. Lectr.
Other Staff: 5 Sr. Clin. Lectrs.

Sociology

Tel: (012) 420 2330 Fax: (012) 342 2873

Kok, Pieter C.   Extraordinary Prof.
Muthien, Yvonne   Hon. Prof.

Oosthuizen, Jacobus S., BD Pret., MA Pret.,
  DrsTh Utrecht, DrsSoc Ley, DPhil Amst.   Prof.;
  Head*
Van Aardt, Carel J.   Assoc. Prof.
Van der Merwe, Adriaan J.   Extraordinary
  Prof.
Van Tonder, Jan L.   Assoc. Prof.
Other Staff: 5 Lectrs.

Statistics

Tel: (012) 420 2523 Fax: (012) 342 3260

Boraine, Hermi   Sr. Lectr.
Crowther, Nicolaas A. S., BSc OFS, MSc
  P.Elizabeth, DSc OFS   Prof.; Head*
Grimbeek, Richard J.   Sr. Lectr.
Groeneveld, Hendrik T.   Prof.
Millard, Salomon M.   Sr. Lectr.
Smit, Christian F.   Prof.
Steyn, Hendrik S.   Extraordinary Prof.
Swanepoel, Andre   Sr. Lectr.
Van Zyl, G. J. J.   Temp. Prof.
Vivier, Francois L.   Prof.
Other Staff: 5 Lectrs.

Surveying and Mapping

Tel: (012) 420 2449 Fax: (012) 432816

De Jager, Pieter C.   Sr. Lectr.
Van der Merwe, Frederik J.   Sr. Lectr.

Tourism Management

Tel: (012) 420 3349 Fax: (012) 362 5194

Francis, Cyril V.   Sr. Lectr.
Heath, Ernie T., MCom Fort Hare, DCom
  P.Elizabeth   Prof.; Head*
Lubbe, Berendien A.   Sr. Lectr.
Wigley, David M.   Extraordinary Prof.
Other Staff: 1 Lectr.

Town and Regional Planning

Tel: (012) 420 3531 Fax: (012) 420 3537

Badenhorst, Marthinus S., BSc Pret., MPhil Rand
  Afrikaans, DPhil Rand Afrikaans   Prof.; Head*
Oranje, Mark C.   Sr. Lectr.
Van Helden, Paul   Assoc. Prof.
Other Staff: 3 Lectrs.

Veterinary Science, see below

Visual Arts and History of Art

Tel: (012) 420 2353 Fax: (012) 420 2698

Duffey, Alexander E.   Assoc. Prof.
Roos, Nicholas O., MA Pret., DPhil Pret.   Prof.;
  Head*
Sauthoff, Marian D.   Assoc. Prof.
Slabbert, Margaret L.   Sr. Lectr.
Other Staff: 4 Lectrs.

Zoology and Entomology

Tel: (012) 420 2539 Fax: (012) 432 3136

Bennett, Nigel C.   Sr. Lectr.
Bester, Marthan N.   Sr. Lectr.
Chown, Steven L.   Prof.
Ferguson, Jan W. H.   Assoc. Prof.
Robinson, Terence J.   Prof.
Schoeman, Adriaan S.   Sr. Lectr.
Scholtz, Clarke H., MSc Pret., DSc Pret.   Prof.;
  Head*
Van Aarde, Rudolph J.   Prof.
Van der Merwe, Meinhardt   Sr. Lectr.
Van Jaarsveld, Albertus S.   Assoc. Prof.
Other Staff: 1 Lectr.; 2 Res. Fellows

DENTISTRY

Community Dentistry

Tel: (012) 319 2911 Fax: (012) 323 7616

Crafford, Elmine   Sr. Lectr.
Kroon, Jeroen   Sr. Lectr.
Prinsloo, Paul M.   Sr. Lectr.
Rossouw, Louis M.   Assoc. Prof.
Snyman, Willem D., MChD Pret., PhD
  Pret.   Prof.; Head*
Van Wyk, Phillippus J.   Assoc. Prof.
White, John G.   Sr. Lectr.
Other Staff: 2 Lectrs.

Diagnostics and Rontgenology

Tel: (012) 319 2911 Fax: (012) 319 2171

Buch, Brian, BScAgric Natal, BDS Witw., MDent Witw. Prof.; Head*
Fortuna, Maria J. Sr. Lectr.
Other Staff: 4 Lectrs.

Maxillo-Facial and Oral Surgery

Tel: (012) 319 2911 Fax: (012) 319 2172

Butow, Kurt W., BSc Rand Afrikaans, MChD Stell., DrMedDent Erlangen-Nuremberg, PhD Pret., DSc Pret. Prof.; Head*
Other Staff: 4 Lectrs.

Oral Pathology and Oral Biology

Tel: (012) 319 2911 Fax: (012) 323 7616

Bredell, Marius G. Sr. Lectr.
De Wet, Elizabeth Sr. Lectr.
Van Heerden, Willem F. P., BChD Pret., MChD Pret., PhD S.Af. Prof.; Head*
Van Niekerk, Petrus J. Sr. Lectr.
Other Staff: 2 Lectrs.

Orthodontics

Tel: (012) 319 2911 Fax: (012) 328 6697

De Muelenaere, Johan J. G. G. Extraordinary Prof.
Grobler, Marthinus Extraordinary Prof.
Mizrahi, Eliakim Extraordinary Prof.
Nel, Stephanus J. P. Extraordinary Prof.
Wiltshire, William A., BChD Pret., MDent Pret., MChD Pret., DSc Pret. Prof.; Head*
Other Staff: 1 Lectr.

Periodontics and Oral Medicine

Tel: (012) 319 2911 Fax: (012) 323 7616

Germishuys, Petrus J. Assoc. Prof.
Lohse, Paul J. Extraordinary Prof.
Petit, Jean-Claude, BDS Congo(Official), LDS Louvain, MDent Witw. Prof.; Head*
Van Heerden, Pieter J. Extraordinary Prof.
Other Staff: 1 Lectr.

Prosthetics and Dental Mechanics

Tel: (012) 319 2911 Fax: (012) 323 7616

Benninghoff, Wilfried Sr. Lectr.
Kemp, Peter L. Prof.
Other Staff: 2 Lectrs.

Restorative Dentistry

Tel: (012) 319 2911 Fax: (012) 326 2754

Becker, Leonard H., MChD Pret. Prof.; Head*
Dannheimer, Manfred F. G. Assoc. Prof.
De Wet, Francois A. Prof.
Driessen, Cornelis H. Assoc. Prof.
Herbst, Dirk Sr. Lectr.
Janse van Vuuren, Pieter A. Assoc. Prof.
Swart, Theunis J. P. Sr. Lectr.
Terblanche, Johan Assoc. Prof.
Other Staff: 4 Lectrs.

MEDICINE

Anaesthesiology

Tel: (012) 354 2386 Fax: (012) 329 8276

Fourie, Pierre J. H. L. Prof.
Hugo, Johannes M., MB ChB Pret., MMed OFS Prof.; Head*
Jacobs, Christina J. Sr. Lectr.
Milner, Analee Sr. Lectr.
Murphy, Julian C. S. Sr. Lectr.
Smith, Francois J. Sr. Lectr.
Other Staff: 4 Lectrs.

Anatomic Pathology

Tel: (012) 354 2386 Fax: (012) 319 4886

Davel, Gerhardus H. Sr. Lectr.
Dreyer, Leonora, MMEd(Path) Pret., MD Pret. Prof.; Head*
Hamersma, Teertse Sr. Lectr.
Van der Hoven, Alida E. Sr. Lectr.
Other Staff: 3 Lectrs.

Anatomy

Tel: (012) 354 2386 Fax: (012) 319 2240

Coetzee, Heleen L. Assoc. Prof.
Grieve, Clayton L. Sr. Lectr.

Liebenberg, Schalk W. Sr. Lectr.
Meiring, Johannes H., MB ChB Pret., MPraxMed Pret. Prof.; Head*
Richards, Penelope A. Assoc. Prof.
Steyn, Maryna Assoc. Prof.
Vorster, Willie Sr. Lectr.
Other Staff: 6 Lectrs.

Cardiology

Tel: (012) 354 2386 Fax: (012) 329 1327

Bobak, Leopold Sr. Lectr.
Myburgh, Dirk P., MB ChB Pret., MSc Pret. Prof.; Head*
Other Staff: 3 Lectrs.

Cardiothoracic Surgery

Tel: (012) 354 2386 Fax: (012) 329 1734

Du Plessis, Dirk J. Prof.
Serfontein, Stephanus J. Sr. Lectr.

Chemical Pathology

Tel: (012) 354 2386 Fax: (012) 328 3600

Elias, John Sr. Lectr.
Hurter, Philip Prof.
Ubbink, Johan B. Prof.
Vermaak, William J. H., BSc Pret., MMed Pret. Prof.; Head*
Other Staff: 1 Lectr.; 1 Sr. Res. Officer; 1 Res. Officer

Community Health

Tel: (012) 354 2386 Fax: (012) 323 8534

Ijsselmuiden, Carolus B., MD Rotterdam, MPH Johns H. Prof.; Head*
Smith, Ferdinand C. A. Sr. Lectr.
Van der Merwe, Antoinette Extraordinary Prof.
Other Staff: 1 Lectr.; 1 Res. Officer

Family Medicine

Tel: (012) 354 2386 Fax: (012) 329 6691

Chapman, Francois Sr. Lectr.
Engelbrecht, Johan C. Sr. Lectr.
Erasmus, Robert J. E., MPraxMed Pret., MD Pret. Prof.; Head*
Heymans, Rik W. J. L. Sr. Lectr.
Heystek, Marthinus J. Sr. Lectr.
Kirkby, Russel E. Sr. Lectr.
Kluyts, Thomas M. Sr. Lectr.
Lalloo, Suraya Sr. Lectr.
Loots, Schalk J. Sr. Lectr.
Marx, Johannes S. S. Sr. Lectr.
Mathews, Peter A. Sr. Lectr.
Meyer, Helgardt P. Prof.
Mhlambi, Sibusiso D. L. A. Sr. Lectr.
Oberholzer, Renier K. Sr. Lectr.
Snyman, Hendrik W. Sr. Lectr.
Other Staff: 9 Lectrs.

Forensic Medicine

Tel: (012) 354 2386 Fax: (012) 324 4886

Saayman, Gert Sr. Lectr.

Haematology

Tel: (012) 354 2386 Fax: (012) 329 1400

Beck, Otto N. Sr. Lectr.
Other Staff: 2 Lectrs.

Human Genetics

Tel: (012) 354 2386 Fax: (012) 323 2788

Jansen van Rensburg, Elizabeth Assoc. Prof.
Other Staff: 2 Res. Officers

Immunology

Tel: (012) 354 2386 Fax: (012) 323 0732

Anderson, Ronald, BSc Glas., MSc Witw., PhD Witw. Prof.; Head*
Medlen, Constance E. Prof.
Myer, Martin S. Sr. Lectr.
Theron, Annette J. Sr. Lectr.
Other Staff: 2 Res. Officers

Internal Medicine

Tel: (012) 354 2386 Fax: (012) 329 1327

Brighton, Stanley W. Assoc. Prof.
Buchel, Elwin H. Sr. Lectr.
Fanjek, Josip Sr. Lectr.

Grimbeek, Johannes F. Sr. Lectr.
Iwanik, Janina M. Sr. Lectr.
Jacyk, Witold K. Prof.
Jones, Ricky Sr. Lectr.
Ker, James A. Assoc. Prof.
Nagel, Gerhardus J. Sr. Lectr.
Potgieter, Cornelius D. Sr. Lectr.
Retief, Johannes H. Sr. Lectr.
Rossouw, Daniel S. Prof.
Van Gelder, Antoine L., MB ChB Pret. Prof.; Head*
Van Rooyen, Renier J. Assoc. Prof.
Visser, Susanna S. Sr. Lectr.
Wentzel, Lars F. Sr. Lectr.
Other Staff: 10 Lectrs.

Medical Microbiology

Tel: (012) 354 2386 Fax: (012) 324 4886

Dove, Michael G. Assoc. Prof.

Medical Oncology

Tel: (012) 354 2386 Fax: (012) 329 1100

De Jager, Lourens C. Sr. Lectr.
Falkson, Carla I. Assoc. Prof.
Falkson, Hendrika C. Assoc. Prof.
Other Staff: 5 Lectrs.; 1 Sr. Res. Officer

Medical Virology

Tel: (012) 354 2386 Fax: (012) 323 5550

Clay, Cornelis G. Sr. Lectr.
Grabow, Wilhelm O. K., DSc Pret. Prof.; Head*
Taylor, Maureen B. Sr. Lectr.

Medicine (General)

Tel: (012) 354 2386 Fax: (012) 319 1351

Chaparro, Felipe Sr. Lectr.
Gericke, Gertruida J. Sr. Lectr.
Grey, Somarie V., MSc Potchef., DSc Pret. Prof.
Prozesky, Detlef R. Assoc. Prof.
Treadwell, Ina Sr. Lectr.
Other Staff: 1 Lectr.

Neurology

Tel: (012) 354 2386 Fax: (012) 329 4764

Bartel, Peter R. Prof.
Mafojane, Ntutu A. Prof.
Schutte, Clara-Maria Sr. Lectr.
Van der Meyden, Cornelis H., MB BCh Witw., MD Pret. Prof.; Head*
Woodward, Warren A. Sr. Lectr.
Other Staff: 1 Lectr.

Neurosurgery

Tel: (012) 354 2386 Fax: (012) 329 4764

1 Lectr.

Nuclear Medicine

Tel: (012) 354 2386

Vacant Posts: 1 Prof./Head*

Nursing

Tel: (012) 354 2386 Fax: (012) 329 6691

Du Rand, Eleonora A. Sr. Lectr.
Malunga, Nondu P. Sr. Lectr.
Van der Westhuizen, Sara J. C. Sr. Lectr.
Van Niekerk, Johanna G. P., MCur Pret., DCur Pret. Prof.; Head*
Van Niekerk, Susan E. Sr. Lectr.
Van Wyk, Neltjie C. Assoc. Prof.
Other Staff: 6 Lectrs.

Obstetrics and Gynaecology

Tel: (012) 354 2386 Fax: (012) 329 6258

De Jonge, Eric T. M. Assoc. Prof.
De Vries, M. F. Sr. Lectr.
De Wet, Gert H. Sr. Lectr.
Howarth, Graham R. Assoc. Prof.
Lamb, Peter J. B. Sr. Lectr.
Lindeque, Barend G., MB ChB Pret., MMed Stell., MD Stell. Prof.; Head*
MacDonald, Angus P. Sr. Lectr.
Mantel, Gerald D. Sr. Lectr.
Pattinson, Robert C. Prof.
Pistorius, Lourens Sr. Lectr.
Other Staff: 3 Lectrs.

Occupational Therapy

Tel: (012) 354 2386 Fax: (012) 354 6006
McAdam, Jennifer C. Sr. Lectr.
Shipham, Imme Sr. Lectr.
Other Staff: 9 Lectrs.

Ophthalmology

Tel: (012) 354 2386 Fax: (012) 320 1352
Grim, Millicent M. Sr. Lectr.
Roux, Paul, MPraxMed Pret., MMed Pret. Prof.;
  Head*

Orthopaedics

Tel: (012) 354 2386 Fax: (012) 329 1517
Burger, Evalina L. Sr. Lectr.
Lindeque, Bennie G. P. Assoc. Prof.
Maritz, Nicolaas G. J., MB ChB Pret., MMed
  OFS Prof.; Head*
Rankin, Kenneth C. Prof.
Other Staff: 8 Lectrs.

Otorhinolaryngology

Tel: (012) 354 2386 Fax: (012) 320 1352
Mulder, Andries A. H. Prof.
Swart, Johannes G., MD Pret. Prof.; Head*
Visser, Pieter F. Sr. Lectr.
Other Staff: 1 Lectr.

Paediatrics

Tel: (012) 354 2386 Fax: (012) 354 1035
Ajusi, Stella F. Sr. Lectr.
Boom, Marie E. J. Sr. Lectr.
Colyn, Emily L. Sr. Lectr.
Delport, Suzanne D. Assoc. Prof.
Fourie, Dirk T. Sr. Lectr.
Hay, Ian T. Prof.
Kruger, Mariana Sr. Lectr.
Malek, Aletta E. Sr. Lectr.
Naude, Stephanus P. E. Sr. Lectr.
Opperman, Johannes C. Sr. Lectr.
Van Biljon, Gertruida Sr. Lectr.
Wittenberg, Dankwart F., MB ChB Cape Town,
  MD Natal Prof.; Head*
Zietsman, Johan Sr. Lectr.
Other Staff: 6 Lectrs.

Pharmacology

Tel: (012) 354 2386 Fax: (012) 319 2411
Blom, Marie W. Sr. Lectr.
Eloff, Jacobus N. Sr. Lectr.
Snyman, Jacques R. Prof.
Sommers, De Klerk, MB ChB Pret., BChD Pret.,
  MD Pret. Prof.; Head*
Van Wyk, Marieta Sr. Lectr.
Other Staff: 1 Lectr.

Physiology

Tel: (012) 354 2386 Fax: (012) 319 2238
Claassen, Nicolaas Sr. Lectr.
Haag, Marianne Sr. Lectr.
Kruger, Marlena C. Assoc. Prof.
Meij, Hester S. Assoc. Prof.
Seegers, Johanna C. Assoc. Prof.
Steinmann, Christiaan M. L. Assoc. Prof.
Van den Bogaerde, Johan B. Prof.
Van Papendorp, Dirk H., MB ChB Pret., PhD
  Stell. Prof.; Head*
Viljoen, Margaretha Assoc. Prof.
Other Staff: 4 Lectrs.

Physiotherapy

Tel: (012) 354 2386 Fax: (012) 354 1226
Eksteen, Carina A. Sr. Lectr.
Van Rooijen, Agatha J., MSc OFS Lectr.;
  Acting Head*
Other Staff: 8 Lectrs.

Psychiatry

Tel: (012) 354 2386 Fax: (012) 319 9617
Bodemer, Wilhelm, MMed Pret., MD
  S.Af.Med. Prof.; Head*
Coetzee, Abraham L. Assoc. Prof.
De Wet, Paul H. Sr. Lectr.
Loen, Adriana E. Sr. Lectr.
Pretorius, Herman W. Assoc. Prof.
Roos, Johannes L. Assoc. Prof.
Other Staff: 6 Lectrs.

Radiation Oncology

Tel: (012) 354 2386 Fax: (012) 329 1302
Friediger, Dan Sr. Lectr.
Louw, C. J. Sr. Lectr.
Nel, Johan S., MB ChB OFS, MMEd(Psych) OFS,
  MFamMEd OFS, MMEd(RadT) Pret. Prof.;
  Head*
Van Rensburg, Ado J. Extraordinary Prof.
Other Staff: 3 Lectrs.

Radiology

Tel: (012) 354 2386 Fax: (012) 329 6763
Gelderman, Gerrit J. Sr. Lectr.
Holl, J. L. Sr. Lectr.
Hugo, Gertina A. Sr. Lectr.
Prinsloo, Simon F., MMed Pret. Prof.; Head*
Van der Merwe, Johanda Sr. Lectr.
Other Staff: 7 Lectrs.

Surgery

Tel: (012) 354 2386 Fax: (012) 329 4589
Becker, Jan H. R., MMed Pret., FCS(SA),
  FRCSGlas, FRCSEd Prof.; Head*
Coetzee, Petrus F. Sr. Lectr.
Ionescu, Gabriël O. Prof.
Karusseit, Victor O. L. Sr. Lectr.
Mokoena, Taole R. Prof.
Pretorius, Jan P. Sr. Lectr.
Schoeman, Bernardus J. Sr. Lectr.
Van Greunen, Andries D. Sr. Lectr.
Other Staff: 3 Lectrs.; 1 Sr. Res. Officer

Urology

Tel: (012) 354 2386 Fax: (012) 329 5152
Reif, Simon, MMed Pret., FCS(SA) Prof.;
  Head*
Sleep, D. J. Prof.
Vercueil, Andre E. Sr. Lectr.
Other Staff: 2 Lectrs.; 1 Sr. Res. Officer

VETERINARY SCIENCE

Anatomy

Tel: (012) 529 8000 Fax: (012) 529 8320
Bezuidenhout, Abraham J., DVSc Pret. Prof.;
  Head*
Groenewald, Hendrik B. Assoc. Prof.
Hornsveld, Marius Sr. Lectr.
Soley, John T. Assoc. Prof.
Turner, Peter H. Sr. Lectr.
Van der Merwe, Nicolaas J. Assoc. Prof.

Animal and Community Health

Tel: (012) 529 8000 Fax: (012) 529 8311
Bath, Garith F. Assoc. Prof.
Gummow, Bruce Assoc. Prof.
Lourens, Dirk C. Prof.
More O'Ferrall, Marianne Sr. Lectr.
Petzer, Inge-Marie Sr. Lectr.
Schultheiss, Willem A. Sr. Lectr.
Spencer, Brian T. Sr. Lectr.
Veary, Courtney M., BVSc Pret.,
  MMEdVet(Hyg) Pret. Prof.; Head*

Medicine

Tel: (012) 529 8000 Fax: (012) 529 8308
Berry, Wayne L. Prof.
Dippenaar, Gertruida Sr. Lectr.
Guglick, Mary A. Sr. Lectr.
Leisewitz, Andrew L. Assoc. Prof.
Lobetti, Remo G. Assoc. Prof.
Milner, Rowan J. Sr. Lectr.
Reyers, Fred Prof.
Shakespeare, Anthony S. Sr. Lectr.
Thompson, Peter N. Sr. Lectr.
Van den Berg, Jacobus S. Prof.
Other Staff: 6 Lectrs.

Pathology

Tel: (012) 529 8000 Fax: (012) 529 8303
Kriek, Nicolaas P. J., MMedVet Pret. Prof.;
  Head*
Lane, Emily Sr. Lectr.
Van der Lugt, Jacob J. Assoc. Prof.
Williams, Mark C. Assoc. Prof.
Other Staff: 1 Lectr.

Pharmacology and Toxicology

Tel: (012) 529 8000 Fax: (012) 529 8304
Botha, Christoffel J. Assoc. Prof.
Swan, Gerald E., BVSc Pret., MMedVet
  Pret. Prof.; Head*

Poultry Diseases

Tel: (012) 529 8000 Fax: (012) 529 8306
Le Roux, Christiaan D., BVSc Pret. Prof.;
  Head*
Odendaal, Michiel W. Sr. Lectr.
Other Staff: 1 Res. Officer

Surgery

Tel: (012) 529 8000 Fax: (012) 529 8307
Bester, Lynette Sr. Lectr.
Booth, Malcolm J. Sr. Lectr.
Coetzee, Gert L. Assoc. Prof.
Fourie, Sheryl L. Sr. Lectr.
Goldin, Jeremy P. Sr. Lectr.
Gottschalk, Roy D. Prof.
Kirberger, Robert M. Prof.
Lambrechts, Nicolaas E. Assoc. Prof.
Lubbe, Anton M. Assoc. Prof.
Olivier, Ann Sr. Lectr.
Scheepers, Elrien Sr. Lectr.
Stegmann, George F. Assoc. Prof.
Van den Berg, Sybrand S., MMedVet
  Pret. Prof.; Head*

Theriogenology

Tel: (012) 529 8000 Fax: (012) 529 8314
Bertschinger, Hendrik J. Prof.
Gerber, David Sr. Lectr.
Irons, Peter C. Sr. Lectr.
Nöthling, Johan O. Assoc. Prof.
Terblanche, Salmon J. Assoc. Prof.
Volkmann, Dietrich H., BVSc Pret., MMedVet
  Pret. Prof.; Head*
Other Staff: 2 Lectrs.

Veterinary Ethology

Tel: (012) 529 8000 Fax: (012) 529 8310
Linde, Robin F. Sr. Lectr.
Odendaal, Johannes S. J., BSc OFS, DVSc Pret.,
  DPhil Pret. Prof.; Head*
Van Dyk, Enette Sr. Lectr.
Wandrag, Daniel B. R. Sr. Lectr.

Veterinary Physiology

Tel: (012) 529 8000 Fax: (012) 529 8317
Boomker, Elizabeth A. Sr. Lectr.
Meintjes, Roy A. Assoc. Prof.
Van der Walt, Johann G., MSc Witw., DSc
  Pret. Prof.; Head*
Other Staff: 1 Lectr.

Veterinary Science (General)

Tel: (012) 529 8000 Fax: (012) 529 8309
Bland-van den Berg, Paul, MMedVet Pret.,
  PhD Prof.
Guthrie, Alan J. Prof.
Other Staff: 1 Lectr.; 1 Res. Officer

Veterinary Tropical Diseases

Tel: (012) 529 8000 Fax: (012) 529 8312
Coetzer, Jacobus A. W., MMedVet Pret. Prof.;
  Head*
Jansen van Vuuren, Moritz Assoc. Prof.
Krecek, Rosina C. Prof.
Meltzer, David G. A. Prof.
Miller, Edgar S. Sr. Lectr.
Penzhorn, Barend L. Prof.
Picard, Jacqueline A. Sr. Lectr.
Schwan, Ernst V. Sr. Lectr.
Stoltsz, Wilhelm H. Sr. Lectr.
Swanepoel, Robert Extraordinary Prof.
Venter, Estelle H. Assoc. Prof.

SPECIAL CENTRES, ETC

Agricultural Extension, South African Institute for

Tel: (012) 420 3246 Fax: (012) 342 2713
Düvel, Gustav H. Prof.†; Dir.*

Applied Materials, Institute of
Fax: (012) 362 5084
Heyns, Anton M. Prof.; Dir.*

Augmentative and Alternative Communication, Centre for
Tel: (012) 420 2035 Fax: (012) 420 3517
Alant, Erna Prof.†; Dir.*

Clinical Pharmacology, Glaxo Institute for
Tel: (012) 354 2386 Fax: (012) 329 4524
Sommers, De Klerk Prof.†; Dir.*

Community Directed Health Research, Hans Snyckers Institute for
Tel: (012) 354 2386 Fax: (012) 329 2256
Christianson, Arnold L. Prof.†; Dir.*

Community Education, Centre for
Tel: (012) 420 2365 Fax: (012) 420 2914
Le Roux, Johann Prof.†; Dir.*

Continuing Theological Education (Dutch Reformed Church), Centre for
Tel: (012) 420 2015 Fax: (012) 420 4016
Vosloo, William Prof.†; Dir.*

Continuing Theological Education (Dutch Reformed Church of Africa), Centre for
Tel: (012) 420 2348 Fax: (012) 420 2887
Beukes, Mattheus J. du P. Prof.
Koekemoer, Johannes H., BA Pret., BD Pret., DD Pret. Prof.†; Dir.*
Steenkamp, Lourens J. S. Prof.

Eco-tourism, Centre for
Tel: (012) 420 3710 Fax: (012) 420 3284
Hattingh, Phillippus S. Prof.†; Dir.*

Economic and Social Reconstruction, Centre for
Tel: (012) 420 4013 Fax: (012) 420 4057
Van Rooyen, Cornelius J. Prof.†; Dir.*

Economic Policy and Analysis, Bureau for
Tel: (012) 420 2413 Fax: (012) 43 3362
Vacant Posts: Prof.†/Dir.*

Environmental Biology and Biological Control, Centre for
Tel: (012) 420 3264 Fax: (012) 420 3266
Kotze, Johannes M. Prof.†; Dir.*

Equine Research Centre
Tel: (012) 529 8000 Fax: (012) 529 8301
Guthrie, Alan J. Prof.†; Dir.*

Financial Analysis, Bureau for
Tel: (012) 420 3371 Fax: (012) 342 2043
Brummer, Leon M. Prof.†; Dir.*
Other Staff: 2 Res. Officers

Hetero-atom Chemistry, Research Centre for
Tel: (012) 420 2512 Fax: (012) 432863
Modro, Tomasz A. Prof.†; Dir.*

Human Rights, Centre for
Tel: (012) 420 3034 Fax: (012) 420 4053
Van der Westhuizen, Johann V. Prof.†; Dir.*

Information Development, Centre for
Tel: (012) 420 2293 Fax: (012) 342 2012
Bothma, Theodorus J. D. Prof.†; Dir.*

Life Sciences, Atomic Energy Institute for
Tel: (012) 319 2427 Fax: (012) 324 4886
Dormehl, Irene C. Assoc. Prof.; Dir.*

Mammal Research Institute
Tel: (012) 420 2066 Fax: (012) 420 2534
Skinner, John D. Prof.; Dir.*
Other Staff: 1 Res. Officer

Micro-Electronics, Carl and Emily Fuchs Institute for
Tel: (012) 420 2952 Fax: (012) 420 3134
Du Plessis, Monuko Prof.†; Dir.*

Missiological and Ecumenical Research, Institute for
Tel: (012) 420 2871 Fax: (012) 420 4016
Kritzinger, Johan J. Prof.†; Dir.*
Other Staff: 2 Lectrs.

Sports Research Institute
Tel: (012) 362 1574 Fax: (012) 362 0463
Kruger, Pieter E. Prof.†Prof.†; Dir.*

Statistical and Survey Methodology, Bureau for
Tel: (012) 420 3646 Fax: (012) 342 3260
Herbst, Deon Dir.*

Stomatological Research, Centre for
Tel: (012) 379 2327 Fax: (012) 323 7616
Botha, Francina S. Sr. Lectr.
Botha, Stephanus J. Assoc. Prof.
Coetzee, Willem J. C. Prof.; Head*

Strategic Studies, Institute for
Tel: (012) 420 2407 Fax: (012) 420 2693
Hough, Michael Prof.†; Dir.*

Technological Innovation, Institute for
Tel: (012) 420 3605 Fax: (012) 342 6521
Pistorius, Carl W. I. Prof.; Dir.*

Wild Life Research, Centre for
Tel: (012) 420 2627 Fax: (012) 362 2034
Bothma, Jacobus du P. Prof.†; Head*

CONTACT OFFICERS

Academic affairs. Acting Registrar: Marais, D. D., MA Pret., DPhil Pret.
Accommodation. Deputy Registrar: Marais, D. D., MA Pret., DPhil Pret.
Admissions (first degree). Deputy Registrar: Marais, D. D., MA Pret., DPhil Pret.
Admissions (higher degree). Deputy Registrar: Marais, D. D., MA Pret., DPhil Pret.
Adult/continuing education. Deputy Registrar: Marais, D. D., MA Pret., DPhil Pret.
Alumni. Head: Cronje, L. J. J., PhD Rand Afrikaans

Archives. Head: Ferreira, Prof. O. J. O., DLitt&Phil S.Af.
Careers. Head: Potgieter, M. J., MEd Pret.
Computing services. Head: Roode, Prof. J. D., PhD Ley.
Development/fund-raising. Director, Marketing: Hendrikz, J., DEd Pret.
Distance education. Head: Jorissen, H. W., PhD Pret.
Equal opportunities. Vice-Principal: De Beer, Prof. C. R., BJur&Art Potchef., LLB Potchef., LLM Rand Afrikaans, LLM W.Cape, DrsJuris Ley., LLD Ley.
Estates and buildings/works and services. Director: Boshoff, L. N., BCom Pret.
Examinations. Deputy Registrar: Marais, D. D., MA Pret., DPhil Pret.
Finance. Director, Finance: Kruger, T. G., BCom Pret., MBA Pret.
General enquiries. Acting Registrar: Marais, D. D., MA Pret., DPhil Pret.
Health services. Head: De Jager, M., MB ChB Pret.
International office. Executive Director: Sinclair, Prof. J. D., BA Witw., LLB Witw., LLD Witw.
Library (chief librarian). Director: Gerryts, Prof. E. D., BA S.Af., MA(Lib) Pret., DLitt&Phil S.Af.
Library (enquiries). Deputy Director: De Bruin, Prof. H., DLib&InfSc OFS
Minorities/disadvantaged groups. Vice-Principal: De Beer, Prof. C. R., BJur&Art Potchef., LLB Potchef., LLM Rand Afrikaans, LLM W.Cape, DrsJuris Ley., LLD Ley.
Personnel/human resources. Director, Personnel: Herholdt, Prof. W. v. d. M., DPhil Pret.
Public relations, information and marketing. Director, Marketing: Hendrikz, J., DEd Pret.
Publications. Director: Hendrikz, J., DEd Pret.
Purchasing. Director: Boshoff, L. N., BCom Pret.
Research. Director: Ofir, Z. M., PhD Stell.
Safety. Head: Strachan, P. J., BSc(Eng) Pret.
Scholarships, awards, loans. Head: Van der Walt, A. J., BA Pret.
Schools liaison. Head: Potgieter, M. J., MEd Pret.
Security. Director: Venter, Y., MBA Pret.
Sport and recreation. Director: Potgieter, G. C.
Staff development and training. Deputy Director, Personnel: Pottas, Prof. C. D., DLitt&Phil Rand Afrikaans
Student union. Dean, Student Affairs: Van der Watt, Prof. P. B., DTh Stell.
Student welfare/counselling. Dean, Student Affairs: Van der Watt, Prof. P. B., DTh Stell.
Students from other countries. Dean, Student Affairs: Van der Watt, Prof. P. B., DTh Stell.
Students with disabilities. Dean, Student Affairs: Van der Watt, Prof. P. B., DTh Stell.
University press. Director: Boshoff, L. N., BCom Pret.
Women. Vice-Principal: De Beer, Prof. C. R., BJur&Art Potchef., LLB Potchef., LLM Rand Afrikaans, LLM W.Cape, DrsJuris Ley., LLD Ley.

[Information supplied by the institution as at 24 March 1998, and edited by the ACU]

RAND AFRIKAANS UNIVERSITY

Founded 1966

Member of the Association of Commonwealth Universities

Postal Address: PO Box 524, Auckland Park, Johannesburg, 2006 South Africa
Telephone: (011) 489 2911 **Fax**: (011) 489 2191 **Cables**: Rauniv **Telex**: 424526 SA
WWW: http://www.rau.ac.za **E-mail formula**: initial(s)firstletter(s)ofsurname@raul.rau.ac.za

VICE-CHANCELLOR AND RECTOR*—Van der Walt, Prof. Johannes C., BA OFS, LLB S.Af., LLD S.Af.
VICE-RECTOR—Botha, Prof. T. Roux, BA Pret., BEd Pret., MEd Pret., DEd Pret.
REGISTRAR (FINANCE)—Mans, Prof. Koert N., BCom S.Af., MCompt S.Af.
REGISTRAR (ACADEMIC)‡—Von Staden, Prof. Paul M. S., BA Pret., BA Stell., MA P.Elizabeth, DLitt&Phil Rand
Afrikaans
REGISTRAR (OPERATIONS)—Labuschagne, Carl D., BCom S.Af.

GENERAL INFORMATION

History. The university was established in 1966.

Admission. to first degree courses (see also South African Introduction). South African Matriculation Certificate with full exemption. Special requirements: vary between faculties.

First Degrees. (see also South African Directory to Subjects of Study) (* = also available with honours). BA*, BA(SocSc), BCom*, BCur, BInf*, BIng, BOptom, BSc*, LLB.

Higher Degrees. (see also South African Directory to Subjects of Study). BEd, LLM, MA, MA(SocSc), MCom, MCur, MEd, MIng, MSc, MPhil, PhD, DCom, DCur, DEd, DIng, DLitt&Phil, DPhil, LLD.

Language of Instruction. Afrikaans and English.

Libraries. 504,442 volumes, 2472 periodicals and 15 special collections.

Fees (annual). R7500–8500.

Academic Year. Two semesters: February–June; July–November.

Statistics (1998). Students: 20,516.

FACULTIES/SCHOOLS

Arts
Tel: (011) 489 2782 Fax: (011) 489 2797
Dean: Naudé, Prof. J. A., BD Pret., MA Pret., DLitt Pret.
Deputy Director: Reynders, P. J.

Economic and Management Sciences
Tel: (011) 489 3144 Fax: (011) 489 2036
Dean: Raubenheimer, Prof. I. v. W. (Naas), MCom Potchef., PhD Purdue
Deputy Director: Steyn, L. C.

Education and Nursing
Tel: (011) 489 2678 Fax: (011) 489 2781
Dean: Lamprecht, Prof. J. C., BA Stell., MEd P.Elizabeth, DEd Rand Afrikaans
Deputy Director: Vermeulen, J. A.

Engineering
Tel: (011) 489 2116 Fax: (011) 489 2054
Dean: van der Merwe, Prof. P.
Deputy Director: Oelofse, T.

Law
Tel: (011) 489 2135 Fax: (011) 489 2049
Dean: van der Merwe, Prof. D., BA Pret., LLB Pret., LLD Pret.
Deputy Director: du Toit, B. J.

Science
Tel: (011) 489 2418 Fax: (011) 489 3207
Dean: van Reenen, Prof. D. D., MSc OFS, PhD Rand Afrikaans

Deputy Director: Dykes, M. G. S.

ACADEMIC UNITS

Accounting
Tel: (011) 489 3153 Fax: (011) 489 2777
Barnes, L. L., BCom Rand Afrikaans Sr. Lectr.
Boshoff, Aletta, MCom Pret. Sr. Lectr.
Botes, Karin, BCom Rand Afrikaans Sr. Lectr.
Coetzee, D., BCom Rand Afrikaans, MCom Rand Afrikaans Prof.
de Jongh, Tessa, BCom Rand Afrikaans Sr. Lectr.
Dempsey, Amanda, MCom Rand Afrikaans Assoc. Prof.
du Toit, Anton, BA OFS, BCompt S.Af., MCom Rand Afrikaans Assoc. Prof.
Griesel, Sonja, BCompt OFS, BCom S.Af., MCom Rand Afrikaans Sr. Lectr.
Hattingh, Karin, BCom Pret. Sr. Lectr.
Jordaan, Keith, BCom Rand Afrikaans Assoc. Prof.
Kellbrick, P. J., BCom OFS Sr. Lectr.
Kocks, E., BCom Stell. Sr. Lectr.
Kriek, J. H., BCom Rand Afrikaans Prof.
Marx, B., BCom OFS, MCom OFS Prof.
Pietersen, Marita E., MCom Rand Afrikaans Assoc. Prof.
Stegman, Nerine, BCom Rand Afrikaans, MCom Rand Afrikaans, DCom Rand Afrikaans Sr. Lectr.
Steyn, Sonja, BCompt S.Af. Sr. Lectr.
Van der Watt, A., BCom Rand Afrikaans Sr. Lectr.
Voogt, T. L., BCom Rand Afrikaans Sr. Lectr.
Vorster, Desiré D., BCom Rand Afrikaans, MCom Rand Afrikaans Prof.; Chairman*

African Languages
Tel: (011) 489 2023 Fax: (011) 489 2797
Du Toit, A. C., MA Rand Afrikaans, DLitt&Phil Rand Afrikaans Sr. Lectr.
Kock, J. H. M., MA Rand Afrikaans, DLitt&Phil Rand Afrikaans Sr. Lectr.
Posthumus, Lionel C., MA OFS, DLitt OFS Prof.; Chairperson*

Afrikaans
Tel: (011) 489 2694 Fax: (011) 489 2797
Beukes, M. P., MA Potchef., DLitt Bophut., BA BPhil Sr. Lectr.
Botha, W. J., BA S.Af., MA S.Af., DLitt&Phil S.Af. Prof.; Chairperson*
Burger, W. D., MA Potchef., PhD Potchef. Assoc. Prof.
Coetzee, A. E., DLitt&Phil Rand Afrikaans, BA MA Assoc. Prof.
Conradie, C. J., BA Stell., MA Stell., DrsLitt Utrecht, PhD Witw. Assoc. Prof.

Biblical Studies
Tel: (011) 489 2337 Fax: (011) 489 2797
Coetzee, J. H., MA S.Af., BD Pret., DD Pret. Assoc. Prof.; Chairperson*
du Rand, J. A., MA OFS, DD Pret. Prof.
Nortjé, S. J., BEd Rand Afrikaans, MA Rand Afrikaans, DLitt&Phil Rand Afrikaans Sr. Lectr.
Viviers, H., BD Pret., DD Pret. Assoc. Prof.

Biochemistry, see Chem. and Biochem.

Botany
Tel: (011) 489 2436 Fax: (011) 489 2411
van Warmelo, K. T., MScAgric Natal, PhD Stell. Prof.
van Wyk, B.-E., MSc Stell., PhD Cape Town Prof.
Whitehead, C. S., BSc Potchef., PhD Rand Afrikaans Prof.; Chairman*

Business Management
Tel: (011) 489 3143 Fax: (011) 489 2827
Bennett, J. Alf, MCom OFS, DCom OFS Assoc. Prof.
Boessenkool, Aart L., BCom Rand Afrikaans, MCom Potchef. Prof.; Chairman*
Conradie, W. M., BA Pret., MBA S.Af., DBA Potchef. Prof.
de Bruyn, Herman E. C., MCom Potchef., DCom Potchef. Prof.
Jooste, Chris J., MCom OFS, DCom OFS Prof.
Koekemoer, C. Ludi, BCom Pret., BCom Rand Afrikaans, MBA Pret., PhD Rhodes Prof.
Kruger, Steven, MCom Potchef., DCom Potchef. Prof.
Lessing, Nic, MCom Potchef., DCom Potchef. Prof.
Swart, Retief, BCom Rand Afrikaans Sr. Lectr.

Chemistry and Biochemistry
Tel: (011) 489 2363 Fax: (011) 489 2605

Biochemistry
Tel: (011) 489 2370
Bornman, L., BSc(Agric) Pret., MSc Witw., PhD Pret. Sr. Lectr.
Dubery, I. A., PhD Rand Afrikaans Prof.

Chemistry
Coetzee, P. P., PhD Stell. Prof.
Holzapfel, C. W., MSc Stell., PhD Manc. Prof.
Kruger, G. J., DSc Potchef. Prof.
Malan, R. E., MSc Rand Afrikaans Sr. Lectr.
van Heerden, F. R., PhD OFS Assoc. Prof.
Williams, D. B. G., PhD Rand Afrikaans Sr. Lectr.

Communication
Tel: (011) 489 2139 Fax: (011) 489 2426
Venter, H. L., MA Rand Afrikaans, DLitt&Phil Rand Afrikaans Sr. Lectr.
Verwey, S., MA Rand Afrikaans, DLitt&Phil Rand Afrikaans Assoc. Prof.; Chairperson*

Computer Science
Tel: (011) 489 2847 Fax: (011) 489 2138
Anderssen, E. C., MSc Rand Afrikaans, MSc Pret., PhD Rand Afrikaans Sr. Lectr.
Ehlers, E. M., PhD Rand Afrikaans Prof.
Eloff, J. H. P., PhD Rand Afrikaans Prof.
Labuschagne, L., MCom Rand Afrikaans Assoc. Prof.
Olivier, M. S., PhD Rand Afrikaans Sr. Lectr.
Smith, T. H. C., MSc Rand Afrikaans, MS Carnegie-Mellon, PhD Carnegie-Mellon Prof.

von Solms, S. H., PhD Rand Afrikaans Prof.; Chairman*

Curriculum Studies

Tel: (011) 489 2666 Fax: (011) 489 2048

Ankiewicz, P. J., MSc Potchef., DEd Potchef. Sr. Lectr.

de Swardt, A. E., BA Rand Afrikaans, DEd Rand Afrikaans Sr. Lectr.

Geyser, H. C., BA Potchef., BA Rand Afrikaans, DEd Rand Afrikaans Assoc. Prof.

Henning, E., BA Potchef., MA Pret., BEd Rand Afrikaans, DPhil Rand Afrikaans Assoc. Prof.

Strauss, J., BSc OFS, BEd Potchef., DEd Rand Afrikaans Prof.; Chairman*

Trümpelmann, M. H., BEd Pret., DPhil Pret., DEd Rand Afrikaans Prof.

van Loggerenberg, M. C., BA Potchef., MEd Potchef., DEd Rand Afrikaans Sr. Lectr.

van Rooyen, H. G., BSc Rand Afrikaans, DEd Rand Afrikaans Prof.

Development Studies

Tel: (011) 489 2859 Fax: (011) 489 2797

Maritz, C. J., MA Potchef., DPhil Potchef. Prof.

van der Waal, C. S., MA Pret., DLitt&Phil Rand Afrikaans Assoc. Prof.; Chairperson*

Economics

Tel: (011) 489 2046 Fax: (011) 489 3039

Botha, Roelof F., MCom Pret., DCom Rand Afrikaans Sr. Lectr.

Greyling, Lorraine, DCom Rand Afrikaans Prof.

Heyns, Jack van der S., BCom Rhodes, MCom S.Af., PhD Natal Prof.; Chairman*

Loots, A. E., MCom Rand Afrikaans, DCom Rand Afrikaans Sr. Lectr.

Schaling, E., PhD Tilburg

Schoeman, C. H., MA Rand Afrikaans, DLitt&Phil Rand Afrikaans Sr. Lectr.

van Zyl, G. (Hardus), DCom Rand Afrikaans Assoc. Prof.

Education and Health, RAU College for

Tel: (011) 489 2213 Fax: (011) 489 2292

Ramusi, Frans M., BA S.Af., BEd Witw., MEd Rand Afrikaans, DEd Rand Afrikaans Dir.*

Educational Sciences

Tel: (011) 489 2055 Fax: (011) 489 2048

Botha, J. H., BA Potchef., MEd Potchef., DEd Rand Afrikaans Sr. Lectr.

Gravett, S. J., BA Potchef., BEd Rand Afrikaans, MEd Rand Afrikaans, DEd Rand Afrikaans Sr. Lectr.

Grobler, B. R., BSc Witw., DEd Rand Afrikaans Assoc. Prof.

Kok, J. C., BA Pret., MEd Pret., DEd P.Elizabeth Prof.

Myburgh, C. P. H., BSc Pret., MCom Rand Afrikaans, DEd Rand Afrikaans Prof.; Chairman*

Smith, D. P. J., MSc Potchef., MEd Rand Afrikaans, DEd Rand Afrikaans Prof.

Smith, J. B., BA Stell., MEd Stell., DEd Rand Afrikaans Assoc. Prof.

Swart, R. E., BA Rand Afrikaans, DEd Rand Afrikaans Sr. Lectr.

van der Merwe, M. P., BA(Ed) Rand Afrikaans, DEd Rand Afrikaans Sr. Lectr.

Energy Studies, Institute for

Tel: (011) 489 2071 Fax: (011) 489 2036

Kotzé, D. J., MCom Stell., PhD Cape Town BP Prof.; Chairman*

Engineering, Civil and Urban

Tel: (011) 489 2342 Fax: (011) 489 2054

Brink, A. B. A., BSc Pret., DSc Pret. Prof.†

Haarhoff, J., MIng Stell., PhD Iowa State, BIng Prof.

Kruger, D., BSc Pret., BIng Pret., MIng Rand Afrikaans Prof.

Legge, T. F. H., BSc(Eng) Witw., MSc Lond. Assoc. Prof.

van den Berg, G. J., BSc Pret., DIng Rand Afrikaans Assoc. Prof.; Chairman*

Engineering, Electrical and Electronic

Tel: (011) 489 2386 Fax: (011) 489 2054

Case, M. J., BSc(Eng) Cape Town, PhD Cape Town Prof.

Cronje, W. A., DIng Rand Afrikaans Sr. Lectr.

Ferreira, H. C., MSc Pret., DSc Pret. Prof.; Chairperson*

Gouws, J., MIng Rand Afrikaans, PhD Wageningen Assoc. Prof.

Hofsajer, I. W., MIng Rand Afrikaans Sr. Lectr.

Lacquet, B. M., DIng Rand Afrikaans Assoc. Prof.

Spammer, S. J., DIng Rand Afrikaans Assoc. Prof.

Swart, P. L., MSc Pret., PhD McM. Prof.

van Wyk, J. D., MSc Pret., DrScTechn T.U.Eindhoven, F(SA)IEE RAU Council Res. Prof., Industrial Electronics

Engineering, Mechanical and Manufacturing

Tel: (011) 489 2147 Fax: (011) 489 2054

Coetzee, G., BEng Pret., MIng Rand Afrikaans, DIng Rand Afrikaans Sr. Lectr.

Katz, Z., MSc Haifa(Technion), DrScTech Haifa(Technion) Morris Gillman Prof., Manufacturing

Laubscher, R. F., MIng Rand Afrikaans Sr. Lectr.

Liebenberg, L., MIng Rand Afrikaans Sr. Lectr.

Meyer, J. P., PhD Pret. Prof.

Pretorius, J., MIng Rand Afrikaans Sr. Lectr.

Pretorius, L., MSc Pret., DEng Pret., F(SA)IME Prof.; Chairperson*

van der Merwe, P., MSc Pret., PhD Missouri Prof.

English

Tel: (011) 489 2063 Fax: (011) 489 2063

Klopper, D. C., MA S.Af., DLitt&Phil S.Af. Sr. Lectr.

MacKenzie, C. H., MA Durban-W., PhD Rhodes Sr. Lectr.

Ryan, R. P., MA Rhodes, PhD Natal Prof.; Chairperson*

Environmental Management, see

Geography and Environmental Management

French

Tel: (011) 489 2063 Fax: (011) 489 2797

Godwin, D. A., MA Rand Afrikaans, Dr3rdCy Aix-Marseilles I Prof.; Chairperson*

Geography and Environmental Management

Tel: (011) 489 2433 Fax: (011) 489 2430

Harmse, J. T., PhD Stell. Assoc. Prof.; Chairman*

Scheepers, L. G. C., DLitt&Phil Rand Afrikaans Sr. Lectr.

van Rensburg, P. A. J., MSc Potchef., PhD Rand Afrikaans Prof.

Wolfaardt, P. J., MA Stell., DLitt&Phil Rand Afrikaans Sr. Lectr.

Geology

Tel: (011) 489 2301 Fax: (011) 489 2309

Ashwal, L. D., BSc N.Y.State, MS Mass., PhD Prin. Prof.

Barton, J. M., PhD McG. Prof.

Beukes, N. J., MSc OFS, PhD Rand Afrikaans Prof.; Chairman*

Cairncross, B., MSc Natal, PhD Witw. Assoc. Prof.

Smit, C. A., PhD OFS Sr. Lectr.

German

Tel: (011) 489 2724 Fax: (011) 489 2797

Knobloch, H.-J., DrPhil Heidel. Prof.; Chairperson*

Greek and Latin Studies

Tel: (011) 489 2735 Fax: (011) 489 2797

Basson, A. F., MA Rand Afrikaans, PhD Aix-Marseilles I Sr. Lectr.

Hendrickx, B., LicAncGreek Leuven, LicByzGreek Leuven, DrPhil Salonika Prof.

Pauw, D. A., MA Pret., DrsLitt&Phil Ley Prof.; Chairperson*

Wolmarans, J. L. P., BD Pret., MA Pret., DD Pret. Sr. Lectr.

History

Tel: (011) 489 2001 Fax: (011) 489 2617

Grundlingh, L. W. F, MA OFS, DLitt&Phil Rand Afrikaans Assoc. Prof.

van Aswegen, H. J., MA Stell., DPhil OFS Prof.; Chairperson*

Verhoef, G., MA Rand Afrikaans, DLitt&Phil Rand Afrikaans Assoc. Prof.

Human Resource Management

Tel: (011) 489 2074 Fax: (011) 489 2710

Coetsee, W. J., BCom Potchef., MCom Potchef. Sr. Lectr.

Crous, F., MCom Rand Afrikaans Sr. Lectr.

Lessing, Barend C., BCom Potchef., MCom Stell., DCom Rand Afrikaans Prof.; Chairman*

Roodt, Gert, BAdmin OFS, MAdmin OFS, DAdmin OFS Assoc. Prof.

Schmidt, Conrad, BCom P.Elizabeth, MCom Rand Afrikaans Sr. Lectr.

Slabbert, J. A. (Kobus), MCom Potchef., DCom Potchef. Prof.

Van Tonder, C. L., BA Rand Afrikaans, BA S.Af., MA Rand Afrikaans Sr. Lectr.

van Vuuren, Leon J., BCom Rand Afrikaans, MCom Rand Afrikaans Sr. Lectr.

Visser, J. D., BSc Stell., MSc Rand Afrikaans, PhD S.Af. Prof.

Information Science

Tel: (011) 489 2183 Fax: (011) 489 2797

Bester, M., MA Potchef., DBibl Potchef. Prof.

du Toit, A. S. A., MBibl Pret. Prof.

van Brakel, P. A., MBibl OFS, DPhil Pret. Prof.; Chairperson*

Latin, see Greek and Latin Studies

Law

Tel: (011) 489 2141 Fax: (011) 489 2049

Barrie, G. N., BA Pret., LLB Pret., LLD S.Af. Prof.

Boshoff, A., BA Rand Afrikaans, LLB Rand Afrikaans, LLM Rand Afrikaans Sr. Lectr.

de Villiers, D. S., BA Pret., LLB Pret., LLD Pret. Prof.

Du Plessis, J. J., LLD Rand Afrikaans Prof.

Giles, G., BA Stell., LLB Witw. Prof.†

Labuschagne, E., BA Pret., LLB Rand Afrikaans, LLM Rand Afrikaans Sr. Lectr.

le Roux, W. P., BIuris Pret., LLB Pret. Prof.†

Malan, F. R., BA Pret., LLB Pret., LLD Pret. Prof.

Malherbe, E. F. J., BA Stell., LLB Stell., LLD Rand Afrikaans Prof.

Neels, J. L., BCom Rand Afrikaans, LLB Rand Afrikaans, LLM Rand Afrikaans Sr. Lectr.

O'Brien, P. H., BCom Rand Afrikaans, LLB Rand Afrikaans, LLM Rand Afrikaans Assoc. Prof.

Olivier, L., BA Stell., LLB Stell., LLM Rand Afrikaans, LLD Rand Afrikaans Assoc. Prof.

Olivier, M. P., BA Pret., LLB Pret., LLD S.Af. Prof.

Otto, J. M., BA Pret., LLB Pret., LLD Pret. Prof.

Rautenbach, I. M., BA Pret., LLB Pret., LLD S.Af. Prof.

Reinecke, M. F. B., BA Pret., LLB Pret. Prof.

Sonnekus, J. C., BA Rand Afrikaans, LLB Rand Afrikaans, LLM Rand Afrikaans, LLD Ley. Prof.

Steenhuisen, E., BA Rand Afrikaans, LLB Rand Afrikaans Sr. Lectr.

van der Walt, J. W. G., BLC Pret., BA Pret., LLB Pret., MA Pret., LLD Rand Afrikaans Prof.

Vorster, H. V., BA Witw., LLB Witw., LLM Witw. Prof.†

Watney, M. M., BA Rand Afrikaans, LLB Rand Afrikaans, LLM Rand Afrikaans, LLD Rand Afrikaans Sr. Lectr.

Zulman, R. H., BCom Witw. Prof.†

Other Staff: 3 Lectrs.

Law Clinic

Tel: (011) 489 2633

Steenhuisen, F., BA Rand Afrikaans, LLB Rand Afrikaans Dir.*

Linguistic and Literary Theory

Tel: (011) 489 2694 Fax: (011) 489 2797

Johl, C. S., BA OFS, MA OFS, DLitt&Phil Rand Afrikaans Assoc. Prof.; Chairperson*
Sweetnam Evans, M. E., BA Rhodes, BA North(S.Af.), MA Rand Afrikaans, DLitt&Phil Rand Afrikaans Sr. Lectr.

Mathematics

Tel: (011) 489 2835 Fax: (011) 489 2874

Broere, I., BSc Pret., PhD Rand Afrikaans Prof.; Chairman*
Burger, I. C., PhD Rand Afrikaans Assoc. Prof.
Buys, A., MSc P.Elizabeth, PhD Rand Afrikaans Prof.
Goranko, V. F., PhD Sofia Assoc. Prof.
Hattingh, J. H., PhD Rand Afrikaans Assoc. Prof.

Mathematics, Applied

Tel: (011) 489 2067 Fax: (011) 489 2616

Solms, F., MSc S.Af., PhD Pret. Sr. Lectr.
Steeb, W-H, DrHabil Kiel Prof.
Villet, C. M., MSc Stell., PhD Rand Afrikaans Prof.; Chairman*

Nursing

Tel: (011) 489 2580 Fax: (011) 489 2257

Botes, A. C., DCur Rand Afrikaans Prof.
Dörfling, C. S., DCur Rand Afrikaans Sr. Lectr.
Gmeiner, A. C., MCur Rand Afrikaans, DCur Rand Afrikaans Sr. Lectr.
Gross, E. J., DCur Rand Afrikaans Sr. Lectr.
Muller, M. E., BACur S.Af., DCur Rand Afrikaans Prof.; Chairman*
Nel, W. E., BSocSc OFS, DCur Rand Afrikaans Sr. Lectr.
Nolte, A. G. W., MSocSc OFS, DLitt&Phil S.Af. Prof.
Poggenpoel, M., BArt&Sc Potchef., MSocSc OFS, DPhil Potchef. Prof.
Roos, S. D., DCur Rand Afrikaans Sr. Lectr.

Optometry

Tel: (011) 489 2423 Fax: (011) 489 2091

Ferreira, J. T., BOptom Rand Afrikaans, PhD Rand Afrikaans Prof.; Chairman*
Harris, W. F., BSc(Eng) Witw., BOptom Rand Afrikaans, PhD Minn. Prof.
Kotze, C. M., BA Rand Afrikaans, BA(Ed) Rand Afrikaans, BCompt S.Af. Dir., Clinic

Philosophy

Tel: (011) 489 2337 Fax: (011) 489 2797

Lötter, H. P. P., BTh Stell., LicTheol Stell., DLitt&Phil Rand Afrikaans Prof.
Rossouw, G. J., BTh Stell., LicTheol Stell., MA Stell., DPhil Stell. Prof.; Chairperson*
Snyman, J. J., MA Rand Afrikaans, DLitt&Phil Rand Afrikaans Prof.

Physics

Tel: (011) 489 2327 Fax: (011) 489 3207

Alberts, H. L., MSc OFS, PhD Rand Afrikaans Prof.
Alberts, V., PhD P.Elizabeth Assoc. Prof.
Saundersen, J. D., MSc Potchef. Sr. Lectr.
Smit, P., PhD Rand Afrikaans Assoc. Prof.
Swanepoel, R., MSc S.Af., PhD Rand Afrikaans Prof.; Chairman*

Political Studies

Tel: (011) 489 2896 Fax: (011) 489 3038

Geldenhuys, D. J., MA Pret., PhD Camb. Prof.; Chairperson*
Sadic, A. Y., MA Stell., PhD Cape Town Sr. Lectr.
Schoeman, M. M. E., MA Rand Afrikaans, PhD Wales Sr. Lectr.
Venter, A. J., MA S.Af., DLitt&Phil S.Af. Prof.
Zybrands, W., BA Pret., LLB S.Af. Prof.

Psychology

Tel: (011) 489 3130 Fax: (011) 489 2797

Burke, A., MA Rand Afrikaans, DLitt&Phil Rand Afrikaans Sr. Lectr.
Gething, N. J., MA Rand Afrikaans Sr. Lectr.
Jooste, M. J. L., MA S.Af., DLitt&Phil S.Af. Sr. Lectr.
Joubert, M. F., MA Pret., DLitt&Phil Rand Afrikaans Assoc. Prof.
Novello, A., MA Rand Afrikaans, DLitt&Phil Rand Afrikaans Sr. Lectr.
Oosthuizen, C. J., MA Stell. Sr. Lectr.
Pretorius, H. G., MA Rand Afrikaans, DLitt&Phil Rand Afrikaans Assoc. Prof.
Schoeman, W. J., BA Pret., BA OFS, MA OFS, DPhil OFS Prof.; Chairman*
Stuart, A. D., MA Rand Afrikaans, DLitt&Phil Rand Afrikaans Assoc. Prof.

Semitic Languages

Tel: (011) 489 2751 Fax: (011) 489 2797

van Rensburg, J. F. J., BD Pret., MA Pret., DLitt Pret. Assoc. Prof.; Chairperson*

Social Science

Tel: (011) 489 2804 Fax: (011) 489 2797

Fouché, C. B., MA Rand Afrikaans, DLitt&Phil Rand Afrikaans Sr. Lectr.
Nel, J. B. S., MA Rand Afrikaans, DLitt&Phil Rand Afrikaans Sr. Lectr.
van Zyl, M. A., MA Rand Afrikaans, PhD Natal Prof.; Chairperson*

Sociology

Tel: (011) 489 2879 Fax: (011) 489 2797

Senekal, A., MA Rand Afrikaans, DLitt&Phil Rand Afrikaans Assoc. Prof.
Uys, J. M., MA Rand Afrikaans, DLitt&Phil Rand Afrikaans Prof.; Chairperson*

Sport and Movement Studies

Tel: (011) 489 3005 Fax: (011) 489 2671

Burnett-Louw, Cora, BA Pret., BA Stell., MA Stell., PhD Stell. Assoc. Prof.
Gouws, Johan S., BSc Pret., DEd S.Af., DCom Rand Afrikaans Prof.; Chairman*
Hollander, Wim J., BSc Rand Afrikaans, DEd Rand Afrikaans Assoc. Prof.
Lombard, A. J. J. (Rian), BSc Stell. Sr. Lectr.
Sierra, Gertrude J., MA Pret. Sr. Lectr.

Statistics

Tel: (011) 489 2848 Fax: (011) 489 2832

Lemmer, H. H., DSc Pret. Prof.
Lombard, F., MSc Pret., PhD Rand Afrikaans Prof.; Chairman*
Strauss, L. J., BSc Pret. Sr. Lectr.

Transport Economics

Tel: (011) 489 2086 Fax: (011) 489 2029

Pretorius, Wynand, MCom Rand Afrikaans, DCom Rand Afrikaans Prof.; Chairman*
Walters, Jackie, MCom Rand Afrikaans, DCom Rand Afrikaans Assoc. Prof.

Zoology

Tel: (011) 489 2441 Fax: (011) 489 3207

Janse van Vuren, J. H., PhD Rand Afrikaans Prof.
Oldewage, A., PhD Rand Afrikaans Assoc. Prof.
Steyn, G. J., PhD Rand Afrikaans Assoc. Prof.
Swanepoel, J. H., DSc Stell. Prof.; Chairman*
van der Bank, F. H., PhD Rand Afrikaans Assoc. Prof.

SPECIAL CENTRES, ETC

European Studies, Centre for

Tel: (011) 489 2896 Fax: (011) 489 3038

Olivier, G. C., MA Pret., DPhil Pret. Prof.; Dir.*

Islamic Studies, Centre for

Fax: (011) 489 2787

Doi, A. R. I., PhD Camb. Prof.; Sr. Researcher

Metropolitan and Regional Administration, Centre for

Tel: (011) 489 2896 Fax: (011) 489 3038

Zybrands, W., BA Pret., LLB S.Af. Prof.; Head*

CONTACT OFFICERS

Academic affairs. Registrar (Academic): Von Staden, Prof. Paul M. S., BA Pret., BA Stell., MA P.Elizabeth, DLitt&Phil Rand Afrikaans
Accommodation. Registrar (Operations): Labuschagne, Carl D., BCom S.Af.
Admissions (first degree). Registrar (Academic): Von Staden, Prof. Paul M. S., BA Pret., BA Stell., MA P.Elizabeth, DLitt&Phil Rand Afrikaans
Admissions (higher degree). Registrar (Academic): Von Staden, Prof. Paul M. S., BA Pret., BA Stell., MA P.Elizabeth, DLitt&Phil Rand Afrikaans
Alumni. Deputy Director: Van Wyk, Gert J., BEd Rand Afrikaans, BA Rand Afrikaans, MEd Rand Afrikaans
Careers. Director: Botha, Prof. Paul P., BA S.Af., MA Rand Afrikaans, MEd Rand Afrikaans, DPhil Potchef.
Computing services. Registrar (Operations): Labuschagne, Carl D., BCom S.Af.
Development/fund-raising. Director: Pretorius, Prof. Johan, BSc Pret., PhD Rand Afrikaans
Distance education. Head: Lamprecht, J. C., BA Stell., MEd P.Elizabeth, DEd Rand Afrikaans
Equal opportunities. Chief Director: De Wet, Willie M.
Estates and buildings/works and services. Registrar (Operations): Labuschagne, Carl D., BCom S.Af.
Examinations. Registrar (Academic): Von Staden, Prof. Paul M. S., BA Pret., BA Stell., MA P.Elizabeth, DLitt&Phil Rand Afrikaans
Finance. Registrar (Finance): Mans, Prof. Koert N., BCom S.Af., MCompt S.Af.
General enquiries. Registrar (Academic): Von Staden, Prof. Paul M. S., BA Pret., BA Stell., MA P.Elizabeth, DLitt&Phil Rand Afrikaans
Health services. Registrar (Operations): Labuschagne, Carl D., BCom S.Af.
Industrial liaison. Chief Director: De Wet, Willie M.
International office. Registrar (Academic): Von Staden, Prof. Paul M. S., BA Pret., BA Stell., MA P.Elizabeth, DLitt&Phil Rand Afrikaans
Library (enquiries). Chief Director: Sander, J., BSc Potchef., BBibl Potchef., MBibl Rand Afrikaans
Minorities/disadvantaged groups. Chief Director: De Wet, Willie M.
Personnel/human resources. Chief Director: De Wet, Willie M.
Public relations, information and marketing. Deputy Director: de Wet, L., BA S.Af.
Publications. Deputy Director: de Wet, L., BA S.Af.
Purchasing. Chief Director: Van Tonder, Rian, BCom S.Af.
Research. Registrar (Academic): Von Staden, Prof. Paul M. S., BA Pret., BA Stell., MA P.Elizabeth, DLitt&Phil Rand Afrikaans
Safety. Registrar (Operations): Labuschagne, Carl D., BCom S.Af.
Scholarships, awards, loans. Chief Director: Van Tonder, Rian, BCom S.Af.
Schools liaison. Director: Botha, Prof. Paul P., BA S.Af., MA Rand Afrikaans, MEd Rand Afrikaans, DPhil Potchef.
Security. Registrar (Operations): Labuschagne, Carl D., BCom S.Af.
Sport and recreation. Chief Director: Gouws, Prof. Johan S., BSc Pret., BEd Potchef., MEd S.Af., DEd S.Af.
Staff development and training. Chief Director: De Wet, Willie M.
Student union. de Jager, Prof. Frederick J., BA Stell., LLB Stell., LLM S.Af., LLD Rand Afrikaans
Student welfare/counselling. de Jager, Prof. Frederick J., BA Stell., LLB Stell., LLM S.Af., LLD Rand Afrikaans

Students from other countries. de Jager, Prof. Frederick J., BA *Stell.*, LLB *Stell.*, LLM *S.Af.*, LLD *Rand Afrikaans*

Students with disabilities. de Jager, Prof. Frederick J., BA *Stell.*, LLB *Stell.*, LLM *S.Af.*, LLD *Rand Afrikaans*

University press. Registrar (Operations): Labuschagne, Carl D., BCom *S.Af.*

[Information supplied by the institution as at 9 July 1998, and edited by the ACU]

RHODES UNIVERSITY

Founded 1951; previously established as Rhodes University College (1904)

Member of the Association of Commonwealth Universities

Postal Address: PO Box 94, Grahamstown, 6140 South Africa
Telephone: (046) 603 8111 **Fax**: (046) 622 5049 **Cables**: Rhodescol **WWW**: http://www.ru.ac.za/
E-mail formula: username@host.ru.ac.za

CHANCELLOR—Relly, G. W. H., MSc *Oxf.*, Hon. LLD *Rhodes*
PRINCIPAL AND VICE-CHANCELLOR*‡—Woods, Prof. David R., BSc *Rhodes*, DPhil *Oxf.*, FRSSAf
VICE-PRINCIPAL—Smout, M. A. H., MSc *Natal*, MA *Newcastle(UK)*, PhD *Lond.*
CHAIRMAN OF COUNCIL—Jones, The Hon. Mr. Justice R. J. W., BA *Rhodes*, LLB *Rhodes*
REGISTRAR—Fourie, Steve, BTh *Rhodes*, BD *Rhodes*, DTh *S.Af.*
PUBLIC ORATOR—Terry, P. D., MSc *Rhodes*, PhD *Camb.*

GENERAL INFORMATION

History. The university was originally established as Rhodes University College in 1904. The decision to create an independent university was taken at the end of the second world war and the university was inaugurated in 1951.

Admission to first degree courses (see also South African Introduction). South African applicants: matriculation exemption issued by the Matriculation Board. International applicants: General Certificate of Education (GCE) O and A levels or equivalent; exemption certificates from the Matriculation Board are also required.

First Degrees (see also South African Directory to Subjects of Study). BA, BA(HMS), BAcc, BBusSc, BCom, BD, BEcon, BFineArt, BJourn, BMus, BPharm, BPrimEd, BSc, BSc(InfSys), BSocSc, BSocSc(SocWork), BTh, LLB.
Courses for BA, BA(HMS) (human movement studies), BCom, BD, BEcon, BSc, BSc(InfSys), BSocSc, BTh last 3 years; BAcc, BBusSc, BFineArt, BJourn, BMus, BPharm, BPrimEd, BSocSc(SocWork), LLB: 4 years.

Higher Degrees (see also South African Directory to Subjects of Study). LLM, MA, MCom, MEcon, MEd, MFineArt, MMus, MPharm, MSc, MSocSc, MTh, PhD, DD, DEcon, DLitt, DMus, DSc, DSocSc, LLD.
Applicants for admission to master's degrees must normally hold an appropriate first degree with honours (first degree without honours is often acceptable); applicants without formal tertiary qualifications who have extensive work experience may also be accepted. PhD: a master's degree.

Libraries. 412,679 volumes; 3400 journals/periodicals (1900 journals/periodicals subscribed to). Specialist libraries: Cory (Africana and items of historical interest).

Fees (1998, annual). Undergraduate: R9350–9900 (arts/humanities); R10,250 (commerce); R9750–10,350 (science). Postgraduate: R4500–7000.

Academic Awards. Various awards ranging in value from R2500 to R6000.

Academic Year (1998). Two semesters: 16 February–26 June; 27 July–11 December.

Income (1997). Total, R106,000,000.

Statistics. Staff: 1229 (545 academic, 684 administrative and other). Students: full-time 4935 (2638 men, 2297 women); part-time 919 (456 men, 463 women); international 782 (386 men, 396 women); total 5854.

FACULTIES/SCHOOLS

Commerce
Tel: (046) 603 8346
Dean: van der Watt, Prof. P., MSc *S.Af.*, PhD *S.Af.*
Secretary: Harwood, G. J.

Education
Tel: (046) 603 8383
Dean: Irwin, Prof. P. R., BA *Natal*, MEd *Natal*, DEd *S.Af.*
Secretary: Gush, J. A.

Humanities
Tel: (046) 603 8350
Dean: Macdonald, Prof. I. A., BA *Rhodes*, MA *Kansas*
Secretary: Murray, D. M.

Law
Tel: (046) 603 8427
Dean: Midgley, Prof. J. R., BCom *Rhodes*, LLB *Rhodes*, PhD *Cape Town*
Secretary: Futuse, L.

Pharmacy
Tel: (046) 603 8495 Fax: (046) 636 1205
Dean: Wilson, B. J., MSc *Sask.*, PhD *Purdue*
Secretary: De Beer, F.

Science
Tel: (046) 603 8098
Dean: Hepburn, Prof. H. R., MS *Louisiana State*, PhD *Kansas*, FRSSAf
Secretary: Guye, S. G.

ACADEMIC UNITS

Accounting
Tel: (046) 603 8201 Fax: (046) 622 5409
Bunting, M. B., BSc(InfProc) *Rhodes*, BCom *Rhodes* Assoc. Prof.; Head*
Maree, K. W., BCom *Rhodes* Sr. Lectr.
Negash, M., BA *Addis Ababa*, MBA *Leuven*, PhD *Brussels* Sr. Lectr.
White, P. P., BCom *Cape Town* Sr. Lectr.

East London Campus
Tel: (0431) 22539 Fax: (0431) 438307
McCole, B. J., MBA *Edin.* Sr. Lectr.
Schulze, M. J., BCom *Rhodes* Sr. Lectr.
Whitfield, S. K., BCom *Rhodes* Assoc. Prof.
Other Staff: 3 Lectrs.

African Languages, see under Langs., Sch. of

Afrikaans and Nederlandic Studies, see under Langs., Sch. of

Anthropology
Tel: (046) 603 8231
de Wet, C. J., MA *Stell.*, PhD *Rhodes* Prof.
Palmer, R. C. G., BA *Durh.*, DPhil *Sus.* Sr. Lectr.
Whisson, M. G., PhD *Camb.* Prof.; Head*
Other Staff: 1 Lectr.

Biochemistry and Microbiology
Tel: (046) 603 8256 Fax: (046) 622 4377
Daya, S., BSc *Durban-W.*, MSc *Rhodes*, PhD *S.Af.Med.* Assoc. Prof., Biochemistry
Duncan, J. R., PhD *Natal* Prof., Biochemistry; Head*
Hendry, D. A., MSc *Stell.*, PhD *Cape Town* Assoc. Prof., Microbiology
Kirby, R., MA *Camb.*, PhD *E.Anglia* Prof., Microbiology
Rose, P. D., BSc *Cape Town*, PhD *Rhodes* Prof., Biotechnology
Whiteley, C. G., PhD *Natal* Assoc. Prof., Biochemistry
Other Staff: 2 Lectrs.; 2 Hon. Fellows

Botany

Tel: (046) 603 8592 Fax: (046) 622 5524

Avis, A. M., PhD Rhodes Sr. Lectr.
Botha, C. E. J., MSc Natal, PhD Natal Prof.; Head*
Lubke, R. A., BSc Rhodes, MSc Keele, PhD W.Ont. Assoc. Prof.
Other Staff: 3 Lectrs.; 2 Res. Assocs.

Chemistry

Fax: (046) 622 5109

Brown, M. E., BSc Witw., PhD Rhodes, FRSSAf Prof., Physical Chemistry
Cosser, R. C., PhD Lond. Sr. Lectr., Physical Chemistry
Davies-Coleman, M. T., BSc Rhodes, PhD Rhodes Assoc. Prof., Organic Chemistry
Kaye, P. T., BSc Natal, BSc S.Af., MSc Natal, DPhil Oxf. Prof., Organic Chemistry; Head*
Nyokong, T., BSc NUL, MSc McM., PhD W.Ont. Assoc. Prof., Physical and Inorganic Chemistry
Other Staff: 3 Lectrs.; 2 Hon. Res. Assocs.

Classics, see under Langs., Sch. of

Computer Science

Tel: (046) 603 8291 Fax: (046) 636 1915

Bangay, S. D., MSc Rhodes, PhD Rhodes Assoc. Prof.
Clayton, P. G., MSc Rhodes, PhD Rhodes Prof.; Head*
Terry, P. D., MSc Rhodes, PhD Camb. Prof.
Wells, G. C., MSc Rhodes Sr. Lectr.
Wentworth, E. P., PhD P.Elizabeth Prof.
Other Staff: 3 Lectrs.

Drama

Tel: (046) 603 8538 Fax: (046) 622 4509

Buckland, A. F., BA Rhodes Assoc. Prof.
Gordon, G. E., BA Natal, MA CNAA Prof.; Head*
Osborne, J. R., BA Natal, MA Rhodes Sr. Lectr.
Other Staff: 2 Lectrs.

Economics and Economic History

Tel: (046) 603 8301 Fax: (046) 622 4509

Antrobus, G. G., MSc(Agric) Natal, PhD Rhodes Prof.; Head*
Nel, H., BCom OFS, DCom P.Elizabeth Prof.
Webb, A. C. M., PhD Rhodes Assoc. Prof.
Other Staff: 4 Lectrs.

East London Campus

Tel: (0431) 22539 Fax: (0431) 438307

Tsegaye, A., BA Addis Ababa, MA Kent, PhD Kent Sr. Lectr.
Other Staff: 2 Lectrs.

Education

Tel: (046) 603 8383 Fax: (046) 622 8028

Euvrard, G. J., BEd S.Af., MA Rhodes, DLitt&Phil S.Af. Head*
Irwin, P. R., BA Natal, MEd Natal, DEd S.Af. Prof.
Kuiper, J., PhD V.U.Amst. Sr. Lectr.
van der Mescht, H., BA P.Elizabeth, MA Rhodes Sr. Lectr.
Other Staff: 6 Lectrs.; 4 Sr. Res. Officers

East London Campus

Tel: (0431) 22539 Fax: (0431) 438307

Mayo, A. L., MEd Hull Sr. Lectr.
McKellar, D. W., BA Natal, BEd Natal, MEd Rhodes, PhD Rhodes Assoc. Prof.; Head, Primary Educn.
Other Staff: 7 Lectrs.

Electronics, see Phys. and Electronics

English

Tel: (046) 603 8400 Fax: (046) 622 5409

Bunyan, D. C., BA Cape Town, MLitt Durh., MPhil Oxf., PhD Rhodes Sr. Lectr.
Cornwell, D. G. N., MA Rhodes, PhD Rhodes Sr. Lectr.

Gouws, J. S., MA Rhodes, DPhil Oxf. Prof.; Head*
Hall, R. F., MA Rhodes, MPhil Oxf., PhD Natal Sr. Lectr.
Jacobson, W. S., BA Lond., PhD Birm. Sr. Lectr.
Smith, M. van W., BA Stell., MA Oxf., MLitt Oxf., PhD Rhodes Prof.
Walters, P. S., BA Rhodes, PhD Rhodes H.A. Molteno Prof.
Other Staff: 4 Lectrs.; 1 Hon. Fellow

East London Campus

Tel: (0431) 22539 Fax: (0431) 438307

Dovey, T. J. M., BA S.Af., MA Oregon, PhD Melb. Sr. Lectr.
Other Staff: 1 Lectr.

English Language, see Linguistics and Engl. Lang.

Entomology, see Zool. and Entomol.

Fine Art

Tel: (046) 318192

Coutouvidis, G. P., BFineArt Rhodes Sr. Lectr.
Haywood, M., BA Manc., MA Northumbria, MPhil RCA Prof.; Head*
Hodnett, N. B. Sr. Lectr.
Oberholzer, P. C. J. Sr. Lectr.
Thorburn, D., MFineArt Rhodes Assoc. Prof.
Verwey, E. W., MFineArt Rhodes Sr. Lectr.
Other Staff: 2 Lectrs.

Fisheries Science, see Ichthyol. and Fisheries Sci.

French, see under Langs., Sch. of

Geography

Tel: (046) 603 8319

Fox, R. C., PhD Strath. Assoc. Prof.; Head*
Lewis, C. A., BA Wales, PhD N.U.I. Prof.
Nel, E. L., BA Rhodes, PhD Rhodes Sr. Lectr.
Rowntree, K. M., MSc Brist., PhD Strath. Assoc. Prof.

East London Campus

Tel: (0431) 22539 Fax: (0431) 438307

1 Lectr.

Geology

Tel: (046) 603 8309

Jacob, R. E., MSc Rhodes, PhD Cape Town Prof.
Marsh, J. S., PhD Cape Town Prof.; Head*
Moore, J. M., PhD Cape Town Prof., Exploration Geology
Other Staff: 3 Lectrs.; 2 Res. Assocs.; 1 Res. Fellow

German, see under Langs., Sch. of

History

Tel: (046) 603 8330

Baines, J. C., BA Lond., BA S.Af., MA Rhodes, PhD Lanc. Sr. Lectr.
Cobbing, J. R. D., BA Lond., PhD Lanc. Sr. Lectr.
Maylam, P. R., BA Rhodes, PhD Qu. Prof.; Head*
Wells, J. C., BA Colorado Coll., MA Yale, PhD Col. Sr. Lectr.

East London Campus

Tel: (0431) 22539 Fax: (0431) 438307

Shell, R. C. H., BA Cape Town, MA Roch., PhD Yale Sr. Lectr.
Other Staff: 2 Lectrs.

Human Movement Studies

Tel: (046) 603 8468

Charteris, J., BA Rhodes, MSc Ill. Prof.
Mackenzie, B. L., MB ChB Pret., MMed Pret. Sr. Lectr.
Scott, P. A., BA(PhysEd) Rhodes, PhD Stell. Assoc. Prof.; Head*
Other Staff: 2 Lectrs.

Ichthyology and Fisheries Science

Tel: (046) 603 8415 Fax: (046) 622 4827

Britz, P. J., BSc Cape Town, PhD Rhodes Sr. Lectr.
Hecht, T., PhD P.Elizabeth Prof., Fisheries Science; Head*
Sauer, W. H. H., PhD P.Elizabeth Sr. Lectr.
Other Staff: 2 Lectrs.; 1 Devel. Officer

Information Systems

Tel: (046) 603 8244

McNeill, J. B., BSc Rhodes Sr. Lectr.
Sewry, D. A., MSc Rhodes, PhD Rhodes Assoc. Prof.; Head*
Other Staff: 2 Lectrs.; 1 Sr. Instr.

East London Campus

Tel: (0431) 22539 Fax: (0431) 438307

Roets, R. A., BSc Cape Town, BA S.Af., MSc Lond., MEd Rhodes Assoc. Prof.
Other Staff: 1 Lectr.; 1 Instr.

Italian, see under Langs., Sch. of (French and Italian)

Journalism and Media Studies

Tel: (046) 603 8336 Fax: (046) 622 8447

Berger, G. J. E. G., BJourn Rhodes, BA Rhodes, BA S.Af., PhD Rhodes Prof.; Head*
Doherty, C. M. W., BA Cape Town, MA Natal Sr. Lectr.
Garman, A. C., BA Witw., MA Natal Sr. Lectr.
Knox, C. M., BA Natal, BA Rhodes, MA Rhodes Sr. Lectr.
Other Staff: 4 Lectrs.

Languages, School of

Tel: (046) 603 8298

Fein, P. L.-M., BA Hull, PhD Lond. Prof.; Head*

African Languages

Tel: (046) 603 8222; (East London Campus)(0431) 22539 Fax: (East London Campus)(0431) 438307

Claughton, J. S., BA Cape Town, MA Camb., PhD Rhodes Sr. Lectr.
Mtuze, P. T., BA Rhodes, MA S.Af., PhD Cape Town Prof., East London Campus
Other Staff: 1 Lectr. (East London Campus)

Afrikaans and Nederlandic Studies

Tel: (046) 603 8226

Meintjes, W. G., PhD Rhodes Sr. Lectr.
Other Staff: 1 Lectr.

Classics

Tel: (046) 603 8272

Snowball, W. D., BSc(Eng) Cape Town, BA Rhodes, MA Lond. Sr. Lectr.
Other Staff: 1 Lectr.

French and Italian

Jaques, F. E., MA Cape Town, PhD Witw. Sr. Lectr.
Other Staff: 1 Lectr.

German

Tel: (046) 318328

Krueger, G. A. L. W., PhD Rhodes Sr. Lectr.
Welz, D. W., DrPhil Hamburg, DLitt Pret. Prof.
Other Staff: 1 Lectr.

Law

Tel: (046) 603 8427 Fax: (046) 622 8960

Barker, G. W., BA Witw., LLB Natal, LLM Bophut. Sr. Lectr.
Campbell, J., BA Cape Town, LLB Cape Town Dir., Legal Aid Clinic
Clark, B. J., BA Rhodes, LLB Rhodes, LLM Camb. Sr. Lectr.
Haydock, J. D., BL Rhodesia, LLB Rhodesia Sr. Lectr.
Meintjes, L., BJuris P.Elizabeth, LLB P.Elizabeth, LLM Rhodes Sr. Lectr.
Midgley, J. R., BCom Rhodes, LLB Rhodes, PhD Cape Town Prof.; Head*

Mqeke, R. B., BJuris Fort Hare, LLB Fort Hare, LLM Rhodes, LLD Fort Hare Prof.
Oelschig, M. J., BL Rhodesia, LLB Rhodesia Sr. Lectr.
Peckham, B. K., BA S.Af., LLM Natal Sr. Lectr.
Plaskett, C. M., BA Natal, LLB Natal, LLM Natal Sr. Lectr.
Other Staff: 2 Lectrs.; 1 Hon. Res. Fellow

East London Campus
Tel: (0431) 22539 Fax: (0431) 438307
Maree, D. A., BA Rhodes, LLB Rhodes Sr. Lectr.
Other Staff: 1 Lectr.

Linguistics and English Language
Barkhuizen, G. P., BA Rhodes, MA Essex, DEd Col. Prof.
Bosch, A. B., BA Stell., PhD Rhodes Prof.
de Klerk, V., MA Rhodes, PhD Cape Town Prof.; Head*
Other Staff: 3 Lectrs.; 1 Hon. Res. Assoc.

Management
Tel: (046) 603 8245
Court, P. W., BSc(Agric) Stell., MBA Witw., PhD Rhodes Sr. Lectr.
Staude, G. E., MBA Cran., PhD Rhodes Raymond Ackerman Prof.; Head*
Other Staff: 4 Lectrs.

East London Campus
Tel: (0431) 22539 Fax: (0431) 438307
2 Lectrs.

Mathematics (Pure and Applied)
Tel: (046) 603 8339
Burton, M. H., BSc Natal, MSc Cape Town, PhD Rhodes Assoc. Prof.
Chadwick, J. J., MSc N.U.I., PhD ANU Sr. Lectr.
Heideman, N. J. H., BSc Cape Town, PhD Wash. Assoc. Prof.
Kotzé, W. J., BSc Stell., PhD McG. Prof.; Head*
Lubczonok, G., MMath Cracow, PhD Silesia Sr. Lectr.
Murali, V., MSc Madr., MSc Wales, PhD Rhodes Assoc. Prof.
Other Staff: 1 Lectr.

Media Studies, see Journalism and Media Studies

Microbiology, see Biochem. and Microbiol.

Music and Musicology
Tel: (046) 603 8489
Lucia, C. E., MA Oxf., PhD Rhodes Head*
Radloff, T. E. K., BA Rhodes, MMus Rhodes, RULM Rhodes, UTLM S.Af., PhD Rhodes Sr. Lectr.
Sholto-Douglas, I. E., MMus Witw., PhD Rhodes Sr. Lectr.
Other Staff: 3 Lectrs.

Pharmaceutical Sciences, School of
Tel: (046) 603 8495 Fax: (046) 636 1205
Dowse, R., PhD Rhodes Sr. Lectr.
Futter, W. T., MCom Rhodes Assoc. Prof.
Glass, B. D., BPharm Rhodes, BSc P.Elizabeth, PhD Rhodes Sr. Lectr.
Haigh, J. M., BSc Rhodes, PhD Cape Town Assoc. Prof., Pharmaceutical Chemistry
Kanfer, I., PhD Rhodes Prof., Pharmaceutics
Parolis, H., PhD Rhodes Prof., Pharmaceutical Chemistry; Head*
Paton, L. T., MSc Rhodes Sr. Lectr.
Potgieter, B., DSc(Pharm) Potchef. Prof., Pharmacology
Robertson, S. S. D., BSc Cape Town, PhD Rhodes Sr. Lectr.
Smith, E. W., PhD Rhodes Sr. Lectr.
Walker, R. B., PhD Rhodes Sr. Lectr.
Wilson, B. J., MSc Sask., PhD Purdue Assoc. Prof.
Other Staff: 4 Lectrs.

Philosophy
Tel: (046) 603 8350
Macdonald, I. A., BA Rhodes, MA Kansas Prof.
Vermaak, M. D., BA Stell., DrsPhil Ley. Sr. Lectr.; Head*
Other Staff: 1 Lectr.

Physics and Electronics
Tel: (046) 603 8450
Baart, E. E., BSc Rhodes, PhD Liv., FRAS Prof., Physics
Grant, R. P. J. S., MSc Rhodes Sr. Lectr.
Nathanson, P. D. K., PhD Natal Sr. Lectr.; Head*
Poole, A. W. V., PhD Rhodes Sr. Lectr.
Poole, L. M. G., MSc Rhodes, PhD Sheff. Assoc. Prof.
Other Staff: 2 Lectrs. ; 1 Res. Officer

Political Studies
Tel: (046) 603 8354 Fax: (046) 622 4345
Ajulu, R., MA NUL, DPhil Sus. Sr. Lectr.
Bischoff, P. H., BA Witw., MA Lanc., PhD Manc. Sr. Lectr.
Fluxman, A. P., MA Witw., PhD Cornell Sr. Lectr.
Southall, R. J., BA Leeds, MA(Econ) Manc., PhD Birm. Prof.; Head*
Other Staff: 4 Lectrs.

Psychology
Tel: (046) 603 8500
Edwards, D. J. A., BA Oxf., PhD Rhodes Prof.
Holmes, R. W., MB ChB Cape Town Assoc. Prof.
Jordan, A. B., BA Rhodes, MSc Cape Town, PhD Rhodes Sr. Lectr.; Dir., Psychol. Clinic
Kelly, K., MA Natal, PhD Rhodes Sr. Lectr.
Stones, C. R., MSc Rhodes, PhD Rhodes Prof.; Head*
Welman, M., MA Cape Town, PhD Rhodes Sr. Lectr.
Other Staff: 6 Lectrs.

East London Campus
Tel: (0431) 22539 Fax: (0431) 438307
Gilbert, A. J., BSocSc Natal, DPhil S.Af. Assoc. Prof.
Other Staff: 2 Lectrs.

Religion and Theology
Tel: (046) 603 8375
Cunningham, T. F., BA Rhodes, MTheol Chic.Theol.Sem. Sr. Lectr., Pastoral Theology
de Villiers, P. G. R., BA Stell., BTh Stell., LTh Stell., DTh Stell., DrsTh Theol.Sch.Kampen Prof., New Testament Studies
Edwards, F., BSc Lond., BD Edin., DPhil Oxf. Assoc. Prof., Systematic Theology; Head*
Gaybba, B. P., STL Pontif.Urb., STD Pontif.Urb. Prof., Systematic Theology
Wakely, A. P. R., BA Trinity(Dub.), PhD Edin. Sr. Lectr., Hebrew and Old Testament Studies
Other Staff: 2 Lectrs.

Social Work
East London Campus
Tel: (0431) 22539 Fax: (0431) 438307
Coughlan, F., BSocSc Rhodes, MSc Lond. Sr. Lectr.; Head*
Other Staff: 2 Lectrs.

Sociology and Industrial Sociology
Tel: (046) 603 8361 Fax: (046) 622 5570
Coetzee, J. K., BD Pret., MA Pret., DPhil Pret. Prof.
Hendricks, F. T., BA W.Cape, MSocSc Uppsala, PhD Uppsala Head*
Other Staff: 5 Lectrs.

East London Campus
Tel: (0431) 22539 Fax: (0431) 438307
Wood, G. T., MA Cape Town, PhD Rhodes Sr. Lectr.
Other Staff: 1 Lectr.

Statistics
Tel: (046) 603 8346
Radloff, S. E., MSc Rhodes, PhD Rhodes Assoc. Prof.; Head*
Szyszkowski, I., PhD Lublin Sr. Lectr.
van der Watt, P., MSc S.Af., PhD S.Af. Prof.
Other Staff: 1 Lectr.

East London Campus
Tel: (0431) 22539 Fax: (0431) 438307
1 Sr. Instr.

Zoology and Entomology
Tel: (046) 603 8525 Fax: (046) 622 4377
Bernard, R. F. T., PhD Natal Prof., Zoology
Brown, C. R., PhD Cape Town Sr. Lectr., Zoology
Craig, A. J. F. K., MSc Cape Town, PhD Natal Assoc. Prof., Zoology
Hepburn, H. R., MS Louisiana State, PhD Kansas, FRSSAf Prof., Entomology
Hodgson, A. N., BSc Liv., PhD Manc. Assoc. Prof., Zoology
Hulley, P. E., MSc Rhodes, PhD Lond. Assoc. Prof., Entomology
McQuaid, C. D., PhD Cape Town Prof., Zoology; Head*
Villet, M. H., PhD Witw. Sr. Lectr., Entomology
Other Staff: 2 Res. Assocs.; 2 Hon. Fellows

SPECIAL CENTRES, ETC

LIRI Technologies
Leather Industries Research Fax: (046) 622 6517
Sweetnam, D. J., BCom S.Af. Dir.*
Other Staff: 20 Leather Scientists

CONTACT OFFICERS
Accommodation. Assistant Dean of Students: L'Ange, I. N., BTh Rhodes
Admissions (first degree). Admissions Officer: Wicks, D.
Admissions (higher degree). Admissions Officer: Wicks, D.
Admissions (higher degree: doctoral). Registrar: Fourie, Steve, BTh Rhodes, BD Rhodes, DTh S.Af.
Alumni. President, Old Rhodian Union: Haigh, E., MSc Rhodes
Archives. Cory Librarian: Rowoldt, S., BSocSc Cape Town
Careers. Student Adviser: Rainier, M. G., BA Rhodes, MEd Rhodes
Computing services. Director, Computing Services: Wilson, D., BA Rhodes, BSc Rhodes
Development/fund-raising. Director, Marketing and Communications: de Villiers, R. A., BA Rhodes
Estates and buildings/works and services. Director, Estates Division: Reynolds, L. M., BCom S.Af.
Examinations. Examinations Officer: Cook, A. J., MA Camb., MA Witw.
Finance. Registrar (Finance): Long, H. A.
General enquiries. Registrar: Fourie, Steve, BTh Rhodes, BD Rhodes, DTh S.Af.
Health services. Sister-in-Charge: Büchner, R. M., BA Rhodes
Industrial liaison. Director of Personnel: Smith, B. M. H., BA Rhodes
International office. Student Adviser: Rainier, M. G., BA Rhodes, MEd Rhodes
Library (chief librarian). Librarian: Ubogu, F. N., BEd Ib., MLS Ib.
Personnel/human resources. Director of Personnel: Smith, B. M. H., BA Rhodes
Public relations, information and marketing. Director, Marketing and Communications: de Villiers, R. A., BA Rhodes
Publications. Director, Marketing and Communications: de Villiers, R. A., BA Rhodes
Purchasing. Registrar (Finance): Long, H. A.
Research. Dean of Research: Parolis, H., PhD Rhodes

Safety. Chief Campus Protection Officer: Charteris, D. M.

Scholarships, awards, loans. Financial Aid Administrator: van Hille, M.

Schools liaison. Senior Schools' Liaison Officer: Norval, S. A., BA(PhysEd) Rhodes, BEd Witw.

Security. Chief Campus Protection Officer: Charteris, D. M.

Sport and recreation. Head, Sports Administration: Andrew, P. H., BA(PhysEd) Rhodes

Staff development and training. Director of Personnel: Smith, B. M. H., BA Rhodes

Student welfare/counselling. Student Adviser: Rainier, M. G., BA Rhodes, MEd Rhodes

Students from other countries. Student Adviser: Rainier, M. G., BA Rhodes, MEd Rhodes

Students with disabilities. Student Adviser: Rainier, M. G., BA Rhodes, MEd Rhodes

CAMPUS/COLLEGE HEADS

East London Campus. (Tel: (0431) 22539; Fax: (0431) 438307.) Director: Marsh, T. A., BEd Cape Town, MSc Cape Town, PhD Rhodes

[Information supplied by the institution as at 19 Februrary 1998, and edited by the ACU]

UNIVERSITY OF SOUTH AFRICA

Universiteit van Suid-Afrika

Founded 1873 as University of the Cape of Good Hope; became University of South Africa 1916

Member of the Association of Commonwealth Universities

Postal Address: PO Box 392, Pretoria, 0003 South Africa
Telephone: (012) 429 3111 **Fax**: (012) 429 3221 **E-mail**: undergrad/student@alpha.unisa.ac.za **Cables**: Unisa
WWW: http://www.unisa.ac.za/

ACTING PRINCIPAL AND VICE-CHANCELLOR*—Melck, Prof. Antony P., BComm Stell., LLB Stell., MComm Stell., MA Camb., DComm Stell., FTCL

ACTING REGISTRAR (FINANCE)—Lenamile, D. O., BCom S.Af., BCompt S.Af., MBA Witw.

VICE-PRINCIPAL (RESEARCH AND PLANNING)—Döckel, Prof. J. A., BSc(Agric) Stell., PhD Iowa

VICE-PRINCIPAL (TUITION)—Maimela, Prof. S. S., BA S.Af., DPhil Harv., MTh

ACTING REGISTRAR (ACADEMIC)—Msimang, Prof. C. T., LLB S.Af., MA S.Af., DLitt&Phil S.Af.

ACTING REGISTRAR (HUMAN RESOURCES)—Van Aswegen, Prof. A., BA Pret., LLB Pret., LLD S.Af.

ACTING REGISTRAR (OPERATIONS)—Mosoma, D. L., BTh S.Af., MTh Prin., PhD Prin.

GENERAL INFORMATION

History. The university was founded in 1873 as the University of the Cape of Good Hope. The present name was adopted in 1916.

The main campus is located on the southern edge of the city of Pretoria.

Admission to first degree courses (see also South African Introduction). Matriculation exemption issued by the South African Matriculation Board.

First Degrees (see also South African Directory to Subjects of Study). BA, BA(Cur), BA(FA), BA(Pol), BA(SW), BAdmin, BBA, BBibl, BCom, BCompt, BDiac, BDiac(MW), BIur, BMus, BPrimEd, BProc, BSc, BSecEd, BTh, LLB.

All courses may be taken part-time or full-time.

Higher Degrees (see also South African Directory to Subjects of Study). BD, LLM, MA, MA(ClinicalPsychology), MA(CounsellingPsychology), MA(Cur), MA(FA), MA(SW), MAdmin, MBibl, MBL, MCom, MCompt, MDiac, MEd, MMus, MPA, MSc, MTh, PhD, DAdmin, DBibl, DBL, DCom, DCompt, DDiac, DEd, DLitt&Phil, DMus, DPA, DPhil, DTh, LLD.

Language of Instruction. English and Afrikaans.

Libraries. 1,500,000 volumes; 7000 periodicals subscribed to; 300,000 other items.

Fees (1999, annual). Undergraduate: R840 (first-year courses); R920 (second-year courses); R1300 (third-year courses). Postgraduate: R2500 (master's degrees); R3500 (doctoral degrees).

Academic Year (1998–1999). January–November. Faculty of economic and management sciences, two semesters: January–May; June–November.

Statistics. Staff: 3399 (1311 academic, 2088 administrative). Students: 124,212 (54,999 men, 69,213 women); international 7875.

FACULTIES/SCHOOLS

Arts

Tel: (012) 429 6228

Dean: Meyer, Prof. W. F., BA Pret., DrPhil Mainz

Economic and Management Sciences

Tel: (012) 429 4569 Fax: (012) 429 3373

Dean: Nel, Prof. P. A., DCom S.Af., DEd S.Af.

Education

Tel: (012) 429 4568 Fax: (012) 429 4000

Dean: McFarlane, Prof. L. R., BSc Stell., BEd Stell., MEd S.Af., DEd S.Af.

Law

Tel: (012) 429 8739 Fax: (012) 429 3343

Dean: Neethling, Prof. J., BA OFS, LLB OFS, LLM McG., LLD S.Af.

Science

Tel: (012) 429 8008 Fax: (012) 429 3434

Dean: McGillivray, Prof. G., BSc Rhodes, PhD Liv.

Theology

Tel: (012) 429 4567 Fax: (012) 429 3332

Dean: Kritzinger, Prof. Johannes N. J., BA Pret., BD Pret., DTh S.Af.

ACADEMIC UNITS

Accountancy, Applied

Tel: (012) 429 4484 Fax: (012) 429 4339

Bakkes, C. Johan, BCom Pret., MCompt S.Af.   Assoc. Prof.

Becker, Hugh M. R., BCom Pret., BCompt S.Af., MCom Rand Afrikaans, DCompt S.Af.   Prof.

Benade, Frans J. C., BSc Rand Afrikaans, BCom Rand Afrikaans   Sr. Lectr.

Bezuidenhout, Jaco J., BCom Pret.   Sr. Lectr.

Coetzee, Karina, BRat Potchef., MCom Potchef., DCompt S.Af.   Sr. Lectr.

Coetzee, S. P., BCom Pret.   Sr. Lectr.

Crafford, Louis, BCompt S.Af.   Sr. Lectr.

Engelbrecht, A. C. (Riaan), BCom Pret., MCom Pret.   Assoc. Prof.

Engelbrecht, Chris, BCom Pret.   Sr. Lectr.

Erasmus, J. Christine, BCom Pret., MComPret.   Sr. Lectr.

Foot, Judith, BCom Pret., MBL S.Af.   Sr. Lectr.

Gerber, J. P., BCom Pret.   Sr. Lectr.

Gericke, Louisa J., BCompt S.Af.   Sr. Lectr.

Goldswain, George K., BCom Rhodes, BCompt S.Af., LLB Rhodes   Assoc. Prof.

Hamel, P. Andre, BCom Rand Afrikaans   Sr. Lectr.

Hancke, J. P. (Kobus), BCom Pret.   Sr. Lectr.

Hattingh, Chris, BSc Pret., BCompt S.Af.   Assoc. Prof.

Hulme, Zahn, BCom Pret.   Sr. Lectr.

Koppeschaar, Z. R., BCom Pret.   Sr. Lectr.

Lötter, T. S., BCom Pret.   Sr. Lectr.

Pienaar, Gina A., BCom Pret.   Sr. Lectr.

Roux, J. M. L. (Koos), BCom Pret.   Sr. Lectr.

Sadler, Elmarie, BCom Pret., MCompt S.Af., DCompt S.Af.   Prof.

Smit, Riëtte, BCom Stell., BCom Pret., MCom Pret.   Assoc. Prof.

Stafleu, Marié, BCom Pret.   Sr. Lectr.

Swanepoel, A. P. (Boela), BCom Potchef., MCompt S.Af.   Sr. Lectr.

Swart, O., BCom Pret. Sr. Lectr.
Van Dyk, Koos C., BCom S.Af., MCom Pret. Assoc. Prof.
Van Rensburg, J. Botha J., BCom Potchef., MCom Pret., DCompt S.Af. Prof.; Head*
Van Rooyen, J. P., BCom Pret. Sr. Lectr.
Van Schalkwyk, Linda, MCom Pret. Sr. Lectr.
Van Staden, J. Marianne, BCompt S.Af., MCompt OFS Sr. Lectr.
Van Wijk, Una, BCom Pret., MSM Purdue Sr. Lectr.
Van Wyk, Attie J. J., BCompt S.Af., MCom Pret. Assoc. Prof.
Verster, H. C. (Elna), BCom Pret. Sr. Lectr.
Von Well, R., BCom Pret. Sr. Lectr.
Williams, George, BCom W.Cape, BCompt S.Af., MBA Nebraska Prof.
Wingard, H. Christa, BCom Pret., MCom Pret. Assoc. Prof.

Accounting

Tel: (012) 429 4411 Fax: (012) 429 3424
Abrie, Willie, MCom Pret., DCom S.Af. Prof.
Beukes, Cecilia J., BCom Stell., BCom Pret., BCom S.Af., MCom Potchef. Sr. Lectr.
Binnekade, Carol S., BCom Pret., MCom Pret. Assoc. Prof.
Boot, Gerrie, BSc S.Af., DCom S.Af. Prof.
Coetzee, Willie J., BCom Pret., BCompt S.Af. Sr. Lectr.
Cronje, P. Marieta, BCom Pret., DCompt S.Af. Prof.
Doussy, Frank, BCom Pret., MCom S.Af. Assoc. Prof.
Du Plessis, Piet C., MCom Potchef., DCom Potchef. Sr. Lectr.
Graham, Charles R., BCom Stell., BCompt S.Af. Sr. Lectr.
Grobbelaar, Albert F., BCom OFS, BCompt S.Af. Prof.; Head*
Grobbelaar, Ettienne, BCom Pret., BCompt S.Af. Sr. Lectr.
Hamel, Edna H., MCom Rand Afrikaans Assoc. Prof.
Howell, Renske, BCom Pret., MCom Pret. Sr. Lectr.
Jonker, Willie D., BCom Potchef., BCompt S.Af., MBA Pret. Sr. Lectr.
Julyan, Frank W., BSc Potchef., DCompt S.Af. Prof.
Julyan, Leonie, BCom Pret., BCompt S.Af. Sr. Lectr.
Koch, Eden, BCom Pret., MCom Pret. Assoc. Prof.
Laubscher, Eugene R., BCom Pret., BCompt S.Af. Sr. Lectr.
Morgan, Judith A., MCom S.Af. Sr. Lectr.
Nel, Chalene, BCom Pret. Sr. Lectr.
Nolte, Louw R., MCom Pret., MBA Pret. Sr. Lectr.
Saenger, Elmarie, BBibl S.Af., BCom Rand Afrikaans, BCompt S.Af., DCom S.Af. Prof.
Saenger, Joe, BCom Rand Afrikaans, BCompt S.Af., MCom S.Af. Sr. Lectr.
Scheepers, Debbie, BCom Pret., BCompt S.Af. Sr. Lectr.
Scott, Deon, BCom Pret., MCom Rand Afrikaans Sr. Lectr.
Smith, Talana, BCom Pret. Sr. Lectr.
Steyn, Ben L., BSc Potchef., BCompt S.Af., MCom S.Af. Prof.
Steyn, Gerrie J., BCom Pret., BCom Rand Afrikaans Sr. Lectr.
Swanepoel, Arrie, BCom Pret. Sr. Lectr.
Swanevelder, Jan J., DCom S.Af. Prof.
Ungerer, Marié, BCom Rand Afrikaans, BCompt S.Af. Sr. Lectr.
Van Rooyen, Annelien A., BCom Pret., MCompt S.Af. Sr. Lectr.
Wandrag, Andre, BCompt S.Af. Sr. Lectr.
Warren, Brian O., MCom Pret. Assoc. Prof.

African Languages

Tel: (012) 429 8200 Fax: (012) 429 3355
Bopape, M. L., BA S.Af., MA S.Af. Sr. Lectr.
Bosch, Sonja E., MA Pret., DLitt&Phil S.Af. Assoc. Prof.

Dembetembe, Norris C., BA Lond., MPhil Lond., PhD Lond. Assoc. Prof.
Finlayson, Rosalie, BA Cape Town, PhD Lond. Prof.
Grobler, Gerhardus M. M., MA Pret., DLitt&Phil S.Af. Prof.
Jones, C. J. J., MA S.Af. Sr. Lectr.
Kgobe, Dominic M., MA S.Af., DLitt&Phil S.Af. Sr. Lectr.
Kosch, Ingeborg M., MA S.Af., DLitt&Phil S.Af. Assoc. Prof.
Kotze, Albert E., BA Pret., MA S.Af. Sr. Lectr.
Le Roux, Jurie C., BA Potchef., MA S.Af. Sr. Lectr.
Louwrens, Louis J., MA Pret., DLitt&Phil Pret. Prof.
Mafela, M. J., BA Natal, MA S.Af., DLitt&Phil S.Af. Assoc. Prof.
Makhambeni, Marjorie N., MA S.Af. Sr. Lectr.
Mampuru, Debrah M., BA S.Af., MA Rand Afrikaans Sr. Lectr.
Mathumba, D. I., MA S.Af., DLitt&Phil S.Af. Assoc. Prof.; Acting Head*
Matsinhe, S. F., BA Dar., MA Lond., MPhil Lond., PhD Lond. Sr. Lectr.
Moeketsi, Rosemary, MA S.Af. Sr. Lectr.
Molefe, Lawrence, MA Natal Sr. Lectr.
Moropa, C. K., MA Fort Hare Sr. Lectr.
Msimang, Christian T., LLB S.Af., MA S.Af., DLitt&Phil S.Af. Prof.
Ntuli, Bhekinkosi D., MA S.Af., DLitt&Phil S.Af. Prof.
Poulos, George, MA Witw., PhD Rhodes Prof.
Ranamane, D. T., BA Natal, BA S.Af., MA Flor. Sr. Lectr.
Raselekoane, N. R., BA Natal, MA S.Af. Sr. Lectr.
Saule, N., BA Fort Hare, DLitt&Phil S.Af. Sr. Lectr.
Sebate, P. M., BEd S.Af., BA S.Af., MA Vista Sr. Lectr.
Sengani, Tom M., BA Natal, MA S.Af. Sr. Lectr.
Serudu, Stephen M., MA S.Af., DLitt&Phil S.Af. Prof.
Shole, J. S. S., BA North(S.Af.), BA S.Af., MA Botswana, DLitt&Phil S.Af. Sr. Lectr.
Sithebe, Z. G., BA UBS, BA S.Af., MA Mich. Sr. Lectr.
Snyman, Jannie W., MA Potchef., PhD Cape Town Prof.
Steyn, Elna C., BA(Ed) Pret., MA Pret. Sr. Lectr.
Swanepoel, Christiaan F., BA OFS, MA Rand Afrikaans, DLitt&Phil Rand Afrikaans Prof.
Taljaard, Petrus C., BA Potchef., MA S.Af., DLitt&Phil S.Af. Sr. Lectr.

Afrikaans

Tel: (012) 429 6308
Coetser, Johannes L., MA S.Af., DLitt&Phil S.Af. Sr. Lectr.
Landman, Kasper J. H., MA S.Af., DLitt&Phil S.Af. Assoc. Prof.
Meiring, Barbara A., MA S.Af., DLitt&Phil S.Af. Sr. Lectr.
Pieterse, Henning J., MA Pret., DLitt&Phil S.Af. Sr. Lectr.
Retief, Rhona, BEd Rand Afrikaans, MA S.Af., DLitt&Phil S.Af. Sr. Lectr.
Roos, Henrietta M., MA Pret., DLitt Pret. Prof.
Spangenberg, Dawid F., MA Stell., DLitt Stell. Assoc. Prof.
Swanepoel, Petrus H., MA Potchef., DLitt Stell. Prof.; Head*
Wiehahn, Rialette, MA Cape Town, PhD Witw. Sr. Lectr.

Anthropology and Archaeology

Tel: (012) 429 6418
Boeyens, Jan C. A., BA Pret., MA Pret., Drs Pret. Sr. Lectr.
De Beer, Frederik C., DPhil Pret. Prof.
De Jongh, Michael, BA Stell., MA P.Elizabeth, PhD Rhodes Prof.; Head*
Herselman, Stephné, BA P.Elizabeth, DLitt&Phil S.Af. Sr. Lectr.
Kruger, Jeanne M., MA S.Af. Sr. Lectr.

Van Heerden, Myra E., MA OFS, DLitt&Phil S.Af. Sr. Lectr.
Van Vuuren, Christo J., DPhil Pret. Sr. Lectr.

Art, see Hist. of Art and Fine Arts

Astronomy, see Maths., Appl. Maths. and Astron.

Auditing

Tel: (012) 429 4388 Fax: (012) 429 3673
Coetzee, Charlotte, BCom Pret. Sr. Lectr.
Ferreira, Laurene, BCompt S.Af. Sr. Lectr.
Joubert, Kobus, BCompt S.Af., BAcc Potchef. Sr. Lectr.
Marais, Marinda, BCompt S.Af. Sr. Lectr.
Odendaal, Elza M., BCom Pret. Sr. Lectr.
Radesich, Lina N., BCom Pret. Sr. Lectr.
Reilly, Yvonne, BCom Pret., BCompt S.Af., MCom S.Af. Sr. Lectr.
Steyn, Blanché, BCom Rand Afrikaans, BCompt S.Af. Sr. Lectr.
Swemmer, Phillip N., MCom Pret., DCom S.Af. Prof.
Theron, Hansja J., BCom OFS, BCompt S.Af., MCom S.Af. Sr. Lectr.
Van Heerden, Bernard, BCompt S.Af., DCom S.Af. Assoc. Prof.
Van Niekerk, Frederik N., BCom Pret. Sr. Lectr.
Visagie, Josias A., BCom Pret., BCompt S.Af. Sr. Lectr.
Vorster, Hendrik J. S., DCom Potchef. Prof.; Head*
Wentzel, Jacobus J., BCom Pret., BCompt S.Af., MCom S.Af. Assoc. Prof.
Yssel, Hester M., BCom Pret., BCompt S.Af. Sr. Lectr.

Business Management, see also Special Centres, etc (Bus. Leadership)

Tel: (012) 429 4212 Fax: (012) 429 3373
Badenhorst, J. A. (Hannie), BCom Potchef., MCom Potchef., DCom Potchef. Prof.
Begemann, Egbert, MCom Potchef., DCom P.Elizabeth Prof.
Beyer, Arthur R., BCom Stell., MCom Stell. Sr. Lectr.
Botha, Johan A. R., BProc S.Af., DCom S.Af. Sr. Lectr.
Brevis, Tersia, MCom Potchef. Sr. Lectr.
Brink, Annekie, BCom Stell., MCom S.Af., DCom S.Af. Sr. Lectr.
Cant, Mike C., MCom Pret., DCom S.Af. Prof.
Cronje, Gerhard J. de J., MBA Pret., DCom Pret. Prof.; Head*
De Klerk, Annette, BCom Pret., MCom S.Af. Sr. Lectr.
Du Toit, Gawie S., MCom S.Af., DCom S.Af. Prof.
Erasmus, Barney J., BMil Stell., BA S.Af., DCom S.Af. Prof.
Ghyoot, Valmond G., MCom S.Af., DCom S.Af. Prof.
Grobler, Pieter A., MCom S.Af., DCom S.Af. Prof.
Hough, Johan, BScAgric OFS, MSc(Agric) Pret., DCom S.Af. Prof.
Krüger, Louis P., BSc Pret., MBA Pret., DBA Pret. Assoc. Prof.
Loubser, F. J. (Erick), BCom Pret., MBA Pret. Sr. Lectr.
Lucas, G. H. G. (Okkie), MCom S.Af., DCom S.Af. Prof.
Machado, Richard, BSc Tulsa, MBA Colorado Sr. Lectr.
Marais, André de K., BAgric Stell., MSc OFS, DCom S.Af. Prof.
Marx, Johan, MCom Potchef., DCom S.Af. Prof.
Palmer, Pat N., BCom Rhodes, MCom S.Af., DCom S.Af. Prof.
Penning, Johan L., MCom Pret., DCom S.Af. Prof.
Rudansky, Sharon, BCom P.Elizabeth, MCom S.Af. Sr. Lectr.
Schoeman, Ronel, BCom Potchef., MCom Potchef. Sr. Lectr.
Smit, Pieter J., MCom OFS, DCom S.Af. Prof.

Steenkamp, Rigard J., BCom Pret., MBA Pret., DCom Pret.   Sr. Lectr.
Strydom, Johan W., MCom Potchef., DCom S.Af.   Prof.
Swart, Nico J., MCom Rand Afrikaans   Sr. Lectr.
Theron, Danie P., BCom Pret., MBA Pret.   Sr. Lectr.
Theron, J. L. (Wikus), BCom Pret., MBA Pret.   Sr. Lectr.
Van Rooyen, Johan H., MCom Rand Afrikaans, DCom Rand Afrikaans   Assoc. Prof.
Vrba, Maré J., BCom Pret., MBL S.Af.   Sr. Lectr.

Chemistry

Tel: (012) 429 8004 Fax: (012) 429 8549

Chemaly, Susan M., PhD Witw.   Sr. Lectr.
Jacobs, Linda A., MSc Pret., PhD Pret.   Sr. Lectr.
Loonat, Mohammed S., MSc Witw., PhD Witw.   Sr. Lectr.
Marsch, Cliff M., MSc Lough., PhD Lough.   Assoc. Prof.
Mphahlele, M. Jack, MSc Pret., PhD Rhodes   Sr. Lectr.
Ogude, N. Audrey, MSc Nair., PhD Witw.   Sr. Lectr.
Paul, Sylvia O., MSc Natal, MPhil S'ton., PhD Witw.   Prof.; Head*
Summers, Gabriel J., MSc Akron, PhD Akron   Prof.

Church History

Tel: (012) 429 4040 Fax: (012) 429 3332

Frank, Gary L., BA C'dia., MDiv Nashotah, PhD St And.   Assoc. Prof.; Head*
Jafta, Liso D., BA(Theol) S.Af., MA Boston, MPhil Drew, PhD Drew   Sr. Lectr.
Millard, Joan A., BTh S.Af., MTh S.Af., DTh S.Af.   Sr. Lectr.

Classics

Tel: (012) 429 6501 Fax: (012) 429 3355

Evans, Richard J., MA Leeds, MPhil Leeds, DLitt&Phil S.Af.   Sr. Lectr.
Kleijwegt, Marc, PhD Ley.   Assoc. Prof.
Lombard, Daniël B., MA S.Af., DLitt&Phil Rand Afrikaans   Prof.; Head*
Mader, Gottfried J., MA Witw., DLitt&Phil S.Af.   Prof.

Communication

Tel: (012) 429 6565 Fax: (012) 429 3346

Angelopulo, George C., MA Rand Afrikaans, DLitt&Phil Rand Afrikaans   Assoc. Prof.
Bredenkamp, Christien J. S., MA S.Af.   Sr. Lectr.
Du Plooy, G. M. (Trudie), MA S.Af., DLitt&Phil S.Af.   Assoc. Prof.
Fourie, Pieter J., MA Potchef., DLitt&Phil S.Af.   Prof.; Head*
Lemon, Jenny, MA S.Af.   Sr. Lectr.
Oosthuizen, Lucas M., MA S.Af.   Sr. Lectr.
Parry, Lynn L., MA S.Af.   Sr. Lectr.
Pitout, Magriet, MA S.Af., DLitt&Phil S.Af.   Sr. Lectr.
Roelofse, J. J. (Koos), MA S.Af., DLitt&Phil S.Af.   Prof.
Siddo, Salifou, DPhil Penn.State   Sr. Lectr.
Sonderling, Stefan, MA S.Af.   Sr. Lectr.
Steinberg, S., MA S.Af., DLitt&Phil S.Af.   Sr. Lectr.
Wigston, D. J., MA S.Af.   Sr. Lectr.

Computer Science and Information Systems

Tel: (012) 429 6122 Fax: (012) 429 3434

Alexander, Patricia M., BSc Cape Town, MSc S.Af.   Chief Researcher
Barnard, Andries, MSc Rand Afrikaans, PhD Rand Afrikaans   Sr. Lectr.
Barrow, John E., MSc(Eng) Witw., PhD S.Af.   Assoc. Prof.
Bornman, Christiaan H., MSc Potchef., DSc Potchef.   Prof.; Head*
Bosua, Rachelle, BSc Pret., MSc S.Af.   Sr. Lectr.
Britz, Katarina, MSc Stell.   Sr. Lectr.
Cloete, Elsabé, BSc Potchef., MSc Potchef.   Sr. Lectr.

De Villiers, Mary R., MEd Pret., MSc S.Af.   Sr. Lectr.
Holland, Ken, BSc Stell., MSc S.Af.   Sr. Lectr.
Kotzé, Paula, MSc Potchef., DPhil York(UK)   Assoc. Prof.
Labuschagne, Willem A., MSc P.Elizabeth, PhD Rand Afrikaans   Prof.
Leenen, Louise, MSc Rand Afrikaans   Sr. Lectr.
Loock, Marianne, BSc Pret., MSc S.Af.   Sr. Lectr.
Meyer, Thomas A., MSc Rand Afrikaans   Sr. Lectr.
Miller, Magdalena G., BSc Potchef., MSc S.Af.   Sr. Lectr.
Olivier, André P. S., BCom Rand Afrikaans, MCom Pret.   Sr. Lectr.
Pistorius, Martha C., MSc OFS   Assoc. Prof.
Pretorius, Laurette, BSc Stell., BSc S.Af., MSc Pret., DSc Potchef.   Assoc. Prof.
Renaud, Karen V., BSc S.Af., MSc S.Af.   Sr. Lectr.
Rosenblatt, Johanna H., BSc Potchef., MSc S.Af.   Sr. Lectr.
Smuts, Walter B., BEng Pret., MEng Pret., PhD Witw.   Assoc. Prof.
Van der Merwe, Aletta J., BSc Rand Afrikaans, MSc Potchef.   Sr. Lectr.
Van der Poll, John A., BSc Stell., MSc S.Af.   Sr. Lectr.
Van Dyk, Tobie J., MBA Pret.
Viljoen, Elizabeth, BSc Stell., MSc S.Af.   Sr. Lectr.

Criminology, see also Special Centres, etc

Tel: (012) 429 6003

Cilliers, Charl H., MA Pret., DLitt&Phil S.Af.   Prof.
Conradie, Herman, MA Potchef., DPhil Potchef.   Prof.
Grobbelaar, Mathys M., MA S.Af.   Sr. Lectr.
Jacobs, Willie J., MA S.Af., DLitt&Phil S.Af.   Sr. Lectr.
Jansen van Vuuren, Jan W., MA S.Af.   Sr. Lectr.
Joubert, Sandra J., MA S.Af., DLitt&Phil S.Af.   Assoc. Prof.
Marais, Coenraad W., MA S.Af., DLitt&Phil S.Af.   Assoc. Prof.
Naudé, C. M. Beaty, MA S.Af., DLitt&Phil S.Af.   Prof.; Head*
Neser, Jan J., MA OFS, DLitt&Phil S.Af.   Prof.
Smit, Bernardus F., MA OFS, DLitt&Phil S.Af.   Prof.
Sonnekus, Eon F., MA Pret., DLitt&Phil S.Af.   Sr. Lectr.
Swart, David N., MA S.Af., DLitt&Phil S.Af.   Sr. Lectr.
Van der Hoven, Anna E., MA S.Af., DLitt&Phil S.Af.   Assoc. Prof.

Development Administration

Tel: (012) 429 6813 Fax: (012) 429 3646

Cornwell, Linda, BA Rand Afrikaans, MA S.Af., DLitt&Phil S.Af.   Assoc. Prof.
De Beer, Frederick C., BA Rand Afrikaans, DLitt&Phil S.Af.   Prof.
Mentz, Johannes C. N., BA Stell., MA Potchef., DLitt&Phil S.Af.   Sr. Lectr.
Stewart, Peter D. S., BA Malawi, BA Witw., MA Nelson, PhD Witw.   Sr. Lectr.
Swanepoel, Hendrik J., DLitt&Phil S.Af.   Prof.; Head*

Economics

Tel: (012) 429 4350 Fax: (012) 429 3433

Akinboade, Oludele A., DPhil Oxf.   Sr. Lectr.
Bekker, Doreen, MCom S.Af.   Sr. Lectr.
Bijker, Arend C., BScAgric Stell., BA S.Af., MCom Pret.   Sr. Lectr.
Boshoff, Johan P., MCom OFS   Sr. Lectr.
Botha, Mariana, BCom Stell., BCom Pret., MCom S.Af.   Sr. Lectr.
Botha, Zichy C., BCom Pret., MCom Rand Afrikaans   Sr. Lectr.
Brown, Gregory P., MCom S.Af.   Assoc. Prof.
Calitz, Estian, DCom Stell.   Prof.
Du Pisanie, Johann A., MCom Pret., MBA Pret., DCom Pret.   Prof.

Fourie, Louis J., MCom OFS, DCom S.Af.   Prof.; Head*
Inggs, Eric J., BJourn Rhodes, MA Rhodes   Sr. Lectr.
Lötter, Johan C., MA Stell.   Sr. Lectr.
Marais, Martin R., BCom Pret., LLB Pret.   Sr. Lectr.
Mohr, Philip J., MCom Stell., DCom Stell.   Prof.
Pringle, William A., BScAgric Natal, BCom S.Af., BCom Rhodes, MCom Witw., DCom S.Af.   Assoc. Prof.
Serfontein, Frederik H. B., BCom Rand Afrikaans, BCom S.Af., MCom S.Af.   Sr. Lectr.
Smith, Johan du P., MCom OFS, DCom OFS   Prof.
Steenekamp, Tjaart J., MCom Pret., DCom S.Af.   Prof.
Torr, Christopher S. W., BSc Stell., BSc Natal, MA S.Af., PhD Rhodes   Prof.
Van der Merwe, Gerrit C., MCom Pret.   Assoc. Prof.
Van der Merwe, Theo, BA Rand Afrikaans, MA S.Af.   Sr. Lectr.
Van Eeghen, P. H., BCom Stell., MEcon Stell., MCom S.Af.   Sr. Lectr.
Viljoen, R. P., BCom P.Elizabeth, BCom Stell., MCom P.Elizabeth   Assoc. Prof.

Educational Studies, see also Further Teacher Educn., Primary Sch. Teacher Educn., and Special Centres, etc. (Educnl. Res., Inst. for)

Tel: (012) 429 4585 Fax: (012) 429 4919

Bergh, A. P., BA Rand Afrikaans, BA Stell., BA S.Af., DEd Pret.   Sr. Lectr.
Bester, G., BSc Potchef., MEd Potchef., DEd S.Af.   Prof.
Bodenstein, H. C. A., BA Pret., MEd S.Af., DEd S.Af.   Prof.
Claassen, J. C., BA OFS, MEd OFS, DEd OFS   Assoc. Prof.
Cockrell, G. A., MA Stell.   Sr. Lectr.
Coetzee, J. H., BA Pret., MEd S.Af., DEd S.Af.   Assoc. Prof.
Coetzer, I. A., BA Potchef., MEd S.Af., DEd S.Af.   Prof.
Crous, S. F. M., BA Potchef., MEd Pret., DEd Pret.   Prof.; Head*
De Meillon, N., BA Pret., MEd Potchef., DEd S.Af.   Sr. Lectr.
De Munnik, E. O., BA S.Af., MEd S.Af., DEd S.Af.   Assoc. Prof.
Du Toit, S. J., BA S.Af., DEd S.Af.   Sr. Lectr.
Higgs, P., BA Witw., MA Wheaton(Ill.), MEd S.Af., DEd S.Af., PhD Natal   Prof.
Hoberg, S. M., BA S.Af., MEd S.Af., DEd S.Af.   Sr. Lectr.
Kruger, A. C. M., BA Pret., MEd S.Af., DEd S.Af.   Sr. Lectr.
Le Roux, J. G., BSc Stell., MEd S.Af., DEd S.Af.   Assoc. Prof.
Lessing, A. C., BCom Potchef., MEd Potchef., MEd S.Af., DEd Rand Afrikaans   Prof.
Mellet, S. M., BSc OFS, MEd S.Af., DEd S.Af.   Assoc. Prof.
Oberholzer, M. O., BA Pret., MA Pret., MEd S.Af., DEd S.Af.   Vice-Dean
Prinsloo, E., BA Pret., MEd Pret., DEd S.Af.   Sr. Lectr.
Roets, H. E., BA Potchef., MEd S.Af.   Assoc. Prof.
Smit, M. E., BA S.Af., MEd Pret., PhD Pret.   Sr. Lectr.
Smith, T. G., BA Stell., MEd P.Elizabeth, PhD Stell.   Sr. Lectr.
Söhnge, W. F., BA Stell., MEd S.Af.   Prof.
Steyn, W., BA Rand Afrikaans, MEd Rand Afrikaans, DEd S.Af.   Sr. Lectr.
Strydom, I., BPrimEd Stell., MEd S.Af., DEd S.Af.   Sr. Lectr.
Van Heerden, E. L., BA Rand Afrikaans, MEd Rand Afrikaans, DEd Rand Afrikaans   Sr. Lectr.
Van Roy, M. P., BSc Potchef., MSc Pret., MEd S.Af.   Prof.
Van Wyk, J. N., BA S.Af., DEd S.Af.   Sr. Lectr.
Van Zyl, A. E., BSc Pret., MEd Pret., DEd S.Af.   Prof.

Visser, P. S., BA Pret., MEd Pret., DEd Pret. Prof.

Wiechers, E., BA Pret., MA Pret., DEd Pret. Prof.

English

Tel: (012) 429 6774 Fax: (012) 429 3355

Andersen, Mitzi C., MA S.Af., DLitt&Phil S.Af. Sr. Lectr.

Batley, Karen E., BA Cape Town, BEd Cape Town, MA Pret., DLitt&Phil S.Af. Assoc. Prof.

Byrne, Deirdre C., BA Natal, MA Natal, DLitt&Phil S.Af. Sr. Lectr.

Curr, Matthew A., MA OFS, MA Lond., PhD Lond. Sr. Lectr.

De Kock, Leon, BA Rand Afrikaans, MA Leeds, DLitt&Phil S.Af. Assoc. Prof.

Ferreira, Jeanette D., BA OFS, MA Camb., DLitt Utrecht Assoc. Prof.

Kilfoil, Wendy R., BA Witw., BA Pret., MA S.Af., DLitt&Phil Rand Afrikaans Assoc. Prof.

Levey, David N. R., BA Pret., MA Witw. Sr. Lectr.

Lloyd, David W., BA Natal, MA S.Af., DLitt&Phil S.Af. Sr. Lectr.

Orr, Margaret H., BA Pret., MA Wash., DLitt&Phil S.Af. Prof.

Rabinowitz, Ivan A., MA Rhodes, DLitt&Phil S.Af. Prof.; Head*

Ryan, Pamela D., BA Natal, MA S.Af., DLitt&Phil S.Af. Prof.

Saycell, Kenneth J., BA Witw., MA Rhodes Sr. Lectr.

Scherzinger, Karen J., MA Natal, DLitt&Phil Witw. Sr. Lectr.

Simpson, Mary-Helen D., PhD Rhodes Sr. Lectr.

Spencer, Brenda, BA Pret., BA S.Af., MA S.Af. Sr. Lectr.

Van Schaik, Pam, BA Natal, MA N.Carolina, DLitt&Phil S.Af. Sr. Lectr.

Viljoen, Leonie, BA S.Af., MA Cape Town Assoc. Prof.

Weinberg, Alan M., BA Witw., MA S.Af., DLitt&Phil S.Af. Prof.

Williams, Michael J., MA Natal, DPhil York(UK) Sr. Lectr.

Environmental Studies, see Geog. and Environmental Studies

French, see Romance Langs.

Further Teacher Education

Tel: (012) 429 4594 Fax: (012) 429 4922

Booyse, Johannes J., MEd S.Af., DEd S.Af. Prof.; Head*

Burger, Sanet, BA(Ed) Pret., MEd S.Af. Sr. Lectr.

Dednam, Anna, BA Pret., MEd Pret., DEd S.Af. Sr. Lectr.

Ferreira, Johanna G., MEd North(S.Af.), DEd S.Af. Assoc. Prof.

Jansen van Rensburg, Jurgens J., BCom OFS, MEd OFS, DEd OFS Assoc. Prof.

Kruger, August G., BA Potchef., MEd Rand Afrikaans, DEd S.Af. Assoc. Prof.

Krüger, Deirdré, BA(Ed) Pret., MEd S.Af. Sr. Lectr.

Landsberg, Emmerentia I., BA Stell., MEd S.Af., MEd Pret. Sr. Lectr.

Lemmer, Eleanor M., BA Stell., MEd S.Af., DEd S.Af. Prof.

Loubser, Carel P., MEd S.Af., DEd S.Af. Assoc. Prof.

Potgieter, Calvyn, BSc Rand Afrikaans, BEd Rand Afrikaans, MEd Rand Afrikaans, DEd S.Af. Prof.

Rossouw, Johanna D., BA Stell., MEd S.Af., DEd S.Af. Sr. Lectr.

Roux, Abel A., MEd S.Af., DEd S.Af. Sr. Lectr.

Schulze, Salomé, BSc Potchef., MEd S.Af., DEd S.Af. Assoc. Prof.

Sonnekus, Inge P., MEd S.Af., DEd S.Af. Sr. Lectr.

Squelch, Joan M., BA S.Af., MEd S.Af., DEd S.Af. Sr. Lectr.

Steyn, Gertruida M., BSc Potchef., MEd S.Af., DEd S.Af. Assoc. Prof.

Wessels, Dirk C. J., BSc OFS, MEd OFS, DEd S.Af. Assoc. Prof.

Woodbridge, Noël B., BSc Cape Town, MEd S.Af., DEd S.Af. Assoc. Prof.

Geography and Environmental Studies

Tel: (012) 429 6013

Ferreira, Sanette, MA Rand Afrikaans, DLitt&Phil S.Af. Sr. Lectr.

Landré, Martin, MS&S Stell., DrsSocGeog Utrecht, DLitt&Phil S.Af. Assoc. Prof.

Liebenberg, Elizabeth C., BA OFS, MA S.Af., DLitt&Phil S.Af. Prof.; Head*

Pienaar, Petrus A., MA P.Elizabeth Sr. Lectr.

Van Rheede van Oudtshoorn, Pieter W., BSc Pret., MSc S.Af. Sr. Lectr.

Vlok, Arnoldus C., MA Stell. Sr. Lectr.

Zietsman, Susanna, BSc Pret., MSc S.Af. Sr. Lectr.

German

Tel: (012) 429 6816

Buchholz, H. Peter, MA Mün., DrPhil Mün., DrPhilHabil Kiel Assoc. Prof.

De Lange, Eike, MA Natal Sr. Lectr.

Misch, Manfred K. E., DrPhil F.U.Berlin Prof.; Head*

History

Tel: (012) 429 6268

Brits, Japie P., BA OFS, MA Potchef., DLitt&Phil S.Af. Prof.

Carruthers, E. Jane, MA S.Af., PhD Cape Town Sr. Lectr.

Cuthbertson, Greg C., MA Cape Town, DLitt&Phil S.Af. Assoc. Prof.

Du Bruyn, Johannes T., MA S.Af. Assoc. Prof.

Eidelberg, Phil G., MA Col., PhD Col. Sr. Lectr.

Grobler, J. C. Hennie, MA Stell., DLitt&Phil S.Af. Assoc. Prof.

Grundlingh, Albert M., MA S.Af., DLitt&Phil S.Af. Assoc. Prof.

Harris, Karin L., MA Stell. Sr. Lectr.

Kew, J. Winston, BA Pret., MA S.Af. Sr. Lectr.

Lambert, John, MA Natal, DLitt&Phil S.Af. Assoc. Prof.

Malan, S. Francois, MA OFS, DLitt&Phil S.Af. Assoc. Prof.

Mouton, Frik A., MA Pret., DLitt&Phil S.Af. Sr. Lectr.

Nöthling, F. J., MA Pret., DLitt&Phil S.Af. Sr. Lectr.

Smith, Ken W., MA S.Af., PhD Rhodes Prof.; Head*

Southey, Nick D., MA Rhodes Sr. Lectr.

Twyman, Lucille J., MA Potchef., DLitt&Phil S.Af. Sr. Lectr.

History of Art and Fine Arts

Tel: (012) 429 6798 Fax: (012) 429 3556

Basson, Eunice L., MA Pret. Sr. Lectr.

Bester, Valerie, MA(FA) S.Af. Sr. Lectr.

Maré, Estelle A., BA Stell., MA Pret., MScS&S Pret., MA S.Af., PhD Witw., DArch OFS Assoc. Prof.

Pretorius, Elfrieda, MA S.Af. Sr. Lectr.

Ross, Wendy, MA(FA) S.Af. Sr. Lectr.

Van der Watt, J. P. (Koos), MA S.Af. Sr. Lectr.

Van Haute, Bernadette M. R., DLitt&Phil S.Af. Sr. Lectr.

Industrial Psychology, see Psychol., Indust.

Information Science

Tel: (012) 429 6071 Fax: (012) 429 3400

Behrens, Shirley J., DBibl S.Af. Sr. Lectr.

De Beer, Carel S., BSc(Agric) Pret., DPhil Pret. Prof.; Head*

Dick, Archie L., BBibl W.Cape, MLS Wash., PhD Cape Town Assoc. Prof.

Gericke, Elizabeth M., BBibl Pret., MBibl S.Af. Sr. Lectr.

Kruger, Jan A., BA Potchef., BA Pret., BEd S.Af., MBibl Rand Afrikaans, DLitt&Phil Rand Afrikaans Prof.

Olén, Sandra I. I., BA Pret., DBibl S.Af. Sr. Lectr.

Poller, Anna C., BA Stell., MBibl S.Af. Sr. Lectr.

Terblanche, Fransie, BEd S.Af., MBibl S.Af. Sr. Lectr.

Theron, Jacobus C., BA OFS, BBibl Stell., MBibl S.Af. Sr. Lectr.

Van der Walt, Thomas B., BA Potchef., BBibl Potchef., BA Pret., BA S.Af., MBibl Rand Afrikaans Sr. Lectr.

Italian, see Romance Langs.

Jurisprudence

Tel: (012) 429 8396 Fax: (012) 429 3442

Church, Joan, BA Witw., BIur S.Af., LLB S.Af., LLD S.Af. Prof.; Head*

Hutchings, Susan, BLC Pret., LLB Pret., LLM S.Af. Sr. Lectr.

Jacobs, Annalize, BLC Pret., BA Pret., LLB Pret. Sr. Lectr.

Nicholson, Caroline M. A., BProc Witw., LLB Witw., LLM S.Af. Sr. Lectr.

Schoeman, Elsabe, BLC Pret., LLB S.Af., LLD S.Af. Sr. Lectr.

Stoop, Ben C., LLB Pret., MA Pret., LLD S.Af. Prof.

Van Blerk, Adrienne E., BIur S.Af., LLB S.Af., LLM Natal, LLD S.Af. Prof.

Van den Bergh, H. (Rena), LLB S.Af., MA S.Af., LLD S.Af. Assoc. Prof.

Van Niekerk, Gardiol J., BA Pret., LLB Pret., LLM S.Af., LLD S.Af. Assoc. Prof.

Van Wyk, Christa W., BA Stell., LLB S.Af., LLM S.Af., LLD S.Af. Prof.

Van Zyl, Lesbury J., BA Cape Town, LLB Stell., LLM S.Af., PhD Rhodes Prof.

Law, Constitutional and Public International

Tel: (012) 429 8339 Fax: (012) 429 3321

Beukes, Margaret, BA Stell., LLD S.Af. Assoc. Prof.

Booysen, Hercules, BIur P.Elizabeth, LLD P.Elizabeth Prof.

Botha, Christo J., BA S.Af., LLB Pret. Assoc. Prof.

Botha, Henk, BLC Pret., LLB Pret., LLM Col. Sr. Lectr.

Botha, Neville J., BIuris Pret., LLB Pret., LLD S.Af. Prof.

Bray, Wilhelmina, BIuris S.Af., LLD S.Af. Assoc. Prof.

Burns, Yvonne M., BIuris S.Af., LLD S.Af. Prof.

Carpenter, Gretchen, BA Pret., BA S.Af., LLB Pret. Prof.

Van Wyk, Dawid H., BIur&Art Potchef., LLB Rand Afrikaans, LLD S.Af. Prof.; Head*

Law, Criminal and Procedural

Tel: (012) 429 8370 Fax: (012) 429 3396

Alheit, Karin, BIur Pret., LLB S.Af., LLD S.Af. Sr. Lectr.

Bekker, Petrus M., BA Pret., LLB Pret., LLD S.Af. Prof.

Faris, John A., BA Pret., LLB S.Af., LLM Cape Town, LLD S.Af. Prof.

Hurter, Estelle, BA Pret., LLB Pret., LLM S.Af., LLD S.Af. Assoc. Prof.

Jansen, Marthie, BA S.Af., LLB S.Af. Sr. Lectr.

Jordaan, Louise, BProc Rand Afrikaans, LLB S.Af., LLD S.Af. Sr. Lectr.

Jordaan, Rita A., BA Pret., LLD S.Af. Prof.

Joubert, Johan J., BA Pret., LLB Pret., LLD S.Af. Assoc. Prof.

Kelbrick, Roshana A., BA Pret., LLB Stell., LLM S.Af., LLD S.Af. Assoc. Prof.

Lötter, Sunette, BA Rand Afrikaans, LLB Rand Afrikaans, LLM Pret., LLD Pret. Assoc. Prof.

Maré, Maria C., BIur&Art Potchef., LLB Potchef., LLD S.Af. Prof.; Head*

Nel, Sanette S., BLC Pret., LLB Pret., LLM S.Af. Sr. Lectr.

Snyman, Carl R., BA OFS, LLB OFS, LLD OFS Prof.

Swanepoel, Johanna P., BIur&Art Potchef., LLB Potchef., LLM S.Af. Assoc. Prof.

Swart, Elizabeth D., BLC Pret., LLB Pret., LLM S.Af. Sr. Lectr.

Terblanche, Stephan S., BJuris Potchef., LLB S.Af., LLD S.Af. Assoc. Prof.

Van der Merwe, Dana P., BJuris P.Elizabeth, LLB S.Af, LLD S.Af. Prof.

Van der Merwe, Emily, BIur S.Af., LLB S.Af. Sr. Lectr.

Law, Indigenous

Tel: (012) 429 8629 Fax: (012) 429 3396

Vorster, Louis P., BIur S.Af., LLB S.Af., DPhil Potchef., Prof.; Head*

Whelpton, Frans P. van R., BA Pret., BIurisS.Af., LLB S.Af., LLD S.Af. Prof.

Law, Mercantile

Tel: (012) 429 8436 Fax: (012) 429 3343

Ailola, Dawid A., LLB Zambia, LLM Zambia, LLM Cornell, PhD Warw. Prof.

Basson, Anneli C., BLC Pret., LLB Pret., LLD S.Af. Assoc. Prof.

Christianson, Mary-Lynn A., BA Cape Town, LLB Natal, LLM Natal Sr. Lectr.

Evans, Roger G., BLC Pret., LLB Pret., LLM Pret. Sr. Lectr.

Franzsen, Riël C. D., BLC Pret., LLB Pret., LLD Stell. Prof.

Garbers, Christoph J., BLC Pret., LLB Pret., BCom S.Af. Sr. Lectr.

Havenga, Michelle K., BA Pret., LLB Pret., LLM S.Af., LLD S.Af. Prof.

Havenga, Peter H., BA Rand Afrikaans, LLM Rand Afrikaans, LLD S.Af. Prof.

Loubser, Annelie, BA Pret., LLB Pret. Sr. Lectr.

Luiz, Stephanie M., BA Natal, LLB Natal, LLM Camb. Assoc. Prof.

Meiring, G. A. (Ina), BA Rand Afrikaans, LLB Rand Afrikaans, LLM Rand Afrikaans Sr. Lectr.

Mischke, Carl, BA Witw., LLB Witw., LLM Heidel., LLD S.Af. Sr. Lectr.

Pistorius, T., BA Pret., LLB S.Af., LLM Pret., LLD Pret. Sr. Lectr.

Pretorius, Japie T., BIur Pret., LLB Natal, LLM Cape Town, LLM Lond., LLD Rand Afrikaans Prof.

Rutherford, Brian R., BA Pret., LLB Pret., LLM Lond. Prof.

Schlemmer, Engela C., BA Rand Afrikaans, LLB Rand Afrikaans, LLM Rand Afrikaans, LLM Mün., LLD Rand Afrikaans Assoc. Prof.

Schulze, Heinrich G., BLC Pret., LLB Pret., LLD S.Af. Sr. Lectr.

Smith, Allistair D., BA Rhodes, LLB Rhodes, PhD Edin. Sr. Lectr.

Strydom, Elize M. L., BA Pret., LLB Pret., LLM S.Af., LLD S.Af. Assoc. Prof.

Swart, Gerrie J., BCom Pret., BIur Pret., LLB S.Af., LLM Stell. Prof.

Van der Linde, Kathleen E., BA Potchef., BIur Potchef., LLB Potchef., LLM S.Af. Sr. Lectr.

Van der Merwe, B. A. (Trix), BA Stell., LLB Stell., LLM S.Af. Sr. Lectr.

Van Niekerk, Johan P., BA Pret., LLB Pret., LLM S.Af., LLM Lond., LLD S.Af. Prof.

Vermaas, Maria R., BLC Pret., LLB Pret., LLM S.Af., LLD S.Af. Sr. Lectr.

Visser, Coenraad J., BCom Stell., LLB Stell., LLM Rand Afrikaans Prof.; Head*

Law, Private

Tel: (012) 429 8418 Fax: (012) 429 3393

Blackbeard, Marié, BProc Pret., LLB Pret., LLD S.Af. Assoc. Prof.

Brink, Paul D., BA Stell., LLB Stell. Sr. Lectr.

Cronjé, Daniël S. P., BA Stell., LLB S.Af., LLM Rand Afrikaans, LLD Rand Afrikaans Prof.

De Jong, Madelene, BLC Pret., LLB Pret. Sr. Lectr.

Floyd, Tomas B., BA Pret., LLB Pret., LLD S.Af. Assoc. Prof.

Hawthorne, Luanda, BA Pret., LLB Pret., LLD Pret. Prof.

Heaton, Jacqueline, BLC Pret., LLB Pret., LLM S.Af. Assoc. Prof.

Jamneck, Juanita, BLC Pret., JLLB Pret., LLD Pret. Sr. Lectr.

Knobel, Johann C., BLC Pret., LLB Pret., LLD S.Af. Sr. Lectr.

Kruger, Johanna M., BIur OFS, LLB OFS Sr. Lectr.

Neethling, Johann, BA OFS, LLB OFS, LLM McG., LLD S.Af. Prof.

Potgieter, Johan M., BIur Rand Afrikaans, LLB Rand Afrikaans, LLM Rand Afrikaans, LLM Harv., LLD S.Af. Prof.

Pretorius, Chris-James, BLC Pret., LLB Pret. Sr. Lectr.

Roos, Annelise, BLC Pret., LLB S.Af., LLM Mich. Assoc. Prof.

Scott, Susan J., BA Pret., LLB Pret., LLD S.Af. Prof.

Steynberg, Loma, BIur Potchef., LLB Potchef., LLM Potchef. Sr. Lectr.

Van Aswegen, Annél, BA Pret., LLB Pret., LLD S.Af. Prof.

Van der Walt, Andries J., BIur Potchef., BA Potchef., LLB Potchef., LLM Witw., LLD Potchef. Prof.

Van Wyk, Adriana M. A., BBibl Pret., LLB S.Af., LLM Witw., LLD S.Af. Prof.

Wiechers, Nikolaas J., BA Pret., LLB S.Af., MA Pret., LLD Pret. Prof.; Acting Head*

Linguistics

Tel: (012) 429 6316 Fax: (012) 429 3355

Barnes, Lawrence A., BA Natal, MA Reading, DLitt&Phil S.Af. Sr. Lectr.

Hendrikse, A. P. (Rusandré), BA Stell., PhD Rhodes Prof.; Head*

Hubbard, E. Hilton, BA Cape Town, MA Reading, MA S.Af., DLitt&Phil S.Af. Prof.

Kruger, Alet, BA Pret., MA S.Af. Sr. Lectr.

Literature, Theory of

Tel: (012) 429 6700

Biermann, Wilhelmina G. J., MA Potchef., DLitt&Phil S.Af. Sr. Lectr.

De Jong, Maria J., MA Rhodes Sr. Lectr.

Gräbe, Regina C., MA P.Elizabeth, DrsLitt Utrecht, DLitt Potchef. Prof.; Head*

Mathematics, Applied Mathematics and Astronomy

Tel: (012) 429 6202 Fax: (012) 429 6064

Alderton, Ian W., MSc S.Af., PhD S.Af. Assoc. Prof.

Bartoszek, Wojciech K., MSc Wroclaw, PhD Wroclaw Assoc. Prof.

Bishop, Nigel T., MA Camb., PhD S'ton. Prof.

Botha, Johan D., MSc Stell., DSc Pret. Sr. Lectr.

Frick, Mariette, MSc ANU, PhD Rand Afrikaans Sr. Lectr.

Heidema, Johannes, Drs Amst., DSc Potchef. Prof.

Mynhardt, Christina M., MSc Rand Afrikaans, PhD Rand Afrikaans Prof.

Naude, Cornelia G., MSc OFS, PhD OFS Sr. Lectr.

Salbany, Sergio de O., MSc Cape Town, PhD Cape Town Prof.

Singleton, Joy E., MSc S.Af. Sr. Lectr.

Smits, Derck P., MSc Natal, PhD Cape Town Assoc. Prof.

Vorster, Stephanus J. R., BSc Pret., MSc S.Af., PhD S.Af. Prof.; Head*

Missiology

Tel: (012) 429 4477 Fax: (012) 429 3332

Botha, Nico A., BA W.Cape, LicTh W.Cape, DrsTh Utrecht, DTh S.Af. Sr. Lectr.

Kritzinger, Johannes N. J., BA Pret., BD Pret., DTh S.Af. Prof.; Head*

Saayman, Willem A., BA OFS, DTh Stell. Prof.

Musicology

Tel: (012) 429 6419 Fax: (012) 429 3400

Davey, Eddie A., UTLM S.Af., BMus Pret., MMus Cape Town Sr. Lectr.

Drury, Jonathan D., BA Kansas, MMus Ill., DPhil Ill. Sr. Lectr.

Geldenhuys, Daniël G., UTLM S.Af., MMus Stell., DMus Stell. Prof.

Geldenhuys, Jolena, UPLM S.Af., UTLM S.Af., BMus Pret., MMus S.Af., DMus S.Af. Sr. Lectr.

King, George T., BA S.Af., MMus S.Af. Sr. Lectr.

Reid, Douglas J., BMus Witw., MLitt Camb., DMus Cape Town Prof.; Acting Head*

Steyn, Gertruida M., MMus OFS, DMus S.Af. Sr. Lectr.

New Testament

Tel: (012) 429 4322 Fax: (012) 429 3332

Botha, J. Eugene, BA Pret., BD Pret., MA Pret., DTh S.Af. Prof.

Botha, Pieter J. J., BA Rand Afrikaans, BD Pret., DD Pret. Prof.

Craffert, Pieter F., BA Pret., BD Pret., DTh S.Af. Assoc. Prof.

De Klerk, Johannes C., BA Pret., BD Pret., DrsTh S.Af. Sr. Lectr.

Du Plessis, Isak J., BD Stell., MA Stell., ThD Theol.Sch.Kampen Prof.

Engelbrecht, Johan, BA Pret., BD Pret., DTh S.Af. Assoc. Prof.; Head*

Gräbe, Pieter J., BA Pret., BD Pret., DD Pret. Assoc. Prof.

Jacobs, Maretha M., BA P.Elizabeth, BTh Stell., DTh S.Af. Sr. Lectr.

Kourie, Celia E. T., BA Lanc., MTh S.Af., DTh S.Af. Assoc. Prof.

Le Roux, Chris R., BA Pret., BD Pret., DTh S.Af. Sr. Lectr.

Lemmer, H. Richard, BA OFS, BTh Stell., DTh S.Af. Assoc. Prof.

Pretorius, Emile A. C., BA OFS, BD Stell., DTh Stell. Prof.

Sebothoma, Wilfred A., BA S.Af., BD Leuven, MA Leuven, PhD Leuven Assoc. Prof.

Van den Heever, Gerhard A., BA Pret., BD Pret., MA S.Af. Sr. Lectr.

Vorster, Johannes N., BA Pret., BD Pret., DD Pret. Prof.

Nursing Science, Advanced

Tel: (012) 429 6131 Fax: (012) 429 6688

Alberts, Ursula U., BCur(I&A) Pret., MA S.Af., DLitt&Phil S.Af. Sr. Lectr.

Bezuidenhout, Marthie C., BCur(I&A) Pret., MCur Rand Afrikaans, DLitt&Phil S.Af. Sr. Lectr.

Booyens, Susanne W., BCur(I&A) Pret., MA S.Af., DLitt&Phil S.Af. Prof.

Botha, Anndi D. H., BCur Pret., MCur Pret., DCur Pret. Sr. Lectr.

Dreyer, J. Marie, MA Potchef., DLitt&Phil S.Af. Prof.

Ehlers, Valerie J., BSocSc Natal, BA S.Af., MA S.Af., DLitt&Phil S.Af. Sr. Lectr.

Human, Sarie P., BCur Pret., MCur Pret. Sr. Lectr.

Jooste, Karien, MA S.Af., DLitt&Phil S.Af. Sr. Lectr.

King, Leatitia J., MA S.Af., DLitt&Phil S.Af. Prof.; Head*

Koch, S. (Poppie), MA S.Af., DLitt&Phil S.Af. Sr. Lectr.

Makhubela-Nkondo, Olga N., BCur S.Af., MA Harv., DLitt&Phil Harv. Sr. Lectr.

Paton, Frieda, BCur Pret., MA S.Af. Sr. Lectr.

Potgieter, Eugené, BCur Pret., MA S.Af., DLitt&Phil S.Af. Sr. Lectr.

Potgieter, Susan, BCur Pret., BA S.Af., MCur Rand Afrikaans, DCur Rand Afrikaans Sr. Lectr.

Tjallinks, J. E. (Nita), BCur Rand Afrikaans, MCur Rand Afrikaans Sr. Lectr.

Troskie, Rosemarie, MA S.Af., DLitt&Phil S.Af. Prof.

Van der Wal, Dirk M., BA S.Af., MA S.Af. Sr. Lectr.

Old Testament

Tel: (012) 429 4711 Fax: (012) 429 3332

Annandale, Joan, BD Pret., DTh S.Af. Sr. Lectr.

Boshoff, Willem S., BA Pret., BD Pret., DDTh S.Af. Sr. Lectr.

Burger, Johannes A., BD Pret., MA Pret., DTh S.Af. Assoc. Prof.

Gous, Ignatius G. P., BA Pret., BD Pret., DTh S.Af. Sr. Lectr.

Heyns, Magdalena, BA Cape Town, BTh S.Af., DLitt&Phil S.Af. Assoc. Prof.

Nel, Willem A. G., BA Rand Afrikaans, BD Pret. Sr. Lectr.

Scheepers, Coenraad L. van W., BD Pret., DTh S.Af. Assoc. Prof.

Scheffler, Eben H., BA Pret., BD Pret., DD Pret. Prof.

Snyman, Gert F., BA Potchef., BA Rand Afrikaans, ThB Potchef., ThM Potchef., DTh S.Af. Sr. Lectr.

Spangenberg, Izak J. J., BTh Stell., MA Stell., DTh S.Af. Assoc. Prof.

Strydom, J. Gerhardus, BA Pret., BD Pret., DTh S.Af. Sr. Lectr.

Van Dyk, Petrus J., BA Pret., BD Pret., BSc S.Af., BSc Pret., BD Pret., DTh S.Af. Prof.; Head*

Van Heerden, Schalk W., BA OFS, BD Pret., MA OFS, DTh S.Af. Assoc. Prof.

Wessels, Jacobus P. H., BA Rand Afrikaans, BD Pret., MA Pret., DTh S.Af. Sr. Lectr.

Wessels, Wilhelm J., BA Pret., BD Pret., DTh S.Af. Prof.

Philosophy

Tel: (012) 429 6888 Fax: (012) 429 3400

Ally, Mashuq, BA Cape Town, MA Durban-W., DPhil Fort Hare Sr. Lectr.

Coetzee, Pieter H., BA S.Af., MA Rhodes Sr. Lectr.

Malherbe, Jeanette G., BA Witw., MA S.Af., MA Kansas Assoc. Prof.

Prinsloo, Erasmus D., MA Pret., DPhil Pret. Prof.; Head*

Voice, Paul, MA Witw., PhD Witw. Sr. Lectr.

Wilkinson, Jennifer R., BA S.Af., MA Witw., DLitt&Phil S.Af. Assoc. Prof.

Physics

Tel: (012) 429 8027 Fax: (012) 429 3434

Basson, Ilsa, MSc S.Af., PhD S.Af. Sr. Lectr.

Reynhardt, Eduard C., MSc OFS, PhD S.Af. Prof.; Head*

Sofianos, Sofianos A., MSc S.Af., PhD S.Af. Prof.

Political Science

Tel: (012) 429 6626

Botha, Susan, MAdmin Pret., DLitt&Phil S.Af. Sr. Lectr.

Faure, Murray A., DAdmin S.Af. Prof.; Head*

Hugo, Pierre J., MSc Brist, DPhil Z'bwe. Prof.

Kotzé, Dirk J., MA Stell., MA Pret., PhD Witw. Sr. Lectr.

Kriek, Anne-Marie, DLitt&Phil S.Af. Sr. Lectr.

Kriek, Dan J., DPhil Pret. Prof.

Labuschagne, Gerhard S., DLitt&Phil S.Af. Assoc. Prof.

Labuschagne, Pieter A. H., LLB S.Af., DPhil OFS Sr. Lectr.

Louw, André du P., MSc Camb., DIur Ley. Assoc. Prof.

Primary School Teacher Education

Barnard, F., BA Potchef., MEd Pret., DEd Pret. Assoc. Prof.

De Witt, M. W., BA Stell., MEd Pret., DEd Pret. Assoc. Prof.

Faber, R. J., BA Pret., MEd S.Af. Sr. Lectr.

Gouws, F. E., BA Pret., MEd Pret., PhD Pret. Sr. Lectr.

Horn, I. H., BSc Rhodes, MEd S.Af., DEd S.Af. Sr. Lectr.

Hugo, A., BA OFS, MEd S.Af. Sr. Lectr.

Le Roux, K., BA Pret., MEd Pret., DEd Pret. Assoc. Prof.

Nieman, M. M., BA Pret., MEd Pret., PhD Pret. Sr. Lectr.

Olivier, A., BCom Stell., MEd S.Af., DEd S.Af. Prof.; Head*

Orr, J. P., BSocSc Natal, MA S.Af. Sr. Lectr.

Pretorius, S. G., BA Stell., MEd S.Af., DEd S.Af. Assoc. Prof.

Van der Linde, C. H., BA S.Af., MEd S.Af., DEd S.Af. Sr. Lectr.

Van Schalkwyk, A., BA Pret., MEd Rand Afrikaans, DEd S.Af. Sr. Lectr.

Van Staden, C. J. S., BA Pret., MEd S.Af., DEd S.Af. Sr. Lectr.

Vorster, P. J., BA Stell., MEd P.Elizabeth, DEd P.Elizabeth Assoc. Prof.

Psychology

Tel: (012) 429 8088 Fax: (012) 429 3414

Appelgryn, Ans E. M., MA S.Af., DLitt&Phil S.Af. Sr. Lectr.

Beyers, Eefke, BA Stell., MA Melb., MA S.Af., DLitt&Phil Stell. Prof.; Head*

Coetzee, Cas H., BA Pret., BSc S.Af., MA P.Elizabeth Sr. Lectr.

Cronjé, Elsjé M., MA Stell., DLitt&Phil S.Af. Sr. Lectr.

Flowers, Dian M., MA Pret. Sr. Lectr.

Fourie, David P., MSc OFS, MA S.Af., PhD S.Af. Prof.

Grieve, Kate W., BSocSc Rhodes, MA S.Af., DLitt&Phil S.Af. Sr. Lectr.

Jordaan, Wilhelm J., BA OFS, BA Stell., MA S.Af. Prof.

Lifschitz, Stan, MA S.Af., DLitt&Phil S.Af. Assoc. Prof.

Meyer, Werner F., BA Pret., DrPhil Mainz Prof.

Moore, Cora, BA Pret., MA S.Af., DLitt&Phil S.Af. Assoc. Prof.

Mynhardt, Johan C., MA Rand Afrikaans, DLitt&Phil S.Af. Assoc. Prof.

Nel, J. A., MA Pret., MA S.Af. Sr. Lectr.

Nieuwoudt, Johan M., MA Stell., DLitt&Phil S.Af. Assoc. Prof.

Plug, C. (Kerneels), BSc Pret., MA S.Af., DLitt&Phil S.Af. Prof.

Rademeyer, Gert, MA OFS, DPhil P.Elizabeth Prof.

Snyders, F. J. A. (Ricky), MA S.Af., DLitt&Phil S.Af. Prof.

Terre Blanche, Martin J., BA Pret., MA S.Af. Sr. Lectr.

Thom, D. P. (Thea), BA Potchef., DLitt&Phil S.Af. Sr. Lectr.

Van Deventer, S. H. (Vasi), MSc Stell., PhD S.Af. Assoc. Prof.

Van Dyk, Alta C., BSocSc OFS, MSc S.Af., DLitt&Phil S.Af. Sr. Lectr.

Van Ede, Dorette M., BA Pret., MA S.Af., DLitt&Phil S.Af. Sr. Lectr.

Van Staden, Fred J., MSc Rand Afrikaans, MA C.U.N.Y, PhD S.Af. Assoc. Prof.

Viljoen, Henning G., MA Potchef., DPhil Pret. Prof.

Willers, Vivien A., MA S.Af., DLitt&Phil S.Af. Sr. Lectr.

Psychology, Industrial

Tel: (012) 429 8003 Fax: (012) 429 8368

Bergh, Ziel C., MA S.Af. Sr. Lectr.

Breed, Marita, MA Potchef., DLitt&Phil S.Af. Sr. Lectr.

Cilliers, Frans V. N., MA Potchef., DPhil Potchef. Prof.

De Koker, Theo H., MSc Lough., MCom Pret. Sr. Lectr.

Flowers, John, MA S.Af., DLitt&Phil S.Af. Prof.

Koortzen, Pieter, MCom Rand Afrikaans Sr. Lectr.

Leary, Michael B., MCom S.Af. Sr. Lectr.

Martins, Nico, MCom OFS, DPhil Pret. Assoc. Prof.

Mauer, Karl F., MA Natal, MA S.Af., DLitt&Phil Rand Afrikaans Prof.

Schreuder, Andries M. G., MAdmin OFS, DAdmin S.Af. Assoc. Prof.; Head*

Theron, Antoinette L., MA Rand Afrikaans, DLitt&Phil S.Af. Assoc. Prof.

Ungerer, Leona M., BA Stell., MA Stell. Sr. Lectr.

Visser, Petrus J., MA Pret., DPhil Pret. Assoc. Prof.

Viviers, Adrian M., MCom Stell., DCom S.Af. Sr. Lectr.

Von der Ohe, Hartmut, MCom Pret. Sr. Lectr.

Vosloo, Salomé E., MCom Pret. Sr. Lectr.

Watkins, Michael L., MA Potchef., DPhil Potchef. Assoc. Prof.

Wolfaardt, Johannes B., MA Pret., DPhil Pret. Assoc. Prof.

Public Administration

Tel: (012) 429 6595

Adlem, Willem L. J., MAdmin Pret., DAdmin S.Af. Prof.

Auriacombe, Christelle J., MAdmin S.Af., DLitt&Phil S.Af. Sr. Lectr.

Brynard, Dirk J., MA Pret., DLitt&Phil S.Af. Prof.; Head*

Ferreira, Gera M., DAdmin Pret. Sr. Lectr.

Nealer, Eric J., MAdmin S.Af., DAdmin S.Af. Sr. Lectr.

Odendaal, Marie-Jane, BAdmin Pret., MAdmin S.Af., DAdmin S.Af. Sr. Lectr.

Pauw, Jacobus C., BA Pret., MA Rand Afrikaans, DLitt&Phil Rand Afrikaans Prof.

Smith, Frank H., DLitt&Phil S.Af. Sr. Lectr.

Ströh, Eduard C., MPA OFS, DAdmin OFS Sr. Lectr.

Uys, Francina, MAdmin Pret., DAdmin S.Af. Assoc. Prof.

Van der Westhuizen, Ernst J., BAdmin OFS, MAdmin Pret., DAdmin S.Af. Assoc. Prof.

Wessels, Jacobus S., BA Pret., MA Pret., DPhil Pret. Assoc. Prof.

Quantitative Management

Tel: (012) 429 4012 Fax: (012) 429 3422

De Villiers, Anton, MSc Pret. Sr. Lectr.

Le Roux, Jeanne, MSc Stell. Sr. Lectr.

Olivier, Ilze, BSc S.Af., MSc Pret. Sr. Lectr.

Potgieter, Petrus H., BSc Pret., MA Kent, PhD Pret. Sr. Lectr.

Swanepoel, Chris J., BSc Rand Afrikaans, MSc Pret., PhD Pret. Assoc. Prof.

Van der Merwe, Carel A., MCom Stell., DCom S.Af. Prof.; Head*

Wolvaardt, J. S. (Kobus), MSc Pret., MSc S.Af., PhD S.Af. Prof.

Religion, Science of, see also New Testament; Old Testament; Theol., Practical; Theol., Systematic, and Theol. Ethics

Tel: (012) 429 4523

Goosen, Daniel P., BCom Pret., BA Pret., BD S.Af., DTh S.Af. Assoc. Prof.

Krüger, Jacobus S., BA Pret., BA S.Af., BD Pret., DrsTh Amst., DTh S.Af. Prof.; Head*

Lubbe, Gerhard J. A., BA Pret., MA Rand Afrikaans, DLitt&Phil S.Af. Assoc. Prof.

Steyn, Helena C., MA S.Af., DLitt&Phil S.Af. Sr. Lectr.

Romance Languages

Tel: (012) 429 6811

Daugherty, Jill D., BA Pret., MA Pret., DU Paris IV Assoc. Prof., French

Maree, M. Cathy, BA N.U.I., MA N.U.I., DLitt&Phil Madrid Prof., Spanish

Meda, Anna R. D., DottLingLett Genoa, MA S.Af., DLitt&Phil S.Af. Assoc. Prof., Italian

Strike, W. Norman, BA Pret., LèsL Aix-Marseilles I, MA Aix-Marseilles I, DLitt&Phil S.Af. Prof., French; Head*

Weinberg, M. Grazia, BA P.Elizabeth, BA S.Af., MA S.Af., DLitt&Phil S.Af. Assoc. Prof., Italian

Russian

Tel: (012) 429 6541

Garmashova, Irina, PhD Moscow Sr. Lectr.

Krzychylkiewicz, Agata A., MA Wroclaw Sr. Lectr.

Semitics

Tel: (012) 429 6812 Fax: (012) 429 3355

Dadoo, Yousuf, MA Durban-W., DLitt&Phil S.Af. Assoc. Prof.

Lübbe, John C., BA Pret., MA S.Af., DLitt&Phil S.Af. Prof.; Head*

Meinster, M. Jansje, BA Pret., MA Rand Afrikaans, DLitt&Phil Rand Afrikaans Assoc. Prof.

Resnick, Max, MA S.Af., DLitt&Phil S.Af. Sr. Lectr.

Vermaak, P. S. (Fanie), BA OFS, BTh Stell., MA Stell., DLitt&Phil S.Af. Assoc. Prof.

Social Work

Tel: (012) 429 6642 Fax: (012) 429 3666

Collins, Kathleen J., MA(SW) Stell., PhD Witw. Sr. Lectr.

Du Toit, Andries S., MA Pret., DPhil
P.Elizabeth Sr. Lectr.
Spies, Glaudina M., MA Pret., DPhil S.Af. Sr.
Lectr.
Van Biljon, Rachel C. W., MA Pret., DPhil
S.Af. Prof.
Van Delft, Willem F., MA Pret.;
MA(ClinicalPsychology) S.Af., DPhil
S.Af. Prof.; Head*

Sociology

Tel: (012) 429 6301
Allais, A. Carol, MA S.Af. Sr. Lectr.
Appelbaum, Karen, BA Witw., BA S.Af., MA
S.Af. Sr. Lectr.
Gelderblom, Derik, MA Stell. Sr. Lectr.
Grobbelaar, Janis I., BSocSc Cape Town, MA Stell.,
DLitt&Phil S.Af. Prof.
Martin, Ruhr, BA Rhodes, MA S.Af. Sr. Lectr.
Mendelsohn, Martin K., BA Witw., PhD
Hamburg Sr. Lectr.
Molamu, Louis, MSc Brad. Sr. Lectr.
Pretorius, Jan C., DPhil Pret. Prof.
Pretorius, Louwrens, BAdmin Pret., MAdmin
Stell., DPhil Stell. Prof.; Head*
Puttergill, Charles H., BA Rand Afrikaans, MA
S.Af. Sr. Lectr.

Spanish, see Romance Langs.

Statistics

Tel: (012) 429 6464 Fax: (012) 429 3434
Bekker, Andriëtte, MSc Rand Afrikaans, PhD
S.Af. Sr. Lectr.
Fresen, John L., MSc Cape Town, PhD Rand
Afrikaans Assoc. Prof.
Katkovnik, Vladimir Y., PhD Leningrad P.I., DSc
Leningrad P.I. Prof.
Markham, Roger, BSc Natal, MSc S.Af., DSc
Pret. Assoc. Prof.
Nieuwoudt, Reina, BSc Pret., MSc S.Af. Sr.
Lectr.
Raath, E. Liefde, MSc Pret., PhD S.Af. Sr. Lectr.
Roux, Jacobus J., MSc OFS, PhD S.Af. Assoc.
Prof.
Steffens, Francois E., MSc Potchef., DSc
Potchef. Prof.; Head*
Yadavilli, V. S. Sarma, MSc Osm., PhD IIT
Madras Prof.

Theology, Practical

Tel: (012) 429 4329 Fax: (012) 429 3332
De Jongh van Arkel, Jan T., BA Stell., BTh Stell.,
ThM Prin., DTh S.Af. Assoc. Prof.
Dreyer, Jaco S., BA Pret., BD Pret., DTh
S.Af. Sr. Lectr.
Heyns, Louis M., BA Stell., BD Stell., DTh
S.Af. Assoc. Prof.; Head*
Pieterse, Hendrik J. C., BA Pret., BD Pret., DTh
Stell. Prof.
Theron, Jacques P. J., BA Pret., BD Pret., DTh
S.Af. Assoc. Prof.
Van Wyk, Agathades G., BSc Pret., DTh
S.Af. Sr. Lectr.
Wolfaardt, Johan A., BA Pret., BD Pret., DTh
V.U.Amst. Prof.

Theology, Systematic, and Theological Ethics

Tel: (012) 429 4420 Fax: (012) 429 3332
Kretzschmar, Louise, BA Witw., MPhil Camb.,
PhD Cape Town Sr. Lectr.
Mosoma, David L., BTh S.Af., MTh Prin., PhD
Prin. Assoc. Prof.
Motlhabi, Mokgethi B. G., MA Chic., PhD
Boston Assoc. Prof.
Olivier, David F., BA Pret., BD Pret., DrsTh
Amst. Prof.
Van Niekerk, Erasmus, BA OFS, BTh Stell.,
DrsTh Theol.Sch.Kampen, DTh S.Af. Prof.;
Acting Head*

Transport Economics

Tel: (012) 429 4027 Fax: (012) 429 4678
Brits, Anton, BCom S.Af., MCom S.Af., DCom
S.Af. Sr. Lectr.
Cronjé, Jacobus N., BCom Rand Afrikaans, BCom
S.Af., MCom S.Af., DCom S.Af. Sr. Lectr.

Shahia, Mrad, BCom Stell., BCom Rand Afrikaans,
MCom S.Af., DCom S.Af. Prof.; Head*
Smuts, Christiaan A., BSc Pret., BCom S.Af., LLB
S.Af., MCom S.Af., DCom S.Af. Prof.
Vorster, Francois N., BCom S.Af., MCom
S.Af. Sr. Lectr.

SPECIAL CENTRES, ETC

Business Leadership, Graduate School of

Tel: (011) 652 0000 Fax: (011) 652 0299
Ackermann, Petrus L. S., BCom S.Af., MSc S.Af.,
PhD S.Af. Prof.
Adendorff, Susan A., BEng Pret., MBA Pret. Sr.
Lectr.
Beaty, David T., BA Tennessee, MA Tennessee, PhD
P.Elizabeth Prof.
Booysen, Annie E., MA Rand Afrikaans, MA
Pret. Sr. Lectr.
Crosbie, Mike H., BSc Witw., BCompt S.Af.,
MBL S.Af. Assoc. Prof.
Du Plessis, Phillipus J., BCom S.Af., MBL S.Af.,
DBL S.Af. Prof.
Erwee, André, BCom S.Af., BCompt S.Af., MBL
S.Af. Sr. Lectr.
Feldman, Joseph A., BSc S.Af., MBA Pret. Sr.
Lectr.
Ferreira, Michael A., BSc Pret., MBL
S.Af. Assoc. Prof.
Hofmeyr, Karl B., BA Rhodes, MBL S.Af., DBL
S.Af. Prof.
Hugo, Willem M. J., DCom S.Af. Prof.; Head*
Joubert, Reinhold J. O., MAAdmin Stell., DCom
Rand Afrikaans Assoc. Prof.
Klerck, Werner G., MSc Pret., MBL S.Af., DBL
S.Af. Prof.
Köster, Manfried J. F., BSc Pret., MBA Pret., PhD
Texas A.& M. Assoc. Prof.
Lenamile, Dikloff O., BCom S.Af., BCompt S.Af.,
MBA Witw. Assoc. Prof.
Makin, Viola, BA Natal, MBL S.Af. Assoc. Prof.
Maritz, Marius J., BCom Pret., BCompt S.Af.,
MBL S.Af., MA Alabama, Assoc. Prof.
Marrian, André G., BSc W.Cape
McLeary, Fred, MCompt S.Af. Prof.
Ngambi-Mubu, Hellicy C., BA Zambia, MBA
Ball Sr. Lectr.
Pellissier, René, BA Stell., MBA Stell. Sr. Lectr.
Pelser, Gert P. J., MSc Pret., MBA Pret., DBL
S.Af. Prof.
Potgieter, Theuns J. E., MCom Pret., DCom
S.Af. Prof.
Rajah, Mahamed, MA Punjab Sr. Lectr.
Rall, Petrus J., MCom Potchef., DCom
Potchef. Prof.
Smit, Albertus J., BCom OFS, MSc
Witw. Assoc. Prof.
Strasheim, Catharina, BSc Pret., MSc S.Af. Sr.
Lectr.
Swanepoel, Barend J., BCom Rand Afrikaans,
MCom S.Af., DCom S.Af. Assoc. Prof.
Van den Berg, Petra H., MCom Stell., MBL S.Af.,
MSc Witw. Prof.
Van Wyk, Marius W., BCom Stell., BA Stell., BA
P.Elizabeth, BProc S.Af., LLB S.Af., LLM Witw.,
LLM S.Af. Assoc. Prof.

Criminology, Institute for

Tel: (012) 429 6608
Prinsloo, J. H., MA S.Af., DLitt&Phil
S.Af. Chief Researcher; Head*

Educational Research, Institute for

Tel: (012) 429 4386 Fax: (012) 429 3444
Kamper, Gerrit D., MA Potchef., MEd Rand
Afrikaans, DEd S.Af. Assoc. Prof.
Swanepoel, C. H., BSc Pret., MEd S.Af., DEd
S.Af. Prof.; Head*

Foreign and Comparative Law, Institute of

Tel: (012) 429 8306 Fax: (012) 429 3321
Schulze, H. C. A. W., DrJur Gött. Prof.; Chief
Researcher
Thomashausen, A. E. A. M., DrIur Kiel Dir.*

Legal Aid Centre

Tel: (012) 429 4092 Fax: (012) 429 4440
Jordaan, Rita A., BA Pret., LLB Pret., LLD
S.Af. Dir.*

Market Research, Bureau of

Tel: (012) 429 3566
Ligthelm, André A., BCom Pret., DComm
Potchef. Prof.
Martins, Johannes H., MCom Pret., DCom
S.Af. Prof.; Head*
Van Wyk, Helgard de J., BComm Stell., MCom
Pret., DCom S.Af. Prof.

Social and Health Sciences, Institute for

Butchart, R. A., BA Cape Town, MA S.Af.,
DLitt&Phil S.Af. Assoc. Prof.
Nell, V., BA Cape Town, MA P.Elizabeth,
DLitt&Phil S.Af. Prof.
Seedat, M. Amine, BA Durban-W., DPhil Durban-
W. Assoc. Prof.; Head*

Theology and Religion, Research Institute for

Tel: (012) 429 4369 Fax: (012) 429 3525
Du Toit, Cornel W., BA Pret., BD Pret., DD
Pret. Prof.; Head*
Landman, Christina, BA Pret., MA S.Af., DTh
S.Af. Chief Researcher
Liebenberg, Jacobus, BA Pret., BD Pret., DTh
Humboldt
Swanepoel, Francois A., BA Witw., DD
Pret. Prof.

CONTACT OFFICERS

Academic affairs. Acting Registrar (Academic):
Msimang, Prof. C. T., LLB S.Af., MA S.Af.,
DLitt&Phil S.Af.
Admissions (first degree). Harding, R. C.,
BTh S.Af.
Admissions (higher degree). Cox, G. W., BA
S.Af.
Adult/continuing education. Vice-Principal
(Tuition): Maimela, Prof. S. S., BA S.Af.,
DPhil Harv., MTh
Alumni. Sprong, J. E., BCom S.Af.
Archives. Coetzee, M. A., BA P.Elizabeth, BA Pret.
Careers. Van Schoor, W. A., MA Stell., MBL
S.Af., DPhil Stell.
Computing services. Weiermans, D. J., BSc
Pret., MSc S.Af.
Consultancy services. Van Schoor, W. A., MA
Stell., MBL S.Af., DPhil Stell.
Credit transfer. Burger, W. P.
Development/fund-raising. Stiglingh, F. J.,
BA Stell., BEd Stell.
Distance education. Vice-Principal (Tuition):
Maimela, Prof. S. S., BA S.Af., DPhil Harv.,
MTh
Equal opportunities. Vakalisa, Prof. N. C. G.,
BSc Fort Hare, BEd S.Af., MEd S.Af., PhD Ohio
State
Estates and buildings/works and services.
Hayes, F. G., MDP S.Af.
Examinations. Beckworth, K. T., BA Natal
Finance. Muller, J. P., BCom Pret.
General enquiries. Acting Registrar
(Academic): Msimang, Prof. C. T., LLB S.Af.,
MA S.Af., DLitt&Phil S.Af.
Health services. Krynauw, J. M., BA Pret.,
BACur S.Af., MACur S.Af.
Industrial liaison. Swanepoel, H. F. J., BCom
S.Af.
Library (enquiries). Willemse, J., MA Pret.
Minorities/disadvantaged groups. Vakalisa,
Prof. N. C. G., BSc Fort Hare, BEd S.Af., MEd
S.Af., PhD Ohio State
Ombudsperson. Swanepoel, H. F. J., BCom
S.Af.
Personnel/human resources. Du Plessis, G.
P., BA Pret.
Public relations, information and marketing.
Stiglingh, F. J., BA Stell., BEd Stell.
Publications. Van der Walt, P., BA Pret.
Purchasing. De Klerk, H. J.

Quality assurance and accreditation. Acting Registrar (Academic): Msimang, Prof. C. T., LLB *S.Af.*, MA *S.Af.*, DLitt&Phil *S.Af.*
Research. Vice-Principal (Research and Planning): Döckel, Prof. J. A., BSc(Agric) *Stell.*, PhD *Iowa*
Safety. Monyai, C., BA *S.Af.*
Scholarships, awards, loans. Hattingh, C. S. J.

Staff development and training. Badenhorst, F. H., BMil *Stell.*, BAdmin *OFS*, MAdmin *OFS*, DAdmin *S.Af.*
Student union. Ngengebule, T., BA *S.Af.*
Student welfare/counselling. Ngengebule, T., BA *S.Af.*
Students with disabilities. Van Schoor, W. A., MA *Stell.*, MBL *S.Af.*, DPhil *Stell.*

University press. Van der Walt, P., BA *Pret.*
Women. Church, Prof. J., BA *Witw.*, BIur *S.Af.*, LLB *S.Af.*, LLD *S.Af.*

[Information supplied by the institution as at 2 October 1998, and edited by the ACU]

UNIVERSITY OF STELLENBOSCH

Founded 1918; previously established as Stellenbosch College (1881) and Victoria College of Stellenbosch (1887)

Member of the Association of Commonwealth Universities

Postal Address: Private Bag X1, Matieland, 7602 South Africa
Telephone: (021) 808 4634, 808 9111 **Fax**: (021) 808 4499 **E-mail**: rk@maties.sun.ac.za/mts@maties.sun.ac.za
Telex: 520 383 **WWW**: http://www.sun.ac.za

CHANCELLOR—Botha, Elize, OMSS, MA *Stell.*, DLitt&Phil *Amst.*, Hon. DLitt *Pret.*, Hon. DLitt *Stell.*
RECTOR AND VICE-CHANCELLOR*—Van Wyk, Prof. Andreas H., BA *Stell.*, LLB *Stell.*, LLD *Ley.*, Hon. LLD *Leuven*
VICE-RECTOR (ACADEMIC AFFAIRS)—Claassen, Prof. Walter T., BTh *Stell.*, MA *Stell.*, DLitt *Stell.*
VICE-RECTOR (OPERATIONS)—Stumpf, Rolf, BA *Pret.*, MA *Pret.*, PhD *S.Af.*
REGISTRAR‡—Kritzinger, Prof. Serf, MSc *Stell.*, MSc *Birm.*, PhD *Birm.*

GENERAL INFORMATION

History. The university was originally established in 1874 as the arts department of Stellenbosch Gymnasium. It achieved separate status in 1881, when Stellenbosch College was founded. It was renamed Victoria College of Stellenbosch in 1887 and became a university under its present name in 1918.

The university is situated about 50km east of Cape Town.

Admission to first degree courses (see also South African Introduction). Recognised South African School Leaving Certificate with matriculation exemption. Certain subjects or combinations of subjects are required for some degree courses. International students may be admitted if a certificate of exemption is issued by the Joint Matriculation Board. International undergraduate students also require a study permit available from the department of home affairs, Pretoria.

First Degrees (see also South African Directory to Subjects to Study) (* = also available with honours; † = only available with honours). BA*, BA(FA)*, BA(FA)(Ed), BA(SW)*, BAcc*, BAdmin†, BAgricAdmin*, BAgric(Ed), BB&A† (business management and administration), BBibl*, BChD, BComm*, BCur*, BD, BDram*, BEcon*, BEng, BFor, BHMS†, BHomeEcon*, BHomeEcon(Ed), BJourn†, BMedSc, BMil*, BMus*, BMus(Ed), BOccTher*, BP&R† (parks and recreation), BPA†, BPrimEd, BSc*, BScAgric*, BScDentSc†, BScDiet, BScFoodSc*, BScFor*, BScForSc†, BScHomeEcon†, BScHomeEcon(Ed), BScHomeEcon(Food), BScMedSc*, BScNCons†, BScPhysio*, BScWoodSc*, BSp&HTher, BTh, LLB, MB ChB.

Most courses normally last a minimum of 4 years, with an additional 1–2 years for honours. BA, BAgricAdmin, BD, BFor, BMil, BSc: minimum 3 years; BAcc, BComm, BEcon: 3 or 4 years; BChD: minimum 5½ years; MB ChB: minimum 6 years.

Higher Degrees (see also South African Directory to Subjects to Study). BEd, BPhil, LLM, MA, MA(FA), MA(SW), MAcc, MAdmin, MAgricAdmin, MBA, MBibl, MChD, MComm, MCur, MD, MDram, MEcon, MEd, MEng, MFamMed, MHMS, MHomeEcon, MJourn, MMed, MMil, MMus, MNutr, MOccTher, MP&R, MPA, MSc, MScAgric, MScDentSc, MScEngSc, MScFoodSc, MScFor, MScForSc, MScHomeEcon, MScMedSc, MScNCons, MScPhysio, MScWoodSc, MTh, MT&RP, MPhil, PhD, PhD(Agric), PhD(AgricAdmin), PhD(Eng), PhDEngSc, PhD(FoodSc), PhD(For), PhDForSc, PhD(HMS), PhD(HomeEcon), PhD(Mil), PhD(NCons), PhD(WoodSc), DAdmin, DComm, DCur, DEd, DEng, DLitt, DMil, DMus, DPhil, DSc, DScAgric, DScFoodSc, DScFor, DScHomeEcon, DScMedSc, DScNCons, DSc(Odont), DScWoodSc, DTh, LLD.

Most courses normally last a minimum of 1 year. MBA, MPA, MPhil, MScMedSc: 1–2 years. MT&RP, DCur, DEd, DMus, DLitt, DPhil, DTh, LLD, PhD, PhD(Agric), PhD(AgricAdmin), PhD(Eng), PhDEngSc, PhD(FoodSc), PhD(For), PhDForSc, PhD(HMS), PhD(HomeEcon), PhD(Mil), PhD(NCons), PhD(WoodSc): minimum 2 years. MFamMed, DAdmin, DComm: minimum 3 years. MMed: 4–5 years.

Language of Instruction. Afrikaans. Other languages may be used where deemed necessary for effective instruction, and in several advanced postgraduate courses English is used.

Libraries. J.S. Gericke Library: 852,130 volumes; 6108 periodicals subscribed to. Five branch libraries: business school, engineering/forestry, medicine, music, and theology.

Fees are calculated according to the course and the number of credits and range from R7300 to R11,800.

Academic Year (1999). Two semesters (four terms): 8 February–26 March; 6 April–24 June; 19 July–10 September; 20 September–9 December.

Income (1998). Total, R383,000,000.

Statistics. Staff (1997): 2111 (869 academic, 1242 administrative). Students (1998): full-time 16,053 (8441 men, 7612 women); part-time 795 (536 men, 259 women); international 628 (384 men, 244 women); total 16,848.

FACULTIES/SCHOOLS

Agricultural Sciences
Tel: (021) 808 4737 Fax: (021) 808 2001
Dean: Hattingh, Prof. Martin J., MSc *Stell.*, DSc *Stell.*
Secretary: Jordaan, Leon, BA *Stell.*

Arts
Tel: (021) 808 2137 Fax: (021) 808 2123
Dean: Van der Merwe, Prof. Izak J., MA *Stell.*, DPhil *Stell.*
Secretary: Loxton, M. C. (Leana), BA *Stell.*

Dentistry
Tel: (021) 931 3379 Fax: (021) 931 2287
Dean: Dreyer, Prof. Wynand P., BDS *Witw.*, PhD *Stell.*
Secretary: Swart, D. C. (Nelis), BA *Stell.*

Economic and Management Sciences
Tel: (021) 808 2248 Fax: (021) 808 2409
Dean: Matthee, Prof. Johan A., BComm *Stell.*
Secretary: Eygelaar, Leon, BA *Stell.*

Education
Tel: (021) 808 2258 Fax: (021) 808 2269
Dean: Park, Prof. Tommy, BSc *Stell.*, DEd *Stell.*
Secretary: De Beer, Johan B., BA *Stell.*, BPA *Stell.*

Engineering
Tel: (021) 808 4204 Fax: (021) 808 4206
Dean: Van der Walt, Prof. P. W., BSc *Stell.*, MEng *Stell.*, PhD(Eng) *Stell.*
Secretary: Pienaar, Minnaar O., BA *OFS*

Forestry
Tel: (021) 808 3323 Fax: (021) 808 3603
Dean: Van Wyk, Prof. Gerrit, BScFor *Stell.*, PhD *N.Carolina State*
Secretary: Pienaar, Minnaar O., BA *OFS*

Law

Tel: (021) 808 4853 Fax: (021) 886 6235

Dean: Fourie, Prof. James S. A., BA Stell., LLB Stell., LLD S.Af.

Secretary: Hanekom, Arie R., BSc Stell., BSc Potchef.

Medicine

Tel: (021) 938 9200 Fax: (021) 938 9558

Dean: Lochner, Prof. Jan d. V., MSc Stell., MB ChB Stell., DSc Stell., FCP(SA)

Secretary: Swart, D. C. (Nelis), BA Stell.

Military Science

Tel: (022) 702 3003 Fax: (022) 702 3060

Dean: Nelson, Prof.; Lt.-Col. Chris, MA OFS, DPhil Stell.

Secretary: Hanekom, Arie R., BSc Stell., BSc Potchef.

Science

Tel: (021) 808 3072 Fax: (021) 808 3680

Dean: Hahne, Prof. Fritz J. W., MSc Pret., PhD Cape Town, FRSSAf

Secretary: Fourie, C. J. (Neels), BEcon Stell.

Theology

Tel: (021) 808 3254 Fax: (021) 808 3251

Dean: Combrink, Prof. H. J. Bernard, BA Pret., BD Pret., ThD Amst.

Secretary: Hanekom, Arie R., BSc Stell., BSc Potchef.

ACADEMIC UNITS

Accountancy

Tel: (021) 808 3428 Fax: (021) 886 4176

Anderson, Geoff E., MBL S.Af. Assoc. Prof.

Booysen, Hanchen, BA Stell., BCompt S.Af. Sr. Lectr.

Brink, P. J., MAcc Stell. Assoc. Prof.

Brown, William, BCom Cape Town, MComm Stell. Prof.

De Villiers, S. S., BCom Pret. Sr. Lectr.

De Wet, Johan J., BComm Stell. Sr. Lectr.

Du Toit, Gerda M., BAcc Stell. Sr. Lectr.

Jacobs, Lisa, BAcc Stell., BComm Stell., MBA Stell. Sr. Lectr.

Koch, Frans J., BMil Stell., BCompt S.Af., MCom S.Af. Sr. Lectr.

Loxton, Leon, BSc Stell., BAcc Stell., MBA Stell. Assoc. Prof.

Matthee, Johan A., BComm Stell. Prof.

Olivier, Pierre, BCompt S.Af., MComm Stell., PhD Stell. Prof.; Chair*

Steyn, B. Wilna, BAcc Stell., BComm Stell. Sr. Lectr.

Van der Walt, W. D., DAcc Stell. Assoc. Prof.

Van Dyk, Danie P., BAcc Stell. Sr. Lectr.

Van Schalkwyk, C. J. (Cobus), BAcc Stell., BComm Stell. Assoc. Prof.

Wessels, Philip L., MComm Stell. Assoc. Prof.

Wiese, Adel, BComm Stell., BCompt S.Af. Sr. Lectr.

Other Staff: 7 Lectrs.

Research: information value of accounting indicators; prediction of corporate failure

Actuarial Science, see Stats. and Actuarial Sci.

African Languages

Tel: (021) 808 2106 Fax: (021) 808 2171

Du Plessis, J. A. (Koos), BA Potchef., MA Pret., DLitt Pret. Prof.

Roux, Justus C., MA Potchef., DLitt Stell. Prof.; Chair*

Visser, Marianna W., DLitt Stell. Sr. Lectr.

Other Staff: 3 Lectrs.

Vacant Posts: 1 Lectr.

Afrikaans and Dutch

Tel: (021) 808 2158 Fax: (021) 808 4336

Britz, Etienne C., MA Stell., LittDrs Amst., DLitt Stell. Sr. Lectr.

De Stadler, Leon G., MA Stell., DLitt Stell. Assoc. Prof.

Gouws, Rufus H., MA Stell., DLitt Stell. Assoc. Prof.

Ponelis, Fritz A., BA Potchef., MA S.Af., MA P.Elizabeth, DLitt&Phil S.Af. Prof., Afrikaans Linguistics; Chair*

Spies, Lina, MA Stell., LittDrs Amst., DLitt Pret. Prof., Literature

Viljoen, Louise, MA Stell., DLitt Stell. Sr. Lectr.

Other Staff: 5 Lectrs.

Afrikaans Cultural History

Tel: (021) 808 2422 Fax: (021) 808 4336

Burden, Mathilda, MA Stell., DPhil Stell. Sr. Lectr.

Vacant Posts: 1 Prof.

Agricultural Economics

Tel: (021) 808 4758 Fax: (021) 808 4336

Kleynhans, Theo E., MScAgric Natal, PhD(Agric) Stell. Sr. Lectr.

Laubscher, Johan, MScAgric Stell., PhD(Agric) Stell. Assoc. Prof.

Lombard, Jan P., MScAgric Stell., PhD(Agric) Stell. Sr. Lectr.

Myburgh, André S., MScAgric Stell., PhD Stell. Sr. Lectr.

Vink, Nick, MScAgric Stell., PhD Stell. Prof.; Chair*

Other Staff: 1 Lectr.

Research: agricultural development; agricultural marketing and business; agriculture in the national economy; agricultural production management; agricultural strategic management

Agronomy and Pastures

Tel: (021) 808 4803 Fax: (021) 887 9273

Agenbag, G. André, MScAgric Stell., PhD(Agric) Stell. Prof.; Chair*

Combrink, Nic J. J., MSc(Agric) Pret., PhD(Agric) Stell. Sr. Lectr.

Pieterse, Petrus J., BSc OFS, MScAgric Stell., PhD Stell. Sr. Lectr.

Research: crop production; hydroponics; soil tillage; veld invaders; weed research

Anatomy, see Medicine

Ancient Near Eastern Studies

Tel: (021) 808 3203 Fax: (021) 808 4336

Claassen, Walter T., BTh Stell., MA Stell., DLitt Stell. Prof.

Cook, Johann, BTh Stell., MA Stell., DLitt Stell. Assoc. Prof.

Cornelius, Izak, MA Stell., MTh Stell., DLitt Stell. Sr. Lectr.

Kruger, Paul A., BTh Stell., MA Stell., DLitt Stell. Assoc. Prof.; Chair*

Van der Merwe, Christo H. J., MA Stell., MTh Stell., DLitt Stell. Eric Sampson Prof., Biblical Hebrew; Sr. Lectr.

Animal Sciences

Tel: (021) 808 4749 Fax: (021) 808 4336

Cruywagen, Chrisjan W., MSc(Agric) Pret., DSc(Agric) Pret. Sr. Lectr.

Hayes, James P., MSc(Agric) Pret., DSc(Agric) Pret. Prof.

Hoffmann, Louw C., MScAgric Stell., PhD(Agric) North(S.Af.) Sr. Lectr.

Poggenpoel, Daan G., MScAgric Stell., PhD(Agric) Stell. Assoc. Prof.

Schoeman, S. J. (Fanie), BSc(Agric) Stell., MScAgric OFS, DScAgric OFS Prof.; Chair*

Other Staff: 1 Lectr.

Research: animal breeding; meat sciences; poultry studies; ruminant nutrition

Archaeology

Tel: (021) 808 3472 Fax: (021) 808 4336

Deacon, Hilary J., BSc Cape Town, MA Cape Town, PhD Cape Town Prof.; Chair*

Other Staff: 1 Hon. Res. Fellow

Art, see Fine Arts, and Sch. Art, Div. of (under Didactics)

Biochemistry

Tel: (021) 808 3038 Fax: (021) 808 3022

Bellstedt, Dirk U., PhD Stell. Sr. Lectr.

Hapgood, Janet P., PhD Cape Town Assoc. Prof.

Hofmeyr, Jan-Hendrik S., PhD Stell. Prof.; Chair*

Rohwer, J. M., MSc Stell., PhD Amst. Sr. Lectr.

Swart, Pieter, PhD Stell. Assoc. Prof.

Other Staff: 3 Lectrs.

Botany

Tel: (021) 808 3068 Fax: (021) 808 3607

Botha, Frikkie C., MSc Potchef., PhD Pret. Prof.

Boucher, Charles, BSc Stell., MSc Cape Town, PhD Stell. Sr. Lectr.

Cramer, Mike D., MSc Witw., PhD Cape Town Sr. Lectr.

Smith, Valdon R., BSc Witw., PhD OFS Prof.; Chair*

Watts, Jeff E., MSc Stell., PhD Stell. Sr. Lectr.

Other Staff: 3 Lectrs.; 1 Sr. Researcher

Vacant Posts: 2 Profs.

Research: plant ecology; plant molecular biology; plant physiology and ecophysiology; plant taxonomy, anatomy and chemotaxonomy

Business, Graduate School of

Tel: (021) 918 4111 Fax: (021) 918 4112

Bendix, D. F. Willy, DCom S.Af. Prof.

Brand, A. Martin, BComm Stell., MCom P.Elizabeth, PhD Stell. Sr. Lectr.

Brown, Chris J., BSc(Eng) Pret., DBA Pret. Assoc. Prof.

Denton, J. Mario, MEcon Stell., MBA Stell. Sr. Lectr.

Gevers, Wim R., MSc(Eng) Cape Town, MBA Stell., PhD Stell. Prof.

Hamman, Willie D., BComm Stell., DBA Stell. Prof.

Loubser, Stephanus, MSc Stell., MBL S.Af. Sr. Lectr.

Oosthuizen, Hein, MCom S.Af., DComm Rand Afrikaans Prof.

Smit, Eon v. d. M., DComm Stell. Prof.; Chair*

Smith, Johan d. P., BSc(Eng) Cape Town, BCom S.Af., MBA Stell., PhD Stell. Sr. Lectr.

Vacant Posts: 1 Sr. Lectr.

Business Management

Tel: (021) 808 2026 Fax: (021) 808 2226

De Villiers, Johan U., BEng Stell., MBA Stell., PhD Witw. Prof.

Doppegieter, Jan J., CandEc Rotterdam, MEcon Stell., PhD Stell. Assoc. Prof.

Du Plessis, Piet G., BCom Pret., BCom S.Af., MBA Pret., DComm Stell. Prof.

Du Toit, M. André, MComm Stell., DComm Stell. Prof.

Hugo, M. M. (Ria), BComm Potchef., MComm Rand Afrikaans, PhD Stell. Sr. Lectr.

Lambrechts, Izak J., MBA Stell., DComm Stell. Prof.

Leibold, Marius, MComm Stell., DComm Stell. Prof.; Chair*

Mostert, F. J. (Erik), MComm Stell., DComm Stell. Prof.

O'Neill, R. Charles, BA Stell., MBA Potchef., PhD Rhodes Sr. Lectr.

Terblanché, Nick S., BCom S.Af., BEcon Stell., MTRP Stell., DPhil Stell. Assoc. Prof.

Other Staff: 5 Lectrs.

Research: advanced distribution trade; cost and revenue determining issues; financial management; investment management; management-labour relations

Chemistry

Tel: (021) 808 3360 Fax: (021) 808 4336

Bartel, Eric E., MSc Stell., PhD Stell. Sr. Lectr.

Bredenkamp, Martin W., MSc Stell., DSc Pret. Sr. Lectr.

Burger, Ben V., MSc Stell., DSc Stell. Prof.; Chair*

Cruywagen, Jo J., MSc Stell., DSc Stell. Prof.
Engelbrecht, Willem J., MSc Stell., DSc
Stell. Prof.
Heyns, J. B. Bernard, BSc Stell., BEd Stell., MSc
Natal, PhD Stell. Sr. Lectr.
Meyer, Connie J., MSc Stell., PhD Stell. Sr.
Lectr.
Raubenheimer, MSc Stell., PhD Stell. Prof.
Sanderson, Ron D., BSc Cape Town, PhD
Akron Prof.
Schneider, Dawie F., MSc Stell., DSc Stell. Prof.
Van der Merwe, S. W. J. (Leon), MSc Stell.,
PhD Stell. Sr. Lectr.
Van Reenen, Albert J., MSc Stell., PhD Stell. Sr.
Lectr.
Wessels, Gawie F. S., MSc OFS, DSc OFS Sr.
Lectr.
Other Staff: 5 Lectrs.; 1 Sr. Researcher
Vacant Posts: 1 Prof.

Classics

Tel: (021) 808 3136 Fax: (021) 808 4336
Claassen, Jo-Marié, MA Stell., DLitt Stell. Assoc.
Prof.
Thom, Johann C., BA Stell., MA Pret., PhD
Chic. Prof.; Chair*
Thom, Sjarlene, MA Stell., DLitt Stell. Sr. Lectr.
Zietsman, J. Christoff, MA Pret., DLitt Pret. Sr.
Lectr.
Other Staff: 2 Lectrs.

Computer Science

Tel: (021) 808 4232 Fax: (021) 808 4416
Cloete, Ian, MSc(Eng) Stell., PhD Stell. Assoc.
Prof.
Gouws, Etienne H., BSc(Eng) Cape Town, PhD
Cape Town Sr. Lectr.
Krzesinski, A. E. (Tony), MSc Cape Town, PhD
Camb. Prof.; Chair*
Uys, Johan B., MSc Stell. Sr. Lectr.
Other Staff: 2 Lectrs.

Consumer Studies: Food, Clothing, Housing

Tel: (021) 808 3398 Fax: (021) 808 4336
Knye, A. Erika, MScHomeEc Stell. Sr. Lectr.
Senekal, Marjanne, MSc Stell., PhD Stell. Sr.
Lectr.
Van Wyk, A. S. (Ria), PhD(HomeEc)
Stell. Assoc. Prof.; Chair*
Visser, E. M. (Bessie), PhD Stell. Prof.
Vosloo, M. Charlyn, MSc Stell., PhD(HomeEc)
Stell. Sr. Lectr.
Other Staff: 7 Lectrs.
Research: clothing and textiles (consumer
behaviour, cultural and physical aspects,
experimental research); dietetics; education
(formal education and non-formal adult
education and community development);
foods; housing

Dentistry, see below

Didactics

Afrikaans, Division of

Tel: (021) 808 2266 Fax: (021) 808 4336
Combrink, Louise E., BA OFS, MA Natal, PhD
Stell. Sr. Lectr.
Smuts, Ria, BA Stell., MA Pret., PhD Stell. Sr.
Lectr.
Other Staff: 2 Lectrs.

Didactics, Division of

Tel: (021) 808 2295 Fax: (021) 808 4336
Carl, Arend E., BA Stell., DEd Stell. Prof.;
Chair*
Jordaan, A. S. (Faan), BSc Stell., DEd Stell. Sr.
Lectr.
Kapp, Chris A., DEd Stell. Prof.
Olivier, Alwyn I., BSc Stell., MEd Stell. Sr.
Lectr.
Park, Tommy, BSc Stell., DEd Stell. Prof.
Roux, Cornelia D., BA Potchef., DPhil Stell. Sr.
Lectr.
Schreuder, Danie R., BSc Stell., BSc S.Af., MEd
S.Af., DEd Stell. Assoc. Prof.
Smit, Mike J., BA Stell., DEd Stell. Sr. Lectr.

Other Staff: 2 Lectrs.
Vacant Posts: 1 Prof.; 1 Sr. Lectr.
Research: computer-based education; educational
leadership; educational technology;
environmental education; general curriculum
studies

English, Division of

Tel: (021) 808 2266 Fax: (021) 808 4336
Swartz, Johan J., BA P.Elizabeth, MEd Stell., DEd
Stell. Sr. Lectr.
Other Staff: 1 Lectr.

School Art, Division of

Tel: (021) 808 2419 Fax: (021) 808 4336
1 Lectr.

Drama

Tel: (021) 808 3216 Fax: (021) 808 4336
Hauptfleisch, Temple, BA OFS, DLitt&Phil
S.Af. Prof.; Chair*
Other Staff: 3 Lectrs.; 1 Lectr.†
Vacant Posts: 1 Sr. Lectr.; 1 Lectr.

Dutch, see Afrikaans and Dutch

Economics, see also Transport Econ. and Logistics

Tel: (021) 808 2247 Fax: (021) 808 2409
De Villiers, A. P., MComm Stell., PhD Stell. Sr.
Lectr.
McCarthy, Colin L., MA Stell., DPhil Stell. Prof.
Schoombee, G. Andries, BCom Pret., MComm
Stell., PhD Stell. Assoc. Prof.
Smit, Ben W., DComm Stell. Prof.
Terreblanche, Sampie J., MA Stell., DPhil
Stell. Emer. Prof.
Van der Berg, Servaas, BCom Natal, MCom
Pret., PhD Stell. Prof.; Chair*
Other Staff: 7 Lectrs.
Research: econometric modelling; economic
systems; economic systems and the history
of economic thought (applied to the South
African situation); regional economic
integration; structural economic change (in
the South African economy)

Education Policy Studies

Educational Administration, Division of

Tel: (021) 808 2419 Fax: (021) 808 4336
Prinsloo, Nic P., BSc Potchef., DEd Pret. Prof.;
Chair*
Van Kradenburg, Lukas P., BA Stell., DEd
Stell. Sr. Lectr.
Other Staff: 1 Lectr.
Research: comparative education; decision-
making; human interaction in educational
organisations; personnel management; policy
analysis and development

Philosophy of Education, Division of

Tel: (021) 808 2291 Fax: (021) 808 4336
Steyn, Johann C., BA Stell., DEd Stell. Prof.
Other Staff: 1 Lectr.
Research: contemporary issues; culture and
community; ideology (ideological paradigms
in education); theory (education as a basic
human phenomenon

Educational Psychology and Specialised Education

Educational Psychology, Division of

Tel: (021) 808 2306 Fax: (021) 808 4336
Cilliers, Charl D., BA Stell., DEd Stell. Prof.;
Chair*
Smit, A. Gerrie, BA Stell., DEd Stell. Sr. Lectr.
Other Staff: 2 Lectrs.
Research: developmental psychology; guidance
and counselling; learning; study skills;
thinking skills

Specialised Education, Division of

Tel: (021) 808 2229 Fax: (021) 808 4336
Engelbrecht, Petra, BA Pret., MEd Pret., PhD
Pret. Prof.

Research: at-risk learners; development of teacher
support teams for learners with special
educational needs; emergent literacy and
reading programmes; hearing-impaired
child; training of teachers in inclusive
education

Engineering, Chemical

Tel: (021) 808 4928 Fax: (021) 808 2059
Aldrich, Chris, BEng Stell., MEng Stell.,
PhD(Eng) Stell. Assoc. Prof.
Bradshaw, Steven M., MSc Natal, PhD
Witw. Assoc. Prof.
Cloete, Frikkie L. D., BSc Cape Town, MSc Natal,
PhD(Eng) Stell. Assoc. Prof.
Els, E. Raymond, BSc Pret., MBL S.Af., MEng
Potchef. Sr. Lectr.
Knoetze, J. H. (Hansie), BEng Stell., PhD(Eng)
Stell. Assoc. Prof.
Lorenzen, Leon, BEng Stell., MEng Stell.,
PhD(Eng) Stell. Prof.; Chair*
Nel, Carel, BSc(Eng) Pret. Sr. Lectr.
Nieuwoudt, Izak, MEng Stell., PhD(Eng)
Stell. Sr. Lectr.
Other Staff: 1 Sr. Researcher
Vacant Posts: 1 Sr. Lectr.

Engineering, Civil

Geotechnics, Technology Management and Transport, Division for

Tel: (021) 808 4352 Fax: (021) 808 4361
Bester, Christo J., BSc Stell., MEng Stell., DEng
Pret. Prof.
Cronjé, Wilhelm B., BSc(Eng) Cape Town, MEng
Stell., PhD(Eng) Stell. Assoc. Prof.
De Wet, Marius, BSc(Eng) Pret., MEng Pret.,
PhD Stell. Sr. Lectr.
Engelbrecht, Johan C., BSc Stell., MEng
Stell. Sr. Lectr.
Schumann, Chris A. W., BSc Stell., MEng
Stell. Sr. Lectr.
Van de Ven, Martin F. C., MSc Delft Prof.

Structural Engineering, Division of

Tel: (021) 808 4352 Fax: (021) 808 4361
Bird, Wyndham W., BSc(Eng) Cape Town, MBA
Cape Town, PhD Cape Town Assoc. Prof.
Dunaiski, Peter E., MEng Stell., PhD(Eng)
Stell. Prof.; Chair of Dept.*
Maritz, Gerhard, BScEng Cape Town Sr. Lectr.
Retief, Johan V., BSc(Eng) Pret., MPhil Lond.,
DSc(Eng) Pret. Prof.
Strasheim, J. A. v. Breda, BSc S.Af., BSc(Eng)
Pret., MEng Stell., MBA Stell. Sr. Lectr.
Van Rooyen, Gert C., BSc OFS, BSc(Eng) Pret.,
MEng Stell. Sr. Lectr.

Water Engineering, Division for

Tel: (021) 808 4352 Fax: (021) 808 4361
Görgens, André H. M., BEng Stell., MSc(Eng)
Stell., PhD Witw. Prof.
Malan, Willie M., BSc Stell., BEng Stell.,
MSc(Eng) Pret. Sr. Lectr.
Rooseboom, Albert, BSc Stell., BEng Stell., DHE
Delft, DSc(Eng) Pret. Prof.
Rossouw, Jan, BSc(Eng) Pret., PhD(Eng) Stell.,
DHE Delft Sr. Lectr.
Sinske, Berndt H., MSc(Eng) Natal, PhD(Eng)
Stell. Sr. Lectr.

Engineering, Electrical and Electronic

Computer and Control, Division for

Tel: (021) 808 4478
Bakkes, Piet J., BSc Stell., BEng Stell., MEng Stell.,
PhD Stell. Sr. Lectr.
Blanckenberg, Mike M., BSc Stell., BEng Stell.,
BEng Pret., PhD Stell. Sr. Lectr.
Milne, Garth W., BScEng Natal, MEng Stell., PhD
Stan. Prof.
Schoonwinkel, Arnold, MEng Stell., MBA Cape
Town, PhD Stan. Prof.; Chair*
Steyn, W. Herman, MEng Stell., MSc Sur., PhD
Stell. Assoc. Prof.

Electrical Power Engineering, Division for

Tel: (021) 808 4478 Fax: (021) 808 4981

Enslin, Johan H. R., BEng *Rand Afrikaans*, MEng *Rand Afrikaans*, DEng *Rand Afrikaans* Prof.

Herman, Ron, BSc(Eng) *Cape Town*, MEng *Stell.*, PhD(Eng) *Stell.* Sr. Lectr.

Holtzhausen, J. P. (Koos), BSc *Stell.*, BEng *Stell.*, MSc(Eng) *Witw.* Sr. Lectr.

Kamper, Martin J., BEng *Stell.*, MEng *Stell.*, PhD *Stell.* Sr. Lectr.

Van der Merwe, Frikkie S., BSc *Stell.*, BEng *Stell.*, MSc *Lond.*, PhD(Eng) *Stell.* Prof.

Vermeulen, H. Johan, BEng *Stell.*, MEng *Stell.*, PhD(Eng) *Stell.* Sr. Lectr.

Electromagnetics, Division for

Tel: (021) 808 4478 Fax: (021) 808 4981

Cloete, John H., BSc *Stell.*, BEng *Stell.*, MSc(Eng) *Calif.*, PhD(Eng) *Stell.* Prof.

Davidson, David B., BEng *Pret.*, MEng *Pret.*, PhD(Eng) *Stell.* Prof.

Palmer, Keith D., BEng *Stell.*, MEng *Stell.* Sr. Lectr.

Electronics, Division for

Tel: (021) 808 4478 Fax: (021) 808 4981

De Swardt, Johan B., BEng *Stell.*, MEng *Stell.*, PhD(Eng) *Stell.* Sr. Lectr.

Meyer, Petrie, BEng *Stell.*, MEng *Stell.*, PhD(Eng) *Stell.* Sr. Lectr.

Perold, Willie J., BEng *Stell.*, MEng *Stell.*, PhD(Eng) *Stell.* Prof.

Reader, Howard C., PhD *Camb.*, BScEng Prof.

Van der Walt, P. W., BSc *Stell.*, MEng *Stell.*, PhD(Eng) *Stell.* Prof.

Other Staff: 1 Lectr.

Signal Processing, Division for

Tel: (021) 808 4478 Fax: (021) 808 4981

Du Preez, Johan A., BEng *Stell.*, MEng *Stell.* Sr. Lectr.

Lourens, Johan G., BEng *Stell.*, MEng *Stell.*, PhD(Eng) *Stell.* Sr. Lectr.

Weber, David M., BEng *Stell.*, MEng *Stell.*, PhD *Carnegie-Mellon* Sr. Lectr.

Engineering, Industrial

Tel: (021) 808 4234 Fax: (021) 808 4245

Bekker, J. F. B., MEng *Stell.* Sr. Lectr.

Du Preez, Nick D., PhD(Eng) *Stell.* Prof.; Chair*

Fourie, C. J. (Neels), BEng *Pret.*, MEng *Stell.* Sr. Lectr.

Michau, Mike, BSc *S.Af.*, BSc(Eng) *Pret.*, MEng *Stell.* Sr. Lectr.

Page, Daan C., MEng *Stell.*, MBA *Pret.*, PhD(Eng) *Stell.* Sr. Lectr.

Van Ryneveld, Willie P., PhD *Witw.* Prof.

Von Leipzig, Konrad H., BCom *S.Af.*, MEng *Stell.* Sr. Lectr.

Vacant Posts: 1 Prof.; 1 Lectr.

Engineering, Mechanical

Fluid Mechanics

Tel: (021) 808 4549

Hoppe, K. Gunther, DrEng *T.U.Berlin* Assoc. Prof.

Strachan, Peter J., MBA *Witw.*, PhD *Leeds* Sr. Lectr.

Thiart, Gerrie D., BEng *Stell.*, MSc *Lond.*, PhD *Stell.* Sr. Lectr.

Von Backström, Theo W., MSc(Eng) *Pret.*, PhD(Eng) *Stell.* Prof.; Chair*

Mechanical Design

Tel: (021) 808 4549

Basson, Anton H., MEng *Stell.*, PhD *Penn.State* Prof.

Els, Danie N. J., BEng *Pret.*, MEng *Stell.* Sr. Lectr.

Taylor, Andrew B., BEng *Stell.*, MScEng *Natal*, PhD *Natal* Sr. Lectr.

Mechanics

Tel: (021) 808 4549

Heese, Johan J., BSc *Stell*, MEng *Stell.* Sr. Lectr.

Pienaar, Dirk v. V., MEng *Stell.* Sr. Lectr.

Terblanche, Eugene, BSc *Stell.*, BEng *Stell.* Sr. Lectr.

Theron, Nicolaas J., MEng *Stell.*, PhD *Rensselaer* Prof.

Van der Westhuizen, K., MEng *Stell.* Sr. Lectr.

Thermodynamics

Tel: (021) 808 4549

Dobson, Robert T., BSc(Eng) *Witw.*, MSc(Eng) *Cape Town*, MBL *S.Af.* Sr. Lectr.

Harms, Thomas M., BSc(Eng) *Cape Town*, MSc(Eng) *Birm.*, PhD(Eng) *Stell.* Sr. Lectr.

Kröger, Detlev G., BSc *Stell.*, BEng *Stell.*, SM *M.I.T.*, ScD *M.I.T.* Prof.

Other Staff: 1 Lectr.

English

Tel: (021) 808 2040

Edmunds, D. Paul, BA *Rhodes*, BA *Brist.*, PhD *S'ton.* Sr. Lectr.

Green, Brian K., MA *Cape Town*, MA *Camb.*, PhD *Cape Town* Sr. Lectr.

Hees, Edwin P. H., BA *Witw.*, MA *S.Af.*, DLitt&Phil *S.Af.* Sr. Lectr.

Henderson, Alistair C. L., BA *Natal*, MPhil *Oxf.* Sr. Lectr.

Heyns, Michiel W., BComm *Stell.*, MA *Stell.*, MA *Camb.*, DLitt *Stell.* Prof.; Chair*

Swart, Marieken, BA *Stell.*, BA *S.Af.*, MA *Stell.* Sr. Lectr.

Other Staff: 5 Lectrs.

Entomology and Nematology

Tel: (021) 808 4775 Fax: (021) 808 4336

Geertsema, Henk, MSc *Stell.*, PhD(Agric) *Stell.* Sr. Lectr.

Giliomee, Jan H., BA *S.Af.*, MTRP *Stell.*, MScAgric *Stell.*, PhD *Lond.* Prof.; Chair*

Meyer, A. J. (Bertus), MScAgric *Stell.*, PhD(Agric) *Stell.* Assoc. Prof.

Pringle, Ken L., MScAgric *Stell.*, PhD(Agric) *Stell.* Sr. Lectr.

Research: ecology (insects and agricultural ecosystems); nematology (host-parasite relationships); pathogenicity, taxonomy); pest management; systematics (emphasis on lepidoptera associated with fynbos)

Environmental Studies, see Geog. and Environmental Studies

Fine Arts

Tel: (021) 808 3052 Fax: (021) 808 4336

Arnold, Marion I., BA *Natal*, BAFA *Natal*, MA *S.Af.*, DLitt&Phil *S.Af.* Sr. Lectr.

Honey, C. Victor R. Sr. Lectr.

Kerr, Gregory J., BA *Witw.*, BA *S.Af.*, BA(FineArts) *S.Af.*, PhD *Georgia* Prof.; Chair*

Smuts, Timo, MA(FineArts) *Cape Town*, DPhil *Stell.* Sr. Lectr.

Other Staff: 2 Lectrs.

Food Science

Tel: (021) 808 3578 Fax: (021) 808 3510

Basson, Dawie S., BCom *S.Af.*, MScFoodSci *Stell.* Sr. Lectr.

Britz, Trevor J., MSc(Agric) *Pret.*, DSc(Agric) *Pret.* Prof.; Head*

Other Staff: 1 Lectr.

Research: environmental management (liquid and solid waste management in the food industry); fermented foods; food processing; near infrared spectroscopy (NIR); propionibacterial aspects

Forest Science

Tel: (021) 808 3295 Fax: (021) 808 3603

Bredenkamp, Brian V., MScFor *Stell.*, PhD *Virginia Polytech.* Prof.

Ellis, Freddie, MScAgric *Stell.*, PhD(Agric) *Stell.* Sr. Lectr.

Theron, J. M. (Kobus), MScFor *Stell.*, PhD(For) *Stell.* Sr. Lectr.

Uys, H. J. Eksteen, MScFor *Stell.*, MBA *Stell.*, PhD(For) *Stell.* Sr. Lectr.

Van Wyk, Gerrit, BScFor *Stell.*, PhD *N.Carolina State* Hans Merensky Prof.; Chair*

Vacant Posts: 1 Prof.; 2 Sr. Lectrs.

Research: dryland forestry; nursery practice; soil-related yield problems; special trials; weed control

Genetics

Tel: (021) 808 4101 Fax: (021) 808 4336

Burger, J. T., BScAgric *Stell.*, PhD *Cape Town* Sr. Lectr.

Louw, J. H. (Bill), MScAgric *Stell.*, PhD *Edin.* Sr. Lectr.

Marais, G. Frans, MScAgric *Stell.*, PhD *N.Dakota*, PhD(Agric) *Stell.* Prof.; Chair*

Warnich, Louise, MScAgric (MedSc) *Stell.*, PhD *Stell.* Sr. Lectr.

Other Staff: 2 Lectrs.

Research: cereal breeding and genetic manipulation of wheat; fish breeding; molecular and cytogenetics; quantitative genetics; statistical inference

Biometry, Unit for

Tel: (021) 808 4744 Fax: (021) 808 4336

Randall, John H., MScAgric *Stell.*, MS *Cornell*, PhD(Agric) *Stell.* Sr. Lectr.

Geography and Environmental Studies

Tel: (021) 808 3218 Fax: (021) 808 4336

De Necker, Pieter H., BA *OFS*, MA *Rand Afrikaans*, DPhil *Stell.* Sr. Lectr.

Van der Merwe, Izak J., MA *Stell.*, DPhil *Stell.* Prof.

Van der Merwe, J. H. (Hannes), DPhil *Stell.* Sr. Lectr.

Van Huyssteen, M. Konrad R., BA *Stell.*, BLitt *Oxf.* Sr. Lectr.

Zietsman, H. Larry, MA *W.Wash.*, DPhil *Stell.* Prof.; Chair*

Other Staff: 3 Lectrs.

Geology

Tel: (021) 808 3219 Fax: (021) 808 3129

Hallbauer, Dieter K., MSc *Freiberg Mining Acad.*, DrRerNat *Mün.* Assoc. Prof.

Le Roux, J. P. (Kobus), MSc *Stell.*, PhD *P.Elizabeth* Assoc. Prof.

Rozendaal, Abraham, MSc *Stell.*, PhD *Stell.* Assoc. Prof.; Chair*

Scheepers, Reyno, MSc *Stell.*, PhD *Stell.* Sr. Lectr.

Other Staff: 1 Lectr.

Vacant Posts: 1 Prof.

History

Tel: (021) 808 2177 Fax: (021) 808 4336

Kapp, Pieter H., MA *Stell.*, MA *Reading*, PhD *Stell.* Prof.; Head*

Venter, Chris, BA *Stell.*, MA *S.Af.*, DLitt&Phil *S.Af.* Sr. Lectr.

Other Staff: 2 Lectrs.

Home Economics, see Consumer Studies: Food, Clothing, Housing

Horticultural Science

Tel: (021) 808 4900 Fax: (021) 808 4336

Jacobs, Gerhard, BSc(Agric) *Pret.*, MScAgric *Natal*, PhD *Natal* Prof.

Rabe, Etienne, BScAgric *Stell.*, MSc(Agric) *Pret.*, PhD *Calif.* Prof.; Chair*

Theron, Karen I., MScAgric *Stell.*, PhD(Agric) *Stell.* Assoc. Prof.

Other Staff: 1 Lectr.

Research: growth and development (of desiduous, citrus and indigenous floricultural crops); post-harvest physiology (apples); spacing, tree training and pruning

Human Movement Studies

Tel: (021) 808 4915 Fax: (021) 808 4817

Blaauw, Johannes H., BEd *Stell.*, MPhysEd *Stell.*, PhD(PhysEd) *Stell.* Assoc. Prof.

Bressan, Elizabeth S., MSPhysEd *Carolina*, PhD *Calif.* Sr. Lectr.

Potgieter, Justus R., MA *Stell.*, MA *Alta.*, MEd *Rhodes*, PhD(PhysEd) *Stell.* Prof.; Chair*

Van der Merwe, Floris J. G., MA *Stell.*, MPhysEd *Stell.*, DPhil *Potchef.* Sr. Lectr.

Other Staff: 6 Lectrs.

Research: exercise physiology; kinanthropometry; perceptual motor aspects; sport history; sport psychology

Industrial Psychology

Tel: (021) 808 3012 Fax: (021) 808 4336
Augustyn, Johan C. D., MComm Stell., DComm Stell. Prof.
Calitz, Coen J., BA Stell., MS Purdue Sr. Lectr.
De Villiers, Willem S., MComm Rand Afrikaans, DComm Rand Afrikaans Sr. Lectr.
Du Toit, Jan B., MA Stell., DPhil Stell. Assoc. Prof.
Duvenage, André, MComm Rand Afrikaans, PhD Stell. Sr. Lectr.
Engelbrecht, Amos S., MComm Stell., PhD Stell. Assoc. Prof.
Tromp, Dave, MComm Potchef., DComm Stell. Prof.; Chair*
Van Wyk, A. J. (Kobus), MComm Stell., DComm Stell. Prof.
Other Staff: 4 Lectrs.
Research: ergonomics; human resources management; occupational psychology; organisational behaviour; psychometics

Information Science

Tel: (021) 808 2423 Fax: (021) 808 4336
Van der Walt, Martin S., DPhil Stell. Sr. Lectr.; Chair*
Other Staff: 2 Lectrs.

Journalism

Tel: (021) 808 3488 Fax: (021) 808 3487
Claassen, George N., MA Pret., DLitt&Phil S.Af. Prof.
Research: broadcast journalism; media-ethics; print journalism; science journalism

Law, Mercantile

Tel: (021) 808 3198 Fax: (021) 886 6235
Butler, David W., BComm Stell., LLD Stell. Prof.; Chair*
De Ville, Esmarie M., BComm Stell., LLM Stell. Sr. Lectr.
Dupper, Ockie C., BA Stell., LLB Cape Town, LLM Harv. Sr. Lectr.
Fourie, James S. A., BA Stell., LLB Stell., LLD S.Af. Prof.
Hugo, Charl F., BA Pret., LLB Pret., LLM S.Af. Prof.
Oosthuizen, P. G., BA S.Af., BIur S.Af., LLB Pret., LLM Pret. Sr. Lectr.
Sutherland, Philip J., BComm Stell., LLB Stell., PhD Edin. Sr. Lectr.
Van Wyk, Andreas H., BA Stell., LLB Stell., LLD Ley. Prof.
Other Staff: 2 Lectrs.
Research: banking law; company law; labour law; law of arbitration

Law, Private and Roman

Tel: (021) 808 3183 Fax: (021) 886 6235
De Vos, Wouter L., BA Rand Afrikaans, LLM Rand Afrikaans, LLD Rand Afrikaans Prof.
De Waal, Marius J., BComm Stell., LLM Stell., LLD Stell. Prof.
Du Plessis, Jacques E., BComm Stell., LLM Stell. Sr. Lectr.
Human, C. Sonia, BMil Stell., LLB Stell. Sr. Lectr.
Loubser, Max M., BA Stell., LLB Stell., DPhil Oxf. Prof.
Lubbe, Gerhard F., BA Stell., LLB Stell., LLM Yale Prof.; Chair*
Pienaar, Juanita M., BJuris Potchef., LLM Potchef., LLD Potchef. Prof.
Van der Merwe, Corné G., BA OFS, LLB OFS, BA Oxf., BCL Oxf., LLD S.Af. Prof.
Other Staff: 1 Lectr.

Law, Public

Tel: (021) 808 3684 Fax: (021) 883 9656
De Waal, H. Johann, BComm Stell., LLM Stell. Sr. Lectr.
Du Plessis, Lourens M., BJur&Comm Potchef., LLB Potchef., BPhil Potchef., LLD Potchef. Prof.; Chair*

Erasmus, M. Gerhard, BJuris OFS, LLB OFS, MA Fletcher, LLD Ley. Prof., Human Rights
Rabie, M. André, BA Pret., LLB Pret., LLD S.Af. Prof.
Van der Merwe, Steph E., BJuris P.Elizabeth, LLB S.Af., LLD Cape Town Prof.
Other Staff: 1 Lectr.
Research: administrative law; constitutional law; criminal law; law of criminal procedure; law of evidence

Linguistics, General

Tel: (021) 808 2010 Fax: (021) 808 2009
Aarons, Debra L., BA Witw., PhD Boston Sr. Lectr.
Botha, Rudi P., MA Stell., LittDrs Utrecht, DLitt Utrecht Prof.; Chair*
Kemp, Mary-Ann, BSc(Log) Cape Town, MA Reading Sr. Lectr.
Le Roux, Cecile, MA Stell. Sr. Lectr.
Vacant Posts: 1 Assoc. Prof.; 1 Lectr.

Management, Public and Development

Includes School for Public Management
Tel: (021) 808 2195 Fax: (021) 808 2114
Burger, A. P. Johan, BArch OFS, MPA Stell., PhD Stell. Sr. Lectr.
Cloete, G. S. (Fanie), BJur Potchef., LLB Rand Afrikaans, MA Stell., PhD Stell. Prof.
Müller, J. J. (Kobus), BSc(Agric) Stell., MPA Stell., PhD Stell. Assoc. Prof.
Schwella, Erwin, BA Stell., MPA Stell., PhD Stell. Prof.; Chair*
Uys, Frederik M., BA Stell., MA Pret., PhD Stell. Sr. Lectr.
Van Rooyen, Andries, MAdmin Stell. Sr. Lectr.
Other Staff: 3 Lectrs.
Research: development management; policy analysis; public management

Mathematics, see also Stats. and Actuarial Sci.

Tel: (021) 808 3282 Fax: (021) 808 4336
Buys, Johan D., MSc Stell., DrWisNat Ley. Sr. Lectr.
De Bruyn, G. F. Cilliers, BSc Stell., PhD Camb. Prof.
De Villiers, Johan M., BSc Stell., PhD Camb. G. B. B. Rubbi Prof.
Green, Barry W., MSc Cape Town, PhD Cape Town Assoc. Prof.
Le Riche, Louis R., BSc S.Af., MSc Stell., PhD Stell. Sr. Lectr.
Maritz, Pieter, MSc OFS, DrWisNat Ley. Assoc. Prof.
Muller, M. Arnold, MSc Stell., PhD Edin. Sr. Lectr.
Rohwer, Carl H., MSc Stell., DSc Potchef. Sr. Lectr.
Van der Merwe, A. Brink, BSc Stell., DPhil Texas A.& M. Sr. Lectr.
Van der Walt, Andries P. J., MSc Potchef., DSc Potchef. Prof.; Chair*
Van Rooyen, G. Willie S., MSc OFS, DrScT Delft Sr. Lectr.
Van Wyk, Leon, MSc Stell., PhD Stell. Prof.
Wild, Marcel, PhD Zür. Sr. Lectr.
Other Staff: 4 Lectrs.

Mathematics, Applied

Tel: (021) 808 4215 Fax: (021) 808 4361
De Kock, Hennie C., PhD Stell. Sr. Lectr.
Du Plessis, J. Prieur, MSc Stell., PhD Stell. Prof.; Chair*
Fourie, Philip d. T., MSc Stell., PhD Rand Afrikaans Sr. Lectr.
Gerber, Marius, BSc Stell., ME Cal.Tech., MA Johns H., MSc Cape Town, PhD Cape Town Assoc. Prof.
MacKinnon, John, MSc Stell., MSc Newcastle(UK) Sr. Lectr.
Theron, Willie F. D., BSc Stell., BSc Oxf., MEng Stell. Sr. Lectr.
Van Vuuren, J. H., MSc Stell., DPhil Oxf. Sr. Lectr.
Other Staff: 2 Lectrs.

Medicine, see below

Microbiology, see also Medicine (Med. Microbiol.), below

Tel: (021) 808 3619 Fax: (021) 808 3611
Dicks, Leon M. T., BSc OFS, MSc Stell., PhD Stell. Assoc. Prof.
Loos, Mike A., MScAgric Stell., PhD Cornell Prof.
Pretorius, I. S. (Sakkie), MScAgric OFS, PhD OFS Prof.
Prior, B. Prof.
Rawlings, M. Prof.
Van Zyl, W. H. (Emile), MSc OFS, PhD Prin. Assoc. Prof.
Other Staff: 1 Lectr.

Military Science, see below

Modern Foreign Languages

Tel: (021) 808 2133 Fax: (021) 808 4336
Köppe, Walter G. H., MA Rand Afrikaans, DLitt Stell. Sr. Lectr.
Kussler, H. Rainer, MA Stell., DLitt Stell. Prof.; Chair*
Other Staff: 4 Lectrs.

Music

Tel: (021) 808 2335 Fax: (021) 808 4336
De Villiers, Juliana E. Sr. Lectr.
Grové, Izak J., MMus OFS, DPhil OFS Prof.
Lüdemann, Winfried A., MMus OFS, DPhil Stell. Sr. Lectr.
Pauw, Niel, MMus Stell., MMus P.Elizabeth Sr. Lectr.
Roux, Magdalena, BMus Pret. Sr. Lectr.
Rycroft, Eric B., FTCL Assoc. Prof.
Smit, M., BA Stell., BMus Stell., BA S.Af., MA Stell., DLitt Stell. Sr. Lectr.
Tamassy, Eva M. Sr. Lectr.
Temmingh, Roelof W., BA Stell., MMus Cape Town, DPhil Stell. Assoc. Prof.
Van Heerden, Petrus, BMus OFS Sr. Lectr.
Other Staff: 11 Lectrs.

Nature Conservation

Tel: (021) 808 3308 Fax: (021) 808 3603
Van Hensbergen, H. J. (Bertie), MA Camb., PhD Camb. Sr. Lectr.; Chair*
Other Staff: 1 Lectr.†
Vacant Posts: 1 Prof.
Research: conservation planning and evaluation; environmental effects of forestry and agriculture; quantitative methods in conservation; recreation and ecotourism planning; wildlife management and utilisation

Oenology and Viticulture

Tel: (021) 808 4785 Fax: (021) 808 4336
Archer, Eben, MScAgric Stell., PhD(Agric) Stell. Assoc. Prof.
Goussard, Pieter G., MScAgric Stell., PhD(Agric) Stell. Prof.; Chair*
Lambrechts, Marius G., MScAgric Stell., PhD(Agric) Stell. Sr. Lectr.
Pretorius, I. S. (Sakkie), MScAgric OFS, PhD OFS Prof., Wine Biotechnology
Other Staff: 1 Lectr.
Research: oenology (aroma composition of grapes, wines and brandies; chemical composition of grapes; optimal ripeness; wine evaluation; wine technology); viticulture (biotechnology; canopy management; choice of terrain; enhancing the environment; mechanisation; plant physiology; soil-climate associations; vegetative propagation and grafting)

Old and New Testament

Tel: (021) 808 3626 Fax: (021) 808 3251
Bosman, Hendrik L., BA Pret., DD Pret. Prof.; Chair*
Combrink, H. J. Bernard, BA Pret., BD Pret., ThD Amst. Prof.
Other Staff: 2 Temp. Lectrs.
Research: contextual hermeneutics (interpretation of Old and New Testament in Africa); hermeneutics (reading strategies of Bible

study groups); historical geography (Wadi and Themed); socio-rhetorical interpretation Matthew; theology of the New Testament (reconciliation in Paul and Matthew)

Philosophy

Tel: (021) 808 2418 Fax: (021) 886 4343

Hattingh, Johan P., MA Stell., DPhil Stell. Assoc. Prof.
Van der Merwe, Willie L., BTh Stell., MA Stell., DPhil Stell. Prof.
Van Niekerk, Anton A., BTh Stell., MA Stell., DPhil Stell. Prof.; Chair*
Other Staff: 2 Lectrs.

Physics

Tel: (021) 808 3391 Fax: (021) 808 4336

Cowley, Anthony A., MSc Pret., DSc Pret. Prof.
De Kock, P. Runan, MSc Stell., PhD Stell. Assoc. Prof.
Eggers, Hans, MSc Pret., PhD Arizona Sr. Lectr.
Geyer, Hendrik B., MSc Rand Afrikaans, PhD Stell. Prof.
Hahne, Fritz J. W., MSc Pret., PhD Cape Town, FRSSAf Prof.
Koen, J. W. (Charlie), MSc Potchef., DSc Stell. Assoc. Prof.
Lombaard, J. C. (Cobus), MSc OFS, PhD P.Elizabeth Sr. Lectr.
Richter, Werner A., MSc Kansas, PhD Stell. Sr. Lectr.
Rohwer, Erich G., MSc Zululand, PhD Stell. Sr. Lectr.
Saayman, Rikus, BEd Stell., MSc Stell., PhD Stell. Sr. Lectr.
Scholtz, Frikkie G., MSc Stell., PhD Stell. Assoc. Prof.
Stander, J. Anton, MSc Stell., PhD Stell. Sr. Lectr.
Van der Westhuizen, Pieter, MSc Stell., PhD Stell. Sr. Lectr.
Visser, Kobus, MSc Stell., PhD Stell. Assoc. Prof.
Walters, Piet E., MSc Stell., DSc Stell. Prof.; Chair*
Other Staff: 1 Lectr.

Physiology, Human and Animal

Tel: (021) 808 3146 Fax: (021) 808 3145

Barry, Danie M., BVSc Pret., MScAgric Stell. Sr. Lectr.
Coetzer, Willem A., MScAgric OFS, PhD(Agric) Stell. Prof.; Chair*
Morgenthal, Johan C., BVSc Pret., PhD(Agric) Stell. Prof.
Myburgh, K. M., BSc(Med) Cape Town, PhD Cape Town Sr. Lectr.
Van Niekerk, Francois E., MSc Stell., PhD(Agric) Stell. Sr. Lectr.
Van Rooyen, Jacques, MSc Stell., PhD Stell. Sr. Lectr.
Other Staff: 4 Lectrs.

Plant Pathology

Tel: (021) 808 4798

Crous, Pedro W., BScFor Stell., MScAgric Stell., PhD OFS Prof.
Hattingh, Martin J., MSc Stell., DSc Stell. Prof.
Holz, Gustav, BSc(Agric) OFS, MScAgric Stell., PhD(Agric) Stell. Prof.; Chair*
Other Staff: 1 Lectr.
Research: host-parasite interactions; integrated disease control; mycology; post-harvest pathology (stone and pome fruit and table grapes); small-grain diseases

Political Science

Tel: (021) 808 2414 Fax: (021) 808 4336

Breytenbach, Willie, MA Pret., DLitt&Phil S.Af. Prof.
Du Toit, Pierre van der P., MA Stell., DPhil Stell. Assoc. Prof.
Gouws, Amanda, MA Rand Afrikaans, PhD Ill. Sr. Lectr.
Kotze, Hennie J., MA S.Af., MA(Econ) Manc., DLitt&Phil Rand Afrikaans Prof.; Chair*
Nel, Philip R., MA Stell., DPhil Stell. Prof.
Other Staff: 3 Lectrs.

Research: democratisation and state-building in Africa; international political economy; political behaviour; South African politics

Practical Theology and Missiology

Tel: (021) 808 3577 Fax: (021) 808 3251

Hendriks, J. Jurgens, BTh Stell., MA Stell., DLitt Stell. Sr. Lectr.
Louw, Daniël J., BTh Stell., MA Stell., DPhil Stell., DTh Stell. Prof.; Chair*
Pauw, C. Martin, BA Pret., MTh Stell., DTh Stell. Prof.
Prins, J. M. G. (Riaan), BA Stell., BD Stell., DTh Stell. Sr. Lectr.
Research: church growth and congregational studies (moral leadership for social transformation); homiletics (preaching and social transformation); missiology (urbanisation in Malawi); pastoral care and counselling (cross-cultural counselling within an African context); youth ministry within the context of post modernity

Psychology, see also Educnl. Psychol. and Spec. Educn., and Indust. Psychol.

Tel: (021) 808 3466 Fax: (021) 808 3584

Kruger, Lou-Marie, BA Stell., MSocSc Cape Town, MA Boston, PhD Boston Sr. Lectr.
Kruijsse, Herman W., PhD Ley. Prof.
Meyer, Johan C., MA Stell., DPhil Stell. Sr. Lectr.
Möller, André T., MA Stell., DPhil Stell. Prof.
Spangenberg, Judora J., MA Stell., DPhil Stell. Sr. Lectr.
Van der Westhuÿsen, T. W. Bodley, MA Stell., DPhil Stell. Prof.; Chair*
Wait, Johnny W. van S., MA Stell., DPhil Stell. Sr. Lectr.
Other Staff: 9 Lectrs.
Vacant Posts: 1 Prof.
Research: child psychology; cognitive behaviour therapy; family psychology; social psychology; vocational psychology

Public Management, School for, see Management, Public and Devel.

Religion, see also Old and New Testament, Practical Theol. and Missiol., and Systematic Theol. and Church Hist. and Church Polity

Tel: (021) 808 2117 Fax: (021) 808 2031

Kinghorn, Johann, BA Pret., DTh Stell. Prof.; Chair*
Lategan, Bernard C., MA OFS, ThD Theol.Sch.Kampen Prof.
Other Staff: 1 Lectr.; 1 Temp. Lectr.

Social Work

Tel: (021) 808 2069 Fax: (021) 808 4336

Cronje, Johan I., MASocWork Stell., DPhil Stell. Assoc. Prof.; Chair*
Green, Sulina, MASocWork Stell., DPhil Stell. Assoc. Prof.
Other Staff: 4 Lectrs.

Sociology

Tel: (021) 808 2420 Fax: (021) 808 2143

Bekker, Simon B., BSc Stell., MA Wayne State, PhD Cape Town Prof.
Groenewald, Corné J., MA Stell., DPhil Stell. Prof.; Chair*
Kritzinger, Andrinetta S., MA Stell., DPhil Stell. Sr. Lectr.
Mouton, Johann, BA Rand Afrikaans, DLitt&Phil Rand Afrikaans Prof.
Sharp, John S., BA Cape Town, PhD Camb. Prof., Anthropology
Other Staff: 3 Lectrs.
Research: computer assisted analysis and presentation of social data; the household, family and gender; labour and industrial relations; race relations; social control and deviance

Soil and Agricultural Water Science

Tel: (021) 808 4788 Fax: (021) 808 4336

Lambrechts, Jan J. N., MScAgric Stell. Sr. Lectr.
Saayman, Dawid, MScAgric Stell. Sr. Lectr.
Other Staff: 1 Researcher
Vacant Posts: 1 Prof.
Research: land suitability and soil amelioration (forestry soils, fruit and wine grape, plant nutrition and environmental effects (of the grapevine); soil classification and genesis; soil physics and irrigation science

Statistics and Actuarial Science

Tel: (021) 808 3244 Fax: (021) 808 4336

Claassen, Mark S., BSc Cape Town Prof.
Conradie, Willie J., MComm Stell., PhD Cape Town Assoc. Prof.
Le Roux, Niel J., MSc Stell., MSc Camb., MSc S.Af., PhD S.Af. Assoc. Prof.
Schoeman, Anton, DComm Stell. Prof.; Chair*
Steel, Sarel J., MSc Stell., PhD Stell. Prof.
Van der Merwe, E. (Lize), BSc Stell., MSc P.Elizabeth, PhD P.Elizabeth Sr. Lectr.
Van Deventer, Pieta J. U., BComm Stell., MSc Cape Town, PhD Cape Town Sr. Lectr.
Other Staff: 5 Lectrs.
Research: discriminant analysis and logistic regression diagnostics and applications; distribution theory and estimation theory; Empirical Bayes (EB) methods; graduation of rates of decrement; nonparametrics

Systematic Theology and Church History and Church Polity

Tel: (021) 808 3258 Fax: (021) 808 3251

Coertzen, Pieter, MA Potchef., MTh Stell., DTh Stell. Prof.
Du Toit, Danie A., BTh Stell., MA Stell., ThDr Amst. Prof.; Chair*
Theron, P. F. (Flip), BA Pret., BD Pret., DD Pret. Assoc. Prof.
Research: church history (ecumenical study of church history); church government (study of principles and systems); ethics (anthropology and ethics); systematic theology (Christian doctrine and culture, reformed theology in the (post)modern period)

Town and Regional Planning

Tel: (021) 808 2152 Fax: (021) 808 4336

Claasen, Piet E., BSc Stell., BEng Stell., MTRP Stell., DPhil Stell. Sr. Lectr.
Muller, J. I. (Anneke), BSc Stell., MTRP Stell. Sr. Lectr.
Pienaar, Willem P., MTRP Stell., DPhil Stell. Sr. Lectr.
Welch, Colin T., BArch Witw., BA S.Af. Prof.; Chair*
Research: environmental behavioural studies; housing, squatting, informal settlement questions and urban renewel; planning law, plan implementation and environmental management systems; regional-urban structural/functional analyses; rural-urban migration issues and concomitant urbanisation problems

Transport Economics and Logistics

Tel: (021) 808 2249 Fax: (021) 808 2409

Pienaar, Wessel J., MEcon Stell., MS(Eng) Calif., DCom S.Af. Prof.; Chair*
Other Staff: 3 Lectrs.
Vacant Posts: 1 Sr. Lectr.
Research: benefit-cost analysis; comparative modal studies; transport costs; transport policy; urban, air, maritime, road transport

Viticulture, see Oenol. and Viticulture

Water Science, see Soil and Agric. Water Sci.

Wood Science

Tel: (021) 808 3318 Fax: (021) 808 3603

Gerischer, Gunther F. R., MScFor Stell., PhD Stell. Emer. Prof.

Steinmann, Dieter E., MSc Aston, PhD Stell. Sr. Lectr.

Vermaas, Hennie F., MScFor Stell., DScFor Stell. Prof.; Chair*

Research: durability testing of exterior surface finishes; kaolin (for coating applications); new fibre sources (sisal as alternative to glassfibre); speciality papers; utilisation of commercial lignins

Zoology

Tel: (021) 808 3236 Fax: (021) 808 4336

Cherry, Michael, BSc Cape Town, DPhil Oxf. Sr. Lectr.

Cook, B. A., BSc Cape Town, PhD Cape Town Sr. Lectr.

Mouton, P. le Fras N. M., MSc Stell., PhD Stell. Sr. Lectr.

Nel, Jan A. J., MSc Stell., DSc Pret. Prof.; Chair*

Reinecke, A. J. (Koot), BProc Potchef., MSc Potchef., DSc Potchef. Prof.

Sirgel, Willem F., MSc Stell., PhD Stell. Sr. Lectr.

Van den Heever, Jurie A., MSc Stell., PhD Stell. Sr. Lectr.

Van Wyk, J. H. (Hannes), MSc Stell., PhD Cape Town Assoc. Prof.

Other Staff: 3 Lectrs.

Research: behavioural ecology, reproductive biology and palaeontology, population genetics, molecular systematics and the physiology of sharks; ecology and general biology of vertebrates and invertebrates (notably small mammals, lizards, birds, snails and earthworms); human impacts on biodiversity and the effects of environmental contaminants (such as pesticides and toxic metals)

DENTISTRY

Tel: (021) 931 2251 Fax: (021) 931 2287

Dreyer, Wynand P., BDS Witw., PhD Stell. Prof.; Head; Dir., Teaching Hosp.*

Roelofse, James A., MB ChB Stell., MMed Stell., PhD Stell. Assoc. Prof., Maxillo-Facial Anaesthesiology

Community Dentistry

Tel: (021) 931 2215 Fax: (021) 931 2287

Chitke, Usuf M. E., BChD W.Cape, MDent Witw., MSc Lond. Assoc. Prof.; Chair*

Louw, Attie J., BScMedSci Stell., MChD Pret. Sr. Lectr.

Research: coronal and root caries; dental fluorosis; fluorides in the prevention of dental disease; periodontal disease profiles; water fluoridation

Dental Prosthetics

Tel: (021) 931 2276 Fax: (021) 931 2287

Geerts, Gretha A. V. M., BChD Stell., MChD Stell. Sr. Lectr.; Chair*

Other Staff: 1 Lectr.

Diagnostics and Clinical Teaching, Division of

Tel: (021) 931 2264 Fax: (021) 931 2287

Dreyer, André G., BChD Pret., MScDentSci Stell. Sr. Lectr.; Head*

Other Staff: 2 Lectrs.

Maxillo-Facial and Oral Surgery

Tel: (021) 931 2223 Fax: (021) 931 2287

Grotepass, Frans W., BChD Pret., MChD Pret. Prof.; Chair*

Van der Westhuijzen, Albertus J., BChD Stell., MChD Stell., FDSRCS Sr. Lectr.

Other Staff: 2 Lectrs.

Maxillo-Facial Radiology

Tel: (021) 931 2241 Fax: (021) 931 2287

Nortjé, Christoffel J., BChD Pret., PhD Stell. Prof.; Chair*

Other Staff: 1 Lectr.

Oral Biology

Tel: (021) 931 2251 Fax: (021) 931 2287

Rossouw, Roelof J., BSc OFS, MMedSc OFS, PhD Stell. Sr. Lectr.

Van Rensburg, Ben G. J., BDS Witw., BSc Witw., MScDentSci Stell. Prof.; Chair*

Oral Hygiene, Division of

Tel: (021) 931 2251 Fax: (021) 931 2287

Van der Linde, Elsa S. M., BA S.Af. Lectr.; Head*

Other Staff: 1 Lectr.

Oral Medicine and Periodontics

Tel: (021) 931 2221 Fax: (021) 931 2287

De Waal, J. (Hanlie), BChD Stell., MDent Witw. Sr. Lectr.; Chair*

Other Staff: 1 Lectr.

Vacant Posts: 1 Prof.

Oral Pathology

Tel: (021) 931 2269 Fax: (021) 931 2287

Phillips, Vincent M., BDS Witw., MChD Stell. Prof.; Chair*

Thompson, Ivor O. C., BChD Pret., MChD Stell. Sr. Lectr.

Orthodontics

Tel: (021) 931 2238 Fax: (021) 931 2287

Harris, Angela M. P., BChD Stell., BScMedSci Stell., MChD Stell. Prof.; Chair*

Restorative Dentistry

Tel: (021) 931 2228 Fax: (021) 931 2287

Louw, Nico P., BChD Pret., MSc Lond., PhD Stell. Prof.; Chair*

Peters, Ruth, BChD Pret., MB ChB Stell., PhD Stell. Prof.

Senekal, Petrus J. C., BChD Pret., MScDentSci Stell. Sr. Lectr.

Other Staff: 2 Lectrs.

MEDICINE

Anaesthesiology

Tel: (021) 938 9226 Fax: (021) 931 7810

Coetzee, André R., MB ChB Stell., MMed Stell., MD Stell., PhD Stell., FFARCS Prof.; Chair*

Coetzee, Johan F., BSc Stell., MB ChB Stell., MMed Stell., PhD Stell. Assoc. Prof.

Miller, Don M., MB ChB Cape Town, PhD Stell. Sr. Lectr.

Payne, Keith, MB ChB Cape Town, MD Stell., FFARCS Sr. Lectr.

Van der Merwe, Wynand L., MB ChB Stell., MMed Stell. Assoc. Prof.

Other Staff: 8 Lectrs.

Anatomy and Histology

Tel: (021) 938 9397 Fax: (021) 931 7810

Chase, Carol C., MSc Stell., PhD Stell. Sr. Lectr.

De Wet, Pierre E., MB ChB Stell. Sr. Lectr.

Du Toit, Don F., MB ChB Stell., PhD Stell., DPhil Oxf., FRCSEd Prof.; Chair*

Other Staff: 1 Emer. Prof.; 3 Lectrs.

Cardio-Thoracic Surgery

Tel: (021) 938 9432 Fax: (021) 931 7810

Rossouw, Gawie J., MB ChB Stell., MMed Stell. Assoc. Prof.; Chair*

Community Health

Tel: (021) 938 9232 Fax: (021) 931 7810

Carstens, Sydney E., MB ChB Stell., MMed Stell. Sr. Lectr.

De Villiers, Barney, MB ChB Stell., MMed Stell. Sr. Lectr.; Chair*

Other Staff: 1 Lectr.

Research: epidemiology and biostatistics; health administration and management; occupational and environmental health

Dermatology

Tel: (021) 938 9111 Fax: (021) 931 7810

Cilliers, Jacques, MB ChB Stell., MSc Stell., MMed Stell., MD Stell. Prof.; Chair*

Jordaan, H. F., MB ChB Stell., MMed Stell. Sr. Lectr.

Other Staff: 1 Lectr.

Family Medicine and Primary Care

Tel: (021) 938 9233 Fax: (021) 931 7810

De Villiers, Pierre J. T., BSc Stell., MB ChB Stell., MFamMed Stell. Assoc. Prof.; Chair*

Van Velden, David P., MB ChB Stell., MPraxMed Pret. Sr. Lectr.

Other Staff: 4 Lectrs.

Research: family medicine (clinical medicine as appropriate on the primary care level; health-seeking behaviour of patients; preventative medicine; provider/patient relationship); practice management/ community medicine (cost effective medicine; epidemiology in primary care family practice; health care to the indigent population; provision of primary health care services; surveillance in family practice)

Forensic Medicine

Tel: (021) 938 9325 Fax: (021) 931 7810

Nel, J. P., MB ChB Pret. Emer. Prof.

Schwär, T. G., MB ChB Pret., MD Heidel. Emer. Prof.

Vacant Posts: 1 Prof.

Human Nutrition

Tel: (021) 938 9259 Fax: (021) 931 7810

Herselman, Marietjie G., MNutr Stell., PhD Stell. Sr. Lectr.

Labadarios, Demetre, BSc Sur., MB ChB Stell., PhD Sur. Prof.; Chair*

Other Staff: 4 Lectrs.

Research: acute phase response; hospital and community malnutrition; micronutrient requirements as altered by the acute phase response; nutritional rehabilitation of children with disease; role of nutrition in the pathogenesis of abruptio placentae

Internal Medicine

Tel: (021) 938 9243 Fax: (021) 931 7810

Bardin, Philip G., MB ChB Stell., FCP(SA) Prof.

Blake, R. Sydney, MB ChB Stell., MMed Stell. Sr. Lectr.

Doubell, Anton F., BSc Stell., MB ChB Stell., MMed Stell., PhD Stell., FCP(SA) Prof.

Hough, F. Stephan, BSc Stell., MB ChB Stell., MMed Stell., MD Stell., FCP(SA) Prof.

Joubert, James R., BSc Stell., MB ChB Stell., MMed Stell., MD Stell., FCP(SA) Prof.; Chair*

Van de Wal, Bernard W., MB ChB Pret., MMed Pret. Sr. Lectr.

Weich, Helmuth F. H., BSc Pret., MEng Pret., MB ChB Pret., MMed Stell., MD Stell. Prof.

Medical Microbiology

Tel: (021) 938 4032 Fax: (021) 931 7810

Bouic, P. J. D., BSc Natal, Drd'Etat Lyon Assoc. Prof.

Joubert, Johan J., BSc Pret., MB ChB Pret., LicSc Ghent, MD Pret., DSc Ghent Prof.; Chair*

Medical Physiology and Biochemistry, see also Physiol., Human and Animal, above

Tel: (021) 938 9390 Fax: (021) 931 7810

Beyers, Albert D., BSc Stell., MB ChB Stell., MMed Stell., DPhil Oxf., FCP(SA) Assoc. Prof.

Daniels, Willie M. U., BSc W.Cape, MSc Stell., PhD Stell. Sr. Lectr.

Koeslag, Johan H., MB ChB Cape Town, PhD Cape Town Assoc. Prof.; Head, Med. Physiol.*

Lochner, Amanda, PhD Stell., DSc Stell. Assoc. Prof.

Spruyt-Beyers, L. L., BSc Potchef., BSc Stell., MB ChB Pret., DPhil Oxf. Sr. Lectr.

Van Helden, Paul D., PhD Cape Town Assoc.
Prof.; Head, Med. Biochem.*
Other Staff: 6 Lectrs.; 12 Med. Researchers

Medical Virology

Tel: (021) 938 9347 Fax: (021) 931 7810

Van Rensburg, E. J., MB ChB Pret., MMed
Witw. Assoc. Prof.; Chair*

Neurosurgery

Tel: (021) 938 9265 Fax: (021) 931 7810

Hartzenberg, H. Bennie, MB ChB Cape Town,
MMed Stell. Assoc. Prof.; Chair*
Other Staff: 1 Lectr.

Nuclear Medicine

Tel: (021) 938 4265 Fax: (021) 931 7810

Klopper, Johannes F., MB ChB Pret., MMed
Stell., MD Stell., FCP(SA) Prof.; Chair*
Other Staff: 2 Lectrs.; 1 Med. Researcher

Nursing Science

Tel: (021) 938 9297 Fax: (021) 931 7810

Bester, M. Estelle, MCur Stell., DCur Stell. Sr.
Lectr.
Stellenberg, Ethelwynn L., BCur W.Cape, MCur
Stell. Sr. Lectr.
Welmann, E. Barene, MCur Pret., DLitt&Phil
S.Af. Prof.; Chair*
Other Staff: 4 Lectrs.

Obstetrics and Gynaecology

Tel: (021) 938 9209 Fax: (021) 931 7810

De Jong, Grietjie, BSc Stell., MB ChB Stell.,
MMed Stell., MD Stell. Sr. Lectr.
Duminy, Paul C., MB ChB Cape Town, MMed
Stell., FRCOG Sr. Lectr.
Franken, Danie R., BSc OFS, MMedSc OFS, PhD
OFS Assoc. Prof.
Kruger, Thinus F., MB ChB Pret., MMed Pret.,
MMed Stell., MD Stell., FRCOG Prof.
Odendaal, Hein J., MB ChB Pret., MMed Stell.,
MD Stell., FRCOG Prof.; Chair*
Schaetzing, A. (Bert), MD Berlin, PhD Stell.,
FRCOG Prof.
Steyn, D. W., MB ChB Stell., MMed Stell. Sr.
Lectr.
Theron, Gerhard B., BSc Stell., MB ChB Stell.,
MMed Stell. Sr. Lectr.
Other Staff: 7 Lectrs.; 12 Med. Researchers

Occupational Therapy

Tel: (021) 938 9305 Fax: (021) 931 7810

Beukes, Susan, BOccThy Stell., BScMedSci
Stell. Sr. Lectr.; Chair*
Smit, M. E., BOccTher Pret., BOccThy Stell.,
MBA Stell. Sr. Lectr.
Other Staff: 4 Lectrs.

Ophthalmology

Tel: (021) 938 9380 Fax: (021) 931 7810

Meyer, David, BSc Potchef., MB ChB Stell., MMed
Stell. Assoc. Prof.; Chair*
Other Staff: 4 Lectrs.

Orthopaedics

Tel: (021) 938 9266 Fax: (021) 931 7810

Vlok, Gert J., MB ChB Stell., MMed Stell. Prof.;
Chair*
Other Staff: 7 Lectrs.

Otorhinolaryngology

Tel: (021) 938 9318 Fax: (021) 931 7810

Gregor, R. Theo, MB BCh Witw., PhD Witw.,
FRCSEd, FACS Prof.; Chair*
Muller, A. M. U. (Lida), BA Pret., MS
Wash. Sr. Lectr.
Russel, Ann F., BA S.Af.,
BA(Speech&HearingTherapy) Witw., MS
Wash., PhD Ill. Sr. Lectr.
Swart, Susan M., MSc Cape Town Sr. Lectr.;
Head, Div. of Speech Pathol. and Audiol.
Other Staff: 4 Lectrs.

Paediatrics and Child Health

Tel: (021) 938 9219 Fax: (021) 931 7810

Beyers, Nulda, MB ChB Stell., MSc(Med) Cape
Town, PhD Stell., FCP(SA) Sr. Lectr.
Cotton, Mark F., MB ChB Stell., MMed Stell.,
FCP(SA) Sr. Lectr.
Donald, Peter R., MB ChB Stell., MD Stell.,
FCP(SA) Assoc. Prof.
Gie, Robert P., MB ChB Stell., MMed Stell.,
FCP(SA) Sr. Lectr.
Henning, Philip A., MB ChB Stell., MMed
Stell. Sr. Lectr.
Hesseling, Pieter B., MB ChB Stell., MMed Stell.,
MD Stell. Prof.; Chair*
Kalis, Neale N., MB ChB Stell., MMed Stell.,
FCP(SA) Sr. Lectr.
Kirsten, Gert F., MB ChB Pret., MMed Pret., MD
Stell., FCP(SA) Sr. Lectr.
Kling, Sharon, MB ChB Cape Town,
FCP(SA) Sr. Lectr.
Nel, Etienne D., BSc Stell., MB ChB Stell., MMed
Stell. Sr. Lectr.
Piek, Christo J., BSc Stell., MB ChB Stell., MMed
Stell. Sr. Lectr.
Pieper, Clarissa H., MB ChB OFS, MMed
Stell. Sr. Lectr.
Schaaf, H. Simon, MB ChB Stell., MMed
Stell. Sr. Lectr.
Schoeman, Johan F., MB ChB Stell., MMed Stell.,
MD Stell., FCP(SA) Assoc. Prof.
Smith, Johan, MB ChB Stell., MMed Stell. Sr.
Lectr.
Van Buuren, A. J. (Tony), BSc Stell., MB ChB
Stell., MMed Stell. Sr. Lectr.
Van der Merwe, Peter L., MB ChB Stell., MMed
Stell., MD Stell., FCP(SA) Prof.
Van Schalkwyk, H. J. S. (Esta), BSc Stell., MB
ChB Stell., MMed Stell. Sr. Lectr.
Wessels, Glynn, MB ChB Stell., MMed Stell., MD
Stell. Sr. Lectr.
Other Staff: 1 Lectr.

Pathology, Anatomical

Tel: (021) 938 4041 Fax: (021) 931 7810

Wranz, Peter A. B., MB ChB Witw., MMed Pret.,
MMed Stell., FRCOG Prof.; Chair*
Other Staff: 7 Lectrs.; 4 Lectrs.†

Pathology, Chemical

Tel: (021) 938 4107 Fax: (021) 931 7810

Taljaard, J. J. Frans, MB ChB Pret., MD
Pret. Prof.; Chair*
Other Staff: 2 Lectrs.; 3 Med. Researchers

Pathology, Haematological

Tel: (021) 938 4610 Fax: (021) 931 7810

Mansvelt, Erna P. G., MB ChB Stell., MMed
Stell., MD Stell. Assoc. Prof.; Chair*
Other Staff: 1 Lectr.; 1 Lectr.†

Pharmacology

Tel: (021) 938 9331 Fax: (021) 931 7810

Müller, Gerbus J., BSc Stell., MB ChB Stell.,
MMed Stell., PhD Stell. Sr. Lectr.
Van der Walt, Ben J., PhD Stell. Chief Scientist
Van Jaarsveld, Piet P., PhD Stell. Prof.; Chair*
Other Staff: 3 Lectrs.; 5 Med. Researchers

Physiotherapy

Tel: (021) 938 9300 Fax: (021) 931 7810

Bester, M. M. (Ria), MSc W.Cape Sr. Lectr.
Crous, Linette C., MSc Stell. Sr. Lectr.
Irwin-Carruthers, Sheena H., MSc Cape
Town Sr. Lectr.; Chair*
Uys, Marietta S., BSc Stell. Sr. Lectr.
Other Staff: 7 Lectrs.

Plastic and Reconstructive Surgery

Tel: (021) 938 9432 Fax: (021) 931 7810

Smit, Christie F., MB ChB Stell., MMed
Stell. Head., Craniofacial Unit
Zeeman, Bennie J. v. R., BSc Stell., MB ChB
Stell., MMed Stell. Prof.; Chair*
Other Staff: 1 Lectr.

Psychiatry

Tel: (021) 938 9227 Fax: (021) 931 7810

Emsley, Robin A., MB ChB Cape Town, MMed
Stell., MD Stell. Prof.; Chair*
Gerber, Mickey F., MA Stell., DPhil Stell. Sr.
Lectr.
Middleton, Tessa I., MA Stell., DPhil Stell. Sr.
Lectr.
Pienaar, Willie P., MB ChB Stell., MMed Stell.,
MD Stell. Sr. Lectr.
Other Staff: 14 Lectrs.; 10 Hon. Lectrs.

Radiation Oncology

Tel: (021) 938 9321 Fax: (021) 931 7810

Böhm, E. Lothar J. F., PhD WI Assoc. Prof.
Smit, Ben J., MB ChB Pret., MMed Cape
Town Prof.; Chair*
Wasserman, Herman J., MSc Stell., PhD
P.Elizabeth Chief Specialist; Med. Physicist
Other Staff: 3 Lectrs.; 4 Med. Researchers

Radiology

Tel: (021) 938 9320 Fax: (021) 931 7810

Scher, Alan T., MB ChB Cape Town, FRCP,
FRCS Prof.; Chair*
Other Staff: 4 Lectrs.

Surgery (General)

Tel: (021) 938 9271 Fax: (021) 931 7810

Groenewald, J. H. (Hannes), MB ChB Pret.,
MMed Stell. Sr. Lectr.
Moore, Sam W., MB ChB Cape Town, MD Cape
Town, FRCSEd Prof.
Van Wyk, Johan A. L., MB ChB Pret., MMed
Pret., FACS Prof.; Chair*
Warren, Brian L., MB ChB Cape Town, MMed
Stell., FCS(SA), FRCSEd Assoc. Prof.
Other Staff: 7 Lectrs.

Urology

Tel: (021) 938 9282 Fax: (021) 931 7810

Heyns, Chris F., MB ChB Stell., MMed Stell.,
PhD Stell., FCS(SA) Prof.; Chair*
Other Staff: 3 Lectrs.; 1 Researcher

MILITARY SCIENCE

Tel: (022) 714 1221 Fax: (022) 714 3824

Accountancy and Auditing

Tel: (022) 714 1221 Fax: (022) 714 3824

Rust, Lt.-Col. L., MComm Stell., DCom
Pret. Chair*
Other Staff: 1 Lectr.

Computer Information Systems

Tel: (022) 714 1221 Fax: (022) 714 3824

Rab, Lt.-Col. D. J. (Kobus), BSc OFS, MEd
OFS Sr. Lectr.; Chair*
Other Staff: 3 Lectrs.

Economics

Tel: (022) 714 1221 Fax: (022) 714 3824

De Wet, Major J. Francois, MCom Pret. Sr.
Lectr.; Chair*
Other Staff: 2 Lectrs.

Industrial Psychology

Tel: (022) 714 1221 Fax: (022) 714 3824

Van Dyk, Lt.-Col. Gielie A. J., BA Stell., BTh
Stell. Chair*
Other Staff: 2 Lectrs.

Mathematics

Tel: (022) 714 1221 Fax: (022) 714 3824

Bezuidenhout, Lt.-Col. Jan G. H., MSc
P.Elizabeth Sr. Lectr.; Chair*
Other Staff: 1 Lectr.

Military Geography

Tel: (022) 714 1221 Fax: (022) 714 3824

Snyman, Lt.-Col. Piet M., MA OFS Sr. Lectr.
Tancred, Cdr. Piet, MEd S.Af., MA Stell., DEd
S.Af. Sr. Lectr.; Chair*
Other Staff: 1 Lectr.

Military Strategy

Tel: (022) 714 1221 Fax: (022) 714 3824

Vreÿ, Lt.-Col. F., MMil Stell.   Chair*
Other Staff: 1 Lectr.

Military Studies, Centre for

Tel: (022) 714 1221 Fax: (022) 714 3824

Du Plessis, Col. Louis, MA Stell., DPhil
   Pret.   Dir.*
Other Staff: 4 Researchers

Military Technology

Tel: (022) 714 1221 Fax: (022) 714 3824

Smit, Lt.-Col. J. P. J., BMil Stell.   Chair*
Other Staff: 2 Lectrs.

Nautical Science

Tel: (022) 714 1221 Fax: (022) 714 3824

Reid, Cdr. Dave W.   Sr. Lectr.; Chair*

Physics

Tel: (022) 714 1221 Fax: (022) 714 3824

Bezuidenhout, Lt.-Cdr. J., BSc Potchef., BEd
   Potchef.   Chair*
Other Staff: 2 Lectrs.

Political Science

Tel: (021) 808 4549

Nelson, Lt.-Col. Chris, MA OFS, DPhil
   Stell.   Prof.
Rust, Lt.-Col. Lino, BA Stell., MA Potchef.   Sr.
   Lectr.; Chair*

Public and Development Management

Tel: (022) 714 1221 Fax: (022) 714 3824

Steele, Roy, BA Stell., MPA Stell.   Sr. Lectr.;
   Head*

SPECIAL CENTRES, ETC

**Academic Development Programmes,
Division for (DADP)**

Tel: (021) 808 3717

Swanepoel, John, BSc S.Af., BEd W.Cape, MEd
   Cape Town, PhD Cornell   Dir.*

**Advanced Manufacturing, Unit for
(SENROB)**

Tel: (021) 808 4327 Fax: (021) 808 4245

Fourie, C. J. (Neels), BEng Pret.   Dir.*

Applied Computer Science, Institute for

Tel: (021) 808 4232 Fax: (021) 808 4416

Krzesinski, A. E. (Tony), MSc Cape Town, PhD
   Camb.   Dir.*

Applied Ethics, Centre for

Tel: (021) 808 2418 Fax: (021) 886 4343

Esterhuyse, Willie P., BTh Stell., MA Stell., DPhil
   Stell.   Head, Unit for Bus. Ethics
Hattingh, Johann P., MA Stell., DPhil
   Stell.   Head, Unit for Environmental Ethics
Van Niekerk, Anton A., BTh Stell., MA Stell.,
   DPhil Stell.   Dir.*; Head, Unit for Bioethics

Bible Translation in Africa, Centre for

Tel: (021) 808 (021) 808 3655 Fax: (021)
   808 3480

Van der Merwe, C. H. J., MA Stell., MTh Stell.,
   DLitt Stell.   Dir.*

Bio-Engineering, Bureau for

Tel: (021) 938 9231 Fax: (021) 931 7810

Coetzee, Johan F., BSc Stell., MB ChB Stell.,
   MMed Stell., PhD Stell.   Dir.*

Chemical Engineering, Bureau for

Tel: (021) 808 4423 Fax: (021) 808 2059

Nel, Carel, BSc(Eng) Pret.   Dir.*

**Children's Literature and Media,
Information Centre for**

Tel: (021) 808 2020 Fax: (021) 808 4336

No staff at present

Contextual Hermeneutics, Centre for

Tel: (021) 808 2027 Fax: (021) 808 2031

Kinghorn, Johann, BA Pret., DTh Stell.   Dir.*

**Continuing Theological Training and
Research, Bureau for**

Tel: (021) 808 3382 Fax: (021) 808 3251

Van der Merwe, Michiel A. V., BTh Stell., MA
   Stell., DTh Stell.   Dir.*
Research: congregation and community (to
   guide congregations in community
   development); faith formation and value
   formation (principles and guidelines);
   liturgy and worship (programmes and
   lectionaries for congregations); practical
   ecclesiology (bridging the division between
   the ideal and reality; responsible citizenship
   (challenging faith communities and their
   value systems)

Cost-Effective Medicine, Centre for

Tel: (021) 938 9243 Fax: (021) 933 3591

Joubert, James R., BSc Stell., MB ChB Stell.,
   MMed Stell., MD Stell., FCP(SA)   Dir.*

**Dictionary of the Afrikaans Language,
Bureau for the**

Tel: (021) 887 3113

No staff at present

**Disabled Care and Rehabilitation,
Centre for**

Tel: (021) 938 9528

Hendry, Jenny A., BA Stell., MScMedSci
   Stell.   Head*

Economic Research, Bureau for (BER)

Tel: (021) 887 2810 Fax: (021) 883 9225

Smit, B. W., DComm Stell.   Dir.*

**Educational Development, Centre for
(CEDUS)**

Tel: (021) 808 2272 Fax: (021) 883 2403

No staff at present

**Electrical and Electronic Engineering,
Centre for**

Tel: (021) 808 4304 Fax: (021) 808 4981

Van der Merwe, Frikkie S., BSc Stell., BEng Stell.,
   MSc Lond., PhD Stell.   Dir.*

**Experimental Phonology, Research Unit
for (RUEPUS)**

Tel: (021) 808 2017 Fax: (021) 808 2171

Roux, Justus, MA Potchef., DLitt Stell.   Dir.*

Futures Research, Institute for (IFR)

Tel: (021) 918 4144 Fax: (021) 918 4146

Breytenbach, Willie J., MA Pret., DLitt&Phil
   S.Af.   Prof.; Co-ordinator for Political
   Studies
Doppegieter, Jan J., PhD Stell.   Prof.; Co-
   ordinator for Energy Studies
Roux, André, PhD Stell.   Dir.*
Van Vuuren, Ester L., BA Stell.   Information
   and Process Manager
Research: future prospects; scenario planning and
   strategic support services for management;
   systems thinking

Geographical Analysis, Centre for

Tel: (021) 808 3103 Fax: (021) 808 2405

Van der Merwe, J. H., MA Stell., DPhil
   Stell.   Dir.*
Research: resource studies; urban studies

Higher and Adult Education, Centre for

Tel: (021) 808 2278 Fax: (021) 808 2270

Kapp, Chris A., BA P.Elizabeth, BA S.Af., DEd Stell.
Research: consultation, mentoring and facilitation
   of processes (transformation, strategic
   planning); instructional and course design;
   instructional and training methods for the
   achievement of effective learning; leadership
   development and training; staff development

Industrial Engineering, Institute for

Tel: (021) 808 4244 Fax: (021) 808 4245

Du Preez, Nick D., PhD Stell.   Dir.*

Industrial Mathematics, Bureau for

Tel: (021) 808 4222 Fax: (021) 808 3778

Du Plessis, J. Prieur, MSc Stell., PhD Stell.   Dir.*

Interdisciplinary Studies, Centre for

Tel: (021) 808 2393 Fax: (021) 808 2023

Mouton, Johann, BA Rand Afrikaans, DLitt&Phil
   Rand Afrikaans   Prof.; Dir.*

**International and Comparative Politics,
Centre for**

Tel: (021) 808 2107 Fax: (021) 808 4336

Kotzé, Hennie J., BA Stell., MA S.Af., MA(Econ)
   Manc., DLitt&PhilRand Afrikaans   Dir.*
Research: comparative research of the political
   challenges facing South Africa; expertise in
   global political and economic trends and
   their implications for Southern Africa

International Business, Centre for

Tel: (021) 808 2216, 913 1837 Fax: (021)
   808 2226, 913 1837

Leibold, Marius, MComm Stell., DComm
   Stell.   Dir.*

**Mathematics and Science Teaching,
Institute for (IMSTUS)**

Tel: (021) 808 3483 Fax: (021) 808 3000

Smit, J. H. (Kosie), MSc Stell., DrWisNat
   Ley.   Dir.*

**Mathematics Education, Research Unit
for (RUMEUS)**

Tel: (021) 808 2286 Fax: (021) 808 2498

Human, Piet G., BSc Stell., MEd Pret., DEd
   Stell.   Dir.*
Research: curriculum studies

**Molecular and Cellular Biology, US/
MNR Centre for**

Tel: (021) 938 9401 Fax: (021) 931 7810

Van Helden, Paul D., PhD Cape Town   Assoc.
   Prof.; Dir.*

**Oral and Dental Research Institute
(ODRI)**

Tel: (021) 931 2246 Fax: (021) 931 2287

Grobler, Sias R., BSc OFS, PhD Stell.   Assoc.
   Prof.
Van der Bijl, Pieter, BSc Cape Town, BChD Stell.,
   BScMedSci Stell., PhD Cape Town   Assoc. Prof.;
   Dir.*

Polymer Science, Institute for

Tel: (021) 808 3172 Fax: (021) 808 4967

Sanderson, Ron D., BSc Cape Town, PhD
   Akron   Dir.*
Van Reenen, Albert J., MSc Stell., PhD Stell.   Sr.
   Lectr.

**Sport and Movement Studies, Institute
for**

Tel: (021) 808 4716 Fax: (021) 808 4817

Malan, Jan H., BCom S.Af., MPhysEd Stell.,
   PhD(HumanMovementSt) Stell.   Dir.*

Structural Engineering, Institute for

Tel: (021) 808 4442 Fax: (021)808 4361

Retief, Johan V., DSc(Eng) Pret.   Dir.*

**Theatre and Performance Studies,
Centre for**

Tel: (021) 808 3216 Fax: (021) 808 3086

Hauptfleisch, Temple, BA OFS, DLitt&Phil
   S.Af.   Dir.*

Theoretical Physics, Institute for

Tel: (021) 808 3658 Fax: (021) 808 4336

Geyer, Hendrik B., MSc Rand Afrikaans, PhD
   Stell.   Prof.; Dir.*

Hahne, Fritz J. W., MSc Pret., PhD Cape Town, FRSSAf   Prof.

Scholtz, Frikkie G., MSc Stell., PhD Stell.   Assoc. Prof.

Thermodynamics and Mechanics, Institute for

Tel: (021) 808 4259 Fax: (021) 808 4958

Kroöger, Detlev G., BSc Stell., BEng Stell., SM M.I.T., ScD M.I.T.   Dir.*

US/MRC Perinatal Mortality Research Unit

Tel: (021) 938 9209 Fax: (021) 931 6595

Odendaal, Hein J., MB ChB Pret., MMed Stell., MD Stell., FRCOG   Dir.*

Wine Biotechnology, Institute for

Tel: (021) 808 4730 Fax: (021) 808 3771

Pretorius, I. S. (Sakkie), MScAgric OFS, PhD OFS   Dir.*

Research: cloning and transformation of wine yeasts; gene regulation and protein secretion in wine yeasts; selection and breeding of brandy yeasts with an enhanced ability for ester formation; selection and breeding of grape cultivar-specific yeast for the production of fruity wine

CONTACT OFFICERS

Academic affairs. Registrar: Kritzinger, Prof. Serf, MSc Stell., MSc Birm., PhD Birm.

Accommodation. Deputy Registrar (Courses): Aspeling, Johan A., MComm Stell.

Admissions (first degree). Deputy Registrar (Courses): Aspeling, Johan A., MComm Stell.

Admissions (higher degree). Deputy Registrar (Courses): Aspeling, Johan A., MComm Stell.

Adult/continuing education. Director, Division of University Education: Botha, Jan, MA Stell., DTh Stell.

Alumni. Senior Director, Marketing and Communication: Visagie, J. J. (Kobus)

Archives. Deputy Registrar (Courses): Aspeling, Johan A., MComm Stell.

Careers. Director, Centre for Student Counselling: Jacobs, C. D., BA Pret., DEd Pret., PhD Pret.

Computing services. Senior Director, Information Technology: Meij, Prof. J. T. (Kobus), MBA Stell., PhD Stell.

Conferences/corporate hospitality. Senior Director, Marketing and Communication: Visagie, J. J. (Kobus)

Credit transfer. Registrar: Kritzinger, Prof. Serf, MSc Stell., MSc Birm., PhD Birm.

Development/fund-raising. Director, US Foundation: Uys, D. Sunley, BA Stell., MBA Stell.

Estates and buildings/works and services. Chief Director, Services and Finance: Basson, Nico J., BComm Stell.

Examinations. Head, Examinations: De Beer, Johan B., BA Stell., BPubAdmin Stell.

Finance. Director, Finance: Lombard, H. A. J. (Manie), BAcc Stell., BComm Stell., BCompt S.Af.

General enquiries. Registrar: Kritzinger, Prof. Serf, MSc Stell., MSc Birm., PhD Birm.

Health services. Malan, Francois B., MB ChB Stell.

International office. Head, International Office: Kotzé, Robert J., BTh Stell., MA Stell.

Language training for international students. Head, International Office: Kotzé, Robert J., BTh Stell., MA Stell.

Library (chief librarian). Senior Director, Library Services: Viljoen, Prof. J. Hennie, BBibl Potchef., MBA Potchef., DBibl OFS

Personnel/human resources. Chief Director, Personnel: Van Wyk, Prof. A. J. (Kobus), MComm Stell., DComm Stell.

Public relations, information and marketing. Senior Director, Marketing and Communication: Visagie, J. J. (Kobus)

Publications. Senior Director, Marketing and Communication: Visagie, J. J. (Kobus)

Purchasing. Director, Commercial Services: Agenbach, Willem A., BComm Stell.

Quality assurance and accreditation. Registrar: Kritzinger, Prof. Serf, MSc Stell., MSc Birm., PhD Birm.

Research. Senior Director, Research: Groenewald, Johann P., MA Stell., DPhil Stell.

Safety. Head, Campus Security: ......

Scholarships, awards, loans (postgraduate). Senior Director, Research: Groenewald, Johann P., MA Stell., DPhil Stell.

Scholarships, awards, loans (undergraduate). Head, Bursaries and Loans: De Beer, Samuel, BA Stell.

Schools liaison. Head, New Students: Van den Heever, P. Leon, BA Stell., BEd Stell.

Security. Head, Campus Security: ......

Sport and recreation. Director, Sports Bureau: Potgieter, J. J. J. (Belius), BA Stell., MHumanMovementSt Stell.

Staff development and training. Director, Staff and Organisation Development: De Jager, Louis C., MComm Stell., DComm *Rand Afrikaans*

Student union. Chief Director, Student Affairs: Du Plessis, Piet G., BCom Pret., BCom S.Af., MBA Pret., DComm Stell.

Student welfare/counselling. Director, Centre for Student Counselling: Jacobs, C. D., BA Pret., DEd Pret., PhD Pret.

Students from other countries. Head, International Office: Kotzé, Robert J., BTh Stell., MA Stell.

Students with disabilities. Chief Director, Services and Finance: Basson, Nico J., BComm Stell.

[Information supplied by the institution as at 15 June 1998, and edited by the ACU]

UNIVERSITY OF TRANSKEI

Postal Address: Private Bag X1, UNITRA, Eastern Cape, South Africa
Telephone: (0471) 302 2111 **Fax**: (0471) 26820 **E-mail**: postmaster@getafix.utr.ac.za
WWW: http://www.utr.ac.za **E-mail formula**: name@getafix.utr.ac.za

PRINCIPAL AND VICE-CHANCELLOR*—Moleah, Prof. Alfred T., BA Lincoln(Pa.), MA C.C.N.Y., PhD N.Y.

REGISTRAR‡—Mqeke, Prof. Richman B., BJuris Fort Hare, LLB Fort Hare, LLM Rhodes, LLD Fort Hare

UNIVERSITY OF VENDA

Founded 1981

Member of the Association of Commonwealth Universities

Postal Address: Private Bag X5050, Thohoyandou, 0950 South Africa
Telephone: (0159) 824757 **Fax**: (0159) 824741, 824742, 824749 **E-mail**: prd@caddy.univen.ac.za
WWW: http://www.univen.ac.za

CHANCELLOR—Ramaphosa, Cyril M., BProc *S.Af.*
VICE-CHANCELLOR AND PRINCIPAL*—Nkondo, Prof. Gessler M., BA *S.Af.*, MA *S.Af.*, MA *Leeds*
DEPUTY VICE-CHANCELLOR AND VICE-PRINCIPAL—Vera, V. N., BA *Lincoln(Pa.)*, MA *Georgetown*, PhD *Union Inst.(Ohio)*
REGISTRAR (ACADEMIC)—Matidza, J. N., BA *S.Af.*, BEd *S.Af.*, MA *S.Af.*

GENERAL INFORMATION

History. Originally established as Venda Branch of the University of the North in 1981, the university gained autonomy in November of that year. It is located in Thohoyandou in the far north-eastern corner of Northern Province.

Admission to first degree courses (see also South African Introduction). Matriculation certificate or certificate of exemption. An entrance test or completion of special courses in certain disciplines may be required. International applicants: certificates or diplomas equivalent to matriculation requirements in candidate's country of origin are generally accepted.

First Degrees (see also South African Directory to Subjects of Study). (* = also available with honours). BA*, BA(Agric), BA(CrimJus)*, BA(Ed), BA(Ed)(Agric), BA(Law), BA(Mus)*, BA(SW), BAdmin*, BCom*, BCur*, BCur(PraxExt), BEcon*, BEnvSc*, BESc, BIur, BProc, BSc*, BSc(Agric)*, BSc(EnvM), BTh, BURP.
Most courses are full-time and normally last 3 years, plus 1 additional year for honours. BA(Ed), BA(Ed)(Agric), BA(SW), BCur(PraxExt), BSc(EnvM), BESc, BProc, BURP: 4 years.

Higher Degrees (see also South African Directory to Subjects of Study). BEd, LLB, LLM, MA, MA(Admin), MA(CrimJus), MA(Mus), MA(SW), MCom, MCurationis, MEcon, MEd, MSc, MSc(Agric), PhD, DAdmin, DEcon, DEd, LLD.
BEd, LLB: 2 years; master's degrees: 1 year full-time; doctorates: 3 years full-time.

Libraries. 80,000 volumes; 900 periodicals subscribed to.

Fees (1998, annual). Undergraduate: R4490 (arts); R4650 (education); R5430 (natural sciences, social sciences); R3710 (all honours degrees, first year), R1870 (further years). Postgraduate: R4220 (master' degrees, first year), R2100 (further years); R5040 (PhD, first year), R2540 (further years); R4530 (other doctorates, first year), R2260 (further years).

Academic Awards. Twelve awards ranging in value from R500 to R5000.

Academic Year (1999). Four terms: 11 January–31 March; 13 April–18 June; 13 July–3 September; 14 September–3 December.

Income (March 1997–February 1998). Total, R67,000,000.

Statistics. Staff: 510 (246 academic, 264 administrative). Students: 6111 (2971 men, 3140 women); international 11 (4 men, 7 women).

FACULTIES/SCHOOLS

Agriculture, Rural Development and Forestry, School of
Dean: Makinde, Prof. M. O., DVM *Ib.*, PhD *Ib.*
Secretary: Ratshitanga, L. N.

Business, Economics and Administrative Sciences, School of
Dean: Nkomo, J. C., BSc *CNAA*, MSc *Sur.*, PhD *Lond.*
Secretary: Cibi, T. G.

Education, School of
Dean: Bayona, Prof. E. L. M., MA(Ed) *S'ton.*, BEd PhD
Secretary: Mutele, T. C.

Environmental Sciences, School of
Dean: Omara-Ojungu, Prof. P. H., BSc *Mak.*, MSc *Wat.*, PhD *Wat.*
Secretary: Budeli, S.

Health Sciences, School of
Dean: Mahoko, Prof. N. S., BA *S.Af.*, MSc(Nursing) *Witw.*
Secretary: Mukhuba, M. W. P.

Human Sciences, School of
Dean: Netshiombo, K. F., BA(SW) *Fort Hare*, MA *Fort Hare*, PhD *S.Af.Med.*
Secretary: Siphorogo, P. J.

Law, School of
Dean: Mawila, P. R., BProc *S.Af.*, LLB *S.Af.*
Secretary: Lewis, M. A.

Mathematics and Natural Sciences, School of
Dean: Djolov, Prof. G. D., BSc *Sofia*, MSc *Sofia*, PhD *St.Petersburg*
Secretary: Nengwenani, M. R.

ACADEMIC UNITS

Accounting and Auditing
Vacant Posts: 1 Prof.; 2 Sr. Lectrs.

African Languages

Afrikaans
Olivier, E. M., MA *Rhodes* Sr. Lectr.
Olivier, S. P., MA *Stell.*, LittDrs *Utrecht*, DLitt *Potchef.* Prof.; Head*

Northern Sotho
Lekganyane, D. N., BA *North(S.Af.)*, BA *Pret.*, MA *Pret.* Head*
Vacant Posts: 1 Prof.

Tshivenda
Khuba, E. A., BA *North(S.Af.)*, MA *North(S.Af.)*, PhD *S.Af.* Prof.
Muloiwa, T. W., BA *S.Af.* Assoc. Prof.
Musehane, N. M., BA *S.Af.*, BA *Venda*, MA *Stell.*, PhD *Stell.* Sr. Lectr.; Head*
Phaswana, E. N., BA *Venda*, BEd *Venda*, MA *Stell.*, MPhil *Cape Town* Sr. Lectr.

Tsonga
Malungana, S. J., BA *S.Af.*, MA *Rand Afrikaans*, DLitt&Phil *Rand Afrikaans* Sr. Lectr.; Head*

Agricultural Economics and Extension
Hartman, S. L., BSc(Agric) *Pret.* Lectr.; Head*

Animal Physiology and Health
Makinde, M. O., DVM *Ib.*, PhD *Ib.* Prof.

Animal Science
Bezuidenhout, B. J., MSc(Agric) *Pret.* Prof.; Head*
Makinde, M. O., DVM *Ib.*, PhD *Ib.* Prof.
Menne, P. F., MSc(Agric) *Pret.* Sr. Lectr.
Nesamvuni, A. E., BSc *Natal*, BSc *Fort Hare*, MSc *Fort Hare*, PhD *Oklahoma State* Sr. Lectr.

Anthropology
Buijs, G. C. V., BA *Natal*, MA *St And.*, PhD *Cape Town* Prof.; Head*
Hanisch, E. O. M., MA *Pret.* Sr. Lectr.

Biochemistry and Microbiology
Du Toit, P. J., MSc *Pret.*, PhD *Rand Afrikaans* Prof.; Head*

Biology
Van der Waal, B. C. W., BSc *Pret.*, PhD *Rand Afrikaans* Prof.; Head*

Botany
Mabogo, D. E. N., BSc *North(S.Af.)*, MSc *Pret.* Sr. Lectr.
Tshivhandekano, R. T., BSc *Venda*, MSc *Cape Town* Lectr.; Head*
Weisser, P. J., MEd *Chile*, PhD *Vienna* Prof.

Business Management
Jacobs, J. H., MCom *Potchef.* Assoc. Prof.; Head*

Chemistry
du Toit, P. J., BSc *Rand Afrikaans*, MSc *Rand Afrikaans*, PhD *Rand Afrikaans* Prof.
Mashimbye, M. J., BSc *Fort Hare*, MSc *Rhodes*, PhD *Natal* Sr. Lectr.
Molepo, M. J., MSc *Hanover*, PhD *Hanover* Sr. Lectr.
van Ree, T., DSc *Pret.* Prof.; Head*
Vijayan, R. P., BSc *Kerala*, MSc *Saug.*, PhD *Saug.* Assoc. Prof.

Contextual Theology and Religion
Leeuw, T., MA *Col.*, PhD *Col.* Sr. Lectr.
Moila, M. P., BTh *S.Af.*, MA *Chic.*, MTh *Luth.Sch.Theol.*, *Chicago*, DTh *Luth.Sch.Theol.*, *Chicago* Prof.; Head*
Moremi, M. M., BTh *North(S.Af.)*, MTh *Northwestern Lutheran* Sr. Lectr.
van der Westhuizen, J. D. N., BA *Pret.*, BD *Pret.* Sr. Lectr.

Criminal Adjectival and Clinical Legal Studies
Maake, S. J., BIur *North(S.Af.)*, LLB *North(S.Af.)*, LLM *Georgetown* Sr. Lectr.
Mawila, P. R., BProc *S.Af.*, LLB *S.Af.* Sr. Lectr.; Head*
Moodley, K., BA *Natal*, LLB *Natal* Sr. Lectr.

Criminal Justice
de Bruyn, J. G., MA *Pret.* Sr. Lectr.
Mukwevho, J. P., BA *S.Af.* Lectr.; Head*

Curriculum Studies and Teacher Education

Mwenesongole, M. W., BA(Educn) Zambia, MA Col., MEd Col., EdD Col. Assoc. Prof.
Ntsandeni, R. F., BA North(S.Af.), MEd Venda Lectr.; Head*
Shrivastava, S. C., BSc Raj., MSc Alld., MEd Raj., MEd Karn., MA Jodh. Sr. Lectr.
Vacant Posts: 2 Profs.

Development Administration, see Public Admin. and Devel. Admin.

Earth Sciences

Mitchev, S. A., BSc Sofia, MSc Sofia, PhD Moscow Sr. Lectr.
Ngirane-Katashaya, G., BSc Nair., MSc Lond., PhD Lond., FRMetS Assoc. Prof.; Head*
Van Biljon, W. J., BSc Pret., MSc Pret., PhD Witw. Visiting Prof.
Vacant Posts: 1 Sr. Lectr.

Ecology and Resource Management

Omara-Ojungu, P. H., BSc Mak., MSc Wat., PhD Wat. Prof.; Head*
Vacant Posts: 1 Prof.; 1 Sr. Lectr.

Economics

Gyeke, A. B., BSc Ghana, MA Virginia, PhD Ohio State Prof.
Mashele, S. H., BA Addis Ababa, MA Inst.Soc.Stud.(The Hague) Sr. Lectr.
Nkomo, J. C., BSc CNAA, MSc Sur., PhD Lond. Assoc. Prof.
Sikhitha, K. M., BA Venda, MA Ohio Sr. Lectr.; Head*
Vacant Posts: 1 Prof.

Education, History and Comparative

Ravhudzulo, M. A., BA North(S.Af.), BEd North(S.Af.), MEd North(S.Af.) Sr. Lectr.; Head*

Education, Mathematics and Science

Seepe, P. S., BScEd Bophut., MSc Witw., PhD Bophut. Assoc. Prof.

Education, Psychology of

Muofhe, L., BA North(S.Af.), BEd North(S.Af.), MEd Witw. Sr. Lectr.
Ngobeli, D. T., BA(SW) North(S.Af.), BA S.Af., BEd S.Af. Lectr.; Head*

Education, Sociology

Flynn, M. T., BSc Lond., MEd Manc., DEd S.Af. Prof.; Head*
Vacant Posts: 1 Sr. Lectr.

English

Forson, B., MA Ghana, PhD Calif. Prof.
Lo Liyong, T., BA Howard, MFA Iowa Prof.
Ramogale, M. M., MA Nott., PhD Nott., BA Prof.; Head*
Yesufu, A. R., BA Nigeria, MA Ib., PhD Indiana Assoc. Prof.

Geography

Musyoki, A., BEd Nair., MA Ohio, PhD Howard Prof., Human Geography; Head*

Saidi, T. A., BSc Malawi, MSc St And., PhD St And.
Vacant Posts: 1 Sr. Lectr.; 2 Lectrs.

History

Hendricks, J. P., BA W.Cape, MA Mich., PhD Mich. Assoc. Prof.
Lukhaimane, E. K., BA S.Af., BA North(S.Af.), MA North(S.Af.) Prof.; Head*
Malunga, W. F., BA North(S.Af.), BA S.Af., MA S.Af. Sr. Lectr.

Horticultural Sciences

Mchau, G. R. A., MSc Pomona, PhD Calif., BSc Head*

Industrial Psychology

No staff at present

Jurisprudence, Legal History and Comparative Law

Kirk-Cohen, A., LLM Gron. Sr. Lectr.; Head*
Makhambeni, S. K. S., BA S.Af., LLB S.Af. Sr. Lectr.

Law, Mercantile

Matlala, D. M., BProc North(S.Af.), LLB Witw., LLM Cape Town, LLM Harv. Sr. Lectr.
Mushasha, M. J., BJuris North(S.Af.), LLB North(S.Af.) Sr. Lectr.; Head*

Law, Private

Parmanand, S. K., BA S.Af., BIuris Durban-W., LLB Durban-W., LLM Penn., PhD Natal Prof.; Head*

Law, Public and International

Choma, H. J., BIur North(S.Af.), LLM Witw. Sr. Lectr.
Haupt, A. J., BA Pret., LLB S.Af. Sr. Lectr.
Kirk-Cohen, A., LLM Gron. Sr. Lectr.; Head*
Mbodla, M., BA(Law) Venda, LLB Witw. Sr. Lectr.

Mathematics, see also Educn., Maths. and Sci.

Kirunda, E. F., PhD Moscow Prof.; Head*

Microbiology, see Biochem. and Microbiol.

Music

Lalendle, L. L. T., BPed Fort Hare, MA(MusEd) Iowa Sr. Lectr.; Head*
Twerefoo, G. O., MSc(Mus) Ill., MEd(Mus) Ill. Assoc. Prof.

Nursing Science

Khusi, P. D., MCur Fort Hare Sr. Lectr.
Rautenbach, C. T., DCur P.Elizabeth Prof.; Head*
Vacant Posts: 1 Assoc. Prof.

Pasture Science

No staff at present

Philosophy

Ramose, M. B., BA S.Af., MSc Lond., PhD Leuven Prof.; Head*

Physics

Djolov, G. D., BSc Sofia, MSc Sofia, PhD St.Petersburg Prof.
Gohil, A. M., BSc Gujar., MSc Saur. Assoc. Prof.; Head*
Matamba, I. P., BSc North(S.Af.), BSc S.Af., MSc Oregon Sr. Lectr.
Sankaran, V., MSc Annam., PhD Annam. Sr. Lectr.
Sikakana, I. Q., MSc Miami(Fla.), PhD Witw. Sr. Lectr.

Political Studies

Kiguwa, S. N. W., BA E.Af., MA Mak., PhD A.Bello Sr. Lectr.; Head*

Psychology, see also Educn., Psychol. of; and Indust. Psychol.

Fourie, A. P., BA Pret., BEd Stell., BA Stell. Sr. Lectr.
Netshiombo, K. F., BA(SW) Fort Hare, MA Fort Hare, PhD S.Af.Med. Sr. Lectr.
Sodi, T. B., BA North(S.Af.), MA(ClinPsych) Witw. Lectr.; Head*

Public Administration and Development Administration

Burger, T. G., MA Rand Afrikaans Assoc. Prof.
Khwashaba, M. P., BAdmin Venda, MAdmin S.Af. Sr. Lectr.
Rickert, D. J. C., MAdmin Pret., PhD Venda Prof.; Head*

Social Work

Thabede, D. G., BA(SW) Zululand, MSW Ohio State Sr. Lectr.; Head*
Vacant Posts: 1 Prof.

Sociology, see also Educn., Sociol.

Gaigher, M. J., BA OFS, MA OFS, DPhil OFS Sr. Lectr.
Mashau, E. M., BSocSc Rhodes, MA Venda Head*

Statistics

Szubarga, A., PhD Lublin Prof.; Head*
Varbanova, M., PhD Bud., MSc Assoc. Prof.

Theology, see Contextual Theol. and Religion

Urban and Regional Planning

Kiamba, J. C., BA Nair., MA Nair., PhD Nott. Assoc. Prof.; Head*

Zoology

Fouche, P. S. O., BSc OFS, BSc Venda Lectr.; Head*
Gaigher, I. G., MSc Pret., PhD Rand Afrikaans Prof.
van der Waal, B. C. W., BSc Pret., PhD Rand Afrikaans Prof.

CONTACT OFFICERS

General enquiries. Director, Public Relations and Development: Kharidzha, Rufus N., BA(SW) North(S.Af.)

[Information supplied by the institution as at 17 July 1998, and edited by the ACU]

VISTA UNIVERSITY

Founded 1982

Postal Address: Private Bag X634, Pretoria, 0001 South Africa
Telephone: (012) 322 8967 **Fax**: (012) 320 0528 **Cables**: VISTA UNIVERSITY **WWW**: http://www.vista.ac.za
E-mail formula: user-id@campus-code.vista.ac.za

VICE-CHANCELLOR*—Africa, Prof. H. P., BA *Natal*, MA *Leeds*, PhD *Tor.*
DEPUTY VICE-CHANCELLOR (ADMINISTRATION)‡—Keto, Prof. C. T., BA *S.Af.*, MA *American(D.C.)*, PhD *Georgetown*

UNIVERSITY OF THE WESTERN CAPE

Member of the Association of Commonwealth Universities

Postal Address: Private Bag X17, Bellville, Western Cape, 7535 South Africa
Telephone: (021) 959 2111, 959 2102 **Fax**: (021) 951 3126 **E-mail**: JSmith@adfin.uwc.ac.za **Cables**: UNIBELL
Telex: 526661

RECTOR AND VICE-CHANCELLOR*—Abrahams, Prof. Cecil A., BA *S.Af.*, MA *New Br.*, PhD
Alta.
VICE-RECTOR—Redlinghuis, Prof. Aubrey C., MA *W.Cape*, DPhil *W.Cape*
VICE-RECTOR—Van De Rheede, Prof. Ikey, MA *W.Cape*, DLitt
EXECUTIVE ASSISTANT TO THE RECTOR—Van Gensen, Alwyn, MA *W.Cape*
REGISTRAR (ACADEMIC)—Smith, Julian F., DLitt

GENERAL INFORMATION

History. The university was founded in 1959 as a constituent college of the University of South Africa. In June 1983 it achieved university status and was renamed the University of the Western Cape (UWC). The university is situated in the northern suburb of the Cape Peninsula.

Admission to first degree courses (see also South African Introduction). Matriculation certificate or certificate of exemption issued by Joint Matriculation Board.

First Degrees (* = also available with honours) († = honours only). BA*, BA(HE)* (human ecology), BA(Law), BA(Mus)*, BA(PhysEd), BA(SW)*, BAdmin*, BBibl*, BBibl(Ed), BChD, BCom*, BCom(Ed), BCur*, BD, BEcon†, BMus, BPharm, BSanOr (oral hygiene), BSc*, BSc(Ed), BTh, LLB.
    Most courses normally last 3 years, with an additional year for honours. BA(HE), BA(SW), BBibl, BBibl(Ed), BCom(Ed), BCur, BPharm, BSc (in dietetics, occupational therapy, physiotherapy), BSc(Ed), BTh, LLB: 4 years. BChD: 5 years.

Higher Degrees. BEd, LLM, MA, MA(HE), MA(SW), MAdmin, MBibl, MChD, MCom, MCur, MEcon, MEd, MPharm, MPsych, MSc, MScD, MTh, MPhil, PhD, DAdmin, DBibl, DCom, DCur, DEcon, DEd, DLitt, DPharm, DPhil, DSc, DTh, LLD.
    Applicants for admission to master's degrees must normally hold an appropriate first degree. Doctorates: master's degree. Most higher degrees normally last 2 years. BEd: 1 year. MA, MA(HE), MA(SW), MAdmin, MCom, MEcon, MEd, MPharm, MPhil, MSc (certain subjects), MTh: 1–2 years.

Language of Instruction. English and Afrikaans.

Libraries. 249,241 volumes; 1438 periodicals.

Fees. Undergraduate. South African Development Community students: US$2060 (commerce, education, law, human sciences, theory); US$2250 (community health services, natural sciences, pharmacy). International students: US$2450 (commerce, education, law, human sciences, theory); US$2690 (community health services, natural sciences, pharmacy).

Academic Awards (1997). Ten awards ranging in value from R10,000 to 100,000.

Academic Year (1998). Two semesters: 22 February–2 July; 26 July–26 November.

Income (1997). Total, R315,739,656.

Statistics. Staff: 1364 (428 academic, 936 non-academic). Students: 11,211 (4833 men, 6378 women).

FACULTIES/SCHOOLS

Arts
Tel: (021) 959 2235, 959 2667 Fax: (021) 959 3636
Dean: Temu, Prof. Arnold J., MA *Oregon*, PhD *Alta.*
Secretary: Thorne, Melony

Community and Health Sciences
Tel: (021) 959 2746, 959 2631 Fax: (021) 959 2755
Dean: Pretorius, Prof. Tyrone B., MA *W.Cape*, DPhil *W.Cape*
Secretary: Coenraad, Ursula

Dentistry
Tel: (021) 328116 Fax: (021) 325050
Dean: Hobdell, Prof. Martin H., BDS *Lond.*, MA *Trinity(Dub.)*, PhD *Lond.*
Secretary: Voight, Esme

Economic and Management Sciences
Tel: (021) 959 2257 Fax: (021) 959 3219
Dean: Kritzinger, Prof. André, MCom *Stell.*
Secretary: Sterris, Bernita

Education
Tel: (021) 959 2276 Fax: (021) 959 2647
Dean: Herman, Prof. Harold D., BSc *S.Af.*, MEd *S.Af.*, DEd *W.Cape*
Secretary: Renecke, Shantal

Law
Tel: (021) 959 2176 Fax: (021) 959 2960
Dean: du Toit, Prof. Darcy, BA *Cape Town*, LLB *Cape Town*, LLD *Ley.*
Secretary: Lottering, Sylvia

Religion and Theology
Tel: (021) 959 2206, 959 2436 Fax: (021) 959 3355
Dean: Cloete, Prof. Walter T. W., BTh *Stell.*, MA *Stell.*, DLitt *Stell.*
Secretary: Cyster, Yvonne

Science
Tel: (021) 959 2762, 959 2255 Fax: (021) 959 2266
Acting Dean: Slammert, Lionel C., MSc *Cape Town*, PhD*Boston*
Secretary: Moodley, Pri

ACADEMIC UNITS

Accounting
Tel: (021) 959 3256 Fax: (021) 959 2578
Albertyn, Dawid S., MCom *Pret.*, MBL *S.Af.* Prof.; Chair*
Elliot, Graham J., BCom *Cape Town*, MCom *Stell.* Assoc. Prof.
Mpuisang, M., BCom *Botswana*, MSc *Stir.*
Van Staden, Chris J., MCom *Stell.* Prof.

Afrikaans and Nederlands
Tel: (021) 959 2113 Fax: (021) 959 2376
Coetzee, Abraham J., MA *Witw.*, PhD *Witw.* Prof.
Conradie, Pieter J. J., MA *Cape Town*, DLitt *W.Cape* Sr. Lectr.
February, Vernon A., BA *Cape Town*, CandLit *Ley.*, DrsLitt&Phil *Ley.* Extraordinary Prof.

Hendriks, Frank S., MA *W.Cape*, DLitt
W.Cape Sr. Lectr.
Van Zyl, Wium J., MA *Stell.*, DrsLitt *Utrecht*,
DLitt *Stell.* Assoc. Prof.; Chair*

Anatomy

Tel: (021) 959 2331 Fax: (021) 959 2338

Heyns, Marise, BSc *Stell.*, MSc *Stell.*, PhD
Stell. Sr. Lectr.
Leonard, Cecil J., BEd *S.Af.*, MSc *W.Cape*, PhD
Cape Town Prof.; Chair*
Smith, Jan H. T., BMedSc *OFS*, MMedSc
OFS Sr. Lectr.
Research: computer-assisted learning in anatomy;
effects of anabolic steroids on
spermatogenesis in the Wistar rat; mollusca
(nudibranchiata: reproductive systems);
teratology (chick embryos, cranial
malformations)

Anthropology/Sociology

Tel: (021) 959 2336 Fax: (021) 959 3401

Ellis, James H. P., BA *W.Cape*, MA *N.Carolina*,
PhD *N.Carolina* Sr. Lectr.
Humphreys, Anthony J., MA *Cape Town*, PhD
Cape Town Sr. Lectr.
Lever, Jeffrey T., BA *Witw.*, BA *Stell.*, MA *Birm.*,
DLitt&Phil *S.Af.* Sr. Lectr.; Chair*
McAllister, Patrick A., PhD *Cape Town* Prof.
Oloyede, Olojide, BSc *Lond.*, MPhil *Essex*, PhD
Uppsala
Prah, Kwesi K., Drs *Amst.*, PhD *Amst.* Prof.

Arabic

Tel: (021) 959 2168 Fax: (021) 959 2376

Ahmed, Mukhtar, BA *Medina*, MA *Rand Afrikaans*
Haron, Muhammed, BA *Durban-W.*, BA *S.Af.*,
MA *Cape Town*, DrsSemSt *V.U.Amst.* Sr.
Lectr.; Chair*
Research: Arabic language and South African
Islam

Biblical Studies and Languages

Tel: (021) 959 2181 Fax: (021) 959 2376

Arendse, Roger A., BA *Cape Town*, MTh *Western
Theol.Sem.* Sr. Lectr.
Cloete, Gerhard D., ThD *Theol.Sch.Kampen* Prof.
Cloete, Walter T. W., BTh *Stell.*, MA *Stell.*, DLitt
Stell. Prof.
Daniels, Jan, BA *W.Cape*, MA *Stell.*, DLitt
Stell. Sr. Lectr.; Chair*
Els, Pieter J. J. S., MA *Stell.*, DTh *Stell.*, DLitt
Stell., PhD *Yale* Prof.
Pretorius, Nicolaas F., MA *Stell.*, MTh *Stell.*,
DLitt *Stell.* Prof.

Biochemistry

Tel: (021) 959 2215 Fax: (021) 959 2266

Channing, Alan, PhD *Natal* Prof.
Hendricks, Denver, PhD *Cape Town* Sr. Lectr.
Rees, David, MA *Oxf.*, DPhil *Oxf.* Prof.; Chair*
Research: oesophageal cancer (studies at
molecular level); plant biotechnology
(disease resistance and crop improvement);
protein structure and function

Botany

Tel: (021) 959 2301 Fax: (021) 959 2266

Aalbers, Johannes, MSc *Stell.* Sr. Lectr.
Keats, Derek W., PhD *Nfld.* Assoc. Prof.
Raitt, Lincoln M., PhD *Stell.* Sr. Lectr.; Chair*

Chemistry

Tel: (021) 959 2262 Fax: (021) 959 3055

Crouch, Andrew M., PhD *C'dia.* Prof.; Chair*
Green, Ivan R., PhD *Cape Town* Prof.
Key, David L., PhD *Lond.* Sr. Lectr.
Linkov, Vladimer, PhD *Stell.* Prof.
Mabusela, Tozamile W., BSc *Fort Hare*, MSc
Rhodes, PhD *Cape Town* Sr. Lectr.
Mapolie, Selwyn F., PhD *Cape Town* Sr. Lectr.

Christian Studies

Tel: (021) 959 2229 Fax: (021) 959 3355

Adonis, Johannes C., BTh *V.U.Amst.*, ThD
V.U.Amst. Prof.; Chair*
Conradie, Ernst M., BA *Stell.*, DTh *Stell.* Sr.
Lectr.

Petersen, Robin M., MA *Cape Town*, PhD
Chic. Sr. Lectr.
Smit, Dirk J., MA *Stell.*, DTh *Stell.* Prof.

Christianity and Society

Tel: (021) 959 2201 Fax: (021) 959 3355

Ackermann, Denise M., MA *Stell.*, DTh
S.Af. Prof.
Boesak, Willem A., MTh *W.Cape*, ThDrs
V.U.Amst., PhD *Cape Town* Prof.
Botman, Russel, BA *W.Cape*, LicTh *W.Cape*, MTh
W.Cape, DTh *W.Cape* Sr. Lectr.; Chair*

Computer Science

Tel: (021) 959 3010 Fax: (021) 959 3055

Norman, Michael J., BSc *W.Cape*, MSc *Cape
Town* Sr. Lectr.
Postma, Stefan W., MSc *Rand Afrikaans*, PhD
S.Af. Prof.; Chair*
Smith, Gideon D., BSc *Pret.*, BSc *S.Af.*, MCom
Cape Town Sr. Lectr.
Vahed, Anwar, BSc *W.Cape*, MSc *Edin.* Sr.
Lectr.
Research: computationally complete program
languages; computer science education;
neural networks; software engineering and
persistant programming languages

Dentistry

Faculty appointments

Tel: (021) 328116 Fax: (021) 325050

Miles, Lionel P., BDS *Rand Afrikaans*,
FDSRCS Prof.†
Shear, Mervin, BDS *Witw.*, MDS *Witw.*,
DSc(Dent) *Witw.*, Hon. LLD *Witw.*, FRCPath,
FRSSAf Prof.†

Dentistry, Community

Tel: (021) 328116 Fax: (021) 323250

Camara, Cecily J., BA *W.Cape*, BEd *W.Cape*, MSc
Newcastle(NSW) Sr. Lectr.
Moola, Mohamed H., BDS *Bom.*, MSc
Lond. Prof.
Mybrugh, Niel G., BChD *Rand Afrikaans*, MChD
W.Cape Sr. Lectr.; Chair*
Yasin-Harnekar, Soreya, BChD *W.Cape*,
MScDent *W.Cape* Sr. Lectr.

Dentistry, Conservative

Tel: (021) 328116 Fax: (021) 325050

Osman, Yusuf I., BChD *W.Cape*, MChD
W.Cape Sr. Specialist; Chair*
Rahbeeni, Riyaaz, BChD *W.Cape* Sr. Lectr.

Dentistry, Prosthetic

Tel: (021) 328116 Fax: (021) 325050

Owen, Peter, BDS *Lond.*, MScDent *W.Cape*,
MChD *W.Cape* Prof.; Chair*
Wilson, Viviene, BChD *W.Cape*, MChD
W.Cape Sr. Lectr.

Didactics

Tel: (021) 959 2442 Fax: (021) 959 2647

Desai, Zubaida K., MA *Lond.* Sr. Lectr.
Gray, Brian V., BSc *Natal*, BEd *Natal*, MEd
W.Cape Sr. Lectr.
Jantjes, Edith M., MA *W.Cape*, PhD
Northwestern Assoc. Prof.; Sr. Lectr.
Julie, Cyril M., MSc *W.Cape*, PhD *Ill.* Prof.
Meerkotter, Dirk A., BA *Pret.*, DEd *Rand
Afrikaans* Prof.; Chair*
Smith, Juliana M., BCom *W.Cape*, BEd *W.Cape*,
MA *Lanc.* Sr. Lectr.

Dietetics Division

Tel: (021) 959 2457, 959 2237, 959 2232
Fax: (021) 959 3686

Mars, Maria, BScDietetics *Stell.* Sr. Lectr.
Wentzel, Edelweiss, MSc *Potchef.* Sr. Lectr.;
Chair*

Earth Sciences

Tel: (021) 959 2223 Fax: (021) 959 3422

Van Bever Donker, Johannes M., Drs *Ley.*, PhD
Cape Town Prof.; Chair*

Economics

Tel: (021) 959 2579 Fax: (021) 959 3201

Adams, Ismail, BCom *S.Af.*, MA *W.Mich.*, MPA
Harv. Sr. Lectr.; Chair*
Huda, Syed N., BA *Dhaka*, MA *Philippines*, PhD
Philippines Sr. Lectr.
Loots, Lieb J., BCom *Rand Afrikaans* Prof.
Van Zyl Wolfaard, Gideon, MCom *Stell.* Sr.
Lectr.

Education, Comparative

Tel: (021) 959 2282 Fax: (021) 959 2647

Herman, Harold D., BSc *S.Af.*, MEd *S.Af.*, DEd
W.Cape Prof.
Sayed, Yusuf M., BA *S.Af.*, MEd *Witw.*, PhD
Brist. Sr. Lectr.; Chair*
Research: impact of information technology in
higher education in South Africa;
investigating postgraduate supervision at
University of the Western Cape; policy
development in South Africa (1994 to
present); policy implementation in South
Africa; school governance and management

Education, Philosophy of

Tel: (021) 959 2450 Fax: (021) 959 2647

Bak, Nelleke, BA(Ed) *Pret.*, BA *Natal*, MA *Cape
Town* Sr. Lectr.
Kallaway, Peter, BA *Rhodes*, BEd *Lond.*, MA
Lond. Prof.; Chair*
Morrow, Wally E., BA *Witw.*, BA *S.Af.*, PhD
Lond. Prof.

Educational Psychology

Tel: (021) 959 2282 Fax: (021) 959 2647

Engelbrecht, J. Levi, BA *W.Cape*, BEd *W.Cape*,
MEd *N.Carolina*, MEd(SpecEd) *W.Cape* Sr.
Lectr.; Chair*
Gouws, Andre, BEd *Stell.*, MA *Stell.*, DEd
W.Cape Prof.
Lazarus, Sandy, BA *S.Af.*, MA *Cape Town*, PhD
Cape Town Assoc. Prof.

English

Tel: (021) 959 2964 Fax: (021) 959 2202

Arendse, Andrew T., BA *W.Cape*, MA *Ball* Sr.
Lectr.
Bunn, David N., BA *Rhodes*, MA *Northwestern*,
PhD *Northwestern* Prof.
Hunter, Eva S., BA *S.Af.*, MA *Cape Town*, PhD
Cape Town Assoc. Prof.
Martin, Julia P., MA *Cape Town* Sr. Lectr.
Nas, Loes, PhD *DrsLit* Sr. Lectr.
Omotoso, Bankole A., BA *Ib.*, PhD *Edin.* Prof.
Parr, Anthony N., BA *York(UK)*, MPhil *York(UK)*,
PhD *Tor.* Assoc. Prof.; Chair*
Taylor, Coleen J., BA *Cape Town*, MA *Cape
Town* Sr. Lectr.
Will, Ruth G., BA *Cape Town*, MA *Cant.* Sr.
Lectr.
Woodward, Wendy V., BA *Rhodes*, MA *Temple*,
PhD *Cape Town* Assoc. Prof.
Research: applied linguistics; early modern travel
writing; feminist theory and criticism and
African women's writing; media studies;
South African literary and cultural studies

English 105

Tel: (021) 959 2964 Fax: (021) 959 2202

No staff at present

French

Tel: (021) 959 2368 Fax: (021) 959 2376

Alant, Jaco, BLC MA PhD Sr. Lectr.
De Meyer, Bernard A., MA *Antwerp* Lectr.;
Chair*

Gender Studies

Tel: (021) 959 2812 Fax: (021) 951 1766

Primo, Natasha, BA *W.Cape*, MRP
Mass. Programme Co-ordinator*

Geography and Environmental Studies

Tel: (021) 959 2259, 959 2421 Fax: (021)
959 3422

Boelhouwers, J. C., MSc *Natal*, PhD *W.Cape* Sr.
Lectr.

McPherson, Elsworth A., MA *W.Cape*, MSc
Edin. Project Manager
Myburgh, David W., MA *Stell.*, PhD *Cape
Town* Assoc. Prof.; Chair*
Taylor, Vincent, BA *Stell.*, MA *Stell.*, DPhil
Stell. Sr. Lectr.
Van Zyl, Jacobus A., MA *Stell.*, DPhil
Stell. Prof.

German

Tel: (021) 959 2404, 959 2368 Fax: (021)
959 2376

Flegg, Anelika B., MA *Stell.* Chair*
Menck, Klaus, BEd *Natal*, MA *Natal*, DLitt
W.Cape Sr. Lectr.
Research: foreign language teaching materials
development; German for special purposes;
translation and interpreting; youth literature

History

Tel: (021) 959 2225, 959 3600 Fax: (021)
959 3598

Abdullah, L., BA *A.Bello*, MA *Ib.*, PhD *Tor.*
Legassick, Martin C., MA *Oxf.*, PhD
Calif. Prof.; Chair*
Minkley, Gary A., BA *Cape Town*, PhD *Cape
Town* Sr. Lectr.
Newton-King, Susan-Jane, BA *Cape Town*, MA
Lond., PhD *Lond.* Sr. Lectr.
Scher, David M., MA *S.Af.*, DPhil *S.Af.* Sr.
Lectr.
Temu, Arnold J., MA *Oregon*, PhD *Alta.* Prof.
Witz, L., BA *Natal*, MA *Witw.*
Research: family, household and slavery in Dutch
South Africa; group area removals in Cape
Town; local history of the Northern Cape
(Upington and Gordonia district); popular
memory (identity, space and place,
production of history, urban history); youth
culture and rebellion in Sierra Leone
1945–98

Human Ecology

Tel: (021) 959 2760 Fax: (021) 959 3686

Cairncross, Anita S., BA *W.Cape*, MPhil
W.Cape Co-ordinator; Lectr.
Cornelissen, Judith J., BA *W.Cape*, MEd
W.Cape Lectr.; Chair*
Daniels, Priscilla S., BA *W.Cape*, BEd *W.Cape*,
MSc *Cornell* Sr. Lectr.
Research: academic development (factors
influencing learners and learning factors
influencing women researchers); AIDS and
HIV (experiences, social and economic
influences, women); community
development (empowering, income
generation through development of
programmes)

Human Movement Studies

Tel: (021) 959 2350 Fax: (021) 959 3688

Burrel, E., BA *Stell.*, MA *Stell.*
Travill, Andre L., BA *Rhodes*, MA *San Diego* Sr.
Lectr.; Chair*

Industrial Psychology

Tel: (021) 959 3184 Fax: (021) 959 3184

Abrahams, Fatima, BEcon *W.Cape*, MEcon
W.Cape Sr. Lectr.; Chair*
Mlonzi, Ezra N., BAdmin *Fort Hare*, BA
P.Elizabeth, MSc *Pace*, MA *Cape Town* Sr. Lectr.
Steyn, Daniel M., BA *Pret.*, MA *Pret.*, PhD
Rhodes Assoc. Prof.

Latin

Tel: (021) 959 2505, 959 2289, 959 2117
Fax: (021) 959 2376

Van Zyl Smit, Elizabeth, MA *Stell.*, DLitt
Stell. Sr. Lectr.; Chair*

Law, Mercantile

Tel: (021) 959 2169 Fax: (021) 959 2960

Du Toit, Darcy, BA *Cape Town*, LLB *Cape Town*,
LLD *Ley.* Prof.
Hamman, D., BA(Law) *Stell.*, LLB *Stell.*, LLM
Cape Town, LLD *Cape Town*
Kotze, Fauree, BA *Stell.*, LLB *Stell.*, LLM
Stell. Sr. Lectr; Chair*

Malherbe, Ethel D., BA *Stell.*, LLB *Stell.* Sr.
Lectr.

Law, Private

Tel: (021) 959 3314, 959 3316 Fax: (021)
959 2960

De Villiers, Francois A., BComm *Potchef.*, LLB
Potchef., LLD *Leuven* Prof.
Martin, Bernard S. C., BA *Natal*, LLB *Natal* Sr.
Lectr.
Sarkin, Jeremy J., BA *Natal*, LLB *Natal*, LLM
Harv. Assoc. Prof.; Sr. Lectr.
Sulaiman, Mubarak A., BA *W.Cape*, LLB *W.Cape*,
LLM *Miami*, DrsIuris *Ley.* Sr. Lectr.
Van Huyssteen, Louis F., BA *Stell.*, LLB *Stell.*,
DrsIuris *Ley.*, LLD *Cape Town* Prof.; Chair*
Research: comparative African customary law;
contract (comparative, constitution,
enforceability, international, socialisation);
law of persons and property (current
issues); legal education; unjustified
enrichment

Law, Public and Adjective

Tel: (021) 959 3299 Fax: (021) 959 2960

De Ville, Jacobus R., BComm *Potchef.*, LLD
Stell. Prof.
De Vos, Pierre F., BComm *Stell.*, LLB *Stell.*, LLM
Stell., LLM *Col.* Sr. Lectr.
Fernandez, Lovell D., BA *W.Cape*, MCJ *N.Y.*,
PhD *Witw.* Prof.
Fredericks, Izak N. A., BA(PubAdmin) *Witw.*,
LLM *Harv.* Sr. Lectr.
Philippe, X., Drd'Etat *Aix-Marseilles III* Visiting
Prof.
Rugege, S., LLB *Mak.*, LLM *Yale*, DPhil
Oxf. Assoc. Prof.
Visser, A. J., BA *Stell.*, LLB *Stell.*, LLM *Stell.*, LLM
Col. Sr. Lectr.
Werle, G., DrJur *Heidel.*, DrJurHabil
Heidel. Visiting Prof.

Law, Public International and
Comparative

Tel: (021) 959 2176 Fax: (021) 959 2960

Moosa, Najma, BA(Law) *W.Cape*, LLB *W.Cape*,
LLM *W.Cape* Sr. Lectr.
Smit, Phillipus C., LLM *Stell.*, LLD *OFS*, DPhil
Stell. Prof.; Chair*

Library and Information Sciences

Tel: (021) 959 2137, 959 3623 Fax: (021)
959 3659

Fredericks, George H., BA *S.Af.*, MBibl *W.Cape*,
DBibl *W.Cape* Sr. Lectr.
Makhubela, Patricia L., BBibl *Zululand*, MLib
Wales Sr. Lectr.
Nzotta, Briggs C., BA *Nigeria*, MA *Lough.*, PhD
Lough. Prof.; Chair*
September, Peter E., BA *W.Cape*, BBibl *W.Cape*,
MA *W.Cape*, MLS *N.Carolina* Sr. Lectr.
Research: education publishing in South Africa;
information literacy in academic institutions;
information services for disadvantaged
communities; librarianship, children's and
youth literature teaching

Linguistics

Tel: (021) 959 2978 Fax: (021) 050 2376

Gough, David H., BA *Rhodes*, PhD *Rhodes* Prof.;
Chair*
Research: academic literacy; language and
gender; language in education;
multilingualism; varieties of English

Management

Tel: (021) 959 2595 Fax: (021) 959 2578

De Vries, Linda E. R., BCom *W.Cape*, MBA
Stell. Sr. Lectr.
Hirschsohn, P., BBusSc *Cape Town*, BCom *S.Af.*,
MSc *Oxf.* Sr. Lectr.
Kritzinger, André, MCom *Stell.* Prof.
May, Christopher J., BCom *W.Cape*, MBA
Stell. Sr. Lectr.; Chair*
Mentoor, Etienne R., MCom *W.Cape* Sr. Lectr.
Visser, Dirk J., BCom *Stell.*, BCom *S.Af.*, MCom
W.Cape Sr. Lectr.

Research: entrepreneurship development;
industrial democracy and industrial relations;
marketing globalisation issues with respect
to South African firms; purchasing strategies
for universities; transformational leadership
in SMMEs

Mathematics and Applied Mathematics

Tel: (021) 959 2023 Fax: (021) 959 3055

Fransman, Andrew, MSc *W.Cape*, MSc *Stell.*, PhD
Amst. Sr. Lectr.
Fray, Richard L., MSc *W.Cape*, MSc *Stell.*, PhD
Stell. Assoc. Prof.
Groenewald, Gilbert J., BSc *W.Cape*, MSc *Ill.*,
MSc *Cape Town*, Drs *V.U.Amst.*, PhD
V.U.Amst. Sr. Lectr.; Chair*
Nel, Willie J. L., BSc *S.Af.*, PhD *Cape Town* Sr.
Lectr.
Nongxa, Gordon L., DPhil *Oxf.* Prof.
Persens, Jan, MSc *S.Af.*, MA *Cornell*, PhD
Cornell Prof.
Slammert, Lionel C., MSc *Cape Town*, PhD
Boston Assoc. Prof.; Sr. Lectr.
Witbooi, Peter J., MSc *W.Cape*, PhD *Cape
Town* Sr. Lectr.

Microbiology

Tel: (021) 959 3028

Africa, Charlene, PhD *Lond.* Sr. Lectr.
Brözel, Volker S., BSc *Stell.*, PhD *Pret.* Sr.
Lectr.; Assoc. Prof.
Davison, Sean, PhD *Otago* Sr. Lectr.; Chair*
Hallett, Arthur F., PhD *Rand Afrikaans*,
FRCPath Prof.

Music

Tel: (021) 959 2320 Fax: (021) 959 2376

Basson, N. J., BEd *Lond.*, BMus *Lond.*, MA *Lond.*,
PhD *Lond.*
Petersen, Alvin B., BMus *Cape Town*, BEd *S.Af.*,
MMus *Cape Town*, MMus *Butler* Sr. Lectr.;
Chair*

Nursing

Tel: (021) 959 2271 Fax: (021) 959 3686

Andrews, Gail V., BA(Cur) *S.Af.*, MCur
W.Cape Sr. Lectr.
Boshoff, Ellen L. D., BA(Cur) *S.Af.*, MCur
W.Cape Sr. Lectr.
Kortenbout, W., PhD *Natal*
Prince, Grace, BA *S.Af.* Sr. Lectr.; Chair*

Occupational Therapy

Tel: (021) 959 2544 Fax: (021) 959 3151

De Jongh, Jo-celene, BOccTher *Stell.* Sr. Lectr.
Janse van Rensburg, Viki C., BOccTher *Stell.*,
MPhil *W.Cape* Sr. Lectr.; Chair*

Oral Biology

Tel: (021) 328116 Fax: (021) 325050

Hartsman, Clive, BChD *Pret.* Sr. Lectr.
Wilding, Rob J. C., BDS *Rand Afrikaans*, MDent
Rand Afrikaans, PhD *W.Cape* Prof.; Chair*

Oral Medicine and Periodontology

Tel: (021) 328116 Fax: (021) 325050

Arendorf, Trevor M., BDS *Witw.*, MMedSci
Sheff., PhD *Wales* Prof.; Chair*
Stephen, Lawrence X. G., BChD *W.Cape* Sr.
Lectr.

Oral Pathology and Anatomical
Pathology

Tel: (021) 328116 Fax: (021) 325050

Hille, Jos J., MDent *Rand Afrikaans*, DDS Prof.;
Chair*

Orthodontics

Tel: (021) 328116 Fax: (021) 325050

Theunissen, Evan T. L., BChD *W.Cape*, MChD
W.Cape Sr. Lectr.; Chair*

Pharmaceutical Chemistry

Tel: (021) 959 2190, 959 3407 Fax: (021)
959 3407

Eagles, Peter F. K., MPharm *W.Cape*, PhD *Cape
Town* Prof.; Chair*

Leng, Henry, BSc *W.Cape*, MPharm *W.Cape*,
MScMedSci *Stell.*, PhD *Cape Town* Sr. Lectr.

Pharmaceutics

Tel: (021) 959 2179 Fax: (021) 959 3407
Russell, Irina, BEd *W.Cape*, BSc *Rhodes*,
BSc(Pharm) *Rhodes*, PhD *Rhodes* Prof.; Chair*

Pharmacology

Tel: (021) 959 2192 Fax: (021) 959 3407
Amabeoku, George J., BSc *Lond.*, MSc *Wales*,
PhD *Nigeria* Sr. Lectr.
Syce, James A., MPharm *W.Cape*, PhD
Kentucky Prof.; Chair*

Pharmacy Practice

Tel: (021) 959 2472 Fax: (021) 959 3407
Butler, Nadine C., BScMedSci *Stell.*, MPharm
W.Cape, PhD *Minn.* Prof.; Chair*
Myburgh, Johannes A., MPharm
W.Cape Assoc. Prof.

Philosophy

Tel: (021) 959 2167 Fax: (021) 959 2376
Abrahams, Jacobus P., MA *W.Cape* Lectr.;
Chair*
Nash, Andrew J., MA *Stell.* Sr. Lectr.

Physics

Tel: (021) 959 2327 Fax: (021) 959 3474
Adams, Danny, MSc *W.Cape*, PhD *Arizona
State* Sr. Lectr.
Carolissen, Randall J., MSc *W.Cape*, PhD
W.Cape Sr. Lectr.
Helm, Hugh, MSc *Cape Town*, PhD *Rhodes* Prof.
Julies, Roderick E., MSc *W.Cape*, PhD *Stell.* Sr.
Lectr.
Knoesen, Dirk, PhD *Stell.* Prof.
Krylov, Igor, MSc *Moscow*, DSc *Moscow* Prof.
Linder, Cedric J., BSc *Rhodes*, EdM *Rutgers*, EdD
Br.Col. Prof.
Lindsay, Robert, BSc *Stell.*, DPhil *Oxf.* Assoc.
Prof.; Chair*

Physiological Sciences

Tel: (021) 959 2183 Fax: (021) 959 3125
Dietrich, Daneel L. L., BSc *W.Cape*, PhD
V.U.Amst. Sr. Lectr.
Martiz, Gert S., BSc *Stell.*, B(B&A) *Stell.*,
MScMedSci *Stell.*, PhD *Stell.* Prof.; Chair*
Van der Horst, Gerhard, MSc *Stell.*, PhD
P.Elizabeth, PhD *Stell.* Prof.

Physiotherapy

Tel: (021) 959 2542, 959 2549 Fax: (021)
959 3125
Amosun, Syei L., BSc *Ib.*, PhD *Ib.* Sr. Lectr.
Mpofu, Ratie M., MSc *S'ton.* Sr. Lectr.; Chair*

Political Studies

Tel: (021) 959 3228 Fax: (021) 959 3621
Maseko, S., BA *W.Cape*, MA *Qu.*
Van Vuuren, Willem L. J., MA *Stell.*, DPhil
Stell. Prof.; Chair*

Psychology, see also Indust. Psychol.

Tel: (021) 959 2283, 959 2453 Fax: (021)
959 2755
Broekmann, Neil C., MA *Stell.*, DPhil
Stell. Prof.; Chair*
Meyer, Joan G. M., BA *S.Af.*, DrsIndPsychol
Amst., PhD *OFS* Assoc. Prof.
Perkel, Adrian K., BA *Witw.*, MA *Natal*, DPhil
W.Cape Sr. Lectr.
Pretorius, Tyrone B., MA *W.Cape*, DPhil
W.Cape Prof.
Simbayi, Assoc. Prof.
Strebel, Ann-Marie, MA *Stell.*, PhD *Cape
Town* Assoc. Prof.

Public Administration

Tel: (021) 959 3169 Fax: (021) 959 2208
Hohls, Orlando E., BA *Stell.* Sr. Lectr.
Lungu, Gatian F., BA *Zambia*, EdM *Harv.*, MPA
Mass., EdD *Harv.* Prof.
Mphaisha, Chisepo J. J., BA *Zambia*, MPA *Pitt.*,
PhD *Pitt.* Sr. Lectr.; Chair*

Radiology and Diagnostics and Maxillo-Facial and Oral Surgery

Tel: (021) 328116 Fax: (021) 325050
Aniruth, Sunil, BChD *W.Cape* Sr. Lectr.
Kariem, G., BChD *W.Cape*, MChD
W.Cape Assoc. Prof.; Chair*
Levendal, Allan, BChD *W.Cape*, BChD *Stell.* Sr.
Lectr.
Parker, Ebrahim, BChD *W.Cape*, MDS
Lond. Prof.

Religious Studies

Tel: (021) 959 2386 Fax: (021) 959 3355
Cornelissen, Jerome K., MA *W.Cape*, STD
W.Cape Lectr.; Chair*

Science and Mathematics Education, School of

Fax: (021) 959 2647
Ogunniyi, Meshach B., BSc(Ed) *A.Bello*,
MSc(Ed) *Wis.*, PhD *Wis.* Dir.; UNESCO
Chair*

Social Work

Tel: (021) 959 2277 Fax: (021) 959 2755
Kotze, Frans G., BA *W.Cape*, MSocSc *Cape Town*,
MSc *Edin.*, DPhil *W.Cape* Sr. Lectr.; Chair*
September, William J., BA(SW) *W.Cape*, MA
Tübingen Sr. Lectr.
Small, Adam, OMSG, BA(SS) *S.Af.*, MA *Cape
Town*, Hon. DLitt *Natal* Prof.

Sociology, see Anthropol./Sociol.

Statistics

Tel: (021) 959 3038 Fax: (021) 959 3055
Blignaut, Renette J., BSc *Rand Afrikaans*, MSc *Cape
Town*, PhD *Pret.* Sr. Lectr.
Breytenbach, Nicolaas J., MSc(Engin) *Calif.*,
PhD *S.Af.* Sr. Lectr.
Chalton, D. O., PhD *Cape Town* Sr. Lectr.;
Chair*
Kotze, Danelle, MSc *S.Af.*, DComm *Stell.* Prof.
Louw, Nelmarie, BSc *Stell.*, DSc *Pret.*, MSc
Potchef. Sr. Lectr.
Wesso, Gilbert R., MCom *W.Cape*, PhD
W.Cape Assoc. Prof.

Xhosa

Tel: (021) 959 2358 Fax: (021) 959 2376
Neethling, Siebert J., MA *P.Elizabeth*, DLitt
Stell. Prof.
Stuurman, Alfred B., MA *Stell.*, BEd
York(UK) Sr. Lectr.; Chair*

Zoology

Tel: (021) 959 2312 Fax: (021) 959 2312
De Villiers, Casper J., PhD *Rhodes* Sr. Lectr.
Hofmeyr, Margaretha D., MSc *Stell.*, PhD *Cape
Town* Sr. Lectr.; Chair*
Veith, Walter J., MSc *Stell.*, PhD *Cape
Town* Prof.

SPECIAL CENTRES, ETC

Adult and Continuing Education, Centre for

Tel: (021) 959 2231, 959 2798, 959 2799
Fax: (021) 959 2481
Walters, Shirley C., BA *Cape Town*, MEd *Manc.*,
PhD *Cape Town* Prof.; Dir.*

Child and Family Development, Institute for

Tel: (021) 959 2602, 959 2603 Fax: (021)
959 2606
Amoateng, Acheampong Y., BA *Ghana*, MA
Baltimore, PhD *Brigham Young* Sr. Lectr.
Lategan, Beatrix M., BEd *Stell.*, MA *S.Af.* Sr.
Lectr.
Sonn, Francis C. T., BA *W.Cape*, BEd *W.Cape*,
MSc *Calif.* Prof.; Dir.*

Community Law Centre

Tel: (021) 959 2950, 959 2951 Fax: (021)
959 2411
Steytler, Nicolaas C., BA *Stell.*, LLB *Stell.*, LLM
Lond., PhD *Natal* Prof.; Dir.*

Education Policy Unit

Tel: (021) 959 2580, 959 2810 Fax: (021)
959 3278
No staff at present

Historical Research/Archives, Institute for

Tel: (021) 959 2616, 959 3162 Fax: (021)
959 3178
Bredekamp, Henry C., MA *W.Cape*, MA
Wesleyan Assoc. Prof.; Dir.*
Odendaal, Andre, MA *Stell.*, PhD *Camb.* Prof.

Legal Aid Clinic

Tel: (021) 959 3421 Fax: (021) 959 2747
Khan, Gadija, BA *Cape Town*, LLB *Cape
Town* Dir.*

Public Health Programme

Tel: (021) 959 2402 Fax: (021) 959 2872
Bility, Khalipha M., MEd *Pitt.*, MPH *Pitt.*, PhD
Pitt. Sr. Lectr.
Heywood, Arthur B., MB ChB *Cape Town*, MPH
Amst. Sr. Lectr.
Sanders, David M., MB ChB *Birm.* Prof.; Dir.*

Southern African Studies, Centre for

Tel: (021) 959 3040 Fax: (021) 959 3041
Vale, Peter, MA *Leic.*, PhD *Leic.* Prof.; Dir.*

Student Counselling, Centre for

Tel: (021) 959 2881, 959 2299 Fax: (021)
959 2882
Naidoo, Anthony V., BA(SW) *W.Cape*, BA
W.Cape, MA *Ball*, PhD *Ball* Sr. Lectr.; Sr.
Student Counsellor
Nicholas, Lionel J., BA(SW) *W.Cape*, BA
W.Cape, MA *Boston*, DPhil *W.Cape* Assoc.
Prof.; Sr. Lectr.; Student Counsellor

CONTACT OFFICERS

Academic affairs. Deputy Registrar:
Gelderbloem, Oswald N., MA *W.Cape*
Accommodation. Nel, Bronnie C., BA *W.Cape*
Admissions (first degree). Admissions Officer:
Davids, Henry S., BA *W.Cape*
Admissions (higher degree). Admissions
Officer: Davids, Henry S., BA *W.Cape*
Alumni. Davids, Shahiem, BA *W.Cape*
Archives. Archivist, Institute for Historical
Research: Loff, Chris J., Drs *Theol.Sch.Kampen*
Computing services. Head, Information
Systems: Pedro, F., BSc
Computing services. Director, Computer
Centre: Wiegers, G., MSc Drs DSc
Development/fund-raising. Director,
Development and Public Affairs:
Pluddemann, Prof. U. R. R., MA DLitt STD
Examinations. Appany, Markham
Finance. Registrar: De Wet, Andre, BCom
General enquiries. Registrar (Academic):
Smith, Julian F., DLitt
Health services. Student Physician: George,
Andre V., MB ChB *Cape Town*, MSc *Cape Town*
Library (chief librarian). University Librarian:
September, P.
Personnel/human resources. Head: Mouton,
Danie R., BA
Publications. Acting Head: Glass, B.
Purchasing. Christians, Howard
Research. Dean: Christie, Prof. Renfrew, BCom
S.Af., BA *Cape Town*, MA *Cape Town*, DPhil *Oxf.*
Safety. Safety Officer: Baatjies, Donald
Schools liaison. Senior Student Counsellor:
Naidoo, Anthony V., BA(SW) *W.Cape*, BA
W.Cape, MA *Ball*, PhD *Ball*
Security. Safety Officer: Baatjies, Donald
Sport and recreation. Head, Sports
Administration: Boshoff, G.
Staff development and training. Van der
Schyff, Anwar

Student welfare/counselling. Senior Student Counsellor: Naidoo, Anthony V., BA(SW)

W.Cape, BA *W.Cape*, MA *Ball*, PhD *Ball*
University press. Head: Lewis, Cedric B., BA

[Information supplied by the institution as at 24 July 1998, and edited by the ACU]

UNIVERSITY OF THE WITWATERSRAND, JOHANNESBURG

Founded 1922; previously established as South African School of Mines (Kimberley) (1896), Transvaal Technical Institute, Transvaal University College, and South African School of Mines and Technology (1910)

Member of the Association of Commonwealth Universities

Postal Address: Private Bag 3, Witwatersrand, 2050 South Africa
Telephone: (011) 716 1111 **Fax**: (011) 716 8030 **Cables**: Uniwits **Telex**: 4-27125SA
WWW: http://www.wits.ac.za

CHANCELLOR—Goldstone, The Hon. Mr. Justice R. J., BA *Witw.*, LLB *Witw.*, Hon. LLD *Witw.*, Hon. LLD *Cape Town*, Hon. LLD *Natal*
VICE-CHANCELLOR AND PRINCIPAL*—Bundy, Prof. Colin J., BA *Natal*, BA *Witw.*, MPhil *Oxf.*, DPhil *Oxf.*
CHAIRMAN OF COUNCIL—Bam, The Hon. Mr. Justice F. C., BA *Cape Town*, BProc *S.Af.*, LLB *S.Af.*
DEPUTY VICE-CHANCELLOR—Kemp, Prof. Alan R., BSc(Eng) *Witw.*, MSc(Eng) *Witw.*, PhD *Camb.*, F(SA)ICE
DEPUTY VICE-CHANCELLOR—Ogunrinade, Prof. Adelani F., MSc *Lond.*, MSc *Brun.*, DVM *Ib.*, PhD *Lond.*
DEPUTY VICE-CHANCELLOR—Tyson, Peter D., BSc *Witw.*, MSc *Witw.*, PhD *Witw.*
DEPUTY VICE-CHANCELLOR—......
REGISTRAR (ACADEMIC)—Swemmer, Derek K., BA *Pret.*, MA *Pret.*, DLitt&Phil *S.Af.*
REGISTRAR (ADMINISTRATION)—......

GENERAL INFORMATION

History. The university achieved full university status in 1922. It is located in Braamfontein, Johannesburg.

Admission to first degree courses (see also South African Introduction). South African applicants under 23 years: matriculation certificate with university exemption. Some faculties set additional requirements, eg admission to BEng course requires higher grade pass in physical science and mathematics. International applicants must obtain exemption from the Matriculation Board. All students must be proficient in English.

First Degrees (see also South African Directory to Subjects of Study;) (* = also available with honours). BA*, BA(DramaticArt), BA(Education), BA(FineArts), BA(FineArts)(Education), BAcc, BAS, BA(SocialWork), BA(Sp&HTherapy), BCom*, BDS, BEconSc*, BMus, BMus(Education), BNurs, BPharm, BPhysEd, BPrimaryEd, BSc*, BSc(Building), BSc(Eng), BSc(LabMed), BSc(OralBiology), BSc(OT), BSc(Physiotherapy), BSc(QS), BSc(TRP), LLB, MB BCh.

All courses are full-time and normally last 4 years, with an additional year full-time or an additional 2 years part-time for honours. BSc(LabMed): 1 year; BA, BCom, BEconSc, BSc: 3 years (BCom: also 4 years part-time); BDS: 5½ years; MB BCh: 6 years.

Higher Degrees (see also South African Directory to Subjects of Study). BArch, BEd, LLM, MA, MA(Audiology), MA(ClinPsych), MA(DramaticArt), MA(FineArts), MA(SocialWork), MA(SpeechPathology), MA(Translation), MArch, MBA, MCom, MDent, MEconSc, MFamMed, MM (management), MMed, MMus, MPH, MPharm, MSc, MSc(Building), MSc(Dent), MSc(DP), MSc(Eng), MSc(Med), MSc(Nursing), MSc(OT), MSc(Physiotherapy), MSc(QS),

MSc(TRP), MUD (urban design), PhD, PhD(Med), DArch, DCom, DEconSc, DEd, DEng, DLitt, DMus, DSc, DSc(Arch), DSc(Building), DSc(BusAd), DSc(Dent), DSc(Eng), DSc(Med), DSc(QS), DSc(TRP), D(TRP), LLD.

Master's courses normally last 1 year full-time or 2 years part-time. BEd: 1 year full-time or 2 years part-time; MSc(Physiotherapy), MSc(Nursing): 1 year full-time or 2½ years part-time; MBA: 1 year full-time or 3 years part-time; MUD: 1½ years full-time or 3 years part-time; BArch, MA(ClinPsych), MA(Translation), MSc(DP): 2 years full-time; MFamMed: 2 years full-time or 3 years part-time; MPH: 2 years full-time or 4 years part-time; MDent, MMed: 3 or 4 years full-time. PhD courses last 2–4 years full-time or 4–6 years part-time. Higher doctorates: awarded on published work.

Libraries. About 1,000,000 items.

Fees. (1998, annual). Undergraduate: R10,480–11,700 (architecture); R8480–R11,940 (arts); R9460–R12,630 (commerce); R8480–R10,520 (education); R9750–R10,910 (engineering); R7370–R15,420 (health sciences); R10,480 (law); R8990–R10,520 (science). Postgraduate: R11,980–R15,950 (architecture); R5910–R13,270 (arts); R12,520 (commerce); R5350–R8230 (education); R950–R14,960 (engineering); R600–R9260 (health sciences); R10,330–R13,810 (law); R10,650–R25,040 (management); R7660 (science); R1420–R4070 (research degrees).

Academic Year (1998). Two terms: 23 February–4 July; 27 July–27 November.

Income (1997). Total, R43,067,000.

Statistics. Staff: 3623 (1110 academic, 2513 administrative and other).

FACULTIES/SCHOOLS

Architecture
Tel: (011) 716 2780 Fax: (011) 403 4657
Dean: Muller, Prof. J. G., BArch *Witw.*, MA *Prin.*
Secretary: Levitan, G.

Arts
Tel: (011) 716 3241 Fax: (011) 339 4524
Dean: Olivier, Prof. Gerrit, BA *Stell.*, MA *Stell.*, LittDrs *Utrecht*, PhD *Witw.*
Secretary: Marx, M.

Commerce
Tel: (011) 716 5300 Fax: (011) 716 5203
Dean: Dagut, Prof. Merton B., BA *Witw.*, MA *Witw.*
Secretary: Variava, M.

Education
Tel: (011) 716 5272 Fax: (011) 403 0613
Dean: Christie, Pam H., BA *Witw.*, MEd *Qld.*, PhD *Qld.*
Secretary: ......

Engineering
Tel: (011) 716 5154 Fax: (011) 716 5476
Dean: Reynders, Prof. Jan P., BSc(Eng) *Witw.*, PhD *Witw.*, F(SA)IEE
Secretary: Attewell, L.

Health Sciences and School Oral Health Sciences
Tel: (011) 647 2510 Fax: (011) 643 4318
Dean: Price, Max, MB BCh *Witw.*, BA *Oxf.*, MSc *Lond.*
Secretary: Holt, L.

Law
Tel: (011) 716 5023 Fax: (011) 339 4733
Dean: Lewis, Prof. Carole M., BA *Witw.*, LLB *Witw.*, LLM *Witw.*
Secretary: Monareng, H. R.

Management

Tel: (011) 488 5623 Fax: (011) 643 2366

Dean: Yeomans, Prof. K. A. H., BA *Keele*, MSc *Keele*, PhD *Aston*, PhD *Witw.*

Secretary: Whiteman, G.

Science

Tel: (011) 716 3167 Fax: (011) 339 3959

Dean: Wright, Prof. C. J., BSc *Witw.*, MPhil *Lond.*, PhD *Witw.*

Secretary: Holmes, M. C.

ACADEMIC UNITS

Accounting

Tel: (011) 716 5472 Fax: (011) 339 7884

de Koker, A. P., BCom *Cape Town*, MCom *Witw.* Prof.

Dickson, P. L., BSc *Witw.* Visiting Prof.; Head*

Farber, S., BCom *Witw.* Assoc. Prof.

Fridman, B. I., BCompt *S.Af.*, MEd *Witw.* Sr. Lectr.

Kolitz, D. L., BCom *Natal*, BCom *S.Af.*, MCom *Witw.* Sr. Lectr.

Kolitz, Maeve A., BCom *Natal*, BA *Natal* Sr. Lectr.

Martin, Albert T., FCA, FCIS Sr. Lectr.

O'Donovan, B., BA *S.Af.*, MCom *Witw.* Sr. Lectr.

Papageorgiiou, E., BCom *Stell.*, BCom *S.Af.*, MCom *Rand Afrikaans* Sr. Lectr.

Steele, Margaret D. F., BAcc *Witw.* Prof.

van Esch, Sandra D. Sr. Lectr.

Other Staff: 2 Principal Tutors; 9 Sr. Tutors; 2 Lectrs.†; 1 Tutor†

Actuarial Science, see Stats. and Actuarial Sci.

African Languages

Tel: (011) 716 3495

Khumalo, J. S. M., BA *S.Af.*, MA *Witw.*, PhD *Witw.* Prof.

Maake, Nhlanhla P., BA *Witw.*, BA *S.Af.*, MLitt *Strath.*, MLitt *Keele*, DLitt&Phil *S.Af.* Prof.; Head*

Yanga, Tshimpaka, Lic *Zaire*, MA *Texas*, PhD *Texas* Visiting Prof.

Other Staff: 1 Visiting Prof.; 1 Lectr.; 2 Sr. Tutors; 3 Tutors

African Literature

Tel: (011) 716 4082

Hofmeyr, I., BA *Witw.*, MA *Witw.*, MA *Lond.*, PhD *Witw.* Prof.

Peterson, B. K. J., BA *Cape Town*, BA *Witw.*, MA *York(UK)* Sr. Lectr.; Head*

Other Staff: 2 Lectrs.; 1 Principal Tutor; 1 Hon. Prof. Res. Fellow

Afrikaans en Nederlands

Tel: (011) 716 3741 Fax: (011) 403 2317

Jansen, Ena, BA *Stell.*, MA *Stell.*, LittDrs *Utrecht*, PhD *Witw.* Sr. Lectr.

Liebenberg, Wilhelm L., BA *Cape Town*, MA *Stell.*, LittDrs *Utrecht*, PhD *Witw.* Sr. Lectr.

Miles, John D., BA *Pret.*, MA *Pret.* Assoc. Prof.; Head*

Olivier, Gerrit, BA *Stell.*, MA *Stell.*, LittDrs *Utrecht*, PhD *Witw.* Prof.

Other Staff: 4 Lectrs.; 1 Hon. Prof. Res. Fellow

Anaesthesia

Tel: (011) 933 1843

Peltz, B., MB BCh *Witw.* Sr. Lectr.; Principal Specialist*

Chris Hani Baragwanath Hospital

Tel: (011) 933 1843

Davis, G., MB BCh *Witw.* Sr. Lectr.

De Bacelar-Gouvei, N. P., MD *Louvain* Sr. Lectr.

Emdon, S., MB BCh *Witw.* Sr. Lectr.

Faria, R. S., MB BCh *Witw.* Sr. Lectr.

Gouws, M., MB ChB *Pret.* Sr. Lectr.

Kuhn, R., MB ChB *Stell.* Sr. Lectr.

Ledlie, H. J., BSc *Witw.*, MB ChB *Pret.* Sr. Lectr.

Liebenberg, C. S., MB ChB *Pret.* Sr. Lectr.

Lipman, J., MB BCh *Witw.* Assoc. Prof.

Lohlun, R. G., MB BCh *Witw.* Sr. Lectr.

Peltz, B., MB BCh *Witw.* Sr. Lectr./Principal Specialist; Acting Head*

Strauss, L., MB BCh *Witw.* Sr. Lectr.

Veliotes, G. D., MB BCh *Witw.*, FCA(SA) Sr. Lectr.

Webb, A. A., MB BCh *Witw.* Sr. Lectr.

Other Staff: 1 Sr. Lectr.; 12 Lectrs.

Coronation Hospital

Tel: (011) 673 4200 Fax: (011) 477 4117

Mistry, B. D., MB BCh *Witw.* Sr. Lectr.

Sieburg, G. W., MB BCh *Witw.* Sr. Lectr.; Principal*

Other Staff: 1 Lectr.

Helen Joseph Hospital

Murfin, T. F., BSc *Pret.*, MB ChB *Pret.* Sr. Lectr.

Other Staff: 3 Lectrs.

Hillbrow Hospital

Tel: (011) 720 1121 Fax: (011) 725 1603

Katz, B., MB BCh *Witw.* Sr. Lectr.

Lines, D., MB BCh *Witw.* Head*

Other Staff: 3 Lectrs.

Johannesburg Hospital

Tel: (011) 488 4343 Fax: (011) 643 4425

Clinton, C., BSc *Witw.*, MB BCh *Witw.* Sr. Lectr.

Edge, K. R., MB BCh *Witw.* Sr. Lectr.

Klein, D. C., BSc *Witw.*, MB BCh *Witw.* Sr. Lectr.

Lundgren, A. C., MB ChB *Cape Town* Sr. Lectr.

Morrell, D. F., MB ChB *Cape Town* Prof.; Head*

Papendorf, MB BCh *Witw.* Sr. Lectr.

Radecka-Basiewicz, D. Sr. Lectr.

Vetten, K. B., MB BCh *Witw.*

Other Staff: 15 Lectrs.

Anatomical Sciences

Tel: (011) 716 2405 Fax: (011) 647 2422

Cowley, Heather M., BSc *Witw.*, PhD *Witw.* Sr. Lectr.

Kramer, Beverley, BSc *Witw.*, PhD *Witw.* Prof.; Head*

Maina, J., BVM *Nair.*, PhD *Liv.* Prof.

Other Staff: 9 Lectrs.; 1 Principal Tutor; 1 Sr. Tutor; 1 Sr. Res. Officer; 1 Res. Assoc.; 6 Lectrs.†; 2 Hon. Lectrs.; 2 Hon. Prof. Res. Fellows; 1 Hon. Res. Fellow; 1 Hon. Res. Assoc.

Research: embryonic differentiation and development; palaeo-anthropology

Archaeology

Tel: (011) 716 4099 Fax: (011) 339 1620

Huffman, T. N., BA *Denver*, MA *Ill.*, PhD *Ill.* Prof.; Head*

Lewis-Williams, J. D., BA *Cape Town*, BA *S.Af.*, PhD *Natal* Prof.

Wadley, L., BA *Cape Town*, MA *Cape Town*, PhD *Witw.* Sr. Lectr.

Other Staff: 1 Lectr.; 1 Res. Officer

Architecture

Tel: (011) 716 2780 Fax: (011) 403 2308

Fitchett, A. S., BArch *Witw.* Sr. Lectr.

Kammeyer, H., BArch *Cape Town*, MArch *Cape Town* Sr. Lectr.; Chairperson*

Low, I. B., BArch *Cape Town*, BArch *Witw.*, MArch *Penn.*, MArch *Witw.* Sr. Lectr.

Other Staff: 1 Visiting Prof.; 8 Lectrs.; 1 Sr. Tutor; 5 Lectrs.†; 3 Tutors†

Biochemistry, see under Biol., Sch. of, and Med. Biochem.

Biology, School of

Hanrahan, S. A., BSc *Witw.*, MSc *Witw.*, PhD *Witw.* Dir.*

Other Staff: 1 Tutor†

Biochemistry

Tel: (011) 716 2115 Fax: (011) 716 4479

Dirr, H., BSc *Rand Afrikaans*, MSc *Rand Afrikaans*, PhD *Rand Afrikaans* Prof.; Head*

McGrath, R. M., BSc *Belf.*, PhD *Belf.* Sr. Lectr.

Other Staff: 2 Lectrs.; 2 Lectrs.†; 1 Hon. Prof. Res. Fellow

Research: protein structure function

Botany

Tel: (011) 716 2251 Fax: (011) 339 1145

Balkwill, K., BSc *Witw.*, PhD *Natal* Sr. Lectr.

Critchley, A., BSc *Portsmouth*, PhD *Portsmouth* Assoc. Prof.

Fletcher, J., BSc *Hull*, PhD *Lond.* Sr. Lectr.

Mycock, D. J., BSc *Natal*, PhD *Natal* Sr. Lectr.

Parkinson, BSc *Newcastle*, MSc *Witw.*, PhD *Witw.* Sr. Lectr.

Pienaar, R. N., BSc *Witw.*, MSc *Witw.*, PhD *Natal* Prof.; Head*

Rogers, K. H., BSc *Natal*, PhD *Natal* Prof.

Sanders, M. R., BSc *Witw.*, MEd *Witw.*, PhD *Cape Town* Sr. Lectr.

Scholes, Mary C., BSc *Witw.*, PhD *Witw.* Sr. Lectr.

Witkowski, E. T. F., BSc *Witw.*, MSc *Witw.*, PhD *Cape Town* Sr. Lectr.

Other Staff: 7 Lectrs.; 1 Tutor

Genetics

Tel: (011) 716 2125 Fax: (011) 403 1735

Dabbs, E. R., BA *Camb.*, MA *Camb.*, PhD *Harv.* Sr. Lectr.; Acting Head*

McLellan, T., SB *M.I.T.*, PhD *M.I.T.*, FLS Sr. Lectr.

Rossouw, F. T., BSc *Lond.*, PhD *Lond.* Sr. Lectr.

Other Staff: 2 Lectrs.

Microbiology

Alexander, Jennifer J., BSc *Witw.*, MA *Texas*, PhD *Chic.* Prof.; Head*

Bey, E. M., PhD *Munich* Hon. Prof.

Rey, Christine M. E., BSc *Witw.*, PhD *Witw.* Sr. Lectr.

von Holy, Alexander, BSc *Witw.*, MSc *Pret.*, PhD *Pret.* Assoc. Prof.

Watson, T. G., PhD *Birm.* Hon. Prof.

Other Staff: 1 Lectr.; 1 Hon. Lectr.; 1 Hon. Res. Assoc.

Zoology

Tel: (011) 716 2410 Fax: (011) 339 2307

Balinsky, B. I., DBiolSc *Kiev*, Hon. DSc *Witw.*, FRSSAf Hon. Prof. Res. Fellow

Brain, C. K., BSc *Cape Town*, PhD *Cape Town*, DSc *Witw.*, FRSSAf Hon. Prof.

Cannone, A. J., BSc *Cape Town*, PhD *Brist.* Assoc. Prof.

Crewe, R. M., BScAgric *Natal*, MScAgric *Natal*, PhD *Georgia*, FRSSAf Prof.

Fabian, B. C., BSc *Witw.*, PhD *Witw.* Prof.

Hanrahan, S. A., BSc *Witw.*, MSc *Witw.*, PhD *Witw.* Assoc. Prof.; Head*

Markus, M. B., BSc *Pret.*, MSc *Pret.*, MSc *Lond.*, PhD *Lond.* Reader

Owen-Smith, R. Norman, BSc *Natal*, MSc *Natal*, PhD *Wis.* Reader

Seely, M. K., BA *Calif.*, PhD *Calif.*, Hon. DSc *Natal* Hon. Prof.

Starfield, A. M., BSc *Witw.*, PhD *Witw.* Hon. Prof.

Thornley, A. L., BSc *Witw.*, PhD *Witw.* Assoc. Prof.

Veale, R. B., BSc *Witw.*, PhD *Witw.* Sr. Lectr.

Other Staff: 4 Lectrs.; 3 Sr. Tutors; 4 Hon. Lectrs.; 1 Hon. Res. Assoc.

Research: African ecology; water in the environment

Botany, see under Biol., Sch. of

Building and Quantity Surveying

Tel: (011) 716 2616 Fax: (011) 339 8175

Morris, J., MSc *Pret.*, DSc *Louvain* Prof.

Nkado, Raymond N., BSc *A.Bello*, MSc *A.Bello*, PhD *Reading* Sr. Lectr.

Schloss, R. I., BSc(QS) *Witw.* Assoc. Prof.; Head*

Other Staff: 4 Lectrs.; 1 Sr. Tutor; 9 Lectrs.†

Business Administration, Graduate School of

Tel: (011) 488 5600 Fax: (011) 643 2336

Abratt, R., BCom Witw., MBA Pret., DBA Pret. Prof.

Anderson, R. T., MBA Cape Town

Bendixen, M., BSc(Eng) Witw., MBL S.Af., PhD Witw. Assoc. Prof.

Binedell, N. A., BCom Rhodes, MBA Cape Town, PhD Wash. Dir.*

Cook, J. T., BA Witw., BA S.Af., MA S.Af., MA Cape Town Sr. Lectr.

Douwes-Dekker, L. C. G., BSocSci Natal, BA S.Af., MA Witw. Prof.

Duffy, N. M., BCom Cape Town, MBL S.Af., DBL S.Af. Prof.

Firer, C., BSc Witw., MBA Witw., PhD Cape Town Prof.

Ford, J. C., BCom Rhodes, MCom Rand Afrikaans Sr. Lectr.

Klein, D., BA Tor., MBA Tor., PhD Tor. Visiting Prof.

Sandler, M., BA Natal, MBA Witw. Sr. Lectr.

Semark, P. M., BSc(Eng) Cape Town, BA S.Af. Sr. Lectr.

Thomas, A., BA Witw., MA Rand Afrikaans, MBA Brun., DLitt&Phil Rand Afrikaans Sr. Lectr.

van Zyl Slabbert, F., BA Stell., MA Stell., PhD Stell. Visiting Prof.

Ward, M., BSc(Eng) Cape Town, MBA Witw., PhD Witw. Sr. Lectr.

Other Staff: 6 Lectrs.; 21 Lectrs.†

Business Economics

Tel: (011) 716 5422 Fax: (011) 339 7835

Benfield, B. C., BCom Witw., PhD Witw. Visiting Prof.

Bethlehem, R., BCom Witw., DCom S.Af. Visiting Prof.

Corder, C. K., BA Camb., MA Camb. Visiting Prof.

Kenney, H. F., BA Cape Town, MSc(Econ) Lond. Sr. Lectr.

Leach, D., BA Penn., PhD Calif. Sr. Lectr.

Reekie, W. D., BCom Edin., PhD Strath. Prof.

Rwigema, H. B., BCom Nair., MBA Nair., PhD Witw. Sr. Lectr.

Solomon, D., BA Cape Town Sr. Lectr.

Vivian, R. W., BSc(Eng)Witw., BProc S.Af., LLB S.Af. Visiting Prof.; Head*

Other Staff: 1 Visiting Lectr.; 2 Lectrs.; 1 Sr. Tutor; 1 Tutor; 2 Lectrs.†

Cardiology

Chris Hani Baragwanath Hospital

Tel: (011) 933 1100 Fax: (011) 933 3135

4 Lectrs.

Johannesburg Hospital

Manga, P., MB BCh Witw., PhD Witw. Prof.; Chief Specialist*

Middlemost, S. J., MB BCh Witw. Sr. Lectr.

Other Staff: 5 Lectrs.

Chemistry

Tel: (011) 716 2219 Fax: (011) 339 7967

Boeyens, J. C. A., BSc OFS, MSc OFS, DSc Pret., FRSSAf Prof.; Head*

Bradley, J. D., BSc Leeds, PhD Lond. Assoc. Prof.

Brink, G., BSc Natal, PhD Natal Assoc. Prof.

Carlton, L., BSc Brist., BSc Exe., PhD Exe. Reader

Coville, N. J., BSc Witw., MSc Witw., PhD McG. Prof.

Cukrowski, I., DChemSc Lublin Sr. Lectr.

de Koning, C., BSc Cape Town, PhD Cape Town Sr. Lectr.

Farrer, H. N., BSc Natal, MSc Natal, DPhil Oxf. Sr. Lectr.

Glasser, L., BSc Cape Town, PhD Lond., FRSChem Prof.

Kiremire, E. M. R., BSc Mak., PhD New Br. Visiting Assoc.

Levendis, D. C., BSc Witw., MSc Witw., PhD Witw. Sr. Lectr.

Marques, H. M., BSc Witw., PhD Witw. Assoc. Prof.

Marsicano, F., BSc Witw., PhD Witw. Sr. Lectr.

Michael, J. P., BSc Witw., PhD Witw. Prof.

Neuse, E. W., BSc Hanover, MSc Hanover, PhD Hanover, DSc Witw. Hon. Prof. Res. Fellow

Nicolaides, C. P., BSc Stell., MSc Stell., DSc Sr. Lectr.

Pillay, A. E., BSc Durban-W., MSc Durban-W., MSc Witw., PhD Lond. Reader

Rollnick, M., BSc Witw., MSc E.Anglia, PhD Witw. Sr. Lectr.

Other Staff: 2 Lectrs.; 3 Sr. Tutors; 1 Res. Officer; 1 Tutor†; 1 Hon. Prof.; 3 Hon. Prof. Res. Fellows

Classics

Tel: (011) 716 3777 Fax: (011) 716 3645

Farron, S. G., BA Col., MA Chic., PhD Col. Assoc. Prof.

Frank, M., BA Cape Town, MLitt St And., PhD St And. Sr. Lectr.

Scott, M., BA Natal, PhD Lond. Sr. Lectr.

Scourfield, J. H. D., MA Oxf., DPhil Oxf. Assoc. Prof.; Head*

Other Staff: 1 Lectr.; 1 Hon. Prof. Res. Fellow

Community Dentistry

Tel: (011) 407 8660 Fax: (011) 339 3036

Rosen, M., BDS Durh., MSc(Dent) Witw. Assoc. Prof.

Rudolph, M. F., BDS Witw., MSc Witw., MPH Harv. Prof.; Head*

Other Staff: 1 Hon. Lectr.

Community Health

Tel: (011) 643 2543 Fax: (011) 642 0733

Gear, J. S. S., BSc Witw., MB BCh Witw., MA Oxf. Sr. Lectr.

Padayachee, G. N., MB BCh Witw., MMed Witw. Sr. Lectr.

Pick, W. M., MB BCh Cape Town, MMed Cape Town Prof.; Head*

Tsotsi, N. M. Sr. Lectr.

Other Staff: 3 Lectrs.; 1 Res. Officer; 2 Lectrs.†; 16 Hon. Lectrs.

Comparative Literature

Tel: (011) 716 4083

Nethersole, R., BA Witw., PhD Witw. Prof.; Head*

Other Staff: 1 Lectr.

Computer Science

Tel: (011) 716 3311 Fax: (011) 339 7965

Baber, R., MSc T.H.Darmstadt Visiting Prof.

Lubinsky, David, BSc Witw., MSc Witw., PhD Rutgers Assoc. Prof.

Machanick, Philip, BSc Natal, BSc Witw., MSc Witw. Sr. Lectr.

Mueller, C. S., BSc Witw., MSc Rand Afrikaans, PhD Witw. Sr. Lectr.; Chairperson*

Neishlos, Hanoch, BSc Latvia, MSc Haifa(Technion), DSc Haifa(Technion) Prof.

Other Staff: 5 Sr. Lectrs.; 1 Principal Tutor; 1 Res. Officer†

Conservative Dentistry

Tel: (011) 407 8644 Fax: (011) 339 3036

Bryer, G. M. Sr. Lectr.

Cohen, J. E. B., BDS Witw. Sr. Lectr.

Exner, H., BChD Pret., MSc Stell., PhD S.Af.Med. Prof.; Head*

Melman, G. E., BDS Witw., MSc(Dent) Witw. Sr. Lectr.

Meyerowitz, A., BDS Witw. Sr. Lectr.

Setzer, S., BDS Witw., MSc(Dent) Witw. Sr. Lectr.

Steltman, A. T., BDS Utrecht Sr. Lectr.

Other Staff: 5 Lectrs.; 3 Jr. Lectrs.; 4 Lectrs.†

Dramatic Art

Tel: (011) 716 3773 Fax: (011) 339 7601

Hagemann, F. R., BA Natal, MA Natal, PhD Natal Sr. Lectr.; Head*

Purkey, M., BA Witw., MA N.Y.State Sr. Lectr.

Steadman, Ian P., BA Natal, MA N.Y.State, PhD Witw. Prof.

Other Staff: 4 Lectrs.; 2 Sr. Tutors; 2 Tutors; 5 Lectrs.†; 2 Tutors†

Economics

Tel: (011) 716 5109 Fax: (011) 339 7755

Cassim, F., BA Kingston(UK), MSc(Econ) Lond. Sr. Lectr.

Dagut, Merton B., BA Witw., MA Witw. Visiting Prof.

Mittermaier, K. H. M., BCom Cape Town, BA Cape Town, PhD Witw. Sr. Lectr.

Simkins, C. E. W., BSc Witw., MA Oxf., PhD Natal Prof.

Strydom, P. D. F., BCom Potchef., MCom Potchef., DCom Potchef., PhD Amst. Visiting Prof.

Zarenda, H., BA Rhodes, MA Witw. Assoc. Prof.

Other Staff: 4 Lectrs.; 2 Sr. Tutors; 2 Tutors; 1 Lectr.†; 2 Tutors†

Economic History, Division of

Tel: (011) 716 5107 Fax: (011) 339 7755

Munro, Katherine, BA Witw. Assoc. Prof.

Other Staff: 1 Lectr.; 1 Sr. Tutor

Education

Tel: (011) 716 5371 Fax: (011) 339 3956

Bapoo, A. H., BSc Witw., PhD Witw. Sr. Lectr.

Basson, R. B., BA Witw., BEd Rhodes, MA Lanc., PhD Oregon Sr. Lectr.

Christie, Pam H., BA Witw., MEd Qld., PhD Qld. Assoc. Prof.

Cross, M., BA Lourenço Marques, MEd Witw. Sr. Lectr.

Enslin, Penelope A., BA Natal, BA Stell., MLitt Camb., MEd Witw., PhD Witw. Prof.

Faulkner, C. J., BEd Brist., MA Sus. Sr. Lectr.

Lelliott, A. D., BSc Durh., MSc Durh. Sr. Lectr.

Pendlebury, Shirley, BA Witw., BEd Witw., MEd Witw., DEd W.Cape Assoc. Prof.; Head*

Roman, A., BA W.Cape Sr. Lectr.

Other Staff: 14 Lectrs.; 2 Principal Tutors; 3 Sr. Tutors; 5 Lectrs.†

Adult Education, Division of

Tel: (011) 716 5230 Fax: (011) 716 3956

Castle, P. J., MEd Witw., PhD Witw. Sr. Lectr.

Russell, D. D., BSc Rhodes Prof.; Dir.*

Other Staff: 1 Principal Tutor; 2 Tutors

Physical Education, Division of

Tel: (011) 716 5718 Fax: (011) 716 6876

Nicholson, Claire M., BA Stell., MA Calif. Sr. Lectr.; Head*

Other Staff: 2 Sr. Tutors; 3 Lectrs.†

Specialised Education, Division of

Tel: (011) 716 5387 Fax: (011) 339 6876

Skuy, Mervyn, BA Witw., MA Witw., DLitt&Phil S.Af. Prof.; Head*

Other Staff: 2 Sr. Tutors; 1 Tutor; 2 Lectrs.†; 1 Tutor†

Endocrinology, see under Health Scis.

Engineering, Civil

Tel: (011) 716 2466 Fax: (011) 339 1762

Ballim, Y., BSc(Eng) Witw., MSc(Eng) Witw., PhD Witw. Sr. Lectr.

Blight, G. E., BSc(Eng) Witw., MSc(Eng) Witw., DSc(Eng) Witw., PhD Lond., DSc(Eng) Lond., F(SA)ICE, FRSSAf Prof.

Dison, L., BSc(Eng) Witw.

Fourie, A. B., BSc(Eng) Witw., MSc(Eng) Witw., PhD Lond. Assoc. Prof.

Gohnert, M., BSc(Civil) Brigham Young, MEM Brigham Young Sr. Lectr.

Hofmeyr, A. G. S., BSc(Eng) Witw., MSc(Eng) Witw. Sr. Lectr.

James, C. S., BSc(Eng) Witw., MS Col., PhD Witw. Assoc. Prof.

Luker, I., BSc Brist., PhD Witw. Sr. Lectr.

Marjanovic, P., BSc(Eng) Glas., MSc(Eng) Glas., MScEng Ill., MSc Calif., PhD Calif. Sr. Lectr.

McCutcheon, R. T., BSc(Eng) Witw., MSc Sus., DPhil Sus. Prof.; Head*

Stephenson, D., BSc(Eng) *Witw.*, MSc(Eng) *Witw.*, PhD *Witw.*, DSc(Eng) *Witw.*, F(SA)ICE, FICE Prof.
Wall, K. C., BSc(Eng) *Cape Town*, MCRP *Cape Town*, MSc(Eng) *Cape Town*, MIndAdmin *Cape Town*, PhD *Cape Town* Hon. Prof.
Other Staff: 4 Lectrs.; 2 Res. Fellows; 1 Res. Officer; 1 Lectr.†
Research: water systems

Engineering, Electrical

Tel: (011) 716 5354 Fax: (011) 403 1929
Aghdasi, F., BSc *Lond.*, MBA *Portland*, PhD *Witw.* Sr. Lectr.
Dwolatzky, B., BSc(Eng) *Witw.*, PhD *Witw.* Sr. Lectr.
Fourie, A., BSc *Witw.*, PhD *Witw.* Sr. Lectr.
Gibbon, G. J., MSc(Eng) *Witw.*, PhD *Witw.* Sr. Lectr.
Hanrahan, H. E., BSc(Eng) *Witw.*, PhD *Witw.* Prof.
Harris, N. G., BSc(Eng) *Witw.*, BSc *Witw.* Sr. Lectr.
Jandrell, I. R., BSc(Eng) *Witw.*, PhD *Witw.* Sr. Lectr.
Landy, C. F., BSc(Eng) *Witw.*, MSc(Eng) *Witw.*, PhD *Witw.* Prof.; Head*
MacLeod, I. M., BSc(Eng) *Witw.*, PhD *Witw.* Prof.
Meyer, A. S., BSc(Eng) *Witw.*, MSc(Eng) *Witw.* Sr. Lectr.
Reynders, Jan P., BSc(Eng) *Witw.*, PhD *Witw.*, F(SA)IEE Prof.
Swarts, F., BSc *Rand Afrikaans*, MSc *Rand Afrikaans*, DSc *Rand Afrikaans* Assoc. Prof.
Turner, M., BSc(Eng) *Witw.*, MSc(Eng) *Witw.*, PhD *Witw.* Assoc. Prof.
Walker, A. J., BSc(Eng) *Witw.*, MSc(Eng) *Witw.*, PhD *Witw.* Assoc. Prof.
Wigdorowitz, B., BSc(Eng) *Witw.*, MSc(Eng) *Witw.*, PhD *Witw.* Sr. Lectr.
Other Staff: 4 Lectrs.; 1 Sr. Res. Officer; 1 Res. Officer; 1 Prof. Asst.; 4 Hon. Lectrs.
Research: power systems engineering

Engineering, Materials, see Engin., Process and Materials, Sch. of

Engineering, Mechanical

Tel: (011) 716 2588 Fax: (011) 339 7997
Chandler, H. D., BSc *Leeds*, MSc *Glas.*, PhD *CNAA* Reader
Dickson, A. J., BSc(Eng) *Witw.*, MSc(Eng) *Witw.* Visiting Prof.
Fielding, E. R., BSc *Aston*, MPhil *Aston* Sr. Lectr.
Jawurek, H. H., BSc(Eng) *Cape Town*, MSc(Eng) *Cape Town*, PhD *Witw.* Sr. Lectr.
Moss, E. A., BSc(Eng) *Witw.*, MSc(Eng) *Witw.*, PhD *Witw.* Assoc. Prof.
Paskaramoorthy, R., BSc *Peradeniya*, PhD *Manit.* Sr. Lectr.
Sandrock, K. C. W., BSc *S.Af.*, BSc *Rand Afrikaans*, MSc *Rand Afrikaans*, MA *Witw.*, MSc(Eng) *Witw.* Sr. Lectr.
Sheer, T. J., BSc(Eng) *Witw.*, MSc(Eng) *Witw.*, PhD *Witw.* Prof.; Head*
Skews, B. W., BSc(Eng) *Witw.*, MSc(Eng) *Witw.*, PhD *Witw.* Prof.
Snaddon, D. R., BSc(Eng) *Witw.*, MBA *Witw.*, PhD *Witw.* Sr. Lectr.
Tully, N., BSc(Eng) *S'ton.*, MA *Oxf.*, PhD *S'ton.* Assoc. Prof.
Other Staff: 6 Lectrs.; 11 Lectrs.†

Engineering, Mining

Tel: (011) 716 5464 Fax: (011) 339 8295
Clark, I., BSc *Strath.*, MSc *Reading*, PhD *Lond.* Visiting Prof.
Clatworthy, G. G., BSc *Witw.*, MSc *Witw.* Sr. Lectr.
Crompton, T. O., BSc *Lond.*, MSc(Eng) *Lond.* Sr. Lectr.
Hardman, D. R., BSc *Newcastle(UK)*, MSc *Newcastle(UK)* Sr. Lectr.
Minnitt, R. C. A., BSc *Witw.*, MSc *Witw.*, PhD *Witw.* Sr. Lectr.

Naismith, W. A., BSc *Newcastle*, MSc *Newcastle*, MBA *Witw.* Sr. Lectr.
Ozbay, M. U., BSc(MinEng) *Middle East Tech.*, MSc(Eng) *Witw.*, PhD *Witw.* Sr. Lectr.
Phillips, H. R., BSc *Brist.*, MSc *Newcastle(UK)*, PhD *Newcastle(UK)* Prof.; Head*
Workman-Davies, C. L., BSc(Eng) *Witw.*, MSc(Eng) *Witw.* Sr. Lectr.
Other Staff: 2 Lectrs.; 1 Sr. Res. Officer; 1 Hon. Res. Assoc.

Engineering, Process and Materials, School of

Tel: (011) 716 2413 Fax: (011) 339 7213
Bryson, A. W., BSc(Eng) *Cape Town*, PhD *Cape Town* Prof.; Head*
Crundwell, F. K., BSc(Eng) *Witw.*, MSc(Eng) *Witw.*, PhD *Witw.* Sr. Lectr.
Eric, R. H., BSc(Eng) *Middle East Tech.*, MSc(Eng) *Middle East Tech.*, PhD *Middle East Tech.* Prof.
Glasser, D., BSc(Eng) *Cape Town*, PhD *Lond.* Prof.
Hildebrandt, Diane, BSc(Eng) *Witw.*, MSc(Eng) *Witw.*, PhD *Witw.* Sr. Lectr.
Koursaris, A., BSc *Aston*, PhD *Witw.* Assoc. Prof.
Letowski, F. K., MSc(Eng) *T.U.Wroclaw*, PhD *T.U.Wroclaw* Sr. Lectr.
Luyckx, S., PhD *Witw.* Assoc. Prof.
Moys, M. H., BSc(Eng) *Witw.*, MSc(Eng) *Natal*, PhD *Natal* Assoc. Prof.
Te Riele, W. A. M., BScEng *Natal*, MScEng *Natal*, PhD *Natal* Visiting Prof.
Tshabala, S. N., BSc(Eng) *Witw.*, MSc(Eng) *Witw.* Sr. Lectr.
Williams, D. A. F., BSc(Eng) *Witw.*, MSc(Eng) *Witw.* Assoc. Prof.
Other Staff: 2 Lectrs.; 1 Res. Officer; 3 Lectrs.†; 1 Hon. Lectr.

English

Tel: (011) 716 2880 Fax: (011) 403 7309
Chaskalson, Lorraine D., BA *Witw.*, PhD *Witw.* Sr. Lectr.
Cheadle, B. D., BA *Witw.*, PhD *Witw.* Prof., Poetry and Poetics
Houliston, V., MA *Cape Town*, DPhil *Oxf.* Sr. Lectr.
Hughes, Geoffrey, MA *Oxf.*, DLitt&Phil *S.Af.* Prof., History of English
Leveson, Marcia I., BA *Cape Town*, BEd *Cape Town*, MA *Witw.*, PhD *Witw.* Assoc. Prof.
Newfield, BA *Witw.*, MA Sr. Lectr.
Orkin, Martin, BA *Witw.*, MA *Lond.*, PhD *Lond.* Assoc. Prof.
Semple, Hilary E., BA *Rhodes*, MA *Witw.* Sr. Lectr.
Sherman, Joseph, BA *Witw.*, MA *Witw.*, PhD *Witw.* Assoc. Prof.
Williams, Merle A., BA *Natal*, PhD *Sheff.* Assoc. Prof.; Head*
Woodward, A. G., MA *Oxf.* Prof.
Other Staff: 8 Lectrs.; 1 Sr. Tutor

English Language Studies, Applied, see under Linguistics

Environmental Studies, see Geog. and Environmental Studies

Family Medicine

Tel: (011) 647 2041 Fax: (011) 647 2558
Celaya, P. Sr. Lectr.
Lonergan, B. F., MB BS *Syd.* Sr. Lectr.
Singleton-Kirby, G. D., MB BCh *Witw.* Sr. Lectr.
Sparks, B. L. W., MB BCh *Witw.*, FRCGP Prof.; Head*
Wallace, R. W. B., MB BCh *Witw.* Sr. Lectr.
Wisniewska, B. E. Sr. Lectr.
Other Staff: 6 Lectrs.; 1 Lectr.†; 72 Hon. Lectrs.

Fine Arts

Tel: (011) 716 3768 Fax: (011) 339 3601
Coetzee, J., BA *Natal*, MA *Witw.* Sr. Lectr.
Crump, A., BA(FineArts) *Cape Town*, MA(FineArts) *Cape Town*, MFA *Calif.* Prof.

Nel, K., BA(FineArts) *Witw.*, MFA *Calif.* Sr. Lectr.
Richards, C. P., BA(FineArts) *S.Af.*, PhD *Witw.* Sr. Lectr.
Schütz, P., BAFineArts *Natal*, MAFineArts *Natal* Sr. Lectr.
Siopis, P., MFA *Rhodes* Assoc. Prof.; Head*
Other Staff: 3 Lectrs.; 1 Sr. Tutor

Genetics, see under Biol., Sch. of, and Human Genetics under Pathol., Sch. of

Geography and Environmental Studies

Tel: (011) 716 2980 Fax: (011) 403 7281
Beavon, K. S. O., BSc *Cape Town*, MSc *Cape Town*, PhD *Witw.* Prof.
Earle, J. L., BA *Cape Town*, BEd *Rhodes* Assoc. Prof.
Hart, G. H. T., BA *Rhodes*, MA *Witw.*, PhD *Witw.* Sr. Lectr.
Rogerson, C. M., BSc *Lond.*, MSc *Witw.*, PhD *Qu.* Prof.; Head*
Other Staff: 3 Lectrs.; 1 Sr. Tutor; 1 Tutor; 1 Hon. Lectr.

Geology

Tel: (011) 716 2608 Fax: (011) 339 1697
Anhaeusser, C. R., BSc *Witw.*, MSc *Witw.*, PhD *Witw.*, DSc *Witw.* Sr. Lectr.
Cawthorn, R. G., BSc *Durh.*, PhD *Edin.* Prof.
Charlesworth, E. G., BSc *Natal*, PhD *Natal* Sr. Lectr.
Hancox, P. J., BSc *Witw.* Visiting Assoc.
McCarthy, T. S., BSc *Witw.*, BSc *Cape Town*, MSc *Cape Town*, PhD *Witw.* Prof.; Head*
Reimold, W. U., PhD *Mün.* Sr. Lectr.
Robb, L. J., MSc *Witw.*, PhD *Witw.* Assoc. Prof.
Viljoen, M. J., BSc *Witw.*, MSc *Witw.*, PhD *Witw.* Prof.
Other Staff: 1 Tutor†

Haematology, see under Pathol. Sch. of

Health Sciences

Chris Hani Baragwanath Hospital (Dermatology)
4 Lectrs.

Endocrinology
Tel: (011) 488 3808
Kalk, W. J., MB BCh *Witw.* Prof.; Chief Specialist*
Other Staff: 3 Lectrs.

Johannesburg, Helen Joseph and Hillbrow Hospitals (Neurology)
Tel: (011) 488 4432 Fax: (011) 488 4459
Fritz, V. U., MB BCh *Witw.*, PhD *Witw.*, FCP(SA) Prof.
Temlett, J. A., MB BCh *Witw.*, MMed *Witw.*, PhD *Witw.*, FCP(SA) Sr. Lectr.
Other Staff: 2 Lectrs.; 8 Lectrs.†

Johannesburg Hospital (Dermatology)
Tel: (011) 488 3644
Schulz, E. Joy, MB ChB *Pret.*, MMed *Pret.* Assoc. Prof.; Principal Specialist*
Other Staff: 1 Lectr.; 2 Jr. Lectrs.; 6 Lectrs.†

History

Tel: (011) 716 2828 Fax: (011) 339 7634
Ally, R. T., BA *Cape Town*, PhD *Camb.* Sr. Lectr.
Bonner, P. L., BA *Nott.*, MA *Lond.*, PhD *Lond.* Prof.
Bratchel, M. E., BA *Camb.*, MA *Camb.*, PhD *Camb.* Sr. Lectr.
Cope, R. L., BA *Natal*, MA *Natal* Sr. Lectr.
Delius, P. N., BA *Lond.*, PhD *Lond.* Assoc. Prof.
Garson, N. G., BA *Witw.*, BA *Camb.*, MA *Witw.*, MA *Camb.* Hon. Prof. Res. Fellow
Hamilton, C. I., BA *Keele*, PhD *Camb.* Sr. Lectr.
Kros, C. J., BA *Witw.*, PhD *Witw.* Sr. Lectr.
La Hausse de Lalouvière, P., BA *Natal*, MA *Cape Town*, PhD *Witw.* Sr. Lectr.
Murray, B. K., BA *Rhodes*, MA *Kansas*, PhD *Kansas*, FRHistS Prof.; Head*

Other Staff: 2 Lectrs.; 1 Sr. Tutor; 1 Hon. Res. Fellow

History of Art

Tel: (011) 716 3440 Fax: (011) 339 6039

Doepel, R. T., BA(FineArts) *Witw.*, MA *Lond.*, PhD *Witw.* Assoc. Prof.

Nettleton, Anitra C. E., BA *Witw.*, MA *Witw.*, PhD *Witw.* Assoc. Prof.

Rankin, Elizabeth A., BA *Witw.*, PhD *Witw.* Prof.; Head*

Other Staff: 2 Lectrs.; 2 Sr. Tutors†; 1 Tutor†

Immunology, see under Pathol., Sch. of

Infectious Diseases, see Clin. Microbiol. and Infectious Diseases under Pathol., Sch. of

Information Systems

Fax: (011) 339 5760

Brodie, Estelle, BSc *Witw.*, MEd *Witw.* Principal Tutor; Chair*

Mende, J. W., BSc *Witw.*, MBL *S.Af.* Sr. Lectr.

Shochot, J., BSc *Witw.* Assoc. Prof.

Sutherland, Frances, BEd *Leeds*, MEd *Witw.*, MCom *Witw.* Sr. Lectr.

Other Staff: 1 Sr. Lectr.; 1 Sr. Tutor; 2 Lectrs.†; 2 Tutors†

International Relations

Tel: (011) 716 2921 Fax: (011) 716 2943

Alden, J. C., BA *Reed*, MA *Fletcher*, PhD *Fletcher* Sr. Lectr.

Shelton, G. L., BA *Witw.*, MA *Witw.*, PhD *Witw.* Sr. Lectr.

Steadman, I. P., BA *Natal*, MA *N.Y.*, PhD *Witw.* Chair*

Zacarias, A. M., BSc *E.Mondlane*, MSc *Lond.*, PhD *Lond.* Sr. Lectr.

Zuzowski, R., MA *ANU*, PhD *La Trobe*, MEc Sr. Lectr.

Other Staff: 2 Lectrs.; 2 Tutors; 1 Lectr.†; 2 Tutors†

Law, School of

Tel: (011) 716 5023 Fax: (011) 339 4733

Abraham, G., BCom *Witw.*, LLB *Witw.* Sr. Lectr.

Brassey, M. S. M., BA *Cape Town*, LLB *Witw.* Prof.

Cassim, F. H. I., LLB *Lond.*, LLM *Lond.* Sr. Lectr.

Chaskalson, A., BCom *Witw.*, LLB *Witw.*, Hon. LLD *Natal*, Hon. LLD *Witw.* Hon. Prof.

Cockrell, A., BA *Cape Town*, LLB *Cape Town* Prof.

Currie, J. B., BA *Witw.*, LLB *Cape Town*, MA *Cape Town* Sr. Lectr.

Davis, D., BCom *Cape Town*, LLB *Cape Town*, MPhil *Camb.* Prof.

Dendy, Mervyn, BCom *Witw.*, LLB *Witw.* Assoc. Prof.

Domanski, A., BSc *Witw.*, LLB *Witw.* Sr. Lectr.

Dugard, C. J. R., BA *Stell.*, LLB *Stell.*, LLB *Camb.*, LLD *Camb.*, Hon. LLD *Natal* Prof.

Goldberg, V., BProc *Witw.*, LLB *Witw.* Sr. Lectr.

Gutto, S., LLB *Nair.*, PhD *Lund* Assoc. Prof.

Itzikowitz, Angela J., BA *Stell.*, LLB *Stell.* Prof.

Jordi, P. R., BA *Witw.*, LLB *Witw.* Sr. Lectr.

Kahn, E., BCom *Witw.*, LLB *Witw.*, LLM *Natal*, LLD *Natal*, Hon. LLD *Cape Town*, Hon. LLD *Witw.*, Hon. LLD *Natal* Hon. Prof. Res. Fellow

Katz, M. M., BCom *Witw.*, LLB *Witw.*, LLM *Harv.* Visiting Prof.

Keightley, R., BA *Natal*, LLB *Natal* Sr. Lectr.

Klaaren, N. J., BA *Harv.*, MA *Cape Town* Sr. Lectr.

Larkin, M. P., BCom *Witw.*, LLB *Witw.* Prof.

Lewis, Carole M., BA *Witw.*, LLB *Witw.*, LLM *Witw.* Prof.

Loots, Cheryl E., BA *Witw.*, LLB *Witw.* Assoc. Prof.

Maharaj, J., BA *S.Af.*, LLB *S.Af.* Sr. Lectr.

Mahomed, Justice J. I., BA *Witw.*, LLB *Witw.* Hon. Prof.

Mosikatsana, T., BA(Law) *NUL*, LLB *Ott.*, MA *Regina* Sr. Lectr.

Paizes, A. P., BCom *Witw.*, LLB *Witw.*, PhD *Witw.* Prof.

Pantazis, A., BA *Witw.*, LLB *Witw.* Sr. Lectr.

Roux, T., BA *Cape Town*, LLB *Cape Town*, PhD *Camb.* Sr. Lectr.

Rudolph, Harold G., BA *Witw.*, LLB *Witw.*, LLM *Witw.* Assoc. Prof.

Skeen, A. StQ., BA *Rhodes*, BL *Rhodesia*, LLB *Rhodesia*, MPhil *Camb.* Prof.; Head*

Smith, N. M., BA *Natal*, LLB *Natal* Sr. Lectr.

Solomon, P., BA *Stell.*, LLB *Stell.* Sr. Lectr.

Zeffertt, D. T., BA *Witw.*, LLB *Witw.* Sr. Lectr.

Other Staff: 4 Lectrs.; 2 Principal Tutors; 8 Sr. Tutors; 1 Lectr.†

Linguistics

Tel: (011) 716 2140 Fax: (011) 716 2474

Traill, A., BA *Witw.*, MLitt *Edin.*, PhD *Witw.* Prof.; Head*

Other Staff: 3 Lectrs.; 2 Hon. Res. Assocs.; 1 Tutor†

Applied English Language Studies, Division of

Tel: (011) 716 2346 Fax: (011) 716 2474

Blight, Norman, BA *Witw.*, BA *S.Af.*, MA *Lond.* Sr. Lectr.

Janks, Hilary, BA *Witw.*, MA *Witw.* Sr. Lectr.; Head*

Ramani, Esther, BA *Madr.*, MA *B'lore.*, MA *Lanc.*, PhD *IISc.* Assoc. Prof.

Other Staff: 5 Lectrs.

Mathematics

Tel: (011) 716 2843 Fax: (011) 403 2017

Adler, J. B., BSc *Witw.*, MEd *Witw.*, PhD *Witw.* Prof.

Driver, Kathleen A., BSc *Witw.*, MS *Stan.*, PhD *Witw.* Assoc. Prof.

Faierman, M., BEng *McG.*, BSc *Lond.*, MA *Tor.*, PhD *Tor.* Ad Hominem Prof.

Hartney, J. F. T., MSc *Nott.*, PhD *Nott.* Sr. Lectr.

Hunt, J. H. V., BSc *Cape Town*, PhD *Warw.* Prof.

Knopfmacher, J. P. L., BSc *Witw.*, MSc *Witw.*, PhD *Manc.*, FRSSAf Prof.

Labuschagne, C. C., BSc *Rand Afrikaans*, DSc *Potchef.* Sr. Lectr.

Laridon, P. E., BA *S.Af.*, BSc *Stell.*, BEd *Cape Town*, MEd *Rand Afrikaans*, DEd *Rand Afrikaans* Assoc. Prof.

Lubinsky, D. S., BSc *Witw.*, MSc *Witw.*, PhD *Witw.* Prof.

Moller, M., DrRerNat *Regensburg*, DrHabil *Regensburg* Reader

Ridley, J. N., BSc *Witw.*, PhD *Lond.* Assoc. Prof.

Schwartzman, Pauline A., BSc *Cape Town*, MSc *S.Af.* Sr. Lectr.

Other Staff: 5 Lectrs.; 3 Principal Tutors; 6 Sr. Tutors; 2 Tutors; 4 Lectrs.†; 1 Sr. Tutor†; 1 Tutor†; 1 Hon. Prof. Res. Fellow; 1 Hon. Lectr.

Mathematics, Computational and Applied

Tel: (011) 716 3923 Fax: (011) 339 7965

Abelman, Shirley, BSc *OFS*, MSc *OFS*, PhD *Potchef.* Sr. Lectr.

Adam, A. A., BSc *S.Af.*, MA *W.Mich.*, PhD *Witw.* Sr. Lectr.

Block, D. L., BSc *Witw.*, MSc *S.Af.*, PhD *Cape Town*, FRAS Assoc. Prof.

Ibragimov, N. H., MSc *Novosibirsk*, PhD *Novosibirsk*, DSc *Novosibirsk* Ad Hominem Prof.

Knopfmacher, A., BSc *Witw.*, PhD *Witw.* Reader

Mahomed, Fazal, BSc *Durban-W.*, BSc *Witw.*, MSc *Witw.*, PhD *Witw.* Sr. Lectr.

Mason, D. P., BSc *Glas.*, DPhil *Oxf.* Prof.; Head*

Naik, K. C., BSc *Witw.*, BEd *Witw.*, MEd *S.Af.*, DEd *S.Af.* Sr. Lectr.

Pendock, N. E., BSc *Witw.*, PhD *Witw.* Sr. Lectr.

Sears, M., BSc *Adel.*, BSc *Flin.*, PhD *Flin.* Hon. Prof.

Sherwell, D., BSc *Witw.*, PhD *St And.* Sr. Lectr.

Wilson, D. B., BSc *Witw.*, MSc *Witw.* Sr. Lectr.

Wong, K. H., BSc *Lond.*, MMath *NSW*, PhD *NSW* Sr. Lectr.

Wright, C. J., BSc *Witw.*, MPhil *Lond.*, PhD *Witw.* Prof.

Young, D. A., BSc *Witw.*, BEd *S.Af.*, MEd *Witw.* Sr. Lectr.

Other Staff: 5 Lectrs.; 1 Sr. Tutor; 1 Lectr.†; 1 Sr. Tutor†

Maxillo-Facial and Oral Surgery

Tel: (011) 407 8642 Fax: (011) 339 3036

Lownie, J. F., BDS *Witw.*, MDent *Witw.* Prof.; Head*

Lownie, M. A., BA *S.Af.*, BDS *Witw.* Sr. Lectr.

Lurie, R., BDS *Witw.*, MDent *Witw.*

Reynecke, J. P., BChD *Pret.* Sr. Lectr.

Smith, I., BDS *Witw.* Assoc. Prof.

Other Staff: 19 Lectrs.

Medical Biochemistry

Tel: (011) 647 2395

Arbuthnot, P. B., BSc *Witw.*, MB BCh *Witw.*, PhD *Witw.* Sr. Lectr.

Davidson, B. C., PhD *Witw.* Sr. Lectr.

Hammond, K. D., BSc *Lond.*, PhD *Witw.* Assoc. Prof.; Head*

Prinz, W., BSc *Witw.*, MBA *Cape Town*, PhD *Witw.* Sr. Lectr.

Other Staff: 1 Lectr.; 1 Hon. Prof. Res. Fellow; 1 Hon. Lectr.

Medicine

Tel: (011) 488 3621 Fax: (011) 643 8777

Bezwoda, W. R., MB BCh *Witw.*, MD *Witw.*, PhD *Witw.*, DSc(Med) *Witw.*, FCP(SA) Prof.

Dubb, A., MB BCh *Witw.* Assoc. Prof.

Feldman, C., MB BCh *Witw.*, PhD *Witw.* Prof.

Fritz, V. U., MB BCh *Witw.*, PhD *Witw.* Prof.

Gallard, M., BSc *Witw.*, MSc *Witw.*, PhD *Witw.* Sr. Lectr.

Huddle, K. R. L., MB BCh *Witw.*, FCP(SA) Prof.

Joffe, B. I., MB BCh *Witw.*, DSc(Med) *Witw.*, FRCP Prof.

Kalk, W. J., MB BCh *Witw.*, FRCP Ad Hominem Prof.

Kew, M. C., MB BCh *Witw.*, MD *Witw.*, PhD *Witw.*, DSc(Med) *Witw.*, FCP(SA), FRCP, FRSSAf Prof.

MacPhail, A. P., BSc *Witw.*, MB BCh *Witw.*, PhD *Witw.*

Manga, P., MB BCh *Witw.*, PhD *Witw.* Prof.

Meyers, A. M., MB BCh *Witw.* Ad Hominem Prof.

Milne, F. J., MB ChB *Cape Town*, MD *Cape Town*, FCP(SA), Hon. FRCP Prof.; Chief Specialist; Head*

Richards, G. A., MB BCh *Witw.*, PhD *Witw.*, FCP(SA) Assoc. Prof.

Sareli, P., MD *Jerusalem* Assoc. Prof.

Schultz, E. J. H., MB ChB *Pret.*, MMed *Pret.* Assoc. Prof.

Segal, I., MB BCh *Witw.*, FRCP Assoc. Prof.

Shires, R., MB BCh *Witw.*, PhD *Witw.* Assoc. Prof.

Temlett, J. A., MB BCh *Witw.*, MMed *Witw.*, PhD *Witw.* Assoc. Prof.

Veriava, Y., MB BCh *Witw.*, FCP(SA) Assoc. Prof.

Other Staff: 1 Sr. Res. Officer; 4 Res. Officers; 1 Res. Fellow†; 2 Res. Officers†; 3 Hon. Prof. Res. Fellows; 1 Hon. Lectr.

Microbiology, see under Biol., Sch. of, and Clin. Microbiol. and Infectious Diseases under Pathol., Sch. of

Modern Languages and Literatures

Tel: (011) 716 3270 Fax: (011) 403 7289

Boisacq, Marie-Jeanne, LèsL *Louvain*, PhD *Witw.* Sr. Lectr.

Cioran, S. D., BA *McM.*, MA *Indiana*, PhD *Lond.*, PhD *Tor.* Visiting Prof.

Dednam, Sabina, BA Witw., BA Cape Town, PhD Witw. Sr. Lectr.

Mariani, Annajulia, MA Witw., DottLett Bologna, PhD Witw. Sr. Lectr.

Rogers, B. G., BA Lond., MA Lond., MA Camb., MLitt Camb., DèsL Paris IV Prof.

Thorpe, Kathleen E., BA Witw., MA Witw., PhD Witw. Sr. Lectr.

Wilson, Rita P. G., BA Witw., MA Witw., PhD Witw. Assoc. Prof.; Head*

Other Staff: 6 Lectrs.

Music

Tel: (011) 716 3970 Fax: (011) 716 2623

Mony, W. A., PhD Witw. Prof.†

Primos, K., BMus S.Af., MMus Witw. Sr. Lectr.; Chair*

van Wyk, C. A., BMus Cape Town, MMus Cape Town, DMus Cape Town Assoc. Prof.

Other Staff: 2 Lectrs.; 5 Sr. Tutors; 3 Practical Music Instrs.; 1 Lectr.†; 7 Tutors†

Neurological Surgery

Tel: (011) 488 2031

Farrell, V. J. R., MB BCh Witw., FRCS Prof.; Head*

Other Staff: 3 Lectrs.

Chris Hani Baragwanath Hospital

Gopal, R., FRCSEd Sr. Lectr.; Principal Specialist*

Other Staff: 1 Lectr.; 1 Lectr.†

Johannesburg Hospital

Farrell, V. J. R., MB BCh Witw. Prof.; Chief Specialist*

Other Staff: 3 Lectrs.

Nuclear Medicine, see under Radiation Services, Dept. of

Nursing Education

Teaching also contributed by staff of other relevant university departments, of the teaching hospitals and of the health authorities; also the Johannesburg College of Education and the B. G. Alexander Nursing College

Tel: (011) 488 4272 Fax: (011) 488 4195

Bruce, J. C. M., BCur W.Cape, BA S.Af., MSc(Nursing) Witw. Sr. Lectr.

Langley, G. C., BA S.Af., MSc(Nursing) Witw. Sr. Lectr.

McInerney, P. A., BSc(Nursing) Witw., MSc(Nursing) Witw. Sr. Lectr.; Chair*

Robertson, Barbara, BCur Pret., BA(Cur) S.Af., MA S.Af., DLitt&Phil S.Af. Prof.

Other Staff: 4 Lectrs.; 1 Sr. Tutor; 1 Tutor; 6 Lectrs.†

Obstetrics and Gynaecology

Tel: (011) 488 3179

Sonnendecker, E. W. W., MB BCh Witw., MMed Pret., FRCOG Prof.; Head*

van Gelderen, C. J., MB ChB Cape Town, FRCOG Prof.

Other Staff: 3 Hon. Lectrs.

Chris Hani Baragwanath Hospital

Tel: (011) 938 1534 Fax: (011) 938 1534

Bareiro-Duarte, M. M., DMC Natnl.Asunción Sr. Lectr.

Bothner, B. K. Sr. Lectr.

Dawood, B. B., MB BCh Witw. Sr. Lectr.

Guidozzi, F., MB BCh Witw. Assoc. Prof.

Hellman, P. R., MB BCh Witw. Sr. Lectr.

Matonhodze, MB ChB Z'bwe. Sr. Lectr.

Mtoba, A. E. M., BSc Fort Hare, MB ChB Natal Sr. Lectr.

Nagar, A., BSc Durban-W., MB ChB Ghana Sr. Lectr.

Naran, V., MB ChB Witw. Sr. Lectr.

Ofori-Amango, K., MB ChB Ghana Sr. Lectr.

Russell, J. Moira, BA Glas., MB ChB Glas., FRCOG Sr. Lectr.

Schackis, R. C., MB ChB Cape Town Sr. Lectr.

Setzen, R., MB BCh Witw. Sr. Lectr.

van Gelderen, C. J., MB ChB Cape Town, FRCOG Prof.; Head*

Other Staff: 15 Lectrs.

Coronation Hospital

Tel: (011) 470 9090 Fax: (011) 470 9092

Adams, R. S., MB BCh Witw. Sr. Lectr.

de Souza, J. J. L., MB ChB Pret. Sr. Lectr.

Hofmeyr, G. J., MB BCh Witw. Prof.; Chief Specialist*

Levin, S. L., MB Witw. Sr. Lectr.

Molingoane, S. J., BSc Fort Hare, MB BCh Witw. Sr. Lectr.

Sridaran, N., MB BS Madr. Sr. Lectr.

Suliman, R. B., MB BS Punjab Sr. Lectr.

Other Staff: 7 Lectrs.

Hillbrow Hospital

Tel: (011) 720 1121

Buthelezi, T. M., MB BCh Witw. Sr. Lectr.

Chrysostomou, A. Sr. Lectr.

Jercovic-Andrin, M., MD Novi Sad

Papacostas, N., MD

Pipingas, A., MD Athens

Other Staff: 2 Lectrs.; 4 Lectrs.†

Johannesburg Hospital

Tel: (011) 488 3170

Amin, G. J. H., MB BS Punjab Sr. Lectr.

Chrisofphers, G. J., MB BCh Witw. Sr. Lectr.

Sonnendecker, E. W. W., MB BCh Witw., MMed Pret., FRCOG Prof.; Head*

van Iddekinge, B., MB BCh Witw., FRCOG Sr. Lectr.

Other Staff: 13 Lectrs.

Occupational Therapy

Tel: (011) 488 3438

Concha, Majorie E., BSc(OT) Witw. Assoc. Prof.; Head*

Other Staff: 2 Lectrs.; 1 Principal Tutor; 2 Sr. Tutors; 8 Lectrs.†; 2 Sr. Tutors†; 1 Tutor†

Odontology, Experimental

Tel: (011) 407 4163 Fax: (011) 339 3036

Cleaton-Jones, P. E., BDS Witw., MB BCh Witw., PhD Witw., DSc Witw. Prof.; Head*

Volchansky, A. L., BDS Durh., PhD Witw. Hon. Prof.

Other Staff: 2 Hon. Lectrs.

Ophthalmology

Tel: (011) 647 2549 Fax: (011) 484 8263

Carmichael, T. R., MB BCh Witw., PhD Witw., FCS(SA) Prof.; Head*

Chris Hani Baragwanath–St John Eye Hospital

Tel: (011) 933 8000

Mthembu, W. T., MB BCh Witw. Sr. Med. Officer*

Other Staff: 5 Lectrs.; 1 Lectr.†

Helen Joseph Hospital

1 Lectr.

Johannesburg Hospital

Tel: (011) 647 2049

Carmichael, T. R., MB BCh Witw., PhD Witw. Head*

Other Staff: 2 Lectrs.; 4 Lectrs.†

Oral Medicine and Periodontology

Tel: (011) 407 8647 Fax: (011) 339 3036

Lemmer, J., BDS Witw. Prof.; Head*

Rachanis, C. C., BA Witw., BSc Witw., BDS Witw., MB ChB Sheff. Sr. Lectr.

Rosen, M., BDS Durh., MSc(Dent) Witw. Assoc. Prof.

Other Staff: 7 Lectrs.†; 1 Hon. Lectr.

Orthodontics

Tel: (011) 407 8530 Fax: (011) 339 3036

Evans, W. G., BDS Witw. Prof.; Head*

Lewin, A., BDS Witw. Hon. Prof.; Res. Fellow

Mizrahi, E., BDS Witw., MSc Manc., PhD Witw. Visiting Prof.

Other Staff: 2 Lectrs.; 12 Lectrs.†; 1 Hon. Prof. Res. Fellow

Orthopaedic Surgery

Tel: (011) 647 2038

Erken, E. H. W., MD, FCS(SA) Prof.; Head*

Ripamonti, U., LMC Milan, MDent Witw., PhD Witw. Hon. Prof.

Other Staff: 1 Reader†; 2 Hon. Lectrs.

Chris Hani Baragwanath Hospital

Tel: (011) 933 1100

Rodrigues, F. A., MD Lisbon Sr. Lectr.

Valentin, R., MD Bucharest Sr. Lectr.

Other Staff: 7 Lectrs.; 8 Lectrs.†

Helen Joseph Hospital

Aden, A. A., MD Somali Natnl. Sr. Lectr.; Head*

Farah, A., MD Somali Natnl. Sr. Lectr.

Marin, J. P. Sr. Lectr.

Munir. M., MB BS Punjab, MB BS Punjab Sr. Lectr.

Rasheed, M. T., MB BS B.Zak. Sr. Lectr.

Younus, A., MB BS B.Zak. Sr. Lectr.

Other Staff: 3 Lectrs.; 2 Lectrs.†

Hillbrow Hospital

Tel: (011) 720 3106

Berzen, H., MB BCh Witw., MChOrth Liv. Sr. Lectr.

Cunningham, S. T., MB BCh Witw. Sr. Lectr.; Principal Med. Officer*

Lichtenberg, M., MD Prague Sr. Lectr.

Mahmood, T., MB BS Punjab Sr. Lectr.

Vaksman, M. Sr. Lectr.

Younis, B., MD Loureno Marques Sr. Lectr.

Other Staff: 3 Lectrs.

Johannesburg Hospital

Erken, E. H. W., MS Munich Prof.; Chief Specialist*

Kabir, H. K., MB BS Chic.Theol.Sem. Sr. Lectr.

Wisniewski, T. F., PhD Gdansk Sr. Lectr.

Other Staff: 11 Lectrs.; 6 Lectrs.†

Natalspruit Hospital

1 Hon. Lectr.

Otorhinolaryngology, see under Surg.

Paediatrics, see also under Surg.

Levin, Solomon E., MB BCh Witw., FRCPEd Prof.

Pettifor, John M., MB BCh Witw., PhD Witw., FCP(SA) Prof.; Head*

Rothberg, A. D., BSc Witw., MB BCh Witw., PhD Witw. Hon. Prof.

Thomson, P. D., MB BCh Witw. Assoc. Prof.

Zwi, K. J., MB BCh Witw., MSc Lond., MMed Witw. Sr. Lectr.

Other Staff: 1 Lectr.†; 1 Hon. Res. Fellow

Chris Hani Baragwanath Hospital

Tel: (011) 933 1297 Fax: (011) 938 9074

Christoforou, A. Sr. Lectr.

Hartman, Ella, MB ChB Stell., FCP(SA) Sr. Lectr.

Jacobs, D. W. C., MB BCh Witw. Sr. Lectr.

Kala, Udai K., MB BCh Witw., FCP(SA) Sr. Lectr.

Pettifor, John M., MB ChB Witw., PhD Witw., FCP(SA) Prof.

Poyiadjis, S. D. Sr. Lectr.

Rodda, John L., MB BCh Witw., FCP(SA) Sr. Lectr.

Other Staff: 23 Lectrs.; 10 Lectrs.†

Research: mineral metabolism; perinatal HIV

Coronation Hospital

Tel: (011) 673 4200

Fullerton, A. J. Sr. Lectr.; Head*

Mayet, Z., BSc S.Af., MB BCh Witw. Sr. Lectr.

Rosen, Eric U., BMus Cape Town, MB ChB Cape Town, MMed Cape Town, MPH Calif. Prof.

Thein, O., MB BS Yangon Sr. Lectr.

Venter, André, MB ChB Pret., MMed Witw., PhD Alta., FCP(SA) Sr. Lectr.

Other Staff: 9 Lectrs.

Johannesburg Hospital

Tel: (011) 488 4246

Cohn, Richard J., MB BCh Witw., FCP(SA) Assoc. Prof.
Cooper, P. A., MB ChB Cape Town Prof.
Davies, V. A., MB BCh Witw. Sr. Lectr.
Hahn, D., MB ChB Cape Town, MMed Witw. Sr. Lectr.; Head*
Jacklin, Lorna B., MB BCh Pret., MMed Pret., FCP(SA) Sr. Lectr.
Koppel, E. E., MB BCh Witw. Sr. Lectr.
Mbamba, K., MD Kinshasa Sr. Lectr.
Scher, L. G., MB BCh Witw. Sr. Lectr.
Schwyzer, R., MB BCh Witw. Sr. Lectr.
Thomson, Peter D., MB BCh Witw., FCP(SA) Assoc. Prof.
Other Staff: 8 Lectrs.; 1 Sr. Tutor; 11 Lectrs.†

Pathology, School of

Klugman, K. P., BSc Witw., MB BCh Witw., MMed Witw., PhD Witw. Prof.; Chief Specialist; Chair*

Anatomical Pathology

Tel: (011) 643 2028 Fax: (011) 643 7031

Cooper, K., BSc Durban-W., MB ChB Natal, DPhil Oxf. Prof.; Head*
Hale, M. J., MB ChB Rhodesia Sr. Lectr.
King, P. C., MB BCh Witw., FRCPath Sr. Lectr.
Leiman, Gladwyn, MB BCh Witw. Assoc. Prof.
Paterson, A. C., MB BCh Witw., PhD Witw. Prof.
Tiltman, A. J., MB ChB Cape Town, MD Cape Town, MMed Cape Town Sr. Lectr.
Verhaart, M. S. J., MB ChB Pret. Sr. Lectr.
Other Staff: 13 Lectrs.

Chemical Pathology

Tel: (011) 643 2021 Fax: (011) 647 2521

Crowther, N. J., BSc Sus., DPhil Sus. Sr. Lectr.
Gray, I. P., MB ChB OFS, MMed OFS Prof.; Head*
Paiker, J. E., MB ChB Pret. Sr. Lectr.
Rowe, Pamela, BSc Birm., MB BCh Birm. Sr. Lectr.
Stewart, M. J., BSc Glas., PhD Glas. Sr. Lectr.
Other Staff: 2 Lectrs.

Clinical Microbiology and Infectious Diseases

Ballard, R. C., PhD Witw. Assoc. Prof.
Crewe-Brown, H. H., BSc Rhodes, MB BCh Witw. Prof.
Fleming, A. F., MB BChir Camb., MA Camb., MD Camb., FRCPath Hon. Prof.
Klugman, K. P., BSc Witw., MB BCh Witw., MMed Witw., PhD Witw. Prof.
Koornhof, H. J., MB ChB Cape Town Hon. Prof. Res. Fellow
Liebowitz, L., BPharm Witw., MB BCh Witw., PhD Witw. Sr. Lectr.
Von Gottberg, A. M., MB BCh Witw. Sr. Lectr.

Forensic Pathology

Heyns, A. D., MB BCh Witw., MD Witw., DSc Witw. Hon. Prof.
Kemp, V. D., MB BCh Witw. Sr. Lectr.; Acting Head*
Other Staff: 4 Lectrs.

Haematology

Heyns, A. D., MB BCh Witw., MD Witw., DSc Witw. Hon. Prof.
Mendelow, B. V., MB BCh Witw., PhD Witw. Prof.; Chief Specialist; Head*
Other Staff: 11 Lectrs.

Human Genetics

Tel: (011) 725 0511

Jenkins, Trefor, MB BS Lond., MD Lond., FRSSAf Prof.; Head*
Kromberg, J. G. R., BA(SocialWork) Witw., MA Witw., PhD Witw. Assoc. Prof.
Makgoba, M. W., MB ChB Natal, DPhil Oxf. Res. Prof.
Ramsay, Michele, BSc(Agric) Stell., MSc Cape Town, PhD Witw. Reader
Other Staff: 6 Lectrs.

Immunology

Wadee, A. A., BSc Tor., MSc(Med) Witw. Prof.; Head*

Oral Pathology, Division of

Altini, M., BDS Witw., MDent Witw. Prof.; Head*
Coogan, M., BSc Pret., MSc Witw., PhD Witw. Sr. Lectr.
Jacobs, Maeve M., BSc Pret., MSc Witw., PhD Witw. Sr. Lectr.

Virology

Tel: (011) 882 9910

Blackburn, N., MPhil Rhodesia Sr. Lectr.
Jupp, Peter G., BSc Cape Town, MSc Witw., PhD Witw., DSc(Med) Witw. Sr. Lectr.
Martin, D. J., MB BCh Witw., MMed Witw. Sr. Lectr.
Schoub, Barry D., MB BCh Witw., MMed Stell., MD Pret., DSc(Med) Witw., FRCPath Prof.; Head*
Swanepoel, Robert, BVSc Pret., PhD Edin. Reader
Other Staff: 2 Lectrs.; 2 Hon. Lectrs.

Periodontology, see Oral Med. and Periodontol.

Pharmacology, Experimental and Clinical

Tel: (011) 643 2042 Fax: (011) 643 5415

Chetty, M., BPharm Durban-W., MSc Rhodes, PhD Durban-W.
Havlik, I., PhD Prague Prof.; Head*
Other Staff: 3 Lectrs.; 1 Sr. Tutor; 1 Res. Officer; 5 Lectrs.†

Pharmacy

Tel: (011) 643 2052

Danckwerts, M. P., MPharm W.Cape, MBL S.Af. Sr. Lectr.
Haasbroek, P. P., BSc Potchef., MSc Potchef. Sr. Lectr.
Moodley, I., BScPharm Durban-W., BSc Lond., PhD Lond. Prof.; Head*
Other Staff: 4 Lectrs.; 2 Lectrs.†

Philosophy

Tel: (011) 716 2757 Fax: (011) 403 1174

Leon, Mark, BA Witw., PhD Lond. Assoc. Prof.; Chairperson*
Pendlebury, Michael J., BA Witw., MA Witw., MA Indiana, PhD Indiana Prof.
Sapire, David M., BSc Witw., BA Witw., BPhil Oxf. Assoc. Prof.
Other Staff: 3 Lectrs.; 1 Tutor†; 1 Hon. Lectr.

Physics, see also Med. Phys. under Radiation Services, Dept. of

Tel: (011) 716 2090 Fax: (011) 339 8262

Carter, J. M., BSc Witw., PhD Witw. Sr. Lectr.
Cole, B. J., BSc Liv., PhD Liv. Assoc. Prof.
Comins, J. D., BSc Natal, PhD Witw. Prof.; Head*
Connell, S. H., BSc Witw., PhD Witw. Sr. Lectr.
Crawford, J. L., BSc Witw. Sr. Lectr.
Derry, T. E., MA Camb., PhD Witw. Reader
du Plessis, P. de V., BSc OFS, MSc OFS, DSc OFS Prof.
Every, A. G., BSc Witw., MSc Witw., PhD Reading Reader
Heiss, W. D., DrRerNat F.U.Berlin Prof.
Hnizdo, V., MSc Prague, PhD Birm. Sr. Lectr.
Hoch, M. J. R., BSc Natal, MSc Natal, PhD St And. Prof.
Joubert, D. P., BSc Stell., MSc Stell., PhD Camb. Sr. Lectr.
Lemmer, R. H., BSc OFS, MSc OFS, PhD Flor., DSc Pret. Prof.
Lowther, J. E., BSc Hull, PhD Hull Prof.
Maaza, M., PhD Paris VI Sr. Lectr.
McLachlan, D. S., BSc Natal, MS Lehigh, PhD Rutgers Prof.

Nabarro, F. R. N., BA Oxf., MA Birm., Hon. DSc Witw., Hon. DSc Cape Town, Hon. DSc Natal Hon. Prof. Res. Fellow
Pollak, H., MA Brussels, PhD Brussels Sr. Lectr.
Price, H. E., BSc Witw., MSc Camb. Sr. Lectr.
Rodrigues, J. A. P., BSc Witw., MSc Brown, PhD Brown Reader
Rutherford, M., BSc(Eng) Lond., PhD Brun. Assoc. Prof.
Tegen, R., MSc Hamburg, PhD Hamburg Assoc. Prof.
van Wyk, J. A., BSc Potchef., MSc Potchef., PhD Witw. Sr. Lectr.
Other Staff: 1 Postdoctoral Res. Fellow; 1 Lectr.; 1 Principal Tutor; 1 Sr. Tutor; 1 Hon. Res. Fellow
Research: condensed matter physics; f-electron magnetism and heavy fermion physics

Physiology

Tel: (011) 643 2560 Fax: (011) 643 2765

Buffenstein, R., BSc Cape Town, PhD Cape Town Sr. Lectr.
Gray, D., BSc Sund., PhD P.Elizabeth Sr. Lectr.
Keegan, D., BSc Lond., MSc Witw., PhD Witw. Sr. Lectr.
Laburn, H. P., BSc Witw., PhD Witw. Ad Hominem Prof.
Mitchell, D., BSc Witw., MSc Witw., PhD Witw., FRSSAf Prof.
Mitchell, G., BSc Witw., BVSc Pret., PhD Witw., DVSc Pret. Prof.; Head*
Norton, G., BSc Witw., MB BCh Witw., PhD Witw. Sr. Lectr.
Rogers, G. G., BSc Witw., MSc Pret., PhD Witw. Assoc. Prof.
Other Staff: 5 Lectrs.; 1 Res. Officer; 1 Lectr.†

Physiotherapy

Tel: (011) 488 3450

Eales, C. J., BSc Witw., MSc Witw. Sr. Lectr.; Head*
Stewart, A., BSc Witw., MSc(Med) Witw. Sr. Lectr.
Other Staff: 1 Lectr.; 1 Sr. Tutor; 3 Lectrs.†; 1 Tutor†; 11 Hon. Lectrs.

Political Studies

Tel: (011) 716 2910

Frankel, P. H., BA Witw., MA Witw., MA Prin., PhD Prin. Sr. Lectr.
Himbara, D., BA York(Can.), PhD Qu. Sr. Lectr.
Hudson, P. A., BA Natal, MèsL Paris Sr. Lectr.
Lodge, Tom, BA York(UK), BPhil York(UK), DPhil York(UK) Assoc. Prof.; Head*
Pines, N. J., BA Witw. Sr. Lectr.
Stadler, A. W., BA Witw., PhD Witw. Prof.
Taylor, R. L., BA Kent, MSc(Econ) Lond., PhD Kent Sr. Lectr.
Other Staff: 2 Lectrs.; 1 Tutor.; 1 Res. Officer; 1 Res. Assoc.

Prosthetic Dentistry

Tel: (011) 407 8514 Fax: (011) 339 3036

Carr, L., BDS Witw., MDent Witw. Sr. Lectr.; Head*
Fouche, BDS Witw., MDent Witw. Sr. Lectr.
Veres, E. M., BDS Witw., MSc(Dent) Witw., MDent Witw. Sr. Lectr.
Other Staff: 9 Lectrs.

Psychiatry

Tel: (011) 647 2026 Fax: (011) 647 2423

Allwood, C. W., BA Rhodes, MB ChB Cape Town, MMed Witw., MD Pret. Sr. Lectr.
Hart, G. A. D., MB ChB Cape Town, MD Natal Hon. Prof.; Acting Head*

Chris Hani Baragwanath Hospital

3 Lectrs.

Helen Joseph Hospital

3 Lectrs.

Johannesburg Hospital

Tel: (011) 488 3553 Fax: (011) 647 2423

Berk, MB BCh Witw., MMed Witw., PhD Pret. Sr. Lectr.; Principal Specialist*

Other Staff: 10 Lectrs.; 4 Lectrs.†

Sterkfontein Hospital

Nchito-Hamukoma, B. C., MB ChB Zambia Sr. Lectr.

Stevenson, C. M., MB ChB Cape Town Lectr.; Chief Specialist*

Vorster, M., MB BCh Witw. Sr. Lectr.

Other Staff: 9 Lectrs.; 1 Lectr.†

Tara, H. Moross Centre

Tel: (011) 783 2010

Allwood, C. W., BA Rhodes, MB ChB Cape Town, MMed Witw., MD Pret. Sr. Lectr.

Other Staff: 10 Lectrs.; 3 Lectrs.†

Psychology

Tel: (011) 716 2550 Fax: (011) 716 2476

Eagle, G. T., BA Natal, MA Natal Prof.

Fisher, J., BSc CNAA, MSc Lough., PhD Witw. Assoc. Prof.

Heuchert, J. W. P., BA Pret., MSc Georgia, MA Boston, PhD Boston Sr. Lectr.

Potter, C. S., BA Witw. Sr. Lectr.

Straker, Gillian, BA Witw., MA Witw., PhD Witw. Prof.; Head*

Watts, Jacqueline, BA Natal, BEd Natal, MA Natal, PhD Witw. Sr. Lectr.

Wortley, R. H., BA S.Af., BA Natal, MA Natal, PhD Witw. Sr. Lectr.

Other Staff: 13 Lectrs.; 1 Sr. Tutor; 7 Tutors; 10 Lectrs.†

Public and Development Management, Graduate School of

Tel: (011) 488 5700 Fax: (011) 643 2336

Ambursley, F., BA Birm., PhD Warw. Sr. Lectr.

Bond, P., BA Swarthmore, PhD Johns H. Sr. Lectr.

Cawthra, G., BA Natal, PhD Lond. Sr. Lectr.; Acting Dir.*

de Coning, C., BA Rand Afrikaans, MA Rand Afrikaans, PhD S.Af.

Fitzgerald, P., BA Witw. Hon. Prof.

Kimani, L., BA San Diego, MSc Calif., MA San Diego Sr. Lectr.

McLennan, A. C., BA Witw., MEd Witw. Sr. Lectr.

Muller, M. W., BSc Witw., MSc Witw., PhD S.Af. Sr. Lectr.

Swilling, M., BA Witw., PhD Warw. Prof.

Tomlinson, R. H., BA Witw., MBA Witw., PhD Witw. Visiting Prof.†

Other Staff: 17 Lectrs.; 4 Hon. Lectrs.

Quantity Surveying, see Bldg. and Quant. Surv.

Radiation Services

Esser, J. D., MB ChB Pret., MMed Witw. Prof.; Head*

Medical Physics

Tel: (011) 488 3517

Keddy, R. J., BSc Pret., MSc Pret., PhD Lond. Prof.; Head*

Other Staff: 1 Lectr.; 3 Hon. Lectrs.

Nuclear Medicine, Division of

Tel: (011) 488 3560 Fax: (011) 488 3592

Esser, J. D., MB ChB Pret., MMed Witw. Prof.; Head*

Other Staff: 2 Lectrs.; 1 Visiting Lectr.†

Radiation Oncology

Tel: (011) 488 2325 Fax: (011) 647 2486

Fainberg, L., MD Tel-Aviv Sr. Lectr.

Laiker, R. H., BSc Witw., MB BCh Witw., MMed Witw. Sr. Lectr.

Other Staff: 7 Lectrs.; 5 Lectrs.†; 1 Hon. Lectr.

Radiology, Diagnostic

Solomon, A., MB BCh Witw., MMed Witw. Visiting Prof.; Acting Head*

Other Staff: 1 Lectr.†; 4 Hon. Lectrs.

Chris Hani Baragwanath Hospital

Tel: (011) 933 1100

Mirwis, J., MB BCh Witw. Sr. Lectr.

Other Staff: 1 Sr. Med. Officer; 1 Lectr.; 1 Lectr.†

Coronation Hospital

Tel: (011) 673 4200

Lucas, S., MB ChB Pret. Sr. Lectr.; Principal Med. Officer*

Other Staff: 1 Lectr.

Helen Joseph Hospital

Tel: (011) 489 0924

Paton, D. F., MB BCh Witw., MA Natal Sr. Lectr.; Principal*

Other Staff: 4 Lectrs.

Hillbrow Hospital

Tel: (011) 720 1121

Buchanan, G. M., MB BCh Witw. Sr. Lectr.

Damant, P., MB ChB Cape Town Sr. Lectr.

Davis, A., BSc S.Afr., MB BCh Witw. Sr. Lectr.

Eitzman, L. M., BCom Witw., MB BCh Witw. Sr. Lectr.

Pater, Z. Sr. Lectr.

Solomon, A., MB BCh Witw., MMed Witw. Sr. Lectr.

Other Staff: 4 Lectrs.

Johannesburg Hospital

Tel: (011) 488 3368

5 Lectrs.; 4 Hon. Lectrs.

Religious Studies

Tel: (011) 716 3416

Domeris, W. R., BA Witw., MA Witw., PhD Durh. Sr. Lectr.

Hellig, J. L., BA Witw., PhD Witw. Assoc. Prof.; Head*

Social Anthropology

Tel: (011) 716 2900

Coplan, D. B., BA Williams, MA Ghana, MA Indiana, PhD Indiana Prof.; Chair*

Hamilton, Carolyn, BA Natal, MA Witw., MA Witw., MA Johns H., PhD Johns H. Sr. Lectr.

James, D., BA Witw., MA Witw., PhD Witw. Sr. Lectr.

Thornton, R. J., BA Stan., MA Chic., PhD Chic. Assoc. Prof.

Other Staff: 1 Visiting Prof.; 1 Lectr.; 1 Sr. Res. Officer; 21 Res. Officers; 1 Lectr.†; 3 Res. Officers†

Social Work

Tel: (011) 716 4142

Drower, Sandra J., BSocSc Cape Town, PhD Cape Town Sr. Lectr.

McKendrick, Brian W., BSocSc Natal, MSocSc Natal, PhD Witw. Prof.; Head*

Other Staff: 5 Lectrs.; 1 Sr. Tutor; †

Sociology

Tel: (011) 716 2897 Fax: (011) 339 8163

Adler, G., BA Calif., PhD Col. Sr. Lectr.

Bozzoli, Belinda, BA Witw., MA Sus., DPhil Sus. Prof.; Head*

Chimere-Dan, O. D., BSc P.Harcourt, MSc Lond., PhD Lond. Sr. Lectr.

Cock, J., BA Rhodes, BSocSc Rhodes, PhD Rhodes Assoc. Prof.

Gilbert, L., BA Jerusalem, MPH Jerusalem Sr. Lectr.

Hyslop, J. R. O., MA Oxf., MA Birm., PhD Witw. Sr. Lectr.

Lazar, D. A. L., BSc Lond., BPhil York(UK), DPhil Oxf. Sr. Lectr.

Morris, E., BA Witw., MA Witw. Sr. Lectr.

Posel, D., BA Witw., DPhil Oxf. Assoc. Prof.

Webster, E. C., BA Rhodes, BPhil York(UK), MA Oxf., PhD Witw. Prof.

Other Staff: 5 Lectrs.; 1 Postdoctoral Res. Fellow; 2 Sr. Tutors; 2 Tutors; 1 Hon. Res. Fellow

Research: sociology of work

Speech Pathology and Audiology

Includes Speech and Hearing Clinic with Unit for Language and Unit for Hearing-Impaired Children

---

Tel: (011) 716 2374 Fax: (011) 716 2403

Penn, Claire, BA(Sp&HTherapy)Witw., PhD Witw. Prof.; Head*

Other Staff: 1 Lectr.; 2 Principal Tutors; 2 Sr. Tutors; 3 Tutors; 1 Sr. Tutor†; 3 Clin. Tutors†; 1 Hon. Prof. Res. Fellow; 1 Hon. Lectr.

Statistics and Actuarial Science

Tel: (011) 716 2790 Fax: (011) 339 1697

Asher, A., BBusSc Cape Town, FIA Prof.; Head*

Fatti, L. P., BSc Witw., MSc Lond., PhD Witw. Prof.

Fridjhon, P., BSc Witw., MA Lanc. Sr. Lectr.

Galpin, Jacqueline S., BSc Witw., MSc S.Af., DSc Potchef. Sr. Lectr.

Kass, G. V., BSc Witw., MSc(Econ) Lond., PhD Witw. Assoc. Prof.

Thomson, R. J., BSc Cape Town Visiting Prof.

Other Staff: 3 Lectrs.; 2 Sr. Tutors; 6 Lectrs.†

Surgery

Tel: (011) 647 2180 Fax: (011) 484 2717

Botha, J. R., MB ChB Pret., FCS(SA) Assoc. Prof.

Cronje, S. L., MB ChB Pret., MMed Pret. Prof.; Chief Specialist

Fait, A. B., BDS Witw. Sr. Lectr.

Kabeya, D. Sr. Lectr.

Levien, L. J., MB BCh Witw., PhD Witw., FCS(SA) Visiting Prof.; Acting Head*

Lownie, J. F., BDS Witw., MDent Witw. Prof.; Chief Specialist

Lownie, M. A., BDS Witw. Sr. Lectr.

Lurie, R., BDS Witw., MDent Witw. Hon. Prof.

Pantanowitz, D., BSc Witw, MB BCh Witw., FCS(SA), FRCSEd Prof.; Chief Specialist

Preston, C. B., BDS Witw., MDent Witw., PhD Witw. Prof.

Reyneke, J. P., BChD Pret., MChD Pret. Sr. Lectr.

Other Staff: 1 Lectr.; 1 Hon. Lectr.; 2 Hon. Res. Assocs.

Accident Service (Johannesburg Hospital)

Alves, H. M. R., MB ChB Pret. Sr. Lectr.

Boffard, K. D., MB BCh Witw. Sr. Lectr.; Principal Specialist*

D'Egidio, A., LMC Rome Sr. Lectr.

Fry, V. G., MB ChB Birm. Sr. Lectr.

Other Staff: 3 Lectrs.; 1 Lectr.†

Cardio-Thoracic Surgery (Johannesburg Hospital)

Cronje, S. L., MB ChB Pret., MMed Pret. Prof.; Chief Specialist*

Sussman, M. J., MB BCh Witw., FCS(SA) Sr. Lectr.

Vanderdonck, K., MD Louvain, FCS(SA) Sr. Lectr.

Other Staff: 5 Lectrs.; 6 Lectrs.†

General Surgery (Chris Hani Baragwanath Hospital)

Balabyeki, M. A., MB ChB Mak. Sr. Lectr.

Florizoone, M. G. C., MD Louvain, FRCSGlas Sr. Lectr.

Hatzitheofilou, C., MD Athens Sr. Lectr.

Kozaczynski, K. C. Sr. Lectr.

Maberti, P. M., LMC Rome Sr. Lectr.

Moyo, J., MB ChB Ghana Sr. Lectr.

Ribeiro, LM Lisbon Sr. Lectr.

Saadia, R., BA S.Af., MD Grenoble, FRCSEd Prof.; Chief Specialist*

Other Staff: 7 Lectrs.

General Surgery (Helen Joseph Hospital)

Pantanowitz, D., BSc Witw., MB BCh Witw., FCS(SA), FRCSEd Prof.; Chief Specialist*

Other Staff: 10 Lectrs.

General Surgery (Hillbrow Hospital)

Berzin, S., MD Latvia, PhD Latvia Sr. Lectr.

Bulabula, K., MB ChB Zaire Sr. Lectr.; Principal Med. Officer*

Other Staff: 6 Lectrs.; 2 Lectrs.†

General Surgery (Johannesburg Hospital)

Botha, J. R., MB ChB Pret., FCS(SA) Assoc. Prof.
Elahi, M., MB BS Punjab Sr. Lectr.
Levien, L. J., MB BCh Witw., PhD Witw., FCS(SA) Prof.; Chief Specialist*
Other Staff: 39 Lectrs.

Otorhinolaryngology (Chris Hani Baragwanath Hospital)

2 Lectrs.; 2 Lectrs.†

Otorhinolaryngology (Helen Joseph Hospital)

1 Lectr.

Otorhinolaryngology (Johannesburg Hospital)

McIntosh, W. A., MB ChB Pret., FCS(SA), FRCSEd, FRCSGlas, FACS Prof.; Chief Specialist*
Other Staff: 6 Lectrs.

Paediatric Surgery (Chris Hani Baragwanath Hospital)

Abrams, M. J., MD Louvain Sr. Lectr.
Da Fonseca, J. M. B., MD Lourenço Marques Sr. Lectr.
Farooq, Q., MB BS A.Iqbal Open Sr. Lectr.
Kazadi, N., MD Kinshasa Sr. Lectr.
Other Staff: 3 Lectrs.

Paediatric Surgery (Johannesburg Hospital)

Davies, M. R. Q., MB ChB Pret., MMed Pret., FCS(SA), FRCS, FRCSEd Prof.
Mahmood, A. J., MB BS Chitt. Sr. Lectr.
Other Staff: 1 Sr. Lectr.; 1 Lectr.

Plastic Surgery (Johannesburg Hospital)

Walker, D. H., FRCSEd Head*
Other Staff: 13 Lectrs.

Transplantation (Johannesburg Hospital)

Oosthuizen, M. M. J., PhD P.Elizabeth Sr. Specialist; Head*
Smith, J. A., DPhil Oxf. Sr. Specialist

Urology (Chris Hani Baragwanath Hospital)

Evans, J. P., MB BS Lond., FRCSEd Sr. Lectr.; Head*
Other Staff: 2 Lectrs.

Urology (Helen Joseph Hospital)

Tupy, M., Dr Bratislava Sr. Lectr.; Principal Med. Officer*

Urology (Johannesburg Hospital)

Kisner, C. D., MB BCh Witw. Sr. Lectr.
Other Staff: 3 Lectrs.; 5 Lectrs.†

Town and Regional Planning

Tel: (011) 716 2810 Fax: (011) 716 2051
Boden, R. T., BArch Witw., MEP Witw., PhD Wash. Sr. Lectr.
Drake, M. F., BA Natal, MA Witw., MSc Strath. Sr. Lectr.
Mabin, A. S., BA Witw., MA Witw., PhD S.Fraser Assoc. Prof.
Muller, J. G., BArch Witw., MA Prin., Prof.; Head*
Other Staff: 2 Lectrs.; 4 Lectrs.†

Translators and Interpreters, Graduate School for

Tel: (011) 716 3509
Meintjes, Elizabeth A., BA Witw., PhD Witw. Sr. Lectr.; Head*
Other Staff: 2 Lectrs.; 3 Lectrs.†

Urology, see under Surgery

Virology, see under Pathol., Sch. of

Zoology, see under Biol., Sch. of

SPECIAL CENTRES, ETC

Academic Development Centre

Tel: (011) 716 3690 Fax: (011) 403 2501
Hillman, J. C., MA Camb. Dir.*

Other Staff: 1 Lectr.

Advanced Social Research, Institute for

Tel: (011) 716 2503
Couzens, T. J., BA Rhodes, MA Oxf., PhD Witw. Prof.
Mangany, C. N., BA S.Af., MA S.Af., DLitt&Phil S.Af. Hon. Prof.
van Onselen, C., BSc Rhodes, BA Witw., DPhil Oxf. Prof.; Dir.*
Other Staff: 1 Sr. Res. Officer

Applied Legal Studies, Centre for

Cheadle, Halton, BA Natal, BProc S.Af., LLB Witw. Prof.
Haysom, Nicholas, BA Natal, LLB Cape Town Assoc. Prof.
Other Staff: 5 Sr. Res. Officers; 1 Res. Fellow; 8 Res. Officers; 1 Sr. Res. Officer†

Brain Function Research Unit

Tel: (011) 647 2359
Mitchell, D., BSc Witw., MSc Witw., PhD Witw., FRSSAf Dir.*
Other Staff: 1 Res. Officer; 1 Hon. Prof. Res. Fellow; 1 Hon. Res. Assoc.

Climatology Research Group

Tel: (011) 716 3400
Tyson, Peter D., BSc Witw., MSc Witw., PhD Witw., FRSSAf Prof.; Dir.*
Other Staff: 1 Sr. Res. Officer; 1 Hon. Res. Assoc.

Condensed Matter Physics Research Unit

Tel: (011) 716 2439 Fax: (011) 339 8262
Hoch, Prof. M. J. R., BSc Natal, MSc Natal, PhD St And. Dir.*
Other Staff: 1 Res. Officer

Economic Geology Research Unit

Tel: (011) 716 2730 Fax: (011) 339 1697
Anhaeusser, C. R., BSc Witw., MSc Witw., PhD Witw., DSc Witw. Prof.; Dir.*
Other Staff: 1 Sr. Res. Officer; 1 Res. Officer; 1 Hon. Prof. Res. Fellow

Education Policy Unit

Tel: (011) 716 5265 Fax: (011) 339 4386
Chisholm, Linda, BA Cape Town, MA Lond., PhD Witw. Dir.*
Other Staff: 2 Res. Officers

Geophysical Research, Bernard Price Institute of, and Geophysics, Department of

Tel: (011) 716 2799
Wright, C., BSc Durh., PhD ANU Prof.; Dir.*
Other Staff: 2 Sr. Res. Officers; 1 Res. Officer

Health Policy, Centre for the Study of

Tel: (011) 647 2627 Fax: (011) 642 0733
Schneider, H., MB ChB Cape Town Dir.*
Other Staff: 1 Sr. Res. Officer; 4 Res. Officers†

Mathematics, Science and Technology Education, Centre for Research and Development in

Tel: (011) 716 4296 Fax: (011) 339 1054
Bradley, J. D., BSc Leeds, PhD Lond. Assoc. Prof.; Dir.*

Mineral Metabolism, MRC–University Research Unit for

Tel: (011) 933 1530 Fax: (011) 938 9074
Pettifor, John M., MB BCh Witw., PhD Witw. Dir.*

Molecular Hepatology Research Unit

Tel: (011) 716 3815
Kew, M. C., MB BCh Witw., MD Witw., PhD Witw., DSc Witw. Sr. Res. Officer; Dir.*
Other Staff: 1 Sr. Res. Officer; 1 Res. Officer

MRC–Bone Research Laboratory

Tel: (011) 647 2144 Fax: (011) 647 2300
Ripamonti, U., MD Milan, MDent Witw., PhD Witw. Res. Officer; Leader*

MRC–University Dental Research Institute

Tel: (011) 407 4163 Fax: (011) 339 3036
Cleaton-Jones, P. E., BDS Witw., MB BCh Witw., PhD Witw., DSc(Dent) Witw. Prof.; Dir.*

Nuclear Sciences, Schonland Research Centre for

Tel: (011) 716 3140 Fax: (011) 339 2144
Annegarn, H. J., BSc Witw., PhD Witw. Assoc. Prof.
Verhagen, B. T. H., BSc Pret., MSc Pret., PhD Witw. Assoc. Prof.
Watterson, J. I. W., BSc Witw., PhD Witw. Assoc. Prof.; Chairperson*
Other Staff: 1 Sr. Res. Officer; 1 Postdoctoral Res. Fellow; 1 Hon. Prof. Res. Fellow

Palaeontological Research, Bernard Price Institute for

Tel: (011) 716 2870 Fax: (011) 339 7367
Wright, C., BSc Durh., PhD ANU Prof.; Dir.*
Other Staff: 2 Sr. Res. Officers; 1 Res. Officer; 1 Hon. Res. Assoc.

Science, College of

Tel: (011) 716 2956 Fax: (011) 339 4908
Keartland, J. M., BSc Witw., PhD Witw. Assoc. Prof.
Rutherford, M., BSc(Eng) Lond., PhD Lond. Assoc. Prof.; Dir.*
Other Staff: 5 Sr. Tutors; 5 Tutors; 1 Res. Officer; 2 Lectrs.†; 3 Tutors†

Sociology of Work Research Unit

Webster, E. C., BA Rhodes, BPhil York(UK), MA Oxf., PhD Witw. Dir.*
Other Staff: 1 Res. Officer

Wits Rural Facility

Tel: (01528) 33991 Fax: (01528) 33992
Gear, John S. S., BSc Witw., MB BCh Witw., DPhil Oxf., FCP(SA) Prof.
White, M. V. G., MSc Leeds Acting Dir.*

CONTACT OFFICERS

Admissions (first degree). Mabanga, Jeannette M.
Admissions (higher degree). Mabanga, Jeannette M.
Adult/continuing education. Russell, Prof. Denzil D., BSc Rhodes
Alumni. Edey, Susan M., BA Witw.
Archives. Arnott, L. Diana, BA Witw.
Careers. Haniff, F. S.
Computing services. Watermeyer, Henry C., BComm Cape Town
Development/fund-raising. Foundation: Steadman, Prof. I. P., BA Natal, MA N.Y.State, PhD Witw.
Estates and buildings/works and services. Williams, Alastair D., BSc(Eng) Cape Town
Examinations. Hammond, Susan E.
Finance. Lee, M. N.
General enquiries. Registrar (Academic): Swemmer, Derek K., BA Pret., MA Pret., DLitt&Phil S.Af.
Health services. Seabrook, Marion, MB BCh Witw., BA S.Af.
Industrial liaison. Crowther, Ian D.
International office. Milliken, Patricia J.
Library (enquiries). Edwards, Heather M., BA Rhodes, MA Witw.
Public relations, information and marketing. Public Relations: McAllister, W. H., BA Natal
Scholarships, awards, loans. Scholarships: Fick, Elizabeth, BEd Sus.
Schools liaison. Kekana, Yvonne S.
Security. Hurst, Clifford J.
Sport and recreation. Sports Administration: Baxter, John S., BA(PhysEd) Rhodes

Staff development and training. Reiner, Gail, BA *Witw.*
Student welfare/counselling. Haniff, F. S.

Students with disabilities. Disabled Students' Programme: Suchon, Dominique

[Information supplied by the institution as at 15 June 1998, and edited by the ACU]

UNIVERSITY OF ZULULAND

Member of the Association of Commonwealth Universities

Postal Address: Private Bag X1001, Kwa-Dlangezwa, Natal, 3886 South Africa
Telephone: (0351) 93911 **Fax**: (0351) 93130 **Telex**: 631311

RECTOR AND VICE-CHANCELLOR*—Dlamini, Prof. Charles R. M.
REGISTRAR—Ndaki, Prof. Byron, BA *S.Af.*, LLB *Fort Hare*

ACADEMIC UNITS

University departments: African Languages, Afrikaans, Agriculture, Anthropology, Applied Mathematics, Biochemistry, Botany, Business Economics, Chemistry, Comparative Law, Constitutional Law, Criminal and Procedural Law, Criminal Justice, Criminology, Didactics, Drama, Economics, Education, Educational Psychology, Engineering, English, French, General Linguistics, Geography, German, History, History of Education, Home Economics, Human Movement Science, Hydrology, Industrial Psychology, Information Technology, Law, Library Science, Mathematical Statistics, Mathematics, Mercantile Law, Missiology, Music, Nursing Science, Philosophy, Philosophy of Education, Physics, Political Science, Private Law, Psychology, Social Work, Sociology, Theology, Water Research, Zoology.

[Information supplied by the institution as at 5 November 1998, and edited by the ACU]

The South African Directory to Subjects of Study follows on p. 1250

SOUTH AFRICA : DIRECTORY

The table below shows which of the institutions indicated provide facilities for study and/or research in the subjects named. The table covers *broad subject areas* only: ie the individual subjects of specialisation in certain professional fields such as education, law, medicine or veterinary science, are not included. In the case of related subject areas which have been grouped together (eg Agronomy/Soil Science), it should be borne in mind that one or more of the subjects may be offered by the institution concerned.

	Cape Town	Medical U. of Southern Africa	Natal	Orange Free State	Port Elizabeth	Potchefstroom	Pretoria	Rand Afrikaans	Rhodes	South Africa	Stellenbosch	Venda	Witwatersrand
Accountancy/Accounting	U		X	X	X	X	X	X	X	X	X	U	X
African Languages/Studies	X		X	X	X	X	X	X	X	X	X	M	X
Afrikaans/Dutch	X		X	X	X	X	X	X	X	X	X	D	X
Agriculture/Agricultural Science			X	X			X				X	U	
Agronomy/Soil Science			X	X			X				X	U	
Animal Science		U	X	X			X		X		X	U	
Anthropology	X		X	X	X		X		X	X	MD	M	U
Arabic										X			
Archaeology	X		U				X			U		U	X
Architecture	X		X	X	X		X						X
Art, History of	X		X	X		M	X			X	X		U
Biochemistry	X	X	X	X	X	X	X	X	X	U	X	U	X
Biology	X	X	X	X			U			U	X	U	X
Botany/Plant Science	X		X	X	X	X	X	X	X	U	X	U	
Building/Construction	X		X	X	X		X						X
Business	X			X	X		X	X	X	X	X	M	
Chemistry	X	X	X	X	X	X	X	X	X	X	X	M	X
Classics/Greek/Latin/Ancient History	X		X	X		X	X	X	X	X	X		X
Computer Science	X	U	X	X	X	X	X	X	X	X	X		X
Dentistry		X					X				X		X
Development Studies			MD		X		U	X	X	X	X		
Drama/Theatre/Dance	X		X	X			X		X		X		
Economics	X		X	X	X	X	X	X	X	X	X	U	X
Economics, Agricultural			X	X			X				X	U	
Education	X		MD	X	X	X	X	X	X	X	X	M	X
Engineering							X	X					
Agricultural			X				X						
Chemical	X		X			X	X				X		X
Civil	X		X				X	X			X		X
Electrical/Electronic	X		X			X	X	X			X		X
Industrial							X				X		X
Mechanical	X		X			X	X	X			X		X
Metallurgical/Materials	X					X	X						X
Mining							X						X
English	X	U	X	X	X	X	X	X	X	X	X	M	X
Environmental Science/Studies	X		X	X		X	U	X	U		X	U	U
Fine Art	X		X	X			X		X	M	X		X
Food Science/Nutrition/Home Economics		X	X	X		X	X				X		
French	X		X	X	X	U	X	X	X	X	X		U
Genetics			X	X			X				X		X
Geography	X		X	X	X	X	X	X	X	X	X	U	X
Geology/Earth Sciences	X		X	X	X		X	X	X	X	U		X
German	X		X	X	X	U	X	X	X	X	X		U
Health Sciences	X	X		X	X		X				X	U	X

TO SUBJECTS OF STUDY

For further information about the individual subjects taught at each institution, please refer to the *Index to Department Names* at the end of the Yearbook, but for full details about subjects/courses offered at universities in the Commonwealth each institution's own official publications must be consulted. U = may be studied for first degree course; M = may be studied for master's degree course; D = research facilities to doctoral level; X = all three levels (UMD). **Note**—the table only includes information provided by institutions currently in membership of the Association of Commonwealth Universities, submitted for this edition of the Yearbook.

	Cape Town	Medical U. of Southern Africa	Natal	Orange Free State	Port Elizabeth	Potchefstroom	Pretoria	Rand Afrikaans	Rhodes	South Africa	Stellenbosch	Venda	Witwatersrand
Hebrew/Semitic Studies	X		U	X		X	X	X	U	X	X		
History	X		X	X	X	X	X	X	X	X	X	U	U
Horticulture			X	X			X				X	U	
Industrial Psychology	X		X	X	X	X	X	X	X	X	X	U	U
Information Science/Studies/Systems	X	U		X	X	X	X	X	X	X	X		X
Italian	X		U								X		X
Journalism/Communication/Media Studies			X	X		X		X	X	X	X		
Law/Legal Studies	X		X	X	X	X	X	X	X	X	X	M	U
Library Science	X		X	X		M	X	X		X			
Linguistics	X		X	X	X	X	X	X	X	X	X	U	X
Management	X		X	X	X	X	X	X		X	X	U	
Mathematics	X	X	X	X	X	X	X	X	X	X	X	M	X
Medicine/Surgery	X	X	X	X			X				X		X
Microbiology	X	X	X	X	X	X	X		X	U	X	U	
Military Science											X		
Music	X		X	X	X	X	X		X	X	X	U	X
Nursing	X	M	X	X	X	X	X	X		X	X	U	X
Optometry		X						X					X
Pharmacy/Pharmaceutical Sciences		X			X	X			X				X
Pharmacology	X		X	X	X	X	M		U		X		X
Philosophy	X		X	X	X	X	X	X	X	X	X	U	X
Physical Education/Human Movement/Sports Studies	X		M	X	X	X	X	X	X		X		X
Physics	X	X	X	X	X	X	X	X	X	X	X	U	X
Physiology	X	X	X	X		X	X		U	U	X		X
Planning, Urban and Regional/Landscape Architecture	X		MD	X	X	X	X						X
Politics/Political Science	X		X	X	X	X	X	X	X	X	X	M	X
Psychology	X	X	X	X	X	X	X	X	X	X	X	M	X
Public Administration	M			X	X	X	X	X	U	X	X	U	X
Religion/Theology	X		X	X	X	X	X	X	X	X	X	M	X
Russian	X										X		
Social Work	X		X	X	X	X	X	X	X	X	X	U	X
Sociology	X		X	X	X	X	X	X	X	X	X	M	X
Statistics	X	X	X	X	X	X	X	X	X	X	X	M	X
Surveying/Quantity Surveying	X		X	X	X		X						X
Teacher Education/Training			MD	X	X	X	X	X	X	U	X	M	X
Veterinary Science		X					X						
Zoology	X		X	X	X	X	X	X	X	U	X	U	X

SOUTH PACIFIC

UNIVERSITY OF THE SOUTH PACIFIC

Established 1968

Member of the Association of Commonwealth Universities

Postal Address: Suva, Fiji
Telephone: 313900, 300830, 300482 **Fax**: 301305 **Cables**: University, Suva **Telex**: FJ 2276
WWW: http://www.usp.ac.fj

CHANCELLOR—Manuella, Tulanga, MBE, GCMG
PRO-CHANCELLOR—Siwatibau, Savenaca, BSc *Well.*, MSc *Auck.*, MA *Sus.*
VICE-CHANCELLOR*—Solofa, Esekia, BSc *Cant.*, MPA *Harv.*
DEPUTY VICE-CHANCELLOR—Chandra, Prof. Rajesh, BA *S.Pac.*, MA *S.Pac.*, PhD
    Br.Col.
PRO-VICE-CHANCELLOR—Lynch, Prof. John D., BA *Syd.*, PhD *Hawaii*
PRO-VICE-CHANCELLOR—......
PRO-VICE-CHANCELLOR—Manoa, Pio, BA *Macq.*
REGISTRAR‡—Pillay, Sarojini D., BSc *Madr.*, BT *Madr.*, MS *Central Mich.*
BURSAR—Dickson, Hugh
UNIVERSITY LIBRARIAN—Williams, Esther W., BA *Well.*, MA *Well.*

GENERAL INFORMATION

History. The university was established in 1968. It has centres in 12 Pacific island countries: Cook Islands, Fiji, Kiribati, Marshall Islands, Nauru, Niue, Samoa, Solomon Islands, Tokelau, Tonga, Tuvalu and Vanuatu, and covers 33,000,000 square km of ocean.

Admission to first degree courses. Fiji Form Seven exam with 250 marks out of 400, and with minimum 50% in English and in specified subjects for particular programmes. Equivalent qualifications, including the university's foundation science programme, and New Zealand Bursary, may also be accepted.

First Degrees. BA, BAgr, BEd, BSc, BTech, LLB.
    All courses are full-time, and most last 3 years. LLB: 4 years.

Higher Degrees. MA, MBA, MSc, PhD.
    MBA: 1 year full-time or 2 years part-time; MA, MSc: 1½–3 years full-time or 2½–5 years part-time; PhD: 3–5 years full-time or 4–7 years part-time.

Language of Instruction. English. English Resources Unit in Centre for the Enhancement of Learning and Teaching is able to assist those for whom English is not their first language.

Libraries. 600,000 volumes; 700 periodicals subscribed to. Special collection: Pacific collection.

Fees (1998). Undergraduate: (regional) F$234–405 per semester course; (non-regional, ie not resident in any member country or in receipt of a third country award) F$820–1370 per semester course; LLB: (regional) F$305 (first year) to VT33,000 (in Vanuatu) per semester course; (non-regional) F$1025–VT77,000 per semester course. Postgraduate (non-regional): F$2000 per course (MBA); F$2050 per semester course (other courses). Thesis fees (annual): F$8200 full-time, F$4100 part-time.

Academic Awards (1997). 43 awards, almost all valued at F$250.

Academic Year (1999). Two semesters: 22 February–25 June; 19 July–19 November (approximate dates).

Income (1998). Total, F$42,296,000.

Statistics. Staff: 1000 (303 academic and comparable staff, 697 other). Students (1997): 4095 women, 5117 men; full-time 3499; part-time 5709; non-regional (international) 128 (66 men, 62 women).

FACULTIES/SCHOOLS

Agriculture, School of
Tel: (685) 21671 Fax: (685) 22933
Head: Pattie, Prof. W. A., BSc *NSW*, PhD *NSW*
Secretary (Alafua Campus): Nagatalevu, Aca, BBS *Massey*

Humanities, School of
Tel: (679) 212370
Head: Thaman, Prof. Konai H., BA *Auck.*, MA *Calif.*, PhD
Administrative Assistant: Kausimae, Paul, BA *S.Pac.*

Law, School of
Tel: (678) 22748 Fax: (678) 22633
Head: Hughes, Prof. Robert, BA *NE*, PhD *NE*
Secretary (Emalus Campus): Ngwele, Ala, BA *S.Pac.*

Pure and Applied Sciences, School of
Tel: (679) 212080 Fax: (679) 302548
Head: Prasad, Surendra, BSc *S.Pac.*, MSc *S.Pac.*, PhD *ANU*
Administrative Assistant: Inia, Marieta, BA *S.Pac.*

Social and Economic Development, School of
Tel: (679) 302413 Fax: (679) 301487
Head: Naidu, Vijay S., DPhil *Sus.*, MA
Administrative Assistant: Seeto, Viniana, BA *S.Pac.*

ACADEMIC UNITS

Accounting and Financial Management
Tel: (679) 212532 Fax: (679) 301487
Nandan, Ruvendra, BCom *Delhi*, MA *S.Pac.*   Sr. Lectr.
Patel, Arvind, BA *S.Pac.*, MCom *NSW*   Sr. Lectr. (on leave)
Prasad, Govind, LLB *Delhi*, BCom *Ban.*, MCom *Ban.*, MA *Raj.*, PhD *Ban.*   Assoc. Prof.
Sharma, M. D., MCom *Agra*, PhD *Agra*   Prof., Banking
White, Michael, BSc(Econ) *Hull*, MSc(Econ) *Lond.*   Prof.; Head*
Other Staff: 7 Lectrs.
Research: accounting standards; performance measurement in public sector; working capital management

Agriculture, School of
Alafua Campus (Western Samoa)
Tel: (685) 21671 Fax: (685) 22933
Ajuyah, Asifo, BSc *Ib.*, MSc *Glas.*, PhD *Alta.*   Sr. Lectr.
Fuatai, L. I., MSc *Cornell*, PhD *Cornell*, BSc   Sr. Lectr.
Johnson, David, BSc *Reading*, MSc *Reading*   Sr. Lectr.
Tofinga, M., MAgr *PNG*, PhD *Reading*   Sr. Lectr.; Acting Head*
Yapa, L., BScAgric *Ceyl.*, MSc *Obihiro*, PhD *Penn.*   Sr. Lectr.
Other Staff: 7 Lectrs.
Research: bio-pesticides; high-yielding, drought and disease resistant Taro varieties; stress and coping strategies among university students

Applied Sciences, Institute of, see Special Centres, etc

Biology
Tel: (679) 212415 Fax: (679) 315601
Newell, P., BSc(Hort) *Lond.*, PhD *Lond.*   Prof.; Head*
Tyagi, A. P., BSc(Ag) *Agra*, MSc(Ag) *Ban.*, PhD *Haryana Ag.*   Sr. Lectr.
Other Staff: 7 Lectrs.
Research: chromosomal analysis; conservation biology; marine biology; molecular genetics; reproductive biology

Business Administration Programme

Tel: (679) 212731 Fax: (679) 303229

Fullerton, Ronald, BA Rutgers, MBA Cornell, MA Harv., PhD Wis.   Prof.; Head*

Olutimayin, Jide, MSc Aston, PhD Lond.   Sr. Lectr.

Business Studies, see also Management and Public Admin.

Tel: (679) 212137 Fax: (679) 301487

Reddy, N., MBA NSW, PhD Auck.   Co-ordinator*

Chemistry

Tel: (679) 212417 Fax: (679) 302548

Aalbersberg, W. G. L., BA Cornell, PhD Calif.   Reader/Assoc. Prof.

Ali, S., MSc PhD   Sr. Lectr.

Bonato, J. A., BSc NSW   Sr. Lectr.

Gangaiya, Philomena, PhD Camb., MSc   Sr. Lectr.

Khurma, Jagjit, BSc Punj.Ag., MSc Punj.Ag., PhD Otago   Sr. Lectr.

Koshy, K. C., MSc Kerala, PhD WI   Reader/Assoc. Prof.

Sotheeswaran, S., BSc Ceyl., PhD Hull, DSc Hull   Prof.; Head*

Other Staff: 6 Lectrs.

Research: environmental amd marine chemistry; food chemistry; natural products and marine natural products chemistry; polymer chemistry

Computing Science, see Maths. and Computing Sci.

Development Studies Centre

Tel: (679) 212297 Fax: (679) 303040

Walsh, Alan C., BA NZ, MA Well., PhD Massey   Prof.; Co-ordinator*

Other Staff: 1 Lectr.

Research: population; rural development; social consequences of economic change and poverty; urbanisation

Economics

Tel: (679) 212547 Fax: (679) 301487

Chand, G., PhD New Sch.Soc.Res., MA   Sr. Lectr.

Forsyth, D., MA Aberd.   Prof.; Head*

Grynberg, R., BEc Monash, MA S.Fraser, PhD McG.   Assoc. Prof./Reader

Sharma, K. L., BSc(Ag) Ud., MSc IARI, PhD Raj.   Sr. Lectr.

Szmedra, Philip, BA Penn.State, MS Georgia, PhD Georgia   Sr. Lectr.

Other Staff: 5 Lectrs.

Research: development economics; economics of technology; human resources development; industrialisation

Education and Psychology

Tel: (679) 212203 Fax: (679) 305053

Baba, T. L., BA NE, MEd Syd., PhD Macq.   Prof.; Head*

Kedrayate, Akanisi, MEd Glas., PhD NE   Sr. Lectr.

Muralidhar, S., BSc Mys., MSc Karn., MSc Keele, PhD Monash   Assoc. Prof./Reader

Schultz, R., BA Adel., MEd Adel., MA Lond.   Sr. Lectr.

Sharma, A., MEd NE, EdD Brist., BA   Sr. Lectr.

Solomona, U. M. P., BMus N.Y.State   Sr. Lectr., Expressive Arts

Sullivan, Terence, BEd Qld., BSocSc Qld., PhD NE   Sr. Lectr.

Thaman, Konai H., BA Auck., MA Calif., PhD   Prof.

Velayutham, T., BSc Madr., MA Ceyl., PhD La Trobe   Assoc. Prof./Reader

Other Staff: 6 Lectrs.

Research: community stress and coping; human development studies; learning difficulties; linguistics; pacific notions of learning

Financial Management, see Acctg. and Financial Management

Food and Textiles

Tel: (679) 212229 Fax: (679) 303413

Jannif-Dean, Jasmine S., MS Wis.   Sr. Lectr.

Schultz, Jimaima T., BAppSc W.Aust.I.T., MSc Otago   Sr. Lectr.

Toganivalu, Vasiti K. V., BS Wash.State, MCN Qld.   Sr. Lectr.; Head*

Research: applied design; applied nutrition; comparative shopping; consumer textiles; recipe development using local foods

Geography

Tel: (679) 212542 Fax: (679) 301487

Ali, Imam, BEd S.Pac., MA S.Pac., PhD ANU   Sr. Lectr.

Nunn, P. D., BSc Lond., PhD Lond.   Prof.; Head*

Thaman, R. R., MA Calif., PhD Calif.   Prof., Pacific Islands Biogeography

Other Staff: 4 Lectrs.

Research: biodiversity; climate change; industrialisation; sea-level rise

History/Politics

Tel: (679) 212083 Fax: (679) 301487

Firth, Stewart, BA Syd., MA ANU, DPhil Oxf.   Prof.; Head*

Other Staff: 8 Lectrs.

Research: Australian foreign policy; Pacific Islands history; Pacific Islands politics

Land Management

Tel: (679) 212469 Fax: (679) 301487

2 Lectrs.

Research: agriculutural valuations; customary land tenure

Law

Tel: (678) 22748 Fax: (678) 27785

Corrin-Care, Jennifer, BA CNAA, MPhil Nott.   Sr. Lectr.

Hardy-Pickering, Sarah, LLB Wales, MA Warw.   Sr. Lectr.

Hughes, Robert, BA NE, PhD NE   Prof.; Head*

Other Staff: 4 Lectrs.; 1 CFTC Fellow

Research: customary law and common law in the South Pacific

Literature and Language

Tel: (679) 212214 Fax: (679) 305053

Gaskell, Ian, BA Wat., MA Tor., PhD Tor.   Prof.

Griffen, Arlene, BA ANU, MA Lond.   Sr. Lectr.

Griffiths, Patrick, BA Witw., PhD Edin.   Sr. Lectr.

Khan, Veena, MA Auck., MA Monash   Sr. Lectr.

Lynch, J. D., BA Syd., PhD Hawaii   Prof.

Manoa, P., BA Macq.   Sr. Lectr.

Mugler, France, Lic Caen, MA Toledo, PhD Mich.   Sr. Lectr.

Prakash, Som, BA Auck., MA Auck., PhD Flin.   Sr. Lectr.

Ricketts, Jane, MA Cant.   Sr. Lectr.

Subramani, BA Cant., MA New Br., PhD   Prof.; Head*

Other Staff: 4 Lectrs.

Research: creative writing; Pacific journalism; Pacific languages; Pacific literature

Management and Public Administration, see also Special Centres, etc (Soc. and Admin. Studies, Inst. of)

Tel: (679) 212134 Fax: (679) 301487

Koirala, Kiran, BCom Tribhuvan, MCom Tribhuvan, PhD Pune   Sr. Lectr.

Reddy, Narendra, BA S.Pac., MBA NSW, PhD Auck.   Sr. Lectr.; Acting Head*

Sarkar, Abu E., BSS Dhaka, MSS Dhaka, PhD Liv.   Sr. Lectr.

Other Staff: 3 Lectrs.

Research: corporate culture; Japanese-style corporations management; public sector reform; total quality management; tourism and small business development

Marine Affairs Programme

Tel: (679) 302338 Fax: (679) 302388

Bidesi, Vina R., BA S.Pac., MSc Kagoshima   Acting Co-ordinator*

Veitayaki, Joeli, MA   Co-ordinator* (on leave)

Other Staff: 1 Lectr.

Research: coastal area management; fisheries economics; management of marine resources; marine natural products; sustainable resource development

Marine Studies

Tel: (679) 212051 Fax: (679) 301490

South, G. R., PhD Liv., DSc Liv.   Prof.; Head*

Other Staff: 4 Lectrs.; 1 Co-ordinator; 1 Operations Manager; 1 Fellow

Research: climate change; coral reefs and atolls; marine natural products; marine pollution; traditional marine tenure

Mathematics and Computing Science

Tel: (679) 212364 Fax: (679) 303455

Adams, Anthony, BSc Manc., MEd Manc., PhD Manc.   Assoc. Prof./Reader; Acting Head*

Deoki, Parul V., BA Auck., BA Ott., MA   Sr. Lectr.

Glasby, Stephen, BSc Syd., PhD Syd.   Sr. Lectr.

Hosack, J., BSc Cal.Tech., MSc Calif., PhD Calif.   Reader/Assoc. Prof.

Klin, Mikhail, BA Kiev, BSc Kiev, MSc Kiev, PhD Kiev   Sr. Lectr.

Osei, K., BSc Ghana, MPhil Lond., PhD Hull   Sr. Lectr.

Pleasants, Anne, BSc Qld., MSc Qld., MPhil Open(UK)   Sr. Lectr.

Pleasants, Peter, BA Cant., MA Cant., MSc Wales, PhD Cant.   Sr. Lectr.

Rao, A. M. S., BSc Mys., BEd Mys., MSc Karn.   Sr. Lectr.

Sharma, D. P., PhD ANU, MSc   Sr. Lectr.

Other Staff: 6 Lectrs.

Research: artificial neural networks; combinatorics; cyclotonic numbers; fourier analysis; photometric stereo techniques

Pacific Studies, Institute of, see Special Centres, etc

Physics

Tel: (679) 212063 Fax: (679) 302548

Garimella, S., MSc And., DrRerNat Mainz   Sr. Lectr.

Khan, M. Jafar, BSc S.Pac., MSc S.Pac., PhD NSW   Sr. Lectr.

Kumar, M., PhD Nott., BSc, FRMetS   Reader/Assoc. Prof.

McArthur, Alastair, BA Strath., PhD Nott.   Prof.; Head*

Prasad, Surendra, BSc S.Pac., MSc S.Pac., PhD ANU   Sr. Lectr.

Todd, Hilary, BSc Durh., PhD Lond.   Sr. Lectr.

Other Staff: 4 Lectrs.

Research: applications of nuclear techniques; energy and the environment; marine physics

Politics, see Hist./Pol.

Population Studies Programme

Tel: (679) 302865 Fax: (679) 302865

Seniloli, Kesaia, MA ANU, PhD ANU, BA   Co-ordinator*

Other Staff: 1 Lectr.

Research: male and young people's attitudes towards family planning; teenage pregnancies

Psychology, see Educn. and Psychol.

Public Administration, see Management and Public Admin.

Social and Administrative Studies, Institute of, see Special Centres, etc

Social Science

Tel: (679) 212651 Fax: (679) 301487

1 Lectr.

Research: social and economic survey in the Pacific

Sociology

Tel: (679) 212136 Fax: (679) 301487

Monsell-Davis, Michael, BA *PNG*, BA *Macq.*, PhD *Macq.* Sr. Lectr.
Naidu, Vijay S., DPhil *Sus.*, MA Assoc. Prof./Reader
Plange, N.-K., BA *Ghana*, MA *Guelph*, PhD *Tor.* Reader; Head*
Other Staff: 5 Lectrs.
Research: child sex abuse; commercial sex and sexual health; ethics and professionalism; male attitudes towards contraception and pregnancy in the South Pacific

Technology

Tel: (679) 212223 Fax: (679) 302567

Aborhey, S. E., BSc *Kumasi*, PhD *NSW* Sr. Lectr.; Acting Head*
Szilvassy, Charles, BEng *T.U.Miskolc*, MSc *Budapest*, PhD *T.U.Miskolc*, DSc *Hungarian Acad.Sc.* Prof.
Other Staff: 5 Lectrs.
Research: building aerodynamics under cyclone conditions; combinational system minimisations; mechanical and microstructural behaviour of steel; quality practices of manufacturing organisations

Textiles, see Food and Textiles

Tourism Studies Programme

Tel: (679) 212688 Fax: (679) 301487

Harrison, David, BSc *Lond.*, PhD *Lond.* Co-ordinator; Head*
Other Staff: 1 Lectr.
Research: development of tourism in the South Pacific; extent of eco-tourism in Fiji; social and cultural impact of luxury island tourism in villages where tourism is developed

SPECIAL CENTRES, ETC

Applied Sciences, Institute of

Tel: (679) 212245 Fax: (679) 300373

Beyer, R., BSc *Strath.*, PhD *Otago* Dir.*
Other Staff: 1 Manager; 3 Fellows
Research: coastal processes; environmental impact of solid and liquid waste management; impact of development on coastal environments; pollution monitoring; water quality and biodiversity

Arts and Culture, Oceania Centre for

Tel: (679) 212832 Fax: (679) 308542

Hau'ofa, Epeli, BA *NE*, MA *McG.*, PhD *ANU* Dir.*

Education, Institute of

Tel: (679) 212361 Fax: (679) 302409

Benson, C. J., MA *Auck.* Dir.*
Other Staff: 1 Co-ordinator; 5 Fellows
Research: assessment/evaluation; basic education literacy; education in the University of the South Pacific region; education policy; quality of education

Justice and Applied Legal Studies, Institute of

Tel: (679) 212801 Fax: 679) 314274

Pulea, Mere, BSocSt *Qld.*, LLB *Lond.*, MPhil *S.Pac.* Dir.*
Other Staff: 3 Fellows
Research: disability law and policy; human rights; legal literacy

Learning and Teaching, Centre for the Enhancement of (CELT)

Tel: (679) 212608 Fax: (679) 307194

Hunter, Bruce, BA *La Trobe*, MA *Monash* Dir.*
Other Staff: 3 Lectrs.
Research: application of information technology; student learning processes

Marine Resources, Institute of

Tel: (677) 30107 Fax: (677) 30258

Pillay, Gunusagaran, BSc *Madr.*, MSc Dir.*
Other Staff: 1 Fellow
Research: mangrove ecology; mangroves

Media Centre

Tel: (679) 212077 Fax: (679) 305779

Farkas, Gerald, BAA *Ryerson*, BA *Tor.*, MCEd *Sask.* Dir.*

Pacific Studies, Institute of

Tel: (679) 212332 Fax: (679) 301594

Ravuvu, A., PhD *Auck.*, MA Prof., Pacific Studies; Dir.*
Other Staff: 3 Fellows
Research: ethnographic projects in Solomon Island and Vanuatu; ethnographic study of kava; Fiji history; governance in Samoa and Vanuatu; publishing of Pacific writing

Research, Extension and Training in Agriculture, Institute of

Tel: (685) 22372 Fax: (685) 22933

Umar, M., BAgrSc *Qld.*, MSc *W.Virginia* Dir.*
Research: agricultural information networks; Taro leaf blight resistant cultivars

Social and Administrative Studies, Institute of

Tel: (679) 212079 Fax: (679) 303229

Ram, Hari, BSc *Delhi* Dir.*
Other Staff: 2 Fellows
Research: commercialisation; corporatisation; privatisation; public sector reform and improvement

University Extension

Tel: (679) 212052 Fax: (679) 300482

Bolabola, Cema, BA *S.Pac.*, MPS *Philippines* Co-ordinator, Continuing Education
Tuimaleali'ifano, Eileen J., MA Co-ordinator
Van Trease, Howard, BA *Calif.*, MA *Calif.State*, PhD *S.Pac.* Dir.*
Research: expected listening and speaking skills for distance students; impact of programmes provided through a university extension centre; impact of satellite technology on distance education; problems faced by distance students

Cook Islands Centre

Tel: (682) 29415 Fax: (682) 21315

Herrmann, John J., MA *ANU*, BA Dir.*
Other Staff: 1 Lectr.

Fiji Centre

Tel: (679) 666800 Fax: (679) 667133

Tubuna, Sakiusa, MEd *NE*, BA Dir.*
Other Staff: 3 Lectrs.

Kiribati Centre

Tel: (686) 21085 Fax: (686) 21419

Tewareka Tentoa, Beta, BEd Dir.*
Other Staff: 1 Lectr.

Marshall Islands Centre

Tel: (692) 625 7279 Fax: (692) 625 7282
1 Lectr.
Vacant Posts: Dir.*

Nauru Centre

Tel: (674) 555 6455 Fax: (674) 444 3774

Gaiyabu, Maria, BEd *S.Qld.* Dir.*

Niue Centre

Tel: (683) 4049 Fax: (683) 4315 (c/o Cable & Wireless)

Talagi, Maru, BA *Auck.*, MA *Auck.* Dir.*

Samoa Centre

Tel: (685) 20874 Fax: (685) 23424

Va'ai, Makerita, BEd Dir.*
Other Staff: 1 Lectr.

Solomon Islands Centre

Tel: (677) 21307 Fax: (677) 21287

Galo, Glyn, MBA *Qld.*, BSc Dir.*
Other Staff: 1 Lectr.

Tonga Centre

Tel: (676) 29240 Fax: (676) 29249

Fukofuka, Salote, BA *NE*, MEd *Canberra* Dir.*
Other Staff: 1 Lectr.

Tuvalu Centre

Tel: (688) 20811 Fax: (688) 20704

Vacant Posts: Dir.*

Vanuatu Centre

Tel: (678) 22748 Fax: (678) 22633

Nirua, Jean-Pierre, BA Dir.*
Other Staff: 3 Lectrs.

CONTACT OFFICERS

Academic affairs. Deputy Registrar: Isala, Prof. Tito, BA *Cant.*, MPubAd *Qld.*
Academic affairs. Deputy Vice-Chancellor: Chandra, Prof. Rajesh, BA *S.Pac.*, MA *S.Pac.*, PhD *Br.Col.*
Accommodation. Provost: Fifita, Filimone, BA *Hawaii*
Admissions (first degree). Deputy Registrar: Isala, Prof. Tito, BA *Cant.*, MPubAd *Qld.*
Admissions (higher degree). Deputy Registrar: Isala, Prof. Tito, BA *Cant.*, MPubAd *Qld.*
Adult/continuing education. Co-ordinator: Bolabola, Cema, BA *S.Pac.*, MPS *Philippines*
Adult/continuing education. Director, University Extension: Van Trease, Howard, BA *Calif.*, MA *Calif.State*, PhD *S.Pac.*
Alumni. Registrar: Pillay, Sarojini D., BSc *Madr.*, BT *Madr.*, MS *Central Mich.*
Archives. University Librarian: Williams, Esther W., BA *Well.*, MA *Well.*
Computing services. Acting Director, Computer Centre: Finau, Kisione, BSc *Hawaii*, MSc *Qld.UT*
Conferences/corporate hospitality. Provost: Fifita, Filimone, BA *Hawaii*
Consultancy services. (Contact the head of the relevant institute/department)
Development/fund-raising. Director of Planning and Development: Mann, Richard, MEcon *Hanover*
Distance education. Director, University Extension: Van Trease, Howard, BA *Calif.*, MA *Calif.State*, PhD *S.Pac.*
Estates and buildings/works and services. Director, Physical Planning: Banner, Ian
Examinations. Deputy Registrar: Isala, Prof. Tito, BA *Cant.*, MPubAd *Qld.*
Finance. Bursar: Dickson, Hugh
General enquiries. Registrar: Pillay, Sarojini D., BSc *Madr.*, BT *Madr.*, MS *Central Mich.*
Health services. Provost: Fifita, Filimone, BA *Hawaii*
Industrial liaison. Registrar: Pillay, Sarojini D., BSc *Madr.*, BT *Madr.*, MS *Central Mich.*
International office. Director of Planning and Development: Mann, Richard, MEcon *Hanover*
International office. Deputy Vice-Chancellor: Chandra, Prof. Rajesh, BA *S.Pac.*, MA *S.Pac.*, PhD *Br.Col.*
Language training for international students. Director, Centre for the Enhancement of Learning and Teaching: Hunter, Bruce, BA *La Trobe*, MA *Monash*
Library (chief librarian). University Librarian: Williams, Esther W., BA *Well.*, MA *Well.*
Personnel/human resources. Personnel Manager: Adair, Kristin, MA *Macq.*
Public relations, information and marketing. Information Officer: Smiles, Seona
Publications. Information Officer: Smiles, Seona
Purchasing. Purchasing Officer: Mataitini, Leba H.
Research. Chairperson, University Research Committee: Sotheeswaran, Prof. Subramaniam, BSc *Ceyl.*, PhD *Hull*, DSc *Hull*

Safety. Registrar: Pillay, Sarojini D., BSc *Madr.*, BT *Madr.*, MS *Central Mich.*

Scholarships, awards, loans. Director of Planning and Development: Mann, Richard, MEcon *Hanover*

Schools liaison. Deputy Registrar: Isala, Prof. Tito, BA *Cant.*, MPubAd *Qld.*

Security. Provost: Fifita, Filimone, BA *Hawaii*

Security. Chief Security Officer: Jiuta, Wilisoni

Sport and recreation. Co-ordinator, Leisure Education: Tuxson, Bob, BS *Adelphi*, MA(ScEd) *Adelphi*

Staff development and training. Registrar: Pillay, Sarojini D., BSc *Madr.*, BT *Madr.*, MS *Central Mich.*

Student union. President, University Student Association: Gautam, Bhoo

Student welfare/counselling. Provost: Fifita, Filimone, BA *Hawaii*

Student welfare/counselling. Student Counsellor: Montu, Elizabeth M., BA *Calif.*, MEd *Hawaii*

Student welfare/counselling. Student Counsellor: Wainikesa, Rev. Laisiasa L., BD *S.Pac.*, MA *Macq.*

Students from other countries. International Students Officer: Konusi, Litia, BA *W'gong.*

CAMPUS/COLLEGE HEADS

Alafua Campus, Apia, Samoa. Head: ......

Emalus Campus, Port Vila, Vanuatu. Head: Lynch, Prof. John D., BA *Syd.*, PhD *Hawaii*

[Information supplied by the institution as at 2 June 1998, and edited by the ACU]

SRI LANKA

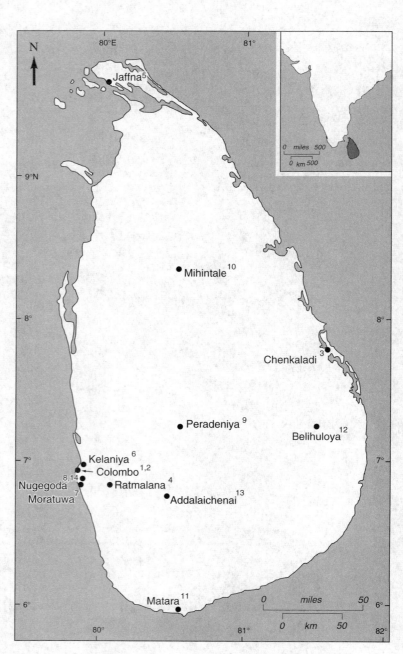

The places named are the seats of the university institutions numbered above

THE UNIVERSITIES OF SRI LANKA

Information compiled by the Committee of Vice-Chancellors and Directors (Sri Lanka) as at 31 October 1998

The University System

The university system in Sri Lanka was established by act of parliament in 1978. There are currently 12 universities functioning under the University Grants Commission (UGC). In addition, two other universities operate outside the ambit of the UGC: Buddhist and Pali University of Sri Lanka and Buddhasravaka Bhikku University, which were established under separate acts of parliament.

In addition, there are institutes affiliated to some universities, which conduct undergraduate or postgraduate degree courses.

Academic Year

This varies from one university to another: some adopt the semester system, and others follow the three-term system.

Pre-University Education

Five years of primary education (or six if pre-school classes are counted) are followed by five years of secondary education culminating in the General Certificate of Education (GCE) ordinary (O) level. Students seeking admission to universities have two years of post-secondary education, with the GCE advanced (A) level serving the purpose of an admission test. The normal admission requirement for technical colleges is a pass at GCE O level.

Admission to First Degree Courses

The minimum requirement is passes in three out of four subjects at GCE A level, provided that the mark in the fourth is not less than 25%. However, admission to university may require higher marks. The UGC sets the admission standard for each university faculty in each district of Sri Lanka.

Method of application. Admissions to the universities under the ambit of the UGC (except the Open University) are effected by the UGC in consultation with the Admissions Committee, comprising the chairman of the UGC and the heads of the universities. The other universities outside the UGC umbrella handle their own admissions.

Finance

Most of the universities in Sri Lanka are almost entirely dependent for their finances on government grants channelled through the UGC. A number of universities have additional sources of income: fee-levying courses, both at postgraduate and at diploma and certificate level; external degrees;

consultations; and charges for hiring playgrounds, gymnasia and halls to outsiders.

In addition fees are levied from undergraduates for examinations, registration, sports, hostels, etc. Universities such as Peradeniya and Colombo also receive fees for accommodation. The Open University obtains most of its income from sources other than the government grant.

The government allocation to the universities for 1998 was Rs3.2 billion for recurrent expenditure and Rs1.1 billion for capital expenditure. The estimates for 1999 approved by parliament are Rs3.3 billion for recurrent and Rs1.3 billion for capital expenditure.

Student finance. While no tuition fees are charged, students repeating examinations and all external students are charged modest registration and examination fees. There is a scheme of state scholarships, the Mahapola scholarships, awarded partly on the basis of academic merit but mainly to students in need of financial assistance. In addition, the UGC gives bursaries of the same value to needy students who do not receive the Mahapola equity scholarships. At present about two-thirds of the undergraduate population receive these scholarships or bursaries. There are also other scholarships awarded by the UGC and the universities on the basis of criteria stipulated by the donors.

Staff and Student Numbers

With the establishment of three new universities in 1997 and a faculty of medical sciences at Sri Jayewardenepura, there has been a substantial increase in the number of students admitted to the universities since 1996–97. In 1997–98 the total number of students who gained admission to the universities was 10,755, of whom 5339 were women. In the year 1999, the total number to gain admission will be approximately 12,000 (double the comparable figure of 6000 in 1989–90).

The approved cadre in respect of all the universities under the UGC is 5288 positions for academic and academic support staff and 8506 positions for non-teaching staff. As at October 1998 the number in position in respect of academic and academic support staff was 4321, of whom 2374 were men. The number of non-teaching staff in position was 7658, of whom 5217 were men.

BUDDHIST AND PALI UNIVERSITY OF SRI LANKA

Founded 1981

Member of the Association of Commonwealth Universities

Postal Address: 214 Bauddhaloka Mawatha, Colombo 7, Sri Lanka
Telephone: (01) 580609, 593604 **Fax**: (01) 580610

CHANCELLOR—Pannasara Poththewela Mahanayaka, Thera, Uththaritara Mahanayaka of the Sri Lanka Ramanya
  Maha Sangha Sabha
VICE-CHANCELLOR*—Vajira, Ven. Prof. Kumburugamuwe, Thera, BA *Vidyal.*, PhD *Ceyl.*
REGISTRAR‡—Wijesekera, S., BA *Ceyl.*
BURSAR—Senenyake, S. A. N. W. S.

GENERAL INFORMATION

History. The university was founded in 1981. It is located at Pitipana North, Homagama, about 20km from Colombo.

Admission to first degree courses (see also Sri Lankan Introduction). General School Certificate (GCE) A level with 4 passes including Pali and Buddhist Studies and an aggregate of not less than 180 marks, or equivalent qualification.

First Degrees (see also Sri Lankan Directory to Subjects of Study). BA: 3 years full-or part-time (general); 4 years part-time (special).

Higher Degrees. (see also Sri Lankan Directory to Subjects of Study). MA, MPhil, PhD.
  Applicants for admission to MA must normally hold an appropriate first degree. MPhil: first degree with at least second class. PhD: appropriate master's degree.

Language of Instruction. Sinhala and English.

Libraries. 15,000 volumes; 300 periodicals subscribed to. Special collections include: Buddha Jayanthi Tripitaka; Burmese Tripitaka; Chinese Tripitaka; Thai Tripitaka.

Fees (1998–99, annual). Undergraduate (international students): £124 (arts). Postgraduate: £248 (MA); £372 (MPhil); £558 (PhD).

Academic Awards (1997–98). 10 awards ranging in value from Rs1000 to Rs5000.

Academic Year (1998–99). 1 January–10 December (three terms).

Income (1997–98). Total, £20,000.

Statistics. Staff: 100 (25 academic, 75 administrative and other). Students: full-time 138; part-time 995; international 151.

FACULTIES/SCHOOLS

Buddhist Studies
Tel: (01) 857782

Dean: Abeynayake, Prof. Oliver, BA *Vidyal.*, PhD *Lanc.*

Language Studies
Tel: (01) 857783

Dean: Wickramasinghe, E. A., BA *Vidyal.*, PhD *Ruhuna*

ACADEMIC UNITS

Buddhist Culture
Tel: (01) 857787

Ekiriyagala Nanda, Ven., Thero, BA *Peradeniya*, MA *Peradeniya*   Head*

Buddhist Philosophy
Tel: (01) 857787

Ittademaliye Indasara, Ven., Thero, BA *Kelaniya*, MA *Delhi*, PhD *Delhi*   Head*

Pali
Tel: (01) 857787

Wegama Piyaratana, Ven., Thero, BA *B&P SLanka*, BEd *Colombo*, MA *B&P SLanka*, MPhil *B&P SLanka*   Head*

Religious Studies and Comparative Philosophy
Tel: (01) 857787

Gallale Sumanasiri, Ven., Thero, BA *Kelaniya*, MA *Delhi*, PhD *Delhi*   Head*
Ratnapure Rahula, Ven., Thero, BA *B&P SLanka*, MPhil *B&P SLanka*   Sr. Lectr.

CONTACT OFFICERS

Academic affairs. Vice-Chancellor: Vajira, Ven. Prof. Kumburugamuwe, Thera, BA *Vidyal.*, PhD *Ceyl.*
Accommodation. Vice-Chancellor: Vajira, Ven. Prof. Kumburugamuwe, Thera, BA *Vidyal.*, PhD *Ceyl.*
Admissions (first degree). Registrar: Wijesekera, S., BA *Ceyl.*
Conferences/corporate hospitality. Vice-Chancellor: Vajira, Ven. Prof. Kumburugamuwe, Thera, BA *Vidyal.*, PhD *Ceyl.*
Consultancy services. Vice-Chancellor: Vajira, Ven. Prof. Kumburugamuwe, Thera, BA *Vidyal.*, PhD *Ceyl.*
Examinations. Registrar: Wijesekera, S., BA *Ceyl.*
Finance. Bursar: Senenyake, S. A. N. W. S.
General enquiries. Registrar: Wijesekera, S., BA *Ceyl.*

Library (chief librarian). Librarian: Amaraweera, J. A., BA *Sri Jay.*, BSc *Vidyod.*
Library (enquiries). Librarian: Amaraweera, J. A., BA *Sri Jay.*, BSc *Vidyod.*
Personnel/human resources. Registrar: Wijesekera, S., BA *Ceyl.*
Public relations, information and marketing. Registrar: Wijesekera, S., BA *Ceyl.*
Publications. Registrar: Wijesekera, S., BA *Ceyl.*
Purchasing. Bursar: Senenyake, S. A. N. W. S.
Research. Dean, Faculty of Buddhist Studies: Abeynayake, Prof. Oliver, BA *Vidyal.*, PhD *Lanc.*
Research. Dean, Faculty of Language Studies: Wickramasinghe, E. A., BA *Vidyal.*, PhD *Ruhuna*
Scholarships, awards, loans. Vice-Chancellor: Vajira, Ven. Prof. Kumburugamuwe, Thera, BA *Vidyal.*, PhD *Ceyl.*
Security. Registrar: Wijesekera, S., BA *Ceyl.*
Sport and recreation. Registrar: Wijesekera, S., BA *Ceyl.*
Staff development and training. Vice-Chancellor: Vajira, Ven. Prof. Kumburugamuwe, Thera, BA *Vidyal.*, PhD *Ceyl.*
Student union. Registrar: Wijesekera, S., BA *Ceyl.*
Student welfare/counselling. Registrar: Wijesekera, S., BA *Ceyl.*
Students from other countries. Registrar: Wijesekera, S., BA *Ceyl.*

AFFILIATED INSTITUTIONS

[Institutions listed by location below provide courses leading to degrees, etc. of the university]

Balagalla. Saraswathie College
Kelaniya. Paramadhamma Institute
Maligakanda. Vidyodaya College
Medagoda. Sri Siddharthodaya Vidyayatanaya
Peliyagoda. Vidyalankara College
Seoul. Korea Buddhist College

[Information supplied by the institution as at 3 March 1998, and edited by the ACU]

UNIVERSITY OF COLOMBO, SRI LANKA

Founded 1979; previously established as Ceylon University College (1921); University of Ceylon (1942);
University of Ceylon, Colombo, (1968); and Colombo Campus of University of Sri Lanka (1972)

Member of the Association of Commonwealth Universities

Postal Address: College House, PO Box 1490, 94 Cumaratunga Munidasa Mawatha, Colombo 03, Sri Lanka
Telephone: (01) 581835, 584695, 585509 **Fax**: (01) 583810 **Cables**: University **Telex**: 22039

CHANCELLOR—Anthonis, P. R., LMS *Ceyl.*, FRCS
VICE-CHANCELLOR*—Lakshman, Prof. Weligamage D., BA *Ceyl.*, DPhil
Oxf.
ACTING REGISTRAR‡—Jinasena, K. G., BA *Ceyl.*
LIBRARIAN—Jayasuriya, S. Chandrawathie, BA *Ceyl.*, MLS *Philippines*
BURSAR—Bandara, Rohini P., BCom *Ceyl.*, FCA

GENERAL INFORMATION

History. Previously established as Ceylon University College (1921), University of Ceylon (1942), University of Ceylon, Colombo (1968), and Colombo Campus of the University of Sri Lanka (1972), the university achieved independent university status under its present name in 1979.

Admission to first degree courses (see also Sri Lankan Introduction). General Certificate of Education (GCE) with passes at A level in three or four approved subjects with a minimum mark of 25% on the fourth subject and a minimum aggregate mark of 180.

First Degrees (see also Sri Lankan Directory of Subjects to Study). BA, BBA, BCom, BSc, LLB, MB BS.
All courses are full-time. BA (general), BSc (general): 3 years. BA (special), BBA, BCom, BSc (special), LLB: 4 years. MB BS: 5 years.

Higher Degrees (see also Sri Lankan Directory of Subjects to Study). LLM, MA, MBA, MCom, MD, MEd, MLS, MSc, MPhil, PhD.
Applicants should normally hold an appropriate first degree with at least second class honours.
MEd, LLM: 1 year. MA, MPhil: 1 year (full-time), 2 years (part-time). PhD: 3 years.

Language of Instruction. Sinhala, Tamil and English.

Libraries. 220,000 volumes; 281 periodicals subscribed to.

Fees. Sri Lankan students: no fees for undergraduates; postgraduate (annual), Rs14,500–Rs45,000.International students (per term): undergraduate, US$550–1400; postgraduate, US$1000–2400.

Academic Awards (annual). 135 awards ranging in value from Rs10,000 to Rs25,000.

Academic Year. 1 October–30 September.

Income (1998). Total, Rs333,057,510.

Statistics. Staff: 514 (462 academic, 52 administrative). Students (full-time): 6744 (3297 men, 3447 women).

FACULTIES/SCHOOLS

Arts
Tel: (01) 500457
Dean: Parakrama, Arjuna, BA *Ceyl.*, PhD *Pitt.*
Secretary: Perera, D. A., BA *Colombo*

Education
Tel: (01) 588812
Dean: Jayasuriya, Chandra L., BA *Ceyl.*,, MEd *S.Carolina*
Secretary: Amarasekera, R., BCom *Sri Jay.*

Graduate Studies
Tel: (01) 502127
Dean: Hettiarachchy, T., BA *Ceyl.*, MA *McM.*, PhD *Lond.*

Law
Tel: (01) 500942
Dean: De Soysa, R. Sharya, LLB *Ceyl.*, LLM *Harv.*, MLitt *Oxf.*
Secretary: Perera, L. L. W., BA *Colombo*

Management and Finance
Tel: (01) 501295
Dean: Gunaratne, P. S. M., BSc *Sri Jay.*, MBA *Colombo*, PhD *Tsukuba*
Secretary: Piyaratne, G., BA *Peradeniya*

Medicine
Tel: (01) 698449 Fax: (01) 691581
Dean: Mendis, Prof. Lalitha N., MB BS *Ceyl.*, PhD *Lond.*
Secretary: Nanayakkara, BCom *Colombo*

Science
Tel: (01) 503148 Fax: (01) 586868
Dean: Abeynayake, Prof. Kanthi, BSc *Ceyl.*, PhD *Lanc.*
Secretary: Gunaratne, R. M., BLE

ACADEMIC UNITS

Anatomy, see Medicine

Arabic and Islamic Studies
Razak, M. I. A., BA *Kelaniya*, MA   Sr. Lectr.

Biochemistry and Molecular Biology, see Medicine

Botany
Tel: (01) 585038
Abeyanayake, Kanthi F., BSc *Ceyl.*, PhD *Lanc.*   Prof.
Hirimburegama, S. S. M. Kshanika, BSc *Colombo*, MPhil *Peradeniya*, PhD *Leuven*   Assoc. Prof.
Hirimburegama, W. K., BSc *Peradeniya*, PhD *Peradeniya*   Sr. Lectr.
Jayasekara, G. A. U., BSc *Colombo*, MSc *Calg.*, PhD *Calg.*   Sr. Lectr.
Perera, R. G., BSc *Cant.*, MSc *Cant.*, PhD *Lond.*   Sr. Lectr.
Seneviratne, A. Sirimawathie, BSc *Ceyl.*, PhD *Lond.*   Sr. Lectr.
Seneviratne, N. G. Indrani, BSc *Colombo*, PhD *Reading*   Sr. Lectr.
Silva, Tara D., BSc *Colombo*, PhD *Reading*   Sr. Lectr.
Tirimanne, T. L. Shamala, BSc *Peradeniya*, PhD *Iowa State*   Sr. Lectr.
Wijesundera, R. L. C., BSc *Ceyl.*, PhD *Brist.*   Prof.; Head*

Chemistry
Tel: (01) 503367
Amerasekera, A. S., BSc *Colombo*, PhD *N.Y.*   Sr. Lectr.

De Alwis, G. K. Hemakanthi, BSc *Colombo*, PhD *Flin.*   Sr. Lectr.
De Costa, M. D. P., BSc *Colombo*, PhD *Dal.*   Sr. Lectr.
De Silva, E. D., BSc *Colombo*, PhD *Hawaii*   Prof.
Deraniyagala, Sriyanthi A., BSc *S.Lanka*, PhD *Dal.*   Sr. Lectr.
Dissanayake, D. P., BSc *Peradeniya*, MPhil *Peradeniya*, PhD *Texas*   Sr. Lectr.
Fernando, S. A., BSc *Colombo*, MPhil *Colombo*, PhD *Arizona*   Sr. Lectr.
Goonesekera, N. C. W., BSc *Colombo*, MSc *Prin.*, PhD *Prin.*   Sr. Lectr.
Gunasekera, Maya B., BSc *Colombo*, PhD *CNAA*   Sr. Lectr.
Gunawardene, H. D., BSc *Ceyl.*, PhD *Salf.*   Prof.
Hewage, Sujatha, BSc *Ceyl.*, PhD *Newcastle(UK)*   Sr. Lectr.; Head*
Mahanama, K. R. R., BSc *Colombo*, MPhil *C.U.N.Y.*, PhD *C.U.N.Y.*   Sr. Lectr.
Wijayaratne, D. Thusita U., BSc *Colombo*, PhD *Arizona*   Sr. Lectr.
Wijesekera, Ramani D., BSc *Colombo*, PhD *ANU*   Sr. Lectr.

Radio Isotope Centre
Tel: (01) 502525
Dharmawardena, K. G., BSc *Ceyl.*, PhD *Camb.*   Dir.
Hewamanna, Rohini, BSc *Ceyl.*, PhD *Lond.*   Sr. Lectr.; Head*
Mahawatte, S. S. B. D. Palee, BSc *Ceyl.*, MSc *S.Lanka*, MSc *Birm.*   Sr. Lectr.

Commerce
Tel: (01) 501294
Dassanayake, D. M. Sunil, BCom *Colombo*, MBA *Asian I.T.*, *Bangkok*   Sr. Lectr.
Gunaratne, P. S. M., BSc *Sri Jay.*, MBA *Colombo*, PhD *Tsukuba*   Sr. Lectr.
Kodagoda, Deepika, BCom *Colombo*, MCom *Panjab*   Sr. Lectr.
Lewke, Bandara G. U., BCom *Colombo*, MBA *Colombo*
Rajapakse, R. M. R. B., BCom *S.Lanka*, MCom *S.Krishna.*   Sr. Lectr.; Head*
Wickramasinghe, D. P., BSc *Sri Jay.*, MCom *Colombo*, MSc *Colombo*, PhD *Manc.*   Sr. Lectr.

Computer Science, see Stats. and Computer Sci.

Demography
Tel: (01) 586111
Amarabandu, W. P., BSc *Ceyl.*, MSc *NSW*   Sr. Lectr.
de Silva, W. I., BDevS *Ceyl.*, MA *ANU*, MA *Colombo*, PhD *ANU*   Assoc. Prof. (on leave)
Dissanayake, D. M. S. S. L., BDevS *Ceyl.*, MA *V.U.Amst.*, PhD *Adel.*   Sr. Lectr. (on leave)
Siddhisena, K. A. P., BA *Ceyl.*, BPhil *Ceyl.*, MA *ANU*, MSc *Mich.*, PhD *Mich.*   Sr. Lectr.; Head*

Economics
Tel: (01) 582666
Abeyratne, A. D. M. S. A., BA *Colombo*, MPhil   Sr. Lectr.

Attanayake, A. M. G. N. K., BSc Ceyl., MA Delhi, PhD Lond.   Sr. Lectr.

Aturupana, D. H. C., BA Colombo, PhD Camb.   Sr. Lectr.

Chandrasiri, K. S., BA Ceyl., BPhil S.Lanka, MA S.Lanka, MBA Hartford   Sr. Lectr.

Dassanayake, S. W. S. B., BA Peradeniya, MA PhD   Sr. Lectr.

De Silva, G. A. Chandani, BA Colombo, DPhil Sus.   Sr. Lectr.

Ranasinghe, M. D. A. L., BA Colombo, MA Thammasat   Sr. Lectr. (on leave)

Rodrigo, P. Chandra, BA Ceyl., PhD Camb.   Prof. (on leave)

Senanayake, S. M. P., BCom Ceyl., MSc Aberd.   Sr. Lectr.

Vidanagama, S. S., BCom Ceyl., MSc Stir.   Sr. Lectr.; Head*

Education, see Humanities Educn., Sci. and Tech. Educn., and Soc. Sci. Educn.

Educational Psychology

Tel: (01) 588812

Abeypala, K. R., BEd Ceyl., MPhil S.Lanka   Sr. Lectr.

Chandradasa, W., BEd S.Lanka, MPhil Colombo

Gunawardena, H. P. R., BA Ceyl., MA Ceyl., PhD Colombo

Jayasuriya, Chandra L., BA Ceyl., MEd S.Carolina   Assoc. Prof.

Perera, L. S., BA Ceyl., MA Ceyl., PhD Moscow   Assoc. Prof.; Head*

Ranawake, D. S., BA Ceyl., BEd Ceyl., MA Ceyl.   Sr. Lectr.

Wijetunge, Swarna, BA Ceyl., MEd Col., PhD Col.   Prof.

English

Tel: (01) 500438

De Mel, F. Niloufer, BA Kelaniya, MA S.Lanka, PhD Kent   Sr. Lectr.

Fernando, M. Siromani, BA Ceyl., PhD Lond.   Prof.; Head*

Parakrama, Arjuna, BA Ceyl., PhD Pitt.   Sr. Lectr.

Geography

Tel: (01) 500458

de Silva, D. H. R. Jayanthi, BA Ceyl., PhD E.Anglia   Assoc. Prof.

Dissanayake, R. M., BA Ceyl.   Sr. Lectr.

Manawadu, L., BA Colombo, MSc Asian I.T., Bangkok   Sr. Lectr.

Rasanayagam, Yogambikai, BA Ceyl., PhD Camb.   Assoc. Prof.; Head*

Srikanthan, R., BA Ceyl., BPhil Ceyl., MA Colombo   Sr. Lectr.

Vitharana, Kanthi, BA Ceyl., MA Iowa, PhD Colombo   Sr. Lectr.

Wanniarachchi, B., BA Colombo, MSc Asian I.T.   Sr. Lectr.

Wilson, W. N., BA Ceyl., BPhil Ceyl., MA S.Lanka   Sr. Lectr.

History and Political Science

Tel: (01) 500433

Ariyaratne, R. A., BA Ceyl., PhD Camb.   Sr. Lectr.

Cooray, M. G. A., BA Ceyl., MPhil Ceyl.   Assoc. Prof.; Head*

Fernando, L. P., BA Peradeniya, MA New Br., PhD Syd.

Jayawardena, S. S. R. B. D. A., BA Ceyl., MA Wash., PhD Wash.   Assoc. Prof.

Karunadasa, W. M., BA Ceyl., LLB Ceyl., MA Lond., PhD S.Lanka   Assoc. Prof.

Leitan, G. R. Tressi, BA Ceyl., MSc(Econ) Lond., PhD Lond.   Assoc. Prof.

Melegoda, Nayani, BA Colombo, MA Colombo, PhD Leeds   Assoc. Prof.

Munasinghe, T. G. Indrani B., BA Ceyl., PhD Lond.   Prof.

Uyangoda, J., BA Ceyl., PhD Hawaii   Sr. Lectr.

Wickramasinghe, Nira K., BA Paris, MA Paris, DPhil Oxf.   Sr. Lectr.

Humanities Education

Atukorala, D. R., BEd Ceyl., BA Ceyl., MA Ceyl.   Sr. Lectr.

de Silva, W. A., BA Ceyl., MEd Birm., PhD Birm.   Sr. Prof.

Kariyawasam, C., BA Lond., BA Ceyl., MEd Ceyl.   Assoc. Prof.; Head*

Weerasinghe, H., BA Lond., PhD Reading   Prof.

Islamic Studies, see Arabic and Islamic Studies

Journalism Unit

Tel: (01) 500431

No staff at present

Law

Tel: (01) 500942

Abeyratne, M. D. Malkanthi, LLB S.Lanka, LLM S.Lanka   Sr. Lectr.

Atapattu, Sumudu A., LLM Camb., PhD Camb.   Sr. Lectr.

Buvanasundaram, Buvanasundari, LLB S.Lanka, MPhil S.Lanka

De Soysa, R. Sharya, LLB Ceyl., LLM Harv., MLitt Oxf.   Assoc. Prof.

Dias, Rev. K. J. F. N., BTh Rome, LLM Lond., MPhil Colombo   Sr. Lectr.

Goonesekera, Savitri W., LLB Ceyl., LLM Harv.   Prof.

Marasinghe, S. Charika, LLB S.Lanka, MLitt Oxf.   Sr. Lectr. (on leave)

Perera, Nirmala, LLB S.Lanka, LLM S.Lanka   Sr. Lectr.; Head*

Purimanasinghe, A. M. Shyami, LLB Colombo, LLM Harv.   Sr. Lectr.

Selvakumaran, N., LLB S.Lanka, LLM S.Lanka   Sr. Lectr.

Thamilamaran, V. T., LLB S.Lanka, LLM S.Lanka   Sr. Lectr.

Udagama, Deepika, LLB S.Lanka, LLM Calif., PhD Calif.   Sr. Lectr.

Vivekananthan, Niranjani, LLB Colombo, MPhil Colombo   Sr. Lectr.

Management Studies

Tel: (01) 501293

Dassanayake, M. S., BSc Sri Jay., MBA Otaru   Sr. Lectr.

De Silva, K. L. S., BSc Sri Jay., MA S.Lanka, PhD Kobe   Sr. Lectr.

Jayaratne, W. M., BA Vidyod., MA New Hampshire   Assoc. Prof.

Jayasinghe, J. A. S. C., BCom Peradeniya, MBA Colombo   Sr. Lectr.; Head*

Rajapakse, H. M. M. Janaki, BCom Colombo, MBA Bangkok   Sr. Lectr.

Ranaweerage, G., BCom Colombo, MCom S.Krishna.   Sr. Lectr.

Mathematics, see also Stats. and Computer Sci.

Tel: (01) 501731

Abeysinghe, J. K. B., BSc Ceyl., MSc Brist.   Sr. Lectr.

Epasinghe, Piyadasa W., BSc Ceyl., PhD Lond.   Sr. Prof.

Jayawardena, D. Romain, BSc Colombo, PhD Carnegie-Mellon   Sr. Lectr.

Karunatilake, A. D. W., MSc Moscow, PhD Moscow   Sr. Lectr.

Premadasa, A. K. K., BSc Colombo, PhD Purdue   Sr. Lectr.

Ramasinghege, W., BSc Colombo, MSc Ohio, PhD Ohio   Sr. Lectr.; Head*

Samaratunga, R. T., BSc Colombo, MScS.Fraser, PhD S.Fraser   Sr. Lectr.

Medicine, see below

Physics

Tel: (01) 584777

Ariyaratne, T. R., BSc S.Lanka, PhD Durh.   Assoc. Prof.; Head*

Daya, D. D. N. B., BSc Colombo, PhD Colombo

de Silva, K. T. L., BSc Colombo, PhD NSW   Assoc. Prof.

Gamalath, K. A. I. Lakmala, BSc Colombo, PhD NSW   Sr. Lectr.

Jayanetti, J. K. D. S., BSc Colombo, PhD C.U.N.Y.   Sr. Lectr.

Jayaratne, K. P. S. C., BSc Colombo, PhD Colombo   Sr. Lectr.

Rosa, S. R. D., BSc Ceyl., MSc Pitt., PhD Pitt.   Sr. Lectr.

Sonnadara, D. U. J., BSc Colombo, MSc Pitt., PhD Pitt.   Sr. Lectr.

Tennakoon, A. B., MSc Moscow, PhD Moscow   Sr. Lectr.

Wijayaratne, W. M. K. P., BSc Colombo, PhD Missouri   Sr. Lectr.

Physiology, see Medicine, below

Political Science, see Hist. and Pol. Sci.

Psychology, see Educnl. Psychol., and Medicine, below

Radio Isotope Centre, see under Chem.

Science and Technical Education

Tel: (01) 503147

Dissanayake, M. W. W., BA Ceyl., MPhil Ceyl.   Sr. Lectr.; Head*

Karunaratne, W. G., BSc Ceyl., MPhil Ceyl.   Sr. Lectr.

Pragnadarsana, W. M., BSc Ceyl., MPhil Colombo

Wanasinghe, J., BSc Ceyl., MSc Cornell, PhD Lond.   Prof.

Sinhala

Tel: (01) 500453

Disanayake, J. B., BA Ceyl., MA Calif., PhD S.Lanka   Prof.

Dissanayake, A. B., BA Ceyl., PhD Amst.   Assoc. Prof.

Jayawardhana, R. P. T., BA Ceyl., PhD Lond.   Assoc. Prof.; Head*

Karunaratne, Kusuma E., BA Ceyl., MA Essex, PhD Ceyl.   Prof.

Kulatunga, Malini, BA Ceyl., PhD Ceyl.   Sr. Lectr.

Paranavitana, Rohini, BA Ceyl., PhD Ceyl., MPhil   Assoc. Prof.

Wickramasinghe, B. K. A., BA Ceyl., PhD Ceyl.   Assoc. Prof.

Wijayawardhana, G. D., BA Ceyl., PhD Ceyl.   Prof.

Wijegunasinghe, Piyaseeli D., BA Ceyl., MA Leeds   Assoc. Prof.

Wijesuriya, W. A. D. S., BA Colombo   Sr. Lectr.

Social Science Education

Tel: (01) 596887

Jayawardena, A. A., BEd Ceyl., MPhil S.Lanka, PhD S.Lanka

Karunasekera, R. P., BCom Ceyl., MPhil S.Lanka   Sr. Lectr.

Kularatne, W. G., BA Ceyl., MA S.Lanka   Sr. Lectr.

Pathirana, J. D., BA Ceyl., MA Ceyl.   Sr. Lectr.; Head*

Rupasinghe, Siripala, BA Ceyl., MPhil Ceyl.   Prof. (on leave)

Sandarasegaram, S., BEd Ceyl., MEd Hiroshima   Assoc. Prof.

Seneviratne, H. M., BA Ceyl., MEd NE   Sr. Lectr.

Sociology

Tel: (01) 500452

Edirisinghe, I. V., BA Ceyl., MA Manc.   Sr. Lectr.

Gunasekera, Suwineetha S., BA Ceyl., BPhil Ceyl., MA Inst.Soc.Stud.(The Hague)   Sr. Lectr.

Herath, S. M. Kamalalochana, BA Colombo, MA Colombo   Sr. Lectr.

Hettiarachchi, T., BA Ceyl., MA McM., PhD Lond.   Assoc. Prof.

Hettige, S. T., BA Ceyl., PhD Monash   Prof.; Head*

Jayathilake, S. Ramanie De S., BA Ceyl., BPhil Ceyl., MPhil Sus., PhD Delhi   Sr. Lectr.

Perera, Sasanka, BA Colombo, PhD Calif. Sr.
Lectr.
Samarasinghe, Gameela, BA Paris IV, MA Paris
IV Sr. Lectr.
Weeramunda, A. J., BA Ceyl., MA Wash., PhD
Wash. Sr. Lectr.

Statistics and Computer Science
Tel: (01) 589123
Fernando, P. N. P., BSc Colombo, MSc Colombo
Karunaratne, Ariyalatha, BSc Colombo Sr.
Lectr.; Head*
Kodikara, N. D., BSc Colombo, MSc Manc., PhD
Manc. Sr. Lectr.
Ranasinghe, D. N., BSc Lond., MSc(Eng) Lond.,
PhD Wales Sr. Lectr.
Samaranayake, V. K., BSc Ceyl., PhD Lond. Sr.
Prof.
Seneviratne, G. P., BSc Colombo, MSc Wales
Sooriyarachchi, M. Roshini, BSc Colombo, MSc
Reading, PhD Reading Sr. Lectr.
Weerasekera, D. R., BSc Colombo, MSc Colombo,
PhD Colombo Sr. Lectr.
Weerasekera, A. R., BSc Colombo, MSc Wales,
PhD Wales Sr. Lectr.
Weerasuriya, B. N. Nandanie, BSc Sri Jay., MSc
Colombo, MPhil Colombo Sr. Lectr.
Wickramasinghe, W. N., BSc Colombo, MSc
Iowa, PhD Kansas Sr. Lectr.

Zoology
Tel: (01) 503397
Dayawansa, P. N., BSc Colombo, PhD Aberd. Sr.
Lectr.
De Silva, Dilrukshi N., BSc Colombo, MSc
Rutgers Sr. Lectr.
Ekaratne, S. U. K., BSc Colombo, PhD
Wales Assoc. Prof.
Jayatunga, Y. N. Amaramali, BSc Colombo,
MPhil Colombo, PhD Lond. Sr. Lectr.
Kotagama, S. W., BSc Colombo, PhD
Aberd. Prof.
Pallewatte, P. K. T. N. Shamala, BSc Colombo,
PhD Lond. Sr. Lectr.
Premawansa, W. S., BSc Kelaniya, PhD
Colombo Sr. Lectr.
Randeniya, Preethi V., BSc Colombo, MSc
Colombo, PhD Colombo Sr. Lectr.
Ratnasooriya, W. D., BSc Colombo, PhD
Strath. Sr. Prof.; Head*
Senanayake, Dhammika G., BSc Colombo, PhD
Manit. Sr. Lectr.
Weerakoon, H. D. K. G. A., BSc Colombo, MSc
Ill., PhD Ill. Sr. Lectr.
Yapa, W. B., BSc Kelaniya, MPhil Colombo, PhD
Munich Sr. Lectr.

MEDICINE
Anatomy
Tel: (01) 695300
Goonewardena, Shanthi, MB BS Ceyl., PhD
Cant. Assoc. Prof.
Jayasekera, M. M. R. W., MB BS Ceyl., PhD
Newcastle(UK) Assoc. Prof.; Head*
Panditharatne, P. S. S., MB BS Ceyl., PhD
Manc. Prof.
Perera, B. J. J. F., MB BS Ceyl., MS
S.Lanka Assoc. Prof.
Satchithanandan, Subhadra, MB BS Ceyl., PhD
Ceyl. Sr. Lectr.
Stephen, Benita E., MB BS Ceyl., FRCS Sr.
Lectr.

Biochemistry and Molecular Biology
Tel: (01) 697485 Fax: (01) 689181
Atukorala, T. M. Sunethra, BSc Ceyl., MSc Ceyl.,
PhD Sur. Assoc. Prof.
Canagaratna, M. C. Pumany, MB BS Ceyl., PhD
Lond. Assoc. Prof.
Chandrasekaran, N. V., BSc Colombo, MSc
Colombo, PhD Colombo Sr. Lectr.
Dharmasena, S. P., BSc Peradeniya, PhD
Wichita Sr. Lectr.
Karunanayake, U. P. E. H., BSc Ceyl., MSc Lond.,
PhD Lond. Prof.; Head*
Mathew, C. P. D. W., BSc Kelaniya, MSc Ceyl.,
PhD S.Lanka Sr. Lectr.

Welihinda, J., BSc Ceyl., PhD Ceyl. Sr. Lectr.

Clinical Medicine
de Mel, W. C. P., MB BS Colombo, MPhil Lond.,
MD S.Lanka Sr. Lectr.
Fernando, D. J. S., MB BS Colombo, MD S.Lanka,
MSc Manc. Sr. Lectr.
Fernando, S. S. D., MB BS Colombo, MD S.Lanka,
PhD Lond. Sr. Lectr.
Jayasinghe, K. S. A., MB BS Ceyl., MD Brist.,
MD S.Lanka Assoc. Prof.
Nanayakkara, L. Seetha H., MB BS Colombo, MD
S.Lanka Sr. Lectr.
Sheriff, M. H. R., MB BS Ceyl., MD Ceyl.,
FRCP Prof.; Head*

Community Medicine
Fernando, Dulitha N., MB BS Ceyl., PhD
Lond. Prof.; Head*
Lankatilleke, M. A. L. K. Nirmala, BSc Ceyl.,
MSc Bangkok Sr. Lectr.
Rajapaksa, Lalani C., MB BS Ceyl., MD
Colombo Sr. Lectr.
Seneviratne, R. Suneetha de, MB BS Ceyl., MD
S.Lanka Sr. Lectr.

Forensic Medicine
Tel: (01) 686142
Fernando, P. R., MB BS Ceyl., MD
S.Lanka Assoc. Prof.; Head*
Perera, H. Jean M., MB BS Colombo, MD
S.Lanka Sr. Lectr.

Microbiology
Tel: (01) 697513
Mendis, Lalitha N., MB BS Ceyl., PhD
Lond. Prof.
Perera, Aurelia J., MB BS Ceyl., MD
S.Lanka Assoc. Prof.; Head*

Obstetrics and Gynaecology
Tel: (01) 501207
Haththotuwa, R. N., MB BS Colombo, MS
S.Lanka Sr. Lectr.
Kaluarachchi, A., MB BS Colombo, MS Colombo
Randeni, C., MB BS Colombo, MS Colombo Sr.
Lectr.
Senanayaka, H. M., MB BS Colombo, MS S.Lanka,
FRCSEd Sr. Lectr.
Seneviratne, H. R., MB BS Ceyl. Prof.; Head*
Wijeratne, Chandrika N., MB BS Colombo, MD
S.Lanka Sr. Lectr.

Paediatrics
Tel: (01) 695300
De Silva, K. H. Shamya, MB BS Ceyl., MD
S.Lanka Sr. Lectr.
Lamabadusuriya, S. P., MB BS Ceyl., PhD Lond.,
FRCP, FRCPEd, FRCPGlas Prof. (on leave)
Mahamitawa, Udayanthi D., MB BS Colombo,
MD S.Lanka Sr. Lectr.
Senanayake, M. Prasanta, MB BS Ceyl., MD
S.Lanka Sr. Lectr.; Head*

Parasitology
Tel: (01) 699284
Ismail, Mohamed M., MB BS Ceyl., MD S.Lanka,
PhD McG. Prof. (on contract)
Karunaweera, N. Nadeera, MB BS Colombo, PhD
Colombo Sr. Lectr.
Naotunne, T. De S., MB BS Colombo, PhD
Colombo Sr. Lectr.; Head*

Pathology
Tel: (01) 691111
Amarasekera, L. R., MB BS Ceyl., PhD
Lond. Prof.; Head*
Angunawela, Preethika, MB BS Ceyl., MD
Colombo, FRCPath Assoc. Prof.
Kumarasinghe, M. Priyanganie, MB BS Ruhuna,
MD S.Lanka Assoc. Prof.
Kurukulasuriya, Arundathi P., MB BS Peradeniya,
MD Colombo Sr. Lectr.
Lokuhetty, M. Dilani S., MB BS S.Lanka Sr.
Lectr.

Pharmacology
Tel: (01) 695230
Abrew, Kusum, MD S.Lanka, MB BS Sr. Lectr.
Fernandopulle, B. M. Rohini, MB BS Ceyl., PhD
Colombo Sr. Lectr.
Jayakodi, R. L., MB BS Ceyl., PhD Alta. Sr.
Lectr.
Weerasuriya, K., MB BS Ceyl.,MD S.Lanka, PhD
Lond. Prof.; Head*

Physiology
Tel: (01) 695230
De Mel, Tara V., MB BS Ceyl., MPhil Lond., MD
Colombo Sr. Lectr.
Dissanayake, S. A., MB BS Ceyl. Sr. Lectr.
Gooneratna, C. de F. W., MB BS Ceyl., PhD,
FRCPEd, FRCP Prof.
Tennakoon, Kamanie H., MB BS Ceyl., PhD
Sheff. Assoc. Prof.; Head*

Psychological Medicine
De Silva, Damani, MB BS Colombo, MD
S.Lanka Sr. Lectr.
Mendis, N., MB BS Ceyl. Prof.; Head*
Perera, H. Niranjala, MB BS Peradeniya Sr.
Lectr.
Samarasinghe, D. S., MB BS Ceyl. Assoc. Prof.

Surgery
Tel: (01) 691111
Dias, M. N. J. R., MB BS Ceyl., MS Colombo,
FRCSEd Sr. Lectr.
Fernando, D. P. A., MB BS Ceyl., FRCSEd,
FRCS Assoc. Prof.
Jayasekera, G. J. B. W., MB BS Ceyl., FRCS,
FRCSEd Assoc. Prof.
Sheriffdeen, A. H., MB BS Ceyl., FRCSEd,
FRCS Prof.; Head*
Wijeratne, S. M., MB BS Colombo, MS
Colombo Sr. Lectr.

CONTACT OFFICERS
Academic affairs. Senior Assistant Registrar:
Thayanithy, Maithili, BA Jaffna
Accommodation. Senior Assistant Registrar:
Wimalasiri, M. M., LLB Colombo
Admissions (first degree). Assistant Registrar:
Sirimathie, W. D.
Admissions (higher degree). Senior Assistant
Registrar: Thayanithy, Maithili, BA Jaffna
Adult/continuing education. Acting Registrar:
Jinasena, K. G., BA Ceyl.
Alumni. Senior Assistant Registrar, Indigenous
Medicine: Talagune, T. K. W. T., BA Jaffna
Archives. Senior Assistant Registrar: Benjamin,
A. Chandra S.
Careers. Senior Assistant Registrar: Ekanayake,
A. C. Subalaximi
Computing services. Director, Institute of
Computer Technology: Epasinghe, Prof. P.
W., BSc Ceyl., PhD Lond.
Consultancy services. Bursar: Bandara, Rohini
P., BCom Ceyl., FCA
Credit transfer. Senior Assistant Bursar:
Dharmasiri, Thimali, BCom Colombo
Development/fund-raising. Bursar: Bandara,
Rohini P., BCom Ceyl., FCA
Distance education. Director, Institute of
Workers' Education: Warakaulle, H. M. N.,
BA Ceyl.
Equal opportunities. Acting Registrar:
Jinasena, K. G., BA Ceyl.
Estates and buildings/works and services.
Works Engineer: Seneviratne, S. S.
Examinations. Senior Assistant Registrar:
Sivalingam, S.
Finance. Bursar: Bandara, Rohini P., BCom
Ceyl., FCA
General enquiries. Acting Registrar: Jinasena,
K. G., BA Ceyl.
Health services. Chief Medical Officer: Peiris,
R. Grace X., MB BS Ceyl., MD S.Lanka
; University Medical Officer: Wasudeva, K. D.
I., MB BS
International office. Senior Assistant Registrar:
Thayanithy, Maithili, BA Jaffna

Library (chief librarian). Librarian: Jayasuriya, S. Chandrawathie, BA *Ceyl.*, MLS *Philippines*

Library (enquiries). Senior Assistant Registrar: Abeywardena, M. Indrani

Minorities/disadvantaged groups. Senior Assistant Registrar: Wimalasiri, M. M., LLB *Colombo*

Ombudsperson. Senior Student Counsellor: Wickramasinghe, Prof. B. K. A.

Personnel/human resources. Senior Assistant Registrar: Jayawardena, Shanthi, BLE *Colombo*

Personnel/human resources (academic). Senior Assistant Registrar: Ekanayake, A. C. Subalaximi

Public relations, information and marketing. Acting Registrar: Jinasena, K. G., BA *Ceyl.*

Publications. Senior Assistant Registrar: Thayanithy, Maithili, BA *Jaffna*

Purchasing. Senior Assistant Bursar: Malalgoda, Damani J.

Research. Senior Assistant Registrar: Thayanithy, Maithili, BA *Jaffna*

Safety. Senior Assistant Registrar: Wimalasiri, M. M., LLB *Colombo*

Scholarships, awards, loans. Assistant Bursar: Mudalige, S.

Schools liaison. Dean of Education: Jayasuriya, Chandra L., BA *Ceyl.*,, MEd *S.Carolina*

Security. Senior Assistant Registrar: Wimalasiri, M. M., LLB *Colombo*

Sport and recreation. Director (Acting), Physical Education: Hewage, N. W.

Staff development and training. Senior Assistant Registrar: Ekanayake, A. C. Subalaximi

Student union. Senior Assistant Registrar: Wimalasiri, M. M., LLB *Colombo*

Student welfare/counselling. Senior Student Counsellor: Wickramasinghe, Prof. B. K. A.

Student welfare/counselling (welfare). Senior Assistant Registrar: Wimalasiri, M. M., LLB *Colombo*

Students from other countries. Senior Assistant Registrar: Wimalasiri, M. M., LLB *Colombo*

Students with disabilities. Senior Assistant Registrar: Wimalasiri, M. M., LLB *Colombo*

CONSTITUENT COLLEGE HEADS

Institute of Computer Science, PO Box 1490, Colombo 3, Sri Lanka. (Tel: (01) 587239, 581245.) Director: Samaranayake, Prof. V. K.

Institute of Indigenous Medicine, Rajagiriya, Sri Lanka. (Tel: (01) 694308, 692385, 397175.) Director: Welihinda, Dr. J

Institute of Workers' Education, PO Box 1558, No 275 Baudhaloka Mawatha, Colombo 7, Sri Lanka. (Tel: (01) 587245.) Director: Warakaulle, H. M. N., BA *Ceyl.*

Postgraduate Institute of Medicine, 160 Norris Cannal Road, Colombo 8, Sri Lanka. (Tel: (01) 697757; Fax: (01) 697757.) Director: Peiris, J. B.

Western Campus, Wewala, Horana, Sri Lanka. (Tel: (034) 61371, 61372.) Rector: Ariyaratne, R. A.

[*Information supplied by the institution as at 11 March 1998, and edited by the ACU*]

EASTERN UNIVERSITY, SRI LANKA

Inaugurated 1986; previously Batticaloa University College, founded 1981

Member of the Association of Commonwealth Universities

Postal Address: Vantharumoolai, Chenkalady, Sri Lanka
Telephone: (065) 40490 **Fax**: (065) 40549, 22302 **E-mail**: postmast@eastu.esn.ac.lk
Cables: Eastern University, Chenkalady, Sri Lanka

CHANCELLOR—......
VICE-CHANCELLOR*—Rajendram, Rev. Prof. Guy F., MA *St.Louis*, MSc *Fordham*, PhD *Calif.*
REGISTRAR—Shanmugam, V., BA *Jaffna*
BURSAR—Brahmachandra, K. N.

GENERAL INFORMATION

History. The university was established in 1986; it was previously Batticaloa University College, founded 1981.
It is located about 16km north of Batticaloa.

Admission to first degree courses (see also Sri Lankan Introduction). Admission is through the University Grants Commission under the national policy.

First Degrees (see also Sri Lankan Directory to Subjects of Study). BA, BBA, BCom, BEcon, BSc, BSc(Acc&FinMgt), BSc(Agric).

Higher Degrees (see also Sri Lankan Directory to Subjects of Study). MPhil, PhD.

Language of Instruction. English and Tamil.

Libraries. 33,293 volumes; 37 journals.

Academic Awards. Eight awards ranging in value from Rs500 to Rs1000.

Academic Year. September/October–July/August.

Income (1997). Total, Rs86,500,000.

Statistics. Staff: 314 (106 academic, 208 administrative). Students: full-time 908 (498 men, 410 women); part-time 562 (327 men, 235 women); total 1470.

FACULTIES/SCHOOLS

Agriculture
Dean: Thedchanamoorthy, K., BScAgric *Peradeniya*, MSc *TN Ag*.

Arts and Culture
Dean: Gunaretnam, V., BA *Jaffna*, MPhil *Jaffna*

Commerce and Management
Acting Dean: Raguragavan, G., BBA *Jaffna*, MBA *Sri Jay*.

Science
Dean: Sabaratnam, Prof. Mano, BSc *Ceyl.*, PhD *Edin*.

ACADEMIC UNITS

Agricultural Economics
Tel: (065) 40530
Ahamed, A. N., BSc *Peradeniya*, MSc *Philippines* Sr. Lectr. (on leave)
Nadarajah, J., BSc *Peradeniya*, PhD *Lond.* Sr. Lectr.; Head*
Other Staff: 1 Lectr.

Agronomy
Tel: (065) 40530
Arulnandhy, V., BScAgric *Peradeniya*, MSc *Texas*, PhD *Lond.* Sr. Lectr.
Mahendran, T., BScAgric *Peradeniya*, PhD *Reading* Sr. Lectr.; Head*

Raveendranath, S., BScAgric *Peradeniya*, PhD *Lond.* Sr. Lectr.
Thedchanamoorthy, K., BScAgric *Peradeniya*, MSc *TN Ag.* Sr. Lectr.
Other Staff: 15 Lectrs.

Animal Science
Tel: (065) 40530
4 Lectrs.

Arabic
Tel: (065) 40165
2 Lectrs.

Botany
Tel: (065) 40528
Jayasingam, T., BSc *Peradeniya*, PhD *Wales* Sr. Lectr.; Head*
Other Staff: 5 Lectrs.

Chemistry
Tel: (065) 40528
Karunakaran, S., BSc *Jaffna*, DPhil *Sus.* Sr. Lectr.; Head*
Manickavasagar, R., BSc *Jaffna*, DPhil *Sus.* Sr. Lectr. (on leave)
Senthilmohan, S. T., BSc *Jaffna*, DPhil *Sus.* Sr. Lectr. (on leave)
Other Staff: 2 Lectrs.

Commerce
Tel: (065) 40214
Logeswaran, N., BCom *Jaffna* Sr. Lectr.; Head*

Other Staff: 3 Lectrs.

Comparative Religion

Tel: (065) 40165

Victor, I. H., BTh *Serampore*, BD *Serampore*, MTh *Serampore*, PhD Sr. Lectr.
Other Staff: 1 Lectr.

Economics

Tel: (065) 40214

Raguragavan J., BA *Jaffna*, MA *Jaffna* Sr. Lectr. (on leave)
Other Staff: 4 Lectrs.

Fine Arts

Tel: (065) 40165

Maunaguru, S., MA *Peradeniya*, PhD *Jaffna* Sr. Lectr. (on leave)
Other Staff: 2 Lectrs.

Geography

Tel: (065) 40165

3 Lectrs.

Islamic Studies

Tel: (065) 40165

No staff at present

Languages

Tel: (065) 40165

Maunaguru, S., MA *Jaffna*, BPhil Sr. Lectr.
Other Staff: 4 Lectrs.

Management

Tel: (065) 40214

Raguragavan, G., BBA *Jaffna*, MBA *Sri Jay.* Sr. Lectr. (on leave)
Other Staff: 5 Lectrs.

Mathematics

Tel: (065) 40528

Pushparajah, S., BSc *Peradeniya*, DPhil *Sus.* Sr. Lectr. (on leave)
Sritharan, T., BSc *Jaffna*, DPhil *Sus.* Sr. Lectr.
Vigneswaran, R., BSc *Jaffna*, DPhil *Sus.* Sr. Lectr.; Head*
Other Staff: 4 Lectrs.

Physics

Tel: (065) 40528

Pathmanathan, N., MSc *Moscow*, DPhil *Sus.* Sr. Lectr.; Head*

Rajendra, J. C. N., BSc *Jaffna*, DPhil *Sus.* Sr. Lectr.
Raymond, S. G., BSc *Jaffna*, DPhil *Sus.* Sr. Lectr.
Other Staff: 3 Lectrs.

Social Sciences

Tel: (065) 40165

Gunaretnam, V., BA *Jaffna*, MPhil *Jaffna* Sr. Lectr.
Thangarajah, C. Y., MA *Peradeniya*, MA *Sus.*, PhD *Roch.* Sr. Lectr.; Acting Head*
Other Staff: 5 Lectrs.

Zoology

Tel: (065) 40528

Dharmaratnam, M., BSc *Jaffna*, DPhil *Sus.* Sr. Lectr.
Sabaratnam, Mano, BSc *Ceyl.*, PhD *Edin.* Prof.
Vinobaba, M., BSc *Jaffna*, DPhil *Sus.* Sr. Lectr.
Vinobaba, P., BSc *Jaffna*, DPhil *Sus.* Head*
Other Staff: 2 Lectrs.

SPECIAL CENTRES, ETC

Computer Unit

Tel: (065) 40166

1 Lectr.; 1 Computer Programmer/Systems Analyst; 1 Computer Programmer; 2 Instrs.

English Language Teaching Unit

3 Instrs.

CONTACT OFFICERS

Academic affairs. Vice-Chancellor: Rajendram, Rev. Prof. Guy F., MA *St.Louis*, MSc *Fordham*, PhD *Calif.*
Accommodation. Assistant Registrar, Welfare: Kandeepan, V., BScAgric *Eastern(Sri Lanka)*
Admissions (first degree). Assistant Registrar, Examinations: Poheenthiran, K., BCom *Jaffna*
Admissions (higher degree). Assistant Registrar, Examinations: Poheenthiran, K., BCom *Jaffna*
Adult/continuing education. Assistant Registrar, Examinations: Poheenthiran, K., BCom *Jaffna*
Alumni. Assistant Registrar, Examinations: Poheenthiran, K., BCom *Jaffna*

Archives. Acting Librarian: Arulnandhy, T., BA *Peradeniya*, MLibSc *B'lore.*
Careers. Vice-Chancellor: Rajendram, Rev. Prof. Guy F., MA *St.Louis*, MSc *Fordham*, PhD *Calif.*
Computing services. Head: Vigneswaran, R., BSc *Jaffna*, DPhil *Sus.*
Development/fund-raising. Bursar: Brahmachandra, K. N.
Estates and buildings/works and services. Works Engineer: Sriskandarajah, N., BScEngin
Examinations. Assistant Registrar, Examinations: Poheenthiran, K., BCom *Jaffna*
Finance. Bursar: Brahmachandra, K. N.
General enquiries. Registrar: Shanmugam, V., BA *Jaffna*
Health services. Consultant Medical Officer: Navaratnam, T.
Library (chief librarian). Acting Librarian: Arulnandhy, T., BA *Peradeniya*, MLibSc *B'lore.*
Library (enquiries). Acting Librarian: Arulnandhy, T., BA *Peradeniya*, MLibSc *B'lore.*
Personnel/human resources. Senior Assistant Registrar: Harris, A. D., BCom *Jaffna*
Public relations, information and marketing. Registrar: Shanmugam, V., BA *Jaffna*
Purchasing. Assistant Bursar, Supplies: Srinivasan, S.
Security. Chief Security Officer: Sivalingam, V., BA *Open S.Lanka*
Sport and recreation. Head, Physical Education: Canagasabey, E. G. J., BSc *Eastern(Sri Lanka)*
Student union. President, Student Union: Nagarajah, T.
Student welfare/counselling. Senior Student Counsellor: Thangarajah, C. Y., BA *Peradeniya*, MA *Sus.*, PhD *Roch.*

CONSTITUENT COLLEGE HEADS

Trincomalee Campus, 315 Dockyard Road, Trincomalee, Sri Lanka. (Tel: (026) 22769.)
Acting Director: Rajendram, Rev. Prof. Guy F., MA *St.Louis*, MSc *Fordham*, PhD *Calif.*

[Information supplied by the institution as at 25 June 1998, and edited by the ACU]

GENERAL SIR JOHN KOTELAWALA DEFENCE ACADEMY

Established 1981; university status 1988

Member of the Association of Commonwealth Universities

Postal Address: Kandawala Estate, Ratmalana, Sri Lanka
Telephone: (01) 635268, 622995, 632028 **Fax**: (01) 605160 **E-mail**: common@kda.ac.lk

CHANCELLOR—Perera, Lt.-Gen. J. E. D., DLitt
COMMANDANT*—Fernando, Commodore E. M. Kumar, MSc Madr.
DIRECTOR OF ACADEMIC STUDIES—Kekulawala, K. R. S. S., BSc Ceyl., PhD ANU
REGISTRAR‡—Jayasuriya, D. G., BCom Ceyl., MPA Sri Jay., MEd Manc.
ACCOUNTANT—Galhena, A. P., BSc Sri Jay. (on leave)
LIBRARIAN—Cooray, S. C. A., BSc Colombo

GENERAL INFORMATION

History. The academy was founded in 1981 and achieved university status in 1988. It is located in Ratmalana, 15km south of Colombo city.

Admission to first degree courses (see also Sri Lankan Introduction). Three General Certificate of Education (GCE) A level passes (aggregate score of 180). Applicants must be Sri Lankan and aged between 18 and 22. Physical standards also apply.

First Degrees (see also Sri Lankan Directory of Subjects to Study). BA, BSc.

Fees. No fees are charged to students. Free accommodation, uniforms and meals are also provided.

Academic Year. Three semesters.

Statistics. Staff: 281 (73 academic; 208 administrative). Students: 300.

ACADEMIC UNITS

Cadet Training Wing

Tel: (01) 622503

Jayasooriya, Lt.-Col. M. P. H.
F.   Commanding Officer; Head*

Computer Science, see Maths., Sci. and Computer Sci.

Engineering, Aeronautical

Tel: (01) 635268, 622995, 632028

Liyanage, E. P. B.   Wing Commdr.; Head*

Engineering, Civil

Tel: (01) 635268, 622995, 632028

Assalaarachchi, P. S. M., BSc Peradeniya, MSc Idaho   Sr. Lectr.; Head*
Bandara, J. M. S. J., MSc Asian I.T., Bangkok, BSc PhD   Prof.†
De Alwis, N. A. D. R., BSc Ceyl., PhD Manc., FIE(SL)   Prof.†
Magedara, G. K. R., MSc P.F.U., Moscow, PhD P.F.U., Moscow   Sr. Lectr.

Pieris, T. A., BSc MSc PhD†
Senerath, D. C. H., BSc Ceyl., MSc Sheff., PhD Birm.   Prof.†

Engineering, Electrical

Tel: (01) 635268, 622995, 632028

Kuruparan, Lt.-Commdr. N., BSc Moratuwa
Wijayatunga, P. D. C., BSc Lond., PhD Lond.   Co-ordinator

Engineering, Electronic

Dias, S. A. D., BSc Moratuwa, MSc Calif., PhD Calif.†
Gunawardena, J. S. A. W., BSc Moratuwa   Co-ordinator†*
Karunadasa, J. P., BSc Moratuwa, MSc Manc., PhD Manc.†
Perera, H. Y. R., BSc S.Lanka, PhD†
Ranaweera, A., BSc Moratuwa, MSc Hawaii, PhD Hawaii†

Engineering, Mechanical and Marine

Tel: (01) 635268, 622995, 632028

Costa, Commdr. M. A. J.   Head*
Karunaratne, G., MSc Moscow, PhD Moscow†
Perera, K. K. C. K., BSc Moratuwa, MSc Calif., PhD Calif.†
Piyasiri, T. A., BSc S.Lanka, MSc Newcastle, PhD Newcastle†
Sirisena, E. J. K. P., BSc Moratuwa, MSc S'ton.   Sr. Lectr.
Tittagala, S. R., BSc S.Lanka, MSc Leeds, PhD Leeds   Co-ordinator†*
Victor Mendis, M., MSc†
Wimalasiri, W. K., BSc Moratuwa, PhD Newcastle(UK)†

Humanities

Tel: (01) 635268, 622995, 632028

Amaradasa, W. M., BA Sri Jay., LLB Colombo   Asst. Lectr.; Head*
Other Staff: 1 Lectr.

Languages

Tel: (01) 635268, 622995, 632028

Gooneratne, A. Y. S. D., BA Ceyl., MA ANU   Head* (on leave)

Parakrama, A., BA Peradeniya, MA Pitt., PhD Pitt.   Co-ordinator†*

Mathematics, Science and Computer Science

Tel: (01) 635268, 622995, 632028

Chandrasiri, L. H. G. S., BSc Tees., MSc Cape Town   Sr. Lectr.; Head*
Samanthilake, P. M. J. U., BSc MSc MCS†
Tilakaratne, M., BSc Colombo, MSc Sri Jay.   Sr. Lectr.
Other Staff: 3 Lectrs.
Research: biodegradable polymers of packing materials; numerical analysis; optimisation techniques

Science, see Maths., Sci. and Computer Sci.

Social Science

Tel: (01) 635268, 622995, 632028

Fonseka, H. N. C., BA Ceyl., MA Ceyl., PhD Ceyl.
Jayawardena, M. M., BA Ceyl., MA Peradeniya   Sr. Lectr.; Head*

CONTACT OFFICERS

Academic affairs. Director of Academic Studies: Kekulawala, K. R. S. S., BSc Ceyl., PhD ANU
General enquiries. Registrar: Jayasuriya, D. G., BCom Ceyl., MPA Sri Jay., MEd Manc.
Library (chief librarian). Librarian: Cooray, S. C. A., BSc Colombo
Library (enquiries). Assistant Librarian: Ranawella, T. C., BSc Kelaniya
Personnel/human resources. Administrative Officer: Pemasisi, K. W., BA Ceyl.
Security. Adjutant: Amarasinghe, Major M. K. M. K.
Students from other countries. Registrar: Jayasuriya, D. G., BCom Ceyl., MPA Sri Jay., MEd Manc.

[Information supplied by the institution as at 28 May 1998, and edited by the ACU]

UNIVERSITY OF JAFFNA, SRI LANKA

Established 1979, previously established as the Jaffna Campus of the University of Sri Lanka 1974

Member of the Association of Commonwealth Universities

Postal Address: Thirunelvely, Jaffna, Sri Lanka
Telephone: (021) 2294, 2006 **Cables**: University, Jaffna

CHANCELLOR—Nadarajah, Emer. Prof. T., BA Camb., MA Camb., PhD Camb., Hon. LLD Colombo, Hon. LittD
VICE-CHANCELLOR*—Balasundarampillai, Prof. Ponnudurai, JP, BA Ceyl., PhD Durh.
REGISTRAR—Kunarasa, K., BA Ceyl., MA Jaffna, PhD Jaffna
BURSAR—Alalasundaram, S. M.
LIBRARIAN—Pararajasingam, R., BSc Madr., MLIS Madr.

GENERAL INFORMATION

History. The university was first established as a campus of the University of Sri Lanka in 1974 and gained independent university status in 1979. It is located about 3km north of Jaffna.

Admission to first degree courses (see also Sri Lankan Introduction). General Certificate of Education (GCE) A level with passes in 4 subjects.

First Degrees (see also Sri Lankan Directory to Subjects of Study). BA, BAdm, BCom, BSc, BSMS, MB BS.

Higher Degrees (see also Sri Lankan Directory to Subjects of Study). Master's degrees, PhD.
Applicants for admission to master's degree courses must hold a relevant first degree with at least second class honours or a relevant first degree and a pass in the university's qualifying exam. PhD: master's or MPhil with no less than 2 years' research component.

Language of Instruction. Exams may be written in Tamil or English. Intensive English language courses available.

FACULTIES/SCHOOLS

Agriculture
Dean: Vijaratnam, R., BSc Ceyl., MSc(AgEng) Asian I.T.,Bangkok

Arts
Dean: Sanmugadas, Prof. A., BA Ceyl., PhD Edin.

Medicine
Dean: Rajendra Prasad, R., MB BS Ceyl., MPhil Jaffna

Science
Dean: Ganesalingam, Prof. V. K., BSc Ceyl, MSc Hawaii, PhD Lond.

ACADEMIC UNITS

Agricultural Biology
Vacant Posts: 2 Sr. Lectrs.

Agricultural Chemistry
Mohanadas, S., BSc Ceyl., PhD Adel.   Sr. Lectr.; Head*
Vacant Posts: 1 Sr. Lectr.

Agricultural Economics
Vacant Posts: 1 Prof.; 1 Lectr.

Agricultural Engineering
Alvappillai, P., BSc Peradeniya, MSc Obihiro   Sr. Lectr.
Vijayaratnam, R., BSc Ceyl., MSc(AgEng) Asian I.T., Bangkok   Sr. Lectr.; Head*

Agronomy
Rajadurai, S., BScAgric Ceyl., MSc(Ag) TN Ag.   Sr. Lectr.
Sellathurai, P., MSc Norway Ag., BSc(Agric)
Vacant Posts: 1 Prof.

Anatomy, see Medicine

Animal Science
Navaratnarajah, A., BVSc Ceyl., MPhil Reading   Sr. Lectr.; Head*
Vacant Posts: 1 Sr. Lectr.

Biochemistry, see Medicine

Botany
Vacant Posts: 1 Prof.; 2 Sr. Lectrs.

Chemistry
Mageswaran, Rajeswary, BSc Ceyl., PhD Sheff.   Sr. Prof.
Saminathan, S., BSc Jaffna, MSc Peradeniya
Sivapalan, N., BSc Jaffna, PhD Camb.   Sr. Lectr.; Head*
Vacant Posts: 1 Prof.; 2 Lectrs.

Christian and Islamic Studies
Matthias, R. A. J., MPhil Rome, MTh Rome, PhD Jaffna   Sr. Lectr.; Head*
Vacant Posts: 1 Sr. Lectr. (Islamic Civilization)

Commerce
Aruloel, K. K., BCom Jaffna, MA Jaffna   Sr. Lectr.
Thevarajah, K., BSc Vidyod., MA   Sr. Lectr.; Head*
Vacant Posts: 1 Prof.; 1 Lectr.

Computer Science
Kanaganathan, S., MSc Ceyl., MSc Liv.   Sr. Lectr.
Mahesan, S., BSc Jaffna, MSc Wales, PhD Wales   Sr. Lectr.
Vacant Posts: 1 Lectr.

Economics
Balakrishnan, N., BA Ceyl., MPhil Leeds   Assoc. Prof.
Manivasagar, V., BA Peradeniya, MA Ban., PhD Ban.   Sr. Lectr.
Sebastiampillai, G. M., BA Mys., MA Annam., MA Jaffna, MPhil Jaffna   Sr. Lectr.
Shanmugalingam, N., BEd Colombo, MA Jaffna, PhD Jaffna   Sr. Lectr.
Sinnathambu, A., BA Jaffna, MA Jaffna   Sr. Lectr. (on leave)
Sivanathan, P., BA Peradeniya, MA Jaffna   Sr. Lectr.
Vacant Posts: 1 Prof.; 2 Sr. Lectrs.

Education
Arulanantham, S., BSc Jaffna, MA Jaffna   Sr. Lectr.
Arumugam, V., BA Ceyl., MPhil Lond.   Prof.; Head*
Jeyarajah, S., BEd Ceyl., MA Colombo, PhD   Sr. Lectr.
Sinnathamby, K., BSc Madr., MA Colombo, MPhil Jaffna   Sr. Lectr.
Vacant Posts: 1 Sr. Lectr.

Engineering
Navaratnarajah, V., BSc(Eng) Ceyl., MEngSc Malaya, PhD City(UK), FICE   Prof.; Head*

English, see Linguistics and Engl.

Fine Arts, see also Special Centres, etc
Vacant Posts: 1 Prof.

Geography
Antonyrajan, A., BA Jaffna, MPhil Jaffna
Balachandran, S., BA Ceyl., MSc Birm.   Assoc. Prof.
Balasundarampillai, P., BA Ceyl., PhD Durh.   Sr. Prof.
Kugabalan, K., BA Ceyl., MA Jaffna, PhD Jaffna   Sr. Lectr.; Head*
Rajendram, K., BA Jaffna, MPhil Jaffna
Rajeswaran, B., BA Peradeniya, MA Jaffna   Sr. Lectr.
Sivachandran, R., BA Ceyl., MA S.Lanka   Sr. Lectr.

Hindu Civilization
Gopalakrishna Iyer, P., BA Ceyl., PhD   Prof.; Head*
Ramanathan, K., BA Colombo, BPhil Colombo, MA Madr.   Sr. Lectr.
Selvanayagam, N., BA Ceyl., BPhil Colombo, MA Jaffna   Sr. Lectr.
Vedanathan, M., MA Jaffna   Sr. Lectr.

History
Krishnakumar, S., MA Jaffna   Sr. Lectr.
Krishnarajah, S., BA Jaffna, MA Mys.   Sr. Lectr.
Pushparatnam, P., BA Jaffna, MA Jaffna   Sr. Lectr.
Sathiyaseelan, S., BA Peradeniya, MA Jaffna   Sr. Lectr.; Head*
Sitrampalam, S. K., BA Ceyl., MA Poona, PhD Poona   Prof.
Vacant Posts: 1 Lectr.

Islamic Studies, see Christian and Islamic Studies

Linguistics and English
Kailainathan, R., BA Colombo, BPhil Colombo, MA Kelaniya   Sr. Lectr., Linguistics
Ramesh, S., BA Jaffna, MA Jaffna   Sr. Lectr., Linguistics (on leave)
Shanmugam, N., BAd Jaffna, MBA Colombo   Sr. Lectr.
Suseendrarajah, S., MA Madr., MA Annam.   Sr. Prof., Linguistics; Head*
Vacant Posts: 3 Sr. Lectrs.

Management
Jeyaraman, D., MBA Delhi, BCom   Sr. Lectr. (on leave)
Nadarajasundaram, M., BA Ceyl., MA   Sr. Lectr.; Head*
Vacant Posts: 1 Prof./Sr. Lectr.; 1 Lectr.

Mathematics and Statistics
Makinan, P., BSc Ceyl., MSc Car.   Sr. Lectr.
Skantharajah, M., BSc Peradeniya, MSc Alta., PhD Alta.   Sr. Lectr.
Srisatkunarajah, S., BSc Jaffna, PhD H.-W.   Sr. Lectr.
Tharmaratnam, V., BSc Ceyl., PhD Lond.   Sr. Prof.
Yogarajah, S., BSc Ceyl.   Sr. Lectr.
Other Staff: 4 Lectrs.
Vacant Posts: 1 Prof.; 3 Lectrs.

Medicine, see below

Microbiology, see Medicine, below

Philosophy

Gnanakumaran, N., BA Kelaniya, PhD RDV, MA Sr. Lectr.; Head*
Krishnarajah, S., MA Ceyl., PhD Moscow Sr. Lectr.
Sivanandamoorthy, K., BA Peradeniya, MA Sr. Lectr.

Physics

Jayanathan, L., BSc Ceyl., PhD Lond. Sr. Lectr.
Kandasamy, K., BSc Ceyl., PhD Keele Assoc. Prof.
Kumaravadivel, R., BSc Ceyl., PhD Brist. Sr. Prof.; Head*
Kunaratnam, K., BSc Ceyl., PhD Lond. Sr. Prof.
Other Staff: 3 Lectrs.
Vacant Posts: 1 Sr. Lectr.; 2 Lectrs.

Physiology, see Medicine, below

Sanskrit

Sivasamy, V., BA Lond., MA Ceyl. Assoc. Prof.; Head*
Sivasanthiran, V., BA Peradeniya, MA Sr. Lectr.

Siddha

Bhavani, G. A. Sr. Lectr. (on leave)
Bhavani, S. Assoc. Prof.
Srikantha, M. C. Sr. Lectr.; Head*
Vacant Posts: 1 Sr. Lectr.

Statistics, see Maths. and Stats.

Tamil

Ragunathan, M., BA Jaffna, MA Jaffna Sr. Lectr.
Sanmugadas, A., BA Ceyl., PhD Edin. Sr. Prof.
Senkathirchelvan, P., BA Jaffna, MPhil Jaffna Sr. Lectr.
Sivalingarajah, S., MA Jaffna, PhD Jaffna Sr. Lectr.
Subramaniam, N., MA Ceyl., PhD Sr. Lectr.; Head*
Vacant Posts: 1 Prof.; 1 Sr. Lectr.

Zoology

Chitravadivelu, K., BSc Lond., MSc Prague, PhD Prague Assoc. Prof.
Ganesalingam, V. K., BSc Ceyl., MSc Hawaii, PhD Lond. Sr. Prof.
Krishnarajah, P., BSc Peradeniya, MPhil Jaffna, PhD Annam. Sr. Lectr.; Head*
Venkatesh, W., BSc Jaffna, MSc Oklahoma Sr. Lectr.
Vacant Posts: 1 Prof. (Marine Biol.)

MEDICINE

Anatomy

Rajendra Prasad, R., MB BS Ceyl., MPhil Jaffna
Vacant Posts: 3 Sr. Lectrs.

Biochemistry

Arasaratnam, V., BSc Madr., MSc Colombo, PhD Assoc. Prof.; Head*
Balasubramaniam, K., BSc Ceyl., PhD Indiana Sr. Prof.
Sivagnanasundram, C., MB BS Ceyl., PhD Lond. Prof.
Vacant Posts: 2 Sr. Lectrs.; 3 Lectrs.

Community Medicine

Sivarajah, N., MB BS Ceyl., MD Syd. Sr. Lectr.; Head*
Vacant Posts: 1 Prof.; 2 Sr. Lectrs.; 2 Lectrs.

Forensic Medicine

Vacant Posts: Prof./ Head*; 1 Sr. Lectr.

Medicine

Ganeshamoorthy, J., MB BS Ceyl. Sr. Lectr.; Head*
Vacant Posts: 1 Prof.

Microbiology

Vacant Posts: 1 Sr. Lectr.

Obstetrics and Gynaecology

Sivasuriya, M., MB BS Ceyl., FRCS, FRCSEd, FRCSGlas, FACS, FRCOG Sr. Prof.; Head*
Vacant Posts: 2 Sr. Lectrs.

Paediatrics

Karunakaran, V. M., MB BS Ceyl. Sr. Lectr.; Head*
Vacant Posts: 1 Prof.; 1 Sr. Lectr.

Parasitology

Vacant Posts: 1 Lectr.

Pharmacology

Vacant Posts: 1 Prof.; 2 Sr. Lectrs; 1 Lectr.

Physiology

Parameswaran, S. V., BSc Mys., MSc Madr., PhD Leeds Sr. Prof.
Vacant Posts: 3 Sr. Lectrs.; 1 Lectr.

Psychiatry

Damian, Rev. S., BTh St Paul(Ott.), MA(Couns) St Paul(Ott.) Lectr.; Head*
Somasundaram, D. J., MB BS Mys., MD Colombo, BA Sr. Lectr. (on leave)
Vacant Posts: 1 Sr. Lectr.

Surgery

Ambalavanar, D. C., MB BS Madr., FRCSEd
Kunanandam, V., MB BS Ceyl., PhD, FRCSEd
Vacant Posts: 1 Prof.; 2 Sr. Lectrs.

SPECIAL CENTRES, ETC

Fine Arts, Ramanathan Academy of

Vacant Posts: 6 Sr. Lectrs.; 4 Asst. Lectrs.

Dance

Jeyarajah, S., BEd S.Lanka, MA S.Lanka, PhD S.Lanka Sr. Lectr.; Head*

Music

Navaratnam, N. V. M., MPhil Jaffna Sr. Lectr.

CONTACT OFFICERS

Academic affairs. Assistant Registrar (Academic): Arudpiragasam, S., BA Ceyl.
Accommodation. Assistant Registrar (Welfare Services): Jeyakumar, J.
Admissions (first degree). Deputy Registrar: Kasinathan, T.
Admissions (higher degree). Assistant Registrar (Academic): Arudpiragasam, S., BA Ceyl.
Adult/continuing education (extra-mural studies). Co-ordinator: Sivachandran, R., BA Ceyl., MA S.Lanka
Adult/continuing education (workers' education). Head, Department of Education: Arumugam, Prof. V., BA Ceyl., MPhil Lond.
Alumni. Assistant Registrar (Welfare Services): Jeyakumar, J.
Archives. Librarian: Pararajasingam, R., BSc Madr., MLIS Madr.

Careers. Senior Assistant Registrar (Establishments): Thankarajah, N., BCom Ceyl.
Computing services. Head, Computer Unit: Somasundaram, K., PhD Camb., BSc
Computing services. Senior Lecturer, Computer Science Department: Mahesan, S., BSc Jaffna, MSc Wales, PhD Lond.
Consultancy services (buildings). Works Engineer (Civil): Thayaparan, S., BSc(Eng) S.Lanka, ME Asian I.T., Bangkok
Consultancy services (research). Professor, Department of Engineering: Navaratnarajah, Prof. V., BSc(Eng) Ceyl., MEngSc Malaya, PhD City(UK), FICE
Development/fund-raising. Bursar: Alalasundaram, S. M.
Distance education. Co-ordinator for External Examinations: Nadarajasundaram, M., BA Ceyl., MA
Estates and buildings/works and services. Works Engineer (Civil): Thayaparan, S., BSc(Eng) S.Lanka, ME Asian I.T., Bangkok
Examinations. Deputy Registrar: Kasinathan, T.
Finance. Bursar: Alalasundaram, S. M.
General enquiries. Parameswaran, K., BA Ceyl.
Health services. University Medical Officer: Sriskantharajah, J., MB BS
Industrial liaison. Works Engineer (Civil): Thayaparan, S., BSc(Eng) S.Lanka, ME Asian I.T., Bangkok
International office. Deputy Registrar: Kasinathan, T.
Library (chief librarian). Librarian: Pararajasingam, R., BSc Madr., MLIS Madr.
Ombudsperson. Chairman, University Council: Balasundarampillai, Prof. P., BA Ceyl., PhD Durh.
Personnel/human resources. Senior Assistant Registrar (Establishments): Thankarajah, N., BCom Ceyl.
Public relations, information and marketing. Senior Student Counsellor: Srisatkunarajah, S., BSc Jaffna, PhD H.-W.
Publications. Deputy Registrar: Kasinathan, T.
Purchasing. Bursar: Alalasundaram, S. M.
Research. Assistant Registrar (Academic): Arudpiragasam, S., BA Ceyl.
Safety. Registrar: Kunarasa, K., BA Ceyl., MA Jaffna, PhD Jaffna
Scholarships, awards, loans. Assistant Registrar (Welfare Services): Jeyakumar, J.
Schools liaison. Assistant Registrar (Administration): Sivanesan, A.
Security. Chief Security Officer: Puthirasigamani, M.
Sport and recreation. Director of Physical Education: ......
Staff development and training. Senior Assistant Registrar (Establishments): Thankarajah, N., BCom Ceyl.
Student welfare/counselling. Assistant Registrar (Welfare Services): Jeyakumar, J.
Students from other countries. Deputy Registrar: Kasinathan, T.
Students with disabilities. Deputy Registrar: Kasinathan, T.
University press. Librarian: Pararajasingam, R., BSc Madr., MLIS Madr.

CONSTITUENT COLLEGE HEADS

Vavuniya Campus. Rector: Balakrishnan, N., BA Ceyl., MPhil Leeds

[Information supplied by the institution as at 8 April 1998, and edited by the ACU]

UNIVERSITY OF KELANIYA, SRI LANKA

Founded 1978; formerly the Vidyalankara University of Ceylon founded 1959, and, from 1972, the Vidyalankara
Campus of the University of Sri Lanka

Member of the Association of Commonwealth Universities

Postal Address: Kelaniya, Sri Lanka
Telephone: (01) 911391, 911397, 911407, 913854-8, 910164 **Fax**: (01) 911569, 911485, 911393
Cables: University, Kelaniya, Sri Lanka

CHANCELLOR—Kusaladhamma, Ven. W., Dharmakeerthi Sri Thero BA *Kelaniya*
VICE-CHANCELLOR*—Bandaranayake, Prof. Senake D., BA *Brist.*, BLitt *Oxf.*, DPhil
Oxf.
DEPUTY VICE-CHANCELLOR—Tilakaratna, Prof. K., BSc *Ceyl.*, MSc *Lond.*, MSc
Camb.
REGISTRAR‡—Amarasinghe, N. B., BA *Vidyod.*
LIBRARIAN—Lankage, Jayasiri, BA *Vidyod.*, MA *Vidyod.*, MLibSc *Ban.*, PhD *Kelaniya*
BURSAR—Hapangama, S. K. J.

GENERAL INFORMATION

History. The University was originally
established in 1875 as Vidyalankara Pirivena, a
centre of learning for Buddhist monks. It was
renamed Vidyalankara University in 1959 and
subsequently became the Vidyalankara Campus
of the University of Ceylon. In 1978, the
university was founded under its present
name.

It is located about 10km north of Colombo.

Admission to first degree courses (see also
Sri Lankan Introduction). Through the
University Grants Commission (UGC) and
authorised agents. Admission is based on
marks obtained at GCE A level exam.
International students with equivalent
qualifications are eligible to apply.

First Degrees (see also Sri Lankan Directory
to Subjects to Study). BA, BCom, BMgt(Acc),
BMgt(HR), BSc, MB BS.

All courses last 3 years.

Higher Degrees (see also Sri Lankan
Directory to Subjects to Study). MA, MCom,
MSc, MPhil, PhD.

All courses normally last 2 years. MA: 1 to
2 years; PhD: 3 years.

Language of Instruction. Sinhalese and
English.

Libraries. 142,230 volumes; 250 periodicals
subscribed to.

Fees (per term). Undergraduate
(international): US$550 (arts); US$1650
(medicine). Postgraduate: US$1000 (arts);
US$2400 (medicine); US$1800 (science).

Academic Year (1997–98). Three semesters:
October–December; January–April; April–June.

Income (1997–98). Total,
Rs267,074,000,000.

Statistics. Staff: 945 (335 academic, 30
administrative, 580 non-academic). Students:
full-time 6392; part-time 792 (441 men, 351
women); total 7184.

FACULTIES/SCHOOLS

Commerce and Management Studies
Tel: (01) 917708 Fax: (01) 914483
Dean: Ananda, J. P., BCom *Peradeniya*, MA *Leeds*

Humanities
Tel: (01) 911913 Fax: (01) 911913
Dean: Palliyaguruge, Prof. Chandrasiri, BA
Vidyal., PhD *S.Lanka*
Assistant Registrar: Jayasekare, Indra

Medicine
Tel: (01) 958317, 958337 Fax: (01) 958337
Dean: De Silva, Prof. H. J., MB BS *Colombo*, MD
Colombo, DPhil *Oxf.*, FRCP, FRCPEd
Assistant Registrar: Kalansuriya, Jayantha

Science
Dean: Wijayaratne, Prof. M. Jayantha S., BSc
S.Lanka, MSc *Mich.*, PhD *Kelaniya*
Assistant Registrar: Herath, Samudrika

Social Sciences
Dean: Amarasekera, A. A. Dayananda, BA
Vidyal., MA *Kelaniya*
Assistant Registrar: Lambert, A.K.

ACADEMIC UNITS

Accountancy and Human Resource Management
Tel: (01) 911164, 911391, 911407, 913854-
8, 910163
Ananda, J. P., BCom *Peradeniya*, MA *Leeds* Sr.
Lectr.
Ariyaratne, J. M. D., BCom *Kelaniya*, MCom
Kelaniya Sr. Lectr.
Dissanayake, D. M. T. B., BSc *Vidyod.*, MPA *Sri
Jay.* Sr. Lectr.
Dissanayake, D. Ranjani, BSc *Vidyod.*, MCom
Colombo Sr. Lectr.
Herath, Vineetha, BSc *Colombo*, MSc *Asian I.T.*,
Bangkok Sr. Lectr.
Ranjanie, R. P. Chitra, BCom *Kelaniya*, MCom
Panjab Sr. Lectr.
Sunil Shantha, A. T. H., BSc *Vidyod.*, MCom
Kelaniya Sr. Lectr.; Head*
Tilakeratne, P. M. C., BCom *Kelaniya*, MCom
Panjab Sr. Lectr.
Other Staff: 5 Lectrs.; 5 Temp. Lectrs.

Anatomy, see Medicine

Archaeology, see also Special Centres, etc
Tel: (01) 911164, 911391, 911397, 911407,
913854-8, 910163
Amarasekera, A. A. Dayananda, BA *Vidyal.*, MA
Kelaniya Sr. Lectr.
Bandaranayake, Senake D., BA *Brist.*, BLitt *Oxf.*,
DPhil *Oxf.* Prof.
Gunawardhane, Prishanta, BA *Kelaniya*, MPhil
Kelaniya
Manathunga, Anura, BA *Kelaniya*, MA *Poona*,
MPhil *Kelaniya* Sr. Lectr.; Head*
Other Staff: 2 Lectrs.

Biochemistry, see Medicine

Botany
Tel: (01) 911164, 911391, 911397, 911407,
913854-8, 910163, 914480
Desapriya, Nelum, BSc *Kelaniya*, MPhil *Kelaniya*,
PhD *Bath* Sr. Lectr.
Gunasekera, S. A., BSc *Ceyl.*, PhD *Birm.* Prof.
(on leave)

Jayasekera, L. R., BSc *Kelaniya*, MSc *Osnabrück*,
PhD *Osnabrück* Assoc. Prof.; Head*
Peris, Bonifus D., MSc *Moscow*, MPhil *Peradeniya*,
PhD *Hawaii* Sr. Lectr.
Senanayake, R. A. Seetha P., BSc *Kelaniya*, MPhil
Reading Sr. Lectr.
Sirisena, D. M., BSc *Kelaniya*, MSc *Calg.*, PhD
Calg. Sr. Lectr.
Other Staff: 2 Lectrs.; 4 Temp. Lectrs.

Buddhist Studies, see Pali and Buddhist
Studies

Chemistry
Tel: (01) 911164, 911391, 911397, 911407,
913854-8, 910163, 914486 Fax: (01)
911916
Arewgoda, C. Malini, BSc *Peradeniya*, PhD
Otago Sr. Lectr. (on leave)
Ariyaratne, J. K. P., BSc *Ceyl.*, PhD *Camb.* Prof.
Goonawardane, Neelakanthi E., BSc *Peradeniya*,
PhD *S'ton.* Assoc. Prof. (on leave)
Liyanage, Janitha A., BSc *Sri Jay.*, PhD
Wales Sr. Lectr.
Navaratne, A. M. A. N., BSc *Peradeniya*, MSc
Hawaii, PhD *Hawaii* Sr. Lectr.
Padmaperuma, Bimali P., BSc *Colombo*, PhD
Ill. Sr. Lectr.
Paranagama, P. A., BSc *Kelaniya*, PhD *Glas.* Sr.
Lectr.
Pathiratne, K. A. S., BSc *Ceyl.*, MSc *Dal.*, PhD
N.Dakota State Sr. Lectr.
Seneviratne, N. A. Kapila P. J., BSc *Kelaniya*,
PhD *Wayne State* Sr. Lectr.
Wickramasinghe, L. Keerthi G., BSc *Ceyl.*, PhD
S.Fraser Sr. Lectr.; Head*
Wimalasena, P. S. Sukumal, BSc *Ceyl.*, MSc
W.Aust. Assoc. Prof.
Other Staff: 10 Lectrs.; 7 Temp. Lectrs.
Research: biochemistry; chemical ecology;
environmental chemistry; natural products

Classical Studies, see Western Classics and
Christian Culture

Commerce and Financial Management
Tel: (01) 911464, 911391, 911397, 911407,
913854-8, 910163, 914485
Jayasena, M. K., BBAd *Vidyod.*, MCom
Kelaniya Sr. Lectr.; Head*
Mettananda, G. G., BSc *Vidyod.*, MCom
Kelaniya Sr. Lectr.
Ubeychandra, E. G., BCom *Kelaniya*, MCom
Kelaniya Sr. Lectr.
Wasantha Kumara, D., BCom *Kelaniya*, MCom
Kelaniya Sr. Lectr.
Other Staff: 6 Lectrs.; 3 Temp. Lectrs.

Economics
Tel: (01) 911164, 911391, 911397, 911407,
913854-8, 910163, 914488
Ariyawansa Dissanayake, M., BA *Vidyal.*, MA
Kelaniya Sr. Lectr.

Bandara, Y. M. S. M., BA Vidyal., MA Shiga Sr. Lectr.
Dharmasena, K., BA Ceyl., MA Ceyl., PhD Lond. Prof.
Herath Banda, M. H. B., BA Vidyod., MA Sri Jay. Sr. Lectr. (on leave)
Hettiarachchi, Upali, BA Peradeniya, MA Kelaniya Sr. Lectr.
Indrani, G. W., BA Vidyal., MA Kelaniya Sr. Lectr.; Head*
Karunanayake, Kamal M., BA Ceyl., PhD Birm. Sr. Lectr.
Karunasena, H. P., BA Vidyal., MA McM. Sr. Lectr.
Pathirage, J. M. P., BA Vidyal., MA Sri Jay. Sr. Lectr.
Podimenike, K. M. P., BCom Peradeniya, MA Kelaniya Sr. Lectr.
Satarasinghe, D. P., BA Vidyal., MA Tokyo Sr. Lectr.
Tennakoon, K. U. A., BA Vidyal., MA Sri Jay. Sr. Lectr. (on leave)
Wijekoon, M. K., BA Vidyod., MA Br.Col. Sr. Lectr.

English
Tel: (01) 911164, 911391, 911397, 911407, 913854-8, 910163
De Silva, M. Lakshmi, BA Ceyl., PhD Kelaniya Sr. Lectr.; Head*
Goonatilleke, D. C. R. A., BA Ceyl., PhD Lanc. Prof.
Gunasekera, Manique, BA Kelaniya, PhD Mich. Sr. Lectr.
Hewabowala, Eisha M. J., BA Kelaniya, MA Sr. Lectr.
Other Staff: 1 Lectr.

Fine Arts
Tel: (01) 911164, 911391, 911397, 911407, 913854-8, 910163
Jayatunga, Mangalika, BA Ceyl., MA Kelaniya Sr. Lectr.
Nandedeva, A. B. D., BA Ceyl., MSc Moratuwa Sr. Lectr.; Head*
Other Staff: 4 Lectrs.

French, see Mod. Langs.

Geography
Tel: (01) 911164, 911391, 911397, 911407, 913854-8, 910163, 914489
Chandrasena, U. A., BA Vidyal., MSc Asian I.T., Bangkok Sr. Lectr.
Dangalle, N. K., BA Ceyl., MA Flin., PhD Peradeniya Prof.
Dharmasiri, R. K. L. M., BA Kelaniya, MA S.Krishna. Sr. Lectr.
Guruge, K. G., BA Vidyal., MA Kelaniya Sr. Lectr.
Harasgama, H. D. A. G., BA Vidyod., MA Sri Jay. Sr. Lectr.
Jayakody, S. K., BA Ceyl., MA Kelaniya Sr. Lectr.
Ratnayake, Ranitha L., BA Vidyod., MA Kelaniya Sr. Lectr.
Wijedasa, M. B., BA Ceyl., PhD Peradeniya Sr. Lectr.; Head*

Hindi
Tel: (01) 911164, 911391, 911397, 911407, 913854-8, 910163 Fax: (01) 911913
Dassanayake, V. Indra, BA Lucknow, MA Lucknow, PhD Lucknow Sr. Lectr.
Palliyaguruge, Chandrasiri, BA Vidyal., PhD S.Lanka Assoc. Prof.; Acting Head*
Other Staff: 2 Lectrs.; 1 Temp. Lectrs.
Research: classical and modern Hindi literature; Hindi folk drama and folklore; Hindi grammar and lexicography

History
Tel: (01) 911164, 911391, 911397, 911407, 913854-8, 910163, 914491
Gunawardena, R. H. R., BA Vidyal., MA Vidyal., PhD Peradeniya Assoc. Prof.; Head*
Illangasinghe, H. B. Mangala, BA Vidyal., MA Vidyal., PhD Lond. Prof.

Karunananda, Ukku B., BA Vidyal., PhD Vidyal. Assoc. Prof.
Kulasekera, K. M. P., BA Vidyal., PhD Lond. Sr. Lectr.
Liyanagamage, Amaradasa, BA Ceyl., PhD Lond. Prof.

Human Resource Management, see
Accty. and Human Resource Management

Industrial Management
Tel: (01) 911164, 911391, 911397, 911407, 913854-8, 910163, 914482 Fax: (01) 914482
Abeysinghe, Dhammika P., BSc Kelaniya, MBA Asian I.T., Bangkok Sr. Lectr.
Jayawardena, D. P. W., BSc Kelaniya, PhD Keele Sr. Lectr.
Munasinghe, Lalithasewa, BSc(Eng) Moratuwa, MSc Strath. Sr. Lectr.; Head*
Peter, Paul L. S., BSc Kelaniya, MSM Georgia Sr. Lectr.
Sunandaraja, Degamboda A. C., BSc(Eng) Moratuwa, MEng Asian I.T., Bangkok Sr. Lectr.
Suriyaarachchi, Rasika H., BScEngin Peradeniya, MA Colombo, MEng Asian I.T., Bangkok Sr. Lectr.
Vidanapathirana, Upali, BA Asian I.T., Bangkok, MSc Asian I.T., Bangkok, MBA Sri Jay. Sr. Lectr.

Library Science
Tel: (01) 911164, 911391, 911397, 911407, 913854-8, 910163
Ranasinghe, P., BA S.Lanka, MLib Sr. Lectr.
Weerasinghe, W. K. M. M. K., BA Kelaniya, MLibSc Panjab Sr. Lectr.; Head*
Weerasooriya, W. A., BA MLib Sr. Lectr.
Research: bibliography; cataloguing; classification; library administration; user survey

Linguistics
Tel: (01) 911164, 911391, 911397, 911407, 913854-8, 910163 Fax: (01) 911913
Kariyakaravana, Sunil M., BA Kelaniya, MA Ott., PhD Cornell Sr. Lectr.
Karunatilake, W. S., BA Ceyl., MA Poona, PhD Cornell Prof.
Nagitha, Ven. K., BA Kelaniya, MA Kelaniya, PhD Edin. Sr. Lectr.; Head*
Premaratne, A. C., BA Vidyal., PhD Lond. Sr. Lectr.
Weerakoon, Hema, BA Ceyl., MA Ceyl., PhD Kelaniya Sr. Lectr.
Wickramasinghe, D. M., BA Ceyl., MA Ceyl., PhD Exe. Assoc. Prof.
Wilson Rajapakse, R. M., BA Vidyal., MA York(UK), MA Kelaniya, PhD Lond. Assoc. Prof.
Other Staff: 2 Lectrs.; 3 Temp. Lectrs.
Research: applied liguistics and language acquisition; lexicography; sign language linguistics; South Asian linguistics; syntax

Mass Communication
Tel: (01) 911164, 911391, 911397, 911407, 913854-8, 910163
Etugala, Ariyaratne, BA Kelaniya, MA Kelaniya, PhD Kelaniya Sr. Lectr.
Gunawardane, H. P. Nihalsiri, BA Vidyal., MA Kelaniya Sr. Lectr.
Kulasekera, Ramani A. A. P., BA Vidyal., MA Kelaniya Sr. Lectr.
Mel, Sunanda M., BA Vidyal., MPhil Lond., PhD Lond. Assoc. Prof.
Piyadasa, Rohana L., BA Kelaniya, MA Kelaniya, PhD Moscow Sr. Lectr.; Head*
Rajapakse, Chandrasiri, BA Vidyal., MA Vidyal., PhD Moscow Sr. Lectr.

Mathematics
Tel: (01) 911164, 911391, 911397, 911407, 913854-8, 910163
Devendra, M. D., BA Kelaniya, PhD Dund. Sr. Lectr.
Dias, N. G. J., BSc Colombo, MSc Belf., PhD Wales Sr. Lectr.

Hewapathirana, Tamara K., BSc S.Lanka, MSc Bath Sr. Lectr.
Kulathunga, D. D. Sarath, BSc Vidyal., MSc Kyushu, PhD Kyushu Sr. Lectr.
Mampitiya, M. A. U., BSc Kelaniya, MSc Ott., PhD Ott. Sr. Lectr.
Piyadasa, R. A. D., BSc Vidyal., MSc Kyushu, PhD Kyushu Sr. Lectr.
Somaratne, K. T., BSc Ceyl., MSc Wales, PhD Wales Sr. Lectr.; Head*
Suriyaarachchi, D. J. C., BSc Ceyl., MSc Manc. Sr. Lectr.
Thillekeratne, K., BSc Ceyl., MSc Lond., MSc Camb. Prof.
Wijegunasekara, M. Carmel, BSc Kelaniya, MSc Wales, PhD Wales Sr. Lectr.
Other Staff: 1 Lectr.

Medicine, see below

Microbiology
Tel: (01) 911164, 911391, 911397, 911407, 913854-8, 910163, 914481
Abeygunawardena, G. A. S. Indika, BSc Kelaniya, MPhil Kelaniya, PhD Kelaniya Sr. Lectr.; Head*
Fernando, G. P. C., MB BS Ceyl. Co-ordinator
Kodikara, C. P., BSc Peradeniya, PhD Copenhagen Sr. Lectr.
Widanapathirana, W. S., BSc Ceyl., MSc H.-W., PhD H.-W. Prof.
Other Staff: 4 Lectrs.
Research: environmental microbiology; food microbiology; microbial technology

Modern Languages
Tel: (01) 911164, 911391, 911397, 911407, 913854-8, 910163, 914494
Amunugama, Sarath T. B., MA Paris, PhD Paris Sr. Lectr., French
Gunasekara, N. Niroshini, BA Kelaniya, MA Montpellier III Sr. Lectr., French; Head*

Paediatrics
Tel: (01) 911164, 911391, 911397, 911407, 913854-8, 910163
No staff at present

Pali and Buddhist Studies, see also Special Centres, etc
Tel: (01) 911164, 911391, 911397, 911407, 913854-8, 910163, 914492
Kariyawasam, Thilak, BA Vidyod., PhD Lanc. Assoc. Prof.
Karunadasa, Y., BA Ceyl., PhD Lond. Prof. (on leave)
Sumanapala, G. D., BA Vidyal., MA Kelaniya Assoc. Prof.; Head*
Wijeratne, Ananda, BA Vidyod., MA Northwestern, PhD Kelaniya Sr. Lectr. (on leave)

Philosophy
Tel: (01) 911164, 911391, 911397, 911407, 913854-8, 910163
Edirisinghe, Daya, BA Vidyod., MA Dongguk Prof., Indian Philosophy; Head*
Kulasena, V. G., BA Ceyl., MA Kelaniya, PhD Ioannina Sr. Lectr.
Piyasiri, Kumar K., BA Ceyl., PhD ANU Sr. Lectr.
Rodrigo, Pushpasiri P. D., BA Vidyod., MA Kelaniya, PhD Kelaniya Sr. Lectr.
Seneviratne, Jayanthi H. D. J., BA Kelaniya, MA Kelaniya, PhD Kelaniya Sr. Lectr.
Wimaladhamma, Ven. K., BA Vidyal., MA Kelaniya Sr. Lectr. (on leave)

Physics
Tel: (01) 911164, 911391, 911397, 911407, 913854-8, 910163, 914495 Fax: (01) 914485, 911916
Amarasekera, C. D., BSc Ceyl., PhD Purdue Sr. Lectr.
Jayakody, J. R. P., BSc Peradeniya, PhD C.U.N.Y. Sr. Lectr.
Jayasuriya, K. A. K. D. D. D., BSc S.Lanka, PhD ANU Sr. Lectr.; Head*

Kalingamudali, S. R. D., BSc Kelaniya, PhD Sheff. Sr. Lectr.

Perera, P. A. A., BSc Colombo, PhD Roch. Sr. Lectr.

Punyasena, M. A., BSc Kelaniya, PhD Alta. Sr. Lectr.

Siripala, W. P., BSc Ceyl., PhD C.U.N.Y. Sr. Lectr.

Sumathipala, H. H., BSc Kelaniya, PhD Peradeniya Sr. Lectr.

Research: electrodeposited copper oxide/copper sulphide thin film solar cells; positron-electron sum-energy spectra for the 238v + 181 system; specific heat of spin glass materials; theoretical studies of hetrojunctional biopolar transisters

Physiology, see Medicine, below

Sanskrit

Tel: (01) 911164, 911391, 911397, 911407, 913854-8, 910163, 914484 Fax: (01) 911913

Dhammaratana, Ven. Induragare, BA Kelaniya, MA B&P SLanka Lectr. (on leave)

Revata, Ven. N., BA Vidyal., MA Nag. Sr. Lectr.; Head*

Sugatharatana, Ven K., BA Kelaniya, MA Kelaniya Sr. Lectr.

Wijesinghe, S. A. G., BA Vidyal., MA Kelaniya Sr. Lectr.

Research: Buddhist sanskrit; Mahayanic philosophy

Sinhala

Tel: (01) 911164, 911391, 911397, 911407, 913854-8, 910163, 914493

Abeysinghe, A. A., BA Ceyl., DPhil York(UK) Assoc. Prof.; Head*

Abeysiriwardane, Ananda, BA Ceyl., MA Ceyl., PhD Kelaniya Assoc. Prof.

Balasooriya, Somaratne, BA Vidyal., PhD Paris Assoc. Prof.

Danansuriya, J., BA Vidyal., MA Kelaniya Sr. Lectr.

Delabandara, T. R. Gamini, BA S.Lanka, MA Kelaniya, PhD Lond. Sr. Lectr.

Dias, Hurson U. G., BA Kelaniya, MA Kelaniya Sr. Lectr.

Goonawardane, N. D., BA Peradeniya, PhD Kelaniya Sr. Lectr.

Kumarasinghe, Kulathilaka, BA S.Lanka, PhD Kelaniya Assoc. Prof.

Palliyaguruge, Chandrasiri, BA Vidyal., PhD S.Lanka Prof.

Parawahera, Nimal, BA Kelaniya, PhD Vic. Sr. Lectr.

Sociology

Tel: (01) 911164, 911391, 911397, 911407, 913854-8, 910163, 914490

Karunaratne, H. W., BA Peradeniya, MA Sri Jay. Sr. Lectr.; Head*

Other Staff: 3 Lectrs.; 5 Temp. Lectrs.

Western Classics and Christian Culture

Tel: (01) 911164, 911391, 911397, 911407, 913854-8, 910163

Abeysinghe, Nihal, LLB Open S.Lanka, MA Kelaniya, LTh Ans., ThD Ans. Sr. Lectr.; Head*

Jayasekera, I. Kamani, BA Kelaniya, MA Kelaniya Sr. Lectr.

Liyanage, Pulsara N., BA Peradeniya, MA Peradeniya Sr. Lectr.

Lowe, N. N. E., BA Kelaniya, MA Sri Jay. Sr. Lectr.

Other Staff: 2 Lectrs.

Research: culture and religion

Zoology

Tel: (01) 911164, 911391, 911397, 911407, 913854-8, 910163, 914479 Fax: (01) 911916, 911485

Amarasinghe, U. S., BSc Kelaniya, MSc Wales, PhD Ruhuna Sr. Lectr.

Costa, H. Henry, BSc Ceyl., PhD Wales Prof.

De Silva, M. P., BSc Colombo, PhD Reading Sr. Lectr.

Fernando, Ivor V. S., BSc Ceyl., MSc Lond., PhD Manc. Sr. Lectr.

Hettiarachchi, Mangalika, BSc Kelaniya, PhD Nigeria Sr. Lectr.

Pathiratne, Asoka, BSc Kelaniya, PhD N.Dakota Sr. Lectr.; Head*

Ratnayake, R. K. S., BSc Kelaniya, MSc Asian I.T., Bangkok, PhD Wales Sr. Lectr.

Wijayaratne, M. Jayantha S., BSc S.Lanka, MSc Mich., PhD Kelaniya Prof.

Research: diseases of fish and shrimps; ecology of Sri Lankan reservoirs; fisheries management; insect pest management

MEDICINE

Tel: (01) 958219, 958039 Fax: (01) 538251

Anatomy

Tel: (01) 985039, 958219 Fax: (01) 958337

Jayasinghe, J. A. P., BDS Peradeniya, MSc Lond., PhD Lond. Sr. Lectr.; Head*

Other Staff: 3 Lectrs.

Research: age changes in bone; osteoporosis placenta in hypertensive disorders of pregnancy

Biochemistry

Tel: (01) 958219, 958039 Fax: (01) 958337

Chakrawarthy, S., BSc Kelaniya, PhD Glas. Sr. Lectr.

Chandrasena, L. G., BSc Liv., PhD Liv., FIChemE Prof.

Kalyananda, M. K. G. S., BSc Peradeniya, MPhil Colombo, MPhil N.Y., PhD N.Y. Sr. Lectr.; Head*

Perera, P. D. T. M., BSc Peradeniya, MSc Kelaniya Sr. Lectr.

Thabrew, I., BSc Colombo, PhD S'ton. Sr. Lectr.

Other Staff: 3 Lectrs.

Research: cellular antioxidants; antioxidants in plant extracts

Community and Family Medicine

Tel: (01) 958219, 958039 Fax: (01) 958251

De Silva, Nandani, MB BS Colombo, MD Colombo Assoc. Prof.

Jayawardane, Pushpa L., MB BS Ceyl., MSc Colombo, MD Colombo Sr. Lectr.

Other Staff: 4 Lectrs.

Forensic Medicine and Medical Law

Tel: (01) 958219, 958039 Fax: (01) 958337

Samarasekera, A. N., MB BS S.Lanka, MD Colombo Sr. Lectr.

Medicine

Tel: (01) 958219, 958039 Fax: (01) 958337

de Silva, H. J., MB BS Colombo, MD Colombo, DPhil Oxf., FRCP, FRCPEd Prof.

Fonseka, M. M. D., MB BS Colombo, MD Colombo Sr. Lectr.

Gunathilake, S. B., MB BS Colombo, MD Colombo, FRCPEd Sr. Lectr.; Head*

Other Staff: 4 Lectrs.

Microbiology

Tel: (01) 958219, 958039 Fax: (01) 958337

Sunil-Chandra, N. P., BVSc S.Lanka, MPhil Peradeniya, PhD Camb. Sr. Lectr.; Head*

Other Staff: 1 Lectr.

Obstetrics and Gynaecology

Tel: (01) 958219, 958039 Fax: (01) 958337

Pathiraya, R. P., MB BS Ruhuna, MS Colombo Sr. Lectr.

Sirisena, J. L. G. J., MB BS Peradeniya, MS Colombo Prof.; Head*

Wijesinghe, P. S., MB BS Peradeniya, MS Colombo, Sr. Lectr.

Other Staff: 1 Lectr.

Research: abdominal hysterectomy; caesarean section; induction of labour; infertility

Paediatrics

Tel: (01) 958219, 958039 Fax: (01) 958337

Gunasekera, D. P., MB BS Colombo, MD Colombo Sr. Lectr.

Jayawardena, D. R. K. C., MB BS Peradeniya, MD Colombo Sr. Lectr.

Karunasekera, K. A. W., MB BS Ruhuna, MMedSc Otago , MD Colombo Sr. Lectr.; Head*

Parasitology

Tel: (01) 958219, 958039 Fax: (01) 958337

De Silva, N. E., MB BS Colombo, MSc Lond., MD Colombo Sr. Lectr.; Head*

Other Staff: 1 Lectr.

Pathology

Tel: (01) 958219, 958039 Fax: (01) 958337

Saparamadu, P. A. M., MB BS Colombo, MD S.Lanka Sr. Lectr.

Wiyesiriwardenam, I. S., MB BS Colombo, MD S.Lanka Sr. Lectr.

Other Staff: 5 Lectrs.

Pharmacology

Tel: (01) 958219, 958039 Fax: (01) 958337

6 Lectrs.

Physiology

Tel: (01) 958251, 956188 Fax: (01) 958251, 958337

Dissanayake, Asoka S., MB BS Ceyl., DPhil Oxf. Assoc. Prof.; Head*

Gunawardena, Palitha, MB BS Colombo, PhD Leeds Sr. Lectr.

Selliah, Siva, MB BS N.C'bo.Med.Coll., MPhil Colombo Sr. Lectr.

Other Staff: 4 Lectrs.

Research: clinical gastrointestinal physiology; electrogastrography, ambulatory manometry and PH cardiovascular and exercise physiology; renal physiology

Psychiatry

Tel: (01) 958337 Fax: (01) 958337

Kuruppuarachchi, K. A. L. A., MB BS Peradeniya, MD Colombo Sr. Lectr.

Other Staff: 2 Lectrs.

Research: alcohol related psychiatric problems; decimerate self harm (DSH); study on old age psychiatric problems

Surgery

Tel: (01) 958219, 958039 Fax: (01) 958337

Ariyarathna, M. H. J., MB BS Colombo, MS Colombo, FRCS, FRCSEd Sr. Lectr.

Deen, K. I., MB BS Peradeniya, MS, FRCS, FRCSEd Sr. Lectr.

Samarasekera, D. N., MB BS Colombo, MS Colombo, FRCS, FRCSEd Sr. Lectr.; Head*

Other Staff: 1 Lectr.

Research: anorectal physiology (ARP); electrogastrography (EGG)

SPECIAL CENTRES, ETC

Aesthetic Studies, Institute of

Tel: (01) 686072, 696971, 691483 Fax: (01) 686071

Abeysiriwardana, Ananda, BA MA PhD Prof.; Dir.*

Archaeology, Postgraduate Institute of

Tel: (01) 503061, 694151, 699623 Fax: (01) 500731

Bandaranayake, Prof. Senake D., BA Brist., BLitt Oxf., DPhil Oxf. Dir.*

Somadewa, D. W. R. K., BA Kelaniya, MPhil Kelaniya Sr. Lectr.

Weerasinghe, Jagath, BFA Kelaniya, MFA Sr. Lectr.

Gampaha Wickramarachchi, Ayurveda Institute of

Tel: (033) 22748, 23787 Fax: (033) 22739

Dissanayaka, Asoka S., MB BS Ceyl., DPhil Oxf. Acting Dir.*
Other Staff: 1 Lectr.

Pali and Buddhist Studies, Postgraduate Institute of

Tel: (01) 501079 Fax: (075) 335369

Abayanansa, K., BA Peradeniya, PhD Kelaniya MA Head, Dept. of Buddhist Culture
Dhammajothi, Ven. K., MA Kelaniya, PhD Kelaniya Head, Dept. of Literary Sources
Kariyawasam, Prof. T., BA S.Lanka, PhD Lanc. Acting Dir.*
Tilakaratne, Asanga, BA Peradeniya, MA Hawaii, PhD Hawaii Head, Dept. of Buddhist Thought

CONTACT OFFICERS

Academic affairs. Senior Assistant Registrar: Poddalgoda, U. G. K., BA S.Lanka
Admissions (first degree). Senior Assistant Registrar: Poddalgoda, U. G. K., BA S.Lanka
Admissions (higher degree). Assistant Registrar: Ranasinghe, G. H., BA Peradeniya
Computing services. Head, Computer Centre: Munasinghe, Lalithseva, BSc(Eng) S.Lanka, MSc Strath.
Estates and buildings/works and services. Works Engineer: Dias, M. N.
Examinations. Deputy Registrar: Christy Silva, L. D. E., BA Vidyal.
Finance. Bursar: Hapangama, S. K. J.
General enquiries. Registrar: Amarasinghe, N. B., BA Vidyod.
Health services. Chief Medical Officer: Jayatissa, J. A. J., MB BS Ceyl.
Library (chief librarian). Librarian: Lankage, Jayasiri, BA Vidyod., MA Vidyod., MLibSc Ban., PhD Kelaniya

Publications. Assistant Registrar: Ranasinghe, G. H., BA Peradeniya
Purchasing. Assistant Bursar: Jayaweera, L. M., BA Sri Jay.
Research. Assistant Registrar: Ranasinghe, G. H., BA Peradeniya
Sport and recreation. Director: Perera, B. L. H., BA Vidyal.
Student welfare/counselling. Head, Medical Faculty Counselling Centre: Kuruppuarachchi, K. A. L. A., MS BS Peradeniya, MD Colombo
Student welfare/counselling (counselling). Chief Student Counsellor: Jayakodi, S. K., BA Ceyl., MA Kelaniya
Student welfare/counselling (welfare). Senior Assistant Registrar: Karunaratne, W. M., BSc

[Information supplied by the institution as at 3 June 1998, and edited by the ACU]

UNIVERSITY OF MORATUWA, SRI LANKA

Founded 1978; formerly the Ceylon College of Technology, founded 1966, and, from 1972, the Katubedda Campus of the University of Sri Lanka

Member of the Association of Commonwealth Universities

Postal Address: Katubedda, Moratuwa, Sri Lanka
Telephone: (01) 645301, 645534 **Fax**: (01) 647622 **Cables**: Ceycoltec **WWW**: http://www.mrt.ac.lk

CHANCELLOR—Clarke, A. C., CBE, BSc Lond., Hon. DSc, FKC, FRAS
VICE-CHANCELLOR*—Karunaratne, Prof. Samarajeewa, BSc(Engin) Ceyl., MSc Glas., FIEE, FIE(SL)
REGISTRAR—De Silva, G. H. D. C., BA Peradeniya
BURSAR—Wijesekera, C., BA Ceyl.
LIBRARIAN—Rubasingam, S., BA Ceyl., MA Lough.

FACULTIES/SCHOOLS

Architecture

Dean: Balasuriya, L., BArch Newcastle(UK), MSc Edin.

Engineering

Dean: Ratnayake, L. L., BSc(Eng) S.Lanka, MSc Birm.

ACADEMIC UNITS

Architecture

Alahakoon, R. Sr. Lectr.
Alwis, L., BArch Melb. Prof.; Dir., Postgrad. Studies
Balasuriya, L., BA Newcastle(UK), MSc Edin. Assoc. Prof.
Balasuriya, S., BArch Newcastle(UK), MSc Edin., MPhil Edin. Sr. Lectr.
Basnayake, N. V. W., BSc(BE) MSc Sr. Lectr.
Chandrasekera, D. P., BSc(BE) S.Lanka, MSc S.Lanka Sr. Lectr.
Dayaratne, K. A. R., BSc(BE) MSc PhD Sr. Lectr.
de Saram, C. J., MSc Sr. Lectr.
de Silva, T. K. N. P., MScArchitecture S.Lanka Assoc. Prof.; Head*
Manawadu, M. S., BSc(BE) S.Lanka, MSc S.Lanka, PhD Kyoto Sr. Lectr.
Perera, L. A. S. R., BSc(BE) S.Lanka, MSc S.Lanka, PhD Bangkok Sr. Lectr.
Prematilaka, M. S., BSc(BE) S.Lanka, MSc S.Lanka Sr. Lectr.

Sri Nammuni, V., BSc(Arch) Newcastle(NSW), MArch Newcastle(NSW) Sr. Lectr.
Weerasinghe, U. G. D., BSc(BE) MSc Sr. Lectr.

Building Economics

de Silva, M. L. D., BSc(BE) MSc Sr. Lectr.
Perera, R. S., BSc Salf., MSc Salf., PhD Salf. Sr. Lectr.
Wedikkara, D. E. R. E., BSc(BE) Sr. Lectr.; Head*

Computer Science and Engineering

Dias, P. G. V., MSc Calif., PhD Calif., BSc(Eng) Sr. Lectr.; Head*

Engineering, Chemical

Amarasinghe, B. M. W. P. K., BSc(Eng) S.Lanka, MSc Manc., PhD Manc. Sr. Lectr.
de Alwis, A. A. P., PhD Camb., BSc(Eng) Sr. Lectr.
Perera, S. A. S., BSc Sr. Lectr.; Head*
Silva, H. D. J., BSc Ceyl., MSc Leeds Assoc. Prof.

Engineering, Civil

Bandara, J. M. S. J., BSc(Eng) PhD Sr. Lectr.
Chandrakeerthi, S. R. de S., BScEngin Ceyl., PhD Sheff. Sr. Prof.
de Alwis, N. A. D. R., BScEngin Ceyl., MSc Manc. Assoc. Prof.
Dias, W. P. S., BSc(Eng) S.Lanka, PhD Lond. Assoc. Prof.
Gunawardena, N. D., MSc Lough., PhD Lough., BSc(Eng) Sr. Lectr.

Hettiarachchi, M. T. P., BSc(Eng) S.Lanka, MSc Lond., PhD Lond. Sr. Lectr.
Hettiarachchi, S. S. L., BSc(Eng) S.Lanka, PhD Lond. Assoc. Prof.; Head*
Jayanandana, A. D. C., PhD Leeds, BSc(Eng) Sr. Lectr.
Jayasinghe, M. T. R., BSc(Eng) S.Lanka, PhD Camb. Sr. Lectr.
Jayawardena, A. K. W., MSc Lough., PhD Lough., BSc(Eng) Sr. Lectr.
Jayaweera, M. W., BSc(Eng) S.Lanka, PhD Sr. Lectr.
Karunaratne, G. H. U., BSc(Eng) S.Lanka, MSc Lond., PhD Sr. Lectr.
Kodikara, G. W., BSc(Eng) S.Lanka, MSc Lough., PhD Sr. Lectr.
Kulatilake, S. A. S., BSc(Eng) PhD Sr. Lectr.
Kumarage, K. A. S., MSc Calg., BSc(Eng) PhD Sr. Lectr.
Nanayakkara, D., BSc(Eng) S.Lanka, M(Eng) Tokyo Sr. Lectr.
Nanayakkara, S. M. A., DEng Tokyo, BSc(Eng) Sr. Lectr.
Pathinathar, S., MPhil Sr. Lectr.
Perera, A. A. D. A. J., MSc Lough., PhD Lough., BSc(Eng) Sr. Lectr.
Priyantha, D. G. N., BSc(Eng) S.Lanka, MSc PhD Sr. Lectr.
Ranasinghe, K. A. M. K., MASc Br.Col., BSc(Eng) PhD Sr. Lectr.
Ratnayake, L. L., BSc(Eng) S.Lanka, MSc Birm. Prof.
Ratnayake, N., BSc(Eng) S.Lanka, MEng Wales Assoc. Prof.

Senarath, D. C. H., BScEngin Ceyl., MEng Sheff., PhD Birm. Sr. Prof.

Tennakoon, B. L., BSc(Eng) Ceyl., PhD Camb. Sr. Prof.

Thilakasiri, H. S., BSc(Eng) S.Lanka, MSc Lond., PhD S.Florida Sr. Lectr.

Weerasekera, I. R. A., BSc(Eng) PhD Sr. Lectr.

Wickramasuriya, S. S., BSc(Eng) S.Lanka, PhD NSW Sr. Lectr.

Wijesekera, N. T. S., BSc(Eng) Peradeniya, MSc Tokyo, PhD Tokyo Sr. Lectr.

Wijeyesekera, D. S., PhD Edin., Hon. DUniv Open(UK), FIE(SL) Sr. Prof.

Engineering, Electrical

Dias, M. P., BScEngin Ceyl., MS Texas A.&M., PhD Texas A.&M. Sr. Lectr.; Head*

Gamage, Lalith D. K. B., BSc(Eng) Moratuwa, PhD Br.Col. Sr. Lectr.

Karunadasa, J. P., BSc(Eng) PhD Sr. Lectr.

Karunaratne, Samarajeewa, BSc(Eng) Ceyl., MSc Glas., FIEE, FIE(SL) Sr. Prof.

Lucas, J. R., BScEngin Ceyl., MSc Manc., PhD Manc., FIEE Prof.; Head*

Nanayakkara, D. P. N., BSc(Eng) Moratuwa, MSc PhD Sr. Lectr.

Perera, H. Y. R., BSc(Eng) S.Lanka, DrIng Sr. Lectr.

Rajakaruna, R. M. A. S., MSc Calg., PhD Tor., BSc(Eng) Sr. Lectr.

Ranaweera, A., MEng Hawaii, PhD Hawaii, BSc(Eng) Sr. Lectr.

Wickramarachchi, N. K., BSc Lond., MSc Lond., PhD Br.Col. Sr. Lectr.

Wijayatunga, R. L. M. P. D. C., BSc(Eng) Lond., PhD Lond. Sr. Lectr.

Engineering, Electronic and Telecommunications

Atukorale, G. S., MS Calif., BSc(Eng) PhD Sr. Lectr.

Dayawansa, Indira J., BSc Ceyl., MSc Wales, PhD Wales Assoc. Prof.

Dias, S. A. D., MS Calif., PhD Calif., BSc(Eng) Sr. Lectr.

Jayasinghe, J. A. K. S., BSc(Eng) PhD Sr. Lectr.; Head*

Punchihewa, G. A. D., BSc(Eng) Moratuwa, MSc T.U.Eindhoven Sr. Lectr.

Physics

Premaratne, L. P. J. P., BSc S.Lanka, MSc Qld. Sr. Lectr.

Engineering Industrial Training

Wijewardena, S. M., BSc(Eng) MEng Sr. Lectr.

Wijewickrama, N. A., BSc(Eng) Moratuwa Sr. Lectr.

Engineering Materials

Gunapala, P. Y., MSc Moscow, PhD Moscow Sr. Lectr.

Jayaratne, M., BSc S.Lanka, DEng Tokyo Sr. Lectr.

Perera, L. M., PhD Qu., BSc(Eng) MSc Sr. Lectr.; Head*

Engineering, Mechanical

Attalage, R. A., BSc(Eng) Moratuwa, MEng Asian I.T., Bangkok, PhD E.S.N.des Mines, Paris Sr. Lectr.

de Silva, P. A., BScEngin Ceyl., MSc Lond., PhD Lond. Sr. Prof.

Karunaratne, G., MSc Moscow, PhD Moscow Sr. Lectr.

Nanayakkara, L. D. J. F., BSc(Eng) S.Lanka, PhD Strath. Sr. Lectr.

Perera, K. K. C. K., BScEng S.Lanka, MSc Calif., PhD Calif. Sr. Lectr.

Sugathapala, A. G. T., BSc S.Lanka, PhD Camb. Sr. Lectr.

Tittagala, S. R., BSc(Eng) S.Lanka, MSc Leeds, PhD Leeds Sr. Lectr.; Head*

Watugala, G. K., BSc(Eng) HK, MPhil HK, MSc Penn., PhD Penn. Sr. Lectr.

Wimalsiri, W. K., BSc(Eng) Moratuwa, PhD Newcastle(UK) Sr. Lectr.

Marine Engineering

Perera, P. A. B. A. R., BSc(Eng) S.Lanka, MSc Newcastle(UK), PhD Newcastle(UK) Sr. Lectr.

Piyasiri, T. A., BSc(Eng) S.Lanka, MSc Newcastle(UK), PhD Newcastle(UK) Sr. Lectr.

Engineering, Mining and Mineral

Dharmaratne, P. G., BSc S.Lanka, MSc Newcastle(UK), PhD Leeds Sr. Lectr.

Fernando, W. L. W., BScEngin Ceyl., MPhil Leeds, PhD Leeds Prof.

Hemalal, P. V. A., MSc Moscow Sr. Lectr.

Senarath, U. G., MSc Moscow, PhD Moscow Sr. Lectr.

Weerawarnakula, S., BSc Ceyl., MPhil Ib. Sr. Lectr.; Head*

Marine Engineering, see under Engin., Mech.

Mathematics

de Silva, G. T. Francis, BSc Ceyl., MSc Lond. Assoc. Prof.

Gunatilake, P. D., BSc Ceyl., MA Camb., PhD Lond., FRAS Prof.

Indralingam, M., BSc S.Lanka, MSc PhD Sr. Lectr.; Head*

Kandasamy, S., BSc Ceyl., BSc Lond., MSc Newcastle(UK), MSc S.Lanka Sr. Lectr.

Physics, see under Engin., Electronic and Telecommunicns.

Polymer Technology

Sivagurunathan, L., BScEngin Ceyl., MSc S.Lanka, PhD CNAA Assoc. Prof.

Subramaniyam, K., BSc Ceyl., MSc CNAA Sr. Lectr.

Technician Studies Division

Saparamadu, A. A. D. D., BSc Ceyl., MEd Leic., MSc Dir.*

Textile and Clothing Technology

De Silva, N. G. H., BSc Ceyl., MSc Leeds Sr. Lectr.

Dissanayake, D. P. D., BSc Ceyl., MSc Leeds Sr. Lectr.

Fernando, E. A. S. K., MSc Ivanovo Textile Technol.Inst., PhD Ivanovo Textile Technol.Inst. Sr. Lectr.

Fernando, L. D., BSc Leeds, PhD Leeds Prof.; Head*

Perera, N., BSc S.Lanka, MSc Leeds, PhD Leeds Sr. Lectr.

Wanigatunga, N. L., MSc T.U.Dresden, MPhil Manc. Sr. Lectr.

Town and Country Planning

Fernando, K. D., BA Ceyl., MSc S.Lanka Sr. Lectr.

Mendis, M. W. J. G., BScEngin Ceyl., MSc Strath., FRTPI Sr. Prof.

Perera, A. L. S., MSc S.Lanka, BA Ceyl. Assoc. Prof.; Dir., Postgrad. Studies; Head*

Senanayake, M. A. P., BSc Colombo, MSc Moratuwa Sr. Lectr.

SPECIAL CENTRES, ETC

Architecture Research Centre

Alwis, L., BArch Melb. Dir.*

Computing Services Centre

Gamage, L. D. K. B., BSc(Eng) Moratuwa, PhD Br.Col. Dir.*

Engineering Research, Centre for

Vacant Posts: Dir.*

English Language Teaching Centre

No staff at present

CONTACT OFFICERS

Academic affairs. Vice-Chancellor: Karunaratne, Prof. Samarajeewa, BSc(Engin) Ceyl., MSc Glas., FIEE, FIE(SL)

Computing services. Director: Gamage, L. D. K. B., BSc(Eng) Moratuwa, PhD Br.Col.

Finance. Bursar: Wijesekera, C., BA Ceyl.

General enquiries. Registrar: De Silva, G. H. D. C., BA Peradeniya

Health services. University Medical Officer: Gunawardena, T., MB BS Ceyl.

Library (chief librarian). Librarian: Rubasingam, S., BA Ceyl., MA Lough.

[Information supplied by the institution as at 22 June 1998, and edited by the ACU]

OPEN UNIVERSITY OF SRI LANKA

Founded 1980

Member of the Association of Commonwealth Universities

Postal Address: PO Box 21, Nawala, Nugegoda, Sri Lanka
Telephone: (01) 853615, 853777, 856201-2 Fax: (01) 436858 E-mail: postmaster@ou.ac.lk
Cables: Open University

CHANCELLOR—Corea, G., MA Camb., DPhil Oxf.
VICE-CHANCELLOR*—Arthenayake, Prof. N. Ranjith, MSc(Eng) P.F.U.,Moscow, MSc Strath., FIE(SL),
FIE(India)
REGISTRAR—de Silva, N. W. S. W. S., JP, BA Vidyod., MPA Sri Jay.
LIBRARIAN—Korale, S. R., BA Ceyl., FLA
BURSAR—Peiris, Trixi F., BA Ceyl.

GENERAL INFORMATION

History. The university was founded in 1980.

Admission to first degree courses (see also Sri Lankan Introduction). Either General Certificate of Education (GCE) A level with at least 3 passes; or completion of levels 1 and 2 of the university's foundation programme.

First Degrees (see also Sri Lankan Directory to Subjects of Study). BA, BEd, BTech(Eng), LLB.

BA: 3 years; BEd, LLB: 4 years; BTech(Eng): 5 years.

Higher Degrees (see also Sri Lankan Directory to Subjects of Study).MEd, MTech, MPhil, PhD.

Applicants for admission to MTech must hold a relevant first degree and have field or industrial experience. MEd: first degree with at least second class honours and merit pass in postgraduate diploma in education; MPhil: good first degree; PhD: master's degree by research, or transfer from MPhil.

MEd: 18 months; MTech, MPhil: minimum 2 years; PhD: minimum 3 years.

Language of Instruction. English. Students may write exams in Sinhala, Tamil or English.

FACULTIES/SCHOOLS

Engineering Technology
Dean: Abeysuriya, A. G. K. de S., BSc(Eng) Ceyl., MSc Leeds, PhD Leeds
Secretary: Diyabedanage, N., BCom Colombo

Humanities and Social Sciences
Dean: Gunawardena, Prof. G. I. C., BA Ceyl., MA Peradeniya, PhD La Trobe
Secretary: Waffa, M.

Natural Sciences
Dean: Fernando, Prof. J. N. O., BSc Ceyl., PhD Lond., FRSChem
Secretary: de Silva, M. W. S., BA Peradeniya

ACADEMIC UNITS

Agricultural and Plantation Engineering
de Silva, C. S., BScAgric Peradeniya, MPhil Peradeniya, PhD Cran.IT Sr. Lectr.
de Silva, R. P., BSc(Eng) Moratuwa, MSc Cran., PhD Cran. Sr. Lectr.
Kulatunga, K. D. G., BSc(Eng) Ceyl. Sr. Lectr.; Head*
Senanayake, S. A. M. N. S., BSc(Eng) Moratuwa, MSc Cran., PhD Cran. Sr. Lectr.
Other Staff: 1 Lectr.
Research: groundwater flow models; irrigation and management; salinity development due to groundwater use; soil analysis and land use patterns; use of groundwater in hard rock aquifer in Sri Lanka

Botany
Amarasinghe, M. D., BSc Peradeniya, MPhil Peradeniya, PhD Salf. Sr. Lectr.

Coomaraswamy, U., BSc Ceyl., PhD Lond. Sr. Prof.; Head*
Jayakody, L. K. R. R., BSc Colombo, PhD Lanc. Sr. Lectr.
Samaranayaka, A. C. I., BSc Ceyl., PhD Lond. Sr. Lectr.
Senaratne, L. K., BSc Colombo, MPhil Open S.Lanka Sr. Lectr.
Weerasinge, T. K., BSc Kelaniya, PhD Kelaniya Sr. Lectr.
Other Staff: 4 Lectrs.

Chemistry
Bandarage, G., BSc Colombo, PhD Alta. Sr. Lectr.
Fernando, J. N. O., BSc Ceyl., PhD Lond., FRSChem Sr. Prof.
Gunaherath, G. M. K. B., BSc Peradeniya, PhD Peradeniya Sr. Lectr.; Head*
Iqbal, S. S., BSc Colombo, PhD Birm. Sr. Lectr.
Jayaratna, K. C., BSc Sri Jay. Sr. Lectr.
Karunaratne, D. N., BSc Colombo, PhD Br.Col. Sr. Lectr.
Kularatne, K. W. S., BSc Ceyl., PhD Aston Sr. Lectr.
Perera, K. S. D., BSc Sri Jay., PhD Belf. Sr. Lectr.
Tantrigoda, R. U., BSc Sri Jay., MPhil Ruhuna Sr. Lectr.
Research: inorganic, organic and organometallic chemistry; ion-atom collisions; natural products chemistry; synthetic chemistry

Computer Engineering, see Engin., Electr./Electronics/Computer

Education
Bopearachchi, K. M. E., BEd Kelaniya, MA Paris, PhD Paris Sr. Lectr.
Fernando, T. S., BA Ceyl., MPhil Open S.Lanka Sr. Lectr.
Gunawardena, G. I. C., BA Ceyl., MA Peradeniya, PhD La Trobe Prof.
Ismail, A. G. H., BEd Ceyl., MA Colombo Sr. Lectr.; Head*
Jaufer, P. C. P., BSc Jaffna Sr. Lectr.
Kudaligama, P. K. D. P., BA Ceyl., MA Colombo, PhD Colombo Sr. Lectr.
Kularatne, N. G., MA Peradeniya, PhD Peradeniya Sr. Lectr.
Lekamge, G. D., BEd Colombo, MPhil Open(UK), PhD Open(UK) Sr. Lectr.
Palihakkara, D. W., BA Ceyl., MA Punjab, PhD Ceyl. Sr. Lectr.
Wickramaratne, V., MA Colombo, MA Ceyl., PhD Ceyl. Sr. Lectr.
Wijeratne, W. A. R., BA Peradeniya, MA Ceyl., MA Colombo, PhD Colombo Sr. Lectr.
Other Staff: 5 Lectrs.

Educational Technology
1 Lectr.

Engineering, Agricultural, see Agric. and Plantation Engin.

Engineering, Civil
Abeysuriya, A. G. K. de S., BSc(Eng) Ceyl., MSc Leeds, PhD Leeds Sr. Lectr.

Costa, R. St. G. S. de, BSc(Eng) Moratuwa, MSc Hiroshima, PhD Hiroshima Sr. Lectr.
Dolage, D. A. R., BSc(Eng) Moratuwa, MSc Reading Sr. Lectr.
Gunasekera, A. U., MSc PhD Sr. Lectr.
Kodikara, P. N., BSc(Eng) Moratuwa, MSc Lough. Sr. Lectr.
Liyanagama, J., MSc Moscow, PhD Moscow Sr. Lectr.; Head*
Pallewatta, T. M., BSc(Eng) Moratuwa, MEng Asian I.T.,Bangkok, PhD Tokyo Sr. Lectr.
Ranasoma, K. I. M., BSc(Eng) Peradeniya, PhD Cant. Sr. Lectr.
Ratnaweera, H. G. P. A., BSc(Eng) Moratuwa, MSc New Jersey I.T., PhD New Jersey I.T. Sr. Lectr.
Sivaprakasapillai, S., BSc Ceyl., MSc Lond., DPhil Oxf. Sr. Lectr.
Tantirimudalige, M. N., BSc(Eng) S.Lanka, MTech Open S.Lanka Sr. Lectr.

Engineering, Electrical/Electronics/Computer
de Silva, N. S., MSc Moscow, MPhil Open S.Lanka Sr. Lectr.
Fonseka, H. C. M., BSc(Eng) S.Lanka, MEng Nagoya I.T. Sr. Lectr.
Gunasena, G. S., BSc(Eng) Moratuwa, MPhil Open S.Lanka Sr. Lectr.
Perera, C. J. S. A. H., BSc(Eng) Moratuwa.. MSc Munich Sr. Lectr.
Ranmuthu, K. T. M., BSc(Eng) Moratuwa, PhD Iowa State Sr. Lectr.
Sriyananda, H., BSc(Eng) Ceyl., MSc Salf., PhD Wales Sr. Prof.
Taldena, D. L., BSc(Eng) Ceyl., ME NSW Sr. Lectr.; Head*
Udagama, L. S., MSc PhD Sr. Lectr.
Other Staff: 4 Lectrs.

Engineering, Mechanical
Dedigamuwa, P. R., BSc(Eng) Moratuwa, MPhil Open S.Lanka Sr. Lectr.
Goonetilleke, H. D., BSc(Eng) S.Lanka, MSc Br.Col., PhD Br.Col. Sr. Lectr.
Jayakody, J. A. M. P., MSc P.F.U.,Moscow, PhD Baumon T.U. Sr. Lectr.
Padmaperuma, G. A. K., MSc Moscow, MTech Brun. Sr. Lectr.
Sarath Chandra, P. D., BSc S.Lanka., MSc Moratuwa Sr. Lectr.; Head*
Wijesundara, A. A. H. P., MSc(Eng) Moscow, PhD Moscow Sr. Lectr.
Wijesundara, W. R. G. A., BSc(Eng) S.Lanka Sr. Lectr.
Other Staff: 3 Lectrs.

Engineering, Philosophy of, see Maths. and Philos. of Engin.

Health Sciences Division
2 Lectrs.

Language Studies
Raheem, R., BA Peradeniya, PhD Leeds Sr. Lectr.; Head*
Ratwatte, H. V. M., BA Peradeniya, MSc Edin., PhD Edin. Sr. Lectr.

Other Staff: 3 Lectrs.

Law

Guneratne, C. E., LLB Colombo, LLM Harv.   Sr. Lectr.; Head*
Rajapaksha, N. G. T., LLB Ceyl., LLM Syd.   Sr. Lectr.
Other Staff: 6 Lectrs.

Management Studies

Gamage, H. R., BSc Colombo, MPA Sri Jay.   Sr. Lectr.; Head*
Rajamantri, S. D., BSc Sri Jay., MCom Colombo   Sr. Lectr.
Sapukotanage, S., BBA Colombo
Senanayake, S. A. D., BSc Kelaniya
Seneviratne, S. J. M. P. U., BBA Colombo
Silva, A. W., BSc Sri Jay., MPA Sri Jay.   Sr. Lectr.
Other Staff: 4 Lectrs.

Mathematics

Arunakirinathar, K., BSc Peradeniya, PhD   Sr. Lectr.
Jayatillake, K. S. E., BA Peradeniya, MSc Iowa State, PhD Texas   Sr. Lectr.
Karunananda, A. S., BSc Colombo, MPhil Open S.Lanka, PhD   Sr. Lectr.; Head*
Perera, W. C. W., BSc Colombo, MSc S.Fraser, PhD S.Fraser   Sr. Lectr.
Sakthivel, S., BSc Reading, MSc Trondheim
Somadasa, H., BA Ceyl., PhD Wales   Sr. Lectr.
Other Staff: 4 Lectrs.
Research: intelligent learning environment for statistics and mathematics; knowledge-based systems; knowledge modelling for expert systems; natural language processing for weather reports and Sinhala grammar

Mathematics and Philosophy of Engineering

de Zoysa, A. P. K., BSc(Eng) S.Lanka, MSc Lond., PhD Colombo   Sr. Lectr.; Head*
Fernando, M. P. W. S., BSc(Eng) S.Lanka   Sr. Lectr.
Jayatilleke, J. A. D. F. M., BSc Colombo
Manohanthan, R., BSc Madr.
Ranasinghe, P. M., BEng
Research: energy/environment; mathematical modelling; philosophy of science

Physics

Abeysinghe, A. A. D. C., BSc Colombo
Fonseka, G. M., BSc Ceyl., MSc Lond., PhD Lond.   Sr. Lectr.
Jayasinghe, E. M., BSc Ceyl., PhD Liv.   Sr. Prof.; Head*
Liyanage, L. S. G., BSc Ceyl., MSc Baylor, PhD Baylor   Sr. Lectr.
Sumathipala, W. L., BSc Ceyl., MSc Hawaii, PhD Hawaii   Sr. Lectr.

Research: atmospheric physics; development of appropriate geophysical method for groundwater exploration in Sri Lanka; electronic structure calculations in transition metal surfaces; magnetic and resistivity methods in location of fractures at Maha Oya thermal spring

Social Studies

Amarasena, G., BA Peradeniya, MA Utah State, MSc Moratuwa, PhD Colorado State   Lectr.; Head*
Kotelawala, D. A., BA Ceyl., PhD Lond.   Asst. Prof.
Mendis, B. M. P., BA Peradeniya, MA Lanc.   Sr. Lectr.
Vidanapathirana, U. B., BA Kelaniya, MSc Asian I.T.,Bangkok   Sr. Lectr.
Wijetunga, L. D. I., BA Peradeniya, MSc Newcastle
Other Staff: 5 Lectrs.

Textile Technology

Delkimburewatta, G. B., MSc T.U.Dresden, MPhil Open S.Lanka   Sr. Lectr.
Disanayake, B. A., BSc Colombo, MPhil Leeds   Sr. Lectr.
Jayananda, G. Y. A. R., MBA Sri Jay., MA Colombo   Sr. Lectr.; Head*
Ovitigala, P., PhD Leeds   Sr. Lectr.
Other Staff: 3 Lectrs.

Zoology

Chandrananda, W. P. N., BSc Peradeniya, PhD Sri Jay.   Sr. Lectr.
Jayasuriya, H. Thusitha R., BSc Colombo, MSc Colombo, PhD Lond.   Sr. Lectr.
Padmalal, U. K. G. K., BSc Colombo, MSc Colombo, PhD   Sr. Lectr.
Ranawake, G. R. R., BSc Colombo, PhD Lond.   Sr. Lectr.
Ratnasiri, N. B., BSc Ceyl., MSc Ill., PhD Ill.   Prof.; Head*
Other Staff: 2 Lectrs.

Other Appointments

In addition, over 500 appointments are made to course teams from among senior university academics and other specialists in public and private sectors, on a part-time basis; visiting staff are also appointed on a similar basis.

CONTACT OFFICERS

Academic affairs. Deputy Registrar: Jayasooriya, S. J., BA Ceyl.
Accommodation. Assistant Registrar, General Administration: Wijesuriya, R. P.
Admissions (higher degree). Deputy Registrar: Jayasooriya, S. J., BA Ceyl.

Adult/continuing education. (Contact the Dean of the appropriate faculty)
Alumni. Secretary, Open University of Sri Lanka Alumni Association: ......
Archives. Registrar: de Silva, N. W. S. W. S., JP, BA Vidyod., MPA Sri Jay.
Computing services. Data Processing Manager: ......
Consultancy services. (Contact the appropriate faculty or the Public Information Office)
Distance education. Director, Educational Technology: Weerasinghe, B., BSc Ceyl., PhD Wales
Estates and buildings/works and services. Assistant Registrar, Capital Works: ......
Examinations. Senior Assistant Registrar: Amarawansa, A. M., BA Kelaniya, MA B&P
Finance. Deputy Bursar: Premaratne, K. M., BA Sri Jay.
General enquiries. Registrar: de Silva, N. W. S. W. S., JP, BA Vidyod., MPA Sri Jay.
Library (chief librarian). Librarian: Korale, S. R., BA Ceyl., FLA
Personnel/human resources. Senior Assistant Registrar, Establishments: Korale, K. V.
Public relations, information and marketing. Director, Public Relations: Bandara, B. W. M. D., MSc Penn., BSc MPhil
Publications. Deputy Director, Operations: Jayasinghe, N., BSc Ceyl.
Purchasing. Senior Assistant Bursar: Ekanayake, P. B.
Quality assurance and accreditation. Deputy Registrar: Jayasooriya, S. J., BA Ceyl.
Research. Director, Educational Technology: Weerasinghe, B., BSc Ceyl., PhD Wales
Safety. Chief Security Officer: ......
Scholarships, awards, loans. Assistant Bursar, Finance: ......
Schools liaison. Director, Regional Educational Services: Gunasekera, T. A. G., MEng Moratuwa, MSc(Eng) PhD
Security. Chief Security Officer: ......
Sport and recreation. Secretary, Welfare Association: ......
Staff development and training. Director, Educational Technology: Weerasinghe, B., BSc Ceyl., PhD Wales
Student welfare/counselling. Chief Student Counsellor: Jayasinghe, Prof. E. M., BSc Ceyl., PhD Liv.
Students from other countries. Director, Public Relations: Bandara, B. W. M. D., MSc Penn., BSc MPhil
University press. Printer: Bananage, D. S. S.

[Information supplied by the institution as at 23 June 1998, and edited by the ACU]

UNIVERSITY OF PERADENIYA, SRI LANKA

Founded 1978; formerly the University of Ceylon, founded 1942 by the incorporation of Ceylon Medical College
(1870) and Ceylon University College (1921); from 1972 the Peradeniya Campus of the University of Sri Lanka

Member of the Association of Commonwealth Universities

Postal Address: Peradeniya, Sri Lanka
Telephone: (08) 388301-5 **Fax**: (08) 388151, 388104 **Cables**: University, Peradeniya

CHANCELLOR—Panabokke, Prof. R. G., MB BS *Ceyl.*, MD *Ceyl.*, PhD *Lond.*,
FRCPath
VICE-CHANCELLOR*—Gunawardana, Prof. R. A. Leslie H., BA *Ceyl.*, PhD
Lond.
REGISTRAR‡—Dissanayake, D. M. W., BA *Ceyl.*
LIBRARIAN—Senadeera, N. T. S. A., BA *Ceyl.*
BURSAR—Kumarage, M. K. S., BCom *Ceyl.*

GENERAL INFORMATION

History. The university was founded in 1942 as University of Ceylon, the result of the merger of Ceylon Medical College and Ceylon University College. It subsequently became Peradeniya Campus of the University of Sri Lanka in 1972 and achieved independent university status in 1978.

Admission to first degree courses (see also Sri Lankan Introduction). Application is through University Grants Commission (UGC) and is based on performance at General Certificate of Education (GCE) A level exam.

First Degrees (see also Sri Lankan Directory of Subjects to Study). BA, BDS, BSc, BScAgric, BScEngin, BVSc, MB BS.
Courses normally last 4 years. BA, BSc: general 3 years; special 4 years. MB BS: 5 years.

Higher Degrees (see also Sri Lankan Directory of Subjects to Study). MA, MSc, MPhil, PhD.
Applicants should hold an appropriate first degree with at least second class honours, or (for arts courses) have passed master's preliminary programme. PhD: master's degree. MA, MSc: 1 year; MPhil: 2 years; PhD: 3 years.

Language of Instruction. Courses in faculty of arts are taught in Sinhala, Tamil and English. Other courses: English.

Libraries. 615,474 volumes.

Fees (1997–98). Undergraduate: Rs325 (medicine, dental and veterinary science); Rs275 (arts, engineering and science). Postgraduate, Sri Lankan students: Rs6000–10,000 (MA, MPhil); Rs15,000–30,000 (PhD). Postgraduate, international students: US$2400 (medical, dental and veterinary science); US$2000 (engineering); US$1800 (agriculture, science); US$1000 (arts). Fees for students from South Asian Association for Regional Cooperation (SAARC) countries are half those for other international students.

Academic Year (1996–97). Three terms.

Income (1998). Total, Rs870,000,000.

Statistics (1997–98). Staff: 2630 (705 academic, 1925 administrative). Students: undergraduate 7890 (4732 men, 3158 women); postgraduate 1850; total 9740.

FACULTIES/SCHOOLS

Agriculture
Dean: Goonasekara, Prof. K. G. A., BScAgric *S.Lanka*, MS *Asian I.T., Bangkok*, PhD *Virginia Polytech.*

Arts
Dean: Dharmadasa, Prof. K. N. O., BA *Ceyl.*, MPhil *York(UK)*, PhD *Monash*

Dental Sciences
Tel: (08) 388045 Fax: (08) 388948
Dean: Ranasinghe, A. W., BDS *Ceyl.*, PhD *Lond.*, MMedSc

Engineering
Tel: (08) 388029, 388322 Fax: (08) 388158
Dean: Ranatunge, Prof. R. J. K. S. K., BSc(Eng) *Ceyl.*, MSc *Birm.*, PhD *Birm.*

Medicine
Tel: (08) 388840 Fax: (08) 232572
Dean: Senanayake, Prof. A. M. A. N. K., MB BS *Ceyl.*, MD *Ceyl.*, FRCPEd

Science
Tel: (08) 388018 Fax: (08) 388018
Dean: Gunewardene, Prof. R. P., BSc *Ceyl.*, PhD *Aberd.*

Veterinary Medicine and Animal Science
Tel: (08) 388205 Fax: (08) 388205
Dean: Kuruwita, Prof. V. Y., BVSc *Ceyl.*, PhD *Massey*

ACADEMIC UNITS
§ = Staff who also teach within the Postgraduate Institute of Agriculture

Agricultural Biology
Ahangama, D., BScAgric *Ceyl.*, MSc *Leip.*, PhD *Texas A.& M.* Sr. Lectr.§
Bandara, D. C., BScAgric *S.Lanka*, MSc *Penn.State*, PhD *Penn.State* Sr. Lectr.§
Bandara, J. M. R. S., BScAgric *Ceyl.*, PhD *Lond.* Prof.§
Herath, H. M. W., MSc *Br.Col.*, PhD *Br.Col.* Prof.§
Perera, A. L. T., BScAgric *Ceyl.*, MSc *Obihiro*, PhD *Birm.* Sr. Lectr.; Head*§
Sumanasinghe, V. A., BScAgric *S.Lanka*, MSc *Penn.State*, PhD *Penn.State* Sr. Lectr.§
Wickramasinghe, I. P., BScAgric *Ceyl.*, MSc *Texas A.& M.*, PhD *Ceyl.* Sr. Lectr.§
Wijayagunasekera, H. N. P., BScAgric *Ceyl.*, MSc *Newcastle(UK)* Sr. Lectr.§

Agricultural Economics
Abeygunawardena, P., BScAgric *Ceyl.*, MSc *Texas A.& M.*, PhD *Texas A.& M.*
Bogahawatta, C., BScAgric *Ceyl.*, MSc *Philippines*, PhD *Texas A.& M.* Prof.§
Gunathilaka, H. M., BScAgric *Ceyl.* Sr. Lectr.
Jogaratnam, T., BA *Ceyl.*, MSc *Tor.*, PhD *Cornell* Prof.§
Kotagama, H. B., BScAgric *S.Lanka*, MSc *Philippines*, PhD *Lond.* Sr. Lectr.; Head*§
Thiruchelvam, S., BScAgric *Ceyl.*, MSc *Obihiro*, PhD *S.Lanka* Sr. Lectr.

Agricultural Engineering
Alahakoon, A. M. P. K., BScEngin *S.Lanka*, MS *Virginia Polytech.*, PhD *Missouri* Sr. Lectr.§
Ariyaratne, A. R., BScAgric *S.Lanka*, MSc *Texas A.& M.*, PhD *Texas A.& M.* Sr. Lectr.§
Basnayake, B. F. A., BSc *Cran.IT*, DrEng *Paris* Sr. Lectr.; Head*§
Goonasekara, K. G. A., BScAgric *S.Lanka*, MS *Asian I.T., Bangkok*, PhD *Virginia Polytech.* Prof.§
Gunawardena, E. R. N., BScAgric *S.Lanka*, MSc *Cran.IT*, PhD *Cran.I.T.* Sr. Lectr.§
Jayatissa, D. N., BScAgric *S.Lanka*, MS *Virginia Polytech.*, PhD *Virginia Polytech.* Sr. Lectr.§
Rambanda, M., BScAgric *S.Lanka*, MSc *Obihiro* Sr. Lectr.

Agricultural Extension
Jayatilake, M. W. A. P., BScAgric *Ceyl.*, MSc *Texas A.& M.* ,PhD *Penn.State* Sr. Lectr.§
Sivayoganathan, C., BScAgric *Ceyl.*, MSc *Qld.*, PhD *Texas A.& M.* Sr. Lectr.; Head*§
Wanigasundara, W. A. D. P., BScAgric *S.Lanka*, PhD *Reading* Sr. Lectr.§
Wickramasuriya, H. V. A., BScAgric *Ceyl.*, MSc *Penn.State*, PhD *Penn.State* Sr. Lectr.§

Agriculture, see Special Centres, etc

Anatomy, see Medicine

Animal Science
Cyril, H. W., BScAgric *Ceyl.*, MSc *Nott.*, PhD *Nott.* Sr. Lectr.; Head*§
Edirisinghe, U. G. de A., MSc *Ceyl.*, PhD *Ceyl.* Sr. Lectr.§
Ibrahim, M. N. M., BScAgric *Ceyl.*, PhD *Melb.* Sr. Lectr.
Jayawardena, V. P., BScAgric *Ceyl.*, MPhil *S.Lanka* Sr. Lectr. (on leave)§
Perera, A. N. F., BScAgric *Ceyl.*, MSc *Virginia Polytech.*, PhD *Virginia Polytech.* Sr. Lectr.§
Perera, E. R. K., BScAgric *Ceyl.*, MSc *Virginia Polytech.*, PhD *Virginia Polytech.* Sr. Lectr.§
Premaratne, S., BScAgric *Ceyl.*, MSc *Virginia Polytech.* PhD *Virginia Polytech.* Sr. Lectr.§
Rajaguru, R. W. A. S. B., BSc(Agr) *Alld.*, MSc *Calif.* Prof.§
Samarasinghe, K., BScAgric *Ceyl.*, MSc *Ceyl.* Sr. Lectr.
Silva, G. L. L. P., BScAgric *S.Lanka*, PhD *Syd.* Sr. Lectr.
Silva, K. F. S. T., BVSc *Ceyl.*, MSc *Arizona*, PhD *Calif.* Sr. Lectr.§

Arabic and Islamic Culture
Ameen, M. I. M., BA *Ceyl.*, MA *Ceyl.* Sr. Lectr.; Head*
Asad, M. N. M. K., BA *Saudi Arabian Inst.*, MLitt *Edin.*, PhD *Edin.* Sr. Lectr.
Casim, A., BA *Libya*, MA *IIU Malaysia* Sr. Lectr.

Archaeology
Gunasekera, D. K., BA *Ceyl.*, MA *Ceyl.*, PhD *Salonika* Sr. Lectr.
Mahinda, Rev. W., BA *Ceyl.*, MA *Ceyl.* Sr. Lectr.; Head*

Seneviratne, S. D. S., BA Delhi, MA J.Nehru U., MPhil J.Nehru U., PhD J.Nehru U. Sr. Lectr.
Tampoe, M. R., BA Ceyl., DPhil Oxf. Sr. Lectr.

Biochemistry, see Medicine

Botany

Tel: (08) 388693 Fax: (08) 388018
Abeygunasekera, Rohini, BSc Ceyl., PhD Lond. Assoc. Prof.
Adikaram, N. K. B., BSc Ceyl., PhD Belf. Assoc. Prof.
Cooray, H. M. V., BSc S.Lanka, PhD Camb. Sr. Lectr.
Dharmasiri, S., BSc S.Lanka, PhD Hawaii Sr. Lectr.
Gunatilleke, C. V. S., BSc Ceyl., PhD Aberd. Assoc. Prof.
Gunatilleke, I. A. U. N., BSc Ceyl., PhD Camb. Assoc. Prof.
Karunaratne, A. M., BSc Ceyl., MSc Nebraska Sr. Lectr.
Kulasooriya, S. A., BSc Ceyl., PhD Lond. Prof.

Buddhist Studies, see Pali and Buddhist Studies

Chemistry

Ariyaratne, K. A. N. S., BSc S.Lanka, PhD Hawaii Sr. Lectr., Inorganic Chemistry
Bandara, B. M. R., BSc Ceyl., PhD ANU Prof., Organic Chemistry
Bandara, H. M. N., BSc Ceyl., MSc Aston, PhD Aston Assoc. Prof., Inorganic Chemistry
Dias, H. W., BSc Ceyl., PhD Leeds Sr. Lectr.
Gunewardene, R. P., BSc Ceyl., PhD Aberd. Sr. Prof., Inorganic Chemistry
Illeperuma, O. A., BSc Ceyl., PhD Arizona Prof., Inorganic Chemistry
Karunaratna, N. L. V. V., BSc S.Lanka, PhD Br.Col. Sr. Lectr., Organic Chemistry
Kumar, Nimal S., BSc Ceyl., PhD Lond. Prof., Organic Chemistry
Kumar, V., BSc Ceyl., DPhil Oxf. Prof., Organic Chemistry
Perera, A. D. L. Chandanie, BSc Ceyl., PhD Tokyo I.T. Sr. Lectr., Physical Chemistry
Perera, J. S. H. Q., BSc Ceyl., PhD Br.Col. Assoc. Prof., Physical Chemistry
Priyantha, H. M. D. N., BSc S.Lanka, PhD Hawaii Sr. Lectr., Physical/Analytic Chemistry
Rajapakse, R. M. G., BSc S.Lanka, PhD Lond. Sr. Lectr., Physical Chemistry
Ranatunga, R. P. J., BSc S.Lanka, PhD Houston Sr. Lectr., Analytic Chemistry
Tennekoon, D. T. B., BSc Ceyl., PhD Wales Prof., Physical Chemistry; Head*
Wannigama, G. P., BSc Ceyl., PhD Camb. Sr. Prof., Organic Chemistry
Wickramasinghe, A., BSc S.Lanka, MPhil Ceyl., PhD Mün. Sr. Lectr., Organic Chemistry

Classical Languages

Arulchelvam, M. M., BA Ceyl., DPhil Oxf. Assoc. Prof.
Handurukande, M. R. M., BA Ceyl., MA Ceyl., MA Camb., PhD Prof.
Pemaratana, Rev. W., BA Ceyl., PhD Ceyl. Sr. Lectr.
Weerakkody, D. P. M., BA Ceyl., PhD Hull Assoc. Prof.; Head*

Commerce, see Econ., Comm. and Stats.

Computer Sciences

No staff at present.

Computer Unit

No staff at present.

Crop Science

De Costa, W. A. J. M., BScAgric S.Lanka, MSc Reading, PhD Reading Sr. Lectr.
Eeswara, J. P., BScAgric S.Lanka Sr. Lectr.
Gunasena, H. P. M., BScAgric Ceyl., PhD Reading Prof.
Jayaweera, C. S., MSc Lincoln(NZ), BScAgric Sr. Lectr.

Malkanthie Menike, D. R. R., BScAgric S.Lanka, MSc Ghent, PhD Kanagawa Sr. Lectr.
Marambe, P. W. M. B. B., BScAgric S.Lanka, MAgr Hiroshima, PhD Hiroshima Sr. Lectr.
Nissanka, N. A. A. S. P., BScAgric S.Lanka, PhD Guelph Sr. Lectr.
Peiris, S., BScAgric Ceyl., MSc Penn., PhD Lond. Sr. Lectr.
Peris, B. C. N., BScAgric Ceyl., MSc Penn.State, PhD Penn.State Sr. Lectr.; Head*
Premaratne, K. P., BScAgric Ceyl., MSc Leip., PhD Berlin Sr. Lectr.
Ranamukarchchi, S. L., BScAgric Ceyl., MSc Penn.State, PhD Penn.State Sr. Lectr.
Sangakkara, U. R., BScAgric Ceyl., PhD Massey Prof.
Senanayake, Y. D. A., BScAgric Ceyl., MSc Louisiana State, PhD Calif. Prof.
Thatill, R. O., BScAgric Ceyl., MSc Philippines, PhD Virginia Polytech. Assoc. Prof.
Wadasinghe, G., BScAgric Ceyl., MSc Lond., PhD S.Lanka Sr. Lectr.

Dental Surgery, see below

Economics, Commerce and Statistics

Abayasekara, C. R., BA S.Lanka, MA Boston, PhD Boston Sr. Lectr.
Abhayaratne, A. S. P., BA Ceyl. Sr. Lectr.
Alfred, M., BCom Ceyl., MPhil Ceyl. Sr. Lectr.
Hewavitharana, B., BA Ceyl., PhD Lond. Prof. (on leave)
Jayanthakumaran, K., BA S.Lanka, MPhil S.Lanka, PhD Brad. Sr. Lectr.
Liyanage, S. G., BA Ceyl., MPhil Colombo Sr. Lectr.
Nandasena, K. M., BCom Ceyl., MBA Yokohama N. Sr. Lectr.
Nigel, J., BA Ceyl., MPhil Ceyl. Sr. Lectr.
Ranasinghe, M., BCom Ceyl., MSc Ceyl., MDE Dal. Sr. Lectr.
Randeniya, P., BA Ceyl., MA Osaka, PhD Osaka Sr. Lectr.
Samarawickrama, N. D., BCom Ceyl., MSc Sur., MA Boston Sr. Lectr.
Sinnathamby, M., BA Ceyl., MA Manc. Assoc. Prof.; Head*
Siripala, D., BA S.Lanka, MSc Thammasat Sr. Lectr.
Tilakaratne, W. M., BA Ceyl., MA Kent, DPhil Sus. Sr. Lectr.

Education

Jayasena, P. H. A. N. S., BA Ceyl., MAEd Ceyl., MA Col., PhD Monash Sr. Lectr.
Liyanage, R. P., BA Ceyl., MA S.Lanka Assoc. Prof.; Head*
Perera, S. J., BSc Ceyl., MEd Brist. Assoc. Prof.
Senadeera, S., MA Ceyl., PhD Ceyl. Sr. Lectr.

Engineering, Agricultural, see Agric. Engin.

Engineering, Chemical

Fernando, W. J. N., BScEngin Ceyl., PhD Lond., FIChemE Prof.; Head*
Shanthini, R., BScEngin S.Lanka, MSc Alta., PhD Luleå Sr. Lectr.

Engineering, Civil

Abayakoon, S. B. S., BSc(Eng) S.Lanka, MASc Br.Col., PhD Br.Col. Sr. Lectr.
Abeyruwan, H., BScEngin Ceyl., MPhil HK Sr. Lectr.
Amirthanathan, G. E., BScEngin Ceyl., MEng Asian I.T., Bangkok, DEng Montpellier II Sr. Lectr.
Dissanayake, U. I., BSc(Eng) Peradeniya, PhD Sheff. Sr. Lectr.
Edirisinghe, A. G. H. J., BSc(Eng) Peradeniya, MEng Ehime, PhD Ehime Sr. Lectr.
Fernando, S. V. M., BSc(Eng) S.Lanka, MEng Asian I.T., Bangkok, PhD Miami Sr. Lectr.
Gusrusinghe, G. S., BSc CNAA, MSc Newcastle Sr. Lectr. (on leave)
Herath, K. R. B., BSc(Eng) S.Lanka, MSc Ill., PhD Calif. Sr. Lectr.
Jayawardana, U. de S., BSc Ceyl., MSc Asian I.T., Bangkok Sr. Lectr.

Keerthisena, H. H. J., BSc(Eng) Ceyl., PhD Ceyl. Sr. Lectr.
Mauroof, A. L. M., BSc(Eng) Peradeniya, MEng Asian I.T., Bangkok, PhD Tokyo Sr. Lectr.
Nandalal, K. D. W., BSc(Eng) Peradeniya, MEng Asian I.T., Bangkok, PhD Wageningen Sr. Lectr.
Ranaweera, M. P., BSc(Eng) Ceyl., PhD Camb. Prof.
Ratnayake, U. R., BSc(Eng) Peradeniya, MEng Asian I.T., Bangkok, DEng Asian I.T., Bangkok Sr. Lectr.
Sathyaprasad, I. M. S., BSc S.Lanka, MEng Asian I.T., Bangkok, DEng Yokohama
Seneviratne, K. G. H. C. N., BSc(Eng) Ceyl., PhD Camb. Prof.; Head*
Somaratna, A. P. N., BSc(Eng) Ceyl., MS Ill., PhD Ill. Sr. Lectr.
Wedage, A. M. P., BSc(Eng) S.Lanka, MEng Asian I.T., Bangkok, PhD Alta. Sr. Lectr.
Weerakoon, W. M. S. B., BSc(Eng) S.Lanka, MEng Tokyo Sr. Lectr.

Engineering, Electrical and Electronic

Ekanayake, E. M. N., MSc Lond., PhD McM., BScEngin Prof. (on leave)
Ekanayake, J. B., PhD Manc., BScEngin Sr. Lectr.
Gunawardena, J. A., BScEngin Ceyl., PhD Camb., MSEE Purdue, FIEE Prof.
Liyanage, K. M., PhD Tokyo, BScEngin Sr. Lectr.
Muthukumarasamy, V., PhD Cant., BScEngin Sr. Lectr.; Head*
Ratnayake, K. B. N., MS Rensselaer, PhD Rensselaer, BScEngin Sr. Lectr.

Engineering Mathematics

Perera, K., BSc Sri Jay., MA N.Y., PhD N.Y. Sr. Lectr.
Samuel, T. D. M. A., BSc Ceyl., MSc Manc., PhD Manc., FIMA Prof.
Siyambalapitiya, S. B., BSc Ceyl., MSc Newcastle(NSW), PhD Newcastle(NSW) Sr. Lectr.; Head*
Walgama, K. S., BScEng Moratuwa, MSc Alta., MEng Philips'(Eindhoven), PhD Luleå Sr. Lectr.

Engineering, Mechanical

Herath, Sobha, PhD Calif., BScEngin MCE Sr. Lectr.
Jayatilake, C. L. V., BScEngin Ceyl., PhD Lond. Prof.
Kahawatta, M. B., DrIng Frib., BSc Sr. Lectr.
Obeysekera, B. R. K., PhD Moscow, MSc(MechEng) Sr. Lectr.
Senevirathe, S. K., BScEngin Ceyl., MSc Leeds Sr. Lectr.
Sumanasiri, K. E. D., PhD Leuven, BScEngin MEng Sr. Lectr.; Head*

Engineering, Production

Devapriya, D. S., BSc(Eng) Ceyl., MEng Asian I.T., Bangkok, PhD Grenoble Sr. Lectr.
Pathirana, S. D., BScEngin Ceyl., MSc Ghent, DEng Tokyo Sr. Lectr.; Head*
Ranatunge, R. J. K. S. K., BSc(Eng) Ceyl., MSc Birm., PhD Birm. Prof.

English, see also Special Centres, etc

de Silva, L., BA Ceyl., MA N.Y.State, PhD N.Texas Sr. Lectr.
Fernando, L. N. A., BA Ceyl., MA Hawaii, PhD Flin. Sr. Lectr.
Halpe, K. A. C. G., BA Ceyl., PhD Brist. Prof.
Perera, S. W., BA Ceyl., MA New Br., PhD New Br. Sr. Lectr.; Head*
Wickramagamage, C. S., BA Ceyl., PhD Hawaii Sr. Lectr.
Wickramasuriya, B. S. S. A., BA Ceyl., MA Lond., PhD Lond., PhD Ceyl. Assoc. Prof.

Food Science and Technology

Illeperuma, D. C. K., BScAgric S.Lanka, MSc S.Lanka, PhD Maryland Sr. Lectr.; Head*
Samarajeewa, U., BSc Ceyl., PhD Ceyl. Prof.
Wijesinghe, D. G. N. G., BScAgric Ceyl., MSc Philippines, PhD Lond. Sr. Lectr.

Geography

Fernando, W. G., BA Ceyl., MA Ceyl., MSc Asian I.T., Bangkok Sr. Lectr.
Gunadasa, J. M., MA Ceyl., DPhil Sus. Assoc. Prof.
Gunawardena, R. S., BA Ceyl., PhD Lond. Assoc. Prof.
Hasbullah, S. H., MA Ceyl., MA Br.Col., PhD Br.Col. Sr. Lectr.
Hennayake, H. A. N. M., PhD Syr. Sr. Lectr.
Hennayake, H. M. S. K., MA Ceyl., PhD Syr. Sr. Lectr.
Indrasena, T. Mendis, MA Ceyl. Sr. Lectr.
Madduma Bandara, Chandrasekera M., BA Ceyl., PhD Camb. Prof.
Mookiah, M. S., MA Ceyl., MSc Wales Sr. Lectr.
Nandakumar, V., MA Ceyl., MSc Tsukuba Sr. Lectr.
Nawfhal, A. S. M., MA Ceyl., MA Tsukuba Sr. Lectr.
Nelson, M. D., BA Ceyl., MSc Asian I.T., Bangkok Sr. Lectr.; Head*
Peiris, G. H., BA Ceyl., PhD Camb. Prof.
Shakoor, W. K. I. M. M., BA Ceyl., MA Ceyl. Sr. Lectr.
Velmurugu, N., MA Ceyl., PhD Ceyl. Sr. Lectr.
Wickramaratna, S. N., BA Ceyl., MA Oregon Sr. Lectr.
Wickrmasinghe, A., BA Ceyl., MSc Sheff., PhD Sheff. Assoc. Prof.
Wickremagamage, P., BA Ceyl., MSc Lond., PhD Lond. Sr. Lectr.

Geology

Dahanayake, K. G. A., BSc Ceyl., Dr3rdCy Nancy Sr. Prof.
Dissanayake, C. B., BSc Ceyl., DPhil Oxf., DSc Oxf. Sr. Prof.
Jayasena, H. A. H., BSc Ceyl., MSc Colorado State Sr. Lectr.
Mathavan, V., BSc Ceyl., PhD Belf. Sr. Lectr.; Head*
Nawaratne, S. W., BSc Ceyl., MSc Laur., PhD Vienna Sr. Lectr.
Perera, L. R. K., MSc Ceyl. Sr. Lectr. (on leave)
Senaratne, A., BSc Ceyl., MSc Lond., PhD Mainz Sr. Lectr.

History

Gajameragedera, B., BA Ceyl., MSc Lond., DPhil Sus. Assoc. Prof.
Gunawardana, R. A. L. H., BA Ceyl., PhD Lond. Prof.
Jayasekera, P. V. J., BA Ceyl., MA Manit., PhD Lond. Assoc. Prof.
Kanapathipillai, V., BA Ceyl., PhD Lond. Sr. Lectr.
Karunatilake, P. V. B., BA Ceyl., PhD Lond. Assoc. Prof.; Head*
Keerawella, G. B., BA Ceyl., MA Windsor, PhD Br.Col. Assoc. Prof.
Kiribamune, S., MA Ceyl., PhD Lond. Prof.
Meththananda, T. P., BA Ceyl., DPhil Oxf. Assoc. Prof.
Pathmanathan, S., BA Ceyl., PhD Lond. Prof.
Siriweera, W. I., BA Ceyl., PhD Lond. Prof.

Islamic Culture, see Arabic and Islamic Culture

Mathematics, see also Engin. Maths.

Dharmadasa, J. P. D., BSc Ceyl., MPhil Lond. Sr. Lectr.
Dissanayake, U. N. B., BSc Ceyl., MSc Alta., PhD Alta. Sr. Lectr.
Perera, A. A. I., BSc S.Lanka, MSc Oslo Sr. Lectr.
Perera, A. A. S., BSc S.Lanka, PhD Albany Sr. Lectr.
Seneviratne, C. M. J., PhD Duisburg Sr. Lectr.
Seneviratne, H. H. G., BSc Ceyl., PhD Lond. Prof.; Head*
Thewarapperuma, P. S. S., BSc Ceyl., MSc Tor., PhD Mich.State Sr. Lectr.
Wijekoon, S. N. M. W. W. M. T. P., BSc S.Lanka, PhD Dortmund Sr. Lectr.

Medicine, see below

Pali and Buddhist Studies

Warnasuriya, K. S., BA S.Lanka, PhD Lond. Sr. Lectr.
Withanachchi, C., BA S.Lanka, BA Camb. Sr. Lectr.; Head*

Philosophy and Psychology

Anes, M. S. M., MA Ceyl. Sr. Lectr.
Dharmasiri, G., BA Ceyl., PhD Lanc. Assoc. Prof.
Gnanissara, Rev. A., MA Ceyl. Sr. Lectr.
Gunaratna, R. D., BA Ceyl., MA Calif., PhD Camb. Assoc. Prof.
Kalansuriya, A. D. P., BA Ceyl., MPhil Reading, PhD Ceyl. Assoc. Prof.; Head*
Mallikarachchi, D. D., MA Ceyl. Sr. Lectr. (on leave)
Nanayakkara, G. D. K., BA Ceyl., PhD Ceyl. Sr. Lectr.
Premasiri, P. D., BA Ceyl., BA Camb., PhD Hawaii Assoc. Prof.
Rajaratnam, M., BA Ceyl., MA Mys. Sr. Lectr.

Physics

Amarasinghe, N. D., BSc S.Lanka, PhD Kent State Sr. Lectr.
Bandaranayake, P. W. S. K., BSc S.Lanka, PhD Lond. Prof.
Careem, M. A., BSc Ceyl., PhD Lond. Prof.; Head*
Disanayake, M. A. K. L., BSc Ceyl., MS Indiana, PhD Indiana Prof.
Hettiarachchi, N. F., BSc Ceyl., PhD Hull Sr. Lectr.
Karunaratne, B. S. B., BSc Ceyl., PhD Warw. Assoc. Prof.
Leelananda, S. A., BSc Ceyl., MSc Lond., PhD Calg. Sr. Lectr. (on leave)
Premaratne, K., BSc Ceyl., MS Hawaii, PhD Hawaii Sr. Lectr.
Wijewardena, R. L., BSc Ceyl., MSc Albany, PhD Albany Sr. Lectr.

Political Science

Amarasinghe, Y. R., BA Ceyl., BPhil York(UK), PhD Lond. Assoc. Prof.
Cader, M. L. A., BA Ceyl., MA ANU Sr. Lectr. (on leave)
Liyanage, K., MA Ceyl., PhD Keio Sr. Lectr.
Navaratne Bandara, A. M., MA Ceyl., DPhil York(UK) Sr. Lectr.
Samaranayake, S. V. D. G., MA Ceyl., PhD St And. Sr. Lectr.
Sivarajah, A., BA Ceyl., MA New Br., PhD Ceyl. Assoc. Prof.
Zoysa, de M. O. A., BA Ceyl., MA Tas. Sr. Lectr.; Head*

Psychology, see Philos. and Psychol.

Sinhalese

Attanayake, H. M., MA Ceyl. Sr. Lectr.
Dhammaloka, Rev. W., MA Ceyl. Sr. Lectr.
Dharmadasa, K. N. O., BA Ceyl., MPhil York(UK), PhD Monash Sr. Prof.
Fernando, G. M. D., BA Ceyl., PhD Humboldt Sr. Lectr.
Gunatilaka, W. M., BA Ceyl., MA Jad. Assoc. Prof.
Meddegama, U. P., BA Ceyl., PhD Lond. Assoc. Prof.
Meegaskumbura, P. B., MA Ceyl., PhD Poona Prof.
Rajakaruna, M. A. D. A., BA Ceyl., MA Waseda, PhD Ceyl. Prof.
Seneviratne, C. A. D. A., BA Ceyl., PhD Halle Prof.; Head*
Soratha, Rev. P., MA Ceyl. Sr. Lectr.
Wijemanne, S. H. M. P., MA Ceyl., PhD Lond. Sr. Lectr.
Wijesriwardena, K. V. A., BA Ceyl. Sr. Lectr.

Sociology

Amarasekera, D. P. D., MA S.Lanka, PhD Calc. Sr. Lectr.
Bandaranayake, P. D., MA Ceyl. Sr. Lectr.

De Silva, M. W. A., BA Ceyl., MSc Asian I.T., Bangkok, PhD Conn. Sr. Lectr.
Herath, H. M. D. R., BA Ceyl., MA Delhi Sr. Lectr.
Pinnawala, S. K., BA Ceyl., MSc Asian I.T., Bangkok, PhD ANU Sr. Lectr.; Head*
Rajakaruna, R. M. H. B., BA Vidyod., MA Ceyl. Sr. Lectr.
Sirisena, W. M., BA Ceyl., MA Calg., PhD ANU Assoc. Prof. (on leave)
Tudor Silva, K., BA Ceyl., PhD Monash Assoc. Prof.

Soil Science

Jayakody, A. N., BSc Leip., MSc Leip., PhD T.U.Berlin Sr. Lectr.
Kumaragamage, D., BScAgric S.Lanka, MPhil S.Lanka, PhD Manit. Sr. Lectr.
Mapa, R. B., BScAgric Ceyl., PhD Hawaii Assoc. Prof.
Nandasena, K. A., BScAgric S.Lanka, MSc S.Lanka, PhD Leuven Sr. Lectr.; Head*
Thenabadu, M. W., BScAgric Ceyl., MS Texas A.& M., PhD Calif. Prof.

Statistics, see Econ., Comm. and Stats.

Tamil

Arunasalam, K., MA Ceyl., PhD Ceyl. Sr. Lectr.; Head*
Kanageratnam, V., MA Ceyl. Sr. Lectr.
Manoharan, T., MA Ceyl. Sr. Lectr.
Nuhuman, M. A. M., BPhil Ceyl., MA Ceyl., PhD Annam., BA Sr. Lectr.
Poologasingha, P., BA Ceyl., DPhil Oxf. Assoc. Prof.
Thilainathan, S., MA Ceyl., MLitt Madr. Prof.

Veterinary Medicine and Animal Science, see below

Zoology

Amarasinghe, F. P., BSc Ceyl., PhD Brist. Assoc. Prof.
Amarasinghe, P. H., BSc S.Lanka, PhD S.Lanka Sr. Lectr.
Breckenridge, W. R., BSc Ceyl., PhD McG. Prof.
De Silva, D. N., BSc Ceyl., MSc Rutgers Sr. Lectr.
de Silva, K. H. G. M., BSc Ceyl., PhD Edin. Prof.
de Silva, P. K., BSc Ceyl., PhD Lanc. Assoc. Prof.
Edirisinghe, J. P., BSc Ceyl., PhD Adel. Sr. Lectr.
Karunaratne, S. H. P. P., BSc S.Lanka, MSc S.Lanka, PhD Lond. Sr. Lectr.
Ranawana, K. B., BSc S.Lanka, MSc N.Y.State, MPhil S.Lanka Sr. Lectr.
Santiapillai, C. V. M., BSc Ceyl., PhD Aberd. Sr. Lectr.
Wijekoon, S., BSc Ceyl., PhD Lond. Sr. Lectr.; Head*

DENTAL SURGERY

Basic Sciences

Fax: (08) 388948

Pitigala Arachchi, A. J., BDS S.Lanka, PhD Brist. Sr. Lectr.; Head*
Wimalasiri, W. R., BSc S.Lanka, PhD S.Lanka Sr. Lectr.

Community Dental Health

Ekanayake, A. N. I., BDS Ceyl., PhD Lond. Prof.; Head*
Ekanayake, S. L., BDS Ceyl., PhD Lond. Sr. Lectr.
Nagaratne, S. P. N. P., BDS Ceyl., MS Sr. Lectr.
Wanigasooriya, N. C., BDS Ceyl. Sr. Lectr.
Wijeyeweera, R. L., BDS Ceyl., PhD N.Y. Sr. Lectr.

Oral Biology Unit

Wimalasiri, W. R., BSc Ceyl., PhD Ceyl. Sr. Lectr.

Oral Medicine and Periodontology

Chandrasekera, A., BDS Ceyl., MPhil
  Peradeniya Sr. Lectr., Periodontology; Head*
Corea, S. M. X., MB BS Ceyl., MD Sr. Lectr.,
  Pharmacology
Rajapakse, P. S., BDS Ceyl., MPhil Peradeniya Sr.
  Lectr., Periodontology
Ranasinghe, A. W., BDS Ceyl., PhD Lond.,
  MMedSc Sr. Lectr.
Sitheeque, M. A. M., BDS Ceyl.,
  FDSRCPSGlas Sr. Lectr.

Oral Pathology

Amaratunga, E. A. P. D., BDS S.Lanka, MSc
  Lond., MS(DentSurg), FDSRCS, FFDRCSI Sr.
  Lectr.
Mendis, B. R. R. N., BDS Ceyl., PhD Brist.,
  FDSRCS, FDSRCSEd, FFDRCSI Prof.; Head*

Oral Surgery

Amaratunge, N. A. de S., BDS Ceyl., PhD Ceyl.,
  FDSRCSEd Prof.; Head*
Weerasinghe, J. U., BDS Ceyl., MS Colombo Sr.
  Lectr.

Prosthetics

Anandamoorthy, T., BDS Ceyl.,
  FDSRCPSGlas Sr. Lectr.

Restorative Dentistry

Wettasinghe, K. A., BDS S.Lanka, MS Col.,
  FDSRCS, FDSRCSEd Sr. Lectr.; Head*

MEDICINE

Anaesthesiology

Tel: (08) 388315 Fax: (08) 232572
Gunawardena, R. H., MB BS Ceyl.,
  FFARCS Assoc. Prof.; Head*

Anatomy

Tel: (08) 388315 Fax: (08) 232572
Amarasinghe, D. M., MB BS Ceyl., MChOrth
  Liv., FRCS Sr. Lectr.
Chandrasekara, M. S., BDS Ceyl., PhD
  Newcastle(UK) Assoc. Prof.; Head*
Nanayakkara, C. D., BDS Ceyl., PhD S.Lanka Sr.
  Lectr.
Sabanayagam, M., BDS Ceyl., PhD Belf. Sr.
  Lectr.
Wikramanayake, Eugene R., MB BS Ceyl., PhD
  Glas. Prof.

Biochemistry

Amarasinghe, A. B. C., PhD Buffalo, BSc
  MS Sr. Lectr.
Atauda, S. B. P., PhD Tokyo, BSc Sr. Lectr.
Fernando, P. H. P., BVSc Ceyl., PhD
  Kagoshima Sr. Lectr.
Gunasekera, S. W., BSc Ceyl., PhD Lond. Sr.
  Lectr.
Perera, P. A. J., BSc Ceyl., PhD Glas. Prof.;
  Head*

Community Medicine

Jayasinghe, A., MB BS Ceyl., Sr. Lectr.
Jayawardena, P. L., MB BS Ceyl., MSc MD Sr.
  Lectr.
Kumarasiri, P. V. R., MB BS Ceyl., MSc
  MD Sr. Lectr.
Nugegoda, D. B., MB BS Ceyl., MSc
  Lond. Assoc. Prof.; Head*

Forensic Medicine

Babapulle, C. J., MB BS Ceyl., PhD Col., PhD
  Peradeniya, MMedSc Prof.; Head*
Ratnayake, R. M. R. S., MB BS Ceyl., PhD
  Sheff. Sr. Lectr.

Medical Education Unit

Tel: (08) 388949 Fax: (08) 232572, 388949
Kasturiaratchi, N. D., MB BS Ceyl., PhD
  Prin. Sr. Lectr.; Dir.*

Medicine

Illangasekera, V. L. U., MB BS Ceyl., MD Ceyl.,
  FRCPEd Sr. Lectr.
Jayasinghe, M. W. C. J., MB BS S.Lanka,
  MD Sr. Lectr.

Mendis, P. B. S., MB BS Ceyl., DM,
  FRCPEd Assoc. Prof.; Head*
Senanayake, A. M. A. N. K., MB BS Ceyl., MD
  Ceyl., FRCPEd Prof.
Shanmuganathan, P. S., MB BS S.Lanka, MD
  S.Lanka Sr. Lectr.

Microbiology

Thevanesan, V., MB BS Ceyl., DM Ceyl. Sr.
  Lectr.; Head*

Nuclear Medicine Unit

Udugama, J. M. C., MB BS S.Lanka Lectr.;
  Head*

Obstetrics and Gynaecology

Amarasinghe, W. I., MB BS Ceyl.,
  FRCOG Assoc. Prof.; Head*
Gunaratne, M., MB BS Ceyl., MS,
  FRCOG Prof.
Jayawardena, J., MA Ceyl., MS Sr. Lectr.
Perera, U. W. H. C. H., MB BS Ceyl. Sr. Lectr.
Samarakoon, E. W., MB BS Ceyl., MS Sr.
  Lectr.

Paediatrics

Abeysekara, C. K., MB BS Ceyl. Sr. Lectr.
Jayasena, Lali, MB BS Ceyl. Sr. Lectr.; Head*
Wijekoon, A. S. B., MB BS Ceyl., MD Sr.
  Lectr.

Parasitology

Edirisinghe, J. S., MB BS Ceyl., MSc Lond., MD
  Col., PhD Lond. Assoc. Prof.
Weilgama, D. J., BVSc Ceyl., MVSc Ceyl., PhD
  Qld. Sr. Lectr.
Wijesundera, M. K. de S., MB BS Ceyl., MSc
  Lond., MD Col., PhD S.Lanka Prof.; Head*

Pathology

Ellepola, S. B., MB BS Ceyl., MD Ceyl. Prof.
Gunawardana, R. T. A. W., MB BS S.Lanka, PhD
  S.Lanka
Rathnayaka, R. M. R. S., MB BS S.Lanka, PhD
  Sheff.
Ratnatunge, N. V. I., MB BS Ceyl., MD Ceyl.,
  PhD Ceyl. Sr. Lectr.; Head*

Pharmacology

Aturaliya, T. N. C., MB BS S.Lanka Sr. Lectr.;
  Head*

Physiology

Balasuriya, P., MB BS Ceyl. Sr. Lectr.; Head*
Rajaratne, A. A. J., BVSc S.Lanka, MPhil S.Lanka,
  PhD Lond. Sr. Lectr.
Udupihille, M., MB BS Ceyl., MPhil Lond.,
  PhD Prof.

Psychiatry

Abeysinghe, D. R. R., MB BS Ceyl., MD
  S.Lanka Sr. Lectr.; Head*
Ratnayake, Priyani U., MB BS Ceyl., MD
  S.Lanka Sr. Lectr.
Rodrigo, E. K., MB BS Ceyl., MD S.Lanka Sr.
  Lectr.

Surgery

Aluwihare, A. P. R., MA Camb., MB BChir
  Camb., MChir Camb., FRCS Prof.; Head*
Amarasinghe, P., MB BS Ceyl., MD Sr. Lectr.
Buthpitiya, A. G., MB BS Ceyl., MS S.Lanka Sr.
  Lectr.
Lamawansa, M. D., MB BS S.Lanka, MS
  S.Lanka Sr. Lectr.
Ratnatunge, P. C. A., MB BS Ceyl.,
  FRCS Assoc. Prof.

VETERINARY MEDICINE AND ANIMAL SCIENCE

Veterinary Clinical Studies

Abeygunawardena, H., BVSc S.Lanka, PhD
  Ill. Sr. Lectr.
De Silva, D. D. N., PhD Camb., BVSc Sr. Lectr.
De Silva, L. N. A., BVSc Ceyl., MPhil Ceyl. Sr.
  Lectr.
Kuruwita, V. Y., BVSc Ceyl., PhD Massey Prof.
Silva, I. D., PhD Calif., BVSc Assoc. Prof.;
  Head*

Veterinary Para-Clinical Studies

Abeynayake, P., BVSc Ceyl., PhD Massey Sr.
  Lectr.
Horadagoda, N. U., BVSc S.Lanka, MVSc
  S.Lanka, PhD Liv. Sr. Lectr.
Mahalingam, S., BVSc Ceyl., MA Tor., PhD
  Edin. Sr. Lectr.; Head*
Rajapakse, R. P. V. J., BVSc S.Lanka, PhD
  Peradeniya Sr. Lectr.
Wettimuny, S. G. de S., BVSc Ceyl., PhD
  Glas. Prof.

Veterinary Pre-Clinical Studies

Abeygunawardena, I. S., BVSc S.Lanka, MSc
  Ill. Sr. Lectr. (on leave)
Abeysinghe, P. M., BSc Wales, PhD Wales Sr.
  Lectr.
Abeysinghe, P. M., BSc S.Lanka, PhD Wales Sr.
  Lectr.
Arambepola, N. K., BVSc S.Lanka, MSc
  S.Lanka Sr. Lectr.
Ariyaratne, H. B. S., BVSc S.Lanka, MPhil
  S.Lanka Sr. Lectr.
Gunawardena, V. K., BVSc Ceyl., PhD Lond. Sr.
  Prof.; Head*
Horadagoda, A., BVSc S.Lanka, MPhil S.Lanka,
  PhD Glas. Sr. Lectr.
Jayasekera, S., BVSc S.Lanka, MSc Utah, PhD
  Utah Sr. Lectr. (on leave)

SPECIAL CENTRES, ETC

Engineering Design Centre

Ekanayake, E. M. N., BScEngin Ceyl., MSc Lond.,
  PhD McM. Dir.*

Engineering Education Unit

Somaratne, A. P. N., MS Ill., PhD Ill.,
  BScEngin Dir.*

Engineering Research Unit

Fernando, S. V. M., BScEng Asian I.T., Bangkok,
  PhD Miami Dir.*

Engineering Workshops

Pathirana, S. D., BScEngin S.Lanka, MSc Ghent,
  DEng Tokyo Dir.*

English Language Teaching Unit

Dharmadasa, S., BA Ceyl. Instr.; Head*

Maha-Illuppallama Training Unit

Jayaweera, C. S., BScAgric S.Lanka, MSc
  Cant. Sr. Lectr.
Pathmarajah, S., BScAgric S.Lanka, MPhil
  Peradeniya, PhD Asian I.T.,Bangkok Sr. Lectr.
Rambanda, M., BScAgric S.Lanka,
  MScAgricEngin Obihiro Sr. Lectr.; Head*

Science Education Unit

Tel: (08) 388693 Fax: (08) 388018
Amerasinghe, Prof. F. P., BSc Ceyl., PhD
  Brist. Dir.*

AGRICULTURE, POSTGRADUATE INSTITUTE OF

See also staff entries marked § in departments
of agric. biol., agric. econ., agric. engin.,
agric. extension and animal sci. above

Agricultural Biology

Adikaram, N. K. B., BSc Ceyl., PhD Belf. Prof.
Gunatilake, I. A. U. N., BSc Ceyl., PhD
  Camb. Prof.

Agricultural Economics, see above

Agricultural Engineering

Abeykoon, S. B. S., BSc(Eng) S.Lanka, PhD
  Br.Col. Sr. Lectr.
Keerthisena, H. H. J., BSc(Eng) Ceyl., PhD
  Ceyl. Sr. Lectr.
Pathmarajah, S., BScAgric S.Lanka, MPhil S.Lanka,
  PhD Asian I.T., Bangkok Sr. Lectr.
Walgama, K. S., BSc(Eng) S.Lanka, MEng
  Philips'(Eindhoven), MSc Alta., PhD Luleå Sr.
  Lectr.

Agricultural Extension

No staff at present.

Animal Science

Ibrahim, M. N. M., BScAgric S.Lanka, PhD   Sr. Lectr.

Common Courses

Dissanayake, U. N. B., BSc Ceyl., MSc Alta., PhD Alta.   Sr. Lectr.
Gunasena, H. P. M., BScAgric Ceyl., PhD Reading   Prof.
Thattil, R. O., BSc Ceyl., MSc Philippines, PhD Virginia Polytech.   Assoc. Prof.
Wickremagamage, P., BA Ceyl., MSc Lond., PhD Lond.   Sr. Lectr.
Wijewardena, R. L., BSc S.Lanka, MS N.Y.State   Sr. Lectr.

Crop Science

De Costa, W. A. J. N., BScAgric S.Lanka, PhD Reading   Sr. Lectr.
Eeswara, J. P., BScAgric S.Lanka, MPhil S.Lanka, PhD Aberd.   Sr. Lectr.
Gunasena, H. P. M., BScAgric Ceyl., PhD Reading   Prof.; Dir. of Inst.*
Jayaweera, C. S., MSc Lincoln(NZ), BScAgric   Sr. Lectr.
Malkanthie Menike, D. R. R., BScAgric S.Lanka, MSc Ghent, PhD Kanagawa   Sr. Lectr.
Marambe, B., BScAgric S.Lanka, MSc Hiroshima, PhD Hiroshima   Sr. Lectr.
Nissanka, N. A. A. S. P., BScAgric S.Lanka, PhD Guelph   Sr. Lectr.
Peiris, S., BScAgric S.Lanka, MSc Penn., PhD Lond.   Sr. Lectr.
Peris, B. C. N., BScAgric Ceyl., MSc Penn.State, PhD Penn.State   Sr. Lectr.
Premaratne, K. P., BScAgric Ceyl., MSc Leip., PhD T.U.Berlin   Sr. Lectr.
Ranamukaarachchi, S. L., BScAgric Ceyl., MMSc Penn.State, PhD Penn.State   Sr. Lectr.
Sangakkara, U. R., BScAgric Ceyl., PhD Massey   Prof.
Senanayake, Y. D. A., BScAgric Ceyl., MSc Louisiana State, PhD Calif.   Prof.
Thattil, R. O., BScAgric Ceyl., MSc Philippines, PhD Virginia Polytech.   Assoc. Prof.
Wadasinghe, G., BScAgric Ceyl., MSc Lond., PhD S.Lanka   Sr. Lectr.

Food Science and Technology

Gamlath, C. G. S., BScAgric S.Lanka, MPhil S.Lanka, PhD Cran.   Sr. Lectr.
Illeperuma, D. C. K., BScAgric S.Lanka, MSc S.Lanka, PhD Maryland   Sr. Lectr.
Perera, P. A. J., BSc Ceyl., PhD Glas.   Prof.
Samarajeewa, U., BSc Ceyl., PhD S.Lanka   Prof.; Head*
Wijesinghe, D. G. N. G., BScAgric S.Lanka, MSc Philippines, PhD Lond.   Sr. Lectr.

Soil Science

Jayakody, A. N., BSc Leip., MSc Leip., PhD Giessen   Sr. Lectr.
Kumaragamage, D., BScAgric S.Lanka, MPhil S.Lanka, PhD Manit.   Sr. Lectr.
Mapa, R. B., BScAgric S.Lanka, MSc Hawaii, PhD Hawaii   Sr. Lectr.
Nandasena, K. A., BScAgric S.Lanka, MSc S.Lanka, PhD Louvain   Sr. Lectr.
Thenabadu, M. W., BSc Ceyl., MSc Texas, PhD Calif.   Prof.

CONTACT OFFICERS

Academic affairs. Senior Assistant Registrar: Abeyratne, K. M. G. W., BA Ceyl., MA S.Lanka
Accommodation. Senior Assistant Registrar: Sirisena, D. K., BA Ceyl.
Admissions (first degree). Assistant Registrar, Registration: Senanayaka, W., BA Ceyl.
Admissions (higher degree). (Contact the Dean of the appropriate faculty)
Adult/continuing education. Student Counsellor: Liyanage, Prof. R. P., BA Ceyl., MA Ceyl.
Alumni. Statistical Officer: Gamage, Hema A., BA Ceyl.
Archives. Registrar: Dissanayake, D. M. W., BA Ceyl.
Careers. Senior Assistant Registrar: Sirisena, D. K., BA Ceyl.
Computing services. Thattil, R. O., BSc Ceyl., MSc Philippines, PhD Virginia Polytech.
Consultancy services. Registrar: Dissanayake, D. M. W., BA Ceyl.
Development/fund-raising. Registrar: Dissanayake, D. M. W., BA Ceyl.
Distance education. Student Counsellor: Liyanage, Prof. R. P., BA Ceyl., MA Ceyl.

Estates and buildings/works and services. Works Engineer: Hewapathirana, S. C., BSc Ceyl.
Examinations. (Contact the Assistant Registrar of the appropriate faculty)
Examinations. Director, External Examinations: Meegaskumbura, Prof. P. B., MA Ceyl., PhD Poona
Finance. Bursar: Kumarage, M. K. S., BCom Ceyl.
General enquiries. Registrar: Dissanayake, D. M. W., BA Ceyl.
Health services. Chief Medical Officer: Amarasiri, S. P., MB BS Ceyl.
Industrial liaison. Dean of Engineering: Ranatunge, Prof. R. J. K. S. K., BSc(Eng) Ceyl., MSc Birm., PhD Birm.
International office. Registrar: Dissanayake, D. M. W., BA Ceyl.
Library (chief librarian). Librarian: Senadeera, N. T. S. A., BA Ceyl.
Personnel/human resources. Senior Assistant Registrar: Ahamed, R., BA Ceyl.
Personnel/human resources (academic). Senior Assistant Registrar: Kulatunga, J. B.
Public relations, information and marketing. Welfare Officer: Ariyaratne, P. H., BA Ceyl.
Public relations, information and marketing. Statistical Officer: Gamage, Hema A.
Publications. Librarian: Senadeera, N. T. S. A., BA Ceyl.
Purchasing. Fernando, G., BA Ceyl.
Quality assurance and accreditation. Registrar: Dissanayake, D. M. W., BA Ceyl.
Research. Senior Assistant Registrar: Abeyratne, K. M. G. W., BA Ceyl., MA S.Lanka
Safety. Chief Security Officer: Ranaweera, G. W.
Scholarships, awards, loans. Vice-Chancellor: Gunawardana, Prof. R. A. Leslie H., BA Ceyl., PhD Lond.
Schools liaison. Student Counsellor: Liyanage, Prof. R. P., BA Ceyl., MA Ceyl.
Security. Chief Security Officer: Ranaweera, G. W.
Staff development and training. Registrar: Dissanayake, D. M. W., BA Ceyl.

[Information supplied by the institution as at 26 February 1998, and edited by the ACU]

RAJARATA UNIVERSITY OF SRI LANKA

Established 1996

Member of the Association of Commonwealth Universities

Postal Address: Mihintale, Sri Lanka
Telephone: (01) 256643, 256645-6 **Fax**: (01) 256511-2

CHANCELLOR—Kelegama, J., BA Ceyl., DPhil Oxf.
VICE-CHANCELLOR*—Siriweera, Prof. Wathuge I., BA Ceyl., PhD Lond.
RECTOR—Kuruwita, Prof. V. Y., BVSc Ceyl., PhD NZ
ACTING REGISTRAR—Dissanayake, B. S. M. S. J., BA Vidyod., MA B&P SLanka
BURSAR—Dassanayake, R. M., BCom Sri Jay.
LIBRARIAN—Jayalal, K. S. B., BSc Ceyl., MSc

FACULTIES/SCHOOLS

Agricultural Sciences

Dean: Upasena, S. H., BSc Moscow, MSc Moscow, PhD Novi Sad

Applied Sciences I

Dean: Tillekeratne, Prof. K., BSc Ceyl., MSc Lond., MSc Camb.

Applied Sciences II

Dean: Herat, Prof. T. R., BSc Colombo, MSc Hawaii, PhD Hawaii

Management Studies
Dean: Weerakoon, Prof. W. T., BEng *Tokyo*, MPhil *Nott.*, PhD *Brunei*

Social Sciences and Humanities
Dean: Wijeratne, Prof. K., BA *Ceyl.*, MA *Ceyl.*, PhD *Ceyl.*

ACADEMIC UNITS

Accounting and Finance
Karunaratne, P. G., BSc *Sri Jay.*, MBA   Sr. Lectr.

Agricultural Engineering, see Food
Technol. and Agric. Engin.

Biological Sciences
Gajameragedara, S. M., BSc *Peradeniya*, MSc *Peradeniya*, MPhil *Peradeniya*   Lectr.; Head*

Business Management
Andarawewa, T. B., BA(BusAdm) *Sri Jay.*   Sr. Lectr.; Head*
Weerakoon, W. T., BEng *Tokyo*, MPhil *Nott.*, PhD *Brunei*   Prof.

Computer Studies, see Indust. Management
and Computer Studies

Finance, see Acctg. and Finance

Food Technology and Agricultural Engineering
Fonseka, T. G. S., BSc *Colombo*, MSc *Kelaniya*, PhD *Nott.*   Prof.; Head*

Horticultural Sciences
Jayasekara, S. J. B. A., BSc *Faisalabad*, PhD *Reading*   Prof.; Head*

Hospitality Management
Tel: (01) 253 5102-3
Hulangamuwa, M. N., BDev   Sr. Lectr.; Acting Head*

Humanities
Paranavitana, K. D., PhD *Moscow*, BA   Sr. Lectr.; Head*

Industrial Management and Computer Studies
No staff at present

Mathematical Sciences
Ekanayake, E. M. P., BSc *Kelaniya*, MSc *Kyushu*, DSc *Kyushu*   Sr. Lectr.; Head*
Tillekeratne, K., BSc *Ceyl.*, MSc *Lond.*, MSc *Camb.*   Visiting Prof.

Nutrition and Community Resource Management
Tel: (01) 253 5102-3
Perera, W. M. K., BSc *Kelaniya*, MPhil *Ruhuna*, PhD *Aberd.*   Sr. Lectr.; Head*

Physical Sciences
Kularatne, K. W. S., BSc *Ceyl.*, PhD *Birm.*   Sr. Lectr.
Ratnasekara, J. L., MSc *Moscow*, PhD *Moscow*   Lectr.; Head*

Plantation Management
Fernandopulle, Malathi, BSc(Agric) PhD   Sr. Lectr.
Jayasekara, N. E. M., BSc *Ceyl.*, PhD *Brunei*   Prof.; Head*

Social Sciences
Navaratne Banda, H. M., BA *Ceyl.*, MSc*Qld.*   Sr. Lectr.; Head*
Wijeratne, K., BA *Ceyl.*, MA *Ceyl.*, PhD*Ceyl.*   Prof.

SPECIAL CENTRES, ETC

Computer Unit
No staff at present

English Language Teaching Unit
No staff at present

CONTACT OFFICERS
General enquiries. Acting Registrar: Dissanayake, B. S. M. S. J., BA *Vidyod.*, MA B&P *SLanka*
Library (chief librarian). Librarian: Jayalal, K. S. B., BSc *Ceyl.*, MSc

[Information supplied by the institution as at 15 July 1998, and edited by the ACU]

UNIVERSITY OF RUHUNA, SRI LANKA

Founded 1984, formerly established as Ruhuna University College, 1979

Member of the Association of Commonwealth Universities

Postal Address: Matara, Sri Lanka
Telephone: (041) 22681-2, 22369 **Fax:** (041) 22683 **Cables:** University of Ruhuna, Sri Lanka, Matara

CHANCELLOR—Pannananda, Ven. P., Nayaka Thero BA *Lond.*, Hon. DLitt *Sri Jay.*
VICE-CHANCELLOR*—Pinnaduwage, Prof. Sathyapala, BScAgric *Ceyl.*, MS *Wis.*, PhD *Wis.*
DEPUTY VICE-CHANCELLOR—Rajapakse, Prof. R. H. S., BScAgric *Ceyl.*, MScAgric *Ceyl.*, PhD *Flor.*
REGISTRAR—Ratnatilake, K. A., BA *Ceyl.*
BURSAR—Yaddehige, G., BSc *Sri Jay.*

GENERAL INFORMATION

History. The university was established as Ruhuna University College in 1979 and achieved full university status in 1984.

Admission to first degree courses (see also Sri Lankan Introduction). General Certificate of Education (GCE) A level in 4 approved subjects with a minimum aggregate mark of 180.

First Degrees (see also Sri Lankan Directory to Subjects of Study). BA(Gen), BA(Spe), BBA, BCom, BSc(Agric), BSc(Gen), BSc(Spe), MB BS.

Higher Degrees (see also Sri Lankan Directory to Subjects of Study). DM, MA, MPhil, PhD.

Language of Instruction. Sinhalese and English.

FACULTIES/SCHOOLS

Agriculture
Dean: Senaratne, R., BScAgric *Ceyl.*, MPhil *Ceyl.*, PhD *Vienna*

Humanities and Social Sciences
Dean: Wawwage, Prof. S., BA *Ceyl.*, MPhil

Medicine
Dean: Mendis, Prof. A. L. S., MB BS *Ceyl.*, PhD *Ruhuna*

Science
Dean: Hettiarachchi, S., BSc *Kelaniya*, PhD *Brussels*

ACADEMIC UNITS

Agricultural Biology
Pathirana, R., MScAgric P.F.U., *Moscow*, PhD P.F.U., *Moscow*   Prof.; Head*
Rajapakse, Prof. R. H. S., BScAgric *Ceyl.*, MScAgric *Ceyl.*, PhD *Flor.*   Sr. Lectr.

Senanayake, S. G. J. N., BScAgric *Ceyl.*, PhD *R.Vet. & Agric.*, *Denmark*   Sr. Lectr.
Other Staff: 1 Lectr.

Agricultural Chemistry
Gunawardene, S. F. B. N., BScAgric *Peradeniya*, MSc *Louvain*   Sr. Lectr. (on leave)
Wijeratne, Vinitha, BScAgric *Ceyl.*, MSc *Ghent*   Sr. Lectr.; Head*
Other Staff: 2 Lectrs.

Agricultural Economics
Amarasinghe, O., BScAgric *Ceyl.*, MSc *Ghent*, PhD *Ghent*   Sr. Lectr.
De Soyza, M., BScAgric *Peradeniya*, MSc *Wageningen*, PhD   Sr. Lectr.
Dharmasena, K. H., BScAgric *Ceyl.*, MPhil *Peradeniya*   Sr. Lectr. (on leave)
Karunadasa, H. R. K. K., BCom *Peradeniya*, MScAgric *Peradeniya*   Sr. Lectr.
Pinnaduwage, S., BScAgric *Ceyl.*, MS *Madison*, MS *Wis.*, PhD *Wis.*   Prof.
Wijeratne, W. M. M. P., BScAgric *Ceyl.*, MSc *Ghent*, PhD *Wageningen*   Prof.; Head*

Other Staff: 1 Lectr,

Agricultural Engineering

Alwis, P. L. A. G., BScAgric Peradeniya, DrIng Montpellier Sr. Lectr.
Weerasinghe, K. D. N., MScAgric P.F.U., Moscow, PhD P.F.U., Moscow Prof.; Head*
Other Staff: 1 Lectr.

Animal Science

Gunawardena, W. W. D. A., BScAgric Ceyl., PhD Sur. Sr. Lectr.; Head*
Pathirana, K. K., BVSc Ceyl., MSc McG., PhD McG. Prof.
Serasinghe, R. Thaksala, BScAgric Ceyl., PhD Sur. Sr. Lectr.
Other Staff: 2 Lectrs.

Biochemistry, see Medicine

Botany

De Silva, M. P., BSc Ceyl., PhD T.H.Aachen Sr. Lectr.; Head*
De Silva, P. H. A. Udul, BSc Kelaniya, PhD Reading Sr. Lectr.
Dissanayake, Nanda P., BSc Peradeniya Sr. Lectr. (on leave)
Hettiarachchi, S., BSc Kelaniya, PhD Brussels Sr. Lectr.
Jayatissa, L. P., BSc Ruhuna, PhD Sr. Lectr.
Samarakoon, S. P., BSc Ceyl., MSc Qld. Sr. Lectr.
Sapumohotti, W. P., BSc Kelaniya, MSc Sr. Lectr.
Other Staff: 3 Lectrs.

Buddhist Studies, see Pali and Buddhist Studies

Business Administration

Dediyagala, N., MSc Brun. Sr. Lectr.
Wickramasinghe, D. P., BSc Sri Jay., MCom Colombo, PhD Manc. Sr. Lectr.
Other Staff: 10 Lectrs.

Chemistry

Dissanayake, A. S., BSc Colombo, PhD Sr. Lectr.
Edissuriya, M., MSc PhD Sr. Lectr.
Pathirana, H. M. K. K., BSc Colombo, PhD Aston Sr. Lectr.
Pathirana, R. N., BSc Peradeniya, MSc S'ton., PhD S'ton. Sr. Lectr.; Head*
Silva, de M. S. W., BSc Peradeniya, PhD Sr. Lectr.
Weerasinghe, M. S. S., BSc Colombo, PhD Sr. Lectr.
Wijayanayake, R. H., BSc Ceyl., PhD Leeds, FRSChem Prof. (on leave)
Other Staff: 9 Lectrs.

Computer Unit

Jayewardana, S. C., BSc Sri Jay., PhD Berne Sr. Lectr.; Head*
Other Staff: 2 Lectrs.

Crop Science

Amerasekera, D. A. B. Nirmala, BScAgric Peradeniya, MSc Leuven Sr. Lectr.
Dayatilake, G. A., BScAgric Ceyl., PhD R.Vet. & Agric.,Denmark Sr. Lectr.
Senaratne, R., BScAgric Ceyl., MPhil Ceyl., PhD Vienna Sr. Lectr.
Serasinghe, P. S. J. W., BScAgric Ceyl., PhD Zür. Sr. Lectr.; Head*
Other Staff: 2 Lectrs.

Economics

Atapattu, D., BA Ceyl., MA McG., PhD McG. Prof.
Dayananda, P. M., BA Vidyal., MPhil Colombo Sr. Lectr.
Dervin, S. K., BA Ruhuna, MA Ruhuna Sr. Lectr.
Hemapala, R., BCom Ceyl., MPhil Ruhuna Sr. Lectr.
Sumanaratna, B. M., BA Peradeniya, MA Ruhuna Sr. Lectr.
Vithanage, P., BA Ceyl., MSc Peradeniya, MPhil Sr. Lectr.; Head*
Other Staff: 10 Lectrs.

Fish Biology

Cumaranatunge, P. R. T., BSc Vidyal., PhD Aston Sr. Lectr.; Head*
Other Staff: 3 Lectrs.

Geography

Edirisinghe, Ghana, BA Ruhuna, MA Ruhuna Sr. Lectr.
Gunadasa, A. D., BA Ceyl., MA Colombo Sr. Lectr. (on leave)
Hewage, P., BA Ceyl., MSc Lond. Sr. Lectr.
Mohamed Ali, Sitty K., BA Ceyl., PhD Durh. Sr. Lectr.
Premadasa, L. A., MA Ceyl., BA Peradeniya, PhD Peradeniya Sr. Lectr.
Ratnayake, L. Kanthi, BA Ceyl., PhD Edin. Prof.
Ratnayake, M., MA Colombo Sr. Lectr.
Razaak, M. M. R., BA Vidyod., MA Colombo Sr. Lectr.; Head*
Senerath, G., MA Colombo Sr. Lectr.
Weerakkody, U. C. de S., BA Vidyod., MSc I.T.C.Enschede Sr. Lectr.
Other Staff: 5 Lectrs.

History

Attanayake, A. S. Anula, BA Ceyl., MA Peradeniya Sr. Lectr. (on leave)
De Silva, M. U., MA Vidyal., PhD Vidyal. Prof.; Head*
Piyasena, S. A., BA Peradeniya, MPhil Ruhuna Sr. Lectr.
Wawwage, S., BA Ceyl., MPhil Sr. Lectr.
Other Staff: 4 Lectrs.

Mathematics

Jayasekara, L. A. L. W., BSc Kelaniya, PhD Kyushu, MSc Sr. Lectr.
Wijayasiri, M. P. A., BSc Vidyal., MSc Brad. Sr. Lectr.; Head*
Other Staff: 8 Lectrs.

Medicine, see below

Microbiology, see Medicine, below

Pali and Buddhist Studies

Dhammajothi, Rev. D., MA Peradeniya Sr. Lectr. (on leave)
Nandawansha, Rev. M., BA Kelaniya, MA PhD Sr. Lectr.
Ruhunuhewa, A. J., MA Paris I, PhD Paris I, BA Sr. Lectr.
Soratha, Rev. M., BA Kelaniya, MA Ceyl. Sr. Lectr.; Head*
Other Staff: 3 Lectrs.

Physics

Dharmaratne, W. G. D., BSc Peradeniya, MSc Tufts, PhD Tufts Sr. Lectr.; Head*
Fernando, C. A. N., MSc Sri Jay., PhD Sr. Lectr.
Kulatunga, A. D. S., BSc Peradeniya, PhD Sr. Lectr.
Samarasekera, P., BSc Kelaniya, PhD Flor. Sr. Lectr.
Yapa, K. K. A. S., BSc Kelaniya, MSc PhD Sr. Lectr.
Other Staff: 5 Lectrs.

Sinhala

Ananda, Rev. K., BA Peradeniya, MA Sr. Lectr.
Dhamminda, Rev. A., BA Vidyal., MA Kelaniya Sr. Lectr. (on leave)
Dharmawathie, R. P., BA Kelaniya, MA Sr. Lectr.
Ekanayake, P. B., MA Vidyod. Sr. Lectr.
Gamlath, S., BA Ceyl., PhD Lond. Prof.; Head*
Kotawalagedara, Angle, MA Peradeniya Sr. Lectr.
Manawadu, S., BA Vidyal. Sr. Lectr.
Pathiraja, D., MA Peradeniya Sr. Lectr. (on leave)
Other Staff: 5 Lectrs.

Sociology

Amarasinghe, S. W., BA Peradeniya, MSc Asian I.T., Bangkok Sr. Lectr.
Jayesinghe, A. K. G., BA Ceyl., MA Colombo Sr. Lectr.; Head*

Ranaweera Banda, R. M., BA Peradeniya, MA Colombo Sr. Lectr.
Other Staff: 5 Lectrs.

Zoology

Amarasinghe, N. J., BSc Ceyl., PhD Sr. Lectr.; Head*
Bogahawatta, Nandanie, MSc Sri Jay., PhD Sr. Lectr.
De Silva, M. P. K. S. K., BSc Kelaniya, MSc Sr. Lectr.
Edirisinghe, H. C., BSc Kelaniya, PhD Sr. Lectr.
Nilakarawasam, N., BSc Colombo, PhD Sr. Lectr.
Senaratne, K. A. D. W., BSc Ceyl., MPhil Lond. Prof.
Wickramasinghe, M. G. Vinitha, BSc Sri Jay., PhD Reading Sr. Lectr.
Other Staff: 5 Lectrs.

MEDICINE

Anatomy

Weerasuriya, T. R., MB BS Peradeniya, DMSc Kyushu Sr. Lectr.; Head*
Wijeratne, D. E., MB BS Ceyl., PhD Lond. Prof.
Other Staff: 5 Lectrs.

Biochemistry

Fernando, M. R., MSc Peradeniya Sr. Lectr.
Jayatilaka, K. A. P. W., MSc Sri Jay., PhD Sr. Lectr.
Pathirana, Chitra, BSc Peradeniya, PhD S'ton. Prof.; Head*
Other Staff: 3 Lectrs.

Community Medicine

Foneseka, Pushpa H. G., MB BS Ceyl., PhD Prof.; Head*
Liyanage, K. D. Chandrani, BSc Baroda, MSc Peradeniya, PhD Ruhuna Sr. Lectr.
Wijesiri, W. A. A., MB BS Colombo Sr. Lectr.
Other Staff: 2 Lectrs.

Forensic Medicine

Chandrasiri, N., MB BS Ceyl., MD S.Lanka, FRCPGlas Prof.; Head*

Medicine

Ariyananda, P. L., MB BS Ceyl., MD Ceyl. Prof.; Head*
De Silva, W. A. S., MB BS S.Lanka, MD Ceyl., FRCPEd Prof.
Mohideen, M. R., MB BS Ceyl., MD Sr. Lectr.
Sarath, L. K. L., MB BS Ceyl. Sr. Lectr. (on leave)
Other Staff: 2 Lectrs.

Microbiology

De Silva, N., MD Colombo, MB BS Sr. Lectr.
Other Staff: 1 Lectr.

Obstetrics and Gynaecology

Collonne, J. R., MB BS Ceyl., MD S.Lanka Sr. Lectr.
Gunasekera, A. G. A. De S., MB BS Ceyl., FRCOG Prof.; Head*
Gunawardena, I. M. R., MB BS Ceyl. Prof.
Samarage, L. H., MB BS Peradeniya, MS Colombo Sr. Lectr.
Other Staff: 2 Lectrs.

Paediatrics

Amarasena, T. S. D., MB BS Ceyl., MD Colombo Sr. Lectr.
De Silva, D. G. H., MB BS Ceyl., MSc Birm. Prof.; Head*
Devasiri, I. V., MB BS Ruhuna, MD Colombo Sr. Lectr.
Fernando, A. D., MB BS Colombo Sr. Lectr.
Jayantha, U. K., MB BS Ruhuna, MD Colombo Sr. Lectr.
Other Staff: 3 Lectrs.

Pathology

Weerasuriya, Mirani V., MB BS Ceyl., DMSc Kyushu Sr. Lectr.; Head*
Other Staff: 4 Lectrs.

Pharmacology

Fernando, Anoja I., MB BS *Ceyl.* Prof.; Head*
Other Staff: 2 Lectrs.

Physiology

Mendis, A. L. S., MB BS *Ceyl.*, PhD
Ruhuna Prof.; Head*
Other Staff: 4 Lectrs.

Psychiatry

Harishchandra, D. V. J., MB BS *Ceyl.* Sr. Lectr.
Jayawardena, M. K. G. R. De S., MB BS
Ceyl. Sr. Lectr.
Other Staff: 1 Lectr.; 1 Clin. Psychologist

Surgery

De Silva, W. A. S. A., MB BS *Ceyl.* Sr. Lectr.
Fernando, F. R., MB BS *Colombo*, FRCSEd Sr.
Lectr.
Fonseka, M. N. T., MB BS *Ceyl.*, FRCSEd,
FRCS Prof.; Head*

Kumara, M. M. A. J., MB BS *Peradeniya* Sr.
Lectr.
Other Staff: 2 Lectrs.

CONTACT OFFICERS

Academic affairs. Assistant Registrar,
Academic Establishment: Mapatuna, M., BA
Sri Jay.
Accommodation. Senior Assistant Registrar,
Student Welfare: Dumindusena, K. D., BA
Ceyl.
Admissions (first degree). Assistant Registrar,
Academic and Publication: Kalugama, P. S.,
BA *Sri Jay.*
Admissions (higher degree). Senior Assistant
Registrar, Examinations: Mudalige, S. C.
Examinations. Senior Assistant Registrar,
Examinations: Mudalige, S. C.
Finance. Bursar: Yaddehige, G., BSc *Sri Jay.*
General enquiries. Registrar: Ratnatilake, K.
A., BA *Ceyl.*

Health services. University Medical Officer:
Weerasinghe, A., MB BS *Ceyl.*
Library (enquiries). Assistant Librarian:
Jayathilaka, M. P., BA *Ceyl.*, MLib *Wales*
Personnel/human resources. Assistant
Registrar, Non Academic Establishments:
Dissanayake, P. S.
Publications. Assistant Registrar, Academic and
Publication: Kalugama, P. S., BA *Sri Jay.*
Scholarships, awards, loans. Senior Assistant
Registrar, Student Welfare: Dumindusena, K.
D., BA *Ceyl.*
Security. Wisumperuma, C. K.
Sport and recreation. Director of Physical
Education: Aluthpatabendige, W.
Student welfare/counselling. Senior Assistant
Registrar, Student Welfare: Dumindusena, K.
D., BA *Ceyl.*

[Information supplied by the institution as at 24 March
1998, and edited by the ACU]

SABARAGAMUWA UNIVERSITY OF SRI LANKA

Established 1995

Member of the Association of Commonwealth Universities

Postal Address: PO Box 02, Belihuloya, Sri Lanka 70140
Telephone: (045) 23515, 23178, 23128 **Fax**: (045) 23128 **E-mail**: belihul@mail.ac.lk

CHANCELLOR—......
VICE-CHANCELLOR*—Somasundara, Prof. J. W. Dayananda, JP, BA *Vidyod.*,
MEc NE
REGISTRAR—Ratnatillake, M. S., BA *Ceyl.*
LIBRARIAN—......
BURSAR—Dharmasena, E. A., BCom *Peradeniya*

GENERAL INFORMATION

History. First established in 1992 as
Sabaragamuwa Province Affiliated University
College, the university was founded in 1995
by the amalgamation of that college with
Buttala Affiliated University College and Uva
Province Affiliated College, and inaugurated in
1996.
It is located in Sabaragamuwa Province,
165km east of Colombo.

Admission to first degree courses (see also
Sri Lankan Introduction). Through University
Grants Commission on the basis of General
Certificate of Education (GCE) A level results.

First Degrees (see also Sri Lankan Directory
to Subjects of Study). BA, BSc.
All courses are full-time and normally last 3
years.

Higher Degrees. Not yet available.

Language of Instruction. Sinhala and
English.

Libraries. Main library: 24,000 volumes; 575
periodicals.

Fees. Home students: no tuition fees.

Academic Year. (1997–98). Two semesters:
10 November–22 March; 3 May–15 August.

Income (1998). Government grant (98.5% of
total income), Rs92,000,000.

Statistics. Staff: 200 (102 academic, 98 non-
academic and administrative). Students (full-
time): 1029 (460 men, 569 women).

FACULTIES/SCHOOLS

Agricultural Sciences
Tel: (057) 45296, 45297 Fax: (057) 45296
Dean: Jayasekara, Prof. M. U., BVSc&AH
E.Pak.Ag., MSc *Sask.*, PhD *Kansas*
Assistant Registrar: Kithsiri, P. V., BCom *Sri Jay.*

Applied Sciences
Tel: (055) 73985-8 Fax: (055) 73987
Dean: Rupasinghe, Prof. M. S., MSc *F.U.Berlin*,
PhD *Mainz*
Assistant Registrar: Samarasinghe, U. J., BSc *Sri
Jay.*

Business Studies
Dean (Acting): Munidasa, M. A., BA *Vidyod.*,
MBA *Sri Jay.*
Assistant Registrar: Kulatunga, K. M. M. P., BA
Sri Jay.

Social Sciences and Languages
Dean: Wijesinha, Prof. Rajiva, BA *Oxf.*, BPhil
Oxf., DPhil *Oxf.*
Assistant Registrar: Kulatunga, K. M. M. P., BA
Sri Jay.

ACADEMIC UNITS

Accountancy and Finance
Siddeek, M. Y. M., BCom *Jaffna*, MBA *Sri
Jay.* Sr. Lectr. (on leave)
Other Staff: 8 Lectrs.

Vacant Posts: 1 Prof.; 3 Sr. Lectrs.
Research: financial markets

Agribusiness Management
Tel: (057) 45296 Fax: (057) 45296
Mahaliyanaarachchi, R. P., MScAgric *Plovdiv*,
PhD *Peradeniya* Sr. Lectr.; Head*
Other Staff: 8 Lectrs.
Vacant Posts: 1 Prof.; 2 Sr. Lectrs.
Research: agricultural extension; gender in
agribusiness; rural sociology

Export Agriculture
Tel: (057) 45296 Fax: (057) 45296
Sandanam, S., BScAgric *Ceyl.*, PhD *Lond.* Prof.;
Head*
Other Staff: 8 Lectrs.
Vacant Posts: 3 Sr. Lectrs.
Research: minituber production in potatoes; soil
erosion under vegetable crops

Finance, see Accty. and Finance

Languages
Amarasekara, C. L., BA *Ceyl.*, MPhil *Lond.*, MA
Reading Sr. Lectr.; Head*
Nageswaran, K., BA *Jaffna*, MA *Jaffna* Sr. Lectr.
Wijesinha, Rajiva, BA *Oxf.*, BPhil *Oxf.*, DPhil
Oxf. Prof.
Wijitha, Rev. Ayagama, BA *Komazawa*, MA
Komazawa Sr. Lectr.
Other Staff: 8 Lectrs.
Research: commonwealth literature; evaluation
and assessment in TESL; literature in
language and teaching; Sri Lankan writing in
English; translations

Livestock Production

Tel: (057) 45296 Fax: (057) 45296

Jayasekara, M. U., BVSc&AH E.Pak.Ag., MSc Sask., PhD Kansas   Prof.

Jayawardene, G. W. L., BVSc Peradeniya, PhD Qld.   Sr. Lectr.; Head*

Other Staff: 8 Lectrs.

Vacant Posts: 1 Prof.; 2 Sr. Lectrs.

Research: farming system research; nutrients in locally available food ingredients; principles of action in medicinal plants; standards for local dairy products; toxic principles in plants

Management Studies

Jayaratne, W. A., BCom Sri Jay., MSc Newcastle(UK)   Sr. Lectr.

Other Staff: 1 Sr. Consultant; 8 Lectrs.

Vacant Posts: 1 Prof.; 3 Sr. Lectrs.

Research: entrepreneurial development; human resources development

Natural Resources

Tel: (055) 73987, 73988 Fax: (055) 73987

Ranaweera, K. K. D. S., MSc Moscow, PhD U.S.S.R.Acad.Sc.   Sr. Lectr.; Head*

Rupasinghe, M. S., MSc F.U.Berlin, PhD Mainz   Prof.

Other Staff: 8 Lectrs.

Vacant Posts: 2 Sr. Lectrs.

Research: bio-diversity; food technology; heat treatment of gem minerals; localisation of gem deposits; plant biotechnology

Physical Sciences

Tel: (055) 73986 Fax: (055) 73987

Perera, Indral K., BSc Ceyl., PhD Hull   Prof.; Head*

Other Staff: 8 Lectrs.

Vacant Posts: 3 Sr. Lectrs.

Research: computer models for various industrial applications; development of solar cells; low cost instrumentation; MALDI mass spectrum

Social Sciences

Samarakoon, J. M. N. G., MSc Kharkov, PhD Kiev   Sr. Lectr.

Somasundara, J. W. Dayananda, BA Vidyod., MEc NE   Prof.

Starkloff, Ralf, BA Mass., MA Brandeis, PhD Brandeis   Sr. Lectr.

Weeratunga, Starkloff N. D., BA Brandeis, MA N.Y.State, PhD Tor.   Head*

Other Staff: 8 Lectrs.

Research: agricultural economics; gender studies; sociology of environment

Surveying Sciences

Salgado, M. P., BSc Ceyl., BSc Camb.   Sr. Consultant; Head*

Other Staff: 1 Sr. Consultant

Vacant Posts: 1 Prof.; 3 Sr. Lectrs.; 5 Lectrs.

CONTACT OFFICERS

Academic affairs. Senior Assistant Registrar: Ranasinghe, A. P., BSc Peradeniya, MSc Birm.

Accommodation. Senior Assistant Registrar: Ranasinghe, A. P., BSc Peradeniya, MSc Birm.

Admissions (first degree). Senior Assistant Registrar: Ranasinghe, A. P., BSc Peradeniya, MSc Birm.

Adult/continuing education. Director, External Services Unit: Wijesinha, Prof. Rajiva, BA Oxf., BPhil Oxf., DPhil Oxf.

Archives. Assistant Librarian: Ratnayake, A. R. M. M., BSc Peradeniya

Careers. Student Counsellor (Careers Guidance): Jayawardana, Fr. A. T., MSc C.U.N.Y.

Computing services. Head, Department of Physical Sciences: Perera, Prof. Indral K., BSc Ceyl., PhD Hull

Consultancy services. Co-ordinator, Projects: Starkloff, Ralf, BA Mass., MA Brandeis, PhD Brandeis

Examinations. Assistant Registrar: Herath, W. M., BA Peradeniya

Finance. Bursar: Dharmasena, E. A., BCom Peradeniya

General enquiries. Registrar: Ratnatillake, M. S., BA Ceyl.

Library (chief librarian). Librarian: ......

Library (enquiries). Assistant Librarian: Neighsoorie, T. N., BA Kelaniya

Personnel/human resources. Senior Assistant Registrar: Rajapaksha, R. M. D. D., BA Vidyod.

Purchasing. Assistant Bursar: Wijesinghe, G. W. A. B., BCom Colombo

Security. Assistant Registrar: Jayasundara, U. A., BA Colombo

Staff development and training. Director, Staff Development: Sandanam, Prof. S., BSc Ceyl., PhD Lond.

Student union. Senior Assistant Registrar: Ranasinghe, A. P., BSc Peradeniya, MSc Birm.

Student welfare/counselling. Chief Student Counsellor: Wijitha, Rev. Ayagama, BA Komazawa, MA Komazawa

University press. Director, Sabaragamuwa University Press: Wijesinha, Prof. Rajiva, BA Oxf., BPhil Oxf., DPhil Oxf.

[Information supplied by the institution as at 3 March 1998, and edited by the ACU]

SOUTH EASTERN UNIVERSITY OF SRI LANKA

Founded 1995

Member of the Association of Commonwealth Universities

Postal Address: Addalaichenai, Sri Lanka 32350
Telephone: (063) 77195 **Fax**: (01) 713048

VICE-CHANCELLOR*—Cader, Abdul, BA Ceyl., MA ANU
REGISTRAR‡—Joufer Sadique, A. L., BSc Jaffna
LIBRARIAN—......
BURSAR—Gulam Rasheed, A.

GENERAL INFORMATION

History. The university was founded in 1995. Its site in Oluvil on the south-eastern coast of Sri Lanka is in the process of development.

First Degrees. BA (general), BA (special), BBA, BCom, BSc(Accty&Fin), BSc (general), BSc (special).

Courses for BA (general), BSc(Accty&Fin) and BSc (general) last 3 years; all others last 4 years.

Academic Year. Two semesters of six months each.

FACULTIES/SCHOOLS

Applied Science

Dean: ......

Arts and Culture

Dean: Kalideen, K. M. H., BA Ceyl., MA Jaffna

Commerce and Management

Dean: ......

ACADEMIC UNITS

Biological Sciences

Srikrishnaraj, K. A., BSc Peradeniya, MSc Colombo, PhD Colombo   Lectr.; Chief Co-ordinator

Other Staff: 4 Lectrs.

Commerce and Accountancy

Ishaq, K., BCom Jaffna, MCom Kerala   Chief Co-ordinator

Other Staff: 3 Lectrs.

Languages and Cultural Studies

Kalideen, K. M. H., BA Ceyl., MA Jaffna   Sr. Lectr.

Other Staff: 6 Lectrs.

Management Studies

4 Lectrs.

Physical Science

4 Lectrs.

Social Science

Balachandran, Prof. S., BA Ceyl., MSc Birm.   (on contract)

Mohamed Ismail, S. M., MSc PhD   Sr. Lectr.

Other Staff: 5 Lectrs.

CONTACT OFFICERS

Academic affairs. Kaleel, M. I. M., BA Peradeniya

Accommodation. Faleel, S. L. M., BA Peradeniya

Admissions (first degree). Careem, M. F. H., BSc Peradeniya, MSc Peradeniya

Computing services. Mahandran, S., BScEngin Peradeniya

Estates and buildings/works and services. Yoosuf, M. M.

Library (enquiries). Library Consultant: Rubasingam, S., BA Ceyl., MA Lough.

Student welfare/counselling. Thayub, A., BCom *Peradeniya*

[*Information supplied by the institution as at 15 February 1998, and edited by the ACU*]

UNIVERSITY OF SRI JAYEWARDENEPURA, SRI LANKA

Founded 1959; originally established as Vidyodaya Pirivena

Member of the Association of Commonwealth Universities

Postal Address: Gangodawila, Nugegoda, Sri Lanka
Telephone: (085) 2695-6, 3191-2 **Fax**: (085) 2604 **Cables**: Unisjay, Sri Lanka

CHANCELLOR—de Silva, Wimala, MA *Lond.*, PhD *Lond.*
VICE-CHANCELLOR*—Wilson, Prof. P., BA *Vidyod.*, MA *ANU*, MA *Penn.*, PhD *Penn.*
REGISTRAR‡—Abeywardene, M., BA *Ceyl.*
ACTING LIBRARIAN—Vidanapathirana, P., BA *Peradeniya*, MLib *NSW*
BURSAR—Ranatunga, D. C., BSc

GENERAL INFORMATION

History. Originally founded as a traditional seat of learning, Vidyodaya Pirivena, the university was established in 1959. It is located about 13km from Colombo.

Admission. to first degree courses (see also Sri Lankan Introduction). Through University Grants Commission on the basis of General Certificate of Education (GCE) A level results.

First Degrees. BA, BCom, BSc, MB BS.
All courses are full-time. BA (general), BSc (general): 3 years; BA (special), BCom, BSc (special): 4 years. MB BS: 5 years.

Higher Degrees. MA, MSc, MPhil, PhD.
Applicants for admission to master's degree courses should hold a relevant first degree with at least second class honours. PhD: MPhil in a relevant subject.
All postgraduate courses last 2 years.

Language of Instruction. Sinhala and English.

Libraries. 140,000 volumes; 650 periodicals subscribed to.

Fees (1998, annual). Undergraduate: US$1650 (arts, management); US$4950 (sciences); US$4950 (medicine). Postgraduate: US$3000 (arts, management); US$6000 (sciences); US$7200 (medicine).

Academic Awards. 35 awards ranging in value from Rs1500 to Rs6000.

Academic Year (1998–99). 1 June–31 May.

Income. (1997). Total, Rs3,233,240.

Statistics. Staff: 951 (402 academic, 549 administrative). Students: full-time 7826 (4214 men, 3612 women); external 10,000 (400 men, 6000 women); part-time 102 (75 men, 27 women); total 17,928.

FACULTIES/SCHOOLS

Applied Science
Tel: (085) 2914

Dean: Dayananda, Prof. R. A., BSc *Ceyl.*, PhD *Wales*
Secretary: Perera, D.

Arts
Tel: (085) 3196

Dean: Kariyawasam, Prof. T., BA *Ceyl.*, MA *Ceyl.*, PhD *Lond.*
Secretary: De Silva, U. L. J.

Management Studies and Commerce
Tel: (085) 3343

Dean: Herath, H. M. A., BPAdm *Vidyod.*, MA *Car.*, PhD *Car.*
Secretary: Gunawardena, E.

Medicine
Tel: (081) 1480

Dean: Jiffry, Prof. M. T. M., BDS *Ceyl.*, MMedSc *Ceyl.*, MSc *Lond.*
Secretary: Gunarathne, K.

Postgraduate Studies
Tel: (085) 2551

Dean: Karunanayake, Prof. M. M., BA *Ceyl.*, BPhil *Liv.*, PhD *Liv.*
Secretary: Rajapakse, D. V.

ACADEMIC UNITS

Accountancy and Financial Management
Gunawardena, K. D., MBA *Colombo*, BSc(BusAdm)   Sr. Lectr.; Head*
Manawaduge, A. S. P. G., MA *Lanc.*, BSc(PubAdm)   Sr. Lectr.
Samarakoon, S. M. L. P., BSc(BusAdm) *Sri Jay.*, MBA *New Hampshire*, PhD *Houston*   Sr. Lectr.
Wickremarachchi, M. W., BA *Vidyod.*, MA *NE*   Sr. Lectr.

Anthropology, see Sociol. and Anthropol.

Archaeology, see Hist. and Archaeol.

Biochemistry, see Med.

Botany
Hettiarachchi, P. L., BSc *Colombo*, PhD *Brussels*   Sr. Lectr.
Nandadasa, H. G., BSc *Ceyl.*, PhD *Leic.*   Sr. Prof.
Ranaweera, S. S., PhD *P.F.U.*, *Moscow*   Sr. Lectr.
Salleem, N., BSc *Vidyod.*, PhD *Bath*   Sr. Lectr.
Tissera, K. M. E. P., BSc *Vidyod.*, PhD *Lanc.*   Sr. Lectr.
Wijeratne, S. C., BSc *Ceyl.*, MPhil *Kelaniya*, PhD *Fukuoka*   Sr. Lectr.

Yapa, P. A. J., BSc *Lond.*, PhD *Lond.*   Sr. Lectr.; Head*

Buddhist Studies, see Pali and Buddhist Studies

Business Administration
Abeyrathna Bandara, W. M., BSc(BusAdm) *S.Lanka*, MBA *Ott.*   Sr. Lectr.
Abeyrathne, G., MA *Dund.*, PhD *Dund.*, BSc(BusAdm)   Sr. Lectr.
Chandrakumara, P. M. K. A., BSc(BusAdm) MBA   Sr. Lectr.
De Silva, D. V. L. B., MBA *Colombo*, BSc(BusAdm) *Sri Jay.*   Sr. Lectr.
Gunatunge, R. S., MBA *Colombo*, BSc(BusAdm)   Sr. Lectr.; Head*
Molligoda, A. G. M. M. N. S. P., MBA *Leuven*, BSc(BusAdm)   Sr. Lectr.
Opatha, H. H. A. D. N. P. K., BSc(BusAdm) *Sri Jay.*, MSc *Sri Jay.*   Sr. Lectr.
Thantrigama, G., BA *Vidyod.*, MA *Leuven*   Sr. Lectr.
Yapa, S. T. W. S., MBA *Sri Jay*, BSc   Sr. Lectr.

Chemistry
Abeysekera, A. M., BSc *Ceyl.*, PhD *Belf.*   Prof.
Bamunuaratchi, A. H. De O., BSc *Vidyod.*, MSc *Calif.*, PhD *NSW*   Prof.
Deraniyagala, S. P., BSc *Ceyl.*, PhD *Dal.*   Sr. Lectr.
Fernando, W. S., BSc *Ceyl.*, PhD *Leic.*   Prof.; Head*
Jayatilleke, W. D. W., BSc *Ceyl.*, MSc *Brad.*   Assoc. Prof.
Mahathanthila, K. C. P., BSc *Vidyod.*, PhD *Ott.*   Sr. Lectr.
Samarasinghe, Shiromi I., BSc *Vidyod.*, PhD *Leeds*   Assoc. Prof.
Silva, W. S. J., BSc   Sr. Lectr.
Sirimanna, V. D. Padmini, BSc *Vidyod.*, PhD *NSW*   Sr. Lectr.
Wijewardena, C. Saroja, BSc *Vidyod.*, PhD *Maryland*   Sr. Lectr.
Wimalasena, B. H. D. J. H., BSc *Ceyl.*, PhD *Dal.*   Sr. Lectr.

Commerce
Dassanayake, D. A. M., BA *Vidyod.*, MBA *Vidyod.*   Sr. Lectr.
Dayarathna, E., BCom *Peradeniya*, MA *Thammasat*   Sr. Lectr.; Head*
Dharmadasa, E. A., BCom *S.Lanka*, MBA *Leuven*   Sr. Lectr. (on leave)

Gunaratna Banda, W. M., MCom Calicut, BCom Sri Jay. Sr. Lectr.

Hirantha, S. W., BCom Sri Jay., MA Essex, PhD Nagoya Sr. Lectr.

Jayasooriya, D. S. P., BSc Sri Jay., MSc Colombo Sr. Lectr.

Naotunne, S. S., BCom Vidyod., MBA Ott. Sr. Lectr.

Silva, W. H. E., MA Lanc., BCom Sr. Lectr.

Warnakulasuriya, B. N. F., BCom Colombo, MBA Colombo Sr. Lectr. (on leave)

Weerakoon Banda, Y. K., BSc(BusAdm) Sri Jay., MBA Colombo Sr. Lectr. (on leave)

Yaparathne, Y. M. W., MBA Sri Jay., BDevS Sr. Lectr.

Cultural Studies, see Langs. and Cultural Studies

Economics

Atukoralage, P., BA Ceyl. Sr. Lectr.

Chandrakumara, D. P. S., BA Peradeniya, MA Kerala Sr. Lectr.

Jayawardena, D., BSc Sri Jay., MA J.Nehru U., Sr. Lectr.

Kodagoda, K. R., BA Ceyl., MSc Lanc. Sr. Lectr.

Purasingha, P. L. T., BA Peradeniya, MA Peradeniya Sr. Lectr.

Rajapaksa, T. W. K., BA Vidyod., MEc NE Sr. Lectr. (on leave)

Sathkumara, M. S., BA Vidyod., MDevelStud Inst.Soc.Stud.(The Hague) Assoc. Prof.

Thantrigama, P. M. S., BA Vidyod., MA Leuven Sr. Lectr.

Thilakaratna, S., BA Ceyl., MA Dal., PhD Qu. Prof. (on leave)

Wickramasinghe, J. W., MEc S.Lanka, MEc NE, PhD S.Lanka Assoc. Prof. (on leave)

Wickremasinghe, G. A. U., BA Sri Jay., MA Thammasat Sr. Lectr.; Head*

Wilson, P., BA Vidyod., MA ANU, PhD Penn. Assoc. Prof.

Environmental Science, see Forestry and Environmental Sci.

Estate Management and Valuation

De Silva, S. S. M., BA Vidyod., MA Vidyod. Sr. Lectr.

Dodankotuwa, J. B., MEng Kobe, BSc(EstMgt&Valn) Sr. Lectr.

Edirisinghe, J., MSc Asian I.T., Bangkok, BSc(EstMgt&Valn) Sr. Lectr.; Head*

Jayarathne, K. A., MSc Asian I.T., Bangkok, BSc(EstMgt&Valn) Sr. Lectr. (on leave)

Karunaratne, K. R. M. T., BSc Ceyl., MSc Moratuwa Sr. Lectr.

Perera, P. K. Y., BSc Lond. Sr. Lectr.

Samarasinghe, H. R. Kanthi, BSc(EstMgt&Valn) Vidyod., MA Leuven Sr. Lectr. (on leave)

Weerakoon, K. G. P. K., BSc(EstMgt&Valn) Sri Jay., MSc Asian I.T., Bangkok Sr. Lectr.

Forestry and Environmental Science

Amarasekera, H. S., BSc Sri Jay., PhD Wales Sr. Lectr.

Ranasinghe, D. M. S. H. K., BSc Kelaniya, MSc Sri Jay., PhD Wales Sr. Lectr.

Singhekumara, B. M. P., BSc Sri Jay., PhD Oxf. Sr. Lectr.

Geography

Abhayaratna, M. D. C., BA Ceyl., MSc Lond. Assoc. Prof.; Head*

Attanayake, D. Chandrawathie, BA Ceyl., MSc Wis., PhD Wis. Assoc. Prof.

Bandaranayake, G. M., BA Sri Jay., MA Sri Jay. Sr. Lectr.

Deheragoda, C. K. M., MSc Sofia, PhD Sofia Sr. Lectr.

Epitawatta, D. S., BA Vidyod., MSc Moratuwa, PhD Sheff. Sr. Lectr.

Karunanayake, M. M., BA Ceyl., BPhil Liv., PhD Liv. Sr. Prof.

Karunaratna, N. L. A., BA Vidyod., PhD Durh. Sr. Lectr.

Katupotha, K. N. J., BA Vidyod., MA Hiroshima Assoc. Prof.

Ulluwishewa, R. K., BA Vidyod., MSc Lond., DrAgric Kyushu Assoc. Prof. (on leave)

Wanasinghe, Y. A. Dammika S., MA Ceyl., PhD Lond. Assoc. Prof.

Wishwakula, U. H. N., BA Sri Jay., MA Sri Jay. Sr. Lectr.

History and Archaeology

Abayawardhana, D. L., BA Vidyod., PhD Paris Assoc. Prof.; Head*

Endagama, Malini, BA Ceyl., PhD Ceyl. Assoc. Prof.

Hettiaratchi, S. B., MA Vidyod., PhD Lond. Assoc. Prof.

Karunatillake, G. K. N. D., MA Sri Jay., BA Sr. Lectr.

Kulatunge, T. G., MA Vidyod. Assoc. Prof.

Vajira, Rev. H., BA Sri Jay., MSc Kelaniya Sr. Lectr.

Languages and Cultural Studies, see also Pali and Buddhist Studies

Gunasinghe, A., BA Vidyod., MA Ban., PhD Sri Jay. Assoc. Prof., Sanskrit and Pali

Gunawardene, A. J., BA Ceyl., MA N.Y., PhD N.Y. Assoc. Prof.

Hettiarachchi, H. A. K., BA Vidyal., MA Alld. Sr. Lectr.

Marasinghe, E. W., BA PhD Prof.; Head*

Nagasundaram, P., MA Peradeniya Sr. Lectr.

Wijetunge, B. M., MA Lucknow, PhD Kanpur Sr. Lectr.

Mathematics

Banneheka, B. M. S. G., BSc Sri Jay., MSc Lond., PhD S.Fraser Sr. Lectr.

Dayananda, R. A., BSc Ceyl., PhD Wales Sr. Prof.

De Silva, T. P., BSc Ceyl., MSc Monash Sr. Lectr.

Dias, P., BSc Sri Jay., MSc Curtin Sr. Lectr.

Edirisuriya, E. A. T. A., MSc Shanghai U.S.T., BSc Sr. Lectr.

Kalukottege, C. J. P., BSc PhD Sr. Lectr.

Liyanage, L. L. M., BSc Colombo, PhD McM. Sr. Lectr.

Makalanda, G. S., BSc Vidyod., MSc Wales Sr. Lectr.

Siriwardane, M. K. N., BSc Ceyl., MSc Flin. Sr. Lectr.; Head*

Weerakoon, Sunethra, BSc Ceyl., MSc Penn., PhD Penn. Sr. Lectr.

Medicine, see below

Pali and Buddhist Studies, see also Langs. and Cultural Studies

Dhammadassi, Rev. N., BA Sri Jay., PhD Lanc. Sr. Lectr.

Moratuwagama, H. M., MPhil Kelaniya, BA Sr. Lectr.

Pannaloka, Rev. M., MA Sri Jay. Sr. Lectr.

Perera, G. A., MA Vidyod., PhD Sr. Lectr.; Head*

Wejebandara, C., BA Peradeniya, PhD Lanc. Assoc. Prof.

Wickramagamage, C., BA Vidyal., PhD Lanc. Sr. Prof. (on leave)

Wimalarathna, Rev. B., BA Vidyod., PhD Lanc. Assoc. Prof. (on leave)

Physics

Abeyratne, C. P. B., BSc PhD Sr. Lectr.

Gunawardena, A. U., BSc Colombo, PhD Louisiana Sr. Lectr.

Jayananda, M. K., BSc Colombo, PhD Sr. Lectr.

Nanayakkara, A. A., BSc Colombo, MS Ohio, PhD Iowa State

Peiris, M. G. C., BSc S.Lanka, MSc Sr. Lectr.

Ranathunga, C. L., BSc MPhil Sr. Lectr.

Tantrigoda, D. A., BSc Ceyl., PhD Durh. Prof.; Head*

Wijeratne, W. D. A. T., BSc Colombo, PhD Wash.State Sr. Lectr.

Public Administration

Ekanayaka, A., BA Vidyod., MPA Vidyod., MA Inst.Soc.Stud.(The Hague) Assoc. Prof. (on leave)

Fernando, H. A. C., MA Leuven Sr. Lectr.

Fernando, R. L. S., MA Manc., BSc(PubAdm) Sr. Lectr.

Herath, H. M. A., BPAdm Vidyod., MA Car., PhD Car. Sr. Lectr.; Head*

Hewapaththu Arachchige, B. J., PhD Well., BSc(PubAdm) Sr. Lectr.

Ramanayake, U. B., MA Leningrad, PhD Leningrad Sr. Lectr. (on leave)

Rathnasekara, B. Y. G., BSc(PubAdm) MCom Sr. Lectr.

Rupasingha, M. L., MA Thammasat, BSc(PubAdm) Sr. Lectr. (on leave)

Samaratunga, S. L. R., BPAdm Vidyod., MA Ott. Sr. Lectr. (on leave)

Weerasinghe, W. N. A. D. C., MA Punjab, BSc(PubAdm) Sr. Lectr.

Wijenayake, A. J., MBA Ott., BSc(PubAdm) Sr. Lectr. (on leave)

Sanskrit, see Langs. and Cultural Studies

Sinhala

Ariyarathne, S., BA Vidyod., PhD Prof.

Dissanayake, D. G., BA Sri Jay., MA Tokai Sr. Lectr.; Head*

Kariyawasam, T., BA Ceyl., MA Ceyl., PhD Lond. Sr. Prof.

Mallawaarachchi, U., BA Vidyod., PhD Paris Sr. Lectr. (on leave)

Wijeratne, M. W. W., BA Vidyod., PhD Sri Jay. Prof.

Wijetunga, R., BA Vidyod., MA Poona, PhD Cornell Prof.

Social Statistics

Herath, H. M. T. N. R., BA Sri Jay., MA Sri Jay. Sr. Lectr.

Jayatissa, W. A., BSc Vidyod., MA Manc., PhD Manc. Prof.

Silva, S. A. C. S., BA Vidyod., MSc Edin. Sr. Lectr.; Head*

Silva, S. K. R., BDevS Vidyod., MA Kent Sr. Lectr.

Wijayasiriwardane, A. M. M. J., BSc Vidyod., MStat I.Stat.I., MEc NE Sr. Lectr.

Sociology and Anthropology

Abayasundere, A. P. N. de S., BA Sri Jay., MA Sri Jay. Sr. Lectr.

Buddhadasa, M. P. A. A., MA Sr. Lectr.

Danapala, W. M., BA Sri Jay., MPhil Sri Jay. Sr. Lectr.

Ganihigama, E. K., BA Vidyod., MA Sr. Lectr.; Head*

Jayasiri, A. A. Jayantha, BA Sri Jay., MA Sri Jay. Sr. Lectr.

Jayasundara, M. W., MA S.Fraser, BA Sr. Lectr.

Perera, B. A. T., BA Vidyod., MA Sr. Lectr.

Perera, H. D. Y. Devika, MA Sri Jay., BA Sr. Lectr. (on leave)

Perera, Swarnalatha M. C., BA Vidyod., MA Sr. Lectr. (on leave)

Ratnapala, B. N., MA Ceyl., PhD Gött. Sr. Prof.

Statistics, see Soc. Stats.

Zoology

Attygala, Manel V. E., BSc Vidyod., PhD E.Anglia Sr. Lectr.

De Alwis, S. M. D. A. U., MSc Bergen, PhD Bergen Sr. Lectr.

De Silva, B. G. D. N. K., PhD Sri Jay., BSc Sr. Lectr. (on leave)

De Silva, K. N., BSc Colombo, PhD Louisiana Sr. Lectr.

Jinadasa, J., MSc Vidyod., PhD Mass. Prof.; Head*

Karunarathne, M. M. S. C., BSc Vidyod., PhD S'ton. Sr. Lectr.

Piyasiri, S., BSc Peradeniya, PhD Vienna Sr. Lectr.

MEDICINE

Anatomy

No staff at present

Biochemistry

Jansz, E. R., BSc *Ceyl.*, PhD *Dal.*   Prof.; Head*
Jayawardene, M. I. F. P., BSc *Ceyl.*, MSc *Ceyl.*, PhD *Ceyl.*   Sr. Lectr.
Peiris, Hemanthe, BVSc *Ceyl.*, MPhil *Ceyl.*, PhD *Qld.*   Sr. Lectr.
Wickramasinghe, S. M. D. N., BSc *Vidyod*, PhD *Maryland*   Sr. Lectr.

Community Medicine and Family Medicine

Perera, M. S. A., MB BS *Ceyl.*, MD *Ceyl.*   Sr. Lectr.
Sivayogan, S., MB BS *Ceyl.*, MD *Ceyl.*   Sr. Lectr.; Head*
Wickramasinghe, A. R., MB BS *Ceyl.*, MPH *Tulane*, PhD *Tulane*   Sr. Lectr.
Wijewardena, K. A. K. K., MB BS *Ceyl.*, MD *Ceyl.*   Prof.

Forensic Medicine

No staff at present

Medicine

Fernando, D. J. S., MB BS *Ceyl.*, MD *Ceyl.*   Prof.
Jayaratne, S. D., MB BS *Ceyl.*, MD *Ceyl.*   Sr. Lectr.; Head*
Kamaladasa, S. Dd., MB BS *Ceyl.*, MD *Ceyl.*   Sr. Lectr.
Wanigasuriya, J. K. P., MB BS *Ceyl.*, MD *Ceyl.*   Sr. Lectr.

Microbiology

Fernando, S., MB BS *Ceyl.*, MSc *Lond.*   Sr. Lectr.; Head*

Obstetrics and Gynaecology

Jayawardena, M. A. J., MB BS *Ceyl.*, MS *Ceyl.*   Prof.; Head*
Weerasekera, D. S., MB BS *Ceyl.*, MS *Ceyl.*, FRCSEd   Sr. Lectr.

Paediatrics

Samarage, D. K., MB BS *Ceyl.*, MD *Ceyl.*   Sr. Lectr.
Warnasuriya, N. D., MB BS *Ceyl.*, FRCP   Prof.; Head*

Parasitology

Ekanayake, S., BSc *Ceyl.*, MSc *Sri Jay.*, PhD *Georgia*   Sr. Lectr.; Head*
Wickramasinghe, D. R., PhD *Ceyl.*, BSc   Sr. Lectr.

Pathology

Wijesiriwardena, I. S., MB BS *Ceyl.*, MD *Ceyl.*   Sr. Lectr.
Withana, R. J., MB BS *Ceyl.*, MD *Ceyl.*   Prof.; Head*

Pharmacology

Fernando, G. H., MB BS *Ceyl.*   Prof.; Head*
Goonetillaka, A. K. E., MB BS *Ceyl.*, MD *Ceyl.*   Sr. Lectr.

Physiology

Jiffry, M. T. M., BDS *Ceyl.*, MMedSc *Ceyl.*, MSc *Lond.*   Prof.
Ruberu, D. K., MB BS *Ceyl.*   Sr. Lectr.; Head*

Psychiatry

Kathriarachchi, S. I., MB BS *Ceyl.*, MD *Ceyl.*   Sr. Lectr.; Head*

Surgery

De Silva, W. M. M., MB BS *Ceyl.*, MS *Ceyl.*, FRCSEd   Sr. Lectr.; Head*
Fernando, D. P. A., MB BS *Ceyl.*, FRCS, FRCSEd   Prof.

SPECIAL CENTRES, ETC

Management, Postgraduate Institute of

Gunapala, N. J., BSc(PubAdm) *Vidyod.*, PhD *Car.*   Dir.*

CONTACT OFFICERS

Academic affairs. Deputy Registrar: De Silva, D. C., BA *Peradeniya*
Accommodation. Assistant Registrar: Herath, W. B., BA *Peradeniya*
Admissions (first degree). Deputy Registrar: De Silva, D. C., BA *Peradeniya*
Admissions (higher degree). Deputy Registrar: De Silva, D. C., BA *Peradeniya*
Adult/continuing education. Senior Assistant Registrar: Muththettuwegedara, J., BA *Kelaniya*
Alumni. Deputy Registrar: De Silva, D. C., BA *Peradeniya*
Computing services. Co-ordinator: Makalande, G. S., BSc *Sri Jay.*, MSc *Wales*
Credit transfer. Bursar: Ranatunga, D. C., BSc
Development/fund-raising. Bursar: Ranatunga, D. C., BSc
Distance education. Senior Assistant Registrar: Muththettuwegedara, J., BA *Kelaniya*
Estates and buildings/works and services. Senior Assistant Registrar: Chandrathilake, D.
Examinations. Assistant Registrar: Hussain, W. H. R., BA *Sri Jay.*
Finance. Bursar: Ranatunga, D. C., BSc
General enquiries. Registrar: Abeywardene, M., BA *Ceyl.*
Health services. Ariyaratne, C. V., MB BS *S.Lanka*
International office. Deputy Registrar: De Silva, D. C., BA *Peradeniya*
Library (chief librarian). Acting Librarian: Vidanapathirana, P., BA *Peradeniya*, MLib *NSW*
Personnel/human resources. Assistant Registrar: Godagama, Dharma, BA *Sri Jay.*
; Deputy Registrar, Administration: Ranaweera, P.
; Assistant Registrar: Gunawardene, E.
Publications. Deputy Registrar: De Silva, D. C., BA *Peradeniya*
Purchasing. Senior Assistant Bursar: Kalubowila, K. A. D. U. P., BDevS *Sri Jay.*
Research. Deputy Registrar: De Silva, D. C., BA *Peradeniya*
Scholarships, awards, loans. Assistant Registrar: Herath, W. B., BA *Peradeniya*
Security. Chief Security Officer: Liyanage, P. R.
Sport and recreation. Director, Physical Education: Rodrigo, E. M. M. N., BA *Colombo*
Student welfare/counselling. Fernando, Prof. W. S., BSc *Ceyl.*, PhD *Leic.*
Students from other countries. Deputy Registrar: De Silva, D. C., BA *Peradeniya*

[*Information supplied by the institution as at 2 March 1998, and edited by the ACU*]

The table below shows which of the institutions indicated provide facilities for study and/or research in the subjects named. The table covers *broad subject areas* only: ie the individual subjects of specialisation in certain professional fields such as education, law, medicine or veterinary science, are not included. In the case of related subject areas which have been grouped together (eg Agronomy/Soil Science), it should be borne in mind that one or more of the subjects may be offered by the institution concerned.

	Buddhist and Pali	Colombo	Eastern	General Sir John K.D.A.	Jaffna	Kelaniya	Open	Peradeniya	Ruhuna	Sabaragamuwa
Accountancy/Accounting		U	U		U	UM			U	U
Agriculture/Agricultural Science			U		U			X	X	U
Agronomy/Soil Science			U		U			X	X	U
Animal Science			U		U			X	X	U
Arabic		U	U					M		
Archaeology						X		X		
Biology		X	X		M				X	
Botany/Plant Science		X	X		M	X		X	X	
Business/Commerce		X	U	U	M	UM		M	UM	U
Chemistry		X	U	U	M	X		X	X	U
Computer Science		X	U	U	M			M	U	U
Dentistry								M		
Economics		X	U	U	M	X	U	X	X	U
Education		X			M		X	M		
Engineering							X	M		
Agricultural							UD	X		
Chemical								M		
Civil				U			X	M		
Electrical/Electronic/Computer				U			UD	M		
Mechanical				U			X	M		
English	U	X	U		U	X	U	X		UM
Finance			U							U
Fine Arts			X		M	X				
Food Science/Nutrition						MD		X		U
Geography			U	U	X	X		X	X	U

TO SUBJECTS OF STUDY

For further information about the individual subjects taught at each institution, please refer to the *Index to Department Names* at the end of the Yearbook, but for full details about subjects/courses offered at universities in the Commonwealth each institution's own official publications must be consulted. U = may be studied for first degree course; M = may be studied for master's degree course; D = research facilities to doctoral level; X = all three levels (UMD). **Note**—the table only includes information provided by institutions currently in membership of the Association of Commonwealth Universities, submitted for this edition of the Yearbook.

	Buddhist and Pali	Colombo	Eastern	General Sir John K.D.A.	Jaffna	Kelaniya	Open	Peradeniya	Ruhuna	Sabaragamuwa
Geology								X		U
Hindi						UM				
History		X		U	M	X		X	X	
Horticulture					U					
Islamic Studies		U	U					M		
Journalism/Communication		U	U			X	U			
Law		X		U			U			
Library Science		M				UM				
Linguistics			U		M	X				
Management		X	U	U	M	X	U		UM	U
Mathematics		X	U	U	M	X		X	X	
Medicine/Surgery		X			U	X		X	X	
Philosophy	X		U		M	X		X		
Physics		X	U	U	M	X		X	X	U
Politics/Political Science		X	U		M			X	U	U
Religion/Theology	U		U		X					
Sinhala	UM	X				X		X	X	U
Sanskrit/Pali	UM				U	X		X	X	
Sociology		X	U		U	UM	UM	X	X	U
Statistics		X	U		U			M	UM	
Tamil			X		X			X		U
Textiles							UD			
Veterinary Science								X		
Zoology		X	U		M	X		X	X	

SWAZILAND

UNIVERSITY OF SWAZILAND

Founded 1982; previously University College of Swaziland, a constituent college of the University of Botswana and Swaziland (1976)

Member of the Association of Commonwealth Universities

Postal Address: Private Bag 4, Kwaluseni, Swaziland, Southern Africa
Telephone: 84011, 85108 **Fax**: 85276 **E-mail**: postmaster@uniswa.sz; postmaster@attic.alt.sz
Cables: Uniswa, Swaziland **Telex**: 2087 WD

CHANCELLOR—Mswati III, H.M. King
VICE-CHANCELLOR*—Makhubu, Prof. Lydia P., BSc S.Af., MSc Alta., PhD Tor., Hon. LLD Wales, Hon. LLD Qu., Hon. LLD St Mary's(Can.), Hon. DSc CNAA, Hon. LLD Bran.
PRO-VICE-CHANCELLOR—Dlamini, Barnabas M., BScAgric Philippines, MSc W.Virginia, PhD Ohio State
REGISTRAR‡—Vilakati, S. S., BA UBLS, MA Ball
LIBRARIAN—Mavuso, Makana R., BA UBLS, MLib Wales
ACTING BURSAR—Dlamini, P. M., BCom Swazi.

GENERAL INFORMATION

History. Founded in 1982, the university was formerly University College of Swaziland, a constituent college of the University of Botswana and Swaziland (founded 1976).

Admission to first degree courses. General Certificate of Education (GCE) O level with at least 6 passes (including English), obtained at no more than 2 sittings.

First Degrees. BA, BA(Law), BCom, BEd, BEng, BNSc, BSc, BSc(Agric), BSc(AgricEd), BSc(HomeEc), LLB.

Higher Degrees. MA (history), MEd, MSc (chemistry), MSc(AgEd), MSc(AgExt).

Libraries. 159,837 volumes; over 1500 journal titles.

Fees (1998–99, annual). Full-time undergraduate: home students E3900 (BA, BCom, BEd, LLB), E4200 (BEng, BSc, BSc(Agric), BSc(AgricEd), BSc(HomeEc)); international students E12,000 (BA, BCom, BEd, LLB), E12,300 (BEng, BSc, BSc(Agric)). Full-time postgraduate: home students E7500 (science), E5600 (other courses); international students E18,600 (science), E17,300 (other courses). Part-time undergraduate: E3000 (institute of distance education); E800 (division of extra-mural studies). Part-time postgraduate: home students E3900 (science), E2950 (other courses); international students E9200 (science), E8500 (other courses).

Academic Year (1998–99). Two semesters: 20 August–11 December; 6 January–23 April.

Income (1997). Total, E59,200,989.

Statistics (1997–98). Staff: 277 (255 academic, 22 administrative). Students: full-time 3023 (1547 men, 1476 women); part-time 405 (194 men, 211 women); international 162.

FACULTIES/SCHOOLS

Agriculture
Tel: 83021 Fax: 83021

Dean: Shongwe, Gideon N., BSc W.Illinois, MSc Guelph, PhD Ohio State
Secretary: Ndabandaba, G.

Commerce
Dean: Khan, Mohammed A., BCom Alig., MCom Alig., PhD Alig.
Secretary: Mamba, L.

Education
Dean: Mkatshwa, T. Daphne, BA UBLS, MA Ball, PhD Penn.
Secretary: Msibi, P

Health Sciences
Acting Dean: Mathunjwa, M. D., BSc New Orleans, MScEd Texas, MPH Texas
Secretary: Dlamini, P.

Humanities
Dean: Simelane, H. S., BA UBS, MA Ohio, PhD Tor.
Secretary: Kunene, T.

Postgraduate Studies
Dean: Kunene, Euphrasia C. L., BA UBLS, MA Calif., PhD Calif.
Secretary: Shongwe, S.

Science
Dean: Mtetwa, Victor S. B., BSc UBLS, DPhil Oxf.
Secretary: Simelane, K.

Social Science
Dean: Ngwisha, J. K., MA Fordham, PhD Brandeis
Secretary: Lokothwayo, P.

ACADEMIC UNITS

Accounting
Khan, Mohammed A., BCom Alig., MCom Alig., PhD Alig. Assoc. Prof.
Kyara, C. A., BA Dar. Lectr.; Head*
Other Staff: 4 Lectrs.

Administrative Studies, see Pol. and Admin. Studies

African Languages and Literature
Kamera, W. D., BA E.Af., MA Cornell, PhD Cornell Assoc. Prof.; Head*
Kunene, Euphrasia C. L., BA UBLS, MA Calif., PhD Calif. Assoc. Prof.
Nwabueze, P. E., BA Nigeria, MA E.Mich., PhD Bowling Green Sr. Lectr.
Other Staff: 3 Lectrs.

Agricultural Economics and Management
Tel: 83021 Fax: 83021

Ama, N. O., BSc Nigeria, MSc Nigeria, PhD Nigeria Sr. Lectr.
Dlamini, Phonias M., BSc Ghana, MSc Nair., PhD Manit. Sr. Lectr.; Head*
Kuhn, R. C., BSc Maryland, MSc Purdue, PhD Purdue Sr. Lectr.
Okorie, F. A., BSc Ib., MSc Cornell, PhD Ib. Prof.
Other Staff: 2 Lectrs.

Agricultural Education and Extension
Tel: 83021 Fax: 83021

Dlamini, Barnabas M., BScAgric Philippines, MSc W.Virginia, PhD Ohio State Assoc. Prof.
Keregero, K. Jackson B., BSc Dar., MSc Wis., PhD Wis. Assoc. Prof.
Mndebele, C. B., BSc W.Virginia, MA W.Virginia, MSc W.Virginia, PhD Virginia Tech. Sr. Lectr.; Head*
Teoh, C., BAgrSc Malaya, MS Philippines, PhD Cornell Sr. Lectr.
Other Staff: 3 Lectrs.

Animal Production and Health
Tel: 83021 Fax: 83021

Dlamini, B. J., BSc Oklahoma State, MSc New Mexico State, PhD Iowa State Lectr.; Head*
Khalifa, Mohammed Y., BSc Alexandria, MSc Tanta, DrDairying Hokkaido Assoc. Prof.
Kumar, B. A., MVSc Agra, BVSc Sr. Lectr.
Ocen, George W., BSc Mak., MSc Aberd. Sr. Lectr.
Other Staff: 4 Lectrs.

Biological Sciences
Karnavar, G. K., BSc Baroda, MSc Baroda, PhD Baroda Prof.
Kunene, I. S., BSc S.Leone, MSc Ib., PhD Texas A.&M. Lectr.; Head*
Nkosi, B. S., BSc UBS, MSc Lond., PhD Lond. Sr. Lectr.
Sesay, A., MSc Iowa State, PhD Iowa State, BScEd Assoc. Prof.
Other Staff: 5 Lectrs.

Business Administration
Joubert, P. N., BCom Swazi., MBA Wales Lectr.; Head*
Other Staff: 5 Lectrs.

Chemistry
Msonthi, J. D., BSc Malawi, PhD Sheff.,
FRSChem   Prof.; Head*
Mtetwa, Victor S. B., BSc UBLS, DPhil
Oxf.   Assoc. Prof.
Other Staff: 5 Lectrs.

Computer Science
Boateng, George K., BSc Lond., PhD Manc.   Sr.
Lectr.; Head*
Jaju, R. P., BSc Lucknow, MSc Lucknow, PhD
Agra   Assoc. Prof.
Other Staff: 3 Lectrs.

Crop Production
Tel: 83021 Fax: 83021
Dlamini, T. O., BSc Calif., MSc Calif.   Sr. Lectr.
Edje, O. T., BSc Mich., MSc Mich., PhD
Iowa   Prof.
Masina, G. T., BSc UBLS, MSc Missouri, PhD
Nair.   Sr. Lectr.
Shongwe, Gideon N., BSc W.Illinois, MSc Guelph,
PhD Ohio State   Sr. Lectr.; Head*
Tunya, G. O., BSc Bath, MSc Mississippi State, PhD
Ill.   Sr. Lectr.
Other Staff: 5 Lectrs.

Curriculum and Teaching
Mkatshwa, T. Daphne, BA UBLS, MA Ball, PhD
Penn.   Sr. Lectr.
Putsoa, E. Bongile, BEd UBLS, BSc S.Af., MA
Adel., DPhil York(UK)   Sr. Lectr.
Rugiireheh-Runaku, J. B. M., BA Mak., MA
Lond.   Sr. Lectr.
Zwane, S. E., BA UBLS, MA Col., MEd Col., EdD
Col.   Lectr.; Head*
Other Staff: 8 Lectrs.

Demography, see Stats. and Demog.

Economics
Elhiraika, A., MA Kent, PhD Glas., BSc   Sr.
Lectr.
Sithole, V. M., BA UBS, MSc Alta.   Lectr.;
Head*
Other Staff: 3 Lectrs.

Education, In-Service
Fax: 84011
Manyatsi, S. E., BSc UBS, MA Lond., PhD
Witw.   Lectr.; Head*
Other Staff: 4 Lectrs.

Education, Primary
Dlamini, Nester S., BA UBS, MEd Ohio, PhD
Ohio   Lectr.; Head*
Other Staff: 4 Lectrs.

Educational Foundations and Management
Adeyinka, A. A., BA Ib., MEd Ib., PhD
Wales   Prof.
Kaikai, C. M., BScEd S.Leone, MA Kent State, PhD
Kent State   Sr. Lectr.
Nxumalo, A. M., BEd UBLS, MA Southern
Nazarene, PhD Kansas   Lectr.; Head*
Other Staff: 3 Lectrs.

Engineering, Electronic, see Phys. and Electronic Engin.

English Language and Literature
Mogekwu, M. E., BA Wis., MA Mich., PhD
Indiana   Sr. Lectr.
Oyegoke, L., BA Ib., MA Ib., PhD Birm.   Sr.
Lectr.; Head*

French, see Mod. Langs.: French

Geography
Mushala, H. M., BA Dar., MA Dar., PhD
Clark   Assoc. Prof.
Simelane, N. O., BA UBLS, MA George
Washington, PhD Clark   Lectr.; Head*
Other Staff: 6 Lectrs.

History
Kanduza, A. M., BA(Ed) Zambia, MA Zambia,
PhD Dal.   Sr. Lectr.; Head*

Kaniki, M. H. Y., BA E.Af., MA Birm., PhD
Birm.   Assoc. Prof.
Sikhondze, B. A. B., BA UBLS, MA Manit., PhD
Lond.   Sr. Lectr.
Simelane, H. S., BA UBS, MA Ohio, PhD Tor.   ,
Sr. Lectr.
Other Staff: 2 Lectrs.

Home Economics
Fax: 83021
Keregero, Miriam M., MSc Wis., PhD Wis.   Sr.
Lectr.
Sibiya, T. E., BSc Tuskegee, MSc Tuskegee, PhD
Guelph   Lectr.; Head*
Other Staff: 4 Lectrs.

Land Use and Mechanisation
Fax: 83021
Manyatsi, A. M., BScAgric Swazi., MSc Cran.,
PhD James Cook   Lectr.; Head*
Mwendera, E. J., BSc Malawi, MSc Cran., PhD
Leuven   Sr. Lectr.
Nath, S., BSc(AgrEngg) Alld., MTech I.I.T., PhD
Kansas State   Sr. Lectr.
Other Staff: 2 Lectrs.

Law
Hlatshwayo, N. A., BA(Law) Swazi., LLB Swazi.,
LLM York(Can.)   Lectr.; Head*
McClain, William, BA Indiana, LLB Indiana, LLM
Lond.   Prof.
Okpaluba, M. C., LLB Lond., LLM Lond., PhD
WI   Prof.
Other Staff: 4 Lectrs.

Mathematics
Phiri, P. A., BSc Zambia, MSc Zambia, PhD
Leeds   Assoc. Prof.; Head*
Valov, Vesko M., MSc Sofia, PhD Sofia   Assoc.
Prof.
Other Staff: 4 Lectrs.

Modern Languages: French
Kockaert, H., BA Louvain, MA Louvain, PhD Rand
Afrikaans   Lectr.; Head*
Other Staff: 2 Lectrs.

Physics and Electronic Engineering
Dlamini, M. D., BSc UBS, MSc Lanc., PhD
Camb.   Sr. Lectr.; Head*
Varkey, A. J., BSc Kerala, MSc Ravi., PhD
Nigeria   Sr. Lectr.
Other Staff: 6 Lectrs.
Vacant Posts: 1 Prof.

Political and Administrative Studies
Dlamini, M. P., BA(Admin) UBLS, MPA Albany,
PhD Durh.   Sr. Lectr.
Magagula, P. Q., BA UBS, MA Dar., PhD
Durh.   Lectr.; Head*
Other Staff: 5 Lectrs.

Religious Studies, see Theol. and Religious Studies

Sociology
Khumalo, P. K., BA Swazi., MA Flin.   Lectr.;
Head*
Ngwisha, J. K., MA Fordham, PhD
Brandeis   Assoc. Prof.
Other Staff: 3 Lectrs.

Statistics and Demography
Sahai, Ashok, BA Lucknow, MA Lucknow, PhD
Lucknow   Prof.
Other Staff: 5 Lectrs.

Theology and Religious Studies
Gillies, F., MA Glas., DPhil Sus.   Prof.
Ndlovu, H. L., BA UBS, MA McCormick, MPhil
Trinity(Dub.), PhD McM.   Lectr.; Head*
Other Staff: 3 Lectrs.

SPECIAL CENTRES, ETC

Computer Centre
Vacant Posts: Manager*

Distance Education, Institute of
Magagula, M. C., BA UBS, BEd Bran., MEd
Manit., EdD Tor.   Dir.*
Other Staff: 3 Lectrs.

Extra-Mural Services, Division of
Mkhwanazi, Almon M., BA UBLS, MSEd
Penn.   Dir.*
Other Staff: 6 Lectrs.

CONTACT OFFICERS
Academic affairs. Assistant Registrar: Masuku,
Richard N., BA Swazi., MPM Carnegie-Mellon
Accommodation. Acting Dean of Student
Affairs: Kunene, M., BEd Swazi.
Admissions (first degree). Assistant Registrar:
Masuku, Richard N., BA Swazi., MPM Carnegie-
Mellon
Admissions (higher degree). Assistant
Registrar: Masuku, Richard N., BA Swazi.,
MPM Carnegie-Mellon
Adult/continuing education. Director,
Division of Extra-Mural Services:
Mkhwanazi, Almon M., BA UBLS, MSEd Penn.
Alumni. Staff Development Fellow: Mabuza,
Theresa P., BA Swazi., MEd Bran.
Careers. Staff Development Fellow: Mabuza,
Theresa P., BA Swazi., MEd Bran.
Computing services. Systems Analyst: Kunene,
Paul F., BSc George Washington, MA George
Washington
Consultancy services. Acting Bursar: Dlamini,
P. M., BCom Swazi.
Development/fund-raising. Acting Bursar:
Dlamini, P. M., BCom Swazi.
Distance education. Director: Magagula, Cisco
M., BA Swazi., BEd Bran., MEd Manit., EdD Tor.
Estates and buildings/works and services.
Physical Planner: ......
Examinations. Assistant Registrar: Masuku,
Richard N., BA Swazi., MPM Carnegie-Mellon
Finance. Acting Bursar: Dlamini, P. M., BCom
Swazi.
General enquiries. Registrar: Vilakati, S. S., BA
UBLS, MA Ball
Health services. Assistant Registrar: Nhlabatsi,
Lindiwe W., BA Swazi., MAM Bowie State
Industrial liaison. Registrar: Vilakati, S. S., BA
UBLS, MA Ball
International office. Acting Dean of Student
Affairs: Kunene, M., BEd Swazi.
Library (chief librarian). Librarian: Mavuso,
Makana R., BA UBLS, MLib Wales
Ombudsperson. Registrar: Vilakati, S. S., BA
UBLS, MA Ball
Personnel/human resources. Registrar:
Vilakati, S. S., BA UBLS, MA Ball
Public relations, information and marketing.
Registrar: Vilakati, S. S., BA UBLS, MA Ball
Publications. Pro-Vice-Chancellor: Dlamini,
Barnabas M., BScAgric Philippines, MSc
W.Virginia, PhD Ohio State
Purchasing. Acting Bursar: Dlamini, P. M.,
BCom Swazi., BA Swazi.
Quality assurance and accreditation. Vice-
Chancellor: Makhubu, Prof. Lydia P., BSc
S.Af., MSc Alta., PhD Tor., Hon. LLD Wales,
Hon. LLD Qu., Hon. LLD St Mary's(Can.),
Hon. DSc CNAA, Hon. LLD Bran.
Research. Pro-Vice-Chancellor: Dlamini,
Barnabas M., BScAgric Philippines, MSc
W.Virginia, PhD Ohio State
Safety. Assistant Registrar: Nhlabatsi, Lindiwe
W., BA Swazi., MAM Bowie State
Scholarships, awards, loans. Registrar:
Vilakati, S. S., BA UBLS, MA Ball
Schools liaison. Acting Dean of Student Affairs:
Kunene, M., BEd Swazi.
Security. Registrar: Vilakati, S. S., BA UBLS,
MA Ball
Sport and recreation. Acting Dean of Student
Affairs: Kunene, M., BEd Swazi.
Staff development and training. Registrar:
Vilakati, S. S., BA UBLS, MA Ball
Student welfare/counselling. Acting Dean of
Student Affairs: Kunene, M., BEd Swazi.
Students from other countries. Acting Dean
of Student Affairs: Kunene, M., BEd Swazi.

Students with disabilities. Acting Dean of Student Affairs: Kunene, M., BEd *Swazi*.

University press. Registrar: Vilakati, S. S., BA *UBLS*, MA *Ball*

CAMPUS/COLLEGE HEADS

Luyengo Campus, PO Luyengo, Swaziland, Southern Africa. (Tel: 83021-4; Fax: 83021) Dean: Shongwe, Gideon N., BSc *W.Illinois*, MSc *Guelph*, PhD *Ohio State*

Mbabane Campus, Box 369, Mbabane, Swaziland. (Tel: 40171, 46242; Fax: 46241.)

Acting Dean: Mathunjwa, M. D., BSc *New Orleans*, MScEd *Texas*, MPH *Texas*

Nazarene Nursing College, PO Box 14, Manzini, Swaziland. (Tel: 54636; Fax: 55077.) Principal: Mulengethwa, W. M., BSc *Boston*, MSc(Nursing) *Howard*

Nazarene Teacher Training College, PO Box 14, Manzini, Swaziland, Southern Africa. Principal: Mavuso, Z. M. , BSc *Swazi*.

Ngwane Teacher Training College, PO Box 474, Nhlangano, Swaziland, Southern Africa. (Tel: 78466; Fax: 78112.) Principal: Dlamini, P., BSc *Bridgewater(Va.)*, MEd *Ohio*

William Pitcher Training College, PO Box 87, Manzini, Swaziland, Southern Africa. (Tel: 52081 Fax: 54690.) Principal: Magagula, P., MEd *Ohio*

[Information supplied by the institution as at 29 July 1998, and edited by the ACU]

TANZANIA

University of Dar es Salaam (p. 1291)   Open University of Tanzania (p. 1296)
Sokoine University of Agriculture (p. 1297)

UNIVERSITY OF DAR ES SALAAM

Founded 1970; originally established as University College, Dar es Salaam, 1961

Member of the Association of Commonwealth Universities

Postal Address: PO Box 35091, Dar es Salaam, Tanzania
Telephone: (051) 410500-8 **Fax**: (051) 43078, 43023 **E-mail**: cado@udsm.ucc.gn.apc.org
Cables: University, Dar es Salaam **Telex**: 41561

CHANCELLOR—Bomani, H.E. Paul, MIPP *Johns H.*
CHAIRMAN OF THE COUNCIL—Kazaura, H.E. F. M.
VICE-CHANCELLOR*—Luhanga, Prof. Matthew L., BSc(Eng) *Calif.State Polytechnic*, MEng *Calif.State Polytechnic*, MPhil *Col.*, PhD *Col.*
CHIEF ACADEMIC OFFICER—Mlama, Prof. Penina O. P., BA(Ed) *Dar.*, MA *Dar.*, PhD *Dar.*
CHIEF ADMINISTRATIVE OFFICER‡—Mkude, Prof. Daniel J., BA *Dar.*, PhD *Lond.*
SECRETARY TO THE COUNCIL—Shundi, Fabia, BA *Lond.*
DIRECTOR, LIBRARY—Nawe, Julita, MA *Lond.*, PhD *Wales*

GENERAL INFORMATION

History. The university was previously founded as a college of the University of London in 1961. In 1963 it became a constitutent college of the University of East Africa. Independent uiversity status was gained in 1970.

Admission to first degree courses. Certificate of Secondary Education Examination (CSEE) or equivalent with passes in 5 approved subjects, and Advanced Certificate of Secondary Education Examination (ACSEE) or equivalent.

First Degrees. BA, BA(Ed), BArch, BCom, BEd, BPharm, BSc, DDS, LLB, MD.
   Most courses are full-time and last 3 to 4 years.

Higher Degrees. LLM, MA, MBA, MMed, MSc, PhD, LLD.

Libraries. 400,000 volumes; 2800 periodicals.

Fees (1998–99, annual). Undergraduate: Tanzanian students Tsh21,000–69,000; international US$4200. Postgraduate (master's): Tanzanian students Tsh290,000; international US$2000.

Academic Awards (1997–98). Awards amounting to total value of Tsh25,713,573.

Academic Year. Three or four terms (depending on faculty), or two semesters (University College of Lands and Architectural Studies): September–August.

Income (1977–98). Total £7,029,702.

Statistics. Staff: 2366 (902 academic, 1464 administrative). Students: 3901.

FACULTIES/SCHOOLS

Arts and Social Sciences
Tel: (051) 410500 Fax: (051) 43395
Dean: Mukandala, Prof. Rwekaza S., MA *Dar.*, PhD *Calif.*
Secretary: Bernard, Mary

Commerce and Management
Tel: (051) 410500 Fax: (051) 43395
Dean: Rutashobya, Lettice H. K., MA *Dar.*, PhD *Dar.*
Secretary: Ndyamukama, G.

Dentistry (Muhimbili University College of Health Sciences)
Tel: (051) 151367 Fax: (051) 151596
Dean: Lembariti, B. S., MSc *Dar.*, PhD *Dar.*, DMD *Semmelweis*
Secretary: Heri, A.

Education
Tel: (051) 410500 Fax: (051) 43016
Dean: Galabawa, J. C., BSc(Ed) *Dar.*, MA *Dar.*, MDS *Inst.Soc.Stud.(The Hague)*, PhD *Alta.*
Secretary: Salehe, Z.

Engineering
Tel: (051) 410500 Fax: (051) 43380
Dean: Masuha, Prof. John R., DrIng *Berlin*
Secretary: Mbotto, E.

Law
Tel: (051) 410500 Fax: (051) 43254
Dean: Mvungi, S. E., LLM *Dar.*, DrIur *Hamburg*

Medicine (Muhimbili University College of Health Sciences)
Tel: (051) 150302 Fax: (051) 151596
Dean: Mhalu, Prof. F. S., MB ChB *E.Af.*
Secretary: Maunmbo, H.

Nursing (Muhimbili University College of Health Sciences)
Tel: (051) 151367 Fax: (051) 151596
Dean: Kohi, Thecla W., BSc(Nursing) *Dal.*, MN *Dal.*
Secretary: Matangho, E.

Pharmacy (Muhimbili University College of Health Sciences)
Tel: (051) 150302 Fax: (051) 151596
Dean: Chambuso, M. H. S., BPharm *Dar.*, MSc *Aston*, DrRerNat *Tübingen*
Secretary: Appolo Tupa

Science
Dean: Nkunya, Prof. M. H. H., MSc *Dar.*, PhD *Dar.*
Secretary: Kulaba, B. S.

ACADEMIC UNITS

Accounting
Tel: (051) 43510
Kitindi, E., MBA *Leuven*, PhD *Vienna Bus.Admin.* Lectr.; Acting Head*

Adult Education and Extension
Tel: (051) 43649 Fax: (051) 43016
Mgulambwa, A. C., BA(Ed) *Dar.*, MA *Dar.*, PhD *Syr.* Sr. Lectr.
Mlekwa, V. M., BA(Ed) *Dar.*, MA *Dar.*, PhD *Alta.* Assoc. Prof.
Mushi, P. A. K., BA(Ed) *Dar.*, MA *Dar.*, PhD *S'ton.* Sr. Lectr.; Head*
Research: critical analysis of adult education; political democratization in Tanzania (a critical analysis of adult education); sustaining literacy and post-literacy in Tanzania

Botany
Tel: (051) 43129 Fax: (051) 43038
Elia, F., MSc *Dar.*, PhD Sr. Lectr.; Head*
Friedricks, J. M., MSc *Kentucky*, PhD *Virginia* Sr. Lectr.

Kivaisi, A. K., BSc Dar., MSc Stockholm, PhD Dar. Assoc. Prof.

Magingo, F. S. S., MSc Dar., PhD Dar. Sr. Lectr.

Mshigeni, K. E., BSc E.Af., PhD Hawaii Prof. (on leave)

Rubindamayugi, M. S. T., PhD Dar., MSc Sr. Lectr.

Rulangaranga, Z. K., MSc Dar., PhD Essex Sr. Lectr.

Semesi, A. K., BSc Dar., PhD Dar. Prof.

Strivastava, V., MSc Lucknow, PhD Lucknow Sr. Lectr.

Research: cultivation of edible mushrooms; marine science; minerals and amino acid composition of algae; rapid regeneration of endangered Tanzanian tree species; terrestrial vegetation ecology

Chemistry

Tel: (051) 410038 Fax: (051) 410039

Jonker, S., MSc Amst., PhD Amst. Sr. Lectr.

Kishimba, M., MSc Dar., PhD Dar. Sr. Lectr.

Lugwisha, E., BSc Dar., MSc E.Anglia, PhD E.Anglia Sr. Lectr.

Mbogo, S. A., MSc Aston, PhD Aston Sr. Lectr.

Mhehe, G., BSc S.Leone, MSc Alta., PhD Dar. Sr. Lectr.

Mhinzi, G. S., MSc Dar., PhD Salf. Sr. Lectr.

Mkayula, L. L., MSc Dar., PhD Salf. Sr. Lectr.; Head*

Mosha, D. M. S., BSc Dar., MSc Dar., PhD Liv. Assoc. Prof.

Mulokozi, A., MSc Munich, PhD Munich, DSc Dar. Prof.

Nkunya, M. H. H., MSc Dar., PhD Dar. Prof.

Othman, O. C., MSc Dar., PhD Dar. Sr. Lectr.

Tibanyenda, N., MSc Dar., PhD Dar. Sr. Lectr.

Research: application of semiochemicals in integrated pest management; chemical analysis of salt lakes; chemical studies of Tanzanian medicinal plants; solid state chemistry and catalysis

Communication Skills, see Foreign Langs. and Linguistics

Curriculum and Teaching

Tel: (051) 43649 Fax: (051) 43016

Chonjo, P. N., BSc(Ed) Dar., MA Dar., PhD S'ton. Sr. Lectr.; Head*

Clegg, A., MSc Oxf., DPhil Oxf.

Katunzi, N. B., MA Dar., PhD Calg. Sr. Lectr. (on leave)

Mahenge, S. T., MA Dar., MEd Alta., PhD Alta. Sr. Lectr.

Mbunda, F. L., BEd Alta., MA Dar., PhD Dar. Prof.

Osaki, K. M., BSc Dar., MA Lond., PhD Alta. Sr. Lectr.

Research: environmental education; evaluation of training programmes; social studies education and curriculum

Dentistry, see Muhimbili University College of Health Sciences

Development Studies, Institute of, see Special Centres, etc

Economic Research Bureau

Tel: (051) 43134 Fax: (051) 48461, 43395

Mabele, R. B. M., BA E.Af., MSc(AgrE) Tennessee, PhD Dar. Assoc. Res. Prof.

Maro, W. E., MSc Karl Marx, PhD T.U.Berlin Sr. Res. Fellow; Dir.*

Moshi, H. P. B., MA Dar., PhD Mün. Assoc. Res. Prof.

Msambichaka, L. A., BSc(Agric) Leip., MSc Leip., PhD Leip. Res. Prof.

Semboja, J. J., MA Dar., PhD Ill. Assoc. Res. Prof.

Tibaijuka, A. K., BSc Dar., MSc Uppsala, PhD Uppsala Assoc. Res. Prof.

Research: economic, cultural and social development of Tanzania and East Africa

Economics

Tel: (051) 43395 Fax: (051) 43395

Amani, H. R., MA Penn., PhD Mich. Assoc. Prof.

Bukuku, E. S. N., MA Dar., PhD Dar. Sr. Lectr. (on leave)

Kapunda, S., MA Tor., MA Dar., PhD Dar. Sr. Lectr.

Mbelle, A. V. Y., MA Dar., PhD Gothenburg Sr. Lectr.

Mtatifikolo, F. P. A., MA Kansas, PhD Kansas Sr. Lectr.

Osoro, E., MA Dar., MSc Ill., PhD Ill. Assoc. Prof.; Head*

Research: environmental economics; fiscal policy issues; industrial economics; macro/micro economic issues; monetary policy

Educational Foundations

Tel: (051) 43649 Fax: (051) 43016, 43395

Ishumi, A. G., BA E.Af., MAEd Harv., PhD Dar. Prof.

Komba, D., BA(Ed) Dar., MA Dar., PhD Col. Assoc. Prof.; Head*

Malekela, G. A., BA(Ed) Dar., MA Dar., PhD Chic. Assoc. Prof.

Puja, Grace K., MA Dar.

Research: appraisal of school-community relations; classroom interaction in primary schools; education in Tanzania; gender disparities in education in Tanzania

Educational Planning and Administration

Tel: (051) 43649 Fax: (051) 43016, 43395

Galabawa, J. C., BSc(Ed) Dar., MA Dar., MDS Inst.Soc.Stud.(The Hague), PhD Alta. Assoc. Prof.

Kiwia, S. N. F., BA(Ed) Dar., MA Brist., PhD Brist. Sr. Lectr.; Head*

Mosha, H. J., BA(Ed) Dar., MA Dar., PhD Alta. Prof.

Research: attitudes and strategies towards education in Tanzania; education in Tanzania; teacher quality and motivation

Educational Psychology

Tel: (051) 43649 Fax: (051) 43016, 43395

Biswalo, Paul M., BA Goshen, PhD Indiana Sr. Lectr.

Mbise, A. S., BA Dar., MA Col., PhD Alta. Assoc. Prof.

Possi, M. K., MA Dar., MA Ball, PhD Ohio State Sr. Lectr.; Head*

Research: childhood developmental milestones in Tanzania; decentralization of education and the role of education in Tanzania; youth educational research and evaluation

Engineering, Chemical and Processing

Tel: (051) 43753 Fax: (051) 43380, 43376

Halfani, M. R., MSc Tor., PhD Leeds Sr. Lectr.

Issangya, A. S., BSc Dar., MSc Leeds Sr. Lectr.

Katima, J., BSc(Eng) Dar., MPhilLough., PhD Leeds Assoc. Prof.

Masanja, MSc Dar., PhD Edin. Sr. Lectr.; Head*

Mbaga, J. P., BSc(Eng) Dar., MSc New Jersey I.T. Sr. Lectr. (on leave)

Migiro, C. L. C., MSc Dar., PhD Trondheim Assoc. Prof.

Mrema, G. D. E., MSc Dar., PhD Trondheim Sr. Lectr.

Sokol, W., MSc Lodz, PhD Gliwice Prof.

Research: bio-chemical and food engineering; environmental protection and hazardous waste treatment and control; extraction and development of natural products; utilization of agricultural and industrial waste

Engineering, Civil

Tel: (051) 43753 Fax: (051) 43380, 43376

Kachroo, R., BSc N.U.I., MSc N.U.I., PhD N.U.I. Assoc. Prof.

Kyulule, A. L., BSc Nair., MSc Zür., DrScTech Zür. Assoc. Prof.

Lema, N. M., BSc(Eng) Dar., MSc Lough. Sr. Lectr.

Lwambuka, L., DrIng Kassel Sr. Lectr.

Mashauri, D. A., MSc Tampere, PhD Tampere Assoc. Prof.; Head*

Mayo, A. W., MSc Dar., MSc Tampere, PhD Tohoku Assoc. Prof.

Mbwette, T. S. A., MSc Dar., PhD Lond. Assoc. Prof.

Mpinzire, S. R., PhD Warsaw Sr. Lectr.

Mrema, A. L., BSc Dar., MSc Strath., PhD Colorado State Sr. Lectr.

Mtalo, F. W., MSc Dar., DrIng Munich Assoc. Prof.

Mwamila, B. L. M., MSc Dar., PhD Stockholm Assoc. Prof.

Mwannzi, F. L. M., MSc Brussels, PhD Brussels Sr. Lectr.

Rwebangira, T., BSc Dar., MSc Birm., PhD Oregon Assoc. Prof.

Segu, W. P., BSc Nair., MSc Lond., PhD Lond. Sr. Lectr.

Research: construction management; highway transportation; hydraulics and water resources

Engineering, Electrical

Tel: (051) 43753 Fax: (051) 43380, 43376

Bagile, B. R. B., MSc Brad., PhD S'ton. Sr. Lectr.

Chambega, D., MSc Moscow, PhD Strath. Sr. Lectr.

Chitamu, P. J., MSc Sur. Sr. Lectr.

Kyaruzi, A. L., MSc Wash., DSc Wash. Sr. Lectr.

Luhanga, Mathew L., BSc Calif., ME Calif., PhD Col. Prof.

Materu, Peter N., BSc(Eng) Dar., MSc Manc., PhD Virginia Polytech. Prof.

Mgombelo, H. R., MSc Leningrad, PhD Brad. Prof.

Mvungi, N. H., MSc Salf., PhD Leeds Sr. Lectr.; Head*

Mwandosya, M. J., BSc Aston, PhD Birm. Prof.

Mwinyiwiwa, B. M. M., MEng McG., PhD McG. Sr. Lectr.

Nzali, A. H., BSc(Eng) Dar., MSc Aston, PhD Dar. Sr. Lectr.

Research: electrical machines and drives; electronics and telecommunications; high voltage and power; measurements and control engineering

Engineering, Mechanical

Tel: (051) 43753 Fax: (051) 43380, 43376

Bisanda, E. T. N., BSc(Eng) Dar., MEng Cran.IT, PhD Bath Assoc. Prof.

John, G. R., BSc Dar., MSc Leeds, PhD Leeds Sr. Lectr.

Kundi, B. A. T., MSc Wat., PhD Wat. Sr. Lectr.; Head*

Majaja, B. A. M., BSc Dar., MSc Calif., PhD Calif. Sr. Lectr.

Masuha, John R., DrIng Berlin Prof.

Mhilu, C. F., MSc Leningrad, PhD Leeds Sr. Lectr.

Mkilaha, I. S. N., MEng Toyohashi, PhD Tokyo Sr. Lectr.

Mshana, J. S., BSc Nair., MASc Ott., PhD Ott. Prof.

Mshoro, I. B., MSc(Eng) Latvia Sr. Lectr.

Mushi, E. M. J., MSc Leeds, PhD Leeds Sr. Lectr.

Mutagahywa, B. M., MSc Dar., PhD Lough. Assoc. Prof.

Nalitolela, N., BSc Dar., MSc Newcastle(UK), PhD Aston Sr. Lectr.

Nyichomba, B., BSc(Eng) Dar., MSc Birm., PhD Birm. Sr. Lectr.

Runyoro, J. J., BSc(Eng) Dar., MSc Cran.IT, PhD Birm. Sr. Lectr.

Tesha, J. V., BSc Dar., MSc Cran.IT Sr. Lectr.

Victor, M. A. M., BSc(Eng) Dar., MSc(Eng) Arizona State Sr. Lectr.

Research: design; energy technology; industrial and production management; materials technology; production engineering

English, see Foreign Langs. and Linguistics

Finance
Tel: (051) 43510

Kaijage, E. S., BA Dar., MBA Leuven, PhD
Sheff. Sr. Lectr.; Head*

Fine and Performing Arts
Tel: (051) 43395 Fax: (051) 43395

Hatar, A., BA Dar., MVA Alta.
Jengo, Elias, BSc Kent State, MA Sir
G.Wms. Assoc. Prof.
Lihamba, Amandina, BA Minn., MFA Yale, PhD
Leeds Prof.; Head*
Mbilinyi, D. Sr. Lectr.
Mlama, Penina O. P., BA(Ed) Dar., MA Dar.,
PhD Dar. Prof.
Research: children's theatre project and festival;
role of traditional media in learning for
change

Foreign Languages and Linguistics
Includes Communication Skills Unit

Tel: (051) 43395 Fax: (051) 43395

Maghway, J. B., MA Dar., MLitt Edin., PhD
Edin. Assoc. Prof., English
Numi, D. M., MA Lanc., PhD Lanc. Sr. Lectr.
Rubagumya, C. M., BA Dar., MA Lanc., PhD
Lanc. Sr. Lectr.; Head*
Rugemalira, J., BA Dar., MA Lanc.., PhD
Calif. Sr. Lectr.
Swilla, I. N., BA Dar., MA Paris IV, PhD
Laval Sr. Lectr., French
Yahya-Othman, S., BA Dar., MA Dar., MA
York(UK), PhD Dar. Sr. Lectr., English
Research: Languages in Contact and in Conflict
in Africa (LICCA); linguistic and cultural
atlas of Tanzania

French, see Foreign Langs. and Linguistics

Geography
Tel: (051) 43395 Fax: (051) 43395

Mbonile, M. J., BA(Ed) Dar., MPhil Cairo, PhD
Liv. Sr. Lectr.; Head*
Misana, Salome B., MA Dar., PhD
Colorado Assoc. Prof.
Rugumamu, W., MSc Reading, MA Dar., PhD
Dar. Assoc. Prof.
Sawio, Fr. C. J., MA N.Y.State, MRP N.Y.State,
PhD Clark Sr. Lectr.
Research: fruit and vegetable marketing in Dar es
Salaam; village land management for
resource conservation in selected villages in
Tanzania

Geology
Tel: (051) 43129 Fax: (051) 43038

Ikingura, J. R., MSc Car., PhD Car. Sr. Lectr.
Kaaya, C. Z., BSc Dar., MSc Dar., DrRerNat
Cologne Sr. Lectr.
Kapilima, S., BSc Dar., MSc Ife, PhD Berl. Sr.
Lectr.
Kinabo, C. P., BSc Lond., DrIng Clausthal Sr.
Lectr.
Maboko, M. A. H., MSc Dar., PhD
Canberra Assoc. Prof.
Malisa, E. J. S., BSc Dar., MSc Ife, PhD
Helsinki Sr. Lectr.
Marobhe, I., MSc Lond., PhD Helsinki Sr. Lectr.
Mbede, E. I., MSc Lond., PhD T.U.Berlin Sr.
Lectr.
Mruma, A. H., MSc Dar., PhD Dar. Sr. Lectr.
Mtakyahwa, M. D., MSc Hamburg, DrRerNat
Hamburg Sr. Lectr.
Muhongo, S., PhD T.U.Berlin, MSc Assoc.
Prof.; Head*
Research: environmental aspects of mining and
industrialization in Tanzania

History
Tel: (051) 410397 Fax: (051) 410395

Chami, F., MA Brown, PhD Uppsala Sr. Lectr.
Kaijage, F. J., BA E.Af., MA Warw., PhD
Warw. Assoc. Prof.
Kimambo, I. N., BA Pacific Lutheran, MA
Northwestern, PhD Northwestern Prof.

Luanda, N. N., MA Dar., PhD Camb. Sr. Lectr.;
Head*
Mlahagwa, J. R., BA E.Af., MA Dar., PhD
Dar. Assoc. Prof.
Tambila, K. I., BA Dar., MA Dar., PhD
Hamburg Assoc. Prof.
Wamba, E., BA Mich., MA Claremont Assoc.
Prof.
Research: history of the University of Dar es
Salaam

Kiswahili, see also Special Centres, etc
Tel: (051) 410500

Besha, Ruth M., BA York(UK), MA Dar., PhD
Dar. Prof.
Kahigi, K. K., MA Dar., PhD Mich.State Sr.
Lectr.
Kezilahabi, E., BA E.Af., MA Dar., PhD
Wis. Assoc. Prof. (on leave)
Madumulla, J. S., MA Leip., PhD Leip. Sr. Lectr.
Mekacha, R. D. K., MA Dar., DPhil Bayreuth Sr.
Lectr.; Head*
Mkude, Rev. Daniel J., BA Dar., PhD
Lond. Prof.
Mochiwa, Z., MA Dar., PhD Ill. Sr. Lectr.
Rubanza, Y. I., MA Dar., PhD Mich.State Sr.
Lectr.
Senkoro, F. E. M. K., MA Alta., MA
Dar. Assoc. Prof.

Law, Constitutional and Administrative
Tel: (051) 48336

Mapunda, A. M., LLM Dar., PhD Warw. Sr.
Lectr.
Mwaikusa, J., LLB Dar., LLM Birm., PhD
Lond. Sr. Lectr.; Head*
Rwezaura, B. A., LLB Mak., LLM Harv., PhD
Warw. Prof. (on leave)
Shivji, LLM Lond., PhD Dar. Prof.

Law, Criminal and Civil
Tel: (051) 48336

Migiro, Rose A., LLM Dar., DrJur Constance Sr.
Lectr.
Wambali, M. K., LLM Dar. Sr. Lectr.; Head*

Law, Economic
Tel: (051) 48336

Gondwe, Z. S., LLM Wis., LLM Dar., SJD
Wis. Assoc. Prof. (on leave)
Kanywanyi, J. L., LLB E.Af., LLM Calif., PhD
Dar. Assoc. Prof.
Luoga, F. D., LLB Dar., LLM Qu. Sr. Lectr.
Mapunda, A. M., LLM Dar., PhD Warw. Sr.
Lectr.; Head*
Mgongo-Fimbo, G., LLB Dar., LLM Lond., PhD
Dar. Assoc. Prof.
Mihyo, P. B., LLM Dar., PhD Dar. Assoc. Prof.
(on leave)
Nditi, N. N. N., LLM Dar., PhD Dar. Sr. Lectr.

Law, International
Tel: (051) 410500

Mahalu, C. R., LLM Dar., DrJur Hamburg Prof.
(on leave)
Mwakyembe, H. G., LLM Dar., LLM Hamburg,
DrIur Hamburg Lectr.; Head*
Peter, C. M., LLM Dar., DrJur Constance Assoc.
Prof.

Legal Theory
Tel: (051) 48336

Mukoyogo, M. C., LLM Dar., DrJur
Constance Sr. Lectr.
Shivji, I. G., LLB E.Af., LLM Lond., PhD
Dar. Prof.
Tenga, R. W., LLM Cornell, LLM Dar., JSD
Cornell Sr. Lectr.
Twaib, F., DrJur Bayreuth, LLM Asst. Lectr.;
Head*

Linguistics, see Foreign Langs. and
Linguistics

Literature
Tel: (051) 43395 Fax: (051) 43395

Mbise, I. R., MA York(Can.), PhD York(Can.) Sr.
Lectr. (on leave)
Njozi, H., MA Dar., PhD Lectr.; Head*

Management, General
Tel: (051) 43510

Katunzi, J. M., MBA Arizona, PhD Lond. Lectr.;
Head*
Saleh, M. I., MSc Prague, PhD Prague Sr. Lectr.
(on leave)
Splettstoesser, D., MBA Cologne, DrRerOec
Linz Sr. Lectr.

Marine Biology, see Zool. and Marine Biol.

Marine Sciences, Institute of, see Special
Centres, etc

Marketing
Tel: (051) 43510

Komba, L. C., MBA Leuven, PhD
Augsburg Lectr.; Head*
Marandu, E. E., BA Dar., MBA Arizona, PhD
Trinity(Dub.) Assoc. Prof.
Okoso-Amaa, K., MSc Helsinki, MSc Moscow, PhD
Uppsala Assoc. Prof.
Rutashobya, Lettice H. K., MA Dar., PhD
Dar. Assoc. Prof.

Mathematics
Tel: (051) 43129 Fax: (051) 43038

Klaasen, G., BA Mich., PhD Nebraska Prof.
Manja, B. A., MSc Dar., PhD E.Anglia Sr. Lectr.
Masanja, V. G., MSc Dar., PhD Berl., DrIng
T.U.Berlin Sr. Lectr.; Head*
Masenge, R. W. P., MSc Oxf., PhD Dar. Prof.
Massawe, E. S., MSc Trinity(Dub.), PhD
Trinity(Dub.) Sr. Lectr.
Mshimba, A. S. A., DrRerNat Halle Prof.
Shayo, L. K., MSc Dar., PhD Lond. Assoc. Prof.

Medicine, see Muhimbili University College
of Health Sciences

Nursing, see Muhimbili University College of
Health Sciences

Performing Arts, see Fine and Performing
Arts

Pharmacy, see Muhimbili University College
of Health Sciences

Physical Education, Sport and Culture
Tel: (051) 43649 Fax: (051) 43016

Kirimbai, R. W., BSc(Ed) E.Af., MSP Leip., MSc
Dar.
Stallman, R. K., MSc Ill., PhD Ill. Prof.; Head*

Physics
Tel: (051) 43129 Fax: (051) 43038

Bilal, M. G., BSc Howard, MA Calif., PhD
Calif. Sr. Lectr. (on leave)
Kainkwa, R. M. R., MSc Dar., PhD Dar. Sr.
Lectr.
Kashinje, S. P., MSc Dar., PhD Dar. Sr. Lectr.
Kivaisi, R. T., MSc Dar., PhD Stockholm Assoc.
Prof.
Kiwanga, C. A., MSc Lanc., PhD Lanc. Sr. Lectr.
Kololeni, Y. I., MSc Dar. Sr. Lectr.
Kondoro, J. W. A., BSc Dar., MSc Flor., PhD
Saar Sr. Lectr.
Kundaeli, H. N., PhD Dar., MSc Sr. Lectr.
Lushiku, E. M., MSc Dar., PhD Dar. Assoc.
Prof.
Makundi, I. N., MSc Dar., PhD Tokyo Sr. Lectr.
Njau, E. C., MSc Dar., PhD La Trobe Prof.;
Head*
Uiso, C. B. S., MSc Dar., PhD Dar. Sr. Lectr.

Political Science and Public Administration

Tel: (051) 43130 Fax: (051) 43395

Baregu, M. L., BA *Brock*, MA *Dar.*, PhD *Stan.* Prof.

Chaligha, A. E., MA *Dar.*, MPA *S.Calif.*, PhD *Claremont* Sr. Lectr.

Kente, M. G., MA *Villanova*, PhD *Duquesne* Sr. Lectr.

Kiondo, A. S., MA *Dar.*, PhD *Tor.* Assoc. Prof.; Head*

Liviga, A. J., MA *Dar.*, PhD *Pitt.* Sr. Lectr.

Meena, Ruth, MA *Dar.* Sr. Lectr.

Mhina, A. K., MA *Dar.*, PhD *Pau* Sr. Lectr.

Mmuya, M., BA(Ed) *Dar.*, MSc *Bath*, PhD *Missouri* Sr. Lectr.

Mukandala, Rwekaza S., MA *Dar.*, PhD *Calif.* Prof.

Mukangara, D. R., MA *Dar.*, PhD *ANU* Sr. Lectr.

Munishi, Gasper K. K., MA *Dar.*, PhD *Wis.* Prof.

Mushi, S. S., BA *Lond.*, MA *Calif.*, PhD *Yale* Prof.

Nyirabu, M., BA *Goshen*, MA *Kent State*, PhD *Kent State* Sr. Lectr.

Research: Research on Education for Democracy in Tanzania (REDET)

Sociology

Tel: (051) 43395 Fax: (051) 43395

Chachage, C. S. L., MA *Dar.*, PhD *Glas.* Assoc. Prof.

Comoro, C. J. B., MA *Dar.*, PhD *Car.* Sr. Lectr.; Head*

Lugalla, J. P., MA *Dar.*, PhD *Bremen* Sr. Lectr. (on leave)

Maghimbi, S., MA *Dar.*, MSc *Lond.*, PhD *Lond.* Assoc. Prof.

Masanja, P., BA *Dar.*, MA *Paris*, PhD *Hull* Sr. Lectr.

Mesaki, B. A., BA *Dar.*, MA *Dar.*, PhD *Minn.* Sr. Lectr.

Musoke, I. K. S., BA *Dar.*., MA *Dar.*, PhD *Mich.* Sr. Lectr.

Omari, Cuthbert K., BD *Rock I.*, STM *N.Y.*, PhD *E.Af.* Prof.

Sivalon, J. B. A., MA *Maryknoll*, MA *Dar.*, MDV *Maryknoll*, PhD *St M.Coll.Tor.* Sr. Lectr.

Tungaraza, F., MA *Dar.*, DrRerPol *Augsburg* Sr. Lectr.

Statistics

Tel: (051) 43395 Fax: (051) 43395

Kamuzora, C. L. A., MA *Penn.*, MA *Dar.*, PhD *Penn.* Prof.

Katapa, Rosalin S., BSc *Dar.*, MA *Car.*, MA *Dar.*, PhD *Tor.* Assoc. Prof.

Mbago, M. C. Y., MA *Dar.*, PhD *Liv.* Assoc. Prof.

Naimani, G. M., MA *Dar.*, PhD *Dar.* Sr. Lectr.; Head*

Rugaimukamu, D. B. M., MA *Dar.*, MSc *S'ton.*, PhD *S'ton.* Sr. Lectr.

Sichona, F. J., MA *Dar.*, PhD *N.Carolina State* Sr. Lectr.

Zoology and Marine Biology

Tel: (051) 43129 Fax: (051) 43038

Howell, K. M., BSc *Cornell*, PhD *Dar.* Prof.

Kasigwa, P. F., MSc *Dar.*, DPhil *Sus.* Sr. Lectr.

Kayumbo, H. Y., MSc *Lond.*, PhD *Dar.* Prof.

Mgaya, Y. D., MSc *Br.Col.*, PhD *N.U.I.* Sr. Lectr.

Nikundiwe, Alfeo M., BSc *Andrews*, MSc *Mich.*, PhD *Mich.* Assoc. Prof. (on leave)

Pratap, H. B., MSc *Gujar.*, PhD *Dar.* Sr. Lectr.

Senzota, R. B. M., MSc *Dar.*, PhD *Texas A.&M.* Assoc. Prof.

Urasa, F. M., MSc *Dar.*, PhD *Dar.* Sr. Lectr.; Head*

Wagner, G. M., MSc *Dar.*, PhD *Dar.* Sr. Lectr.

Yarro, J. G., MSc *Dar.*, PhD *Dar.* Sr. Lectr.

SPECIAL CENTRES, ETC

Computing Centre

Tel: (051) 410500 Fax: (051) 43380, 43376

Koda, G. R., MSc *Dar.*, MSc *Car.* Sr. Lectr.

Mutagahywa, B. M., MSc *Dar.*, PhD *Lough.* Dir.*

Twaakyondo, H. M., MEng *Shinshu*, PhD *Shinshu* Sr. Lectr.

Development Studies, Institute of

Tel: (051) 410500 Fax: (051) 43258, 43016, 43393

Chambua, S. E., MA *Car.*, MA *Dar.*, PhD *Car.* Sr. Lectr.

Halfani, M. S., MA *Dar.*, PhD *Tor.* Sr. Lectr. (on leave)

Koda, Bertha, MA *Dar.* Sr. Lectr. (on leave)

Kweka, A. N., PhD *Dar.* Assoc. Prof.

Mbilinyi, Marjorie, BSc *Cornell*, MA *Stan.*, PhD *Dar.* Prof.

Mlawa, H., MA *Dar.*, DPhil *Sus.* Prof.

Mongula, B. S., MA *Car.*, MA *Dar.* Sr. Lectr.

Mpangala, G., BA *Dar.*, MA *Dar.*, PhD *Leip.* Assoc. Prof.

Ngaiza, Magdalena K., MA *Dar.*, MLS *Lough.* Sr. Lectr. (on leave)

Ngware, S. S., MA *Dar.*, MA *Minn.*, PhD *Minn.* Assoc. Prof.

Nkonoki, S. R., BEd *E.Af.*, MA *Leeds*, PhD *Dar.* Prof.

Othman, H. M., LLM *Moscow*, PhD *Dar.* Prof.

Rugumamu, S. M., MA *Dar.*, MA *Maryland*, PhD *Maryland* Prof.

Shao, I., MA *Dar.*, PhD *Dar.* Assoc. Prof.; Dir.*

Kiswahili Research, Institute of

Tel: (051) 43757

Khamis, A. M., BA *E.Af.*, MPhil *York(UK)*, PhD *Hawaii* Res. Prof.

Massamba, D. P. B., BA(Ed) *Dar.*, MA *Dar.*, MA *Indiana*, PhD *Indiana* Assoc. Res. Prof.

Mdee, J. S., MA *Dar.*, PhD *Leip.* Assoc. Prof.

Mlacha, S. A. K., MA *Moscow*, PhD *Lond.* Assoc. Res. Prof.; Dir.*

Mulokozi, M. M., BA *Dar.*, PhD *Dar.* Assoc. Res. Prof.

Mwansoko, H. J. M., MA *Moscow*, DPhil *York(UK)* Assoc. Res. Prof.

Marine Sciences, Institute of

Tel: (054) 30741, 32128 Fax: (054) 33050

Francis, J., BSc *Dar.*, PhD *Flin.* Res. Fellow; Acting Dir.*

Production Innovation, Institute of

Tel: (051) 43376 Fax: (051) 43376

Kaunde, O., MSc *Leeds*, PhD *Leeds*

Research: cassava project; food processing technology; mining and mineral processing technology; sugar project

Resource Assessment, Institute of

Tel: (051) 43393 Fax: (051) 43393

Kauzeni, A. S., MSc *W.Virginia*, PhD *Dar.* Prof.

Kikula, Idris S., MSc *Dar.*, PhD *Griff.* Prof.

Mujwahuzi, M. R., BA *E.Af.*, MA *Clark*, PhD *Clark* Assoc. Prof.

Mwalyosi, R. B. B., MSc *Dar.*, PhD *Agric.Coll.Norway* Assoc. Prof.

Shishira, E. K., MSc *Sheff.*, PhD *Sheff.* Sr. Res. Fellow; Dir.*

Research: man–land interrelations

MUHIMBILI UNIVERSITY COLLEGE OF HEALTH SCIENCES

DENTISTRY

Tel: (051) 151367 Fax: (051) 151596

Oral Surgery and Pathology

Shubi, F. M., DDS *Inst.Med.Moscow*, PhD *Inst.Med.Moscow*, MD *Donets Inst.Med.* Lectr.; Head*

Preventive and Community Dentistry

Tel: (051) 151367, 46163

Hiza, J. R., MD *Leningrad* Sr. Lectr.

Mabelya, L., MD *Moscow*, MSc *Lond.* Sr. Lectr.; Head*

Nyandindi, U., MDent *Dar.*, PhD *Dar.* Sr. Lectr.

Restorative Dentistry

Tel: (051) 151367, 46163

Lembariti, B. S., MSc *Dar.*, PhD *Dar.*, DMD *Semmelweis* Assoc. Prof.

Nyerere, J. W., MDent *Dar.*, DDS *Dar.* Lectr.; Head*

MEDICINE

Tel: (051) 150302, 46163 Fax: (051) 151596

Anaesthesiology

Tel: (051) 151367, 46163

Matekere, N. J., MB ChB *E.Af.*, MMed *Dar.* Sr. Lectr.

Mwafongo, V. V., MD *Dar.*, MMed *Dar.* Sr. Lectr.; Head*

Anatomy and Histology

Tel: (051) 151367, 46163

Magori, C. C., MD *Dar.*, PhD *Lond.* Assoc. Prof.

Mtui, E. P. J., MMed *N.U.I.*, MD *Dar.* Assoc. Prof.

Ngassapa, D., DSc *Kuopio*, DDS *Timisoara*, MSc *Nijmegen* Assoc. Prof.; Head*

Biochemistry

Tel: (051) 151367, 46163

Jahazi, B. L., MSc *Jerusalem*, MD *Dar.*, PhD *Chic.* Sr. Lectr.

Nyambo, T. B. N., MSc *Brussels*, MD *Dar.* Lectr.; Head*

Chemistry, Clinical

Tel: (051) 151367, 46163

Chuwa, L. M., MSc *Sur.*, MD *Dar.* Sr. Lectr.

Kabyemela, E. A. R., MD *Dar.*, MSc *Dar.* Asst. Lectr.; Acting Head*

Haematology and Blood Transfusion

Tel: (051) 151367, 46163

Magesa, P. M., MD *Dar.*, MMed *Dar.* Sr. Lectr.; Head*

Histopathology and Morbid Anatomy

Tel: (051) 151367, 46163

Kaaya, E. E., MSc *Dar.*, PhD *Karolinska* Sr. Lectr.

Kitinya, J. N., MB ChB *E.Af.*, MMed *Dar.*, PhD *Kyushu* Prof.; Head*

Mgaya, E. M., MD *Dar.*, MMed *Dar.*, MSc *Dar.* Sr. Lectr.

Mwakyoma, H. A., MD *Dar.*, MSc *Dar.* Sr. Lectr.

Medicine, Internal

Tel: (051) 151367, 46163

Lwakatare, J. M., MB ChB *E.Af.* Sr. Lectr.

Maro, E. E., MD *Dar.*, MMed *Dar.* Sr. Lectr.

Matuja, W. B. M., MB ChB *E.Af.* Assoc. Prof.; Head*

Mtulia, I. A. T., MB ChB *E.Af.*, MMed *Dar.* Assoc. Prof. (on leave)

Mugusi, F. S., MMed *Dar.*, MD *Dar.* Sr. Lectr.

Mwakyusa, D. H., MB ChB *E.Af.*, MMed *Dar.* Prof.

Pallangyo, K. J., MD *Dar.*, MMed *Dar.* Prof.

Swai, A. B., MD *Dar.*, MMed *Dar.* Prof.

Medicine, Traditional, Institute of, see

Special Centres, etc

Microbiology/Immunology

Tel: (051) 151367, 46163

Lyamuya, E. F., MD *Dar.*, MMed *Dar.* Sr. Lectr.

Maselle, S. Y., MB ChB *E.Af.* Prof.

Matee, M. I., DDS *Dar.*, MSc *Dar.*, PhD *Dar.* Sr. Lectr.

Mhalu, F. S., MB ChB *E.Af.* Prof.

Mwakagile, D. S. M., MD *Dar.*, MMed *Dar.* Sr. Lectr.; Head*

Shao, J. F., MSc *Brun.*, MD *Dar.* Prof. (on leave)

Obstetrics/Gynaecology

Tel: (051) 151367, 46163

Kilewo, C. D. S., MMed *Dar.*, MD Sr. Lectr.

Massawe, S. N., MD *Dar.*, MMed *Dar.*, MEd *Manc.* Sr. Lectr.

Mgaya, Hans N., MB ChB *E.Af.*, MMed *Dar.* Prof.

Ngwale, K. E. W., MD *Dar.*, MMed *Dar.* Sr. Lectr.

Urassa, E. N., MD *Dar.*, MMed *Dar.* Assoc. Prof.; Head*

Ophthalmology

Tel: (051) 151367, 46163

Kinabo, N. N., MB BS *Agra*, MMed *Dar.* Assoc. Prof.

Masesa, D. E., MB ChB *E.Af.*, MSc *Dar.* Sr. Lectr.; Head*

Sangawe, J. L., MB ChB *E.Af.*, MD *All India IMS* Prof.

Orthopaedics and Trauma

Tel: (051) 151367, 46163

Kahamba, J. F., MMed *Dar.*, MD Sr. Lectr.

Kessi, E. M., MSc *Dar.*, MD *Dar.*, MMed *Dar.* Sr. Lectr. (on leave)

Mhina, R. I., MMed *Dar.*, MSc *Dar.* Sr. Lectr.

Museru, L. M., MSc *Dar.*, MD *Dar.*, MMed *Dar.* Sr. Lectr.; Head*

Otorhinolaryngology

Tel: (051) 151367, 46163

Minja, B. M., MB ChB *E.Af.*, MMed *Dar.*, MSc *Dar.* Assoc. Prof.

Moshi, N. H., MD *Dar.*, MMed *Dar.*, MSc *Dar.* Sr. Lectr.; Head*

Ole-Lengine, L., MMed *Dar.*, MSc *Dar.* Sr. Lectr.

Paediatrics and Child Health

Tel: (051) 151367, 46163

Kalokola, F. M., MD *Dar.*, MMed *Dar.* Sr. Lectr.; Head*

Manji, K. P., MMed *Dar.* Sr. Lectr.

Massawe, A. W., MD *Dar.*, MMed *Dar.* Sr. Lectr.

Mbise, R. L., MB ChB *E.Af.*, MMed *Dar.*, MSc *Dar.* Assoc. Prof.

Msengi, A. E., MD *Dar.*, MMed *Dar.* Assoc. Prof.

Mwaikambo, Esther, MMed *Dar.*, MD *P.F.U.*, *Moscow* Assoc. Prof.

Pharmacology, Clinical

Tel: (051) 151367, 46163

Jande, M. B., BPharm *Dar.*, MSc *Manc.*, PhD *Trinity(Dub.)* Sr. Lectr.

Kongola, G. W., MMed *Dar.*, MSc *Manc.*, PhD *Manc.* Assoc. Prof.

Maselle, A. Y., MD *Dar.*, MSc *Brad.*, PhD *Brad.* Assoc. Prof.; Head*

Mwaluko, G. M. P., MB ChB *E.Af.*, MSc *Manc.*, PhD *Manc.* Assoc. Prof. (on leave)

Sayi, J., MD *Dar.*, PhD *N.U.I.* Sr. Lectr.

Physiology

Tel: (051) 151367, 46163

Masesa, Z. E., MB ChB *E.Af.*, PhD *Lond.* Sr. Lectr.; Head*

Mashalla, Y. J. S., MD *Dar.*, PhD *Dar.* Sr. Lectr.

Mtabaji, J. P., MB ChB *E.Af.*, PhD *Newcastle(UK)* Prof.

Ntongwisangu, J. H., MB ChB *E.Af.*, PhD *Leeds* Sr. Lectr.

Psychiatry

Tel: (051) 151367, 46163

Hogan, M., MPhil *York*, PsyD *Chic.* Sr. Lectr.

Kaaya, Sylvia F., MD *Dar.*, MSc *Manc.* Sr. Lectr.; Head*

Kilonzo, Gad P., MB ChB *E.Af.*, MMed *Dar.*, MD *Br.Col.*, FRCPCan Assoc. Prof.

Mbatia, J., MD *Dar.*, MSc *Manc.* Sr. Lectr.

Sangiwa, M. G., MD *Dar.* Sr. Lectr.

Public Health, Institute of, see Special Centres, etc

Radiology

Tel: (051) 151367, 46163

Gabone, J. A., MD *Dar.*, MMed *Nair.* Lectr.; Head*

Kazema, R. R., MD *Dar.*, MMed *Nair.* Sr. Lectr.

Surgery

Tel: (051) 151367, 46163

Abond, M., MD *Dar.*, MMed *Dar.* Sr. Lectr.

Aziz, M. R., MD *Dar.*, MMed *Dar.* Sr. Lectr.

Carneiro, P., MD *Dar.*, MMed *Dar.* Assoc. Prof.

Hassan Amir, MB BS *Kashmir* Assoc. Prof.

Kisanga, R. E., MB ChB *E.Af.*, MMed *Dar.* Sr. Lectr.

Lema, L. E. K., MB ChB *E.Af.*, MMed *Dar.* Prof.

Mbembati, MD *Dar.*, MMed *Dar.* Sr. Lectr.

Mcharo, O. N., MD *Dar.*, MMed *Dar.* Sr. Lectr.

Mkony, C. A., MD *Dar.*, MMed *Dar.* Assoc. Prof.; Head*

Sayi, E. N., MD *Dar.*, MMed *Dar.* Sr. Lectr.

Shija, J. K., MB ChB *E.Af.*, FRCSEd Prof.

Yongolo, C. M., MD *Dar.*, MMed *Dar.* Sr. Lectr.

NURSING

Tel: (051) 151367, 46163 Fax: (051) 151596

Basic Nursing Education

Kohi, Thecla W., BSc(Nursing) *Dal.*, MN *Dal.* Lectr.; Head*

PHARMACY

Tel: (051) 151367, 46163 Fax: (051) 151596

Chemistry, Medicinal

Chambuso, M. H. S., BPharm *Dar.*, MSc *Aston*, DrRerNat *Tübingen* Lectr.; Head*

Kigodi, P. G. K., BPharm *Dar.*, PhD *Aston* Sr. Lectr. (on leave)

Pharmaceutical Microbiology

Kagashe, G. A. B., BPharm *Dar.*, PhD *N.U.I.* Lectr.; Acting Head*

Pharmaceutics

Sam, E. N., BPharm *Dar.*, MSc *Leuven* Lectr.; Head*

Temu, M. J., BPharm *Dar.*, MSc *Leuven*, PhD *Leuven* Sr. Lectr.

Pharmacognosy

Ngassapa, O., BPharm *Dar.*, PhD *Chic.* Sr. Lectr.; Head*

Nshimo, C. M., MSc *Wales*, PhD *Chic.* Sr. Lectr.

SPECIAL CENTRES, ETC

Development Studies, Institute of

Tel: (051) 151367, 46163 Fax: (051) 151596

Kiwara, A. D., MD *Dar.*, MA *Dar.*, PhD *Conn.* Sr. Lectr.; Dir.*

Traditional Medicine, Institute of

Tel: (051) 151367, 46163 Fax: (051) 151596

Mahuna, R. L. A., MSc *Dar.*, PhD *Dar.* Assoc. Res. Prof.; Dir.*

ALLIED HEALTH SCIENCES, INSTITUTE OF

Tel: (051) 151367, 46163 Fax: (051) 151596

Senya, S. S., BPharm *Dar.* Dir.*

Environmental Health Sciences, School of

(Muhimbili Medical Centre)

Mrema, G. N. Head*

Medical Laboratory Technology, School of

(Muhimbili Medical Centre)

Mhoja, J. W. Head*

Nurse Teachers, School of

Ndakidemi, R. M. Head*

Pharmacy, School of

Mauga, E. A. S. K., BPharm *Dar.* Head*

Radiography, School of

(Muhimbili Medical Centre)

Ndolele, L. Head*

PRIMARY HEALTH CARE AND CONTINUING HEALTH EDUCATION, INSTITUTE OF

Tel: (051) 151367, 46163 Fax: (051) 151596

Mtango, F. D. E., MD *Kharkov*, MSPH *Loma Linda* Sr. Lectr.; Dir.*

Epidemiology and Biostatistics

Killewo, J. Z. J., MB ChB *E.Af.*, MSc *Lond.* Assoc. Prof.

Mnyika, K. S., MSc *Dar.*, PhD *Dar.* Sr. Lectr.; Head*

PUBLIC HEALTH, INSTITUTE OF

Tel: (051) 151367, 46163 Fax: (051) 151596

Leshabari, M. T., MA *Dar.*, DrSc *Johns H.* Assoc. Prof.; Dir.*

Behavioural Sciences

Leshabari, M. T., BSc *Dar.*, MA *Dar.*, PhD *Lond.* Assoc. Prof.

Lwihula, G. K., MA *Dar.*, MSc *Lond.*, PhD *Lond.* Sr. Lectr.; Head*

Muhondwa, E. P. Y., MA *Dar.*, PhD *Nott.* Assoc. Prof. (on leave)

Community Health

Msamanga, G. I., MD *Dar.*, MSc *Harv.*, DSc *Harv.* Sr. Lectr.

Rongo, L. M. B., BSc(Eng) *Dar.* Lectr.; Head*

Parasitology/Medical Entomology

Kihamia, C. M., MB ChB *E.Af.*, MSc *Liv.*, MMed *Dar.* Prof.; Head*

Minjas, J. N., BSc *Dar.*, MSc *Liv.*, PhD *Liv.* Prof.

Prenyi, Z., MSc *Lond.*, PhD Sr. Lectr.

CONTACT OFFICERS

Academic affairs. Chief Academic Officer: Mlama, Prof. Penina O. P., BA(Ed) *Dar.*, MA *Dar.*, PhD *Dar.*

Accommodation. Acting Dean of Students: Maghimbi, Musa Y., BA *E.Af.*

Admissions (first degree). Principal Manpower Management Officer, Admissions Office: Njau, Adela E., BA *Dar.*

Admissions (higher degree). Director of Postgraduate Studies: Materu, Prof. Peter N., MSc *Manc.*, PhD *Virginia Polytech.*

Alumni. Senior Insurance Officer: Ntake, B. M., BA *Dar.*

Careers. Chief Academic Officer: Mlama, Prof. Penina O. P., BA(Ed) *Dar.*, MA *Dar.*, PhD *Dar.*

Careers. Chief Administrative Officer: Mkude, Prof. Daniel J., BA *Dar.*, PhD *Lond.*

Computing services. Director, Computing Centre: Mutagahywa, B. M., MSc *Dar.*, PhD *Lough.*

Consultancy services. Director, University Consultancy Bureau: Rugumamu, Prof. S. M., MA *Dar.*, MA *Maryland*, PhD *Maryland*

Development/fund-raising. Chief Administrative Officer: Mkude, Prof. Daniel J., BA *Dar.*, PhD *Lond.*

Distance education. Vice-Chancellor, Open University of Tanzania: Mmari, Prof. Geoffrey R. V., BA *N.Iowa*, MA *N.Iowa*, PhD *Dar.*

Equal opportunities. Chief Administrative Officer: Mkude, Prof. Daniel J., BA *Dar.*, PhD *Lond.*

Estates and buildings/works and services. Estates Manager: Rubaratuka, I. A., MSc *Kiev*, PhD *Kiev*

Examinations. Senior Principal Administrative Officer: Mohamed, Miskia N. A., BA *Dar.*, MPA *Indiana*

Finance. Acting Bursar: Tesha, T. S.

General enquiries. Secretary to the Council: Shundi, Fabia, BA *Lond.*

Health services. Medical Officer-in-Charge: Mroso, D. M., MD *Dar.*, MMed *Dar.*

Industrial liaison. Acting Public Relations Officer: Macha J. G. M., BEd *Dar.*, MA *Dar.*

International office. Principal Manpower Management Officer, Admissions Office: Njau, Adela E., BA *Dar.*

International office. Senior Manpower Management Officer, Co-operation, Links and Projects Section: Mshigeni, Neema G., MPA *Liv.*

Library (chief librarian). Director, Library: Nawe, Julita, MA *Lond.*, PhD *Wales*

Minorities/disadvantaged groups. Chief Administrative Officer: Mkude, Prof. Daniel J., BA *Dar.*, PhD *Lond.*

Personnel/human resources. Principal Manpower Management Officer: Jaka, R. L.

Public relations, information and marketing. Acting Public Relations Officer: Macha J. G. M., BEd *Dar.*, MA *Dar.*

Publications. Principal Manpower Management Officer, Research and Publications Section: Muze, Agnes S., BA *Dar.*, MPhil *Stir.*

Purchasing. Chief Supplies Officer: Hatibu, R.

Quality assurance and accreditation. Acting Chief Internal Auditor: Mlingi, C. M., BA *Dar.*, MBA *Dar.*

Research. Principal Manpower Management Officer, Research and Publications Section: Muze, Agnes S., BA *Dar.*, MPhil *Stir.*

Safety. Chief Administrative Officer: Mkude, Prof. Daniel J., BA *Dar.*, PhD *Lond.*

Scholarships, awards, loans. Director of Postgraduate Studies: Materu, Prof. Peter N., MSc *Manc.*, PhD *Virginia Polytech.*

Schools liaison. Chief Academic Officer: Mlama, Prof. Penina O. P., BA(Ed) *Dar.*, MA *Dar.*, PhD *Dar.*

Security. Chief Administrative Officer: Mkude, Prof. Daniel J., BA *Dar.*, PhD *Lond.*

Sport and recreation. Acting Principal Games Coach: Gogomoka, L. H.

Staff development and training. Senior Manpower Management Officer: Macha, Mary, BA *Dar.*, MPA *Liv.*

Student welfare/counselling. Acting Dean of Students: Maghimbi, Musa Y., BA *E.Af.*

Students from other countries. Principal Manpower Management Officer, Admissions Office: Njau, Adela E., BA *Dar.*

Students from other countries. Senior Manpower Management Officer, Co-operation, Links and Projects Section: Mshigeni, Neema G., MPA *Liv.*

Students with disabilities. Acting Dean of Students: Maghimbi, Musa Y., BA *E.Af.*

University press. Director: Mwitta, N. G., MSc *Odessa*, PhD *Leeds*

Women. Chief Administrative Officer: Mkude, Prof. Daniel J., BA *Dar.*, PhD *Lond.*

CAMPUS/COLLEGE HEADS

Muhimbili University College of Health Sciences, PO Box 65001, Dar es Salaam, Tanzania. (Tel: (051) 150331, 150302, 151367; Fax: (051) 151596.) Principal: Mtabaji, Prof. J. P., MB ChB *E.Af.*, PhD *Newcastle(UK)*

University College of Lands and Architectural Studies, PO Box 35176, Dar es Salaam, Tanzania. (Tel: (051) 71263-4, 71272; Fax: (051) 75448, 75479.) Principal: Nikundiwe, Prof. Alfeo M., BSc *Andrews*, MSc *Mich.*, PhD *Mich.*

[Information supplied by the institution as at 5 June 1998, and edited by the ACU]

OPEN UNIVERSITY OF TANZANIA

Founded 1992

Member of the Association of Commonwealth Universities

Postal Address: PO Box 23409, Dar es Salaam, Tanzania
Telephone: (051) 668992, 668820, 668835, 668445, **Fax**: (051) 668759 **E-mail**: avu@out.udsm.ac.tz

CHANCELLOR—Malecela, Hon. J. S., BCom *Bom.*, Hon. DHum *Hardin-Simmons*
CHAIRMAN OF COUNCIL—Mramba, Hon. B. P., BA *Mak.*, MSc *City(UK)*
VICE-CHANCELLOR*—Mmari, Prof. Geoffrey R. V., BA *N.Iowa*, MA *N.Iowa*, PhD *Dar.*
DEPUTY VICE-CHANCELLOR (ACADEMIC)—Komba, Prof. Donatus, BA(Ed) *Dar.*, MA *Dar.*, PhD *Col.*
REGISTRAR‡—Chale, Egino M., BA(Ed) *Dar.*, MA *Dar.*, PhD *Lond.*

GENERAL INFORMATION

History. The university was established in 1992. It is located at Msasani, in the north of Dar es Salaam, and has 21 regional centres throughout Tanzania.

Admission to first degree courses. Certificate of Secondary Education, or East African Certificate of Education O level or equivalent, with passes in 5 approved subjects, and Advanced Certificate of Secondary Education or an equivalent diploma or certificate approved by the university.

First Degrees. BA, BCom, BSc, LlB.

Higher Degrees. Not yet available.

Libraries. 20,000 volumes.

Fees. Home students: Tsh70,000 (first year); Tsh72,000 (subsequent years). International students: US$1263 (first year); US$1120 (subsequent years).

Income (1997–98, estimated). Total, Tsh650,000,000.

Statistics. Staff: 180 (136 academic, 44 administrative). Students: 4806.

FACULTIES/SCHOOLS

Arts and Social Sciences
Dean: Kapalatu, S. S., MA *Leningrad*, MA *Ott.*

Education
Acting Dean: Mkuchu, S. G. V., BA(Ed) *Dar.*, MA *Dar.*

Law
Acting Dean: Mukoyogo, M. C., LLB *Dar.*, LLM *Dar.*, DrJur *Constance*

Science, Technology and Environmental Sciences
Dean: Mhoma, J. R. L., DVM *Kiev*, MSc *James Cook*, PhD *Murd.*, MSc

ACADEMIC UNITS
Arranged by Faculties

Arts and Social Sciences
Kapalatu, S. S., MA *Leningrad*, MA *Ott.* Sr. Lectr.

Education
No staff at present

Law
Mukoyogo, M. C., LLB *Dar.*, LLM *Dar.*, DrJus *Constance*

Science, Technology and Environmental Studies
Mhoma, J. R. L., DVM *Kiev*, MSc *James Cook*, PhD *Murd.*, MSc Sr. Lectr.
Ndaalio, Gaspar, BSc *N.U.I.*, MSc *Tor.*, PhD *Tor.* Prof.

CONTACT OFFICERS

Academic affairs. Deputy Vice-Chancellor (Academic): Komba, Prof. Donatus, BA(Ed) *Dar.*, MA *Dar.*, PhD *Col.*

Admissions (first degree). Deputy Vice-Chancellor (Academic): Komba, Prof. Donatus, BA(Ed) *Dar.*, MA *Dar.*, PhD *Col.*

Alumni. Registrar: Chale, Egino M., BA(Ed) *Dar.*, MA *Dar.*, PhD *Lond.*

Credit transfer. Deputy Vice-Chancellor (Academic): Komba, Prof. Donatus, BA(Ed) *Dar.*, MA *Dar.*, PhD *Col.*

Development/fund-raising. Vice-Chancellor: Mmari, Prof. Geoffrey R. V., BA N.Iowa, MA N.Iowa, PhD Dar.

Distance education. Deputy Vice-Chancellor (Academic): Komba, Prof. Donatus, BA(Ed) Dar., MA Dar., PhD Col.

Estates and buildings/works and services. Registrar: Chale, Egino M., BA(Ed) Dar., MA Dar., PhD Lond.

Examinations. Deputy Vice-Chancellor (Academic): Komba, Prof. Donatus, BA(Ed) Dar., MA Dar., PhD Col.

Finance. Registrar: Chale, Egino M., BA(Ed) Dar., MA Dar., PhD Lond.

General enquiries. Registrar: Chale, Egino M., BA(Ed) Dar., MA Dar., PhD Lond.

Health services. Registrar: Chale, Egino M., BA(Ed) Dar., MA Dar., PhD Lond.

Library (enquiries). Deputy Vice-Chancellor (Academic): Komba, Prof. Donatus, BA(Ed) Dar., MA Dar., PhD Col.

Personnel/human resources. Registrar: Chale, Egino M., BA(Ed) Dar., MA Dar., PhD Lond.

Public relations, information and marketing. Vice-Chancellor: Mmari, Prof. Geoffrey R. V., BA N.Iowa, MA N.Iowa, PhD Dar.

Publications. Deputy Vice-Chancellor (Academic): Komba, Prof. Donatus, BA(Ed) Dar., MA Dar., PhD Col.

Purchasing. Registrar: Chale, Egino M., BA(Ed) Dar., MA Dar., PhD Lond.

Quality assurance and accreditation. Deputy Vice-Chancellor (Academic): Komba, Prof. Donatus, BA(Ed) Dar., MA Dar., PhD Col.

Research. Deputy Vice-Chancellor (Academic): Komba, Prof. Donatus, BA(Ed) Dar., MA Dar., PhD Col.

Scholarships, awards, loans. Deputy Vice-Chancellor (Academic): Komba, Prof. Donatus, BA(Ed) Dar., MA Dar., PhD Col.

Security. Registrar: Chale, Egino M., BA(Ed) Dar., MA Dar., PhD Lond.

Staff development and training. Vice-Chancellor: Mmari, Prof. Geoffrey R. V., BA N.Iowa, MA N.Iowa, PhD Dar.

Student welfare/counselling. Dean of Students: Muyinga, E. G. M., MA Reading

CAMPUS/COLLEGE HEADS

Dar es Salaam Regional Centre, PO Box 13224, Dar es Salaam, Tanzania. (Tel: (051) 43941-2.) Director: Kimaty, H., BScAgric Agric.Univ.Gödöllö

Dodoma Regional Centre, PO Box 1944, Dodoma, Tanzania. (Tel: (061) 22345.) Director: Kinshanga, D. Y., BEd Alta., MA(Ed) Dar., PhD Alta.

Mbeya Regional Centre, PO Box 2803, Mbeya, Tanzania. (Tel: (065) 2589.) Director: Swai, L. N. A., BA(Ed) Dar., MA Dar.

Morogoro Regional Centre, PO Box 2062, Morogoro, Tanzania. (Tel: (056) 4219.) Director: Mfangavo, F. Y. K., BEd Dar., MEd Lagos

Moshi Regional Centre, PO Box 517, Moshi, Tanzania. (Tel: (055) 53472.) Director: Meena, A. S., BA N.Iowa, MA New Hampshire, PhD Dar.

Mtwara Regional Centre, PO Box 322, Mtwara, Tanzania. (Tel: (059) 3352.) Director: Mmuni, C. A., BSc(Ed) Dar., MSc Dar.

Mwanza Regional Centre, PO Box 2281, Mwanza, Tanzania. (Tel: (068) 2314.) Director: Shungu, H. A., BA(Ed) Dar., MA(DS) Dar.

Regional Services. Director: Mfangavo, F. Y., BA(Ed) Dar., MEd Lagos

Songea Regional Centre, PO Box 338, Songea, Tanzania. (Tel: (0635) 2550.) Director: Chale, B., BA(Ed) Dar., MA Dar.

Tabora Regional Centre, PO Box 1204, Tabora, Tanzania. (Tel: (062) 3099.) Director: Dasu, M. M., BA(Ed) Dar., MA Dar.

Zanzibar Regional Centre, PO Box 2599, Zanzibar, Tanzania. (Tel: (053) 32827, 33079.) Director: Kissassi, G. R., BA(Ed) Dar., MA Dar.

[Information supplied by the institution as at 18 February 1998, and edited by the ACU]

SOKOINE UNIVERSITY OF AGRICULTURE

Founded 1984

Member of the Association of Commonwealth Universities

Postal Address: PO Box 3000, Chuo Kikuu, Morogoro, Tanzania
Telephone: (056) 3511-4 **Cables**: Uniagric, Morogoro **Telex**: 55308 UNIVMOG TZ

CHANCELLOR—Kassum, Hon. Al-Noor
CHAIRMAN OF THE UNIVERSITY COUNCIL—Muhammed, Prof. Saleh I., BVM&S Edin., MSc Colorado, PhD Colorado
VICE-CHANCELLOR*—Lwoga, Prof. Anselm B., BSc(Agric) Mak., PhD Wales
DEPUTY VICE-CHANCELLOR/PRESIDENT, ALUMNI—Msolla, Prof. P. M., BVM Nair., PhD Glas.
REGISTRAR—Mkoba, S. P

FACULTIES/SCHOOLS

Agriculture
Dean: Bangu, N. T. A., BSc E.Af., MSc Mak., PhD Dar.

Forestry
Dean: Chamshama, S. A. O., MSc(For) Dar., PhD Dar.

Veterinary Medicine
Dean: Mosha, R. D., BVM Nair., PhD Copenhagen Agric., MVM

ACADEMIC UNITS

Agricultural Economics and Agribusiness
Kashuliza, A. K., BSc(Agric) Dar., MSc Guelph, PhD Lond. Sr. Lectr.
Minde, I. J., BSc(Agric) Dar., MSc(AgricEcon) Dar., PhD Mich.State Sr. Lectr. (on leave)
Mlambiti, M. E., BSc(Agric) E.Af., MSc W.Virginia, PhD Dar. Assoc. Prof.; Head*
Mlay, G. I., BSc(Agric) Dar., MSc Oklahoma State, PhD Oklahoma State Sr. Lectr. (on leave)

Rugambisa, J. I. B., BA Dar., MSc Wis., PhD Ill. Sr. Lectr. (on leave)

Agricultural Education and Extension
Hadjivayanis, G. G., BSc(Agric) Dar., MA Dar. Sr. Lectr.
Lupanga, I. J., BSc(Agric) Mak., MSc W.Virginia, PhD Cornell Sr. Lectr. (on leave)
Mattee, A. Z., BSc(Agric) Dar., MSc Wis., PhD Wis. Sr. Lectr.; Head*
Mlozi, M. R. S., MSc(Agric) W.Virginia, PhD Br.Col. Sr. Lectr.
Mollel, N. M., BSc(Agric) Dar., MSc Ill., PhD Ill. Sr. Lectr.
Mvena, Z. S. K., BSc(Agric) Dar., MSc Missouri, PhD Missouri Sr. Lectr.
Rutachokozibwa, V., BSc(Agric) Dar., MSc Iowa State, PhD Iowa State Sr. Lectr.
Rutatora, D. F., BSc(Agric) Dar., MSc Guelph, PhD Tor. Sr. Lectr.

Agricultural Engineering and Land Planning
Dihenga, H. O., BSc(Agric) Dar., MSc Çran.IT, PhD Mich. Sr. Lectr.
Hatibu, N., BSc Cran.IT, PhD Newcastle(UK) Sr. Lectr.

Kayombo, B., BSc(Agric) Dar., MSc Cran.IT, PhD Assoc. Prof.; Head*
Kihupi, N. T., BSc(Agric) Dar., MSc Cran.IT, PhD Sr. Lectr.
Mahoo, H. F., BSc Dar., MSc S'ton., PhD Sr. Lectr.
Makungu, P. S. J., BSc(Eng) Dar., MSc Melb., PhD Newcastle Sr. Lectr.
Simalenga, T. E., BSc(Eng) Dar., MSc Newcastle(UK), PhD Copenhagen Sr. Lectr. (on leave)

Animal Science and Production
Katule, A. N. N., BSc(Agric) Dar., MSc Dar., PhD Sr. Lectr.
Kifaro, G. C., PhD Sokoine Ag., MSc(Agric) Sr. Lectr.
Kimambo, A. E., BSc(Agric) Dar., MSc Adel., PhD Aberd. Sr. Lectr.
Kurwijila, R. L. B., BSc(Agric) Dar., MSc Nair., PhD E.T.H.Zürich Assoc. Prof.; Head*
Lekule, F. P. M., BSc(Agric) Dar., MSc Dar., PhD Assoc. Prof.
Mtenga, L. A., BSc(Agric) Dar., MSc Reading, PhD Reading Prof.
Shem, M. N., BSc(Agric) Dar., MSc Guelph, PhD Edin. Sr. Lectr.

Urio, N. A., BSc(Agric) Dar., MSc Dar., PhD Dar. Assoc. Prof.

Crop Science and Production

Lana, A. F., BSc Wis., MSc Ohio State, PhD Mass. Prof.
Mabagala, R. B., BSc(Agric) Dar., MSc Mich., PhD Mich. Sr. Lectr.
Maingu, Z. E., BSc(Agric) Dar., MSc Reading, PhD Reading Sr. Lectr.
Minjas, A. N., BSc(Ed) Dar., MSc Dar., PhD Br.Col. Assoc. Prof. (on leave)
Misangu, R. N., BSc(Agric) Dar., MSc Dar. Sr. Lectr. (on leave)
Mphuru, A. N., BSc E.Af., MSc W.Virginia, PhD Dar. Assoc. Prof. (on leave)
Nchimbi-Msolla, S., BSc(Agric) Dar., MSc Wis., PhD Wis. Sr. Lectr.
Reuben, S. O. W. M., BSc(Agric) Dar., MSc Guelph, PhD Wales Sr. Lectr.
Rweyemamu, C. L., BSc(Agric) Dar., MSc Alta., PhD Mich. Sr. Lectr.
Sakia, R. M. N., BA Dar., MSc Guelph, PhD Hohenheim Sr. Lectr. (on leave)
Sibuga, K. P., BSc(Agric) Dar., MSc Guelph, PhD Nair. Assoc. Prof.; Head*
Tarimo, A. J. P., BSc(Agric) Dar., MSc Br.Col., PhD Qld. Sr. Lectr.
Teri, J. M., BSc(Agric) Mak., MSc Cornell, PhD Cornell (on leave)

Development Studies Institute, see

Special Centres, etc

Economics, see Agric. Econ. and

Agribusiness; Forest Econ.

Food Science and Technology

Bangu, N. T. A., BSc E.Af., MSc Mak., PhD Dar. Sr. Lectr.
Keregero, M. M., MSc Wis., PhD Wis. Sr. Lectr. (on leave)
Laswai, H. S., BSc(Agric) Dar., MSc Reading, PhD Reading Sr. Lectr.
Maeda, E. E., BSc(Agric) Dar., MSc Dar., PhD Utah Sr. Lectr.
Mtebe, K., BSc(Agric) Dar., MSc Mass., PhD Reading Sr. Lectr.; Head*
Tiisekwa, B. P. M., BSc Dar., MSc Reading, PhD Ghent Sr. Lectr. (on leave)

Forest Biology

Chamshama, S. A. O., MSc(For) Dar., PhD Dar. Assoc. Prof.
Lulandala, L. L. L., MSc(For) Dar., PhD Sr. Lectr.; Head*
Madoffe, S. S., BSc(For) Dar., PhD Agric.Coll.Norway, DSc Agric.Coll.Norway, MSc(For) Sr. Lectr.
Maganga, S. L. S., BSc(For) Dar., MSc Idaho, PhD Idaho Sr. Lectr.
Maliondo, S. M. S., BSc(For) Dar., MSc Wales, PhD New Br. Sr. Lectr.
Mugasha, A. G., BSc(For) Dar., MSc Lake., PhD Alta. Sr. Lectr.
Temu, R. P. C., PhD Uppsala, BSc(For) Sr. Lectr.

Forest Economics

Kaoneka, A. R. S., PhD Agric.Coll.Norway, MSc(For) Sr. Lectr.
Kowero, G. S., MSc(For) Dar., MSc Calif., PhD Dar. Prof. (on leave)
Monela, G. C., MSc(For) Sr. Lectr. (on leave)
O'Kting'ati, A., MSc(For) Dar., MSc Mich., PhD Assoc. Prof.; Head*

Forest Engineering

Abeli, W. S., MSc(For) Dar., PhD Assoc. Prof.; Head*
Ole-Meiludie, R. E. L., MSc(For) Dar., PhD Dar. Assoc. Prof. (on leave)

Forest Mensuration and Management

Malimbwi, R. E., MSc(For) Dar., PhD Aberd. Sr. Lectr.; Head*
Mgeni, A. S. M., MSc(For) Dar., PhD Wales Prof.

Temu, A. B., BSc(Forestry) Mak., MSc(For) Dar., PhD Dar. Prof. (on leave)

Land Planning, see Agric. Engin. and Land

Planning

Soil Science

Kilasara, M., BSc(Agric) Dar., MSc Reading, PhD Paris VI Sr. Lectr.
Mnkeni, P. N. S., BSc(Agric) Dar., MSc McG., PhD McG. Assoc. Prof.
Mrema, J. P., BSc(Agric) Dar., MSc Reading, PhD Sr. Lectr.; Head*
Msaky, J. J. T., BSc(Agric) Dar., MSc Calif., PhD Paris VI Sr. Lectr.
Msanya, B. M., BSc(Agric) Dar., MSc Ghent, PhD Ghent Sr. Lectr.
Msumali, G. P., BSc(Agric) Dar., MSc Manit., PhD Reading Sr. Lectr.
Salema, M. P., BSc(Agric) Dar., PhD W.Aust. Assoc. Prof.
Semoka, J. M. R., BSc(Agric) Dar., MSc Calif., PhD Calif. Sr. Lectr.
Semu, E., BSc(Agric) Dar., MSc Guelph, MSc Mich., PhD Dar. Sr. Lectr.
Shayo-Ngowi, A. J., BSc Uppsala, MSc Wash. State, PhD Newcastle(UK) Sr. Lectr.

Veterinary Medicine, see below

Wood Utilization

Hamza, F. K. S., BSc(For) Dar., PhD Hohenheim, MSc(For) Sr. Lectr.
Iddi, S., MSc(For) Dar., PhD Wales Assoc. Prof.
Ishengoma, R. C., MSc(For) Dar., DSc Agric.Coll.Norway Assoc. Prof.; Head*

VETERINARY MEDICINE

Veterinary Anatomy

Assey, R. J., BVSc Dar., PhD R.Vet.& Agric., Denmark, MVM Sr. Lectr.
Mbassa, G. K., BVM Nair., PhD Copenhagen Agric., MVM Assoc. Prof.; Head*

Veterinary Medicine and Public Health

Kambarage, D. M., BVSc Dar., PhD Brist., MVM Assoc. Prof.; Head*
Kazwala, R. R., MVM Trinity(Dub.), BVSc Sr. Lectr. (on leave)
Lyaku, J. R., MSc Edin., PhD Edin., BVSc Sr. Lectr. (on leave)
Msolla, P. M., BVM Nair., PhD Glas. Prof.
Mtambo, M. M. A., PhD Glas., BVM Sr. Lectr.

Veterinary Microbiology and Parasitology

Gwakisa, P. S., MSc Moscow, PhD Moscow Assoc. Prof.
Jiwa, S. F. H., BVM Nair., PhD Uppsala Prof.
Kassuku, A. A., BVM Nair., MSc Edin., PhD Copenhagen Agric. Assoc. Prof.; Head*
Kilonzo, B. S., MSc Lond., PhD Dar. Prof.
Kimbita, E. N., MVSc Liv., PhD Sokoine Ag., BVM Sr. Lectr.
Machang'u, R. S., MSc(Vet) Cluj, DVM Giessen, PhD Guelph Sr. Lectr.
Maeda-Machang'u, BVM Nair., PhD Edin. Assoc. Prof.
Minga, U. M., BVM Nair., MSc Ill., PhD Copenhagen Agric. Assoc. Prof.
Silayo, R. S., BVM Nair., MSc Edin., PhD Edin. Assoc. Prof.

Veterinary Pathology

Maselle, R. M., DPVM Copenhagen Agric., DVM Cluj-Napoca Agric., PhD Copenhagen Agric., MVM Sr. Lectr.
Matovelo, J. A., BVSc Dar., DSc Oslo Assoc. Prof.; Head*
Mwamengele, G. L. M., BVSc Dar., PhD Copenhagen, MVM Sr. Lectr.
Semuguruka, W. D., BVMS Glas., MSc Ill., PhD Copenhagen Agric. Assoc. Prof.

Veterinary Physiology, Biochemistry, Pharmacology and Toxicology

Mosha, R. D., BVM Nair., PhD Copenhagen Agric., MVM Assoc. Prof.
Mutayoba, B. M., BVSc Dar., MSc Nair., PhD Glas. Sr. Lectr.
Ngomuo, A. J., BVM Nair., MVM Glas., PhD Sur. Sr. Lectr.; Head*
Pereka, A. E., BVSc Dar., MVM N.U.I., PhD Copenhagen Agric. Sr. Lectr.

Veterinary Surgery, Obstetrics and Reproduction

Batamuzi, E. K., BVSc Dar., MVM Sr. Lectr. (on leave)
Bittegeko, S. B. P., MVM Sr. Lectr. (on leave)
Kessy, B. M., BVM Nair., PhD Lond. Assoc. Prof.
Mgasa, M. N., BVM Nair., PhD Copenhagen Agric., MVM Assoc. Prof.; Head*
Mgongo, F. O. K., BVM Nair., MSc Nair., DrMedVet Munich Prof.
Nkya, R., MSc Moscow, PhD Moscow Sr. Lectr.

SPECIAL CENTRES, ETC

Basic Science Unit

Mgeni, A. S. M., MSc(For) Dar., PhD Wales Prof.; Co-ordinator

Communication Skills Section

Neke, S. M., BA(Ed) Dar., MA Wales Lectr.; Co-ordinator (on leave)
Other Staff: 2 Lectrs.

Computer Centre

Katule, A. N. N., BSc Dar., MSc(Agric) Dar., PhD Sokoine Ag. Sr. Lectr.; Dir.*
Sakia, R. M. N., BA Dar., MSc Guelph, PhD Hohenheim Sr. Lectr. (on leave)

Continuing Education, Institute of

Keregero, K. J. B., BSc(Agric) Dar., MSc Wis., PhD Wis. Assoc. Prof. (on leave)
Lugeye, S. C., BSc(Agric) N.Carolina, MSc Reading, PhD N.U.I. Sr. Lectr.; Dir.*

Development Studies Institute

Kapinga, D. S., BA(Ed) Dar., MA Dar. Sr. Lectr. (on leave)
Kasimila, J. B., BA(Ed) Dar., MA Dar., PhD Bamberg Sr. Lectr.; Dir.*
Kihiyo, V. B. M. S., BSc(For) Dar., PhD Sokoine Ag., MSc(For) Sr. Lectr.
Kyulule, V. L., BA(Ed) Dar., MA Dar., MSc N.U.I., PhD Qld. Sr. Lectr.
Ngasongwa, J. A., MSc Prague, MA Dar., PhD E.Anglia Sr. Lectr. (on leave)

CONTACT OFFICERS

Academic affairs. Deputy Vice-Chancellor: Msolla, Prof. P. M., BVM Nair., PhD Glas.
Accommodation. Registrar: Mkoba, S. P
Accommodation. Dean of Students: Mwampamba, E. N., MSc Bucharest, PhD Leip.
Admissions (first degree). Principal Administrative Officer (Admissions): Lubela, P. L.
Admissions (higher degree). Director, Research and Postgraduate Studies: Kinabo, L. D. B., BVSc Dar., MVM Sokoine Ag., PhD Glas.
Adult/continuing education. Director, Institute of Continuing Education: Lugeye, S. C., BSc(Agric) N.Carolina, MSc Reading, PhD N.U.I.
Alumni. President, Alumni: Msolla, Prof. P. M., BVM Nair., PhD Glas.
Computing services. Director, Computer Centre: Katule, A. M., BSc Dar., MSc(Agric) Dar., PhD Sokoine Ag.
Consultancy services. Co-ordinator, Bureau for Agricultural Consultancy and Agricultural Services (BACAS): Mdoe, N. S. Y. S., BSc(Agric) Dar., MSc Guelph, PhD Reading

Consultancy services. Co-ordinator, Forestry Consultancy (FORCUNSULT): Malimbwi, R. E., BSc *Dar.*, MSc(For) *Dar.*, PhD *Aberd.*

Estates and buildings/works and services. Estates Manager: Kingwalu, D., BSc *Dar.*

Examinations. Senior Administrative Officer (Examinations): Mtapa, J. K., BA *Dar.*

Finance. University Bursar: Kapungu, A. M.

General enquiries. Registrar: Mkoba, S. P

Health services. Resident Medical Officer: Mangi, W. Z.

Library (chief librarian). Director, Sokoine National Agricultural Library (SNAL): Chiduo, E. V., BA *E.Af.*

Personnel/human resources. Principal Administrative Officer (Personnel): Kavishe, P. R., MA *Calif.Baptist*, PhD *Calif.Baptist*

Public relations, information and marketing. Principal Public Relations Officer: Msagati, K. A.

Research. Director, Research and Postgraduate Studies: Kinabo, L. D. B., BVSc *Dar.*, MVM *Sokoine Ag.*, PhD *Glas.*

Safety. Chief Security Officer and Head, Security Department: Kombe, E.

Sport and recreation. Senior Games Tutor and Head, Sports Department: Mlinda, E.

Staff development and training (academic staff). Senior Administrative Officer, Recruitment and Academic Staff Development: Nyangaka, W. S., BA *Dar.*

Staff development and training (administrative staff). Principal Administrative Officer (Personnel): Kavishe, P. R., MA *Calif.Baptist*, PhD *Calif.Baptist*

Student union. President, Sokoine University of Agriculture Students' Organisation (SUASO): Temu, V.

Student welfare/counselling. Dean of Students: Mwampamba, E. N., MSc *Bucharest*, PhD *Leip.*

[Information supplied by the institution as at 28 December 1995, and edited by the ACU]

UGANDA

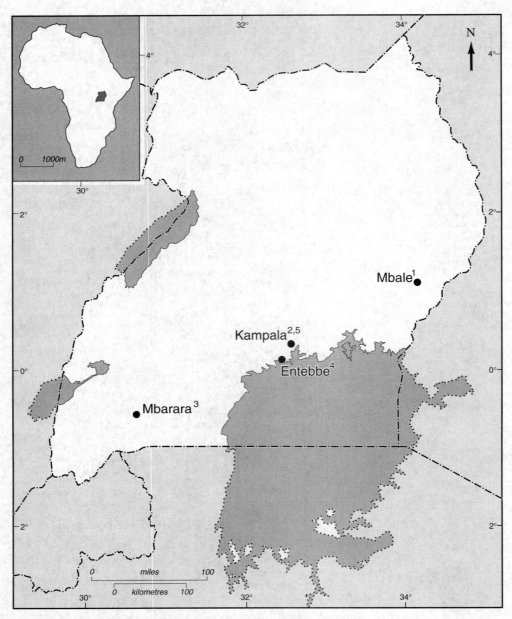

The places named are the seats of the university institutions numbered above

ISLAMIC UNIVERSITY IN UGANDA

Founded 1988

Member of the Association of Commonwealth Universities

Postal Address: PO Box 2555, Mbale, Uganda
Telephone: (045) 33417, 33502 **Fax**: (045) 254576 **E-mail**: abkasozi@imul.com **Telex**: 66176 ISLUNIV UG

CHAIRMAN OF UNIVERSITY COUNCIL/CHANCELLOR—Jassim Al-Hijji, H.E. Sheikh Youssuf
RECTOR*—Adamu, Prof. Mahdi, BA *A. Bello*, MA *A.Bello*, PhD *Birm.*
VICE-RECTOR (ACADEMIC AFFAIRS, FINANCE AND ADMINISTRATION)—Kasozi, Prof. A. B. K., BA *E.Af.*, MA *Calif.*, PhD *Calif.*
UNIVERSITY SECRETARY‡—Sengendo, Ahmad K., BSc *Mak.*, MScEd *Kansas*, PhD *Kansas*
ACTING ACADEMIC REGISTRAR—Kabali, S., BA *Medina*, MA *Medina*
BURSAR—Kipanga, Assad A., MBA *Dar.*
LIBRARIAN—Ansari, M. Tariq, BLibSc *Alig.*, MSc *Alig.*

GENERAL INFORMATION

History. The university was opened in 1988. It is located in Mbale Town, Mbale District, Eastern Uganda.

Admission to first degree courses. O level certificate and at least 2 principal passes at A level.

First Degrees. BA, BBS, BPA, BSc.
Students may choose single or combined honours within BA and BSc categories.
The following subjects may be studied at first degree level: Arabic studies, biochemistry, botany, business studies, chemistry, computer science and application, economics, education, environmental studies, geography, history, Islamic studies, language/literature/linguistics, mass communication, mathematics, microbiology, physics, political science, public administration, Shariah, sociology, sociology and Dawah, statistics, zoology.

Higher Degrees. MA, MBA, MPA, PhD.

Language of Instruction. English, except for Arabic studies and Islamic studies (Arabic) and French and Kiswahili (the relevant language).

Fees (1999, annual). Undergraduate: BSc, US$684; all other courses, US$384. Postgraduate: US$984.

Academic Year. October–July.

Statistics. Staff: 81. Students: 966.

FACULTIES/SCHOOLS

Arts and Social Sciences
Dean: Tigiti, Prof. S. Y. Sengo, BA *Dar.*, MA *Khart.*, PhD *Khart.*

Education
Dean: Ssesanga, A. Karim, BA(Ed) *Mak.*, MA(Ed) *Mak.*

Islamic Heritage
Dean: Roshash, M. A. A., LLM *Khart.*, PhD *Bayero*

Management Studies
Dean: Olum, Yasin, BA *Mak.*, MA *Manc.*, PhD *Newcastle(UK)*

Science
Dean: Allam, M. A., BSc *Cairo*, MSc *Cairo*, PhD *Cairo*

ACADEMIC UNITS

Arabic Studies
Hussain, M. S., MA *Bayero*, PhD *Bayero* Assoc. Prof.; Head*

Arts and Social Science
Gimui, K., MScEd *N.Illinois* Sr. Lectr.
Kasozi, A. B. K., BA *E.Af.*, MA *Calif.*, PhD *Calif.* Prof.
Ngozi Ibrahim, BA *Dar.*, MA *Dar.* Sr. Lectr.
Serwanga, J., BA *Islamic Uganda*, MA *Mak.* Asst. Lectr.; Head*
Swai, Bonaventure, BA *Dar.*, DPhil *Sus.* Prof.
Tigiti, S. Y. Sengo, BA *Dar.*, MA *Khart.*, PhD *Khart.* Prof.

Education
Ssesanga, A. Karim, BA(Ed) *Mak.*, MA(Ed) *Mak.* Head*

Islamic Studies and Sharia
Roshash, M. A. A., LLM *Khart.*, PhD *Bayero* Assoc. Prof.; Head*

Management Studies
Atikoro, P., BSc *Portland*, MBA *Portland* Assoc. Prof.
Olum, Yasin, BA *Mak.*, MA *Manc.*, PhD *Newcastle(UK)* Head*
Sendaro, A. M., BA *E.Af.*, MA *Dar.*, PhD *Dar.* Assoc. Prof.
Wahab, M. A., MCom *Dhaka* Assoc. Prof.

Science
Allam, M. A., BSc *Cairo*, MSc *Cairo*, PhD *Cairo* Sr. Lectr.; Head*
Ansari, A. S., MPhil *Alig.*, PhD *Alig.* Sr. Lectr.
Maher Muhammad Ibrahim El-Dessouky, BSc *Cairo*, MSc *Cairo*, PhD *Cairo* Prof.
Masihur Rahman, BSc *Alig.*, MSc *Alig.*, MPhil *Alig.*, PhD *Alig.* Sr. Lectr.
Muhammad Saquib, BSc *Alig.*, MSc *Alig.*, PhD *Alig.* Sr. Lectr.
Opyene Eluk, P., BSc *Mak.*, MA *Kent* Sr. Lectr.
Sekimpi, P. S. N. A., MSc *Arizona*, PhD *Arizona* Sr. Lectr.

SPECIAL CENTRES, ETC

Postgraduate Studies Programme
Sendaro, A. M., BA *E.Af.*, MA *Dar.*, PhD *Dar.* Assoc. Prof.; Acting Dir.*

Remedial Studies Programme
Yusuf, U. A., LLB *Medina*, MA *Ib.* Lectr.; Head*

Vocational Training Centre
Kasule, U. A., BA *Mak.*, MA *Mak.* Assoc. Prof.; Head*

CONTACT OFFICERS

Academic affairs. Acting Academic Registrar: Kabali, S., BA *Medina*, MA *Medina*
Accommodation. Co-ordinator: Samaali, Abasi, BA *Mak.*, MEd *Mak.*
Admissions (first degree). Acting Academic Registrar: Kabali, S., BA *Medina*, MA *Medina*
Development/fund-raising. Rector: Adamu, Prof. Mahdi, BA *A. Bello*, MA *A.Bello*, PhD *Birm.*
Estates and buildings/works and services. Assistant University Engineer: Namunyere, Kassim, BSc(Eng) *Mak.*
Examinations. Acting Academic Registrar: Kabali, S., BA *Medina*, MA *Medina*
Finance. Vice-Rector (Academic Affairs, Finance and Administration): Kasozi, Prof. A. B. K., BA *E.Af.*, MA *Calif.*, PhD *Calif.*
General enquiries. University Secretary: Sengendo, Ahmad K., BSc *Mak.*, MScEd *Kansas*, PhD *Kansas*
Health services. University Medical Officer: Kassi, Eryasa, MB ChB *Mak.*
International office. Rector: Adamu, Prof. Mahdi, BA *A. Bello*, MA *A.Bello*, PhD *Birm.*
Library (chief librarian). Librarian: Ansari, M. Tariq, BLibSc *Alig.*, MSc *Alig.*
Personnel/human resources. University Secretary: Sengendo, Ahmad K., BSc *Mak.*, MScEd *Kansas*, PhD *Kansas*
Public relations, information and marketing. Public Relations Officer: Kaye, Hussein, BA *Al-Azhar*
Publications. University Secretary: Sengendo, Ahmad K., BSc *Mak.*, MScEd *Kansas*, PhD *Kansas*
Purchasing. Bursar: Kipanga, Assad A., MBA *Dar.*
Research. Rector: Adamu, Prof. Mahdi, BA *A. Bello*, MA *A.Bello*, PhD *Birm.*
Scholarships, awards, loans. Acting Academic Registrar: Kabali, S., BA *Medina*, MA *Medina*
Security. Security Officer: Nsereko, Salim
Sport and recreation. Chairman of Sports Committee: Alonga, S. Othman, BA *Medina*, MA *Khart.*
Staff development and training. Rector: Adamu, Prof. Mahdi, BA *A. Bello*, MA *A.Bello*, PhD *Birm.*
Student union. Co-ordinator: Samaali, Abbas, BA *Mak.*, MEd *Mak.*
Student welfare/counselling. Co-ordinator: Samaali, Abasi, BA *Mak.*, MEd *Mak.*
Students from other countries. Acting Academic Registrar: Kabali, S., BA *Medina*, MA *Medina*

[Information supplied by the institution as at 1 March 1998, and edited by the ACU]

MAKERERE UNIVERSITY

Inaugurated 1970; previously established as Makerere College (1922) and Makerere University College (1949)

Member of the Association of Commonwealth Universities

Postal Address: PO Box 7062, Kampala, Uganda
Telephone: (041) 532631-4 Fax: (041) 533640 E-mail: postmaster@muk.ac.ug Cables: Makunika Telex: 61351

CHANCELLOR—H.E. The President of Uganda and Commander in Chief of the Armed Forces (ex officio)
CHAIRMAN OF COUNCIL—Matovu, David, BSc MSc PhD
VICE-CHANCELLOR*—Ssebuwufu, Prof. John P. M., BSc Mak., PhD Belf., Hon. EdD Ohio State
DEPUTY VICE-CHANCELLOR—Epelu-Opio, Prof. J., BVSc Nair., MSc Nair., PhD Mak.
UNIVERSITY SECRETARY AND SECRETARY TO COUNCIL—Tibarimbasa, Avitus K. M., BSc Mak., MEd Manc.
ACADEMIC REGISTRAR—Hyuha, Mukwanason A., BSc Mak., MA S.Fraser, PhD Alta.
DEAN OF THE UNIVERSITY—Kihuguru, G. B., BA Lond.
BURSAR—Byambabazi, Ben, BCom Mak., MBA Mak.
UNIVERSITY LIBRARIAN—Mugasha, J., BSc E.Af., MSLS Ohio

FACULTIES/SCHOOLS

Agriculture and Forestry
Dean: Sabiiti, E. N., BSc(Agric) Mak., MSc(Agric) Mak., PhD Brun.

Arts
Dean: Ndoleriire, O., BA Paris IV, MA Paris IV, PhD Paris IV

Business School
Dean: Wasswa Balunywa, BCom Delhi, MBA Delhi

Education
Dean: Ssekamwa, C. J., BA E.Af., MA Mak., PhD Mak.

Industrial and Fine Arts, Margaret Trowell School of
Dean: Kwesiga, P. K., BA(FA) Mak., MA(FA) Mak.

Law
Dean: Oloka-Onyango, J., LLB Mak., LLM Harv., SJD Harv.

Medicine
Dean: Sewankambo, N. K., MB ChB MMed MPH

Science
Dean: Luboobi, Prof. L. S., BSc E.Af., MSc Tor., PhD Adel.

Social Sciences
Dean: Kwesiga, Joy, BA Mak., MA PhD

Technology
Dean: Higenyi, J. K. D., BScEng Nair., MSc Rice, PhD Rice

Veterinary Medicine
Dean: Katunguka, E. R., BVM Mak., MSc Trinity(Dub.), PhD Glas.

ACADEMIC UNITS

Accounting, see Finance and Acctg.

Agricultural Economics
Hyuha, T., BA S.Fraser, MSc Alta. Sr. Lectr.; Acting Head*
Other Staff: 8 Lectrs.; 2 Asst. Lectrs.

Agricultural Engineering
Sentongo-Kibalama, J., BSc Mak., MEngSc Melb., PhD Ohio Sr. Lectr.; Head*
Other Staff: 1 Lectr.; 5 Asst. Lectrs.

Agricultural Extension Education
Semana, A. R., BSc Wis., MSc Mak. Sr. Lectr.; Acting Head*
Other Staff: 6 Lectrs.; 3 Asst. Lectrs.

Animal Science
Bareeba, F. B., BSc Mak., MSc Mak., PhD Manit. Assoc. Prof.; Head*

Kiwuwa, G. H., BSc(Agric) Lond., MSc Ill., PhD Cornell Prof.
Mutetikka, D. B., BSc Mak., MSc Nair., PhD Ohio Sr. Lectr.
Okot, M. W., BSc W.Virginia, MSc(Agric) Mak., PhD Mak. Sr. Lectr.
Other Staff: 4 Lectrs.; 2 Asst. Lectrs.

Architecture
Nawangwe, B., MSc(Arch) Kiev, PhD Kiev, BArch Sr. Lectr.; Head*
Other Staff: 6 Lectrs.; 10 Asst. Lectrs.

Art, see Indust. Art and Des.; Sculpture

Art History, see Printing and Art Hist.

Biochemistry
Bimenya, G. S., BSc Mak., MSc Mak., PhD Mak. Sr. Lectr.
Carasco, J. F., BSc Mak., MSc Birm., PhD Durh. Assoc. Prof.
Kabayo, J. P., BSc Mak., MSc Mak., PhD Brist. Sr. Lectr.; Head*
Kakonge, J. B., BSc St.And., BSc Sheff., PhD Newcastle(UK) Assoc. Prof.
Rutesasisra, A., BSc Mak., MSc Mak. Sr. Lectr.
Other Staff: 2 Lectrs.; 5 Asst. Lectrs.

Botany
Bukenya-Ziraba, R., BSc Mak., MSc Ghana, PhD Mak. Assoc. Prof.
Buruga, J. H., BSc E.Af., MSc E.Af., MSc Liv. Assoc. Prof.
Kakudidi, E. K. Z., BSc Mak., MSc ANU Herbarium Curator
Kasenene, J. M., BSc Mak., MSc Mak., PhD Mich. Sr. Lectr.
Kashambuzi, J. T., BSc Mak., MSc Mak. Sr. Lectr.
Male, M., BSc Mak., MSc Mak. Sr. Lectr.; Head*
Oryem-Origa, H., BSc Mak., MSc Mak., PhD Mak. Sr. Lectr.
Taligoola, H. K., BSc E.Af., PhD Nott. Prof.
Other Staff: 7 Lectrs.; 2 Asst. Lectrs.; 2 Lectrs.†

Business Administration, see under Marketing and Management

Chemistry
Kiremire, B. T., BSc Mak., MSc Mak., PhD Windsor Assoc. Prof.
Mbabazi, J., BSc Mak., MSc Mak., PhD Mak. Sr. Lectr.
Mpango, G. B., BSc Mak., MSc Mak., PhD Wat. Sr. Lectr.
Mukasa, S., BSc E.Af., PhD Mak. Sr. Lectr.; Head*
Nyangababo, J. T., BSc Mak., MSc Mak., PhD Mak. Assoc. Prof.
Nyanzi, S. A., BSc Mak., MSc Nair., PhD Sr. Lectr.
Silike-Murumu, J., BSc E.Af., MSc Mak., PhD Mak. Sr. Lectr.

Ssekaalo, H., BSc Lond., MSc Lond., PhD Nair. Prof.
Other Staff: 5 Lectrs.; 2 Asst. Lectrs.

Computer Science, Institute of, see Special Centres, etc

Crop Science
Adipala-Ekwamu, BSc(Agric) Mak., MSc(Agric) Mak., PhD Ohio Assoc. Prof.
Kyamanywa, S., BSc Mak., PhD Mak. Sr. Lectr.
Magambo, M. J. S., BA Lake Forest, MSc Howard, PhD Nair. Sr. Lectr.
Ogenga-Latigo, M., BSc Mak., MSc Nair., PhD Mak. Assoc. Prof.
Osiru, D. S., BSc Mak., MSc Mak., PhD Mak. Prof.; Head*
Owera, S. A. P., BSc Mak., PhD Wales Sr. Lectr.
Rubaihayo, P. R., BSc Lond., MSc Mak., PhD Ill. Prof.
Sabiiti, E. N., BSc(Agric) Mak., MSc(Agric) Mak., PhD Brun. Assoc. Prof.
Ssekabembe, C., BSc Mak., MSc Mak., PhD Ohio Sr. Lectr.
Other Staff: 3 Lectrs.; 1 Asst. Lectr.

Curriculum, Teaching and Media
Komakech, L., BA Lond., MSc Indiana Sr. Lectr.
Mungoma-Mwalye, P., BEd E.Af., MEd Ib. Sr. Lectr.; Head*
Other Staff: 5 Lectrs.; 2 Asst. Lectrs.

Dance and Drama, see Music, Dance and Drama

Economics
Ddumba-Sentamu, J., BA Mak., MA Wat., PhD Mak. Sr. Lectr.; Head*
Mubazi, J. K. E., BA Mak., MA Kent Sr. Lectr.
Ssemogerere, G., BA Vassar, MA Duke, PhD Duke Sr. Lectr.
Other Staff: 15 Lectrs.; 3 Asst. Lectrs.; 1 Consultant

Education, see Curric., Teaching and Media; Educnl. Foundations and Management; Educnl. Psychol.; Higher Educn.; Lang. Educn.; Sci. and Tech. Educn.; Soc. Scis. and Arts Educn.

Educational Foundations and Management
Munakukaama, J. Nsereko, BA E.Af., MPhil Nott. Sr. Lectr.; Head*
Odaet, C. F., BA Mak., MA Lond. Prof.; Head*
Ssekamwa, C. J., BA E.Af., MA Mak., PhD Mak. Assoc. Prof.
Other Staff: 7 Lectrs.

Educational Psychology
Baguma, P. K., BSc Mak., MSc Lond. Sr. Lectr.
Mayengo, R. K., BSc Howard, MSc Pitt. Sr. Lectr.
Munene, J., BA Mak., MSc Sheff., MSc W.Aust., PhD Lond. Assoc. Prof.

Opolot, A. Jethro, MA Edin., MEd Birm., MSc Birm., PhD Birm. Prof.

Owens, V. L., BA Wash., MEd Wash. Lectr.; Acting Head*

Other Staff: 5 Lectrs.; 7 Asst. Lectrs.

Engineering, Agricultural, see Agric. Engin.

Engineering, Civil

Kiggundu, B. M., BSc(Eng) New Mexico, MSc Carnegie-Mellon, PhD New Mexico Sr. Lectr.; Head*

Musoke, A. E. M., BSc(Eng) Mak., MBdgSc Syd. Sr. Lectr.

Other Staff: 6 Lectrs.; 3 Asst. Lectrs.

Engineering, Electrical

Kaluuba, L. L., BSc(Eng) Mak. Sr. Lectr.; Head*

Kasangaki, V. B. A., BSc(Eng) Mak., MSc Sus., PhD Temple Sr. Lectr.

Lugujjo, E., BSc Mak., MSc(Eng) Cal.Tech., PhD Cal.Tech. Assoc. Prof.

Musaazi, M. K., BSc(Eng) Mak., MSc(Eng) Lond., PhD Sr. Lectr.*

Tusubira, F. F., BSc(Eng) Mak., MSc New Br., PhD S'ton. Sr. Lectr.

Other Staff: 3 Lectrs.; 3 Asst. Lectrs.

Engineering, Mechanical

Byaruhanga, J. K., BSc(Eng) Mak., PhD NSW Sr. Lectr.

Higenyi, J. K. D., BScEng Nair., MSc Rice, PhD Rice Assoc. Prof.

Turyagyenda, J. B. T., ME P.F.U., Moscow, MSc P.F.U., Moscow, MBA Sr. Lectr.; Head*

Other Staff: 7 Lectrs.; 2 Asst. Lectrs.

Engineering Mathematics

Tickodri-Togboa, S. S., BSc(Eng) Odessa, MSc(Eng) Odessa, PhD Odessa Sr. Lectr.; Head*

Other Staff: 1 Lectr.

Urban Planning

1 Lectr.

Environment and Natural Resources, Institute of, see Special Centres, etc

Finance and Accounting

Kakuru, J., BCom MAcct Lectr.; Acting Head*

Wasswa Balunywa, BCom Delhi, MBA Delhi Sr. Lectr.

Other Staff: 1 Lectr.; 8 Staff Devel. Fellows; 2 Lectrs.†

Food Science and Technology

Ameny, M. A., BSc Mak., MSc Wales, PhD Lagos State Sr. Lectr.

Kikafunda, J. K., BSc Mak., MSc Sask., Reading Lectr.; Acting Head*

Other Staff: 9 Lectrs.; 3 Asst. Lectrs.

Forestry

Banana, A. Y., BSc Mak., MSc Calif., PhD ANU Sr. Lectr.

Byaruhanga, T. K., BSc Mak., MSc Mak. Sr. Lectr.

Gombya, S. S. W., BSc Mak., MSc Edin. Sr. Lectr.

Kaboggoza, J. R. S., BSc Mak., MSc Calif., PhD Calif. Sr. Lectr.; Head*

Obua, J., BSc Mak., MSc Wales, PhD Wales Sr. Lectr.

Ruyooka, R. D. A., BSc Wales, PhD ANU Prof.

Other Staff: 4 Lectrs.; 2 Asst. Lectrs.

Geography

Basalirwa, C. P. K., BSc Dar., MSc Nair., MSc N.U.I., PhD Nair. Sr. Lectr.

Nyakaana, J. B., BA Mak., MA Mak., PhD Amst. Sr. Lectr.

Sengendo, H., BA Mak., MA Leeds, PhD Nott. Lectr.; Acting Head*

Tukahirwa, J. M., BSc Mak., MSc E.Anglia, PhD Mak. Sr. Lectr.

Were, J. W., BA N.Y.State, MA N.Y.State Sr. Lectr.

Other Staff: 5 Lectrs.; 1 Asst. Lectr.; 3 Lectrs.†

Geology

Barifaijo, E., BSc N.Carolina, MSc N.Carolina Sr. Lectr.

Biryabarema, M., BSc Mak., MSc Mak. Sr. Lectr.

Muwanga, A., BSc Mak., MSc Mak. Lectr.; Head*

Other Staff: 2 Lectrs.; 1 Asst. Lectr.; 1 Lectr.†

Higher Education

Ocitti, J. P., BEd E.Af., MA Mak., PhD Dar. Prof.

Ssekamwa, C. J., BA E.Af., MA Mak., PhD Mak. Assoc. Prof.

Tiberondwa, A., BSc Lond., MA Col., PhD Dar. Sr. Lectr.

Other Staff: 1 Lectr.

History

Mulira, J., BA E.Af., MA Prin., PhD Prin. Assoc. Prof.

Okalany, D. H., BA Mak., MA Mak. Sr. Lectr.

Tibenderana, P. K., BA E.Af., PhD Ib. Prof.; Head*

Other Staff: 8 Lectrs.

Industrial Art and Design

Kwesiga, P. K., BA(FA) Mak., MA(FA) Mak. Sr. Lectr.

Other Staff: 4 Lectrs.; 1 Asst. Lectr.

Language Education

Nabukenya, M., BA Mak., MEd Mak. Sr. Lectr.; Head*

Nsibambi, R., BA Lond., MA Edin. Sr. Lectr.

Other Staff: 8 Lectrs.; 7 Asst. Lectrs.

Languages, Institute of

Byakutaga, S., BA Mak., MA Victoria Sr. Lectr.

Kalema, BA E.Af., MA Reading, PhD Reading Sr. Lectr.

Matovu, K., BA Mak., MA Nair., PhD Mak. Sr. Lectr.

Mukama, R., BA E.Af., MA E.Af., PhD York Prof.

Muranga, M. J. K., BA Mak., PhD Bayreuth Sr. Lectr.; Dir.*

Natukunda-Togboa, E. R., BA Mak., MA Mak., PhD Aix-Marseilles I Sr. Lectr.

Ndoleriire, A. K., BA Paris IV, MA Paris IV, PhD Paris IV Assoc. Prof.

Walusimbi, L., PhD Calif. Assoc. Prof.

Other Staff: 6 Lectrs.; 10 Asst. Lectrs.

Law and Jurisprudence

Ekirikubinza, L., LLB Mak., LLM Copenhagen, PhD Copenhagen Sr. Lectr.

Jjuuko, F. W., LLB Mak., LLM Mak. Assoc. Prof.

Kakooza, J. M. N., BCL N.U.I., LLB N.U.I., MLitt Oxf. Prof.

Nagitta, D., LLB Mak., LLMNott. Lectr.; Acting Head*

Tamale, S. R., LLB Mak., LLM Harv., PhD Minn. Sr. Lectr.

Other Staff: 2 Lectrs.

Law, Commercial

Bakibinga, D. J., LLB Mak., MA Lond., PhD Lond. Prof.

Kigula, J., LLB Mak., LLM Warw. Sr. Lectr.; Head*

Musisi, A. S., LLB Mak., LLM Dar. Sr. Lectr.

Tumwine-Mukubwa, G. P., LLB Dar., LLM York(Can.), LLD York(Can.) Assoc. Prof.

Other Staff: 5 Lectrs.

Law, Public and Comparative

Barya, J. J., LLB Mak., LLM Warw., PhD Warw. Sr. Lectr.; Head*

Katalikawe, J., LLB Lond., LLM Harv., MA Tufts, PhD Lond. Sr. Lectr.

Ntambirweki, J., LLB Mak., LLM Nair. Sr. Lectr.

Okumu-Wengi, R., LLB Dar., LLM Brussels Sr. Lectr.

Other Staff: 6 Lectrs.

Library and Information Science, East African School of, see Special Centres, etc

Literature and Mass Communication

Literature

Ejiet, A., BA Mak., MA Mak. Sr. Lectr.

Kiyimba, A., BA Mak., MLitt Strath. Sr. Lectr.; Acting Head*

Wangusa, Timothy, BA E.Af., MA Leeds, PhD Mak. Prof.

Other Staff: 8 Lectrs.; 1 Asst. Lectr.; 1 Sr. Res. Fellow

Mass Communication

5 Lectrs; 4 Asst. Lectrs.; 2 Hon. Lectrs.

Marketing and Management

Sejjaaka, Samuel, BCom Mak., MSc Strath. Lectr.; Acting Head*

Other Staff: 1 Lectr.; 7 Staff Devel. Fellows; 3 Lectrs.†

Business Administration

MBA Programme

22 Staff Members

Mass Communication, see Literature and Mass Communicn.

Mathematics

Luboobi, L. S., BSc E.Af., MSc Tor., PhD Adel. Prof.

Mangheni, P. J., BSc Mak., MA Oxf., MSc Oxf., DPhil Oxf. Sr. Lectr.; Head*

Mugambi, P. E., BSc Lond., MSc S'ton., PhD Roch. Prof.

Other Staff: 9 Lectrs.; 1 Lectr.†; 2 Hon. Lectrs.

Medicine, see below

Music, Dance and Drama

Adolu-Otajoka, Z., BSc Oregon, MM Oregon Sr. Lectr.; Head*

Mbowa, R., BA E.Af., MA Leeds Assoc. Prof.

Tamusuza, L., BA Mak., MA Bel. Assoc. Prof.

Other Staff: 5 Lectrs.

Philosophy

Beyaraza, BA Mak., MA Mak., PhD Bayreuth Sr. Lectr.

Dalfovo, A. T., BPhil Mak., PhD Mak., PhD Brun. Prof.; Head*

Kaboha, P., BA Lond., MA E.Af. Sr. Lectr.

Kigongo, J. K., BA Mak., MA Mak., PhD Mak. Sr. Lectr.

Other Staff: 4 Lectrs.

Physics

Banda, E. J. K. B., BSc E.Af., MA Roch., PhD Roch. Assoc. Prof.

Heisel, W., PhD Regensburg Sr. Lectr.

Ilukor, Odeke J., BSc Lond., PhD Roch. Prof.

Kaahwa, Y., BSc E.Af., MSc Alta., PhD NSW Prof.

Kwizera, P., PhD M.I.T. Assoc. Prof.

Mugambe, E. K. S., BSc Cal.Tech., DPhil Oxf. Assoc. Prof.

Odong-Edimu, C. W., BSc Mak., MSc Mak. Sr. Lectr.

Otiti, Tom, BSc Mak., MSc Reading Sr. Lectr.

Twesigomwe, E. M., BSc Mak., MSc Nair., PhD Mak. Sr. Lectr.; Head*

Other Staff: 7 Lectrs.

Political Science and Public Administration

Akiiki-Mujaju, B., BA Mak., MA Col., PhD Col. Prof.; Head*

Byarugaba, F. E., BA Mak., MA Mak., PhD Mak. Assoc. Prof.

Gingyera-Pincywa, A. A. G., BA Lond., MA Chic., PhD Lond. Prof.

Tangri, R., BA Leic., MSc Edin., PhD Edin. Assoc. Prof.

Other Staff: 11 Lectrs.; 2 Asst. Lectrs.

Population Studies, see Special Centres, etc (Stats. and Appl. Econ., Inst. of)

Printing and Art History

Ifee, F. X., BA(FA) Mak., MA(FA) Mak. Lectr.; Head*
Musango, G. F., MEd Sr. Lectr.
Sengendo, P. C. N., MA(FA) Mak. Assoc. Prof.
Sserulyo, I., MA(FA) Mak. Sr. Lectr.
Other Staff: 2 Lectrs.; 2 Asst. Lectrs.

Religious Studies

Byaruhanga-Akiiki, Rev. A. B. T., BA Notre
   Dame(Ind.), MA Holy Cross(Wash.), PhD
   E.Af. Prof.
Kabazzi-Kisirinya, BA Pontif.Urb., MA Pontif.Urb.,
   PhD Greg. Sr. Lectr.
Katahweire, Rev. Canon E. K., MDiv Prin., MTh
   Prin. Sr. Lectr.
Rutiba, Rev. E., BD Colgate-Roch., PhD Mak.,
   MTh Assoc. Prof.
Tinkasimire, T., BA Mak., MA Portland, PhD
   Gonzaga Lectr.; Acting Head*
Other Staff: 5 Lectrs.; 2 Asst. Lectrs.; 1 Visiting
   Lectr.; 1 Hon. Lectr.

Science and Technical Education

Mulemwa, J. N., BSc Mak., PhD Belf. Sr. Lectr.
Olango, P. O., BSc Mak., MA Bayreuth Sr.
   Lectr.; Head*
Other Staff: 6 Lectrs.; 4 Asst. Lectrs.

Sculpture

Naggenda, F. X., MA(FA) Munich Assoc. Prof.
Other Staff: 4 Lectrs.; 3 Asst. Lectrs.

Social Sciences and Arts Education

Balyejusa Ngobi, P., BA Chic., MA Chic. Sr.
   Lectr.
Mazinga, T. K. M., MEd Mak. Assoc. Prof.;
   Head*
Ocitti, J. P., BA E.Af., MA Mak., PhD Dar. Prof.
Odada, M., BA E.Af., MA Mak., PhD
   Mak. Assoc. Prof.
Tamwesigire, Rev. S., BA Mak., MA Lond. Sr.
   Lectr.
Other Staff: 8 Lectrs.; 3 Asst. Lectrs.

Social Work and Social Administration

Dufite-Bizimana, BA Mak., MSc Wales,
   PhD Lectr.; Acting Head*
Sengendo, J., BA Mak., MA S.Fraser, PhD
   Mak. Sr. Lectr.
Wandera-Nabaho, A., BA Mak., MA Mak., PhD
   Mak. Sr. Lectr.
Other Staff: 7 Lectrs.; 7 Asst. Lectrs.

Sociology

Kirumira, E. K., BA Mak., MA Exe., PhD
   Copenhagen Sr. Lectr.; Head*
Kisamba-Mugerwa, C., BA Mak., MA Nair. Sr.
   Lectr.
Mbaaga, F., BSc Alta., MSc Alta. Sr. Lectr.
Rwabukwali, C., BA Mak., MPA Arizona, MSc
   Case W.Reserve, PhD Case W.Reserve Sr. Lectr.
Other Staff: 7 Lectrs.; 4 Asst. Lectrs.

Soil Science

Aniku, J. R. F., BSc Alexandria, MSc Ghent, PhD
   Ohio Sr. Lectr.; Head*
Bekunda, M. A., BSc Mak., MSc Wageningen, PhD
   ANU Sr. Lectr.
Kitungulu-Zake, J. Y., BSc Mich., MSc Mich.,
   PhD Ohio Prof.
Ochwoh, V. O. A., BSc Mak., MSc Mak. Sr.
   Lectr.
Tumuhairwe, J., BSc Mak., MSc WI Sr. Lectr.
Other Staff: 5 Lectrs.; 2 Asst. Lectrs.

Statistics and Applied Economics, Institute of, see Special Centres, etc, below

Surveying

Batungi, N. A., BSc Nair., MSc Lagos Sr. Lectr.;
   Head*
Other Staff: 9 Lectrs.; 3 Asst. Lectrs.; 1 Lectr.†

Veterinary Medicine, see below

Women's Studies

Mcnairn, R. Assoc. Prof.; Commonwealth
   Expert; Head*
Other Staff: 8 Lectrs.

Zoology

Banage, W. B., BSc Lond., PhD Durh. Prof.
Baranga, D. D., BSc Mak., MSc Mak., PhD
   Mak. Sr. Lectr.
Basuta-Isabirye, G., BSc Mak., MSc Mak., PhD
   Mak. Sr. Lectr.
Kaddu, J. B., BSc E.Af., MSc Liv., PhD
   Nair. Assoc. Prof.
Kangwagye, T. N., BSc Lond., PhD E.Af. Assoc.
   Prof.
Kasoma, P. M. B., BSc Mak., MSc Mak., PhD
   Camb. Sr. Lectr.
Kizito, Y. S., BSc Mak., MSc Mak. Sr. Lectr.
Makanga, B., BSc Dar., MSc Mak., PhD
   Mak. Assoc. Prof.; Head*
Masaba, S., BA Calif., MSc Wales, PhD
   Wales Assoc. Prof.
Muyingo-Kezimbira, A., BSc Mak., MSc Mak.,
   PhD Mak. Sr. Lectr.
Okwakol, M. J. N., BSc Mak., MSc Mak., PhD
   Mak. Assoc. Prof.
Other Staff: 3 Lectrs.

MEDICINE

Anaesthesia

Bukwirwa, W. H., MB ChB Mak., MMed
   Mak. Lectr.; Head*
Other Staff: 1 Lectr.; 1 Hon. Lectr.

Anatomy

Luboga, S., MB ChB Mak., MMed Mak. Sr.
   Lectr.
Nzarubara, G. R., MB ChB Mak., MMed
   Mak. Assoc. Prof.; Head*
Other Staff: 2 Lectrs.; 2 Asst. Lectrs.; 3 Hon.
   Lectrs.

Child Health and Development Centre

Jessica, J. A., MB ChB MMed Lectr.; Dir.*
Other Staff: 1 Lectr.

Community Practice

Ndoboli, F. W., MB ChB MMed Lectr.;
   Head*
Other Staff: 2 Lectrs.

Dentistry

Ecec, S., BDS Lond. Assoc. Prof.; Head*
Other Staff: 2 Lectrs.; 2 Asst. Lectrs.

Ear, Nose and Throat

Tumweheire, G. O., MB ChB Mak., MMed
   Mak. Hon. Lectr.; Head*
Other Staff: 2 Lectrs.; 3 Hon. Lectrs.

Medical Illustration

Serumaga Sr. Med. Illustrator; Head*
Other Staff: 1 Sr. Asst. Med. Illustrator; 3 Asst.
   Med. Illustrators

Medicine

Freers, O. J., MB ChB Munich, MMed
   MTropMed MD Sr. Lectr.
Mugerwa, R. D., MB ChB Mak., MMed
   Mak. Prof.; Acting Head*
Okello, D., MB ChB Mak., MMed Mak. Sr.
   Lectr.
Otim, A. M., MB ChB Mak., MMed Mak., MD
   Mak., FRCP Prof.
Tabasoboke Katabira, E., MB ChB Mak. Sr.
   Lectr.; Head*
Other Staff: 4 Lectrs.; 1 Visiting Lectr.; 18
   Hon. Lectrs.

Microbiology

Aisu, T. O., MB ChB MMed Sr. Lectr.; Head*
Mercedes, C., BSc MD Sr. Lectr.
Munube, MB ChB, FRCPath Prof.
Other Staff: 3 Lectrs.; 1 Asst. Lectr.

Nursing

Mbabali, Specioza, MSN Lectr.; Head*
Other Staff: 3 Lectrs.

Obstetrics/Gynaecology

Kakande, H. W., MB ChB Mak., MMed
   Mak. Sr. Lectr.
Lule, J. C., MB ChB Mak., MMed Mak.,
   MSc N. Sr. Lectr.
Miiro, F. A., MB BS Bom., MB ChB Bom.,
   FRCOG Prof.; Head*
Mirembe, F., MB ChB Mak., MMed Mak., PhD
   Mak. Sr. Lectr.
Other Staff: 3 Lectrs.; 13 Hon. Lectrs.

Ophthalmology

Medi Kawuma, A., MB ChB Mak. Sr. Lectr.
Mwaka, F. P., MB ChB Mak., MMed Sr. Lectr.;
   Head*
Other Staff: 3 Lectrs.; 3 Hon. Lectrs.

Orthopaedics

3 Lectrs.; 2 Hon. Lectrs.

Paediatrics

Jitta, J. S., MB ChB MMed Sr. Lectr.
Karamagi, C. A., MB ChB MMed Sr. Lectr.
Mukasa, J. S., MB ChB MMed Sr. Lectr.;
   Head*
Ndugwa, C. M., MB ChB MMed Prof.
Tumwine, J., MB ChB MMed Sr. Lectr.
Other Staff: 4 Lectrs.; 1 Nutritionist; 11 Hon.
   Lectrs.

Pathology

Byarugaba, W., MSc Cologne, PhD Cologne,
   BSc Sr. Lectr.
Odida, M., MB ChB MMed Sr. Lectr.
Owor, R., MB ChB E.Af., MD E.Af.,
   FRCPath Prof.
Wabinga, H. R., MB ChB MMed Sr. Lectr.
Wamukota, M. W., MD Jerusalem,
   MMed Assoc. Prof.; Head*
Other Staff: 1 Hon. Lectr.

Pharmacology and Therapeutics

Anokbongo, W. W., PhD Brad., MSc
   MD Prof.; Head*
Nawerere, Y., MSc Lond., MB ChB Sr. Lectr.
Ogwal-Okeng, J. W., MB ChB MSc Sr. Lectr.
Other Staff: 1 Asst. Lectr.

Pharmacy

Adome, Odoi, BPharm Delhi, MSc Delhi,
   PhD Sr. Lectr.; Head*
Odyek, Olwa, BSc MSc PhD Assoc. Prof.
Owino, E., MSc PhD Sr. Lectr.
Other Staff: 7 Lectrs.; 1 Asst. Lectr.

Physiology

Nakiboneka Mazzi, J. N., MB ChB Mak., MSc
   Mak. Lectr.; Acting Head*
Okullo, J. H., MB ChB Mak., MSc Lond. Sr.
   Lectr.
Walumbe, J. M., MB ChB Mak., MSc
   Lond. Prof.
Other Staff: 3 Lectrs.

Psychiatry

Nakasi, G., MB ChB Mak., MMed Mak. Sr.
   Lectr.
Ovuga, E. B. L., MB ChB Mak., MMed
   Mak. Sr. Lectr.; Head*
Rwegellera, G., MB ChB E.Af., MPhil Assoc.
   Prof.
Tugumisirize, J., MB ChB Mak., MMed
   Mak. Sr. Lectr.
Other Staff: 1 Lectr.; 3 Asst. Lectrs.; 4 Hon.
   Lectrs.

Public Health, Institute of

Bazeyo, M., MB ChB MPH Sr. Lectr.
Kakitahi, J. T., MB ChB Mak., MSc Mak.,
   MPH Assoc. Prof.
Konde-Lule, Y. K., MB ChB MPH Sr. Lectr.
Ndungutse, D., MB ChB Mak., MPH Mak. Sr.
   Lectr.
Oryema-Lalobo, M., BSc MPH Sr. Lectr.
Serwadda, D., MB ChB MMed MPH Sr. Lectr.

Wabwire-Manghen, MB ChB *Mak.*, MMed
Mak. Sr. Lectr.; Head*
Zirabamuzaale, C., MB ChB MPH Sr. Lectr.
Other Staff: 5 Lectrs.; 1 Hon. Lectr.

Radiology
Kasozi, H., MD Prof.
Kawoya, M. G., MB ChB MMed Sr. Lectr.;
Head*
Mugambe, Kigula, MB ChB MMed Sr. Lectr.
Other Staff: 4 Lectrs.

Surgery
Kakande, I., MB ChB MMed Assoc. Prof.
Kijjambu, S., MB ChB MMed Sr. Lectr.;
Head*
Omaswa, F. G., MB ChB MMed, FRCS Assoc.
Prof.; Consultant
Other Staff: 6 Lectrs.; 18 Hon. Lectrs.

VETERINARY MEDICINE

Veterinary Anatomy
Bukenya, E. M. F., BSc *E.Af.*, MSc *Mak.* Sr.
Lectr.
Dranzoa, C., BSc *Mak.*, MSc *Mak.*, PhD
Mak. Sr. Lectr.
Muwazi, R. T., BVM *Mak.*, MSc *Mak.*, PhD
Mak. Sr. Lectr.; Head*
Other Staff: 2 Lectrs.; 1 Lectr.†

Veterinary Medicine
Katunguka, K. E., BVM *Mak.*, MSc Trinity(Dub.),
PhD *Glas.* Assoc. Prof.
Mukiibi, J. Sr. Lectr.
Mwambu, P. M., MSc *Nair.* Sr. Lectr.; Head*
Omara-Opyene, BVM *Khart.*, MSc *Nair.* Sr.
Lectr.
Other Staff: 2 Asst. Lectrs.

Veterinary Parasitology and Microbiology
Lubega, G. W., BVM *Mak.*, MSc *McG.*, PhD
McG. Assoc. Prof.
Nyeko, J. P. H., BVM *Mak.*, MSc *Mak.*, PhD
Mak. Sr. Lectr.
Rubaire-Akiiki, C., BVM *Nair.*, MSc *Nair.* Sr.
Lectr.; Head*
Wafula, Z. O., BVSc *E.Af.*, MSc *Mak.* Sr. Lectr.
Other Staff: 3 Lectrs.

Veterinary Pathology
Aruo, S. K., BVSc *Qld.* Sr. Lectr.
Ojok-Lonzy, BVM *Mak.*, PhD *Mak.*, DrVetMed
Giessen Assoc. Prof.; Head*
Other Staff: 1 Lectr.

Veterinary Physiological Sciences
Okello, K. L., BVM *Nair.*, MSc *Mak.* Sr. Lectr.
Other Staff: 3 Lectrs.; 1 Asst. Lectr.

Veterinary Public Health and Preventive Medicine
Opuda-Asibo, J., BVM *Mak.*, MSc *Minn.*, PhD
Minn. Prof.; Head*
Other Staff: 4 Lectrs.; 2 Asst. Lectrs.

Veterinary Surgery and Reproduction
Acon, J., BVS *Mak.*, MSc *Flor.*, PhD *Mak.* Assoc.
Prof.
Koma, L. M. P. K., BVM *Mak.*, MPhil *Edin.* Sr.
Lectr.; Head*
Other Staff: 5 Lectrs.; 1 Asst. Lectr.

Wildlife and Animal Resources Management
Dranzoa, C., BSc *Mak.*, MSc *Mak.*, PhD
Mak. Sr. Lectr.; Acting Head*
Okello, K. L., BVM *Nair.*, MSc *Mak.* Sr. Lectr.
Siefert, L., DrVetMed *Hanover* Sr. Lectr.
Other Staff: 2 Lectrs.; 1 Hon. Lectr.

SPECIAL CENTRES, ETC

Computer Science, Institute of
Mulira, J. N., BA *Mak.*, MSc *Lond.* Acting Dir.*
Other Staff: 6 Lectrs.; 2 Asst. Lectrs.

Environment and Natural Resources, Institute of
Jackel, N., PhD *Gött.* Sr. Lectr.
Kasoma, P., BSc *Mak.*, MSc *Mak.*, PhD
Camb. Sr. Lectr.; Acting Dir.*
Pomeroy, D. E., MA *Camb.*, PhD *Adel.* Prof.;
Deputy Dir.
Other Staff: 5 Lectrs.; 1 Asst. Lectr.; 1 Res.
Fellow

Human Rights and Peace Centre (HURIPEC)
Oloka-Onyango, J., LLB *Mak.*, LLM *Harv.*, SJD
Harv. Assoc. Prof.
Tindifa, S. B., LLB *Mak.*, LLM *Lund* Lectr.;
Acting Dir.*
Other Staff: 3 Lectrs.

Library and Information Science, East African School of (EASLIS)
Abidi, S. A. H., MA *Agra*, MLibSc *Delhi*, BA
PhD Dir.*
Kigongo-Bukenya, MA Sr. Lectr.
Other Staff: 2 Lectrs.; 2 Asst. Lectrs.

Makerere University Agricultural Research Institute, Kabanyolo (MUARIK)
Bekunda, M. A., BSc *Mak.*, MSc *Wageningen*, PhD
ANU Acting Dir.*
Other Staff: 3 Asst. Farm Managers

Social Research, Makerere Institute of
Munene, J., BA *Mak.*, MSc *Sheff.*, MSc *Wales*,
PhD *Lond.* Assoc. Prof.; Acting Dir.*
Other Staff: 1 Sr. Res. Fellow; 8 Res. Fellows;
4 MISR Res. Assocs.

ADULT AND CONTINUING EDUCATION, INSTITUTE OF

Adult and Communications Studies
Kakooza, T., BSc *Wales*, MEd *Mak.*, PhD
Mak. Sr. Lectr.
Katahoire, A., BA *Hull*, MEd *Glas.* Sr. Lectr.
Okech, A., BA *E.Af.*, STL *Rome*, LèsL *Besançon*,
MèsL *Besançon* Sr. Lectr.; Head*
Other Staff: 4 Lectrs.

Community Education and Extra-Mural Studies
Atim, D. K., BA *Mak.*, MEd *NE* Sr. Lectr.
Openjuru, G., BA *Mak.*, MEd *Mak.* Lectr.;
Head*
Other Staff: 4 Lectrs.

Distance Education
Bbuye, J., BA *Mak.*, MEd *Mak.* Lectr.; Head*
Sentongo, Nuwa, BA *E.Af.*, MA *Indiana* Sr.
Lectr.; Dir. of Inst.*
Other Staff: 2 Lectrs.; 1 Editor

STATISTICS AND APPLIED ECONOMICS, INSTITUTE OF

Planning and Applied Statistics
Atuhaire, L. K., BStat *Mak.*, MSc *S'ton.*, PhD
S'ton. Sr. Lectr.
Kibirige, G. W., BSc *Mak.*, MSc *Mak.*, MA
Ott. Sr. Lectr.; Dir. of Inst.*
Sekibobo, A., BStat *Mak.*, MStat *Mak.* Sr. Lectr.
Other Staff: 10 Lectrs.; 1 Lectr.†

Population Studies
Ntozi, J. P. N., BSc *Mak.*, MSc *Mak.*, PhD
Lond. Prof.
Ssekamatte, S. J., BA *Mak.*, PhD *Brown* Sr.
Lectr.; Head*
Other Staff: 7 Lectrs.; 2 Asst. Lectrs.; 1
Commonwealth Expert

Statistical Methods
Byamugisha, A., BStat *Mak.*, MSc *Sheff.* Lectr.;
Head*
Mugisha, X. R., BA *Dar.*, PhD Assoc. Prof.;
Assoc. Dir. of Inst.
Tulya-Mulika, BSc *E.Af.*, PhD *Sheff.* Prof.
Other Staff: 8 Lectrs.; 1 Asst. Lectr.; 1 Lectr.†

CONTACT OFFICERS

Academic affairs. Academic Registrar: Hyuha,
Mukwanason A., BSc *Mak.*, MA *S.Fraser*, PhD
Alta.
Accommodation. Dean of Students: Ekudu-
Adoku, John, BSc *Mak.*
Admissions (first degree). Deputy Academic
Registrar (Admissions): Bazanye-Nkangi, G.,
BSc *Mak.*, MEd *NE*
Admissions (higher degree). Deputy Registrar:
Okello, J. G., BA *Mak.*, MSc *Sur.*
Adult/continuing education. Senior Lecturer:
Katahoire, A., BA *Hull*, MEd *Glas.*
Archives. University Librarian: Mugasha, J.,
BSc *E.Af.*, MSLS *Ohio*
Careers. Senior Assistant Registrar: Bukenya,
A., BA *Mak.*
Computing services. Director of Computer
Science: Katiti, E. B., BSc *CNAA*, MSc *Essex*,
PhD *Essex*
Development/fund-raising. Acting Director:
Kalema, E., BA *Mak.*
Distance education. Director, Institute of
Adult and Continuing Education: Odurkene,
J. N., BA *E.Af.*, MLitt *Oxf.*
Estates and buildings/works and services.
Senior Assistant Engineer: Kerali, G. A.,
BSc(Eng) *Mak.*, MSc
Examinations. Deputy Academic Registrar:
Kiiza, P. N., BA *Mak.*
Finance. Bursar: Byambabazi, Ben, BCom *Mak.*,
MBA *Mak.*
General enquiries. Academic Registrar:
Hyuha, Mukwanason A., BSc *Mak.*, MA
S.Fraser, PhD *Alta.*
Health services. Acting Director, University
Hospital: Bosa, Jane, MB ChB *Mak.*
Industrial liaison. Lecturer: Byaruhanga, J. K.,
PhD
Library (chief librarian). University Librarian:
Mugasha, J., BSc *E.Af.*, MSLS *Ohio*
Ombudsperson. Legal Officer: Lubwama-
Musisi, J., LLB *Mak.*
Personnel/human resources. Senior Assistant
Secretary, Personnel: Lubwama, F. J. Y., BA
Mak., MA *Lond.*
Public relations, information and marketing.
Acting Public Relations Officer: Mayegai, H.,
BA *Mak.*
Publications. Senior Assistant Registrar:
Karindiriza, E. S. K., BA(Educn) *Mak.*, MEd
Mak.
Purchasing. Senior Assistant Bursar
(Purchasing): Mugamba, R., BCom *Mak.*,
MBA
Research. Senior Assistant Registrar:
Karindiriza, E. S. K., BA(Educn) *Mak.*, MEd
Mak.
Scholarships, awards, loans. Academic
Registrar: Hyuha, Mukwanason A., BSc *Mak.*,
MA *S.Fraser*, PhD *Alta.*
Security. Deputy Vice-Chancellor: Epelu-Opio,
Prof. J., BVSc *Nair.*, MSc *Nair.*, PhD *Mak.*
Sport and recreation. Principal Sports Tutor:
Mugisha, E. N. B., BScEd *N.Y.State*, MScEd
N.Y.State
Staff development and training. Deputy
Registrar (Staff Development): Kigenyi, T.
N., BSc *Mak.*
Student welfare/counselling. Principal
Counsellor: Matovu, P. C., BA(Educn) ThM
MA PhD
Students from other countries. Deputy
Academic Registrar (Admissions): Bazanye-
Nkangi, G., BSc *Mak.*, MEd *NE*

CAMPUS/COLLEGE HEADS

Institute of Teacher Education, Kyambogo.
Principal: Lutalo-Bosa, A., BSc *Lond.*, MSc
McG., PhD *McG.*
Kyambogo Polytechnic. Principal: Rwendeire,
A. J. J., BSc *Mak.*, PhD
Uganda College of Commerce. Principal:
Rwambulla, W., MSc

[*Information supplied by the institution as at June 1998,
and edited by the ACU*]

MBARARA UNIVERSITY OF SCIENCE AND TECHNOLOGY

Founded 1989

Member of the Association of Commonwealth Universities

Postal Address: PO Box 1410, Mbarara, Uganda
Telephone: (0485) 20782-3 Fax: (0485) 20782 E-mail: must@ugu.healthnet.org Cables: MUST UGA
(Overseas Office: (Liaison Office: PO Box 7062, Kampala. Telephone: (041) 533162))

CHANCELLOR—H.E. the President of Uganda, and Commander in Chief of the Armed Forces
(ex officio)
VICE-CHANCELLOR*—Kayanja, Prof. Frederick I. B., BVetMed Lond., MSc Lond., PhD E.Af.
ACADEMIC REGISTRAR—Bazirake, S. B., BA E.Af.
UNIVERSITY SECRETARY‡—Kibirige, C. K., MB ChB Kalinin
UNIVERSITY BURSAR—Tushabomwe-Kazooba, BCom Mak., MBA Birm.

GENERAL INFORMATION

History. The university was founded in 1989. It is located in Mbarara, 260km southwest of Kampala.

Admission. to first degree courses. General Certificate of Education (GCE) O level and passes in at least 2 A levels at the same sitting, or equivalent qualifications. International applicants who do not possess A levels must have completed at least one year of a relevant university course.

First Degrees. BDevSc, BSc(Ed), BScCompt, MB ChB.
Most courses last 3 years. MB ChB: 5 years.

Higher Degrees. MD, MMed, MSc, PhD.
MD, MSc: minimum 2 years; MMed: minimum 3 years; PhD: minimum 4 years.

Libraries. 15,000 volumes; 15 periodicals subscribed to.

Fees. (1998–99). Undergraduate: home students Ush2,120,000 (medicine), Ush1,400,000 (all other courses); international students US$3400 (medicine), US$2000 (all other courses). Postgraduate: US$1400 (sciences).

Academic Year. Most courses: three terms; medicine: four terms. October–December; January–March; April–June; (fourth term) June–August.

Income (1998–99, estimated). Ush1,343,902,000.

Statistics. (1997–98). Staff: 506 (54 academic, 452 hospital and administrative). Students: full-time 334 (249 men, 85 women); international 6 (4 men, 2 women).

FACULTIES/SCHOOLS

Medicine
Tel: (0485) 20786
Dean: Mutakooha, E. K., MB ChB Mak., MMed Mak.

Science Education
Tel: (0485) 20851
Dean: Barranga, Prof. J., BSc(Ed) Mak., MSc Mak., PhD Mak.

ACADEMIC UNITS

Anatomy
Kayanja, F. I. B., BVetMed Lond., MSc Lond., PhD E.Af. Prof.
Labrada, Carmen A., MD Camagёy Assoc. Prof.; Head*
Other Staff: 2 Lectrs.; 2 Asst. Lectrs.

Biochemistry
Isharaza, W. K., MSc Mak., PhD Brussels Assoc. Prof.; Head*
Mohamoud, S., BSc Dijon, PhD Dijon Assoc. Prof.
Other Staff: 1 Lectr.; 1 Asst. Lectr.

Development Studies
Mbabazi, Pamela, BA Mak., MA Leeds, MA Ghana
Other Staff: 1 Lectr.; 1 Asst. Lectr.

Internal Medicine
Pepper, James L., BSc Mich.State, MSc Dayton, DO Mich.State Prof.
Socorro, Felipe, MD Havana Prof.; Head*
Other Staff: 1 Lectr.; 1 Asst. Lectr.

Mathematics
Wanjala, P., BSc Mak., MSc Mak Lectr.; Head*
Other Staff: 2 Lectrs.

Microbiology and Parasitology
Kigaye, M. K., BSc Tuskegee, DVM Tuskegee, MSc Cornell Assoc. Prof.; Head*
Tamara, Teresa, MD Havana Assoc. Prof.
Other Staff: 1 Lectr.

Obstetrics/Gynaecology
Herpay, G., MD Debrecen Prof.; Head*
Wasswa, G. M., MB ChB Mak., MMed Mak. Sr. Lectr.
Other Staff: 1 Lectr.; 1 Asst. Lectr.

Paediatrics and Child Health
Dobreva-Vaptzarova, D., MD Sofia Prof.; Head*
Other Staff: 1 Lectr.; 1 Asst. Lectr.

Pathology
Perez Padilla, Eduardo, MD Camagüey Assoc. Prof.; Head*
Other Staff: 2 Lectrs.

Pharmacology
Makanga, M. M., MB ChB Mak., MSc Liv. Lectr.; Head*
Other Staff: 2 Lectrs.

Physics
Ssozi, T., BSc Mak., MSc Mak. Lectr.; Head*
Other Staff: 2 Lectrs.

Physiology
Begumya, Y. R., BSc Mak., MB BS Khart. Prof.; Head*
Mukiibi, N., MSc Moscow, PhD Moscow Assoc. Prof.
Murphy, Oliver, MB BCh BAO Trinity(Dub.) Prof.
Other Staff: 1 Lectr.; 1 Asst. Lectr.

Psychology/Psychiatry
Van Duyl, Marjolein, MD Limburg Assoc. Prof.; Head*
Other Staff: 1 Asst. Lectr.

Public Health
Kabakyenga, J., MB ChB Mak., MSc Leeds Lectr.; Head*
Yidong Jin, MD Beijing, MMed Beijing Visiting Prof.
Other Staff: 2 Lectrs.; 3 Lectrs.†

Surgery
El Baz, Elfriede, DrMed Gött. Prof.; Head*
Mutakooha, E. K., MB ChB Mak., MMed Mak. Sr. Lectr.
Rodriguez Garcia, Hortensia, MD Havana Assoc. Prof.
Other Staff: 5 Lectrs.

SPECIAL CENTRES, ETC

Tropical Forest Conservation, Institute of
Malenky, Richard, BS N.Y.State, MS Chic., PhD N.Y.State Dir.*

CONTACT OFFICERS

Academic affairs. Academic Registrar: Bazirake, S. B., BA E.Af.
Accommodation. Dean of Students: Katungwensi-Rubimbwa, BA Mak., MA Lond.
Admissions (first degree). Senior Assistant Registrar: Kibirige, J. L., BA Mak., MA Mak.
Admissions (higher degree). Academic Registrar: Bazirake, S. B., BA E.Af.
Alumni. Senior Assistant Registrar: Opio, Okello F., BA Mak., MA Mak.
Estates and buildings/works and services. University Engineer: Besigiroha, N., BScEng E.Af.
Examinations. Senior Assistant Registrar: Opio, Okello F., BA Mak., MA Mak.
Finance. University Bursar: Tushabomwe-Kazooba, BCom Mak., MBA Birm.
General enquiries. Academic Registrar: Bazirake, S. B., BA E.Af.
Library (chief librarian). Librarian: Kamihanda, Lawrence, BLIS Mak.
Personnel/human resources. University Secretary: Kibirige, C. K., MB ChB Kalinin
Publications. Senior Assistant Registrar: Opio, Okello F., BA Mak., MA Mak.
Purchasing. Senior Assistant Bursar: Tumwesigye, Deogratius, BCom Mak.
Research. Academic Registrar: Bazirake, S. B., BA E.Af.
Sport and recreation. Sports Tutor: Tumwesigye, Charles, BScAgric Mak., MEd Mak.
Staff development and training. Academic Registrar: Bazirake, S. B., BA E.Af.

[Information supplied by the institution as at 13 August 1998, and edited by the ACU]

NKUMBA UNIVERSITY

Postal Address: PO Box 237, Entebbe, Uganda
Telephone: (042) 20134 **Fax**: (041) 321448

VICE-CHANCELLOR*—Senteza Kajubi, Prof. William, MA Chic.
REGISTRAR‡—Kasasa, David C., BA Mak.

UGANDA MARTYRS UNIVERSITY

Founded 1993

Member of the Association of Commonwealth Universities

Postal Address: PO Box 5498, Kampala, Uganda
Telephone: (0481) 21894 **Fax**: (0481) 21898 **E-mail**: umu@imul.com
WWW: http://www.fiuc.org/umu/umu.html

CHANCELLOR—Chairman, Uganda Episcopal Conference (ex officio)
PATRON—His Eminence Cardinal Archbishop of Kampala Archdiocese (ex officio)
CHAIRMAN OF COUNCIL—Oyanga, His Lordship Bishop Joseph
VICE-CHANCELLOR*—Lejeune, Michel, LLD Louvain
DEPUTY VICE-CHANCELLOR—Kanyandago, Peter, BTh Louvain, MA Louvain, PhD Louvain
REGISTRAR‡—Onyango, Bernard, MA Lond.

GENERAL INFORMATION

History. The university was founded in 1993. It is a Catholic institution.

Admission to first degree courses. Uganda Certificate of Education with at least 2 subjects at A level. Post-secondary diplomas are also considered.

First Degrees. BA, BBAM (business administration and management), BSc.
All courses are full-time and last 3 years.
The following subjects may be studied at first degree level: business administration and management, computer science, development, economics, ethics, mathematics, statistics.

Higher Degrees. MA in ethics, development and African studies (1 year).

Libraries. 16,000 volumes; 2000 periodicals. Special collection: African Research Documentation Centre (ARDC).

Fees (1998–99, annual). Undergraduate: US$2760. Postgraduate: US$3310.

Academic Year (1998–99). Two semesters: 28 September–24 January; 25 January–4 June.

Income (1996–97). Total, US$448,502.

Statistics. Staff: 45 (24 academic, 21 administrative). Students: full-time 188 (83 men, 105 women); international 6.

FACULTIES/SCHOOLS

Business Administration and Management

Dean: Haflett, Marie-Esther, BA Detroit, MA Detroit, MA Notre Dame(Ind.), PhD Notre Dame(Ind.)
Secretary: Nakyagaba, Sarah

ACADEMIC UNITS

Accounting and Finance

Ssenyonjo, Vincent M. M., MSc Reading, BCom   Sr. Lectr.
Other Staff: 6 Lectrs; 2 Lectrs.†

African Studies, see Ethics and African Studies

Business Law

Nalyanya, Matthias, LLB Mak., LLM Lond.   Sr. Lectr.; Head*

Computer Science

2 Lectrs.

Development Studies

No staff at present.

Economics and Mathematics

Haflett, Marie-Esther, BA Detroit, MA Detroit, MA Notre Dame(Ind.), PhD Notre Dame(Ind.)   Sr. Lectr.
Other Staff: 2 Lectrs.

Ethics and African Studies

Carabine, Deirdre, BA Belf., MA Belf., PhD Belf., PhD N.U.I.   Asst. Prof.; Head*
Kanyandago, Peter, BTh Louvain, MA Louvain, PhD Louvain   Asst. Prof.
Other Staff: 1 Lectr.

Extra-Mural Studies

Heidenreich-Naganda, Cecilia, BA Mak., MEd Dund., PhD Bayreuth   Lectr.; Head*
Other Staff: 1 Lectr.

Hospital Administration and Management

Zirembuzi, George, MD Padua. MMed Mak.   Lectr.; Head*
Other Staff: 1 Lectr.; 2 Lectrs.†

Law, see Bus. Law

Management and Marketing

4 Lectrs.

SPECIAL CENTRES, ETC

African Research and Documentation Centre

Kanyandago, Peter, BTh Louvain, MA Louvain, PhD Louvain   Head*
Other Staff: 1 Res. Co-ordinator

Ethics and Development Studies, Institute of

Carabine, Deirdre, BA Belf., MA Belf., PhD Belf., PhD N.U.I.   Dir.*
Other Staff: 4 Lectrs.

CONTACT OFFICERS

Academic affairs. Registrar: Onyango, Bernard, MA Lond.
Accommodation. Campus Warden: Mugabi, Christopher, BBAM Uganda Martyrs
Admissions (first degree). Registrar: Onyango, Bernard, MA Lond.
Admissions (higher degree). Registrar: Onyango, Bernard, MA Lond.
Adult/continuing education. Lecturer: Heidenreich-Nganda, Cecilia, BA Mak., MEd Dund., PhD Bayreuth
Alumni. Vice-Chancellor: Lejeune, Michel, LLD Louvain
Archives. Deputy Vice-Chancellor: Kanyandago, Peter, BTh Louvain, MA Louvain, PhD Louvain
Computing services. Lecturer: Ramjit, Vladimir, BSc Lond., MSc Manc., MSc Lond., MPhil Lond.
Credit transfer. Registrar: Onyango, Bernard, MA Lond.
Development/fund-raising. Vice-Chancellor: Lejeune, Michel, LLD Louvain

Distance education. Lecturer: Heidenreich-Nganda, Cecilia, BA Mak., MEd Dund., PhD Bayreuth

Equal opportunities. Registrar: Onyango, Bernard, MA Lond.

Estates and buildings/works and services. Estates Officer: Ssembatya, Lawrence

Examinations. Registrar: Onyango, Bernard, MA Lond.

Finance. Vice-Chancellor: Lejeune, Michel, LLD Louvain

General enquiries. Registrar: Onyango, Bernard, MA Lond.

Health services. Nurse: Mwagale, Sr. Specioza

International office. Vice-Chancellor: Lejeune, Michel, LLD Louvain

Library (enquiries). Assistant Librarian: Luswejje, Aaron, BLIS Mak.

Minorities/disadvantaged groups. Deputy Vice-Chancellor: Kanyandago, Peter, BTh Louvain, MA Louvain, PhD Louvain

Personnel/human resources. Registrar: Onyango, Bernard, MA Lond.

Public relations, information and marketing. Registrar: Onyango, Bernard, MA Lond.

Publications. Vice-Chancellor: Lejeune, Michel, LLD Louvain

Purchasing. Purchasing Officer: Tamale, Dominic

Quality assurance and accreditation. Registrar: Onyango, Bernard, MA Lond.

Research. Vice-Chancellor: Lejeune, Michel, LLD Louvain

Safety. Estates Officer: Ssembatya, Lawrence

Scholarships, awards, loans. Vice-Chancellor: Lejeune, Michel, LLD Louvain

Schools liaison. Assistant Lecturer: Muhwezi, Augustin, LLB Mak.

Security. Campus Warden: Mugabi, Christopher, BBAM Uganda Martyrs

Sport and recreation. Deputy Vice-Chancellor: Kanyandago, Peter, BTh Louvain, MA Louvain, PhD Louvain

Staff development and training. Vice-Chancellor: Lejeune, Michel, LLD Louvain

Student union. Deputy Vice-Chancellor: Kanyandago, Peter, BTh Louvain, MA Louvain, PhD Louvain

Student welfare/counselling. Deputy Vice-Chancellor: Kanyandago, Peter, BTh Louvain, MA Louvain, PhD Louvain

Students from other countries. Deputy Vice-Chancellor: Kanyandago, Peter, BTh Louvain, MA Louvain, PhD Louvain

Students with disabilities. Campus Warden: Mugabi, Christopher, BBAM Uganda Martyrs

University Press. Owa-Mataze, Nduhukire, BA(Ed) Dar., MA Essex

University press. Vice-Chancellor: Lejeune, Michel, LLD Louvain

[Information supplied by the institution as at 18 February 1998, and edited by the ACU]

UNITED KINGDOM

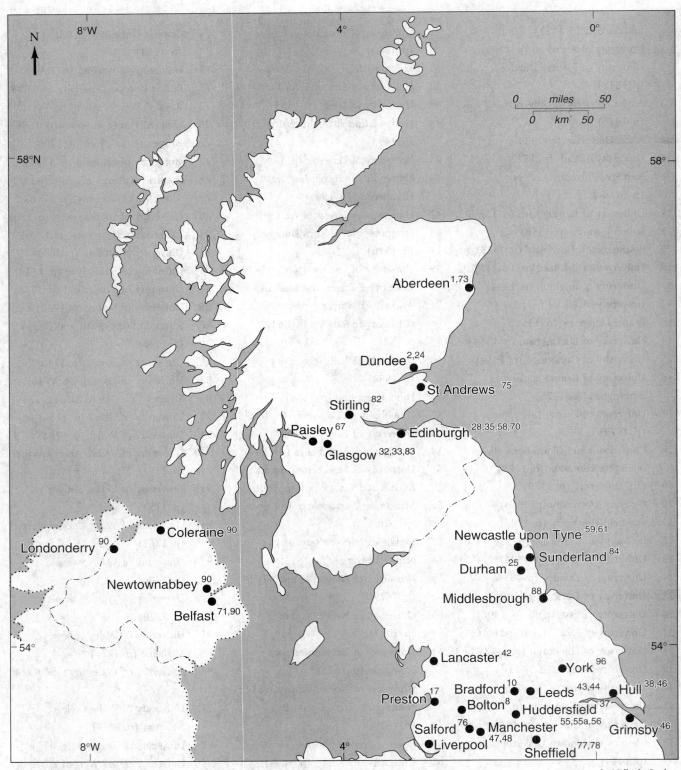

N

8°W   4°   0°

0   miles   50

0   km   50

58°N   58°

Aberdeen [1,73]

Dundee [2,24]

St Andrews [75]

Stirling [82]

Paisley [67]

Edinburgh [28,35,58,70]

Glasgow [32,33,83]

Coleraine [90]

Londonderry [90]

Newcastle upon Tyne [59,61]

Sunderland [84]

Newtownabbey [90]

Durham [25]

Belfast [71,90]

Middlesbrough [88]

54°   54°

Lancaster [42]

York [96]

Bradford [10]   Leeds [43,44]   Hull [38,46]

Preston [17]

Bolton [8]   Huddersfield [37]

Salford [76]   [55,55a,56]

Manchester [47,48]   Grimsby [46]

Liverpool   Sheffield [77,78]

8°W   4°

The places named are the seats of the university institutions in Northern England, Northern Ireland and Scotland numbered on p. 1309. For university institutions in the Midlands, Southern England and Wales, see next page

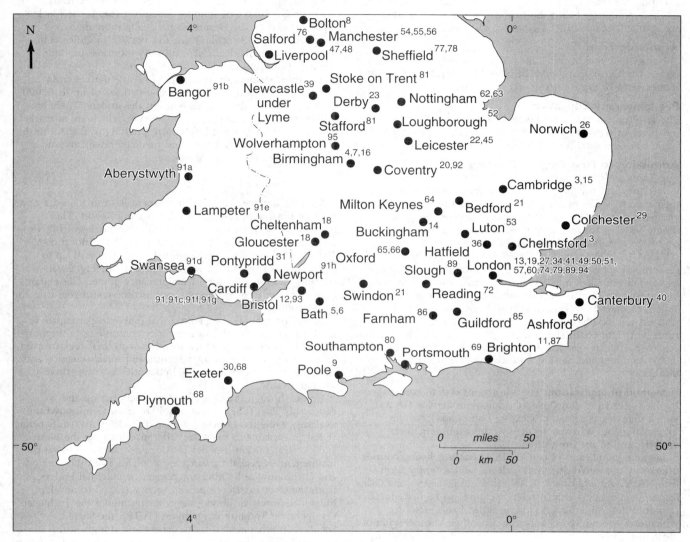

N

Bolton [8]
Salford [76] Manchester [54,55,56]
Liverpool [47,48] Sheffield [77,78]
Stoke on Trent [81]
Bangor [91b] Newcastle [39]
under Derby [23] Nottingham [62,63]
Lyme
Stafford [81] Loughborough [52]
Wolverhampton [95] Leicester [22,45]
Norwich [26]
Birmingham [4,7,16]
Coventry [20,92]
Aberystwyth [91a]
Cambridge [3,15]
Lampeter [91e] Milton Keynes [64] Bedford [21]
Cheltenham [18] Buckingham [14] Luton [53] Colchester [29]
Gloucester [18] Hatfield [36] Chelmsford [3]
Swansea [91d] Pontypridd [31] Oxford [65,66] London [13,19,27,34,41,49,50,51,
Newport [91h] Slough [89] 57,60,74,79,89,94]
Cardiff Swindon [21] Reading [72]
91,91c,91f,91g Bristol [12,93] Canterbury [40]
Bath [5,6] Farnham [86] Guildford [85] Ashford [50]
Southampton [80] Brighton [11,87]
Poole [9] Portsmouth [69]
Exeter [30,68]
Plymouth [68]

miles 50
km 50

The places named are the seats of the university institutions in the Midlands, Southern England and Wales numbered on p. 1309. For university institutions in Northern England, Northern Ireland and Scotland, see previous page

THE UNIVERSITIES OF THE UNITED KINGDOM

Information compiled by the Committee of Vice-Chancellors and Principals of the Universities of the United Kingdom as at 18 November 1998

The University System

There are 90 university institutions in the United Kingdom, counting the federal universities of London and Wales each as single institutions (113 if the constituent parts of the latter two are counted separately).

Academic Year

The academic year in the United Kingdom begins in September/October and ends in June. Most institutions operate a three-term or two-semester system.

Pre-University Education

The government-maintained education system and the independent sector together provide 13 years of primary and secondary education for all children in the United Kingdom.

Admission to First Degree Courses

Applicants are free to apply to their own choice of British universities and colleges, and the institutions are free to make their own selection of students: there is no automatic entitlement to a place and entry is competitive. Entry for 'home' undergraduates, domiciled in Britain, is based largely on results obtained in the General Certificate of Education (GCE) A Level Examination. For 'mature students' over 21 at the time of application, alternative qualifications and previous experience are taken into account. International students may be assessed on the basis of performance in the examination system of their own countries. In addition, international students are usually required to provide evidence of ability to read, write and comprehend the English language. This can be achieved either by passing a British Council Test, or equivalent, or by attending and passing a suitable course at the accepting university.

Method of application. The admissions system is managed by the Universities and Colleges Admissions Service (UCAS), which operates as a central 'clearing house' and provides information and advisory services to the applicants, their advisers, and to the institutions.

Intending applicants obtain *The UCAS Handbook* listing courses offered by the universities and colleges, and an entry form from UCAS. An additional UCAS publication, *University and College Entrance*, is a detailed annual reference guide to higher education opportunities. Applicants decide on up to five courses for which they would like to apply, and list their choices without indicating an order of preference. Completed applications are usually returned to UCAS by December of the year preceding the start of courses, but later applications are accepted. UCAS is responsible for processing the applications and sending copies to each institution to allow selection. Conditional offers made by the institutions are notified to UCAS, who in turn notify the applicants. Once public examination results are available, usually in August of the entry year, institutions decide which conditional applicants satisfy the entry requirements. A sophisticated clearing process is available from late August to match some of the unsuccessful applicants to courses with available places.

Finance

With the exception of Buckingham, British universities are largely financed, directly or indirectly, from government sources. Under the stimulus of reduced funding from government and its positive policy of encouraging universities to seek more private support, however, there has been an increase in endowment income in recent years.

A large element in university income is external research income. Research income is obtained from three sources. The main source continues to be research studentships and fellowships, and grants, from six research councils. Research council funds are derived entirely from the government. The second source of research funds is charitable foundations, many of which are related to medical research. The third source is contract research, with increasingly larger sums coming from European Union research programmes and from industry.

The major source of funding for universities is the block grant, funded by the Department for Education and Employment, the Scottish Office and the Welsh Office, and distributed to individual universities by the three funding councils (for England, Wales and Scotland).

The third element in universities' income derives from tuition fees. As from 1998 a means-tested fee of up to £1000 is charged and is the responsibility of the student. There are differential fees for international students, which are at market rates and are set at three levels corresponding to courses in the arts, sciences and technology, and medicine, dentistry and veterinary medicine respectively.

Student finance. The UK government has introduced a new funding scheme in response to the Dearing Report. This recommended that students, as major beneficiaries of higher education, should make a contribution to their tuition costs. The scheme includes a means-tested contribution of up to £1000 per year to tuition fees by full-time undergraduate students and the abolition of maintenance grants. These grants have been replaced by an enhanced income-contingent loan for 1999–2000.

British postgraduate students are also able to participate in the loan scheme but the vast majority continue to be supported by maintenance grants which together with their fees are paid by the research councils for scientists and social scientists and by the British Academy for the humanities as competitive student awards.

Grants through the Commonwealth Scholarship and Fellowship Plan (CSFP) are available to assist Commonwealth students, while the Overseas Research Students Awards Scheme (ORS) is available to meet the difference between the home and overseas tuition fees but provides no assistance towards maintenance. Specialist awards are available from the Foreign and Commonwealth Office for present or potential leaders; from the Overseas Development Agency (ODA) to develop human resources in developing countries under the Technical Co-operation Training Programme (TCTP), the Shared Scholarship Scheme and, more generally, through British Council Fellowships. Many of these latter awards are for limited periods only and do not often enable a degree to be obtained. All overseas students are required to provide any university which accepts them with evidence that they can support themselves financially throughout their courses.

Staff and Student Numbers

In 1997–98 there were about 1,702,000 students at the higher education level in United Kingdom publicly-funded higher education institutions. Mature students represented 53% overall of first-year students in higher education, 30% of first-year full-time students and 90% of first-year part-time students. International students represented 11% of all higher education students.

Further Information

FEE. *Progress report on the new student support arrangements in higher education from 1998/99.* 1998.

DfEE. *Investing in the future: supporting students in higher education.* 1997.

UCAS/CVCP. *Higher education: the facts, figures and fiction.* 1997.

Higher Education Statistics Agency (HESA). *Reference volume, students in higher education institutions 1996/7.* 1998.

UNIVERSITY OF ABERDEEN

Founded 1495

Member of the Association of Commonwealth Universities

Postal Address: Aberdeen, Scotland AB24 3FX
Telephone: (01224) 272000 **Fax**: (01224) 487048 **Cables**: Aberdeen University **Telex**: 73458
WWW: http://www.abdn.ac.uk

CHANCELLOR—Wilson of Tillyorn, Lord, GCMG, PhD *Lond.*, Hon. LLD *Aberd.*, Hon. DLitt *Syd.*
PRINCIPAL AND VICE-CHANCELLOR*—Rice, Prof. C. Duncan, MA *Edin.*, PhD *Edin.*, FRHistS
SENIOR VICE PRINCIPAL—Macdonald, Prof. I. R., MA *St And.*, PhD *Aberd.*
VICE-PRINCIPAL—Forrester, Prof. A. R., BSc *H-W*, PhD DSc, FRSEd, FRSChem
VICE-PRINCIPAL—Catto, Prof. G. R. D., MD *Aberd.*, DSc *Aberd.*, FRCP, FRCPEd, FRCPGlas
VICE-PRINCIPAL—Sloane, Prof. P. J., BA(Econ) *Sheff.*, PhD *Strath.*
VICE-PRINCIPAL—Roberts, J. G., MA *St And.*, PhD *Aberd.*
VICE-PRINCIPAL—Houlihan, Prof. D. F., BSc *Brist.*, PhD *Brist.*
VICE-PRINCIPAL—Logan, Prof. S. D., BSc *St.And.*, PhD *St.And.*
RECTOR—......
SECRETARY—Cannon, S., MA *Dund.*
DIRECTOR OF INFORMATION SYSTEMS AND SERVICES—Pryor, G. H. S., BA *Hull*
ASSOCIATE DIRECTOR OF INFORMATION SYSTEMS AND SERVICES AND LIBRARIAN—McLaren, C. A., BA *Lond.*, MPhil
Lond.

GENERAL INFORMATION

History. The university was founded by Bishop William Elphinstone in 1495.

Admission. to first degree courses (see also United Kingdom Introduction). Through Universities and Colleges Admissions Service (UCAS). Basic requirement is Scottish Certificate of Education (SCE) highers, General Certificate of Education (GCE) A levels, or International Baccalaureate. Other qualifications (eg Scottish Vocational Education Certificates (SCOTVEC), Higher National Certificates and Diplomas (HNCs/HNDs), Scottish Vocational Qualifications (SVQs), General National Vocational Qualifications (GNVQs), and international qualifications) are also recognised.

First Degrees. BD, BEng, BLE, BScEng, BSc, BTechnol, BTh, LLB, MA, MEng, MB ChB.

Most degrees normally last 4 years, though students with appropriate qualifications may be admitted to second or subsequent years. MB ChB: normally 5 years.

Higher Degrees. ChM, LLM, MBA, MChOrth, MD, MEd, MLE, MLitt, MMedSci, MRad (radiology), MSc, MScEcon, MScEntr (entrepreneurship), MTh, MPhil, PhD, DD, DLitt, DMus, DSc, LLD.

Applicants for admission to master's degrees must normally hold an appropriate first degree with at least second class honours. PhD: appropriate first or master's degree. ChM, DLitt, DMus, DSc, LLD, MD: awarded on published work.

Master's degree courses normally last 12 months full-time or 24 months part-time; PhD: normally 33 months full-time or 60 months part-time.

Language of Instruction. English. Five-week intensive pre-sessional courses available (tuition free to those paying overseas fees and who have been admitted to a full-time course).

Libraries. Over 1,050,000 volumes; over 250,000 maps; over 600 periodicals subscribed to. Special holdings include the Aberdeen Bestiary (mediaeval illuminated manuscript).

Fees (1998–99, annual). Undergraduate: £6480 (arts); £8580 (sciences); £15,720 (clinical medicine). Postgraduate: UK/EU students £4350 (MLE), £2610 (all other courses); international students £6480 (arts),

£8850 (MLE, sciences), £15,720 (clinical medicine).

Academic Year (1999–2000). Three terms: 21 September–17 December; 10 January–24 March; 17 April–9 June.

Income. Total, £106,000,000.

Statistics. Staff: 2700 (1400 academic, 1300 non-academic). Students: 11,050.

FACULTIES/SCHOOLS

Arts and Divinity
Tel: (01224) 272084 *Fax:* (01224) 272082
Dean: Roberts, J. G., MA *St And.*, PhD *Aberd.*

Medicine and Medical Sciences
Tel: (01224) 618818 *Fax:* (01224) 840708
Dean: Logan, Prof. S. D., BSc *St.And.*, PhD *St.And.*

Science and Engineering
Tel: (01224) 272081 *Fax:* (01224) 272082
Dean: Houlihan, Prof. D. F., BSc *Brist.*, PhD *Brist.*

Social Sciences and Law
Tel: (01224) 272080 *Fax:* (01224) 272082
Dean: Sloane, Prof. P. J., BA(Econ) *Sheff.*, PhD *Strath.*

ACADEMIC UNITS

Accountancy
Tel: (01224) 272205 *Fax:* (01224) 272214
Buckland, R., MA *Camb.*, MPhil *York(UK)* Prof.; Head*
Fraser, Patricia, MA PhD Abtrust Prof., Finance and Investment Management
Heald, D. A., BA *Leic.* Prof.
McEwen, G. T., MA *Kansas*, MA *Aberd.*, DPhil *Oxf.* Hon. Prof.
Percy, J. P. Hon. Prof.
Roberts, Clare, BSc *S'ton.*, MSc *S'ton.*, PhD *Glas.* Prof.
Thomson, Lydia, DPhil *Oxf.*, MA *Oxf.*, MA *Newcastle(UK)* Sr. Lectr.
Research: financial reporting; operations and structure of capital markets; public sector and regulated sector accounting

Agriculture
Tel: (01224) 274122 *Fax:* (01224) 273731
Bremner, J. M., BSc PhD ScD Hon. Prof.
English, P. R., BScAgr PhD Reader, Animal Science
Galbraith, H., BSc *Strath.*, PhD Sr. Lectr., Animal Science

Heath, S. B., BSc *Reading*, PhD *Reading* Sr. Lectr.
Hutchinson, J. S. M., BSc *Nott.*, PhD *Nott.* Sr. Lectr., Animal Science
Lomax, M. A., BSc *Newcastle(UK)*, PhD *Reading* Strathcona-Fordyce Prof.; Head*
Naylor, R. E. L., PhD *Wales*, DSc *Wales* Prof., Crop Science
Seddon, B., BSc *Manc.*, PhD *Manc.* Sr. Lectr., Agricultural Microbiology
Slee, R. W., BA *Camb.*, PhD Sr. Lectr., Agriculture and Rural Economics
Thomson, K. J., MSc *Lond.*, MS *Iowa*, MA Prof., Agriculture and Rural Economics
Research: animal science; crop science and microbiology; rural economics

Art, see Hist. of Art

Biology, Molecular and Cell
Tel: (01224) 274172 *Fax:* (01224) 273144
Booth, I. R., BSc *Liv.*, PhD *Wales* Prof.
Booth, Nuala A., BSc *N.U.I.*, PhD *Wales* Sr. Lectr.
Brown, A. J. P., BSc PhD Prof.
Docherty, K., BSc *St And.*, PhD *Edin.* Macleod-Smith Prof.
Fothergill, J. E., BSc *Brist.*, PhD *Brist.*, FRSEd Prof.
Glover, L. Anne, BSc *Edin.*, MPhil *Camb.*, PhD *Camb.* Sr. Lectr.
Gooday, G. W., BSc *Brist.*, PhD *Brist.*, FRSEd Prof.
Gow, N. A. R., BSc *Edin.*, PhD Prof.
Haites, Neva E., BSc *Qld.*, MB ChB Prof.
Hamilton, W. A., BSc *Glas.*, PhD *Glas.*, FIBiol, FRSEd Prof.†
Harold, F. M. Hon. Prof.
Harris, W. J., BSc *St And.*, PhD *Dund.* Prof.
Jeffery, J., MA *Oxf.*, DSc *Oxf.*, DPhil *Oxf.*, FRSEd, FIBiol, FRSChem Prof.
Long, W. F., BSc *Lond.*, MSc PhD Sr. Lectr.
Melvin, W. T., BSc *Glas.*, PhD *Glas.* Sr. Lectr.
Pearson, C. K., BSc *Liv.*, PhD *Liv.* Sr. Lectr.
Poole, N. J., BSc *Lond.*, PhD *Lond.* Hon. Prof.
Prosser, J. I., BSc *Lond.*, PhD *Liv.* Prof.; Head*
Shaw, D. J., BSc *St And.*, PhD *St And.* Prof.
Skinner, E. R., BSc *Birm.*, PhD *Lond.* Reader
Trayhurn, P., BSc *Reading*, DPhil *Oxf.* Hon. Prof.
Williamson, F. B., BSc *Edin.*, PhD *Edin.* Sr. Lectr.
Wilson, B. S., BSc *Nott.*, PhD *Nott.* Sr. Lectr.
Research: microbiology; molecular and cell pathology; molecular medicine

Biomedical Physics and Bioengineering
Tel: (01224) 681818 *Fax:* (01224) 685645
Allen, A. R., BSc *Birm.*, DPhil *Sus.* Sr. Lectr., Information Technology

Heaton, B., BSc Manc., MSc Salf., PhD   Sr. Lectr.

Hukins, D. W. L., BSc Lond., PhD Nott., DSc Nott.   MacRobert Prof.

Hutchison, J. M. S., BSc PhD   Reader

Hutchison, Margaret A., BSc Durh., MSc St And., PhD   Reader

Lurie, D. J., MSc Lond., PhD Lond., BSc   Sr. Lectr.

Sharp, P. F., BSc Durh., PhD, FIP   Prof.; Head*

Undrill, P. E., BSc Lond., PhD   Sr. Lectr.

Research: free radical imaging; magnetic resonance imaging; radiation protection; radionuclide imaging; retinal imaging

Biomedical Sciences

Tel: (01224) 273006 Fax: (01224) 273019

Ashford, M. L. J., BSc PhD   Prof., Pharmacology

Cameron, N. E., BSc E.Anglia, DPhil Sus.   Sr. Lectr.

Cotter, Mary A., BSc Birm., PhD Birm.   Sr. Lectr.

Hawksworth, Gabrielle M., BSc Leeds, PhD Lond.   Prof.

Kidd, C., BSc Durh., PhD Durh., FIBiol   Regius Prof., Physiology; Head*

Logan, S. D., BSc St And., PhD St And.   Prof., Neuroscience

Macdonald, A. G., BSc Brist., PhD Brist., DSc   Reader

McCaig, C. D., BSc Edin., PhD Glas.   Sr. Lectr.

Milton, A. S., DSc Oxf.   Prof.†, Pharmacology

Pertwee, R. G., MA Oxf., DPhil Oxf.   Reader

Scott, R. H., BSc Nott., PhD Nott.   Sr. Lectr.

Trayhurn, P., BSc Reading, DPhil Oxf.   Hon. Prof.

Wallace, Heather M., BSc Glas., PhD   Sr. Lectr.

Vacant Posts: Regius Prof. (Anat.)

Research: cellular, developmental and integrative neuroscience; membrane and cellular physiology and pharmacology

Celtic, see under Mod. Langs.

Chemistry

Tel: (01224) 272943 Fax: (01224) 272921

Alford, N. M.   Hon. Prof.

Cameron, G. G., BSc Glas., PhD Glas., DSc, FRSEd, FRSChem   Prof.

Forrester, A. R., BSc H.-W., PhD DSc, FRSEd, FRSChem   Prof.

Ingram, M. D., BSc Liv., PhD Liv., DSc, FRSChem   Prof.

Marr, I. L., MSc PhD   Sr. Lectr.

McQuillan, G. P., BSc Lond., PhD Lond.   Sr. Lectr.; Head*

Turner, A. B., BSc Brist., PhD Brist., FRSChem   Sr. Lectr.

Wardell, J. L., BSc Lond., PhD Lond.   Reader

West, A. R., BSc Wales, PhD DSc, FRSChem   Prof.

Research: cement chemistry; environmental and analytical chemistry; glass chemistry; polymer chemistry; solid state chemistry

Computing Science

Tel: (01224) 272296 Fax: (01224) 273422

Fothergill, A. Patricia, MA Camb.   Sr. Lectr.

Gray, P. M. D., MA Camb., DPhil Oxf.   Prof.

Hunter, J. R. W., BSc Edin., DPhil Sus.   Sr. Lectr.

Sleeman, D. H., BSc Lond., PhD Lond., FRSEd   Prof.; Head*

Research: application of artifical intelligence to design and manufacturing engineering; constraints and optimisation; intelligent software agents; machine discovery; object-oriented databases and constraints

Defence Studies, see Special Centres, etc

Divinity with Religious Studies

Tel: (01224) 272380 Fax: (01224) 273750

Ellingworth, P., BA Camb., MA Oxf., PhD   Hon. Prof.

Fergusson, D. A. S., MA Glas., BD Edin., DPhil Oxf.   Prof.; Head*

Johnstone, W., MA Glas., BD Glas.   Prof.

Main, A., TD, STM N.Y., MA BD PhD   Sr. Lectr.

Marshall, I. H., BA Camb., MA BD PhD   Prof.

Stephens, W. P., MA Camb., BD Camb., DrScRel Stras.   Prof.

Thrower, J. A., BLitt Oxf., MA Durh., PhD   Prof.

Research: church history; Hebrew and Semitic languages; history of religions; New Testament; practical theology

Economic History, see Hist.

Economics

Tel: (01224) 272167 Fax: (01224) 272181

Elliot, R. F., BA Oxf., MA Leeds   Prof.

Kemp, A. G., MA   Prof.

Kidd, M. P., BA Brist., MA Essex, PhD Qu.   Sr. Lectr.

Lee, C. H., MA Camb., MLitt Camb.   Prof.

McAvinchey, I. D., BSc Belf., MA Manc., PhD Manc.   Sr. Lectr.

Newlands, D. A., MA Edin., MSocSc Birm.   Sr. Lectr.

Sloane, P. J., BA(Econ) Sheff., PhD Strath.   Jaffrey Prof.; Head*

Research: economics of energy and natural resources; labour economics; regional economics

Engineering

Tel: (01224) 272820 Fax: (01224) 272497

Allen, A. R., BSc Birm., DPhil Sus.   Sr. Lectr.

Baker, M. J., BSc Lond.   Prof.

Chandler, H. W., BSc Sheff., PhD Sheff.   Jackson Prof.

Deans, W. F., BSc Strath., PhD Strath.   Sr. Lectr.

Gorman, D. G., BSc Strath., PhD Strath., FIMechE   Prof.

Hutchinson, J. M., BA Oxf., DPhil Oxf.   Reader

Jones, C. J., BSc Leeds, PhD Leeds   Sr. Lectr.

Penman, J., BSc H.-W., PhD Dund., FIEE   Prof.; Head*

Player, M. A., MA Oxf., DPhil Oxf., FIP   Prof.

Rodder, A., BScEng PhD   Prof.

Spracklen, C. T., BSc Manc., PhD Leic.   Prof.

Sumptner, J. I., BSc Lond., PhD Lond., FIMechE   Hon. Prof.

Vas, P., BSc Bud., MSc Bud., PhD Bud., DSc   Prof.

Watson, J., PhD St And.   Sr. Lectr.

Willetts, B. B., MA Camb., PhD   Prof.

Research: civil and environmental engineering; electromechanical systems; electronics and communications; imaging and optical technology; materials

English

Tel: (01224) 272625 Fax: (01224) 272624

Alexander, Flora M., BLitt Oxf., MA   Sr. Lectr.

Alexander, J. H., MA Oxf., BLitt Oxf., DPhil Oxf.   Reader

Coates, P.   Reader

Gilmour, R., MA Camb., PhD Edin.   Reader

Hewitt, D. S., MA Edin., PhD   Prof.

McClure, J. D. R., MA Glas., MLitt Edin.   Sr. Lectr.

Milton, C., MA PhD   Sr. Lectr.

Porter, J. W., MA St.And., BMus Edin.   Prof.

Ray, M. S., MA Manc., PhD Manc.   Sr. Lectr.

Roberts, J. G., MA St And., PhD Aberd.   Sr. Lectr.; Head*

Ronberg, G., BA Aarhus, MLitt Oxf.   Sr. Lectr.

Rousseau, G. S., BA Amherst, MA Prin., PhD Prin.   Regius (Chalmers) Prof.

Schlicke, P. Van W., BA Stan., PhD Calif.   Sr. Lectr.

Tait, Isobel M., MA Edin., PhD Edin.   Sr. Lectr.

Watson, G. J. B., BA Belf., BLitt Oxf.   Prof.

Vacant Posts: 1 Prof.

Research: the Enlightenment; Renaissance literature; Romantic and Victorian writing and culture; Scottish and Irish literature; women's studies

Forestry

Tel: (01224) 272678 Fax: (01224) 272685

Holmes, G. D., CB, DSc Wales, FRSEd   Hon. Prof.

Miller, Hugh G., OBE, BScFor PhD DSc, FIBiol, FRSEd   Prof.; Head*

Mitchell, C. P., BSc Sur., PhD Stir.   Reader

Parry, W. H., BSc Wales, PhD Wales   Sr. Lectr.

Petty, J. A., MA Oxf., PhD Leeds, DSc   Reader

Woodward, S., BSc Hull, PhD Lond.   Sr. Lectr.

Research: forest planning; forest policy; silviculture; tropical forest research; wood supply research

French, see under Mod. Langs.

Geography

Tel: (01224) 272328 Fax: (01224) 272331

Benn, D. I., BSc Leic., PhD   Sr. Lectr.

Bryden, J. M., BSc Glas., PhD E.Anglia   Prof.

Chapman, K., BA Birm., PhD Birm.   Prof.; Head*

Clapperton, C. M., MA Edin., PhD Edin.   Prof.

Clark, B. D., MA Liv.   Prof.

Farrington, J. H., BSc Hull, PhD Hull   Sr. Lectr.

Gemmell, A. M. D., PhD Glas., BSc   Sr. Lectr.

Mather, A. S., BSc PhD   Prof.

Smith, J. S., MA PhD   Sr. Lectr.

Williams, N. J., BSc Wales, PhD Wales   Sr. Lectr.

Wood, M., BSc   Sr. Lectr.

Wright, R., BSc Glas., BSc(PhysEng) I.T.C.Delft, MS Mich.   Sr. Lectr.

Research: economic and social change in advanced economies; environmental policy; management and mapping; physical environment; rural development

Geology and Petroleum Geology

Tel: (01224) 273433 Fax: (01224) 272785

Ashcroft, W. A., MSc Birm., PhD Birm., BSc, FGS   Sr. Lectr.

Hurst, A., PhD Reading, BSc, FGS   Prof., Petroleum Geoscience

Pearson, M. J., BSc Sheff., PhD Sheff.   Sr. Lectr.

Rice, C. M., BSc Sheff., PhD Sheff.   Sr. Lectr.

Simmons, M. D., BSc Plym., PhD Plym.   Sr. Lectr.

Trewin, N. H., BSc Brist., PhD Keele, FGS   Reader

Walkden, G. M., BSc Manc., PhD Manc.   Sr. Lectr.; Head*

Williams, B. P. J., BSc Wales, PhD Wales, FGS   Prof., Petroleum Geology

Vacant Posts: Kilgour Prof.

Research: geodynamics and petrogenesis; palaeo-environmental studies; petroleum geoscience

German, see under Mod. Langs.

History

Tel: (01224) 272456 Fax: (01224) 272203

Bridges, R. C., BA Keele, PhD Lond.   Prof.

Brotherstone, W. T. C., BA Camb.   Sr. Lectr.

Dukes, P., BA Camb., MA Wash., PhD Lond.   Prof.

Macinnes, A. I., MA St And., PhD Glas.   Burnett-Fletcher Prof.

Payne, P. L., BA Nott., PhD Nott.   Prof., Economic History

Perren, R., BA Nott., PhD Nott.   Sr. Lectr., Economic History

Tyson, R. E., MA Manc.   Sr. Lectr., Economic History

Vacant Posts: 2 Profs.

Research: comparative contemporary labour history; diet, death and diseases; non-anglocentric British history; the North Sea and Baltic world; Scotland and the Americas

History of Art

Tel: (01224) 272458

Gash, J. M., MA Lond., MA Oxf.   Sr. Lectr.; Head*

Mannings, D. M., BA Lond., PhD Lond.   Sr. Lectr.

Research: eighteenth–twentieth century British art; Italian art 1300–1800; mediaeval art; Scottish architecture

International Relations, see Pol. and Internat. Relns.

Land Economy

Tel: (01224) 273670 Fax: (01224) 273487

Adams, C. D., MA Camb., MCD Liv.   Reader
Cullen, I., PhD   Hon. Prof.
Keouah, T.   Sr. Lectr.
MacGregor, B. D., BSc Edin., MSc H.-W., PhD Camb.   MacRobert Prof.
Nanthakumaran, N., BSc Ceyl., BSc Reading   Sr. Lectr.
Rowan-Robinson, R. J., MA Kent, LLM   Prof.; Head*
Shucksmith, D. M., MA Camb., MSc Newcastle(UK), PhD Newcastle(UK)   Prof.
Watchman, P. Q., LLD   Hon. Prof.
Research: land development and policy; property investment and market analysis; rural housing and rural development

Law

Tel: (01224) 272440 Fax: (01224) 272442

Anton, A. E., CBE, MA LLB, FRSEd, FBA   Hon. Prof.
Beaumont, P. R., LLB Glas., LLM Dal.   Prof.
Blaikie, J., LLB Edin., MA Edin., PhD   Sr. Lectr.
Carey Miller, D. L., BA Natal, LLB Natal, LLM Edin., PhD   Prof.
Cusine, D. J., LLB Glas.   Hugh McLennan Prof.
Duff, P. R., LLB Edin., PhD   Sr. Lectr.
Evans-Jones, R., PhD Edin., LLB   Prof.
Forte, A. D. M., LLB MA   Prof.
Gane, C. H. W., LLB Edin.   Prof.; Head*
Hope, Rt. Hon. Lord   Hon. Prof.
Ireland, R. D., QC, LLB Edin., MA Oxf.   Hon. Prof.
Lessels, D., LLB Dund., BPhil Hull   Sr. Lectr.
Lyall, F., LLB Aberd., MA Aberd., LLM McG., PhD Aberd.   Prof.
O'Donnell, D., LLB   Sr. Lectr.
Pearson, Judith J. H., LLB Edin., LLM Lond.   Sr. Lectr.
Risk, Sheriff Principal D. J.   Hon. Prof.
Ross, Margaret L., LLB   Sr. Lectr.
Walker, N.   Prof.
Research: civil law; commercial law; criminal law and criminal justice; environmental law; European Union law

Mathematical Sciences

Tel: (01224) 272740 Fax: (01224) 272607

Archbold, R. J., MA Camb., PhD Newcastle(UK)   Reader
Clark, R. C.   Sr. Lectr.
Crabb, M. C., MA Oxf., MSc Oxf., DPhil Oxf.   Reader
Craw, I. G., MA Camb., PhD Camb.   Sr. Lectr.
Garthwaite, P. H., MA Oxf., MSc Wales, PhD Wales   Sr. Lectr.
Hall, G. S., BSc Newcastle(UK), PhD Newcastle(UK)   Reader
Hubbuck, J. R., MA Camb., MA Oxf., DPhil Oxf., FRSEd, FIMA   Prof.
Jollife, I. T., BSc Sus., DPhil Sus.   Prof.; Head*
Maclachlan, C., BSc St And., PhD Birm.   Sr. Lectr.
Sheehan, J., BSc Wales, PhD Wales   Sr. Lectr.
Vacant Posts: 1 Prof.
Research: computer vision; general relativity; pure mathematics; statistics

Medicine, see below

Microbiology, see Medicine (Med. Microbiol.), below

Modern Languages, School of

Celtic

Tel: (01224) 272549 Fax: (01224) 272562

Meek, D. E., MA Camb., PhD Glas., FRHistS   Prof.

O'Boyle, C. J. M., MA Belf., PhD Belf.   Prof.; Head*
Research: Gaelic language; mediaeval Celtic literature; modern Irish literature; Scottish Gaelic literature

French

Tel: (01224) 272163 Fax: (01224) 272562

Britton, Celia M., BA Camb., PhD Essex   Carnegie Prof.
Dunkley, J., MA Exe., PhD Exe.   Sr. Lectr.
Hartley, D. J., BA Lond., PhD Lond.   Sr. Lectr.
Roach, J., BA Keele, PhD Keele   Sr. Lectr.
Saunders, Alison M., BA Durh., PhD Durh.   Prof.; Head*
Research: cinema and cultural studies; eighteenth-century theatre; emblem literature; mediaeval and Renaissance studies; twentieth-century fiction

German

Tel: (01224) 272486 Fax: (01224) 272494

Burgess, G. J. A., BA Lond., MPhil Lond., PhD   Reader
Fennell, Barbara. A., BSc Sur., PhD Sur.   Sr. Lectr.
Thomaneck, J. K. A., JP, DrPhil Kiel, MEd   Prof.; Head*
Research: computer-assisted textual analysis (including single-language and parallel concordancing); exile studies; German literature 1600–present (especially Baroque, classical and twentieth-century); German Democratic Republic studies; linguistics

Spanish

Tel: (01224) 272549 Fax: (01224) 272562

Harris, D. R., MA Nott., PhD Hull   Prof.
Macdonald, I. R., MA St And., PhD Aberd.   Prof.; Head*
Research: culture of post-Franco transition; modern Latin American narrative; modern Spanish narrative; twentieth-century poetry; visual representation and feminist theory in Spanish America

Petroleum Geology, see Geol. and Petroleum Geol.

Philosophy

Tel: (01224) 272366

Cameron, J. R., MA St And., BPhil And.   Regius Prof.†, Logic
Dower, N., BA Oxf., MA Leeds, PhD Aberd.   Sr. Lectr.; Head*
Graham, L. C., MA St.And., MA Durh., PhD Durh.   Regius Prof., Moral Philosophy
Matthews, E. H., MA Oxf., BPhil Oxf.   Prof.
Research: aesthetics; epistemology and philosophy of science; ethics and moral philosophy; history of philosophy; logic

Physiology, see Biomed. Scis.

Plant and Soil Science

Tel: (01224) 272692 Fax: (01224) 272703

Alexander, I. J., BSc Edin., PhD Edin.   Regius Prof., Botany
Billett, M. F., BSc Edin., PhD Lond.   Sr. Lectr.
Cresser, M. S., BSc Lond., PhD Lond.   Prof.
Killham, K. S., BSc Sheff., PhD Sheff.   Prof.; Head*
Mullins, C. E., BA Essex, MSc Essex, PhD Essex   Sr. Lectr.
Swaine, M. D., BSc Wales, PhD Wales   Sr. Lectr.
Vacant Posts: Regius Prof.
Research: environmental microbiology; plant/microbe interactions; plant physiology; soil physical environment; soil and water quality

Politics and International Relations

Tel: (01224) 272714 Fax: (01224) 272181

Arter, D., BA Manc., MPhil Hull   Prof., Nordic Politics
Criddle, B. J., BA Keele, MA Leic.   Reader
Dower, N., BA Oxf., MA Leeds, PhD   Sr. Lectr.
Jordan, A. G., MA Strath., PhD Strath.   Prof.

Salmon, T. C., MA Aberd., MLitt Aberd., PhD St And.   Prof., International Relations
Urwin, D., MA Manc., PhD Strath.   Prof.
Wyllie, J. H., BA Stir., MA Lanc.   Sr. Lectr.
Research: European integration; Nordic politics; parties, elections and interest groups; public policy; security studies

Psychology

Tel: (01224) 272227 Fax: (01224) 273426

Crawford, J. R., BSc Stir., MSc PhD   Reader
de Renzi, E.   Hon. Prof.
Della Sala, S. F., MD Milan, PhD Milan   Prof.
Deregowski, J. B., BSc(Eng) Lond., BA Lond., PhD Lond., DSc, FBPsS, FRSEd   Prof.
Dominowski, R. L., AB De Paul, PhD   Sr. Lectr.
Flin, Rhona, MA PhD   Prof.
Gilhooly, K. J., MA Edin., MSc Stir., PhD Stir., FBPsS   Sr. Lectr.
Gray, C. D., BSc Belf., PhD Belf.   Sr. Lectr.
Kinnear, P. R., MSc Edin., PhD   Sr. Lectr.
Logie, R. H., BSc Lond., PhD Lond.   Prof.
Parker, D. M., BA Durh., PhD Durh.   Reader
Salzen, E. A., BSc Edin., PhD Edin.   Anderson Prof.†
Shepherd, J. W., BSc Lond.   Reader; Head*
Research: applied psychology; development psychology; memory and thinking; neuropsychology; social psychology

Religious Studies, see Div. with Religious Studies, and Special Centres, etc

Sociology

Tel: (01224) 272760

Blaikie, J. A. D., MA Camb., PhD Lond.   Sr. Lectr.
Bonney, N. L., JP, BSc(Econ) Lond., MA Chic., PhD Chic.   Sr. Lectr.
Bruce, S., BA Stir., PhD Stir.   Prof.; Head*
Hepworth, J. M., BA Hull   Reader
Twine, F. E., MA Essex   Sr. Lectr.
Vacant Posts: 1 Prof.
Research: development, culture, identity and environmentalism in the Arctic; family, work and society in East and West (comparative studies); historical sociology of the family; Northern Ireland conflict and sociology of religion; sociology of the body, sexuality and ageing

Soil Science, see Plant and Soil Sci.

Spanish, see under Mod. Langs.

Zoology

Tel: (01224) 272861 Fax: (01224) 272396

Boyle, P. R., BSc Wales, PhD Auck.   Prof.
Chappell, L. H., BSc Leeds, PhD Leeds, FIBiol   Reader
Cowey, C. B., BSc Newcastle(UK), BA Oxf., MA Oxf., DSc Durh.   Hon. Prof.
Fry, C. H., BA Camb., MA Camb., PhD Nigeria, DSc Aberd.   Hon. Prof.
Gorman, M. L., BSc PhD   Sr. Lectr.
Holliday, Sir Frederick G. T.   Hon. Prof.
Houlihan, D. F., BSc Brist., PhD Brist.   Prof.; Head*
Jenkins, D., MA Camb., DPhil Oxf., DSc Oxf., FRSEd   Hon. Prof.
McIntyre, A. D., CBE, DSc Glas., FRSEd   Hon. Prof.
Mordue, Jennifer A., MSc Sheff., PhD Lond.   Sr. Lectr.
Mordue, W., PhD Sheff., DSc Sheff., FRSEd, FIBiol   Prof.
Patterson, I. J., DPhil Oxf., DSc   Sr. Lectr.
Pike, A. W., BSc Wales, PhD Wales   Sr. Lectr.
Priede, I. G., BSc Wales, PhD Stir.   Reader
Racey, P. A., MA Camb., PhD Lond., DSc, FIBiol   Regius Prof.
Raffaelli, D. G., BSc Leeds, PhD Wales   Sr. Lectr.
Secombes, C. J., BSc Leeds, PhD Hull   Sr. Lectr.
Speakman, J. R., BSc Stir., PhD Stir.   Sr. Lectr.
Staines, B. W., BSc Lond., PhD Aberd.   Hon. Prof.
Steele, J. H., DSc, FRS, FRSEd   Hon. Prof.
Usher, M. B., BSc Edin., PhD Edin.   Hon. Prof.

Young, M. R., BSc Birm., PhD Birm.   Sr. Lectr.
Research: dynamic processes of animal
   populations; fundamental and applied
   animal physiology; marine and fisheries
   science

MEDICINE

For subjects of first 2 years—Anatomy, etc—
see Biomedical Sciences, above

Anaesthetics

Tel: (01224) 681818
No staff at present

Biomedical Physics and Bioengineering,
   see above

Cardiology

Tel: (01224) 681818
No staff at present

Child Health

Tel: (01224) 681818 Fax: (01224) 663658
Golden, Barbara E., BSc Belf., MB BCh BAO
   Belf., MD Belf.   Sr. Lectr.
Helms, P. J. B., MB BS Lond., PhD Lond.,
   FRCP   Prof.; Head*
Research: migraine; nutrition and inflammation;
   paediatric respiratory health and disease

Clinical Biochemistry

Tel: (01224) 681818
Ross, I. S., MB ChB PhD   Clin. Sr. Lectr.†;
   Head*
Vacant Posts: 1 Prof.

Dental Surgery

Tel: (01224) 681818
No staff at present

Dermatology

Tel: (01224) 681818
No staff at present

Environmental and Occupational
   Medicine

Tel: (01224) 681818 Fax: (01224) 662990
Cherrie, J. W., BSc Edin.   Sr. Lectr.
Maughan, R. J., BSc PhD   Prof.
Ross, J. A. S., PhD Lond., MB ChB, FFARCS   Sr.
   Lectr.
Seaton, A., CBE, BA Camb., MD Camb., FRCP,
   FRCPEd   OMS Prof.; Head*
Watt, S. J., BSc Lond., MB BS Lond.   Sr. Lectr.
Research: hyperbaric medicine; occupational
   studies

Forensic Medicine, see Pathol.

General Practice and Primary Care

Tel: (01224) 681818
Brebner, J. A.   Sr. Lectr.
Hannaford, C. P.   Prof., Primary Care
McKie, Linda, BA Ulster, MSc Bath, PhD
   Durh.   Sr. Lectr.
Ritchie, L. D., MSc Edin., BSc MD   James
   Mackenzie Prof.; Head*
Taylor, R. J., MD, FRCGP   Sr. Lectr.
Research: balance of care and guidelines studies;
   deprivation and health equality; micro-
   computer-based information systems;
   palliative and cancer care; prevention and
   health promotion

Genito-Urinary Medicine

Tel: (01224) 681818
No staff at present

Geriatric Medicine

Tel: (01224) 681818
No staff at present

Haematology

Tel: (01224) 681818
No staff at present

Medical Microbiology

Tel: (01224) 681818 Fax: (01224) 685604
Cash, P., BSc Wales, PhD Glas.   Sr. Lectr.
McKenzie, H., BSc Strath., MB ChB Glas., PhD
   Strath.   Sr. Lectr.
Pennington, T. H., MB BS Lond., PhD
   Lond.   Prof.; Head*
Research: bacteriological, virological and electron
   microscopy investigations

Medicine and Therapeutics

Tel: (01224) 681818 Fax: (01224) 699884
Bennett, N. B., MD, FRCP, FRCPath   Reader
Cassidy, J., MB ChBGlas., MSc Glas., MD
   Glas.   Prof., Oncology
Catto, G. R. D., MD Aberd., DSc Aberd., FRCP,
   FRCPEd, FRCPGlas   Prof.
Galloway, D. B., MB ChB, FRCPEd, FRCP   Sr.
   Lectr.
Golden, M. H. N., BSc Belf., MB BCh
   Belf.   Wellcome Trust Prof.
Greaves, M.   Prof., Haematology
Haites, Neva E., BSc Qld., PhD Qld., MB
   ChB   Prof.
Hawksworth, Gabrielle M., BSc Leeds, PhD
   Lond.   Prof.
Kulkarni, V., MB BS MSc PhD, FRCA,
   FFARCS   Sr. Lectr.
Little, J., BA Camb., MA Camb., PhD   Prof.,
   Epidemiology
McLay, J. S., BPharm Lond., PhD Lond., MB
   ChB   Sr. Lectr.
McLeod, H. L., BSc Wash., PharmD
   Phil.Pharm.   Sr. Lectr.
Norman, J. N., MB ChB MD PhD DSc, FRCS,
   FIBiol   Prof.†
Ogston, D., MA MD PhD DSc, FIBiol, FRCP,
   FRCPEd, FRSEd   Prof., Clinical Medicine
Petrie, James C., CBE, MB ChB, FRCPEd,
   FRCP   Prof., Clinical Pharmacology
Power, D. A., MB BS W.Aust., MD   Sr. Lectr.
Ralston, S. H., MD   Prof.
Rees, A. J., MB ChB Liv., MSc Lond.,
   FRCP   Regius Prof.
Reid, D. M., MB ChB MD, FRCP   Sr. Lectr.
Seymour, D. G., BSc Birm., MD Birm.,
   FRCP   Prof.
Turner, A. N., MA Camb., BM BCh Oxf., PhD
   Lond.   Sr. Lectr.
Vickers, M. A., MA BM ChB DM   Sr. Lectr.
Webster, J., BMedBiol MD, FRCPEd   Sr. Lectr.
Webster, N. R., BSc MB ChB PhD,
   FRCA   Prof.
Research: anaesthetics and intensive care; blood
   transfusion; bone research; care of the
   elderly; clinical pharmacology

Mental Health

Tel: (01224) 681818 Fax: (01224) 685157
Alexander, D. A., MA Dund., PhD St And.   Sr.
   Lectr.
St Clair, D., BA Oxf., BM BCh Oxf., MPhil
   Edin.   Sr. Lectr.
Walker, L. G., MA PhD   Sr. Lectr.
Whalley, I. J., MB BS Newcastle(UK), MD
   Newcastle(UK)   Crombie-Ross Prof.; Head*
Wischik, C. M., BA Adel., MB BS S.Aust.,
   BMedSci S.Aust., PhD Camb.   Prof.,
   Psychiatric Geratology
Vacant Posts: Thompson Prof. (Psychother.)
Research: genetic epidemiology of severe mental
   illnesses; management of post-traumatic
   stress syndrome; psychiatric genetics;
   psychosocial aspects of cancer; psychosocial
   costs of genetic and other screening
   programmes

Obstetrics and Gynaecology

Tel: (01224) 681818
Abramovich, D. R., MB BS Syd., PhD Liv.,
   FRCOG   Reader
Campbell, Doris M., MD   Sr. Lectr.
Graham, Wendy, BSc DPhil   Dir., Dugald
   Baird Centre
Hamilton, M. P. R., MD Glas.   Sr. Lectr.
Templeton, A. A., MD, FRCOG   Regius Prof.;
   Head*

Research: gynaecological oncology; obstetric and
   gynaecological health services and
   epidemiological research; reproductive
   biology and medicine

Ophthalmology

Tel: (01224) 681818 Fax: (01224) 663002
Forrester, J. V., MD Glas., FRCSEd,
   FRCSGlas   Cockburn Prof.; Head*
Research: clinical and basic science study of
   human and experimental models of
   uveoretinitis, pathogenesis of idiopathic
   eveitis and alternative methods of
   suppressing immune response; cytokine
   production and regulation and ocular
   inflammation; diabetes, retinal disease,
   inflammation, autoimmunity and
   immunology of the eye; factors affecting
   corneal wound healing (especially the role
   of small electric fields applied to corneal
   epithelium, fibroblasts and endothelium);
   molecular events associated with
   pathogenesis of diabetic retinopathy, glucose
   transport mechanisms of the retina and role
   of growth factors in development of retinal
   neovascularisation

Otolaryngology

Tel: (01224) 681818
No staff at present

Pathology

Tel: (01224) 681818 Fax: (01224) 663002
Ewen, S. W. B., MB ChB PhD, FRCPath   Sr.
   Lectr.
Gray, Elizabeth S., MB ChB, FRCPath   Sr.
   Lectr.
Grieve, J. H. K., MB ChB   Sr. Lectr., Forensic
   Medicine
Murray, G. I., MB ChB PhD   Sr. Lectr.
Scott, G. B., MB ChB, FRCPath   Sr. Lectr.
Simpson, J. G., MB ChB PhD,
   FRCPath   Reader
Thompson, W. D., MB ChB Glas., PhD
   Glas.   Sr. Lectr.
Walker, F., PhD Glas., MD Glas.,
   FRCPath   Regius Wilson Prof.; Head*
Wheatley, D. N., BSc Lond., PhD Lond., DSc,
   FIBiol   Reader, Cell Pathology
Research: colon cancer; gut lecithin interaction
   and signal transduction; histochemistry;
   molecular pathology; polyamines and the
   gut

Pharmacology, see Biomed. Scis., above

Psychiatry, see Mental Health

Public Health

Tel: (01224) 681818 Fax: (01224) 662994
Cairns, J. A., MA York(UK), MPhil
   York(UK)   Dir., Health Econ. Res. Unit;
   Head*
Donaldson, C. R., BA Nott., MSc York(UK),
   PhD   Prof.
Grant, A. M., BA Oxf., BM BCh Oxf., MA Oxf.,
   MSc Lond., DM Oxf.   Prof.; Dir., Health
   Services Res. Unit
Grimshaw, J. M., MB ChB Edin.   Lectr.;
   Programme Dir., Health Services Res. Unit
Ludbrook, Anne, BA York(UK), MSc
   York(UK)   Sr. Lectr.; Consultancy Dir., Health
   Econ. Res. Unit
Russell, Elizabeth M., MD Glas., FRCP   Prof.
Smith, W. C., MDDund., PhD Dund.,
   FRCP   Reader
Research: cohort studies and record linkage;
   epidemiology of infectious diseases;
   evidence-based health care; genetic
   epidemiology and genetic counselling;
   health outcomes and disability;

Radiology

Tel: (01224) 681818
Gilbert, Fiona J., MB ChB Glas., FRCR,
   FRCPSGlas, FRCPEd   Roland Sutton Prof.
Murray, Alison D., MB ChB, FRCR   Sr. Lectr.

Research: avascular necrosis; breast imaging including screening, magnetic resonance imaging and positron emission tomography; implementation of guidelines; low back pain; ovarian screening

Radiotherapy

Tel: (01224) 681818
No staff at present

Rheumatology

Tel: (01224) 681818
No staff at present

Surgery

Tel: (01224) 681818
Ah-See, A. K., ChM, FRCSEd   Sr. Lectr.
Binnie, N. R., BSc *Edin.*, MB ChB *Edin.*, MD *Edin.*, FRCS   Sr. Lectr.
Eremin, O., MD *Melb.*, FRACS, FRCSEd   Regius Prof.; Head*
Heys, S. B., BMedBiol MD, FRCS   Sr. Lectr.
Hutchison, J. D., MB ChB *Dund.*, PhD, FRCS   Sir Harry Pratt Prof., Orthopaedic Surgery
Maffuli, N., MD *Naples*, MS *Lond.*, PhD   Sr. Lectr.
McLauchlan, J., MB BS *Lond.*, ChM, FRCSEd   Clin. Reader, Orthopaedic Surgery
Weir, J., MB BS *Lond.*, FRCPEd, FRCP   Clin. Prof.
Research: behavioural oncology; immunotherapy and gene therapy; orthopaedic surgery; surgical nutrition; surgical oncology

Thoracic Medicine

Tel: (01224) 272000
No staff at present

Other Appointments

Honorary Research Appointments

Hawkins, A. D., BSc *Brist.*, PhD *Brist.*, FRSEd   Hon. Res. Prof., Fisheries and Oceanography
James, W. P. T., MA *Lond.*, MD *Lond.*, DSc *Lond.*, FRCP, FRCPEd, FIBiol, FRSEd   Hon. Res. Prof., Physiology of Nutrition
Maxwell, T. J., BSc *Edin.*, PhD *Edin.*   Hon. Prof., Land Use Systems Research
Poole, N. J., BSc *Lond.*, PhD *Lond.*   Hon. Indust. Prof., Microbiology

SPECIAL CENTRES, ETC

Conoco Natural History Centre

Tel: (01224) 493288
Browning, Annabel R., BA *Oxf.*   Devel. Co-ordinator

Continuing Education, Centre for

Tel: (01224) 272447 Fax: (01224) 272478
Canning, R., BA *H.-W.*, MA *Brighton*   Vocational Training Co-ordinator
Cudworth, C. J., BSc *Durh.*, PhD *Durh.*, MA *Trinity(Dub.)*   Dir., Summer Sch. for Access
Dalgarno, M. T., MA PhD   Dir.*
Omand, D., MSc *Strath.*, MA   Continuing Educn. Organiser
Paterson, D. R., BSc   Continuing Educn. Organiser

Simenton, Deborah L., MA *Arizona*, PhD *Essex*   Continuing Educn. Organiser

Cultural History Group

Tel: (01224) 272620
Fisher, N. W., PhD   Dir.*

Defence Studies, Centre for

Tel: (01224) 272710 Fax: (01224) 272181
Greenwood, D. E., MA *Liv.*   Dir.*

Educational Research, Centre for

Tel: (01224) 272729 Fax: (01224) 273442
Darling, J. E. M., MA *Edin.*, MLitt *Edin.*, PhD   Sr. Lectr.; Head*
Hendry, L. B., MEd *Leic.*, MSc *Brad.*, PhD, FBPsS   Prof.†
Kiger, Alice M., BA *Towson State*, MA *Morgan*, MSc *Edin.*, PhD *Edin.*   Sr. Lectr.

History, Languages and Culture of the North of Scotland, Elphinstone Institute for the Study and Promotion of

Tel: (01224) 272996 Fax: (01224) 272728
Porter, Prof. J.   Dir.*

Language Centre

Tel: (01224) 272535
Trengove, G. R., MA *Oxf.*   Dir.*

Nordic Studies, Centre for

Tel: (01224) 272714 Fax: (01224) 272181
Arter, D.   Prof.; Dir.*

Religions, Centre for the Study of

Tel: (01224) 272380 Fax: (01224) 273750
Thrower, J. A., MA *Durh.*, BLitt *Oxf.*, PhD   Dir.*

Rural Development Research, Arkleton Centre for

Tel: (01224) 273901 Fax: (01224) 273902
Bryden, Prof. J. M., BSc *Glas.*, PhD *E.Anglia*   Co-Dir.*
Shucksmith, Prof. D. M., MA *Camb.*, MSc *Newcastle(UK)*, PhD *Newcastle(UK)*   Co-Dir.*

Scottish Studies, Centre for

Tel: (01224) 272342
Smith, J. S.   Dir.*

Teaching of Philosophy and Reasoning Skills in Schools, Centre for Research into

Tel: (01224) 272369
Graham, Prof. L. G., MA *St And.*, MA *Durh.*, PhD *Durh.*   Dir.*

CONTACT OFFICERS

Academic affairs. Academic Registrar: Murray, P. J., MA *St And.*, PhD *Edin.*
Accommodation. Accommodation Officer: Fraser, Moira
Admissions (first degree). Assistant Secretary: Kay, Christine
Admissions (higher degree). Administrative Officer (Postgraduate Office): Ingram, Lorna, BSc *Edin.*, MSc *Aberd.*
Adult/continuing education. Director of Continuing Education: Dalgarno, M. T., MA *Aberd.*, PhD *Aberd.*

Alumni. Alumnus Officer: Charnock, Rachel, MA
Archives. Associate Curator, Special Collections and Archives: Anderson-Smith, Myrtle, MA *Aberd.*
Careers. Head of Careers Service: Madden, J. L. A., BA *Nott.*, MA *York(UK)*
Consultancy services. Director of AURIS RESEARCH: Stevenson-Robb, F., MA *CNAA*
Credit transfer. Assistant Secretary: Kay, Christine
Development/fund-raising. Taylor, R.
Distance education. Director of Continuing Education: Dalgarno, M. T., MA *Aberd.*, PhD *Aberd.*
Estates and buildings/works and services. Director of Estates: Wight, H.
Examinations. Assistant Secretary, Examinations and Timetabling: Park, Maggie
Finance. Director of Finance: Ord, M. J., MA
General enquiries. Secretary: Cannon, S., MA *Dund.*
Health services. Chief Medical Officer: Irvine, William, MB ChB
Industrial liaison. Director of AURIS RESEARCH: Stevenson-Robb, F., MA *CNAA*
International office (Far East). Director (International), Student Recruitment Services: Marshall, A. G., BScAgr *Aberd.*, MS *Calif.*, PhD *Aberd.*
International office (North America). Director (International), Student Recruitment Services: Smith, E. A., CBE, MA *Aberd.*, PhD *Aberd.*
Library (chief librarian). Associate Director of Information Systems and Services and Librarian: McLaren, C. A., BA *Lond.*, MPhil *Lond.*
Personnel/human resources. Director of Personnel Services: Shaw, Maureen, MA *Aberd.*
Public relations, information and marketing. Executive Director of Public Relations: Christine, C. K., MA *Aberd.*
Publications. Public Relations Officer: Godfrey-Brown, A., BA *CNAA*
Purchasing. Purchasing Officer: McKinnon, G.
Safety. Security Officer: ......
Scholarships, awards, loans. Deputy Registry Officer: Duggan, S. V., TD, BEd *Aberd.*
Schools liaison. Director, Student Recruitment Services: Carter, J. C., BA *Lond.*, PhD *Lond.*, FRHistS
Security. Security Officer: ......
Sport and recreation. Director of Physical Education and Recreation: Marsden, Elizabeth
Student welfare/counselling. Head of Counselling Service: Lloyd, Siobhan
Students from other countries. Director (International), Student Recruitment Services: Smith, E. A., CBE, MA *Aberd.*, PhD *Aberd.*
Students from other countries. Director (International), Student Recruitment Services: Marshall, A. G., BScAgr *Aberd.*, MS *Calif.*, PhD *Aberd.*
Students with disabilities. University Regent: Powell, J., PhD

[Information supplied by the institution as at 25 September 1998, and edited by the ACU]

UNIVERSITY OF ABERTAY DUNDEE

Founded 1994; previously established as Dundee Technical Institute 1888

Member of the Association of Commonwealth Universities

Postal Address: Bell Street, Dundee, Scotland DD1 1HG
Telephone: (01382) 308000 **Fax**: (01382) 308877 **WWW**: http://www.tay.ac.uk
E-mail formula: initial.surname@abertay-dundee.ac.uk

CHANCELLOR—Airlie, The Earl of, KT, GCVO
PRINCIPAL AND VICE-CHANCELLOR*—King, Prof. Bernard, MSc *Aston*, PhD *Aston*, FIBiol
VICE-PRINCIPAL—McGoldrick, Prof. James, BA *G.Caledonian*
ASSISTANT PRINCIPAL EXTERNAL RELATIONS—Wright, Grahame A., BA(Econ) *Newcastle(UK)*, MPhil *Camb.*
ASSISTANT PRINCIPAL FINANCE AND ADMINISTRATION‡—Hogarth, David J., MA *Edin.*, LLB *Edin.*
HEAD OF INFORMATION SERVICES—Lloyd, I. G., BA *Strath.*

GENERAL INFORMATION

History. Established in 1888 as Dundee Technical Institute, the university was granted its charter in 1994.

It is located in the city of Dundee, adjacent to the Tay Estuary.

Admission to first degree courses (see also United Kingdom Introduction). Through Universities and Colleges Admissions Service (UCAS). The university welcomes applications from students with or without formal educational qualifications. Minimum Scottish Certificate of Education (SCE) requirements: 5 passes, 3 at higher grade and 2 at standard grade (including English and mathematics). Mature students (over 21): accredited prior learning and/or accredited prior experiential learning. International applicants: qualifications equivalent to those listed above and proficiency in English.

First Degrees (see also United Kingdom Directory to Subjects of Study) BA, BSc, BEng.

All courses may be studied full- or part-time. BA, BSc: 3 or 4 years full-time; BEng: 4 years full-time. Some courses include an additional year's work placement.

Higher Degrees (see also United Kingdom Directory to Subjects of Study). MBA, MEng, MSc, MPhil, PhD, DBA.

Applicants for admission to master's degrees must normally hold an appropriate first degree and/or have relevant work experience.

MSc: 1 year full-time or 2 years part-time; MPhil: minimum 2 years full-time or 4 years part-time; PhD: minimum 3 years full-time or 6 years part-time.

Libraries. 100,000 volumes; 800 periodicals subscribed to. Special collections: Faculty of Procurators and Solicitors (law); Dundee and Tayside Local Collection.

Fees (1997–98). Undergraduate: (home students) £750 (acccountancy and law, management), £750—1600 (social and health sciences), £1600 (construction and law, computing, engineering, molecular and life sciences); international students £5250 (acccountancy and law, management), £5250–5950 (social and health sciences), £5250–6700 (engineering), £5950 (construction and law, computing, molecular and life sciences). Postgraduate: (home students) £2540 (MEng, MSc, MPhil, PhD), £3500 (MBA, DBA); (international students) £5950 (MEng, MSc, MPhil, PhD), £5900 (MBA, DBA).

Academic Awards (1997-98) 132 awards ranging in value from £80 to £1000.

Academic Year (1998–99). 2 semesters: 21 September–29 January; 8 February–28 May.

Income (1997-98). Total, £20,523,000.

Statistics. Staff: 515 (275 academic, 240 administrative). Students: full-time 3444 (1748 men, 1696 women); part-time 783 (371 men, 412 women); international 517 (305 men, 212 women); total 4227.

ACADEMIC UNITS
Arranged by Schools

Accountancy and Law
Tel: (01382) 308400 Fax: (01382) 308400

Downes, J. J., LLB *Dund.* Div. Leader, Law
Jelly, R. G., BA *Strath.*, MBA *Edin.* Head*
Lane, D., BA *Open(UK)*, BSc *Lond.*, MSc *Lond.* Div. Leader, Management Accounting and Finance
McCallum, C., BA *Strath.*, MAcc *Glas.* Sr. Lectr.
Murphie, J., LLB *Dund.* Sr. Lectr.
Rennie, E. D., BA *Strath.*, MAcc *Glas.* Div. Leader, Financial Accounting
Seenan, A. J., BEd *Aberd.*, MAcc *Dund.* Sr. Lectr.
Tunney, J. G., BA *Trinity(Dub.)*, LLM *Lond.* Sr. Lectr.
Willsdon, J. A., BA *H.-W.* Sr. Lectr.

Computing
Tel: (01382) 308600 Fax: (01382) 308877

File, P. E., BA *S.Methodist*, BA *Open(UK)*, MSc *Dund.*, PhD *Texas* Sr. Lectr.
Fraser, C., MSc *Strath.*, PhD *Strath.* Sr. Lectr.
Lawson, A. B., MA *Aberd.*, MSc *Qu.*, MPhil *Leeds*, PhD *St And.* Sr. Lectr.
Lucas, T. N., BSc *Wales*, PhD *Wales* Sr. Lectr.
Marshall, I. M., BSc *H.-W.*, BA *Open(UK)*, PhD *Abertay* Head*
Miller, C. J., BSc *Nott.*, PhD *Nott.* Sr. Lectr.
Milne, A. C., MSc *St And.* Sr. Lectr.
Natanson, L. D., BSc *St And.*, PhD *Abertay* Sr. Lectr.
Paris, R. B., BSc *Manc.*, PhD *Manc.*, FIMA Sr. Lectr.
Rutherford, G. S. W., BSc *Lond.*, MSc *Dund.* Sr. Lectr.
Samson, W. B., BSc *St And.*, MSc *H.-W.*, PhD *Edin.* Reader
Smith, N. M., BSc *Abertay*, MBA *Abertay* Sr. Lectr.

Construction and Environment
Tel: (01382) 308102 Fax: (01382) 308104

Ashley, R. M., BSc *CNAA*, MPhil *CNAA* Prof.
Blackwood, D. J., BSc *CNAA*, MSc *Lough.*, PhD *Abertay* Sr. Lectr.
Gow, H. A., MSc *H.-W.*, FRICS Sr. Lectr.
Jefferies, C., BSc *Leeds*, MSc *Birm.*, PhD *Abertay* Div. Leader, Environmental Engineering
Morton, C. W., MSc *H.-W.*, FRICS Div. Leader, Construction Economics and Management
Munday, J. G. L., BSc *Dund.*, PhD *Dund.* Head*
Oduyemi, K. O. K., BSc *Birm.*, PhD *Birm.* Sr. Lectr.
Preston, R. J., BTech *Brad.*, MSc *Brad.*, PhD *Brad.* Div. Leader, Construction Engineering
Sarkar, S., BTech *Kharagpur*, PhD *Leeds* Prof.
Spence, I. M., BSc *Dund.*, PhD *Dund.* Sr. Lectr.
Other Staff: 19 Staff Members

Dundee Business School, see Special Centres, etc

Engineering
Tel: (01382) 308231 Fax: (01382) 308261

Bradley, D. A., BTech *Brad.*, PhD *Brad.* Prof.
Fraser, C. J., BSc *CNAA*, PhD *CNAA*, FIMechE Reader
Gay, C. H., BSc *CNAA* Sr. Lectr.
Gillespie, W. A., BSc *Glas.*, DPhil *Glas.* Prof.
Longair, I. M., BSc *CNAA*, MPhil *CNAA* Sr. Lectr.
Main, C., BSc *Edin.*, PhD *Edin.* Reader
Martin, P. F., BSc *Newcastle(UK)*, PhD *Durh.* Prof.; Head*
McWhannell, D. C., BSc *Edin.*, PhD *Edin.*, FIMechE Sr. Lectr.
Milne, J. S., BSc *Strath.*, FIMechE Emer. Prof.
Other Staff: 16 Lectrs.
Research: amorphous semiconductors; machines; mechatronics; photonics; power systems

Health Sciences, see Soc. and Health Scis.

Law, see Accty. and Law

Life Sciences, see Molecular and Life Scis.

Management
Tel: (01382) 308476 Fax: (01382) 308475

Delcloque, Philippe E., LèsL LèsSc MèsL MèsSc DèsL Sr. Lectr.
Edward, K. I. M., BSc *Glas.*, MSc *Cran.IT*, MBA *H.-W.* Sr. Lectr.
Hotho, S., PhD *Gött.* Sr. Lectr.
Howe, W. S., BA *Strath.*, MSc *Lough.*, PhD *CNAA* Head*
Kirk, R. D., MA *Aberd.*, MPhil *Glas.* Sr. Lectr.
Pemble, Robert J., BA *Nott.*, MA *Nott.* Sr. Lectr.
Robson, I., BA *Newcastle(UK)*, MBA *Strath.* Sr. Lectr.

Molecular and Life Sciences
Tel: (01382) 308651 Fax: (01382) 308663

Benson, E. E., BSc *Nott.Trent*, PhD *Nott.Trent* Reader
Bremner, D. H., BSc *H.-W.*, MBA *Strath.*, PhD *H.-W.* Reader
Bruce, A., BSc *CNAA*, PhD *CNAA* Res. Dir.
Gartland, K. M. A., BSc *Leeds*, PhD *Nott.*
Palfreyman, J. W., BSc *Lond.*, DPhil *Sus.* Reader
Ross, D. A., BSc *Strath.*, PhD *Strath.* Prof.; Head*
Walker, G. M., BSc *H.-W.*, PhD *H.-W.* Reader
Wishart, G. J., BSc *Dund.*, PhD *Dund.* Reader
Wylde, L., BSc *Kent*, PhD *Kent* Sr. Lectr.
Other Staff: 17 Staff Members
Research: avian physiology; microbial biotechnology; molecular biotechnology; plant conservation; wood technology

Social and Health Sciences
Tel: (01382) 308725 Fax: (01382) 223121

Cook, M.J., MA *Aberd.*, PhD *Dund.* Sr. Lectr.
Dawson, D., BSc *Lond.*, MSc *Strath.* Sr. Lectr.
Di Domenico, C., MA *Edin.*, PhD *Ib.* Sr. Lectr.

Leishman, J. L., MEd Dund. Sr. Lectr.
McGillivray, A., MA St And., MPhil Dund. Sr. Lectr.
McNair, M. C., BA Open(UK) Sr. Lectr.
Moir, J., BEd Dund., MEd Dund., PhD CNAA, PhD St And. Sr. Lectr.
Morison, M. J., BSc Edin., MSc Lond., PhD QM Edin. Sr. Lectr.
Siler, P. A., BA Portland, MSc Portland, PhD Edin. Sr. Lectr.
Swanston, M. T., MA Camb., PhD Dund. Prof.; Head*

SPECIAL CENTRES, ETC

Dundee Business School
Tel: (01382) 322260 Fax: (01382) 322290
Dowling, Martin J., BSc Manc., MA Keele Sr. Lectr.
Martin, G., BA CNAA, MSc Strath., MBA H.-W. Dir.*

Wastewater Technology Centre (WWTC)
Tel: (01382) 308117 Fax: (01382) 308117
Ashley, R. M., BSc CNAA, MPhil CNAA Prof.; Head*
Blackwood, D. J., BSc CNAA, MSc Lough., PhD Abertay Bus. Manager
Jefferies, C., BSc Leeds, MSc Birm., PhD Abertay Dir., Engin.

Wood Technology, Scottish Institute for (SIWT)
Tel: (01382) 308930
Bruce, A., BSc CNAA, PhD CNAA Res. Dir.
Sinclair, Derek, BSc Abertay, PhD Abertay Industry Manager
Research: biodeterioration

CONTACT OFFICERS
Academic affairs. Vice-Principal: McGoldrick, Prof. James, BA G.Caledonian
Accommodation. Depute Secretary: Keir, E., BA Abertay
Admissions (first degree) (post application). Administrative Officer: Galloway, Kenneth

Admissions (first degree) (pre application). Information and Recruitment Officer: McEwan, J.
Admissions (higher degree). Academic Services Officer: Teppett, Jonathan L., BA Wales, PhD Wales
Admissions (higher degree) (post application). Administrative Officer: Galloway, Kenneth
Admissions (higher degree) (pre application). Information and Recruitment Officer: McEwan, J.
Alumni. Information and Recruitment Officer: Middleton, Carol-Anne
Archives. Administrative Officer: Galloway, Kenneth
Careers. Careers Adviser: Tait, Christopher, BA Abertay
Computing services. Head of Information Services: Lloyd, I. G., BA Strath.
Consultancy services. Senior Industrial Liaison Officer: Higgins, R., MA Oxf., DPhil Oxf.
Credit transfer. Vice-Principal: McGoldrick, Prof. James, BA G.Caledonian
Development/fund-raising. Assistant Principal External Relations: Wright, Grahame A., BA(Econ) Newcastle(UK), MPhil Camb.
Equal opportunities. Assistant Principal Finance and Administration: Hogarth, David J., MA Edin., LLB Edin.
Estates and buildings/works and services. Assistant Principal Finance and Administration: Hogarth, David J., MA Edin., LLB Edin.
Examinations. Administrative Officer: Galloway, Kenneth
Finance. Director of Finance: Lamb, Caroline
General enquiries. Assistant Principal Finance and Administration: Hogarth, David J., MA Edin., LLB Edin.
Health services. Director, Student Services Unit: Whelan, Margaret, BA Stir.
Industrial liaison. Senior Industrial Liaison Officer: Higgins, R., MA Oxf., DPhil Oxf.
International office. International Recruitment Officer: Conway, Colette, BA G.Caledonian
Library (chief librarian). Head of Information Services: Lloyd, I. G., BA Strath.
Minorities/disadvantaged groups. Assistant Principal External Relations: Wright,

Grahame A., BA(Econ) Newcastle(UK), MPhil Camb.
Ombudsperson. Assistant Principal Finance and Administration: Hogarth, David J., MA Edin., LLB Edin.
Personnel/human resources. Personnel Officer: Morgan, A. C., BA Open(UK), MBA Dund.
Public relations, information and marketing. Assistant Principal External Relations: Wright, Grahame A., BA(Econ) Newcastle(UK), MPhil Camb.
Publications. Senior Information and Recruitment Officer: Pullen, Frank F.
Purchasing. Director of Finance: Lamb, Caroline
Purchasing. Procurement Officer: Kirkpatrick, Mary, BA H.-W.
Quality assurance and accreditation. Vice-Principal: McGoldrick, Prof. James, BA G.Caledonian
Research. Vice-Principal: McGoldrick, Prof. James, BA G.Caledonian
Research. Academic Services Officer: Teppett, Jonathan L., BA Wales, PhD Wales
Safety. Safety Officer: Prophet, C.
Scholarships, awards, loans. Vice-Principal: McGoldrick, Prof. James, BA G.Caledonian
Schools liaison. Information and Recruitment Officer: Balfour, Lesley
Staff development and training. Vice-Principal: McGoldrick, Prof. James, BA G.Caledonian
Staff development and training. Training and Development Officer: Sisman, Craig, MA Edin., MSc Strath.
Student union. President: Kilpatrick, Michael
Student welfare/counselling. Director, Student Services Unit: Whelan, Margaret, BA Stir.
Students from other countries. Senior Student Counsellor: Jackson, P. A. K., BA Camb.
Students with disabilities. Student Counsellor: Ritchie, Ailsa J., MA Aberd.
University press. Assistant Principal External Relations: Wright, Grahame A., BA(Econ) Newcastle(UK), MPhil Camb.

[Information supplied by the institution as at 11 February 1998, and edited by the ACU]

ANGLIA POLYTECHNIC UNIVERSITY

Founded 1992; previously established as Anglia Polytechnic 1989

Postal Address: Victoria Road South, Chelmsford, Essex, England CM1 1LL
Telephone: (01245) 493131 **Fax**: (01245) 490835 **WWW**: http://www.anglia.ac.uk

VICE-CHANCELLOR AND CHIEF EXECUTIVE*——Malone-Lee, Mike, CB, MA Oxf.

ASTON UNIVERSITY

Incorporated by Royal Charter as the University of Aston in Birmingham 1966; officially renamed 1997; originally established as Birmingham Municipal Technical School 1895

Member of the Association of Commonwealth Universities

Postal Address: Aston Triangle, Birmingham, England B4 7ET
Telephone: (0121) 359 3611 **E-mail**: support@aston.ac.uk
Cables: Aston University, Aston Triangle, Birmingham, England B4 7ET **WWW**: http://www.aston.ac.uk
E-mail formula: initials.surname@aston.ac.uk

CHANCELLOR—Cadbury, Sir Adrian, MA *Camb.*, Hon. LLD *Brist.*, Hon. DSc *Cran.IT*, Hon. DSc *Aston*
PRO-CHANCELLOR—Bett, Sir Michael, CBE, MA *Camb.*, Hon. DBA *Liv.J.Moores*
VICE-CHANCELLOR*—Wright, Prof. Michael T., BSc *Aston*, PhD *Aston*, FIEE, FIMechE, FIMA, Hon. FEng
SENIOR PRO-VICE-CHANCELLOR—Tighe, Prof. Brian J., BSc *Aston*, PhD *Aston*, FRSChem
PRO-VICE-CHANCELLOR—Reeves, Prof. Nigel B. R., OBE, MA *Oxf.*, DPhil *Oxf.*
PRO-VICE-CHANCELLOR—Hewitt, Fred, BA *Brist.*, PhD *Brist.*
TREASURER—Harford, Sir Timothy, Bt., MA *Oxf.*
UNIVERSITY SECRETARY-REGISTRAR‡—Packham, R. David A., BA *Manc.*
DIRECTOR OF FINANCE AND BUSINESS SERVICES—Dhariwal, Guppy, BSc *Newcastle(UK)*
DIRECTOR OF LIBRARY AND INFORMATION SERVICES—Smith, Nick R., BSc *S'ton.*, MSc *Sheff.*, PhD *S'ton.*

GENERAL INFORMATION

History. The university was founded in 1895 as Birmingham Municipal Technical School and gained its university charter in 1966.

Admission to first degree courses (see also United Kingdom Introduction). Through Universities and Colleges Admissions Service (UCAS).

First Degrees (see also United Kingdom Directory to Subjects of Study). BEng, BSc, MChem, MEng, MPharm.
BEng, BSc: 3 years or 4 years (sandwich); MPharm: 4 years; MChem, MEng: 4 years or 5 years (sandwich).

Higher Degrees (see also United Kingdom Directory to Subjects of Study). MBA, MSc, MPhil, PhD.
Applicants for admission to master's degrees must hold a good first degree. In addition, MBA: at least three years' work experience; MSc (certain subjects): relevant professional experience. MPhil, PhD: relevant first degree with first or upper second class honours.

Language of Instruction. English. Modern languages courses are partly taught in French and German, as applicable.

Libraries. 253,062 volumes; 1608 periodicals subscribed to.

Fees (1998–99, annual). Home undergraduate: £500–1000 (classroom-based courses); £850–1000 (laboratory-based courses). International undergraduate: £3350–6700 (classroom-based courses); £4450–8900 (laboratory-based courses). Home postgraduate: £1600–8750 (taught programmes); £2610 (research programmes). International postgraduate: £1600–10,500 (classroom-based programmes); £4225–8900 (laboratory-based programmes).

Academic Awards (1996–97). 87 awards ranging in value from £150 to £7990.

Academic Year (1998–99). Three terms: 4 October–12 December; 10 January–20 March; 18 April–26 June.

Income (1997–98). Total, £42,000,000.

Statistics. Staff: 1128 (343 academic, 785 administrative/support). Students: full-time 5222 (2773 men, 2449 women); part-time 923 (550 men, 373 women); international 773; total 6145.

FACULTIES/SCHOOLS

Engineering and Applied Science
Fax: (0121) 359 8482

Dean: Miller, J. David, MA *Camb.*, PhD *Camb.*
Secretary: Candlin, Julia

Life and Health Sciences
Tel: (0121) 359 3621 Fax: (0121) 359 0733

Dean: Irwin, Prof. William J., BPharm *Lond.*, PhD *Lond.*, DSc *Lond.*, FRSChem, FRPharmS
Secretary: Taylor, Julie

Management, Languages and European Studies
Fax: (0121) 333 5708

Dean: Davis, Prof. Edward W., MASt *And.*
Secretary: Yelland, Denise

ACADEMIC UNITS

Aston Business School
Fax: (0121) 333 5774

Bainbridge, David I., BSc *Wales*, PhD *CNAA* Reader
Bennett, David J., MSc *Birm.*, PhD *Birm.* Prof.
Botschen, Günter, MBA *Innsbruck*, PhD *Innsbruck* Sr. Lectr.
Bovaird, Anthony G., BSc *Belf.*, MA *Lanc.* Sr. Lectr.
Burcher, Peter G., BSc *Birm.*, PhD Sr. Lectr.
Cox, Anthony J., BSc *Brist.*, MBA *Warw.*, PhD *Birm.*, FIP Sr. Lectr.
Davis, Edward W., MA St *And.* Lloyds Bank Prof., Business Finance
Edwards, John S., BA *Camb.*, PhD *Camb.* Sr. Lectr.
Egan, Sir John, BSc *Lond.*, MSc(Econ) *Lond.*, Hon. DSc *Aston* Visiting Prof.
Ellwood, Sheila M., BSc *Wales*, MSc PhD Sr. Lecr.
Greenley, Gordon E., BA *Open(UK)*, MSc *Salf.*, PhD *Salf.* Prof.
Hooley, Graham J., BSc *Warw.*, PhD *Warw.* Prof., Marketing
Johnson, David M., BA *Nott.*, MEc *Monash* Sr. Lectr.; Dir., Undergrad. Studies
Lewis, Colin D., BSc *Brist.*, MSc *Birm.*, PhD *Birm.* Prof., Operations Management
Loveridge, Raymond J., MA *Camb.*, MSc *Lond.* Prof., Manpower Management; Dir., Res. and Doctoral Programmes
Oakley, Mark H., BSc *Newcastle(UK)*, PhD *Aston* Dir., Postgrad. Studies
Parker, David, BSc(Econ) *Hull*, MSc *Salf.*, PhD *Cran.* Prof.
Saunders, John A., BSc MBA PhD Prof., Marketing; Head*
Shackleton, Vivian J., BSc *Wales*, PhD *Wales* Sr. Lectr.
Smith, Chris, BA *CNAA*, PhD *Brist.* Sr. Lectr.

Smith, Dennis, MA *Camb.*, MSc *Lond.*, PhD *Leic.* Reader
Smith, John, BA *Lond.* Visiting Prof.
Steward, H. Frederick, BSc *Manc.*, MSc *Manc.*, PhD *Manc.* Sr. Lectr.
Tricker, Michael J., BA *Birm.* Sr. Lectr.
Watt, John C., BSc(Econ) *Lond.*, MA *Edin.* Sr. Lectr.
Research: management and information systems; marketing and business strategy; organisation studies; public services management; technology and innovation

Chemistry, Applied, see Engin., Chem., and Appl. Chem.

Engineering, Chemical, and Applied Chemistry
Fax: (0121) 359 4094

Amass, Allan J., BSc *Birm.*, PhD *Birm.*, FRSChem Sr. Lectr.
Bridgwater, Tony V., BScTech *Manc.*, MSc PhD DSc Prof.
Butterworth, David, BSc(Eng), FEng, FIChemE Visiting Prof.
Homer, John, PhD *Birm.*, DSc *Leeds*, FRSChem Prof.
Jenkins, John D., BA *Open(UK)*, BSc *Birm.*, PhD *Birm.* Sr. Lectr.
Lopez-Merono, Jose, BSc MSc PhD Visiting Prof.
McWhinnie, William R., PhD *Lond.*, DSc *Lond.*, FRSChem Prof.
Miller, J. David, MA *Camb.*, PhD *Camb.* Sr. Lectr.
Mumford, Clive J., BSc *Birm.*, PhD DSc Reader
Slater, Nigel K. H., MA *Camb.*, PhD *Camb.* Prof.; Head*
Smith, Eric L., BScTech *Manc.*, MScTech *Manc.*, PhD *Manc.* Reader
Tighe, Brian J., BSc PhD, FRSChem Prof.
Research: bio-energy research into thermal biomass conversion; chemical and pharmaceutical manufacturing; development of fundamental nuclear magnetic resonance techniques; polymer and bio-materials; polymer sunthesis

Engineering, Civil and Mechanical
Fax: (0121) 333 3389

Foot, Nigel I. S., BSc *Leeds*, MEng *Liv.* Sr. Lectr.
Garvey, Seamus D., PhD Reader
Hayns, Mike R., OBE, BSc *Leic.*, PhD *Leic.* Powergen Prof.
Hedges, Pete D., MA *Camb.*, MSc *Birm.*, PhD Sr. Lectr.
Kettle, Roger J., BSc *Sur.*, MSc *Sur.*, PhD *Sur.* Prof.; Head*
Moore, Philip, BSc *Birm.*, PhD *Brun.*, FRAS Sr. Lectr.

Norris, W. Toby, MA, FIEE   Prof.
Page, Chris L., MA *Camb.*, PhD *Camb.*,
    FICE   Prof.
Penny, John E. T., BSc(Eng) *Lond.*, PhD,
    FIMA   Sr. Lectr.
Short, Neil R., BSc *Sur.*, PhD *Leeds*   Sr. Lectr.
Thornton, Colin, BSc PhD   Reader
Traill, Alasdair L., MA *St And.*   Sr. Lectr.
Wood, Jonathan, BSc PhD, FIStructE   Visiting
    Prof.
Research: dynamics control and vibration;
    engineering materials and structures;
    environmental systems; integrated design
    and manufacture; materials and processes in
    engineering alloys

Wolfson Heat Treatment Centre

Fax: (0121) 359 8910

Hick, Alan J., BSc *Birm.*, FIM   Manager*

Engineering, Electronic, and Computer Science

Fax: (0121) 333 6215

Bennion, Ian, BSc *Glas.*, FIEE   Prof.
Blow, G. Keith, MA *Camb.*, PhD
    Camb.   Visiting Prof.
Bounds, David J., BSc *Manc.*, PhD
    Manc.   Visiting Prof.
Buus, Jens, MSc PhD DSc   Visiting Prof.
Cardwell, Michael J., BSc *Lond.*, PhD *Lond.*,
    FIEE   Prof.; Head*
Carpenter, Geof F., BSc *Lond.*, PhD *Lond.*   Sr.
    Lectr.
Doran, Nicholas J., BSc *Reading*, PhD *Reading*,
    FIEE   Prof.
Feigenbaum, Edward, BSc *Carnegie-Mellon*, PhD
    Carnegie-Mellon   Visiting Prof.
Grimes, Norman W., PhD *Brist.*, DSc
    Brist.   Reader
Hinton, Geoffrey, BA *Camb.*, PhD
    Edin.   Visiting Prof.
Holding, David J., BSc(Eng) *Lond.*, PhD *Lond.*,
    FIEE   Sr. Lectr.
Lowe, David, BSc *Warw.*, PhD *Warw.*   Prof.
Opper, Manfred, PhD *Giessen*   Reader
Saad, David, MSc *Tel-Aviv*, PhD *Tel-Aviv*   Reader
Sullivan, John, BSc PhD DSc   Reader
Research: information technology: design and
    use; neural computing and pattern
    recognition; new optical phenomena;
    photonics; surface science

Engineering, Mechanical and Electrical

Fax: (0121) 333 5809

Health and Safety Unit

Booth, Richard T., MSc *Lond.*, PhD *Warw.*,
    FIMechE   Prof.; Dir.*
Cahill, Michael, BSc, FIEE, FIMechE   Visiting
    Prof.
Research: risk assessment and management

German, see Langs. and European Studies

Human Biology, see Psychol. and Human
    Biol.

Languages and European Studies

Fax: (0121) 359 6153

Ager, Dennis E., BA *Lond.*, PhD *Salf.*   Prof.
Chilton, Paul A., MA *Oxf.*, DPhil *Oxf.*   Prof.;
    Head*
Görner, Rüdiger, BA *Lond.*, MA *Tübingen*, PhD
    Sur.   Prof., German
Haselbach, Dieter, DPhil *Marburg*   Reader
Knowles, Frank E., MA *Oxf.*, MSc *Salf.*   Prof.,
    Language
Moores, Pamela M., MA *Camb.*, PhD *Leic.*   Sr.
    Lectr.
Reeves, Nigel B. R., OBE, MA *Oxf.*, DPhil
    Oxf.   Prof.

Research: European societies and cultures;
    language and society

Language Studies Unit

Fax: (0121) 359 2725

Richards, Keith E., BA *Liv.*, MSc PhD   Lectr.;
    Head*
Research: analysis of discourse; content-based
    language learning; development of a
    pedagogic description of journal articles;
    investigation into task-based activity;
    redesign of foreign language teacher
    education

Mathematics, Applied, see Engin.,
    Electronic, and Computer Sci.

Pharmaceutical Sciences

Fax: (0121) 359 0733

Akhtar, Saghir, BSc *Leic.*, PhD *Bath*   Reader
Billington, David C., BSc *Warw.*, PhD *Warw.*,
    FRSChem   Prof.; Head*
Handley, Sheila L., BPharm *Lond.*, PhD   Sr.
    Lectr.
Irwin, William J., BPharm *Lond.*, PhD *Lond.*, DSc
    Lond., FRSChem, FRPharmS   Prof.
Lambert, Peter A., BSc *Lond.*, PhD *Lond.*, DSc
    Lough.   Sr. Lectr.
Martin, Ian L., BSc *Birm.*, PhD *Birm.*   Prof.
Schwalbe, Carl H., AM *Harv.*, PhD *Harv.*   Sr.
    Lectr.
Tisdale, Mike J., BSc *Hull*, PhD *Lond.*, DSc
    Lond.   Prof.
Wilson, Keith A., BSc PhD   Sr. Lectr.
Research: cancer biochemistry; drug delivery;
    medicinal chemistry; microbiology;
    pharmacology

Psychology and Human Biology

Bailey, Clifford J., BSc *Sheff.*, PhD   Sr. Lectr.
Davies, D. Roy, BA *Brist.*, PhD *Brist.*,
    FBPsS   Reader
Harding, Graham F. A., BSc *Lond.*, PhD *Birm.*,
    DSc, FBPsS   Prof., Clinical Neurophysiology
Perris, Alan D., BSc *Sheff.*, PhD *Sheff.*   Reader,
    Cell Physiology
Rimmer, Jim J., BSc *Durh.*, PhD *Durh.*   Sr.
    Lectr.
Stammers, Robert B., BSc *Hull*, PhD *Hull*,
    FBPsS   Reader
Research: clinical neurophysiology; human
    performance and cognition; immunology;
    social and developmental psychology

Vision Sciences

Fax: (0121) 333 4220

Barnes, Derek A., MSc   Sr. Lectr.; Head*
Foster, David H., BSc *Lond.*, PhD *Lond.*, DSc
    Lond., FIMA, FIP   Prof.
Fowler, Colin W., BSc *Wales*, PhD   Sr. Lectr.
Gilmartin, Bernard, BSc *City(UK)*, PhD
    City(UK)   Reader
Wild, John M., BSc *City(UK)*, MSc PhD   Sr.
    Lectr.
Research: clinical neurophysiology; opthalmic
    and physiological optics; visual
    psychophysics and computational vision

SPECIAL CENTRES, ETC

Combined Honours Studies

Fax: (0121) 359 4334

Dennis, J. Keith, BSc *Nott.*, PhD *Nott.*,
    DSc   Dir.*

Continuing Professional and Managerial Studies, Institute of

Fax: (0121) 359 6427

Gregory, David G., MA *Oxf.*, MSocSc
    Birm.   Dir.*

CONTACT OFFICERS

Accommodation. Head of Residential and
    Catering Services: Cutler, Alan M.
Admissions (first degree). Senior Assistant
    Registrar: Walter, John G., BA *CNAA*
Admissions (higher degree). Senior Assistant
    Registrar: Walter, John G., BA *CNAA*
Adult/continuing education. Director,
    Institute of Continuing Professional and
    Managerial Studies: Gregory, David G., MA
    Oxf., MSocSc *Birm.*
Alumni. Alumni Relations Officer: Pymm,
    Sarah E., BA *Bourne.*
Archives. Senior Assistant Registrar: Walter,
    John G., BA *CNAA*
Careers. Head, Schools Liaison and Careers:
    Comfort, Stewart, BSc *Lough.*
Computing services. Director of Finance and
    Business Services: Dhariwal, Guppy, BSc
    Newcastle(UK)
Development/fund-raising. Director of
    Marketing and Communications: Betteridge,
    Paula, BA *Hull*
Distance education. Director, Institute of
    Continuing Professional and Managerial
    Studies: Gregory, David G., MA *Oxf.*. MSocSc
    Birm.
Equal opportunities. Personnel Officer:
    Walley, Annie M., BA *CNAA*
Estates and buildings/works and services.
    Director of Estates and Buildings: Carthy,
    Walter
Examinations. Senior Assistant Registrar:
    Walter, John G., BA *CNAA*
Finance. Director of Finance and Business
    Services: Dhariwal, Guppy, BSc *Newcastle(UK)*
General enquiries. University Secretary-
    Registrar: Packham, R. David A., BA *Manc.*
Health services. Honorary University
    Physician: Nye, Matthew N-L., MB ChB *Sheff.*
International office. International Student Co-
    ordinator: Crumpton, Dennis, BSc *Lond.*, PhD
    Aston, FIP, FIEE
Library (chief librarian). Director of Library
    and Information Services: Smith, Nick R.,
    BSc *S'ton.*, MSc *Sheff.*, PhD *S'ton.*
Personnel and human resources. Director of
    Human Resources: Thomas, Keith, BA
    E.Anglia
Public relations, information and marketing.
    Director of Marketing and Communications:
    Betteridge, Paula, BA *Hull*
Publications. Director of Marketing and
    Communications: Betteridge, Paula, BA *Hull*
Purchasing. Director of Finance and Business
    Services: Dhariwal, Guppy, BSc *Newcastle(UK)*
Quality assurance and accreditation. Pro-
    Vice-Chancellor: Reeves, Prof. Nigel B. R.,
    OBE, MA *Oxf.*, DPhil *Oxf.*
Safety. Safety Adviser: Branston, David S.
Scholarships, awards, loans. Senior Assistant
    Registrar: Walter, John G., BA *CNAA*
Schools liaison. Head, Schools Liaison and
    Careers: Comfort, Stewart, BSc *Lough.*
Sport and recreation. Physical Recreation
    Officer: Draper, Vic C.
Staff development and training. Head of Staff
    Development: Doidge, John, BSc *Lond.*, MSc
Student union. Permanent Secretary: Edgson,
    Mal, BSc *Aston*
Student welfare/counselling. University
    Counsellor: Fearnside, Suzanne, BA *Plym.*
Students from other countries. International
    Student Co-ordinator: Crumpton, Dennis,
    BSc *Lond.*, PhD *Aston*, FIP, FIEE
Students with disabilities. Senior Assistant
    Registrar: Walter, John G., BA *CNAA*

*[Information supplied by the institution as at 1 April
1998, and edited by the ACU]*

UNIVERSITY OF BATH

Founded 1966 as Bath University of Technology; originally established as Merchant Venturers Technical College
(1894)

Member of the Association of Commonwealth Universities

Postal Address: Claverton Down, Bath, England BA2 7AY
Telephone: (01225) 826826 **Fax**: (01225) 462508 **Telex**: 449097 **WWW**: http://www.bath.ac.uk
E-mail formula: initial.surname@bath.ac.uk

CHANCELLOR—Tugendhat of Widdington, Baron Kt., MA *Camb.*
PRO-CHANCELLOR—Embleton, David T., BSc *Leic.*
PRO-CHANCELLOR—Maitland, Sir Donald, GCMG, OBE, MA *Edin.*
PRO-CHANCELLOR—......
VICE-CHANCELLOR*—VandeLinde, Prof. V. David, BS *Carnegie-Mellon*, MS *Carnegie-Mellon*, PhD
Carnegie-Mellon
DEPUTY VICE-CHANCELLOR—Lunt, Prof. George G., MSc *Birm.*, PhD *Birm.*
TREASURER—Buchanan, Sir Robin
REGISTRAR‡—Bursey, Jonathan A., BA *Durh.*, MSc *CNAA*
BURSAR—Thomas, Brian
DIRECTOR OF FINANCE—Aderyn, Diane, BA *Newcastle(UK)*, MA(Econ) *Manc.*
LIBRARIAN—Nicholson, Howard, MA *Sus.*

GENERAL INFORMATION

History. The university was originally established as Merchant Venturers Technical College in 1894, receiving university status in 1966.

Admission to first degree courses (see also United Kingdom Introduction). Through Universities and Colleges Admissions Service (UCAS).

First Degrees (see also United Kingdom Directory to Subjects of Study). BA, BEng, BSc, MBioc, MChem, MEng, MMath, MPharm, MPhys.
All courses are full-time and normally last 3 years, or 3 years plus 1 year industrial placement. Undergraduate master's degrees: 4 years, or 4 years plus 1 year industrial placement.

Higher Degrees (see also United Kingdom Directory to Subjects of Study). MA, MBA, MEd, MSc, MPhil, PhD.
Applicants for admission to postgraduate degrees must normally hold an appropriate first degree with at least second class honours. PhD candidates are registered in the first instance for MPhil.
MA, MBA, MEd, MSc: 1 year full-time or 2 years part-time; MPhil: 1–3 years full-time or 2–4 years part-time; PhD 2–4 years full-time or 3–5 years part-time.

Libraries. 420,000 volumes; 2200 periodicals subscribed to. Specialist libraries: European Documentation Centre; Holburne of Menstrie Museum and Crafts Study Centre Library; Royal Bath and West and Southern Counties Society. Special collection: Pittman (shorthand and orthographic systems, initial teaching alphabet).

Fees (1997–98, annual). Undergraduate and postgraduate: £6450 (arts); £8500 (sciences). MBA: £11,000.

Academic Year (1998–99). Two semesters: 23 September–29 January; 8 February–18 June.

Income (to 31 July 1997). Total, £69,300,000.

Statistics. Staff: 848 (642 academic, 206 administrative). Students: full-time 5624 (3226 men, 2398 women); part-time 1124 (790 men, 334 women); international 1423 (835 men, 588 women).

FACULTIES/SCHOOLS

Access and Continuing Studies
Tel: (01225) 323546 Fax: (01225) 826709
Dean: Calderhead, Prof. James J., MA *Dund.*, PhD *Stir.*

Engineering and Design
Tel: (01225) 323525 Fax: (01225) 323255
Dean: Burrows, Prof. Clifford R., BSc *Wales*, PhD *Lond.*, DSc(Eng) *Lond.*, FIMechE
Executive Assistant: Anstee, Judith M., BA *Leeds*

Humanities and Social Sciences
Tel: (01225) 826013 Fax: (01225) 826113
Dean: Jamieson, Prof. Ian M., BSc *Sur.*, PhD *Sur.*
Executive Assistant: Jacobs, Suzanne M., BA *Sus.*

Management, School of
Tel: (01225) 826111 Fax: (01225) 826861
Head: Bayliss, Prof. Brian T., BSc(Econ) *Lond.*, PhD *Birm.*
Secretary: ......

Science
Tel: (01225) 826772 Fax: (01225) 323353
Dean: Davies, Prof. David J. G., MSc *Manc.*, PhD *Manc.*, FPS
Executive Assistant: Bird, Elizabeth, BA *Lond.*

ACADEMIC UNITS

Architecture and Civil Engineering
Tel: (01225) 826357 Fax: (01225) 826691
Ballantyne, Andrew N., MA *Sheff.*, PhD *Sheff.* Sr. Lectr.
Barnes, Michael R., BSc *Manc.*, MSc *Manc.*, MA *Manc.*, PhD *City(UK)* Prof., Civil Engineering
Clegg, Peter, MA *Camb.*, MEd Visiting Prof.†
Day, Alan K., BArch *Glas.*, PhD *CNAA* Prof., Architecture; Head*
Dickson, Michael, BA MS Visiting Prof.†
Ford, S. Max, CBE Visiting Prof.†
Frewer, Richard J. B., MA *Camb.* Prof., Architecture
Hart, Vaughan A., MPhil *Camb.*, PhD *Camb.*, BSc BArch Reader
Shalev, David, OBE, BArch *Haifa(Technion)* Prof.†, Architecture
Tavernor, Robert W., BA *CNAA*, PhD *Camb.* Prof., Architecture
Other Staff: 1 Sr. Lectr.†; 9 Lectrs.
Research: architectural history: treatises, British Renaissance architecture, the picturesque; computer modelling: urban form, energy monitoring, software development; lightweight structures: computer modelling, wind loading, dome structures; window and cladding technology: building envelope, integrity and construction, physics

Biology and Biochemistry
Tel: (01225) 826407 Fax: (01225) 826779
Acharya, K. Ravindra, BSc *Mys.*, MSc *B'lore.*, PhD *B'lore.* Prof.
Atkinson, Anthony, BSc *Manc.*, PhD *Manc.* Visiting Prof.†
Beeching, John R., BA *Durh.*, BSc *Wales*, PhD *Warw.* Sr. Lectr.
Charnley, Anthony K., BSc *Durh.*, PhD *Durh.* Reader
Clarkson, John M., BSc *Nott.*, PhD *Lond.* Sr. Lectr.
Cooper, Richard M., MSc *Lond.*, PhD *Lond.* Reader
Danson, Michael J., BSc *Leic.*, PhD *Leic.* Prof.
Eisenthal, Robert S., AB *Amherst*, PhD *N.Carolina* Reader
Franks, Nigel R., BSc *Leeds*, PhD *Leeds* Prof., Animal Behaviour and Ecology
Harrison, Roger, MA *Camb.*, PhD *Birm.* Reader
Henshaw, Graham G., BSc *Liv.*, PhD *Liv.* Prof.†, Plant Biology
Holman, Geoffrey D., BSc *S'ton.*, PhD *S'ton.* Prof.
Hough, David W., BSc *Manc.*, DPhil *Sus.* Reader
Hurst, Laurence D., BA *Camb.*, DPhil *Oxf.* Prof., Evolutionary Genetics
Lowe, C. R., BSc PhD Visiting Prof.
Marsh, P., BSc PhD Visiting Prof.†
Rayner, Alan D. M., MA *Camb.*, PhD *Camb.* Reader
Rees, Anthony R., MA *Oxf.*, MSc *Oxf.*, DPhil *Oxf.* Prof., Biochemistry
Reynolds, Stuart E., MA *Camb.*, PhD *Camb.* Prof.; Head*
Roberts, R. J., BSc PhD Visiting Prof.†
Sharp, R. J. Visiting Prof.†
Sharpiro, R., BS PhD Visiting Prof.†
Slack, Jonathan M. W., BA *Oxf.*, PhD *Edin.* Prof., Cell and Molecular Biology
Taylor, Garry L., BSc *Lond.*, PhD *Lond.* Reader
Wheals, Alan E., BSc *Leic.*, PhD *Leic.* Sr. Lectr.
Whish, William J. D., BSc *Lond.*, PhD *Wat.* Sr. Lectr.
Wolstenholme, Adrian J., BSc *Lond.*, PhD *Camb.* Sr. Lectr.
Wonnacott, Susan J., MSc *Lond.*, PhD *Lond.* Reader, Neuroscience
Wright, Sidney J. L., BSc *Wales*, PhD *Wales* Sr. Lectr.
Other Staff: 10 Lectrs.; 1 Reader†
Research: biobial pathogenicity; developmental biology; enzyme structure and function cell biology; neuroscience; structural molecular biology

Business, see Management, Sch. of

Chemistry
Tel: (01225) 826130 Fax: (01225) 826231
Bewick, Alan, BSc *Manc.*, PhD *Manc.*   Visiting
Prof.†
Brisdon, Brian J., BSc *S'ton.*, PhD *S'ton.*   Reader
Campbell, Malcolm M., BSc *Glas.*, PhD *Glas.*,
FRSChem, FRSEd   Prof. Fellow†
Green, Michael, BSc *Hull*, PhD *Lond.*, DSc
Brist.   Prof.
Mann, Stephen, MSc *Manc.*, DPhil *Oxf.*   Prof.
Molloy, Kieran C., BSc *Nott.*, PhD *Nott.*   Reader
Osguthorpe, David J., BSc *Sheff.*, PhD
Manc.   Reader
Parker, Stephen C., BSc *Lond.*, PhD
Lond.   Reader
Peter, Laurence M., BSc *S'ton.*, PhD *S'ton.*   Prof.
Price, Gareth J., BSc PhD   Sr. Lectr.
Sainsbury, Malcolm, PhD DSc,
FRSChem   Prof.; Head*
Williams, Ian H., BSc *Sheff.*, PhD *Sheff.*   Prof.
Williams, Jonathan M. J., BSc *York(UK)*, DPhil
Oxf.   Prof.
Other Staff: 8 Lectrs.; 1 Sr. Lectr.†

Economics and International Development
Fax: (01225) 826381
Bowles, Roger A., BSc   Reader
Collard, David A., MA *Camb.*   Prof., Economics
Cullis, John G., MA *Leeds*, MSc
York(UK)   Reader
Heady, Christopher J., BA *Camb.*, MA *Yale*,
MPhil *Yale*, PhD *Camb.*   Prof., Applied
Economics
Hudson, John R., BSc *Lond.*, MA *Warw.*, PhD
Warw.   Reader
Jones, Philip R., MA *Leic.*, PhD *Leic.*   Reader
Lawson, Colin W., MSc(Econ) *Lond.*, PhD
Lond.   Sr. Lectr.
Markandya, Anil, BA *York(UK)*, MSc *Lond.*, PhD
Lond.   Prof., Quantitive Economics; Head*
Wood, Geoffrey D., BA *Sus.*, MPhil *Sus.*,
PhD   Reader
Other Staff: 10 Lectrs.

Education
Tel: (01225) 826225 Fax: (01225) 826113
Haydn, Mary C., BSc *S'ton.*, MPhil *Bath*   Sr.
Lectr.
Johnson, Rita, BA *Manc.*, MPhil *Sheff.Hallam*   Sr.
Lectr.
Lauder, Hugh, BSc *Lond.*, MA *Lond.*, PhD
Camb.   Prof.
Scott, William A. H., BSc *Leeds*, PhD *Leeds*   Sr.
Lectr.; Head*
Stables, Andrew, BA *Lond.*, PhD *Bath*   Sr. Lectr.
Thompson, John J., CBE, MA *Oxf.*, MA *Camb.*,
PhD *CNAA*, FRSChem   Prof.
Walker, George R., OBE, MA *Oxf.*, MSc
Oxf.   Visiting Prof.†
Other Staff: 17 Lectrs.; 1 Sr. Lectr.†
Research: culture and environment; education
policy, innovation and change; international
and comparative education; professional
learning

Engineering, Aeronautical, see Engin.,
Mech.

Engineering, Chemical
Tel: (01225) 826338 Fax: (01225) 826894
Andrew, Sydney P. S., BSc DSc, FRS,
FEng   Visiting Prof.†
Chaudhuri, Julian B., BSc *Lond.*, PhD
Reading   Sr. Lectr.
Crittenden, Barry D., BSc *Birm.*, PhD *Birm.*,
FIChemE   Prof.
England, Richard, MSc *Wales*, PhD *Wales*   Sr.
Lectr.
Field, Robert W., MA *Camb.*, PhD
Camb.   Reader
Greaves, Malcolm, BTech *Lough.*, PhD *Lough.*,
FIChemE   Prof.
Guy, Keith W. A., BSc *Lond.*, MSc *Lond.*, PhD
Lond.   Visiting Prof.†

Howell, John A., MA *Camb.*, PhD *Minn.*,
FIChemE   Prof., Biochemical Engineering
Hubble, John, BSc PhD   Reader
Kolaczkowski, Stanislaw T., BSc PhD   Prof.;
Head*
Plucinski, Pawel, MSc *Warsaw*, PhD *Warsaw*,
DrHabil *Munich*   Sr. Lectr.
Thomas, William J., PhD *Lond.*, DSc *Wales*,
FIChemE   Prof.†
Tonge, G. M.   Visiting Prof.†
Other Staff: 6 Lectrs.
Research: advanced separation processes;
biochemical engineering; environmental
chemical engineering; reaction engineering

Engineering, Civil, see Archit. and Civil
Engin.

Engineering, Electronic and Electrical
Tel: (01225) 826327 Fax: (01225) 826305
Aggarwal, Raj K., BEng *Liv.*, PhD *Liv.*   Reader
Balchin, Martin J., BSc *Lond.*, PhD *Lond.*   Sr.
Lectr.
Bolton, Brian, MSc *Manc.*, PhD   Sr. Lectr.
Dunn, Roderick W., BSc PhD   Sr. Lectr.
Fowkes, A., FIEE
Gosling, William   Visiting Prof.†
Hill, Roland J., BEng *Liv.*, PhD *Liv.*   Reader
Johns, Allan T., PhD DSc   Prof.†, Electrical
Engineering
Leonard, Paul J., BSc *Aberd.*, PhD *Lond.*   Sr.
Lectr.
Monro, Donald M., MASc *Tor.*, PhD
Lond.   Prof., Electronics
Moore, Philip J., BEng *Lond.*, PhD   Sr. Lectr.
Pennock, Stephen R., BSc *Liv.*, PhD   Sr. Lectr.
Redfern, Miles A., BSc *Nott.*, PhD *Camb.*   Sr.
Lectr.
Rodger, David, BSc(Eng) *Aberd.*, PhD
Aberd.   Prof.
Sarma, Jayanta, BETelE *Jad.*, MS *Ill.*, PhD
Leeds   Reader
Shepherd, Peter R., BEng *Sheff.*, PhD *CNAA*   Sr.
Lectr.
Watson, Peter, BSc *Durh.*, PhD *Durh.*   Head*
Other Staff: 9 Lectrs.
Research: electrical engineering: electrical
machines, traction, nmr magnets, power
electronics; electromagnetics: three-
dimensional finite elements, electromagnetic
design and prototypes; electronics and
communications: microwave circuits,
optoelectronic devices, radiocommunication,
signal-processing; information systems:
image processing, video and audio
compression; power and energy systems:
electrical power systems, generation,
transmission, control

Engineering, Mechanical
(with Aeronautical, Systems and Manufacturing
Engineering)
Tel: (01225) 826115 Fax: (01225) 826928
Bowyer, Adrian, BSc *Lond.*, PhD *Lond.*   Sr.
Lectr.
Bramley, Alan N., BEng *Liv.*, PhD *Liv.*,
FIMechE   Prof.
Clift, Sally E., BSc *Birm.*, PhD *Birm.*   Sr. Lectr.
Culley, Stephen J., BSc *Brist.*   Sr. Lectr.
Darling, Jocelyn, BSc *Bath*, PhD *Bath*   Sr. Lectr.
Edge, G.   Visiting Prof.†
Edge, Kevin A., BSc PhD DSc, FIMechE   Prof.;
Head*
Hammond, Geoffrey P., MSc *Cran.IT*   Prof.
Hawley, John G., BSc *Sheff.Hallam*, PhD *Exe.*   Sr.
Lectr.
Henderson, James F., BSc(Eng) *Lond.*, PhD
Brist.   Sr. Lectr.
Hunt, Giles W., BSc(Eng) *Lond.*, MSc(Eng)
Lond., PhD *Lond.*   Prof.
Keogh, Patrick S., BSc *Nott.*, PhD *Manc.*   Sr.
Lectr.
Medland, Anthony J., PhD *CNAA*,
FIMechE   Prof.
Mileham, Anthony R., BSc *CNAA*, PhD
CNAA   Sr. Lectr.
Miles, Anthony W., MSc *Cape Town*   Reader

Mullineux, Glen, MA *Oxf.*, MSc *Oxf.*, DPhil
Oxf.   Reader
Owen, John M., BSc *Durh.*, DPhil *Sus.*   Prof.
Rees, David A., BSc *Lond.*, PhD *Brist.*   Reader
Swadling, S.   Visiting Prof.†
Tilley, Derek G., BSc PhD   Sr. Lectr.
Vaughan, Nicholas D., BSc *Brist.*, PhD *Brist.*   Sr.
Lectr.
Whitfield, Arnold, MSc *Manc.*, PhD
Manc.   Reader
Other Staff: 12 Lectrs.
Research: aerospace engineering; automotive
engineering; design and manufacture; fluid
power systems; structures

European Studies and Modern Languages
Tel: (01225) 826471 Fax: (01225) 826099
Brooks, William S., BA *Newcastle(UK)*,
PhD   Reader, French
Bull, Anna, Dottlett *Naples*, MA *Reading*, PhD
Reading   Prof., Italian; Head*
Butler, Geoffrey P. G.   Emer. Visiting Prof.†
Eatwell, Roger, MA *Oxf.*, DPhil *Oxf.*   Reader
Gillespie, David C., BA *Leeds*, PhD
Leeds   Reader, Russian
Goodbody, Axel H., BA *Trinity(Dub.)*, MA *Kiel*,
DrPhil *Kiel*   Sr. Lectr., German
Howorth, Jolyon, BA *Manc.*, PhD *Reading*   Prof.,
French
Marsh, Rosalind J., MA *Camb.*, DPhil
Oxf.   Prof., Russian
Milner, Susan E., BSc *Aston*, PhD *Aston*   Sr.
Lectr., French Studies
Szarka, Joseph P., BA *Liv.*, PhD *Camb.*   Sr.
Lectr., French with Management
Tate, George D., BA *Trinity(Dub.)*, MA *McM.*,
PhD *Warw.*   Reader, German
Wagstaff, Peter J., MA *Exe.*, PhD *Exe.*   Sr.
Lectr., French
Wallace, Ian, MA *Oxf.*, BLitt *Oxf.*   Prof.,
German
Other Staff: 17 Lectrs.
Research: cross-national European and nation-
specific research (France, Germany, Italy,
Russia) including: employment, business
and European integration; European cultural
developments; media and communication
including contemporary European film;
social identities and political cultures

French, see European Studies and Mod.
Langs.

German, see European Studies and Mod.
Langs.

Italian, see European Studies and Mod. Langs.

Management, School of
Tel: (01225) 826742 Fax: (01225) 826473
Arthurs, Alan J., BSc *Birm.*, MA *Warw.*, PhD
Birm.
Barbour, Anthony K., BSc *Birm.*, PhD
Birm.   Visiting Prof.†
Bate, Stuart P., BA *Sheff.*, PhD *Lond.*   Sr. Lectr.
Bayliss, Brian T., BSc(Econ) *Lond.*, PhD
Birm.   Prof., Business Economics; Head*
Britton, Andrew, BA *Oxf.*, MSc *Lond.*   Visiting
Prof.†
Butt, Philip A., BA *Oxf.*, DPhil *Oxf.*   Reader
Fineman, Stephen, BA *Strath.*, MPhil *Strath.*, PhD
Lond.   Prof.
Ford, Ivan D., MSc *Brad.*, PhD *Manc.*   Prof.,
Marketing
Gabriel, Yiannis   Sr. Lectr.
Green, Rodney H., BTech *Lough.*, MA *Lanc.*, PhD
Lanc.   Reader
Lamming, Richard C., BSc *Aston*   Prof.,
Purchasing and Supply
Macdonald, K. H.   Visiting Prof.†
Maraj, J. A., BA PhD, FRICS   Visiting Prof.†
Marshall, Judi A., BA *Manc.*, PhD *Manc.*   Prof.
Morgan, Eleanor J., BSc(Econ) *Lond.*, MA
Mass.   Sr. Lectr.
Parfitt, R. T., BPharm PhD,
FRPharmS   Visiting Prof.†

Pickering, John F., BSc Lond., MSc Manc., PhD Lond., DSc Lond. Prof.†

Purcell, John, MA Camb., MSc Lond. Prof.

Reason, Peter W., BA Camb., PhD Ohio Sr. Lectr.

Ritter, Thomas, PhD

Tomkins, Cyril R., BA Brist., MSc Lond. Prof.†, Business Finance

Vass, Peter, MSc(Econ) Lond. Sr. Lectr.

Wilkinson, Barry, BA Warw., MSc Aston, PhD Aston Prof.

Other Staff: 21 Lectrs.; 1 Teaching Fellow

Research: decision and information systems: IS for strategic and competitive advantage; international regulation and policy: regulated industries, the environment, international business; logistics, supply and strategic networks: chain management, business-to-business marketing; work and employment: human resources management in strategic and organisational context

Materials Science and Engineering

Tel: (01225) 826196 Fax: (01225) 826098

Almond, Darryl P., BSc Lond., PhD Lanc. Prof.

Ansell, Martin P., BSc Sus., PhD Lond. Sr. Lectr.

Harris, Bryan, PhD Camb., DSc Birm., FIP, FIM Prof.

McEnaney, Brian, BSc Hull, PhD Hull, FRSChem Prof.

Packham, David E., BSc Durh., PhD City(UK) Sr. Lectr.

Scott, Victor D., PhD Lond., DSc Lond., FIM, FIP Prof.†

Stevens, Ronald, BSc Wales, PhD Wales Prof.; Head*

Other Staff: 4 Lectrs.; 1 Sr. Lectr.†

Research: carbon and graphite; ceramics and coatings; composite materials; materials characterisation and evaluation; timber science and engineering

Mathematical Sciences

Tel: (01225) 826989 Fax: (01225) 826492

Britton, Nicholas F., BA Oxf., MSc Oxf., DPhil Oxf. Sr. Lectr.

Brooke, Naurice M., BSc Lond., PhD Lond. Sr. Lectr.

Budd, Christopher J., MA Camb., DPhil Oxf. Prof., Applied Mathematics

Burstall, Francis E., MA Aberd., MSc Warw., PhD Warw. Reader

Burton, Geoffrey R., BSc Lond., PhD Lond. Reader

Chatfield, Christopher, BSc Lond., PhD Lond. Reader

Davenport, James H., MA Camb., PhD Camb. Prof., Information Technology

Draper, David, BS N. Carolina, MA Calif., PhD Calif. Reader

Fitch, John P., MA Camb., PhD Camb. Prof., Software Engineering

Fraenkel, Ludwig W., MSc Tor., MA Camb., FRS Prof.†

Galaktionov, Victor A., MD PhD Prof.

Graham, Ivan G., MA Edin., PhD NSW Reader

Jennison, Christopher, BSc Camb., MS Cornell, PhD Cornell Prof., Statistics

Logemann, Hartmut, DrRerNat Bremen Reader

Morton, Keith W., BA Oxf., PhD Prof.

Movchan, Alexander B., MSc Leningrad, PhD Leningrad Reader

Padget, Julian A., BSc Leeds, PhD Sr. Lectr.

Richardson, Daniel S., PhD Brist., BSc Sr. Lectr.

Rogers, Leonard C. G., BA Camb., PhD Camb. Prof., Probability

Ryan, Eugene P., BE N.U.I., PhD Camb. Prof., Mathematics

Smith, Geoffrey C., MA Oxf., MSc Warw., PhD UMIST Sr. Lectr.

Spence, Alastair, MSc Edin., DPhil Oxf., FIMA Prof., Numerical Analysis

Toland, John F., BSc Belf., MSc Sus., DPhil Sus. Prof., Mathematics

Wallis, Peter J. L., BSc Lond., DPhil Oxf. Reader

Walton, Keith, MA Camb., PhD Camb. Sr. Lectr.

Williams, David, MA Oxf., DPhil Oxf., FRS Prof., Mathematics

Willis, J. R. Visiting Prof.†

Willis, Philip J., BSc Sus., MSc Essex, DPhil Sus. Prof.; Head*

Wood, Andrew T., BA Camb., PhD Open(UK) Sr. Lectr.

Other Staff: 17 Lectrs.

Medicine, Postgraduate

Tel: (01225) 826400 Fax: (01225) 323833

Blake, David R., MB ChB, FRCP Prof.

Horrocks, Michael, MB BS Lond., MS Lond., FRCS Compass Prof., Surgery; Hon. Consultant Surgeon; Head*

Lewis, Peter A., BTech Lough., PhD Birm. Sr. Lectr.

McHugh, Neil J., MB ChB Otago, MD Otago, FRACP Sr. Lectr.; Hon. Consultant Rheumatologist

Milner, Philip C., BA Camb., MB ChB Sheff., MBA Lond. Prof.†, Public Health

Morris, Christopher J., BSc Lond., MSc Birm., PhD Lond. Reader

Other Staff: 1 Lectr.; 1 Reader†

Pharmacy and Pharmacology

Fax: (01225) 826114

Beresford, Jon N., BSc Aston, PhD Sheff. Sr. Lectr.

Blagbrough, Ian S., BSc Nott., PhD Nott. Sr. Lectr.

Byron, Peter R., BSc Manc., PhD Manc. Visiting Prof.†

Collins, Anthony J., MB ChB Brist., BSc MD PhD Sr. Lectr.

Gigg, Roy H. Visiting Prof.†

Hall, Nicolas D., MA Camb., PhD Lond. Reader

Moss, Stephen H., BPharm Nott., MSc PhD Sr. Lectr.

Notarianni, Lidia J., BSc E.Anglia, MSc Lond., PhD Lond. Sr. Lectr.

Potter, Barry V. L., MA Oxf., DPhil Oxf. Prof., Pharmaceutical Chemistry

Pouton, Colin W., PhD Lond., BPharm Sr. Lectr.

Redfern, Peter H., BPharm Nott., PhD Nott., DSc Prof.

Roach, A. G., BSc PhD Visiting Prof.†

Sansom, David M., BSc Brist., PhD Brist. Sr. Lectr.

Staniforth, John N., BSc Aston, PhD Aston Prof.

Threadgill, Michael D., BA Camb., PhD Camb. Sr. Lectr.

Tyrrell, Rex M., BPharm Bath, PhD Bath Prof.

Westwick, John, BSc CNAA, PhD Lond. Prof., Pharmacology; Head*

Williams, Kenneth I., BSc Lond., PhD Lond. Sr. Lectr.

Woodward, Brian, BSc PhD Sr. Lectr.

Other Staff: 11 Lectrs.; 1 Sr. Lectr.†

Physics

Tel: (01225) 826837 Fax: (01225) 826110

Bending, Simon J., BA Camb., PhD Stan. Reader

Bird, David M., BA Camb., PhD Camb. Prof.

Bullett, David W., MA Camb., PhD Camb. Prof.; Head*

Cronin, Nigel J., BSc Lond., PhD Lond. Prof.

Davies, John J., MA Oxf., DPhil Oxf. Prof.

Humphrey, Victor F., BSc Brist., PhD Brist. Sr. Lectr.

Russell, Philip St. J., BA Oxf., DPhil Oxf. Prof.

Salmon, Philip S., BSc Brist., PhD Brist. Sr. Lectr.

Saunders, George A., BSc Lond., PhD Lond., FIP Prof.

Squire, Patrick T., BSc Lond., PhD Bath Sr. Lectr.

Walker, Alison B. Sr. Lectr.

Other Staff: 12 Lectrs.

Psychology

Tel: (01225) 826817 Fax: (01225) 826752

Collins, H. M. Visiting Prof.†

Gooding, David C., MA Dal., DPhil Oxf. Prof.

Haste, Helen E., BA Lond., MPhil Sus., PhD Prof.; Head*

Lewis, Alan, BSc Wales, PhD Wales Reader

Skevington, Suzanne M., BSc Wales, PhD Wales Reader

Other Staff: 4 Lectrs.; 1 Sr. Lectr.†

Research: applied social psychology; economic and political psychology; health psychology; science, culture and communication

Russian, see European Studies and Mod. Langs.

Social and Policy Sciences

Tel: (01225) 826089 Fax: (01225) 826381

Carlen, Patricia C., BA Lond., PhD Lond. Prof., Sociology

Cressey, Peter, MA York(UK) Sr. Lectr.

Gough, Ian R., BA Camb. Prof., Social Policy

Gould, Nicholas G., MA Sus., MSc Oxf., PhD Sr. Lectr.

Illsey, R. Visiting Prof.†

Jones, Bryn, BA Lond., PhD Liv. Sr. Lectr.

Kerslake, Andrew S., BA CNAA Sr. Lectr.

Millar, Jane I., BA Sus., MA Brun., DPhil York(UK) Prof., Social Policy; Head*

Room, Graham J., MA Oxf., DPhil Oxf. Prof.

Rose, Michael J., BA Camb., MA Camb., PhD Camb. Prof.†

Vagero, D. Visiting Prof.†

Webb, S. Visiting Prof.†

Other Staff: 9 Lectrs.; 1 Sr. Lectr.†

Research: politics: mass communication; sociology: criminology and sociology of law; social policy: welfare state and welfare policy in Europe; social work: equality and health, children and families

SPECIAL CENTRES, ETC

Action Research in Professional Practice, Centre for

Tel: (01225) 826792 Fax: (01225) 826473

Reason, P. W., BA Camb., PhD Ohio Dir.*

Other Staff: 1 Prof.; 1 Lectr.

Architecture, Centre for Advanced Studies in (CASA)

Tel: (01225) 826357 Fax: (01225) 826691

Hart, Vaughan A., MPhil Camb., PhD Camb., BSc BArch Reader; Dir.*

Analysis of Social Policy, Centre for the

Tel: (01225) 826141 Fax: (01225) 826381

Millar, Prof. Jane I., BA Sus., MA Brun., DPhil York(UK) Dir.*

Other Staff: 2 Profs.; 1 Lectr.

Research: policy and changing family patterns; priority setting and rationing in the NHS; social policy and economic competitiveness; social policy, poverty and social exclusion in Europe; strategies of different regulatory structures in defining and monitoring standards

Applied Electromagnetics Research Centre

Tel: (01225) 826327 Fax: (01225) 826305

Rodger, Prof. David, BSc(Eng) Aberd., PhD Aberd. Dir.*

Development Studies, Centre for

Tel: (01225) 826736 Fax: (01225) 826381

Wood, Geoffrey D., BA Sus., MPhil Sus., PhD Dir.*

Drug Formulation Studies, Centre for (CDFS)

Tel: (01225) 826776

Meakin, Brian J., BPharm Lond. Dir.*

Economic Psychology, Centre for

Tel: (01225) 826582 Fax: (01225) 826752

Lewis, A., BSc Wales, PhD Wales Dir.*

Research: altruism and charitable giving; economic perception, attitudes, preferences; gender and household decision-making; morals and markets: ethical investing

Electron Optics, Centre for

Tel: (01225) 826681 Fax: (01225) 826098

Stevens, Prof. Ronald, BSc *Wales*, PhD *Wales* Dir.*

Research: electron beam analysis, particularly flow atomic number elements

Environment, International Centre for the

Tel: (01225) 826156 Fax: (01225) 826157

Warhurst, Prof. Alyson, BSc *Brist.*, MSc *Sus.*, DPhil *Sus.* Dir.*

Research: clean technology and integrated environmental management; corporate strategy and public policy towards the environment; management of natural resources

Environmental Education Theory and Practice, Centre for Research in

Tel: (01225) 826648 Fax: (01225) 826113

Scott, William A. H., BSc *Leeds*, PhD *Leeds* Dir.*

European Research Institute

Tel: (01225) 826490 Fax: (01225) 826987

Lawson, Colin, MSc(Econ) *Lond.*, PhD *Lond.* Sr. Lectr.; Dir.*

Other Staff: 1 Prof.; 1 Visiting Prof.; 2 Readers

Research: contemporary European politics, economics, society and culture

Executive Development, Centre for

Tel: (01225) 826726 Fax: (01225) 826210

Ford, Prof. I. D., MSc *Brad.*, PhD *Manc.* Dir.*

Extremophile Research, Centre for

Tel: (01225) 826509 Fax: (01225) 826779

Danson, Prof. Michael J., BSc *Leic.*, PhD *Leic.* Dir.*

Other Staff: 1 Prof.; 1 Reader; 1 Sr. Lectr.

Research: enzymes from extremophiles: stability, structure and function; enzymes in biotechnology; extremophiles: micro-organisms living in extreme environments; microbial biodiversity and evolution

Fiscal Studies, Centre for

Tel: (01225) 826839 Fax: (01225) 826381

Bowles, R., MSc *York(UK)*, BSc Dir.*

Health, Institute of

Tel: (01225) 826400 Fax: (01225) 323833

Milner, Prof. Philip C., BA *Camb.*, MB ChB *Sheff.*, MBA *Lond.* Dir.*

Higher Education Management, International Centre for

Tel: (01225) 826628 Fax: (01225) 826543

Mawditt, Richard M., OBE, MSc Dir.*

Other Staff: 2 Visiting Profs.

Research: comparative higher education management structures; design of education databases; higher education management in developing countries; knowledge and industry; performance and achievement in British schools

History of Technology, Science and Society, Centre for the

Including National Cataloguing Unit for the Archives of Con Scientists

Tel: (01225) 826839 Fax: (01225) 826381

Buchanan, Prof. R. A., OBE, MA *Camb.*, PhD *Camb.*, FRHistS Dir.*

Holburne Museum and Crafts Study Centre

Tel: (01225) 466669 Fax: (01225) 333121

Roscoe, Barley, BA *Brist.* Curator*

Mathematical Biology, Centre for

Tel: (01225) 826989 Fax: (01225) 826492

Britton, Nicholas F., BA *Oxf.*, MSc *Oxf.*, DPhil *Oxf.* Sr. Lectr.; Dir.*

Media Technology Research Centre

Tel: (01225) 826989 Fax: (01225) 826492

Willis, Prof. Philip J., BSc *Sus.*, MSc *Essex*, DPhil *Sus.* Dir.*

Medical Engineering, Bath Institute of

Tel: (01225) 824084 Fax: (01225) 824111

Lillicrap, Prof. Stephen C., BSc *Lond.*, DSc *Lond.* Dir.*

Research: cryosurgery; rehabilitation engineering; rehabilitation robotics; surgical instruments

Membrane Application Centre

Tel: (01225) 826 6117 Fax: (01225) 826894

Field, Robert W., MA *Camb.*, PhD *Camb.* Reader; Dir.*

National Cataloguing Unit for the Archives of Contemporary Scientists

Tel: (01225) 323522 Fax: (01225) 826229

Harper, Peter, BA PhD Dir.*

Neuroscience, Centre for

Tel: (01225) 826797 Fax: (01225) 826114

Redfern, Prof. Peter H., BPharm *Nott.*, PhD *Nott.*, DSc, FRPharmS Dir.*

Research: amino-acid receptors in nematodes; assessment of quality of life in the mentally ill; melanin-concentrating hormone in fish; neurochemistry of circadian clocks; nicotinic receptors, dopamine and reward systems

Power Transmission and Motion Control, Centre for

Tel: (01225) 826932 Fax: (01225) 323255

Burrows, Prof. Clifford R., BSc *Wales*, PhD *Lond.*, DSc(Eng) *Lond.*, FIMechE Dir.*

Other Staff: 1 Prof.

Research: control of energy transmission systems; electro-hydraulic and hydromechanical power transmission; fluid power systems design and analysis; modelling and computer simulation; pump flowripple and system noise

School Improvement, Centre for

Tel: (01225) 826225 Fax: (01225) 826113

Lauder, Prof. Hugh, BSc *Lond.*, MA *Lond.*, PhD *Camb.* Dir.*

Science Studies, Centre for

Tel: (01225) 826335 Fax: (01225) 826381

Gooding, David C., MA *Dal.*, DPhil *Oxf.* Dir.*

Social Services Research and Development Unit (SSRADU)

Tel: (01225) 484088 Fax: (01225) 330313

Kerslake, Andrew S., BA *CNAA* Dir.*

Strategic Information Systems, Centre for Research into

Tel: (01225) 826856 Fax: (01225) 826473

Barnes, Stuart Acting Dir.*

Other Staff: 2 Visiting Profs.; 2 Lectrs.

Research: emerging technologies: tracking the business impact of new information technologies; evaluation of IT investments; information management: methods of defining organisational information needs; outsourcing: investigating role of outsourcing as part of competitive strategies

Strategic Purchasing and Supply, Centre for Research into

Tel: (01225) 826536 Fax: (01225) 826473

Lamming, Prof. Richard C., BSc *Aston* Dir.*

Education in an International Context, Centre for the Study of (CEIC)

Tel: (01225) 826225 Fax: (01225) 826113

Thompson, Prof. John J., CBE, MA *Oxf.*, MA *Camb.*, PhD *CNAA*, FRSChem Dir.*

Library and Information Networking, UK Office for

Tel: (01225) 826254

Dempsey, Lorcan, BA Dir.*

Window and Cladding Technology, Centre for

Tel: (01225) 826506 Fax: (01225) 826556

Ledbetter, Stephen R., BSc *Dund.*, PhD Dir.*

Research: building management: supply chain analysis, failure mode and effects analysis; building materials: glass, finishes, metals, durability; building physics: condensation, photovoltaics, advanced glazings; facade engineering: weathertightness, construction, performance, specification; structural engineering: structural use of glass, facade structure interaction

Women's Studies Centre

Tel: (01225) 826876 Fax: (01225) 826099

Haste, Prof. Helen E., BA *Lond.*, MPhil *Sus.*, PhD Dir.*

Other Staff: 1 Prof.; 1 Lectr.

Research: feminist methodology, gender and culture; gender and social welfare; women in contemporary Europe: society, culture; women in management; women's psychology and health

Work and Employment Research Centre

Tel: (01225) 826742 Fax: (01225) 826473

Purcell, Prof. John, MA *Camb.*, MSc *Lond.* Dir.*

CONTACT OFFICERS

Academic affairs. Registrar: Bursey, Jonathan A., BA *Durh.*, MSc *CNAA*

Admissions (first degree). Director of Admissions: Driscoll, Diana L., BSc *Loyola(Ill.)*, BA *Lond.*, MA *Lond.*

Admissions (higher degree). Director of Admissions: Driscoll, Diana L., BSc *Loyola(Ill.)*, BA *Lond.*, MA *Lond.*

Adult/continuing education. Director of Continuing and Distance Education: Bilham, Timothy D., MA *Camb.*

Alumni. Graduate Relations Officer: Savva-Coyle, Ghika, BA *Reading*

Archives. Registrar: Bursey, Jonathan A., BA *Durh.*, MSc *CNAA*

Careers. Careers Advisor: Davidson, James E. M., LLB *Lond.*

Computing services. Director of Computing Services: Harlow, John

Consultancy services. Director of Finance: Aderyn, Diane, BA *Newcastle(UK)*, MA(Econ) *Manc.*

Credit transfer. Director of Admissions: Driscoll, Diana L., BSc *Loyola(Ill.)*, BA *Lond.*, MA *Lond.*

Development/fund-raising. Development Director: Leighton, A. Jeremy, MA *Camb.*

Distance education. Director of Continuing and Distance Education: Bilham, Timothy D., MA *Camb.*

Equal opportunities. Director of Personnel: Hill, Peter J., BSc *Lough.*, MSc *CNAA*

Estates and buildings/works and services. Director of Estates: Moore, A., BSc *CNAA*

Examinations. Senior Assistant Registrar: Harris, John, BA *Lond.*, PhD *Lond.*

Finance. Director of Finance: Aderyn, Diane, BA *Newcastle(UK)*, MA(Econ) *Manc.*

General enquiries. Registrar: Bursey, Jonathan A., BA *Durh.*, MSc *CNAA*

Health services. Medical Officer: Bennett, Jennifer, MB ChB *Aberd.*

Health services. Medical Officer: Reid, Catriona, MB ChB *Edin.*

International office. International Students' Officer: Currie, Leslie L., MA *Glas.*

Library (chief librarian). Librarian: Nicholson, Howard, MA *Sus.*

Ombudsman. Postgraduate Ombudsman: Redfern, Prof. Peter H., BPharm *Nott.*, PhD *Nott.*, DSc

Personnel/human resources. Director of Personnel: Hill, Peter J., BSc *Lough.*, MSc *CNAA*

Public relations, information and marketing. Director of Public Relations: ......

Publications. Director of Public Relations: ......

Purchasing. Supplies Officer: Browne, Roger, BA *Trinity(Dub.)*

Quality assurance and accreditation. Registrar: Bursey, Jonathan A., BA *Durh.*, MSc *CNAA*

Safety. Safety Officer: Adams, Peter, BEng

Scholarships, awards, loans. Student Loans Officer: Woosey-Griffin, Marica R. S., BSc *Liv.*

Schools liaison. Director of Admissions: Driscoll, Diana L., BSc *Loyola(Ill.)*, BA *Lond.*, MA *Lond.*

Security. Head of Security: Hicks, Adrian

Sport and recreation. Director of Sports Development and Recreation: Roddy, Ged, BA *Birm*

Staff development and training. Head of Staff Development: Hole, Catherine, BSc *Manc.*, MSc *Brist.*, PhD *Brist.*

Student union. General Manager: Robinson, Ian W., BA *CNAA*

Student welfare/counselling. Student Counsellor: Davies, Elizabeth V., MA *Edin.*

Students from other countries. International Students' Officer: Dewhurst, Carla J., BA *Leic.*

Students with disabilities. Dean of Students: Edwards, Leila, BA *CNAA*, MSc *CNAA*

University press. Librarian: Nicholson, Howard, MA *Sus.*

[*Information supplied by the institution as at 29 September 1998, and edited by the ACU*]

BATH SPA UNIVERSITY COLLEGE

Founded 1983 as Bath College of Higher Education; renamed 1997

Postal Address: Newton Park, Newton St Loe, Bath, England BA2 9BN
Telephone: (01225) 875875 **Fax**: (01225) 875444 **E-mail formula**: firstinitialsurname@bathspa.ac.uk

DIRECTOR AND CHIEF EXECUTIVE*—Morgan, Frank, BA *Lond.*, MSc *City(UK)*
ASSISTANT DIRECTOR AND CLERK TO THE BOARD OF GOVERNORS‡—Dewberry, Anthony E.

UNIVERSITY OF BIRMINGHAM

Founded 1900; previously established as Mason Science College 1880, and incorporated as Mason University College 1898

Member of the Association of Commonwealth Universities

Postal Address: Edgbaston, Birmingham, England B15 2TT
Telephone: (0121) 414 3344 **Fax**: (0121) 414 3971 **Telex**: 333762 **WWW**: http://www.bham.ac.uk
E-mail formula: initials.surname@bham.ac.uk

VISITOR—Elizabeth, H.M. The Queen
CHANCELLOR—Jarratt, Sir Alex, CB, BCom *Birm.*, Hon. DSc *Cran.IT*, DUniv *Brun.*, Hon. LLD *Birm.*, Hon. DUniv *Essex*
PRO-CHANCELLOR—Burman, R. S., CBE, BSc *Birm.*, Hon. LLD *Birm.*
DEPUTY PRO-CHANCELLOR—Bettinson, J. R., LLB *Birm.*, Hon. LLD *Birm.*
TREASURER—Foster, K. J., BA *Nott.*, Hon. LLD *Birm.*, FCA
DEPUTY TREASURER—Lancaster, J., MA *Oxf.*
VICE-CHANCELLOR AND PRINCIPAL*—Irvine, Prof. J. Maxwell, BSc *Edin.*, MSc *Mich.*, PhD *Manc.*, Hon. DSc *William & Mary*, Hon. DEd *R.Gordon*, Hon. DUniv *Edin.*, Hon. LLD *Aberd.*, FRAS, FIP, FRSEd, Hon. FRCSEd
VICE-PRINCIPAL—Westbury, Prof. D. R., BSc *Oxf.*, MA *Oxf.*, BM BCh *Oxf.*, DM *Oxf.*
PRO-VICE-CHANCELLOR—Snaith, Prof. M. S., BAI *Trinity(Dub.)*, MA *Trinity(Dub.)*, MSc *Trinity(Dub.)*, ScD *Trinity(Dub.)*, PhD *Nott.*, FICE
PRO-VICE-CHANCELLOR—Young, Prof. F. M., BA *Lond.*, MA *Camb.*, PhD *Camb.*, Hon. DD *Aberd.*
PRO-VICE-CHANCELLOR—Clarke, Prof. M. G., MA *Sus.*
REGISTRAR AND SECRETARY‡—Allen, David J., BA *Wales*, MEd *Wales*
LIBRARIAN AND DIRECTOR OF INFORMATION SERVICES—Field, C. D., MA *Oxf.*, DPhil *Oxf.*

GENERAL INFORMATION

History. The university was founded in 1900. It is located about 4km from the centre of Birmingham.

Admission to first degree courses (see also United Kingdom Introduction). Through Universities and Colleges Admissions Service

(UCAS). General Certificate of Education (GCE) A levels or equivalent qualifications, and English language proficiency (eg General Certificate of Secondary Education (GCSE) grade C). Certain courses have specific subject requirements.

First Degrees (see also United Kingdom Directory to Subjects of Study). BA, BCom,

BDS, BEd, BEdStudies, BEng, BLitt, BMedSc, BMus, BNurs, BSc, BTheol, LLB, MB ChB, MEng, MSci.

All courses are full-time and normally last 3 years. BA/BCom/BSc/LLB with languages: 4 years; BDS, MB ChB: 5 years. LLB honours in legal studies (first degree for graduate entry): 2 years.

Higher Degrees (see also United Kingdom Directory to Subjects of Study). BD, BPhil, LLM, MA, MBA, MD, MEd, MJur, MLitt, MMath, MMus, MNatSc, MPH, MPhys, MSc, MPhil, PhD, ClinPsyD, DD, DDS, DEng, DLitt, DMus, DSc, EdD, ThD.

Applicants for admission to postgraduate courses should normally hold a good first degree from a recognised institution.

MA, MSc: normally 12 months full-time or 24 months part-time; MPhil: normally 1 or 2 years; doctorates: normally 3 years.

Libraries. About 2,000,000 volumes; about 3,000,000 manuscript and archival items.

Fees (annual). Undergraduate (1997–98): £750 (classroom-based courses); £1600 (laboratory/workshop-based courses); £2800 (clinical medical and dental). Postgraduate, home/EU students (1997–98): £2540 full-time; £1270 part-time; £635 (self-financing part-time). Postgraduate, international students (1998–99): £6700 (non-laboratory-based courses); £8900 (laboratory-based courses); £16,200 (clinical courses).

Academic Year (1998–99). Two semesters: 28 September–22 January; 25 January–18 June.

Income (1996–97). Total, £209,593,000.

Statistics. Staff: 2426 (2158 teaching and research, 268 academic-related administrative). Students: full-time 16,078 (8424 men, 7654 women); part-time 2782 (1072 men, 1710 women); international 3194 (1884 men, 1310 women).

FACULTIES/SCHOOLS

Arts, Commerce and Social Science, and Education and Continuing Studies
Tel: (0121) 414 6607 Fax: (0121) 414 5349
Dean: Spencer, Prof. K. M., MA Liv.
Secretary: Major, K.

Engineering
Tel: (0121) 414 7452 Fax: (0121) 414 3149
Dean: Knott, Prof. J. F., BMet Sheff., ScD Camb., FRS, FEng, FIM, FIMechE
Secretary: May, B.

Law
Tel: (0121) 414 6312 Fax: (0121) 414 3585
Dean: Feldman, Prof. D. J., BA Oxf., BCL Oxf.
Secretary: Kimmins, P.

Medicine and Dentistry
Tel: (0121) 414 4046 Fax: (0121) 414 7149
Dean: Doe, Prof. W. F., BM Syd., MSc Lond., FRCP, FRCPA
Secretary: Taylor, J.

Science
Tel: (0121) 414 5469 Fax: (0121) 414 7680
Dean: Blake, Prof. J. R., BSc Adel., PhD Camb., FIMA
Secretary: Harris, J.

ACADEMIC UNITS
Arranged by Schools

Accounting and Finance, see under Business

American and Canadian Studies, see under Hist. Studies

Archaeology, see Anc. Hist. and Archaeol. under Hist. Studies

Astronomy, see Phys. and Astron.

Biochemistry
Tel: (0121) 414 5400 Fax: (0121) 414 3982
Briggs, D. E., MA Camb., PhD Lond., DSc Birm. Sr. Lectr.

Busby, S. J. W., MA Camb., DPhil Oxf. Prof.
Candy, D. J., BSc Leeds, PhD Leeds Sr. Lectr.
Chipman, J. K., BSc Leic., PhD Reading, FIBiol Sr. Lectr.
Cole, J. A., MA Camb., DPhil Oxf. Prof., Microbial Physiology
Coleman, R., PhD Birm., DSc Birm. Prof., Medical Biochemistry
Heath, J. K., BSc Glas., MA Oxf., DPhil Oxf. Prof.
Jackson, J. B., BSc Brist., PhD Brist. Prof., Bioenergetics
Kirk, C. J., BSc Lond., PhD Lond. Reader; Royal Soc. Res. Fellow
Kuhn, N. J., MA Oxf., DPhil Oxf. Reader
Levine, B. A., BA Oxf., DPhil Oxf. Reader, Biophysics
Michell, R. H., PhD Birm., DSc Birm., FRS Royal Soc. Res. Prof.
Strain, A. J., BSc St And., PhD Lond. Sr. Lectr.
Trayer, I. P., PhD Birm., DSc Birm. Prof.; Head*
Waring, R. H., MA Camb., PhD Birm., DSc Birm. Reader, Human Toxicology
Wharton, C. W., BSc Lond., PhD Lond. Reader, Biophysics
Wheatley, M., BSc Lond., PhD Nott. Sr. Lectr.
Young, T. W., BSc Sheff., PhD Sheff. Sr. Lectr.
Other Staff: 8 Lectrs.; 33 Res. Fellows; 10 Res. Assocs.; 3 Hon. Lectrs.; 4 Hon. Res. Fellows; 1 Hon. Res. Assoc.
Research: eukaryotic cell regulation; mechanisms of cellular toxicity; microbial gene regulation and function; protein structure and function

Biological Sciences
Tel: (0121) 414 5924 Fax: (0121) 414 5925
Bale, J. S., BSc Newcastle(UK), PhD Newcastle(UK) Prof., Environmental Biology
Block, W. Hon. Prof.
Brown, N. L., BSc Leeds, PhD Leeds, FIBiol, FRSChem Prof., Molecular Genetics and Microbiology; Head*
Butler, P. J., BSc S'ton., PhD E.Anglia, FIBiol Mason Prof., Comparative Physiology
Callow, J. A., BSc Sheff., PhD Sheff., FIBiol Mason Prof., Botany
Caten, C. E., BSc Reading, PhD Birm. Reader, Fungal Genetics
Crute, I. R., BSc Newcastle(UK), PhD Newcastle(UK) Hon. Prof.
Dennis, C., BSc Sheff., PhD Sheff. Hon. Prof.
Ford-Lloyd, B. V., BSc Birm., PhD Birm. Sr. Lectr.
Franklin, F. C. H., BSc Wales, PhD Wales Reader, Plant and Molecular Biology
Green, J. R., BA Camb., PhD Camb. Sr. Lectr.
Jones, G. H., BSc Wales, PhD Wales Reader, Cytogenetics
Jones, H. G., BA Camb., PhD ANU Hon. Prof.
Kearsey, M. J., BSc Wales, PhD Reader, Biometrical Genetics
Leadbeater, B. S. C., PhD Lond., DSc Lond. Reader, Protistology
Macaskie, L. E., BSc Lond., PhD Lond. Reader, Microbiology
Newbury, H. J., BSc Leeds, PhD Leeds Sr. Lectr.
Payne, C. C., BA Oxf., MA Oxf., DPhil Oxf. Hon. Prof.
Penn, C. W., BSc Liv., PhD CNAA Reader, Microbiology
Pooni, H. S., MSc Punj., PhD Birm. Sr. Lectr.
Pullin, A. S., BSc Warw., MSc Durh., PhD CNAA Sr. Lectr.
Stephen, J., BSc Aberd., PhD Aberd. Sr. Lectr.
Sweet, C., BSc Wales, PhD Wales, DSc Wales Sr. Lectr.
Taylor, E. W., BSc S'ton., PhD S'ton., FIBiol Prof., Animal Physiology
Thomas, C. M., MA Oxf., DPhil Oxf. Prof., Molecular Genetics
Williams, J. T., MA Camb., PhD Wales, DSc Zür., FIBiol Hon. Prof., Plant Genetic Resources
Woakes, A. J., BSc Brist., PhD Birm. Sr. Lectr.
Wood, K. R., BSc Oxf., MA Oxf., DPhil Oxf. Sr. Lectr.

Other Staff: 14 Lectrs.; 29 Res. Fellows; 6 Res. Assocs.; 1 Reader†; 5 Hon. Sr. Lectrs.; 11 Hon. Lectrs.; 6 Hon. Res. Fellows
Research: animal cell and molecular physiology; environmental and population biology; microbial molecular genetics; plant genetics; plant molecular cell sciences

Business
Tel: (0121) 414 6225 Fax: (0121) 414 7380
Rickwood, C. P., BCom Birm., MSc Lond. Head of Sch.*

Accounting and Finance
Tel: (0121) 414 6530 Fax: (0121) 414 6678
Fry, M. J., BSc Lond., PhD Lond., MA Calif. Tokai Bank Prof.†, International Finance
Jones, R. H., MA Lanc., PhD Lanc. Prof., Public Sector Accounting; Head*
Murinde, V., BA Mak., MSc Wales, PhD Wales Sr. Lectr.
Rickwood, C. P., BCom Birm., MSc Lond. Prof., Management Accounting
Samuels, J. M., BCom Birm. Prof., Business Finance
Theobald, M. F., BSc Lond., MA Manc., PhD Manc., FCA KMPG Prof.
Thomas, A. P., BA Open(UK), PhD Birm. Sr. Lectr.
Other Staff: 7 Lectrs.; 1 Res. Assoc.; 1 Sr. Lectr.†; 1 Lectr.†; 1 Hon. Res. Fellow
Research: corporate finance; development finance; international accounting; international finance; public sector accounting

Commerce
Tel: (0121) 414 6690 Fax: (0121) 414 6707
Bagozzi, R. P., MSc Colorado, MBA Wayne State, PhD Northwestern Hon. Prof.
Burton, J., BA Wales, MSc(Econ) Lond. Prof., Business Administration
Clark, P. A., BA Leic., PhD Lough. Prof.
Cox, A. W., BA Lanc., MA Mich., PhD Essex Prof., Business Strategy and Procurement Management
Driver, J. C., BSc Hull, MA Manc., PhD Birm. Sr. Lectr.
Hanlon, J. P., BSc(Econ) Hull, MA(Econ) Manc., PhD Birm. Sr. Lectr.
Kavanagh, N. J., BCom Trinity(Dub.), MA Trinity(Dub.) Sr. Lectr., Industrial Economics
Littlechild, S. C., BCom Birm., PhD Texas Hon. Prof.
Oughton, C. P., BA E.Anglia, PhD Camb. Sr. Lectr.; Dir., Res. Centre for Indust. Strategy
Siebert, W. S., BA Cape Town, MSc Lond., PhD Lond. Prof., Labour Economics
Slater, J. R., BSc&BCom Birm. Sr. Lectr.; Dir., Grad. Centre for Bus. Admin.
Sugden, R., BA(Law) Sheff., MA Warw., PhD Warw. Prof.; Head*
Tann, J., MA Manc., PhD Leic. Prof.†
Wilkes, F. M., BSocSc Birm., PhD Birm. Prof., Business Investment and Management
Other Staff: 14 Lectrs.; 9 Res. Fellows; 2 Res. Assocs.; 1 Sr. Lectr.†; 4 Hon. Sr. Res. Fellows; 10 Hon. Res. Fellows
Research: business competition and competition policy; industrial relations and labour economics; industrial strategy; organisational management and innovation; trade and investment linkages between East Asia and Europe

Byzantine, Ottoman and Modern Greek Studies, Centre for, see under Hist. Studies

Canadian Studies, see American and Canadian Studies under Hist. Studies

Chemistry
Tel: (0121) 414 4361 Fax: (0121) 414 4403
Burdon, J., PhD Birm., DSc Birm. Reader, Organic Chemistry

Coe, P. L., PhD Birm., DSc Birm.   Reader, Organofluorine Chemistry
Edwards, P. P., BSc Salf., PhD Salf., FRSChem   Prof., Inorganic Chemistry; Head*
Greaves, C., MA Oxf., DPhil Oxf.   Prof., Solid State Chemistry
Harris, K. D. M., BSc St And., PhD Camb.   Prof., Structural Chemistry
Harrison, R. M., BSc Birm., PhD Birm., DSc Birm., FRSChem, FRMetS   Prof.
Higgitt, J.   Sr. Lectr.
Hriljac, J. A., BSc Ill., PhD Northwestern   Sr. Lectr.
Jones, C. J., BSc Sheff., PhD Sheff.   Sr. Lectr.
Knowles, P. J., BA Camb., PhD Camb.   Prof., Theoretical Chemistry
Lehrle, R. S., PhD Birm., DSc Birm., FRSChem   Reader, Physical Chemistry
Parsons, I. W., PhD Birm., DSc Birm.   Sr. Lectr.
Percy, J. M., BSc Lond., PhD Camb.   Sr. Lectr.
Philp, D., PhD Aberd., PhD Birm.   Sr. Lectr.
Smith, I. W. M., MA Camb., PhD Camb., FRSChem, FRS   Mason Prof.
Somers, P. J., BSc Birm., DSc Birm.   Sr. Lectr.
Tuckett, R. P., BA Camb., PhD Camb.   Sr. Lectr.
Other Staff: 14 Lectrs.; 37 Res. Fellows; 5 Res. Assocs.; 1 Sr. Lectr.†; 1 Hon. Sr. Res. Fellow; 2 Hon. Res. Fellows
Research: metal (non-metal transition); oligosaccharide systems; solid state chemistry (high temperature superconductors); structural, dynamic and chemical properties of solids; theory of molecular electronic structure

Classics, see under Humanities

Computer Science
Tel: (0121) 414 4773 Fax: (0121) 414 4281
Barnden, J. A., MA Camb., DPhil Oxf.   Prof.
Bocca, J. B., BSc Chile, MSc St And., PhD S'ton.   Prof.†
Claridge, E., MSc Gdansk, PhD Birm.   Sr. Lectr.
Dodd, W. P., BSc PhD   Sr. Lectr.†
Edmondson, W. H., BSc Sur., MA Essex, PhD Lond.   Sr. Lectr.
Horne, P. J., BSc Lond., PhD Lond.   Sp. Prof.
Jarratt, P., BSc Manc., PhD Brad., FIMA   Prof.†
Jung, A., PhD T.H.Darmstadt   Prof.; Head*
Sloman, A., BSc Cape Town, DPhil Oxf.   Prof., Artificial Intelligence and Cognitive Science
Other Staff: 16 Lectrs.; 3 Res. Fellows; 2 Res. Assocs.; 1 Sr. Lectr.†; 2 Hon. Sr. Res. Fellows; 2 Hon. Res. Fellows
Research: artificial intelligence and cognitive science; evolutionary and emergent behaviour intelligence and computation; image, understanding and computer vision; theory of computation

Continuing Studies
Tel: (0121) 414 3413 Fax: (0121) 414 5619
Bowl, R. E. E., BA Reading, MA Sus., MA Warw.   Sr. Lectr., Social Policy
Henderson, W., MA Glas., MA Sus., DPhil Sus.   Sr. Lectr., Economics
Hicks, C. M., BA Exe., MA Exe., PhD Aston   Sr. Lectr., Psychology
Hunt, L.-A., MA Edin., MA Lond., PhD Lond.   Sr. Lectr., History of Art
Martin, G. R., BSc Sur., PhD Exe., DSc Sur.   Prof., Avian Sensory Science; Head*
Nixon, S., BA(Econ) Sheff., MPhil Sheff.   Sr. Lectr., Applied Social Studies
Tudor Jones, G., MA Camb., MA Calif., PhD Birm.   Reader, High Energy Physics
Wheeler, S. J., BA Newcastle(UK), MA Warw.   Sr. Lectr.
Wright, A. W., BSc(Econ) Lond., DPhil Oxf.   Reader, British Political Thought
Other Staff: 9 Lectrs.; 1 Sr. Lectr.†; 1 Hon. Lectr.; 1 Hon. Sr. Res. Fellow
Research: employers' responses to employee stress; environmental and regional studies; industrial history and industrial archaeology; role of approved social workers

Cultural Studies, see under Soc. Scis.

Dentistry, see below

Development Administration, see under Public Policy

Drama and Theatre Arts, see under Humanities

Earth Sciences
Tel: (0121) 414 6751 Fax: (0121) 414 4942
Barker, R. D., MSc Nott., PhD Nott., FGS   Sr. Lectr.
Chambers, A. D., BSc Durh., PhD Durh.   Sr. Lectr.
Coope, G. R., BSc Manc., MSc Manc., PhD DSc   Hon. Prof.
Gaskarth, J. W., BSc Leeds, MSc McG., PhD Sask., FGS   Sr. Lectr.
Hallam, A., MA Camb., PhD Camb., FGS, FIBiol   Lapworth Prof.†
Hawkes, D. D., BSc Lond., MSc Lond., PhD Lond., FGS   Prof., Geological Science
Hutton, D. H. W., BSc Belf., PhD Belf., Hon. MA Trinity(Dub.)   Prof.
Lloyd, J. W., BSc Brist., PhD Brist., DSc Brist., FGS, FICE   Prof., Hydrogeology
MacKay, R., BSc Lond., PhD Newcastle(UK)   Prof., Hydrogeology
Tellam, J. H., BSc S'ton., MSc S'ton., PhD S'ton.   Reader, Hydrogeology
Thomas, A. T., BSc Keele, PhD Camb.   Sr. Lectr.
Turner, P., DSc Wales, PhD Leic., FGS   Reader, Sedimentology
Westbrook, G. K., BSc Lond., PhD Durh., FRAS, FGS   Prof., Geophysics; Head*
Other Staff: 12 Lectrs.; 4 Res. Fellows; 2 Res. Assocs.; 1 Hon. Lectr.; 7 Hon. Res. Fellows; 1 Hon. Res. Assoc.
Research: evolutionary palaeobiology and marine palaeoecology; groundwater resources; contaminant transport modelling, hydrochemistry; igneous and metamorphic petrology and metallogenesis; marine and environmental geophysics, palaeomagnetism; orogenic processes and basin studies

Economics, see under Soc. Scis.

Education
Tel: (0121) 414 4866 Fax: (0121) 414 4865
Brighouse, T., BA Oxf., MA Oxf., DLitt Exe., Hon. EdD CNAA, Hon. DUniv C.England, Hon. DUniv Open(UK)   Hon. Prof.
Burton, L. M., BSc Lond., PhD Lond.   Prof.†
Butt, G. W., MA Lond., MA Oxf.   Sr. Lectr.
Butterfield, S., PhD Birm.   Sr. Lectr.
Chitty, C. W., BA Lond., PhD Lond.   Reader, Modern History
Daniels, H. R. J., BSc Liv., PhD Lond.   Prof., Special Education, and Education and Educational Psychology
Davies, M. L., BA Exe., MEd Birm., PhD Birm.   Prof., International Education
Evans, P.   Hon. Prof.
Gregory, S., BSc Leic., MA Nott., PhD Nott.   Sr. Lectr.
Grimmitt, M. H., BEd Lond., PhD Lond.   Reader, Religious Education
Harber, C. R., BA Reading, MA Leic., PhD Birm.   Reader, International Education
Hull, J. M., BA Melb., BEd Melb., MA Camb., PhD Birm., Hon. DTheol Fran.   Prof., Religious Education
Jordan, R. R., BSc Lond., MSc Lond., MA CNAA   Sr. Lectr.
Lock, R. J., BSc Aberd., PhD Leeds, FIBiol   Sr. Lectr.
Miller, C. J., MSc Lond., PhD Open(UK)   Sr. Lectr.
O'Hanlon, C., BA Belf., DPhil Ulster   Sr. Lectr.
Osler, A. H., BA Leeds, MA Leeds, PhD Birm.   Sr. Lectr.
Ranson, P. R. S., BSc(Econ) Lond., MA Reading, DSocSc Birm.   Prof.
Ribbins, P. M., BA Leic., BSc(Econ) Lond., MA Lond., PhD Birm.   Prof., Education Management

Riding, R. J., BSc Hull, PhD Birm., FBPsS   Reader, Educational Psychology
Rutherford, R. J. D., BSc Durh., PhD Durh., PhD Birm.   Sr. Lectr.
Smith, C. J., JP, BA Manc., MEd Liv., PhD Birm.   Sr. Lectr.
Tebbutt, M. J., BSc Nott., FIP   Sr. Lectr.
Thomas, H. R., BA Manc., MEd Manc., PhD Birm.   Prof., Economic of Education; Head*
Tilstone, C., MEd Leic., MA(Ed) Leic.   Sr. Lectr.
Tobin, M. J., BA Lond., PhD Birm., DLit Lond., FBPsS   Reader, Special Education
Wade, C. B., BA Nott., BA Open(UK), MA Leeds, PhD Birm.   Prof., English in Education
Watts, R. E., BA Lond., MA Leic., PhD Leic.   Sr. Lectr.
Williams, E. A., BEd Lond., MA Birm., PhD Birm.   Sr. Lectr.
Other Staff: 1 Sr. Lectr.; 35 Lectrs.; 10 Res. Fellows; 12 Hon. Lectrs.; 4 Hon. Sr. Res. Fellows; 15 Hon. Res. Fellows; 2 Hon. Res. Assocs.
Research: early literacy, reading and oral ability; evaluation and development of professional practice across a range of special educational needs; integration of children with Down's Syndrome in mainstream schools; teaching and assessment of mathematics and science

Engineering, Chemical
Tel: (0121) 414 5330 Fax: (0121) 414 5324
Al-Rubeai, M., BSc Baghdad, PhD Lond.   Reader, Biotechnology
Arrowsmith, A., BSc Sheff., PhD Sheff.   Sr. Lectr.
Ashton, N. F., BSc Birm., PhD Birm., FIChemE   Sr. Lectr.
Barker, A. J., BA Camb., PhD Lond.   Sr. Lectr.; Dir., Postgrad. Studies
Biddlestone, A. J., BSc Birm., PhD Birm., FIChemE   Prof.; Head*
Blackburn, S., BSc CNAA, MSc Birm., PhD Birm.   Sr. Lectr.
Campbell, A. P., BSc Strath., DSc Strath.   Sr. Lectr.
Emery, A. N., MSc Birm.   Sr. Lectr.
Fryer, P. J., MA Camb., MEng Camb., PhD Camb., FIChemE   Prof.
King, R., BSc Wales, PhD Lough.   Hon. Prof.
Lyddiatt, A., BSc Durh., PhD Durh.   Prof., Process Biotechnology
Nienow, A. W., PhD Lond., DSc Lond., FEng, FIChemE   Prof., Biochemical Engineering
Rowson, N. A., BSc Leeds, PhD Leeds   Sr. Lectr.
Seville, J. P. K., MA Camb., MEng Camb., PhD Sur., FIChemE   Prof.
Thomas, C. R., BA Camb., MA Camb., PhD Lond.   Prof., Biochemical Engineering; Dir., Biochem. Engin. Res.
Veasey, T. J., BSc Birm., PhD Birm.   Sr. Lectr.
Warner, N. A., DSc NSW, FEng, FIM, FIChemE   Prof., Minerals Engineering
Winterbottom, J. M., BSc Hull, PhD Hull   Reader, Catalytic Reaction Engineering
Other Staff: 6 Lectrs.; 2 Sr. Res. Fellows; 18 Res. Fellows; 12 Res. Assocs.; 2 Hon. Sr. Lectrs.; 3 Hon. Lectrs.; 5 Hon. Sr. Res. Fellows; 3 Hon. Res. Fellows; 1 Hon. Res. Assoc.
Research: biochemical engineering; environmental engineering; food process engineering; materials processing

Engineering, Civil
Tel: (0121) 414 5049 Fax: (0121) 414 3675
Ash, J. E., BSc Nott., PhD Birm.   Sr. Lectr.
Chan, A. H., BSc HK, MPhil HK, PhD Wales   Reader, Computational Engineering
Clark, L. A., BEng Sheff., PhD Sheff., FIStructE, FEng, FICE   Prof., Structural Engineering
Dawe, D. J., BSc Wales, PhD Wales, DSc Wales   Prof., Structural Mechanics
Forster, C. F., BSc Hull, PhD Wales, DEng, FIChemE   Reader, Public Health Engineering
Freer-Hewish, R. J., BTech Brad., PhD Birm.   Sr. Lectr.
Hamlin, M. J., CBE, BSc Brist., LLD St And.   Hon. Prof.

Hoare, D. J., BSc Birm., MSc Birm. Sr. Lectr.

Horsington, R. W., BSc Brist. Sr. Lectr.

Hughes, B. P., PhD DSc DEng, FIStructE, FICE Emer. Prof.†

Ingold, T. S., BSc Lond., MSc Lond., PhD Sur., FICE, FGS Hon. Prof.

Kerali, H. G. R., BSc(Eng) Mak., MSc Birm., PhD Birm. Sr. Lectr.

Knight, D. W., BSc(Eng) Lond., MSc Aberd., PhD Aberd. Reader, Hydraulics and Fluid Mechanics

Little, G. H., MSc Camb., PhD Camb. Sr. Lectr.

Madelin, K. B., MSc Birm., FICE Prof.

Perry, J. G., BEng Liv., MEng Liv., PhD Manc., FICE Beale Prof.; Head*

Rushton, K. R., BSc Manc., PhD DSc Emer. Prof.

Seymour, D. E., BA S'ton., PhD S'ton., MA(Econ) Manc. Sr. Lectr.

Snaith, M. S., MA Trinity(Dub.), BAI Trinity(Dub.), MSc Trinity(Dub.), ScD Trinity(Dub.), PhD Nott., FICE Prof., Highway Engineering

West, J. R., BSc St And., PhD Dund. Reader, Coastal and Water Engineering

Other Staff: 12 Lectrs.; 7 Res. Fellows; 5 Res. Assocs.; 1 Sr. Lectr.†; 6 Hon. Lectrs.; 4 Hon. Sr. Res. Fellows; 4 Hon. Res. Fellows; 1 Hon. Res. Assoc.

Research: computational solid and fluid mechanics; environmental management (water engineering); infrastructure management including transportation and structures

Engineering, Electronic and Electrical

Tel: (0121) 414 4285 Fax: (0121) 414 4291

Atkins, P. R., BSc Birm., MPhil(Eng) Birm. Sr. Lectr.

Brdys, M. A., MSc Warsaw, PhD Warsaw, DSc Warsaw, FIMA Sr. Lectr.

Coates, R. F. W., BSc S'ton., PhD Belf. Prof.

Constantinou, C. C., BEng Birm., PhD Birm. Sr. Lectr.

Edwards, J. A., PhD Birm. Sr. Lectr.

Evans, P. D., BSc(Eng) Lond., PhD Lond., FIEE Prof.; Head*

Goodman, C. J., MA Camb., PhD Camb. Reader, Traction Systems

Hall, P. S., BSc Sheff., MSc Sheff., PhD Sheff., FIEE Prof., Communication Engineering

Lancaster, M. J., BA Bath, PhD Bath Reader, Microwave Engineering

Mehler, M. J., BSc PhD, FIEE Hon. Prof.

Mellitt, B., BTech Lough., Hon. DTech Lough., FIEE, FIMechE, FEng Hon. Prof., Electronics

Norton, J. P., MA Camb., PhD Lond. Prof., Control Engineering

Parsons, A. T., BSc Brist., MSc Brist., PhD Brist. Hon. Prof.

Sharples, M. Prof., Educational Technology

Other Staff: 17 Lectrs.; 16 Res. Fellows; 8 Res. Assocs.; 1 Reader†; 3 Sr. Lectrs.†; 5 Hon. Lectrs.; 2 Hon. Res. Fellows; 6 Hon. Res. Assocs.

Research: communications engineering; education technology; electronic materials and devices; power electronics and traction systems

Engineering, Manufacturing and Mechanical

Tel: (0121) 414 4215 Fax: (0121) 414 3958

Aspinwall, D. K., MSc Birm. Sr. Lectr.

Bakhtar, F., BSc PhD DSc, FIMechE Hon. Prof.

Ball, A. A., BSc Lond., PhD E.Anglia Prof., Engineering Design; Head*

Dean, T. A., MSc Lond., PhD Birm. Prof., Manufacturing Engineering

Haley, K. B., BSc Birm., PhD Birm., FIMA, FIEE Prof., Operational Research

Hartley, P., BSc Aston, PhD Birm. Reader, Plasticity

Hodgson, D. C., BSc Birm., PhD Birm. Sr. Lectr.

Hooke, C. J., BSc Birm., PhD Birm., DEng Reader, Applied Mechanics

Jackson, R. R. P., BSc Lond. Hon. Prof.

Jones, B., MSc Aston, PhD, FIMechE Sr. Lectr.

King, T. G., BSc Lond., MDes RCA, PhD, FIEE Prof., Mechanical Engineering

Loftus, M., BSc H.-W., MSc H.-W., PhD Birm., PhD H.-W. Sr. Lectr.

Megaw, E. D., BA Camb., MSc Camb., PhD Camb. Sr. Lectr.

Neal-Sturgess, C. E., BSc CNAA, PhD Birm., FIMechE Jaguar Prof., Automotive Engineering

Quick, N. J., BSc Salf., MSc Cran., MBA Birm., FIEE Sr. Lectr.

Randle, J. N., FIMechE, FEng Hon. Prof., Automotive Engineering; Dir. of Automotive Engin. Res.

Tobias, A. M., PhD Nott., BSc Nott. Sr. Lectr.

Walton, D., BTech Lough., PhD Brist. Prof., Mechanical Engineering

Winterton, R. H. S., BA Camb., PhD Camb., DEng Sr. Lectr.

Wyszynski, M. L., MSc Warsaw, PhD Warsaw Sr. Lectr.

Other Staff: 18 Lectrs.; 15 Res. Fellows; 14 Res. Assocs.

Research: CAD (surface modelling), CAM for industry; control and mechanics (high speed machinery); engineered surfaces (design, manufacture, characterisation, testing); machining (high speed and non-conventional); metalforming (net-shape, light alloy, aerospace)

English, see under Humanities

French Studies, see under Humanities

Geography

Tel: (0121) 414 5544 Fax: (0121) 414 5528

Bradshaw, M. J., MA Calg., PhD Br. Col., BSc Sr. Lectr.

Daniels, P. W., BSc Lond., PhD Lond. Prof.; Head*

Ford, R. G., BSc Lond., MSc Northwestern Sr. Lectr.

Gerrard, A. J. W., BSc Lond., PhD Lond. Reader, Geomorphology

Gregory, K. Hon. Prof.

Gurnell, A. M., BSc Exe., PhD Exe. Prof., Physical Geography

Gwynne, R. N., MA Oxf., BPhil Liv., PhD Liv. Reader, Latin American Development

Lawler, D. M., BA Wales, PhD Wales Sr. Lectr.

McGregor, G. R., MSc Auck., PhD Cant. Sr. Lectr.

Milner, A., BSc Aston, MSc Lond., PhD Lond. Sr. Lectr.

Petts, G. E., BSc Liv., PhD S'ton. Prof., Physical Geography

Shaw, D. J. B., BA Lond., PhD Lond. Reader, Russian Geography

Slater, T. R., BA Hull, PhD Hull Reader, Historical Geography

Thornes, J. E., BSc Manc., MSc Manc., PhD Lond., FRMetS Reader, Applied Meteorology

Whitehand, J. W. R., BA Reading, PhD Reading, DSc Reading Prof., Urban Geography

Other Staff: 15 Lectrs.; 1 Res. Fellow; 4 Res. Assocs.; 2 Hon. Sr. Res. Fellows; 9 Hon. Res. Fellow; 1 Hon. Res. Assoc.

Research: conservation ecology, freshwater ecology and palaeoecology; hydrological processes and the fine sediment transfer process; meteorology and climatology; Russian Far East: resource frontier for the Pacific century; urban morphology

Geology, see Earth Scis.

German Studies, see under Humanities, Sch. of

Greek, Modern, see Byzantine, Ottoman and Mod. Greek Studies under Hist. Studies

Health Sciences, see below

Health Services Management, see under Public Policy

Hispanic Studies, see under Humanities

Historical Studies

Tel: (0121) 414 6627 Fax: (0121) 414 7685

Limbrey, S. P., BA Lond., PhD Lond. Prof., Environmental Archaeology; Head of Sch.*

American and Canadian Studies

Tel: (0121) 414 5740 Fax: (0121) 414 6866

Harding, B. R., MA Oxf., PhD Brown Sr. Lectr.

Lucas, W. S., BA Vandebilt, PhD Birm. Sr. Lectr.; Head*

Simmons, R. C., MA Camb., PhD Calif. Prof., American History

Other Staff: 5 Lectrs.; 1 Res. Fellow; 1 Hon. Res. Fellow

Research: history, film and television; international history and US foreign policy; urban studies; US and Canadian literature and film; US colonial history

Ancient History and Archaeology

Tel: (0121) 414 5497 Fax: (0121) 414 3595

Blockley, M. R., MA Leic. Sr. Lectr.

Esmonde Cleary, A. S., BA Lond., DPhil Oxf., FSA Sr. Lectr.

Hunter, J. R., BA Durh., PhD Durh., FSA Prof.; Head*

Leahy, M. A., MA Camb., PhD Camb. Sr. Lectr.

Limbrey, S., BSc Lond., PhD Lond. Prof., Environmental Archaeology; Head of Sch.*

Livingstone, A., MA Camb., PhD Birm. Reader, Assyriology

Wardle, K. A., MA Camb., PhD Lond., FSA Sr. Lectr.

Other Staff: 10 Lectrs.; 1 Sr. Res. Fellow; 7 Res. Fellows; 4 Res. Assocs.; 1 Reader†; 4 Hon. Lectrs.; 2 Hon. Sr. Res. Fellows; 3 Hon. Res. Fellows; 1 Hon. Fellow; 1 Hon. Res Assoc.

Research: archaeology and environmental science; British and European archaeology (field techniques, methodologies); classical world (social and economic history); Egyptology and Near Eastern studies (archaeology, language and literature); Greek archaeology (material culture, urbanism)

Byzantine, Ottoman and Modern Greek Studies, Centre for

Tel: (0121) 414 5775 Fax: (0121) 414 6866

Bryer, A. A. M., MA Oxf., DPhil Oxf., FSA Prof., Byzantine Studies

Goldstein, E. D., MA Tufts, PhD Camb., FRHistS Prof., International History

Haldon, J. F., MA Birm., PhD Birm. Prof., Byzantine History; Dir.*

Murphey, R., MA Chic., PhD Chic. Sr. Lectr.

Tziovas, D. P., BA Ioannina, PhD Birm. Prof., Modern Greek Studies

Other Staff: 1 Lectr.; 1 Instr.; 1 Sr. Lectr.†; 1 Hon. Sr. Res. Fellow; 10 Hon. Res. Fellows; 1 Hon. Res. Assoc.

Research: Byzantine language and literature; late Roman/Byzantine history; modern Greek culture, language, literature; nineteenth-and twentieth-century Balkan/East Mediterranean history; nineteenth- and twentieth-century great power/international diplomacy

History of Art

Tel: (0121) 414 7330 Fax: (0121) 414 3370

Verdi, R., BA Mich., MA Chic., PhD Lond. Prof.

West, S. C., BA Virginia, PhD St And. Sr. Lectr.; Head*

Other Staff: 3 Lectrs.; 1 Hon. Res. Fellow

Research: British visual culture; European painting (1500-1930); history of collecting; Italian and German modernism; Italian Renaissance architecture

Medieval History

Tel: (0121) 414 5736 Fax: (0121) 414 3656

Bassett, S. R., BA Birm., PhD Birm., FSA Sr. Lectr.

Brooks, N. P., MA Oxf., DPhil Oxf., FSA, FBA, FRHistS Prof., Medieval History; Head*

Dyer, C. C., BA Birm., PhD Birm.,
FRHistS Prof., Medieval Social History
Swanson, R. N., MA Camb., PhD Camb.,
FRHistS Reader, Medieval Church History
Wickham, C. J., MA Oxf., DPhil Oxf.,
FRHistS Prof., Early Medieval History
Other Staff: 4 Lectrs.; 1 Hon. Reader; 1 Hon.
Lectr.; 1 Hon. Res. Fellow
Research: Anglo-Saxon England; English
mediaeval archaeology and landscape
history; English social and economic history;
late mediaeval church and society; late
mediaeval Spain

Modern History

Tel: (0121) 414 5736 Fax: (0121) 414 3656

Bourne, J. M., BA Leic., PhD Leic., FRHistS Sr.
Lectr.
Breuilly, J. J., BA York(UK), DPhil York(UK),
FRHistS Prof.; Head*
Briggs, J. H. Y., MA Camb., FRHistS,
FSA Hon. Prof.
Chinn, C. S. A., BA Birm., PhD Birm. Sr. Lectr.
Cust, R. P., BA Lond., PhD Lond., FRHistS Sr.
Lectr.
Garside, W. R., BA Leeds, PhD Leeds,
FRHistS Prof., Economic and Social History
Grenville, J. A. S., BA Lond., PhD Lond.,
FRHistS Emer. Prof.
Ives, E. W., BA Lond., PhD Lond., FSA,
FRHistS Emer. Prof., English History
Jones, P. M., BA Leeds, DPhil Oxf. Prof.,
French History
Lukowski, J. T., BA Camb., PhD Camb. Sr.
Lectr.
Marsh, P., BA Tor., PhD Camb., LittD
Camb. Hon. Prof.
Randall, A. J., BA Birm., MA Sheff., PhD
Birm. Prof., English Social History
Robinson, R. A. H., MA Oxf., DPhil Oxf.,
FRHistS Reader, Iberian History
Schwarz, L. D., BA Oxf., DPhil Oxf. Sr. Lectr.
Other Staff: 10 Lectrs.; 3 Hon. Lectrs.; 2 Hon.
Sr. Res. Fellows; 1 Hon. Res. Fellow
Research: Mediterranean history (1500–1800);
nineteenth-and twentieth-century Germany;
nineteenth-and twentieth-century social and
urban history; society and politics of
seventeenth-century England; twentieth-
century military history

Theology

Tel: (0121) 414 5666 Fax: (0121) 414 6866

Ambler, R. A., BA Manc., MA Manc., PhD
Birm. Sr. Lectr.
Lartey, E. Y., BA Ghana, PhD Birm. Sr. Lectr.
McLeod, D. H., BA Camb., PhD Camb. Prof.,
Church History
Nielsen, J. S., MA Lond., PhD Beirut Hon. Prof.
Norton, G. J., BA Trinity(Dub.), PhD
Trinity(Dub.), LSS Rome Sr. Lectr.
Parker, Rev. D. C., MTheol St And., ThD
Ley. Sr. Lectr.
Parratt, J. K., BD Lond., PhD Lond. Sr. Lectr.
Turner, D. A., BA N.U.I., MA N.U.I., DPhil
Oxf.; Head*
Ustorf, W., DrTheol Hamburg, DrTheolHabil
Heidel. Prof., Mission
Young, F. M., BA Lond., MA Camb., PhD Camb.,
Hon. DD Aberd. Edward Cadbury Prof.
Other Staff: 5 Lectrs.; 1 Res. Fellow; 22 Hon.
Lectrs.; 1 Hon. Sr. Res. Fellow; 8 Hon.
Tutors
Research: Holocaust studies and Christian-Jewish-
Islamic relations; late antique/mediaeval and
Syriac/Western theology; practical, pastoral
theologies, anthropology, ritual, mission;
synoptic problem, biblical texts and
manuscripts/versions; systematic, contextual,
philosophical, Third World theologies

West African Studies, Centre of

Tel: (0121) 414 5128 Fax: (0121) 414 3228

Barber, K. J., BA Camb., PhD Ife Reader,
African Popular Culture
Brown, S., BA CNAA, MA Sus., PhD Wales Sr.
Lectr.
Hughes, A., BA Wales Dir.*

McCaskie, T. C., MA Aberd., MA Ghana, PhD
Camb. Sr. Lectr.
Other Staff: 3 Lectrs.; 1 Res. Fellow; 1 Hon.
Fellow; 3 Hon. Sr. Res. Fellows; 1 Hon. Res.
Fellow; 4 Hon. Res. Assocs.
Research: African/Caribbean literature and
Yoruba studies; history of Asante (Ghana),
Borgu (Benin) and Islam (Mali); migration/
urbanisation and gender development in
Ghana; natural resources management in
Nigeria and Sierra Leone; politics of Pan-
Africanism: re-democratisation of small
states in Gambia

Humanities

Tel: (0121) 414 5994 Fax: (0121) 414 7250

Dent, N. J. H., BA Camb., PhD Camb. Prof.;
Head of Sch.*

Classics

Tel: (0121) 414 5773 Fax: (0121) 414 7174

Barker, A. D., MA Oxf., MA Camb., PhD
Oxf. Prof.
Costa, C. D. N., MA Oxf., BPhil Oxf. Prof.;
Head*
Dowden, K., MA Oxf. Sr. Lectr.
Other Staff: 2 Lectrs.; 2 Hon. Lectrs.
Research: Greek and Roman religion, mythology,
novels; Greek music, musical theory and
musical discourse; late Greek fictional letters;
Latin poetry, Hellenistic poetry, epic;
rhetoric and historiography, gender in
antiquity

Drama and Theatre Arts

Tel: (0121) 414 5998 Fax: (0121) 414 5998

Adamson, A. J., BMus Birm. Sr. Lectr.
Alexander, W. Hon. Prof.
Crow, B., MA St And., MA New Br., PhD
Brist. Sr. Lectr.
Edgar, D., BA Manc. Prof.†, Playwriting
Studies
Kaplan, J. H., BA Penn., MA Tor., PhD
Tor. Prof.; Head*
Wright, Sir Peter, CBE, Hon DLitt Hon. Prof.
Other Staff: 4 Lectrs.; 1 Reader†; 1 Hon. Sr.
Lectr.; 1 Hon. Sr. Res. Fellow
Research: modern and contemporary British
theatre; play-writing studies; Russian theatre;
Victorian and Edwardian theatre; women's
theatre

English, Department of

Tel: (0121) 414 5673 Fax: (0121) 414 5668

Coulthard, R. M., BA Sheff., PhD Birm. Prof.,
English Language and Linguistics
Davies, L. A., BA Wales, MA Birm. Prof.;
Head*
Edden, V. J., MA Birm., PhD Birm. Sr. Lectr.
Ellis, S. P., BA Lond., PhD Lond. Sr. Lectr.
Faulkes, A. R., MA Oxf., BLitt Oxf., DrPhil
Iceland Prof., Old Icelandic
Lodge, David J., CBE, MA Lond., PhD,
FRSL Hon. Prof., Modern English Literature
Sinclair, J. M., MA Edin. Prof.†, Modern
English Language
Small, I. C., BA Reading, PhD Reading Prof.,
English Literature
Storey, M. G., MA Oxf., BLitt Oxf. Prof.,
English Literature
Thornton, R. K. R., MA Manc., PhD
Manc. Prof.†, English Studies
Toolan, M., MA Edin., DPhil Oxf. Prof.,
Applied English Linguistics
Walsh, M., MA Oxf., BPhil Oxf., PhD
Tor. Reader, English Literature
Wilcher, R., BA Oxf., MA Birm., PhD Birm. Sr.
Lectr.
Other Staff: 12 Lectrs.; 1 Res. Fellow; 1 Res.
Assoc.; 2 Hon. Sr. Res. Fellows; 13 Hon.
Res. Fellows; 2 Hon. Res. Assocs.
Research: bibliography and history of book
production; corpus research: exploiting
computerised language; early modernisms
(literature, culture, modernity (1870–1920);
forensic linguistics (language description as
courtroom evidence); Shakespeare studies
(text, performance, contexts)

English for International Students Unit

Tel: (0121) 414 5697 Fax: (0121) 414 3600

Hewings, M. J., BA S'ton., MA Birm.,
PhD Dir.*
Johns, T. F., BA Camb. Sr. Lectr.
Other Staff: 6 Lectrs.; 1 Res. Assoc.; 1 Sr.
Lectr.†

English Language Studies, Centre for

Tel: (0121) 414 3239 Fax: (0121) 414 3298

Kennedy, C. J., BA Lond., MA Lanc. Sr. Lectr.;
Dir.*
Other Staff: 6 Lectrs.; 1 Sr. Lectr.†

French Studies

Tel: (0121) 414 5965 Fax: (0121) 414 5966

Birkett, J., MA Oxf., DPhil Oxf. Prof.
Brook, L. C., BA Brist., PhD Brist. Sr. Lectr.
Callander, M. M., MA Manc., PhD Manc. Sr.
Lectr.
Cornick, M., MA Warw., PhD Warw. Sr. Lectr.
Cousins, R. F. W., BA Birm., PhD Birm. Sr.
Lectr.
Crossley, E. C. D., BA Wales, PhD Wales Prof.,
19th Century French Studies
Hughes, A., BA Lond., PhD Lond. Sr. Lectr.
Mason, S. M., BA Lond., PhD Lond. Sr. Lectr.
Perkins, A. W., BA Lond., PhD Lond. Sr. Lectr.
Pickup, I., BA Leeds, PhD Leeds Sr. Lectr.
Wood, D. M., BA Lond., PhD Camb. Prof.,
French Literature; Head*
Other Staff: 6 Lectrs.; 1 Sr. Lectr.†; 1 Hon. Sr.
Lectr.
Research: computerised concordance of
mediaeval Occitan; cultural studies; film and
media studies; women's studies and gender
studies; works of Montesquieu and Benjamin
Constant

German Studies

Tel: (0121) 414 6173 Fax: (0121) 414 4213

Butler, M. G., MA Camb., PhD CNAA Prof.,
Modern German Literature; Head*
Dodd, W. J., BA Leeds, MA Manc., PhD Leeds Sr.
Lectr.
Hill, D. D., BA Trinity(Dub.), BA Oxf., DPhil
Oxf. Sr. Lectr.
Klapper, J. M., BA Oxf., MLitt Oxf., PhD
Birm. Sr. Lectr.
Perraudin, M. F., MA Camb., PhD Birm. Sr.
Lectr.
Speirs, R. C., MA Aberd., PhD Stir. Prof.
van der Will, W., DPhil Cologne Prof., Modern
German Studies
Other Staff: 4 Lectrs.
Research: German education; Kafka's imagery
and novels; language pedagogy; post-1945
German literature; contemporary German/
Swiss literature

Hispanic Studies

Tel: (0121) 414 6035 Fax: (0121) 414 6035

Dadson, T. J., BA Leeds, PhD Camb. Prof.;
Head*
Flitter, D. W., MA Oxf., DPhil Oxf. Sr. Lectr.
Odber de Baubeta, P. A., MA Glas., PhD
Glas. Sr. Lectr.
Other Staff: 5 Lectrs.; 1 Sr. Lectr.†; 1 Hon.
Lectr.; 1 Hon. Res. Fellow
Research: Galician (sociolinguistics, translation
studies); golden age poetry, drama, cultural
history, textural editing; Latin American
fiction, gender and Chicano studies;
mediaeval textual editing and chronicles;
Romanticism and modern historiography,
poetry and fiction

Italian Studies

Tel: (0121) 414 5930 Fax: (0121) 414 5930

Caesar, M. P., MA Camb. Prof.; Head*
Other Staff: 3 Lectrs.
Research: autobiography; Leopardi, Romanticism
and nineteenth-century studies; modern and
contemporary writing (all genres); theatre
and music since the Renaissance; women's
history

Music

Tel: (0121) 414 5781 Fax: (0121) 414 5781

Banfield, S. D., MA *Camb.*, DPhil *Oxf.* Elgar Prof.; Head*

Harrison, D. J. T., BA *York(UK)*, DPhil *York(UK)* Reader, Composition and Electroacoustic music

Hoyland, D. V., BA *Hull*, DPhil *York(UK)* Sr. Lectr.

Meikle, R. B., BMus *Glas.*, MA *Glas.*, PhD *Cornell* Sr. Lectr.

Timms, C. R., MA *Camb.*, MMus *Lond.*, PhD *Lond.* Peyton and Barber Prof.

Vick, G. Hon. Prof.

Whenham, E. J., BMus *Nott.*, MA *Nott.*, DPhil *Oxf.* Reader, Music History

Other Staff: 2 Lectrs.; 1 Res. Fellow; 1 Hon. Sr. Lectr.; 2 Hon. Sr. Res. Fellows; 1 Hon. Res. Fellow

Research: British music (nineteenth and twentieth century); composition; early music, including performance practice; nineteenth-century music, including performance practice; popular musical theatre

Philosophy

Tel: (0121) 414 5658 Fax: (0121) 414 5668

Dent, N. J. H., BA *Camb.*, PhD *Camb.* Prof.

Falk, B., BA *Lond.* Sr. Lectr.

McCulloch, G. W., BA *Leic.*, BPhil *Oxf.*, DPhil *Oxf.* Prof.; Head*

Noonan, H. W., MA *Camb.*, PhD *Camb.* Reader, Philosophical Logic

Other Staff: 5 Lectrs.

Research: Greek ethics (Socrates, Plato and Aristotle); metaphysics (essentialism, causation, counterfactuals and possible worlds); phenomenology of content; philosophy of language and mind

Russian Language and Literature

Tel: (0121) 414 6044 Fax: (0121) 414 7280

Briggs, A. D. P., MA *Camb.*, PhD *Lond.* Prof.†; Head

Tait, A. L., MA *Camb.*, PhD *Camb.* Sr. Lectr.

Other Staff: 3 Lectrs.; 1 Sr. Lectr.†; 1 Hon. Res. Fellow

Research: contemporary Slavonic philology; nineteenth-century Russian literature; Russian language, computer-assisted language learning; twentieth-century Russian poetry

Shakespeare Institute

Tel: (01789) 293138 Fax: (01789) 414992

Holland, P. D., MA *Birm.*; PhD *Camb.* Prof.; Dir.*

Jackson, R. B., MA *Oxf.*, PhD *Birm.* Sr. Lectr.

Jowett, J. D., MA *Newcastle(UK)*, PhD *Liv.* Sr. Lectr.

Other Staff: 2 Lectrs.; 10 Hon. Fellows; 1 Hon. Res. Fellow

Icelandic, Old, see English under Humanities

Italian Studies, see under Humanities

Law

Tel: (0121) 414 3637 Fax: (0121) 414 3585

Arnull, A. M., BA *Sus.*, PhD *Leic.* Wragge Prof., European Law

Baldwin, J., BSocSc *Birm.*, PhD *Sheff.* Prof., Judicial Administration

Borrie, Rt. Hon. Lord, LLM *Manc.*, Hon. LLD *Manc.*, Hon. LLD *CNAA* Hon. Prof.

Crawford, C., LLM *Edin.* Sr. Lectr.

Ellis, E. D., MA *Camb.*, LLM *Birm.*, PhD *Birm.* Prof., Public Law

Feldman, D. J., BA *Oxf.*, BCL *Oxf.* Barber Prof., Jurisprudence; Head*

Harvey, B. W., MA *Camb.*, LLM *Camb.* Prof., Property Law

Hodgin, R. W., LLM *Leeds* Sr. Lectr.

Lloyd-Bostock, S. M. A., BA *Reading*, MA *Oxf.*, DPhil *Oxf.* Sr. Lectr.

Lonbay, J. L., LLB *Dund.*, PhD *Florence* Sr. Lectr.

Mackie, K., MA *Lond.*, PhD *Nott.* Hon. Prof.

Manchester, C. D., LLB *Lond.*, PhD *Birm.* Sr. Lectr.

McBride, M. J., LLB *Camb.*, LLB *Birm.* Sr. Lectr.

Meisel, F., LLB *Leeds* Sr. Lectr.

Miller, C. J., BA *Nott.*, LLM *Nott.* Prof., English Law

Moodie, P. C. E., BA *Camb.* Sr. Lectr.

Mustill, Rt. Hon. Lord, QC, MA *Camb.*, LLD *Camb.* Hon. Prof.

Perrins, B., MA *Camb.*, PhD *Birm.* Sr. Lectr.

Salter, D. R., LLB *Birm.* Sr. Lectr.

Scott, I. R., LLB *Melb.*, PhD *Lond.* Barber Prof.

Shute, S. C., LLB *Kingston(UK)*, BCL *Oxf.*, MA *Oxf.* Sr. Lectr.

Simester, A. P., BCom *Auck.*, LLB *Auck.*, DPhil *Oxf.* Sr. Lectr.

Woodman, G. R., BA *Camb.*, LLB *Camb.*, PhD *Camb.* Reader, Comparative Law

Other Staff: 15 Lectrs.; 1 Sr. Res. Fellow; 3 Hon. Lectrs.; 2 Hon. Fellows

Research: criminal justice; European law: community and convention; judicial administration and procedure; public law and legal theory; socio-legal studies

Institute of European Law

Tel: (0121) 414 6298 Fax: (0121) 414 3585

Lonbay, J. L., LLB *Dund.*, PhD *Florence* Dir.*

Other Staff: 1 Hon. Res. Fellow

Institute of Judicial Administration

Tel: (0121) 414 6285 Fax: (0121) 414 3585

Baldwin, Prof. J., BSocSc *Birm.*, PhD *Sheff.* Dir.*

Other Staff: 1 Sr. Res. Fellow

Local Government Studies, see under Public Policy

Mathematics and Statistics

Tel: (0121) 414 6587 Fax: (0121) 414 3389

Blake, J. R., BSc *Adel.*, PhD *Camb.*, FIMA Prof., Applied Mathematics

Brookes, C. J., BSc *Manc.*, MSc *Manc.*, PhD DSc Hon. Prof.

Critchley, F., MA *Camb.*, DPhil *Oxf.* Prof., Statistics

Cunninghame-Green, R. A., MA *Oxf.*, PhD *Leic.*, DSc *Leic.*, FIMA Prof., Industrial Mathematics

Curtis, R. T., MA *Camb.*, PhD *Camb.* Reader, Combinatorial Algebra; Head*

Gardiner, A. D., BSc *S'ton.*, MSc *Warw.*, PhD *Warw.* Reader, Mathematics and Mathematics Education

Gunson, J., MA *Camb.*, PhD *Camb.* Sr. Lectr.

Hoare, A. H. M., BA *Oxf.*, DPhil *Oxf.* Reader, Algebra

Holder, R. L., BSc *Lond.* Sr. Lectr.

King, A. C., BSc *Leeds*, PhD *Leeds* Prof., Applied Mathematics

Kyle, J., BSc *Glas.*, PhD *Newcastle(UK)* Sr. Lectr.

Lawrance, A. J., BSc *Leic.*, PhD *Leic.*, MSc *Wales* Prof., Statistics

Patil, P. N., BSc *Poona*, MSc *Poona*, PhD *N.Carolina* Reader, Statistics

Wagner, A. Hon. Prof.

Wilson, J. S., MA *Camb.*, PhD *Camb.*, ScD *Camb.* Mason Prof., Pure Mathematics

Wilson, R. A., MA *Camb.*, PhD *Camb.* Reader, Group Theory

Other Staff: 22 Lectrs.; 6 Res. Fellows; 4 Hon. Sr. Res. Fellows; 1 Hon. Res. Fellow

Research: cavitation bubble dynamics and underwater explosions; dynamical systems and chaos; finite classical and sporadic groups; general finite groups and associated geometrics; medical and industrial statistics

Medicine, see below

Metallurgy and Materials

Tel: (0121) 414 5220 Fax: (0121) 414 5232

Abell, J. S., BSc *Reading*, PhD *Sur.*, DSc *Birm.* Reader, Electronic and Magnetic Materials

Aindow, M., BEng *Liv.*, PhD *Liv.* Sr. Lectr.

Bell, T., BEng *Liv.*, PhD *Liv.*, FIM Hanson Prof., Metallurgy

Bowen, P., MA *Camb.*, PhD *Camb.* Prof., Mechanical Metallurgy

Campbell, J., OBE, MA *Camb.*, MMet *Sheff.*, PhD *Camb.*, DEng *Birm.*, FEng, FIM T&N Prof.†, Casting Technology

Cockayne, B., BSc PhD Hon. Prof.

Dillamore, I. L., PhD DSc, FEng, FIM Hon. Prof.

Edington, J. W., DSc, FEng Hon. Prof.

Farr, J. P. G., BSc *Birm.*, PhD *Birm.* Sr. Lectr.

Hall, M. G., BMet *Sheff.*, PhD *Birm.* Sr. Lectr.

Harris, I. R., BSc *Birm.*, PhD *Birm.*, DSc *Birm.*, FIM, FEng Prof., Materials Science; Head*

Hay, J. N., BSc *Glas.*, PhD *Glas.*, DSc *Birm.*, FRSChem Reader, Polymer Chemistry

Jones, I. P., MA *Camb.*, PhD *Birm.* Prof., Physical Metallurgy

Knott, J. F., BMet *Sheff.*, ScD *Camb.*, FRS, FEng, FIM, FIMechE Feeney Prof.

Loretto, M. H., BMet *Sheff.*, DSc, FIM, FIP Prof., Materials Science and Technology; Dir., Interdisciplinary Res. Centre in Materials for High Performance Applicns.

Marquis, P. M., BSc *Sur.*, PhD Prof., Biomaterials

Mills, N. J., MA *Camb.*, MSc *Cran.*, PhD *Birm.*, DEng Reader, Polymer Engineering

Oates, G., BSc PhD, FEng, FIM Hon. Prof.

Ponton, C. B., BSc(Eng) *Lond.*, PhD *Lond.* Sr. Lectr.

Wise, M. L. H., BSc *Birm.*, PhD *Birm.*, FIM Sr. Lectr.

Young, J. M., BSc *Wales*, PhD *Wales* Sr. Lectr.

Other Staff: 6 Lectrs.; 1 Sr. Res. Fellow; 21 Res. Fellows; 2 Res. Assocs.; 1 Sr. Res. Fellow†; 1 Hon. Lectr.; 1 Hon. Consultant; 3 Hon. Sr. Res. Fellows; 4 Hon. Res. Fellows; 1 Hon. Res. Assoc.

Research: biomaterials; ceramics; electrometallurgy; magnetic materials; microstructural characterisation

Music, see under Humanities

Philosophy, see under Humanities, Sch. of

Physics and Astronomy

Tel: (0121) 414 4568 Fax: (0121) 414 4577

Batty, C. J., BSc *Birm.*, PhD *Birm.*, DSc *Birm.* Hon. Prof.

Beddoe, A. Hon. Prof.

Beynon, T. D., MSc *Manc.*, PhD *Lond.*, DSc *Manc.*, FIP Prof.†, Applied Physics

Charles, M. W., PhD *Leic.*, DSc *Leic.*, FIP Reader, Radiation Physics

Clarke, N. M., PhD *Lond.*, DSc *Lond.*, FIP Sr. Lectr.

Close, F. E., BSc *St.And.*, DPhil *Oxf.* Hon. Prof.

Cox, G. F., BA *Camb.*, PhD *Camb.* Sr. Lectr.

Cruise, A. M., BSc *Lond.*, PhD *Lond.* Prof., Astrophysics and Space Research; Head*

Darlington, C. N. W., MA *Camb.*, PhD *Camb.* Sr. Lectr.

Dowell, J. D., BSc PhD, FRS, FIP Prof., Elementary Particle Physics

Durrani, S. A., BA *Punjab*, MSc *Punjab*, PhD *Camb.*, DSc, FIP Reader, Radiation Physics

Elliott, K. H., BSc *Lond.*, MSc *Manc.*, PhD *Manc.*, FRAS Sr. Lectr.

Elsworth, Y. P., BSc *Manc.*, PhD *Manc.* Sr. Lectr.

Eyles, C. J., BSc *Lond.*, PhD *Lond.* Sr. Lectr.

Forgan, E. M., MA *Camb.*, PhD Prof., Condensed Matter Physics

Fulton, B. R., BSc PhD Reader, Nuclear Physics

Garvey, J., BSc *Glas.*, PhD *Glas.*, FIP Reader, Particle Physics

Gough, C. E., MA *Camb.*, PhD *Camb.* Prof.†, Condensed Matter Physics

Gunn, J. M. F., BSc *Edin.*, PhD *Camb.*, FIP Prof., Theoretical Physics

Hopewell, J. W., BSc *Hull*, MA *Oxf.*, PhD *Lond.* Hon. Prof.

Humphreys, R., MA *Camb.*, PhD *Bath* Hon. Prof.

Isaak, G. R., BSc Melb., PhD Melb., FIP, FRAS Prof.†

Jones, R. C., BSc Manc., PhD Manc. Sr. Lectr.

Kenyon, I. R., MA Oxf., DPhil Oxf., DSc Oxf., FIP Reader, Particle Physics

Kinson, J. B., DSc PhD, FIP Prof., High Energy Physics

Langford, J. I., BSc(Eng) Lond., PhD Wales, DSc Lond. Reader, Powder Diffraction

Lerner, I. V., PhD Moscow Reader, Theoretical Physics

Long, M. W., BA Camb., PhD Lond. Sr. Lectr.

Lowe, J., BSc PhD Sr. Lectr.

Muirhead, C. M., BSc CNAA, PhD CNAA Sr. Lectr.

Nelson, J. M., MSc Rand Afrikaans, DPhil Oxf., FIP Prof., Nuclear Physics

Palmer, R. E., BA Camb., MA Camb., PhD Camb. Prof., Experimental Physics

Ponman, T. J., BSc Warw., PhD Sr. Lectr.

Rae, A. I. M., BSc Edin., PhD W.Aust. Reader, Quantum Physics

Ray, B. Hon. Prof.

Simnett, G. M., BSc Lond., PhD Lond., FRAS Prof., High Energy Astrophysics

Skinner, G. K., BSc PhD, FRAS Reader, High Energy Astrophysics

Tungate, G., BSc Birm., PhD Sr. Lectr.

Watkins, P. M., BSc Birm., PhD Birm. Sr. Lectr.

Weaver, D. R., MA Camb., PhD Camb., FIP Sr. Lectr.

Wilson, J. A., BSc Aberd., PhD Lond. Sr. Lectr.

Other Staff: 16 Lectrs.; 5 Sr. Res. Fellows; 44 Res. Fellows; 6 Res. Assocs.; 2 Sr. Lectrs.†; 1 Reader†; 1 Sr. Res. Fellow†; 2 Hon. Sr. Lectrs.; 3 Hon. Lectrs.; 3 Hon. Sr. Res. Fellows; 9 Hon. Res. Fellows

Research: astrophysics and space research; condensed matter physics; nanoscale physics; nuclear physics; particle physics

Political Science and International Studies, see under Soc. Scis.

Psychology

Tel: (0121) 414 4932 Fax: (0121) 414 4897

Birchwood, M. J., BSc Hull, MSc PhD Hon. Prof.

Booth, D. A., MA Oxf., BSc Oxf., BA Lond., PhD Lond., DSc, FBPsS Prof.

Broks, P., BA Sheff., MSc Oxf., DPhil Oxf. Sr. Lectr.

Browne, K. D., BSc Lond., PhD CNAA Sr. Lectr.

Cochrane, R., BA Wales, PhD Wales, FBPsS Prof.

Cushway, D. J., BA Reading, MSc Reading, PhD Reading Sr. Lectr.

Dent, H., BA Hull, MPhil Lond., PhD Nott. Sr. Lectr.

Georgeson, M. A., MA Camb., DPhil Sus. Prof.

Greville-Harris, M. W., BSc Sus., PhD Brist. Sr. Lectr.

Griffin, C. E., BSc Aston, PhD Aston Sr. Lectr.

Humphreys, G. W., BSc Brist., PhD Brist., FBPsS Prof., Cognitive Psychology

Lamberts, K., BSc Leuven, PhD Leuven, LicPsych Sr. Lectr.

MacRae, A. W., BSc Edin., PhD Wales Sr. Lectr.

Mitchell, I. J., BSc Sheff., DPhil Sus. Sr. Lectr.

Mitchell, P. L., BSc Liv., PhD Liv. Sr. Lectr.

Oliver, C., BSc Lough., MPhil Edin., PhD Lond. Sr. Lectr.

Olson, A. C., BS Johns H., MA Johns H., PhD Johns H. Sr. Lectr.

Orford, J. F., MA Camb., PhD Lond., FBPsS Prof., Clinical and Community Psychology

Ostapiuk, E. B., BA Trinity(Dub.), MSc Sp. Prof.

Riddoch, M. J., BSc Lond., PhD Lond. Sr. Lectr.

Robinson, E. J., BSc Lond., PhD Lond., FBPsS Prof., Developmental Psychology

Thomas, G. V., BSc Wales, PhD Nott., FBPsS Prof.; Head*

Trower, P. E., BSc Brist., MSc Leeds, PhD Brist., FBPsS Sr. Lectr.

Wing, A. M., BSc Edin., PhD McM. Prof., Human Movement

Other Staff: 12 Lectrs.; 14 Res. Fellows; 10 Res. Assocs.; 2 Hon. Sr. Lectrs.; 7 Hon. Lectrs.; 4 Hon. Sr. Res. Fellows; 19 Hon. Res. Fellows

Research: applied social and criminological psychology; clinical and health psychology; developmental psychology; neuropsychology and neuroscience; perception and cognition

Public Policy

Tel: (0121) 414 4986 Fax: (0121) 414 4989

Clarke, Prof. M. G., MA Sus. Head of Sch.*

Hood, C., BA York(UK), BLitt Glas., DLitt York(UK), FBA Hon. Prof.

Marcau, G. Hon. Prof.

Stoker, G. ., BA Manc., PhD Manc. Hon. Prof.

Other Staff: 1 Lectr.; 2 Hon. Sr. Res. Fellow

Research: government and administration in developing countries; health policy and management; housing and urban regeneration; public management; UK local government

Development Administration

Tel: (0121) 414 4987 Fax: (0121) 414 4989

Amis, P. H., BSc Brist., PhD Kent Sr. Lectr.

Batley, R. A., BSocSc Birm., MA Durh., DPhil Sus. Prof.; Head*

Campbell, A., BA Brist., PhD Brun. Sr. Lectr.

Curtis, D. M. E., BA Trinity(Dub.), PhD Kent Dir.*

Davey, K. J., OBE, MA Oxf., MSocSc Birm., FRSA Prof.

Devas, C. N., BA Warw., MCD Liv. Sr. Lectr.

Hubbard, M. E. V., MA Sus., DPhil Sus. Sr. Lectr.

Nickson, R. A., BA Camb. Sr. Lectr.

Shepherd, A. W., BA Camb., PhD Camb. Sr. Lectr.

Slater, R. P., BA Durh., PhD Lond. Sr. Lectr.

Other Staff: 7 Lectrs.; 3 Res. Fellows; 2 Hon. Sr. Fellows; 3 Hon. Fellows

Research: environmental management: environmental policy process; good governance: regulation and enabling roles of government; local government: decentralisation and strengthening; non-government organisations: changes in administration and practice; sustainable development: urban and peri-urban management

Health Services Management

Tel: (0121) 414 7050 Fax: (0121) 414 7051

Baines, D. L., BA York(UK), MSc York(UK) Sr. Lectr.

Barnes, M., BA Sus., MA Sheff., PhD Sheff. Sr. Lectr.

Ham, C. J., BA Kent, MPhil Kent, PhD Brist. Prof., Health Policy and Management; Head*

McIver, S. A., BSc York(UK), PhD York(UK) Sr. Lectr.

Mullen, P. M., MSc(Eng) Lond. Sr. Lectr.

Raftery, J. P., BA S'ton., MA Trinity(Dub.), PhD Lond. Prof., Health Economics

Spurgeon, P. C., BSc S'ton., PhD Lond. Prof.

Other Staff: 6 Lectrs.; 1 Sr. Fellow; 2 Sr. Res. Fellows; 3 Res. Fellows; 1 Res. Assoc.; 1 Hon. Sr. Res. Fellow; 2 Hon. Sr. Fellow; 2 Hon. Fellows; 4 Hon. Res. Fellows

Research: financial management; health care planning; health policy; human resource management; information and resource management

Local Government Studies

Tel: (0121) 414 4986 Fax: (0121) 414 4989

Clarke, M. G., MA Sus. Prof., Local Government Management

Coulson, A. C., MA Camb., PhD Camb. Sr. Lectr.

Game, C. H., BA Manc., MA Essex Sr. Lectr.

Gibson, J. G., BA Leeds, MSc Lond., PhD Birm. Sr. Lectr.

Newman, J. E., BA Open(UK), PhD Open(UK) Sr. Lectr.

Puffitt, R. G., MA Kent Sr. Lectr.

Raine, J. W., BA Wales, PhD Wales Sr. Lectr.; Head*

Richards, S., BA Liv., MA Essex Prof., Public Management

Rogers, S. A., BA Hull, MSocSc Birm. Sr. Lectr.

Skelcher, C. K., BSc Manc., MSocSc Birm. Sr. Lectr.

Spencer, K. M., MA Liv. Prof., Local Policy

Watt, P. A., BA Leeds, DPhil York(UK) Sr. Lectr.

Other Staff: 9 Lectrs.; 4 Hon. Res. Fellows; 1 Hon. Sr. Res. Fellow; 1 Hon. Res. Fellow

Research: community governance and local authority leadership; competition and contracting public services; democratic systems and processes; public sector management (UK and international); social care management

Urban and Regional Studies

Tel: (0121) 414 5021 Fax: (0121) 414 3279

Duffield, M. R., BA Sheff., PhD Birm. Sr. Lectr.

Groves, R., MTech Brun. Sr. Lectr.

Mullins, D., BA Oxf., MA Brist. Sr. Lectr.

Murie, A. S., BA S'ton., MSc Lond. Prof.; Head*

Niner, P. M., BA Brist., BPhil Glas. Sr. Lectr.

Wheeller, B. A., BA Wales, BPhil Liv., MA Nott., MPhil Sur. Sr. Lectr.

Other Staff: 12 Lectrs.; 1 Sr. Res. Fellow†; 2 Hon. Lectrs.; 2 Hon. Res. Fellows

Research: housing studies and housing policy; leisure and tourism; local economic development; urban and regional planning; urban policy

Russian and East European Studies, see under Soc. Scis.

Russian Language and Literature, see under Humanities

Shakespeare Institute, see under Humanities

Social Sciences

Tel: (0121) 414 6630 Fax: (0121) 414 6630

Bailey, D. E., BSc Warw., MSc Oxf. Sr. Lectr.

Mullineux, A. W., BA Liv., MSc Lond., PhD CNAA Prof., Money and Banking; Head of Sch.*

Cultural Studies and Sociology

Tel: (0121) 414 6060 Fax: (0121) 414 6061

Gabriel, J. G., BA Liv., PhD Liv. Sr. Lectr.; Head*

Gray, A., BA Leeds, DPhil York(UK) Sr. Lectr.

Larrain, J., BTheol Birm., LicSoc C.U.Chile, MA Sus., DPhil Sus. Prof.†, Social Theory

Wright, S. A., BA Durh., DPhil Oxf. Sr. Lectr.

Other Staff: 6 Lectrs.; 1 Sr. Lectr.†

Research: domestic technologies; ethnicity and racism; gender; socially contested forms of labour; urban culture, locality and place

Economics

Tel: (0121) 414 6640 Fax: (0121) 414 7377

Backhouse, R. E., BSc Brist., PhD Birm. Prof., History and Philosophy of Economics

Barrett, C. R., BA Oxf., BSc Cape Town Sr. Lectr.

Burridge, P., BSc Brist., MA Kent Sr. Lectr.

Dickinson, D. G., BA Manc., PhD Sheff. Sr. Lectr.

Fender, J., MA Oxf., DPhil Oxf. Reader, Macroeconomics

Kelsey, D., MA Oxf., DPhil Oxf. Prof., Economic Theory

Mullineux, A. W., BA Liv., MSc Lond., PhD CNAA Prof., Money and Banking; Head of Sch.*

Sen, S., MA Calc., PhD Warw., MSocSc Birm. Prof., Development Economics; Head*

Sinclair, P. J. N., MA Oxf., DPhil Oxf. Prof.

Other Staff: 11 Lectrs.; 3 Res. Fellows; 1 Sr. Lectr.†; 2 Hon. Sr. Res. Fellows; 1 Hon. Res. Fellow

Research: economic development, particularly north/south economic relations; history of economic thought; international economic integration; monetary policy; trade policy in trading blocks

Political Science and International Studies

Tel: (0121) 414 6526 Fax: (0121) 414 3496

Croft, S. J., MSc S'ton., PhD S'ton. Prof., International Relations
Furlong, P. F., MA Oxf., PhL Rome, PhD Reading Reader, Italian Politics
Jennings, J. R., BA Wales, MA Wales, DPhil Oxf. Reader, Political Theory
Marsh, D., BA Wales, PhD Exe. Prof.; Head*
Navari, C. B., BA Col., MSc Lond., PhD Birm. Sr. Lectr., Political Science
Preston, P. W., BA Leeds, PhD Leeds Reader, Political Sociology
Redmond, J., MSc Wales, PhD Warw. Prof., European Studies
Siew, V. Hon. Prof.
Terriff, T. R., MA Calg., PhD Lond. Sr. Lectr., Political Science
Other Staff: 11 Lectrs.; 1 Res. Fellow; 1 Sr. Lectr.†; 2 Hon. Sr. Lectrs.; 2 Hon. Sr. Res. Fellows; 1 Hon. Res. Fellow
Research: American foreign and defence policies; British politics; British security policy; modern political thought; political economy of the European Union

Russian and East European Studies

Tel: (0121) 414 6346 Fax: (0121) 414 3423

Allison, R. A., BA Exe., DPhil Oxf. Sr. Lectr. (on leave)
Amann, R., MSocSc Birm., PhD Birm. Prof., Soviet Politics (on leave)
Batt, J. R., BSocSc Birm., PhD Birm. Sr. Lectr.
Cooper, J. M., BSc(Econ) Bath, PhD Birm. Prof., Russian Economic Studies; Dir.*
Hanson, P., MA Camb., PhD Birm. Prof., Soviet Economics
Perrie, M. P., MA Edin., MA Birm. Reader, Russian History
Pilkington, H. A., MSocSc Birm., PhD Birm. Sr. Lectr.
Rees, E. A., BA York(UK), PhD Birm. Sr. Lectr.
Other Staff: 5 Lectrs.; 1 Sr. Res. Fellow; 5 Res. Fellows; 1 Res. Assoc.; 6 Hon. Sr. Res. Fellows; 10 Hon. Res. Fellows
Research: post-communist politics in Russia, Central and Eastern Europe; Russian economic transformation; Russian society; Soviet history; Ukraine

Social Policy and Social Work

Tel: (0121) 414 5708 Fax: (0121) 414 5726

Barnes, M., BA Sus., MA Sheff., PhD Sheff, Sr. Lectr.
Davis, A., BA York(UK), MSc Lond. Prof., Social Work; Head*
Deakin, N. D., MA Oxf., DPhil Sus. Prof., Social Policy and Administration
Doling, J. F., BA Lond., MSc Birm., PhD Birm. Prof., Housing Studies
Jones-Finer, C. J., MA Oxf., PhD Lond. Reader, Comparative Social Policy
Ryburn, M. R., MA Cant., MSc Lond., PhD Sr. Lectr.
Other Staff: 12 Lectrs.; 1 Res. Fellow; 3 Hon. Lectrs.; 4 Hon. Fellows; 4 Hon. Res. Fellows; 1 Hon. Res. Assoc.
Research: social policy analysis; social service organisation and management; social work theory and practice

Spanish, see under Humanities (Hispanic Studies)

Sport and Exercise Sciences

Tel: (0121) 414 4115 Fax: (0121) 414 4121

Brown, M. D., BSc Birm., PhD Birm. Sr. Lectr.
Carroll, D., BSc Edin., PhD ANU Prof., Applied Psychology
Gleeson, M., BSc Birm., PhD CNAA Sr. Lectr.
Jenkins, G. G. H., BSc(Soc) Lond., MSc(Econ) Lond. Sr. Lectr.

Jones, D. A., BSc Lond., PhD Lond. Prof.; Head*
Lakie, M. D., BSc Edin., PhD Edin. Sr. Lectr.
Other Staff: 9 Lectrs.; 2 Res. Fellows; 2 Res. Assocs.; 1 Hon. Lectr.; 3 Hon. Res. Fellows; 1 Hon. Res. Assoc.
Research: cardiovascular circulatory control; health psychology; motor control (biomechanical and psychological aspects); muscle fatigue and damage

Statistics, see Maths. and Stats.

Urban and Regional Studies, see under Public Policy

DENTISTRY

Tel: (0121) 236 8611 Fax: (0121) 625 8815

Anderson, R. J., BSc Lond., BDS Lond., PhD Lond., DDS John Humphreys Prof., Dental Public Health; Head*
Chapple, I. L. C., BDS Newcastle(UK), PhD Birm., FDSRCS Sr. Lectr.
Davenport, J. C., BDS Brist., PhD Birm., FDSRCS Prof., Primary Dental Care
Frame, J. W., BDS Glas., MSc Manc., PhD Manc., FDSRCS Prof.†, Oral Surgery
Hamburger, J., BDS Birm., MSc, FFDRCSI Sr. Lectr.
Laird, W. R. E., BDS Glas., DDS Glas, FDSRCPSGlas, FDSRCS Prof., Prosthetic Dentistry
Lumley, P. J., BDS Dund., MDentSc Birm., FDSRCPSGlas Sr. Lectr.
Marchment, G., BA Open(UK), PhD Birm. Sr. Lectr.
Marquis, P. M., BSc Sur., PhD Prof., Biomaterials; Dep. Dir.
Matthews, J. B., BSc Leeds, MSc Birm., PhD Birm. Sr. Lectr.
Rippin, J. W., BDS Birm., PhD Birm. Sr. Lectr.
Rock, W. P., MBE, JP, DDS, FDSRCS Sr. Lectr.
Saxby, M. S., DDS, FDSRCSEd Sr. Lectr.
Shaw, L., BDS Lond., PhD Lond., FDSRCS Sr. Lectr.
Shortall, A. C. C., BDS Belf., DDS, FDSRCPSGlas, FFDRCSI Sr. Lectr.
Smith, A. J., BSc Liv., PhD Liv. Reader, Oral Biology
Walmsley, A. D., BDS Manc., MSc Manc., PhD Manc., FDSRCPSGlas Sr. Lectr.
Other Staff: 38 Lectrs.; 4 Instrs.; 2 Res. Fellows; 2 Res. Assocs.; 22 Hon. Sr. Lectrs.; 25 Hon. Lectrs.; 1 Hon. Res. Fellow; 1 Hon. Res. Assoc.
Research: development and evaluation of biomaterials; mechanisms and applications of dental tissue repair; mechanisms and prevalence of dental erosion; pathogenesis of oral diseases; provisions and needs involved in primary dental care

HEALTH SCIENCES

Tel: (0121) 414 6893 Fax: (0121) 414 3158

Wrightson. P. A., BA Open(UK), MSocSc Birm. Head of Sch.*
Other Staff: 1 Lectr.; 1 Res. Fellow; 1 Res. Assoc.
Research: education in health care; health maintenance and rehabilitation; health psychology; mental health; primary care

Nursing

Tel: (0121) 414 6893 Fax: (0121) 414 3158

Clifford, C. M., MSc Manc., DPhil Birm. Jenny Jones Prof., Nursing; Head of Res.*
Nolan, P. W., BA Open(UK), BEd Manc., MEd Brist., PhD Bath Sr. Lectr.
van den Akker, O. B. A., BSc Lond., PhD Lond. Sr. Lectr.
Wild, D. J. W., BA Open(UK), MSc Birm. Sr. Lectr.
Other Staff: 14 Lectrs.; 2 Hon. Sr. Lectrs.; 16 Hon. Lectrs.; 1 Hon. Tutor

Physiotherapy

Tel: (0121) 627 2020 Fax: (0121) 627 2021

Wrightson, P. A., BA Open(UK), MSocSc Birm. Sr. Lectr.; Head of Sch.*
Other Staff: 14 Lectrs.

MEDICINE

Tel: (0121) 414 4046 Fax: (0121) 414 4036

Boyle, P., BSc Glas., PhD Glas. Hon. Prof.
Doe, W. F., BM Syd., MSc Lond., FRCP, FRCPA Prof.; Head of Sch.*
Farndon, P. A., BSc MB BS, FRCP Hon. Prof.
London, D. R. Hon. Prof.
Stewart, A. Hon. Prof.
Other Staff: 1 Res. Fellow

Anatomy

Tel: (0121) 414 6814 Fax: (0121) 414 6815

Jenkinson, E. J., BSc Brist., PhD Wales Prof., Experimental Immunology
Owen, J. J. T., MA Oxf., BSc Liv., MD Liv., FRS Sands Cox Prof.; Head*
Shuttleworth, J., BSc Birm., PhD Birm. Sr. Lectr.
Turner, B. M., BSc Lond., PhD Lond. Prof., Experimental Genetics
Other Staff: 8 Lectrs.; 7 Res. Fellows; 1 Res. Associate; 1 Hon. Res. Associate
Research: cell cycle and protein kinases; gene expression, chromatin structure and histone acetylation; thymocyte, development, signalling and cell interactions

Biomedical Science and Biomedical Ethics

Tel: (0121) 414 3616 Fax: (0121) 414 6979

Morton, D. B., BVSc Brist., PhD Liv., MRCVS, FIBiol Prof.; Head*
Moss, P., MA Camb., MB BS Oxf. Prof.
Other Staff: 1 Lectr.
Research: ethical decisions at the end of life; ethics of animal use and animal welfare; ethics of therapy abatement; health care management ethics

Cancer Studies, Institute of

Tel: (0121) 414 4471 Fax: (0121) 414 4486

Ferry, D. R., BSc Birm., MB ChB Birm., PhD Birm. Sr. Lectr.
Gallimore, P. H., PhD Birm., MSc, FIBiol, FRCPath Prof.
Grand, R. J. A., BSc Sheff., PhD Leeds, DSc Birm. Reader, Experimental Cancer Studies
Gray, R., MA Oxf., MSc Oxf. Prof., Medical Statistics
James, N. D., BSc Birm., MB BS Birm., PhD Birm., FRCR Sr. Lectr.
Kerr, D. J., MSc Glas., MB ChB Glas., MD Glas., PhD Glas. Prof., Clinical Oncology; Clinical Head of Institute
Poole, C., BA Camb., MB BChir Camb. Macmillan Sr. Lectr.
Rea, D. W., BSc Brist., MB BS Lond. Sr. Lectr.; Consultant
Rickinson, A. B., MA Camb., PhD Camb. Prof.; Head*
Seymour, L., BSc Birm., PhD Birm. Sr. Lectr.
Taylor, A. M. R., BSc Lond., PhD Lond. Prof., Cancer Genetics
Wakelam, M. J. O., BSc Birm., PhD Birm. Prof., Molecular Pharmacology
Young, L. S., BSc Birm., PhD Birm. Prof., Cancer Biology
Other Staff: 2 Lectrs.; 39 Res. Fellows; 11 Res. Assocs.; 18 Sr. Clin. Lectrs.; 1 Hon. Sr. Lectr.; 1 Hon. Clin. Lectr.; 1 Hon. Sr. Res. Fellow; 2 Hon. Res. Fellows; 1 Hon. Res. Assoc.
Research: DNA tumour virus systems; gene regulation; genetic analysis of susceptibility to cancer; genetic and protein engineering

Cardiovascular Medicine

Tel: (0121) 414 3713 Fax: (0121) 414 1045

Gammage, M. D., MD Birm., FRCP Reader
Littler, W. A., MD Liv., FRCP Sir Melville Arnott British Heart Foundation Prof.; Head*

Townend, J. N., BSc Birm., MD Birm. Sr. Lectr.
Other Staff: 2 Lectrs.; 4 Res. Fellows; 11 Hon. Sr. Clinical Lectrs.; 3 Hon. Res. Fellows

Clinical Neuroscience

Tel: (0121) 472 1311 Fax: (0121) 627 2105
Cruikshank, G. S., BSc PhD MB BS, FRCS FRCSEd Prof., Neurosurgery
Francis, D. A., BSc Manc., MD Birm. Sr. Lectr.
Jackowski, A., BSc Lond., MB BS Lond., MD Lond., FRCS Sr. Lectr.
Pall, H. S., MD Brist. Sr. Lectr.
Traub, R. D., BA Prin., MD Penn. Prof.
Williams, A. C., MD Birm., FRCP Bloomer Prof., Clinical Neurology; Head*
Winer, J. B., MB Birm.., BSc Lond. Sr. Lectr.
Other Staff: 1 Lectr.; 17 Hon. Sr. Clin. Lectrs.; 2 Hon. Clin. Lectrs.; 1 Hon. Sr. Res. Fellow; 2 Hon. Res. Fellows; 1 Hon. Res. Assoc.
Research: identifying risk factors for the neuro-degenerative diseases; immune mechanisms in neuropathy and multiple sclerosis; neurosurgical practice, particularly with reference to advanced technology; xenobiotic enzymes at a biochemical or molecular level

Epidemiology, see Public Health and Epidemiol.

General Practice

Tel: (0121) 414 3766 Fax: (0121) 414 6571
Cooke, M. W., MB ChB Birm., FRCSEd Sr. Lectr.
Gill, P. S., BM S'ton., DCh Lond. Sr. Lectr.
Hobbs, F. D. R., MB ChB Brist., FRCGP Prof.; Head*
Mant, J. W. F., MA Camb., MSc Lond., MB BS Lond. Sr. Lectr.
Morgan, D. R., MB ChB Glas., MD, FRCGP, FRCPGlas Sr. Lectr.
Parle, J. V., MB ChB Birm., FRCGP Sr. Lectr.
Skelton, J., BA Liv., MA Leeds Sr. Lectr.
Other Staff: 11 Lectrs.; 16 Res. Fellows; 4 Res Assocs.; 3 Sr. Lectrs.†; 1 Hon. Sr. Lectr.; 18 Hon Sr. Clin. Lectrs.; 2 Hon. Fellows; 21 Hon. Clin. Lectrs.; 1 Hon. Res. Fellow; 10 Hon. Tutors
Research: cancer screening; cardiovascular medicine; clinical guideline implementation; diagnostic technologies and computer decision support; gastro-intestinal medicine

Geriatric Medicine

Tel: (0121) 627 8266 Fax: (0121) 627 8304
O'Mahoney, D., MD Trinity(Dub.) Sr. Lectr.
Sinclair, A. J., MB BS Lond., BSc Lond., MD Lond., MSc Syd., FRCP Charles Hayward Prof.; Head*
Other Staff: 3 Lectrs.; 1 Res. Fellow; 10 Hon. Sr. Clin. Lectrs.
Research: cardiovascular reflexes in older people; diabetes; respiratory medicine; stroke rehabilitation

Immunology

Tel: (0121) 414 4065 Fax: (0121) 414 3599
Bradwell, A. R., MB ChB Birm., FRCP, FRCPath Sr. Lectr.
Brown, G., MA Oxf., BSc Lond., PhD Lond. Reader
Drayson, M. T., BSc Manc., MB ChB Manc., PhD Manc. Sr. Lectr.
Gordon, J., BSc S'ton., PhD S'ton., DSc Birm. Prof., Cellular Immunology
Jefferis, R., BSc Birm., PhD Birm., DSc Birm. Prof., Molecular Immunology
Lane, P. J. L., PhD Birm., MB ChB Edin. Sr. Lectr.
MacLennan, I. C. M., BSc Lond., MB BS Lond., PhD Lond., FRCPath Prof.; Head*
Thompson, R. A. Hon. Prof.
Other Staff: 2 Lectrs.; 1 Royal Soc. Univ. Sr. Res. Fellow; 1 Sr. Res. Fellow; 15 Res. Fellows; 3 Res. Assocs.; 1 Reader†; 2 Hon. Sr. Clin. Lectrs.; 2 Hon. Clin. Lectrs.; 1 Hon. Res. Fellow

Research: b-cell system; cellular basis of antibody production and pathological consequences of malfunction; development of immunodiagnostic reagents; regulation of haemopoietic cell differentiation

Infection

Tel: (0121) 414 6945 Fax: (0121) 414 3454
Buchan, A., BSc Aberd., PhD Aberd. Sr. Lectr.
Cane, P. A., BSc Brist., PhD Brist. Sr. Lectr.
Catty, D., BSc Birm., MSc Birm., PhD Birm. Res. Dir.
Geddes, A. M., CBE, MB ChB Edin., FRCP, FRCPEd Prof.; Head*
Gill, M. J., BSc Lond., MB ChB Leeds, PhD Lond. Sr. Lectr.
Piddock, L. J. V., BSc CNAA, PhD CNAA Sr. Lectr.
Skinner, G. R. B., MD ChB Glas., DSc Birm., FRCPath, FRCOG Sr. Lectr.
Wise, R., MD, FRCPath Hon. Prof.
Other Staff: 2 Lectrs.; 3 Res. Fellows; 3 Res. Assocs.; 26 Hon. Sr. Clinical Lectrs.; 1 Hon. Lectr.; 2 Hon. Clin. Lectrs.; 1 Hon. Sr. Res. Fellow; 5 Hon. Res. Fellows; 4 Hon. Res. Assocs.
Research: antimicrobial immunity; action mechanisms of and resistance mechanisms to antimicrobial agents; microbial diseases; neisseria; susceptibility to anti-viral drugs

Intensive Care, see Surgery, Anaesth. and Intensive Care, Inst. of

Medicine

Tel: (0121) 414 4046 Fax: (0121) 414 4036
Adams, D. H., MB BChir Camb., MD Camb., FRCP Prof., Hepatology
Bain, S., MA Camb., MB BS Lond. Sr. Lectr.
Barnett, A. H., BSc Lond., MD Lond., FRCP Prof., Diabetic Medicine
Beevers, D. G., MD Lond., FRCP Prof.
Doe, W. F., BM Syd., MSc Lond., FRCP, FRCPA Prof.; Head of Sch.*
Dunne, F. P., MB BCh BAO N.U.I., MD Birm., PhD Birm. Sr. Lectr.
Elias, E. E., BSc Lond., MB BS Lond., FRCP Hon. Prof., Hepatology
Franklyn, J. A., MD ChB Birm., PhD Birm., FRCP Prof.
Gough, S. C. L., MB ChB Leeds, MD Leeds Sr. Lectr.
Heath, D. A., MB ChB Birm., FRCP Reader
Hewison, M., BSc CNAA, PhD Lond. Sr. Lectr.
Jankowski, J. A. Z., MB ChB Glas., MD Dund. Sr. Lectr.
Kendall, M. J., MD, FRCP Reader
Langman, M. J. S., BSc Lond., MD Lond., FRCP William Withering Prof.
Llewellyn-Jones, C. G., MB BCh Wales, MD Wales Sr. Lectr.
Logan, A., BSc Lond., PhD Lond. Reader
Miller, M. R., BSc Lond., MD Lond., FRCP Sr. Lectr.
Mutimer, D. J., MB BS Melb. Sr. Lectr.
Ramsden, D. B., BScTech Manc., MSc Manc., PhD Brad., FRSChem Sr. Lectr.
Savage, C. O., MD Birm., PhD Birm. Sr. Lectr.
Sheppard, M. C., MB ChB Cape Town, PhD Cape Town, FRCP Prof.; Head*
Singh, S., MB ChB Birm. Sr. Lectr.
Stewart, P. M., MB ChB Edin., MD Edin., FRCP Prof.
Stockley, R. A., MD DSc, FRCP Hon. Prof., Respiratory Medicine
Other Staff: 7 Lectrs.; 1 Sr. Res. Fellow; 29 Res. Fellows; 14 Res. Assocs.; 1 Sr. Lectr.†; 1 Hon. Reader; 3 Hon. Sr. Lectrs.; 79 Hon. Sr. Clin. Lectrs.; 5 Hon. Lectrs.; 4 Hon. Clin. Lectrs.; 5 Hon. Sr. Res. Fellows; 32 Hon. Res. Fellows; 2 Hon. Res. Assocs.
Research: cancer (clinical and scientific); endocrinology, especially thyroid disease; immunology/infection and the human immune response; neurosciences (clinical and scientific)

Obstetrics and Gynaecology

Tel: (0121) 627 2695 Fax: (0121) 414 1576
Afnan, M. A. M., MB BS Lond. Sr. Lectr.
Gee, H., MD ChB Liv. Sr. Lectr.
Kehoe, S. T., BA Trinity(Dub.), MB BCh Trinity(Dub.) Sr. Lectr.
Kilby, M. D., MB BS Lond., MD Nott. Sr. Lectr.
Luesley, D. M., MA Camb., MD ChB Camb. Prof., Gynaecological Oncology
Newton, J. R., MD Lond., FRCOG Lawson Tait Prof.
Whittle, M. J., MD Manc., FRCPGlas, FRCOG Dame Hilda Lloyd Prof., Fetal Medicine; Head*
Other Staff: 4 Lectrs.; 1 Sr. Res. Fellow; 4 Res. Fellows; 39 Hon. Sr. Clin. Lectrs.; 1 Hon. Clin. Lectr.; 1 Hon. Res. Fellow
Research: foetal anaemia; foetal endocrinology; placental pathiophysiology; twin-to-twin transfusion syndrome; ultrasound diagnosis of foetal anomalies

Occupational Health, Institute of

Tel: (0121) 414 6030 Fax: (0121) 414 6217
Aw, T. C., MB BS Malaya, MSc Sing., MSc Lond., PhD Lond., FRCPCan, FRCP Sr. Lectr.
Beach, J. R., MB BS Newcastle(UK) Sr. Lectr.
Gardiner, K., BSc CNAA, PhD CNAA Sr. Lectr.
Harrington, J. M., CBE, MSc Lond., MD Lond., FRCP, FACE Birmingham Hospital Saturday Fund Prof.; Head*
Sorahan, T. M., BSc Birm., PhD Birm. Reader, Occupational Epidemiology
Spurgeon, A., BSc S'ton., PhD Birm. Sr. Lectr.
Other Staff: 3 Lectrs.; 1 Sr. Res. Fellow; 3 Res. Fellows; 1 Res. Assoc.; 2 Hon. Sr. Lectrs.; 12 Hon. Sr. Clin. Lectrs.; 1 Hon. Lectr.; 4 Hon. Clin. Lectrs.; 4 Hon. Sr. Res. Fellows; 2 Hon. Res. Fellows
Research: occupational cancer (cohort studies); occupational hygiene (retrospective exposure assessments); occupational medicine (audit, sensitisation and lung disease); occupational psychology (effects of chemicals, neuro behaviour)

Paediatrics and Child Health

Tel: (0121) 454 4851 Fax: (0121) 454 5383
Booth, I. W., BSc Lond., MSc Lond., MB BS Lond., MD Lond., FRCP Leonard Parsons Prof.; Head*
Bundey, S., MB BChir Camb., FRCP Prof., Clinical Genetics
Green, S. H., MA Camb., MB BChir Camb., FRCP Sr. Lectr.
Hulten, M. A., MD Lund, MD Stockholm, PhD Stockholm Hon. Prof., Cytogenetics
Kelly, D. A., MB ChB BAO Trinity(Dub.), MD Trinity(Dub.) Hon. Prof.
Knutton, S., BSc Birm., PhD Birm. Sr. Lectr.
Lander, A. D., MB BS Lond., PhD Lond., FRCS, FRCSEd Sr. Lectr.
Latif, F., BSc Liv., PhD Lond. Sr. Lectr.
Maher, E. R., BSc Manc., MB ChB Manc., MD Manc. Prof., Medical Genetics
Mann, J. R., MB BS, FRCP Hon. Prof.
McConville, C. M., BSc Belf., PhD Belf. Sr. Lectr.
Moy, R. J. D., BA Camb., MB BChir Camb., MD Camb. Sr. Lectr.
Murphy, M. S., BSc N.U.I., MB BCh BAO N.U.I., MD N.U.I. Sr. Lectr.
Tarlow, M. J., MB BS Lond., MSc Lond., FRCP Sr. Lectr.
Webb, T. P., BSc Birm., PhD Birm. Sr. Lectr.
Wright, S. E., MB BChir Camb., FRCP Prof.†
Other Staff: 6 Lectrs.; 1 Sr. Res. Fellow; 11 Res. Fellows; 2 Res. Assocs.; 92 Hon. Readers; 1 Hon. Sr. Clin. Lectr.; 1 Hon. Lectr.; 4 Hon. Clin. Lectrs.; 2 Hon. Sr. Res. Fellows; 3 Hon. Res. Fellows; 2 Hon. Res. Assocs.
Research: clinical genetics/cytogenetics DNA structure and function; multifactorial inheritance; nutrition/gastroenterology; paediatric liver disease and transplantation

Child Health, Institute for

Booth, Prof. I. W., BSc Lond., MB BS Lond., MSc Lond., MD Lond., FRCP Dir.*
Other Staff: 1 Hon. Lectr.; 2 Hon. Sr. Res. Fellows; 1 Hon. Res. Fellow; 1 Hon. Res. Assoc.

Pathology

Tel: (0121) 414 4017 Fax: (0121) 414 4019
Barber, P. C., BA Oxf., BM BCh Oxf., DPhil Oxf. Sr. Lectr.
Howie, A. J., MB BChir Camb., MD Camb., MA Camb. Sr. Lectr.
Hubscher, S. G., MB ChB Sr. Lectr.
Jones, E. L., MD Birm., FRCPath Leith Prof.; Head*
Rushton, D. I., MB ChB Manc., FRCPath Sr. Lectr.
Sanders, D. S. A., MB ChB Dund. Sr. Lectr.
Young, J. A., MB BCh BAO Trinity(Dub.), MD Trinity(Dub.), FRCPath Sr. Lectr.
Other Staff: 2 Lectrs.; 1 Res. Assoc.; 22 Hon. Sr. Clin. Lectrs.; 2 Hon. Res. Fellows
Research: cadherin expression in oral and oesophageal cancer; cell differentiation and growth; EBV in nasopharyngeal tumours and lymphomas; haemolytic uraemic syndrome in children; liver allograft rejection grading and diagnosis

Pharmacology

Tel: (0121) 414 4507 Fax: (0121) 414 4509
Barnes, N. M., BSc Brad., PhD Wales Sr. Lectr.
Bowery, N. G., Laur Florence, PhD Lond., DSc Lond. Prof.; Head*
Davies, W. E., BSc Wales, PhD Wales Sr. Lectr.
Key, B. J., BSc Birm., PhD Birm. Sr. Lectr.
Lacey, M. G., BSc Sus., PhD Brist. Sr. Lectr.
Other Staff: 2 Lectrs.; 11 Res. Fellows; 3 Res. Assocs.; 1 Hon. Sr. Res. Fellow; 3 Hon. Res. Fellows; 1 Hon. Res. Assoc.
Research: auditory function; biochemical and molecular pharmacology; cardiovascular pharmacology; cellular electrophysiology

Physiology

Tel: (0121) 414 6906 Fax: (0121) 414 6919
Comis, S. D., BSc Lond., PhD Birm. Sr. Lectr.
Coote, J. H., BSc Lond., PhD Lond., DSc Birm., FIBiol Bowman Prof.; Head*
Cummins, P., BSc Reading, PhD Birm. Sr. Lectr.
Egginton, S., BSc Birm., PhD St And. Sr. Lectr.
Harris, M. C., BSc CNAA, PhD Lond. Sr. Lectr.
Jefferys, J. G. R., BSc Lond., PhD Lond. Prof., Neuroscience
Johns, E. J., BSc S'ton., PhD S'ton., DSc Birm. Prof., Renal Science
Kumar, P., BSc Birm., DPhil Oxf. Sr. Lectr.
Lote, C. J., BSc Manc., PhD Manc. Reader, Renal Physiology
Lovick, T. A., BSc Birm., PhD Birm. Sr. Lectr.
Marshall, J. M., BSc Birm., PhD Birm. Prof., Cardiovascular Science
Nash, G. B., BSc Manc., PhD Lond. Reader, Cardiovascular Rheology
Osborne, M. P., PhD Birm., DSc Birm. Reader, Neurobiology
Ross, H. F., BSc Aberd. Sr. Lectr.
Smith, M. E., BSc Birm., DSc Birm., PhD Reader, Experimental Neurology
Westbury, D. R., BCh Oxf., BSc Oxf., MA Oxf., DM Oxf. Prof.
Other Staff: 5 Lectrs.; 18 Res. Fellows; 5 Res. Assocs.; 1 Hon. Sr. Lectr.; 2 Hon. Lectrs.; 3 Hon.Sr. Res. Fellows; 7 Hon. Res. Fellows; 2 Hon. Res. Assocs.
Research: cardiorespiratory control during hypoxia; cellular basis of atheroma or angiogenesis; nervous control of heart and circulation; neuronal mechanisms in epilepsy and prion diseases; renin-angiotensin system, kidney and hypertension

Psychiatry

Tel: (0121) 627 2844 Fax: (0121) 427 2832
Betts, T. A., MB ChB Birm. Sr. Lectr.
Brockington, I. F., MD Camb., MPhil Lond., FRCP, FRCPsych Prof.; Head*

Clarke, D. J., MB ChB, FRCPsych Sr. Lectr.
Corbett, J. A., MB BS Lond., FRCPsych, FRCP Prof., Developmental Psychiatry
Craddock, N. J., MA Camb., MB ChB Birm., MMedSc Birm., PhD Wales Prof., Molecular Psychiatry
Humphreys, M. S., BDS Sr. Lectr.
Reed, A., MB BS Lond. Sr. Lectr.
Remschmidt, H., MD Erlangen, PhD Tübingen Sp. Prof.
Sashidharan, S. P., MB BS Madr., MPhil Edin., PhD Edin. Prof., Community Psychiatry
Vostanis, P., MA Athens Sr. Lectr.
Other Staff: 2 Lectrs.; 2 Sr. Res. Fellows; 3 Res. Fellows; 4 Res. Assocs.; 51 Hon. Sr. Clin. Lectrs.; 9 Hon. Clin. Lectrs.; 1 Hon. Tutor; 5 Hon. Sr. Res. Fellows; 2 Hon. Res. Fellows; 4 Hon. Res. Assocs.
Research: biological investigation and mental handicap syndromes; biology of Down's Syndrome; mental illness in motherhood; molecular psychiatry; psychiatric genetics

Public Health and Epidemiology

Tel: (0121) 414 6767 Fax: (0121) 472 1122
Birt, C. A., BA Camb., MA Camb., MSc Manc., MB BChir Camb., FRCP Sr. Lectr.; Consultant
Burls, A. J. E., MSc Lond., MB BS Lond. Sr. Lectr.; Consultant
Cheng, K. K., BSc HK, MB BS HK, PhD Camb. Prof.; Head*
Hawkins, M. M., MSc Sus., DPhil Oxf. Reader, Maternal and Child Epidemiology
Hyde, C. Sr. Lectr.
Lawrence, P. T., BSc Lond., MSc C.England Sr. Health Devel. Advisor
Lilford, R. J., PhD Lond., MB BCh, FRCOG, FRCP Hon. Prof.
MacArthur, C., BSc Salf., BSc Manc., PhD Manc. Reader, Maternal and Child Epidemiology
Marshall, T., MBE, MSc Lond. Sr. Lectr.
Stevens, A. J., BA Camb., MA Nott., MSc Lond., MB BS Lond. Prof., Public Health
Stewart, A., MD, FRCP Hon. Prof.
Walters, S., MB BS Lond. Sr. Lectr.
Other Staff: 2 Lectrs.; 1 Sr. Res. Fellow; 8 Res. Fellows; 8 Res. Assocs.; 1 Sr. Lectr. Consultant†; 1 Sr. Lectr.†; 1 Hon. Sr. Lectr.; 18 Hon. Sr. Clin. Lectrs.; 2 Hon. Lectrs.; 8 Hon. Clin. Lectrs.; 2 Hon. Sr. Res. Fellows; 2 Hon. Res. Assocs.
Research: cancer epidemiology; health services, particularly health care evaluation; maternal and child health; respiratory and environmental epidemiology

Rheumatology

Tel: (0121) 414 6778 Fax: (0121) 414 6794
Bacon, P. A., MA Camb., MB BChir Camb., FRCP Arthritis and Rheumatism Council Prof.; Head*
Bowman, S. J., BSc Lond., MB BS Lond. Sr. Lectr.
Gordon, P. C., MA Camb., MB BS Lond. Sr. Lectr.
Salmon, M., BSc, PhD Reader, Experimental Rheumatology
Southwood, T. R., BM BS Flin., FRACP Sr. Lectr., Paediatric Rheumatology
Young, S. P., BSc Lond., PhD Lond. Sr. Lectr.
Other Staff: 4 Lectrs.; 7 Res. Fellows; 4 Res. Assocs.; 5 Hon. Sr. Clin. Lectrs.; 2 Hon. Clin. Lectrs.; 1 Hon. Res. Assoc.
Research: human t-cell differentiation and memory; paediatric rheumatology; t-cell signal transduction in disease; t-cells in autoimmunity; vasculitis and connective tissue diseases

Surgery, Anaesthesia and Intensive Care, Institute of

Tel: (0121) 414 4046

Anaesthesia and Intensive Care

Tel: (0121) 627 2060 Fax: (0121) 627 2062
Bion, J. F., MB BS Lond., MD Lond., FRCA Reader, Intensive Care Medicine
Clutton-Brock, T. H., MB ChB Brist., FRCA Sr. Lectr.
Cooper, G. M., MB ChB Birm., FRCA Sr. Lectr.
Hutton, P., BSc Birm., MB ChB Birm., PhD Birm., FRCA Hickman Prof.; Dir.*
Stokes, M. A., BM BS Nott., BMedSc Birm., FRCA Sr. Lectr.
Other Staff: 4 Lectrs.; 2 Res. Fellows; 59 Hon. Sr. Clin. Lectrs.
Research: cardiac anaesthesia; clinical measurement; day case anaesthesia; intensive care; paediatric anaesthesia

Surgery

Tel: (0121) 627 2276 Fax: (0121) 472 1230
Alpar, E. K., MD Ankara, MChOrth Liv., FRCSEd Sr. Lectr.
Keighley, M. R. B., MS Lond., FRCS Barling Prof.; Head*
McMaster, P. Hon. Prof.
Morton, D. G., MD Birm., FRCS Sr. Lectr.
Murray, P. I., MB BS Lond., PhD Amst., FRCS Prof., Ophthalmology
Philips, S., MB ChB Birm., FRCS Sr. Lectr.
Radley, S., MB ChB Birm., MD Birm., FRCS Clin. Consultant Sr. Lectr.
Temple, J. G., ChM Liv., FRCS Hon. Prof.
Haldon, J. F., MA PhD Head*
Other Staff: 3 Lectrs.; 12 Res. Fellows; 79 Hon. Sr. Clin. Lectrs.; 1 Hon. Tutor; 1 Hon. Sr. Res. Fellow; 7 Hon. Res. Fellows; 2 Hon. Res. Associates
Research: faecal DNA as a possible screening tool; large bowel screening; molecular changes in colorectal cancer; post-obstetric bowel incontinence; surgery of inflammatory bowel disease

SPECIAL CENTRES, ETC

Fine Arts, Barber Institute of

Tel: (0121) 414 7333 Fax: (0121) 414 3370
Verdi, Prof. R., BA Mich., MA Chic., PhD Lond. Dir.*

German Studies, Institute for

Tel: (0121) 414 7182 Fax: (0121) 414 7329
Hyde-Price, A. G., BEcon Wales, PhD Kent Sr. Lectr.
Jeffery, C. A., BA Lough., PhD Lough. Reader
Kaser, M., MA Camb., DLitt Oxf., Hon. DSocSc Camb. Hon. Prof.
Marsh, D., BA Oxf. Hon. Prof.
Paterson, W. E., MA St And., MSc Lond., PhD Lond., FRSEd Prof.; Dir.*
van der Will, W., DPhil Cologne Prof.
Watson, A., CBE Hon. Prof.
Other Staff: 2 Res. Fellows; 1 Res. Assoc.
Research: economic and governance and policy in Germany; German cultural studies; politics and government of unified Germany; role of Germany within the European Union; twentieth-century German history

Humanities, Institute for Advanced Research in the

Tel: (0121) 414 5655 Fax: (0121) 414 3852
Boulton, J. T., BA Durh., BLitt Oxf., PhD Nott., Hon DLitt Durh., Hon DLitt Nott., FBA, FRSL Hon. Dir.*
Other Staff: 45 Hon. Fellows

Ironbridge Institute

Tel: (0121) 414 2274 Fax: (0121) 414 3595
Blockley, M. R., MA Leic. Programme Dir.*

Japan Centre

Tel: (0121) 414 3269 Fax: (0121) 414 3270
Watson, C. J., BA Brist. Dir.*
Other Staff: 1 Lectr.; 1 Lang. Tutor; 2 Japanese Instrs.

Research: comparative urban and housing policy; countryside management; Japan and the European Union: Asia-Europe Meeting (ASEM); Nepal; women in Asia

Materials for High Performance Applications, Interdisciplinary Research Centre in

Tel: (0121) 414 5215 Fax: (0121) 414 3441

Cheng, J., BSc *Hunan*, MSc *Anhui*, PhD *Anhui* Hon. Prof.

Li, X. Hon. Prof.

Loretto, M. H., BMet *Sheff.*, DSc *Birm.*, FIM, FIP Prof., Materials Science and Technology; Dir.*

Other Staff: 6 Sr. Res. Fellows; 36 Res. Fellows; 8 Res. Assocs.; 2 Hon. Sr. Res. Fellows; 5 Hon. Res. Fellows; 1 Hon. Res. Assoc.

Research: alloy development; ceramic processing; melting/casting; process modelling; spray farming

Public and Environmental Health, Institute for

Tel: (0121) 414 6774 Fax: (0121) 472 1122

Harrison, Prof. R. M., BSc *Birm.*, PhD *Birm.*, DSc *Birm.*, FRSChem, FRMetS Dir.*

Other Staff: 1 Sr. Lectr.; 2 Lectrs.; 3 Res. Fellows; 1 Res. Assoc.; 9 Hon. Lectrs.; 2 Hon. Res. Fellows

CONTACT OFFICERS

Academic affairs. Academic Registrar and Director of Planning: Denner, P. W., BA *Durh.*, MSocSc *Durh.*,

Admissions (first degree). Director of Admissions Liaison: Ash, J. E., BSc *Nott.*, PhD *Birm.*

Admissions (higher degree). Director of Admissions Liaison: Ash, J. E., BSc *Nott.*, PhD *Birm.*

Adult/continuing education. Head of School of Continuing Studies: Martin, Prof. G. R., BSc *Sur.*, PhD *Exe.*

Alumni. Director of Communications and Alumni Relations: Thomas, J. M., BA *Lond.*

Archives. University Archivist: Penney, C. L., BA *Brist.*

Careers. Director of Careers Centre: Maynard, R. A., BSc *Birm.*, PhD *Birm.*

Computing services. Assistant Director of Information Services: Hendry, J. A., BSc *Glas.*, PhD *Glas.*

Conferences/corporate hospitality. Assistant Director of Estate Management: Pringle, G.

Consultancy services. Director of Research Support and Business Development: Bushaway, R. W., BA *S'ton.*, PhD *S'ton.*

Credit transfer. Academic Registrar and Director of Planning: Denner, P. W., BA *Durh.*, MSocSc *Durh.*,

Development/fund-raising. Development Adviser to the Vice-Chancellor: Jarratt, Prof. P., BSc *Manc.*, PhD *Brad.*, FIMA

Distance education. Distance Education Co-ordinator, School of Education: Miller, C. J., MSc *Lond.*

Equal opportunities. Deputy Director of Staffing Services: Usherwood, J., BA *Manc.*

Estates and buildings/works and services. Director of Estate Management: Addison, J. P., BSc *CNAA*

Examinations. Academic Registrar and Director of Planning: Denner, P. W., BA *Durh.*, MSocSc *Durh.*,

Finance. Director of Finance: Ball, G.

General enquiries. Registrar and Secretary: Allen, David J., BA *Wales*, MEd *Wales*

Health services. University Medical Officer: Raichura, V., MB BS *Lond.*

Industrial liaison. Director of Research Support and Business Development: Bushaway, R. W., BA *S'ton.*, PhD *S'ton.*

International office. Director of International Affairs: ......

Language training for international students. Director of English for International Students Unit: Hewings, M. J., BA *S'ton.*, MA *Birm.*, PhD

Library (chief librarian). Librarian and Director of Information Services: Field, C. D., MA *Oxf.*, DPhil *Oxf.*

Personnel/human resources. Director of Staffing Services: Scott, P. J. F., BA *Manc.*

Public relations, information and marketing. Director of Public Affairs: Albrighton, F. C., BA *Reading*

Publications. Director of Communications and Alumni Relations: Thomas, J. M., BA *Lond.*

Purchasing. University Purchasing Officer: Higgins, B. J.

Quality assurance and accreditation. Head of Academic Policy Support and Quality Assurance: Bosworth, J. R. B., MA *Camb.*

Research. Director of Research Support and Business Development: Bushaway, R. W., BA *S'ton.*, PhD *S'ton.*

Safety. Director of Health and Safety Unit: Harrison, D. I., BSc *St And.*, MSc *Strath.*

Scholarships, awards, loans. Academic Registrar and Director of Planning: Denner, P. W., BA *Durh.*, MSocSc *Durh.*,

Schools liaison. Director of Admissions Liaison: Ash, J. E., BSc *Nott.*, PhD *Birm.*

Security. Security Manager: Butler, M. J.

Sport and recreation. Assistant Director of Estate Management (Sports and Recreation Facilities): Madeley, K. A., BA *Birm.*, MA *Birm.*

Staff development and training. Director of Staff Development: Heyes, L. R., BA *Birm.*

Student union. General Manager, Guild of Students: Yeates, D.

Student welfare/counselling. Director of Student Support and Counselling Service: Rickinson, B., BA *Qld.*

Students from other countries. International Students Support Officer: Hannabuss, F., BA *Leic.*

Students with disabilities. Disability Co-ordinator: Williams, D., BA *Birm.*

University press. Managing Editor, University Press: Whittaker, V.

[Information supplied by the institution as at 12 March 1998, and edited by the ACU]

BOLTON INSTITUTE

Founded 1982

Additional Member of the Association of Commonwealth Universities

Postal Address: Deane Road, Bolton, England BL3 5AB
Telephone: (01204) 528851 Fax: (01204) 399074 E-mail: enquiries@bolton.ac.uk
WWW: http://www.bolton.ac.uk

PRINCIPAL*—Temple, Mollie, BA MA
VICE-PRINCIPAL—Gardner, Wilf, BSc *Newcastle(UK)*
VICE-PRINCIPAL—......
HEAD OF FINANCE AND CLERK TO THE GOVERNORS—Hubbard, Colin F., BA *Manc.*
REGISTRAR—Kingsbury, Paul A., BA *Liv.*
HEAD OF LEARNING SUPPORT SERVICES (LIBRARY, MEDIA AND COMMUNICATIONS SKILLS)—Scholefield, Alan J., BSc *Lond.*, PhD *Sheff.*

GENERAL INFORMATION

History. The institute was established in 1982 as a result of the merger of Bolton Institute of Technology (established 1964) and Bolton College of Education (Technical) (established 1946). In 1989 the institute became an independent higher education corporation.

It is located in the centre of Bolton, approximately 18km north-west of Manchester.

Admission to first degree courses (see also United Kingdom Introduction). All applicants must apply through Universities and Colleges Admissions Service (UCAS). International applicants: national equivalent of UK qualifications are generally accepted.

First Degrees (see also United Kingdom Directory of Subjects to Study). BA, BEd, BEng, BSc.

Courses normally last 3 years full-time or 4 years part-time. Sandwich programmes: 4

years (including 1 year placement). BEd: 1 year (for appropriately qualified international students).

Higher Degrees (see also United Kingdom Directory of Subjects to Study). MA, MEd, MSc, MPhil, PhD.

Applicants to master's degree courses should hold an appropriate first degree or equivalent qualification. For direct entry to PhD programmes: appropriate master's degree or equivalent qualification.

Master's programmes are normally 1 year full-time or 2 years part-time (minimum). MPhil: 18 months full-time or 3 years part-time; PhD: 3 years full-time or 6 years part-time.

Libraries. 138,000 volumes; 1300 periodicals subscribed to.

Fees (1998–99, annual). Undergraduate: UK students £1000; international students £5500 (arts), £6200 (science/technology). Postgraduate (taught courses): UK students £2750 (arts), £3500 (science/technology); international students £6150. Postgraduate (research): UK students £2540; international students £6450.

Academic Awards (1996–97). 76 grants made to UK students of between £200 and £500, 14 grants to international students totalling £2300.

Academic Year (1999–2000). Two semesters: 27 September–11 February; 14 February–30 June.

Income (1996–97). Total, £25,868,000.

Statistics. Staff: 727 (315 academic, 412 support). Students: full-time 4200; part-time 2800; international 300.

FACULTIES/SCHOOLS

Arts, Science and Education
Fax: (01204) 903338

Dean: Marsh, Peter, BA Manc.Met., MA(Econ) Manc., PhD Manc.
Faculty Support Manager: Birtwistle, Hilary

Bolton Business School
Fax: (01204) 900516

Dean: Kitson, Prof. Alan, BA Nott., PhD Nott.
Faculty Support Manager: Selous-Hodges, Rosslynne, BSc Bolton IHE

Technology
Fax: (01204) 381107

Dean: Horrocks, Prof. A. Dick, BA Oxf., PhD E.Anglia
Faculty Support Manager: Michaelides, Roula, BSc Athens, MSc Sur., MSc Birm.

ACADEMIC UNITS
Arranged by Faculties

Arts, Sciences and Education
Fax: (01204) 903338

Andrews, Brid M., BEd Reading, MA Sheff. Sr. Lectr.
Ashworth, Barbara A., MDes Liv. Sr. Lectr.
Bailey, Joe, BSc Salf., MSc Manc. Sr. Lectr.
Barrow, Corrinne J., BA Liv., PhD Liv. Sr. Lectr.
Bath, Des, BA Open(UK), MEd Sheff. Principal Lectr.
Benton, Ann F., BA CNAA Sr. Lectr.
Billington, W. Frank, BEng Liv. Sr. Lectr.
Campbell, Prof. Rob J., BA Manc., PhD Manc. Principal Lectr.
Clark, Alan K. Sr. Lectr.
Cowie, Caroline, BA CNAA Sr. Lectr.
Eastham, Veronica, BA C.Lancs., MA C.Lancs. Sr. Lectr.
Eubank, Ken, BEd Manc., MSc Manc. Sr. Lectr.
Farrell, Vince, BA Manc., MA Manc. Sr. Lectr.

Fisher, Ken L., BA Open(UK), MSc Bolton IHE, MEd Brad. Sr. Lectr.
France, Terry, BA Open(UK), MEd Wales Sr. Lectr.
Glover, Prof. Jon M., BA Leeds, MPhil Leeds Subj. Group Leader
Gomoluck, Karen, BA Essex Sr. Lectr.
Goodridge, Frank, BSc Lond. Sr. Lectr.
Greenwood, Trevor F. Sr. Lectr.
Hahlo, Ken G., BA Witw., PhD Open(UK), MSocSc Sr. Lectr.
Hannavy, John, PhD Manc.Met Prof.; Subj. Group Leader
Hardman, Margaret A., BSc Sur., PhD Strath. Principal Lectr.
Hargrave, Malcolm Sr. Lectr.
Harwood, Derek, BSc Salf. Principal Lectr.
Hebenton, Christine A., BA Hull, MSc Manc. Sr. Lectr.
Hill, Nigel J., MSc Dund., PhD CNAA Sr. Lectr.
Holden-Smith, Jean M., BA Bolton IHE, MEd Bolton IHE Sr. Lectr.
Hosey, Geoff R., BSc Manc., PhD Bolton IHE Subj. Group Leader
Howell, Richard, BSc Newcastle(UK), PhD Newcastle(UK) Sr. Lectr.
Humphreys, Mike, BSc Leeds Sr. Lectr.
Kavanagh, Ann, BSc Manc.Met., MSc Edin. Sr. Lectr.
King, John M., BA Lond., MA Lanc. Sr. Lectr.
Lee, Chas W., BA Camb., PhD Lanc. Subj. Group Leader
Lofthouse, Trevor B. Sr. Lectr.
Luckin, Prof. Bill E., BA Oxf., MSc Lond. Sr. Lectr.
Mallalieu, Barbara E., BSc Bolton IHE, MSc Salf. Principal Lectr.
Martin, Chris, BSc Lond., PhD Lond. Principal Lectr.
McGhee, Patrick, MA Glas., DPhil Oxf. Subj. Group Leader
Moss, Beryl Sr. Lectr.
Nettleton, Rob J., BNurs Manc. Sr. Lectr.
Noble, Rod S., BSc Edin., PhD Edin. Sr. Lectr.
Norman, Marie, BA CNAA Sr. Lectr.
Parker, Ian, BA CNAA, PhD S'ton Prof.
Paterson, Joyce L., BA CNAA Sr. Lectr.
Phillips, Tom E., BSc Lond., MSc Nott., PhD Manc. Subj. Group Leader
Platt, Richard J., BA CNAA, MDes RCA Sr. Lectr.
Ranyard, Rob H., BSc Stir., PhD Stir. Principal Lectr.
Rigley, Mary, BSc Manc. Sr. Lectr.
Sargent, Doug Sr. Lectr.
Scott, Mark G., BSc Sheff., PhD Lanc. Principal Lectr.
Shields, Colin Sr. Lectr.
Simpson, Steve C. J., BA Camb., MA Camb., MSc Salf. Sr. Lectr.
Smith, Christopher J., BEd Manc. Sr. Lectr.
Stephenson, Pat, MSc Aston Sr. Lectr.
Stern-Gillet, Prof. Suzanne M. F., Lic Liège, PhD Liège Principal Lectr.
Tigwell, Ros E., BA Liv., MPhil Liv. Sr. Lectr.
Unsworth, Glynn, BA Open(UK) Sr. Lectr.
Unwin, Nick L., BPhil Oxf., MA Oxf., DPhil Oxf. Sr. Lectr.
Walker, Roy E., BA Exe., MEd Manc. Sr. Lectr.
Webb, Keith F., BSc Lond., MA York, MA Subj. Group Leader
Whalley, Geoff Sr. Lectr.
Whitehouse, Roger A., BA Oxf., MA Warw. Sr. Lectr.
Whittaker, Joe, BEd CNAA, MEd Manc. Sr. Lectr.
Wilkie, Neil M., BA CNAA Sr. Lectr.
Williamson, E. Janis, BA Belf., PhD Belf. Sr. Lectr.
Wood, Alan R., MEd CNAA Sr. Lectr.
Wood, D. Barry, BA Reading, MA McM., MA Essex Principal Lectr.
Wrench, David J., BA Wales, PhD Wales Principal Lectr.
Other Staff: 58 Lectrs.; 3 Res. Fellows
Research: art and design; biology and environmental studies; education, health and

community studies; humanities: history, literature and philosophy; psychology

Bolton Business School
Fax: (01204) 900516

Armistead, Derek, BSc Lond. Sr. Lectr.
Barrett, R. W., BA Manc. Sr. Lectr.
Beveridge, Mike, BSc CNAA Sr. Lectr.
Blower, John H., BEd Liv., MEd CNAA, MSc CNAA Principal Lectr.
Burkinshaw, Susan F., BA CNAA Sr. Lectr.
Connor, Joe P., BA Sheff. Sr. Lectr.
Cooke, Geoff, BA Open(UK) Sr. Lectr.
Dawes, Frank, BSc Lanc., MSc City(UK) Dir., Centre for Enterprise and Management
Dewhurst, Amanda J., BA Lond. Sr. Lectr.
Diskin, Pat J., BSc CNAA Sr. Lectr.
Elliott, Brian B. R., MA Lanc. Sr. Lectr.
Elliott, Terry P., BSc Manc. Sr. Lectr.
Eyles, David, BA Open(UK) Sr. Lectr.
Fallone, Andrew, BSc CNAA, MSc Lough. Sr. Lectr.
Ford, Margaret, BA CNAA Sr. Lectr.
Glen, John, BSc Wales, MSc Salf. Sr. Lectr.
Gosling, Julie, BSc Salf. Sr. Lectr.
Greenwood, Bob P., BA Hull, MSc Salf. Principal Lectr.
Hall, John, BSc Manc., MSc Liv., MSc Salf. Principal Lectr.
Haydock, Wes, BSc CNAA, MSc Lond. Principal Lectr.
Higson, Phil J. Sr. Lectr.
Höpfl, Prof. Heather J., BA Open(UK), PhD Lanc. Principal Lectr.
Hornby, Patricia, BA Liv., MSc Sheff. Sr. Lectr.
Joynson, Richard H., BSc Strath. Sr. Lectr.
Leigh, Margaret J., BA York(UK) Sr. Lectr.
Lowe, Mike J., MA Sheff. Sr. Lectr.
MacGregor, David I., BA CNAA, MBA C.Lancs. Sr. Lectr.
Moran, Peter J., BSc Brad., PhD Hull Sr. Lectr.
Morgan, Dan W., BA Brad. Dir., Centre for Sport and Leisure
Murphy, Roy E., BA Hull, BSc Lond. Sr. Lectr.
Narasimhan, Nash, BSc Mys., MSc Manc., BEng Sr. Lectr.
Naylor, Pat A., BA Reading, MSc Manc. Sr. Lectr.
Orchard, E. Bill, BSc Lond., MA Manc., MSc Salf. Sr. Lectr.
Scott, A. Tony, BA Birm., MSc Manc. Sr. Lectr.
Simmons, A. Barry, BSc Salf. Sr. Lectr.
Smith, Ruth, BSc Manc., MA CNAA Sr. Lectr.
Smith, Tim M., BA Lanc., MSc Salf. Sr. Lectr.
Taylor, Peter G. M., MSc Manc., FCA Sr. Lectr.
Terry, Neil W., BSc Salf. Sr. Lectr.
Turton, Shirley A., BSc Hull Sr. Lectr.
Watson, J. Ian, BEd Manc. Sr. Lectr.
Whittaker, Nick, MSc Sheff.Hallam Sr. Lectr.
Wilkinson, John K., BA Open(UK) Sr. Lectr.
Williamson, Jim B., BSc CNAA Sr. Lectr.
Woodburn, Brian A., BA CNAA, LLB Lond., MSc Salf. Principal Lectr.
Research: enterprise research (action research, applied, flexible learning, management); informatics (new technology, risk, systems environments); social organisation (critical management, ethics, geo-politics, post-modernism, sexuality)

Education, see Arts, Scis. and Educn.

Sciences, see Arts, Scis. and Educn.

Technology
Fax: 01204 381107

Adamson, Mark, BSc City(UK) Sr. Lectr.
Anand, Prof. Subash C., BSc Punjabi, MSc Manc., PhD Manc. Principal Lectr.; Fac. Dir. of Res.
Aykroyd, Les, BA Brad., MSc CNAA Sr. Lectr.
Bateson, David R., BSc Salf. Sr. Lectr.
Beddard, J. Dave S., BSc Manc., MSc Manc. Sr. Lectr.
Binkley, John P., BSc CNAA, PhD CNAA Sr. Lectr.
Bullman, Peter J. M., BA Camb. Principal Lectr.
Busby, Keith P., BA Brad. Subj. Group Leader

Cherry, Dave J., BA Open(UK), MSc Cran.IT   Sr. Lectr.

Chirwa, E. Clive, BSc Zambia, MSc Cran.IT, MSc Volgograd, PhD Cran.   Principal Lectr.

Chittenden, Andrew M., BSc Manc., PhD UMIST   Sr. Lectr.

Clough, Brian A., BA CNAA   Sr. Lectr.

Coleman, Julian, BEng Wales, MSc Wales   Sr. Lectr.

Convey, Harold J., BTech Brun.   Principal Lectr.

Cornthwaite, Alan   Subj. Group Leader

Cowey, Derek, BSc CNAA, MSc Strath.   Sr. Lectr.

Cropper, A. Ernie, BSc Leeds, MPhil Leeds   Sr. Lectr.

Dodds, Dennis, BSc Salf., MSc Salf., PhD Salf.   Principal Lectr.

Duncan, Malcolm, BSc Bolton IHE   Sr. Lectr.

Eggleton, Robert, BSc Leeds   Sr. Lectr.

England, Jim, BEng Liv.   Sr. Lectr.

Fairbank, Richard, BSc Manc.   Principal Lectr.

Fairclough, Phil H., BSc CNAA   Sr. Lectr.

Farrell, Peter   Sr. Lectr.

Garrison, Phil M., BSc Birm.   Sr. Lectr.

Greenhalgh, John, BSc CNAA, MSc CNAA   Sr. Lectr.

Halfpenney, J. Ray, BEd Lanc.   Sr. Lectr.

Hall, Michael A., BSc CNAA, MSc Salf.   Sr. Lectr.

Hall, Mike E., BSc Manc., MSc Manc., PhD Manc.   Sr. Lectr.

Hartley, Andrew J., BSc Manc., MSc Salf., PhD Manc.   Subj. Group Leader

Henderson, Brian, BSc CNAA   Sr. Lectr.

Hill, Dave J., BA Brad., MSc Manc.   Principal Lectr.

Holland, Dennis A., BSc Salf.   Sr. Lectr.

Holmes, Dave A., BSc Brad., PhD Brad.   Sr. Lectr.

Holmes, Keith, BSc Leeds, MSc Leeds, PhD Leeds   Principal Lectr.

Howarth, Bill   Sr. Lectr.

Howarth, Michael, BSc CNAA   Sr. Lectr.

Jackson, Roger G., BSc Manc., PhD UMIST   Sr. Lectr.

Jamson, Steve, BSc Leeds   Sr. Lectr.

Jenkins, J. Andrew, BSc Salf.   Sr. Lectr.

Lloyd, Norman J., BSc Manc., MSc Manc.   Sr. Lectr.

Marks, Peter I., BSc Portsmouth, FRICS   Sr. Lectr.

Martin, Peter, BSc Wales, MSc Salf.   Sr. Lectr.

Matthews, Steve A., BSc Bolton IHE, MSc Salf.   Sr. Lectr.

McMahon, Paul H., BSc CNAA, PhD CNAA   Sr. Lectr.

McMahon, Steve W.   Sr. Lectr.

Minta, Chris H., BA Open(UK), MBA Open(UK)   Sr. Lectr.

Miraftab, Mohsen, BSc Manc., MSc Manc., PhD UMIST   Sr. Lectr.

Muskett, John H., BEng Liv.   Principal Lectr.

Myler, Peter, BSc CNAA, MSc Manc., PhD UMIST   Subj. Group Leader

Nedwell, J. Claire, BSc Brad.   Sr. Lectr.

Nwagboso, Chris, MSc Aston, MSc CNAA, PhD Salf.   Sr. Lectr.

Olubodun, Olufemi F., BSc Ife., MSc Ife.   Sr. Lectr.

Ormerod, Jeff, BSc Salf.   Principal Lectr.

Over, Victor G., BSc Manc., MSc Durh., FGS   Sr. Lectr.

Palin, David J., BSc Leeds, MSc Lond.   Sr. Lectr.

Patel, Zubair, BEng CNAA, BSc Bolton IHE   Sr. Lectr.

Pederson, Brian, BA CNAA   Sr. Lectr.

Pickering, John R., BSc Leeds   Sr. Lectr.

Quinn, Tony, MSc Lough   Principal Lectr.

Reveley, Ian G., BTech Manc., MSc Essex   Sr. Lectr.

Richards, Andy F., BSc Lond., PhD Lond.   Principal Lectr.

Riley, Michael J., BSc Brad.   Sr. Lectr.

Rowe, Trevor, BTech Brad.   Sr. Lectr.

Sarsby, Prof. Bob W., BSc Manc., MSc Manc., PhD Manc., FICE   Reader

Seal, David R., BSc Lond.   Sr. Lectr.

Seeds, Roger, BSc CNAA   Sr. Lectr.

Sinclair, Martin, BSc Manc.   Sr. Lectr.

Sullivan, Richard, BSc CNAA   Sr. Lectr.

Tonge, Andrew D., BSc Bolton IHE, MSc Manc.   Sr. Lectr.

Ward, Tim, BSc Wales   Sr. Lectr.

Waters, Barbara, BA CNAA, MSc Salf.   Sr. Lectr.

Yates, Philip   Sr. Lectr.

Other Staff: 15 Lectrs.; 7 Res. Fellows

Research: automobile electronics; engineering materials; environmental engineering; microelectronics; textile materials and processes

CONTACT OFFICERS

Academic affairs. Head of Academic Affairs: Birkett, Paul E., BA Lond., PhD CNAA

Accommodation. Residential Services Manager: Burgess, Sara E.

Alumni. Head of Marketing and Public Relations: Hughes-Jones, Heather, BA Manc., MPhil Lond.

Careers. Senior Careers Advisor: James, M. Ann

Computing services. Head of Learning Support Services (Academic Computer Services): Scholefield, Alan J., BSc Lond., PhD Sheff.

Consultancy services. Dean of Technology: Horrocks, Prof. A. Dick, BA Oxf., PhD E.Anglia

Credit transfer. CATS/Quality Audit Co-ordinator: Birkett, Paul E., BA Lond., PhD CNAA

Development/fund-raising. Vice-Principal: Gardner, Wilf, BSc Newcastle(UK)

Equal opportunities. Associate Dean, Faculty of Arts, Sciences and Education: Killen, Tom, BA Wales, MEd Manc.

Estates and buildings/works and services. Property Services Manager: Stevens, David, BA Open(UK)

Examinations. Head of Academic Affairs: Birkett, Paul E., BA Lond., PhD CNAA

Finance. Head of Finance and Clerk to the Governors: Hubbard, Colin F., BA Manc.

General enquiries. Assistant to the Principal: Clarke, Ged, BA Tees.

Industrial liaison. Dean of Technology: Horrocks, Prof. A. Dick, BA Oxf., PhD E.Anglia

International office. Head of International Office: Fishwick, David

Library (chief librarian). Head of Learning Support Services (Library, Media and Communications Skills): Scholefield, Alan J., BSc Lond., PhD Sheff.

Personnel/human resources. Head of Human Resources: Cain, Bruce W., BA Sheff.

Public relations, information and marketing. Head of Marketing and Public Relations: Hughes-Jones, Heather, BA Manc., MPhil Lond.

Publications. Head of Learning Support Services (Library, Media and Communications Skills): Scholefield, Alan J., BSc Lond., PhD Sheff.

Purchasing. Purchasing Manager: Bullough, Mike

Quality assurance and accreditation. Head of Academic Affairs: Birkett, Paul E., BA Lond., PhD CNAA

Research. Director of Faculty Research: Anand, Prof. Subash, BSc Punjabi, MSc Manc., PhD Manc.

Safety. Health and Safety Adviser: Jenkins, Frank R.

Scholarships, awards, loans. Registrar: Kingsbury, Paul A., BA Liv.

Schools liaison. Schools and Colleges Liaison Officer: Davey, Earl R. K., BA CNAA,

Security. Campus Services Manager: Heydon, Wendy A.

Sport and recreation. Director, Centre for Sport and Leisure: Morgan, Dan W., BA Brad.

Staff development and training. Staff Development Officer: Harris, Richard J., BSc Lond., MA Lanc.

Student welfare/counselling. Head of Student Services: Parker, Mike J., BSc Sheff., PhD Sheff.

Students with disabilities. Information Officer: Anthony, Denise M., BA Hull

[Information supplied by the institution as at 3 March 1998, and edited by the ACU]

BOURNEMOUTH UNIVERSITY

Founded 1992; previously established as Bournemouth Polytechnic, 1990

Member of the Association of Commonwealth Universities

Postal Address: Talbot Campus, Fern Barrow, Poole, Dorset, England BH12 5BB
Telephone: (01202) 524111 **Fax**: (01202) 513293 **E-mail**: Postmaster@Bournemouth.ac.uk
WWW: http://www.bournemouth.ac.uk **E-mail formula**: initialsurname@bournemouth.ac.uk

CHANCELLOR—Cox, Baroness C. A., of Queensbury
PRO VICE-CHANCELLOR—Higginson, Sir Gordon, BSc Leeds, PhD Leeds, FEng
VICE-CHANCELLOR*—Slater, Prof. Gillian L., BA Oxf., MSc Oxf., MA Oxf., DPhil Oxf., FIMA
PRO VICE-CHANCELLOR (FINANCE AND CORPORATE DEVELOPMENT)—Conder, Prof. Richard, BA Hull, MSc Bath
PRO VICE-CHANCELLOR (ACADEMIC)—Light, Prof. Paul, BA Camb., MA Nott., MA Camb., PhD Camb.
DIRECTOR OF HUMAN RESOURCES—Riordan, M. G., BA N.U.I., BD Maynooth
REGISTRAR AND CLERK TO THE UNIVERSITY BOARD‡—Richardson, Noel D. G., BA Trinity(Dub.)

FACULTIES/SCHOOLS

Business, School of
Fax: (01202) 595036
Head: Jones, Prof. O. D., BSc Leic.
Secretary: Eccleston, N.

Conservation Sciences, School of
Fax: (01202) 595255
Head: Brown, Prof. B. J. H., BSc Lond., PhD Bath
Secretary: Drew, L.

Design, Engineering and Computing, School of
Tel: (01202) 595078 Fax: (01202) 595314
Head: Knight, D., MSc Lond.
Secretary: Copper, D.

Finance and Law, School of
Tel: (01202) 595187 Fax: (01202) 595261
Head: Grief, Prof. N., BA PhD
Secretary: Mussell, S.

Health and Community Studies, Institute of
Tel: (01202) 504319 Fax: (01202) 504326
Head: Nattrass, H., BA
Secretary: Commings, J.

Media Arts and Communication, Institute of
Fax: (01202) 595530
Acting Head: Howard, D.
Secretary: Rose, S.

Service Industries, School of
Tel: (01202) 590017 Fax: (01202) 595562
Head: Jones, Prof. P. A., BSc Sur., MPhil Sur.
Secretary: Treen, D.

ACADEMIC UNITS

Accounting and Finance
Tel: (01202) 595187 Fax: (01202) 595261
Allerston, A., BA Bourne., MSc S'ton. Sr. Lectr.
Bollen, D. G., BA Open(UK) Sr. Lectr.
Bolt, T., BA Sr. Lectr.
Broad, M. J., BA Bourne. Sr. Lectr.
Cornes, D. M., MSc S'ton. Sr. Lectr.
Davies, F. L. G., BA Keele, MSc Stir. Sr. Lectr.
Day, R. G., MSc Lond., MPhil Sr. Lectr.
Fitz-John, P., MBA Cran.IT Principal Lectr.
Hardwick, P., BA York(UK), MA Qu., PhD S'ton. Prof., Financial Services
Hatch, M. D., BSc Liv. Principal Lectr.
Howell, K., BSc Wales Sr. Lectr.
Jones, M., BA Warw. Sr. Lectr.
Langmead, J., BA Essex, MA S'ton., MSc S'ton. Sr. Lectr.
Little, J., BSc Liv. Sr. Lectr.
Marshall, D. M., MBA S'ton. Sr. Lectr.
Maughan, W., BA NZ, MSc PhD Sr. Lectr.
McElroy, T. J., BA Manc., MSc Lond. Head of Dept.*
Miller, A. M., BA Lanc. Sr. Lectr.

Molson, K. Sr. Lectr.
Navare, MBA Principal Lectr.
Newall, J. A., BA CNAA, MSc Lond., MSc Wis. Principal Lectr.
Porter, E. L. E., BA CNAA, MSc Stir. Sr. Lectr.
Sayles, B., BA Durh. Sr. Lectr.
Segal, A., BSc Lond., MA Sr. Lectr.
Short, T. E., MBA City(UK), FCA Principal Lectr.
Songi, M., BA Camb., MA Camb. Sr. Lectr.
Trevett, D. S., BSc Warw., MA Bourne. Sr. Lectr.
Wells, D. H., BA Newcastle(UK), MA CNAA Sr. Lectr.

Communication and Marketing
Tel: (01202) 595026 Fax: (01202) 595530
Bradshaw, D. C., MA Oxf. Sr. Lectr.
Brown, R., MSc Nott. Sr. Lectr.
Campbell, Angela M., PhD Ohio State Head*
Cownie, Fiona J., BA Reading Sr. Lectr.
Daymon, Christine, MBA Kent Sr. Lectr.
Dermody, J., BA Lond., PhD Brist. Sr. Lectr.
Ellis, J. C. P., BA Camb., MA Birm. Prof.
Giddings, R. L., MLitt Brist., PhD Keele Reader
McManus, T., BSc City(UK), MA Brun. Sr. Lectr.
Milton, P., MA Camb. Sr. Lectr.
Moloney, K., BSc Lond. Principal Lectr.
Murtha, M., MPhil Lond. Principal Lectr.
Noble, P., BSc Brist. Sr. Lectr.
O'Brien, K. M. Sr. Lectr.
Platt, Carole, BSc Lanc. Sr. Lectr.
Povey, M. L., MA Lanc., MSt Oxf. Sr. Lectr.
Wylie, S. E. Sr. Lectr.

Computer Animation
Tel: (01202) 595026 Fax: (01202) 595530
Bell, S., BA CNAA, PhD Lough. Sr. Lectr.
Cominos, Prof. P., PhD CNAA Head*
Hardie, P. F. Principal Lectr.
King, A. J., MPhil CNAA Sr. Lectr.
Rudge, A. P., BA CNAA, MA RCA Sr. Lectr.
Scanlan, L. Principal Lectr.

Computing
Tel: (01202) 595078 Fax: (01202) 595314
Bale, D. W., BSc Lond. Sr. Lectr.
Bray, I. K., BA Open(UK) Sr. Lectr.
Chapman, Sally C., BSc Leeds Sr. Lectr.
Cooper, R. G., BSc Reading, PhD Hull Sr. Lectr.
Craven, J., BA Portsmouth, MSc Brun. Principal Lectr.
Hole, Linda S., BEd Brist., DPhil Sus. Sr. Lectr.
Hukins, G. N., MA Lond., MSc CNAA Sr. Lectr.
Hurne, Janice C., BSc Wales, MSc CNAA Sr. Lectr.
Jones, M., BSc CNAA, MSc Warw. Principal Lectr.
Lefley, M., BSc Leic., MSc Newcastle(UK), PhD CNAA Sr. Lectr.
Machura, M., MSc PhD Sr. Lectr.
Main, A. Principal Lectr.
Milsom, F. D., DPhil Sus., BSc Sr. Lectr.
Muir, J., MA Lond., MA S'ton., MSc City(UK) Sr. Lectr.
Rolfe, R. W., PhD Kent Sr. Lectr.

Sahandi, M. R., MSc Brad., PhD Brad., BSc Principal Lectr.
Shepperd, M. J., BA Exe., MSc Aston, PhD Open(UK) Prof.
Webster, S., MSc CNAA Sr. Lectr.
Wilson, J. V., BSc Lond., MA Sus., MSc Leic. Sr. Lectr.

Conservation Science
Tel: (01202) 595516 Fax: (01202) 595255
Andrews, K., BSc Sheff., MA Brad., PhD Sheff.
Astin, B., BSc Bath, PhD Brist.
Barker, K. M., BA Birm., MA Lond. Sr. Lectr.
Beavis, J., BSc Open(UK), MSc Reading, PhD Reading Reader
Brisbane, M. A., BA S'ton., FSA Reader
Brown, Prof. B. J. H., BSc Lond., PhD Bath Head of Sch.*
Cox, M., BA CNAA, BA Open(UK), PhD Lond. Sr. Lectr.
Darvill, J., PhD S'ton. Prof., Archaeology
Fox, J. H., BSc Leeds Sr. Lectr.
Gale, J., BA Nott.
Heeps, C., PhD CNAA Sr. Lectr.
Hill, R., BSc Lond., MA Qld.
Induni, B. Sr. Lectr.
James, B., BSc Bourne.
Kneller, P., MPhil CNAA
Maltby, J. M., BA Sheff., MA Sheff. Sr. Lectr.
May, V. J., BA S'ton., MSc S'ton., FRMetS Prof.
Merrington, G., BSc Lond., PhD Lond.
Morris, Patricia A., BA Manc., MA Wales Sr. Lectr.
Russell, M., BA Lond.
Ryan, C., BSc Leic., MA Manc. Sr. Lectr.
Schofield, D. J. Sr. Lectr.
Shah, A., BSc Sheff., MSc Napier
Smith, H., BSc Sheff., PhD Sheff.
Winder, L., BSc S'ton., PhD S'ton. Course Leader
Wood, C., BSc Lond., PhD Leic.

Electronics
Tel: (01202) 595078 Fax: (01202) 595314
Benyon-Tinker, G., BA Camb., MSc Sus., DPhil Sus. Sr. Lectr.
Boucouvalas, A. C., BSc Newcastle(UK), MSc Lond., PhD Lond. Reader
Claremont, D., BSc Lond., MSc Strath., DPhil Sus. Principal Lectr.
Doody, Claire, BSc Nott., MSc Aberd. Sr. Lectr.
Eadie, D. W., BSc Glas. Sr. Lectr.
Murphy, C. J., BSc CNAA Sr. Lectr.
Roach, J. P., MSc Wales Head*
Sanderson, J. G., BSc Wales Sr. Lectr.
Teal, M. K., BSc Birm., MSc Lond. Sr. Lectr.
Veness, P. J. Sr. Lectr.
Webber, K., MSc City(UK) Principal Lectr.

Finance, see Acctg. and Finance

Food and Hospitality Management
Tel: (01202) 595017 Fax: (01202) 595562
Adams, Debra, BSc Sr. Lectr.
Alder, H., BSc Sur. Head*
Allen, R., BA Reading, MA Leeds Sr. Lectr.
Anderton, R., BA Kent, MA CNAA Sr. Lectr.

Boer, A., BA Hudd., MBA Brun. Sr. Lectr.
Braham, B. R. Sr. Lectr.
Calver, S., BSc Sur., MBA City(UK) Principal Lectr.
Conlan, M. N., BA Glas. Sr. Lectr.
Creed, P. G., BSc Manc. Sr. Lectr.
Cullis, A., MBA Bourne. Sr. Lectr.
Cuthbertson, R. W., BSc Lanc. Sr. Lectr.
Edwards, Prof. J. S., PhD Sur. Sr. Lectr.
Ferrone, L. R., BA Open(UK) Sr. Lectr.
Hall, C. A., MA Sus. Principal Lectr.
Hayman, K. G., BA Leeds Sr. Lectr.
Hudson, P., BSc Brist. Sr. Lectr.
McSavage, J., BSc Glas., MSc Salf., MSc S'ton. Sr. Lectr.
Pierson, B. J., MSc Reading, PhD Lond. Reader
Randall, Linda M., BSc Sr. Lectr.
Reeve, W. G., BA Open(UK) Sr. Lectr.
Schafheitle, J., MPhil Bourne. Sr. Lectr.
Senior, I., MBA Strath. Sr. Lectr.; Dir. of Studies
Symonds, C., BSc Lond., MPhil Lond. Sr. Lectr.

Health and Community Studies Research
Tel: (01202) 504319 Fax: (01202) 504326
Coles, C., BSc Leic., MA Sus., DPhil S'ton. Prof.
Holloway, I. M., BEd Lond., PhD Lond. Reader
Thomas, P. Reader

Human Resource Management
Tel: (01202) 504214 Fax: (01202) 298321
Donnelly, E., MA Thames V., MSc Lond. Sr. Lectr.
Eldridge, J. A., BA Wales Sr. Lectr.
Kiely, Julia, BSc Ulster, PhD Aston Reader
Leathes, R. de M., MA Camb., MSc Lond. Principal Lectr.
Marsden, Lynn, BA Open(UK), PhD S'ton. Sr. Lectr.
Orpen, C., BA Rhodes, BA Natal, PhD Cape Town Reader
Preget, L., BA PhD Sr. Lectr.
Prescott, Jean M., BSc Birm., MSc Salf., PhD S'ton. Sr. Lectr.
Shiel, Christine, BA Dir. of Studies*

Information Systems
Tel: (01202) 595413 Fax: (01202) 595151
Atkinson, R. W., MPhil Sr. Lectr.
Bobeva, M. V., MSc Sofia, MSc Leeds Sr. Lectr.
Butterfield, H. Sr. Lectr.
Day, J., BSc Lough., MBA Hull Sr. Lectr.
Hennell, Cheryl D., MSc Kingston(UK) Sr. Lectr.
Hollocks, Prof. B. W., PhD S'ton. Sr. Lectr.
Roushan, G., MBA Strath. Sr. Lectr.
Sanders, S., BA Keele, MSc Kingston(UK) Sr. Lectr.
Tansey, S. D., BA Exe., MSc Lond., MSc City(UK), MPhil Bath Sr. Lectr.
Wateridge, J. V., BA Manc., PhD Brun. Sr. Lectr.

International Communication
Tel: (01202) 595330 Fax: (01202) 595224
Beetham, W., BA
Carter, R. J., BA Lond. Sr. Lectr.
Geoghegan, C., MA Keele, DèsL Picardie, BA Principal Lectr.
Lewis, H. M. A., LèsL Paris, MA Edin. Principal Lectr.
Ridolfo, Mark
Rios de Garcia, Carmen, LicFil&Lett MA
Robinson, Jane, BA
Southam, J., BSc MA
Woodhall, M., BA Brist., MA Birm. Head*

Law
Tel: (01202) 595187 Fax: (01202) 595261
Astbury, N. S., BA Durh. Sr. Lectr.
Boxer, N. M. Sr. Lectr.
Cavill, K. H., LLB S'ton., LLM S'ton. Sr. Lectr.
Copp, S. E., LLB Exe. Sr. Lectr.
Dilley, R. K., LLB S'ton. Sr. Lectr.
Dowding, D., LLM Lond. Principal Lectr.
Hunter, M., QC Visiting Prof.
Kaistha, S., LLB Nott. Sr. Lectr.

Letza, S., MSc Manc., PhD Brad. ICSA Prof., Corporate Governance
McGuinness, K. P., BA Windsor, MA Tor., DJur Tor. Steele Raymond Prof.
Mitchell, K., LLB Lond.
Mytton, E. A., BA Bourne., BA CNAA, LLM S'ton. Sr. Lectr.
Nasser, S., BSc Sus., MA Sus., MA CNAA, LLM Camb., MBA Bourne. Dir. of Studies
Paine, J., BA Sheff. Sr. Lectr.
Palka, K., BA Sus. Sr. Lectr.
Riley, J., BA Camb., MA Sr. Lectr.
Soetendrop, R., BA CNAA, LLM S'ton. Head*
Vigor, Julie A., BA Leic., LLM S'ton. Sr. Lectr.
Walsh, P. D., LLB Lond. Sr. Lectr.
Weston, S., BA Kingston(UK), LLM Leic. Sr. Lectr.

Marketing, see Communicn. and Marketing

Media Production
Tel: (01202) 595026 Fax: (01202) 595530
Auckland, J., BA CNAA, MSc Wales Sr. Lectr.
Deutsch, Prof. S. F., BMus S.Methodist, MA Calif. Principal Lectr.
Foster, J. Principal Lectr.
Hanson, D. M., BA S'ton. Sr. Lectr.
Hurmusiadis, V., MA Bourne. Sr. Lectr.
Legge, P. W., BA Witw., BA S.Af. Principal Lectr.
Lush, D. R., BSc Kingston(UK) Sr. Lectr.
Murray, R. S., BA Sheff. Sr. Lectr.
Parsons, M. G., MPhil Leic. Sr. Lectr.
Richards, N., BA Oxf. Sr. Lectr.
Vince, J. Prof.
Wallace, S., BA Sr. Lectr.
Wensley, C. J., MA Exe. Head*
Zhang, J. J., BSc MSc PhD Sr. Lectr.

Nursing and Midwifery
Tel: (01202) 504319 Fax: (01202) 504326
Andrewes, C., BSc Lond. Co-ordinator
Barr, W. A., BSc Glas., PhD Glas. Co-ordinator
Benbow, W., BA Open(UK), MSc S.Bank Sr. Lectr.
Burrows, E., BEd CNAA, MPhil Bourne. Sr. Lectr.
Carr, E., BSc Sur., MSc Lond. Sr. Lectr.
Dowding, Christine, MSc S'ton. Sr. Lectr.
Edwards, B., BSc Bourne. Sr. Lectr.
Galvin, Kate, BSc Res. Co-ordinator
Gosby, Janice, MEd S'ton. Co-ordinator
Graham, Iain W. Head*
Hall, K., BSc Ulster Sr. Lectr.
Halliday, L., BA Open(UK) Sr. Lectr.
Halliwell, D., BSc Bourne. Sr. Lectr.
Harrison, M. S. Co-ordinator
Jones, J., BA Open(UK), MSc Manc., PhD S'ton. Sr. Lectr.
Lewis, P. A., BSc MSc Co-ordinator
Matthews, C., MSc S'ton. Sr. Lectr.
Mercer, A., BSc Brist., MA Sr. Lectr.
Ratcliffe, B., BSc CNAA, MSc Sr. Lectr.
Scammell, J., BA Open(UK), MSc Sr. Lectr.
Todres, L. A., BSocSc MSocSc PhD Sr. Lectr.
Townes, J. M., MA Lond. Sr. Lectr.
Wheeler, Stephanie J., BSc CNAA Sr. Lectr.
Willis, S., BA Open(UK) Sr. Lectr.

Product Design and Manufacture
Tel: (01202) 595078 Fax: (01202) 595314
Edwards, P., MSc Lond. Sr. Lectr.
Hills, Judi D., BA CNAA, MSc Cran.IT Sr. Lectr.
Hills, N. M., BSc CNAA Sr. Lectr.
Hogarth, P., BTech Lough. Prof., Design, Engineering and Computing
Humphries, T. M. B., BSc Lond., MPhil Sur. Sr. Lectr.
Rodgers, A. M. Sr. Lectr.
Roe, T. M., BA CNAA, MDes RCA Sr. Lectr.
Saidpour, S. H., BSc CNAA, PhD Lough. Sr. Lectr.
Tabeshfar, K., PhD S'ton. Head*
Wilson, A., BSc Lond., MSc Exe., MSc Cran.IT Principal Lectr.

Psychology, Applied
Tel: (01202) 595078 Fax: (01202) 595314
Burns, R., BSc Edin. Principal Lectr.
Cowley, C. K., BA Wales Sr. Lectr.
Griffin, G. F., BA Birm., MSc Warw. Head*
Hallam, J., BSc Brad., PhD Aston Principal Lectr.
Taylor, J., BSc Portsmouth, PhD Portsmouth Sr. Lectr.

Social Work and Community Studies
Tel: (01202) 504319 Fax: (01202) 504326
Brimble, M. J., BSc Brist., MSc S'ton., PhD Wales Sr. Lectr.
Brown, K. L., BSc Lond., MSc Lond. Sr. Lectr.
Hume, Susan V., MA Brun. Head*
White, R., BSc Lond., MA Brun. Sr. Lectr.

Strategic Management
Tel: (01202) 595078 Fax: (01202) 595314
Armistead, Prof. C. G., BSc Manc., PhD Manc. Head*
Blee, M. A., MBA Bourne Sr. Lectr.
Ellis, J. M., MBA Sheff., PhD Manc. Principal Lectr.
Feeney, J. A., MBA Cran.IT, PhD Sheff. Principal Lectr.
Gill, J. D., BA Sheff. Sr. Lectr.
Harvey, Christine L., MBA Bath, BSc Sr. Lectr.
Jay, T. Sr. Lectr.
Johnsen, Rhona, BA Strath. Sr. Lectr.
Marsden, A. G. Principal Lectr.
Nwabueze, Uche, PhD Sheff. Sr. Lectr.
Smales, B. J., BA Manc., BSc Lond., MA Reading Sr. Lectr.

Tourism and Retail Management
Tel: (01202) 595017 Fax: (01202) 595562
Beer, S. C., BSc Reading Sr. Lectr.
Brooks, C. L., BSc Lond., PhD Edin. Sr. Lectr.
Cooper, C., BSc Lond., PhD Lond. Dir. of Res.
Edwards, J. R., BSc Aston, MSc Birm., PhD CNAA Reader
Freeth, N. C. J., BA Open(UK), MPhil Sur. Sr. Lectr.
Gush, Jacqueline, BA Manc. Sr. Lectr.
Harris, Christine M., MSc Lough. Sr. Lectr.
Jackson, C., BA Staffs., MSc Lough. Sr. Lectr.
Jolley, A. I., BA CNAA Sr. Lectr.
Ladkin, A., BA Leic., MSc Sur.
Lawson, F., MSc Salf., PhD Sur.
Linzer, D. J. Sr. Lectr.
McIntyre, C. M., BSc Glas. Project Leader
Morgan, M., BA Liv., BPhil Liv. Sr. Lectr.
Robbins, D. K., BSc CNAA, MSc CNAA Sr. Lectr.
Vaughan, D. R., BSc Hull, MSc Bath, PhD Edin. Principal Lectr.
Wanhill, S., BA Wales, PhD Wales Travelbag Prof., Tourism
Westlake, J., BSc Lond., MSc Lond. Dir. of Continuing Educn. and Devel.
Wilkes, K. R., BA Wales, PhD Liv. Head*
Other Staff: 1 Res. Fellow

CONTACT OFFICERS
Academic affairs. Head of Academic Services: Jones, O. D., BA CNAA, PhD CNAA
Accommodation. Accommodation Officer: Marshall, J.
Admissions (first degree). Deputy Registrar: Gutierrez, A.
Admissions (higher degree). Deputy Registrar: Gutierrez, A.
Adult/continuing education. Deputy Registrar: Gutierrez, A.
Alumni. Head of Marketing Services: Cretton, L.
Archives. Deputy Registrar: Gutierrez, A.
Careers. Learner Support Unit: Brooke, P.
Computing services. Head of Computer Centre: Hall, C. J., DPhil Sus.
Consultancy services. Head of Marketing Services: Cretton, L.
Development/fund-raising. Head of Marketing Services: Cretton, L.

Equal opportunities. Personnel Officer: Watts, B. J., BA *CNAA*

Estates and buildings/works and services. Head of Estates Group: Kirkwood, D., BSc

Examinations. Examinations Officer: Forbes, G., BA *Reading*

Finance. Head of Accounting Services: Allan, R., MA *Oxf.*

General enquiries. Registrar and Clerk to the University Board: Richardson, Noel D. G., BA *Trinity(Dub.)*

Industrial liaison. Director of Human Resources: Riordan, M. R., BA *N.U.I.*, BD *Maynooth*

International office. Parsons, L.

Library (chief librarian). Head of Library and Information Services: Ball, D. J. T.

Minorities/disadvantaged groups. Lilley, J.

Personnel/human resources. Director of Human Resources: Riordan, M. R., BA *N.U.I.*, BD *Maynooth*

Public relations, information and marketing. Head of Marketing Services: Cretton, L.

Publications. Registrar and Clerk to the University Board: Richardson, Noel D. G., BA *Trinity(Dub.)*

Purchasing. Purchasing Manager: Lifford, D.

Quality assurance and accreditation. Head of Academic Programmes: Hunt, A. M., BA *Birm.*

Research. Head of Research: Light, Prof. P., BA *Camb.*, MA *Nott.*, PhD *Camb.*

Safety. Head of Estates Group: Kirkwood, D., BSc

Scholarships, awards, loans. Deputy Registrar: Gutierrez, A.

Schools liaison. Head of Marketing Services: Cretton, L.

Security. Head of Estates Group: Kirkwood, D., BSc

Sport and recreation. Head of Sport: Dower, D.

Staff development and training. Personnel Officer: Watts, B. J., BA *CNAA*

Student union. General Manager, Student Union: James, A.

Student welfare/counselling. Head of Counselling: ......

Students from other countries. Deputy Registrar: Gutierrez, A.

Students with disabilities. Deputy Registrar: Gutierrez, A.

[*Information supplied by the institution as at 17 June 1998, and edited by the ACU*]

UNIVERSITY OF BRADFORD

Founded 1966; originally established as Bradford Technical College in 1882

Member of the Association of Commonwealth Universities

Postal Address: Richmond Road, Bradford, West Yorkshire, England BD7 1DP
Telephone: (01274) 232323 **Fax**: (01274) 305340 **Telex**: 896827 TACS G **WWW**: http://www.brad.ac.uk
E-mail formula: initials.surname@bradford.ac.uk

CHANCELLOR—Lockwood of Dewsbury, The Baroness, Hon. LLD *Strath.*, Hon. DLitt
PRO-CHANCELLOR—Ashdown, Tom W. G., MSc *Leeds*, FTI
PRO-CHANCELLOR—Jerome, Alan H., MA *Camb.*
VICE-CHANCELLOR AND PRINCIPAL*—Bell, Prof. Colin R., BA *Keele*, MScEcon *Wales*, FRSEd
DEPUTY VICE-CHANCELLOR—Costall, Prof. Brenda, BPharm PhD DSc
PRO-VICE-CHANCELLOR—Green, Prof. John N., MA *Camb.*, DPhil *York(UK)*
PRO-VICE-CHANCELLOR—Mellors, Prof. Colin, MA *Sheff.*, PhD
REGISTRAR AND SECRETARY‡—Andrew, Nick J., BA *Camb.*
LIBRARIAN—Stevenson, Malcolm B., BSc *Leeds*, MA *Lond.*, PhD *Leeds*

FACULTIES/SCHOOLS

Engineering and Physical Sciences
Dean: Gardiner, Prof. John G., MSc *Birm.*, PhD *Birm.*

Health and Environmental Sciences
Dean: Alderson, Prof. Grace, PhD *Newcastle(UK)*

Social Sciences and Humanities
Dean: Waton, Alan, BA *Sus.*

ACADEMIC UNITS

Accounting, see Management Centre

Archaeological Sciences
Tel: (01274) 233559 Fax: (01274) 235190
Heron, C., BTech *Wales*, PhD *Wales* Sr. Lectr.
Jones, Rick F. J., BA *Manc.*, PhD *Lond.*, FSA Reader
O'Connor, Terence P., BSc *Lond.*, PhD *Lond.* Sr. Lectr.
Pollard, A. Mark, BA *York(UK)*, DPhil *York(UK)* Prof.; Head*
Roberts, Charlotte, BA *Leic.*, MA *Sheff.*, PhD *Sheff.* Sr. Lectr.

Biomedical Sciences
Tel: (01274) 235520 Fax: (01274) 309742
Alderson, Grace, PhD *Newcastle(UK)* Prof.
Baker, Terry G., BSc *Wales*, PhD *Birm.*, DSc *Edin.*, FRSEd, FIBiol Prof.; Head*

Gardner, Michael L. G., PhD *Edin.*, DSc *Edin.*, FIBiol Prof.
Randall, Valerie A., BSc *Sheff.*, PhD *Sheff.* Sr. Lectr.
Schallreuter, Karin, PhD *Hamburg*, MD Prof.
Wood, John M., BSc *Leeds*, PhD *Leeds* Prof.

Clinical Oncology Unit
Tel: (01274) 233226
Bibby, Michael C., MSc *Wales*, PhD Reader
Double, John A., BTech *Brun.*, PhD *Lond.*, DSc *Lond.* Prof.; Sci. Co-Dir.*

Computing
Tel: (01274) 233 9925 Fax: (01274) 233920
Kouvatsos, Demetres D., BSc *Athens*, MSc *Manc.*, PhD *Manc.* Reader
Torsun, Imad S., BSc *Manc.*, MTech *Manc.*, PhD *Manc.* Prof.; Head*

Development and Project Planning Centre
Tel: (01274) 233975 Fax: (01274) 235280
Anacoui, Farhad, BSc *Teheran*, MA *Lanc.*, PhD *Cran.*
Cusworth, John W., BSc *Wales*, MA *Leeds* Sr. Lectr.; Head*
Dennis, Carolyne J., BSc *Lond.*, BPhil *York(UK)*, PhD *Birm.* Sr. Lectr.
Franks, Thomas R., BA *Camb.*, MA *Camb.* Sr. Lectr.
Tribe, Michael A., BA *Sheff.*, MA *E.Af.*, PhD *Brad.*

Weiss, John, MA *Camb.*, DPhil *Sus.* Prof.
Wilson, Frank A., BSc *Leeds*, MPhil *Leeds*, PhD Sr. Lectr.

Economics, see Management Centre, and Soc. and Econ. Studies

Engineering, Chemical
Tel: (01274) 233678 Fax: (01274) 235700
Bailes, Phil J., BSc *Newcastle(UK)*, PhD *Newcastle(UK)*, FIChemE Reader; Head*
Benkreira, Hadj, BTech MSc PhD Sr. Lectr.
Bickley, Roger I., BSc *Exe.*, PhD *Exe.* Sr. Lectr., Physical Chemistry
Edwards, Howell G. M., BSc *Oxf.*, MA *Oxf.*, DPhil *Oxf.* Prof., Structural Chemistry
Godfrey, Jim C., BEng *Adel.*, MSc *Adel.*, PhD Sr. Lectr.
Harnby, Norman, BSc *Lond.*, PhD Sr. Lectr.
Henry, Robert M., BSc *Lond.*, MSc PhD Sr. Lectr., Control
Maitland, Derek J., BSc *Belf.*, PhD *Belf.* Sr. Lectr., Organic Chemistry
Slater, Michael J., BSc *Lond.*, PhD, FIChemE Sr. Lectr.
Walls, John R., BSc(Eng) *Lond.*, PhD *Lond.*, FIChemE Prof.
Woodcock, Leslie V., MA *Camb.*, PhD *Lond.*, FRSChem Prof.

Engineering, Civil and Environmental
Tel: (01274) 233871 Fax: (01274) 233888
Boot, Jess C., BTech PhD Sr. Lectr.

Garrity, Stephen W., BSc Nott. Sr. Lectr.
Hothersall, David C., BSc Sheff., PhD
Salf. Reader
Hughes, David, BSc Portsmouth, PhD Sur. Sr.
Lectr.
Toropov, U. Vassili, MSc Gorky State, PhD
Moscow Reader

Engineering, Electrical

Tel: (01274) 234100 Fax: (01274) 234054

Alder, Chris, BSc City(UK), MSc PhD Sr.
Lectr., Information Systems
Barton, Steve K., BSc(Eng) Lond., MSc
Essex Prof.
Bowron, Peter, BSc Birm., PhD Newcastle(UK),
FIEE Reader
Earnshaw, Rae, BSc Leeds, PhD Leeds Prof.;
Head*
Excell, Peter S., BSc Reading, PhD Reader;
Head*
Gardiner, John G., MSc Birm., PhD
Birm. Prof., Electronic Engineering
Green, Roger J., BSc Manc., PhD Sr. Lectr.
Howson, David P., BSc Brist. Prof.
Hunter, Ian A., BSc Leeds, PhD Leeds Sr. Lectr.
McCurrie, Robert A., BSc Sheff., PhD Sheff.,
FIP Sr. Lectr.
McEwan, Neil J., MA Camb., PhD
Manc. Reader
Rodriguez-Tellez, José, BSc CNAA, MPhil
PhD Sr. Lectr.
Simmons, John G., BSc Lond., MSc Temple, PhD
Lond., DSc Lond. Prof.

Engineering, Mechanical and Manufacturing

Tel: (01274) 234500 Fax: (01274) 234525

Bartlett, Hayden, BSc CNAA, PhD Sr. Lectr.
Bolton, John D., BSc Aston, PhD CNAA Sr.
Lectr.
Bruun, Hans H., MSc T.U.Denmark, PhD
T.U.Denmark
Coates, Phil D., BSc Lond., MSc Leeds, PhD
Leeds Prof., Polymer Engineering
Day, Andrew J., MA Camb., PhD Lough. Prof.
Seale, William J., BEng Wales, MSc Birm.
Thew, Martin, BSc Lond. Prof.
Whalley, Robert, BSc Durh., MSc Manc., PhD
Manc. Prof.; Head*
Wronski, Andrew, BSc Lond., PhD Lond.,
DSc(Eng) Lond., FIM Prof., Engineering
Materials

English, see Soc. and Econ. Studies

Environmental Science

Tel: (01274) 234230 Fax: (01274) 234231

Copperthwaite, Nigel H., BSc PhD Sr. Lectr.,
Geography
French, Mike J., BSc Lond., PhD Lond.,
FRSChem Lectr.; Head*
Seaward, Mark R. D., BSc Birm., MSc Nott., PhD
DSc, FLS, FIBiol Prof., Environmental
Biology

European Studies

Tel: (01274) 233829 Fax: (01274) 235550

Cole, Alistair M., BSc Lond., DPhil Oxf. Reader
Dyson, Kenneth H. F., MSc(Econ) Lond., PhD
Liv., FRHistS Prof.
Espindola, Roberto, Egresado Chile, MA
F.L.A.C.S.O., Chile Sr. Lectr., Politics
Featherstone, Kevin, MA Essex, PhD
Manc. Prof., Politics
Hiden, John W., BA Hull, PhD Lond. Prof.
Lane, A. Thomas, MA Camb. Sr. Lectr.,
History; Head*
Medhurst, Kenneth N., MA Edin., PhD
Manc. Visiting Prof., European Political
Studies
Mellors, Colin, MA Sheff., PhD Prof., Politics

French, see Mod. Langs.

Geography, see Environmental Sci.

German, see Mod. Langs.

Health Studies, School of

Fax: (01274) 386340

Lucas, Jeffery, BSc Lond., MPhil Lond., PhD
Lond. Prof.; Head of Sch.*

Health Care Studies

Fax: (01274) 236302

Harrigan, Patricia, BA Open(UK), MSc
York(UK) Head*
Kenworthy, Doreen, MSc Brad. Sr. Lectr.
Kitwood, Tom M., BA Camb., MSc PhD Sr.
Lectr., Philosophy

Midwifery

Fax: (01274) 236302

No staff at present

Nursing

Fax: (01274) 236302

Archibong, Uduak E., BSc Nigeria, PhD Hull Sr.
Lectr. (Res.)
Armitage, Gerrard, BSc Hudd. Sr. Lectr.
Bryant, Timothy P., BEd E.Anglia Sr. Lectr.
Coates, David, BA Brad., MSc Brad. Sr. Lectr.
Keyzer, Dirk M., MSc Manc., PhD Lond. Prof.;
Head*
Smith, Isabel, BSc Leeds, MA Leeds Sr. Lectr.
Whitemoss, Beverley J., BSc CNAA Sr. Lectr.

Physiotherapy

Fax: (01274) 236390

Spedding, J. Charmaine, BA Open(UK), MEd
Nott. Sr. Lectr.

Radiography

Fax: (01274) 236390

Milner, Stephen C., BA Open(UK) Head

Industrial Technology

Tel: (01274) 234239 Fax: (01274) 391333

Lloyd, David W., BSc Lond., MPhil CNAA, PhD
Manc. Prof.; Head*
McColm, Ian J., BSc Manc., DPhil Oxf. Prof.
Stylios, George, MSc Leeds, PhD Leeds Prof.

Interdisciplinary Human Studies

Tel: (01274) 233986 Fax: (01274) 720494

Carling, Alan H., BA Camb., MA Essex, PhD
Essex Sr. Lectr., Sociology
Fellows, D. Roger, BA Warw., BPhil Oxf., MA
Calg. Sr. Lectr., Philosophy; Head*
MacDonald, Graham F., BA Witw., BPhil
Oxf. Sr. Lectr., Social Philosophy
O'Hear, Anthony, MA Warw., PhD
Warw. Prof., Philosophy
Smith, Ken E., MA Oxf., BPhil Oxf., PhD
Wales Sr. Lectr., Humanities/Literature

Literature, see Interdisciplinary Human
Studies

Management Centre

Tel: (01274) 234382 Fax: (01274) 546866

Butler, Richard J., BSc(Eng) S'ton., MSc Lough.,
PhD Ill. Prof., Organisational Analysis
Hogarth-Scott, Sandra, BA Melb., MBA PhD Sr.
Lectr.
Hope, Christine A., BSc PhD Sr. Lectr.
Jobber, David, BA Manc., MSc Warw.,
PhD Prof., Marketing
Lowes, Brian, MPhil PhD Sr. Lectr.,
Managerial Economics
Luffman, George A., BA Nott., MSc Manc.,
PhD Sr. Lectr., Managerial Economics
Mirza, Hafiz R., BA Lanc., MPhil CNAA Prof.,
Managerial Economics
Molander, Christopher F., BA Liv., PhD Sr.
Lectr., Organisational Analysis
Muhlemann, Alan P., MSc Hull, PhD
Manc. Prof., Operations
Oakland, John S., PhD Salf. Exxon Chem.
Prof., Total Quality Management
Ostell, Alastair E., BSc Leeds, DPhil Sus. Sr.
Lectr., Psychology

Pass, Christopher L., BSc(Econ) Hull,
MPhil Reader, Managerial Economics
Pike, Richard H., MA Lanc., PhD,
FCA Provident Financial Group Prof.,
Finance and Accounting
Porter, Leslie J., BSc Lond., MSc Sur., MBA Sheff.,
PhD Sur. Prof., Quality Management
Price, David H. R., BSc Lond., PhD
Glas. Reader, Management Science
Randell, George A., BSc Nott., MSc Lond., PhD
Lond. Prof., Organisational Behaviour
Sanderson, Stuart M., MSc Sr. Lectr.,
Managerial Economics
Sparkes, John R., BA Wales, MScEcon Wales,
PhD Prof., Managerial Economics
Taylor, David S., BSc Leeds, PhD Sr. Lectr.,
Psychology
Taylor, William A., BSc Belf., MSc Belf., PhD
Belf. Prof.
Weir, David T. H., MA Oxf. Prof.; Dir.*
Wilson, Neil, BA Nott., PhD Nott. Prof., Credit
Management
Winterton, Jonathan C. A., MSc Lond.,
BTech Sr. Lectr., Industrial Relations
Zairi, Mohammed, BSc Aston, MSc Aston Prof.

Mathematics

Tel: (01274) 234288

Graves-Morris, Peter R., BA Oxf., PhD Camb.,
DSc Oxf., FIMA Prof.
Jerwood, David, BSc Hull, PhD Sheff.
Tupholme, Geoff E., BSc Sheff., PhD
E.Anglia Sr. Lectr.
Wood, Alastair S., BSc St And., PhD St And. Sr.
Lectr.

Midwifery, see under Health Studies, Sch. of

Modern Languages

Tel: (01274) 234619 Fax: (01274) 235590

Allison, Margaret E., BA Leeds, MèsL
Bordeaux Sr. Lectr., French
Amodia, José E., LicDer Oviedo, BA Lond. Sr.
Lectr., Spanish
Bridger, Susan C., BA PhD Sr. Lectr., Russian
Finlay, Francis J., BA Newcastle(UK), PhD
Newcastle(UK) Sr. Lectr., German
Green, John N., MA Camb., DPhil
York(UK) Prof., French
Griffiths, Brian T., MBE, BA Nott. Sr. Lectr.,
French
Heathcote, Owen N., BA Lond., PhD Lond. Sr.
Lectr., French
Meinhof, Ulrike H., MA Munich, PhD
Essex Prof., Cultural Studies
Russell, John, BSc Sur., PhD Birm. Lectr.,
Russian; Head*
Williams, Arthur, MA Keele Sr. Lectr., German

Nursing, see under Health Studies, Sch. of

Optometry

Tel: (01274) 234640 Fax: (01274) 235570

Buckingham, Terry J., MSc Aston, PhD
Aston Sr. Lectr.
Douthwaite, William A., PhD Wales, MSc Sr.
Lectr.
Elliott, David B., BSc Brad., PhD Brad. Sr. Lectr.
Jenkins, Tom C. A., MScTech Manc., PhD Sr.
Lectr.
Pierscionek, Barbara K., BSc Melb., PhD
Melb. Sr. Lectr.
Whitaker, David J., BSc Brad., PhD
Brad. Reader
Winn, Barry, BSc Glas., PhD Glas. Prof.; Head*

Peace Studies

Tel: (01274) 235235 Fax: (01274) 235240

Bujra, Janet M., MSc Lond., PhD Lond. Sr. Lectr.
Chalmers, Malcolm G., BA Camb., MA
E.Anglia Sr. Lectr.
Dando, Malcolm R., BSc St And., PhD St
And. Prof.
Gallagher, Tom G., BA Manc., PhD
Manc. Reader
Greene, Owen J., BSc Brist., PhD Sr. Lectr.
Gregory, Shaun R., BSc Nott. Sr. Lectr.

Ramsbotham, Oliver P., BA Oxf., PhD   Sr. Lectr.

Rogers, Paul F., BSc Lond., PhD Lond.   Prof.; Head*

Woodhouse, Tom, BA Leeds, PhD Leeds   Sr. Lectr.

Pharmacy

Tel: (01274) 234661 Fax: (01274) 235600

Barry, Brian W., DSc Manc., PhD Lond., FPS, FRSChem   Prof., Pharmaceutical Technology

Beedham, Christine, BPharm PhD   Sr. Lectr., Pharmaceutical Chemistry

Brown, John E., BPharm Lond., MSc Lond., PhD CNAA   Sr. Lectr., Pharmaceutical Chemistry

Chrystyn, Henry, MPharm PhD   Glaxo Prof., Pharmacy Practice

Clark, Brian J., MSc H.-W., PhD H.-W.   Sr. Lectr.

Costall, Brenda, BPharm PhD DSc   Prof., Neuropharmacology

Fell, Anthony F., BPharm Lond., PhD H.-W., FRSChem   Prof., Pharmaceutical Chemistry

Kelly, M. Elizabeth, BTech PhD   Sr. Lectr., Pharmacology

Linley, Peter A., BPharm Lond., PhD   Sr. Lectr., Pharmacognosy

Marshall, Kay, BPharm Brad., PhD Brad.   Sr. Lectr., Pharmacology

McCurrie, Janice R., BSc Sheff., PhD Sheff.   Sr. Lectr., Physiology

Naylor, Ian L., BPharm Brad., MSc Brad., PhD Brad.   Sr. Lectr., Pharmacology

Naylor, Robert J., BPharm PhD DSc   Prof., Pharmacology; Head*

Obrenovitch, T. P., MSc Lyons, PhD Lyons   Sr. Lectr., Pharmacology

Purvis, John R., BPharm PhD   Sr. Lectr.

Smith, John A., BPharm Lond., PhD Lond.   Sr. Lectr., Pharmaceutical Chemistry

Williams, A. C., BSc CNAA, PhD Brad.   Sr. Lectr., Pharmaceutical Technology

Wiseman, David, BSc Manc., PhD   Sr. Lectr., Pharmaceutics

Wood, Diana, BSc CNAA, PhD Strath.   Sr. Lectr., Pharmacology

York, Peter, BSc Manc., PhD Lond., FRSChem   Prof., Pharmaceutical Technology

Other Staff: 1 Reader†; 1 Sr. Lectr.†

Philosophy, see Interdisciplinary Human Studies

Physiotherapy, see under Health Studies, Sch. of

Politics, see European Studies

Psychology, see Management Centre, and Soc. and Econ. Studies

Radiography, see under Health Studies, Sch. of

Russian, see Mod. Langs.

Social and Economic Studies

Tel: (01274) 234800 Fax: (01274) 235295

Ahmad, Waqar I., BA Open(UK), PhD   Sr. Lectr.

Burkitt, Brian, BA Leeds, PhD Leeds   Sr. Lectr., Economics

Harrison, John R., MA Sheff.   Sr. Lectr., English

Husband, Charles H., BA Strath., PhD   Prof., Social Psychology

Littlejohn, Gary M., MA Glas., PhD Glas., MSc Lond.   Reader, Sociology

Milgate, Maurice, MEc Syd., MA Essex, PhD Camb.   Prof., Economics; Head*

Waton, Alan, BA Sus.   Sr. Lectr., Sociology

Social Studies, Applied

Tel: (01274) 233502 Fax: (01274) 235690

Duncan, Simon S., BA Camb., PhD Camb.   Reader

Macey, Marie, BA Open(UK), MEd Manc.   Sr. Lectr.

Moxon, Eileen M., BA Belf.   Sr. Lectr.; Head*

Sociology, see Interdisciplinary Human Studies, and Soc. and Econ. Studies

Spanish, see Mod. Langs.

SPECIAL CENTRES, ETC

Computer Centre

Tel: (01274) 233304 Fax: (01274) 304354

Houghton, Stanley J., BSc Lond., PhD   Dir.*

Continuing Education, Centre for

Tel: (01274) 233221 Fax: (01274) 235360

Jowitt, J. Anthony, BSc Leeds, MPhil Leeds, PhD Leeds   Acting Dir.*

Language Unit

Tel: (01274) 235208 Fax: (01274) 235207

Harding, Graham, BA Sheff., MA Leeds   Dir.*

Teaching Quality Enhancement Group

Tel: (01274) 233293

Pickles, Clare P., BSc Aston, MEd Hudd.   Educnl. Devel. Adviser

CONTACT OFFICERS

Academic affairs. Academic Secretary: Town, John, BA Camb.

Accommodation. Director of Residences and Catering: Johnson, Von, BEd Leeds Met.

Admissions (first degree). Head of Admissions and Schools Liaison: Ash, Roger, BSc Reading, PhD Reading

Admissions (higher degree). Assistant Registrar: Knifton, D. Kevin, BA Oxf.

Adult/continuing education. Acting Director: Jowitt, J. Anthony, BSc Leeds, MPhil Leeds, PhD Brad.

Archives. Librarian: Stevenson, Malcolm B., BSc Leeds, MA Lond., PhD Leeds

Careers. Head: Carney, Bernard J., BSc Liv.

Computing services. Director: Houghton, Stanley J., BSc Lond., PhD

Equal opportunities. Equal Opportunities Officer: Lankford, Maeve, BA N.U.I., MA N.U.I., PhD Brad.

Estates and buildings/works and services. Estates and Buildings Officer: Fairweather, Colin R., FRICS

Examinations. Administrative Assistant: Beaumont, Jenny, BSc Edin.

Finance. Director: Hull, David

General enquiries. Registrar and Secretary: Andrew, Nick J., BA Camb.

Health services. Senior Medical Officer and Occupational Health Adviser: Gill, Jane, BSc Manc., MB ChB Manc.

Industrial liaison. Director of Research Support and Industrial Liaison: Johnson, Neil, BA Salf., MSc Salf.

International office. Head of International Officer: Jennings, David, BA York(UK)

Library (chief librarian). Librarian: Stevenson, Malcolm B., BSc Leeds, MA Lond., PhD Leeds

Personnel/human resources. Director: Bunting, Paul, BA Keele

Public relations, information and marketing. Head: Coffey, Suzanne, BA Lond.

Publications. Head of Student Recruitment Services and Print Production: Waller, John C., BSc Brist., MPhil

Purchasing. Purchasing Officer: Wilson, Stephen D.

Safety. Safety Advisor: Williams, John H., BSc Lond.

Scholarships, awards, loans. Senior Assistant Registrar: Buck, Nick J., BA Wales

Schools liaison. Head of Student Recruitment and Schools Liaison: Ash, Roger, BSc Reading, PhD Reading

Security. Fairweather, Colin R., FRICS

Sport and recreation. Teasdale, J. Steve, BTech

Staff development and training. Adviser: Sayers, Pete, BA Newcastle(UK), MA Lanc., MSc Lanc.

Student welfare/counselling. Students' Union Welfare Officer: Chadwick, Hazel C.

Student welfare/counselling. Student Counsellor: Ashdown, Marjorie

Students from other countries. Adviser to International Students: Benkreira, H., BTech MSc PhD

Students with disabilities. Co-ordinator: Uszkurat, Carol A., BA CNAA, PhD Warw.

University press. Head: Coffey, Suzanne, BA Lond.

CAMPUS/COLLEGE HEADS

Bradford and Ilkley Community College, Great Horton Road, Bradford, West Yorkshire BD7 1AY, United Kingdom. Principal: Gallagher, Dr. Paul J., MSc PhD, FIEE

[Information supplied by the institution as at 27 March 1998, and edited by the ACU]

UNIVERSITY OF BRIGHTON

Founded 1992; previously established as Brighton Polytechnic, 1970

Postal Address: Mithras House, Lewes Road, Brighton, England BN2 4AT
Telephone: (01273) 600900 **Fax**: (01273) 642010 **E-mail**: admissions@brighton.ac.uk
WWW: http://www.brighton.ac.uk **E-mail formula**: initials.surname@brighton.ac.uk

DIRECTOR*—Watson, Prof. D. J., MA Camb., MA Penn., PhD Penn.
DEPUTY DIRECTOR AND CLERK TO THE BOARD‡—House, David E., BA E.Anglia

---

UNIVERSITY OF BRISTOL

Founded 1909; previously established as University College, Bristol, 1876

Member of the Association of Commonwealth Universities

Postal Address: Senate House, Tyndall Avenue, Bristol, England BS8 1TH
Telephone: (0117) 928 9000 **Fax**: (0117) 925 1424 **Cables**: University, Bristol BS8 1TH
WWW: http://www.bris.ac.uk
E-mail formula: firstname.surname@bristol.ac.uk or initial.initial.surname@bristol.ac.uk

VISITOR—Elizabeth, H.M. The Queen
CHANCELLOR—Morse, Sir Jeremy, KCMG, MA Oxf., Hon. DSc Aston, Hon. DLitt City(UK), Hon. LLD Brist.
PRO-CHANCELLOR—Wall, Sir Robert, MA
PRO-CHANCELLOR—Durie, T. P.
PRO-CHANCELLOR—Clarke, Stella R., JP, Hon. LLD Brist.
VICE-CHANCELLOR*—Kingman, Sir John, MA Camb., MA Oxf., ScD Camb., DSc Oxf., Hon. DSc Sus., Hon. DSc S'ton.,
  Hon. DSc W.England, Hon. LLD Brist., FRS
DEPUTY VICE-CHANCELLOR—Pickering, Prof. B. T., PhD Brist., DSc Brist., Hon. MD Bucharest
PRO-VICE-CHANCELLOR—Evans, Prof. D. V., BSc Manc., PhD Manc.
PRO-VICE-CHANCELLOR—Partington, Prof. T. M., BA Camb., LLB Camb.
CHAIRMAN OF COUNCIL—Woolley, J. Moger, BSc Brist.
TREASURER—Clark, D., MA Camb., MSc Lond.
LIBRARIAN—Ford, M. Geoffrey, BSc Leic., MSc Sheff.
DIRECTOR OF COMPUTING—Grant, Alan R., BSc Lond.
REGISTRAR—Parry, J. H. M., MA Oxf.

GENERAL INFORMATION

History. The university was created by the merger in 1893 of University College, Bristol (established 1876) and Bristol Medical School (1833). During negotiations for a university charter these institutions were joined by Merchant Venturers' Technical College (1885; previously Bristol Trade and Mining School), which later became the university's faculty of engineering. The university received its charter in 1909.

Admission to first degree courses (see also United Kingdom Introduction). United Kingdom applicants: through Universities and Colleges Admissions Service (UCAS). Five approved subjects in General Certificate of Secondary Education (GCSE) and General Certificate of Education (GCE) A level with at least 2 subjects at A level, or 4 approved subjects in GCSE and A level with 3 subjects at A level, or 4 approved subjects in A level and Advanced Supplementary (AS) level with 2 subjects at A level (no subject to be counted at both levels). The following qualifications are regarded under certain conditions as equivalent to GCE: Scottish Certificate of Education (SCE), Higher National Certificate/Diploma (HNC/HND), International Baccalaureate (IB), kitemarked Access course, Open University credits. International applicants: most European and Commonwealth matriculation exams and

sufficient command of English (eg satisfactory score in English Language Testing Service test).

First Degrees (see also United Kingdom Directory to Subjects of Study) († = honours only). BA†, BDS, BEng†, BSc†, BVSc, LLB, MB ChB, MEng, MSci.

All courses are full-time and normally last 3 years; courses involving study abroad or industrial placements last 4 years. MEng, MSci: 4 years; BDS, BVSc, MB ChB: 5 years (6 years if preliminary course is necessary).

Higher Degrees (see also United Kingdom Directory to Subjects of Study). ChM, LLM, MA, MBA, MCD, MD, MEd, MLitt, MMus, MSc, MSW, MPhil, PhD, DDS, DEng, DLitt, DMus, DSc, EdD, LLD.

Applicants for admission to higher degrees must normally be graduates of a UK university or, subject to Senate's approval, of any other university. DMus awarded on musical composition; DEng, DSc, LLD awarded on published work.

Libraries. 1,250,000 volumes; 6500 periodicals subscribed to. Special collections include: Brunel (railway engineering); business history; election addresses (British parliamentary history); Eyles (geology); Gladstone Library (political pamphlets); medical history; Penguin Books and Hamish Hamilton Archives (publishers' archives); Wiglesworth (ornithology).

Fees (1997–98, annual). Undergraduate: £750 (arts); £1600 (science); £2800 (clinical). Postgraduate: £2540 (UK students); £6690 (arts, international students); £8798 (science, international students); £16,303 (clinical, international students).

Academic Awards (1997–98). 96 awards ranging in value from £3600 to £7800.

Academic Year (1998–99). Three terms: 28 September–11 December; 8 January–19 March; 19 April–18 June.

Income (1996–97). Total, £158,706,000.

Statistics. Staff: 2388 (1926 academic, 462 administrative). Students: full-time 11,611 (6012 men, 5599 women); part-time 966 (471 men, 495 women); international 1132 (564 men, 568 women); total 12,577.

FACULTIES/SCHOOLS

Arts

Dean: Liversidge, Michael J. H., BA Lond., FSA
Assistant Registrar (Arts): Straker, Judy M. E., BA CNAA

Engineering

Dean: Blockley, Prof. David I., BEng Sheff., PhD Sheff., DSc Brist., FEng, FIStructE, FICE
Faculty Administrator: Knox, Jennifer L., BSc Glas.

Law

Dean: Bailey-Harris, Prof. Rebecca J., BCL Oxf., MA Oxf.
Faculty Administrator: McDermott, S. J., BSc Brist.

Medicine

Dean: Holbrook, Prof. J. J., BSc Birm., PhD Birm., DSc Brist., Hon. DSc Barcelona, FRSChem
Faculty Administrator: Bryson, A. R., MA Aberd.

Science

Dean: Beringer, Prof. John E., CBE, BSc Edin., PhD E.Anglia, FIBiol
Faculty Administrator: Worsfold, G., BA CNAA

Social Sciences

Dean: Hodder-Williams, Prof. Richard, MA Oxf.
Faculty Administrator: McDermott, S. J., BSc Brist.

ACADEMIC UNITS

Accounting, see Econ.

Agricultural Sciences, see below

Anatomy

Brown, M. W., MA Camb., PhD Camb. Reader
Carrington, S. D., BVM&S Edin., PhD Liv. Sr. Lectr.
Clarke, G., BPharm Lond., PhD Lond. Sr. Lectr.
Collingridge, Graham L., BSc Brist., PhD Lond. Prof.; Head*
Henley, Jeremy M., BSc Aston, PhD Lond. Reader
Ingram, C. D., BSc Bath, PhD Camb. Reader
Musgrave, J. H., MA Oxf., PhD Camb., FSA Sr. Lectr., Oral Biology
Nicholson, Helen D., BSc MD ChB Sr. Lectr.
Wakerley, J. B., BSc Nott., PhD Reader
Other Staff: 8 Lectrs.; 1 Sr. Res. Fellow; 2 Res. Fellows; 1 Res. Fellow†; 2 Hon. Res. Fellows

Archaeology

Harrison, Richard J., MA Camb., PhD Harv., FSA Reader; Head*
Parker, Anthony J., MA Oxf., DPhil Oxf., FSA Sr. Lectr.
Warren, Peter M., BA Wales, MA Camb., PhD Camb., FSA Prof., Ancient History and Classical Archaeology
Other Staff: 3 Lectrs.

Art, see Hist. of Art

Biochemistry

Fax: (0117) 928 8274
Banting, G., BSc Salf., PhD CNAA Reader
Brady, Robert L., BSc Macq., DPhil York(UK) Reader
Denton, R. M., MA Camb., PhD Camb., DSc Prof.; Head*
Griffiths, W. T., BSc Wales, PhD Wales Reader
Gutfreund, H., PhD Camb., FRS Emer. Prof., Physical Biochemistry; Sr. Res. Fellow
Halestrap, A. P., MA Camb., PhD DSc Prof.
Halford, S. E., PhD DSc Prof.
Hall, L., BSc Leeds, PhD Leic. Reader
Hayes, M. L., BDS Lond., MSc Lond., PhD Liv. Sr. Lectr., Oral Biology
Holbrook, J. J., BSc Birm., PhD Birm., DSc Brist., Hon. DSc Barcelona, FRSChem Prof.
McGivan, J. D., BA Camb., PhD Reader
Rivett, Ann J., BSc Birm., PhD Camb. Reader
Tanner, M. J. A., MA Camb., PhD Camb. Prof.
Wood, P. M., MA Camb., PhD Camb., DSc Sr. Lectr.
Other Staff: 5 Lectrs.; 2 Sr. Res. Fellows; 8 Res. Fellows

Biological Sciences

Fax: (0117) 925 7374
Avery, R. A., BSc PhD Sr. Lectr., Zoology
Beckett, A., BSc Wales, PhD Wales, DSc Brist. Reader, Electron Microscopy/Mycology

Beringer, John E., CBE, BSc Edin., PhD E.Anglia, FIBiol Prof., Molecular Genetics
Cuthill, I. C., MA Camb., DPhil Oxf. Reader
Goldsmith, A. R., BSc Wales, PhD Leic. Reader, Zoology
Harris, S., PhD Lond., DSc Brist. 2nd Lord Dulverton Memorial Prof., Environmental Sciences
Hayes, P. K., BSc Wales, PhD Wales Sr. Lectr., Botany
Haynes, L. W., BSc S'ton., PhD S'ton. Sr. Lectr., Neurobiology
Houston, A. I., MA Oxf., DPhil Oxf. Prof., Theoretical Biology
Jones, G., BSc Lond., PhD Stir. Reader
Lazarus, C. M., BSc E.Anglia, PhD Sr. Lectr., Molecular Genetics
Martin, M. H., BSc Sheff., PhD Camb. Sr. Lectr., Botany
Miller, P. J., BSc Liv., PhD Liv., DSc Brist. Reader, Zoology
Pinfield, N. J., BSc Wales, PhD Wales Sr. Lectr., Botany
Rayner, J. M. V., MA Camb., PhD Camb. Prof., Zoology
Roberts, A. M., BA Camb., PhD Calif. Prof., Zoology
Round, F. E., PhD Birm., DSc Birm. Emer. Prof.†; Sr. Res. Fellow, Phycol.
Stobart, A. K., BSc Durh., PhD Newcastle(UK) Prof., Plant Biochemistry
Strong, L., BSc Sheff., PhD Sheff. Sr. Lectr., Entomology
Tinsley, R. C., BSc Leeds, PhD Leeds Prof., Zoology; Head*
Wall, R. L., BSc Durh., MBA Open(UK), PhD Liv. Reader, Zoology
Walsby, A. E., BSc Birm., PhD Lond. Melville Wills Prof., Botany
Other Staff: 6 Lectrs.; 1 Sr. Res. Fellow; 3 Res. Fellows; 1 Hon. Sr. Res. Fellow†; 4 Hon. Res. Fellows†

Chemistry

Fax: (0117) 925 1295
Alder, R. W., MA Oxf., DPhil Oxf., DSc, FRSChem Prof., Organic Chemistry
Allan, N. L., MA Oxf., DPhil Oxf. Sr. Lectr., Chemical Physics
Ashfold, M. N. R., BSc Birm., PhD Birm. Prof., Physical Chemistry
Balint-Kurti, G. G., MA Camb., PhD Col. Reader, Theoretical Chemistry
Connelly, N. G., BSc Sheff., PhD Sheff., DSc, FRSChem Prof., Inorganic Chemistry
Cosgrove, T., MSc Manc., PhD Manc., DSc Brist. Prof., Physical Chemistry
Cox, A. P., BSc Birm., PhD Birm., DSc, FRSChem Reader, Physical Chemistry
Dixon, R. N., BSc Lond., PhD Camb., ScD Camb., FRSChem, FRS Emer. Prof.†; Sr. Res. Fellow
Eglinton, Geoffrey, PhD Manc., DSc Manc., FRS Emer. Prof.†; Sr. Res. Fellow, Organic Geochem.
Evershed, R. P., BSc CNAA, PhD Keele Reader
Field, D., BSc Newcastle(UK), PhD Camb. Reader, Physical Chemistry
Gallagher, T. C., BSc Wales, PhD Liv., FRSChem Prof., Organic Chemistry
Goodfellow, Robin J., MA Oxf., DPhil Oxf. Sr. Lectr., Inorganic Chemistry
Goodwin, J. W., PhD Reader, Physical Chemistry
Jeffery, J. C., BSc Warw., PhD Warw. Reader, Inorganic Chemistry
Jennings, Barry R., PhD S'ton., DSc S'ton., FRSChem, FIP Visiting Indust. Prof.†
Knox, S. A. R., PhD DSc, FRSChem Alfred Capper Pass Prof., Inorganic Chemistry; Head*
Maher, J. P., BSc Lond., PhD Lond. Sr. Lectr., Inorganic Chemistry
Maxwell, J. R., BSc Glas., PhD Glas., DSc, FRS Emer. Prof.†, Organic Geochemistry; Sr. Res. Fellow
McCleverty, J. A., BSc Aberd., PhD Lond. Prof., Inorganic Chemistry

Nickless, G., BSc PhD Reader, Analytical Chemistry
Norman, Nicholas C., BSc Brist., PhD Brist. Reader, Inorganic Chemistry
Orpen, A. G., BSc Cape Town, PhD Camb. Prof., Structural Chemistry
Ottewill, Ronald H., OBE, BSc Lond., MA Camb., PhD Camb., PhD Lond., FRS, FRSChem Emer. Prof.†; Sr. Res Fellow, Phys. Chem.
Pringle, P. G., BSc Leic., PhD Leeds Reader, Inorganic Chemistry
Richardson, R. M., BSc PhD Reader, Physical Chemistry
Simmonds, I. G., BSc Lond., PhD Houston Visiting Indust. Prof.†
Simpson, T. J., DSc Edin., PhD Prof., Organic Chemistry
Tadros, Tharwat F., MSc Alexandria, PhD Alexandria Visiting Indust. Prof.†
Timms, P. L., BA Oxf., BSc Oxf., DPhil Oxf. Reader, Inorganic Chemistry
Vincent, B., PhD DSc Leverhulme Prof.
Willis, Christine L., BSc Lond., DPhil Sus. Sr. Lectr., Organic Chemistry
Wormald, C. J., BSc Nott., PhD Reading, DSc, FRSChem Reader, Chemical Thermodynamics
Other Staff: 12 Lectrs.; 8 Res. Fellows; 1 Hon. Sr. Res. Fellow†; 5 Hon. Res. Fellows†

Classics and Ancient History

Fax: (0117) 928 8678
Betts, J. H., BA Lond., FSA Sr. Lectr.; Head*
Buxton, R. G. A., MA Camb., PhD Camb. Prof., Greek Language and Literature
Edwards, C. H., MA Camb., PhD Camb. Sr. Lectr.
Fowler, Robert L. H., MA Tor., DPhil Oxf. Henry Overton Wills Prof., Greek
Gould, John P. A., MA Oxf., MA Camb., FBA Emer. Prof.; Sr. Res. Fellow†
Kennedy, D. F., MA Trinity(Dub.), PhD Camb. Sr. Lectr.
Martindale, C. A., MA Oxf., BPhil Oxf., PhD Brist. Prof., Latin
Rudd, W. J. N., MA Trinity(Dub.), PhD Trinity(Dub.) Emer. Prof.†; Sr. Res. Fellow, Latin
Other Staff: 6 Lectrs.

Computer Science

Fax: (0117) 928 8128
Barron, I. M., MA Camb., DSc CNAA Visiting Indust. Prof.†
Hughes, G., BSc Liv., MSc Aston, FIEE Dir., Safety Systems Res. Centre
Lewis, E., BSc PhD Sr. Lectr.
Lloyd, J. W., MSc Newcastle(NSW), PhD ANU Prof.
May, M. D., MA Camb., DSc S'ton., FRS Prof.; Head*
Paddon, D. J., BSc Wales, PhD Wales, MSc Reading Sr. Lectr.
Taylor, J. M., MA Camb., PhD Camb., FIEE Visiting Indust. Prof.†
Thomas, B. T., MSc Lond., PhD Lond. Prof.
Thomas, M., BSc Lond. Visiting Indust. Prof.†
Other Staff: 11 Lectrs.; 1 Res. Fellow; 1 Sr. Lectr.†

Continuing Education

Fax: (0117) 925 4975
Aston, M. A., BA Birm., FSA Prof.†, Landscape Archaeology
Bird, Elizabeth, MA Oxf., DPhil Sus. Sr. Lectr.; Head*
Costen, M. D., MA Oxf., PhD Brist., FSA Sr. Lectr.
Feest, A., BSc Exe., PhD Brist. Sr. Lectr., Environmental and Health Studies
Fowler, Rowena S. M., MA Birm., PhD Camb. Sr. Lectr.
Hardy, P. G., BSc Manc., PhD Manc. Sr. Lectr.
Hill, D. J., BSc Sheff., DPhil Oxf., FIBiol Sr. Lectr.
Jessup, C. F. H., MA Oxf. Sr. Lectr.
Lane, B., BA Liv. Sr. Lectr.
Smith, D., MA Oxf. Sr. Lectr.

Thomas, E. J., MA Oxf., MSc Lond., PhD Manc. Prof.
Other Staff: 5 Staff Tutors; 1 Staff Tutor†

Dentistry, see Oral and Dental Science, below

Drama

Fax: (0117) 928 8251

Adams, J. R. J., BA Exe. Sr. Lectr.
Adler, J., BA Manc. Manager†, Glynne Wickham Studio Theatre
Attenborough, Lord, CBE, Hon. DLitt Leic., Hon. DLitt Kent, Hon. DLitt Sus., Hon. DCL Newcastle(UK), Hon. LLD Dickinson Coll. Visiting Indust. Prof.†
Berghaus, G., DrPhil F.U.Berlin Reader
Brandt, G. W., BA Lond., MA Manit. Emer. Prof.†; Sr. Res. Fellow
Braun, E., MA Camb., PhD Camb. Emer. Prof.†; Sr. Res. Fellow
Marshall, J. G., BEd Leeds, MA Leeds Sr. Lectr.
Rose, D. Visiting Indust. Prof.†
Thumim, Janet B., PhD Lond. Sr. Lectr., Film and TV
White, M. E., BA Newcastle(UK), MA Birm. Prof., Theatre; Head*
Wickham, G. W. G., MA Oxf., DPhil Oxf., Hon. DLitt Lough., Hon. DLitt South Emer. Prof.†; Sr. Res. Fellow
Other Staff: 2 Lectrs.

Economics

Fax: (0117) 928 8577

Ashton, D. J., MA Oxf., MA Lanc., BA Open(UK), PhD Warw. Prof., Accounting Finance
Attfield, C. L. F., MA Essex Prof.
Brewer, A. A., MA Camb. Reader
Burgess, S. M., MA Camb., DPhil Oxf. Reader
Chesher, A. D., BSocSc Birm. Prof., Econometrics; Head*
Demery, D., BScEcon Wales Reader
Duck, N. W., MA Manc., PhD Manc. Reader
Green, S., BSc Brist. Sr. Lectr.
Grout, P. A., BA Newcastle(UK), MSc Lond., PhD Essex Prof., Political Economy
Jewitt, I. D., BA Sheff., DPhil York(UK) Prof.
Propper, C., BSc Brist., MSc Oxf., DPhil York(UK) Prof.
Rees, Hedley J. B., BSc Nott., PhD Nott. Sr. Lectr.
Smith, Richard J., MA Camb., MA Essex, PhD Camb. Prof.
Tonks, Ian, BA CNAA, MA Warw., PhD Warw. Prof.
Tweedie, D. J., BCom Edin., BA Edin., PhD Edin. Visiting Indust. Prof.†
Winter, D. F., BA Oxf., MA Penn. Sr. Lectr., Econometrics
Other Staff: 10 Lectrs.; 1 Sr. Lectr.†; 1 Hon. Res. Fellow†

Education, School of

Fax: (0117) 925 1537

Beveridge, Michael C., BA Manc., PhD Manc. Prof.
Broadfoot, Patricia M., BA Leeds, MEd Edin., PhD Open(UK) Prof.
Claxton, Guy L., BA Camb., DPhil Oxf. Visiting Prof.†
Crossley, M. W., BEd Keele, MA Lond., PhD La Trobe Sr. Lectr.
Furlong, V. John, BA CNAA, MA Camb., PhD City(UK) Prof.; Head*
Garrett, R. M., MA Keele, PhD Keele Sr. Lectr.
Hall, Valerie J., BA Manc., MA Oregon, MA Essex, PhD Essex Sr. Lectr.
Hill, T. R., BA Open(UK), MEd Dir., Academic Devel.
Hoyle, E., BSc Lond., MA Lond. Emer. Prof.†; Sr. Res. Fellow
McMahon, Agnes J., BA Lond., MEd Trinity(Dub.) Sr. Lectr.
Meadows, Sara A. C., BSc Lond., PhD Lond. Sr. Lectr.
Pollard, Andrew J., BA Leeds, MEd Sheff., PhD Sheff. Prof.

Squirrell, Gillian C., MA Kent, PhD Brist., BA Dir., Prison Educn.
Sutherland, Rosamund J., BSc Brist., PhD Lond. Prof.
Other Staff: 13 Lectrs.; 4 Res. Fellows; 1 Sr. Lectr.†; 7 Lectrs.†

Engineering

Fax: (0117) 925 1154

Peters, H. Visiting Indust. Prof.†
Shears, M., BSc Lond., MS Calif., FEng R.A.E. Visiting Indust. Prof.†, Principles of Engineering Design
Other Staff: 4 Lectrs.

Engineering, Aerospace

Balmford, D. E. H., OBE, BSc Durh., FEng, FRAeS Visiting Indust. Prof.†
Barrett, R. V., BSc PhD Sr. Lectr.
Birdsall, D. L., BASc Br.Col., PhD Sr. Lectr.
Fiddes, P., BSc Lond. Prof., Aerodynamics
Knibb, Terence F., BSc Lond. Visiting Prof.†
Lowson, M. V., BSc S'ton., PhD S'ton., FEng, FRAeS Sir George White Prof.; Head*
Moses, R. T., BSc PhD Sr. Lectr., Continuing Education
Wisnom, M. R., BSc Lond., PhD Prof., Aircraft Structures
Other Staff: 9 Lectrs.; 1 Sr. Res. Fellow; 1 Res. Fellow; 1 Reader†; 2 Sr. Lectrs.†; 1 Hon. Sr. Res. Fellow†

Engineering, Civil

Fax: (0117) 928 7783

Blockley, David I., BEng Sheff., PhD Sheff., DSc Brist., FEng, FIStructE, FICE Prof.
Cluckie, BSc Sur., MSc Birm., PhD Birm., FICE, FRMetS Prof., World-Wide Water Management
Davies, J. C., BSc Aston, PhD Aston R.A.E. Visiting Indust. Prof.†
Davis, J. P., BSc S'ton., PhD Reader, Hydroinformatics
Godfrey, P. S., BSc Visiting Indust. Prof.†
Hoyt, J. W., PhD Calif. Visiting Prof.†
Key, D. E., BSc Lond., PhD S'ton., FIStructE Visiting Indust. Prof.†
Lings, M. L., MA Oxf., MSc Lond. Sr. Lectr., Geotechnical Engineering
Loveless, J. H., MSc Lond., PhD Lond. Sr. Lectr.
Morgan, R. G., BSc Manc. Sr. Lectr.
Muir Wood, A. M., MA Camb., FRS, FEng, FICE Prof.; Head*
Nash, D. F. T., MA Camb., MSc Lond. Sr. Lectr.
Sellin, R. H. J., BSc Brist., PhD Brist., DSc Brist., FICE Emer. Prof.†; Sr. Res. Fellow
Severn, R. T., CBE, DSc Lond., FICE, FEng Emer. Prof.†; Sr. Res. Fellow
Smith, J. W., BSc Edin., PhD Sr. Lectr.
Taylor, C. A., BSc Leeds Reader
Woodman, N. J., BSc Wales, MSc Manc., PhD Sr. Lectr.
Other Staff: 7 Lectrs.; 1 Sr. Res. Fellow; 2 Res. Fellows

Engineering, Electrical and Electronic

Fax: (0117) 925 5265

Barton, M. H., BSc Kent, PhD Wales Sr. Lectr., Microelectronics
Beach, M. A., BSc York(UK), PhD Brist. Sr. Lectr.
Betteridge, F., PhD Birm., DSc Birm. Visiting Indust. Prof.†
Bowes, S. R., PhD Leeds, FIEE, FIMechE Prof.
Bull, D. R., BSc Exe., MSc Manc., PhD Wales Prof., Signal Processing
Copping, A. J., PhD Lough., BSc Sr. Lectr.
Dagless, E. L., BSc Sur., PhD Sur., FIEE Imperial Group Prof., Microelectronics
Elliott, C. J., MA Camb., PhD Camb., FRAeS Visiting Indust. Prof.†
Gowar, J., MA Oxf., MSc Lond. Sr. Lectr.
Grant, D. A., BSc Manc., PhD Reader
Horne, N., PhD Camb., BSc, FEng, FIEE Visiting Indust. Prof.†
Leakey, D. M., BSc Lond., PhD Lond., FIEE, FEng Visiting Indust. Prof.†

Martin, W. E., MS San Diego, PhD Calif. Visiting Indust. Prof.†
McGeehan, J. P., BEng Liv., PhD Liv. Prof., Communications Engineering; Head*
Railton, C., BSc Lond., PhD Bath Reader, Information Technology
White, Ian H., MA Camb., PhD Camb. Prof., Optical Communication Systems
Other Staff: 7 Lectrs.; 3 Res. Fellows; 1 Reader†

Engineering Mathematics

Baldwin, J. F., MSc Leic., DSc Prof., Artificial Intelligence
Bickley, D. T., MA Camb., PhD Camb. Sr. Lectr.; Head*
Clements, R. R., MA Camb., PhD Camb. Reader
Hogan, S. J., MA Camb., PhD Camb., FIMA Prof., Mathematics
Martin, T. P., BSc Manc., PhD Sr. Lectr.
Pilsworth, B. W., BSc PhD Sr. Lectr.
Richardson, A. T., BSc Durh., MSc Newcastle(UK), PhD Newcastle(UK) Reader
Sims Williams, J. H., MA Camb., MEng Sheff. Sr. Lectr.
Wright, J. H., BSc S'ton., PhD S'ton., MSc Lond. Sr. Lectr.
Other Staff: 5 Lectrs.; 1 Sr. Lectr.†

Engineering, Mechanical

Fax: (0117) 929 4423

Adams, R. D., PhD Camb., DSc(Eng) Lond., FIMechE Prof.; Head*
Brett, P. N., BSc Bath, PhD Bath Sr. Lectr.
Butterworth, D., BSc Lond., FIChemE, FEng Visiting Indust. Prof.†
McMahon, C. A., BSc Sr. Lectr.
Morgan, J. E., BSc Exe., PhD Exe. Sr. Lectr.
Pearce, T. R. A., BSc PhD Dir., Inst. of Grinding Technol.
Poulter, R., BSc Newcastle(UK), PhD Newcastle(UK) Sr. Lectr.
Quarini, G. L., BSc Lond., PhD Lond. Zeneca Prof., Process Engineering
Smith, D. J., BSc Newcastle(UK), PhD Lond. Prof.
Stoten, D. P., BSc Salf., PhD Camb. Prof., Dynamics & Control
Wragg, J. D., CBE, BSc Lond., DEng, FIMechE, FRAeS Visiting Indust. Prof.†
Other Staff: 6 Lectrs.; 2 Res. Fellows; 2 Lectrs.†; 1 Hon. Res. Fellow†

Food Refrigeration and Process Engineering

James, S. J., BA Open(UK) Dir.*
Other Staff: 1 Res. Fellow

English

Burrow, J. A., MA Oxf., FBA Winterstoke Prof.†
Hopkins, D. W., MA Camb., PhD Leic. Reader, English Poetry
Lyon, J. McA., MA St And., PhD Camb. Sr. Lectr.
McDonald, D. P., MA Oxf., DPhil Oxf. Reader
Meale, Carol M., BA York(UK), DPhil York(UK) Reader, Medieval Studies
Stokes, Myra F. K., MA PhD Sr. Lectr.
Tomlinson, A. C., MA Camb., MA Lond., Hon. DLitt Keele, Hon. DLitt Colgate, Hon. DLitt New Mexico, FRSL Emer. Prof.†; Sr. Res. Fellow
Webb, E. T., MA Trinity(Dub.), DPhil Oxf. Prof.; Head*
Other Staff: 10 Lectrs.; 1 Res. Fellow

French

Fax: (0117) 928 8922

Bolster, R. H., MA Trinity(Dub.), DU Paris Sr. Lectr.
Forbes, Jill E., BA Manc., DPhil Oxf. Ashley Watkins Prof.
Forman, E. R. B., MA Oxf., DPhil Oxf. Sr. Lectr.; Head*
Freeman, E., MA Oxf., BLitt Oxf. Sr. Lectr.
Freeman, Michael J., BA Leeds, PhD Leeds Prof.
Mason, H. T., BA Wales, AM Middlebury, DPhil Oxf. Emer. Prof.†; Sr. Res. Fellow
Parkin, J., BA Oxf., PhD Glas. Sr. Lectr.
Reynolds, Deirdre A., BA Trinity(Dub.), Maîtrise Paris I, PhD E.Anglia Sr. Lectr.

Sampson, R. B. K., MA *Camb.*, MA *Manc.* Sr.
Lectr.
Other Staff: 6 Lectrs.; 2 Sr. Lectrs.†

Geography

Fax: (0117) 928 7878
Anderson, M. G., BSc *Nott.*, PhD *Camb.*, DSc
Brist., FICE Prof.†
Bailey, J. O., BSc Sr. Lectr.
Bamber, Jonathan L., BSc *Brist.*, PhD *Camb.* Sr.
Lectr.; Dir., Centre for Remote Sensing
Bassett, K. A., BA *Birm.*, PhD *Brist.* Sr. Lectr.
Cloke, P. J., BA *S'ton.*, PhD *Lond.* Prof.
Glennie, P. D., MA *Camb.*, PhD *Camb.* Sr.
Lectr.
Haggett, P., CBE, MA *Camb.*, PhD *Camb.*, ScD
Camb., Hon. DSc *York(Can.)*, Hon. DSc *Durh.*,
Hon. LLD *Brist.*, FBA Prof.†
Hepple, L. W., MA *Camb.*, PhD *Camb.* Sr.
Lectr.
Hoare, A. G., MA *Camb.*, PhD *Camb.* Sr. Lectr.
Johnston, Ronald J., MA *Manc.*, PhD
Monash Prof.
King, Anthony D., MA *Sheff.*, MA *S.Carolina*, PhD
Brun. Visiting Indust. Prof.†
Leyshon, Andrew, BA *Wales*, PhD
Wales Reader
Longley, P. A., BSc PhD Prof.
Smart, P. L., MSc *Alta.*, BSc PhD Reader
Thrift, N. J., BA *Wales*, PhD Prof.; Head*
Tranter, M., BSc *E.Anglia*, PhD *E.Anglia* Reader
Trenter, Neil A., BSc *Lond.*, MSc *Birm.*, FGS,
FICE Visiting Indust. Prof.†
Whatmore, Sarah J., BA *Lond.*, PhD
Lond. Reader
Other Staff: 7 Lectrs.; 1 Res. Fellow; 2 Hon.
Res. Fellows†

Geology

Fax: (0117) 928 3385
Bailey, D. K., BSc *Lond.*, MA *Trinity(Dub.)*, PhD
Lond. Emer. Prof.†; Sr. Res. Fellow
Benton, M. J., BSc *Aberd.*, PhD
Newcastle(UK) Prof., Vertebrate Palaeontology
Briggs, D. E. G., BA *Trinity(Dub.)*, MA *Camb.*,
PhD *Camb.* Prof., Palaeontology; Head*
Carroll, M. R., BSc *Long Island*, MSc *Brown*, PhD
Brown Reader
Hancock, P. L., BSc *Durh.*, PhD *Durh.* Prof.,
Neotectonics
Hawkins, A. B., BSc *Brist.*, PhD *Brist.*, DSc
Brist. Reader, Engineering Geology
Kearey, P., BSc *Durh.*, PhD *Durh.* Sr. Lectr.,
Applied Geophysics
Palmer, M. R., BSc *E.Anglia*, PhD *Leeds* Reader,
Earth Sciences
Parkes, R. J., BEd *Birm.*, PhD *Aberd.* Prof.,
Geomicrobiology
Ragnarsdottir, K. V., BSc *Iceland*, MS *Northwestern*,
PhD *Northwestern* Sr. Lectr.
Robinson, D., BSc *Lond.*, PhD *Durh.* Sr. Lectr.
Sparks, R. S. J., BSc *Lond.*, PhD *Lond.*,
FRS Chaning Wills Prof.
Walker, George P. L., MSc *Belf.*, PhD *Leeds.*, DSc
Lond., Hon. DSc *Iceland* Visiting Indust.
Prof.†
Wood, B. J., BSc *Lond.*, MSc *Leeds*, PhD
Newcastle(UK) Prof., Earth Sciences
Other Staff: 5 Lectrs.; 6 Res. Fellows; 1 Lectr.†;
1 Res. Fellow†; 3 Hon. Res. Fellows†

German

Fax: (0117) 929 1901
Hibberd, J. L., MA *Oxf.*, BLitt *Oxf.*, PhD
Brist. Reader; Head*
Reiss, H. S., MA *Trinity(Dub.)*, PhD
Trinity(Dub.) Emer. Prof.†; Sr. Res. Fellow
Shaw, F., MA *Manc.*, DrPhil *Bonn* Emer. Prof.†;
Sr. Res. Fellow
Skrine, P. N., MA *Camb.*, DU *Stras.* Prof.†
Other Staff: 7 Lectrs.

Health Science, see Sport, Exercise and
Health Sci.

Hispanic, Portuguese and Latin
American Studies

Fax: (0117) 934 9860
Brookshaw, D. R., BA *Lond.*, PhD *Lond.* Reader;
Head*
Costeloe, Michael P., BA *Durh.*, PhD
Newcastle(UK), FRHistS Prof.
Minter, G. G., BA *Leeds* Sr. Lectr.
Other Staff: 5 Lectrs.; 1 Lectr.†

Historical Studies

Fax: (0117) 928 8276
Alford, B. W. E., BSc(Econ) *Lond.*, PhD
Lond. Prof.; Head*
Antonovics, A. V., BA *Oxf.*, DPhil *Oxf.* Sr.
Lectr.
Clay, C. G. A., MA *Camb.*, PhD *Camb.* Prof.,
Economic History
Coates, P. A., MA *St And.*, PhD *Camb.* Sr.
Lectr., International History
Doyle, W., MA *Oxf.*, DPhil *Oxf.*, Hon. DU
Bordeaux, FRHistS Prof.
Hutton, R. E., MA *Camb.*, DPhil *Oxf.*,
FRHistS Prof.
Lowe, R., PhD *Lond.*, BA Prof., Contemporary
History
MacLeod, Christine, BA *Oxf.*, PhD *Camb.* Sr.
Lectr.
Merridale, C. A., MA *Camb.*, PhD *Birm.* Sr.
Lectr.
Middleton, R. A. H., BA *Manc.*, PhD
Camb. Reader, Political Economy
Pemble, J. C., MA *Camb.*, PhD *Lond.* Reader
Richardson, P. J., BA *E.Anglia* Sr. Lectr.
Ryder, A. F. C., MA *Oxf.*, DPhil *Oxf.*,
FRHistS Emer. Prof.†; Sr. Res. Fellow
Tulloch, H. A., BSc(Econ) *Lond.*, PhD
Camb. Sr. Lectr.
Whittam, J. R., MA *Oxf.*, BPhil *Oxf.*, PhD *Lond.*,
FRHistS Sr. Lectr.
Other Staff: 7 Lectrs.

History of Art

Lilley, E. D., BA *Lond.*, MPhil *Lond.* Sr. Lectr.;
Head*
Liversidge, Michael J. H., BA *Lond.*, FSA Sr.
Lectr.
Smith, M. Q., MA *Camb.*, PhD *Glas.* Sr. Lectr.
Smith, P. G., BA *Lond.*, PhD *Lond.* Sr. Lectr.
Other Staff: 2 Lectrs.; 1 Lectr.†; 1 Res. Fellow†

Italian

Fax: (0117) 928 8143
Bryce, Judith H., MA *Aberd.*, PhD *Aberd.* Prof.;
Head*
Parry, Margaret M., BA *Wales*, MA *Oxf.*, PhD
Wales Sr. Lectr.
Other Staff: 3 Lectrs.

Latin American Studies, see Hispanic,
Portuguese and Latin American Studies

Law, see also Professl. Legal Studies

Fax: (0117) 925 1870
Bailey-Harris, Rebecca J., BCL *Oxf.*, MA
Oxf. Prof.
Borkowski, J. A., LLB *Lond.* Sr. Lectr.
Clarke, D. N., MA *Camb.*, LLB *Camb.* Prof.;
Head*
Davis, G. C., BA *Wales* Prof., Socio-Legal
Studies
Evans, M. D., MA *Oxf.*, DPhil *Oxf.* Sr. Lectr.
Furey, N. E., LLM *Lond.* Prof., Finance Law
Furmston, M. P., MA *Oxf.*, BCL *Oxf.*, LLM
Birm. Prof.
Greer, S. C., BA *Oxf.*, MSc *Lond.*, PhD
Belf. Reader
Hill, J. D., LLB *Birm.*, LLM *Camb.* Prof.
Kerridge, J. R., MA *Camb.*, LLB *Camb.* Reader
Morgan, Rodney E., BSc *S'ton.* Prof., Criminal
Justice
Parkinson, J. E., BA *Oxf.* Prof.
Partington, T. M., BA *Camb.*, LLB *Camb.* Prof.
Sanders, Andrew H. L., LLB *Warw.*, MA
Sheff. Prof., Criminal Law and Criminology

Stanton, K. M., BA *Oxf.*, BCL *Oxf.* Prof.
Sufrin, Brenda E., LLB *Birm.* Reader
Other Staff: 23 Lectrs.

Mathematics

Fax: (0117) 928 7999
Boyd, W. G. C., BSc *Dund.*, PhD *Dund.* Sr.
Lectr.; Head*
Chatters, A. W., BSc *Birm.*, PhD *Leeds* Reader
Collins, E. J., BSc *Leeds*, MSc *Manc.*, PhD
Manc. Sr. Lectr., Statistics
Drazin, P. G., BA *Camb.*, PhD *Camb.* Henry
Overton Wills Prof.
Evans, David V., BSc *Manc.*, PhD *Manc.* Prof.
Green, P. J., BA *Oxf.*, MSc *Sheff.*, PhD
Sheff. Prof., Statistics
Griffel, D. H., BSc *Birm.*, PhD *Cal.Tech.* Sr.
Lectr.
Hutton, Anthony G., MSc *Wales* Visiting
Indust. Prof.†, Mathematics and Mechanical
Engineering
Keating, Jonathan P., BA *Oxf.*, PhD *Brist.* Prof.,
Mathematical Physics
Maslov, V. P., PhD *Moscow* Visiting Prof.†
McNamara, J. M., MA *Oxf.*, DPhil *Oxf.*, MSc
Sus. Prof., Mathematics and Biology
Peregrine, D. H., BA *Oxf.*, PhD *Camb.* Prof.,
Applied Mathematics
Rickard, J. C., MA *Camb.*, PhD *Lond.* Reader,
Pure Mathematics
Schofield, A. H., BA *Camb.*, PhD *Lond.* Prof.,
Pure Mathematics
Shepherdson, John C., MA *Camb.*, ScD *Camb.*,
FBA Emer. Prof.†; Sr. Res. Fellow
Silverman, B. W., MA *Camb.*, PhD *Camb.*, ScD
Camb. Prof., Statistics
Slater, M., BA *Oxf.*, PhD *Chic.* Reader
van den Berg, Michiel, MSc *Delft*, PhD
Gron. Prof., Pure Mathematics
Welch, P. D., BSc *Lond.*, MSc *Oxf.*, DPhil
Oxf. Reader, Pure Mathematics
Winters, K. H., BSc *Newcastle(UK)*, PhD
Durh. Visiting Prof.†
Woods, Andrew W. Prof., Applied
Mathematics
Zaturska, Maria B., BSc *Lond.*, PhD *Lond.* Sr.
Lectr.
Other Staff: 15 Lectrs.; 1 Res. Fellow; 1
Lectr.†; 1 Hon. Sr. Res. Fellow†

Medicine, see below

Music

Fax: (0117) 954 5027
Jenkins, W. G., MA *Camb.*, MusB *Camb.*, PhD
Camb., FRCO Sr. Lectr.
Samson, Thomas J., BMus *Belf.*, PhD
Wales Stanley Hugh Badock Prof.
Thomas, W. H., MA *Durh.* Sr. Lectr.; Head*
Warren, R. H. C., MA *Camb.*, MusD
Camb. Emer. Prof.†; Sr. Res. Fellow
Other Staff: 2 Lectrs.; 1 Reader†

Oral and Dental Science, see below

Philosophy

Graham, K., BA *Lond.*, BPhil *Oxf.*, PhD Prof.
Harrison, A., BPhil *Oxf.*, BA Sr. Lectr.
Morton, A., BA *McG.*, PhD *Prin.* Prof.
Welbourne, M., BPhil *Oxf.*, MA *Oxf.* Sr. Lectr.;
Head*
Woodfield, A. R., MA *Oxf.*, DPhil *Oxf.*, MLitt
Edin. Reader
Other Staff: 7 Lectrs.; 1 Lectr.†

Physics, see also Chem.

Fax: (0117) 925 5624
Alam, M. A., MSc *Halle*, PhD *E.Anglia*,
FIP Reader
Alcock, J. W., BSc *Birm.*, PhD *Birm.* Sr. Lectr.
Allen, M. P., MA *Oxf.*, DPhil *Oxf.* Prof.
Atkins, E. D. T., BSc *Wales*, PhD *Leeds*,
DSc Melville Wills Prof.
Barham, P. J., BSc *Warw.*, MSc PhD Reader
Berry, Sir Michael, BSc *Exe.*, PhD *St And.*,
FRS Royal Soc. Res. Prof.

Birkinshaw, Mark, MA Camb., PhD Camb., FRAS William P. Coldrick Prof., Cosmology and Astrophysics
Cherns, D., MA Camb., MA Oxf., PhD Camb. Reader
Cottingham, W. N., BSc Birm., PhD Birm. Reader
Dickens, Robert J., BSc Lond., DPhil Sus. Visiting Prof.†
Dingley, D. J., BSc Lond., PhD Lond. Visiting Prof.†
Enderby, J. E., CBE, BSc Lond., PhD Lond., Hon. DSc Lough., FIP, FRS Emer. Prof.†; Sr. Res. Fellow
Evans, R., BSc Birm., PhD, FIP Prof.
Flewitt, Peter E. J., PhD Lond., DSc Lond. Visiting Prof.†
Foster, B., BSc Lond., DPhil Oxf., FIP Prof.
Gyorffy, B. L., BS Yale, PhD Yale Prof.
Hannay, J. H., BA Camb., PhD Camb. Reader
Hayden, S. M., MA Camb., PhD Camb. Reader
Henshaw, D. L., BSc Lond., PhD Nott. Prof.
Hillier, R. R., BSc PhD Sr. Lectr.
Hurle, D. T. J., PhD S'ton., DSc S'ton. Visiting Indust. Prof.†
Keller, Andras, PhD Brist., FRS Emer. Prof.†; Sr. Res. Fellow
Lang, A. R., MSc Lond., PhD Camb., FRS Emer. Prof.†; Sr. Res. Fellow
McCubbin, N. A., BSc Oxf., DPhil Oxf. Visiting Prof.†
Miles, M. J., MSc Birm., PhD Birm. Reader
Neilson, G. W., BSc H.-W., MSc Toledo(Ohio), PhD Mass., FIP Reader
Nye, J. F., PhD Camb., FRS Emer. Prof.†; Sr. Res. Fellow
Odell, J. A., BSc PhD Reader
Smith, V. J., MA Oxf., PhD Reader
Springford, M., BSc Durh., PhD Hull Henry Overton Wills Prof.; Head*
Steeds, J. W., BSc Lond., PhD Camb., FRS Prof.
Other Staff: 11 Lectrs.; 2 Sr. Res. Fellows; 11 Res. Fellows; 1 Lectr.†; 1 Hon. Sr. Res. Fellow†; 1 Hon. Res. Fellow†

Physiology

Fax: (0117) 928 8923

Armstrong, D. M., BA Oxf., BSc Oxf., PhD ANU Prof.
Bush, B. M. H., BSc Natal, MSc Rhodes, PhD Camb. Reader
Denton, Sir Eric, CBE, BA Camb., PhD Aberd., ScD Camb., FRS Hon. Prof.†
Headley, P. M., BVSc BSc PhD Prof.
Jones, Roland S. G., BSc Brad., MA Oxf., PhD Wales Reader
Lawson, Sally N., BSc PhD Reader
Levi, A. J., BSc Leeds, MB ChB Leeds, PhD Leeds Reader
Lewis, D. M., BA Camb., MB BChir Camb., PhD Lond. Reader
Lisney, S. J. W., BSc BDS PhD Sr. Lectr., Oral Biology; Head*
Lumb, B. M., BSc Birm., PhD Birm. Sr. Lectr.
Matthews, B., BDS Lond., PhD Prof.
Meech, R. W., PhD S'ton., DSc S'ton. Reader
Ranatunga, K. W., BSc S.Lanka, PhD Sr. Lectr.
Ridge, R. M. A. P., BSc S'ton., PhD S'ton. Sr. Lectr.
Woolley, D. M., BVSc Liv., PhD Edin. Sr. Lectr.
Other Staff: 3 Lectrs.; 3 Sr. Res. Fellows; 3 Res. Fellows; 1 Res. Fellow†; 1 Hon. Res. Fellow†

Policy Studies, School for

Tel: (0117) 974 1117 Fax: (0117) 973 7308

Bartlett, W. J., BA Camb., MSc Lond., PhD Liv. Reader, Social Economics
Boddy, M. J., BA Camb., PhD Camb. Prof., Urban and Regional Studies
Bullock, R., BA Leic., MA Essex, PhD Brist. Prof., Child Welfare Research
Caddick, B. F., BASc Br.Col., MA S.Fraser, PhD Sr. Lectr.
Davies, T. M., MA Edin. Sr. Lectr.
Doyal, Lesley, BA Lond., MSc Lond. Prof., Health and Social Care

Forrest, R. S., MSocSc Birm., PhD Prof., Urban Studies
Harrison, Lyn, BSc Manc., PhD Sr. Lectr.
Hillyard, P. A. R., BSocSc Trinity(Dub.), MA Keele, PhD Brist. Sr. Lectr.
Johnson, Malcolm L., BA Leic. Prof., Health and Social Policy
Land, Hilary, BSc Brist. Prof., Family Policy and Child Welfare; Head*
MacDonald, G. M., BA Oxf., MSc Oxf. Prof., Social Work and Applied Social Studies
Millham, S. L., OBE, MA Camb. Emer. Prof.†; Sr. Res. Fellow
Quinton, David L., BA Camb., PhD Lond. Prof., Psychosocial Development
Rees, Teresa L., BA Exe., PhD Wales Prof., Labour Market Studies
Smith, R. C., BA Oxf. Reader, Policy Studies
Taper, Prof. Toby T., BA E.Anglia Visiting Prof.†
Townsend, Peter B., BA Camb., Hon. DU Essex, Hon. DUniv Open(UK), Hon. DLitt Tees. Emer. Prof.; Sr. Res. Fellow
Whiteside, Noel, BA Liv., PhD Liv. Reader, Public Policy
Other Staff: 15 Lectrs.; 1 Sr. Res. Fellow; 8 Res. Fellows; 6 Lectrs.†; 3 Res. Fellows†

Politics

Fax: (0117) 973 2133

Carver, T. F., BA Col., DPhil Oxf. Prof., Political Theory
Crouch, M., MA Wales Sr. Lectr.
Hodder-Williams, Richard, MA Oxf. Prof.
Little, R., BSc Lond., MA Lehigh, PhD Lanc. Prof., International Politics; Head*
Pridham, G. F. M., MA Camb., PhD Lond. Prof., European Politics
Sanford, G., MPhil Lond., PhD Lond., BA Sr. Lectr.
Other Staff: 8 Lectrs.; 1 Sr. Lectr.†

Portuguese, see Hispanic, Portuguese and Latin American Studies

Professional Legal Studies

Fax: (0117) 925 6717

Annand, Ruth E., BA Durh. Prof.; Head*
Other Staff: 9 Lectrs.; 1 Hon. Sr. Res. Fellow†

Psychology

Fax: (0117) 928 8588

Baddeley, Alan D., BA Lond., MA Prin., PhD Camb., FRS Hon. Prof.†
Conway, M. A., BSc Lond., PhD Open(UK) Prof.; Head*
Duck, S. W., MA Oxf., PhD Sheff., FAPsS Visiting Prof.†
Frankish, C. R., MA Camb., PhD Camb., BA Liv. Sr. Lectr.
Freeman, N. H., BA Camb., PhD Camb., FBPsS Reader
Gathercole, Susan E., BSc York, PhD City(UK) Prof.
Gregory, R. L., CBE, MA Camb., DCs Brist., Hon. LLD Brist., Hon.DUniv Open(UK), Hon. DUniv Stir., FRS, FRSEd, Emer. Prof.†; Sr. Res. Fellow
Robinson, W. P., MA Oxf., DPhil Oxf., FBPsS Prof., Social Psychology
Routh, D. A., BSc Lond. Sr. Lectr.
Smith, A. P., BSc Lond., PhD Lond. Prof.
Other Staff: 8 Lectrs.; 1 Res. Fellow; 1 Sr. Lectr.†; 1 Hon. Sr. Res. Fellow†; 6 Hon. Res. Fellows†

Religious Studies, see Theol. and Religious Studies

Russian

Fax: (0117) 929 0712

Basker, M. G., BA Oxf. Sr. Lectr.
Cornwell, N. J., BA Lond., PhD Belf. Prof.
McVay, G., BA Oxf., DPhil Oxf. Prof.†, Russian Literature
Offord, D. C., PhD Lond. Prof., Russian Intellectual History; Head*
Porter, R. C., BA Leeds Reader

Other Staff: 1 Lectr.

Sociology

Fax: (0117) 970 6022

Bradley, H. K., BA Brist., BSc Leic., PhD Durh. Sr. Lectr.
Fenton, C. S., BA Hull, MA McM., PhD Duke Sr. Lectr.; Head*
Flanagan, K. D., MA Minn., BSocSc N.U.I., DPhil Sus. Reader
Levitas, Ruth A., BA Sheff., PhD Sheff. Sr. Lectr.
Modood, T., MA Durh., PhD Wales Prof., Sociology, Politics and Public Policy
Nichols, W. A. T., MA Hull, DSc Prof.
Walby, Sylvia T., BA Reading, MA Essex, PhD Essex Prof.
Other Staff: 5 Lectrs.; 2 Lectrs.†

Spanish, see Hispanic, Portuguese and Latin American Studies

Sport, Exercise and Health Science

Fax: (0117) 946 7748

Reeves, R. A., MEd Dir.*
Riddoch, C. J., BA Open(UK), PhD Belf., MEd Sr. Lectr.

Statistics, see Maths.

Theology and Religious Studies

Fax: (0117) 929 7850

D'Costa, G., BA Birm., PhD Camb. Sr. Lectr.
Gill, S. P., MA Oxf. Sr. Lectr.; Head*
King, Ursula M., STL Paris, MA Delhi, PhD Lond. Prof.
Williams, P. M., BA Sus., DPhil Oxf. Reader, Indo-Tibetan Studies
Williams, Rowan D., MA Camb., DPhil Oxf., DD Oxf. Visiting Prof.†
Other Staff: 4 Lectrs.; 1 Res. Fellow

Veterinary Science, see Clinical Veterinary Science, below

AGRICULTURAL SCIENCES

at Long Ashton

Tel: (01275) 392181 Fax: (01275) 394007

MacMillan, J., BSc Glas., PhD Glas., DSc Brist., FRS Emer. Prof.†; Sr. Res. Fellow
Shewry, P. R., PhD DSc Prof.; Head, Long Ashton Res. Stn.*
Other Staff: 2 Sr. Res. Fellows; 26 Res. Fellows

CLINICAL VETERINARY SCIENCE

Fax: (0117) 928 9505

Badger, Susan F. Dir., Vet. Nursing Unit
Crispin, Sheila M., BSc Wales, MA Camb., VetMB Camb., PhD Edin. Sr. Lectr., Veterinary Medicine
Duffus, W. P. H., BVSc Liv., PhD Liv., MA Camb. Prof., Veterinary Medicine; Head*
Gruffydd-Jones, T. J., BVetMed Lond., PhD Reader, Small Animal Medicine
Harbour, D. A., BSc Liv., PhD Liv. Sr. Lectr., Veterinary Virology
Holt, P. E., BVMS Glas., PhD, FRCVS Sr. Lectr.
Johnson, K. A. Prof., Companion Animal Studies
Long, Susan E., BVMS Glas., PhD Glas. Sr. Lectr.
Nicol, Christine J., BA Oxf., DPhil Oxf. Reader, Animal Welfare
O'Brien, J. K., MVB Trinity(Dub.), PhD Camb. Sr. Lectr., Large Animal Medicine
Perry, G. C., BSc Wales, PhD Wales Sr. Lectr., Animal Husbandry
Stokes, C. R., BSc S'ton., PhD Lond. Prof., Mucosal Immunology
Taylor, F. G. R., BVSc Liv., PhD Sr. Lectr., Equine Medicine
Waterman-Pearson, Avril E., BVSc PhD, FRCVS Prof., Veterinary Anaesthesia
Webster, A. J. F., MA Camb., VetMB Camb., PhD Glas. Prof., Animal Husbandry
Other Staff: 16 Lectrs.; 3 Sr. Res. Fellows; 11 Res. Fellows; 1 Sr. Lectr.†; 2 Lectrs.†; 1 Res. Fellow†; 2 Hon. Sr. Res. Fellows; 3 Hon. Res. Fellows†

MEDICINE
For subjects of first 2 years—Anatomy, etc—see above
Campbell, Alastair V., BD Edin., MA Edin., ThD San Francisco Prof., Ethics in Medicine
Other Staff: 1 Lectr.

Clinical Medicine

Anaesthesia

Fax: (0117) 926 8674

Black, A. McL. S., BM BCh Oxf., MA Oxf., DPhil Oxf., FCAnaesth, FFARACS Consultant Sr. Lectr.
Howell, S. J., BA Camb., MB BS Lond., MSc Lond., FRCA Consultant Sr. Lectr.
Prys-Roberts, C., MA Oxf., DM Oxf., PhD Leeds, FCAnaesth, FFARACS Prof.
Other Staff: 1 Lectr.; 1 Hon. Clin. Reader†; 53 Hon. Sr. Clin. Lectrs.†; 1 Hon. Lectr.†; 1 Hon. Res. Fellow†

Child Health

Fax: (0117) 928 5010

Baum, J. D., MB ChB Birm., MA Birm., MSc Lond., MD Birm., FRCP Prof.
Carswell, F., BSc Glas., MB ChB Glas., MD Brist., PhD Leeds Reader
Dunn, P. M., MB BChir Camb., MA Camb., MD Camb., FRCP Emer. Prof.†; Sr. Res. Fellow
Fleming, Peter J., MB ChB Brist., FRCPCan Hon. Prof.†
Golding, M. Jean, MA Oxf., PhD Lond., DSc Brist. Prof.
Hamilton-Shield, J. P., MB ChB Brist. Consultant Sr. Lectr.
Henderson, Alexander J. W., MB ChB Manc., MD Manc. Consultant Sr. Lectr.
Hunt, L. P., BSc Brist., MSc Manc., PhD Manc. Sr. Lectr., Medical Statistics
Mott, M. G., MB ChB Brist., DSc Brist., FRCP Prof., Paediatric Oncology
Oakhill, A. Hon. Prof.†, Childhood Leukaemia and Transplantation
Stanley, O. H., MA Camb., MD Camb. Consultant Sr. Lectr.
Thoresen, K., PhD Oslo Consultant Sr. Lectr.
Tizard, Elaine J., MB BS Lond. Consultant Sr. Lectr.
Other Staff: 1 Lectr.; 2 Sr. Res. Fellows; 1 Res. Fellow; 2 Res. Fellows†; 1 Hon. Clin. Reader†; 10 Hon. Sr. Clin. Lectrs.†; 6 Hon. Res. Fellows†; 1 Hon. Sr. Lectr.

Clinical Radiology

Fax: (0117) 928 2319

Jones, Angela J., BM S'ton., FRCR Consultant Sr. Lectr.
Rees, Michael R., BSc E.Anglia, MB ChB Sheff., FRCR Prof.
Wells, P. N. T., PhD DSc, FIEE, FEng Hon. Prof.†
Other Staff: 28 Hon. Sr. Clin. Lectrs.†

Laryngology, Rhinology and Otology

Tel: (0117) 721 5411

6 Hon. Sr. Clin. Lectrs.†

Medicine

Fax: (0117) 928 7628

Anstee, D. J. Hon. Prof.†, Transfusion Sciences
Barry, R. E., BSc MD, FRCP Consultant Sr. Lectr.
Bingley, P. J., MB BS Lond., MD Lond. Consultant Sr. Lectr., Diabetic Medicine
Dawbarn, D., BSc Bath, PhD Reader, Care of the Elderly
Dayan, C. M., MB BS Lond., MA Oxf., PhD Lond. Consultant Sr. Lectr.
Dow, Lindsey, MB BS Lond., DM S'ton. Consultant Sr. Lectr.
Gale, Edwin A. M., MB BChir Camb., FRCP Prof., Diabetic Medicine
Kirwan, J. R., BSc Lond., MB BS Lond., MD Lond. Reader, Rheumatology

Langton Hewer, R., MB BS Lond., FRCP Hon. Prof.†, Neurology; Sr. Res. Fellow
Levy, A., BMedSci Nott., BM BS Nott., PhD Lond. Consultant Sr. Lectr.
Lightman, S. L., MB BChir Camb., MA Camb., PhD Camb., FRCP Prof.
Mathieson, Peter W., MB BS Lond., PhD Camb. Prof., Renal Medicine
McArdle, C. A., BSc CNAA, PhD CNAA Sr. Lectr.
Millar, Ann B., MB ChB Liv., MD Liv. Consultant Sr. Lectr.
Murphy, David, BSc Edin., PhD Lond. Prof., Experimental Medicine
Norman, Michael R., BSc Lond., PhD Lond., FRCPath Sr. Lectr.
Probert, C. S. J., MB ChB Birm., MD Leic. Consultant Sr. Lectr.
Tobias, Jonathan H., BA Camb., MB BS Lond., MD Lond., PhD Lond. Consultant Sr. Lectr.
Vann Jones, J., MB ChB Glas., PhD Glas., FRCP Hon. Prof.†
Wilcock, G. K., BSc Lond., BM BCh Oxf., DM Oxf., FRCP Prof., Care of the Elderly
Wynick, David, BSc Lond., MB BS Lond., MD Lond., PhD Open(UK) Consultant Sr. Lectr.
Other Staff: 11 Lectrs.; 2 Sr. Res. Fellows; 9 Res. Fellows; 47 Hon. Sr. Clin. Lectrs.; 1 Hon. Clin. Reader†; 3 Hon. Res. Fellows†

Obstetrics and Gynaecology

Fax: (0117) 927 2792

Cahill, David J., MB BCh BAO N.U.I., MD Brist. Consultant Sr. Lectr.
Glew, Susan S., BSc Manc., MB ChB Manc., MD Manc. Consultant Sr. Lectr.
Gordon, Uma D., MB BS S.Venkat. Consultant Sr. Lectr.
Holmes, C. H., BSc E.Anglia, PhD Nott. Sr. Lectr.
Hull, Michael G. R., MB BS Lond., MD Lond., FRCOG Prof.
Jenkins, Julian M., DM S'ton. Consultant Sr. Lectr.
Soothill, Peter W., BSc Lond., MB BS Lond., MD Lond. Prof.
Stirrat, G. M., MB ChB Glas., MA Oxf., MD Lond., FRCOG Prof.
Thein, A. T. A., MB BS Rangoon, PhD Lond. Sr. Lectr.
Wardle, P. G., MB ChB MD, FRCS, FRCOG Consultant Sr. Lectr.
Other Staff: 2 Lectrs.; 1 Sr. Res. Fellow; 1 Lectr.†; 22 Hon. Sr. Clin. Lectrs.†; 2 Hon. Res. Fellows†

Oncology

Forbes, Karen, MB ChB Birm. Consultant Sr. Lectr., Palliative Medicine
Hanks, Geoffrey W. C., BSc Lond., MB BS Lond., FRCP, FRCPEd Prof., Palliative Medicine
Hawkins, Robert E., MB BS Lond., MA Camb., PhD Open(UK) Prof.
Other Staff: 2 Macmillan Lectrs.; 1 Sr. Res. Fellow; 1 Reader†; 1 Sr. Lectr.†; 2 Sr. Res. Fellows†; 11 Hon. Sr. Clin. Lectrs.†; 2 Hon. Res. Fellows†

Ophthalmology

Fax: (0117) 925 1421

Easty, D., MD Manc., FRCS Prof.
Sparrow, J. M., MB BCh Witw., DPhil Oxf., FRCS Consultant Sr. Lectr.
Other Staff: 2 Lectrs.; 1 Sr. Res. Fellow; 3 Res. Fellows; 1 Res. Fellow†; 1 Hon. Clin. Reader†; 5 Hon. Sr. Clin. Lectrs.†; 1 Hon. Lectr.†

Primary Care

Mant, D., MB ChB Birm., MA Camb., MSc Lond. Hon. Prof.†
Salisbury, C. J., MB ChB Brist., MSc Lond., FRCGP Consultant Sr. Lectr.
Sharp, D. J., MA Oxf., BM BCh Oxf., PhD Lond., FRCGP Prof.; Head*
Other Staff: 3 Lectrs.; 1 Lectr.†

Psychiatry

Fax: (0117) 925 9709

Evans, J., MB ChB Birm. Consultant Sr. Lectr.
Harrison, Glynn L., MB ChB Dund., MD Dund., FRCPsych Norah Cooke Hurle Prof.
Morgan, H. G., MA Camb., MD Camb., FRCP, FRCPsych Emer. Prof.†; Sr. Res. Fellow
Mumford, D. B., MA Camb., MPhil Edin., MB ChB MD Consultant Sr. Lectr.
Nutt, D. J., BA Camb., MB BChir Camb., DM Oxf., FRCPsych Prof., Psychopharmacology
Russell, J. A. O., BM BCh Oxf., MA Oxf., FRCPsych Reader
Skultans, Vieda, BA Lond., PhD Wales Sr. Lectr.
Other Staff: 3 Lectrs.; 1 Sr. Res. Fellow; 2 Res. Fellows; 64 Hon. Sr. Clin. Lectrs.†; 4 Hon. Lectrs.†; 2 Hon. Res. Fellows†

Surgery

Fax: (0117) 925 2736

Alderson, D., MB BS Newcastle(UK), MD Newcastle(UK), FRCS Prof., Gastrointestinal Surgery
Angelini, G. D., MD Siena, MCh Wales, FRCS Prof., Cardiothoracic Surgery
Birchall, Martin A., MB BChir Camb., MA Camb., MD Camb., FRCS Consultant Sr. Lectr., Ear, Nose and Throat
Coakham, H. B., BSc Lond., MB BS Lond., FRCP, FRCS Hon. Prof.†, Neurosurgery
Cunningham, James L., BSc Strath., PhD Brist. Sr. Lectr.
Farndon, J. R., BSc Newcastle(UK), MB BS Newcastle(UK), MD Newcastle(UK), FRCS Prof.
Hardy, J. R. W., BSc Lond., MB BS Lond., MD Lond., FRCSEd, FRCS Consultant Sr. Lectr., Orthopaedic Surgery
Holly, Jeffrey M. P., BSc Lond., PhD Lond. Prof.
Jackson, M., MB BS Lond., FRCSEd, FRCS Consultant Sr. Lectr.
Lear, P. A., MB BS Lond., FRCS Consultant Sr. Lectr., Transplantation
Learmonth, Ian D., MB ChB Stell., FRCS, FRCSEd, FCS(SA) Prof., Othopaedic Surgery
Mitchell, J. P., CBE, TD, MB ChB Lond., MS Lond., FRCSEd, FRCS Hon. Prof.†, Urology
Newby, Andrew C., MA Camb., PhD Wales British Heart Foundation Prof.
Smith, F. C. T., BSc Birm., MB ChB Birm., FRCS, FRCSEd, FRCSGlas Consultant Sr. Lectr., Vascular Surgery
Suleiman, Mohammed S., BSc Beirut, PhD Essex Sr. Lectr.
Thomas, Michael G., BSc Lond., MB BS Lond., FRCS Consultant Sr. Lectr.
Other Staff: 8 Lectrs.; 7 Res. Fellows; 1 Lectr.†; 2 Res. Fellows†; 4 Hon. Clin. Readers†; 53 Hon. Clin. Sr. Lectrs.†; 1 Hon. Sr. Res. Fellow†; 2 Hon. Res. Fellows†

Transplantation Sciences

Tel: (0117) 959 5340 Fax: (0117) 950 6277

Bradley, B. A. de B., MB ChB Birm., MA Camb., PhD Birm., FRCPath Prof.
Hows, Jill M., MB BS Lond., MSc Lond., MD Lond., FRCP, FRCPath Prof., Clinical Haematology
Other Staff: 3 Res. Fellows

Pathology and Microbiology

Fax: (0117) 928 7896

Bennett, P. M., BSc Glas., PhD Glas. Reader, Bacteriology
Berry, P. J., BA Camb., MB BChir Camb. Prof., Paediatric Pathology
Billington, W. D., BSc Wales, MA Oxf., PhD Wales Reader, Reproduction Immunology
Brown, K. W., MA Camb., MSc Birm., PhD Birm. Sr. Lectr.
Cartwright, K. A. V. Hon. Prof.†
Charles, Adrian, MB BChir Camb., MA Camb. Consultant Sr. Lectr.
Chopra, I., MA Trinity(Dub.), PhD DSc Visiting Indust. Prof.†
Collins, C. M. P., BA Camb., MB BChir Camb. Consultant Sr. Lectr., Histopathology
Davies, J. D., MB BS Lond., MD Lond., FRCPath Consultant Sr. Lectr.

Day, M. J., BSc Murd., BVMS Murd., PhD Murd., FRCVS Sr. Lectr.
Elson, C. J., BSc Edin., PhD Edin. Prof., Immunology
Grinsted, J. E., MA Camb., PhD Camb. Sr. Lectr.
Hill, T. J., BVSc PhD Reader, Virology
Hirst, Timothy R., BSc Kent, DPhil York(UK) Prof., Microbiology
Howe, T. Gilbert B., MA Trinity(Dub.), PhD Trinity(Dub.) Sr. Lectr.
Love, S., MB ChB Witw., PhD Lond. Hon. Prof.†
Millar, M. R., MB ChB MD Consultant Sr. Lectr.
Moorghen, M., BSc St And., MB ChB Manc. Consultant Sr. Lectr., Histopathology
Morgan, A. J., BSc Bath, PhD Camb. Reader
Paraskeva, C., BSc Manc., DPhil Oxf. Prof., Experimental Oncology
Pearson, G. R., BVMS Glas., PhD Belf. Sr. Lectr., Veterinary Pathology
Porter, Helen J., BSc St And., MD ChB Manc. Consultant Sr. Lectr.
Poste, G. H., BVSc PhD DSc, FRCVS, FRCPath, FRS Visiting Indust. Prof.†
Pullen, A. M., BSc Bath, PhD Camb. Sr. Lectr.
Reeves, D. S., MB BS Lond., MD Brist., FRCPath Hon. Prof.†
Sheffield, E. A., DM S'ton. Consultant Sr. Lectr., Histopathology
Silver, I. A., MA Camb., FRCVS Emer. Prof.†, Anatomy; Sr. Res. Fellow
Standen, G. R., BPharm Nott., BMedSci Nott., BM BS Nott., PhD Lond. Consultant Sr. Lectr., Haematology
Steward, C. G., MA Camb., MB BCh Oxf. Consultant Sr. Lectr.
Sykes, Sir Richard B., DSc, FRS Visiting Indust. Prof.
Virji, M., BSc Leeds, PhD Leeds Prof.
Wraith, David C., BSc Newcastle(UK), PhD Lond. Prof.; Head*
Other Staff: 6 Lectrs.; 11 Res. Fellows; 1 Reader†; 15 Hon. Sr. Clinical Lectrs.†; 4 Hon. Res. Fellows†

Pharmacology

Fax: (0117) 925 0168

Erecinska, M., MD Gdansk, PhD Warsaw Visiting Prof.
Garland, C. J., BSc S'ton., PhD Lond. Reader
Henderson, G., BSc Glas., MA Camb., PhD Aberd. Prof.; Head*
Hill, R., BPharm Lond., PhD Lond. Visiting Indust. Prof.†
Marrion, N. V. Sr. Lectr.
Roberts, C. J. C., MB BS Lond., MD, FRCP Consultant Sr. Lectr., Clinical Pharmacology
Roberts, P. J., BSc Dund., PhD Prof., Neurochemical Pharmacology
Taberner, P. V., BSc Edin., MSc S'ton., PhD S'ton. Sr. Lectr.
Watkins, J. C., MSc W.Aust., PhD Camb., FRS Hon. Prof.
Other Staff: 5 Lectrs.; 3 Res. Fellows

Primary Care, see under Clin. Med.

Psychiatry, see under Clin. Med.

Radiology, see Clin. Radiol. under Clin. Med.

Social Medicine

Fax: (0117) 928 7340

Ben-Shlomo, Yoav, MB BS Lond., MSc Lond. Consultant Sr. Lectr.
Davey Smith, George, MA Oxf., MB BChir Camb., MSc Lond., MD Camb. Prof.
Dieppe, P. A., BSc Lond., MB BS Lond., MD Lond., FRCP Hon. Prof.†
Donovan, Jenny L., BA Liv., PhD Lond. Sr. Lectr.
Frankel, S. J., BM BCh Oxf., MA Oxf., DM Oxf., PhD VCamb. Prof.; Head*
Gunnell, D. J., MB ChB Consultant Sr. Lectr.
Ness, A. R. Sr. Lectr.

Peters, T. J., MSc Oxf., PhD Exe. Reader, Medical Statistics
Other Staff: 6 Lectrs.; 1 Res. Fellow; 2 Lectrs.†

ORAL AND DENTAL SCIENCE

For subjects of first 2 years—Anatomy, etc—see above

Fax: (0117) 928 4150

Addy, M., BDS Wales, MSc Wales, PhD Wales, FDSRCS Prof., Periodontol
Cowpe, Jonathan G., BDS Manc., PhD Dund., FDSRCSEd Prof., Oral Surgery
Crawford, P. J. M., BDS Sheff., MScD Wales, FDSRCSEd Consultant Sr. Lectr., Paediatric Dentistry
Eveson, J. W., PhD Glas., BDS, FDSRCPSGlas, FRCPath Reader, Oral Pathology
Harrison, A., TD, BDS Wales, PhD Wales, FDSRCS Prof., Dental Care for the Elderly; Head*
Jandt, Klaus D., DerRerNat T.U.Hamburg-Harburg Sr. Lectr.
Jenkinson, H. F., BSc Warw., PhD Nott. Prof., Oral Microbiology
Matthews, R. W., BDS Newcastle(UK), PhD Newcastle(UK), MDS Sr. Lectr.
Meredith, N., BDS Lond., MSc Lond., PhD Lond., FDSRCS Consultant Sr. Lectr.
Moran, J. M., BDS Wales, MScD Wales, PhD Wales, FDSRCS Consultant Sr. Lectr.
Prime, S. S., BDS Birm., PhD Melb., FDSRCPSGlas Prof., Experimental Pathology
Rees, J. S., BDS Wales, MScD Wales, PhD Wales, FDSRCSEd Consultant Sr. Lectr., Restorative Dentistry
Sandy, J. R., BDS Lond., MSc Lond., PhD Lond., FDSRCS, FDSRCSEd Reader, Orthodontics
Stephens, C. D., BDS Lond., MDS, FDSRCS Prof., Child Dental Health
Other Staff: 17 Lectrs.; 2 Res. Fellows; 2 Lectrs.†; 1 Res. Fellow†; 10 Hon. Sr. Clin. Lectrs.†; 5 Hon. Res. Fellows†

Other Appointments

Medical and Dental Postgraduate Studies

Fax: (0117) 928 4526

Seel, D., BDS Manc., FDSRCS, FRCS, FRCA Dent. Postgrad. Dean†
West, R. J., MB BS Lond., MD Lond., FRCP Prof.†, Postgraduate Medical Education

SPECIAL CENTRES, ETC

Advanced Studies, Institute of

Anderson, Malcolm G. Prof.; Co-Dir.†
Haggett, Peter, CBE, MA Camb., PhD Camb., ScD Camb., Hon. DSc York(Can.), Hon. DSc Durh., Hon. LLD Brist., FBA Prof.†; Dir.*

Deaf Studies, Centre for

Kyle, J. G., MA Glas., MSc Stir., PhD Lond. Dir.*
Other Staff: 2 Lectrs.; 2 Lectrs.†

Interface Analysis Centre

Allen, G. C., BSc S'ton., PhD Brist., DSc Brist., FRSChem Prof.
Steeds, J. W., BSc Lond., PhD Camb., FIP, FRS Prof.; Dir.*
Other Staff: 1 Sr. Res. Fellow; 2 Res. Fellows

International Business, Graduate School of

Tel: (0117) 973 7695 Fax: (0117) 973 7687

Cunningham, Catherine M., BA Liv. Dir.*
De Neufville, Richard, PhD M.I.T. Visiting Prof.†
Friedman, A. L. Dir. of Res.†
Kruse-Kempen, Eigil, MA Reading, MSc Lond. Visiting Prof.†
Lisle, Edmond A., MA Oxf., PhD Paris Visiting Prof.†

Posner, Michael V., CBE, MA Oxf., Hon. LLD Brist. Visiting Prof.†
Russo, Celia D. M., MA Oregon, DèsSc Paris Visiting Prof.†

Learning and Research Technology, Institute of

Hobbs, Philip J., BSc Bath Dir.*
Price, S. N., BSc CNAA Project Dir.
Williams, P. J., BSc Brist., PhD Brist. Project Dir.

University Language Centre

Satchell, BA CNAA, MEd Brist. Dir.*
Other Staff: 4 Lectrs.; 1 Lectr.†

CONTACT OFFICERS

Academic affairs. Academic Registrar: Franklin, Jim, BSc Leeds, PhD Leeds
Accommodation. Accommodation and Welfare Officer: Ryan, Andrea M.
Admissions (first degree). Admissions Officer: Walker, Catherine D., BA Open(UK)
Adult/continuing education. Director of Continuing Education: Huntley, Ian D., BA Essex, PhD Essex, FIMA
Alumni. Development Director: Lockhart, Alisdaire N., BSc Lond., MSc Wales, PhD Lond.
Careers. Head of Careers Advisory Service: Goodman, Jeffrey A., BA Lond.
Computing services. Director of Computing: Grant, Alan R., BSc Lond.
Development/fund-raising. Development Director: Lockhart, Alisdaire N., BSc Lond., MSc Wales, PhD Lond.
Equal opportunities. Secretary to Equal Opportunity Advisory Group: Clapham, Jennifer M., MA St And.
Estates and buildings/works and services. Bursar: Adamson, David M., MA Camb., FICE
Examinations. Examinations Officer: Horton, Preston G.
Finance. Finance Director: Crawford, Ian
General enquiries. Registrar: Parry, J. H. M., MA Oxf.
Health services. Medical Officer-in-Charge, Students' Health Service: Butler, Anthony V. J., MB ChB Brist.
Industrial liaison. Head of Research Support and Industrial Liaison: Hill, Adrian N., BSc Lond.
International office. Director of International Affairs: Jones, Tim L., BA Oxf.†
Library (chief librarian). Librarian: Ford, M. Geoffrey, BSc Leic., MSc Sheff.
Personnel/human resources. Personnel Director: Maslin, Christopher A., MBA City(UK)
Public relations, information and marketing. Information Officer: Rayner, Andrea, MA Camb.
Publications. Information Officer: Rayner, Andrea, MA Camb.
Purchasing. Purchasing Officer: Garvey, Robert W., BA CNAA
Quality assurance and accreditation. Senior Assistant Registrar: Clarke, Gillian, MSc City(UK)
Research. Director of Research Development Service: O'Prey, Paul G., PhD Brist.
Safety. University Safety Officer: Lewis, John D., BSc Liv., MPhil Lond.
Scholarships, awards, loans. Student Finance Officer: Watson, Ann T.
Security. Security Officer: Dewhurst, James L.
Sport and recreation. Director, Sport, Exercise and Health Science: Reeves, Robert A., MEd Brist.
Staff development and training. Director, Staff Training and Development: Hughes, Paul, BA Leeds, MSc CNAA
Student union. Permanent Secretary: Milkins, Edward T., MA Brist.
Student welfare/counselling. Director, Student Counselling Service: Booth, Rosemary P. E., BA Lond.
Students from other countries. Adviser to Overseas Students: Jayne, Patricia

University press. Information Officer: Rayner, Andrea, MA *Camb.*

CAMPUS/COLLEGE HEADS

Baptist College, The Promenade, Clifton, Bristol BS8 3NG. Principal: Haymes, Rev. Brian, BA *Brist.*, PhD *Exe.*

Trinity College, Stoke Hill, Bristol BS9 1JP. (Tel: (0117) 968 2803.) Principal: Gillett, Rev. Canon David K., BA *Leeds*, MPhil *Leeds*

Wesley College, Henbury Hill, Bristol BS10 7QD. (Tel: (0117) 959 1320.) Principal: Richardson, Rev. N. G., BA *Camb.*, MA *Oxf.*, MLitt *Brist.*, PhD *Brist.*

[Information supplied by the institution as at 17 February 1998, and edited by the ACU]

BRUNEL UNIVERSITY

Founded 1966; previously established as a Regional College (1957) and designated a College of Advanced Technology (1962)

Member of the Association of Commonwealth Universities

Postal Address: Uxbridge, Middlesex, England UB8 3PH
Telephone: (01895) 274000 **Fax**: (01895) 232806 **Telex**: 261173G **WWW**: http://www.brunel.ac.uk/
E-mail formula: firstname.surname@brunel.ac.uk

VISITOR—Keene, The Hon. Mr. Justice, QC
CHANCELLOR—Wakeham, The Rt. Hon. Lord, JP, FCA
PRO-CHANCELLOR—Trier, P. E., CBE, MA *Camb.*, MSc *Brun.*, Hon. DTech *Brun.*, FEng, FIEE, FIP, FIMA
CHAIRMAN OF COUNCIL—Kempner, Prof. Tom, BSc(Econ)
VICE-CHANCELLOR AND PRINCIPAL*—Sterling, Prof. Michael J. H., BEng *Sheff.*, PhD *Sheff.*, DEng *Sheff.*, Hon. DEng *Sheff.*, FEng, FIEE, FIP, FIMA
VICE-PRINCIPAL—Cave, Prof. Martin, MA *Oxf.*, DPhil *Oxf.*
PRO-VICE-CHANCELLOR—Billett, Prof. Eric H., MA *Camb.*, DPhil *Oxf.*
PRO-VICE-CHANCELLOR—Sarhadi, Prof. Mansoor, BSc *Reading*, MSc *Lond.*, PhD *Lond.*

GENERAL INFORMATION

History. The university was established in 1966 as one of ten new universities created from colleges of advanced technology in the mid-1960s. Shoreditch College (now Runnymede Campus) merged with the university in 1981, and West London Institute (now Osterley and Twickenham campuses) in 1995.

Admission to first degree courses (see also United Kingdom Introduction). Through Universities and Colleges Admissions Service (UCAS). General Certificate of Secondary Education (GCSE) in English, or equivalent, and 2 or 3 General Certificate of Education (GCE) A levels, or equivalent (such as Business and Technology Education Council (BTEC), General National Vocational Qualifications (GNVQ), International Baccalaureate or overseas exams). Mature students (over 21 years old) may offer alternative qualifications.

First Degrees (see also United Kingdom Directory to Subjects of Study). BA, BEng, BSc, LLB.
 Courses usually last 3 years full-time or 4 years with work placement. Some courses may be taken part-time (4–6 years); some require a 1-year foundation programme.

Higher Degrees (see also United Kingdom Directory to Subjects of Study). LLM, MA, MBA, MEng, MSc, MPhil, PhD, DBA, EdD, EngD.
 Applicants for admission to master's degrees should hold an appropriate first degree, or equivalent qualification. Doctorates: good first degree or master's degree.
 Taught master's degrees: 1 year full-time or 2 years part-time; MPhil: 1 year full-time or 3 years part-time; doctorates: 3 years full-time or minimum 4 years part-time.

Language of Instruction. English. Pre-entry EFL courses available.

Libraries. 400,000 volumes; 3000 periodicals subscribed to.

Fees (1997–98, annual). Undergraduate: UK/EU residents, £750–1600 (full-time), £375–800 (part-time); Isle of Man/Channel Islands residents, £4450–6645 (full-time); non-UK/EU residents, £6370–8450 (full-time), £3185–4225 (part-time). Taught postgraduate courses (full-time): UK/EU residents, £3540 (MA in design strategy and innovation), £10,250 (MBA), £2540 (all other courses); non-UK/EU residents, £6370–8450. Taught postgraduate courses (part-time): UK/EU residents, £1270–1500 (most courses); non-UK/EU residents, £3185–4225 (most courses). Research programmes: UK/EU residents, £2540 (full-time), £1640 (part-time and external); non-UK/EU residents, £6370–8450 (full-time), £2100 (external), £3825–5070 (part-time).

Academic Year (1999–2000). Two semesters: 27 September–28 January; 7 February–9 June.

Income. Total, £74,489,000.

Statistics. Staff: 2047 (923 academic, 1124 adminstrative). Students: full-time 10,135 (5725 men, 4410 women); part-time 2935 (1621 men, 1314 women); international 739; total 13,070.

FACULTIES/SCHOOLS

Arts
Tel: (0181) 891 0121 Fax: (0181) 891 8270
Dean: Wootton, Prof. David, MA *Camb.*, MSc *Oxf.*, PhD *Camb.*, FRHistS
Secretary: ......

Professional Education
Tel: (0181) 891 0121 Fax: (0181) 891 8270
Dean: Thomas, Prof. Linda, BSc *Wales*, MEd *Wales*, PhD *Lond.*
Secretary: ......

Science
Dean: Newbold, Prof. Robert, BSc *Aston*, PhD *Lond.*, FIBiol
Secretary: Kruger, M.

Social Sciences
Dean: Wood, Prof. Adrian G. W., BA *CNAA*, MA *Lanc.*, PhD
Secretary: Woodhead, D.

Technology
Dean: Aitchison, Prof. Colin S., BSc, FIEE
Secretary: Jackson, Elaine

ACADEMIC UNITS
American Studies, see under Arts

Arts
Tel: (0181) 891 0121 Fax: (0181) 891 2161
Other Staff: 33 Lectrs.; 100 Lectrs.†

American Studies and History
Giles, Arthur, BA *S'ton.*, MTh *Lond.* Sr. Lectr.
Kingwell, Nicholas, BA *Lond.* Sr. Lectr.
Kleinberg, Susan, BA *Pitt.*, MA *Pitt.*, PhD *Pitt.* Principal Lectr.
Matthews, Geoffrey, BA *Oxf.*, MA *Oxf.*, PhD *Lough.* Reader
Morgan, Kenneth, BA *Leic.*, DPhil *Oxf.* Principal Lectr.

English
Moran, Maureen, BA *Calg.*, MA *Calg.*, PhD *Lond.* Principal Lectr.; Head*
Smith, Peter, BA *Camb.*, MA *Leic.* Sr. Lectr.

Performing Arts

Aplin, John, BA *Wales*, MA *Wales*, PhD *Reading* Sr. Lectr.
Edwards, Barry, BA *Sus.*, MA *Essex* Reader
Ginman, John, BA *Warw.* Sr. Lectr.
Hunt, Leon, BEd *Birm.*, MA *E.Anglia* Sr. Lectr.
McKim, Ross, MA *Sur.* Sr. Lectr.
McLarnon, Oliver, MA *Lond.* Sr. Lectr.

Biology and Biochemistry

Tel: (01895) 203090 Fax: (01895) 274348
Arrand, Janet E., BSc PhD Prof.
Dickson, Ian R., BA *Camb.*, MA *Camb.*, MSc *Brad.*, PhD *Lond.*, FIBiol Reader
Newbold, Robert, BSc *Aston*, PhD *Lond.*, FIBiol Prof.; Head*
Sumpter, John P., BSc *Wales*, PhD *Wales*, FIBiol Prof.
Tyler, Charles R., MSc *Aston*, PhD *Aston* Sr. Lectr.
Other Staff: 11 Lectrs.; 26 Lectrs.†

Business Studies

Tel: (0181) 891 0121 Fax: (0181) 891 8291
Aston, John, MBA *Brun.* Sr. Lectr.
Bogard, Montague, BCom *Birm.*, MSc *Lond.*, FCA Sr. Lectr.
Childerhouse, Ken, BSc *Lond.* Sr. Lectr.
Cockett, William A., BSc *Lond.*, MSc *Brun.*, PhD *Brun.* Sr. Lectr.; Head*
Finer, Anne, BSc *Lond.* Sr. Lectr.
Jarvis, Christopher, BA *Birm.*, MSc Sr. Lectr.
Other Staff: 24 Lectrs.; 15 Lectrs.†

Design

Tel: (01784) 431341 Fax: (01784) 472879
Brickwood, Alan, MDes Prof. (on secondment from DTI)
Isherwood, Peter, MA *Lond.* Prof.; Head*
Stroud, Ray R., MTech *Brun.*, PhD *Brun.* Sr. Lectr.
Turnock, Paul, BA *Lond.*, MDes *RCA* Sr. Lectr.
Wright, David, BSc *Lond.*, PhD *Warw.* Sr. Lectr.
Other Staff: 8 Lectrs.; 4 Teaching Assocs.; 1 Prof.†; 1 Sr. Lectr.†; 4 Lectrs.†

Earth Sciences, see Geog. and Earth Scis.

Economics and Finance

Fax: (01895) 203384
Antoniou, Anthony, BA *CNAA*, MSc *York(UK)*, DPhil *York(UK)* Prof.; Head*
Barr, David, BSc *Lond.*, MSc *Lond.*, PhD *Lond.* Prof.
Bennett, Paul B., MA *Trinity(Dub.)*, MA *Calif.* Sr. Lectr.
Burningham, David J., MA *Camb.*, PhD Sr. Lectr.
Buxton, Martin, BA *Leic.*
Cave, Martin, BA *Oxf.*, MA *Oxf.* Prof.
Martin, Chris, BSc *Brist.*, MSc *Lond.*, PhD *Durh.* Reader
Parker, Simon, BSc *Wales*, PhD *Lond.* Reader
Other Staff: 14 Lectrs.; 7 Lectrs.†

Education, School of

Tel: (0181) 891 0120 Fax: (0181) 744 2960
Barlex, David, BSc *Leic.*, PhD *Leic.* Sr. Lectr.
Day, Michael, BA *CNAA*, MPhil *Lond.*, PhD *Lond.* Sr. Lectr.
Fisher, Robert, BA *Lond.* Sr. Lectr.
Garner, Philip, BA *Wales*, MA *Lond.*, PhD *Lond.* Sr. Lectr.
Gregory, Gerald, BA *Lond.*, MA *Lond.*, PhD *Lond.* Sr. Lectr.
Hodkinson, Steven, BA *Manc.*, PhD *Manc.* Prof.; Head*
Jeffrey, Robert, BSc *S'ton.*, MPhil *Nott.* Principal Lectr.
Koshy, Valsa, BSc *Kerala*, MA *Keele*, MPhil *Lond.* Sr. Lectr.
Longman, Christopher, BA *Open(UK)*, MA *Lond.* Sr. Lectr.
Smithers, Alan, BSc *Lond.*, MEd *Manc.*, MSc *Brad.*, PhD *Lond.*, PhD *Brad.* Prof.
Thomas, Linda, BSc *Wales*, MEd *Wales*, PhD *Lond.* Prof.

Other Staff: 27 Lectrs.; 11 Lectrs.†

Engineering, Electrical and Electronic

Tel: (01895) 203223 Fax: (01895) 258728
Aitchison, Colin S., BSc Prof.
Hunter, Arthur, BSc *Lond.*, MSc *Lond.*
Irving, Michael, PhD *Sheff.* Prof.
Lea, R. Mike, MSc *Lond.*, FIEE Prof.
Marsh, John F., BSc *Aston*, PhD *Brist.* Sr. Lectr.
Mehta, Pratab A., BSc *St And.*, PhD *Brist.* Reader
Richardson, Julian, MSc *Manc.*, PhD *Manc.* Sr. Lectr.
Song, Yong-Hua, BEng *Chengdu Sci.& Technol.*, PhD *Beijing* Prof.
Stonham, T. John, MSc *Kent*, PhD *Kent* Prof.; Head*
Other Staff: 20 Lectrs.; 1 Prof.†

Engineering, Mechanical

Fax: (01895) 256392
Brown, Chris, BSc *Leeds* Sr. Lectr.
Henshall, John, BA *Camb.*, MA *Camb.*, PhD *Camb.* Prof.
Isat, Ibrahim, BSc *Lond.*, PhD *Lond.* Reader
Ladommatos, Nicos, MSc *Lond.*, PhD *Lond.* Prof.; Head*
Mokhtarzadeh-Behghan, Mohammad-Reza, BSc *Arya-Mehr*, MSc *Lond.*, PhD *Lond.* Sr. Lectr.
Reynolds, Alan J., BASc *Tor.*, PhD *Lond.* Prof.
Stolarski, Tom A., MSc *Gdansk*, PhD *Gdansk*, DSc *Cracow* Prof.
Tassou, Savvas, BSc *CNAA*, MBA *Westminster*, PhD *Westminster* Reader
Wrobel, Luiz, MSc *Brazil*, PhD *S'ton.* Prof.
Yettram, Alan L., BA *Trinity(Dub.)*, BAI *Trinity(Dub.)*, ScD *Trinity(Dub.)* Prof.
Other Staff: 14 Lectrs., 6 Lectrs.†

Engineering Systems, see Manufacturing and Engin. Systems

English, see under Arts

Environmental Sciences, see Phys. and Environmental Scis., Inst. of

Finance, see Econ. and Finance

Geography and Earth Sciences

Tel: (01895) 203215 Fax: (01895) 203217
Firth, Callum, BSc *Wales*, PhD *Coventry* Sr. Lectr.; Head*
Other Staff: 9 Lectrs.; 7 Lectrs.†

Government

Tel: (01895) 203333 Fax: (01895) 812595
Glees, P. Anthony, MA *Oxf.*, BPhil *Oxf.*, MPhil *Oxf.*, DPhil *Oxf.* Reader
Kogan, Maurice, MA *Camb.*, DLitt Prof.†, Government and Social Administration
Packwood, G. F. L., BA *Leic.*, MEd *Reading* Sr. Lectr.
Pollitt, Christopher, MA *Oxf.*, PhD *Lond.* Prof.
Tomlinson, James, BSc *Lond.*, PhD *Lond.* Prof.; Head*
Webb, Paul, BA *Nott.*, MSc *Lond.*, PhD *Florence* Sr. Lectr.
Other Staff: 7 Lectrs., 4 Lectrs.†

Health Studies

Tel: (0181) 891 0121 Fax: (0181) 847 2030
Anderson-Ford, David, LLB *Liv.* Sr. Lectr.
De Souza, Lorraine, BSc *Brist.*, MSc *Newcastle(UK)*, PhD *Lond.* Prof.
Farrow, Alexandra, BSc *Lond.*, MSc *Wales*, *Brist.* Sr. Lectr.
LeMay, Andree, BSc *Lond.*, PhD *Lond.* Sr. Lectr.; Acting Head*
MacDonald, Theodore, BSc *McG.*, MSc *Col.*, PhD *Glas.*, DMed, FAPS Sr. Lectr.
Marsland, David, BA *Camb.*, MA *Camb.*, PhD *Brun.* Prof.; Reader
Naylor, Sandra, MEd *Brun.* Sr. Lectr.
Waters, Bernadette, MA *Lond.* Sr. Lectr.
Wilson, Lesley, BSc *Newcastle(UK)* Sr. Lectr.
Other Staff: 49 Lectrs.; 8 Lectrs.†

History, American, see under Arts

Human Sciences

Fax: (01895) 237573
Adams, Parveen, BA *Lond.* Sr. Lectr.
Irwin, G. Alan, BSc *Salf.*, MSc *Manc.*, PhD *Manc.* Sr. Lectr.
Kuper, Adam J., BA *S.Af.*, PhD *Camb.* Prof.
Lynch, Michael E., BSc *Cornell*, PhD *Calif.* Prof.
Ray, Colette, BA *Wales*, PhD *Wales* Sr. Lectr.
Richardson, John T. E., BA *Oxf.*, DPhil *Sus.*, FBPsS Prof.†
Robinson, Ian C., MA *Nott.* Sr. Lectr.
Toren, Christina, BSc *Lond.*, MPhil *Lond.*, PhD *Lond.* Sr. Lectr.
Woolgar, Stephen, MA *Camb.*, DPhil *York(UK)* Prof.; Head*
Wright, Michael J., BA *Camb.*, PhD *Camb.* Prof.
Other Staff: 20 Lectrs.; 1 Lectr.†

Information Systems and Computing

Tel: (01895) 203374 Fax: (01895) 251686
Elliman, Anthony D., BTech PhD Sr. Lectr.
Neal, Leslie R., BSc *Nott.*, PhD *Nott.* Sr. Lectr.
O'Keefe, Robert, BSc *Lanc.*, PhD *S'ton* Prof.
Paul, Ray J., BSc *Hull*, MSc *Hull*, PhD *Hull* Prof.; Head*
Other Staff: 23 Lectrs.; 13 Lectrs.†

Languages

Tel: (01895) 203073 Fax: (01895) 203073
Hayes, Karin, BA *Lond.*, MA *Thames V.* Lectr.; Head*
Other Staff: 2 Lectrs.

Law

Fax: (01895) 810476
Choo, Andrew, BCom *NSW*, LLB *NSW*, DPhil *Oxf.* Lectr.
Corbett, Claire, BSc *Lond.*, MPhil *Camb.*, PhD *Lond.* Sr. Lectr.
Easton, Susan, BSc *Wales*, MA *Lond.*, PhD *S'ton.* Sr. Lectr.
King, Michael, BA *Lond.*, LLM *Warw.* Prof.
Loveland, Ian D., BA *Warw.*, DPhil *Oxf.* Prof.; Head*
Morris, Gillian, LLB *Brist.*, PhD *Camb.* Prof.
Piper, Christine, BA *Brist.*, MA *Lond.*, PhD *Lond.* Sr. Lectr.
Polden, Patrick, BA *Reading*, PhD *Reading* Sr. Lectr.
Rawlings, Philip, PhD *Hull* Sr. Lectr.
Stanko, Elizabeth, BA *N.Y.*, PhD *N.Y.* Prof.
Other Staff: 13 Lectrs.; 10 Lectrs.†

Management Studies

Tel: (01895) 203122 Fax: (01895) 203149
Dickson, Keith, BE *NZ*, MSc *Birm.* Sr. Lectr.
McLoughlin, Ian P., BA *Kent*, PhD *Bath* Reader; Head*
Sims, David B., BA *Portsmouth*, MA *Leeds*, PhD *Bath* Prof.
Woods, Adrian G. W., BA *CNAA*, MA *Lanc.*, PhD Prof.
Other Staff: 11 Lectrs.; 4 Lectrs.†

Manufacturing and Engineering Systems

Tel: (01895) 203300 Fax: (01895) 812556
Balachandran, Wamedeva, BSc *Ceyl.*, MSc *Brad.*, PhD *Brad.* Prof.
Butler, Clive, BSc *Manc.*, MSc *Lond.*, PhD *Lond.* Reader
Clark, Colin, BSc *CNAA*, PhD *Lond.* Prof.
Grieve, Robert J., BSc *Salf.*, MSc *Manc.*, PhD *Manc.* Reader
Griffiths, Brian J., MTech PhD, FIEE, FIMechE Reader
Gunasekaran, Angapur, BE *Madr.*, ME *Madr.*, PhD *Bom.* Sr. Lectr.
Hindi, Khalil, BEng *Beirut*, MSc *Manc.*, PhD *Manc.* Prof.
Jones, Brian E., BSc *Manc.*, MSc *Manc.*, PhD *Manc.*, DSc *Manc.* Hewlett Packard Prof., Manufacturing Metrology
Middleditch, Alan E., MSc *Manc.*, MS *Carnegie-Mellon*, PhD *Carnegie-Mellon* Prof.

Peirce, E. Alan, MTech   Sr. Lectr.
Powell, Roger, BEng Sheff., PhD Durh.   Sr.
    Lectr.
Rakowski, Richard, BSc Lond., MSc Lond., PhD
    Lond.   Sr. Lectr.
Rees, David, MA MSc PhD   Sr. Lectr.
Sarhadi, Mansoor, BSc Reading, MSc Lond., PhD
    Lond.   Prof.; Head*
Sivalaganathan, Sangarappillai, MSc Birm., PhD
    Lond.   Sr. Lectr.
Other Staff: 9 Lectrs.; 2 Lectrs.†

Materials Technology

Fax: (01895) 812636
Evans, Julian R. G., BSc Birm., PhD
    Bath   Reader
Folkes, Michael J., MSc Brist., PhD Brist.   Prof.;
    Head*
Hornsby, P. R., BSc CNAA, PhD   Sr. Lectr.
Ralph, Brian, MA Camb., PhD Camb., Hon. ScD
    Camb., FIM, FIP   Prof.
Vesely, Drahomir, DrRerNat Prague, CSc
    Prague   Reader
Other Staff: 7 Lectrs.; 1 Lectr.†

Mathematics and Statistics

Tel: (01895) 203304 Fax: (01895) 203303
Chandler-Wilde, Simon, BSc Lond., MSc
    Newcastle(UK), PhD Brad.   Sr. Lectr.
Darby-Dowman, Kenneth, BSc Brad., MSc Brun.,
    PhD Brun.   Sr. Lectr.
Goodall, Gerald W., BSc Birm., MBA Brun.   Sr.
    Lectr.
Mitra, Guatum, BEE Jad., MSc Lond., PhD
    Lond.   Prof.; Head*
Newby, John C., BA Keele, PhD Dund.,
    FIMA   Sr. Lectr.
Rawlins, Anthony D., BSc Aston, MSc Sur., PhD
    Sur.   Reader
Twizell, Edward H., BSc Wales, MA York(Can.),
    PhD CNAA   Prof.
Whiteman, John R., BSc St And., PhD Lond.,
    FIMA   Prof.
Other Staff: 14 Lectrs.; 6 Lectrs.†

Performing Arts, see under Arts

Physical and Environmental Sciences,
Institute of

Fax: (01895) 256844
Cave, Martin, MA Oxf., DPhil Oxf.   Chairman*
Other Staff: 6 Lectrs.; 40 Lectrs.†

Environmental Research, Centre for

Donaldson, John D., BSc Aberd., PhD Aberd., DSc
    Lond.   Prof.; Head*
Grimes, Sue M., BSc Lond., MBA Lond., PhD
    Lond.   Sr. Lectr.

Physical Sciences, Centre for

Beynon, John, BSc Wales, PhD Wales   Sr. Lectr.
Coombes, Robert G., BSc Lond., PhD Lond.,
    FRSChem   Sr. Lectr.
Hobson, Peter R., BSc Lond., PhD Lond.   Sr.
    Lectr.
Watts, Stephen J., BSc Lond., PhD Lond.   Reader

Social Work

Tel: (0181) 891 0121 Fax: (0181) 891 2858
Aymer, Catherine, BSc Sus., MSc Aberd.   Sr.
    Lectr.
Beresford, Peter, BA Oxf., BLitt Oxf.   Reader
Trevillion, Steven, BSc Lond., MLitt
    Oxf.   Reader; Head*
Other Staff: 25 Lectrs.; 20 Lectrs.†

Sport Sciences

Tel: (0181) 891 0121 Fax: (0181) 891 8211
Hunter, John, MA Leeds   Sr. Lectr.
Radford, Peter F., PhD Glas., MSc   Prof.;
    Head*
Sharp, Norman, PhD Glas.   Prof.
Terry, Peter, BA Brun., MA Vic.(Tor.), PhD
    Kent   Sr. Lectr.
Other Staff: 17 Lectrs.; 9 Lectrs.†

Statistics, see Maths. and Stats.

SPECIAL CENTRES, ETC

Applied Simulation Modelling, Centre
for

Fax: (01895) 251686
Paul, Prof. Ray J., PhD Hull   Dir.*

Bio-Engineering, Brunel Institute for

Tel: (01895) 271206 Fax: (01895) 274608
Sutherland, Ian, PhD Brist.   Prof.; Dir.*

Computational Mathematics, Brunel
Institute of

Tel: (01895) 203270 Fax: (01895) 203303
Whiteman, Prof. John R., BSc St And., PhD
    Lond., FIMA   Dir.*

Consumer and Commercial Law,
Centre for

Fax: (01895) 810476
Woodroffe, Prof. Geoffrey, MA Camb.   Dir.*

Criminal Justice Research, Centre for

Fax: (01895) 810476
Stanko, Elizabeth, BA N.Y., PhD N.Y.   Prof.;
    Dir.*

Design Research Centre

Tel: (01784) 431341 Fax: (01784) 472879
Inns, Tom G., PhD   Dir.*

Education and Employment Research,
Centre for

Tel: (0181) 891 0121 Fax: (0181) 891 8270
Smithers, Alan, BSc Lond., MEd Manc., MSc Brad.,
    PhD Lond., PhD Brad.   Prof.; Dir.*

Health Economics Research Group

Buxton, Martin, BA Leic.   Prof.; Dir.*

Health, Sickness and Disablement,
Centre for the Study of

Tel: (01895) 203306 Fax: (01895) 237573
Robinson, Ian C., MA Nott.   Dir.*

Information Environments, Centre for

Rosenberg, D.   Dir.*

Innovation, Culture and Technology,
Centre for Research into

Tel: (01895) 203121 Fax: (01895) 203155
Hine, Christine, BA Oxf., MSc York(UK), DPhil
    York(UK)   Acting Dir.*
Woolgar, Prof. Stephen W., MA Camb.,
    PhD   Head*

Law, the Child and the Family, Centre
for the Study of

Fax: (01895) 810476
King, Michael, BA Lond., LLM Warw.   Jt. Dir.*
Piper, Christine, BA Brist., PhD   Jt. Dir.*

Lifelong Learning Centre

Tel: (01895) 235332 Fax: (01895) 811737
Jones, Anne, BA Lond.   Prof.; Head*

Living Information Systems Thinking,
Centre for

Paul, Ray J., BSc Hull, MSc Hull PhD Hull

Manufacturing Metrology, Brunel
Centre for

Fax: (01895) 812556
Jones, Barry E., PhD Manc., DSc Manc.   Prof.;
    Dir.*

Materials Processing, Wolfson Centre
for

Bevis, Michael J., BSc Lond., PhD Lond.,
    FIP   Prof.; Dir.*

Neotectonics Research Centre

Firth, Callum, BSc Wales, PhD Coventry   Dir.*

Neural and Evolutionary Systems,
Centre for

Dracopolous, Dimitri, PhD   Dir.*

Neural Computing Applications, Centre
for

Tel: (01784) 431341 Fax: (01784) 472879
Harris, Tom, BSc Brun., PhD Brun.   Dir.*

Power Systems, Brunel Institute of

Tel: (01895) 203209 Fax: (01895) 258728
Irving, Prof. Malcolm, PhD Sheff.   Dir.*

Public Policy and Practice, Centre for
the Evaluation of

Tel: (01895) 203334 Fax: (01895) 247697
Kogan, Prof. Maurice, MA Camb., DLitt   Co-
    Dir.*
Pollitt, Prof. Christopher, MA Oxf., PhD
    Lond.   Co-Dir.*

Rehabilitation, Centre for Research in

Tel: (0181) 891 0121 Fax: (0181) 891 8211
de Souza, Lorraine, BSc Brist., MSc Newcastle(UK),
    PhD Lond.   Dir.*

Water Operational Research Centre

Powell, Roger, BEng Sheff., PhD Durh.   Dir.*

Youth Work Studies, Centre for

Tel: (0181) 891 0121 Fax: (0181) 744 2960
Day, Michael, BA CNAA, MPhil   Dir.*

CONTACT OFFICERS

Academic affairs. Academic Secretary:
    Alexander, John B.
Accommodation (Twickenham/Osterley).
    Accommodation Officer: Alward, A.
Accommodation (Uxbridge/Runnymede).
    Accommodation Officer: Gee, Angela
Admissions (first degree). Admissions Officer:
    Callaway, William
Admissions (higher degree). Assistant
    Registrar: Callaway, William
Adult/continuing education. Director: Jones,
    Anne, BA Lond.
Alumni. Curley, Sue
Careers. Head of Careers Services: Wolff,
    Jonathan
Computing services. Director: Broadbent,
    Alan, BSc Wales
Conferences/corporate hospitality.
    Tomlinson, Valerie
Consultancy services. Director, Research
    Services: MacFarlane, Christine
Credit transfer. Senior Assistant Registrar:
    Weale, Juliet, BA Lond.
Distance education. (Contact the appropriate
    Course Director)
Estates and buildings/works and services.
    Director of Estates: ......
Examinations. Senior Assistant Registrar:
    Pickess, Kevin
Finance. Director of Finance: Clifford, John,
    FCA
General enquiries. Le Marquand, Philippa
Health services. Director, University Health
    Services: Sedgwick, John P., MB BS Lond.
International office. Director, International
    Office: Browne, Caroline, BA Nott.
Language training for international students.
    Hayes, Karen
Library (chief librarian). Head of Library
    Services: Thompson, Beryl-Ann, BSc Aberd.
Personnel/human resources. Director of
    Personnel and Staff Development: Brant,
    Sarah, BSc Wales, MA Warw.
Public relations, information and marketing.
    Director, External Relations: Billett, Prof. Eric
    H., MA Camb., DPhil Oxf.
Publications. Publications Officer: Bevis,
    Marianne E., BA Lond.
Purchasing. Purchasing Officer: Babe, Peter

Quality assurance and accreditation. Senior Assistant Registrar: Weale, Juliet, BA *Lond.*
Research. Director, Research Services: MacFarlane, Christine
Safety. Head, Safety and Site Services: Champion, John, MSc *Brun.*
Scholarships, awards, loans. Senior Assistant Registrar: Westaway, Bob
Schools liaison. Head, Student Recruitment: Hall, Robert A.
Security. Head, Safety and Site Services: Champion, John, MSc *Brun.*
Sport and recreation. Director: Brightwell, Mike, BA *Nott.*, MSc *Lough.*
Student welfare/counselling. Head of Counselling: McNulty, Geoff

Students from other countries. Director, International Office: Browne, Caroline, BA *Nott.*
Students with disabilities. University Disablement Officer: ......
University press. Manager: Leach, Gary

CAMPUS/COLLEGE HEADS

Osterley Campus, Borough Road, Isleworth, Middlesex, England TW7 5DU. (*Tel:* (0181) 891 0121; *Fax:* (0181) 891 8211.) Warden: ......

Runnymede Campus, Englefield Green, Egham, Surrey, England TW20 0JZ. (*Tel:*

(01784) 431341; *Fax:* (01784) 472879.) Warden: ......

Twickenham Campus, Gordon House, 300 St Margarets Road, Twickenham, Middlesex, England TW1 1PT. (*Tel:* (081) 891 0121; *Fax:* (0181) 891 8270.) Warden: ......

[Information supplied by the institution as at 27 March 1998, and edited by the ACU]

UNIVERSITY OF BUCKINGHAM

Founded 1973

Postal Address: Buckingham, England MK18 1EG
Telephone: (01280) 814080 **Fax**: (01280) 822245 **E-mail**: solo@bucksuni.demon.co.uk

VICE-CHANCELLOR*—Taylor, Prof. Robert H., BA *Ohio*, MA *Antioch*, PhD *Cornell*
SECRETARY AND REGISTRAR—Elder, John, MAppSci *Glas.*

UNIVERSITY OF CAMBRIDGE

Founded in the 13th century

Member of the Association of Commonwealth Universities

Postal Address: The Old Schools, Trinity Lane, Cambridge, England CB2 1TN
Telephone: (01223) 337733 **Fax**: (01223) 332332 **WWW**: http://www.cam.ac.uk

CHANCELLOR—Edinburgh, H.R.H. The Duke of, KG, KT, OM, GBE, Hon. LLD *Camb.*, Hon. LLD *Edin.*, Hon. LLD *Malta*, Hon. LLD *Wales*, Hon. DSc *Delhi*, Hon. DSc *Salf.*, Hon. Dr *RCA*, FRS, Hon. Fellow of Trinity College
VICE-CHANCELLOR*—Broers, Prof. Sir Alec, CBE, BSc *Melb.*, BA *Camb.*, PhD *Camb.*, ScD *Camb.*, Hon. DEng *Glas.*, Hon. DSc *Warw.*, FRS, FEng, FIEE, FIP
HIGH STEWARD—Runcie, The Rt. Rev. Lord, MA *Camb.*, Hon. DD *Camb.*, Hon. Fellow of Trinity Hall
PRO-VICE-CHANCELLOR—Needham, Prof. Roger M., MA *Camb.*, PhD *Camb.*, Hon. DSc *Kent*, FRS, Feng (Wolfs.)
PRO-VICE-CHANCELLOR—Lonsdale, Anne M., MA *Oxf.*, MA *Camb.* (New H.)
DEPUTY HIGH STEWARD—Richardson, The Rt. Hon. the Lord, MBE, MA *Camb.*, LLB *Camb.*, Hon. LLD *Camb.*, Hon. DSc *City(UK)*, Hon. Fellow of Caius College
COMMISSARY—Oliver, The Rt. Hon. the Lord, QC, Hon. LLD *Camb.*, BA, Hon. Fellow of Trinity Hall
ORATOR—Bowen, Anthony J., MA (Jes.)
REGISTRARY‡—Mead, Timothy J., BSc *Lond.*, PhD *Camb.*
SECRETARY GENERAL OF THE FACULTIES—Livesey, David A., BSc *Lond.*, MA *Camb.*, PhD *Camb.* (Emm.)
LIBRARIAN—Fox, Peter K., BA *Lond.*, MA *Sheff.*, MA *Camb.* (Selw.)
TREASURER—Womack, Joanna M., MA *Camb.* (Trin.H.)
DIRECTOR OF THE FITZWILLIAM MUSEUM AND MARLAY CURATOR— Robinson, D. Duncan, MA *Yale*, MA *Camb.* (Cla.)

GENERAL INFORMATION

History. The university was founded in the thirteenth century. Statutes granted to the university by Elizabeth I remained in force for 300 years, and were replaced twice in the nineteenth century and again in 1926. The

university has 31 constituent colleges, each of which is a separate foundation with its own statutes. The fellows of the colleges provide the majority of the teaching staff of the university.

Admission to first degree courses (see also United Kingdom Introduction). Through

Universities and Colleges Admission Service (UCAS) and the university's individual colleges. United Kingdom students: General Certificate of Education (GCE) A level with several high passes. International students: normally a degree from a university in the student's home country.

First Degrees (see also United Kingdom Directory to Subjects of Study). BA, BEd, BTh, BVetMed, MB BChir, MusB.

BA, BTh, MusB: 3 years; BEd: 4 years; MB BChir: 5 years; BVetMed: 6 years.

Higher Degrees (see also United Kingdom Directory to Subjects of Study). BD, LLM, MA, MBA, MChir, MEd, MEng, MLitt, MSc, MSci (natural sciences), MStud, MPhil, PhD, DD, LittD, LLD, MD, MusD, ScD.

MA: awarded without examination to members of the university of a certain standing. MEng, MSci: awarded after 4-year honours courses in various triposes. Higher doctorates: awarded on published work (also possible for PhD).

LLM: 1 year; MBA, MPhil: 1–2 years; MEd, MLitt, MSc, MStud: 2 years; PhD: 3 years; BD, MChir: minimum 5 years after first degree.

Libraries. University library: 4,892,000 printed books; 1,162,000 serials; 142,000 manuscripts; 1,075,800 maps; 1,215,000 microforms. Faculty and departmental libraries: several million items, including historic collections. College libraries: historical collections, manuscripts and current literature.

Fees (1998–99, annual). Undergraduate: £1000 (UK/EC). Postgraduate: £2610 (UK/EC); £6606–16,014 (international).

Academic Year (1999–2000). Three terms: 5 October–3 December; 18 January–17 March; 25 April–16 June. Courses are also taught during July–early August.

Income (1996–97). Total, £282,400,000.

Statistics. Staff: over 4170 academic/academic-related; approximately 2900 assistant/support; 500 fellows of colleges not employed by the university. Students (1997–98): total 15,821 (8742 men, 7079 women); international, approximately 2100.

ACADEMIC UNITS

Anatomy, see also Veterinary Studies

Tel: (01223) 333750 Fax: (01223) 333786
Bray, Sarah J., BA MPhil PhD   Lectr. (Down.)
Burton, Graham J., MB BCh Oxf., MA Camb., MD Camb.   Lectr. (S.Joh.)
Dyball, R. E. J., MA Camb., VetMB Camb., PhD Brist., ScD Camb.   Lectr. (Fitz.)
Edgley, S. A., BSc Brist., MA Camb., PhD Brist.   Lectr. (S.Joh.)
Ferguson-Smith, Anne C., BSc Glas., MS Yale, PhD Yale   Lectr. (Darw.)
Grandage, John, BVetMed Lond., MA Camb.   Univ. Clin. Vet. Anatomist (S.Cat.)

Hardie, Roger C., BA Camb., PhD ANU   Lectr.
Harris, William A., BA Calif., PhD Cal.Tech.   Prof. (Cla.)
Hastings, M. H., BSc Liv., PhD Liv.   Lectr.
Herbert, J., BSc Birm., MB ChB Birm., PhD Lond., MA   Reader, Neuroendocrinology (Cai.)
Holt, Christine E., BSc Sus., PhD Lond.   Lectr.
Johnson, Martin H., MA PhD   Prof., Reproductive Sciences; Head* (Chr.)
Keynes, Roger J., MA MB BChir   Lectr. (Trin.)
Navaratnam, Visvanathan, MB BS Ceyl., PhD   Lectr. (Chr.)
Parkin, Ian, MB ChB Aberd.   Univ. Clin. Vet. Anatomist (Rob.)
Roberts, Angela C., BSc Sus., PhD Camb.   Lectr. (Gir.)
Schofield, P. N., MA Oxf., DPhil Oxf.   Lectr. (Gir.)
Sofroniew, M. V., BSc Loyola(Calif.), MD Munich, DPhil Oxf.   Reader, Neuroanatomy (Jes.)
White, R. A. H., BA Oxf., DPhil Oxf.   Lectr.
Other Staff: 3 Sr. Tech. Officers; 1 Assoc. Lectr.

Anglo-Saxon, Norse and Celtic

Tel: (01223) 335070 Fax: (01223) 335079
Bibire, Paul A., BA Wales, BPhil Oxf., MA   Lectr.
Dumville, David N., PhD Edin., MA, FRHistS   Prof., Palaeography and Cultural History (Gir.)
Keynes, Simon D., MA PhD LittD   Reader, Anglo-Saxon History (Trin.)
Lapidge, Michael, MA Alta., MA Camb., PhD Tor., LittD   Elrington and Bosworth Prof.; Head* (Cla.)
Mhaonaigh, Máire, MA N.U.I., PhD N.U.I.   Lectr. (S.Joh.)
Orchard, Andrew P. M., MA Oxf., PhD   Lectr. (Emm.)
Padel, Oliver J., MLitt Edin., MA Camb., LittD Camb.   Lectr. (Pet.)

Anthropology, Biological

Tel: (01223) 335454 Fax: (01223) 335460
Foley, Robert A., MA PhD   Lectr. (King's)
Lee, Phyllis C., BA Stan., PhD Camb.   Lectr. (Down.)
Mascie-Taylor, C. G. Nicholas, MA PhD ScD   Reader; Head* (Chur.)

Anthropology, Social

Tel: (01223) 334599 Fax: (01223) 334748
Goody, Esther N., BA Ohio, PhD ScD   Lectr. (New H.)
Hart, J. Keith, MA PhD   Lectr.
Howe, Leopold E. A., BSc Birm., PhD Edin., MA   Lectr. (Darw.)
Hugh-Jones, Stephen P., MA PhD   Lectr.; Head* (King's)
Humphrey, Caroline, MA PhD   Reader, Asian Anthropology (King's)

Lewis, Gilbert A., BM BCh Oxf., MA Oxf., MA Camb., PhD Lond.   Lectr. (S.Joh.)
Macfarlane, Alan D. J., MA Oxf., MA Camb., DPhil Oxf., PhD   Prof., Anthropological Science (King's)
Strathern, Marilyn, MA PhD, FBA   William Wyse Prof. (Gir.)
Watson, Helen E., BA Belf., PhD   Lectr. (S.Joh.)

Arabic, see also Islamic Studies

Tel: (01223) 335106 Fax: (01223) 335110
Khalidi, Tarif, MA Oxf., PhD Chic.   Sir Thomas Adams's Prof. (King's)
Postgate, J. Nicholas, MA, FBA   Prof., Assyriology (Trin.)
Other Staff: 2 Lang. Teaching Officers

Aramaic

Tel: (01223) 335106 Fax: (01223) 335110
Snaith, J. G., MA Oxf., MA Camb., BD Lond.   Lectr. (Wolfs.)

Archaeology, see also Classics

Tel: (01223) 333500 Fax: (01223) 333503
Chakrabarti, Dilip K., MA Calc., PhD Calc.   Lectr.
French, Charles A. I., BA Wales, MA Lond., PhD Lond.   Lectr. (Gir.)
Hills, Catherine M., BA Durh., MA Camb., PhD Lond.   Lectr. (Newn.)
Hodder, Ian R., BA Lond., PhD, FBA   Prof., Prehistory (Darw.)
Jones, Martin K., MA PhD   George Pitt-Rivers Prof., Archaeology Science; Head*
Mellars, Paul A., MA PhD ScD, FBA, FSA   Prof., Prehistory and Human Evolution (Corp.)
Renfrew, Lord, MA Camb., PhD Camb., ScD Camb., Hon. LittD Sheff., Hon. Dr Athens, FSA, FBA   Disney Prof. (Jes.)
Sørensen, Marie L. S., BA Aarhus, CandPhil Aarhus, PhD Camb.   Lectr. (Jes.)
Stoddart, Simon K. F., MA Camb., PhD Camb.   Lectr. (King's)

Archaeology and Anthropology, Museum of

Tel: (01223) 333516 Fax: (01223) 333503
Phillipson, David W., MA PhD, FSA   Reader, African Prehistory; Curator and Dir.* (Cai.)
Other Staff: 3 Sr. Asst. Curators

Architecture

Tel: (01223) 332950 Fax: (01223) 332960
Baker, N. V., BSc Lond., PhD Lond., MA   Lectr. (S.Edm.)
Bullock, N. O. A., MA PhD   Lectr. (King's)
Carl, P. W., MArch Prin., MA   Lectr.
Carolin, P. B., MA Lond., MA Camb.   Prof.; Head* (Corp.)
Echenique, Marcial, DrArch Barcelona, MA   Prof., Land Use and Transport Studies (Chur.)
Hogben, Patrick G. O'N., MA   Lectr. (Magd.)
McNeur, Lorna A., BArch Cooper Union, MA MPhil   Lectr. (L.Cav.)
Penz, François-André, PhD Camb.   Asst. Dir. of Res. (Darw.)
Ray, N. J., MA   Lectr. (Jes.)
Saint, Andrew J., BA Oxf., MPhil Lond., FRIBA   Prof.
Sergeant, J. F. H., MA   Lectr. (Rob.)
Spence, Robert J. S., MSc Cornell, MA PhD   Reader, Architectural Engineering (Magd.)
Steemers, Koen A., BSc Bath, MPhil Camb., PhD Camb.   Lectr.
Vesely, D., PhD Prague, MA   Lectr.

Astronomy, Institute of, see also Phys.

Tel: (01223) 337548 Fax: (01223) 337523
Carswell, R. F., BSc Otago, MSc Br.Col., DPhil Sus.   Reader
Clarke, Catherine J., MA Camb., DPhil Oxf.   Lectr. (Cla.)

The abbreviation in round brackets after a teacher's name denotes the college of which the teacher is a present fellow. The names of fellows of the colleges who do not hold an academic appointment within the university's teaching departments are listed below under 'The Colleges' section. The names of the colleges are indicated by abbreviations as follows:

Chr.	Christ's College	Magd.	Magdalene College
Chur.	Churchill College	New H.	New Hall
Cla.	Clare College	Newn.	Newnham College
Cla.H.	Clare Hall	Pemb.	Pembroke College
Corp.	Corpus Christi College	Pet.	Peterhouse
Darw.	Darwin College	Qu.	Queens' College
Down.	Downing College	Rob.	Robinson College
Emm.	Emmanuel College	Selw.	Selwyn College
Fitz.	Fitzwilliam College	Sid.	Sidney Sussex College
Gir.	Girton College	S.Cat.	St Catharine's College
Cai.	Gonville and Caius College	S.Edm.	St Edmund's College
Hom.	Homerton College	S.Joh.	St John's College
Hug.	Hughes Hall	Trin.	Trinity College
Jes.	Jesus College	Trin.H.	Trinity Hall
King's	King's College	Wolfs.	Wolfson College
L.Cav.	Lucy Cavendish College		

Note—For fellows of college the usual postal address is the college, and for other staff the university department, laboratory, museum, etc.

Efstathiou, George P., MA Oxf., MA Camb., PhD Durh., FRS, FIP, FRAS   Prof., Astrophysics (King's)

Eggleton, P. P., BSc Edin., MA Edin., PhD   Asst. Dir. of Res. (Corp.)

Ellis, Richard S., BSc Lond., DPhil Oxf.   Plumian Prof., Astronomy and Experimental Philosophy; Dir.* (Magd.)

Gilmore, G. F.   Reader, Astrophysics

Gough, Douglas O., MA PhD   Prof., Theoretical Astrophysics (Chur.)

Griffin, R. F., MA PhD ScD   Reader, Observational Astronomy (S.Joh.)

Hewett, P. C., BSc Edin., MA Camb., PhD Edin.   Asst. Dir. of Res., John Couch Adams Astronomer (Corp.)

Lahav, Ofer, BSc Tel-Aviv, MSc Ben Gurion, PhD   Lectr. (S.Cat.)

Lynden-Bell, Donald, MA PhD, FRS   Prof., Astrophysics (Cla.)

Mackay, C. D., BSc Edin., PhD   Asst. Dir. of Res. (Corp.)

McMahon, Richard G., BSc Belf.   Asst. Dir. of Res.

Parry, Ian R., BSc St And., MSc Sus., PhD Durh.   Asst. Dir. of Res.

Perry, Judith J., BCE C.U.N.Y., MS N.Y.Polytech., PhD N.Y.Polytech.   Asst. Dir. of Res. (Newn.)

Pringle, James E., MA PhD   Reader, Theoretical Astronomy (Emm.)

Willstrop, R. V., MA PhD   Sr. Asst. Observer

Astrophysics, see Astron., Inst. of

Biochemistry, see also Medicine

Tel: (01223) 333600 Fax: (01223) 333345

Blundell, Sir Tom, BA Oxf., DPhil Oxf., FRS   Sir William Dunn Prof.; Head* (Sid.)

Brand, M. D., BSc Manc., PhD Brist., MA   Reader, Cellular Biochemistry (Gir.)

Brindle, Kevin M., BA Oxf., DPhil Oxf.   Lectr. (Fitz.)

Broadhurst, Richard W., MA Oxf., DPhil Oxf.   Asst. Dir. of Res.

Carrington, D. M., BA PhD   Lectr. (S.Joh.)

Dupree, Paul, MA Camb., PhD Camb.   Lectr.

Ellar, D. J., BSc Leeds, PhD Syr., MA ScD   Reader, Microbial Biochemistry (Cai.)

Evans, Philip A., BA Oxf., DPhil Oxf.   Lectr. (New H.)

Hesketh, T. R., BSc Lond., PhD Lond., MA   Lectr. (Selw.)

Howe, C. J., MA PhD   Lectr. (Corp.)

Jackson, Antony P., MA Oxf., PhD Camb.   Lectr. (Sid.)

Jackson, R. J., MA PhD   Reader, Biochemical of Nucleic Acids (Pemb.)

Laue, E. D., MA Camb., MA CNAA, PhD CNAA   Lectr. (S.Joh.)

Leadlay, Peter F., MA Oxf., DPhil Oxf., PhD   Reader, Molecular Enzymology (Cla.)

Martin, B. Richard, BSc Brist., PhD Brist., MA   Lectr. (Emm.)

Metcalfe, James C., MA PhD   Prof., Mammalian Cell Biochemistry (Darw.)

Packman, L. C., BSc Leic., PhD Leic.   Asst. Dir. of Res.

Perham, R. N., MA PhD ScD, FRS   Prof., Structural Biochemistry (S.Joh.)

Reynolds, Peter E., MA PhD   Lectr. (Magd.)

Rubery, P. H., MA PhD ScD   Lectr. (Down.)

Salmond, George P. C., BSc Strath., PhD Warw.   Prof., Molecular Microbiology

Smith, C. W. J., BSc Brist., PhD Lond.   Lectr.

Standart, Nancy M., MA Camb., PhD Wales   Lectr.

Thomas, Jean O., CBE, MA Wales, MA Camb., PhD Wales, ScD, FRS   Prof., Macromolecular Biochemistry (New H.)

Thorne, Christopher J. R., MA Camb., PhD Camb.   Lectr. (S.Cat.)

Tolkovsky, Aviva M., MSc Jerusalem, PhD Jerusalem   Lectr.

Biotechnology, Institute of

Tel: (01223) 334160 Fax: (01223) 334162

Bruce, Neil C., BSc CNAA, PhD Kent   Lectr. (Trin.H.)

Hall, E. A. H., BSc Lond., PhD Lond., MA   Lectr. (Qu.)

Lowe, Christopher R., BSc Birm., PhD Birm.   Dir.* (Trin.)

Murray, J. A. H., MA   Lectr. (King's)

Celtic, see Anglo-Saxon, Norse and Celtic

Chemistry

Tel: (01223) 336454 Fax: (01223) 336362

Abell, Christopher, MA PhD   Lectr. (Chr.)

Amos, Roger D., BSc Glas., DPhil York(UK)   Asst. Dir. of Res.

Attfield, J. P., BA Oxf., DPhil Oxf.   Lectr. (Jes.)

Davies, P. B., BSc Liv., MA PhD   Reader, Spectroscopy (Corp.)

Duer, Melinda J., MA Camb., PhD Camb.   Lectr. (Rob.)

Elliott, Stephen R., MA PhD   Reader, Solid State Chemistry Physics (Trin.)

Fersht, A. R., MA PhD, FRS   Prof., Inorganic Chemistry (Cai.)

Fleming, I., MA PhD ScD   Reader, Organic Chemistry (Pemb.)

Freeman, R., MA Oxf., DPhil Oxf., DSc Oxf., ScD Camb., FRS   Prof. (Jes.)

Gerloch, Malcolm, BSc Lond., PhD Lond., MA ScD   Reader, Inorganic Chemistry (Trin.H.)

Gill, Peter M. W., MSc Auck., PhD ANU   Lectr.

Handy, Nicholas C., MA Camb., PhD Camb., ScD Camb., FRS   Prof., Quantum Chemistry (S.Cat.)

Hansen, Jean-Pierre, LèsSPhys Liège, PhD Paris XI   Prof., Chemistry

Holmes, Andrew B., MSc Melb., PhD Lond., MA   Reader, Org. and Polymer Chem.; Dir., Melville Lab. for Polymer Synthesis (Cla.)

Husain, D., DSc Manc., MA PhD ScD   Reader, Physical Chemistry (Pemb.)

Jefferson, D. A., MA PhD   Lectr. (Cai.)

Johnson, Brian F. G., BSc Nott., MA Camb., PhD Nott., FRS   Prof., Inorganic Chemistry (Fitz.)

Jones, R. L., MA Oxf., DPhil Oxf.   Lectr. (Qu.)

Jones, W., BSc Wales, PhD Wales   Lectr. (Sid.)

Keeler, J. H., MA Oxf., DPhil Oxf., PhD, FRSChem   Lectr. (Selw.)

King, David A., BSc Witw., PhD Witw., ScD E.Anglia, FRS   Prof., Physical Chemistry; Head* (Down.)

Kirby, A. J., MA PhD, FRS   Prof., Bio-organic Chemistry (Cai.)

Klenerman, David, MA Camb., PhD Camb.   Asst. Dir. of Res. (Chr.)

Klinowski, J., MSc Cracow, PhD Cracow, PhD Lond., MA   Asst. Dir. of Res.

Lambert, R. M., BA Oxf., DPhil Oxf., MA   Reader, Physical Chemistry (King's)

Leeper, Finian J., MA PhD   Lectr. (Emm.)

Ley, Steven V., BSc Lough., MA Camb., PhD Lough., DSc Lond., FRS, FRSChem   BP Prof., Organic Chemistry (Trin.)

Mays, M. J., MA PhD   Lectr. (Down.)

McDonald, Ian R., BSc Hull, PhD Nott., MA ScD   Lectr. (Trin.)

Moratti, Stephen C., BSc Auck., MSc Auck., PhD Auck.   Lectr. (Corp.)

Paterson, I., BSc St And., PhD   Reader, Organic Chemistry (Jes.)

Pyle, John A., BSc Durh., DPhil Oxf., PhD   Reader, Atmospheric Chemistry (S.Cat.)

Raithby, Paul R., BSc Lond., MA Camb., PhD Lond., ScD Camb.   Lectr. (S.Cat.)

Rawson, Jeremy M., BSc Durh., PhD Durh.   Lectr. (Magd.)

Rayment, T., BSc Durh., MSc Oxf., DPhil Oxf.   Lectr. (Gir.)

Sanders, J. K. M., BSc Lond., MA PhD, FRSChem, FRS   Prof. (Selw.)

Snaith, R., BSc Durh., PhD Durh., MA   Lectr. (S.Joh.)

Sprik, Michiel, MSc Amst., PhD Amst.   Lectr.

Staunton, J., BSc Liv., PhD Liv., MA   Reader, Organic Chemistry (S.Joh.)

Stone, Anthony J., MA PhD   Reader, Theoretical Chemistry (Emm.)

Warren, Stuart G., MA PhD   Lectr. (Chur.)

Williams, Dudley H., BSc Leeds, PhD Leeds, MA ScD, FRS   Prof., Biological Chemistry (Chur.)

Wright, D. S., BSc Strath., PhD   Lectr. (Cai.)

Zhou, Wuzong, BA Fudan, PhD Camb.   Asst. Dir. of Res.

Other Staff: 1 Asst. Lectr.; 1 Sr. Tech. Officer; 2 Tech. Officers; 1 Computer Officer

Chinese

Tel: (01223) 335106 Fax: (01223) 335110

Daruvala, Susan F., BA Leeds, MSc Lond., MA Chic., PhD Chic.   Lectr.

Lewis, M. E., MA Chic., PhD Chic.   Lectr.

McDermott, J. P., MA Oxf., BA Yale, PhD Camb.   Lectr. (S.Joh.)

McMullen, D. L., MA Camb., PhD Camb., FBA   Prof. (S.Joh.)

Van de Ven, Hans J., BA Ley., PhD Harv.   Lectr. (S.Cat.)

Yuan, Boping, MSc Edin., PhD Edin.   Lectr.

Classics

Tel: (01223) 335152

Austin, Colin F. L., MA Oxf., MA Camb., DPhil Oxf., FBA   Reader, Greek Language and Literature (Trin.H.)

Beard, W. Mary, MA Camb., PhD Camb.   Lectr.; Curator, Museum of Classical Archaeol. (Newn.)

Cartledge, Paul A., MA Oxf., DPhil Oxf., PhD   Reader, Greek History (Cla.)

Clackson, James P. T., MA Camb., PhD Camb.   Lectr. (Gir.)

Denyer, Nicholas C., MA Oxf.   Lectr. (Trin.)

Diggle, J., MA Camb., PhD Camb., LittD Camb., FBA   Prof., Greek and Latin (Qu.)

DuQuesnay, I. M. Le M., BA Birm.   Lectr. (Jes.)

Easterling, Patricia E., MA Camb.   Regius Prof., Greek (Newn.)

Goldhill, S. D., MA Camb., PhD Camb.   Lectr. (King's)

Hardie, Philip R., MA Oxf., MPhil Lond., PhD Camb.   Lectr. (New H.)

Henderson, J. G. W., BA Oxf., MA Camb., DPhil Oxf., PhD Camb.   Reader, Latin Literature (King's)

Hopkins, M. K., MA Camb., FBA   Prof., Ancient History (King's)

Horrocks, Geoffrey C., MA Camb., PhD Camb.   Prof., Comparative Philology

Hunter, R. L., BA Syd., MA Camb., PhD Camb.   Reader, Greek and Latin Literature (Pemb.)

Hurst, Henry R., MA Camb.   Lectr. (Chur.)

Kelly, Christopher M., PhD Camb.   Lectr. (Corp.)

Killen, J. T., MA Trinity(Dub.), MA Camb., PhD   Prof., Mycenean Greek (Jes.)

Lloyd, Sir Geoffrey, MA Camb., PhD Camb., FBA   Prof., Ancient Philosophy and Science (Darw.)

Millett, P. C., MA PhD   Lectr. (Down.)

Patterson, John R., MA Oxf., DPhil Oxf., PhD   Lectr. (Magd.)

Reeve, M. D., MA Oxf., MA Camb., FBA   Kennedy Prof., Latin (Pemb.)

Schofield, M., DPhil Oxf., MA PhD   Reader, Ancient Philosophy (S.Joh.)

Sedley, D. N., MA Oxf., MA Camb., PhD Lond., FBA   Prof., Ancient Philosophy (Chr.)

Snodgrass, Anthony M., MA Oxf., MA Camb., DPhil Oxf., PhD   Laurence Prof., Classical Archaeology (Cla.)

Spivey, Nigel J., MA PhD   Lectr. (Emm.)

Voutsaki, Sofia, BA Athens, MPhil Camb., PhD Camb.   Lectr. (Newn.)

Wardy, Robert B. B., BA Yale, MA PhD   Lectr. (S.Cat.)

Computer Laboratory

Tel: (01223) 334600

Anderson, Ross J., MA Camb., PhD

Bacon, Jean M., BSc Lond., MSc CNAA, MA Camb., PhD C.N.A.A.   Lectr. (Jes.)

Briscoe, E. J., BA Lanc., PhD   Lectr. (Gir.)

Clocksin, William F., BA Evergreen, MA Oxf., MA Camb., PhD Camb. Lectr. (Trin.H.)
Crosby, Simon A., BSc Cape Town, MSc Stell., PhD Camb. Lectr. (Fitz.)
Daugman, John, BA Harv., PhD Harv. Lectr.
Dodgson, Neil A., BSc Massey, PhD Camb. Lectr. (Emm.)
Gordon, M. J. C., BA Camb., PhD Edin. Prof., Computer-Assisted Reasoning
Greaves, David J., MA Camb., PhD Camb. Lectr. (Corp.)
Hopper, A., BSc Wales, PhD Prof., Computer Technology (Corp.)
King, Frank H., MA PhD Lectr. (Chur.)
Leslie, Ian M., MASc Tor., PhD Lectr. (Chr.)
Milner, Arthur J. R. G., BA Camb., Hon. DSc Gothenburg, FRS, FRSEd Prof., Computer Science; Head* (King's)
Moody, J. K. M., MA Camb., PhD Camb. Lectr. (King's)
Mycroft, A., MA Camb., PhD Edin., ScD Camb. Lectr. (Rob.)
Needham, Roger M., MA Camb., PhD Camb., Hon. DSc Kent, FRS Prof., Computer Systems (Wolfs.)
Norman, Arthur C., MA PhD Lectr. (Trin.)
Paulson, Laurence C., BSc Pasadena, PhD Stan., MA Lectr. (Cla.)
Pitts, Andrew M., MA PhD Reader, Theoretical Computer Science (Darw.)
Pulman, S. G., BA Lond., MA Essex, PhD Essex Reader, Computational Linguistics
Richards, M., BA PhD Lectr. (S.Joh.)
Robinson, P., MA PhD Lectr. (Cai.)
Sayers, Michael D., BSc Sus., DPhil Sus., MA Dir., Univ. Computing Service (Emm.)
Sparck Jones, Karen I. B., MA PhD Reader, Computers and Information
Westwood, Brian A., MA PhD Dep. Dir., Univ. Computing Service (Chur.)
Other Staff: 7 Sr. Computer Officers; 51 Computer Officers

Criminology, Institute of

Tel: (01223) 335360 Fax: (01223) 335356
Bennett, T. H., BA Kent, PhD Kent Lectr. (Wolfs.)
Bottoms, A. E., MA Oxf., MA Camb., PhD Sheff. Wolfson Prof.; Dir.* (Fitz.)
Farrington, D. P., MA PhD Prof., Psychology Criminology
Gelsthorpe, Loraine R. R., BA Sus., MPhil Camb., PhD Camb. Lectr. (Pemb.)
Grounds, Adrian T., BMedSci Nott., BM BS Nott. Lectr. (Darw.)
Morris, Allison, LLB Edin., LLM Col., MA Camb., PhD Camb. Reader, Criminal Justice (Cai.)
Thomas, David A., MA Camb., LLD Camb. Reader, Criminal Justice (Trin.H.)
Wikstrom, Per-Olof, BA Stockholm, PhD Stockholm Lectr.

Divinity, see also Hebrew, Hist., and Rabbinics

Tel: (01223) 332590 Fax: (01223) 332582
Bockmuehl, M. N. A., BA Br.Col., MDiv Regent Coll.(Br.Col.), MCS Regent Coll.(Br.Col.), PhD Camb. Lectr. (Fitz.)
Carleton Paget, James N. B., MA Camb., PhD Camb. Lectr. (Pet.)
Chester, A. N., MA Oxf., MA Camb., PhD Camb. Lectr. (Selw.)
Davies, G. I., MA Oxf., PhD Camb. Reader, Old Testament Studies (Fitz.)
Dell, Katharine J., BA Oxf., DPhil Oxf. Lectr. (S.Cat.)
Duffy, Eamon, BA Hull, PhD Camb., DD Camb. Reader, Church History (Magd.)
Ford, D. F., MA PhD Regius Prof. (Selw.)
Hebblethwaite, Rev. B. L., BD Camb., MA Oxf., MA Camb. Lectr. (Qu.)
Hedley, Douglas, BA Oxf., MSt Oxf., PhD Munich Lectr.
Horbury, W., MA Oxf., MA Camb., PhD Reader, Jewish and Early Christian Studies (Corp.)
Lash, Rev. N. L. A., MA PhD DD Norris-Hulse Prof. (Cla.H.)

Lipner, J. J., PhD Lond., MA Lectr. (Cla.H.)
Lohr, Winnich A., BA Bonn, PhD Bonn Lectr.
Milbank, A. J., BA Oxf., PhD Birm., MA Reader, Philosophical Theology (Pet.)
Rex, Richard A. W., MA Camb., PhD Camb. Lectr. (Qu.)
Soskice, Janet M., BA Cornell, MA Sheff., DPhil Oxf. Lectr. (Jes.)
Thompson, D. M., BD Camb., MA Camb., PhD Camb., FRHistS Lectr. (Fitz.)
Watts, Fraser N., MA Oxf., MSc Lond., PhD Lond. Lectr. (Qu.)
Wickham, L. R., MA PhD Lectr.
Winter, Timothy J., MA Camb. Lectr., Islamic Studies

Dutch, see Other Langs.

Earth Sciences

Tel: (01223) 333400 Fax: (01223) 333450
Bickle, M. J., DPhil Oxf. Reader, Tectonics
Butterfield, Nicholas J., BSc Alta., PhD Harv. Lectr.
Carpenter, M. A., MA PhD Reader, Mineralogy and Mineral Physics (Magd.)
Chinner, Graham A., BSc Adel., PhD Lectr. (Trin.)
Conway Morris, S., BSc Brist., MA PhD, FRS Prof., Evolutionary Palaeobiology (S.Joh.)
Dickson, J. A. D., BSc Lond., PhD Lond. Reader, Carbonate Diagensis
Dove, M. T., BSc Birm., PhD Birm. Lectr.
Elderfield, Henry, BSc Liv., MA Camb., PhD Liv., ScD Camb. Reader, Geochemistry (S.Cat.)
Farnan, Ian, BSc E.Anglia, PhD E.Anglia Lectr.
Friend, Peter F., MA PhD Lectr. (Darw.)
Gibson, Sally A., BSc Sheff., PhD CNAA Lectr.
Haines, A. John, MSc Well., PhD Camb. Reader, Geodesy and Geophysics
Hobbs, R. W., PhD Durh. Asst. Dir. of Res.
Holland, T. J. B., MA Oxf., DPhil Oxf., PhD Lectr.
Jackson, J. A., MA PhD Reader, Active Tectonics (Qu.)
McCave, I. N., MA Oxf., DSc Oxf., PhD Brown, ScD, FGS Woodwardian Prof., Geology; Head* (S.Joh.)
McKenzie, D. P., MA PhD, FRS Prof., Earth Sciences (King's)
Miller, Jack A., BSc Hull, MSc Birm., ScD, FGS Asst. Dir. of Res. (Chur.)
Norman, D. B., BSc Leeds, PhD Lond. Curator; Sedgwick Museum
Priestley, K. F., MS Wash., PhD Nevada Asst. Dir. of Res. (Qu.)
Pyle, David M., MA PhD Lectr. (S.Cat.)
Redfern, Simon A. T., MA Camb., PhD Camb. Lectr. (Jes.)
Reed, S. J. B., BSc S'ton., PhD Asst. Dir. of Res.
Rickards, R. Barrie, BSc Hull, PhD Hull, MA ScD Reader, Palaeobiology (Emm.)
Salje, Ekhard K. H., PhD Hanover, MA, FRS Prof., Mineral Physics (Darw.)
Schultz, A., ScB Brown, MA Camb., PhD Wash. Lectr. (S.Edm.)
Shackleton, Nicholas J., MA Camb., PhD Camb., ScD Camb. Prof., Quaternary Palaeoclimatology
Shen, Andy H.-T., BS Taiwan Chinese, PhD Cornell Lectr.
Sinha, M. C., BSc Liv., PhD Asst. Dir. of Res.
Smith, A. G., PhD Prin., MA Reader, Geology (S.Joh.)
White, N. J., BA Trinity(Dub.), PhD Asst. Dir. of Res.
White, R. S., MA PhD, FRS Prof., Geophysics (S.Edm.)
Woodcock, Nigel H., BSc Manc., MSc Lond., PhD Lond., MA Lectr. (Cla.)
Other Staff: 1 Sr. Asst. in Res.; 1 Asst. Lectr.; 3 Sr. Tech. Officers; 3 Computer Officers

Economics and Politics, see also Econ., Appl.; Hist.; Land Economy; and Soc. and Pol. Scis.

Tel: (01223) 335200 Fax: (01223) 335475

Anderlini, L., BSc Rome, MPhil PhD Asst. Dir. of Res. (S.Joh.)
Brown, W. A., BA Oxf. Montagu Burton Prof., Industrial Relations (Wolfs.)
Buiter, Willem H., MA Camb., MA Yale, PhD Yale Prof., International Macroeconomics (Trin.)
Chang, H.-J., BA Seoul, MPhil PhD Asst. Dir. of Devel. Studies (Wolfs.)
Coutts, K. J., MA Asst. Dir. of Res. (Selw.)
Dasgupta, P., BSc Delhi, BA PhD, FBA Prof., Economics (S.Joh.)
Dutta, Jayasri, BA Calc., MA Delhi, PhD Delhi Asst. Dir. of Res. (Chur.)
Eatwell, Lord, AM Harv., MA Camb., PhD Harv. Lectr. (Qu.)
Edwards, J. S. S., BPhil Oxf., MA Oxf., MA Camb., PhD Reader, Economics
Evans, R. A., BA Oxf., MSc Lond., MA Lectr. (S.Joh.)
Hara, Chiaki, MA Tokyo, MA Harv., PhD Harv. Lectr. (Chur.)
Harris, C. J., MA Oxf., DPhil Oxf. Prof., Economics (King's)
Harvey, Andrew C., BA York(UK), MSc Lond. Prof., Econometrics (Corp.)
Hess, Gregory D., BA Calif., MA Johns H., PhD Johns H. Lectr. (S.Joh.)
Horrell, Sara H., BSc Bath, MPhil Camb., PhD Camb. Lectr. (New H.)
Hughes, A., MA Camb. Lectr. (Sid.)
Humphries, K. Jane, MA Cornell, MA Camb., PhD Cornell Reader, Economics and Economic History (Newn.)
Lawson, A., MSc Lond., MA PhD Lectr.
Meeks, Geoffrey, PhD Edin., BA Lectr. (Darw.)
Mirrlees, Sir James A., MA Edin., MA Camb., PhD Camb., Hon. DLitt Warw. Prof., Political Economics (Trin.)
Ogilvie, Sheilagh C., MA St And., PhD Lectr.
Palma, J. G. P., BSc Pontif.Chile, DPhil Oxf., PhD Lectr.
Pesaran, M. Hashem, BSc Salf., PhD Prof., Economics (Trin.)
Peterson, A. William A., MA PhD Lectr. (Chr.)
Robertson, D., MA Camb., MSc Lond., PhD Lond. Lectr. (Pemb.)
Rowthorn, R. E., BA Oxf., MA Prof., Economics (King's)
Ryan, P., PhD Harv., MA Lectr. (King's)
Sabourian, H., MSc Lond., MA PhD Lectr. (King's)
Satchell, Stephen E., BA NSW, MCom NSW, MA Syd., MA Camb., PhD Lond. Lectr. (Trin.)
Seabright, Paul B., MA Oxf., DPhil Oxf. Asst. Dir. of Res. (Chur.)
Singh, A., BA Panjab, MA Howard, MA Camb., PhD Calif. Prof., Economics (Qu.)
Solomou, S. N., MSc Lond., PhD Lectr. (Pet.)
Sutherland, Alister, MA Oxf., MA Yale, MA Camb. Lectr. (Trin.)
Trevithick, J. A., MSc(Econ) Lond., MA Lectr. (King's)
Wells, J. R., MA PhD Lectr.
Whittington, G., BSc(Econ) Lond., MA PhD, FCA Prof., Financial Accounting (Fitz.)
Wright, Stephen H., BA Camb. Asst. Dir. of Res.
Other Staff: 1 Sr. Asst. in Res.; 1 Computer Officer

Economics, Applied

Tel: (01223) 335200 Fax: (01223) 335299
Barker, T. S., MA Edin., MA Camb., PhD Sr. Res. Officer
Garratt, Anthony G., BSc Wales, PhD Lond. Sr. Res. Officer
Green, Richard J., BA Camb., MPhil Camb., PhD Camb. Sr. Res. Officer (Fitz.)
Holly, M. J. Sean, BA Reading, PhD CNAA Dep. Dir. (Fitz.)
Newbery, David M. G., MA PhD, FBA Prof.; Dir.* (Chur.)
Pratten, Clifford F., BA Brist., MA Sr. Res. Officer (Trin.H.)
Shin, Yongcheol, MA Hankuk Foreign, PhD Mich. Sr. Res. Officer

Sutherland, Holly E., BA   Sr. Res. Officer
(New H.)
Weeks, Melvyn J., BA *Reading*, MA *Ill.*, PhD
Penn.   Sr. Res. Officer
Wilkinson, S. F., MA PhD   Sr. Res. Officer
(Gir.)
Other Staff: 1 Res. Officer

Education, Faculty of

Tel: (01223) 332888 Fax: (01223) 332894,
332876

Adams, Anthony L. E., MA *Camb.*   Lectr.
(Wolfs.)
Arnot, Madeleine M., MA *Edin.*, PhD
Open(UK)   Lectr. (Jes.)
Bage, Grant J., MA *Camb.*, MLitt *Camb.*   Lectr.
Bowers, A. J., BA *Open(UK)*, MEd *Manc.*, MSc
Lond.   Lectr.
Conner, Colin, BEd *Sus.*, MA *Lond.*, PhD
Lond.   Lectr. (Hug.)
Cooper, Paul W., BA *Stir.*, MEd *Dund.*, PhD
Birm.   Lectr.
Counsell, Christine E., MA *Edin.*, MEd
Brist.   Lectr.
Dadds, Marion, BEd *Lanc.*, MA *Camb.*, MEd
Nott., PhD *E.Anglia*   Lectr.
Dee, Lesley M., MEd *Ill.*   Lectr.
Drummond, Mary J., BA *Oxf.*, MA
Camb.   Lectr.
Evans, M. J., BA *E.Anglia*, PhD *Warw.*   Lectr.
Fielding, M., BEd *Brist.*, MA *Lond.*, MA
Camb.   Lectr.
Frost, David, BEd *Lond.*, MA *Kent*, PhD
E.Anglia   Lectr.
Gardner, P. W., BA *E.Anglia*, MA *E.Anglia*, DPhil
Sus., MA   Lectr. (S.Edm.)
Hargreaves, D. H., MA PhD   Prof. (Wolfs.)
Hart, Susan, BA *Paris*, MA *Lond.*, MA
Camb.   Lectr.
James, Mary E., BEd *Sus.*, MA *Lond.*, MA *Camb.*,
PhD *Open(UK)*   Lectr.
Jennison, Brenda M., BSc *Lond.*, MA   Lectr.
(Chur.)
Lister, Robert W., MA *Camb.*   Lectr.
McIntyre, Donald I., MA *Edin.*, MEd *Edin.*, MA
Oxf.   Prof.; Head* (Hug.)
McLaughlin, Colleen M., MEd *Wales*,
BEd   Lectr.
McLaughlin, T. H., BEd *Lond.*, PhD *Lond.*, MA
Lond., MA *Camb.*   Lectr. (S.Edm.)
Raffan, John G. A., BSc *Belf.*, MA *Camb.*   Lectr.
(Hug.)
Rouse, M. D., BEd *CNAA*, MA *Lond.*, MA
Camb.   Lectr.
Ruthven, Kenneth B. H., MA *Oxf.*, MA *Camb.*,
PhD *Stir.*   Lectr. (Hug.)
Sebba, Judy, BA *Sus.*, MA *Manc.*, MA
Camb.   Lectr.
Walford, R. A., BSc(Econ) *Lond.*, BD *Lond.*, MA
Northwestern, MA *Camb.*   Lectr. (Wolfs.)
West, M., BA *Lond.*, MA *Camb.*   Lectr.
Whitehead, Joan M., BA *Wales*, PhD *Open(UK)*,
MA   Lectr. (Wolfs.)

Egyptology

Tel: (01223) 335106 Fax: (01223) 335110

Kemp, Barry J., BA *Liv.*, MA *Camb.*   Reader
(Wolfs.)
Ray, J. D., MA *Camb.*   H. Thompson Reader
(Selw.)

Engineering

Tel: (01223) 332600 Fax: (01223) 332662

Al-Tabbaa, Abir, BSc *Brist.*, MPhil *Camb.*, PhD
Camb.   Lectr. (Sid.)
Amaratunga, Gehan A. J., PhD *Camb.*   Prof.
Babinsky, Holger, PhD *Cran.*   Lectr. (Magd.)
Barlow, Claire Y., MA *Camb.*, PhD
Camb.   Lectr. (Newn.)
Beaumont, P. W. R., BSc *Sur.*, DPhil *Sus.*,
MA   Lectr. (Wolfs.)
Bligh, T. P., MSc *Witw.*, PhD *Witw.*   Lectr.
(Cai.)
Bolton, Malcolm D., MSc *Manc.*, MA
PhD   Reader, Geotechnical Engineering
(Chur.)

Britter, R. E., BE *Monash*, PhD *Monash*,
MA   Reader, Environmental Fluid Dynamics
(Pemb.)
Brunton, John H., MSc *Birm.*, PhD   Lectr.
(Chur.)
Burgoyne, Christopher J., MSc *Lond.*, PhD *Lond.*,
MA   Lectr. (Emm.)
Calladine, C. R., SM *M.I.T.*, MA ScD, FICE, FRS,
FEng   Prof., Structural Mechanics (Pet.)
Campbell, Archibald M., MA PhD   Reader,
Superconductivity Engineering (Chr.)
Cant, R. Stewart, BSc *St And.*, PhD *Cran.*   Lectr.
(Selw.)
Cardwell, D. A., BSc *Warw.*, MA *Camb.*, PhD
Warw.   Lectr. (Fitz.)
Carroll, J. E., MA PhD ScD, FEng   Prof. (Qu.)
Cebon, D., BE *Melb.*, PhD   Lectr. (Qu.)
Cipolla, R., MA *Camb.*, MSE *Penn.*, MEng *Tokyo*,
DPhil *Oxf.*, PhD *Camb.*   Reader, Information
Engineering (Jes.)
Clarkson, P. John, MA *Camb.*, PhD
Camb.   Lectr. (Trin.H.)
Collings, N., BSc *Brist.*, PhD   Reader, Applied
Thermodynamics (Rob.)
Cosh, A. D., BA PhD   Lectr. (Qu.)
Cowley, Martin D., BA PhD   Lectr. (Trin.)
Cumpsty, N. A., BSc *Lond.*, MA PhD   Prof.,
Aerothermal Technology (Pet.)
Davidson, Peter A., BSc *Aberd.*, PhD
Camb.   Lectr. (Chur.)
Dawes, W. N., MA PhD   Francis Mond Prof.,
Aeronautical Engineering (Chur.)
Denton, John D., BA PhD, FEng   Prof.,
Turbomachinery Aerodynamics (Trin.H.)
Dowling, Ann P., MA *Camb.*, PhD *Camb.*,
FEng   Prof., Mechanical Engineering (Sid.)
Ffowcs Williams, John E., BSc *S'ton.*, MA *Camb.*,
PhD *S'ton.*, ScD *Camb.*, FEng   Rank Prof.
(Emm.)
Fitzgerald, William J., MSc *Birm.*, PhD
Birm.   Lectr. (Chr.)
Flack, Timothy J., BSc *Lond.*, PhD *Lond.*   Lectr.
(King's)
Fleck, N. A., MA PhD   Reader, Mechanics of
Materials (Pemb.)
Garnsey, Elizabeth W., BA *Oxf.*, PhD *Calif.*,
MA   Lectr. (Cla.H.)
Gee, Andrew H., MA *Camb.*, PhD *Camb.*   Lectr.
(Qu.)
Gill, C. G., MA *Warw.*, MA *Camb.*   Lectr.
(Wolfs.)
Glover, K., BSc *Lond.*, SM *M.I.T.*, PhD *M.I.T.*,
MA, FRS   Prof. (Sid.)
Godsill, Simon J., MA *Camb.*, PhD *Camb.*   Lectr.
(Corp.)
Graham, William R., BA *Camb.*, MA *Camb.*, PhD
Camb.   Lectr. (Trin.)
Greenwood, J. A., MA PhD   Reader, Tribology
(Pet.)
Gregory, Michael J., BSc *S'ton.*, MA
Camb.   Prof., Manufacturing Engineering
(Chur.)
Guest, Simon D., MA *Camb.*, PhD *Camb.*   Lectr.
(Trin.H.)
Hodgson, G. M., BSc *Manc.*, MA *Camb.*, MA
Manc.   Lectr.
Hodson, H. P., MA PhD   Lectr. (Gir.)
Holburn, D. M., MA PhD   Lectr. (Cai.)
Holden, Tony, BSc *Lond.*, PhD *Lond.*   Asst. Dir.
of Res.
Hope, C. W., MA *Oxf.*, PhD   Lectr. (Cla.H.)
Hunt, Hugh E. M., BE *Melb.*, PhD   Lectr.
(Trin.)
Hynes, T. P., MA PhD   Lectr. (S.Joh.)
Johnson, Aylmer L., MA   Lectr. (Cla.)
Jones, David R. H., MA PhD   Lectr. (Chr.)
Jones, Matthew R., BSc *Newcastle(UK)*, PhD
Reading   Lectr. (Darw.)
Kingsbury, Nicholas G., MA PhD   Lectr.
(Trin.)
Longley, J. P., BA PhD   Lectr. (Sid.)
Lu, Tian J., PhD *HK*, PhD *Harv.*   Lectr.
Maciejowski, J. M., BSc *Sus.*, MA PhD   Lectr.
(Pemb.)
Madabhusi, Santa-Phani G., BTech *Nehru Tech.*,
PhD *Camb.*   Lectr. (Chur.)
Mair, Robert J., MA *Camb.*, PhD *Camb.*, FEng,
FICE   Prof. (S.Joh.)

Maloney, Christopher E., MA PhD   Lectr.
(Cla.)
Marić, Svetislav V., BS *Novi Sad*, MS *Roch.*, PhD
Roch.   Lectr. (Sid.)
McConnel, R. E., ME *Cant.*, DPhil *Oxf.*,
PhD   Lectr. (S.Joh.)
McFarlane, Duncan C., BE *Melb.*, PhD
Camb.   Lectr. (S.Joh.)
McMahon, R. A., MA PhD   Lectr. (Corp.)
McRobie, Frank A., BSc *Brist.*, MSc *S'ton.*   Lectr.
Mears, R. J., BA *Oxf.*, PhD *S'ton.*   Lectr.
(Pemb.)
Middleton, Campbell R., BE *Tas.*, MSc *Lond.*,
PhD *Camb.*   Asst. Dir. of Res. (King's)
Migliorato, Piero, DottFis *Rome*   Reader,
Physical Electronics (Trin.)
Milne, William I., BSc *St And.*, PhD *Lond.*,
MA   Prof., Electrical Engineering (Chur.)
Moore, David F., PhD *Stan.*, MA   Lectr.
(Trin.H.)
Morgan, Neil A., BA *Lond.*, MBA *Wales*   Lectr.
Morley, Christopher T., BA PhD   Lectr. (Trin.)
Neely, Andrew D., BEng *Nott.*, PhD
Nott.   Lectr. (Chur.)
Newland, D. E., ScD *M.I.T.*, ScD *Camb.*, MA,
FEng, FIMechE   Prof.; Head* (Selw.)
Niranjan, M., BSc *Peradeniya*, PhD   Lectr. (Rob.)
O'Shaughnessy, Nicholas J. O., BA *Lond.*, MPhil
Oxf., MBA *Col.*, MPhil *Camb.*   Lectr. (Hug.)
Organ, A. J., BSc *Birm.*, MASc *Tor.*, PhD *Birm.*,
MA   Lectr. (Down.)
Palmer, Patrick R., BSc *Lond.*, PhD *Lond.*,
MA   Lectr. (S.Cat.)
Parks, Geoffrey T., BA *Camb.*, PhD
Camb.   Lectr. (Jes.)
Payne, F. P., MA PhD   Lectr. (King's)
Pellegrino, S., LaurCivIng *Naples*, MA
PhD   Reader, Structural Engineering (Corp.)
Platts, Kenneth W., MA *Camb.*, PhD
Camb.   Lectr. (Fitz.)
Platts, M. J., BA   Lectr.
Plumb, R. S. G., MA PhD   Lectr. (Pet.)
Prager, R. W., MA PhD   Lectr. (Qu.)
Probert, David R., MA *Camb.*   Lectr.
Rayner, Peter J. W., PhD *Aston*, MA   Reader,
Information Engineering (Chr.)
Richards, R. J., BSc *Lond.*, PhD   Lectr. (Down.)
Robertson, John, BA *Camb.*, PhD *Camb.*   Lectr.
(Chur.)
Robertson, Paul A., MA *Camb.*, PhD
Camb.   Lectr. (Jes.)
Robinson, Anthony J., MPhil *Camb.*, PhD
Camb.   Lectr.
Scholtes, Stefan, PhD *Karlsruhe*   Lectr.
Shercliff, Hugh R., MA *Camb.*, PhD
Camb.   Lectr. (Gir.)
Sleath, John F. A., MA PhD   Reader, Coastal
Engineering (Emm.)
Smith, J. Derek, MA PhD   Lectr. (Emm.)
Smith, M. C., MA MPhil PhD   Reader, Control
Engineering (Cai.)
Soga, Kenichi, BSc *Kyoto*, MEng *Kyoto*, PhD
Calif.   Lectr. (Chur.)
Spreadbury, Peter J., MA MSc   Lectr. (Emm.)
Stronge, W. J., BSc *Oregon*, MS *Calif.*, PhD
Stan.   Reader, Applied Mechanics (Jes.)
Sutcliffe, Michael P. F., MA *Camb.*, PhD
Camb.   Lectr. (S.Cat.)
Travis, Adrian R. L., MA PhD   Lectr. (Cla.)
Vanderbeck, François, BSc *Louvain*, MSc
M.I.T.   Lectr.
Vinnicombe, Glenn, MA *Camb.*, PhD
Camb.   Lectr.
Wallace, K. M., BSc *Manc.*, MA   Lectr. (Selw.)
Welland, M. E., BSc *Leeds*, MSc *Brist.*, PhD *Brist.*,
MA   Reader, Nanoscale Science (S.Joh.)
Williams, J. A., MA PhD   Lectr. (Rob.)
Woodhouse, James, MA PhD   Reader,
Structural Dynamics (Cla.)
Woodland, P. C., MA MPhil   Lectr. (Pet.)
Young, J. B., MSc *Birm.*, PhD *Birm.*,
MA   Reader, Thermodynamics and Fluid
Mechanics (King's)
Young, Stephen J., MA *Camb.*, PhD
Camb.   Prof., Information Engineering
(Emm.)
Other Staff: 2 Asst. Lectrs.; 2 Sr. Des.
Engineers; 2 Des. Engineers; 2 Sr. Tech.

Officers; 1 Sr. Computer Officer; 8 Computer Officers

Engineering, Chemical

Tel: (01223) 334777 Fax: (01223) 334796

Barrie, Patrick J., MA Camb., PhD Camb.   Lectr.

Bridgwater, John, MSE Prin., ScD, FIChemE, FEng   Shell Prof.; Head* (S.Cat.)

Chase, Howard A., MA PhD   Reader, Biochemical Engineering (Magd.)

Gladden, Lynn F., BSc Brist., PhD Brist.   Reader, Process Engineering Science (Rob.)

Hayhurst, A. N., MA PhD ScD   Reader (Qu.)

Mackley, M. R., BSc Leic., MSc Brist., PhD Brist., MA   Reader (Rob.)

Middelberg, Anton P. J., BE Adel., PhD Adel.   Lectr.

Nedderman, Ronald M., MA MEng PhD   Lectr. (Trin.)

Paterson, W. R., BSc Edin., PhD Edin.   Lectr.

Rielly, C. D., BSc Lond., MA   Lectr. (Pet.)

Scott, D. M., MA PhD   Lectr.   (Fitz.)

Skelton, Robert L., MA Camb.   Lectr. (Magd.)

Thorpe, Rex B., MA MEng PhD   Lectr. (Chur.)

Wilson, D. Ian, MA Camb., MEng Camb., PhD Br.Col.   Lectr. (Jes.)

Other Staff: 3 Asst. Lectrs.; 1 Sr. Tech. Officer; 1 Tech. Officer; 1 Computer Officer

English, see also Anglo-Saxon, Norse and Celtic

Tel: (01223) 335070 Fax: (01223) 335075

Adamson, Sylvia M., MA   Lectr.

Axton, Marie H., BA Harv., MA Camb., PhD Camb.   Lectr. (Newn.)

Axton, Richard P., MA PhD   Lectr. (Chr.)

Barton, Anne, BA Bryn Mawr, PhD, FBA   Prof. (Trin.)

Beadle, H. Richard L., DPhil York(UK), MA   Lectr. (S.Joh.)

Beer, Gillian P. K., BLitt Oxf., MA Oxf., MA Camb., LittD Camb., FBA   King Edward VII Prof., English Literature (Cla.H.)

Brown, Gillian, PhD Edin., MA   Prof., English as an International Language (Cla.)

Burrow, C. J., DPhil Oxf., MA   Lectr. (Cai.)

Casey, J. P., MA PhD   Lectr. (Cai.)

Chothia, Jean K., BA Durh., PhD   Lectr. (Selw.)

Collini, S. A., MA Yale, MA Camb.   Reader, Intellectual History and English Literature (Cla.H.)

Donaldson, C. Ian E., BA Melb., MA Oxf.   Prof. (King's)

Ellmann, Maud, DPhil Oxf., MA   Lectr. (King's)

Erskine-Hill, Howard H., BA Nott., PhD Nott., MA LittD, FBA, FAHA, FRSEd   Prof., Literary History (Pemb.)

Glen, Heather J., BA Syd., MA PhD   Lectr. (New H.)

Griffiths, Eric, MA PhD   Lectr. (Trin.)

Harvey, John R., MA PhD   Lectr. (Emm.)

Heath, S. C., MA PhD   Reader, Cultural Studies (Jes.)

Kerrigan, J. F., MA Oxf.   Lectr. (S.Joh.)

Leask, N. J., BA Oxf., PhD   Lectr. (Qu.)

Long, Mike D., MA PhD   Lectr. (Chur.)

Luckett, Richard, MA PhD   Lectr. (Magd.)

Mann, Jill L., MA Oxf., MA PhD, FBA   Prof., Mediaeval and Renaissance English (Gir.)

Manning, Susan L., MA Camb., PhD Camb.   Lectr. (Newn.)

Mengham, R., MA Camb., PhD Edin.   Lectr. (Jes.)

Milne, Andrew G., BA Camb., PhD Camb.   Lectr., Drama and Poetry

Page, C. H., BA Oxf., DPhil York(UK)   Reader, Mediaeval Literature and Music (Sid.)

Parker, G. Frederick, MA PhD   Lectr. (Cla.)

Poole, Adrian D. B., MA PhD   Reader, English and Comparative Literature (Trin.)

Prynne, Jeremy H., MA   Lectr. (Cai.)

Quayson, L. Ato, BA Ghana, PhD Camb.   Lectr. (Pemb.)

Rathmell, John C. A., MA PhD   Lectr. (Chr.)

Sanders, J. W., BA Melb., PhD Brist., MA   Lectr. (Selw.)

Simpson, W. J., BA Melb., MPhil Oxf., PhD Camb.   Lectr. (Gir.)

Tanner, P. A., MA PhD   Prof., English and American Literature (King's)

Wheeler, Kathleen M., MA Mich., PhD   Lectr. (Darw.)

Windeatt, Barry A., MA Camb., PhD Camb., LittD Camb.   Reader, Medieval Literature (Emm.)

Wright, Laura C., MA Edin., DPhil Oxf.   Lectr. (L.Cav.)

Other Staff: 1 Asst. Lectr.

Fine Arts, see Hist. of Art

French

Tel: (01223) 335009 Fax: (01223) 335062

Bayley, Peter J., MA PhD   Drapers Prof. (Cai.)

Bennett, Wendy M., MA Oxf., MA Camb., DPhil Oxf., PhD   Lectr. (Qu.)

Collier, P. J., BA Lond., PhD Lond., MA   Lectr. (Sid.)

Ford, Philip J., MA PhD   Lectr. (Cla.)

Gaunt, Simon B., BA Warw., PhD Warw.   Lectr. (S.Cat.)

Hammond, Nicholas G., MA Rhodes, DPhil Oxf.   Lectr. (Cai.)

Huot, Sylvia, BA Calif., PhD Prin.   Lectr. (Pemb.)

Jondorf, Gillian, MA PhD   Lectr. (Gir.)

Jones, Mari C., BA Wales, MPhil PhD   Lectr. (Pet.)

Kay, Helen S., MA Reading, MA Oxf., DPhil Oxf., PhD   Reader; Head* (Gir.)

Kenny, Neil F., MA Camb., DPhil Oxf.   Lectr. (Chur.)

Mander, Jenny S., MA Camb., PhD Camb.   Lectr. (Newn.)

Martin, A. J., MA Sus., PhD   Lectr.

Prendergast, C. A. J., BPhil Oxf., MA Oxf., MA Camb., PhD   Prof., Modern French Literature (King's)

Wilson, Emma F., MA PhD   Lectr. (Corp.)

Other Staff: 1 Lector

Genetics

Tel: (01223) 333999 Fax: (01223) 333992

Ashburner, Michael, MA PhD ScD, FRS   Prof. (Chur.)

Barrett, J. A., BSc Wales, PhD Liv.   Lectr.

Evans, M. J., MA Camb., PhD Lond., ScD Camb.   Prof., Mammalian Genetics

Furner, I. J., BSc Sus., PhD Calif.   Lectr.

MacDonald, Donald W. B., BSc Aberd., MA Camb., PhD E.Anglia   Lectr.; Head* (Wolfs.)

Majerus, Michael E. N., BSc Lond., PhD Lond., MA   Lectr. (Cla.)

O'Donald, Peter, MA PhD ScD   Lectr. (Emm.)

O'Kane, Cahir J., PhD Trinity(Dub.), MA   Lectr. (Chur.)

Oliver, Philip, BSc Reading, PhD Kent, MA   Lectr. (S.Cat.)

Summers, D. K., DPhil Oxf., MA PhD   Lectr. (Cai.)

Other Staff: 1 Sr. Tech. Officer

Geography

Tel: (01223) 333399 Fax: (01223) 333392

Adams, W. M., MSc Lond., MA PhD   Lectr. (Down.)

Baker, Alan R. H., BA Lond., PhD Lond., MA   Lectr. (Emm.)

Bayliss-Smith, T. P., MA PhD   Lectr. (S.Joh.)

Bennett, Robert J., MA Camb., PhD Camb., FBA   Prof., Geography (S.Cat.)

Billinge, Mark D., MA PhD   Lectr. (Magd.)

Cliff, Andrew D., BA Lond., MA Northwestern, MA Camb., PhD Brist., DSc Brist., FBA   Prof., Theoretical Geography (Chr.)

Corbridge, S. E., BA Camb., PhD Camb.   Lectr., South-Asian Geography (Sid.)

Duncan, James S., BA Hanover, MA Syr., PhD Syr.   Lectr. (Emm.)

Gibbard, Philip L., BSc Sheff., PhD Camb.   Lectr. (S.Joh.)

Glasscock, Robin E., BA Lond., PhD Lond., MA   Lectr. (S.Joh.)

Howell, P. M. R., BA PhD   Lectr. (Down.)

Kearns, Gerard P., BA Camb., PhD Camb.   Lectr. (Jes.)

Keeble, David E., MA PhD   Lectr. (S.Cat.)

Martin, Robert L., MA PhD   Lectr. (S.Cat.)

McDowell, Linda M., MPhil Lond., MA Camb., PhD Lond.   Lectr. (Newn.)

Oppenheimer, Clive M. M., MA Camb., PhD Open(UK)   Lectr. (Sid.)

Owens, Susan E., MA Camb., PhD E.Anglia   Lectr. (Newn.)

Radcliffe, Sarah A., BSc Lond., PhD Liv.   Lectr. (New H.)

Richards, K. S., MA PhD   Prof., Geography; Head* (Emm.)

Smith, G. E., BA Strath., PhD Glas., MA   Lectr. (Sid.)

Spencer, Thomas, MA PhD   Lectr. (Magd.)

Trudgill, Stephen T., BSc Brist., PhD Brist.   Lectr. (Rob.)

Willis, Ian C., BSc CNAA, PhD   Lectr. (S.Cat.)

Other Staff: 3 Asst. Lectrs.; 1 Tech. Officer

Geology, see Earth Scis.

German

Tel: (01223) 335037 Fax: (01223) 335062

Boyle, Nicholas, MA PhD   Reader, German Literary and Intellectual History; Head* (Magd.)

Chinca, M. G., MA PhD   Lectr. (Trin.)

Hutchinson, Peter, PhD Lond., MA   Lectr. (Trin.H.)

Llewellyn, R. Terence, BA Wales, PhD   Lectr. (Chr.)

Midgley, D. R., BA Oxf., DPhil Oxf., PhD Camb.   Lectr. (S.Joh.)

Minden, M. R., MA PhD   Lectr. (Jes.)

Nisbet, H. B., MA Edin., MA Camb., PhD Edin.   Prof., Modern Languages (Sid.)

Paulin, Roger C., MA NZ, MA Camb., DrPhil Heidel., LittD   Schröder Prof. (Trin.)

Stewart, Mary E., MA Oxf., MA Camb., DPhil Oxf., PhD   Lectr. (Rob.)

Webber, Andrew J., MA Camb., PhD Camb.   Lectr. (Chur.)

Whaley, J., MA PhD   Lectr. (Cai.)

Other Staff: 1 Asst. Lectr.; 2 Lectors

Greek, Modern, see Other Langs.

Hebrew

Tel: (01223) 335106 Fax: (01223) 335110

Domb, Risa, BA Lond., PhD Lond., MA   Lectr., Modern Hebrew (Gir.)

Gordon, Robert P., MA Camb., PhD Camb.   Regius Prof. (S.Cat.)

Khan, Geoffrey A., BA Lond., PhD Lond.   Lectr. (Wolfs.)

Snaith, J. G., MA Oxf., MA Camb., BD Lond.   Lectr. (Wolfs.)

Hindi

Tel: (01223) 335106 Fax: (01223) 335110

1 Sr. Lang. Teaching Officer

History, see also Anglo-Saxon, Norse and Celtic, and Classics, and Japanese, and S. Asian Hist.

Tel: (01223) 335340 Fax: (01223) 335968

Abulafia, D. S. H., MA Camb., PhD Camb., LittD Camb.   Reader, Mediterranean History (Cai.)

Andrew, C. M., MA PhD   Prof., Modern and Con History (Corp.)

Badger, A. J., PhD Hull, MA   Paul Mellon Prof., American History (Sid.)

Bayly, Christopher A., MA Oxf., DPhil Oxf., PhD, FBA   Vere Harmsworth Prof., Imperial and Naval History (S.Cat.)

Biagini, Eugenio F., PhD Pisa   Lectr.

Blanning, T. C. W., MA Camb., PhD Camb.   Prof., Modern European History (Sid.)

Brading, David A., MA Lond., MA Camb., PhD Lond., LittD Camb.   Reader, Latin-American History (Cla.H.)

Bradshaw, B. I., BD Pontif.Athen.Angelicum, MA N.U.I., MA Camb., PhD   Lectr. (Qu.)

Burke, U. Peter, MA Oxf., MA Camb. Prof., Cultural History (Emm.)

Carpenter, M. Christine, MA PhD Reader, Medieval English History (New H.)

Chandavarkar, Rajnarayan S., BA PhD Lectr. (Trin.)

Clarke, P. F., MA PhD LittD, FBA, FRHistS Prof., Modern British History (S.Joh.)

Daunton, Martin J., BA Nott., PhD Kent Prof., Economic History (Chur.)

Dobson, R. Barrie, MA Oxf., DPhil Oxf., PhD, FSA, FRHistS, FBA Prof., Medieval History (Chr.)

Evans, Gillian R., MA Oxf., DLitt Oxf., PhD Reading, LittD, FRHistS Lectr.

Figes, Orlando G., BA PhD Lectr. (Trin.)

Garnsey, P. D. A., BA Syd., MA Oxf., DPhil Oxf., PhD Prof., History of Classical Antiquity (Jes.)

Gatrell, V. A. C., MA PhD Lectr. (Cai.)

Goldie, Mark A., BA Sus., MA Camb., PhD Camb. Lectr. (Chur.)

Harper, Timothy N., MA Camb., PhD Camb. Lectr. (Magd.)

Hatcher, M. J., BSc(Econ) Lond., MA Camb., PhD Lond., LittD Camb. Prof., Economics and Social History (Corp.)

Hilton, A. J. Boyd, MA Oxf., MA Camb., DPhil Oxf., PhD, FRHistS Reader, Modern British History (Trin.)

Hont, I., MA Bud., MA Camb., PhD Bud. Lectr. (King's)

Hopkins, Anthony G., BA Lond., PhD Lond. Prof., Commonwealth History (Pemb.)

Hyam, Ronald, MA PhD LittD Reader, British Imperial History (Magd.)

Iliffe, J., MA PhD LittD Prof., African History (S.Joh.)

Kaplanoff, M. D., BA Yale, MA PhD Lectr. (Pemb.)

Lonsdale, John M., MA PhD Reader, African History (Trin.)

Lovatt, R. W., MA Oxf., MA Camb., DPhil Oxf., PhD Lectr. (Pet.)

McKendrick, Neil, MA Camb. Reader (Cai.)

McKitterick, Rosamond D., BA W.Aust., MA Camb., PhD Camb., LittD Camb., FRHistS Prof., Early Medieval European History (Newn.)

Morrill, J. S., MA Oxf., DPhil Oxf., PhD, FRHistS, FBA Reader, Early Modern History (Selw.)

Outhwaite, R. B., BA Nott., PhD Nott., MA Lectr. (Cai.)

Parry, J. P., MA PhD Lectr. (Pemb.)

Reynolds, David J., MA PhD Reader, International History (Chr.)

Riley-Smith, Jonathon S. C., MA Camb., PhD Camb. Dixie Prof., Ecclesiastical History (Emm.)

Seal, Anil, MA PhD Lectr. (Trin.)

Shepard, J. E. B., MA Oxf., PhD Lectr., Russian History (Pet.)

Skinner, Quentin R. D., MA, FBA Regius Prof., Modern History (Chr.)

Smith, Richard M., BA Lond., MA Oxf., PhD Camb., FBA Reader, Historical Demography; Dir., Cambridge Group for Hist. and Population of Soc. Structure (Down.)

Spufford, P., MA PhD LittD Reader, Economic History (Qu.)

Stedman Jones, G., MA Oxf., MA Camb., DPhil Oxf. Prof., Political Science (King's)

Steinberg, Jonathan, BA Harv., MA PhD Reader, Modern European History (Trin.H.)

Szreter, S. R. S., MA PhD Lectr. (S.Joh.)

Thompson, John A., MA PhD Lectr. (S.Cat.)

Tombs, R. P., MA PhD Lectr. (S.Joh.)

Trebilcock, R. C., MA Lectr. (Pemb.)

Winter, J. M., BA Col., PhD Reader, Modern History (Pemb.)

Wood, Betty C., BA Keele, MA Lond., MA Camb., PhD Penn. Lectr. (Gir.)

Wrightson, K. E., MA PhD Reader, English Social History (Jes.)

Other Staff: 5 Asst. Lectrs.; 1 Computer Officer

History and Philosophy of Science

Tel: (01223) 334540 Fax: (01223) 334554

Forrester, J. P., MA PhD Reader, History and Philosophy of the Sciences

French, R. K., MA Oxf., DPhil Oxf., PhD Lectr., History of Medicine; Dir., Wellcome Unit (Cla.H.)

Jardine, Nicholas, MA PhD Prof., History and Philosophy of the Sciences (Darw.)

Kusch, Martin P. H., MA Oulu, PhD Oulu Lectr.

Lipton, P., BA Wesleyan, BPhil Oxf., DPhil Oxf. Prof.; Head* (King's)

Schaffer, Simon J., MA Harv., MA Camb., PhD Reader (Darw.)

Secord, J. A., BA Pomona, PhD Prin. Lectr.

Taub, Liba, BA Tulane, MA Chic., MA Oklahoma, PhD Oklahoma Curator, Whipple Museum

History of Art

Tel: (01223) 332950 Fax: (01223) 332960

Binski, Paul, MA Camb., PhD Camb. Lectr. (Cai.)

Gage, J. S., BA Oxf., PhD Lond. Reader, History of Western Art

Joannides, P. E. A., MA PhD Lectr. (Cla.H.)

Massing, J. M., MHistArt Stras., Dr Stras., MA Reader; Head* (King's)

Watkin, D. J., MA PhD LittD Reader, History of Architecture (Pet.)

Indian Studies

Tel: (01223) 335106 Fax: (01223) 335110

Kahrs, E. G., MA Oslo, PhD Oslo Lectr. (Qu.)

Industrial Relations, see Econ. and Pol.

Islamic Studies, see also Arabic

Tel: (01223) 335106 Fax: (01223) 335110

Bennison, Katharine N., MA Camb., MA Harv., PhD Lond. Lectr.

Melville, C. P., MA PhD Lectr. (Pemb.)

Musallam, B. F., MA Beirut, PhD Harv. Lectr. (King's)

Italian

Tel: (01223) 335038 Fax: (01223) 335062

Boyde, P., MA PhD Serena Prof. (S.Joh.)

Caesar, Ann, BA Kent, PhD Lond., MA Lectr.; Head* (Corp.)

Cox, Virginia, BA PhD Lectr. (Chr.)

Forgacs, D. A., BA Oxf., MPhil Oxf., DottLett Pisa Lectr. (Cai.)

Gordon, Robert S. C., BA Oxf., PhD Camb. Lectr. (Cai.)

Kirkpatrick, R., BA Oxf., PhD Lectr. (Rob.)

Other Staff: 1 Sr. Lang. Teaching Officer

Japanese

Tel: (01223) 335106 Fax: (01223) 335110

Bowring, R. J., MA PhD LittD Prof., Modern Japanese Studies (Down.)

Kornicki, P. F., MA Oxf., MSc Oxf., DPhil Oxf. Reader, Japanese History and Bibliography (Rob.)

Large, S. S., BA Harv., MA Mich., MA Camb., PhD Mich. Reader, Modern Japanese History (Wolfs.)

Morris, Mark R., BA Col., PhD Harv. Lectr. (Trin.)

Swenson-Wright, John H., BA Oxf., DPhil Oxf. Lectr.

Whittaker, D. H., BA Tokyo, PhD Lond. Lectr. (Cla.H.)

Other Staff: 1 Sr. Lang. Teaching Officer; 1 Lector

Land Economy

Tel: (01223) 337147 Fax: (01223) 337130

Cathie, J., BA Strath., MLitt St And., PhD Strath., MA Asst. Dir. of Res. (Wolfs.)

Dixon, M. J., BA Oxf., MA Lectr. (Rob.)

Fennell, Shailaja, MA Delhi, MPhil Delhi, MPhil Camb. Asst. Dir., Development Studies (Jes.)

Fingleton, Bernard, BA Wales, MPhil Camb., PhD Wales Lectr.

Grant, Malcolm J., LLD Otago Prof.; Head* (Cla.)

Hodge, I. D., BSc Reading, PhD Lond. Gilbey Lectr.

Howarth, David R., MA Yale, MA Camb., LLM Yale, MPhil Yale Lectr. (Cla.)

McCombie, J. S. L., MA McM., MA Camb., PhD Lectr. (Down.)

McFarquhar, A. M. M., MA PhD Lectr.

McHugh, P. G., LLB Well., LLM Sask., PhD Lectr. (Sid.)

Moore, B. C., MSc(Econ) Lond., MA Asst. Dir. of Res. (Down.)

Nicholls, Derek C., MA Camb., PhD Camb. Gurney Lectr. (Fitz.)

Patel, Kanaklata, BSc Lond., MA Essex, PhD Essex Lectr. (Magd.)

Pearce, Barry J., JP, BSc Wales, MA PhD Lectr. (Magd.)

Renwick, Alan W., BSc Lond., PhD Newcastle(UK) Sr. Asst. in Res. (Hug.)

Spash, Clive L., BA Stir., MA Br.Col., PhD Wyoming Lectr.

Tyler, Peter, MA Camb., PhD Camb. Lectr. (S.Cat.)

Whitehead, C. M. E., BSc Lond., PhD Lond. Dir., Property Res. Unit

Languages, Modern and Mediaeval, see separate langs., Linguistics, and Other Langs.

Latin-American Studies, see Hist., and Spanish and Portuguese

Latin, Classical, see Classics

Latin, Mediaeval, see Other Langs.

Law, see also Criminol.

Tel: (01223) 330033 Fax: (01223) 330055

Allan, T. R. S., BCL Oxf., MA Oxf., MA Camb. Reader, Legal and Constitutional Theory (Pemb.)

Allison, John W. F., LLM Camb., MPhil Camb., PhD Camb. Lectr. (Qu.)

Allott, Philip J., MA LLM Reader, International Public Law (Trin.)

Andrews, Neil H., BA Oxf., BCL Oxf., MA Lectr. (Cla.)

Bainham, Andrew W. E., LLM Camb., PhD Camb. Lectr. (Chr.)

Baker, John H., LLB Lond., MA Camb., PhD Lond., LLD Camb., FBA Prof., English Legal History (S.Cat.)

Barnard, Catherine S., MA Camb., LLM European Univ.Inst. Lectr. (Trin.)

Beatson, Jack, BCL Oxf., MA Oxf., MA Camb. Rouse Ball Prof., English Law (S.Joh.)

Bridge, S. N., MA Lectr. (Qu.)

Cheffins, Brian R., LLB Vic.(BC), LLM Camb. Prof., Corporate Law

Clarke, M. A., MA LLB PhD Reader, Commercial Contract Law (S.Joh.)

Collier, John G., MA LLB Lectr. (Trin.H.)

Cornish, William R., LLB Adel., BCL Oxf., FBA Herchel Smith Prof., Intellectual Property Law (Magd.)

Crawford, J. R., BA Adel., LLB Adel., DPhil Oxf. Whewell Prof., International Law (Jes.)

Cripps, Yvonne M., LLB Vic.(Tor.), LLM Well., PhD Reader (Emm.)

Dashwood, Arthur A., BA Rhodes, MA Oxf. Prof., European Law (Sid.)

Deakin, S. F., MA PhD Lectr. (Pet.)

Fentiman, R. G., BCL Oxf., MA Oxf., MA Camb. Lectr. (Qu.)

Ferran, Eilis V., MA PhD Lectr. (S.Cat.)

Fleming, David W., MA LLB Lectr. (Trin.H.)

Forsyth, C. F., BSc Natal, LLB Natal, LLB Camb., PhD Lectr. (Rob.)

Glazebrook, P. R., MA Oxf., MA Camb. Lectr. (Jes.)

Gray, Christine D., MA Camb., PhD Camb. Lectr. (S.Joh.)

Gray, Kevin J., MA PhD LLD Prof. (Trin.)

Harpum, C., MA LLB Lectr. (Down.)

Hedley, Stephen W., LLB *Camb.*, MA *Oxf.* Lectr. (Chr.)

Hepple, Bob A., QC, LLD *Camb.* Prof. (Cla.)

Hooley, Richard J. A., MA *Camb.* Lectr. (Fitz.)

Hopkins, J. A., MA LLB Lectr. (Down.)

Johnston, David E. L., MA PhD Regius Prof., Civil Law (Chr.)

Jones, Gareth H., QC, LLM *Harv.*, MA LLD, FBA Downing Prof., Laws of England (Trin.)

Keown, I. J., DPhil *Oxf.*, MA Lectr. (Qu.)

Kramer, Matthew H., BA *Cornell*, JD *Harv.*, PhD *Camb.* Lectr. (Chur.)

Lowe, A. V., LLM *Wales*, MA *Wales*, PhD *Wales* Reader, International Law (Corp.)

Marks, Susan R., BA *Syd.*, LLB *Syd.*, LLM Lectr. (Emm.)

Marston, G., LLM *Lond.*, PhD *Lond.*, MA Lectr. (Sid.)

Munday, R. J. C., MA PhD Lectr. (Pet.)

Nolan, Richard C., MA *Camb.* Lectr. (S.Joh.)

Oakley, Antony J., MA LLB Lectr. (Trin.H.)

Oldham, Mika P. C., MA PhD Lectr. (Jes.)

Palmer, Stephanie, LLM Lectr. (Gir.)

Rogerson, Philippa J., MA PhD Lectr. (Cai.)

Sharpston, Eleanor V. E., MA Lectr. (King's)

Simmonds, N. E., MA LLM PhD Reader, Jurisprudence (Corp.)

Smith, A. T. H., LLM *Cant.*, PhD Prof. (Cai.)

Spencer, J. R., MA LLB Prof. (Selw.)

Thornton, Rosamund E., MA PhD Lectr. (New H.)

Tiley, J., BCL *Oxf.*, MA *Oxf.*, MA *Camb.* Prof., Law of Taxation (Qu.)

Virgo, G. J., MA Lectr. (Down.)

Weir, J. Tony, MA Reader (Trin.)

Other Staff: 3 Asst. Lectrs.; 1 Computer Officer

Linguistics

Tel: (01223) 335010 Fax: (01223) 335062

Hawkins, Sarah, BSc *S'ton.*, PhD Lectr. (Cla.H.)

Law, Vivien A., BA *McG.*, PhD *Camb.* Lectr. (Trin.)

Lyons, Christopher G., MA *Camb.* Lectr.

Matthews, P. H., MA LittD, FBA Prof. (S.Joh.)

McMahon, April M. S., MA *Edin.*, MA *Camb.*, PhD *Edin.* Lectr. (Selw.)

Nolan, F. J. D., MA PhD Lectr.; Head*

Other Staff: 1 Asst. Lectr.

Management Studies, Judge Institute of

Tel: (01223) 337051 Fax: (01223) 339701

Barker, Richard G., BA *Oxf.*, MPhil *Camb.* Lectr. (Wolfs.)

Bartholomew, Susan L., BA *Tor.*, MBA *Tor.*, PhD *Tor.* Lectr. (L.Cav.)

Brown, Andrew D., BA *Oxf.*, MSc *Sheff.*, PhD *Sheff.* Lectr.

Child, J., MA PhD ScD Guinness Prof. (S.Joh.)

Collier, Jane, BSc *Lond.*, PhD *Birm.*, MA Lectr. (L.Cav.)

Dawson, Sandra J. N., BA *Keele*, MA *Camb.* KPMG Prof.; Head* (Jes.)

Dempster, Michael A. H., BA *Tor.*, MA *Oxf.*, MS *Carnegie Tech.*, PhD *Carnegie Tech.* Prof.

Dissanaike, Gishan R., BA *Peradeniya*, MPhil *Camb.*, PhD *Camb.* Lectr.

Hendry, J. L., MSc *Lond.*, PhD *Lond.*, MA Dir., MBA Course (Gir.)

Lambrecht, Bart M. A. C., MPhil *Camb.* Lectr.

Nolan, Peter H., MA *Camb.*, MSc *Lond.*, PhD *Lond.* Sinyi Prof., Chinese Management (Jes.)

Oliver, Nick, MA *Edin.*, PhD *Open(UK)* Reader

Pitelis, C. N., BA *Panteios*, MA *Warw.*, PhD *Warw.* Lectr. (Qu.)

Roberts, J. D., BSc *Manc.*, PhD *Manc.* Lectr.

Steinberg, Richard, BA *Reed*, MMath *Wat.*, MBA *Chic.*, PhD *Wat.* Lectr.

Other Staff: 1 Computer Officer

Materials Science and Metallurgy

Tel: (01223) 334300 Fax: (01223) 334567

Bhadeshia, Harshad K. D. H., BSc CN*AA*, PhD Reader, Physical Metallurgy (Darw.)

Blamire, Mark G., MA *Camb.*, PhD *Camb.* Asst. Dir. of Res. (Hug.)

Boothroyd, C. B., MA PhD Asst. Dir. of Res.

Bristowe, Paul D., BSc *E.Anglia*, PhD *Sur.* Lectr.

Burstein, Gordon T., MA *Auck.*, MSc *Auck.*, PhD *Auck.* Asst. Dir. of Res.

Cameron, Ruth E., MA PhD Lectr. (L.Cav.)

Clegg, William J., BSc *Manc.*, DPhil *Oxf.* Lectr. (Selw.)

Clyne, T. W., MA PhD Reader, Mechanics of Materials (Down.)

Evetts, J. E., MA PhD Reader, Device Materials (Pemb.)

Fray, Derek J., BSc *Lond.*, MA *Camb.*, PhD *Lond.* Prof., Materials Chemistry (Fitz.)

Glowacki, Bartlomiej A., MSc *Wrocław*, PhD *Polish Acad.Sc.* Asst. Dir. of Res.

Goldbeck-Wood, Gerhard, PhD *Brist.* Asst. Dir. of Res.

Greer, A. L., MA *Camb.*, PhD *Camb.* Reader, Microstructural Kinetics (Sid.)

Humphreys, C. J., BSc *Lond.*, MA *Oxf.*, PhD Goldsmiths' Prof., Materials Science (Selw.)

Hutchings, I. M., MA PhD Reader, Tribology (S.Joh.)

Knowles, David M., MA *Camb.*, PhD *Camb.* Lectr. (Fitz.)

Knowles, Kevin M., DPhil *Oxf.*, MA Lectr. (Chur.)

Kumar, Ramachandran V., BTech *Bom.*, PhD *McM.* Lectr.

Leake, J. A., MA PhD Lectr. (S.Joh.)

Little, John A., MA PhD Lectr. (S.Cat.)

Midgley, Paul A., MSc *Brist.*, PhD *Brist.* Asst. Dir. of Res.

Reed, Roger C., MA *Camb.*, PhD *Camb.* Asst. Dir. of Res.

Wallach, E. R., MSc *Qu.*, MA PhD Lectr. (King's)

Windle, Alan H., BSc(Eng) *Lond.*, PhD Prof., Materials Science; Head* (Trin.)

Withers, Philip J., MA PhD Lectr. (Trin.H.)

Other Staff: 2 Sr. Tech. Officers; 1 Tech. Officer

Mathematics, Applied, and Theoretical Physics

Tel: (01223) 337900 Fax: (01223) 337918

Burgess, A., BSc *Lond.*, PhD *Lond.*, MA Lectr. (Wolfs.)

Cowley, S. J., MA PhD Lectr. (Selw.)

Crighton, D. G., PhD *Lond.*, MA ScD, FRS Prof., Applied Mathematics; Head* (S.Joh.)

D'Eath, P. D., MA PhD Lectr.

Dalziel, Stuart B., BE *Auck.*, PhD *Camb.* Asst. Dir. of Res.

Davis, Anne C., BSc *Lond.*, PhD *Brist.* Reader, Theoretical Physics (King's)

Dougherty, J. P., MA PhD Stokes Lectr. (Pemb.)

Drummond, I. T., BSc *Edin.*, MA *Edin.*, PhD Reader, Mathematical Physics (Rob.)

Gibbons, G. W., MA PhD Prof., Theoretical Physics

Goddard, Peter, MA *Camb.*, PhD *Camb.*, ScD, FRS Prof., Theoretical Physics (S.Joh.)

Green, M. B., MA PhD, FRS John Humphrey Plummer Prof., Theoretical Physics (Cla.H.)

Harding, R. D., MA PhD Asst. Dir. of Res. (Selw.)

Hawking, Stephen W., CBE, CH, BA *Oxf.*, MA PhD Hon. ScD, FRS Lucasian Prof. (Cai.)

Haynes, P. H., MA PhD Lectr. (Qu.)

Hinch, E. John, MA PhD Reader, Fluid Mechanics (Trin.)

Horgan, R. R., BSc *Reading*, DPhil *Oxf.*, PhD *Camb.* Lectr. (Sid.)

Hudson, J. A., MA PhD Reader, Elastodynamics (Jes.)

Huppert, H. E., BSc *Syd.*, MSc *ANU*, MSc *Calif.*, PhD *Calif.*, MA ScD, FRS Prof., Theoretical Geophysics (King's)

Iserles, A., MA Reader, Numerical Analysis of Differential Equations

Jensen, Oliver E., MA *Camb.*, PhD *Camb.* Asst. Dir. of Res. (Cai.)

Kent, Adrian P. A., MA *Camb.*, PhD *Camb.* Asst. Dir. of Res.

Landshoff, Peter V., MA PhD Prof., Mathematical Physics (Chr.)

Linden, Noah, MA *Lond.*, PhD *Lond.* Asst. Dir. of Res. (Jes.)

Linden, P. F., BSc *Adel.*, MSc *Flin.*, PhD Reader, Geophysical Fluid Dynamics (Down.)

Lister, John R., MA *Camb.*, PhD *Camb.* Lectr. (Trin.)

Macfarlane, A. J., MSc *Edin.*, PhD *Lond.*, MA Reader, Mathematical Physics (S.Joh.)

MacKay, Robert S., MA *Camb.* Prof., Nonlinear Dynamics

Manton, Nicholas S., MA PhD Reader, Mathematical Physics (S.Joh.)

Mason, Helen E., BSc *Lond.*, PhD *Lond.*, MA Asst. Dir. of Res. (S.Edm.)

McIntyre, M. E., BSc *Otago*, PhD, FRS Prof., Atmospheric Dynamics

Moffatt, H. Keith, BA *Camb.*, PhD *Camb.*, ScD *Camb.*, FRS Prof., Mathematical Physics (Trin.)

Nikiforakis, Nikolaos, BSc *Manc.*, MSc *Cran.IT*, PhD *Cran.IT* Asst. Dir. of Res.

Osborn, Hugh, BSc *Lond.*, PhD *Lond.*, MA Reader, Theoretical Physics (Trin.)

Peake, Nigel, MA *Camb.*, PhD *Camb.* Lectr. (Emm.)

Pedley, Timothy J., MA *Camb.*, PhD *Camb.*, ScD *Camb.* Prof., Fluid Mechanics (Cai.)

Powell, M. J. D., ScD, FRS John Humphrey Plummer Prof., Applied Numerical Analysis (Pemb.)

Proctor, Michael R. E., MA *Camb.*, PhD *Camb.*, ScD *Camb.* Reader, Astrophysical Fluid Dynamics (Trin.)

Rallison, John M., MA PhD Lectr. (Trin.)

Shellard, Edward P. S., BSc *Syd.*, PhD *Camb.* Lectr.

Siklos, Stephen T. C., MA *Camb.*, PhD *Camb.* Asst. Dir. of Res.

Spivack, Mark, BSc *Wales*, MSc *Manc.*, PhD *Manc.* Asst. Dir. of Res. (Rob.)

Stewart, J. M., MA PhD Lectr. (King's)

Townsend, P. K., PhD *Brandeis*, MA Reader

Turok, Neil G., MA *Camb.*, PhD *Lond.* Prof., Mathematical Physics (Cla.H.)

Weiss, Nigel O., MA PhD ScD Prof., Mathematical Astrophysics (Cla.)

Whelan, Colm T., MSc *N.U.I.*, PhD *Camb.* Asst. Dir. of Res.

Williams, Ruth M., MA *Camb.*, PhD *Lond.* Asst. Dir. of Res. (Gir.)

Willis, John R., MA *Camb.*, PhD *Lond.*, FIMA, FRS Prof., Theoretical Solid Mechanics (Fitz.)

Worster, M. Grae, MA PhD Asst. Dir. of Res. (Trin.)

Other Staff: 3 Computer Officers

Mathematics, Pure, and Mathematical Statistics

Tel: (01223) 337999 Fax: (01223) 337920

Allan, Graham R., MA PhD Reader, Functional Analysis (Chur.)

Altham, Patricia M. E., MA *Camb.*, PhD *Camb.* Lectr. (Newn.)

Baker, Alan, BSc *Lond.*, MA PhD, FRS Prof. (Trin.)

Beardon, A. F., BSc *Lond.*, PhD *Lond.*, MA Reader (S.Cat.)

Carne, T. K., MA PhD Lectr. (King's)

Coates, John H., BSc *ANU*, PhD, FRS Sadleirian Prof., Pure Mathematics (Emm.)

Corti, Alessio, BSc *Pisa*, PhD *Utah* Lectr. (Emm.)

Croft, H. T., MA PhD Lectr. (Pet.)

Garling, D. J. H., MA PhD ScD Reader, Mathematical Analysis (S.Joh.)

Gowers, W. Timothy, BA *Camb.*, PhD *Camb.* Prof. (Trin.)

Grimmett, G. R., MA *Oxf.*, MSc *Oxf.*, DPhil *Oxf.* Prof., Mathematical Statistics; Dir., Stat. Lab.

Grojnowski, Ian, BSc *Syd.*, PhD *M.I.T.* Lectr.

Hyland, J. M. E., MA Oxf., MA Camb., DPhil Oxf., PhD Reader (King's)
Johnstone, P. T., MA PhD ScD Reader, Foundations of Mathematics (S.Joh.)
Kelly, Frank P., BSc Durh., MA PhD, FRS Prof., Mathematics of Systems (Chr.)
Kennedy, Douglas P., BA Trinity(Dub.), MS Stan., PhD Stan., MA Lectr. (Trin.)
Körner, Thomas W., MA PhD ScD Reader, Analysis (Trin.H.)
Lickorish, W. B. R., MA PhD ScD Prof., Geometric Topology; Head* (Pemb.)
Nekovar, Jan, BSc Prague, PhD Czech Acad.Sc. Lectr. (Chr.)
Norris, James R., MA Oxf., DPhil Oxf. Lectr. (Chur.)
Pitts, Susan M., MA Camb., MSc Lond., PhD Lond. Lectr. (Newn.)
Roseblade, J. E., BA PhD Reader, Algebra (Jes.)
Saxl, Jan, BSc Brist., MA Camb., MSc Oxf., DPhil Oxf., PhD Camb. Lectr. (Cai.)
Segal, G. B., BSc Syd., MA Oxf., DPhil Oxf., PhD Camb., FRS Lowndean Prof., Astronomy and Geometry (S.Joh.)
Shepherd-Barron, Nicholas I., PhD Warw., BA Reader, Algebraic Geometry (Trin.)
Sparrow, C. T., MA PhD Lectr. (King's)
Suhov, Y. M., MA Moscow, MA Camb., PhD Moscow Reader, Probability (S.Joh.)
Thomas, C. B., BA PhD Lectr. (Rob.)
Thomason, Andrew G., MA PhD Lectr. (Cla.)
Wassermann, Antony J., PhD Penn., MA Lectr. (Chr.)
Weber, Richard R., MA Camb., PhD Camb. Prof., Mathematics for Operational Research (Qu.)
Whiteside, D. T., BA Brist., PhD Prof., History of Mathematics and Exact Sciences
Wilson, Pelham M. H., MA PhD Reader, Algebraic Geometry (Trin.)
Young, G. Alastair, BSc Edin., PhD Lectr. (Emm.)
Other Staff: 2 Computer Officers

Medicine, see below

Metallurgy, see Materials Sci. and Metall.

Mineralogy, see Earth Scis.

Music
Tel: (01223) 335184 Fax: (01223) 335067
Bowers, R. D., MA Oxf., MA Camb., PhD E.Anglia Lectr. (Jes.)
Butt, John A., MA Camb., MPhil Camb., PhD Camb. Lectr. (King's)
Castelvecchi, Stefano, MA Chic., PhD Chic. Lectr.
Cross, Ian R. M., BSc City(UK), PhD City(UK) Lectr. (Wolfs.)
Davis, Ruth F., BMus Lond., MFA Prin., MA Lectr. (Corp.)
Ennis, Martin W., MA Camb., MPhil Camb., PhD Lectr. (Gir.)
Fenlon, Iain A., BMus Reading, MA Birm., MA Camb., PhD Reader, Historical Musicology (King's)
Goehr, Alexander, MA Prof. (Trin.H.)
Holloway, R. G., MA PhD MusD Lectr. (Cai.)
Jones, A. V., MA Oxf., MA Camb., DPhil Oxf., PhD Lectr. (Selw.)
Rankin, Susan K., MMus Lond., MA PhD Lectr. (Emm.)
Sutcliffe, William D., BMus Auck., MA Auck., MPhil PhD Lectr. (S.Cat.)
Wood, Hugh B., MA Oxf. Lectr. (Chur.)

Norse, see Anglo-Saxon, Norse and Celtic

Other Languages
Tel: (01223) 335038 Fax: (01223) 335062
Dronke, E. P. M., MA NZ, MA Oxf., MA Camb. Prof., Mediaeval Latin Literature (Cla.H.)
Holton, D. W., MA Oxf., DPhil Oxf., PhD Lectr., Modern Greek; Head* (Selw.)
Strietman, Elzelina G. C., CandLitt Gron., MA Lectr., Dutch (New H.)

Pathology
Tel: (01223) 333695 Fax: (01223) 333346
Affara, Nabeel A., BSc Edin., MA Camb., PhD Glas. Lectr. (Hug.)
Ajioka, James W., BS Utah, PhD N.Y. Lectr. (Jes.)
Arno, Jeanne, BA Oxf., BM BCh Oxf., MA Lectr. (Trin.H.)
Blackwell, Jenefer M., BSc W.Aust., PhD W.Aust. Glaxo Prof., Molecular Parasitology (Newn.)
Bowyer, D. E., MA PhD Lectr. (Fitz.)
Brierley, I., BSc Leeds, DPhil York(UK) Lectr.
Brown, T. D. K., BA Oxf., PhD Leic. Lectr.
Clark, M. R., BSc Lond., PhD Lectr.
Coleman, Nicholas, BSc Brist., MB ChB Brist., PhD Camb. Lectr. (Down.)
Collins, V. Peter, MB BCh BAO N.U.I., MD Stockholm, FRCPI Prof., Histopathology
Cooke, Anne, BSc Glas., DPhil Sus. Reader, Immunology (King's)
Dunne, D. W., BSc Brist., PhD Lond. Lectr.
Edwards, Paul A. W., MA PhD Lectr. (Cla.)
Efstathiou, S., BA Leeds, PhD Lectr.
Holmes, N. J., BA PhD Lectr.
Hughes, Colin, BSc Kent, PhD Kent Reader, Microbiology (Trin.)
Kelly, Adrian, BSc Lond., MPhil Lond., PhD Lond. Lectr.
Kingston, I. B., BSc Brist., PhD Brist. Lectr.
Koronakis, Vasilios, MSc Athens, PhD Graz Lectr.
Le Page, R. W. F., MA PhD Lectr. (Cai.)
Loke, Y. W., MA MD Reader, Reproductive Immunology (King's)
McKee, T. A., BSc Glas., MB ChB Glas., PhD Glas. Clin. Lectr.
Minson, A. C., BSc Birm., PhD ANU, MA Prof., Virology (Wolfs.)
Mitchinson, Malcolm J., MA MD Lectr. (Cla.)
Reyburn, Hugh T., BVMS Glas., PhD Edin. Lectr.
Stanley, Margaret A., BSc Lond., PhD Brist., MA Reader, Epithelial Biology (Chr.)
Thirunavukkarasu, Sathia, MB ChB Leeds, MA Lectr. (Pemb.)
Trowsdale, John, BSc Birm., PhD Birm. Prof., Immunology
Xuereb, John H., MD Malta, MD Newcastle(UK), MA Camb. Lectr. (S.Cat.)
Yates, J. R. W., MA Oxf., MA Camb., MB BS Lond. Lectr.
Other Staff: 13 Assoc. Lectrs.; 1 Sr. Tech. Officer; 1 Superintendent of Dept.

Pharmacology
Tel: (01223) 334000 Fax: (01223) 334040
Callingham, B. A., BPharm Lond., PhD Lond., MA, FPS Lectr. (Qu.)
Cuthbert, Alan W., BSc St And., BPharm Lond., MA Camb., PhD Lond., Hon. LLD Dund., Hon. DSc De Mont., Hon. DSc Aston, FRS Sheild Prof.; Head* (Fitz.)
Edwardson, J. M., MA PhD Lectr. (Fitz.)
Fan, T.-P. D., BSc Lond., PhD Lond. Lectr.
Ferguson, Douglas R., ChB Brist., MD Brist., MA Lectr. (Chr.)
Henderson, Robert M., BSc Lond., MA Camb., PhD Lond. Lectr. (Emm.)
Hiley, C. Robin, MA PhD Lectr. (New H.)
Hladky, S. B., BA Dartmouth, MA PhD Lectr. (Jes.)
Irvine, R. F., BA Oxf., PhD, FRS Prof., Molecular Pharmacology
Matthews, E. K., BPharm Nott., PhD Lond., MA Reader (S.Joh.)
Morton, A. Jennifer, BSc Otago, PhD Otago Lectr. (Newn.)
Murrell-Lagnado, Ruth D., BSc Lond., PhD Camb. Lectr. (Newn.)
Richardson, P. J., MA Oxf., PhD Lectr. (Sid.)
Taylor, C. W., MA PhD Reader, Cellular Pharmacology
Thorn, Peter, BSc Nott., MSc Edin., PhD Edin. Lectr.
Waring, M. J., MA PhD ScD Reader, Chemotherapy (Jes.)
Young, J. M., MA PhD Lectr. (Selw.)

Philology, Romance, see Spanish and Portuguese

Philosophy, see also Classics, and Hist. and Philos. of Sci.
Tel: (01223) 335090 Fax: (01223) 335091
Altham, J. E. J., MA PhD Lectr. (Cai.)
Craig, Edward J., MA PhD, FBA Prof., Modern Philosophy (Chur.)
Geuss, Raymond, BA Col., PhD Col. Lectr.
Harrison, T. R., MA PhD Reader (King's)
Heal, Barbara J., MA PhD Reader (S.Joh.)
James, Susan D. T., MA PhD Lectr. (Gir.)
Mellor, D. Hugh, MSc Minn., MA PhD ScD, FBA Prof. (Darw.)
Oliver, Alexander D., MA Camb., MA Yale, MPhil Yale, PhD Camb. Lectr. (Qu.)
Olson, Eric T., BA Reed, PhD Syr. Lectr.
Scott, Dominic J., MA PhD Lectr. (Cla.)

Physics, see also Maths., Appl., and Theoret. Phys.
Tel: (01223) 337200 Fax: (01223) 363263
Adkins, C. J., MA PhD Lectr. (Jes.)
Ahmed, H., BSc Lond., PhD Camb., ScD Camb. Prof., Microelectronics (Corp.)
Alexander, P., MA PhD Lectr. (Jes.)
Allison, W., BSc Lond., MA Camb., PhD Lond. Lectr. (Fitz.)
Ansorge, R. E., MA PhD Asst. Dir. of Res. (Down.)
Baldwin, J. E., MA PhD, FRS Prof., Radioastronomy (Qu.)
Ball, R. C., MA PhD Reader (Cai.)
Batley, J. Richard, DPhil Oxf., MA Lectr. (Chr.)
Bland, J. A. C., MA PhD Lectr. (Selw.)
Brown, L. M., BASc Tor., PhD Birm., MA ScD, FRS Prof. (Rob.)
Butcher, R. J., MA PhD Lectr. (Cai.)
Carter, Janet R., MA PhD Reader (Newn.)
Chaudhri, M. Munawar, MSc Panjab, PhD Asst. Dir. of Res., Surface Physics (Darw.)
Cleaver, J. R. A., MA PhD Asst. Dir. of Res. (Fitz.)
Cooper, John R., BSc Lond., PhD Lond. Asst. Dir. of Res. (Darw.)
Donald, Athene M., MA PhD Reader, Experimental Physics (Rob.)
Duffett-Smith, P. J., MA PhD Lectr. (Down.)
Field, John E., OBE, BSc Lond., PhD, FRS Prof., Applied Physics (Magd.)
Ford, C. J. B., MA PhD Lectr. (Gir.)
Friend, R. H., MA PhD, FRS Cavendish Prof. (S.Joh.)
Gibson, Valerie, BSc Sheff., DPhil Oxf. Lectr. (Trin.)
Green, David A., MA Camb., PhD Camb. Lectr. (Chur.)
Gull, S. F., MA PhD Reader (S.Joh.)
Hasko, David G., BSc Lond., PhD Lond. Asst. Dir. of Res.
Hills, Richard E., PhD Calif., BA Prof., Radio Astronomy (S.Edm.)
Hopkinson, Ian, BSc Brist., PhD Durh. Asst. Dir. of Res.
Howie, Archie, BSc Edin., PhD, FRS Prof. (Chur.)
Hughes, H. P., BSc Lond., PhD Lectr. (S.Joh.)
Jones, G. A. C., BSc Wales, PhD Wales, MA Lectr. (Rob.)
Josephson, Brian D., Hon. DSc Wales, Hon. DSc Exe., MA PhD, FRS Prof. (Trin.)
Julian, Stephen R., BSc Tor., MSc Tor., PhD Tor. Lectr. (Trin.)
Lasenby, A. N., MSc Lond., PhD Manc., MA Reader (Qu.)
Liang, W. Y., BSc Lond., PhD Prof., Superconductivity (Cai.)
Linfield, Edmund H., MA Camb., PhD Camb. Asst. Dir. of Res.
Littlewood, Peter B., BA Camb., PhD Camb. Prof. (Trin.)
Longair, M. S., BSc St And., Hon. LLD Dund., MA PhD, FRAS, FRSEd Jacksonian Prof., Natural Philosophy; Head* (Cla.H.)

Lonzarich, Gilbert G., BA *Calif.*, MS *Minn.*, PhD *Br.Col.*, MA, FRS   Prof., Condensed Matter Physics (Trin.)

MacKay, David J. C., BA *Camb.*, PhD *Calif.*   Lectr. (Darw.)

Marseglia, Elisabeth A., BA *Delaware*, MA *Johns H.*, MA *Camb.*, PhD *McM.*   Asst. Dir. of Res. (Fitz.)

Melrose, John R., BSc *Wales*, PhD *Wales*   Asst. Dir. of Res.

Monthoux, Philippe H., MS *Ill.*, PhD *Ill.*   Asst. Dir. of Res.

Needs, R. J., BSc *Brist.*, PhD   Lectr. (Rob.)

Nicholls, J., BA   Asst. Dir. of Res.

Padman, Rachael, BEng *Monash*, PhD *Camb.*   Asst. Dir. of Res. (Newn.)

Parker, M. A., BA *Oxf.*, PhD *Lond.*   Lectr. (Pet.)

Payne, M. C., MA PhD   Lectr.

Pepper, Michael, BSc *Reading*, PhD *Reading*, MA ScD, FRS   Prof. (Trin.)

Phillips, Richard T., MA PhD   Lectr. (Cla.)

Rajagopal, Gunaretnam, MSc *Malaya*, PhD *Georgia I.T.*   Asst. Dir. of Res.

Rennie, A. R., MA PhD   Asst. Dir. of Res. (Jes.)

Ritchie, D. A., MA *Oxf.*, DPhil *Sus.*   Asst. Dir. of Res. (Rob.)

Saunders, R. D. E., BSc *Brist.*, MSc *Leic.*, PhD   Asst. Dir. of Res.

Scott, P. F., BSc *Birm.*, MA PhD   Asst. Dir. of Res. (Sid.)

Simons, Benjamin D., MA *Camb.*, PhD *Camb.*   Lectr. (S.Joh.)

Smith, Charles G., BSc *St And.*, PhD *Camb.*   Lectr. (Cla.H.)

Waldram, J. R., MA PhD   Lectr. (Pemb.)

Walker, Ian R., BSc *Br.Col.*, MSc *S.Fraser*, PhD *Camb.*   Asst. Dir. of Res.

Ward, D. R., MA PhD   Lectr. (Qu.)

Warner, M., MA PhD   Reader (Corp.)

Warner, P. J., BSc *Sus.*   Asst. Dir. of Res.

Webber, Bryan R., MA *Oxf.*, MA *Camb.*, PhD *Calif.*   Reader, Theoretical Physics (Emm.)

White, T. O., BS *Alabama*, PhD *Purdue*   Lectr. (King's)

Withington, Stafford, BEng *Brad.*, PhD *Manc.*   Asst. Dir. of Res. (Down.)

Other Staff: 3 Sr. Assts. in Res.; 5 Sr. Tech. Officers; 10 Tech. Officers; 2 Computer Officers

Physiology, see also Veterinary Studies

Tel: (01223) 333899 Fax: (01223) 333840

Barnes, Richard J., MB BChir MA PhD   Lectr. (Emm.)

Brown, John, MA MB BChir   Lectr. (Trin.)

Carpenter, R. H. S., MA PhD   Lectr. (Cai.)

Colledge, William H., BSc *Lond.*, PhD *Lond.*   Lectr.

Crawford, Andrew C., MA PhD, FRS   Prof., Neurophysiology (Trin.)

Dickson, Suzanne L., MA *Camb.*, PhD *Camb.*   Lectr. (Pet.)

Edwards, A. V., MA VetMB PhD ScD, FRCVS   Reader, Neuroendocrine Physiology (Fitz.)

Fawcett, J. W., BA *Oxf.*, MB BS *Lond.*, PhD *Lond.*   Lectr. (King's)

Findlay, Alan L. R., MA VetMB PhD   Lectr. (Chur.)

Fowden, Abigail L., MA PhD   Reader, Perinatal Physiology (Gir.)

Giussani, Dino A., BSc *Lond.*, PhD *Lond.*   Lectr. (Cai.)

Hickson, J. C. D., MA PhD   Lectr., Veterinary Physiology (Pemb.)

Hill, Adrian E., BSc *Durh.*, MA *Camb.*, PhD *Lond.*   Lectr. (Wolfs.)

Hillier, A. P., MA PhD   Lectr. (Selw.)

Huang, Christopher L.-H., BM BCh *Oxf.*, MA *Oxf.*, MA *Camb.*, MD PhD ScD   Reader, Cellular Physiology (New H.)

Lamb, Trevor D., BE *Melb.*, MAppSc *Melb.*, PhD ScD, FRS   Prof., Neuroscience (Darw.)

Lew, V. L., MD *Buenos Aires*, MA   Asst. Dir. of Res.

Matthews, H. R., MA PhD   Lectr. (S.Joh.)

Robinson, Hugh P. C., MA *Camb.*, PhD *Camb.*   Lectr.

Robson, J. G., MA PhD   Reader, Neurophysiology (Cai.)

Rogers, J. H., MA MB BChir   Lectr.

Sage, Stuart O., MA *Camb.*, PhD *Camb.*   Lectr. (Qu.)

Schwiening, Cristof J., BSc *Brist.*, PhD *Brist.*   Lectr.

Surani, M. Azim H., BSc *Lond.*, MSc *Strath.*, PhD, FRS   Mary Marshall and Arthur Walton Prof., Physiology of Reproduction (King's)

Tapp, Roger L., MA PhD   Lectr. (Cla.)

Thomas, Roger C., BSc *S'ton.*, MA *Camb.*, PhD *S'ton.*, FRS   Prof.; Head* (Down.)

Tolhurst, David J., MA PhD   Lectr. (Emm.)

Winter, Ian M., BA *Sus.*, DPhil *Sus.*   Lectr.

Woods, R. I., MA *Oxf.*, MA *Camb.*, DPhil *Oxf.*   Lectr. (Sid.)

Other Staff: 1 Computer Officer

Plant Sciences

Tel: (01223) 333900 Fax: (01223) 333953

Bennett, K. D., MA PhD   Asst. Dir. of Res.

Briggs, D., MA   Lectr.; Curator of Herbarium (Wolfs.)

Carr, J. P., BSc *Liv.*, PhD *Liv.*   Lectr.

Davies, Julia M., BSc *Wales*, PhD *Liv.*   Lectr.

Echlin, P., BSc *Lond.*, PhD *Penn.*, MA   Lectr. (Cla.H.)

Gilligan, C. A., BA *Oxf.*, MA   Reader, Mathematical Biology (King's)

Gray, J. C., BSc *Birm.*, PhD *Birm.*, MA   Prof., Plant Molecular Biology (Rob.)

Grubb, Peter J., MA PhD ScD   Reader, Ecology (Magd.)

Hanke, D. E., BA *Oxf.*, PhD   Lectr. (Jes.)

Johnstone, K., BSc *Leeds*, PhD   Lectr. (Qu.)

Leigh, Roger A., BSc *Wales*, PhD *Wales*, FIBiol   Prof., Botany; Head*

MacRobbie, Enid A. C., PhD *Edin.*, MA ScD   Prof., Plant Biophysics (Gir.)

Parker, John S., MA *Oxf.*, DPhil *Oxf.*   Prof., Plant Cytogenetics

Smith, Alison G., BSc *Brist.*, MPhil PhD   Lectr. (Corp.)

Tanner, E. V. J., MA PhD   Lectr. (Cai.)

Tester, Mark A., BSc *Adel.*, PhD   Lectr. (Chur.)

Other Staff: 2 Tech. Officers (Botanic Garden)

Polar Research

(Scott Polar Research Institute)

Tel: (01223) 336540 Fax: (01223) 336549

Rees, W. Gareth, MA PhD   Asst. Dir. of Res. (Chr.)

Richards, Keith S., MA *Camb.*, PhD *Camb.*   Dir.* (Emm.)

Vitebsky, Piers G., PhD *Lond.*, MA   Asst. Dir. of Res.

Wadhams, P., MA *Camb.*, PhD *Camb.*, ScD *Camb.*   Reader, Polar Studies (Chur.)

Political Science, see Econ. and Pol., and Soc. and Pol. Scis.

Portuguese, see Spanish and Portuguese

Psychology, Experimental

Tel: (01223) 333552 Fax: (01223) 333564

Bradley, Brendan P., MSc *Aberd.*, MA *Camb.*, PhD *Lond.*   Lectr. (Hug.)

Dickinson, A., BSc *Manc.*, DPhil *Sus.*   Reader, Comparative Psychology (Trin.)

Dunnett, Steven B., BSc *Lond.*, MA PhD   Reader, Neurobiology (Cla.)

Eimer, Martin, MA *Bielefeld*, DrPhil *Bielefeld*   Lectr.

Everitt, B. J., BSc *Hull*, MA *Camb.*, PhD *Birm.*   Prof., Behavioural Neuroscience (Down.)

Laming, D. R. J., MA PhD   Lectr.

Mackintosh, N. J., MA *Oxf.*, DPhil *Oxf.*, PhD, FRS   Prof.; Head* (King's)

McCarthy, Rosaleen A., BSc *Leic.*, PhD *Leic.*   Lectr. (King's)

McLaren, Ian P. L., MA *Camb.*, PhD *Camb.*   Lectr. (Emm.)

Mollon, John D., BA *Oxf.*, DPhil *Oxf.*, MA   Reader (Cai.)

Monsell, S., MA *Oxf.*, DPhil *Oxf.*   Lectr. (Pemb.)

Moore, B. C. J., MA PhD   Prof., Auditory Perception (Wolfs.)

Robbins, T. W., MA PhD   Prof., Cognitive Neuroscience (Down.)

Russell, J., MA *Oxf.*, PhD *Lond.*   Lectr.

Whittle, P., BA PhD   Lectr. (Gir.)

Rabbinics

Tel: (01223) 332590 Fax: (01223) 332582

de Lange, Nicholas R. M., MA *Oxf.*, DPhil *Oxf.*, PhD   Lectr. (Wolfs.)

Radioastronomy, see Phys.

Russian, see Slavonic Studies

Sanskrit

Tel: (01223) 335106

Smith, John D., MA PhD   Lectr. (Chur.)

Scandinavian Studies

Ries, Paul, MA PhD   Lectr. (Darw.)

Slavonic Studies

Tel: (01223) 335007

Cross, A. G., AM *Harv.*, LittD *E.Anglia*, MA PhD, FBA   Prof. (Fitz.)

Franklin, Simon C., DPhil *Oxf.*, MA PhD   Lectr. (Cla.)

Gömöri, George T., BLitt *Oxf.*, MA   Lectr. (Darw.)

Howlett, Jana R., BA *Sus.*, DPhil *Oxf.*, MA PhD   Lectr. (Jes.)

Kelly, Aileen M., MA PhD   Lectr. (King's)

Ward, C. E., BEd *Lond.*, MA *Lanc.*, PhD *E.Anglia*   Lectr.; Acting Head* (Rob.)

Other Staff: 1 Lang. Teaching Officer

Social and Political Sciences

Tel: (01223) 334520

Barber, J. D., MA PhD   Lectr., Politics (King's)

Blackburn, Robert M., PhD *Liv.*, MA   Reader, Sociology (Cla.)

Burchell, Brendan J., BSc *Birm.*, PhD *Warw.*   Lectr. (Magd.)

Dunn, J. M., MA   Prof., Political Theory (King's)

Duveen, G. M., BSc *Sur.*, MSc *Strath.*, DPhil *Sus.*   Lectr. (Corp.)

Fraser, Colin, MA *Aberd.*, PhD *Brist.*   Lectr., Social Psychology (Chur.)

Good, D. A., BA *Sus.*, PhD   Lectr., Social Psychology (King's)

Hawthorn, G. P., BA *Oxf.*, MA   Reader (Cla.H.)

Hay, Dale F., BA *Allegheny*, PhD *N.Carolina*   Lectr. (Sid.)

Ingham, Geoffrey K., BA *Leic.*, PhD *Camb.*   Lectr. (Chr.)

Jobling, Raymond G., BA *Liv.*, MA *Camb.*   Lectr. (S.Joh.)

Jones, Gill E., BA *Reading*, MSc *Sur.*, PhD *Sur.*   Asst. Dir. of Res.

Lane, Christel O., BA *Essex*, MA *Camb.*, PhD *Lond.*   Lectr. (S.Joh.)

Lane, David S., BSocSc *Birm.*, PhD   Reader, Sociology (Emm.)

Lehmann, A. D., DPhil *Oxf.*   Asst. Dir. of Devel. Studies

Mazey, Sonia P., BA *Leic.*, MA *Camb.*, DPhil *Oxf.*   Lectr. (Chur.)

Mitchell, Juliet C. W., MA *Oxf.*   Lectr. (Jes.)

Prandy, K., BSc *Lond.*, BA *Open(UK)*, PhD *Liv.*, MA   Asst. Dir. of Res. (Fitz.)

Richards, M. P. M., MA PhD   Prof., Family Research and Human Development; Head*

Scott, Jacqueline L., BA *Sus.*, MA *Mich.*, PhD *Mich.*   Asst. Dir. of Res. (Qu.)

Thompson, Helen, BA *Warw.*, MA *Virginia*, PhD *Lond.*   Lectr. (Cla.)

Thompson, John B., BA *Keele*, PhD *Camb.*   Reader, Sociology (Jes.)

Other Staff: 2 Asst. Lectrs.

South Asian History

Johnson, Gordon, MA Camb., PhD Camb. Lectr. (Wolfs.)

Spanish and Portuguese

Tel: (01223) 335038

Boldy, Steven R., MA PhD Lectr., Latin-American Studies (Emm.)

Close, A. J., PhD Trinity(Dub.), MA Lectr.

Kantaris, E. Geoffrey, BA Camb., PhD Camb. Lectr. (S.Cat.)

Keown, Dominic, PhD Sheff. Lectr. (Fitz.)

Lisboa, Maria M. G., BSc Lond., MA Nott., PhD Nott. Lectr. (S.Joh.)

McKendrick, Melveena C., BA Lond., MA PhD Reader, Spanish Literature and Society (Gir.)

Pountain, C. J., MA PhD Lectr., Romance Philology (Qu.)

Sinclair, Alison S., MA PhD Reader, Modern Spanish Literature and International History (Cla.)

Smith, Paul J., MA PhD Prof.; Head* (Trin.H.)

Other Staff: 1 Sr. Lang. Teaching Officer

Statistics, see Maths., Pure, and Mathl. Stats.

Theology, see Div.

Veterinary Studies, see below

Zoology, see also Veterinary Studies, below

Tel: (01223) 336600

Akam, Michael E., BA Camb., DPhil Oxf. Prof.; Dir., Museum of Zool. (King's)

Amos, William, BA Oxf., PhD Camb. Lectr.

Barnes, Richard S. K., BSc Lond., PhD Qld., MA Lectr. (S.Cat.)

Bate, C. M., BA Oxf., PhD Reader, Development Biology (King's)

Bateson, Patrick P. G., MA Camb., PhD Camb., ScD Camb., FRS Prof., Ethology (King's)

Boutilier, R. G., MA Camb., MSc Acad., PhD E.Anglia Lectr. (Sid.)

Burrows, M., ScD Camb., MA PhD, FRS Prof.; Head* (Wolfs.)

Cheek, Timothy R., BSc Sheff., PhD Liv. Lectr. (Gir.)

Clutton-Brock, Timothy H., MA PhD ScD Prof., Animal Ecology (Magd.)

Corbet, Sarah A., MA Camb., PhD Camb. Lectr. (Newn.)

Davies, N. B., MA Oxf., MA Camb., DPhil Oxf., FRS Prof., Behavioural Ecology (Pemb.)

Ellington, C. P., BA Duke, MA PhD Reader (Down.)

Flowerdew, John R., BSc Wales, MA Camb., DPhil Oxf. Lectr. (Wolfs.)

Foster, William A., MA PhD Lectr.; Curator (Insects), Museum of Zool. (Cla.)

Friday, A. E., MA PhD Lectr.; Curator (Vertebrates) (Corp.)

Grenfell, B. T., BSc Lond., MSc York(UK), DPhil York(UK) Lectr.

Gurdon, Sir John, BA Oxf., DPhil Oxf., Hon. DSc Oxf., FRS John Humphrey Plummer Prof., Cell Biology (Magd.)

Hedwig, Berthold G., BSc Cologne, PhD Gött. Asst. Dir. of Res.

Jackson, Stephen P., BSc Leeds, PhD Edin. Prof., Biology

Johnstone, Rufus A., BA Oxf., DPhil Oxf. Lectr.

Keverne, E. B., BSc Lond., PhD Lond., MA Reader, Behavioural Neuroscience; Dir., Sub-dept. of Animal Behaviour (King's)

Laskey, Ronald A., MA Oxf., DPhil Oxf., PhD, FRS Charles Darwin Prof., Animal Embryology (Darw.)

Laughlin, S. B., PhD ANU, MA Reader (Chur.)

McCabe, B. J., BSc Leeds, PhD Lond., MA Lectr. (Rob.)

Other Staff: 1 Sr. Tech. Officer; 1 Computer Officer

MEDICINE

Faculty of Clinical Medicine—for Anatomy, Pathology, Pharmacology, Physiology, see above

Tel: (01223) 336700

Allen, Christopher M. C., MA Camb., MB BChir Camb., MD Camb., FRCP Clin. Dean (Wolfs.)

Biggs, John S. G., MB BS Melb., MA Camb., MD Aberd., FRCOG Regional Postgrad. Dean (Sid.)

Carpenter, Thomas A., MA PhD Lectr. (Cla.H.)

Cox, Dennis, MB BS Lond. Asst. Dir. of Studies in Gen. Practice (Wolfs.)

Hall, Laurance D., BSc Brist., PhD Brist., MA Herchel Smith Prof., Medicinal Chemistry (Emm.)

Khaw, Kay-Tee, MSc Lond., MA MB BChir Prof., Clinical Gerontology (Cai.)

Males, Anthony G., MA Camb., MB BChir Camb. Asst. Dir. of Studies in Gen. Practice (Corp.)

Perry, John R., MB BCh Wales, FRCGP Asst. Dir., Studies in Gen. Practice (Newn.)

Siklos, Paul W. L., BSc Lond., MA Camb., FRCP Assoc. Dean

Stark, John E., MD, FRCP Assoc. Dean (Emm.)

White, Anthony J. S., MA MB BChir Asst. Dir., Studies in Gen. Practice (S.Joh.)

Other Staff: 122 Assoc. Lectrs.; 2 Sr. Tech. Officers; 2 Tech. Officers; 1 Computer Officer

Biochemistry, Clinical

Tel: (01223) 336792

Hales, C. N., MD PhD, FRCP, FRS Prof.; Head* (Down.)

Kealey, G. T. E., BSc Lond., MB BS Lond., MA Camb., DPhil Oxf. Lectr.

Luzio, J. P., MA PhD Reader, Molecular Membrane Biology (S.Edm.)

Siddle, Ken, MA PhD Serono Prof., Molecular Endocrinology (Chur.)

Genetics, Medical

Tel: (01223) 333692

Bobrow, Martin, CBE, MB BCh Witw., DSc Witw., FRCP, FRCPath Prof.; Head*

Ffrench Constant, Charles K., MA Camb., MB BChir Camb. Lectr.

Todd, John A., BSc Edin., PhD Camb. Prof. (Cai.)

Other Staff: 2 Clin. Lectrs.

Haematology

Tel: (01223) 336820

Allain, J.-P., MD Paris, PhD Paris Prof., Transfusion Medicine

Barker, C. R., BSc Nott., PhD Nott., MA Lectr.

Carrell, R. W., MBSc Cant., MB ChB NZ, MA PhD, FRSNZ, FRCP, FRCPath Prof.; Head* (Trin.)

Karpas, A., DrVetMed Zür., MA ScD Asst. Dir. of Res. (Wolfs.)

Lee, Helen, BSc N.Y., MSc Oxf., PhD N.Y. Reader, Biomedical Technology (L.Cav.)

Ouwehand, W. H., MD Amst., PhD Amst. Lectr.

Rees, J. K. H., MB BCh Wales, MA Lectr. (Wolfs.)

Williamson, Lorna M., BSc Edin., MD Edin. Lectr.

Medicine

Tel: (01223) 336844

Alexander, G. J. M., MB ChB Brist., MA Camb. Lectr.

Brown, M. J., MSc Lond., MD Prof., Clinical Pharmacology (Cai.)

Compston, David A. S., MB BS Lond., PhD Lond., FRCP Prof., Neurology (Jes.)

Compston, Juliet E., BSc Lond., MD Lond., FRCP, FRCPath Lectr.

Cox, T. M., BS Lond., MSc Lond., MD Lond., MD Camb., MA, FRCP Prof. (Sid.)

Gareth Jones, J., MB BCh Wales, MD Birm., FRCP Prof., Anaesthesia

Gaston, John S. H., BM BCh Oxf., MA Oxf., PhD Brist., FRCP Prof., Rheumatology

Kenwrick, Susan J., BSc Nott., PhD Lond. Lectr. (Hug.)

Lachmann, Peter J., MA PhD ScD, FRCP, FRS Sheila Joan Smith Prof., Tumour Immunology (Chr.)

Lever, Andrew M. L., BSc Wales, MD Wales Lectr. (Pet.)

Lockwood, Christopher M., BA Camb., MB BChir Camb., FRCP, FRCPath Reader

Lomas, David A., BMedSci Nott., BM BS Nott., PhD Camb. Lectr.

Menon, D. K., MD Madr., FFARCS Lectr.

O'Rahilly, Stephen, MB BCh N.U.I., MD N.U.I. Prof., Metabolic Medicine (Chur.)

Peters, Sir Keith, MB BCh Wales, MA, FRCP Regius Prof., Physic (Chr.)

Scolding, Neil J., BSc Wales, MB BCh Wales, PhD Wales Lectr.

Sinclair, J. H., BSc Essex, PhD Essex Lectr.

Sissons, J. G. Patrick, MA Camb., MD Lond., FRCP Prof.; Head* (Darw.)

Smith, Ken G. C., BMedSc Melb., MB BS Melb., FRACP Lectr.

Spillantini, Maria G., BSc Florence, PhD Camb. Lectr., Neurology (Cla.H.)

Sterling, Jane C., MA Camb., MB BChir Camb., PhD Camb. Lectr. (Newn.)

Weissberg, P. L., MB ChB Birm., MD Birm. Prof., Cardiovascular Medicine (Wolfs.)

Other Staff: 4 Clin. Lectrs.

Medicine, Community

Baxter, P. J., MSc Lond., MD Lond. Consultant Occupnl. Physician

Brayne, Carol E. G., MB BS Lond. Lectr. (Darw.)

Cox, Brian D., MA Camb., PhD Lond. Lectr. (Wolfs.)

Davies, Tom W., BA Camb., MB BChir Camb., MD Camb. Lectr. (Wolfs.)

Day, Nicholas E., MA Oxf., MA Camb., PhD Aberd. Prof., Public Health; Head* (Hug.)

Easton, Douglas F., MA Camb., PhD Lond. Lectr.

Edwards, A. W. F., MA PhD ScD Reader, Biometry (Cai.)

Hanka, R., MSc Prague, PhD Strath., MA Lectr. (Wolfs.)

Himsworth, Richard L., MD, FRCP Prof., Health Research and Development (Gir.)

Kinmonth, Ann-Louise, MA Camb., MB BChir Camb., MSc Lond., MD Camb., FRCGP, FRCP Prof., General Practice (New H.)

Palmer, Christopher R., MA Oxf., MS N.Carolina, PhD N.Carolina Asst. Dir. of Res. (Hug.)

Powles, J. W., MB BS Syd., FRCP Lectr.

Medicine, History of, see Hist. and Philos. of Sci.

Obstetrics and Gynaecology

Tel: (01223) 336881

Charnock-Jones, David S., BSc Lond., PhD Camb. Lectr.

Dalton, K. J., BSc Lond., MB BS Lond., DPhil Oxf., PhD Lectr. (S.Cat.)

Prentice, A., BSc Glas., MB ChB Glas., MA Camb. Lectr.

Smith, S. K., MB BS Lond., MD Lond., MA Prof.; Head* (Fitz.)

Thornton, Steven, MA Camb., DM S'ton. Lectr.

Other Staff: 1 Clin. Lectr.

Oncology

Tel: (01223) 336800

Burnet, Neil G., MA Camb., MD Camb. Lectr.

Earl, Helena M., MB BS Lond., PhD Lond. Lectr.

Philpott, Anna, MA Camb., PhD Camb. Lectr. (Selw.)

Ponder, Bruce A. J., MA Camb., MB BChir Camb., PhD Lond., FRCP Cancer Res.

Campaign Prof., Clinical Oncology; Head*
(Jes.)

Paediatrics

Tel: (01223) 336885

Hawkins, John R., BSc *Newcastle(UK)*, PhD
Leic. Lectr.
Hughes, I. A., MD *Wales*, MA, FRCP Prof.;
Head* (Cla.H.)
Morley, C. J., MA MD Lectr.
Tait, A. D., MA Lectr. (Wolfs.)
Other Staff: 3 Clin. Lectrs.

Psychiatry

Tel: (01223) 336965

Baron-Cohen, Simon, BA *Oxf.*, MPhil *Lond.*, PhD
Lond. Lectr. (Trin.)
Berrios, G. E., BM BCh *San Marcos*, MA *Oxf.*, MA
Camb. Lectr. (Rob.)
Bolton, P. F., BSc *Lond.*, MB BS *Lond.*, MA
Camb. Lectr., Child and Adolescent
Psychiatry
Dowson, J. H., MA MB BChir Lectr. (Qu.)
Goodyer, I. M., MD *Lond.* Prof., Child and
Adolescent Psychiatry (Wolfs.)
Holland, A. J., BSc *Lond.*, MB BS *Lond.*, MPhil
Lond. Lectr., Mental Handicap
Huppert, F. A., PhD Lectr.
Paykel, E. S., MD *NZ*, MD *Camb.*, FRCP,
FRCPEd, FRCPsych Prof.; Head* (Cai.)
Sahakian, Barbara J., BA *Mt. Holyoke*, PhD
Camb. Lectr., Neuropsychology
Other Staff: 2 Clin. Lectrs.

Public Health Institute

Tel: (01223) 330300

Day, Prof. Nicholas E., MA *Oxf.*, MA *Camb.*,
PhD *Aberd.* Dir.* (Hug.)

Radiology

Tel: (01223) 336890

Berman, L. H., MB BS *Lond.*, FRCP Lectr.
Dixon, A. K., MA MB BChir, FRCR Prof.;
Head* (Pet.)
Lomas, D. J., MA MB BChir, FRCR Lectr.
Other Staff: 1 Clin. Lectr.

Surgery

Tel: (01223) 336980

Bolton, Eleanor M., BSc *Lond.*, PhD *Glas.* Asst.
Dir. of Res.
Bradley, J. Andrew, MB ChB *Leeds*, PhD
Glas. Prof.
Friend, Peter J., MA MB BChir MD,
FRCS Lectr. (Magd.)
Jamieson, N. V., MB BS *Lond.*, MA MD,
FRCS Lectr., Transplant Surgery
Pickard, John D., MA MB MChir, FRCS,
FRCSEd Bayer Prof., Neurosurgery (S.Cat.)
Rushton, Neil, MB BS *Lond.*, MA *Camb.*, MD
Camb., FRCS Lectr. (Magd.)
White, D. J. G., BSc *Sur.*, PhD Lectr.
Other Staff: 1 Clin. Lectr.

VETERINARY STUDIES

Central Biomedical Services

Tel: (01223) 336767

North, David C., BVetMed *Lond.* Addtnl.
Named Vet. Surgeon; Dep. Dir.
Vacant Posts: Named Vet. Surgeon/Dir.*

Clinical Veterinary Medicine

Tel: (01223) 337600

Allen, William R., BVSc *Syd.*, PhD *Camb.* Jim
Joel Prof., Equine Reproduction (Rob.)
Bathe, Andrew P., MA *Camb.*, VetMB
Camb. Equine Surgeon
Blacklaws, Barbara A., BSc *Aberd.*, PhD
Camb. Lectr. (Newn.)
Blakemore, W. F., BVS *Brist.*, PhD *Lond.*, MA
ScD Reader (Wolfs.)
Bostock, D. E., MA VetMB Lectr. (Wolfs.)
Broom, Donald M., MA PhD Colleen Macleod
Prof., Animal Welfare (S.Cat.)
Bujdoso, R., BSc *Leic.*, PhD Lectr.
Cockcroft, Peter D., MA *Camb.*, VetMB
Camb. Lectr.

Connan, R. M., BVetMed *Lond.*, MA
PhD Lectr. (Wolfs.)
Dobson, Jane M., BVetMed *Lond.*, MA *Camb.*,
DVetMed *Lond.* Lectr. (Darw.)
Dunn, J. K., BVM&S *Edin.*, MVSc *Sask.*,
MA Lectr.
Evans, R. J., MA VetMB PhD Lectr. (Gir.)
Field, H. J., BSc *Lond.*, PhD *Brist.*, MA Lectr.
(Qu.)
Heath, M. F., MA PhD Lectr.
Herrtage, M. E., BVSc *Liv.*, MA Lectr.
(S.Edm.)
Holmes, M. A., MA PhD VetMB Lectr.
Houlton, J. E. F., MA VetMB Univ. Surgeon
Jackson, P. G. G., BVM&S *Edin.*, MA,
FRCVS Univ. Physician (S.Edm.)
Jeffcott, L. B., BVetMed *Lond.*, MA *Camb.*, PhD
Lond., DVSc *Melb.*, FRCVS Prof., Veterinary
Clinical Studies; Dean of Vet. Sch.; Head*
(Pemb.)
Jefferies, A. R., MA VetMB Univ. Pathologist
(Gir.)
Lloyd, Sheelagh S., MVB *Trinity(Dub.)*, PhD
Penn. Lectr. (Wolfs.)
Maskell, Duncan J., MA *Camb.*, PhD
Camb. Marks and Spencer Prof., Farm
Animal Health, Food Science and Food
Safety
McConnell, I., BVMS *Glas.*, MA PhD Prof.,
Veterinary Pathology
Miller, E. L., MA PhD Lectr. (Wolfs.)
Phillips, Clive J. C., BSc *Rd'g.*, PhD *Glas.* Lectr.
Sargan, D. R., PhD *Lond.*, MA Lectr.
Slater, Julian D., BVM&S *Edin.*, PhD
Camb. Lectr. (Gir.)
Stout, Tom A. E., MA *Camb.*, VetMB
Camb. Lectr.
Taylor, Polly M., MA *Camb.*, VetMB *Camb.*, PhD
Camb. Lectr. (Gir.)
Tiley, Laurence S., BSc *Manc.*, PhD
Reading Lectr.
White, R. A. S., BVetMed *Lond.* Lectr.
Wise, D. R., MA PhD VetMB Lectr.
Other Staff: 2 Assoc. Lectrs.; 2 Sr. Tech.
Officers; 1 Univ. Asst. Anaesthetist; 1 Univ.
Asst. Pathologist; 2 Univ. Asst. Physicians; 2
Univ. Asst. Surgeons; 1 Asst. in Res.

Veterinary Anatomy

Tel: (01223) 333847

Brackenbury, J. H., BSc *Brist.*, PhD Lectr.
(Wolfs.)
Chivers, David J., MA PhD Lectr. (Selw.)

Veterinary Physiology

Tel: (01223) 333817

Hickson, J. C. D., MA PhD Lectr. (Pemb.)

SPECIAL CENTRES, ETC

Aerial Photography, Committee for

Tel: (01223) 334578 Fax: (01223) 334400

Vacant Posts: Curator*

African Studies, Centre of

Tel: (01223) 334396

Hart, J. Keith, MA PhD Dir.*

Brain Repair, MRC Centre for

Tel: (01223) 331160 Fax: (01223) 331174

Compston, David A. S., MB BS *Lond.*, PhD *Lond.*,
FRCP Chairman* (Jes.)
Other Staff: 1 Sci. Dir.; 1 Sr. Tech. Officer

Business Research, ESRC Centre for

Tel: (01223) 335244 Fax: (01223) 335768

Hughes, Alan, MA *Camb.* Dir.*

Cancer and Developmental Biology,
Wellcome Trust and Cancer
Research Campaign Institute of

Tel: (01223) 334088 Fax: (01223) 334089

Gurdon, Prof. Sir John, BA *Oxf.*, DPhil *Oxf.*,
Hon. DSc *Oxf.*, FRS Chairman* (Magd.)

Continuing Education

Tutors appointed by the Board of Continuing
Education Studies

Tel: (01954) 210636 Fax: (01954) 210677

Howes, Graham A. K., MA Tutor (Trin.H.)
Kalnins, Mara I. Tutor (Corp.)
Lord, Evelyn A., BA *Open(UK)*, PhD *Leic.* Tutor
Mason, Richard V., MA *Camb.*, PhD
Brist. Tutor (Wolfs.)
Padfield, Christopher J., MA PhD Sr. Staff
Tutor (Trin.H.)
Sewell, M. J., MA PhD Tutor (Selw.)

English and Applied Linguistics,
Research Centre for

Tel: (01223) 332340 Fax: (01223) 330253

Blevins, James P., BA *Bishop's*, PhD *Mass.* Asst.
Dir. of Res.
Brown, Gillian, PhD *Edin.*, MA Prof.; Dir.*
(Cla.)
Malmkjaer, Kirsten S., BA *Birm.*, PhD
Birm. Asst. Dir. of Res.
Tsimpli, Ianthi-Maria, BA *Athens*, PhD
Lond. Asst. Dir. of Res.
Williams, John N., BA *Durh.*, PhD *Camb.* Asst.
Dir. of Res.

Industrial Liaison Office, Wolfson

Tel: (01223) 334756 Fax: (01223) 332797

Jennings, Richard C., BSc *Sus.*, DPhil *Sus.* Dir.*

International Studies, Centre of

Tel: (01223) 335333 Fax: (01223) 335397

Vacant Posts: Prof.; Dir.*

Language Centre

Tel: (01223) 335040 Fax: (01223) 335040

Esch, Edith M., MA *Camb.*, PhD *Open(UK)* Dir.*
(L.Cav.)
Other Staff: 1 Sr. Tech. Officer; 1 Sr. Lang.
Adviser; 1 Lang. Adviser

Latin-American Studies, Centre of

Tel: (01223) 335390 Fax: (01223) 335397

Lehmann, A. D., DPhil *Oxf.* Dir.*

Mathematical Sciences, Isaac Newton
Institute for

Tel: (01223) 335999 Fax: (01223) 330508

Moffatt, H. Keith, BA *Camb.*, PhD *Camb.*, ScD
Camb., FRS Dir.* (Trin.)
Other Staff: Visiting Rothschild Profs.

Medical Genetics, Centre for

Tel: (01223) 331154 Fax: (01223) 331206

Vacant Posts: Dir.*

Middle Eastern Studies, Centre of

Tel: (01223) 335103 Fax: (01223) 335110

Khalidi, Prof. Tarif, MA *Oxf.*, PhD *Chic.* Dir.*
(King's)

South Asian Studies, Centre of

Tel: (01223) 338094 Fax: (01223) 316913

Johnson, Gordon, MA *Camb.*, PhD *Camb.* Dir.*
(Wolfs.)
Other Staff: 2 Grad. Staff

THE COLLEGES

In the following lists name entries are included
only for fellows and other staff of the
colleges who do not hold an academic
appointment within the university's teaching
departments. Fellows who are members of
staff of the teaching departments have name
entries above under 'Academic Units', and
are represented here by a composite entry
only (eg Other Staff: 16 Fellows).

CHRIST'S COLLEGE

Tel: (01223) 334900 Fax: (01223) 334967

Baker, Stuart N., BA Camb.   Fellow
Barham, Paul, PhD Camb.   Fellow
Barker, Douglas C., BSc Edin., PhD Edin., MA   Fellow
Bayly, Susan M., PhD   Tutor; Fellow
Bowkett, Kelvin M., BSc Wales, MA PhD   Sr. Tutor; Fellow
Brindle, Peter, MPhil Camb.   Domestic Bursar; Fellow
Coombe, David E., MA PhD   Fellow
Courtney, Cecil P., BA Belf., DPhil Oxf., PhD Camb., LittD Camb.   Emer. Reader; Fellow
Cromartie, Alan, BA Camb., PhD Camb.   Fellow
Cuomo, Serafina, MPhil Camb., PhD   Fellow
Diamond, Robert, MA PhD   Fellow
Gay, Nicholas J. A., BSc Leeds, PhD   Tutor; Fellow
Hild, Matthias, PhD   Fellow
Hunt, Robert, PhD   U. Lectr., Applied Mathematics and Theoretical Physics; Fellow
Izzet, Vedia, PhD Camb.   Fellow
Kempton, Albert E., MA PhD   Fellow
Kornberg, Sir Hans, MA Oxf., DSc Oxf., PhD Sheff., Hon. DSc Warw., Hon. DSc Leic., Hon. DSc Bath, Hon. DSc Strath., Hon. DSc Sheff., Hon. DSc Cinc., Hon. DU Essex, Hon. DrMed Leip., ScD, FRS, Hon. FRCP   Life Fellow
Lewitter, Lucjan R., MA PhD   Emer. Prof., Slavonic Studies; Fellow
Loke, Terence, PhD Camb.   Fellow
Maunder, C. Richard F., MA PhD   Fellow
Moyes, Craig, PhD   U. Lectr., French; Fellow
Munro, Alan J., MA Camb., PhD Camb.   Master*
O'Higgins, Paul, LLD Trinity(Dub.), MA Trinity(Dub.), MA Camb., PhD   Fellow
Parker, C. Alan, BSc   Bursar; Fellow
Perrey, Beate, PhD Camb.   Fellow
Plumb, Sir John, Hon. DLitt Leic., PhD LittD, FSA, FBA, FRHistS   Emer. Prof., Modern English History; Fellow
Shute, Charles C. D., MA MB BChir MD   Emer. Prof., Histology; Fellow
Stark, Alex, MA Camb., PhD Camb.   Fellow
Sykes, Peter, BSc Manc., MA PhD   Fellow
Vahey, Shaun P., BA MA PhD   Fellow
Wilson, John S., MA PhD ScD   Life Fellow
Winter, Alan, PhD   Lectr.; Fellow
Yale, David E. C., MA LLB, FBA   Emer. Reader, Law; Fellow
Other Staff: 32 Fellows

CHURCHILL COLLEGE

Tel: (01223) 336000 Fax: (01223) 336180

Abrahams, Ray G., MA PhD   Fellow
Acheson, Roy M., MA Oxf., MA Trinity(Dub.), BM BCh Oxf., DM Oxf., ScD Trinity(Dub.), ScD Camb., MD, FRCP   Fellow
Allchin, F. Raymond, BA Lond., PhD Lond., MA, FBA   Fellow
Allen, Michael J., MA   Bursar; Fellow
Barbrook, Adrian C., PhD Camb.   Fellow
Barnes, John A., DPhil Oxf., MA, FBA   Fellow
Barnett, J. (Bill), MA, FRSL, FRHistS   Fellow
Bishop, Dorothy V. M., MPhil Lond., MA Oxf., DPhil Oxf.   Fellow
Boksenberg, Alec, CBE, BSc Lond., PhD Lond., FRS, FRAS   Hon. Prof., Experimental Astronomy; Fellow
Bondi, Sir Hermann, KCB, MA, FRS   Emer. Prof.; Fellow
Boyd, Sir John, KCMG, MA Yale, MA Camb.   Master*
Brendon, Piers, MA Kent, PhD Kent   Keeper of the Archives; Fellow
Broers, Sir Alec N., BSc Melb., BA PhD ScD, FRS, FEng, FIEE   Vice-Chancellor; Fellow
Callear, Tony B., PhD Birm., MA Camb., MA   Fellow
Campbell, R. Colin, MA PhD   Fellow
Chatterjee, V. Krishna K., MB BChir   Fellow

Cribb, Tim J. L., MA   Coll. Lectr., English; Fellow
Crisp, Adrian J., MA MD, FRCP   U. Assoc. Lectr., Medicine; Fellow
Dixon, Bill G., MA PhD   Tutorial Bursar and Tutor for Rooms; Fellow
Edwards, Robert G., CBE, PhD Edin., DSc Wales, MA, FRS   Fellow
Elia, Marinos, MB ChB Manc., MD Oxf., MD Manc., FRCP   Fellow
Fitzmaurice, Andrew K., MA NSW, PhD Camb.   Fellow
Gaskell, Phil H., BSc Lond., PhD Lond.   Fellow
George, Hywel, OBE, CMG, BA Wales, MA   Fellow
Hahn, Frank H., BSc(Econ) Lond., PhD Lond., DLitt Athens, DPhil Athens, MA, FBA   Fellow
Hawkes, Christopher M., MA Camb., DPhil Oxf.   Fellow
Hawthorne, Sir William, CBE, MA ScD, FRS, FEng, FIMechE   Emer. Prof., Applied Thermodynamics; Fellow
Hewish, A., MA Camb., PhD Camb., ScD Camb., FRS   Fellow
Hey, Richard W., MA PhD   Fellow
Hoskin, Michael A., MA Lond., PhD   Fellow
Kelly, Anthony, ScD, FRS   Fellow
Kendall, David G., MA Oxf., MA Camb., ScD, FRS   Fellow
Keynes, Richard D., CBE, MA PhD ScD, FRS   Emer. Prof., Physiology; Fellow
King, Anny N., LicLet Paris IV, MèsL Paris IV   Sr. Lang. Adviser; Fellow
Knott, John F., PhD ScD, FRS, FEng   Fellow
Levene, Charles I., MB BS Lond., MD Lond., DSc Lond., MA ScD, FRCPath   Fellow
Livesley, R. Ken, PhD Manc., MA   Fellow
McQuillen, Kenneth, MA PhD   Fellow
Northeast, Christine H., MA   Fellow
Palmer, Andrew C., PhD Camb., FRS, FEng   Fellow
Richens, Paul N., MA Camb.   Asst. Dir. of Res., Architecture; Fellow
Roberts, Gareth, PhD   Fellow
Ryall, Ron W., BSc Lond., PhD ANU, MA   Fellow
Schofield, Andrew N., MA PhD, FEng, FRS   Prof., Engineering; Fellow
Spencer, Jane, MA Camb., PhD Camb.   Tutor for Admissions; Fellow
Squire, Leonard C., BSc Brist., PhD Brist., MA ScD   Fellow
Squire, Peter S., MA PhD   Fellow
Steiner, George, BA Chic., MA Harv., DPhil Oxf., PhD, FRSL   Fellow
Stern, David L., MA Prin., PhD Prin.   Fellow
Steven, Donald H., MA VetMB   Fellow
Thompson, John G., PhD Chic., MA, FRS   Fellow
Thurlow, Jeremy R., MPhil Camb.   Fellow
Tippett, Maria, PhD Lond., Hon. LLD Windsor, FRSCan   Fellow
Tizard, Richard H., MA Oxf., MA Camb., FIEE   Fellow
Tozer, David J., MA Camb., PhD Camb.   Fellow
Tristram, Andrew G., BSc St And., PhD   Fellow
Turner, H. A. F., BSc Lond., PhD Manc., MA   Fellow
Wallace, Debra J., PhD Camb.   Fellow
Walters, D. Eurof, PhD Wales   Fellow
Wells, Martin J., MA ScD   Fellow
Whittaker, Richard, PhD Camb., MA   Fellow
Whittle, Peter, MSc NZ, DrPhil Uppsala, MA, FRS   Fellow
Williams, Keith R., BSc Lond., MA   Fellow
Other Staff: 47 Fellows

CLARE COLLEGE

Tel: (01223) 333200 Fax: (01223) 333219

Baesens, Claude, DrSciPhys Brussels   Coll. Lectr., Mathematics; Fellow
Black, William W., PhD Leeds, MA   Fellow, Geology
Bown, Michael G., MA PhD   Fellow, Crystallography

Brown, Timothy C., MA   Dir., Music; Fellow
Chilton, John P., MA PhD   Fellow, Metallurgy
Cooper, Brian, MA   Fellow, Engineering
Derrer, Samuel, PhD Camb., BSc   Res. Fellow, Organic Chemistry
Foyster, Elizabeth A., PhD Durh.   Tutor, History; Res. Fellow
Freeman, Elizabeth M., MA LLB   Lectr., Law; Fellow
Gooder, Richard D., MA PhD   Coll. Lectr., English; Tutor; Forbes Librarian; Fellow
Greenham, Neil C., BA Camb., PhD Camb.   Sr. Asst. in Res., Physics; Fellow
Harris, Rachel M., BA Camb., PhD Camb.   Univ. Lang. Teaching Officer, Oriental Studies; Fellow
Hartley, David F., MA PhD   Fellow, Computing
Heine, Volker, MSc NZ, PhD, FRS   Emer. Prof., Theoretical Physics; Fellow
Holister, F. Darnton, MA(Archit) Harv., MA   Fellow
Hunt, R. Timothy, MA PhD, FRS   Fellow, Biochemistry
Jagger, Christopher N., MA PhD   Res. Fellow, Mathematics
Knewstubb, Peter F., MA PhD   Fellow
Knighton, Tessa W., MA PhD   Coll. Lectr., Spanish; Fellow
Lipstein, Kurt, PhD LLD   Emer. Prof., Law; Fellow
Lucas, Alan, MA MB BChir PhD   Fellow
Matthews, Robert C. O., CBE, MA Oxf., MA Camb., FBA   Emer. Prof., Economics; Fellow
Moore, Terence H., MA Calif., MA Camb., PhD Calif.   Tutor; Fellow
Moule, Rev. Charles F. D., CBE, MA, FBA   Emer. Prof., Theology; Fellow
Northam, John R., MA PhD   Emer. Prof., English and Drama; Fellow
O'Hanlon, Rosalind, MA PhD   Coll. Lectr., History; Admissions Tutor (Arts); Fellow
Reddaway, W. Brian, CBE, MA, FBA   Emer. Prof., Economics; Fellow
Reed, Adam D. E., BA Otago, MA Otago, PhD Camb.   Res. Fellow, Social Anthropology
Riley, Kenneth F., MA PhD   U. Lectr., Physics; Tutorial Bursar; Fellow
Robinson, D. Duncan, MA Yale, MA Camb.   Dir., Fitzwilliam Museum and Marlay Curator; Fellow
Ruel, Malcolm J., BLitt Oxf., MA Camb., DPhil Oxf.   Fellow, Social Anthropology
Schofield, Roger S., MA PhD   Dir., Hist. Population Studies Group; Fellow
Smale-Adams, Brian A. W., MA   Fellow
Smiley, Timothy J., MA PhD   Knightbridge Prof., Philosophy; Fellow
Squires, David R., BA Oxf., MPhil Oxf.   Coll. Lectr., Economics; Fellow
Swinton, Andrea M., BA Tas., PhD   Res. Fellow, Classical Archaeology
Thompson, Brig. Timothy K., MA   Coll. Bursar; Steward; Fellow
Turpin, Colin C., MA LLB   Emer. Reader, Public Law; Fellow
Wells, Rev. Jo B., BA Durh., MA Camb., MA Minn., PhD Durh.   Dean; Fellow
West, Richard G., MA PhD ScD, FRS   Emer. Prof., Botany; Fellow
Willmer, E. Neville, MA ScD, FRS   Fellow, Histology
Wright, Gordon H., MA MD   Fellow, Anatomy
Other Staff: 36 Fellows

CLARE HALL

Tel: (01223) 332360 Fax: (01223) 332333

Apter, Terri E., MA Edin., MA Camb., PhD   Tutor; Fellow
Ashbourn, Joanna M. A., MA   Fellow
Ashby, Michael F., CBE, MA PhD, FRS   Royal Soc. Prof.; Fellow
Bruck, Joanna, MA Camb., PhD Camb.   Fellow

Burnstone, Daniel K., MA *Camb.*, PhD *Camb.* Fellow

Carlyon, Robert P., BSc *Sus.*, PhD *Camb.* Fellow

Carman, Richard J., PhD *Camb.*, MPhil Res. Fellow

Cass, Sir Geoffrey A., MA *Oxf.*, MA *Camb.* Fellow

Chandler, Claire J., BSc *Birm.*, PhD *Edin.* Res. Fellow

Galanidou, Nena, MSc *S'ton.*, BA PhD Res. Fellow

Hintze, Almut, MPhil DPhil Fellow

Hughes, Ieuan A., MA MD, FRCP, FRCPCan Fellow

Jarron, T. Edward L. Bursar; Fellow

Kennedy, Karen L., BSc PhD Fellow

Lawes, Richard J., BA DPhil Fellow

Luff, Rosemary M., BSc *St And.*, PhD Steward; Fellow

McCoy, Airlie, PhD Fellow

Mould, Ruth M., PhD Fellow

Murthi, Mamta, DPhil Fellow

Napolitano, Valentina, MPhil PhD Fellow

Proud, William G., PhD Fellow

Quevedo, Fernando, BSc PhD Fellow

Randall, Andrew D., BSc *Brist.*, PhD *Brist.* Fellow

Rhodes, Daniella, PhD Asst. Praelector; Fellow

Rubinsztein, Judy, MB ChB Fellow

Schertler, Gebhard, PhD *Munich* Fellow

Shackleton, Sir Nicholas J., MA PhD ScD, FRS Fellow

Shogimen, Takashi, LLB PhD Fellow

Singh, Meena V., MSc *Camb.*, PhD *Camb.* Fellow

Stewart, Murray J., BSc *Syd.*, PhD *Syd.*, MA Praelector; Fellow

Woollard, Alison C. S., DPhil Fellow

Other Staff: 18 Fellows

CORPUS CHRISTI COLLEGE

Tel: (01223) 338000 Fax: (01223) 338061

Bailey, Mark D., BA *Camb.*, PhD *Camb.* Domus Bursar; Bursar of Leckhampton; Fellow

Beattie, Paul D., PhD *Camb.* Sr. Tutor; Fellow

Brookes, C. J. B., MA PhD Fellow

Bruce, D. J., BSc *Reading*, PhD *Reading*, MA Fellow

Bulag, U. E., MPhil *Camb.*, PhD *Camb.* Res. Fellow, Social Anthropology

Burton, Jonathan W. Res. Fellow

Chadwick, M. P., BSc *Nott.* Pfizer Res. Fellow, Gene Therapy

Coombs, R. R. A., BSc *Edin.*, MD PhD ScD, FRS Fellow

Dawson, Diane A., MA *Calif.* Life Fellow

Dewhirst, D. W., MA PhD Fellow

Erickson, Charlotte J., MA *Cornell*, MA *Camb.*, PhD *Cornell* Life Fellow

Faber, T. E., MA PhD Life Fellow

Green, F. M., BA *Durh.*, PhD *Camb.* Dep. Tutor for Advanced Students; Fellow

Harley-Mason, J., MA ScD Life Fellow

Haslam, J. G., BSc *Birm.*, MA *Camb.*, MLitt Admissions Tutor; Fellow

Hazleman, B. L., MB BS *Lond.*, MA, FRCS, FRCP Assoc. Lectr., Clinical Medicine; Dir., Rheumatol. Res. Unit, Addenbrooke's Hosp.; Fellow

Kempf, A., PhD *Munich* Res. Fellow, Physics

Lewis, P. R., MA *Oxf.*, MA *Camb.*, DPhil *Oxf.*, ScD Fellow

Longuet-Higgins, H. C., MA *Oxf.*, MA *Camb.*, DPhil *Oxf.*, Hon. DUniv *York(UK)*, Hon. DU *Essex*, Hon. DSc *Brist.*, Hon. DSc *Sus.*, FRS, FRSEd Life Fellow

Maull, D. J., PhD *Lond.*, MA Reader, Engineering; Fellow

Mayhew, Robert J. Res. Fellow

McCrum, Michael W., MA *Camb.* Life Fellow

Mills, D. E., BA *Lond.*, PhD *Lond.*, MA Life Fellow

Morgan, Rev. R. W., MA *Oxf.*, MA *Camb.* Life Fellow

Page, R. I., PhD *Nott.*, MA *Sheff.*, MA *Camb.*, LittD Life Fellow

Pryce, Rev. R. M., BA *Sus.*, MA Tutor; Dean of Chapel; Fellow

Rackham, O., MA PhD Fellow

Ratcliffe, F. W., CBE, JP, MA *Manc.*, MA *Camb.*, PhD *Manc.* Librarian; Fellow

Regan, D., PhD Res. Fellow, Experimental Psychology

Roach, J. P. C., MA PhD Life Fellow

Robinson, H. P. C., MA PhD Fellow

Sherratt, Yvonne K., BA MPhil Res. Fellow, Philosophy

Stopford, P. R., MA Bursar; Fellow

Strachan, H. F. A., MA PhD Life Fellow

Styler, Rev. G. M., MA Precentor Emer.; Life Fellow

Tanner, M. K., MA PhD Fellow

Tubbs, P. K., MA PhD Life Fellow

Wilkins, N. E., BA *Nott.*, PhD *Nott.*, MA Life Fellow

Woodhead, A. G., MA, FSA Life Fellow

Wrigley, Prof. Sir Tony, MA *Camb.*, PhD *Camb.*, FBA Emer. Prof.; Master*

Zutshi, Patrick N. R., MA *Camb.*, PhD *Camb.*, FSA U. Archivist; Fellow

Other Staff: 29 Fellows

DARWIN COLLEGE

Tel: (01223) 335660 Fax: (01223) 335667

Beck, John M., BA *E.Anglia*, MA *Lond.*, PhD *Camb.* Adrian Res. Fellow

Bishop, Christopher M., BA *Oxf.*, PhD *Edin.* Fellow, Microsoft Research

Boulter, Catherine, PhD *CNAA* Assoc. Dean, Genetics; Fellow

Bourriau, Janine D., BA *Lond.*, MA, FSA Archivist; Fellow

Branson, Nicholas J. B. A., MA *Camb.*, PhD *Camb.* Dep. Registrary; Coll. Secretary; Fellow

Clack, Jennifer A. C., BSc *Newcastle(UK)*, MA *Camb.*, PhD *Newcastle(UK)* Fellow

Cocke, Thomas H., PhD, FSA Fellow

Cone, Margaret, MPhil PhD Asst. Dir. of Res., Oriental Studies; Fellow

Cooper, Andrew I., BSc *Nott.*, PhD *Nott.* Res. Fellow

Doran, Chris J. L., BA *Camb.*, PhD *Camb.* Schlumberger Res. Fellow

Fabian, Andrew C., BSc *Lond.*, PhD *Lond.*, FRS Royal Soc. Res. Prof., Astronomy; Vice-Master; Fellow

Grigorieff, Nikolaus, MSc *Brist.*, PhD *Brist.* Res. Fellow

Henderson, Richard, BSc *Edin.*, PhD, FRS Dir., MRC Lab. of Molecular Biology; Fellow

Iwasawa, Kazushi, BSc *Nagoya*, MSc *Nagoya*, PhD *Nagoya* Charles and Katharine Darwin Res. Fellow

James, Ronald G., BSc *Lond.*, PhD Asst. Dir. of Res., Engineering; Fellow

Joshi, Mark S., BA *Oxf.*, PhD *M.I.T.* U. Asst. Lectr., Pure Mathematics and Mathematical Statistics; Fellow

Leedham-Green, Elisabeth S., BLitt *Oxf.*, MA *Oxf.*, MA *Camb.*, DPhil *Oxf.*, PhD, FSA Praelector; Asst. Keeper of the Univ. Archives; Fellow

Nagai, Kiyoshi, PhD MRC Lab. of Molecular Biol.; Fellow

Patterson, Karalyn E., PhD *Calif.* Res. Psychologist; MRC Appl. Psychol. Unit; Fellow

Prentice, Andrew M., PhD Sr. Scientist; MRC Dunn Clin. Nutr. Unit; Fellow

Ridderbos, Katinka M. Adrian Res. Fellow, Philosophy

Scheidel, Walter, MA *Vienna*, PhD *Vienna* Moses and Mary Finley Res. Fellow, Ancient History

Shore, Heather, BA *Lond.*, MA *Lond.*, PhD *Lond.* Moses and Mary Finley Res. Fellow, History

Sweeney, Sean T., BSc *CNAA*, MPhil *Leic.* Res. Fellow

Teo, Edward H. K., BSc *Flin.*, PhD *Camb.* Res. Fellow

Thompson, Andrew R., MBE, BA *Brist.*, MPhil *Camb.* Bursar; Fellow

White, Chester, MBE, BSc *Oxf.*, BM BCh *Oxf.*, MA PhD Fellow

Whitehead, Roger G., BSc *Leeds*, PhD *Leeds*, MA Dir., Dunn Nutritional Lab.; Fellow

Woolfson, Adrian, BM BCh *Oxf.*, PhD *Camb.* Charles and Katharine Darwin Res. Fellow

Other Staff: 26 Fellows

DOWNING COLLEGE

Tel: (01223) 334800 Fax: (01223) 62279

Barrand, M. A., BSc *Lond.*, PhD *Lond.* Asst. Tutor for Grads.; Fellow, Pharmacology

Davies, Meryl G., BA *Lond.* Res. Fellow, Modern Japanese Studies

Evans, P. D., ScD Tutor, Physiology; Fellow

Fleet, Stephen G., MA PhD Vice Master; Fellow

Gatzouras, Dimitrios, MSc PhD Fellow, Mathematics

Haniff, C. A., BA PhD Fellow, Radio Astronomy

James, Ian R., BA *Warw.*, MA *Warw.*, PhD *Camb.* Fellow, French

Kinsey, B. R. L., BD *Lond.*, MTh *Lond.* Chaplain; Steward; Fellow

Kobine, J. Jonathan, BSc *Edin.*, DPhil *Oxf.* Fellow, Applied Mathematics

Ledgeway, Adam N., BA *Salf.*, MA *Manc.*, PhD *Manc.* U. Lectr., Linguistics; Fellow

Lintott, Susan E., MA *Camb.*, PhD *Kent* Bursar; Fellow

MacGregor, Lucy M., MA *Camb.*, PhD *Camb.* Res. Fellow, Earth Sciences

Phillips, C. L., BA *Qu.*, MA *Tor.*, PhD Tutor, English; Fellow

Schneider, Rolf M., PhD *Heidel.* U. Lectr., Classics; Fellow

Scott, J. H., BA PhD History Librarian; Fellow

Stibbs, Richard J., MA *Camb.* U. Computer Officer; Praelector; Fellow

Topping, I. B., MA Domestic Bursar; Fellow

Wachsmann, Nikolaus D., BSc *Lond.*, MPhil *Camb.*, PhD *Lond.* Res. Fellow, History

Wales, D. J., MA PhD Fellow, Chemistry

Other Staff: 26 Fellows

EMMANUEL COLLEGE

Tel: (01223) 334200 Fax: (01223) 334426

Aldred, Jonathan S., MA *Camb.*, MPhil *Camb.* Res. Fellow

Bilek, Marcela M. M., BSc *Syd.* Fellow

Bleloch, Andrew L., MSc *Witw.*, PhD Sr. Asst. in Res. in Cavendish Lab., Physics; Fellow

Bower, Edward A., MA VetMB PhD Fellow

Brewer, Derek S., MA *Oxf.*, MA *Camb.*, PhD *Birm.*, Hon. LLD *Keio*, Hon. LLD *Harv.*, Hon. DLitt *Birm.*, Hon. DUniv *York(UK)*, Hon. DèsL *Paris IV*, LittD, FSA Fellow

Caddick, Jeremy L., MA *Camb.* Dean; Fellow

Coleman, Robert G. G., MA *NZ*, MA *Camb.* Emer. Prof.; Fellow

Cupitt, Rev. Don, MA Fellow

Douglas-Fairhurst, Robert, PhD *Camb.* Fellow

Doye, Jonathan P. K., MA *Camb.* Res. Fellow

Duffy, David C., BA Fellow

Evans, Gerard D., MA *Camb.*, PhD *Camb.* Fellow

Gales, Mark J. F., PhD *Camb.* Fellow

Git, Yoav, BA *Camb.* Fellow

Grant, John W., MB ChB *Aberd.*, MD *Aberd.* Consultant, Addenbrooke's Hosp.; Fellow

Grave, Walter W., CMG, Hon. LLD McM., Hon. LLD Camb., MA PhD   Fellow
Gray, Ronald D., MA PhD   Fellow
Gross, M. J., MA PhD   Bursar; Fellow
Herissone, Rebecca C., BA Lond., MMus Lond., PhD   Fellow
Hunter, Daniel A. D., BSc LLB   Fellow
Janousch, Andreas E., MPhil Camb.   Fellow
Jarvis, David A., PhD Lanc.   Fellow
Lewis, Paul A., MA Camb., MPhil Camb.   Res. Fellow
Livesey, David A., BSc Lond., MA Camb., PhD Camb.   Sec. Gen. of the Facs.; Fellow
Moran, Dominic P., BA   Fellow
Morgan, Benjamin A. C., DPhil Oxf.   Tutor; Fellow
Noetinger, Élise I. C., MA Kent   Fellow
Oakley, Stephen P., MA PhD   Tutor; Fellow
Pickstock, Catherine J. C., MA Camb., PhD Camb.   Fellow
Plevy, Neil R., MA Camb.   Devel. Dir.; Supernumerary Fellow
Polonsky, Rachel A., BA Oxf., DPhil Oxf.   Fellow
Pratt, David R., BA Camb.   Res. Fellow
Reddaway, John L., MA, FIMechE   Fellow
Rehding, Alexander, MPhil Camb.   Res. Fellow
Rickard, Peter, MA Oxf., DPhil Oxf., PhD LittD   Fellow
Sansom, Ian E., DPhil Oxf.   Fellow
St John of Fawsley, Lord, MA Oxf., MA Camb., PhD Lond., LittD Camb., DLitt Oxf., SJD Yale, Hon. DD Susquehanna, Hon. DLitt Brist., Hon. LLD Leic., FRSL, Hon. Fellow of St Edmund's College, Hon. Fellow of Fitzwilliam College   Vice Master; Fellow
Stubbings, Frank H., MA PhD, FSA   Fellow
Thoday, John M., BSc Wales, PhD ScD, FRS   Fellow
Thrush, Brian A., MA PhD ScD, FRS   Emer. Prof., Physics Chemistry; Fellow
Törzök, Judit, MA Bud.   Res. Fellow
Townsend, Alan A., MSc Melb., PhD, FRS   Fellow
van Houts, Elizabeth M. C., MA Camb., PhD Gron.   U. Lectr., History; Fellow
Williams, Sir David, Hon. QC, LLB Camb., LLM Calif., MA Oxf., MA Camb., Hon. DLitt W.Jewell, Hon. DLitt Lough., Hon. DLitt Davidson, Hon. LLD Hull, Hon. LLD Syd., Hon. LLD Nott., Hon. LLD Liv., Hon. LLD McG., Hon. LLD De Mont., Hon. LLD Duke   Prof., Law; Fellow
Wills, Andrew J., BSc S'ton.   Res. Fellow
Other Staff: 39 Fellows

FITZWILLIAM COLLEGE

Tel: (01223) 332000 Fax: (01223) 464162
Alford, Stephen A., MA StAnd., PhD StAnd.   Res. Fellow, History
Annett, Lucy E., PhD Lond.   Coll. Lectr., Psychology; Fellow
Ashby, Alison M., BSc E.Anglia, PhD Durh.   Royal Soc. Res. Fellow, Plant Sciences; Fellow
Blackburn, J. M., BA Oxf., MA Camb., DPhil Oxf.   Royal Soc. Res. Fellow, Chemistry; Fellow
Chalmers, Hero A., BA Oxf., DPhil Oxf.   Coll. Lectr., English; Tutor; Dir. of Studies in Engl.; Fellow
Clark, Alan, MA Camb., PhD Camb.   Principal Asst. Registrary; Fellow
Coles, J. M., MA Camb., PhD Edin., ScD Camb., FBA, FSA   Life Fellow
Duncan, Nancy G., MA Syr., PhD Syr.   Coll. Lectr., Geography; Fellow
Everard, Judith A., BA W.Aust., PhD Camb.   Res. Fellow, History
Horrox, Rosemary E., MA Camb., PhD Camb., FRHistS   Coll. Lectr., History; Dir. of Studies in Hist.; Sec. of Governing Body; Fellow
Houghton, Conor J., MSc N.U.I.   Res. Fellow, Applied Mathematics

Hudson, Alan C., BSc Brist., PhD Camb.   Coll. Lectr., Geography; Asst. Dir. of Studies in Geography; Fellow
Hudson, Harry J., MA Camb., PhD Sheff.   Life Fellow
Joysey, K. A., MA Camb., PhD Lond., ScD   Life Fellow
Kelly, R., DU Lyons, MA   Life Fellow
Kerridge, D., MA PhD   Life Fellow
Kirkland, A. I., MA PhD   Asst. Dir. of Studies in Chemistry; British Ramsay Memorial Res. Fellow
Landy, B., MA   Sr. Computer Officer, Computer Laboratory; Dean of Coll.; Fellow
Lane, Stuart N., MA Camb., PhD Camb.   U. Asst. Lectr., Geography; Dir. of Studies in Geog.; Tutor; Fellow
Leigh, John D., MA Camb.   U. Asst. Lectr., French; Dir. of Studies in Mod. and Mediev. Langs.; Fellow
Lethbridge, R. D., MA McM., MA Camb., PhD   Life Fellow
McAuley, Derek R., BA Camb., PhD Camb.   Asst. Dir., Microsoft Res. Ltd.; Fellow
New, D. A. T., PhD Lond., MA ScD   Life Fellow
Nex, C. M. M., MSc Sus., MA PhD   Computer Officer, Physics; Asst. Dir. of Studies in Maths. for Nat. Sci.; Fellow
Nicol, A. D. I., CBE, BSc Manc., MA PhD   Life Fellow
Padfield, Nicola M., MA Oxf.   Coll. Lectr., Law; Admissions Tutor (Arts); Tutor; Fellow
Parkins, Helen M., BA Leic., PhD Leic.   Res. Fellow, Classics
Pearl, D. S., LLB Birm., MA LLM PhD   Life Fellow
Pooley, G. G., MA PhD   Sr. Res. Assoc., Physics; Dir. of Studies in Nat. Sci. (Physical); Fellow
Porter Goff, R. F. D., MA Camb., PhD Leic.   Life Fellow
Potter, M. D., MA Camb., DPhil Oxf.   Coll. Lectr., Pure Mathematics; Tutor; Dir. of Studies in Maths.; Leathersellers' Fellow
Pratt, C. L., MA   Bursar; Fellow
Smith, K. C. A., MA PhD   Life Fellow
Stanton, Graham N., BD Otago, MA Otago, PhD Camb.   Lady Margaret's Prof., Divinity; Fellow
Vira, Bhaskar, MPhil Camb.   U. Asst. Lectr., Environmental Economics; Fellow
von Hirsch, Andrew, AB Harv., LLB Harv., Hon. LLD Uppsala   Hon. Prof., Penal Theory and Penal Law; Steward; Fellow
Walker, G. J., MA PhD   Life Fellow
Wayper, C. L., MA PhD   Life Fellow
Weeds, Helen F., MPhil Oxf., DPhil Oxf.   Res. Fellow, Economics
Widdis, Emma K., MPhil Camb.   U. Asst. Lectr., Slavonic Studies; Fellow
Other Staff: 30 Fellows

GIRTON COLLEGE

Tel: (01223) 338999 Fax: (01223) 338896
Abrahams, Peter, MB BS Lond., FRCS   Supernumerary Fellow
Barden, Dennis, MA Camb., PhD Camb.   Tutor; Fellow
Barker, Kathleen E., MBE, MA Camb., Hon. DSocSc HK   Registrar of Roll; Bye-Fellow
Bray, Kenneth N. C., MA Camb., MSE Prin., PhD S'ton., BA   Emer. Prof.; Prof. Fellow
Campbell, Juliet J. d'A., CMG, MA Oxf., MA Camb.   Mistress*
Cartwright, Dame Mary L., DBE, MA Oxf., MA Camb., DPhil Oxf., Hon. LLD Edin., Hon. DSc Leeds, Hon. DSc Hull, Hon. DSc Wales, Hon. DSc Oxf., ScD, FRS   Life Fellow
Clackson, Sarah J., MA Camb., PhD Camb.   Fellow
Davies, John E., BSc Monash, MA Camb., PhD Monash   Fellow
Doyle, Richard, BSc Witw., PhD   Res. Fellow

Duke, Alison, MA Camb.   Registrar Emer. of the Roll; Life Fellow
Dusinberre, Juliet A. S., MA Oxf., MA Camb., PhD Warw.   Fellow
Fernihough, Anne, MA Oxf., PhD Camb.   Tutor; Fellow
Gandy, Frances, BA Open(UK), MA Camb.   Librarian; Tutor; Fellow
Gay y Blasco, Paloma, MA Madrid, PhD Madrid   Res. Fellow
Gillies, Sheila M., MA Camb.   Life Fellow
Godby, Rex, MA Camb., PhD Camb.   Supernumerary Fellow
Grove, Jean M., MA Camb., PhD Camb.   Life Fellow
Hadley, C. K., MA MSc   Bye-Fellow
Hall, Leslie W., BSc Lond., MA Camb., PhD Lond.   Life Fellow
Harker, Janet E., MSc Syd., MA Camb., PhD Manc., ScD   U. Lectr., Zoology; Fellow
Hopkins, Charity A., MA Camb., LLB   Tutor; Sec. to Council; Fellow
Jeffreys, Lady, MA Camb., PhD Camb.   Life Fellow
Jinpa, Thupten, BA Camb.   Res. Fellow
Jolowicz, Poppy, MA Camb., LLB   Life Fellow
Jordan, Meredith J. T., BSc Syd., PhD Syd.   Res. Fellow
Kelsey, Christine H., MA Camb., PhD Camb.   U. Lectr., Earth Sciences; Fellow
Lane Perham, Nancy J., PhD Camb., DPhil Oxf., Hon. LLD Dal., ScD   Grad. Tutor; Fellow
Leadbeater, Nicholas E., BSc Nott.   Res. Fellow
Lowther, Deborah, MA Camb.   Bursar; Fellow
Marks, John, MD Lond., MA Camb., FRCP, FRCPath   Life Fellow
Marrian, Elizabeth M., MA Camb., MD   Life Fellow
McMullen, John, MA Camb., LLB PhD   Bye-Fellow, Law
Megaw, Helen D., MA Camb., ScD   Life Fellow
Natali, Alfredo G., BA Florence   U. Sr. Lang. Teaching Officer; Fellow
Oates, Joan L., PhD Camb.   Life Fellow
Randall, Roland E., MSc McG., MA Camb., PhD Camb.   Tutor; Fellow
Reid, Alastair J., MA Camb., PhD Camb.   Fellow
Riley, Julia M., MA Camb., PhD Camb.   Admissions Tutor; Fellow
Ross, Colin F., MA Camb., PhD Camb.   Fellow
Runde, Jochen, MPhil Camb., PhD Camb.   Grad. Tutor; Fellow
Sparks, Peter C. J., MA Camb.   Domestic Bursar; Fellow
Thompson, Dorothy J., MA Camb., PhD Camb.   Fellow
Udrea, Florin, MSc Warw., PhD Camb.   Res. Fellow
Vogt, Marthe L., DrMed Berl., DrPhil Berl., PhD Camb., Hon. DSc Edin., PhD Hon. ScD, FRS   Life Fellow
Warnock, Baroness, DBE, MA Oxf.   Life Fellow
Wright, Elizabeth, DPhil Oxf., MA PhD   Life Fellow
Other Staff: 32 Fellows

GONVILLE AND CAIUS COLLEGE

Tel: (01223) 332400 Fax: (01223) 332456
Alexander, Gavin R., MA Camb., MPhil Camb., PhD Camb.   Fellow
Baddeley, Michelle, BA Qld., MPhil Camb., PhD Camb.   Fellow
Bauer, Lord, MA ScD, FBA   Fellow
Bierman, Gavin M., BSc PhD   Fellow
Booij, Wilfrid E., MSc T.H.Twente   Fellow
Brett, Annabel S., MA Camb., PhD Camb.   U. Lectr., History; Fellow
Brooke, Prof. Christopher N. L., CBE, MA LittD, FBA, FSA, FRHistS   Fellow
Bullen, Air Vice-Marshall Reginald, CB, GM, MA   Fellow
Bunyan, Anita S., BA Trinity(Dub.), PhD Camb.   Fellow
Calaresu, M., MA W.Ont., PhD Camb.   Fellow

Deane, Julie P., MA *Camb.* Devel. Officer, Registrary; Fellow

Dimmick, Jeremy N., MA *Camb.*, MPhil *Camb.* Fellow

Duncan-Jones, Richard P., MA PhD, FBA Fellow

Edwards, Sir Samuel, Hon. DSc *Bath*, MA PhD, FRS Fellow

Evans, Jonathan M., MA PhD Fellow

Fink, Thomas, BSc *Cal.Tech.* Fellow

Fitzsimons, James T., Hon. MD *Lausanne*, MA MD PhD ScD, FRS Fellow

Ford, John D., MA *Glas.*, LLM *Penn.*, PhD Fellow, Law

Goodhart, Charles B., MA PhD Fellow

Gray, Peter, MA PhD ScD, FRSChem, FRS Fellow

Grierson, Philip, Hon. LittD *Leeds*, Hon. LittD *Ghent*, MA LittD, FSA, FBA Fellow

Halstead, Michael P., MA PhD Chief Exec. and Sec. Gen., Local Exams. Syndicate; Fellow

Harland, W. Brian, MA Fellow

Harper, Elizabeth M., MA PhD Tutor; Fellow

Herd, Ian R. Domestic Bursar; Fellow

Heslop, Prof. Thomas A., BA *Lond.*, PhD *Lond.*, FSA Fellow

Hill, R., ScD, FRS Fellow

Ingram, David G. W., MA Fellow

Liu, Yunkang, MSc *Zhongshan* Fellow

Macpherson, William J., MA *Aberd.*, PhD Fellow

Maddrell, Simon H. P., MA PhD ScD, FRS Fellow

Marnette, Sophie, CandLic *Brussels*, PhD *Calif.* Fellow

Martin, Konrad J., PhD *McG.*, MD *Munich*, MA Fellow

Mukherji, Subha, BA *Oxf.*, MPhil *Camb.*, PhD *Camb.* Fellow

Netz, Reviel, BA *Tel-Aviv*, MA *Tel-Aviv* Fellow

O'Shaughnessy, Kevin M., BM BCh MA DPhil Fellow

Patel, K. J., MB BS *Lond.*, PhD Fellow

Porteous, John, OBE, MA Sr. Bursar; Fellow

Prichard, Michael J., LLB MA Fellow

Ram, Capt. Thomas G. A., MA Domestic Bursar; Fellow

Rotherham, Craig, LLB *Cant.*, LLM *Yale*, PhD *Camb.* U. Lectr., Law; Fellow

Schofield, Andrew J., BA Fellow

Sealy, Leonard S., MA *NZ*, LLM *NZ*, PhD *Emer.* Prof.; Fellow

Secher, David S., MA PhD Tutor for Grads.; Fellow

Shoenberg, D., MBE, BA PhD, FRS Fellow

Tabor, David, ScD, FRS Fellow

Thwaites, J. J., MA *Oxf.*, MA *Camb.*, PhD Fellow

Timms, Edward F., MA PhD Fellow

Tuck, Stephen G. N., MA *Camb.* Fellow

Umbach, Maiken, MA *Camb.*, PhD *Camb.* Fellow

Wade, Prof. Sir William, QC, MA LLD, FBA Fellow

Webber, Geoffrey A., MA *Oxf.*, DPhil *Oxf.* Precentor; Dir. of Coll. Music; Fellow

Wood, Michael D., MA PhD Fellow

Wood, Rachel A. W., BSc *Brist.*, PhD *Open(UK)* Tutor; Fellow

Woodroffe, Rosemary B., MA *Oxf.*, DPhil *Oxf.* Fellow

Other Staff: 47 Fellows

HOMERTON COLLEGE

Tel: (01223) 507111 Fax: (01223) 507120

Gray, John M., MA *Oxf.*, MEd *Harv.*, DPhil *Sus.* Res. Dir.

Hopkins, John, BMus *Wales*, MMus *Wales* Admissions Tutor

Morrison, Ian H., MSc *Belf.*, MEd *Lond.*, PhD *Lond.* Dir., Undergrad. Programmes

Pretty, Kate, MA *Camb.*, PhD *Camb.* Principal*

Rudduck, Jean, BA *Lond.*, PhD *E.Anglia* Res. Dir.

Webb, Linda, BSc *Lond.*, MSc *Oxf.* Admissions Tutor

Younger, Michael R., MA *Lond.* Dir., Postgrad. Programmes

Other Staff: 1 Sr. Tutor.; 1 Admissions Tutor; 1 Undergrad. Tutor; 1 Grad. Tutor

HUGHES HALL

Tel: (01223) 334893 Fax: (01223) 311179

Barker, John H., LLM *Camb.*, LLM *McG.* Fellow

Boast, Robin B., MA *Denver*, PhD *Camb.* Fellow

Booth, Martin B., MA *Camb.*, MA(Education) *Reading*, PhD *Reading* Fellow

Carter, Lionel J., BSc(Econ) *Lond.*, MSc *Lond.*, PhD *Camb.* Sec.-Librarian, Centre of S. Asian Studies; Fellow

Crossland, William A., BSc *Lond.* N. Telecom Res. Prof., Photonics; Fellow

Davis, Pamela B., BA *Indiana*, MPhil *Camb.*, PhD *Camb.* Fellow

Dawson, Frank G., BA *Prin.*, LLB *Yale*, MA *Harv.*, PhD *Camb.* Fellow

Forster, Thomas E., BA *E.Anglia*, MA *E.Anglia*, PhD *Camb.* Fellow

Franklin, Michael J., MA *Camb.*, PhD *Camb.* Fellow

Igel, Heiner, PhD *Paris* Res. Fellow

Johnston, William B., MA *Oxf.*, MA *Camb.*, MS *Carnegie-Mellon* Bursar; Fellow

Lambert, Jean F., BA *Lond.*, BA *Open(UK)*, MA *Camb.* Tutor; Librarian; Fellow

Lemons, Tony D., BA *Open(UK)*, MA *Camb.* Dir. of Phys. Educn.; Fellow

Li, Ziyou, BSc *Fudan*, PhD *Camb.* Res. Fellow

Matthewson, Murray H., MB ChB *Otago*, MA *Camb.*, FRCS Assoc. Lectr., Clinical Medicine; Fellow

McVeigh, Keith J. A., MA *Oxf.*, MA *Camb.* Under-Librarian (University Library); Fellow

Mogg, Karin, BSc *Sus.*, MSc *Sur.*, MA *Camb.*, PhD *Lond.* Tutor; Fellow

Mukaetova-Ladinska, Elizabeta B., MD *Skopje*, MSc *Skopje*, PhD *Camb.* Res. Fellow

Norris, Elizabeth A., BA *Lond.*, MA *Lond.*, MA *Camb.* Fellow

Pinnock, Sally M., BA *Manc.*, MA *Camb.* Secretary, Sch. of Clin. Med.; Fellow

Pirrie, Rev. S. Robin, BA *Kent*, MA *Camb.* Tutor; Fellow

Richards, Peter, MA *Camb.*, MD *Camb.*, PhD *Lond.* President

Rigney, James R., MA *Syd.*, DPhil *Oxf.* Res. Fellow

Robertson, Ian, BSc *Glas.*, MPhil *Lond.*, PhD *Lond.* Fellow

Rodgers, Anthony K., BA *Camb.* Asst. Dir., Estates; Fellow

Sinclair Brown, Nicholas, LLB *Leic.* Fellow

Story, E. Patricia, BA *Lond.*, MA *Camb.* Admissions Tutor; Life Fellow

Tomaselli, Sylvana P., BA *Br.Col.*, MA *York(Can.)* Fellow

Turner, R. Ann, MA *Oxf.*, MA *Camb.*, PhD *Camb.* Fellow

Wakeford, Richard E., BA *Sus.* Fellow

Weller, Marc, MALD *Tufts* Fellow

Other Staff: 14 Fellows

JESUS COLLEGE

Tel: (01223) 339339 Fax: (01223) 339313

Bowen, Anthony J., MA *Camb.* Orator, Classics; Fellow

Cham, Tat J., BA *Camb.*, PhD *Camb.* Res. Fellow

Collingham, Elizabeth M., BA *Sus.*, MA *York(UK)*, PhD *Camb.* Res. Fellow

Fisher, Paul J., MA *Camb.*, PhD *Edin.*, FCA Sr. Bursar; Fellow

Gaberdiel, Matthias R., PhD *Camb.* Res. Fellow

Grant, Charlotte H., MA *Lond.*, PhD *Camb.* Fellow

Jenkins, T. D., MA *Oxf.*, MLitt *Oxf.*, BA Dean of Chapel; Fellow

Keefe, Rosanna J., BA *Camb.*, MPhil *Camb.*, PhD *Camb.* Res. Fellow

Kochloukova, Dessislava H. Res. Fellow

Nolan, P. H., MSc *Lond.*, PhD *Lond.*, MA Sinyi Prof., Chinese Management; Fellow

Osborne, Vivienne R. Domestic Bursar; Fellow

Papadakis, Nikolaos, MEng *Athens* Res. Fellow

Renfrew, A. Colin, ScD Disney Prof., Archaeology; Dir., McDonald Inst. Archaeol. Res; Fellow

Rider, B. A. K., LLB *Lond.*, MA *Camb.*, PhD *Lond.*, Hon. LLD *Penn.*, MA Fellow

Roopnaraine, Terence R. R., BA *Harv.*, PhD *Camb.* Res. Fellow

Saslaw, W. C., AB *Prin.*, MA PhD Fellow

Scott-Warren, Jason E., BA *Camb.*, MPhil *Camb.*, PhD *Camb.* Res. Fellow

Shaw-Taylor, Leigh M., BA *Open(UK)*, MSc *Oxf.* Res. Fellow

Tooze, J. Adam, BA *Camb.*, PhD *Lond.* U. Asst. Lectr., History; Fellow

Wilson, J. C., MA PhD Tutorial Adviser; Fellow

Withington, Philip J., BA Res. Fellow

Other Staff: 45 Fellows

KING'S COLLEGE

Tel: (01223) 331100 Fax: (01223) 331315

Adkins, Tessara S., MA PhD Fellow, Geography

Annan, Rt. Hon. Lord, OBE, Hon. DLitt *York(Can.)*, Hon. DU *Essex*, MA Fellow

Aparicio, Samuel A. J. R., BM BCh *Oxf.*, MA Fellow, Molecular Biology

Aunger, Robert, BA *S.Florida*, PhD *Calif.* Fellow, Cognition and Evolution

Avery, P. W., BA *Lond.*, MA Fellow, Persian

Balfour, W. E., PhD *Edin.*, MA Fellow, Physiology

Barter, I. S., MA LLB First Bursar; Fellow

Berry, Philippa J., DPhil *Sus.*, MA Fellow, English

Brenner, Sydney, CH, MSc *Witw.*, MB BCh *Witw.*, DPhil *Oxf.*, PhD *Camb.*, FRS Hon. Prof., Genetic Medicine; Fellow

Brown, Andrew S., MA *Camb.*, PhD *Camb.* U. Asst. Lectr., French; Fellow

Brown, D. McG., BSc *Glas.*, ScD, FRS Emer. Reader, Organic Chemistry; Fellow

Cleobury, S. J., MA MusB Dir. of Music; Fellow

Colclough, D. P., MA DPhil Fellow, English

de Bolla, P. L., MA PhD Fellow, English

de Castro, E. B. V. Prof., Latin American Studies

Dixon, H. B. F., MA PhD ScD Fellow

Giddens, Anthony Prof., Sociology; Fellow

Godley, Hon. W. A. H., MA Prof., Applied Economics; Fellow

Hibbert, A. B., MA Fellow, History

Hook, K. A., MA Domus Bursar; Fellow

Hoyle, Rebecca B., MA PhD Fellow, Applied Maths

Jin, Guoping, BA *Wuhan*, MA *Beijing*, PhD Fellow, Mathematics

Jones, Aled W. Fellow, Astronomy

Jones, P. M., MA *Oxf.* Librarian; Fellow

King, A. Fellow, Medicine

Klasen, S. Fellow, Economic History

Kleczkowski, A. S., PhD Fellow, Mathematical Biology

Laidlaw, James A., MA *Camb.*, PhD *Camb.* U. Asst. Lectr., Social Anthropology; Fellow

Lane, Melissa S., AB *Harv.*, BA *Camb.*, MPhil *Camb.*, PhD U. Asst. Lectr., History; Fellow

Lepora, Nathan F., MA PhD Fellow, Theoretical Physics

Lummis, Sarah C. R., BSc *Bath*, PhD Fellow, Neurophysiology

Macpherson, R. E., MA Fellow, Mathematics

McCann, G. K., BA *Kent*, PhD U. Asst. Lectr., Social and Political Sciences; Fellow

Moggridge, Geoffrey D., MA *Camb.*, PhD *Camb.* U. Asst. Lectr., Chemical Engineering; Fellow

Omitowoju, Rosanna S., MA Fellow, Classics

Parry, Bronwyn C. Fellow

Parry, D. A., BSc *Brist.*, PhD Fellow, Zoology

Patterson, Ian, MA Fellow, English

Pattison, Rev. G. L., BD *Edin.*, MA *Edin.*, PhD *Durh.* Dean; Fellow

Payne, D. J., MA PhD U. Lectr., Engineering; Admissions Tutor; Fellow

Pratt, Ian A., MA Fellow, Computer Science

Rees, Sir Martin, MA PhD, FRS Prof., Astronomy; Fellow

Rothschild, Emma, MA *Oxf.* Fellow, Politics

Rylands, G. H. W., CH, CBE, MA Hon. LittD Fellow, English

Salt, G., BSc *Alta.*, ScD *Harv.*, ScD *Camb.*, FRS Emer. Reader, Zoology; Fellow

Sampson, Elisa, BA *Oxf.* Fellow, Hispanic Studies

Sonenscher, M., BA *Warw.*, PhD *Warw.* Fellow, History

Swales, Erika M., DPhil *Basle* Fellow, German

Williams, B. A. O. Prof., Philosophy; Fellow

Wylie, J. J. Fellow, Geology and Mathematics

Zeeman, Nicolette, MA Fellow, English

Other Staff: 59 Fellows

LUCY CAVENDISH COLLEGE

Tel: (01223) 332190 Fax: (01223) 332178

Abulafia, Anna B., Drs *Amst.*, PhD *Amst.*, MA Coll. Lectr., History; Sr. Tutor; Fellow

Curry, Alison J., BSc *Lond.*, PhD *Lond.* Fellow

Hawthorn, Ruth, MA *Essex*, MA *Camb.* Admissions Tutor; Fellow

Houghton, M. Christine, BA *Ulster* Domestic Bursar; Fellow

Lawrence, Marie C., MA PhD Fellow

Mackintosh, Ellen, MA Fellow

Martin, Jessica, MA *Camb.*, PhD *Camb.* Grad. Tutor; Fellow

Penston, Margaret, BSc *Edin.*, MSc *Sus.*, DPhil *Sus.* Fellow

Perry of Southwark, Baroness, Hon. LLD *Aberd.*, Hon. DEd *Wolv.*, Hon. LLD *S.Bank*, Hon. LLD *Bath*, Hon. DLitt *Sus.*, MA President*

Rawlings, Susan E., BA *Lond.*, MA Praelector; Dep. Sec., Bd. of Continuing Educn.; Warden of Madingley Hall; Fellow

Renfrew, Jane M. (Lady Renfrew of Kaimsthorn), MA PhD Coll. Lectr., Archaeology; Fellow

Sheppard, Jennifer M., MA *Bryn Mawr*, PhD *Bryn Mawr* Fellow

Squire, Nathalie, MA Fellow

Tee, L., MA Coll. Lectr., Law; Tutor; Fellow

Tiley, Jillinda M., MA *Oxf.*, MA *Camb.* Fellow

Traub, Lindsey M., MA *Lond.*, PhD Coll. Lectr., English; Vice-Pres.; Fellow

Tucker, Elizabeth M., PhD *Lond.*, DSc *Lond.*, MA Fellow

Vassilika, Eleni, MA PhD Keeper of Antiquities; Fitzwilliam Museum; Fellow

Vinnicombe, Alison A., BA *Leeds* Registrar; Fellow

Wheeler, Joyce, MA PhD Fellow

Other Staff: 8 Fellows

MAGDALENE COLLEGE

Tel: (01223) 332100 Fax: (01223) 462589

Alboussiere, Thierry, PhD Fellow

Aragón-Salamanca, Alfonso, PhD Sr. Res. Fellow

Bennett, R. F., MA LittD Emer. Fellow

Best, Victoria J. L., BA MPhil Res. Fellow

Bourne, Neil K., MA PhD Sr. Res. Fellow

Carpenter, Michael A., MA PhD Reader, Mineralogy and Mineral Physics; Jt. Dir. of Studies (Nat. Sci. (Phys.)); Fellow

Deakin, Brian M., MA *Oxf.*, MA *Camb.* Emer. Fellow

Dias, R. W. Michael, MA LLB Emer. Fellow

Dwight, John B., MA MSc Emer. Fellow, Engineering

Finlay, Rev. Hueston E., BAI *Trinity(Dub.)*, BTh *Trinity(Dub.)*, MA *Trinity(Dub.)* Dir. of Studies (Theology); Chaplain; Fellow

Grainger, David J., MA PhD Sr. Res. Fellow

Hughes, M. E. Jane, MA PhD Dir. of Studies (Engl.); Admissions Tutor (Undergrads.); Fellow

Jones, Neil G., MA *Camb.*, LLM *Camb.*, PhD *Camb.* U. Asst. Lectr., Law; Dir. of Studies (Law); Fellow

Kawamami, Akane, BA *Oxf.*, DPhil *Oxf.* Dir. of Studies, Modern Languages; Fellow

Kilner, Rebecca M., PhD Res. Fellow

Kolbert, His Honour Judge C. F., MA PhD Emer. Fellow

Lyne, Raphael T. R., MA MPhil PhD Res. Fellow

Martin, Stuart, MA PhD Dir. of Studies (Maths.); Fellow

McDowell, Natasha, BA Res. Fellow

Morris, Roger B., MA PhD Fellow

Murphy, Denis J. H., MA Bursar; Tutor; Fellow

Murray, Natalie H., BA Res. Fellow

Nellist, Peter D., MA *Camb.*, PhD *Camb.* Res. Fellow

Oulton, Sir Derek (Anthony Maxwell), GCB, QC, MA PhD Life Fellow

Stevens, John E., CBE, MA PhD, FBA Emer. Prof., English; Emer. Fellow

Tobin, Nicholas J. Domus Bursar; Steward; Fellow

Ward, Angela, BA LLB PhD Fellow

Other Staff: 28 Fellows

NEW HALL

Tel: (01223) 762100 Fax: (01223) 352941

Acton, Elizabeth, MA PhD Dir. of Studies, Engineering and Management Sciences; Fellow

Appleby, Bridget M., BA *Camb.*, DPhil *Oxf.* Res. Fellow, Zoology

Ardavan, Houshang, BSc *M.I.T.*, PhD Coll. Lectr., Mathematics; Fellow

Baert, Patrick J. N., DPhil *Oxf.* Coll. Lectr., Social and Political Sciences; Fellow

Barton, Penelope J., MA PhD Coll. Lectr. in Earth Sciences; Exec. Grad. Tutor; Fellow

Bearcroft, Philip W. P., MA MB BChir, FRCR Fellow, Neuroscience

Benson, Susan N., MA PhD Coll. Lectr., Social Sciences; Tutor; Fellow

Blyth, Caroline M., DPhil *Oxf.* British Academy Res. Fellow, English

Butcher, Geoffrey W., BA *Oxf.*, PhD *Camb.* Coll. Lectr., Pathology; Fellow

Chau, Pak-Lee, MPhil *Camb.*, PhD *Camb.*, MB BChir Coll. Lectr., Biochemistry; Fellow

Ellington, Stephanie K. L., BSc *Lond.*, PhD Coll. Lectr., Physiology; Tutor for Admissions; Fellow

Filippucci, Paola, BA *Sheff.*, PhD Tutor; Res. Fellow, Soc. Anthropol.

Guthrie, John D., MA *W.Aust.*, PhD Coll. Lectr., German; Fellow

Hamilton, Darren G., BSc *Lond.*, PhD *S'ton.* Coll. Lectr., Chemistry; Fellow

Harris, Harriet E., MA *Lond.*, PhD *Lond.* Coll. Lectr. in Cell Biol.; Tutor; Maplethorpe Fellow

Henson, Frances M. D., MA *Camb.*, VetMB *Camb.*, PhD *Camb.* Tutor in Physiology and Veterinary Medicine; Fellow

Herring, Jonathan J. W., BA *Oxf.*, BCL *Oxf.* Coll. Lectr., Law; Fellow

Hessayon, Ariel Y., BA *Oxf.*, PhD *Camb.* Res. Fellow, History

Hinde, Joan S., MSc *Brown*, PhD *Brown*, MA ScD Coll. Lectr., Psychology; Tutor; Vice-Pres.; Fellow

Ledeneva, Alena V., BA *Novosibirsk*, MPhil *Camb.*, PhD *Camb.* Res. Fellow, Social and Political Sciences

Lonsdale, Anne M., MA *Oxf.*, MA *Camb.* President*

Malone, Caroline A. T., MA *Camb.*, PhD *Camb.* Fellow, Archaeology

Rodenburg, John M., BA *Exe.*, PhD Fellow, Physics

Rohani, Pejman, PhD *Camb.* Res. Fellow, Zoology

Saxton, W. Owen, MA PhD Coll. Lectr., Physics; Praelector; Tutor; Fellow

Selby, Alexander P., MA PhD Res. Fellow, Mathematics

Sinnatamby, Ruchira, MA MB BChir, FRCR Fellow, Anatomy

Smith, Emma, BA *Oxf.*, DPhil *Oxf.* Coll. Lectr., English; Schools Liaison and Access Officer; Fellow

Stevenson, Christopher A. E. T., MA Fellow

Tadmor, Naomi, MA *Jerusalem*, PhD Coll. Lectr., History; Kitson-Clark Fellow

Townsend, Susan C., BA *Sheff.*, PhD *Sheff.* British Academy Res. Fellow, Oriental Studies

Venkitaraman, Ashok R., MB BS *Madr.*, MA *Camb.*, PhD *Lond.* Prof. Fellow, Immunology

Wilson, Alison M., BA *Brist.*, MSc *Lond.*, MLitt Coll. Librarian; Fellow

Wilson, Penelope B., MA *Edin.*, MA *Camb.*, DPhil *Oxf.* Coll. Lectr., English; Sr. Tutor; Fellow

Wright, Nicholas R. M., BA *Sheff.* Bursar; Fellow

Wylie, R. Neville, BA *Lond.*, MPhil PhD Dean, Hist.; British Academy Res. Fellow

Other Staff: 13 Fellows

NEWNHAM COLLEGE

Tel: (01223) 335700 Fax: (01223) 359155

Brown, Sarah, MA *Camb.*, PhD *Brist.* Res. Fellow, English

Crown, June, MA *Camb.*, MB BChir *Camb.*, MSc *Lond.* Assoc. Fellow

De Waal, Clarissa, MA *Edin.*, MPhil *Camb.*, PhD *Camb.* Tutor; Fellow

Dex, Shirley, BA *Keele*, MSc *Brist.*, PhD *Keele* U. Lectr., Management Studies; Fellow

Drury, Clare, MA *Oxf.*, MA *Camb.* Sr. Tutor; Tutor; Fellow

Edgcombe, Katherine, MA *Camb.* Financial Tutor; Tutor; Fellow

Etheridge, Joanne, BSc *Melb.*, PhD *Melb.* Res. Fellow, Solid State Physics

Fleet, Kate, BA *Lond.*, PhD *Lond.* Curator, Skilliter Centre for Ottoman Studies; Tutor; Fellow

Friday, Laurie E., MA *Exe.*, PhD *Exe.* Coll. Lectr., Ecology; Grad. Tutor; Tutor; Fellow

Gilbert, Lynne, MA *Camb.*, MB BChir *Camb.*, PhD *Brist.* Fellow

Gooder, Jean M., MA *Camb.* Coll. Lectr., English; Fellow

Greer, Germaine, BA *Melb.*, MA *Syd.*, PhD *Camb.* Spec. Coll. Lectr., English; Fellow

Haskell, Yasmin A., BA *Syd.*, PhD *Syd.* Res. Fellow, Renaissance Literature

Hawley, Katherine, BA *Oxf.*, MPhil *Camb.* Res. Fellow, Philosophy of Science

Hicks, Carola M., MA *Edin.*, PhD *Edin.* Fellow

Hodder, Deborah K., MA *Lond.*, MA *Camb.* Coll. Librarian; Fellow

Holness, Marion B., MA *Camb.*, PhD *Camb.* U. Asst. Lectr., Earth Sciences; Coll. Lectr.; Fellow

Hudson, Maria, MA *Camb.*, MA *Warw.* Coll. Lectr., Economics; Fellow

Hunt, Felicity M., BA *Thames V.*, MA *Essex*, PhD *Camb.* U. Asst. Registrary; Fellow

Ignatovich, Olga, BSc *Minsk* Res. Fellow, Molecular Biology

Jaszczolt, Katarzyna M., MA *Lodz*, MPhil *Lodz*, DPhil *Oxf.* U. Asst. Lectr., Linguistics; Tutor; Coll. Lectr. in Linguistics; Fellow

Lasenby, Joan, MA *Camb.*, PhD *Camb.* Coll. Lectr., Engineering; Fellow

Lipton, Diana, BA *Oxf.*, PhD *Camb.* Admissions Tutor; Tutor; Fellow

MacDougall, Jane, BA MB BChir Consultant, Addenbrooke's Hosp.; Fellow

McMahon, Augusta, BA *Bryn Mawr*, MA *Chic.*, PhD *Chic.* Grad. Tutor; Tutor; Fellow

Morgan, Teresa J., MA *Camb.*, PhD *Camb.* Tutor; Res. Fellow, Classics

Mullinger, Ann M., MA *Camb.*, PhD *Camb.* Coll. Lectr., Zoology; Fellow

O'Neill, Onora S., CBE, MA *Oxf.*, MA *Camb.*, PhD *Harv.*, FBA Principal*

Ridley, Rosalind, MA *Camb.*, PhD *Lond.*, ScD *Camb.* Tutor; Fellow

Scadden, Deirdre, BSc *Otago*, PhD *Camb.* Res. Fellow, Molecular Biology

Sergeant, Carol, MA *Camb.*, MBA *City(UK)* Assoc. Fellow

Seville, Catherine A., BMus *Lond.*, LLM *Camb.*, MA *Camb.* Coll. Lectr., Law; Fellow

Sutherland, Gillian R., MA *Oxf.*, MA *Camb.*, DPhil *Oxf.*, PhD *Camb.* Coll. Lectr., History; Fellow

Taub, Liba, BA *Tulane*, MA *Chic.*, PhD *Oklahoma* Curator, U. Whipple Museum; Tutor; Fellow

Zanna, Antonella, BA *Bari.* Res. Fellow, Mathematics

Other Staff: 25 Fellows

PEMBROKE COLLEGE

Tel: (01223) 338100 *Fax:* (01223) 338163

Baskey, Nicholas S., BA *Yale*, MBA *Ohio State* Treasurer and Bursar; Fellow

Bodenhorn, B. A., BA *Mich.*, MPhil PhD Coll. Lectr., Social and Political Science; Asst. Tutor; Fellow

Cardoso, Silvana S. S., BA *Oporto*, PhD *Camb.* U. Asst. Lectr., Chemical Engineering; Fellow

Chamblin, H. Andrew, BA *Rice*, MSc *Oxf.* Drapers' Res. Fellow, Applied Mathematics

Cooper, Nigel R., MA *Camb.*, DPhil *Oxf.* Drapers' Res. Fellow, Physics

Edwards, G. R., BA *Wales*, PhD *Lond.* Jean Monnet Dir. of European Studies; Asst. Tutor; Fellow

Franklin, Robin J. M., BSc *Lond.*, VetMB *Lond.*, PhD *Camb.* Asst. Tutor; Smith Kline Beecham Fellow, Vet. Med.

Grimstone, A. V., MA PhD U. Lectr., Zoology; President; Asst. Tutor; Fellow

Herbison, A. E., MB ChB *Otago*, PhD *Camb.* Principal Res. Scientist; Babraham Inst. Fellow, Neuroendocrinology

Hickson, J. C. D., MA PhD U. Lectr., Veterinary Physiology; Asst. Tutor; Fellow

Hutton, W. S., TD, MA Fellow

Janes, Dominic T. S., BA *Oxf.*, PhD *Camb.* Drapers' Res. Fellow, History

Johnson, L. P., BA *Durh.*, DrPhil *Kiel*, MA Emer. Reader; Fellow

Kenderdine, S., MA PhD Praelector; Fellow

Kinsella, Sharon E., BSc *Lond.*, DPhil *Oxf.* Daiwa-Calbee Res. Fellow, Japanese Studies

Kuczynski, M. G., MA Coll. Lectr., Economics; Asst. Tutor; Fellow

Lingwood, Rebecca J., MA *Camb.*, PhD *Camb.* Maudsley Res. Fellow, Engineering

Livanios, Dimitrios, BA *Salonika*, DPhil *Oxf.* Georgakis Res. Fellow, Modern Greek Studies

Lyons, Malcolm C., MA PhD LittD Emer. Prof.; Fellow

MacKay, Niall J., BA *Camb.*, PhD *Durh.* Stokes' Res. Fellow, Applied Mathematics

Majid, S. H., MA *Harv.*, PhD *Harv.* Fellow, Applied Mathematics

McBride, Nicholas J., BA *Oxf.* James Campbell Fellow, Law

McRae, Susan B., BSc *Car.*, MSc *Wat.*, PhD *Camb.* Drapers' Res. Fellow, Behavioral Ecology

Meissner, Torsten, MA *Bonn*, PhD *Camb.*, DPhil *Oxf.* U. Lectr., Classics; Fellow

Raingold, Howard P., MA Devel. Dir.; Fellow

Smith, G. C., MA Fellow

Stobbs, Susan H., MA *Camb.* Admissions Tutor for Sci.; Asst. Tutor; Fellow

Tomkys, Sir Roger, KCMG, MA *Oxf.*, MA *Camb.* Master*

Watchorn, Rev. B., MA Dean and Chaplain; Asst. Tutor; Fellow

Wilcockson, C. G., MA *Oxf.*, MA *Camb.* Coll. Lectr., English; Asst. Tutor; Fellow

Wilkinson, Timothy D., BEng *Cant.*, PhD *Cant.*, PhD *Camb.* Sir Henry Jones British Gas Res. Fellow, Engineering

Wormald, M. R., BA *Oxf.* Coll. Lectr., English; Dep. Tutor; Fellow

Young, Christopher J., MA *Camb.*, PhD *Camb.* U. Asst. Lectr., German; Asst. Tutor; Fellow

Other Staff: 33 Fellows

PETERHOUSE

Tel: (01223) 338200 *Fax:* (01223) 337578

Brown, W. A., MA PhD Res. Fellow, Chemistry

Crowther, R. A., MA PhD, FRS Supernumerary Fellow, Natural Science

Golding, M. S., MA Admissions Tutor for Undergrads.; Librarian; Fellow

Jackson, S. E., PhD Supernumerary Fellow, Chemistry

Jones, M. H., MA *Oxf.* Res. Fellow, History

Köhler, Anna, PhD Res. Fellow, Solid State Physics

Langmore, N. E., BSc *ANU*, PhD Res. Fellow, Zoology

Lipman, E. W. J., BA *Col.* Res. Fellow, History

McCaughan, Gareth J., PhD Res. Fellow, Pure Maths

McLeod, A. S., BSc *Edin.*, PhD *Camb.* Rolls Royce/Frank Whittle Res. Fellow, Chemical Engineering

Murison, A. H., MA Bursar; Fellow

Pattenden, P., MA *Camb.*, MA *Oxf.*, DPhil *Oxf.*, PhD Coll. Lectr., Classics; Sr. Tutor; Admissions Tutor for Postgrads.; Fellow

Rucklidge, A. M., BASc *Tor.*, SM *M.I.T.*, PhD Bye Fellow, Applied Mathematics

Shephard, D. S., PhD *Edin.* Royal Soc. Smithson Res. Fellow, Inorganic Chemistry

Simms, B. P., MA PhD Coll. Lectr., History; Admissions Tutor for Undergrads.; Fellow

Skaer, R. J., MA PhD Coll. Lectr., Natural Science; Praelector; Fellow

Stacey, A. M., MA *Camb.*, PhD Res. Fellow, Mathematics

Stott, Kelvin R. Res. Fellow, Biochemical Protein Engineering

Thomas, Prof. Sir John Meurig, PhD *Wales*, DSc *Wales*, Hon. LLD *Wales*, Hon. DLitt *CNAA*, Hon. DSc *H.-W.*, Hon. DSc *Birm.*, Hon. DUniv. *Open(UK)*, MA ScD, FRS Master*

Turner, D. M., MA PhD U. Lectr., Land Economy; Fellow

Wallace, J. M. B., MA PhD Fellow, English

Ward, G. J., MA *Oxf.*, PhD Coll. Lectr., Philosophy; Dean; Fellow

Waters, S. L., BA Res. Fellow, Biomathematics

Other Staff: 22 Fellows

QUEENS' COLLEGE

Tel: (01223) 335511 *Fax:* (01223) 335522

Beament, Sir James, MA ScD, FRS Fellow

Bowett, Sir Derek, CBE, QC, PhD *Manc.*, MA LLD, FBA Fellow

Brown, Georgia E., MA *Oxf.*, MPhil *Oxf.*, DPhil *Oxf.* Fellow

Buler, Oliver, MSE *Mich.*, PhD Bye Fellow, Applied Mathematics

Challinor, Anthony D., BA *Camb.* Res. Fellow

Coaker, T. H., BSc *Lond.*, MA PhD Steward; Fellow

Gagne, Christophe, MLitt *St.-Etienne* Bye Fellow, French

Glover, Beverley J., BSc *St And.* Res. Fellow

Green, J. T., MA PhD Fellow

Hart, Rev. H. St J., MA BD Fellow

Hewson, Stephen F., MA Res. Fellow, Mathematics; Paterson Award Fellow

Holloway, J., DLitt *Aberd.*, DPhil *Oxf.*, MA *Oxf.*, MA *Camb.*, LittD, FRSL Fellow

Holmes, Rev. J. M., MA VetMB PhD Chaplain; Dean; Fellow

Llewellyn Smith, Stefan G., MA *Camb.*, PhD *Camb.* Res. Fellow

Macleod, M. D., MA PhD Fellow

Milgate, Murray J., MEc *Syd.*, MA *Essex*, PhD *Camb.* Fellow

Oxburgh, Sir E. Ronald, MA *Prin.*, MA *Oxf.*, MA *Camb.*, PhD *Prin.*, Hon. DSc *Paris*, FRS Fellow

Parmée, D., MA Fellow

Phillips, W. A., MA PhD Fellow

Polkinghorne, Rev. J. C., MA *Camb.*, ScD *Camb.*, FRS Fellow

Prentis, J. M., MSc *Lond.*, PhD *Lond.*, MA Fellow

Smithson, Michael, LLB *Lond.* Univ. Devel. Dir.; Fellow

Spearing, A. C., MA Fellow

Spence, Peter E., BA *Alta.*, MA *W.Ont.*, PhD Bye Fellow, Modern History

Stein, P. G., Hon. DrJur *Gött.*, PhD *Aberd.*, MA LLB, FBA Fellow

Thompson, Rupert J. E., MA *Camb.*, PhD *Camb.* Res. Fellow

Thorne, K. J. I., MA PhD Sr. Tutor; Fellow

Thurschwell, Pamela, BA *Yale*, MA *Sus.*, PhD *Cornell* Res. Fellow, English; Michael Greet Field Fellow

Walker, R. D. H., MA PhD Jr. Bursar; Fellow

Wright, I. R., MA Fellow

Other Staff: 41 Fellows

ROBINSON COLLEGE

Tel: (01223) 339100 *Fax:* (01223) 351794

Affuso, Luisa, BSc *Naples*, MSc *Warw.*, PhD *Waik.* Fellow

Bamforth, Nicholas, BA *Oxf.* Fellow

Brett, Martin, DPhil *Oxf.*, MA Sr. Tutor; Fellow

Brooks, Peter N., MA *Camb.*, PhD *Camb.* U. Lectr., Divinity; Fellow

Donald, Athene M., MA PhD Reader, Experimental Physics; Fellow

du Sautoy, Marcus P. F., BA *Oxf.*, DPhil *Oxf.* Res. Fellow

Guild, Elizabeth M., MA *St And.*, MA *Camb.*, PhD Admissions Tutor; Fellow

Hooker, Morna D., MA *Brist.*, MA *Oxf.*, MA *Camb.*, PhD *Manc.*, DLitt *Brist.*, DD Lady Margaret's Prof., Divinity; Fellow

Jarvis, S. P., PhD Fellow

Kerr, D. A. H., CBE Sr. Bursar; Fellow

Lewis, Lord, MA *Camb.*, MSc *Manc.*, PhD *Nott.*, DSc *Lond.*, ScD *Camb.*, Hon. Doc *Rennes*, Hon. DUniv *Open(UK)*, Hon. DUniv *Kingston(UK)*, Hon.DSc *Bath*, Hon. DSc *E.Anglia*, Hon. DSc *Nott.*, Hon. DSc *Keele*, Hon. DSc *Durh.*, Hon. DSc *Leic.*, Hon. DSc *Birm.*, Hon. DSc *Wat.*, Hon. DSc *Manc.*, Hon. DSc *Wales*, Hon. DSc *Sheff.*, Hon. DSc *Cran.IT*, Hon. DSc *Edin.*, Hon. DSc *HK*, FRS Emer. Prof., Inorganic Chemistry; Warden*

Love, Rosalind C., PhD Fellow

McDonald, Maryon E., BA *Lond.*, DPhil *Oxf.* Fellow

McKie, D. S., MA PhD Fellow

Merridale, Catherine A., MA *Camb.*, PhD *Birm.* Res. Fellow

Murk Jansen, Saskia M., MA Camb., PhD
  Camb. Grad. Tutor; Praelector; Fellow
Myers, J. R., LLB Liv., MA Jr. Bursar.; Fellow
Nolan, William P., BSc Lond., PhD
  Camb. Fellow
Payne, Jennifer S., MA Camb. Fellow
Rudy, I. A., MA PhD Fellow
Smith, Julie E., MA Oxf., MPhil Oxf., DPhil
  Oxf. Fellow
Suttie, R. P., PhD Edin. Res. Fellow
Thom, D., MA Warw., MA Camb., PhD
  CNAA Fellow
Walsh, C. A., MSc Dund., BA PhD Res. Fellow
Weiss, Judith E., BA Rhodes, MA PhD Fellow
Yuan, J., BSc Lond., PhD Fellow
Other Staff: 31 Fellows

SELWYN COLLEGE

Tel: (01223) 335846 Fax: (01223) 335837

Ahmed, Akbar S., BA Punjab, BSocSc Birm., PhD
  Lond., MA Fellow
Beber, Massimo M., Laurea Sacred Heart(Milan),
  MPhil Fellow
Berger, Sir Peter, KCB, DSC Fellow
Brinton, Sal V., MA Bursar; Fellow
Brock, William R., MA PhD, FBA Fellow
Chadwick, W. Owen, OM, KBE, MA DD,
  FBA Emer. Regius Prof., Modern History;
  Fellow
Cook, Sir Alan, MA PhD ScD, FRS,
  FRSEd Emer. Jacksonian Prof., Natural
  Philosophy; Fellow
Cook, Graham P., BSc Lond., PhD
  Camb. Fellow
Cranfield, Nicholas W. S., MA Oxf., DPhil Oxf.,
  PhD Camb. Dean of Chapel; Chaplain;
  Precentor; Fellow
Fox, Peter K., BA Lond., MA Sheff., MA
  Camb. Univ. Librarian; Fellow
Grimley, Daniel M., MA MPhil Fellow
Harrison, Sir David, CBE, MA Camb., PhD
  Camb., ScD Camb., Hon. DUniv Keele, Hon.
  DSc Exe., FEng, FRSChem Master*
Kim, Keechang, LLB Seoul, LLM Chic., PhD
  Camb. Fellow
Manning, Mark R., MA PhD Fellow
Matheson, James M. R., MA Sr. Computer
  Officer, Information (Engineering); Tutor;
  Fellow
Muir, Ian D., MA PhD Fellow
O'Sullivan, Janet A., MA U. Asst. Lectr., Law;
  Tutor; Fellow
Panić, Micá, MA Sheff., MA Camb., PhD Fellow
Plumley, Rev. Jack M., BA Durh., MLitt Durh.,
  MA Prof. Emer., Egyptology; Fellow
Reynolds, Andrew W. M., MA Oxf., DPhil
  Oxf. Tutor; Fellow
Smith, David L., MA PhD, FRHistS Tutor for
  Admissions; Fellow
Sweet, Rev. John P. M., MA Oxf., MA Camb.,
  DD Lambeth Fellow
Taylor, Andrew M., BA Lond., MA Lond.,
  PhD Fellow
Tilby, Michael J., MA PhD Sr. Tutor; Fellow
Titmuss, Simon, MA Fellow
Vlasto, Alexis P., MA PhD Fellow
Welbourn, Donald B., MA, FEng, FIMechE,
  FIEE Fellow
Whitaker, Robert H., MA MB BChir MChir
  MD, FRCS Fellow
Willis, Katherine J., BSc S'ton., PhD Tutor;
  Royal Soc. Fellow
Other Staff: 28 Fellows

SIDNEY SUSSEX COLLEGE

Tel: (01223) 338800 Fax: (01223) 338884

Beales, D. E. D., MA Camb., PhD Camb., LittD
  Camb., FBA Fellow
Bhalla, Ajit S., BA Punjab, MA Delhi, PhD
  Manc. U. Lectr.; Fellow
Bohr, Annette, MA Harv. Fellow

Bramall, Chris M., MA Camb., PhD
  Camb. Tutor; Fellow
Buchli, Victor A., BA PhD Fellow
Castor, Helen R., BA PhD Camb. Tutor; Fellow
Chorley, Richard J., MA Oxf. Prof.; Fellow
Clark-King, Rev. Ellen J., MA Camb. Chaplain;
  Jr. Proctor; Fellow
Clemmow, P. C., MA Camb., PhD
  Camb. Fellow
Eskin, Michael, BA C'dia., MA Munich, PhD
  Rutgers Fellow
Gizeli, Electra, BSc Athens, MSc Lond., PhD
  Camb. Fellow
Hennings, M. A., DPhil Oxf., PhD Camb. Sr.
  Tutor; Admissions Tutor; Fellow
Horn, Gabriel, BSc Birm., MD Birm., MA Camb.,
  ScD Camb., FRS Master*
Hutchison, Rev. H. P., MA Oxf., MA
  Camb. Fellow
Jackson, J. Clare L., BA Camb., MA Camb., PhD
  Wales Fellow
Mayall, James B. L., BA Camb. Prof.,
  International Relations; Fellow
Northcote, D. H., PhD Lond., ScD, FRS Prof.;
  Fellow
Parish, C., MB ChB Manc., MA, FRCS,
  FSA Keeper of Records; Fellow
Partington, Richard J., BA Fellow
Perrett, Sarah E. D., MA Camb. Fellow
Pollitt, Michael G., DPhil Oxf. U. Lectr.; Dean;
  Fellow
Preston, Claire E., MPhil Yale, DPhil Oxf., PhD
  Camb. Newton Trust Lectr.; Admissions
  Tutor; Fellow
Switzer, J. F. Q., MA Fellow
Tawfik, Dan S., BSc Jerusalem, PhD
  Weizmann Fellow
Thornely, J. W. A., MA Fellow
Turner, Stephen R. E., BA Fellow
Viles, Thomas C., BA Harv., LLM
  Camb. Praelector; Fellow
Walker, John E., BA Oxf., DPhil Oxf.,
  FRS Fellow
Whittington, H. B., DSc Birm., MA, FRS Prof.;
  Fellow
Wilson, A. L., BA Oxf. Fellow
Wyatt, T. S., MA MLitt Fellow
Zernicka-Goetz, Magdalena, MSc Warsaw, PhD
  Warsaw Fellow
Other Staff: 30 Fellows

ST CATHARINE'S COLLEGE

Tel: (01223) 338300 Fax: (01223) 338340

Aldridge, David C., MA PhD Res. Fellow,
  Zoology
Bates, John, BSc Lanc., PhD Camb. Res. Fellow,
  Computer Sciences
Berend, Nora, PhD Col. MPhil Res. Fellow,
  History
Buckle, Abigail M. S., BA Manc., MEd
  Manc. Tutor, Social and Political Sciences;
  Fellow
Bulkeley, Harriet A., BA Camb., PhD
  Camb. Res. Fellow, Geography
Clark, Christopher M., BA PhD Coll. Lectr.,
  History; Tutor; Fellow
Crawford, Charles M. C., MA Camb. Fellow;
  Bursar and Domestic Bursar
Dance, Richard W., BA Res. Fellow,
  Mediaeval History
Davenport, Anthony P., BSc Lond., MA Lond.,
  PhD Lond. Lectr., Clinical Pharmacology;
  Fellow
Davies, Robert P., BSc PhD Res. Fellow,
  Chemistry
Dew, Nicholas, BA Oxf., MSc Oxf. Res.
  Fellow, History
English, Sir Terence, KBE, MB BS Lond., MA
  Camb., FRCS, FRCP Master*
Ferran, Eilis V., MA PhD U. Lectr., Law;
  Fellow
Gilbert, Geoffrey I., MA Aberd., PhD
  Camb. Res. Fellow, English
Gonda, Caroline, MA Camb., PhD Camb. Coll.
  Lectr., English; Tutor; Fellow

Goodhew, Rev. David, DPhil Chaplain;
  Fellow
Hartle, Paul N., MA PhD Coll. Lectr., English;
  Admissions Tutor; Fellow
Kitson, Michael, BA Coll. Lectr., Economics;
  Financial Tutor; Fellow
McNay, Kirsty, MPhil Camb., PhD Camb. Res.
  Fellow, Economics
Melikan, Rose A., BA Mich., MA Chic., JD Chic.,
  PhD Coll. Lectr., Law; Fellow
Message, Michael A., MA MB BChir
  PhD Fellow
Roberts, Gareth O., BA Oxf., PhD Warw. U.
  Lectr., Mathematics; Fellow
Vassiliadis, Vassilios, BA Athens, PhD Lond. U.
  Lectr., Chemical Engineering; Fellow
Vassilicos, John C., PhD U. Lectr., Applied
  Mathematics; Fellow
Watt, James W. A., BA Camb., PhD Camb. Res.
  Fellow, English
Wothers, Peter D., MA Camb., PhD Camb. Res.
  Fellow, Chemistry
Yim, Louis W. K., BEng Strath., PhD Camb.,
  DPhil Res. Fellow, Engineering
Other Staff: 34 Fellows

ST EDMUND'S COLLEGE

Tel: (01223) 336250 Fax: (01223) 336111

Bache, B. W., BA Oxf., MA PhD U. Lectr.,
  Geography; Fellow
Bailer-Jones, Coryn, BA Oxf., PhD Camb. Res.
  Fellow
Boniface, Simon J., MD Lond., BSc MB
  BS Fellow
Bunbury, Judith M. R., BSc Durh., PhD
  Camb. Res. Fellow
Cook, G. M. W., MSc Nott., PhD,
  FRSChem U. Assoc. Lectr., Anatomy; Vice-
  Master; Fellow
Heap, Prof. Robert B., CBE, BSc Nott., PhD
  Nott., Hon. DSc Nott., ScD, FIBiol, FRSChem,
  FRS Master*
McHugh, Rev. F. P., MA Oxf., PhD Fellow
Mitton, S. A., MA Oxf., MA Camb.,
  PhD Editorial Dir. (Sci. and Reference
  Publishing), Univ. Press; Fellow
Morrissey, Mary E., BA Trinity(Dub.), MLitt
  Trinity(Dub.) Res. Fellow
Murphy, M. C., MEconSc N.U.I., MA PhD Sr.
  Tutor
O'Dochartaigh, Caitríona, BA N.U.I., MA
  N.U.I. Res. Fellow
O'Flynn, Bernadette M., BA N.U.I.,
  MA Personnel Officer (Asst. Staff Office);
  Fellow
O'Keeffe, Bernadette M., BSc Lond., PhD
  Lond. Res. Fellow
Paul, Douglas J., BA Camb., PhD Camb. Res.
  Fellow
Rex, Susan A., LLB Lond., PhD Camb. Res.
  Fellow
Robson, Rev. M., PhD Dean; Admissions
  Tutor
Stanley, Brian, BA Camb., MA Camb., PhD
  Camb. Fellow
Tudor, J., MB BS Lond., MA, FRCR Fellow
Valls, Helen, BA Lond., MA Reading, MA Tor.,
  PhD Tor. Res. Fellow
Zajac, Natascha E., BA Res. Fellow
Other Staff: 11 Fellows

ST JOHN'S COLLEGE

Tel: (01223) 338600 Fax: (01223) 338727

Alexander, J. A., MA PhD ScD, FSA Fellow
Armstrong, W. D., OBE, MA PhD Fellow
Arnold, Neil S., BA Camb., PhD Camb. U.
  Lectr., Geography; Fellow
Bambrough, J. R., MA Fellow
Barrowclough, Diana V. O., MA Auck., MPhil
  Camb. Fellow, Economics
Bertram, G. C. L., MA PhD Fellow

Bleehen, N. M., CBE, BSc Oxf., BM BCh Oxf., MA Oxf., MA Camb., FRCR, FRCP Fellow
Brookes, A. M. P., MA Fellow
Budden, K. G., MA PhD, FRS Fellow
Charles, J. A., BSc Lond., MA ScD, FEng Fellow
Colwell, S. M., MA PhD Tutor; Fellow
Connell, Philip J., BA Liv. Fellow
Cowburn, Russell P., MA Camb. Fellow
Crook, J. A., MA Fellow
Elliott, Sophia N., BA McG., MPhil Camb., PhD Camb. Fellow
Emerton, Rev. J. A., MA Oxf., MA Camb., Hon. DD Edin., DD, FBA Fellow
Evans, G. C., MA PhD ScD Fellow
Frogley, Michael R., BSc Kingston(UK), PhD Camb. Fellow
Gardner, Philippa A., MA Oxf., PhD Edin. Fellow, Computer Science
Goody, J. R., MA PhD ScD, FBA Fellow
Green, R. A., BSc Lond., PhD Fellow
Guest, G. H., CBE, MusD Lambeth, MA MusB, FRCO Fellow
Harrison, Simon J., BA Oxf., MA Camb., PhD Camb. Fellow
Hinde, Prof. R. A., CBE, MA Oxf., DPhil Oxf., ScD, FRS Fellow
Hollick, F. S. J., MA PhD Fellow
Horrocks, G. C., MA Camb., PhD Camb. Prof., Philology; Fellow
Howard, Deborah J., MA PhD, FSA Reader, Architectural History; Librarian, Fac. of Architecture and History of Art; Fellow
Hutchison, J. B., MSc Natal, PhD Natal, PhD Camb., ScD Fellow
James, E. D., MA PhD Fellow
Jewell, P. A., BSc Reading, MA PhD, FIBiol Fellow
Johnson, C. M. P., MA PhD Fellow
Keen, Catherine M., BA Camb., PhD Camb. Fellow
Laven, Mary R., BA Camb., MA Lond., PhD Leic. U. Asst. Lectr., History; Fellow
Lee, A. G., MA Fellow
Linehan, P. A., MA PhD, FRHistS Fellow
Macintosh, Rev. A. A., MA DD Dean; President; Fellow
Mao, Yong, BA Camb., PhD Camb. Fellow
Matthewman, J. H., MA PhD Fellow, Engineering
McClay, Catherine I., BEng Lond., PhD Camb. Fellow
Metaxas, A. C., BSc Lond., PhD Lond., MA Tutor; Fellow, Engin.
Milsom, S. F. C., QC, MA, FBA Fellow
Ní Mhaonaigh, Máire, MA N.U.I., PhD N.U.I. U. Lectr., Anglo-Saxon, Norse and Celtic; Tutor; Fellow
Plaisted, Katrina C., BSc Lond., PhD Camb. U. Lectr., Psychology; Fellow
Prince, R. H., PhD Lond., MA ScD Fellow
Ravelhofer, Barbara Fellow
Reid, G. A., MA PhD Sr. Bursar; Fellow
Robinson, C. J., CVO, MA Oxf., MusB Oxf., FRCO Organist and Dir. of Music; Fellow
Robinson, Col. R. H., OBE, MA Domestic Bursar; Fellow
Rublack, Ulinka C., MA Hamburg, PhD Camb. U. Asst. Lectr., History; Fellow
Saville, A. J., MA Sheff., MA Camb. Librarian; Fellow
Shah, Paul A., BA Camb. Fellow
Smithies, F., BA PhD Fellow
Spencer, Jonathan B., BSc S'ton., PhD S'ton. Fellow, Chemistry
Watson, G. G., MA Oxf., MA Camb. Fellow
Whitmarsh, Timothy J. G., MA Camb., MPhil Camb. Fellow
Wight, D. G. D., MA MB BChir Assoc. Lectr., Pathology; Fellow
Wilkes, M. V., MA PhD Hon. ScD, FRS, FEng Fellow
Wood, Rupert A., BA Lond., PhD Camb. Affiliated Lectr., Modern and Mediaeval Languages; Fellow
Zimmermann, R. Arthur Goodhart Prof., Legal Science (1998-99); Fellow

Other Staff: 64 Fellows

TRINITY COLLEGE

Tel: (01223) 338400 Fax: (01223) 338564

Adeye, Adekunle O., MPhil Camb., PhD Camb. Fellow
Allen, W. Sidney, MA PhD, FBA Fellow
Arcus, Vickery L., PhD Camb. Fellow
Ashmead, John, MA PhD Fellow
Atiyah, Sir Michael, OM, Hon. DSc Bonn, Hon. DSc Warw., Hon. DSc Durh., Hon. DSc St And., Hon. DSc Trinity(Dub.), Hon. DSc Chic., Hon. DSc Edin., Hon. DSc Essex, Hon. DSc Lond., Hon. DSc Sus., Hon. DSc Ghent, Hon. DSc Helsinki, Hon. DSc Reading, Hon. DSc Leic., Hon. DSc Rutgers, Hon. DSc Salamanca, Hon. DSc Wales, Hon. DSc Qu., Hon. DSc Keele, Hon. DSc Birm., Hon. DMath Wat., Hon. DMaths Lebanese, Hon. Doctorat Montr., Hon. DUniv Open(UK), Hon. DSc UMIST, Hon. DSc Prague, Hon. DSc Oxf., Hon. DSc Chinese HK, Hon. DSc Brown, MA PhD Hon. ScD, FRS, Hon. FEng ; Fellow
Balasubramanian, Shankar, MA Camb., PhD Camb. Fellow, Organic Chemistry
Barlow, Horace B., MA MB BChir ScD, FRS Fellow
Barrett, Paul M., BA Camb. Fellow
Batchelor, George K., Hon. ScD Grenoble, Hon. ScD T.U. Denmark, Hon ScD Mich., Hon. DSc McG., MSc Melb., PhD, FRS Fellow
Battye, Richard A., MA Camb., PhD Camb. Fellow
Berridge, Sir Michael, BSc Lond., PhD Camb., FRS Hon. Prof., Cell Signalling; Fellow
Borcherds, Richard E., MA Camb., PhD Camb. RS Res. Prof., Mathematics; Fellow
Bradfield, John R. G., CBE, MA PhD Hon. LLD Fellow
Bray, Joseph D., BA Camb., PhD Camb. Fellow
Browne, Rev. Arnold S., MA Oxf., MSc Sur., PhD Camb. Dean of Chapel; Fellow
Carrell, Robin W., BSc Cant., MB ChB NZ, MA PhD, FRSNZ, FRCP, FRCPath Prof., Haematology; Fellow
Cassels, John W. S., MA Edin., PhD, FRS Fellow
Champernowne, David G., MA Oxf., MA Camb., FBA Fellow
Collinson, Patrick, CBE, PhD Lond., Hon. DLitt Kent, Hon. DLitt Trinity(Dub.), Hon. LittD Sheff., Hon. DUniv York(UK), MA, FBA, FRHistS Fellow
Cox, Anthony, R. W. Fellow
Davidson, John F., Hon. DSc Aston, Hon. DSc Toulouse, MA PhD ScD, FEng, FRS Fellow
Dawe, Roger D., MA PhD LittD Lectr., Classics; Fellow
Duke, Thomas A. J., MA Camb., PhD Camb. Res. Royal Soc. Fellow, Physics; Fellow
Easterling, H. John, MA Sec. of Council; Fellow
Fairbrother, Jeremy R. F., MA Oxf., MBA Manc., DPhil Oxf., PhD Camb.. Sr. Bursar; Fellow
Ferrari, Ronald L., BSc Lond., MA Camb., ScD Camb. Fellow
Fox, Eustace N., MA ScD Fellow
Gaskell, J. Philip W., MA PhD LittD Fellow
Glauert, Richard H., MA PhD Fellow
Glynn, Ian M., MA MB BChir MD PhD, FRS Fellow
Green, Andrew G., MA Camb. Fellow
Green, Dennis H., DrPhil Basle, MA, FBA Fellow
Hamer, Neil K., MA PhD Fellow
Handley, Eric W., CBE, Hon. Dr Athens, MA, FBA Fellow
Hare, Ivan C., LLB Lond., BCL Oxf., MA Camb. U. Asst. Lectr., Law; Steward; Fellow
Haselwimmer, R. Kurt W., MA Camb. Fellow
Hopkinson, Neil, MA PhD Lectr., Classics; Tutor; Fellow
Horton, Julian A., MA Camb., MPhil Camb. Fellow

Hunt, Julian C. R., MA Camb., PhD Camb., FRS Hon. Prof., Fluid Mechanics; Fellow
Huxley, Sir Andrew, OM, Hon. MD Humboldt, Hon. MD Saar, Hon. DSc Brun., Hon. DSc Harv., Hon. DSc Hyd., Hon. DSc Keele, Hon. DSc Maryland, Hon. DSc Penn., Hon. DSc Sheff., Hon. DSc Leic., Hon. DSc Lond., Hon. DSc St And., Hon. DSc Aston, Hon. DSc W.Aust., Hon. DSc Oxf., Hon. LLD Birm., Hon. LLD Dund., Hon. DUniv York(UK), Hon. DHL N.Y., Hon. Dr Marseilles, Hon. ScD E.Anglia, Hon. ScD Camb., MA, Hon. FEng, FRS Fellow
Johnson, Paley, MA PhD ScD Fellow
Jolowicz, J. Anthony, QC, Hon. Dr. Mexico Natnl., MA Fellow
Kabir, Ananya J. Fellow
Kelley, David J., MA PhD Fellow
Khalfa, Jean, MA Lectr., French; Fellow
Khmelnitskii, David E., PhD Moscow Fellow
Kusakawa, Sachiko, MPhil Camb., PhD Camb. Asst. Lectr., History and Philosophy of Science; Fellow
Lackenby, Marc, BA Camb. Fellow
Laslett, T. Peter R., CBE, Hon. DUniv Open(UK), MA LittD, FBA Fellow
Lauterpacht, Elihu, CBE, QC, MA Camb., LLM Camb. Hon. Prof., International Law; Fellow
Longuet-Higgins, Michael S., MA PhD, FRS Fellow
Marenbon, John A., BA PhD Lectr., History of Philosophy; Fellow
Marlow, Richard K., MA MusB PhD, FRCO Dir. of Music; Fellow
Marrian, Denis H., CVO, MSc Manc., MA PhD Praelector; Fellow
Maule, Jeremy F., MA Oxf., MA Lond. Lectr., English; Fellow
McKitterick, David J., MA Camb., LittD Camb., FBA Tutor; Librarian; Fellow
McLachlan, Andrew D., MA PhD ScD, FRS Fellow
Merton, Patrick A., MA MB BChir MD, FRS, FRCP Fellow
Mitchell, Brian R., MA Aberd., PhD Fellow
Natarajan, Priyamvada Fellow
Neild, Robert R., MA Fellow
Neuberger, Michael S., MA Lond., PhD Lond., FRS Lectr., Cellular Biology; Fellow
Panagopoulos, Christos, PhD Camb. Fellow
Perry, Malcolm J., MA PhD Lectr., Mathematics; Fellow
Quinn, Michael J., PhD Camb. Fellow
Radzinowicz, Sir Leon, Hon. LLD Leic., Hon. LLD Edin., LLD Rome, LLD Cracow, LLD Camb., MA, FBA Fellow
Read, Charles J., MA PhD Lectr., Mathematics; Fellow
Riordan, Oliver M., MA Camb. Fellow
Roth, Sir Martin, Hon. ScD Trinity(Dub.), Hon. ScD Indiana, MD Camb., MD Lond., MA, FRCP, FRCPsych, FRS Fellow
Runciman, Lord, CBE, MA, FBA Fellow
Salingar, Leo G., MA Fellow
Sen, Amartya K., MA Camb., PhD Camb., Hon. DLitt Oxf., Hon. DLitt Stockholm Hon. DHumLitt Bard, Hon. Dr Kiel, FBA Master
Serjeantson, Richard W., MPhil Camb. Fellow
Simm, A. Paul, CBE, MPhil Jr. Bursar; Fellow
Squires, Gordon L., MA PhD Fellow
Striker, Gisela, DrPhil Gött. Laurence Prof., Ancient Philosophy; Fellow
Taras-Semchuk, J. P. Damian, BA Camb. Fellow
Tobias, Steven M., MA Camb., PhD Camb. Fellow
Unwin, P. Nigel T., PhD, FRS Fellow
Webber, M. Teresa J., MA Oxf., MPhil Oxf. Lectr., Palaeography; Fellow
Weeds, Alan G., MA PhD ScD Lectr., Biochemistry; Fellow
Wingfield, Paul, BA MPhil PhD Lectr., Music; Tutor; Fellow
Winter, Gregory P., CBE, MA PhD, FRS Fellow
Other Staff: 64 Fellows

TRINITY HALL

Tel: (01223) 332500 Fax: (01223) 332537

Adams, Nicholas S., MA *Camb.*, PhD *Camb.* Res. Fellow, Social Theory and Theology

Ancarani, Lorenzo U., PhD Res. Fellow, Physics

Calne, Sir Roy, MS *Lond.*, MA, FRCS, FRS Prof., Surgery; Prof. Fellow

Collins, Douglas L. Campaign Dir.; Supernumerary Fellow

Elliott, Charles M., MA PhD Dean; Chaplain; Staff Fellow

Harrison, Nicholas D., MA *Camb.*, PhD *Camb.* U. Asst. Lectr., French; Tutor; Staff Fellow

Hobson, Michael P., MA *Camb.*, PhD *Camb.* Fellow, Astrophysics

Hollfelder, Florian, MPhil *Camb.* Res. Fellow, Bio-organic Chemistry

Lennard, John C., MA DPhil Newton Trust Lectr., English; Staff Fellow, Engl.

Liebling, Alison, MA PhD Tutor; Staff Fellow, Criminol.

Lloyd, Stephen L. Res. Fellow, Materials Science

Lyons, Sir John, MA *Camb.*, PhD *Camb.*, LittD *Camb.*, FBA Master*

Montgomery, James E., MA *Glas.*, PhD *Glas.* Staff Fellow, Oriental Studies

Pope, Susan E., MA *Camb.* Bursar; Steward; Staff Fellow

Raban, Sandra G., MA PhD Sr. Tutor; Staff Fellow, Hist.

Rubenstein, David, MD *Lond.*, MA, FRCP Assoc. Lectr., Medicine; Staff Fellow

Slater, Wendy N., MA *Manc.* Res. Fellow, Modern Russian History and Politics

Wlodarczyk, Marta A. H., MPhil *Camb.*, PhD *Camb.* Res. Fellow, Greek Philosophy

Womack, Joanna M., MA *Camb.* U. Treasurer; Prof. Fellow

Other Staff: 24 Fellows

WOLFSON COLLEGE

Tel: (01223) 335900 Fax: (01223) 335908

Baker, Anne M. E., MA *Camb.*, PhD *Camb.* Jr. Res. Fellow, Crystallography

Brown, Jason P., PhD *Camb.* Wolfson-Parke-Davies Jr. Res. Fellow, Neuroscience

Buchan, Iain E., BSc *Liv.*, MB ChB *Liv.* Sr. Res. Fellow, Medical Informatics; Fellow

Chang, N. Jennifer, PhD *Camb.* Universities China Committee Fellow, Chinese History and Language

Chatterji, Joya, PhD *Camb.* Sr. Res. Fellow, History; Fellow

Clode, D. M., BSc *Birm.*, PhD *Birm.* Fellow

Collins, L. A., LLB *Col.*, LLB *Camb.*, MA *Camb.*, LLD *Camb.*, FBA Fellow

Davis, Jennifer S., BA *Sarah Lawrence*, MSc *Lond.*, PhD *Boston* Sr. Res. Fellow, Law

Day, I., MSc *Natal*, PhD Rolls-Royce Fellow, Engineering

Dupree, Marguerite W., DPhil *Oxf.* Fellow

Edwards, O. M., MD *Lond.*, MA Assoc. Lectr., Medicine; Fellow

Emerton, Norma, MA *Oxf.*, PhD *Camb.* Sr. Tutor, History of Science; Fellow

Franks, D., BSc *Birm.*, PhD Sec., Sch. of Biol. Scis.; Fellow

Gatiss, J., MA U. Lectr., Engineering; Fellow

Gonzalez, Maria I., PhD *Camb.* Wolfson-Parke-Davies Jr. Res. Fellow, Neuroscience

Harte, Thomas P., MSc *Edin.* Jr. Res. Fellow, Computer Science

Henderson, J. S., BA *Newcastle(UK)*, PhD *Lond.* Wellcome Trust Fellow, History of Population and Social Structure

Hepworth, Mark B., PhD *Brist.* Wolfson-Parke-Davies Jr. Res. Fellow, Neuroscience

Hughes, John, MA *Camb.*, Dr *Liège*, PhD *Lond.*, FRS Hon. Prof., Neuropharmacology; Dir., Parke-Davis Res. Unit; Fellow

Hyndman, Patricia, LLM *Lond.* Fellow, Law

Johnson, E., MA *Essex* Fellow

Kirkman, W. P., MA *Oxf.*, MA *Camb.* Dir., Press Fellow Programme; Fellow

Lee, Aaron M., PhD *Camb.* Jr. Res. Fellow, Theoretical Chemistry

Lee, E. Stewart, MEng *McG.*, PhD *Tor.* Res. Prof., Centre for Communications Systems Research; Fellow

Lovatt, Marie, PhD Tutor; Fellow

Maunder, J. W., MSc *Lond.*, PhD *Lond.* Dir., Med. Entomol. Centre; Fellow

McCallum, D. P. F., MA Sr. Asst. Registrary, Bd. of Grad. Studies; Fellow

Mead, Timothy, PhD *Camb.* U. Registrary; Fellow

Meier, Sonja, LLM *Lond.* Asst. Lectr., Law; Fellow

Naughton, J. Dep. Dir., Press Fellow Programme; Fellow

Orsini, Francesca U. Asst. Lectr., Oriental Studies; Fellow

Peabody, Norbet, AM *Harv.*, PhD *Harv.* Grad. in Res., South Asian Studies; Fellow

Reid, Alison M., PhD *Durh.* Wolfson-Parke-Davis Jr. Res. Fellow, Neuroscience

Rennie, G. W. J., MA *Aberd.*, MA *Camb.* Sr. Asst. Registrary; Fellow

Rhodes James, Sir Robert, MA *Oxf.* Fellow

Richardson, Michael E., MA *Camb.* Sec. and Dir., Continuing Education; Fellow

Seagrave, J. R., BA *Durh.*, MA *Camb.*, MA *Oxf.*, PhD *Birm.* Bursar; Fellow

Shaw-Miller, Lindsey, MA *Camb.* Speelman Fellow, Dutch and Flemish Art

Shepherd, M. E., MA PhD Jr. Res. Fellow, Historical Geography

Smith, S. Tyrell, BSc *Wales*, MA *Camb.*, PhD *Brist.* Dep. Sec., Local Examinations Syndicate; Fellow

Stelmashenko, Nadia A., PhD *Camb.* Jr. Res. Fellow, Physics

Thornton, John M. C., PhD *Wales* Wolfson-Hitachi Fellow, Microelectronics

Todd, Christopher J., MA *Camb.*, PhD *Durh.* Sr. Res. Assoc., Community Medicine; Fellow

West, Janet, MA PhD Fellow

Wilkinson, I. M. S., BSc *Manc.*, MD *Manc.*, MA, FRCP Assoc. Lectr., Clinical Medicine; Fellow

Wilson, Anthony K., MA *Camb.* Chief Exec., Cambridge Univ. Press; Fellow

Wilson, D. V., MSc *Durh.*, PhD *Brad.*, MA Fellow

Wilson, David R., BLitt *Oxf.*, MA *Oxf.*, MA *Camb.*, FSA Curator, Aerial Photography; Fellow

Other Staff: 48 Fellows

CONTACT OFFICERS

Academic affairs. Secretary General of the Faculties: Livesey, David A., BSc *Lond.*, MA *Camb.*, PhD *Camb.* (Emm.)

Accommodation. Secretary, Accommodation Syndicate: Blanning, Nicky

Admissions (first degree). Newbould, Anne, BA *Manc.*

Admissions (higher degree). Brown, Katherine L., BA *Oxf.*, MA *Lond.*

Adult/continuing education. Secretary and Director, Continuing Education: Richardson, Michael E., MA *Camb.* (Wolfs.)

Alumni. Jardine, Jenny

Archives. University Archivist: Zutshi, Patrick N. R., MA *Camb.*, PhD *Camb.*, FSA (Corp.)

Careers. Secretary, Careers Service: Raban, Antony J., MA *Camb.* (Corp.)

Computing services. University Computer Officer: Stibbs, Richard J., MA *Camb.* (Down.)

Consultancy services. Director: Jennings, Richard C., BSc *Sus.*, DPhil *Sus.*

Credit transfer. Principal Assistant Registrary: Clark, Alan, MA *Camb.*, PhD *Camb.* (Fitz.)

Development/fund-raising. Director, Development Office: Smithson, Michael (Qu.)

Distance education. Secretary and Director, Continuing Education: Richardson, Michael E., MA *Camb.* (Wolfs.)

Equal opportunities. Assistant Registrary: Hunt, Felicity, MA *Essex*, PhD *Camb.* (Newn.)

Estates and buildings/works and services. Acting Director, Estate Management and Building Service: Bienias, Michael R., BA *Oxf.*

Examinations. Deputy Registrary: Branson, Nicholas J. B. A., MA *Camb.*, PhD *Camb.* (Darw.)

Finance. Deputy Treasurer: Mardles, Peter J., MA *Camb.* (S.Edm.)

General enquiries. Administrative Officer: Baker, Susannah M., MA *Camb.*

Health services. Administrative Officer: Garrod, Yvonne B., BSc *St And.*, PhD *St And.* (Wolfs.)

Industrial liaison. Director: Jennings, Richard C., BSc *Sus.*, DPhil *Sus.*

International office. Moss, Matthew N. H., MA *Camb.*

Library (chief librarian). Librarian: Fox, Peter K., BA *Lond.*, MA *Sheff.*, MA *Camb.* (Selw.)

Library (enquiries). Head of Reader Services: Harper, Anthony C., BSc *Newcastle(UK)*

Public relations, information and marketing. Administrative Officer: Baker, Susannah M., MA *Camb.*

Publications. Administrative Officer: Baker, Susannah M., MA *Camb.*

Quality assurance and accreditation. Principal Assistant Registrary: Rennie, Graeme W. J., MA *Aberd.*, MA *Camb.*

Safety. Williams, John H., MSc *Lond.*, MA *Camb.* (Hug.)

Scholarships, awards, loans. Principal Assistant Registrary: Benton, Alice M., MA *Camb.*

Schools liaison. Newbould, Anne, BA *Manc.*

Sport and recreation. Director of Physical Education: Lemons, Tony D., BA *Open(UK)*, MA *Camb.* (Hug.)

Staff development and training. Newbold, Linda, BA *Leic.*, MA *Camb.* (Wolfs.)

Student union. President, Cambridge University Students' Union

Student welfare/counselling. Head: Phippen, Charles M., BSc *Kent*

Students from other countries. Moss, Matthew N. H., MA *Camb.*

Students with disabilities. Administrative Officer: Garrod, Yvonne B., BSc *St And.*, PhD *St And.* (Wolfs.)

University press. Deputy Chief Executive and Managing Director, Publishing Division: Mynott, R. Jeremy, MA *Camb.*, PhD *Camb.* (Corp.)

Women. Assistant Registrary: Hunt, Felicity, MA *Essex*, PhD *Camb.* (Newn.)

CAMPUS/COLLEGE HEADS

Christ's College, Cambridge, England CB2 3BU. (Tel: (01223) 334900; Fax: (01223) 334967.) Master: Munro, Alan J., MA *Camb.*, PhD *Camb.*

Churchill College, Cambridge, England CB3 0DS. (Tel: (01223) 336000; Fax: (01223) 336180.) Master: Boyd, Sir John, KCMG, MA *Yale*, MA *Camb.*

Clare College, Cambridge, England CB2 1TL. (Tel: (01223) 333200; Fax: (01223) 333219.) Master: Hepple, Prof. Bob A., QC, BA *Witw.*, LLB *Witw.*, LLB *Camb.*, MA *Camb.*, LLD *Camb.*

Clare Hall, Cambridge, England CB3 9AL. (Tel: (01223) 332360; Fax: (01223) 332333.) President: Beer, Prof. Dame Gillian P. K., BLitt *Oxf.*, MA *Oxf.*, MA *Camb.*, LittD *Camb.*, FBA

Corpus Christi College, Cambridge, England CB2 1RH. (Tel: (01223) 338000; Fax: (01223) 338061.) Master: Wrigley, Prof. Sir Tony, MA *Camb.*, PhD *Camb.*, FBA

Darwin College, Cambridge, England CB3 9EU. (Tel: (01223) 335600; Fax: (01223) 335667.) Master: Lloyd, Prof. Sir Geoffrey, MA *Camb.*, PhD *Camb.*, FBA

Downing College, Cambridge, England CB2 1DQ. (Tel: (01223) 334800; Fax: (01223) 467934.) Master: King, Prof. David A., BSc Witw., PhD Witw., ScD E.Anglia, FRS

Emmanuel College, Cambridge, England CB2 3AP. (Tel: (01223) 334200; Fax: (01223) 334426.) Master: Ffowcs Williams, Prof. John E., BSc S'ton., MA Camb., PhD S'ton., ScD Camb., FEng

Fitzwilliam College, Cambridge, England CB3 0DG. (Tel: (01223) 332000; Fax: (01223) 464162.) Master: Cuthbert, Prof. Alan W., BSc St And., BPharm Lond., MA Camb., PhD Lond., Hon. LLD Dund., DSc De Mont., Hon. DSc Aston, FRS

Girton College, Cambridge, England CB3 0JG. (Tel: (01223) 338999; Fax: (01223) 338896.) Mistress: Strathern, Prof. Marilyn, MA Camb., PhD Camb., FBA

Gonville and Caius College, Cambridge, England CB2 1TA. (Tel: (01223) 332400; Fax: (01223) 332456.) Master: McKendrick, Neil, MA Camb.

Homerton College, Cambridge, England CB2 2PH. (Tel: (01223) 411141; Fax: (01223) 411622.) Principal: Pretty, Kate, MA Camb., PhD Camb.

Hughes Hall, Cambridge, England CB1 2EW. (Tel: (01223) 334893; Fax: (01223) 311179.) President: Richards, Peter, MA Camb., PhD Lond., MD Camb., FRCP

Jesus College, Cambridge, England CB5 8BL. (Tel: (01223) 339339; Fax: (01223) 324910.) Master: Crighton, Prof. D. G., PhD Lond., MA ScD, FRS

King's College, Cambridge, England CB2 1ST. (Tel: (01223) 350411; Fax: (01223) 314019.) Provost: Bateson, Prof. Patrick P. G., MA Camb., PhD Camb., ScD Camb., FRS

Lucy Cavendish College, Lady Margaret Road, Cambridge, England CB3 0BU. (Tel: (01223) 332190; Fax: (01223) 332178.) President: Perry of Southwark, Baroness, Hon. LLD Aberd., Hon. DEd Wolv., Hon. LLD S.Bank, Hon. LLD Bath, Hon. DLitt Sus., MA

Magdalene College, Cambridge, England CB3 0AG. (Tel: (01223) 332100; Fax: (01223) 63637.) Master: Gurdon, Prof. Sir John, BA Oxf., DPhil Oxf., Hon. DSc Oxf., FRS

New Hall, Cambridge, England CB3 0DF. (Tel: (01223) 762100; Fax: (01223) 352941.) President: Lonsdale, Anne M., MA Oxf., MA Camb.

Newnham College, Cambridge, England CB3 8DF. (Tel: (01223) 335700; Fax: (01223) 357898.) Principal: O'Neill, Onora S., CBE, MA Oxf., MA Camb., PhD Harv., FBA

Pembroke College, Cambridge, England CB2 1RF. (Tel: (01223) 338100; Fax: (01223) 338163.) Master: Tomkys, Sir Roger, KCMG, MA Oxf., MA Camb.

Peterhouse, Cambridge, England CB2 1RD. (Tel: (01223) 338200; Fax: (01223) 337578.) Master: Thomas, Prof. Sir John Meurig, PhD Wales, DSc Wales, Hon. LLD Wales, Hon. DLitt CNAA, Hon. DSc H.-W., Hon. DSc Birm., Hon. DUniv. Open(UK), MA ScD, FRS

Queens' College, Cambridge, England CB3 9ET. (Tel: (01223) 335511; Fax: (01223) 335522.) President: Eatwell, Lord, AM Harv., MA Camb., PhD Harv.

Selwyn College, Cambridge, England CB3 9DQ. (Tel: (01223) 335846; Fax: (01223) 335837.) Master: Harrison, Sir David, CBE, MA Camb., PhD Camb., ScD Camb., Hon. DUniv Keele, Hon. DSc Exe., FEng, FRSChem

Sidney Sussex College, Cambridge, England CB2 3HU. (Tel: (01223) 338800; Fax: (01223) 338884.) Master: Horn, Prof. Gabriel, BSc Birm., MD Birm., MA Camb., ScD Camb., FRS

St Catharine's College, Cambridge, England CB2 1RL. (Tel: (01223) 338300; Fax: (01223) 338340.) Master: English, Sir Terence, KBE, MB BS Lond., MA Camb., FRCS, FRCP

St Edmund's College, Cambridge, England CB3 0BN. (Tel: (01223) 336250; Fax: (1223) 336111.) Master: Heap, Prof. Robert B., CBE, BSc Nott., PhD Nott., Hon. DSc Nott., ScD, FIBiol, FRSChem, FRS

St John's College, Cambridge, England CB2 1TP. (Tel: (01223) 338600; Fax: (01223) 337720.) Master: Goddard, Prof. Peter, MA Camb., PhD Camb., ScD, FRS

Trinity College, Cambridge, England CB2 1TQ. (Tel: (01223) 338400; Fax: (01223) 338564.) Master: Sen, Amartya K., MA Camb., PhD Camb., Hon. DLitt Oxf., Hon. DLitt Stockholm, Hon. DHumLitt Bard, Hon. Dr Kiel, FBA

Trinity Hall, Cambridge, England CB2 1TJ. (Tel: (01223) 332500; Fax: (01223) 332537.) Master: Lyons, Sir John, MA Camb., PhD Camb., LittD Camb., FBA

Wolfson College, Cambridge, England CB3 9BB. (Tel: (01223) 335900; Fax: (01223) 335908.) President: Johnson, Gordon, MA Camb., PhD Camb.

[Information supplied by the institution as at 1 July 1998, and edited by the ACU]

UNIVERSITY OF CENTRAL ENGLAND IN BIRMINGHAM

Founded 1991; previously established as Birmingham Polytechnic, 1971

Member of the Association of Commonwealth Universities

Postal Address: Perry Barr, Birmingham, England B42 2SU
Telephone: (0121) 331 5595 **Fax**: (0121) 331 6358 **E-mail**: recruitment@uce.ac.uk
WWW: http://www.uce.ac.uk

PRO-CHANCELLOR AND CHAIRMAN OF THE BOARD OF GOVERNORS—Shaw, Frank L., JP, BCom, FCA, FCIS
VICE-CHANCELLOR*—Knight, Peter C., CBE, BSc York(UK), DPhil York(UK), Hon. DUniv York(UK), Hon. DSc Aston, FRAS
PRO-VICE-CHANCELLOR—Walkling, Prof. Philip H., BA MEd
PRO-VICE-CHANCELLOR—Tidmarsh, Prof. David H., BSc PhD, FIMechE
SECRETARY AND REGISTRAR—Penlington, Maxine, BA

GENERAL INFORMATION

History. The university, previously established as Birmingham Polytechnic (1971), was founded in 1991. The university's seven teaching campuses are scattered across Birmingham. The main campus, Perry Barr, is situated 5km north of the city centre.

First Degrees (see also United Kingdom Directory of Subjects to Study). BA, BEd, BEng, BSc, LLB.

Most courses may be taken full- or part-time. Full-time: 3 years; part-time: 3–6 years.

Higher Degrees (see also United Kingdom Directory of Subjects to Study). MA, MBA, MSc, MPhil, PhD.

MA: 1–2 years full-time or 2–4 years part-time; MBA: 1 year full-time or 2 years part-time; MPhil: 3 years full-time or 4 years part-time; PhD: 5 years full-time or 6 years part-time.

Language of Instruction. English. International applicants must pass an English entry test before being accepted on a course. Language lessons are available for those who need extra help once enrolled.

Libraries. Main library: over 300,000 volumes; about 1200 journals subscribed to.

Academic Year (1998–99). 21 September–11 December; 4 January–26 March; 19 April–25 June.

Income (1997–98). Total, £78,153,000.

Statistics. Staff (1998): 2563 (1087 academic, 1476 administrative/support). Students (1997–98): 23,883 (10,305 men, 13,578 women; 11,586 full-time, 12,297 part-time), including international 625.

FACULTIES/SCHOOLS

Birmingham Institute of Art and Design

Tel: (0121) 331 5801 Fax: (0121) 331 7814
Dean: Durman, Prof. Mick, MA MPhil
Secretary: Pitt, Marilyn

Built Environment

Tel: (0121) 331 5100 Fax: (0121) 356 9915
Dean: Low, Prof. Jim A., BArch MSc PhD
Secretary: Ross, Wendy

Business School

Tel: (0121) 331 5200 Fax: (0121) 331 6366
Dean: Pardesi, Prof. Upkar
Secretary: Oliver, Carol

Computing and Information Technology

Tel: (0121) 331 5600
Dean: Elkin, Prof. Judith C., BA, FLA

Conservatoire

Tel: (0121) 331 5901 Fax: (0121) 331 5906
Dean: Caird, Prof. George, MA, FRAM
Secretary: Cox, Andrea

Education

Tel: (0121) 331 6100
Dean: Buchanan, Prof. Stewart, BA MSc
Secretary: Summers, Hazel

Engineering and Computer Technology

Tel: (0121) 331 5401 Fax: (0121) 331 6315
Dean: Rogers, Prof. Graham, BSc MSc
Secretary: Smith, Patricia

Health and Community Care

Tel: (0121) 331 5500 Fax: (0121) 331 6306
Dean: Hitchen, Prof. Judith M., BSc PhD
Secretary: Gascoigne, Joy

Law and Social Sciences

Tel: (0121) 331 5901 Fax: (0121) 331 5906
Dean: Rouse, Prof. John, BA MA MSc
Secretary: Hill, Christine

ACADEMIC UNITS

Accountancy

Andrews, J. M., BCom MPhil   Sr. Lectr.
Bromiley, T.   Sr. Lectr.
Byrne, P. J., BSc, FCA   Sr. Lectr.
Calvert, P. M., FCA   Sr. Lectr.
Carpenter, D. J., BSc *Leeds*   Sr. Lectr.
Carter, G. M., BSc   Sr. Lectr.
Eve, J., BA MEd   Sr. Lectr.
Forth, G., BA MSocSc   Sr. Lectr.
Goulding, J. W., MBA *Aston*   Principal Lectr.
Grieve, K. M., BSc, FCA   Sr. Lectr.
Hayward, M. J., MEd MBA   Principal Lectr.
Jarvis, W. J., MSc   Principal Lectr.; Dep.
  Head*
Johnson, J. A., BSc   Sr. Lectr.
Jones, D., JP   Sr. Lectr.
Langford, B.   Sr. Lectr.
Mann, T.   Sr. Lectr.
Morgan, G. J., BA *Leic.*, MA *Lanc.*, PhD
  Warw.   Sr. Lectr.
Sergeant, M., BSc MBA   Sr. Lectr.
Stafford, A. P., BA   Principal Lectr.
Stokes-Harrison, D. N., FCA   Sr. Lectr.
Ullathorne, A. E., BA *Nott.*, MA *C.England*,
  FCA   Sr. Lectr.

**Advanced Manufacturing Technology,
School of**

Draper, Alan, BSc MSc PhD   Course Dir.
Gray, David, MSc   Sr. Academic; Course Dir.
Holden, Nick, BSc   Sr. Lectr.
Kempson, John, BSc, FIEE   Head*
Kumar, Krishna, BTech MSc PhD   Course Dir.
McQueen, Keith, MSc PhD   Sr. Academic;
  Course Dir.
Meakin, Dave   Course Dir.
Nagpal, Baldev, MEng PhD   Sr. Lectr.
Shirvani, Bez, BSc PhD   Sr. Lectr.
Snaith, B., MSc PhD   Sr. Lectr.

Art, see also Birmingham Inst. of Art and
Design

Blundell, S.   Course Dir.
Davies, T., MPhil MA   Course Dir.
Holland, M., MA   Head of Painting
Hughes, Prof. A.   Head*
Inglis, J., MA   Sr. Lectr., Fine Art Painting
Jones, N., BA   Sr. Officer/Workshop Manager
Mabb, D., MA   Course Dir.
Permar, R., MA   Head of Sculpture
Swift, J., MA PhD   Prof.; Head, Sch. of Art
  Educn.
Vaudeau, J., MA   Head of Printmaking

Theoretical and Historical Studies, School of

Noszlopy, G.   Course Leader
Quickenden, K.   Head*

Birmingham Conservatoire

Tel: (0121) 331 5901
Cross, A.   Course Dir.
Daw, S.   Principal Lectr.
Holroyd, M.   Co-ordinator
Johnson, P.   Head, P.G. Studies
Racz, M.   Course Dir.

Organ Studies

Bruce-Payne, D., BMus, FRCO   Sr. Lectr.
Saint, D., BA BMus, FRCO   Sr. Lectr.; Head*

Birmingham Institute of Art and Design

**Fashion, Textiles and Three-Dimensional
Design**

Beard, D.   Sr. Lectr., Industrial Design
Chapman, P., BA   Sr. Lectr., Interior Design
Clarke, M.   Sr. Lectr., Theatre Design
Cookesy, R., BA   Sr. Lectr., Furniture
Doona, L.   Sr. Lectr., Theatre Design
Edge, S.   Sr. Lectr., Interior Design
Fothergill, A., BA   Sr. Lectr., Embroidery
Gale, C., BA PhD   Sr. Lectr., Computer Aided
  Design
Goodall, T.   Sr. Lectr.
Griffiths, G.   Sr. Lectr., Interior Design
Hastings, M.   Sr. Lectr., Industrial Design
Hodgetts, K.   Sr. Lectr.
Jerrard, R., MDes *RCA*, PhD   Principal Lectr.,
  Design Management
Jones, C.   Sr. Lectr., Industrial Design
Law, J.   Sr. Lectr.
Little, M.   Sr. Lectr., Constructed Textiles
Malem, W., MBA   Sr. Lectr., Fashion
Malkin, N., MA   Sr. Lectr., Ceramics and Glass
Manning, B.   Sr. Lectr., Fashion
Margan, J.   Principal Lectr., Printed Textiles
Puxley, D., MA   Principal Lectr., Ceramics and
  Glass
Rowe, D., MDes *RCA*   Sr. Lectr., Furniture
Snell, R., MA   Principal Lectr., Furniture
Suntharalingham, P., BSc   Sr. Lectr., Computer
  Aided Design
Tranbusti, B.   Sr. Lectr., Fashion
Vernon, M.   Sr. Lectr., Printed Textiles
Waddell, G.   Sr. Lectr., Fashion
Welsh, C.   Sr. Lectr., Embroidery
Whiles, M.   Principal Lectr., Constructed
  Textiles
Wilkinson, R., BA   Sr. Lectr., Furniture
Woolley, Prof. M., MDes *RCA*, BA
  PhD   Principal Lectr., Design Research

Foundation and Community Studies

Tel: (0121) 331 5775
Allen, T.   Sr. Lectr.
Bradley, S.   Sr. Lectr.
Crutchley, B.   Sr. Lectr.
Davies, K.   Sr. Lectr.
Hind, E.   Sr. Lectr.
Wilson, D.   Sr. Lectr.

Jewellery, School of

Amatt, A.   Sr. Lectr.
Fisher, J. S.   Sr. Lectr.
Kynes, J.   Sr. Lectr.
Slusarczuk, P.   Sr. Lectr.

Built Environment, Faculty of

Architecture, School of

Madden, P.   Head*

Housing, School of

Adamczuk, Henryk   Sr. Lectr.
Coatham, Veronica   Head*
Dixon, Andrew   Sr. Lectr.
Griffiths, Mary   Sr. Lectr.
Hill, Anne   Sr. Lectr.
Turkington, Richard   Sr. Lectr.; Dir. of Res.

Landscape Architecture, School of

Cassidy, D.   Head*

Planning, School of

Chapman, D. W.   Prof.; Head*
Dickins, I. S. J., BSc(Eng) MSc   Centro
  Principal Lectr.
Hammersley, R., BSc MCD PhD   Principal
  Lectr.
Ingram, M. I., BA   Sr. Lectr.
Jackson, M., BA MSc   Principal Lectr.
Jones, H., BSc(Econ) MSocSci   Sr. Lectr.
Pratt, D.   Sr. Lectr.
Tate, J. C., BSc(Econ) MA   Sr. Lectr.
Wood, C., BSc MA   Sr. Lectr.

Property and Construction

Badman, J., BSc MSc   Head*
Barrett, P. A., LLB   Sr. Lectr.
Blackburn, R. W., BSc   Sr. Lectr.
Blakey, J. A., BSc   Sr. Lectr.
Boyle, C. F., BEng BSc MSc MSocSci   Sr. Lectr.
Cemm, S. J.   Sr. Lectr.
Crofts, J. D., BSc   Sr. Lectr.
Davies, J. E. D., MSc   Sr. Lectr.
Dent, P.   Sr. Lectr.
Grimmett, D. L., BSc LLM   Principal Lectr.
Jordan, R., BSc LLB   Sr. Lectr.
Kelley, G. A.   Sr. Lectr.
Livette, M., MBA   Sr. Lectr.
Madill, W., BSc   Sr. Lectr.
McCabe, S., BSc MSc   Sr. Lectr.
Mitchell, R. J., BSc   Sr. Lectr.
Morgan, S.   Sr. Lectr.
Orr, K.   Sr. Lectr.
Rudge, D.   Sr. Lectr.
Rumball, M. A., BSc   Principal Lectr.
Russell, J.   Sr. Lectr.
Sansom, R.   Principal Lectr.
Schafir, R., BSc MSc PhD   Sr. Lectr.
Shabha, G.   Sr. Lectr.
Templeton, R., BSc   Sr. Lectr.
Thompson, B. C., MBA   Sr. Lectr.
Uzzell, G. D.   Sr. Lectr.
Yarnell, A., BSc   Sr. Lectr.

Business School

Business

Alexander, J.   Principal Lectr.
Barlow, G. L., MBA MSc   Sr. Lectr.
Boait, J. E., BSc MSc   Sr. Lectr.
Bowles, M. L., BA PhD   Sr. Lectr.
Curwin, J., BA MSc MBA   Principal Lectr.
Fletcher, B., BA(Econ) MA(Econ)   Course Dir.
Furnival, J. B., BA MBA   Principal Lectr.
Haq, M. A., MS *Indiana*, MA PhD   Sr. Lectr.
Johnson, J., BA DrPhil   Head*
Jones, B. G., MSc   Sr. Lectr.
Lukeman, A. E., BA MA   Sr. Lectr.
Martin, C. J., MA *Camb.*   Principal Lectr.
McCann, M. V., BA   Sr. Lectr.
Walker, P. K., BA(Econ) MBA   Sr. Lectr.

Economics

Embley, Paul E., BA *Leic.*, MA *Leic.*   Sr. Lectr.
Fortey, David W., BSocSc *Birm.*   Sr. Lectr.
Goodkin, Debbie, BA MSc   Sr. Lectr.
Haywood, Susan, BAEcon *CNAA*, MA *Leic.*   Sr.
  Lectr.
Jarman, Howard W., BSc(Econ) *Lond.*, MSc
  Wales, PhD *Lough.*   Sr. Lectr.
Mabbett, Alan J., BA MSc   Principal Lectr.
McDonagh, John, BSc *Lond.*, MSc *Lond.*   Sr.
  Lectr.

Nayar, Narinder, MSocSc Birm., PhD Birm.   Sr. Lectr.

O'Sullivan, George, BA Camb., MA Camb., MSc Birm., MEd Birm.   Principal Lectr.

Ramsay, David I., BSc(Econ) Birm., MSocSc Birm.   Head*

Romp, Graham, BScEcon S'ton., MAEcon Warw.   Sr. Lectr.

Seth, Manohar, MA Punjab, LLB Punjab, PhD Birm.   Sr. Lectr.

Wilkinson, John, BA E.Anglia, MA Leic.   Sr. Lectr.

Finance

Bentley, P.   Sr. Lectr.
Burley, T., BSc MSc   Sr. Lectr.
Coulson, J., BA Camb., MSc Warw.   Sr. Lectr.
Curry, S. J., BA MA   Principal Lectr.
Davis, J., MA   Sr. Lectr.
Foard, D. N., BSc   Sr. Lectr.
Hooper, J. G., MBA   Sr. Lectr.
Hukwulobelu, O.   Sr. Lectr.
Hussain, J. G., BA MSocSc PhD   Sr. Lectr.
Morris, R., LLB   Sr. Lectr.
Pickford, J.   Sr. Lectr.
Underhill, T., BA   Sr. Lectr.
Whittington, D., BA   Sr. Lectr.
Winstone, D. R., BA MA   Head*

Management

Bray, J.   Sr. Lectr.
Foss, P.   Sr. Lectr.
Meachem, L.   Head*
Wild, A.   Sr. Lectr.

Marketing and Languages

Armstrong, B. L. A., BA MBA   Sr. Lectr.
Baty, R., BA MSc   Principal Lectr.
Bolton, D., BA LLB MBA   Sr. Lectr.
Chapman, L., BA   Sr. Lectr.
Frame, A., BA Durh., MA CNAA   Sr. Lectr.
Gomez-Sanchez, G., LicFilos&Let Granada, MA Birm., MIntS Birm.   Sr. Lectr.
Hillin, G., MBA   Sr. Lectr.
Jones, L., MA Oxf., MPhil Lond.   Sr. Lectr.
Laycock, P.   Sr. Lectr.
Liddicott, C., BA Hull, LèsL Nantes, LèsL Lille   Sr. Lectr.
MacKay, S., BA MBA   Principal Lectr.
Moffatt, I., MA Glas.   Sr. Lectr.
Page, J.   Principal Lectr.
Richardson, J. M., BSc MPhil   Sr. Lectr.
Robinson, G.   Sr. Lectr.
Rosindale, L., BA Open(UK)   Sr. Lectr.
Tavares, S., BA   Sr. Lectr.
Wyde, I., LLB Lond., MBA Aston   Sr. Lectr.

Clinical Nursing Studies, School of

Atkins, D.   Sr. Lectr.
Atkins, K.   Sr. Lectr.
Dodson, A.   Sr. Lectr.
England, A.   Sr. Lectr.
Fitzgibbon, S.   Sr. Lectr.
Hall, J.   Sr. Lectr.
Harley, J.   Sr. Lectr.
Harvey, M.   Sr. Lectr.
Jones, S.   Sr. Lectr.
Kitchen, K.   Sr. Lectr.
Malem, F.   Sr. Lectr.
O'Grady, K.   Sr. Lectr.
Philpott, R.   Sr. Lectr.
Phipps, H.   Sr. Lectr.
Prittaway, D.   Sr. Lectr.
Rickard, N.   Sr. Lectr.
Saunders, P.   Sr. Lectr.
Stevens, P.   Sr. Lectr.
Symonds, B.   Sr. Lectr.
Viney, T.   Sr. Lectr.
Vint, P.   Sr. Lectr.
Walton, J.   Sr. Lectr.
Whittle, T.   Sr. Lectr.
Williams, L.   Head*
Winning, D.   Sr. Lectr.
Wragg, K.   Sr. Lectr.

Computer Science, School of

Campbell, William, MA MSc   Sr. Lectr.
Clarke, Robert, BSc   Principal Lectr.
Cresswell, Ian, BSc PhD   Sr. Lectr.

Elkington, John H., BA MA MSc   Principal Lectr.
Etheridge, David M., BSc MPhil PhD   Sr. Lectr.
Lewis, Anthony D., BSc   Sr. Lectr.
Ratcliffe, Martyn, BSc MSc   Sr. Lectr.
Riley, Richard, BSc MSc   Head*
Sarna, S., BSc MSc   Sr. Lectr.
Simpson, Rupert, BSc MSc PhD   Sr. Lectr.
Wilkinson, David, BSc MSc   Sr. Lectr.
Winfield, Michael J., MTech   Principal Lectr.

Continuing Care and Community Nursing, School of

Abrahams, A.   Sr. Lectr.
Barnes, E.   Sr. Lectr.
Beattie, J.   Sr. Lectr.
Bennett, C.   Sr. Lectr.
Brown, R.   Principal Lectr.
Chilton, S.   Sr. Lectr.
Coad, R.   Sr. Lectr.
Cunnliffe, P.   Sr. Lectr.
Gossett, J.   Sr. Lectr.
Green, B.   Sr. Lectr.
Hull, A.   Sr. Lectr.
Inman, C.   Sr. Lectr.
Jacob, F.   Sr. Lectr.
Jukes, M.   Sr. Lectr.
Kippax, C.   Sr. Lectr.
Mirden, D.   Sr. Lectr.
Nevin, G.   Sr. Lectr.
Nugent, B.   Sr. Lectr.
O'Rourke, M.   Sr. Lectr.
O'Shea, K.   Sr. Lectr.
Pajak, E.   Head*
Parry, B.   Principal Lectr.
Saxon, A.   Sr. Lectr.
Stafford, M.   Sr. Lectr.
Temple, A.   Sr. Lectr.
Wills, M.   Sr. Lectr.

Design, see Birmingham Inst. of Art and Des.

Education, Faculty of

Armstrong, S., BA   Programme Dir., Initial Teacher Training
Baptiste, G., MA   Lectr.; Co-ordinator
Biddulph, J., MA   Course Dir.; Lectr.
Cholmondeley, A., BA BSc MA   Dir., Sch. of Environmental Studies and Humanities; Lectr.
Coll, H., BA MEd   Dir., Sch. of Arts; Course Dir.; Lectr.
Davis, D., MEd   Course Dir.; Lectr.
Dewhirst, S., BA   Course Dir.; Lectr.
Finlow, S., BEd MEd   Course Dir.; Lectr.
Franklin, D., BEd PhD   Course Dir.; Lectr.
Hatcher, R., BA MA PhD   Res. Dir.; Course Dir.; Lectr.
Hill, C., BEd   Dir., Sch. of Lang. Studies and Vocational Trg.; Lectr.
Hoskyns, J., BA DPhil   Course Dir.; Lectr.
Norman, K., BA MAEd   Dir., Independent Learning Dept.; Lectr.
Rathbone, M., BPhil(Ed) MPhil   Programme Dir.; Lectr.
Rennalls, Y., BSc MSc   Course Dir.; Lectr.
Slater, S., BA BSc   Lectr.; Co-ordinator
Turner, J., BA   Course Dir.; Lectr.
Watkins, A., BEd   Lectr.; Co-ordinator
Watt, D., BA MA MEd   Course Dir.; Lectr.
Webster, F., BA   Course Dir.; Lectr.

Engineering, Electronics and Software, School of

Beddow, Ian, BSc   Course Dir.
Buzza, Phil, BSc   Sr. Lectr.
Dixey, Alan, MSc   Sr. Lectr.
Edwards, John, BSc PhD   Principal Lectr.
Emmett, Stan, BSc(Eng) MSc   Sr. Lectr.
Haigh, D.   Sr. Lectr.
Handley, S.   Course Dir.
Higginson, Prof. A., BSc PhD   Principal Lectr.
Lobban, P., BSc   Course Dir.
Martin, Jim, BEng   Sr. Lectr.
Morley-Smith, D., BSc   Head*
Noble, Chris, BSc   Sr. Lectr.
Stokes, Andy, BSc PhD   Course Dir.
Ullermayer, Lazlo, BSc MSc PhD   Sr. Lectr.
Whitehouse, Keith, BSc PhD   Sr. Lectr.

Wilcox, Tony, PhD   Sr. Lectr.
Wilkes, Mike, BSc   Programme Dir.
Workman, Neil, BSc   Sr. Lectr.

Engineering, Mechanical and Environmental, School of

Ashman, D., BSc PhD   Course Dir.
Atkinson, Gordon, BSc MSc PhD   Head*
Brunt, Mike, BSc PhD   Sr. Academic; Course Dir.
Daniels, M.   Principal Lectr.
Davenport, Tom, BA MSc   Sr. Lectr.
Davies, Haydn, BSc PhD   Course Dir.
Grant, Sandy, BSc   Course Dir.
Hayes, David, MSc PhD   Course Dir.
Keyworth, A., MSc PhD   Course Dir.
Mason, Peter, BA   Course Dir.
Smith, Brian, BA   Sr. Lectr.
Thomas, Kerry, BSc MSc   Course Dir.
Walker, Neil, BSc MSc PhD   Principal Lectr.
Watkins, Alison, BA   Sr. Lectr.

Engineering Systems and Information Technology, School of

Athwal, Cham, BSc MSc PhD   Sr. Lectr.
Burden, T.   Sr. Lectr.
Dewhurst, Chris, BTech   Course Dir.
Elson, Bruce, MSc   Sr. Lectr.
Evans, Derek, BA   Course Dir.
Foster, Ron, BSc PhD   Principal Lectr.
Griffiths, John, BSc MSc MEd   Sr. Lectr.
Millward, Andrew, BA MSc   Course Dir.
Oakes, Ian, BSc MSc   Head*
Paton, Dan, MA PhD   Course Dir.
Phelan, Alan, BA MSc PhD   Sr. Lectr.
Potter, Nigel, BA MBA   Sr. Lectr.
Salt, John, BSc MSc, FIEE, FIMechE   Principal Lectr.
Simpson, Will, BA   Course Dir.
Squires, George, BSc MSc MBA   Course Dir.

English, School of

Aughterson, Kate, BA DPhil   Course Dir.
Jackson, Prof. Howard, BA MA PhD   Course Dir.
Littlewood, Derek, BA MA PhD   Course Dir.
Miller, Mick, BA MA PhD   Course Dir.
Smallwood, Philip, MA MPhil PhD   Head*

Fashion, see under Birmingham Inst. of Art and Des.

Health and Community Care, Faculty of

Health and Policy Studies, School of

Abudarham, S., MSc PhD   Principal Lectr.
Anderson, H.   Sr. Lectr.
Brand, S., BSc PhD   Sr. Lectr.
Denny, E., BSc MA   Sr. Lectr.
Filby, M., BSc MA PhD   Head*
Gorman, H., LLB MSocSci   Sr. Lectr.
Hubbard, J., BSc MPhil   Sr. Lectr.
Hughes, M., BSc PhD   Sr. Lectr.
Hurd, A., BSc MA   Sr. Lectr.
Jones, P.   Sr. Lectr.
Kornreich, BS MS   Sr. Lectr.
Lindsay, J., BA MA PhD   Sr. Lectr.
McCarrick, D., MSc MA   Sr. Lectr.
Mohabeersingh, C., MSc   Principal Lectr.
Murray, M., BA MSc   Sr. Lectr.
Nettleton, J., BSc MPhil   Sr. Lectr.
Rabiee, BSc MSc PhD   Sr. Lectr.
Reilly, O., BSc   Sr. Lectr.
Righton, T., BA MSc   Sr. Lectr.
Shute, B., BA MA PhD   Sr. Lectr.
Shute, C., BA MA PhD   Sr. Lectr.
Smith, R., BA PhD   Sr. Lectr.
Stobert, L.   Sr. Lectr.
Thompson, M.   Sr. Lectr.

Social Work and Rehabilitation Studies, School of

Belgrave, W., BA CNAA, MA Leic.   Course Dir.
Doel, M., BA Oxf., MA Oxf.   Head*
Dyson, I.   Course Dir.
Ford, E., BSc Wales   Sr. Lectr.
Gordon, R., BA Nott., MSocSc Birm.   Course Dir.

Gurney, A., MSocSc Birm., MA Edin. Course Dir.
Haywood, P. Course Dir.
Irvine, J., BA Sr. Lectr.
Kumari, K., MA Warw. Sr. Lectr.
Richards, Novlett, MEd Sr. Lectr.
Sylvester, Val, MSc C.England Sr. Lectr.

Information Studies, School of

Butcher, D. R., BA Sr. Lectr.
Chivers, B. E., BA Sr. Lectr.
Denham, D., BLib Sr. Lectr.
Elkin, Prof. Judith C., BA, FLA Head*
Foster, W. T., BSc Sr. Lectr.
Gash, S., BA MA Sr. Lectr.
Hall, B. M., MLS Sr. Lectr.
Hart, C., BA MA(Econ) PhD Sr. Lectr.
Rafferty, P. M. R., MA MSc Sr. Lectr.
Reardon, D. F., BSc Principal Lectr.
Reid, B. J., BA Sr. Lectr.

Information Systems Management, School of

Bhogal, Jagdev, BSc MPhil Sr. Lectr./Lectr.
Clarkson, Janet Sr. Lectr./Lectr.
Dingley, Sharon, BSc PhD Sr. Lectr./Lectr.
Hidderley, Rob G., BA Principal Lectr./Sr. Academic
Kirkham, Sandi, BA MSc Head*
Miller, David, BA Principal Lectr./Sr. Academic
Perkins, John, BA Sr. Lectr./Lectr.
Robson, Alan, BSc Sr. Lectr./Lectr.
Shepherd, Bob, BSc Principal Lectr./Sr. Academic
Trounce, Richard J. A., BA MSc PhD Principal Lectr./Sr. Academic
Wakefield, Allan, BSc Sr. Lectr./Lectr.
Wright, Warren, BSc Sr. Lectr./Lectr.

Law, School of

Arrand, M., LLB Sr. Lectr.
Bladen, S., BA Sr. Lectr.
Byrne, A., LLB Sr. Lectr.
Chatterton, D., LLB MPhil Sr. Lectr.
Daines, C., BA MASc(Soc) Principal Lectr.
Denham, P., BA LLB Sr. Lectr.
Flavel, W., LLB MA Principal Lectr.
Friedrich, K., LLB Sr. Lectr.
Gerrard, M., BA Sr. Lectr.
Harris, P., BA LLM Sr. Lectr.
Hartley, D., MA Oxf. Sr. Lectr.
Hopkins, B. Sr. Lectr.
Humphreys, V., LLB LLM Sr. Lectr.
James, T., BA Sr. Lectr.
Killingley, J., LLB MSc Sr. Lectr.
Kirvan, S., LLB MA Sr. Lectr.
Mulvihill, P., LLB Sr. Lectr.
Oakes, A., BA Sr. Lectr.
Peaple, S., BA Oxf., MA Oxf. Sr. Lectr.
Platts, A. Sr. Lectr.
Saunders, O., LLB LLM Sr. Lectr.
Spencer, M., BA LLM Principal Lectr.
Thomas, M., BA LLM Sr. Lectr.
Tighe, M., LLB Head*
Treloar, H., LLB Sr. Lectr.
Turnbull, A., LLB LLM Sr. Lectr.
Whittle, L., LLB LLM Sr. Lectr.
Woodward, P., LLB Principal Lectr.
Wright, G., LLB MA Sr. Lectr.

Media and Communication, School of

Kemp, Diane, BA Lectr., Radio/Video; Course Dir.
Pilling, Rod, BA MA Head*
Wall, Tim, BA MA Lectr., Media; Course Dir.
Windows, Peter, BA Lectr., Radio; Sr. Academic; Course Dir.

Music, see Birmingham Conservatoire

Nursing Studies, School of

Badger, T. Sr. Lectr.
Bisnauth, R. Sr. Lectr.

Brookes, D. Sr. Lectr.
Butler, K. Sr. Lectr.
Chippendale, M. Sr. Lectr.
Clarke, V. Sr. Lectr.
Clay, B. Sr. Lectr.
Cobley, R. Sr. Lectr.
Cooper, C. Sr. Lectr.
Cresswell, J. Sr. Lectr.
Doyle, C. Sr. Lectr.
Glaze, P. Sr. Lectr.
Goodall, J. Sr. Lectr.
Hart, J. Sr. Lectr.
Haynes, S. Sr. Lectr.
Honeyman, T. Sr. Lectr.
Hulbert, J. Sr. Lectr.
Hunt, L. Sr. Lectr.
Johnson, G. Sr. Lectr.
Mallaber, C. Head*
Manion, J. Sr. Lectr.
McComiskie, A. Sr. Lectr.
Mitchell, C. Sr. Lectr.
Moloney, B. Sr. Lectr.
Moore, L. Sr. Lectr.
Morley, P. Sr. Lectr.
Nankoo, A. Sr. Lectr.
Orford, J. Sr. Lectr.
Page, J. Sr. Lectr.
Philpott, S. Sr. Lectr.
Rakha, D. Sr. Lectr.
Rawstorne, D. Sr. Lectr.
Rich, F. Sr. Lectr.
Royle, L. Sr. Lectr.
Stack, D. Sr. Lectr.
Turner, P. Sr. Lectr.
Twcross, A. Sr. Lectr.

Podiatry, School of

Ashford, R. Head*

Public Policy

Barnes, C., BA PhD Sr. Lectr.
Cremin, M., BA MA Sr. Lectr.
Cunliffe, J., BA PhD Sr. Lectr.
Holden, C. Sr. Lectr.
Isaac-Henry, Prof. K., BSc MSocSci PhD Principal Lectr.
Johnson, E., BA MA PhD Sr. Lectr.
Martin, P., BA Principal Lectr.
Morgan, G., BSc MA Principal Lectr.
Painter, Prof. C., BA PhD Head*
Sharp, D., BSc MA Sr. Lectr.
Williams, K., BA MEd Sr. Lectr.

Radiography, West Midlands School of

Baker, M. I., MSc Sr. Lectr.
Cole, D. S., BA Open(UK), MSc Sr. Lectr.
Coppendale, L., MSc Sr. Lectr.
Hughes, N. J., MA Sr. Lectr.
Klem, R. P., MEd Head*
Lawler, M., BA Open(UK), MSc Sr. Lectr.
Sterry, L., MSc Sr. Lectr.
Turner, S., MSc Sr. Lectr.
Walker, S. J., MSc Sr. Lectr.

Sociology, School of

Aldred, Steve, BA Sr. Lectr.
Canaan, Joyce, BA MA PhD Sr. Lectr.
Ditch, Michael, BSc MA Sr. Lectr.
Joshi, Shirley, BSocSci MSocSc Principal Lectr.
Mandrell, Terry, BA MLit MEd Sr. Lectr.
O'Sullivan, Sean, BA MPhil Sr. Lectr.
Roper, Bill, BA Sr. Lectr.
Smith, George, BA PhD Sr. Lectr.
Staunton, Neil, BA PhD Sr. Lectr.
Vannelli, Prof. Ron, BA MA PhD Head*

Textiles, see under Birmingham Inst. of Art and Des. (Fashion, Textiles and Three-Dimensional Des.)

Women's Health Studies, School of

Amos, D. Sr. Lectr.
Bamfield, T. Sr. Lectr.
Bodin, P. Sr. Lectr.

Clarke, E. Sr. Lectr.
Dover, S. Sr. Lectr.
Hayes, L. Sr. Lectr.
Howells, P. Sr. Lectr.
Hunt, S. Head*
Jones, S. Sr. Lectr.
Kingscott, A. Sr. Lectr.
Long, E. Sr. Lectr.
McDonnel, C. Sr. Lectr.
Midgley, C. Sr. Lectr.
Moore, S. Sr. Lectr.
Shortt, S. Sr. Lectr.
Simms, M. Sr. Lectr.

CONTACT OFFICERS

Academic affairs. Pro-Vice-Chancellor: Walkling, Prof. Philip H., BA MEd
Accommodation. Director of Accommodation, Building and Catering Services: Bradley, Steve
Admissions (first degree). Head of Recruitment Unit: Lewis, Susan
Admissions (higher degree). Head of Recruitment Unit: Lewis, Susan
Careers. Careers Counsellor: Ireland, Peter
Computing services. Director of Information Services: Abel, Mike
Conferences/corporate hospitality. Conference Officer: Bowers, Christine
Consultancy services. Pardesi, Prof. Upkar, MPhil PhD
Equal opportunities. Head of Student Services: Rowley, Russell
Estates and buildings/works and services. Director of Estates: Rhodes, Graham
Finance. Director of Finance: Spilsbury, Richard
General enquiries. Secretary and Registrar: Penlington, Maxine, BA
Health services. Head of Student Services: Rowley, Russell
Industrial liaison. Dean, Faculty of Engineering and Computer Technology: Rogers, Prof. Graham, BSc MSc
International office. International Officer: Turner, Anthony
Library (chief librarian). Director of Information Services: Andrews, Judith
Minorities/disadvantaged groups. Head of Student Services: Rowley, Russell
Personnel/human resources. Director of Personnel: Mee, David
Public relations, information and marketing. Pro-Vice-Chancellor: Tidmarsh, Prof. David H., BSc PhD, FIMechE
Public relations, information and marketing. Director of University Marketing Unit: Ward, Sue, BA MSc
Publications. Marketing Officer: Lewis, Jason, BA
Purchasing. Wright, David
Quality assurance and accreditation. Head of Quality Assurance and Audit: Boyne, Ros
Research. Baylie, Julia
Schools liaison. Schools Liaison Officer: Hurd, Josie
Security. Chief Security Officer: Watkins, Des
Staff development and training. Training Officer: Evans, Roy
Student union. President, Union of Students: Greaves, Ben
Student welfare/counselling. Head of Student Services: Rowley, Russell
Students from other countries. International Officer: Turner, Anthony
Students with disabilities. Head of Student Services: Rowley, Russell
University press. Design and Print Manager: Read, Malcolm

[Information supplied by the institution as at 19 March 1998, and edited by the ACU]

UNIVERSITY OF CENTRAL LANCASHIRE

Founded 1992; previously established as Preston Polytechnic 1973; later Lancashire Polytechnic

Postal Address: Preston, Lancashire, England PR1 2HE
Telephone: (01772) 201201 **Fax**: (01772) 892911 **E-mail**: reception@uclan.ac.uk **Telex**: 677409 (UCLANG)
WWW: http://www.uclan.ac.uk **E-mail formula**: user.i.d@uclan.ac.uk

VICE-CHANCELLOR*—.....
SECRETARY‡—Ackroyd, Pam M., BA *Newcastle(UK)*, MA *Lanc.*

CHELTENHAM AND GLOUCESTER COLLEGE OF HIGHER EDUCATION

Established 1990

Postal Address: PO Box 220, The Park, Cheltenham, Gloucestershire, England GL50 2QF
Telephone: (01242) 532825 **Fax**: (01242) 256759 **E-mail**: admissions@chelt.ac.uk
WWW: http://www.chelt.ac.uk

DIRECTOR*—Trotter, J., OBE, BD MA MSc
REGISTRAR‡—Beard, T.

CITY UNIVERSITY

Founded 1966; previously established as Northampton Polytechnic Institute 1894, and Northampton College of Advanced Technology 1957

Member of the Association of Commonwealth Universities

Postal Address: Northampton Square, London, England EC1V 0HB
Telephone: (0171) 477 8000 **Fax**: (0171) 477 8560 **WWW**: http://www.city.ac.uk
E-mail formula: initial(s).surname@city.ac.uk

CHANCELLOR—The Lord Mayor of London (*ex officio*)
PRO-CHANCELLOR AND CHAIRMAN OF THE COUNCIL—Newall, Sir Paul, TD, MA
DEPUTY PRO-CHANCELLOR AND VICE-CHAIRMAN OF THE COUNCIL—Stonefrost, M. F., CBE
VICE-CHANCELLOR AND PRINCIPAL*—Rhind, Prof. David W., BSc *Brist.*, PhD *Edin.*, DSc *Lond.*, Hon. DSc *Lough.*, Hon. DSc *Brist.*, Hon. DSc *S'ton.*, FRICS
TREASURER—Reeves, C. R.
PRO-VICE-CHANCELLOR—Charlwood, Fred J., BSc(Eng) *Lond.*, MSc PhD
PRO-VICE-CHANCELLOR—Dockray, Prof. Martin S., LLB *Hull*, PhD *Lond.*
PRO-VICE-CHANCELLOR—Haines, Prof. Chris R., BSc *Lond.*, MSc *Lond.*, PhD, FIMA
PRO-VICE-CHANCELLOR—Grammenos, Prof. Costas T., OBE, BA *Athens*, MSc *Wales*
SECRETARY—O'Hara, Michael M., MA *Camb.*
ACADEMIC REGISTRAR‡—Seville, Adrian H., MA *Camb.*, PhD *Edin.*
LIBRARIAN—McGuirk, John A., MA *Camb.*

GENERAL INFORMATION

History. The university was founded in 1894 as Northampton Polytechnic Institute. In 1957 it was renamed Northampton College of Advanced Technology and became a university under its present name in 1966.
It is located in central London.

Admission to first degree courses (see also United Kingdom Introduction). Through Universities and Colleges Admissions Service (UCAS). Applicants whose first language is not English must provide evidence of a command of English language suitable for degree level studies.

First Degrees (see also United Kingdom Directory of Subjects to Study). BA, BEng, BMus, BSc, LLB, MEB (European business), MEng, MMath.

Higher Degrees (see also United Kingdom Directory of Subjects to Study). MA, MBA, MHM (health management), MSc, MPhil, PhD, DClinPsych, DCounPsych, DMA (musical arts).

Libraries. 236,000 volumes; 97,000 volumes of periodicals. Specialist libraries include Cyril Kleinwort (arts policy, business management).

Fees (annual). Undergraduate. United Kingdom/European Union students (1998-99): £1000 (subject to legislation). International students (1997-98): £3950 (foundation courses); £6450 (arts); £7250 (engineering); £8550 (science); £8750 (optometry).

Academic Year (1998-99). Three terms: 5 October–11 December; 11 January–19 March; 19 April–25 June.

Income (1996-97). Total, £69,300,000.

Statistics. Staff: 1334 (590 academic and research); 593 administrative and technical; 151 manual/maintenance). Students: full-time 6157; part-time 2078; total 8235.

FACULTIES/SCHOOLS

Business

Fax: (0171) 477 8781

Dean: Hannah, Prof. Leslie, CBE, BA MA DPhil PhD, FEng
Personal Assistant: Hosking, Denise

Engineering

Fax: (0171) 477 8101

Dean: Wootton, Prof. L. Roger, BSc City(UK), PhD City(UK), FEng, FICE
Personal Assistant: Lawrence, Barbara

Health Sciences, Institute of

Director: Carson, Prof. Ewart R., BSc St And., MSc Lond., PhD City(UK), DSc City(UK), FIEE
Secretary: Brown, Sharon

Informatics

Fax: (0171) 477 8586

Dean: Osmon, Prof. Peter E., BSc Lond., PhD Lond., FIEE
Administrator: Baillie, Lucia

Mathematics, Actuarial Science and Statistics

Fax: (0171) 477 8572

Dean: Haberman, Prof. Steven, MA Camb., PhD, FIA, FIMA
Personal Assistant: Parris, Marilyn

Nursing and Midwifery, St Bartholomew School of

Tel: (0171) 505 5709 Fax: (0171) 505 5705

Dean: Studdy, Susan J., MA Lond.
Personal Assistant: Dyer, Pat

Social and Human Sciences

Fax: (0171) 477 8580

Dean: Miller, Stephen H., BSc Lond., PhD Lond.
Secretary: Toop, Krystyna

ACADEMIC UNITS

Accounting and Finance

Tel: (0171) 477 8631 Fax: (0171) 477 8648

Citron, D., MA Camb., MSc Lond., MBA McG., FCA   Sr. Lectr.
Lasfer, M., BSc MSc PhD   Reader
Levis, M., BA Jerusalem, MSc PhD   Prof., Finance; Head*
Selim, G. M., MCom Cairo, PhD Cairo   Prof., Internal Auditing
Sudarsanam, P. S., MSc Madr., PhD   Prof.
Taffler, R. J., BSc(Econ) Lond., MSc Lond., PhD   Prof.
Thomas, D. C., MCom MSc
Other Staff: 3 Lectrs.

Actuarial Science and Statistics

Allan, J. N., BSc Edin., FFA   Visiting Prof., Actuarial Science
Benjamin, B., BSc PhD, FIA   Prof. Emer.
Booth, P. M., BA Durh., FIA   Sr. Lectr.
Chadburn, R. G., BSc PhD, FIA   Sr Lectr.
Clarkson, R. S., BSc, FFA, FIMA   Visiting Prof.

Daykin, C. D., MA, FIA
Haberman, Steven, MA Camb., PhD, FIA, FIMA   Prof., Actuarial Science
Newby, M. J., BSc Sus., MSc Sus., PhD Brad.   Prof., Statistical Science
Puzey, A. S., MA Camb., PhD, FIA   Sr. Lectr.
Renshaw, A. E., BSc Wales, PhD Wales   Sr. Lectr.
Verrall, R. J., MA Camb., MSc Lond., PhD, FIMA   Reader
Winterbottom, A., BSc Reading, MSc Lond., PhD City(UK)   Visiting Prof., Statistics
Wolstenholme, L. C., BSc City(UK)., PhD Sur., FIMA   Sr. Lectr.; Head*
Other Staff: 7 Lectrs.; 2 Res. Fellows

Aeronautics, see Engin., Mech., and Aeronautics

Arts Policy and Management

Tel: (0171) 477 8751 Fax: (0171) 477 8887

Boylan, P. J., BSc Hull, PhD Leic., FGS   Prof.
Hammet, M., MA Leeds, PhD   Sr. Lectr.
Moody, E. H., MA Lond., PhD   Sr. Lectr.; Head*
Pick, J. M., BA Leeds, MA Birm., PhD   Prof. Emer.
Quine, M. W., MA St And.   Sr. Lectr.
Other Staff: 5 Lectrs.; 2 Sr. Res. Fellows

Banking and Finance

Tel: (0171) 477 8741 Fax: (0171) 477 8881

Batchelor, Roy. A., MA Glas.   Midland Bank Prof.
Capie, Forrest H., BA Auck., MSc Lond., PhD Lond.   Prof., Economic History
Chrystal, K. Alec, BA Exe., MA Essex, PhD Essex   Prof., Monetary Economics; Head*
Gemmill, Gordon T., BSc Lond., MSc Liv., MA Mich.State, PhD Mich.State   Prof., Finance
Heffernan, Shelagh, BA Tor., DPhil Oxf.   Prof.
Pepper, Gordon T., CBE, MA Camb., FIA   Prof., Financial Markets
Phylaktis, Kate, BSc Brun., MSc(Econ) Lond., PhD   Reader
Res, Zannis, BSc(Eng) Minn., MA(Econ) Minn.   Sr. Lectr.
Rybczynski, Tad M., BCom Lond., MSc(Econ) Lond.   Visiting Prof.
Salmon, M., BA MSc   Deutsche Morgan Grenfell Prof., Financial Markets
Wood, Geoffrey E., MA Aberd., MA Essex   Prof., Economics

Clinical Communication Studies

Tel: (0171) 477 8281 Fax: (0171) 477 8577

Byng, S., PhD Lond.   Prof., Communication Disability; Head*
Chiat, S., PhD Lond.   Sr. Lectr.
Clarke, L., BSc Lond.   Dir., Clin. Educn.
Law, J., PhD City(UK)   Sr. Lectr.
Pring, T., PhD Lond.   Sr. Lectr.
Woll, B., PhD Brist.   Prof., Sign Language and Deaf Studies
Other Staff: 14 Lectrs.; 4 Clin. Staff

Computing

Tel: (0171) 477 8405, 477 8432 Fax: (0171) 477 8587

Bolton, D. J., BSc Lond.   Sr. Lectr.
Cohen, B., BSc Glas.   Prof., Computing
Das, S. K., BSc Sur., MSc Manc.   Sr. Lectr.
Gilbert, D. R., BSc Brist., MEd Brist., MSc Lond., PhD   Sr. Lectr.
Hammersley, P., BSc MA   Visiting Prof.
McCann, J., BSc DPhil   Sr. Lectr.
Osmon, Peter E., BSc Lond., PhD Lond., FIEE   Prof., Computer Systems
Till, D. R., BA Oxf., MSc Lond.   Reader
Other Staff: 11 Lectrs.; 4 Res. Fellows

Continuing Education

Connell, T. J., MA Oxf., BPhil Liv.   Sr. Lectr.; Dir., Div. of Langs.
Davies, P. A., MSc PhD   Reader
Haines, Chris R., BSc MSc PhD, FIMA   Prof., Mathematics Education

Lewis, A. J., BA Durh., MSc E.Lond.   Sr. Lectr.; Head*
Other Staff: 5 Lectrs.

Economics

Tel: (0171) 477 8503 Fax: (0171) 477 8580

Cubbin, John S., MA Camb., MA Warw., PhD S.Fraser   Prof.
Glycopantis, D., MSc(Econ) Athens, PhD Lond.   Prof.; Head*
Hadri, K., BSc PhD   Sr. Lectr.
Harbury, Colin D., BCom Lond., PhD Wales   Visiting Prof.
Holl, Peter, BSc(Econ) Lond., MA Sus., PhD   Sr. Lectr.
McGuire, Alistair J., BA Edin., MLitt Aberd., PhD Aberd.   Prof.
Pilbeam, K., BA PhD   Sr. Lectr.
Prais, S. J., MCom Birm., PhD Camb.   Visiting Prof.
Price, Simon, BSc Brist., MSc Lond., PhD Essex   Prof.
Rybczynski, T., BCom Lond., MSc(Econ) Lond.   Visiting Prof.
Other Staff: 7 Lectrs.

Engineering, Civil

Fax: (0171) 477 8570

Atkinson, J. H., MSc Lond., PhD Lond., FICE, FGS   Prof., Soil Mechanics
Barrett, A., BSc(Eng), FICE   Visiting Prof.
Boswell, L. F., PhD Leeds   Prof.; Head*
Chamberlain, D. A., MSc Lond., BSc   Sr. Lectr.
Chaplin, J. R., BSc Brist., PhD Brist., FICE   Prof., Hydraulics
Cooke, G. M. E., BSc PhD   Visiting Prof.
Coop, M. R., BSc Lond., DPhil Oxf.   Sr. Lectr.
Cooper, M. A. R., BSc Brist., FRICS, FICE   Prof., Engineering Surveying
D'Mello, C., BSc Sus., DPhil Sus.   Sr. Lectr.
Denton, A. A., MA PhD, FEng, FIMechE   Visiting Prof.
Fookes, P. G., BSc PhD DSc, FGS, FEng   Visiting Prof.
Forno, Colin, BSc PhD   Visiting Prof.
Garas, F. K., BSc PhD, FIStructE   Visiting Prof.
Lewin, J., FICE, FIMechE   Visiting Prof.
Morris, W. J., PhD   Visiting Prof.
Savvidou, C., BSc Athens, PhD Camb.   Visiting Prof.
Simpson, B., MA PhD   Visiting Prof.
Speare, P. R. S., MA Camb., PhD Lond.   Sr. Lectr.
Supple, W. J., BSc(Eng) PhD   Visiting Prof.
Taplin, D. M. R., MA DPhil DSc   Visiting Prof.
Taylor, R. N., MA Camb., MPhil Camb., PhD Camb.   Prof., Geotechnical Engineering
Tolloczko, J. J. A., BSc PhD   Visiting Prof.
Tromans, P. S., BA MA PhD   Visiting Prof., Principles of Design
Virdi, K. S., BSc Agra, BTech IIT Bombay, ME Roor., PhD Lond., FICE, FIStructE   Prof., Structural Engineering
Wolf, P. O., BSc(Eng), FEng, FICE   Visiting Prof.
Younis, B. A., BEng Wales, MSc Lond., PhD Lond.   Sr. Lectr.
Other Staff: 5 Lectrs.

Engineering, Electrical, Electronic and Information

Tel: (0171) 477 8130 Fax: (0171) 477 8568

Allibone, T. E., CBE, DSc Sheff., PhD Sheff., PhD Camb., Hon. DSc, FRS, FIP, FIEE, FEng   Visiting Poynton Prof.
Brook, R. A., BSc Brist., MSc Lond.   Visiting Prof.
Comley, R. A., BSc PhD   Sr. Lectr.
Ellis, T. J., BSc Kent, PhD Lond.   Reader
Finkelstein, L., OBE, DSc Lond., FEng, FIP, FIEE   Prof., Measurement and Instrumentation
Grattan, K. T. V., BSc Belf., PhD Belf., DSc, FIP, FIEE   Prof., Measurement and Instrumentation; Head*
House, H., BSc(Eng) Lond., PhD Lond.   Visiting Prof., High Voltage Engineering

Karcanias, N., BSc *Athens*, MSc *Manc.*, PhD *Manc.*, DSc, FIMA   Prof., Control Theory of Design
Meggitt, B., BBSc MSc PhD   Visiting Prof.
Palmer, A. W., BE *Cant.*, MPhil PhD   Prof., Electrical Engineering
Rahman, B. M. A., BScEng *B'desh.Engin.*, MSc *B'desh.Engin.*, PhD *Lond.*   Prof., Electrical Engineering
Roberts, P. D., BEng *Sheff.*, PhD *Belf.*, DSc, FIEE   Prof., Control Engineering
Thomas, P., BSc, FIEE   Visiting Prof.
Weight, J. P., MPhil PhD   Reader
Other Staff: 8 Lectrs.; 7 Res. Fellows

Engineering Management
Tel: (0171) 477 8366
Payne, Andrew C., MA *Lond.*, BSc(Eng) *Lond.*   Sr. Lectr.

Engineering, Mechanical, and Aeronautics
Tel: (0171) 477 8108 Fax: (0171) 477 8566
Banerjee, J. Ranjan, BE *Calc.*, MTech *Kharagpur*, PhD *Cran.IT*   Reader
Done, George T. S., BSc(Eng) *Lond.*, PhD *Brist.*, FRAeS   Prof., Aeronautics
Fry, Martin, MSc *Cran.*, FIMechE   Visiting Prof.
Henry, Frank S., BSc *Lond.*, MS *Rutgers*, PhD   Sr. Lectr.
Leyman, Clive, BSc(Eng) *Lond.*, FRAeS   RAE Visiting Prof., Principles of Engineering Design
Lush, Peter A., BSc *Brist.*, PhD *Brist.*, FRAeS   Sr. Lectr.
Martin, Peter R., BSc, FIMechE   Visiting Prof.
Mintz, Barry, MSc *Birm.*, PhD *Birm.*, DEng, FIM   Prof., Engineering Materials
Neve, Ray S., MSc(Eng) *Lond.*, PhD, FRAeS   Sr. Lectr.
Peake, David J., BSc *Brist.*, MSc *Brist.*, PhD *Brist.*, PhD *Car.*, FRAeS   Prof., Aeronautics and Fluid Dynamics; Head, Centre for Aeronautics
Smith, Ian K., BSc(Eng) *Lond.*, PhD *Lond.*, FIMechE   Prof., Applied Thermodynamics
Stosic, Nikola, DSc   Royal Academy of Engin. Prof., Positive Displacement Compressor Technology
Thorley, A. R. David, BSc *City(UK)*, MPhil *Lond.*, PhD *City(UK)*, FIMechE   Prof., Fluid Engineering; Head*
Tozer, Bryan A., BSc *Liv.*, PhD *Liv.*, FIP, FIEE   Visiting Prof.
Wootton, L. Roger, BSc *City*, PhD *City(UK)*, FEng, FICE   Prof., Engineering
Other Staff: 5 Lectrs.; 1 Res. Fellow

Finance, see Acctg. and Finance; Banking and Finance; Shipping, Trade and Finance

Human Computer Interface Design, Centre for
Maiden, N. A. M., BA PhD   Sr. Lectr.; Dir.*
Sutcliffe, Alistair G., MA *Camb.*, PhD *Wales*   Prof., Systems Engineering
Other Staff: 2 Res. Fellows

Human Resource Management and Organisational Behaviour
Tel: (0171) 477 8641 Fax: (0171) 477 8546
Downs, S., BSc, FBPsS   Visting Prof.
Hendry, C., BA *Lond.*, MSc *Sheff.*, PhD *CNAA*   Centenary Prof., Organisational Behaviour; Head*
Herriot, P., BA MEd PhD, FBPsS   Visting Prof.
Lessem, R. S., MSc *Lond.*, MBA *Harv.*, PhD   Reader
Rajan, A., MA *Essex*   Visiting Prof.
Rosewell, BA MA   Visiting Prof.
Vielba, C., BA BPhil PhD   Sr. Lectr.
Williams, A. P. O., MA *Lond.*, PhD *Lond.*, FBPsS   Prof., Occupational Psychology
Other Staff: 2 Lectrs.; 2 Res. Fellows

Information Engineering, see Engin., Electr., Electronic and Information

Information Science
Tel: (0171) 477 8381 Fax: (0171) 477 8584
Bawden, David, BSc *Liv.*, MSc *Sheff.*, PhD *Sheff.*, FIInfSc   Sr. Lectr.
Blick, A. R., FIInfSc   Visiting Prof.
Jones, Susan, BA *Lond.*, MSc *Lond.*   Sr. Lectr.
Keen, E. M., MSc, FLA   Visiting Prof.
Nicholas, David, MPhil *N.Lond.*, PhD *City(UK)*   Sr. Lectr.; Head*
Robertson, Stephen E., MA *Camb.*, PhD *Lond.*, MSc, FIInfSc   Visiting Prof.
Other Staff: 4 Lectrs.; 1 Res. Fellow

Investment, Risk Management and Insurance
Tel: (0171) 477 8694 Fax: (0171) 477 8885
Barone-Adesi, G., PhD   Visiting Prof.
Bland, D., BA MLitt PhD, FIM   Visiting Prof.
Dickinson, G. M., BA(Econ) *Manc.*, DPhil *Sus.*   Prof., International Insurance
Dinenis, E., BA *Athens*, MA *Manc.*, PhD *Lond.*   Lectr.; Head*
Melnick, A., PhD   Visiting Prof.
Nakajima, C., BA MA PhD   Sr. Lectr.
Parsons, C., BA *Hull*, LLB   Sr. Lectr.
Ratcliff, A. R. N., FIA   Visiting Prof.
Robinson, A., PhD   Visiting Prof.
Young, P., PhD   Visiting Prof.
Other Staff: 6 Lectrs.

Journalism
Tel: (0171) 477 8221 Fax: (0171) 477 8594, 8574
Allen, Rod   Head*
Christmas, Linda   Sr. Lectr.
Jones, Bob, BA *Birm.*   Sr. Lectr.
Keeble, R., BA PhD   Sr. Lectr.
Stephenson, Hugh, MA *Oxf.*   Prof.
Worcester, R. M., BSc   Visiting Prof.
Other Staff: 6 Lectrs.

Law
Adams, J., LLB *Brist.*   Visiting Prof.
Bennett, G. J., MA *Camb.*   Visiting Prof.
Burn, E. H., BCL *Oxf.*, MA *Oxf.*, Hon.DCL   Prof.
Davies, J. W., LLB *Birm.*, BCL *Oxf.*, MA *Oxf.*   Visiting Prof.
Dockray, M. S., LLB *Hull*, PhD *Lond.*   Prof.
Elagab, O., BA *CNAA*, LLM *Lond.*, DPhil *Oxf.*   Reader
Glazebrook, P. R., MA *Oxf.*, MA *Camb.*   Visiting Prof.
Hopkins, J. A., MA *Camb.*, LLB *Camb.*   Visiting Prof.
Moore, V., LLB LLM   Visiting Prof.
Phillips, M., MA LLM Hon.DCL   Visiting Prof.
Purdue, M., LLB *Lond.*, LLM *Lond.*   Prof.
Ryan, C. L., LLB *Well.*, LLM *Well.*   Prof.; Head*
Scanlan, G. P., LLB *Sheff.*   Sr. Lectr.
Other Staff: 8 Lectrs.

Management, see Human Resource Management and Orgnl. Behaviour; Management Systems and Information

Management Systems and Information
Tel: (0171) 477 8629 Fax: (0171) 477 8628
Charlwood, Fred J., BSc(Eng) *Lond.*, MSc PhD   Sr. Lectr.
Chelsom, John V., BSc *Lond.*   Visiting Prof.
Handy, Laurence J., MA *Camb.*, PhD *Camb.*   Visiting Prof.
Holtham, C. W., MA *Oxf.*, MSocSc *Birm.*   Bull Prof., Information Management; Head*
Janes, F. Ross, BTech *Brun.*, MSc PhD   Sr. Lectr.
Leeming, A., BSc *Lond.*, MSc   Sr. Lectr.
Reavill, Lawrie R. P., MA *CNAA*, BSc *Lond.*, PhD *Lond.*, FIChemE   Sr. Lectr.
Roberts, Peter C., BA *Camb.*   Visiting Prof.
Other Staff: 3 Lectrs.

Marketing
Tel: (0171) 477 8747 Fax: (0171) 477 8546
Baker, M., BA   Visiting Prof.
Bruce, I., BSocSc *Birm.*   Visiting Prof.
Collins, M., BSc(Econ) *Lond.*   Market Res. Soc. Prof., Marketing Research
Johne, F. A., BA *Liv.*, MPhil PhD   Prof., Marketing; Head*
Leat, D., BSc(Econ) PhD   Visiting Prof.
Tyrell, R., MA MSc   Visiting Prof.
White, J., BA *Nott.*, MA *Lond.*, PhD *Lond.*   Visiting Prof.
Other Staff: 4 Lectrs.

Mathematics
Tel: (0171) 477 8452 Fax: (0171) 477 8597
Bowtell, Graham, MSc *Hull*, PhD *Lond.*   Sr. Lectr.
Bryan, Alan C., MSc *Lond.*, PhD   Sr. Lectr.
Daniels, Peter G., BSc *Brist.*, PhD *Lond.*, DSc *Lond.*   Prof., Applied Mathematics
Eagles, Peter M., MA *Camb.*, MSc *Lond.*, PhD *Lond.*   Visiting Prof.
Jaswon, Maurice A., MA *Trinity(Dub.)*, PhD *Birm.*, FIMA   Emer. Prof.
Martin, Paul P., BSc *S'ton.*, PhD *S'ton.*   Prof., Mathematical Physics
Mathon, Jiri, PhD *Prague*   Prof., Mathematical Physics; Head*
Stanley, Terence E., BSc *Aberd.*, MSc *Newcastle(UK)*, PhD *Lond.*   Sr. Lectr.
Villeret, M. A., PhD   Reader
Other Staff: 3 Lectrs.

Music
Tel: (0171) 477 8284 Fax: (0171) 477 8576
Emmerson, Simon, BA *Camb.*, PhD *City(UK)*   Reader
Euba, A., BA MA DPhil, FTCL   Visiting Prof.
Samuel, Rhian, BA *Reading*, BMus *Reading*, AM *Wash.(Mo.)*, PhD *Wash.(Mo.)*   Prof.
Smalley, Denis, BMus *Well.*, MusB *Cant.*, DPhil *York(UK)*   Prof.; Head*
Stanton, Steve, BA *York(UK)*, DPhil *York(UK)*   Sr. Lectr.
Troup, M., DPhil Hon.LLD, FRCArt   Visiting Prof.
Other Staff: 4 Lectrs.; 1 Res. Fellow

Nursing and Midwifery, see St Bartholomew School of Nursing and Midwifery

Optometry and Visual Science
Tel: (0171) 477 8339 Fax: (0171) 477 8355
Arden, Geoffrey B., MB BS *Lond.*, PhD   Visiting Prof.†
Barbur, John L., BSc *Lond.*, MSc *Lond.*, PhD *Lond.*   Prof.
Birch, Jenny, BSc *Aston*, MPhil *Lond.*   Sr. Lectr.
Buckley, R. J., BM BCh MA, FRCS   Prof., Ocular Medicine
Douglas, Ron H., BSc *Sus.*, PhD *Stir.*   Reader
Edgar, David F., BSc *Belf.*, BSc *Lond.*   Sr. Lectr.
Fahle, M., BSc MSc MD PhD   Head*
Fletcher, R. J., MSc   Emer. Prof.
Obstfeld, Henri, MPhil *Lond.*   Sr. Lectr.
Pearson, R. M. (Dick), MPhil *Lond.*   Sr. Lectr.
Port, Mike J. A., MSc *Aston*   Sr. Lectr.
Ruskell, G. L., MSc DSc   Emer. Prof.
Thomson, W. David, PhD *Lond.*, BSc   Sr. Lectr.
Woodward, E. Geoffrey, PhD *City(UK)*   Prof.
Other Staff: 5 Lectrs.

Philosophy, Division of
Grieder, A., PhD   Reader; Head*
Rickman, H. P., MA DPhil   Reader
Other Staff: 1 Lectr.

Property Valuation and Management
Tel: (0171) 477 8214 Fax: (0171) 477 8573
Hattersley, W. M., BSc MSc MA, FRICS   Visting Prof.
Herd, G. R. C., MSc *Reading*, FRICS   Sr. Lectr.
Johnson, T. A., BSc, FRICS   Visting Prof.
Rodney, W. H., MSc, FRICS   Head*

Venmore-Rowland, P., MA *Reading*, BSc *Reading*, MSc, FRICS Prof.
Other Staff: 1 Lectr.

Psychology

Tel: (0171) 477 8521 Fax: (0171) 477 8581

Ayton, P., BSc PhD Reader
Bor, Robert, BA *Witw.*, MA *S.Af.*, DPhil *S.Af.* Prof.
Bowler, Dermot M., BA *Trinity(Dub.)*, MSc *Lond.*, PhD *Lond.* Sr. Lectr.
Gardiner, John M., BSc *Lond.*, PhD *Lond.* Prof.
Golombok, Susan E., BSc *Glas.*, MSc *Lond.*, PhD *Lond.* Prof.
Hampton, James A., BA *Camb.*, PhD *Lond.* Reader; Head*
Hines, Melissa, BA *Prin.*, MA *Calif.*, PhD *Calif.* Prof.
Honess, T., BSc PhD Reader
Kaminska, Zofia, BSc *Lond.*, PhD *Lond.* Sr. Lectr.
Kuczmierczyk, Andrew R., BA *Keele*, MSc *Georgia*, PhD *Georgia* Sr. Lectr.
Legg, Charles R., BSc *Lond.*, MSc *City(UK)*, DPhil *Oxf.* Sr. Lectr.
Miller, Stephen H., BSc *Lond.*, PhD *Lond.* Sr. Lectr.
Watts, Mary H., BSc *Lond.*, MA *Kent*, PhD *City(UK)* Sr. Lectr.
Other Staff: 8 Lectrs.; 3 Res. Fellows

Radiography

Tel: (0171) 505 5678 Fax: (0171) 505 5691

Cherry, P., MSc Sr. Lectr.
Edie, J., MEd Sr. Lectr.
Hicks, R. W., BA MSc Head*
McClellan, M., BSc MSc Sr. Lectr.
Other Staff: 13 Lectrs.; 7 Clin. Lectrs.

Shipping, Trade and Finance

Tel: (0171) 477 8671 Fax: (0171) 477 8895

Grammenos, C. T., BA *Athens*, MSc *Wales* Prof.; Head*
Griffiths, Lord,, MSc(Econ) *Lond.* Visiting Prof.
Kavussanos, M., BSc(Econ) MSc PhD Sr. Lectr.
Other Staff: 2 Lectrs.

Sociology

Tel: (0171) 477 8527 Fax: (0171) 477 8558

Barrett, M. V., BA *Durh.*, MA *Sus.*, DPhil *Sus.* Prof.
Barron, R. D., BA *Well.*, MA *Essex* Sr. Lectr.
Cockburn, C. Prof. Res. Fellow
Coyle, A., BSocSc *Birm.*, PhD *Warw.* Prof.
Feuchtwang, S., BA *Oxf.*, MA *Lond.*, PhD *Lond.* Prof.
Grieder, A., PhD *Brist.* Reader
Hills, J., BSc *Manc.*, MA *Essex*, PhD *Essex* Prof.
Rattansi, A., MA *Manc.*, PhD *Camb.* Reader
Rose, H., BA PhD Visiting Prof.
Tumber, H., MA *Essex*, PhD Head*
Tunstall, C. J., MA *Camb.* Prof.
Vogler, C., BEd *CNAA*, MSc *CNAA*, PhD *CNAA* Sr. Lectr.
Wiggins, Richard, BA *Kent*, MSc *Lond.*, PhD *Lond.* Reader
Willetts, Peter, BA *Keele*, MSc *Strath.*, PhD *Strath.* Reader
Other Staff: 1 Lectr.; 1 Res. Fellow

Software Reliability, Centre for

Bloomfield, R., MA Visiting Prof.
De Neumann, B., MSc Visiting Prof.
Fenton, N. E., BSc *Lond.*, MSc *Sheff.*, PhD *Sheff.* Prof., Software Engineering
Littlewood, B., MSc *Lond.*, PhD Prof., Computer Science; Dir.*
Malcolm, R., MA Visiting Prof.
Strigini, Lorenzo Reader
Other Staff: 2 Lectrs.; 3 Res. Fellows

Statistics, see Actuarial Sci. and Stats.

Strategy and International Business

Tel: (0171) 477 8645 Fax: (0171) 477 8628

Algie, J., BA MA Visiting Prof.

Baden-Fuller, Charles, BA *Oxf.*, MA *Cornell*, PhD *Lond.* Prof.
Choi, C. J., MPA *Harv.*, MBA *Europ.Inst.Bus.Admin.*, MPhil *Oxf.*, DPhil *Oxf.* Gyosei Prof., International Business Policy; Head*
Harrison, P., MSc PhD Visiting Prof.
Mathur, S. S., BTech IIT *Kanpur*, MSc *Lond.*, PhD *Lond.* Sr. Lectr.
Miller, C. J. M., BSc MA PhD Sr. Lectr.
Nakajima, C., BA *Keio*, MA *Keio* Sr. Lectr.
Raimond, P., BA *Manc.*, MBA *Manc.*, PhD *Manc.* Sr. Lectr.
Other Staff: 1 Lectr.; 4 Res Fellows

Visual Science, see Optom. and Visual Sci.

ST BARTHOLOMEW SCHOOL OF NURSING AND MIDWIFERY

Tel: (0171) 505 5700 Fax: (0171) 505 5717

Creber, B., MSc Sr. Lectr.; Dir., Post-Registration Studies
Fitzgerald, L., BA(Econ) PhD Prof., Health Services Research; Dir., Res.
Goreham, C., BSc MPhil Sr. Lectr.; Dir., Pre-Registration Studies

Adult Nursing

Ball, C., MSc Sr. Lectr.
Cox, C., BSc MSc MA PhD Head*
Manning, A., MSc Sr. Lectr.
Meyer, J., BSc MSc PhD Reader
Monaghan, A., MA Sr. Lectr.
Rawlings-Anderson, K., BA MSc Sr. Lectr.
Other Staff: 26 Lectrs.; 2 Res. Fellows

Applied Behavioural and Biological Sciences

Pryce, A., BA MSc Sr. Lectr.
Vickers, J., BSc MSc Sr. Lectr.
Yarwood,.D., BSc MSc Head*
Other Staff: 26 Lectrs.

Children's Nursing

Lane, M., MSc Head*
Sheldon, L., BSc MSc Sr. Lectr.
Other Staff: 6 Lectrs.

Community and Primary Health Care

Mayor, V., BSc BEd Head*
Naik, A., BSc MA Sr. Lectr.
Other Staff: 6 Lectrs.

Continuing Educational and Academic Standards

Freeth, D., BSc MPhil PhD Sr. Lectr.
Holroyd, D., MAEd Head*
Parker, P., BA MAEd Sr. Lectr.
Woods, S., MSc Sr. Lectr.
Other Staff: 2 Lectrs.

Mental Health Nursing

Bowers, L., BSc MA PhD Prof., Psychiatric Nursing
Sourial, S., BA MSc Head*
Other Staff: 12 Lectrs.

Midwifery

Opoku, D., BEd MA Head*
Sandall, J. Reader
Other Staff: 8 Lectrs.

SPECIAL CENTRES, ETC

Actuarial Research Centre

Tel: (0171) 477 8467 Fax: (0171) 477 8572

Haberman, Prof. Steven, MA *Camb.*, PhD, FIA, FIMA Professor; Dir.*

Applied Vision Research Centre

Tel: (0171) 477 8331 Fax: (0171) 477 8355

Barbur, Prof. J. L., BSc *Lond.*, MSc *Lond.*, PhD *Lond.* Dir.*

Communications Policy and Journalism Research Unit

Tel: (0171) 477 8512 Fax: (0171) 477 8558

Tumber, H., MA *Essex*, PhD Dir.*

Continuing Education Research Unit

Tel: (0171) 477 8254 Fax: (0171) 477 8256

Haines, Chris R., BSc MSc PhD, FIMA Prof., Mathematics Education; Dir.*

Control Engineering Research Centre

Tel: (0171) 477 8133 Fax: (0171) 477 8568

Karcanias, Prof. N., BSc *Athens*, MSc *Manc.*, PhD *Manc.*, DSc, FIMA Dir.*
Roberts, Prof. P. D., BEng *Sheff.*, PhD *Belf.*, DSc, FIEE Dir.*

Engineering Surveying, Photogrammetry and Highways Research Centre

Tel: (0171) 477 8149 Fax: (0171) 477 8570

Cooper, Prof. M. A. R., BSc *Brist.*, FRICS, FICE Dir.*

Family and Child Psychology Research Centre

Tel: (0171) 477 8510 Fax: (0171) 477 8582

Golombok, Prof. S. E., BSc *Glas.*, MSc *Lond.*, PhD *Lond.* Dir.*

Gender, Ethnicity and Social Change Research Centre

Tel: (0171) 477 8527 Fax: (0171) 477 8558

Barrett, Prof. M. V., BA *Durh.*, MA *Sus.*, DPhil *Sus.* Dir.*

Geotechnical Engineering Research Centre

Tel: (0171) 477 8154 Fax: (0171) 477 8571

Taylor, R. N., MA *Camb.*, MPhil *Camb.*, PhD *Camb.* Prof.; Dir.*

Health Management Group

Tel: (0171) 477 8798 Fax: (0171) 477 8595

Iles, Valerie M., BPharm *Wales*, MSc *Lond.* Sr. Lectr.; Dir.*
Meads, G., MA MSc(Tech) Visiting Prof.
Other Staff: 2 Lectrs.

Health Sciences, Institute of

Tel: (0171) 477 8370 Fax: (0171) 477 8579

Carson, Prof. Ewart R., BSc *St And.*, MSc *Lond.*, PhD *City(UK)*, DSc *City(UK)*, FIEE Dir.*

Interactive Systems Research Centre

Tel: (0171) 477 8380 Fax: (0171) 477 8584

Robertson, Prof. S. E., MA *Camb.*, PhD *Lond.*, MSc, FIInfSc Dir.*

Interoperable Systems Research Centre

Tel: (0171) 477 8401 Fax: (0171) 477 8587

Osmon, Prof. Peter E., BSc *Lond.*, PhD *Lond.*, FIEE Dir.*

Low-dimensional Magnetic Structures Research Unit

Tel: (0171) 477 8459 Fax: (0171) 477 8597

Mathon, Prof. J., PhD *Prague* Dir.*

Measurement and Information in Medicine Research Centre

Tel: (0171) 477 8370 Fax: (0171) 477 8579

Carson, Prof. Ewart R., BSc *St And.*, MSc *Lond.*, PhD *City(UK)*, DSc *City(UK)*, FIEE Prof., System Science; Dir.*
Cramp, Derek G., BA *Trinity(Dub.)*, MPhil *Lond.*, PhD *Lond.* Visiting Prof.
Hennessy, Tom R., MSc *Cape Town*, PhD *Cape Town*, FIMA Sr. Lectr.
Hill, Dennis W., MSc *Lond.*, PhD *Lond.*, DSc(Eng) *Lond.*, FIEE, FIP Visiting Prof.
Moonman, Eric, OBE, MSc *Manc.* Visiting Prof.
Sönksen, Peter H., MB BS *Lond.*, MD *Lond.*, FRCP Visiting Prof.
Wilkins, Les J., BSc(Eng) *Lond.*, MSc *Brun.*, PhD *City(UK)*, FIEE Sr. Lectr.; Dir.*
Other Staff: 1 Lectr.; 2 Res. Fellows

Measurement and Instrumentation Research Centre

Tel: (0171) 477 8120 Fax: (0171) 477 8568

Finkelstein, Prof. L., OBE, DSc *Lond.*, FIP, FIEE, FEng Dir.*

Grattan, Prof. K. T. V., BSc *Belf.*, PhD *Belf.*, DSc, FIP, FIEE Dir.*

Ocean Engineering Research Centre

Tel: (0171) 477 8140 Fax: (0171) 477 8570

Boswell, Prof. L. F., PhD *Leeds* Dir.*

Personnel Research and Enterprise Development Unit

Tel: (0171) 477 8641 Fax: (0171) 477 8546

Williams, Prof. A., MA *Lond.*, PhD *Lond.*, FBPsS Dir.*

Positive Displacement Compressor Technology, Centre for

Smith, Ian K., BSc(Eng) *Lond.*, PhD *Lond.*, FIMechE Prof., Applied Thermodynamics; Co-Dir.*

Stosic, Nikola, DSc Royal Academy of Engin. Prof.; Co-Dir.*

Property Investment Research Unit

Tel: (0171) 477 8218 Fax: (0171) 477 8573

Matysiak, G. A., MSc *CNAA* Dir.*

Rehabilitation Resource Centre

Tel: (0171) 477 8377 Fax: (0171) 477 8356

Floyd, M., BSc *Edin.*, PhD *Brun.* Reader; Dir.*
Other Staff: 1 Lectr.; 2 Res Fellows

Structures Research Centre

Tel: (0171) 477 8142 Fax: (0171) 477 8570

Virdi, Prof. K. S., BSc *Agra*, BTech IIT Bombay, ME *Roor.*, PhD *Lond.*, FICE, FIStructE Dir.*

Thermo-Fluids Engineering Research Centre

Tel: (0171) 477 8109 Fax: (0171) 477 8566

Thorley, Prof. A. R. D., MPhil *Lond.*, BSc PhD, FIMechE Dir.*

Voluntary Sector and Not-For-Profit Management, Centre for

Tel: (0171) 477 8667 Fax: (0171) 477 8880

Bruce, Prof. I., BSocSc *Birm.* Hon. Dir.*

CONTACT OFFICERS

Academic affairs. Academic Registrar: Seville, Adrian H., MA *Camb.*, PhD *Edin.*

Accommodation. Director of Accommodation: ......

Admissions (first degree). Undergraduate Admissions Officer: Broom, Richard, BA *Liv.*, MA *Liv.*

Admissions (higher degree). (Contact the head of the appropriate department)

Adult/continuing education. Head, Department of Continuing Education: Lewis, A. J., BA *Durh.*, MSc *E.Lond.*

Alumni. Alumni and Publications Officer: Richardson, Lesley, BSc *Flor.*

Archives. Librarian: McGuirk, John A., MA *Camb.*

Careers. Head of Careers: Cohen, Ruth, BA *Lond.*

Computing services. Director of Computing Services: Vinograd, David, MS *N.Y.*

Development/fund-raising. Secretary: O'Hara, Michael M., MA *Camb.*

Equal opportunities. Director, Academic Services: Owen, Frances, BA *E.Anglia*, MSc *Lond.*

Estates and buildings/works and services. Director: Ostle, Barry

Examinations. Examinations Officer: ......

Finance. Director of Finance: Toop, Frank, BA *N.U.I.*

General enquiries. Secretary: O'Hara, Michael M., MA *Camb.*

Health services. Senior Physician: Rajah, Christine, MB BS *Lond.*

International office. Senior Assistant Registrar: Morris, Christopher, BA *Wales*, MA *York(UK)*

Library (chief librarian). Librarian: McGuirk, John A., MA *Camb.*

Personnel/human resources. Head of Personnel: Dunn, Robin

Public relations, information and marketing. Information Officer: Guess, Kate, BSc *City(UK)*

Publications. Publications Officer: Dry, Christopher, BA *Manc.*

Purchasing. Tibble, John, BA *Lond.*

Quality assurance and accreditation. Director, Academic Services: Owen, Frances, BA *E.Anglia*, MSc *Lond.*

Research. Tinson, Andrea

Safety. Safety Officer: Wilson, Tug

Schools liaison. Senior Assistant Registrar: Sanders, Monica, BA *S'ton.*

Security. General Services Manager: Da Silva, Helio

Sport and recreation. Head of Recreation: Biggar, Sue

Staff development and training. Staff Development and Training Officer: Garrett, Helen, BA *Birm.*, MA *Lond.*

Student union. General Manager: Parkes, Rob, BA *CNAA*

Student welfare/counselling. Student Adviser: Johnson, Sarah, BA *CNAA*

Students from other countries. Senior Assistant Registrar: Morris, Christopher, BA *Wales*, MA *York(UK)*

Students with disabilities. Disability Liaison Officer: Gibberd, Debbie, BA *CNAA*

[*Information supplied by the institution as at 20 July 1998, and edited by the ACU*]

COVENTRY UNIVERSITY

Founded 1992; previously established as Lanchester Polytechnic 1970, Coventry (Lanchester) Polytechnic 1980 and Coventry Polytechnic 1987

Member of the Association of Commonwealth Universities

Postal Address: Priory Street, Coventry, England CV1 5FB
Telephone: (01203) 631313 **Fax**: (01203) 838793

CHAIR OF GOVERNORS—Libby, T. A., MA *St And.*, MBA *Col.*
DEPUTY CHAIR OF GOVERNORS—Marsh, G. R., BEng
VICE-CHANCELLOR*—Goldstein, Michael, CBE, BSc *CNAA*, PhD *CNAA*, DSc *Lond.*, FRSChem
PRO-VICE-CHANCELLOR—Bellamy, Prof. Norman W., BEng *Sheff.*, PhD *Sheff.*
PRO-VICE-CHANCELLOR (RESEARCH)—Pryce, Prof. Robert J., BSc *Brist.*, PhD *Brist.*
PRO-VICE-CHANCELLOR (QUALITY)—Thomas, Prof.Gareth, BA *Exe.*, PhD *Exe.*
SECRETARY—Arlidge, Lynda
ACADEMIC REGISTRAR—Gledhill, John, PhD *Lond.*
LIBRARIAN—Noon, Patrick, BA *CNAA*, MBA *Leic.*

GENERAL INFORMATION

History. The university was originally founded as the School of Design, a predecessor to the School of Art and Design, in 1843. It changed its title to university following the 1992 Further and Higher Education Act.

The university is situated in Coventry city centre.

First Degrees (see also United Kingdom Directory to Subjects of Study). BA, BEng, BSc, LLB, MEng, MSci.

Courses normally last 3 years full-time or the equivalent part-time. MEng, MSci: 4 or 5 years; sandwich courses: 4 years.

Higher Degrees (see also United Kingdom Directory to Subjects of Study). MA, MSc, MPhil, PhD.

Taught master's courses last 12 months full-time. Part-time and research courses vary.

Libraries. Specialist libraries: art and design; nursing; performing arts.

Academic Year (1998–99). Three terms: 28 September–18 December; 11 January–26 March; 26 April–18 June.

FACULTIES/SCHOOLS

Art and Design, Coventry School of
Tel: (01203) 838542 Fax: (01203) 838667
Dean: Tovey, Prof. Michael, MDes RCA
Secretary: Madden, Susan

Built Environment, School of
Tel: (01203) 838257 Fax: (01203) 838590
Dean: Pratt, Prof. Christopher, PhD S'ton.
Secretary: Burr, Joan

Coventry Business School
Tel: (01203) 838412 Fax: (01203) 838400
Dean: Morris, David, BA Keele, MA McM., PhD Warw.
Secretary: MacDonald, Ingrid

Engineering, School of
Tel: (01203) 838365 Fax: (01203) 553007
Dean: Smith, Prof. Edward, BSc Leeds, MSc Leeds, PhD Leeds
Secretary: ......

Health and Social Sciences, School of
Tel: (01203) 838357 Fax: (01203) 838784
Dean: Pennington, Donald, PhD Warw.
Secretary: Lissaman, Jane

International Studies and Law, School of
Tel: (01203) 838000 Fax: (01203) 838679
Dean: Hartley, Paul, PhD Leeds
Secretary: ......

Mathematical and Information Sciences, School of
Tel: (01203) 838564 Fax: (01203) 838585
Dean: James, Glyn, BSc Wales, PhD Warw., FIMA
Secretary: Dinza, Jazz

Natural and Environmental Sciences, School of
Tel: (01203) 838684 Fax: (01203) 838282
Dean: O'Connor, Patrick, MSc Durh.
Secretary: Cahill, April

ACADEMIC UNITS
Arranged by Schools

Art and Design, Coventry School of
Tel: (01203) 838248 Fax: (01203) 838667
Barker, P., BSc CNAA   Sr. Lectr.
Beardsmore, P. J.   Sr. Lectr.
Bennett, R. C., BA Willamette, MA Penn., MPhil CNAA, PhD Penn.   Sr. Lectr.
Best, C.   Sr. Lectr.
Birch, A., BA CNAA, MA CNAA   Sr. Lectr.
Birtley, N.   Sr. Lectr.
Browne, D., BA Leeds   Principal Lectr.
Cannatella, H. J., MDes RCA   Sr. Lectr.
Devane, J., BA CNAA, MA RCA   Sr. Lectr.
Downey, John W., BA Camb., PhD Camb.   Sr. Lectr.
Edge, D., BA Salf., MA Lough.   Sr. Lectr.
Evans, M.   Sr. Lectr.
French, D., BA Essex, MSc Lough.   Head of Subj. Group
Grant, D., BA CNAA   Sr. Lectr.
Hann, Jennifer, MA CNAA   Head of Subj. Group
Harrison, Sandra, BA Brist.   Sr. Lectr.
Harvey, Miranda, BA Reading   Sr. Lectr.
Havers, A., MA CNAA   Sr. Lectr.
Hellaby, J.   Sr. Lectr.
Hides, D. S., BA Leic.   Sr. Lectr.
Hill, Valerie, BA Wales, MA Warw.   Sr. Lectr.
Hostler, J.   Sr. Lectr.
James, C. A.   Sr. Lectr.
Journeaux, J., BA Humb.   Head of Subj. Group
Lee, M. J., BA CNAA   Sr. Lectr.
McGuigan, G., BSc Brad., MPhil Leeds, PhD Leic.   Reader
Mermoz, G., MItal Aix-Marseilles I, MHistArt Aix-Marseilles I   Sr. Lectr.

Newman, R. M., BSc Birm., MSc Tees.
Owen, J., BA CNAA, MA RCA   Sr. Lectr.
Ramskill, R.   Sr. Lectr.
Richards, C., MPhil CNAA, PhD RCA   Prof.
Salisbury, J., BA Keele   Sr. Lectr.
Saunders, R., BA Pratt   Sr. Lectr.
Saunders, S., BA CNAA
Sherlock, G.   Sr. Lectr.
Spaak, R. A., BA CNAA, MA CNAA   Sr. Lectr.
Super, K., BA CNAA   Sr. Lectr.
Sutton, Rachel H.   Sr. Lectr.
Thompson, K., BA CNAA   Sr. Lectr.
Thussu, Dil K.   Sr. Lectr.
Toynbee, J., BA Coventry   Principal Lectr.
Vanner, G., MTech Lough.   Sr. Lectr.
Whatley, Sarah   Sr. Lectr.
Wilby, P., BA CNAA, MPhil CNAA   Head of Subj. Group
Yeadon, J., MA RCA   Sr. Lectr.
Other Staff: 4 Assoc. Sr. Lectrs.; 2 Assoc. Lectrs.

Built Environment
Tel: (01203) 838166 Fax: (01203) 838166
Beck, M. S., BSc CNAA   Head of Subj. Group
Briscoe, D., BCom Birm.   Sr. Lectr.
Broadbent, D., BSc Lond., MSc Brad.   Sr. Lectr.
Chapman, K., MSc Cran.IT   Head of Subj. Group
Claisse, P., BA Oxf., PhD Leeds   Head of Subj. Group
Cross-Rudkin, P., MBA Strath., MA Camb.   Sr. Lectr.
Davies, J., BSc Wales, MSc Wales   Sr. Lectr.
Greengrass, P., BSc Newcastle(UK)   Sr. Lectr.
Lee, C., BA Manc.   Sr. Lectr.
Morgan, S., BSc   Sr. Lectr.
Moseley, Leslie A.   Sr. Lectr.
Penn, S., BSc Durh.   Sr. Lectr.
Rizzuto, J., BSc CNAA, MSc Kingston(UK)   Sr. Lectr.
Saidani, M., PhD Nott.   Sr. Lectr.
Simons, M., MSc Brist.   Sr. Lectr.
Tasker, R., BSc Manc.   Sr. Lectr.
Wright, J. A., MSc H.-W.   Sr. Lectr.

Coventry Business School
Tel: (01203) 838410 Fax: (01203) 838400
Adcock, D., BSc Edin., MSc Lond.   Principal Lectr.
Bayley, Vida, BA Northwestern, MA Lond.   Sr. Lectr.
Beech, J., BA Camb., MBA Camb.   Sr. Lectr.
Bird, L., BSc Lond., MBA W.England   Sr. Lectr.
Blight, D., BA CNAA, MSc Lond.   Principal Lectr.
Bono, C., MSc S.Bank   Sr. Lectr.
Braithwaite, T., MA Leic.   Sr. Lectr.
Carter, K., BSocSc Birm.   Reader, Urban and Regional Planning
Cashian, P., BA Keele   Head of Subj. Group
Chadwick, S., BA CNAA, MA De Mont.   Sr. Lectr.
Clowes, J., BEd Leeds, MSc Mass.   Sr. Lectr.
Collis, C., BA Wales, MA McM.   Principal Lectr.
Cook, S., BA Lond., MSc S'ton.   Sr. Lectr.
Deakin, Ann, BA Leeds   Sr. Lectr.
Donnelly, T., BA Strath., PhD Aberd.   Head of Subj. Group
Eaton, B. D., BA Oxf., PhDWarw.   Sr. Lectr.
Evans, R., MSc Lond.   Sr. Lectr.
Farnell, R., BA Manc., MPhil CNAA   Sr. Lectr.
Finlay, D. C., BCom Birm., MBA Nott.   Head of Subj. Group
Ghosh, D., MA Calc., MA Essex, PhD Leic.   Sr. Lectr.
Goodall, G., BA Durh., MSc Birm., MSocSc Birm.   Sr. Lectr.
Gore, C.   Assoc. Dean
Gray, K. E., BA Oxf., MPhil CNAA   Sr. Lectr.
Green, J., MSc Aston   Sr. Lectr.
Greenwood, B. D.   Sr. Lectr.
Guest, J., BA CNAA, MA E.Anglia   Sr. Lectr.
Halborg, A., BSc Lond., MBA City(UK)   Principal Lectr.
Hammersley, Geraldine, MA Leic.   Sr. Lectr.
Haslam, P., BSc Manc., MBA Aston   Sr. Lectr.
Heaviside, R.   Sr. Lectr.

Hibbert, M. S., BA Hull, MA Brun.   Sr. Lectr.
Horsman, S., BA CNAA, MBA Warw.   Sr. Lectr.
Hughes, Joan, MA Edin.   Sr. Lectr.
Hughes, S., BA Wales, MA Manc.   Sr. Lectr.
Jeffery, B.; MSc   Sr. Lectr.
Johnson, D.   Sr. Lectr.
Kelly, M., MA Tor.   Sr. Lectr.
Kinross, R.   Sr. Lectr.
Lindsay, G. E., BA CNAA, MA De Mont.   Sr. Lectr.
Maynard, Jennifer, BSc Exe.   Sr. Lectr.
Meyrick, B., BA Strath., MBA Coventry   Sr. Lectr.
Mofid, K., MA Windsor, PhD Birm.   Sr. Lectr.
Newman, S., BA Lanc.   Sr. Lectr.
O'Sullivan, M., MA Leic.   Sr. Lectr.
Old, J., BSc Lond.   Principal Lectr.
Panther, J., BA Oxf., MSc Warw.   Principal Lectr.
Parker, G., MA Warw., BA   Sr. Lectr.
Petrochilos, G., BA Athens, MA Lond., PhD Birm.   Sr. Lectr.
Proctor, R., BA Lond., MBA Warw.   Sr. Lectr.
Redhead, K., BSc Brad., MA Leeds, MSc Lond., MPhil Warw.   Principal Lectr.
Robertson, M. J., BSc Warw., MA Warw.   Sr. Lectr.
Rodgers, T., BA Stir., MSc York   Sr. Lectr.
Rogers, R., BA CNAA, MBA CNAA, PhD Nott.   Sr. Lectr.
Rosser, M., BA Essex, MA Warw.   Principal Lectr.
Sandhu, R., BA CNAA, MSc Brad.   Sr. Lectr.
Sara, G., BSc Lond.   Head of Subj. Group
Saunders, M., MA Trinity(Dub.)   Principal Lectr.
Skipper, A. C., BA E.Anglia, MA Warw.   Sr. Lectr.
Steven, Noreen V., BA Belf.   Sr. Lectr.
Sullivan, M. N., BSc Manc., MBA Manc.   Sr. Lectr.
Tanna, S., BSc Lond., MSc Lond., PhD CNAA   Sr. Lectr.
Tapp, A., BSc Birm., PhD Birm.   Sr. Lectr.
Thandi, S., BSc Hull, MSc Lond.   Sr. Lectr.
Tyrrell, Julia, BSc Lough., MBA Coventry   Sr. Lectr.
Urwin, G., BA CNAA, MBA Aston   Sr. Lectr.
Weber, Marit, BA E.Anglia   Sr. Lectr.
Yavash, Perihan, BA CNAA, MSc Lond.   Sr. Lectr.
Other Staff: 3 Res. Fellows

Design, see Art and Des., Coventry Sch. of

Engineering
Tel: (01203) 838888 Fax: (01203) 553007
Aaron, P., BSc Liv.   Principal Lectr.
Abdel-Gayed, R.   Sr. Lectr.
Al-Daiani, A., BSc Wales, MSc Birm., PhD Birm.   Principal Lectr.
Anderson, R. D., BSc CNAA, MSc Lough.   Principal Lectr.
Bacon, M., PhD CNAA   Sr. Lectr.
Bailey, David, BSc Salf., MSc Sheff.   Sr. Lectr.
Baker, M. D.   Sr. Lectr.
Balmer, L., BSc Durh., MSc Warw., PhD Warw.   Sr. Lectr.
Batchelor, A. R., BSc Newcastle(UK), PhD Leeds   Sr. Lectr.
Bate, S., BSc Sheff., PhD   Sr. Lectr.
Baxter, J., MSc CNAA   Sr. Lectr.
Benjamin, S., BSc Lond., PhD Lond.   Reader
Blake, M., BSc CNAA   Sr. Lectr.
Bland, C., MEng Wales   Principal Lectr.
Blount, G., MSc Leeds, PhD Leeds   Prof., Engineering Design
Blundell, M., BSc CNAA, MSc Lond.   Sr. Lectr.
Bray, K., BSc CNAA   Sr. Lectr.
Brindley, J., BSc Aston   Sr. Lectr.
Brooke, W. C., BA Warw., MA Coventry   Sr. Lectr.
Burnham, K. J., BSc CNAA, MSc CNAA, PhD CNAA   Reader
Bush, S., BEng Hull   Sr. Lectr.
Cotton, W., BSc Aston   Principal Lectr.
Crofts, W., BA Open(UK)   Sr. Lectr.
Crowley, Patricia, BA Coventry, MSc Coventry   Sr. Lectr.
Cubillo, J., BSc Salf., MA Lanc.   Sr. Lectr.

Danks, J., BSc Birm., PhD CNAA Principal Lectr.

Darkins, P., BSc Lond., PhD Lond.

Davies, J., MSc Wales Sr. Lectr.

Duffill, R., MSc Birm. Principal Lectr.

Dunn, I. K., BEng CNAA Sr. Lectr.

Dunn, W., BSc Glas., BA Open(UK) Sr. Lectr.

Evatt, M., BA Open(UK) Sr. Lectr.

Fisher, M., BSc Birm., MSc Manc., PhD Manc. Sr. Lectr.

Foyer, P., BSc Nott. Visiting Prof.

Gallois, P., BSc Aston, FIEE Head of Subj. Group

Garner, Wendy, BEng Manc. Sr. Lectr.

Gilbert, J., BTech Lough., MSc Sr. Lectr.

Goodyer, J., BEng CNAA Sr. Lectr.

Griffiths, P., BSc Birm. Principal Lectr.

Harb, S., PhD Manc., BSc MSc Sr. Lectr.

Helps, J., BA Essex, PhD Leeds Sr. Lectr.

Hesketh, T., BSc Salf. Sr. Lectr.

Hickin, R. H., BSc Warw.

Hookes, D., BA Camb., PhD Lond. Sr. Lectr.

Jarvis, R., BA MSc Sr. Lectr.

Jawaid, Ashraf, BSc Lahore UET, MSc Birm., PhD Birm. Prof.; Assoc. Dean

Jerrams, S., MSc Warw. Sr. Lectr.

Jinks, R., BEng CNAA Sr. Lectr.

Johnson, M., BSc Birm., MSc Aston, MSc Warw. Sr. Lectr.

Johnson, T., BSc Salf. Sr. Lectr.

Jones, R. M., BSc CNAA, PhD CNAA Sr. Lectr.

Justham, J. Sr. Lectr.

Kneebone, S., BEng Sheff., MSc Coventry, PhD Coventry Head of Unit

Kondrat, M. W., BSc CNAA, PhD CNAA Sr. Lectr.

Lewis, C., BSc Birm., PhD CNAA, FIEE Reader, Control Engineering

Lewis, M., BEng CNAA Sr. Lectr.

Lloyd, D., BSc Salf., MPhil CNAA Principal Lectr.

Mahtani, J., BSc Liv., MSc Warw. Sr. Lectr.

Manning, A., BSc City(UK) Principal Lectr.

Mansfield, R., BA Open(UK) Sr. Lectr.

Mather, D. Head of Unit

Matthew, M. I., MSc Aston, PhD Coventry Sr. Lectr.

Maydew, Mark, BSc CNAA, MSc Warw. Sr. Lectr.

Mayes, C., BSc CNAA Sr. Lectr.

McCaffery, K., BSc Salf. Sr. Lectr.

McCaskie, C., OBE, BEng Liv., FEng, FIMechE Visiting Prof.

Mercer, R., BSc Leeds, PhD Leeds Principal Lectr.

Middleton, G., BSc Lond., MSc CNAA Sr. Lectr.

Miller, R., BSc Edin. Sr. Lectr.

Page, C., BSc Nott., PhD Nott. Reader, Manufacturing Systems

Perry, R., MA Camb. Sr. Lectr.

Phillips, B., BA Camb. Head of Subj. Group

Poole, N., BSc Leeds Sr. Lectr.

Porter, B., BSc Sr. Lectr.

Pye, T., BA CNAA Sr. Lectr.

Rhodes, R., BSc Sheff. Sr. Lectr.

Richards, O., BSc Wales, PhD Wales Sr. Lectr.

Rider, R. J., BSc CNAA, PhD CNAA Sr. Lectr.

Roberts, T., BSc Nott., PhD CNAA Principal Lectr.

Robotham, A., BSc Leeds, PhD Open(UK) Sr. Lectr.

Saunders, D., BSc CNAA Principal Lectr.

Singh, G., BSc Lond. Sr. Lectr.

Smith, G., BSc Lond., MSc Birm., FIEE Sr. Lectr.

Southey, P., BSc CNAA Sr. Lectr.

Spraggett, S., BSc CNAA, PhD CNAA Head, SME Unit

Srikanthan, T., BSc Sr. Lectr. (on leave)

Steeple, D., MA Camb., PhD Nott. Principal Lectr.

Thorpe, S., BEng Liv. Principal Lectr.

Tubman, K., MEng Liv., PhD Liv. Sr. Lectr.

Watmore, R. E., BSc Lond. Sr. Lectr.

West, M., BEng Liv., PhD CNAA Head of Subj. Group

Wheeler, R. J., BSc Birm., MSc Aston Principal Lectr.

White, P., BSc Nott., PhD Nott. Reader, Thermofluid Dynamics

Whorwood, J., MSc Aston Head of Subj. Group

Winn, P., BSc Sr. Lectr.

Wood, D. G. Head, SME Unit

Wood, R., MSc CNAA Sr. Lectr.

Young, R., BSc Durh. Sr. Lectr.

Other Staff: 3 Lectrs.

Environmental Sciences, see Nat. and Environmental Scis.

Health and Social Sciences

Tel: (01203) 838338 Fax: (01203) 838784

Adams, F., BSc Ulster, PhD Ulster Sr. Lectr.

Alcock, C., BA CNAA, MA Warw. Sr. Lectr.

Allen, D. M., BA CNAA Sr. Lectr.

Alleyne-Belgrave, Verlyn, BA CNAA, MSc Manc. Principal Lectr.

Archer, K. L. Sr. Lectr.

Asby, S., BSc CNAA Sr. Lectr.

Astley-Cooper, Jean, BSc Edin. Sr. Lectr.

Barlow, J. H. Prof.

Barnes, K. V., BSc Coventry, MSc Coventry, PhD Leic. Sr. Lectr.

Barrett, A., BSc Wales, MA W.Ont. Sr. Lectr.

Bato, C. P., BA Philippines Sr. Lectr.

Berney, K., BSc Sr. Lectr.

Bluteau, P. A. Sr. Lectr.

Brew, J. M., BA Nott., BA Lond. Sr. Lectr.

Brown, Maureen, BSc CNAA, MSc Warw. Sr. Lectr.

Bywaters, P., MA Oxf. Head of Subj. Group

Canning, D., LLB Sr. Lectr.

Carney, P. Sr. Lectr.

Cassidy, A. J., BSc Ulster, DPhil Ulster Sr. Lectr.

Chamley, C., BA Lond. Sr. Lectr.

Clouder, Lynne, BSc Birm. Sr. Lectr.

Cook, M., BA Exe. Sr. Lectr.

Copping, J., BA Open(UK), BPT Alta. Sr. Lectr.

Corbett, S., BSc Hudd. Sr. Lectr.

Cross, Dawn Sr. Lectr.

Cullen, S. M., BSc Wolv. Sr. Lectr.

Daley, Claudette, BA CNAA, MSc Aston Sr. Lectr.

Davies, B. M., BSc Coventry Sr. Lectr.

Denny, H. A., MA Warw. Sr. Lectr.

Dignon, A. M., BA Brighton, BSc Leic. Sr. Lectr.

Dowding, L. L., BA Oxf., MEd Warw. Sr. Lectr.

Elliot, Faith, BA Leeds Sr. Lectr.

Field, L. T., MA Coventry Sr. Lectr.

Flemming, R. E., BA Oxf., MA Warw. Sr. Lectr.

Fuller, Sarah, BA CNAA, MA Lond. Sr. Lectr.

Gilbert, F. M., BA Oxf. Sr. Lectr.

Godfrey, S., BSc Coventry, MSc Coventry Sr. Lectr.

Gopee, L. N., BA Oxf., MEd Warw. Sr. Lectr.

Gough, Anna, BSc Oulu, PhD Brad. Sr. Lectr.

Green, Ann, MSc Liv. Sr. Lectr.

Griggs, E., BSc Brist., DPhil York(UK) Sr. Lectr.

Gurden, Helen, BA Sus., MPhil Warw. Sr. Lectr.

Hall, J., BSc Wolv. Sr. Lectr.

Hanlon, Angela, BA CNAA Sr. Lectr.

Harrison, Karen, BEd CNAA, MSc Aston Head of Subj. Group

Heames, Ruth Head of Subj. Group

Heeney, S. L. Sr. Lectr.

Hernandez, M. E., MEd Warw. Sr. Lectr.

Hewison, Alistair, BSc Birm., MA Warw. Head of Subj. Group

Hill, P. M., BA Oxf. Sr. Lectr.

Hirsch, Maureen, BA Exe., MA Brun. Sr. Lectr.

Hopkins, A. E., BA Wolv., BA Wales, MSc Manc.

Horner, L., BA CNAA, MSc Aston

Jackson, Joanna, BA Open(UK), MSc Lough. Sr. Lectr.

Jacob-Lloyd, H. Sr. Lectr.

Jayram, R., BA CNAA Principal Lectr.

Jeffery, Bridget, MSc Wolv. Sr. Lectr.

Jones, Lynda Sr. Lectr.

Jones, N. G., BA Leic. Sr. Lectr.

King, E. M., BA Lough.

Lambon, Nicola, MA Keele Sr. Lectr.

Law, S. M., BSc Wales Sr. Lectr.

Lilley, Pauline, BSc C.England Sr. Lectr.

Loach, W., BA Hull, MPhil Birm. Sr. Lectr.

Macey, S., MSc Lond. Sr. Lectr.

Marchbank, Jennifer, BA Strath., MA CNAA, PhD Strath. Sr. Lectr.

McGregor, F. M., BSc Sr. Lectr.

McKenna, C., BSc Leeds Sr. Lectr.

McNabb, C. M., BA Warw. Sr. Lectr.

Mills, Natalie, BSc Warw., BEd Warw., MEd Warw. Sr. Lectr.

Minett, R., BA CNAA, MA Warw. Head of Subj. Group

Navarro, D. C., MA Warw. Sr. Lectr.

O'Neill, S. J., BA Nott., BSc Coventry Sr. Lectr.

Odedra, S., BA CNAA

Parker, J., BEd Brad., MSc Coventry Sr. Lectr.

Parra-Ramirez, G., BA Warw. Sr. Lectr.

Pehl, L., BSc Lond., MSc S.Bank Sr. Lectr.

Pritchard, Jacqueline, BSc Open(UK) Head of Subj. Group

Rodney, C., BA Open(UK), MSc Aston Sr. Lectr.

Rushton, A. Sr. Lectr.

Sandwell, Mary, BSc Wolv. Sr. Lectr.

Scott, C. A., BSc Coventry, MSc Coventry Sr. Lectr.

Scullion, P. A., BSc C.England Sr. Lectr.

Shanley, J. M., BA CNAA, MSc Brun. Sr. Lectr.

Shannon, J. T., BA Oxf. Sr. Lectr.

Sharp, K., BSc Lond., PhD Edin. Head of Subj. Group

Sim, J., BA Durh., MSc CNAA Principal Lectr.

Singh, Gurnam, MSc Brad. Sr. Lectr.

Smith, M., BA Newcastle(UK) Sr. Lectr.

Stanton, Angela, MA Warw., PhD Warw. Principal Lectr.

Stapleton, J. A., BA Oxf. Sr. Lectr.

Steed, Anita Sr. Lectr.

Sterling, C. M., BA Stir., MSc Roehampton IHE, PhD Stir. Principal Lectr.

Wade, Mary, MSc City(UK) Sr. Lectr.

Waine, W. T., MSc Reading Sr. Lectr.

Wallis, P. A., BSc Nene, MEd Warw. Sr. Lectr.

Ward, Karen, BSc CNAA Sr. Lectr.

Waterrold, J., BA Sheff., MSc Sur. Sr. Lectr.

Webb, A. K., BSc Wolv. Sr. Lectr.

Whitehead, Kathy, BA CNAA Sr. Lectr.

Wilde, R., BA Wales Head of Subj. Group

Wildman, S., BA Hull, MA Sheff. Sr. Lectr.

Willden, S. M., BA Oxf. Sr. Lectr.

Other Staff: 6 Assoc. Sr. Lectrs.; 15 Lectrs.; 3 Assoc. Lectrs.

Information Sciences, see Mathl. and Information Scis.

International Studies and Law

Tel: (01203) 838176 Fax: (01203) 838679

Astley, Sonja Sr. Lectr.

Blain, Marion, BEd Glas. Sr. Lectr.

Bradley, Margaret, MA Manc., MPhil Leeds Sr. Lectr.

Brobbey, B., LLM Lond., PhD Lond. Principal Lectr.

Campbell, Lesley, BSc Wales Sr. Lectr.

Chubarov, A., PhD Moscow Sr. Lectr.

Corness, P., BA Lond., MA Warw. Principal Lectr.

Dandy, Dorothy, BA Lond. Sr. Lectr.

Devis, Pauline M., BA Coventry Sr. Lectr.

Dunne, J., BA Liv. Sr. Lectr.

Forbes, N., BA Hull, MA Lond., PhD Kent Sr. Lectr.

Foster, S., BA CNAA, LLM Lond. Principal Lectr.

Gingell, R., LLB Warw. Sr. Lectr.

Goulbourne, Selina, LLB S'ton., LLM Lond. Principal Lectr.

Grantham, D., MA Sus. Sr. Lectr.

Haydon, D., MèsL Nice Sr. Lectr.

Henderson, I., BA Oxf., MA Edin., PhD Edin. Principal Lectr.

Hocking, B., BA Brist., MA Leic., PhD Lond., MPhil Prof., International Relations

Hoskyns, Catherine, MA Oxf. Prof.

Jeffree, Debra, LLB CNAA Principal Lectr.

Johnson, J. A., LLB Coventry, MA Leic.

Jones, D., BA Wales, MA Lond., MA Birm. Principal Lectr.

Jones, H., MA Oxf., MPhil S'ton. Sr. Lectr.
Katalikawe, J., LLB Lond., LLM Harv., MA Tufts, PhD Lond. Sr. Lectr.
Kay, R., BA Oxf. Sr. Lectr.
Kohler-Ridley, Monika, BA Warw. Sr. Lectr.
Magee, F., BA Leeds Sr. Lectr.
Matthews, K., BSc Lond. Sr. Lectr.
May, R., BSc Lond. Head of Subj. Group
McKay, N., LLB CNAA Sr. Lectr.
Mitchell, B., LLB Birm. Reader
Montague, J., LLB Warw., MA CNAA Sr. Lectr.
Orsini-Jones, Marina, DottLett Bologna, MA Warw. Sr. Lectr.
Page, Caroline, BA Reading, PhD Reading Sr. Lectr.
Panesar, S., LLB Coventry, LLM Warw. Sr. Lectr.
Parkin, Dorothy, BA Lond., MA Warw. Sr. Lectr.
Parra-Ramirez, G., BA Warw. Sr. Lectr.
Perkin, C., BA CNAA, LLM Birm. Principal Lectr.
Roberts, C., BA Lond., MPhil Warw. Sr. Lectr.
Semafumu, S., LLM Warw. Sr. Lectr.
Shaw, G., MA S'ton. Sr. Lectr.
Smith, G. W., BA Dund., MA Dund., PhD Lough. Head of Subj. Group
Smith, M. P., MA Warw. Sr. Lectr.
Squires, N., LLM Warw. Sr. Lectr.
Steventon, B., BA Bath Sr. Lectr.
Talbot, I., BA Lond., PhD Lond. Reader
Vickery, Susan, BA Sr. Lectr.
Vollans, T., LLB Leeds Sr. Lectr.
Wells, G., MA Oxf., MA Birm. Sr. Lectr.
Wilcox, Lynne, BSc Aston Sr. Lectr.
Wilkinson, R., BA E.Anglia, MSc Aston Sr. Lectr.
Williams, M. T., LLB Sheff. Sr. Lectr.
Other Staff: 1 Assoc. Sr. Lectr.; 3 Lectrs.; 2 Assoc. Lectrs.

Mathematical and Information Sciences

Tel: (01203) 838673 Fax: (01203) 838585

Adams, R., BA Oxf., MSc Warw. Sr. Lectr.
Amin, S. A., MPhil Brun., PhD Lough. Sr. Lectr.
Aspinall, B., BSc Durh. Head of Subj. Group
Baker, B., MSc Lond., PhD Lond. Sr. Lectr.
Barrett, K., BSc Lond., PhD Lond. Reader, Computational Mathematics
Baxter, J., BA Sheff., MSc Warw. Principal Lectr.
Betteley, I., BSc Birm. Sr. Lectr.
Bowman, P., BSc Manc. Sr. Lectr.
Carson, R., BA Salf., PhD Brist. Sr. Lectr.
Chantler, A., BSc Lond. Principal Lectr.
Chapman, D., BSc CNAA Sr. Lectr.
Chapman, M., BSc Warw., PhD Warw. Sr. Lectr.
Cook, R., BSc Liv., MSc CNAA Sr. Lectr.
Croft, A., BSc Lond., MSc Warw., PhD CNAA Principal Lectr.
Dil, A., BSc Maryland, PhD Lough. Sr. Lectr.
Gatward, R., BA Open(UK), MSc CNAA Sr. Lectr.
Giannasi, F., BA Open(UK), BSc Newcastle(UK), MSc Birm. Sr. Lectr.
Gleeson, J., BSc Aston, MSc Sr. Lectr.
Glendinning, Irene, BSc CNAA Sr. Lectr.
Godwin, A., BSc Reader, Computer Science
Goodall, D., BSc CNAA, MSc Dund., PhD Bath Sr. Lectr.
Hamer, D. N., BSc CNAA Principal Lectr.
Hobson, A., BSc Wales, MSc Birm. Sr. Lectr.
Hodder, S., BSc CNAA, MPhil CNAA Sr. Lectr.
Hough, D., BSc Manc., MSc Brun., PhD Brun. Sr. Lectr.
Humphries, P., BSc Lond., MSc Warw., PhD Warw. Sr. Lectr.
Hunt, D., BSc Nott., PhD Nott. Principal Lectr.
James, Anne E., BSc Aston, PhD Aston Principal Lectr.
Johnston, C., BSc Belf., MSc Birm., PhD Brad. Sr. Lectr.
Jones, R., BSc Wales Sr. Lectr.
Kenning, G., BA Lond., BA Open(UK)., MA Essex, MSc Open(UK), MEd Open(UK) Sr. Lectr.
King, Virginia, BA Lanc. Sr. Lectr.
Lawson, D., BA Oxf., DPhil Oxf. Sr. Lectr.
Lennon, H., BSc Lond. Head of Subj. Group

Leyland, Valerie, MBA Warw. Sr. Lectr.
Lockett, F., MA Camb., PhD Warw. Sr. Lectr.
Low, R., MA Aberd., DPhil Oxf. Sr. Lectr.
Mashoudy, H., MSc Lond., PhD Warw. Sr. Lectr.
Monk, K., BA Open(UK), MSc Birm. Sr. Lectr.
Morgan, L., MSc Manc. Sr. Lectr.
Neal, Maureen, BSc Brist. Assoc. Dean
Newman, R., BSc Birm. Sr. Lectr.
O'Neil, M., MSc Wales Principal Lectr.
Obray, C., BSc Sheff., MSc City(UK), PhD City(UK) Principal Lectr.
Odetayo, M. O., MSc Lond., PhD Glas. Sr. Lectr.
Payne, Lisa, BSc E.Anglia, MSc CNAA Sr. Lectr.
Poppleton, M., BSc Witw., MSc Aston Sr. Lectr.
Prince, Sandra, BA CNAA, MSc Oxf. Sr. Lectr.
Railton, A., BSc Lond. Sr. Lectr.
Reeves, C., BSc CNAA, MPhil CNAA Sr. Lectr.
Reeves, Jane, BSc NSW, PhD NSW Sr. Lectr.
Robinson, Helen, BA Camb., MSc Warw. Sr. Lectr.
Shanmugalimgum, S., BSc Ceyl., MSc Sheff. Sr. Lectr.
Shields, D., BSc Lough., PhD Lough. Reader, Control Theory
Smith, E., BSc Manc., MSc Brist., PhD Brist. Sr. Lectr.
Solomon, R., BA Open(UK), MEd Birm. Sr. Lectr.
Stavrinides, A., BSc Lond., PhD Birm. Principal Lectr.
Steele, N., MSc S'ton., FIMA Head of Subj. Group
Tabor, J., BSc Lond., PhD Lond. Principal Lectr.
Talbot, D., BSc Bath, PhD Bath Sr. Lectr.
Tatham, E., BA Open(UK), MSc CNAA Sr. Lectr.
Taylor, D., BA Leeds, MSc Leeds
Tyrrell, S. E., LLB Lond., MA Camb.
Vella, C., BSc Birm., MSc CNAA Sr. Lectr.
Webster, M., MSc Lond., MA Sus. Principal Lectr.
Wilkin, J., BSc Sheff. Sr. Lectr.
Wilson, M., MA Camb., MSc Warw., FIMA Sr. Lectr.
Wright, Christine, BSc CNAA Sr. Lectr.
Yan, S. Y., BSc Beijing Sr. Lectr.
Zhang, B., PhD Glas. Sr. Lectr.
Other Staff: 2 Lectrs.

Natural and Environmental Sciences

Tel: (01203) 838694 Fax: (01203) 838282

Abyaneh, M., PhD S'ton. Sr. Lectr.
Al-Daffaee, H., BSc Baghdad Sr. Lectr.
Arthurs, M., BSc Belf., PhD Belf. Sr. Lectr.
Baban, S., BSc Baghdad, MSc Baghdad, PhD E.Anglia Sr. Lectr.
Barrett, Hazel, BA Sus., MA Birm., PhD Birm. Sr. Lectr.
Bourne, W., BSc Durh., PhD Newcastle(UK) Head of Subj. Group
Brooks, S., BSc Lond. Principal Lectr.
Browne, Angela, BA Sheff., MA Newcastle(UK), PhD Sr. Lectr.
Carey, R., BSc Nott., PhD Nott. Prof., Magnetic Materials
Clark, D., BSc Brad., MA Sus., PhD Wales Reader, Human Geography; Head of Subj. Group
Conlon, Jane, MSc Manc., PhD Open(UK) Dir., TABEISA Project
Covency, J., BSc Lond., PhD Warw. Sr. Lectr.
Crisp, D., BSc Brist., PhD Brist. Sr. Lectr.
Dawson, A., BSc Aberd., MSc Louisiana State, PhD Edin. Reader, Quaternary Science
Duckers, L., BSc E.Anglia, PhD E.Anglia Principal Lectr.
Economides, H. P., BSc Lond., PhD Lond. Assoc. Dean
Fagbemi, O., PhD Ib. Sr. Lectr.
Foster, I., BSc Lond., PhD Exe. Prof., Geomorphology
Halstead, Alison, BSc Lond., PhD Lond. Head of Subj. Group
Harris, P., BSc Bath, PhD Glas. Prof., Plant Science
Harrison, S., BSc Leic., PhD CNAA Sr. Lectr.

Henderson, Janey, BSc Aberd., MSc Manc., PhD Durh. Sr. Lectr.
Heptinstall, J., BSc Sheff., PhD Sheff. Sr. Lectr.
Hubbard, P. J., BA Birm., PhD Birm. Sr. Lectr.
Ilbery, B., BA Wales, PhD Wales Prof., Human Geography
Jackson, Roselyn, BSc Durh., MSc Sheff., PhD S'ton. Sr. Lectr.
Javed, T., BSc Salf., PhD Salf. Sr. Lectr.
Jones, R., BSc Durh., PhD Durh. Principal Lectr.
Keen, D., BSc Lond., PhD Lond. Reader, Quaternary Palaeontology
Kirk, D., BSc Birm., PhD Birm. Principal Lectr.
Langlands, Beata, BSc Glas., PhD Glas. Sr. Lectr.
Lorimer, P., BSc Lond., PhD Lond. Reader, Physical Chemistry
Marsh, D., BSc Lond., PhD Lond. Principal Lectr.
Mason, T., BSc S'ton., PhD S'ton. Prof., Chemistry
Mian, R., BSc Liv., PhD Birm. Sr. Lectr.
Mighall, T., BSc Keele Sr. Lectr.
Morrow, R. J., BSc Ulster, MSc E.Anglia, PhD E.Anglia Sr. Lectr.
Newman, A., MSc CNAA Sr. Lectr.
Nicholls, P., MA Lond., PhD Lond. Principal Lectr.
Norris, G., BA Keele Sr. Lectr.
Parker, N., BSc Brist., PhD CNAA Sr. Lectr.
Peterson, I., BSc Syd., MSc Syd. Prof., Molecular Electronics
Smith, D., BA Manc., PhD Edin. Prof., Geography
Smith, H., BSc Edin., MSc Aberd., PhD Edin. Sr. Lectr.
Smith, S. J., BSc Exe., PhD Open(UK) Sr. Lectr.
Sturdee, A., BSc Aberd., PhD Leeds Principal Lectr.
Tomlinson, W., MSc Manc., PhD Manc. Reader, Materials
Turner, A. P., BA Coventry Sr. Lectr.
Viney, I., BSc Nott., PhD Nott. Sr. Lectr.
Walton, D., BSc Sus., DPhil Sus. Reader, Applied Chemistry
Whitehouse, Diane, BSc Newcastle(UK), PhD Lond. Sr. Lectr.
Other Staff: 6 Lectrs.; 3 Assoc. Lectrs.

Social Sciences, see Health and Soc. Scis.

CONTACT OFFICERS

Academic affairs. Academic Registrar: Gledhill, John, PhD Lond.
Accommodation. Manager of Residences: Whitlock, David
Alumni. Director of Corporate Affairs: Macrae, Cyrrhian, BA Manc.
Careers. Deputy Director of Student Services: Barlow, Marshall, BA Salf.
Computing services. Director of Computing Services: Dimmer, Paul, BSc Lond., PhD Leic.
Consultancy services. Director of Commercial Affairs: Roberts, Eulian, BSc MBA PhD
Estates and buildings/works and services. Director of Estates: Woolhead, William
Finance. Director of Finance: Law, Graham
General enquiries. Secretary: Arlidge, Lynda
International office. Director of International Affairs: O'Sullivan, Ann
Library (chief librarian). Librarian: Noon, Patrick, BA CNAA, MBA Leic.
Personnel/human resources. Director of Personnel: Skinner, Andrew, BA Lond.
Public relations, information and marketing. Director of Corporate Affairs: Macrae, Cyrrhian, BA Manc.
Quality assurance and accreditation. Pro-Vice-Chancellor (Quality): Thomas, Prof. Gareth, BA Exe., PhD Exe.
Research. Pro-Vice-Chancellor (Research): Pryce, Prof. Robert J., BSc Brist., PhD Brist.
Students with disabilities. Disabilities Officer: Boctusz, Helen

[Information supplied by the institution as at 4 March 1998, and edited by the ACU]

CRANFIELD UNIVERSITY

Incorporated by Royal Charter, 1969 as Cranfield Institute of Technology, and retitled Cranfield University in 1993; previously established as the College of Aeronautics, 1946

Member of the Association of Commonwealth Universities

Postal Address: Cranfield, Bedfordshire, England MK43 0AL
Telephone: (01234) 750111 **Fax**: (01234) 750972 **Telex**: 825072 CITECH G **WWW**: http://www.cranfield.ac.uk
E-mail formula: initial(s)surname@cranfield.ac.uk (for Silsoe–silsoe.cranfield.ac.uk;
for Shrivenham–rmcs.cranfield.ac.uk)

VISITOR—Kent, H.R.H. The Duke of , KG, GCMG, GCVO, FEng, FRS
CHANCELLOR—Vincent of Coleshill, The Lord , GBE, KCB, DSO, FIMechE, FRAeS
PRO-CHANCELLOR—Gill, Sir Anthony, BSc(Eng) *Lond.*, Hon. DSc *Cran.*, Hon. DSc *S'ton.*, Hon. DSc *Warw.*, Hon. DEng *Birm.*, FIMechE, FIEE, FEng
TREASURER—Baldwin. B. A., FCA
VICE-CHANCELLOR*—Hartley, Prof. Frank R., BA *Oxf.*, MA *Oxf.*, DPhil *Oxf.*, DSc *Oxf.*, FRSChem, FRAeS
PRO-VICE-CHANCELLOR—Hutchinson, Prof. Philip, BSc *Durh.*, PhD *Newcastle(UK)*
DEPUTY VICE-CHANCELLOR—Fletcher, Prof. R. S., BScTech *Manc.*, PhD *Lond.*, FRAeS
DEPUTY VICE-CHANCELLOR—Hutchinson, Prof. Philip, BSc *Durh.*, PhD *Newcastle(UK)*
DIRECTOR OF PERSONNEL—Delger, Patricia A., MA *Leic.*
DIRECTOR OF FINANCE—Bate, David H., FCA

GENERAL INFORMATION

History. The university has its origins in the College of Aeronautics established in 1946. It was incorporated by royal charter as Cranfield Institute of Technology in 1969, and the present name was adopted in 1993.

The university has campuses at Cranfield and Silsoe in Bedfordshire; it is also responsible for the academic work at the Royal Military College of Science at Shrivenham in Oxfordshire.

Admission to first degree courses (see also United Kingdom Introduction). Through Universities and Colleges Admissions Service (UCAS). Passes in 5 separate subjects in the General Certificate of Secondary Education (GCSE) (grade C or above) or General Certificate of Education (GCE), of which 2 must be at A level and 1 must be in English. Qualifications judged equivalent to these are also acceptable.

First Degrees (see also United Kingdom Directory to Subjects of Study). BEng, BSc.

Courses are full-time and normally last 3 years.

Higher Degrees (see also United Kingdom Directory to Subjects of Study). MA, MBA, MDA (defence administration), MRes, MSc, MPhil, PhD, DSc, EngD.

Applicants must normally hold an appropriate first degree with at least second class honours, or equivalent.

Libraries. 405,250 volumes; 1745 periodicals subscribed to. Special collections: Conservation Trust (at Silsoe).

Academic Year. 1 October–30 September.

Income (1996–97). Total, £99,101,000.

Statistics. Staff: 1783 (414 academic). Students: full-time 2270; part-time 759; international 767; total 3029.

FACULTIES/SCHOOLS

Agricultural Engineering, Food Production and Rural Land Use
Tel: (01525) 863289

Dean: Carr, Prof. Michael K. V., BSc *Nott.*, PhD *Nott.*

Defence Science, Technology and Management
Tel: (01793) 782551

Dean: Mays, Prof. Geoff C., BSc *Brist.*, PhD *Dund.*

Engineering
Dean: Sanderson, Prof. Michael L., MSc *Manc.*, PhD *Manc.*

Management
Dean: Vinnicombe, Susan M., MA *Lanc.*, PhD *Manc.*

Manufacturing Technology and Production Management
Dean: Corbett, Prof. John, MSc *Cran.*, FIMechE, FIEE

Science and Technology
Dean: Stephenson, Prof. Tom, BSc *York(UK)*, PhD *Lond.*

ACADEMIC UNITS

Accounting, see Management, Sch. of

Aeronautics, College of
Fax: (01234) 752149

Alamdari, F., MSc *Cran.*, PhD *Cran.* Sr. Lectr.
Allerton, D. J., BSc *CNAA*, PhD *Camb.*, FIEE, FRAeS GEC Prof., Avionics
Bowling, Tom S., BSc *Lond.* Sr. Lectr.
Cook, Michael V., BSc *S'ton.*, MSc *Cran.*, FRAeS, FIMA Sr. Lectr.
Devine, Mike L., BSc *CNAA*, MSc *Newcastle(UK)* Sr. Lectr.
Eshelby, Martin E., BSc *Glas.*, PhD *Cran.*, FRAeS Sr. Lectr.
Fielding, John P., MSc *Cran.*, PhD *Cran.*, FRAeS Prof., Aerospace Technology
Garry, Kevin P., BSc *S'ton.*, MSc *Cran.*, PhD *Cran.* Sr. Lectr.
Golding, Robert J., MSc *Cran.* Sr. Lectr.
Guenov, Marin D., PhD *Napier* Sr. Lectr.
Harris, Ian, MA *Camb.*, FRMetS Reader, Wind Engineering
Lewis, David J. G., BSc *Wales* Sr. Lectr.
Loughlan, Joe, MSc *Strath.*, PhD *Strath.* Reader
Morrell, Peter S., MA *Camb.*, MS *M.I.T.* Sr. Lectr.
Morris, Alan J., BSc *Manc.*, MSc *Colorado*, PhD *Camb.* Prof., Computational Structural Analysis
Muir, Helen C., OBE, MA *St And.*, PhD *Lond.* Prof., Aerospace Psychology
Poll, D. Ian A., BSc(Eng) *Lond.*, PhD *Cran.*, FRAeS, FEng Prof.; Head*
Qin Ning, MEng *Nanjing Aeron.Inst.*, PhD *Glas.* Sr. Lectr.
Snow, John E., BSc *S'ton.*, MSc *Cran.* Sr. Lectr.
Taylor, A. Frank, BSc *Reading*, FRAeS Sr. Lectr.
Thomasson, Peter G., MSc Sr. Lectr.
Williams, George, PhD *Cran.* Sr. Lectr.

BioScience and Technology, Institute of
Fax: (01234) 752401

Magan, Naresh, BSc *Exe.*, MSc *Exe.*, PhD *Reading* Sr. Lectr.
Turner, Tony P. F., BSc *CNAA*, MSc *Kent*, PhD *CNAA* Prof., Bio-sensor Technology; Head*
Warner, Philip J., BSc *Lond.*, PhD *Kent* Prof., Industrial Molecular Biology

Finance, see Management, Sch. of

Industrial and Manufacturing Science, School of
Fax: (01234) 752159

Allen, David M., BSc *Wales*, PhD *Wales* Reader
Allen, Peter M., BSc *Hull*, PhD *Hull* Res. Prof.
Allwood, Robert L., BSc *Reading*, PhD *H.-W.* Sr. Lectr.
Ashwell, Geoffrey J., BSc *Nott.*, PhD *Nott.*, FRSChem Prof., Molecular Electronics
Baines, Timothy S., MSc *Cran.*, PhD *Cran.* Sr. Lectr.
Barnes, John A., BSc *Lond.* Sr. Lectr.
Billingham, John, BSc *Birm.*, PhD *Warw.*, FIM Prof., Marine Technology; Head*
Blackman, Stephen A., BSc *Wales*, MSc *Cran.* Sr. Lectr.
Bucknall, Clive B., MA *Camb.*, PhD *Camb.*, ScD *Camb.*, FIM Prof., Polymer Science
Chubb, John P., BSc *Newcastle(UK)*, PhD *Newcastle(UK)* Sr. Lectr.
Corbett, John, MSc *Cran.*, FIMechE, FIEE Prof., Precision Engineering
Cordey-Hayes, Martin, BSc *Wales*, PhD *Birm.* Prof., Technology Policy
Cousins, Steve H., BSc *Durh.*, PhD *Open(UK)* Assoc. Prof.
Darlington, Michael W., BSc *S'ton.*, PhD *S'ton.*, FIM Reader
Deasley, Peter J., BSc *Nott.*, PhD *Nott.*, FIEE Prof., Mechatronics
Dickenson, Richard P., BSc *Warw.*, MSc *Sur.*, PhD *Westminster* Sr. Lectr.
Evans, Stephen, BSc *Bath*, PhD *Bath* Sr. Lectr.
Fan, I., BSc *HK*, PhD *Cran.* Sr. Lectr.
Fuller, Graham D., MPhil *Cran.* Sr. Lectr.
Gee, Anthony E., BSc *Reading*, PhD *Reading* Sr. Lectr.
Groves, Gwynn, BSc *City(UK)*, MSc *Cran.* Sr. Lectr.
Irving, Philip, BSc *Birm.*, PhD *Birm.* Prof., Helicopter Damage Tolerance
Jared, Graham E. M., BA Reader
Judd, Simon J., BSc *Bath*, MSc *S'ton.*, PhD *Cran.* Sr. Lectr.
Kay, John M., BSc *Nott.*, PhD *Nott.*, FIEE Prof., Manufacturing Systems Engineering
McMaster, R. S., MSc *Cran.*, PhD *Cran.* Sr. Lectr.

Newman, Victor, BA Manc., PhD Bath   Sr. Lectr.

Nicholls, John R., BSc(Eng) Lond., PhD Lond.   Prof., Coatings Technology

Partridge, Ivana K., MA Camb., PhD Cran.   Sr. Lectr.

Richardson, Ian M., BSc E.Anglia, MSc Sheff., PhD Cran.   Sr. Lectr.

Robinson, Michael J., BSc Leeds, PhD Leeds   Reader

Rogerson, John H., MA Camb., PhD Cran.   Prof., Quality Systems

Rooney, E. Margaret, BSc Newcastle(UK), PhD Cran.   Sr. Lectr.

Sackett, Peter, MSc Manc., PhD UMIST   Prof.

Shaw, Trevor W., BSc Wales, PhD Wales   Sr. Lectr.

Soltan, H., BSc Aston, MSc   Sr. Lectr.

Sprague, Linda, MBA Boston, DBA Harv.   Prof.†

Spurrier, John, MA Camb., PhD Leeds   Sr. Lectr.

Stephenson, David J., BSc York(UK), PhD Lond.   Prof.

Stephenson, Tom, BSc York(UK), PhD Lond.   Lorch Prof., Water Sciences

Strutt, John E., BSc Sus., DPhil Sus.   Sr. Lectr.

Wainwright, Charles, BEng CNAA, PhD UMIST   Sr. Lectr.

Webster, Norman, DSc Lond.   Sr. Lectr.

Whatmore, Roger W., MA Camb., PhD Camb.   Royal Academy of Engineering Prof., Engineering Nanotechnology

Williams, David F., MSc Cran.   Sr. Lectr.

Wu, Bin, BSc Brunei, PhD Brun.   Sr. Lectr.

Management, School of

Tel: (01234) 751122 Fax: (01234) 751806

Barrow, Colin, MBA   Sr. Lectr.

Black, Ian G., BA Nott.   Sr. Lectr.

Bowman, Cliff, BA Liv., MBA Liv.   Prof., Business Strategy

Brewster, Chris J., BA(Econ) Sheff., PhD Lond.   Prof., European Human Resource Management

Buckley, Adrian, MSc Brad., FCA   Prof., International Financial Management

Butcher, David J., BA Leeds, MA Leeds, PhD Brad.   Sr. Lectr.

Buttle, Francis, BSc Manc., MA Lanc., PhD Lanc.   Prof., Marketing

Christopher, Martin G., BA Lanc., MSc Brad., PhD Cran.   Prof., Marketing and Logistics Systems

Clark, Graham R., BSc Leeds, MSc Lond.   Sr. Lectr.

Drake, Jacqueline, BA Exe., MBA   Sr. Lectr.†

Edwards, Chris, MA Sheff., PhD Strath.   Prof., Management Information Systems

Fishwick, Frank, MA(Econ) Manc., PhD Cran.   Reader, Managerial Economics

Gordon, Colin, BA Lond.   Sr. Lectr.

Grimshaw, David, BSc Hull, MPhil CNAA, PhD Warw.   Sr. Lectr.

Hatch, Mary Jo, MBA Indiana, PhD Stan.   Prof., Organisation Theory

Hope-Hailey, Veronica R., BA York(UK), MSc Aston, PhD Aston   Sr. Lectr.

James, Kim, BSc   Sr. Lectr.

Jenkins, M., BA Hudd., MSc Cran., PhD Cran.   Sr. Lectr.

Johnson, Gerry, BA Lond., PhD Aston   Prof., Strategic Management

Kakabadse, Andrew, BSc Salf., MA Brun., PhD Manc., FBPsS   Prof., Management Development

Knox, Simon D., BSc Sheff., PhD Sheff.   Prof., Brand Marketing

Lambert, Robert D., MSc Bath   Sr. Lectr.

Ludlow, J. Ron, MBA Cran.   Sr. Lectr.

Mapes, John, MA Camb., MTech Brun.   Sr. Lectr.

McDonald, Malcolm H. B., MA Oxf., MSc Brad., PhD Cran.   Prof., Marketing Strategy

Meldrum, Michael J., BA Manc.Met., MBA Cran.   Sr. Lectr.

Murray, Leo G., MA Glas.   Prof.; Dir.*

Myddelton, David R., MBA Harv., FCA   Prof., Finance and Accounting

Nellis, Joe G., BSc(Econ) Ulster, MA Warw., PhD Cran.   Prof., International Management Economics

New, Colin C., MA Camb., MSc Lond., PhD Lond.   Prof., Manufacturing Strategy

Payne, Adrian F. T., MSc Aston, MEd Melb., PhD Melb.   Prof., Services and Relationships Marketing

Peter, Melvyn J., MSc Cran.   Sr. Lectr.

Porter, Brenda, BSc Hull, PhD Massey   Sr. Lectr.

Randlesome, Colin C., BA Nott., MA Nott.   Sr. Lectr.

Rickard, Sean M., BSc Lond., MSc Lond., MBA Cran.   Sr. Lectr.

Rushton, Alan S., BA Warw., MSc Cran.   Sr. Lectr.

Saw, Richard J., MA Camb., MA Lanc.   Sr. Lectr.

Scott, Melvyn D., MBA Cape Town   Sr. Lectr.

Srikanthan, S., MBA   Sr. Lectr.

Steele, W. Murray B., BSc Glas., MSc Glas., MBA Cran.   Sr. Lectr.

Sweeney, Mike T., MSc Bath   Prof., Operations Management

Tallman, M., BSc U.S.Military Acad., PhD Calif.   Sr. Lectr.

Tyson, Shaun J. J., BA Lond., PhD Lond.   Prof., Human Resource Management

Vinnicombe, Susan M., MA Lanc., PhD Manc.   Reader

Ward, John M., MA Camb., FCA   Prof., Strategic Information Systems

Wright, Derek S., MSc Cran., PhD Cran., BTech   Sr. Lectr.

Manufacturing, see Indust. and Manufacturing Sci., Sch. of

Mechanical Engineering, School of

Fax: (01234) 750728

Badr, Ossama M. H., BSc Cairo, PhD Cran.   Sr. Lectr.

Bannister, Roy H., MSc Aston, PhD Aston   Sr. Lectr.

Batty, William J., MSc PhD   Sr. Lectr.

El-Zafrany, Ali M., MSc Cran., PhD Cran., BSc(Eng)   Sr. Lectr.

Elder, Robin L., BSc Lond., PhD Leic.   Prof., Compressor Technology

Greenhalgh, Douglas A., BSc Newcastle(UK), PhD Newcastle(UK)   Prof., Non-Intrusive Measurement of Combustion and Flow

Hemp, John, BSc Manc., DPhil Oxf.   Sr. Lectr.

Hutchinson, Philip, BSc Durh., PhD Newcastle(UK)   Prof., Statistical Fluid Mechanics; Head*

Moss, J. Barrie, BSc Leeds, MSc Cran., PhD Cran., FIMechE   Prof., Thermofluids and Combustion

Newborough, Marcus, MSc Cran., PhD Cran.   Sr. Lectr.

Pilidis, Pilidis, BSc Glas., MBA Glas., PhD Glas.   Sr. Lectr.

Ramsden, Ken W., BSc CNAA, MSc   Sr. Lectr.

Robertson, A. John, BSc(Eng) Lond.   Sr. Lectr.

Rubini, Philip A., BSc Sheff., PhD Sheff.   Sr. Lectr.

Sanderson, Michael L., MSc Manc., PhD Manc.   Prof., Fluid Instrumentation

Sharp, Robin S., BSc Leeds, MSc Cran.   Prof., Automotive Product Engineering

Singh, Riti, BSc Delhi   Prof., Gas Turbine Engineering

Tatam, Ralph P., BSc Exe., PhD CNAA   Reader

Thompson, Christopher P., MA Oxf., MSc Oxf., PhD Bergen   Sr. Lectr.

Tomlinson, Michael A., BSc CNAA, MPhil CNAA   Sr. Lectr.

Yeung, H. C., BSc(Eng) HK, PhD Newcastle(UK)   Sr. Lectr.

SHRIVENHAM SITE

Tel: (01793) 782551 Fax: (01793) 783878

Defence Technology, College of

Tel: (01793) 782551 Fax: (01793) 783878

Aitchison, Joyce M., MA Oxf., DPhil Oxf., FIMA   Sr. Lectr.

Aitken, James E., PhD Camb.   Sr. Lectr.

Akhaven, Jacqueline, BSc S'ton., MPhil S'ton., PhD S'ton.   Sr. Lectr.

Avery, Alan J., BSc S'ton., PhD S'ton.   Sr. Lectr.

Bailey, Alan, BSc Brist., PhD Brist., FRSChem   Prof., Applied Chemistry

Bathe, Mike R., BSc Reading, MSc Sus.   Sr. Lectr.

Bellamy, Christopher D., BA Oxf., MA Lond., PhD Edin.   Reader

Bellamy, Tony J., BSc Birm., PhD Birm.   Reader

Bellerby, John M., BSc York(UK), PhD Camb.   Sr. Lectr.

Berridge, Pamela M., MBA Oxf.Brookes   Sr. Lectr.

Brown, Alexander, PhD Belf., DSc Nott., FIMechE   Prof., Power Plants and Propulsion

Cartwright, M., BSc Lond., PhD Lond.   Sr. Lectr.

Clark, Kevin P. D., BSc Lond., FRSChem   Sr. Lectr.

Colyer, Ron E., BSc Brist., PhD Brist., FIEE   Sr. Lectr.

Crowley, Anna B., MA Oxf., MSc Oxf., DPhil Oxf.   Prof., Ballistics

Dacre, Brian, BSc Sheff., PhD Sheff.   Sr. Lectr.

Dahele, Jash S., PhD HK   Reader

Doig, Alastair, BSc Leeds   Sr. Lectr.

Edwards, Mike R., BSc(Eng) Lond., PhD Lond.   Sr. Lectr.

Edwards, Morfydd G., BSc Lond., MTech Brun.   Sr. Lectr.

Friend, Cliff M., BSc Sur., PhD Sur.   Prof., Materials and Medical Sciences

Gibbons, G. Edward, BSc Hull, MA Leic.   Sr. Lectr.

Goyder, Hugh G. D., BSc S'ton., PhD S'ton.   Sr. Lectr.

Harrison, A., BA Open(UK), MSc City(UK), PhD Open(UK)   Sr. Lectr.

Hetherington, John G., MA Camb., PhD Cran.   Prof., Engineering Design

Hill, Peter C. J., BSc Birm., PhD Lond., FIEE   Prof., Information Systems Engineering

Hilton, Brian J., BA Edin., PhD Edin.   Sr. Lectr.

Hollis, James E. L., BSc Lond., PhD Lond.   Sr. Lectr.

Holmes, Edward R., MA Camb., PhD Reading   Prof., Military and Security Studies

Holwell, Susan E.   Sr. Lectr.

Howard, M. John, BA Keele, PhD Sheff.   Sr. Lectr.

Hunter, John M. D., BA Camb.   Sr. Lectr.

Hutchinson, Philip, BSc Durh., PhD Newcastle(UK)   Prof., Statistical Fluid Mechanics; Head*

Iremonger, Michael J., BSc(Eng) Lond., PhD Lond., FIMechE   Sr. Lectr.

James, Jimmy R., BSc Lond., PhD Lond., DSc Lond., FIMA, FIEE, FEng   Prof., Electromagnetic Systems Engineering

Jones, Berwyn L., BSc Lond., PhD Lond.   Sr. Lectr.

Knowles, Kevin, BSc Exe., PhD Exe.   Sr. Lectr.

Lawton, Bryan, BSc Salf., PhD Salf.   Reader

Lee, Martin P., BA Lond., MSc Keele   Sr. Lectr.

Matthews, Ron G., BSc Aston, MSc Wales, MBA Warw., PhD Glas.   Sr. Lectr.

Mays, Geoff C., BSc Brist., PhD Dund.   Prof., Civil Engineering

McGuigan, Stuart J., BSc Aston, PhD Aston, FIMechE   Sr. Lectr.

McLellan, Peter R., BSc Brist., PhD Brist.   Sr. Lectr.

Moore, David, MBA Wales   Sr. Lectr.

Moss, Peter J., BSc Lond., PhD   Sr. Lectr.

Moulding, Michael R., BSc Sur.   Prof., Software Engineering

Murray, Stephen G., BSc Manc., PhD Manc., FRSChem   Reader, Explosives Technology

Probert, Stephen K., BA Open(UK), BA Warw., MPhil Northumbria   Sr. Lectr.

Robertson, John D. A., PhD Brun.   Sr. Lectr.

Rogers, Keith D., BSc *Wales*, PhD *Wales* Sr. Lectr.
Sammes, Tony J., BSc *Lond.*, MPhil *Lond.*, PhD *Lond.* Prof., Computer Science
Smith, Peter D., MA *Oxf.*, MSc *Oxf.* Sr. Lectr.
Smith, Rod N. L., BSc *Lanc.*, MSc *Brun.*, PhD *CNAA*, FIMA Sr. Lectr.
Szmelter, Joanne M., PhD *Wales* Sr. Lectr.
Taylor, Trevor, BSc *Lond.*, MA *Lehigh*, PhD *Lond.* Prof.
White, Brian A., BSc *Leic.*, MSc *Manc.*, PhD *Manc.* Prof., Control and Guidance
Whitford, Ray, BSc *CNAA* Sr. Lectr.
Whitworth, Ian R., MA *Camb.* Sr. Lectr.

SILSOE SITE

Agriculture, Food and Environment, School of

Tel: (01525) 863000 Fax: (01525) 863001

Bascombe, Maurice L. A., BSc *Lond.* Sr. Lectr.
Carr, Michael K. V., BSc *Nott.*, PhD *Nott.* Prof., Irrigation Agronomy
Carter, Richard C., MA *Camb.*, MSc *S'ton.*, FGS Sr. Lectr.
Clarke, Brian, BSc *Salf.*, PhD *Lond.* Sr. Lectr.
Crawford, Ian M., BA *Brad.* Sr. Lectr.
Godwin, Richard J., BSc *CNAA*, MS *Ill.*, PhD *Reading* Prof., Agricultural Machine Technology
Howsam, Peter, BSc *Manc.*, PhD *Manc.*, FGS Sr. Lectr.
Kay, Melvyn G., BSc *Leeds*, MSc *Lond.* Sr. Lectr.

Kilgour, John, BSc *Reading*, MSc *Durh.* Sr. Lectr.
Leeds-Harrison, Peter B., BSc *CNAA*, PhD *Reading* Reader, Soil and Water Management
Morgan, Roy P. C., BA *S'ton.*, MA *Lond.*, PhD *Malaya* Prof., Soil Erosion Control
Morris, Ed R., BSc *Edin.*, PhD *Edin.*, FRSChem Prof., Food Structure and Processing
Morris, Joe, BSc *Reading*, MSc *Lond.*, PhD Reader, Rural Resource Economics
Parkin, C. Steve, MSc *Lough.*, PhD *Lough.* Sr. Lectr.
Radley, R. Bill, BSc *Nott.*, PhD *Nott.* Prof., Agricultural Production Technology; Head*
Spoor, Gordon, MSc *Durh.* Prof., Applied Soil Physics
Stenning, Brian C., BSc *Reading* Sr. Lectr.†
Stephens, William, BSc *Edin.*, MSc *Cran.*, PhD *Cran.* Sr. Lectr.
Taylor, John C., MS *Iowa*, PhD *Iowa* Prof., Land Resources Monitoring
Thompson, Keith E., MSc *Cran.* Sr. Lectr.
Weatherhead, E. Keith, BA *Oxf.*, MA *Oxf.* Sr. Lectr.

CONTACT OFFICERS

Accommodation. Facilities Director: Robinson, Peter S., FRICS
Admissions (first degree). Academic Registrar, Shrivenham: Frank, Ann M., BA *Lond.*
Archives. Archivist: Harrington, John D., MA *Lond.*
Careers. Head, Student Services, Silsoe: Harding, Peter G., MSc *CNAA*

Computing services. Director, Computer Centre, Cranfield campus: Hulley, Elaine, BSc *Aston*
Estates and buildings/works and services. Facilities Director: Robinson, Peter S., FRICS
Finance. Director of Finance: Bate, David H., FCA
Personnel/human resources. Director of Personnel: Delger, Patricia A., MA *Leic.*
Purchasing. Facilities Director: Robinson, Peter S., FRICS
Schools liaison. Academic Registrar, Shrivenham: Frank, Ann M., BA *Lond.*
Security. Facilities Director: Robinson, Peter S., FRICS
Staff development and training. Director of Personnel: Delger, Patricia A., MA *Leic.*

CAMPUS/COLLEGE HEADS

Shrivenham Site, Cranfield University, Royal Military College of Science, Shrivenham, Swindon, Wiltshire SN6 8LA, United Kingdom. (Tel: (01793) 782551; Fax: (01793) 783878.) Principal: Hutchinson, Prof. Philip, BSc *Durh.*, PhD *Newcastle(UK)*
Silsoe Site, School of Agriculture, Food and the Environment, Cranfield University, Silsoe, Bedfordshire MK45 4DT, United Kingdom. (Tel: (01525) 863000; Fax: (01525) 863001.) Head: Radley, Prof. R. Bill, BSc *Nott.*, PhD *Nott.*

[Information supplied by the institution as at 6 March 1998, and edited by the ACU]

DE MONTFORT UNIVERSITY

Granted university status 1992; previously established as Leicester Polytechnic, 1969

Member of the Association of Commonwealth Universities

Postal Address: The Gateway, Leicester, England LE1 9BH
Telephone: (0116) 255 1551 **Fax**: (0116) 257 7616 **E-mail**: postmaster@uk.ac.dmu
WWW: http://www.dmu.ac.uk

CHANCELLOR—Whitmore, Sir Clive, GCB, CVO, BA *Camb.*
CHAIRMAN OF THE BOARD OF GOVERNORS—Clarke, M., MA, FCA
PRO-CHANCELLOR—White, J. G., CBE, BA *Manc.*, PhD *Manc.*
PRO-CHANCELLOR—Whitehead, J. M. S., CBE, JP
CHIEF EXECUTIVE AND VICE-CHANCELLOR*—(until 31 July 1999) Barker, Prof. Kenneth, CBE, BMus *Lond.*, MA *Sus.*, Hon. DSc *Moscow State T.U.* , Hon. DUniv *St. Petersburg Technol.&Design*, FTCL
CHIEF EXECUTIVE AND VICE-CHANCELLOR*—(from 1 August 1999) Tasker, Prof. Philip, BSc PhD, FIP, FRSChem
PRO-VICE-CHANCELLOR—Swanick, Prof. Brian H., BEng *Liv.*, PhD *Liv.*, FIEE
PRO-VICE-CHANCELLOR—Brown, Prof. M. A., BSc *Nott.*, PhD *Nott.*
PRO-VICE-CHANCELLOR—Chiddick, Prof. D. M., MSc *Cran.IT*, FRICS
PRO-VICE-CHANCELLOR—Scott, Prof. M., MA *Wales*, PhD *De Mont.*
PRO-VICE-CHANCELLOR—Tasker, Prof. Philip, BSc PhD, FIP, FRSChem
CLERK TO THE BOARD OF GOVERNORS—Hayter, Alison C., BA *Brist.*
ACADEMIC REGISTRAR‡—Critchlow, Eugene, BA *Leic.*, MA *Sheff.*

FACULTIES/SCHOOLS

Agriculture and Horticulture, School of
Head: Moverley, Prof. J., MA *Camb.*

Applied Arts and Design, School of
Head: Shacklock, Prof. V., BA *CNAA*, MA *Sheff.*, FRTPI

Applied Sciences, School of
Head: Linford, Prof. R. G., MA *Oxf.*, DPhil *Oxf.*, FRSChem

Arts and Multi-Disciplinary Studies, School of
Head: Oxley, Prof. D. P., BSc *Sheff.*, PhD *Sheff.*, FIP

Built Environment, School of
Head: Field, Prof. B., BSc *City(UK)*, MA *Brun.*, MPhil *Camb.*

Business, School of
Head: Coyne, Prof. J., BA *Nott.*

Computing Sciences, School of
Head: Luker, Prof. P., BSc *Lond.*, MSc *City(UK)*, PhD *Brad.*

Design and Manufacture, School of
Head: Sullivan, P., MBA *CNAA*

Education, School of
Head: Walden, Prof. P., BA *Wales*, MA *Lond.*

Engineering and Manufacture, School of

Head: Chapman, Prof. G. M., PhD Nott., FIMechE

Health and Community Studies, School of

Head: Saks, Prof. M. P., BA Lanc., MA Kent, PhD Lond.

Humanities and Social Sciences, School of

Acting Head: Saunders, Carol, MA Leic.

Law, School of

Head: Card, Prof. Richard I. E., LLB Nott., LLM Birm.

Physical Education, Sport and Leisure, School of

Head: Slack, Trevor, BPE Alta., MA Alta., PhD Alta.

Social Sciences, School of

Acting Head: Thewlis, Prof. Peter J., BSc Salf., MScTech Sheff., PhD CNAA

ACADEMIC UNITS

Academic Development

School of Agriculture and Horticulture, Lincoln Campus

Ducker, A. J.   Sr. Lectr., Agriculture
Heald, J. M.   Sr. Lectr., Business Management
Henderson, T. A.   Sr. Lectr., Special Needs
May, K. D.   Sr. Lectr., Agriculture
McGurk, H. M.   Sr. Lectr., Agriculture
Odell, J. L.   Sr. Lectr., Poultry
Wilson, H., BA Open(UK)   Sr. Lectr., Leisure and Tourism

Accounting and Finance

Tel: (0116) 257 7259 Fax: (0116) 251 7548
Anderson, D. A., BA(Econ), FCA   Sr. Lectr.
Carte, A., FCA   Sr. Lectr.
Christison, I., MSc   Principal Lectr.
Cockfield, R., MA MSc   Sr. Lectr.
Dungworth, S. R., BA   Principal Lectr.
Hill, A., MSc   Principal Lectr.
Holland, L., BSc   Principal Lectr.
Illidge, R., BA MBA   Principal Lectr.
Lane, S., BA   Sr. Lectr.
Lodhia, K., MBA   Sr. Lectr.
Mear, F., MBA   Principal Lectr.
Patel, A., BA BCom   Principal Lectr.
Pierce-Brown, B.   Principal Lectr.
Pierce-Brown, R., BA   Sr. Lectr.
Russell, D., MSc   Principal Lectr.
Scott, P., BA DPhil   Principal Lectr.
Thody, R. S., MSc, FCA   Principal Lectr.
Vickerstaff, B., FCA   Sr. Lectr.
Wilkinson-Riddle, G., BA, FCA   Prof.; Head*

Adult and Continuing Education

School of Agriculture and Horticulture, Lincoln Campus

Rhoden, M. M.   Sr. Lectr., Adult Education; Manager*

Agriculture and Horticulture

Further and Higher Education

Tel: (01400) 272521 Fax: (01400) 272722
Atkins, C., BEd MA   Sr. Lectr., Education
Bound, C. L. T., MEd   Acting Head*
Braybrooks, V. A.   Sr. Lectr., Food Technology
Butler, R., BSc   Acting Programme Manager, Agriculture
Cheffins, N. J., BSc PhD   Head*
Cowell, A. M.   Sr. Lectr., Forestry
Curry, M., BSc Wales, PhD Essex   Sr. Lectr., Equine Studies
Franklin, H. A.   Sr. Lectr., Floristry
Geering, R., BVetMed   Sr. Lectr., Equine Studies
Ginns, J. W.   Sr. Lectr., Engineering/Mechanisation
Goodger, S., BSc   Programme Manager, Agriculture

Hall, S. J. G., BA Camb., MA Camb., PhD Camb.   Prof., Animal Science
Lambert, Y., BSc Liv., MSc Wales   Sr. Lectr., Equine Science
Lawson, M.   Programme Manager, Business Studies (Further Education)
Leggett, C., BA Middx.   Head*
Locke, N. R.   Sr. Lectr., Equine Studies
Marley, A. P., BA CNAA   Sr. Lectr., Business Studies (Higher Education)
McClements, J., BSc Belf.   Sr. Lectr., Animal Care/Behavioural Studies
Mills, D., BVSc Brist.   Sr. Lectr., Behavioural Studies
Rowbottom, N.   Sr. Lectr., Horticulture
Widdicombe, R., BSc PhD   Sr. Lectr., Landscape Ecology
Williams, G., BA PhD   Sr. Lectr., Equine Studies
Wilson, H., BA Open(UK)   Sr. Lectr.; Programme Manager, Rural Leisure

Architecture

Tel: (0116) 257 7415 Fax: (0116) 250 6311
Archibold, J. A., BA   Sr. Lectr.
Boys, J., MSc   Sr. Lectr.
Brierley, E. S., MArch Strath.   Sr. Lectr.
Brindley, T. S., BA PhD   Principal Lectr.
Cakin, S., MArch Kansas State, PhD Strath.   Sr. Lectr.
Cawthorne, D., BSc Dund., PhD   Principal Lectr.
Cowles, R. M., BSc Bath, BArch Bath   Sr. Lectr.
Curl, J. S., PhD Lond., FSA   Prof.
Doidge, C. W., MSc Lond., PhD Lond.   Principal Lectr.
Ford, B., MA   Prof.
Henderson, D. G., MPhil CNAA   Prof.; Head*
Lee, J. E., MSc Lough.   Principal Lectr.
Lyons, A. R., MA Camb., MSc Warw., PhD Leic.   Principal Lectr.
Moyles, B. F., MSc Lough.   Sr. Lectr.
Muirhead, T., DottArch Florence   Principal Lectr.
Patterson, R., BA Camb., MA Prin.   Sr. Lectr.
Richardsen, M.   Principal Lectr.
Ryan, S. J., BA Kingston(UK)   Sr. Lectr.
Short, R.   Principal Lectr.
Weston, R., BA BArch MLA   Principal Lectr.
Other Staff: 1 Sr. Res. Fellow

Arts and Associated Studies

Lincoln Campus

Bingham, Jayne, BA CNAA   Academic Unit Manager
Foster, Peter   Academic Unit Manager
James, Keith, BA Staffs.   Course Leader
Measures, Colin   Academic Unit Manager
Peacock, Diane   Head*
Ridsdale, Roy, MDes RCA   Academic Unit Manager
Thomas, Sue, BA Essex, MA Leic.   Academic Unit Manager

Arts and Humanities

Bedford Campus

Badley, Margaret, BA Wales, MA CNAA   Sr. Lectr., History
Blanchard, Bob, BA Durh., MA CNAA   Sr. Lectr., Sociology
Boast, Brigitte, BEd CNAA   Sr. Lectr., Performing Arts
Brown, Phil, BA Essex, MA Essex   Sr. Lectr., Sociology
Day, G., BA Essex, MA Wales   Section Leader
Dowson, Jane, MA Leic.   Sr. Lectr., English and Cultural Studies
Faherty, M., BA Wis., MA Wis., PhD Wis.   Sr. Lectr.
Graham, Fiona, BA CNAA, MA Lond.   Sr. Lectr., Performing Arts
Jones, David, BEd S'ton., MSc Oxf.   Subject Leader/Sr. Lectr., Performing Arts
Manning, Paul, BSc CNAA, MA Essex, PhD Camb.   Sr. Lectr.
Randall, Adrian, BA Newcastle(UK), PhD Newcastle(UK)   Section Leader/Sr. Lectr., European Studies

Sibbald, Ray, BA Liv.   Sr. Lectr., History
Smart, Richard, BA Oxf., MA Oxf., MEd Leic.   Section Leader/Sr. Lectr., History
Spindler, Michael, BA York(UK), MA Lanc., PhD Lanc.   Sr. Lectr., English and Cultural Studies
Stevens, Sarah, BA Open(UK), MA CNAA   Sr. Lectr., Performing Arts
Stoneham, Geraldine, BA ANU, MA Leeds, PhD Leeds   Sr. Lectr.
Walker, Alistair, BA Edin., MLitt Edin., MA York(UK)   Sr. Lectr., English and Cultural Studies
Walsh, Clare, MA St And., MLing Manc., MPhil Birm.   Sr. Lectr.
Wood, Carole, BA Leic., MA Nott.   Sr. Lectr., English and Cultural Studies

Biological Sciences

Barghchi, M., BSc Shiraz, MSc Lond., PhD Nott.   Sr. Lectr.
Barker, R. D. J., MA Camb., PhD Durh.   Sr. Lectr.
Cummins, J. M., BA Oxf.   Sr. Lectr.
Dewhurst, F., BSc Sheff., PhD Sheff., FRSChem   Principal Lectr.
Fowler, J. A., BSc Wales, PhD Wales   Principal Lectr.
Hector, T. H.   Sr. Lectr.
Jenkins, N., BSc Lond., PhD Wales   Prof.
Jenkins, R. O., BSc CNAA, PhD CNAA   Principal Lectr.
Leach, C. K., BSc Liv., PhD Liv.   Principal Lectr.
Oldham, R. S., BSc Sheff., PhD W.Ont.   Prof.
Salter, Alison L.   Sr. Lectr.
Stewart, K. M., BSc Glas., PhD Glas.   Sr. Lectr.
Waller, A. R., MSc Qld., PhD Sur.   Sr. Lectr.
Weston, G. D., BA Camb., PhD Wales.   Principal Lectr.

Building Studies

Tel: (0116) 257 7412 Fax: (0116) 257 7440
Adams, O. A., BSc Ill., MSc Kansas, PhD Lond.   Sr. Lectr.
Ashley, M. J.   Sr. Lectr.
Ebohon, O. J., BA CNAA, MA Leic., PhD Leic.   Sr. Lectr.
McArthur, H., BA Camb., MA Camb., PhD Lough.   Principal Lectr.
Moore, D. R., BSc CNAA, PhD CNAA   Sr. Lectr.
Seden, Rev. M. R., BSc Manc., MSc Manc., PhD Salf.   Principal Lectr.; Acting Head*
Taki, A. H., BSc Salf., MSc Salf., PhD Salf.   Sr. Lectr.
Wood, E. J., MSc Lond., FRICS   Sr. Lectr.

Building Surveying

Tel: (0116) 257 7424 Fax: (0116) 257 7440
Ashton, R. G., BSc Manc., MA Sheff.   Sr. Lectr.
Brunskill, R. W., OBE, BA Manc., MA Manc., PhD Manc.   Visiting Prof.†
Chanter, M. B., BSc CNAA, MSc Warw.   Principal Lectr.
Lager, J. E. V.   Sr. Lectr.
Lamberini, D., DottLett Siena   Visiting Prof.†
Morris, L., BA Wales   Sr. Lectr.
Reville, Jill M., MA Camb.   Sr. Lectr.
Stanley, J., LLB CNAA   Sr. Lectr.
Swallow, P. G., FRICS   Prof.; Head*
Watts, C. J., BA CNAA, BTP CNAA   Sr. Lectr.
Williamson, P. D., MSc Lough.   Sr. Lectr.
Other Staff: 1 Sr. Res. Fellow

Chemistry

Tel: (0116) 257 7102 Fax: (0116) 257 7135
Adama-Acquah, R. W., BSc CNAA, MSc Lond.   Sr. Lectr.
Armitage, D. A., BSc Leic., PhD Leic.   Sr. Lectr.
Ayub, M., BSc CNAA, MSc Manc., PhD Brun.   Sr. Lectr.
Bayliss, S. C., BSc Lond., PhD Camb.   Prof.
Comyn, J., BSc Brist., PhD Leeds, FRSChem   Visiting Prof.
Cope, B. C., PhD CNAA, FIM   Principal Lectr.
Craig, P. J., BSc Manc., PhD Brist., FRSChem   Prof.; Head*
Dahm, R. H., BSc Wales, PhD Lond.   Sr. Lectr.
Evans, J. A., BSc Lond., PhD Lond., FRSChem   Principal Lectr.

Fox, M. F., BSc Lond., PhD Lond., FRSChem   Principal Lectr.
Glasse, M. D., PhD, FIM, FRSChem   Principal Lectr.
Groves, C. L., PhD CNAA   Sr. Lectr.
Hagan, P., BSc E.Anglia, PhD E.Anglia   Sr. Lectr.
Hao Quan, BSc China UST, PhD Chinese Acad.Sc.   Sr. Lectr.
Huddersman, K., BSc Lond., PhD Lond.   Sr. Lectr.
Kadhim, N. J., MSc Salf., PhD CNAA   Sr. Lectr.
Latham, R. J., BSc Lough., PhD Lough., FRSChem   Principal Lectr.
Laurie, S. H., BSc Wales, PhD Wales, FRSChem   Prof.
Lawson, G., BSc Kent, PhD Kent   Principal Lectr.
Linford, R. G., MA Oxf., DPhil Oxf., FRSChem   Prof.
Pavlidis, V. H., MPhil CNAA, PhD CNAA   Sr. Lectr.
Pett, C., BSc Leic., PhD Leic.   Principal Lectr.
Symons, M. C. R., PhD Lond., DSc Lond., FRS   Sr. Lectr.
West, D. E., BSc Brist., PhD Brist., FRSChem   Principal Lectr.
Woodland, E. D., BSc Nott., PhD Nott.   Sr. Lectr.

Computer and Information Sciences

Tel: (01908) 843431 Fax: (01908) 834948
Abraham, Ann, MSc Brun.   Sr. Lectr.
Beckhoum, Kamal, PhD Cran.   Sr. Lectr.
Clapworthy, Gordon, BSc Lond., MSc City(UK), PhD Lond.   Principal Lectr., Research
Cochrane, Lynda, BSc CNAA, PhD CNAA   Sr. Lectr.
Constable, Ian B., MA Camb., MSc CNAA   Sr. Lectr.
Cowell, John R., BSc Nott., MPhil Lough., PhD Nott.Trent   Principal Lectr.
Jefferin, Pat, BEd Trent, MSc Lough.   Sr. Lectr.
Kiely, Brian, BSc Liv., MSc Lond.   Principal Lectr.
Lander, Rachel, BSc Lond., MSc Lond.   Sr. Lectr.
McRobb, Steve, BA Leic., MSc CNAA   Sr. Lectr.
Perkins, Graham R., BSc Lond.   Sr. Lectr.
Savory, Clive, BSc CNAA, MSc City(UK)   Sr. Lectr.
Stacey, Martin, BA Oxf., MS Carnegie-Mellon, PhD Aberd.   Sr. Lectr.
Stowell, Frank A., MA Lanc., PhD Lanc.   Prof.; Head*
Wu, J. Zimmin, BA E.China Normal, MSc Lough.   Sr. Lectr.
Xia, Shuanghua, BSc Xian Jiaotong, PhD Manc.   Sr. Lectr.

Computer Science

Tel: (0116) 257 7476 Fax: (0116) 254 1891
Amin, I., MSc Lough.   Sr. Lectr.
Bramer, B., BTech Brad., PhD Brad.   Principal Lectr.
Callaghan, J. M., MSc   Sr. Lectr.
Chapman, T., FCA   Principal Lectr.
Coats, R., BSc Durh., PhD Durh.   Principal Lectr.
Czarnecki, C., MPhil CNAA, PhD De Mont.   Principal Lectr.
Dowson, Monica, MPhil Leic., PhD Leic.   Principal Lectr.
Essendal, T., BSc Middle East T.U., PhD Aston   Sr. Lectr.
Foxon, B. N. T., TD, OBE, BSc Belf., MSc Sur.   Principal Lectr.
Garnett, Kathryn, BSc   Sr. Lectr.
Hand, C. P., BSc Manc.   Sr. Lectr.
Innocent, P. R., BSc Liv., MSc Lough., PhD Lough.   Principal Lectr.
Istance, H., BSc Lough., MSc   Principal Lectr.
Jones, Judith, PhD   Sr. Lectr.
Kocura, Eva, BSc City(UK)   Sr. Lectr.
Littlewood, M., BSc CNAA   Sr. Lectr.
Luker, P., BSc Lond., MSc City(UK), PhD Brad.   Prof.
Messer, P., MSc Strath.   Principal Lectr.; Acting Head*
O'Callaghan, A., BA Kent, MSc CNAA   Sr. Lectr.
Platt, Amelia, BSc De Mont., PhD De Mont.   Principal Lectr.

Richardson, Diane, BSc Keele, MSc Manc.   Sr. Lectr.
Rumsby, S. M. I., BSc Lond., MSc City(UK)   Sr. Lectr.
Sexton, I., BSc Leeds   Sr. Lectr.
Skipper, M., BSc   Sr. Lectr.
Smallwood, D., BSc CNAA, MSc Oxf.   Sr. Lectr.
Smith, I. M., BSc CNAA   Principal Lectr.
Vlaeminke, I., BSc Birm., MSc Brist.   Principal Lectr.
Watson, T., BSc   Sr. Lectr.
Williamson, N., BSc Leeds, BSc CNAA   Sr. Lectr.
Yang, H., BSc Jilin, MPhil Jilin, PhD Durh.   Principal Lectr.
Zarzycki, L., BSc Leeds   Sr. Lectr.
Zedan, H., BSc Cairo, MSc Brist., PhD Brist.   Prof.

Contextual and Associated Studies

School of Applied Art and Design, Lincoln Campus

Bingham, Jayne, BA   Sr. Lectr.
Brown, Veronica, BA Sheff.Hallam   Sr. Lectr.
Greenwood, John, BSc Wales   Sr. Lectr.
Lord, John, BA Newcastle(UK), PhD Leeds   Sr. Lectr.
Moran, Gerard, BA Lond., MA Reading, PhD Lond.   Head*
Thomas, Sue, BA Essex, MA Leic.   Sr. Lectr.
Walton, Peter, BA Durh.   Sr. Lectr.

Corporate Strategy

Tel: (0116) 257 7269 Fax: (0116) 251 7548
Azhashemi, M., BSc Lahore UET, MSc Manc.   Sr. Lectr.
Balderson, S., BSc Leic., MEd Sheff.   Principal Lectr.
Britton, C., BA CNAA, MSc Lond.   Principal Lectr.
Duffy, K., BA CNAA, MA Warw.   Principal Lectr.
Egan, Colin, BA CNAA, MBA Brad., PhD Trinity(Dub.)   Prof.
Elliott, D., BA Warw., MBA CNAA   Principal Lectr.
Foley, P. D., BSc S'ton., MEd Sheff., PhD CNAA   Prof.; Head*
Galloway, R. L., BSc Durh., MSc Aston   Principal Lectr.
Gregory, P. E., BA Warw., MA Wayne State   Principal Lectr.
Kaur, Parmjit, BA CNAA, MA Leic.   Sr. Lectr.
Murphy, A., BA(Econ) CNAA, MBA Aston   Principal Lectr.
Patton, D., BA Nott.   Principal Lectr.
Rees, A., BSc Wales, MA Leic.   Principal Lectr.
Rendall, J., BSc Lond., MA Reading   Principal Lectr.
Rouse, Michael, BA Calg.   Sr. Lectr.
Rowbotham, F., LLB CNAA, MBA Warw.   Sr. Lectr.
Swartz, E. M., BA Cape Town, BA Rhodes   Sr. Lectr.
Tattersall, R., BSc Sheff.   Sr. Lectr.
Williams, D. M., MA C.N.A.A   Principal Lectr.
Worthington, I., BA Lanc., PhD Lanc.   Principal Lectr.
Zvesper, A., BSc(Econ) Lond., MBA Lond.   Sr. Lectr.

Design and Associated Studies

Lincoln Campus

Bramston, David, BA CNAA, MA CNAA   Course Leader
Craggs, Tamar, BA CNAA   Course Leader
Dickinson, Yvonne   Sr. Lectr.
Fabian, Tim   Course Leader
Foster, Peter   Sr. Lectr.
Garnett, Elizabeth   Sr. Lectr.
Middleton, Paul, BA CNAA   Head*
Parkin, Anna   Course Leader
Pemberton, Howard   Sr. Lectr.
Puzzovio, Carolyn   Sr. Lectr.
Reynolds, Kevin   Course Leader
Ridsdale, Roy   Sr. Lectr.
Ryder, Dian, MDes RCA   Subject Leader
Simpson, Neil   Acting Subject Leader

Wakefield, Yvonne, BA CNAA   Acting Subject Leader
Whittaker, Maxine   Academic Unit Manager

Design, Industrial and Graphic

Tel: (0116) 257 7570 Fax: (0116) 257 7574
Cook, J. H., MDes RCA   Head*
Ford, P. B., BA   Principal Lectr.
Greensides, C. J., MSc   Principal Lectr.
Harding, N., MDes RCA   Sr. Lectr.
Hartwell, D.   Sr. Lectr.
Hill, G., MSc MA(Des)   Sr. Lectr.
Hooper, J. S., BEd   Sr. Lectr.
Hull, E., BA   Sr. Lectr.
Martin, P., BA   Principal Lectr.
Mills, N.   Sr. Lectr.

Design Management

Tel: (0116) 257 7570 Fax: (0116) 257 7574
Avery, J., BA   Sr. Lectr.
Barnes-Powell, Tina, BA MA MSc DPhil   Principal Lectr.
Chipps, Richard, BA MA   Sr. Lectr.
Coe, B., MDes   Principal Lectr.
Hawkes, John, BSc   Sr. Lectr.
Higgett, N., BSc MA   Principal Lectr.
Holland, R., MSc   Principal Lectr.
Hubbard, Bill, BA MSc   Sr. Lectr.
MacTavish, R., BSc   Principal Lectr.
Myerson, Jeremy, MA RCA   Assoc. Prof.
Robertson, A. D., MA RCA   Principal Lectr.
Stewart, J., BA MBA   Sr. Lectr.
Woudhuysen, James, BSc   Assoc. Prof.

Drama, see Arts and Humanities

Economics

Tel: (01908) 834977 Fax: (01908) 834879
Anand, Paul, BA Nott., MSc Lond., DPhil Oxf.   Reader
Fleetwood, Stephen, BA CNAA, MPhil Camb., PhD Camb.   Sr. Lectr.
Ghatak, Anita, MA Calc., PhD Leic.   Prof.
Girardin, Eric, BA Paris IV, MPhil Camb., Dr Paris IV   Prof.
Lee, Frederic, BA Frostburg, MPhil Rutgers, PhD Rutgers   Reader
Parsons, Stephen, BSc S'ton., PhD S'ton.   Principal Lectr.
Pashkoff, Susan, BA N.Y.State, MA New Sch.Soc.Res., PhD New Sch.Soc.Res.   Sr. Lectr.
Riach, Peter A., BCom Melb., PhD Lond.   Prof.; Head*
Waterton, Robert, BA Camb., MA Leic.   Principal Lectr.
Williams, Michael, BA E.Anglia, MSc Lond., PhD Amst.   Sr. Lectr.

Education

Bedford Campus

Allison, Brian, PhD Reading   Emer. Prof.
Atherton, James, MLitt Lanc., MEd Manc., PhD Manc.   Principal Lectr.
Brennan, John, BA Liv., MEd Leic.   Sr. Lectr.
Brookes, Colin A., MPhil Birm.   Sr. Lectr.
Bruntlett, Steve, BA Leeds, MA Leic.   Sr. Lectr.
Clarke, Hilary, MA Lond.   Sr. Lectr.
Elton, Georgina, BSc Lond., MA Leic.   Sr. Lectr.
Falconer, Andrew, BA Open(UK)   Sr. Lectr.
Fletcher, Martin, BEd   Sr. Lectr.
Frecknall, Paul, BEd Warw.   Sr. Lectr.
Grugeon, Elizabeth, MA Lond.   Sr. Lectr.
Hubbard, Lorraine, MPhil Exe.   Sr. Lectr.
Huckle, John, MA Lond.   Principal Lectr.
Hutson, Don G., MEd Manc.   Sr. Lectr.
Ireland, Tony, MES Leic.   Sr. Lectr.
Lawless, Sheila, MA Camb., MPhil Nott.   Sr. Lectr.
Lea, M. O., BA MA   Sr. Lectr.
Leask, Marilyn, MPhil E.Anglia   Principal Lectr.
Littleford, Peter, BSc Lond., MA Lond.   Sr. Lectr.
Mould, Ian   Sr. Lectr.
Rix, Chris, MPhil Nott.   Sr. Lectr.
Roddis, Maggie, MA Leic.   Sr. Lectr.
Sampson, John, MA Lond.   Principal Lectr.
Strangwick, Roger, MA E.Anglia   Principal Lectr.

Wilcockson, David, BEd CNAA, MPhil
Cran.   Sr. Lectr.
Wilder, Peter, MA Cant., MSc Lond.   Sr. Lectr.
Wilkinson, Graham, BA Open(UK)   Sr. Lectr.
Wilson, Steve, BEd MA   Professl. Devel.
Manager
Wooldridge, David, BSc City(UK)   Sr. Lectr.
Wooldridge, Irene, BEd Lond., MA E.Anglia   Sr.
Lectr.
Yeomans, Robin, BA Birm., MEd E.Anglia   Sr.
Lectr.

Engineering, Electronic and Electrical

Tel: (0116) 257 7087 Fax: (0116) 257 7052
Aggoun, A., PhD Nott.   Sr. Lectr.
Al-Akaidi, M., PhD Lough.   Principal Lectr.
Boardman, John, BEng Liv., PhD Liv.,
FIEE   Prof.
Chowanietz, Eric G., BSc CNAA, PhD
Leic.   Principal Lectr.
Cole, Orlando G., BSc CNAA   Sr. Lectr.
Coulbeck, Bryan, MSc Lough., PhD Sheff.,
FIEE   Emer. Prof.
Davies, N.   Sr. Lectr.
Duffy, A., MEng Wales, PhD Nott.   Sr. Lectr.
Hargreaves, Martin, BEng Liv., MEng Sheff.   Sr.
Lectr.
Haydock, L., PhD   Visiting Prof.
Hills, Ray, BSc Brist., FIEE   Visiting Prof.
Ivins, Jon R., BA Open(UK)   Sr. Lectr.
Low, Foong W., PhD Sheff.   Principal Lectr.
Mann, I., BEng Coventry, MSc Nott.   Sr. Lectr.
McCormick, Malcolm, MEng Sheff., FIEE   Prof.;
Head*
Mesias, Gerado   Sr. Lectr.
Norris, Peter, BSc Leic.   Sr. Lectr.
Phillips, Nicholas J., BSc Lond., FIP   Prof.
Sharma, Harry C., MSc Lough., PhD
CNAA   Principal Lectr.
Titterington, Bob F., BEng Liv., MSc
Lough.   Principal Lectr.
Ulanicki, Bogumil, PhD T.U.Warsaw, DSc
T.U.Warsaw   Reader
Urwin, Paul, PhD Liv.   Principal Lectr.
Other Staff: 4 Sr. Res. Fellows

Engineering, Mechanical and Manufacturing

Tel: (0116) 257 7091 Fax: (0116) 257 7052
Abdalla, H., BSc Menoufia, MSc Menoufia, PhD De
Mont.   Sr. Lectr.
Ahmed, M. S., BSc Birm., PhD Birm.   Visiting
Prof.
Dickens, P. M., BSc CNAA   Prof.
Few, P. C., MEng Liv., PhD Bath,
FIMechE   Principal Lectr.
Halls, M., MSc CNAA   Sr. Lectr.
Jackson, M. D., BSc Manc.   Sr. Lectr.
Knight, J. A. G., BSc Leic., MSc Lough., PhD
Nott., Hon. DUniv Kaunas U.T.,
FIMechE   Prof.; Head*
Lawrence, R., BTech, FIMechE   Principal Lectr.
Lees, A., BSc Birm., MSc Cran.IT   Sr. Lectr.
Lindley, D., BSc PhD, FEng, FIMechE   Visiting
Prof.
Maycock, K., BSc CNAA, PhD De Mont.   Sr.
Lectr.
Moore, P., BTech Lough., PhD Lough.,
FIEE   Prof.
Nash, R., BSc St And., PhD Dund., FRAS   Sr.
Lectr.
Nazha, M. A. A., BSc Lond., MSc Lond., PhD
Lond.   Principal Lectr.
Newlyn, H. A., BSc Lond., PhD CNAA   Sr. Lectr.
Pancholi, H., BSc Brun.   Sr. Lectr.
Paradise, M. G. A., BSc PhD   Visiting Prof.
Picken, D. J., MA Camb., PhD CNAA,
FIMechE   Emer. Prof.
Prettyjohns, R. C., PhD Wales   Sr. Lectr.
Price, F. C., BSc Nott., FIMechE   Visiting Prof.
Prickett, P. J., MPhil Lough.   Sr. Lectr.
Singh, U. K., MEng Liv., PhD Liv.,
BScEng   Prof.
Stockton, D. J., BSc CNAA, MSc Lough., PhD
Lough.   Principal Lectr.
Vaughan, I. F., BSc Aston, FIEE   Visiting Prof.

English, Media and Cultural Studies, see also Arts and Humanities

Fax: (0116) 257 7199
Briggs, Julia, BLitt Oxf.   Prof.
Cheetham, D., MA Camb.   Sr. Lectr.
Chibnall, S. J., BA Lond., PhD Lond.   Sr. Lectr.
Davison, Peter, BA Lond., MA Lond., PhD
Syd.   Visiting Prof.
Richardson, R. M., MA Hull   Sr. Lectr.
Saunders, Carol, MA Leic.   Sr. Lectr.
Wells, P., BA Reading, PhD Reading   Sr. Lectr.
Whelehan, Imelda, BA Kent, MA Nott.   Sr.
Lectr.
Zurbrugg, Nicholas, BA E.Anglia, DPhil
Oxf.   Prof.; Head*

European Studies, see Arts and Humanities, and Langs. and European Studies and Centre for Lang. Instrucn.

Health and Continuing Professional Studies

Tel: (0116) 257 7736 Fax: (0116) 257 7708
Amoroso, Jasmin, BA Nott.Trent   Sr. Lectr.
Bentley, Helen, MSc Nott.   Sr. Lectr.
Brand, Pauline, BA Open(UK), MSc
Manc.Met.   Sr. Lectr.
Carter, Ellen, BSc C.England, MA Lough.   Sr.
Lectr.
Cook, Ray   Sr. Lectr.
Dalby, David, MA Keele   Sr. Lectr.
Davis, Catherine C., BA Open(UK), MA
Leeds   Principal Lectr.
Dyson, Simon M., BSc Leic., MPhil
Warw.   Principal Lectr.
Fowler, John, BA Open(UK), MA Lough.   Sr.
Lectr.
Geary, Martyn, BA York(UK)   Sr. Lectr.
Goodrich, Nigel, BSc Coventry   Sr. Lectr.
Ham-Ying, Silvia, BSc Leic., MSc
Lond.   Principal Lectr.
Harding, Vasanta, BA De Mont.   Sr. Lectr.
Leatham, R. Jacqueline, MA S'ton.   Sr. Lectr.
Moore, Kathleen A., BA CNAA, MA Warw.   Sr.
Lectr.
Prowse, Julie, BSc Lond., MA Leeds   Sr. Lectr.
Ruane, Sally, BA Durh., MA Liv., PhD Durh.   Sr.
Lectr.
Starling, Jennie, BA Open(UK)   Sr. Lectr.
Todd, Keith   Sr. Lectr.
Watterson, Andrew E., BA Nott., PhD
Brist.   Head*
Wilkinson, Carol, BA Open(UK), MSc Wales   Sr.
Lectr.
Vacant Posts: Sr. Lectr./Lectr.

Historical and International Studies

Tel: (0116) 257 7320 Fax: (0116) 257 7199
Freeman, C., MA Oxf.   Principal Lectr.
Holt, R., BA Oxf., DPhil Oxf.   Prof.†
Jamplew, W., BA S'ton., PhD Edin.   Prof.
Jones, K. T., MA Wales   Principal Lectr.
Lanfranchi, P., BA Montpellier, MPhil Montpellier,
PhD European Univ.Inst.   Prof.
Martin, J., BSc Lough., MPhil Lough., PhD
Reading   Sr. Lectr.
Myles, Janet, BA CNAA, PhD CNAA   Principal
Lectr.
Panayi, P., BA CNAA, PhD Sheff.   Sr. Lectr.
Rimmer, J. F., BA CNAA   Sr. Lectr.
Roenisch, Rowan P. M., BA Lond.   Sr. Lectr.
Sadler, D., BA CNAA, MSocSc Birm.   Sr. Lectr.
Scott, Margaret, MA Glas., MA Lond., PhD
Lond.   Sr. Lectr.
Singh, G., MA Warw., BSc Lond., PhD Lond.   Sr.
Lectr.
Thoms, D. W., BSc(Econ) Lond., MA Kent, PhD
Brun.   Prof.; Head*

Human Communication

Tel: (0116) 257 7756 Fax: (0116) 257 7708
Bixley, Morag D., BSc CNAA   Sr. Lectr.
Grundy, Kim F., MA Leeds   Principal Lectr.
Grunwell, P., BA Leeds, MA Leeds, PhD
Reading   Prof.; Head*
Harding, Anne, PhD De Mont.   Sr. Lectr.

Hiles, D. R., BSc Hull, MSc McG., PhD
McG.   Principal Lectr.
Hill, Heather M., MSc Lond.   Sr. Lectr.
Noon, Elizabeth, BSc Leic., PhD Leic.   Sr. Lectr.
Rowley, D. T., BA Reading   Principal Lectr.
Vacant Posts: 1 Lectr.†

Human Resource Management

Tel: (0116) 257 7207 Fax: (0116) 251 7548
Beardwell, Ian J., BSc Lond., MSc Lond., PhD
Lond.   Prof., Industrial Relations
Buchanan, David A., BA H.-W., PhD
Edin.   Prof., Organisational Behaviour
Clark, Ian A. F., BA Leic., MA CNAA, MA Warw.,
PhD Leeds   Principal Lectr.
Claydon, Tim J., BSc Brist., MSc(Econ) Lond.,
PhD Kent   Principal Lectr.; Head*
Collin, Audrey, BA Exe., PhD Lough.   Reader
Davies, Linda, BA Strath., MBA Sheff.Hallam   Sr.
Lectr.
Doyle, Mike, BA Open(UK), MA CNAA   Sr.
Lectr.
Golding, Nicky, BA Wales, MSc Aston   Sr. Lectr.
Harris, John, BA Leic.   Sr. Lectr.
Hetherington, Angela P., BA Open(UK), MSc
Cran.IT, PhD Cran.IT   Sr. Lectr.
Holden, Len T., BSc Lond., MPhil Open(UK), PhD
Cran.   Principal Lectr.
Marlow, Sue, BA Warw., MA Warw.   Sr. Lectr.
O'Doherty, Damian P., BA Newcastle(UK), MA
Warw.   Sr. Lectr.
Roberts, Ian, BSc Warw., MA Warw.   Sr. Lectr.
Smith, Mic, BSc Lond., MBA CNAA   Sr. Lectr.
Storey, Julie, BA Leeds, MA De Mont.   Principal
Lectr.
Wilson, Roy, BA Wales, MBA CNAA   Principal
Lectr.
Wright, Mary, BA CNAA, MBA Lough.   Sr.
Lectr.
Young, Richard, BA Montr., BEd Montr., MEd
McG.   Visiting Prof.

Independent Study, Centre for

School of Arts and Multi-Disciplinary Studies
Tel: (0116) 257 7015 Fax: (0116) 257 7625
Cork, Alison M., LLB Newcastle(UK)   Head*

Industrial Relations, see Human Resource Management

Information Science, see Computer and Information Scis.

Information Systems

Tel: (0116) 257 7471 Fax: (0116) 254 1891
Al-Maliki, I., BSc Edin., MSc Strath., PhD
Strath.   Sr. Lectr.
Bennett, J., BSc(Econ) Lond., MSc Leic.   Sr.
Lectr.
Bennett, S., BA Camb., MPhil Lough.   Principal
Lectr.
Berry, P. A., BSc St And., MSc Aston, PhD
Aston   Principal Lectr.
Burns, J., MSc Lough., BA Open(UK)   Sr. Lectr.
Cox, D., BSc S'ton., MSc Aston   Sr. Lectr.
Farmer, R., BSc Warw.   Principal Lectr.
Fidler, Christine S., BSc York(UK), DPhil
York(UK)   Principal Lectr.
Howe, D. R., MA Oxf., DPhil Sus.   Prof.;
Head*
Howley, R., BSc Wales, MSc Leic.   Sr. Lectr.
Larner, A.   Sr. Lectr.
Leigh, M., BSc Wales, BA Open(UK)   Sr. Lectr.
McBride, N., BSc Lond., PhD Lond.   Principal
Lectr.
Oldroyd, Pauline, MSc Essex   Principal Lectr.
Platt, J., BA Leic., MBA Strath.   Sr. Lectr.
Prior, Mary, BA Lanc., MSc Aston   Sr. Lectr.
Roberts, N., BSc Lough., MSc Leic.   Sr. Lectr.
Robinson, Barbara A., BA Open(UK)   Principal
Lectr.
Rogerson, S., BSc Dund.   Principal Lectr.
Sherwood, T., BA Essex   Sr. Lectr.
Skelton, J., BSc Sheff.   Sr. Lectr.
Thornton, S., BSc Manc., PhD Manc., MSc
Birm.   Principal Lectr.
Watts, B. M., BSc Lond., MSc Reading, MSc
Leic.   Sr. Lectr.

Wood, C., BDS *Lond.*, MSc *Leic.* Sr. Lectr.
Wroe, M., MSc *Leic.* Sr. Lectr.

International Studies, see Hist. and
Internat. Studies

Land Management

Tel: (0116) 257 7435 Fax: (0116) 257 7440
Abbott, Tim J. Sr. Lectr.
Brown, Tim J., BSc Principal Lectr.
Carter, Elizabeth S. J., BSc Sr. Lectr.
Carter, Norma A. C., BA Principal Lectr.
Dobbin, Mervyn, BSc PhD Sr. Lectr.
Hay, H., BA MPhil Sr. Lectr.
Head, Donald Sr. Lectr.
Hill, Martin P., MA *Camb.*, MSocSc,
FRICS Head*
King, Peter, BSc PhD Sr. Lectr.
Lawson, Russell E. M., BA *Oxf.*, BA *Camb.*, MA
Oxf. Sr. Lectr.
Luithlen, Lutz H., PhD Sr. Lectr.
Mathieson, Robert, BA *Oxf.*, MA *Oxf.*,
MPhil Sr. Lectr.
Maxted, William M., MSc Sr. Lectr.
Mollart, Richard G., BSc MA Sr. Lectr.
Oxley, Michael J., BSc(Econ) MSc PhD Prof.
Porter, Trudi J. Sr. Lectr.
Staffell, Colin, FRICS Sr. Lectr.
Strachan, Joan M., BSc PhD Sr. Lectr.
Tomlins, Richard, BA Sr. Lectr.
Warren, Marcus, MA Sr. Lectr.

Languages and European Studies and
Centre for Language Instruction

Tel: (0116) 257 7240 Fax: (0116) 257 7265
Golland, A., BSc *Leic.*, PhD *Leic.*
Jordan, B., BA *Liv.*, PhD *Liv.* Prof.
Randall, A., BA *Durh.*, PhD *Newcastle(UK)* Sr.
Lectr.
Thiem, E., BA *Hull*, MEd Principal Lectr.
Watson, M. N., BA *Nott.*, PhD Principal
Lectr.; Head*

Law, see also Professional Legal Studies

Tel: (0116) 257 7177 Fax: (0116) 257 7186
Cameron, Euan D., MA *Camb.* Principal Lectr.
Card, Richard I. E., LLB *Nott.*, LLM *Birm.* Prof.
Davis, Martin R., LLB *Nott.* Principal Lectr.
Harvey, Barbara A., LLB *CNAA*, LLM *Leic.* Sr.
Lectr.
Hawke, Neil, LLB *Hull*, PhD *Nott.* Prof.
Hillier, Tim, LLB *Lond.*, LLM *Sheff.* Sr. Lectr.
Hughes, David, LLB *Liv.*, LLM *Camb.* Prof.
Jones, Brian L., MA *Camb.*, LLB *Camb.* Prof.
Lockton, Deborah J., LLB *Nott.*, MPhil
CNAA Principal Lectr.
Mackay, Ronnie D., BA *CNAA*, MPhil
Leic. Prof.
Marriott, Jenny, LLB *CNAA*, MA *Nott.* Sr.
Lectr.
Marston, John, LLB *Leic.* Principal Lectr.
Matthew, Veronica A., LLB *CNAA*, BA
Leeds Principal Lectr.
Mulholland, J. Mary, LLB *CNAA* Principal
Lectr.
Oughton, David W., LLB *Lond.*, MPhil
CNAA Prof.
Price, David P. T., BA *CNAA* Principal Lectr.
Reville, Nicholas R., LLB *Lond.*, LLM *Keele* Sr.
Lectr.
Ross, Lynne, LLB *Warw.* Sr. Lectr.
Shorrock, Kathleen A., BA *CNAA* Sr. Lectr.
Upson, Joan E., LLB *CNAA*, LLM *Sheff.* Sr.
Lectr.
Ward, Anthony, LLM *Lond.*, PhD *CNAA* Sr.
Lectr.
Ward, Richard W., LLB *Lond.* Prof.; Head*

Marketing

Tel: (0116) 257 7203 Fax: (0116) 251 7548
Baron, P. J., BSc *Durh.*, MSc *Calif.* Prof.; Head*
Bradford, M., BA *Durh.* Sr. Lectr.
Brodenck, A., BEd *St.Patrick's(Dub.)*, BA *Dublin
City*, MPhil *Glas.* Sr. Lectr.
Chaudhry, S., MBA *Brun.* Principal Lectr.
Garton, P. A., BA *Lough.*, MBA *Lough.* Sr. Lectr.
Hartley, R. A., BA *Nott.*, MBA Principal Lectr.

Holmes, I. J., BCom *Newcastle(NSW)*, MA
Warw. Principal Lectr.
Hudson, D., BA *Brighton*, MBA *City* Sr. Lectr.
Phillips, H., BSc *Sur.* Sr. Lectr.
Pickton, D. W., MA *Lanc.* Principal Lectr.
Rickard, L., BA *N.Carolina*, MIA
Sch.Internat.Training, Vermont Sr. Lectr.
Starkey, M. W., BSc *Newcastle(UK)*, MBA
Nott. Sr. Lectr.
Vaughan-Jones, C., MA *Lanc.* Sr. Lectr.
Wright, S., MBA *Warw.* Principal Lectr.

Mathematical Sciences

Tel: (0116) 257 7473 Fax: (0116) 250 6114
Andrews, C. P., MSc *Warw.*, MSc *Sheff.*, MSc
Open(UK) Sr. Lectr.
Birkenhead, R., BSc *York(Can.)*, MSc *Calg.* Sr.
Lectr.
Blackledge, J. M., BSc *Lond.*, PhD *Lond.*,
FIMA Prof.; Head*
Crane, C. M., BSc *Sheff.*, PhD *Sheff.* Principal
Lectr.
Davison, R., BSc *Newcastle(UK)*, PhD
Cran.IT Principal Lectr.
Evans, G. A., MA *Oxf.*, DPhil *Oxf.*, DSc *Lough.*,
FIMA Prof.
Gregson, M. J., BSc *Oxf.*, MSc *Nott.*, PhD
Leic. Sr. Lectr.
Hoskins, R. F., BSc *Lond.*, MSc *Lond.* Prof.
Howkins, M., BTech *Brun.*, FIMA Sr. Lectr.
Jaffar, M. J., MSc *Baghdad*, MPhil *Lond.*, PhD
Leeds Sr. Lectr.
John, R. I., BSc *Leic.*, MSc *Manc.* Principal
Lectr., Operational Research
Owen, A., BSc *Sheff.* Sr. Lectr., Operational
Research
Palmer, A. F., MSc *Wales* Principal Lectr.,
Operational Research
Pugh, P. T., BSc *Leic.* Sr. Lectr., Operational
Research
Smith, R., BSc *Manc.*, MSc *Leic.* Principal Lectr.
Storey, C., BSc *Lond.*, DSc *Lond.*, FIMA Prof.
Storry, D. J. T., MA *Edin.*, MA *Calif.*, PhD
Lough. Sr. Lectr.
Taylor, J. B., MSc *Wales*, MSc *Leic.* Sr. Lectr.
Thompson, R. M., BSc *Birm.*, MSocSc *Birm.*,
MSc *Warw.* Principal Lectr., Operational
Research
Yardley, P. J., BSc *S'ton.*, PhD *S'ton.* Principal
Lectr.

Media Studies, see Engl., Media and Cultural
Studies

Medical Statistics

Tel: (0116) 257 7472 Fax: (0116) 250 6114
Denne, J. S., BSc *Durh.*, MSc *Camb.*, PhD
Bath Sr. Lectr.
Donev, A. N., BSc *Sofia*, PhD *Lond.* Sr. Lectr.
du Boulay, E. P. G. H., CBE, FRCR,
FRCP Prof.
Hubbard, S. J., BSc *CNAA*, MSc *Leic.* Sr. Lectr.
James, C., BSc *Liv.*, PhD *Liv.* Sr. Lectr.
Jones, B., BSc *Bath*, MSc *Reading*, PhD *Kent* Prof.
Koch, G., BSc *Ohio State*, MSc *Ohio State*, PhD
N.Carolina Prof.
Lawson, M., BSc *Leic.*, MSc *Leic.* Sr. Lectr.
Lewis, J. A., MA *Oxf.*, DPhil *Oxf.* Prof.
Lindsey, J. K., BMath *Wat.*, PhD *Lond.* Prof.
Teather, B. A., BSc *Nott.*, MSc *Leic.*, PhD
CNAA Principal Lectr.
Teather, D., BSc *City(UK)*, MSc *Lond.*, PhD
CNAA Prof.; Head*
Wills, K. M., BSc *Leic.*, MPhil *Leic.* Sr. Lectr.
Other Staff: 1 Sr. Res. Fellow

Nursing and Midwifery

Tel: (0116) 257 7769 Fax: (0116) 257 7708
Ackbarally, Rafik, BA *Leic.* Sr. Lectr., Applied
Social and Biological Sciences
Andrews, Cindy, BA *Open(UK)* Sr. Lectr.,
Applied Social and Biological Sciences
Ash, Carol, MBA *Birm.* Sr. Lectr., Nursing
Autar, Ricky, BA *Open(UK)*, MSc *C.England* Sr.
Lectr., Applied Social and Biological Sciences
Barr, Rosemary J., MBA *Open(UK)* Sr. Lectr.,
Nursing

Beebeejaun, Ali, BSc *Coventry* Sr. Lectr.,
Nursing
Beretta, Ruth, BSc *C.England*, MA *Leic.* Sr.
Lectr., Nursing
Bonomaully, Giotto, BSc *Open(UK)* Sr. Lectr.,
Applied Social and Biological Sciences
Brimson, Maggie, BA *Open(UK)* Sr. Lectr.,
Applied Social and Biological Sciences
Bryant, Bernadette, BA *Leic.* Sr. Lectr.,
Midwifery
Buchanan, Eileen, BA *Leic.* Sr. Lectr., Applied
Social and Biological Sciences
Butt, Caroline Sr. Lectr., Nursing
Chevannes, Mel, BA *Open(UK)*, MA *Warw.*, PhD
Keele Prof.; Head*
Chooramun, Jack, BA *Coventry*, MSc *Coventry* Sr.
Lectr., Applied Social and Biological Sciences
Crothers, Sam, BSc *Leic.* Sr. Lectr., Applied
Social and Biological Sciences
Dale, Heather, BSc *Coventry* Sr. Lectr., Nursing
Denholm, Barbara, BA *Open(UK)* Sr. Lectr.,
Applied Social and Biological Sciences
Dooher, Jim, MA *Lough.* Sr. Lectr., Applied
Social and Biological Sciences
East, David Sr. Lectr., Nursing
Ellison, Jacqueline, BSc *Leic.* Sr. Lectr.,
Applied Social and Biological Sciences
Fletcher, Beverley, BA *Leic.* Sr. Lectr., Nursing
Ford, Kelvin, BA *Leic.*, MA *Warw.* Sr. Lectr.,
Applied Social and Biological Sciences
Genders, Nicky, BA *Leic.*, MA *Leic.*, MPhil *Leic.*,
PhD *Leic.* Sr. Lectr., Applied Social and
Biological Sciences
Gregory, Anthony, BA *Lanc.*, MA *Warw.* Sr.
Lectr., Applied Social and Biological Sciences
Hamilton, Patricia M., BA *Manc.*, MSc
Keele Principal Lectr., Midwifery
Harris, Tina, BSc *Wolv.* Sr. Lectr., Midwifery
Heath, Samantha, MA *Wolv.* Sr. Lectr.,
Nursing
Huag, Pak, MA *Birm.* Sr. Lectr., Midwifery
Hung, Pak, BSc *Wolv.* Sr. Lectr., Midwifery
Iddisah, Charles, BA *Open(UK)*, MA *Lough.* Sr.
Lectr., Applied Social and Biological Sciences
Jackson, Karen, MSc *Derby* Sr. Lectr., Nursing
Johnson, Sandra, BSc *C.England* Sr. Lectr.,
Nursing
Long, Norman, BEd *CNAA*, MEd *Wolv.* Sr.
Lectr., Nursing
Marie, Phillipe, BA *Leic.*, MA *Warw.* Sr. Lectr.,
Applied Social and Biological Sciences
Maurimootoo, Sam, MSc *Leeds Met.* Sr. Lectr.,
Applied Social and Biological Sciences
Mazhindu, Debbie, BA *Portsmouth* Sr. Lectr.,
Nursing
McHugh, Nessa, MA *Lough.* Sr. Lectr.,
Midwifery
McLean, Moira Sr. Lectr., Midwifery
Neill, Sarah, BSc *Sheff.*, MSc *Lond.* Sr. Lectr.,
Applied Social and Biological Sciences
Pertab, Danny, BSc *C.England*, MA *Coventry* Sr.
Lectr., Nursing
Pleasance, Paul, MEd *Leic.* Principal Lectr.;
External Liaison Co-ordinator
Power, Kevin, MA *Leic.* Sr. Lectr., Nursing
Reece, Judith H., BA *Open(UK)*, BA *Manc.* Sr.
Lectr., Applied Social and Biological Sciences
Rendall, Linda, BA *Leic.* Sr. Lectr., Nursing
Rigby, Paul Sr. Lectr., Nursing
Robson, Elizabeth, MSc *Lough.* Sr. Lectr.,
Midwifery
Rudd, Ian, BSc *Open(UK)*, MA *Leic.* Sr. Lectr.,
Applied Social and Biological Sciences
Rushby, Kenneth, BEd *Hudd.* Sr. Lectr.,
Nursing
Salter, Nick, BSc *Lond.* Sr. Lectr., Nursing
Schober, Jane E., MSc *Wales* Principal Lectr.,
Nursing
Smith, Jeni, BA *Leic.*, MA *Lond.* Sr. Lectr.,
Applied Social and Biological Sciences
Smith, Raymond, BA *Leic.* Sr. Lectr., Nursing
Stone, Bernard Sr. Lectr., Nursing
Sweeney, John F., MSc *Manc.* Principal Lectr.;
Quality, Equality and Devel. Co-ordinator
Sweetland, Yvonne, MSc *Manc.* Sr. Lectr.,
Midwifery
Tait, Thomas, MA *York(UK)* Sr. Lectr., Applied
Social and Biological Sciences

Turner, Maureen, MA *Keele* Sr. Lectr., Applied Social and Biological Sciences
Walker, Patricia, MBA *Open(UK)* Sr. Lectr., Midwifery
Watson, Naomi, MSc *Aston* Sr. Lectr., Nursing
Wearne, Graham, BA *Leic.* Sr. Lectr., Applied Social and Biological Sciences
West, Janet, MA *Leeds* Sr. Lectr., Midwifery
Whittaker, Norma, BA *Leic.* Sr. Lectr., Nursing
Wood, Alan Sr. Lectr., Nursing
Young, Donna, BA *Open(UK)* Principal Lectr., Applied Social and Biological Sciences; Leader

Operational Research, see Mathl. Scis.

Performing Arts, see Visual and Performing Arts

Pharmacy
Andrew, M. H. E., BSc *Nott.*, PhD Principal Lectr.
Aulton, M. E., BPharm *Lond.*, PhD *Lond.* Prof.
Billany, M. R., BSc(Pharm) *CNAA* Principal Lectr.
Burke, M. D., BSc *Lond.*, PhD *Sur.* Prof.; Head*
Collett, D. M., BPharm *Lond.*, PhD *Lond.* Principal Lectr.
Eden, J., BSc *CNAA* Sr. Lectr.
Hainsworth, A. H., MA *Camb.*, PhD *Chic.* Sr. Lectr.
Hall, G., BSc *Strath.*, PhD *Strath.* Sr. Lectr.
Jaroskiewicz, E. M. M., BSc *Warsaw*, MSc *Kent*, PhD *Nott.* Sr. Lectr.
O'Neill, J. G., BSc *Leeds*, MSc *Wales*, PhD *CNAA* Sr. Lectr.
Patterson, L. H., BSc *CNAA*, PhD *Lond.* Prof.
Piacentini, L. C., BSc *Strath.*, PhD *Strath.* Sr. Lectr.
Potter, G. A., BSc *Manc.*, PhD *Lond.* Sr. Lectr.
Proudfoot, S. G., BSc *Leeds*, PhD *Leeds* Principal Lectr.
Smith, G., BPharm *Bath*, PhD *CNAA* Sr. Lectr.
Stanford, J. B., MPharm *Wales* Sr. Lectr.
Stanley, L. A., BA *Oxf.*, PhD *Edin.* Sr. Lectr.
Taylor, M. J., BSc *CNAA*, MSc *Lond.*, PhD *Nott.* Sr. Lectr.
Taylor, P. M., BSc *Bath*, PhD *CNAA* Sr. Lectr.
Twitchell, A. M., BSc(Pharm) *CNAA*, PhD *CNAA* Sr. Lectr.
Westwood, N., BPharm *Lond.*, PhD *Lond.* Sr. Lectr.
Whiting, P. H., BSc *Lond.*, PhD *Hull*, DSc *Hull* Sr. Lectr.
Woolley, J. G., BSc *Manc.*, PhD *Nott.* Sr. Lectr.

Physical Education, Sport and Leisure
Bedford Campus
Tel: (01234) 793268 Fax: (01234) 793440
Amis, J., BSc *Birm.*, MA *Dal.* Sr. Lectr., Sport
Bonser, Rob, BA *York(UK)*, DPhil *York(UK)* Sr. Lectr., Sport
Bott, Jenny Sr. Lectr., Sport
Carpenter, Paul, BSc *CNAA*, MS *Calif.* Sr. Lectr., Sport
Craig, Peter, BEd Sr. Lectr., Sport
Day, J. Sr. Lectr., Sport
Eassom, Simon, BEd *Warw.*, MA *Alta.* Sr. Lectr., Sport
Elkington, Helen Sr. Lectr., Sport
Hall, Howard, BA *Staffs.*, MS *N.Texas* Sr. Lectr., Sport
Harwood, Michael, BSc *Lough.*, MSc *Lough.* Sr. Lectr., Sport
Hewett, T. Sr. Lectr., Sport
Kelly, E. Sr. Lectr., Sport
Kerr, Alistair, BSc *City(UK)*, MA *Lond.*, MSc *Hudd.* Sr. Lectr., Sport
Leah, Jean Sr. Lectr., Sport
Lockwood, Andrea, BEd *Miami*, MEd Sr. Lectr., Sport
Roberts, Ken, BSc *CNAA*, MPhil *Wales* Sr. Lectr., Sport
Sherlock, Joyce, BA *Sheff.*, PhD *Lond.* Sr. Lectr., Sport
Slack, Trevor, BPE *Alta.*, MA *Alta.*, PhD *Alta.* Head*

Winter, Ed, BEd *Lough.*, MSc *Lough.*, PhD *Lough.* Sr. Lectr., Sport
Youngs, R., BEd *CNAA* Sr. Lectr., Sport
Other Staff: 1 Sr. Res. Fellow

Physics, Applied
Tel: (0116) 257 7137 Fax: (0116) 257 7135
Adama-Acquah, R. W., BSc *CNAA*, MSc *Lond.*, PhD *Lond.* Sr. Lectr.
Bayliss, Susan C., BSc *Lond.*, PhD *Camb.* Principal Lectr.
Kadhim, N. J., BSc *Salf.*, MSc *Salf.*, PhD *CNAA* Sr. Lectr.
Thurstans, R. E., BSc *Birm.*, MSc *Birm.*, PhD *CNAA* Principal Lectr.

Plant Science, see Special Centres, etc

Professional Legal Studies
Tel: (0116) 257 7177 Fax: (0116) 257 7186
Allen, Helen, LLB *Birm.* Sr. Lectr.
Anderson, Emma, LLB *Sheff.* Sr. Lectr.
Bragg, Alison M., LLB *Leic.* Sr. Lectr.
Cook, M. C., BA *CNAA* Head*
Crutchley, Kay H., BA *CNAA* Sr. Lectr.
Gray, A., LLB *CNAA* Sr. Lectr.
Green, Kimbra, LLB *Lanc.* Sr. Lectr.
Hibbert, P. R., LLB *Manc.* Prof.
Hipwell, G. J., LLB *E.Anglia* Sr. Lectr.
Keefe, F. M., BA *CNAA* Principal Lectr.
Mummery, Eileen, BA *Manc.*, LLB *CNAA* Sr. Lectr.
Packer, M. W., BA *CNAA*, LLM *Lond.* Principal Lectr.
Thorpe, Sarah R., MA *Camb.* Sr. Lectr.
Thurston, J. M. R. T., LLB *Newcastle(UK)* Principal Lectr.
Wilcock, Stephen, LLB *Sheff.* Sr. Lectr.
Zambartas, Louise, LLB *Birm.* Sr. Lectr.

Public Policy and Managerial Studies
Tel: (0116) 257 7780 Fax: (0116) 257 7795
Baggott, I. R., BA *York(UK)*, PhD *Hull* Reader
Beuret, Kristine, BSc *Lond.* Sr. Lectr.
Clarke, M. L., BScEcon *Wales*, MPhil *S'ton.*, PhD *Lond.* Principal Lectr.
Denscombe, M., BSc *Lond.*, PhD *Leic.* Prof.
Goldfarb, B. M., BA *Leic.*, MPhil *Nott.* Sr. Lectr.
Gray, C. J., BA *CNAA* Principal Lectr.
Greenwood, J. R., BA *Keele*, PhD *Reading* Prof.
Hall, R., MA *Manc.* Principal Lectr.
Harley, Sandra, BA *Sus.*, PhD *Brist.* Sr. Lectr.
Lambie, G. R., MA *Liv.*, BA *Warw.*, PhD *Warw.* Principal Lectr.
Leach, S. N., BSocSc *Birm.*, MSocSc *Birm.* Prof.
Lowe, P. E., BA *Wales*, MA *Leic.* Sr. Lectr.
Lowndes, V., BSc *Brist.*, MPhil *Sus.*, PhD *Strath.* Prof.
Norris, E. W., BSc *Brist.* Sr. Lectr.
O'Donovan, C., BA *Hull*, MA *Warw.* Sr. Lectr.
Robins, L. J., BSc *S'ton.*, PhD *S'ton.* Principal Lectr.
Saks, Maj-Lis H., BSc *CNAA*, MSc(Econ) *Lond.* Sr. Lectr.
Stott, A. W., BA(Econ) *Manc.*, MA *McG.* Sr. Lectr.
Wilson, D. J., BPhil *Liv.*, BA *Warw.*, PhD *Warw.* Prof.; Head*
Other Staff: 1 Sr. Res. Fellow

Social and Community Studies
Tel: (0116) 257 7796 Fax: (0116) 257 7708
Batchelor, D. J., BSc *Oregon*, MSc *Lough.* Principal Lectr., Youth/Community Studies
Fabes, R. C., MEd *Leic.* Sr. Lectr., Youth/Community Studies
Howson, C., BA *Leic.*, MA *Warw.* Sr. Lectr., Youth/Community Studies
Johns, Robert, BA *Wales*, MA *Brun.* Sr. Lectr., Social Work
Joseph, J. M., BSc *Birm.*, MA *Reading* Sr. Lectr., Youth/Community Studies
Kent, Julie, BA *Kent*, MA *Nott.* Sr. Lectr., Social Work
Knight, Charlotte Sr. Lectr., Social Work

McIntosh-Stewart, Linda, BSc *Dund.*, MA *Dund.* Sr. Lectr., Social Work
Payne, Christopher, BA *Durh.*, MA *Brun.* Prof.†
Payne, Malcolm, BA *E.Anglia* Sr. Lectr., Youth/Community Studies
Ruegger, Maria, BA *CNAA* Sr. Lectr., Social Work
Sedgewick, Andrew, BSc *S'ton.*, MA *CNAA* Sr. Lectr., Social Work
Stewart, M., BA *Open(UK)* Sr. Lectr., Social Work
Sullivan, Elizabeth, BA *Open(UK)* Sr. Lectr., Social Work
Sutton, D. Carole, BA *Lond.*, MSc *Leic.*, PhD *Leic.* Principal Lectr., Social Work
Taylor, G., MA *CNAA* Sr. Lectr., Social Work
Tyler, Mary J., BSc *Wales*, MA *CNAA* Principal Lectr., Youth/Community Studies
Unwin, Hilary F., MA *Leic.* Principal Lectr., Social Work
Ward, D., LLB *Manc.*, MA *Nott.* Prof.; Head*
Weston, T. P., BA *Brad.* Sr. Lectr., Social Work

Sociology, see Arts and Humanities

Sport, see Phys. Educn., Sport and Leisure

Statistics, see Mathl. Scis., and Med. Stats.

Textiles and Fashion
Tel: (0116) 257 7570 Fax: (0116) 257 7574
Blissett, T. B., BSc Sr. Lectr.
Bradshaw, Mark S. B., BSc *De Mont.*, PhD Sr. Lectr.
Cassidy, C. Sr. Lectr.
Cooper, J. S., BSc Sr. Lectr.
Curran, S. D., BA Sr. Lectr.
Dunn, H., BA *CNAA* Sr. Lectr.
Fagan, R. Principal Lectr.
Fozzard, G. J. W., BSc MSc PhD Sr. Lectr.
Harwood, R., BScTech PhD, FRSChem Head*
Hutchings, T., MA *RCA* Sr. Lectr.
Mee, J., MA Sr. Lectr.
Miller, T. D. Sr. Lectr.
Morgan, P. W., MDes *RCA* Principal Lectr.
Pollard, J., FTI Sr. Lectr.
Spencer, D. J., FTI Sr. Lectr.
Wignall, K. R., BA *Leeds* Sr. Lectr.
Williams, John, BSc *S'ton.*, PhD *Cran.IT* Sr. Lectr.

Visual and Performing Arts

Performing Arts
Arnold, N. J. M., BA *Oxf.*, DPhil *Oxf.* Sr. Lectr.
Hugill, A., MA *Keele* Sr. Lectr.
Huxley, M. R., BEd *Keele*, MA *Leeds* Sr. Lectr.
MacDonald, C., BA *Leeds* Sr. Lectr.
Maughan, C. C., BSc *Aberd.* Sr. Lectr.
Patterson, M. W., MA *Oxf.*, DPhil *Oxf.* Prof.; Head*
Stevens, J. S., BA *Nott.* Sr. Lectr.
Witts, N. V., BA *Leeds* Prof.
Other Staff: 1 Sr. Res. Fellow

Visual Arts
Boast, B. Sr. Lectr.
Gray, D. J., BA *CNAA* Sr. Lectr.
Hale, M. T. Sr. Lectr.
Jones, D., PhD Principal Lectr.
Kinnell, F. Sr. Lectr.
Kirkwood, I., BA *Lond.* Sr. Lectr.
Lancaster, L., BA *CNAA*, MA *RCA* Sr. Lectr.
Stevens, S. Sr. Lectr.
Tebby, S., BA *Lond.*, PhD *Lond.* Prof.
Turnell, K., MA *CNAA* Sr. Lectr.
Welsford, A. Sr. Lectr.
Wilman, R. H., BA *Leeds* Sr. Lectr.

Youth and Community Studies, see Soc. and Community Studies

SPECIAL CENTRES, ETC

Energy and Sustainable Development, Institute of

Tel: (0116) 257 7401 Fax: (0116) 250 6125

Bowman, Neil T., BSc CNAA, PhD Lond.   Prof.; Dir.*

Lomas, Kevin, BSc PhD   Prof.; Dep. Dir.

Plant Science Research, Norman Borlaug Institute for

Tel: (0116) 257 7776

Chen, D. F., BSc Shanxi, MSc Shanghai, PhD Camb.   Sr. Lectr.

Elliott, Malcolm C., BSc Wales, PhD Wales, FIBiol   Prof.; Dir.*

Scott, N. W., BSc Leeds, PhD Newcastle(UK)   Sr. Lectr.

Slater, A., BSc Edin., PhD Glas.   Sr. Lectr.

CONTACT OFFICERS

Academic affairs. Pro-Vice-Chancellor: Swanick, Prof. Brian H., BEng Liv., PhD Liv., FIEE

Accommodation. Accommodation Officer: Wolf, Sue

Admissions (first degree). Head, Admissions Division (Academic Registry): Maddox, Anne E., BA Leic.

Admissions (higher degree). Head, Admissions Division (Academic Registry): Maddox, Anne E., BA Leic.

Adult/continuing education. Pro-Vice-Chancellor: Swanick, Prof. Brian H., BEng Liv., PhD Liv., FIEE

Alumni. Alumni Officer: Wilson, M. R. J.

Careers. Head of Careers Advisory Service: Nichol, Doug M., BA Open(UK)

Computing services. Head, Division of Learning Development: Collier, Prof. M. W., MA St And.

Credit transfer. Director, HE Access Unit: Kirkman, Irene, BA Lond.

Development/fund-raising. Pro-Vice-Chancellor: Tasker, Prof. Philip, BSc PhD, FIP, FRSChem

Distance education. Head, Centre for Independent Studies: Cork, Alison M., LLB Newcastle(UK)

Equal opportunities. Personnel Services Manager: Richens-Green, J.

Estates and buildings/works and services. Head of Property Services: Stevens, Susan, BSc PhD

Examinations. Head, Examinations and Academic Awards Division (Academic Registry): Hilton, Alison J., BA Lanc.

Finance. Director of Finance: Hefford, T., MBA

General enquiries. Academic Registrar: Critchlow, Eugene, BA Leic., MA Sheff.

Health services. Senior Receptionist: Straker, Anne

Industrial liaison. Pro-Vice-Chancellor: Tasker, Prof. Philip, BSc PhD, FIP, FRSChem

International office. Recruitment Officer: Charles, Alison, BA Kent

Library (chief librarian). Head of Library, Information and Networking Services: Adams, Roy J., MLS Lough., FLA

Personnel/human resources. Director of Personnel: Smith, R., BA

Public relations, information and marketing. Director of External Relations: Harris-Bridge, Marianne, BA Lough.

Publications. Director of External Relations: Harris-Bridge, Marianne, BA Lough.

Purchasing. Purchasing Officer: Dobson, Kevin, BA

Quality assurance and accreditation. Head of Quality Management: Cox, P. M., BA CNAA

Research. Head, Research Unit: Farmer, Julie M., BA Leic.

Safety. Health and Safety Officer: Weston, R.

Scholarships, awards, loans. Head, Admissions Division (Academic Registry): Maddox, Anne E., BA Leic.

Schools liaison. Director of External Relations: Harris-Bridge, Marianne, BA Lough.

Security. Security Manager: Jordan, David M., LLB CNAA

Sport and recreation. Head, Centre for Physical Education and Recreation: Keighley, John S., BA Wales, MA Leeds

Student union. Acting Head, School of Social Sciences: Thewlis, Prof. Peter J., BSc Salf., MScTech Sheff., PhD CNAA

Student welfare/counselling (counselling). Counselling Services Administrator: Lovering, Diane

Student welfare/counselling (welfare). General Manager, Student Services: Sanders, L., BA Leeds

Students from other countries. Administrative Assistant, Admissions Division (Academic Registry): Pole, Andrea M., BA CNAA

Students with disabilities. General Manager, Student Services: Sanders, L., BA Leeds

[Information supplied by the institution as at 3 March 1998, and edited by the ACU]

UNIVERSITY OF DERBY

Established 1993; founded as Derbyshire College of Higher Education, 1983

Postal Address: Kedleston Road, Derby, England DE22 1GB
Telephone: (01332) 622222 **Fax**: (01332) 294861 **E-mail**: postmaster@derby.ac.uk
WWW: http://www.derby.ac.uk **E-mail formula**: initials.surname@derby.ac.uk

VICE-CHANCELLOR*—Waterhouse, Prof. Roger W., MA
PRO VICE-CHANCELLOR AND REGISTRAR‡—Fry, Jennifer M., BSc

UNIVERSITY OF DUNDEE

Founded 1967, previously established as University College, Dundee in 1881, later as Queen's College

Member of the Association of Commonwealth Universities

Postal Address: Dundee, Scotland DD1 4HN
Telephone: (01382) 344000 **Fax**: (01382) 201604 **Cables**: Dundee University **Telex**: 9312110826 DU G
WWW: http://www.dundee.ac.uk **E-mail formula**: initials.surname@dundee.ac.uk

CHANCELLOR—Black, Sir James W., MB ChB St And., Hon. LLD Dund., FRS, FRSEd, FRCP
PRINCIPAL AND VICE-CHANCELLOR*—Graham-Bryce, Ian J., BSc Oxf., MA Oxf., DPhil Oxf., FRSChem, FRSEd
VICE-PRINCIPAL—Swinfen, Prof. David B., MA Oxf., DPhil Oxf., FRHistS
DEPUTY PRINCIPAL—......
DEPUTY PRINCIPAL—Grinyer, Prof. John R., MSc Lond., FCA
DEPUTY PRINCIPAL—Howie, Prof. Peter W., MB ChB Glas., MD Glas., FRCOG, FRCPGlas, FRSEd
RECTOR—Slattery, Tony, MA Camb.
SECRETARY OF THE UNIVERSITY‡—Seaton, Robert, MA Glas., LLB Edin.
LIBRARIAN—Bagnall, John M., MA Camb.
FINANCE OFFICER—Walker, Robin S.

GENERAL INFORMATION

History. The university was established in 1967.

It has a main campus near the city centre, a medical school and school of nursing and midwifery campus 5km from the city centre, and a second campus of the school of nursing and midwifery in Kirkcaldy, 50km from Dundee.

Admission to first degree courses (see also United Kingdom Introduction). Through Universities and Colleges Admission Service (UCAS). International applicants should satisfy either UK entry requirements or those for a comparable course at a university in their own country.

First Degrees. BA, BAcc, BArch, BDes, BDS, BEng, BFin, BMid, BMSc, BN, BSc, LLB, MA, MB ChB, MEng, MSci.

Higher Degrees. LLM, MAcc, MBA, MD, MDes, MDSc, MEd, MFA, MFM, MMEd, MMSc, MOrthS, MPH, MSc, MSSc, MSW, MPhil, PhD, DDSc, DLitt, DSc.

Postgraduates should hold a UK first degree or equivalent from their own country.

Libraries. 550,000 volumes; over 3800 periodicals subscribed to.

Fees (1998–99, annual). International students: £5900 (arts); £6200 (studio-based courses); £7900 (laboratory-based courses); £10,100 (pre-clinical); £16,000 (clinical medicine/dentistry).

Academic Awards. Eighty awards ranging in value from £80 to £5300.

Academic Year (1999–2000). Three terms: 4 October–17 December; 10 January–17 March; 17 April–23 June.

Income (1996–97). Total, £90,094,000.

Statistics. Staff: 2830 (including 616 academic, 489 administrative). Students: full-time 8387 (3606 men, 4781 women); part-time 1885 (810 men, 1075 women); international 1095 (657 men, 438 women).

FACULTIES/SCHOOLS

Arts and Social Sciences
Tel: (01382) 344177 Fax: (01382) 345527
Dean: Jones, Prof. Huw R., BA Wales, MA Wales
Secretary: Tricker, Alan S., BSc Sheff., PhD Sheff.

Duncan of Jordanstone College
Tel: (01382) 345213 Fax: (01382) 345203
Dean: Barr, William W., BA Open(UK)
Secretary: Macpherson, Helen A., MA Dund.

Law and Accountancy
Tel: (01382) 345140 Fax: (01382) 345094
Dean: Lyon, Robert A., MA Dund.
Secretary: Ardron, Susan A., MBA Dund.

Medicine and Dentistry
Tel: (01382) 632763 Fax: (01382) 644267
Dean: Levison, Prof. David A., MB ChB St And., MD Lond., FRCPath
Secretary: Williamson, Walter M., BA Open(UK), MPhil Lough., MBA Leeds

Science and Engineering
Tel: (01382) 344182 Fax: (01382) 345519
Dean: Boxer, Prof. David H., BSc Brist., PhD Brist.
Secretary: Findlay, Graeme R. W., MA Dund.

ACADEMIC UNITS

Accountancy and Business Finance
Tel: (01382) 344193 Fax: (01382) 224419
Bebbington, Kathryn, BCom Cant., MCom Cant.   Sr. Lectr.
Gray, Robert H., BSc Hull, MA Manc., FCA   Prof., Accountancy and Information Systems
Grinyer, John R., MSc Lond., FCA   Prof., Accountancy
Innes, John, BCom Edin., PhD Edin.   Prof., Accountancy; Head*
Lee, Thomas A., MSc Strath., DLitt Strath.   Hon. Prof.
Lonie, A. Alasdair, MA Glas.   Sr. Lectr.
Lowden, Gordon S., MA Camb., LLB St And.   Hon. Prof.
Lyon, Robert A., MA Dund.   Sr. Lectr.
Nixon, William A. J., BCom N.U.I., MBA Warw., PhD Dund., FCA   Sr. Lectr.
Power, David M., BComm N.U.I., MSc Lond., PhD Dund.   Prof., Business Finance
Russell, Alexander, BSc Dund., PhD Dund.   Sr. Lectr.
Sinclair, Crawford D., BSc St And.   Sr. Lectr.
Stout, George A., MA Edin.   Hon. Prof.
Other Staff: 7 Lectrs.; 1 Hon. Lectr.; 1 Temp. Lectr.†
Research: financial markets; financial reporting: theory and practice; management accounting and auditing; social and environmental accounting

Anatomy and Physiology
Tel: (01382) 344206 Fax: (01382) 345514
Dawson, David L., BA Adams, MA S.Illinois, PhD S.Illinois   Sr. Lectr.
Lane, E. Birgitte, BSc Lond., PhD Lond., FRSEd   Cox Prof., Anatomy and Cell Biology
Leslie, Grant C., BSc St And., PhD   Sr. Lectr.
Part, Nicholas J., BSc St And., PhD Dund.   Sr. Lectr.

Proud, Christopher G., BSc Brist., PhD Dund.   Prof., Biochemical Physiology
Rennie, Michael J., BSc Hull, MSc Manc., PhD Glas., FRSEd   Symers Prof.
Sturrock, Robert R., MB ChB St And., DSc Dund.   Prof., Anatomy
Tickle, Cheryll A., BA Camb., PhD Glas.   Prof., Developmental Biology
Ward, Martyn R., BSc Newcastle(UK), PhD Newcastle(UK)   Sr. Lectr.; Head*
Weijer, Cornelis J., MBiol Utrecht, PhD Utrecht   Sr. Lectr.
Williams, Jeffrey G., BSc Lond., PhD Lond.   Prof., Developmental Biology
Other Staff: 7 Lectrs.; 6 Hon. Lectrs.; 1 Temp. Sr. Lectr.†
Research: cell cycle and apoptosis; cell structure and morphogenesis; membrane transport mechanisms; neurophysiology; whole body metabolism

Architecture
Tel: (01382) 345261 Fax: (01382) 203631
Heathcote, Barry   Lectr.; Head*
Lockhart, Gordon, MA Edin., MArch N.Y.State   Sr. Lectr.
McKean, Charles, BA Brist., FRIBA, FRIAS   Prof.
Pirnie, William J., BArch H.-W., MSc H.-W.   Sr. Lectr.
Roberts, Angus   Sr. Lectr.
Other Staff: 5 Lectrs.; 1 Temp. Sr. Lectr.; 3 Temp. Lectrs.; 2 Temp Lectrs.†
Research: architectural history and conservation; design and practice initiatives; technology initiatives; urban investigation

Biochemistry
Tel: (01382) 344880 Fax: (01382) 322558
Blow, John J., BSc Edin., PhD Camb.   Sr. Lectr.
Booth, Roger, BSc Liv., PhD Liv.   Sr. Lectr.
Boxer, David H., BSc Brist., PhD Brist.   Prof., Microbial Biochemistry
Cohen, Patricia T., BSc Lond., PhD Lond.   Reader
Cohen, Philip, BSc Lond., PhD Lond., FRS, FRSEd   Prof., Enzymology
Crocker, Paul R., BA Camb., PhD Lond.   Sr. Lectr.
Downes, Charles P., PhD Birm., FRSEd   Prof.; Head*
Fairlamb, Alan H., BSc Edin., MB ChB Edin., PhD Edin., FLS   Prof.
Ferguson, Michael A. J., BSc Manc., PhD Lond., FRSEd   Prof., Molecular Parasitology
Flavell, Andrew J., BSc Sheff., PhD Sheff.   Sr. Lectr.
Hardie, David G., MA Camb., PhD H.-W., FRSEd   Prof., Cellular Signalling
Kernohan, John C., MA Camb., PhD Camb.   Sr. Lectr.

Lamond, Angus I., BSc *Glas.*, PhD *Camb.*, FRSEd Prof., Biochemistry
Lane, David P., BSc *Lond.*, PhD *Lond.*, FRSEd Prof., Molecular Oncology
Lilley, David J. M., BSc *Durh.*, MSc *Lond.*, PhD *Durh.*, FRSEd Prof., Molecular Biology
Quinlan, Roy A., BSc *Kent*, PhD *Kent* Sr. Lectr.
Ragan, Charles I., BA *Camb.*, PhD *Brist.* Hon. Prof.
Stansfield, David A., BSc *Wales*, PhD *Wales* Sr. Lectr.
Stark, Michael J. R., MA *Camb.*, PhD *Leic.* Reader
Watts, Colin, BSc *Brist.*, DPhil *Sus.* Prof., Immunobiology
Other Staff: 1 Lectr.; 2 Hon. Lectrs.; 1 Temp Sr. Lectr.; 3 Temp. Lectrs.
Research: cancer research; cell biology; immunobiology; molecular biology and molecular genetics; molecular parasitology

Biological Sciences

Tel: (01382) 344765 Fax: (01382) 322318
Codd, Geoffrey A., BTech *Brad.*, PhD *Brad.*, FIBiol Prof., Microbiology
Eddy, F. Brian, BSc *Lond.*, PhD *Brist.* Reader
Gadd, Geoffrey M., BSc *Wales*, PhD *Wales*, DSc *Wales*, FIBiol Prof., Microbiology
Herbert, Rodney A., BTech *Brad.*, PhD *Aberd.*, FRSEd Prof., Microbial Ecology; Head*
Hillman, John R., BSc *Wales*, PhD *Wales*, FIBiol, FRSEd Hon. Prof.
Hopkins, David W., BSc *CNAA*, PhD *Newcastle(UK)* Sr. Lectr.
Horrobin, David F., MA *Oxf.*, BM BCh *Oxf.*, DPhil *Oxf.* Hon. Prof.
Hubbard, Stephen F., MSc *Lond.*., DPhil *Oxf.* Sr. Lectr.
Hutchison, Christopher J., BSc *Sus.*, PhD *Lond.* Sr. Lectr.
Jones, Allan M., BSc *Wales*, PhD *Wales*, FLS Sr. Lectr.
Oliver, Roy F., BSc *Hull*, PhD *Birm.*, DSc *Birm.*, FIBiol Reader, Zoology
Raven, John A., MA *Camb.*, PhD *Camb.*, Hon. PhD *Umeå*, FRS, FRSEd Boyd Baxter Prof., Biology
Riley, John, BSc *Leeds*, PhD *Leeds* Sr. Lectr.
Rowell, Peter, BSc *Liv.*, PhD *Liv.* Sr. Lectr.
Weyers, Jonathan D. B., BSc *Glas.*, PhD *Glas.* Sr. Lectr.
Wilson, Thomas M. A., BSc *Edin.*, PhD *Camb.* Hon. Prof.
Other Staff: 5 Lectrs.; 10 Hon. Sr. Lectrs.; 25 Hon. Lectrs.; 1 Temp. Lectr.
Research: animal cell and molecular biology; animal ecology; applied and environmental microbiology; plant ecophysiology and molecular biology

Chemistry

Tel: (01382) 344328 Fax: (01382) 345517
Barnes, John C., BSc *Wales*, PhD *Wales*, DSc *Dund.*, FRSChem Sr. Lectr.
Bell, Stephen, BSc *St And.*, PhD *St And.*, FRSChem Sr. Lectr.
Brimacombe, John S., PhD *Birm.*, DSc *Birm.*, DSc *Dund.*, FRSChem, FRSEd Roscoe Prof.
Dines, Trevor J., BTech *Brad.*, PhD *Brad.*, FRSChem Sr. Lectr.
Horspool, William M., BSc *Strath.*, PhD *Glas.*, DSc *Dund.*, FRSChem, FRSEd Reader
Hunter, Geoffrey, BSc *Sheff.*, PhD *Newcastle(UK)*, FRSChem Prof.; Head*
Miller, John A., BSc *Glas.*, PhD *Strath.*, FRSChem, FRSEd Hon. Prof.
Murray, Alistair W., BSc *Aberd.*, PhD *Aberd.* Sr. Lectr.
Rochester, Colin H., BSc *Lond.*, PhD *Lond.*, DSc *Lond.*, FRSChem, FRSEd Baxter Prof.
Other Staff: 1 Lectr.; 5 Hon. Lectrs.; 1 Temp. Lectr.; 1 Temp. Lectr.†
Research: biological chemistry; heterogeneous catalysis and surface chemistry; materials science; molecular recognition

Computing, Applied

Tel: (01382) 344145 Fax: (01382) 345509
Arnott, John L., BSc *Hull*, MSc *S'ton.*, PhD *Dund.* Reader
Newell, Alan F., BSc *Birm.*, PhD *Birm.*, FIEE, FRSEd Prof., Electronics and Microcomputer Systems; Head*
Parkes, Stephen M., BSc *Lanc.*, MSc *Lanc.*, PhD *Wales* Sr. Lectr.
Ricketts, Ian W., BSc *Dund.*, PhD *Dund.* Reader
Other Staff: 5 Lectrs.; 1 Hon. Lectr.
Research: computer-supported interpersonal communication; extra-ordinary human-computer interaction; information technology for assisting disabled and elderly people; medical informatics; telecommunication service provision and access

Dentistry, see below

Design, see also Fine Art and Des.

Tel: (01382) 345290 Fax: (01382) 201378
Ashcroft, Roland J., MA *CNAA* Sr. Lectr.
Carr, Richard, MA *Oxf.* Sr. Lectr.
Follett, Georgina L. P., BA *CNAA*, MDes *RCA* Prof.; Head*
Herbert, David J., BA *Open(UK)* Sr. Lectr.
Morris, Roger C., MA *RCA* Sr. Lectr.
Schenk, Pamela M., BA *Newcastle(UK)*, PhD *Manc.* Sr. Lectr.
Shelley, Janet, MDes *RCA* Sr. Lectr.
Starszakowna, Norma Prof.
Taylor, Andrew Sr. Lectr.
Other Staff: 9 Lectrs.; 3 Temp Sr. Lectrs.; 2 Temp. Lectrs.; 2 Temp. Lectrs.†
Research: textile design; three-dimensional design; visual communication

Economic Studies

Tel: (01382) 344371 Fax: (01382) 344691
Chatterji, Monojit, BA *Bom.*, MA *Camb.*, PhD *Camb.* Bonar Prof., Applied Economics; Head*
Dewhurst, John H. L., BA *Camb.*, MA *Kent*, PhD *Dund.* Sr. Lectr.
Jones, Stephen R. H., BSc *Lond.*, PhD *Lond.* Sr. Lectr.
Lythe, Charlotte M., MA *St And.* Sr. Lectr.
Molana, Hassan H., BA *Teheran*, MA *Essex*, PhD *S'ton.* Prof., Economics
Montagna, Catia, Laur *Parma*, MPhil *Glas.*, PhD *Dund.* Sr. Lectr.
Other Staff: 6 Lectrs.; 6 Hon. Lectrs.; 1 Temp. Lectr.†
Research: environmental economics; industrial organisations; international and regional economics; labour economics; new institutional economics

Education and Lifelong Learning, Institute for

Tel: (01382) 344935 Fax: (01382) 221057
Cooke, Anthony J., MA *Manc.* Sr. Lectr.
Hartley, J. David, BA *Winn.*, MEd *Nott.*, PhD *Exe.* Prof., Educational Theory and Policy
Siann, Gerda, BSc *Cape Town*, MSc *Zambia*, PhD *Edin.*, FBPsS Prof., Gender Relations
Swinfen, Prof. David B., MA *Oxf.*, DPhil *Oxf.*, FRHistS Acting Head*
Other Staff: 7 Lectrs.; 1 Temp. Lectr.
Research: analysis of educational policy; comparative education; educational ethics; history of education; lifelong learning

Engineering, Civil

Tel: (01382) 344341 Fax: (01382) 344816
Davies, Michael C. R., BSc *Lond.*, MPhil *Camb.*, PhD *Camb.*, FGS Prof.
Davies, Peter A., BSc *Newcastle(UK)*, PhD *Newcastle(UK)*, FRSEd Prof., Fluid Dynamics; Head*
Dhir, Ravindra K., BSc *Durh.*, PhD *Sheff.*, FGS Prof., Concrete Technology
Hamlin, Michael J., CBE, BSc *Brist.*, Hon. LLD *St And.*, Hon. LLD *Dund.*, Hon. DEng *Birm.*, FEng, FICE, FRSEd Hon. Prof.

Hewlett, P. C., BSc *Lond.*, PhD *Lond.*, FRSChem Hon. Prof.
Horner, R. Malcolm W., BSc *Lond.*, PhD *Lond.* Prof.
Jones, Martyn R., BSc *CNAA*, PhD *Dund.*, FGS Sr. Lectr.
Subedi, Nutan K., BSc *Ranchi*, PhD *Strath.*, FIStructE Sr. Lectr.
Vardy, Alan E., BSc *Leeds*, PhD *Leeds*, FICE Res. Prof.†
Other Staff: 1 Hon. Sr. Lectr.; 3 Hon. Lectrs.; 1 Temp. Lectr.
Research: concrete technology and construction; construction management; fluid mechanics and public health engineering; geotechnical and structural engineering; structural performance of bridges

Engineering, Electronic and Manufacturing, see Phys., Appl., and Electronic and Manufacturing Engin.

English

Tel: (01382) 344412 Fax: (01382) 345503
Newton, Kenneth M., MA *Glas.*, PhD *Edin.* Prof., Literary Theory
Robb, David S., MA *Aberd.*, PhD *Edin.* Sr. Lectr.
Skretkowicz, Victor, BA *McM.*, MA *New Br.*, PhD *S'ton.* Sr. Lectr.
Smith, I. C., MA *Aberd.*, Hon. DLitt *Aberd.*, Hon. DLitt *Glas.*, Hon. LLD *Dund.* Hon. Prof.
Smith, Stanley W., MA *Camb.*, PhD *Camb.* Prof.
Ward, Geoffrey, MA *Camb.* Prof., English Literature; Head*
Watt, Robert J. C., MA *Aberd.*, MLitt *Oxf.* Sr. Lectr.
Wolfreys, Julian L., BA *Sus.*, MA *Clark*, DPhil *Sus.* Sr. Lectr.
Wynn-Davies, Marion, BA *Wales*, PhD *Lond.* Sr. Lectr.
Other Staff: 9 Lectrs.
Research: eighteenth-, nineteenth-and twentieth-century literature; literary computing; Old and Middle English; Renaissance, Scottish, American and post-colonial literature; textual studies

Fine Art

Tel: (01382) 345226 Fax: (01382) 200983
Fisher, Gareth R. Sr. Lectr.
Forbes, Ronald Sr. Lectr.
Howard, Ian, MA *Edin.* Prof.
Kempsell, Jake Sr. Lectr.
Maclean, William Prof.
Modeen, Mary, BA *Alma*, BFA *Alma*, MA *Missouri*, MFA *Louisiana* Sr. Lectr.
Robb, Alan, MA *RCA* Prof.; Head*
Shemilt, Elaine, BA *CNAA*, MA *RCA* Sr. Lectr.
Watson, Arthur J. Sr. Lectr.; Dir.*
Other Staff: 5 Lectrs.; 2 Temp. Lectrs.; 15 Temp. Lectrs.†
Research: artist-led publishing; lens-based art; painting, printmaking and sculpture; performance; site-specific and environmental art

Fine Art and Design

General Course
Tel: (01382) 345251 Fax: (01382) 200983
Hunter, Richard Sr. Lectr.; Dir.*
Other Staff: 2 Lectrs.

Geography

Tel: (01382) 344434 Fax: (01382) 344434
Duck, Robert W., BSc *Dund.*, PhD *Dund.* Sr. Lectr.
Findlay, Allan, MA *Aberd.*, PhD *Durh.* Prof.
Jones, Huw R., BA *Wales* Prof., Population Geography; Head*
Werritty, Alan, MA *Camb.*, MSc *Penn.State*, PhD *Camb.*, FRSEd Prof., Physical Geography
Other Staff: 8 Lectrs.; 1 Hon. Lectr.; 1 Temp. Lectr.
Research: environmental assessment and change; geomorphology; hydrological studies; marine, estuarine and coastal studies;

population geography and development geography

History

Tel: (01382) 344512 Fax: (01382) 345506

Cornwall, John M., BA Leeds, PhD Leeds, FRHistS Sr. Lectr.

Davey, Christopher J., BA Lond. Sr. Lectr.

Gowland, David A., BA Manc., PhD Manc. Sr. Lectr.; Head*

Harris, Robert, BA Durh., DPhil Oxf., FRHistS Sr. Lectr.

MacDonald, Murdo J. S., MA Edin., PhD Edin. Prof.†, History of Scottish Art

Machin, George I. T., MA Oxf., DPhil Oxf., FRHistS Prof., British History

Smout, T. Christopher, MA Camb., PhD Camb., FRSEd Hon. Prof.

Swinfen, David B., MA Oxf., DPhil Oxf., FRHistS Prof., Commonwealth History

Whatley, Christopher A., BA Strath., PhD Strath., FRHistS Prof., Scottish History

Other Staff: 5 Lectrs.; 1 Temp. Lectr.; 1 Temp. Lectr.†

Research: British political and social history; colonial America; Eastern Europe and Russia; European Union; Scottish social and economic history

Law

Tel: (01382) 344764 Fax: (01382) 226905

Belcher, C. Alice, BSocSc Keele, MPhil Camb., PhD Manc. Sr. Lectr.

Bissett-Johnson, Alastair, LLB Nott., LLM Mich. Prof., Private Law

Brand, D. A., LLB Dund. Sr. Lectr.

Cameron, Peter D., LLB Edin., PhD Edin. Prof.†, International Energy Law and Policy

Crowson, Phillip C. F., BA Camb. Hon. Prof.

Davies, Peter, BA Warw., MSc Lond. Hon. Prof.

Ervine, W. Cowan H., BA Trinity(Dub.), LLB Trinity(Dub.), LLM Lond. Sr. Lectr.

Ferguson, Pamela R., LLB Glas., PhD Dund Sr. Lectr.

McBryde, William W., LLB Edin., PhD Glas., LLD Edin., FRSEd Prof., Scots Law

McManus, James J., LLB Edin., PhD Dund. Sr. Lectr. (on leave)

Moody, Susan R., BA Trinity(Dub.) Sr. Lectr.

Page, Alan C., LLB Edin., PhD City(UK) Prof., Public Law

Palmer, Keith F., BSc Birm., PhD Birm. Prof.†

Raitt, Fiona E., LLB Edin. Sr. Lectr.

Reid, Colin T., MA Oxf., LLB Camb. Prof., Environmental Law; Head*

Ross, Rt. Hon. Lord, QC, MA Edin., LLB Edin., Hon. LLD Dund., Hon. LLD Edin., Hon. DUniv H-W, FRSEd Hon. Prof.

Stevens, P., BA Camb., MA Lond., PhD Lond. Prof., Petroleum Policy and Economics

Walde, Thomas W., BL Fran., LLM Harv., PhD Fran. Prof., International Economic, Energy and Natural Resources Law

Ward, Ian, BA Keele, LLM Tor., PhD Camb. Prof.

White, Robin M., JP, LLB St And., LLM Lond. Sr. Lectr.

Zamora, Armando, MSc Bogota, MBA Lausanne Sr. Lectr.

Other Staff: 8 Lectrs.; 1 Temp. Sr. Lectr.; 4 Temp. Lectrs.

Research: alternative dispute resolution; charity law; criminal law and justice; energy, petroleum and mineral law and policy; environmental law

Management and Consumer Studies

Tel: (01382) 345354 Fax: (01382) 200047

Anderson, Annie, BSc CNAA, PhD Aberd. Prof., Food Choice

Calder, Moira B., BSc Sur., MBA Edin. Sr. Lectr.

Colquhoun, Anne, BA CNAA Sr. Lectr.

Cunningham, Brian, BA Strath. Sr. Lectr.

Lederer, Peter Hon. Prof.

Lyon, H. Philip, BSc Lond., MA Essex, PhD Wales Sr. Lectr.; Head*

Vickers, Terence G., BSc Brist., MBA Dund., PhD Brist., FRSChem Sr. Lectr.

Other Staff: 8 Lectrs.; 1 Temp. Lectr.; 4 Temp. Lectrs.†

Research: ageing society; food choice; management

Mathematics

Tel: (01382) 344471 Fax: (01382) 345516

Brown, Richard A., BSc Durh., MSc Newcastle(UK), PhD Newcastle(UK) Sr. Lectr.

Chaplain, Mark A., BSc Dund., PhD Dund. Sr. Lectr.

Cloude, Shane R., BSc Dund., PhD Dund. Hon. Prof.

Fletcher, Roger, MA Camb., PhD Leeds, FIMA, FRSEd Baxter Prof.

Goodman, Timothy N. T., BA Camb., MSc Warw., DPhil Sus. Prof., Applied Analysis; Head*

Griffiths, David F., BSc Wales, PhD Wales, FIMA Reader

Sleeman, Brian D., BSc CNAA, PhD Lond., DSc Dund., FIMA, FRSEd Hon. Prof.

Smith, Paul D., BSc Adel., PhD Camb., FIMA Reader

Thomas, David P., BSc Liv., PhD Liv., FIMA Sr. Lectr.

Watson, George A., BSc Edin., MSc Edin., PhD ANU, FIMA, FRSEd Prof., Numerical Analysis

Other Staff: 4 Lectrs.; 1 Sr. Lectr.†; 1 Hon. Lectr.

Research: acoustics and electromagnetics; approximation theory; mathematical biology; optimisation; statistics and numerical analysis

Medicine, see below

Nursing and Midwifery, see Medicine, below

Philosophy

Tel: (01382) 344538 Fax: (01382) 224140

Davey, Jeremy R. N., BA York(UK), MA Sus., DPhil Sus. Sr. Lectr.

Harris, Nigel G. E., BSc Brist., BA Leeds, BPhil Oxf. Sr. Lectr.

Kemal, Salim, BA CNAA, MA Lond., PhD Camb. Prof.; Head*

O'Neill, Basil C., MA Oxf., BPhil Oxf. Sr. Lectr.

Other Staff: 3 Lectrs.; 1 Temp. Lectr.†

Research: artificial intelligence; Buddhism and Islam; computer logic; modern continental philosophy; philosophy of visual arts

Physics, Applied, and Electronic and Manufacturing Engineering

Tel: (01382) 344395 Fax: (01382) 202830

Anderson, James M., BSc Edin., PhD Edin. Sr. Lectr.

Cairns, James A., BSc Glas., PhD Glas., DSc Glas., FRSChem, FRSEd Prof., Microelectronics and Materials Science

Cameron, Ian D. Hon. Prof.

Cracknell, Arthur P., MA Camb., MA Oxf., MSc Sing., DPhil Oxf., FIP, FRSEd Carnegie Prof., Physics

Fitzgerald, Alexander G., BSc St And., PhD Camb., DSc Dund., FIP, FRMetS, FRSEd Prof., Analytical Electron Microscopy; Head*

Gibson, Peter F., BSc Leic. Hon. Prof.

Gibson, Roderick A. G., BSc Dund., PhD Dund. Sr. Lectr.

Hewit, James R., BSc Edin., MSc Wales, PhD Lough., FIMechE Prof., Mechanical and Manufacturing Engineering

Lawrenson, Brian, BSc Hull, MSc Hull Sr. Lectr.

Low, John N., BSc St And., MSc Dund., PhD Dund. Sr. Lectr.

Makin, Brian, BSc(Eng) S'ton., PhD S'ton., FIEE, FIP, FRSEd Watson Watt Prof., Electrical Engineering

Middleton, David E. S., BSc Strath., MSc Birm. Sr. Lectr.

Powell, M. J., BA Camb., PhD Camb. Hon. Prof.

Ramsay, Bruce, BSc St And., PhD Sr. Lectr.

Storey, Brian E., BSc Nott., PhD Nott. Sr. Lectr.

Vaughan, Robin A., BSc Nott., PhD Nott. Sr. Lectr.

Young, David E., BSc CNAA Hon. Prof.

Other Staff: 11 Lectrs.; 1 Sr. Lectr.†; 11 Hon. Lectrs.

Research: amorphous materials; analytical electron microscopy and surface analysis; applied electrostatics; electrical power engineering; environmental physics; mechatronics; medical engineering

Physiology, see Anat. and Physiol.

Political Science and Social Policy

Tel: (01382) 344656 Fax: (01382) 344675

Black, Anthony J., MA Camb., PhD Camb. Prof., History of Political Thought

Dunphy, Richard A. R., BA Trinity(Dub.), MA N.U.I., PhD Florence Sr. Lectr.

MacQueen, Norman J. D., BA Ulster, MSc Lond., DPhil Ulster Sr. Lectr.

Smith, Brian C., BA Exe., MA McM., PhD Exe. Prof.; Head*

Spicker, Paul S., MA Oxf., MSc Lond., PhD Lond. Sr. Lectr.

Other Staff: 4 Lectrs.; 1 Temp. Lectr.†

Research: development politics; European politics; international relations; political thought; social policy and politics of gender

Psychology

Tel: (01382) 344622 Fax: (01382) 229993

Bennett, Robert M. J., BA Reading, PhD Lond. Sr. Lectr.

Harley, Trevor A., BA Camb., PhD Camb. Sr. Lectr.

Kennedy, Robert A., BA Birm., PhD Birm., FBPsS, FRSEd Prof.; Head*

Matthews, Gerald, BA Camb., PhD Camb. Reader

Murray, Wayne S., BSc Monash, PhD Monash Sr. Lectr.

Seymour, Philip H. K., BA Oxf., MEd St And., PhD Dund. Prof., Cognitive Psychology

Todman, John B., BSc Birm., PhD Dund. Sr. Lectr.

Topping, Keith J., BA Sus., MA Nott., PhD Sheff., FBPsS Sr. Lectr.

Wade, Nicholas J., BSc Edin., PhD Monash Prof., Visual Psychology

Wilkes, Allan L., BSc Manc., BSc Oxf. Sr. Lectr.

Willatts, Peter B., BSc Lond., PhD Lond. Sr. Lectr.

Wilton, Richard N., BSc Brist., PhD Exe. Sr. Lectr.

Other Staff: 6 Lectrs.

Research: cognitive and social development; ingestive behaviour; psychophysiology of attention and emotion; reading and language; social identity processes

Social Work

Tel: (01382) 344647 Fax: (01382) 221512

Baldwin, Norma, BA Manc., MPhil Warw. Prof., Child Care and Protection; Head*

Hogg, James H., BA Reading, PhD Reading Prof., Profound Disabilities

Williams, Brian P., BA Hull, MA Brist. Prof.

Other Staff: 3 Lectrs.; 1 Lectr.†; 2 Hon. Lectrs.; 1 Temp. Sr. Lectr.†

Research: child care and protection; community care; criminial justice services

Television and Imaging

Tel: (01382) 345352 Fax: (01382) 345329

Edlund, Richard Hon. Prof.

Johnson, Nigel M., BA CNAA Sr. Lectr.

Partridge, Stephen, BA CNAA Prof., Media Art; Head*

Other Staff: 5 Lectrs.; 5 Hon. Lectrs.; 1 Temp. Sr. Lectr.; 1 Temp. Lectr.

Research: computer imaging; digital visual effects; interactive art and time-based art; media art; multimedia and internet

Town and Regional Planning

Tel: (01382) 345236 Fax: (01382) 204234

Edgar, William M., BA Belf., MPhil Lond.   Sr. Lectr.

Jackson, Anthony A., BA Camb., MSc Reading   Sr. Lectr.

Lloyd, Michael G., BA Sheff., MSc Aberd.   Res. Prof., Planning Research

Mawson, John, BSc Lond., MPhil Lond.   Prof.; Head*

Moir, John, BSc Aberd., PhD Dund.   Sr. Lectr.

Pollock, S. H. Alan, BSc Dund., MSc Dund.   Sr. Lectr.

Roberts, Peter W., BA Leic., MA Newcastle(UK)   Prof.†, European Strategic Planning

Skea, Ralph G., PhD Dund.   Sr. Lectr.

Other Staff: 8 Lectrs.; 1 Temp. Lectr.†

Research: housing and social policy; local economic development; regeneration and urban conservation; regional planning: governance of cities and regions; rural planning and the environment

DENTISTRY

Dental School

Tel: (01382) 345984 Fax: (01382) 225163

Cadden, Samuel W., BSc Glas., BDS Glas., PhD Brist.   Sr. Lectr.

Chisholm, Derrick M., BDS Glas., PhD Glas., FDSRCPSGlas, FDSRCSEd   Boyd Prof.

Drummond, John R., BMSc Dund., BDS Dund., PhD Dund.   Sr. Lectr.

Duguid, Robert, BA York.(U.K.), MSc Newcastle(UK), DPhil York.(U.K.)   Sr. Lectr.

Erskine, Richard B., BDS St And., MDSc Dund., FDSRCSEd   Sr. Lectr.

Evans, Dafydd J. P., BDS Lond., PhD Lond., FDSRCS   Sr. Lectr.

Gilbert, Angela D., BDS Edin., PhD Edin., FDSRCSEd   Sr. Lectr.

Grieve, Andrew R., BDS St And., DDS Birm., FDSRCSEd   Prof.

Lloyd, Charles H., BSc Birm., PhD Birm.   Reader

Mossey, Peter A., BDS Dund., PhD Glas., FDSRCS, FFDRCSI   Sr. Lectr.

Newton, James P., BDS Dund., BSc St And., PhD St And.   Sr. Lectr.

Ogden, Graham R., BDS Sheff., MDSc Dund., PhD Dund., FDSRCPSGlas   Sr. Lectr.

Pine, Cynthia M., BDS Manc., PhD Manc.   Sr. Lectr.

Pitts, Nigel B., BDS Lond., PhD Lond., FDSRCS, FDSRCSEd   Prof.; Head*

Radford, John R., BDS Lond., PhD Lond., FDSRCS   Sr. Lectr.

Saunders, Elizabeth M., BDS St And., PhD Dund.   Sr. Lectr.

Schor, Ana Maria, PhD Camb.   Reader

Schor, Seth L., BA Chic., PhD Rockefeller   Prof., Oral Cell Biology

Scott, Brendan J. J., BSc Lond., BDS Lond., PhD Lond., FDSRCSEd   Sr. Lectr.

Stirrups, David R., BDS Sheff., BA Open(UK), MSc CNAA, FDSRCS, FDSRCPSGlas   Prof., Orthodontics

Yemm, Robert, BDS Brist., BSc Brist., PhD Brist., FDSRCSEd   Prof.

Other Staff: 3 Lectrs.; 9 Hon. Sr. Lectrs.; 7 Hon. Lectrs.; 3 Temp. Sr. Lectrs.; 5 Temp. Lectrs.

Research: conservative dentistry; dental surgery; odontology; oral pathology; public dental health

MEDICINE

(for pre-clinical subjects—Anat., etc., see above)

Anaesthesia

Tel: (01382) 632175

Wildsmith, John A. W., MB ChB Edin., MD Edin., FRCA   Prof.; Head*

Other Staff: 27 Hon. Sr. Lectrs.; 1 Temp. Lectr.

Research: acute pain; intensive care therapy; neuroanaesthesia; obstetric anaesthesia; regional anaesthesia and analgesia

Biomedical Research Centre

Tel: (01382) 632621 Fax: (01382) 669993

Elcombe, Clifford R., BSc Sur., PhD Sur.   Sr. Lectr.

Friedberg, Thomas H., PhD Mainz   Sr. Lectr.

Hayes, John D., BSc Edin., PhD Edin.   Prof.

Meek, David W., BSc Glas., PhD Glas.   Sr. Lectr.

Wolf, C. Roland, BSc Sur., PhD Sur., FRSEd   Imperial Cancer Res. Fund Prof., Molecular Pharmacology

Other Staff: 2 Lectrs.; 2 Hon. Lectrs.; 2 Temp. Lectrs.

Research: cancer research; chemoprotection; drug metabolism; gene expression; stress responses and signal transduction

Cardiovascular Epidemiology Unit

Tel: (01382) 632283 Fax: (01382) 641095

Tunstall Pedoe, Hugh, MA Camb., MD Camb., FRCP, FRCPEd   Prof.; Dir.*

Other Staff: 1 Hon. Lectr.; 1 Temp. Sr. Lectr.†

Research: trends of coronary heart disease in different populations

Child Health

Tel: (01382) 632179 Fax: (01382) 645783

Hume, Robert, BSc Edin., MB ChB Edin., PhD Edin., FRCPEd   Prof., Developmental Medicine

Mehta, Anil, MB BS Lond., MSc Lond.   Sr. Lectr.

Mukhopadhyay, Somnath, MB BS Calc.   Sr. Lectr.

Olver, Richard E., BSc Lond., MB BS Lond., FRCP   James Mackenzie Prof.; Head*

Tarnow-Mordi, William O., BA Camb., MB BChir Camb.   Reader

Other Staff: 2 Lectrs.; 12 Hon. Sr. Lectrs.; 5 Hon. Lectrs.; 2 Temp. Sr. Lectrs.; 1 Temp. Lectr.

Research: foetal development; growth and metabolism; lung biology in health and disease; perinatal health

Clinical Pharmacology and Therapeutics

Tel: (01382) 632161 Fax: (01382) 667120

Davey, Peter G., MD Lond.   Reader

Lipworth, Brian J., BSc St And., MB ChB Manc., MD Manc., FRCP   Sr. Lectr.

MacDonald, Thomas M., BSc Aberd., MB ChB Dund., MD Dund., FRCP   Reader

McDevitt, Denis G., MD Belf., DSc Belf., FRCP, FRCPI, FRCPEd   Prof., Clinical Pharmacology; Head*

McEwen, John, MB ChB St And., PhD Dund., FRCP   Hon. Prof.

Struthers, Allan D., BSc Glas., MB ChB Glas., MD Glas., FRCP, FRCPGlas, FRCPEd   Prof., Clinical Pharmacology

Other Staff: 1 Lectr.; 1 Hon. Sr. Lectr.; 1 Hon. Lectr.; 2 Temp. Lectrs.

Research: adverse drug reaction monitoring; cardiovascular clinical research (chronic heart failure); clinical pharmacology of B3 adrenoceptors; pharmacoeconomics; respiratory medicine (asthma, pulmonary circulation)

Clinical Skills Centre

Ledingham, Iain M., MB ChB Glas., MD Glas., FRCS, FRSEd, FRCPGlas, FIBiol   Prof.; Head*

Dermatology

Tel: (01382) 632240 Fax: (01382) 646047

Ferguson, J., BSc St And., MB ChB   Hon. Sr. Lectr.; Head*

Other Staff: 5 Hon. Sr. Lectrs.; 1 Hon. Lectr.; 1 Temp. Lectr.

Research: development of phototherapy and photochemistry; drug/chemical photosensitisation; photocarcinogenesis

Epidemiology and Public Health

Tel: (01382) 632124 Fax: (01382) 644197

Alder, Elizabeth M., BSc Aberd., PhD Edin.   Sr. Lectr.

Crombie, I. K., BSc Edin., MSc Sheff., PhD Glas.   Reader

Florey, Charles du V., BA Camb., MD Camb., MPH Yale, FRCPEd   James Mackenzie Prof.; Head*

James, Philip B., MB ChB Liv., PhD Liv.   Sr. Lectr.

Ruta, Danny A., MB BS Lond., MSc Lond., PhD Aberd.   Sr. Lectr.

Other Staff: 2 Lectrs.; 11 Hon. Sr. Lectrs.; 2 Hon. Lectrs.

Research: environmental health; epidemiology, including child development; health service research, including audit; hyperbaric medicine, especially deep sea diving

Forensic Medicine

Tel: (01382) 200794 Fax: (01382) 322094

Pounder, Derrick J., MB ChB Birm., FRCPA   Prof.; Head*

Sadler, David W., MB ChB Sheff.   Sr. Lectr.

Research: forensic medicine for human rights; forensic toxicology

General Practice

Tel: (01382) 644425 Fax: (01382) 480330

Bain, Douglas J. G., MD Aberd., PhD Aberd., FRCGP, FRCPEd   Prof.; Head*

Sullivan, Francis M., MB ChB Glas., PhD Glas., FRCPGlas, FRCGP   Prof., General Practice and Primary Care

Other Staff: 2 Lectrs.; 2 Sr. Lectrs.†; 1 Hon. Sr. Lectr.; 10 Hon. Lectrs.; 1 Temp. Lectr.

Research: asthma care in the community; frail and elderly; outcomes of day care surgery; prescribing through pharmacies; team care in general practice

Medical Education, Centre for

Tel: (01382) 631972 Fax: (01382) 645748

Davis, Margery H., MB ChB Glas.   Sr. Lectr.

Harden, Ronald M., MD Glas., FRCPGlas, FRCS, FRCP   Prof.; Dir.*

Rogerson, Elizabeth C. B., MA Dund.   Sr. Lectr.

Other Staff: 4 Temp. Lectrs.; 1 Temp. Lectr.†

Research: computer-assisted learning; curriculum design and planning; distance learning; evaluation methods; techniques of teaching and learning

Medical Microbiology

Tel: (01382) 632166 Fax: (01382) 641907

Kerr, Michael A., BSc Leeds, PhD Leeds, FRCPath   Prof., Infection and Immunity; Head*

Old, David C., BSc Edin., PhD Edin., DSc Dund., FIBiol, FRCPath   Reader

Parratt, David, MB ChB St And., MD Dund., FRCPath   Sr. Lectr.

Other Staff: 2 Lectrs.; 3 Hon. Sr. Lectrs.; 1 Hon. Lectr.

Medical Oncology

Rankin, Elaine M., BSc St And., MB ChB Manc., MD Manc.   Prof.; Head*

Medical Physics

Tel: (01382) 632700 Fax: (01382) 640177

Lerski, Richard A., BSc Edin., PhD St And.   Hon. Sr. Lectr.; Head*

Other Staff: 10 Hon. Lectrs.; 1 Temp. Sr. Lectr.†

Research: magnetic resonance imaging; novel medical electronics; nuclear medicine techniques; radiation physics; radiobiology and biophysics

Medicine

Tel: (01382) 632457 Fax: (01382) 660675

Belch, Jill J. F., MD Glas., FRCPGlas   Prof., Vascular Medicine

Forbes, C. D., MD Glas., DSc Glas., FRCP, FRCPEd, FRCPGlas, FRSEd   Prof.; Head*

McMurdo, Marion E. T., MD Dund., FRCPEd Prof., Ageing and Health

Morris, Andrew D., MB ChB Glas., MSc Glas., MD Glas. Sr. Lectr.

Newton, Ray W., BSc Edin., MB ChB Edin., FRCPEd, FRCPGlas Hon. Prof.

Paterson, Colin R., MA Oxf., MSc Oxf., DM Oxf., FRCPEd Sr. Lectr.

Roberts, Richard C., BM BCh Oxf., MA Oxf., DPhil Oxf., FRCPEd Sr. Lectr.

Ross, Peter E., MSc Dund., PhD Dund. Sr. Lectr.

Other Staff: 33 Hon. Sr. Lectrs.; 7 Hon. Lectrs.; 4 Temp. Lectrs.

Research: ageing and health; cardiology; neurology; rheumatology and connective tissue; vascular medicine

Molecular and Cellular Pathology

Tel: (01382) 633120 Fax: (01382) 566933

Baty, John D., BSc Manc., PhD Keele, FRSChem Sr. Lectr.

Bowen, David T., MA Camb., MB BChir Camb., MD Camb. Sr. Lectr.

Burchell, Brian, BSc St.And., PhD Dund. Prof., Medical Biochemistry

Coughtrie, Michael W. H., BSc Dund., PhD Dund. Sr. Lectr.

Fuller-Pace, Frances V., PhD Edin. Sr. Lectr.

Hall, Peter A., BSc Lond., MB BS Lond., MD Lond., PhD Lond. Prof., Cellular Pathology

Hopwood, David, BSc Leeds, MB ChB Leeds, MD Leeds, PhD St And., FRCPath Reader

Kay, Richard A., MB ChB Manc., PhD Edin. Sr. Lectr.

Kernohan, Neil M., MB ChB Aberd., PhD Aberd. Sr. Lectr.

Levison, David A., MB ChB St And., MD Lond., FRCPath Prof., Pathology

Pippard, Martin J., BSc Birm., MB ChB Birm., FRCP, FRCPath Prof., Haematology; Head*

Ross, Peter E., MSc Dund., PhD Dund. Sr. Lectr.

Woof, Jennifer M., BSc Sheff., PhD Sheff. Sr. Lectr.

Other Staff: 1 Lectr.; 17 Hon. Sr. Lectrs.; 13 Hon. Lectrs.; 3 Temp. Lectrs.

Research: cancer and cell nucleus; clinical diagnosis; inherited disease; molecular immunology; molecular toxicology and metabolism

Neurology, Surgical

Gentleman, Douglas de R., BSc Glas., MB ChB Glas., FRCS, FRCSGlas Hon. Sr. Lectr.; Head*

Other Staff: 2 Hon. Sr. Lectrs.

Research: image guidance and neuronavigation; outcome of cervical fusion; outcome of severe head injuries; ruptured intracranial aneurysm; stereotactic neurosurgery

Nursing and Midwifery

Tel: (01382) 632304 Fax: (01382) 641738

Drummond, John S., MEd Dund. Sr. Lectr.; Head of Div.

Elliott, Lawrence, MA Glas., PhD Glas. Sr. Lectr.; Dir.

Forbes, Eleanor C., BA Open(UK), MBA Glas. Sr. Lectr.

Glen, Sally, MA Lond. Prof.; Head*

Muir, David S., BA Open(UK), MBA Edin. Sr. Lectr.

Ryan, Desmond P., BA Oxf., DPhil Sus. Sr. Lectr.; Dir.

Tulloch, Alexis M. N., BA Open(UK), MEd Dund. Sr. Lectr.; Head of Div.

Other Staff: 5 Lectrs.; 1 Hon. Sr. Lectr.; 2 Hon. Lectrs.; 2 Temp. Sr. Lectrs.; 3 Temp. Lectrs.

Obstetrics and Gynaecology

Tel: (01382) 632147 Fax: (01382) 566617

Babubhas, Narendra K., MB ChB St And., FRCOG Hon. Prof.

Burchell, Ann, BSc Dund., PhD Dund. Reader

Chien, Patrick F. W., MB ChB Dund., MD Dund. Sr. Lectr.

Duncan, Ian D., MB ChB St And., FRCOG Reader

Howie, Peter W., MB ChB Glas., MD Glas., FRCOG, FRCPGlas, FRSEd Prof.; Head*

Mires, Gary J., MB ChB Dund., MB Dund. Sr. Lectr.

Other Staff: 1 Lectr.; 13 Hon. Sr. Lectrs.; 6 Hon. Lectrs.

Research: embryonic and foetal development; in vitro fertilisation; pre-term labour; pregnancy-induced hypertension; regulation of blood glucose levels

Ophthalmology

Tel: (01382) 633196 Fax: (01382) 660130

McGhee, Charles N. J., BSc Glas., MB ChB Glas., FRCS Prof.; Head*

Other Staff: 4 Hon. Sr. Lectrs.; 3 Hon. Lectrs.; 1 Temp. Lectr.

Orthopaedic and Trauma Surgery

Tel: (01382) 322803 Fax: (01382) 202460

Abel, Eric W., BSc Wales, MSc Sur., PhD Dund., FIMechE Sr. Lectr.

Clift, Benedict A., BMSc Dund., MB ChB Dund., FRCSEd Sr. Lectr.

Dent, John A., MB ChB Dund., MMedEd Dund., MD Dund., FRCSEd Sr. Lectr.

Rowley, David I., BMedBiol Aberd., MB ChB Aberd., MD Sheff., FRCSEd, FRCSGlas Prof.; Head*

Other Staff: 1 Lectr.; 15 Hon. Sr. Lectrs.; 4 Hon. Lectrs.; 3 Temp. Lectrs.

Research: clinical gait analysis; foot pressure analysis; knee, hip and shoulder replacements; prosthetics and orthotics; rehabilitation engineering

Otolaryngology

Tel: (01382) 632726 Fax: (01382) 632816

Blair, R. L., MB ChB Edin., FRCS, FRCSCan, FRCSEd, FACS Hon. Sr. Lectr.; Head*

Other Staff: 7 Hon. Sr. Lectrs.

Pharmacology and Neurosciences

Tel: (01382) 632161 Fax: (01382) 667120

Balfour, David J. K., BSc St And., PhD St And. Reader

Breen, Kieran C., BSc N.U.I., PhD N.U.I. Sr. Lectr.

Caulfield, Malcolm P., BSc Lond., PhD Lond. Sr. Lectr.

Lambert, Jeremy J., BSc Strath., MSc Strath., PhD Strath. Prof., Neuropharmacology

Nicholls, David G., MA Camb., PhD Brist., FRSEd Prof., Neurochemistry

Peters, John A., BSc Sus., PhD Nott. Sr. Lectr.

Stevenson, Ian H., BSc St And., PhD St And., FRSEd Prof., Pharmacology; Head*

Other Staff: 2 Hon. Sr. Lectrs.; 1 Hon. Lectr.; 2 Temp. Lectrs.

Research: experimental psychopharmacology; ligand gated ion channels; mitochondria and neuronal cell death; neurosteroids; protein glycosylation

Psychiatry

Tel: (01382) 633111

Coghill, David R., BSc Edin., MB ChB Edin. Sr. Lectr.

Durham, Robert C., BA Oxf., MPhil Lond., PhD Indiana Sr. Lectr.

Matthews, Keith, MB ChB Aberd., MD Aberd. Prof.

May, David R., BA Brist., PhD Aberd. Sr. Lectr.

Reid, Ian C., BMedBiol Aberd., MB ChB Aberd., PhD Edin. Prof.; Head*

White, Christopher de B., MD Lond. Sr. Lectr.

Other Staff: 26 Hon. Sr. Lectrs.; 8 Hon. Lectrs.; 1 Temp. Lectr.

Research: behavioural neuroscience; mapping brain activity in psychiatric disorder; neurosurgery for psychiatric disorder; sociology of learning disorders

Radiology, Diagnostic

Tel: (01382) 632651

McCulloch, Alan S., MB ChB Aberd., FRCR Hon. Sr. Lectr.; Head*

Other Staff: 13 Hon. Sr. Lectrs.

Radiotherapy and Oncology

Tel: (01382) 633902 Fax: (01382) 632885

Munro, Alastair J., BSc St And., MB ChB Dund., FRCR Prof., Radiation Oncology; Head*

Other Staff: 2 Hon. Sr. Lectrs.

Surgery

Tel: (01382) 632174 Fax: (01382) 641795

Cuschieri, Sir Alfred, MD Malta, ChM Liv., FRCS, FRCSEd, FRCPGlas, FIBiol Prof.; Head*

Dunkley, M. Peta, MB BS Lond., FRCS Sr. Lectr.

Preece, Paul E., MB BCh Wales, MD Wales, FRCS, FRCSEd Reader

Shimi, Sami M., BSc Dund., MB ChB Dund., FRCS Sr. Lectr.

Steele, Robert J. C., BSc Edin., MB ChB Edin., MD Edin., FRCSEd, FRCS Prof., Surgical Oncology

Thompson, Alastair M., BSc Edin., MB ChB Edin., MD Edin., FRCSEd Sr. Lectr.

Other Staff: 1 Lectr.; 18 Hon. Sr. Lectrs.; 1 Hon. Lectr.; 3 Temp. Lectrs.

Research: gastrointestinal cell biology; hepatic cryotherapy; minimal access surgery; photodiagnosis

SPECIAL CENTRES, ETC

Applied Language Studies, Centre for

Tel: (01382) 344535 Fax: (01382) 227858

Adamson, Robin, BA Qld., BPhil St And., PhD Edin. Sr. Lectr.†; Head

Other Staff: 2 Lectrs.; 2 Temp. Lectrs.; 2 Temp. Lectrs.†

CONTACT OFFICERS

Academic affairs. Academic Secretary: Francis, Ian K., BA Exe., MA Keele, PhD Exe.

Accommodation. Bursar of Residences: Anderson, Graham, BA Strath.

Admissions (first degree). University Admissions Officer: Black, G. Gordon, BSc Edin.

Admissions (higher degree). Senior Administrative Assistant: Duncan, M. M.

Adult/continuing education. Acting Director: Swinfen, Prof. David B., MA Oxf., DPhil Oxf., FRHistS

Alumni. Development Director: Mackenzie, Allen R.

Careers. Director of Careers Service: Campbell, Richard M., BSc Glas.

Computing services. Director of Information Technology Services: Murphy, Richard S. D., BSc E.Anglia, MSc Lond.

Consultancy services. Director of Research and Innovation Services: Houston, J., MSc CNAA

Credit transfer. Academic Secretary: Francis, Ian K., BA Exe., MA Keele, PhD Exe.

Development/fund-raising. Development Director: Mackenzie, Allen R.

Distance education. Chair, Distance Learning Forum: Rogerson, Elizabeth C. B., MA Dund.

Equal opportunities. Assistant Personnel Officer: Poor, Leonie, BSc Lanc.

Estates and buildings/works and services. Director of Estates and Buildings: Copeland, Peter B. P., BSc CNAA, FIMechE

Examinations. Academic Secretary: Francis, Ian K., BA Exe., MA Keele, PhD Exe.

Finance. Finance Officer: Walker, Robin S.

General enquiries. Secretary of the University: Seaton, Robert, MA Glas., LLB Edin.

Health services. Medical Adviser: Dymock, Thomas, MB ChB Dund.

Industrial liaison. Director of Research and Innovation Services: Houston, J., MSc CNAA

International office. Director of Admissions and Student Recruitment: Craig, Gordon, BA Strath.

Library (chief librarian). Librarian: Bagnall, John M., MA Camb.

Minorities/disadvantaged groups. Head of Student Advisory Service: Donaldson, Irene

Personnel/human resources. Director of Personnel Services: Milne, Pamela A., MA *Glas.*, MBA *Dund.*

Public relations, information and marketing. Pope, Carol, BA *Stir.*

Publications. Assistant Secretary: Gerrie, Roy M., MA *Aberd.*

Purchasing. Purchasing Manager: Cruikshank, J.

Quality assurance and accreditation. Monaghan, Eric D., BSc *Dund.*, PhD *Dund.*

Research. Deputy Secretary: George, David R. W., MA *Oxf.*

Scholarships, awards, loans. Academic Secretary: Francis, Ian K., BA *Exe.*, MA *Keele*, PhD *Exe.*

Schools liaison. Director of Admissions and Student Recruitment: Craig, Gordon, BA *Strath.*

Security. Director of Estates and Buildings: Copeland, Peter B. P., BSc *CNAA*, FIMechE

Sport and recreation. Director of Physical Education: Ewing, Brian G., BEd *Glas.*, MSc *Strath.*

Staff development and training. Staff Development Officer: Anderson, James M., BSc *Edin.*, PhD *Edin.*†

Student union. General Manager: Sloan, Christopher

Student welfare/counselling (counselling). Student Counsellor: Halpin, Nicholas R., BA *Durh.*, MA *Camb.*, PhD *Dur.*

Student welfare/counselling (welfare). Head of Student Advisory Service: Donaldson, Irene

Students from other countries. Head of Student Advisory Service: Donaldson, Irene

Students with disabilities. Co-ordinator: Shaw, Di, MA *Dund.*

Women. Assistant Personnel Officer: Poor, Leonie, BSc *Lanc.*

CAMPUS/COLLEGE HEADS

Duncan of Jordanstone College, Perth Road, Dundee, Scotland DD1 4HT. (Tel: (01382) 223261; Fax: (01382) 227304.) Dean: Barr, William W., BA *Open(UK)*

Ninewells Medical School, Ninewells, Dundee, Scotland DD1 9SY. (Tel: (01382) 660111; Fax: (01382) 644267.) Dean: Levison, Prof. David A., MB ChB *St And.*, MD *Lond.*, FRCPath

School of Nursing and Midwifery (Dundee), Ninewells, Dundee, Scotland DD1 9SY. (Tel: (01382) 660111; Fax: (01382) 644267.) Dean: Glen, Prof. Sally, MA *Lond.*

School of Nursing and Midwifery (Fife), Forth Avenue, Kirkcaldy, Fife, Scotland KY2 5YS. (Tel: (01592) 268888; Fax: (01592) 642910.) Associate Dean: Muir, David S., BA *Open(UK)*, MBA *Edin.*

[Information supplied by the institution as at 23 March 1998, and edited by the ACU]

UNIVERSITY OF DURHAM

Founded 1832

Member of the Association of Commonwealth Universities

Postal Address: Old Shire Hall, Durham, England DH1 3HP
Telephone: (0191) 374 2000 **Fax:** (0191) 374 7250 **Telex:** (BT Bureau Service): 317210
WWW: http://www.dur.ac.uk
E-mail formula: initials.surname@durham.ac.uk *or*, if one first name only, then in full

VISITOR—The Rt. Rev. The Lord Bishop of Durham (*ex officio*)
CHANCELLOR—Ustinov, Sir Peter, CBE, Hon. DLitt, FRSL
VICE-CHANCELLOR AND WARDEN*—Calman, Prof. Sir Kenneth, KCB, BSc *Glas.*, MD *Glas.*, PhD *Glas.*, FRCSGlas, FRCP, FRCPEd, FRCGP, FRCR, FRCSEd, FRCPath, FRSEd
PRO-VICE-CHANCELLOR AND SUB-WARDEN—Prestwich, Prof. Michael C., MA *Oxf.*, DPhil *Oxf.*, FRHistS, FSA
PRO-VICE-CHANCELLOR—Gower, Barry S., BSc *Leic.*, DPhil *Oxf.*
PRO-VICE-CHANCELLOR—Anstee, Prof. John H., BSc *Nott.*, PhD *Nott.*
CHAIRMAN OF COUNCIL—Hawley, Robert, BSc *Durh.*, PhD *Durh.*, DSc *Newcastle(UK)*, Hon. DSc *Durh.*, FEng, FIEE, FIMechE
REGISTRAR AND SECRETARY‡—Hayward, John C. F., MA *Oxf.*
TREASURER—Lubacz, Paulina, BA *CNAA*
LIBRARIAN—Hall, John T. D., BA *Manc.*, MA *Camb.*, PhD *Manc.*

GENERAL INFORMATION

History. The university was founded in Durham in 1832. From 1852 until Newcastle became a separate university in 1963 there were also students in Newcastle upon Tyne.

Admission to first degree courses (see also United Kingdom Introduction). International students: high levels in International Baccalaureate or European Baccalaureate or, in many cases, qualifications acceptable for university entrance in applicant's own country.

First Degrees (see also United Kingdom Directory to Subjects of Study). BA, BEng, BSc, LLB, MEng, MMath, MSci.

Courses normally last 3 years full-time. Courses including a foreign language or European studies: 3 years plus 1 year abroad; MEng, MMath, MSci: 4 years full-time.

Higher Degrees (see also United Kingdom Directory to Subjects of Study). BD, LLM, MA, MBA, MEd, MJur, MLitt, MMus, MSc, MTheol, MPhil, PhD, DD, DLitt, DMus, DSc, EdD.

Applicants for admission must normally hold a good honours degree in an appropriate subject.

LLM, MA, MBA, MJur and MSc last 1 year full-time; MTheol: 1 year full-time at Durham or 2 semesters full-time at University of Tübingen; MEd, MLitt, MMus, MPhil: 2 years full-time; PhD: 3 years full-time; EdD: 3 calendar years full-time; BD, DD, DLitt, DMus, DSc: awarded on published work. All degrees except BD, LLM, DD, DLitt, DMus and DSc may be taken by combinations of full-time and part-time study.

Libraries. 600,000 volumes; 3200 periodicals subscribed to. Special collections include: Abbas Hilmi II (Middle East); archives of Durham Cathedral (monastic to 1539) and Diocese; Durham bishopric estate; Earl Grey (political); Malcolm MacDonald (political and diplomatic); mediaeval manuscripts; modern literary manuscripts (including Basil Bunting poetry archive); north-east local collection (including family papers); seventeenth-century English printing; Sudan archive (political).

Fees. Home students: £750 (undergraduate arts); £1600 (undergraduate science); £2540 (full-time postgraduate); £7950 (MBA internal). International students: £6415 (arts and social sciences); £8540 (science); £9500 (MBA internal).

Academic Awards (1998–99). Thirty-three postgraduate awards totalling £163,020.

Academic Year (1998–99). Three terms: 7 October (5 October for new undergraduates)–9 December; 11 January–19 March; 26 April–25 June.

Income (1996–97). Total, £92,000,000.

Statistics. Staff: 718 (568 academic, 150 administrative). Students: full-time 8157 (3972 men, 4185 women); part-time 476 (163 men, 313 women); international 1321; total 9954.

FACULTIES/SCHOOLS

Arts

Tel: (0191) 374 2929

Dean: Manning, Prof. Peter D., BA Durh., PhD Durh.

Secretary: Allison, Margaret E.

Science

Tel: (0191) 374 7024 Fax: (0191) 374 7479

Dean: Unsworth, Prof. Anthony, BSc Salf., MSc Leeds, PhD Leeds, DEng Leeds, FIMechE

Secretary: Cutmore, Janet

Social Sciences

Tel: (0191) 374 7607

Dean: Palmer, Prof. Joy A., MEd Birm., MA Stan., PhD Durh.

Secretary: Allison, Margaret E.

ACADEMIC UNITS

Anthropology

Tel: (0191) 374 2841 Fax: (0191) 374 2870

Barton, Robert A., BSc Brist., MSc Lond., PhD St.And. Reader

Bilsborough, Alan, MA Camb., DPhil Oxf. Prof.; Head*

Carrier, James G., BA Virginia, MA Virginia, PhD Lond. Reader

Carrithers, Michael B., MA Conn., DPhil Oxf. Prof.

Layton, Robert H., BSc Lond., MPhil Lond., DPhil Sus. Prof.

Panter-Brick, Catherine, MA Oxf., MSc Oxf., DPhil Oxf. Reader

Sillitoe, Paul, MA Durh., PhD Camb. Prof.

Wilder, William D., AB Harv., MA Lond., PhD Lond. Sr. Lectr., Anthropology of Middle East

Other Staff: 19 Lectrs.

Applied Social Studies, Centre for

Tel: (0191) 374 7241

Carpenter, John S. W., BSc Brist. Prof.; Head*

Other Staff: 4 Lectrs.; 1 Res. Fellow

Research: community mental health services; family support services; older people's social welfare and health; professionals and interprofessional education

Archaeology

Tel: (0191) 374 3625 Fax: (0191) 374 3619

Bailiff, Ian K., BSc Sus., MSc Oxf. Reader

Bintliff, John L., MA Camb., PhD Camb., FSA Reader

Caple, Christopher, BSc Wales, PhD Brad. Sr. Lectr.

Casey, P. John, BA Wales, FSA Reader

Chapman, John C., BA Lond., PhD Lond. Reader

Harding, Anthony F., MA Camb., PhD Camb., FSA Prof.

Haselgrove, Colin C., BSc Sus., MA Camb., PhD Camb., FSA Prof.

Johnson, Matthew H., MA Camb., PhD Camb. Reader

Millett, Martin J., BA Lond., DPhil Oxf., FSA Prof.; Head*

Price, A. Jennifer, BA Wales, PhD Wales, FSA Reader

Rowley-Conwy, Peter A., MA Camb., PhD Camb. Reader

Todd, Malcolm, BA Wales, MA Oxf., MA Bonn, DLitt Wales, FSA Prof.†

Other Staff: 6 Lectrs.; 8 Res. Fellows; 1 Lectr.†

Research: archaeology from late antiquity to capitalism; chronometry, geoarchaeology and environmental studies; emergence of complex societies in prehistory; Graeco-Roman world and its neighbours; numismatic studies

Astronomy, see Phys.

Biological Sciences

Tel: (0191) 374 7573 Fax: (0191) 374 2417

Angelides, Kimon J., BA Lawrence, PhD Calif. Prof., Animal Cell Biology

Anstee, John H., BSc Nott., PhD Nott. Prof.

Bowler, Kenneth, BSc Hull, PhD Hull Prof., Animal Physiology

Croy, Ronald R. D., BSc Edin., PhD Aberd. Reader

Edwards, Robert, BSc Bath, PhD Lond. Reader

Evans, Peter R., MA Camb., PhD Camb., DPhil Oxf. Prof., Zoology

Gatehouse, John A., BA Oxf., DPhil Oxf. Reader

Hoelzel, A. Rus, BA Portland, MSc Sus., PhD Camb. Reader

Horton, John D., BSc Hull, PhD Hull Reader, Immunology

Huntley, Brian, MA Camb., PhD Camb. Prof.

Jahoda, Colin A. B., BSc Dund., PhD Dund. Reader

Lindsay, Steven W., BSc Wales, PhD Lond. Reader

Lindsey, Keith, BA Oxf., PhD Edin. Prof., Plant Molecular Biology

Shaw, Charles H., BSc Leeds, PhD Lond. Sr. Lectr.

Slabas, Antoni R., BSc Lond., DPhil Oxf. Prof., Plant Sciences

Watson, Martin D., BSc S'ton., PhD S'ton. Sr. Lectr.

Whitton, Brian A., MA Oxf., PhD Lond. Reader, Botany

Other Staff: 24 Lectrs.; 2 Res. Fellows; 1 Reader†; 1 Sr. Lectr.†; 3 Lectrs.†

Research: animal cell biology; ecology; neurobiology; plant and animal developmental biology; plant molecular biology and biochemistry

Business, see Special Centres, etc (Univ. Bus. Sch.)

Chemistry

Tel: (0191) 374 3128 Fax: (0191) 374 3745

Badyal, Jas-Pal S., BA Camb., PhD Camb. Prof.

Brooke, Gerald M., PhD Birm., DSc Birm. Reader

Bryce, Martin R., BSc CNAA, DPhil York(UK) Prof.

Chambers, Richard D., PhD Durh., DSc Durh., FRS, FRSChem Prof.

Crampton, Michael R., PhD Lond., DSc Lond., FRSChem Reader

Dillon, Keith B., MA Oxf., DPhil Oxf. Reader

Feast, W. James, BSc Sheff., PhD Birm., FRS, FRSChem Prof.

Harris, Robin K., MA Camb., PhD Camb., ScD Camb., FRSChem Prof.

Howard, Judith A. K., CBE, DSc Brist., DPhil Oxf., FRSChem Prof.

Hutson, Jeremy M., MA Oxf., DPhil Oxf. Prof.

Kilner, Melvyn, BSc Nott., PhD Nott., FRSChem Reader

Marder, Todd B., BSc M.I.T., PhD Calif. Prof.

O'Hagan, David, BSc Glas., PhD S'ton. Sr. Lectr.

Parker, David, MA Oxf., DPhil Oxf., FRSChem Prof.

Richards, Randal W., BSc Salf., PhD Salf., DSc Salf., FRSChem Prof.

Williams, D. Lyn H., PhD Lond., DSc Lond., FRSChem Prof.

Other Staff: 6 Lectrs.; 4 Res. Fellows; 1 Lectr.†; 3 Temp. Lectrs.

Research: materials and macromolecules; structure and spectroscopy; synthesis and reactivity; synthesis involving fluorination and organofluorine compounds; theoretical and computational chemistry

Chinese, see E. Asian Studies

Classics and Ancient History

Tel: (0191) 374 2070 Fax: (0191) 374 7338

Dickinson, Oliver T. P. K., MA Oxf., DPhil Oxf., FSA Reader

Hunt, E. David, MA Oxf., DPhil Oxf. Sr. Lectr.

Moles, John L., MA Oxf., DPhil Oxf. Prof.; Head*

Rhodes, Peter J., MA Oxf., DPhil Oxf., FBA Prof., Ancient History

Rowe, Christopher J., MA Camb., PhD Camb. Prof., Greek

Woodman, Anthony J., BA Durh., PhD Camb. Prof., Latin

Other Staff: 4 Lectrs.

Community and Youth Work, see Sociol. and Soc. Policy

Computer Science

Tel: (0191) 374 2630 Fax: (0191) 374 2560

Bennett, Keith H., MSc Manc., PhD Manc., FIEE Prof.

Boldyreff, Cornelia, BA Leeds, MPhil Durh., PhD Durh. Sr. Lectr.

Garigliano, Roberto, BA Genoa, MSc Lond., DPhil Oxf. Prof.; Head*

Luo, Zhaohui, MSc Changsha I.T., PhD Edin. Reader

Munro, Malcolm, BSc Leic., MSc Liv. Sr. Lectr.

Robson, David J., MSc Sheff., MSc Hull, MA Durh., PhD Hull Sr. Lectr.

Other Staff: 6 Lectrs.

Research: natural language engineering; planning in artificial intelligence; program and system comprehension; software evolution and maintenance; software visualisation

East Asian Studies

Tel: (0191) 374 3231 Fax: (0191) 374 3242

Barnes, Gina L., BA Colorado, MA Mich., MA Camb., PhD Mich. NSK Prof., Japanese Studies; Head*

Dillon, Michael S., BA Leeds, PhD Leeds Sr. Lectr., Modern Chinese History

Other Staff: 4 Lectrs.

Research: East Asian art and archaeology (China/Japan/Korea/Tibet); Japanese/Chinese business language and culture; Japanese/Chinese language and literature (traditional and contemporary); modern Japanese history (US/Japanese relations); traditional and modern Chinese history (Islam, Ming/Qing cultural studies)

Economics

Tel: (0191) 374 7272 Fax: (0191) 374 7289

Darnell, Adrian C., BA Durh., MA Warw. Prof.

Evans, J. Lynne, BA Newcastle(UK), PhD Newcastle(UK) Sr. Lectr.

Holmes, Philip R., BA CNAA, MA Newcastle(UK), PhD Brun. Prof.

Johnson, Peter S., BA Nott., PhD Nott. Prof.

Thomas, R. Barry, BA Liv., MA(Econ) Manc., PhD Manc. Reader; Head*

Wilson, Rodney J. A., BSc(Econ) Belf., PhD Belf. Prof.

Other Staff: 4 Lectrs.; 1 Sr. Lectr.†

Research: applied econometrics studies; economics of tourism, heritage and arts; financial economics/corporate finance/international finance; industrial economics and small business; Islamic economics

Education, School of

Tel: (0191) 374 3559 Fax: (0191) 374 3506

Bond, Timothy N., BA Durh. Sr. Lectr.

Byram, Michael S., MA Camb., PhD Camb. Prof.

Farrow, Stephen J., BSc Wales, PhD Liv. Sr. Lectr.

Fitz-Gibbon, Carol T., BSc Lond., MA Calif., PhD Calif. Prof.

Fleming, Michael P., BA Durh., PhD Durh. Sr. Lectr.

Galloway, David M., MA Oxf., MSc Lond., PhD CNAA Prof.; Head*
Gott, Richard, BSc Leeds, MA Leeds, PhD Leic. Prof.
Ingram, John H., BSc CNAA, MEd Leic., PhD Lond. Sr. Lectr.
McGuiness, John B., MA Camb., MA Durh. Sr. Lectr.
Morrison, Keith R. B., BEd Liv., MEd Newcastle(UK), PhD Durh. Sr. Lectr.
Newton, Lynn D., BEd Durh., MA Durh., PhD Newcastle(UK) Sr. Lectr.
Palmer, Joy A., MEd Birm., MA Stan., PhD Durh. Prof.
Smith, Richard D., BA Oxf., MEd Birm. Sr. Lectr.
Thompson, Linda A., BPhil Birm., MA Birm., PhD Durh. Sr. Lectr.
Tymms, Peter B., MA Camb., MEd Newcastle(UK), PhD Camb. Reader
Other Staff: 28 Lectrs.; 3 Lectrs.†
Research: assessment and 'value-added' in schools; counselling and values in education; curriculum analysis; policy studies in education; subject knowledge in early childhood

Engineering, School of

Tel: (0191) 374 3927 Fax: (0191) 374 2550
Appleton, Ernest, MSc Salf., PhD Salf. Prof.
Bettess, Peter, MSc Lond., PhD Durh. Prof.
Bumby, James R., BSc Durh., PhD Durh. Reader
Clarke, Peter H., BSc Hull, PhD Hull Sr. Lectr.
Dominy, Robert G., BSc CNAA, PhD Lond. Sr. Lectr.
Gregory-Smith, David G., MA Camb., PhD Camb. Reader
He, Li, MSc Beijing, PhD Camb. Reader
Maropoulos, Paul, MSc Manc., PhD UMIST Reader
Mars, Philip, MSc Newcastle(UK), PhD CNAA, FIEE Prof.
Petty, Michael C., PhD Lond., DSc Sus. Prof.; Head*
Preece, Clive, BSc Durh., PhD Newcastle(UK) Sr. Lectr.
Purvis, Alan, BSc Leeds, PhD Camb. Prof.
Scott, Richard H., MSc Lond., PhD Durh., FIStructE Reader
Selby, Alan R., BSc Brist., PhD Brist. Reader
Spooner, Edward, BSc Lond., PhD Aston Prof.
Swift, James S., BSc Leeds Sr. Lectr.
Toll, David G., BSc Wales, PhD Lond. Sr. Lectr.
Unsworth, Anthony, BSc Salf., MSc Leeds, PhD Leeds, DEng Leeds, FIMechE Prof.
Wood, David, BSc Hull, PhD Hull Sr. Lectr.
Other Staff: 11 Lectrs.; 2 Temp. Lectrs.
Research: biomedical engineering; electronic systems; industrial automation; molecular electronics and microelectronics; telecommunication networks

English Studies, see also Linguistics and Engl. Lang.

Tel: (0191) 374 2730 Fax: (0191) 374 7471
Clark, Timothy J. A., BA Oxf., DPhil Oxf. Reader
Clemit, Pamela A., MPhil Oxf., DPhil Oxf. Reader
Fuller, David S., BA Sheff., BLitt Oxf. Reader
McKinnell, John S., MA Oxf. Reader
O'Neill, Michael S. C., MA Oxf., DPhil Oxf. Prof.; Head*
Reeves, Gareth E., BA Oxf., MA Stan., PhD Stan. Reader
Robertson, Fiona, MA Oxf., MPhil Oxf., DPhil Oxf. Reader
Sanders, Andrew L., BA Exe., MLitt Camb., PhD Lond. Prof.
Watson, J. Richard, MA Oxf., PhD Glas. Prof.
Waugh, Patricia, BA Birm., PhD Birm. Prof.
Other Staff: 7 Lectrs.; 1 Sr. Lectr.†; 1 Lectr.†; 1 Temp. Lectr.
Research: editing (all periods from mediaeval to modern); literary theory (aesthetics, ethics, feminism, historicism, post-structuralism); mediaeval studies (Chaucer, drama, myth,

romance); modernist poetry and prose (H. D., T. S. Eliot, James Joyce, Virginia Woolf, W. B. Yeats); Romantic Studies 1780–1830

French, see under Mod. European Langs., Sch. of

Geography

Tel: (0191) 374 2462 Fax: (0191) 374 2456
Allison, Robert J., BA Hull, PhD Lond. Reader
Amin, Ash, BA Reading, PhD Reading Prof.
Atkins, Peter J., MA Camb., PhD Camb. Sr. Lectr.
Blake, Gerald H., JP, MA Oxf., PhD S'ton. Prof.†
Blakemore, Michael J., BA Manc. Prof.
Burt, Timothy P., BA Camb., MA Car., PhD Brist. Prof.†
Donoghue, Daniel N. M., BSc Aberd., PhD Durh. Sr. Lectr.
Evans, Ian S., MA Camb., MS Yale, PhD Camb. Sr. Lectr.
Hudson, Raymond, BA Brist., PhD Brist. Prof.
Lewis, Jim R., MA Camb. Sr. Lectr.
Pocock, Douglas C. D., MA Nott., PhD Nott. Reader
Rigg, Jonathan D., BA Lond., PhD Lond. Reader
Roberts, Brian K., BA Birm., PhD Birm. Prof.
Sadler, David, BA Durh., PhD Durh. Reader
Shennan, Ian, BSc Durh., PhD Durh. Prof.; Head*
Simmons, Ian G., BSc Lond., PhD Lond., DLitt Durh., FSA Prof.
Townsend, Alan R., MA Camb. Reader
Townsend, Janet G., MA Oxf., DPhil Oxf. Sr. Lectr.
Other Staff: 15 Lectrs.; 1 Sr. Lectr.†; 2 Temp. Lectrs.†
Research: development studies (cultural/historical geography, gender); European integration (urban/regional change); geomorphology (drylands, hillslopes, hydrology, sediments, uplands); quaternary (environmental change, human impact, palaeoceanography, sea-level change, stratigraphy); remote sensing (geographical information systems)

Geological Sciences

Tel: (0191) 374 2520 Fax: (0191) 374 2510
Foulger, Gillian R., MA Camb., MSc Durh., PhD Durh. Reader
Goulty, Neil R., MA Oxf., PhD Camb. Reader
Holdsworth, Robert E., BSc Liv., PhD Leeds, FGS Sr. Lectr.
Pearce, Julian A., BA Camb., PhD E.Anglia, FGS Reader
Searle, Roger C., MA Camb., PhD Newcastle(UK) Prof., Geophysics; Head*
Thompson, Robert N., MA Oxf., DPhil Oxf., DSc Oxf., FGS Prof., Geology
Tucker, Maurice E., BSc Durh., PhD Reading, FGS Prof.†
Turner, Brian R., BSc Hull, MSc Witw., PhD Witw., FGS Sr. Lectr., Geology
Other Staff: 10 Lectrs.; 1 Lectr.†

German, see under Mod. European Langs., Sch. of

Health Studies, Centre for

Tel: (0191) 374 2313 Fax: (0191) 374 7010
Cheung, Philip, BA Open(UK), MA(Ed) S'ton., PhD S'ton. Dir.*
Hungin, A. Pali S., MB BS Newcastle(UK), FRCGP Prof.†
Other Staff: 1 Lectr.
Research: health information studies (training in resource evaluation for research); maternal studies (obstacles to breastfeeding, pregnancy loss); primary health services (management of preventive and clinical care); public understanding of health (enabling self-care); smoking and young people (causes, practice and deterrents)

History, see also E. Asian Studies

Tel: (0191) 374 2013 Fax: (0191) 374 4754

Britnell, Richard H., MA Camb., PhD Camb., FRHistS Prof.
Brooks, Christopher W., BA Prin., DPhil Oxf., FRHistS Reader
Bythell, Duncan, MA Oxf., DPhil Oxf., FRHistS Sr. Lectr.
Frame, Robin F., MA Trinity(Dub.), PhD Trinity(Dub.), FRHistS Prof.
Harris, Howell J., MA Oxf., DPhil Oxf. Reader
Harvey, Margaret M., MA Oxf., DPhil Oxf., FRHistS Sr. Lectr.
Heesom, Alan J., MA Camb., FRHistS Sr. Lectr.
Michie, Ranald C., MA Aberd., PhD Aberd. Prof.
Prestwich, Michael C., MA Oxf., DPhil Oxf., FRHistS, FSA Prof.
Ratcliffe, Donald J., MA Oxf., BPhil Oxf., PhD Durh., FRHistS Sr. Lectr.
Rogister, John M. J., BA Birm., DPhil Oxf., FRHistS Sr. Lectr.
Rollason, David W., MA Oxf., PhD Birm., FSA, FRHistS Prof.; Head*
Williamson, Philip A., MA Camb., PhD Camb., FRHistS Reader
Other Staff: 6 Lectrs.; 1 Sr. Lectr.†; 1 Lectr.†; 1 Temp. Lectr.†
Research: American history; mediaeval British history; mediaeval European history; modern British history; modern European history

History, Ancient, see Classics and Anc. Hist.

Immunology, see Biol. Scis.

Islamic Studies, see Middle Eastern and Islamic Studies, Centre for

Italian, see under Mod. European Langs., Sch. of (Spanish and Italian)

Law

Tel: (0191) 374 2033 Fax: (0191) 374 2044
Allen, Thomas F. W., BA Qu., LLB Dal., LLM Lond. Sr. Lectr.
Cullen, Holly A., BCL McG., LLB McG., LLM Essex Sr. Lectr.
Emery, Carl T., LLB Camb., MA Camb. Sr. Lectr.
Fenwick, Helen M., BA Newcastle(UK), LLB CNAA Sr. Lectr.
Greaves, Rosa-Maria, LLB Leeds, LLM Exe. Allen and Overy Prof.
Leigh, Ian D., LLB Wales, LLM Wales Prof.
Priest, Jacqueline A., LLB Hull Sr. Lectr.
Sullivan, G. Robert, LLB Wales, LLM Lond. Prof.
Teff, Harvey, MA Oxf., LLM Lond., PhD Lond. Prof.
Warbrick, Colin J., MA Camb., LLB Camb., LLM Mich. Prof.; Head*
Other Staff: 6 Lectrs.; 1 Res. Fellow†
Research: computers and law; European Community law; human rights; international law; law and medicine

Linguistics and English Language, see also Engl. Studies

Tel: (0191) 374 2641 Fax: (0191) 374 2685
Davenport, Michael J. S., MA Edin. Lectr.; Head*
Emonds, Joseph, BA Iowa, MA Kansas, PhD M.I.T. Prof.
Grundy, Peter, BA Leeds, MPhil Camb. Sr. Lectr.
Schwartz, Bonnie D., BA Indiana, MA S.Calif., PhD S.Calif. Reader
Tallerman, Maggie O., BA Hull, PhD Hull Sr. Lectr.
Other Staff: 3 Lectrs.
Research: ELT methodology; first and second language acquisition; phonological theory; syntactic theory

Mathematical Sciences

Tel: (0191) 374 2349 Fax: (0191) 374 7388
Armstrong, M. Anthony, MSc Birm., PhD Warw. Sr. Lectr.
Bolton, John, BSc Liv., PhD Liv. Sr. Lectr.
Coleman, John P., MSc N.U.I., PhD Lond., FIMA Sr. Lectr.

Corrigan, F. Edward, MA *Camb.*, PhD *Camb.*, FRS Prof.

Dorey, Patrick E., BA *Oxf.*, PhD *Durh.* Reader

Fairlie, David B., BSc *Edin.*, PhD *Camb.* Prof.

Goldstein, Michael, MSc *Oxf.*, DPhil *Oxf.* Prof., Statistics

Kearton, Cherry, MA *Camb.*, PhD *Camb.*, ScD *Camb.* Reader, Pure Mathematics

Mansfield, Paul, BA *Oxf.*, PhD *Camb.* Reader

Pennington, Michael R., BSc *Edin.*, PhD *Lond.*, FIP Prof., Mathematical Sciences and Physics

Penrose, Mathew D., BA *Camb.*, PhD *Edin.* Reader

Reznikov, Alexander, MA *Kiev*, PhD *Tel-Aviv* Prof.

Scholl, Anthony J., MA *Oxf.*, MSc *Oxf.*, DPhil *Oxf.* Prof., Pure Mathematics; Head*

Stirling, W. James, MA *Camb.*, PhD *Camb.*, FIP Prof., Mathematical Sciences and Physics

Ward, Richard S., MSc *Rhodes*, DPhil *Oxf.* Prof.

Woodward, Lyndon M., MA *Oxf.*, DPhil *Oxf.* Sr. Lectr.

Zakrzewski, Wojciech J. M., MSc *Warsaw*, PhD *Camb.* Prof.

Other Staff: 12 Lectrs.; 2 Lectrs.†; 6 Temp. Lectrs.

Research: applied mathematics and mathematical physics; numerical analysis; pure mathematics; statistics and applied probability

Middle Eastern and Islamic Studies, Centre for

Tel: (0191) 374 2822 Fax: (0191) 374 2830

Anderson, Ewan W., MA *Manc.*, MA *Oxf.*, MEd *Newcastle(UK)*, PhD *Newcastle(UK)*, PhD *Durh.*, DPhil *York(UK)* Prof.

Ehteshami, Anoushiravan, BA *CNAA*, PhD *Exe.* Reader, International Relations; Head*

Niblock, Timothy C., BA *Oxf.*, DPhil *Sus.* Prof.

Starkey, Paul G., MA *Oxf.*, DPhil *Oxf.* Sr. Lectr.

Other Staff: 3 Lectrs.; 1 Sr. Lectr.†; 2 Lectrs.†; 1 Temp. Lectr.

Research: Arabic language, literature, linguistics; international relations and strategic studies; modern and contemporary Islam; political economy of the Middle East; women's studies

Modern European Languages, School of

Tel: (0191) 374 2713 Fax: (0191) 374 2716

French

Baguley, David, BA *Nott.*, MA *Leic.*, DUniv *Nancy* Prof.

Britnell, Jennifer J., BA *Lond.*, PhD *Lond.* Reader

Garnham, Barry G., MA *Manc.*, PhD *Durh.* Sr. Lectr.

Lloyd, Christopher D., MA *Oxf.*, PhD *Warw.* Sr. Lectr.; Head of Sch.*

Maber, Richard G., MA *Oxf.*, DPhil *Oxf.* Sr. Lectr.

Moss, J. Ann, MA *Camb.*, PhD *Camb.* Prof.

Whyte, Peter J., MA *Camb.*, PhD *Camb.* Sr. Lectr.

Other Staff: 4 Lectrs.

Research: mediaeval French literature; nineteenth-century literature and history; seventeenth-century literature; sixteenth-century literature and thought (French/Latin); twentieth-century literature and culture

German

Good, Colin H., BA *Brist.*, PhD *Brist.* Prof.

Musolff, Andreas, MA *Düsseldorf*, DrPhil *Düsseldorf* Sr. Lectr.

Other Staff: 4 Lectrs.

Research: language of politics, history and media; literature and intellectual history, eighteenth to twentieth centuries; mediaeval and Renaissance writing; metaphor in discourse of the EU; narrative theory

Spanish and Italian

Archer, Robert, BA *Durh.*, DPhil *Oxf.* Prof.

Other Staff: 3 Lectrs.; 2 Lectrs.†; 1 Temp. Lectr.

Research: Latin American cinema; mediaeval Catalan literature; mediaeval Spanish literature; modern Latin American literature; modern Spanish literature

Music

Tel: (0191) 374 3221 Fax: (0191) 374 3219

Dibble, Jeremy C., BA *Camb.*, PhD *S'ton.* Reader; Head*

Greer, David C., MA *Oxf.*, MusD *Trinity(Dub.)* Prof.

Manning, Peter D., BA *Durh.*, PhD *Durh.* Prof.

Paddison, Max H., MA *Exe.*, PhD *Exe.* Reader

Provine, Robert C., MA *Harv.*, PhD *Harv.* Prof.

Other Staff: 4 Lectrs.

Research: composition; electro-acoustics and music technology; ethnomusicology; music theory and analysis; musicology

Philosophy

Tel: (0191) 374 7641 Fax: (0191) 374 7635

Cooper, David E., MA *Oxf.*, BPhil *Oxf.* Prof.

Gower, Barry S., BSc *Leic.*, DPhil *Oxf.* Sr. Lectr.

Knight, David M., MA *Oxf.*, DPhil *Oxf.* Prof., History and Philosophy of Science

Lowe, E. Jonathan, MA *Camb.*, DPhil *Oxf.* Prof.; Head*

Maehle, A.-Holger, DrMed *Bonn*, DrMedHabil *Gött.* Wellcome Trust Res. Fellow/Reader

Other Staff: 4 Lectrs., 2 Temp. Lectrs.

Research: aesthetics and moral philosophy; Continental philosophy; history of science and medicine; metaphysics and philosophy of mind; philosophy of science

Physics

Tel: (0191) 374 2167 Fax: (0191) 374 3749

Abram, Richard A., BSc *Manc.*, PhD *Manc.*, FIP Prof.

Bloor, David, BSc *Lond.*, PhD *Lond.*, FIP Prof., Applied Physics

Brinkman, Andrew W., BSc *Nott.*, PhD *Nott.* Reader

Davies, Roger L., BSc *Lond.*, PhD *Camb.*, FRAS Prof., Astronomy

Flower, David R., BSc *Lond.*, PhD *Lond.* Prof.

Fong, Richard, BA *Camb.*, PhD *Maryland*, FRAS Sr. Lectr.

Frenk, Carlos S., BSc *Mexico Natnl.*, PhD *Camb.*, FRAS Prof., Astronomy

Glover, E. W. Nigel, BA *Camb.*, PhD *Durh.* Reader

Hatton, Peter D., BSc *Leic.*, PhD *Leic.* Reader

Lucey, John R., BSc *Leic.*, DPhil *Sus.* Sr. Lectr.

Martin, Alan D., BSc *Lond.*, PhD *Lond.*, FIP Prof., Theoretical Physics

Maxwell, Christopher J., BSc *Lond.*, PhD *Lond.* Sr. Lectr.

Monkman, Andrew P., BSc *Lond.*, PhD *Lond.* Reader

Orford, Keith J., TD, BSc *Durh.*, PhD *Durh.*, FIP, FRAS Reader

Osborne, John L., BSc *Durh.*, PhD *Durh.*, FRAS Sr. Lectr.

Pennington, Michael R., BSc *Edin.*, PhD *Lond.*, FIP Prof., Mathematical Sciences and Physics

Scarrott, S. Michael, BSc *Birm.*, PhD *Birm.* Reader

Shanks, Thomas, MSc *Lond.*, PhD *Durh.* Reader

Sharples, Raymond M., BSc *St And.*, PhD *Edin.* Reader

Stephenson, F. Richard, BSc *Durh.*, MSc *Newcastle(UK)*, PhD *Newcastle(UK)*, DSc *Newcastle(UK)*, FRAS Prof. Fellow

Stirling, W. James, MA *Camb.*, PhD *Camb.*, FIP Prof., Mathematical Sciences and Physics

Tanner, Brian K., MA *Oxf.*, DPhil *Oxf.*, FIP Prof.; Head*

Turver, K. Edward, TD, BSc *Leeds*, PhD *Leeds*, FIP, FRAS Prof.

Other Staff: 16 Lectrs.; 9 Res. Fellows; 2 Temp. Lectrs.

Research: astronomy; atomic and molecular physics; condensed matter physics; high energy paricle theory

Politics

Tel: (0191) 374 2811 Fax: (0191) 374 7630

Armstrong, J. David, BSc *Lond.*, MSc(Econ) *Lond.*, PhD *ANU* Prof.

Kennedy-Pipe, Caroline, BA *Wales*, MScEcon *Wales*, DPhil *Oxf.* Res. Reader

Reynolds, Charles, BA *Wales* Sr. Lectr.

Williams, Robert J., JP, BA *Nott.*, MPhil *Nott.* Sr. Lectr.; Head*

Other Staff: 9 Lectrs.; 2 Lectrs.†

Research: East Asia and development issues; European integration; good governance, political culture and transitions; history of political thought; international relations

Psychology

Tel: (0191) 374 2614 Fax: (0191) 374 7474

Campbell, Anne C., BA *Reading*, DPhil *Oxf.* Reader

Cooper, Steven J., BSc *Manc.*, PhD *Lond.*, DSc *Birm.*, DSc *Manc.* Prof.; Head*

Drewett, Robert F., BA *Hull*, DPhil *Oxf.* Reader

Findlay, John M., MA *Camb.*, PhD *Camb.* Prof.

Heywood, Charles A., BSc *St And.*, DPhil *Oxf.* Prof.

Little, Hilary J., BSc *Manc.*, MSc *Manc.*, PhD *Manc.* Prof., Psychopharmacology

Stevenson, Rosemary J., BSc *Lond.*, PhD *Lond.* Reader

Other Staff: 6 Lectrs.; 1 Res. Fellow; 1 Temp. Lectr.

Research: behavioural neuroscience (memory processes); cognitive psychology (language and memory); developmental psychology (attachment and autism); psychopharmacology (addiction and appetite); vision (eye movements and cognition)

Slavonic Studies/Ustinov Institute

Tel: (0191) 374 2687 Fax: (0191) 374 2684

Warner, Elizabeth A., MA *Edin.*, PhD *Edin.* Prof.

Other Staff: 2 Lectrs.; 1 Lectr.†; 1 Temp. Lectr.

Research: gender issues under socialism; modern Russian language; nineteenth-and twentieth-century Russian history; Russian literature of later nineteenth century; Russian traditional culture and ethnography

Sociology and Social Policy

Tel: (0191) 374 2311 Fax: (0191) 374 4743

Boyne, Roy D., BSocSc *Birm.*, PhD *Leeds* Prof.†

Byrne, David S., BA *Newcastle(UK)*, MSc(Econ) *Lond.*, PhD *Durh.* Sr. Lectr., Social Policy and Administration

Chaney, David C., MSocSc *Birm.*, PhD *Durh.* Prof.

Ellison, Nicholas, BA *S'ton.*, MA *Sus.*, MSc *Lond.*, PhD *Lond.* Lectr.; Head*

Fuller, Steve W., BA *Col.*, MPhil *Camb.*, PhD *Pitt.* Prof.

Hobbs, Richard F., BEd *Lanc.*, MSc *Lond.*, PhD *Sur.* Prof.

Jeffs, Anthony J., BPhil *Birm.*, MA *York(UK)* Sr. Lectr., Community and Youth Work

Taylor, Ian R., BA *Durh.*, PhD *Sheff.* Prof.†

Williams, Robin, BSc(Soc) *Lond.* Sr. Lectr.

Other Staff: 7 Lectrs.; 2 Lectrs.†; 1 Temp. Lectr.

Spanish, see under Mod. European Langs., Sch. of

Statistics, see Mathl. Scis.

Theology

Tel: (0191) 374 2061 Fax: (0191) 374 4744

Astley, Rev. Jeffrey, MA *Camb.*, PhD *Durh.* Hon. Prof. Fellow, Practical Theology and Christian Education

Barton, Rev. Stephen C., BA *Macq.*, MA *Lanc.*, PhD *Lond.* Sr. Lectr.
Brown, Rev. Canon David W., MA *Edin.*, DPhil *Oxf.*, PhD *Camb.* Van Mildert Prof., Divinity
Davies, Rev. Douglas J., BA *Durh.*, MLitt *Oxf.*, PhD *Nott.* Prof.†
Dunn, James D. G., MA *Glas.*, BD *Glas.*, BD *Camb.*, PhD *Camb.*, DD *Camb.* Lightfoot Prof., Divinity; Head*
Gilley, Sheridan W., BA *Qld.*, PhD *Camb.* Reader
Hayward, C. T. Robert, MA *Durh.*, DPhil *Oxf.* Reader
Jenkins, Rt. Rev. David E., MA *Oxf.*, Hon. DD *Durh.* Hon. Prof.
Loades, Ann L., BA *Durh.*, MA *McM.*, PhD *Durh.* Prof., Divinity
Louth, Andrew, MA *Camb.*, MA *Oxf.*, MTh *Edin.*, DD *Oxf.* Prof., Patristic and Byzantine Studies
Sagousky, Rev. Nicholas, BA *Oxf.*, BA *Nott.*, PhD *Camb.* Hon. Prof. Fellow
Other Staff: 7 Lectrs.; 1 Lectr.†
Research: ethics, sociology of religion; New Testament theology, Jewish pseudepigrapha, hermeneutics; Old Testament, Israelite history, early Judaism; patristic theology, Augustine, Reformation, modern church history; systematic theology, philosophy of religion, feminism

SPECIAL CENTRES, ETC

Language Centre
Tel: (0191) 374 3716 Fax: (0191) 374 7790
Pugh, Anthony C., BA *Lond.*, PhD *Lond.* Dir.*
Other Staff: 1 Lectr.

University Business School
Tel: (0191) 374 2211 Fax: (0191) 374 3748
Atterton, Timothy I., BA *CNAA* Exec. Dir., Small Bus. Centre
Burns, Sir Terence, BA(Econ) *Manc.*, Hon. DSc *Durh.* Hon. Prof.
Clarke, Ian M., BA *Wales*, PhD *ANU* Prof., Retail Marketing
Cockerill, T. Anthony J., BA *Leeds*, MPhil *Leeds*, PhD *Manc.* Prof., Business Management and Economics; Dir.*
Dixon, Robert, MA *Leic.* Prof.
Fuller, Edward C., MSc *Warw.* Dir., Knowledge Systems
Gibb, Allan A., OBE, BA(Econ) *Manc.*, PhD *Durh.* Prof., Small Business Studies
Gray, Andrew G., BA *Exe.* Prof., Public Sector Management
Hall, Richard, MA *Camb.*, PhD *Newcastle(UK)* Prof., Operations and Procurement Strategy
Jervis, V. T. Paul, BSc *Sus.* Dir., Exec. Educn.
Manley, Peter S., BA *Lond.*, FCA Sr. Lectr.
McClelland, W. Grigor, MA *Oxf.*, Hon. DCL *Durh.* Hon. Visiting Prof., Business Administration
Miller, Susan J., BA *CNAA*, MBA *Brad.*, PhD *Brad.* Sr. Lectr.
Sieff, The Hon. David Hon. Visiting Prof., European Business Strategy
Smith, Denis, BEd *Manc.*, MSc *Manc.*, MBA *Sheff.Hallam*, PhD *Manc.* Prof., Management
Stoker, David, BA *Manc.*, PhD *Manc.* Dir., Taught Degree Programmes
Other Staff: 10 Lectrs.
Research: entrepreneurship and enterprise development; finance, accounting and applied economics; public sector management; strategy, risk and crisis management; supply-chain management

COLLEGE OF ST HILD AND ST BEDE
Tel: (0191) 374 3000 Fax: (0191) 374 4740
Davies, Rev. Douglas J., BA *Durh.*, MLitt *Oxf.*, PhD *Nott.* U. Prof.†, Theology; Principal*
Pearson, J. Alan, BSc *Wales*, PhD *Wales* U. Lectr.†, Biological Sciences; Vice-Principal
Other Staff: 34 Tutors†

COLLINGWOOD COLLEGE
Tel: (0191) 374 4500 Fax: (0191) 374 4595
Blake, Gerald H., JP, MA *Oxf.*, PhD *S'ton.* U. Prof.†, Geography; Principal*
Martin, Nigel, MA *Camb.*, PhD *Camb.* U. Lectr.†, Mathematics; Vice-Principal
Other Staff: 31 Tutors†

GREY COLLEGE
Tel: (0191) 374 2900 Fax: (0191) 374 2992
Hillery, David, BA *Durh.*, PhD *Durh.* Vice-Master; Sr. Tutor
Watts, Victor E., MA *Oxf.* U. Sr. Lectr.†, English; Master*
Other Staff: 29 Tutors†

HATFIELD COLLEGE
Tel: (0191) 374 3163 Fax: (0191) 374 7472
Burt, Timothy P., BA *Camb.*, MA *Car.*, PhD *Brist.* U. Prof.†, Geography; Master*
Wetton, Barrie E., MA *Keele* Sr. Tutor
Other Staff: 28 Tutors

ST AIDAN'S COLLEGE
Tel: (0191) 374 3269 Fax: (0191) 374 4749
Ashworth, John S., BA(Econ) *Manc.*, MA(Econ) *Manc.* U. Sr. Lectr.†; Principal*
Yarwood, Alan, BSc *Liv.*, PhD *Liv.* U. Sr. Lectr.†, Biological Sciences; Vice-Principal
Other Staff: 25 Tutors†

ST CHAD'S COLLEGE
Tel: (0191) 374 3364 Fax: (0191) 386 3422
Cassidy, Rev. Joseph P. M., BA *C'dia.*, MA *Detroit*, STB *Tor.*, MDiv *Tor.*, PhD *Ott.*, ThD *St Paul(Ott.)* Principal*
Other Staff: 11 Tutors†

ST CUTHBERT'S SOCIETY
Tel: (0191) 374 3400 Fax: (0191) 374 4753
Robertson, Bernard, BSc *Durh.* Vice-Principal
Stoker, Samuel G. C., BA *Durh.*, MEd *Durh.* U. Schs. Liaison Officer†; Principal*
Other Staff: 17 Tutors†

ST JOHN'S COLLEGE
Tel: (0191) 374 3500 Fax: (0191) 374 3573
Croft, Rev. Steven J. L., MA *Oxf.*, PhD *Durh.* Warden of Cranmer Hall
Day, David V., BA *Lond.*, MEd *Nott.*, MTh *Nott.* Principal*
Masson, Margaret J., MA *Aberd.*, PhD *Durh.* Sr. Tutor
Other Staff: 7 Tutors; 21 Tutors†

ST MARY'S COLLEGE
Tel: (0191) 374 7119 Fax: (0191) 374 7473
Crossley, Elizabeth G., BA *Durh.* Sr. Tutor
Kenworthy, Joan M., MA *Oxf.*, BLitt *Oxf.* Principal*
Other Staff: 26 Tutors†

THE GRADUATE SOCIETY
Tel: (0191) 374 2863 Fax: (0191) 374 2868
Richardson, Michael, BSc *Hull*, PhD *Hull* U. Reader†, Botany; Principal*
Rowell, Michael J., BSc *Newcastle(UK)*, PhD *Newcastle(UK)* Sr. Tutor; Dep. Principal
Other Staff: 9 Tutors†

TREVELYAN COLLEGE
Tel: (0191) 374 3700 Fax: (0191) 374 3789
Todd, Malcolm, BA *Wales*, MA *Oxf.*, MA *Bonn*, DLitt *Wales*, FSA U. Prof.†, Archaeology; Master*
Other Staff: 28 Tutors†

UNIVERSITY COLLEGE
Tel: (0191) 374 3856 Fax: (0191) 374 7470
Pritchard, Francis W., LLB *Wales* U. Sr. Computing and Admin. Officer, Law; Admissions Tutor
Thomas, R. Barry, BA *Liv.*, MA(Econ) *Manc.*, PhD *Manc.* U. Reader, Economics; Admissions Tutor
Tucker, Maurice E., BSc *Durh.*, PhD *Reading*, FGS U. Prof., Geological Sciences; Master*
Other Staff: 26 Tutors†

UNIVERSITY COLLEGE, STOCKTON ON TEES
Tel: (01642) 618020 Fax: (01642) 618345
Bilsborough, Alan, MA *Camb.*, DPhil *Oxf.* U. Prof., Anthropology; Academic Dir., Human Sciences
Bowler, Kenneth, BSc *Hull*, PhD *Hull* U. Prof., Animal Physiology; Academic Dir., Biomed. Scis.
Boyne, Roy D., BSocSc *Birm.*, PhD *Leeds* U. Prof., Sociology and Social Policy; Vice-Principal and Academic Dir., European Studies
Evans, Peter R., MA *Camb.*, PhD *Camb.*, DPhil *Oxf.* U. Prof., Zoology; Academic Dir., Environmental Scis.
Gott, Richard, BSc *Leeds*, MA *Leeds*, PhD *Leic.* U. Prof., Education; Academic Dir., Educn.
Hayward, John C. F., MA *Oxf.* Principal*
Lewis, Jim R., MA *Camb.* U. Sr. Lectr., Geography; Vice-Principal
Lowe, Robert L., BA *Durh.* Sr. Tutor and Head of Student Services

VAN MILDERT COLLEGE
Tel: (0191) 374 3900 Fax: (0191) 374 3974
Patterson, George, MA *Oxf.* Vice-Principal and Sr. Tutor
Taylor, Ian R., BA *Durh.*, PhD *Sheff.* U. Prof.†, Sociology; Principal*
Other Staff: 32 Tutors†

CONTACT OFFICERS

Academic affairs. Academic Registrar: Hogan, John V., BA Lanc., MA Sus., DPhil Sus.

Accommodation. Sales and Marketing Manager: Hunter-Ellis, Dawn, MA Camb.

Admissions (first degree). Assistant Registrar: Forrest, Victoria F., MA Camb., MSc Sheff.

Admissions (higher degree). Administrative Officer: Rowell, Michael J., BSc Durh., PhD Newcastle(UK)

Adult/continuing education. Director of Continuing Education at University College, Stockton: Shelley, Vivian M., PhD Salf.

Alumni. Officer: Simpson, Lorraine, MBA Durh.

Archives. Chief Clerk: Moffat, Andrée P.

Careers. Director of Careers Advisory Service: May, Rennie, BSc Nott., PhD Liv.

Computing services. Director of Information Technology Service: Stinson, Iain, BSc Lond., MSc Lond.

Conferences/corporate hospitality. Sales and Marketing Manager: Hunter-Ellis, Dawn, MA Camb.

Consultancy services. Assistant Treasurer: White, John R., BA Durh.

Credit transfer. Academic Registrar: Hogan, John V., BA Lanc., MA Sus., DPhil Sus.

Development/fund-raising. Development Officer: Hayter, J. Scott W., BA RMC, MEd Brock

Distance education. Academic Registrar: Hogan, John V., BA Lanc., MA Sus., DPhil Sus.

Equal opportunities. Director of Personnel: Boyd, Jack, MA Glas.

Estates and buildings/works and services. Director of Estates and Buildings: Metcalfe, Richard J., BA Durh., MA Durh.

Examinations. Examinations Officer: Halpin, Joseph, Hon. MA Durh.

Finance. Treasurer: Lubacz, Paulina, BA CNAA

General enquiries. Registrar and Secretary: Hayward, John C. F., MA Oxf.

Health services. Medical Adviser: Charters, John W., MB ChB Manc.

Industrial liaison. Durham Knowledge House Manager: Timothy D. Scott, BSc Durh.

International office. Director of International Office: Hobbs, Jenny, MBE, MA Camb.

Language training for international students. Director of Language Centre: Pugh, Anthony C., BA Lond., PhD Lond.

Library (chief librarian). Librarian: Hall, John T. D., BA Manc., MA Camb., PhD Manc.

Library (enquiries). Sub-Librarian (Reader Services): Watchman, Eric C., BA Manc.

Minorities/disadvantaged groups. Academic Registrar: Hogan, John V., BA Lanc., MA Sus., DPhil Sus.

Personnel/human resources. Director of Personnel: Boyd, Jack, MA Glas.

Public relations, information and marketing. Director of Marketing and Corporate Communications: Slee, Peter R. H., BA Reading, PhD Camb., FRHistS

Publications. Secretary to Deputy Registrar and Secretary: Merchant, P. Ann

Purchasing. Head of Procurement: Johnson, Melinda J., BSc York(UK), MBA Durh.

Research. Deputy Registrar and Secretary: Stewart, Ian M., MA Oxf.

Safety. Safety Adviser and Radiation Protection Officer: Kell, Robert L., BSc Leeds, MSc Manc., PhD Dund.

Scholarships, awards, loans. Academic Registrar: Hogan, John V., BA Lanc., MA Sus., DPhil Sus.

Schools liaison. Schools Liaison Officer: Stoker, Samuel G. C., BA Durh., MEd Durh.

Security. Facilities Manager: Harris, Roger

Sport and recreation. Director of Sport: Warburton, Peter A., BA Durh., PhD Hull

Staff development and training. Director of Personnel: Boyd, Jack, MA Glas.

Student union. Academic Registrar: Hogan, John V., BA Lanc., MA Sus., DPhil Sus.

Student welfare/counselling. University Senior Counsellor: Fraser, M. Ruth, MA Edin.

Students from other countries. Director of International Office: Hobbs, Jenny, MBE, MA Camb.

Students with disabilities. Senior Adviser, Service for Students with Hearing and Other Disabilities: Collins, Margaret P., BSc Durh., PhD Newcastle(UK)

Women. Personnel Officer: Storer, Lucy J., BA CNAA

Women. Personnel Officer: Wood, Barbara

CAMPUS/COLLEGE HEADS

University College, Stockton on Tees, University Boulevard, Thornaby, Stockton on Tees, England TS17 6BH. (Tel: (01642) 618020; Fax: (01642) 618345.) Principal: Hayward, John C. F., MA Oxf.

[Information supplied by the institution as at 13 July 1998, and edited by the ACU]

UNIVERSITY OF EAST ANGLIA

Incorporated by Royal Charter 1964

Member of the Association of Commonwealth Universities

Postal Address: Norwich, England NR4 7TJ

Telephone: (01603) 456161 Fax: (01603) 458553 Cables: UEANOR, Norwich WWW: http://www.uea.ac.uk

E-mail formula: name@uea.ac.uk

VISITOR—Elizabeth, H.M. The Queen
CHANCELLOR—Allen, Prof. Sir Geoffrey, PhD, FRS, FEng, FRSChem, FIP
PRO-CHANCELLOR—Colman, T. J. A., JP, Hon. DCL
PRO-CHANCELLOR—Frostick, R. C., MA LLM Hon. DCL
VICE-CHANCELLOR*—Watts, Vincent, OBE, BA Camb., MSc Birm., FCA
CHAIRMAN OF COUNCIL—McCall, David, CBE
PRO-VICE-CHANCELLOR—Woodhams, Prof. F. W. D., BSc Exe., PhD Exe.
PRO-VICE-CHANCELLOR—Davis, Prof. J. C., MA Manc., FRHistS
PRO-VICE-CHANCELLOR—Bridges, Prof. D., BA Oxf., MA Lond., PhD Lond.
REGISTRAR AND SECRETARY‡—Paulson-Ellis, M. G. E., OBE, MA Camb., FCA
LIBRARIAN—Baker, D. M., MA Kent, MMus Lond., MLS Lough., PhD Lough., FLA, FRCO

GENERAL INFORMATION

History. The university was established in 1964. It is located on the outskirts of Norwich.

Admission to first degree courses (see also United Kingdom Introduction). Applicants must fulfil the general entrance requirement and any special requirement for the course. International students: qualifications accepted for admission to universities in student's own country together with an approved English

language qualification. European qualifications, including International or European Baccalaureate, must include an English language element.

First Degrees (see also United Kingdom Directory to Subjects of Study). BA, BEd, BEng, BSc, LLB, MChem, MMath.

Most full-time courses last 3 years; MChem, MMath: 4 years. Certain programmes may also be taken by part-time study.

Higher Degrees (see also United Kingdom Directory to Subjects of Study). LLM, MA, MBA, MEd, MMus, MSc, MPhil, PhD, ClinPsyD, DLitt, DSc, DSW, EdD, LLD, MD.

Applicants for admission to master's-level degrees must normally hold an appropriate first degree with at least second class honours. MPhil and doctorates: an appropriate first degree with at least second class honours or, in some cases, an appropriate master's degree and/or professional experience. MD and PhD: also awarded on published work; DLitt, DSc and LLD: awarded on published work.

Master's degrees: 1 year full-time, 2 years part-time; MPhil: 2 years full-time, 4 years part-time; doctorates: 3 years full-time, 6 years part-time.

Libraries. 750,000 books; over 2000 journal titles.

Fees. United Kingdom and European Union students: undergraduate £1000; postgraduate £2610. International students, undergraduate and postgraduate: £6450–6980 (arts/social sciences/mathematics); £8400 (science and engineering).

Academic Awards (1997–98). 77 awards ranging in value from £25 to £5000.

Academic Year (1998–99). Two semesters: 17 September–22 January; 25 January–11 June.

Income (1996–97). Total, £67,644,000.

Statistics. Students: full-time 7095, part-time 2630; total 9725.

FACULTIES/SCHOOLS

Biological Sciences, School of
Tel: (01603) 592760 Fax: (01603) 592250
Dean: Dawson, A. P., MA Camb., PhD Camb.
Secretary: Goffin, L.

Chemical Sciences, School of
Tel: (01603) 592005 Fax: (01603) 259396
Dean: Andrews, Prof, D. L., BSc Lond., PhD Lond.
Secretary: Larwood, J.

Development Studies, School of
Tel: (01603) 592330 Fax: (01603) 451999
Dean: Jenkins, R. O., BA Camb., DPhil Sus.
Secretary: Cushan, J.

Economic and Social Studies, School of
Tel: (01603) 592099 Fax: (01603) 250434
Dean: Kemp-Welch, A., BSc Lond., PhD Lond.
Secretary: Allen, M.

Education and Professional Development, School of
Tel: (01603) 592620 Fax: (01603) 593446
Dean: Aspland, R. W. B., BA Open(UK), MA E.Anglia, MSc CNAA
Secretary: Harding, H.

English and American Studies, School of
Tel: (01603) 592274 Fax: (01603) 507728
Dean: Sales, R. B., BA E.Anglia, PhD Camb.
Secretary: Striker, V.

Environmental Sciences, School of
Tel: (01603) 592842 Fax: (01603) 507719
Dean: Vine, Prof. F. J., BA Camb., PhD Camb., FRS
Secretary: Flack, C.

Health, School of
Tel: (01603) 592389 Fax: (01603) 593166
Dean: Pearce, Prof. S., BA Oxf., MPhil Lond., PhD Lond.
Secretary: Kemp, K.

History, School of
Tel: (01603) 592795 Fax: (01603) 593519
Dean: Church, Prof. R. A., BA Nott., PhD Nott., FRHistS
Secretary: Sparks, J.

Information Systems, School of
Tel: (01603) 592800 Fax: (01603) 593674
Dean: Glauert, J. R. W., BA Camb., MSc Manc., PhD Camb.
Secretary: Horncastle, N.

Law, School of
Tel: (01603) 592526 Fax: (01603) 250245
Dean: Miller, Prof. J. G., LLM Wales, LLM Camb., PhD Camb.
Secretary: Hodges, B.

Management, School of
Tel: (01603) 593340 Fax: (01603) 593343
Dean: Fletcher, Prof. K. P., MA Lanc., PhD Strath.
Secretary: Sinclair, P.

Mathematics, School of
Tel: (01603) 592849 Fax: (01603) 259515
Dean: Janacek, G. J., BSc MSc PhD
Secretary: Mason, A.

Modern Languages and European Studies, School of
Tel: (01603) 592159 Fax: (01603) 250599
Dean: Carr, M. G., BA Wales
Secretary: Gallard, R.

Music, School of
Dean: Aston, Prof. P. G., DPhil York(UK)

Physics, School of
Tel: (01603) 592005 Fax: (01603) 259515
Dean: Andrews, Prof. D. L., BSc Lond., PhD Lond.
Secretary: Larwood, J.

Social Work, School of
Tel: (01603) 593566 Fax: (01603) 593552
Dean: Thoburn, Prof. J., BA ReadingMSW LittD
Secretary: Barrett, A.

World Art Studies and Music, School of
Tel: (01603) 593596 Fax: (01603) 593642
Dean: Cocke, R. H. St. G., BA Oxf., PhD Lond.
Secretary: Beatty, S.

ACADEMIC UNITS
Arranged by Schools

American Studies, see Engl. and American Studies

Art, see World Art Studies and Museol.

Biological Sciences
Tel: (01603) 592269 Fax: (01603) 592250
Aidley, D. J., MA Camb., PhD Camb.   Sr. Lectr.
Bell, D., BSc PhD   Sr. Lectr.
Davy, A. J., BSc Lond., PhD Lond.   Sr. Lectr.
Duncan, G., BSc Aberd., MSc PhD   Reader
Edwards, D., MA PhD   Prof., Biology
Flavell, R. B., BSc Birm., PhD   John Innes Prof., Biology
Greenwood, C., BSc Sheff., PhD Sheff.   Prof., Biology
Hewitt, G. M., PhD Birm., DSc Birm.   Prof., Biology
Hopwood, D. A., MA Camb., PhD Camb., DSc Glas., FRS, FIBiol   John Innes Prof., Genetics
James, Richard, BSc Lond., PhD Lond.   Sr. Lectr.
Johnston, A. W. B., BSc Edin., PhD Edin.   Prof., Biology
Kleanthous, C., BSc Leic., PhD Leic.   Sr. Lectr.
Leg, E. J. A., BA DPhil   Sr. Lectr.
Lewis, B. G., BSc PhD   Sr. Lectr.
Murphy, G., BSc Birm., PhD Birm.   Prof., Cell Biology
Noble-Nesbitt, J., MA Camb., PhD Camb.   Sr. Lectr.
Sutherland, W. J., BSc Liv., PhD Liv.   Prof., Biology
Turner, J. G., BSc Leeds, MSc Missouri, PhD Missouri   Sr. Lectr.
Warn, R. M., MA Oxf., DPhil Oxf.   Sr. Lectr.
Watkinson, A. R., BA York(UK), PhD Wales   Prof., Ecology
Wildon, D. C., BScAgr Syd., PhD Syd.   Sr. Lectr.

Chemical Sciences
Tel: (01603) 592705 Fax: (01603) 259396
Andrews, D. L., BSc Lond., PhD Lond.   Prof.; Dean*
Cannon, R. D., BA Oxf., DPhil Oxf., DSc Oxf.   Reader
Cook, M. J., BSc Birm., PhD Birm.   Prof., Chemistry
Haines, A. H., BSc Birm., PhD Birm.   Reader
Jones, R. A., BSc Oxf., MA Oxf., PhD Camb., ScD Camb., FRSChem   Reader
Maskill, R., BA Oxf., PhD Kent   Sr. Lectr.
McKillop, A., PhD Glas., DSc Glas.   Prof., Chemistry
Moore, G. R., BSc CNAA, MSc Lond., DPhil Oxf.   Prof., Chemistry
Powell, Anne K., BSc Manc., PhD Manc.   Reader
Robinson, B. H., BSc Manc., DPhil Oxf.   Prof., Chemistry
Russell, D. A., BSc PhD   Sr. Lectr.
Sodeau, J. R., MSc S'ton., PhD S'ton.   Reader
Stephenson, G. R., MA Camb., PhD Camb.   Reader
Thomson, A. J., BA Oxf., DPhil Oxf., FRS   Prof., Chemistry
Other Staff: 1 Sr. Res. Officer

Development Studies
Tel: (01603) 592807 Fax: (01603) 451999
Barnett, A. S., BA Hull, MA(Econ) Manc., PhD Manc.   Prof.
Biggs, S. D., BSc Lond., MS Ill., PhD Calif.   Sr. Lectr.
Blaikie, P. M., MA Camb., PhD Camb.   Prof.
Brown, K., BSc MSc PhD   Sr. Lectr.
Cameron, J., MA Essex   Sr. Lectr.
Coleman, G., MA Manc.   Sr. Lectr.
Edwards, C. B., BA Nott., PhD   Sr. Lectr.
Ellis, F. T., BSc Reading, MSc Lond., DPhil Sus.   Reader
Holmstrom, M. N., MA Oxf., DPhil Oxf.   Sr. Lectr.
Howell, Jude A., BA York(UK), DPhil Sus.   Sr. Lectr.
Jackson, Cecile, BSc Lond., PhD Lond.   Sr. Lectr.
Jenkins, R. O., BA Camb., DPhil Sus.   Reader; Dean*
Livingstone, I., BA Sheff., MA Yale   Prof., Development Economics
Pearson, Ruth E., BA Camb., MA Sus., DPhil Sus.   Sr. Lectr.
Seddon, J. D., MA Camb., PhD Lond.   Prof.
Stocking, M. A., BA Oxf., MPhil Lond., PhD Lond.   Reader
Sumberg, J., BSc MSc PhD   Sr. Lectr.
Thoburn, John T., BA Leic., MA Leic., PhD Alta.   Reader

Ecology, see Biol. Scis.

Economic and Social Studies
Tel: (01603) 592723 Fax: (01603) 250434
Bellaby, P., BA Camb., PhD Camb.   Sr. Lectr., Sociology
Cubitt, R., BA Oxf., MA Oxf., MPhil Oxf., DPhil Oxf.   Reader, Economics
Davies, S. W., BA Warw., MA Warw., PhD Warw.   Prof., Economics
Fisher, A. E., BSocSc Birm., DLitt E.Anglia   Sr. Lectr., Philosophy
Goodwin, B. L., BA Oxf., MA Oxf., DPhil Oxf.   Prof., Politics
Hargreaves-Heap, S. P., BA Oxf., PhD Calif.   Sr. Lectr., Economics
Hollis, J. M., JP, MA Oxf.   Prof., Philosophy
Kemp-Welch, A., BSc Lond., PhD Lond.   Sr. Lectr., Politics; Dean*
O'Hagan, T. D. B., BA Oxf., MA Oxf., DPhil Oxf.   Sr. Lectr., Philosophy
Parikh, A., MCom Bom., MSc(Econ) Lond.   Prof., Economics
Scott, A., BA Essex, PhD Leeds   Sr. Lectr., Sociology
Starmer, C. V., BA CNAA, MA E.Anglia, PhD E.Anglia   Sr. Lectr., Economics
Street, J. R., BA Warw., DPhil Oxf.   Sr. Lectr., Politics

Sugden, R., BA York(UK), MSc Wales Prof., Economics
Vesper, J. R. Z., BA PhD Sr. Lectr.

Education and Professional Development

Tel: (01603) 592856 Fax: (01603) 593446

Aspland, R. W. B., BA Open(UK), MA E.Anglia., MSc CNAA Lectr.; Dean*
Barnes, R. H., PhD E.Anglia Sr. Lectr.
Bridges, D., BA Oxf., MA Lond., PhD Lond. Prof.
Cockburn, A. D., BSc St And., MSc Strath., PhD E.Anglia Prof.
Elliott, J., MPhil Lond. Prof.
Goodson, I., BSc DPhil Prof.
Haylock, D. W., MA Oxf., MEd Lond., PhD Lond. Sr. Lectr.
Kushner, S., BSc PhD Sr. Lectr.
MacLure, Margaret V., MA Edin., DPhil York(UK) Reader
Norris, N. F. J., BA E.Anglia, PhD E.Anglia Sr. Lectr.
Phillips, T., MPhil PhD Sr. Lectr.
Schostak, J. F., BA CNAA, MSc Brad., PhD E.Anglia Prof.
Thorne, B., MA Camb. Prof.
Tickle, L., BEd Keele, MA Keele, PhD E.Anglia Sr. Lectr.

English and American Studies

Tel: (01603) 592810 Fax: (01603) 507728

Barr, C. J. A., BA Camb., BA York(UK) Sr. Lectr.
Bigsby, C. W. E., MA Sheff., PhD Nott. Prof., American Studies
Clark, R., BA Essex, PhD Essex Sr. Lectr.
Cook, J., BA Camb., MA Sr. Lectr.
Crockatt, R., MA DPhil Sr. Lectr.
Higson, A. D., BEd Brist., MA Leic., PhD Kent Sr. Lectr.
Homberger, E. R., BA Calif., MA Chic., PhD Camb. Reader
Hyde, G. M., MA Camb., MA Essex, LittD Sr. Lectr.
Lawton, D. A., MA Oxf., DPhil York(UK) Prof.
Lloyd-Smith, A. G., MA Sus., PhD Indiana Sr. Lectr.
Motion, A., BA MA MLitt Prof.
Sage, Lorna, BA Durh., MA Birm. Prof.
Sage, V. R. L., BA Durh., MA Birm., PhD Reader
Sales, R. B., BA Camb., BA E.Anglia, PhD Camb. Prof.; Dean*
Thompson, R. F., MA Oxf. Reader
Todd, Janet, BA Camb., PhD Flor. Prof., English Literature
Womack, P., BA Oxf., PhD Edin. Sr. Lectr.
Yarrow, R., BA Reading, MA Manc., PhD Manc. Sr. Lectr.
Vacant Posts: 1 Prof.; 1 Lectr.

Environmental Sciences

Tel: (01603) 592836 Fax: (01603) 507719

Alexander, J., BSc Brist., PhD Leeds Sr. Lectr.
Andrews, J., BSc PhD Sr. Lectr.
Atkinson, T. C., BSc Brist., PhD Brist. Reader
Ball, D. J., BSc Exe., DPhil Sus. Reader
Bateman, I. J., BSc MA PhD Reader
Bentham, C. G., MA Camb. Reader
Bigg, G. R., BSc Adel., PhD Adel. Sr. Lectr.
Brimblecombe, P., BSc Auck., MSc Auck., PhD Auck. Prof.
Burton, P. W., MA Camb., PhD Durh. Reader
Chroston, P. N., BSc Wales, PhD Wales Sr. Lectr.
Corbett, B. M., BSc MSc Sr. Demonstrator
Davies, T. D., BSc Sheff., PhD Sheff. Prof.
Dent, D. L., BSc Durh., MSc Durh., PhD E.Anglia Sr. Lectr.
Hassall, M., BSc Leeds, PhD Leeds Sr. Lectr.
Haynes, R. M., BA Brist., PhD Penn. Sr. Lectr.
Hey, R. D., BSc Brist., PhD Camb. Reader
Heywood, K. J., BSc PhD Sr. Lectr.
Jickells, T. D., BSc Reading, MSc S'ton., PhD S'ton. Reader
Jones, P., BA MSc PhD Reader
Kelly, M., BSc PhD Reader
Liss, P. S., BSc Durh., PhD Wales Prof.

Lovett, A., BA Wales, PhD Wales Sr. Lectr.
Maher, B. A., BSc Liv., PhD Liv. Sr. Lectr.
O'Riordan, T., MA Edin., MS Cornell, PhD Camb. Prof.
Palutikof, J., BSc PhD Reader
Penkett, S. A., BSc Leeds, PhD Leeds Prof.
Plane, J. M. C., MA Camb., PhD Camb. Reader
Tovey, N. K., MA Camb., PhD Camb. Reader
Turner, R. K., BA Wales, MA Leic. Prof.
Vincent, C. E., BSc Lond., PhD S'ton. Reader
Vine, F. J., BA Camb., PhD Camb., FRS Prof.; Dean*
Watkinson, A. R., BA York(UK), PhD Wales Prof.
Watson, A. J., BSc Lond., PhD Reading Prof.
Other Staff: 1 Sr. Fellow; 1 Sr. Res. Felllow; 1 Sr. Res. Assoc.; 1 Sr. Demr.

European Studies, see Mod. Langs. and European Studies

Health

Tel: (01603) 593244 Fax: (01603) 593166

Pearce, S., BA Oxf., MPhil Lond., PhD Lond. Prof., Health Psychology; Dean*

Health Policy and Practice

Tel: (01603) 593309 Fax: (01603) 593604

Appleby, J., BA Essex, MSc York(UK) Sr. Lectr.
Haynes, R. M., BA Brist., PhD Penn. Sr. Lectr.
Mugford, M., BA Stir., DPhil Oxf. Sr. Lectr.
Reynolds, S. A., BSc Wales, MSc Leic., PhD Sheff. Sr. Lectr.
Other Staff: 2 Hon. Sr. Lectrs.

Nursing and Midwifery

Tel: (01603) 421422 Fax: (01603) 421430

Jerosch, C., MSc Sr. Lectr.
Richardson, B., MSc PhD Sr. Lectr.
Willson, M., BA Open(UK), MSc Salf. Sr. Lectr.; Dir.*

Occupational Therapy and Physiotherapy

Tel: (01603) 593083 Fax: (01603) 593166

Routledge, J. M., MEd Leeds Sr. Lectr.; Dir.*
Stephenson, R. C., BA MSc Sr. Lectr.
Watson, M., MSc Sr. Lectr.
Willson, M., BA Open(UK), MSc Salf. Sr. Lectr.

History

Tel: (01603) 593521 Fax: (01603) 593519

Acton, E. D. J., BA York(UK), PhD Camb. Prof.
Casey, J. G., BA Belf., PhD Camb., FRHistS Sr. Lectr.
Charmley, J. D., BA Oxf., DPhil Oxf. Sr. Lectr.
Church, R. A., BA Nott., PhD Nott., FRHistS Prof.; Dean*
Davis, J. C., MA Manc., FRHistS Prof.
Fairclough, A., BA PhD Prof.
John, M. F., MA Oxf., DPhil Oxf. Prof.
Logan, O., MA PhD, FRHistS Sr. Lectr.
Munting, R. D., BA(Econ) Sheff., PhD Birm. Sr. Lectr.
Sanderson, J. M., MA Camb., PhD Camb. Reader
Searle, G. R., MA Camb., PhD Camb. Prof.
Short, R., MA DPhil Sr. Lectr.
Wilson, R. G., BA Leeds, PhD Leeds, FRHistS Sr. Lectr.
Wilson, S., MA Camb., PhD Camb. Reader

Information Systems

Tel: (01603) 592801 Fax: (01603) 592674

Aldridge, R., BSc PhD Sr. Lectr.
Arnold, D. B., MA Camb., PhD Camb. Prof.
Bangham, J. A., BSc Lond., PhD Lond. Reader
de Cogan, D., BA Trinity(Dub.), PhD Trinity(Dub.) Reader
Dearnley, P. A., BSc(Econ) Lond., PhD E.Anglia Sr. Lectr.
Dowsing, R. D., PhD Lond. Sr. Lectr.
Forrest, A. R., BSc Edin., PhD Camb. Prof.
Glauert, J. R. W., BA Camb., MSc Manc., PhD Camb. Sr. Lectr.; Dean*
Mayhew, Pamela J., BSc E.Anglia, PhD E.Anglia Sr. Lectr.
McKeown, G. P., MSc Manc., PhD Manc. Sr. Lectr.

Rayward-Smith, V. J., MA Oxf., PhD Lond. Prof.
Razaz, M., BSc Teheran, MSc Manc., PhD Lond. Sr. Lectr.
Sleep, M. R., BSc Brist., PhD Brun. Prof.
Smith, G. D., BSc H.-W., MSc E.Anglia, PhD E.Anglia Sr. Lectr.
Tattersall, G. D., BTech Brad. Sr. Lectr.
Woodhams, F. W. D., BSc Exe., PhD Exe. Prof., Electronic Systems Engineering

Law

Fax: (01603) 250245

Ball, Caroline, LLB Brist., PhD Brist. Sr. Lectr.
Banakas, E. K., LLB Athens, PhD Camb. Sr. Lectr.
Miller, J. G., LLM Wales, LLM Camb., PhD Camb. Prof.; Dean*
Morgan, J., LLB LLM PhD Sr. Lectr.
Naldi, G. J., LLM Birm., PhD Birm. Sr. Lectr.
Pattenden, Rosemary D., BCom NSW, LLB NSW, DPhil Oxf. Reader
Smith, I. T., MA Camb., LLB Camb. Prof.
Stallworthy, M., MA Oxf., LLM Lanc. Dir., Professl. Legal Educn.
Thomas, D. R., LLB Wales, MA Sheff. Prof.
Thomas, G. H., LLB Wales, BCL Oxf. Sr. Lectr.

Management

Tel: (01603) 592316 Fax: (01603) 593343

Brown, T. L. T., MA Dir.
Fletcher, K. P., MA Lanc., PhD Strath. Prof.; Dean*
Jones, C. S., MSc Warw., PhD Hull Prof.
Williams, B. C., BSc Lond., PhD E.Anglia Sr. Lectr.
Witcher, B. J., BA Leic., PhD Stir. Sr. Lectr.

Mathematics

Tel: (01603) 592597 Fax: (01603) 259515

Camina, A. R., BSc Lond., PhD Lond. Reader
Evans, D., BA DPhil Reader
Everest, G. R., BSc Lond., PhD Lond. Sr. Lectr.
Janacek, G. J., BSc MSc PhD Sr. Lectr.; Dean*
Johnson, J. A., BSc Manc., PhD Camb. Prof.
Morland, L. W., BSc Manc., PhD Manc., FIMA Prof.
Riley, N., BSc Manc., PhD Manc., FIMA Prof.
Scott, N. H., BA Camb., MSc PhD Sr. Lectr.
Siemons, I. J., PhD Lond. Sr. Lectr.
Walpole, L. J., BSc Cant., PhD Camb. Sr. Lectr.
Zalesskii, A. E., PhD Belorussian State Prof.

Modern Languages and European Studies

Tel: (01603) 592749 Fax: (01603) 250599

Carr, M. G., BA Wales Sr. Lectr.; Dean*
Fletcher, J. W. J., MA Camb., Dr3rdCy Toulouse Prof., European Literature
Garton, Janet, MA Camb. Sr. Lectr.
Hale, T., BA MA PhD Dir.
Kenning, M. M., LèsL PhD Sr. Lectr.
Lodge, K. R., BA Manc., PhD Sr. Lectr.
Robinson, M. G., BA E.Anglia, PhD Camb. Prof., Scandinavian Studies
Scott, C., MA Oxf., DPhil Oxf., FBA Prof., European History
Sebald, W. G., LèsL Frib., MA Manc., PhD Prof., European Literature
Shaffer, Elinor S., BA Chic., MA Oxf., MA Camb., PhD Col., FBA Reader
Short, R. S., MA Camb., DPhil Sus. Sr. Lectr.

Museology, see World Art Studies and Museol.

Music

Tel: (01603) 592450 Fax: (01603) 250454

Aston, P. G., DPhil York(UK) Prof.; Dean*
Chadd, D. F. L., MA Oxf. Sr. Lectr.

Philosophy, see Econ. and Soc. Studies

Physics

Tel: (01603) 592843 Fax: (01603) 259515

Champeney, D. C., MA Oxf., DPhil Oxf. Sr. Lectr.
Coleman, P. G., BSc Lond., PhD Lond. Prof.

Davies, J. J., MA Oxf., DPhil Oxf. Prof.
Silbert, M., LenF La Plata, DenF La Plata Reader
Watts, B. R., MA Camb., PhD Camb. Sr. Lectr.
Wolverson, D., MA PhD Sr. Lectr.
Other Staff: 1 Sr. Fellow

Politics, see Econ. and Soc. Studies

Professional Development, see Educn. and
Professl. Devel.

Social Studies, see Econ. and Soc. Studies

Social Work
Tel: (01603) 592068 Fax: (01603) 593552
Ball, M. C., LLB Brist. Sr. Lectr.
Boswell, G. R., MA Keele, PhD Liv. Sr. Lectr.
Davies, M. B., BA Liv., PhD Lond. Prof.
Howe, D. K., BSc Durh., MA Nott., PhD Prof.
Keene, J. M., BA Sus., PhD Wales Sr. Lectr.
Stone, N. A., LLB Exe., LLB Camb., LLM Col.,
MA Nott. Sr. Lectr.
Thoburn, J., BA Reading, MSW LittD Prof.;
Dean*

Sociology, see Econ. and Soc. Studies

World Art Studies and Museology
Tel: (01603) 592817 Fax: (01603) 593642
Cocke, R. H. St. G., BA Oxf., PhD Lond. Sr.
Lectr.; Dean*
Grieve, A. I., BA Lond., PhD Lond. Sr. Lectr.
Heslop, T. A., BA Lond., FSA Sr. Lectr.
Hodges, R. A., OBE, BA S'ton., PhD S'ton.,
FSA Prof.
Hooper, S., BSc PhD Dir.
Johnson, N., MA Dir.
Jordanova, L., BA Camb., MA Essex, PhD Camb.,
FRHistS Prof.
McWilliam, N. F., MA Oxf., DPhil Oxf. Sr.
Lectr.
Mitchell, J. B., BA Penn., FSA Sr. Lectr.
Muthesius, S., DPhil Marburg Reader
Onians, J. B., BA Camb., PhD Lond., FSA Prof.

SPECIAL CENTRES, ETC

Applied Research in Education, Centre for
Tel: (01603) 592638 Fax: (01603) 451412
Elliott, Prof. J., MPhil Lond. Dir.*

Arts of Africa, Oceania and the Americas, Sainsbury Research Unit for the
Tel: (01603) 592498 Fax: (01603) 259401
Hooper, S. J. P., BSc Brad., PhD Camb. Dir.*

Audio Visual Centre
Tel: (01603) 592833 Fax: (01603) 507721
Browne, C.

Climatic Research Unit
Tel: (01603) 592088 Fax: (01603) 507784
Davies, Prof. T. D., BSc Sheff., PhD Sheff. Dir.*

Computing Centre
Tel: (01603) 592390 Fax: (01603) 593467
Roper, J. P. G., BSc Durh. Dir.*

Continuing Education, Centre for
Tel: (01603) 593016 Fax: (01603) 250035
Brown, A. L. T., MA Oxf. Dean*

Counselling Studies, Centre for
Tel: (01603) 592651
Thorne, B., MA Camb. Dir.*

East Anglian Studies, Centre of
Tel: (01603) 592667 Fax: (01603) 592660
Wilson, R. G., BA Leeds, PhD Leeds,
FRHistS Dir.*

Economics Research Centre
Tel: (01603) 593423 Fax: (01603) 250434
Sugden, R., BA York(UK), MSc Wales,
FBA Prof.; Dir.*

English Language and British Studies, Centre for
Tel: (01603) 592977 Fax: (01603) 250559
Horncastle, C. W., BA Wales Co-Dir., English
Language*

Overseas Development Group
Tel: (01603) 457880 Fax: (01603) 505262
Coleman, G. Managing Dir.*

Public Choice Studies, Centre for
Tel: (01603) 592067 Fax: (01603) 250434
Street, J. R., BA Warw., DPhil Oxf. Dir.*

Religious Education, Keswick Hall Centre for Research and Development in
Tel: (01603) 593179 Fax: (01603) 507728
Rudge, L., BA E.Anglia, MA E.Anglia Dir.*

Visual Arts Education, Applied Research in
Tel: (01603) 592465 Fax: (01603) 259401
Sekules, V., BA Lond., PhD Lond. Dir.*
Tickle, L.

Visual Arts, Sainsbury Centre for
Tel: (01603) 592466 Fax: (01603) 259401
Johnson, N., MA Dir.*

CONTACT OFFICERS

Academic affairs. Academic Registrar: Rich, A.
H., BA Manc., PhD Manc.
Accommodation. Accommodation Manager:
Winter, C. K.
Admissions (first degree). Assistant Registrar:
Perowne, Naomi C., BA Reading
Admissions (higher degree). Deputy
Academic Registrar: Brind, J. C., MA Camb.
Adult/continuing education. Dean, Centre for
Continuing Education: Brown, A. L. T., MA
Oxf.
Alumni. Public Relations and Development
Manager: Cutress, L., BA CNAA
Careers. Director, Careers Centre: McGilvray,
I., BSc

Computing services. Director, Computing
Centre: Roper, J. P. G., BSc Durh.
Credit transfer. Assistant Registrar: Greatrix,
P., MA Edin.
Development/fund-raising. Public Relations
and Development Manager: Cutress, L., BA
CNAA
Distance education. McBride, R., PhD E.Anglia
Estates and buildings/works and services.
Director of Estates and Buildings: Goodall, R.
G.
Examinations. Assistant Registrar: Williams, L.
M., BA Open(UK)
Finance. Director of Finance: Morland, C. W.
General enquiries. Registrar and Secretary:
Paulson-Ellis, M. G. E., OBE, MA Camb., FCA
Health services. Senior Partner: Coathup, Dr.
P. A.
Industrial liaison. Director: Brown, A. L. T.,
MA Oxf.
International office. Assistant Registrar:
Perowne, Naomi C., BA Reading
Library (chief librarian). Librarian: Baker, D.
M., MA Kent, MMus Lond., MLS Lough., PhD
Lough., FLA, FRCO
Personnel/human resources. Director of
Personnel and Registry Services: Beck, J. R.
L., BA York(UK)
Public relations, information and marketing.
Director of Communications: Preece, Alan,
BA Open(UK)
Publications. Editor: Walisiewicz, M.
Purchasing. Purchasing Officer: Deans, C. G.
Quality assurance and accreditation. Senior
Administrative Assistant: Clarke, A. S., BA
E.Anglia, MA E.Anglia
Research. Deputy Academic Registrar: Brind, J.
C., MA Camb.
Safety. Director, Safety Services: Thomas, R.
N., BSc Lond.
Scholarships, awards, loans. Assistant
Registrar: Morton, L., BA Durh., BPhil Oxf.
Schools liaison. Schools and Colleges Liaison
Officer: Beard, J., BA E.Anglia
Security. Superintendent, Security Services:
Morson, M.
Sport and recreation. Director, Physical
Recreation: Nicholls, K., BEd Lond., MA Leeds
Staff development and training. Staff
Development and Training Officer: Goodall,
Ruth E., BA York(UK)
Student union. Communications Officer:
Watson, A.
Student welfare/counselling. Dean of
Students: Matheson, C. C., BSc St And., PhD
St And.
Student welfare/counselling. Director,
Student Counselling: Thorne, B. J., MA Camb.
Students from other countries. Dean of
Students: Matheson, C. C., BSc St And., PhD
St And.
Students with disabilities. Dean of Students:
Matheson, C. C., BSc St And., PhD St And.
University press. Press Officer: Ogden, Anne,
BA Liv.

*[Information supplied by the institution as at 23 February
1998, and edited by the ACU]*

UNIVERSITY OF EAST LONDON

Established 1992; founded as North East London Polytechnic, 1970; incorporated as the Polytechnic of East London, 1989

Member of the Association of Commonwealth Universities

Postal Address: Romford Road, London, England E15 4LZ
Telephone: (0181) 590 7722, 590 7000 Fax: (0181) 519 3740 WWW: http://www.uel.ac.uk
E-mail formula: initials.surname@UEL.AC.UK

CHAIRMAN OF GOVERNORS—White, Don, FIMechE
VICE-CHANCELLOR*—Gould, Prof. Frank W., BA Lond., MA NSW
SECRETARY AND REGISTRAR‡—Ingle, Alan, BA
HEAD OF LEARNING SUPPORT SERVICES/LIBRARIAN—Doust, Janet, BA MA

GENERAL INFORMATION

History. The university was founded as North East London Polytechnic in 1970, incorporated as the Polytechnic of East London in 1989, and gained its current title in 1992.

Admission to first degree courses (see also United Kingdom Introduction). Through Universities and Colleges Admissions Service (UCAS).

First Degrees (see also United Kingdom Directory to Subjects of Study). BA, BEng, BSc, LLB, MEng.

Single honours programmes are normally available full-time, lasting 3 years. MEng, extended degrees (which include a foundation year): 4 years full-time. Part-time options and sandwich courses are widely available, as is the option to study a combination of 2 or 3 subjects.

Higher Degrees (see also United Kingdom Directory to Subjects of Study). LLM, MA, MBA, MSc, MPhil, PhD.

Applicants for admission to master's degrees must normally hold a first degree, a postgraduate diploma or equivalent, or have had substantial experience or employment in a relevant field.

Master's degree courses normally last 1 year full-time or 2 years part-time.

Fees (1998–99). Home undergraduate: £145 (per single unit on modular undergraduate degree scheme); £4675 (design foundation course, annual). International undergraduate (annual): £6200 (full-time).

Academic Year (1999–2000). Three terms: 27 September–17 December; 10 January–7 April; 1 May–7 July.

FACULTIES/SCHOOLS

Design, Engineering and the Built Environment
Dean: Ellis, Prof. Christopher, PhD

East London Business School
Dean: Knowles, Philip, MSc

Science and Health
Dean: Doonan, Prof. Shawn, DSc

Social Sciences
Dean: Rustin, Prof. Michael J., MA

ACADEMIC UNITS

Accounting, see under E. London Bus. Sch.

Architecture
Fax: (0181) 849 3686
Coates, Paul S. Sr. Lectr.
Ford, Peter Sr. Lectr.
Salter, Peter Prof.; Head*
Thompson, Michael W., MSc Sr. Lectr.
Weaver, Nicholas K., MA Principal Lectr.

Art and Design
Fax: (0181) 849 3694
Barrett, M., MA Sr. Lectr.
Brunell, Geoffrey R., MA RCA Principal Lectr.
Dawson, C. Sr. Lectr.
Duncan, Andrea Sr. Lectr.
Dyall, D. Principal Lectr.
Elinor, Gillian, MA Principal Lectr.; Head*
Fraser-Steele, Stanford Sr. Lectr.
O'Pray, Michael E. Sr. Lectr.
Ruffhead, Andrew N., BA Sr. Lectr.
Sinden, Tony Sr. Lectr.

Business Studies, see under E. London Bus. Sch.

Cultural Studies
Fax: (0181) 849 3538
Alexander, Sally A., BA Sr. Lectr.
Blake, Andrew J., MA PhD Sr. Lectr.
Chase, Robert, MA PhD Principal Lectr.
Greenway, S. Sr. Lectr.
Hargreaves, J. Sr. Lectr.
Holly, Mike J. Sr. Lectr.
Horne, P., MA Sr. Lectr.
Humm, Prof. Maggie, BA CNAA, PhD CNAA Principal Lectr.
Lewis, Reina Sr. Lectr.
Nava, Mica, BSc PhD Sr. Lectr.
O'Shea, Alan, MA Head*
Parker, Prof. R. Kenneth S., MA Principal Lectr.
Radstone, Susanna Sr. Lectr.
Stubbs, Olive Sr. Lectr.
Venn, Couze, BA PhD Sr. Lectr.

East London Business School
Fax: (0181) 534 8332

Accounting
Fax: (0181) 590 7799
Bashir, Tariq Sr. Lectr.
Clingan, John Sr. Lectr.
Cooper, J. Sr. Lectr.
Everitt, Mary Sr. Lectr.
Ewers, David Sr. Lectr.
Johnston, R. Sr. Lectr.
Kelsey, B. Sr. Lectr.
Lawrence, S. Sr. Lectr.
Len Hing, C. Sr. Lectr.
Malinowski, C. Sr. Lectr.
Norkett, Paul Subj. Group Leader*
O'Connor, William Sr. Lectr.
Stirk, Ian Sr. Lectr.
Tobbell, Graham Sr. Lectr.

Business Information Systems
Fax: (0181) 590 7799
Anthony, R. Sr. Lectr.
Carter, A. Sr. Lectr.
Carter, J. Sr. Lectr.
Everitt, Michael Principal Lectr.
Hind, Robert Sr. Lectr.
Kretsis, M. Sr. Lectr.
Lynch, J. Sr. Lectr.
Martin, Steven Sr. Lectr.
Richardson, M. Sr. Lectr.
Smith, William Subj. Group Leader*

Woolliams, Peter Prof.

Business Policy
Fax: (0181) 590 7799
Church, D. Sr. Lectr.
Cooper, M. Sr. Lectr.
De, P. Sr. Lectr.
Godwin, Terence Principal Lectr.
Isaac, Ian Sr. Lectr.
Mezen, R. Sr. Lectr.
Neale, A. Principal Lectr.
Pirie, Ian Principal Lectr.
Sandiland, David Sr. Lectr.

Education Management
Fax: (0181) 534 8332
Ewers, Christine Sr. Lectr.
John, C. Principal Lectr.
Lyons, Geoffrey Subj. Group Leader*

Human Resource Management
Fax: (0181) 590 7799
Barry, Jim Sr. Lectr.
Chandler, John Sr. Lectr.
Ellis, A. Sr. Lectr.
Fenwick, P. Sr. Lectr.
Holloway, M. Sr. Lectr.
Honour, Trudie Principal Lectr.
Murton, A. Sr. Lectr.
Stenning, Winifred Sr. Lectr.

Marketing
Fax: (0181) 590 7799
Donovan, D. Sr. Lectr.
Madill, Colin Subj. Group Leader*
Taylor, P. Sr. Lectr.
Waters, Patrick Sr. Lectr.

Public Sector Management
Fax: (0181) 590 7799
Binns, D. Sr. Lectr.
Eglin, Gregory Principal Lectr.
Hamilton, Judith Sr. Lectr.
O'Hara, Rory Sr. Lectr.
Pinfield, David Principal Lectr.
Rowswell, Maurice Sr. Lectr.

Economics
Fax: (0181) 590 7799
Arestis, Prof. Philip, MA MSc PhD
Bain, Keith, BA NSW, MPol Sr. Lectr.
Boyd, D. A. C. Sr. Lectr.
Fenn, Douglas R., JP, MA Sr. Lectr.
Glickman, Murray L. Principal Lectr.
Lee, M. Sr. Lectr.
Lowe, P., BA Sr. Lectr.
Marshall, M. G. Sr. Lectr.
Mottershead, Peter, BA MSc Sr. Lectr.
Skuse, Frank E., BComm MEc Head*
Vis, Rudi J., MSc PhD Principal Lectr.
Wright, G. M., BA MSc Sr. Lectr.

Education Management, see under E. London Bus. Sch.

Education Studies
Fax: (0181) 590 7799
DaCosta, Cornel, MSc PhD Principal Lectr.
Digings, P. M. Sr. Lectr.

Dineen, Georgina L., MSc   Principal Lectr.
Graham, James D., MA BEd   Head*
Hoyles, Martin, MA   Sr. Lectr.
Owen, C. M.   Sr. Lectr.
Paine, C. D.   Sr. Lectr.
Parker, Vivien M., MA   Sr. Lectr.
Pittaway, G. A.   Sr. Lectr.
Slater, A.   Sr. Lectr.
Trushell, J. M.   Sr. Lectr.
Vincent, Denis R., MA   Reader
Woods, Patricia M., BA   Sr. Lectr.

Engineering, Civil

Fax: (0181) 590 7799

Al Naib, Shafik K., BSc PhD, FICE   Prof.; Head*
Day, S. J. G., BEng MEngSc   Sr. Lectr.
Ford, G. J., MSc   Sr. Lectr.
Freeman, Richard J., BSc   Sr. Lectr.
Ionnou, Costas S., MSc   Sr. Lectr.
King, D. E. C.   Sr. Lectr.
Ludgate, Peter J., BEng   Sr. Lectr.
Noor, Faz A., BEng PhD   Principal Lectr.
Smith, P. S., MSc BEng   Sr. Lectr.
Wijeyesekera, D. C., MSc PhD, FGS   Reader

Engineering, Electrical and Manufacturing

Fax: (0181) 590 7799

Bailey, W. N., MEng PhD   Sr. Lectr.
Brook, Ian C., BSc PhD   Sr. Lectr.
Chanerley, Andrew A., MSc   Sr. Lectr.
Costa, George, MSc   Sr. Lectr.
Dodds, Prof. Stephen J., MSc PhD   Reader
Goodfellow, John E., BSc PhD   Principal Lectr.
Hosny, Wada N., MSc   Sr. Lectr.
Kemp, Ray A., MTech   Sr. Lectr.
Lawrence, Prof. Charles C., BSc PhD   Reader
Leeson, M. S., BEng PhD   Sr. Lectr.
Malhotra, Venn N., BChem MTech PhD   Sr. Lectr.
Perryman, Roy, PhD   Head*
Sale, Prof. Roger   Principal Lectr.
Slawson, Alan J.   Sr. Lectr.
Smith, Martin C., MSc   Sr. Lectr.
Weerasinghe, V. M., MSc PhD   Sr. Lectr.

Environmental and Mathematical Sciences

Attridge, Terence H., PhD   Sr. Lectr.
Ayres, Ruth, PhD   Sr. Lectr.
Boulter, Prof. Michael C., BSc PhD, FGS   Principal Lectr.
Colman, W. J. A., MSc   Sr. Lectr.
Corke, David, BSc PhD   Sr. Lectr.
De Jong, Wim, Cand *Ley.*, Dr *Ley.*, FIMA   Sr. Lectr.
Evans, John, BSc   Sr. Lectr.
Harris, James A., PhD   Reader
Hubbard, Richard N. L.   Sr. Lectr.
Insole, Joan M., BSc   Sr. Lectr.
Jardine, Fred H., MSc PhD   Sr. Lectr.
Kynicos, Costas, BSc   Sr. Lectr.
McCall, John S., MSc   Sr. Lectr.
Murphy, Prof. Gene E., MSc PhD   Principal Lectr.
Murphy, J. J.   Sr. Lectr.
Peel, Michael H., BA PhD   Sr. Lectr.
Rostron, John   Sr. Lectr.
Snow, Prof. Keith R., BSc PhD   Principal Lectr.; Head*
Taghavikhonsary, M.   Sr. Lectr.
Waite, James A., BSc PhD, FRSChem   Principal Lectr.

Fashion: Design with Marketing

Fax: (0181) 590 7799

Branigan, Dawn   Sr. Lectr.
Carter, Helen   Sr. Lectr.
Goodworth, Valerie A.   Principal Lectr.

Health Sciences

Armstrong, M. B.   Sr. Lectr.
Atkinson, Karen   Sr. Lectr.
Bahl, Daman K., BA MSc   Principal Lectr.
Beeston, Sarah, MA BEd   Head*
Bithell, Christine P., MA   Principal Lectr.

Bone, Anthony A. J., MPhil MA   Principal Lectr.
Callaghan, P., BSc   Sr. Lectr.
Churcher, E. M.   Sr. Lectr.
Cooke, M., BSc   Sr. Lectr.
Coutts, Fiona J.   Sr. Lectr.
Evers, Rachel M., BA   Sr. Lectr.
Gidney, A. R., BSc PhD   Sr. Lectr.
Goodfellow, Barbara E., BA   Sr. Lectr.
Houston, Melsa, BA   Sr. Lectr.
James, Joyce, BA   Sr. Lectr.
Jobling, Margot   Sr. Lectr.
Mantle, M. Jill   Sr. Lectr.
Percival, K. A.   Sr. Lectr.
Ranasingehe, P.   Sr. Lectr.
Rastall, Maggie J.   Sr. Lectr.
Reed, M. A.   Sr. Lectr.
Ryan, Susan E.   Sr. Lectr.
Scott, Oona, PhD   Sr. Lectr.
Simmons, S. M., MSc   Principal Lectr.
Thomson, D. J., MSc   Sr. Lectr.
Veness, B. J.   Sr. Lectr.

Human Relations

Bradbury, P. S.   Principal Lectr.
Cree, W. A., BA   Sr. Lectr.
Fletcher, J. L., BA   Sr. Lectr.
Hollows, Anne   Principal Lectr.
Lyons, Karen H., MA   Principal Lectr.
Quammie, Sari E.   Sr. Lectr.
Richards, Barry, PhD   Prof.; Head*
Smee, M., PhD   Sr. Lectr.
Thomas, Alison M., PhD   Sr. Lectr.
Treacher, Amal, BA   Sr. Lectr.

Human Resource Management, see under E. London Bus. Sch.

Innovation Studies

Bandyopadhyay, M., MSc   Sr. Lectr.
Biggs, S.   Sr. Lectr.
De Miranda, Alvaro T., MSc   Head*
Hargreaves, A. W.   Sr. Lectr.
Henwood, Felicity J., BA MSc PhD   Sr. Lectr.
Marcelle, G.   Sr. Lectr.
Miller, N., PhD   Principal Lectr.
O'Malley, T. P., BA   Sr. Lectr.
Ormrod, S. C.   Sr. Lectr.
Poynter, Gavin, MA   Principal Lectr.
Richardson, Malcolm   Sr. Lectr.
Stepulevage, Linda, MSc   Sr. Lectr.
Thomas, Graham S., BA   Sr. Lectr.
Webster, Juliet L. I., BSc PhD   Sr. Lectr.
Wyatt, Sally M. E., MA   Principal Lectr.

Institutional Studies, Centre for

Fax: (0181) 849 3678

Locke, Michael, BA   Reader
Pratt, Prof. John, BSc   Reader; Head*

Law

Fax: (0181) 590 7799

Brown, B., PhD   Prof.
Cardan, B.   Sr. Lectr.
Fairweather, Fiona, LLB   Sr. Lectr.
Green, Kate M., LLB PhD   Principal Lectr.
Griffiths, A. J.   Sr. Lectr.
Hobby, C. O.   Sr. Lectr.
Levy, Sharon I., LLB   Sr. Lectr.
Lim, H., LLB MA   Sr. Lectr.
McArthur, Ronald H., LLM MBA   Sr. Lectr.
Moore, Maurice F., LLM   Sr. Lectr.
Pickford, E. J.   Sr. Lectr.
Strawson, John, BA   Sr. Lectr.
Sumner, Prof. Colin, PhD   Head*
Togbor, S.   Sr. Lectr.
Topping, R. M.   Sr. Lectr.
Tuitt, D. A.   Sr. Lectr.
Van Bruggen, Brigid, LLB   Sr. Lectr.
Vernon, Stuart K. H., JP, LLB MA   Principal Lectr.
Wilson, A. P.   Sr. Lectr.

Life Sciences

Fax: (0181) 849 3499

Adams, Kenneth J., PhD   Principal Lectr.
Bradman, W. R. W., MSc   Sr. Lectr.
Bunn, David N., BSc PhD   Principal Lectr.

Freeman, Patricia C., BSc PhD   Sr. Lectr.
Hide, Denis, BSc PhD   Principal Lectr.
Humber, David P., PhD   Head*
Humphreys, J. M., BSc PhD   Sr. Lectr.
Jakobson, Michael E., PhD MSc BA   Sr. Lectr.
Jones, K. D.   Sr. Lectr.
Marshall, P.   Sr. Lectr.
Melamed, Mark D., MSc PhD   Reader
Moffett, B. F.   Sr. Lectr.
Morinan, Alun, MSc PhD   Principal Lectr.
Mottley, John, MSc PhD   Sr. Lectr.
Poole, P. L., BSc PhD   Sr. Lectr.
Roberts, Prof. A. V., BSc PhD   Principal Lectr.
Rogers, P. D.   Sr. Lectr.
Rowley, David A., BSc PhD   Sr. Lectr.
Salmon, D. M. W., PhD MSc   Sr. Lectr.
Sieber, Vivien   Sr. Lectr.
Smith, Roland G., PhD BSc   Sr. Lectr.
Steele, W. H., PhD   Sr. Lectr.
Sturman, Gillian M., PhD   Principal Lectr.
Watkins, David K., BSc PhD   Sr. Lectr.
Webb, G. P., MSc PhD   Sr. Lectr.
Wright, John D., BSc PhD   Sr. Lectr.

Marketing, see under E. London Bus. Sch.

Mathematical Sciences, see Environmental and Mathl. Scis.

Psychology

Fax: (0181) 849 3697

Baker, Martyn C., BA   Sr. Lectr.
Bayne, Rowan S., MA PhD   Sr. Lectr.
Berry, Colin, BSc PhD   Principal Lectr.
Bimrose, Jennifer M. F.   Principal Lectr.
Boyle, Mary E., MA PhD   Sr. Lectr.
Brill, Cynthia, MA   Sr. Lectr.
Burton, Andrew, BA PhD   Sr. Lectr.
Burton, Esme, BA MSc   Sr. Lectr.
Clifford, Brian R., PhD   Prof.
Fine, M. L., BA MSc   Sr. Lectr.
Fullerton, Clare   Sr. Lectr.
Govier, Ernest, BSc   Principal Lectr.
Green, P. S., BSc   Sr. Lectr.
Horton, Ian E., MA   Sr. Lectr.
Kwiatkowski, Richard M.   Sr. Lectr.
Merry, Anthony W.   Sr. Lectr.
Noyes, E. J., BSc   Sr. Lectr.
Parrott, Andrew C., BSc PhD   Sr. Lectr.
Rose, David, PhD   Prof.; Head*
Sage, R. M., MSc   Sr. Lectr.
Tribe, R. J. N.   Sr. Lectr.
Vitkovitch, M., BSc PhD   Sr. Lectr.
Wilden, Sally, BA   Sr. Lectr.
Wolfendale, Prof. Sheila, BA MSc, FBPsS   Principal Lectr.
Woollett, Prof. E. Anne, PhD   Reader

Public Sector Management, see under E. London Bus. Sch.

Social Politics and Languages

Fax: (0181) 590 7799

Craig, L. J., MA   Sr. Lectr.
Fenn, Douglas, MA   Sr. Lectr.
Fogelman, Frances, BA   Sr. Lectr.
Fogelman, John, MA   Head*
Kenworthy, Joanne N., MA   Sr. Lectr.
Lee, M.   Sr. Lectr.
Pitts, Gerard A., BA   Sr. Lectr.
Simpson, John, MA   Sr. Lectr.

Sociology

Fax: (0181) 590 7799

Butler, Timothy S. C., MA PhD   Principal Lectr.
Cannon, R. J., MA   Sr. Lectr.
Chamberlayne, Prudence M., MSc PhD   Principal Lectr.
Filtzer, Donald, PhD   Sr. Lectr.
Grimwood, Cordelia, MPhil   Sr. Lectr.
Grundy, Alan D.   Sr. Lectr.
Harrison, Prof. Barbara   Head*
Kelly, Aidan, MA   Principal Lectr.
Kirton, D.   Sr. Lectr.
Noble, Denise E., BA   Sr. Lectr.
Sims, Lionel D., MA MSc   Sr. Lectr.
Virdee, G., BA   Sr. Lectr.

White, Alan P., BA PhD   Sr. Lectr.

Surveying, School of

Fax: (0181) 849 2918

Brimicombe, Allan, PhD   Head*
Brown, Graham M., BSc   Principal Lectr.
Bullard, Richard K., MSc PhD, FRICS   Reader
Dare, Peter J., BSc   Sr. Lectr.
Dixon-Gough, Robert W.   Sr. Lectr.
Fisher, Roger   Principal Lectr.
Gorham, Prof. Barry J., MSc PhD   Reader
Hobbs, Frank   Sr. Lectr.
Hollinshead, Graham H.   Sr. Lectr.
Home, Robert K., MA PhD   Sr. Lectr.
Huang, Yi Dong   Sr. Lectr.
Latham, Richard J., BSc   Sr. Lectr.
Ralphs, Martin
Whitehouse, Sharon   Sr. Lectr.
Whiting, Brian M., BSc PhD, FRAS   Sr. Lectr.

SPECIAL CENTRES, ETC

Access and Advice

Fax: (0181) 849 3477

Chiswick, Lynne, MSc   Principal Lectr.; Head*
Clark, Stephanie J.   Sr. Lectr.
Wailey, Anthony P., PhD   Sr. Lectr.

Antibody and Cell Biology Research Unit

Melamed, Mark, MSc PhD   Dir.*

Chemotherapy Research Unit (CRU)

Fax: (0181) 555 1971

Edwards, Prof. David I., PhD, FRSChem   Dir.*

Cognitive Neuropsychology Research Unit

Fax: (0181) 849 3697

Burton, Andrew, BA PhD   Dir.*

Environmental Science Research Unit

Harris, James A., PhD   Dir.*

Industrial Metrology Research Unit (IMRU)

Fax: (0181) 849 2918

Gorham, Prof. Barry J., MSc PhD   Dir.*

Information Technology

Fax: (0181) 590 7799

Beaver, Rae E.   Sr. Lectr.

Boden, K. G.   Sr. Lectr.
Diss, Jacqueline, BSc   Sr. Lectr.
Gowers, Kenneth G., BSc   Sr. Lectr.
Hooker, Alan A.   Sr. Lectr.
Jones, A. B.   Sr. Lectr.

Media Communications Research Unit

Fax: (0181) 849 3697

Berry, Colin, BSc PhD   Dir.*
Clifford, Brian R., BA MSc   Dir.*

Microbial Technology Research Group

Rowley, David, PhD   Dir.*

Neuropharmacology Research Group

Morinan, Alun, PhD   Dir.*

New Ethnicities Research Group

Fax: (0181) 590 7799

Cohen, Philip   Dir.*

Paleobiology Research Unit

Boulter, Prof. Michael, BSc PhD, FGS   Dir.*

Parasitology Research Unit

Humber, David, PhD   Dir.*

Plant Biotechnology Research Group

Roberts, Andrew V., BSc PhD   Dir.*

Recreation and Sports Studies

Fax: (0181) 590 7799

Ryder, Bernard R.   Head*
Yates, Michael S.   Sr. Lectr.

Student Services

Fax: (0181) 590 7799

Hoskins, W. Donald, PhD   Principal Lectr.
MacArthur, Iain R. M., BA MSc   Head*
Wyatt, Maggie   Sr. Lectr.

CONTACT OFFICERS

Academic affairs. Vice-Chancellor: Gould, Prof. Frank W., BA Lond., MA NSW
Accommodation. Residential Services Manager: Salmon, Roberta
Adult/continuing education. Head of Access and Advice Unit: Chiswick, Lynne, MSc
Alumni. Alumni Officer: Minshaw, Graham
Archives. Dye, Paul, MSc
Careers. Head of Careers Service: Francis, Anne
Computing services. Head of Information Technology: Freimanis, Al

Consultancy services. Laycock, Martyn
Equal opportunities. Secretary and Registrar: Ingle, Alan, BA
Estates and buildings/works and services. Director of Finance and Estates: Fowlie, Derek
Examinations. Secretary and Registrar: Ingle, Alan, BA
Finance. Director of Finance and Estates: Fowlie, Derek
General enquiries. Secretary and Registrar: Ingle, Alan, BA
International office. Head of International Office: Parry, Graham
Library (chief librarian). Head of Learning Support Services/Librarian: Doust, Janet, BA MA
Minorities/disadvantaged groups. Special Needs Advisor: Parker, Viv, BA
Personnel/human resources. Head of Personnel Services: Beeton, Sheila, MSc
Public relations, information and marketing. Head of Communications and Publicity: Hodgson, Christine, MA
Publications. Head of Communications and Publicity: Hodgson, Christine, MA
Purchasing. Nash, Theresa
Quality assurance and accreditation. Head, Quality Assurance Unit: Burrows, Alison
Research. Senior Administrative Officer: Woodhouse, David
Safety. Secretary and Registrar: Ingle, Alan, BA
Scholarships, awards, loans. Secretary and Registrar: Ingle, Alan, BA
Schools liaison. Schools and Colleges Liaison Officer: Sorrell, Patrick, BSc MPhil
Security. Director of Finance and Estates: Fowlie, Derek
Sport and recreation. Head of Recreation and Sports Studies: Ryder, Bernard, BSc
Staff development and training. Head of Personnel Services: Beeton, Sheila, MSc
Student union. Secretary and Registrar: Ingle, Alan, BA
Student welfare/counselling. Academic Secretary: Millard, Sheila
Students with disabilities. Special Needs Advisor: Parker, Viv, BA
University press. Head of Communications and Publicity: Hodgson, Christine, MA

[Information supplied by the institution as at 11 February 1998, and edited by the ACU]

UNIVERSITY OF EDINBURGH

Founded 1583

Member of the Association of Commonwealth Universities

Postal Address: Old College, South Bridge, Edinburgh, Scotland EH8 9YL
Telephone: (0131) 650 1000 **Fax**: (0131) 650 2147 **Cables**: University, Edinburgh **Telex**: 727442 (UNIVED G)
WWW: http://www.ed.ac.uk

CHANCELLOR—Edinburgh, H.R.H. The Duke of, KG, KT, OM, GBE, Hon. LLD *Edin.*, Hon. LLD *Malta*, Hon. LLD
   Wales, Hon. DSc *Delhi*, Hon. DSc *Salf.*, Hon. Dr *RCA*, FRS
PRINCIPAL AND VICE-CHANCELLOR*—Sutherland, Prof. Sir Stewart, BA *Camb.*, MA *Aberd.*, MA *Camb.*, Hon. LHD
   Wooster, Hon. LHD *Virginia*, Hon. LLD *Aberd.*, Hon. LLD *N.U.I.*, Hon. DLitt *Richmond Coll.*, Hon. DLitt *Wales*, Hon. Dr
   Uppsala, Hon. Dr *N.Y.*, FBA, FRSEd
VICE-PRINCIPAL—Bell, Prof. Colin, BA *Keele*, MScEcon *Wales*, FRSEd
VICE-PRINCIPAL—Ibbett, Prof. Roland N., MSc PhD, FRSEd
VICE-PRINCIPAL—Anderson, Prof. Michael, MA *Camb.*, PhD, FBA, FRSEd
VICE-PRINCIPAL—Field, G. Richard, BSc *Lond.*, PhD *Lond.*
RECTOR—Colquhoun, John
LIBRARIAN/UNIVERSITY LIBRARIAN—Mowatt, Ian R. M., BPhil MA, FLA
SECRETARY TO THE UNIVERSITY‡—Lowe, Martin J. B., BSc *St And.*, PhD *St And.*
DEPUTY SECRETARY—Cornish, Melvyn, BSc *Leic.*
DEPUTY SECRETARY—Longstaff, F. M., BA *Birm.*, MA *Well.*
DIRECTOR OF FINANCE—Sutherland, George O.
DIRECTOR OF ESTATES AND BUILDINGS—Currie, A., FRICS
DIRECTOR OF PERSONNEL—Wallace, Christina E., BA *Stir.*

GENERAL INFORMATION

History. The university was originally
founded in 1583 as the College of Edinburgh,
or Tounis College, by the town council of
Edinburgh under the charter of King James VI.

Admission to first degree courses (see also
United Kingdom Introduction). Through
Universities and Colleges Admission Service
(UCAS).

First Degrees (see also United Kingdom
Directory to Subjects of Study). BA, BArch,
BCom, BD, BEng, BMus, BSc, BScMedSci,
BScSocSci, BScVetSc, BTech, BVM&S, LLB, MA,
MB ChB, MEng.

Higher Degrees (see also United Kingdom
Directory to Subjects of Study). LLM, MA
(offered at Moray House Institute), MBA, MEd,
MLitt, MMus, MPhil, MRes, MSc, MSW, MTh,
PhD, DD, DDS, DLitt, DMus, DPsychol, DSc,
DVM&S, LLD, MD.
   Applicants for admission to master's degrees
must normally hold an appropriate first degree
with at least second class honours, or have
appropriate equivalent professional experience.
PhD: at least upper second class honours; DDS,
MD, DPsychol, DVM&S: awarded on
submission of a thesis; DD, DLitt, DMus, DSc,
LLD: awarded on published work.
   Taught master's: 1 year full-time of 2–6
years part-time; MPhil/MLitt: 2 years full-time
or 3–5 years part-time; PhD: 3 years full-time
or 4–6 years part-time.

Libraries. 2,369,535 volumes; 9541
periodicals subscribed to. Special collections
include: Drummond (archaeology and
geography); Erskine (medical); New College
(divinity); Reid (music); Darwin (biological
sciences).

Fees (1998–99, annual). Home
undergraduate students: £1000 (all courses).
International undergraduate and postgraduate
students: £6780 (arts (some postgraduate
courses have separate fees)); £8910 (science);
£16,200 (clinical/medicine).

Academic Year (1998–99). Three terms: 8
October–18 December; 11 January–19 March;
20 April–25 June.

Income (1996–97). Total, £226,050,000.

Statistics. Staff: 2589 (2094 academic, 495
administrative). Students: full-time 15,924;
part-time 1921; international 2965.

FACULTIES/SCHOOLS

Arts
Tel: (0131) 650 3568 Fax: (0131) 650 6536
Dean: Dow, Frances D., DPhil *York(UK)*, MA,
   FRHistS
Secretary: Rodgers, P. A., MA

Divinity
Tel: (0131) 650 8900 Fax: (0131) 650 6579
Dean: Forrester, Rev. Prof. Duncan B., MA
   St.And., DPhil *Sus.*, BD
Secretary: McGuire, Paul F., BA *NE*, MBA *Exe.*

Education
Dean: Kirk, Prof. Gordon, MA *Glas.*, MEd *Glas.*,
   PhD

Law
Tel: (0131) 650 2006 Fax: (0131) 662 4902
Dean: Usher, Prof. John A., LLB *Newcastle(UK)*
Secretary: Bell, W. A.

Medicine
Tel: (0131) 650 3192 Fax: (0131) 650 6525
Dean: Bird, Prof. C. C., MB ChB *Glas.*, PhD
   Glas., FRCPath, FRCPEd, FRSEd, FRCSEd
Secretary: Mackay, S. M., MA *St And.*

Music
Tel: (0131) 650 2427 Fax: (0131) 650 2425
Dean: Kimbell, Prof. David R. B., MA *Oxf.*,
   DPhil *Oxf.*
Secretary: Godwin, Lenora J., BA

Science and Engineering
Tel: (0131) 650 5759 Fax: (0131) 650 5738
Dean: Boulton, Prof. Geoffrey S., PhD *Birm.*,
   DSc *Birm.*, FRS, FRSEd
Secretary: ......

Social Sciences
Tel: (0131) 650 4088 Fax: (0131) 650 6512
Dean: Cohen, Prof. A. P., BA *S'ton.*, MSc *S'ton.*,
   PhD *S'ton.*, FRSEd
Secretary: Hulme, J. E., MA

Veterinary Medicine
Tel: (0131) 650 6130 Fax: (0131) 650 6511
Dean: Miller, Prof. Hugh R. P., BVMS *Glas.*,
   PhD *Glas.*

Secretary: Hackel, J.

ACADEMIC UNITS

Accounting and Business Method
Tel: (0131) 650 8335 Fax: (0131) 650 8337
Hatherley, D. J., BSc *Wales*, MAcc *Glas.*,
   FCA   Prof., Accounting
Lapsley, I. McL., BCom PhD   Prof.,
   Accountancy; Head*
Llewellyn, S. E., BA *CNAA*, MSc *Stir.*   Sr. Lectr.
Macleod, J. S., LLM *Glas.*   Hon. Prof.
Marrian, I.   Visiting Prof.
McDougall, Alex B., BSc   Visiting Prof.
Mitchell, F., BCom   Prof., Management
   Accounting
Walker, S. P., BA *Kent*, PhD   Sr. Lectr.
Yoshikawa, T.   Visiting Prof.
Other Staff: 5 Lectrs.; 1 Res. Assoc.
Research: auditing; management accounting;
   public sector accounting

African Studies, Centre of
Tel: (0131) 650 3878 Fax: (0131) 650 6535
Allen, C. H., MA *Oxf.*   Sr. Lectr., Politics
Barnard, Alan J., BA MA PhD   Reader, Social
   Anthropology
Griffiths, Anne, LLB PhD   Sr. Lectr., Private
   Law
Jedrej, M. C., MA PhD   Sr. Lectr., Social
   Anthropology
King, Kenneth J., BA *Camb.*, PhD   Prof.
   Institute for the Study of Education and
   Society
Neff, Stephen C., AB LLM   Sr. Lectr., Public
   International Law
Nugent, Paul C., BA *Cape Town*, MA *Lond.*, PhD
   Lond.   Sr. Lectr., History
Walls, Andrew F., OBE, MA *Oxf.*, BLitt *Oxf.*,
   DD   Hon. Prof. Centre for the Study of
   Christianity in the non-Western World
Other Staff: 8 Lectrs.

Anatomy
Tel: (0131) 650 3111 Fax: (0131) 650 6545
Bard, Jonathan, MA *Camb.*, PhD *Manc.*   Reader
Findlater, G. S., BSc PhD   Sr. Lectr.
Glasby, M. A., MA *Camb.*, MSc *Oxf.*, BM BCh
   Oxf., FRCS, FRCSEd   Reader
Kaufman, M. H., MA *Camb.*, PhD *Camb.*, MB
   ChB DSc, FRCPEd   Prof.
Kristmundsdottir, BSc PhD   Sr. Lectr.
Shaw, J. P., BDS PhD   Sr. Lectr.; Head*
Other Staff: 4 Lectrs.; 3 Res. Assocs.

Research: comparative anatomy; embryology; histology; mammalian development; topographical anatomy

Archaeology

Tel: (0131) 650 2501 Fax: (0131) 662 4094

Bonsall, J. C., BA *Sheff.*   Sr. Lectr.
Harding, D. W., MA *Oxf.*, DPhil *Oxf.*, FRSEd   Abercromby Prof.
Midgley, Magdalena S., MA PhD   Sr. Lectr.
Peltenburg, E. J., BA *Birm.*, PhD *Birm.*, FSA   Prof.
Ralston, I. B. M., MA PhD   Sr. Lectr.
Watkins, T. F., BA *Birm.*, PhD *Birm.*, FSA   Sr. Lectr.; Head*
Other Staff: 1 Lectr.; 2 Res. Fellows
Research: aerial photography; artefact analysis; early development of industry in Scotland; environmental reconstruction; landscape archaeology

Architecture

Tel: (0131) 650 2306 Fax: (0131) 650 8019

Coyne, A. R., BArch PhD   Prof., Architecture Computing
Filor, S. W.   Sr. Lectr.
Gilmour, A.   Sr. Lectr.
Macdonald, A. J., BSc PhD   Sr. Lectr.; Head*
McLachlan, F., MA   Sr. Lectr.
Pedreschi, R. F., BSc *Strath.*, PhD   Sr. Lectr.
Raman, P. G., BArch *Madr.*, PhD   Sr. Lectr.
Russell, T. M., BArch *Sheff.*, PhD *Sheff.*   Sr. Lectr.
Talbot, R. D., BSc *Sheff.*, PhD   Sr. Lectr.
Whyte, I. B., BA *Nott.*, MPhil *Nott.*, MA *Leeds*, PhD *Camb.*   Prof., Architectural History
Other Staff: 6 Lectrs.; 1 Res. Assoc.
Vacant Posts: Forbes Prof.

Art (Fine Art)

Tel: (0131) 650 4124 Fax: (0131) 650 6638

Bury, K. M., MA *Camb.*, MA *Lond.*   Sr. Lectr.
Campbell, Jean P., MA PhD   Sr. Lectr.
Cowling, Elizabeth G., BA *Oxf.*, MA *Lond.*   Sr. Lectr.
Dallapiccola, Anna L.   Hon. Prof.
Hammer, Martin A., BA *Lond.*
Higgitt, J. C., MA *Oxf.*, MA *Lond.*, FSA   Sr. Lectr.; Head*
Hillenbrand, R., MA *Camb.*, DPhil *Oxf.*, FRSEd   Prof., Islamic Art
Howarth, D. J., MA *Camb.*, PhD *Camb.*   Sr. Lectr.
Jones, M., MA   Hon. Prof.
Macmillan, J. D., MA *St And.*, PhD   Prof., History of Scottish Art
Tarr, Roger P., MA *Oxf.*   Sr. Lectr.
Thomson, Richard, BA MA PhD   Watson Gordon Prof.
Tolley, T. S., BA *E.Anglia*, PhD *E.Anglia*   Sr. Lectr.
Other Staff: 4 Hon. Fellows

Astronomy, see Phys. and Astron.

Biochemistry

Tel: (0131) 650 3717 Fax: (0131) 650 3711

Apps, D. K., MA *Camb.*, PhD *Camb.*   Reader
Ashley, R. H., MB BS *Lond.*, MSc PhD   Sr. Lectr.
Boyd, A., BSc *Leeds*, PhD *Leic.*   Sr. Lectr.
James, Allan, BSc PhD   Reader
Nimmo, I. A., MA *Camb.*, PhD   Sr. Lectr.; Head*
Phillips, J. H., MA *Camb.*, PhD *Camb.*   Prof., Biology Teaching
Sawyer, Lindsay, BSc PhD, FRSChem   Sr. Lectr.
van Heyningen, S., MA *Camb.*, PhD *Camb.*, FRSChem   Sr. Lectr.; Dir., Biol. Teaching Orgn.
Walkinshaw, M. D., BSc PhD   Prof., Structural Biochemistry
Other Staff: 3 Lectrs.; 1 Univ. Fellow; 1 Sr. Res. Fellow; 6 Res. Fellows; 7 Res. Assocs.; 1 Hon. Sr. Lectr.; 7 Hon. Fellows
Vacant Posts: 1 Prof.

Research: characterisation of ion channels; mechanism of secretion and protein traffic in eukaryotic cells; structure and function of chromatin and the cytoskeleton; structure, assembly and function of biological macromolecules

Biological Sciences, Division of, see Cell and Molecular Biol., Inst. of.; Cell, Animal and Population Biol., Inst. of.; and Ecol. and Resource Management, Inst. of

Business Studies, see also Acctg. and Bus. Method

Tel: (0131) 650 3826 Fax: (0131) 668 3053

Adams, Andrew T., BSc MSc   Sr. Lectr.
Ansell, J. I., MSc PhD   Sr. Lectr.
Coke, S., MA *Oxf.*   Morrison Prof., International Business
Crook, J. N., BA *Lanc.*, MSc *Wales*   Reader
Dawson, J. A., BSc *Lond.*, MPhil *Lond.*, PhD *Nott.*   Prof., Marketing; Head*
Draper, Paul, BA *Exe.*, MA *Reading*, PhD *Stir.*   Prof., Finance and Investment
Fleck, J., MSc *Manc.*, MA BSc   Prof., Organisation of Industry and Commerce
Glen, J. J., BSc *Glas.*, MSc *Strath.*, PhD   Sr. Lectr.
Henley, J. S., BSc *Lond.*, PhD *Lond.*   Prof., International Management
Kerley, Richard, BA   Sr. Lectr.
McCrone, Gavin, CB, MA *Camb.*, MSc *Wales*, PhD *Glas.*, Hon. LLD *Glas.*, FRSEd   Visiting Prof.
McCue, Joseph A., BA   Visiting Prof.
Molina, A. H., MPhil PhD   Reader
Terry, N. G., BSc *Hull*, MSocSc *Birm.*, MPhil *Bath*   Sr. Lectr.
Thomas, L. C., MA *Oxf.*, DPhil *Oxf.*, FRSEd   Prof., Management Science
Thompson, Paul, BA *Liv.*, PhD *Liv.*   Prof., Management
White, P. J., BA *Strath.*, MSc *Strath.*   Sr. Lectr.
Other Staff: 20 Lectrs.; 1 Univ. Fellow; 1 Res. Fellow; 2 Res. Assocs.; 5 Hon. Fellows
Research: finance, business economics and international management; management of innovation and technology; management science; marketing; organisational studies and industrial behaviour

Canadian Studies, Centre of

Tel: (0131) 650 4129 Fax: (0131) 650 4130

Coates, Colin M., BA MA PhD   Lectr.; Dir.*
Martin, G. W., MA *Camb.*, PhD *Camb.*   Prof.

Cell and Molecular Biology, Institute of (ICMB)

Tel: (0131) 650 5366 Fax: (0131) 668 8650

Beggs, Jean D., BSc PhD   Prof. Fellow
Bird, A. P., BSc *Sus.*, PhD, FRS, FRSEd   Buchanan Prof., Genetics
Bond, D. J., BSc *Wales*, PhD *Camb.*   Sr. Lectr.
Bownes, Mary, BSc *Sus.*, DPhil *Sus.*   Prof., Developmental Biology
Coulson, A. F. W., MA *Oxf.*, DPhil *Oxf.*   Sr. Lectr.
Deacon, J. W., BSc *Hull*, PhD *Camb.*   Sr. Lectr.
Donachie, W. D., BSc *Birm.*, PhD   Prof., Bacterial Genetics
Earnshaw, W., BA *Colby*, PhD *M.I.T.*   Prof. Fellow
Fantes, P. A., MA *Camb.*, PhD *Leic.*   Reader
Finnegan, D. J., BSc *Adel.*, PhD   Prof., Molecular Genetics; Head*
Fry, S. C., BSc *Leic.*, PhD *Leic.*, FRSEd   Prof., Plant Biochemistry
Hayward, R. S., BSc *Belf.*, PhD *Belf.*   Sr. Lectr.
Henderson, D. M., CBE, BSc, FRSEd, FLS   Hon. Prof.
Ingram, D. S., BSc MA PhD ScD, FIBiol, FLS, FRSEd   Hon. Prof.
Kilbey, B. J., BSc *Lond.*, PhD *Lond.*, DSc, FRSEd   Reader
Masters, Millicent, BS *Queens, N.Y.*, MS *Calif.*, PhD *Calif.*   Reader
Melton, D. W., MA *Camb.*, PhD *Camb.*   Reader

Murray, Sir Kenneth, BSc PhD, FRCPath, FRS, FRSEd   Res. Prof., Molecular Biology
Murray, Noreen, BSc *Lond.*, PhD *Birm.*, FRS, FRSEd   Prof., Molecular Genetics
Read, N. D., BSc PhD   Reader
Reid, G. A., PhD *Dund.*, BSc   Reader
Smith, P. M., BSc *Birm.*, PhD *Birm.*   Sr. Lectr.
Smith, S. M., BSc *Leic.*, MA *Indiana*, PhD *Warw.*   Sr. Lectr.
Sutherland, I. W., PhD DSc   Prof., Microbial Physiology
Trewavas, A. J., BSc *Lond.*, PhD *Lond.*, FRSEd   Prof., Plant Biochemistry
Other Staff: 8 Lectrs.; 1 Endowment Fellow; 4 Sr. Res. Fellows; 48 Res. Fellows; 25 Res. Assocs.; 14 Hon. Fellows
Vacant Posts: Regius Prof. (Bot.)
Research: eukaryotic molecular genetics; gene expression and development; plant physiology and biochemistry; prokaryotic molecular genetics; structure and function of macromolecules

Cell, Animal and Population Biology, Institute of (ICAPB)

Tel: (0131) 650 5454 Fax: (0131) 650 6564

Barton, N. H., BA *Camb.*, PhD *E.Anglia*, FRS   Prof. Fellow
Bulfield, G. J., BSc *Leeds*, PhD, FRSEd   Hon. Prof.
Corbet, P. S., BSc *Reading*, DSc *Reading*, PhD *Camb.*, ScD *Camb.*, FRSEd, FIBiol   Hon. Prof.
Cosens, D. J., BSc *Durh.*, PhD *Durh.*   Sr. Lectr.
Deag, J. M., BSc *Leic.*, PhD *Brist.*   Sr. Lectr.
French, V. K., BSc *Sus.*, DPhil *Sus.*   Sr. Lectr.
Hill, W. G., BSc *Lond.*, MS *Calif.*, PhD DSc, FRSEd, FRS   Prof., Animal Genetics; Head, Div. of Biol. Scis.
Illius, A. W., PhD *Nott.*, BSc   Sr. Lectr.
Inchley, C. J., BSc PhD   Sr. Lectr.
Jones, K. W., BSc PhD   Reader
Jones, P. J., BSc *Exe.*, DPhil *Oxf.*   Sr. Lectr.
Leigh-Brown, A. J., BSc *Lond.*, PhD *Leic.*   Reader
Maddy, A. H., MSc *Lond.*, PhD *Lond.*   Sr. Lectr.
Maizels, R. M., BSc PhD   Prof., Zoology; Head*
McBride, J. S., MSc PhD   Sr. Lectr.
Preston, P., BSc PhD   Sr. Lectr.
Rogers, M. E., MA *Oxf.*, MS *Yale*, PhD *Yale*   Sr. Lectr.
Saunders, D. S., BSc *Lond.*, PhD *Lond.*   Prof., Insect Physiology
Truman, D. E. S., BA *Camb.*, PhD *Camb.*, FIBiol   Sr. Lectr.
Walliker, D., BA *Oxf.*, PhD *Lond.*   Hon. Prof.
Other Staff: 4 Lectrs.; 2 Sr. Res. Fellows; 23 Res. Fellows; 19 Res. Assocs.; 1 Hon. Sr. Lectr.; 19 Hon. Fellows
Research: behaviour; ecology; genetics; immunology; physiology

Celtic

Tel: (0131) 650 3622 Fax: (0131) 650 3626

Black, R. I., MA *Glas.*   Sr. Lectr.
Gillies, W., BA *Oxf.*, MA, FRSEd   Prof.; Head*
Other Staff: 2 Lectrs.; 3 Hon. Fellows
Research: Celtic language and peoples; early Irish art and literature; Gaelic and Irish literature

Chemistry

Tel: (0131) 650 4742 Fax: (0131) 650 4743

Baxter, R. L., BSc *Glas.*, PhD *Glas.*   Reader
Chapman, Stephen K., BSc *Newcastle(UK)*, PhD *Newcastle(UK)*   Prof., Biological Inorganic Chemistry
Donovan, Robert J., BSc *Wales*, PhD *Camb.*, FRSChem, FRSEd   Prof., Physical Chemistry
Farmer, John G., BSc *Glas.*, PhD *Glas.*, FRSChem   Sr. Lectr.
Flitsch, Sabina L., MA *Oxf.*, DPhil *Oxf.*   Reader
Fluendy, M. A. D., MA *Oxf.*, DPhil *Oxf.*, DSc, FRSChem, FRSEd   Reader
Gosney, Ian, BSc *ANU*, PhD *ANU*   Reader
Gould, R. O., BA *Mass.*, PhD *St And.*, FRSChem   Reader
Harrison, Andrew, MA *Oxf.*, DPhil *Oxf.*   Reader

Langridge-Smith, P. R. R., BSc Brist., PhD Brist. Reader
Lawley, Kenneth, MA Oxf., DPhil Oxf. Reader
McDougall, G. S., BSc E.Anglia, PhD Glas. Sr. Lectr.
McKendrick, Kenneth G., DPhil Oxf., BSc Sr. Lectr.
McNab, Hamish, BSc St And., PhD St And. Reader
Paton, R. Michael, BSc St And., PhD St And. Reader
Ramage, Robert, PhD Glas., DSc Glas., MSc, FRSChem, FRSEd, FRS Forbes Prof., Organic Chemistry; Head*
Rankin, David W. H., MA Camb., PhD Camb., FRSEd Prof., Structural Chemistry
Sadler, Ian H., BSc Lond., PhD Lond. Reader
Sadler, Peter J., MA Oxf., DPhil Oxf. Crum Brown Prof.
Sharp, J. T., PhD Lond., DSc Lond., FRSChem Reader
Tasker, Peter A., MA MA DPhil, FRSChem Prof., Industrial Chemistry
Tennant, George, BSc Glas., PhD Glas., FRSChem, FRSEd Reader
Turner, Nick, BSc DPhil Reader
Yellowlees, Lesley J., BSc PhD Sr. Lectr.
Other Staff: 10 Lectrs.; 1 Sr. Res. Fellow; 1 Univ. Fellow; 24 Res. Fellows; 8 Res. Assocs.; 2 Hon. Lectrs.; 8 Hon. Fellows

Chinese, see E. Asian Studies

Classics

Tel: (0131) 650 3582

Davies, Glenys M., BA Lond., PhD Lond. Sr. Lectr.
Hood, Allan B. E., MA St And., BPhil Oxf. Sr. Lectr.
Howie, J. Gordon, MA Glas. Sr. Lectr.
Nicoll, W. S. M., MA Camb., PhD Camb. Sr. Lectr.; Head*
Richardson, John S., MA DPhil, FRSEd Prof.
Ridgway, D. W. R., BA Lond., FSA Reader
Rutter, N. K., MA Camb., PhD Lond. Sr. Lectr.
Strachan, J. C. G., MA Sr. Lectr.
Other Staff: 4 Lectrs.; 1 Univ. Fellow; 3 Hon. Fellows

Cognitive Science, Computer Science,
see under Engin. and Informatics, Sch. of

Continuing Education, Centre for

Tel: (0131) 650 4400 Fax: (0131) 667 6097

Gillen, C., BSc Glas., BA Open(UK), MEd Aberd., PhD Glas., FGS Sr. Lectr.
Macdonald, Murdo J. S., MA PhD Sr. Lectr.
Miller, J., BSc Manc., PhD Manc. Sr. Lectr.
Schuller, T. E., MA Oxf. Prof.; Dir.*
Other Staff: 4 Lectrs.; 2 Lectrs.†

Criminology, see Law and Society

Curriculum Studies (Arts and Humanities)

Aldridge, Jeffrey P., BA Durh. Sr. Lectr.
Carver, David, MA Camb., MEd Edin. Sr. Lectr.
Martin, Brian, BA Essex, MEd Edin. Sr. Lectr.
Mills, Marion Sr. Lectr.
Starsmeare, David, BA Wales Sr. Lectr.
Wallace, Michael J., MA Glas., MLitt Edin., PhD Edin. Sr. Lectr.

Curriculum Studies (Science, Technology, Mathematics and Computing)

Tel: (0131) 651 6046 Fax: (0131) 557 5430

Baptie, Robin, MA Edin., MSc H-W Sr. Lectr.
Barrett, Peter J., BA Open(UK) Sr. Lectr.
Conlon, Tom, BSc Lond., MSc Glas., PhD Sr. Lectr.
Frame, John, BA Stir., MSc Sr. Lectr.
Goldie, Margaret Sr. Lectr.
Long, Allison E. Sr. Lectr.
Quickfall, Michael, BSc Manc., BA Open(UK), BA Edin. Sr. Lectr.
Thomson, David Sr. Lectr.
van der Kuyl, Anthony, MA Dund. Sr. Lectr.

Divinity

Tel: (0131) 650 8900 Fax: (0131) 650 6579

Auld, Rev. A. Graeme, BD Aberd., MA Aberd., PhD Aberd., DLitt Aberd. Prof., Hebrew Bible
Brown, S. J., BA Ill., MA Chic., PhD Chic. Prof., Ecclesiastical History
Forrester, Rev. Duncan B., MA St And., DPhil Sus., BD Prof., Christian Ethics
Hayman, A. P., BA Durh., PhD Durh. Sr. Lectr.
Hurtado, L. W., MA PhD Prof., New Testament Language, Literature and Theology
Kee, A. A., MA Glas., BD Glas., STM U.T.S.(N.Y.), PhD N.Y. Prof., Religious Studies
Kerr, D. A., BA MA DPhil Prof., Christianity in non-Western World
Lyall, Rev. D., STM Yale, BSc BD PhD Sr. Lectr.
Mackey, J. P., BA N.U.I., LPh Maynooth, DD Maynooth, STL Maynooth, PhD Belf. Prof., Theology
McDonald, Rev. J. Ian H., MA Glas., BD Glas., MTh Glas., PhD Reader
Mealand, David L., MA Oxf., MLitt Brist., PhD Sr. Lectr.
Northcott, M. S., BA Durh., MA Durh., PhD CNAA Sr. Lectr.
Page, Rev. Ruth, MA St And., BD Otago, DPhil Oxf. Sr. Lectr.
Ross, Rev. Andrew C., STM U.T.S.(N.Y.), MA BD PhD, FRHistS Sr. Lectr.
Sutherland, Sir Stewart, BA Camb., MA Aberd., MA Camb., Hon. LHD Wooster, Hon. LHD Virginia, Hon. LLD Aberd., Hon. LLD N.U.I., Hon. DLitt Richmond Coll., Hon. Dr Uppsala, FBA Prof., Philosophy of Religion
Templeton, Rev. D. A., BA Camb., BD Glas., PhD Glas. Sr. Lectr.
Vanhoozer, K. J., PhD Camb., BA MDiv Sr. Lectr.
Walls, A. F., OBE, MA Oxf., BLitt Oxf. Hon. Prof., Christianity in non-Western World
Whaling, F., MA Camb., ThD Harv., PhD Prof., Study of Religion
Wright, D. F., MA Camb. Sr. Lectr.
Wyatt, Rev. N., BA BD MTh PhD Sr. Lectr.
Other Staff: 9 Lectrs.; 1 Sr. Lectr.†; 1 Lectr.†; 3 Hon. Fellows

East Asian Studies

Tel: (0131) 650 4227 Fax: (0131) 651 1258

Astley, Ian, BA DPhil Sr. Lectr.
McDougall, Bonnie S., MA Syd., PhD Syd. Prof., Chinese; Head*
Other Staff: 4 Lectrs.; 2 Hon. Fellows

Ecology and Resource Management, Institute of

Tel: (0131) 535 4051, 650 6708 Fax: (0131) 667 2601, 662 0478

Appleby, Michael C., BSc Brist., PhD Camb. Sr. Lectr.
Atkinson, David, BSc PhD, FIBiol Hon. Prof.
Bulfield, G. J., BSc Leeds, PhD, FRSEd Hon. Prof.
Cannell, Melvin G. R., DSc PhD Hon. Prof.
Ennos, Richard, MA Camb., PhD Liv. Sr. Lectr.
Grace, J., BSc Sheff., PhD Sheff., FRSEd Prof., Environmental Biology
Hanley, Nick, BA Stir., PhD Newcastle(UK) Prof., Agricultural Resource Management
Heal, O. W., BSc Durh., PhD Durh., FIBiol Hon. Prof.
Hillman, J. R., BSc Wales, PhD Wales, FLS, FIBiol, FRSEd Hon. Prof.
Hinks, C. E., BSc Newcastle(UK), PhD Newcastle(UK) Sr. Lectr.
Hughes, Gareth, BA York(UK), DPhil York(UK) Sr. Lectr.
Jarvis, P. G., MA Oxf., PhD Sheff., FilDr Uppsala, FRSEd, FIBiol Prof., Forestry and Natural Resources
Last, Fred, PhD Lond., DSc Lond., FRSEd Hon. Prof.
Maxwell, T. J., BSc PhD Hon. Prof.
Moncrieff, J. B., BSc Nott., PhD Nott. Reader

Monteith, J. L., BSc PhD Hon. DSc, FRS, FRSEd Hon. Prof.
Muetzelfeldt, R. I., BA Oxf., PhD Sr. Lectr.
Russell, Graham, BSc Nott., PhD Nott. Sr. Lectr.
Simmonds, N. W., ScD, FRSEd, FIBiol Hon. Prof.
Smith, Keith A., BSc Durh., PhD Reading
Thomas, P. C., BSc Wales, PhD Wales, FIBiol, FRSEd Hon. Prof.
Turner, M. R., BSc Reading, PhD Reading Sr. Lectr.
Whittemore, C. T., BSc Newcastle(UK), PhD Newcastle(UK), DSc, FIBiol, FRSEd Prof., Agriculture and Rural Economics; Head*
Wilson, Ronald M., BSc Glas., MSc Aberd., PhD Aberd. Sr. Lectr.
Other Staff: 14 Lectrs.; 10 Res. Fellows; 11 Res. Assocs.; 2 Hon. Sr. Lectrs.; 21 Hon. Lectrs.; 16 Hon. Fellows

Economics

Tel: (0131) 650 8361 Fax: (0131) 650 4514

Clark, S. J., MSc Lond., PhD Sr. Lectr.; Head*
Fransman, M. J., MA Witw., DPhil Sus. Prof.
George, Donald A. R., BSc Sus., BPhil Oxf. Sr. Lectr.
Hughes, G. A., BA PhD Hon. Prof.
Koop, Gary, PhD Tor. George Watson's and David Stewart's Prof., Political Economy
Main, Brian, BSc St And., MA St And., MBA Calif., PhD Calif. Prof.
Sayer, Stuart, BA Oxf., BPhil Oxf. Sr. Lectr.
Snell, A. J., BSc Hull, PhD Warw. Reader
Steel, Mark, BA Antwerp, MA Louvain, PhD Louvain Prof.
Other Staff: 5 Lectrs.; 1 Res. Assoc.; 1 Hon. Fellow

Education and Society

Tel: (0131) 651 6019 Fax: (0131) 651 6018

Cosford, Brian D., BSc(SocialSciences) S'ton., MPhil Sur. Sr. Lectr.
Draper, Janet M., BA Stir., MBA Edin. Sr. Lectr.
Jonathan, Ruth M., BA Liv., MA Leic., PhD Prof.
King, Kenneth J., BA Camb., PhD Prof., International and Comparative Education
Mallinson, Ian Sr. Lectr.
McLaughlin, Patrick, BA Stir., PhD Stir. Sr. Lectr.
McNie, Robert W., MA Edin., MEd Glas. Sr. Lectr.
Raffe, David J., BA Oxf., BPhil Oxf. Prof.
Sharp, Stephen, BA Sheff., MSc Stir., PhD Liv. Sr. Lectr.
Taylor, Warwick B., MA Chic., BA Sr. Lectr.

Education and Society, Institute for the Study of

Tel: (0131) 650 4211 Fax: (0131) 667 4335

Entwistle, N. J., BSc Sheff., PhD Aberd., FilDr Gothenburg, FBPsS Bell Prof.
Jonathan, Ruth M., BA Liv., MA Leic., PhD Prof., Educational Theory and Policy
King, Kenneth J., BA Camb., PhD Prof., International and Comparative Education
Roffe, David J., BA Oxf., BPhil Oxf. Prof., Sociology of Education; Co-Dir.*
Thomson, G. O. B., MEd Glas., MA PhD Prof., Educational Psychology; Co-Dir.*
Other Staff: 2 Lectrs.; 4 Res. Fellows; 1 Sr. Res. Assoc.; 5 Res. Assocs.; 1 Hon. Fellow

Education, Community

Tel: (0131) 651 6120 Fax: (0131) 557 3458

Kirkwood, Colin, MA Glas., MSc Sr. Lectr.
Martin, Ian S., BA MSc Sr. Lectr.
McCulloch, K. H., MEd Sr. Lectr.
Tett, Lyn, MEd H-W, BA Sr. Lectr.

Education, Higher and Further

Tel: (0131) 650 4131 Fax: (0131) 650 6956

Entwistle, Noel J., BSc Sheff., PhD Aberd., Hon. FilDr Gothenburg, FBPsS Prof.
Haywood, J., BSc PhD Sr. Lectr.
Hounsell, Dai, BA PhD Co-Dir.*

Education, Physical, Sport and Leisure Studies

Coalter, Fred, MSc   Sr. Lectr.
Collins, Dave, BEd Lond., MSc Penn.State, PhD Sur.   Prof.
Dunnett, Anne S. W. L., BA Edin., MSc Edin.   Sr. Lectr.
Early, Phyllis   Sr. Lectr.
Higgins, Peter, BSc Kent, MSc Lond., PhD Aberd.   Sr. Lectr.
Jackson, Lorna, BSc Glas., MEd Glas., MBA Edin.   Sr. Lectr.
Maile, Andrew J., BA Birm., MA Leeds   Sr. Lectr.
Reid, Andrew, MA Glas., MEd Glas.   Sr. Lectr.
Squire, Patrick J., MA Birm.   Sr. Lectr.
Williams, Arwyn M., BA Open(UK), MSc Sur.   Sr. Lectr.

Education, Special, see Equity Studies and Special Educn.

Educational Theory and Practice

Tel: (0131) 651 6430 Fax: (0131) 557 4962
Adams, Frank R., MEd Glas.   Sr. Lectr.
Cameron-Jones, Margot, MA Edin., MEd Edin.   Prof.
Carr, David, BA Leeds, MA Lond.   Reader
Fraser, Helen, MA Aberd.   Sr. Lectr.
Kidd, Jim, MA St And., MEd Dund., PhD Edin.   Sr. Lectr.
Munn, Pamela, MA Aberd., MLitt Aberd.   Prof.
Parton, N. T., BA Stir., MEd Stir.   Sr. Lectr.
Paterson, Lindsay, MA Aberd., PhD   Prof.
Skinner, Don, BSc Edin., MEd Edin.   Sr. Lectr.
Turner, David L., BA Open(UK), MEd Edin.   Sr. Lectr.

Engineering and Informatics, School of

Tel: (0131) 650 5736

Artificial Intelligence

Tel: (0131) 650 3090, 650 2700 Fax: (0131) 650 6899, 650 6516
Bishop, Christopher M., BA Oxf., PhD   Prof., Computer Science
Bundy, Alan R., BSc Leic., PhD Leic., FRSEd   Prof., Automated Reasoning
Fisher, Robert B., BS Cal.Tech., MS Stan., PhD   Sr. Lectr.
Hallam, John, MA Oxf., PhD   Sr. Lectr.
Mellish, C. S., BA Oxf., PhD   Reader
Pain, H. G., BA Wales, PhD   Sr. Lectr.
Ritchie, Graeme, BSc Dund., MA Essex, PhD   Lectr.
Ross, Peter, MA Camb., MSc Lond., PhD Lond.   Sr. Lectr.; Head*
Thompson, Henry S., MA Calif., MS Calif., PhD Calif.   Reader
Other Staff: 5 Lectrs.; 5 Res. Fellows; 2 Res. Assocs.; 5 Hon. Fellows
Research: automated reasoning; intelligent robotics; knowledge-based systems; natural language processing; non-symbolic artificial intelligence

Chemical Engineering

Tel: (0131) 650 4860 Fax: (0131) 650 6551
Bañares-Alcántara René, BS MS PhD   Reader
Christy, John R. E., MA Camb., PhD, FIChemE   Sr. Lectr.
Davidson, John M., BSc Lond., PhD Lond.   Sr. Lectr.
Glass, D. H., BSc Manc., PhD Camb., FIChemE   Sr. Lectr.; Head*
Metcalfe, Ian S., BSc MA PhD   Prof.
Ponton, J. W., BSc PhD, FIChemE   ICI Prof.
Pritchard, Colin L., MA Camb., PhD Delhi, FIChemE   Sr. Lectr.
Seaton, Nigel A., BSc PhD   Prof., Interfacial Engineering
Other Staff: 6 Lectrs.; 1 Lectr.†; 4 Res. Fellows; 4 Res. Assocs.; 1 Hon. Fellow
Research: advanced holographic techniques; catalysis; fluid dynamics; process intensification in biotechnology; safety engineering

Civil and Environmental Engineering

Tel: (0131) 650 5720, 650 5717 Fax: (0131) 650 6781
Drysdale, D. D., PhD Camb., BSc   Reader; Dir., Fire Safety Engin. Unit
Forde, Michael C., BEng Birm., MSc Birm., PhD Birm., FIEE   Tarmac Prof.; Head*
McConnachie, Gordon L., MSc Strath., BSc   Sr. Lectr.
Ooi, Jin Y., BEng Auck., PhD Syd.   Sr. Lectr.
Ponniah, D. A., BSc Ceyl., MEng Glas., PhD Glas.   Sr. Lectr.
Rotter, J. Michael, MA Camb., PhD Syd., FIEAust   Prof.
Sinha, Braj P., BSc Patna, PhD, FICE, FIStructE   Reader
Wardlaw, R. B., BSc Strath., PhD Strath.   Sr. Lectr.
Other Staff: 7 Lectrs.; 2 Univ. Fellows; 4 Res. Fellows; 2 Res. Assocs.; 5 Hon. Fellows

Cognitive Science, Centre for

Tel: (0131) 650 4667 Fax: (0131) 650 6626
Klein, E. H., BA Camb., MA Reading, PhD Camb.   Reader; Head*
Stenning, Keith, MA PhD   Prof., Human Communications
Willshaw, David, MA Camb., MSc Lond., PhD   Hon. Prof.
Other Staff: 4 Lectrs.; 8 Res. Fellows
Research: cognitive processing; logic and formal semantics; multimodal communication and virtual environments; natural language processing; neural networks and computational neuroscience

Computer Science

Tel: (0131) 650 5128 Fax: (0131) 667 7209
Abramsky, Samson, MA PhD   Prof., Theoretical Computer Science
Anderson, Stuart, BSc H-W   Sr. Lectr.
Brebner, Gordon, BSc PhD   Sr. Lectr.
Burstall, R. M., BA Camb., MSc Birm., PhD Birm., FRSEd   Prof.
Fourman, M. P., BSc Brist., MSc Oxf., DPhil Oxf.   Prof., Computer Systems/Software; Head*
Ibbett, Roland N., MSc PhD, FRSEd   Prof.
Jerrum, M. R., MA Camb., PhD   Reader
Plotkin, G. D., BSc Glas., PhD, FRS, FRSEd   Prof., Computation Theory
Pooley, R. J., BSc Brist., MSc Brad.   Sr. Lectr.
Rees, D. J., BSc Lond., PhD   Sr. Lectr.
Sannella, D. T., BSc Yale, MSc Calif., PhD   Reader
Stirling, C. P., MA Oxf., DPhil Oxf.   Prof., Computation Theory
Other Staff: 19 Lectrs.; 11 Res. Fellows; 4 Res. Assocs.; 1 Lectr.†; 7 Hon. Fellows
Research: communication protocols; computational complexity; computer architecture and systems; computer graphics; very large scale integration (VLSI)

Electrical Engineering

Tel: (0131) 650 5565 Fax: (0131) 650 6554
Denyer, Peter, BSc Lough., PhD, FIEE   Prof., Integrated Engineering
Dripps, Jimmy, BSc Belf., PhD Strath.   Sr. Lectr.
Ewen, Peter J. S., BSc PhD   Sr. Lectr.
Flynn, Brian W., BSc PhD   Sr. Lectr.
Grant, Peter M., BSc H.-W., PhD, FIEE   Prof., Electronic Signal Processing
Hannah, J. M., BSc Strath., PhD   Sr. Lectr.
Jack, M. A., MSc H.-W., PhD, FIEE   Prof., Electronic Systems
Jordan, J. R., MSc Sur., PhD, FIEE   Prof., Electronic Instrumentation; Head*
Kelly, R. G., BSc PhD   Sr. Lectr.
Macpherson, D. E., BSc PhD   Sr. Lectr.
McLaughlin, S., BSc PhD   Reader
Mulgrew, Bernie, BSc Belf., PhD   Reader
Murray, Alan F., BSc PhD   Prof., Neural Electronics
Reekie, H. M., BSc PhD   Sr. Lectr.
Reeves, C. M., BSc PhD   Sr. Lectr.
Renshaw, D., BSc MSc PhD   Sr. Lectr.
Snell, A. J., BSc PhD   Sr. Lectr.

Underwood, Ian, BSc Glas., MSc Strath., PhD   Sr. Lectr.
Wallace, A. R., BSc PhD   Sr. Lectr.
Walton, Anthony J., MSc Newcastle(UK), PhD   Prof., Microelectronic Manufacturing
Whittington, H. W., BSc Strath., PhD Strath., FIEE   Prof., Electrical Power Engineering
Other Staff: 7 Lectrs.; 1 Sr. Res. Fellow; 10 Res. Fellows; 12 Res. Assocs.; 6 Hon. Fellows

Mechanical Engineering

Tel: (0131) 650 5684 Fax: (0131) 667 3677
Alder, George M., MA Camb., PhD   Sr. Lectr.
Easson, W. J., BSc PhD   Reader; Head*
McGeough, J. A., BSc Glas., PhD Glas., DSc Aberd., FIEE, FIMechE, FRSEd   Regius Prof.
Mill, Frank G., BSc   Sr. Lectr.
Roberts, J. W., BSc PhD   Sr. Lectr.
Salter, S. H., MA Camb., FRSEd   Prof., Engineering Design
Other Staff: 4 Lectrs.; 1 Sr. Res. Fellow; 4 Res. Fellows; 3 Endowment Fellows; 2 Res. Assocs.; 8 Hon. Fellows
Research: dynamic systems; fluid dynamics; manufacturing planning; manufacturing processes; surface engineering

English Language

Tel: (0131) 650 3628 Fax: (0131) 650 6883
Anderson, J. M., MA PhD, FBA   Prof.
Britton, D. A., BA Durh.   Sr. Lectr.
Colman, Frances, MA Syd., DPhil Oxf.   Reader
Giegerich, H. J., MA Mainz, PhD   Prof., English Linguistics
Jones, C., MA Glas., BLitt Glas., FRSEd   Forbes Prof.; Head*
Macleod, N., MA   Sr. Lectr.
Other Staff: 2 Lectrs.; 1 Hon. Fellow

English Literature

Tel: (0131) 650 3620 Fax: (0131) 650 6898
Bell, Bill R., BSc MA PhD   Sr. Lectr.
Bevan, Jonquil, MA Oxf., DPhil Oxf.   Reader
Campbell, Ian, MA Aberd., PhD   Prof., Scottish and Victorian Literature
Carpenter, Sarah M., MA Oxf., DPhil Oxf.   Sr. Lectr.
Christianson, Aileen, MA Aberd.   Sr. Lectr.
Craig, R. C., MA PhD   Reader; Head*
Day, A., MA Leic., PhD Leic.   Sr. Lectr.
Ermarth, Elizabeth, MA PhD   Saintsbury Prof.
Jack, R. D. S., MA Glas., PhD Glas., DLitt Glas.   Prof., Scottish and Medieval Literature
Nicholson, C. E., BA Leeds   Reader
Pullin, Faith, BA Birm., MA Lond.   Sr. Lectr.
Savage, R. T., MA Camb., PhD Camb.   Sr. Lectr.
Stevenson, Randall, MA Oxf., MLitt Oxf.   Reader
Other Staff: 7 Lectrs.; 6 Hon. Fellows
Vacant Posts: Regius Prof. (Rhetoric and Engl. Lit.)

Equity Studies and Special Education

Tel: (0131) 651 6433 Fax: (0131) 651 6511
Brennan, Mary   Sr. Lectr.
Buultjens, Marianna A., MA Glas.   Sr. Lectr.
Diniz, Fernando A., MEd Manc.   Sr. Lectr.
Landon, John, MA Camb.   Sr. Lectr.
Lloyd, Gwynedd   Sr. Lectr.
Wishart, Jennifer G., MA PhD   Prof.

Europa Institute

Tel: (0131) 650 2038 Fax: (0131) 662 0883
Edward, D. A. O., CMG, QC, MA Oxf., LLB, FRSEd   Hon. Prof.
Lane, R. C., MA Car., DPhil Oxf.   Sr. Lectr.
Scott, A. G., MA   Sr. Lectr.
Usher, John A., LLB Newcastle(UK)   Prof., European Institutions
Other Staff: 3 Lectrs.; 2 Hon. Fellows
Research: agricultural law; constitutional law; EC employment law; European Union law

Fine Art, see Art (Fine Art)

French

Tel: (0131) 650 8420, 650 8421 Fax: (0131) 650 8408

Aspley, Keith R., BA *Leeds*, PhD Sr. Lectr.
Barron, B. D., MA PhD Sr. Lectr.; Head*
Bennett, Philip E., MA *Oxf.* Reader
Dayan, Peter T., MA *Oxf.*, DPhil *Oxf.* Sr. Lectr.
Martin, G. D., MA *Oxf.*, BLitt *Oxf.* Sr. Lectr.
Renwick, J. P., MA *Oxf.*, MA *Camb.*, PhD *Glas.*, DLitt *Glas.*, FRHistS Prof.
Revie, Ian, MA PhD Sr. Lectr.
Runnalls, Graham A., MA *Exe.*, DLitt Prof., French Medieval Theatre
Sharratt, P., BA *Durh.*, MLitt *Durh.*, PhD Reader
Wakely, Richard G., BA *Oxf.*, LèsL *Lille*, LèsL *Stras.*, PhD Sr. Lectr.
Other Staff: 3 Lectrs.; 1 Endowment Fellow; 5 Hon. Fellows

Geography

Tel: (0131) 650 2565 Fax: (0131) 650 2524

Bondi, Elizabeth, PhD *Manc.*, MA Sr. Lectr.
Collins, L., BA *Hull*, MA *Tor.*, PhD *Tor.* Sr. Lectr.
Furley, Peter A., MA *Oxf.*, DPhil *Oxf.* Prof., Tropical Biogeography
Hughes, C. G., BA MA Sr. Lectr.
Kirby, R. P., BSc *Lond.*, MSc *McG.*, PhD Sr. Lectr.
Metcalfe, S. E., BA *Camb.*, MA *Camb.*, DPhil *Oxf.* Reader
Penrose, J. M., BA *McG.*, MA *McG.*, PhD *Tor.* Sr. Lectr.
Rose, Gillian, BA PhD Sr. Lectr.
Smith, Susan J., MA *Oxf.*, DPhil *Oxf.* Ogilvie Prof.
Sugden, D. E., BA *Oxf.*, DPhil *Oxf.* Prof.; Head*
Summerfield, M. A., MA *Oxf.*, DPhil *Oxf.* Prof., Geomorphology
Withers, C. W. J., BSc *St And.*, PhD *Camb.* Prof.
Other Staff: 8 Lectrs.; 7 Res. Fellows; 1 Endowment Fellow; 2 Res. Assocs.; 7 Hon. Fellows
Research: geographical information systems and environmental modelling; global geomorphology and environmental change; identity and cultural politics; socio-economic and welfare restructuring

Geology and Geophysics

Tel: (0131) 650 4843 Fax: (0131) 668 3184

Banks, R. J., MA *Camb.*, PhD *Camb.*, FRAS Sr. Lectr.
Boulton, Geoffrey S., PhD *Birm.*, DSc *Birm.*, FRS, FRSEd Regius James Hutton Prof.
Clarkson, Euan N. K., MA *Camb.*, PhD *Camb.*, DSc, FRSEd Reader
Crampin, S., BSc *Lond.*, PhD *Camb.*, FRSEd, FRAS Hon. Prof.
Dixon, J. E., BA *Camb.*, PhD *Camb.* Sr. Lectr.
Fitton, J. G., BSc *Durh.*, PhD *Durh.*, FGS Reader
Ford, C. E., BSc *Leic.*, PhD *Reading* Sr. Lectr.
Graham, Colin M., BSc PhD, FGS, FRSEd Prof., Experimental Geochemistry
Harley, Simon L., BSc *NSW*, MA *Tas.*, DPhil *Oxf.* Prof., Lower Crustal Processes
Harte, Ben, MA *Camb.*, PhD *Camb.*, FRSEd Prof., Metamorphism
Hipkin, Roger G., BSc *Lond.*, PhD *Newcastle(UK)*, FRSEd Sr. Lectr.
Hobbs, B. A., BSc *Exe.*, PhD *Exe.*, FRAS Sr. Lectr.
Kroon, D., MSc *Lond.*, PhD *Lond.* Reader
Main, Ian G., BSc *St And.*, MSc *Durh.*, PhD Reader
Parsons, Ian, BSc PhD, FRSEd Prof., Mineralogy
Pearce, R. G., BSc *Manc.*, PhD *Newcastle(UK)* Sr. Lectr.
Price, N. B., BSc *Wales*, PhD *Wales*, FRSEd Reader
Robertson, A. H. F., MA *Camb.*, PhD *Leic.*, BSc, FRSEd Prof.

Scrutton, R. A., BSc *Durh.*, PhD *Camb.*, FGS Reader; Head*
Thompson, R., BSc *Reading*, PhD *Newcastle(UK)* Reader
Tudhope, Sandy, BSc PhD Sr. Lectr.
Underhill, John R., BSc PhD Sr. Lectr.
Upton, B. G. J., MA *Oxf.*, DPhil *Oxf.*, FRSEd Prof., Petrology
Whaler, Kathryn A., BSc PhD, FRSEd Prof.
Ziolkowski, A. M., MA *Camb.*, PhD *Camb.*, MSc *Lond.*, FRSEd Prof., Petroleum Geoscience
Other Staff: 8 Lectrs.; 3 Sr. Res. Fellows; 18 Res. Fellows; 2 Univ. Fellows; 9 Res. Assocs.; 11 Hon. Fellows
Research: evolving response of lithosphere to stress and heat; global environmental change; mass transfer processes in mantle and crust; origin and character of reservoirs

German and Russian

Tel: (0131) 650 3635, 650 3670 Fax: (0131) 650 3604

Barker, Andrew W., MA PhD Prof., Austrian Studies; Head*
Buck, T., MA *S'ton.* Sr. Lectr.
Falchikov, Michael G., BA *Oxf.* Sr. Lectr.
Gaskill, P. H., MA *Camb.*, PhD *Camb.* Sr. Lectr.
Scheunemann, D., MA *Heidel.*, DrPhil *Heidel.* Prof.
Webster, William T., MA PhD Sr. Lectr.
Other Staff: 3 Lectrs.; 1 Res. Assoc.; 2 Hon. Fellows

Hispanic Studies

Tel: (0131) 650 3674 Fax: (0131) 650 6536

Lowe, Jennifer, BA *Lond.*, PhD *Lond.* Lectr.; Head*
Williamson, E. H., MA PhD Prof.
Other Staff: 4 Lectrs.

History

Tel: (0131) 650 3783 Fax: (0131) 650 3784

Anderson, Robert D., MA *Oxf.*, DPhil *Oxf.*, FRHistS Prof., Modern History
Angold, M. J., BA *Oxf.*, DPhil *Oxf.*, FRHistS Prof., Byzantine History
Bailey, P. J., BA *Leeds*, MA *Lond.*, PhD *Br.Col.*, FRHistS Reader
Brown, J., MA *Lond.*, PhD *Lond.*, FRHistS Sr. Lectr.
Brown, T. S., PhD *Nott.*, MA, FRHistS Reader
Day, Alan F., BA *S'ton.*, MA *Johns H.*, MA *McM.*, PhD *Johns H.*, FRHistS Sr. Lectr.
Dickinson, Harry T., MA *Durh.*, PhD *Newcastle(UK)*, DLitt, FRHistS Richard Lodge Prof.
Dickson, M. Gary, AB *Stan.*, MA *Yale*, PhD, FRHistS Sr. Lectr.
Dow, Frances D., DPhil *York(UK)*, MA, FRHistS Sr. Lectr.
Duffield, Ian, BA *Lond.*, BA *Edin.*, PhD Sr. Lectr.
Edwards, O. Dudley, BA *N.U.I.*, FRHistS Reader
Fielden, K., BA *Lond.*, PhD *Camb.* Sr. Lectr.
Gooding, J. E., MA *Oxf.* Sr. Lectr.
Goodman, A. E., MA *Oxf.*, BLitt *Oxf.*, FRHistS Prof., Medieval and Renaissance History; Head*
Jeffreys-Jones, Rhodri, BA *Wales*, PhD *Camb.*, FRHistS Prof., American History
Larkin, Maurice J. M., MA *Camb.*, PhD *Camb.*, FRHistS Richard Pares Prof.
Mackenney, Richard S., MA *Camb.*, PhD *Camb.*, FRHistS Reader
Nugent, Paul C., BA *Cape Town*, MA *Lond.*, PhD *Lond.* Sr. Lectr.
Phillipson, N. T., MA *Aberd.*, BA *Camb.*, PhD *Camb.*, FRHistS Reader
Rothwell, V. H., BA *Nott.*, PhD *Leeds*, FRHistS Reader
Stephenson, A. Jill R., MA PhD, FRHistS Reader
Other Staff: 7 Lectrs.; 1 Lectr.†; 1 Hon. Fellow

History, Economic and Social

Tel: (0131) 650 3843 Fax: (0131) 650 6645

Anderson, Michael, MA *Camb.*, PhD, FBA, FRSEd Prof., Economic History
Blanchard, I. S. W., BSc(Econ) *Lond.*, PhD *Lond.* Prof., Medieval Economic History
Chick, M. J., MA *Camb.*, PhD Sr. Lectr.
Davidson, Roger, MA *Camb.*, PhD, FRHistS Reader
Greasley, David G., BA *Liv.*, BPhil *Liv.*, PhD *Liv.* Reader
Morris, R. J., BA *Oxf.*, DPhil *Oxf.* Prof.; Head*
Nenadic, Stana, BA *Strath.*, PhD *Glas.* Sr. Lectr.
Palairet, M. R., MA PhD Sr. Lectr.
Turner, Elspeth M., MA Sr. Lectr.
Other Staff: 5 Lectrs.; 1 Res. Fellow; 1 Hon. Fellow

History, Scottish

Tel: (0131) 650 4030 Fax: (0131) 650 4042

Breeze, D. J., BA PhD, FSA, FRSEd Hon. Prof.
Lynch, Michael, MA *Aberd.*, PhD *Lond.*, FRHistS Sir William Fraser Prof.; Head*
Other Staff: 3 Lectrs.; 3 Hon. Fellows
Research: Scottish history of all periods; urban history and comparative history

Informatics, see Engin. and Informatics, Sch. of

Islamic and Middle Eastern Studies

Tel: (0131) 650 4182 Fax: (0131) 650 6804

Hillenbrand, Carole, BA *Oxf.*, MA *Camb.*, PhD Reader; Head*
McDonald, Michael V., MA *Camb.*, PhD Sr. Lectr.
Suleiman, M. Y. I. H., BA *Jordan*, BA *Durh.*, PhD *St And.* Iraq Prof., Arabic and Islamic Studies
Other Staff: 4 Lectrs.; 5 Hon. Fellows
Research: Arabic language, linguistics and literature; history and politics of the Middle East; Islamic history and political thought; Islamic law

Italian

Tel: (0131) 650 3646 Fax: (0131) 650 6536

Usher, J., BA *Reading* Prof.; Head*
Other Staff: 3 Lectrs.

Language Studies, Applied, Institute for

Tel: (0131) 650 6200 Fax: (0131) 667 5927

Glendinning, Eric H., MA Sr. Lectr.; Dir.*
Other Staff: 4 Lectrs.; 1 Res. Assoc.
Research: analysing language needs of business and industry; teaching and learning English as a foreign language; teaching and learning for special purposes; teaching and learning modern languages

Law and Society, Centre for

Tel: (0131) 650 2025, 650 2033 Fax: (0131) 662 4902

Bankowski, Zenon, LLB *Dund.* Prof., Legal Theory
MacCormick, D. Neil, MA *Glas.*, MA *Oxf.*, Hon. LLD *Uppsala*, LLD, FRSEd, FBA Regius Prof., Public Law
Smith, David J., MA Prof., Criminology
Young, P. J., BSc *Lond.*, MA *Sheff.*, PhD Sr. Lectr.; Head*
Other Staff: 3 Lectrs.; 1 Res. Fellow; 1 Res. Assoc.; 1 Hon. Fellow
Research: deviance and punishment; medical jurisprudence; philosophy of law and studies in legal reasoning; sociological and historical analysis; studies in sexuality and gender

Law: Legal Practice Unit

Tel: (0131) 650 2004 Fax: (0131) 662 4902

Barr, Alan R., MA LLB Sr. Lectr.; Dir*
Other Staff: 1 Lectr.

Law, Private

Tel: (0131) 650 2017, 650 2344 Fax: (0131) 662 4902

Black, Robert, LLM *McG.*, LLB, FRSEd Prof., Scots Law
Brodie, J. D., LLB PhD Sr. Lectr.
Cairns, John W., LLB PhD Reader
Eden, Sandra M., BA *Kent*, LLB Sr. Lectr.
Gretton, George L., BA *Durh.*, LLB Lord President Reid Prof.; Head*
Griffiths, Anne M. O., LLB PhD Sr. Lectr.
Leslie, R. D., BA *Cape Town*, LLM *Cape Town*, PhD Sr. Lectr.
MacQueen, Hector L., LLB PhD, FRSEd Prof.
McCall-Smith, R. A. A., LLB PhD Prof., Medical Law
Murray, John, MA LLB Dickson Minto Prof.
Reid, K. G. C., MA *Camb.*, LLB Prof., Property Law
Other Staff: 8 Lectrs.; 1 Lectr.†; 6 Hon. Fellows
Research: commercial and company law; contract; family law; law of delict and legal history; property law

Law, Public

Tel: (0131) 650 2056 Fax: (0131) 662 0724
Finnie, Wilson, LLB *Aberd.* Sr. Lectr.
Himsworth, C. M. G., BA *Camb.*, LLB *Camb.* Reader
Munro, Colin R., LLB *Aberd.*, BA Prof.; Head*
Other Staff: 2 Lectrs.
Research: administrative law; constitutional laws and government; housing law and health law; human rights and civil liberties; welfare law

Law, Public International

Tel: (0131) 650 2053 Fax: (0131) 662 0724
Boyle, A. E., BA BCL Prof.; Head*
Gilmore, William C., LLM *Lond.*, LLM *Edin.*, MA *Car.*, PhD *Lond.* Prof., International Criminal Law
Neff, Stephen C., AB *Harv.*, JD *Virginia*, LLM Sr. Lectr.
Other Staff: 1 Lectr.; 1 Hon. Fellow

Linguistics

Tel: (0131) 650 3961 Fax: (0131) 650 3962
Bard, E. G., BA *Smith*, MA *Harv.*, MLitt *Harv.*, PhD *Harv.* Sr. Lectr.
Cann, Ronnie, BA *Lond.*, DPhil *Sus.* Sr. Lectr.
Hurford, James R., BA *Camb.*, PhD *Lond.* Prof., General Linguistics
Isard, S. D., BA *Harv.*, MA *Calif.* Reader
Ladd, D. R., MA *Cornell*, PhD *Cornell* Prof.
Miller, J. E., MA PhD Prof., Linguistics and Spoken Language; Head*
Other Staff: 2 Lectrs.; 2 Res. Fellows; 2 Hon. Fellows

Linguistics, Applied

Tel: (0131) 650 3864 Fax: (0131) 650 6526
Howatt, A. P. R., MA Sr. Lectr.
Joseph, John E., MA PhD Prof.; Head*
Mitchell, W. Keith, MA Sr. Lectr.
Sorace, Antonella, MA *Los Angeles*, PhD Reader
Other Staff: 1 Lectr.; 1 Hon. Fellow

Mathematics and Statistics

Tel: (0131) 650 5060 Fax: (0131) 650 6553
Aitken, C. G. G., PhD *Glas.*, BSc Reader
Arthur, Derek W., DPhil *Oxf.*, BSc Sr. Lectr.
Bailey, Toby, MA *Camb.*, DPhil *Oxf.* Sr. Lectr.
Braden, H. W., BSc *Syd.*, PhD *Camb.* Sr. Lectr.
Byatt-Smith, J. G., BSc *Brist.*, PhD *Brist.* Sr. Lectr.
Carbery, A., BA *Oxf.*, PhD *Calif.* Colin MacLaurin Prof., Mathematics
Davie, A. M., BA *Camb.*, PhD *Dund.* Prof., Mathematical Analysis
Duffy, J. C., MSc *Reading*, BSc Sr. Lectr.
Gilbert, A. D., MA *Camb.*, PhD *Camb.* Sr. Lectr.
Gillespie, Prof. T. Alastair, BA *Camb.*, PhD, FRSEd Prof., Mathematical Analysis
Gyöngy, I. J., PhD *Moscow* Reader
Heggie, Douglas S., MA *Camb.*, PhD *Camb.*, FRSEd Prof., Mathematical Astronomy
Hulse, J. A., MA *Camb.*, PhD *Camb.* Sr. Lectr.
Lenagan, T. H., BSc *Lond.*, PhD *Leeds* Reader
Leonard, T., BSc MSc PhD Prof., Statistics

Lyons, T. J., MA *Camb.*, DPhil *Oxf.*, FRSEd Hon. Prof.
Macintyre, A. J., MA PhD, FRS Prof., Mathematical Logic
Martin, John, MA PhD Sr. Lectr.; Head*
McKinnon, Ken, BSc *Glas.*, PhD *Camb.* Reader
Meldrum, John D. P., MA *Camb.*, PhD *Camb.* Reader
O'Carroll, Liam, MSc *Belf.*, PhD *Belf.* Reader
Parker, D. F., MA *Camb.*, PhD *Nott.*, FRSEd Prof., Applied Mathematics
Patterson, H. D., DSc, FRSCan, FIMA, FRSEd Hon. Prof.
Prentice, Michael J., BSc *Manc.* Sr. Lectr.
Racliffe, Nicholas J., BSc *Sus.*, PhD Visiting Prof.
Ranicki, A. A., MA *Camb.*, PhD *Camb.*, FRSEd Prof., Algebraic Surgery
Rees, E. G., MA *Camb.*, MA *Oxf.*, PhD *Warw.*, FRSEd Prof.
Richardson, S., MA *Camb.*, PhD *Camb.* Reader
Searl, J. W., BSc *S'ton.* Sr. Lectr.
Sinclair, A. M., BSc *Witw.*, MSc *Rhodes*, PhD *Newcastle(UK)*, FRSEd Prof., Operator Algebras and Mathematical Analysis
Smyth, C. J., BA *ANU*, MA *Adel.*, PhD *Camb.* Reader
Other Staff: 16 Lectrs.; 3 Res. Fellows; 1 Endowment Fellow; 3 Res. Assocs.; 5 Hon. Fellows

Medical Physics and Medical Engineering

Tel: (0131) 537 1000 Fax: (0131) 537 2801
Brash, Harry M., BSc PhD Sr. Lectr.
Marshall, Ian, MA PhD Sr. Lectr.
McDicken, Norman, BSc PhD Prof.; Head*
Other Staff: 2 Res. Fellows; 1 Res. Assoc.; 3 Lectrs.†; 12 Hon. Fellows

Medicine, see below

Meteorology

Tel: (0131) 650 5101 Fax: (0131) 662 4269
Duncan, C. N., BSc PhD Sr. Lectr.; Head*
Harwood, Robert S., BSc *Lond.*, PhD *Lond.*, FRMetS Prof., Atmospheric Physics
Weston, K. J., BSc *Brist.*, PhD *Lond.* Sr. Lectr.
Other Staff: 1 Lectr.; 5 Res. Fellows; 4 Res. Assocs.
Research: computer-aided learning; observational and modelling studies of the middle atmosphere; ocean modelling and surface air pollution

Middle Eastern Studies, see Islamic and Middle Eastern Studies

Music

Tel: (0131) 650 2427 Fax: (0131) 650 2425
Harper, E. J., MA *Oxf.*, BMus *Oxf.* Reader
Kimbell, David R. B., MA *Oxf.*, DPhil *Oxf.* Prof.; Head*
Kitchen, John P., MA *Glas.*, BMus *Glas.*, PhD *Camb.*, FRCO Sr. Lectr.
Monelle, Raymond, MA *Oxf.*, BMus *Lond.*, PhD Reader
Nelson, Peter W., MA *Glas.*, BMus *Glas.*, MMus Sr. Lectr.
O'Regan, Noel, MSc *N.U.I.*, BMus *N.U.I.*, PhD Sr. Lectr.
Osborne, N., BA *Oxf.*, BMus *Oxf.* Reid Prof.
Turnbull, Michael, MA *Oxf.*, DPhil *Oxf.* Sr. Lectr.
Williams, Peter F., MusB MA PhD, Hon. FRCO Hon. Prof.
Other Staff: 2 Lectrs.; 1 Lectr.†; 1 Hon. Fellow

Nursing Studies

Tel: (0131) 650 3889 Fax: (0131) 650 3891
Mander, Rosemary, MSc PhD Sr. Lectr.
Melia, Kathleen M., BNurs *Manc.*, PhD Prof.; Head*
Tierney, Alison J., BSc PhD Prof., Nursing Research
Watson, Roger, PhD *Sheff.*, BSc Sr. Lectr.
Whyte, Dorothy A., BA *Open(UK)*, PhD Sr. Lectr.

Other Staff: 7 Lectrs.; 2 Res. Assocs.; 2 Lectrs.†; 1 Hon. Fellow
Research: cancer nursing and palliative care; community care and primary-secondary care interface; nursing and health care of elderly people; women's health

Philosophy

Tel: (0131) 650 3661 Fax: (0131) 650 6536
Haksar, V. N., BA *Delhi*, MA *Oxf.*, DPhil *Oxf.*, FRSEd Reader
Hope, V. M., MA PhD Sr. Lectr.
Jones, Peter, MA *Camb.*, FRSEd Prof.
Lewis, Peter, BA *Wales* Sr. Lectr.
Madell, Geoffrey, BA *Oxf.*, PhD *Lond.* Sr. Lectr.
Menlowe, Michael A., BA *Pitt.*, BLitt *Oxf.*, LLB Sr. Lectr.
Milne, Peter, MSc PhD Reader
Priest, S. M., BA *Lanc.*, MA *Camb.* Sr. Lectr.
Scaltsas, Theodore, BSc *Oxf.*, MA *Oxf.*, DPhil *Oxf.* Reader; Head*
Williamson, Timothy, MA *Oxf.*, MA *Trinity(Dub.)*, DPhil *Oxf.*, FBA, FRSEd Prof., Logic and Metaphysics
Other Staff: 3 Lectrs.; 2 Hon. Fellows
Vacant Posts: 1 Prof.

Physics and Astronomy, see also Med. Phys. and Med. Engin.

Tel: (0131) 650 5249, 668 8356 Fax: (0131) 650 7174, 668 8356
Barnes, Francis H., BSc PhD Sr. Lectr.
Bowler, K. C., BSc *Lond.*, DPhil *Sus.*, FIP Reader
Brand, P. W. J. L., PhD DSc, FRAS, FRSEd Prof., Astrophysics
Branford, D., BSc *Hull*, PhD *Manc.*, FIP Reader
Bruce, A. D., BSc PhD Reader
Campbell, D. Murray, BSc PhD Sr. Lectr.
Cates, Michael, MA PhD Prof., Natural Philosophy
Fancey, N. E., BSc PhD Sr. Lectr.
Galloway, Robert B., BSc PhD, FIP Sr. Lectr.
Greated, C. A., BSc *Lond.*, PhD *S'ton.*, FIP, FIMA, FRSEd Prof., Fluid Dynamics; Dir., Fluid Dynamics Unit
Heavens, Alan F., MA *Camb.*, PhD *Camb.* Reader
Hossack, William J., BSc *Lond.*, MSc *Lond.*, PhD *Lond.* Sr. Lectr.
Kenway, Richard D., BSc *Exe.*, DPhil *Oxf.*, FRSEd Tait Prof., Mathematical Physics; Head*
Lawrence, Andrew, BSc PhD, FRAS, FRSEd Regius Prof., Astronomy
McComb, W. D., MSc *Manc.*, PhD *Manc.*, FIP Prof., Statistical Physics
McKirdy, A. S., BSc *Glas.* Sr. Lectr.
Nelmes, R. J., MA *Camb.*, ScD *Camb.*, PhD, FRSEd Prof., Physical Crystallography
Pawley, G. S., MA *Camb.*, PhD *Camb.*, FRSEd, FRS Prof., Computational Physics
Peach, K. J., BSc PhD Prof., Particle Physics Experiment
Peacock, J. A. Hon. Prof.
Pendleton, B. J., BSc DPhil Sr. Lectr.
Poon, W. C. K., MA *Camb.*, PhD *Camb.* Sr. Lectr.
Pusey, P. N., MA *Camb.*, PhD *Pitt.*, FIP, FRS, FRSEd Prof.
Shotter, Alan C., BSc *Lond.*, DPhil *Oxf.*, FIP, FRSEd Prof., Experimental Physics
Vass, D. G., BSc PhD Reader
Woods, P. J., BSc *Manc.*, PhD *Manc.* Reader
Other Staff: 15 Lectrs.; 22 Res. Fellows; 1 Univ. Fellow; 14 Res. Assocs.; 2 Hon. Fellows

Physiology

Tel: (0131) 650 2860 Fax: (0131) 650 6527
Dutia, Manyank B., BSc *Lond.*, PhD *Glas.* Sr. Lectr.
Ellis, David, BSc *Leic.*, PhD *Leic.* Sr. Lectr.
Flatman, Peter W., MA *Camb.*, PhD *Camb.* Sr. Lectr.
Leng, Gareth, BSc *Warw.*, MSc *Birm.*, PhD *Birm.* Prof., Experimental Physiology
Price, D. J., DPhil *Oxf.*, BSc MB ChB Reader

Ribchester, Richard R., BSc Durh., PhD
 Newcastle(UK) Sr. Lectr.
Russell, John A., BSc MB ChB PhD Reader;
 Head*
Watson, W. E., MD Lond., DPhil Oxf.,
 FRCS Prof.
Wright, M. O., MB ChB Manc., FRCSEd Sr.
 Lectr.
Other Staff: 6 Lectrs.; 8 Res. Fellows; 8 Res.
 Assocs.; 1 Endowment Fellow†; 2 Hon.
 Fellows
Research: developmental biology; membrane and
 cell biology; neuroendocrinology; synaptic
 plasticity and repair biology

Politics

Tel: (0131) 650 4457 Fax: (0131) 650 6546
Allen, C. H., MA Oxf. Sr. Lectr.
Anderson, Malcolm, MA Oxf., DPhil Oxf.,
 FRSEd Prof.
Brown, Alice, MA PhD Prof.
Buckley, M. E. A., BA Leic., MSc Lond.,
 PhD Reader
Clark, Martin, MA Camb., PhD Lond. Reader
Hayward, Tim, BA Warw., MA Warw., DPhil
 Warw. Sr. Lectr.
Hutchings, Kimberley, BSc Brist., MA Sus., PhD
 Sus. Sr. Lectr.
Irving, R. E. M., MA Oxf., DPhil Oxf. Reader
Keat, R. N., BA BPhil Prof., Political Theory;
 Head*
McAllister, Richard A., MA Camb. Sr. Lectr.
Raab, C. D., BA Col., MA Yale Reader
Other Staff: 6 Lectrs.; 3 Hon. Fellows

Psychology

Tel: (0131) 650 3440 Fax: (0131) 650 3461
Caryl, P. G., MA Camb., PhD Sr. Lectr.
Deary, Ian J., BSc MB ChB PhD,
 FRCPEd Prof., Differential Psychology
Donaldson, Morag L., MA PhD Sr. Lectr.;
 Head*
Grieve, R., MA PhD Prof.
Lee, David N., MA Camb., PhD Lond.,
 FRSEd Prof., Perception, Action and
 Development
MacLeod, Hamish A., BSc PhD Sr. Lectr.
McGonigle, B. O., BA Belf., PhD Belf. Reader
Morris, Robert L., BS Pitt., PhD Duke Koestler
 Prof., Parapsychology
Pitcairn, Tom K., BSc Wales, PhD Birm. Sr.
 Lectr.
Wright, Peter, MA Oxf., DPhil Oxf. Sr. Lectr.
Other Staff: 7 Lectrs.; 4 Res. Fellows; 1
 Endowment Fellow; 2 Res. Assocs.; 1
 Lectr.†; 5 Hon. Fellows
Research: behavioural psychology; clinical
 psychology; cognitive psychology;
 developmental psychology; social psychology

Russian, see German and Russian

Sanskrit

Tel: (0131) 650 4182 Fax: (0131) 650 6804
Brockington, J. L., MA Oxf., DPhil
 Oxf. Reader; Head*
Dundas, P., MA Sr. Lectr.

Scandinavian Studies

Tel: (0131) 650 4026
Graves, P. A., MA Aberd. Sr. Lectr.; Head*
Other Staff: 2 Lectrs.

Scottish Studies, School of

Tel: (0131) 650 4167 Fax: (0131) 650 4163
Fraser, I. A., MA Sr. Lectr.
Mackay, Margaret A., BA Tor., PhD Sr. Lectr.;
 Dir.*
Macleod, Morag, MA Sr. Lectr.
Shaw, John W., BA Harv., MA Harv., PhD
 Harv. Sr. Lectr.
Other Staff: 1 Lectr.; 3 Res. Fellows; 9 Hon.
 Fellows
Vacant Posts: 1 Prof.

Social Anthropology

Tel: (0131) 650 3932 Fax: (0131) 650 3945
Barnard, Alan J., BA Wash., MA McM., PhD
 Lond. Reader
Carsten, J. F., BSc Lond., PhD Lond. Sr. Lectr.
Cohen, A. P., BA S'ton., MSc S'ton., PhD S'ton.,
 FRSEd Prof.
Good, A., BSc PhD Sr. Lectr.; Head*
Jedrej, M. C., MA PhD Sr. Lectr.
Spencer, Jonathan, AM Chic., DPhil Oxf.,
 MA Sr. Lectr.
Other Staff: 10 Lectrs.; 3 Hon. Fellows

Social Policy

Tel: (0131) 650 3923 Fax: (0131) 650 3919
Adler, Michael E., BA Oxf., AM Harv. Prof.,
 Socio-Legal Studies
Dey, Ian, PhD Brist., MA Sr. Lectr.
Fraser, Neil M., BA Oxf., BPhil Oxf. Sr. Lectr.
Parry, Richard H., MA Strath., MSc Strath. Sr.
 Lectr.
Robertson, Alex, MA Aberd., PhD Reader
Sinfield, Adrian, BA Oxf. Prof.
Wasoff, Fran, MA Penn., PhD Penn. Sr. Lectr.;
 Head*
Other Staff: 3 Res. Assocs.; 4 Hon. Fellows
Research: criminal justice; social philosophy;
 social policy; social security; unemployment

Social Sciences, Research Centre for

Tel: (0131) 650 6384 Fax: (0131) 650 6399
Bechoffer, F., MA Camb. Prof., Social Research
Williams, R. A., MA Camb., MSc Aston, PhD
 Aston Sr. Lectr.; Dir.*
Other Staff: 1 Sr. Res. Fellow; 1 Res. Fellow; 2
 Res. Assocs.; 1 Hon. Fellow

Social Work

Tel: (0131) 650 3915 Fax: (0131) 650 3911
Clark, Chris, BSc Birm., PhD Sr. Lectr.
Davidson, Ralph, MA Sr. Lectr.
Waterhouse, L. A. M., BA MSW Prof.; Head*
Whyte, W. T., MA Sr. Lectr.
Other Staff: 4 Lectrs.; 1 Res. Assoc.; 3 Lectrs.†

Sociology

Tel: (0131) 650 4001 Fax: (0131) 650 3989
Bell, Colin, BA Keele, MScEcon Wales,
 FRSEd Prof.
Bloor, David, BA Keele, MA Camb., PhD Reader
Faulkner, W., MSc Sus., DPhil Sus. Sr. Lectr.
Henry, John, BA Leeds, MPhil Leeds, PhD
 Open(UK) Sr. Lectr.
Holmwood, J. M., MA Camb. Reader
Jamieson, Lynn H. A., MA PhD Sr. Lectr.;
 Head*
Jeffery, Patricia M., MA Camb., MA Nott.,
 PhD Reader
Jeffery, Roger, MA Camb., MSc Brist., PhD Sr.
 Lectr.
MacInnes, John, MA PhD Sr. Lectr.
MacKenzie, Donald A., BSc PhD Prof.
McCrone, David, MA MSc Prof.
McGlew, T. J., BSc Holy Cross, MA Brown Sr.
 Lectr.
Orr, John, BSc Birm., PhD Prof.
Raffel, Stanley H., AB Col., PhD Sr. Lectr.
Webb, J., BSc Hull, PhD Nott. Sr. Lectr.
Other Staff: 1 Res. Fellow; 2 Hon. Fellows

Statistics, see Maths. and Stats.

Theology, see Div.

Veterinary Medicine, see below

MEDICINE

(for subjects of first 2 years—Anat., etc. see
 above)

Anaesthetics

Tel: (0131) 536 3672 Fax: (0131) 536 3679
Drummond, Gordon B., MB ChB MA,
 FRCA Sr. Lectr.
Spence, A. A., MD Glas., FCAnaesth, FRCPGlas,
 FRSEd Prof.; Head*

Other Staff: 1 Lectr.; 2 Res. Fellows; 1 Res.
 Assoc.; 3 Sr. Lectrs.†; 33 Clin. Teaching
 Staff; 12 Hon. Sr. Lectrs.; 1 Hon. Fellow

Biochemistry, Clinical

Tel: (0131) 536 2698 Fax: (0131) 536 2758
Beckett, G. J., BSc Manc., PhD Reader
Mason, J. Ian, BSc PhD, FRCPath Prof.
Simpson, Daniel, BSc PhD, FRSChem Sr.
 Lectr.
Smith, Alistair F., MA Camb., MD BChir Camb.,
 FRCPEd, FRCPath Sr. Lectr.; Head*
Walker, Simon W., MA Oxf., MB BS Lond.,
 DM Sr. Lectr.
Other Staff: 2 Lectrs.; 1 Res. Assoc.; 5 Hon. Sr.
 Lectrs.; 1 Hon. Fellow
Research: drug detection, measurement and
 metabolism; gene expression; lipidology;
 molecular basis of organogenesis

Child Life and Health

Tel: (0131) 536 0690 Fax: (0131) 536 0821
Belton, Neville R., BSc Birm., PhD Birm. Sr.
 Lectr.
Cutting, William A. M., MB ChB,
 FRCPEd Reader
Hoare, P., MA Oxf., DM BCh Oxf. Sr. Lectr.
McIntosh, Neil, BSc Lond., MB BS Lond., FRCP,
 FRCPEd Edward Clark Prof.; Head*
Midgley, P., MB ChB Sr. Lectr.
Minns, Robert A., JP, MB BS Qld., PhD,
 FRCPEd Sr. Lectr.
Wilson, D. C., MD Sr. Lectr.
Other Staff: 2 Lectrs.; 1 Res. Fellow; 8 Sr.
 Lectrs.†; 15 Clin. Teaching Staff; 17 Hon. Sr.
 Lectrs.; 3 Hon. Fellows

Dental Education

Tel: (0131) 536 4970 Fax: (0131) 536 4971
Sutcliffe, P., MChD PhD, FDSRCSEd Prof.,
 Preventive Dentistry
Other Staff: 1 Sr. Lectr.†; 13 Hon. Sr. Lectrs.;
 4 Hon. Fellows

Dermatology

Tel: (0131) 536 2042 Fax: (0131) 229 8769
Hunter, J. A. A., OBE, BA Camb., MD,
 FRCPEd Grant Prof.; Head*
Other Staff: 2 Lectrs.; 1 Univ. Fellow; 2 Sr.
 Lectrs.†; 5 Clin. Teaching Staff; 1 Hon.
 Fellow
Research: cytokines; human papillomavirus; in
 vitro skin models; langerhans cells;
 photoimmunology and skin diseases

General Practice

Tel: (0131) 650 2675, 650 2676 Fax: (0131)
 650 2681
Howie, J. G. R., CBE, MD ChB Glas., PhD
 Aberd., FRCGP, FRCPEd James Mackenzie
 Prof.; Head*
Murray, Scott A., MB ChB Aberd. Sr. Lectr.
Porter, A. Mike D., BA Durh., MPhil Durh. Sr.
 Lectr.
Thomson, Donald M., BSc MB ChB, FRCPEd,
 FRCGP Sr. Lectr.
Other Staff: 2 Lectrs.; 1 Sr. Res. Fellow; 8 Res.
 Fellows; 5 Res. Assocs.; 1 Sr. Lectr.†; 53
 Clin. Teaching Staff; 1 Hon. Sr. Lectr.; 3
 Hon. Fellows
Research: general practice; health economics;
 medical sociology; nursing; psychology

Genito-Urinary Medicine, see under Med.

(Royal Infirmary)

Geriatric Medicine, see under Med. (Royal

Infirmary)

Human Genetics, see under Med. (W. Gen.

Hosp.)

Medical Education, Centre for

Tel: (0131) 650 2607, 650 2609 Fax: (0131)
 662 0580
Fleming, Stewart, BSc MD, FRCPath Sr. Lectr.
Muir, A. L., MD, FRCPEd, FRCR,
 FRCSEd Prof.; Dir.*

Watson, G. R., BSc MA PhD   Sr. Lectr.
Wright, M. O., MB ChB, FRCSEd   Sr. Lectr.
Other Staff: 1 Sr. Lectr.†; 2 Hon. Sr. Lectrs.

Medical Microbiology

Tel: (0131) 650 3161, 650 3169 Fax: (0131) 650 6531

Amyes, S. G. B., MSc Reading, PhD Lond., DSc Lond., FIBiol, FRCPath   Prof., Microbial Chemotherapy; Head*
Blackwell, Cecelia C., BS Louisiana State, PhD Stan., DSc, FRCPath   Sr. Lectr.
Crawford, D. H., MD PhD DSc   Robert Irvine Prof.
Fraser, Andrew G., BSc MD   Sr. Lectr.
Govan, J. R. W., BSc PhD DSc   Reader
Miles, Rex S., MB ChB, FRCPath   Sr. Lectr.
Norval, Mary, PhD DSc   Reader
Ogilvie, Marie M., BSc MD   Sr. Lectr.
Poxton, Ian R., BSc PhD DSc   Reader
Ross, Philip W., TD, MD Aberd., FLS, FIBiol, FRCPath, FRCPEd   Reader
Simmonds, P., BM PhD   Sr. Lectr.
Stewart, John, BSc PhD   Sr. Lectr.
Sutherland, Sheena, MB ChB, FRCPath   Sr. Lectr.
Other Staff: 6 Lectrs.; 7 Res. Fellows; 3 Res. Assocs.; 4 Clin. Teaching Staff; 8 Hon. Sr. Lectrs.; 1 Hon. Fellow
Research: bacteriology; chemotherapy; microbial immunology; virology

Medical Physics and Medical Engineering, see above

Medical Radiology

Tel: (0131) 536 2809 Fax: (0131) 229 9106

Allan, P. L., BSc Lond., MB BS Lond., FRCPEd, FRCR   Sr. Lectr.; Head*
Best, Jonathan, MSc Lond., MB ChB MSc, FRCPEd, FRCR   Forbes Prof.
Other Staff: 1 Lectr.; 2 Sr. Lectrs.†; 30 Clin. Teaching Staff; 1 Hon. Sr. Lectr.

Medical Statistics, see under Public Health Scis.

Medicine (Royal Infirmary)

Tel: (0131) 536 2234 Fax: (0131) 229 2948

Brash, Harry M., BSc PhD   Sr. Lectr.
Cumming, Allan D., BSc MB ChB, FRCP   Sr. Lectr.
Dransfield, I., BSc PhD   Sr. Lectr.
Hayes, Peter C., BMSc Dund., MB ChB Dund., PhD, FRCPEd   Sr. Lectr.
Heading, Robert C., BSc MD, FRCPEd   Reader
Turner, A. Neil, BM BCh MA PhD, FRCP   Prof., Nephrology
Turner, Marc, MB BS PhD   Sr. Lectr.
Other Staff: 3 Lectrs.; 1 Res. Fellow; 2 Res. Assocs.; 4 Readers†; 6 Sr. Lectrs.†; 18 Clin. Teaching Staff; 20 Hon. Sr. Lectrs.; 3 Hon. Fellows
Vacant Posts: 1 Prof.

Cardiovascular Research Unit

Tel: (0131) 536 2742 Fax: (0131) 536 2744

Fox, K. A. A., BSc MB ChB, FRCP   Prof.
Riemersma, Rudolph A., MSc Ley., PhD   Sr. Lectr.
Other Staff: 2 Lectrs.; 1 Sr. Res. Fellow; 1 Res. Fellow; 2 Res. Assocs.; 1 Clin. Teaching Staff Member; 3 Hon. Sr. Lectrs
Research: altered lipid metabolism in ischaemic heart disease; antioxidant mechanisms; cardiovascular ultrasound; thrombolysis; thrombosis

Genito-Urinary Medicine Unit

Tel: (0131) 536 2097 Fax: (0131) 229 8769

1 Sr. Lectr.†; 2 Hon. Sr. Lectrs.
Research: epidemiology of HIV infection; sexually transmissible infections; sexually transmissible intestinal protozoal infections

Geriatric Medicine Unit

Tel: (0131) 536 4535 Fax: (0131) 536 4536

Currie, C. T., BSc MB ChB, FRCPEd   Sr. Lectr.

Other Staff: 1 Res. Fellow; 1 Res. Assoc.; 2 Sr. Lectrs.†; 24 Clin. Teaching Staff; 6 Hon. Sr. Lectrs.; 1 Hon. Fellow
Research: dementia; dizziness; nutrition; stroke; trauma in the elderly

Otolaryngology Unit

Tel: (0131) 536 3747 Fax: (0131) 229 8769

Maran, A. G. D., MD, FRCSEd, FACS, FRCPEd   Prof.†; Head*
Other Staff: 1 Res. Fellow; 1 Clin. Teaching Staff Member; 3 Hon. Sr. Lectrs.
Research: acoustics; swallowing; voice

Respiratory Medicine Unit

Tel: (0131) 536 2263 Fax: (0131) 536 2274

Douglas, Neil J., MD ChB, FRCPEd   Prof., Respiratory and Sleep Medicine
Haslett, Chris, BSc MB ChB, FRCP, FRCPEd   Prof.; Head*
Lamb, J. R., BDS BA MA PhD, FRCPath   Prof., Respiratory Science
MacNee, W., MD Glas., FRCPEd, FRCPGlas   Prof., Respiratory and Environmental Medicine
Warren, Patricia M., BSc Sheff., PhD Sheff.   Sr. Lectr.
Other Staff: 2 Lectrs.; 3 Sr. Res. Fellows; 12 Res. Fellows; 1 Res. Assoc.; 2 Sr. Lectrs.†; 1 Hon. Sr. Lectr.; 2 Hon. Fellows
Research: bronchial asthma; chronic obstructive pulmonary disease; environmental lung diseases; lung cancer and inflammatory diseases of the lung; sleep apnoea

Medicine (Western General Hospital)

Tel: (0131) 537 1867 Fax: (0131) 537 1012

Ansell, John, BSc Nott., PhD   Prof., Experimental Haematology
Butler, Peter C., MB ChB Birm., FRCPEd   Prof., Diabetic Medicine
Ferguson, Anne, BSc Glas., MB ChB Glas., FRCP, FRCPath, FRSEd   Prof., Gastroenterology; Head*
Parker, Alistair C., BSc PhD MB ChB, FRCPath, FRCPEd   Sr. Lectr.
Seckl, Jonathan R., BSc Lond., MB BS Lond., PhD Lond., FRCPEd   Moncrieff Arnott Prof.
Sutherland, G. R., MB ChB, FRCP   Sr. Lectr.
Williams, B. C., BSc St And., PhD Dund.   Sr. Lectr.
Other Staff: 4 Lectrs.; 10 Res. Fellows; 6 Res. Assocs.; 1 Reader†; 6 Sr. Lectrs.†; 5 Clin. Teaching Staff; 11 Hon. Sr. Lectrs.; 6 Hon. Fellows

Clinical Pharmacology Unit

Tel: (0131) 332 1205 Fax: (0131) 343 6017

Webb, David J., MB BS Lond., MD, FRCP, FRCPEd   Christison Prof., Therapeutics and Clinical Pharmacology
Other Staff: 2 Res. Fellows; 2 Hon. Fellows
Research: characterisation of cardiovascular actions of drugs; pathophysiology of cardiovascular disease

Human Genetics Unit

Tel: (0131) 651 1041 Fax: (0131) 537 1059

Bonthron, D. T., MA Camb., MB BChir Camb.   Sr. Lectr.
Brock, David J. H., BA Oxf., PhD Cape Town, FIBiol, FRCPEd, FRSEd   Prof.; Dir.*
Porteous, David J., BSc PhD   Hon. Prof.
Other Staff: 1 Lectr.; 7 Res. Fellows; 2 Res. Assocs.; 1 Sr. Lectr.†; 1 Hon. Sr. Lectr.; 1 Hon. Fellow

Rheumatology Unit

Tel: (0131) 537 1797 Fax: (0131) 537 1032

Nuki, G., MB BS Lond., FRCP, FRCPEd   Prof.; Head*
Other Staff: 1 Lectr.; 1 Res. Assoc.; 1 Sr. Lectr.†; 1 Hon. Sr. Lectr.

Neurosciences, Clinical

Tel: (0131) 537 1000 Fax: (0131) 537 2561

Dennis, M. S., MB BS Lond., MD Lond., FRCPEd   Reader
Kelly, P. A. T., PhD Glas., BSc   Sr. Lectr.
Sandercock, Peter, MA Oxf., DM Oxf., FRCPEd   Reader
Wardlaw, J. M., BSc MB ChB, FRCR   Sr. Lectr.
Warlow, Charles, BA Camb., MD Camb., FRCP, FRCPEd, FRCPGlas   Prof.; Head*
Whittle, Ian R., MD Adel., PhD, FRACS, FRCSEd   Forbes Prof., Surgical Neurology
Other Staff: 1 Lectr.; 4 Res. Fellows; 3 Res. Assocs.; 6 Sr. Lectrs.†; 2 Hon. Sr. Lectrs.; 1 Hon. Fellow

Obstetrics and Gynaecology

Tel: (0131) 229 2575 Fax: (0131) 229 2408

Aitken, R. J., BSc Lond., MSc Wales, PhD Camb.   Hon. Prof.
Baird, David T., BA Camb., MB ChB DSc, FRCPEd, FRCOG, FRSEd   MRC Clin. Res. Prof.
Boddy, K., MB BS Durh., FRCOG   Sr. Lectr.
Bramley, T. A., BSc Birm., PhD Birm.   Sr. Lectr.
Calder, Andrew, MD Glas., FRCPGlas, FRCPEd, FRCSEd   Prof.; Head*
Critchley, H. O. D., BSc MD ChB, FRCOG   Sr. Lectr.
Hillier, Stephen G., MSc Leeds, PhD Wales, DSc, FRCPath   Prof., Reproductive Endocrinology
Johnstone, F. D., MD Aberd.   Sr. Lectr.
McNeilly, A. S., BSc Nott., PhD Reading, DSc, FRSEd   Hon. Prof.
West, John D., BSc E.Anglia, PhD   Sr. Lectr.
Other Staff: 2 Lectrs.; 10 Res. Fellows; 2 Res. Assocs.; 3 Sr. Lectrs.†; 10 Clin. Teaching Staff; 15 Hon. Sr. Lectrs.; 3 Hon. Fellows
Research: foetal and utero-placental physiology; genetics and developmental biology; gynaecological oncology; reproductive endocrinology; telemedicine

Oncology, Clinical

Medical Oncology

Tel: (0131) 332 2471 Fax: (0131) 332 8494

Jodrell, Duncan, MSc DM   Sr. Lectr.
Miller, W. R., BSc Leeds, PhD Leeds, DSc   Prof., Experimental Oncology
Smyth, J. F., MA Camb., MD Camb., MSc Lond., FRCP, FRCPEd   Prof.
Other Staff: 1 Sr. Lectr.†; 1 Hon. Sr. Lectr.; 3 Hon. Fellows
Research: brain tumours; functional neurosurgery; head injury; spongiform encephalopathy; stroke

Radiation Oncology

Tel: (0131) 332 2471 Fax: (0131) 332 8494

Gregor, Anna, FRCPEd, FRCR   Sr. Lectr.
Price, Allan, MB ChB Wales, PhD Lond., FRCR   Prof.
Other Staff: 1 Lectr.; 2 Clin. Teaching Staff; 3 Hon. Sr. Lectrs.; 4 Hon. Fellows

Ophthalmology, see under Surg.

Orthopaedic Surgery

Tel: (0131) 536 4667 Fax: (0131) 536 4754

Gibson, J. N. A., MD, FRCSEd   Sr. Lectr.
Gillespie, W. J., BSc MB MS, FRCSEd, FRACS   George Harrison Law Prof.; Head*
Other Staff: 2 Lectrs.; 2 Sr. Lectrs.†; 9 Clin. Teaching Staff; 11 Hon. Sr. Lectrs.; 2 Hon. Fellows

Rehabilitation Studies Unit

Tel: (0131) 537 9076 Fax: (0131) 537 9030

2 Sr. Lectrs.; 2 Res. Fellows; 1 Res. Assoc.; 1 Hon. Sr. Lectr.; 2 Hon. Fellows
Vacant Posts: 1 Prof.
Research: amputation; brain injury; cardiac disorders; stroke

Otolaryngology, see under Surg.

Pathology

Tel: (0131) 650 3001 *Fax:* (0131) 650 6528

Al-Nafussi, Awatif I., DPhil *Oxf.*, MB ChB, FRCPath   Sr. Lectr.
Anderson, T. J., MB ChB *Glas.*, PhD *Glas.*, FRCPath, FRSEd   Reader
Arends, Mark J., BSc MB ChB PhD   Sr. Lectr.
Bell, Jeanne E., BSc MD, FRCPath   Reader
Bird, C. C., MB ChB *Glas.*, PhD *Glas.*, FRCPath, FRCPEd, FRSEd, FRCSEd   Prof.
Duvall, E., MA *Oxf.*, DPhil *Oxf.*, MB ChB, FRCPath   Sr. Lectr.
Fleming, Stewart, BSc *Glas.*, MD *Glas.*, FRCPath   Sr. Lectr.
Gilmour, H. M., MB ChB, FRCPath   Sr. Lectr.
Grigor, Ken M., BSc *Glas.*, MD, FRCPath   Sr. Lectr.
Harrison, D. J., BSc MB ChB   Reader
Hooper, M. L., MA *Camb.*, PhD *Camb.*, FRSEd   Prof., Molecular Pathology
Howie, Sarah E. M., BSc *St And.*, PhD *Lond.*   Sr. Lectr.
Ironside, James W., MB ChB, FRCPath   Sr. Lectr.
Krajewski, A. S., BSc MB ChB PhD, FRCPath   Sr. Lectr.
Lammie, G. Alistair, BA MB BChir PhD   Sr. Lectr.
McGoogan, Euphemia, MB ChB *Aberd.*, FRCPath   Sr. Lectr.
McLaren, Kathryn M., BSc MB ChB, FRCPath, FRCSEd, FRCPEd   Sr. Lectr.
Piris, J., DPhil *Oxf.*, LicenMedCh, FRCPath   Sr. Lectr.
Reid, W. A., BSc MD, FRCPath   Sr. Lectr.
Salter, Donald M., BSc MB ChB   Sr. Lectr.
Wharton, S. B., BSc MB BS MSc   Sr. Lectr.
Williams, Alistair R. W., BSc MD   Sr. Lectr.
Wyllie, Andrew H., BSc *Aberd.*, MB ChB *Aberd.*, PhD, FRCPath, FRSEd, FRS, FRCPEd   Prof., Experimental Pathology; Head*
Other Staff: 1 Lectr.; 17 Res. Fellows; 6 Res. Assocs.; 1 Lectr.†; 4 Clin. Teaching Staff; 1 Hon. Sr. Lectr.; 5 Hon. Fellows

Forensic Medicine Unit

Tel: (0131) 650 4518, 650 3283 *Fax:* (0131) 650 6529

Busuttil, A., MD *Malta*, FRCPath, FRCPEd   Prof.
Research: child abuse; drug misuse; fatal house fires; sudden infant death syndrome; vehicular collisions

Pharmacology

Tel: (0131) 650 8274 *Fax:* (0131) 650 6530

Donaldson, I. M. L., MA *Oxf.*, BSc MB ChB, FRCPEd   Prof.
Fink, G., MA *Oxf.*, DPhil *Oxf.*, MB BS *Melb.*, MD *Melb.*, FRSEd   Hon. Prof.
Harmar, A. J., MA PhD   Hon. Prof.
Kelly, J. S., MA *Camb.*, BSc MB ChB PhD, FRCPEd, FRSEd   Prof.
McQueen, D. S., BPharm *Lond.*, PhD *Lond.*, DSc   Reader
Morris, R. G. M., MA *Oxf.*, DPhil *Oxf.*, FRS, FRSEd   Prof.
Olverman, Henry J., BSc *Glas.*, PhD *Camb.*   Sr. Lectr.
Poyser, Norman L., BPharm *Lond.*, PhD DSc   Sr. Lectr.; Head*
Walker, Jamieson, BSc PhD   Sr. Lectr.
Wilson, Norrie, BSc PhD, FRSChem   Sr. Lectr.
Other Staff: 3 Lectrs.; 8 Res. Fellows; 8 Res. Assocs.; 15 Hon. Fellows

Pharmacology, Clinical, see under Med. (W. Gen. Hosp.)

Psychiatry

Tel: (0131) 537 6267 *Fax:* (0131) 447 6860

Blackwood, D. H. R., MB ChB PhD, FRCP, FRCPsych   Reader
Ebmeier, Klaus P., MD *Aberd.*   Prof.
Hoare, P., MA *Oxf.*, DM *Oxf.*   Sr. Lectr.
Johnstone, Eve C., MD *Glas.*, FRCPEd, FRCPGlas, FRCPsych   Prof.; Head*

Kendell, R. E., MA MD, FRCP, FRCPsych   Hon. Prof.
Muir, Walter J., BSc MB ChB   Sr. Lectr.
Owens, D. G. Cunningham, MD ChB, FRCPGlas, FRCPsych   Sr. Lectr.
Power, Mick, BSc MSc DPhil   Prof., Clinical Psychology
Sharpe, Michael, MA   Sr. Lectr.
Thomson, Lindsay D. G., MB ChB MPhil   Sr. Lectr.
Other Staff: 8 Lectrs.; 11 Res. Fellows; 6 Res. Assocs.; 3 Sr. Lectrs.†; 19 Clin. Teaching Staff; 18 Hon. Sr. Lectrs.; 9 Hon. Fellows

Public Health Sciences

Tel: (0131) 650 3221, 650 3222 *Fax:* (0131) 650 6909

Agius, R. M., MD, FRCP, FRCPEd   Sr. Lectr.
Alexander, Freda E., BA MSc PhD   Reader
Amos, Amanda, BA *Camb.*, PhD *Camb.*, MSc   Sr. Lectr.
Campbell, H., BSc MSc MD, FRCPEd   Sr. Lectr.
Cunningham-Burley, BSc *Birm.*, PhD *Aberd.*   Sr. Lectr.
Forbes, John F., BA *Calif.*, MSc *York(UK)*, PhD   Sr. Lectr.
Fowkes, F. G. R., MSc *Lond.*, MSc *Edin.*, MB ChB PhD, FRCPEd   Prof., Epidemiology; Head*
Other Staff: 1 Bruce and John Usher Prof.; 5 Lectrs.; 4 Res. Fellows; 5 Res. Assocs.; 1 Sr. Lectr.†; 7 Clin. Teaching Fellows; 7 Hon. Sr. Lectrs.; 22 Hon. Fellows

Medical Statistics Unit

Tel: (0131) 650 3225 *Fax:* (0131) 650 3224

Murray, Gordon D., MA *Camb.*, PhD *Glas.*   Prof.
Prescott, Robin J., BSc *Reading*, MSc *S'ton.*, PhD *Liv.*   Sr. Lectr.
Other Staff: 2 Res. Fellows; 1 Res. Assoc.; 1 Hon. Fellow
Research: epidemiology; health promotion/education; health service research; medical statistics; occupational and environmental health

Radiodiagnosis, see Med. Radiol.

Rehabilitation Studies, see under Orthop. Surg.

Respiratory Medicine, see under Med. (Royal Infirmary)

Rheumatology, see under Med. (W. Gen. Hosp.)

Surgery

Tel: (0131) 536 3819 *Fax:* (0131) 228 2661

Bradbury, Andrew W., BSc MD, FRCSEd   Sr. Lectr.
Carter, Sir David C., MD *St And.*, FACS, FRCS, FRCSEd, FRCSGlas   Regius Prof.
Dunlop, M. G., MB ChB MD, FRCS   Reader
Fearon, K. C. H., MB ChB *Glas.*, FRCSGlas   Reader
Garden, O. J., BSc MD, FRCSEd, FRCSGlas   Prof., Hepatobiliary Surgery
Habib, Fouad K., BA *Utah*, PhD *Leeds*, FRSChem   Reader
James, Keith, BSc *Birm.*, PhD *Birm.*, DSc, FRSEd, FRCPath, FIBiol   Prof., Immunology
MacKinlay, G. A., MB BS *Lond.*, FRCS, FRCSEd   Sr. Lectr.
McArdle, C. S., MD, FRCS, FRCSEd, FRCSGlas   Prof.; Head*
Mealy, Kenneth, BA MD   Sr. Lectr.
Miller, W. R., BSc *Leeds*, PhD *Leeds*, DSc   Prof., Experimental Oncology
Ross, J. A., BSc *Strath.*, PhD *Strath.*   Sr. Lectr.
Ruckley, C. V., MB ChM, FRCPEd, FRCSEd   Prof., Vascular Surgery
Siriwardena, A. K., MB ChB MD, FRCS, FRCSEd   Sr. Lectr.
Other Staff: 2 Lectrs.; 1 Sr. Res. Fellow; 6 Res. Fellows; 1 Endowment Fellow; 3 Res. Assocs.; 3 Sr. Lectrs.†; 29 Clin. Teaching Staff; 18 Hon. Sr. Lectrs

Research: breast disease; colorectal cancer; hepatic and renal transplantation; hepatobiliary and pancreatic surgery; urogenital tract disease

Ophthalmology Unit

Tel: (0131) 536 3769 *Fax:* (0131) 536 3735

Bartholomew, R. S., BA *Camb.*, MB BChir *Camb.*, FRCSEd   Sr. Lectr.
Other Staff: 1 Res. Fellow; 1 Clin. Teaching Staff; 2 Hon. Fellows
Vacant Posts: 1 Prof.
Research: anti-glaucoma drugs; epidemiology of cataract; genetic eye diseases; glaucoma; neuro-opthalmology

Otolaryngology Unit

Tel: (0131) 536 3747 *Fax:* (0131) 229 8769

Maran, A. G. D., MD, FRCSEd, FACS   Prof.
Other Staff: 1 Res. Fellow; 1 Clin. Teaching Staff Member; 2 Hon. Sr. Lectrs.

VETERINARY MEDICINE

Pre-clinical Veterinary Sciences

Tel: (0131) 650 6100, 650 6085 *Fax:* (0131) 650 6576

Arbuthnott, Gordon W., BSc *Aberd.*, PhD *Aberd.*   Hon. Prof.
Brophy, Peter J., BSc *Lond.*, PhD *Lond.*, FIBiol   Mary Dick Prof., Veterinary Anatomy and Cell Biology
Brown, A. G., BSc MB ChB PhD, FRSEd, FIBiol   Prof., Veterinary Physiology; Head*
Cottrell, D. F., BVSc *Liv.*, MSc PhD   Sr. Lectr.
Duggan, A. W., BSc *Qld.*, MD *Qld.*, PhD *ANU*, FRSEd   Prof., Veterinary Pharmacology
Fleetwood-Walker, S. M., BSc *Birm.*, MSc *Birm.*, PhD *Birm.*   Sr. Lectr.
Kempson, Susan A., BSc *Leeds*, PhD *Liv.*   Sr. Lectr.
Macdonald, A. A., BSc *Glas.*, PhD MVD   Sr. Lectr.
Martin, R. J., BVSc *Liv.*, PhD   Reader
McLelland, J., BVMS *Glas.*, MVSc *Liv.*, PhD *Liv.*   Reader
Molony, V., BVSc *Liv.*, MSc *Cornell*, PhD *Liv.*, PhD *Edin.*   Reader
Pettigrew, G. W., BSc PhD   Reader
Short, A. D., MA *Oxf.*, BSc *Oxf.*, BM BCh *Oxf.*, PhD *Oxf.*   Sr. Lectr.
Other Staff: 4 Lectrs.; 8 Res. Fellows; 5 Res. Assocs.; 2 Hon. Fellows
Vacant Posts: Mary Dick Prof. (Vet. Physiol.)
Research: biochemistry; cell-membrane studies; comparative anatomy and physiology; developmental biology; veterinary anatomy

Tropical Animal Health

Tel: (0131) 650 6216 *Fax:* (0131) 445 5099

Brown, Duncan, BVM&S   Prof. Fellow
Edelsten, Martyn, BVMS MSc   Sr. Lectr.
Fielding, Denis, BSc MSc PhD   Sr. Lectr.
Hunter, A. G., BVM&S   Sr. Lectr.
Smith, A. J., MSc *Nott.*, PhD *Lond.*   Sr. Lectr.
Spooner, Roger L., OBE, BVetMed *Lond.*, MA *Camb.*, PhD *Camb.*   Hon. Prof.
Taylor, David W., BSc *S'ton.*, PhD *Camb.*   Prof.; Head*
Woodhouse, Mark E. J., BA MSc PhD   Prof., Veterinary Public Health and Quantitative Epidemiology
Other Staff: 1 Lectr.; 2 Sr. Res. Fellows; 6 Res. Fellows; 5 Res. Assocs.; 3 Lectrs.†; 6 Hon. Fellows

Veterinary Clinical Studies

Tel: (0131) 650 6281, 650 6061 *Fax:* (0131) 650 6588, 650 6577

Burnie, A. G., BVM&S   Sr. Lectr.; Dir., Small Animal Clinic
Corcoran, Brendan M., PhD   Sr. Lectr.
Cuddeford, D., BSc *Lond.*, MSc *Aberd.*, PhD   Sr. Lectr.
Dixon, P. M., MVB *N.U.I.*, PhD   Sr. Lectr.
Doxey, D. L., PhD BVM&S   Sr. Lectr.
Halliwell, R. E. W., MA *Camb.*, VetMB *Camb.*, PhD *Camb.*   William Dick Prof.; Head*

Kelly, J. M., BVM&S   Sr. Lectr.
Mayhew, Ian G., BVSc PhD   William Dick
  Prof., Veterinary Surgery
McGorum, B. C., BSc   Sr. Lectr.
Miller, Hugh R. P., BVMS *Glas.*, PhD
  Glas.   William Dick Prof., Clinical Studies
Penny, C. D., BVM&S   Lectr.; Dir., Large
  Animal Practice
Scott, P. R., BVM&S MPhil, FRCVS   Sr. Lectr.
Simpson, James W., BVM&S MPhil   Sr. Lectr.
Stead, A. C., BVMS *Glas.*, FRCVS   Sr. Lectr.
Thoday, K. L., BVetMed *Lond.*, PhD   Sr. Lectr.
Thrusfield, M. V., BVMS *Glas.*, MSc *Birm.*,
  FIBiol   Sr. Lectr.
Van den Brock, A. H. M., BVSc *Liv.*,
  FRCVS   Sr. Lectr.
Watson, E. D., BVM&S MVM PhD,
  FRCVS   Reader
Other Staff: 19 Lectrs.; 1 Sr. Res. Fellow; 4
  Res. Fellows; 1 Univ. Fellow; 2 Res. Assocs.;
  14 Hon. Fellows
Research: diagnosis, treatment and prevention of
  diseases in animals

Veterinary Pathology

Tel: (0131) 650 6173 Fax: (0131) 650 6511
Aitken, I. D., OBE, BVMS PhD Hon.
  DVM&S   Hon. Prof.
Dalziel, R. G., BSc *Glas.*, PhD *Glas.*   Sr. Lectr.
Else, R. W., BVSc *Brist.*, PhD *Brist.*   Sr. Lectr.
Fazakerley, John K., BSc PhD   Sr. Lectr.
Harkiss, G. D., PhD *Camb.*, BSc   Reader
Hopkins, J., BSc *Liv.*, PhD *Lond.*   Reader
Nash, A. A., BSc MSc PhD   Prof.; Head*
Other Staff: 5 Lectrs.; 8 Res. Fellows; 3 Res.
  Assocs.; 9 Hon. Fellows
Research: diagnostic pathology; immunology;
  neurobiology; pathogenesis of bacterial
  infection; virology

SPECIAL CENTRES, ETC

Artificial Intelligence Applications Institute (AIAI)

Tel: (0131) 650 2732 Fax: (0131) 650 6513
Tate, B. A., BA *Lanc.*, PhD   Dir.*
Other Staff: 1 Res. Assoc.

Genome Research, Centre for

Tel: (0131) 650 5890 Fax: (0131) 667 0164
Bishop, J. O., BSc PhD, FRSEd   Prof.,
  Molecular Cell Biology
Smith, A. G., BA *Oxf.*, PhD   Dir.*
Other Staff: 3 Sr. Res. Fellows; 12 Res.
  Fellows; 6 Res. Assocs.

Scottish Universities Research and Reactor Centre, see under University of Glasgow

Teaching, Learning and Assessment, Centre for

Tel: (0131) 650 4131 Fax: (0131) 650 6956
Forster, Fred, BSc *Brist.*, PhD *Brist.*   Co-Dir.*
Haywood, J., BSc *Open(UK)*, PhD *Open(UK)*   Sr.
  Lectr.
Hounsell, D., BA *Lond.*, PhD *Lanc.*   Co-Dir.*
Other Staff: 1 Res. Fellow

CONTACT OFFICERS

Academic affairs. Deputy Secretary: Longstaff,
  F. M., BA *Birm.*, MA *Well.*
Accommodation. Director of Accommodation
  Services: Cole, T. F., BA *Sus.*
Admissions (first degree). Senior
  Administrative Officer: Bruce, Linda M. S.,
  MA *Aberd.*, PhD *Aberd.*
Admissions (higher degree). Senior
  Administrative Officer: Garner, Vanessa L.
  C., BA *Brist.*
Adult/continuing education. Director, Centre
  for Continuing Education: Schuller, Prof.
  Tom, MA *Oxf.*
Alumni. Director, Development and Alumni
  Services: Tilley, Catrin, BSc
Archives. Sub-Librarian: Wilson, Arnott T.,
  MA
Careers. Director, Careers Service: Porrer,
  Robert A., MA *Oxf.*
Computing services. Director, Computing
  Services: Gilmore, Brian A. C., BSc MPhil
Conferences/corporate hospitality. Cole, J.
  F., BA *Sus.*
Consultancy services. Director of Research
  Services: Smailes, Bob, MBA PhD
Credit transfer. Senior Administrative Officer:
  Bruce, Linda M. S., MA *Aberd.*, PhD *Aberd.*
Development/fund-raising. Director,
  Development and Alumni Services: Tilley,
  Catrin, BSc
Equal opportunities. Equal Opportunities
  Officer: Larson, Marion, MA
Estates and buildings/works and services.
  Director of Estates and Buildings: Currie, A.,
  FRICS
Examinations. Director of Registry: Cattanach,
  Donald M., LLB
Finance. Director of Finance: Sutherland,
  George O.
General enquiries. Secretary to the University:
  Lowe, Martin J. B., BSc *St And.*, PhD *St And.*
Health services. Physician-in-Charge:
  Harrison, Nadine, MB ChB
Industrial liaison. Director of Research
  Services: Smailes, Bob, MBA PhD
International office. Director, International
  Office: Barron, Thomas J., MA *Aberd.*, PhD
  Lond.

Language training for international students.
  Glendenning, Eric H., MA
Library (chief librarian). Librarian/University
  Librarian: Mowatt, Ian R. M., BPhil MA, FLA
Personnel/human resources. Director of
  Personnel: Wallace, Christina E., BA *Stir.*,
  MEd *Dund.*, MPhil *Dund.*
Public relations, information and marketing.
  Director, Information and Public Relations
  Services: Footman, Raymond A., BA *Wales*
Publications. Director, Information and Public
  Relations Services: Footman, Raymond A.,
  BA *Wales*
Purchasing. Director of Procurement:
  Chadwick, Thomas D., BSc *Glas.*
Quality assurance and accreditation. Vice-
  Principal: Bell, Prof. Colin, BA *Keele*, MScEcon
  Wales, FRSEd
Research. Director of Research Services:
  Smailes, Bob, MBA PhD
Safety. Director, Health and Safety: Sykes,
  Peter J., BSc *St And.*, PhD *St And.*
Scholarships, awards, loans. Senior
  Administrative Officer: Bruce, Linda M. S.,
  MA *Aberd.*, PhD *Aberd.*
Schools liaison. Director, Schools Liaison
  Service: Hutcheson, Sandy
Security. Chief Security officer: Mackintosh,
  William B.
Sport and recreation. Director, Physical
  Education: Chainey, Alan, BSc
Staff development and training. Director of
  Personnel: Wallace, Christina E., BA *Stir.*
Student union. President, EUSA: Dalrymple,
  Bob
Student welfare/counselling (counselling).
  Head, Student Counselling Service: McDevitt,
  Craig, MA *St And.*
Student welfare/counselling (welfare).
  Director: Porrer, Robert A., MA *Oxf.*
Students from other countries. Director,
  International Office: Barron, Thomas J., MA
  Aberd., PhD *Lond.*
Students with disabilities. Special Needs
  Officer: Butson, Pat, BA
University press. Executive Chairman,
  Edinburgh University Press: Martin, David,
  BSc

CAMPUS/COLLEGE HEADS

New College, The Mound, Edinburgh,
  Scotland EH1 2LU. Principal: Page, Rev.
  Ruth, MA *St.And.*, BD *Otago*, DPhil *Oxf.*
Scottish Agricultural College: Edinburgh,
  The King's Buildings, West Mains Road,
  Edinburgh, Scotland EH9 3JG. Principal:
  Thomas, Prof. P. C., BSc *Wales*, PhD *Wales*,
  FIBiol

*[Information supplied by the institution as at 13 May
1998, and edited by the ACU]*

UNIVERSITY OF ESSEX

Established 1965

Member of the Association of Commonwealth Universities

Postal Address: Wivenhoe Park, Colchester, England CO4 3SQ
Telephone: (01206) 873333 **Fax**: (01206) 873598 **Cables**: University Colchester **WWW**: http://www.essex.ac.uk

VISITOR—Slynn of Hadley, The Rt. Hon. the Lord, Hon. LLD Hon. DCL
CHANCELLOR—Nolan of Brasted, The Rt. Hon. Baron, MA
PRO-CHANCELLOR—Beckett, Sir Terence, KBE, Hon. DSc(Econ) *Lond.*, Hon. DSc *Cran.IT*, Hon. DSc *H.-W.*, Hon. DTech *Brun.*, Hon. DU *Essex*, FEng, FIMechE
PRO-CHANCELLOR—Hart, R. D., OBE, BSc *Wales*, Hon. DU *Essex*
PRO-CHANCELLOR AND CHAIR OF COUNCIL—Waine, The Rt. Rev. John, BA *Manc.*
VICE-CHANCELLOR*—Crewe, Prof. Ivor M., BA *Oxf.*, MSc *Lond.*
TREASURER—Thomson, S., CBE
PRO-VICE-CHANCELLOR (ACADEMIC)—Crossick, Prof. G. J., MA *Camb.*, PhD *Lond.*
PRO-VICE-CHANCELLOR (RESEARCH)—Sanders, Prof. D. J., BSc *Lough.*, MA PhD
PRO-VICE-CHANCELLOR (SOCIAL AND TECHNICAL SUPPORT)—Massara, Prof. R. E., BA PhD, FIEE
REGISTRAR AND SECRETARY‡—......
LIBRARIAN—Butler, R., BSc *Aberd.*, MSc *Sheff.*

GENERAL INFORMATION

History. The university was established in 1965. It is located about 3km from Colchester.

Admission to first degree courses (see also United Kingdom Introduction). Through Universities and Colleges Admissions Service (UCAS). At least 2 passes in General Certificate of Education (GCE) A level, and 3 passes (Grade C or better) in General Certificate of Secondary Education (GCSE), or equivalent qualifications.

First Degrees (see also United Kingdom Directory to Subjects of Study). BA, BEng, BSc, LLB, MEng, MMaS (mathematical sciences).
BA, BEng, BSc, LLB: 3 years full-time or 4 years full-time (including 1 year of study abroad, or, for BSc, 1 year industrial placement). BEng, MMaS, MEng: 4 years full-time.

Higher Degrees (see also United Kingdom Directory to Subjects of Study). LLM, MA, MEnv, MSc, MPhil, PhD.
Applicants for admission to postgraduate degrees should hold a first degree with at least second class honours, or equivalent qualification.
Master's degrees: 1 year full time or two years part-time; MPhil: 2 years full-time or equivalent part-time (candidates with first degree), or 1 year full-time or equivalent part-time (candidates with master's degree); PhD: minimum 3 years full-time (candidates admitted with a first degree) or minimum 2 years (candidates with master's degree).

Language of Instruction. English. Full-time English language courses may be taken before degree study.

Libraries. Over 715,000 books, pamphlets and microforms.

Fees (1997–98). Undergraduate: £6310 (non-laboratory-based courses); £8350 (laboratory-based courses). Postgraduate: home/EU students: £2540; international students: £6310 (arts), £8350 (sciences).

Academic Year (1998–99). Three terms: 8 October–19 December; 18 January–27 March; 26 April–3 July.

Income (1996–97). Total, £50,083.

Statistics (1997-98). Staff: 1395 (including 484 teaching and research staff). Students: 5710.

FACULTIES/SCHOOLS

Graduate School
Tel: (01206) 872984 Fax: (01206) 872794
Dean: Sherer, Prof. Michael J., BA(Econ) *Manc.*, MA(Econ) *Manc.*, FCA

Humanities and Comparative Studies, School of
Tel: (01206) 872973 Fax: (01206) 872794
Dean: Radford, Prof. Andrew, BA *Camb.*, PhD *Camb.*

Law, School of
Tel: (01206) 872967 Fax: (01206) 872794
Dean: McCormack, Prof. Gerard, BCL *Trinity(Dub.)*, LLM *Trinity(Dub.)*

Mathematical and Computer Sciences, School of
Tel: (01206) 872773 Fax: (01206) 872794
Dean: Lowden, Barry G. T., MSc *Lond.*

Science and Engineering, School of
Tel: (01206) 872921 Fax: (01206) 872794
Dean: Gray, Prof. Timothy R. G., BSc *Nott.*, PhD *Nott.*, FIBiol

Social Sciences, School of
Tel: (01206) 872284 Fax: (01206) 872794
Dean: Richmond, Prof. James, MA *Glas.*, MSc(Econ) *Lond.*

ACADEMIC UNITS

Accounting, Finance and Management
Tel: (01206) 872546 Fax: (01206) 873429
Arnold, Anthony J., MSc *Brad.*, PhD *Lond.*, FCA Prof.
Chia, Robert, MA *Lanc.*, PhD *Lanc.* Prof.
Laughlin, Richard C., MSocSc *Birm.*, PhD *Sheff.*, FCA Prof.
Manson, Stuart, BA *Strath.*, MBA *Strath.* Sr. Lectr.
Sherer, Michael J., BA(Econ) *Manc.*, MA(Econ) *Manc.*, FCA Royal London Prof.
Sikka, Prem N., BA *Open(UK)*, MSc *Lond.*, PhD *Sheff.*, FCA Prof.
Wearing, Robert T., MSc *Lond.*, BA PhD, FCA Reader; Head*
Other Staff: 5 Lectrs.
Research: auditing; finance; financial reporting; regulation; management

Art History and Theory
Tel: (01206) 872200 Fax: (01206) 873003
Ades, J. Dawn, BA *Oxf.*, MA *Lond.* Prof.
Fraser, Valerie, MPhil *Lond.*, BA PhD Reader
Goubert, J. Sarah, MA *Lond.*, PhD *Lond.* Sr. Lectr.
Iversen, Margaret D., BA *Wellesley*, MLitt *Edin.*, PhD Reader; Head*
Lubbock, Julius A., BA *Camb.*, MA *Lond.* Reader
Nash, John M. Reader
Puttfarken, Thomas, DrPhil *Hamburg* Prof.
Vergo, Peter J., MA *Camb.*, PhD *Camb.* Prof.
Other Staff: 3 Lectrs.
Research: aesthetics and the visual arts (idealism to post-modernism); art and film studies; gallery studies; history and theory of modern art and architecture; Latin American and pre-Colombian art and architecture

Biological Sciences
Tel: (01206) 872248
Bailey, Graham S., BSc *Lond.*, PhD *Lond.* Sr. Lectr.
Baker, Neil R., BSc *Liv.*, PhD *Liv.* Prof.; Head*
Bowden, Keith, BSc *Hull*, DSc *Hull*, PhD *Hull*, FRSChem Prof.†
Cherry, Richard J., MA *Oxf.*, PhD *Sheff.* Prof.†
Colbeck, Ian, MSc *Lond.*, PhD *Lanc.* Reader
Gorrod, John, PhD *Lond.*, DSc *Lond.* Visiting Prof.
Gray, Timothy R. G., BSc *Nott.*, PhD *Nott.*, FIBiol Prof.†
Long, Stephen P., BSc *Reading*, PhD *Leeds* Prof.
Mason, Christopher F., BSc *Sheff.*, DPhil *Oxf.* Reader
Morison, James I. L., BSc *Lanc.*, PhD *Edin.* Sr. Lectr.
Mullineaux, Prof. P., BSc *Wales*, PhD *Wales* Visiting Prof.
Nedwell, David B., BSc *Wales*, PhD *Wales* Prof.
Nicolls, P., BA *Camb.*, PhD *Camb.*, DSc *Camb.* Visiting Prof.
O'Farrell, Minnie K., BSc *Sus.*, DPhil *Sus.* Sr. Lectr.
Raines, Christine A., BSc *Glas.*, PhD *Glas.* Sr. Lectr.
Stanway, Glyn, BSc *Lond.*, PhD *Lond.* Sr. Lectr.
Thornalley, Paul J., BSc *UMIST*, DPhil *Oxf.* Reader
Wilson, Michael T., MSc *E.Anglia*, PhD *E.Anglia* Prof.
Other Staff: 13 Lectrs.; 2 Readers†; 1 Sr. Lectr.†
Research: biochemistry (haem and metalloproteins, membranes, oxidative stress); cell and molecular biology (cell cycle, immunology, membrane biology, virology); ecology (aquatic and terrestrial ecosystems, conservation, ecological genetics); environmental microbiology (climate change, soils, estuarine and marine); plant biology (climate change, environmental stress, photosynthesis)

Computer Science

Tel: (01206) 872790 Fax: (01206) 872788

De Roeck, Anne N., LicGermFil *Leuven*, MSc Sr. Lectr.; Head*
Doran, James E., MA *Oxf.* Prof.
Henson, Martin C., BSc *S'ton.*, MSc Sr. Lectr.
Herbert, A., BSc *Leeds*, PhD *Camb.* Visiting Prof.
Lavington, Simon H., MSc *Manc.*, PhD *Manc.*, FIEE Prof.
Lowden, Barry G. T., MSc *Lond.* Sr. Lectr.
Oliver, John, BSc *Durh.*, PhD *Camb.* Prof.
Reynolds, T. Jeff, BA *Oxf.*, MSc *Wales*, PhD *Wales* Sr. Lectr.
Scott, Paul D., MA *Oxf.*, MSc *Lond.*, DPhil *Sus.* Sr. Lectr.
Standeven, John, MSc *Manc.*, PhD *Manc.* Sr. Lectr.
Steel, Sam W. D., BA *Camb.*, PhD *Edin.* Sr. Lectr.
Tsang, Edward P. K., BBA *HK*, MSc PhD Reader
Turner, Raymond, BSc *Lond.*, MA *Lond.*, PhD *Lond.* Prof.
Other Staff: 10 Lectrs.; 1 Reader†
Research: artificial intelligence; distributed information management systems; logic and formal methods; numerical computation; robotics and intelligent machines

Economics

Tel: (01206) 872728 Fax: (01206) 872724

Bailey, Roy E., MA Sr. Lectr.
Burdett, Kenneth, BA *CNAA*, MSc *Lond.*, PhD *Northwestern* Prof.
Chambers, Marcus J., MA PhD Prof.
Coles, Melvyn G., BA *Camb.*, MSc *S'ton.*, PhD *Prin.* Prof.
Goenka, Aditya, BA *Bom.*, MS *Cornell*, PhD *Cornell* Reader
Hatton, Timothy J., BA *Warw.*, PhD *Warw.* Prof.; Head*
Keen, Michael J., BA *Oxf.*, MPhil *Oxf.* Prof.
Lahiri, Sajal, PhD *I.Stat.I.* Prof.
McAuley, Alastair N. D., BSc(Econ) *Lond.* Reader
Muthoo, Abhinay, BSc *Lond.*, MPhil *Camb.*, PhD *Camb.* Prof.
Richmond, James, MA *Glas.*, MSc(Econ) *Lond.* Prof.
Other Staff: 12 Lectrs.; 5 Temp. Lectrs.
Research: econometrics (theoretical and applied); economic theory (particularly game theoretic applications); international trade and development; labour economics (theoretical and applied); public economics and public finance

Electronic Systems Engineering

Tel: (01206) 872435 Fax: (01206) 872900

Childs, I., BSc *Camb.*, PhD *Camb.*, FIEE Visiting Prof.
Clark, Adrian F., BSc *Newcastle(UK)*, PhD *Lond.* Sr. Lectr.
Clark, J. L., BS *New Mexico*, MSc *Idaho*, PhD *New Mexico* Visiting Prof.
Cochrane, P., BSc *CNAA*, MSc PhD, FIEE Visiting Prof.
Crawford, D., BA MSc PhD Visiting Prof.
Dennis, Timothy J., BA PhD Sr. Lectr.
Dilworth, Ian J., BSc *Kent*, PhD Sr. Lectr.
Downton, Andrew C., BSc *S'ton.*, PhD *S'ton.* Prof.
Ghanbari, Mohammad, BSc *Arya-Mehr*, MSc PhD Prof.
Hawksford, Malcolm O. J., BSc *Aston*, PhD *Aston*, FIEE Prof.
Jones, Edwin V., BSc *CNAA*, MSc PhD Sr. Lectr.
Lind, Larry F., BS *Virginia Polytech.*, MS *New Mexico*, PhD *Leeds*, FIEE Prof.
Mack, Robert J., BSc(Eng) *Lond.* Sr. Lectr.
Massara, Robert E., BA PhD, FIEE Prof.
Mirshekar-Syahkal, Dariush, BSc *Teheran*, MSc *Lond.*, PhD *Lond.* Reader
Nicol, R., BA PhD, FIEE Visiting Prof.
Noakes, Peter D., BSc *Lond.* Sr. Lectr.
O'Mahony, Michael J., BSc PhD Prof.; Head*

Pearson, Donald E., BSc(Eng) *CapeT.*, PhD *Lond.*, FIEE Prof.
Ritchie, Gordon J., BSc *St And.*, PhD, FIEE Sr. Lectr.
Saul, P., BSc *Durh.*, PhD *Durh.*, FIEE Visiting Prof.
Siddiqui, A. Shamim, BSc *H.-W.*, PhD *H.-W.* Sr. Lectr.
Walker, Stuart D., BSc *Manc.*, MSc PhD Sr. Lectr.
Other Staff: 9 Lectrs.
Research: communication networks (ATM, photonic/optical networks, radio systems); electronics (audio, design automation, microwaves, signal processing); multimedia and vision (image analysis, multimedia, video, virtual reality)

Finance, see Acctg., Finance and Management

Government

Tel: (01206) 872759 Fax: (01206) 873970

Anglade, Christian, LèsL *Toulouse* Sr. Lectr.
Barker, Anthony P., BA *Nott.*, MA *Nott.* Reader
Budge, Ian, MA *Edin.*, PhD *Yale* Prof.
Clarke, P. Barry, BA *Keele*, MA *Lanc.*, PhD *Manc.* Sr. Lectr.
Foweraker, Joseph W., BA *Camb.*, DPhil *Oxf.* Prof.
Frank, Peter J., BA *Leeds* Res. Prof.†
Freeman, Michael A., BA *Camb.*, LLB *Stan.*, PhD Reader
King, Anthony, BA *Qu.*, MA *Oxf.*, DPhil *Oxf.* Prof.
Kirchner, Emil J., MA *Case W.Reserve*, PhD *Case W.Reserve* Prof.
Laclau, Ernesto, LicHist *Buenos Aires*, PhD Prof.†
McKay, David H., BSc *Hull*, MA PhD Prof.
Millard, L. Frances E., BA *Earlham*, MA *Col.*, PhD *Col.* Sr. Lectr.
Neary, Ian J., BA *Sheff.*, DPhil *Sus.* Prof.
Newton, Kenneth, BA *Exe.*, PhD *Camb.* Prof.
Randall, M. Victoria, BA *Camb.*, MSc *Lond.*, PhD *Lond.* Reader
Richardson, Jeremy J., BA *Keele*, MA(Econ) *Manc.*, PhD *Manc.* Prof.
Sanders, David J., BSc *Lough.*, MA PhD Prof.
Scarbrough, Elinor M., BA *Manc.*, MA PhD Sr. Lectr.
Walker, Rachel S., BA *CNAA*, MA PhD Sr. Lectr.
Ward, Hugh D., BA PhD Reader
Weale, Albert P., BA *Camb.*, PhD *Camb.* Prof.; Head*
Other Staff: 5 Lectrs.; 1 Lectr.†; 2 Temp. Lectrs.
Research: democracy (elections, performance, practices, principles); European and UK public policy (ethics, environment, transport, welfare); international relations and comparative politics (decision-making, democratization, global commons, minorities, peacekeeping); pan-European (expansion, parties, public attitudes, security, union); political theory (autonomy, citizenship, human rights, social mobilization)

History

Tel: (10206) 872303 Fax: (01206) 873757

Crossick, Geoffrey J., MA *Camb.*, PhD *Lond.* Prof.
Davies, Joan M., BA *Lond.*, PhD *Lond.* Sr. Lectr.
Fletcher, Anthony J., MA *Oxf.*, FRHistS Prof.
Hamnett, Brian R., MA *Camb.*, PhD *Camb.* Prof.
Krikler, Jeremy, BA *Cape Town*, DPhil *Oxf.* Sr. Lectr.
Martin, Geoffrey H., CBE, MA *Oxf.*, DPhil *Oxf.*, Hon. DU Res. Prof.†
Smith, Stephen A., BA *Oxf.*, PhD *Birm.* Prof.
Venn, Fiona M., BA *Brist.*, PhD *Brist.* Sr. Lectr.
Walter, John. D., MA *Camb.*, MA *Penn.* Sr. Lectr.; Head*
Woolf, Stuart J., MA *Oxf.*, DPhil *Oxf.*, *Camb.*, DLitt *Oxf.* Prof.†
Other Staff: 7 Lectrs.; 1 Sr. Lectr.†

Language and Linguistics

Tel: (01206) 872196 Fax: (01206) 872198

Atkinson, R. Martin, BSc *Manc.*, MSc *Sus.*, PhD *Edin.* Prof.
Clahsen, Harald, MA *Wuppertal*, PhD *Wuppertal* Prof.
Cook, Vivian J., MA *Oxf.*, PhD Reader
Hawkins, Roger D., MA *Edin.*, PhD *Camb.* Sr. Lectr.
Jones, Michael A., BA *Sus.*, LèsL *Paris* Reader
McDonough, Jose E., BA *Keele*, MA *Birm.*, MA Sr. Lectr.
Radford, Andrew, BA *Camb.*, PhD *Camb.* Prof.
Roca, Ignacio M., LicenDer *Compostela*, LicenFilRom *Barcelona*, MA PhD Prof.
Sadler, Louisa G., BA *Sus.*, MA PhD Sr. Lectr.; Head*
Scholfield, Philip J., BA *Camb.* Sr. Lectr.
Spencer, Andrew J., BSc *Sus.*, PhD Sr. Lectr.
Tatham, Marcel A. A., BA *Leeds*, PhD *Leeds* Prof.
Widdowson, Henry G., MA *Camb.*, PhD *Edin.* Prof.†
Other Staff: 7 Lectrs.; 2 Temp. Lectrs.
Research: applied linguistics and English language teaching; computational linguistics; language acquisition and psycholinguistics; social aspects and dimensions of language; syntax, morphology and phonology (generative/constraint-based)

Law

Tel: (01206) 872586 Fax: (01206) 873428

Anderman, Steven D., BA *C.U.N.Y.*, LLB *Yale*, MSc *Lond.* Birkett Long Prof.
Boyle, C. Kevin, LLB *Belf.* Prof.
Dine, Janet, LLB *Lond.*, PhD *Lond.* Prof.
Gilbert, Geoffrey S., LLB *Leic.*, LLM *Virginia*, SJD *Virginia* Prof.
Gobert, James J., BA *Cornell*, JD *Duke* Prof.
Hamilton, Carolyn P., LLB *Brist.* Reader
Hampson, Françoise J., LLB *Newcastle(UK)* Prof.
Leader, Sheldon L., BA *Yale*, BA *Oxf.*, DPhil *Oxf.* Prof.
McCormack, Gerard, BCL *Trinity(Dub.)*, LLM *Trinity(Dub.)* Prof.
Peers, Steven J., BA *McM.*, LLB *W.Ont.*, LLM *Lond.* Sr. Lectr.
Rodley, Nigel S., LLB *Leeds*, LLM *Col.*, LLM *N.Y.*, PhD Prof.
Sherr, Avrom, PhD *Warw.* Visiting Prof.
Stone, Peter A., LLB *Camb.*, MA *Camb.* Reader
Sunkin, Maurice, LLM *Lond.* Prof.; Head*
Watt, Robert A., BA *CNAA*, BCL *Oxf.* Sr. Lectr.
Other Staff: 11 Lectrs.
Research: European law (EU law, Eastern Europe); human rights (humanitarian law, international human rights); law of enterprises (commercial, company and labour law); legal theory (criminology, jurisprudence); public law (administrative law, governance/regulation, judicial review)

Linguistics, see Lang. and Linguistics

Literature

Tel: (01206) 872604 Fax: (01206) 872620

Barker, Francis A., MA *Oxf.*, PhD Prof.
Brotherston, J. Gordon, BA *Leeds*, PhD *Camb.* Res. Prof.
Burnett, Leon, BA *Wales*, MA PhD Sr. Lectr.; Head*
Gray, Richard J., MA *Camb.*, PhD *Camb.*, FBA Prof.
Howard, Roger, MA Sr. Lectr.
Hulme, Peter, BA *Leeds*, PhD Prof.
Jordan, Elaine, BA *Oxf.*, PhD Reader
Kaye, Jacqueline, BA *Lond.*, MPhil *Lond.*, PhD Sr. Lectr.
Livingstone, Angela M., MA *Camb.*, PhD *Camb.* Res. Prof.
Pearson, Gabriel, MA *Oxf.* Prof.†
Stevenson, Kay G., BA *Agnes Scott*, MA *Calif.*, PhD *Yale* Sr. Lectr.
Other Staff: 10 Lectrs.; 1 Temp. Lectr.

Management, see Acctg., Finance and Management

Mathematics

Tel: (01206) 873040 Fax: (01206) 873043

Dowden, John M., MA Camb., PhD   Reader
Fremlin, David H., BA Camb., PhD Camb.   Reader
Higgins, Peter M., BA ANU, BSc Tas., PhD Monash   Sr. Lectr.
Holt, Anthony R., MA Oxf., DPhil Oxf.   Prof.; Head*
Mazumdar, Ravi, BTech IIT Bombay, MSc Lond., PhD Calif.   Prof.
Upton, Graham J. G., BSc Leic., MSc Birm., PhD Birm.   Reader
Other Staff: 5 Lectrs.

Philosophy

Tel: (01206) 872703 Fax: (01206) 873377

Critchley, Simon J., MPhil Nice, BA PhD   Reader
Dews, Peter K., BA Camb., PhD S'ton., MA   Prof.; Head*
Sacks, Mark D., BA Jerusalem, PhD Camb.   Reader
Sorell, Thomas E., BA McG., DPhil Oxf.   Prof.
Other Staff: 7 Lectrs.
Research: continental philosophy (Hegel, Kant and twentieth-century developments); ethics (applied ethics); philosophy and art (literature and the visual arts); philosophy and psychoanalysis; social and political philosophy (critical theory and human rights)

Physics

Tel: (01206) 872851

Adams, Michael J., BSc Lond., MSc Wales, PhD Wales   Prof.; Head*
Allen, L., PhD Lond., DSc Lond., FIP   Visiting Prof.
Babiker, Mohammad, BSc Khart., MSc Sus., DPhil Sus.   Prof.
Balkan, A. Naci, BSc Ankara, PhD Glas.   Reader
Barber, David J., BSc Brist., PhD Brist.   Visiting Prof.
Barr, Hugh C., BSc St And., PhD Wales   Reader
Boyd, T. James M., BSc Belf., PhD Belf., FIP   Prof.†
Hall, Thomas A., BSc Nott., PhD Lond.   Reader
Hughes, Thomas P., BSc Wales, FIP   Visiting Prof.
Kapadia, Phiroze D., BSc Manc., MSc Lond., PhD Lond.   Res. Prof.†
Loudon, Rodney, MA Oxf., DPhil Oxf., FRS   Prof.†
Parker, Terence J., BSc Lond., PhD Lond.   Prof.
Ridley, Brian K., BSc Durh., PhD Durh., FIP   Res. Prof.†
Smith, Stephen R. P., MA Oxf., DPhil Oxf.   Reader
Tallents, Gregory J., BSc NE, PhD ANU   Reader
Tilley, David R., BA Camb., PhD Camb.   Res. Prof.
Vickers, Anthony J., BSc Lanc., PhD Lanc.   Sr. Lectr.
Other Staff: 2 Lectrs.
Research: lasers and plasmas (inertial confinement fusion and X-ray lasers); non-linear optics and quantum optics; semi-conductors (low-dimensional structures and devices); spectroscopy (solid state spectroscopy of thin films and surfaces)

Psychology

Tel: (01206) 873591 Fax: (01206)873590

Fox, Elaine M., BA N.U.I., PhD N.U.I.   Sr. Lectr.
Joseph, Stephen A., BSc Ulster, MSc Lond., PhD Lond.   Sr. Lectr.

Masterson, Jacqueline, BSc CNAA, PhD Lond.   Sr. Lectr.
Meddis, Raymond, BA Lond., PhD Lond.   Prof.; Head*
Temple, Christine M., BSc St And., MA Calif., DPhil Oxf.   Prof.
Wilkins, Arnold J., BA Lond., PhD Lond.   Prof.
Other Staff: 6 Lectrs.
Research: cognition (attention, language, memory, perception, reasoning); cognitive neuropsychology (amnesia, aphasia, dyslexia); developmental psychology and neuropsychology; health/social psychology (stress and trauma); sensory perception (psycho acoustics, vision)

Sociology

Tel: (01206) 873049 Fax: (01206) 873410

Benton, Edward, BA Leic., BPhil Oxf., PhD   Prof.
Busfield, N. Joan, MA St And., MA PhD   Prof.
Coxon, Anthony P. M., BA Leeds, PhD Leeds   Res. Prof.
Craib, Ian E., BA Lond., PhD Manc.   Prof.
Davidoff, Leonore, BA Oberlin, MA Lond., PhD   Res. Prof.†
Glucksmann, Miriam A., BA Lond., PhD Lond.   Prof.; Head*
Lockwood, David, CBE, BSc(Econ) Lond., MA Camb., PhD Lond., FBA   Res. Prof.†
Marsden, Dennis, MA Camb.   Prof.
Morris, Lydia, BA Keele, PhD Lond.   Prof.
Plummer, Kenneth J., BSc Lond., PhD Lond.   Prof.
Scott, Alison M., MA Edin., PhD   Reader
Scott, John P., BSc Lond., PhD Strath.   Prof.
South, Nigel, BA Middx., MA Middx., PhD Middx.   Prof.
Thompson, Paul R., MA Oxf., DPhil Oxf.   Res. Prof.†
Woodiwiss, Anthony B., BA Leeds, MSc Lond., PhD   Prof.
Other Staff: 11 Lectrs.

SPECIAL CENTRES, ETC

Data Archive

Tel: (01206) 872001 Fax: (01206) 872033
Vacant Posts: Dir.*

Psychoanalytic Studies, Centre for

Tel: (01206) 873745

Hinshelwood, Robert L., BSc Lond., MB BS Lond., FRCPsych   Prof.†
Papadopoulos, Rene K., PhD Cape Town   Prof.†
Raphael-Leff, Joan, BA Tel-Aviv, MSc Lond.   Prof.†
Samuels, Andrew, DHumL Santa Barbara   Prof.†

Social and Economics Research, University of Essex Institute for

Tel: (01206) 872957 Fax: (01206) 873151

Berthoud, Richard, BA Oxf.   Prof.
Booth, Alison L., BA NSW, MA Syd., MSc Lond., PhD Lond.   Prof.
Ermisch, John F., BS Wis., MA Kansas, PhD Kansas   Prof.
Gershuny, Jonathan I., BSc Lough., MA Oxf., MSc Strath., DPhil Sus.   Prof.; Dir.*
Jenkins, Stephen P., BA Otago, DPhil York(UK)   Prof.
Micklewright, J., BA Exe., PhD Lond.   Visiting Prof.
Pahl, Raymond, MA Camb., PhD Lond.   Visiting Prof.
Rose, David, BA Wales, PhD   Res. Prof.
Verma, Vijay, BTech Kharagpur, MSc Lond., PhD Camb.   Res. Prof.†
Research: demographic research on families and households; income inequality and social stratification; longitudinal analysis of the labour market; longitudinal survey and statistical methods; time use and domestic work

CONTACT OFFICERS

Academic affairs. Academic Registrar: Collett, Moira H. R., BA York(UK)
Accommodation. Academic Registrar: Collett, Moira H. R., BA York(UK)
Admissions (first degree). Admissions Officer: Walker, P. D. A., BA Lond.
Admissions (higher degree). Admissions Officer: Walker, P. D. A., BA Lond.
Adult/continuing education. Director of Continuing Education: Tillett, J. G., PhD Lond., DSc Lond., FRSChem†
Alumni. Director of External Relations: Lister, R., BA York(UK)
Careers. Careers Officer: Symons, Joanna M., BA Warw., MA
Computing services. Director of Information Systems: Powers, J. S., BA Camb.
Development/fund-raising. Director of External Relations: Lister, R., BA York(UK)
Equal opportunities (staff). Personnel Officer: Sample, M. Ellen
Equal opportunities (students). Academic Registrar: Collett, Moira H. R., BA York(UK)
Estates and buildings/works and services. Estates Officer: Nightingale, A. R., FRICS
Examinations. Academic Registrar: Collett, Moira H. R., BA York(UK)
Finance. Director of Finance: Gorringe, J. P.
General enquiries. Registrar and Secretary: ......
Health services. Personnel Officer: Sample, M. Ellen
Industrial liaison. Industrial Liaison Officer: Huston, W., BSc Belf.
International office. Director of Overseas Relations: Oliver, Prof. J., BSc Durh., PhD Camb.
Library (chief librarian), Library (enquiries). Librarian: Butler, R., BSc Aberd., MSc Sheff.
Personnel/human resources. Personnel Officer: Sample, M. Ellen
Public relations, information and marketing. Director of External Relations: Lister, R., BA York(UK)
Publications. Publications Officer: Illsley, Monica, LLB
Purchasing. Purchasing Manager: Mason, K.
Quality assurance and accreditation. Assistant Registrar: Harrison, Rosemary, BA Lond., MA Lond.
Research. Pro-Vice-Chancellor (Research): Sanders, Prof. D. J., BSc Lough., MA PhD
Safety. Fire and Safety Officer: Donaldson, J. L.
Scholarships, awards, loans. Academic Registrar: Collett, Moira H. R., BA York(UK)
Schools liaison. Director of External Relations: Lister, R., BA York(UK)
Security. Security Officer: Hughes, G. F.
Sport and recreation. Director of Physical Recreation: Rustage, A. F., BA Open(UK), MBA Essex
Staff development and training. Staff Development Officer: Hewes, I. R., BA Liv., MBA City(UK)
Student union. General Manager: Harris, Peter
Student welfare/counselling. Senior Administrative Assistant: Jones, Angela, BA
Students from other countries. Senior Administrative Assistant: Jones, Angela, BA
Students with disabilities. Senior Administrative Assistant: Jones, Angela, BA

[Information supplied by the institution as at May 1998, and edited by the ACU]

UNIVERSITY OF EXETER

Founded 1955; previously established as the University College of the South West of England, 1922

Member of the Association of Commonwealth Universities

Postal Address: Northcote House, The Queen's Drive, Exeter, Devon, England EX4 4QJ
Telephone: (01392) 263263 **Fax**: (01392) 263108 **Cables**: University Exeter **Telex**: 42894 EXUNIV G
WWW: http://www.ex.ac.uk **E-mail formula**: initial.surname@exeter.ac.uk

VISITOR—Elizabeth, H.M. The Queen
CHANCELLOR—Richards, Sir Rex, DSc Oxf., Hon. DSc, FRS, FRSChem, Hon. FRCP, Hon. FRAM, FBA
PRO-CHANCELLOR—Day, E. R., JP, MA Camb.
PRO-CHANCELLOR—Lorenz, Margaret E., BA Lond.
VICE-CHANCELLOR*—Holland, Sir Geoffrey, KCB, BA Oxf., MA Oxf., Hon. LLD Sheff.
DEPUTY VICE-CHANCELLOR—Atkinson, Prof. Keith, BSc Wales, PhD Wales, FGS
DEPUTY VICE-CHANCELLOR—Bennett, Prof. Neville, BEd Lanc., PhD Lanc.
DEPUTY VICE-CHANCELLOR—Newitt, Prof. Malyn D. D., BA Oxf., PhD Lond., FRHistS
TREASURER—Hardyman, N. T., CB, MA Oxf.
REGISTRAR AND SECRETARY‡—Powell, Ian H. C., MA Birm.
LIBRARIAN—Paterson, Alasdair T., MA Edin., MA Sheff.

GENERAL INFORMATION

History. Established as University College of the South West of England in 1922, the university was founded under its present name in 1955.

The main site overlooks the city of Exeter. The School of Education occupies a second site in Exeter and the Camborne School of Mines is situated in West Cornwall.

Admission to first degree courses (see also United Kingdom Introduction). Through Universities and Colleges Admissions Service (UCAS). Part-time students apply direct to the university. General entrance requirement: 2 passes at General Certificate of Education (GCE) A level (or equivalent qualifications), together with acceptable levels of literacy and numeracy.

First Degrees (see also United Kingdom Directory to Subjects of Study). BA, BA(Ed), BEd, BEng, BMus, BSc, BSc(Ed), LLB, LLB(Eur), MChem, MEng, MMath, MPhys, MStat.

Full-time degrees normally last 3 years. Modern language degrees and degrees with European study: 3 years plus 1 year abroad. MChem, MEng, MMath, MPhys, MStat: 4 years.

All undergraduate degrees may be taken on a part-time basis by arrangement with the department concerned.

Higher Degrees (see also United Kingdom Directory to Subjects of Study). LLM, MA, MBA, MEd, MEng, MEng(Eur), MMus, MPhil, MSc, PhD.

Applicants must normally hold an appropriate first degree with at least second class honours. The majority of courses last 1 year full-time or 2 years part-time; PhD: normally 3 years full-time or up to 7 years part-time.

Language of Instruction. English. Pre-sessional and in-sessional courses are available for students whose first language is not English.

Libraries. 1,000,000 books and journals; over 3000 periodicals subscribed to. Responsible for running: Cathedral Library (possesses the Exeter Book, the Exeter Domesday Book and many other rare examples from the medieval and early modern periods); Devon and Exeter Institution Library (West Country materials and nineteenth-century periodicals). Special collections include: personal library of Sir John Betjeman.

Fees. Undergraduate (1998–99, annual): UK students up to £1000; international students £6645 (arts-based subjects), £8325 (science/engineering-based subjects). Postgraduate (1997–98, annual): UK students £2540 (basic fee); international students £6870 (arts-based subjects), £8550 (science-based subjects).

Academic Year (1998-99). Three terms: 5 October–11 December; 11 January–19 March; 26 April–2 July.

Income (1996-97). Total, £74,900,000.

Statistics. Staff: 981 (895 academic, 86 administrative). Students: full-time 7846 (6734 undergraduate, 1112 postgraduate); part-time 1778 (922 undergraduate, 856 postgraduate); international 778; total: 10,402.

FACULTIES/SCHOOLS

Faculty of Academic Partnerships

Dean: Forsythe, William J., MA Camb., MPhil Exe., PhD Exe.

Faculty of Postgraduate Studies

Dean: Overton, Prof. Mark, BA Exe., MA Camb., PhD Camb.

Faculty of Undergraduate Studies

Dean: Narayanan, Ajit, BSc Aston, PhD Exe.

ACADEMIC UNITS

Accountancy, see Business and Econ., Sch. of

Adult Education, see Continuing and Adult Educn.

Agricultural Economics Unit, see under Business and Econ., Sch. of

Arabic and Middle East Studies, see under Mod. Langs., Sch. of

Archaeology, see Geog. and Archaeol., Sch. of

Biological Sciences, School of

Tel: (01392) 264674 Fax: (01392) 263700
Anderson, Jonathan M., BSc Exe., PhD Lond. Prof., Ecology
Brown, J. Anne, BSc Wales, PhD Sheff. Reader, Fish Physiology
Bryant, John A., MA Camb., PhD Camb., FIBiol Prof.
Clarkson, D. T., PhD Exe., DSc Exe. Visiting Prof., Plant Physiology
Dinan, Laurence N., BSc Liv., PhD Liv. Sr. Lectr.
Harris, Tegwyn, BSc Wales, PhD Exe. Sr. Lectr.
Kennedy, Clive R., PhD Liv., DSc Liv. Prof., Parasitology; Head*

Lappin-Scott, Hilary M., BSc Warw., PhD Warw. Reader, Environmental Microbiology
Littlechild, Jennifer A., PhD Lond. Reader, Biological Chemistry
Macnair, Mark R., BA Camb., MA Camb., PhD Liv. Prof., Evolutionary Genetics
Pitt, Dennis, PhD Birm., DSc Birm. Reader, Plant Pathology
Roddick, James G., BSc Glas., PhD Glas. Sr. Lectr.
Stebbings, Howard, BSc St And., PhD St And. Reader, Cell Biology
Talbot, Nicholas J., BSc Wales, PhD E.Anglia Reader
Willetts, Andrew J., BSc Liv., PhD Liv. Reader, Applied Microbiology
Wootton, Robin J., BSc Lond., PhD Lond. Sr. Lectr.
Other Staff: 7 Lectrs.; 13 Res. Fellows; 5 Hon. Res. Fellows
Research: molecular biology and biochemistry; physiological ecology and genetics; physiology; terrestrial and aquatic ecology

Business and Economics, School of

Tel: (01392) 263218 Fax: (01392) 263242
Adair, John, BLitt Oxf., MA Camb., PhD Lond. Visiting Prof., Leadership
Blaug, Mark, BA Qu., BA N.Y., MA Col., PhD Col., FBA Visiting Prof.†
Bulkley, I. George, MA Essex, PhD Calif. Prof.
Collier, Paul A., BSc Aston, PhD Exe., FCA Sr. Lectr., Accountancy
Cooke, Terry E., BSc(Econ) Lond., PhD Exe., FCA Prof., Accounting
de Meza, David E., BSc(Econ) Lond., MSc Lond. Prof.
Gifford-Gifford, Mark A., MA Camb., MPhil Lond., FCA Sr. Lectr., Accountancy
Gregory, Alan, MSc Lond. Prof., Business and Finance
James, Simon R., BSc(Econ) Lond., MSc Lond., MA Open(UK), MBA Open(UK), LLM Leic. Reader
Jones, Ian, PhD Lond.Bus. Visiting Prof.
Luther, Robert G., BCom Natal, MA Exe. Sr. Lectr.
Maloney, John, BA Camb., PhD Nott. Sr. Lectr.
McInerney, John P., OBE, BSc(Agric) Lond., PhD Iowa Glanely Prof., Agricultural Policy
Myles, Gareth D., BA Warw., MSc(Econ) Lond., DPhil Oxf. Prof.
Phillips, Garry D. A., BA Sheff., MSc S'ton. Prof., Econometrics
Timbrell, Martin C., MA Camb., MA Warw. Sr. Lectr.; Head*
Tippett, Mark, BCom Newcastle(NSW), PhD Edin. Prof., Accounting
Wren-Lewis, Simon, MA Camb., MSc Lond. Bertie Black Prof., Business and Economics

Other Staff: 20 Lectrs.; 12 Res. Fellows; 11 Lectrs.†

Research: accounting; business and management; economics and econometrics; finance

Agricultural Economics Unit

Tel: (01392) 263836 Fax: (01392) 263852

Howe, Keith S., BScEcon Wales, MPhil Lond., PhD Exe.   Sr. Lectr.
McCorriston, Steven, BA Strath., MSc Reading   Reader
McInerney, John P., OBE, BSc(Agric) Lond., PhD Iowa   Glanely Prof., Agricultural Policy; Dir.*
Other Staff: 2 Res. Fellows

Camborne School of Mines, see Mines, Camborne Sch. of

Chemistry, School of

Tel: (01392) 263489 Fax: (01392) 263434

Bruce, Duncan W., BSc Liv., PhD Liv., FRSChem   Prof., Inorganic Chemistry; Head*
Coldham, Ian, BA Cant.CCC, PhD Cant.CCC   Sr. Lectr.
Fowler, Patrick W., BSc Sheff., PhD Sheff.   Prof., Theoretical Chemistry
Kite, Ken, BSc Leeds, PhD Leeds, FRSChem   Sr. Lectr.
Legon, Anthony C., PhD Lond., DSc Lond., FRSChem   Prof., Physical Chemistry; EPSRC Sr. Fellow
Littlechild, Jennifer A., PhD Lond.   Reader, Biological Chemistry
Moodie, Roy B., PhD Lond., DSc Lond., FRSChem   Reader, Physical-Organic Chemistry
Moody, Christopher J., PhD Liv., DSc Lond.   Prof., Organic Chemistry
Orrell, Keith G., BScTech Manc., PhD Manc., DSc Manc., FRSChem   Reader, Spectroscopy
Osborne, Anthony G., BSc Hull, PhD Lond., FRSChem   Sr. Lectr.
Rosseinsky, David R., MSc Rhodes, PhD Manc., DSc Manc., FRSChem   Reader, Physical Chemistry
Sandall, John P. B., BSc Lond., PhD Lond., FRSChem   Sr. Lectr.
Shipman, Michael, BSc Lond., PhD Lond.   Sr. Lectr.
Slade, Robert C. T., MA Oxf., DPhil Oxf., FRSChem   Reader, Materials Chemistry
Stead, Keith, MA Oxf., DPhil Oxf.   Sr. Lectr.; Dir., Labs.
Steiner, Eric, MSc Manc., PhD Manc.   Sr. Lectr.
Other Staff: 8 Lectrs.; 12 Res. Fellows; 4 Hon. Res. Fellows

Research: co-ordination and metal-organic chemistry; kinetics and mechanism; materials chemistry; organic and bio-organic chemistry; theoretical chemistry

Classics and Theology, School of

Classics and Ancient History

Tel: (01392) 264202 Fax: (01392) 264377

Braund, David C., MA Camb., PhD Camb.   Prof., Mediterranean and Black Sea History
Gill, Christopher J., MA Camb., PhD Yale   Prof., Ancient Thought
Postlethwaite, Norman, MA Sheff., PhD Sheff.   Sr. Lectr.; Head of Sch.*
Seaford, Richard A. S., MA Oxf., DPhil Oxf.   Prof., Greek Literature
Wilkins, John M., MA Camb., PhD Camb.   Sr. Lectr.
Wiseman, T. Peter, MA Oxf., DPhil Oxf., Hon. DLitt Durh., FBA, FSA   Prof.
Other Staff: 3 Lectrs.; 4 Res. Fellows; 1 Lectr.†

Research: Greek literature of the archaic and classical period; ideas of personality in the ancient world; Latin literature and ritual; Latin literature and science; relations of Greece and north-eastern Europe

Theology

Tel: (01392) 264241 Fax: (01392) 264377

Catchpole, David R., MA Oxf., PhD Camb.   St Luke's Foundation Prof.
Logan, Rev. Alistair H. B., MA Edin., BD Edin., ThM Harv., PhD St And.   Sr. Lectr.
Other Staff: 3 Lectrs.; 1 Lectr.†; 2 Hon. Lectrs.; 4 Hon. Res. Fellows

Research: New Testament; Old Testament; philosophy/ethics; systematics

Computer Science, see Engin. and COmputer Sci., Sch. of

Continuing and Adult Education

Tel: (01392) 411905 Fax: (01392) 436082

Benn, Roseanne C., MSc Lond.   Sr. Lectr.; Head*
Fieldhouse, Roger T., BA Reading, PhD Leeds   Prof., Adult Education
Other Staff: 4 Lectrs.; 2 Lectrs.†

Research: adult education; archaeology; biology/psychology; historical studies; literary studies

Drama and Music, School of

Drama

Tel: (01392) 264580 Fax: (01392) 411949

McCullough, Christopher J., BA CNAA, MA Leeds   Head of Sch.*
Read, Leslie Du S., BA Manc.   Sr. Lectr.
Thomson, Peter W., MA Camb.   Prof.
Other Staff: 3 Lectrs.; 1 Lectr.†; 3 Hon. Res. Fellows

Research: actor and character in performance; ancient Greek theatre performance and stages; Brecht, Meyerhold and political theatre; gender and performance; Shakespeare's stage then and now

Music

Tel: (01392) 263810 Fax: (01392) 263815

Grange, Philip R., BA York(UK), DPhil York(UK)   Reader, Composition
Langham Smith, Richard, BA York(UK)   Reader, Music
Sandon, Nicholas J., BMus Birm., PhD   Prof.
Other Staff: 3 Lectrs.; 1 Lectr.†

Research: composition; early music (especially editing); eighteenth-, nineteenth-and twentieth-century music

Economics, see Business and Econ., Sch. of

Education, School of

Tel: (01392) 264888 Fax: (01392) 264788

Ackland, John W., BSc(Soc) Lond., MPhil Sus.   Sr. Lectr.
Armstrong, Neil, BEd Lough., MSc Lough., PhD Exe., FIBiol   Prof., Health and Exercise Science
Balding, John W., MA Camb., MSc Nott.   Sr. Lectr.
Bennett, S. Neville, BEd Lanc., PhD Lanc.   Prof.
Bloomer, J. Martin, MEd Brist., PhD Exe.   Sr. Lectr.
Bolt, A. Brian, BSc Lond.   Sr. Lectr.
Boutcher, Stephen H., MSc Dal., PhD Arizona   Sr. Lectr.
Burden, Robert L., BA Hull, PhD Exe., FBPsS   Reader, Educational Psychology
Burghes, David N., BSc Sheff., PhD Sheff.   Prof.
Carré, Clive G., MSc Brist., PhD Exe.   Sr. Lectr.
Cockett, Stephen J., BA(Mus) Manc., MPhil Exe.   Sr. Lectr.
Copley, Terence D., BA Nott.   Prof., Religious Education
Crossman, Jane, BSc MSc PhD   Visiting Prof.
Cunliffe, Leslie   Sr. Lectr.
Davis, Nicola E., BSc Edin., PhD Belf.   Prof., Educational Telematics
Day, Mick G., BSc Lond., PhD Exe.   Sr. Lectr.
Desforges, Charles W., BSc Lond., PhD Lanc.   Prof.; Head*
Ernest, Paul, BSc Sus., MSc Lond., PhD Lond., FIMA   Reader, Mathematics Education
Fines, John, MA PhD, FRHistS   Visiting Prof.
Fox, Geoff, MA Oxf.   Sr. Lectr.

Fox, Kenneth R., BSc Lond., MS Kansas, PhD Arizona   Reader, Exercise and Public Health
Fox, Richard M. H., BSc Lond., MA Sus., MEd Exe., PhD Exe.   Sr. Lectr.
Golby, Michael J., MA Exe., PhD Exe.   Reader
Green, Margaret D., MA   Visiting Prof.
Hobbs, David A., MA Camb.   Sr. Lectr.
Holden, Cathie, BA Wales, MPhil CNAA   Sr. Lectr.
Hughes, Martin, BA Oxf., PhD Edin.   Prof.
MacLeod, Fiona, BA Open(UK), PhD Exe.   Sr. Lectr.
Midwinter, Eric, MA Camb., DPhil York(UK), Hon. DUniv Open(UK)   Visiting Prof.
Neather, Edward J., MA Camb., MEd Exe.   Sr. Lectr.
Nichol, Jon D., MA Camb., PhD Camb.   Reader, History in Education
Peacock, Alan, BSc Manc., DPhil Ulster   Sr. Lectr.
Preece, Peter F. W., MA Oxf., PhD Exe., FIP   Prof.
Radnor, Hilary A., BA Glas., MA Sus., PhD Lond.   Reader, Educational Policy
Somers, John W., MEd Exe.   Sr. Lectr.
Sparkes, Andrew C., BEd Lough., PhD Lough., MA Durh.   Prof., Social Theory
Taylor, William H., MA Aberd., MEd Aberd., MS Kansas, PhD Exe.   Sr. Lectr.
Thacker, V. John, BSc Edin., PhD Exe.   Sr. Lectr.
Trend, Roger D., BA Sheff., MSc Keele, PhD Exe.   Sr. Lectr.
Underwood, A. Martin, PhD Exe.   Sr. Lectr.
Williams, Marion D., BSc St And., MEd HK   Sr. Lectr.
Wood, Elizabeth A., BA CNAA, MEd Leeds   Sr. Lectr.
Wragg, Edward C., BA Durh., MEd Leic., PhD Exe., Hon. DUniv Open, Hon. DU Strath.   Prof.
Wray, David J., BA Hull, MSc Lanc.   Reader, Literacy in Education
Other Staff: 54 Lectrs.; 14 Res. Fellows; 1 Hon. Lectr.; 11 Hon. Res. Fellows; 6 Temp. Lectrs.†

Research: curriculum development and evaluation; literacy and language; teaching and learning; teaching English as a second and as a foreign language; telematics and new technology in education

Engineering and Computer Science, School of

Computer Science

Tel: (01392) 264061 Fax: (01392) 264067

Ford, Lindsey, BSc Lanc., PhD Exe.   Sr. Lectr.
Gibbons, Peter, BA Oxf., BPhil Oxf., DPhil Oxf.   Visiting Prof.
Milne, Wendy J., BSc Nott., PhD Nott.   Sr. Lectr.
Narayanan, Ajit, BSc Aston, PhD Exe.   Sr. Lectr.
Partridge, Derek, BSc Lond., PhD Lond.   Prof.
Turner, Stephen J., MA Camb., MSc Manc., PhD Manc.   Sr. Lectr.
Other Staff: 7 Lectrs.; 3 Computer Devel. Officers; 3 Res. Fellows; 4 Hon. Res. Fellows

Research: artificial intelligence and cognitive science; media computing; neural computing; parallel systems; visualisation and visual programming

Engineering

Tel: (01392) 263628 Fax: (01392) 217965

Ashcroft, Stan J., BSc Leeds, PhD Leeds   Sr. Lectr.
Belmont, Michael R., BSc Wales, PhD Wales   Sr. Lectr.
Boyle, John D., MA Camb., MSc Lond.   Sr. Lectr.
Davies, Thomas W., BScTech Sheff., PhD Sheff., FIChemE   Prof., Thermofluids Engineering
Evans, Kenneth E., BSc Lond., PhD Camb.   Prof., Materials Engineering
Grainger, Peter, BSc Reading, MSc Lond., PhD Exe., FGS   Sr. Lectr.
Harvey, William J., BSc Leeds, PhD Leeds, FICE   Prof., Civil Engineering

Hills, P. Robin, BSc(Eng) Lond., MSc Birm. Sr. Lectr.

Hooper, Bill R. M., BSc Exe., PhD Exe. Sr. Lectr.

Horwood, J. Michael K., BSc Exe., PhD Exe. Lectr.; Head, Microprocessor Unit

Kalaugher, Patrick G., MA Oxf., BSc Lond., FGS Sr. Lectr.

Knezević, Jezdimir, BEng Belgrade, MSc Belgrade, DSc Belgrade Reader, Reliability and Logistics Engineering

Lee, A. J. Clive, BSc Nott., PhD Nott. Reader, Bioengineering

Matthews, John J., MA Camb. Sr. Lectr.

Maunder, Edward A. W., MA Camb., PhD Lond. Sr. Lectr.

Owens, David H., BSc Lond., PhD Lond., FIEE, FIMA Prof., Systems and Control Engineering; Head of Sch.*

Patrick, Michael A., BScTech Sheff., PhD Sheff. Sr. Lectr.

Robinson, John, MSc Cran., PhD S'ton. Hon. Indust. Res. Prof.

Walters, Godfrey A., MA Camb., PhD Liv. Reader, Water Systems Engineering

Woollons, David J., BSc Brist., PhD Brist., FIEE Prof., Engineering Science

Wragg, A. Anthony, BSc Manc., PhD Manc., FIChemE Prof., Electro Chemical Engineering

Other Staff: 13 Lectrs.; 8 Res. Fellows; 1 Lectr.†; 8 Hon. Res. Fellows

Research: control and computational engineering; electronic and systems engineering; materials and process engineering; structure and infrastructure

English, School of

Tel: (01392) 264263 Fax: (01392) 264361

Brooks, Chris L., BA Manc., DPhil Oxf. Sr. Lectr.

Corbin, Peter F., BA Birm., PhD Birm. Sr. Lectr.

Faulkner, Peter, MA Camb., MA Birm. Reader, Modern English Literature

Gagnier, Regenia, BA Calif., PhD Calif. Prof., English Literature

Glasscoe, Marion, MA Edin., MA Lond., FSA Sr. Lectr.

Hartmann, Reinhard R. K., BSc Vienna, MA S.Illinois, DCom Vienna Reader, Applied Linguistics

Henry, Avril K., MA Oxf., DPhil Oxf. Prof., English Medieval Culture

Lawson-Peebles, Robert, MA Sus., DPhil Oxf. Sr. Lectr.

New, Peter J., MA Camb. Sr. Lectr.; Head*

Petrie, Duncan J., MA Edin., PhD Edin. Sr. Lectr.

Quartermaine, Peter N., BA Exe., PhD Exe. Sr. Lectr.

Roberts, Gareth J., BA Lond., PhD Lond. Sr. Lectr.

Sedge, Douglas, MA Wales, PhD Wales Sr. Lectr.

Spencer, Jane, BA Hull, DPhil Oxf. Sr. Lectr.

Swanton, Michael J., BA Durh., MSc Bath, PhD Durh., FSA, FRHistS Prof., English Medieval Studies

Tamplin, Ronald N., MA Oxf. Sr. Lectr.

Other Staff: 9 Lectrs.; 1 Lectr.†; 1 Temp. Lectr.

Research: critical theory; lexicography; historiography of witchcraft studies; modern and medieval English literature

French, see under Mod. Langs., Sch. of

Geography and Archaeology, School of

Archaeology

Tel: (01392) 264350 Fax: (01392) 264377

Coles, Bryony J., BA Brist., MPhil Lond., FSA Prof., Prehistoric Archaeology

Coles, John M., BA Tor., MA Camb., PhD Edin., FBA Hon. Prof., Archaeology

Higham, Robert A., BA Exe., PhD Exe., FSA, FRHistS Sr. Lectr., Archaeology

Maxfield, Valerie A., BA Leic., PhD Durh., FSA Reader, Roman Archaeology

Other Staff: 2 Lectrs.; 2 Hon. Res. Fellows

Research: archaeology of the Roman provinces; historic landscape archaeology; history and archaeology of medieval castles; material culture studies including lithics; wetland archaeology, predominantly from the mesolithic to the medieval period

Geography

Tel: (01392) 263341 Fax: (01392) 263342

Brown, Antony G., BSc Lond., PhD S'ton. Reader, Physical Geography and Geoarchaeology

Caseldine, Christopher, MA St And., PhD St And. Reader, Environmental Change; Head of Sch.*

Chadwick, B., BSc Lond., PhD Lond., FGS Sr. Lectr., Earth Science

Cullingford, Robin A., MA Edin., PhD Edin. Sr. Lectr.

Ford, Nicholas J., BA Wales, PhD Wales Sr. Lectr.

Gilg, Andrew W., MA Edin. Reader, Human Geography

Kain, Roger J. P., BA Lond., PhD Lond., FBA, FSA Montefiore Prof.

Little, Jo K., BA Wales, PhD Reading Sr. Lectr.

Quine, Timothy A., BSc Lond., PhD Strath. Sr. Lectr.

Shaw, Gareth, BSc Hull, PhD Hull Reader, Human Geography

Walling, Desmond E., BA Exe., PhD Exe. Reardon Smith Prof.

Webb, Bruce W., BSc Exe., PhD Exe. Reader, Physical Geography

Williams, Allan M., BScEcon Wales, PhD Lond. Prof., Human Geography and European Studies

Other Staff: 5 Lectrs.; 10 Res. Fellows; 7 Hon. Res. Fellows

Research: historical geography; hydrology; quaternary/geoarchaeology; rural geography; tourism and services

German, see under Mod. Langs., Sch. of

Historical, Political and Sociological Studies, School of

History

see also Classics and Anc. Hist. (under Classics and Theol., Sch. of), and under Educn., Sch. of

Tel: (01392) 264297 Fax: (01392) 264377

Barry, Jonathan, MA Oxf., DPhil Oxf., FRHistS Sr. Lectr.; Head of Sch.*

Black, Jeremy M., MA Camb., PhD Durh., FRHistS Prof.

Booth, Alan E., BA Kent, PhD Kent Sr. Lectr.

Burt, Roger, BSc(Econ) Lond., PhD Lond., FRHistS, FGS Prof., Mining History

Coleman, Bruce I., MA Camb., PhD Camb., FRHistS Sr. Lectr.

Critchley, John S., BA Nott., PhD Nott. Sr. Lectr.

Donald, Moira, BA Leeds, PhD Leeds Sr. Lectr.

Duffy, Michael D., MA Oxf., DPhil Oxf., FRHistS Sr. Lectr.

Lewis, Robert A., MA Edin., PhD Birm. Sr. Lectr.

Melling, Joseph L., BSc Brad., PhD Glas., FRHistS Sr. Lectr.

Newitt, Malyn D. D., BA Oxf., PhD Lond., FRHistS Sr. Lectr.

Noakes, Jeremy D., MA Oxf., DPhil Oxf., FRHistS Prof.

Orme, Nicholas I., MA Oxf., DPhil Oxf., DLitt Oxf., FSA, FRHistS Prof.

Overton, Mark, BA Exe., MA Camb., PhD Camb. Prof.

Smith, Joseph, BA Durh., PhD Lond., FRHistS Reader, American Diplomatic History

Thorpe, Andrew J., BA Birm., PhD Sheff. Sr. Lectr.

Other Staff: 5 Lectrs.; 7 Hon. Res. Fellows

Research: Africa; Asia; mediaeval and modern Britain and Europe; the Americas

Politics

Tel: (01392) 263164 Fax: (01392) 263305

Castiglione, Dario, DottFil Palermo, MA Sus., DPhil Sus. Sr. Lectr.

Doern, G. Bruce, BComm Manit., MA Car., PhD Qu. Prof., Public Policy

Dumper, Michael, BA Lanc., MPhil Lanc., PhD Exe. Sr. Lectr.

Hampsher-Monk, Iain W., BA Keele, FSA Prof., Political Theory

Rush, Michael D., BA Sheff., PhD Sheff. Prof.

Stanyer, Jeffrey, BA Oxf., BPhil Oxf. Sr. Lectr.

Szajkowski, Bogalan, MA Manc., PhD Wales Prof., Pan-European Politics

Wilks, Stephen R. M., BA Lanc., PhD Manc., FCA Prof.

Other Staff: 7 Lectrs.; 1 Hon. Lectr.; 13 Hon. Res. Fellows

Research: European democracy; international politics; Middle East politics; political theory; public policy and administration

Sociology

Tel: (01392) 263276 Fax: (01392) 263285

Barnes, S. Barry, BA Camb., MSc Leic., MA Essex Prof.

Davie, Grace R. C., BA Exe., PhD Lond. Sr. Lectr.

DeNora, Tia, BA Westchester, MA Calif., PhD Calif. Sr. Lectr.

Snowden, Robert, BA PhD Prof., Family Studies

Vincent, John A., BA Sus., DPhil Sus. Sr. Lectr.

Walsh, Dermot P., BA Lond., MSc Lond., PhD Lond. Sr. Lectr.

Witkin, Robert W., BA Leeds, PhD Exe. Sr. Lectr.

Other Staff: 5 Lectrs.; 1 Res. Fellow; 4 Hon. Res. Fellows

Research: culture and technology of reproduction; culture, knowledge and expertise; theoretical and methodological problems of sociology

Italian, see under Mod. Langs., Sch. of

Law, School of

Tel: (01392) 263371 Fax: (01392) 263196

Betten, Lammy, LLM Utrecht, PhD Utrecht Prof., European Law

Bridge, John W., LLM Brist., PhD Brist. Prof., Public Law; Head*

Coombes, John M., LLB Exe. Sr. Lectr.

Drury, Robert R., LLB Newcastle(UK) Sr. Lectr.

Economides, Kim M., BA CNAA, LLM Lond. Reader

English, Peter, LLB Lond., LLM Northwestern Sr. Lectr.

Hicks, Andrew R., LLB S'ton., LLM Sing. Sr. Lectr.

Honeyball, Simon E., LLB Birm., PhD Birm. Sr. Lectr.

Jaffey, Anthony J. E., BA Cape Town, LLB Cape Town, BCL Oxf. Sr. Lectr.

Perrott, David L., BCL Oxf., LLB Exe. Reader, Business Law

Pugsley, David F., BCL Oxf., MA Oxf. Sr. Lectr.

Shrubsall, Vivien J., LLB Leeds Prof.; Dir., Centre for Legal Practice

Stebbings, Chantal, LLB Exe., PhD Exe. Reader, Modern Legal History

Tettenborn, Andrew M., MA Camb., LLB Camb. Bracton Prof.

Other Staff: 17 Lectrs.; 1 Lectr.†; 3 Hon. Res. Fellows

Research: commercial and environmental law; European and international law; professional legal studies

Linguistics, Applied, see Engl., Sch. of

Mathematical Sciences, School of

Tel: (01392) 264464 Fax: (01392) 264460

Bailey, Trevor C., MSc Lond., PhD Exe. Sr. Lectr.

Bassom, Andrew P., BA Oxf., PhD Exe. Reader, Applied Mathematics

Cremona, John E., MA *Oxf.*, DPhil
Oxf. Reader, Number Theory
Firby, Peter A., BSc *Sheff.*, PhD *Sheff.* Sr. Lectr.
Jones, Christopher A., BA *Camb.*, PhD *Camb.*,
ScD *Camb.*, FRAS Prof., Applied
Mathematics
Krzanowski, Wojcek J., BSc *Leeds*, PhD
Reading Prof., Statistics; Head of Sch.*
Lawrence, Clive J., BSc *Exe.* Sr. Lectr.
Maskell, Stephen J., BA *Oxf.*, MSc *Manc.*, PhD
Manc. Sr. Lectr.
Munford, Alan G., BSc *Brist.*, PhD *S'ton.* Sr.
Lectr.
Read, Kenneth L. Q., MA *Camb.*, PhD *Exe.* Sr.
Lectr.
Soward, Andrew M., PhD *Camb.*, ScD *Camb.*,
FRS Prof., Applied Mathematics
Stratton, Anthony E., BA *Keele*, PhD *Lond.*,
FIMA Sr. Lectr.
Tizzard, Keith, BSc *Brist.* Sr. Lectr.
Townley, Stuart B., BSc *Warw.*, PhD
Warw. Reader, Dynamics and Control
Vámos, Peter, PhD *Sheff.*, DSc *Sheff.* Prof., Pure
Mathematics
Zhang, Keke, BSc *Nanjing*, MSc *Calif.*, PhD
Calif. Reader, Geophysical and
Astrophysical Fluid Dynamics
Other Staff: 13 Lectrs.; 2 Res. Fellows; 2 Hon.
Res. Fellows
Research: computational number theory; control
theory; fluid dynamics; multivariate
statistics; stochastic modelling

Medicine, see Postgrad. Med. and Health
Scis., Sch. of

Mines, Camborne School of

Tel: (01209) 267198 *Fax:* (01209) 716977
Atkinson, Keith, BSc *Wales*, PhD *Wales*,
FGS Prof., Mining Geology; Head*
Bristow, Colin, BSc *Brist.*, MSc *Exe.*,
FGS Visiting Prof.
Hancock, Richard J., BSc *Lond.*, MSc *Birm.* Sr.
Lectr.
Phillips, C. Victor, BSc *Birm.*, PhD *Birm.* Sr.
Lectr.
Pirrie, Duncan, BSc *CNAA*, PhD *CNAA* Sr.
Lectr.
Scott, Peter W., BSc *Newcastle(UK)*, PhD *Lond.*,
FGS Prof., Industrial Geology
Stead, Douglas, BSc *Exe.*, MSc *Leeds*, PhD *Lond.*,
FGS Prof., Geomechanics
Williams, Richard A., BSc(Eng) *Lond.*, PhD
Lond., FIChemE Royal Academy/RTZ Prof.,
Minerals Engineering
Other Staff: 18 Lectrs.; 3 Res. Fellows; 10
Hon. Res. Fellows
Vacant Posts: 2 Profs. (Mining Engineering)
Research: environmental research; fundamental
and applied geology; geomechanics and
mining engineering; minerals, particle and
colloid engineering

Modern Languages, School of

Arabic and Middle East Studies

Tel: (01392) 264036 *Fax:* (01392) 264035
Al-Qasimi, His Highness Shaikh Sultan bin
Mohammed Visiting Prof.
El-Enany, Rasheed, BA *Cairo*, PhD Reader,
Modern Arabic Literature
Other Staff: 2 Lectrs.; 2 Hon. Res. Fellows
Research: history; Islam; linguistics; literature;
poetry

French

Tel: (01392) 264222 *Fax:* (01392) 264377
Cameron, Keith C., BA *Exe.*, LèsL *Rennes*, DU
Rennes Prof., French and Renaissance Studies
Cook, Malcolm C., BA *Warw.*, PhD
Warw. Prof., French 18th Century Studies
Davison, Ray, BA *Leeds*, MPhil *Leeds* Sr. Lectr.
Hayward, Susan, MA *Exe.*, PhD *Exe.* Prof.
Kearns, James, MA *Warw.*, PhD *Warw.* Lectr.;
Head of Sch.*
Orr, Mary M., MA *St And.*, PhD *Camb.* Reader
Sorrell, Martin R. M., BA *Oxf.*, MA
Kent Reader, French and Translation Studies

Other Staff: 9 Lectrs.; 6 Lectors; 3 Hon. Res.
Fellows
Research: French cinema; French literature and
culture from earliest times to present day;
French thought from the Renaissance to the
present day; literary translation;
sociolinguistics of French

German

Tel: (01392) 264335 *Fax:* (01392) 264339
Hanson, William P., MA *Wales* Sr. Lectr.
Lewis, Derek R., BA *Lond.*, MPhil *Lond.* Sr.
Lectr.
McKenzie, John R. P., MA *Manc.*, PhD *Exe.* Sr.
Lectr.
Robertshaw, Alan T., BA *Durh.*, PhD *Durh.* Sr.
Lectr.
Sharpe, Lesley, MA *Oxf.*, DPhil *Oxf.* Prof.
Yates, W. Edgar, MA *Camb.*, PhD *Camb.* Prof.
Other Staff: 5 Lectrs.; 3 Lectors
Research: Austrian literature of the nineteenth
and twentieth centuries; literature of the
classical period (particularly medieval lyric
poetry, Schiller, Oswald von Wolkenstein);
literature of the Reformation and Baroque
era; post-war fiction

Italian

Tel: (01392) 264214 *Fax:* (01392) 264215
Bruni, Roberto L., DottLett *Pisa* Sr. Lectr.
Davie, R. Mark, MA *Camb.*, PhD *Reading* Sr.
Lectr.
Diffley, Paul B., MA *Oxf.*, DPhil *Oxf.* Prof.
Quartermaine, Luisa, DottLett *Milan* Sr. Lectr.
Other Staff: 1 Lectr.; 1 Lector
Research: contemporary Italian literature and
society; Dante's writings; Italian book
publishing; late Renaissance literature and
humanism; vernacular literature of the
fourteenth and fifteenth centuries

Russian

Tel: (01392) 264310 *Fax:* (01392) 264300
Cockrell, C. Roger S., BA *Lond.*, PhD *Exe.* Sr.
Lectr.
Pursglove, D. Michael, MA *Camb.*, BPhil
Oxf. Sr. Lectr.
Richards, David J., MA *Oxf.*, BLitt *Oxf.* Reader
Other Staff: 2 Lectrs.; 1 Lector
Research: Gothic literature; 1920s Russian
literature; nineteenth-century Russian
literature; post-revolutionary Russian
literature; Russian women writers

Spanish

Tel: (01392) 264245 *Fax:* (01392) 264377
Calcraft, Raymond P., BPhil *St And.*, MA *St
And.* Sr. Lectr.
Hitchcock, Richard, MA *St And.*, PhD *St
And.* Reader, Hispano-Arabic Studies
Longhurst, C. Alex, BA *Exe.*, PhD *Exe.* Prof.
Williams, Lynn, BA *Lond.*, PhD *Lond.* Sr. Lectr.
Other Staff: 4 Lectrs.; 2 Lectors
Research: contemporary Spanish society; Golden
Age Spanish literature; Latin American
literature; medieval Spain; modern Spanish
literature

Music, see Drama and Music, Sch. of

Physics, School of

Tel: (01392) 264151 *Fax:* (01392) 264111
Barnes, William L., BSc *Exe.*, PhD *Exe.* Sr.
Lectr.
Bradberry, Geoffrey W., BSc *Leic.*, PhD
Leic. Sr. Lectr.
Clark, Michael G., MA *Camb.*, PhD *Camb.* Hon.
Res. Prof.
Cousins, Christopher S. G., MA *Oxf.* Sr. Lectr.
Cousins, John E., BSc *Nott.*, PhD *Nott.* Sr.
Lectr.
Inkson, John C., BSc *Manc.*, MA *Camb.*, PhD
Camb., ScD *Camb.* Prof., Theoretical Physics;
Head*
Jones, Bob, BSc *Manc.*, MSc *Wales*, PhD *Wales*,
Hon. FD *Umeå* Reader, Theoretical Physics
Preist, Trevor W., BSc *Brist.*, PhD *Brist.* Sr.
Lectr.

Sambles, J. Roy, BSc *Lond.*, PhD *Lond.* Prof.,
Experimental Physics
Savchenko, Alexander K., MSc *Moscow Physico-
Tech.*, PhD *Russian Acad.Sc.*, DSc *Russian
Acad.Sc.* Reader, Condensed Matter Physics
Srivastava, Gyaneshwar P., PhD *Ban.*, DSc
Ban. Reader, Theoretical Semiconductor
Physics
Summers, Iain R., MA *Oxf.*, PhD *Lond.* Sr.
Lectr.
Usher, Alan, MA *Oxf.*, DPhil *Oxf.* Sr. Lectr.
Vennart, William, BSc *Brist.*, PhD
Nott. Reader, Medical Physics
Whyte, Thomas D., BSc *Lond.*, PhD *Lond.* Sr.
Lectr.
Wyatt, Adrian F. G., BSc *Brist.*, DPhil
Oxf. Prof.
Other Staff: 7 Lectrs.; 10 Res. Fellows; 3
Experimental Officers; 8 Hon. Res. Fellows
Research: medical physics; quantum fluids;
semiconductor physics; thin films and
interfaces

Politics, see Hist., Pol. and Sociol. Studies,
Sch. of

Postgraduate Medicine and Health Sciences, School of

Tel: (01392) 403146 *Fax:* (01392) 432223
Anthony, Peter P., MB BS *Lond.*,
FRCPath Prof., Clinical Histopathology
Ernst, Edzard, MD *Munich*, PhD *Munich*,
FRCP Laing Prof., Complementary
Medicine
Halpin, David, MA *Lond.*, MB BS *Lond.*, DPhil
Oxf. Sr. Lectr.
Kirby, Brian J., MB ChB *Leeds*, FRCP Reader,
Medicine; Dep. Dir.
Pearce, Vaughan, MB BS *Lond.*, BSc *Lond.*,
FRCP Sr. Lectr.
Pereira Gray, Denis J., OBE, MA *Camb.*, MB
BChir *Camb.*, FRCGP Prof., General Practice
Rowland, Christopher G., BSc *Wales*, MB BS
Lond., FRCR Sr. Lectr.
Simpson, Roderick H. W., BSc *St And.*, MB ChB
Dund., MMed Sr. Lectr.
Tooke, John E., MA *Oxf.*, MSc *Oxf.*, DM
Oxf. Prof., Vascular Medicine; Head of
Sch.*
Other Staff: 4 Hon. Sr. Lectrs.

Child Health

Tel: (01392) 403149 *Fax:* (01392) 403158
Quinn, Michael W., BA *Trinity(Dub.)*, MB BCh
BAO *Trinity(Dub.)*, MD *Trinity(Dub.)* Sr. Lectr.
Tripp, John H., BSc *Lond.*, MB BS *Lond.*, MD
Lond., FRCP Sr. Lectr.
Other Staff: 1 Lectr.; 1 Res. Fellow; 1 Hon. Sr.
Lectr.; 1 Hon. Res. Fellow
Research: behaviourally effective sex education;
effects of family breakdown on children;
pathophysiological responses to pain in the
neonate; peer-led health education; quality
of life estimation in childhood

Clinical Science

Tel: (01392) 403045
Halpin, David, MA *Lond.*, MB BS *Lond.*, DPhil
Oxf. Sr. Lectr.
Kirby, Brian J., MB ChB *Leeds*, FRCP Reader,
Medicine
McLeod, Ken, MB ChB *Aberd.*, MD *Aberd.* Sr.
Lectr.
Pearce, Vaughan, MB BS *Lond.*, BSc *Lond.*,
FRCP Sr. Lectr.
Quinn, Michael W., BA *Trinity(Dub.)*, MB BCh
BAO *Trinity(Dub.)*, MD *Trinity(Dub.)* Sr. Lectr.
Simpson, Roderick H. W., BSc *St And.*, MB ChB
Dund., MMed Sr. Lectr.
Taylor, Rod, BSc *Glas.*, PhD *Glas.* Sr. Lectr.
Other Staff: 1 Hon. Sr. Lectr.
Research: biological chemistry; cell and
molecular biology; children's health and
exercise; clinical measurement; clinical
microvascular research

Complementary Health

Tel: (01392) 424989 Fax: (01392) 424989

Ernst, Edzard, MD *Munich*, PhD *Munich* Laing Prof., Complementary Medicine
Other Staff: 8 Res. Fellows
Research: acupuncture; homeopathy; phytomedicine; placebo effect; spinal manipulation

General Practice

Tel: (01392) 403020 Fax: (01392) 432223

Bolden, Keith J., MA *Camb.*, MB BChir *Camb.*, FRCGP Sr. Lectr.
Goble, Rita, BA *Exe.*, PhD *Exe.* Sr. Lectr.
Hall, Michael S., BSc *Lond.*, MB BS *Lond.*, FRCGP Sr. Lectr.
Hopkins, Robin J., BSc *Brist.*, MB ChB *Brist.*, MPhil *Exe.* Sr. Lectr.
Lewis, Anthony P., BSc *Open(UK)*, MA *Camb.*, MB BChir *Camb.*, FRCGP Sr. Lectr.
Marshall, Martin, BSc *Lond.*, MB BS *Lond.*, MSc *Exe.* Sr. Lectr.
Pereira Gray, Denis J., OBE, MA *Camb.*, MB BChir *Camb.*, FRCGP Prof.
Other Staff: 8 Lectrs.; 9 Res. Fellows; 14 Hon. Res. Fellows
Research: comparative study of disability; depression in primary care; quality assurance; teenage pregnancy; the therapeutic relationship

Mental Health

Lloyd, Keith, MSc(Econ) *Lond.*, MB BS *Lond.*, MSc *Lond.* Sr. Lectr.
Other Staff: 2 Lectrs.; 4 Res. Fellows; 2 Hon. Lectrs.; 1 Hon. Res. Fellow
Research: common mental disorders in primary care; ethnicity and mental illness; health services research; severe mental illness; suicide

Research and Development Support

Tel: (01392) 403055 Fax: (01392) 403042

Taylor, Rod, BSc *Glas.*, PhD *Glas.* Sr. Lectr.
Tooke, John E., MA *Oxf.*, MSc *Oxf.*, DM *Oxf.* Prof.; Head*
Other Staff: 3 Lectrs.; 1 Res. Fellow

Social Work and Probation Studies

Tel: (01392) 263311 Fax: (01392) 263305

Forsythe, William J., MA *Camb.*, MPhil *Exe.*, PhD, FRHistS Reader, Historical Criminology
Sheldon, Brian, MPhil *Birm.*, PhD *Leic.* Prof.; Dir., Centre for Evidence-Based Social Services
Other Staff: 2 Lectrs.; 1 Reader†; 2 Lectrs.†; 1 Hon. Res. Fellow
Research: British childcare policy and practice; evidence-base in social care; history of British prisons, lunatic asylums and workhouses 1500-1939; psychology and social work; social policy and social welfare worldwide

Vascular Medicine

Tel: (01392) 403064 Fax: (01392) 432223

Hattersley, Andrew T., MA *Camb.*, BM BCh *Oxf.*, DM *Oxf.* Sr. Lectr.
McLeod, Ken, MB ChB *Aberd.*, MD *Aberd.* Sr. Lectr.
Shore, Angela C., BSc *Newcastle(UK)*, PhD *Newcastle(UK)* Reader
Tooke, John E., MA *Oxf.*, MSc *Oxf.*, DM *Oxf.*, FRCP Prof.; Head of Sch.*
Other Staff: 1 Lectr.; 4 Res. Fellows; 1 Hon. Res. Fellow
Research: clinical and physiological studies of patients with genetic sub-types of diabetes; molecular genetics of non-insulin dependent diabetes; normal microvascular physiology; patho-physiology of diabetic microvascular complications; treatment strategies in patients with complications

Psychology, School of

Tel: (01392) 264626 Fax: (01392) 264623

Eiser, Christine, BSc *Brist.*, PhD *Brist.* Reader, Health Psychology
Eiser, J. Richard, MA *Oxf.*, PhD *Lond.*, FBPsS Prof.
Gordon, Ian E., BSc PhD, FBPsS Sr. Lectr.
Herbert, Martin, MA *Natal*, PhD *Lond.* Prof., Clinical and Community Psychology
Howe, Michael J. A., BA *Sheff.*, PhD *Sheff.*, FBPsS Prof.
Kay, Harry, CBE, MA *Camb.*, MA *Oxf.*, PhD *Camb.*, Hon. DSc *Exe.*, Hon. DSc *Sheff.* Hon. Prof.
Kay, Janice M., BA *Newcastle(UK)*, PhD *Camb.* Sr. Lectr.
Kline, Paul, BA *Reading*, MEd *Aberd.*, PhD *Manc.*, DSc *Manc.* Prof., Psychometrics
Lea, Stephen E. G., MA *Camb.*, PhD *Camb.*, FBPsS Prof.
Mitchell, Don C., BSc *Manc.*, PhD *Manc.* Sr. Lectr.
Nichols, Keith A., MSc *Leeds* Sr. Lectr.
Slater, Alan M., BSc *Wales*, PhD *Durh.* Sr. Lectr.
Webley, Paul, BSc *Lond.*, PhD *Lond.* Reader, Economic Psychology; Head*
Other Staff: 11 Lectrs.; 3 Lectrs.†; 3 Hon. Lectrs.; 5 Hon. Res. Fellows
Research: cognitive psychology and cognitive science; health, community and clinical psychology; social and economic psychology

Russian, see under Mod. Langs., Sch. of

Sociology, see Hist., Pol. and Sociol. Studies, Sch. of

Spanish, see under Mod. Langs., Sch. of

Theology, see Classics and Theol., Sch. of

SPECIAL CENTRES, ETC

Arab Gulf Studies, Centre for

Tel: (01392) 264024 Fax: (01392) 264023

Mahdi, Kamil A., BA *Manc.*, MSocSc *Birm.*, PhD *Birm.* Temp. Dir.*
Other Staff: 2 Res. Fellows; 9 Hon. Res. Fellows
Research: development studies; economics; modern history; politics; social studies

Children's Health and Exercise Research Centre

Tel: (01392) 264937 Fax: (01392) 264706

Armstrong, Prof. Neil, BEd *Lough.*, MSc *Lough.*, PhD *Exe.*, FIBiol Dir.*
Other Staff: 1 Res. Fellow
Research: assessment and interpretation of physiological responses to exercise in relation to growth and maturation; coronary prevention in children, including diet, body composition, lipid profile, blood pressure and lifestyle; role of physical exercise and training in the promotion of health and well-being; sex differences in young people's attitude to exercise; young people's physical activity patterns

Complementary Health Studies, Centre for

Tel: (01392) 264496 Fax: (01392) 433828

Mills, Simon Y., MA *Camb.* Lectr.; Dir.; Head*
Other Staff: 1 Lectr.; 1 Lectr.†; 1 Res. Fellow
Research: acupuncture and other oriental medicines; herbal medicine; relationship between orthodox and complementary medicine; relationship between patient and practitioner; use of complementary medicine in hospices

Cornish Studies, Institute of

Tel: (01872) 263457 Fax: (01872) 223449

Payton, Philip J., BSc *Brist.*, PhD *Adel.*, PhD *CNAA*, FRHistS Reader; Dir.*

Other Staff: 1 Lectr.; 4 Hon. Res. Fellows
Research: Celtic studies; culture; education; history; territorial politics

Dictionary Research, Centre for

Tel: (01392) 264302 Fax: (01392) 264377

Hartmann, Reinhard R. K., BSc *Vienna*, MA *S.Illinois*, DComm *Vienna* Dir.*
Other Staff: 3 Hon. Res. Fellows
Research: all aspects of lexicography, with special reference to the user perspective

Earth Resources, Centre for

Tel: (01392) 263901 Fax: (01392) 263907

Grainger, Peter, BSc *Reading*, MSc *Lond.*, PhD *Exe.*, FGS Dir.*
Other Staff: 3 Experimental Officers; 1 Res. Fellow; 10 Hon. Res. Fellows
Research: airborne dust characterisation; groundwater recharge assessment; mining impact assessment; slope instability; soil gas geochemistry for geological fault detection, seismic hazard zonation and volcanic risk

Educational Development and Co-operation, Centre for

Tel: (01392) 264865 Fax: (01392) 411274

Bloomer, Martin J., MEd *Brist.*, PhD *Exe.* Dir.*
Other Staff: 2 Res. Fellows
Research: Central and Eastern Europe (education); curriculum development; European education policy; evaluation; professional development

Energy and the Environment, Centre for

Tel: (01392) 264144 Fax: (01392) 264111

Wyatt, Prof. Adrian F. G., BSc *Brist.*, DPhil *Oxf.* Dir.*
Other Staff: 3 Res. Fellows
Research: building acoustics; computational methods; energy in building; environmental campaigns; waste strategies

English Language, Centre for

Tel: (01392) 264282 Fax: (01392) 264277

Nuttall, John C., BA *Lond.*, MA *Wales* Lectr.; Dir.*
Other Staff: 2 Lectrs.†

European Legal Studies, Centre for

Tel: (01392) 263380 Fax: (01392) 263381

Betten, Prof. Lammy, LLM *Utrecht*, PhD *Utrecht* Dir.*
Research: effects of European Community law in the UK and other member states

European Studies, Centre for

Tel: (01392) 263371 Fax: (01392) 263196

Lewis, Robert A., MA *Edin.*, PhD *Birm.* Dir.*
Szajkowski, Bogdan, MA *Manc.*, PhD *Wales* Dir.*
Other Staff: 1 Hon. Res. Fellow
Research: economy of the European Union; European history; modern European society; pan-European politics

Evidence-based Social Services, Centre for

Tel: (01392) 263323 Fax: (01392) 263324

Little, Michael, BA *Birm.*, PhD *Lanc.* Visiting Prof.
Macdonald, Geraldine, BA *Oxf.*, MSc *Oxf.* Visiting Prof.
Sheldon, Brian, MPhil *Birm.*, PhD *Leic.* Prof.; Dir.*
Research: evaluations of critical appraisal skill training for social care staff; matching needs and services for children; rehabilitation work with frail, elderly people; translation of results of existing research into service and practice development; training of foster carers in the management of challenging behaviours

Foreign Language, Centre for

Tel: (01392) 264293 Fax: (01392) 264377
Lewis, Derek R., BA Lond., MPhil Lond.   Dir.*
Other Staff: 2 Lectrs.†

History of Cinema and Popular Culture, Bill Douglas Centre for the

Tel: (01392) 264352 Fax: (01392) 264361
Petrie, Duncan, MA Edin., PhD Edin.   Dir.*
Other Staff: 1 Res. Fellow; 1 Hon. Res. Fellow
Research: cinema history; relationship between cinema and pre-cinema; social impact of cinema

Industrial Reliability, Cost and Effectiveness, Centre for Management of

Tel: (01392) 263639 Fax: (01392) 263620
Blanchard, Benjamin S., BSc Roch., MBA Roch.   Visiting Prof.
Knezević, Jezdimir, BEng Belgrade, MSc Belgrade, DSc Belgrade   Reader, Reliability and Logistics Engineering; Dir.*
Other Staff: 2 Lectrs.; 6 Hon. Res. Fellows
Research: design for life cycle; life cycle engineering and economics; reliability, maintainability and supportability; software reliability and fault tolerant computing; systems engineering and logistics

Innovation in Mathematics Teaching, Centre for

Tel: (01392) 264707 Fax: (01392) 499398
Burghes, Prof. David N., BSc Sheff., PhD Sheff.   Dir.*
Other Staff: 1 Res. Fellow; 2 Hon. Res. Fellows
Research: enhancing mathematics teaching and learning and raising expectations in the UK; implementing a mathematics enhancement programme in UK schools and evaluating its effect on raising attainment and understanding; monitoring attainment of pupils aged 14-16 in seventeen countries to determine factors giving rise to enhanced mathematics teaching and learning

Leadership Studies, Centre for

Tel: (01392) 413023 Fax: (01392) 434132
Adair, John, BLitt Oxf., MA Camb., PhD Lond.   Visiting Prof.
Hooper, R. Alan, MA Exe.   Dir.*
Other Staff: 4 Hon. Univ. Fellows
Research: development of strategic leadership; leadership and management education; leadership of change; leading multicultural organisations; organisation culture

Legal Practice, Centre for

Tel: (01392) 263156 Fax: (01392) 263196
Shrubsall, Vivien J., LLB Leeds   Prof.; Dir.*
Other Staff: 8 Lectrs.
Research: practical application of the law and the provision of legal services, particularly in employment taxation, litigation and professional legal ethics

Maritime Historical Studies, Centre for

Tel: (01392) 264324 Fax: (01392) 264377
Duffy, Michael, MA Oxf., DPhil Oxf., FRHistS   Dir.*
Other Staff: 9 Hon. Res. Fellows
Research: British maritime history; maritime archives; naval history

Medical History and Related Social Studies, Centre for

Tel: (01392) 263297 Fax: (01392) 263297
Melling, Joseph L., BSc Brad., PhD Glas., FRHistS   Dir.*
Other Staff: 3 Res. Fellows
Research: comparative history of welfare; disease management in the twentieth century; gender and health; history of insanity; history of medical statistics and patient records

Mediterranean Studies, Centre for

Tel: (01392) 264280
Wilkins, John M., MA Camb., PhD Camb.   Dir.*
Research: archaeology; cultural studies; history and ancient history; identity; romance languages

Population Studies, Institute of

Tel: (01392) 263800 Fax: (01392) 490870
2 Lectrs.; 2 Res. Fellows; 1 Lectr.†; 3 Hon. Res. Fellows
Vacant Posts: Dir.*
Research: improving and developing contraceptive and reproductive health technologies; sexual and reproductive behaviour; strengthening family planning provision

South Western Historical Studies, Centre for

Tel: (01392) 263333 Fax: (01392) 263342
Burt, Prof. Roger, BSc(Econ) Lond., PhD Lond., FGS, FRHistS   Dir.*
Kain, Prof. Roger J. P., BA Lond., PhD Lond., FBA   Chairman*
Research: historical atlas of the South-West; local and regional history of south-west England

Systems and Control Engineering, Centre for

Tel: (01392) 263689 Fax: (01392) 217965
Owens, Prof. David H., BSc Lond., PhD Lond., FIEE, FIMA   Dir.*
Other Staff: 1 Res. Fellow; 1 Hon. Res. Fellow
Research: systems dynamics and control; use of dynamics and control techniques in improved process understanding, improved design and improved operation

Teaching and Learning, Centre for Research on

Tel: (01392) 264796 Fax: (01392) 264792
Bennett, Prof. Neville, BEd Lanc., PhD Lanc.   Dir.*
Desforges, Prof. Charles, BSc Lond., PhD Lanc.   Dir.*
Hughes, Prof. Martin, BA Oxf., PhD Edin.   Dir.*
Wragg, Prof. Edward C., BA Durh., MEd Leic., PhD Exe., Hon. DUniv Open(UK), Hon. DUniv Strath.   Dir.*
Research: effective literacy teaching; effective practice in teaching and learning from early childhood to higher education; role of parents in early learning; role of play in early learning; teaching skills in higher education and employment

Telematics, Centre for

Tel: (01392) 264758 Fax: (01392) 493761
Davis, Nicola E., BSc Edin., PhD Belf.   Prof.; Dir.*
Other Staff: 5 Res. Fellows; 1 Hon. Res. Fellow
Research: distance learning and Information and Communication Technology (ICT); ICT and teacher training; ICT and wider professional development; ICT in education; multimedia and communications in education and training

Wetland Research

Tel: (01392) 264351 Fax: (01392) 263377
Brown, Antony G., BSc Lond., PhD S'ton.   Reader, Physical Geography and Geoarchaeology
Coles, Bryony J., BA Brist., MPhil Lond., FSA   Prof.; Dir.*
Research: conservation and excavation of wetland archaeology; wetland archaeology; wetland conservation and management; wetland palaeoecology; wetlands and environmental change

Women's Studies, Centre for

Tel: (01392) 264363
Hanscombe, Gillian, BA Melb., MA Monash, DPhil Oxf.   Dir.*
Other Staff: 4 Hon. Res. Fellows
Research: domestic violence; feminist theory; hypertext writing workshops; women and education; women and modernism

CONTACT OFFICERS

Academic affairs. Academic Secretary: Harvey, Philip, BSc CNAA, PhD Durh.
Accommodation. Accomodation Officer: Newton, Betty
Admissions (first degree). Admissions Officer: Hoad, Pamela A.
Admissions (higher degree). Assistant Registrar (Postgraduate Admissions): Kingdom, D. Liz, BA Lond.
Adult/continuing education. Director, Department of Continuing and Adult Education: Benn, Roseanne C., BSc Lond., MSc Lond.
Alumni. Alumni Officer: Padget, Nicola, BSc Exe.
Archives. Modern Records Clerk: Cross, Suzie
Careers. Information Officer: Lovegrove, Shirley
Computing services. Deputy Director, Information Technology Services: Ellison, Paul A., BSc Aston
Consultancy services. Corporate Manager, Exeter Enterprises Ltd: Letcher, Diana
Credit transfer. Director, Department of Continuing and Adult Education: Benn, Roseanne C., BSc Lond., MSc Lond.
Development/fund-raising. Development Officer: Baines, Jill, BA Sheff., BPhil Liv., MA CNAA
Distance Education. Director, Department of Continuing and Adult Education: Benn, Roseanne C., BSc Lond., MSc Lond.
Equal opportunities. Equal Opportunities Co-ordinator: Bergondo-Castro, Maggie, BA Wales, MA Lanc.
Estates and buildings/works and services. Director of Buildings and Estate: Alcock, Robert J., BA Brist.
Examinations. Senior Assistant Registrar (Examinations): Welland, Deborah A., BSc Reading, MBA Exe.
Finance. Assistant Director of Finance: Woodcock, Stephen R., BSc Aston, FCA
General enquiries. Registrar and Secretary: Powell, Ian H. C., MA Birm.
Health services. Principal Medical Officer: Thomas, Kate, MB BS Lond.
Industrial liaison. Business Relations Officer: Fielding, Sean, BA Lond.
International office. International Officer: Dean, Christopher N. J., BSc Aston
Library (chief librarian). Librarian: Paterson, Alasdair T., MA Edin., MA Sheff.
Minorities/disadvantaged groups. Equal Opportunities Co-ordinator: Bergondo-Castro, Maggie, BA Wales, MA Lanc.
Minorities/disadvantaged groups. Advisor to Disabled Students: Ford, Deirdre J., BA Birm., MSc Oxf.
Ombudsperson. Equal Opportunities Co-ordinator: Bergondo-Castro, Maggie, BA Wales, MA Lanc.
Personnel/human resources. Administrative Officer: Knowles, David A.
Public relations, information and marketing. Press Officer: Franklin, Stuart D., BA S'ton.
Publications. Publications Officer: Pollard, Ann, BSc Brist.
Purchasing. Supplies Officer, Central Stores: Sweeney, Peter
Quality assurance and accreditation. Deputy Vice-Chancellor: Newitt, Prof. Malyn D. D., BA Oxf., PhD Lond., FRHistS
Research. Assistant Registrar (Postgraduate Admissions): Kingdom, D. Liz, BA Lond.

Research (funding). Assistant Registrar (Research and External Support Unit): Loughlin, Helen, BA CNAA

Safety. Safety Officer: Adams, Paul H., BSc Reading, PhD Reading

Scholarships, awards, loans. Assistant Registrar (Research and External Support Unit): Loughlin, Helen, BA CNAA

Schools liaison. Schools Liaison Officer: Fisk, Jonathan, BEng Exe.

Security. Security Officer: Paddon, Mike

Sport and recreation. Assistant Superintendent (Sports Halls): Todd, Kenneth A.

Staff development and training. Director, Staff Development Unit: Buckingham, David J., BSc(Eng) S'ton., PhD S'ton.

Student union. Permanent Secretary to the Guild of Students: Fishwick, Simon

Student welfare/counselling. Senior Counsellor: Halpern, Lisa

Student welfare/counselling. Welfare Co-ordinator: Lawrence, Rose

Students from other countries. Secretary, International Office: Shand, Linda

Students with disabilities. Advisor to Disabled Students: Ford, Deirdre J., BA Birm., MSc Oxf.

University press. Publisher for the University Press: Baker, Simon C., BA Camb.

Women. Equal Opportunities Co-ordinator: Bergondo-Castro, Maggie, BA Wales, MA Lanc.

[Information supplied by the institution as at 10 March 1998, and edited by the ACU]

UNIVERSITY OF GLAMORGAN

Founded 1992; previously established as South Wales and Monmouthshire School of Mines 1913, Glamorgan College of Technology 1958 and Polytechnic of Wales 1970

Member of the Association of Commonwealth Universities

Postal Address: Pontypridd, Wales CF37 1DL
Telephone: (01443) 480480 **Fax**: (01443) 480558 **WWW**: http://www.glam.ac.uk

VICE-CHANCELLOR*—Webb, Prof. Adrian L., BSocSc Birm., MSc(Econ) Lond., DLitt Lough.
UNIVERSITY SECRETARY—Bracegirdle, J. L., BA BPhil MEd
DIRECTOR OF PLANNING AND PROGRAMMES—Hobson, Prof. Leslie, BA MSc MA PhD
DIRECTOR OF RESOURCES—Porter, Prof. J., OBE, BSc, FIEE, FRAeS
ACADEMIC REGISTRAR—O'Shea, J. T., BSc(Econ)
FINANCIAL CONTROLLER—Williams, Huw R., LLB
LIBRARIAN/HEAD OF LEARNING RESOURCES CENTRE—Atkinson, P. Jeremy, BSc MPhil

GENERAL INFORMATION

History. The university was founded in 1992. It was previously established as South Wales and Monmouthshire School of Mines (1913), Glamorgan College of Technology (1958), and the Polytechnic of Wales (1970).

It is located about 15km west of Cardiff.

Admission to first degree courses (see also United Kingdom Introduction). Through Universities and Colleges Admissions Service (UCAS). International applicants are considered on an individual basis.

First Degrees (see also United Kingdom Directory to Subjects of Study). BA, BEng, BSc, LLB, MEng, MMath.

All courses last 3 years full-time or 4 years sandwich.

Higher Degrees (see also United Kingdom Directory to Subjects of Study). LLM, MA, MBA, MSc, PhD.

Applicants should normally hold a first degree with honours and/or appropriate work experience.

LLM, MA, MBA, MSc: 1 year full-time or 3–4 years part-time.

Language of Instruction. English. Pre-sessional English language course available for students wishing to improve their skills.

Libraries. 223,340 volumes; 1745 periodicals.

Fees (1998, full-time). Undergraduate: £1000 (home); £5900 (international, band 1); £6300 (international, band 2). Postgraduate: £2610 (home); £6300 (international).

Academic Year (1998–99). Two semesters: 21 September–22 January; 25 January–28 May.

Three terms: 14 September–11 December; 4 January–26 March; 19 April–11 June.

Income (1997). Total, £57,000,000.

Statistics. Staff: 1017 (475 academic, 542 administrative and support). Students: full-time 10,931; part-time 6217; total 17,148.

ACADEMIC UNITS

Accounting and Mathematics, School of

Tel: (01443) 482255 Fax: (01443) 482711

Ameen, Jamal R. M., BSc Baghdad, MSc Baghdad, PhD Warw. Sr. Lectr./Lectr.

Burrows, A. W., BBS Massey, MBS Massey, MA Nebraska, PhD Nebraska Prof.

Christopher, Jeffrey, MA(Econ) Manc. Sr. Lectr./Lectr.

Coombs, Hugh M., BScEcon Wales, MPhil Principal Lectr.

Davies, Marlene, BScEcon Wales Sr. Lectr./Lectr.

Gordon, Dan V., BSc Lond., MSc Wales, MSc Bath Sr. Lectr./Lectr.

Gracia, Louise, BA Glam. Sr. Lectr./Lectr.

Griffiths, Mark G., BSc Lond., MSc Wales Sr. Lectr./Lectr.

Hayward, John, BSc Lond., PhD Lond., FRAS Sr. Lectr./Lectr.

Hobbs, David C., MBA Strath. Sr. Lectr./Lectr.

James, Lisa, BA Glam. Sr. Lectr./Lectr.

Jenkins, David E., BA Wales, MSocSc Birm. Principal Lectr.

Jones, David M., MA Oxf., MSc Wales, PhD Camb. Principal Lectr.

Jones, Mark S., BSc Wales, PhD Wales Sr. Lectr./Lectr.

Jones, Wendy, BSc Wales Sr. Lectr./Lectr.

Knight, David G., BSc Wales, PhD Wales Sr. Lectr./Lectr.

Lane, Alison, BA Lanc. Sr. Lectr./Lectr.

Lloyd, Sherrianne, BSc Wales, PhD Wales Principal Lectr.

Lowe, Brian C., BSc Wales, MSc Liv. Sr. Lectr./Lectr.

Marriott, Pru, BA Glam. Sr. Lectr./Lectr.

Martin, Ian W., BSc Lanc., MSc Oxf. Sr. Lectr./Lectr.

McCarthy, Simon, BScEcon Wales Sr. Lectr./Lectr.

Porch, M. G., BSc Wales Sr. Lectr./Lectr.

Roach, Paul A., BSc Wales, PhD Wales Sr. Lectr./Lectr.

Ryley, Prof. Alan, BSc CNAA, MSc Salf., PhD Salf., FIMA Head*

Shellard, Elaine Sr. Lectr./Lectr.

Smith, Derek H., BSc Wales, PhD S'ton., FIMA Prof.

Smith, Pat M., BSc Leeds, MSc Open(UK) Sr. Lectr./Lectr.

Ware, Jonathan A., BSc CNAA, MSc CNAA, PhD Glam. Sr. Lectr./Lectr.

Williams, Hywel D., BA Glam. Sr. Lectr./Lectr.

Williams, Mel C., MSc Bath Sr. Lectr./Lectr.

Williams, Rowland W., BSc Wales, PhD Wales Principal Lectr.

Wiltshire, Ron J., BSc Kent, PhD Kent, FIMA, FIP Reader

Applied Sciences, School of

Tel: (01443) 482108 Fax: (01443) 482285

Ansari, B. M. Sr. Lectr./Lectr.

Ashton, T. Sr. Lectr./Lectr.

Babecki, R., MSc PhD Sr. Lectr.

Bailey, D. M. Sr. Lectr./Lectr.

Baker, R., BSc Sr. Lectr.

Baskerville, S., BSc PhD Sr. Lectr.

Berry, A. J., BSc PhD Sr. Lectr.

Blakemore, F. B., MSc Principal Lectr.

Burton, K. W. C., BSc PhD, FRSChem Principal Lectr.

Davies, A., BSc Sr. Lectr.

Davies, C., BSc Sr. Lectr.

Davies, L. J., BSc PhD Sr. Lectr.

Davies, P. Sr. Lectr./Lectr.

Dixon, J. R., BSc PhD, FRSChem   Prof.; Head*
Emes, P. J., BSc PhD   Sr. Lectr.
Evans, E. W., BSc PhD   Sr. Lectr.
Gilson, C. D., BSc PhD   Sr. Lectr.
Griffiths, I. W., BSc PhD   Sr. Lectr.
Hall, P. G., BSc PhD   Sr. Lectr.
Harris, A. J.   Sr. Lectr./Lectr.
Hawkes, F. R., BSc PhD   Principal Lectr.
Hogg, S. I., MSc PhD   Sr. Lectr.
Johnson, T. P., BSc Liv., PhD St And.   Sr. Lectr./Lectr.
Jones, S. D. R.   Sr. Lectr./Lectr.
Kell, T., BSc PhD   Principal Lectr.
King, S.   Sr. Lectr./Lectr.
Lee, C. W., MSc PhD   Principal Lectr.
Lewis, R. H., BSc PhD   Sr. Lectr.
Leyshon, P. R., BSc PhD   Principal Lectr.
Ling, S., BSc PhD   Sr. Lectr./Lectr.
Matthews, R. T., FRICS   Sr. Lectr.
McIntyre, P. S., BSc PhD   Principal Lectr.
Morgan, E., BSc PhD   Sr. Lectr.
Morton, J. L.   Sr. Lectr./Lectr.
Nuttall, F. E., MSc Lough.   Sr. Lectr./Lectr.
Powell, G. T., BSc PhD   Sr. Lectr.
Price, R. D., BSc   Sr. Lectr.
Quince, M., BSc   Geol. Curator
Ramsey, E. D., BSc PhD   Sr. Lectr.
Rees, G. J.   Sr. Lectr./Lectr.
Roberts, G. T., BSc PhD   Principal Lectr.
Thomas, A., MSc PhD   Sr. Lectr.
Thomas, M. C.   Sr. Lectr./Lectr.
Williams, J. M., BSc PhD   Sr. Lectr.
Williams, S. R. P.   Sr. Lectr./Lectr.
Worthington, H., PhD   Sr. Lectr.

Built Environment, School of

Tel: (01443) 482171 Fax: (01443) 482169

Anderson, W. C., BSc Wales   Sr. Lectr./Lectr.
Barber, P. L. R., FRICS   Sr. Lectr./Lectr.
Barthorpe, S. B., BSc Manc.   Sr. Lectr./Lectr.
Bennett, R., BA   Sr. Lectr./Lectr.
Bowler, R. J., MSc   Sr. Lectr./Lectr.
Dallimore, D.   Sr. Lectr./Lectr.
Davies, J.   Sr. Lectr./Lectr.
Davies, P. H.   Sr. Lectr./Lectr.
Delpak, R., MSc Wales, PhD Wales, FIStructE, FIMA   Principal Lectr.
Djialli, D. A., BSc Wales   Principal Lectr.
Francis, T. J., MSc Strath.   Sr. Lectr./Lectr.
Geens, A. J., BEng S.Bank   Sr. Lectr./Lectr.
Gibbons, P., MSc Brun.   Sr. Lectr./Lectr.
Graham, M. S., MSc Manc., PhD Manc.   Principal Lectr.
Gronow, Stuart A., BSc MA   Prof.
Hibberd, Peter R., MSc, FRICS   Prof.
Hillier, D., BA MA PhD   Sr. Lectr./Lectr.
Hirst, C.   Sr. Lectr./Lectr.
Hodgson, J., BSc Glam.   Sr. Lectr./Lectr.
Horsfield, J. A.   Sr. Lectr./Lectr.
Howells-Davies, J.   Principal Lectr.
Hughes, T. B., MSc , FRICS   Principal Lectr.
Ing, D. V.   Sr. Lectr./Lectr.
James, D. M.   Sr. Lectr./Lectr.
Jenkins, S., BA   Sr. Lectr./Lectr.
Jones, G. E., BA   Sr. Lectr./Lectr.
Jones, G. I., MSc Durh.   Principal Lectr.
Jones, J. P., MSc Wales, PhD Wales   Sr. Lectr./Lectr.
Lavender, S. D., BA MA   Sr. Lectr./Lectr.
Leverton, P. J., BSc MPhil   Principal Lectr.
McGorrigan, P. T., BSc Wales   Principal Lectr.
Mofor, L. A.   Sr. Lectr./Lectr.
Moore, D. B.   Sr. Lectr./Lectr.
Mustapha, F. H., MSc Brun., PhD Bath   Principal Lectr.
Neale, R. H., BSc Nott., MSc Lough.   Prof.; Head*
O'Hara, C., BSc Wales   Sr. Lectr./Lectr.
Penn, R. G., BArch Liv.   Principal Lectr.
Plimmer, F. A. S., MPhil , FRICS   Sr. Lectr./Lectr.
Prescott, G., MA   Principal Lectr.
Pugh, D. K., BSc Wales, MPhil Wales   Principal Lectr.
Rayment, A. R., BSc Wales   Sr. Lectr./Lectr.
Rees, P. T., BSc Wales   Sr. Lectr./Lectr.
Richards, L. A., BSc MBA   Sr. Lectr./Lectr.

Robinson, R. B., BSc Wales, PhD Wales, FGS   Sr. Lectr./Lectr.
Sabir, B. B., MSc Wales, PhD Wales   Sr. Lectr./Lectr.
Siddall, R. J., BEng(Tech) Wales, MSc Lough.   Sr. Lectr./Lectr.
Summerill, J.   Sr. Lectr./Lectr.
Tann, D. B., MSc Wales, BSc(Eng)   Sr. Lectr./Lectr.
Taylor, A. P., MEd, FRICS   Principal Lectr.
Taylor, J. L., MSc Wales   Principal Lectr.
Thomas, D. J., BA MSc   Sr. Lectr./Lectr.
Wild, S., MSc Newcastle(UK), PhD Newcastle(UK)   Reader
Williams, J. S., BSc Wales   Sr. Lectr./Lectr.
Williams, T., BSc MPhil   Sr. Lectr./Lectr.

Business School

Tel: (01443) 482330 Fax: (01443) 482380

Allard, G. M., BA Liv., MSc Staffs.,   Sr. Lectr./Lectr.
Anthony, P. D.   Sr. Lectr./Lectr.
Berrow, Teresa, BSc   Sr. Lectr./Lectr.
Bignall, Kay   Sr. Lectr./Lectr.
Blackey, H. E.   Sr. Lectr./Lectr.
Blythe, Jim, BA   Sr. Lectr./Lectr.
Brooksbank, David   Sr. Lectr./Lectr.
Broomfield, Mary, BA   Sr. Lectr./Lectr.
Clarke, Andre, BSc   Sr. Lectr./Lectr.
Cohen, David, BCom MPhil   Reader
Colebourne, David, BA MSc   Sr. Lectr./Lectr.
Connolly, Michael   Prof.; Dir.*
Copely, John, BScEcon MA MEd   Sr. Lectr./Lectr.
Crandon, Garth, BA MSc(Econ)   Sr. Lectr./Lectr.
Daunton, Lyn, MSc   Sr. Lectr./Lectr.
Davies, Paul, BA   Sr. Lectr./Lectr.
Davies, Trevor, BA   Principal Lectr.
Dessant, Jefferey, BA MSc(Econ) MBA   Head of Div.
Dimond, B. C.   Prof. Res. Fellow
Driscoll, Terry, MSc(Econ)   Sr. Lectr./Lectr.
Edwards, Julia, MSc PhD   Sr. Lectr./Lectr.
Evans, David, BSc   Sr. Lectr./Lectr.
Farrell, Catherine, BA   Sr. Lectr./Lectr.
Fitzgibbon, Karen   Sr. Lectr./Lectr.
Fosterjohn, Andy, BA   Sr. Lectr./Lectr.
Fox, Denis, MSc   Sr. Lectr./Lectr.
Grey, Antonia, BEd   Sr. Lectr./Lectr.
Gunn, Rod, BSc MBA PhD   Reader
Hall, Robert, BSc MBA   Sr. Lectr./Lectr.
Hamilton, Robert, BA   Sr. Lectr./Lectr.
Hedges, P.   Sr. Lectr./Lectr.
Hole, C.   Sr. Lectr./Lectr.
Huish, J. M., BSc Lond., MSc(Econ) Lond.   Sr. Lectr./Lectr.
Hurlow, Sarah, BA   Sr. Lectr./Lectr.
Hutcheson, Graham   Sr. Lectr./Lectr.
James, Chris, BSc PhD   Sr. Lectr./Lectr.
James, R.   Sr. Lectr./Lectr.
Jarvis, Martin, MSc   Sr. Lectr./Lectr.
Jenkins, Hugh, MSc   Principal Lectr.
Jones, Alan, LLM MSc(Econ)   Principal Lectr.
Jones, Catherine, BA   Sr. Lectr./Lectr.
Jones-Evans, D., BSc Wales, MSc Manc., PhD Aston   Prof.
Jones, Heather, BA   Sr. Lectr./Lectr.
Jones, Norah   Principal Lectr.
Jones, Norman, BA MSc   Principal Lectr.
Jones, Robert, BSc MSc   Sr. Lectr./Lectr.
Kilibarda, Penny, BSc   Sr. Lectr./Lectr.
Laffin, M.   Chair*
Law, Jennifer, BA   Sr. Lectr./Lectr.
Luffrum, Peter, BSc(Econ) BA MA(Econ)   Principal Lectr.
McCarthy, Phillip, BA MSc   Principal Lectr.
McDonald, Kevin, BSc(Econ)   Sr. Lectr./Lectr.
Morgan, Colin, BA MSc   Sr. Lectr./Lectr.
Morgan, Robert, MSc(Econ)   Principal Lectr.
Morgan, W. A., MBA Glam.   Sr. Lectr./Lectr.
Morse, Leighton   Sr. Lectr./Lectr.
Moskvin, A.   Sr. Lectr./Lectr.
O'Sullivan, D.   Sr. Lectr./Lectr.
Parselle, Virginia, BSc(Econ)   Sr. Lectr./Lectr.
Patterson, Maurice, BA   Sr. Lectr./Lectr.
Peattie, Sue, MA   Sr. Lectr./Lectr.
Pickernell, D. G., BSc Wales   Sr. Lectr./Lectr.

Pownall, I. E., BSc Lough., MA Limerick   Sr. Lectr./Lectr.
Preece, Terry, MBA   Sr. Lectr./Lectr.
Randall, Peter, MSc(Econ) MSc   Principal Lectr.
Robinson, Gordon, BA   Sr. Lectr./Lectr.
Smith, G. A.   Sr. Lectr./Lectr.
Snee, H. R.   Sr. Lectr./Lectr.
Sparkes, A.   Sr. Lectr./Lectr.
Talbot, Colin, MSc PhD   Sr. Lectr./Lectr.
Talbot, J. L.   Sr. Lectr./Lectr.
Thomas, Alys, BA Wales, MA Wales, PhD Wales   Sr. Lectr./Lectr.
Thomas, Paul, BA MSc   Principal Lectr.
Thomas, Robyn, BSc   Sr. Lectr./Lectr.
Trotman-Dickenson, D. I.   Prof. Res. Fellow
Waters, Ken, BSc(Tech) MBA   Sr. Lectr./Lectr.
Watkins, E. J.   Sr. Lectr./Lectr.
White, Philip   Sr. Lectr./Lectr.
Williams, W. H.   Sr. Lectr./Lectr.
Woldie, Astede, BA MSc MSoc PhD   Sr. Lectr./Lectr.
Young, Judith, BA MSc(Comp) MSc(SocSci)   Sr. Lectr./Lectr.

Computer Studies

Tel: (01443) 482277 Fax: (01443) 482715

Abdelmoty, A. I., BSc MSc PhD   Sr. Lectr./Lectr.
Beynon-Davies, P., BSc Wales, PhD Wales   Principal Lectr.
Blyth, A. J. C., MSc Newcastle(UK)   Sr. Lectr./Lectr.
Cox, D. W. J., MSc Wales, BSc   Sr. Lectr./Lectr.
Cunliffe, D. J., BA Sus., PhD Edin.   Sr. Lectr./Lectr.
Davies, P., BSc CNAA   Sr. Lectr./Lectr.
Davies, R. A., BSc Wales, MSc Wales, PhD Wales   Sr. Lectr./Lectr.
Dorey, M., BSc Glam.   Sr. Lectr./Lectr.
Evans, D., BSc Wales   Principal Lectr.
Evans, G. V., BSc Manc.   Principal Lectr.
Eyres, D. E., BSc Lond., MSc Essex   Principal Lectr.
Farthing, D. W., BSc Glam.   Sr. Lectr./Lectr.
Fletcher, G. P., BSc Lond., PhD Lough.   Sr. Lectr./Lectr.
Furse, E., BA Open(UK), BSc Sus., PhD Nott.   Sr. Lectr./Lectr.
Hanlon, J. G., BSc Wales, MSc CNAA   Sr. Lectr./Lectr.
Hodson, P. J., BSc CNAA, MSc Open(UK)   Head*
Hutchings, T. D., BSc CNAA   Sr. Lectr./Lectr.
Inglis, I. R., BA Macq., MSc Birm., PhD Flin.   Sr. Lectr./Lectr.
Jones, B. F., BSc Manc., PhD Nott.   Reader
Jones, C. B., BSc Brist., PhD Newcastle(UK)   Prof.
Kidner, D., BSc CNAA, PhD CNAA   Sr. Lectr./Lectr.
Large, R., BSc Wales   Sr. Lectr./Lectr.
Lewis, S. F. L., BSc CNAA   Sr. Lectr./Lectr.
McPhee, D., BEd Wales, MPhil CNAA   Sr. Lectr./Lectr.
Moon, J., BSc CNAA   Sr. Lectr./Lectr.
Morris, C. W., BSc Exe., MSc Wales   Sr. Lectr./Lectr.
Norris, K., BSc CNAA   Sr. Lectr./Lectr.
Reddy, M., BSc Durh., MSc Manc.   Sr. Lectr./Lectr.
Rees, C., BA Glam.   Sr. Lectr./Lectr.
Rees, D. C., BSc CNAA, MSc CNAA   Sr. Lectr./Lectr.
Sheppard, D., PhD Wales   Sr. Lectr./Lectr.
Tudhope, D., BSc Wales, PhD Wales   Sr. Lectr./Lectr.
Verheyden, K., BSc Salf.   Sr. Lectr./Lectr.
Watkins, M., BSc Lond.   Principal Lectr.
Wright, G. G. L., BA Camb., MA Camb.   Principal Lectr.
Vacant Posts: 1 Prof.

Electronics and Information Technology

Tel: (01443) 482523 Fax: (01443) 482541

Abdul-Wahab, M. D., BSc PhD   Principal Lectr.
Al-Nuaimi, M. O., BSc PhD, FIEE   Prof.

Beaujean, D. A., MSc PhD   Principal Lectr.
Dooley, L. S., MSc PhD   Sr. Lectr./Lectr.
Egan, J. T., BSc   Sr. Lectr./Lectr.
Evans, D. C.   Sr. Lectr./Lectr.
Gardner, P. F., BSc MTech   Sr. Lectr./Lectr.
Gardner, S., BSc MPhil   Sr. Lectr./Lectr.
Hamill-Keays, W. J. P., BEM, MSc   Principal Lectr.
Hammett, T. P. J., MPhil   Sr. Lectr./Lectr.
Hammouden, A. M.   Sr. Lectr./Lectr.
Jayne, M. G., MSc PhD   Principal Lectr.
Jones, D. L., BSc PhD   Principal Lectr.
Jones, D. R., BSc MPhil   Sr. Lectr./Lectr.
McCabe, M. A., BTech MPhil   Sr. Lectr./Lectr.
Mehenni, B., BEng MSc PhD   Sr. Lectr./Lectr.
Morgan, C., BSc PhD   Sr. Lectr./Lectr.
Morgan, S. B., BSc   Principal Lectr.
Otung, I. E.   Sr. Lectr./Lectr.
Payne, R. R., BSc PhD   Principal Lectr.
Pennington, A. W., BSc   Sr. Lectr./Lectr.
Price, M. H., BSc PhD   Sr. Lectr./Lectr.
Rees, D., BSc PhD, FIEE   Reader
Rees, S. J., BSc(Eng)   Sr. Lectr./Lectr.
Shewring, I., BEng MSc   Sr. Lectr.
Stone, R. E., BSc MPhil   Sr. Lectr./Lectr.
Thomas, E. J. C., BSc MBA   Sr. Lectr./Lectr.
Watson, R. V., BSc BA   Sr. Lectr./Lectr.
Williams, R. J., MPhil   Principal Lectr.
Witting, P. A., BSc MTech, FIEE   Prof.; Head*

Engineering, Mechanical and Manufacturing

Tel: (01443) 482202 Fax: (01443) 482231

Appleton, Peter R., BSc Manc.   Sr. Lectr.
Biffin, Martin, BSc Wales, PhD Wales   Sr. Lectr.
Blythe, D., BSc CNAA   Sr. Lectr.
Board, M. J. P.   Principal Lectr.
Collins, Steven G., BSc Glam.   Sr. Lectr.
Evans, Peter R., BSc CNAA   Sr. Lectr./Lectr.
Franklin, K. L., BSc Wales, PhD   Sr. Lectr.
Garwood, David R., MSc Manc.   Sr. Lectr.
Gordon, Rae S., MSc Cran., PhD Cran., BSc   Sr. Lectr.
Griffiths, T. J., BEng(Tech) Wales, PhD Glam.   Principal Lectr.
Guile, A. W.   Sr. Lectr./Lectr.
Hague, W. M., BSc Strath.   Sr. Lectr.
Hawkes, Prof. D. L., BSc Wales, PhD Glam.   Reader
Higgins, Steven, BEng Wales   Principal Lectr.
Lloyd, S.   Principal Lectr.
Maksaud, T.   Sr. Lectr./Lectr.
Powell, Steven, BSc   Sr. Lectr.
Premier, Giuliano C., BSc Glam.   Sr. Lectr.
Smith, John A., MPhil   Reader
Story, Dawn L., BSc Wales, PhD Wales   Sr. Lectr.
Thomas, Michael J., BEng Wales, MEd Wales   Principal Lectr.
Thomas, Stephen L., BSc Glam.   Sr. Lectr.
Ward, John, BSc Wales   Prof.; Head*
White, G., BMet Sheff., MMet Sheff., PhD Sheff.   Sr. Lectr.
Wilcox, S. J., BSc Wales, PhD H.-W.   Sr. Lectr.

Humanities and Social Sciences, School of

Tel: (01443) 282353 Fax: (01443) 482138

Abousnnouga, N. G.   Sr. Lectr./Lectr.
Adamson, David L., BScEcon Wales   Principal Lectr.
Allan, S. R.   Sr. Lectr./Lectr.
Amuda, A. A.   Sr. Lectr./Lectr.
Ayisi, F. I.   Sr. Lectr./Lectr.
Baron Cohen, Dan J., BA Oxf., MLitt Oxf.   Sr. Lectr.
Barton, A. J.   Sr. Lectr./Lectr.
Beddoe, D.   Prof. Res. Fellow
Beynon, John, BA Wales, MA Lond., PhD Wales   Reader
Blandford, Steve J., BA Lond., MA Keele   Principal Lectr.
Boardman Jacobs, S.   Sr. Lectr./Lectr.
Bond, T. J., BA Wales   Sr. Lectr./Lectr.
Brewer-Wilcox, Teri F., BA Calif., PhD Calif.   Sr. Lectr.
Clark, Andrew C. T., BA Wales, MA Wales   Principal Lectr.

Cole, A. M.   Sr. Lectr./Lectr.
Croll, A. J.   Sr. Lectr./Lectr.
Crowley, K. J.   Sr. Lectr./Lectr.
Curtis, Tony, BA Wales, MFA Vermont   Prof.
Davies, Cennard, BA Wales, MA Wales   Reader
Davies, Marie-Christine, LèsL Lille   Sr. Lectr.
Davies, W. Basil, MA Wales   Principal Lectr.
Dunkerley, David, BScEcon Wales, MScEcon Wales, PhD Wales   Prof.
Eldridge, E. J.   Sr. Lectr./Lectr.
Elias, J. Hefin, BSc(Econ) Lond., BD Wales   Sr. Lectr.
England, A.   Sr. Lectr./Lectr.
Evans, C.   Sr. Lectr./Lectr.
Faulkner, S. E.   Sr. Lectr./Lectr.
Gemie, S.   Sr. Lectr./Lectr.
Granfield, Alun J., BA Wales, PhD Wales   Principal Lectr.
Griffiths, M.   Sr. Lectr./Lectr.
Gruffydd, L. A.   Sr. Lectr./Lectr.
Hagopian, P.   Sr. Lectr./Lectr.
Hand, R. J.   Sr. Lectr./Lectr.
Handley, J. F.   Sr. Lectr./Lectr.
Hill, Alan J., BA Wales   Sr. Lectr.
Hutson, Susan, BA Sus., MPhil Sus., DPhil Sus.   Sr. Lectr.
Jackson, R. C.   Sr. Lectr./Lectr.
James, Allan, BA Wales, MA Wales   Principal Lectr.
Joinson, A. N.   Sr. Lectr./Lectr.
Jones, Rod, MPhil Lond.   Sr. Lectr.
Jordan, Glenn H., BA Stan., MA Stan.   Sr. Lectr.
Keehan, B.   Sr. Lectr./Lectr.
Knowles, Pamela M., BA Wales, PhD Lond.   Sr. Lectr.
Le Bihan-Smith   Sr. Lectr./Lectr.
Lewis, C. W.   Prof.
Majumdar, Margaret, BA MA PhD   Principal Lectr.
Manjon, J. E.   Sr. Lectr./Lectr.
Mannsaker, Frances M., BA Nott., PhD Nott.   Head*
Masson, U.   Sr. Lectr./Lectr.
Mayer, P. A.   Sr. Lectr./Lectr.
McNorton, Maggy, BEd Brist.   Principal Lectr.
Mercer, Peter A., BA Exe., MEd Wales   Principal Lectr.
Meredith, Christopher L., BA Wales   Sr. Lectr.
Middlehurst, Robert, BA Lond., MA Lanc.   Sr. Lectr.
Morris, Ieuan R., MA RCA, BA   Sr. Lectr.
Naamani, C.   Sr. Lectr./Lectr.
Nurse, C. L.   Sr. Lectr./Lectr.
O'Hara, M. P.   Sr. Lectr./Lectr.
O'Malley, Tom, BA Birm.   Sr. Lectr.
Odiari, S.   Sr. Lectr./Lectr.
Oerton, Sarah J., BA Kent, MA Wales, MSc Open(UK), PhD Open(UK)   Sr. Lectr.
Pearson, Rose, BA Leeds, MSc Wales   Sr. Lectr.
Price, A.   Sr. Lectr./Lectr.
Prince, Jane, BSc Wales, MSc Lond.   Sr. Lectr.
Pritchard, G. D.   Sr. Lectr./Lectr.
Reader, W. R., BSc CNAA, MSc CNAA, DPhil York(UK)   Sr. Lectr./Lectr.
Roberts, M. E.   Sr. Lectr./Lectr.
Robins, Timothy, BSc CNAA   Sr. Lectr.
Rowson, Richard H., BA Lond.   Principal Lectr.
Salisbury, Alan, MA RCA   Principal Lectr.
Schoene-Harwood, B. J.   Sr. Lectr./Lectr.
Slater, R., BA Sus., MPhil   Sr. Lectr./Lectr.
Smith, A.   Sr. Lectr./Lectr.
Smith, David, BA Sus., MA Sus., MSc Open(UK)   Principal Lectr.
Striff, E. E.   Sr. Lectr./Lectr.
Stuart, E. B.   Sr. Lectr./Lectr.
Thompson, A.   Sr. Lectr./Lectr.
Travis, G. David, BSc PhD   Sr. Lectr.
Traynor, M. J.   Sr. Lectr./Lectr.
Vernon, Gabrielle, BA CNAA, MSc Lond.   Sr. Lectr.
Wallace, Jeff, BA Newcastle(UK), MA Kent, PhD Kent   Sr. Lectr.
Walters, J. Roderick, BA Oxf., MA Oxf.   Sr. Lectr.
Wardak, A. A.   Sr. Lectr./Lectr.
Wiblin, I. A.   Sr. Lectr./Lectr.
Wilson, M.   Sr. Lectr./Lectr.
Woodley, Frances, MA Manc.   Sr. Lectr.

Workman, Lance, BA Keele, DPhil Sus.   Sr. Lectr.
Wynn, Neil, MA Edin., PhD Open(UK)   Reader
Young, John, BA Wales, MEd Wales   Sr. Lectr.

Information Technology, see Electronics and Information Technol.

Law School

Tel: (01443) 483005 Fax: (01443) 483008

Brand, Patricia A., BA Lond.   Sr. Lectr./Lectr.
Calderwood, David A., BA Wales, MA Wales   Principal Lectr.
Chapman, G. A.   Sr. Lectr./Lectr.
Counsell, Karen M., LLB Wales, MSc Wales   Sr. Lectr./Lectr.
D'Sa, Rose M., LLB Birm., PhD Birm.   Prof.
Davies, Shan C., LLB Wales   Sr. Lectr./Lectr.
Doherty, Michael J., MA Hull   Sr. Lectr./Lectr.
Dowrick, Brian, LLB Wales   Sr. Lectr./Lectr.
East, R.   Principal Lectr.
Evans, Michelle, LLB Wales   Sr. Lectr./Lectr.
Griffiths, Gerwyn Ll. H., LLB CNAA   Sr. Lectr./Lectr.
Griffiths, Ivor, LLB Wales   Sr. Lectr./Lectr.
Griffiths, S. M.   Prof.; Head*
James, C. A.   Sr. Lectr./Lectr.
Jones, Catherine A., BA Wales   Sr. Lectr./Lectr.
Keyse, M. J., BA Wales   Sr. Lectr./Lectr.
Litton, Kriston M., LLB CNAA   Sr. Lectr./Lectr.
Mahmood, Irfan, LLB Lond., LLM Brist.   Sr. Lectr./Lectr.
McCartney, Annie, LLB Wales, MSc Lond.   Sr. Lectr./Lectr.
Morris, Claire E., LLB Wales, BA   Sr. Lectr./Lectr.
Newman, Veronica, BA Portsmouth   Sr. Lectr./Lectr.
Owen, W. R., LLB Birm.   Sr. Lectr./Lectr.
Picton, V.   Sr. Lectr./Lectr.
Power, Helen P. C., BA York(UK), LLM Brist.   Sr. Lectr./Lectr.
Pryce-Brown, Tim, LLB Wales   Sr. Lectr./Lectr.
Spurin, Corbett H., LLB CNAA, LLM Wales   Sr. Lectr./Lectr.
Tovey, Gwyn, LLB CNAA   Sr. Lectr./Lectr.
Williams, A. Mark, LLB Brist.   Sr. Lectr./Lectr.
Williams, Julie, BSc Wales, LLB Wales, MSc Wales   Sr. Lectr./Lectr.
Yeates, V. A.   Sr. Lectr./Lectr.

Mathematics, see Acctg. and Maths., Sch. of

Nursing and Midwifery Studies

Tel: (01443) 482635 Fax: (01443) 482646

Achilles, John D., BA Glam.   Principal Lectr.
Baines, Peter J., BEd   Sr. Lectr.
Bale, Barbara F., MSc Sur.   Principal Lectr.
Beech, Ian, BA   Sr. Lectr.
Bence, Jeffrey P., MSc(SocialSciences) S'ton.   Sr. Lectr.
Bennett, Glynnis, MSc   Sr. Lectr.
Binks, Edna M.   Sr. Lectr.
Black, Damien J., BEd   Sr. Lectr.
Botting, Deborah, BSc MN   Sr. Lectr.
Broom, Mark, MN   Sr. Lectr.
Constantine, Sue, BA   Sr. Lectr.
Cowpe, Marianne, BA Open(UK)   Sr. Lectr.
Davies, J.   Sr. Lectr./Lectr.
Davies, Kevin, MA Wales   Sr. Lectr.
Davies, Moira L.   Sr. Lectr.
Davies, Nancy L., BEd   Sr. Lectr.
Davies, P. D.   Sr. Lectr./Lectr.
Elley, Katherine   Sr. Lectr.
Evans, Lynwen E.   Sr. Lectr.
Evans, Robert   Sr. Lectr.
Goff, Ann E.   Sr. Lectr.
Guyatt, Clive, BEd   Principal Lectr.
Harris, Lyne, TD, MN Wales   Sr. Lectr.
Harris, Susan E., BSc CNAA, MN   Sr. Lectr.
Hill, Janne L. G., MEd Wales   Sr. Lectr.
Horne, Agnes   Sr. Lectr.
Houlihan, G. D.   Sr. Lectr./Lectr.
Howell, Janet M., BSc(Econ)   Sr. Lectr.
Jenkins, R. I.   Sr. Lectr./Lectr.
John, Marie E., MSc Wales   Sr. Lectr.
Jones, Jame M.   Sr. Lectr.
Jones, Sian, BA Lond., LLM Wales   Sr. Lectr.

Kneath-Jones, J. A.
Lado, Amode, BA *Open(UK)*, MSc *Glam.* Sr. Lectr.
Lewis, Elfed, BA *Lampeter*, BSc(Econ) *Lond.* Sr. Lectr.
Lipp, Allyson Sr. Lectr.
MacDonald, D. G. Sr. Lectr./Lectr.
Mansell, D. A. Sr. Lectr.
Mead, D. M., MSc *Manc.*, PhD *Wales* Head*
Moran, Lorraine A., BEd MPhil Principal Lectr.
Morse, Vanessa R. Sr. Lectr.
Nicke, John A. E. Sr. Lectr.
Osborne, P. A. Sr. Lectr.
Phillips, P. Drewe, MEd *Wales* Sr. Lectr.
Preece, Wayne P., MPhil Sr. Lectr.
Pugh, Alwyn Sr. Lectr.
Rogers, Andrew, BEd MSc Principal Lectr.
Semmens, Vivienne C., MSc *Wales* Sr. Lectr.
Semple, Martin J., MSc *Wales* Sr. Lectr.
Sinfield, Mair Sr. Lectr.
Smith, Mary E., BA *Open(UK)* Sr. Lectr.
Stephenson, Marian E., BScNursing MN Principal Lectr.
Thomas, Irene E., MSc(Econ) Sr. Lectr.
Thomas, Nancy M., MA *Wales* Sr. Lectr.
Thomas, R. Sr. Lectr./Lectr.
Torrance, C. Prof.
Walker, G. M. Sr. Lectr./Lectr.
Walters, Dorothy N. M. Sr. Lectr.
Watkins, Janice, BA *Open(UK)*, LLM Sr. Lectr.
White, Pat V., BEd Sr. Lectr.
Williams, Elizabeth, BN *Wales* Sr. Lectr.
Willock, J. H. Sr. Lectr./Lectr.
Woolley, Norman N., MN Sr. Lectr.

Social Sciences, see Humanities and Soc. Scis., Sch. of

SPECIAL CENTRES, ETC

Built Environment, Centre for Research in the
Tel: (01443) 482708 Fax: (01443) 482660
Hibberd, Peter R., MSc, FRICS Dir.*
Jenkins, David H., BSc MPhil Sr. Lectr./Lectr.

Health and Social Care, Welsh Institute of
Iredoue, R. Sr. Lectr./Lectr.

CONTACT OFFICERS

Academic affairs. Director of Planning and Programmes: Hobson, Prof. Leslie, BA MSc MA PhD
Accommodation. Accommodation Officer: Maidment, Patricia
Admissions (first degree). Senior Administrative Officer (Admissions): Davies, Julie
Admissions (higher degree). Senior Administrative Officer (Admissions): Davies, Julie
Adult/continuing education. Curriculum Development Manager/Head of Education Development Unit: Saunders, Danny J., BA MSc
Archives. Senior Administrative Officer (Quality): Zobole, Nikki, BA
Careers. Senior Careers Adviser: Evans, Euros J., BA
Computing services. Head, Information Services Department: Cobley, Ron, MEd *Wales*
Consultancy services. Managing Director, University of Glamorgan Commercial Services: Lea, Dave A., BSc MPhil
Distance education. Curriculum Development Manager/Head of Education Development Unit: Saunders, Danny J., BA MSc
Equal opportunities. Assistant Academic Registrar: ......
Estates and buildings/works and services. Head of Estates Services: Woodruff, Alun J., BA
Examinations. Senior Administrative Officer (Examinations): Withers, Pam
Finance. Financial Controller: Williams, Huw R., LLB
General enquiries. University Secretary: Bracegirdle, J. L., BA BPhil MEd
Health services. Nursing Officer: Osmond, Althea, BA
Industrial liaison. Managing Director, University of Glamorgan Commercial Services: Lea, Dave A., BSc MPhil
Library (chief librarian). Librarian/Head of Learning Resources Centre: Atkinson, P. Jeremy, BSc MPhil
Personnel/human resources. Head of Personnel Services: Morgan, Kevin E., MSc
Purchasing. Purchasing Manager: Thomas, D. Alan
Quality assurance and accreditation. Assistant Academic Registrar: Rainsbury, Diane, BSc
Research. Assistant Academic Registrar: McIntyre, Denise, BA
Safety. Health and Safety Officer: Curtis, John

Scholarships, awards, loans. Head, Student Services: Aldridge, Barrie J., BSc MA
Security. Head of Estates Services: Woodruff, Alun J., BA
Sport and recreation. Head, Sport and Recreation Centre: Williams, Tudor
Staff development and training. Assistant Head of Personnel Services (Training): Jones, Neil
Student union. President: Blunden, J.
Student welfare/counselling. Head, Student Services: Aldridge, Barrie J., BSc MA
Students from other countries. Head, Student Services: Aldridge, Barrie J., BSc MA
Students with disabilities. Student Adviser (Special Needs): Evans, Amanda, BA
Women. Deputy President, Women: Parry-Davies, Sian

CAMPUS/COLLEGE HEADS

Aberdare College. Principal: Roberts, Chris, BA MSc
Barry College. Principal: Wilmore, Trevor, BSc
Bridgend College of Technology. Principal: Wylie, Keith
Carmarthenshire College of Technology and Art, Alban Road, Llanelli, Dyfed, Wales SA15 1NG. Principal: Price, Ieuan, MSc(Eng), FIMechE
Coleg Powys, Llanidloes Road, Newtown, Powys, Wales SY16 1BE. Principal: Stephenson, John, MA MSc
Evangelical Theological College of Wales. Principal: Davies, Eryl, BA BD MA PhD
Gwent Tertiary College, College Road, Ebbw Vale, Gwent, Wales NP3 6LE. Principal: Robinson, Brian, BSc MSc
Gwynedd Technical College. Principal: Edwards, Haydn, BSc PhD, FRSChem
Llandrillo College. Principal: Evans, Huw, BSc MPhil
Merthyr Tydfil College. Principal: Marsh, Frank, MEd
Neath College. Principal: Trebilcock, Robin, BSc MSc
Pontypridd College. Principal: Cocks, Jeffrey, BA MEd
Swansea College, Tycoch, Swansea, West Glamorgan, Wales SA2 9EB. Principal: Lewis, Cyril M., OBE, MSc ME
Ystrad Mynach College, Twyn Road, Ystrad Mynach, Hengoed, Mid Glamorgan, Wales CF8 7XR. Principal: Brooks, Don, BA MEd

[Information supplied by the institution as at 26 May 1998, and edited by the ACU]

UNIVERSITY OF GLASGOW

Founded 1451

Member of the Association of Commonwealth Universities

Postal Address: Glasgow, Scotland G12 8QQ
Telephone: (0141) 339 8855 **Telex**: 777070 UNIGLA **WWW**: http://www.gla.ac.uk
E-mail formula: name@website.gla.ac.uk

CHANCELLOR—Fraser, Sir William K., GCB, MA *Glas.*, LLB *Glas.*, Hon. LLD, FRSEd
PRINCIPAL AND VICE-CHANCELLOR*—Davies, Prof. Sir Graeme, BE NZ, MA *Camb.*, PhD NZ, ScD *Camb.*, Hon. LLD
   Liv., Hon. DMet *Sheff.*, Hon. DSc *Nott.*, Hon. DEng *Manc.Met.*, FEng, FRSEd, Hon. FRSNZ, Hon. FTCL
VICE-PRINCIPAL (DIRECTOR OF INFORMATION SERVICES)—Allison, Prof. A. C., BSc *Belf.*, PhD
VICE-PRINCIPAL—Holmes, Prof. Peter H., BVMS PhD
VICE-PRINCIPAL—Bone, Prof. J. Drummond, MA *Glas.*
VICE-PRINCIPAL—Trainor, Prof. Richard H., BA *Brown*, MA *Oxf.*, MA *Prin.*, DPhil *Oxf.*, FRHistS
VICE-PRINCIPAL—Green, Prof. David R., BSc *Glas.*, MS *Calif.*, PhD *Glas.*
RECTOR—Wilson, Richard, OBE, Hon. DLitt *G.Caledonian*
DEAN OF FACULTIES—Duncan, Prof. Archibald A. M., FRHistS, FRSEd
SECRETARY OF THE UNIVERSITY COURT‡—Mackie, Dugald M., MA *Edin.*
DIRECTOR OF FINANCE—Yuille, Michael, BAcc *Glas.*
CLERK OF SENATE—Whitehead, Prof. Rex R., MSc *Melb.*, PhD *Melb.*, DSc *Glas.*, FRSEd
LIBRARIAN AND KEEPER OF HUNTERIAN BOOKS AND MANUSCRIPTS—......
CLERK OF THE GENERAL COUNCIL—Black, J. Michael, BA *Durh.*

GENERAL INFORMATION

History. Founded in 1451, the university moved to its current campus on Gilmorehill, in the west end of the city of Glasgow, in 1870. The university's veterinary school is located 8km from the main campus, on the Garscube estate.

Admission to first degree courses (see also United Kingdom Introduction). United Kingdom applicants: through Universities and Colleges Admissions Service (UCAS). International applicants: apply to the appropriate faculty admissions office.

First Degrees. BA, BAcc, BArch, BCommEdCommDev (community education and community development), BD, BDS, BEd, BEng, BES, BFLS, BN, BSc, BSc(DentSci), BSc(MedSci), BSc(VetSci), BTechnol, BTheol, BVMS, LLB, MA, MA(AppSocSci), MA(SocSci), MB ChB, MEng, MSc.

Most courses are full-time and normally last four years. BCommEdCommDev, BES, BSc: 3 years; BVMS, MB ChB, MEng: 5 years.

Higher Degrees. LLM, MAcc, MArch, MBA, MCC, MDes, MFA, MLitt, MM, MMus, MPH, MPhil, PhD, DClinPsy, DDS, DEng, DLitt, DMus, DSc, DVM, DVS, LLD, MD.

Applicants for admission to master's degrees must normally hold an appropriate first degree with at least second class honours. PhD: appropriate master's degree or equivalent; DEng, DLitt, DMus, DSc, DVM, DVS, LLD: awarded on published work.

Courses leading to a higher degree are normally 1–2 years full-time for a master's degree and 3 years full-time for a PhD. Part-time study/research also available.

Libraries. 1,700,000 million volumes; almost 10,000 current periodicals subscribed to. Special collections: European Documentation Centre for the European Union; Council of Europe publications.

Fees (1998–99, annual). United Kingdom students (undergraduate): £1000. International students: £6730 (arts); £8800 (science); £13,240 (MB ChB); £12,500 (BVMS); £16,320 (BDS clinical courses); £9980 (postgraduate non-clinical courses in medicine); £16,320 (postgraduate clinical courses in dentistry, medicine, and veterinary medicine).

Academic Awards (1997–98). 26 university postgraduate scholarships with a value of £7844.

Academic Year (1998–99). Three terms: 8 October–18 December; 11 January–19 March; 19 April–25 June.

Income (1996–97). Total, £191,000,000.

Statistics. Staff: 1699 (1318 academic, 381 administrative). Students: full-time 17,911; part-time 4518 (1836 men, 2682 women); international 1222 (690 men, 532 women); total 22,429.

FACULTIES/SCHOOLS

Arts
Tel: (0141) 330 5253 Fax: (0141) 330 4537
Dean: Ward, Prof. Mark G., BA *Lond.*
Clerk: Macdonald, Robert, MA *Glas.*

Divinity
Tel: (0141) 330 5155 Fax: (0141) 330 4943
Dean: Hunter, Rev. Alastair G., BD *Glas.*, MSc *Glas.*
Clerk: Macdonald, Robert, MA *Glas.*

Engineering
Tel: (0141) 330 5222 Fax: (0141) 330 6004
Dean: Murray-Smith, Prof. David J., MSc *Aberd.*, PhD
Clerk: Simpson, John, MA *Glas.*

Law and Financial Studies
Tel: (0141) 330 5865 Fax: (0141) 330 5140
Dean: Thomson, Prof. Joseph M., LLB, FRSEd
Clerk: Wilson, A. Elizabeth, BSc *Glas.*

Medicine
Tel: (0141) 330 4249 Fax: (0141) 330 5440
Dean: Whiting, Prof. Brian, MD *Glas.*, FRCPGlas
Clerk: Spurway, Alison K., MA *Glas.*

Science
Tel: (0141) 330 6574 Fax: (0141) 330 4371
Dean: Webb, Prof. Geoffrey, BSc *Hull*, PhD *Hull*, DSc, FRSChem, FRSEd
Clerk: McNeil, Iain C.

Social Sciences
Tel: (0141) 330 4690 Fax: (0141) 330 3547
Dean: Slaven, Prof. Anthony, BLitt MA
Clerk: Boyle, Linda, BSc

Veterinary Medicine
Tel: (0141) 330 5701 Fax: (0141) 330 5701
Dean: Wright, Prof. Norman G., BVMS *Glas.*, PhD *Glas.*, DVM *Glas.*, FIBiol, FRCPath, FRSEd
Clerk: Mathieson, Thomas W.

ACADEMIC UNITS

Accounting and Finance
Tel: (0141) 330 4138 Fax: (0141) 330 4442
Adams, Carol A. H., BA *Stir.*, MSc *Lond.*   Sr. Lectr.
Emmanuel, C. R., BSc *Wales*, MA *Lanc.*, PhD *Lanc.*   Ernst and Young Prof.
Garrod, N., BSc *Manc.*, PhD *Manc.*   Prof., Accountancy
Harte, G. F., MSc *Lond.*, MAcc *Glas.*   Sr. Lectr.
Holland, J. B., BSc *Aston*, MBA *Liv.*, PhD   Prof.; Head*
Rees, William P., MSA, FCA   Prof.
Shackleton, J. Kendrick, MSc *Brad.*   Sr. Lectr.
Shaw, Sir John C., CBE, BL *Edin.*   Visiting Prof.
Other Staff: 6 Lectrs.
Research: comparative international accounting; corporate finance (market valuation and investor relations); corporate governance in Britain and Europe; developments in corporate reporting; educational and professional research

Adult and Continuing Education
Tel: (0141) 330 4394 Fax: (0141) 330 3525
Kelly, Elinor A., BA *Lond.*, MPhil *Lond.*, PhD *Manc.*   Sr. Lectr.
MacDonald, J. G., BSc PhD   Sr. Lectr.
Slowey, Maria, BComm *Trinity(Dub.)*, MLitt *Trinity(Dub.)*   Prof.; Dir.*
Other Staff: 14 Lectrs.
Research: access to higher and further education; continuing vocational education, professional development and personal development; equal opportunities issues; issues of higher education policy and practice; work-based learning

Agriculture
Scottish Agricultural College
Tel: (01292) 520 331 Fax: (01292) 521 119
Thomas, P. C., BSc *Wales*, PhD *Wales*, FIBiol   Prof.; Head*
Research: animal and public health; clean technology; economic and social systems; farming systems; plant and crop science

Archaeology
Tel: (0141) 330 5690 Fax: (0141) 330 8044
Chapman, J. C.   Reader

Hanson, W. S., BA Manc., PhD Manc., FSA Sr. Lectr.

Jones, Richard E., CBE, BSc Kent, MSc Warw., PhD Wales, FSA Sr. Lectr.

Knapp, A. Bernard, BA Akron, MA Calif., PhD Calif. Reader

Morris, Christopher D., BA Durh., FSA Prof.; Head*

Other Staff: 5 Lectrs.

Research: archaeological theory and material culture studies; archaeology of mediaeval Britain; Mediterranean archaeology (society, landscape and technology); Roman frontier and Roman-native interactions; social history/prehistory of Scottish highlands and islands

Architecture, Mackintosh School of

Tel: (0141) 353 4686 Fax: (0141) 353 4703

Lever, W. F., MA Oxf., DPhil Oxf. Prof.

MacCallum, Charles H. A. Prof.; Head*

Art, see Hist. of Art

Astronomy, see Phys. and Astron.

Biomedical and Life Sciences, Institute of

Tel: (0141) 330 2032 Fax: (0141) 330 4758

Adams, Roger L. P., MA Oxf., DPhil Oxf., FRSEd Prof., Nucleic Acid Biochemistry

Barnes, W. J. P., BSc St And., PhD St And. Sr. Lectr.

Barry, J. David, BSc PhD Prof., Molecular Parasitology

Baxendale, R. H., BSc PhD Sr. Lectr.

Beeley, Josie A., MSc Manc., PhD Manc. Sr. Lectr., Oral Biochemistry

Birkbeck, T. H., BSc Birm., PhD Birm. Reader

Blackshaw, Susanna E., BSc Birm., PhD Wales Sr. Lectr.

Bowes, B. G., BSc Lond., PhD Lond. Sr. Lectr.

Boyle, Frances C., BSc PhD Sr. Lectr.

Brett, C. T., BA Camb., PhD Camb. Sr. Lectr.

Burton, R. F., BA Camb., PhD Lond. Sr. Lectr.

Campbell, Ailsa M., BSc Edin., PhD Reader

Carman, W. F., MB BCh Witw., MMed Witw. Sr. Lectr.

Clements, J. B., BSc Belf., PhD Belf., FRSEd Prof., Virology

Clutterbuck, A. John, BSc Sheff., PhD Sheff. Sr. Lectr.

Cogdell, R. J., BSc Brist., PhD Brist., FRSEd Hooker Prof.

Coggins, J. R., MA Oxf., PhD Ott. Prof.

Cohen, B. L., BSc Lond., PhD Edin. Sr. Lectr.

Cook, B., BSc Lond., PhD Ill. Sr. Lectr.

Coombs, G. H., BSc Lond., PhD Lond. Prof.

Coote, J. G., BSc Leeds, PhD Leeds Reader

Coutts, J. R. T., BSc St And., PhD St And. Reader, Obstetrics

Crampton, Julian M. Prof., Molecular Entomology

Crompton, David W. T., MA Camb., PhD Camb., ScD Camb., FIBiol, FRSEd John Graham Kerr Prof.

Crozier, A., BSc Durh., PhD Lond. Reader

Curtis, A. S. G., MA Camb., PhD Edin. Prof.

Cushley, W., BSc PhD Sr. Lectr.

Davies, P. S., BSc Wales, PhD Sr. Lectr.

Davies, R. W., MA Camb., PhD Camb. Robertson Prof.

Dickson, J. H., MA Camb., PhD Camb., BSc Prof.

Douglas, L. Julia, BSc Newcastle(UK), PhD Newcastle(UK) Sr. Lectr.

Dow, Jocelyn W., BSc NZ, PhD N.Y. Sr. Lectr.

Dow, Julian A., MA Camb., PhD Camb. Reader

Downie, J. R., PhD Lond., BSc Sr. Lectr.

Dunn, J. S., BSc Glas., MB ChB Glas., PhD Glas. Sr. Lectr.

Edwards, J. G., BSc Lond., PhD Lond. Sr. Lectr.

Elder, H. Y., BSc PhD Reader

Elliott, R. M., BSc Sur., DPhil Oxf. Personal Prof.

Ferrell, W. R., MB ChB PhD Sr. Lectr.

Fewson, Charles A., BSc Nott., PhD Brist., FIBiol Prof., Microbial Chemistry; Head*

Freer, J. H., BSc Durh., MSc Nott., PhD Birm. Prof.

Furness, R. W., BSc Durh., PhD Durh. Reader

Gilmore, D. P., BSc NZ, PhD Lond. Sr. Lectr.

Gladden, Margaret, MB BS Lond., PhD Liv. Reader

Goddard, J. P., BSc Newcastle(UK), PhD Newcastle(UK) Sr. Lectr.

Gould, Gwyn W., BSc S'ton., PhD S'ton. Prof.

Hagan, Paul, BSc PhD Sr. Lectr.

Hansell, M. H., BA Trinity(Dub.), DPhil Oxf. Sr. Lectr.

Hillman, J. R., BSc PhD, FLS, FIBiol, FRSEd Visiting Prof.

Hodgins, M. B., BSc Manc., PhD Sr. Lectr.

Holmes, O., MSc Lond., MB BS Lond., DSc Sr. Lectr.

Houslay, M. D., BSc Manc., PhD Camb. Gardiner Prof.

Houston, D. C., BSc Brist., DPhil Oxf. Reader

Huntingford, Felicity A., BA Oxf., DPhil Oxf. Prof.

Ingram, D. S., BSc Hull, PhD Hull, MA Camb., ScD Camb. Visiting Prof.

Jacobs, H. T., BA Camb., MA Camb., PhD Glas. Reader

Jenkins, G. I., BSc Liv., PhD Leeds Sr. Lectr.

Johnson, Keith, MB ChB BSc PhD Prof., Genetics

Kaiser, K., BSc CNAA, PhD Edin. Reader

Kennedy, Malcolm W., BSc PhD Prof., Infection Biology

Kusel, John R., BA Camb., PhD Camb. Prof., Cellular Biochemistry

La Thangue, Nicholas B., BSc Birm., MSc Reading, PhD Lond. Cathcart Prof.

Lawrence, A. J., BSc Lond., PhD Lond. Sr. Lectr.

Leader, David P., MA Oxf., DPhil Oxf. Sr. Lectr.; Grieve Lectr.

Leake, R. E., MA Oxf., DPhil Oxf. Reader

Lindsay, J. G., BSc PhD Titular Prof.

MacKay, S., BSc Birm., PhD Birm. Sr. Lectr.

Mackenna, Beverly R., MB ChB PhD Sr. Lectr.

MacLean, M., BSc Edin., PhD Edin. Reader

Martin, William, BSc PhD Prof., Cardiovascular Pharmacology

Mauldin, I., BSc Newcastle(UK), MSc Birm., PhD Lond. Prof.

Maxwell, D. J. Welcome Trust Sr. Lectr.

Maxwell, William L., BSc Brist., PhD Brist. Sr. Lectr.

McCruden, Elizabeth A. B., BSc MB ChB Sr. Lectr.

McGeoch, Duncan J., BSc PhD, FRSEd Hon. Prof.

McGrath, J. C., BSc PhD Prof.

Meadows, P. S., MA Camb., BA Open(UK), FIBiol Sr. Lectr.

Miller, D. J., BSc Leic., PhD Leic. Reader

Milligan, G., BSc Birm., PhD Nott. Reader

Milner-White, E. J., BSc Aberd., PhD Lond. Sr. Lectr.

Mitchell, Timothy J. Prof., Microbiology

Monaghan, Patricia, PhD Durh., BSc Prof.

Moores, Geoffrey R., BSc Lond., PhD Sr. Lectr.

Morris, B. J., BA Camb., PhD Brist. Sr. Lectr.

Murphy, K. J., BSc Liv., PhD Liv. Sr. Lectr.

Mutrie, Nanette, MEd Glas., PhD Penn.State Sr. Lectr.

Neil, D. M., MA Camb., PhD Camb. Sr. Lectr.

Nimmo, H. G., MA Camb., PhD Camb. Prof.

Orchardson, R., PhD Brist., BSc BDS Sr. Lectr.

Parton, R., BSc Birm., PhD Birm. Sr. Lectr.

Payne, A. P., BSc Reading, PhD Birm. Prof.

Phillips, R. S., BSc Lond., PhD Camb., FIBiol Prof.

Pollock, D., MSc PhD Sr. Lectr.

Rosenberg, J. R., AB Calif., PhD Calif. Prof.

Shaw Dunn, J., BSc MB ChB PhD Sr. Lectr.

Skett, P., BSc Liv., FilDr R.Karolinska Sr. Lectr.

Smith, Godfrey L., BSc PhD Prof.

Smith, R. A., MA Oxf., PhD S'ton. Sr. Lectr.

Spurway, Neil C., MA Camb., PhD Camb. Prof., Exercise Physiology

Stewart-Tull, Duncan E. S., MA Trinity(Dub.), PhD Prof., Microbial Immunology

Stone, T. W., PhD Aberd., BPharm Lond., DSc Lond. Prof.

Strang, Robin H. C., BSc St And., PhD Edin. Sr. Lectr.

Sutcliffe, R. G., BSc Manc., PhD Edin. Sr. Lectr.

Taylor, A. C., BSc Liv., PhD Liv. Reader

Thompson, R., BSc Brist., PhD Edin. Sr. Lectr.

Tippett, R., BA Keele, MSc Qu., PhD Brist. Sr. Lectr.

Turner, C., BSc Lond., PhD Lond. Sr. Lectr.

Vickerman, K., PhD Lond., DSc Lond., FRSEd, FRS Regius Prof.

Wardlaw, Alastair C., MSc Manc., PhD Manc., DSc Prof.; Res. Fellow

Wheeler, C. T., BSc Liv., PhD Liv. Sr. Lectr.

Wilkins, Malcolm B., PhD Lond., DSc Lond., FRSEd Regius Prof., Botany

Wilson, J., BSc Sus., PhD Lond. Sr. Lectr.

Other Staff: 45 Lectrs.

Research: biochemistry and molecular biology (cancer, cell signalling and membrane biology, molecular medicine, proteins, enzymes and X-ray crystallography, transcriptional and cell cycle control); environmental and evolutionary biology (ecophysiology, fish behaviour and ecology, ornithology, taxonomy and biodiversity); infection and immunity (microbiological pathogenesis, pathogen immunity); molecular genetics (animal models of human disease, human genetics); neuroscience and biomedical systems (cardiovascular studies/heart failure, neuroscience, sports and exercise science)

Business School

Hunter, Sir Laurence, CBE, DPhil Oxf., MA, FRSEd Prof.; Head*

Pignatelli, Frank, MA MEd Prof.†

Celtic

Tel: (0141) 330 4222

O Dochartaigh, Cathair N., BA Belf., MA Belf., PhD Aberd. Prof.; Head*

Other Staff: 3 staff members

Research: early mediaeval Scottish history; mediaeval Gaelic and Welsh literatures; Irish and Scottish Gaelic dialectology; Scottish Gaelic literature

Chemistry

Tel: (0141) 330 6661 Fax: (0141) 330 4888

Barron, L. D., BSc Lond., DPhil Oxf. Prof.

Campbell, K. C., BSc Durh., PhD Durh. Sr. Lectr.

Carnduff, J., BSc PhD Sr. Lectr.

Colvin, E. W., BSc PhD Reader

Connolly, J. D., PhD DSc Prof.

Cooper, A., BSc Manc., PhD Manc. Reader

Cross, R. J., BSc Durh., PhD Durh. Sr. Lectr.

Duncan, H. J., BSc PhD Reader

Dymond, J. H., MA Oxf., DPhil Oxf. Reader

Farrugia, L. J., BA Oxf., PhD Brist. Sr. Lectr.

Fryer, J. R., BTech Brun., PhD DSc Reader

Gilmore, C. J., BSc Brist., PhD Brist. Reader

Hill, R. A., MA PhD Sr. Lectr.

Isaacs, N. W., BSc Qld., PhD Qld. Joseph Black Prof.

Klapötke, Thomas M., DrRerNatHabil, FRSChem Ramsay Prof.

Kocienski, P., PhD Edin. Regius Prof.

MacNicol, D. D., DSc PhD Reader

Manojlovic-Muir, Ljubica, BSc Belgrade, PhD Belgrade Reader

Muir, K. W., BSc PhD Reader

Peacock, R. D., BSc St And., PhD Dund., FRSChem Reader

Pulford, I. D., BSc PhD Sr. Lectr.

Robins, D. J., BSc Exe., PhD Exe., DSc Prof.

Tyler, J. K., BSc Birm., PhD Birm. Reader

Webb, Geoffrey, BSc Hull, PhD Hull, DSc, FRSChem, FRSEd Prof.

Webster, B. C., BA Oxf., PhD Sr. Lectr.

White, D. N. J., BSc Wales, DPhil Sus. Reader

Winfield, John M., BSc Lond., PhD Prof.; Head*

Other Staff: 13 Lectrs.

Research: agricultural, food and environmental chemistry; biophysical and physical chemistry; heterogenous catalysis and solid state chemistry; inorganic chemistry; organic chemistry

Classics

Tel: (0141) 330 5695 Fax: (0141) 330 4459

Garvie, A. F., MA Edin., MA Camb.   Reader
Green, Roger P. H., MA BLitt   Prof.; Head*
MacDowell, D. M., MA Oxf., FRSEd,
   FBA   Prof., Greek
Moignard, Elizabeth A., MA Oxf., DPhil
   Oxf.   Sr. Lectr.
Other Staff: 4 Lectrs.
Research: Greek and Roman history; Greek art
   and archaeology; Greek literature (comedy,
   epic, oratory, tragedy); post-classical Latin
   literature and Christian thought; Roman
   comedy (fiction and mime)

Computing Science

Tel: (0141) 330 4256 Fax: (0141) 330 4913

Atkinson, M. P., MA Camb., PhD Camb.,
   FIEE   Prof.
Black, Andrew   Visiting Prof.
Cooper, R., MSc PhD   Sr. Lectr.
Holt, N.   Visiting Prof.
Irving, R. W., BSc PhD   Sr. Lectr.
Johnson, Christopher W., BA MA MSc
   DPhil   Sr. Lectr.
Kamarradine, F., BSc Essex, MSc Essex   Reader
Melham, T. F., BSc Calg., PhD Camb.   Sr. Lectr.
Morris, J., BA Trinity(Dub.), BAI Trinity(Dub.),
   MSc Trinity(Dub.), PhD Trinity(Dub.)   Sr. Lectr.
Narasimhalu, D.   Visiting Prof.
Patterson, J. W., BSc PhD   Sr. Lectr.
Peyton Jones, S. L., MA Camb.   Prof.
Siebert, J., BSc PhD   Sr. Lectr.
Thomas, M., BSc Stir., PhD St And.   Sr. Lectr.
van Rijsbergen, C. J., BSc W.Aust., PhD
   Camb.   Prof.
Watt, Prof. D. A., BSc PhD   Prof.
Welland, R. C., BSc Reading, MSc Lond.   Sr.
   Lectr.; Head*
Other Staff: 17 Lectrs.
Research: formal methods (verification protocol
   analysis types); human-computer interaction
   (animation accident analysis); multi-media
   systems (information retrieval three-
   dimensional modelling); programming
   language implementation (functional
   programming optimisation)   .

Czech, see Slavonic Langs. and Lits.

Dairy Science

Hannah Research Institute

Tel: (01292) 674000 Fax: (01292) 671052

Peaker, M., BSc Sheff., PhD HK   Hannah Prof.;
   Head*
Research: animal welfare; foetal and neonatal
   programming and development; food
   quality and safety; mammary gland and milk
   secretion; nutrient partitioning

Dentistry, see below

Divinity, see Theol. and Religious Studies

Economic and Social History, see Hist.,
   Econ. and Soc.

Economics

Tel: (0141) 330 4618 Fax: (0141) 330 4940

Bain, A. D., MA Camb., PhD Camb.   Visiting
   Prof.
Hay, F. G., MA   Sr. Lectr.
Huff, W. G., MSc Penn., PhD Penn.   Sr. Lectr.
MacLennan, M. C., MA   Prof.
Malley, James R., MPhil Glas., PhD Glas.,
   BA   Sr. Lectr.
Milne, R. G., MA Edin.   Sr. Lectr.
Muscatelli, V., MA   Daniel Jack Prof.; Head*
Noorbakhsh, F., PhD Birm., BSocSci
   Natnl.Iran   Sr. Lectr.
Skinner, A. S., MA BLitt, FBA, FRSEd   Adam
   Smith Prof.
Smith, L. D., BSc Lond.   Prof., Agricultural
   Economics
Stevenson, A. A., MA   Sr. Lectr.

Varoufakis, Y.   Prof.
Wooton, Ian, MA St. And., MPhil Col., PhD
   Col.   Prof.
Other Staff: 8 Lectrs.
Research: applied econometric techniques;
   interaction of business cycles and growth;
   international trade and imperfectly
   competitive markets; modelling
   macroeconomic performance; monetary
   economics and financial markets

Education, see also Adult and Continuing
   Educn.

Tel: (0141) 330 4407 Fax: (0141) 330 5451

Baron, S. R., BA Nott, MEd Manc.   Sr. Lectr.
Mackenzie, M. L., MA MEd   Sr. Lectr.
McGettrick, Bartholomew J., OBE, BSc
   MEd   Hon. Prof.
Scobie, Rev. G. E. W., MSc Brist., MA Birm.,
   PhD   Sr. Lectr.
Wilkinson, J. Eric, BSc St And., MEd Dund.,
   PhD   Sr. Lectr.; Head*
Other Staff: 2 Lectrs.
Research: governance, regulation and
   accountability; knowledge, communication
   and learning; social inclusion and exclusion

Electronics and Electrical Engineering

Tel: (0141) 330 5218 Fax: (0141) 330 4907

Aitchison, J. S., BSc H.-W., PhD H.-W.   Sr.
   Lectr.
Anderson, J. S., BSc St And.   Visiting Prof.
Arnold, J. M., BEng Sheff., PhD Sheff.   Prof.
Assenov, A., BSc Sofia, PhD Bulgarian
   Acad.Sc.   Reader
Barker, J. R., BSc Edin., MSc Durh., PhD
   Warw.   Prof.
Barlow, A. J., BSc Lond., PhD Lond.   Prof.
Beaumont, S. P., MA Camb., PhD Camb.   Prof.;
   Head*
Cooper, Jonathan M., BSc S'ton., MSc Cran.IT,
   PhD Cran.IT   Sr. Lectr.
Davie, H. J., BSc Edin., PhD Edin.   Sr. Lectr.
Davies, J. H., MA Camb., PhD Camb.   Sr. Lectr.
De La Rue, R. M., BSc Lond., PhD Lond., MASc
   Tor.   Prof.
Doughty, G. F., BA Open(UK), PhD   Sr. Lectr.
Harrison, G., BSc(Eng) Lond., PhD Lond.   Sr.
   Lectr.
Ironside, C. N., BSc H.-W., PhD H.-W.   Reader
Laybourn, P. J. R., MA Camb., PhD Leeds   Prof.
Marsh, John H., BA Camb., MEng Liv., PhD
   Sheff.   Prof., Optoelectronic Systems
Miller, T. J. E., PhD Leeds, BSc   Prof.
Murray-Smith, David J., MSc Aberd., PhD   Prof.
O'Reilly, John, PhD Belf., DSc Belf.   Prof.,
   Control Engineering
Portnoi, E. L.   Visiting Prof.
Richter, J., BSc Lond., PhD Lond.   Sr. Lectr.
Sewell, J. I., BSc Durh., PhD Newcastle(UK)   Prof.
Shanks, I. A., PhD CNAA, BSc, FRS   Visiting
   Prof.
Sharman, Kenneth C., BSc Strath., PhD
   Strath.   Sr. Lectr.
Stanley, C. R., BEng Sheff., PhD S'ton.   Prof.
Wilkinson, C. D. W., MA Oxf., PhD Stan.,
   FRSEd   James Watt Prof.
Williamson, J. G., BSc Edin., PhD Sheff.   Sr.
   Lectr.
Winning, D. J., BSc PhD   Sr. Lectr.
Other Staff: 14 Lectrs.
Research: advanced software for electric motors/
   drives; bioelectronics (cellular engineering,
   molecular electronics, sensing); control
   aerospace and electro-mechanical systems;
   nanoelectronic device design (simulation
   and assessment); robotics

Engineering, Aerospace

Tel: (0141) 330 3575 Fax: (0141) 330 5560

Coton, F. N., BSc PhD   Sr. Lectr.
Galbraith, R. A. McD., BSc CNAA, PhD
   Camb.   Shoda Prof., Aerospace Systems;
   Head*
Goodchild, C., BSc Essex, MSc Cran.IT   Sr. Lectr.
Hurst, D., BSc S'ton., PhD S'ton.   Sr. Lectr.
McInnes, Colin R., BSc PhD   Reader

Richards, B. E., BSc Lond., PhD Lond.   Mechan
   Prof.
Smrcek, L.   Sr. Lectr.
Other Staff: 10 Lectrs.
Research: aeroelasticity; aircraft design; air traffic
   management systems; CFD and unsteady
   aerodynamics; helicopter flight mechanics

Engineering, Civil

Tel: (0141) 330 5201 Fax: (0141) 330 4557

Agar, T. J. Alan, BSc Belf., PhD Belf.   Sr. Lectr.
Bhatt, P., BE Mys., ME B'lore., PhD   Sr. Lectr.
Bicanic, Nenad J. N.   Regius Prof.; Head*
Davies, T. G., BSc Wales, PhD Wales   Sr. Lectr.
Ervine, D. A., BSc Belf., PhD Belf.   Prof.
Herbertson, J. G., PhD Strath., BSc   Sr. Lectr.
Pender, G., BSc Strath., PhD Strath.   Sr. Lectr.
Phillips, D. V., BSc Birm., MSc Wales, PhD
   Wales   Sr. Lectr.
Wheeler, Simon J., MA Camb., DPhil
   Oxf.   Cormack Prof.
Other Staff: 7 Lectrs.
Research: geotechnical research (constitutive
   modelling, microscopy, piling foundations,
   unsaturated soils); structural research (bridge
   mechanics, concrete failure, direct design,
   finite elements, particulate modelling); water
   (biology, dams, estuary behaviour, hydraulic
   structures, river flooding, sediment,
   transport)

Engineering, Electrical, see Electronics and
   Electr. Engin.

Engineering, Mechanical

Tel: (0141) 330 5914 Fax: (0141) 330 4343

Cartmell, M., BSc Edin., PhD Edin.   Prof.
Chatwin, C. R., MSc Birm., PhD Birm.   Sr.
   Lectr.
Cowling, Michael J.   Prof.
Fairlie-Clarke, A. C., BSc Strath., PhD Strath.   Sr.
   Lectr.
Gawthrop, P. J., MA Oxf., DPhil Oxf.   Wylie
   Prof.
Green, G., BSc PhD   Sr. Lectr.
Hancock, J. W., BSc Birm., PhD   Prof.; Head*
Hodgkiess, T., BSc Manc., PhD Manc.   Sr. Lectr.
Howell, J., BEng Sheff.   Sr. Lectr.
Hunt, K. J., BSc Strath., PhD Strath.   Prof.
McGregor, R. C., MSc Leeds, PhD Leeds   Reader
Scott, B. F., BSc Birm., PhD Birm.   James Watt
   Prof.
Watson, I., BSc S.Bank, PhD Glas.   Sr. Lectr.
Whittaker, Arthur R., MSc Birm., PhD
   Birm.   Sr. Lectr.
Other Staff: 12 Lectrs.
Research: control; design; dynamics; laser and
   optical systems engineering; marine
   technology materials (including fracture
   mechanics and corrosion)

Engineering, Ocean, see Naval Archit. and
   Ocean Engin.

English Language

Tel: (0141) 330 6340 Fax: (0141) 330 8030

Caie, G. D., MA Aberd., MA McM., PhD
   McM.   Prof.
Kay, Christian J., MA Edin., AM
   Mt.Holyoke   Prof.; Head*
MacMahon, M. K. C., BA Durh., PhD   Prof.
Smith, Jeremy J., BA Lond., BPhil Oxf.,
   PhD   Reader
Other Staff: 6 Lectrs.
Research: historical English language (Old and
   Middle English, codicology, dialectology,
   onomastics, historical linguistics); literary
   and linguistic computing; modern English
   language (discourse analysis, grammar,
   lexicography, phonetics, phonology
   semantics, sociolinguistics, stylistics); Scots

English Literature, see also Scottish Lit.

Tel: (0141) 330 5296 Fax: (0141) 330 4601

Bank, D. A., BA NZ   Reader
Cronin, R., BA Oxf., BLitt Oxf.   Reader; Head*
Cummings, R. M., BLitt Oxf., MA   Sr. Lectr.

Gillespie, S. F., MA Camb., PhD Camb. Sr. Lectr.
Grant, R. A. D., MA Camb., PhD Camb. Reader
Hobsbaum, P. D., MA Camb., PhD Sheff. Prof.
Hook, A. D., MA Edin., PhD Prin. Bradley Prof.
Kemp, Sandra, BA Oxf., DPhil Oxf. Sr. Lectr.
Lyons, P. G., MA Trinity(Dub.) Sr. Lectr.
Porter McMillan, Dorothy, MA Sr. Lectr.
Prickett, A. T. S., MA Camb., PhD Camb. Regius Prof.
Wu, Duncan, MA Oxf., DPhil Oxf. Reader
Other Staff: 15 Lectrs.
Research: the early modern period/Renaissance; European modernism (especially France, England); Irish and intercultural studies; literature and translation; romanticism

Fine Art, see Hist. of Art

French Language and Literature

Tel: (0141) 330 5642 Fax: (0141) 330 4234
Birks, Renée O., LèsL Paris Sr. Lectr.
Campbell, J., BA Belf., PhD Sr. Lectr.
Davies, P. V., BA Leic., PhD Leic. Sr. Lectr.
Dickson, W. J., MA Aberd. Sr. Lectr.
Jimack, Christine M., BA Lond., MPhil Lond. Sr. Lectr.
Kennedy, A. J., MA PhD Prof.
Lloyd, Heather, BA Belf., PhD Sr. Lectr.
Newton, L. Joy, BA Leeds, PhD Lond. Reader
Peacock, N. A., MA Wales Prof.; Head*
Rawles, Alison R., BA Brist., PhD Brist. Sr. Lectr.
Smethurst, C., MA Oxf., BLitt Oxf. Marshall Prof.
Steel, J., Drd'Etat Paris, MA Reader
Woollen, C. Geoffrey, BA Birm., PhD Reader
Other Staff: 9 Lectrs.
Research: French culture, language, cinema and politics; mediaeval and Renaissance French literature (including emblems); seventeenth to twentieth-century literature and thought

Geography and Topographic Science

Tel: (0141) 330 4782 Fax: (0141) 330 4894
Bishop, Paul, BA PhD Prof.
Briggs, John A., BA Lond., PhD Wales Prof., Geography
Dickinson, G. J., BSc PhD Sr. Lectr.
Drummond, Jane E., BSc MEngin PhD Sr. Lectr.
Evans, David J. A., BA Wales, MSc Nfld., PhD Alta. Sr. Lectr.
Hansom, James D., MA Aberd., PhD Aberd. Reader
Lowder, Stella M., BA Nott., PhD Liv. Sr. Lectr.
Morris, A. S., BA Oxf., MA Maryland, PhD Wis. Prof.
Paddison, Ronan, BA Durh., PhD Aberd. Prof.; Head*
Philo, Christopher, BA Camb., PhD Camb. Prof.
Shearer, J. W., MA Aberd., MSc Sr. Lectr.
Tait, David A., BSc Glas., BSc I.T.C.Delft Sr. Lectr.
Thompson, I., BA Durh., PhD Durh., MA Indiana Prof.
Other Staff: 7 Lectrs.
Research: developing countries (environment/development, urbanisation, marketing); geographic information systems/digital mapping (design, maintenance and visualisation); geomorphological processes (mega-landscape evolution, fluvial coastal and glacial processes); political/cultural geography (power/resistance, decentralisation)

Geology and Applied Geology

Tel: (0141) 330 5441 Fax: (0141) 330 4817
Braithwaite, C. J. R., BSc Lond., PhD Lond., FGS Sr. Lectr.
Burton, C. J., BSc Exe., PhD Exe., FGS Sr. Lectr.
Couples, G. D., BSc MA PhD Sr. Lectr.
Curry, G. B., BA Trinity(Dub.), PhD Lond. Reader

Gribble, C. D., BSc Aberd., PhD Edin. Sr. Lectr.; Head*
Hall, A. J., BSc Edin., PhD Durh. Sr. Lectr.
Haszeldine, R. S., BSc Edin., PhD Strath. Sr. Lectr.
Ingham, J. K., BSc Hull, PhD Hull, FGS Sr. Lectr.; Sr. Curator
Keen, Michael C., BSc Leic., PhD Leic. Sr. Lectr.
Owen, A. W., BSc Durh., PhD Sr. Lectr.
Ramsay, D. M., BSc PhD, FGS, FRSEd Prof.
Russell, M. J., BSc Lond., PhD Durh. Dixon Prof.
Smythe, D. K., BSc PhD, FGS Britoil Prof.
Tanner, P. W. G., BSc Sheff., PhD Lond., FGS Sr. Lectr.
Other Staff: 6 Lectrs.
Research: crustal processes and environments; palaeobiology

German Language and Literature

Tel: (0141) 330 5377 Fax: (0141) 330 3512
Bishop, Paul C., BA Oxf. Sr. Lectr.
Stephenson, R. H., BA Lond., PhD Lond. Prof.
Ward, Mark G., BA Lond. Prof.
Watt, R. H., MA Edin., PhD Edin. Sr. Lectr.; Head*
Other Staff: 4 Lectrs.
Research: age of enlightenment (classicism, romanticism); ethnograph (comparative literature, cultural studies, feminism); mediaeval culture and literature; modern German thought; twentieth-century literature and culture

Hetherington Language Centre

Tel: (0141) 330 4134 Fax: (0141) 339 1119
Woodruff, Stephen Manager
Other Staff: 2 Staff Members

Hispanic Studies

Tel: (0141) 330 5335 Fax: (0141) 339 1119
Donnelly, P. J., MA Oxf., DPhil Oxf. Sr. Lectr.
Gonzalez, M. A., BA Leeds Sr. Lectr.
Harland, M. C., MA Lond. Sr. Lectr.
Mackenzie, Ann L., MA Ivy McClelland Res. Prof.; Head*
Walters, D. Gareth, BA Wales, PhD Wales Stevenson Prof.
Other Staff: 2 Lectrs.
Research: Catalan literature (mediaeval and modern poetry); Latin American studies (culture, literature, music); language (CALL lexicography translation); modern Spanish poetry (Lorca, Machado and contemporaries); Spanish golden age literature (drama, ideas, poetry, prose)

History, Economic and Social

Tel: (0141) 330 5992 Fax: (0141) 330 4889
Crowther, Margaret A., BA Adel., DPhil Oxf. Prof.
Durie, A. J., MA Edin., PhD Edin. Sr. Lectr.
French, M. J., BA E.Anglia, MSc Lond., PhD Lond. Sr. Lectr.; Head*
Gordon, Eleanor, MA Edin., PhD Sr. Lectr.
Munro, J. F. S., MA PhD Prof.
Slaven, Anthony, MA BLitt Prof., Business History
Stokes, R. G., BA MA Sr. Lectr.
Other Staff: 6 Lectrs.
Research: British economic policy since 1945; business history (financial institutions, business and state); social history (crime, gender, history, medical)

History of Art

Tel: (0141) 330 5677 Fax: (0141) 330 8013
Gibbs, R. J., BA Lond. Sr. Lectr.
Stirton, Paul A. W., MA Edin., MA Lond. Sr. Lectr.
Tait, A. A. H., PhD Camb. Richmond Prof.
Other Staff: 7 Lectrs.
Research: Chinese and related areas of art and decorative arts; eighteenth-century architecture and landscape in Britain and Italy; impressionism and post-impressionism painting in Britain and Europe; Italian art of

the thirteenth and fourteenth centuries; theory and aesthetics of twentieth-century art

History of Medicine, see Wellcome Hist. of Med. Unit

History, School of

Tel: (0141) 330 4087 Fax: (0141) 330 5056
Bates, David R., BA Exe., PhD Exe. Edwards Prof.; Head*
Black, C. F., MA Oxf., BLitt Sr. Lectr.
Brown, A. L., DPhil Oxf., MA, FRHistS Hon. Prof. Res. Fellow
Cowan, Edward J., MA Edin. Prof.
Dixon, Simon M., MA Camb. Sr. Lectr.
Dunn, Marilyn, MA Edin., PhD Edin. Sr. Lectr.
Glassey, L. K. J., MA Oxf., DPhil Oxf. Sr. Lectr.
Hope, Nicholas, MA Oxf., DPhil Oxf. Reader
Kirk, J., MA Edin., PhD Edin., DLitt Edin., FRHistS Reader
Larner, John P., MA Oxf. Hon. Prof.
Mawdsley, E., MA Chic., PhD Lond. Reader
Munck, T., MA St. And., PhD E.Anglia Sr. Lectr.
Smith, A. G. R., PhD Lond., MA Prof.
Strachan, H. F. A., MA Camb., PhD Camb. Prof.
Thomson, J. A. F., MA Edin., DPhil Oxf. Prof.
Other Staff: 15 Lectrs.
Research: ecclesiastical history; the Enlightenment; late mediaeval and Renaissance Italy; mediaeval western Europe (Scotland, France, the Normans); warfare

Islamic Studies, see Arabic and Islamic Studies

Italian

Tel: (0141) 330 4135
Millar, Eileen A., MA PhD Prof.; Head*
Other Staff: 4 Lectrs.
Research: Italian Renaissance literature; Italian romanticism; Italian resistance to fascism; twentieth-century Italian history and literature; twentieth-century Italian poetry

Law

Tel: (0141) 330 6075 Fax: (0141) 330 5140
Attwooll, Elspeth M. M., LLB St And., MA St And. Sr. Lectr.
Burrows, Noreen, LLB Edin., PhD Edin. Prof., European Law
Crearer, L., LLB Glas. Prof.
Davidson, Fraser P. Prof.
Fergus, T. D., MA LLB PhD Sr. Lectr.
Forrester, I. S., QC, MA LLM MCL Visiting Prof.
Goldberg, D. J. A., LLB Sr. Lectr.
Gordon, W. M., MA Aberd., LLB Aberd., PhD Aberd. Douglas Prof., Civil Law
Grant, John P., LLM Penn. Prof.
Maxton, J. K. Sr. Lectr.
McLean, Sheila A. M., LLB MLitt PhD, FRSEd Internat. Bar Prof., Law and Ethics in Medicine
Mullen, T. J., LLM Harv., LLB Sr. Lectr.
Murdoch, J. L., LLM Calif., LLB Sr. Lectr.; Head*
Örücü, A. Esin, BA Istanbul, LLB Istanbul, PhD Istanbul Prof.
Prosser, J. A. W., LLB Liv. John Millar Prof.
Rennie, Robert, LLB Glas., PhD Glas. Prof., Conveyancing
Robinson, Olivia F., MA Oxf., PhD Lond. Reader
Scobbie, Iain G. M., LLB Edin., LLB Camb., PhD Camb. Sr. Lectr.
Sutherland, Elaine E., LLM Br.Col., LLB Sr. Lectr.
Thomson, Joseph M., LLB, FRSEd Regius Prof.
Villiers, C., LLB Hull, LLM Lond. Sr. Lectr.
Other Staff: 17 Lectrs.
Research: family child law and criminal responsibility; legal history and Roman law; medical law and ethics (including biotechnology); public international law

(including cultural heritage); public utility, European and media regulation

Management Studies

Tel: (0141) 330 4131 Fax: (0141) 330 5669

Beaumont, P. B., BEcon Glas., MEcon Glas., PhD Glas. Prof.

Beirne, Martin J., BA CNAA, MSc Strath., PhD Strath. Sr. Lectr.

Boddy, D., BSc(Econ) Lond., MA Lanc. Reader

Francis, F. A. S., BSc Prof., Corporate Strategy

Huczynski, A. A., BSc(Soc) Lond. Sr. Lectr.

Lander, Ronald, MSc Visiting Prof.

Lewis, J. W., BSc(Eng) Lond., MSc Sr. Lectr.

Macbeth, D. K., MSc Strath. Prof., Manufacturing Management

Martin, R., MA Oxf., DPhil Oxf. Prof., Organisational Behaviour; Head*

McGregor, A., BAcc Glas., MA Glas. Prof.

Moutinho, L. A., BA Sheff., MA Sheff., PhD Sheff. Prof.

Mouwen, Cornelis A. M., PhD Visiting Prof.

Paton, R. A., MSc Strath. Sr. Lectr.

Southern, G., MSc Birm., PhD Sr. Lectr.

Timms, Peter, MBE Visiting Prof.

Wilson, J. M., BTech BSc MA MBA PhD Sr. Lectr.

Other Staff: 6 Lectrs.

Research: Europe management (design management, organisational change, strategy, training and employment research, transformation); marketing (computer applications, cross-cultural marketing research); operations management (supply chain management OB/HRM-C&E)

Mathematics

Tel: (0141) 330 5176 Fax: (0141) 330 4111

Anderson, I., MA St And., PhD Nott. Reader

Baker, Andrew J., BSc Manc., PhD Manc. Reader

Brown, K. A., MSc Warw., PhD Warw., BSc Prof.

Cohen, S. D., BSc PhD Reader

Fearn, D. R., BSc St And., PhD Newcastle(UK) Prof.; Head*

Haughton, D. M., BSc Bath, PhD Bath Sr. Lectr.

Hoggar, S. G., BSc Birm., MSc Warw., PhD Warw. Sr. Lectr.

Lindsay, K. A., MSc Oxf., DPhil Oxf., BSc Sr. Lectr.

Mason, A. W., BSc PhD Sr. Lectr.

Nair, M. K., BA Oxf., PhD Nott. Sr. Lectr.

Nimmo, J. J. C., BSc Leeds, PhD Leeds Sr. Lectr.

Odoni, R. W. K., BSc Exe., PhD Camb. Prof.

Ogden, R. W., MA Camb., PhD Camb. George Sinclair Prof.

Pride, S. J., BSc Monash, PhD ANU Prof.

Smith, P. F., MA Aberd., MSc Aberd., PhD Leeds Prof.

Spain, Philip G., BA Camb., PhD Sr. Lectr.

Spence, E., BSc PhD Reader

Steiner, R. J., MA Camb., PhD Camb. Sr. Lectr.

Stothers, W. W., PhD Camb., BSc Sr. Lectr.

Straughan, B., MSc Newcastle(UK), PhD H.-W. Simpson Prof.

Tomkinson, M. J., MSc Newcastle(UK), PhD Newcastle(UK) Sr. Lectr.

Wassermann, A. S., MA Camb., PhD Camb. Reader

Webb, J. R. L., BSc Sus., DPhil Sus. Prof.

Weiglhofer, Werner S., DrTechn Graz Sr. Lectr.

Whitelaw, T. A., PhD Camb., BSc Sr. Lectr.

Other Staff: 12 Lectrs.

Research: algebra; applied mathematics; elasticity (electromagnetism, fluids, magnetohydrodynamics); non-linear differential equations; solitons (integrable systems)

Medicine, see below

Music

Tel: (0141) 330 4093 Fax: (0141) 330 8018

Arnold, S., BA S'ton., PhD S'ton., MA Nott. Sr. Lectr.

Edwards, W. A., MA Camb., MusB Camb., PhD Camb. Sr. Lectr.

Hair, G. B., MMus Melb., PhD Sheff. Gardiner Prof.

Rycroft, Marjorie E., MA Aberd., PhD Aberd. Sr. Lectr.; Head*

Other Staff: 1 Lectr.

Research: composition and twentieth-century composers; computer applications including artificial intelligence; early music; Russian music and criticism; Scottish music and musicians

Naval Architecture and Ocean Engineering

Tel: (0141) 330 4322 Fax: (0141) 330 5917

Barltrop, Nigel D. P., BSc John Elder Prof.; Head*

Das, P. K., BE Burd., MSc Burd., PhD Burd. Sr. Lectr.

Winkle, I. E., BSc Newcastle(UK) Sr. Lectr.

Other Staff: 3 Lectrs.

Research: computational fluid dynamics (manoeuvring and model testing, slamming and deck wetness); dynamics of fixed and offshore structures (ro-ro survivability, structural adhesives reliability and fatigue analysis, wind engineering); optimisation in design (marine vehicle performance at design stage, resistance and propulsion)

Philosophy

Tel: (0141) 330 5692 Fax: (0141) 330 4112

Borowski, E. J., BPhil Oxf., MA Sr. Lectr.

Broadie, Alexander, MA Edin., BLitt PhD, FRSEd Prof., Logic and Rhetoric

Downie, R. S., BPhil Oxf., MA, FRSEd Prof.

Edwards, J. S., BA Brist., PhD Edin., BPhil Sr. Lectr.

Hale, Robert L. V., BA BPhil Prof., Metaphysical Philosophy

Knowles, D. R., BA Oxf., MLitt Sr. Lectr.; Head*

Meikle, Scott, BA Brist., PhD Brist. Reader

Shaw, P. D., BA Wales, BPhil Oxf. Sr. Lectr.

Stalley, R. F., MA Oxf., BPhil Oxf. Prof.

Telfer, Elizabeth A., MA Oxf., BPhil Oxf. Reader

Zangwill, Nicholas, BA Brist., MA Lond., PhD Lond. Sr. Lectr.

Other Staff: 10 Lectrs.

Research: epistemology, metaphysics, philosophy of mind/psychology; history of philosophy (ancient, mediaeval, Scottish enlightenment); meta-normative and applied ethics; philosophies of logic, language, mathematics, science; political philosophy

Physics and Astronomy

Tel: (0141) 330 4709 Fax: (0141) 334 9029

Barbour, I. M., BSc PhD Reader

Bluck, B. J., BSc Wales, PhD Wales, DSc, FGS FRSEd Prof.

Brown, John C., DSc PhD, FRSEd Regius Prof., Astronomy

Bussey, P. J., MA Camb., PhD Camb. Sr. Lectr.

Chapman, J. N., BA Camb., PhD Camb., FRSEd Prof.

Clarke, D., MSc Manc., PhD Manc. Reader

Craven, A. J., MA Camb., PhD Camb. Reader

Cumming, J., BSc PhD Sr. Lectr.

Davies, A. T., MA Edin., PhD Camb. Sr. Lectr.

Davies, Christine T. H., BA Camb., MA Camb., PhD Camb. Reader

Drever, R. W. P., BSc PhD, FRSEd Visiting Prof.

Ferrier, R. P., MA Camb., BSc St And., PhD St And., FRSEd Prof.

Froggatt, C. D., BSc Birm., PhD Camb. Reader

Green, R. M., MA Oxf., PhD Sr. Lectr.

Hall, S. J., MSc Belf., PhD Belf. Sr. Lectr.

Hough, J. S., BSc PhD, FRAS, FRSEd Prof.

Kellie, J. D., BSc PhD Sr. Lectr.

Land, D. V., BSc PhD Sr. Lectr.

Ledingham, K. W. D., BSc PhD Reader

Long, A. R., BA Camb., PhD Camb. Reader

Lynch, J. G., BSc PhD Sr. Lectr.

MacGregor, I. J. D., BSc PhD Sr. Lectr.

MacLeod, A. M., BSc PhD Sr. Lectr.

Negus, P. J., BSc PhD Sr. Lectr.

Newton, G. P., BSc H.-W., DPhil Sus. Sr. Lectr.

Owens, R. O., MA Oxf., DPhil Oxf. Prof.

Robertson, Norna A., BSc PhD Sr. Lectr.

Saxon, D. H., MA Oxf., DPhil Oxf., DSc Oxf., FRSEd Kelvin Prof.; Head*

Singhal, R. P., MSc Lucknow, PhD Sask. Sr. Lectr.

Smith, K. M., BSc PhD Prof.

Ward, H., BSc PhD Sr. Lectr.

Watt, A., MA Aberd., PhD Aberd. Sr. Lectr.

Other Staff: 9 Lectrs.

Research: astronomy/astrophysics (cosmology, plasmas, solar physics); femtosecond lasers; gravitational waves (advanced detectors); nuclear physics (electron scattering); particle physics (experimental, CERN DESY detectors, lattice theory)

Politics

Tel: (0141) 330 5130 Fax: (0141) 330 5071

Berry, C. J., BA Nott., PhD Lond. Prof.

Corrin, C., BA Open(UK), BA E.Anglia, DPhil Oxf. Sr. Lectr.

Crook, R. C., MA Durh., PhD Lond. Sr. Lectr.

Girvan, Brian, BA N.U.I., MA N.U.I., PhD N.U.I. Sr. Lectr.

Kellas, J. G., MA Aberd., PhD Lond. Prof.

Lessnoff, M. H., MA Oxf., BPhil Oxf. Reader

Lloyd-Jones, I. D., MA Camb., PhD Camb. Sr. Lectr.

Lockyer, A. A., BA Leic., MA Sheff. Sr. Lectr.

Miller, W. L., MA Edin., PhD Newcastle(UK) Edward Caird Prof.

O'Toole, Barry J., BA Durh., MSc Strath., PhD Strath. Sr. Lectr.

Peterson, John C., BSc MA PhD Sr. Lectr.

White, S. L., MA Trinity(Dub.), MA Oxf., DPhil Oxf., PhD Prof.; Head*

Other Staff: 4 Lectrs.

Research: British and Scottish politics; comparative politics (especially Eastern Europe, EU, Latin America, West Africa); political theory (conceptual and historical); public opinion (surveys and methodology)

Psychology

Anderson, Anne H., MA PhD Sr. Lectr.

Brown, R. I. F., MA MEd Sr. Lectr.

Burton, A. Michael, BSc PhD Prof.; Head*

Bushnell, Ian W. R., BA Strath., PhD Camb. Sr. Lectr.

Dimigen, Gisela, PhD Rhodes Sr. Lectr.

Draper, S. W., BSc Sus., DPhil Sus., MSc Manc. Sr. Lectr.

Garrod, S. C., BA Oxf., MA Prin., PhD Prin. Prof.

Gillies, J. B., MA PhD Sr. Lectr.

Jones, B. T., BSc Durh., PhD Edin. Sr. Lectr.

Kilbom, Kerry E., BA Oregon, PhD Calif. Sr. Lectr.

Mayes, Gillian, MA PhD Sr. Lectr.

Moxey, Linda, MA Glas., MSc Glas., PhD Glas. Sr. Lectr.

O'Donnell, P. J., MA Sr. Lectr.

Sanford, A. J., BSc Leeds, PhD Camb. Prof.

Other Staff: 10 Lectrs.

Research: health (addiction, dysfunction and remediation); language (lexical sentence and task analyses); neuroscience (diurnal rhythms, psychopharmacology); perception (motion, scene, object and face recognition); vision (cortical and retinal visual systems)

Religious Studies, see Theol. and Religious Studies

Russian and East European Studies, Institute of, see also Slavonic Langs. and Lits.

Lowenhardt, John, MA PhD Prof.; Head*

Ticktin, H., BA BSc Reader

White, J. D., MA PhD Reader

Other Staff: 3 Lectrs.

Research: Central and East European economics;
history and historiography; politics and
transition; social structure (USSR and
successor states)

Scottish Literature

Tel: (0141) 330 5093 Fax: (0141) 330 4537
Gifford, T. D. M., MA PhD   Prof.; Head*
Other Staff: 4 Lectrs.
Research: eighteenth-century Scottish literature;
literature of the Renaissance and
Reformation; mediaeval Scottish literature;
pastoral and the Scottish tradition; poetry of
the sixteenth-century

Slavonic Languages and Literatures, see
also Russian and E. European Studies, Inst.
of

Dunn, J. A., MA Oxf., DPhil Oxf.   Sr. Lectr.
Fronek, J., MA Lanc., PhD   Sr. Lectr., Czech
Kirkwood, M., MA Lanc., MA Glas.   Prof.;
Head*
Other Staff: 6 Lectrs.
Research: censorship (Polish and Russian
censorship); central European/Russian media
(control of information, media ownership);
comparative drama (Polish/English
playwrights/dramaturgical history);
lexicography (Czech-English/English-Czech
dictionaries); Russo-Hispanic cultural links
(cross-cultural literary and intellectual
influences)

Social Policy and Social Work

Tel: (0141) 330 5029 Fax: (0141) 330 8035
Asquith, S., MA St And., PhD Edin.   Prof.;
Head*
Barr, A., BSocSc Birm., PhD   Sr. Lectr.
Hill, Malcolm, MA Oxf., PhD Edin.   Prof.
McIntosh, J. R. B., MA Aberd., PhD Aberd.   Sr.
Lectr.
McKeganey, Neil, BA MSc PhD   Prof.
Taylor, R. C., BA Durh., PhD Durh.   Prof.
Other Staff: 10 Lectrs.
Research: children and society; community care;
community development; disability studies;
drug misuse

Sociology

Tel: (0141) 330 5981 Fax: (0141) 330 8022
Charsley, S. R., MA Camb., MA(Econ) Manc.,
PhD   Sr. Lectr.
Eldridge, J. E. T., BSc(Econ) Lond., MA
Leic.   Prof.
Evans, D. T., BA(Econ) Sheff.   Sr. Lectr.
Ferguson, H., MA Edin., PhD   Reader
Fowler, Bridget, BA Leeds, PhD   Sr. Lectr.
Frisby, D. P., BSc Lond., DSSc Belf., PhD   Prof.
Furlong, A.   Reader
Madigan, Ruth, MA Leeds   Sr. Lectr.
Miles, R. F., BSc Bath, PhD   Prof.; Head*
Moorhouse, H. F., BA Leic., MSc(Econ)
Lond.   Sr. Lectr.
O'Brien, P. J., MA   Sr. Lectr.
Philo, G., BSc Brad., PhD   Reader
Other Staff: 6 Lectrs.
Research: criminology and socio-legal studies;
modernity, leisure, sport and consumption;
social anthropology (caste and religion);
sociologies of media, racism and migration;
youth education and employment

Spanish, see Hispanic Studies

Statistics

Tel: (0141) 330 4386 Fax: (0141) 330 4814
Aitchison, T. C., BSc   Sr. Lectr.
Bowman, A. W., BSc   Prof.
Breeze, P., BSc Lond.   Sr. Lectr.; Head*
Ford, I., BSc PhD   Prof.
Gilmour, W. H., MSc   Sr. Lectr.
McColl, J. H., MA MSc   Sr. Lectr.
Molchano, I., PhD   Reader
Scott, E. Marian, BSc PhD   Sr. Lectr.
Titterington, D. M., BSc Edin., PhD Camb.,
FRSEd   Prof.
Torsney, B., BSc Strath., MSc Lond., PhD   Sr.
Lectr.

Other Staff: 2 Lectrs.
Research: biostatistics; environmetric and non-
parametric modelling; image processing and
spatial patterns; neural networks;
optimisation and optimal design of
experiments

Theatre, Film and Television Studies

Tel: (0141) 330 5162 Fax: (0141) 330 4142
Billington, Sandra, BA Camb., PhD
Camb.   Reader
Caughie, J. M., MA   Prof.
Craven, I., BA Exe., PhD Exe.   Sr. Lectr.
Giesekam, G. J., BA Syd., BPhil Oxf.   Sr. Lectr.
Kuhn, Annette, MA Sheff., PhD Lond.   Reader
McDonald, Janet B. I., MA, FRSEd   Prof.
Pearson, A. G., BA Hull   Sr. Lectr.; Head*
Schumacher, C., BA Brist.   Reader
Other Staff: 7 Lectrs.

Theology and Religious Studies

Tel: (0141) 330 6524 Fax: (0141) 330 4943
Barclay, J. M. G., MA Camb., PhD Camb.   Sr.
Lectr.
Carroll, R. P., MA Trinity(Dub.), PhD Edin.   Prof.
Hazlett, Rev. W. I. P., BA Belf., BD St And.,
DrTheol Mün.   Sr. Lectr.
Houston, Rev. J., MA Oxf., BD Oxf., DPhil
Oxf.   Sr. Lectr.
Hunter, Rev. Alastair G., BD Glas., MSc
Glas.   Sr. Lectr.; Head*
Jasper, David, BA Camb., MA Oxf., BD Oxf., PhD
Durh.   Prof.
Newlands, G. M., MA Edin., BD Edin., PhD
Edin.   Prof.
Riches, Rev. J. K., MA Camb.   Prof., Divinity
and Biblical Criticism
Other Staff: 8 Lectrs.
Research: the Bible and literary theory; Islamic
law and Sufism; New Testament and early
Judaism; systematic, apologetic and practical
theology; Reformation and Scottish church
history

Topographic Science, see Geog. and
Topographic Sci.

Urban Studies

Tel: (0141) 330 5993 Fax: (0141) 330 4668
Beaumont, Philip B., MEc Monash, PhD   Prof.,
Industrial Relations
Goodlad, Robina, MA Aberd., MPhil   Sr. Lectr.,
Housing Studies
Gulliver, S., BSc   Visiting Prof.
Kearns, A. J., BA Camb.   Sr. Lectr., Housing
Studies; Head*
Kemp, Peter A., BSc S'ton., MPhil Glas., DPhil
Sus.   Prof., Housing and Urban Studies;
Dir., CHRUS
Lever, W. F., MA Oxf., DPhil Oxf.   Prof.
Maclennan, D., CBE, MA MPhil   Prof., Urban
Studies
McCrone, R. G. L., MA Camb., MSc Wales, PhD
LLB   Prof.
Munro, Moira, MSc York(UK)   Sr. Lectr.
Parr, J. B., BSc(Econ) Lond., PhD Wash.   Prof.,
Applied Economics
Turok, Ivan N., BSc Brist., MSc Wales, PhD
Reading   Prof., Urban Economic Development
Woolfson, C. A., BA Strath., PhD Strath.   Sr.
Lectr., Applied Sociology
Other Staff: 8 Lectrs.
Research: housing aspects of social policy; real
estate economics and finance; social
exclusion; urban change and policy; urban
neighbourhoods and governance

Veterinary School and Hospital

Tel: (0141) 330 5738 Fax: (0141) 942 7215
Research: bacteriology; developmental and
reproduction biology; molecular oncology;
molecular parasitology; virology/
retrovirology

Veterinary Clinical Studies

Tel: (0141) 330 5738 Fax: (0141) 942 7215
Bennett, David   Prof., Small Animal Clinical
Studies

Cameron, E. R., BVMS   Sr. Lectr.
Carmichael, S.   Sr. Lectr.
Duncan, James L., BVMS Glas., PhD Glas.   Prof.
Eckersall, P. D., BSc Liv., PhD Edin., MBA   Sr.
Lectr.
Griffiths, I. R., BVMS PhD, FRCVS   Prof.,
Neurology
Harvey, M. J. A., BVMS PhD   Sr. Lectr.
Jarrett, Ruth F., MB ChB   Sr. Lectr.
Little, C. J., BVMS PhD   Sr. Lectr.
Love, S., BVMS   Prof., Equine Clinical Studies
Reid, Jacqueline, BVMS PhD   Sr. Lectr.
Sullivan, M., BVMS   Sr. Lectr.
Thompson, H., BVMS PhD   Sr. Lectr.
Other Staff: 10 Lectrs.

Veterinary Molecular Parasitology

Tel: (0141) 3300 4875
Barry, J. D.   Prof.
Other Staff: 1 Lectr.

Veterinary Parasitology

Tel: (0141) 330 5755 Fax: (0141) 330 5603
Devaney, Eileen, BSc Glas., PhD Liv.   Sr. Lectr.
Tait, A., BSc PhD   Prof.; Head*
Other Staff: 2 Lectrs.

Veterinary Pathology

Tel: (0141) 330 5773 Fax: (0141) 330 5602
Jarrett, J. O., BVMS PhD   Prof.
McNeil, Pauline E., BVMS PhD   Sr. Lectr.
Neil, J. C., BSc PhD   Prof.
Nicholson, L., BSc Aberd., PhD Glas.   Sr. Lectr.
Onions, D. E., BVSc Brist., PhD   Prof.; Head*
Pirie, H. M., BVMS PhD, FRCPath   Prof.
Roberts, M., BSc PhD   Sr. Lectr.
Steele, W. B., BVMS   Sr. Lectr.
Taylor, D. J., MA Camb., VetMB Camb., PhD
Camb.   Reader, Veterinary Microbiology
Other Staff: 1 Lectr.

Veterinary Pre-Clinical Studies

Aughey, Elizabeth, BVMS   Sr. Lectr.
Boyd, J. S., BVMS PhD   Prof.
Nolan, Andrea M., MVB Trinity(Dub.), PhD
Brist.   Sr. Lectr.
O'Shaughnessy, P. J., PhD Brist., BSc   Sr. Lectr.
Solomon, Sarah E., BSc PhD   Prof.
Wright, Norman G., BVMS Glas., PhD Glas.,
DVM Glas., FRCPath, FRSEd, FIBiol   Prof.
Other Staff: 9 Lectrs.

Wellcome History of Medicine Unit

Tel: (0141) 330 6071 Fax: (0141) 330 8011
Geyer-Kordesch, Johanna, MA Mass., PhD
Mass.   Dir.*

DENTAL SCHOOL

Tel: (0141) 211 9701 Fax: (0141) 331 2798
Bagg, J., BDS Edin., PhD Edin., FDSRCSEd   Sr.
Lectr.
Beeley, Josie A., MSc Manc., PhD Manc.   Sr.
Lectr.
Brocklebank, Laetitia, BDS Lond., MSc Lond.,
FRACDS   Sr. Lectr.
Burke, F. J. Trevor, BDS Belf., MDS Belf., MSc
Manc., DDS Manc.   Prof., Dental Primary Care
Creanor, S. L., BDS PhD   Sr. Lectr.
Kerr, W. J. S., MDS Belf., FDSRCSEd,
FFDRCSI   Prof.
Kinane, D. F., BDS Edin., PhD Edin.,
FDSRCSEd   Prof.
Lamb, A. B., DDS, FDSRCPSGlas   Sr. Lectr.
Lyons, M. F., BDS Otago, MSc Lond.,
FDSRCPSGlas   Sr. Lectr.
MacDonald, D. G., RD, BDS PhD,
FDSRCPSGlas, FRCPath   Prof., Oral
Pathology
MacFarlane, T. Wallace, DDS, FDSRCPSGlas,
FRCPath   Prof., Oral Microbiology; Dean*
Macpherson, Lorna M. D., BDS PhD,
FRCDCan   Sr. Lectr.
McCrossan, J., BDS, FDSRCPSGlas   Sr. Lectr.
Millett, Declan T., BDSc Trinity(Dub.), DDS
Newcastle(UK)   Sr. Lectr.
Moos, K. F., BDS MB BS, FRCS   Hon. Clin.
Prof.

Rennie, J. S., BDS PhD, FDSRCPSGlas   Sr.
   Lectr.
Saunders, W. P., BDS Lond., PhD Dund.,
   FDSRCSEd   Prof.
Stenhouse, D., DDS, FDSRCPSGlas   Sr. Lectr.
Stephen, K. W., BDS DDSc, FDSRCS   Prof.,
   Community Dental Health
Wray, D., BDS MB ChB MD, FDS   Prof., Oral
   Medicine
Other Staff: 2 Lectrs.; 17 Clin. Lectrs.

MEDICINE

For subjects of first 2 years—Anatomy, etc, see
Biomedical and Life Sciences, Institute of,
above

Tel: (0141) 330 5921 Fax: (0141) 330 5440

Research: cardiovascular research (vascular
biology, cardiovascular physiology and
pathophysiology); cancer (molecular and
cellular biology of human tumours, cancer
therapy); immunology (cellular and
molecular mechanisms of immune system,
vaccine design, cytokine and gene therapy);
neuroscience (genetic susceptibility to
stroke, chronic neurological disease);
developmental sciences (reproductive health,
child health and medical genetics); health of
communities (nursing and midwifery
studies, community care, primary care)

Anaesthesia

Tel: (0141) 221 2698 Fax: (0141) 337 2969

Asbury, A. J., MB ChB Birm., PhD   Reader;
   Head*
Fitch, W., BSc Edin., MB ChB Edin., PhD,
   FFARCS, FRCPGlas   Prof.
Kenny, G. N. C., BSc MD, FFARCS   Prof.
Other Staff: 13 Clin. Lectrs.

Bacteriology

Tel: (0141) 211 4000

Alcock, S. R., MB ChB   Sr. Lectr.
Gemmell, C. G., BSc PhD   Reader; Head*
Platt, D. J., BSc Lond., PhD   Sr. Lectr.
Other Staff: 1 Lectr.; 1 Clin. Lectr.

Cardiac Surgery

Tel: (0141) 304 4730 Fax: (0141) 552 0897

Belcher, Philip R., MB BS Lond., MD Lond.,
   FRCS   Prof.
Naik, Surendra K., FRCS   Sr. Lectr.
Wheatley, D. J., MD ChM Cape Town   Prof.;
   Head*
Other Staff: 2 Clin. Lectrs.

Child and Adolescent Psychiatry

Tel: (0141) 201 0223 Fax: (0141) 201 0837

Barton, Joanne   Acting Head*

Child Health

Tel: (0141) 201 0000 Fax: (0141) 201 0837

Donaldson, M. D. C., MB ChB Brist.   Sr. Lectr.
Drummond, Margaret B., MB ChB Edin.   Sr.
   Lectr.
McGowan, D. A., MDS Belf., PhD Lond.,
   FDSRCS, FFDRCSI, FDSRCPSGlas   Prof., Oral
   Surgery
Paton, J. Y., MD Leic., BSc MB ChB   Sr. Lectr.
Stone, David, BSc MB ChB MD   Sr. Lectr.
Tappin, David, MBBS MD   Sr. Lectr.
Weaver, Lawrence T., BA MA MD   Samson
   Gemmell Prof.; Head*
Other Staff: 2 Clin. Lectrs.

Dermatology

Tel: (0141) 330 4012 Fax: (0141) 330 4008

Edward, M., BSc H.-W., PhD H.-W.   Sr. Lectr.
Hodgins, M. B., BSc Manc.   Sr. Lectr.
MacKie, Rona M., MD, FRCP, FRCPath   Prof.;
   McCall Anderson Lectr.; Head*
Tillman, D. M., BSc MB ChB PhD   Sr. Lectr.
Other Staff: 1 Clin. Lectr.

Forensic Medicine and Science

Tel: (0141) 330 4574 Fax: (0141) 330 4602

Al-Alousi, Louay M.   Sr. Lectr.
Anderson, R. A., BSc PhD   Sr. Lectr.

Black, Marjorie, MB ChB Glas.   Sr. Lectr.
Cromie, Alan J., MB BCh BAO   Sr. Lectr.
MacFarlane, Jeannette H., BSc MB ChB   Sr.
   Lectr.
Oliver, J. S., BSc PhD   Sr. Lectr.
Smith, H., BSc PhD   Prof.
Vanezis, Peter, MB ChB Brist., MD Brist., PhD
   Lond., FRCPath   Regius Prof.; Head*
Other Staff: 1 Clin. Lectr.

General Practice

Tel: (0141) 332 8118 Fax: (0141) 353 3402

Murray, T. S., MB ChB PhD   Prof.; Head*
Watt, Graham C. M., BMedBiol Aberd., MB ChB
   Aberd.   Norie-Miller Prof.
Wood, S. F., MD   Sr. Lectr.
Stott, David J., MD Glas.   David Cargill Prof.
Other Staff: 5 Clin. Lectrs.

Haematology

Rowan, R. M., MB ChB Edin., FRCPGlas   Sr.
   Lectr.; Head*

Immunology

Western Infirmary

Tel: (0141) 211 2251 Fax: (0141) 337 3217

Brock, J. H., MA Camb., MSc Newcastle(UK), PhD
   Reading   Reader
Harnett, M., BSc Glas., PhD Glas.   Reader
Kirkwood, E. M., BSc MB ChB   Reader
Liew, F. Y., BSc Monash, PhD ANU, DSc
   ANU   Prof.; Head*
Mowat, A. M., MB ChB PhD   Sr. Lectr.
Stott, D. I., BSc Manc., PhD Camb.   Sr. Lectr.
Other Staff: 1 Lectr.

Medical Cardiology

Tel: (0141) 211 4000

Cobbe, S. M., MA Camb., MD Camb.,
   FRCP   Walton Prof.; Head*
Hutton, I., MD, FRCPGlas   Reader
Lorimer, A. R., MB ChB MD, FRCPGlas, FRCP,
   FRCPEd   Hon. Clin. Prof.
Macfarlane, P. W., BSc PhD, FRSEd   Prof.
Rankin, A. C., BSc MD   Sr. Lectr.
Other Staff: 2 Lectrs.

Medical Genetics

Tel: (0141) 201 0365

Connor, J. M., BSc Liv., MD Liv.   Burton Prof.;
   Head*
Lyall, F., BSc PhD   Sr. Lectr.
Wilcox, D. E., BSc MB ChB   Sr. Lectr.

Medicine

Tel: (0141) 211 4000

Allison, Marjorie E. M., BSc MD, FRCPEd,
   FRCPGlas   Sr. Lectr.
Field, M. A., MD   Sr. Lectr.
Franklin, Ian M., BSc MB ChB PhD, FRCPath,
   FRCPGlas, FRCP   Prof., Transfusion
   Medicine
Lawson, David H., CBE, MD   Hon. Clin. Prof.
Lowe, G. D. O., MD, FRCPGlas, FRCPEd   Prof.
McKillop, J. H., BSc PhD, FRCPGlas   Muirhead
   Prof.; Head*
Reid, Daniel, MD   Hon. Prof.
Stott, David J., MD Glas.   David Cargill Prof.
Sturrock, R., MD, FRCPGlas FRCP   McLeod/
   ARC Prof.
Thomson, J. A., MD PhD, FRCP
   FRCPGlas   Reader
Other Staff: 2 Lectrs.; 3 Clin. Lectrs.

Medicine and Therapeutics

Tel: (0141) 211 2000 Fax: (0141) 339 2800

Allen, Janet M., BSc Lond., MB BS Lond., MD
   Lond.   Prof., Molecular Medicine
Brodie, Martin J., MD   Hon. Prof.
Connell, J., MB ChB MD, FRCPGlas   Prof.
Dargie, Henry J., MB ChB, FRCPGlas   Hon.
   Prof.
Davies, D. L., MD, FRCP, FRCPGlas   Sr. Lectr.
Dominiczak, Anna F., MD Gdansk Med.Acad., MD
   Glas.   Prof.
Elliott, H. L., MD   Sr. Lectr.
Fallon, Marie T.   Marie Curie Sr. Lectr.,
   Palliative Medicine

Hillis, W. S., MB ChB, FRCPGlas   Reader
Lees, K. R., BSc MD   Reader
Lever, A. F., MB ChB   Hon. Prof.
McColl, K. E. L., MD, FRCP   Prof.
McInnes, G. T., BSc MD, FRCPGlas   Sr. Lectr.
Meredith, P. A., BSc Strath., PhD   Reader
Murray, Lilian, BSc MSc PhD   Sr. Lectr.
Reid, J. L., MA Oxf., BM BCh Oxf., DM Oxf.,
   FRCPGlas, FRCP   Regius Prof.; Head*
Semple, P. F., MB ChB, FRCP   Sr. Lectr.
Welsh, John, BSc MB ChB   Dr. Olav Kerr
   Prof., Palliative Medicine
Whiting, Brian, MD Glas., FRCPGlas   Prof.
Other Staff: 13 Clin. Lectrs.

Neurology

Tel: (0141) 201 1100

Barnett, S. C, BSc   Sr. Lectr.
Behan, P. O., MD, FACP, FRCP, FRCPGlas,
   FRCPI   Prof.
Bone, I., MB ChB   Hon. Prof.
Brown, M., BSc PhD   Prof.
Kennedy, P. G. E., MD PhD, FRCP,
   FRCPGlas   Burton Prof.; Head*
Willison, H. J., MB BS Lond., PhD   Sr. Lectr.
Other Staff: 2 Lectrs.; 24 Clin. Lectrs.

Neuropathology

Tel: (0141) 201 1100

Graham, D. I., MB ChB PhD, FRCPath, FRCP,
   FRSEd   Prof.; Head*
Nicoll, J. A. R., BSc MB ChB   Sr. Lectr.

Neurosurgery

Tel: (0141) 201 1100

Dunn, L. T.   Sr. Lectr.
Papanstassiou, V., MB ChB, FRCS   Sr. Lectr.
Teasdale, G. M., MB BS Durh., FRCSEd,
   FRCP   Prof.; Head*

Nursing and Midwifery Studies

Tel: (0141) 330 4051 Fax: (0141) 330 8039

Carter, Diana E., BA Open(UK), MSc   Sr. Lectr.
Hillan, Edith M., MSc Strath., PhD   Sr. Lectr.
Ibbotson, T., BSc PhD   Sr. Lectr.
Smith, Lorraine N., BScN Ott., MEd Manc., PhD
   Manc.   Prof.; Head*
Other Staff: 13 Lectrs.

Obstetrics and Gynaecology

Tel: (Queen Mother's Hospital) (0141) 201
   0568, (Royal Infirmary) (0141) 211 4000
Fax: (Queen Mother's Hospital) (0141) 357
   3610

Cameron, I. T., MA Camb., MD Edin.,
   BSc   Regius Prof.
Coutts, J. R. T., BSc St And., PhD St
   And.   Reader
Greer, I. A., MD   Muirhead Prof.; Head*
Hepburn, Mary, BSc Edin., MD Edin.   Sr. Lectr.
Lumsden, Mary Ann, BSc Lond., MB BS Lond.,
   MD Lond.   Sr. Lectr.
Norman, Jane   Sr. Lectr.
Other Staff: 1 Lectr.; 3 Clin. Lectrs.

Oncology

Medical Oncology

Tel: (0141) 330 4161 Fax: (0141) 330 4127

Brown, Robert, BSc PhD   Reader
Evans, T. R., MB BS Lond., MD   Sr. Lectr.
Freshney, R. I., BSc PhD   Sr. Lectr.
Kaye, S. B., BSc Lond., MD Lond., FRCP   Cancer
   Research Campaign Prof.; Head*
Vassey, P., MB ChB   Sr. Lectr.
Wyke, J. A., MA Camb., VetMB Camb., PhD
   Lond.   Hon. Prof.
Other Staff: 4 Clin. Lectrs.

Radiation Oncology

Tel: (0141) 330 4161 Fax: (0141) 330 4127

Barrett, Ann, MD Lond., FRCR   Prof.; Head*
Rampling, Roy, MSc Lond., MB BS Lond., PhD
   Lond., FRCR   Sr. Lectr.
Twelves, Chris J., MB ChB BMedSci MD   Sr.
   Lectr.

Ophthalmology

Tel: (0141) 211 2099 Fax: (0141) 339 7485

Kirkness, C. M., BMedBiol Aberd., MB ChB
  Aberd., FRCSEd Tennent Prof.; Head*
Lee, W. R., MD Manc., FRCPath, FRSEd Prof.

Orthopaedics

Tel: (0141) 211 2000

Gregoris, Peter, MS PhD Sr. Lectr.
Hamblen, D. L., MB BS Lond., PhD, FRCS,
  FRCSEd, FRCSGlas Prof.; Head*
Waddell, G. A. B., BSc MB ChB MD, FRCSGlas,
  FRCSEd Hon. Prof.
Other Staff: 1 Clin. Lectr.

Otolaryngology

Tel: (0141) 211 4000

Browning, G. G., MD, FRCSEd,
  FRCSGlas Prof.; Head*
Gatehouse, S. Hon. Clin. Prof.
Swan, I. R. C., MD, FRCSEd Sr. Lectr.

Paediatrics, see Surg. Paed.

Pathological Biochemistry

Tel: (0141) 211 4000 Fax: (0141) 553 1703

Clark, B., BSc PhD Sr. Lectr.
Cook, B., BSc Lond., PhD Ill. Sr. Lectr.,
  Biochemistry
Fell, G. S., BSc PhD, FRCPath Prof.
Logan, R. W., MB ChB BSc, FRCPath,
  FRCP Sr. Lectr.
Percy-Robb, I., MB ChB Edin., PhD Edin. Prof.
Shepherd, J., BSc MB ChB PhD Prof.; Head*

Pathology

Tel: (0141) 211 2732

Behan, Wilhelmina M. H., MB ChB Brist.,
  FRCPath Sr. Lectr.
Going, J. J., BSc Edin., MB ChB Edin., PhD
  Edin. Sr. Lectr.
Lee, F. D., MB ChB St And., MD Dund., FRCPath,
  FRCPGlas Hon. Clin. Prof.
Lee, W. R., MD Manc., FRCPath Prof.†
Lindop, G. B. M., BSc MB ChB Sr. Lectr.
MacSween, R. N. M., BSc MD, FRCPGlas,
  FRCPEd, FRCPath, FRSEd, FIBiol Prof.;
  Head*
McNicol, Anne Marie, BSc MD Reader
More, I. A. R., BSc MB ChB PhD Sr. Lectr.
Reid, R. P., BSc MB ChB Sr. Lectr.
Rowan, R. M., MB ChB Edin. Sr. Lectr.
Other Staff: 1 Lectr.

Physics, Clinical

Tel: (0141) 211 2942 Fax: (0141) 339 1563

Elliott, A. T., BA Stir., PhD DSc, FIP Prof.;
  Head*

Postgraduate Medical Education

Tel: (0141) 330 4736 Fax: (0141) 330 6298

Calman, K. C., MD PhD Visiting Prof.
MacKay, N., CBE, MD, FRCPGlas,
  FRCPEd Prof.; Head*
Murray, T. S., MB ChB PhD, FRCGP,
  FRCP Prof.
Other Staff: 1 Lectr.

Psychological Medicine, see also Child and
  Adolescent Psychiat.

Atkinson, Jacqueline M., BA Hull, PhD Hull Sr.
  Lectr.
Bond, Sir Michael, MD Sheff., PhD Sheff.,
  FRCSEd, FRCPGlas, FRCPsych Prof.
Espie, Colin A., BSc MAppSci PhD,
  FBPsS Prof., Clinical Psychology
Jahoda, A., BSc MSc PhD Sr. Lectr.
Livingston, Martin G., MD Sr. Lectr.
Millar, Keith, BA Stir., PhD Dund., FBPsS Prof.
Other Staff: 2 Lectrs.; 2 Clin. Lectrs.

Public Health

Tel: (0141) 330 4039 Fax: (0141) 330 5018

Atkinson, Jacqueline M., BA Hull, PhD Hull Sr.
  Lectr.

Capewell, Simon, MB BS Newcastle(UK), MSc
  Edin., MD Newcastle(UK) Sr. Lectr.
Hanlon, Philip W., BSc Glas., MB ChB Glas.,
  MD Glas. Sr. Lectr.
Jones, R. B., BSc Lond., MSc Reading, PhD
  Nott. Sr. Lectr.
Knill-Jones, R. P., MB BChir Camb., MA Camb.,
  MSc Lond., FRCP Sr. Lectr.
Macdonald, E. B., MB ChB Sr. Lectr.
McEwen, J., MB ChB St And. Henry Mechan
  Prof.; Head*
Petch, Alison J., BA Camb., MA Sheff., PhD
  Edin. Reader
Reid, Margaret E., MA Aberd., PhD Reader
Other Staff: 3 Lectrs.; 2 Clin. Lectrs.

Surgery

Tel: (Royal Infirmary) (0141) 211 4000,
  (Western Infirmary) (0141) 211 2650
  Fax: (Western Infirmary) (0141) 334 1826

Angerson, W., BA Oxf., DPhil Sus. Reader
Bradley, J. Andrew, MB ChB Leeds, PhD Glas.,
  FRCSGlas Hon. Prof.
Cooke, T. G., MD Liv., FRCS, FRCSGlas St.
  Mungo Prof.; Head, Royal Infirmary*
Gallagher, G., BSc Strath., PhD Strath. Sr. Lectr.
George, W. D., MB BS Lond., MS Lond. Prof.;
  Head, Western Infirmary*
Harper, A. M., MD Prof., Wellcome Surgical
  Research Unit
Horgan, P., MB ChB Sr. Lectr.
MacPherson, S. G., MB ChB, FRCSGlas Sr.
  Lectr.
McArdle, C. S., MD ChB Hon. Prof.
O'Dwyer, P., MB BS Lond., FRCSI Reader
Purushotham, A. D., MB BS Madr., MD Sr.
  Lectr.
Reid, Iona, MB BCL BAO MD, FRCS Sr. Lectr.
Stuart, Robert C., MB BCh BAO MCH,
  FRCSI Sr. Lectr.
Other Staff: 2 Lectrs.; 6 Clin. Lectrs.

Surgical Paediatrics

Tel: (0141) 201 0170 Fax: (0141) 201 0858

Carachi, R., MD PhD Sr. Lectr.
Young, D. G., MB ChB Prof.; Head*

SPECIAL CENTRES, ETC

Scottish Universities Research and
  Reactor Centre

Consortium of 3 universities (Edinburgh,
  Glasgow and Strathclyde), with 2 associate
  members (Aberdeen and St Andrews)

Tel: (013552) 23332 Fax: (013552) 29898

Banford, H. M., BSc Glas., PhD Strath. Sr.
  Lectr.
Cook, G. T., BSc Glas., PhD Glas. Sr. Lectr.
East, B. W., BSc Durh., PhD Kent Sr. Lectr.
Fallick, A. E., BSc Glas., PhD Glas. Prof.,
  Isotope Geosciences
Mackenzie, A. B., BSc Glas., PhD Glas. Sr.
  Lectr.
Sanderson, D. C. W., BSc Durh., MPhil Brad.,
  PhD CNAA Sr. Lectr.
Scott, R. D., BSc Edin., PhD Edin. Dir.*
Other Staff: 6 Lectrs.
Research: aerial detection of radioactivity; mass
  spectrometry (application to life sciences
  and isotope geosciences); measurement of
  environmental radioactivity; testing of
  irradiated foodstuffs

CONTACT OFFICERS

Academic affairs. Clerk of Senate: Whitehead,
  Prof. Rex R., MSc Melb., PhD Melb., DSc Glas.,
  FRSEd
Accommodation. Director: Campbell, Neil,
  BSc Edin.
Admissions (first degree). Director, Central
  Admissions Service: Brown, James J., BA
  PhD

Admissions (higher degree). Director, Central
  Admissions Service: Brown, James J., BA
  PhD
Adult/continuing education. Director, Adult
  and Continuing Education: Slowey, Prof.
  Maria, BComm Trinity(Dub.), MLitt
  Trinity(Dub.)
Alumni. Alumni Relations Officer,
  Development Campaign Office:
  Montgomery, Diane
Archives. University Archivist (acting):
  Richmond, Lesley
Careers. Director, Careers Service: Mercer,
  John, BSc Dund.I.T.
Computing services. Director, Computing
  Service: McCormick, Linda M. L., BSc
Credit transfer. Head of Registry: Lowther,
  Christine R., BA
Development/fund-raising. Acting Director,
  Development Campaign: Bell, Catherine R.
Distance education. Head, Department of
  Education: Wilkinson, J. Eric, BSc St And.,
  MEd Dund., PhD
Equal opportunities. Equal Opportunities
  Monitoring Officer: Webb, Angela
Estates and buildings/works and services.
  Director, Estates and Buildings: Wilson,
  Robert B., MBA
Finance. Director of Finance: Yuille, Michael,
  BAcc Glas.
General enquiries. Head of Registry: Lowther,
  Christine R., BA
Health services. Medical Officer: Hamilton,
  Gordon M., MB ChB Glas.
Library (chief librarian). Librarian and
  Keeper of Hunterian Books and Manuscripts:
  ......
Library (enquiries). Librarian and Keeper of
  Hunterian Books and Manuscripts: ......
Personnel/human resources. Director,
  Personnel Services: Denton, David D., MA
  Camb.
Public relations, information and marketing.
  Press Officer: Brown, Mike, MA Dund.
Publications. Publications Assistant: Bell, Lynn
Purchasing. Director of Procurement: Holmes,
  C. Robert
Quality assurance and accreditation. Director,
  Quality Assurance Office: Emanuel, Ronald
  V., BSc Glas., PhD Glas., FRSChem
Research. Director, Research and Enterprise:
  Garner, Cathy, MA Edin., PhD Edin.
Safety. Safety Officer: Rankine, Andrew O.,
  BSc Glas., PhD Glas., FRSChem
Scholarships, awards, loans. Clerk to the
  Senate Office: McGill, Patricia M., MA Edin.
Security. Central Services Manager: Edgar,
  Laurence W.
Sport and recreation. Director: McNeish,
  Sharon, BEd MSc
Staff development and training. Deputy
  Director of Personnel Services: Chandler,
  Jean F.
Student welfare/counselling. Counsellor,
  Student Counselling and Advisory Service:
  Kelly, Janette, MB ChB Glas.
Students with disabilities. Special Needs
  Adviser: Sillars, Kate, BA†

CAMPUS/COLLEGE HEADS

Glasgow School of Art, 67 Renfrew Street,
  Glasgow G3, Scotland, United Kingdom.
  Director: Cameron, Dugald
Scottish Agricultural College, Auchincruive,
  Ayr KA6 5HW, Scotland, United Kingdom.
  Principal: Thomas, Phillip C., BSc Wales, PhD
  Wales, FIBiol
St Andrew's College, Duntocher Road,
  Bearsden, Glasgow G61 4QA, Scotland,
  United Kingdom. Principal: McGettrick,
  Bartholomew J., OBE, BSc MEd

[Information supplied by the institution as at 29 May
1998, and edited by the ACU]

GLASGOW CALEDONIAN UNIVERSITY

Founded 1993; previously established as The Queen's College, Glasgow 1875 and Glasgow Polytechnic 1971

Member of the Association of Commonwealth Universities

Postal Address: City Campus, Cowcaddens Road, Glasgow, Scotland G4 0BA
Telephone: (0141) 331 3000 **Fax**: (0141) 331 3005 **Telex**: 779341

CHANCELLOR—Nickson, The Lord David, KBE, DUniv
CHAIRMAN OF COURT—Campbell, Malcolm
PRINCIPAL AND VICE-CHANCELLOR*—Johnston, Ian A., CB, BSc Birm., PhD Birm.
VICE-PRINCIPAL—Bush, Prof. Peter W., BA PhD
VICE-PRINCIPAL—Phillips, Prof. John C., BSc, FIMA
SENIOR ASSISTANT PRINCIPAL—Finch, Peter B., BA(Econ)
HEAD OF ACADEMIC ADMINISTRATION‡—Ferguson, E. Brendan, BSc
DEPUTY HEAD OF ACADEMIC ADMINISTRATION—Struthers, A. Ian

GENERAL INFORMATION

History. The university was founded in 1993 by the merger of The Queen's College, Glasgow and Glasgow Polytechnic. It comprises two campuses: Park Campus in the west end of Glasgow; and City Campus, the main campus, in the heart of the city.

Admission to first degree courses (see also United Kingdom Introduction). Through Universities and Colleges Admissions Service (UCAS).

First Degrees (see also United Kingdom Directory of Subjects to Study). BA, BEng, BSc.
Most courses are full-time and last 3–5 years.

Higher Degrees (see also United Kingdom Directory of Subjects to Study). LLM, MBA, MSc, MPhil, PhD.
Courses last up to 5 years.

Libraries. 304,200 volumes; 2016 serials subscribed to. Special collections include: Norman and Janey Buchan, Scottish and Northern Book Distribution Centre, Norrie McIntosh, and Mike Scott (all left-wing politics and labour movement); Queen's College (cookery and home economics); RSSPCC Archive (child welfare and abuse); Anti-Apartheid Movement in Scotland Archive; Heatherbank Museum of Social Work (book library, photo library, ephemera and resources library, journals and periodicals library). Custodianship of Gallagher Memorial Library (left-wing politics).

Fees (1997–98). Undergraduate: UK students band 1 £750, band 2 (laboratory-based) £1250–1600; international students £6060. Postgraduate: UK students £2490; international students £6075–8050.

Academic Year (1998–99). Two semesters: 21 September–22 January; 1 February–28 May.

Income (1996–97). Total, £57,000,000.

Statistics. Staff: 870 academic (including research), 561 support, 227 manual. Students: full-time 10,867 (4462 men, 6405 women); part-time 3265 (1360 men, 1905 women); international 770 (416 men, 354 women); total 14,132.

FACULTIES/SCHOOLS

Business
Tel: (0141) 331 3129 Fax: (0141) 331 3172
Dean: Taylor, Prof. John, BSc(Econ) MSc(Econ)
Secretary: Peoples, Patricia

Health
Tel: (0141) 331 3624 Fax: (0141) 331 3500
Dean: Dickson, Prof. Gordon, MLitt Glas., PhD CNAA
Personal Assistant: Donald, Ruth

Science and Technology
Tel: (0141) 331 3115 Fax: (0141) 331 3778
Dean: Chisholm, Prof. Colin, BSc Strath., PhD St And.
Personal Assistant: Crech, D.

ACADEMIC UNITS

Accounting, see Finance and Acctg.

Biological Sciences
Tel: (0141) 331 3209 Fax: (0141) 331 3208
Aido, Kofi E., MSc PhD   Sr. Lectr.
Blackstock, Jim, BSc PhD   Sr. Lectr.
Craft, John, BSc PhD   Prof.
Darby, F. Joseph, BSc PhD   Sr. Lectr.
Howarth, Richard J., MPhil   Sr. Lectr.
Knowler, Prof. John T., PhD, FIBiol   Head*
MacDonald, Allan, BSc PhD   Reader
Macham, Leo, BSc PhD   Sr. Lectr.
Wilkie, Iain, BSc PhD   Sr. Lectr.
Wood, Les, BSc PhD   Sr. Lectr.

Building and Surveying
Tel: (0141) 331 3629 Fax: (0141) 331 3696
Akintoye, Akintola, BSc MSc PhD   Sr. Lectr.
Bonnar, Irene, BSc(Comm)   Sr. Lectr.
Galbraith, Graham, BSc MSc PhD   Sr. Lectr.
Hardcastle, Cliff, BSc MSc PhD   Head*
Kennedy, Peter, MSc   Sr. Lectr.
Madden, Harry   Sr. Lectr.
Palmer, Angela, MSc PhD   Sr. Lectr.

Business Administration
Tel: (0141) 331 3179 Fax: (0141) 331 3193
Barr, Stephen, MSc Glas.   Sr. Lectr.
Doswell, Prof. Andrew, MSc Portsmouth, PhD S'ton.   Sr. Lectr.
Jordan, Michael, MSc Brad.   Sr. Lectr.
Reid, Vivien, MBA Strath.   Acting Head*
Other Staff: 6 Lectrs.; 2 Lectrs.†; 3 Temp. Lectrs.
Research: business process re-engineering; effect of technology on small professional businesses; impact of networks on managers

Community Health, see Nursing and Community Health

Computer Studies
Tel: (0141) 331 3279 Fax: (0141) 331 3277
Cartwright, Geoffrey, BSc St And., MTech Brun., PhD St And.   Sr. Lectr.
Gray, Edwin, BA Strath., MSc   Sr. Lectr.; Asst. Head
Leaning, John, MA Camb., MSc Lond.   Sr. Lectr.
Newman, Julian, BA Oxf.   Reader
Stewart, Grace, BSc Glas.   Sr. Lectr.

Consumer Studies
Tel: (0141) 337 4353 Fax: (0141) 337 4420
Campbell, Gillian, MSc Strath.   Head*
Clack, Ed, BA H.-W.   Sr. Lectr.
Clarke, Prof. Ian, BSc PhD   Reader
Daly, Jan, BA Strath.   Sr. Lectr.
Lochhead, Malcolm, BA CNAA   Sr. Lectr.

MacArthur, Sheena, BA Open(UK), MSc Glas.   Sr. Lectr.
McLean, Morag, BA Strath., MSc Strath.   Sr. Lectr.
Moore, Christopher, MA Glas., MBA Stirling   Sr. Lectr.

Economics
Tel: (0141) 331 3309 Fax: (0141) 331 3293
Arnot, Robert, BSc Lond., PhD Glas.   Sr. Lectr.
Bailey, Stephen, MA Dund., MLitt Dund., PhD Strath.   Prof.
Cooper, John, BA Strath., PhD Strath.   Sr. Lectr.
Dow, Alexander, MA St And., MA S.Fraser, PhD Manit.   Prof.; Head*
Hutton, Alan, BCom Leeds, MA Leeds   Sr. Lectr.
Leahy, James, BA Strath.   Sr. Lectr.
McKay, Pat, BSc Herts., MEd Stir.   Sr. Lectr.
Riddington, Geoffrey, BA Sus., PhD Wales, MPhil   Sr. Lectr.
Smith, Peter, MA Oxf., MLitt Glas.   Reader
Sproull, Alan, BAStrath., MPhil Glas., PhD Glas.   Reader

Energy and Environmental Technology
Tel: (0141) 331 3300 Fax: (0141) 331 3370
Baird, James, BSc PhD   Prof.
Campbell, Thomas, BSc Strath., PhD Strath., FIMechE   Prof.; Head*
Crowther, John, BA Oxf., DPhil Oxf.   Sr. Lectr.
Cullen, Martin, BSc Paisley, MBA Paisley   Sr. Lectr.
Doyle, John, MA MSc   Sr. Lectr.
El Sharif, Mahmoud R., MSc Glas.   Reader
Hytiris, Nicholas, BSc Strath., MSc Strath, PhD Strath., FGS   Sr. Lectr.
Taylor, Gavin, MSc PhD, FIMechE   Sr. Lectr.

Engineering
Tel: (0141) 331 3529 Fax: (0141) 331 3690
Allan, Malcolm, BSc Strath., PhD G.Caledonian   Sr. Lectr.
Burns, George R., BSc Strath., PhD Strath.   Sr. Lectr.
Champaneri, Ramesh, BSc Aston, MPhil Northumbria   Sr. Lectr.
Davidson, John C., BSc Glas., PhD Strath.   Sr. Lectr.
Gordon, David R., BSc Strath., PhD Strath.   Sr. Lectr.
Kemp, Ian J., BSc Strath., PhD Strath.   Reader
Kirkwood, Prof. Daniel, BSc Strath., PhD Strath., FIM   Head*
McLeod, Colin F., MSc Manc.   Sr. Lectr.
Mehta, Phiroze, BSc Bom., BSc Glas., MSc Paisley   Sr. Lectr.
Temple, Bryan K., BTech Brad., PhD Leeds   Sr. Lectr.
Westwood, Tom, BSc Glas., MSc Strath.   Sr. Lectr.

Entrepreneurial Studies
Tel: (0141) 337 4028 Fax: (0141) 337 4500
Weaver, Prof. Richard Y., MBA   Head*

Environmental Technology, see Energy and Environmental Technol.

Finance and Accounting

Tel: (0141) 331 3360 Fax: (0141) 331 3171
Forbes, David J., BA PhD
Fraser, Ian A. M., MA   Reader
Godfrey, Alan D., BA G.Caledonian   Prof.; Head*
Henry, William M.   Sr. Lectr.
Keddie, Jean L., MAcc   Sr. Lectr.
McArthur, Archie, MA   Sr. Lectr.
McChlery, Stuart, BA   Sr. Lectr.
McKendrick, Ennis J., MA MPhil   Sr. Lectr.
Paudyal, Prof. Krishna, MSc MBA PhD   Sr. Lectr.
Rolfe, Thomas F., MAcc G.Caledonian   Sr. Lectr.
Other Staff: 20 Lectrs.; 1 Sr. Res. Fellow; 12 Res. Fellows

Financial Services, see Risk and Financial Services

Hospitality, Tourism and Leisure Management

Tel: (0141) 337 4254 Fax: (0141) 337 4141
Bell, Irene, MA Glas., MSc Strath.   Programme Leader/Lectr.
Biggam, Maggie, MSc Strath.   Sr. Lectr.
Boyd, Morag, BA Open(UK)   Sr. Lectr.
Foley, Malcolm, MSc Edin.   Reader
Hinds, Debbie, MSc Strath.   Programme Leader/Lectr.
Kent, Roy, BA Strath., MSc Strath.   Programme Leader/Lectr.
Lennon, John J., BSc Oxf.Brookes, MPhil Strath.   Reader
Leslie, David, BA Strath., MPhil Ulster   Reader
Littlejohn, David, BA Strath., MSc Manc.   Prof.
Macfarlane, Dorothy, BA Paisley   Programme Leader/Lectr.
Maxwell, Gillian, BA Strath., MPhil Strath.   Programme Leader/Sr. Lectr.
McPherson, Gayle, BA H.-W.   Programme Leader/Lectr.
Scott, Bernadette, BA MPhil   Programme Leader/Lectr.
Stewart, Donald, BA Open(UK), MSc Strath., PhD Glas.   Programme Leader/Sr. Lectr.
Other Staff: 2 Lectrs.
Vacant Posts: Head*

Language and Media

Tel: (0141) 331 3259 Fax: (0141) 331 3264
Blain, Neil, BA Stir., PhD Strath.   Sr. Lectr.
Fermor, John, BA S'ton., PhD S'ton.   Sr. Lectr.
Hutchison, David, MA Glas., MLitt Glas.   Sr. Lectr.
O'Donnell, H., MA Glas., PhD Glas.   Reader
Ross, Margaret, MA Glas., MLitt Glas., MèsL   Sr. Lectr.
Scott, W. T., MA Glas., PhD Sheff.   Prof.; Head*

Law and Public Administration

Tel: (0141) 331 3429 Fax: (0141) 331 3798
Charlton, Jacqueline, BA Liv.   Head*
Chisholm, Marcella, LLM Nan.   Sr. Lectr.
Mackie, Robert, BA Strath., MSc Strath.
Maharg, Paul, LLB Glas., MA Glas., PhD Edin.
Pyper, Bobby, MA Glas., PhD Glas.   Reader
Younis, Tal, BSc Birm., MEd Birm., PhD Birm.   Reader

Management

Tel: (0141) 331 3410 Fax: (0141) 331 3269
Campbell, Colin, BA Strath.   Sr. Lectr.
Carlisle, Brian, BSc Stir., MSc Strath., PhD Strath.   Sr. Lectr.
Cousins, John, MSc Bath, MLitt H.-W.   Sr. Lectr.
Hill, Sandra, MBA G.Caledonian   Sr. Lectr.
McDougall, Marilyn, MA Glas., MEd Sheff.   Sr. Lectr.
McKay, John, BA Strath., MEd Stir.   Head*
Penlington, John, BSc Newcastle, MA Manc.   Sr. Lectr.
Vaughan, Elizabeth, BA Strath., MSc Strath.   Sr. Lectr.

Mathematics

Bradley, Roy, BSc Durh,, MSc Newcastle(UK), PhD Glas., FIMA   Prof.; Head*
Cook, Jean, BSc Lond., MA Ill., PhD Ill.   Sr. Lectr.
Gomatam, Jagannathan, BSc Madr., MSc Madr., PhD Syr.   Prof.
Hamson, Michael J., MSc Lond., MPhil Lond., FIMA   Sr. Lectr.
Jha, Vikram, MSc Lond., PhD Lond.   Reader
Macauley, Alexander B., BSc Strath., MSc Strath.   Sr. Lectr.
McAllister, Sandra A., BSc Belf., BSc Strath.   Sr. Lectr.
McFadyen, Angus K., BSc Paisley, MSc Strath.   Sr. Lectr.
Williamson, Geoffrey H., BSc Lough.   Sr. Lectr.
Other Staff: 19 Lectrs; 2 Res. Fellows; 3 Lectrs.†

Media, see Lang. and Media

Nursing and Community Health

Tel: (0141) 331 3467 Fax: (0141) 331 3575
Fleming, Valerie, PhD   Sr. Lectr.
McIntosh, Jean, BSc PhD   Prof.
Parfitt, Barbara, MSc MCommH PhD   Prof.; Head*
Reid, Gerald W., BA MSc   Sr. Lectr.
Schartau, E., BA MLitt   Sr. Lectr.

Occupational Therapy

Tel: (0141) 337 4726 Fax: (0141) 337 4910
Carnduff, Ann E. J., BA   Head of Div.*

Physical Sciences

Tel: (0141) 331 3669 Fax: (0141) 331 3653
Ansell, Raymond O., BSc Lond., PhD Newcastle(UK)   Reader
Bather, P. A., DPhil York(UK)   Sr. Lectr.
Campbell, Michael, BSc Paisley, PhD Glas.   Reader
Crowther, John M., BA Oxf., DPhil Oxf.   Sr. Lectr.
Eadie, Andrew S., BSc Glas., PhD G.Caledonian   Sr. Lectr.
Fortune, J. D., BSc Glas., MSc Aberd., PhD Glas.   Sr. Lectr.
Jones, Mark G., BSc Greenwich, PhD Greenwich   Sr. Lectr.
McPherson, Ian, BA Open(UK), BSc Aberd., PhD Strath.   Sr. Lectr.
Phillips, Geoffrey L., OBE, MSc Glas., FRSChem   Visiting Prof.
Pugh, Prof. John R., BSc Glas., PhD Glas.   Head*
Other Staff: 2 Sr. Lectrs.; 8 Lectrs.; 2 Sr. Res. Fellows; 2 Res. Fellows; 3 Lectrs.†
Research: analytical science and measurement; bulk solids handling technology

Physiotherapy, Podiatry and Radiography

Tel: (0141) 337 4775 Fax: (0141) 337 4701
Baird, Stuart A., BSc Brighton   Sr. Lectr.
Brydson, Gillian, BSc CNAA, MSc G.Caledonian   Sr. Lectr.
Burrow, J. Gordon, MPhil Strath., BA   Sr. Lectr.
Campbell, Robert, MSc G.Caledonian   Sr. Lectr.
Grant, Margaret, MSc Liv.
Meredith, Catherine, BA Open(UK), MPH Glas.
Myles, Prof. Sandra, BA Open(UK), MEd Stir.   Head*
O'Donnell, Maureen, BSc Sund.
Stachura, Kay, BA Open(UK), MSc Stir.

Clinical Research Centre

Tel: (0141) 337 4751, 4801
No staff at present

Podiatry, see Physiother., Podiatry and Radiog.

Psychology

Tel: (0141) 331 3119 Fax: (0141) 331 3636
Cooke, David, BSc St And., MSc Newcastle(UK), PhD Glas., FBPsS   Prof.†
Durndell, A., BSc Lond., PhD Aberd.   Sr. Lectr.
Forbes, Douglas, MA Aberd., PhD Aberd.   Sr. Lectr.
Furnell, J. R. G., LLB Dund., MA Aberd., PhD Stir., FBPsS   Prof.
Mitchell, Margaret C., MA Glas., MSc Calg., PhD Glas.   Reader
Needs, A., BA Wales, DPhil York(UK)
Parker, Denis, BA Durh., PhD Durh., FBPsS   Prof.; Head*
Rotheiler Elke   Sr. Lectr.
Tuohy, Alan, BSc Lond., PhD Strath.   Sr. Lectr.
Wrennall, Mike, BSc Lond., MPhil Lond.   Sr. Lectr.
Vacant Posts: 1 Lectr.

Public Administration, see Law and Public Admin.

Radiography, see Physiother., Podiatry and Radiog.

Risk and Financial Services

Tel: (0141) 331 3159 Fax: (0141) 331 3229
Drennan, Lynn, BA Strath.   Sr. Lectr.
Gao, Simon S., BA Shaanxi, MA Shaanxi, PhD Rotterdam   Sr. Lectr.
Munro, Harry, MBA Strath.   Head*
Watson, Alan B., MPhil G.Caledonian   Sr. Lectr.
Research: financial risk management; insurance in developing countries; leasing in emergency markets; risk managment in public sectors; social security and pensions

Social Sciences

Tel: (0141) 331 3437 Fax: (0141) 331 3439
Bleicher, Josef, BSc Leeds, PhD Leeds   Reader
Charlton, Roger, BSc Sheff., MA Sheff.   Reader
Culbert, John, BSc Strath.   Sr. Lectr.
Donald, David, BA Strath.   Sr. Lectr.
Hughes, William G., BA Aberd., PhD Aberd.   Sr. Lectr.
McFarland, Elaine, MA Glas., PhD Glas.   Sr. Lectr.
Thompson, William, MA Strath., PhD Strath.   Reader
Walsh, David, MA Glas., MPhil Glas.   Head*

Social Work

Tel: (0141) 331 3104
Brodie, Ian J., BA MPhil   Sr. Lectr.

Surveying, see Bldg. and Surv.

Tourism and Leisure Management, see Hospitality, Tourism and Leisure Management

Vision Sciences

Tel: (0141) 331 3379 Fax: (0141) 331 3387
Button, Norman, BSc Glas., PhD Glas.   Sr. Lectr.
Doughty, Michael, BSc Lond., MSc Warw., PhD Lond.   Prof.
Heron, Gordon, MSc Manc., PhD Manc.   Sr. Lectr.
McCulloch, Daphne L., OD Wat., PhD Indiana   Sr. Lectr.
Tomlinson, Prof. Alan, MSc Brad., PhD Manc.   Prof.; Head*
Wright, Lesley, BEd   Sr. Lectr.

SPECIAL CENTRES, ETC

Continuing Education, Centre for

Fax: (0141) 331 3518
Fearn, Richard, BSc MA PhD   Sr. Lectr.
Gallacher, Jim, MA MSc   Head*

McGrane, Jim, BSc *Strath.* Sr. Lectr.

Learning and Teaching Innovation, Centre for

Tel: (0141) 331 1271 Fax: (0141) 332 8214

Drysdale, Jan, BSc *Dund.*, MSc *Strath.*, MBA *Strath.* Sr. Lectr.

Mackie, Robert, BA *Strath.*, MSc *Strath.* Sr. Lectr.

Mayes, Terry, BSc *Brist.*, PhD *Newcastle(UK)* Prof.; Head*

CONTACT OFFICERS

Academic affairs. Head of Academic Administration: Ferguson, E. Brendan, BSc

Accommodation. Lamberton, Angelina, MA *G.Caledonian*

Admissions (first degree and postgraduate). Student Administration Manager: Aitken-Orun, Catherine, BSc *Strath.*

Admissions (higher degree). Murray, Sybil, BA

Adult/continuing education. McGrane, Jim, BSc *Strath.*

Alumni. Bailey, Kirsty

Archives. McCallum, Carole, BA *Stir.*

Careers. Assistant Head of Student Services Department: McAleese, George, BA *Strath.*

Computing services. Head, Information Technology Support Centre: White, Ian, BSc *Edin.*

Conferences/corporate hospitality. Barton, June

Consultancy services (Faculty of Business). McFarlane, John, MPhil

Consultancy services (Faculty of Science and Technology). Chisholm, Prof. Colin U., BSc *Strath.*, PhD *St And.*

Credit transfer. Fearn, Richard, BSc *Aston*, MA *Essex*, PhD *E.Anglia*

Development/fund-raising. Bannerman, Sara

Distance education. Workbased Learning and Research/Development: Gallagher, Jim, MA *Glas.*, MSc *Lond.*

Equal opportunities. Head of Personnel: Lysaght, Janette, MBA *G.Caledonian*

Estates and buildings/works and services. Scott, George

Examinations. Blaber, Jean

Finance. Head of Finance Office: Boyle, John

General enquiries. Deputy Head of Academic Administration: Struthers, A. Ian

Health services. Anderson, Alex, MB ChB

International office. Carey, Prof. Roger, BA *Wales*, MA *Wales*

Library (chief librarian). Head of Library: Haythornthwaite, Jo, BA *Strath.*, PhD *Strath.*, FLA, FIInfSc

Personnel/human resources. Head of Personnel: Lysaght, Janette, MBA *G.Caledonian*

Public relations, information and marketing. Director of Marketing and Public Relations: Conn, Ian, BA *Open(UK)*, MBA *Strath.*

Publications. Marketing Communications Officer: Cavani, John, BA *CNAA*

Publications. Director of Marketing and Public Relations: Conn, Ian, BA *Open(UK)*, MBA *Strath.*

Purchasing. Pritchard, Anne, BA

Quality assurance and accreditation. Head of Academic Administration: Ferguson, E. Brendan, BSc

Research. Administrative Officer: Aitchison, Linda, BA *G.Caledonian*

Safety. Bullock, Alistair

Scholarships, awards, loans. Student Administration Manager: Aitken-Orun, Catherine, BSc *Strath.*

Schools liaison. Schools and Colleges Liaison Officer: Gray, Paul, BA *G.Caledonian*

Sport and recreation. Menzies, Corinne, BA *Strath.*

Staff development and training. Head, Department of Quality Enhancement: ......

Student welfare/counselling. Head of Student Services: Troup, Gill, BA *Edin.*, MA *Aberd.*, MSc *Edin.*, MBA *G.Caledonian*

Students from other countries. Director, International Office: Carey, Prof. Roger, BA *Wales*, MA *Wales*

Students with disabilities. Student Adviser: McAllister, Chris, MA *Aberd.*

[*Information supplied by the institution as at 16 March 1998, and edited by the ACU*]

UNIVERSITY OF GREENWICH

Founded 1992

Member of the Association of Commonwealth Universities

Postal Address: Bexley Road, Eltham, London, England SE9 2PQ
Telephone: (0181) 331 8000 **Fax**: (0181) 331 8876 **WWW**: http://www.gre.ac.uk

CHANCELLOR—Young, Rt. Hon. the Baroness
PRO-CHANCELLOR—Warren, Keith G., BSc(Eng) PhD, FIEE
VICE-CHANCELLOR*—Fussey, David E., BA *Camb.*, MA *Camb.*, PhD *Warw.*, FIMechE
DEPUTY VICE-CHANCELLOR—McWilliam, John D. A., OBE, FRICS
PRO-VICE-CHANCELLOR—Humphreys, John, MSc MEd
SECRETARY TO THE UNIVERSITY—Charles, J. M., MA
ACADEMIC REGISTRAR—Rose, Christine H., MSc
DIRECTOR OF FINANCE—Denton, R.
UNIVERSITY LIBRARIAN—Heathcote, D. A., MA
DIRECTOR OF ACADEMIC DEVELOPMENT—Allen, Robert M., BA(Econ) PhD
DIRECTOR OF COMPUTING SERVICES—Cooper, G. A., MSc
DIRECTOR OF PERSONNEL—Brockett, R. J., BA MA

GENERAL INFORMATION

History. The university was founded in 1992. It was previously established as Thames Polytechnic which was originally founded in 1890 as Woolwich Polytechnic Young Men's Christian Institution. The university has four campuses based in London and Kent.

Admission to first degree courses (see also United Kingdom Introduction). Through the Universities and Colleges Admissions Service (UCAS). General Certificate of Secondary Education (GCSE), or equivalent qualification, with passes in 3 approved subjects and passes in 2 subjects at A level. International applicants: equivalent qualifications. Students whose first language is not English must normally pass

either English language at GCSE or an approved test in English (eg IELTS).

First Degrees (see also United Kingdom Directory to Subjects of Study). BA, BEng, BSc, LLB.

Higher Degrees (see also United Kingdom Directory to Subjects of Study). MA, MBA, MSc.

Libraries. 500,000 volumes.

Fees (1998–99, annual). Undergraduate: £1000 (home students); £6950 (international students). Postgraduate: £2610–8800 (home students); £6950–9450 (international students).

Academic Year (1998–99). Three terms: 21 September–18 December; 18 January–26 March; 19 April–25 June. Two semesters: 21 September–29 January; 1 February–4 June.

Income (1996–97). Total, £83,800,000.

Statistics (1996–97). Students: full-time 11,757 (6104 men, 5653 women); part-time 6785 (3482 men, 3303 women); international 527; total 18,542.

ACADEMIC UNITS

Arranged by Schools

Architecture and Landscape

Tel: (0181) 331 9100 Fax: (0181) 331 9105

Bennetts, J. B. Principal Lectr.

Blackett, Heather, MA   Sr. Lectr.
Charlton, R., MA   Sr. Lectr.
Clarke, G. R. I., LLB   Sr. Lectr.
Cleiford, A. J., BA MSc   Sr. Lectr.
Conrad, A., MSc   Sr. Lectr.
Daniell, Gillian, MA   Sr. Lectr.
Delage, Corine C. F., MLA *Harv.*   Head*
Gilby, H., BA   Sr. Lectr.
Goode, P., MA DPhil   Sr. Lectr.
Holden, R., BA   Sr. Lectr.
Jones, Carol   Sr. Lectr.
Kinnear, Lynn, BA   Sr. Lectr.
Linden, F. A.   Principal Lectr.
Marda, Nelly, MSc   Sr. Lectr.
Pillans, G. N., BSc PhD   Sr. Lectr.
Quiney, A. P., MA PhD   Prof.
Seijo, R. E.   Sr. Lectr.
Shokoohy, M., MSc PhD, FRAS   Sr. Lectr.
Stringer, P. M.   Sr. Lectr.
Tatum, I. G., BA   Sr. Lectr.
Turner, T. H. D., MA   Sr. Lectr.

Business

Fax: (0181) 331 9005
Atkin, Rod, BA MA   Sr. Lectr.
Barnett, D., MA   Sr. Lectr.
Baynes, P. T., BA   Principal Lectr.
Begley, A. P., BA(Econ)   Sr. Lectr.
Burke, I. F.   Sr. Lectr.
Bysouth, A. J., MSc   Principal Lectr.
Carter, Polly C., MA   Sr. Lectr.
Carty, R., BSc MBA   Sr. Lectr.
Catchpowle, Leslie J., BA MSc   Sr. Lectr.
Darlington, S. D., BA   Principal Lectr.
Dennison, P. H., BSc MBA   Sr. Lectr.
Dickson, M. K., MA   Sr. Lectr.
Druker, Jan M., BA PhD   Principal Lectr.
Ellis, H., BA PhD   Sr. Lectr.
Galton, K., MEd   Principal Lectr.
Gould, J. J., BA MA   Principal Lectr.
Hand, N. G., BComm MSc   Sr. Lectr.
Hayes, D. M.   Sr. Lectr.
Holtom, K. G., MA   Principal Lectr.
Housden, M. J., BA   Sr. Lectr.
Hughes, D. A., BEd   Sr. Lectr.
Hugill, C. W., BSc   Sr. Lectr.
Jones, C. A.   Sr. Lectr.
Kemp, A. V. C.   Sr. Lectr.
Ledgerwood, J. G., BA PhD   Reader
Lee, G.   Sr. Lectr.
Lewis, B. K., BSc   Sr. Lectr.
Mackerrell, D. K. D.   Principal Lectr.
Mayor, R. J.   Sr. Lectr.
Mead, D. S.   Sr. Lectr.
Millar, Susan M., BA MA   Head*
Mould, C. A., BA   Principal Lectr.
Newland, D. J., BSc   Sr. Lectr.
Nicholls, Helen J., MA   Principal Lectr.
Owen, G. N., BA   Sr. Lectr.
Slater, A.   Sr. Lectr.
Street, B. P., BA   Sr. Lectr.
Tilley, I., MSc PhD   Reader
Turnbull, D. K., BA MSc   Sr. Lectr.
Vellam, Iwona, BA   Sr. Lectr.
White, G. K., MA   Sr. Lectr.
Williams, D. E., BA   Sr. Lectr.
Williams, L. D., BSc BA MBA   Principal Lectr.
Yeshin, A. D., BScComm BSc(Econ)   Sr. Lectr.

Chemical and Life Sciences

Fax: (0181) 331 8305
Barnes, J. D., BSc PhD   Sr. Lectr.
Blackburn, R., MSc PhD, FLS   Sr. Lectr.
Briggs, Elizabeth M., BSc PhD,
  FRSChem   Principal Lectr.
Brown, G. W., BSc PhD, FRSChem   Sr. Lectr.
Bruce, I. J., MSc PhD   Prof.
Charlwood, Katherine A., BSc PhD   Sr. Lectr.
Chowdhry, B. Z., MSc PhD   Prof.
Chowdrey, C., BSc PhD   Sr. Lectr.
Deane, R., BSc PhD   Reader
Edwards, M., MSc   Sr. Lectr.
Evans, I. H., MSc PhD   Reader
Goss-Sampson, M. A., MA PhD   Sr. Lectr.
Hannaford, A. J., BSc PhD, FRSChem   Sr.
  Lectr.
Harvey, Patricia J., BSc PhD   Reader
Henson, Rev. R. C., BSc PhD   Principal Lectr.

Marshall, R. A. G., MA PhD   Sr. Lectr.
Metcalfe, E., BSc PhD, FRSChem   Prof.; Head*
Moulton, Ruth J., BA PhD   Sr. Lectr.
Newbery, J. E., BSc MA PhD,
  FRSChem   Principal Lectr.
Peakin, G. J., BSc PhD   Principal Lectr.
Prashad, D. N., BSc PhD   Reader
Riby, P. J., BSc PhD   Sr. Lectr.
Rogers, V., BSc PhD   Sr. Lectr.
Savoy, L., BA PhD   Sr. Lectr.
Smith, A. R. W., BSc PhD   Reader
Thomas, M. J. K., BSc PhD   Sr. Lectr.
Thomas, R., PhD   Sr. Lectr.
Todd, M., BSc PhD   Sr. Lectr.
Vecht, A., MSc, FGS, FIP, FRSChem   Prof.
Vidgeon, E. A., PhD   Sr. Lectr.
Whittle, S. J., BSc PhD   Sr. Lectr.
Withnall, R., MA MSc PhD   Sr. Lectr.

Computing and Mathematical Sciences

Fax: (0181) 331 8665
Ackroyd, A., MA MSc   Sr. Lectr.
Ades, Y., MSc   Sr. Lectr.
Agha, M., BA MSc PhD   Principal Lectr.
Al-Zobadie, A., MSc PhD   Sr. Lectr.
Bacon, Elizabeth A., BSc PhD   Sr. Lectr.
Bailey, C. J., BSc PhD   Sr. Lectr.
Bramwell, M. C., MSc   Sr. Lectr.
Chadwick, D. R., BSc   Sr. Lectr.
Clipsham, P. S., BSc   Sr. Lectr.
Cowell, D. F., BSc PhD   Sr. Lectr.
Cross, M., PhD DSc, FIMA   Prof.
Edwards, D., BSc PhD   Sr. Lectr.
Everett, M. G., BSc MSc DPhil   Prof.; Head*
Fedorec, A. M., BSc   Sr. Lectr.
Finney, Kate, MSc   Sr. Lectr.
Fryer, M., BSc   Principal Lectr.
Galea, E., BSc PhD   Prof.
Gates, J., MSc PhD   Sr. Lectr.
Hodges, L. C., MSc   Sr. Lectr.
Hudson, M., BA MSc(Econ)   Sr. Manager/
  Principal Lectr.
Ibrahim, M., MSc   Principal Lectr.
Jeffers, J.   Visiting Prof.
Jolliffe, Flavia R., BSc   Sr. Lectr.
Knight, B., BA MSc PhD   Prof.
Knight, Joan, BEd MSc   Sr. Lectr.
Koulopoulos, C., MSc PhD   Sr. Lectr.
Lai, C.-H., BSc PhD, FIMA   Sr. Lectr.
Livadas, Lelia, MSc   Sr. Lectr.
Lynch, D., BA MSc   Sr. Lectr.
Major, Elaine, BSc   Sr. Lectr.
Malcolm, Jan M., BSc   Sr. Lectr.
Mann, A. J. S., MA   Sr. Lectr.
McKenzie, Sati, MSc PhD   Sr. Lectr.
Morris, P. N., MSc   Sr. Lectr.
Patel, M. K., MSc PhD   Reader
Patel, Swatee, MSc   Sr. Lectr.
Pericleous, K., BSc PhD   Prof.
Perry, J.   Visiting Prof.
Planitz, M., BA MSc PhD, FIMA   Sr. Lectr.
Rennolls, K., MSc   Prof.
Rima, Monique   Sr. Lectr.
Soper, A. J., BA MSc PhD   Sr. Lectr.
Stanley, A. J., BA MSc   Sr. Lectr.
Strusevich, V., PhD   Reader
Tambyrajah, A., BSc PhD   Principal Lectr.
Tyler, Francine M., BSc PhD   Principal Lectr.
Tyler, T. F., MSc   Sr. Lectr.
Windall, G., BSc PhD   Sr. Lectr.
Woollard, C. C., BSc PhD   Principal Lectr.

Construction Management, see Land and
  Construcn. Management

Earth and Environmental Sciences

Baxter, A. N., BSc PhD, FGS   Prof., Earth
  Sciences; Head*
Bussell, M. A., BA PhD, FGS   Principal Lectr.
Carey, Paula J., BSc PhD, FGS   Principal Lectr.
Coker, P. D., BSc MPhil PhD   Sr. Lectr.
Doyle, P., BSc PhD, FGS   Reader
Edwards, S., BSc PhD, FGS   Sr. Lectr.
Fisher, B. E. A., MA PhD   Res. Prof.
Gale, A. S., BSc PhD, FGS   Prof., Geology
George, G. T., BSc PhD, FGS   Sr. Lectr.
Grindrod, A. J., BSc, FGS   Sr. Lectr.
Harvey, Katherine, BA PhD   Sr. Lectr.

Helm, D. G., BSc PhD   Principal Lectr.
Horne, D. J., MSc PhD, FGS   Reader
Jones, P. C., BA PhD   Sr. Lectr.
Key, C. H., BSc PhD   Sr. Lectr.
King, R. M., BSc PhD   Sr. Lectr.
Leharne, S. A., BSc PhD   Principal Lectr.
Manby, G. M., BSc PhD   Reader
Merritt, Q.   Sr. Lectr.
Platten, I. M., BSc PhD, FGS   Sr. Lectr.
Scott, R. A. M., BSc PhD   Sr. Lectr.
Simon, R., MSc PhD   Sr. Lectr.

Education, see also Post Compulsory Educn.
  and Trg.

Tel: (0181) 331 9500 *Fax:* (0181) 331 9504
Austin, R. L., PhD   Sr. Lectr.
Barnes, T. J., MA   Principal Lectr.
Barron, P. D., BSc BEd   Sr. Lectr.
Bland, R., BA   Sr. Lectr.
Brook, D. J. P., MA MSc   Sr. Lectr.
Browne, G. J. M., BSc MA   Sr. Lectr.
Cobb, D. H., MA   Sr. Lectr.
Coggins, G. F., BSc MA, FIMA   Sr. Lectr.
Davies, J. L., BA   Sr. Lectr.
Dolden, R. M., BSc   Sr. Lectr.
Draper, M. W., MA   Principal Lectr.
Driscoll, T. J., MA(Ed)   Sr. Lectr.
Durrell, J., BEd   Sr. Lectr.
Farmer, G. T., BA MSc MBA   Principal Lectr.
Fisher, F. G., MEd   Principal Lectr.
Gerrish, Elizabeth, BEd   Sr. Lectr.
Gibson, A. J., MEd   Sr. Lectr.
Goddard, W. D., MEd MPhil   Sr. Lectr.
Golden, J. W., BHum   Sr. Lectr.
Good, K. W., BEd   Sr. Lectr.
Harland, Linda A., BA MEd   Principal Lectr.
Hobson, Mollie, MA   Sr. Lectr.
Huish, Barbara A.   Sr. Lectr.
Janikoun, Jan K., BEd MBA   Sr. Lectr.
Kinchington, Francia, MA BEd   Sr. Lectr.
Lloyd, Christine M., BEd MA PhD   Sr. Lectr.
Mayes, Jo, MSc   Sr. Lectr.
Momen, A., MA   Sr. Lectr.
Murphy, C. T., BSc PhD   Sr. Lectr.
Peck, Joan, BSc   Sr. Lectr.
Reeves, C. G., BHum MEd   Sr. Lectr.
Robertson, Judith A., MA   Sr. Lectr.
Sanders, Pat G., MA   Sr. Lectr.
Sharp, M. W., BEd   Sr. Lectr.
Sheath, G. V., BA MSc   Sr. Lectr.
Smith, Penny A., BEd   Sr. Lectr.
Springate, D. T., BSc MEd   Sr. Lectr.
Steele, Suzanna, BEd MA   Sr. Lectr.
Street-Porter, Rosalind, BA   Principal Lectr.
Townsend, Ruth E., BA   Sr. Lectr.
Webster, K., BA MA   Sr. Lectr.
Wright, M. W., MSc   Sr. Lectr.
Young, R. M., MA MSc   Principal Lectr.
Vacant Posts: Head*

Engineering

Tel: (0181) 331 8600 *Fax:* (0181) 331 8605
Amadi-Echendu, J. E., MSc DPhil   Sr. Lectr.
Ashenden, S. J., BSc PhD   Sr. Lectr.
Barnes, R. N., BScEng   Principal Lectr.
Bright, R. E., BScEng   Sr. Lectr.
Ford, M.   Sr. Lectr.
May, C. A., MSc PhD   Sr. Lectr.
Mehdian, M., MSc PhD   Sr. Lectr.
Reed, R. A., BSc PhD   Prof.; Head*
Seals, R. C., BSc PhD   Principal Lectr.
Smith, G. R., BSc MPhil   Sr. Lectr.
Smith, M. J., MSc   Sr. Lectr.
Vaezi-Nejad, S. M., BScEng MSc PhD   Reader
Whapshott, Grazyna F., MSc   Sr. Lectr.
Yan, Y., BEng MSc PhD   Sr. Lectr.

Health

Tel: (0181) 331 9150 *Fax:* (0181) 331 9160
Barry-Shevlin, Patsy   Principal Lectr., Nursing
Beeby, Jayne, BSc   Sr. Lectr., Nursing
Billington, Mary, BA   Sr. Lectr., Midwifery
Borthwick, Hazel, BSc   Sr. Lectr., Nursing
Bruneau, B., BA   Sr. Lectr., Health and Social
  Care
Chojnacka, Irena   Sr. Lectr., Nursing
Chummun, Harry, BSc   Sr. Lectr., Nursing
Clawson, Lynne, BSc   Sr. Lectr., Midwifery

Cleaver, Karen, BEd MSc   Principal Lectr., Nursing
Coopamah, Seenee   Sr. Lectr., Nursing
Crapnell, Denis, BEd MSc   Principal Lectr., Nursing
Dalton-O'Connor, Ann   Sr. Lectr., Nursing
Dass, Luchuman   Principal Lectr., Nursing
Delaney, Ros, BSc   Sr. Lectr., Midwifery
Downie, Carol, MSc   Principal Lectr., Health and Social Care
Freeman, Susan, BA   Principal Lectr., Health and Social Care
Fuller, Liz, BA   Sr. Lectr., Nursing
Gousy, Mamood, BEd MSc   Principal Lectr., Nursing
Graham, Lesley, BSc   Sr. Lectr., Nursing
Hackman, Sam, MA   Sr. Lectr., Health and Social Care
Haulkhory, Ram, BEd   Sr. Lectr., Nursing
Heptinstall, Tina, BSc   Sr. Lectr., Midwifery
Holliday, Mary, MA   Sr. Lectr., Midwifery
Hoppin, Beverley, BEd MSc   Sr. Lectr., Health and Social Care
Jordan, Gillian, BA MSc   Sr. Lectr., Health and Social Care
Jumnoodoo, Boni, BEd MA   Principal Lectr., Health and Social Care
Lahiff, John, BSc   Principal Lectr., Nursing
Lawes, Chew Yeen, MA   Principal Lectr., Midwifery
Le Rolland, Pat A., BA   Principal Lectr., Health and Social Care
Luchman, Anita   Sr. Lectr., Nursing
Maharajh, Asha, MSc   Sr. Lectr., Nursing
Marques, Jo   Principal Lectr., Nursing
Meek, Rhona, BA   Sr. Lectr., Nursing
Morey, Sally   Sr. Lectr., Nursing
Mounty, Maureen, BSc   Sr. Lectr., Nursing
Nickson, Caroline, BA   Principal Lectr., Midwifery
Ootim, Billy, BSc MSc   Sr. Lectr., Health and Social Care
Parker, David, BN MA   Principal Lectr., Nursing
Pass, Patricia, BSc   Principal Lectr., Health and Social Care
Peters, Randolph, BSc   Sr. Lectr., Nursing
Poligadoo, Appannah, BEd MA   Principal Lectr., Nursing
Pope, Rosemary, BSc PhD   Principal Lectr., Health and Social Care
Ramnawaz, Gary, MSc   Sr. Lectr., Health and Social Care
Ramnawaz, Sheila, BA   Sr. Lectr., Nursing
Redfern, Morag   Sr. Lectr., Nursing
Reuyl, Liz, MA   Sr. Lectr., Health and Social Care
Rogers, John, BSc   Sr. Lectr., Nursing
Rose, Gwen, BA   Sr. Lectr., Nursing
Rose, Pat, BSc MSc   Sr. Lectr., Nursing
Rumley, Mandy, BA MSc   Sr. Lectr., Nursing
Seamons, Sue   Sr. Lectr., Health and Social Care
Spencer, Lynne, MA(Ed)   Sr. Lectr., Midwifery
Spittles, Heather, BSc   Principal Lectr., Nursing
Steele, Dianne   Sr. Lectr., Midwifery
Sumoreeah, Lyn   Principal Lectr., Nursing
Sutton, Paul, BA   Sr. Lectr., Nursing
Theodore, Andre, BSc MSc   Sr. Lectr., Nursing
Thorne, Linda, MA   Principal Lectr., Health and Social Care
Tiran, Denise   Principal Lectr., Health and Social Care
Veeramah, Ven, BSc MSc(Econ) MSc(SocRes)   Principal Lectr., Health and Social Care
Warburton, Judy   Principal Lectr., Health and Social Care
Woodward, Lynn, MA   Sr. Lectr., Health and Social Care

Humanities

Tel: (0181) 331 8988 Fax: (0181) 331 8805
Alsford, M., BA PhD   Sr. Lectr.
Alsford, Sally, BA PhD   Sr. Lectr.
Brown, Carolyn M. H., MA PhD   Sr. Lectr.
Campbell, N., MA PhD   Sr. Lectr.

Cannon, T. G., BA MSc MPhil   Reader
Cooper, T. J., BLitt MA PhD   Sr. Lectr.
Dawson, A., BScEcon PhD   Sr. Lectr.
Duke, F., MA MSc   Principal Lectr.
Dunne, J., MA PhD   Sr. Lectr.
Foster, A. J., BA MScEcon PhD   Reader
Geraghty, D. M., BA MSc   Sr. Lectr.
Golding, S., MA PhD   Reader
Goodger, B. C., BScEcon PhD   Sr. Lectr.
Grayson, Gail, BA MPhil   Sr. Lectr.
Humm, P., BA MPhil   Sr. Lectr.
Jenkins, G. P. W., MA   Sr. Lectr.
John, Angela V., MA PhD   Prof.
Joyce, Vicky, MA PhD   Sr. Lectr.
Leach, Bridget, MA   Sr. Lectr.
Leggett, Denise, BA MEd   Sr. Lectr.
Lindop, F. J., BA MPhil   Sr. Lectr.
Mendes, J. P., BA PhD   Sr. Lectr.
Partridge, A. J., BA PhD   Principal Lectr.
Ryan, M. C., MA   Prof.
Stigant, E. P., BA MA   Head*
Williams, J. R., BA DPhil   Reader
Wingrove, P. A., BA MAEcon   Sr. Lectr.
Woodhead, D. J., BA MAEcon PhD   Principal Lectr.
Zell, M. L., MA PhD   Sr. Lectr.

Land and Construction Management

Tel: (0181) 331 9330 Fax: (0181) 331 9305
Allan, S., MSc   Principal Lectr.
Anderson, L. A., BSc, FRICS   Head*
Balchin, P., BSc(Econ) PhD   Reader
Bull, G., MA DPhil   Sr. Lectr.
Burchess, D.   Sr. Lectr.
Burrows, C., BSc   Sr. Lectr.
Bushell, Fiona L., BSc   Sr. Lectr.
Coffey, M., MSc, FRICS   Sr. Lectr.
Cooper, R. A., BA   Sr. Lectr.
Dalton, P. M., BSc   Principal Lectr.
Davis, Maxine, BSc MA   Sr. Lectr.
Degroote, K. M., MSc   Principal Lectr.
Eagle, M. J., BSc   Sr. Lectr.
Ewin, G., MSc, FRICS   Sr. Lectr.
Falconer, E., MSc   Principal Lectr.
Fantie, Shirley, BSc   Sr. Lectr.
Forrester, Pauline M., MA   Sr. Lectr.
Frankland, J. W., MSc   Sr. Lectr.
Grant, A., BSc   Sr. Lectr.
Habgood, Veronica A., MSc   Sr. Academic/Principal Lectr.
Heath, Samantha, BSc   Sr. Lectr.
Holder, A. T., BSc MBA PhD   Sr. Lectr.
Isaac, D. W. L., BSc(Econ) MSc, FRICS   Prof.
Johnson, K. P., MSc, FRICS   Principal Lectr.
Jones, K. G., BSc PhD   Sr. Lectr.
Jones, R., FRICS   Sr. Lectr.
Lewis, G. M., MSc PhD   Sr. Lectr.
Mandlik, J. E., BSc(Eng)   Sr. Lectr.
Manning, J., PhD   Principal Lectr.
McDonald, T., BSc   Principal Lectr.
McKillop, D., MSc MBA   Sr. Lectr.
Parsons, G., BSc(EstMan) MSc   Principal Lectr.
Rahman, S., MAArch   Sr. Lectr.
Rhoden, M. D., MA   Sr. Lectr.
Watson, J., MA   Sr. Lectr.

Landscape, see Archit. and Landscape

Languages Unit

De Peon Davila, J. L., MA   Sr. Lectr.
Delbourgo, Francoise, BA   Sr. Lectr.
Dold, Brigitte, MA   Sr. Lectr.
Whitehead, Margaret, BA   Sr. Lectr.

Law

Tel: (0181) 331 9583 Fax: (0181) 331 8473
Barrett, F. H., LLB   Sr. Lectr.
Chambers, D., MA MSc DPhil   Prof.; Head*
Dobson, P., LLB   Visiting Prof.
Everett, K., LLB   Sr. Lectr.
Fitzgerald, M. G., LLB   Sr. Lectr.
French, M. P., LLM   Principal Lectr.
Gaborak, Margaret J., LLM   Sr. Lectr.
Hacking, Susan, MA   Sr. Lectr.
Harding, G., LLM PhD   Visiting Prof.
Horder, J. R., BSc DPhil   Sr. Lectr.
Lloyd, S., LLB   Sr. Lectr.
Ottley, M., LLM   Sr. Lectr.

Pawlowski, M., LLB   Sr. Lectr.
Phillips, E. P., LLB   Principal Lectr.
Sankar, R., LLB   Sr. Lectr.
Shields, G., BSc LLM   Sr. Lectr.
Taylor, M. L., LLM   Sr. Lectr.
Vaughan, P., LLB

Mathematical Sciences, see Computing and Mathl. Scis.

Midwifery, see Health

Nursing, see Health

Post Compulsory Education and Training

Tel: (0181) 331 9236 Fax: (0181) 331 9235
Atkinson, C., BA MEd   Sr. Lectr.
Bailey, W., MA   Principal Lectr.
Baldry, R., BScEng   Sr. Lectr.
Boyer, R., MEd   Principal Lectr.
Bradley, S., BEd   Sr. Lectr.
Brophy, J., MEd MSc PhD   Principal Lectr.
Burton, Julia, BSc MEd   Sr. Lectr.
Butterworth, Chris, BA MAEd   Sr. Lectr.
Chandler, Barbara, MA   Sr. Lectr.
Cotton, Julie, BSc MA   Principal Lectr.
Cox, Anne, BSc MA   Sr. Lectr.
Craft, M., PhD   Res. Prof.
Garner, L., BA PhD   Sr. Lectr.
Grant, Pat, MSc BEd   Sr. Lectr.
Griffin, Anne, BA MAEd   Principal Lectr.
Hall, D., BScEcon   Principal Lectr.
Hall, Lynda, BA   Sr. Lectr.
Jones, Diana, MA BEd   Sr. Lectr.
Lewis, D. A., BA MSc   Principal Lectr.
Marsh, K., MA   Sr. Lectr.
McNay, Iain, BA   Prof.; Head*
Parsons, V., BA MSc MEd, FIMA   Sr. Lectr.
Quinn, F., BA MSc   Principal Lectr.
Robson, Jocelyn, MA PhD   Principal Lectr.
Ryan, M., MEd   Sr. Lectr.
Webb, E., MA MEd   Sr. Lectr.
Wood, K., BSc MA MPhil   Sr. Lectr.

Social Sciences

Tel: (0181) 331 8902 Fax: (0181) 331 8905
Acton, T. A., MA DPhil   Reader
Anthias, Floya, MScSoc PhD   Prof.
Arora, K. C., BA BSc MA MPhil   Sr. Lectr.
Ayres, R. I., BAEcon MScEcon PhD   Principal Lectr.
Caffrey, Susan, MScSoc   Sr. Lectr.
Caldwell, Lesley K., MA PhD   Sr. Lectr.
Corney, Rosalind, MSc PhD   Prof.
Demetre, J. D., BA PhD   Sr. Lectr.
Fox, R. G., BA   Sr. Lectr.
Freeman, A., BSc MA   Sr. Lectr.
Hood-Williams, J., BEd MA   Sr. Lectr.
Kelly, M. P. T., BA MPhil PhD   Prof.; Head*
Kitromilides, J., BScEcon MAEcon PhD   Principal Lectr.
Megarry, T. W., BSc MA   Sr. Lectr.
Oliver, M. J., BA PhD   Prof.
Riley, J., MScEcon   Sr. Lectr.
Roarty, M. J., BA MSc   Sr. Lectr.
Yuval-Davis, Nira, MA DPhil   Prof.

CONTACT OFFICERS

Academic affairs. Academic Registrar: Rose, Christine H., MSc
Accommodation. Services Manager: Chandler, J., BA
Admissions (first degree). Fisher, Peter
Admissions (higher degree). Fisher, Peter
Adult/continuing education. Access and Progression Co-ordinator: Kumrai, Rajni
Alumni. Stephenson, Martin, BA
Archives. Assistant Academic Registrar: Hill, Henry
Careers. Senior Careers Adviser: Humphrys, Gay, BA MA
Computing services. Director of Computing Services: Cooper, G. A., MSc
Consultancy services. Director of Commercial Development: Plant, J. E., BSc, FRSChem

Credit transfer. Director of Academic Development: Allen, Robert M., BA(Econ) PhD

Development/fund-raising. Director of Commercial Development: Plant, J. E., BSc, FRSChem

Equal opportunities. Director of Personnel: Brockett, R. J., BA MA

Estates and buildings/works and services. Director of Estates and Building Services: Adams, Susan J.

Examinations. Assessment and Examinations Officer: Dineen, Yvonne, PhD

Finance. Director of Finance: Denton, R.

General enquiries. Secretary to the University: Charles, J. M., MA

Health services. Head of Student Services: Street-Porter, Rosalind, BA

Industrial liaison. Director of Commercial Development: Plant, J. E., BSc, FRSChem

International office. Wallis, Steve E., BSc MSc

Library (chief librarian). University Librarian: Heathcote, D. A., MA

Minorities/disadvantaged groups. Head of Student Services: Street-Porter, Rosalind, BA

Ombudsperson. Academic Registrar: Rose, Christine H., MSc

Personnel/human resources. Director of Personnel: Brockett, R. J., BA MA

Public relations, information and marketing. Head of Public Relations Unit: Jones, Caron

Publications. Head of Public Relations Unit: Jones, Caron

Publications. Director of University Press: Seymour, C., BSc PhD

Purchasing. Director of Finance: Denton, R.

Quality assurance and accreditation. Pro-Vice-Chancellor: Humphreys, John, MSc MEd

Research. Director of Research: Cross, Prof. M., PhD DSc, FIMA

Safety. Safety Advisor: Bernard, Bronwen, BSc

Scholarships, awards, loans. Stevenson, May

Schools liaison. School and College Liaison Officer: Burrows, Brigitte S.

Security. Security Manager: Checkley, D. R., LLB

Sport and recreation. Director of Estates and Building Services: Adams, Susan J.

Sport and recreation. Student Union Sports Officer: Fitzgerald, Clare

Staff development and training. Director of Personnel: Brockett, R. J., BA MA

Student welfare/counselling. Head of Student Services: Street-Porter, Rosalind, BA

Student welfare/counselling. Head of Counselling Services: Stein, Suzannah

Students from other countries. Dean, Dartway: Wills, Prof. D. J., MPhil, FRICS

Students from other countries. Dean, Combined Studies: Spence, Mary F., BA MBA

Students with disabilities. Head of Student Services: Street-Porter, Rosalind, BA

University press. Director of University Press: Seymour, C., BSc PhD

[Information supplied by the institution as at July 1998, and edited by the ACU]

HERIOT-WATT UNIVERSITY

Incorporated by Royal Charter 1966; originally established (1821) as Edinburgh School of Arts

Member of the Association of Commonwealth Universities

Postal Address: Edinburgh, Scotland EH14 4AS
Telephone: (0131) 449 5111 **Fax**: (0131) 449 5153 **WWW**: http://www.hw.ac.uk
E-mail formula: initials.surname@hw.ac.uk

CHANCELLOR—Mackay of Clashfern, The Rt. Hon. The Lord, BA Camb., LLB Edin., MA Edin., Hon. LLD Dund., Hon. LLD Strath., Hon. LLD Aberd., Hon. LLD St And., Hon. LLD Camb., Hon. LLD Virginia, Hon. LLD Newcastle(UK), Hon. DUniv, Hon. FRCSEd, Hon. FICE, FRSEd

PRINCIPAL AND VICE-CHANCELLOR*—Archer, Prof. John S., BSc City(UK), PhD Lond., FEng, FRSEd

VICE-PRINCIPAL—Brown, Prof. Charles M., BSc Birm., PhD Birm., DSc Birm., FIBiol, FRSEd

ASSISTANT PRINCIPAL (STUDENT ADMISSIONS AND RESEARCH ASSESSMENT EXERCISE STRATEGY)—O'Farrell, Prof. P. N., BA Trinity(Dub.), PhD Trinity(Dub.)

ASSISTANT PRINCIPAL (LEARNING STRATEGIES)—Leitch, Prof. R. R., BSc PhD, FIEE

ASSISTANT PRINCIPAL (EXTERNAL)—Owen, Prof. D. G., BD Lond., MA Camb., PhD Camb., FICE

CHAIRMAN OF COURT—Brown, E., LLB St And., MA St And.

SECRETARY OF THE UNIVERSITY‡—Wilson, P. L., BSc Glas., MA Lond.

DIRECTOR OF FINANCE—Paterson, Stephen L. L., BA H-W

LIBRARIAN—Breaks, Michael L., BA Leeds

GENERAL INFORMATION

History. The university was founded in 1966; it traces its origins back to the Edinburgh School of Arts established in 1821.

Admission to first degree courses (see also United Kingdom Introduction). Through Universities and Colleges Admissions Service (UCAS). Normally Scottish Certificate of Education (SCE) Highers, General Certificate of Education (GCE) A levels or Irish Leaving Certificate. Further education qualifications also accepted; applications from mature students encouraged.
International students: contact the university's international office.

First Degrees. BA, BSc, MChem, MEng, MPhys.

Higher Degrees. MBA, MEng, MSc, MTM (technology management), MPhil, PhD.

Language of Instruction. English. Short courses in English as a foreign language available.

Libraries. 111,000 volumes; 1500 periodicals.

Fees (1997–98; annual). Undergraduate: £750 (science and management, except physics); £1600 (engineering and physics). Postgraduate: £2400 (home/EC students); £6500–8500 (international students).

Academic Awards (1996–97). Fifty awards ranging in value from fees-only to full scholarship.

Academic Year (1998–99). Three terms: 5 October–12 December; 12 January–20 March; 20 April–26 June.

Income (1996–97). Total, £64,784,000.

FACULTIES/SCHOOLS

Art and Design
Dean: Docherty, Michael

Economic and Social Studies
Dean: Weetman, Prof. Pauline, BA Oxf., BSc(Econ) Lond., PhD Glas.

Engineering
Dean: Owen, Prof. D. G., BD Lond., MA Camb., PhD Camb., FICE

Environmental Studies
Dean: Anderson, Ernie

Science
Dean: McCutcheon, Prof. J. J., CBE, MA Camb., DSc Liv., PhD, FFA, FRSEd

Textiles
Tel: (01896) 753351 Fax: (01896) 758965
Dean: Brydon, Donald L., BSc St And., PhD St And., FRSChem

ACADEMIC UNITS

Accountancy, see under Management, Sch. of

Actuarial Mathematics and Statistics
Tel: (0131) 451 3201 Fax: (0131) 451 3249
Currie, I. D., BSc St And., PhD H-W Sr. Lectr.

Macdonald, A. S., BSc *Glas.*, PhD *H-W*,
FFA   Sr. Lectr.
McCutcheon, J. J., CBE, MA *Camb.*, DSc *Liv.*,
PhD, FFA, FRSEd   Prof., Actuarial Studies
Mollison, D., MA *Camb.*, PhD *Camb.*, ScD
Camb.   Prof., Applied Probability
Scott, W. A., MA *Aberd.*, PhD *Dund.*, FFA   Sr.
Lectr.
Waters, H. R., MA *Oxf.*, DPhil *Oxf.*, FIA   Prof.;
Head*
Wilkie, A. D., MA *Camb.*, FFA, FIA   Hon.
Prof.†
Zachary, S., MA *Camb.*, PhD *Durh.*   Sr. Lectr.
Research: mortality studies; permanent health
insurance; risk theory; statistical education

Architecture, School of, see Edinburgh
College of Art

Art, Edinburgh College of, see below

Biological Sciences

Tel: (0131) 451 3187 Fax: (0131) 451 3009
Austin, B., BSc *Newcastle(UK)*, PhD *Newcastle(UK)*,
DSc *H-W*   Prof.
Bamforth, C. W., BSc PhD DSc   Indust. Prof.
Brown, Charles M., BSc *Birm.*, PhD *Birm.*, DSc
Birm., FIBiol, FRSEd   Prof., Microbiology
Campbell, I., BSc *Edin.*, PhD *Edin.*   Sr. Lectr.
Catley, B. J., MA *Oxf.*, PhD *Lond.*   Sr. Lectr.
Kingston, P. F., BSc *Lond.*   Sr. Lectr.
Mitchell, W. J., BSc *Aberd.*, PhD *Aberd.*   Sr.
Lectr.
Moore, C. G., BSc *Liv.*, PhD *Liv.*   Sr. Lectr.
Palmer, G. H. O., BSc *Leic.*, PhD *Edin.*,
DSc   Prof.
Priest, F. G., BSc *Newcastle(UK)*, PhD *Birm.*, DSc
H-W   Prof.; Head*
Slaughter, J. C., BSc *Liv.*, PhD *E.Anglia*,
DSc   Reader
Stark, J. R., BSc *H-W*, PhD *Edin.*, DSc *H-W*   Sr.
Lectr.†
Stewart, G. G., BSc *Wales*, PhD *Wales*, DSc
Bath   Prof.
Wilkinson, M., BSc *Liv.*, PhD *Liv.*   Sr. Lectr.
Research: brewing and distilling; environmental
biology; marine ecology; microbial
physiology; molecular biology

Building Engineering, see Engin., Bldg., and
Surv.

Business Organisation, see under
Management, Sch. of

Chemistry

Tel: (0131) 451 3217 Fax: (0131) 451 3180
Bailey, P. D., MA *Oxf.*, DPhil *Oxf.*,
FRSChem   Prof., Organic Chemistry
Cowie, J. M. G., BSc *Edin.*, PhD *Edin.*, DSc *Edin.*,
FRSChem, FRSEd   Prof., Chemistry of
Materials
Davidson, J. L., BSc *CNAA*, PhD *Glas.*   Reader
John, P., BSc *Wales*, PhD *Wales*, DSc
Wales   Prof.
Johnson, C. A. F., BSc *Birm.*, PhD *Birm.*   Sr.
Lectr.
Lindsell, W. E., MA *Oxf.*, DPhil *Oxf.*,
FRSChem   Sr. Lectr.
McCullough, K. J., BSc *Strath.*, PhD *Strath.*   Sr.
Lectr.
Parker, J. E., BSc *Birm.*, PhD *Birm.*,
FRSChem   Sr. Lectr.
Pfab, J., DrRerNat *T.H.Munich*   Prof.
Preston, P. N., BSc *Nott.*, PhD *Manc.*,
DSc   Reader
Steedman, W., BSc *Glas.*, PhD *Glas.*,
FRSChem   Sr. Lectr.
Walker, I. C., BSc *Edin.*, PhD *Edin.*   Sr. Lectr.
Welch, Alan J., BSc *Lond.*, PhD *Lond.*,
FRSChem   Prof.; Head*
Wightman, R. H., MA *Camb.*, PhD *Camb.*,
FRSChem   Sr. Lectr.
Other Staff: 2 Sr. Lectrs.; 7 Lectrs.; 2 Lectrs.†
Research: organic synthesis of medically
important compounds; organometallic and
co-ordination chemistry; polymers and new
materials; spectroscopy

Combined Studies, Centre for

Tel: (0131) 451 3470 Fax: (0131) 451 3473
Charlesworth, S. G., MA *Camb.*   Dir.*
McAleese, R., MA PhD   Prof.
Research: cognition and learning; concept
mapping; learning skills; self-regulation

Economics, see under Management, Sch. of

Engineering, Building, and Surveying

Fax: (0131) 451 3161
Banfill, Phillip F. G., BSc *S'ton.*, PhD *Liv.*   Prof.
Cantley, W. R. B.   Indust. Prof.†
Cheesman, P. G., MSc   Sr. Lectr.
Craik, R. J. M., BSc MSc PhD   Prof.
Hinks, A. J., BSc *H-W*, MA *Salf.*, PhD
Edin.   Reader
Kelly, J. R., BSc *Aston*, MPhil *Reading*   Sr. Lectr.
Swaffield, J. A., BSc *Brist.*, MPhil *City(UK)*, PhD
City(UK)   Watson Prof., Building
Engineering; Head*
Torrance, J. S.   Indust. Prof.†
Webb, R. S., BEng *Liv.*, MSc *Lond.*   Sr. Lectr.
Research: acoustics and vibration; building
services; construction technology

Engineering, Chemical, see Engin., Mech.
and Chem.

Engineering, Civil and Offshore

Tel: (0131) 451 3143 Fax: (0131) 451 3170
Cairns, J., BSc *Glas.*, PhD *Glas.*   Sr. Lectr.
Fordyce, D. S. E., BSc MSc   Sr. Lectr.
Grant, I., BSc *Edin.*, PhD *Edin.*, FIP   Prof.,
Offshore Engineering
Haldane, D., BSc   Sr. Lectr.
Jowitt, P. W., BSc(Eng) *Lond.*, PhD *Lond.*,
FICE   Prof., Civil Engineering Systems;
Head*
Linfoot, B. T., BEng *Liv.*   Sr. Lectr.
May, I. M., BEng *Brad.*, MSc *Warw.*, PhD
Warw.   Prof., Civil Engineering
McCarter, W. J., BSc *Edin.*, PhD *Edin.*   Reader
Paul, M. A., BA *Open(UK)*, BSc *E.Anglia*, PhD
E.Anglia, FGS   Prof., Engineering and
Environmental Geology
Paxton, R. A., MBE, MSc, FICE   Hon. Prof.
Peacock, J. D., BSc *Durh.*, PhD *Durh.*,
FRSEd   Hon. Prof.†
Side, J. C., BSc *H-W*, PhD *H-W*, FRICS   Sr.
Lectr.
Walker, S., BSc *Manc.*, PhD *Manc.*   Hon. Prof.†
Wilson, A., OBE, FIP   Hon. Prof.†
Wolfram, J., BSc *Reading*, BSc *Newcastle(UK)*, PhD
Strath.   Total Oil Marine Prof., Offshore
Research and Development
Other Staff: 13 Lectrs.; 1 Sr. Res. Assoc.
Research: environmental resource management;
materials engineering; oilfield chemistry;
reliability and safety; structural engineering

Engineering, Computing and Electrical

Tel: (0131) 451 3328 Fax: (0131) 451 3327
Chantler, M. J., BSc *Glas.*, PhD *H-W*   Sr. Lectr.
Clarke, R. J., BTech *Lough.*, MSc *Lough.*, PhD
Lough., BA *Open*   Prof., Electronic
Engineering; Head*
Close, A. M., BSc *H-W*   Sr. Lectr.
Davis, R. H., BSc *Belf.*, PhD *Belf.*   Sr. Lectr.
Etherington, P. H., BA *Camb.*, MSc *H-W*   Sr.
Lectr.
Helszajn, J., OBE, DSc *H-W*, DEng *Leeds*, FEng,
FRSEd, FIEE   Prof., Microwave
Holt, P. O., BA *Iceland*, PhD *Nott.*   Sr. Lectr.
Kilgour, A. C., BSc *Glas.*, PhD *Glas.*   Prof.†,
Human Computer Interaction
Lane, D. M., BSc *H-W*, PhD *H-W*   Prof.
Leitch, R. R., BSc *H-W*, PhD *H-W*, FIEE   Prof.,
Systems Engineering
Linett, L. M., BSc MSc PhD   Reader
Michaelson, G. J., BA *Essex*, MSc *St And.*, PhD *H-
W*   Sr. Lectr.
Russell, G. T., BSc *Durh.*, PhD *Newcastle(UK)*,
FIEE   Prof., Electrical and Electronic
Engineering
Sangster, A. J., BSc(Eng) *Aberd.*, MSc *Aberd.*, PhD
Aberd., FIEE   Prof., Microwave Engineering
Wallace, A. M. F., BSc *Edin.*, PhD *Edin.*   Prof.

Williams, B. W., BSc *Adel.*, BE *Adel.*, MEngSc
Adel., PhD *Camb.*   Prof., Electrical
Engineering
Williams, M. H., BSc *Rhodes*, PhD *Rhodes*, DSc
Rhodes   Prof., Computer Science
Other Staff: 22 Lectrs.; 1 Sr. Lectr.†; 2 Lectrs.†
Vacant Posts: 1 Prof.
Research: databases and information systems;
dependable systems; intelligent systems
engineering; ocean systems engineering;
vision and image processing

Engineering, Electrical, see Engin.,
Computing and Electr.

Engineering, Mechanical and Chemical

Fax: (0131) 451 3129
Addlesee, A. J., MA *Camb.*, PhD   Sr. Lectr.
Brown, R. D., BSc *Lond.*, MSc *S'ton.*,
FIMechE   Sr. Lectr.
Cornwell, Keith J., BSc *City(UK)*, PhD *Lond.*,
DEng *H-W*, FIMechE   Prof., Engineering
Heat Transfer
Davies, J. B. C., BSc *Manc.*, MSc *H-W*, PhD *H-
W*   Sr. Lectr.
Docherty, R., BSc *Strath.*, PhD *Strath.*   Hon.
Prof.
Hartnup, G. C., BSc(Eng) *Lond.*, MPhil *Sur.*   Sr.
Lectr.
Hill, R. G., BSc *Edin.*   Sr. Lectr.
MacFarlane, A., BSc *Aberd.*   Royal Academy of
Engineering Visiting Prof.
Macpherson, S., LLB *Sheff.*   Hon. Prof.
Muller, W. H., DrRerNat *Berlin*   Reader
Murray, J. L., BSc MSc, FIMechE   Prof. Emer.,
Computer-Aided Engineering
Murray, K. R., BSc   Sr. Lectr.
Ni, X.-W., BSc *Chongqing*, PhD *Leeds*   Sr. Lectr.
Oliver, R., BSc *H-W*, PhD *H-W*,
FIChemE   Hon. Prof.
Reay, D. A., MSc *Brist.*, BSc   Visiting Prof.†
Reuben, R. L., BSc *Strath.*, PhD *Open(UK)*   Prof.,
Materials Engineering
Roberts, K. J., BSc *CNAA*, PhD *CNAA*, FIChemE,
FRSChem   Prof., Chemical Processing
Simmons, J. E. L., BSc *Birm.*, PhD *Camb.*, FIEE,
FIMechE   Prof., Mechanical Engineering;
Head*
Steel, J. A., BSc *H-W*, MSc *H-W*, PhD *H-W*   Sr.
Lectr.
Topping, B. H. V., BSc *City(UK)*, PhD *City(UK)*,
FIMA   Prof., Computational Mechanics
Waldie, B., BSc *Durh.*, PhD *Newcastle(UK)*,
FIChemE   Prof., Chemical and Offshore
Process Engineering
Other Staff: 17 Lectrs.; 3 Academic-Related
Staff; 18 Res. Assocs.
Vacant Posts: 1 Prof.
Research: computational mechanics; engineering
design, manufacture and assembly;
molecular and interface engineering;
surfaces, materials and monitoring;
thermodynamics, heat transfer and process
fluid mechanics

Engineering, Offshore, see Engin., Civil
and Offshore

Engineering, Petroleum

Tel: (0131) 451 3128 Fax: (0131) 451 3127
Corbett, Patrick W. M., BSc *Exe.*, MSc *Lond.*,
PhD *H-W*   Sr. Lectr.
Dake, L. P., OBE, BSc *Glas.*   Hon. Prof.†
Danesh, A., BSc *Abadan*, PhD *Manc.*   Visiting
Prof.
Davies, D., BSc *Exe.*, PhD *Exe.*   Sr. Lectr.
Everett, P., BSc *Edin.*   Hon. Prof.†
Kingston, P., BSc *Oxf.*   Hon. Indust. Prof.†
Peden, Prof. James M., BSc MEng PhD   Dir.*
Smart, B. D. G., BSc *Strath.*, PhD *Strath.*   Prof.;
Head*
Sorbie, K. S., BSc *Strath.*, DPhil *Sus.*   Prof.
Stewart, G., BSc *Edin.*, PhD *Newcastle(UK)*   Prof.†
Tehrani, A. D. H., BSc *Teheran*   Hon. Prof.†
Todd, A. C., BTech *Lough.*, PhD *Lough.*,
FIChemE   Prof.
Tweedie, J. A., BSc *Edin.*, MSc *Stir.*   Sr. Lectr.

Research: drilling and production; flow in porous media; production chemistry; reservoir description and simulation; rock mechanics

Finance, see under Management, Sch. of (Accty. and Finance)

French, see Langs.

German, see Langs.

Landscape Architecture, see Edinburgh College of Art, below

Languages
Fax: (0131) 451 3079
Halliday, J., MA St And. Sr. Lectr., Russian
Laffling, J. D., BA Brist., PhD CNAA Sr. Lectr., German
Lang, M. F., LèsL Rennes, MA Aberd., MèsL Rennes, PhD Aberd. Prof., French; Head*
Mason, I., BA Lond., PhD Lond. Prof., Interpreting and Translation
Research: computer applications; European politics; linguistics; teaching methodology; theory and practice of interpreting and translating

Management, School of
Hare, Paul G., BA Camb., DPhil Oxf. Prof.; Head*
Haslam, J., BA PhD Prof.
McKinnon, A. C., MA Aberd., MA Br.Col., PhD Lond. Prof.
Schaffer, M. E., MA Stan., MSc Lond. Prof.

Accountancy and Finance
Tel: (0131) 451 3294 Fax: (0131) 449 3008
Baillie, J., MA Glas. Hon. Prof.†
Brown, E., MA St And., LLB St And. Hon. Prof.†
Christie, A. J. M., BAcc Glas. Hon. Prof.†
Fraser, M., BCom Edin. Sr. Lectr.
Hirst, I. R. C., BA Oxf., MBA Cornell, PhD Chic. Prof., Finance
Leslie, J., BA MLitt Sr. Lectr.
Ward, J. M. Hon. Prof.†
Weetman, Pauline, BA Oxf., BSc(Econ) Lond., PhD Glas. Prof.
Research: corporate accounting; corporate finance; financial analysis; financial markets; financial reporting

Business Organisation
Fax: (0131) 451 3296
Clarkson, A. H., MA Camb., MSc Brad. Sr. Lectr.
Cooper, C. L., BS Calif., MBA Calif., MSc Manc., PhD Leeds Visiting Prof.†
Craig, V., LLB Edin. Prof.
Keenan, A., BA Strath., PhD Birm. Prof.
Shaw, W. N., BSc Strath., MBA Strath., PhD Strath. Sr. Lectr.
Tayeb, M., BA Teheran, MLitt Oxf., PhD Aston Sr. Lectr.
Wedderburn, A. A. I., MA Oxf., PhD H-W, FBPsS Prof. Fellow; Head*
Vacant Posts: 1 Prof.; 1 Lectr.
Research: business law; entrepreneurship; international business; logistics; stress management

Economics
Tel: (0131) 451 3491 Fax: (0131) 451 3498
Mair, D., MA St And., PhD Prof.
Moore, J. H., BA Camb., MSc Lond., PhD Lond. Prof.
O'Farrell, Patrick N., BA Trinity(Dub.), PhD Trinity(Dub.) Prof.
Simpson, L. D., BA Leic., MA Leic. Sr. Lectr.
Torrance, T. S., MA Aberd., PhD Edin. Sr. Lectr.
Welham, P. J., BA Leeds, PhD Leeds Sr. Lectr.
Wyatt, G. J., BA Keele, DPhil York(UK) Reader
Vacant Posts: 1 Lectr.
Research: artificial intelligence and graph presentation of economic models; business

services; development economics; economics of transition; post-Keynesian public finance

Mathematics, see also Actuarial Maths. and Stats.
Tel: (0131) 451 3229 Fax: (0131) 451 3249
Beevers, C. E., BSc Manc., PhD Manc. Prof.
Brown, K. J., BSc Aberd., PhD Dund., FRSEd Prof.
Carr, J., BSc Bath, MSc Oxf., DPhil Oxf., FRSEd Prof.
Eilbeck, J. C., BA Oxf., PhD Lanc., FIMA, FRSEd Prof., Scientific Computation
Hills, R. N., BSc Lond., PhD Lond. Reader
Howie, J., BSc St And., PhD Lond., FRSEd Prof.; Head*
Johnston, D. A., BA Camb., PhD Lond. Sr. Lectr.
Knops, R. J., BSc Nott., PhD Nott., FRSEd Prof.
Kuskin, S., MSc Moscow, PhD Russian Acad.Sc. Prof.
Lacey, Prof. A. A., MA Oxf., MSc Oxf., DPhil Oxf., FRSEd Prof.
McGuire, G. R., BSc Edin., MSc Dund., PhD Dund. Sr. Lectr.
Penrose, O., BSc Lond., PhD Camb., FIMA, FRS Prof.
Prince, A. R., MA Oxf., DPhil Oxf., MSc Col. Sr. Lectr.
Rynne, B. P., BSc Manc., PhD Dund. Reader
Sherratt, J. A., BA Camb., DPhil Oxf. Emer. Prof.
Other Staff: 11 Lectrs.; 1 Res. Assoc.; 2 Computing Officers; 1 Software Prodn. Officer; 1 Lectr.†; 2 Temp. Lectrs.
Vacant Posts: 2 Lectrs.
Research: differential equations; mathematical biology; mechanics and fluid mechanics; numerical analysis and scientific computation; pure mathematics

Physics
Tel: (0131) 451 3020 Fax: (0131) 451 3136
Abraham, E., BSc Buenos Aires, PhD Manc. Sr. Lectr.
Baker, H. J., BSc Manc., PhD Manc. Reader
Cavenett, B. C., BSc Adel., PhD Adel., FIP, FRSEd V.G. Semicon Prof., Optoelectronic Materials
Elliott, C. T., BSc Manc., PhD Manc., FRS Hon. Visiting Prof.†
Greenaway, H. H., BSc Brun., PhD Lond. Visiting Prof.
Hall, D. R., BSc Manc., MPhil Lond., PhD Case W.Reserve, FIP, FIEE, FRSEd Prof., Optoelectronics
Harrison, R. G., BSc Lond., PhD Lond., FRSEd Prof.
Jones, J. D. C., BSc Wales, PhD Wales Prof.
Kar, A. K., MSc Delhi, MSc Essex, PhD Essex Reader
Lewis, K. L., BSc Brist., PhD Brist. Visiting Prof.
MacKenzie, H. A., BSc Strath.., PhD Sr. Lectr.
Peckham, G. E., MA Camb., PhD Camb. Prof.
Pidgeon, C. R., BSc Reading, PhD Reading, FIP, FRSEd Prof., Semiconductor Physics; Head*
Prior, K. A., MA Camb., PhD Camb. Sr. Lectr.
Taghizadeh, M. R., BSc Meshed, MSc Meshed, MSc Essex, PhD Reader
Tooley, F. A. P., BSc St And., PhD Sr. Lectr.
Walker, A. C., BA Essex, MSc Essex, PhD Essex, FIP, FRSEd OCLI Prof., Modern Optics
Wherrett, B. S., BSc Reading, PhD Reading, FRSEd Prof., Theoretical Physics
Wilson, J. I. B., BSc Durh., PhD Durh. Prof.
Research: computational and theoretical physics; lasers; non-linear optics; optoelectronic computing; semiconductor physics

Planning and Housing, School of, see Edinburgh College of Art, below

Russian, see Langs.

Statistics, see Actuarial Maths. and Stats.

Surveying, see Engin., Bldg. and Surv.

Textiles, see Scottish College of Textiles, below

SPECIAL CENTRES, ETC

Brewing and Distilling, International Centre for
Tel: (0131) 451 3184 Fax: (0131) 449 7459
Stewart, Prof. Graham G., BSc Wales, PhD Bath, DSc Bath Dir.*
Research: cereals; yeast

Economic Reform and Transformation, Centre for
Tel: (0131) 451 3494 Fax: (0131) 451 3498
Hare, Prof. Paul G., BA Camb., DPhil Oxf.
Schaffer, Prof. Mark E., AB Harv., MA Stan., MSc Lond., PhD Lond.
Other Staff: 1 Lectr.; 5 Res. Assocs.
Research: economics of transition: Eastern and Central Europe, former Soviet Union and China

Edinburgh Business School
Tel: (0131) 451 3090 Fax: (0131) 451 3002
Kennedy, G., BA Strath., MSc Strath., PhD Brun. Prof. Fellow
Lothian, N., BA H-W Prof.
Lumsden, Prof. K. G., MA Edin., PhD Stan. Prof. Fellow; Dir.*
Mackay, Sir Donald, MA Edin., DUniv Stir. Prof. Fellow†
Peacock, Sir Alan, DSC, MA St And., Hon. DUniv Stir., Hon. DEcon Zür., Hon. DSc Buckingham, Hon. DSc(ScoSci) Edin., Hon. LLD St And., Hon. LLD Dund., FRSEd, FBA Hon. Res. Prof., Public Finance
Roberts, A., MBA Lond., PhD Lond., FCIS Sr. Lectr.
Scott, A., MA Edin., MSc Edin., PhD Prof. Fellow

Learning Technology Centre
Rist, Roger J., BSc Nott., PhD Nott. Dir., Academic Support and Devel.
Spence, A. A. Dir., Multi-Media Prodn.

Mathematical Sciences, International Centre for
Tel: (0131) 220 1777 Fax: (0131) 220 1053
Dart, Tracey, MA Camb. Exec. Dir.*

Orkney Water Test Centre
Tel: (01856) 70451 Fax: (01856) 70473
Hartmann, T. J. G., BSc Manager*

Technology Management, Institute of
Tel: (0131) 451 3192 Fax: (0131) 451 3193
Alexander, C., BSc Edin., MBA H-W Dir.*
Other Staff: 4 Business Execs.

EDINBURGH COLLEGE OF ART
Associated College

Architecture, School of, see also Landscape Archit.
Tel: (0131) 221 6071-2 Fax: (0131) 221 6006
Forsyth, L., BArch MSc
Napper, A., BSc Durh. Dir.*
Somerville, A., BArch, FRIAS

Design and Applied Arts, School of
Tel: (0131) 221 6121-2 Fax: (0131) 221 6004
Flavell, M. R. Sr. Lectr.
Franks, A. M. Prof.; Head*
Mitchell, L. G. Sr. Lectr.

Drawing and Painting, School of
Tel: (0131) 221 6063 Fax: (0131) 221 6003
Docherty, Michael Sr. Lectr.
Fairgrieve, J. H. Sr. Lectr.
Hodge, M. Reader

Main, K. Reader; Head*
Onwin, G. M. K. Sr. Lectr.

Humanities

Tel: (0131) 221 6141 Fax: (0131) 221 6001
King, D. I., MA Edin. Sr. Lectr.

Landscape Architecture, see also Archit., Sch. of

Tel: (0131) 221 6091-2 Fax: (0131) 221 6005
Aspinall, P. A., MSc Edin., PhD Edin. Reader
Murray, J. S., BLD MSc
Ward Thompson, C. J., BSc S'ton. Head*

Planning and Housing, School of

Tel: (0131) 221 6162 Fax: (0131) 221 6163
Bramley, Glen R., BSc Brist., PhD Brist. Prof.
Hague, C. B., MA Camb. Prof.
Lyddon, W. D. C., CB, BA Lond., Hon. DLitt, FRTPI Hon. Prof.†
Munro, M., BA MSc Prof.
Prior, A. A., MLitt Glas., BSc Head*
Rosenburg, L. S., AB Johns H., MCP Penn., PhD Penn. Sr. Lectr.

Sculpture, School of

Tel: (0131) 221 6087 Fax: (0131) 221 6001
Harvey, J. Prof.; Head*
Scott, G. W. Prof.

Visual Communication, School of

Tel: (0131) 221 6138 Fax: (0131) 221 6001
Dodds, R. G., MA Oxf., MEd Exe. Sr. Lectr.
MacGregor, B. Prof.; Head*

SCOTTISH COLLEGE OF TEXTILES

Associated College

Management Studies

Tel: (01896) 753351 Fax: (01896) 758965
Forrest, G. N., BSc Strath., MBA Strath. Sr. Lectr.
McCulloch, A. M., BSc Glas. Sr. Lectr.
Paul, R., MBA Strath. Sr. Lectr.
Taylor, C., BSc Glas. Sr. Lectr.

Textiles

Christie, R., BSc St And., PhD St And. Sr. Lectr.
Mather, R. R., BA Camb., PhD Birm. Sr. Lectr.
McInnes, I. M., BA CNAA Sr. Lectr.
McKenna, D., MSc Strath. Sr. Lectr.
Morgan, K. M., MA Camb., DPhil York(UK)
Walker, R., BA Sr. Lectr.
Walker, V., BSc Brad. Sr. Lectr.
Wardman, R. H., BTech Brad., PhD Brad. Head*

Weedall, P., BSc Hull, PhD Brad. Sr. Lectr.

CONTACT OFFICERS

Academic affairs. Vice-Principal: Brown, Prof. Charles M., BSc Birm., PhD Birm., DSc Birm., FIBiol, FRSEd
Academic affairs. Assistant Principal (Student Admissions and Research Assessment Exercise Strategy): O'Farrell, Prof. P. N., BA Trinity(Dub.), PhD Trinity(Dub.)
Accommodation. Brown, Allan, BD
Admissions (first degree). Admissions Officer: McLean, Patricia S., BA CNAA
Admissions (first degree). Director of Recruitment and Admissions: Lister, Elizabeth, BSc
Admissions (higher degree). Postgraduate Officer: Glen, Jane
Adult/continuing education. Director, Centre for Continuing Education: Inglis, Thomas A., BSc Strath., MEng
Alumni. Development and Alumni Officer: Richardson, Sandy L., MA Aberd., MBA Edin.
Archives. Archivist: Jones, Ann, BA York(UK), MArAd Liv.
Careers. Director, Careers Advisory Service: Dane, Margaret H., BA Open(UK), MA St And.
Computing services. Director, Computing Services: Rundell, David R., BSc St And., MSc
Consultancy services. Director, Unilink/ Research Grants and Contracts Office (Finance Office): Ross, I. Grant
Credit transfer. Senior Assistant Registrar: Coleman, Norma-Ann, MA St And.
Development/fund-raising. Director, Institutional Development Division: Boak, David S., BSc PhD
Estates and buildings/works and services. Director, Estate and Building Services: Kerr, Peter G.
Examinations. Examinations Officer: Gregor, K.
Finance. Vice-Principal: Brown, Prof. Charles M., BSc Birm., PhD Birm., DSc Birm., FIBiol, FRSEd
Finance. Director of Finance: Paterson, Stephen L. L., BA H-W
General enquiries. Secretary of the University: Wilson, P. L., BSc Glas., MA Lond.
Health services. Physician-in-Charge, University Health Service: de Lima, Victor, MB ChB Edin.
Industrial liaison. Director, Unilink/Research Grants and Contracts Office (Finance Office): Ross, I. Grant
International office. Director, Institutional Development Division: Boak, David S., BSc PhD

Library (chief librarian). Librarian: Breaks, Michael L., BA Leeds
Ombudsperson. Secretary of the University: Wilson, P. L., BSc Glas., MA Lond.
Personnel/human resources. Director of Personnel: Cooke, Harvey W., BSc Lond.
Public relations, information and marketing. Press Officer: Dempster, Caroline, BSc Edin.
Publications. Publications Officer: Sampson, Miles, MA Edin.
Purchasing. Supplies Officer: Allardyce, Ralph L.
Quality assurance and accreditation. Senior Assistant Registrar: Coleman, Norma-Ann, MA St And.
Research. Assistant Principal (Student Admissions and Research Assessment Exercise Strategy): O'Farrell, Prof. P. N., BA Trinity(Dub.), PhD Trinity(Dub.)
Safety. Assistant Director (Central Support Services), Estate and Building Services: Lang, Derek G. C.
Scholarships, awards, loans. Parkinson, Ralph, MA
Schools liaison. Director of Recruitment and Admissions: Lister, Elizabeth, BSc
Security. Assistant Director (Central Support Services), Estate and Building Services: Lang, Derek G. C.
Sport and recreation. Director, Sport and Exercise: Fitchett, M. A., BSc
Staff development and training. Training and Staff Development Officer: Sibbald, Anne, BA
Student welfare/counselling. Director, Student Welfare Services: McKeand, W. Donald
Students from other countries. Director, Institutional Development Division: Boak, David S., BSc PhD
Students with disabilities. Adviser for Students with Special Needs: Trotman, Ann

CAMPUS/COLLEGE HEADS

Edinburgh College of Art, Lauriston Place, Edinburgh, Scotland EH3 9DF. (Tel: (031) 221 6000.) Principal: Rowan, Prof. A. J., MA Oxf., PhD Camb., Hon. FRIAS, FRSEd
Scottish College of Textiles, Netherdale, Galashiels, Selkirkshire, Scotland TD1 3HF. (Tel: (01896) 753351; Fax: (01896) 758965.) Head of School: Brydon, Donald L., BSc St And., PhD St And., FRSChem

[Information supplied by the institution as at 22 May 1998, and edited by the ACU]

UNIVERSITY OF HERTFORDSHIRE

Established 1992; previously established as Hatfield Technical College 1952, Hatfield College of Technology 1959 and Hatfield Polytechnic 1969

Member of the Association of Commonwealth Universities

Postal Address: College Lane, Hatfield, Hertfordshire, England AL10 9AB
Telephone: (01707) 284000 **Fax**: (01707) 284115 **Telex**: 262413 **WWW**: http://www.herts.ac.uk
E-mail formula: initials.surname@herts.ac.uk

CHANCELLOR—MacLaurin, Lord, Hon. DUniv *Stir.*, Hon. LLD *Herts.*
PRO-CHANCELLOR AND CHAIRMAN OF BOARD OF GOVERNORS—McGown, James F.
VISITOR—Archer, Mary D., MA *Oxf.*, MA *Camb.*, PhD *Lond.*, Hon. DSc *Herts.*
VICE-CHANCELLOR*—Buxton, Prof. Neil K., MA *Aberd.*, PhD *H.-W.*
PRO-VICE-CHANCELLOR—Hanahoe, Prof. T. H. P., PhD *CNAA*, FIBiol
PRO-VICE-CHANCELLOR—Wilson, R. J. T., BSc *Reading*, MA *Lanc.*, PhD *Walden*
SECRETARY AND REGISTRAR‡—Jeffreys, Peter G., BA *Wales*, MEd *Wales*
DIRECTOR OF FINANCE—Neville, Terry M.
DIRECTOR OF LEARNING AND INFORMATION SERVICES—Wingate-Martin, Diana, BA *Lond.*

GENERAL INFORMATION

History. The institution was established in 1952 and became successively a technical college, a college of technology and a polytechnic, before receiving its university status in 1992.

The main campus is at Hatfield, 16 km north of London, with other campuses at Hertford, Watford and St Albans.

Admission to first degree courses (see also United Kingdom Introduction). Applications for full-time or sandwich first degree courses should be made through the Universities and Colleges Admissions Service (UCAS).

First Degrees (see also United Kingdom Directory to Subjects of Study). BA, BEd, BEng, BSc, LLB.

Most courses are full-time, some with a sandwich year out, and normally last for 3 or 4 years.

Higher Degrees (see also United Kingdom Directory to Subjects of Study). LLM, MA, MBA, MChem, MPhys, MRes, MPhil, PhD, DLitt, DSc, LLD.

Applicants for admission to master's degrees must normally hold an appropriate first degree with at least second class honours. MPhil, PhD: good honours or master's degree; DLitt, DSc, LLD: awarded on published work.

MPhil: 2 years full-time or 3 years part-time; PhD: 3–4 years full-time or 5–6 years part-time.

Libraries. 4060 periodicals subscribed to.

Fees (annual). Home students: £1000 (undergraduate); £2610 (postgraduate). International students: £6450–£6650 (postgraduate).

Academic Awards (1997–97). 209 awards ranging in value from £5 to £40.

Academic Year (1998–99). Two semesters: 28 September–29 January (18 weeks, integral vacation three weeks); 1 February–4 June (18 weeks, integral vacation three weeks).

Income (1997–98). Total, £85,101,000.

Statistics. Staff: 702 academic, 718 administrative. Students: full-time 8048; sandwich 5082; part-time 5475; international (non-European) 1391; 8712 men, 9894 women.

FACULTIES/SCHOOLS

Art and Design
Tel: (01707) 285301 Fax: (01707) 285312
Dean: McIntyre, C., BA *CNAA*
Secretary: Mettam, Stella

Business
Tel: (01707) 285401 Fax: (01707) 285409
Dean: Fletcher, Prof. Ben C., BA *Keele*, DPhil *Oxf.*
Secretary: Firman, Denise

Engineering and Information Sciences
Tel: (01707) 284100 Fax: (01707) 284781
Dean: Lines, Prof. Peter D., BSc *City(UK)*, MSc *Essex*, FIEE
Secretary: Carvall, Cathy

Health and Human Sciences
Tel: (01707) 284400 Fax: (01707) 284415
Dean: Turner, Paul R., BA *Oxf.*
Secretary: Smith, Wendy

Humanities and Education
Tel: (01707) 285601 Fax: (01707) 285681
Dean: Holderness, Prof. Graham, MA *Oxf.*, PhD *Sur.*, DLitt *Herts.*
Secretary: Hubbard, Hilary

Interdisciplinary Studies
Tel: (01707) 285200 Fax: (01707) 285202
Dean: Weir, Alan, BA *Keele*
Secretary: Peck, Sue

Law
Tel: (01707) 286 3211 Fax: (01707) 286 3205
Dean: Tribe, Prof. Diana, LLB *Birm.*, MEd *Manc.*
Secretary: Strange, Connie

Natural Sciences
Dean: Bardon, Prof. Keith S., BA *Wales*, PhD *Wales*
Secretary: Hawkins, Pat

ACADEMIC UNITS

Art and Arts Therapies
Fax: (01707) 285310
Adams, S. R. Sr. Lectr.
Baggaley, R. Sr. Lectr.
Brown, P., BA *CNAA* Sr. Lectr.
Byrnes, Alice Sr. Lectr.
Dalwood, Alison, BA *Newcastle(UK)*, MFA *Reading* Sr. Lectr.
Dokter, Dirkje, MSc Sr. Lectr.
Dubowski, J. K., BA *Leeds*, PhD *Leeds* Principal Lectr.
Fuller, J., BA *Lond.* Sr. Lectr.
Gersie, Alida Principal Lectr.
Glasman, Judy, BA *Lond.* Academic Manager; Head*
Johnson, S. R., BA *Sus.*, MPhil *Lond.*, DPhil *Oxf.* Sr. Lectr.
Jones, P. R., MA *Sus.* Sr. Lectr.
Lanham, R., BA *Humb.* Sr. Lectr.
Leworthy, R. Sr. Lectr.
Seaton, D. Principal Lectr.
Shortt, Linka J., BA *Lough.*, MA *Newcastle(UK)* Principal Lectr.
Smy, E. Sr. Lectr.
Wainwright, R., BA *Exe.*, MPhil *Lond.* Sr. Lectr.
Wright, M. J., BA *Liv.* Sr. Lectr.
Research: art history (design, nineteenth-century French painting, twentieth-century Soviet art); art therapies (art therapy and autism, efficacy studies in arts therapies for people with learning difficulties, story-telling and therapy, theoretical developments in drama therapy); design (design, philosophy and the diagrammatical, product design and information technology user interface, rapid prototyping); fine art (fine art and new technologies, fine art/craft interface, site-specific art

Biosciences
Fax: (01707) 285046
Bailey, D., BSc *Wales*, PhD *St And.* Sr. Lectr.
Boffey, S. A., MA *Camb.*, PhD *Camb.*, FIBiol Academic Manager
Bugeja, V., BSc *Lond.*, PhD *Lond.* Sr. Lectr.
Chissick, H. H., BPharm *Lond.*, PhD *Lond.* Sr. Lectr.
Doyle, K., BSc *Trinity(Dub.)*, PhD *Trinity(Dub.)* Sr. Lectr.
Farid, Nadir R., MB BS *Khart.*, FRCP, FACP
Fox, Rachel M., BSc *Sund.*, PhD *Sund.* Sr. Lectr.
Gaffney, Patrick J., BSc *N.U.I.*, MSc *N.U.I.*, MSc *Reading*, PhD *Ohio*
Griffiths, D. G., BSc *S'ton.*, PhD *Kent* Sr. Lectr.
Hayes, Ann, BSc *Nott.*, PhD *Lond.* Visiting Prof.
Jenkins, Margaret R., BSc *Liv.*, MSc *Warw.* Sr. Lectr.
Jones, H., BSc *Wales*, PhD *Wales* Sr. Lectr.
Le Roux, Norman, BSc *Lond.*, MSc *Newcastle(UK)* Visiting Prof.
Longstaff, A., BSc *Lond.*, PhD *Open(UK)* Sr. Lectr.
McMullan, N., BSc *Salf.*, PhD *Trinity(Dub.)* Sr. Lectr.
Parsons, Michael E., BPharm *Lond.*, PhD *Lond.* Prof.†, Pharmacy
Peterson, D. W., BA *Minn.*, PhD *Minn.* Sr. Lectr.
Slater, R. J., BSc *Leeds*, PhD *Nott.* Academic Manager
Smith, R. N., BSc *Nott.*, PhD *Nott.* Academic Manager
Stanbury, P. F., BSc *Wales*, MSc *Lond.* Principal Lectr.
Walker, J. M., BSc *Lond.*, PhD *Lond.* Prof.; Head*
Wilkinson, J., BSc *Sheff.*, PhD *Newcastle(UK)* Principal Lectr.
Williams, Susan P., BSc *Brist.*, BSc *CNAA* Sr. Lectr.
Research: medicinal chemistry; molecular biology and biotechnology; physiology and pharmacology

Business and Finance

Fax: (01707) 285455

Bromberg, M. D., BSc *Aston*, PhD *Lond.* Academic Manager
Bryant, Tina A. Principal Lectr.
Byass, Edwina Principal Lectr.
Byne-Grey, Elizabeth V., BSc *Sur.* Sr. Lectr.
Carey, Sandra, MSc *Sur.* Sr. Lectr.
Carr, N., BSc *St And.*, PhD *Exe.* Sr. Lectr.
Crimes, B., BA *W.England* Sr. Lectr.
Dunton, H. G., BA *Manc.* Principal Lectr.
Fisher, C. W., BA *CNAA* Sr. Lectr.
Forrester, J. W., MPhil *CNAA* Academic Manager; Head*
Francis, A., BA *De Mont.*, MA *Warw.* Sr. Lectr.
Gayfer, J. Principal Lectr.
Healy, Geraldine M., MSc *Lond.* Principal Lectr.
Hughes, M., BSc *Manc.* Sr. Lectr.
Johnston, S. H., BA *Belf.*, MA *CNAA* Sr. Lectr.
Kerr, E. Sr. Lectr.
Newman, P., BSc *Lond.* Sr. Lectr.
Rosier, M. J., BSc *Lond.*, MSc *City(UK)* Academic Manager
Shevlane, Nicola A., BA *Salf.* Sr. Lectr.
Smith, David, BA *Leic.*, MA *Lond.*, PhD *Lond.* Visiting Prof.
Spencer, T. Sr. Lectr.
Spurr, I. G., BA *CNAA*, MPhil *City(UK)* Principal Lectr.
Wellstead, M. C., BA *CNAA*, MSc *Lond.* Sr. Lectr.
Research: local democracy and policy-making; restructuring the Polish economy; schoolteachers' attitudes; women in the labour market in the UK and South America; workaholism and organisational culture

Computer Science

Fax: (01707) 284303

Adams, R. G., MSc *Leic.*, MSc *CNAA*, PhD *CNAA* Principal Lectr.
Ambrosiadou, Barbara, BSc *Leeds*, MSc *Manc.*, PhD *UMIST* Sr. Lectr.
Baillie, Jean, MSc *CNAA*, PhD *CNAA* Sr. Lectr.
Barrett, R., MSc *CNAA* Principal Lectr.
Bateman, Andrew, BSc *Warw.* Sr. Lectr.
Berkout, Mariette, MSc *Gron.*, MSc *Herts.* Sr. Lectr.
Britton, C., BA *S'ton.*, MSc *CNAA* Principal Lectr.
Brown, J. A. F., BA *Exe.*, MSc *Sheff.* Principal Lectr.
Chapman, R. D., MSc *Sus.* Sr. Lectr.
Christianson, D. B., MSc *Well.*, DPhil *Oxf.* Academic Manager
Crouch, R., MA *CNAA* Sr. Lectr.
Davey, N., MSc *Lond.*, MSc *Brun.* Principal Lectr.
Davies, M. J., BA *Durh.* Academic Manager
Davis, J. A., BSc *Lond.*, MTech *Brun.* Academic Manager; Head*
Davis, M., MSc *CNAA* Sr. Lectr.
Davis, S. J., BA *Open(UK)*, MSc *CNAA* Sr. Lectr.
Derrick, A. J., MA *Camb.* Principal Lectr.
Dickerson, R. G., BA *E.Anglia*, MSc *Lond.* Principal Lectr.
Finlay, B. J., MA *Camb.*, MSc *Lond.* Sr. Lectr.
Frank, R. J., MSc *Lond.* Principal Lectr.
French, T. Sr. Lectr.
George, Stella J., BSc *Nott.*, PhD *Exe.* Sr. Lectr.
Hewitt, Jill, BA *E.Anglia*, MSc *CNAA* Academic Manager
Hinton, Pamela, BSc *Wales* Sr. Lectr.
Hunt, S., MSc *CNAA* Sr. Lectr.
Jefferies, Amanda, BA *Lond.*, MSc *Herts.* Sr. Lectr.
Jones, F. Sr. Lectr.
Lam, W., BSc *Salf.*, PhD *Lond.* Sr. Lectr.
Loomes, M. J., BSc *Bath*, PhD *Sur.* Prof.
Malcolm, J. A., MA *Camb.* Sr. Lectr.
Nichols, G. S., MSc *Brun.* Sr. Lectr.
Oliver, R. G., BSc *Hull*, PhD *Hull* Principal Lectr.
Pearson, D., MSc *Manc.* Sr. Lectr.
Potter, Benjamin, MA *Herts.* Sr. Lectr.
Pye, Lynette, BA *Stir.*, MSc *Cran.* Sr. Lectr.
Quick, P. C., MA *Camb.* Sr. Lectr.

Sapsford-Francis, J., MSc *CNAA* Principal Lectr.
Shankararaman, Venky, BTech *Cochin*, PhD *Strath.* Sr. Lectr.
Smith, D. E., MSc *Lond.* Sr. Lectr.
Steven, G. B., MSEE *Prin.*, PhD *Manc.* Principal Lectr.
Stobo, J. R., BA *Oxf.*, MSc *CNAA* Principal Lectr.
Tiwari, Ashok, MSc *Cran.*, MBA *Lond.* Sr. Lectr.
Trainis, S., BEd *Leeds*, MSc *CNAA* Sr. Lectr.
Ward, Joan, BA *Lanc.*, MSc *CNAA* Sr. Lectr.
Webb, S. A., BA *Calif.*, MSc *Kent*, MSc *CNAA* Sr. Lectr.
Wood, M. F., MSc *CNAA* Sr. Lectr.

Design and Foundation Studies

Arnold, P. Principal Lectr.
Biggs, M. A. R., BA *Lond.*, MA *Manc.* Principal Lectr.
Cooke, F. M. Sr. Lectr.
Dorey, R. W. Sr. Lectr.
Goatman, M. C. Principal Lectr.
Gray, P. G. Sr. Lectr.
Holder, B. P. Principal Lectr.
Lewis, Tessa, BA *Leic.* Sr. Lectr.
Lindley, Julian, BA *CNAA* Sr. Lectr.
Mann, S. R., MPhil *CNAA* Principal Lectr.
Marden, Adrian, BA *CNAA* Academic Manager; Head*
Meredith, Anthony, BA *CNAA* Sr. Lectr.
Mitchell, I. Sr. Lectr.
Peacock, A. D., BEd *Camb.* Principal Lectr.
Pinn, A. J. Sr. Lectr.
Sibley, Peter Sr. Lectr.
Ward, Nathan, BA *CNAA*, MA *RCA* Sr. Lectr.
Research: design, philosophy and the diagrammatical; product design and information technology user interface; rapid prototyping

Economics, Statistics and Decision Sciences

Fax: (01707) 285489

Adams, J. C., BSc *Hull*, MPhil *Kent* Academic Manager; Head*
Andrews, D., BSc *Hull*, MA *Essex* Sr. Lectr.
Barrientos, A., PhD *Kent* Principal Lectr.
Barrientos, Stephanie, PhD *Kent* Sr. Lectr.
Boniface, D., MA *Edin.*, MSc *Lond.* Principal Lectr.
Boussofiane, A. E. A., PhD *Lanc.* Sr. Lectr.
Bradbury, Pamela, BSc *Lond.* Sr. Lectr.
Cottee, Michaela, BSc *CNAA*, MSc *Lond.*, PhD *Open(UK)* Sr. Lectr.
Currie, F., BSc *Strath.* Sr. Lectr.
De Maria, E., MSc *Lond.* Sr. Lectr.
Eames, Margaret A., BSc *Manc.*, MSc *Lond.* Sr. Lectr.
Hardy, Jane, BSc *Bath* Sr. Lectr.
Kraithman, D. A., BSc *Hull*, MA *Sus.* Principal Lectr.
Langford, Ann, MSc *Wales*, BSc Sr. Lectr.
Rainnie, A., BA *York(UK)*, PhD *CNAA* Principal Lectr.
Seamark, Christine, BSc *Sus.* Sr. Lectr.
Shah, P. P., MSc *Lond.* Sr. Lectr.
Spencer, Neil, BSc *Reading*, MSc *S'ton.*, PhD *Lanc.* Sr. Lectr.
Thomas, D. G., BA *CNAA*, MSc *Lond.* Sr. Lectr.
Tofallis, C., PhD *Lond.* Sr. Lectr.
Wigodsky, P., MSc *Lond.*, PhD *CNAA* Sr. Lectr.
Research: gender equality and ethical trading; management of scientific research in pharmaceutical industry; pension reform in Latin America; restructuring the Polish economy; teachers' careers under New Labour

Education

Fax: (01707) 285626

Bloomfield, P. A., BSc *E.Anglia* Sr. Lectr.
Burchell, Helen, MSc *Lond.* Principal Lectr.
Connolly, W. J., BSc *Manc.*, MA *Lond.* Sr. Lectr.
Cook, C. D., MA *Lond.* Academic Manager; Head*
De Boo, F. Sr. Lectr.

Duncan, Diane, BEd *CNAA*, MA *Sus.*, PhD *Warw.* Sr. Lectr.
Emery, T., BSc *Hull* Sr. Lectr.
Gidley, Patricia, BPhil *Warw.*, MA *Luton* Sr. Lectr.
Hill, B., MA *Sus.*, MPhil *Lond.* Principal Lectr.
Jarvis, Joy, BEd *Exe.*, MA *Herts.* Sr. Lectr.
Jones, E. T., BA *Lond.*, MA *McM.*, MA *Keele* Sr. Lectr.
Lilley, Patricia R., BEd *Lond.* Principal Lectr.
McCrae, J. K., BSc *Leeds* Sr. Lectr.
Mercer, A. W. B., BA *Open(UK)*, MEd *Sheff.* Sr. Lectr.
Miller, Linda K., MA *Lond.*, MPhil Principal Lectr.
Oakes, Christine, BEd *Sus.* Sr. Lectr.
Powell, S. D., PhD *Birm.*, BEd Principal Lectr.
Rawlings, Bernice M., BA *Manc.* Sr. Lectr.
Read, Mary E., MA *Open(UK)* Principal Lectr.
Redmore, Alison M., BSc *Lond.* Sr. Lectr.
Rees, Mary E., BPhil *Exe.* Sr. Lectr.
Revitt, Shirley L., BSc *Nott.* Sr. Lectr.
Scrivens, Gillian I., BEd Sr. Lectr.
Shah, Sneh, BA *Camb.*, MA *Nair.*, PhD *Lond.* Principal Lectr.
Short, G. A., BA *Leeds*, MEd *CNAA* Sr. Lectr.
Simmons, Melani, BA *Liv.*, MA *Sur.* Sr. Lectr.
Smith, Gillian R., MA *Lond.* Sr. Lectr.
Smith, R., BA *Warw.*, MEd *Leic.* Principal Lectr.
Thomas, Keith Sr. Lectr.
Thomas, N., CBE Visiting Prof.
Thornton, Mary E., MA *Lond.*, PhD *Lond.* Principal Lectr.
Turner-Bisset, R., BA *E.Anglia*, PhD *Exe.* Sr. Lectr.
Warren, Valerie N., BSc *Lond.* Sr. Lectr.
Woolhouse, Marian, MA *Lond.* Sr. Lectr.
Other Staff: 5 Sr. Lectrs.†
Research: autism; equal opportunities; literacy; teaching and learning

Engineering, Aerospace, Civil and Mechanical

Fax: (01707) 285086

Al-Zubaidy, S., MSc *Liv.*, PhD *Herts.* Visiting Prof.
Armstrong, M. G., BSc *Salf.* Sr. Lectr.
Arnaouti, C., BSc *Lond.*, PhD *Aston* Reader
Badi, M. N. M., MSc *Lond.*, PhD *Lond* Sr. Lectr.
Bonner, D. G., BSc *Leeds* Academic Manager
Bullen, P. R., BSc *Lond.*, MSc *Birm.*, PhD *S'ton.*, FIMechE, FRAeS Prof.; Head*
Byrne, Liz, BSc *Brist.*, MPhil *CNAA* Sr. Lectr.
Campbell, Alan, BSc *Glas.* Sr. Lectr.
Chana, J. S., BSc *Lond.* Sr. Lectr.
Chrysanthou, Andreas, BSc *Lond.*, PhD *Lond.* Sr. Lectr.
Cook, N. J., BSc *Brist.*, PhD *Brist.*, DSc *Brist.*, FIStructE, FICE Visiting Prof.
Day, D. J., BEng *Herts.*, PhD *Herts.* Sr. Lectr.
Fenner, R. A., BSc *Newcastle(UK)*, PhD *CNAA* Principal Lectr.
Germany, David, BSc *Lough.*, MSc *Cran.* Sr. Lectr.
Green, P. C., BEng *CNAA*, PhD *CNAA* Sr. Lectr.
Guo, Shijun, MSc *Northwestern P.U.(Xi'an)*, PhD *Herts.* Sr. Lectr.
Haddleton, F. L., BSc *Aston*, PhD *Aston* Principal Lectr.
Harrington, M. J., BSc *Lond.*, BEng *Herts.* Sr. Lectr.
Hart, K. J., BSc *Sus.* Sr. Lectr.
Hemingway, N. G., MPhil *Sur.*, PhD *CNAA* Principal Lectr.
Holdo, A. E., BSc *CNAA*, PhD *CNAA* Principal Lectr.
Ilyas, M., BSc *Alig.*, MEng *Liv.*, PhD *Liv.* Sr. Lectr.
Jawad, S. A. W., PhD *Brun.*, BSc Sr. Lectr.
Johnson, G., BA *Lond.* Visiting Prof.
King, J., BSc *CNAA*, FIMechE Visiting Prof.
Lewis, A. P. L., MA *Oxf.*, MSc *Cran.IT* Principal Lectr.
Marriott, M. J., MA *Camb.*, MSc *Lond.* Sr. Lectr.
Mays, I. D., BSc *Reading*, PhD *Reading* Visiting Prof.

McKay, Neil, BEng Strath. Sr. Lectr.

Nasser, S., BSc Baghdad, MSc Leeds, PhD Leeds Sr. Lectr.

Palmer, R. M., BEng CNAA Sr. Lectr.

Peters, J., BEng Herts. Sr. Lectr.

Philpott, David R., BSc Brist., PhD CNAA Sr. Lectr.

Price, D. R., BA, FRAS Sr. Lectr.

Rofe, B. H., BA Camb., MA Camb., FICE Visiting Prof.

Sands, T. B., BSc Sr. Lectr.

Sayigh, A. A. M., BSc Lond., PhD Lond. Visiting Prof.

Surendran, P. N., MSc Manc., PhD CNAA Principal Lectr.

Taylor, Penelope, BSc Coventry, MSc Warw. Principal Lectr.

Tiu, W. P., BSc Lond., PhD City(UK) Sr. Lectr.

White, W. R., BSc Leeds, PhD Leeds Visiting Prof.

Wibberley, B. L., MSc CNAA Sr. Lectr.

Wilkinson, R. Sr. Lectr.

Wong, A., BSc Edin., PhD Edin. Sr. Lectr.

Other Staff: 2 Sr. Lectrs.†

Engineering, Electrical/Electronic

Akhan, M. B., MSc Birm., PhD Birm. Sr. Lectr.

Alukaidey, T., BSc Baghdad, MSc Brun., PhD Brun. Academic Manager

Ariyaeeinia, A. M., BEng Teheran, MSc Keele, PhD CNAA Sr. Lectr.

Barrett, R., BSc Birm., PhD CNAA, FIEE Emer. Prof.

Bass, Julian, BSc Wales, PhD Sheff. Sr. Lectr.

Bussell, R. L., BSc Sur. Sr. Lectr.

Clark, J. M., BSc Lough. Visiting Prof.

Cloutman, R. W. G., BSc Lond. Principal Lectr.

Cookson, M. J., BSc Newcastle(UK), PhD Lond. Visiting Prof.

Dykes, E., BSc CNAA, PhD Lond. Principal Lectr.

Gordon, J., MA Camb., PhD CNAA Visiting Prof.

Gordon, R., BSc CNAA Principal Lectr.

Jackson, P. F., MSc Nott. Principal Lectr.

Jefferies, B., PhD Camb. Academic Manager; Head*

Kyffin, R. K., BSc Wales Sr. Lectr.

Lauder, D. M., BSc Essex Sr. Lectr.

Lee, David, BSc Nott., MPhil Staffs., PhD Lond., PhD Glam. Sr. Lectr.

Lord, P. I., BSc Essex Sr. Lectr.

Luk, Patrick, BSc CNAA Sr. Lectr.

Patel, B., BSc Lond., MSc CNAA, PhD Lond. Principal Lectr.

Phillips, S. H., BSc Leeds Sr. Lectr.

Randall, P. A., BSc Lond. Sr. Lectr.

Sun, Yichuang, BSc Dalian, MSc Dalian, DPhil York(UK) Principal Lectr.

White, C. E., BSc Lond., PhD CNAA Principal Lectr.

Environmental Sciences

Allen-Williams, L. J., BSc Lond., PhD Lond. Principal Lectr.

Blumhof, Jennifer R., MA CNAA Sr. Lectr.

Burton, Marie A. S., BSc Aberd., PhD Lond. Sr. Lectr.

Cheshire, D. A., BSc S'ton. Sr. Lectr.

Copp, G. H., BSc Trent, MSc Delft, PhD Lyons Principal Lectr.

Dickinson, Janet, BA Manc. Sr. Lectr.

Duff, Charles C., BSc Durh. Visiting Prof.

Finch, Adrian, BSc Durh., PhD Edin. Sr. Lectr.

Foster, J., BSc Wales, PhD Wales Principal Lectr.

Gardiner, J. L., BSc Lond., PhD S'ton., FICE Visiting Prof.

Hall, Avice M., BSc Leic., MSc Exe., PhD Exe. Sr. Lectr.

Higgs, D., BSc Wales, PhD Wales Sr. Lectr.

Pearlman, D. J. Sr. Lectr.

Smith, Marie A. S., BSc Adel., PhD Lond. Reader

Sokhi, R. S., BSc Birm., MSc Aston, PhD Aston Sr. Lectr.

Steeley, G. C., OBE, BA Oxf., FRTPI Visiting Prof.

Teeuw, R. M., BSc Nott., PhD Stir. Sr. Lectr.

Todd, Ian, BSc Wales, PhD Wales Sr. Lectr.

Warrington, S., BA Camb., PhD Lanc. Principal Lectr.

Other Staff: 1 Principal Lectr.†; 2 Sr. Lectrs.†

Research: atmospheric science; clean technology; environmental management and policy; landscape and ecology

Finance, see Business and Finance

Health and Social Care

Fax: (01707) 285237

Alexander, G., BA CNAA, MA CNAA Sr. Lectr.

Brownbill, A., BSc Sur. Sr. Lectr.

Buckroyd, Julia M., MA St And., MA McM., PhD Camb. Principal Lectr.

Campbell, G., BA CNAA Sr. Lectr.

Cloudsdale, Stephen J., BA Open(UK) Sr. Lectr.

Cosis Brown, H., BA CNAA, MA Sus. Academic Manager; Head*

Doel, L. Sr. Lectr.

Dwyer, A. M. Sr. Lectr.

Fearns, Debra, BA CNAA Sr. Lectr.

Goatly, Ruth, LLB Leic. Principal Lectr.

Green, R., MA CNAA Sr. Lectr.

Greensmith, Katherine A., BSc Sur., MSc Sur. Sr. Lectr.

Hansen, G., CandPsych Copenhagen Sr. Lectr.

Kelly, J. Sr. Lectr.

Kidd, A. Sr. Lectr.

Lee, S., MSc Lond., MA Brun. Sr. Lectr.

Lewis, D. R. Sr. Lectr.

Li, Kam W. I., BSc Lond. Sr. Lectr.

Littlechild, B., MA CNAA Principal Lectr.

McCaffrey, M. Sr. Lectr.

Mitchell, Y. Sr. Lectr.

Morton-Smith, J., BSc Bridgeport, MEd Springfield Sr. Lectr.

Payne, Helen Sr. Lectr.

Paynter, Marilyn J., BEd Sus. Sr. Lectr.

Ponapalam, B. Sr. Lectr.

Randle, Alan, MSc Hull Sr. Lectr.

Roche, J. P., BA Trinity(Dub.), MSc Lond. Sr. Lectr.

Rostom, Manjit K., MSc City(UK) Principal Lectr.

Salauroo, Mohamed A., BSc Manc. Sr. Lectr.

Sooben, Roja D. Sr. Lectr.

Taylor, Karen J. Sr. Lectr.

Weinrabe, D. P., BEd CNAA Principal Lectr.

Whatton, Susan S. Sr. Lectr.

Wysling, G. D., BA CNAA, MSc Aston Sr. Lectr.

Other Staff: 1 Sr. Lectr.†

Humanities

Fax: (01707) 285611

Allen, Rosemary K. Sr. Lectr.

Brown, D. E., MA Lond., DPhil Sus. Prof.

Clutterbuck, A. H., BEd Camb., MSc Sus. Sr. Lectr.

Coates, P., MA Sus., PhD Lond. Principal Lectr.

Cragoe, M. F., BA Lond., MA Wales, DPhil Oxf. Sr. Lectr.

Gatland, P., MA Oxf., MA Lond., PhD Lond. Principal Lectr.

Goose, N. R., BA Kent, PhD Camb. Academic Manager; Head*

Gowing, Laura, BA Oxf., PhD Lond. Sr. Lectr.

Green, D. C., MA Lond. Sr. Lectr.

Holderness, Graham, MA Oxf., PhD Sur., DLitt Herts. Prof.

Hutto, D. D., BA Marist, MPhil St And. Sr. Lectr.

Hutton, Sarah C., BA Camb., PhD Lond. Principal Lectr.

Leinonen, Eeeva K., BSc Aston, MPhil Exe., PhD Leic. Principal Lectr.

Lippitt, J., BSc Manc., MLitt Durh. Sr. Lectr.

MacKinnon, K., BSc Lond., MA Lond., PhD Lond. Visiting Prof.

Monaghan, J., MA Glas., DPhil Fran. Principal Lectr.

Monteith, Sharon J., BA E.Anglia Principal Lectr.

Parke, T. H., BA Reading, MA Lond., PhD Reading Principal Lectr.

Pechey, G., BA Natal Sr. Lectr.

Riley, Stephanie, BA Open(UK), MA Middx. Sr. Lectr.

Singleton, Jane, BA Exe., DPhil Sus. Sr. Lectr.

Southgate, S. J. Sr. Lectr.

Tegal, Susan, BA Vassar, MSc Lond., PhD Lond. Principal Lectr.

Thomson, A., MA Camb., PhD Lond. Academic Manager

Turner, G. J., MA Lond. Academic Manager

Turner, L. Sr. Lectr.

Other Staff: 1 Sr. Lectr.†

Research: history (countryside, demography, film, masculinities, Wales, women); linguistics (bilingual language acquisition, disordered, normal, pragmatics); literature (early modern, modernism, postmodernism: colonial, post-colonial); philosophy (epistemology, ethics, metaphysics, mind, religion and science)

Interdisciplinary Studies

Arter, Catherine J., BA CNAA Principal Lectr.

Harridge-March, S., MA Westminster Sr. Lectr.

Herbert, Ailsa E., BA Wales, MA Wales Sr. Lectr.

Kynnersley, J. Principal Lectr.

Lockett, P. E., MA Camb. Principal Lectr.; Head*

Pinn, K., BSc CNAA, MA Herts. Sr. Lectr.

Winder, J., MSc Lond., PhD Herts. Sr. Lectr.

Wright, K. Marcella, BA Durh. Sr. Lectr.

Languages, see Mod. Langs.

Law

Fax: (01707) 283205

Barnes, Lee A., LLB CNAA Sr. Lectr.

Bell, Cedric, LLB Birm., LLM Birm., PhD Birm. Visiting Prof.

Carey, Penelope J., LLB Sur. Sr. Lectr.

Foster, Ilaine V. J., BA CNAA, LLM Camb. Sr. Lectr.

Hackett, M. Sr. Lectr.

Kay, Frances, BA CNAA, LLM Lond. Sr. Lectr.

Korgaonkar, Gillian J. A., LLM Lond. Principal Lectr.

Martin, Rhea S. L., JP, LLB Lond., MA Brun. Visiting Prof.

Morcowitz, Isaac, BProc Cape Town Sr. Lectr.

O'Brien, J., LLB Camb., MA Camb., LLM Lond. Sr. Lectr.

Pandya, H. Sr. Lectr.

Parry, P. W., LLB CNAA, MSc Lond. Principal Lectr.

Percival, Mary E., LLB Lond., LLM Harv. Sr. Lectr.

Reay, Rosamund, BA Keele, MA Brun. Sr. Lectr.

Rendell, Catherine A., BA Durh., BCL Durh. Sr. Lectr.

Rice, S. S., BA Camb. Sr. Lectr.

Singh, H., LLB Wales, LLM Lond. Sr. Lectr.

Slee, D., BA Kent, LLM Lond. Sr. Lectr.

South, D. Colleen, LLB Exe. Sr. Lectr.

Stockdale, E., LLB Lond., BSc Lond., LLM Lond., PhD Lond. Visiting Prof.

Tongue, Penny, BA Lond., LLM Lond. Principal Lectr.

White, R. Sr. Lectr.

Other Staff: 1 Sr. Lectr.†

Management and Business Information Systems

Fax: (01707) 285410

Barnett, H. C., MSc Lough. Principal Lectr.

Bywaters, D. S., BA Essex, MA Middx. Sr. Lectr.

Clark, Brian R., BA Birm., BSc Lond., MBA Brad. Academic Manager; Head*

Culkin, N., BA CNAA Principal Lectr.

Dnes, Anthony, BA Leic., MLitt Aberd., PhD Edin. Academic Manager

Evans, Jenny, MA CNAA Sr. Lectr.

Fowler, M. Sr. Lectr.

Fraser, P. J., MA Edin., MSc Lond. Sr. Lectr.

Goodwin, Brian, BSc McG., BA Oxf., MSc McG., PhD Edin. Visiting Prof.

Herman, M. J., MSc City(UK) Sr. Lectr.

Hobson, J. B. Principal Lectr.

Jones, R., BSc Wales, MSc Birm. Sr. Lectr.

Kelvin, A., PhD *Wales*, MA Sr. Lectr.
Kirkbride, P. Visiting Prof.
Morris, Clare, MA *Oxf.*, MSc *Brist.*, PhD *Brist.* Academic Manager
Noble, Dorothea, BA *Manc.* Sr. Lectr.
Randle, K. R., BSc *Bath*, BPhil *Liv.* Principal Lectr.
Robins, Karen E., BSc *Lough.*, MSc *Sus.* Sr. Lectr.
Shearer, P. R., MSc *S'ton.* Sr. Lectr.
Stacey, R. D., MSc *Lond.*, PhD *Lond.* Prof.
Stevens, Richard A. Visiting Prof.
Taylor, Susan, BA *N.U.I.*, MA *N.U.I.*, MSc *Birm.*, PhD *Nott.* Principal Lectr.
Other Staff: 1 Principal Lectr.†; 1 Sr. Lectr.†
Research: Bayes linear influence diagrams for forecasting, planning and control; Bayesian decision support systems for management; development of holistic non-linear feedback framework for understanding innovative management; management of research teams in pharmaceutical industry; 'virtual team-working' using groupware technologies and organisational dynamics

Manufacturing Systems

Fax: (01707) 284256

Ball, G. J., MPhil *Lond.*, FIMechE Sr. Lectr.
Beamish, J. C., BSc *Lanc.*, PhD *Lanc.* Principal Lectr.
Dawkins, K. T., BSc *CNAA* Sr. Lectr.
Esmail, K. Sr. Lectr.
Fowler, Moyra A., BSc *CNAA* Sr. Lectr.
Harland, G., BSc *Leeds*, MSc *Lough.*, FIEE Head*
Hayes, Robin S. Sr. Lectr.
Jones, M. H., BSc *CNAA* Principal Lectr.
Khoudian, P., BSc *CNAA* Principal Lectr.
Lane, R., BSc *Brun.*, MSc *Cran.*, PhD *Cran.* Sr. Lectr.
Lumkin, P. J. Sr. Lectr.
McAndrew, I. R., BA *Open(UK)* Sr. Lectr.
Mitchell, L. Sr. Lectr.
Ngum, S. Sr. Lectr.
O'Sullivan, J. M., BSc *Wales*, MSc *Sheff.*, MA *Open(UK)*, PhD *CNAA* Principal Lectr.
Page, T. Sr. Lectr.
Parkinson, B., BA *CNAA* Principal Lectr.
Pearce, D. M., BSc *CNAA* Sr. Lectr.
Portway, S. M. Sr. Lectr.
Wilson, R. A., BSc *CNAA*, MSc *Lond.* Principal Lectr.

Mathematics

Bartholomew Biggs, M. C., BSc *Exe.*, PhD *Lond.* Reader
Beddiaf, Salah S., BSc *Annaba*, MSc *Dund.* Sr. Lectr.
Busolini, D. T., BSc *Manc.*, MSc *Lond.*, MPhil *Reading* Principal Lectr.
Davies, A. J., BSc *S'ton.*, MSc *Lond.*, PhD *Lond.*, FIMA Prof.; Head*
Dixon, L. C. W., MA *Camb.*, PhD *Camb.* Emer. Prof.
Fitzharris, A. M., BSc *CNAA*, MSc Principal Lectr.
Georgiou, A., BSc *Lond.*, PhD *Lond.* Sr. Lectr.
Parkhurst, S. Sr. Lectr.
Ranzetta, R. F. D., MA *Oxf.*, MSc *Lond.*, FIMA Academic Manager
Samuels, P., MSc *Lond.*, PhD *Lond.*, FIMA Sr. Lectr.
Singh, Kuldeep, BSc *Lond.*, MSc *Lond.* Sr. Lectr.
Stansfield, G. Sr. Lectr.

Midwifery and Child

Fax: (01707) 285299

Blunden, Rosemary, BA *Open(UK)* Sr. Lectr.
Boyle, Sally A. Principal Lectr.
Charles, Michele Sr. Lectr.
Condell, Kathryn, BA *CNAA*, MSc *Nott.* Sr. Lectr.
Deane-Gray, Tandy A. S. Sr. Lectr.
Dolby, E. Sr. Lectr.
Entwistle, Fransesca Sr. Lectr.
Fay, Gillian P. Sr. Lectr.
Hallworth, Christine Academic Manager; Head*
Harwood, Patricia, BA *Open(UK)* Sr. Lectr.

Karstadt, Lyn, BA *Open(UK)* Principal Lectr.
Lawrence, Christine, BSc *Lond.* Principal Lectr.
Loveluck, J. Sr. Lectr.
Mead, Joanne Sr. Lectr.
Mead, Marianne M. P., BA *Open(UK)* Principal Lectr.
Miller, Susan M. Sr. Lectr.
Rogers, Catherine A. Sr. Lectr.
Russell-Johnson, H. M. F. Sr. Lectr.
Shaw, Mary A. Sr. Lectr.
Taylor, Wendy J. Sr. Lectr.
Thompson, F., BSc *Lanc.* Sr. Lectr.
Tobias, Joleen Sr. Lectr.
Tomlin, Margaret D. Sr. Lectr.
Turner, Janette A. Sr. Lectr.
Walker, Ruth Sr. Lectr.
Whiting, Lisa S., BA *Manc.* Sr. Lectr.
Wildeman, T. F. C. Sr. Lectr.
Yearley, C. Sr. Lectr.

Modern Languages

Fax: (01707) 285241

Beck, Siegrid Sr. Lectr.
Boak, Helen L., BA *Manc.*, PhD *Manc.* Academic Manager; Head*
Bowden, Jill D., BA *Leeds* Sr. Lectr.
Bradley, Janette E., BA *Reading*, MA *Lond.* Sr. Lectr.
Buchan, Marion, BA *Lond.*, MPhil *Lond.* Sr. Lectr.
Duplain, Nicole G. M., LèsL *St.-Etienne*, Maîtrise *St.-Etienne* Sr. Lectr.
Gillett, A. J., BSc *Durh.*, MA *Kent* Principal Lectr.
O'Sullivan, Mary M., BA *Lond.* Sr. Lectr.
Parry, Patricia M., BA *Lond.* Sr. Lectr.
Slater, Anne M., LèsL *Lyons* Sr. Lectr.
Zakrzewski, Vanessa M., BSc *Salf.* Sr. Lectr.

Nursing and Adult Health

Almond, P., BSc *Herts.* Sr. Lectr.
Andrews, Elaine P., BA *Open(UK)* Academic Manager; Head*
Byrne, Geraldine S. M., BA *Sus.*, PhD *Northumbria* Principal Lectr.
Cahill, Martha J., BSc Sr. Lectr.
Comerasamy, Jacqueline C., BA *CNAA*, MSc *City(UK)* Sr. Lectr.
Cumber, Christine E. Principal Lectr.
Gault, Christine A. Principal Lectr.
Goulden, Barbara A., BSc *Manc.* Sr. Lectr.
Gray, Carole Academic Manager
Greeno, S., BSc *Herts.* Sr. Lectr.
Knopp, N., BSc *CNAA*, MSc *S.Bank* Sr. Lectr.
Lancaster, J. C., BSc *Reading* Sr. Lectr.
Nair, M. Sr. Lectr.
Orpwood, Jean M. F., BSc *Lond.* Sr. Lectr.
Peate, I. Sr. Lectr.
Roberts, Susan C., BSc *Brun.* Sr. Lectr.
Rodin, Melissa J. Sr. Lectr.
Say, J., BSc *Liv.* Sr. Lectr.
Smith, Kim P. Sr. Lectr.
Worthington, Judith M. Sr. Lectr.
Yagambrun, S., MA *E.Anglia* Sr. Lectr.

Nursing and Paramedic Studies

Appleton, J., BA *CNAA*, MSc *Lond.* Sr. Lectr.
Birkinhead, Patricia A., BSc *Greenwich* Sr. Lectr.
Birtles, Ann P. Sr. Lectr.
Brown, Dorothy A., BA Sr. Lectr.
Dean, G. P., BSc Principal Lectr.
Denham, Michael J., BChir *Camb.*, MA *Camb.*, MD *Camb.*, FRCP Visiting Prof.
Dykes, E., BSc *CNAA*, PhD *Lond.* Principal Lectr.
Edwards, S., MSc *City(UK)* Sr. Lectr.
Flynn, Frances C., BSc Sr. Lectr.
Harwood, C., BA *Open(UK)* Academic Manager
Hayes, D. A. Sr. Lectr.
Hunt, W. B., PhD *Nott.* Academic Manager; Head*
Jones, Indra, BA *Manc.* Sr. Lectr.
Kai, Luk C. S. Sr. Lectr.
Lewis, Deborah Sr. Lectr.
Machen, I., BA *CNAA*, MA *Herts.* Sr. Lectr.
McMorran, P. Sr. Lectr.
Mehta, L. Sr. Lectr.
Montague, Susan, BSc *Sur.* Principal Lectr.
Rhodes, L. J., BSc *Herts.* Sr. Lectr.

Richards, A., BA *Open(UK)* Sr. Lectr.
Simmons, K. L., BSc *CNAA*, MSc *City(UK)* Principal Lectr.
Smith, Jane A. Sr. Lectr.
Thayre, Karen W. Sr. Lectr.
Weston, Janet F., BA *CNAA*, BSc Sr. Lectr.
Williams, J., BSc *Sur.* Sr. Lectr.
Williams, Laurien E. Sr. Lectr.
Wood, Patricia L., MA *Open(UK)* Sr. Lectr.

Observatory

Fax: (01707) 284644

Kitchin, C. R., BA BSc, FRAS Dir.*

Physical Sciences

Fax: (01707) 284644

Appleton, Q., BSc *Lond.* Sr. Lectr.
Bailey, T. H., BA *Open(UK)*, MSc *Durh.* Principal Lectr.
Banford, L., PhD *Durh.* Sr. Lectr.
Bevan, C. D., BSc *CNAA*, PhD *CNAA* Visiting Prof.
Beynon, D., MA *Camb.* Visiting Prof.
Carr, P., MSc *Lond.*, PhD *CNAA* Sr. Lectr.
Cox, M., MSc *Lond.*, PhD *Lond.* Prof.
Evans, Michael B., BSc *Lond.*, PhD *Lond.*, FRSChem Prof. Emer.
Evans, S. J., BSc *Wales*, PhD *CNAA* Sr. Lectr.
Fish, Sir Hugh, CBE, BSc *Leeds* Visiting Prof.
Flett, D., BSc *Aberd.* Visiting Prof.
Frearson, M. J., MA *Camb.*, PhD *Camb.* Sr. Lectr.
Gardiner, J. L., BSc *Lond.*, PhD *S'ton.*, FICE Visiting Prof.
Gemlyn, R., BSc *Wales*, PhD *Wales*, PhD *Camb.*, DSc *Wales* Prof. Emer.
Hall, S. J., MSc *Birm.*, PhD *Wales* Sr. Lectr.
Hemming, Karl, BSc *Salf.*, PhD *Salf.* Sr. Lectr.
Horwell, D. C., BSc *Lond.*, PhD *Leic.* Visiting Prof.
Hough, J. H., BSc *Leeds*, PhD *Leeds* Prof.; Head*
Ismail, F. M. D., BSc *Salf.*, PhD *Salf.* Sr. Lectr.
Knapen, J. Sr. Lectr.
Le Roux, N. W., MSc *Newcastle(UK)*
Ludlow, I. K., BSc *Lond.*, PhD *Leeds* Reader
McCall, D., BSc *Bath*, PhD *CNAA* Sr. Lectr.
Nowell, D. V., PhD *Salf.*, FRSChem Prof. Emer.
Piggott, B. Reader
Pryce-Jones, T., BSc *Wales*, MSc *CNAA*, PhD *CNAA*, FRSChem Principal Lectr.
Pye, P. L., DPhil *Sus.* Sr. Lectr.
Shaw, J. A., BSc *Sheff.*, PhD *Sheff.* Sr. Lectr.
Sheriff, T. S., BSc *Lond.*, PhD *Lond.* Sr. Lectr.
Steeley, G., OBE, BA *Oxf.*, FRTPI Visiting Prof.
Van Der Zee, P., PhD *Lond.* Sr. Lectr.
Research: astronomy; light scattering and particle characterisation; microfluidics and microengineering; optical monitoring and imaging techniques in medicine; theoretical physics

Physiotherapy

Fax: (01707) 284977

Alltree, J. R., MSc *Lond.* Sr. Lectr.
Bailey Metcalfe, Alison, BS *Delaware*, MSc *Lond.* Sr. Lectr.
Beeton, K., BSc *CNAA* Sr. Lectr.
Chappell, Judith A., MSc *Liv.* Principal Lectr.
Davis, Diana H. Sr. Lectr.
Higgins, Jill R. Principal Lectr.
McGovern, D. Sr. Lectr.
Perry, Sarah Sr. Lectr.
Potter, Jacqueline Sr. Lectr.
Upjohn, S. Sr. Lectr.
Watson, Tim, BSc *CNAA*, PhD *Sur.* Academic Manager; Head*

Post Registration Nursing

Fax: (01707) 284954

Culley, Fiona C., BSc *Brun.* Sr. Lectr.
Davidson, M. Sr. Lectr.
Dawson, Deborah, BSc *CNAA* Sr. Lectr.
Dearden, Henrietta M., BA *York(UK)* Sr. Lectr.
Dietmann, John C., BA *Chic.*, MA *Chic.* Sr. Lectr.

Fisher, V. P., MSc Sur.   Academic Manager
Flanagan, Madeleine   Principal Lectr.
Fletcher, J.   Sr. Lectr.
Flynn, Sheila   Sr. Lectr.
Ford, K.   Sr. Lectr.
Froggatt, K., BSc Durh.   Sr. Lectr.
Goodman, C.   Sr. Lectr.
Grace, S. M.   Sr. Lectr.
Hemming, Laureen J., BA Open(UK)   Sr. Lectr.
Hodge, Deborah, BSc Manc.   Principal Lectr.
Holt, Ian, BA Manc., MSc Manc.   Sr. Lectr.
Holt, Paula   Sr. Lectr.
Horner, Catherine T., BSc Lough.   Sr. Lectr.
Hunter, Cheri   Principal Lectr.
Jenner, Elizabeth A., BSc Sur.   Principal Lectr.
Kempson, Audrey   Sr. Lectr.
Knight, Denise A., BSc CNAA, MSc Lond.   Sr. Lectr.
Law, Carol E.   Sr. Lectr.
Lovett, K.   Sr. Lectr.
McGregor-Cheers, Jean M., BA Open(UK)   Sr. Lectr.
O'Connell, Rachel G.   Sr. Lectr.
Offredy, Maxine   Sr. Lectr.
Palmer, Lynn, BSc Lond.   Sr. Lectr.
Read, Ann E.   Sr. Lectr.
Richardson, Marion L., BD Lond.   Sr. Lectr.
Rosenfeld, Virginia, BSc Manc.   Sr. Lectr.
Smart, Jacqueline, BA Open(UK)   Academic Manager; Head*
Taylor, V., BSc Herts., MSc Sur.   Sr. Lectr.
Tunbridge, S.   Sr. Lectr.
Turney, C.   Sr. Lectr.
Unerman, Evelyn, BSc Manc.   Sr. Lectr.
Walton, A. G., BEd CNAA   Academic Manager
Whelan, J.   Sr. Lectr.
Whitfield, Andrew, BSc Ulster, MSc Herts.   Sr. Lectr.
Wilson, Desiree A., MSc Sur.   Principal Lectr.
Wilson, Patricia, BEd CNAA   Sr. Lectr.
Windo, Mary P.   Sr. Lectr.
Other Staff: 1 Sr. Lectr.†

Psychology

Fax: (01707) 285073

Austin, N. G., BSc Liv., BSc Lond.   Principal Lectr.
Clarke, A., CBE, BA Reading, PhD Lond., FBPsS, FRCPsych   Visiting Prof.
Dittrich, W., DSc Marburg   Sr. Lectr.
Done, D. J., BA Leic., PhD Wales   Academic Manager
Gilbert, David B., BSc CNAA, PhD Birm.   Sr. Lectr.
Hasan, Patricia J., BSc CNAA   Principal Lectr.
Henderson, L., MA Glas., PhD Wat.   Emer. Prof.
Hilton, D., BA Sus., DPhil Oxf.   Sr. Lectr.
Holland, Angela E., MSc CNAA   Sr. Lectr.
Jones, Fiona A., BA Nott., MA Brun., MSc CNAA   Sr. Lectr.
Kornbrot, Diana E., BSc Brist., MSc Lond., MA Col., PhD Col.   Reader
Messer, D. J., BSc Reading, PhD Strath.   Prof.
Miller, Linda R., MSc Lond., PhD Wales   Sr. Lectr.
Murphy, Robin, BA Belf., MA McG., PhD McG.   Sr. Lectr.
Petrie, Helen L., BA Melb., MSc Lond., PhD Lond.   Sr. Lectr.
Ridley, D., BSc Lond.   Principal Lectr.
Smith, Pamela, BA Lond.   Principal Lectr.
Starr, Beryl S., BSc Lond., PhD Lond.   Academic Manager; Head*
Vallee-Tourangeau, F., BA McG., MA Penn., PhD McG.   Sr. Lectr.
Winter, D., BSc Durh., MSc Newcastle(UK), PhD Durh.   Visiting Prof.
Wiseman, R., BSc Lond., PhD Edin.   Sr. Lectr.
Wolke, D., BSc Kiel, MSc Lond., PhD Lond.   Prof.
Young, R.   Principal Lectr.
Research: health and disability (ageing, health promotion, stress); human-computer interaction (visual impairment, web technology); longitudinal development (cognition, disability, language, pre-term, sleeping); neuropsychology/psychopharmacology (Alzheimer's, motor,

Parkinson's, stroke); thinking (cognitive and social judgement and decisions, inference)

Radiography

Fax: (01707) 284977

Davidson, Jennifer, BSc CNAA   Sr. Lectr.
Fernando, Regina, MSc City(UK)   Principal Lectr.
Gradwell, Mark, BSc Kingston(UK), MSc Kingston(UK)   Sr. Lectr.
Henderson, Julia, MSc Sur.   Principal Lectr.
High, Janet, BSc CNAA   Principal Lectr.
Murray, Susan   Sr. Lectr.
Pearce, Vivian M.   Sr. Lectr.
Price, R., MSc Lanc.   Academic Manager; Head*
Prime, N. J., BA Open(UK), MA Keele   Sr. Lectr.
Vospar, M.   Sr. Lectr.

Social Sciences

Fax: (01707) 284799

Andrews, G.   Sr. Lectr.
Cousins, Christin R., BSc Sur., MA Nott., MPhil Lond.   Principal Lectr.
Dale, D. W., BSc CNAA, MSc Lond.   Principal Lectr.; Head*
Doughty, G. P., BA CNAA, MSc Lond.   Sr. Lectr.
Heather, Judy, BSc Lond., MSc Sur.   Principal Lectr.
Hewitt, M. V., BSc Lond., MA Essex   Sr. Lectr.
Hooper, A. F., BA Sus., PhD Lond.   Sr. Lectr.
James, D., BA CNAA   Sr. Lectr.
Killeen, J. F., BSc Aston, MPhil Lond.   Sr. Lectr.
Neal, D., BA Sus., MSc CNAA   Sr. Lectr.
Nicholas, A. N., BSc Lond., BPhil York(UK), MSc Manc.   Principal Lectr.
Turton, J. R., MSc Lond.   Principal Lectr.
Woolley, Penny A. F., MSc Lond.   Sr. Lectr.
Research: democracy and politics of the EU; evaluation of vocational, educational guidance and careers education; poverty, work and welfare in Europe (unemployment and health); professional groups within the NHS and the internal market; reforming the welfare state

SPECIAL CENTRES, ETC

Analytical Services, Centre for

O'Sullivan, Helen   Dir.*

Biodeterioration Centre

Smith, N., BSc Nott., PhD Nott.   Dir.*

Engineering Research and Development Centre

Fax: (01707) 284185

Kaye, Prof. P., BSc CNAA, PhD CNAA   Dir.*

Environmental Services Unit

Higgs, D., BSc Wales, PhD Wales   Dir.*
Research: conservation management and advice; environmental management and audits; geographic information systems; insect infestation and identification advice; plant growth and phytotoxicity trials

Information Management and Technology, Centre for (CIMTECH Ltd)

Hendley, A. M.   Dir.*

Local Employment Studies Unit

Rainnie, A., BA York(UK), PhD CNAA   Dir.*
Research: gender equality and ethical trading; management of scientific research in the pharmaceutical industry; pension reform in Latin America; restructuring of the Polish economy; teachers' careers under New Labour

Music Centre

Blinko, T.   Sr. Lectr.
Burrell, H. J., BMus Belf., MA Nott.   Prof.; Head*
Dearden, I., BA Leeds, MMus E.Anglia, PhD City(UK)   Sr. Lectr.

Parry, D. M. G., MA Oxf.   Sr. Lectr.
Research: artistic (composition, performance); critical and aesthetic; technological (software development, human-computer interaction and sound cognition)

Numerical Optimisation Centre

Dixon, Prof. L., MA Camb., PhD Camb.   Dir.*
Research: automatic differentiation (efficient automatic implementation of reverse differentiation); neural networks (approximation of continuous objective functions); new algebraic systems (accurate arithmetic and intervals for global optimisation); non-linear programming (software for large constrained problems); unconstrained optimisation (design of software for minimising functions)

Perrott-Warrick Research Unit

Tel: (01707) 284628

Wiseman, Richard, BSc Lond., PhD Edin.   Head*
Research: luck and intuition; psychology of lying and deception; psychology of the paranormal

Primary and Community Care, Centre for Research in

Tel: (01707) 285249 Fax: (01707) 285995

Townsend, Joy   Dir.*
Research: adolescent health promotion in primary care; care attendant post-discharge schemes for over 75s; literature reviews in health care; methodology for prioritising health technology assessments; nurse-led primary care of older people

Sensory Disabilities Research Unit

Tel: (01707) 285058 Fax: (01707) 285059

Petrie, Helen, BA Melb., MSc Lond., PhD Lond.   Head*
Research: access to WWW for disabled people; design and evaluation of computer interfaces; psychology of disability; technology for disabled and elderly users

Wolke Research Group

Tel: (01707) 285262 Fax: (01707) 284042

Wolke, Dieter, BSc Kiel, MSc Lond.   Prof.; Head*

CONTACT OFFICERS

Academic affairs. Academic Registrar: Clark, Jeannette, BA Lond., MA CNAA
Accommodation. Head of Residential Services: Thorp, Amanda, BA Hull
Admissions (first degree). Assistant Registrar (Admissions): O'Callaghan, Penny, BA Oxf., MA Reading
Admissions (higher degree). Assistant Registrar (Research Degrees): Caras, Lilian, BA CNAA
Adult/continuing education. Adult Guidance Administrator: Goodchild, Margaret
Alumni. Development Committee Manager: ......
Archives. Director of Learning and Information Services: Wingate-Martin, Diana, BA Lond.
Careers. Senior Careers Adviser: Rhys-Williams, Julian L., BA Sus.
Computing services. Assistant Director (Campus Information Services): Wroot, Andrew, BSc Alta., MSc Alta., PhD Lond.
Computing services. Head of Management Services: Short, Tom, BSc Lond., MSc CNAA
Consultancy services. Director of External Relations: Levine, Kathleen, BSc Lond.
Development/fund-raising. Development Committee Manager: ......
Equal opportunities. Equal Opportunities Officer: Wright, Marcella, BA Durh.
Estates and buildings/works and services. Director of Estates: Parris, Stephen, FRICS
Examinations. Assistant Registrar (Examinations and Conferments): McElroy, Sheila, BA CNAA
Finance. Director of Finance: Neville, Terry M.

General enquiries. Secretary and Registrar: Jeffreys, Peter G., BA *Wales*, MEd *Wales*

Health services. Director of Student Services: Ball, David, BSc *CNAA*

Industrial liaison. Director of External Relations: Levine, Kathleen, BSc *Lond.*

International office. Director, International Office: Casey, Peter S., BSc *CNAA*, MSc *Aston*

Library (enquiries). Administrative Manager: Irving, Avril, BA *Lanc.*, MSc *City(UK)*

Minorities/disadvantaged groups. Equal Opportunities Officer: Wright, Marcella, BA *Durh.*

Personnel/human resources. Director of Personnel: Lott, Patricia

Public relations, information and marketing. Public Relations Manager: Emsley, Brian

Publications. Editorial Manager: Davies, Valerie, BA *Keele*

Purchasing. Purchasing Officer: Wakeling, Jill

Quality assurance and accreditation. Director of Academic Quality: Lines, Prof. Peter D., BSc *City(UK)*, MSc *Essex*, FIEE

Quality assurance and accreditation. Assistant Registrar (Academic Quality): Clarke, Kate, MA *Reading*, PhD *Reading*

Research. Director of Research and Research Degrees: Holderness, Prof. Graham, MA *Oxf.*, PhD *Sur.*, DLitt *Herts.*

Safety. Director of Health and Safety: Thomas, Clive, BA *Open(UK)*

Scholarships, awards, loans. Academic Registrar: Clark, Jeannette, BA *Lond.*, MA *CNAA*

Schools liaison. UK Development Manager: Ward, Geoffrey, BSc *Lond.*

Sport and recreation. Deputy Head of Sport and Physical Recreation: Cornish, Keith, BA *Open(UK)*

Staff development and training. Training Officer: Bryant, Linda

Student union. General Manager: Fletcher, Rachel, BSocSc *Birm.*

Student welfare/counselling. Director of Student Services: Ball, David, BSc *CNAA*

Student welfare/counselling. Head Counsellor: Smith, Eileen, MA *St And.*, MA *Birm.*

Students from other countries. Director, International Office: Clark, Brian, BA *Birm.*, BSc *Lond.*, MBA *Brad.*

Students with disabilities. Director of Student Services: Ball, David, BSc *CNAA*

Students with disabilities. Disabled Students' Officer: Cooper, Sally, BA *Open(UK)*, BA *Oxf.*

University press. Public Relations Manager: Emsley, Brian

Women. Equal Opportunities Officer: Wright, Marcella, BA *Durh.*

[Information supplied by the institution as at 17 July 1998, and edited by the ACU]

UNIVERSITY OF HUDDERSFIELD

Established 1992; previously established as Huddersfield Technical College 1896, Huddersfield College of Technology 1958, and Huddersfield Polytechnic 1970

Member of the Association of Commonwealth Universities

Postal Address: Queensgate, Huddersfield, England HD1 3DH
Telephone: (01484) 422288 **Fax**: (01484) 516151 **Telex**: 518299 **WWW**: http://www.hud.ac.uk
E-mail formula: initial.surname@hud.ac.uk

CHANCELLOR—Hall, Sir Ernest, OBE, Hon. DUniv *York(UK)*, Hon. DLitt *Brad.*, Hon. DArt *W.England*, Hon. DUniv *Leeds Met.*, Hon. LLD *Leeds*

VICE-CHANCELLOR AND PRINCIPAL*—Tarrant, Prof. John R., BSc *Hull*, PhD *Hull*

DEPUTY VICE-CHANCELLOR/CHAIRMAN OF EQUAL OPPORTUNITIES COMMITTEE—Arthur, Prof. Fenwick, BSc *Durh.*, MSc *Aston*, PhD *Aston*

PRO VICE-CHANCELLOR (ACADEMIC AFFAIRS)—Evans, Prof. Brendan J., BA *Manc.*, MEd *Manc.*, PhD *Manc.*

REGISTRAR AND SECRETARY‡—Andrew, Margaret H., BA *E.Anglia*

DIRECTOR OF FINANCE—Smelt, Paul A., FCA

DIRECTOR OF LIBRARY SERVICES—Sykes, Philip, BA *Oxf.*

ACADEMIC REGISTRAR—Jeffs, Vivien P., BSc *Birm.*, MSc *Leeds*, PhD *Newcastle(UK)*

DIRECTOR OF ESTATES AND FACILITIES—Tait, Richard, LLB *Lond.*

GENERAL INFORMATION

History. The university's history dates back to the formation of the Young Men's Mental Improvement Society in 1841, later renamed the Mechanics' Institution (1844), Huddersfield Technical School & Mechanics' Institution (1894) and Huddersfield Technical College (1896). In 1958 the institution expanded to become Huddersfield College of Technology, and in 1970 a merger with Oastler College of Education created Huddersfield Polytechnic. The polytechnic was enlarged in 1974 by its absorption of Huddersfield College of Education. The institution was established as a university in 1992.

The university is situated almost entirely in the centre and immediate suburbs of the town of Huddersfield.

Admission to first degree courses (see also United Kingdom Introduction). Through Universities and Colleges Admissions Service (UCAS). General Certificate of Education (GCE) and General Certificate of Secondary Education (GCSE) with passes in 2 subjects at GCE A level and in 3 other subjects at GCSE (grade C or above). Wide range of equivalent

qualifications accepted. Additional course requirements are specified in the university's prospectus.

Mature entrants lacking formal educational qualifications: either by completion of a recognised access course or by satisfying the university that they will be able to benefit from the proposed course.

International students: qualifications judged equivalent to those specified above. Applicants whose first language is not English will be required to demonstrate proficiency in English.

First degrees (see also United Kingdom Directory to Subjects of Study). BA, BEd, BEng, BMus, BSc, LLB, MChem, MEng.

BMus and LLB courses last 3 years full-time; BA, BEng and BSc: 3 years full-time or 4 years sandwich; MChem: 4 years full-time; MEng: 5 years sandwich. BA, BEd, BEng, BSc and LLB may also be taken part-time.

Higher degrees (see also United Kingdom Directory to Subjects of Study). MA, MBA, MEd, MSc, MPhil, PhD.

Applicants for admission must normally hold an appropriate first degree or equivalent (for MPhil with at least second class honours). PhD: an appropriate master's degree; EdD:

normally a higher degree or professional qualification.

MA, MBA, MEd and MSc courses last 12 months full-time or equivalent part-time. MSc in geographical information systems and in multimedia and education offered by distance learning; EdD: 24 months part-time taught programme, with research element extending beyond this period; MPhil, PhD: minimum 24 months full-time, 36 months part-time.

Language of instruction. English. A lecturer in English as a foreign language assists international students.

Libraries. 379,163 volumes and other holdings; 1800 periodicals subscribed to. Special collections: George Henry Wood (social, political and economic history); John Yudkin (food and nutrition); local history (West Riding of Yorkshire); historic journals and newspapers (many relating to politics).

Fees. Home students (1998–99): undergraduate, £1000; postgraduate, £2630 (excluding MBA and postgraduate diploma in legal practice for which a full-cost fee is charged). International students (1997–98): postgraduate taught courses, £6825. Research programmes: £5650 (arts, business); £6360 (sciences, computing, engineering).

Academic awards (1997–98). 154 awards and prizes, in the form of cash amounts given to students, ranging in value from £25 to £500.

Academic year (1998–99). Three terms: 21 September–18 December; 11 January–26 March; 19 April–2 July.

Income (1997). Total, £62,167,000.

Statistics (as at 1 January 1998). Staff: 1265 (595 academic (excluding part-time staff and visiting professors), 670 administrative). Students: full-time, higher education 10,141 (5021 men, 5120 women), further education 33; part-time, higher education 4929 (1841 men, 3088 women), further education 343; international 711; total 16,157.

FACULTIES/SCHOOLS

Applied Sciences, School of

Tel: (01484) 472169 Fax: (01484) 472182

Dean: Page, Prof. Michael I., PhD *Glas.*, DSc *CNAA*, FRSChem
Secretary: Heslop, Angela

Computing and Mathematics, School of

Tel: (01484) 472150 Fax: (01484) 421106

Dean: Lee, Prof. Barry S., BA *Camb.*, MA *Camb.*, MEd *Manc.*
Secretary: Elliot, Diana V.

Design Technology, School of

Tel: (01484) 472289 Fax: (01484) 472940

Dean: Calderbank, Geoffrey, BArch *Strath.*, MSc *Strath.*
Secretary: Shaw, Judith

Education and Professional Development, School of

Tel: (01484) 478239 Fax: (01484) 514784

Dean: Somekh, Prof. Bridget E. M., BA *Trinity(Dub.)*, MA *E.Anglia*, PhD *E.Anglia*
Secretary: Ryan, Adele

Engineering, School of

Tel: (01484) 472574 Fax: (01484) 451883

Dean: Stout, Prof. Kenneth J., MSc *Cran.*, PhD *CNAA*, DSc *CNAA*
Secretary: Ainley, Petronella M.

Huddersfield University Business School

Tel: (01484) 472742 Fax: (01484) 473174

Dean: Smith, David, BA *CNAA*, MSc *Salf.*
Secretary: Monaghan, Doreen

Human and Health Sciences, School of

Tel: (01484) 472036 Fax: (01484) 472794

Dean: Frost, Prof. Susan A., BA *Open(UK)*, MPhil *Bath*
Secretary: Jarvis, Geraldine

Music and Humanities, School of

Tel: (01484) 472242 Fax: (01484) 472655

Dean: Taylor, David, BA *Oxf.*, DPhil *Oxf.*, FRHistS
Secretary: Furmedge, Sheila

ACADEMIC UNITS

Arranged by Schools

Accountancy, see under Huddersfield Univ. Business Sch.

Applied Sciences

35 Lectrs.†

Chemical and Biological Sciences

Tel: (01484) 472169 Fax: (01484) 472182

Ardrey, Robert E., BSc *Sur.*, PhD *Sur.* Sr. Lectr.
Balac, Pauline A., BSc *Sheff.*, PhD *Sheff.* Sr. Lectr.

Barnes, Philip A., BSc *Wales*, PhD *Brist.* Prof.; Head*
Bowtell, Sophie A., BA *Camb.*, PhD *Leeds* Sr. Lectr.
Bridgeland, Eric S., BSc *Reading*, PhD *Leic.* Sr. Lectr.
Brown, David R., BSc *Birm.*, PhD *Leic.* Reader
Clemenson, Peter I., MSc *Salf.*, PhD *Wales* Sr. Lectr.
Garrood, Anthony C., BSc *Newcastle(UK)*, PhD *Liv.* Sr. Lectr.
Golshekan, Hamid R., MEng *Brad.*, PhD *Brad.* Sr. Lectr.
Gowling, Eric W., BSc *Sheff.*, PhD *Sheff.*, FRSChem Sr. Lectr.
Jewsbury, Roger A., BSc *Brist.*, PhD *Brist.*, FRSChem Principal Lectr.
Lahmers, Harry, BSc *Manc.*, MSc *Manc.* Sr. Lectr.
Lamont, Christine L. A., BSc *Bath*, PhD *S'ton.* Sr. Lectr.
Laws, Andrew P., BSc *Lanc.*, DPhil *Sus.*, FRSChem Sr. Lectr.
Leonard, Michael N., BSc *Nott.*, PhD *Nott.* Sr. Lectr.
Martin, Philip, BA *Oxf.*, MA *Oxf.*, PhD *Camb.* Sr. Lectr.
Mortimer, Michael G., BSc *Leeds*, PhD *Leeds* Sr. Lectr.
Peagram, M. Visiting Prof.
Ramsden, D. Visiting Prof.
Saul, Michael W., BA *Camb.*, DPhil *Sus.* Sr. Lectr.
Southam, Richard M., MA *Oxf.*, DPhil *Oxf.* Sr. Lectr.
Vann, Anthony R., BSc *Wales*, PhD *Wales* Sr. Lectr.
Research: analytical chemistry (development of sensors and mass-spectrometer interfaces); biomolecular sciences (design and synthesis of therapeutic agents); catalysis (characterisation, preparation and application, heterogeneous catalysis); environmental sciences (bioremediation of land and water); thermal analysis

Food, Nutrition and Hospitality Management

Tel: (01484) 472012 Fax: (01484) 472562

Ball, Stephen D., BSc *Manc.*, MPhil *Hudd.* Sr. Lectr.
Guevara, Leo V., BSc *Leeds*, PhD *Leeds* Sr. Lectr.
Hawkins, Malcolm W., BA *CNAA*, MBA *Hudd.* Sr. Lectr.
Hunt, Clive, BSc *Lond.*, MPhil *CNAA*, PhD *CNAA* Sr. Lectr.
Lawson, John M., BSc *Lond.* Sr. Lectr.
Marshall, Valerie M. E., BSc *Aberd.*, PhD *Reading* Prof.; Head*
Mazurkiewicz, Margaret, BA *Strath.* Principal Lectr.
Mennell, David E. Sr. Lectr.
Smith, Alan G., BSc *Sheff.* Sr. Lectr.
Thompson, Elizabeth J., BSc *CNAA* Sr. Lectr.
Turner, Margaret Sr. Lectr.
Waite, James A., BA *Open(UK)* Sr. Lectr.
West, Ann, BSc *Lond.* Principal Lectr.
Williams, Alistair J. D., BSc *CNAA* Sr. Lectr.
Research: customer usage of hotels; database analysis of UK hotel groups; decision processes in hospitality operational management; internationalisation of hotel groups; managerial career trajectories in international hotel groups

Geographical and Environmental Sciences

Tel: (01484) 472384 Fax: (01484) 472347

Couch, Ian R., BA *Nott.*, MA *Manc.*, PhD *Manc.* Principal Lectr.; Head*
Etherington, David, MA *Durh.* Sr. Lectr.
Gunn, John, BSc *Wales*, PhD *Auck.* Prof.
Hunt, Christopher O., BA *Sheff.*, MSc *Sheff.*, PhD *Wales* Sr. Lectr.
Jones, Anne M., BSc *Lond.*, DPhil *Oxf.* Sr. Lectr.
Labadz, Jillian C., BSc *Nott.*, PhD *CNAA* Sr. Lectr.
Meaton, Julia, BA *CNAA*, PhD *CNAA* Sr. Lectr.

Reeve, Derek E., BA *Manc.*, MA *Manc.*, MSc *Brad.* Principal Lectr.
Thompson, Bernice, BSc *Sheff.*, PhD *Sheff.* Sr. Lectr.
Trescott, Anthony S., BSc *Lond.*, PhD *Lond.* Sr. Lectr.
Tufnell, Lance, BA *Durh.*, PhD *Newcastle(UK)* Sr. Lectr.
Wood, Adrian P., BA *Durh.*, PhD *Liv.* Principal Lectr.
Research: environmental change; hydrology and geomorphology; karst (hydrology, geomorphology and ecology); resource management and sustainable development; urban, economic and social geography

Limestone Research Group

Gunn, John, BSc *Wales*, PhD *Auck.* Prof.; Dir.*
Hunt, Christopher O., BA *Sheff.*, MSc *Sheff.*, PhD *Wales* Sr. Lectr.

Transport and Logistics

Tel: (01484) 472614 Fax: (01484) 473019

Bamford, Colin G., BA *Leeds* Prof.; Head*
Hubbard, Nicholas J., BSc *Liv.*, MPhil *Brad.*, PhD *Brad.* Sr. Lectr.
Murray, William, BA *CNAA*, MSc *Cran.IT*, PhD *Hudd.* Sr. Lectr.
Whiteing, Anthony E., BSc *Hull*, MA *Leeds*, PhD *Leeds* Sr. Lectr.
Research: commercial vehicle accident reduction (risk management for commercial vehicle operations); economics of rail freight privatisation (opportunities for competition and 'open access'); improving efficiency in vehicle fleet management (monitoring and management of fuel consumption); skills required for success in logistics management; urban freight problems and policies (balancing efficient operation and environmental considerations)

Water and Environmental Management, Centre for

Tel: (01484) 472643

Labadz, Jillian C., BSc *Nott.*, PhD *CNAA* Dir., Applied Sciences*

Architecture, see under Des. Technol.

Behavioural Sciences, see under Human and Health Scis.

Biological Sciences, see Chem. and Biological Scis. under Appl. Scis.

Business, see Huddersfield Univ. Business Sch.

Chemical Sciences, see under Appl. Scis.

Communication Arts, see under Music and Humanities

Computing and Mathematics

Tel: (01484) 472150 Fax: (01484) 421106

Computing Science

Dench, David J., BSc *St And.*, MSc *Manc.* Sr. Lectr.
Downs, Denise, BA *Lanc.*, MA *Open(UK)*, MSc *Manc.* Sr. Lectr.
Ellis, Geoffrey P., BSc *Manc.*, MSc *Manc.* Sr. Lectr.
Graba, Jan P., BA *Sheff.*, MSc *Sheff.* Sr. Lectr.
Grundy, Anne R., BSc *Reading*, MSc *CNAA* Sr. Lectr.
Hood, Peter W. L., BSc *CNAA* Sr. Lectr.
Jackson, Adrian R., BSc *Manc.*, MSc *Aston*, DPhil *York(UK)* Principal Lectr.
Lodge, William T., BSc *Manc.* Sr. Lectr.
McCluskey, Thomas L., BSc *Newcastle(UK)*, MSc *Warw.*, PhD *City(UK)* Prof.; Head*
McHattie, Allan D., BSc *Newcastle(UK)* Sr. Lectr.
Simpson, Ronald M., MA *Aberd.*, MPhil *Leeds*, MSc *Lond.* Sr. Lectr.
Smith, Martin, BA *Open(UK)*, BSc *Hull*, MSc *Lanc.*, MSc *Sheff.*, PhD *Manc.* Sr. Lectr.
Other Staff: 5 Lectrs.†

Research: artificial intelligence and formal methods (Artform); software engineering

Information Systems

Copley, Malcolm G., BA *Leeds*   Sr. Lectr.
Gregory, Mark R., BSc *Reading*, MSc *CNAA*   Sr. Lectr.
Haslam, Sue, BSc *Salf.*   Sr. Lectr.
Mansell, Gilbert J., BA *Open(UK)*, MSc *Aston*, MPhil *Aston*   Principal Lectr.; Head*
Pollitt, A. Stephen, BSc *CNAA*, PhD *CNAA*   Principal Lectr.
Pringle, Robert N., MSc *Sheff.*   Sr. Lectr.
Wade, Stephen J., BSc *CNAA*, MSc *Sheff.*, PhD *Sheff.*   Sr. Lectr.
Watson, David M., BSc *Hull*, PhD *Hull*   Principal Lectr.
Wraith, Peter C., BSc *Aston*, MSc *Aston*   Sr. Lectr.
Other Staff: 5 Lectrs.†
Research: database access research; teaching company programmes

Interactive Technology

Elsom-Cook, Mark T., BSc *Manc.*, MSc *Warw.*, PhD *Warw.*   Sr. Lectr.; Head*
Finlay, Janet E., BA *York(UK)*, MSc *York(UK)*, DPhil *York(UK)*   Sr. Lectr.
Kirby, Mark A. R., BSc *Manc.*, MA *Lanc.*, PhD *Hudd.*   Principal Lectr.
Marsden, Philip H., BSc *Hudd.*, PhD *Manc.*   Sr. Lectr.
Sapherson, Marshall S., BA *Brist.*   Sr. Lectr.
Stepney, Roy J., LLB *Warw.*, MSc *Lanc.*   Sr. Lectr.
Ward, Robert D., BA *Hull*, MSc *Manc.*, PhD *Hull*   Sr. Lectr.
Wrightson, Ann M., BA *Camb.*, MA *Camb.*   Sr. Lectr.
Other Staff: 4 Lectrs.†
Vacant Posts: 1 Sr. Lectr.
Research: human-computer interaction; multimedia and education

Mathematics and Statistics

Baker, Paul C., BSc *Sheff.*, MSc *Hull*, MSc *Sheff.*, PhD *Sheff.*   Sr. Lectr.
Blacktop, Jonathan, BA *York(UK)*, MSc *Sheff.*, PhD *Sheff.*   Sr. Lectr.
Booth, Dexter J., BSc *Wales*, MSc *Wales*, PhD *Vic.(BC)*, FIMA   Sr. Lectr.
Daniels, Sandra, MSc *Leeds*, PhD *Leeds*   Sr. Lectr.
Ferguson, Donald, BSc *Glas.*   Sr. Lectr.
Griffin, Graham K., BSc *Durh.*, MSc *Newcastle(UK)*, PhD *Brad.*   Principal Lectr.
Ingleby, Michael, BA *Camb.*, PhD *McM.*   Principal Lectr.
Mason, John C., BA *Oxf.*, MA *Oxf.*, DPhil *Oxf.*   Prof.; Head*
Parkin, Jane, BA *Oxf.*, MA *Oxf.*, MSc *Sheff.*   Sr. Lectr.
Priestley, John B., BA *Open(UK)*, MSc *Sheff.*   Sr. Lectr.
Pryce, Linda, BSc *Liv.*, MSc *CNAA*   Sr. Lectr.
Rawlins, Ian, BA *Oxf.*, MA *Oxf.*, MSc *Sheff.*   Sr. Lectr.
Roome, M. Antonia, BA *Stir.*   Sr. Lectr.
Talbot, Christopher J., BSc *Manc.*, PhD *Brad.*   Sr. Lectr.
Taylor, Sonia A., BEd *Leeds*, MSc *CNAA*   Sr. Lectr.
Turner, John K., BSc *Wales*, PhD *Newcastle(UK)*   Sr. Lectr.
Other Staff: 1 Lectr.; 2 Lectrs.†
Research: data advisory service; numerical and neural computing (Connect)

Design Technology

Tel: (01484) 472289 Fax: (01484) 472940

Architecture

Tel: (01484) 472289 Fax: (01484) 472940
Bush, Jonathon G.   Sr. Lectr.
Carling, Denis, BA *CNAA*, MSc *Leeds*   Sr. Lectr.
Dale, Julia E. S., BA *Newcastle(UK)*, BArch *Wales*, MA *Nott.*   Sr. Lectr.
Edwards, Brian, MSc *H-W*, PhD *Glas.*   Prof.
Fellows, Richard A., MPhil *York(UK)*   Principal Lectr.; Head*

Hales, D., BA *Hudd.*   Sr. Lectr.
Hall, Richard N., BArch *Liv.*, MA *Sheff.*   Sr. Lectr.
Halstead, Graham, BSc *CNAA*   Sr. Lectr.
Hartley, Stuart A.   Sr. Lectr.
Hippisley-Cox, Charles I., BA *Sheff.*, BSc *Sheff.*   Sr. Lectr.
Jones, Roy, BSc *Birm.*   Sr. Lectr.
Nicholls, Richard, BSc *CNAA*, MSc *Manc.*   Sr. Lectr.
Price, Helen A., BA *CNAA*, BSc *Salf.*, MA *Keele*   Sr. Lectr.
Riley, Janine D., BSc *Edin.*   Sr. Lectr.
Sibley, Magda, BSc *Sheff.*, PhD *Sheff.*   Sr. Lectr.
Wood, P.   Sr. Lectr.
Wood, Susan, MA   Sr. Lectr.
Other Staff: 6 Sr. Lectrs.†
Research: building conservation technologies and management practices in architecture; sustainability in design; third world development

Design

Almond, Kevin, MDes *RCA*, BA   Sr. Lectr.
Atkinson, Paul, BSc *CNAA*   Sr. Lectr.
Beale, Joanna M., BA *CNAA*   Sr. Lectr.
Clarkson, Gary, BA *Westminster*   Sr. Lectr.
Edwards, Robert J.   Sr. Lectr.
Gill, Harry, MSc *Manc.*   Sr. Lectr.
Howard, Christopher J., BA *CNAA*   Sr. Lectr.
Little, Beverley A., BA *Lough.*, MA *RCA*   Sr. Lectr.
Lyons, Agnes M. M., BA *Manc.*, MA *Salf.*   Sr. Lectr.
Moscovitch, Timothy J., BA *Lough.*, MDes *RCA*   Prof.; Head*
Oliver, Michael G.   Sr. Lectr.
Short, Jaqueline M., BA *CNAA*   Sr. Lectr.
Short, Margot, BA *Leeds*   Sr. Lectr.
Swann, David M., MDes *CNAA*, MA *RCA*   Sr. Lectr.
Tancock, David J., BSc *City(UK)*, MSc *Cran.IT*   Sr. Lectr.
Other Staff: 2 Lectrs.; 9 Sr. Lectrs.†
Research: history of local products and services; methodologies to test and develop the concept of innovation in design

Textiles

Tel: (01484) 472114
Annable, Raymond G., BSc *Leeds*, PhD *Leeds*   Sr. Lectr.
Atkinson, Catherine E.   Principal Lectr.
Beever, Christopher J., BSc   Sr. Lectr.
Bland, Douglas   Sr. Lectr.
Pearson, John S., BSc *Leeds*, MPhil *Leeds*, PhD *Leeds*   Principal Lectr.
Ritchie, Jane   Sr. Lectr.
Shearer, Allan J.   Sr. Lectr.
Squires, Paul L., BA *Lond.*   Sr. Lectr.
Other Staff: 2 Lectrs.; 14 Sr. Lectrs.†
Vacant Posts: 1 Sr. Lectr.†
Research: evolution of new finishes for textile products in areas such as crease resistance and reduction of UV light penetration; production of new materials from textile waste

Economics, see under Huddersfield Univ. Business Sch.

Education and Professional Development, see also Human and Health Scis. (Careers Guidance, and Continuing Professl. Educn.)

Tel: (01484) 428239 Fax: (01484) 514784
Ashmore, Melvyn J., BA *Leic.*, MEd *Manc.*   Sr. Lectr.
Brady, David B., BSc *Brist.*, MSc *Leeds*, PhD *Brist.*   Sr. Lectr.
Breckin, Michael J., BA *Lond.*, PhD *Lond.*   Principal Lectr.; Head, Devel. (Internat. Devel. Centre)
Butroyd, Robert, BA *Hull*   Sr. Lectr.
Crawford, Roger A., BSc *Hull*, MSc *Brad.*   Sr. Lectr.

Cullingford, Cedric I., BA *Camb.*, MA *Tor.*, MA *Oxf.*, MPhil *Oxf.*, MPhil *Lanc.*   Prof.; Head, Devel. (Res.)
Eccles, Peter, BEd *Leeds*   Sr. Lectr.
Fisher, Roy, BA *Wales*, MSc *Brad.*, MPhil *Leeds*   Sr. Lectr.
Gibson, F. Anne, BA *Sus.*   Sr. Lectr.
Guggenheim, Michael J., BSc *Brist.*   Sr. Lectr.
Gunn, Stanley E., BA *Keele*, MSc *Brad.*   Sr. Lectr.
Harris, Gill M., BSc *Reading*, PhD *CNAA*   Principal Lectr.; Head, Devel. (Staffing and Staff Devel.)
Harris, M. Ann, BA *Newcastle(UK)*, MA *Newcastle(UK)*   Sr. Lectr.
Herrick, Cathryn E., BSc *Aston*, MSc *Aston*, PhD *Aston*   Sr. Lectr.
Jarvis, Christine A., BA *Warw.*, MA *Warw.*   Principal Lectr.; Head, Devel. (Teaching)
Jones, Helen M. F., BA *Leeds*, MEd *Leeds*   Sr. Lectr.
Lord, David, BSc *Nott.*, MSc *Manc.*, PhD *Manc.*   Sr. Lectr.
Lundy, Suzanne, BA *Stir.*   Sr. Lectr.
Mitchell, Philip G., BA *Wales*, MEd *Liv.*   Sr. Lectr.
Morrison, C. Mary, BA *Camb.*, MA *Camb.*   Sr. Lectr.
Neve, David J., BEd *CNAA*, MEd *Hudd.*   Sr. Lectr.
Newbold, David E., BA *Camb.*, BA *Manc.*, MA *Camb.*, MLitt *Oxf.*, DPhil *Oxf.*   Prof.; Head, Devel. (Policy)
Notley, Martin W. J., MEd *Warw.*   Sr. Lectr.
Oliver, Paul, BEd *CNAA*, MPhil *Leeds*, PhD *CNAA*   Principal Lectr.; Head, Devel. (Curric.)
Ollin, Ros E., BA *Warw.*   Sr. Lectr.
Pearson, Lesley, BMus *Hull*, MEd *Leeds*   Sr. Lectr.
Powell, Loraine A., BEd *Lanc.*, MSc *Sheff.*   Sr. Lectr.
Rosier, Carolyn S., BSc *Brad.*, MA *Lanc.*   Sr. Lectr.
Sanderson, Peter J., BA *Camb.*, MPhil *York(UK)*   Sr. Lectr.
Swift, Helen D., BA *CNAA*, MA *York(UK)*   Principal Lectr.; Head, Devel. (Continuing Professl. Devel.)
Swindells, David F., BEd *CNAA*, MEd *Hudd.*   Sr. Lectr.
Thompson, David L., BA *Camb.*, MA *Kent*   Sr. Lectr.
Thompson, Ronald, BA *Lond.*   Sr. Lectr.
Turner, Alwyn, BA *Open(UK)*   Sr. Lectr.
Other Staff: 1 Reader†; 3 Sr. Lectrs.†; 3 Principal Lectrs.†; 1 Lectr.†
Vacant Posts: 1 Sr. Lectr.
Research: culture and education; information, technology and education; lifelong and continuing education; school improvement; vocational and professional education

Engineering

Tel: (01484) 472574 Fax: (01484) 451883
2 Res. Fellows; 8 Lectrs.†
Vacant Posts: 1 Lectr.
Research: analogue and digital electronics, optical and mobile communications; manufacturing systems (process mapping, planning and scheduling, PDM and program management); mechanical engineering (braking systems, noise reduction and flow measurement); ultra precision engineering (error avoidance and correction, metrology, surface characterisation)

Electronic and Electrical Engineering

Tel: (01484) 472319
Benaissa, Mohammed, PhD *Newcastle(UK)*   Sr. Lectr.
Daykin, Christopher I., BA *Camb.*, MA *Camb.*   Sr. Lectr.
Faraj, Abdul-Jabbar I., BSc *Leeds*, PhD *Leeds*   Sr. Lectr.
Fenn, Sebastian T. J., BSc *Wales*, MSc *CNAA*, PhD *Hudd.*   Sr. Lectr.

Harris, James K., BTech Brad., MSc Manc. Sr.
Lectr.
Lewis, Michael, BEng Sheff., PhD
Sheff. Principal Lectr.
Lucas, Gary P., BSc Brist., MSc Manc., PhD
Manc. Principal Lectr.
Marland, David, BSc Wales Sr. Lectr.
Mather, Peter J., BEng Hudd., PhD Hudd. Sr.
Lectr.
Mehrdadi, Behrooz, BSc Brad., MSc Brad., PhD
Brad. Sr. Lectr.
Phillips, George C. H., BA Oxf., MA Oxf., MSc
Newcastle(UK), MSc Sheff. Sr. Lectr.
Raczkowycz, Julian, BSc Manc., PhD CNAA Sr.
Lectr.
Sibley, Martin J. N., BSc CNAA, PhD CNAA Sr.
Lectr.
Taylor, David, BSc CNAA, PhD CNAA Reader
Thorn, Michael T., BSc Birm., PhD
Birm. Principal Lectr.
Ward, Stephen, BSc CNAA, PhD CNAA Head*
Wassell, Ian J., BEng Lough., BSc Lough., PhD
S'ton. Sr. Lectr.
Wright, Selwyn E., MSc S'ton., PhD
S'ton. Brook Crompton Prof.

Mechanical and Manufacturing Systems Engineering

Tel: (01484) 472128

Baron, John K., MSc Manc. Sr. Lectr.
Barrans, Simon M., BSc Manc. Sr. Lectr.
Blunt, Liam A., BSc Coventry, PhD
Coventry Reader
Bullingham, John M., BSc Manc., MSc Manc.,
PhD Lond. Emer. Prof.
Cerns, Christopher Visiting Prof.
Chandler, Jeffrey R., BSc CNAA, MSc Manc., PhD
CNAA Sr. Lectr.
Fieldhouse, John D., BSc CNAA, PhD Hudd. Sr.
Lectr.
Ford, Derek G., MSc Herts., PhD Hudd. Reader
Hall, David M., BSc Lough., PhD Lough. Sr.
Lectr.
Johnson, Anthony D., BSc CNAA Sr. Lectr.
Kelly, Philip F., BSc CNAA, MSc CNAA, PhD
Hudd. Principal Lectr.
Little, David Prof.
Mavromihales, Michael, BSc CNAA, MPhil
CNAA Sr. Lectr.
McMurtry, Christopher Visting Prof.
Munro, Robert G., BSc Durh., MA Camb., PhD
Camb. Prof.
Postlethwaite, Scott, BSc CNAA, PhD Hudd. Sr.
Lectr.
Rao, Vasudeva H., BE And., MTech Kharagpur,
PhD Kharagpur Prof.
Sherwin, Keith, BSc Wales, PhD CNAA Sr.
Lectr.
Ubbi, Kuldip S., BEng Brad. Sr. Lectr.
Weston, William, BSc Lond., PhD CNAA Head*

Environmental Sciences, see Geog. and
Environmental Scis. under Appl Scis.

Finance, see Accty. and Finance under
Huddersfield Univ. Business Sch.

**Food, Nutrition and Hospitality
Management**, see under Appl. Scis.

Geographical Sciences, see under Appl.
Scis.

History, see under Music and Humanities

Huddersfield University Business School

Tel: (01484) 472742 Fax: (01484) 473174

Accountancy and Finance

Tel: (01484) 472327 Fax: (01484) 473062

Cowton, Christopher J., BA Sheff., MScEcon
Wales Prof.
Derwin, Garry A., BSc Nott., MSc Brist., PhD
Brist. Sr. Lectr.
Drake, Julie E., BA CNAA Sr. Lectr.
Drury, Colin, BA Open(UK), MBA Brad. Prof.
Fidler, Wayne, BA CNAA Sr. Lectr.

Gallagher, Irene D., BA Open(UK), FCA Sr.
Lectr.
Leach, Willliam J., BA CNAA, MBA Hudd. Sr.
Lectr.
McGrath, Pamela A., BA CNAA Sr. Lectr.
Mehafdi, Messaoud, MSc Manc., PhD CNAA Sr.
Lectr.
Murphy, Vivienne M., BA CNAA Sr. Lectr.
Teviotdale, Wilma W., BA Strath.,
FCA Principal Lectr.; Head*
Thompson, Paul, BSc Warw. Sr. Lectr.
Thompson, Susan, BA Sheff. Sr. Lectr.
Trotter, Eileen, BA Stir. Sr. Lectr.
Other Staff: 12 Lectrs.†
Research: accounting and financial ethics;
accounting education; management
accounting and control

Economics and Business Studies

Tel: (01484) 472206 Fax: (01484) 473062

Anchor, John R., BSc Manc., PhD
Manc. Principal Lectr.; Head*
Barton, Christopher A., BSc Brad., MA Kent Sr.
Lectr.
Buckley, Martin W., BCom Leeds, MA Sheff. Sr.
Lectr.
Cafferty, Peter, BA Leeds, MA Leeds, MSc
Lond. Sr. Lectr.
Carr, Andrew, BA CNAA Sr. Lectr.
Casserley, Damian J., BA Leeds, MA Leeds,
MSc(Econ) Lond. Sr. Lectr.
Day, Janine C., BSc Hull, MBA Hudd. Sr. Lectr.
Day, John, BSc Hull, MSc Salf. Sr. Lectr.
Hardaker, Glenn, BA CNAA Sr. Lectr.
Kenny, Brian, MSc Aston, PhD Salf. Prof.
Kuhanen, Ismo M. Sr. Lectr.
Lodge, J. Martin Sr. Lectr.
Marsh, G., MA Oxf., MA Warw. Visiting Prof.
Oldroyd, Michael E., BSc Hull, MA Leeds Sr.
Lectr.
Rowles, Kevin J., BA Leeds, MA Leeds Sr. Lectr.
Simister, Leslie T., BA Manc., PhD
Manc. Principal Lectr.
Thompson, John L., BA CNAA, MBA
Cran.IT Prof.
Trick, Robert R., BA Lond. Principal Lectr.
Turner, Colin, BSc Exe., MA Exe. Sr. Lectr.
Warmington, Robert V., BA Warw., MA
McM. Principal Lectr.
Welford, Richard J., BA CNAA, MA CNAA, PhD
Warw. Prof.
Other Staff: 8 Lectrs.†
Vacant Posts: 3 Lectrs.
Research: corporate environment management;
entrepreneurship; European business
strategy; strategic change

Law

Tel: (01484) 472192 Fax: (01484) 472279

Clayton, Georgina A., BA Oxf., LLM Leic. Sr.
Lectr.
Coidan, Nicholas A., LLB S'ton., LLM Lond. Sr.
Lectr.
Cook, Carol A., LLB CNAA Sr. Lectr.
Fairhurst, John, BA CNAA Sr. Lectr.
Foxcroft, Lynne C., LLB CNAA Sr. Lectr.
Lazer, Susan, LLB Leeds Sr. Lectr.
Murphy, Martin B., BA Camb., MA Camb. Sr.
Lectr.
Norris, Terence L., BA Nott., LLM Leic. Sr.
Lectr.
Pitt, Gwyneth J., LLB CNAA Prof.; Head*
Richards, Paul H., LLB CNAA, PhD
CNAA Principal Lectr.
Sagar, David P., LLB Leeds, LLM Leeds Sr. Lectr.
Turner, Christopher J., LLB Nott. Sr. Lectr.
Ware, Susan P., LLB Sheff., LLM Exe. Sr. Lectr.
Wild, Vivienne M., LLB Leeds Sr. Lectr.
Wolstencroft, Timothy G., BA Durh., MA
CNAA Principal Lectr.
Wood, Anne E., LLB CNAA Sr. Lectr.
Wragg, Diane M., BA Sus., LLM
Hudd. Principal Lectr.
Other Staff: 2 Lectrs.
Vacant Posts: 1 Sr. Lectr.; 7 Lectrs.†
Research: civil liberties; employment and
discrimination law; European Community

law; international economic and energy law;
medical law and ethics

Management

Tel: (01484) 472026 Fax: (01484) 473174

Abell, Donald, BA Oxf. Sr. Lectr.
Broadhead, A. David, BSc CNAA Sr. Lectr.
Carmichael, Janis L., BSc Brad. Sr. Lectr.
Cook, John A., BSc Brad., MSc Strath., PhD
Nott. Sr. Lectr.
Dunn, John, BA Durh., MSc Brad., MA Leic. Sr.
Lectr.
Duxbury, William, BA Keele, BA Open(UK) Sr.
Lectr.
Edwards, David J., BA Open(UK), PhD
Cran.IT Sr. Lectr.
Foot, Margaret D., BA Newcastle(UK), MA Alta.,
MBA York(Can.) Sr. Lectr.
Gibbs, Sylvia, BA E.Anglia, MSc(Econ) Lond.,
MBA Brad. Sr. Lectr.
Graham, Richard J., BA Keele, MA E.Anglia Sr.
Lectr.
Handley, Janet, BA CNAA, MSc Hudd. Sr. Lectr.
Hook, Caroline M., BA Leeds, MEd CNAA Sr.
Lectr.
Rickwood, Anthony G., BSc Lond., MA
Lanc. Sr. Lectr.
Rollinson, Derek J., BA Open(UK), MBA Aston,
PhD Aston Principal Lectr.
Routledge, Christopher W., BSc Newcastle(UK),
MSc Lough., PhD Lough. Principal Lectr.
Stansfield, Lynda M., BSc CNAA, LLB Lond., MSc
Bolton IHE Sr. Lectr.
Waddington, Michael E., MPhil Birm., PhD
Hudd. Head*
Wilson, Hazel J., MBA Brad. Sr. Lectr.
Other Staff: 4 Lectrs.; 5 Lectrs.†
Research: change and human resource
management; human resource management;
management; management stategy; research
and action learning

Marketing

Tel: (01484) 472746 Fax: (01484) 472896

Aldred, Anthony, BA Wales, MSc Manc. Sr.
Lectr.
Carroll, Angela, BA CNAA, MSc Salf. Sr. Lectr.
Crowther, Geoffrey, BA Sheff., MSc Brad. Sr.
Lectr.
Forbes, Giles R., BSc Wales, MBA Brad. Sr.
Lectr.
Harness, David R., BSc Aston Sr. Lectr.
Harvey, David J., BA CNAA Sr. Lectr.
Jackson, Howard E., MBA Brad. Sr. Lectr.
Johnson, Terence, BSc Wales Sr. Lectr.
Jones, Glynis, MA C.Lancs. Sr. Lectr.
Marr, Norman E., MSc Cran.IT, PhD
Cran.IT Prof.; Head*
Parsons, M. Visiting Prof.
Reynolds, Paul L., BA CNAA, MSc Manc. Sr.
Lectr.
Varley, Rosemary, BA CNAA Sr. Lectr.
Withey, Frank, BA CNAA, MA Leeds Sr. Lectr.
Other Staff: 2 Lectrs; 3 Lectrs.†
Research: communications; database marketing;
financial services; leisure consumer research;
retailing

Human and Health Sciences

Tel: (01484) 472036 Fax: (01484) 472794

Behavioural Sciences, Division of

Tel: (01484) 472265

Arevalo, Mavis, BSc CNAA, MSc Brad. Sr. Lectr.
Burr, Vivien, BA CNAA, PhD CNAA Sr. Lectr.
Butt, Trevor W., BSc Leeds, MSc Leeds Sr. Lectr.
Cliff, Dallas R., MA Sus., PhD Manc. Principal
Lectr.
Garwood, Jeanette, BSc Lond., MSc Edin., DPhil
Oxf. Sr. Lectr.
Gibbs, Graham, BSc S'ton., MSc Kent Sr. Lectr.
Hickling, Keith, BSc Hudd. Principal Lectr.
Kelly, Nancy, BSc CNAA, MSc CNAA Sr. Lectr.
King, Nigel, BA Kent, PhD Sheff. Sr. Lectr.
Leach, C., BA Hull, BA Open(UK), MSc Leeds, PhD
Hull Visiting Prof.
McAuley, James W., BSc Ulster, PhD
Leeds Reader

Pease, Kenneth, BA Lond., MA Manc., PhD Manc. Prof.

Roberts, Brian, BA CNAA, LLM Sheff., PhD Birm. Sr. Lectr.

Robinson, David N., BEd Manc., BSc CNAA, MSc Sheff. Sr. Lectr.

Sparks, Geoffrey H., BSc Lond., MSc Birm. Principal Lectr.; Head*

van Kemenade, Rudyard J. J., BA Rhodes, MSc Lond., MA Brad. Sr. Lectr.

Other Staff: 1 Lectr.; 1 Visiting Res. Fellow

Research: autobiographical memory; health psychology; personal construct psychology; nationalism; social identity

Careers Guidance

Tel: (01484) 472036

Bretherick, Graham, LLB Hull Sr. Lectr.
Hunter, Christine, BA Sheff. Sr. Lectr.
Norton, Debra S., BA CNAA Sr. Lectr.
Other Staff: 1 Lectr.†
Research: British careers market

Continuing Professional Education

Tel: (01924) 814788 Fax: (01924) 814952

Arthurs, Joyce, BEd Brad., MEd Leeds Sr. Lectr.
Bowers, Patricia A., BA Open(UK), BEd Manc., MA Leeds Sr. Lectr.
Chirema, Kathleen, BA Open(UK), MA Leeds Sr. Lectr.
Delbridge, Bronwyn, BEd Leeds Sr. Lectr.
Donley, Linda, BA Leeds Principal Lectr.
Durkan, Patricia M., BSc Hudd. Sr. Lectr.
Farrell, Jane S., BSc Hudd. Sr. Lectr.
Farrell, Winifred, BEd Brad., MEd Hudd. Sr. Lectr.
Gething, Linda, BA Leeds Sr. Lectr.
Gren, Elizabeth R., BSc Hudd. Sr. Lectr.
Hauxwell, Jonathan M., BSc Leic. Principal Lectr.
Heaton, Margaret, BSc Leeds, MA York(UK) Sr. Lectr.
Hepworth, Sylvia, BA Open(UK), MEd Hudd. Principal Lectr.
Hirst, Ian, BA Open(UK), MSc Hudd. Head*
Jones, James Sr. Lectr.
Joyce, Patrick, BSc Hudd., MSc Hudd. Sr. Lectr.
Leach, Ann, BSc Hudd. Sr. Lectr.
Mills, Valerie, BSc Hudd. Sr. Lectr.
Padgett, Katherine, BSc Leeds Sr. Lectr.
Roche, Tracy, BSc Hudd. Sr. Lectr.
Smith, Carole, BA Open(UK) Sr. Lectr.
Smith, Linda Sr. Lectr.
Smith, Martin E. Principal Lectr.
Snowden, Michael, BSc Leeds, MA Manc. Sr. Lectr.
Straw, James A. Sr. Lectr.
Taylor, Brian, BA Lanc., MEd Leeds Sr. Lectr.
Thurgood, Graham, MSc Aston Sr. Lectr.
Wallis, Timothy J., BSc Hudd. Sr. Lectr.
Westwood, Linda, BA CNAA Sr. Lectr.
Williams, Jane, BSc Hudd. Sr. Lectr.
Wood, Barbara, BEd Leeds, MSc Leeds Sr. Lectr.
Wordsworth, Stephen L., BA Hudd. Sr. Lectr.
Other Staff: 2 Lectrs.; 5 Practitioners/Lectrs.

Health, Social Work and Community Studies, Division of

Tel: (01484) 472541

Balen, Rachel, BA Leeds, MA Brad. Sr. Lectr.
Ball, Dorothy M., BA CNAA, MA Brad. Sr. Lectr.
Bindless, Linda, BA Open(UK), MA Manc. Sr. Lectr.
Blyth, Eric D., BA York(UK), MA Brun. Reader
Bradshaw, Peter L., BMus Manc., MA Leeds Prof.
Brooke, Shelagh M., BSc Aston, PhD Liv. Sr. Lectr.
Firth, Janet E., MEd Hudd. Sr. Lectr.
Hayles, Michelle, BA Sus., MA Brad. Sr. Lectr.
Jordan, William, BA Oxf., MA Oxf. Prof.
Karban, Kathryn E., BA Reading, MA Sheff. Sr. Lectr.
Kazi, Mansoor A. F., BSc Lond., MA Hull Sr. Lectr.
Makin, Philip, BA Leeds, MA Nott. Sr. Lectr.
Masson, Helen C., BA Nott. Principal Lectr.

O'Byrne, Patrick, MA Brad. Sr. Lectr.
Parkin, Wendy P., BA Brad. Principal Lectr.
Parton, Nigel A., BA Brad., MA Essex Prof.
Playle, John F., BSc Hudd., MSc Hudd. Sr. Lectr.
Rae, Rosemary J., BSc CNAA, MSc Lond. Sr. Lectr.
Raynes, Norma, BA Lond., MSc Manc., PhD Lond. Prof.
Richards, Christopher, BSc Lond. Sr. Lectr.
Seed, Ann, BSc Leeds Met., PhD CNAA Principal Lectr.
Topping, Anne E., BSc Sur. Sr. Lectr.
Wolff, Penelope R., BSc Liv., MBiol CNAA, PhD CNAA Sr. Lectr.
Research: cancer care; care in the community; child care and child protection; evaluation of human services; infertility and surrogacy

Midwifery, Division of

Tel: (01924) 213712 Fax: (01924) 814542

Deery, Ruth M., BSc Hudd. Sr. Lectr.
Holt, Alison, BSc Manc. Sr. Lectr.
Hughes, Deborah, BA York(UK), MA York(UK) Sr. Lectr.
Jarvis, Yvonne, BEd Leeds Met., MSc Leeds Met. Sr. Lectr.
Jones, Patricia A., BSc Hudd. Sr. Lectr.
Lessing-Turner, Georgina H. S., BA Manc., MA Manc. Sr. Lectr.
McGuire, Glenys, BSc Manc. Sr. Lectr.
Phillips, Mari A., BA Open(UK), MEd Hudd. Sr. Lectr.
Pickles, Alison, MA C.Lancs. Sr. Lectr.
Powell, Jane D., MA Manc. Principal Lectr.
Simpson, Marion O., MEd Leeds Sr. Lectr.
Wood, Helen, BSc Hudd. Principal Lectr.

Nursing

Tel: (01924) 465105 Fax: (01484) 450839

Allsopp, Tom, BSc Hudd. Sr. Lectr.
Armstrong, Barry, BEd Leeds Met. Sr. Lectr.
Ascroft, Biljiana, BEd Sarajevo, MEd Hudd. Principal Lectr.
Belk, Dennis, BA Brad. Sr. Lectr.
Burton, Robert, BSc CNAA, MEd Hudd. Sr. Lectr.
Cheung, Sui, BEd Leeds Met. Sr. Lectr.
Cranmer, Pam, BSc CNAA, MA Leeds Sr. Lectr.
Dew, Niall, BSc Hudd. Sr. Lectr.
Doggett, Cathy, BEd Leeds Met., MEd Leeds Met. Head*
Ellis, Rona, BSc Hudd. Sr. Lectr.
Foo, Shih Liang, BA Manc.Met., MSc Manc. Sr. Lectr.
Francis, Richard Sr. Lectr.
Gannon, Judy, BSc Hudd. Sr. Lectr.
Goonoo, Bhye F., BA Open(UK), MSc Open(UK) Sr. Lectr.
Howden-Leach, Hazel, MSc Sheff.Hallam Sr. Lectr.
Kieran, Brian Principal Lectr.
Leckey, Jill, BSc Leeds Met. Sr. Lectr.
Lee, Tony, BA Open(UK) Sr. Lectr.
Machin, David, BEd Leeds Sr. Lectr.
Mawdsley, Josephine, BA Brad. Sr. Lectr.
Meadows, Jill, BEd CNAA Sr. Lectr.
Mills, Joe, BA Hudd., MPhil Hudd. Sr. Lectr.
Mountain, Gary, BA Sheff.Hallam, MA Leeds Sr. Lectr.
Nhemachena, Jean, BSc Brighton, MSc Sur. Sr. Lectr.
Quashie, Charles, MA Lanc. Sr. Lectr.
Rangeley, Hazel, MA York(UK) Sr. Lectr.
Rodak, Jenny, BSc Hudd., MEd Nott. Sr. Lectr.
Shaw, Sue, BEd Hudd., MA Sheff. Sr. Lectr.
Shuttleworth, Margaret, BEd CNAA Sr. Lectr.
Spencer, Britt, BEd CNAA Principal Lectr.
Spilsbury, Hilary, BSc Hull, MA Sheff.Hallam Sr. Lectr.
Thomas, Paul, BSc Leeds Sr. Lectr.
Thurgood, Graham, MSc Aston Sr. Lectr.
Tramposch, Val, BA Sheff.Hallam Sr. Lectr.
Ward, Keith, BSc Hudd. Sr. Lectr.
Watson, David, BSc CNAA Sr. Lectr.
Wilbourn, Veronica, BA Open(UK) Sr. Lectr.

Physiotherapy, Division of

Tel: (01924) 212275

Buttling, Pauline, BSc Leeds Sr. Lectr.
Fletcher-Cook, Phyl, MEd Leeds Sr. Lectr.
Freeburn, Margaret Sr. Lectr.
Johnstone, Jane C., MSc Hull Sr. Lectr.
Robinson, Gillian M. Sr. Lectr.
Stignant, Mark, BSc Liv. Sr. Lectr.
Thornton, Sandra E., MEd Leeds Principal Lectr.; Head*
Weeks, Susan M., BA Lough., MA Lough. Sr. Lectr.
Research: computer-based learning; fibre optics and spinal movement; virtual reality modelling

Podiatry

Tel: (01484) 472201

Davies, Christopher S., BSc Salf., MEd Sr. Lectr.
Pickard, James M., MSc Salf. Sr. Lectr.
Renwick, Penelope A., MA Leeds Principal Lectr.; Head*
Other Staff: 4 Lectrs.
Research: clinical podiatry; gait analysis

Law, see under Huddersfield Univ. Business Sch.

Management, see under Huddersfield Univ. Business Sch.

Marketing, see under Huddersfield Univ. Business Sch.

Mathematics, see Computing and Maths.

Midwifery, see under Human and Health Scis.

Music and Humanities

Tel: (01484) 472242 Fax: (01484) 472655
116 Lectrs.†
Vacant Posts: 1 Lectr.

Communication Arts, Division of

Tel: (01484) 472606

Arragon, Jean-Claude, MA Leeds Sr. Lectr.
Bembridge, Paul U., BA York(UK), MPhil York(UK) Sr. Lectr.
Foot, Robert, BA Wales, MA Alta., PhD Alta. Sr. Lectr.
Hemsley, Michael J., BA E.Anglia, MA Warw. Sr. Lectr.
Holden, Catherine J., BA E.Anglia, PhD E.Anglia Sr. Lectr.
Jeffries, Leslie E., BA Reading, PhD Leeds Principal Lectr.
Kelly, Stephen F., BSc Lond. Sr. Lectr.
Leahy, Stephen Visiting Prof.
Maidment, Brian E., BA Wales, MA Wales, PhD Leic. Prof.; Head, Engl.*
Meredith, Christopher J., BA Manc. Sr. Lectr.
Nicholson, Stephen J., BA Exe., MA Lanc., PhD Leeds Sr. Lectr.
Prior, Christopher N., BA Camb., MA Camb. Sr. Lectr.
Ridley, Glynis B., MA Edin., DPhil Oxf. Sr. Lectr.
Robertson, Hugh G., BA Camb., MA Camb. Principal Lectr.; Head, Media/Theatre Studies*
Townsend, Peter W., BA Birm., MA Birm. Sr. Lectr.
Williams, Granville,, BA Leeds MA Exe. Sr. Lectr.
Williams, T. Glynn, BA Wales Principal Lectr.
Research: cultural theory, popular culture, conversation analysis; feminist linguistic theory; literature (critical linguistics, Irish, post-colonial theory, stylistics, text analysis); theatre (physical forms of actor training, psychopathology of performance art, theatre in educational and community settings, twentieth-century British political theatre)

History, Division of

Tel: (01484) 472359

Cullum, Patricia H., BA *Keele*, MA *York(UK)*,
DPhil *York(UK)* Sr. Lectr.
Davies, Peter J., BSc *CNAA* Sr. Lectr.
Gurney, Peter J., BA *Sus.*, MA *Sus.*, DPhil
Sus. Sr. Lectr.
Laybourn, Keith, BSc *Brad.*, MA *Lanc.*, PhD *Lanc.*,
FRHistS Prof.
Stafford, Pauline, BA *Oxf.*, MA *Oxf.*, DPhil *Oxf.*,
FRHistS Prof.
Taithe, Bertrand O., PhD *Manc.* Sr. Lectr.
Taylor, David, BA *Oxf.*, DPhil *Oxf.*,
FRHistS Principal Lectr.; Head*
Woodfine, Philip L., BA *Camb.*, MA *Camb.*, PhD
Hudd., FRHistS Principal Lectr.
Research: gender and women's history,
particularly mediaeval; labour history,
Labour Party, co-operative movement;
medical history, nineteenth and twentieth
centuries; political history, sixteenth to
eighteenth centuries

Music

Tel: (01484) 472003 Fax: (01484) 472656

Bryan, John H., BA *York(UK)* Principal Lectr.
Clarke, J. Michael, BA *Durh.*, PhD
Durh. Principal Lectr.
Cummings, Graham H., BMus *Birm.*, MA *Birm.*,
PhD *Birm.* Sr. Lectr.
Fox, Christopher, BA *Liv.*, BMus *S'ton.*, DPhil
York(U.K.) Sr. Lectr.
Holloway, Michael L., BMus *Manc.* Sr. Lectr.
Jarvis, E. Keith, BA *Oxf.*, MA *Oxf.*,
FRCO Principal Lectr.
Lawson, Peter J., BA *Oxf.*, BMus *Oxf.*, MA
Oxf. Principal Lectr.; Head*
Steinitz, Richard J., MA *Camb.*, MMus *Ill.* Prof.
Webb, Barry E. R., BA *Camb.*, MA
Camb. Principal Lectr.
Wilkins, Margaret L., BMus *Nott.* Sr. Lectr.
Research: computer music and computer-assisted
learning; contemporary (composition,
electroacoustic, musicology); gender issues;
Handel in London; historically aware
performance practice (eighteenth century)

Politics, Division of

Tel: (01484) 472359

Bryson, Valerie, BA *Kent*, PhD *Kent*, MA
Manc. Sr. Lectr.
Stafford, Prof. William, BA *Oxf.*, MA *Oxf.*, DPhil
Oxf., FRHistS Reader
Taylor, Andrew J., BA *Manc.*, PhD *Sheff.* Prof.
Timmins, Graham, BA *CNAA*, MPhil *Glas.* Sr.
Lectr.; Head, Pol./Hist./Langs.*
Research: British politics (parties and policy-
making); international politics (international
organisations); political theory (gender and
feminist); West European politics
(integration); world politics (food security)

Nursing, see under Human and Health Scis.

Physiotherapy, see under Human and Health
Scis.

Podiatry, see under Human and Health Scis.

Social Work, see Health, Soc. Work and
Community Studies under Human and
Health Scis.

Statistics, see Maths. and Stats. under
Computing and Maths.

Textiles, see under Des. Technol.

Transport and Logistics, see under Appl.
Scis.

CONTACT OFFICERS

Academic affairs. Pro Vice-Chancellor
(Academic Affairs): Evans, Prof. Brendan J.,
BA *Manc.*, MEd *Manc.*, PhD *Manc.*
Accommodation. Accommodation Officer:
Bowser, Diana
Admissions (first degree). Assistant Registrar
(Admissions): McGregor, Linda
Admissions (higher degree). Assistant
Registrar (Admissions): McGregor, Linda
Adult/continuing education. Lee, Prof. Barry
S., BA *Camb.*, MA *Camb.*, MEd *Manc.*
Alumni. International and European Alumni
Administrative Assistant: Park, Julie A., BA
Hudd.
Careers. Head of Careers Advisory Service:
Gilworth, Robert, BA *CNAA*
Computing services. Director of Computing
Services: Jordan, Andrew P. H., BSc *Lond.*,
MSc *Manc.*, PhD *Manc.*
Conferences/corporate hospitality. Wragg,
Joan
Consultancy services. Regional Development
Director: Mullen, Bede, BA *Warw.*
Credit transfer. Learning Development Co-
ordinator: Latimer, Richard W., LLB *Lond.*,
MA *Manc.*
Development/fund-raising. Regional
Development Director: Mullen, Bede, BA
Warw.
Equal opportunities. Deputy Vice-Chancellor/
Chairman of Equal Opportunities Committee:
Arthur, Prof. Fenwick, BSc *Durh.*, MSc *Aston*,
PhD *Aston*
Estates and buildings/works and services.
Director of Estates and Facilities: Tait,
Richard, LLB *Lond.*
Examinations. Assistant Registrar
(Examinations): Shaw, Amanda, BA *CNAA*
Finance. Deputy Director of Finance: Thorpe,
David, BA *CNAA*
General enquiries. Academic Registrar: Jeffs,
Vivien P., BSc *Birm.*, MSc *Leeds*, PhD
Newcastle(UK)
Health services. University Senior Medical
Officer: Varley, Yvonne W., BSc *Lond.*, BM
S'ton.

Industrial liaison. Regional Development
Director: Mullen, Bede, BA *Warw.*
International office. Director: Sweeney,
Eammon, BSc *CNAA*, MA *Wales*, MBA *Hudd.*
Language training for international students.
Hemsley, Michael J., MA *Warw.*
Library (chief librarian). Director of Library
Services: Sykes, Philip, BA *Oxf.*
Library (enquiries). Assistant Director of
Library Services: Hart, Elizabeth, BA *Leic.*,
FLA
Minorities/disadvantaged groups. Head of
Welfare Support: Moran, Anne, BA *Leeds Met.*
Ombudsperson. (Contact the appropriate Dean
or Director/Head of Service or the Vice-
Chancellor and Principal)
Personnel/human resources. Head of Payroll
and Establishment Office: Sutcliffe, Robert I.,
BA *Open(UK)*
Public relations, information and marketing.
Head of Publicity and Media Relations:
Williams, Philip, BA *Leeds*, MA *Leeds*
Publications. Publications Manager: Hirstle,
Ian
Purchasing. Purchasing Co-ordinator:
Thompson, John
Quality assurance and accreditation. Training
and Quality Services: Lundy, Suzanne, BA
Stir.
Research. Assistant Academic Registrar:
Davison, Judith A., BEd *Keele*
Safety. Health and Safety Adviser:
Boryslawskyj, Michael, PhD *CNAA*
Scholarships, awards, loans. Assistant
Registrar (Student Records and Registration):
......
Schools liaison. Pedley, Julie, BA *Leeds*
Security. Security Officer: Tain, Graham
Sport and recreation. Sports Supervisor:
Smith, Laurie
Staff development and training. Director,
Quality and Staff Development Group:
Lemon, Prof. Nigel F., BSc *Hull*, PhD *Hull*
Student union. President, University of
Huddersfield Student Union: Bartlett, Roisin
Student welfare/counselling (counselling).
Forbes, Maggie, BA *Reading*
Student welfare/counselling (welfare).
Director of Student Services: Wilcock, Rev.
Paul T., BA *Brist.*, MA *Leeds*
Students from other countries. Advisor to
Overseas Students: Iqbal, M., MSc *Punjab*,
MPhil *CNAA*, PhD *CNAA*
Students with disabilities. Head of Welfare
Support: Moran, Anne, BA *Leeds Met.*
Women. Deputy Vice-Chancellor/Chairman of
Equal Opportunities Committee: Arthur,
Prof. Fenwick, BSc *Durh.*, MSc *Aston*, PhD
Aston

[Information supplied by the institution as at 2 February
1998, and edited by the ACU]

UNIVERSITY OF HULL

Founded 1954; previously established as University College of Hull 1928

Member of the Association of Commonwealth Universities

Postal Address: Hull, England HU6 7RX
Telephone: (01482) 346311 **Fax**: (01482) 465936 **Telex**: 52530 **WWW**: http://www.hull.ac.uk

VISITOR—Elizabeth, H.M. The Queen
CHANCELLOR—Armstrong of Ilminster, The Lord, GCB, CVO, MA LLD
PRO-CHANCELLOR AND CHAIRMAN OF COUNCIL—Robinson, J., BSc Birm., FEng, FIChemE
PRO-CHANCELLOR EMERITUS—Farrell, T. H. F., TD, CBE, LLB Lond., Hon. LLD
PRO-CHANCELLOR—Black, W., LLD
PRO-CHANCELLOR—Barker, P. W., CBE, DSc(Econ)
VICE-CHANCELLOR*—Dilks, Prof. David N., BA Oxf., Hon. DrHist Russian Acad.Sc., FRHistS, FRSL
TREASURER—Pettifer, V. M.
PRO-VICE-CHANCELLOR—Kopp, P. E., BSc Stell., DPhil Oxf.
PRO-VICE-CHANCELLOR—King, Prof. V. T., BA Hull, MA Lond., PhD Hull
PRO-VICE-CHANCELLOR—Walker, Prof. R. W., BSc Hull, PhD Hull, FRSChem
PRO-VICE-CHANCELLOR—Lloyd, Prof. H. A., BA Wales, DPhil Oxf., FRHistS
REGISTRAR AND SECRETARY‡—Lock, David, BSc Bath, MPhil Bath, FCIS
LIBRARIAN AND DIRECTOR OF ACADEMIC SERVICES—Heseltine, Richard G., BA Sus., DPhil Sus.

GENERAL INFORMATION

History. The university was established in 1928 as a college of the University of London and achieved its independence in 1954.

Admission to first degree courses (see also United Kingdom Introduction). Through Universities and Colleges Admissions Service (UCAS). Candidates whose native language is not English will normally be expected to possess a recognised qualification in English Language or to submit acceptable evidence of proficiency.

First Degrees (see also United Kingdom Directory to Subjects to Study). BA, BEng, BMus, BSc, BScEcon, BTh, LLB, MChem, MEng, MMath, MPhys.

Higher Degrees (see also United Kingdom Directory to Subjects to Study). BPhil, LLM, MA, MBA, MEd, MMus, MSc, MScEcon, MPhil, PhD, ClinPsyD, DD, DLitt, DMus, DSc, DSc(Econ), EdD, LLD, MD, PsyD.

BPhil, LLM, MA, MBA, MEd, MMus, MSc, MScEcon, MPhil: 1 year full-time; ClinPsyD: 1 year full-time plus 2 years part-time; MD: 1 year full-time or equivalent part-time; PsyD: 2 years part-time; EdD, PhD: 3 years full-time or 4 years part-time. DD, DLitt, DSc, DMus, DSc(Econ), LLD: by submitted work.

Language of Instruction. English. Pre-sessional English language courses available.

Libraries. 930,000 volumes; 3700 periodicals subscribed to; 59 electronic databases subscribed to. Special collections include: Philip Larkin; Stevie Smith (lecturer); Hull Grammar School; Holy Trinity Hull (local history); Labour history (political history); extensive map collection. The archives include collections from Hotham of South Dalton, Sykes of Sledmere, the Carleton Estate, Ellerman's Wilson Line.

Fees (1998–99, annual). Undergraduate: UK/EU students £1000; international students £6200 (arts), £8200 (science). Postgraduate: UK/EU students £ 2610 (arts), £2610 (science), £7000–10,000 (MBA programmes); international students £6200 (arts), £8200 (science), £7000–10,000 (MBA programmes).

Academic Awards. Over 100 awards ranging in value from £100 to £900.

Academic Year (1998–99). Two semesters: 28 September–30 January; 8 February–12 June.

Income (1997–98). Total, £25,000,000.

Statistics. Staff: 596 (530 academic, 66 administrative). Students: full-time 8100 (3240 men, 4860 women); part-time 5375 (2042 men, 3333 women); international 2055 (780 on campus, 1275 distance-taught).

FACULTIES/SCHOOLS

Arts
Tel: (01482) 465860 Fax: (01482) 465991
Dean: Best, A. D., BA Durh., PhD Exe.
Secretary: Escreet, P.

Engineering and Mathematics
Tel: (01482) 466662 Fax: (01482) 466660
Dean: Collinson, Prof. C. D., BSc Lond., PhD Lond.
Secretary: Low, D.

Health
Tel: (01482) 466716 Fax: (01482) 466682
Dean: Horsman, Prof. A., MA Leeds, PhD Leeds, DSc Oxf., FIP
Secretary: Foster, L.

Science/Environment
Tel: (01482) 465509 Fax: (01482) 465932
Dean: Sewell, D. F., BA Sheff., PhD Sheff.
Secretary: Muzaffar, M.

Social Science
Tel: (01482) 466629 Fax: (01482) 466099
Dean: von Prondzynski, Prof. Ferdinand, BA Trinity(Dub.), LLB Trinity(Dub.), PhD Camb.
Secretary: Wilson, V.

ACADEMIC UNITS

Accounting, Business and Finance
Tel: (01482) 466300 Fax: (01482) 466377
Briston, R. J., BSc(Econ) Lond., FCA   Price Waterhouse Prof.
Jones, C. J., MSc Brad., PhD CNAA   Sr. Lectr.
Kedslie, M. J. M., BA H-W, PhD Hull   Sr. Lectr.
Maunders, K. T., BA Hull   Prof.
Paudyal, K., BA Tribhuvan, MBA Tribhuvan, MSc Strath., PhD Strath.   Prof.
Prodhan, B. K., MSc Lond., PhD Glas.   Sr. Lectr.
Saadouni, B., BA Algiers, MSc Strath.   Sr. Lectr.; Dep. Head*
Other Staff: 4 Lectrs.
Research: accounting education; corporate governance; ethical, environmental and cultural issues; European and international financial reporting; international capital marketing

American Studies
Tel: (01482) 465303 Fax: (01482) 465303
Abramson, E. A., BA N.Y., MA Iowa, PhD Manc.   Sr. Lectr.
Ashworth, J., BA Lanc., MLitt Lanc., DPhil Oxf.   Prof.; Head*
Taylor, P. A. M., MA Camb., PhD Camb.   Emer. Prof.
Virden, J., BA Wash., MA Wash., PhD Wash.   Sr. Lectr.
White, J., BA Manc., MA Mich., PhD Hull   Reader
Other Staff: 2 Lectrs.
Research: history (immigration, nineteenth and twentieth centuries, civil and black protests, women's history); literary and cultural studies (Jewish American fiction, Anglo-American literature and visual art, women's literature, poetry, film and short story)

Asian Studies, see Pol. and Asian Studies

Biological Sciences
Tel: (01482) 465198 Fax: (01482) 465458
Armstrong, W., BSc Hull, PhD Hull, DSc Hull, FIBiol   Prof.
Carvalho, G. R., BSc Lond., MSc Wales, PhD Wales   Prof.
Dawes, E. A., PhD Leeds, DSc Leeds, FIBiol, FRSChem   Emer. Prof.†
Dickinson, F. M., BSc Sheff., PhD Sheff.   Sr. Lectr.
Elliott, M., BSc Lond., PhD Stir., FIBiol   Sr. Lectr.
Goulder, R., BSc Hull, PhD Hull, DSc Hull   Sr. Lectr.
Large, P. J., BSc Sheff., DPhil Oxf., DSc Hull, FIBiol   Reader
McFarlane, I. D., BSc Brist., PhD Brist.   Sr. Lectr.
Ratledge, C., BScTech Manc., PhD Manc., FRSChem, FIBiol   Prof.
Robinson, J., BSc Nott., PhD Edin.   Sr. Lectr.
Seymour, A. L., BA Oxf., MA Oxf., PhD   Sr. Lectr.
Threlfall, D. R., PhD Liv., DSc Liv., FIBiol   Prof.; Head*
Uglow, R. F., BSc Wales, PhD Wales   Sr. Lectr.
Other Staff: 10 Lectrs.
Research: aquatic and wetland biology, aquatic plant physiology, microbiology, zooplankton, environment; bioscience, invitro fertilization, heart biochemistry, muscle physiology; biotechnology, lipids, terpenes, biopolymers, formation technology, biotransformations; molecular biology, fungal genetics, molecular evolution, parasitology, mycobacteria; molecular ecology, fish population genetics,

ancient DNA, biodiversityaquatic and
wetland biology

Business, see Acctg., Business and Finance

Chemistry

Tel: (01482) 465461 Fax: (01482) 466410

Aveyard, R., BSc Sheff., PhD Sheff. Prof.
Baldwin, R. R., MA Camb., PhD Lond.,
  FRSChem Emer. Prof.
Binks, P. B., BSc Hull, PhD Hull Sr. Lectr.
Chipperfield, J. R., MA Camb., PhD Camb.,
  FRSChem Reader
Ewing, D. F., BSc St And., PhD St And. Sr.
  Lectr.
Fletcher, P. D. I., BSc Lond., PhD Kent Prof.
Goodby, J. W., BSc Hull, PhD Hull, DSc Hull,
  FRSChem Prof.
Haswell, S. J., BSc CNAA, PhD CNAA Sr. Lectr.
Lacey, D., BSc CNAA, PhD CNAA Reader
Mackenzie, G., BTech Brad., PhD Brad.,
  FRSChem Reader
McDonnell, D. G., BSc Hull, PhD Hull Hon.
  Prof.
Sinn, E., BA Syd., BSc Syd., MSc Syd., PhD NSW,
  FRSChem, FRACI Prof.; Head*
Townshend, A., BSc Birm., PhD Birm., DSc
  Birm., FRSChem Prof.
Toyne, K. J., BSc Manc., PhD Hull,
  FRSChem Prof.
Walker, R. W., BSc Hull, PhD Hull,
  FRSChem Prof.
Westwood, R., BSc Hull, PhD Hull,
  FRSChem Prof.†
Other Staff: 15 Lectrs.†
Research: analytical chemistry and chemometrics
  (process analysis, microanalytical systems,
  chemiluminescence, immobilised reagents,
  microwave-enhanced reactors); biological
  chemistry (synthesis, hetercyclic chemistry,
  drug design, nucleosides); heterogeneous
  chemistry (colloid science, surface
  chemistry, surfactants, clean-technology,
  asymmetric synthesis); inorganic chemistry
  (bio-inorganic, crystallography, fullerenes,
  EXAFS, metallomesogens, matrix-isolation,
  co-ordination chemistry); liquid crystals and
  advanced organic materials (non-linear
  optics, electrorheological fluids,
  ferroelectrics, liquid crystal polymers,
  photochromics)

Comparative and Applied Social
  Sciences

Tel: (01482) 466215 Fax: (01482) 466366

Bottomley, A. K., MA Camb., PhD Camb. Prof.
Forster, P. G., MA(Econ) Manc., PhD Hull Sr.
  Lectr.
James, A., BA Durh., PhD Durh. Reader
Mullard, M., BA Portsmouth, MPhil S'ton., PhD
  Hull Sr. Lectr.
Okely, J., BA Oxf., MA Oxf., DPhil Oxf. Prof.
O'Neill, N. J., BA York(UK), PhD Hull Sr.
  Lectr.; Head*
Prout, A., BA Keele, MA Keele, PhD Keele Reader
Zvekic, U., LLB Belgrade, MA Denver, PhD
  Belgrade Hon. Prof.
Other Staff: 5 Lectrs.; 1 Lectr.†
Research: criminal justice and crime control;
  cultural economics of identity; disability and
  health; gender/sexuality and the life course;
  social study of childhood

Computer Science

Tel: (01482) 465951 Fax: (01482) 466666

Brookes, G. R., MA Camb., MSc Manc., PhD
  Glas. Prof.
Griffiths, J. G., MSc Leeds, PhD Salf. Sr. Lectr.
Phillips, R., BSc Manc., PhD Manc. Prof.;
  Head*
Visvalingham, M., BA Malaya, PhD Hull Sr.
  Lectr.
Other Staff: 10 Lectrs.
Research: graphics and visualisation; medical
  engineering; software technology

Drama

Tel: (01482) 466210

Meech, A. J., BA Manc., MA Brist. Sr. Lectr.;
  Head*
Peacock, D. K., BA Leeds, PhD Exe. Sr. Lectr.
Walton, J. M., MA St And., PhD Hull Prof.
Other Staff: 5 Lectrs.; 1 Lectr.†
Research: British, German, African American
  and Classical Greek and Roman theatre;
  theory and practice (folk theatre,
  pantomime, political theory, unscripted
  drama, set design, the director)

Dutch Studies

Tel: (01482) 465893 Fax: (01482) 465898

King, P. K., MA Lond., MA Camb. Emer. Prof.
Schludermann, B., BA McG., MA Manit., PhD
  Camb. Prof.
Vismans, R. M., MA Manc., CandEng V.U.Amst.,
  PhD V.U.Amst. Sr. Lectr.; Head*
Other Staff: 1 Lectr.
Research: Dutch gender studies; medieval Dutch
  culture (German-Dutch language mix);
  modern Dutch language studies (functional
  grammar of Dutch)

Economic Studies

Tel: (01482) 466206 Fax: (01482) 466216

Dobson, S. M., BSc Hull, MA CNAA, PhD
  CNAA Sr. Lectr.
Nield, K. H., BA Leeds Sr. Lectr.
Pearson, R., MA Edin., PhD Leeds Sr. Lectr.
Reid, D. A., BA Birm., PhD Birm. Sr. Lectr.
Richardson, P. D., BA Manc., MA Manc. Prof.
Saville, J., BSc(Econ) Lond. Emer. Prof.
Tremayne, A. R., BSc(Econ) Lond., MSc
  Lond. Prof.
Turner, M. E., BSc Lond., PhD Sheff. Prof.
Woodward, D. M., BA Manc., MA Manc. Prof.
Other Staff: 12 Lectrs.; 1 Lectr.†
Research: applied microeconomics; economic
  history (constructing long-run databases,
  seventeenth to nineteenth centuries);
  international macroeconomics; public
  choice/decision making under uncertainty

Engineering

Tel: (01482) 466222 Fax: (01482) 466533

Cummings, A., BSc Lond., MSc Liv., PhD Liv.,
  DEng Liv., FIMechE, FIEE Prof.
Ekere, N. N., BEng Nigeria, MSc Lough., PhD
  UMIST Prof.
Fagan, M. J., BSc Exe., PhD Exe. Sr. Lectr.
Haywood, Stephanie K., BA Oxf., PhD
  CNAA Sr. Lectr.
Hurst, K. S., BSc CNAA, MSc Hull, PhD Hull Sr.
  Lectr.
James, R. D., BSc S'ton., PhD CNAA, FIMechE,
  FIEE Sr. Lectr.
Judah, S. R., BEng Jab., MSc Lond., PhD
  Lond. Sr. Lectr.
Lunn, B., BA Oxf. Reader
Matthews, A., BSc Salf., PhD Salf. 3M Prof.
Patton, R. J., BEng Sheff., MEng Sheff., PhD
  Sheff. Prof.
Pulko, S. H., BSc Lond., PhD Nott. Sr. Lectr.
Riley, N. G., BEng Sheff., MSc Essex Sr. Lectr.
Selke, K. K. W., BSc Hull, PhD Hull Sr. Lectr.
Swift, K. G., BSc Salf., MSc Salf., PhD Lucas
  Prof.
Waddington, C. P., MA Camb., PhD Camb. Sr.
  Lectr.
Other Staff: 6 Lectrs.
Research: communications; control, design and
  analysis, field dynamics, VLSI;
  manufacturing systems; materials,
  techniques, devices

English

Tel: (01482) 465309 Fax: (01482) 465641

Booth, J., BA Oxf., BLitt Oxf. Reader
Headlam Wells, R. H., BA Leeds, BLitt Oxf., PhD
  Hull Reader
Hoyles, F. J., MA Camb., PhD Hull Sr. Lectr.
Hutson, L. M., BA Oxf., DPhil Oxf. Prof.
Scase, W. L., BA Kent, DPhil Oxf. Sr. Lectr.

Sinyard, N. R., BA Hull, MA Manc. Sr. Lectr.;
  Head*
Stoneman, P. M., BA Lond., MA Lond. Sr. Lectr.
Woodcock, B., BA Leic., PhD Leic. Sr. Lectr.
Wymer, R. G. E., BLitt Oxf., MA Oxf. Sr.
  Lectr.
Other Staff: 6 Lectrs.; 2 Lectrs.†
Research: contemporary culture from the post-
  colonial Anglophone literatures to science
  fiction and film; medieval and Renaissance
  periods; nineteenth and twentieth centuries;
  women's studies

European Studies

Tel: (01482) 465043 Fax: (01482) 465020

Morgan, P. J., MA Camb., PhD Reading Sr.
  Lectr.
Wintle, M. J., MA Camb., PhD Hull Sr. Lectr.;
  Head*
Other Staff: 2 Lectrs.
Research: contemporary European history with
  special reference to foreign policy; European
  political economy with special reference to
  information and communication; Italian
  history and Dutch history; technologies

Finance, see Acctg., Business and Finance

French

Tel: (01482) 465990 Fax: (01482) 465345

Curtis, D. E., BTh Hull, MA Manc. Sr. Lectr.
Hindley, A., BA Hull, PhD Hull Sr. Lectr.;
  Head*
Jamieson, D. M., BPhil Oxf., MA Glas. Sr.
  Lectr.
Levy, B. J., MA Edin., PhD Edin. Reader
Noreiko, S. F., BA S'ton., MPhil S'ton. Sr. Lectr.
Rigby, S. A., BPhil Oxf., MA Oxf. Prof.
Smith, Pauline M., BA Lond., PhD Lond. Prof.
Strugnell, A. R., BA Exe., PhD Exe. Reader
Williams, D. A., BA Oxf., BPhil Oxf. Prof.
Other Staff: 4 Lectrs.
Research: cultural studies (popular culture, the
  media and cinema); language studies
  (telematics, simultaneous interpreting,
  speech-encoding in French pronunciation
  acquisition, Old French–English dictionary,
  European multilingual dictionary); literary
  studies (mediaeval literature, Renaissance
  literature and modern literature)

Geography

Tel: (01482) 465377 Fax: (01482) 466340

Boehmer-Christiansen, S. A., BA Adel., MA Sus.,
  DPhil Sus. Reader
Bradley, P. N., BSc Lond., MSc Lond., PhD
  Camb. Sr. Lectr.
Davidson, R. N., MA Glas., PhD Glas. Sr. Lectr.
Ellis, S., MSc Reading, PhD Reading Sr. Lectr.;
  Head*
Frostick, L. E., BSc Leic., PhD E.Anglia Prof.
Gibbs, D. C., BA Manc., PhD Manc. Prof.
Hardisty, J., BSc Lond., MSc Wales, PhD
  Hull Prof.
Pedley, H. M., BSc Leic., PhD Hull Sr. Lectr.
Sibley, D., BA Liv., MA S.Illinois, PhD
  Camb. Reader
Spooner, D. J., MA Camb., PhD Camb. Sr.
  Lectr.
Watts, D., BA Lond., MA Calif., PhD
  McG. Reader
Other Staff: 10 Lectrs.
Research: catchment and coastal dynamics
  (sediment flux); environmental policy and
  resource management; palaeoenvironments
  and environmental change (wetland
  archaeology, palaeogenetics, climate
  change); restructuring, governance and
  exclusion (economic restructuring, urban
  sustainability, social exclusion); waste and
  water pollution

German

Tel: (01482) 465356

McCobb, T., BA Hull, PhD Hull Head*
Turner, D., MA Lond., PhD Hull Reader
Other Staff: 2 Lectrs.

Research: early twentieth-century German and Austrian literature (narrative fiction); language studies (bilingual machine-readable valency dictionary); reception of medieval German literature in the twentieth century

Health, see below

Hispanic Studies

Tel: (01482) 465360 Fax: (01482) 465360

Beardsell, P. R., MA *Manc.*, PhD *Sheff.* Prof.
Jones, J. A., BA *Leeds*, PhD *Leeds* Sr. Lectr.; Head*
Powell, B. J., BA *Birm.*, PhD *Camb.* Sr. Lectr.
Other Staff: 2 Lectrs.
Research: applied linguistics (computer-assisted language learning); Latin American studies (twentieth-century Spanish American literature, postcolonial studies and education); Spanish peninsular studies (modern Spanish literature, literature in the Golden Age and mediaeval literature

History

Tel: (01482) 465344 Fax: (01482) 466126

Ambler, R. W., BA *Lond.*, PhD *Hull*, FRHistS Sr. Lectr.
Ayton, A. C., BA *Hull*, PhD *Hull* Sr. Lectr.
Bernasconi, J. G., BA *Brist.*, MA *Lond.*, FSA Lectr.; Head*
Burgess, G., MA *Well.*, PhD *Camb.* Reader
Flint, V. I. J., BA *Oxf.*, DPhil *Oxf.*, FRHistS Prof.
Hoppen, K. T., MA *N.U.I.*, PhD *Camb.*, FRHistS Prof.
Lewis, M. J. T., MA *Camb.*, PhD *Camb.*, FSA Sr. Lectr.
Lloyd, H. A., BA *Wales*, DPhil *Oxf.*, FRHistS Prof.
Neave, D., BA *Lanc.*, MPhil *York(UK)*, PhD *Hull*, FSA Sr. Lectr.
Omissi, D. E., BA *Lanc.*, MA *Lond.*, PhD *Lond.* Sr. Lectr.
Palmer, J. J. N., BA *Oxf.*, BLitt *Oxf.*, PhD *Lond.*, FRHistS Reader
Price, J. L., BA *Lond.*, PhD *Lond.* Sr. Lectr.
Other Staff: 5 Lectrs.
Research: Atlantic history; British and European history (especially France and the Low Countries); Indian and South-East Asian history; maritime history

Italian

Tel: (01482) 465993

Williams, Pamela A., BA *Wales*, PhD *Camb.* Sr. Lectr.; Head*
Other Staff: 3 Lectrs.; 1 Prof.†
Research: historical studies (eighteenth-century Tuscany); language studies (computer-assisted language learning, advanced translation, grammar); literary studies (literature of the Middle Ages, the Renaissance and the nineteenth and twentieth centuries, children's literature)

Law

Tel: (01482) 465861 Fax: (01482) 466388

Baxter, C. R., LLB *Leeds* Sr. Lectr.
Birkinshaw, P. J., LLB Prof.; Head*
Carby-Hall, J. R., RD, LLB *Aberd.*, MA *Aberd.*, PhD *Hull*, DLitt *Northland* Sr. Lectr.
Charlesworth, A., LLB *Warw.* Sr. Lectr.
Freestone, D. A. C., LLM *Lond.*, LLB *Hull* Prof.
Graham, C., BA *Sus.*, LLM *Lond.* Prof.
Lucy, W. N. R., LLB *Leeds*, MJur *Manc.*, MA(Econ) *Manc.* Sr. Lectr.
McCoubrey, H., MA *Camb.*, PhD *Nott.* Prof.
Parry, D. L., BA(Law) *Sheff.* Sr. Lectr.
Parry, M. L., LLB *Leic.* Reader
Subedi, S. P., LLB *Tribhuvan*, MA *Tribhuvan*, LLM *Hull* Sr. Lectr.
Other Staff: 14 Lectrs.; 1 Lectr.†
Research: family law; housing law and policy; international law, including international economics law; legal and social theory; public law, including European public law

Learning, Institute for

Centre for Educational Studies

Tel: (01482) 465988 Fax: (01482) 466133

Andrews, R. J., BA *Oxf.*, MA *Oxf.*, PhD *Hull* Prof.; Head*
Bottery, M. P., BA *Oxf.*, MEd *Hull*, PhD *Hull* Sr. Lectr.
Moore, J. L., BSc *Birm.*, MPhil *Nott.*, MSc PhD Sr. Lectr.; Organiser for In-service Educn.
Squires, G., MA *Camb.*, PhD *Edin.* Sr. Lectr.
Whitehead, M., BA *Durh.*, PhD *Hull* Sr. Lectr.
Other Staff: 6 Lectrs.
Research: educational values and ethics (religious education, spirituality and education, ethics, gender); physical and mental health education (counselling, drugs education, physical education); special educational needs (differences in learning, acquisition of thinking skills); teacher and professional education (teacher education, informal learning, workers' education)

Centre for Lifelong Learning

Tel: (01482) 465988 Fax: (01482) 466133

Somerton, M. F., BA *Manc.* Sr. Lectr.
Vulliamy, D. L., BA *Lanc.*, MA *Warw.* Sr. Lectr.; Head*
Other Staff: 4 Lectrs.
Research: teacher and professional education (teacher education, informal learning, workers' education)

Centre for Professional Development and Training in Education

Tel: (01482) 465989 Fax: (01482) 466133

Chesters, G., MA *Wales* Prof.; Head*
Hornby, G., BSc *Leeds*, MA *NZ* Sr. Lectr.
Milne, P. S., MA *Aberd.* Sr. Lectr.
Other Staff: 12 Lectrs.; 1 Sr. Lectr.†
Research: educational values and ethics (religious education, spirituality and education, ethics, gender); physical and mental health education (counselling, drugs education, physical education); teacher and professional education (teacher education, informal learning, workers' education)

Management

Tel: (01482) 466330 Fax: (01482) 466236

Carter, P., BA *Essex*, MA *Lanc.* Sr. Lectr.
Flood, R. L., BSc *Lond.*, PhD *Lond.* Sir Q. W. Lee Prof.
Keys, P., BSc *St And.*, PhD *Hull* Sr. Lectr.; Head*
Wharton, F., BSc *Manc.* Sr. Lectr.
Other Staff: 6 Lectrs.
Research: management and systems science (methodological issues, critical management science, community operational research, management information systems, project management); organisational studies (management ethics, organisational behaviour, post-modern organisation theory, management and organisational learning)

Mathematics

Tel: (01482) 465885 Fax: (01482) 466218

Beckett, P. M., MA *Oxf.*, PhD Reader
Bingham, M. S., MSc *Sheff.*, PhD *Sheff.* Sr. Lectr.
Brzezniak, Z., PhD *Cracow* Reader
Busch, P., MSc *Cologne*, PhD *Cologne* Reader
Cutland, N. J., MA *Camb.*, PhD *Brist.* Prof.; Head*
Dunning-Davies, J., BSc *Liv.*, PhD *Wales* Sr. Lectr.
Howarth, J. A., MSc *Brist.*, PhD *Brist.* Sr. Lectr.
Kopp, P. E., BSc *Stell.*, DPhil *Oxf.* Prof.
Pearson, D. B., BA *Camb.*, PhD *Camb.*, ScD *Camb.* Prof.
Scott, T., BSc *Lond.*, PhD *Lond.* Sr. Lectr.
Shaw, R., BA *Camb.*, PhD *Camb.*, ScD *Camb.* Leverhulme Emer. Prof.
Sproston, J. P., MA *Camb.*, PhD *Newcastle* Sr. Lectr.

Taylor, F. E., BSc *Manc.*, MSc *Manc.*, PhD *Durh.* Hon. Prof.
Wisher, S. J., MPhil *City(UK)*, PhD *City(UK)* Sr. Lectr.
Other Staff: 6 Lectrs.; 1 Lectr.†
Research: applied mathematics; pure mathematics; statistics

Music

Tel: (01482) 465998 Fax: (01482) 465998

Dale, C., MusB *Manc.*, MMus *Lond.*, PhD *Reading* Sr. Lectr.
Ford, A. D., BMus *Birm.* Sr. Lectr.
Newbould, B., BMus *Brist.*, MA *Brist.* Prof.; Head*
Sadler, A. G., BMus *Nott.* Sr. Lectr.
Other Staff: 2 Lectrs.; 1 Lectr.†
Research: baroque (especially the French baroque); classical periods (especially Schubert); Gregorian chant; mediaeval Renaissance; performance practice

Philosophy

Tel: (01482) 465995 Fax: (01482) 466122

Almond, B. M., BA *Lond.*, MPhil *Lond.* Prof.
Gilbert, P. H., MA *Camb.* Sr. Lectr.
Lamarque, P. V., BA *E.Anglia*, BPhil *Oxf.* Ferens Prof.; Head*
Lennon, Kathleen, BA *Kent*, BPhil *Oxf.*, DPhil *Oxf.* Sr. Lectr.
Other Staff: 3 Lectrs.; 1 Lectr.†
Research: aesthetics; ethics/applied philosophy; history of philosophy; philosophy of language; philosophy of the mind

Physics

Tel: (01482) 465501 Fax: (01482) 465606

Dyer, P. E., BSc *Hull*, PhD *Hull*, FIP Prof.; Head*
Greenough, R. D., BSc *Sheff.*, PhD *Sheff.* Reader
Hogg, J. H. C., BSc *Hull*, PhD *Hull* Sr. Lectr.
Moghissi, K., BSc *Geneva*, MD *Geneva*, MSChir *Geneva*, FRCS, FRCSEd Hon. Prof.
Nicholls, J. E., BSc *Lond.*, PhD *Lond.* Reader
O'Neill, M., BSc *N.U.I.*, PhD *Strath.* Sr. Lectr.
Scott, C. G., BSc *Hull*, PhD *Hull* Sr. Lectr.
Other Staff: 5 Lectrs.
Research: chemical physics (lasers, spectroscopy, novel materials, theoretical underpinning); lasers and applications (ablation, medical, analysis, carbon dioxide/excimer lasers); magnetics (magnetism, magnetoelastic, amorphous, thin films, sensors, actuation, control); organic ptoelectronics (light-emitting polymers, liquid crystals, alignment theory); semiconductor physics (theory, spectroscopy, x-ray analysis, electrical characterisation)

Politics and Asian Studies

Tel: (01482) 466209 Fax: (01482) 466208

Burgess, M. D., BA *CNAA*, MA *Leic.*, PhD *Leic.* Reader
Christie, J. W., PhD *Lond.*, BA Hon. Prof.
Gray, C., BA *WI*, DPhil *Oxf.* Prof.
Grove, E. J., MA *Aberd.*, MA *Lond.*, PhD *Hull* Sr. Lectr.
Harris, R. J., BA *Leeds*, MA *McM.* Prof.
Huxley, T. J., MA *Oxf.*, MScEcon *Wales*, PhD *ANU* Sr. Lectr.
King, V. T., BA *Hull*, MA *Lond.*, PhD *Hull* Prof.
McNeill, T. P., BA *Belf.*, MA *Essex* Sr. Lectr.; Head*
Norton, P., BA *Sheff.*, MA *Penn.*, PhD *Sheff.* Prof.
O'Sullivan, N. K., BSc(Econ) *Lond.*, PhD *Lond.* Prof.
Page, E. C., BA *CNAA*, MSc *Strath.*, PhD *Strath.* Prof.
Parekh, B., BA *Bom.*, MA *Bom.*, PhD *Lond.* Prof.
Parnwell, M. J. G., BA *Hull*, PhD *Hull* Sr. Lectr.
Sutton, P. K., BSc *S'ton.*, MLitt *Glas.*, PhD *Manc.* Reader
Tarling, N., BA *Camb.*, MA *Camb.*, PhD *Camb.*, LittD *Camb.*, FRAS, FRHistS Hon. Prof.
Other Staff: 17 Lectrs.; 2 Lectrs.†

Research: politics (political economy, European Union politics, strategic studies, international relations, political philosophy, British politics, West European politics, Third World politics, the former Soviet Union, Indian politics); South East Asia (development, problems, policy, politics, security, international relations); history (modern, archaeology); religion

Psychology

Tel: (01482) 466154 Fax: (01482) 465599

Crawshaw, C. M., BSc S'ton., PhD S'ton. Sr. Lectr.

Empson, J. A. C., BA Sheff., PhD Sheff. Sr. Lectr.

Flowers, K. A., MA Camb., PhD Camb. Sr. Lectr.

Hockey, G. R., BSc Leic., PhD Camb. Prof.

Hoghughi, M., BA Hull, PhD Durh., FBPsS Hull and Holderness Hon. Prof.; Community Lectr. in Learning Disability

Horrell, R. I., BA Camb., PhD Sheff. Sr. Lectr.

Phillips, J. P. N., BA Open(UK), MA Oxf., MSc Open(UK), PhD Lond., FBPsS Reader

Sheridan, M. R., BSc Hull, PhD Hull Head*

Singleton, C. H., BA Nott., PhD Nott., FBPsS Sr. Lectr.

Williams, D. I., BSc Hull, PhD Hull, FBPsS Sr. Lectr.

Other Staff: 10 Lectrs.

Research: application of psychology to medicine (psychogynaecology, sleep, movement disorders, pain); human factors and cognitive ergonomics (work design, performance, human computer systems); psychological health and lifestyle (stress, wellbeing, drugs, sport/exercise, coping); psychological testing and assessment (psychometrics, dyslexia screening, cognitive/physical difficulties)

Scandinavian Studies

Tel: (01482) 465015

Holmes, P. A., BA Hull, PhD Hull Reader; Head*

Morris, B. A., BA Lond., PhD Lond. Sr. Lectr.

Other Staff: 3 Lectrs.

Research: medieval Swedish culture (Saint Birgitta of Sweden); modern Swedish novel (Sven Delblanc, Vilhelm Moberg); Swedish and Danish language studies

Social Sciences, see Compar. and Appl. Soc. Scis.

Theology

Tel: (01482) 465997 Fax: (01482) 466122

Grabbe, L. L., MA Pasadena, PhD Claremont Prof.; Head*

North, J. L., BA Lond., MA Oxf., PhD Durh. Sr. Lectr.

Other Staff: 1 Lectr.; 2 Lectrs.†

Research: biblical studies; church history; Indian religions

HEALTH

Community and Health Studies, School of

Tel: (01482) 465820

Harrison, L., MA Essex Sr. Lectr.; Head*

Research: issues relating to risk and vulnerability

Institute of Health Studies

Tel: (01482) 465820 Fax: (01482) 466402

Alaszewski, A. M., BA Camb., MA Camb., PhD Camb. Prof.; Head*

Malin, V. R. M., BA Open(UK), MSc Hull Sr. Lectr.

Other Staff: 1 Lectr.

Social Work

Tel: (01482) 466228 Fax: (01482) 466306

Bradley, G., BA Nott., MA Nott. Head*

Burke, P. C., BA Open(UK), MSc Sur. Sr. Lectr.

Harrison, L. R., MA Essex Sr. Lectr.

Manthorpe, G., BA York, MA Hull Sr. Lectr.

Other Staff: 3 Lectrs.; 1 Lectr.†

Medicine, School of

Tel: (01482) 674456 Fax: (01482) 675539

Cleland, J. G. F. Clin. Prof./Consultant

Morice, A. H., MA Camb., MD Camb. Clin. Prof./Consultant

Stafford, N. D., MB ChB, FRCS Clin. Prof./Consultant; Head*

Other Staff: 2 Lectrs.

Academic Surgical Unit

Tel: (01482) 623225 Fax: (01482) 623274

Duthie, G. S., MD Edin., BMedBio FRCSEd Clin. Sr. Lectr./Consultant

Kerin, M. J., ChM Edin., FRCSEd, FRCSI Clin. Sr. Lectr./Consultant

McCollum, P. T., BA MB BCh BAO MCh Clin. Prof./Consultant

Monson, J. R. T., MB, BCh, BAO Trinity(Dub.), MD, FRCSI, FACS, FRCS Clin. Prof./Consultant; Head*

Other Staff: 7 Clin. Lectrs.; 1 Lectr.

Research: anorectal trauma; neorectal dynamics; neural networks (prognosticate in patients with colorectal cancer)

Centre for Magnetic Resonance Investigations

Tel: (01482) 674072 Fax: (01482) 320137

Turnbull, L. W., BSc Edin., MB ChB Edin., MD Edin. Clin. Prof./Consultant

Research: cancer research (breast, prostate, uterus, colorectal, brain)

Centre for Metabolic Bone Disease

Tel: (01482) 675302 Fax: (01482) 675301

Purdie, D. W., MD, FRCOG, FSA Clin. Prof./Consultant; Head*

Other Staff: 2 Clin. Lectrs.

Research: determination of the prevalence and incidence of osteoporosis and related fractures in the Yorkshire population; development of primary care prediction of osteoporosis; development of selective oestrogen receptor modulators (SERMs); status on the natural history of perimenopausal bone loss; studies on the accuracy and precision of bone mineral densitometry

Clinical Psychology

Tel: (01482) 465933 Fax: (01482) 466155

Clement, S., BSocSc MSc Sr. Lectr.; Head*

Research: Alzheimer's disorder, detection management and carer support; measures and organisation for people with long-term disabilities; psychological aspects of anaesthesia

Institute of Rehabilitation and Therapies

Tel: (01482) 675046 Fax: (01482) 675046

Moffett, J, MSc Sr. Lectr.

Research: back pain; cardiac rehabilitation; chronic fatigue syndrome; chronic pain; muscular skeletal disorders

Medical Physics

Tel: (01482) 675311 Fax: (01482) 702147

Langton, C. M., BSc Hull, MSc Aberd., PhD Hull Sr. Lectr.

Research: clinical studies (trials for preventative and therapeutic agents); stimulation (ultrasound propagation in cancellous bone); technology development (propensity to fall)

Medicine

Tel: (01482) 675365 Fax: (01482) 675370

Atkin, S. L., BSc Newcastle(UK), MB BS Liv., PhD Liv. Clin. Sr. Lectr./Consultant; Head*

Masson, E. A., BSc St And., MB ChB MD Clin. Sr. Lectr./Consultant

Research: breast cancer; cytokine production by human anterior pituitary adenomas; diabetic neuropathy (collagen sub-types in human sural nerve); tumour radiosensitisation

Obstetrics and Gynaecology

Tel: (01482) 676655 Fax: (01482) 676646

Killick, R. S., BSc Lond., MB BS Lond., MD Lond., FRCOG Clin. Prof./Consultant; Head*

Lindow, S. W., MB ChD MMed, FRCOG Clin. Sr. Lectr./Consultant

Other Staff: 3 Clin. Lectrs.

Research: human physiology (explanations of function, novel imaging techniques); obstetrics (epidural analgesia, sphincter imaging)

Oncology

Lind, M. J. Clin. Prof./Consultant

Otolaryngology and Head and Neck Surgery

Tel: (01482) 674456 Fax: (01482) 675539

Ell, S., BSc MB, FRCS Clin. Sr. Lectr./Consultant

Stafford, N. D., MB ChB, FRCS Clin. Prof./Consultant; Head*

Research: counselling of patients in head and neck cancer; molecular aspects of tumours of the larynx and pharynx; prediction of prognosis in head and neck cancer

Psychiatry

Tel: (01482) 466756 Fax: (01482) 654256

Mortimer, A. M., BSc MB ChB MMedSci Clin. Prof./Consultant; Head*

Research: antipsychotic trials; high-dose neuroleptics; schizophrenia

Public Health and Primary Care

Tel: (01482) 466047 Fax: (01482) 441408

Campion, P. D., MA Oxf., PhD Liv., BM BCh, FRCGP Clin. Prof./Consultant; Head*

Meadows, K. A., BA PhD Sr. Lectr.

Summerton, N., MA Oxf., MPH Leeds, BM BCh Clin. Sr. Lectr./Consultant

Research: chronic fatigue syndrome; ischaemic heat disease; problems of couples undergoing fertility treatment; quality of life in diabetes; sexual health in young people

Nursing, School of

Tel: (01482) 466695 Fax: (01482) 466694

Snowley, G., BSc Sheff., MEd Nott. Head*

Research: cancer care; cardiac rehabilitation; delivery of acute healthcare; learning disabilities

Postgraduate Studies and Continuing Professional Education

Tel: (01482) 464561 Fax: (01482) 466683

Buckingham, L., BSc MBA Head*

Porock, D. C. Sr. Lectr.

Other Staff: 6 Lectrs.

Radiology

Vacant Posts: 1 Prof.

Undergraduate and Pre-Registration Nursing and Midwifery Studies

Tel: (01482) 465241 Fax: (01482) 466686

Gates, R. J., BEd CNAA, MSc Open(UK) Sr. Lectr.; Head*

SPECIAL CENTRES, ETC

Accounting and Finance

International Accounting Research, Centre for

Tel: (01482) 466363 Fax: (01482) 466377

Briston, Prof. R. J., BSc(Econ) Lond., FCA Dir.*

International Management Centre

Tel: (01482) 466390 Fax: (01482) 466399

Levett, B., MA Camb. Lectr.; Dir.*

Applied Electronics, Centre for

Tel: (01482) 465777

No staff at present

Estuarine and Coastal Studies, Institute of

Tel: (01482) 465503 Fax: (01482) 465001
De Jonge, V. N., PhD Hon. Prof.
Elliott, Michael, BSc Lond., PhD Stir. Prof.;
  Dir.*

European Public Law, Institute of

Tel: (01482) 465917 Fax: (01482) 466388
Birkinshaw, Prof. P. J., LLB Hull Dir.*

European Union Studies, Centre for

Bradley, G., BA Nott., MA Nott. Co-Dir.
Burgess, Michael, BA CNAA, PhD Leic.,
  MA Co-Dir.
Francis, Ray, BA W.Aust. Co-Dir.
Freestone, David A. C., LLB Hull, LLM
  Lond. Co-Dir.
Gilbert, Paul, MA Camb. Co-Dir.
Harris, Robert, BA Leeds, MA McM. Co-Dir.
Heseltine, R. G., BA Sus., DPhil Sus. Co-Dir.
Magone, José, MPhil Vienna, DPhil Vienna Co-
  Dir.
McNeill, T. P., MA Essex, BA Co-Dir.
Morris, Justin, BA Lond. Co-Dir.
O'Neill, Norman J., BA York(UK), PhD
  Hull Co-Dir.
Page, Edward C., BA CNAA, MSc Strath., PhD
  Strath. Co-Dir.
von Prondzynski, Ferdinand, BA Trinity(Dub.),
  LLB Trinity(Dub.), PhD Camb. Co-Dir.

Language Institute

Tel: (01482) 465616 Fax: (01482) 466180
Aub-Buscher, Gertrud E., MA Edin., DU
  Stras. Academic Dir.*
Best, Alan D., BA Durh., PhD Exe. Dir.
Marsh, Debra, BSc Aston, MEd Leeds Head of
  EFL
Other Staff: 1 Lectr.
Research: (applied) linguistics; language
  learning; language technology and discourse

Legislative Studies, Centre for

Norton, Prof. P., BA Sheff., MA Penn., PhD
  Sheff. Dir.*

Modern Languages, Computers in Teaching Initiative Centre for

Chesters, G., MA Wales Prof.; Dir.*
Research: CTI (use of technology in language
  learning); Eurocall (language learning
  technology); TELL (development of software
  for language learning)

Surface Engineering, Research Centre in

Tel: (01482) 466474 Fax: (01482) 466477
Matthews, Prof. Allan, BSc Salf., PhD Salf.,
  FIMechE, FIEE Dir.*

Systems Studies, Centre for

Tel: (01482) 857544 Fax: (01482) 857544
Flood, Prof. R. L., BSc City(UK), PhD
  City(UK) Dir.*

Teaching and Learning, Centre for

Tel: (01482) 466588
Woolston, C. J., BSc E.Anglia, PhD E.Anglia Sr.
  Lectr.; Head*

Teaching and Learning Support, Centre for

Heseltine, R. G., BA Sus., DPhil Sus. Dir.*
Pears, B. Head, Audio Visual Centre
Woolston, C. J., BSc E.Anglia, PhD
  E.Anglia Educnl. Devel. Team Co-ordinator

University of Hull International Fisheries Institute

Tel: (01482) 466433 Fax: (01482) 470129
Cowx, I., BSc Liv., PhD Exe. Sr. Lectr.
Crean, K., BSc CNAA, MSc Lond. Sr. Lectr.;
  Dep. Dir.
Haywood, K. H., BSc Lond., MSc Birm.,
  PhD Dir.*
Palfreman, D. A., BSc Oxf., MA E.Anglia,
  PhD Sr. Lectr.
Ridgway, S., BSc CNAA, BA Open(UK) Sr. Lectr.

CONTACT OFFICERS

Accommodation. Accommodation Officer:
  Fincham, J. Carl, BA Hull
Admissions (first degree). Administrative
  Assistant: Dowling, Sheila C., BSc Bath
Admissions (higher degree). Administrative
  Assistant: Dowling, Sheila C., BSc Bath
Adult/continuing education. Acting Director,
  Centre for Continuing Education,
  Development and Training: Vulliamy,
  Daniel, BA Lanc., MA Warw., LLM Leic.
Alumni. Alumni Officer: Stephenson, Susan
  M., BSc Hull
Archives. Archivist: Dyson, Brian, BSc Salf.,
  MScEcon Wales
Careers. Head of Careers and Appointments
  Service: Franks, John C., BA Hull
Computing services. Librarian and Director of
  Academic Services: Heseltine, Richard G., BA
  Sus., DPhil Sus.
Consultancy services. IPR Consultant: Halford,
  Nigel, MBA Hull
Credit Transfer. Administrative Assistant:
  Burton, Tim

Distance education. Walker, Christopher H.,
  MA
Estates and buildings/works and services.
  Estates Development Officer: Farr, Richard,
  JP, BA Wales
Estates and buildings/works and services.
  Estates Maintenance Officer: Mackenzie,
  Robert G., BSc Strath.
Estates and buildings/works and services.
  Director of Estates: Coy, F. Alan, BSc CNAA
Finance. Director of Finance: Soutter, David,
  BA Oxf., MA Oxf.
General enquiries. Registrar and Secretary:
  Lock, David, BSc Bath, MPhil Bath, FCIS
Industrial liaison. IPR Consultant: Halford,
  Nigel, MBA Hull
International office. Assistant Registrar:
  Newham, Derek, BA Kent
Library. Librarian and Director of Academic
  Services: Heseltine, Richard G., BA Sus.,
  DPhil Sus.
Ombudesperson. Applegarth, Susan M., BSc
  Reading
Personnel/human resources. Senior Personnel
  Officer: Parsons, Stephen J., BD Lond.
Public relations, information and marketing.
  Public Relations Officer: Dumsday, James H.,
  BA Leeds
Publications. Publications Manager: Bull,
  Martin
Purchasing. Purchasing Officer: Gurling, Susan
  E. A.
Quality assurance and accreditation.
  Applegarth, Susan M., BSc Reading
Research. Director, Research Office: Fentem,
  A., BA Oxf., PhD Manc.
Safety. University Safety Officer: Watson,
  David H.
Scholarships, awards, loans. Examinations
  Officer: Clark, Joanne, BA Manc.
Schools liaison. Schools Liaison Officer: Jones,
  Hilary A., BA Hull
Security. Security Officer: Lilley, Barry
Staff development and training. Plumb, Kate,
  MSc S.Bank
Student welfare/counselling. Page, Steve, BA
  York(UK), MEd Leeds
Students from other countries. Assistant
  Registrar: Newham, Derek, BA Kent
Students with disabilities. Tuck, David
University press. Innes, Glen, BA Brighton

CAMPUS/COLLEGE HEADS

Bishop Grosseteste College, Newport,
  Lincoln, England LN1 3DY. (Tel: (01522)
  527347; Fax: (01522) 530243.) Principal
  (Dean): Baker, E.

[Information supplied by the institution as at August
1998, and edited by the ACU]

UNIVERSITY OF KEELE

Founded 1962; previously established as University College of North Staffordshire

Member of the Association of Commonwealth Universities

Postal Address: Staffordshire, England ST5 5BG
Telephone: (01782) 621111 **Fax**: (01782) 613847 **E-mail**: s.j.morris@keele.ac.uk or rda20@keele.ac.uk
Telex: 36113 UNKLIB G **WWW**: http://www.keele.ac.uk

VISITOR—Elizabeth, H.M. The Queen
CHANCELLOR—Moser, Sir Claus, KCB, CBE, Hon. DSc(SocialSciences) S'ton., Hon. DSc Leeds, Hon. DSc City(UK),
    Hon. DSc Sus., Hon. DUniv Sur., Hon. DUniv Keele, Hon. DUniv York(UK), Hon. DTech Brun., FBA
PRO-CHANCELLOR—Stafford,The Rt. Hon. the Lord
DEPUTY PRO-CHANCELLOR—......
DEPUTY PRO-CHANCELLOR—Wood, A. F.
VICE-CHANCELLOR*—Finch, Prof. Janet V., BA Lond., PhD Brad., Hon. DLitt W.England
DEPUTY VICE-CHANCELLOR—Vincent, Prof. David M., BA York(UK), PhD Camb., FRHistS
PRO VICE-CHANCELLOR—Sloboda, Prof. J. A., MA Oxf., PhD Camb., FRHistS
PRO VICE-CHANCELLOR—Wilks, Prof. Graham, BSc Manc., PhD Manc.
HONORARY TREASURER—Edmunds, David, BA
SECRETARY AND REGISTRAR—Morris, Simon J., BA Durh.
DIRECTOR OF ACADEMIC AFFAIRS—Slade, Edward F., BSc Nott., PhD Keele, FIP
DIRECTOR OF FINANCE—Rigg, Paul R., BA CNAA
DIRECTOR OF INFORMATION SERVICES—Foster, Allan, BA Open(UK), FIInfSc
DIRECTOR OF PERSONNEL—Price, Jane F.

GENERAL INFORMATION

History. The university was founded as University College of North Staffordshire in 1949, to become the University of Keele in 1962.

Admission to first degree courses (see also United Kingdom Introduction). Through Universities and Colleges Admissions Service (UCAS). General Certificate of Secondary Education (GCSE)/General Certificate of Education (GCE): minimum 5 subjects with 2 at A level. International Baccalaureate: minimum 26 points; European Baccalaureate: minimum 60%. Other qualifications may be considered provided they satisfy senate.

First Degrees (see also United Kingdom Directory to Subjects of Study). BA, BMid (midwifery), BN, BSc, LLB.

Higher Degrees (see also United Kingdom Directory to Subjects of Study). LLM, MA, MBA, MCh(Orth.), MD, MLitt, MS, MSc, MPhil, PhD.

Libraries. 500,000 volumes.

Fees. Home/EC students: £750 (undergraduate non-science); £1600 (undergraduate science); £2540 (postgraduate); £6000 (MBA). International students: £5800 (undergraduate foundation); £6200 (undergraduate combination of social sciences and humanities); £7200 (undergraduate combination of one social sciences or humanities plus one laboratory subject); £8000 (undergraduate combination of two laboratory subjects); £6200 (postgraduate); £8500 (MBA).

Academic Awards. 32 awards totalling £372,000.

Academic Year (1997–98). Two semesters: 29 September–23 January; 26 January–12 June.

Income. Total, £52,750,000.

Statistics. Staff: 1046 (560 academic, 486 administrative). Students: full-time 5589 (2272 men, 3317 women); part-time 4213; international (full-time) 706 (309 men, 397 women); total 9802.

FACULTIES/SCHOOLS

Health and Medicine, Faculty of
Dean: Templeton, Prof. John R., MB BCh BAO Belf., FRCSCan

Humanities, Faculty of
Dean: Bell, Prof. Ian F. A., BA Reading, PhD Reading

Natural Sciences, Faculty of
Dean: Williams, Prof. Graham D., BSc Leic., PhD Wales, FGS

Social Sciences, Faculty of
Dean: Dugdale, Prof. Anthony M., BCL Oxf., MA Oxf.

ACADEMIC UNITS

American Studies
Tel: (01782) 583010 Fax: (01782) 583460
Bailey, Christopher J., MA Oxf., DPhil Oxf. Sr. Lectr.
Bell, Ian F. A., BA Reading, PhD Reading Prof., American Literature
Bonwick, Colin C., MA Oxf., PhD Maryland, FRHistS Prof.
Crawford, Martin S., BA Keele, MPhil Oxf., DPhil Oxf. Reader
Dumbrell, John W., MA Camb., MA Keele, PhD Keele Sr. Lectr.
Ellison, Mary L., BA Lond., PhD Lond. Reader
Garson, Robert A., BA Sus., PhD Lond. Reader; Head*
Godden, Richard L., BA Kent, PhD Kent, MA Sus. Prof.
Mills, Stephen F., BA Keele, MA Maryland Sr. Lectr.
Swann, Charles S. B., MA Camb., PhD Camb. Reader

Biological Sciences
Tel: (01782) 583028 Fax: (01782) 630007
Arme, Christopher, BSc Leeds, PhD Leeds, DSc Keele, FIBiol Prof.; Head*
Chevins, Peter F. D., BSc Leeds, PhD Leeds Dir., Laboratories
Duncan, Ruth, BSc Liv., PhD Keele Visiting Prof.
Hurd, Hilary, BSc Wales, PhD Keele Sr. Lectr.
Morgan, Noel G., BSc Leic., PhD Leic. Prof., Biochemistry
Ward, Richard D., BSc Lond., MSc Lond., PhD Lond. Prof.
Williams, Gwyn T., BSc Warw., DPhil Sus. Prof.

Chemistry
Tel: (01782) 583037 Fax: (01782) 712378
Catlow, Richard, MA Oxf., DPhil Oxf. Visiting Prof.
Fitch, Andrew N., MA Oxf., DPhil Oxf. Sr. Lectr. (on leave)
Greaves, G. Neville, BSc St And., PhD Camb. Visiting Prof.
Heywood, Brigid R., BSc Manc., PhD Liv. Prof.
Howell, James A. S., MSc Vic.(BC), PhD Camb. Prof.
Jackson, Robert A., BSc Lond., PhD Lond. Sr. Lectr.
Kendall, Kevin, BA Lond., PhD Camb., FRS Prof., Material Science
Long, D. A., MA
Ramsden, Christopher A., BSc Sheff., PhD Sheff., DSc Sheff., FRSChem Prof., Organic Chemistry
Truscott, T. George, BSc Wales, PhD Wales, DSc Wales, FRSChem, FRSEd Prof., Physical Chemistry; Head*

Classics
Tel: (01782) 583049 Fax: (01782) 584256
Sharrock, Alison R., BA Liv., PhD Camb. Sr. Lectr.; Head*
Todd, Stephen C., MA Camb., PhD Camb. Sr. Lectr.

Communication and Neuroscience
Tel: (01782) 583057 Fax: (01782) 583055
Ainsworth, William A., BSc Lond., PhD Keele Prof.
Evans, Edward F., BSc Birm., MB ChB Birm., PhD Birm., DSc Birm., FRCP Prof., Auditory Physiology
Hackney, Carole M., BSc Manc., PhD Manc. Prof.; Head*

Computer Science
Tel: (01782) 583446 Fax: (01782) 713082
Bostock, S. J., BSc Manc., MSc Manc., PhD Manc. Dir., Information Technol.
Brereton, O. Pearl, BSc Sheff., PhD Keele Sr. Lectr.
Budgen, David, BSc Durh., PhD Durh. Prof., Software Engineering; Head*
Deen, S. Misbah, MSc Dacca, PhD Lond. Prof.
Worboys, Michael F., BSc Reading, MSc Brist., PhD Birm. Prof.

Criminology
Tel: (01782) 583084 Fax: (01782) 584269
Hope, Timothy J., BA Leeds, MSc Lond., PhD Lond. Prof.

Jefferson, Anthony, J., BEd Lough MA
Birm. Prof.; Head*
Sparks, J. Richard, BA Camb., MPhil Camb., PhD
Camb. Prof.

Earth Sciences

Tel: (01782) 583172 Fax: (01782) 584116

Fairchild, Ian J., BSc Nott., PhD Nott.,
FGS Prof.
Floyd, Peter A., BSc Leic., PhD Birm.,
FGS Reader
Park, R. Graham, BSc Glas., PhD Glas.,
FGS Prof., Tectonic Geology
Rowbotham, George, BSc Durh., PhD Durh.,
FGS Sr. Lectr.
Torrens, Hugh S., BA Oxf., PhD Leic.,
FGS Reader
Williams, Graham D., BSc Leic., PhD Wales,
FGS Prof.
Winchester, John A., MA Oxf., DPhil Oxf.,
FGS Sr. Lectr.
Young, R. Paul, BSc Lond., MSc Newcastle(UK),
PhD CNAA, FGS Prof.; Head*

Economics

Tel: (01782) 583091

Bladen-Hovell, Robin C., BSc Wales, MA(Econ)
Manc. Prof.; Head*
Cornes, Richard C., BSc S'ton., MSc S'ton., PhD
ANU Prof.
Devereux, Michael P., BA Oxf., MSc Lond., PhD
Lond. Prof., Finance
Hartley, Roger, BA Camb., PhD Camb. Prof.,
Operational Research
Lawrence, Peter R., MA Sus., PhD Leeds Sr.
Lectr.
Rosenthal, Leslie, BSc S'ton., MA Essex, PhD
Essex Sr. Lectr.
Symons, Elizabeth, MSc S'ton., PhD S'ton. Sr.
Lectr.
Tribe, Keith P., BA Essex, PhD Camb. Reader
Walker, Ian, BA Liv., MA Warw. Prof.
Worrall, Timothy S., BA Liv., MA Essex, PhD
Liv. Prof.

Education

Tel: (01782) 583114

Bale, John R., BSc(Econ) Lond., MPhil
Lond. Reader
Brighouse, Timothy, MA Oxf. Visiting Prof.
Cleland, Gilian P., BPhil Lond. MA
Open(UK) Prof.; Professl. Devel./Educn.
Management Co-ordinator
Gleeson, Denis, BSc Oxf., MA Lond. Dir.,
Research; Head*
Hari, Maria Hon. Prof.
Maden, Margaret, BA Leeds Prof.; Dir., Centre
for Successful Schs.
Ozga, Jenifer T., BA Aberd., MEd Aberd., PhD
Open(UK) Prof.
Wringe, Colin A., BA Oxf., MA Lond., PhD
Lond. Reader

Electronics, see Phys.

English Language and Literature

Tel: (01782) 583138 Fax: (01782) 713468

Kelly, Gary, BA Tor., BA Oxf., DPhil Oxf. Prof.
Larrissy, Edward T., MA Oxf., DPhil
Oxf. Prof.; Head*
Swigg, Richard, BA Liv., PhD Brist. Sr. Lectr.
Trodd, Anthea N., MA Lond. Sr. Lectr.

Environmental Social Studies
(Geography)

Tel: (01782) 584307 Fax: (01782) 584144

Dwyer, Denis J., BA Lond., PhD Lond. Prof.†
Ekins, Paul W., BSc Lond., MSc Lond., MPhil
Brad. Sr. Lectr., Environmental Policy Unit
Kivell, Philip T., BSc Lond., PhD Keele Reader
Phillips, Anthony D. M., BA Lond., PhD
Lond. Reader
Proops, John L. R., BA Keele, PhD Keele Prof.,
Environmental Policy Unit
Redclift, Michael, BA Sus., DPhil Sus. Prof.;
Head*
Turton, Brian J., BSc Nott., PhD Nott. Sr. Lectr.

French, see under Mod. Langs.

German, see under Mod. Langs.

Health Planning and Management

Tel: (01782) 583191 Fax: (01782) 711737

Cropper, Stephen A., BSc Dund., PhD Wales Sr.
Lectr.
Dyson, Roger F., BA Keele, PhD Leeds Hon.
Prof.
Lee, Kenneth, BSc(Econ) Hull, MA Keele Prof.;
Dir.*
Ong, Pauline, BN Nijmegen, BEd Nijmegen, MA
Nijmegen, PhD Manc. Reader
Paton, Calum R., MA Oxf., MPP Harv., DPhil
Oxf. Prof.
Scrivens, Ellie, BA Exe., PhD Lond. Prof.

History

Tel: (01782) 583195 Fax: (01782) 583195

Clavin, Patricia M., BA Lond., PhD Lond. Sr.
Lectr.
Crook, Malcolm H., BA Wales, PhD
Lond. Reader; Head*
Hughes, Ann L., BA Liv., PhD Liv.,
FRHistS Prof.
Jackson, Peter, MA Camb., PhD Camb.,
FRHistS Sr. Lectr.
McInnes, Angus J. D. M., MA Wales, PhD
Keele Sr. Lectr.
Morgan, Philip J., BA Lond., PhD Lond. Sr.
Lectr.
Roseman, Mark, MA Camb., PhD Warw. Sr.
Lectr.
Studd, J. Robin, BA Leeds, PhD Leeds,
FRHistS Sr. Lectr.
Townshend, Charles J. N., MA Oxf., DPhil Oxf.,
FRHistS Prof.
Vincent, David M., BA York(UK), PhD Camb.,
FRHistS Prof.

Human Resource Management and
Industrial Relations

Tel: (01782) 583254 Fax: (01782) 584271

Burchill, Frank, BA Leeds Prof.; Head*
Lyddon, David, BA Oxf., MSc(Econ) Lond., PhD
Warw. Sr. Lectr.
Seifert, Roger V., BA Oxf., MSc(Econ) Lond.,
PhD Lond. Prof.

International Relations

Tel: (01782) 583088 Fax: (01782) 583088

Danchev, Alexander, MA Oxf., PhD Lond. Prof.
James, Alan M., BSc(Econ) Lond. Prof.†
Keohane, Daniel J., BA Sus., MA Warw. Sr.
Lectr.
Linklater, Andrew, MA Aberd., BPhil Oxf., PhD
Lond. Prof.
Suganami, Hidemi, BA Tokyo, MScEcon Wales,
PhD Lond. Sr. Lectr.; Head*
Thornberry, Patrick, LLB CNAA, LLM Keele, PhD
Keele Prof.

Law

Tel: (01782) 583218 Fax: (01782) 583228

Cocks, Raymond C., BA Camb. Prof.; Head*
Dugdale, Anthony M., BCL Oxf., MA
Oxf. Prof.
Haley, Michael A., LLB Liv., LLM Leic. Reader
Herman, Didi, BA Tor., LLB Tor., PhD
Wales Reader
McEwan, Jenny A., LLB Exe., BCL Oxf. Prof.
Olowofoyeku, Abimbola A., LLB Lagos, LLM
Lond., PhD Lond. Sr. Lectr.
Stychin, Carl F., BA Alta., LLB Tor., LLM
Col. Sr. Lectr.

Management

Tel: (01782) 583089 Fax: (01782) 584272

Cooper, Robert C., BA Reading, PhD Liv. Prof.
Forrester, Paul L., BSc Aston, PhD Aston Sr.
Lectr.
Hassard, John S., BA Lanc., MSc Aston, PhD
Aston Prof.
Munro, Rolland J. B., BA Stir., PhD
Edin. Reader

Pearson, Gordon J., BSc Warw., PhD Manc. Sr.
Lectr.; Head*
Proctor, R. Anthony, MA Lanc., MPhil Warw.,
PhD Manc. Sr. Lectr.

Mathematics

Tel: (01782) 583257 Fax: (01782) 584268

Chapman, Christopher J., BA Camb., MA Camb.,
PhD Brist. Reader
Fu, Yibin, BSc Changsha Railway Inst., MSc
E.Anglia, PhD E.Anglia Sr. Lectr.
Grieve, Andrew P., BSc S'ton., MSc S'ton., PhD
Nott. Hon. Prof.
Jones, J. Mary, MSc Lond., PhD Manc. Sr. Lectr.
Jones, Peter W., MSc Reading, PhD Wales Prof.
Quinney, Douglas A., BSc Nott., MSc Oxf.,
DPhil Oxf. Reader
Smith, Peter, BSc Nott., PhD Nott. Prof.
Walker, Keith, MA Camb. Sr. Lectr.
Wilks, Graham, BSc Manc., PhD Manc. Prof.;
Head*
Willmott, Andrew J., BSc Brist., MSc E.Anglia,
PhD E.Anglia Prof.

Medicine, Postgraduate, see below

Medicines Management

Tel: (01782) 584133 Fax: (01782) 713586

Blenkinsopp, Alison, BPharm Brad., PhD
Aston Dir., Educn. and Res.
Chapman, Stephen R., BSc Liv., PhD
Lond. Prof.; Dir., Prescribing Analysis
Fitzpatrick, Raymond W., BSc Manc., PhD
Manc. Sr. Lectr.
Frisher, M., BA PhD Sr. Lectr.
Heeley, David Impact Project Manager
Mucklow, John C., MB ChB Birm., MD Birm.,
FRCP Sr. Lectr.

Modern Languages

French

Tel: (01782) 584075 Fax: (01782) 584078

Gaffney, John, BA Sus., MA Sus., DPhil
Sus. Prof.
Holmes, Diana, BA Sus., MèsL Paris, DPhil
Sus. Prof.; Head*
Johnson, Christopher M., BA Lond., PhD
Camb. Sr. Lectr.

German

Tel: (01782) 583282 Fax: (01782) 583441

Kolinsky, Eva W., DrPhil F.U.Berlin Prof.

Russian

Tel: (01782) 583290 Fax: (01782) 584238

Andrew, Joseph M., BA Oxf. Prof.
Polukhina, Valentina, BA Tula, MA Moscow, PhD
Keele Prof.
Reid, Robert E., BA Birm. Sr. Lectr.

Music

Tel: (01782) 583295

Firsova, Elena Visiting Prof.; Composer in
Residence
Nicholls, David R., MA Camb., PhD
Camb. Prof.
Smirnov, Dmitri Visiting Prof.; Composer in
Residence
Vaughan, Michael P., BA CNAA, PhD Nott. Sr.
Lectr.; Head*

Neuroscience, see Communicn. and
Neurosci.

Nursing and Midwifery

Hollins, M. Sandra, BEd CNAA Head,
Midwifery Studies
Latham, David R., BA Manc.Met. Head, Post-
Registration Nursing Studies; Head*
Traylor, Sarah E. A., BA Staffs. Head, Pre-
Registration Nursing Studies
White, Edward G., MSc Cran., MSc Sur., PhD
Manc. Prof.

Philosophy

Tel: (01782) 583304 Fax: (01782) 583399

Gallois, André, BA Sus., BPhil Oxf. Prof.

McNaughton, David A., BA *Newcastle(UK)*, BPhil *Oxf.* Prof.; Head*
Rogers, G. A. John, BA *Nott.*, PhD *Keele* Prof.

Physics

Tel: (01782) 583326 Fax: (01782) 711093

Challis, Richard E., BSc(Eng) *Lond.*, PhD *Lond.* Prof., Electronics
Dugdale, David E., BSc *Manc.*, MSc *Lond.*, PhD *Durh.* Sr. Lectr.
Evans, Aneurin, BSc *Wales*, PhD *Wales*, FRAS Prof.; Head*
Fuller, Watson, BSc *Lond.*, PhD *Lond.*, FIP Prof.
Gillan, Michael J., BA *Oxf.*, DPhil *Oxf.*, FIP Prof., Theoretical Physics
Gould, Robert D., BA *Lanc.*, MSc *Lanc.*, PhD *Brun.* Sr. Lectr., Electronics
Greenhough, Trevor J., BSc *Nott.*, MSc *Sur.*, PhD *Sur.* Reader
Hagen, Mark E., BSc *S'ton.*, PhD *Edin.* Sr. Lectr.
Lainé, Derek C., PhD *S'ton.*, DSc *S'ton.*, FIP, FIEE Prof.†, Molecular Physics
Mahendrasingam, Arumugam, BSc *S.Lanka*, PhD *Keele* Sr. Lectr.
Pattinson, E. Barrie, BSc *Wales*, PhD *Wales*, FIP Sr. Lectr.
Pigram, William J., BSc *Lond.*, PhD *Lond.* Sr. Lectr.
Strange, Paul, BSc *Lond.*, PhD *Lanc.* Sr. Lectr.
Wood, Janet H., BSc *Leic.*, PhD *Camb.* Reader

Physiotherapy

Tel: (01782) 584190 Fax: (01782) 584255

Bailey, Margaret J., BA *Open(UK)*, MSc *Liv.* Lectr.; Head, Postgrad. Studies; Acting Head, Res.
Lowe, Jennifa M. Lectr.; Clin. Educn. Co-ordinator
Place, Marilyn, MEd *Manc.* Lectr.; Head, Undergrad. Studies; Head*
Smith, Julius W., BA *Durh.*, MSc *S.Bank*, PhD *Keele* Prof.

Politics

Tel: (01782) 583452 Fax: (01782) 583452

Canovan, Margaret E., MA *Camb.*, PhD *Camb.* Prof.
Dobson, Andrew N. H., BA *Reading*, DPhil *Oxf.* Prof.
Horton, John, MSc(Econ) *Wales* Reader; Head*
O'Kane, Rosemary H. T., BA *Essex*, MA *Essex*, PhD *Lanc.* Sr. Lectr.
Waller, D. Michael, BA(Econ) *Manc.*, MA *Oxf.* Prof.; Dir., European Studies

Psychology

Tel: (01782) 583380 Fax: (01782) 583387

Cullen, Christopher, BA *Wales*, PhD *Wales*, FBPsS Prof.
Gellatly, Angus R. H., MA *Dund.*, PhD *Lond.* Sr. Lectr.; Head*
Hutt, S. John, BA *Manc.*, MA *Oxf.* Emer. Prof.†
Sloboda, John A., MA *Oxf.*, PhD *Lond.*, FBPsS Prof.

Russian, see under Mod. Langs.

Social Studies, Applied

Tel: (01782) 584063 Fax: (01782) 584069

Bernard, Miriam, BA *Keele*, PhD *Keele* Reader
Biggs, Simon J., BSc *City(UK)*, PhD *Lond.* Reader
McLeod, John A., MA *Edin.*, PhD *Edin.* Prof.; Head*
Phillipson, Christopher R., BA *CNAA*, PhD *Durh.* Prof.

Sociology and Social Anthropology

Tel: (01782) 583355 Fax: (01782) 584151

Law, John, BScEcon *Wales*, PhD *Edin.* Prof.; Head*
Werbner, Pnina, BA *Jerusalem*, MA *Manc.*, PhD *Manc.* Reader; Res. Fellow

Visual Arts

Tel: (01782) 583491 Fax: (01782) 583487

Frascina, Francis A., BA *CNAA* Prof.; Head*

Harris, Jonathan P., BA *Sus.*, PhD *CNAA* Sr. Lectr.

POSTGRADUATE MEDICINE

Tel: (01782) 716047 Fax: (01782) 747319

Temple, J. G., ChM *Birm.*, FRCS Hon. Dean

Biomedical Engineering and Medical Physics

El-Haj, A. J., BA *Hull*, MSc *Manc.*, PhD *Aberd.* Sr. Lectr.; Head*
Smith, David, BA *Keele*, PhD *Birm.*, DSc *Birm.*, Hon. DSc *Keele*, FIP, FRS Visiting Prof.

Epidemiology

Bridgeman, Stephen, MPH MD, FRCSEd, FRCSGlas Sr. Lectr.
Croft, Peter, BA *Birm.*, MB ChB *Birm.*, MSc *Lond.*, MD *Birm.* Prof.†; Head*
Davies, Simon J., BSc *Lond.*, MB BS *Lond.* Sr. Lectr.
Hassell, Andrew B., MB ChB *Manc.*, MD *Manc.* Sr. Lectr.
Hawkins, C., BM BS *Nott.*, DM *Nott.* Sr. Lectr.
Hill, Simon, MB BS *Newcastle*, FRCP Sr. Lectr.
Melville, Colin A. S., MB ChB *Aberd.* Sr. Lectr.
Pantin, Charles F. A., MB BS *Lond.*, MSc *Camb.*, PhD *Camb.* Sr. Lectr.
Rajaratnam, Giri, MB BS *Lond.*, MSc *Lond.* Sr. Lectr.
Roffe, Christine
Russell, Gavin I., MB ChB *Birm.*, MD *Leic.* Sr. Lectr.
Samuels, M., BSc *Lond.*, MB BS *Lond.*, MD *Lond.* Sr. Lectr.
Scarpello, John H. B., MB BCh *Wales*, MD *Wales*, FRCP Sr. Lectr.
Spencer, S. A., BMedSci *Nott.*, BM BS *Nott.*, DM *Nott.* Sr. Lectr.
Spiteri, Monica, PhD *Lond.* Sr. Lectr.

Geriatric Medicine

Crome, Peter, MB BS *Lond.*, MD *Lond.*, PhD *Lond.*, FRCP, FRCPEd, FRCPGlas Prof.†

Medicine

Clayton, Richard N., BSc *Lond.*, MB BS *Lond.*, MD *Birm.*, FRCP Prof.†; Head*
Southall, David P., MB BS *Lond.*, MD *Lond.*, FRCP Prof.†, Paediatrics

Obstetrics and Gynaecology

Johanson, Richard B., BSc *St And.*, MA *St And.*, MD *Camb.* Sr. Lectr.
O'Brien, P. M. Shaughn, MB BCh *Wales*, MD *Wales* Prof.†; Head*
Redman, Charles E., MB ChB *Manc.*, MD *Manc.*, FRCOG, FRCS Sr. Lectr.

Pathology and Molecular Medicine, Centre for

Strange, Richard L., BSc *Lond.*, PhD *Lond.* Prof.†; Dir.*

Primary Health Care, Centre for

Charlton, Roger, BA *Open(UK)*, MB ChB *Birm.*, MPhil *Nott.* Sr. Lectr.
McGuinness, Brian W., MB ChB *Liv.*, MD *Liv.*, FRCGP Prof.†

Psychiatry

Acuda, Stanley W., MB ChB, FRCPsych Sr. Lectr.
Cox, John L., BM BCh *Oxf.*, MA *Oxf.*, DM *Oxf.*, FRCPsych, FRCPEd Prof.†; Head*
Foreman, David, MB ChB *Brist.*, MSc *Manc.* Sr. Lectr.
Henshaw, C., MB ChB *Aberd.* Sr. Lectr.

Surgery

Deakin, Mark, MB ChB *Liv.*, ChM *Liv.*, FRCS Sr. Lectr.
Elder, James B., MB ChB *Glas.*, MD *Glas.*, FRCS Prof.†; Head*
Smith, Ian, BSc *Lond.*, MB BS *Lond.*, FRCA Sr. Lectr.
Worrall, Steven, BDS *Birm.*, MB ChB *Birm.*, FDSRCS, FRCS Sr. Lectr.

Surgery, Orthopaedic

Neal, Nicholas C., MB ChB *Birm.*, FRCSEd
Redmond, A. O., OBE, MB ChB *Manc.*, MD *Manc.*, FRCPGlas, FRCSEd Prof.
Richardson, James B., MB ChB *Aberd.*, MD *Aberd.*, FRCSEd Prof.†
Templeton, John R., MB BCh BAO *Belf.*, FRCSCan Prof.†; Head*
Thomas, Peter B. M., MB BS *Lond.*, FRCS, FRCSEd Sr. Lectr.

SPECIAL CENTRES, ETC

Continuing and Professional Education

Pike, Christopher R., MA *Edin.* Dir.*

CONTACT OFFICERS

Academic affairs. Director of Academic Affairs: Slade, Edward F., BSc *Nott.*, PhD *Keele*, FIP
Accommodation. Accommodation Services Manager: Ford, Barbara
Admissions (first degree). Head of Admissions: Thorley, H. A., BA *Oxf.*
Admissions (higher degree). Head of Admissions: Thorley, H. A., BA *Oxf.*
Adult/continuing education. Director, Centre for Continuing and Professional Education: Pike, Christopher R., MA *Edin.*
Alumni. Alumni Co-ordinator: Parry, Cedric H. T., BA *Wales*
Alumni. Public Relations Assistant, Graduate Liaison Programme: Garner, Susan, BA *Staffs.*
Careers. Head of Careers Service: Hardy, Holly, BA *Lanc.*
Computing services. Director of Information Services: Foster, Allan, BA *Open(UK)*, FIInfSc
Consultancy services. Head of Secretariat and Research Development: Anderson, Sarah, BA *Lanc.*, MLitt *Lanc.*, PhD *Birm.*
Credit transfer. Director of Programmes and Deputy Director, Academic Affairs: Law, David S., BA *Sus.*, MPhil *Glas.*, PhD *Keele*
Development/fund-raising. Head of Public Relations: Bridgett, Susan J., BA *Lond.*, MA *Lond.*
Distance education. Director, Centre for Continuing and Professional Education: Pike, Christopher R., MA *Edin.*
Equal opportunities. Personnel Manager: Miller, Judith M., BA *Leeds*
Examinations. Head of Examinations and Records: Hart, Diane, MSc *Hull*
Finance. Director of Finance: Rigg, Paul R., BA *CNAA*
General enquiries. Head of Public Relations: Bridgett, Susan J., BA *Lond.*, MA *Lond.*
Health services. Medical Officer: Mairs, T. David, MB BCh BAO *Belf.*
International office. Head of International Office: Kratz, Annette, BSc *Aston*, PhD *Aston*
Library (chief librarian). Director of Information Services: Foster, Allan, BA *Open(UK)*, FIInfSc
Personnel/human resources. Director of Personnel: Price, Jane F.
Public relations, information and marketing. Head of Public Relations: Bridgett, Susan J., BA *Lond.*, MA *Lond.*
Publications (general). Head of Public Relations: Bridgett, Susan J., BA *Lond.*, MA *Lond.*
Publications (prospectuses). Director of Programmes and Deputy Director, Academic Affairs: Law, David S., BA *Sus.*, MPhil *Glas.*, PhD *Keele*
Purchasing. Purchasing Manager: Warburton, Leon A.
Quality assurance and accreditation. Director of Programmes and Deputy Director, Academic Affairs: Law, David S., BA *Sus.*, MPhil *Glas.*, PhD *Keele*
Research. Head of Research Support: Anderson, Sarah, BA *Lanc.*, MLitt *Lanc.*, PhD *Birm.*
Safety. Safety Advisor: Rosiek, Clive W., BSc *Wales*

Scholarships, awards, loans. Director of
Academic Affairs: Slade, Edward F., BSc
Nott., PhD *Keele*, FIP
Schools liaison. Recruitment Officer: Hicks,
Amanda, BA *Oxf.*
Security. Security Officer: Toplass, Roy P.
Sport and recreation. Leisure Centre Manager:
Burchell, Christopher D., BEd *CNAA*

Staff development and training. Staff
Training and Development Manager: Padin,
John
Student union. General Manager: McCormack,
Martyn, BSc *Brun.*
Students from other countries. Head of
International Office: Kratz, Annette, BSc
Aston, PhD *Aston*

Women. Personnel Manager: Miller, Judith M.,
BA *Leeds*

*[Information supplied by the institution as at 5 March
1998, and edited by the ACU]*

UNIVERSITY OF KENT AT CANTERBURY

Founded 1965

Member of the Association of Commonwealth Universities

Postal Address: Canterbury, Kent, England CT2 7NZ
Telephone: (01227) 764000 **Fax**: (01227) 452196 **Cables**: Unikent, Canterbury **Telex**: 965449 UKCLIB G
WWW: http://www.ukc.ac.uk/ **E-mail formula**: initials.surname@ukc.ac.uk

VISITOR—Canterbury, His Grace The Lord Archbishop of
CHANCELLOR—Tickell, Sir Crispin, GCMG, KCVO, DCL
PRO-CHANCELLOR—Brabourne,The Rt. Hon. the Lord, CBE, DCL
DEPUTY PRO-CHANCELLOR—Swire, Sir John, CBE, MA Hon. LLD
DEPUTY PRO-CHANCELLOR—Chipperfield, Sir Geoffrey, KCB
VICE-CHANCELLOR*—Sibson, Prof. Robin, MA *Camb.*, PhD *Camb.*
DEPUTY VICE-CHANCELLOR—Freedman, Prof. Robert B., MA *Oxf.*, DPhil *Oxf.*
PRO-VICE-CHANCELLOR—Slater, Prof. John B., MA *Oxf.*, DPhil *Oxf.*, FIMA
PRO-VICE-CHANCELLOR—De Friend, Richard H. M., BA *Kent*, LLM *Lond.*, LLM
Yale
TREASURER—Bird, James, MA Trinity(Dub.), MBA *Stan.*, DCL
DEPUTY TREASURER—Dunning, Alister A., LLB *Lond.*
SECRETARY AND REGISTRAR‡—McHard, Nick, BSc *Lond.*, MA *CNAA*
LIBRARIAN—Coutts, Margaret, MA *Glas.*, MA *Sheff.*

GENERAL INFORMATION

History. The university was founded in 1965.
It is situated on the outskirts of Canterbury.

Admission to first degree courses (see also
United Kingdom Introduction). All applicants
should apply through the Universities and
Colleges Admissions Service (UCAS). Normal
entry requirements: 3 A levels, or equivalent
qualifications.

First Degrees (see also United Kingdom
Directory to Subjects to Study). BA, BBA,
BEng, BSc, LLB, MChem, MComp, MEng,
MManSci, MPhys.
　Most courses are full-time and last at least 3
years. MChem, MComp, MEng, MManSci,
MPhys, sandwich courses, courses with a year
abroad or foundation year: 4 years.

Higher Degrees (see also United Kingdom
Directory to Subjects to Study). LLM, MA,
MBA, MBS, MClinSci, MEBA (European
business administration), MEBS (European
business studies), MRes, MSc, MSurg, MTh,
MPhil, PhD, MD, DClinSci.
　Applicants should normally hold an
appropriate first or second class honours
degree.
　Master's degrees: 1 year full-time, 2 years
part-time; MPhil: 2 years full-time, 3 years
part-time; PhD: 3 years full-time, 4 years part-
time; MClinSci/DClinSci: up to 6 years part-
time.

Libraries. Over 1,000,000 books, periodicals,
pamphlets, slides and microforms. Special
collections: Melville, Pettingell, Reading
Rayner, playbills (drama); Weatherill papers
(parliamentary practices and procedures);
Crow collection (ballad and song,

bibliography, English renaissance, proverbs and
language); Maddison (seventeenth to
nineteenth-century science and technology);
Farquharson (Greek and Roman
classics,1800–1939); Lloyd George (part of his
private library); Kent local history; modern
first editions; modern poetry.

Fees (annual). Undergraduates (1998–99):
UK and EU students up to £1000; overseas
(non-EU) students £6630 (non-laboratory
courses), £8650 (laboratory courses).
Postgraduates full-time (1997–98): UK and EU
students £2540; overseas (non-EU) students
£6435 (non-laboratory courses), £8395
(laboratory courses). Postgraduates part-time
(1997–98): non-laboratory research degrees
£1120; non-laboratory coursework degrees
£1070; laboratory research degrees £1200;
laboratory coursework degrees £1120. MBA
full-time (1997–98): UK and EU students
£7000; overseas (non EU) students £9000.
MBA part-time (1997–98): £467 per unit
(minimum of 6 units in first year).

Academic Awards. 83 prizes awarded.

Academic Year (1999–2000). Three terms:
11 October–17 December; 17 January–24
March; 26 April–4 July.

Income (1995–96). Total, £68,567,000.

Statistics. Staff: 1700. Students: full-time
7239; part-time 2848; other 1979; total
12,066.

FACULTIES/SCHOOLS
Humanities
Dean: Nightingale, David R., MA *Oxf.*

**Science, Technology and Medical
Studies**
Dean: Fuller, Ursula, MA *Camb.*, MA *Kent*

Social Sciences
Dean: Hann, Prof. Christopher M., BA *Oxf.*,
PhD *Camb.*

ACADEMIC UNITS
Accounting, see Canterbury Bus. Sch.

Anthropology
Colclough, Neville T., BA *Oxf.*, PhD *Lond.*　Sr.
Lectr.
Corbin, John, BA *Lond.*, PhD　Sr. Lectr.
Ellen, Roy F., BSc *Lond.*, PhD *Lond.*　Prof.,
Anthropology and Human Ecology; Head*
Fischer, Michael D., MA *Texas*, PhD *Texas*　Sr.
Lectr.
Hann, Christopher M., BA *Oxf.*, PhD
Camb.　Prof., Social Anthropology
Kemp, Jeremy H., BA *Lond.*, PhD *Lond.*　Sr.
Lectr.
Stirling, A. Paul, MA *Oxf.*, DPhil *Oxf.*　Prof.;
Res. Fellow
Watson, C. William, BA *Brist.*, MA *Hull*, PhD
Camb.　Sr. Lectr.

Arts and Image Studies, School of

Art, History and Theory of
Fax: (01227) 827846
Bann, Stephen, MA *Camb.*, PhD *Camb.*　Prof.,
Modern Cultural Studies
Cardinal, Roger, MA *Camb.*, PhD *Camb.*　Prof.,
Literature and Visual Studies
Clarke, Graham, MA *Essex*, PhD *Essex*　Reader

Communications and Image Studies

Cardinal, Roger, MA Camb., PhD Camb. Prof., Literary and Visual Studies
Reason, David A., BA Essex Sr. Lectr.
Sharratt, Bernard, MA Camb., PhD Camb. Reader, English and Cultural Studies

Drama and Theatre Studies

Anderson, Michael, BA Brist. Prof., Drama
Baugh, Christopher, BA Manc., MA Manc. Prof., Drama; Head*
Davis, Jill, BA Hull Sr. Lectr.
Oddey, Alison J. L., BA Exe., MA Leeds Sr. Lectr.

Film Studies

Christie, Ian Prof.
Cowie, Elizabeth J., BA S'ton. Sr. Lectr.

Psychoanalytic Studies

Reason, David A., BA Essex Sr. Lectr.
Stanton, Martin, BA Sus., DPhil Oxf. Sr. Lectr.

Biosciences

Fax: (01227) 763912
Baines, Anthony J., BSc Lond., PhD Lond. Sr. Lectr.
Blower, Philip, BA Camb., DPhil Sus. Sr. Lectr.
Bull, Alan T., BSc Leic., PhD Leic., FIBiol Prof., Microbiology Technology
Bunch, Alan W., BSc Liv., PhD Sr. Lectr.
Burns, Richard G., MSc Wales, PhD Lond. Prof., Environmental Microbiology; Head*
Freedman, Robert B., MA Oxf., DPhil Oxf. Prof., Biochemistry
Jarvis, Simon M., BSc Nott., PhD Camb. Reader, Biochemistry
Jeffries, Peter, BSc Lond., PhD Lond. Reader, Mycology
Proud, Christopher, BSc Brist., PhD Dund. Prof., Cell and Molecular Biology
Stacey, Ken Emer. Prof., Molecular Biology
Strange, Philip G., MA Camb., PhD Camb. Prof., Neuroscience
Tuite, Michael F., BSc Lond., DPhil Oxf. Prof., Molecular Biology; Chairman, Res. Sch. of Bioscis.

Business, see Canterbury Bus. Sch.

Canterbury Business School

Fax: (01227) 761187
Bevan, John M., MA Oxf. Sr. Lectr.
Cheng, Russell C. H., MA Camb., PhD Bath Prof., Operational Research
Fuller, Michael F., MA Camb. Sr. Lectr.
Hale, Chris, BA Keele, MSc PhD Prof., Criminology
Hughes, James J., BSc(Econ) Hull Prof., Industrial Relations and Human Resource Management
Lam, Alice C. L., BSc HK, MA Waseda, PhD Lond. Sr. Lectr.
MacDonald, M. Graeme, LLM Lond., MA, FCA Reader, Accounting and Taxation
Morris, Barbara, BSc Manc., PhD Brun. Sr. Lectr.
Rutherford, Brian A., BA Exe., PhD Prof., Accounting; Head*
Scase, Richard, BA Leic., MA Leic., PhD Kent Prof., Sociology and Organisational Behaviour
Sharp, John A., MA Camb., PhD Brad. Prof., Management

Communications, see under Arts and Image Studies, Sch. of

Computing Laboratory

Fax: (01227) 762811
Brown, Heather, BSc Brist. Prof., Electronic Publishing
Brown, Peter J., BA Camb., MA N.Carolina, PhD Camb. Prof., Computer Science
Eager, Bob D., BSc Essex, MSc Essex Sr. Lectr.
Hanna, F. Keith, BSc Brist., PhD Camb. Reader, Formal Design Methods

Hopkins, Tim, BSc S'ton., PhD Liv. Reader, Numerical Computing
Johnson, Leslie, BA York(UK), PhD Brun. Prof., Information Management
Jones, Richard E., MA Oxf., MSc Sr. Lectr.
Kemp, Zarine P., BCom Bom., BSc(Econ) Lond. Sr. Lectr.
Linington, Peter F., MA Camb., PhD Camb. Prof., Computer Communication
Makinson, Gordon, BSc St.And., PhD Liv., FIMA Sr. Lectr.
Slater, John B., MA Oxf., DPhil Oxf., FIMA Prof.; Dir.*
Spratt, Brian, BSc Nott., PhD Durh., FIMA Emer. Prof., Computing
Thompson, Simon J., MA Camb., DPhil Oxf. Sr. Lectr.
Turner, David A., MA Oxf., DPhil Oxf. Prof., Computation
Welch, Peter H., BSc Warw., PhD Warw. Prof., Parallel Computing
Wilson, Eve, BSc Leeds Sr. Lectr.

Drama and Theatre Studies, see Arts and Image Studies, Sch. of

Economics

Cannon, Colin, BSc Hull, MSocSc Birm., PhD Manc. Sr. Lectr.
Carruth, Alan A., BA Stir., MA Warw., MSc Strath. PhD Warw. Prof.
Sinclair, M. Thea, MA Reading, PhD Reading Sr. Lectr.
Thirlwall, Anthony P., BA Leeds, MA Clark, PhD Leeds Prof., Applied Economics
Vickerman, Roger W., MA Camb., DPhil Sus. Prof., Regional and Transport Economics*

Electronic Engineering Laboratory

Fax: (01227) 456084
Ashworth, David G., BSc Manc., PhD Manc., FRAS Reader, Solid State Electronics
Collier, R. J., BSc S'ton., PhD S'ton., FIEE Sr. Lectr.; Dir., Electr. Engin. Lab.
Davies, P. A., BSc PhD Prof., Optical Communications*
Fairhurst, M. C., BSc PhD Prof., Computer Vision
Jastrzebski, A. K., MSc Warsaw Reader
Kelly, S. W., MSc Sr. Lectr.
Langley, R. J., BSc PhD Prof., Antenna Systems
Little, L. T., MA Camb., PhD Camb., FRAS Prof., Millimetre Wave Astronomy
Macdonald, G. H., MA Camb., PhD Camb., FRAS Sr. Lectr.
Parker, E. A., MA Camb., PhD Camb., FRAS Prof., Radio Communications
Pepper, M. G., BSc PhD Sr. Lectr.
Sobhy, M. I., BSc Cairo, PhD Leeds, FIEE Prof., Electronics
Walczowski, L. T., BSc Lond., PhD Sr. Lectr.
Waller, W. A. J., BSc Sur., MSc Sr. Lectr.

English, School of

Tel: (01227) 827461 Fax: (01227) 827001
Andrews, Malcolm Y., MA Camb., PhD Lond. Prof., Victorian and Visual Studies
Brown, Peter, BA Sus., DPhil York(UK) Sr. Lectr.
Carabine, Keith, MA Leeds, MA Yale, MLitt Yale, PhD Yale Sr. Lectr.
Claridge, G. Henry, BA Warw., MA Ill. Sr. Lectr.
Docherty, Thomas, MA Glas., DPhil Oxf. Prof., English Literature
Edmond, Rod S., BA Well., BPhil Oxf. Sr. Lectr.
Ellis, David G., MA Camb., PhD Camb. Prof.
Gurnah, Abdulrazak, BEd Lond., PhD Kent Sr. Lectr.
Hutchinson, Stuart, MA Leeds Sr. Lectr.
Innes, Lyn, BA Syd., MA Oregon, PhD Cornell Prof., Postcolonial Literatures*
Irwin, Michael, BA Oxf., BLitt Oxf. Prof., English Literature

James, W. Louis G., MA Oxf., DPhil Oxf. Prof., Victorian and Modern Literature
Montefiore, Janet, BA Oxf., BPhil Oxf., PhD Kent Sr. Lectr.
O'Connor, Marion F., BA Tor., MPhil Lond., PhD Lond. Sr. Lectr.
Scofield, Martin P., BA Oxf., BPhil Oxf. Sr. Lectr.

European Culture and Languages, School of

Tel: (01227) 823638 Fax: (01227) 823641

Classical Studies

Anderson, Graham, MA Glas., MPhil N.U.I., DPhil Oxf. Prof., Classics
Barlow, Shirley A., MA Camb., PhD Lond. Sr. Lectr.
Blagg, Thomas F. C., MA Oxf., PhD Lond., FSA Sr. Lectr., Archaeology
Keaveney, Arthur P., MA N.U.I., PhD Hull Sr. Lectr.
Ward, Anthony, MA Camb., PhD Nott. Sr. Lectr., Archaeology

English Language and Linguistics

Bex, Anthony R., MA Sus. Sr. Lectr.
Danilewicz, Christina Lectr.; Dir., Engl. Lang. Unit

French

Bell, Sheila M., MA Glas., PhD Glas. Sr. Lectr.
Bell, William M. L., MA Oxf. Sr. Lectr.
Flower, John, MA St And., PhD Reading Prof.
Robinson, Philip E. J., BA Wales, PhD Wales Reader, 18th Century French Studies
Shaw, David J., BA Sheff., PhD Sheff. Sr. Lectr.

German

Coggle, Paul A., BA Lond. Sr. Lectr.
Durrani, Osman, MA Oxf., DPhil Oxf. Prof.; Head of Sch.*
Kane, B. Martin, BA Leeds, PhD Birm. Reader, Modern German Studies
Raraty, Maurice M., BA Keele, MA Trinity(Dub.), PhD Sheff. Sr. Lectr.

Italian

No staff at present

Philosophy

Cherry, Christopher M., BA Camb., BPhil Oxf. Reader, Moral Philosophy
Norman, Richard J., BA Camb., PhD Lond. Prof., Moral Philosophy; Head*
Radford, Colin J., BSc Lond., DPhil Oxf. Res. Prof.
Sayers, Sean P., MA Camb., PhD Kent Reader
Skillen, Anthony J., BA Syd., BLitt Oxf. Reader

Spanish

Lough, Frank, MA Glas., PhD Salf. Sr. Lectr.

Theology and Religious Studies

Court, John M., BA Durh., PhD Durh. Sr. Lectr.
Gill, Robin, BD Lond., MSocSc Birm., PhD Lond. Michael Ramsey Prof., Modern Theology

Film Studies, see under Arts and Image Studies, Sch. of

French, see under European Culture and Langs., Sch. of

German, see under European Culture and Langs., Sch. of

Government, see Pol. and Internat. Relns.

History

Armstrong, Walter A., BA Birm., PhD Birm., FRHistS Prof., Economics and Social History
Birmingham, David, BA Lond., PhD Lond. Prof., Modern History
Bolt, Christine A., BA Lond., PhD Lond. Prof., American History
Copley, Antony R. H., MA Oxf., MPhil Oxf., FRHistS Reader

Cunningham, Hugh St. C., MA Camb., DPhil Sus. Prof., Social History; Head*
Ditchfield, Grayson M., BA Durh., PhD Camb., FRHistS Sr. Lectr.
Dolby, Alex, MSc Well., AM Prin. Sr. Lectr.
Eales, Richard G., MA Camb. Sr. Lectr.
Fincham, Kenneth C., BA Oxf., PhD Lond. Sr. Lectr.
Fortescue, William A. I., BA Oxf., MA Qu., PhD Lond. Sr. Lectr.
Gameson, Richard, MA Oxf., DPhil Oxf. Sr. Lectr.
Omrod, David, BSc(Econ) Lond., PhD Camb., FRHistS Sr. Lectr.
Potter, David L., BA Durh., PhD Camb. Sr. Lectr.
Rosman, Doreen M., BA Keele, PhD Keele Sr. Lectr.
Smith, Crosbie, MA Camb., PhD Camb. Reader, History and Cultural Studies
Turley, David M., MA Camb., PhD Camb. Sr. Lectr.
Welch, David A., BA Wales, PhD Lond. Prof., Modern European History

International Relations, see Pol. and Internat. Relns.

Italian, see under European Culture and Langs., Sch. of

Kent Law School

Fax: (01227) 827831

Carr, Indira, PhD Reader
Conaghan, Joanne A. F., BA Oxf., BCL Oxf. Sr. Lectr.
Diesfeld, Kate, DrJuris Lectr.; Dir., Mental Health Law Clinic
Howarth, William, BA Keele, LLM Wales Cripps Harries Hall ISAUR UK Prof., Environmental Law
Ireland, Paddy W., BA Kent Sr. Lectr.
Mansell, Wade, BA Well., LLM Well. Sr. Lectr.
Rubin, Gerry R., LLB Glas., MA Sus., PhD Warw. Prof.; Head*
Samuel, Geoffrey Prof.
Slaughter, Marty, BA Wis., MA Wis., PhD Wis., JD Calif. Reader
Uglow, Steve P., BA Oxf., BCL Oxf. Reader
De Friend, Richard H. M., LLM Lond., LLM Yale, BA Sr. Lectr.

Learning Disability, see Tizard Centre

Management Science, see Canterbury Bus. Sch.

Mathematics and Statistics, Institute of

Actuarial Science
No staff at present

Mathematics
Fax: (01227) 827932

Chisholm, J. Roy S., BA Oxf., MA Oxf., DPhil Oxf. Emer. Prof., Applied Mathematics
Clarkson, Peter A., BA Oxf., MA Oxf., DPhil Oxf. Prof.
Common, Alan K., BSc Lond., PhD Lond., FIP Prof., Applied Mathematics; Head*
Shackell, John R., BSc Nott., PhD Kent Reader, Symbolic Computation
Woodcock, Chris F., MA Oxf., DPhil Oxf. Sr. Lectr.

Statistics
Bassett, Eryl E., BA Oxf., MSc Wales, PhD Wales Sr. Lectr., Statistics
Brown, Philip J., BSc Leic., MSc Wales, PhD Lond. Pfizer Prof., Medical Statistics
Kenward, Michael G., BSc Birm., MSc Reading, PhD Reading Reader
Morgan, Byron J. T., BSc Lond., PhD Camb. Prof., Applied Statistics
Preece, Donald A., MA St And., PhD, FIMA Hon. Prof.
Tong, Howell, MSc Manc., PhD Manc. Prof.
Yao, Qiwei, MSc Nanjing, PhD Wuhan Sr. Lectr.

Mental Health Services, see Tizard Centre

Philosophy, see European Culture and Langs., Sch. of

Physical Sciences, School of

Chemistry
Tel: (01227) 462594 Fax: (01227) 827724

Beezer, Anthony E., BA Keele, MSc Manc., PhD Keele, DSc Keele Prof., Applied Chemistry; Head*
Benfield, Robert, MA Camb., PhD Camb. Sr. Lectr.
Boyle, L. Laurence, BSc Oxf., MA Oxf., DPhil Oxf. Sr. Lectr.
Chadwick, Alan V., BSc Manc., PhD Manc. Prof., Physical Chemistry
Connor, Joseph A., MA Camb., PhD Manc., FRSChem Prof., Inorganic Chemistry
Cragg, R. Harry, BSc Manc., PhD Manc., FRSChem Reader, Inorganic Chemistry
Creighton, John A., MA Oxf., DPhil Oxf. Reader, Chemical Spectroscopy
Davidson, R. S., DSc Leeds, PhD Leeds Prof., Applied Chemistry
Hyde, Richard Prof., Medicinal Chemistry
Jones, Richard G., MSc NZ, PhD Leeds, FRSChem Reader, Polymer Chemistry
Mitchell, John C., MSc S.Illinois, PhD Duke Sr. Lectr.
Todd, John F. J., BSc Leeds, PhD Leeds, FRSChem Prof., Mass Spectroscopy
Wallis, John D., MA Oxf., DPhil Oxf. Sr. Lectr.
Went, Michael J., BSc Brist., PhD Brist. Sr. Lectr.
Wright, John D., MA Oxf., DPhil Oxf. Reader

Physics
Fax: (01227) 827558

Dore, John C., BSc Birm., PhD Birm. Prof., Condensed Matter Physics
Jackson, David A., BSc S'ton., PhD Lond., FIP Prof., Applied Optics
Kay, L., BSc Manc., PhD Manc. Sr. Lectr.
McDonnell, J. A. M., BSc Manc., PhD Manc., FRAS Prof., Space Physics
Newport, Robert J., BSc Leic., PhD Leic. Prof., Materials Physics; Head*
Niblett, D. H., MA Oxf., DPhil Oxf. Sr. Lectr.
Pannell, Chris N., BSc Kent, PhD Kent Reader, Optics
Powles, Jack G., MSc Manc., PhD Manc., DèsSc Paris, FIP Emer. Prof.
Rickayzen, Gerald, BSc Lond., PhD Camb., FIP Emer. Prof., Theoretical Physics
Ryder, Lewis H., MA Oxf., PhD Edin. Sr. Lectr.
Smith, Mark E., MA Camb., PhD Warw. Reader
Strange, John H., BSc Lond., PhD Lond., FIP Prof., Experimental Physics
Zarnecki, John C., MA Camb., PhD Lond. Reader, Space Science

Politics and International Relations

Frost, Mervyn, BA Stell., MA Stell., DPhil Oxf., DPhil Stell. Prof., International Relations
Groom, A. J. R., BSc(Econ) Lond., MA Lehigh, DèsScPol Geneva Prof., International Relations*
McLellan, David T., MA Oxf., DPhil Oxf. Prof., Political Theory
Sakwa, Richard, BA Lond., PhD Birm. Prof., Russian and European Politics
Seymour-Ure, Colin K., MA Oxf., MA Car., DPhil Oxf. Prof., Government
Webb, Keith, BA Keele, MSc Strath. Sr. Lectr.
Williams, Andrew J., BA Keele, DèsScPol Geneva Reader, International Relations

European Studies
Church, Clive H., BA Exe., PhD Lond. Jean Monnet Prof.
Stevens, Anne, MA Camb., MSc(Econ) Lond., PhD Lond. Prof.

Psychology
Fax: (01227) 827030

Abrams, W. Dominic J., BA Manc., MSc Lond., PhD Prof., Social Psychology
Brown, Rupert J., BSc Edin., PhD Brist. Prof., Social Psychology*
Clark, Noel K., BA PhD Sr. Lectr.
Forrester, Mike A., MSc Strath., PhD Strath. Sr. Lectr.
Leekam, Sue, BA Open(UK), DPhil Sus. Sr. Lectr.
Quine, Lyn, BA PhD Reader, Health Psychology
Rutter, Derek R., BA Nott., PhD Nott. Prof., Health Psychology
Stephenson, Geoffrey, BA Nott., PhD Nott. Prof., Social Psychology
Weekes, Brenda, BA Melb., MClinPsych Macq., PhD Macq. Sr. Lectr.

Religious Studies, see European Culture and Langs., Sch. of

Social and Public Policy and Social Work
Fax: (01227) 827246, 824014

Baldock, John C., BA Oxf., MA Reader, Social Policy and Administration
Butler, John R., MA Nott., PhD Prof., Health Service Studies
George, Vic, MA Nott., PhD Nott. Prof.†, Social Policy and Social Work
Jenkins, William I., BSc Lond., PhD Lond. Reader, Public Policy and Management
Munday, Brian R., MA Oxf. Dir., Soc. Work Studies
Pahl, Jan, MA Camb., PhD Kent Prof., Social Policy*
Pickvance, Chris G., MA(Econ) Manc. Prof., Urban Studies
Sayers, Janet V., MA Camb., PhD Prof., Psychoanalytical Psychology
Taylor-Gooby, Peter F., BA Brist., MPhil York(UK), PhD Prof., Social Policy
Twigg, Julia, BA Durh., MSc Lond., PhD Lond. Reader, Social Policy
Vickerstaff, Sarah, BSc Leic., PhD Leeds Sr. Lectr.

Sociology
Evans, Mary S., MSc(Econ) Lond., DPhil Sus. Prof., Women's Studies; Head*
Furedi, Frank, BA McG., MA Lond., PhD Lond. Reader
Morgan, David G., BA Hull Sr. Lectr.
Rootes, Christopher A., BA Qld., BPhil Oxf. Sr. Lectr.

Spanish, see under European Culture and Langs., Sch. of

Statistics, see under Maths. and Stats., Inst. of

Tizard Centre
Learning Disability and Mental Health Services

Fernando, Suman, MA Camb., MD Camb. Sr. Lectr.
Mansell, Jim M., MScEcon Wales Prof., Applied Psychology of Learning Disability; Dir.*
McGill, Peter, BSc Glas., MPhil Lond. Sr. Lectr.
Murphy, Glynis H., BA Oxf., MA Birm., PhD Lond. Reader, Applied Psychology of Learning Disability
Williams, Jennie A., MSc Exe., PhD Brist. Sr. Lectr.

Women's Studies, see Sociol.

SPECIAL CENTRES, ETC

American Studies, Centre for
Turley, David A., BA Wales, PhD Lond. Dir.*

Applied Ethics, Centre for

Gill, R., BD Lond., MSocSc Birm., PhD Lond. Prof.; Dir.*

Applied Statistics Research Unit

North, Philip M., MSc Sus., PhD Dir.*
Pearce, S. Clifford, BSc Lond., PhD Lond., DSc Hon. Prof., Biometry

Cartoons and Caricature, Centre for the Study of

Vacant Posts: Dir.*

Colonial and Postcolonial Research, Centre for

Edmond, Rod, BA Well., BPhil Oxf. Dir.*

Conservation and Ecology, Durrell Institute of

Harrop, Stuart, LLB Leeds Prof., Wildlife Management Law
Leader-Williams, Nigel, BVSc Liv., PhD Camb. Prof., Biodiversity Management
Swingland, Ian R., BSc Lond., PhD Edin., FIBiol Prof., Conservation Biology; Founding Dir.*
Walkey, Michael, BSc Durh., PhD Durh. Exec. Dir.

Economic History, Centre for

Armstrong, A., BA Birm., PhD Birm., FRHistS Prof.
Crompton, Gerald, MA Camb. Dir.*

European Regional and Transport Economics, Centre for

Vickerman, Roger W., MA Camb., DPhil Sus. Prof.; Dir.*

Geography, Centre for

Whyman, John, BSc(Econ) Lond., PhD Kent Head*

Group Processes, Study of

Abrams, Dominic, BA Manc., MSc Lond., PhD Kent Prof.; Dir.*
Brown, Rupert J., BSc Edin., PhD Brist. Prof., Social Psychology
Clark, Noel, BA Kent, PhD Kent Sr. Lectr.

Health Behaviour, Centre for Research in

Abrams, Dominic, BA Manc., MSc Lond., PhD Prof., Social Psychology
Quine, Lyn, BA PhD Reader
Rutter, Derek, BA Nott., PhD Nott. Dir.*
Stephenson, Geoffrey, BA Nott., PhD Nott. Prof., Social Psychology

Health Services Studies, Centre for

Butler, J. R., MA Nott., PhD Prof.
Calnan, M. W., BSc CNAA, MSc Brist., PhD Prof.; Dir.*
Carpenter, I., BSc MD, FRCP, FRCPEd Sr. Lectr., Health Care of the Elderly
Forsythe, M., MB BS Lond., MSc Lond. Prof. Fellow, Public Health
Opit, L. J., BSc Warw., MB BS Adel., FRCS, FRACS Emer. Prof., Community Medicine

History and Cultural Studies of Science, Unit for the

Smith, C. W., MA Camb., PhD Camb. Sr. Lectr.; Dir.*

Kent Energy Economics Research Group

Peirson, John, BA Camb., PhD Dir.*

Kent Law Clinic

Fitzpatrick, John F., BA Oxf. Lectr.; Dir.*
Partridge, J., BA Liv., DrPhil Regensburg Dir.*

Materials Research, Centre for

Chadwick, Alan, BSc Manc., PhD Manc. Prof., Physical Chemistry
Jones, Richard G., MSc NZ, PhD Leeds, FRSChem Dir.*
Newport, Robert J., BSc Leic., PhD Leic. Prof., Materials Physics
Smith, Mark E., MA Camb., PhD Warw. Reader
Wright, John D., MA Oxf., DPhil Oxf. Reader

Medicine and Health Sciences, Kent Institute of

Colchester, Alan, BA BM BCh PhD, FRCP Reader, Neurosciences and Computing
Cook, Christopher Prof., Psychiatry of Alcohol Misuse
Rake, M., BSc Lond., MB BS Lond., FRCP Dir.*

Modern Cultural Studies, Centre of

Bann, S., MA Camb., PhD Camb. Dir.*

Part-time Study, Unit for the Support and Development of

Harrison, A., BA Leic., MA Kent Dir.*

Personal Social Services Research Unit

Fax: (01227) 827038
Challis, David J., BA York(UK), MSc Manc., PhD Reader, Social Work and Social Care; Asst. Dir.
Davies, Bleddyn P., MA Camb., DPhil Oxf. Prof., Social Policy; Dir.*
Judge, Ken Prof., Social Policy

Propaganda, Study of

Welch, David A., BA Wales, PhD Lond. Prof.; Dir.*

Social and Political Movements, Centre for the Study of

Rootes, C., BA Qld., BPhil Oxf. Dir.*

Social Research, Institute for

Morgan, D., BA Hull Dir.*

Social Services, European Institute of

Munday, B., MA Oxf. Dir.*

Space Sciences and Astrophysics, Unit for

Kay, L., BSc Manc., PhD Manc. Sr. Lectr.
Little, L. T., MA Camb., PhD Camb., FRAS Prof., Millimetre Wave Astronomy
McDonnell, J. A. M., BSc Manc., PhD Manc., FRAS Prof., Space Sciences; Dir.*
Niblett, D. H., MA Oxf., DPhil Oxf. Sr. Lectr.
Zarnecki, John C., MA Camb., PhD Lond. Reader, Space Science

Tourism Research Centre

Sinclair, Thea, MA Reading, PhD Reading Sr. Lectr.; Dir.*

Urban and Regional Studies Unit

Pickvance, Chris G., MA(Econ) Manc. Prof.; Dir.*

Women's Studies, Centre for

Evans, Mary, MSc(Econ) Lond., DPhil Sus. Prof.; Dir.*

CONTACT OFFICERS

Academic affairs. Director of Academic Administration and Deputy Registrar: Reilly, John E., MA Edin., MA Lond.
Accommodation. Accommodation Officer: Goss, Derek
Admissions (first degree). Assistant Registrar: King, Jennifer, MA Kent

Admissions (higher degree). Assistant Registrar: Hughes, Mary P., BSc Syr., MA S'ton.
Adult/continuing education. Director, Unit for the Support and Development of Part-time Study: Harrison, Ann, BA Leic., MA Kent
Alumni. Alumni Relations Officer: Burn, Killara, BA Calif.
Careers. Head of Careers Advisory Service: Greer, John W., MA Trinity(Dub.)
Computing services. Deputy Director of Services: Caul, Des J.
Development/fund-raising. Director of Communications and Development Office: Motion, Joanna, BA Oxf., MA Oxf.
Equal opportunities. Equal Opportunities Officer: Allcock, Ann, BSc Sur.
Estates and buildings/works and services. Estates and Buildings Officer: Burton, John E., BA Open(UK)
Examinations. Senior Assistant Registrar: Gibbs, John A., BSc Newcastle(UK), MSc Warw., PhD Warw.
Finance. Director of Finance: Everitt, Denise R., BA Kent
General enquiries. Secretary and Registrar: McHard, Nick, BSc Lond., MA CNAA
Health services. Head of Student Health Service (Senior Partner): Bowhay, Alyson, BSc Lond., MB BS Lond., MS Lond.
International office. Director of International Office: Cross, Pamela A., BA Lanc.
Library (chief librarian). Librarian: Coutts, Margaret, MA Glas., MA Sheff.
Minorities/disadvantaged groups. Equal Opportunities Officer: Allcock, Ann, BSc Sur.
Personnel/human resources. Director of Personnel: Mitson, Rolf
Public relations, information and marketing. Director of Public Relations: Harrison, Helen, BA
Publications. Publications Manager: Saunders, Hilary, BA Warw.
Purchasing. Purchasing Officer: Gallop, C., BSc Lond.
Research. Research Grants and Contracts Officer: Bentley, Ann, MA St And.
Safety. Safety Officer and Radiation Protection Officer: Chadwick, Ann, BSc Lond., PhD Manc.
Schools liaison. Executive Officer, Schools and Colleges Liaison: Aspinall, Susan
Sport and recreation. Director of Sport and Recreation: Wilkins, Michael, BA
Student welfare/counselling. Supervisor, Counselling Service: Klinefelfer, P., BA Calif., MA Calif., MA Sus.
Students from other countries. Director of International Office: Cross, Pamela A., BA Lanc.
Students with disabilities. Assistant Registrar: Anderson, Margaret, LLB Glas.

CAMPUS/COLLEGE HEADS

Darwin College. Master: Eager, Bob D., MSc Essex, BSc
Eliot College. Master: Pollard, Bruce, BAppEc NE, MEc NE, FCPA
Keynes College. Master: Keen, Lynda, BA Kent, MA Kent, MBA Lond., PhD Kent
Rutherford College. Master: Hutchinson, Stuart, MA Leeds

[Information supplied by the institution as at 6 February 1998, and edited by the ACU]

KINGSTON UNIVERSITY

Founded 1992; previously established as Kingston Science, Art and Technical Institute 1899, Kingston College of Technology 1962, and Kingston Polytechnic 1970

Member of the Association of Commonwealth Universities

Postal Address: River House, 53-57 High Street, Kingston upon Thames, Surrey, England KT1 1LQ
Telephone: (0181) 547 2000 **Fax**: (0181) 547 7178 **WWW**: http://www.king.ac.uk
E-mail formula: initial.surname@kingston.ac.uk

CHANCELLOR—Lampl, Sir Frank, KBE, Hon. Dr Brno, Hon. DUniv Kingston(UK)
CHAIRMAN OF THE BOARD OF GOVERNORS AND PRO-CHANCELLOR—Seth, Andrew, BA Oxf., MA Oxf., Hon. DUniv Kingston(UK)
VICE-CHANCELLOR (AND CHIEF EXECUTIVE)*—Scott, Prof. Peter, BA Oxf., Hon. LLD Bath, Hon. DLitt CNAA, Hon. FUMIST
DEPUTY VICE-CHANCELLOR—Gipps, Prof. Caroline, BSc Brist., MSc Lond., PhD Lond.
UNIVERSITY SECRETARY—Abdullah, Raficq, MA Oxf.
PRO-VICE-CHANCELLOR (EXTERNAL AFFAIRS)—Mercer, Anthony J. H., BSc Oxf., MA Oxf., DPhil Oxf., FRSChem
FINANCE DIRECTOR—Butcher, Terence M.
PERSONNEL DIRECTOR—Lanchbery, Elizabeth C., BA

GENERAL INFORMATION

History. The university's origins date from the establishment of Kingston Science, Art and Technical Institute in 1899. Kingston Polytechnic was created in 1970 by the merger of Kingston College of Art and Kingston College of Technology. Gypsy Hill College of Education joined the polytechnic in 1975. It attained university status in 1992.

The university has four campuses located in the outskirts of London.

Admission to first degree courses (see also United Kingdom Introduction). Through Universities and Colleges Admissions Service (UCAS).

First Degrees (see also United Kingdom Directory to Subjects of Study). BA, BEng, BMus, BSc, LLB, MChem, MEng, MPhys, MTeach.

Many courses are offered full-or part-time; some are sandwich courses.

Higher Degrees (see also United Kingdom Directory to Subjects of Study). LLM, MA, MArch, MBA, MEd, MSc, MPhil, PhD, DBA.

Applicants for admission to master's degree courses and for MPhil/PhD should normally hold an appropriate first degree. DBA: master's degree.

Master's degrees usually last 2 years part-time, though some courses may be taken 1 year full-time. PhD: 33 months full-time or 45 months part-time; DBA: 4 years part-time.

Libraries. 745,607 volumes; 2216 periodicals subscribed to. Special collection: art and design.

Fees (1998–99, annual). Undergraduate: home students £1000; international students £7250 (laboratory-based), £5750 (other courses). Postgraduate, international students: £5750–7250 (arts, business, social sciences); £7250–10,990 (science and technology).

Academic Awards. Up to 100 scholarships of £1000 each awarded annually.

Academic Year (1998–99). Term/semester dates are course-specific but fall within the following periods: 21 or 28 September–11 or 18 December; 4 or 11 January–26 March; 12 or 19 April–2 July.

Income (1996–97). Total, £73,132,000.

Statistics. Staff: 1464. Students: full-time 11,576 (6014 men, 5562 women); part-time 4137 (1929 men, 2208 women); international 1534.

FACULTIES/SCHOOLS

Business
Tel: (0181) 547 7228 Fax: (0181) 547 7024
Executive Dean: Miles, Prof. David, BA
Secretary: Otterwell, Sue

Design
Tel: (0181) 547 7061 Fax: (0181) 547 7069
Executive Dean: Grant, Keith W., MA
Secretary: Gardner, Elizabeth

Healthcare Sciences (joint faculty with St George's Hospital Medical School, University of London)
Tel: (0181) 725 2155 Fax: (0181) 725 2159
Executive Dean: Pittilo, Prof. Michael R., BSc PhD, FIBiol, FLS
Secretary: Bunyan, Debbie

Human Sciences
Tel: (0181) 547 7291 Fax: (0181) 547 7292
Executive Dean: Cunningham, Gail R., MA DPhil
Secretary: Graham, Pauline

Science
Tel: (0181) 547 7421 Fax: (0181) 547 7437
Executive Dean: Davis, Prof. Reg, PhD DSc, FRSChem
Secretary: Lowe, Joy

Technology
Tel: (0181) 547 7987 Fax: (0181) 547 7971
Executive Dean: Roberts, Prof. John J., BSc(Eng) PhD, FIStructE, FICE
Secretary: Affleck, Pat

ACADEMIC UNITS
Arranged by Schools

Accounting and Finance
Tel: (0181) 547 7353 Fax: (0181) 547 7026
Erman, O. K., BSc(Econ) MSc, FCA Principal Lectr.
Holland, C. J., BSc(Soc) MSc, FCA Principal Lectr.
Jarvis, R. W., BA Prof., Accounting; Head*
Lipman, Hyman Principal Lectr.
Myers, V. J., MA, FCA Principal Lectr.
Parker, G. F. P., BA MSc, FCA Principal Lectr.
Rinsler, Ann L., BSc Principal Lectr.
Other Staff: 4 Sr. Lectrs.; 2 Lectrs.; 1 Sr. Lectr.†

Aeronautical Engineering, see Engin., Mech., Aeronaut. and Prodn.

Architecture
Tel: (0181) 547 7193 Fax: (0181) 547 7186
Bell, T. J. E., MA Principal Lectr.

Brown, Patricia J., BSc Principal Lectr.
Butler, Gary Principal Lectr.
Farren Bradley, Judith V. Principal Lectr.
French, Hilary Sr. Lectr.
Jacob, J. P., BA BArch Prof.; Head*
Lee, Susan A., MA Principal Lectr.
Martin-Quirk, H. R. N., MA Camb., MSc Principal Lectr.
Other Staff: 2 Sr. Lectrs.; 5 Sr. Lectrs.†
Research: green audit built environment

Art, see Fine Art

Art and Design History
Tel: (0181) 547 7112
Kelly, C. Jane, MA Principal Lectr.
Lloyd, Frances A., MA Head*
McDermott, Catherine E., MA Reader
Other Staff: 2 Sr. Lectrs.†; 3 Lectrs.†
Research: collecting and curating in art and design -Dorich House

Business Strategy and Development
Tel: (0181) 547 7454 Fax: (0181) 547 7026
Evans, R. J., MSc, FCA Principal Lectr.
Foster, M. John, MSc Principal Lectr.
Haywood, J. J., BSc(Econ) MPhil Principal Lectr.
Matthews, R. D. C., BA(Econ) MSc(Econ) Prof., International Business Policy; Reader
Samouel, P., BA MSc DBA Head*
Thurbin, P. J., MSc Principal Lectr.
Other Staff: 7 Sr. Lectrs.

Chemistry, Applied
Tel: (0181) 547 7536 Fax: (0181) 547 7562
Bland, W. J., PhD Leic., FRSChem Principal Lectr.
Coleman, R. Visiting Prof.
Eadington, Daphne, MSc Lond. Principal Lectr.
Foot, P. J. S., MSc S'ton., PhD Brighton Prof.; Reader
Jones, Keith Prof.; Principal Lectr.
Kealey, D., PhD Lond. Principal Lectr.
Skinner, G. A., BSc Leic., DPhil Principal Lectr.
Vincent, A., JP, PhD Lond., FRSChem Principal Lectr.
Watson, R. A., BSc PhD Principal Lectr.
Wells, C. H. J., PhD Edin., DSc, FRSChem Prof., Chemistry; Head*
Wyer, J., BSc PhD Principal Lectr.
Other Staff: 10 Sr. Lectrs.; 2 Sr. Lectrs.†
Research: materials research group -polymers; pharmaceutical and medicinal chemistry

Combined Studies
Tel: (0181) 547 7346
Painting, D. A., BA Principal Lectr.
Spencer, P. J., BA MPhil Head*
Other Staff: 1 Sr. Lectr.†

Computer Science and Electronic Systems

Tel: (0181) 547 7659 Fax: (0181) 547 7824

Augarde, L. W. B., BSc(Eng) MSc Principal Lectr.
Bali, H. N., MSc PhD Principal Lectr.
Bloxham, P. A., BSc(Eng) MSc Principal Lectr.
Cotter, J. M., BA BSc Principal Lectr.
Cramer, N. J., MSc Principal Lectr.
Forte, P. W., BSc MA DPhil Reader
Geake, T. H., MA MSc Principal Lectr.
Goodge, M. E., BSc MPhil Principal Lectr.
Jones, G. A., BSc PhD Reader
Kirkby, Barbara A., MSc Principal Lectr.
Malyan, R. R., BA MSc PhD Principal Lectr.
Stockwell, R. J., BSc(Eng) MTech Principal Lectr.
Wallin, P. I., BSc Principal Lectr.
White, G., BSc MPhil Principal Lectr.
Wilkinson, G., FRICS Prof.; Head*
Other Staff: 11 Sr. Lectrs.; 2 Lectrs.
Research: automated visual surveillance; virtual environments -navigating through remote environments over the internet

Design, see Art and Des. Hist., Graphic Des., and Three-Dimensional Des.

Economics

Tel: (0181) 547 7335 Fax: (0181) 547 7388

Auerbach, P. R., MA PhD Reader
Daly, V. D., MSocSc Head*
French, C. J., MA PhD Principal Lectr.
Ghatak, Subrata, BA Calc., MSc Lond., PhD Lond. Prof., Applied Economics
Humm, A. L., BA MSc PhD Principal Lectr.
Hyett, A. J., MSc(Econ) PhD Principal Lectr.
Nugent, J. A., MSc(Econ) Principal Lectr.
Pollock, Catherine M., BA MSc PhD Principal Lectr.
Shaw, A. W., MSc(Econ) Principal Lectr.
Other Staff: 9 Sr. Lectrs.; 1 Lectr.; 3 Sr. Lectrs.†
Research: factor mobility (capital and labour flows)

Education

Tel: (0181) 547 7635 Fax: (0181) 547 7116

Blair, Celia, BEd MA Principal Lectr.
Bowell, Pamela, BPhil Principal Lectr.
Crisp, S. A., BEd MA Principal Lectr.
Farrell, P. Bernie, MA Principal Lectr.
Fine, Carol A., BEd Liv., MEd Lond. Principal Lectr.
Gibson, M. R., MA PhD Head*
Grieves, K. R., BEd PhD Reader
Johnson, G. F., MPhil Principal Lectr.
Jones, B. L., BEd MA Principal Lectr.
Jones, Cynthia E. C., BA MPhil Principal Lectr.
Lomax, Pamela M., BSc MA PhD Prof., Educational Research
Manning, Janet M., BA Lond., MA(Ed) Open(UK) Principal Lectr.
Osborne, J. D., MA PhD Principal Lectr.
Robson, K., BSc Principal Lectr.
Stammers, Peter B., BA Open(UK), MA Lond.Inst. Head, In-service Teacher Training
Other Staff: 16 Sr. Lectrs.; 1 Lectr.; 5 Sr. Lectrs.†
Research: African and Caribbean teachers and pupils; primary mathematics education

Electronic Systems, see Computer Sci. and Electronic Systems

Engineering, Civil

Tel: (0181) 547 7242 Fax: (0181) 547 7972

Armstrong, James H., BSc, FICE, FGS Visiting Prof.
Bromhead, E. N., MSc PhD, FGS Prof., Geotechnical Engineering
Gardner, M. J., MSc PhD Principal Lectr.
Harris, A. J., MSc, FGS Principal Lectr.
O'Reilly, M., BEng LLB PhD Prof.; Head*
Ryan, E. C., MSc Principal Lectr.
Shepherd, K. L., BSc PhD Principal Lectr.

Somerville, George Visiting Prof.
Other Staff: 7 Sr. Lectrs.; 1 Researcher; 1 Sr. Lectr.†
Research: concrete and masonry

Engineering, Mechanical, Aeronautical and Production

Tel: (0181) 547 7949 Fax: (0181) 547 7992

Karwatzki, John M., MPhil PhD, FIMechE Principal Lectr.
Lilley, P. A., MA Principal Lectr.
Roome, R. L., MSc Principal Lectr.
Self, Andrew W., MSc, FIEE Prof., Manufacturing Engineering; Head*
Stephenson, Pauline M., MSc Principal Lectr.
Vasudevan, M. S., BSc PhD, FRAeS Principal Lectr.
Wagstaff, P. G., BSc(Met) MSc Principal Lectr.
Welch, C. S., MSc PhD Principal Lectr.
Other Staff: 15 Sr. Lectrs.; 5 Teaching Company Assocs.
Research: re-engineering flowmeter conditioners in petrochemical and food industries; simulation and control centre

English Literature, see Humanities

Fashion

Tel: (0181) 547 7101 Fax: (0181) 547 7098

Griffiths, I., BA Manc., MDes RCA Prof.; Head*
Russell, Laura M., BA Principal Lectr.
Other Staff: 1 Sr. Lectr.; 2 Sr. Lectrs.†
Research: fashion theory -imaging fashion

Finance, see Acctg. and Finance

Fine Art

Tel: (0181) 547 7128 Fax: (0181) 547 7041

Dellow, Jeffrey, MA Principal Lectr.
Russell, B. J., MA Lond. Prof.; Head*
Yule, A. A. Reader
Other Staff: 4 Sr. Lectrs.†

Foundation Studies

Tel: (0181) 547 7090

Stafford, P., BA Dir.*
Other Staff: 1 Sr. Lectr.; 2 Sr. Lectrs.†

French, see Langs.

Geography

Tel: (0181) 547 7502 Fax: (0181) 547 7497

Gant, R. L., BA PhD Principal Lectr.
Holmes, J. A., DPhil Oxf. Reader
Linsey, T. K., PhD Principal Lectr.
Robinson, Guy M., BSc DPhil Prof.; Head*
Taylor, Rosalind M., BSc PhD Principal Lectr.
Walford, N. S., BA Sus., PhD Lond. Principal Lectr.
Other Staff: 7 Sr. Lectrs.; 8 Lectrs.
Research: geoarchaeology; palaeoenvironmental change; remote sensing

Geological Sciences

Tel: (0181) 547 7524 Fax: (0181) 547 7497

Clemens, John D., PhD, FRMIT Prof., Geosciences
Grocott, J., BSc PhD, FGS Reader
Jarvis, I., BSc DPhil, FGS Reader
Moody, Richard Emer. Prof.
Petford, N., BSc PhD Sr. Lectr.
Rankin, A. H., BSc PhD, FGS Prof., Applied Geology; Head*
Sutcliffe, P. J. C., BSc PhD, FGS Principal Lectr.
Thomas, Neil, BSc PhD Principal Lectr.
Treloar, P. J., BSc PhD, FGS Reader
Other Staff: 5 Sr. Lectrs.; 1 Lectr.
Research: regional geology of the Indochina region; remote sensing; structural geology/magmatic arc tectonics

German, see Langs.

Graphic Design

Tel: (0181) 547 7135 Fax: (0181) 547 7148

Hudd, Penelope A. Head*

Kennard, Malcolm, MA Principal Lectr.
Love, B. F. A., MA Principal Lectr.
Other Staff: 1 Sr. Lectr.; 1 Sr. Researcher; 3 Sr. Lectrs.†
Research: sustainability in art and design

History, see Humanities

History of Ideas, see Humanities

Human Resource Management

Tel: (0181) 547 7220 Fax: (0181) 547 7026

Blackburn, R. A., MA PhD Midland Bank Prof., Small Business Studies; Reader
Edwards, Christine Y., BA MSc Prof., Industrial Relations; Head*
Gourlay, S. N., MA PhD Principal Lectr.
Mitchell, D. M., MSc Principal Lectr.
Morris, H. J., MSc Principal Lectr.
Oldfield, Agi I., MSc Principal Lectr.
Pidduck, Jasmine L., BA Principal Lectr.
Smith, Lesley J., BEd Principal Lectr.
Willey, B. H., MA Principal Lectr.
Woodall, M. Jean, BA PhD Prof., Human Resource Development; Reader
Other Staff: 4 Sr. Lectrs.; 1 Sr. Lectr.†
Research: industrial performance; quality management and employee responses

Humanities

Tel: (0181) 547 7305 Fax: (0181) 547 7292

Beck, P. J., BSc(Econ) PhD Prof., International History
Brivati, Brian L., PhD Reader, History
Clarke, J. J., MA Reader, History of Ideas
Corner, M. N., MA Principal Lectr., English Literature
Glanville, G. H., MA PhD Principal Lectr., History
Ibbett, P. J., BA MPhil Head, History of Ideas*
Mepham, J. K., BA Reader, English Literature
Rogers, David L., BA Arkansas, MA Arkansas, MPhil Rutgers, PhD Rutgers Principal Lectr.
Other Staff: 6 Sr. Lectrs.; 1 Lectr.; 1 Researcher; 3 Lectrs.†
Research: society and politics; Taoism and Western thought

Industrial Relations, see Human Resource Management

Information Systems

Tel: (0181) 547 7690 Fax: (0181) 547 7887

Briggs, J. H., BSc(Eng) Prof., New Media Design; Reader
Gelepithis, P. A. M., PhD Principal Lectr.
Lindsay, J. M., BA BLS Reader
Marks, S. M., MSc Principal Lectr.
Rapley, Elizabeth A., MSc Principal Lectr.
Saxby, B. J. L. Head*
Stewart, R. W., BA Reader
Tompsett, C. P., MA Principal Lectr.
Warner, Christine L., MSc Principal Lectr.
Wills, C. C., MA Principal Lectr.
Other Staff: 10 Sr. Lectrs.; 1 Teaching Company Assoc.
Research: virtual environments

Languages

Tel: (0181) 547 7288 Fax: (0181) 547 7392

Brick, Noelle M. C., LèsL MA Principal Lectr., French
Burke, Claire S. A., BA PhD Principal Lectr., German
Cobb, Christopher Emer. Prof., Spanish
Lawlor, Teresa A., BA MPhil Head, Spanish*
Loschmann, Martin F. K. Reader, German
Nectoux, François Prof., French
Rothwell, Libby, BA Principal Lectr.
Spaas, Lieve, MA PhD Prof., French
Wilks, Clarissa F., BA Oxf., MA Lond. Principal Lectr., French and German
Other Staff: 7 Sr. Lectrs.; 3 Sr. Lectrs.†; 1 Lectr.†

Law

Tel: (0181) 547 7322 Fax: (0181) 547 7038

Holmes, Mary, LLB MA   Principal Lectr.
Holmes, R. J., LLB   Principal Lectr.; Head*
Riedel, Eibe   Visiting Prof.
Sacks, Vera J., BA LLB   Reader
Thompson, J., LLB   Principal Lectr.
Tolmie, Fiona, BA LLM   Principal Lectr.
Upex, R. V., MA LLM   Prof.
Other Staff: 10 Sr. Lectrs.; 2 Lectrs.; 4 Sr.
   Lectrs.†
Research: civilist legal systems

Life Sciences

Tel: (0181) 547 7592 Fax: (0181) 547 7562

Mackintosh, D., BSc PhD   Principal Lectr.
Manly, R., BSc PhD   Head*
McGuckin, C. P., BSc DPhil   Sr. Lectr.
McNaughton, Lars R.   Prof., Sport
Mikhailidis, Dimitri   Visiting Prof.
Russell, Angela J., MSc PhD   Reader
Seddon, A. M., PhD   Principal Lectr.
Weaire, P. J., BSc PhD   Principal Lectr.
Other Staff: 6 Sr. Lectrs.; 6 Lectrs.; 1 Sr.
   Lectr.†
Research: exercise physiology

Marketing

Tel: (0181) 547 7226 Fax: (0181) 547 7026

Collins, P. B., MSc(Econ) MPhil   Principal
   Lectr.
Davies, D. G., BA MSc(Econ)   Principal Lectr.
East, J. R., BA(SocSc) DPhil   Prof., Consumer
   Behaviour; Principal Lectr.
Eldred, J. G., BSc   Principal Lectr.
Hogg, Annik V., BA(Econ)   Head*
Kalafatis, S. P., BA MPhil PhD   Reader
Lomax, A. Wendy, BSc   Reader
Masikunas, G. D., MA   Principal Lectr.
Robinson, Helen R., BA   Principal Lectr.
Rolls-Willson, Gillian M., BA   Principal Lectr.
Other Staff: 3 Sr. Lectrs.
Research: marketing and consumer behaviour;
   relationship marketing

Mathematics

Tel: (0181) 547 7922 Fax: (0181) 547 7497

Bidgood, Penelope L., BSc MSc PhD   Principal
   Lectr.
Cox, Maurice G., BSc PhD, FIMA   Visiting
   Prof.
Lyle, Svetlana, BSc PhD   Principal Lectr.
Morris, John L. L.   Prof.; Head*
Soan, P. H., MSc PhD   Principal Lectr.
Other Staff: 5 Sr. Lectrs.; 5 Lectrs.
Research: applications for neural networks

Midwifery, see Nursing and Midwifery

Music

Tel: (0181) 547 7118

Bate, J. R., BMus MA, FRCO, FTCL   Principal
   Lectr.
Beeson, R. A., BA BMus PhD   Principal Lectr.
Gartrell, Carole A., BMus PhD   Principal Lectr.
Ho, E. S., BA DMus, FTCL   Prof.; Head*
Jones, K. J., BA MPhil PhD   Reader
Searby, M. D., MMus, FTCL   Principal Lectr.
Other Staff: 2 Sr. Lectrs.; 1 Sr. Lectr.†
Research: ethnomusicology -gamelan research;
   recursive algorithms for music generation

Nursing and Midwifery

Tel: (0181) 725 2155 Fax: (0181) 725 2159

Cheng, Linda, BA   Principal Lectr.
Collington, Val, BSc MSc   Head of Midwifery
Coppard, Susan P., MSc   Principal Lectr.
Fergy, Susan P., BEd   Principal Lectr.
Forte, Denise, MSc   Principal Lectr.
Gale, Julia, BSc   Principal Lectr.
Gault, Iris, BSc MSc   Principal Lectr.
Jones, Soraya, BSc MSc   Principal Lectr.
McLaren, Susan, BSc PhD   Prof., Nursing
Mohammed, Nizam I., BEd MBA
   MSc   Principal Lectr.
Pedley, Gillian, BSc MSc   Principal Lectr.

Ross, Fiona, BSc PhD   Prof., Primary Care
   Nursing
Rush, Susan C., MSc   Principal Lectr.
Seymour, Maggi, BA   Principal Lectr.
Sheidan, Margaret V.   Principal Lectr.
Spurway, Maggie, MSc   Principal Lectr.
Start, Kath, BSc MSc   Head of Post-registration
   Nursing
Strong, Susan E., BSc   Head of Pre-registration
   Nursing
Tennant, Shirley, BA   Principal Lectr.
Watkins, Yvonne, MSc   Head of Physiotherapy
Webb, Patricia A.   Principal Lectr.
Other Staff: 68 Sr. Lectrs.; 16 Sr. Lectrs.†
Research: nutrition; primary care

Operations Management and Quantitative Methods

Tel: (0181) 547 7214 Fax: (0181) 547 7452

Browne, D. A., BSc MSc MSc(Econ)   Principal
   Lectr.
Ennals, J. R., MA   Prof., Business Information
   Technology; Head*
Fitzgerald, S. J., BSc(Econ) MA   Principal
   Lectr.
List, M. J., BA MSc   Principal Lectr.
Molyneux, S. P., MSc   Principal Lectr.
Russell, D. J., MSc   Principal Lectr.
Skok, W., MSc PhD   Principal Lectr.
Walters, B. N., BSc PhD   Principal Lectr.
Other Staff: 6 Sr. Lectrs.

Physics, Applied

Tel: (0181) 547 7432 Fax: (0181) 547 7562

Augousti, A. T., BSc PhD   Reader
Bishop, R. J., MSc PhD   Principal Lectr.
Briers, J. D., MSc PhD, FIP   Prof., Applied
   Optics; Head*
Flowers, A. G., BSc MA PhD   Principal Lectr.
Koenders, M. A., MSc PhD   Prof., Theoretical
   Mechanics
Other Staff: 3 Sr. Lectrs.; 1 Teaching Company
   Assoc.
Research: multidimensional datasets

Politics, see Soc. Sci.

Radiography

Tel: (0181) 547 7399 Fax: (0181) 547 7562

Francis, Geraldine, BSc   Principal Lectr.
Lock, Nicholas, MSc   Principal Lectr.
Morgan, Graham, BA MA   Head*
Other Staff: 7 Sr. Lectrs.; 1 Lectr.†

Social Science

Tel: (0181) 547 7319 Fax: (0181) 547 7388

Bailey, J. P., BA MSc   Prof., Sociology; Head*
Chapman, M. A., BA(Soc)
   MSc(Econ)   Principal Lectr.
Gordon, I. A., MA   Reader
Hawkins, M. J., BSc PhD   Reader
Pond, R. J., MSc(Soc)   Principal Lectr.
Roberts, M. A., MA *Leeds*   Sr. Lectr.
Showstack-Sassoon, Anne F., BA PhD   Prof.,
   Politics
Sullivan, T. J., BSc(Econ) MSc   Principal Lectr.
Weightman, K. O., BA(SocSc)   Principal Lectr.
Other Staff: 6 Sr. Lectrs.; 4 Lectrs.; 1 Lectr.†
Research: French economy

Social Work

Tel: (0181) 547 7072

Donnelly, P., BA MSc   Head*
Hodgson, D. R., BA MA   Principal Lectr.
Jenkins, Lily V.   Sr. Lectr.; Practice Devel.
   Tutor
Lindsay, J. F., MA MSc   Principal Lectr.
Tompsett, Hilary M., BPhil MA   Principal
   Lectr.; Acting Head*
Other Staff: 4 Sr. Lectrs.

Spanish, see Langs.

Surveying

Tel: (0181) 547 7070 Fax: (0181) 547 7087

Bennett, T. P., BSc   Principal Lectr.
Gillett, Alan H.   Visiting Prof.
Sayce, Sarah L., BSc, FRICS   Head*

Zwirner, W. G. O., MPhil   Reader
Other Staff: 6 Sr. Lectrs.; 2 Sr. Lectrs.†

Three-Dimensional Design

Tel: (0181) 547 7165

Ordish, N. F., BA *CNAA*, MDes *RCA*   Head*
Scott, P. F., MDes *RCA*   Principal Lectr.
Warren, M. D., MDes *RCA*   Principal Lectr.
Other Staff: 3 Sr. Lectrs.; 2 Sr. Lectrs.†
Research: sustainability in art and design

SPECIAL CENTRES, ETC

European Research Centre

Fax: (0181) 547 7388

Showstack-Sassoon, Prof. Anne F., BA
   PhD   Dir.*

Kingston Language Export Centre

Fax: (0181) 547 7392

Lawlor, Teresa, BA MPhil   Dir.*

Kingston Regional Management Centre

Fax: (0181) 547 7024

Miles, Prof. David, BA   Dir.*

Kingston University Enterprises Ltd

Tel: (0181) 547 8130 Fax: (0181) 547 8132

Mercer, Anthony J. H., BSc *Oxf.*, MA *Oxf.*,
   DPhil *Oxf.*, FRSChem   Acting Managing
   Dir.*

Kingston University Service Company Limited

Tel: (0181) 547 7138

Shedden, Ray   Managing Dir.*

Simulation and Control Centre

Fax: (0181) 547 7992

Self, Prof. Andrew W., MSc, FIEE   Dir.*

Small Business Research Unit

Blackburn, R. A., MA PhD   Head*
Other Staff: 1 Sr. Lectr.; 1 Sr. Researcher; 4
   Researchers
Research: owner-manager and family firms;
   small businesses

CONTACT OFFICERS

Academic affairs. Deputy Vice-Chancellor:
   Gipps, Prof. Caroline, BSc *Brist.*, MSc *Lond.*,
   PhD *Lond.*
Accommodation. Head of Accommodation:
   Churchouse, Christine
Admissions (first degree). Head of
   Admissions Office: Milner-Walker, Diana
Admissions (higher degree) (research). Head
   of Research Office: Carver, Kaye, BA *Reading*
**Admissions (higher degree) (taught
   courses)**. Head of Admissions Office:
   Milner-Walker, Diana
Adult/continuing education. Pro-Vice-
   Chancellor (Lifelong Learning): Miles, Prof.
   David, BA
Alumni. Events and Alumni Manager:
   Thomson, Emma, BA
Careers. Head of Careers Advisory Service:
   Horgan, Shauna S., BA *Portsmouth*, MA *Sur.*
Computing services. Head of Computing
   Services: Kingston, F. Gerry, BSc *Belf.*, PhD
   Lond.
Conferences/corporate hospitality. Events
   and Alumni Manager: Thomson, Emma, BA
Consultancy services. Pro-Vice-Chancellor
   (External Affairs): Mercer, Anthony J. H.,
   BSc *Oxf.*, MA *Oxf.*, DPhil *Oxf.*, FRSChem
Credit transfer. Head of Academic Services:
   Roberts, Larry H., BSc PhD
Development/fund-raising. Pro-Vice-
   Chancellor (External Affairs): Mercer,
   Anthony J. H., BSc *Oxf.*, MA *Oxf.*, DPhil *Oxf.*,
   FRSChem
Equal opportunities. Personnel Director:
   Lanchbery, Elizabeth C., BA

Estates and buildings/works and services.
Deputy Vice-Chancellor: Gipps, Prof.
Caroline, BSc Brist., MSc Lond., PhD Lond.

Examinations. Head of Examinations Office:
Johnston, Doreen

Finance. Finance Director: Butcher, Terence M.

General enquiries. University Secretary:
Abdullah, Raficq, MA Oxf.

Health services. Head of Health and
Counselling: Winter, Marcia

International office. Head of International
Relations: Coulter, Diana M., BA Brist.

Library (chief librarian). Head of Library and
Media Services: Pollard, Nik P., BA

Minorities/disadvantaged groups. Dean of
Students: Hopkins, Kenneth V. J., BA Lond.,
BD Lond., PhD Hull

Ombudsperson. Head of Student Life Office:
Powell, David, LLB Nott.

Personnel/human resources. Personnel
Director: Lanchbery, Elizabeth C., BA

Public relations, information and marketing.
Head of Marketing and Public Relations:
Thorne, Trevor, BA Leeds

Publications. Head of Marketing and Public
Relations: Thorne, Trevor, BA Leeds

Purchasing. Finance Director: Butcher, Terence
M.

Quality assurance and accreditation. Head of
Academic Services: Roberts, Larry H., BSc
PhD

Research. Head of Research Office: Carver,
Kaye, BA Reading

Safety. Personnel Director: Lanchbery,
Elizabeth C., BA

Scholarships, awards, loans. Dean of Students:
Hopkins, Kenneth V. J., BA Lond., BD Lond.,
PhD Hull

Schools liaison. Recruitment and Admissions
Manager: Graham, Bennett

Security. Managing Director, Kingston
University Service Company Ltd: Shedden,
Ray

Sport and recreation. Director of Sport:
Hayter, James, BEd Exe.

Staff development and training. Personnel
Director: Lanchbery, Elizabeth C., BA

Student welfare/counselling. Head of Health
and Counselling: Winter, Marcia

Students from other countries. Head of
Recruitment: Hewitt, Rachel, BA

Students with disabilities. Special Needs Co-
ordinator: Norowzian, Mary

Women. Personnel Director: Lanchbery,
Elizabeth C., BA

[Information supplied by the institution as at 28 August
1998, and edited by the ACU]

UNIVERSITY OF LANCASTER

Founded 1964

Member of the Association of Commonwealth Universities

Postal Address: University House, Lancaster, England LA1 4YW
Telephone: (01524) 65201 **Fax**: (01524) 63806 **Telex**: 65111 LANCUL G **WWW**: http://www.lancs.ac.uk
E-mail formula: initial.surname@lancs.ac.uk

VISITOR—Elizabeth, H.M. The Queen
CHANCELLOR—Alexandra, H.R.H. Princess , The Hon. Lady Ogilvy, GCVO
PRO-CHANCELLOR—Heron, J. Brian, MA Camb.
VICE-CHANCELLOR*—Ritchie, Prof. William, OBE, BSc Glas., PhD Glas., FRSEd, FRICS
DEPUTY VICE-CHANCELLOR—......
PRO-VICE-CHANCELLOR—Abercrombie, Prof. Nicholas, BA Oxf., MSc(Econ) Lond., PhD
Lanc.
PRO-VICE-CHANCELLOR—Davies, Prof. Richard B., MA Camb., MSc Birm., PhD Brist.
SECRETARY‡—Lamley, Stephen A. C., MA Camb.
LIBRARIAN—Whiteside, Jacqueline M., MA Oxf.

GENERAL INFORMATION

History. The university was founded in 1964.
It is located 3km south of the city of
Lancaster.

Admission to first degree courses (see also
United Kingdom Introduction). Through
Universities and Colleges Admissions Service
(UCAS). At least 2 passes at General Certificate
of Education (GCE) A level and evidence of
competence in English language. Additional
requirements specified for each scheme of
study.

First Degrees (see also United Kingdom
Directory to Subjects of Study). BA, BBA,
BEng, BMus, BSc, LLB, MEng, MMath, MPhys,
MStat.
All courses are full-time and normally last 3
years. Some courses (principally languages,
management) last 4 years.

Higher Degrees (see also United Kingdom
Directory to Subjects of Study). MA, MBA,
MMus, MRes, MSc, MPhil, PhD, DLitt, DSc.
Most courses are available full-or part-time.
Full-time master's degree courses: 12 months.

Language of Instruction. English. Pre-
sessional remedial courses available from
institute of English language education.

Libraries. 900,000 items; 3000 periodicals
subscribed to.

Fees. (1997–98). Undergraduate: £750 (band
I); £1600 (band II). Postgraduate: home
students, minimum £2540; international
students, £6283 (non-science), £8307
(science).

Academic Awards (1997–98). Eight awards
of up to £7500 each.

Academic Year (1998–99). Three terms: 2
October–11 December; 8 January–19 March;
16 April–25 June.

Income (1996–97). Total, £73,941,000.

Statistics. (1996–97). Staff: 821 academic,
175 administrative/library/computing.
Students: 9715 (5001 men, 4714 women).

FACULTIES/SCHOOLS

Applied Sciences
Dean: Carter, Prof. Richard G., MA Camb., PhD
Wales
Secretary: Thorley, Alexander J., BA Durh.

Arts and Humanities
Dean: Henig, Ruth B., BA Lond., PhD Lanc.
Secretary: Agius, Steven J. R., BA Leic., MA Lanc.

Environmental and Natural Sciences
Dean: Ayres, Prof. P. G., BA Camb., PhD Reading
Secretary: Thorley, Alexander J., BA Durh.

Management
Dean: Watson, Stephen R., MA Camb., PhD
Camb.
Secretary: Bolton, Allan R., BA E.Anglia, MBA
Aston

Postgraduate Studies
Dean: ......
Secretary: Pardee, Rosamund L., BA William &
Mary, MA York(UK)

Research
Dean: Diggle, Prof. Peter J., BSc Liv., MSc Oxf.,
PhD Newcastle(UK)
Secretary: McClintock, Marion E., BA Durh.

Social Sciences
Dean: McKinlay, Prof. Robert D., BSocSc Birm.,
DPhil York(UK)
Secretary: Farron, Timothy, BA Newcastle(UK)

ACADEMIC UNITS

Accounting and Finance
O'Hanlon, John F., BA Hull, MA Lanc.,
FCA   Reader
Otley, David T., MA Camb., MTech Brun., PhD
Manc.   Peat Marwick McLintock Prof.

Peasnell, Kenneth V., MSc(Econ) Lond., PhD
Lanc., FCA   Prof.
Pope, Peter F., BCom Liv., MA Lanc.   Prof.
Taylor, Stephen J., BA Camb., MA Lanc., PhD
Lanc.   Prof.; Head*
Other Staff: 5 Lectrs.
Vacant Posts: 1 Lectr.
Research: financial reporting; financial series;
statistical modelling

Applied Social Science

Clough, Roger J., MA Camb., MPhil Lond., PhD
Brist.   Hon. Prof.
Graham, Hilary, MA York(UK), DPhil
York(UK)   Prof.
Hadley, Roger D., BSc(Econ) Lond., PhD
Lond.   Hon. Prof.
Smith, David B., MA Oxf., BPhil Exe.   Prof.;
Head*
Soothill, Keith, BA Exe., PhD Lond.   Prof.
Stewart, Gillian M., BA Oxf.   Sr. Lectr.
Thorpe, David H., BA Birm., PhD Lanc.   Prof.
Wise, Susan, MA Manc., PhD Manc.   Sr. Lectr.
Other Staff: 4 Lectrs.; 1 Res. Fellow
Research: child care; community care; criminal
justice

Art

Davies, Gerald, BA CNAA, MArt RCA   Sr. Lectr.
Whiteley, Nigel S., BA Wales, PhD Lanc.   Prof.;
Head*
Other Staff: 3 Lectrs.
Research: cultural criticism; graphic art;
theorised practice

Behaviour in Organisations

Ackroyd, Stephen C., BA Newcastle(UK),
MSc(Econ) Lond.   Prof.
Blackler, Frank H. M., BA Brist., MPhil
Lond.   Prof.
Reed, Michael I., BSc Wales, PhD Wales   Prof.
Whitaker, Alan, BA Birm.   Sr. Lectr.; Head*
Other Staff: 2 Lectrs.
Vacant Posts: 1 Sr. Lectr.; 1 Lectr.
Research: knowledge, work and competitive
advantage

Biological Sciences, see Environmental and
Biol. Scis., Inst. of

Chemistry, see Phys. and Chem., Sch. of

Computing

Blair, Gordon S., BSc Strath., PhD Strath.   Prof.
Garside, Roger G., MA Camb.   Sr. Lectr.
Hutchison, David, BSc Edin., MTech Brun., PhD
Strath.   Prof.
Mariani, John A., BSc Strath., PhD Strath.   Sr.
Lectr.
Parkes, Alan P., BSc CNAA, PhD Lanc.   Sr. Lectr.
Rodden, Thomas A., BSc Strath., PhD
Lanc.   Prof.
Sawyer, Peter H., BSc Lanc., PhD Lanc.   Sr.
Lectr.
Shepherd, W. Douglas, BSc Lond.   Prof.
Sommerville, Ian F., BSc Strath., MSc St And.,
PhD St And.   Prof.; Head*
Other Staff: 5 Lectrs.; 1 Sr. Res. Fellow; 17
Res. Assocs.
Research: co-operative systems engineering;
distributed multimedia

Continuing Education

Percy, Keith A., BSc Lond., MA Camb., MA Nott.,
PhD Lanc.   Prof.; Dir.*
Other Staff: 7 Staff Tutors
Research: post-compulsory and adult education

Creative Writing

2 Tutorial Fellows; 1 Lectr.†

Economics

Balasubramanyam, V. N., MA Mys., AM Ill.,
PhD Ill.   Prof.
Bradley, Steven, BA Leeds, MA Lanc., PhD
Lanc.   Sr. Lectr.
Ingham, Hilary, BSc Lough., MA Manc., PhD
Glas.   Sr. Lectr.
Johnes, Geraint, BSc Bath, MSc PhD   Sr. Lectr.

Kirby, Maurice W., BA Newcastle(UK), PhD
Sheff.   Reader; Head*
Rose, Mary B., BA Liv., MA Manc., PhD
Manc.   Sr. Lectr.
Rothschild, Robert, MA Cape Town   Sr. Lectr.
Sapsford, David R., BSc Leic., MPhil Leic., PhD
Leeds   Prof.
Snowden, P. Nicholas, BCom Liv., MA Leeds,
PhD Leeds   Sr. Lectr.
Taylor, James, MA Liv., PhD Lanc.   Prof.
Westall, Oliver M., BSc(Econ) Lond.   Sr. Lectr.
Other Staff: 6 Lectrs.
Research: business history; international business;
regional and educational economics

Education, see Continuing Educn.

Educational Research

Deem, Rosemary, BA Leic., MPhil Leic., PhD
Open(UK)   Prof.
Fulton, K. A. Oliver, MA Oxf., MA Calif., PhD
Lanc.   Prof.
Goodyear, Peter M., BSc Ulster, DPhil
Ulster   Prof.
Knight, Peter, BA Oxf., MA Lanc., PhD Lanc.   Sr.
Lectr.
Rogers, Colin G., BA Sheff., PhD Leic.   Sr. Lectr.
Saunders, Murray, BA Essex, MA Lanc., PhD
Lanc.   Reader; Head*
Smith, Leslie, BA Lond., PhD Leic.   Sr. Lectr.
Summerfield, A. Penelope, MA Sus., DPhil
Sus.   Prof.
Other Staff: 7 Lectrs.; 1 Sr. Res. Fellow; 7 Res.
Assocs.
Research: gender; learning technology; post-
compulsory; psychology of learning

Engineering

Bradshaw, Alan, BSc Nott., PhD Nott.   Prof.
Carter, Richard G., MA Camb., PhD
Wales   Prof.
Dawson, David, MSc Manc.   Sr. Lectr.
Dorey, Anthony P., BA Camb., PhD S'ton.,
FIEE   Hon. Prof.
French, Michael J., MA Camb., MSc Lond.,
FIMechE   Hon. Prof.
Honary, Braham, BSc Mashhad, MSc Kent, PhD
Kent   Prof.
Seward, Derek W., BSc Salf., MSc Brad.   Sr.
Lectr.
Turvey, Geoffrey J., BSc Birm., MSc Lond., PhD
Birm.   Sr. Lectr.
Other Staff: 10 Lectrs.; 2 Res. Officers; 12 Res.
Assocs.; 1 Sr. Lectr.†; 3 Lectrs.†
Research: communications; electronics;
mechatronics

English, see also Linguistics and Mod. Engl.
Lang.

Carroll, David R., BA Durh., MA Lond., PhD
Durh.   Hon. Prof.
Cosslett, A. Therese, BA Oxf., BPhil Oxf., DPhil
Oxf.   Sr. Lectr.
Dutton, A. Richard, MA Camb., PhD
Nott.   Prof.
Easton, Alison M. J., MA Edin., DPhil Sus.   Sr.
Lectr.
Hanley, Keith A., MA Oxf., BLitt Oxf., PhD
Lanc.   Prof.
Hewison, Robert, MA Oxf., DLitt Oxf.   Prof.†
Horsley, Lee S., BA Minn., MPhil Reading, PhD
Birm.   Sr. Lectr.
Pearce, Lynne, BA Hull, MA Wales, PhD
Birm.   Sr. Lectr.
Pinkney, Tony A., BA Brist., MA Warw.   Sr.
Lectr.
Sharpe, Anthony E., MA Camb., PhD Camb.   Sr.
Lectr.; Head*
Twycross, Margaret A., MA Oxf., BLitt
Oxf.   Prof.
Wheeler, Michael D., MA Camb., PhD
Lond.   Prof.
Wilson, Richard F., BA York(UK), DPhil
York(UK)   Prof.
Other Staff: 6 Lectrs.
Research: mediaeval and Renaissance; nineteenth
and twentieth centuries; women's writing

Environmental and Biological Sciences, Institute of

Andrew, Sarah M., BSc Lond., PhD Nott.   Sr.
Lectr.
Ayres, P. G., BA Camb., PhD Reading   Prof.,
Biological Sciences
Berry, Roger J., BA Oxf., MD Oxf., DPhil Oxf.,
FRCP   Hon. Prof.†
Beven, Keith J., BSc Brist., PhD E.Anglia   Prof.,
Environmental Sciences
Binley, Andrew M., BSc Aston, PhD Aston   Sr.
Lectr., Environmental Sciences
Chotai, Arankamar, BSc Bath, PhD Bath   Sr.
Lectr., Environmental Sciences
Davies, J. Eric D., BSc Wales, PhD Wales   Sr.
Lectr., Environmental Scis.
Davies, William J., BSc Reading, PhD
Wis.   Prof., Biological Sciences
Davison, William, BSc Newcastle(UK), PhD
Newcastle(UK), FRSChem   Prof.,
Environmental Sciences
Fryer, Geoffrey, PhD Lond., DSc Lond.,
FRS   Hon. Prof.
Hamilton-Taylor, John, BSc Wales, PhD
Edin.   Reader, Environmental Sciences
Hetherington, Alistair M., BSc St And., PhD St
And.   Prof., Biological Sciences
Hewitt, C. Nicholas, BA Lanc., PhD Lanc.   Prof.,
Environmental Sciences; Head*
Hornung, Michael, BSc Durh., PhD Durh.   Hon.
Prof., Biological Sciences
Huddart, Henry, BSc Durh., PhD Durh.   Reader,
Biological Sciences
Jones, Keith, BSc Nott., PhD Lond.   Sr. Lectr.,
Biological Sciences
Jones, Kevin C., BSc Lond., PhD Lond.   Prof.,
Environmental Sciences
Jones, Roger I., BSc E.Anglia, DPhil Ulster   Sr.
Lectr., Biological Sciences
Lea, Peter J., PhD Liv., DSc Liv., FIBiol   Prof.,
Biological Sciences
Macdonald, Raymond, PhD Edin., DSc Edin.,
FGS, FRSEd   Prof., Environmental Sciences
Malloch, Andrew J. C., MA Camb., PhD
Camb.   Sr. Lectr., Biological Sciences
Mansfield, Terence A., BSc Nott., PhD Reading,
FRS   Prof.†, Biological Sciences
McMillan, Trevor J., BSc Lanc., PhD
Lanc.   Prof., Biological Sciences
Nieduszynski, Ian A., BSc Leeds, PhD
Leeds   Reader, Biological Sciences; Head*
Piearce, Trevor K., BSc Wales, PhD Wales   Sr.
Lectr., Biological Sciences
Pinkerton, Harry, BSc Strath., PhD Lanc.,
FGS   Sr. Lectr., Environmental Sciences
Rodwell, John S., BSc Leeds, PhD S'ton.   Prof.
Shepherd, John B., BSc Manc., PhD
Manc.   Reader, Environmental Sciences
Smith, R. John, BSc Sheff., PhD
Newcastle(UK)   Sr. Lectr., Biological Sciences
Talling, John F., PhD Leeds, DSc Leeds,
FRS   Hon. Prof.†, Biological Sciences
Thomson, Alan, BSc Open(UK), MA Oxf., DPhil
Oxf., BSc, FRSChem   Sr. Lectr., Biological
Sciences
Wellburn, Alan R., PhD Liv., DSc Liv.   Prof.,
Biochemistry
Whittaker, John B., BSc Durh., PhD Durh., DSc
Durh.   Prof., Biological Sciences
Wilson, Lionel, BSc Birm., PhD Lond., FRAS,
FGS   Hon. Prof., Environmental Sciences
Young, Peter C., BTech Lough., MSc Lough., MA
Camb., PhD Camb.   Prof., Environmental
Sciences
Other Staff: 15 Lectrs.; 9 Res. Fellows; 15 Res.
Assocs.; 2 Teaching Fellows
Research: environmental chemistry; hydrology;
medical, plant and environmental biology;
systems and control; volcanology

European Languages and Cultures

Cheles, Luciano, BA Reading, MPhil Essex   Sr.
Lectr., Italian
Keefe, Terence, BA Lond., MA Leic.   Prof.,
French
Nott, David O., MA Camb.   Sr. Lectr., French
Payne, J. Philip, MA Camb., MLitt Camb., PhD
Camb.   Prof., German

Quainton, Malcolm D., BA Exe., PhD
Exe. Prof., French
Rossi, Paolo L., MA Glas. Sr. Lectr., Italian
Whitton, David W., BA Durh., PhD
Durh. Prof., French; Head*
Other Staff: 12 Lectrs. (French 4, Italian 2,
Spanish 3); 1 Teaching Fellow (German); 1
Sr. Lectr.†; 1 Hon. Reader (German)
Research: applied linguistics; contemporary,
romantic and Renaissance literature; film and
theatre; socio-cultural studies

Finance, see Acctg. and Finance

French, see European Langs. and Cultures

Geography

Auty, Richard M., BA Reading, MA Tor., PhD
Lond. Sr. Lectr.
Carling, Paul A., BSc Leic., PhD Wales Prof.
Chapman, Graham P., BA Camb., PhD
Camb. Prof.; Head*
Clark, Gordon, MA Edin., PhD Edin. Sr. Lectr.
Flowerdew, Robin T. N., MA Oxf., MS
Northwestern, PhD Northwestern Sr. Lectr.
Gatrell, Anthony C., BSc Brist., MS Penn., PhD
Penn. Prof.
Park, Christopher C., BSc Ulster, PhD Exe. Sr.
Lectr.
Pooley, Colin G., BA Liv., PhD Liv. Prof.
Pringle, Ada W., BA Hull, PhD Hull Sr. Lectr.
Vincent, Peter J., BSc Sheff., PhD Durh. Sr.
Lectr.
Whyte, Ian D., MA Edin., PhD Edin., DSc
Edin. Prof.
Other Staff: 4 Lectrs.
Research: environment; health, migration;
hydrodynamics and sedimentology

German, see European Langs. and Cultures

History

Blinkhorn, R. Martin, BA Oxf., AM Stan., DPhil
Oxf., FRHistS Prof.
Brooke, John H., MA Camb., PhD Camb. Prof.,
History of Science
Constantine, Stephen, BA Oxf., DPhil Oxf.,
FRHistS Sr. Lectr.
Evans, Eric J., MA Oxf., PhD Warw.,
FRHistS Prof.; Head*
Grant, Alexander, BA Oxf., DPhil Oxf. Reader
Harman, Peter M., BA Oxf., BSc Oxf., MA
Camb., PhD Leeds Reader, History of Science
Heale, Michael J., BA Manc., DPhil Oxf. Prof.
Henig, Ruth B., BA Lond., PhD Lanc. Sr. Lectr.
MacKenzie, John M., MA Glas., PhD Br.Col.,
FRHistS Prof.
Merriman, Marcus H., BA Bowdoin, PhD Lond.,
FSA Sr. Lectr.
Mullett, Michael A. A., BA Wales, MLitt Camb.,
PhD Lanc. Sr. Lectr.
Phillips, Gordon A., MA Oxf., DPhil Oxf. Sr.
Lectr.
Pumfrey, Stephen, BA Camb., MA Yale, PhD
Yale Sr. Lectr.
Richards, Jeffrey M., MA Camb., FRHistS Hon.
Prof.
Shennan, Joseph H., BA Liv., PhD Camb.,
FRHistS Hon. Prof.
Smith, Roger, MA Camb., PhD Camb. Reader,
History of Science
Stringer, Keith J., MA Camb., PhD Camb., FSA,
FRHistS Reader
Walton, John K., MA Oxf., PhD, FRHistS Prof.
Winchester, Angus J. L., BA Durh., PhD
Durh. Sr. Lectr.
Winstanley, Michael J., BA Oxf., MA PhD,
FRHistS Sr. Lectr.
Wood, Alan T., BA Oxf. Sr. Lectr.
Other Staff: 7 Lectrs.
Research: history of science; international and
imperial history; social and cultural history

Independent Studies

Wakeford, John R., BA Nott., PhD Brun. Sr.
Lectr.†; Dir.*
Other Staff: 1 Programme Dir.; 1 Lectr.; 1
Teaching Fellow

International Relations, see Pol. and
Internat. Relns.

Italian, see European Langs. and Cultures

Law

Macnair, Michael, MA Oxf., BCL Oxf., DPhil
Oxf. Sr. Lectr.
Moran, Leslie J., LLB Sheff., MA Sheff. Sr. Lectr.
Picciotto, Solomon, BA Oxf., JD Chic. Prof.
Rowe, Peter, LLB Belf., LLM Lond., PhD
Liv. Prof.; Head*
Salter, Michael G., LLB S'ton., PhD Sheff. Sr.
Lectr.
Sugarman, David, LLB Hull, LLM Camb., LLM
Harv., SJD Harv., FRHistS Prof.
Other Staff: 9 Lectrs.
Research: comparative and international law;
gender and family; history of law; legal
theory

Linguistics and Modern English Language

Alderson, J. Charles, MA Oxf., PhD Edin Prof.
Allwright, Richard L., BA Reading, MLitt Edin.,
PhD Lanc. Sr. Lectr.
Barton, David P., BA Sus., MA Essex, PhD
Lond. Sr. Lectr.
Fairclough, Norman L., MA Lond. Prof.
Ivanič, Rosalind E., BA Brist., MA Lanc., PhD
Lanc. Sr. Lectr.
Johnson, Keith, MA Oxf., MA Essex, PhD
Essex Sr. Lectr.
Katamba, Francis X., BA Mak., PhD Edin. Prof.;
Head*
Knowles, Gerald, MA Camb., PhD Leeds Sr.
Lectr.
Leech, Geoffrey N., MA Lond., PhD Lond.,
FBA Prof.†
Myers, Gregory A., BA Claremont, MA Col., PhD
Col. Sr. Lectr.
Short, Michael H., BA Lanc., MA Birm., PhD
Lanc. Prof.
Siewierska, Anna M., MA Melb., PhD
Melb. Prof.
Other Staff: 5 Lectrs.
Research: computer corpus; formal and
descriptive linguistics; stylistics

Management Learning

Burgoyne, John G., BSc Lond., MPhil Lond., PhD
Manc. Prof.; Head*
Easterby-Smith, Mark P. V., BSc Durh., PhD
Durh. Sr. Lectr.
Fox, Steven, BA CNAA, PhD Manc. Sr. Lectr.
Hodgson, Vivien, BSc Birm., PhD Sur. Sr.
Lectr.
Lee, Monica M., BSc Lanc., PhD Open(UK) Sr.
Lectr.
Reynolds, P. Michael, MB ChB Edin., PhD
Durh. Sr. Lectr.
Other Staff: 2 Lectrs.
Research: social learning process

Management Science

Brown, David H., MA Lanc. Sr. Lectr.
Checkland, Peter B., MA Oxf. Hon. Prof.
Eglese, Richard W., BA Camb., MA Lanc. Sr.
Lectr.
Fildes, Robert, BA Oxf., MA Calif., PhD
Calif. Prof.
Kingsman, Brian G., MA Camb., PhD Prof.
Mercer, Alan, MA Camb., PhD Lond. Hon.
Prof.
Pidd, Michael, BTech Brun., MSc Birm. Prof.;
Head*
Rand, Graham K., BSc Liv. Sr. Lectr.
Worthington, David J., BSc Birm., MSc Reading,
PhD Reading Sr. Lectr.
Wright, Michael B., BA Oxf., MSc Oxf. Sr.
Lectr.
Other Staff: 4 Lectrs.
Vacant Posts: 2 Lectrs.
Research: operational research and management;
systems and information

Marketing

Araujo, Luis M. P. M., LMechEng Oporto, MA
Lanc., PhD Lanc. Sr. Lectr.
Easton, Geoffrey, BSc Brist., PhD Lond. Prof.;
Head*
Other Staff: 5 Lectrs.; 3 Lectrs.†
Vacant Posts: 2 Lectrs.
Research: industrial networks; quantitative
marketing

Mathematics and Statistics

Chetwynd, Amanda G., MSc Nott., PhD
Open(UK) Sr. Lectr.
Coles, Stuart G., BSc Sus., MSc Sheff., PhD
Sheff. Sr. Lectr.
Diggle, Peter J., BSc Liv., MSc Oxf., PhD
Newcastle(UK) Prof.
Henderson, Robin, BSc Newcastle(UK), PhD
Edin. Sr. Lectr.
Jameson, Graham J. O., MA Camb., PhD
Edin. Sr. Lectr.
Power, Stephen C., BSc Lond., PhD Edin. Prof.
Tawn, Jonathan A., BSc Lond., PhD Sur. Prof.
Towers, David A., BSc Newcastle(UK), PhD
Leeds Sr. Lectr.
Tunnicliffe-Wilson, Granville, BA Camb.,
PhD Reader; Head*
Whittaker, Joseph C., MSc Lond., PhD Lond. Sr.
Lectr.
Other Staff: 3 Lectrs.; 8 Res. Assocs.
Research: analysis and algebra; statistical
modelling of complex data

Music

Bray, Roger W., MA Oxf., DPhil Oxf. Prof.
Harrison, Bernard, BMus N.U.I., MA N.U.I.,
DPhil Oxf. Lectr.; Head*
McCaldin, Denis J., BSc Nott., BMus Birm., PhD
Nott. Prof.
Woodley, Ronald, MusB Manc., DPhil Oxf. Sr.
Lectr.
Other Staff: 2 Lectrs.; 1 Res. Assoc.
Research: analysis; late mediaeval and 18th
century music

Organisational Behaviour, see Behaviour
in Orgns.

Philosophy

Hammond, Michael A., MA St And., MPhil
Sus. Lectr.; Head*
Holland, Alan J., MA Oxf., BPhil Oxf. Sr. Lectr.
Howarth, Jane, MBA Lond., DPhil Oxf. Sr.
Lectr.
O'Neill, John F., MA Lanc., PhD Lanc. Reader
Pratt, Vernon F. J., BA Manc., BPhil Oxf. Sr.
Lectr.
Stewart, M. Alexander, MA St And., PhD
Penn. Prof.†
Other Staff: 2 Lectrs.
Research: aesthetic; continental; environmental;
ethical; intellectual

Physics and Chemistry, School of

Clegg, Arthur B., MA Camb., MA Oxf., PhD
Camb., FIP Hon. Prof., Nuclear Physics
Ebdon, John R., BSc Birm., PhD Birm. Prof.
Guénault, Anthony M., MA Camb., PhD Camb.,
FIP Prof.
Huckerby, Thomas N., BSc Birm., PhD Birm.,
DSc Reader
Hughes, Gareth, MA Oxf., DPhil Oxf. Reader
Krier, Anthony, BSc Sheff., PhD Hull Sr. Lectr.
Lambert, Colin J., BSc Hull, PhD Hull Prof.
Lyth, David H., BSc Manc., PhD Lond. Sr. Lectr.
McClintock, Peter V. E., DSc Belf., DPhil Oxf.,
FIP Prof.; Head*
Pickett, George R., BA Oxf., DPhil Oxf. Prof.
Ratoff, Peter N., BA Oxf., PhD Lond. Reader
Sloan, Terence, BSc Liv., PhD Liv. Prof.
Soutar, Ian, BSc Strath., PhD Strath. Prof.
Tucker, Robin W., MA Camb., PhD Camb.,
FIP Prof.
Wigmore, J. Keith, MA Oxf., DPhil Oxf.,
FIP Reader
Other Staff: 13 Lectrs.; 2 Sr. Res. Fellows; 17
Res. Assocs.; 4 Res. Officers; 3 Hon. Sr.
Lectrs.

Research: clean materials (chemistry); low temperature; materials (physics); particle physics

Politics and International Relations

Bellany, Ian, MA Oxf., DPhil Oxf. Prof.
Clapham, Christopher S., MA Oxf., DPhil Oxf. Prof.
Cohan, Alvin S., MA Miami(Fla.), PhD Georgia Sr. Lectr.
Denver, David T., MA Glas., BPhil Dund. Reader
Dillon, G. Michael, BA Liv., MA Dal., PhD Lanc. Prof.
Gates, David, MA Dund., DPhil Oxf. Sr. Lectr.
Hands, H. T. Gordon, BA Oxf., BPhil Oxf. Sr. Lectr.; Head*
Höpfl, Harro M. W., MSc(Econ) Lond., PhD Lanc. Sr. Lectr.
King, Preston, BA Fisk, MSc Lond., PhD Lond. Prof.
McKinlay, Robert D., BSocSc Birm., DPhil York(UK) Prof.
Nonneman, Gerd A. J., MA Exe., PhD Exe. Sr. Lectr.
Price, Russell J., MA Well. Sr. Lectr.
Other Staff: 6 Lectrs.; 6 Hon. Res. Fellows
Research: comparative international; defence; electoral studies; theory

Psychology

Bremner, J. Gavin, BSc St And., DPhil Oxf. Prof.; Head*
Condor, Susan G., BA Wales, PhD Brist. Sr. Lectr.
Gilmour, Robin, MA Glas., MPhil Glas. Sr. Lectr.
Hay, Dennis C., BSc Aberd., PhD Aberd. Sr. Lectr.
Hitch, Graham J., MA Camb., MSc Sus., PhD Camb. Prof.
Hopkins, J. Brian, BA Ill., MSc Ill., PhD Leeds Prof.
Lewis, Charles N., BA Lanc., MA Nott., PhD Nott. Reader
Morris, Peter E., BA Exe., PhD Exe., FBPsS Prof.
Ormerod, Thomas C., BSc Leeds, PhD CNAA Sr. Lectr.
Ridgway, James, BSc Sheff., MSc Stir., PhD Lanc. Reader
Smyth, Mary M., BA Dub., MSc Leic., PhD Leic., FBPsS Reader
Subbotsky, Eugene V., PhD Moscow, DSc Moscow Reader
Walker, Peter S., BSc Lond., PhD Lond. Sr. Lectr.
Other Staff: 5 Lectrs.
Research: child development; cognition; infancy; memory

Religious Studies

Cunningham, Adrian M., MA Camb. Sr. Lectr.
Heelas, Paul L. F., MA Oxf., DPhil Oxf. Reader
Morris, Paul M., BA Well., MA McM. Sr. Lectr.
Roberts, Richard, BA Lanc., BD Camb., MA Camb., PhD Edin. Prof.
Samuel, Geoffrey B., MA Oxf., PhD Camb. Prof.
Sawyer, Deborah F., BA Newcastle(UK), MLitt Newcastle(UK), PhD Lanc. Sr. Lectr.
Segal, Robert, BA Wesleyan, MA Prin., PhD Prin. Reader
Smith, David J., BA Oxf., DPhil Oxf. Sr. Lectr.
Waines, David, BA Manit., BA Lond., MA McG., PhD McG. Prof., Islamic and Middle Eastern Studies; Head*
Other Staff: 4 Lectrs.; 1 Reader†
Research: eastern and western traditions; method and theory

Social Science, Applied, see Appl. Soc. Sci.

Sociology

Abercrombie, Nicholas, BA Oxf., MSc(Econ) Lond., PhD Lanc. Prof.
Currie, Catherine C., BSc(Soc) Lond., MSc(Econ) Lond. Sr. Lectr.

Franklin, Sarah, BA Smith, MA Kent, MA N.Y., PhD Birm. Sr. Lectr.
Heald, Suzette S., BSc Lond., PhD Lond. Sr. Lectr.
Hughes, John A., BSocSc Birm., PhD Lanc. Prof.
Jessop, Robert D., BA Exe., MA Camb., PhD Camb. Prof.
McNeil, Maureen, BA Tor., MA Wat., PhD Camb. Reader
Penn, Roger D., BA Camb., MA Brown, PhD Camb. Reader
Ray, Lawrence J., BA Lanc., MA Sus., DPhil Sus. Reader
Sayer, R. Andrew, BA Lond., MA Sus., DPhil Sus. Reader
Shapiro, Daniel Z., MA Oxf. Prof.; Head*
Skeggs, Beverley, BA York(UK), PhD Keele Sr. Lectr.
Urry, John R., MA Camb., PhD Camb. Prof.
Warde, Alan, BA Camb., MA Durh., PhD Leeds Prof.
Other Staff: 1 Lectr.
Vacant Posts: 4 Lectrs.
Research: culture; environment; gender; political economy; technology and work

Spanish, see European Langs. and Cultures

Statistics, see Maths. and Stats.

Theatre Studies

Harris, Geraldine M., MA Manc. Lectr.; Head*
Kershaw, Barrie R., BA Manc., MA Hawaii, PhD Exe. Prof.
Shevtsova, Maria, BA Syd., PhD Syd. Prof.
Other Staff: 4 Lectrs.
Research: performance; practice as research

SPECIAL CENTRES, ETC

Accounting, International Centre for Research in

Peasnell, Kenneth V., MSc(Econ) Lond., PhD Lanc. Prof.
Pope, Prof. Peter F., BCom Liv., MA Lanc. Dir.*
Research: accounting and finance; theoretical and empirical

Applied Statistics, Centre for

Crouchley, Robert, BSc Lough., MSc Wales, PhD Wales, PhD Lond. Sr. Lectr.
Davies, Richard B., MA Camb., MSc Birm., PhD Brist. Prof.
Francis, Brian J., BSc Lond., MSc Sheff. Sr. Lectr.; Dir.*
Other Staff: 2 Lectrs.; 8 Res. Assocs.
Research: statistical modelling of complex data

Computer Support for Co-operative Working, Centre for Research in

Shapiro, Prof. Daniel Z., MA Oxf. Dir.*
Research: social organisation of work

Cultural Research, Institute for

Dillon, G. Michael, BA Liv., MA Dal., PhD Lanc. Dir.*
Research: cultures of modern societies

Education and Training, Centre for the Study of

Saunders, Murray S., BA Essex, MA Lanc., PhD Lanc. Dir.*
Other Staff: 2 Sr. Res. Fellows; 5 Res. Officers
Research: policy and practice; upper secondary and post-compulsory

Engineering Design, Centre for

Bradshaw, Prof. Alan, BSc Nott., PhD Nott. Dir.*
Research: development of discipline in engineering design

English Language Education, Institute for

McGovern, John J., BA S'ton., MSc Edin. Dir.*
Other Staff: 1 Assoc. Dir.; 8 Lectrs.

Environmental Change, Centre for the Study of

Grove-White, Robin B., BA Oxf. Dir.*
Wynne, Brian E., MA Camb., PhD Camb., MPhil Edin. Prof.
Research: global and local environmental knowledge

Environmental Systems and Statistics, Centre for Research in

Young, Prof. Peter C., BTech Lough., MSc Lough., MA Camb., PhD Camb. Dir.*
Research: environmental systems and statistics

Health Research, Institute for

Gatrell, Prof. Anthony C., BSc Brist., MS Penn., PhD Penn. Dir.*

Lancaster University Archaeological Unit

Newman, Richard, BA Wales, PhD Wales Dir.*
Other Staff: 6 Field Officers
Research: local, regional and national archaeological sites

Management School: Development Division

Davis, Julia M., BA Exe. Prof.; Fellow
Mackness, John R., BSc Nott., PhD Lanc. Sr. Teaching Fellow; Dir.*
Other Staff: 1 Lectr.; 4 Sr. Teaching Fellows; 5 Teaching Fellows

North-West Regional Studies, Centre for

Roberts, Elizabeth A. M., BA Brist., PhD Dir.*
Other Staff: 4 Hon. Res. Fellows

Peace Studies, Richardson Institute for

Miall, A. Hugh, BA Oxf., PhD Lanc. Dir.*
Other Staff: 1 Hon. Lectr.
Research: conflict resolution; peace and conflict

Polymer Centre

Ebdon, Prof. John R., BSc Birm., PhD Birm. Dir.*
Other Staff: 1 Res. Fellow
Research: polymer science, especially polymer chemistry

Ruskin Programme

Hewison, Robert, MA Oxf., DLitt Oxf. Prof.†
Wheeler, Prof. Michael D., MA Camb., PhD Lond. Dir.*
Research: John Ruskin and his circle

Science Studies and Science Policy, Centre for

Shove, Elizabeth, BA York, DPhil York Dir.*
Research: public knowledge of science; risk

Training and Development, Centre for

O'Brien, Jane, MA Oxf. Head*
Other Staff: 3 Programme Managers

Women's Studies, Institute for

McNeill, Maureen, BA Tor., MA Wat., PhD Camb.
Other Staff: 2 Lectrs.; 1 Sr. Lectr.†

CONTACT OFFICERS

Academic affairs. Academic Registrar: McClintock, Marion E., BA Durh.
Admissions (first degree). Undergraduate Admissions Officer: Gillison, Jess M., BSc Wales
Admissions (higher degree). Postgraduate Admissions Officer: Willes, Heather A., BA Lond.
Adult/continuing education. Director: Percy, Keith A., BSc Lond., MA Camb., MA Nott., PhD
Alumni. Alumni Officer: Fay, Emily A., BA

Archives. Academic Registrar: McClintock, Marion E., BA Durh.

Careers. Head of Careers Service: Knaggs, Lesley, BA Nott., BEd Nott., MA Nott.

Computing services. Director, Information Services: Macklin, Janice E., BSc Manc.

Conferences/corporate hospitality. Director: Christian, Eric M.

Equal opportunities. Director, Personnel Services: Walshe, Valerie C., BA Warw.

Estates and buildings/works and services. Director: Phillips, Ernest

Examinations. Head, Student Registry: Wareing, Lesley, BA Lanc.

Finance. Director: McGregor, Euan T., BCom Edin.

General enquiries. Secretary: Lamley, Stephen A. C., MA Camb.

Health services. Medical Officer: Burr, R. H., MB BS Newcastle(UK)

International office. International Officer: Withrington, John K. B., BA Camb., MA Leic., DPhil York(UK)

Language training for international students. Director: McGovern, John J., BA S'ton., MSc Edin.

Library (enquiries). Sub-Librarian: Clark, Winifred R., MA Sheff., BA

Library (enquiries). Sub-Librarian: Hutchinson, Michael B., BA MSc

Personnel/human resources. Director, Personnel Services: Walshe, Valerie C., BA Warw.

Public relations, information and marketing. Press Officer: Tyrrell, Victoria L., BA CNAA

Purchasing. Head, Strategic Purchasing: Holt, Hilary, MBA Lanc.

Quality assurance and accreditation. Academic Registrar: McClintock, Marion E., BA Durh.

Research. Academic Registrar: McClintock, Marion E., BA Durh.

Safety. Safety and Radiation Protection Officer: Madeley, Anthony T., MSc Aston

Scholarships, awards, loans. Student Support Officer: Brennan, Sylvia A., BA CNAA

Schools liaison. Admissions Liaison Officer: Gould, Roger S., BA Lanc., MA Open(UK)

Security. Head: Evans, Anthony G., BA Open(UK)

Sport and recreation. Director, Sport and Physical Recreation: Cinnamond, Stanley T., BA Ulster

Staff development and training. Training and Development Officer: Wareham, Theresa K., BA CNAA, MA

Student union. General Manager: Elliott, Peter R., BA Lanc., MBA Strath.

Student welfare/counselling. Counsellor: Elder, John, BA Oxf., MSc Birm.

Students from other countries. International Officer: Withrington, John K. B., BA Camb., MA Leic., DPhil York(UK)

Students with disabilities. Special Needs Adviser: Quinn, Christine

CAMPUS/COLLEGE HEADS

Bowland College. Principal: Saunders, Ian J., BSc Glas., MSc PhD

Cartmel College. Principal: Hughes, Prof. John A., BSocSc Birm., PhD Lanc.

Furness College. Principal: Clements, Janet E., MA Edin.

Fylde College. Principal: Thomson, Alan, BA Oxf., DPhil Oxf.

Grizedale College. Principal: Cinnamond, Stanley T., BA Ulster

Lonsdale College. Principal: Neal, Robert A.

Pendle College. Principal: Whitaker, Alan, BA Birm.

The County College. Principal: Widden, Martin B., MA Camb.

The Graduate College. Principal: Park, Christopher C., BSc Ulster, PhD Exe.

[Information supplied by the institution as at 14 March 1998, and edited by the ACU]

UNIVERSITY OF LEEDS

Founded 1904; previously established 1884, by amalgamation of the Leeds School of Medicine (1831) with the Yorkshire College of Science (1874)

Member of the Association of Commonwealth Universities

Postal Address: Leeds, England LS2 9JT

Telephone: (0113) 243 1751 **Fax:** (0113) 233 6017 **E-mail:** office@scf.leeds.ac.uk **Telex:** 556473 UNILDS G
WWW: http://www.leeds.ac.uk

VISITOR—Elizabeth, H.M.The Queen
CHANCELLOR—Kent, H.R.H. The Duchess of, GCVO, Hon. LLD
PRO-CHANCELLOR—Roberts, Colonel A. C., MBE, TD, JP, MPhil PhD, FIBiol
VICE-CHANCELLOR*—Wilson, Prof. Alan G., MA Camb., FBA
PRO-VICE-CHANCELLOR (INFORMATION TECHNOLOGY)—Taylor, Prof. Chris M., BSc(Eng) Lond., MSc Leeds, PhD Leeds, DEng Leeds, FEng, FIMechE
PRO-VICE-CHANCELLOR (RESEARCH)—May, Prof. Anthony D., MA Camb., FICE
PRO-VICE-CHANCELLOR (TEACHING)—Chapman, Prof. Anthony J., BSc Leic., PhD Leic., FBPsS
PRO-VICE-CHANCELLOR (STAFF)—Hill, Joyce M., BA Lond., DPhil York(UK)
TREASURER—Stone, Arthur, OBE
REGISTRAR AND SECRETARY‡—Robinson, David S., BA Leeds, PhD Leeds
LIBRARIAN—Brindley, Lynne J., BA Reading, MA Lond.

GENERAL INFORMATION

History. The antecedents of the university were Leeds School of Medicine, founded in 1831, and Yorkshire College of Science, founded in 1874. These combined in 1884, eventually to form a constituent part of the federal Victoria University (founded 1887). The university received its charter in 1904.

Admission to first degree courses (see also United Kingdom Introduction). Through Universities and Colleges Admissions Service (UCAS). Acceptable levels of literacy are required for all degree programmes, together with specified requirements for individual degree programmes.

First Degrees (see also United Kingdom Directory to Subjects of Study). BA, BBc,

BChD, BEng, BMus, BSc, LLB, MB ChB, MChem, MEng, MGeog, MGeol, MGeophys.

Higher Degrees (see also United Kingdom Directory to Subjects of Study). MA, MBA, MDentSci, MEd, MHSc, MMedSc, MMus, MPsychother, MSc, MSc(Eng), PhD.

Libraries. Over 2,500,000 items.

Fees (1998–99). International students (undergraduate and postgraduate): £6390 (arts); £7440 (combined); £8480 (science); £15,6000 (clinical). United Kingdom students (postgraduate): £2610.

Academic Awards (1997–98). 401 awards ranging in value from £2000 to £15,000.

Academic Year (1998–99). Two semesters: 28 September–22 January; 25 January–18 June.

Income (1996–97). Total, £230,187,000.

Statistics. Staff: 6172 (2486 academic, 3686 administrative, etc). Students: full-time 19,909 (9863 men, 10,046 women); part-time 3188 (1219 men, 1969 women); international 3704 (2139 men, 1565 women); total 23,097.

FACULTIES/SCHOOLS

Arts, Research School and Faculty of

Research Dean: Macklin, Prof. John J., BA Belf., PhD Belf.

Secretary: Aston, Denise

Biological Sciences, Research School and Faculty of

Research Dean: Henderson, Prof. Peter J. F., BSc Brist., MA Camb., PhD Brist.

Business, Law, Education and Social Sciences, Research School and Faculty of

Research Dean: Pearman, Prof. Alan D., BSocSc Birm., MA Leeds, PhD Leeds

Earth and Environment, Research School and Faculty of

Research Dean: McDonald, Prof. Adrian T., BSc Edin., PhD Edin.

Engineering, Research School and Faculty of

Research Dean: Fisher, Prof. John, BSc Birm., PhD Glas., DEng Leeds, FIMechE

Mathematical and Physical Sciences, Rsearch School and Faculty of

Research Dean: Brindley, John, BSc Lond., PhD Lond.

Medicine, Dentistry, Psychology and Health, Research School and Faculty of

Research Dean: Smith, Prof. Michael A., BSc Brist., MSc Aberd., PhD Edin., FIP

ACADEMIC UNITS

§ = Fixed-Term Appointment

Arabic and Middle Eastern Studies

Tel: (0113) 233 3421 Fax: (0113) 233 3426

Agius, Dionisius A., MA Tor., PhD Tor. Sr. Lectr.
Netton, Ian R., BA Lond., PhD Exe. Prof.; Head*
Shivtiel, A., MA Jerusalem, PhD Camb. Sr. Lectr.
Sirriyeh, Hussein M., MA Beirut, DPhil Oxf. Sr. Lectr.
Other Staff: 4 Lectrs.; 1 Visiting Res. Fellow

Art, see Fine Art

Astronomy, see Phys. and Astron.

Biochemistry and Molecular Biology, School of

Tel: (0113) 233 3112 Fax: (0113) 233 3167

Baldwin, S. A., MA Camb., PhD Camb. Reader, Biochemistry
Berry, Alan, BSc S'ton., PhD S'ton. Sr. Lectr.
Blair, G. E., BSc Edin., PhD Warw. Reader, Biochemistry
Booth, A. G., BSc Leeds, PhD Leeds Sr. Lectr.
Brown, Stanley B., BSc Durh., PhD Newcastle(UK) Yorkshire Cancer Res. Campaign Prof.
Findlay, J. B. C., BSc Aberd., PhD Leeds Prof., Biochemistry
Hames, B. D., BSc Brist., PhD Leic. Reader, Developmental Biochemistry
Henderson, P. J. F., BSc Brist., MA Camb., PhD Brist. Prof., Biochemistry
Higgins, S. J., BA Oxf., DPhil Oxf. Sr. Lectr.
Hooper, N. M., BSc Leeds, PhD Leeds Sr. Lectr.
Knowles, P. F., BSc Sheff., PhD Sheff. Prof., Biophysical Chemistry
Knox, J. Paul, BSc Newcastle(UK), PhD Wales Sr. Lectr.
Lydon, J. E., BSc Leeds, PhD Leeds Sr. Lectr.
Mackie, W., BSc Edin., PhD Edin. Sr. Lectr.
McPherson, M. J., BSc Leeds, PhD Leeds Sr. Lectr.
Millner, P. A., BSc Leeds, PhD Leeds Sr. Lectr.
Packter, N. M., BSc Liv., PhD Liv. Sr. Lectr.
Parish, J. H., MA Oxf., DPhil Oxf. Sr. Lectr.
Phillips, S. E. V., BSc Lond., PhD Lond. Astbury Prof., Biophysics
Turner, A. J., MA Camb., PhD Camb. Prof., Biochemistry; Head*
Walker, J. H., BSc Nott., PhD Nott. Sr. Lectr.

Wood, Edward J., MA Oxf., DPhil Oxf. Reader, Biochemistry
Other Staff: 7 Lectrs.

Biology

Tel: (0113) 233 2880, 233 2828 Fax: (0113) 233 3091, 233 2835

Alexander, R. McN., MA Camb., PhD Camb., DSc Wales, FIBiol, FRS Prof., Zoology
Altringham, John D., BA York(UK), PhD St And. Reader, Comparative Physiology
Atkinson, Howard J., BSc Newcastle(UK), PhD Newcastle(UK) Prof., Nematology
Baumberg, Simon S., BA Oxf., DPhil Oxf. Prof., Bacterial Genetics
Butlin, Roger K., MA Camb., PhD Nott. Reader, Evolutionary Biology
Coates, David, BSc Leeds, PhD E.Anglia Sr. Lectr.
Compton, Stephen G., BSc Hull, PhD Hull Sr. Lectr.
Cove, David J., MA Camb., PhD Camb., FIBiol Prof., Genetics
Cuming, Andrew C., BA Oxf., PhD Camb. Sr. Lectr.
Feare, Christopher J., BSc Leeds, PhD Leeds Visiting Prof.
Forbes, J. Michael, PhD Leeds, DSc Nott. Prof., Agricultural Sciences
Gill, E. Margaret, BSc Edin., BA Open(UK), PhD Massey Visiting Prof.
Gilmartin, Philip M., BSc Leeds, PhD Warw. Sr. Lectr.
Grahame, John W., BSc WI, PhD Wales Sr. Lectr.
Greenwood, Duncan J., BSc Liv., PhD Aberd., DSc Aberd., FRS Visiting Prof.
Hardy, Anthony J., MA Oxf., PhD Aberd. Visiting Prof.
Hill, Stephen A., BSc Reading, PhD Reading Visiting Prof.
Hollingdale, Michael R., BSc Liv., PhD Lond. Prof., Parasitology; Head*
Hope, Ian A., BA Oxf., PhD Edin. Sr. Lectr.
Isaac, R. Elwyn, BSc Wales, PhD Wales Reader, Invertebrate Neuro-Endocrinology
Knox, J. Paul, BSc Newcastle(UK), PhD Wales Sr. Lectr.
Meyer, Peter, PhD Cologne Prof., Plant Genetics
Mill, Peter J., BSc Nott., PhD Birm., DSc Birm. Sr. Lectr.
Pilbeam, David J., BSc Lond., PhD Lond. Sr. Lectr.
Price, Nicholas R., BSc Lanc., PhD Lanc. Visiting Prof.
Radford, Alan, BSc Leeds, MSc McM., PhD McM. Sr. Lectr.
Rodway, Richard G., BSc Lond., PhD Birm. Sr. Lectr.
Sastry, Gummaluru R. K., MS Wis., PhD Wis. Sr. Lectr.
Shorrocks, B., BSc Leic., PhD Manc. Prof., Population Biology
Smith, Judith E., BSc Edin., PhD Camb. Sr. Lectr.
Stanley, Peter I., BSc Lond., PhD Lond. Visiting Prof.
Stockley, Peter G., BSc Lond., PhD Camb. Prof., Biological Chemistry
Symonds, Herbert W., BVetMed Lond. Sr. Lectr.
Turner, John R. G., BSc Liv., DPhil Oxf., DSc Oxf. Prof., Evolutionary Genetics
Wootton, John C., BSc Brist., PhD Brist. Sr. Lectr. (on leave)
Other Staff: 15 Lectrs.; 34 Res. Fellows; 3 Sr. Res. Fellows; 11 Hon. Lectrs.; 4 Hon. Res. Fellows

Business, see Leeds Univ. Business Sch.

Ceramics, see under Materials, Sch. of

Chemistry, School of

Tel: (0113) 233 6566 Fax: (0113) 233 6565

Bartle, Kevin D., PhD Leeds Prof.
Beddard, Godfrey, BSc Lond., PhD Lond. Prof., Chemical Physics

Bochmann, Manfred, PhD Lond., FRSChem Prof., Inorganic and Structural Chemistry
Boden, Neville, BSc Liv., PhD Liv. Prof.
Bushby, Richard J., BSc Lond., DPhil Oxf. Reader, Organic Chemistry
Calder, Alan, CBE, BSc Aberd., PhD Aberd. Visiting Prof.
Campbell, Simon F., BSc Birm., PhD Birm. Visiting Prof.
Clifford, Anthony A., BA Oxf., BSc Oxf., DPhil Oxf., DSc Oxf. Reader, Physical Chemistry
Davidson, Alan H., BA Camb., PhD Camb. Visiting Prof.
Fisher, Julie F., BSc Lanc., PhD Liv. Sr. Lectr.
Fishwick, Colin W. G., BSc Liv., PhD Liv. Sr. Lectr.
Gans, Peter, BSc Lond., PhD Lond. Sr. Lectr.
Gibb, Terence C., BSc Durh., PhD Newcastle(UK) Reader, Inorganic Chemistry
Greatrex, R., MSc Newcastle(UK), PhD Newcastle(UK), FRSChem Sr. Lectr.
Griffiths, John F., BSc Liv., PhD Liv., DSc Liv. Reader, Physical Chemistry
Griffiths, Trevor R., BSc S'ton., PhD S'ton., FRSChem Sr. Lectr.
Grigg, Ronald E., PhD Nott. Prof., Organic Chemistry
Herbert, Richard B., BSc Cape Town, PhD Leeds, DSc Leeds Reader, Bio-Organic Chemistry
Johnson, A. Peter, MSc Manc., PhD Manc. Prof., Computational Chemistry; Dir., Inst. for Computer Applicns. in Molecular Scis.
Johnson, Anthony F., BSc Nott., PhD Nott. Prof., Polymer Science and Technology
Kee, Terence P., BSc Durh., PhD Durh. Sr. Lectr.
Kennedy, J. D., BSc Lond., PhD Lond., FRSChem Reader, Inorganic Chemistry
Newton, Roger F., BSc Lond., PhD Lond. Visiting Prof.
Pilling, Michael J., MA Camb., PhD Camb., FRSChem Prof., Physical Chemistry; Head*
Rayner, Christopher M., BSc Liv., PhD Liv. Sr. Lectr.
Scott, Stephen K., BSc Leeds, PhD Leeds Prof., Mathematical Chemistry
Shaw, Bernard L., BSc Manc., PhD Manc., FRS, FRSChem Res. Prof., Inorganic and Structural Chemistry
Whitaker, Ben J., BSc Sus., DPhil Sus. Sr. Lectr.
Other Staff: 4 Lectrs.; 30 Res. Fellows; 6 Hon. Lectrs.

Chinese Studies, see E. Asian Studies

Classics, School of

Tel: (0113) 233 3537

Cairns, Francis, MA Glas., MA Oxf., PhD Liv. Prof., Latin Language and Literature
Heath, Malcolm F., MA Oxf., DPhil Oxf. Reader, Greek Language and Literature
Maltby, Robert, MA Camb., PhD Camb. Sr. Lectr.; Chairman*
Other Staff: 6 Lectrs.; 2 Hon. Lectrs.
Vacant Posts: 1 Prof. (Greek Lang. and Lit.)

Colour Chemistry and Dyeing

Tel: (0113) 233 2930 Fax: (0113) 233 2947

Burkinshaw, Stephen M., BSc Brad., PhD Brad. Sr. Lectr.
Griffiths, John, BSc Birm., PhD Birm. Sr. Lectr.
Guthrie, James T., PhD Salf., FRSChem Prof., Polymer and Surface Coatings Science and Technology
Lewis, David M., BSc Leeds, PhD Leeds, FRSChem Prof.; Head*
Nobbs, James H., BSc Leeds, PhD Leeds Sr. Lectr.
Oakes, John, BSc Leic., PhD Leic. Visiting Prof.
Other Staff: 2 Lectrs.; 1 Sr. Res. Fellow; 8 Res. Fellows; 5 Hon. Lectrs.

Computer Studies, School of

Tel: (0113) 233 5430 Fax: (0113) 233 5468

Artificial Intelligence

Boyle, Roger D., BA York(UK), DPhil York(UK) Sr. Lectr.
Cohn, Anthony G., BSc Essex, PhD Essex Prof., Automated Reasoning
Hogg, David C., BSc Warw., MSc W.Ont., DPhil Sus. Prof.; Head of Div. and Sch.*
Millican, Peter J. R., MA Oxf., BPhil Oxf. Sr. Lectr.
Smith, Barbara M., BSc Lond., MSc Sheff., PhD Leeds Sr. Lectr.
Other Staff: 4 Lectrs.; 1 Sr. Res. Fellow; 6 Res. Fellows

Computer Science

Berzins, Martin, BSc Leeds, PhD Leeds, FIMA Reader, Computational Partial Differential Equations
Birtwhistle, Graham M., BSc Sheff., PhD Sheff., DSc Sheff. Prof., Formal Methods
Brodlie, Kenneth W., BSc Edin., MSc Dund., PhD Dund. Sr. Lectr.
Davy, John R., BA Oxf., MSc Manc., PhD Leeds Sr. Lectr.
Dew, Peter M., BTech Brad., PhD Brad. Prof.; Head*
Dyer, Martin E., BSc Leeds, MSc Lond., PhD Leeds Prof., Theoretical Computer Science
Jesty, Peter H., BSc(Eng) Leeds, MSc Leeds Sr. Lectr.
Jimack, Peter K., BSc Brist., PhD Brist. Sr. Lectr.
Other Staff: 5 Lectrs.; 1 Advisory Fellow

Operational Research and Information Systems

Gough, Thomas G., MA Oxf., FCIS Sr. Lectr.
Grimshaw, David J., BSc(Econ) Hull, MPhil CNAA, PhD Warw. Sr. Lectr.
Proll, Leslie G., BSc Liv., PhD Liv. Sr. Lectr.
Roberts, Stuart A., BSc Sus., PhD Lond. Sr. Lectr.
Wren, Anthony, MA Edin. Prof., Scheduling and Constraint Management; Head*
Other Staff: 4 Lectrs.

Continuing Education, School of

Tel: (0113) 233 3221 Fax: (0113) 233 3246
Chase, Malcolm S., BA York(UK), MA Sus., DPhil Sus. Sr. Lectr.
Forrester, Keith P., BA Leeds, PhD Leeds Sr. Lectr.
Frost, Nicholas P., BA Wales, MA Warw. Sr. Lectr.
Gardiner, Jean, BA Camb., MSc Lond. Sr. Lectr.
Harrison, Barry J. D., MA Oxf. Sr. Lectr.
Spencer, R. Luke, BA Lond. Sr. Lectr.
Taylor, Richard K. S., MA Oxf., PhD Prof.; Dir.*
Ward, Kevin, BSocSc N.U.I., MPhil Brad. Sr. Lectr.
Zukas, Miriam, BSc Exe. Sr. Lectr.
Other Staff: 7 Lectrs.; 3 Lectrs.†

Dentistry, see below

Earth Sciences, School of

Tel: (0113) 233 5222 Fax: (0113) 233 5259
Baker, Peter E., BSc Sheff., DPhil Oxf., FGS Prof.
Best, James, BSc Leeds, PhD Lond. Reader, Experimental Sedimentology
Briden, James C., MA Oxf., PhD Canberra, FGS, FRAS Visiting Prof.
Butler, Robert, BSc Leeds, PhD Wales Reader, Orogenic Geology
Cann, Johnson R., BA Camb., PhD Camb., ScD Camb., FRS Prof.
Cliff, Robert A., BA Oxf., DPhil Oxf., FGS Lectr.
Fairhead, J. Derek, BSc Durh., MSc Newcastle(UK), PhD Newcastle(UK), FRAS Prof., Applied Geophysics
Francis, Jane E., BSc S'ton., PhD S'ton. Sr. Lectr.
Gubbins, David, BA Camb., PhD Camb., FRS Prof., Geophysics
Hencher, Stephen R., BSc Lond., PhD Lond. Sr. Lectr. (on secondment)

Hudson, John A., BSc H.-W., PhD Minn. Visiting Prof.
Knipe, Robert J., BSc Wales, MSc Lond., PhD Lond. Prof., Structural Geology
Krom, Michael D., MA Camb., PhD Edin. Reader, Marine and Environmental Geochemistry
Leeder, Michael R., BSc Durh., PhD Reading, FGS Prof., Sedimentology; Head*
Lumsden, Alistair C., BSc Durh., MSc Newcastle(UK), FGS Sr. Lectr.
McCaig, A. M., BA Camb., PhD Camb., MSc W.Ont. Sr. Lectr.
Raiswell, Robert W., MSc Liv., PhD Liv. Prof., Sedimentary Geochemistry
Stuart, Graham W., BSc Leic., PhD Reading Sr. Lectr.
Wilson, B. Marjorie, BA Oxf., MA Calif., PhD Leeds Sr. Lectr.
Yardley, Bruce W. D., BSc Exe., PhD Brist., FGS Prof., Metamorphic Geochemistry
Other Staff: 13 Lectrs.; 4 Sr. Res. Fellows; 17 Res. Fellows

East Asian Studies

Tel: (0113) 233 3460 Fax: (0113) 233 6741
Benton, Gregor, MA Camb., PhD Leeds Prof., Chinese Studies
Davin, Delia, BA Leeds, PhD Leeds Reader, Chinese Social Studies; Head*
Francks, Penelope G., BA Camb., MSc Lond., PhD Lond. Sr. Lectr.
Hook, B. G., BA Lond. Sr. Lectr.
Hunter, Alan, BA Leeds, PhD Leeds Sr. Lectr.
Rimmington, D., MA Camb. Prof.
Williams, Mark B., MA Oxf., MA Calif., PhD Calif. Sr. Lectr.

Economic Studies, see Leeds Univ. Business Sch.

Education, School of

Tel: (0113) 233 4545 Fax: (0113) 233 4541
Anning, Angela J. E., BA Leeds, MEd Leic. Sr. Lectr.
Asher, Colin, BA Leeds, PhD Leeds Sr. Lectr.
Bates, Inge, BA Birm., PhD Leeds Prof., Education and Work
Beard, Roger F., BA Open(UK), PhD Brun. Reader, Literacy Education
Beveridge, Sally E., BA Manc., PhD Manc. Sr. Lectr.
Chambers, Gary M., BA Belf., MA Lond., PhD Leeds Sr. Lectr.
Coleman, P. Hwyel, MA Oxf., MA Lanc. Sr. Lectr.
Donnelly, James F., BSc Lond., MEd Leeds, PhD Leeds Sr. Lectr.
Edwards, Anne, BA Wales, MEd Wales, PhD Wales Prof., Primary Education
Higham, J. J. S., BA Leeds, MEd Leeds Sr. Lectr.
Jarvis, Jennifer I., BA Keele, MA Lond. Sr. Lectr.
Jenkins, Edgar W., JP, BSc Leeds, MEd Leeds, FRSChem Prof., Science Education Policy
Self, John A., BA Camb., MSc Leeds, PhD Leeds Prof., Knowledge Based Systems
Sharp, Paul R., BA Leeds, MEd Leeds, PhD Leeds Sr. Lectr.
Shorrocks-Taylor, Diane, BA Leic., MA Leeds, PhD Leeds Sr. Lectr.
Stibbs, Andrew, BA Camb., MA Durh. Sr. Lectr.
Sugden, D. A., MSc Calif., PhD Calif. Prof., Special Needs in Education; Chairman*
Tomlinson, Peter D., BPhil Louvain, MA Oxf., MA Tor., PhD Tor. Sr. Lectr.
Welford, A. Geoffrey, BSc Reading, MSc York(UK) Sr. Lectr.
Wiegand, Patrick A., BSc Lond., MA Lond. Sr. Lectr.
Williams, Ralph P., BA Wales, MA Lond. Sr. Lectr.
Other Staff: 25 Lectrs.; 3 Sr. Res. Fellows; 3 Res. Fellows; 1 Lectr.†; 1 Hon. Lectr.

Energy, see Fuel and Energy

Engineering, Chemical

Tel: (0113) 233 2404 Fax: (0113) 233 2405
Amooie-Foumeny, Esmail, MSc Leeds, PhD Leeds Prof., Process Modelling
Dowd, Peter A., BSc NE, MSc Montr., PhD Leeds Prof.; Acting Head*
McGreavy, Colin, BSc Leeds, MEng Yale, DEng Yale, FIChemE Prof.
Roberts, John R., BSc Visiting Prof.
Other Staff: 6 Lectrs.; 2 Res. Fellows; 5 Hon. Lectrs.
Vacant Posts: 1 Prof.

Engineering, Civil

Tel: (0113) 233 2269 Fax: (0113) 233 2265
Barton, John, BSc Leeds Sr. Lectr.§
Beeby, Andrew W., BSc Lond., PhD Lond. Instn. of Struct. Engineers Prof., Structural Design
Bonsall, Peter W., BA Oxf. Prof., Transport Planning
Brooks, Jeffrey J., BSc Leeds, PhD Leeds Sr. Lectr.
Cabrera, Joseph G. Prof., Civil Engineering Materials
Dalton, Donald C., MA Camb., MSc Sur. Sr. Lectr.
Dixon, J. Ross, BSc CNAA Sr. Lectr.
Garner, John B., BScTech Manc. Sr. Lectr.
Horan, Nigel J., BSc Salf., MSc Hull, PhD Hull Reader, Public Health Engineering
Leake, Gerald R., MSc Birm. Sr. Lectr.
Male, Stephen P., MSc H.-W., PhD H.-W. Balfour Beatty Prof., Building Engineering and Construction Management; Head*
Mara, Duncan D., BSc St And., PhD Dund., FICE, FIBiol Prof.
May, Anthony D., MA Camb., FICE Prof., Transport Engineering
Megson, T. H. Gordon, BSc Lond., PhD Leeds Sr. Lectr.
Narayanan, Nary, BE Madr., MSc Lond., FIStructE Visiting Prof.
Smith, Nigel J., BSc Birm., MSc Manc., PhD Manc. Prof., Construction Project Management
Smyth, Hilary C., BA Newcastle(UK), BArch Newcastle(UK) Sr. Lectr.
Stentiford, Edward I., MA Camb., MSc Leeds Biwater Prof., Public Health Engineering
Tight, Miles R., BSc Liv., PhD Lond. Sr. Lectr.
Tinker, John A., BSc Aston, MSc Manc., PhD Salf. Sr. Lectr.
Uren, John, BSc Leeds, PhD Leeds Sr. Lectr.
Wainwright, Peter J., BSc Aston, PhD Aston Sr. Lectr.
Watson, Alastair S., PhD Brad. Sr. Lectr.
Other Staff: 12 Lectrs.; 6 Res. Fellows; 1 Hon. Lectr.

Engineering, Electronic and Electrical, School of

Tel: (0113) 233 2000 Fax: (0113) 233 2032
Bernstein, Dennis, ScB Brown, MS Mich., PhD Mich. Visiting Prof.
Corda, Jasmin, MSc Zagreb, PhD Leeds Sr. Lectr.
Daly, Peter, BSc Glas., PhD Glas., FIEE Prof.
Darnell, Michael, PhD Camb., FIEE, FIMA Prof.
Fan, Pingzhi, PhD Hull, MSc Visiting Prof.
Howes, Michael J., BSc Leeds, PhD Leeds, FIEE Prof., Electronic Engineering
Hoyle, Brian S., BSc CNAA, MPhil CNAA, PhD CNAA Prof., Vision and Image Systems
Hughes, Austin, BSc Brist., PhD Brist. Sr. Lectr.; Head*
Itoh, Tatsuo, PhD Ill. Visiting Prof.
Lockhart, Gordon B., MSc Aberd., PhD Lond. Sr. Lectr.
McLernon, Desmond C., BSc Belf., MSc Belf., PhD Lond. Sr. Lectr.
Miles, Robert E., BSc Lond., PhD Lond. Sr. Lectr.

Nelson, John C. C., BSc *Manc.*, PhD *Leeds*   Sr. Lectr.

Nightingale, Stephen J., PhD *Kent*, FIEE   Visiting Prof.

Pollard, Roger D., BSc *Leeds*, PhD *Leeds*   Prof., High Frequency Measurements

Rhodes, J. David, OBE, BSc *Leeds*, PhD *Leeds*, DEng *Brad.*, FIEE   Indust. Prof.†

Snowden, Christopher M., BSc *Leeds*, PhD *Leeds*, FIEE   Prof., Microwave Engineering; Chairman*

Stephenson, J. Michael, BSc *Leeds*, PhD *Leeds*, FIEE   Reader, Electrical Drives

Strangeways, Hal J., BSc *Lond.*, PhD *S'ton.*, FRAS   Reader, Electromagnetic Wave Propagation

Van Graas, Frank, BSEE *Delft*, MSEE *Delft*, PhD *Ohio*   Visiting Prof.

Wilson, David A., BSc(Eng) *Lond.*, PhD *Camb.*   Reader, Control Engineering

Other Staff: 8 Lectrs.; 14 Res. Fellows

Engineering, Mechanical

Tel: (0113) 233 2186 Fax: (0113) 242 4611

Barton, David C., BSc *Brist.*, MSc *Manc.*, PhD *Manc.*   Sr. Lectr.

Bradley, Derek, BSc *Leeds*, PhD *Leeds*, FRS, FIMechE   Emer. Res. Prof.

Childs, Thomas H. C., MA *Camb.*, PhD *Camb.*, FIMechE   Prof., Manufacturing Engineering

Coney, John E. R., BSc(Eng) *Lond.*, MSc *Birm.*, PhD *Leeds*, FIMechE   Sr. Lectr.

Coy, Richard C., BSc *Leic.*, PhD *Aston*   External Prof.

Crolla, David A., DTech *Lough.*, PhD *Lough.*, FIMechE   Prof., Automotive Engineering; Head*

David, Timothy, BSc *Leeds*, PhD *Leeds*   Sr. Lectr.

De Pennington, Alan, OBE, MSc *Manc.*, PhD *Manc.*   Prof., Computer Aided Engineering

Dearnley, Peter A., BSc *Birm.*, PhD *Birm.*   Sr. Lectr.

Dowson, Duncan, CBE, BSc *Leeds*, PhD *Leeds*, DSc *Leeds*, Hon. DTech *Chalmers*, Hon. DSc *I.N.S.A.Lyons*, FEng, FRS, FIMechE   Emer. Res. Prof.

Fisher, John, BSc *Birm.*, PhD *Leeds*, DEng *Glas.*   Prof., Mechanical Engineering

Gaskell, Philip H., BSc *Leeds*, PhD *Leeds*   Sr. Lectr.

Juster, Neal P., BSc *Leeds*, PhD *Leeds*   Sr. Lectr.

McKnight, Jim   External Prof.

Sheppard, Christopher G. W., BSc *Leeds*, PhD *Leeds*   Prof., Applied Thermodynamics and Combustion Science

Taylor, Christopher M., BSc(Eng) *Lond.*, MSc *Leeds*, PhD *Leeds*, DEng *Leeds*, FIMechE   Prof., Tribology

Taylor, Richard S., BSc *Wolv.*   Visiting Prof.

Wroblewski, Michael, MB ChB *Leeds*, FRCSEd   External Prof.

Other Staff: 13 Lectrs.; 16 Res. Fellows

Engineering, Mining, see Mining and Mineral Engin.

English, School of

Tel: (0113) 233 4739 Fax: (0113) 233 4774

Banham, Martin J., MA *Leeds*   Prof., Drama and Theatre Studies; Dir., Workshop Theatre (on leave)

Barnard, John, MA *Oxf.*, BLitt *Oxf.*   Prof., English Literature (on leave)

Boon, Richard P., BA *Sheff.*, PhD *Sheff.*   Sr. Lectr.

Brennan, Michael G., MA *Oxf.*, MA *Camb.*, DPhil *Oxf.*   Sr. Lectr.

Brown, Richard H., BA *Lond.*, PhD *Lond.*   Sr. Lectr.

Butler, Martin H., MA *Camb.*, PhD *Camb.*   Reader, Renaissance Drama

Chew, Shirley, BA *Sing.*, PhD *Sing.*, BPhil *Oxf.*   Prof., Commonwealth and Post-Colonial Literature

Ewbank, Inga-Stina, BA *Minn.*, FilKand *Gothenburg*, MA *Sheff.*, PhD *Liv.*   Prof., English Literature (on leave)

Fairer, David, MA *Oxf.*, DPhil *Oxf.*   Reader, 18th-Century Poetry (on leave)

Felsenstein, Frank, BA *Leeds*, PhD *Leeds*   Reader, 18th-Century Studies

Gidley, Mick, BA *Manc.*, MA *Chic.*, DPhil *Sus.*   Prof., American Literature

Hammond, Paul, MA *Camb.*, PhD *Camb.*   Prof., 17th-Century Literature

Hill, Joyce M., BA *Lond.*, DPhil *York(UK)*   Prof., English Language and Medieval English Literature

Hunter, Lynette A. C., BA *Qu.*, MA *Leic.*, PhD *Edin.*   Reader, Rhetoric

Johnson, Lesley A., MA *Liv.*, PhD *Lond.*   Sr. Lectr.

Jones, Vivien M., MA *Oxf.*, DPhil *Oxf.*   Sr. Lectr.

Lindley, David, BA *Oxf.*, BPhil *Oxf.*   Reader, Renaissance Literature; Chairman*

Massa, Ann R., MA *Edin.*, PhD *Manc.*   Sr. Lectr.

McTurk, Rory W., MA *Oxf.*, BPhilol *Iceland*, PhD *N.U.I.*   Reader; Icelandic Studies

Meredith, Peter, MA *Oxf.*   Prof., Mediaeval Drama

Richards, David, MA *Camb.*, MA *Lond.*, PhD *Camb.*   Sr. Lectr.

Stead, Alistair J., BA *Oxf.*, BLitt *Oxf.*   Sr. Lectr.

Todd, Loreto, MA *Belf.*, MA *Leeds*, PhD *Leeds*   Reader, International English (on leave)

Wales, Katie, BA *Lond.*   Prof., Modern English Language

Wawn, Andrew, BA *Birm.*, PhD *Birm.*   Reader, English and Icelandic Studies

Whale, John C., BA *Leeds*, PhD *Leeds*   Sr. Lectr.

Other Staff: 13 Lectrs.; 2 Res. Fellows; 2 Hon. Readers; 1 Hon. Lectr.

Fine Art

Tel: (0113) 233 5260 Fax: (0113) 245 1977

Atkinson, Terence H.   Reader

Hay, Kenneth G., BA *Leeds*, MA *Wales*, PhD *Wales*   Head*

Orton, Lionel F., MA *Lond.*   Reader, Art History and Theory

Pollock, Griselda F. S., BA *Oxf.*, MA *Lond.*, PhD *Lond.*   Prof., Social and Critical Histories of Art

Rifkin, Adrian D., MA *Oxf.*   Prof.; Head*

Siegfried, Susan L., BA *Wellesley*, MA *Harv.*, MA *Oxf.*, PhD *Harv.*   Prof., Art History

Other Staff: 7 Lectrs.; 2 Res. Fellows; 1 Hon. Lectr.

Food Science, Procter Department of

Tel: (0113) 233 2958 Fax: (0113) 233 2982

Davenport, Robert R., MSc *Brist.*, PhD *Brist.*   External Prof.

Dickinson, Eric, BSc *Sheff.*, PhD *Sheff.*, DSc   Prof., Food Colloids

Georgala, Douglas L., CBE, BSc *Stell.*, PhD *Aberd.*   External Prof.

Gilbert, John, MSc *Leeds*, PhD *Leeds*   Visiting Prof.

Gould, Grahame W., BSc *Brist.*, PhD *Aberd.*   External Prof.

Gramshaw, John W., BSc *Nott.*, PhD *Nott.*   Sr. Lectr.

Horne, David, PhD *Edin.*, BSc   Visiting Prof.

Moseley, Bevan E. B., BSc *Brist.*, PhD *Lond.*, PhD *Camb.*   External Prof.

Robinson, David S., BSc *Manc.*, PhD *Manc.*   Prof.

Wedzicha, Bronislaw L., BSc *Lond.*, PhD *Lond.*   Prof.; Head*

Other Staff: 5 Lectrs.; 6 Res. Fellows; 5 Hon. Lectrs.

French Language and Literature

Tel: (0113) 233 3479 Fax: (0113) 233 3477

Atack, Margaret K., BA *Lond.*, PhD *Lond.*   Prof. (on leave)

Coward, David A., BA *Lond.*, PhD *Lond.*   Prof., Modern French Literature; Head*

Dolamore, C. E. J., BA *Wales*   Sr. Lectr.

Hintze, Marie-Anne M. J., LèsL *Lille*   Sr. Lectr.

Killick, Rachel, BA *Oxf.*, PhD *Leeds*   Sr. Lectr.

Looseley, David L., BA *Exe.*, PhD *Exe.*   Sr. Lectr.

Roe, David, MA *Oxf.*, DPhil *Oxf.*   Sr. Lectr.

Rothwell, Andrew J., MA *Oxf.*, DPhil *Oxf.*   Sr. Lectr.

Shaw, David C., MA *Exe.*   Sr. Lectr.

Silverman, Maxim, BA *E.Anglia*, PhD *Kent*   Sr. Lectr.

Todd, F. Christopher C., BA *Lond.*, PhD *Lond.*   Reader, 18th Century French Literature

Other Staff: 8 Lectrs.

Vacant Posts: 1 Prof. (French Lang. and Romance Philol.)

Fuel and Energy

Tel: (0113) 233 2498 Fax: (0113) 244 0572

Andrews, Gordon E., BSc *Leeds*, PhD *Leeds*   Prof., Combustion Engineering

Clarke, Andrew G., MA *Oxf.*, DPhil *Oxf.*, FRSChem   Sr. Lectr.

Gibbs, Bernard M., BScTech *Sheff.*, PhD *Sheff.*   Sr. Lectr.

Hampartsoumian, Edward, BSc *Leeds*, PhD *Leeds*   Sr. Lectr.

McIntosh, Andrew C., BSc *Wales*, PhD *CNAA*   Reader, Combustion Theory

Pourkashanian, Mohamed, MSc *Leeds*, PhD *Leeds*   Reader, High Temperature Combustion Processes

Williams, Alan, CBE, BSc *Leeds*, PhD *Leeds*, FRSChem   Livesey Prof., Fuel and Combustion Science; Head*

Williams, Paul T., BSc *Lond.*, MSc *Leeds*, PhD *Leeds*, FGS   Reader, Environmental Engineering

Other Staff: 5 Lectrs.; 1 Sr. Res. Fellow; 10 Res. Fellows; 5 Hon. Lectrs.

Geography, School of

Tel: (0113) 233 3300 Fax: (0113) 233 3308

Ashworth, Philip, BSc *Wales*, PhD *Stir.*   Sr. Lectr.

Atkinson, Kenneth, BA *Durh.*, MSc *Aberd.*, PhD *Durh.*   Sr. Lectr.

Clarke, Graham P., BA *Wales*, PhD *Leeds*   Sr. Lectr.

Clarke, Martin C., BA *Leeds*, PhD *Leeds*   Prof., Geographic Modelling

Grainger, Alan, BSc *Birm.*, MSc *CNAA*, MPhil *CNAA*, DPhil *Oxf.*   Sr. Lectr.

Kirkby, Michael J., MA *Camb.*, PhD *Camb.*   Prof., Physical Geography

Kneale, Pauline E., BSc *Lond.*, PhD *Brist.*   Sr. Lectr.

Leigh, Christine M., BA *Leeds*, PhD *Leeds*   Prof., Virtual Working Environments

Macklin, Mark G., BSc *Wales*, PhD *Wales*   Reader, Fluvial Environmental Change

McDonald, Adrian T., BSc *Edin.*, PhD *Edin.*   Yorkshire Water Prof., Environmental Management

Openshaw, Stanley, BA *Newcastle(UK)*, PhD *Newcastle(UK)*   Prof., Human Geography

Phillips, Deborah A., BA *Lond.*, MA *Br.Col.*, PhD *Camb.*   Sr. Lectr.

Preston, David A., BA *Sheff.*, MSc *Ill.*, PhD *Lond.*   Sr. Lectr.

Rees, Philip H., MA *Camb.*, MA *Chic.*, PhD *Chic.*   Prof., Population Geography

Stillwell, John C. H., BA *Leeds*, PhD *Leeds*   Sr. Lectr.; Chairman*

Wilson, Alan G., MA *Camb.*, FBA   Prof., Urban and Regional Geography

Other Staff: 14 Lectrs.; 1 Sr. Res. Fellow; 6 Res. Fellows; 1 Lectr.†

Geology, see Earth Scis., Sch. of

German Language and Literature

Tel: (0113) 233 3508 Fax: (0113) 233 3508

Beddow, Michael, MA *Camb.*, PhD *Camb.*   Prof.

Byrn, Richard F. M., MA *Trinity(Dub.)*, PhD *Leeds*   Sr. Lectr.

Chambers, Helen E., MA *Glas.*, PhD *Glas.*   Sr. Lectr.

Donald, Sydney G., MA *St And.*, PhD *St And.*   Sr. Lectr.; Head*

Grave, Christian, DPhil *Berl.*   Visiting Prof.

Tailby, John E., MA *St And.*, BPhil *St And.*   Sr. Lectr.

Other Staff: 2 Lectrs.; 1 Res. Fellow

Health, Nuffield Institute for, see Medicine

History and Philosophy of Science, see under Philos.

History, School of

Tel: (0113) 233 3586 *Fax:* (0113) 234 2759

Ancient History

2 Lectrs.

Medieval History

Childs, Wendy R., MA *Camb.*, PhD *Camb.*   Reader

Loud, Graham A., MA *Oxf.*, DPhil *Oxf.*   Sr. Lectr.

Palliser, David M., MA *Oxf.*, DPhil *Oxf.*   Prof.

Wood, Ian M., MA *Oxf.*, DPhil *Oxf.*   Prof., Early Medieval History

Modern History

Black, Robert D., BA *Chic.*, PhD *Lond.*   Reader, Renaissance History

Bridge, F. Roy, BA *Lond.*, PhD *Lond.*   Prof., Diplomatic History

Cecil, Hugh P., MA *Oxf.*, DPhil *Oxf.*   Sr. Lectr.

Challis, Christopher E., BA *Brist.*, PhD *Brist.*, FSA   Reader

Childs, John C. R., BA *Hull*, PhD *Lond.*   Prof., Military History

Gooch, John, BA *Lond.*, PhD *Lond.*   Prof., International History

Green, Simon J. D., MA *Oxf.*, DPhil *Oxf.*   Sr. Lectr.

Morison, John D., MA *Oxf.*   Sr. Lectr.; Chairman*

Parker, David, BA *Liv.*, PhD *Liv.*   Sr. Lectr.

Spiers, Edward M., MA *Edin.*, PhD *Edin.*   Prof., Strategic Studies

Tinios, P. Ellis, BA *Harv.*, MPhil *Leeds*, PhD *Mich.*   Sr. Lectr.

Whiting, Richard C., MA *Oxf.*, DPhil *Oxf.*   Sr. Lectr.

Wilson, Keith M., BA *Oxf.*, DPhil *Oxf.*   Reader, International History

Wright, Anthony D., MA *Oxf.*, DPhil *Oxf.*   Sr. Lectr.

Other Staff: 4 Lectrs.; 1 Hon. Lectr.

Icelandic Studies, see Engl., Sch. of

Information Systems, see under Computer Studies

Italian

Tel: (0113) 233 3630

Andrews, Richard A., MA *Oxf.*   Prof.

Bullock, Alan O., MA *Oxf.*, PhD *Leeds*   Reader, Italian Literature

Richardson, Profesor Brian F., MA *Oxf.*, MPhil *Lond.*   Prof.; Head*

Other Staff: 2 Lectrs.

Law

Tel: (0113) 233 5033 *Fax:* (0113) 233 5056

Ackers, H. Louise, BSc *Lond.*, MA *Lond.*, PhD *Lond.*   Sr. Lectr.

Bell, John S., MA *Camb.*, DPhil *Oxf.*   Prof., Public and Comparative Law

Cardwell, Michael N., MA *Oxf.*   Sr. Lectr.

Crawford, T. Adam, BA *Warw.*, MPhil *Camb.*   Sr. Lectr.

McGee, Andrew, BA *Oxf.*, BLL   Prof., Business Law

McMullen, John, MA *Camb.*, PhD *Camb.*   Prof.†, Labour Law

Rogers, W. V. Horton, MA *Camb.*   Prof., English Law

Seago, Peter J., JP, LLM *Nott.*   Sr. Lectr.

Shaw, Josephine, MA *Camb.*, MPhil *Brist.*   Prof., European Law

Walker, Clive P., LLB *Leeds*, PhD *Manc.*   Prof., Criminal Justice

Wheeler, Sally, BA *Oxf.*, DPhil *Oxf.*   Prof., Law, Business and Society

Other Staff: 18 Lectrs.

Leeds University Business School

Tel: (0113) 233 4466 *Fax:* (0113) 233 4465

Allinson, Christopher W., BSc *Brad.*, MA *Leeds*, PhD *Brad.*   Sr. Lectr.

Bowers, John K., BA *Oxf.*   Reader, Applied Economics

Buckley, Peter J., BA *York(UK)*, MA *E.Anglia*, PhD *Lanc.*   Prof., International Business

Burgess, Thomas F., MBA *Brad.*, PhD *Leeds*   Sr. Lectr.

Casson, Mark C., BA *Brist.*   Visiting Prof., International Business

Chartres, John A., MA *Oxf.*, DPhil *Oxf.*   Prof., Business and Economic Studies

Clegg, L. Jeremy, BA *Nott.*, PhD *Reading*   Sr. Lectr.

Collins, Michael, BSc(Econ) *Lond.*, PhD *Lond.*   Prof., Financial History

Fowkes, Anthony S., BA *Leeds*, PhD *Leeds*   Sr. Lectr.

Gerrard, William, MA *Aberd.*, MPhil *Camb.*, DPhil *York(UK)*   Reader, Economics

Glaister, Keith W., BA *Leic.*, MA *Lanc.*, MBA *Brad.*, PhD *Brad.*   Sr. Lectr.

Green, Francis, BA *Oxf.*, MSc *Lond.*, PhD *Lond.*   Prof., Economics

Hayes, John, BSc(Econ) *Hull*, PhD *Leeds*   Prof., Management Studies

Hodgkinson, Gerard P., BA *Wolv.*, MSc *Hull*, PhD *Sheff.*   Sr. Lectr.

Honeyman, Katrina, BA *York(UK)*, PhD *Nott.*   Sr. Lectr.

Jones, Anthony J., MCom *Birm.*   Dir., Undergrad. Studies

Keasey, Kevin, BA *Durh.*, MA *Newcastle(UK)*, PhD *Newcastle(UK)*   Leeds Permanent Building Soc. Prof., Financial Services

Lewis, Paul, MA *Liv.*, PhD *Leeds*   Sr. Lectr.

Lynch, J. E., MA *Oxf.*, MSc *Brad.*, PhD *Brad.*   Yorkshire Bank Prof., Marketing and Strategic Management

Mackie, Peter J., BA *Nott.*   Prof., Transport Studies

Maule, A. John, BA *Durh.*, PhD *Dund.*   Sr. Lectr.

Moizer, Peter, MA *Oxf.*, MA(Econ) *Manc.*, PhD *Manc.*, FCA   Prof., Accounting

Moon, P., BA *Oxf.*, PhD *Warw.*   Sr. Lectr.

Mucchielli, Jean-Louis, MA *Paris*, PhD *Paris*   Visiting Prof.

Nash, Christopher A., BA *Reading*, PhD *Leeds*   Prof., Transport Economics

Nolan, Peter, BA *E.Anglia*, MSc *Lond.*   Montague Burton Prof., Industrial Relations

O'Donnell, Kathleen, BA *E.Anglia*, MSc(Econ) *Lond.*, PhD *Lond.*   Sr. Lectr.

Oakland, John S., PhD *Salf.*   Visiting Prof.

Ogden, Stuart G., BA *Oxf.*, MA *Warw.*   Prof., Accounting and Organisational Analysis

Pearman, Alan D., BSocSc *Birm.*, MA *Leeds*, PhD *Leeds*   Prof., Management Decision Analysis

Sawyer, Malcolm C., BA *Oxf.*, MSc(Econ) *Lond.*   Prof., Economics

Thwaites, Desmond, BSc *CNAA*, MBA *Brad.*, PhD *Brad.*   Sr. Lectr.

Tolliday, Stephen W., BA *Camb.*, PhD *Camb.*   Prof., Economic History

Tsakalotos, Euclid, MA *Oxf.*, MPhil *Sus.*, DPhil *Oxf.*   Visiting Prof.

Turnbull, P. J., BA *Leeds*, MA *Warw.*   Reader, Industrial Relations

Watson, Robert, BA *Hull*, PhD *Manc.*   Prof., Finance and Accounting

Wilson, John F., BA *Manc.*, PhD *Manc.*   Sr. Lectr.

Woolmer, Kenneth J., BA *Leeds*   Acting Chairman*

Michell, Paul C. N., BSc(Econ) *Lond.*, PhD *Brun.*   Prof., Marketing and Media

Marginson, Paul, BA *Camb.*, MA *Warw.*, PhD *Warw.*   Prof., Human Resource Management and Employment Relations

Other Staff: 35 Lectrs.; 6 Res. Fellows; 11 Hon. Lectrs.

Linguistics and Phonetics

Tel: (0113) 233 3563 *Fax:* (0113) 233 3566

Fox, Anthony T. C., MA *Edin.*, PhD *Edin.*   Sr. Lectr.; Head*

Other Staff: 4 Lectrs.

Vacant Posts: 1 Prof. (Linguistics)

Management, see Leeds Univ. Business Sch.

Materials

Tel: (0113) 233 2348 *Fax:* (0113) 242 2531

Ceramics

Jha, Animesh, PhD *Lond.*   Reader, Materials Processing

Milne, Steven J., BSc *Aberd.*, PhD *Aberd.*   Sr. Lectr.

Rand, Brian, MSc *Durh.*, PhD *Newcastle(UK)*, FIM   Prof.; Head*

Riley, Frank L., BSc *Leeds*, PhD *Leeds*, FIM   Prof., Ceramic Processing

Other Staff: 10 Res. Fellows

Metallurgy

Cochrane, Robert C., BSc *Birm.*, PhD *Birm.*   British Steel Prof.

Edmonds, David V., BSc *Birm.*, MA *Camb.*, MA *Oxf.*, PhD *Birm.*, FIM   Prof.; Head of Div.*

Gee, Robert, MSc *Manc.*, PhD *Manc.*   Sr. Lectr.

Hammond, Christopher, MA *Camb.*, PhD *Leeds*   Sr. Lectr.

Other Staff: 2 Lectrs.; 5 Res. Fellows

Mathematical Studies, Applied

Tel: (0113) 233 5110 *Fax:* (0113) 242 9925

Barnett, Stephen, MSc *Manc.*, PhD *Lough.*, DSc *Manc.*, FIMA   Visiting Prof.

Bloor, Malcolm I. G., BSc *Manc.*, PhD *Manc.*   Reader, Applied Mathematics

Brindley, John, BSc *Lond.*, PhD *Lond.*   Prof., Applied Mathematics

Cole, Eric A. B., BSc *Wales*, PhD *Wales*   Sr. Lectr.

Elliott, Lionel, BSc *Manc.*, PhD *Manc.*   Sr. Lectr.

Falle, Samuel A. E. G., BA *Camb.*, MSc *Sus.*, DPhil *Sus.*   Prof., Astrophysical Fluid Dynamics; Head*

Fordy, Alan P., MSc *Lond.*, PhD *Lond.*   Prof., Nonlinear Mathematics

Heggs, Peter J., BSc *Leeds*, PhD *Leeds*   Visiting Prof.

Hill, Nicholas A., MSc *Lond.*, PhD *Lond.*   Sr. Lectr.

Hughes, David W., MA *Oxf.*, PhD *Camb.*   Prof., Applied Mathematics

Ingham, Derek B., PhD *Leeds*, DSc *Leeds*, FIMA   Prof., Applied Mathematics

Kelmanson, Mark A., BSc *Leeds*, PhD *Leeds*   Sr. Lectr.

Merkin, John H., MSc *Manc.*, PhD *Manc.*   Prof., Applied Mathematics

Nijhoff, Frank W., MSc *Ley.*, PhD *Ley.*   Reader, Applied Mathematics

Pedley, Timothy J., ScD *Camb.*, FIMA, FRS   Visiting Prof.

Rubio, Julio E., ED *Chile*, MS *Stan.*, PhD *Brooklyn*   Reader, Applied Mathematics

Sleeman, Brian D., BSc *Lond.*, PhD *Lond.*, DSc *Dund.*   Prof., Applied Mathematics

Wilson, Michael J., MA *Camb.*, PhD *Camb.*   Reader, Applied Mathematics

Other Staff: 8 Lectrs.; 1 Sr. Res. Fellow; 13 Res. Fellows; 1 Hon. Lectr.

Vacant Posts: 1 Prof. (Maths. for Appl. Sci.)

Mathematics, Pure

Tel: (0113) 233 5140 *Fax:* (0113) 233 5145

Allenby, Reginald B. J. T., MScTech *Manc.*, PhD *Wales*   Sr. Lectr.

Carter, Sheila, MSc *Liv.*, PhD *Liv.*   Sr. Lectr.

Cooper, S. Barry, BA *Oxf.*, PhD *Leic.*   Prof., Pure Mathematics

Crawley-Boevey, William W., BA *Camb.*, PhD *Camb.*   Reader, Algebra

Dales, H. Garth, MA *Camb.*, PhD
  Newcastle(UK) Prof.
Hart, Robert, MA *Edin.*, MSc *Sheff.*, DSc
  Leeds Sr. Lectr.
Lance, E. Christopher, MA *Camb.*, PhD
  Camb. Prof.; Head*
McConnell, John C., BSc *Belf.*, PhD *Leeds* Prof.
McPherson, H. Dugald, MA *Oxf.*, DPhil
  Oxf. Reader, Mathematical Logic
Partington, Jonathan R., MA *Camb.*, PhD
  Camb. Reader, Functional Analysis and
  Systems Theory
Robson, J. Christopher, BSc *Durh.*, PhD
  Leeds Prof.
Truss, John K., BA *Camb.*, PhD *Leeds* Reader,
  Group Theory and Combinatorics
Wainer, Stanley S., MSc *Leeds*, PhD *Leeds* Prof.;
  Head*
Wood, John C., BA *Oxf.*, MSc *Warw.*, PhD
  Warw. Reader, Differential Geometry
Other Staff: 2 Lectrs.; 1 Principal Teaching
  Fellow; 3 Res. Fellows

Medicine, see below

Metallurgy, see under Materials

Middle Eastern Studies, see Arabic and
Middle Eastern Studies

Mining and Mineral Engineering

Tel: (0113) 233 2787 Fax: (0113) 246 7310
Dowd, Peter A., BSc *NE*, MSc *Montr.*, PhD
  Leeds Prof., Mining Engineering; Head*
Dunn, Robert B., BEng *Sheff.*, FEng Visiting
  Prof.
Farmer, Ian, BSc *Nott.*, PhD *Sheff.*, DEng
  Sheff. Visiting Prof.
Farthing, Tom, OBE, MA *Camb.*, PhD *Camb.*,
  FIM, FIMechE Visiting Prof.
Fowell, Robert J., BSc *Leic.*, MEng *Sheff.*, PhD
  Newcastle(UK) Reader, Mining Engineering
Fray, Derek J., BSc(Eng) *Lond.*, MA *Camb.*, PhD
  Lond., FEng Visiting Prof.
Poole, Colin, BSc *Leeds*, PhD *Leeds* Sr. Lectr.
Rice, Neville M., MSc *Witw.*, PhD *Lond.* Sr.
  Lectr.
Wade, Lindsay, BSc *Wales*, MSc(Eng) *Witw.*,
  PhD *Witw.* Sr. Lectr.
Walton, Geoffrey, BSc *Brist.*, PhD
  Nott. Visiting Prof.
Other Staff: 4 Lectrs.; 2 Res. Fellows; 3 Hon.
  Lectrs.

Music

Tel: (0113) 233 2583 Fax: (0113) 233 2586
Barber, Graham D., BA *E.Anglia*, MMus *E.Anglia*,
  FRCO Sr. Lectr.; Head*
Cooper, David G., BA *Leeds*, DPhil *York(UK)* Sr.
  Lectr.
Rastall, G. Richard, MA *Camb.*, MusB *Camb.*,
  PhD *Manc.* Reader
Rushton, Julian G., MusB *Camb.*, MA *Camb.*,
  DPhil *Oxf.* West Riding Prof.
Wilby, Philip, BA *Oxf.*, BMus *Oxf.* Sr. Lectr.
Other Staff: 1 Lectr.; 1 Res. Fellow

Philosophy

Tel: (0113) 233 3260 Fax: (0113) 233 3265
Cantor, Geoffrey N., BSc *Lond.*, PhD
  Lond. Prof., History of Science
Christie, John R., MA *Edin.* Sr. Lectr.
French, Stephen D., BSc *Newcastle(UK)*, PhD
  Lond. Sr. Lectr.
Hodge, M. Jonathan, BA *Camb.*, MS *Wis.*, PhD
  Harv. Sr. Lectr.
Holdcroft, David, MA *Camb.* Prof.
Jackson, Jennifer C., MA *Qu.* Sr. Lectr.
Le Poidevin, Robin D., MA *Oxf.*, PhD
  Camb. Sr. Lectr.
Lewis, Harry A., MA *Oxf.*, PhD *Stan.* Sr. Lectr.
Megone, Christopher B., BA *Oxf.*, DPhil
  Oxf. Sr. Lectr.
Millican, Peter J. R., MA *Oxf.*, BPhil *Oxf.*, PhD
  Leeds Sr. Lectr.
Parry, S. James, BA *Wales*, MEd *Manc.*, MA
  Leeds Sr. Lectr.; Head*
Ross, George MacD., MA *Camb.* Sr. Lectr.

Simons, Peter M., BSc *Manc.*, MA *Manc.*, PhD
  Manc. Prof.
Other Staff: 9 Lectrs.; 1 Res. Fellow; 5 Hon.
  Lectrs.

History and Philosophy of Science Division

Tel: (0113) 233 3262
Cantor, G. N., BSc *Lond.*, PhD *Lond.* Prof. (on
  leave)
Christie, J. R. R., MA *Edin.* Sr. Lectr.
French, S. R. D., BSc *Newcastle(UK)*, PhD
  Lond. Lectr.; Chairman of Div.*
Hodge, M. J. S., BA *Camb.*, MS *Wis.*, PhD
  Harv. Sr. Lectr.
Other Staff: 2 Lectrs.; 1 Wellcome Res. Lectr.;
  1 Hon. Lectr.†; 2 Hon. Lectrs.

Phonetics, see Linguistics and Phonetics

Physics and Astronomy

Tel: (0113) 233 3860 Fax: (0113) 233 3900
Batchelder, D. N., BA *Williams(Mass.)*, MSc *Ill.*,
  PhD *Ill.* Prof.
Brereton, M. G., BSc *Liv.*, DPhil *Sus.* Reader,
  Theoretical Polymer Physics
Clarke, A. R., BSc *Lond.*, PhD *Lond.* Sr. Lectr.
Davies, G. R., BSc *Brist.*, PhD *Brist.* Prof.,
  Polymer Science
Duckett, R. A., MSc *Brist.*, PhD *Brist.* Sr. Lectr.
Dyson, John E., BSc *Lond.*, PhD *Manc.*, DSc
  Manc., FRAS Prof., Astronomy
Greig, D., BSc *St And.*, PhD *Aberd.* Prof.
Henderson, James R., BSc *Well.*, PhD *Well.* Sr.
  Lectr.
Hickey, B. J., BA *Leeds*, BSc *Leeds*, PhD *Leeds* Sr.
  Lectr.
Hillas, A. M., BSc *Leeds*, PhD *Leeds* Prof.
Howson, M. A., BSc *Leeds*, PhD *Leeds* Prof.,
  Condensed Matter Physics
Jakeways, R., BSc *Lond.*, PhD *Exe.* Sr. Lectr.
Klein, Philip G., MSc *Lanc.* Sr. Lectr. (on
  secondment)
Lawrie, Ian D., BA *Oxf.*, DPhil *Sus.* Sr. Lectr.
Lloyd-Evans, J., BSc *Leeds*, PhD *Leeds* Sr. Lectr.
McLeish, T. C. B., MA *Camb.*, PhD
  Camb. Prof., Polymer Physics
Morgan, G. J., BSc *Manc.*, MSc *St And.*, PhD
  Lond., FIP Cavendish Prof.
Pitt, G. David, BSc *Glas.*, MSc *Newcastle(UK)*, PhD
  Newcastle(UK), DSc *Glas.* Visiting Prof.
Savage, Michael D., BSc *Manc.*, PhD *Leeds* Prof.,
  Thin Liquid Films and Coatings
Ward, Ian M., MA *Oxf.*, DPhil *Oxf.*, FRS Res.
  Prof.§
Watson, Alan A., BSc *Edin.*, PhD *Edin.*,
  FRAS Prof.; Chairman*
Wiser, Nathan, BSc *Wayne State*, PhD
  Chic. Visiting Prof.
Other Staff: 7 Lectrs.; 17 Res. Fellows

Politics

Tel: (0113) 233 4382 Fax: (0113) 233 4400
Beetham, D., BA *Oxf.*, MA(Econ) *Manc.*, PhD
  Manc. Prof.†
Bell, D. S., MA *Aberd.*, MSc *S'ton.*, DPhil
  Oxf. Prof., French Government and Politics
Bromley, Simon J., BA *Camb.*, PhD *Camb.* Sr.
  Lectr.
Bush, R. C., BA *CNAA*, MA *Leeds*, PhD *Leeds*
  Lectr.; Head*
Cerny, Philip G., BA *Kenyon*, PhD *Manc.* Prof.,
  International Political Economy
Cliffe, L. R., BA *Nott.* Prof.
Fry, G. K., BSc(Econ) *Lond.*, PhD *Lond.* Prof.,
  British Government and Administration
Lord, C. J., MA *Oxf.*, PhD *Lond.* Sr. Lectr.
Nossiter, Tom, BA *Oxf.*, DPhil *Oxf.* Visiting
  Prof.
Ramsay, Maureen A., BA *Manc.*, PhD *Manc.* Sr.
  Lectr.
Schwartzmantel, John J., BA *Oxf.*, BPhil *Oxf.*,
  PhD *Leeds* Sr. Lectr.
Sergeyev, Viktor M. Visiting Prof.
Szeftel, M., BA *Cape Town*, MA *Zambia*, PhD
  Manc. Sr. Lectr.
Theakston, K., BSc(Econ) *Lond.*, PhD
  Lond. Reader, Government

Wilson, Irene B., MA *Edin.*, PhD
  Nijmegen Visiting Res. Prof.
Other Staff: 2 Lectrs.; 1 Sr. Res. Officer; 1 Res.
  Officer; 4 Lectrs.†; 3 Hon. Lectrs.

Portuguese, see Spanish and Portuguese

Psychology

Tel: (0113) 233 5724 Fax: (0113) 233 5749
Blundell, John E., BSc *Leeds*, PhD *Lond.*,
  FBPsS Prof., Psychobiology; Head*
Chapman, Anthony J., BSc *Leic.*, PhD *Leic.*,
  FBPsS Prof.
Child, Dennis, OBE, BSc *Lond.*, MEd *Leeds*, PhD
  Brad., FBPsS Visiting Prof.
Connor, Mark T., BSc *Lanc.*, PhD *Birm.* Sr.
  Lectr.
Davies, P., BSc *Brad.*, PhD *Aberd.* Sr. Lectr.
Feldman, M. Philip, BA *Manc.*, PhD *Lond.*,
  FBPsS Visiting Prof.
Fielding, Dorothy M., MSc *Leeds*, PhD
  Leeds Visiting Prof.
Hendrie, C. A., BA *CNAA*, PhD *Brad.* Sr. Lectr.
Hewison, Jenny, BA *Camb.*, MSc *Lond.*, PhD
  Lond. Sr. Lectr.
Holloway, Wendy, BA *Sheff.*, PhD
  Lond. Reader, Gender Relations
Howes, A. Mark, BSc *Aston* Sr. Lectr.
Roach, Peter J., MA *Oxf.*, PhD *Reading* Visiting
  Prof.
Rodgers, R. J., BSc *Belf.*, PhD *Belf.* DSc *Belf.*,
  FBPsS Prof., Behavioural Psychology
Sheehy, Noel P., MA *Trinity(Dub.)*, PhD *Wales*,
  FBPsS Visiting Prof.
Shimmin, Sylvia B., BSc *Lond.*, FBPsS Visiting
  Prof.
Stratton, P. M., BSc *Leic.*, BSc *Lond.*, PhD *Sheff.*,
  FBPsS Sr. Lectr.
Other Staff: 11 Lectrs.; 1 Principal Res. Fellow;
  3 Sr. Res. Fellows; 1 Res. Officer; 1 Lectr.†;
  6 Res. Fellows†; 2 Hon. Sr. Lectrs.†; 1 Hon.
  Lectr.

Religious Studies, see Theol. and Religious
Studies

Russian and Slavonic Studies

Tel: (0113) 233 3285 Fax: (0113) 233 3287
Collins, David N., BA *Leeds*, PhD *Leeds* Sr.
  Lectr.; Head*
Holman, M. J. de K., MA *Oxf.* Prof.
Other Staff: 2 Lectrs.; 1 Lectr.†

Science (Joint Honours)

Tel: (0113) 233 2691 Fax: (0113) 233 2689
Hatton, C. J., BSc *Leeds*, PhD *Leeds* Dir.*

Slavonic Studies, see Russian and Slavonic
Studies

Social Policy and Sociology

Tel: (0113) 233 4418 Fax: (0113) 233 4415
Bagguley, Paul, BA *E.Anglia*, MA *Sus.*, DPhil
  Sus. Sr. Lectr.
Barnes, Colin, BA *Leeds*, PhD *Leeds* Sr. Lectr.
Baylies, Carolyn L., BA *Calif.*, MS *Wis.*, PhD
  Wis. Sr. Lectr.
Deacon, Alan J., BSc(Soc) *Lond.*, PhD
  Lond. Prof., Social Policy
Foster-Carter, A. G., BA *Oxf.* Sr. Lectr.
Harding, Lorraine M., BA *Sheff.*, MA *Brun.* Sr.
  Lectr.; Head*
Harrison, M. L., MA *Camb.*, PhD *Camb.* Sr.
  Lectr.
Law, Ian G., BA *Liv.*, PhD *Liv.* Sr. Lectr.
Mann, Kirk, BA *Leeds*, PhD *Leeds* Sr. Lectr.
Mason, Jennifer, BSc *S'ton.*, PhD *Kent* Sr. Lectr.
Mercer, G., BA *Durh.*, MA *S.Fraser*, PhD
  Strath. Sr. Lectr.
Pawson, R. D., BA *Essex*, PhD *Lanc.* Sr. Lectr.
Smart, Carol C., BSc(Soc) *Lond.*, MA *Sheff.*, PhD
  Sheff. Prof., Sociology
Walby, Sylvia, BA *Reading*, MA *Essex*, PhD
  Essex Prof., Sociology
Williams, Fiona, BSc *Lond.*, PhD
  Open(UK) Prof., Social Policy
Other Staff: 3 Lectrs.; 2 Res. Fellows; 1 Lectr.†;
  4 Res. Fellows†

Spanish and Portuguese

Tel: (0113) 233 3516

Corkill, David, BA York(UK), MA Liv., PhD
Essex   Sr. Lectr.
Drinkwater, Judith, MA Camb.   Head*
Macklin, J. J., BA Belf., PhD Belf.   Cowdray
Prof., Spanish
Other Staff: 7 Lectrs.; 1 Sr. Lectr.†; 1 Lectr.†

Statistics

Tel: (0113) 233 5101 Fax: (0113) 233 5102

Kent, J. T., BA Harv., PhD Camb.   Prof.
Mardia, K. V., MSc Bom., MSc Poona, PhD Raj.,
PhD Newcastle(UK), DSc Newcastle(UK)   Prof.,
Applied Statistics; Head*
Redfern, E. J., BSc St And., MSc Sheff.   Sr. Lectr.
Taylor, C. C., MSc Lond., PhD Lond.   Sr. Lectr.
Other Staff: 5 Lectrs.

Textile Industries

Tel: (0113) 233 3700 Fax: (0113) 233 3704

Brunnschweiler, David, OBE, MScEng,
FTI   Visiting Prof.
Dobb, M. G., BSc Leeds, PhD Leeds   Sr. Lectr.
East, G. C., BSc Liv., PhD Liv.   Sr. Lectr.
Hann, M. A., BA Leeds, MPhil Leeds, PhD Leeds,
FTI   Reader, International Design
Harlock, S. C., BSc Leeds, PhD Leeds   Sr. Lectr.
Jackson, K. C., BA Leeds, MSc Brad., FTI   Sr.
Lectr.
Johnson, D. J., MSc Leeds, PhD Leeds, FIP   Prof.,
Fibre Science
Kilduff, Peter D. F., BA Leeds, PhD Leeds   Sr.
Lectr.
Lawrence, C. A., BSc CNAA, PhD Brad.   Prof.,
Textile Engineering; Head*
Mukhopadhyay, Samir K., MTech Delhi, PhD
UMIST   Sr. Lectr.
Thomson, G. M.   Sr. Lectr.
Tomka, J. G., CSc Czech Acad.Sc., FTI   Sr. Lectr.
Other Staff: 4 Lectrs.; 5 Res. Fellows; 1 Sr.
Lectr.†; 1 Lectr.†

Theology and Religious Studies

Tel: (0113) 233 3644 Fax: (0113) 233 3654

Elliott, J. K., BA Wales, DPhil Oxf., DD
Wales   Prof., New Testament Textual
Criticism
Hastings, Adrian, MA Oxf., ThD Rome, DD
Edin.   Emer. Res. Prof.§
Knott, Kim, MA Leeds, PhD Leeds   Sr. Lectr.;
Head*
McFayden, A. I., BA Birm., PhD Birm.   Sr.
Lectr.
Robinson, Neal, MA Oxf., PhD Birm.   Sr. Lectr.
Willmer, H., MA Camb., PhD Camb.   Prof.
Other Staff: 4 Lectrs.; 5 Lectrs.†; 3 Hon.
Lectrs.†

Transport Studies, Institute for, see also
Leeds Univ. Business Sch.; and Engin., Civil

Tel: (0113) 233 5326 Fax: (0113) 233 5334

Bonsall, P. W., BA Oxf.   Prof., Transport
Planning
Daly, Andrew, BA Oxf., PhD Birm.   Visiting
Prof.
Fowkes, A. S., BA Leeds, PhD Leeds   Sr. Lectr.
Mackie, Profesor P. J., BA Nott.   Prof.; Dir.*
May, Anthony D., MA Camb.   Prof., Transport
Engineering
Nash, C. A., BA Reading, PhD Leeds   Prof.,
Transport Economics
Tight, M. R., BSc Liv., PhD Lond.   Sr. Lectr.
Van Vliet, D., BSc McG., PhD Camb.   Sr. Lectr.
Other Staff: 1 Lectr.; 1 Sr. Lectr.†; 2 Lectrs.†; 3
Principal Res. Fellows†; 7 Sr. Res. Fellows†;
10 Res. Fellows†

Zoology, see Biol.

DENTISTRY

Child Dental Health

Tel: (0113) 233 6137 Fax: (0113) 233 6165

Cook, P. A., BChD Leeds, MDSc Leeds,
FDSRCPSGlas   Sr. Clin. Lectr.,
Orthodontistry; Head*

Curzon, M. E. J., BDS Lond., MSc Roch., PhD
Lond., FDSRCS, FRCDCan   Prof., Children's
and Preventative Dentistry
Williams, Sonia A., BDS Lond., MDSc Leeds, PhD
Lond.   Sr. Lectr.
Other Staff: 3 Lectrs.

Dental Surgery

Tel: (0113) 233 6121 Fax: (0113) 233 6165

Corrigan, A. M., BDS Lond., BM S'ton.,
FDSRCPSGlas, FRCSEd   Clin. Lectr., Oral
Surgery; Head*
Goldberg, Jerold S., BS Cleveland, DDS
Cleveland   Visiting Prof.
Hume, W. J., BDS Edin., PhD Manc.,
FDSRCPSGlas, FDSRCPSGlas, FRCPath   Prof.,
Oral Pathology; Dean, Dent. Sch.; Dir. of
Leeds Dent. Inst.
Main, D. M. G., BDS St And., PhD Lond.   Sr.
Lectr., Oral Medicine
Other Staff: 3 Lectrs.

Oral Biology

Tel: (0113) 233 6159 Fax: (0113) 233 6165

Devine, Deirdre, BSc Reading, PhD Lond.   Sr.
Lectr.
Kirkham, Jennifer, BSc CNAA, PhD Leeds   Sr.
Lectr.
Marsh, Philip D., BSc Sheff., PhD Lond.   Prof.†,
Oral Microbiology
Robinson, C., BSc Leeds, PhD Leeds   Prof.;
Head*
Shore, Roger C., BSc Leeds, MPhil CNAA, PhD
Brist.   Sr. Lectr.
Other Staff: 2 Lectrs.

Restorative Dentistry

Tel: (0113) 233 6129 Fax: (0113) 233 6165

Basker, R. M., BDS Lond., DDS Birm.   Prof.,
Dental Prosthetics
Clerehugh, D. Valerie, BDS Manc., PhD
Manc.   Sr. Lectr.
Glyn-Jones, J. C., BDS Lond., PhD Birm.,
FDSRCS   Sr. Lectr.; Head*
Martin, D. M., BDS Edin., MDSc Leeds,
FDSRCSEd   Sr. Lectr.
Watson, C. J., BDS Wales, PhD Wales,
FDSRCS   Sr. Lectr.
Other Staff: 12 Lectrs.

MEDICINE

Behavioural Sciences, see Psychiat. and
Behavioural Scis., Div. of

Clinical Sciences, Division of

Barker, M. C. J., BSc Nott., PhD Leeds   Sr.
Lectr., Medical Physics; Chairman*
Boylston, A. W., BA Yale, MD Harv.,
FRCPath   Prof., Pathology
Bridges, L. R., BSc Lond., MB BS Lond.   Sr.
Lectr., Pathology
Burns, Philip A., BSc Edin., PhD Edin.   Sr.
Lectr., Pathology
Cowen, Arnold R., BSc Nott.   Sr. Lectr.,
Pathology
Dixon, M. F., MD Edin., FRCPath   Reader,
Gastrointestinal Pathology
Evans, J. A., BSc Leeds, MSc Aberd., PhD
Wales   Sr. Lectr., Medical Physics
Forman, David, BA Keele, PhD S'ton.   Prof.,
Cancer Epidemiology
Haward, Robert A., ChB Brist.   Prof., Cancer
Studies
Hay, A. W. M., BSc Lond., PhD Lond.   Reader,
Chemical Pathology and Immunology
Jones, R. G., MA Oxf., BM BCh Oxf., DM
Oxf.   Sr. Lectr., Chemical Pathology and
Immunology
Markham, A. F., MB BS Lond., PhD Birm., DSc
Birm.   West Riding Med. Res. Trust Prof.
Quirke, P., BM S'ton., PhD Leeds   Prof.,
Molecular Pathology
Schorah, C. J., BSc Sheff., PhD Lond.   Sr. Lectr.,
Chemical Pathology and Immunology
Smith, M. A., BSc Brist., MSc Aberd., PhD Edin.,
FIP   Prof., Medical Physics; Dir., Bone and
Body Composition Res. Group

Wells, M., BSc Manc., MD Manc.,
FRCPath   Prof., Gynaecology Pathology
Wild, Christopher P., BSc Manc., PhD
Manc.   Prof., Molecular Epidemiology
Other Staff: 7 Lectrs.

General Practice and Public Health
Medicine, Division of

Cartwright, R. A., MA Camb., MB BChir Camb.,
PhD Durh.   Leukaemia Res. Fund Prof.,
Cancer Epidemiology
Connelly, J. B., MB BS Newcastle(UK), MSc
Lond.   Sr. Lectr., Public Health Medicine
Franks, A. J., BSc Edin., MD Edin., FRCPath   Sr.
Lectr., Public Health Medicine
Harris, C. M., MEd Manc., MB ChB Liv.,
FRCGP   Prof., General Practice
Lubben-Dinkelaar, Marianne, BSc Ley., MD Ley.,
MPH Leeds   Sr. Lectr., Public Health
Medicine
Robinson, Michael, MA Camb., MSc Lond., MB
BS   Sr. Lectr., Public Health Medicine
Thistlethwaite, Jill, BSc Lond., MB BS Lond.   Sr.
Lectr., Community-based Teaching
Walley, J. D., MB BS Newcastle(UK), MSc
Liv.   Sr. Lectr., Public Health Medicine
Williams, D. R. R., BSc Lond., MB BS Lond., MA
Camb., PhD Durh.   Prof., Epidemiology and
Public Health; Chairman*
Other Staff: 5 Letcrs.; 2 Sr. Lectrs.†

Healthcare Studies, School of

Rye, David, BA Open(UK)   Visiting Prof.

Academic Pharmacy Practice, Division of

Tel: (0113) 243 2799 Fax: (0113) 243 6860
3 Lectrs.

Applied Health Sciences, Division of

Tel: (0113) 243 2799 Fax: (0113) 243 6095
5 Sr. Lectrs. (2 Healthcare, 3 Nursing); 23
Lectrs. (1 Healthcare, 22 Nursing); 3
Lectrs.† (Nursing)

Development of Nursing Practice and Policy,
Centre for

Tel: (0113) 242 2411 Fax: (0113) 242 2042

Hamer, Susan, BA Northumbria, MA
York(UK)   Centre Co-ordinator

Imaging, Division of

Tel: (0113) 243 8614
2 Sr. Lectrs. (1 Radiog., 1 Radiother.); 6
Lectrs. (Radiother.); 1 Sr. Lectr.†
(Ultrasound); 2 Lectrs.† (Ultrasound)

Midwifery, Division of

Tel: (0113) 233 6888 Fax: (0113) 244 9730

Renfrew, Mary J., BSc Edin., PhD Edin.   Prof.;
Head*
Other Staff: 1 Sr. Lectr.; 6 Lectrs.; 2 Lectrs.†

Nursing, Division of

Tel: (01943) 876151 Fax: (01943) 870676
6 Sr. Lectrs.; 35 Lectrs.; 11 Lectrs.†

Medicine, Division of

Alison, D. L., MB ChB Glas., MD Glas., MSc
Lond.   Robert Ogden-Macmillan Sr. Lectr.,
Oncology and Palliative Studies
Ball, S. B., MA Camb., MB BChir Camb., PhD
Leeds, FRCP   British Heart Foundation Prof.,
Cardiology
Balmforth, Anthony J., BSc Lanc., PhD Lanc.   Sr.
Lectr., Cardiovascular Studies
Banks, Rosamonde E., BSc St And., MSc Sur.,
PhD St And.   Sr. Lectr., Cancer Studies
Batten, T. F. C., BSc Sheff., PhD Sheff.   Sr.
Lectr., Cardiovascular Studies
Bird, H. A., MA Camb., MB BChir Camb., MD
Camb., FRCP   Prof., Pharmacological
Rheumatology
Brownjohn, A., MB BS Lond., FRCP   Sr. Lectr.,
Medicine
Bullimore, D. W. W., BSc Brist., MD Brist.   Sr.
Lectr., Medicine

Chamberlain, M. Anne, BSc Lond., MB BS Lond., FRCP   Charterhouse Prof., Rheumatological Rehabilitation

Davies, J. A., MD Aberd., FRCP   Prof., Clinical Education

Ellis, F. R., MB ChB Manc., PhD Leeds, FRCA   Prof., Anaesthesia

Emery, Paul, MB BChir Camb., MA Camb., MD Camb., FRCP   Arthritis and Rheumatism Council Prof., Rheumatology

Feely, M. P., MD N.U.I., FRCPI   Sr. Lectr., Clinical Pharmacology

Goldspink, D. F., PhD Newcastle(UK), DSc Newcastle(UK)   Prof., Cell Biology

Grant, P. J., MB ChB Brist., MD Brist.   Prof., Molecular Vascular Medicine

Hainsworth, R., MB ChB Leeds, PhD Leeds, DSc Leeds   Prof., Applied Physiology

Hall, Alistair S., MB ChB Leeds, PhD Leeds   Sr. Lectr., Cardiovascular Studies

Heatley, R. V., MD Wales, FRCP   Sr. Lectr., Medicine

Helliwell, Philip, MA Oxf., MB BCh Oxf., MD Oxf., PhD Leeds, FRCP   Sr. Lectr., Rheumatology

Hopkins, P. M., MB BS Lond., FRCA   Sr. Lectr., Anaesthesia

Howdle, Peter D., BSc Leeds, MD Leeds, FRCP   Prof., Clinical Education; Chairman*

Isaacs, John D., BSc Lond., MB BS Lond., PhD Lond.   Sr. Lectr., Rheumatology

Johnson, Peter W. M., MA Camb., MD Cam.   Imperial Cancer Res. Fund Sr. Lectr.

Mary, D. S. G., MB ChB Baghdad, PhD Leeds, FRCP   Sr. Lectr., Cardiovascular Studies

McWilliam, P. N., BSc Dund., PhD Glas.   Reader, Cardiovascular Studies

Miloszewski, K. J. A., BSc Leeds, MD Leeds, FRCP   Sr. Lectr., Medicine

Moayedi, Paul   Sr. Lectr., Medicine

Morrison, J. F. J., MD Leeds   Sr. Lectr., Clinical Pharmacology

Neuman, Vera, MD   Sr. Lectr., Rehabilitation

Perren, T. J., MB BS Lond., MD Lond.   Imperial Cancer Res. Fund Sr. Lectr., Cancer Studies

Prentice, C. R. M., BA Camb., MD Camb., FRCPGlas   Prof., Medicine

Seedhom, B. B., BSc Assiut, PhD Leeds   Reader, Bioengineering

Selby, P. J., MA Camb., MB BChir Camb., MD Camb., FRCP   Yorkshire Cancer Res. Campaign Prof., Cancer Medicine; Dir., ICRF Cancer Med. Res. Unit

Seymour, Matthew T., MA Camb., MD Lond.   ICRF Sr. Lectr., Cancer Studies

Tan, L.-B., BSc Sing., MB BChir Camb., DPhil Oxf.   Mautner/British Heart Foundation Sr. Lectr., Cardiovascular Studies

Trejdosiewicz, L. K., BSc Exe., PhD Birm.   Sr. Lectr., Immunology in Relation to Medicine

Vaughan, P. F. T., MA Oxf., DPhil Oxf.   Reader, Neurochemistry

Veale, Douglas, MB BCh Trinity(Dub.), MD Trinity(Dub.)   Sr. Lectr., Rheumatology

Vucevic, Michael, MB ChB Birm., FRCA   Sr. Lectr., Anaesthesia

Wales, J. K., MD Wales, FRCP   Sr. Lectr., Medicine

Weston, Clive F. M., MB BCh Wales   Sr. Lectr., Cardiovascular Studies

Other Staff: 9 Lectrs.

Microbiology

Tel: (0113) 233 5647 Fax: (0113) 233 5638

Adams, D. G., BSc Liv., PhD Liv.   Sr. Lectr.

Adams, David J., BSc Edin., PhD Aberd.   Sr. Lectr.

Chopra, Ian, MA Trinity(Dub.), PhD Brist., DSc Brist.   Prof.

Cove, J. H., BSc Lond., PhD CNAA   Sr. Lectr.

Evans, E. G. V., BSc Wales, PhD Glas., FIBiol, FRCPath   Prof., Medical Mycology

Halliburton, I. W., BSc Glas., PhD Glas.   Reader, Virology

Hawkey, P. M., BSc E. Anglia, MB BS Lond., MD Brist., FRCPath   Prof., Medical Microbiology

Heritage, J., BA York(UK), DPhil Sus.   Sr. Lectr.

Holland, K. T., BSc Leeds, PhD Leeds, FIBiol   Prof., Microbiology; Head*

Ingham, Eileen, BSc Leeds, PhD Leeds   Sr. Lectr.

Kerr, K. G., MB ChB Manc., BSc St And., MD Manc.   Sr. Lectr.

Killington, R. A., BSc Birm., PhD Birm.   Sr. Lectr.

Knapp, Jeremy S., BSc Hull, PhD Wales   Sr. Lectr.

Lacey, R. W., MA Camb., MD Camb., PhD Brist., FRCPath   Visiting Prof.

Rowlands, David J., BSc Lond., PhD S'ton.   Prof., Molecular Virology

Wilcox, Mark H., BM BS Nott., BMedSci Nott., MD Nott.   Sr. Lectr.

Other Staff: 2 Lectrs.; 3 Hon. Lectrs.

Nuffield Institute for Health

Tel: (0113) 233 6633 Fax: (0113) 246 0899

Alimo-Metcalfe, Beverly M., BEd Leeds, MSc Brad., MBA Brad., PhD Brad.   Prof., Leadership Studies§

Barker, Carol E., BSc Lond., PhD Lond.   Sr. Lectr.; Head, Internat. Div.§

Collins, C. D., BSc Lond., MSocSc Birm., PhD Birm.   Sr. Lectr.§

Connelly, James, MB BS Newcastle(UK), MSc Newcastle(UK)   Sr. Lectr.

Green, A. T., BA Oxf., MA Sus.   Sr. Lectr.§

Hunter, D. J., MA Edin., PhD Edin.   Prof., Health Policy and Management; Dir.*

Long, A., BA Leeds, MSc Sheff., MPhil Leeds   Sr. Lectr.§

Robinson, M., MA Camb., MSc Lond., MB BS   Sr. Lectr.

Ruck, Nicola F., BA Oxf., MSc Lond.   Sr. Lectr.§

Smith, Iain, MB Edin., BSc Edin., MPH, FRCP   Sr. Lectr.§

Walley, J., MB BS Newcastle(UK), MSc Liv.   Sr. Lectr.

Williams, D. R. R., MA Camb., PhD Durh., FRCP   Prof., Epidemiology and Public Health

Wistow, G., BA Hull, MSocSc Birm.   Prof., Health and Social Care

Other Staff: 10 Lectrs.†; 1 Hon. Reader; 15 Hon. Lectrs.

Obstetrics and Gynaecology, Division of

Bromham, D. I. R., BSc Lond., MB BS Lond., PhD Lond.   Sr. Lectr.

Cuckle, H., BA Leeds, MSc Oxf., DPhil Oxf.   Prof., Reproductive Epidemiology

Drife, J. O., MD Edin., FRCSEd, FRCOG   Prof.

Duffy, Sean R. G., MD Glas., FRCS   Sr. Lectr.

Gosden, Roger, BSc Brist., PhD Camb., DSc Edin., FIBiol   Prof., Reproductive Biology

Johnson, N., BM BS Nott., FRCS   Sr. Lectr.

Landon, Christine R., MB ChB Leeds, MD Leeds   Sr. Lectr.

Thornton, J. G., MD Leeds   Reader

Walker, James J., MD Glas., FRCP, FRCOG   Prof.; Chairman*

Other Staff: 5 Lectrs.; 1 Sr. Lectr.†

Paediatrics and Child Health, Division of

Brocklebank, J. T., MB BS Durh., FRCP   Reader, Paediatric Nephrology

Dear, P. R. F., MD Lond., FRCP   Sr. Lectr.

Levene, M. I., MD Lond., FRCP   Prof.; Chairman*

Meadow, Sir Roy, MA Oxf., BM BCh Oxf., FRCP   Prof.

Murdoch-Eaton, Deborah G., MB BS Lond.   Sr. Lectr.

Puntis, J. W. L., BM S'ton.   Sr. Lectr., Obstetrics and Gynaecology

Other Staff: 8 Lectrs.

Pharmacology

Tel: (0113) 233 4311 Fax: (0113) 233 4331

Bowmer, C. J., BSc Liv., PhD Liv.   Sr. Lectr.; Head*

Brown, David A., BSc Lond., PhD Lond., FRS   Visiting Prof.

Gent, J. P., MA Camb., PhD Nott.   Sr. Lectr.

Hughes, I. E., BSc Leeds, PhD Leeds   Sr. Lectr.

Shepperson, Nicholas, BSc Leeds, PhD Lond.   Visiting Prof.

Triggle, D. J., BSc PhD   Visiting Prof.

Wray, D. A., BA Camb., MSc Lond., DPhil Oxf.   Prof.

Yates, M. S., BSc Liv., PhD Liv.   Sr. Lectr.

Other Staff: 5 Lectrs.

Physiology

Tel: (0113) 233 4225 Fax: (0113) 233 4228

Boyett, M. R., BSc E. Anglia, PhD Lond.   Prof.

Henderson, Zaineb, BSc Lond., PhD Camb.   Reader, Integrative Neuroscience

Holden, A. V., BA Oxf., PhD Alta.   Reader, General Physiology

Hunter, M., BSc Newcastle(UK), PhD Manc.   Reader, Epithelial Phyisiology

Karim, F., MB BS Dacca, MPhil Karachi, PhD Leeds   Reader, Cardiovascular Physiology

King, Anne E., BSc Aberd., PhD S'ton.   Sr. Lectr.

Morrison, J. F. B., MB ChB Edin., BSc Edin., PhD Edin., FRCSEd   Prof.

Orchard, C. H., BSc Lond., PhD Lond.   Prof.

Potts, D. J., BPharm Lond., PhD   Sr. Lectr.

Rayfield, Kathleen M., BSc Sheff., MBA Open(UK), PhD Sheff.   Sr. Lectr.; Head*

Whitaker, Elaine M., BSc Dund., MSc Leeds, PhD Leeds   Sr. Lectr.

Winlow, W., BSc Newcastle(UK), PhD St And.   Reader, Invertebrate Neuroscience

Withington, Deborah J., BSc Nott., PhD Birm.   Sr. Lectr.

Other Staff: 7 Lectrs.; 5 Hon. Lectrs.

Psychiatry and Behavioural Sciences, Division of

Aldridge, Jan, BA Wales, MSc Glas., PhD Wales   Sr. Lectr., Clinical Psychology

Butler, A. W. J., BA Brad., MA Wales, MA Leeds   Sr. Lectr., Mental Health Social Work

Cottrell, D. J., MA Oxf., MB BS Lond.   Prof., Child and Adolescent Psychiatry

Dabbs, A. R., BA Manc., FBPsS   Sr. Lectr., Clinical Psychology

Green, David R., BA Wales, MSc Leeds   Sr. Lectr., Clinical Psychlogy

Hill, A. J., BSc Leeds, PhD Leeds   Sr. Lectr., Behavioural Sciences

Lynch, S. P. J., MB ChB Manc.   Sr. Lectr., Psychiatry

Mindham, Richard H. S., MD Lond., FRCPEd, FRCPsych   Nuffield Prof., Psychiatry

Morley, S. J., BSc Lond., MPhil Lond., PhD Lond., FBPsS   Prof., Clinical Psychology

Owens, D. W., BSc Leeds, MD Leeds   Sr. Lectr., Psychiatry

Pieri, Lorenzo, BSc St And., MB ChB Manc.   Sr. Lectr., Medical Communication Skills

Shapiro, David A., BA Oxf., MSc Lond., PhD Lond., FBPsS   Prof., Clinical Psychology

Sims, A. C. P., MA Camb., MD Camb., FRCPsych, FRCPEd   Prof., Psychiatry

Snaith, R. P., MD Lond., FRCPsych   Sr. Lectr., Psychiatry

Worrall, Anne, MB ChB Leeds   Sr. Lectr., Child and Adolescent Psychiatry

Other Staff: 4 Lectrs.; 6 Sr. Lectrs.†; 2 Lectrs.†

Public Health Medicine, see Gen. Practice and Public Health Med., Div. of

Surgery, Division of

Dickson, R. A., MB ChB Edin., MA Oxf., ChM Edin., DSc Edin., FRCS, FRCSEd   Prof., Orthopaedic Surgery

Guillou, P. J., BSc Leeds, MD Leeds, FRCS   Prof.; Chairman*

Johnston, D., MD ChM Glas., FRCSEd, FRCSGlas, FRCS   Prof.

Limb, David, BSc Lond.   Sr. Lectr., Orthopaedic Surgery

Martin, Iain G., MB ChB Leeds, FRCS   Sr. Lectr.

McMahon, M. J., MB ChB Sheff., PhD Birm., ChM Sheff., FRCS   Prof.

Millner, P. A., BSc Leeds, MB ChB Leeds, FRCS   Sr. Lectr., Orthopaedic Surgery

Somers, Shaw S., BSc Leeds, MD Leeds, FRCS   Sr. Lectr.

Windsor, Alistair, MB BS Lond., FRCS, FRCSEd   Sr. Lectr.
Other Staff: 5 Lectrs. (2 Orthop. Surg.)

Other Appointments

Honorary Medical Staff (of Divisions)
Axon, Anthony T. R., MD Lond., FRCP   Hon. Prof., Gastroenterology
Bishop, D. Timothy, MSc Brist., PhD Sheff.   Hon. Prof., Pathology
Cunliffe, W. J., BSc Manc., MD Manc., FRCP   Hon. Prof., Dermatology
Davison, Alexander M., RD, BSc Edin., MD Edin., FRCP, FRCPEd   Hon. Prof., Renal Medicine
Kester, Ralph, MD Cape Town, FRCS   Hon. Prof., Vascular Surgery
Mueller, Robert F., MB BS Lond., BSc Lond.   Hon. Prof., Clinical Genetics
Mulley, G. P., MB ChB   Hon. Prof., Medicine of the Elderly
Whicher, John T., MB BChir Camb., MA Camb., MSc Lond.   Hon. Visiting Prof., Molecular Pathology
Other Staff: 1 Hon. Reader (Paed. Oncol.)

SPECIAL CENTRES, ETC

African Studies Unit
Tel: (0113) 233 5069
Bush, R., BA CNAA, MA Leeds, PhD Leeds   Dir.*

Archaeological Studies, Centre for
Tel: (0113) 233 3545
Macklin, Mark G., BSc Wales, PhD Wales   Dir.*

Architecture and the Decorative Arts, Centre for
Arnold, Dana, BA Lond., MSc Lond.   Dir.*

Bibliography and Textual Criticism, Institute of
Barnard, Prof. J., MA Oxf., BLitt Oxf.   Dir.*

Biomechanics and Medical Engineering, Centre for Studies in
Tel: (0113) 233 5146
Fisher, Prof. J., BSc Birm., PhD Glas.   Dir.*

Business and Professional Ethics, Centre for
Tel: (0113) 233 3280
Jackson, Jennifer C., MA Qu.   Dir.*

Business History, Centre for
Tel: (0113) 233 4474
Tolliday, Prof. S. W., BA Camb., PhD Camb.   Dir.*

Business Law and Practice, Centre for the Study of
Tel: (0113) 233 5039
McGee, Andrew, BA Oxf., BLL   Prof., Public and Comparative Law

Canadian Studies, Centre for
Tel: (0113) 233 4022
Todd, Roy, BA Leeds, PhD Brad.   Dir.*

Combustion and Energy Studies, Centre for
Tel: (0113) 233 2506
Pilling, Prof. Michael J., MA Camb., PhD Camb., FRSChem   Dir.*

Communications Studies, Institute of
Tel: (0113) 233 5800 Fax: (0113) 233 5808
Pronay, Prof. N., BA Wales, FRHistS   Dir.*

Computational Fluid Dynamics, Centre for
Tel: (0113) 233 5113
Ingham, Prof. D., BSc Leeds, PhD Leeds, DSc Leeds, FIMA   Dir.*

Computer Analysis of Language and Speech, Centre for
Tel: (0113) 233 5761
Atwell, E. S., BA Lanc.   Dir.*

Criminal Justice Studies, Centre for
Tel: (0113) 233 5022
Walker, Prof. C. P., PhD Manc., LLB   Dir.*

Cultural Studies, Centre for
Tel: (0113) 233 5267
Pollock, Prof. Griselda F. S., BA Oxf., MA Lond., PhD Lond.   Dir.*

Decision Research, Centre for
Tel: (0113) 233 2614
Pearman, Prof. Alan D., BSocSc Birm., MA Leeds, PhD Leeds   Dir.*

Democratization Studies, Centre for
Tel: (0113) 233 4481
Beetham, Prof. D., BA Oxf., MA(Econ) Manc., PhD Manc.   Dir.†*

Development Studies, Centre for
Tel: (0113) 233 4393 Fax: (0113) 233 6784
Baylies, Carolyn L., BA Calif., MS Wis., PhD Wis.   Dir.*

Education, Centre for Policy Studies in
Tel: (0113) 233 4656
Nolan, Peter J., BA E.Anglia, MSc Lond.   Dir.*

European Studies, Centre for
Tel: (0113) 233 4441 Fax: (0113) 233 6784
Lodge, Juliet, BA CNAA, MA Reading, MPhil Reading, PhD Hull, DLitt Reading   Dir.*

Family, Kinship and Childhood, Centre for Research on
Smart, Carol, BSc(Soc) Lond., MA Sheff., PhD Sheff.   Dir.*

Human Biology, Centre for
Tel: (0113) 233 4337 Fax: (0113) 233 4344
Soames, Roger W., BSc Lough., PhD Lough.   Sr. Lectr.; Dir.*

Industrial Policy and Performance, Centre for
Tel: (0113) 233 4481 Fax: (0113) 233 4400
Nolan, Prof. Peter J., BA E.Anglia, MSc Lond.   Dir.*

International Studies, Institute for
Tel: (0113) 233 6780 Fax: (0113) 233 6784
Kennedy-Pipe, Caroline, BA Wales, MScEcon Wales, DPhil Oxf.   Dir.*

Jewish Studies, Centre for
Tel: (0113) 233 5197 Fax: (0113) 245 1977
Frojmovic, Eva, BA Freib., MA Munich, PhD Munich   Dir.*

Law in Europe, Centre for the Study of
Tel: (0113) 233 5065
Shaw, Prof. Jo, MA Camb., MPhil Brist.   Dir.*

Leeds Environment Centre
Tel: (0113) 233 6461 Fax: (0113) 233 6716
Mobbs, Prof. Stephen, BSc Leeds, PhD Leeds   Dir.*

Manufacturing and Information Systems Engineering, Keyworth Institute of
Tel: (0113) 233 2147 Fax: (0113) 233 2162
de Pennington, Prof. A., OBE, MSc Manc., PhD Manc.   Dir.*

Medical Imaging Research, Centre for
Tel: (0113) 243 2799
Hogg, Prof. D. C., BSc Warw., MSc W.Ont., DPhil Sus.   Dir.*

Medieval Studies, Centre for
Tel: (0113) 233 3620
Hill, Prof. Joyce M., MA Lond., DPhil York(UK)   Dir.*

Military History, Centre for
Childs, Prof. John C. R., BA Hull, PhD Lond.   Dir.*

Molecular Recognition Centre
Tel: (0113) 233 3022
Phillips, Prof. S. E. V., BSc Lond., PhD Lond.   Dir.*

Nano-Device Modelling, Centre for
Cole, Eric A. B., BSc Wales, PhD Wales   Dir.*

Natural Gas Engineering, Centre for
Williams, Prof. Alan, CBE, BSc Leeds, PhD Leeds   Dir.*

Non-Linear Studies, Centre for
Tel: (0113) 233 5115
Fordy, Prof. Allan P., MSc Lond., PhD Lond.   Dir.*

Photobiology and Photodynamic Therapy, Centre for
Tel: (0113) 233 3166
Brown, Prof. Stanley B., BSc Durh., PhD Newcastle(UK)   Dir.*

Physical Education and Sports Science, Centre for Studies in
Tel: (0113) 233 5080 Fax: (0113) 233 5083
Lindsay, M. R., BSc(Eng) Oklahoma, MPhil Strath., PhD Strath.   Dir.*

Plant Biochemistry and Biotechnology, Centre for
Tel: (0113) 233 2863
Atkinson, Prof. H. J., BSc Newcastle(UK), PhD Newcastle(UK)   Dir.*

Policy Studies in Education, Centre for
Edwards, Prof. Anne, BA Wales, MEd Wales, PhD Wales   Dir.*

Polymer Science and Technology, Interdisciplinary Research Centre in
Universities of Leeds, Bradford (B), Durham (D)
Tel: (0113) 233 3810 Fax: (0113) 233 3846
Coates, P. D., BSc Lond., MSc Leeds, PhD Leeds, FIMechE   Prof., Polymer Engineering(B)
Davies, G. R., BSc Brist., PhD Brist.   Prof., Polymer Physics
Duckett, R. A., MSc Brist., PhD Brist.   Sr. Lectr.
Feast, Prof. W. J., BSc Sheff., PhD Birm., FRSChem   Dir.*(D)
Johnson, A. F., BSc Nott., PhD Nott.   Prof.
Klein, P. G., MSc Lanc., PhD Lanc.   Sr. Lectr.
Richards, R. W., BSc Salf., PhD Salf., FRSChem   Prof., Polymer Chemistry(D)

Psychological Therapies Research Centre
Tel: (0113) 233 1955 Fax: (0113) 233 1956
Barkham, Michael, BEd Sus., MA Camb., PhD Brighton   Sr. Lectr.
Shapiro, Prof. David A., BA Lond., MSc Lond., PhD Lond., FBPsS   Dir.*

Russian, Eurasian and Central European Studies, Leeds University Centre for
Holman, Prof. Michael J. de K., MA Oxf.   Dir.*

Science and Mathematics Education, Centre for Studies in

Tel: (0113) 233 4611

Jenkins, Prof. Edgar J. P., BSc Leeds, MEd Leeds   Dir.*

Self-Organising Molecular Systems, Centre for

Tel: (0113) 233 6453

Boden, Prof. N., BSc Liv., PhD Liv.   Dir.*

Skin Research, Centre for

Tel: (0113) 233 5647 Fax: (0113) 233 5638

Ingham, Eileen, BSc Leeds, PhD Leeds   Dir.*

Theoretical Computer Science, Centre for

Tel: (0113) 233 5447

Cohn, Prof. A. G., BSc Essex, PhD Essex   Dir.*

Tribology, Institute of

Tel: (0113) 233 2155

Taylor, Prof. Christopher M., BSc(Eng) Lond., MSc Leeds, PhD Leeds, DEng Leeds   Dir.*

University Computing Service

Tel: (0113) 233 5401 Fax: (0113) 233 5411

Carter, Ed J., BSc CNAA   Head, Network Services

Chidlow, S., BSc Sheff., PhD Sheff.   Head, Unix Support

Duke, A. J., BSc Leeds, PhD Leeds   Dir.*

Johnson, M. C., BSc Leic.   Head, PC Support

Nicholson, P., BSc Leeds, MSc Lond.   Head, Applications Software

Virtual Working Environments, Centre for

Leigh, Prof. Christine M., BA Leeds, PhD Leeds   Dir.*

CONTACT OFFICERS

Academic affairs. Pro-Vice-Chancellor (Teaching): Chapman, Prof. Anthony J., BSc Leic., PhD Leic., FBPsS

Accommodation. Director of Residential and Commercial Services: Irving, David L.

Admissions (first degree). Schools and Colleges Liaison Officer: Smith, Leonard M., BSc Brist., MSc Leeds

Admissions (higher degree). Senior Assistant Registrar: Findlay, Jacqueline Y., BA Warw., MA Birm.

Adult/continuing education. Director, School of Continuing Education: Taylor, Prof. Richard K. S., MA Oxf., PhD Leeds

Alumni. Alumni Relations Development Officer: Glennon, Jayne, BA Leeds

Archives. Assistant Librarian: Shipway, Mark, BA York(UK), PhD Manc.

Careers. Director of Careers Service: Siddall, Richard M., BSc Lond., PhD Camb.

Computing services. Assistant Director: Duke, A. Jonathan, BSc Leeds, PhD Leeds

Consultancy services. Managing Director, ULIS: Williams, Ederyn, BA Open(UK), MA Camb., DPhil Oxf.

Credit transfer. Further Education Development Officer: Burnley, Keith G., BSc Warw., MPhil Leeds

Development/fund-raising. Director of Development: Copland, Keith

Equal opportunities. Equal Opportunities Officer: Harper, Susan, BA Liv.

Estates and buildings/works and services. Assistant Director (Estates and Building Maintenance): Sladdin, D. Robert, FRICS

Examinations. Senior Assistant Registrar: Brooks, C. Andrew G., BSc Leic., PhD Leic.

Finance. Finance and Commercial Director: Smith, Berenice, BA Oxf.Brookes

General enquiries. Registrar and Secretary: Robinson, David S., BA Leeds, PhD Leeds

Health services. Administrative Assistant: Veale, Janice

Industrial liaison. Managing Director, ULIS: Williams, Ederyn, BA Open(UK), MA Camb., DPhil Oxf.

International office. International Officer: Baker, David, BA CNAA

Library (chief librarian). Librarian: Brindley, Lynne J., BA Reading, MA Lond.

Library (enquiries). Senior Administrative Officer: Hilton, Valerie

Minorities/disadvantaged groups. Director of Human Resources: Knight, Matthew, MA Camb.

Personnel/human resources. Director of Human Resources: Knight, Matthew, MA Camb.

Publications. Publications Officer: Mazzoleni, Susan C., BSc Brist.

Purchasing. Purchasing Co-ordinator: Branon, Tim, BA Nott.Trent

Quality assurance and accreditation. Director of Teaching Quality Assurance Unit: Hodgson, Kath, MEd Leeds, PhD Leeds

Research. Pro-Vice-Chancellor (Research): May, Prof. Anthony D., MA Camb., FICE

Safety. University Safety Officer: Singleton, Brian, BSc Strath., PhD Strath.

Scholarships, awards, loans. Senior Assistant Registrar: Findlay, Jacqueline Y., BA Warw., MA Birm.

Schools liaison. Schools and Colleges Liaison Officer: Smith, Leonard M., BSc Brist., MSc Leeds

Security. Director of Security: Blanchflower, George

Sport and recreation. Director, Physical Education Service: Lindsay, Michael R., BSc(Eng) Oklahoma, MPhil Leeds, PhD Strath.

Staff development and training. Director: Hatton, Penelope M., MA Leeds

Student union. Administration USE Officer: Sobel, Alexander

Student welfare/counselling. Senior Student Counsellor: Humphrys, Nigel R., BA CNAA, MSEd Maine(USA)

Students from other countries. International Officer: Baker, David, BA CNAA

Students with disabilities. Disabilities Officer: Russell, Judith, MSc CNAA

University press. Smith, Helena, BSc Manc.

Women. Director of Human Resources: Knight, Matthew, MA Camb.

CAMPUS/COLLEGE HEADS

Askham Bryan College, Askham Bryan, York, England YO2 3PR. (Tel: (01904) 772277; Fax: (01904) 702629.) Principal: Bennett, R.

Barnsley College, Church Street, Barnsley, England S70 2AX. (Tel: (01226) 730191; Fax: (01226) 216470.) Chief Executive: Eade, D.

Bretton Hall, West Bretton, Wakefield, West Yorkshire, England WF4 4LG. (Tel: (01924) 830261; Fax: (01924) 830521.) Principal: Bell, Prof. G. H.

College of Ripon and York St John, Lord Mayor's Walk, York, England YO3 7EX. (Tel: (01904) 656771; Fax: (01904) 612512.) Principal: Butlin, Prof. R. A.

College of the Resurrection, Mirfield, West Yorkshire, England WF14 0BW. (Tel: (01924) 490441; Fax: (01924) 492738.) Acting Principal: Guiver, Rev. Fr. G.

Doncaster College, Waterdale, Doncaster, England DN1 3EX. (Tel: (01302) 553553; Fax: (01302) 553559.) Principal: Ashurst, Dr. T. B.

Leeds College of Art and Design, The Jacob Kramer Building, Blenheim Walk, Leeds, England LS2 9AQ. (Tel: (0113) 243 3848; Fax: (0113) 244 5916.) Principal: Wigan, E.

Leeds College of Music, St Peter's Square, 3 Quarry Hill, Leeds, England LS2 7PD. (Tel: (0113) 222 3400; Fax: (0113) 243 8798.) Principal: Hoult, D.

Northern School of Contemporary Dance, 98 Chapeltown Road, Leeds, England LS7 4BH. (Tel: (0113) 262 5359; Fax: (0113) 237 4585.) Principal: Senior, N.

Trinity and All Saints College, Brownberrie Lane, Horsforth, Leeds, England LS18 5HD. (Tel: (0113) 283 7100; Fax: (0113) 283 7200.) Principal: Turnbull, Dr. G. L.

[Information supplied by the institution as at 27 February 1998, and edited by the ACU]

LEEDS METROPOLITAN UNIVERSITY

Founded 1970 as Leeds Polytechnic; received university status 1992

Member of the Association of Commonwealth Universities

Postal Address: Calverley Street, Leeds, England LS1 3HE
Telephone: (0113) 283 2600 **Fax**: (0113) 283 3142 **E-mail**: mwilkinson@lmu.ac.uk
WWW: http://www.lmu.ac.uk **E-mail formula**: initialsurname@lmu.ac.uk

VICE-CHANCELLOR*—Wagner, Prof. Leslie, BA(Econ) *Manc.*, MA(Econ) *Manc.*
DEPUTY VICE-CHANCELLOR—Griffiths, Frank
DEPUTY VICE-CHANCELLOR—Hitchins, Geoff
SECRETARY AND CLERK TO THE BOARD OF GOVERNORS‡—Wilkinson, Mike
DIRECTOR OF FINANCE—Collins, Geoff

GENERAL INFORMATION

History. The university was originally founded as Leeds Polytechnic in 1970 and gained university status in 1992. It has two campuses: City, in the centre of Leeds; and Beckett Park, 5km from the city centre.

Admission to first degree courses (see also United Kingdom Introduction). Normally through Universities and Colleges Admissions Service (UCAS).

First Degrees (see also United Kingdom Directory to Subjects of Study). BA, BEng, BSc, LLB.

Courses may be taken full-time (normally 3 years), part-time (normally 6–8 years) or on a sandwich basis (normally 3 years plus 1 year industrial placement).

Higher Degrees (see also United Kingdom Directory to Subjects of Study). LLM, MA, MBA, MSc, MPhil, PhD, DEng, DLitt, DSc, DTech, EdD, LLD.

Applicants for admission to postgraduate courses must either hold a relevant degree or must have other qualifications and relevant work experience.

Courses last 1–4 years.

Libraries. 373,000 volumes; 1787 periodicals subscribed to. Specialist collection: European Documentation Centre.

Academic Year (1998–99). Two semesters: 28 September–29 January; 8 February–11 June.

Income (1996–97). Total, £72,100,000.

Statistics. Staff: 2145 (897 academic, 928 administrative, 320 manual/craft). Students: full-time/sandwich 11,170 (5842 men, 5328 women); part-time 9699; international 1098 (581 men, 517 women).

FACULTIES/SCHOOLS

Business
Tel: (0113) 283 7503 Fax: (0113) 283 7508
Dean: Green, David
Personal Assistant: Pegler, Kate

Cultural and Education Studies
Fax: (0113) 283 3163
Dean: Osborne, Allan, BA York(UK), MA York(UK), MSc Sheff.Hallam
Personal Assistant: Fletcher, Maureen

Health and the Environment
Fax: (0113) 283 3190
Dean: Bale, Prof. R. John, MSc
Personal Assistant: Huby, Michelle

Information and Engineering Systems
Fax: (0113) 283 3110
Dean: Taylor, Prof. Gaynor, BSc Manc., MSc Manc., PhD Manc.
Personal Assistant: ......

ACADEMIC UNITS

Business, see Leeds Business Sch.

Cultural and Education Studies

Cultural and Education Central
Fax: (0113) 283 3163
Osborne, Allan, BA York(UK), MA York(UK), MSc Sheff.Hallam Dean

Cultural Studies
Fax: (0113) 283 3112
Bekker, Pieter, BA Witw., PhD Leeds Principal Lectr.
Brown, Ronald, BA CNAA, MA Sus. Sr. Lectr.
Caygill, Matthew, BA Leeds, MA York(UK) Sr. Lectr.
Douglas, Janet, BA MA Sr. Lectr.
Farrar, Maxim, BA Leeds Sr. Lectr.
Griffin, Prof. Gabrielle, BA Leic., MA Lond., PhD Leic. Head*
Gunn, Simon, BA Lanc., MA Lanc., PhD Manc. Principal Lectr.
Hall, Alison, BSc Lough. Principal Lectr.
Johnston, Gordon, BSc Lond., MA Leeds, PhD Leeds Principal Lectr.
Leeks, Wendy, BA Leeds, PhD Leeds Sr. Lectr.
Satterthwaite, Jerome, BA Open(UK), BA Leeds, MPhil Leeds, MEd Leeds Principal Lectr.
Stinson, Marie, BA Leeds, PhD Leeds Sr. Lectr.
Tseelon, Efrat, BSc Lond., MA Jerusalem, DPhil Oxf. Sr. Lectr.

Leisure and Sports Studies
Fax: (0113) 283 3710
Abrams, Jeffrey, BSc N.Y.State, MA Kent Principal Lectr.
Adams, Gordon, BA CNAA Sr. Lectr.
Baker, Ruth, BA MSc Sr. Lectr.
Bramham, Peter, BSc Lond., MA Essex, MA CNAA, PhD Leeds Sr. Lectr.
Brown, Helen, BSc Lough., MA Sheff. Principal Lectr.
Butterly, Ronald, BEd Liv., MA Leeds, PhD Leeds Sr. Lectr.
Carroll, Sean Sr. Lectr.
Cooke, Carlton, BSc Birm., PhD Birm. Principal Lectr.
Flintoff, Anne, BEd Leeds, MA Leeds, PhD Open(UK) Principal Lectr.
Hartley, Hazel, BEd Leeds, MEd Leeds Sr. Lectr.
Jackson, David, BSc Brad. Sr. Lectr.
Latham, Nicola, BSc CNAA, MSc Leeds Met. Sr. Lectr.
Lavalee, David, BA Boston Coll., MEd Harv., PhD W. Aust. Sr. Lectr.
Lloyd, Edward, BSc Wash.State, MEd Leeds Principal Lectr.
Long, Jonathan, BSc Brist., MA McM. Principal Lectr.
McKinney, George, BA Open(UK), MSc Birm. Head*
Miller, Stuart Sr. Lectr.
Nesti, Mark, BA Leeds, MA Alta. Sr. Lectr.
Newell, Susan, BSc Lough., MSc Brad. Sr. Lectr.
Newton, John, MA Mich., PhD Mich. Sr. Lectr.
Pringle, Andy, BA Staffs., MA Leeds Met. Sr. Lectr.

Scraton, Prof. Sheila, BEd Liv., PhD Open(UK) Principal Lectr.
Snowden, Irena, BA Newcastle(UK) Sr. Lectr.
Spink, John, BA Leeds, MA Manit. Sr. Lectr.
Tomlinson, Pat Principal Lectr.
Totten, Michael, BA Brad., MA Leeds Met. Sr. Lectr.
Trueman, Terence, BA CNAA, MSc Salf. Sr. Lectr.
Twinem, Janette, BPhil Exe. Sr. Lectr.
Wolsey, Christopher, BA Staffs., MA Sheff., MEd Nott. Sr. Lectr.

Professional Education and Development
Fax: (0113) 283 3181
Anderson, Viv, BA Exe., MSc Sr. Lectr.
Barrett, Francis, BA MA Sr. Lectr.
Beasley, Elizabeth, BEd CNAA, MEd Sr. Lectr.
Bennett, Horace, BA MSc Principal Lectr.
Betts, Janet, BA Manc., BA Liv. Sr. Lectr.
Clegg, Susan, BSc Lond., MSc Brad., MA Leeds Principal Lectr.
Dean, Jacqueline, BA Natal, MEd Exe. Sr. Lectr.
Ellison, Linda, MSc CNAA Principal Lectr.
Flecknoe, Mervyn, BSc Lond., MA York(UK) Sr. Lectr.
Holmes, Gary, BA MSc Head*
Konrad, John, BSc Hull, MEd Leic. Sr. Lectr.
Mee, John, MA Leeds Sr. Lectr.
Morgan, Andrew, BA Leeds, MA Manc. Principal Lectr.
Poole, Iain, BA Lond., MEd Leeds, MA E.Anglia Principal Lectr.
Rawnsley, Stuart, BSc Brad., PhD Brad. Principal Lectr.
Reid, Sylvia, MSc CNAA Sr. Lectr.
Shaw, Eileen, BEd Leeds, MEd Leeds, PhD Leeds Sr. Lectr.
Sutcliffe, Nick, BSc Leic., MEd Leeds Sr. Lectr.
Tarbitt, Valerie Sr. Lectr.
Tomlinson, Harry, BA Open(UK), MA Oxf., MSc Manc. Principal Lectr.

Teaching and Education Studies
Fax: (0113) 283 7410
Adam, Jill, BEd Sr. Lectr.
Allison, Yvonne Sr. Lectr.
Balchin, Peter, BSc Lond. Sr. Lectr.
Belcher, Christopher, BSc Lond., MA Lond. Sr. Lectr.
Botsaris, Nicholas, BEd CNAA Principal Lectr.
Bowles, Andrew, BEd CNAA Sr. Lectr.
D'Sena, Peter, BA S'ton., MPhil Open(UK) Sr. Lectr.
Dickson, Linda, BSc Exe., MEd Lond. Sr. Lectr.
Doherty, Jonathan, BA MEd Sr. Lectr.
Gilchrist, Denise, BEd CNAA Principal Lectr.
Gray, Michael, BEd Leeds, BA Open(UK), MEd Sheff. Sr. Lectr.
Hamilton, Philippa, BEd CNAA Sr. Lectr.
Hawkin, Wendy, BEd Reading, MA Lond. Principal Lectr.
Hurst, Paul Sr. Lectr.
Jones, Glyn, BA Leeds, MA York(UK) Principal Lectr.
Keay, Jeanne, BEd CNAA, MEd Sheff. Principal Lectr.
Lindsay, Vivienne, BEd Leeds, MEd Edin. Sr. Lectr.

Little, David   Sr. Lectr.
Macdermott, Julie, BA CNAA   Sr. Lectr.
Marshall, Paul, BEd E.Anglia, MSc Leeds   Sr. Lectr.
Martin, Paul, BA Oxf., MA Leeds   Sr. Lectr.
McManus, Michael, BA Open(UK), MEd Leeds   Principal Lectr.
Myers, Julia, BA Wales, MEd Exe.   Sr. Lectr.
Nuttall, Wendy, BA Durh., MA Manc.   Head*
Tanner, Julia, BSc Salf., MEd Keele   Sr. Lectr.
Thomas, Vernon, BEd   Sr. Lectr.
Trist, Helen, MEd Leeds   Sr. Lectr.
Tweedie, Christine, MSc CNAA   Sr. Lectr.
Valli, Yasmin, MA Lanc.   Sr. Lectr.
Warren, Susan, BA Open(UK), MEd CNAA   Principal Lectr.
Welch, Susan E., BSc Birm., BSc CNAA, MSc CNAA   Principal Lectr.

Tourism and Hospitality Management, School of

Fax: (0113) 283 3111

Blackwell, Ruth, BA E.Anglia, MA Warw.   Sr. Lectr.
Busby, Roger, BA Open(UK), MSc Leeds   Sr. Lectr.
Church, Ivor, BSc CNAA, MPhil Leeds Met.   Sr. Lectr.
Clarkson, L. Barry, BSc CNAA, MSc Brad.   Sr. Lectr.
Coll, Patricia   Sr. Lectr.
Cullen, Peter, BSc MA   Sr. Lectr.
Curland, Susan, MBA Leeds   Sr. Lectr.
Dewhurst, Peter, BA Newcastle(UK), MSc Salf., PhD   Sr. Lectr.
Eaglen, Andrew   Sr. Lectr.
Fitzgerald-Moore, Deborah, BSc CNAA   Sr. Lectr.
Harris, Vicky, BA Open(UK), MA   Head*
Hawkin, Rosemary, BSc Lond., MSc Wis., MBA Leeds Met.   Sr. Lectr.
Hodgson, Isabell   Sr. Lectr.
Jameson, Stephanie, BA CNAA, MPhil   Sr. Lectr.
Jones, Steven, MSc   Sr. Lectr.
Jowett, Val, MSc Sheff.   Sr. Lectr.
Lincoln, Guy, BSc CNAA   Sr. Lectr.
Machin, Alan   Sr. Lectr.
Margerison, John, BA York(UK), MA Leeds   Sr. Lectr.
McKellan, Sue, BSc MSc   Principal Lectr.
Newman, Andrew   Sr. Lectr.
Parsons, Anthony, BSc Nott., PhD Nott.   Principal Lectr.
Pearson, Catherine, BEd CNAA   Principal Lectr.
Piso, Anne-Marie, MA   Sr. Lectr.
Rodger, Carole, BA CNAA   Sr. Lectr.
Shacklock, Raisa, BEd MSc   Principal Lectr.
Sheard, Michael, BSc Leeds   Principal Lectr.
Thomas, Rhodri, BA MA   Principal Lectr.
Tum, Julia, MBA   Sr. Lectr.
Walsh, Stella, BEd Leeds, MEd Leeds   Sr. Lectr.
Ward, David, MBA Brad., MPhil Brad., MSc Leic.   Principal Lectr.
Welch, Susan J., BSc Leeds   Principal Lectr.
Whitworth, Graham, MSc   Sr. Lectr.
Xie, Guozhong, BSc Shanghai, MSc Leeds, PhD Leeds   Sr. Lectr.

Health and the Environment

Fax: (0113) 283 3190

Bale, R. John, MSc   Willmott Dixon Prof., Construction Management

Applied Social Sciences, School of

Batson, Brian, MSc   Sr. Lectr.
Bray, Monica, BA MPhil   Sr. Lectr.
Brown, Fraser   Sr. Lectr.
Charlton, Marion L.   Sr. Lectr.
Cheesman, Brian E., BA Leeds, MA Leeds   Principal Lectr.
Chiosso, Rosamond, BA MA   Sr. Lectr.
Crookston, R. Ian, BA Hull, PhD Reading   Sr. Lectr.
Elleschild, Lyvinia, BA CNAA, MA Brad.   Sr. Lectr.
Foster, Sally A., BA Leeds, MA Leeds, MSc Manc.   Sr. Lectr.

Freeman, Alan, BSc Lond., MPhil   Sr. Lectr.
Fryer, Marilyn, BA PhD, FBPsS   Sr. Lectr.
Heselwood, Barry C., BA BLing   Sr. Lectr.
Irving, Zoe   Sr. Lectr.
Keighley, David A., BSc Wales, MSc Lond., PhD Leeds   Sr. Lectr.
Lavery, Gerard, BA CNAA, MA Warw.   Sr. Lectr.
Lee, Wendy   Sr. Lectr.
Llewellyn, M. Ann, BA Leeds, PhD Leeds   Sr. Lectr.
Mobbs, Kenneth L., BA Leeds, MA Lanc., MA York(UK)   Sr. Lectr.
Moran, Gerald F., BA Liv., MSc Lond.   Sr. Lectr.
Palmer, Susan P., BA Open(UK)   Principal Lectr.
Paul, Stephen, BA Brad., MSc CNAA   Sr. Lectr.
Peters, Michael, BA Leeds   Sr. Lectr.
Rennie, Stephen A.   Sr. Lectr.
Ross, Alison J., MA Leeds, MPhil Sheff.   Head
Sayers, Stephen F., BA York(UK), DPhil York(UK)   Sr. Lectr.
Smalle, Yvette, MA   Sr. Lectr.
Spoor, Christopher, BSc Edin.   Sr. Lectr.
Taylor, Lynne, BSc   Sr. Lectr.
Tharratt, Penny, BSc MA   Sr. Lectr.
Walley, Edward D., BA Lond., MEd Leeds, MA York(UK)   Head
Whittington, Brian, BSc Birm., PhD Brad.   Head of Sch.*
Wilce, Merlin, BSc Hull, MA Manc., MA Leeds   Principal Lectr.
Wobbaka, Patrick N., BA CNAA, MBA Brad.   Sr. Lectr.

Art, Architecture and Design, School of

Fax: (0113) 283 3190

Anderson, John   Sr. Lectr.
Baldwin, Alistair, BA   Sr. Lectr.
Bicknell, John, BA   Sr. Lectr.
Bowen, Lloyd, BA   Sr. Lectr.
Brien, Alyson, BA CNAA, MA   Sr. Lectr.
Brier, John, MBA   Sr. Lectr.
Cain, Judith B.   Sr. Lectr.
Dunnigan, Brian, MA Edin.   Sr. Lectr.
Edwards, Andrew, BA   Sr. Lectr.
Ellis, Peter   Sr. Lectr.
Evans, Adrian, BA   Sr. Lectr.
Felix, Robert, BA PhD   Principal Lectr.
Gardiner, Penny   Sr. Lectr.
Gething, Fleure, BA   Sr. Lectr.
Gray, Len, BA MA   Sr. Lectr.
Hainsworth, Prof. George   Principal Lectr.
Harding-Hill, Steve, BA MA   Sr. Lectr.
Hassall, Joanne, BA   Sr. Lectr.
Heywood, Ian, BA Lond., DPhil York(UK)   Principal Lectr.
Hodson, Jo   Sr. Lectr.
Hoffman, A. Steven, BA   Sr. Lectr.
Horton, Derek, MA PhD   Sr. Lectr.
Howes, Jaki, BA   Principal Lectr.
Julier, Guy, BA MA   Sr. Lectr.
Kappa, Juha   Principal Lectr.
Knighton, Edwin J., BA   Principal Lectr.
Knudsen, Erik   Sr. Lectr.
Logan, Paul, BA   Sr. Lectr.
Lowe, Robert J., MA PhD   Principal Lectr.
Macdonald, Ian   Principal Lectr.
Mayfield, Wendy, BSc Lough., MPhil Nott.   Principal Lectr.
Mayson, William L., BA   Sr. Lectr.
McCallion, Brian   Sr. Lectr.
Millard, Andrew V., BSc PhD   Sr. Lectr.
Millard, Lesley, BSc Hudd.   Sr. Lectr.
Morant, Steven A., BA MA   Sr. Lectr.
Morgan, Alice   Sr. Lectr.
Morgan, Jill, BA Wales   Principal Lectr.
O'Brien, Kevin, BA MA   Sr. Lectr.
Oswin, Pamela   Sr. Lectr.
Peacock, Briton R.   Sr. Lectr.
Rees, Anthony L., BA   Principal Lectr.
Rodgers, Anne, BSc   Sr. Lectr.
Ross, John C., BA MA   Principal Lectr.
Royffe, Christopher D., MA   Head*
Sandle, C. Douglas, BA Leeds   Principal Lectr.
Simpkins, Nigel B., BA Leeds   Sr. Lectr.
Simson, Alan J.   Sr. Lectr.
Sykes, Sandy C., BA CNAA, MA   Sr. Lectr.
Taylor, Alistair B., BSc   Principal Lectr.

Teasdale, Geoffrey G.   Principal Lectr.
Temple, Nick, MA   Sr. Lectr.
Thwaites, Kevin, BA   Sr. Lectr.
Treen, Colin, BA PhD   Reader
Wakefield, John R., BA MA   Sr. Lectr.
Wharton, Jenny, BA   Sr. Lectr.
Wilson-Lambeth, Andrew, BA   Sr. Lectr.
York, Denise R., BA Natal, MA Natal   Sr. Lectr.

Built Environment, School of the

Fax: (0113) 283 3190

Allmendinger, Philip, BSc PhD   Sr. Lectr.
Bates, Mike, BSc MSc   Sr. Lectr.
Bell, Malcolm, MSc   Principal Lectr.
Bingel, Pawel R., BSc Leeds, MSc Leeds, PhD Leeds   Sr. Lectr.
Colledge, Barbara, BSc   Head*
Cook, Andrew E., BSc   Sr. Lectr.
Douglas, Ian, BA MPhil MA   Sr. Lectr.
Dunn, Michael H., BSc LLB   Sr. Lectr.
Edwards, Janice, BSc   Sr. Lectr.
Ellis, Robert C., BSc CNAA, MSc Lough., FRICS   Principal Lectr.
Emmitt, Steve   Sr. Lectr.
English, John G., BSc   Sr. Lectr.
Garbett, Christopher, BSc   Sr. Lectr.
Gordon, Peter B., BSc   Sr. Lectr.
Hargreaves, Robert C., BSc MSc   Principal Lectr.
Harrington, John R., BSc   Sr. Lectr.
Hart, Trevor J., BA   Sr. Lectr.
Haughton, Prof. Graham F., BA PhD   Principal Lectr.
Highfield, David, BSc MPhil   Sr. Lectr.
Hirst, Paul, BSc PhD   Sr. Lectr.
Ho, Suet Y., BSc MSc   Sr. Lectr.
Jeffrey, John, BSc   Sr. Lectr.
Keel, David A., BSc   Principal Lectr.
Kettle, Jane, BSc MA   Sr. Lectr.
Knight, Jeffrey T.   Sr. Lectr.
May, Graham, BA MA   Principal Lectr.
Moran, Celia A., BSc MA   Principal Lectr.
Pearce, David G., BSc MSc   Sr. Lectr.
Rodgers, David G., BSc LLB   Sr. Lectr.
Rogers, Stephen P., BSc   Sr. Lectr.
Smales, Lindsay M., BA PhD   Sr. Lectr.
Sturges, John L., MSc   Sr. Lectr.
Thomas, Kevin, BSc MPhil   Sr. Lectr.
Turpin-Brooks, Sue, BSc MPhil   Sr. Lectr.
Whitehead, Paul G., BSc MSc   Sr. Lectr.
Whitney, David, BA MPhil   Principal Lectr.
Wood, Gerard D., BSc   Principal Lectr.

Health and Community Care, School of

Clegg, Philip L., BA Lond., MSc Sur.   Sr. Lectr.
Copeman, June P., BSc Lond., MSc Lond., MEd Leeds Met.   Sr. Lectr.
Delaney, Faith G., BSc MSc   Sr. Lectr.
Dimmock, Gary W., BA Liv., MA Sheff.   Principal Lectr.
Dixey, Rachel A., BA PhD   Sr. Lectr.
Fatchett, Anita B., BA Leeds, MA Leeds   Sr. Lectr.
Green, Jacqueline, BSc Lond., MSc Leeds Met.   Sr. Lectr.
Joyce, Lesley A., BPhil MSc   Sr. Lectr.
Lowry, Michael, BEd CNAA, MEd Curtin   Sr. Lectr.
Merrick, Susan, BSc Leeds Met.   Sr. Lectr.
Norton, Lavinia, BSc MA   Sr. Lectr.
Nutman, Peter N., BA MA PhD   Head of Sch.*
Piercy, Jennifer M., BA Open(UK), MA Leeds   Head*
Sherwin, Susan A.   Sr. Lectr.
Slavin, S. Fiona, BSc Hudd.   Sr. Lectr.
Thomas, Terence V., BA Hull   Sr. Lectr.
Tilford, Sylvia, BSc Lond., MA Leeds   Head*
Trenchard, Stephen, BA Manc.   Sr. Lectr.
Vincent, Jane, BSc   Sr. Lectr.
Walker, Diane F., BA   Sr. Lectr.
White, Alan K., BSc Sur., MSc Leeds Met.   Sr. Lectr.

Health Sciences, School of

Airey, William, BA CNAA, PhD CNAA   Sr. Lectr.
Alexander, Michael D., PhD Lond.   Head*
Aslett-Bentley, Avril D., BSc Sheff., MSc Lond.   Sr. Lectr.
Auty, P. Linda, BSc Leeds, MPhil Leeds   Sr. Lectr.

Brown, Pauline J., BEd *Warw.* Sr. Lectr.
Caswell, Alison M., BSc PhD Sr. Lectr.
Chaplin, Robin, BSc Sr. Lectr.
Cooper, Keith J., BSc *Hull*, MSc *Nott.*, PhD
  Nott. Principal Lectr.
Cram, Alan G., BSc PhD, FRSChem Sr. Lectr.
Daltrey, Diana C., BSc *Lond.*, PhD *Nott.* Head
  of Sch.*
Davies, Derek, BSc MA MSc Sr. Lectr.
Dewhurst, David G., BSc *Sheff.*, PhD Reader
Edmondson, Alan S., BSc PhD Sr. Lectr.
Gairn, Catherine M., BSc Sr. Lectr.
Hartford, Trudy, BSc PhD Sr. Lectr.
Johnson, Mark I., BSc *Leeds*, PhD
  Newcastle(UK) Sr. Lectr.
Lee, Jennifer M., BA MSc Head*
Mera, Steven L. Sr. Lectr.
Mitchell, Signe E., BA *Uppsala* Sr. Lectr.
Moran, Terence P., BSc LLB LLM Sr. Lectr.
Mwanje, Zach Sr. Lectr.
Richardson, Adrian P., BSc DPhil Sr. Lectr.
Sanderson, Catherine, BSc *Newcastle(UK)*, PhD
  Open(UK) Sr. Lectr.
Sharples, Paul Sr. Lectr.
Smalley, Neil Sr. Lectr.
Unsworth, Bridget A., BSc *Bath*, PhD *Brad.* Sr.
  Lectr.
Wilkinson, Jacqueline Sr. Lectr.
Young, Michael, BA Sr. Lectr.

Information and Engineering Systems

Computing

Fax: (0113) 283 3182

Balls, Timothy, BSc Sr. Lectr.
Beard, David J., BSc *Aston*, MSc *Aston* Sr. Lectr.
Calvert, Maurice, BSc *Leeds*, PhD *Leeds* Sr. Lectr.
Coxhead, John F., MPhil *CNAA* Sr. Lectr.
Dacre, Anthony N., BA *Oxf.*, MSc *Lond.*, MA
  Oxf. Principal Lectr.
Dodman, Edward A., BSc *Lond.*, MSc *Leeds*,
  MPhil *Leeds* Principal Lectr.
Doney, Paul Sr. Lectr.
Duddell, David, BA *Brist.*, PhD *Brist.* Sr. Lectr.
Ellyard, John, BSc *Lough.* Sr. Lectr.
Harland, David M., BA *Oxf.*, BA *Open(UK)*, MSc
  York(UK) Sr. Lectr.
Harvey, John, BSc *Liv.* Principal Lectr.
Hobbs, David J., BSc *Sus.*, MSc *Sus.*, MSc
  York(UK), PhD *CNAA* Sr. Lectr.
Jennings, Neil, BA *Open(UK)* Principal Lectr.
Jones, Richard J., BSc *Wales* Principal Lectr.
Kemp, Douglas J., BA *Leeds*, MSc
  Leeds Principal Lectr.
Kennedy, Nairn F., BSc *Glas.*, PhD *Glas.* Sr.
  Lectr.
Martin, Ian, BSc *CNAA* Sr. Lectr.
McGrath, A. C. Paul, BSc
  Newcastle(UK) Principal Lectr.
Moore, David J., BA *E.Anglia*, MA *E.Anglia*, MSc
  York(UK), PhD *Leeds Met.* Sr. Lectr.
Newbury, Paul Sr. Lectr.
Old, Julian Sr. Lectr.
Pattinson, Colin, BSc *Leeds*, PhD *Leeds* Sr. Lectr.
Rayner, Bernard, BA *Oxf.*, BA *Open(UK)* Sr.
  Lectr.
Semmens, Lesley T., BSc *Lond.*, MSc *Brad.* Sr.
  Lectr.
Sharp, Simon Sr. Lectr.
Strachan, Rebecca Sr. Lectr.
Thorpe, John K. Sr. Lectr.
Willis, Neil, BSc *Sheff.* Sr. Lectr.; Head*
Willoughby, H. Lynette, BSc *Sur.*, MSc
  Brad. Sr. Lectr.

Engineering

Fax: (0113) 283 3110

Carter, Peter S., BSc *Manc.*, PhD *Manc.* Sr.
  Lectr.
Conway, Paul A., BEng PhD Principal Lectr.
Cope, Nicholas, BSc *Salf.*, PhD *S'ton.* Sr. Lectr.
Cowey, Jeffrey E., MSc *Manc.*, PhD *Essex*,
  FIEE Principal Lectr.
Crispin, Alan J., BSc *E.Anglia*, PhD
  E.Anglia Principal Lectr.
Darwish, Mostafa, BSc *Cairo*, PhD *Brun.* Sr.
  Lectr.

Folley, Duncan A., BSc *Salf.*, MSc *Salf.* Sr.
  Lectr.
Gledhill, David, BSc Sr. Lectr.
Harrison, Michael J., BA MA Sr. Lectr.
Hartwell, Peter J. Sr. Lectr.
Long, J. Anthony Sr. Lectr.
Marsh, Rodney, MSc *CNAA*, PhD *CNAA* Head*
Maybury, Alan, BSc PhD Principal Lectr.
Mercer, Francis, BSc *CNAA*, MSc *Nott.* Sr.
  Lectr.
O'Toole, Bernard M., MSc Principal Lectr.
Parker, Stephen, BSc *Bath*, MSc *CNAA* Sr.
  Lectr.
Ratcliff, Paul, MSc *CNAA* Sr. Lectr.
Reed, Edward W., BA *Camb.*, MA *Camb.*,
  PhD Sr. Lectr.
Rush, Gary E., PhD *Leeds* Sr. Lectr.
Scorer, Alexander P., BSc Sr. Lectr.
Singh, Balbir Sr. Lectr.
Sutton, Terence W., BA *Hull*, BSc *Lond.*, MSc
  Lond., MSc *Hull*, PhD *Hull* Sr. Lectr.
Tasker, Joy Sr. Lectr.
Taylor, Peter L., BTech *Brad.* Sr. Lectr.
Ward, Robert L., BSc MPhil PhD Sr. Lectr.
Waterworth, Geoffrey Sr. Lectr.
Webb, David C., BSc *CNAA*, DPhil *York(UK)*,
  FRAS Principal Lectr.
Whitbread, Martin J., MPhil
  Open(UK) Principal Lectr.
Wilkinson, Stephen P., BSc *CNAA*, PhD Sr.
  Lectr.

Information and Engineering Systems Central

Fax: (0113) 283 3110

Taylor, Prof. Gaynor, BSc *Manc.*, MSc *Manc.*,
  PhD *Manc.* Dean
Webster, John A., BSc *Sheff.* Dep. Dean

Information Management

Fax: (0113) 283 3182

Bailey, Trevor Sr. Lectr.
Black, Alistair, BA *Lond.*, MA *Lond.*, PhD
  CNAA Sr. Lectr.
Blake, John D., BSc *Leic.*, MSc *Newcastle(UK)* Sr.
  Lectr.
Broughton, Linda M., BSc *Leeds* Sr. Lectr.
Brunt, Rodney M., BA *Belf.* Sr. Lectr.
Bryant, Prof. Anthony, BA *Camb.*, MA *Camb.*,
  MSc *Brad.*, PhD *Lond.*
Burke, Alan, BSc *Sheff.*, MSc *Lanc.* Sr. Lectr.
Cockerill, Steve Sr. Lectr.
Cookson, Anne I., BA *Nott.* Sr. Lectr.
Crann, Melvyn P., BA *Open(UK)* Sr. Lectr.
Douglas, John Sr. Lectr.
Durham, Martin Sr. Lectr.
Gibbs, Sally E., BA *Wales*, MA *CNAA* Sr. Lectr.
Grogan, John Sr. Lectr.
Hall, John, BA *Belf.* Sr. Lectr.
Hamill, John Sr. Lectr.
Heyworth, H. Lee, BSc *Leeds* Sr. Lectr.
Hirst, Stuart L., MSc *Birm.* Sr. Lectr.
Howard, Alan W., BSc *Nott.*, MSc *Salf.* Sr.
  Lectr.
Leek, Colin, BSc *Newcastle(UK)* Sr. Lectr.
Livesey, J. Brian, BSc *Leeds*, PhD *Leeds* Principal
  Lectr.
Mills, Alan F., BSc *Leeds*, LLB *CNAA*, MSc
  Leeds Head*
Moon, Joanna, MA *Edin.*, MBA *Edin.* Sr. Lectr.
Muddiman, David J., BA *Leic.*, MSc
  Open(UK) Sr. Lectr.
Nicholls, Paul Sr. Lectr.
Nottingham, Annett Sr. Lectr.
Orange, Graham, MA Sr. Lectr.
Poulter, Alan Sr. Lectr.
Robinson, Lesley A., BSc *Sheff.*, MSc *Sheff.* Sr.
  Lectr.
Savage, John P., MSc *Reading* Sr. Lectr.
Smith, David S. Principal Lectr.
Steadman, Chris Sr. Lectr.
Strickler, Linda Sr. Lectr.
Towers, Keith, BSc *Wales*, MSc *Liv.* Principal
  Lectr.
Trayhurn, Deborah, BEd *Camb.* Principal
  Lectr.
Urwin, Jackie, BA *CNAA* Sr. Lectr.
Uttley, Patricia M., BEd *Lond.*, MEd
  Leeds Principal Lectr.

Vasconcelos, Ana Sr. Lectr.
Vilinskis, Karen Sr. Lectr.
Walker, Steve Sr. Lectr.
Williams, Leonard T., BSc *Aston*, MBA
  Brad. Principal Lectr.
Young, Jane Sr. Lectr.

Language Study, Centre for

Fax: (0113) 274 5966

Languages

Tel: (0113) 283 7440 *Fax:* (0113) 274 5966,
  283 3189

Alesso-Waywell, Lucia M., PhD *Turin* Sr.
  Lectr.
Foster, Bernard, BA *Hull*, LèsL *Lille*, MA *CNAA*,
  PhD *Bath* Principal Lectr.
Jones, Elspeth, BA *Reading*, MA *Lond.* Dir.*
Keinhorst, Wolfgang Sr. Lectr.
Killick, David, BEd *Leeds*, MEd *Leeds* Principal
  Lectr.
Leconte, Marie-Odile, PhD *Amiens* Principal
  Lectr.
Mallinson, J. Stephen, BA *Lond.* Sr. Lectr.
Mathie, Gillian, BA *Nott.* Sr. Lectr.
Roy, James, MA *Reading* Sr. Lectr.
Turnbull, Sarah, MA *Lond.* Sr. Lectr.
Webb, Graham, BA *CNAA* Principal Lectr.
Zoellner, Ricarda Principal Lectr.

Leeds Business School

Accounting and Finance

Fax: (0113) 283 3245

Booth, Richard, MA, FCA Principal Lectr.
Britton, Ann E., BA *Hull* Principal Lectr.
Burnup, John T., MSc *Brad.* Principal Lectr.
Combs, Alan M., BA *Leic.*, MSc *Leic.* Sr. Lectr.
Foster, John W. Principal Lectr.
Guy, Peter, MSc Head*
Henderson, Roger, BA MBA Reader
Knight, David L., BA Sr. Lectr.
Lambell, Jill, BSc Sr. Lectr.
Manners, John M., FCA Sr. Lectr.
O'Sullivan, Colin, BA Sr. Lectr.
Shead, Janet, BA Sr. Lectr.
Silberstein, Martin B. Sr. Lectr.
Smith, Richard J., MBA *Brad.* Principal Lectr.
Waterson, Christopher, BA MEd Principal
  Lectr.
Wood, Peter M., BEd, FCA Sr. Lectr.

Business Central

Fax: (0113) 283 3221

Green, David Dean
Greenhalgh, Anthony, BSc MSc Acting Dep.
  Dean

Business Strategy

Fax: (0113) 283 3227

Allis, Ann Principal Lectr.
Chippindale, Peter M., BSc *Brad.* Sr. Lectr.
Clark, Thomas, BSc *Birm.*, MA *Warw.*, PhD
  Warw. Prof., Corporate Governance
Drake, Eric, BA Sr. Lectr.
Duprey, Clive, BTech *Brad.*, MBA
  Brad. Principal Lectr.
Gregory, Anne, BA Head*
Hughes, Graham, MA Sr. Lectr.
Palihawadana, Dayananda, BSc *Colombo*, PhD
  Glas. Sr. Lectr.
Payne, Elaine, BA Principal Lectr.
Robertson, Martyn R., FCA Sr. Lectr.
Sheard, Marie-Paul Sr. Lectr.
Tench, Ralph Sr. Lectr.
Theaker, Alison, BA *York(UK)*, MA *Leeds
  Met.* Principal Lectr.
Toth, John L. Sr. Lectr.
Webster, Philip A., MA Sr. Lectr.
Whittaker, Lesley, BA MBA Principal Lectr.
Williams, Gareth, BA MBA Principal Lectr.
Yeomans, Elizabeth, BA *S'ton.*, MSc *Stir.* Sr.
  Lectr.

Economics, Policy and Information Analysis

Fax: (0113) 283 3245

Allen, John M., BA PhD Sr. Lectr.
Beachill, Robert, BA MA Sr. Lectr.

Hamilton, Leslie, BA MSc   Sr. Lectr.
Helman, Basil   Principal Lectr.
Jones, Christopher M., BSc   Principal Lectr.
Judge, Prof. Eamonn J., BA Leeds, MA Sheff.   Principal Lectr.
Leach, Robert F., BA Oxf., BSc Lond.   Principal Lectr.
Otter, Dorron, BA Oxf., MA Leeds   Sr. Lectr.
Sheehan, Brendan M., BA MPhil   Sr. Lectr.
Shutt, John, BSc MPhil   Prof., Regional Business Development
Stead, David R., BSc Lond., MEd Leeds   Sr. Lectr.
Stewart, Gerald, BA Brad., MBA Brad.   Principal Lectr.
Sutherland, Robert J., BA Strath., MSc Manc.   Reader
Thompson, Frank, BA MA   Sr. Lectr.
Watson, Colin, BA Leeds, BA Manc.   Sr. Lectr.
Wetherley, Paul A., BA MA PhD   Principal Lectr.; Acting Head*
Wilson, Derrick, BA   Sr. Lectr.

Human Resource Management

Fax: (0113) 283 3227

Barras, Judith, BA Birm., MA Lanc.   Sr. Lectr.
Blakeborough, Margaret I., BSc Lanc., MA Lanc.   Sr. Lectr.
Burrell, Catherine, BA MBA   Sr. Lectr.
Davies, David, BSc MSc MA   Sr. Lectr.
Finnigan, Valerie   Sr. Lectr.
Gold, Jeffrey, BA   Sr. Lectr.
Griffiths, Robert O., BA MSc   Sr. Lectr.
Hamblett, John W.   Sr. Lectr.
Holden, Richard J., BA PhD   Principal Lectr.
Jones, Stephen W., MBA   Principal Lectr.
Kelly, Michael J., BA MSc   Head*
McCauley, Patrick T., BA MSc   Sr. Lectr.
Michaud, Ann, BA Leeds, MBA Brad.   Sr. Lectr.
Sinclair, Lynda, BA   Sr. Lectr.
Thackray, John, BA Leeds   Principal Lectr.
Warhurst, Russell P., BA Liv., MA PhD   Sr. Lectr.
Watson, Stuart, BA   Sr. Lectr.
Wolstenholme, Eric, BSc Nott., PhD Nott.   Visiting Prof.

Law

Fax: (0113) 283 3206

Askew, Melissa, LLB Newcastle(UK)   Sr. Lectr.
Balchin, Daphne, LLB Birm.   Sr. Lectr.
Birtwistle, Timothy, BA   Principal Lectr.
Cousins, Lynn, LLB Lond.   Sr. Lectr.
Creasey, Julian, BA Oxf.   Principal Lectr.
Gale, Christopher J., LLB Wales   Sr. Lectr.
Harwood, Michael, BA Camb., LLB Camb.   Sr. Lectr.
Hawker, John R., BA Oxf.   Principal Lectr.
Johnson, Sandra, LLB MA   Sr. Lectr.
Joyce, Pauline, BA   Principal Lectr.

Kirkbride, James   Head*
Lister, Robin, BA Oxf.   Sr. Lectr.
Manzoor, Tasnim, LLB   Sr. Lectr.
Martin, Derek H., LLB Belf.   Principal Lectr.
Moxon, Hilary, BA MA   Principal Lectr.
Myers, Maxine, LLB   Sr. Lectr.
Payn, Terence L., BA Newcastle(UK), LLM Lond.   Sr. Lectr.
Shaw, Darren, LLB   Sr. Lectr.
Silberstein, Sandra J., LLB Leeds   Sr. Lectr.
Walker, Bridget, BA Durh.   Principal Lectr.
Wolstencroft, Patricia A., LLB LLM   Sr. Lectr.
Wood, Adrian, BA   Sr. Lectr.

Policy Research Institute

Fax: (0113) 283 3224

Burden, Thomas A., BSc MA   Principal Lectr.
Campbell, Prof. Michael P., BA Sheff., MA Lanc., MA Leeds   Dir.*
Close, Paul, BA MA PhD   Sr. Lectr.

CONTACT OFFICERS

Academic affairs. Academic Registrar: Orange, Cath
Accommodation. Accommodation Officer: Webster, Ann, BA CNAA
Admissions (first degree). Admissions Officer: Somerville, Martine, LLB Leeds
Admissions (higher degree). Admissions Officer: Somerville, Martine, LLB Leeds
Adult/continuing education. Access and Lifelong Learning Manager: Molloy, Steve, BSc Lond., PhD Leeds
Alumni. Student Recruitment and Promotions Manager: Braham, David, BA Sheff.Hallam
Archives. Assistant University Secretary: Rushall, Martin, BA Leeds, MA Leeds
Careers. Careers and Placements Manager: Marsland, Phillip, BA CNAA
Computing services. Computing Services Manager: Driver, Josie
Conferences/Corporate Hospitality. Conference Co-ordinator: Dodds, Sally
Consultancy services. Head, External Business Development Centre: Rodgers, Peter
Credit transfer. Access and Lifelong Learning Manager: Molloy, Steve, BSc Lond., PhD Leeds
Development/fund-raising. Media and Public Relations Manager: Leech, Emma, BA Hudd.
Distance education. Director, Learning Support Services: Heap, John, BSc Manc.
Equal opportunities. Director of Human Resources: Pashley, Steve, BA Leeds Met.
Estates and buildings/works and services. Director of Estates: Hudson, Trevor
Examinations. Senior Awards and Examinations Officer: Bradley, Sue, BA Leeds Met.
Finance. Director of Finance: Collins, Geoff

General enquiries. Assistant University Secretary: Rushall, Martin, BA Leeds, MA Leeds
Health services. Senior Nursing Officer: Lord, Brenda
Industrial liaison. Head, External Business Development Centre: Rodgers, Peter
International office. Media and Public Relations Manager: Leech, Emma, BA Hudd.
Language training for international students. Director, Centre for Language Study: Jones, Elspeth, BA Reading, MA Lond.
Library (chief librarian). Library Services Manager: Payne, Philip, BA Northumbria
Ombudsperson. Secretary and Clerk to the Board of Governors: Wilkinson, Mike
Personnel/human resources. Director of Human Resources: Pashley, Steve, BA Leeds Met.
Public relations, information and marketing. Media and Public Relations Manager: Leech, Emma, BA Hudd.
Publications. Head of Communications and External Relations: Shields, Mark, BA Lanc., MPhil Hull, MBA Brad.
Purchasing. Purchasing and Environment Officer: Briggs, Mike
Quality Assurance and Accreditation. Academic Quality and Assurance Manager: Stoney, Clare, MSc
Research. Head, Research Development: Green, Howard, BA Camb., MA Camb., PhD Reading
Safety. Senior Health and Safety Officer: Richold, Chris
Scholarships, awards, loans. Assistant University Secretary: Rushall, Martin, BA Leeds, MA Leeds
Schools liaison. Education Liaison and Promotions Officer: Moore, Joyce
Security. Security Manager: Haines, Peter
Sport and recreation. University Head of Sport: Talbot, Prof. Margaret, OBE, BEd Sus., MA Leeds, PhD Birm.
Staff development and training. Staff Development Manager: Triller, Fiona
Student welfare/counselling. Student Services Manager: Smith, Carol, BA Lond.
Students from other countries. Student Services Manager: Smith, Carol, BA Lond.
Students with disabilities. Student Services Manager: Smith, Carol, BA Lond.
University press. Media and Public Relations Manager: Leech, Emma, BA Hudd.

[Information supplied by the institution as at 20 March 1998, and edited by the ACU]

UNIVERSITY OF LEICESTER

Founded 1921

Member of the Association of Commonwealth Universities

Postal Address: University Road, Leicester, England LE1 7RH
Telephone: (0116) 252 2522 **Fax**: (0116) 252 2200 **Cables**: University Leicester **Telex**: 347250 LEICUN G
WWW: http://www.le.ac.uk **E-mail formula**: username@le.ac.uk

VISITOR—Elizabeth, H.M. The Queen

CHANCELLOR—Atiyah, Sir Michael, OM, MA Camb., PhD Camb., Hon. DSc Leic., FRS

PRO-CHANCELLOR—Foster, John C., OBE, MA Oxf.

PRO-CHANCELLOR—......

VICE-CHANCELLOR*—(until September 1999) Edwards, Kenneth J. R., BSc Reading, MA Camb., PhD Wales, Hon. LLD Belf., Hon. DSc Reading, Hon. DSc Lough., Hon. MA Leic.

VICE-CHANCELLOR*—(from 1 October 1999) Burgess, Prof. Robert, BA Durh., PhD Warw.

TREASURER—Cinderby, Gerald A.

PRO-VICE-CHANCELLOR—Beeby, Prof. John L., MA Camb., PhD Camb.

PRO-VICE-CHANCELLOR—Blakeley, Prof. Asa G. H., BM BCh Oxf., MA Oxf., DPhil Oxf.

PRO-VICE-CHANCELLOR—Fearon, Prof. Peter S., BA Liv.

REGISTRAR AND SECRETARY‡—Julian, Keith J., MA Camb.

LIBRARIAN—Hobbs, Timothy D., MA Exe., PhD Camb.

GENERAL INFORMATION

History. The university was founded in 1921 and was granted its royal charter in 1957. It is located in the East Midlands, about 160km from London.

Admission to first degree courses (see also United Kingdom Introduction). Through Universities and Colleges Admissions Service (UCAS). Minimum requirement: General Certificate of Education (GCE) A levels or equivalent qualification.

First Degrees (see also United Kingdom Directory to Subjects of Study). BA, BEng, BSc, LLB, MB ChB, MChem, MEng, MGeol, MMath.
All courses are full-time and normally last 3 years or 4 years sandwich. MB ChB: 5 years.

Higher Degrees (see also United Kingdom Directory to Subjects of Study). LLM, MA, MSc, MPhil, PhD, DClinPsy, EdD.
Applicants for admission to postgraduate degrees should normally hold a good first degree or equivalent qualification.

Language of Instruction. English. Preparatory English language courses offered during the year, plus 4-week pre-sessional English language course.

Libraries. Over 1,000,000 volumes; 3084 periodicals subscribed to. Specialist collections include: English local history; Orton papers.

Fees (1998–99, annual). Home/EU students: undergraduate £1000, postgraduate £2610. International students (undergraduate and postgraduate): £6330 (arts); £8415 (sciences); £7350 (MBA); £15,600 (clinical).

Academic Awards (1997–98). Ten open scholarships of £2000 per year; three full scholarships (British Chevening/Leicester University) to Indian students.

Academic Year (1998–99). Three terms: 28 September–18 December; 18 January–26 March; 3 May–25 June. Two semesters: 28 September–29 January; 1 February–25 June.

Income (1996–97). Total, £112,000,000.

Statistics. Staff: 3056 (673 academic, 729 academic-related, 1654 support). Students: full-time 8657 (4174 men, 4483 women); part-time 1263; distance learning 5279; international (non-EU) 856; total 15,199.

FACULTIES/SCHOOLS

Arts

Tel: (0116) 252 2679 Fax: (0116) 252 5213

Dean: (1996–2000) Pearce, Prof. Susan M., MA Oxf., PhD S'ton., FSA

Secretary: Howe, Beth, BSc Birm.

Education and Continuing Studies

Tel: (0116) 252 3688 Fax: (0116) 252 3653

Dean: (1998–2002) Fogelman, Prof. Kenneth R., BA Keele, FBPsS

Secretary: Lacey, Anthony J., BEd Durh., MA Lond.

Law

Tel: (0116) 252 2363 Fax: (0116) 252 5023

Dean: (1995–99) Woodliffe, John C., LLB Hull, LLM Lond.

Secretary: Paisey, Holly, BA CNAA

Medicine

Tel: (0116) 252 2969 Fax: (0116) 252 3013

Dean: Harris, Prof. Frank, CBE, MB ChB Cape Town, MMed Cape Town, MD Cape Town, FRCP, FRCPEd

Secretary: Jones, Peter K., BSc(SocSci) S'ton.

Science

Tel: (0116) 252 5012 Fax: (0116) 252 2770

Dean: (1997–99) Brammar, Prof. William J., BSc Lond., PhD Lond.

Secretary (Biological Sciences): Davies, Rosemary F., BA Exe.

Secretary (Physical Sciences): Hopkins, Rachel E.

Social Science

Tel: (0116) 252 2842 Fax: (0116) 252 5073

Dean: (1998–2002) Pyle, Prof. David J., BA York(UK), MSc Brist., PhD Leic.

Secretary: Cox, Neil A., BA Leic.

ACADEMIC UNITS

Archaeological Studies, School of

Tel: (0116) 252 2611 Fax: (0116) 252 5005

Barker, Graeme W. W., MA Camb., PhD Camb., FSA   Prof.; Head of Sch.*

Ancient History Division

Tel: (0116) 252 2777 Fax: (0116) 252 5016

Foxhall, Lin, BA Bryn Mawr, MA Penn., PhD Liv.   Reader; Head*

Shipley, D. Graham J., MA Oxf., DPhil Oxf.   Sr. Lectr.

Other Staff: 1 Lectr.

Research: gender and women in antiquity; Hellenistic world; landscape and landuse in Greece and Italy; social/economic history of classical antiquity; towns and cities in Greece and Italy

Archaeology Division

Tel: (0116) 252 2611 Fax: (0116) 252 5005

Brown, Anthony E., MA Oxf., FSA   Sr. Lectr.

Mattingley, David J., BA Manc., PhD Manc., FSA   Reader; Head*

Palmer, Marilyn, MA Oxf., PhD Leic., FSA   Reader

Parsons, David, BA Durh., PhD Leic., FSA   Sr. Lectr.

Ruggles, Clive L. N., MA Camb., DPhil Oxf., FRAS, FRAI, FSA   Sr. Lectr.

Young, Robert, BA Wales, PhD Durh., FBA   Sr. Lectr.

Other Staff: 9 Lectrs.; 1 Hon. Lectr.

Research: colonial archaeology (ancient and modern); environmental archaeology; historical archaeology; landscape archaeology (prehistoric and industrial); professional archaeology and heritage management

Astronomy, see Phys. and Astron.

Biochemistry

Tel: (0116) 252 3471 Fax: (0116) 252 3369

Bagshaw, Clive R., BSc Birm., PhD Brist.   Reader

Brammar, William J., BSc Lond., PhD Lond.   Prof.

Cohen, Gerald M., BSc Leeds, PhD Minn.   Hon. Prof., Biochemistry Toxicology

Cooper, Ronald A., BSc Birm., PhD Birm.   Sr. Lectr.

Critchley, David R., BSc Brist., PhD Brist.   Prof.; Head*

Cundliffe, Eric, MA Camb., PhD Camb., ScD Camb.   Prof.

Eperon, Ian C., BSc Brist., PhD Camb.   Reader

Gescher, Andreas J., BSc Fran., PhD Würzburg, DSc Aston   Hon. Prof., Biochemical Toxicology

Harrison, Timothy M., BSc Wales, PhD Camb.   Sr. Lectr.

Lian, Lu-Yun, BSc W.Aust., PhD Warw.   Sr. Lectr., Biological NMR Spectroscopy

Liddington, Robert C., BA Oxf., DPhil York(UK)   Prof., X-ray Crystallography

Maxwell, Anthony, BSc Lond., PhD Brist.   Prof.

Roberts, Gordon C. K., BSc Lond., PhD Lond.   Prof., Biological NMR Spectroscopy

Rowe, Arthur J., MA Camb., PhD Camb.   Sr. Lectr., Electron Microscopy

Sampson, Jeffrey, BSc Sus., DPhil Sus.   Sr. Lectr.

Smith, Lewis L., BSc CNAA, PhD CNAA   Hon. Prof., Biochemical Toxicology

Other Staff: 5 Lectrs.; 1 Hon. Reader; 6 Hon. Lectrs.; 2 Sr. Lectrs.†; 1 Lectr.†

Research: antibiotic synthesis and mechanisms of action; eukaryotic molecular cell biology; molecular enzymology, protein engineering; signal transduction, growth control and cancer; structural biochemistry, NMR, X-ray crystallography

Biology

Tel: (0116) 252 3344 Fax: (0116) 252 3330

Cockburn, William, BSc *Durh.*, PhD *Newcastle(UK)* Sr. Lectr.

Gornall, Richard J., BSc *St And.*, MSc *Birm.*, PhD *Br.Col.* Sr. Lectr.; Curator of Bot. Gdns. and Herbarium

Harper, David M., MA *Oxf.*, PhD *Dund.*, FLS Sr. Lectr.

Harris, Robert R., BSc *S'ton.*, PhD *S'ton.* Sr. Lectr.

Hart, Paul J. B., BSc *Liv.*, BA *Open(UK)*, PhD *Liv.* Reader

Shelton, Peter M. J., BSc *St And.*, PhD *ANU* Sr. Lectr.

Smith, Harry, BSc *Manc.*, PhD *Wales*, DSc *Manc.*, Hon. DSc *Aix-Marseilles*, FIBiol Prof., Botany

Smith, Robert H., BA *York(UK)*, MSc *Reading*, PhD *Reading* Prof., Environmental Biology; Head*

Stace, Clive A., BSc *Lond.*, PhD *Lond.*, DSc *Lond.* Prof., Plant Taxonomy

Walker, Muriel H., BSc *St And.*, PhD *St And.*, FLS Sr. Lectr.

Whitelam, Garry C., BSc *Leeds*, PhD *Reading* Prof., Plant Molecular Physiology

Other Staff: 4 Lectrs.; 1 Prof.†

Research: antibody production in plants; developmental biology of animals and plants; environmental biology and molecular ecology; photomorphogenesis in plants; plant taxonomy, biosystematics and cytology

Chemistry

Tel: (0116) 252 2100 Fax: (0116) 252 3789

Atkinson, Robert S., BSc *Nott.*, PhD *Nott.* Sr. Lectr.

Blandamer, Michael J., BSc *S'ton.*, PhD *S'ton.*, DSc *S'ton.*, FRSChem Prof., Physical Chemistry

Cullis, Paul M., BSc *Exe.*, DPhil *Oxf.*, FRSChem Prof., Organic Chemistry; Head*

Harger, Martin J. P., BSc *St And.*, DSc *St And.* Reader

Hillman, A. Robert, BSc *Lond.*, DPhil *Oxf.* Prof., Physical Chemistry

Holloway, John H., BSc *Birm.*, PhD *Birm.*, DSc *Birm.*, FRSChem Prof., Inorganic Chemistry

Jenkins, Paul R., BSc *Wales*, PhD *Wales* Sr. Lectr.

Kocovsky, Pavel, MSc *Prague*, PhD *Prague*, DSc *Leic.* Reader

Malpass, John R., BSc *Birm.*, PhD *Birm.*, FRSChem Sr. Lectr.

Russell, David R., BSc *Lond.*, PhD *Glas.* Sr. Lectr.

Other Staff: 9 Lectrs.; 2 Readers†; 1 Sr. Lectr.†; 1 Hon. Prof.; 4 Hon. Lectrs.

Research: biological chemistry and biomolecular sciences; electrochemistry; fluorine chemistry; gas phase chemistry and earth observation science; organic synthesis and synthetic methods; organometallic chemistry and homogeneous catalysis

Computer Science, see Maths. and
Computer Sci.

Ecology, see Biol.

Economics, see also Hist., Econ. and Soc.

Tel: (0116) 252 2887 Fax: (0116) 252 2908

Baker, Alan J., MA *Edin.*, PhD *Leic.* Sr. Lectr.

Bradley, Ian G., MA *Camb.* Sr. Lectr.

Charemza, Wojciech, DrEcon *Gdańsk*, DrHabEcon *Gdańsk* Prof.

Deadman, Derek F., BA *Leeds*, MA(Econ) *Manc.* Sr. Lectr.

Fielding, David J., BA *Oxf.*, MPhil *Oxf.*, DPhil *Oxf.* Sr. Lectr.

Fraser, Clive D., BSocSci *Birm.*, PhD *S'ton.* Prof.

Jackson, Peter M., BA *Strath.*, PhD *Stir.* Prof.

Lee, Kevin C., BA *Sheff.*, MSc *Brist.*, PhD *Lond.* Prof.

Pudney, Stephen E., BSc(Econ) *Leic.*, MSc *Lond.* Tyler Prof.; Head*

Pyle, David J., BA *York(UK)*, MSc *Brist.*, PhD *Leic.* Prof.

Thompson, R. Stephen, BSc(Econ) *Hull*, MA *Newcastle(UK)*, PhD *Newcastle(UK)* Prof.

Other Staff: 1 Sr. Lectr.; 11 Lectrs.

Research: analysis of macro-economic performance; applied macro-and micro-econometrics; consumer demand; income distribution; operation of labour markets

Education, School of, see also Special
Centres, etc (Adult Educn.)

Tel: (0116) 252 3688 Fax: (0116) 252 3653

Bush, Anthony W., BSocSci *Birm.*, MA *Brun.* Prof., Education Management

Busher, Hugh C., BA *Manc.*, MEd *Birm.*, PhD *Leeds* Sr. Lectr.

Cortazzi, Martin, BEd *Reading*, MA *Reading*, PhD *Leic.* Sr. Lectr.

Fogelman, Kenneth R., BA *Keele*, FBPsS Prof.

Galton, Maurice J., BSc *Durh.*, MSc *Newcastle(UK)*, MEd *Leeds*, PhD *Leic.* Prof.

Jarvis, Christine J., BSc *Birm.* Sr. Lectr.

Knight, Roger, BA *Camb.* Sr. Lectr.

Merry, Roger, BA *Keele*, MSc *Aston*, PhD *Aston* Sr. Lectr.

Moyles, Janet R., MEd *Warw.* Sr. Lectr.

Whiteside, Martin T., BA *Leic.*, MEd *Leic.* Sr. Lectr.; Dir.*

Other Staff: 18 Lectrs.; 1 Sr. Lectr.†; 4 Lectrs.†

Research: applied linguistics and TESOL; educational applications of ICT; education management and school improvement; pedagogy in the primary school; science education

Engineering

Tel: (0116) 252 2559 Fax: (0116) 252 2619

Coats, Christopher M., BSc *Leeds*, PhD *Leeds* Sr. Lectr.

Cocks, Alan C. F., BSc *Leic.*, PhD *Camb.* Prof.

Dissado, Leonard A., BSc *Lond.*, PhD *Lond.*, DSc *Lond.* Reader

Folkard, Geoffrey K., BSc *Edin.*, MSc *Lond.*, PhD *Lond.* Sr. Lectr.

Fothergill, John C., BSc *Wales*, MSc *Wales*, PhD *Wales* Sr. Lectr.

Gostelow, J. Paul, BEng *Liv.*, MA *Camb.*, MA *Lond.*, PhD *Liv.*, DEng *Liv.*, FIEAust, FRAeS Prof., Thermofluids

Gu, Da Wei, BA *Fudan*, MSc *Shanghai Jiaotong*, PhD *Lond.* Sr. Lectr.

Jones, N. Barrie, BSc *Manc.*, MEng *McM.*, DPhil *Sus.*, FIEE Prof.

Ponter, Alan R. S., BSc *Lond.*, MA *Camb.*, MS *Brown*, PhD *Lond.* Prof.

Postlethwaite, Ian, BSc(Eng) *Lond.*, MA *Oxf.*, PhD *Camb.*, FIEE, FIMechE Prof.; Head*

Spurgeon, Sarah K., BSc *York(UK)*, DPhil *York(UK)*, FIMA Sr. Lectr.

Other Staff: 17 Lectrs.; 1 Sr. Lectr.†

Research: bioengineering, transducers, signal processing (diagnostics, measurements); control systems (industrial applications, nonlinear, robust); electrical power (dielectrics, electronics) radio systems; mechanics of materials (microstructure, performance, processing); thermofluids (turbomachinery, unsteady flows)

English

Tel: (0116) 252 2620 Fax: (0116) 252 2065

Campbell, Gordon R., MA *Qu.*, DPhil *York(UK)*, FRHistS Prof.

Hanson, Clare, BA *Oxf.*, MA *Reading*, PhD *Reading* Reader

Myers, William F. T., MA *Oxf.*, BLitt *Oxf.* Prof.

Newey, Vincent A., MA *Oxf.*, BLitt *Oxf.*, PhD *Liv.* Prof.; Head*

Rosslyn, Felicity M., MA *Camb.*, PhD *Camb.* Sr. Lectr.

Shattock, E. Joanne, BA *New Br.*, MA *Leeds*, PhD *Lond.* Prof.

Stannard, Martin J., BA *Warw.*, MA *Sus.*, DPhil *Oxf.* Prof.

Walker, Greg M., BA *S'ton.*, PhD *S'ton.*, FRHistS Reader

Warren, Roger B., MA *Oxf.*, BLitt *Oxf.* Sr. Lectr.

Other Staff: 7 Lectrs.

Research: contemporary literature and cultural theory; mediaeval literature; nineteenth-century literature, Romantic and Victorian; Renaissance literature (in particular reign of Henry VIII and Shakespeare)

French, see Mod. Langs., Sch. of

Genetics

Tel: (0116) 252 3438 Fax: (0116) 252 3378

Cashmore, Annette M., BSc *Sus.*, PhD *CNAA* Sr. Lectr.

Dalgleish, Raymond W. M., BSc *Glas.*, PhD *Lond.* Sr. Lectr.

Dover, Gabriel A., BA *Lond.*, BSc *Leeds*, PhD *Camb.*, ScD *Camb.* Prof.

Jeffreys, Sir Alec J., BA *Oxf.*, DPhil *Oxf.*, DSc *Open(UK)*, FRS, FLS, FRCPath, Hon. FRCP Wolfson Res. Prof.

Ketley, Julian M., BSc *Birm.*, PhD *Birm.* Reader

Kryiacou, Charalamros P., BSc *Birm.*, PhD *Sheff.* Prof.

Meacock, Peter A., BSc *Newcastle(UK)*, MSc *Newcastle(UK)*, PhD *Leic.* Sr. Lectr.

Orr, Elisha, BSc *Jerusalem*, PhD *Jerusalem* Sr. Res. Lectr.

Wilkins, Brian M., MA *Oxf.*, DPhil *Oxf.* Reader; Head*

Other Staff: 2 Lectrs.; 2 Sr. Lectrs.†

Research: behavioural and developmental genetics; human and medical genetics; microbial genetics and the molecular basis of pathogenicity; mutation, genetic variability and evolutionary genetics

Geography

Tel: (0116) 252 3822 Fax: (0116) 252 3854

Bowler, Ian R., BA *Liv.*, PhD *Liv.* Reader

Fisher, Peter F., BSc *Lanc.*, MSc *Reading*, PhD *CNAA* Reader

Lewis, Gareth J., MA *Wales*, PhD *Leic.* Prof.

Millington, Andrew C., BSc *Hull*, MA *Colorado*, DPhil *Sus.* Prof.; Head*

Parsons, Anthony J., BA *Sheff.*, MSc *Sheff.*, PhD *Reading* Prof.

Robinson, Geoffrey, MA *Camb.* Sr. Lectr.

Smalley, Ian J., PhD *Lond.* Hon. Prof., Applied Geomorphology

Strachan, Alan J., MA *Edin.*, MS *Wis.*, PhD *Edin.* Sr. Lectr.

Turnock, David, MA *Camb.*, PhD *Camb.* Reader

Williams, Colin C., BSc *CNAA*, MPhil *Birm.* Sr. Lectr.

Other Staff: 13 Lectrs.

Research: environmental processes and change in low latitudes; geographical information systems (GIS) and earth observation (EO); restructuring of economies and societies

Geology

Tel: (0116) 252 3933 Fax: (0116) 252 3918

Aldridge, Richard J., BSc *S'ton.*, PhD *S'ton.*, FGS Prof.; Head*

Clements, Roy G., BSc *Leic.*, PhD *Hull*, FGS Principal Curator

Harvey, Peter K. H., BSc *Brist.*, PhD *Brist.*, FGS Sr. Lectr.

Hill, Ian A., BSc *Leic.*, MSc *Birm.*, PhD *Birm.*, FGS Sr. Lectr.

Hudson, John D., MA *Camb.*, PhD *Camb.*, FGS Prof.

Lovell, Michael A., BSc *Reading*, MSc *Wales*, PhD *Wales*, FGS Reader

Maguire, Peter K. H., BSc *Edin.*, PhD *Durh.*, FRAS Sr. Lectr.

Parrish, Randell R., BA *Middlebury*, BSc *Br.Col.*, PhD *Br.Col.* Prof.†, Isotope Geology

Saunders, Andrew D., BSc *Sheff.*, MSc *Birm.*, PhD *Birm.*, FGS Prof.

Siveter, David J., BSc Leic., PhD Leic. Reader
Tarney, John, BSc Durh., PhD Durh., FGS F.
W. Bennett Prof.
Windley, Brian F., BSc Liv., PhD Exe., DSc Leic.,
FGS Prof.
Other Staff: 10 Lectrs.; 1 Adjunct Lectr.; 1
Prof.†; 1 Sr. Lectr.†
Research: borehole research (interpretation of
wireline logs); geochemistry, mantle plumes
and crustal evolution; palaeontology
(microfossils and exceptionally preserved
fossils); seismic investigations of the earth's
crust; tectonic processes in mountain belts

German, see Mod. Langs., Sch. of

History

Tel: (0116) 252 2800 Fax: (0116) 252 3986
Ball, Stuart R., MA St And., PhD St And.,
FRHistS Reader
Bonney, Rev. Richard J., MA Oxf., DPhil Oxf.,
FRHistS Prof., Modern History; Head*
Cull, Nicholas J., BA Leeds, PhD Leeds Prof.,
American Studies
Hartley, Terence E., BA Lond., PhD Lond.,
FRHistS Sr. Lectr.
Housley, Norman J., MA Camb., PhD Camb.,
FRHistS Prof.
Johnson, David T., MA Oxf. Sr. Lectr.
Other Staff: 1 Prof.; 7 Lectrs.; 1 Lectr.†; 1 Res.
Lectr.†; 1 Hon. Lectr.†
Research: contemporary history; early modern
history; mediaeval European history;
religious and political pluralism and the
history of the Holocaust; United States
history

History, Ancient, see under Archaeol.
Studies, Sch. of

History, Economic and Social

Tel: (0116) 252 2588 Fax: (0116) 252 5081
Bowen, Huw V., BA Wales, PhD Wales,
FRHistS Sr. Lectr.; Head*
Clark, Peter A., MA Oxf., FSA, FRHistS Prof.
Cottrell, Phillip L., BSc(Econ) Hull, PhD
Hull Prof.
Dewey, Clive J., MA Camb., PhD Camb. Reader
Fearon, Peter S., BA Liv. Prof.
Rodger, Richard G., MA Edin., PhD Edin. Sr.
Lectr.
Williams, David M., MA Liv. Sr. Lectr.
Other Staff: 5 Lectrs.
Research: area studies of India and the USA;
British imperial economic and social history;
British social and urban history; European
economic and social history; modern
business, financial and maritime history

History, English Local

Tel: (0116) 252 2762 Fax: (0116) 252 5769
Fox, Harold S. A., BA Lond., MA Camb., PhD
Camb. Sr. Lectr.; Head*
Snell, Keith D. M., MA Camb., PhD
Camb. Reader
Other Staff: 1 Marc Fitch Res. Fellow
Vacant Posts: 1 Prof.
Research: English provincialism AD 410–2000;
English surnaming and surnames; rural
history (culture, economy, society); south-
west England (landscape, mediaeval
societies)

History of Art

Tel: (0116) 252 2866 Fax: (0116) 252 5128
Lindley, Phillip G., MA Camb., PhD Camb.,
FSA Reader; Head*
Watkins, Nicholas G. G., BA Lond., MPhil
Lond. Reader
Yarrington, Alison W., BA Reading, PhD Camb.,
FSA Prof.
Other Staff: 2 Lectrs.
Research: British art 1700–1900; European art
1890–1990; European art and architecture
1500–1770; Gothic and Renaissance
architecture and art; sculpture c. 1750–1914

Law

Tel: (0116) 252 2363 Fax: (0116) 252 5023
Allen, David K., MA Oxf., LLM McG. Sr. Lectr.
Bonner, David, LLB Leic., LLM Qu. Sr. Lectr.
Bourn, Colin J., BSc(Econ) Lond. Sr. Lectr.
Bradney, Anthony G. D., LLB Hull, BA
Open(UK) Sr. Lectr.
Buck, Trevor G., LLB CNAA, LLM Lanc. Sr.
Lectr.
Clarkson, Christopher M. V., BA Cape Town, LLB
Cape Town, LLM Lond. Prof.; Head*
Cownie, Fiona C., BA Brist., LLB Leic., LLM
Lond. Sr. Lectr.
Everton, A. Rosemarie, LLM Birm., PhD
Birm. Sr. Lectr.
Finch, John D., BA Oxf., BCL Oxf. Sr. Lectr.
Holyoak, Jonathon H., BA Camb. Sr. Lectr.
Neal, Alan C., LLB Warw., LLM Lond., LLM Leic.,
DGLS Stockholm Prof.
Pollard, David W., LLB Leeds Sr. Lectr.
Ross, Malcolm G., LLB Warw., MPhil Leic. Jean
Monet Sr. Lectr.
Shaw, Malcolm N., LLB Liv., LLM Jerusalem, PhD
Keele Sir Robert Jennings Prof., International
Law
Snaith, Ian, BA Keele, MA Manc. Sr. Lectr.;
Ironsides Ray & Vials Fellow
Thompson, Mark P., LLB Leic., LLM Keele Prof.
White, Robin C. A., MA Oxf., LLM
Virginia Prof.
Woodliffe, John C., LLB Hull, LLM Lond. Sr.
Lectr.
Other Staff: 19 Lectrs.; 1 Prof.†; 2 Lectrs.†
Research: criminal law and criminal justice;
European law; intellectual property and
international trade; international law and
human rights; real property and equitable
obligations

Mass Communication Research Centre

Tel: (0116) 252 3863 Fax: (0116) 252 3874
Boyd-Barrett, J. Oliver, BA Exe., PhD
Open(UK) Sr. Lectr.
Linné, Olga, FilLic Stockholm Sr. Lectr.
Negrine, Ralph M., BA Kent, PhD Leic. Sr.
Lectr.
Sreberny-Mohammadi, Annabelle, MA Camb.,
MA Col., MPhil Col., PhD Col. Prof.; Dir.*
Other Staff: 1 Res. Prof.; 6 Lectrs.
Research: globalization, new information and
communication technologies and gender;
international communication; media,
identity and representation; political
communication; science, health, risk and the
environment

Mathematics and Computer Science

Tel: (0116) 252 3882 Fax: (0116) 252 3915
Ainsworth, Mark, BSc Durh., PhD Durh. Reader
Levesley, Jeremy, BSc Manc., PhD Coventry Sr.
Lectr.
Light, William A., BSc Sus., MA Lanc., PhD
Lanc. Prof.
Robinson, Geoffrey R., BA Lanc., MSc Oxf.,
DPhil Oxf. Prof.; Head*
Stewart, Iain A., MA Oxf., PhD Lond.,
FIMA Prof., Computer Science
Thomas, Richard M., MA Oxf., MSc Oxf., DPhil
Oxf. Prof.
Watters, John F., BSc Liv., PhD Lond. Sr. Lectr.
Other Staff: 1 Reader; 15 Lectrs.; 2 Lectrs.†
Research: computer science (automata,
complexity, distributed sytems, logic,
semantics); numerical analysis
(approximation theory, eigenvalue
problems, finite elements); pure
mathematics (algebraic topology,
representation theory, ring theory); statistics
(medical statistics, reliability)

Medicine, see below

Microbiology and Immunology, see
Medicine, below

Modern Languages, School of

Tel: (0116) 252 2683 Fax: (0116) 252 3633
Fawcett, Peter R., MA Oxf., DPhil Oxf. Sr.
Lectr., French; Head*
Graves, Peter J., BA Lond., MA Brown Sr. Lectr.,
German
Gregory, Stewart, MA Oxf., DPhil Oxf. Reader,
French
Kenworthy, H. Martin, MA Leeds Dir., Engl.
Lang. Teaching Unit
Littlejohns, Richard, MA Oxf., MLitt Oxf., PhD
Birm. Prof., German
Rolfe, Christopher D., MA Wales Sr. Lectr.
Other Staff: 10 Lectrs.; 1 Lectr.†
Research: applied linguistics and CALL; editing
of texts and correspondences; Francophone
studies, especially Quebec; mediaeval
studies; modern European literature and
culture

Museum Studies

Tel: (0116) 252 3963 Fax: (0116) 252 3960
Hooper-Greenhill, Eilean R., BA Reading, MA
Lond., PhD Lond. Sr. Lectr.; Head*
Pearce, Susan M., MA Oxf., PhD S'ton.,
FSA Prof.
Other Staff: 5 Lectrs.
Research: material culture studies; museum
culture studies; museum education and
communication; museum history and
historiography; museums as agents of social
regeneration

Physics and Astronomy

Tel: (0116) 252 3575 Fax: (0116) 252 2770
Beeby, John L., MA Camb., PhD Camb. Prof.,
Theoretical Physics
Cooke, Brin A., BSc Leic., PhD Leic. Sr. Lectr.
Cowley, Stanley W. F., BSc Lond., PhD
Lond. Prof., Solar-Planetary Physics
Davis, Edward A., BSc Birm., MA Camb., PhD
Reading, FIP Prof., Experimental Physics
Evans, R. Emyr, BSc Wales, PhD Wales Sr.
Lectr.
Fraser, George W., BSc Aberd., PhD
Leic. Reader
Gurman, Stephen J., BSc S'ton., PhD Camb. Sr.
Lectr.
Howe, Robert A., BSc Lond., PhD Sheff. Sr.
Lectr.
Jameson, Richard F., MA Oxf., DPhil Oxf. Sr.
Lectr.
King, Andrew R., MA Camb., PhD Camb. Prof.,
Astrophysics; PPARC Sr. Fellow
Lester, Mark, BSc Sheff., PhD Sheff. Sr. Lectr.
Llewellyn-Jones, David T., MA Oxf., MSc M.I.T.,
PhD M.I.T. Prof., Earth Observation Science
Maksym, Piotr A., BA Camb., MSc Leic., PhD
Warw. Reader
Norris, Colin, BSc Reading, PhD Reading Prof.,
Surface Physics
Pounds, Kenneth A., CBE, BSc Lond., PhD Lond.,
Hon. DUniv York(UK), Hon. DSc Lough., FRS,
FIP Prof., Space Physics; Head*
Raine, Derek J., MA Camb., PhD Camb. Sr.
Lectr.
Robinson, Terence R., BSc Birm., MSc Leic., PhD
Leic. Prof., Space Plasma Physics
Stewart, Gordon C., BSc St And., PhD St
And. Reader
Ward, Martin J., BSc Lond., MA Camb., MSc Sus.,
DPhil Sus. Prof., Astronomy
Warwick, Robert S., BSc Birm., PhD
Manc. Reader
Wells, Alan A., BSc Lond., MSc Lond. Prof.,
Space Technology
Other Staff: 10 Lectrs.; 1 Prof.†; 1 Sr. Lectr.†;
1 Hon. Sr. Lectr.; 1 Hon. Lectr.
Research: astronomy and cosmology; condensed
matter physics; solar-terrestrial interactions
and space plasmas; space instrumentation; x-
ray astronomy

Politics

Tel: (0116) 252 2707 Fax: (0116) 252 5082

Berridge, Geoffrey R., BA Durh., MA Sus., PhD Durh. Prof., International Politics

Borthwick, Robert L., BA Nott., PhD Nott. Sr. Lectr.

Hoffman, John A., BA Cape Town, MA Sus., DPhil Sus. Reader

Melissen, Jan, BA Amst., MPhil Amst., PhD Gron., FRHistS Sr. Lectr.

Monar, Jorg, LèsL Paris, MA Munich, DrPhil Munich, DrRerPol Florence Prof.

Young, John W., BA Nott., PhD Camb., FRHistS Prof.; Head*

Other Staff: 9 Lectrs.

Research: British foreign policy and European security; early-modern theories of property, morals, politics; European Union institutions and policy-making; sovereignty and self, gender, order; theory and practice of diplomacy

Public Order, Scarman Centre for the Study of

Tel: (0116) 252 2458 Fax: (0116) 252 3944

Benyon, John T., BA Warw. Prof., Political Studies; Dir.*

Gill, Martin L., BA CNAA, MA CNAA Sr. Lectr.

Willis, Andrew S., BA York(UK) Sr. Lectr.

Other Staff: 12 Lectrs.

Research: crime and its causes; crime prevention and security management; policing issues; public order and collective violence; risk assessment and disaster management

Psychology

Tel: (0116) 252 2170 Fax: (0116) 252 2067

Beech, John R., BSc City(UK), MPhil Reading, DPhil Ulster, FBPsS Sr. Lectr.

Colley, Ann M., BA Sheff., PhD Sheff. Prof.; Head*

Colman, Andrew M., MA Cape Town, PhD Rhodes, FBPsS Reader

Davies, Graham M., BA Hull, PhD Hull, DSc Hull, FBPsS Prof.

Foreman, Nigel P., BSc Brad., PhD Nott. Sr. Lectr.

Gillett, Raphael T., MA Glas., MSc Stir., PhD Stir., FBPsS Sr. Lectr.

Hargreaves, David J., BSc Durh., PhD Durh., FBPsS Reader

Hollin, Clive R., BSc Lond., PhD Lond., FBPsS Reader

Joseph, Michael H., BSc Lond., MA Camb., PhD Lond. Prof., Behavioural Neuroscience

McCrea, Celia W., BA Belf., PhD Lond. Sr. Lectr.

Miller, Edgar, BSc Hull, MA Camb., MPhil Lond., PhD Hull, FBPsS Prof., Clinical Psychology

Other Staff: 13 Lectrs.; 1 Hon. Reader

Research: applied cognitive psychology; clinical psychology; forensic and legal psychology; neurosciences; social behaviour and development

Social Work, School of

Tel: (0116) 252 3766 Fax: (0116) 252 3748

Aldgate, P. Jane, MA Edin., MA Oxf., PhD Edin. Prof.

Hurd, Geoffrey E., MA Leic. Sr. Lectr.

Jones, Jocelyn C., BA Warw., MA Warw. Sr. Lectr.; Dir.*

Page, Robert, BA Kent, PhD Kent Sr. Lectr.

Ward, Harriet, MA St And., PhD Brist. Sr. Lectr.

Other Staff: 2 Lectrs.; 1 Sr. Lectr.†; 5 Lectrs.†; 1 Practice Co-ordinator†

Research: child protection; children and families social work; research-based social work practice; social policy; social work theory

Sociology

Tel: (0116) 252 2738 Fax: (0116) 252 5259

Ashton, David N., BA Leic. Prof.

Crompton, Rosemary, BSc Lond. Prof.

Dunning, Eric G., BSc(Econ) Lond., MA Leic. Prof.

Fulcher, D. James, BA Camb., MSc Lond., PhD Leic. Sr. Lectr.

Holloway, Sydney W. F., BA Lond. Sr. Lectr.

Hurd, Geoffrey E., MA Leic. Sr. Lectr.

Jewson, Nicholas D., BScEcon Wales, MA Leic. Sr. Lectr.

Layder, Derek R., BSc(Soc) Leic., PhD Lond. Reader

Murphy, Patrick J., BA Leic. Sr. Lectr.

O'Connell Davidson, Julia, BSc Bath, PhD Brist. Reader

Phizacklea, Anne M., BA Exe., MA McM., PhD Exe. Prof.

Waddington, Ivan H., BA Leic. Sr. Lectr.

Westwood, Sallie, BSc(Soc) Lond., PhD Camb. Prof.; Head*

Williams, John, BA Leic. Football Trust Sr. Res. Lectr.

Other Staff: 5 Lectrs.

Research: gender, sexuality, and globalisation; racism, ethnicity and migration; realist social theory; sport (particularly football), leisure and culture; women's employment and the changing labour force

MEDICINE

Tel: (0116) 252 2966 Fax: (0116) 252 3013

Cookson, John B., MB ChB Birm., MD Leic., FRCP Hon. Sr. Lectr.; Clin. Sub-Dean

Evans, David M., BSc Sur., PhD Leic., FIP Prof., Medical Physics

Harris, Frank, CBE, MB ChB Cape Town, MMed Cape Town, MD Cape Town, FRCP, FRCPEd Prof.; Dean

Heney, David, MB ChB Cape Town, MD Leeds Sr. Lectr., Paediatric Oncology and Basic Medical Education

Howard, Laurence J. P., BSc Nott., PhD Leic. Sr. Lectr.; Pre-Clinical Sub-Dean

Panerai, Ronney B., BSc Rio Grande do Sul, MSc Rio de Janeiro, PhD Lond. Sr. Lectr., Medical Physics

Smith, Graham, BSc Lond., MD Lond., FRCA Prof.; Sub-Dean

Walls, John, MB ChB Leeds, FRCP Hon. Prof.; Postgrad. Dean

Other Staff: 2 Lectrs. (1 Med. Phys., 1 Med. Educn.)

Research: developing magnetic resonance imaging techniques; development and evaluation of clinical measurements; Doppler ultrasound instrumentation and signal processing; modelling physiological systems; ultrasound image processing

Anaesthesia

Tel: (0116) 285 5291 Fax: (0116) 285 4487

Atcheson, Robert, MB BS Lond., MD Leic., FRCA Sr. Lectr.

Buggy, Donal J., MSc Trinity(Dub.), MB, FFARCSI Sr. Lectr.

Duthie, David J. R., MB ChB Aberd., MD Sheff., FRCA Sr. Lectr.

Rowbotham, David J., MB ChB Sheff., MD Sheff., FRCA Prof.

Smith, Graham, BSc Lond., MD Lond., FRCA Prof.; Head*

Thompson, Jonathan P., BSc Leic., MB ChB Leic., FRCA Sr. Lectr.

Other Staff: 4 Lectrs.; 1 Hon. Sr. Lectr.

Research: acute pain after surgery (novel pharmacological treatments); chronic pain (iontophoretic drug delivery); electronic data collection (universal serial bus interfaces); lung mechanics (surgical patients with chronic lung disease); second messenger systems (cell membrane signalling)

Cell Physiology and Pharmacology

Tel: (0116) 252 2922 Fax: (0116) 252 3996

Boarder, Michael R., BSc Lond., MSc Sus., PhD Lond. Sr. Lectr.

Challiss, R. A. John, BSc Bath, DPhil Oxf. Sr. Lectr.

Law, Robert O., BSc Brist., MA Camb., PhD Brist. Sr. Lectr.

Nahorski, Stefan R., BSc S'ton., PhD CNAA Prof.; Head*

Standen, Nicholas B., MA Camb., PhD Camb. Prof.

Stanfield, Peter R., MA Camb., PhD Camb., ScD Camb. Prof.

Other Staff: 1 Visiting Prof.; 6 Lectrs.; 1 Hon. Reader; 1 Hon. Sr. Lectr.; 2 Hon. Lectrs.

Research: cardiovascular physiology (arterial resistance vessels, vasodilation); cell signalling (intracellular calcium, phosphoinositides); electrophysiology (inwardly rectifying potassium-channels); neurophysiology (arthritis, auditory processing, inflammation); receptors (adrenoceptors, matabotropic glutamate receptors, muscarinic acetycholine)

Child Health

Tel: (0116) 252 3262 Fax: (0116) 252 3282

Field, David J., MB BS Lond., MD Nott., FRCP, FRCPEd Prof.

Grigg, Jonathan M., BSc Lond., MB BS Lond., MD Lond. Sr. Lectr.

Harris, Frank, CBE, MB ChB Cape Town, MMed Cape Town, MD Cape Town, FRCP, FRCPEd Prof., Paediatrics

Kotecha, Sailesh, MA Camb., MB BS Lond. Sr. Lectr.

O'Callaghan, Christopher L. P., BMedSci Nott., MB BS Nott., DM Nott., FRCP Sr. Lectr.

Silverman, Michael, MB BChir Camb., MA Camb., MD Camb., FRCP Prof.; Head*

Wailoo, Michael P., MB ChB Manc., MD Manc., FRCP Sr. Lectr.

Other Staff: 4 Lectrs.; 1 Hon. Lectr.

Research: aerosol medicine; childhood asthma (especially pre-school children); ciliary function in CNS and lungs; developmental cardio-pulmonary physiology; inflammatory processes in childhood lung disease

Epidemiology and Public Health

Tel: (0116) 252 3155 Fax: (0116) 252 3272

Abrams, Keith R., BSc Warw., MSc Leic., PhD Liv. Sr. Lectr., Medical Statistics

Clarke, Michael, MB BS Lond., FRCP Prof.; Head*

Jagger, Carol, BSc Leeds, MSc Leeds, PhD Leic. Sr. Lectr.

Jones, David R., BA Camb., MSc E.Anglia, PhD E.Anglia Prof., Medical Statistics

McGrother, Catherine W., MB BS Newcastle(UK) Sr. Lectr.

Parker, Gillian, BA Liv., PhD Birm. Nuffield Prof., Community Care

Other Staff: 1 Visiting Prof.; 7 Lectrs.; 1 Hon. Sr. Lectr.; 4 Hon. Lectrs.

Research: causes and treatment of urinary incontinence; development of registers for learning disabilities and diabetes mellitus; evaluation of obstetrics and neonatal services; methodological studies; physical and mental functioning of old people

General Practice and Primary Health Care

Tel: (0116) 258 4871 Fax: (0116) 258 4982

Fraser, Robin C., MB ChB Aberd., MD Aberd., FRCGP Prof.; Head*

McKinley, Robert K., BSc Belf., MB BCh BAO Belf., MD Belf., FRCGP Sr. Lectr.

Wilson, Andrew D., MB BS Newcastle(UK), MD Newcastle(UK) Sr. Lectr.

Other Staff: 1 Lectr.; 6 Lectrs.†; 1 Hon. Sr. Lectr.

Research: educational research; interface care; health promotion in the consultation; provision of primary care services

Eli Lilly National Medical Clinical Audit Centre

Tel: (0116) 258 4873 Fax: (0116) 258 4982

Baker, Richard H., MB BS Lond., MD Lond., FRCGP Dir.*

Cheater, Francine M., MA St And., PhD Nott. Sr. Lectr.

Other Staff: 2 Lectrs.; 2 Lectrs.†; 1 Hon. Lectr.

Research: development of audit protocols; evaluation of audit; implementing change in clinical performance; measurement of patients' views; multidisciplinary teamwork/ quality of care

Medicine and Therapeutics

Tel: (0116) 252 3182 Fax: (0116) 252 3273

Barnett, David B., MD *Sheff.*, FRCP   Prof., Clinical Pharmacology

Camp, Richard D. R., MB ChB *Cape Town*, PhD *Lond.*, FRCP   Prof., Dermatology

de Bono, David P., MA *Camb.*, MD *Camb.*, FRCPEd   British Heart Foundation Prof., Cardiology; Head*

Fotherby, Martin D., BSc *Lanc.*, MB ChB *Leic.*   Sr. Lectr., Medicine for the Elderly

Harris, Kevin P. G., MB BS *Lond.*, MA *Camb.*, MD *Leic.*, FRCP   Sr. Lectr., Nephrology

Maxwell, Simon R. J., BSc *Birm.*, MB ChB *Birm.*   Sr. Lectr., Clinical Pharmacology

Ng, Leong L., MA *Camb.*, MD *Camb.*, FRCP   Reader, Clinical Pharmacology

Norman, Robert I., BSc *Leic.*, PhD *Lond.*   Sr. Lectr., Medical Biochemistry

Parker, Stuart G., MB BS *Newcastle(UK)*, MD *Newcastle(UK)*   Sr. Lectr., Medicine for the Elderly

Playford, Raymond J., MB BS *Lond.*, PhD *Lond.*, FRCP   Prof., Gastroenterology

Pohl, Jürgen E. F., BSc *Melb.*, MB BS *Melb.*, FRCP   Sr. Lectr.

Potter, John F., BMedSci *Nott.*, DM *Nott.*, FRCP   Prof., Medicine for the Elderly

Samani, Nilesh J., BSc *Leic.*, MB ChB *Leic.*, MD *Leic.*, FRCP   Prof., Cardiology

Stafford, Peter J., BSc *Lond.*, MB BS *Lond.*, MD *Lond.*   Sr. Lectr., Cardiology

Swales, John D., MA *Camb.*, MD *Camb.*, FRCP   Prof. (on leave)

Thurston, Herbert, BSc *Manc.*, MD *Manc.*, FRCP   Prof., Vascular Medicine

Trembath, Richard C., BSc *Lond.*, MB BS *Lond.*   Prof., Medical Genetics

Walls, John, MB ChB *Leeds*, FRCP   Hon. Prof., Nephrology

Wardlaw, Andrew J., BA *Camb.*, MB BChir *Camb.*, PhD *Lond.*, FRCP   Sr. Lectr., Respiratory Medicine

Williams, Bryan, BSc *Lond.*, MB BS *Lond.*, MD *Leic.*, FRCP   Prof.

Woods, Kent L., MA *Camb.*, MD *Camb.*, ScM *Harv.*, FRCP   Prof., Therapeutics

Other Staff: 1 Visiting Prof.; 7 Lectrs.; 1 Hon. Reader; 11 Hon. Sr. Lectrs.; 2 Hon. Lectrs.

Research: biology of gastrointestinal disease; hypertension and coronary disease at all ages; immuno-and cell biology of skin diseases and asthma; renal pathophysiology and cell biology; vascular cell and molecular biology and genetics

Microbiology and Immunology

Tel: (0116) 252 2951 Fax: (0116) 252 5030

Andrew, Peter W., BSc *Wales*, PhD *Wales*   Prof., Microbiology Pathogenesis

Browning, Michael J., BSc *Glas.*, BM BCh *Oxf.*, PhD *Glas.*   Sr. Lectr.

Grant, William D., BSc *Edin.*, PhD *Edin.*   Prof., Environmental Microbiology

Myint, Stephen H., MB BS *Lond.*, MD *Lond.*   Prof., Clinical Microbiology

Nicholson, Karl G., MB BS *Lond.*, MD *Lond.*, FRCP   Sr. Lectr., Infectious Diseases

Schwaeble, Wilhelm J., DrRerNat *Mainz*   Reader, Immunology

Shaw, William V., BA *Williams(Mass.)*, MD *Col.*   Prof., Chemical Microbiology

Sheldon, Peter J. H., MB ChB *Birm.*, MD *Birm.*, FRCP   Sr. Lectr., Clinical Immunology

Whaley, Keith, MB BS *Newcastle(UK)*, MD *Newcastle(UK)*, PhD *Glas.*, FRCP, FRCPath   Prof., Immunology

Williams, Peter H., BSc *Lond.*, PhD *E.Anglia*   Prof., Microbiology; Head*

Other Staff: 2 Visiting Profs.; 1 Univ. Fellow; 5 Lectrs.; 1 Hon. Lectr.

Research: clinical microbiology (molecular techniques for diagnosis and epidemiology); environmental microbiology (bacterial survival in extreme environments); immunology (allergy, inflammation, pathogenesis of auto-immune disease); microbial pathogenicity (molecular cell biology of virulence mechanisms)

Obstetrics and Gynaecology

Tel: (0116) 252 3160 Fax: (0116) 252 3154

Al-Azzawi, Farook, MB ChB *Baghdad*, MA *Camb.*, PhD *Strath.*, FRCOG   Sr. Lectr.

Bell, Stephen C., BSc *W.Aust.*, PhD *Liv.*   Reader, Reproductive Biochemistry

Halligan, Aiden W. F., MA *Trinity(Dub.)*, MB BCh BAO *Trinity(Dub.)*, MD *Trinity(Dub.)*   Prof., Fetal Maternal Medicine

Konje, Justin C., MB BS *Ib.*, MD *Leic.*   Sr. Lectr.

Taylor, David J., MB BS *Newcastle(UK)*, MD *Newcastle(UK)*, FRCOG   Prof.; Head*

Other Staff: 3 Lectrs.; 1 Hon. Sr. Lectr.

Research: decidua in menstruation and pregnancy; exogenous hormone action and the menopause; fetal determinants of adult cardiovascular disease; infection, fetal membranes and pre-term birth; pre-eclampsia and hypertensive disorders in pregnancy

Oncology

Tel: (0116) 258 7597 Fax: (0116) 258 7599

Heney, David, MB ChB *Cape Town*, MD *Leeds*   Sr. Lectr., Paediatric Oncology and Basic Medical Education

O'Byrne, Kenneth J., MB BCh BAO *Trinity(Dub.)*   Sr. Lectr.

Steward, William P., MB ChB *Manc.*, PhD *Manc.*, FRCPCan, FRCPGlas   Prof.; Head*

Research: angiogenesis (focus on angiogenesis inhibition to treat cancer); chemoprevention (preclinical and clinical evaluation); new drug development

Ophthalmology

Tel: (0116) 258 6291 Fax: (0116) 255 8810

Thompson, John R., BSc *Exe.*, PhD *Open(UK)*   Sr. Lectr., Epidemiology

Woodruff, Geoffrey H. A., BSc *Lond.*, MB BS *Lond.*, FRCSEd   Sr. Lectr.

Other Staff: 1 Lectr.

Vacant Posts: 1 Prof.

Research: epidemiology (including cataract, diabetic retinopathy and ARMD); paediatric ophthalmology (including amblyopia and ophthalmic genetics)

Orthopaedic Surgery

Tel: (0116) 256 3012 Fax: (0116) 232 1702

Harper, William M., MB ChB *Leic.*, MD *Leic.*, FRCSEd   Prof., Orthopaedic Trauma Surgery; Head*

Triffitt, Paul D., BM BCh *Oxf.*, MA *Oxf.*, MD *Leic.*, FRCS   Sr. Lectr.

Other Staff: 1 Lectr.; 1 Hon. Sr. Lectr.

Research: outcome assessment following fractures in the elderly; strategies to treat hip fractures

Pathology

Tel: (0116) 252 3221 Fax: (0116) 252 3274

Furness, Peter N., BA *Camb.*, BM BCh *Oxf.*, PhD *Nott.*   Sr. Lectr.

Herbert, Karl E., BSc *Brunel*, PhD *Lond.*   Sr. Lectr.

Jones, J. Louise, BSc *Leic.*, MB ChB *Leic.*   Sr. Lectr., Breast Cancer

Lauder, Ian, MB BS *Newcastle(UK)*, FRCPath   Prof.; Head*

Lunec, Joseph, BSc *Lond.*, PhD *Lond.*   Prof., Chemical Pathology

McKeever, Patricia A., MB BCh BAO *Belf.*   Sr. Lectr.

Pringle, James H., BSc *CNAA*, PhD *Warw.*   Sr. Lectr.

Walker, Rosemary A., MB ChB *Birm.*, MD *Birm.*, FRCPath   Reader, Histopathology

West, Kevin P., BSc *Leic.*, MB ChB *Leic.*   Sr. Lectr.

Other Staff: 4 Lectrs.; 1 Hon. Sr. Lectr.; 3 Hon. Lectrs.

Research: breast cancer research; molecular pathology; molecular toxicity; renal research

Pharmacology, see Cell Physiol. and Pharmacol.

Pre-Clinical Sciences

Tel: (0116) 252 3021 Fax: (0116) 252 5072

Blakeley, Asa G. H., BM BCh *Oxf.*, MA *Oxf.*, DPhil *Oxf.*   Prof., Applied Physiology

England, Marjorie A., BA *Lawrence*, PhD *Lond.*   Sr. Lectr.

Gulamhusein, Amirali P., BSc *Mak.*, PhD *Lond.*   Sr. Lectr.; Head*

Howard, Laurence, JP, BSc *Nott.*, PhD *Leic.*   Sr. Lectr.

Ockleford, Colin D., BSc *St And.*, PhD *St And.*   Sr. Lectr.

Petersen, Stewart A., MA *Camb.*, PhD *Edin.*   Sr. Lectr.

Scott, Jonathan J. A., BSc *Durh.*, PhD *Durh.*   Sr. Lectr.

Tunstall, John, BSc *Durh.*, PhD *St And.*   Sr. Lectr.

Other Staff: 2 Lectrs.; 1 Hon. Lectr.

Research: human fetal membrane cell pathology; microscopy and image analysis; palaeopathology; sensory co-ordination of motor systems; vertebrate embryology

Psychiatry

Tel: (0116) 252 3240 Fax: (0116) 252 3293

Brugha, Terry S., MB BCh BAO *N.U.I.*, MD *N.U.I.*   Sr. Lectr.

Cameron, Douglas, BSc *Glas.*, MB ChB *Glas.*, MD *Glas.*, FRCPsych   Sr. Lectr., Substance Misuse

Dennis, Michael S., MB BCh *Wales*   Sr. Lectr., Psychiatry for Elderly

Dogra, Nisha, BM *S'ton.*   Sr. Lectr., Child Psychiatry

Duggan, Conor F., BSc *NUI*, MB BCh BAO *NUI*, PhD *NUI*, MD *NUI*   Prof., Forensic Mental Health

Lindesay, James E. B., MA *Oxf.*, DM *Oxf.*   Prof., Psychiatry for Elderly; Head*

Palmer, Robert L., MB BS *Lond.*, FRCPsych   Sr. Lectr.

Parkin, Andrew, BMedSci *Nott.*, BM BS *Nott.*   Sr. Lectr., Child Psychiatry

Prettyman, Richard J., MB ChB *Leic.*   Sr. Lectr., Psychiatry for the Elderly

Reveley, Michael A., BA *Texas*, MD *Texas*, PhD *Lond.*, FRCPsych   Prof.

Other Staff: 6 Lectrs.; 2 Hon. Sr. Lectrs.; 2 Hon. Lectrs.

Vacant Posts: 1 Prof.

Research: child and adolescent psychiatry; forensic mental health; psychiatry (alcohol/ substance abuse, eating disorders, neuropsychiatry, social/epidemiological); psychiatry for the elderly

Public Health, see Epidemiol. and Public Health

Radiology

Tel: (0116) 258 6719 Fax: (0116) 258 6721

Cherryman, Graham R., MB ChB *Cape Town*, FRCR   Prof.; Head*

Wilcock, David J., BA *Camb.*, MB BChir *Camb.*, MChir *Camb.*, FRCR   Sr. Lectr.

Other Staff: 1 Lectr.; 1 Hon. Sr. Lectr.

Research: echoplanar imaging in stroke; function MRI psychiatry and visual deficits; hepatic and oncological cross-sectional imaging; structural and functional cardiac MRI; structural MRI of cognitive impairment

Surgery

Tel: (0116) 252 3252 Fax: (0116) 252 3179

Bell, Peter R. F., MB ChB *Sheff.*, MD *Sheff.*, FRCS, FRCSGlas   Prof.; Head*

Galiñanes, Manuel, MD *Salamanca*, PhD
Lond.   Reader, Cardiac Surgery
James, Roger F. L., BSc *Sus.*, MSc *Lond.*, PhD
McG.   Reader, Immunology
London, Nicholas J. M., MB ChB *Birm.*, MD
Leic., FRCS   Prof.
Nicholson, Michael L., BMedSci *Nott.*, BM BS
Nott., MD *Leic.*, FRCS   Prof., Transplant
Surgery
Rew, David A., MB BChir *Camb.*, MA *Camb.*,
MChir *Camb.*, FRCS   Sr. Lectr.
Other Staff: 1 Visiting Prof.; 5 Lectrs.; 3 Hon.
Sr. Lectrs.; 2 Hon. Lectrs.
Research: vascular surgery and transplantation

Therapeutics, see Med. and Therapeutics

SPECIAL CENTRES, ETC

Adult Education
Tel: (0116) 252 5911 *Fax:* (0116) 252 5909
Berryman, Julia C., BSc *Aberd.*, PhD   Sr. Lectr.
Brown, Anthony E., MA *Oxf.*, FSA   Sr. Lectr.
Carter, Robert, BA *Leic.*, PhD *Brist.*   Sr. Lectr.;
Head*
Colls, Robert M., BA *Sus.*, DPhil *York(UK)*   Sr.
Lectr.
Harper, David M., MA *Oxf.*, PhD *Dund.*,
FLS   Sr. Lectr.
Jacobs, Michael D., MA *Oxf.*   Sr. Lectr.
Parsons, David, BA *Durh.*, PhD *Leic.*, FSA   Sr.
Lectr.
Other Staff: 6 Lectrs.; 1 Prof.†; 1 Sr. Lectr.†
Research: archaeology, architectural and social
history; ecology (pearlands and water
habitats); labour process, class analysis, trade
unions; music, drama and literature;
psychological research on parenthood and
parenting

American Studies, Centre for
Tel: (0116) 252 2803 *Fax:* (0116) 252 3986
Cull, Nicholas, BA *Leeds*, PhD *Leeds*   Prof.; Dir.*
Research: American poetry; film, literature and
society; gender, sexualities and identity in
literature; US foreign policy, media and
propaganda; US social history (women's and
African American)

Applied Psychology, Centre for
Tel: (0116) 252 2481 *Fax:* (0116) 252 3994
Hollin, Clive R., BSc *Lond.*, PhD *Lond.*,
FBPsS   Reader
McCrea, Celia W., BA *Belf.*, PhD *Lond.*   Sr.
Lectr.
Miller, Prof. Edgar, BSc *Hull*, BA *Camb.*, MPhil
Lond., PhD *Hull*, FBPsS   Dir.*
Other Staff: 4 Lectrs.; 1 Hon. Reader; 7 Hon.
Lectrs.
Research: clinical psychology; forensic and legal
psychology

Archaeological Services, Leicester University
Tel: (0116) 252 2848 *Fax:* (0116) 252 2614
Buckley, Richard J., BA *Durh.*   Dir.*
Research: archaeology of buildings; artefactual
analysis; landscape archaeology; study of
past environments; urban archaeology

Biological NMR Spectroscopy Centre
Tel: (0116) 252 2938 *Fax:* (0116) 252 3995
Lian, Lu-Yun, BSc *W.Aust.*, PhD
Warw.   Manager
Roberts, Prof. Gordon C. K., BSc *Lond.*, PhD
Lond.   Dir.*
Research: drug-metabolising enzymes; NMR
methods for studying proteins; protein-DNA
interactions; protein structure and dynamics;
structures of signalling proteins

Community Care Studies Unit, Nuffield
Tel: (0116) 252 5422 *Fax:* (0116) 252 5423
Parker, Prof. Gillian, BA *Liv.*, PhD *Birm.*   Head*
Other Staff: 1 Lectr.

Research: boundaries in health and social care;
evaluation of community care policy/
practice; inequalities in health and social
care; population forecasting for community
care needs

Computers in Teaching Initiative Centre for Geography, Geology and Meteorology
Tel: (0116) 252 3827 *Fax:* (0116) 252 3854
Robinson, Geoffrey, MA *Camb.*   Dir.*
Research: technologies to support teaching and
learning

Diplomacy, Centre for the Study of
Tel: (0116) 252 2797 *Fax:* (0116) 252 5082
Berridge, Prof. Geoffrey R., BA *Durh.*, MA *Sus.*,
PhD *Durh.*   Dir.*
Research: database on formal diplomatic
relations; diplomatic theory from Machiavelli
to Kissinger; economic diplomacy; history of
the resident embassy; inter-disciplinary
perspectives on diplomacy

Disability and the Arts, Richard Attenborough Centre for
Tel: (0116) 252 2455 *Fax:* (0116) 252 5165
Hartley, Eleanor, BA *Liv.*, MA *Leic.*, PhD
Leic.   Dir.*
Other Staff: 3 Lectrs.
Research: art and touch education; art education
and care training; choreography and dance
analysis; classical music of the African
diaspora; dance and physical disability

Early-Modern Studies, Centre for
Tel: (0116) 252 2800 *Fax:* (0116) 252 3986
Davidson, Nicholas S., BA *Camb.*   Dir.*
Research: British and Continental history; focus
on gender, religion, class, age; history of
medicine and science; interdisciplinary and
comparative approach to period; studies of
social and cultural dissent

Ethnicity Research Centre
Tel: (0116) 252 2749 *Fax:* (0116) 252 5259
Jewson, Nicholas O., BScEcon *Wales*, MA
Leic.   Dir.*
Research: equal opportunities policies and
practices; ethnic communities and urban
contexts; ethnicity and health care; ethnicity
employment and labour markets; ethnicity,
nationalisms and identities

European Economic Studies, Centre for
Tel: (0116) 252 2757 *Fax:* (0116) 252 5129
Charemza, Wojciech, DrEcon *Gda(ac)nsk*,
DrHabEcon *Gda(ac)nsk*   Dir.*
Other Staff: 1 Lectr.
Research: economic analysis of East European
transition/European integration; European
economic research

European Politics and Institutions, Centre for
Tel: (0116) 252 2714 *Fax:* (0116) 252 5082
Monar, Prof. Jorg, LèsL *Paris IV*, MA *Munich*,
DrPhil *Munich*, DrRerPol *Florence*   Dir.*
Research: British politics and European
integration; co-operation in justice and
home affairs; eastern enlargement of the
European Union; European security and
defence policy; European Union institutions
and policy-making

Football Research, Sir Norman Chester Centre for
Tel: (0116) 252 2741 *Fax:* (0116) 252 2746
Phizacklea, Prof. Anne, BA *Exe.*, MA *McM.*, PhD
Exe.   Dir.*
Williams, John, BA *Leic.*   Res. Sr. Lectr.
Research: ethnicity (community, history,
identity, racism); fan cultures (consumption,
creativity, fashion, hooliganism);
globalisation (migration, mobility, transnational identities); modernisation (change,
marketing, new football, relocation,

tradition); women (community, gender,
playing careers, sexuality)

Forensic Pathology, Centre for
Tel: (0116) 258 6581 *Fax:* (0116) 255 2482
Bouch, D. Clive, BSc *Edin.*, MB ChB *Edin.*   Dir.*
Other Staff: 1 Hon. Lectr.
Research: dating of human remains

History of Religions, Inter-Faith Dialogue and Pluralism, Centre for the
Tel: (0116) 252 2800 *Fax:* (0116) 252 3986
Bonney, Rev. Prof. Richard J., MA *Oxf.*, DPhil
Oxf., FRHistS   Dir.*
Research: Christian-Jewish-Muslim relations
(Islam and the West); Holocaust/genocidal
conflict in world perspective; inter-faith
relations in the Indian sub-continent; issues
in pluralism and cultural identity; issues of
social harmony/minority rights

Holocaust Studies, Stanley Burton Centre for
Tel: (0116) 252 2800 *Fax:* (0116) 252 3986
Paulsson, Gunnar S., BA *Car.*, MA *Tor.*   Dir.*
Research: Anglo-Jewry and the Holocaust;
Holocaust experiences in individual
European states; media studies (press and
radio); post-Holocaust experience
(restitution and resettlement); societies that
were destroyed

Labour Market Studies, Centre for
Tel: (0116) 252 5950 *Fax:* (0116) 252 5953
Ashton, Prof. David, BA *Leic.*   Dir.*
Other Staff: 1 Deputy Dir.; 3 Lectrs.
Research: business reorganisation; employers'
training policies and practices; growth of
non-standard forms of employment; national
human resource and training systems; work-
related and work-based learning

Macromolecular Hydrodynamics, National Centre for
Tel: (0116) 252 3471 *Fax:* (0116) 252 5260
Rowe, Arthur J., MA *Camb.*, PhD *Camb.*   Dir.*
Research: analytical ultracentrifugation (AUC) of
proteins; differential refractometric
(Schlieren) optics for AUCs; solution studies
of motility proteins; structural studies of
bacterial toxins; theory of concentration
dependence of sedimentation

Management Centre
Tel: (0116) 252 3952 *Fax:* (0116) 252 3949
Jackson, Prof. Peter M., BA *Strath.*, PhD
Stir.   Dir.*
Scarbrough, Harry, BA *Durh.*, MBA *Brad.*, PhD
Aston   Prof., Organisational Analysis
Other Staff: 8 Lectrs.
Research: human resource management and
development; industrial relations and
organisational behaviour; public sector
performance management; SME innovation
and technology management; strategic
planning for co-operative organisations

Management, Law and Industrial Relations, International Centre for
Tel: (0116) 252 2370 *Fax:* (0116) 252 2699
Bourn, Colin J., BSc(Econ) *Lond.*   Dir.*
Neal, Prof. Alan C., LLB *Warw.*, LLM *Lond.*, LLM
Leic.   Dir.*
Research: discrimination in the labour market;
employment law; European social law;
health and safety

Mechanisms of Human Toxicity, Centre for
Tel: (0116) 252 5525 *Fax:* (0116) 252 5616
Roberts, Prof. Gordon C. K., BSc *Lond.*, PhD
Lond.   Dir.*
Woods, Prof. Kent L., MA *Camb.*, ScM *Harv.*,
MD *Camb.*, FRCP   Dir., Clin. Programmes

Other Staff: 1 Lectr.; 4 Hon. Profs.; 8 Hon. Lectrs.

Research: apoptosis; biomonitoring of exposure to carcinogens; genetic susceptibility to effects of toxins; mechanisms of chemical carcinogenesis; neurotoxicology

Midlands Regional Research Laboratory

Tel: (0116) 252 3825 Fax: (0116) 252 3854

Strachan, Alan J., MA *Edin.*, MS *Wis.*, PhD *Edin.* Dir.*

Research: academic support for spatial information systems; fuzzy land information for environmental remote systems; Project Argus (visualisation in the spatial sciences); urban information systems; virtual field course

Public Sector Economics Research Centre

Tel: (0116) 252 3950 Fax: (0116) 252 3949

Fraser, Prof. Clive D., BSocSci *Birm.*, PhD *S'ton.* Dir. of Res.

Jackson, Prof. Peter M., BA *Strath.*, PhD *Stir.* Dir.*

Other Staff: 1 Lectr.

Research: crime, law, taxation; economics of public good provision; informal economy; public sector economies

Quebec Studies, Centre for

Tel: (0116) 252 2694 Fax: (0116) 252 3633

Rolfe, Christopher D., MA *Wales* Dir.*

Research: culture and society of Quebec; Quebec model

Space Research Centre

Tel: (0116) 252 3491 Fax: (0116) 252 2464

Cole, Richard E., MA *Camb.*, PhD *Lond.*, MBA *De Mont.* Manager

Wells, Prof. Alan A., BSc *Lond.*, MSc *Lond.* Prof.*

Research: advanced x-ray sensors and infra-red for space astronomy; climate-related research using satellite and other data; low temperature x-ray imaging spectroscopy; modelling and data analysis of the ocean-atmosphere system; space instrumentation system design and development

Sport and Society, Centre for Research into

Tel: (0116) 252 5939 Fax: (0116) 252 5720

Dunning, Prof. Eric G., BSc(Econ) *Lond.*, MA *Leic.* Dir.*

Murphy, Patrick J., BA *Leic.* Dir.*

Waddington, Ivan H., BA *Leic.*, PhD *Leic.* Dir.*

Other Staff: 1 Lectr.

Research: sport and health; sports and drugs; sports and race; sports and violence

Urban History, Centre for

Tel: (0116) 252 2378 Fax: (0116) 252 5062

Clark, Prof. Peter A., MA *Oxf.*, FSA, FRHistS Dir.*

Research: European urban history; small towns; urban education and housing; urban history methodology

Victorian Studies Centre

Tel: (0116) 252 3943 Fax: (0116) 252 2065

Shattock, Prof. E. Joanne, BA *Newcastle(UK)*, MA *Leeds*, PhD *Lond.* Dir.*

Research: Dickens; labour history; nineteenth-century sculpture; regional culture; Victorian theatre

CONTACT OFFICERS

Academic affairs. Academic Registrar: Williams, Katherine E., BA *Reading*

Accommodation. Director of Residential and Conference Services: Wragg, Timothy R., MA *CNAA*, MBA *Leic.*

Admissions (first degree). Sr. Assistant Registrar: Graham, Janet, BA *Leic.*, MA *Leic.*

Admissions (higher degree). Principal Assistant Registrar: Masterman, S. Louise, BA *Manc.*

Adult/continuing education. Secretary (Department of Adult Education/Faculty of Education and Continuing Studies): Lacey, Anthony J., BEd *Durh.*, MA *Lond.*

Alumni. Alumni and Fund Raising Officer: Allen, Peter, BA *Lond.*

Archives. Archivist: Clark, Jennifer D., BA *Brist.*†

Careers. Head of Careers Service: Grant, Ann E., MA *Camb.*, PhD *Camb.*, FSA

Computing services. Director: Wilson, John D., BSc *Birm.*

Conferences/corporate hospitality. Conference Sales and Marketing Manager: Myatt, Rebecca

Credit transfer. Sr. Assistant Registrar: Graham, Janet, BA *Leic.*, MA *Leic.*

Development/fund-raising. Alumni and Fund Raising Officer: Allen, Peter, BA *Lond.*

Distance education. Principal Assistant Registrar: Masterman, S. Louise, BA *Manc.*

Equal opportunities. Staff Welfare and Equal Opportunities Officer: McPhail, Fiona H. R., BA *Lanc.*, MA *Warw.*

Estates and buildings/works and services. Director: Britton, Simon P., BSc *Manc.*, FRICS

Examinations. Assistant Registrar: Forshaw, Damian, BA *Durh.*

Finance. Director: Wright, Martin D., BA *Open(UK)*, MA *Oxf.*

General enquiries. Registrar and Secretary: Julian, Keith J., MA *Camb.*

Health services. Director: Jethwa, Ashok, MB ChB *Brist.*

Industrial liaison. Business Development Officer: Murray, Catherine M., BSc *Salf.*†

International office. Principal Assistant Registrar: Pearson, Anthony C. E., BA *Kent*

Language Training for International Students. Director of Language Services Unit: Kenworthy, H. Martin, BA *Leeds*, MA *Leeds*

Library (chief librarian). Librarian: Hobbs, Timothy D., MA *Exe.*, PhD *Camb.*

Library (enquiries). Information Services Librarian: Rawlinson, Stephen, BSc *S'ton.*

Minorities/disadvantaged groups. Staff Welfare and Equal Opportunities Officer: McPhail, Fiona H. R., BA *Lanc.*, MA *Warw.*

Ombudsperson. Registrar and Secretary: Julian, Keith J., MA *Camb.*

Personnel/human resources. Head of Personnel Office: Hodgson, Ronald G., BA *Leic.*

Public relations, information and marketing. Director of Press and Publications: Mirza, Ather A., BA *Leic.*

Publications. Director of Press and Publications: Mirza, Ather A., BA *Leic.*

Research. Director: Davis, Keith M. C., BSc *Nott.*, PhD *Nott.*

Safety. Director: Widdowson, David, BSc *Newcastle(UK)*, PhD *Sheff.*

Scholarships, awards, loans. Senior Administrative Assistant: Mann, Julia, BA *Warw.*†

Schools liaison. Senior Administrative Assistant: Wetzig, Jacquelyn M.

Security. Security Officer: Blandford, Graham

Sport and recreation. Manager: Hide, Colin P., BEd *Warw.*, MA *Birm.*

Staff development and training. Director: Beasley, Nigel A., BA *Nott.*, PhD *Nott.*

Student union. Union Manager: Kirk, Philip

Student welfare/counselling. Senior Student Welfare Officer: Taylor, Clare F., BA *Leic.*

Students from other countries. Principal Assistant Registrar: Pearson, Anthony C. E., BA *Kent*

Students with disabilities. Senior Student Welfare Officer: Taylor, Clare F., BA *Leic.*

Women. Staff Welfare and Equal Opportunities Officer: McPhail, Fiona H. R., BA *Lanc.*, MA *Warw.*

[*Information supplied by the institution as at 31 March 1998, and edited by the ACU*]

UNIVERSITY OF LINCOLNSHIRE AND HUMBERSIDE

Founded 1992 as University of Humberside; previously established as Hull School of Art (1861), Humberside
College of Higher Education (1982), and Humberside Polytechnic (1991); present name adopted 1996

Member of the Association of Commonwealth Universities

Postal Address: Cottingham Road, Kingston upon Hull, England HU6 7RT
Telephone: (01482) 440550 **Fax**: (01482) 471343 **E-mail formula**: initialsurname@humber.ac.uk

CHAIRMAN OF GOVERNORS AND CHANCELLOR—Hooper, H., CBE
VICE-CHANCELLOR/CHIEF EXECUTIVE*‡—King, Prof. Roger P., BSc(Econ) *Lond.*, MSocSci *Birm.*
SENIOR DEPUTY VICE-CHANCELLOR, RESOURCES—Holt, John, MA *Leeds*
DEPUTY VICE-CHANCELLOR—Bardon, Keith, BA *Wales*, PhD *Wales*
PRO-VICE-CHANCELLOR, QUALITY COMMISSIONER—Crothall, Derek, BA *Hull*
PRO-VICE-CHANCELLOR, SYSTEMS AND CLIENT SERVICES—Whittingham, Jim, PhD *Sheff.*, BSc
HEAD OF LEARNING SUPPORT (LIBRARIES)—Foster, Mike, PhD *Hull*
REGISTRAR—Marks, F. S.

GENERAL INFORMATION

History. The University of Humberside was founded in 1992. Previously established as Hull School of Art (1861), Humberside College of Higher Education (1982), and Humberside Polytechnic (1991), the university adopted its present name in 1996.

It comprises three campuses located in Grimsby, Hull and Lincoln.

Admission to first degree courses (see also United Kingdom Introduction). Through Universities and Colleges Admissions Service (UCAS). Minimum English language requirements for international applicants: O Level/GCSE grade C, ELTS score 6.0, TOEFL score 550.

First Degrees (see also United Kingdom Directory to Subjects of Study). BA, BEng, BSc.

Most courses last 3 years. BEng foundation course: 1 year; sandwich courses: 4 years.

Higher Degrees (see also United Kingdom Directory to Subjects of Study). MA, MBA, MEd, MSc, DBA, EdD.

Academic Year. September–July.

Statistics. Students: undergraduate 9151 (full-time 7427, part-time 1724); postgraduate 1301; non-degree 1272; total 11,724.

FACULTIES/SCHOOLS

Applied Science and Technology, School of
Dean: Barlow, Philip, PhD *Leeds*
Secretary: Burley, Sarah

Architecture, Hull School of
Acting Dean: Jones, Chris

Art and Design, Hull School of
Dean: Bush, Roger

Economics and International Studies, School of
Dean: Barnes, Prof. Ian, MA *Hull*

Engineering and Information Technology, School of
Dean: Stokes, Roland, MSc *Lough.*, BSc
Secretary: Henderson, Julie

Hull Business School
Dean: Jackson, Prof. Michael, MA *Lanc.*
Secretary: Gibbs, Doreen

Management, Lincoln School of
Dean: Jackson, Prof. Michael, MA *Lanc.*
Secretary: Gibbs, Doreen

Media and Communications, School of
Dean: Cosker, Phil, BScEcon *Wales*

Policy Studies, School of
Dean: Arnold, Prof. Peter, MA *York(UK)*

Social Sciences and Professional Studies, School of
Dean: Lockwood, John, MA *Leeds*

ACADEMIC UNITS
Arranged by Schools

Accountancy, see under Hull Bus. Sch.

Applied Science and Technology
Fax: (01472) 751404 Fax: (01472) 315099
Beers, Paul

Environmental Studies
Fax: (01472) 315099
Butler, David   Named Award Leader, BA Environmental Studies
Doughty, Mark
Esser, John   Head*
Gilbert, Alan   Named Award Leader, HNC
Grantham, David
Latus, Mike
Marriott, Alan
Parkinson, Keith
Powell, Alan   Named Award Leader, BA Environmental Studies
Sanchez, John

Food Science and Technology
Ahmad, John   Named Award Leader, Modular Food Studies
Birkett, John   Named Award Leader, Modular Food Studies
Boyce, William
Breen, Brendan
Cassidy, Phil   Named Award Leader, Postgrad./MSc Food Safety and Quality Management; Postgrad. Programme Leader (Food)
Garthwaite, Tony
Gennard, Dorothy   Named Award Leader, Modular Food Studies
Grigor, John
Hallam, Ellie
Hanna, John   Head*
Hole, Mike   Programme Manager (Food)
Knowles, Mike
Meldrum, Richard   Named Award Leader, Postgrad./MSc Food Technology
Miskin, Dave
Morris, Ann
Nolan, Marie   Named Award Leader, HND/HNC Food Science/Technology
Proudlove, Keith   Named Award Leader, Modular Food Studies
Quantick, Peter
Radcliffe, Clive
Smith, Peter
Swanney, Geoff
Taylor, Prof. Tony
Warburton, Gordon   Named Award Leader, HND/HNC Food Science/Technology

Ward, Adrian   Named Award Leader, Modular Food Studies

Architecture, Hull School of
Arnold, Norman
Clark, George
Colquhoun, Ian
Cottrell, Derek   Assoc. Dean
Earl, Andy
Etherton, David   Field Leader
Hansford, Bridget
Hay, Chris   Named Award Leader
Hodges, David
Hornsby, Gary   Named Award Leader
Jenkins, Kathie   Named Award Leader
Kent, Roger
Latham, Alan   Named Award Leader
Lomholt, Jane
Matthews, Geoff
McConnell, Richard
Oakenfull, Michael
Raynor, David
Sodagar, Behzad
Squire, Paul
Sully, Tony
Todd, David   Named Award Leader
Watt, Kathleen

Art and Design, Hull School of
Atkinson-Dell, Peter   Field Leader; Named Award Leader
Beaumont, Nick
Bradshaw, Stuart
Chamberlain, Walter   Named Award Leader
Charnley, Clare
Cole, Richard
Czarnecki, Gina
Dyson, Gillian
Eisenenmann, Marcus
Emberton, Anne
Fearnley, Brian
Finn, Colin
Gates, Eleanor
Gawthrop, Rob   Named Award Leader
Harkness, Allan
Humphreys, Sarah
Jeffery, Alan
Longworth, John
Miszewska, Anna
Morley, Catherine
Mowbray, Joanna
Owen, Peter
Phippard, Pat
Ringe, Simon
Silverman, Lynn
Thomas, Alan
Warren, Carol
Wolmark, Jenny   Named Award Leader
Wright, Alexa
Vacant Posts: 1 Field Leader

Business, see Hull Bus. Sch., and under Management, Lincoln Sch. of

Communications, see under Media and Communicns.

Economics and International Studies

Barnes, Pam
Clarke, P.
Good, Max
Gray, David
Mearman, Andrew
Randerson, Claire
Seawright, David
Strange, Gerard
Turner, C.

Engineering and Information Technology

Fax: (01482) 463783

Engineering

Fax: (01482) 463783

Blencoe, Roger †
Childs, Amanda, BA MSc Sr. Lectr.; Named Award Leader
Cockram, David †
Collins, John †
Deverell, John, BSc MPhil Sr. Lectr.; Field Leader
Dickinson, Martin
Evans, Frank †
Gilbert, I. Gordon, BSc Sr. Lectr.; Field Leader
Goodwin, Gerry
Hassan, Jaffar, BSc MSc PhD Sr. Lectr.; Named Award Leader
Hodgson, Simon
Horler, Greg
Packard, Paul, BSc MSc Sr. Lectr.
Singer, George
Smith, Alan, BSc MSc Sr. Lectr.; Named Award Leader
Thomson, John †
Tomlinson, Stuart †
Tranter, David Named Award Leader
Ward, Robert †
West, Tony †

Information Technology

Fax: (01482) 463783

Amyes, David †
Blaza, Sonia, MPhil *Sheff.Hallam*, BEng Sr. Lectr.; Named Award Leader
Chapman, Mel †
Crosbie, Sandra, BSc Sr. Lectr.; Placements Officer
Hill, Caroline
Hollingworth, John, BA MSc Sr. Lectr.; Named Award Leader
Lewak, John, MBA Sr. Lectr.; Named Award Leader
Myers, Malcolm, BSc *Manc.*, PhD *Hull* Sr. Lectr.; Named Award Leader
Perry, Ian Named Award Leader
Reeve, Paul
Robson, Wendy
Saich, Virginia, BSc MSc Sr. Lectr.; Named Award Leader
Spencer, Terry

Environmental Studies, see under Appl. Sci. and Technol.

Finance, see Accty. and Finance under Hull Bus. Sch.

Food Science and Technology, see under Appl. Sci. and Technol.

Health Studies, see under Soc. Scis. and Professional Studies

Hull Business School, see also under Management, Lincoln Sch. of

Fax: (01482) 463599

Accountancy and Finance

Fax: (01482) 463575

Bellamy, Malcolm
Berridge, David

Boczko, Tony
Fell, Lindsay Named Award Leader
Fijalkowski, Peter
Landen, Ian
Memmott, John
Mould, Pat
Murphy, John Head*
Pliener, Martin
Smales, Peter
Smith, David
Thompson, Tim
Varlow, Peter Named Award Leader

Business Management

Fax: (01482) 463828

Berrow, Terry
Burdett-Conway, Angela
Clannachan, Sharon
Coggon, Brian
Davison, Leigh Head*
Dent, Christopher
Flynn, John
Harrison, Lynda
Johnson, Debra
McPherson, Campbell
Meyer, Hugh
Milner, Brian
Murtagh, Tom
Tether, Philip
Thompson, Chris

Human Resource and Administrative Management

Fax: (01482) 463784

Agyeman, Sam
Cagney-Watts, Helen
Currie, David
Dobson, Fred
Grimble, Maureen
Headlam-Wells, Jenny
Kellie, Jean
Maksymiw, Wolodymyr
McElwee, Gerard Head of External Business Unit
McGivern, Janet
Milsom, Brian
Nason, Joe
Osuch, Doreen Head*
Pattison, David
Pike, Christopher
Reeve, Diane
Thompson, Jane

International Marketing

Fax: (01482) 463048

Cardyn, George
Cox, Val
De Bel, Marc
Dean, Diane
Evans, David
Forte, Peter Head*
Lowensberg, Daniel
Spickett-Jones, Graham Named Award Leader, Marketing
Teale, Mark
Witty, Joanna

Modern Languages

Bissonauth-Bedford, Anu
Coverdale-Jones, Patricia
Gervais, Chantel
Johnson, Sheelagh
Picard, Nigel
Scott, Ian Head*

Humanities, see under Media and Communicns.

Information Technology, see Engin. and Information Technol.

Law, see under Soc. Scis. and Professional Studies

Management, Lincoln School of, see also under Hull Bus. Sch.

Tel: (01482) 438828 *Fax:* (01482) 299985

Applied Development Studies, Centre for

Tel: (01522) 882000

Carlton, Andy
Finlayson, Dennis
Friend, John
Gregory, Amanda Head*

Business Policy

Tel: (01522) 882000

Clarke, Peter
Croft, Robin
Good, Max
Gray, David
Lancaster, Geoff
Loughlin, Linda
Marchant, Alan Leader*
Mearman, Andrews
White, Brian

Information Systems

Tel: (01522) 882000 *Fax:* (01522) 886032

Brayshaw, Mike
Castell, Adrian
Edgar-Nevill, Denis Leader*
James, Mathew
Warren, Lorraine
Zhi-Chang Zhu

International Educational Leadership and Management Centre

Tel: (01522) 882000

Davies, Brent Leader*
O'Sullivan, Fergus Named Award Leader, MBA and MSc Education Management
Thody, Angela Named Award Leader, EdD
West-Burnham, John Named Award Leader, Education Management

Organisational Analysis

Tel: (01522) 882000

Brooke, Carole
Hitchen, Linda
O'Brien, Paula
Pritchard, Craig

Marketing, see Internat. Marketing under Hull Bus. Sch.

Media and Communications

Communications

Tel: (01522) 882000 *Fax:* (01522) 886021

Dubois, Diane
Hildyard, Rupert
Kenyon, David
Lewczuk, Alex A.
McLaurin, Allen Head*
Nayer, Bhaskaran
Redpath, Philip Named Award Leader
Tate, Alison

Humanities

Tel: (01522) 882000 *Fax:* (01522) 886021

Dixon, John
Hill, Kate
Langran, Phillip Named Award Leader
McCracken, Penny Head*
Nield, Barbara
Swan, Philip
Walker, Andrew Named Award Leader
Ziegler, Harry

Media

Tel: (01522) 882000 *Fax:* (01522) 886021

Bellamy, Christine
Booth, Jerry Head*
Dexter, Christine
Galton, Graeme Named Award Leader
Garland, Ros
Georgiou, Darryl
Greene, Roger
Healey, Mike
Holden, John
Mason, Mike
Mendelle, Noe Named Award Leader
Reiners, Colin
Richards, Tony
Rudd, Bryan

Tirohl, Blu
Wilson, Deborah

Modern Languages, see under Hull Bus.
Sch.

Policy Studies

Social Policy

Bochel, Catherine
Bochel, Hugh   Named Award Leader; Leader*
Bouandel, Youcef
Briggs, Jacqueline
Brown, Sally
Cooper, Charles
Craig, Gary
Gillespie, Gill
Spink, Bill
Wiles, Melvyn

Tourism

Bahaire, Tim
Bull, Adrian
Cuthill, Vivienne
Elliot-White, Martin
Finn, Mick
Knight, Martin
Lewis, Alison
Morpeth, Nigel
Voase, Richard
Walton, Mike   Named Award Leader; Leader*

Social Sciences and Professional Studies

Health Studies

Birchenall, Peter   Named Award Leader;
Leader*
Clayton, John
Farr, Janet
Lee, Derek

Law

Bankole, Cole
Fitzpatrick, Edmund   Named Award Leader;
Leader*
Forbes, Malcolm
Jameson, Jill
Jones, Kelvin   Named Award Leader,
Criminology
Lawson, Ann
McCann, Liam
McLaughlin, Clive
Ryland, Diane
Summan, Sandhla
Whittle, Alan

Psychology

Allinson, Lesley
Barnecutt, Peter
Bromnick, Rachel
Coates, Peter
Goddard, Paul
Guernina, Zoubida
Pfeffer, Karen   Named Award Leader
Robertson, Colin   Named Award Leader
Wilson, Garry
Wilson, John
Vacant Posts: 1 staff member

Social Science

Billington, Ros
Blackburn, Don   Leader*
Conway, Stephen
Emptage, Tricia
Fitzsimons, Annette   Named Award Leader,
Applied Social Science
Macdonald, Paul
Maxwell, Maureen
McCorry, Stephen
Norton, Paul
Sutcliffe, Christine
Swallow, Brian
Waller, K.

Social Work

Adams, Robert
Bethell, Jackie   Named Award Leader, Practice
Teaching
Crimmens, David   Named Award Leader,
Community and Youth Work Diploma
Golightly, Malcolm   Leader*
Matthews, Trevor
O'Sullivan, Terry   Named Award Leader,
DipSW
Petrie, Steph
Smith, Clare   Named Award Leader,
Counselling
Smythe, Peter
Strickland, Tom   Named Award Leader,
Managing Care Services
Vaughan, Gerry
Vacant Posts: 1 Named Award Leader; 1 other
staff member

Tourism, see under Policy Studies

SPECIAL CENTRES, ETC

Food Research Centre

Warren, Peter   Dir.*

CONTACT OFFICERS

Academic affairs. Director of Academic
Development: Holmes, George
Accommodation. Residential Services Manager:
Buckby, David
Careers. Senior Careers Advisor: Gibbeson, Ian
Computing services. Director, Computing and
Network Services: Jones, Martyn
Computing services. Director, Management
Information Systems Services: Blackett, Val
Distance education. Director, Open Learning
Institute: Humphreys, Steve
Estates and buildings/works and services.
Director, Estates and Facilities: Mullaney,
David
Finance. Director, Financial Services: Feller,
Ian
General enquiries. Registrar: Marks, F. S.
Health services. Health Centre: Miller, Mary
International office. Director, Open Learning
Institute: Humphreys, Steve
Library (chief librarian). Director of Learning
Support: Foster, Mike, PhD Hull
Library (enquiries). Academic Services
Manager, Learning Support: Dyson, Philippa
Personnel/human resources. Manager,
Personnel: Fill, Jane
Personnel/human resources. Director,
Human Resources: Lyne de Ver, Erzsi
Public relations, information and marketing.
Director, Marketing: Cook, Sheila
Quality assurance and accreditation. Director,
Quality and Student Services: Corfield, Prof.
George
Research. Director, Research: Arnold, Prof.
Peter
Safety. Health and Safety Officer: Wood, Rob
Schools liaison Humberside. Education
Liaison Officer: Spencer, Ann
Schools liaison Lincoln. Ridings, Prof. Arthur
Student welfare/counselling. Student
Counselling: Mathers, Eunice

CAMPUS/COLLEGE HEADS

Lincoln University Campus, Brayford Pool,
Lincoln, England LN6 7TS. Head: King, Prof.
Roger P., BSc(Econ) *Lond.*, MSocSci *Birm.*

[*Information supplied by the institution as at March
1998, and edited by the ACU*]

UNIVERSITY OF LIVERPOOL

Founded 1903; previously established as the University College, Liverpool 1881

Member of the Association of Commonwealth Universities

Postal Address: Liverpool, England L69 3BX
Telephone: (0151) 794 2000 **Fax**: (0151) 708 6502 **E-mail**: liverpool.ac.uk or liv.ac.uk (SUN network)
Cables: University, Liverpool **WWW**: http://www.liv.ac.uk **E-mail formula**: initials.surname@liverpool.ac.uk
or surnameinitials@liverpool.ac.uk or firstname.surname@liverpool.ac.uk

VISITOR—Elizabeth, H.M. The Queen
CHANCELLOR—Owen, The Rt. Hon. the Lord, CH, BA *Camb.*, MB BChir *Camb.*, MA *Camb.*
PRO-CHANCELLOR—Mould, Anthony M., JP, Hon. LLD *Liv.*
PRESIDENT OF THE COUNCIL—Holden, Lawrence, LLB
VICE-PRESIDENT OF THE COUNCIL—Booth, Dame Margaret, LLB *Lond.*, LLM *Lond.*, Hon. LLD *Liv.*
VICE-CHANCELLOR*—Love, Prof. Philip N., CBE, LLB *Aberd.*, MA *Aberd.*, Hon. LLD *Abertay*, Hon.
   LLD *Aberd.*
TREASURER—Potts, Michael S., FCA
DEPUTY-TREASURER—Thelwall Jones, Graham M., MA PhD
PRO-VICE-CHANCELLOR—Fisher, Prof. John R., BA *Lond.*, MPhil *Lond.*, PhD *Liv.*, FRHistS
PRO-VICE-CHANCELLOR—Tarn, Prof. John N., OBE, BArch *Durh.*, PhD *Camb.*, FRHistS, FSA
PRO-VICE-CHANCELLOR—Williams, Prof. David F., PhD *Birm.*, DSc *Birm.*, FIM
REGISTRAR‡—Carr, Michael D., MA *Durh.*
LIBRARIAN—Thomson, Frances M., MA *Glas.*, BLitt *Glas.*

GENERAL INFORMATION

History. The university was originally established in 1881 as University College, Liverpool, in response to a petition presented on behalf of the citizens of Liverpool, and gained university status in 1903.

Most of the university's buildings are located near the centre of Liverpool.

Admission to first degree courses (see also United Kingdom Introduction). Normally General Certificate of Education (GCE) A levels or equivalents (including Scottish and Irish Certificates, International or European Baccalaureate, Malaysian STPM, Hong Kong A levels, etc.). Each course has its own formal entry requirements, including literacy and numeracy requirements. Candidates whose first language is not English must provide evidence of proficiency in English, such as British Council IELTS test.

First Degrees. BA, BClinSci, BDS, BEd, BEng, BN, BSc, BTh, BVSc, LLB, MB BCh.

BClinSci: 1 year intercalated, following at least 2 years of MB BCh; BEd, BTh: 3 years; BA: 3 or 4 years full-time, or 7 years part-time; BEng, BSc, LLB: 3 or 4 years; BN: 4 years; BDS, BVSc, MB ChB: 5 years.

Higher Degrees. BPhil, ChM, LLM, MA, MArch, MBA, MCD, MChOth, MCommH, MD, MDentSci, MDes, MDS, MEd, MPhil, PhD, DClinPsychol, DEng, DLitt, DSc, DVSc, LLD.

Applicants for admission to master's degree courses and PhD must normally hold an appropriate first degree with at least second class honours; equivalent professional experience may be acceptable in some cases. DEng, DLitt, DSc, DVSc, LLD: awarded on the basis of published work to graduates of this university of at least 7 years' standing.

Most courses last 1 year full-time or 2 years part-time. ChM, MD, MDS: by thesis; MBA, MCommH: full-time only; MDentSci, MDes: part-time only; MCD: 2 years full-time; DClinPsychol: 3 years full-time; MChOth: 4 years part-time; MPhil: minimum 1 year full-time or minimum 2 years part-time; PhD: minimum 2 years full-time or 4–7 years part-time.

Language of Instruction. English. Intensive pre-sessional courses available through Applied English Language Studies Unit.

Libraries. 1,400,000 volumes; 5000 periodicals subscribed to. Special collections include: Cunard Steamship Company; Gypsy (including archive of Gypsy Lore Society); mediaeval and early Renaissance manuscripts; Science Fiction Foundation; social work (including Barnardo's); Stapledon (life and works of Olaf Stapledon).

Fees (1997–98, annual). Undergraduate: UK/EU students £750 (arts), £1600 (sciences), £2800 (clinical); international students £6106 (arts), £8211 (sciences), £14,843 (clinical). Postgraduate: £6106–6606 (arts); £3284–8211 (sciences); £2464–14,843 (clinical).

Academic Awards (1998–99). Fifty international scholarships covering tuition fees for up to three years.

Academic Year (1998–99). Two semesters: 28 September–29 January; 1 February–11 June.

Income (1996–97). Total, £156,922,000.

Statistics. Staff: 4117 (1451 academic, 710 administrative, 1956 other). Students: full-time 12,007 (6104 men, 5903 women); part-time 1627 (747 men, 880 women); international 1334 (765 men, 569 women); total 13,634.

FACULTIES/SCHOOLS

Arts
Tel: (0151) 794 6902 Fax: (0151) 794 2454
Dean: Clark, Prof. Stephen R. L., MA *Oxf.*, DPhil *Oxf.*
Sub-Dean: Wilde, Richard C., BA *Nott.*

College Studies
Tel: (0151) 794 5669 Fax: (0151) 794 2060
Dean: Chubb, James C., BSc *Liv.*, PhD *Liv.*
Director of College Partnerships: Millward, Joanna M. E., BMus *Wales*, MA *Keele*

Dental Studies
Tel: (0151) 706 5203 Fax: (0151) 706 5845
Dean: Scott, Prof. John, BDS *Liv.*, PhD *Liv.*, FDSRCS, FDSRCSEd, FRCPath
School Administrator: Culkin, Maria, MA

Engineering
Tel: (0151) 794 6801 Fax: (0151) 794 4930
Dean: Goodhew, Prof. Peter J., PhD *Birm.*, DSc *Birm.*, FIP, FIM
Sub-Dean: Settle, J. Grahame, MSc *Liv.*

Law
Tel: (0151) 794 2807 Fax: (0151) 794 2829
Dean: Jones, Prof. Michael A., BA *Keele*, LLM *W.Ont.*, PhD *Liv.*

Faculty Administrator: Gray, Philip, BA *Liv.*

Medicine
Tel: (0151) 706 4275 Fax: (0151) 706 5667
Dean: Johnson, Prof. Peter M., MA *Oxf.*, PhD *Lond.*, DSc *Oxf.*, FRCPath
Administrative Sub-Dean: Bridgett, Gillian A., BA *Wales*

Science
Tel: (0151) 794 6903 Fax: (0151) 794 3646
Dean: Harris, Prof. Anthony L., BSc *Wales*, PhD *Wales*, FRSEd
Sub-Dean: Settle, J. Grahame, MSc *Liv.*

Social and Environmental Studies
Tel: (0151) 794 6901 Fax: (0151) 794 2465
Dean: Batey, Prof. Peter W. J., BSc *Sheff.*, MCD *Liv.*, PhD *Liv.*, FRTPI
Sub-Dean: Whitfield, Ian R., MA *Oxf.*

Veterinary Science
Tel: (0151) 794 4281 Fax: (0151) 794 6005
Dean: Gaskell, Prof. Christopher J., BVSc *Brist.*, PhD *Brist.*
Assistant Registrar: Finch, Elizabeth A., MA *Liv.*

ACADEMIC UNITS

Accounting, see Econ. and Acctg.

Anatomy, see Medicine (Human Anat. and Cell Biol.)

Archaeology, Classics and Oriental Studies, School of
Tel: (0151) 794 2449 Fax: (0151) 794 2442
Blumenthal, Henry J., MA *Camb.*, PhD *Camb.* Gladstone Prof., Greek
Clark, E. Gillian, MA *Oxf.*, DPhil *Oxf.* Sr. Lectr.
Davey, Peter J., BD *Lond.*, BPhil *Liv.*, PhD *Liv.* Reader
Davies, John K., MA *Oxf.*, DPhil *Oxf.*, FBA, FSA Rathbone Prof., Ancient History and Classical Archaeology
Eyre, Christopher J., MA *Oxf.*, DPhil *Oxf.* Sr. Lectr.
Gowlett, John A. J., MA *Camb.*, PhD *Camb.* Reader
Jones, Fred M. A., BA *Newcastle(UK)*, MA *Leeds*, PhD *St And.*
Mee, Christopher B., BA *Brist.*, PhD *Lond.* Charles W. Jones Sr. Lectr.
Millard, Alan R., MA *Oxf.*, MPhil *Lond.*, FSA Rankin Prof., Hebrew and Ancient Semitic Languages
Seager, Robin J., MA *Oxf.* Reader
Shaw, John, BSc *Liv.*, PhD *Liv.* Prof.

Slater, Elizabeth A., MA Camb., PhD
  Camb. Prof., Archaeology; Head*
Taylor, Joan J., BA Penn., PhD Camb. John
  Rankin Reader
Tuplin, Christopher J., MA Oxf., DPhil Oxf. Sr.
  Lectr.
Other Staff: 11 Lectrs.; 1 Fellow; 1 Res.
  Fellow; 1 Hon. Lectr.; 2 Hon. Sr. Fellows; 8
  Hon. Res. Fellows
Research: ancient Near East and Egypt;
  archaeological science; classical Greece and
  Rome; hominid archaeology and European
  prehistory; medieval and post-medieval
  British archaeology

Architecture and Building Engineering,
see also Civic Des.

Tel: (0151) 794 2604 Fax: (0151) 794 2605
Carter, David J., MSc Manc., PhD Liv. Sr. Lectr.
Dunster, David, BA Lond. Roscoe Prof.,
  Architecture; Head*
Gibbs, Barry M., BSc Sheff., MA Sheff., PhD
  Aston Prof.
Oldham, David J., MSc Manc., DPhil
  York(UK) Prof., Building Engineering
Pepper, Simon M., PhD Essex, FSA Prof.
Tarn, John N., OBE, BArch Durh., PhD Camb.,
  FRHistS, FSA Prof., Architecture
Thistlewood, David J., MSc Newcastle(UK), PhD
  Liv. Prof.
Other Staff: 2 Visiting Profs.; 13 Lectrs.; 2 Sr.
  Fellows; 5 Fellows; 1 Univ. Teacher†; 1
  Hon. Lectr.; 4 Hon. Sr. Fellows
Research: acoustics and noise control; aesthetics;
  building technology; computer-aided
  architectural design; design history

Biological Sciences, School of

Tel: (0151) 794 4477 Fax: (0151) 794 4475
Barraclough, Barry R., BSc Leeds, PhD Leeds Sr.
  Lectr.
Begon, Michael E., BSc Leeds, PhD Leeds Prof.,
  Environmental and Evolutionary Biology
Brand, Andrew R., BSc Hull, PhD Hull Sr.
  Lectr.
Britton, George, BSc Sheff., PhD Sheff. Reader
Chubb, Jimmy C., BSc Liv., PhD Liv. Reader
Collin, Hamish A., BSc Nott., DPhil Sus. Sr.
  Lectr.
Collins, Julian C., BSc Lond., PhD E.Anglia Sr.
  Lectr.
Cossins, Andrew R., BSc Durh., PhD
  Durh. Prof.
Crampton, Julian M., BSc Sus., PhD
  Warw. Prof., Molecular Biology; Head*
Dunbar, Robin I. M., BA Oxf., PhD Brist. Prof.
Duncan, Christopher J., BSc Lond., PhD Lond.,
  FIBiol Prof., Zoology
Easterby, John S., BSc Lond., PhD Lond. Sr.
  Lectr.
Eaton, John W., BSc Brist., PhD Brist. Sr. Lectr.
Edwards, Clive, BSc Wales, PhD Wales Reader
Edwards, Steven W., BSc Wales, PhD
  Wales Reader
Eggleston, Paul, BSc Birm., PhD Birm. Sr.
  Lectr.
Ensor, David M., BSc Liv., PhD Sheff. Reader
Goad, Lionel J., BSc Liv., PhD
  Manc. Leverhulme Reader, Biochemistry
Green, Christopher D., BA Oxf., DPhil Oxf. Sr.
  Lectr.
Hardwick, Keith, BSc Sheff., PhD Sheff. Sr.
  Lectr.
Hartnoll, Richard G., PhD Liv., DSc
  Liv. Reader
Haslam, John M., BA Oxf., DPhil Oxf. Sr.
  Lectr.
Johnson, Michael S., BSc Lond., PhD Liv. Prof.
Maden, Brian E. H., MB BChir Camb., PhD
  Camb., DSc Glas., FRSEd Johnston Prof.,
  Biochemistry
Manning, John T., BSc Lond., MSc Liv., PhD
  Liv. Sr. Lectr.
Marrs, Robert H., BA Stir., PhD Stir., DSc
  Stir. Bulley Prof., Applied Plant Biology
McCarthy, Alan J., BSc Bath, PhD Brad. Sr.
  Lectr.

McLennan, Alexander (Sandy) G., BSc Glas.,
  PhD Aberd., FIBiol Reader
McNeilly, Thomas, BSc Wales, PhD Wales Sr.
  Lectr.
Merry, Brian J., BSc Hull, MSc Leeds, PhD
  Hull Sr. Lectr.
Mortimer, A. Martin, BSc Wales, PhD
  Wales Reader
Moss, Brian, BSc Brist., PhD Brist., DSc
  Brist. Holbrook Gaskell Prof., Botany
Norton, Trevor A., BSc Liv., PhD Liv.,
  FRSEd Prof., Marine Biology; Dir., Port
  Erin Marine Lab.
Parker, Geoffrey A., BSc Brist., MA Camb., PhD
  Brist., FRS Derby Prof., Zoology
Pearson, Howard W., BSc Lond., PhD Lond. Sr.
  Lectr.
Putwain, Philip D., BSc Wales, PhD Wales Sr.
  Lectr.
Rees, Huw H., BSc Wales, PhD Wales Prof.
Ritchie, Donald A., BSc Leic., PhD Lond., FRSEd,
  FIBiol Prof., Genetics
Rudland, Philip S., MA Camb., PhD Camb.,
  FRCPath, FIBiol Prof., Biochemistry
Saunders, Jonathan R., BSc Brist., PhD
  Brist. Prof.
Stanisstreet, Martin, BSc S'ton., PhD Brist. Sr.
  Lectr.
Strike, Peter, BSc Sus., PhD Newcastle(UK) Prof.
Thompson, David J., BA York(UK), DPhil
  York(UK) Reader
Thorpe, John P., BSc St And., PhD
  Wales Reader
Tomsett, A. Brian, BSc Sheff., PhD Camb. Sr.
  Lectr.
Turner, Philip C., BSc Leeds, PhD Edin. Sr.
  Lectr.
Other Staff: 8 Visiting Profs.; 23 Lectrs.; 4 Sr.
  Fellows; 7 Fellows; 15 Hon. Lectrs.; 7 Hon.
  Sr. Fellows; 1 Hon. Res. Fellow; 1 Temp.
  Lectr.
Research: applied ecology and population
  biology; cellular recognition and signalling;
  marine biology; molecular and
  environmental microbiology; molecular
  medicine and genetics

Catalan, see Hispanic Studies

Chemistry

Tel: (0151) 794 3525 Fax: (0151) 794 3588
Abraham, Raymond J., PhD Birm., DSc
  Birm. Prof.
Bethell, Donald, BSc Lond., PhD Lond. Prof.,
  Physical Organic Chemistry
Cooper, David L., BA Oxf., DPhil Oxf. Reader
Cosstick, Richard, BSc Birm., PhD Birm. Sr.
  Lectr.
Derouane, Eric G., BA Liège, MA Prin., DrSc
  Liège Prof.
Eastmond, Geoffrey C., BSc Liv., PhD
  Liv. Reader
Gilchrist, Thomas L., BSc Lond., PhD
  Lond. Reader
Greeves, Nicholas, MA Camb., PhD Camb. Sr.
  Lectr.
Heaton, Brian T., DPhil Sus., DSc Sus.,
  FRSChem Grant Prof., Inorganic Chemistry
Holloway, Stephen, BSc Leic., PhD Leic. Prof.,
  Chemical Physics
Johnstone, Robert A. W., PhD Sheff., DSc Sheff.,
  FRSChem Prof.
Richardson, Neville V., BA Oxf., DPhil
  Oxf. Prof.; Dir., Interdisciplinary Res.
  Centre in Surface Sci.
Roberts, Stanley M., PhD Salf., DSc Salf.,
  FRSChem Heath Harrison Prof., Organic
  Chemistry; Head*
Schiffrin, David J., BSc Buenos Aires, PhD
  Birm. Brunner Prof., Physical Chemistry
Other Staff: 4 Visiting Profs.; 12 Lectrs.; 4 Sr.
  Fellows; 1 Fellow; 3 Hon. Sr. Fellows; 1
  Hon. Res. Fellow
Research: computer-assisted learning in
  chemistry; physical, organic and inorganic
  chemistry; surface science and catalysis

Civic Design

Tel: (0151) 794 6919 Fax: (0151) 794 3125
Batey, Peter W. J., BSc Sheff., MCD Liv., PhD
  Liv., FRTPI Lever Prof., Town and Regional
  Planning
Brown, Peter J. B., BEng Liv., MCD Liv., PhD
  Liv. Sr. Lectr., Transport Studies
Kirkby, Richard J. R., BSc Brist., PhD Brist. Sr.
  Lectr.
Madden, Moss, MEng Liv., MCD Liv., PhD
  Liv. Prof., Planning and Regional Science;
  Head*
Massey, David W., BA Leic., PhD Camb. Sr.
  Lectr.
Other Staff: 1 Visiting Prof.; 3 Lectrs.; 2
  Fellows; 1 Lectr.†; 3 Hon. Sr. Fellows; 1
  Hon. Res. Fellow
Research: environmental planning and
  management; planning and development in
  Pacific Asia; urban and regional analysis;
  urban design and development

Classics, see Archaeol., Classics and Oriental
  Studies, Sch. of

Communication Studies, see Pol. and
  Communicn. Studies, Sch. of

Computer Science

Tel: (0151) 794 3703 Fax: (0151) 794 3715
Bench-Capon, Trevor J. M., BA Oxf., DPhil
  Oxf. Sr. Lectr.
Charlton, Colin C., MSc Liv. Sr. Lectr.
Diaz, Bernard M., BSc Lond., PhD Lond. Sr.
  Lectr.
Gibbons, Alan M., BSc Nott., PhD Warw. Prof.;
  Head*
Leng, Paul H., BSc Lond., MSc Liv. Sr. Lectr.
Rytter, Wojciech, MSc Warsaw, PhD
  Warsaw Prof.
Shave, Michael J. R., MA Oxf., PhD Brist. Prof.
Taylor, Malcolm J., BSc Salf., MSc Manc., PhD
  Manc. Sr. Lectr.
Woodward, Martin R., BSc Nott., PhD Nott. Sr.
  Lectr.
Other Staff: 9 Lectrs.; 1 Sr. Fellow; 3 Temp.
  Lectrs.
Research: algorithmics; information systems and
  software engineering; knowledge processing

Computing Services

Tel: (0151) 794 3752 Fax: (0151) 794 3759
Schonfelder, J. Lawrence, MSc Melb., PhD
  Lond. Dir.*
Other Staff: 41 Sr. Staff

Continuing Education, Centre for

Tel: (0151) 794 6900 Fax: (0151) 794 2544
Derricott, Raymond, BA Nott., MEd Nott. Dir.*
Wright, Rodney C., MA Oxf., DPhil
  Oxf. Deputy Dir.
Other Staff: 1 Lectr.; 1 Manager; 2 Fellows; 1
  Hon. Sr. Fellow; 3 Hon. Fellows

Dentistry, School of, see below

Earth Sciences

Tel: (0151) 794 5150 Fax: (0151) 794 5170
Atherton, Michael P., PhD Sheff., DSc
  Sheff. Reader
Chester, Roy, BSc Manc., PhD Manc. Prof.,
  Oceanography
Crimes, Thomas P., BSc Liv., PhD Liv.,
  FGS Reader
Elliott, Trevor, BSc Wales, DPhil Oxf. George
  Herdman Prof., Geology
Flint, Steven S., BSc Aston, PhD Leeds Sr. Lectr.
Harris, Anthony L., BSc Wales, PhD Wales,
  FRSEd Prof., Geology
Hunter, Robert H., BSc Durh., PhD Durh. Sr.
  Lectr.
Kokelaar, Brian P., BSc Wales, MSc Oxf., PhD
  Wales Reader
Kusznir, Nicholas J., BSc Durh., PhD
  Durh. Prof., Geophysics; Head*
Marshall, James D., BSc Sheff., PhD Leic. Sr.
  Lectr.

Paul, Christopher R. C., MA Camb., PhD Camb. Prof.

Piper, John D. A., BSc Brist., PhD Lond. Reader

Preston, Martin R., BSc Liv., PhD Liv. Sr. Lectr.

Shaw, John, BSc Liv., PhD Liv. Prof.

Styles, Peter, BA Oxf., PhD Newcastle(UK) Sr. Lectr.

van den Berg, C. M. G. (Stan), MSc Wageningen, PhD McM. Reader

Walsh, John J., BSc Trinity(Dub.), PhD N.U.I. Sr. Lectr.

Wheeler, John, BA Camb., PhD Leeds Sr. Lectr.

Other Staff: 6 Visiting Profs.; 8 Lectrs.; 1 Sr. Demonstrator; 3 Sr. Fellows; 6 Fellows; 3 Hon. Sr. Fellows; 1 Hon. Sr. Res. Fellow; 1 Hon. Res. Fellow; 2 Temp. Lectrs.

Research: geodynamics; geology; geophysics; oceanography; palaeoceanography, palaeoecology and palaeobiology

Economic and Social History, see Hist., Econ. and Soc.

Economics and Accounting

Tel: (0151) 794 3035 Fax: (0151) 794 3028

Hojman, David E., BSc Chile, LEconSc Chile, PhD Edin. Sr. Lectr.

Morris, Richard C., BA Brist., MSc Lond., FCA Prof., Accounting

Thomas, W. Arthur, BSc(Econ) Lond., MA Wales, PhD Liv. Sr. Lectr.; Acting Head*

Wynn, Robert F. K., BSc Reading, BA Reading, MAgrSc Reading, PhD Reading Sr. Lectr.

Other Staff: 11 Lectrs.; 1 Sr. Fellow; 2 Fellows; 1 Tutor†; 1 Hon. Sr. Fellow

Research: accounting and finance; microeconomics; theoretical and applied macroeconomics

Education

Tel: (0151) 794 6970 Fax: (0151) 794 2512

Beattie, Nicholas M., MA Camb., MA Essex, PhD Liv. Reader; Head*

Boyes, Edward, BSc Liv., MEd Liv., PhD Liv. Sr. Lectr.

Harrop, Sylvia A., BSc(Econ) Lond., MEd Manc., PhD Liv., FRHistS Sr. Lectr.

Hartnett, Anthony J. P., BSc Lond., MA Lond., PhD Liv. Sr. Lectr.

McLean, K. Robin, MA Camb., PhD Liv. Sr. Lectr.

Russell, Terence J., BA MEd PhD Prof.; Dir., Centre for Res. and Devel. in Primary Sci. and Technol.

Other Staff: 1 Visiting Prof.; 9 Lectrs.; 2 Sr. Fellows; 6 Fellows; 3 Lectrs.†; 6 Hon. Sr. Fellows; 1 Hon. Res. Fellow; 3 Temp. Lectrs.

Research: evaluation and assessment; general educational aspects; primary science and technology

Engineering

Tel: (0151) 794 4670 Fax: (0151) 794 4675

Bacon, David J., PhD Lond., DSc Lond., FIM, FIP Prof.; Head*

Manufacturing Engineering and Industrial Management

Tel: (0151) 794 4681 Fax: (0151) 794 4693

Hon, K. K. Bernard, MSc Birm., PhD Birm., FIEE Prof., Manufacturing Systems; Head*

Kehoe, Dennis F., BSc(Eng) Lond., PhD Liv. Sr. Lectr.

Other Staff: 1 Visiting Prof.; 5 Lectrs.; 1 Visiting Sr. Fellow; 2 Hon. Lectrs.; 1 Hon. Sr. Fellow

Research: advanced manufacturing; industrial management; intelligent manufacturing; manufacturing systems; rapid prototyping

Materials Science and Engineering

Tel: (0151) 794 4670 Fax: (0151) 794 4675

Bacon, David J., PhD Lond., DSc Lond., FIM, FIP Prof.; Head*

Cantwell, Wesley J., BSc S'ton., MSc Lond., PhD Lond. Sr. Lectr.

Goodhew, Peter J., PhD Birm., DSc Birm., FIP, FIM Henry Bell Wortley Prof., Materials Engineering

Kiely, Christopher J., BSc Brist., PhD Brist. Sr. Lectr.

Noble, Frank W., BEng Liv., PhD Liv., FIM Sr. Lectr.

Pond, Robert C., MSc Brist., PhD Brist., FIP Prof.

Tatlock, Gordon J., BSc Brist., PhD Brist., FIP Reader

Other Staff: 2 Visiting Profs.; 2 Lectrs.; 1 Sr. Fellow; 2 Fellows; 2 Hon. Res. Fellows

Research: inorganic materials (semiconductors and catalysis); metals and alloys; polymers and composites

Mechanical Engineering

Tel: (0151) 794 4802 Fax: (0151) 794 4848

Blachut, Jan, PhD Cracow, DSc(Eng) Reader

Cleaver, John W., BA Nott., PhD S'ton. Sr. Lectr.

Escudier, Marcel P., PhD Lond., DSc Lond., FIMechE Harrison Prof.; Head*

Johnson, Mark W., MA Camb., PhD Camb. Sr. Lectr.

Jones, Norman, PhD Manc., DSc Manc., FIMechE A.A. Griffith Prof.

Moffat, Douglas G., BSc Strath., FIMechE Reader

Moreton, David N., BSc CNAA, PhD Liv. Sr. Lectr.

Mottershead, John E., BSc CNAA, PhD CNAA Alexander Elder Prof., Applied Mechanics

Owen, Ieuan, BSc Wales, PhD Wales, FIMechE Reader

Sproston, John L., BSc Liv., PhD Liv. Reader

Other Staff: 9 Lectrs.; 1 Hon. Sr. Fellows

Research: impact mechanics; laser materials processing; marine hydrodynamics; process fluid mechanics; vibrations, structural integrity and automatic control

Engineering, Building, see Archit. and Bldg. Engin.

Engineering, Civil

Tel: (0151) 794 5237 Fax: (0151) 794 5218

Ali, Kamil H. M., MEng Liv., PhD Liv. Sr. Lectr.

Bungey, John H., MSc Lond., PhD Liv. Prof.; Head*

Burrows, Richard, BEng Liv., PhD Liv. Reader

Hedges, Terry S., MEng Liv., FRMetS Sr. Lectr.

King, George J. W., MSc(Eng) Lond., PhD Liv. Sr. Lectr.

Millard, Steven G., BEng Leic., PhD Warw. Sr. Lectr.

O'Connor, Brian A., BEng Liv., PhD Liv., FICE Prof., Maritime Civil Engineering

Templeman, Andrew B., BEng Liv., PhD Liv. Prof.

Tickell, R. Geoffrey, BSc Brist. Sr. Lectr.

Other Staff: 10 Lectrs.; 1 Visiting Lectr.; 2 Hon. Lectrs.; 2 Hon. Res. Fellows

Research: environmental civil engineering; maritime civil engineering; structures and soil mechanics

Engineering, Clinical, see Medicine

Engineering, Electrical, and Electronics

Tel: (0151) 794 4539 Fax: (0151) 794 4540

Amaratunga, Gehan A. J., BSc Wales, PhD Camb. Prof., Electrical Engineering

Austin, Brian A., MSc(Eng) Witw., PhD Witw., FIEE, F(SA)IEE Sr. Lectr.

Eccleston, William, MSc Lond., PhD Lond., FIEE Robert Rankin Prof., Electronic Engineering

Fang, Michael T. C., BA Camb., DPhil Oxf. Prof., Applied Electromagnetism

Hall, Stephen, BSc Liv., PhD Liv. Sr. Lectr.

Jones, Gordon R., BSc Wales, PhD Liv., DSc Wales, FIEE Prof.

Lucas, James, PhD Lond., DSc Lond. Prof.

Parsons, J. David, BSc Wales, DSc(Eng) Lond., FEng, FIEE David Jardine Prof., Electrical Engineering; Head*

Smith, Jeremy S., BEng Liv., PhD Liv. Sr. Lectr.

Stuart, Robert A., BSc Birm., PhD Birm. Sr. Lectr.

Taylor, Stephen, BSc(Eng) Lond., MEng Liv., PhD Liv. Sr. Lectr.

Vourdas, Apostolos, BEng Athens, PhD Manc., DSc Manc., FIP Reader

Williams, E. Malcolm, BSc Wales, PhD Wales, FIP Sr. Lectr.

Wu, Qing-Hua (Henry), MSc Huazhong U.S.T., PhD Belf. Prof., Electrical Engineering

Other Staff: 4 Visiting Profs.; 10 Lectrs.; 1 Sr. Fellow; 1 Hon. Lectr.; 7 Hon. Sr. Fellows

Research: intelligence and engineering automation; plasma and intelligent optical monitoring; radio communications and signal processing; robotics and free electron lasers; solid state electronics

English Language and Literature

Tel: (0151) 794 2734 Fax: (0151) 794 2730

Bate, A. Jonathan, MA Camb., PhD Camb. King Alfred Prof., English Literature; Head*

Bawcutt, Nigel W., MA Liv., PhD Liv. Reader

Burns, Edward J., BA Oxf., DPhil Oxf. Sr. Lectr.

Davis, Philip M., BA Camb., PhD Camb. Reader

Everest, Kelvin D., BA Reading, PhD Reading Andrew Cecil Bradley Prof., Modern English Literature

Hoey, Michael P., BA Lond., PhD Birm. Baines Prof., English Language

Mills, A. David, MA Manc., PhD Manc. Prof.

Seed, David, MA Camb., MA Leic., PhD Hull Reader

Wogan-Browne, Jocelyn G., BA Melb., BPhil Oxf. Sr. Lectr.

Other Staff: 1 Visiting Prof.; 13 Lectrs.; 1 Sr. Fellow; 2 Res. Fellows; 8 Fellows; 1 Univ. Teacher†; 2 Hon. Sr. Fellows; 1 Hon. Res. Fellow; 1 Temp. Lectr.

Research: medieval studies, Shakespeare, the Renaissance and romanticism; science fiction; textual editing and discourse analysis; Victorian studies

Esperanto

Tel: (0151) 794 2458

1 Lectr.†

French

Tel: (0151) 794 2741 Fax: (0151) 794 2357

Ainsworth, Peter F., MA Manc., Dr3rdCy Paris Prof.

Burgess, Glyn S., MA Oxf., MA McM., DU Paris Prof.; Head*

Gunny, Ahmad, BA Lond., PhD Lond. Sr. Lectr.

Howe, Alan, BA Wales Sr. Lectr.

Unwin, Timothy A., MA Camb., MA Exe., PhD Exe. James Barrow Prof.

Waller, Richard E. A., MA Oxf., DPhil Oxf. Sr. Lectr.

Other Staff: 4 Lectrs.; 3 Tutors; 1 Sr. Fellow; 1 Res. Fellow; 1 Lectr.†

Research: eighteenth century studies; French theatre; medieval studies; the nouveau roman; the Renaissance

Geography

Tel: (0151) 794 2839 Fax: (0151) 794 2866

Bloemendal, Jan, BA Liv., PhD Liv. Sr. Lectr.

Chester, Rev. David K., BA Durh., PhD Aberd. Reader

Dearing, John A., BSc Manc., PhD Liv. Prof.

Gould, William T. S., MA St And. Prof.; Head*

Harvey, Adrian M., BSc Lond., PhD Lond. Reader

Lloyd, Peter E., MA Birm. Prof., Urban Geography

Meegan, Richard A., BScEcon Wales, MA Reading Sr. Lectr.

Plater, Andrew J., BSc Wales, PhD Nott. Sr. Lectr.

Smith, David W., MA *Wales*, PhD *HK* Prof., Economic Geography

Woods, Robert I., MA *Camb.*, DPhil *Oxf.* John Rankin Prof.

Other Staff: 1 Visiting Prof.; 11 Lectrs.; 4 Sr. Fellows; 2 Fellows; 1 Hon. Sr. Fellow

Research: environmental change; environmental processes; population studies; urban and regional development studies

Geology, see Earth Scis.

Geophysics, see Earth Scis.

German

Tel: (0151) 794 2352 Fax: (0151) 794 2537

Rosenhaft, Eve, BA *McG.*, PhD *Camb.* Sr. Lectr.

Simpson, James, BA *Liv.*, PhD *Liv.* Lectr.; Acting Head*

Other Staff: 3 Lectrs.; 3 Tutors; 1 Hon. Sr. Fellow

Research: German law; modern German literary studies; social and cultural history

Greek, see Archaeol., Classics and Oriental Studies, Sch. of

Hebrew and Ancient Semitic Languages, see Archaeol., Classics and Oriental Studies, Sch. of

Hispanic Studies, see also Latin American Studies, Inst. of

Tel: (0151) 794 2775 Fax: (0151) 794 2785

Higgins, James, MA *Glas.*, LèsL *Lyons*, PhD *Liv.* Prof., Latin American Literature

Marfany, Joan-Luis, LicenFil&Let *Barcelona*, PhD *Barcelona* Reader, Spanish and Catalan

Severin, Dorothy S., AM *Harv.*, PhD *Harv.* Gilmour Prof., Spanish; Head*

Wright, Roger H. P., MA *Oxf.*, BLitt *Oxf.*, PhD *Liv.* Prof., Spanish

Other Staff: 4 Lectrs.; 3 Tutors; 1 Hon. Tutor; 1 Hon. Sr. Fellow

Research: Spanish-American and Portuguese-African literature; Spanish, Catalan and Portuguese literature; Spanish cinema; Spanish linguistics/philology

History

Tel: (0151) 794 2394 Fax: (0151) 794 2366

Allmand, Christopher T., MA *Oxf.*, DPhil *Oxf.*, FRHistS, FSA Prof.; Head*

Belchem, John C., BA *Sus.*, DPhil *Sus.*, FRHistS Prof.

Booth, Paul H. W., BA *Sheff.*, MA *Liv.* Sr. Lectr.

Clough, Commendatore Cecil H., MA *Oxf.*, DPhil *Oxf.*, FRHistS, FSA Reader

Cobban, Alan B., MA *Aberd.*, MA *Camb.*, PhD *Camb.*, FRHistS Reader

Dutton, David J., BA *Lond.*, PhD *Lond.*, FRHistS Sr. Lectr.

Elliott, Marianne, BA *Belf.*, DPhil *Oxf.*, FRHistS Andrew Geddes and John Rankin Prof., Modern History

Jewell, Helen M., MA *Oxf.*, PhD *Leeds*, FRHistS Sr. Lectr.

Kermode, Jennifer I., BA *York(UK)*, PhD *Sheff.* Sr. Lectr.

Quintrell, Brian W., MA *Manc.*, PhD *Lond.*, FRHistS Sr. Lectr.

Other Staff: 5 Lectrs.; 1 Sr. Fellow; 3 Fellows; 2 Res. Fellows; 1 Reader†; 1 Hon. Lectr.; 8 Hon. Sr. Fellows; 1 Temp. Lectr.

Research: archive studies; British and European history; European colonisation in Asia; local, Irish and Manx history; North-American history

History, Economic and Social

Tel: (0151) 794 2413 Fax: (0151) 794 2423

Anderson, Bruce L., MA *Liv.* Sr. Lectr.

Finch, M. Henry J., MA *Oxf.*, MA *McM.*, PhD *Liv.* Sr. Lectr.

Hudson, Patricia, BSc(Econ) *Lond.*, DPhil *York(UK)* Prof.

Lee, W. Robert, MA *Oxf.*, DPhil *Oxf.* Chaddock Prof.; Head*

Miller, Rory M., MA *Camb.*, PhD *Camb.* Sr. Lectr.

Other Staff: 7 Lectrs.; 3 Fellows; 2 Lectrs.†; 1 Univ. Res. Fellow†; 2 Hon. Sr. Fellows; 1 Hon. Fellow

Research: business and labour history; comparative industrialisation; social and demographic change

Irish Studies, Institute of

Tel: (0151) 794 3831 Fax: (0151) 794 3836

Cox, W. Harvey, MA Trinity(Dub.), MSc(Econ) *Lond.* Deputy Dir.

Elliott, Marianne, BA *Belf.*, DPhil *Oxf.*, FRHistS Prof.; Dir.*

Other Staff: 1 Visiting Prof.; 3 Lectrs.; 1 Fellow; 9 Hon. Fellows

Research: history of ideas; migration and the Irish diaspora; nationalism and ethnicity: Northern Ireland/Ulster; regional cultures and economic development; social exclusion and inclusion

Latin American Studies, Institute of, see also Hispanic Studies

Tel: (0151) 794 3079 Fax: (0151) 794 3080

Fisher, John R., BA *Lond.*, MPhil *Lond.*, PhD *Liv.*, FRHistS Prof., Latin American History; Dir.*

Hojman, David E., BEconSc *Chile*, PhD *Edin.* Sr. Lectr., Economics

Howard-Malverde, Rosaleen E., BA *Leeds*, PhD *St And.* Sr. Lectr.

Miller, Rory M., MA *Camb.*, PhD *Camb.* Sr. Lectr., Economic and Social History

Other Staff: 3 Lectrs.; 1 Sr. Fellow; 1 Lectr.†; 1 Univ. Teacher†; 2 Hon. Sr. Fellows; 2 Hon. Res. Fellows

Research: economic history; linguistics and literature; politics; social anthropology and sociology

Law

Tel: (0151) 794 2816 Fax: (0151) 794 2829

Arora, Anu, LLB *Birm.*, PhD *Birm.* Prof.

Doyle, Brian J., LLM *Lond.*, PhD *Salf.* Prof.

Jones, Michael A., BA *Keele*, LLM *W.Ont.*, PhD *Liv.* Hills Dickinson Davis Campbell Prof.; Head*

Lyon, Christina M., LLB *Lond.* Prof., Common Law

Macleod, John K., LLB *Nott.*, PhD *Manc.* Prof.

McGoldrick, Dominic, LLB *Nott.*, PhD *Nott.* Sr. Lectr.

Morris, Anne E., LLB *Liv.* Sr. Lectr.

Neuwahl, Nanette A. E. M., Drs *Ley.*, PhD *European Univ.Inst.* Prof., European Law

Nott, Susan M., LLB *Wales*, BCL *Durh.* Sr. Lectr.

Thompson, William B., LLB *Belf.*, MLitt *Oxf.* Sr. Lectr.

Other Staff: 2 Visiting Profs.; 14 Lectrs.; 1 Reader†; 1 Hon. Sr. Fellow; 3 Hon. Res. Fellows

Research: charity law; child law; English law; international and European law; medical law and bioethics

Management, see Public Admin. and Management, Liverpool Inst. of

Marine Biology, see Biol. Scis., Sch. of

Materials Science, see under Engin.

Mathematical Sciences

Tel: (0151) 794 4062 Fax: (0151) 794 4061

Appleby, Peter G., BSc *Cant.*, BE *Cant.*, PhD *Cant.* Reader

Backhouse, Nigel B., MA *Oxf.*, DPhil *Oxf.* Sr. Lectr.

Ball, Michael A., BA *Camb.*, PhD *Camb.* Sr. Lectr.

Bhansali, Rajendra J., BCom *Bom.*, BSc *Lond.*, PhD *Lond.* Prof.

Boffey, T. Brian, MSc *Liv.*, PhD *Lond.* Sr. Lectr.

Bowers, Roger G., BSc *Lond.*, PhD *Lond.* Sr. Lectr.

Bruce, J. William, MSc *Lond.*, PhD *Liv.* Prof.; Head*

Doman, Brian G. S., MA *Oxf.*, DPhil *Oxf.* Sr. Lectr.

Giblin, Peter J., BSc *Lond.*, PhD *Lond.* Reader

Goryunov, Victor V., PhD *Moscow* Sr. Lectr.

Humphreys, John F., BSc *Manc.*, PhD *Manc.* Reader

Irving, Alan C., BSc *Glas.*, PhD *Durh.* Reader

Jack, D. Ian, BA *Camb.*, PhD *Camb.* Sr. Lectr.

Jones, D. R. Timothy, BA *Oxf.*, DPhil *Oxf.* Prof.

Kermode, Mark W., BSc *Liv.*, PhD *Liv.*, FRS Sr. Lectr.

Message, Peter J., MA *Camb.*, PhD *Camb.*, FRAS Reader

Michael, Christopher, MA *Oxf.*, DPhil *Oxf.*, FIP Prof., Theoretical Physics

Morton, Hugh R., MA *Camb.*, PhD *Camb.* Reader

Newstead, Peter E., BA *Camb.*, PhD *Camb.* Sr. Lectr.

Rees, S. Mary, BA *Oxf.*, MSc *Oxf.*, PhD *Warw.* Sr. Lectr.

Wall, C. Terence C., BA *Camb.*, PhD *Camb.*, FRS Prof.

Other Staff: 1 Visiting Prof.; 15 Lectrs.; 9 Sr. Fellows; 2 Advanced Fellows; 2 Hon. Lectrs.; 4 Hon. Sr. Fellows; 1 Temp. Lectr.

Research: algebra; biomathematics; singularity theory; statistics and operational research; theoretical physics

Medicine, see below

Music

Tel: (0151) 794 3096 Fax: (0151) 794 3141

Blezzard, Judith H., BA *Leeds*, BMus *Leeds*, PhD *Leeds*, FSA Sr. Lectr.

Horn, R. David W., MA *Oxf.* Sr. Lectr.

Orledge, Robert N., MA *Camb.*, PhD *Camb.* Prof.

Tagg, Philip D., BA *Camb.*, FilDr *Gothenburg* Sr. Lectr.

Talbot, Michael O., MA *Camb.*, MMus *Camb.*, PhD *Camb.*, FBA James and Constance Alsop Prof.

Williamson, John G., MA *Glas.*, DPhil *Oxf.* Sr. Lectr.; Head*

Other Staff: 2 Lectrs.; 5 Fellows; 1 Hon. Lectr.

Research: contemporary and popular music; English Renaissance; European music, 1850-1950; Italian baroque

Nursing, see Medicine, below

Oceanography, see Earth Scis.

Oriental Studies, see Archaeol., Classics and Oriental Studies, Sch. of

Philosophy

Tel: (0151) 794 2787 Fax: (0151) 794 2789

Clark, Stephen R. L., MA *Oxf.*, DPhil *Oxf.* Prof.

McGhee, Michael J., BA *Lond.*, PhD *Lond.* Lectr.; Head*

Robinson, Howard M., BA *Oxf.*, MA *Nott.* Reader

Other Staff: 4 Lectrs.; 1 Res. Fellow; 1 Hon. Sr. Fellow; 9 Hon. Res. Fellows

Research: ancient philosophy; applied ethics; epistemology; metaphysics; philosophy of religion

Physical Education, see Medicine (Movement Sci. and Phys. Educn.), below

Physics

Tel: (0151) 794 3370 Fax: (0151) 794 3444

Andrews, Peter T., MSc *NZ*, PhD *Liv.* Reader

Booth, Paul S. L., BSc *Liv.*, PhD *Liv.*, FIP Prof.

Bowcock, Themis J. V., BA *Oxf.*, PhD *Lond.* Sr. Lectr.

Butler, Peter A., BSc *Lond.*, PhD *Liv.* Reader

Carroll, Leo J., BSc *Liv.*, PhD *Liv.* Sr. Lectr.

Dainton, John B., MA Oxf., DPhil Oxf., FIP   Prof.
Dickson, Dominic P. E., MSc Wales, PhD Liv., FIP   Reader
Fry, John R., MA Oxf., PhD Birm.   Reader
Gabathuler, Erwin, MSc Belf., PhD Glas., Hon. Dr Uppsala, FRS, FIP   Sir James Chadwick Prof., Experimental Physics; Head*
Gamet, Ray, BSc Liv., PhD Liv.   Reader
Hall, Ian, MA Oxf., DPhil Oxf.   Sr. Lectr.
Hayman, Peter J., BSc Durh., PhD Durh.   Sr. Lectr.
Houlden, Michael A., BSc Liv., PhD Liv.   Sr. Lectr.
Jackson, J. Neil, BSc Liv., PhD Liv., FIP   Reader
James, Arthur N., MA Camb., PhD Camb., FIP   Reader
Jones, Graham D., BSc Manc., PhD Liv.   Sr. Lectr.
Nolan, Paul J., BSc Lond., PhD Liv.   Reader
Stirling, William G., BSc PhD, FIP   Prof., Experimental Physics
Thomas, Michael F., BSc Oxf., DPhil Oxf.   Reader
Twin, Peter J., OBE, BSc Liv., PhD Liv., FIP, FRS   Lyon Jones Prof.
Weightman, Peter, BA Keele, PhD Keele, FIP   Prof.
Other Staff: 1 Visiting Prof.; 4 Lectrs.; 2 Sr. Fellows; 2 Advanced Fellows; 3 Fellows; 2 Hon. Sr. Fellows
Research: condensed matter physics; high energy physics; nuclear structure physics

Physiology, see Medicine, below

Politics and Communication Studies, School of

Tel: (0151) 794 2890 Fax: (0151) 794 3948
Corner, John R., MA Camb.   Prof.
Femia, Joseph V., BA Col., DPhil Oxf.   Reader
Kavanagh, David A., MA Manc.   Prof.
Munslow, Barry, BA Manc., PhD Manc.   Prof.
Padgett, Stephen, BA York(UK), PhD Kent   Prof., Politics; Head*
Pollack, Benny, BA Chile, MA Northeastern, PhD Liv.   Prof., Latin American and Spanish Politics
Richardson, Kay P., BA E.Anglia, MA Birm., PhD Birm.   Sr. Lectr.
Other Staff: 7 Lectrs.; 2 Sr. Fellows; 2 Fellows; 1 Res. Fellow; 1 Hon. Sr. Fellow; 1 Temp. Lectr.
Research: broadcasting policy; current affairs television; European Union policy and politics; political science and philosophy

Psychology

Tel: (0151) 794 2957 Fax: (0151) 794 2945
Canter, David V., BA Liv., PhD Liv., FBPsS, FAPA   Prof.
Davies, Ann D. M., BA Liv., PhD Liv., FBPsS   Sr. Lectr.
Donald, Ian, BA CNAA, MSc Sur., PhD Aston   Sr. Lectr.
Goudie, Andrew J., BA Oxf., MSc Wales, PhD Liv.   Reader
Hanley, J. Richard, MA Dund., PhD Lanc.   Sr. Lectr.
Latto, Richard M., MA Camb., PhD Camb., FBPsS   Sr. Lectr.; Head*
Lovie, Alexander D., BA Leeds, PhD Lond., FBPsS   Sr. Lectr.
Thornton, Everard W., BSc Durh., PhD Durh.   Sr. Lectr.
Wagstaff, Graham F., BA Newcastle(UK), PhD Newcastle(UK)   Reader
Other Staff: 6 Lectrs.; 1 Hon. Res. Fellow; 1 Lectr.†
Research: applied social psychology; behavioural neuroscience; cognition and neuropsychology; health psychology

Public Administration and Management, Liverpool Institute of

Tel: (0151) 794 2911 Fax: (0151) 794 2909
Davies, Morton R., BA Wales   Prof.; Dir.*
Drummond, Helga, BA Leeds, PhD Leeds   Prof.

Other Staff: 4 Lectrs.; 1 Fellow; 1 Hon. Sr. Fellow; 2 Temp. Lectrs.
Research: European Union; government policy; organisation and reform; politics of South Africa; public management

Sociology, Social Policy and Social Work Studies

Tel: (0151) 794 2995 Fax: (0151) 794 2997
Clarke, Michael J., BA E.Anglia, MA Manc., PhD Durh.   Sr. Lectr.
Corby, Brian C., BA Lond.   Sr. Lectr.
Delantly, Gerard, MA N.U.I., PhD N.U.I.   Sr. Lectr.
Jones, Christopher, BA CNAA, PhD Durh.   Prof., Social Policy and Social Work; Head*
Kingdom, Elizabeth F., MA St And., PhD Liv.   Sr. Lectr.
Lane, Anthony D., BA Liv.   Reader
Moore, Robert S., BA Hull, PhD Durh.   Eleanor Rathbone Prof., Sociology
Munck, Ronaldo P., BA Essex, PhD Essex   Sr. Lectr.
Roberts, Kenneth, BSc(Soc) Lond., MSc(Econ) Lond.   Prof.
Vacant Posts: Charles Booth Prof.
Research: city, community and policy; globalisation, regulation and citizenship

Spanish, see Hispanic Studies

Veterinary Science, see below

DENTISTRY, SCHOOL OF

Clinical Dental Sciences

Tel: (0151) 706 5000 Fax: (0151) 706 5845
Adams, Derek, MDS Liv., FDSRCSEd   Sr. Lectr., Dental Prosthetics
Appleton, John, JP, BDS Lond., PhD Lond.   Sr. Lectr., Oral Anatomy
Cunningham, John, MDS Liv., FDSRCSEd   Sr. Lectr.
Field, Elizabeth A., MDS Manc., FDSRCS   Sr. Lectr.
Field, John K., BDS Liv., MA Trinity(Dub.), PhD Wales   Sr. Lectr.
Ireland, Robert S., BDS Liv.   Prof., Primary Dental Care
Last, Keith S., BDS Lond., MSc Lond., PhD, FDSRCS   Sr. Lectr., Periodontology
Lee, George T. R., MDS Liv., FDSRCPSGlas   Sr. Lectr.
Lennon, Michael A., BDS Liv., MDS Manc., FDSRCSEd   Prof., Public Dental Health; Head*
Mair, Lawrence H., BDS Liv., PhD Liv.   Sr. Lectr.
Martin, Michael V., BA Open(UK), BDS Birm., PhD Birm.   Sr. Lectr.
Pender, Neil, BDS Wales, MScD Wales, PhD, FDSRCSEd   Sr. Lectr.
Scott, John, BDS Liv., PhD Liv., FDSRCS, FDSRCSEd, FRCPath   Louis Cohen Prof., Oral Diseases
Watts, Andrew, BDS PhD   Prof., Restorative Dentistry
Woolgar, Julie A., BDS Birm., PhD   Sr. Lectr.
Other Staff: 18 Lectrs.; 2 Sr. Fellows; 1 Sr. Lectr.†; 14 Lectrs.†; 21 Hon. Lectrs.; 3 Hon. Res. Fellows; 29 Hon. Clin. Lectrs.
Research: aerorespiratory tract cancers; cariology, oral microbiology and pathology; dental materials; dental public health and primary care; ultrastructural research

MEDICINE

at Royal Liverpool Univ. Hosp.

Anaesthesia

Tel: (0151) 706 4008 Fax: (0151) 706 5884
Booker, Peter D., MB BS Lond., FRCA   Sr. Lectr., Paediatric Anaesthesia
Hunter, Jennifer M., MB ChB St And., PhD Liv., FRCA   Reader
Jones, Ronald S., JP, MVSc Liv., DrMedVet Berne, DVSc Pret., FIBiol, FRCVS   Head*

Other Staff: 4 Lectrs.; 33 Clin. Lectrs.†; 3 Hon. Lectrs.; 2 Hon. Sr. Fellows; 1 Hon. Res. Fellow; 1 Hon. Clin. Tutor
Research: development of anaesthetic equipment; measures of the depth of anaesthesia; neuromuscular blockading drugs; paediatric anaesthesia

Child Health

Tel: (0151) 252 5695
Carty, Helen M. L., MB ChB N.U.I., FRCR   Prof., Paediatric Radiology
Choonara, Imti A., MD Liv.   Sr. Lectr.
Cooke, Richard W. I., MD Lond., FRCP   Prof., Paediatric Medicine; Head*
Ellis, I. H., BSc Lond., MB BS Lond.   Sr. Lectr., Clinical Genetics
Lloyd, David A., MChir Camb., FCS(SA), FACS, FRCS   Prof., Paediatric Surgery
Losty, Paul D., MD Trinity(Dub.), FRCS   Sr. Lectr., Paediatric Surgery
Rintala, R., MD Helsinki   Sr. Lectr., Paediatric Surgery
Rogers, M. G. H., MB BS Lond., MA Camb.   Sr. Lectr.
Ryan, Stephen, MD Leeds   Sr. Lectr.
Smith, Colin S., MB ChB Liv., FRCP   Sr. Lectr.
Smyth, Ros E., MB BS Lond., MA Camb., MD Camb.   Sr. Lectr.
Weindling, A. Michael, BSc Lond., MA Lond., MD Lond., FRCP   Prof.
Other Staff: 1 Visiting Prof.; 2 Lectrs.; 2 Res. Fellows; 67 Clin. Lectrs.†; 4 Hon. Lectrs.; 2 Hon. Res. Fellows; 1 Hon. Clin. Tutor
Research: chronic lung disease and cystic fibrosis; clinical and molecular genetics; developmental anatomy of the gastrointestinal tract; human foetal metabolism; neurophysiology of the newborn

Clinical Chemistry

Tel: (0151) 706 4232 Fax: (0151) 706 5813
Diver, Michael J., MSc W.Ont., PhD Liv.   Sr. Lectr.
Fraser, William D., BSc Glas., MD Glas.   Sr. Lectr.
Shenkin, Alan, BSc Glas., MB ChB Glas., PhD Glas., FRCP, FRCPath   Prof.; Head*
Other Staff: 1 Lectr.; 8 Clin. Lectrs.†; 1 Hon. Res. Fellow
Research: cytokines; endocrinology; molecular genetics of hyperlipidaemia; pepsin structure and function; thyroid biochemistry

Clinical Engineering

Tel: (0151) 706 4200 Fax: (0151) 706 5803
How, Thien V., BSc Sus., PhD Liv.   Sr. Lectr.
Williams, David F., PhD Birm., DSc Birm., FIM   Prof.; Head*
Other Staff: 3 Lectrs.; 1 Lectr.†; 4 Hon. Lectrs.; 1 Hon. Sr. Fellow
Research: biocompatability of biomaterials; medical device design; quantitative assessment procedures for biocompatability evaluation; vascular bioengineering

Clinical Psychology

Tel: (0151) 794 5529 Fax: (0151) 794 5537
Bentall, Richard P., BSc Wales, MClinPsychol Liv., PhD Wales   Prof.; Head*
Blackburn, Ronald, MA Camb., MSc Birm., PhD S'ton.   Prof., Clinical and Forensic Psychology Studies
Humphries, Gerry M., BSc Reading, MClinPsychol Liv., PhD Lond.   Sr. Lectr.
McGuire, James, MA Glas., MSc Leeds, PhD Leic.   Sr. Lectr.
Salmon, Peter, BA Oxf., DPhil Oxf., MSc Leeds   Reader
Other Staff: 6 Lectrs.; 4 Hon. Lectrs.; 2 Hon. Sr. Fellows
Research: forensic psychology; health psychology; psychological factors in dentistry; psychopathology, primarily psychotic phenomena

Dermatology, see Med.

Genito-Urinary Medicine, see Med. Microbiol. and Genito-Urinary Med.

Geriatric Medicine

Tel: (0151) 706 4062 Fax: (0151) 706 4064

Gosney, Margot A., MD Liv.   Sr. Lectr.

Lye, Michael D. W., MD Leeds, FRCP   Prof.†; Head*

Other Staff: 1 Lectr.; 12 Clin. Lectrs.†; 1 Hon. Lectr.; 1 Hon. Sr. Fellow

Research: assessment of innovative drugs in elderly patients; interaction of ageing and age-related pathology

Haematology

Tel: (0151) 706 4311 Fax: (0151) 706 4311

Cawley, John C., MD Leeds, PhD Camb., FRCP, FRCPath   Prof.†; Head*

Clark, Richard E., MA Camb., MD Lond., FRCP   Sr. Lectr.

Toh, Cheng-Hock, MD Sheff.   Sr. Lectr.

Other Staff: 2 Lectrs.; 2 Clin. Lectrs.†; 6 Hon. Lectrs.

Research: gene therapy in chronic myeloid leukaemia; influence of microenvironment on cell survival; interaction of proteases with endothelial receptors; migratory behaviour of malignant B cells

Health Care Education

Tel: (0151) 794 4293

Bligh, John G., BSc St And., MB ChB Manc., MMedEd Dund., FRCGP   Prof., Medical Education; Head*

Bradley, Paul L., MB ChB leeds, FRCGP   Sr. Lectr., Dir., Clinical Skills Lab.

Gibbs, Trevor J., MB ChB Liv., MMedSci Leeds, FRCGP   Sr. Lectr., Primary Care Education

Other Staff: 3 Lectrs.; 1 Sr. Res. Fellow; 1 Res. Fellow; 1 Clin. Teacher†; 4 Hon. Lectrs.; 1 Hon. Res. Fellow

Research: cancer education; factors influencing learning in clinical practice; interprofessional learning in health care education; socialisation during medical school life; teaching of clinical skills

Human Anatomy and Cell Biology

Tel: (0151) 794 5455 Fax: (0151) 794 5517

Cobbold, Peter H., BSc Newcastle(UK), PhD Newcastle(UK)   Prof.; Head*

Connolly, Robert C., BSc Wales   Sr. Lectr.

Crompton, Robin H., BSc Lond., AM Harv., PhD Harv.   Sr. Lectr.

Edgar, David H., BA Oxf., DPhil Oxf.   Sr. Lectr.

Gallagher, James A., BSc Newcastle(UK), MSc Aberd., PhD Camb.   Reader

Howard, C. Vyvyan, MB ChB Liv., PhD Liv.   Sr. Lectr.

Marshall-Clarke, Stuart, PhD Lond.   Sr. Lectr.

Richards, R. Clive, BSc Wales, PhD Liv.   Sr. Lectr.

Other Staff: 1 Visiting Prof.; 9 Lectrs.; 1 Sr. Demonstrator; 2 Sr. Fellows; 1 Res. Fellow; 1 Lectr.†; 1 Univ. Teacher†; 5 Hon. Sr. Demonstrators; 2 Hon. Sr. Fellows; 3 Hon. Res. Fellows

Research: cell signalling; cellular pathphysiology; evolutionary biology; molecular mechanisms of cell growth and differentiation

Immunology

Tel: (0151) 706 4353 Fax: (0151) 706 5814

Barnes, Roger M. R., MB BS Lond., PhD Lond., FRCPath   Sr. Lectr.

Christmas, Stephen E., MA Oxf., PhD Oxf.; Acting Head*

Johnson, Peter M., MA Oxf., PhD Lond., DSc Oxf., FRCPath   Prof.

Other Staff: 4 Lectrs.; 1 Clin. Lectr.†; 2 Hon. Sr. Res. Fellows; 2 Hon. Res. Fellows

Research: applied research in allergy; lymphocyte-endothelial cell interactions; reproductive immunology; T cell and cytokine immunology; tumour and transplantation immunology

Medical Imaging

Sluming, Vanessa A., MSc Liv.   Sr. Lectr.

Whitehouse, Graham H., MB BS Lond., FRCR, FRCP   Prof.†, Diagnostic Radiology; Head*

Other Staff: 5 Lectrs.; 1 Lectr.†; 21 Clin. Lectrs.†

Research: body composition and imaging methods; clinical applications of ultrasound; image analysis; magnetic resonance imaging; psychological effects of imaging

Medical Microbiology and Genito-Urinary Medicine

Tel: (0151) 706 4381 Fax: (0151) 706 5805

Baxby, Derrick, BSc Liv., PhD Liv., FRCPath   Sr. Lectr.

Birley, Humphrey D. E., BA Camb., MB BS Lond.   Sr. Lectr.

Hart, C. A. Tony, BSc Lond., MB BS Lond., PhD Lond., FRCPath   Prof.†; Head*

Schultz, Thomas F., MD PhD   Jefferiss Prof., Genito-Urinary Medicine

Shears, Paul, BSc Reading, MB BS Lond., MD Liv.   Sr. Lectr.

Smith, Godfrey W., MB BChir Camb., MA Camb.   Sr. Lectr.

Tong, C-Y. William, MB BS HK, MSc Lond., FRCP   Sr. Lectr.

van Saene, H. K. F. (Rick), MD Leuven, PhD Gron.   Sr. Lectr.

Other Staff: 2 Lectrs.; 10 Clin. Lectrs.†; 2 Hon. Lectrs.; 1 Hon. Sr. Fellow; 6 Hon. Sr. Res. Fellows; 8 Hon. Res. Fellows

Research: antimicrobials and antibiotic resistance; gastro-intestinal infections; genital tract infections; latent and persistent viral infections; respiratory tract infection

Medicine

Tel: (0151) 706 4070 Fax: (0151) 706 5802

Benbow, Susan J., MB ChB Brist.   Sr. Lectr., Diabetes and Endocrinology

Calverley, Peter M., MB ChB Edin.   Prof., Rehabilitation Medicine

Costello, Richard W. K., MB ChB   Sr. Lectr.

Friedmann, Peter S., BA Camb., MD Camb., FRCP   Prof., Dermatology; Acting Head*

Gill, Geoffrey V., BA Open(UK), MSc Newcastle(UK), MD Newcastle(UK), FRCP   Sr. Lectr., Diabetes and Endocrinology

Green, John A., BSc Glas., MB ChB Glas.   Sr. Lectr.

Grierson, Ian, BSc Glas., PhD Glas.   Littlewoods Prof., Experimental Ophthalmology

Griffiths, Richard D., BSc Lond., MD Lond.   Sr. Lectr.

Hiscott, Paul S., MB BS Lond., PhD Lond., FRCS   Sr. Lectr.

Jackson, Malcolm J., PhD Lond., DSc Sur.   Prof., Cellular Pathophysiology

Lombard, Martin G., BSc Lond., MD N.U.I.   Sr. Lectr.

Moots, Robert J., BSc Lond., MB BS Lond., PhD CNAA   Sr. Lectr.

Rhodes, Jonathan M., MA Camb., MD Camb., FRCP   Prof.

Sharpe, Graham R., MB ChB Leeds, BA Open(UK)   Sr. Lectr., Dermatology

Warenius, Hilmar M., MB BChir Camb., MA Camb., PhD Camb., FRCR   Cancer Res. Campaign Prof., Oncology Research

Widowson, Peter S., BSc Newcastle(UK), PhD Manc.   Sr. Lectr.

Wilding, John P. H., DM S'ton., BMed   Sr. Lectr.

Wilkinson, David G., BSc Edin., MB ChB Edin., MPhil Edin., FRCP, FRCPsych   Prof., Liaison Psychiatry

Williams, Gareth, MA Camb., MD Camb., FRCP   Prof.

Other Staff: 2 Visiting Profs.; 9 Lectrs.; 2 Lectrs.†; 71 Clin. Lectrs.†; 11 Hon. Lectrs.; 4 Hon. Sr. Res. Fellows; 1 Hon. Sr. Fellow; 9 Hon. Res. Fellows; 1 Temp. Sr. Lectr.

Research: clinical physiology and metabolism; diabetes and neuroendocrinology; mucosal pathophysiology; oncology; ophthalmology

Movement Science and Physical Education

Tel: (0151) 794 3221 Fax: (0151) 794 3229

Brodie, David A., BEd Nott., MSc Lough., PhD Lough.   Prof.; Head*

Other Staff: 3 Lectrs.

Research: biomechanics; exercise physiology; kinanthropometry; motor skill; paediatric physiology

Neurological Science

Tel: (0151) 529 4592 Fax: (0151) 525 3857

Baker, G. A., MA PhD   Sr. Lectr.

Chadwick, David W., DM Oxf.   Prof., Neurology; Head*

Hart, Ian K., BSc Glas., MB ChB Glas., PhD Lond.   Sr. Lectr.

Moore, A. Peter, MD Birm.   Sr. Lectr.

Smith, Steven J., BSc Leeds, MB ChB Leeds   Sr. Lectr.

Other Staff: 1 Lectr.; 23 Clin. Lectrs.†; 1 Hon. Lectr.; 3 Hon. Res. Fellows

Research: neuroimmunology, neurophysiology, neuroendocrinology and neuro-oncology; neuropsychology and epilepsy; neurorehabilitation; neurovascular research

Nursing

Tel: (0151) 794 6913 Fax: (0151) 794 5678

Carlisle, Caroline, BA Open(UK), MSc Edin.   Sr. Lectr.; Head*

Other Staff: 5 Lectrs.; 1 Tutor; 1 Hon. Visiting Prof.; 6 Hon. Lectrs.; 1 Hon. Sr. Res. Fellow; 1 Temp. Lectr.

Research: clinical decision making; HIV and AIDS; mental health and mentally disordered offenders; patient participation in treatment decisions; research utilisation in nursing

Obstetrics and Gynaecology

Tel: (0151) 702 4101 Fax: (0151) 702 4024

Alfirevic, Zarko, MD Zagreb, MRSci Zagreb   Sr. Lectr.

Garden, Anne S., MB ChB Aberd., FRCOG   Sr. Lectr.

Gosden, Christine M., BSc Edin., PhD Edin.   Prof., Medical Genetics

Lewis-Jones, D. Iwan, MD Liv.   Sr. Lectr.

Neilson, James P., BSc Edin., MD Edin.   Prof.; Head*

Other Staff: 3 Lectrs.; 37 Clin. Lectrs.†; 1 Hon. Lectr.; 1 Hon. Sr. Res. Fellow; 4 Hon. Res. Fellows

Research: clinical epidemiology; foetomaternal and perinatal medicine; gene expression in human development; paediatric gynaecology; tropical obstetrics and gynaecology

Occupational Therapy

Tel: (0151) 794 5725 Fax: (0151) 794 5719

Martin, Judith M., MEd Liv.   Sr. Lectr.; Head*

Other Staff: 6 Lectrs.; 2 Lectrs.†; 1 Hon. Res. Fellow

Research: disability issues; efficacy of occupational therapy; interprofessional education

Oncology, see Med.

Ophthalmology, see Med.

Orthopaedic and Accident Surgery

Tel: (0151) 706 4122

Frostick, Simon P., MA DM, FRCS   Prof.; Head*

Kemp, G. J., MA Oxf., DM Oxf.   Sr. Lectr.

Other Staff: 9 Clin. Lectrs.†; 2 Hon. Lectrs.; 1 Hon. Res. Fellow

Research: bone cell biology; clinical data-based research; magnetic resonance spectroscopy of human muscle; shoulder dysfunction; sports medicine and sports physiology

Orthoptics

Tel: (0151) 794 5733 Fax: (0151) 794 5781

Stephenson, M. Gail   Sr. Lectr.; Head*

Other Staff: 3 Lectrs.; 1 Lectr.†; 3 Hon. Lectrs.

Research: neuro-physiology of eye movements; reading disorders; visual development; especially in premature infants; visual effects from prolonged VDU exposure

Otolaryngology

Tel: (0151) 706 4051 Fax: (0151) 706 5847

Jones, Andrew S., MD Wales, FRCSEd   Prof., Otorhinolaryngology

Other Staff: 1 Lectr.; 7 Clin. Lectrs.†; 2 Hon. Lectrs.

Research: head and neck oncology; nasal physiology

Paediatrics, see Child Health

Parasitology, see Trop. Med., Sch. of

Pathology

Tel: (0151) 706 4484 Fax: (0151) 706 5859

Foster, Christopher S., BSc Lond., PhD Lond., MD Lond.   George Holt Prof.; Head*

Gosney, John R., BSc Liv., MD Liv.   Reader

Helliwell, Timothy R., MA Camb., MD Camb.   Reader

Herrington, C. Simon, MB BS Lond., MA Camb., MA Oxf., DPhil Oxf.   Sr. Lectr.

Hiscott, Paul S., MB BS Lond., PhD Lond., FRCS   Sr. Lectr.

Kokai, G. K., DM Szeged, DS Belgrade   Sr. Lectr.

McDicken, Ian W., MD Glas.   Sr. Lectr.

Nash, John R. G., BM BCh Oxf., DPhil Oxf.   Sr. Lectr.

Sloane, John P., MB BS Lond., FRCPath   Prof.

Smith, Peter H., BSc Liv., PhD Liv.   Sr. Lectr.

Other Staff: 1 Lectr.; 4 Hon. Lectrs.; 1 Hon. Res. Fellow

Research: gastroenterological pathology; gynaecological pathology; immunocytochemistry; lymphoreticular pathology; molecular pathology

Forensic Pathology

Tel: (0151) 706 4301

Johnson, C. Paul, BSc Liv., MB ChB Liv.   Sr. Lectr.; Head*

Wilson, C. A., MB ChB Sheff.   Sr. Lectr.

Research: forensic pathology; sudden cardiac death

Pharmacology and Therapeutics

Tel: (0151) 794 6812 Fax: (0151) 794 5540

Back, David J., BSc Liv., PhD Liv.   Prof.

Barry, Michael G., BSc N.U.I., MB BCh BAO N.U.I.   Sr. Lectr.

Barton, Stuart B., BA Oxf., BM BCh Oxf., DPhil Oxf.   Sr. Lectr.

Breckenridge, Alistair M., CBE, BSc St And., MD Dund., MSc Lond., FRCP, FRCPEd, FRSEd   Prof., Clinical Pharmacology; Head*

Coker, Susan J., MSc Strath., PhD Strath.   Sr. Lectr.

Coleman, John W., BSc Lond., PhD Lond.   Reader

Edwards, I. Geoffrey, BSc Birm., PhD Manc.   Sr. Lectr.

Kitteringham, Neil R., BSc Aberd., PhD Aberd.   Sr. Lectr.

Lindup, W. Edward, BPharm Wales, PhD Sur.   Sr. Lectr.

McLean, W. Graham, BSc Glas., PhD Brist.   Reader

Park, B. Kevin, BSc Liv., PhD Liv.   Prof.

Pirmohamed, Munir, MB ChB Liv., PhD Liv.   Sr. Lectr.

Walley, Thomas J., MB BCh BAO N.U.I., MD N.U.I.   Glaxo Prof., Clinical Pharmacology

Ward, Stephen A., BSc Aston, PhD Liv.   Sr. Lectr.

Winstanley, Peter A., MD Liv.   Reader

Other Staff: 1 Visiting Prof.; 1 Lectr.; 1 Lectr.†; 3 Hon. Lectrs.; 2 Hon. Sr. Fellows; 12 Hon. Res. Fellows

Research: drug metabolism; mechanisms of adverse drug reactions; pharmacoepidemiology and pharmacoeconomics; pharmacology of anti-AIDS drugs; pharmacology of antimalarial drugs

Physiology

Tel: (0151) 794 5322 Fax: (0151) 794 5327

Burgoyne, Robert D., BSc Birm., PhD Birm.   Prof.

Dimaline, Rodney, BSc Liv., PhD Liv.   Reader

Dockray, Graham J., BSc Nott., PhD Nott.   Prof.

Gallacher, David V., BSc Glas., BDS Glas.   Reader

Petersen, Ole H., MD Copenhagen   George Holt Prof.; Head*

Tepikin, Alexei, BSc Moscow, PhD Kiev   Sr. Lectr.

Varro, Andrea, MD Szeged, PhD Budapest   Sr. Lectr.

Wray, Susan C., BSc Lond., PhD Lond.   Prof.

Other Staff: 4 Lectrs.; 1 Res. Fellow; 2 Hon. Sr. Fellows; 2 Hon. Res. Fellows

Research: calcium signalling; cell function and regulation; cellular roles of novel proteins; control of smooth muscle function; physiological role of peptide hormones

Physiotherapy

Tel: (0151) 794 5741 Fax: (0151) 794 5740

Thornton, Eileen, BA Open(UK), MEd Liv.   Sr. Lectr.; Head*

Other Staff: 4 Lectrs.; 2 Lectrs.†; 1 Hon. Lectr.; 28 Hon. Clin. Tutors

Research: curriculum planning, delivery and evaluation; physiotherapy interventions in cardiovascular/respiratory problems; physiotherapy interventions in management of musculoskeletal problems

Primary Care

Tel: (0151) 794 5597 Fax: (0151) 794 5604

Bundred, Peter E., MB BS Lond., MD   Sr. Lectr.

Dowrick, Christopher F., BA Oxf., MB ChB Manc., MSc Lond., MD Liv.   Prof.; Head*

Other Staff: 1 Visiting Prof.; 5 Lectrs.; 2 Lectrs.†; 7 Hon. Lectrs.; 25 Hon. Clin. Tutors.; 4 Hon. Res. Fellows

Research: detection of depression; heart disease; primary care epidemiology

Psychiatry

Tel: (0151) 706 4149 Fax: (0151) 709 3765

Blackburn, Ronald, MA Camb., MSc Birm., PhD S'ton.   Prof., Clinical and Forensic Psychological Studies

Copeland, John R. M., MA Camb., MD Camb., FRCP, FRCPsych   Prof.†; Clin. Lectr., Head*

Forth, Michael W., MB BS Lond., FRCPsych   Sr. Lectr.

Gowers, Simon G., BSc Lond., MB BS Lond., MPhil Lond.   Prof., Adolescent Psychiatry

Hill, Jonathan W., BA Camb., MB BChir Camb.   M.R.H.A. Prof., Child and Developmental Psychiatry

Sharma, Vimal K., MB BS Raj., PhD Liv., MD   Sr. Lectr., Psychiatry in Primary Care

Swinton, Mark, BSc Lond., MD Lond.   Sr. Lectr., Forensic Psychiatry

Wilkinson, David G., BSc Edin., MPhil Edin., MB ChB Edin., FRCPEd, FRCPsych   Prof., Liaison Psychiatry

Wilson, Kenneth C. M., MB ChB Liv., MPhil Lond.   Prof., Psychiatry of Old Age

Other Staff: 4 Lectrs.; 2 Fellows; 1 Lectr.†; 18 Clin. Lectrs.†; 2 Hon. Sr. Res. Fellows; 5 Hon. Res. Fellows

Research: adult functioning and developmental processes; conduct disordered young children; dementia in old age; forensic psychology; personality disorders; psychosocial and psychiatric consequences of sexual abuse

Public Health

Tel: (0151) 794 5576 Fax: (0151) 794 5588

Bellis, Mark   Sr. Lectr., Sexual Health and Substance Misuse Epidemiology

Bruce, Nigel G., MB BS Lond., MSc Lond., PhD Lond.   Sr. Lectr.

Maudsley, Gillian, MB ChB Liv.   Sr. Lectr.

Platt, Mary Jane, MB BS Lond., MPH   Sr. Lectr.

Scott-Samuel, Alex J. R., MB ChB Liv., MCommH Liv.   Sr. Lectr.

Williams, Evelyn M. I., MA Camb., MD Lond.   Sr. Lectr.; Acting Head*

Other Staff: 2 Visiting Profs.; 4 Lectrs.; 1 Fellow; 1 Lectr.†; 12 Hon. Lectrs.; 1 Hon. Res. Fellow

Research: epidemiology (cancer, substance misuse, HIV/AIDS, suicide); health inequalities and economics of health care rationing; health promotion approaches to nutrition; history of public health; perinatal, infant and childhood health and disability

Surgery

Tel: (0151) 706 4170

Leinster, Samuel J., BSc Edin., MB ChB Edin., MD Liv., FRCSEd   Prof.

McCulloch, Peter G., MB ChB Aberd., MD, FRCS   Sr. Lectr.

Neoptolemos, John P., MB BChir Camb., MA Camb., MD Leic., FRCS   Prof., Surgery; Head*

Slavin, John P., BSc Lond., MB BS Lond., FRCS   Sr. Lectr.

Sutton, Robert, BA Durh., MB BS Lond., DPhil Oxf., FRCS   Sr. Lectr.

Other Staff: 1 Visiting Prof.; 3 Lectrs.; 63 Clin. Lectrs.†; 1 Hon. Lectr.; 10 Hon. Res. Fellows

Research: cancer research (clinical trials, genetic treatment, molecular and cellular pathogenesis); surgical gastroenterology (acute pancreatitis, mechanisms of soft tissue injury, portal hypertension)

Therapy Radiography

Tel: (0151) 794 5750

Burgess, Kathryn, MB Lond.   Sr. Lectr.; Head*

Other Staff: 3 Lectrs.; 1 Lectr.†

Research: CBL in radiotherapy degree programmes; descriptive epidemiology of cancer in the elderly; minimising side effects of radiography; psychosocial aspects of cancer care

Tropical Medicine, School of

Tel: (0151) 708 9393 Fax: (0151) 708 8733

Ashford, Richard W., PhD Lond., DSc Lond., FIBiol   Prof.

Barnish, Guy, BSc Lond., MCommH Liv., PhD Liv.   Sr. Lectr.

Beeching, Nicholas J., BM BCh Oxf., MA Oxf., FRACP   Sr. Lectr.

Bianco, E. (Ted), BSc Lond., PhD Lond., FIBiol   Walter Myers Prof., Parasitology

Birley, Martin H., MSc Warw., MS Ill., PhD Lond.   Sr. Lectr.

Brabin, Bernard J., MB ChB Manc., MSc Lond., PhD Lond., FRCPCan   Sr. Lectr.

Chance, Michael L., MSc E.Anglia, PhD E.Anglia   Sr. Lectr.

Coulter, J. Brian S., BA Trinity(Dub.), MD Trinity(Dub.), FRCPI   Sr. Lectr.

Edwards, I. Geoffrey, BSc Birm., PhD Manc.   Sr. Lectr.

Garner, Paul A., MD Lond.   Sr. Lectr.

Gilks, Charles F., MB BS Lond., MA Camb., MSc Lond., DPhil Oxf.   Sr. Lectr.

Haran, David, BSc MEd PhD DTM   Sr. Lectr.

Hommel, Marcel, MD Stras., PhD Liv.   Alfred Jones and Warrington Yorke Prof.

Kröeger, Axel, DrMed Hamburg, MSc Lond., PhD Heidel.   Middlemass Hunt Prof., International Community Health

Macfarlane, Sarah B. J., BA Lanc., MSc Lond.   Reader

Marshall, Ian, BSc Wales, PhD Wales   Sr. Lectr.

Martinez, Javier, MB BChir MCommH   Sr. Lectr.

Molyneux, David H., MA Camb., PhD Camb., DSc Camb., FIBiol   Prof., Tropical Health Sciences; Dir.*

Molyneux, Malcolm E., MB BChir Camb., MA Camb., MD Salf., FRCP   Prof.

Shears, Paul, BSc Reading, MB BS Lond.   Sr. Lectr.

Smith, David H., MB BS, FRCP   Sr. Lectr.
Squire, S. Bertie, BSc Lond., MD Camb.   Sr. Lectr.
Theakston, Robert D. G., MSc Leeds, PhD Liv.   Reader
Townson, Harold, MSc PhD   Selwyn Lloyd Prof., Medical Entomology
Trees, A. J. (Sandy), BVM&S Edin., PhD Edin.   Prof., Veterinary Parasitology
Other Staff: 5 Visiting Profs.; 15 Lectrs.; 3 Clin. Lectrs.†; 2 Sr. Fellows; 1 Hon. Sr. Res. Fellow
Research: international health; molecular biology and immunology; parasite and vector biology; tropical medicine

VETERINARY SCIENCE

Veterinary Anaesthesia

Tel: (0151) 706 4002 Fax: (0151) 706 5884
Jones, Ronald S., JP, MVSc Liv., DrMedVet Berne, DVSc Pret., FIBiol, FRCVS   Prof.
Other Staff: 1 Lectr.; 2 Residents; 1 Demonstrator
Research: cardiovascular function and anaesthesia in horses; muscle relaxants in anaesthesia; new inhalant anaesthetic agents; stress and anaesthesia in horses and cattle

Veterinary Clinical Science and Animal Husbandry

Tel: (0151) 794 6026 Fax: (0151) 794 6028
Edwards, G. Barrie, BVSc Liv., DVetMed Lond., FRCVS   Prof., Equine Studies; Head*

Animal Husbandry, Division of

Tel: (0151) 794 6101 Fax: (0151) 794 6017
Dobson, Hilary, PhD Liv., DSc Liv.   Prof., Veterinary Reproduction; Head of Div.*
Lawrence, Timothy L. J., MSc Reading, PhD Liv., FIBiol, FLS   Reader
Other Staff: 1 Lectr.; 1 Hon. Sr. Fellow
Research: breeding and nutrition of sheep; fertility, stress and welfare; nutrition and growth in farm animals; reproductive endocrinology

Equine Studies, Division of

Tel: (0151) 794 6071 Fax: (0151) 794 6034
Cox, John E., BSc Lond., BVetMed Lond., PhD Liv., FRCVS   Sr. Lectr.
Edwards, G. Barrie, BVSc Liv., DVetMed Lond., FRCVS   Prof., Equine Studies; Head of Div.*
Knottenbelt, Derek C., DVM&S Edin.   Sr. Lectr.
Riggs, Christopher M., BSc Brist., BVSc Brist., PhD Lond.   Sr. Lectr.
Other Staff: 2 Lectrs.; 2 Residents; 1 Hon. Res. Fellow
Research: aetiology and surgery of intestinal obstructions; endocrinology and seasonality in stallions; equine orthopaedics; equine parasitology and epidemiology; equine respiratory and alimentary tracts

Farm Animal Studies, Division of

Tel: (0151) 794 6029 Fax: (0151) 794 6065
Cripps, Peter J., BSc Brist., BVSc Brist., MSc(Epid) Lond., PhD Brist.   Sr. Lectr.
Morgan, Kenton L., VetMB Camb., MA Camb., PhD Brist.   Prof., Epidemiology; Head of Div.*
Ward, W. Robert, BVSc Brist., PhD Liv.   Sr. Lectr.
Other Staff: 4 Lectrs.; 1 Lectr.†; 4 Hon. Lectrs.; 3 Hon. Sr. Fellows
Research: clinical epidemiology; dairy cattle lameness; ectoparasites and tick-borne diseases; mastitis; nutrition; reproduction

Small Animal Studies, Division of

Tel: (0151) 794 4290 Fax: (0151) 794 4304
Carter, Stuart D., BSc Bath, PhD Bath   Sr. Lectr.
Gaskell, Christopher J., BVSc Brist., PhD Brist.   Prof.; Head of Div.*
Walton, Gus S., BVSc Brist.   Sr. Lectr.
Other Staff: 5 Lectrs.; 4 Residents; 1 Hon. Lectr.; 1 Hon. Sr. Fellow

Research: feline and canine virology; immunology of cat, dog and horse arthritides; small animal medicine and surgery; small animal nutrition

Veterinary Parasitology, see Medicine (Trop. Med., Sch. of)

Veterinary Pathology

Tel: (0151) 794 4265 Fax: (0151) 794 4268
Bennett, Malcolm, BVSc Liv., PhD Liv.   Sr. Lectr.
Bradbury, Janet M., MSc St And., PhD Liv.   Reader
Carter, Stuart D., BSc Bath, PhD Bath   Sr. Lectr.
Dixon, John B., VetMB Camb., MA Camb., PhD Lond.   Reader
Hewicker-Trautwein, Marion, BVSc Hanover, DrMedVet Hanover, DrMedHabil   Sr. Lectr.
Jones, Richard C., PhD Liv., DSc Birm.   Reader
Kelly, Donald F., BVSc Brist., MA Camb., PhD Camb., FRCPath   Prof.; Head*
Other Staff: 3 Lectrs.; 2 Residents; 1 Sr. Fellow; 1 Reader†; 1 Hon. Lectr.; 4 Hon. Sr. Fellows
Research: electron microscopy; histopathology; immunocytochemistry; infectious diseases; virology

Veterinary Preclinical Sciences

Tel: (0151) 794 4229 Fax: (0151) 794 4243
Cooke, Robert G., BSc Liv., PhD Liv.   Sr. Lectr.
Eisner, David A., BA Camb., DPhil Oxf.   Prof., Veterinary Biology; Head*
O'Neill, Stephen C., BSc Glas., PhD Glas.   Sr. Lectr.
Shirazi-Beechey, Soraya P., BS Mich., PhD Lond.   Sr. Lectr.
Vaillant, Camille R., BSc Wales, PhD Liv.   Sr. Lectr.
Other Staff: 4 Lectrs.; 3 Hon. Sr. Fellows; 1 Hon. Sr. Res. Fellow
Research: mechanisms of contraction in cardiac and smooth muscle; molecular biology and physiology; peptide systems; somatosensory processing

SPECIAL CENTRES, ETC

African Studies, Centre for

Tel: (0151) 794 2989
Gould, William T. S., MA St And.   Prof.; Deputy Dir.
Roberts, Penelope A., MA Camb., PhD Camb.   Dir.*
Research: agriculture and the food crisis; energy and development; gender and health issues; population change; Southern African issues

Applied English Language Studies Unit

Tel: (0151) 794 2734 Fax: (0151) 794 2291
Hoey, Prof. Michael P., BA Lond., PhD Birm.   Dir.*
Research: discourse analysis; language teaching

Archive Studies, Centre for

Tel: (0151) 794 2390 Fax: (0151) 794 2366
Williams, Caroline M., BA Lond.   Dir.*
Research: archive studies; records and information management

Cancer Tissue Bank

Tel: (0151) 706 4354
Gosney, John R., BSc Liv., MD Liv.   Dir.*

Central and Eastern European Studies, Centre for

Tel: (0151) 794 2415
Lee, Prof. F. W. Robert, MA Oxf., DPhil Oxf.   Dir.*
Research: life under the former socialist regimes; politics of agricultural protection; rural unemployment and rural regeneration; socio-economic transformation

Child, the Family and the Law, Centre for the Study of the

Tel: (0151) 794 2818
Lyon, Prof. Christina M., LLB Lond.   Dir.*

Clinical Tropical Medicine, Wellcome Trust Centre for Research in

Tel: (0151) 708 9393
Molyneux, Prof. Malcolm E., MB BChir Camb., MA Camb., MD Salf., FRCP   Dir.*

Comparative Infectious Diseases, Centre for

Tel: (0151) 794 6015 Fax: (0151) 794 6005
Bennett, Malcolm, BVSc Liv., PhD Liv.   Dir.*
Research: descriptive and theoretical epidemiology; immunopathogenesis; molecular taxonomy; pathological, microbial and clinical diagnostics; vaccine design

Environmental Radioactivity Research Centre

Tel: (0151) 794 4020 Fax: (0151) 794 4061
Appleby, Peter G., BSc Cant., BE Cant., PhD Cant.   Dir.*
Research: dating of lake and estuarine sediments and peat cores; monitoring of radioactive discharges; nuclear waste geology; studies of Chernobyl fallout

European Population Studies, Centre for

Tel: (0151) 794 2857
Siddle, David J., BA Durh., MLitt Durh., PhD Durh.   Dir.*
Research: changing role of the family; comparative urban population of Western Europe; migration; social and occupational change

Health and Community Care Research Unit

Tel: (0151) 794 5503 Fax: (0151) 794 5434
Perkins, Elizabeth, BSc Hull, MSc Manc., PhD Manc.   Dir.*
Research: care in the community; continuing care and rehabilitation services

Health Studies, Latin-American Centre for

Tel: (0151) 708 2222 Fax: (0151) 708 8733
Kroëger, Prof. Axel, DrMed Hamburg, MSc Lond., PhD Heidel.   Dir.*

Human Ageing, Institute of

Tel: (0151) 794 5079 Fax: (0151) 794 5077
Merry, Brian J., BSc Hull, MSc Leeds, PhD Hull   Sr. Lectr., Biological Gerontology
Sherratt, Catherine, MA Liv.   Trg. Manager
Wilson, Kenneth C. M., MB ChB Liv., MPhil Lond.   Prof.; Dir.*
Other Staff: 2 Lectrs.; 2 Fellows; 1 Asst. Dir.†; 1 Hon. Lectr.; 1 Hon. Sr. Res. Fellow; 2 Hon. Res. Fellows
Research: biological processes of normal ageing; epidemiology of Alzheimer's disease; health, well-being and quality of life; housing and care of the elderly; prevalence and outcome of cognitive decline

Impact Research Centre

Tel: (0151) 794 4874 Fax: (0151) 794 4892
Jones, Prof. Norman, PhD Manc., DSc Manc., FIMechE   Dir.*
Research: emplosion loading of structures; response of structural membranes under large impact loads; structural crashworthiness and transportation safety

Innovative Catalysis, Leverhulme Centre for

Tel: (0151) 794 3582 Fax: (0151) 794 3589
Derouane, Prof. Eric G., BA Liège, MA Prin., DrSc Liège   Dir.*

Magnetic Resonance and Image Analysis Research Centre

Tel: (0151) 794 5632 Fax: (0151) 794 5635
Roberts, J. Neil, MSc Aberd., PhD Wales Sr. Lectr.
Whitehouse, Prof. Graham H., MB BS Lond., FRCR FRCP Dir.*
Other Staff: 1 Hon. Sr. Res. Fellow
Research: foetal imaging; functional imaging of invertebral disc disease; physiology of human muscle fatigue; tissue characterisation and quantification of brain morphology

Manx Studies, Centre for

Tel: (01624) 673074 Fax: (01624) 661299
Davey, Peter J., BD Lond., BPhil Liv., PhD Liv. Dir.*
Research: Manx archaeology; Manx culture and language; Manx environment; Manx history; Manx politics, economics and tourism

Marine and Coastal Studies, Centre for

Leah, Richard T., BSc E.Anglia, PhD E.Anglia Dir.*

Medicine, Law and Bioethics, Institute of

Tel: (0151) 794 3087 Fax: (0151) 794 2884
Jones, Prof. Michael A., BA Keele, LLM W.Ont., PhD Liv. Dir.*
Research: drug regulation; medical litigation; NHS reforms and resource allocation; public health; reproductive medicine

Medieval Studies, Centre for

Tel: (0151) 794 2389 Fax: (0151) 794 2366
Scott, Thomas, BA Camb., PhD Camb., FRHistS Dir.*
Research: interdisciplinary studies: literature, history and archaeology

Muscle Research Centre

Tel: (0151) 706 4077 Fax: (0151) 706 5802
Jackson, Prof. Malcolm J., PhD Lond., DSc Sur. Dir.*
Research: investigation of adults and children with disorders of muscle

Popular Music, Institute of

Tel: (0151) 794 3101 Fax: (0151) 794 2566
Horn, R. David W., MA Oxf. Dir.*
Research: civic music policy initiatives; popular music making in Merseyside; popular music, tourism and urban regeneration

Port and Maritime History, Centre for

Tel: (0151) 794 2415
Lee, Prof. W. Robert, MA Oxf., DPhil Oxf. Dir.*
Research: ancillary occupations; changing structure of commerce and trade; dock management; Merseyside's maritime history -social and community context

Primary Science and Technology, Centre for Research in

Tel: (0151) 794 3270 Fax: (0151) 794 3271
Russell, Prof. Terence J., BA Manc., MA Sus. Dir.*
Research: development of curriculum and training materials; implementation of science curriculum in England; public understanding of science and technology

Proudman Oceanographic Laboratory

Affiliated Institution
Tel: (0151) 653 8633 Fax: (0151) 652 3950

McCartney, Prof. Brian S., BSc Birm., PhD Birm., FIEE Dir.*

Quaternary Environmental Research Centre

Tel: (0151) 794 3463 Fax: (0151) 794 3464
Shaw, Prof. John, BSc Liv., PhD Liv. Dir.*
Research: cavity detection and risk assessment; climatic change from magnetic measurements; environmental effects of magnetic fields; environmental monitoring instrumentation development; environmental pollution monitoring

Surface Science, Interdisciplinary Research Centre in

Tel: (0151) 794 3870 Fax: (0151) 708 0662
Richardson, Prof. Neville V., BA Oxf., DPhil Oxf. Dir.*
Research: behaviour of oxide surfaces; complex molecules at surfaces; gas-surface reaction dynamics; interfaces and semiconductor surface chemistry; surface science and catalysis design

Tropical Clinical Pharmacology, Centre for

Tel: (0151) 794 5543
Breckenridge, Prof. Alistair M., CBE, BSc St And., MB ChB St And., MD Dund., MSc Lond., FRCP Dir.*
Research: pharmacology of antimalarial drugs

Tropical Medical Microbiology, Centre for

Tel: (0151) 706 4396
Shears, Paul, BSc Reading, MB BS Lond., MD Dir.*

CONTACT OFFICERS

Academic affairs. Academic Secretary: Jones, Keith H., MA Camb.
Accommodation. Welfare and Accommodation Adviser: Wyn-Jones, Carys
Admissions (first degree). Head, Schools, Colleges and International Liaison and Admissions Service: Pickering, Ian A., BSc Hull, PhD Hull
Admissions (higher degree). (Contact the faculty concerned)
Adult/continuing education. Director, Centre for Continuing Education: Derricott, Raymond, BA Nott., MEd Nott.
Alumni. Director of Administrative Services: Buss, Ray G., MA Oxf., PhD Reading
Archives. University Archivist: Allan, Adrian R., BA Durh.
Careers. Centre for Careers and Academic Practice: Merry, Anne M., BSc Hull, MSc Leeds, PhD Hull
Computing services. Administrator, Computing Services: Bryson, C. Anne, BA Open(UK), MPhil Open(UK)
Consultancy services. Director, Research Support and Industrial Liaison: Prior, David L., BEng Liv., PhD Liv.
Credit transfer. Academic Secretary: Jones, Keith H., MA Camb.
Development/fund-raising. Director of Administrative Services: Buss, Ray G., MA Oxf., PhD Reading
Distance education. Assistant Registrar, Continuing Professional Development: Stewart, Carol
Equal opportunities. Director of Personnel: Rutherford, Susan J., BSc Leic.
Estates and buildings/works and services. Director of Estates: Doyle, Kevin P., BSc(Eng) CNAA

Examinations. Senior Assistant Registrar, Student and Examinations Division: Walker, Gary, BSc Liv., PhD Liv.
Finance. Director of Finance: Sandbach, John C.
General enquiries. Registrar: Carr, Michael D., MA Durh.
Health services. Practice Manager, Student Health Service: ......
Industrial liaison. Director, Research Support and Industrial Liaison: Prior, David L., BEng Liv., PhD Liv.
International office. Director of International Liaison/Director of College Partnerships: Millward, Joanna M. E., BMus Wales, MA Keele
Library (chief librarian). Librarian: Thomson, Frances M., MA Glas., BLitt Glas.
Minorities/disadvantaged groups. Director of Personnel: Rutherford, Susan J., BSc Leic.
Personnel/human resources. Director of Personnel: Rutherford, Susan J., BSc Leic.
Public relations, information and marketing (information and marketing). Director, Research Support and Industrial Liaison: Prior, David L., BEng Liv., PhD Liv.
Public relations, information and marketing (public relations). Public Relations Officer: Bamber, David T., BCom Liv.
Publications. Editorial and Publishing Office: Hill, Richard W. F., MA LIv.
Purchasing. Purchasing Officer: Beard, Geoffrey M., BTech Lough., BA Open(UK)
Quality assurance and accreditation. Senior Assistant Registrar, Quality Assurance Unit: Brook, Anne C., BA Lond.
Research. Director, Research Support and Industrial Liaison: Prior, David L., BEng Liv., PhD Liv.
Safety. Safety Adviser: Bowes, Christopher M., BA Camb., PhD Lond.
Scholarships, awards, loans (international students). Director of International Liaison/ Director of College Partnerships: Millward, Joanna M. E., BMus Wales, MA Keele
Scholarships, awards, loans (loans). Student Loans Officer: Flint, S.
Scholarships, awards, loans (scholarships, awards). Administrative Assistant, Student and Examinations: Hewison, Frances M., BA Hull
Schools liaison. Director, Schools and Colleges Liaison: Kelly, Graham, BScEcon Wales
Security. General Manager, Operational Services: Blythe, K. William
Staff development and training. Litherland, Moragh B., BA Hull
Student union. General Manager, Guild of Students: Jenkins, M. P.
Student welfare/counselling. Head of the Counselling Service: ......
Students from other countries. International Students' Adviser: Spencer, Susan, BA Birm.
Students with disabilities. Welfare and Accommodation Adviser: Wyn-Jones, Carys
University press. Assistant Registrar: Bloxsidge, Robin J. C., BA Liv.

CAMPUS/COLLEGE HEADS

Liverpool Hope University College, Hope Park, Liverpool, England L16 9JD. (Tel: (0151) 737 3000; Fax: (0151) 737 3100.) Rector: Lee, Prof. Simon, BA LLM
University College Chester, Cheyney Road, Chester, England CH1 4BJ. (Tel: (01244) 375444; Fax: (01244) 373379.) Principal: Wheeler, Prof. Timothy, BSc Wales, PhD CNAA

[Information supplied by the institution as at March 1998, and edited by the ACU]

LIVERPOOL JOHN MOORES UNIVERSITY

Founded 1992; previously established as Liverpool Polytechnic 1970

Member of the Association of Commonwealth Universities

Postal Address: Rodney House, 70 Mount Pleasant, Liverpool, England L3 5UX
Telephone: (0151) 231 2121 **WWW**: http://www.livjm.ac.uk **E-mail formula**: initial(s).surname@LIVJM.AC.UK

CHANCELLOR—Moores, John, CBE, DL
VICE-CHANCELLOR AND CHIEF EXECUTIVE*—Toyne, Prof. Peter, BA Brist., DEd DL
PROVOST—Latto, Prof. Jennifer, BA Camb., MA Camb.
BURSAR—Bickerstaffe, J. Allan, FCIS
REGISTRAR AND SECRETARY AND CLERK TO THE BOARD‡—Wild, Alison

GENERAL INFORMATION

History. The university was founded in 1823 as the Liverpool Mechanics' and Apprentices' Library. In 1970 many of the colleges formed in the intervening years were merged to become Liverpool Polytechnic, and in 1992 the university was given its current title.

Admission to first degree courses (see also United Kingdom Introduction). Through Universities and Colleges Admissions Service (UCAS). UK nationals: normally a minimum of 5 passes at General Certificate of Secondary Education (GCSE) including mathematics and English language, and 2 A levels or equivalent.

International applicants: certified academic achievement equivalent to UK entry requirements. Where English is a second language: TOEFL score of 550–600, IELTS 6 or equivalent.

First Degrees (see also United Kingdom Directory to Subjects of Study). BA, BEd, BEng, BSc, LLB.

All courses are full-time and normally last 3 years. BEng/BA (business): 3 years plus 1 year industrial placement. Selected courses are available part-time.

Higher Degrees (see also United Kingdom Directory to Subjects of Study). MA, MBA, MSc, MPhil, PhD.

Applicants to master's degree courses must normally hold a relevant first degree. PhD: appropriate master's degree with relevant research component.

MSc: 1 year full-time or 2–3 years part-time; MBA: 2 years full-time or 4 years part-time; MPhil: 1–2 years full-time, 2–4 years part-time.

Libraries. 500,000 volumes; 2500 periodicals subscribed to; 660,000 miscellaneous items.

Fees (1998–99, annual). Undergraduate: £1000; sandwich courses £500. Postgraduate: home students £2610 full-time; international students £6170 (taught MA), £6950 (taught MSc), £5800 (international banking, economics and finance), £6952 (MBA), £5800 (arts, by research), £6480 (engineering and science, by research).

Academic Year (1998–99). Two semesters: 7 September–18 December; 25 January–28 May.

Income (1997–98). Total, £88,400,000.

Statistics. Staff: 2443 (870 academic, 1573 administrative and other). Students: full-time 13,020 (6589 men, 6431 women); part-time 6649 (2931 men, 3718 women); international 1579 (936 men, 643 women); total 21,248.

FACULTIES/SCHOOLS

Arts and Professional Studies, Division of

Tel: (0151) 231 3920 Fax: (0151) 231 3539
Chair: Evans, Prof. Roger, BSc Wales, MA Warw., PhD Birm.

Education, Health and Social Science, Division of

Tel: (0151) 231 4099 Fax: (0151) 258 1593
Chair: Jacks, Prof. E. Jane, BEd Manc., MEd Manc.

Engineering and Science, Division of

Tel: (0151) 231 2042 Fax: (0151) 207 3224
Chair: Wheeler, Prof. Peter E., BSc Durh., PhD Durh.

ACADEMIC UNITS

Arranged by Divisions and Schools

ARTS AND PROFESSIONAL STUDIES, DIVISION OF

Tel: (0151) 231 3579, 231 3586 Fax: (0151) 709 4957

Built Environment

Tel: (0151) 231 3579 Fax: (0151) 709 4952
Al-Khaddar, Rafid M. Lectr./Sr. Lectr.
Al-Nageim, Hassan K. Lectr./Sr. Lectr.
Alexander, David A. Lectr./Sr. Lectr.
Boughey, L. Joseph Lectr./Sr. Lectr.
Brindle, Helen Lectr./Sr. Lectr.
Brown, Gary P. Lectr./Sr. Lectr.
Brown, Peter K. Principal Lectr.
Cantwell, Michael A. Lectr./Sr. Lectr.
Clelland, Douglas Prof., Architecture
Clucas, Richard H. Lectr./Sr. Lectr.
Couch, Christopher R., MSc Lond. Prof.
Curd, Eric F. Reader
Dunlea-Jones, Patrick Lectr./Sr. Lectr.
Eden, Nicholas B. Lectr./Sr. Lectr.
Fortune, Christopher J. Lectr./Sr. Lectr.
Fowles, Steven Lectr./Sr. Lectr.
Garner, Robert Lectr./Sr. Lectr.
Glover, Susan J. Lectr./Sr. Lectr.
Haslem, Robert F. Lectr./Sr. Lectr.
Hodgkinson, Robert D. Sch. Head of Undergrad. Programmes
Horgan, Bernice M. Lectr./Sr. Lectr.
Howard, Christopher A. Lectr./Sr. Lectr.
Hugill, David Lectr./Sr. Lectr.
Ireland, Jeremy Lectr./Sr. Lectr.
Jackson, Robert P. Principal Lectr.
Jagger, David M. Prof.
Johnson, Jaqueline A. Lectr./Sr. Lectr.
Jones, George A. Lectr./Sr. Lectr.
Kirke, Edward J. Lectr./Sr. Lectr.
Kirsten, Louise M. Lectr./Sr. Lectr.
Kokosalakis, Jennifer Lectr./Sr. Lectr.
Lesley, Lewis J. S., BSc Lond., PhD Strath. Prof., Transport Studies
Lo, Philip Lectr./Sr. Lectr.
Longworth, Edward J. Lectr./Sr. Lectr.
Lunney, Frances Lectr./Sr. Lectr.
MacDonald, Robert G. Reader
Melaine, Yassine Lectr./Sr. Lectr.
Migos, Athanassios Lectr./Sr. Lectr.
Miller, Peter Lectr./Sr. Lectr.
Morgan, Peter H., BA Leic., PhD Wales Prof.; Head*
Murray, William Lectr./Sr. Lectr.
Nutt, Michael A. Lectr./Sr. Lectr.
Owen, Peter R. Lectr./Sr. Lectr.
Parry, James J. Lectr./Sr. Lectr.
Rayner, Alison J. Lectr./Sr. Lectr.

Riley, Michael L. Lectr./Sr. Lectr.
Ross, Andrew D. Principal Lectr.
Rostron, Jack R. Lectr./Sr. Lectr.
Rowlinson, Kevin M. Lectr./Sr. Lectr.
Ruddock, Felicite M. Lectr./Sr. Lectr.
Seavor, Kenneth R. G. Lectr./Sr. Lectr.
Springer, Stephen J. Lectr./Sr. Lectr.
Sturrock, Neil S. Lectr./Sr. Lectr.
Sudenham, Helen L. Lectr./Sr. Lectr.
Swanson, Alan G. Lectr./Sr. Lectr.
Tremear, Christopher H. Lectr./Sr. Lectr.
Vakiris, Constantine Lectr./Sr. Lectr.
Wall, Douglas C. Principal Lectr.
Whitelegg, John Prof., Environmental Studies
Williams, Aled W. Lectr./Sr. Lectr.
Williams, Delyth W., BA Wales, LLB Liv. Prof., Estate Management
Williams, Peter N. Principal Lectr.
Wordsworth, Paul R. Principal Lectr.
Wright, Linda P. Lectr./Sr. Lectr.
Wroot, Ian Lectr./Sr. Lectr.
Other Staff: 2 Lectrs.; 1 Sr. Lectr.†

Law, Social Work and Social Policy

Tel: (0151) 231 3911 Fax: (0151) 231 3908
Actobino, Biko Lectr./Sr. Lectr.
Baxter, Gerald P. Lectr./Sr. Lectr.
Brooman, Simon D. Lectr./Sr. Lectr.
Burke, Beverley J. Lectr./Sr. Lectr.
Carter, Keith W. Lectr./Sr. Lectr.
Chappelle, Diane Lectr./Sr. Lectr.
Charley, Janette P. Lectr./Sr. Lectr.
Charlesworth, Lorrie R. Lectr./Sr. Lectr.
Clifford, Derek J. Lectr./Sr. Lectr.
Cooke, Peter J. Principal Lectr.
Council, Bronwen J. Principal Lectr.
Cunningham, Lynda Lectr./Sr. Lectr.
Evans, Roger, BSc Wales, MA Warw., PhD Birm. Prof.; Head*
Fagan, Noel J. Lectr./Sr. Lectr.
Fargher, Fiona L. Lectr./Sr. Lectr.
George, Susan I. Principal Lectr.
Gill, Peter Reader
Harris, Neville S. Prof., Law
Harrison, Philomena Lectr./Sr. Lectr.
Harvey, Anthony R. Lectr./Sr. Lectr.
Hughes, Michael J. Lectr./Sr. Lectr.
Jones, Dick P., LLB Lond., MA CNAA Reader
Jones, Stephen R. Lectr./Sr. Lectr.
Kershaw, Sheila Lectr./Sr. Lectr.
Lauterburg, Dominique M. Lectr./Sr. Lectr.
Legge, Deborah J. Lectr./Sr. Lectr.
Lower, Michael L. P. Lectr./Sr. Lectr.
Mair, George I. U. Prof., Criminal Justice
Mayhew, John R. Principal Lectr.
Nairns, Janice Lectr./Sr. Lectr.
Newman, Eileen T. Lectr./Sr. Lectr.
Platten, William J. Lectr./Sr. Lectr.
Pope, Paula Lectr./Sr. Lectr.
Preston-Shoot, Michael Prof., Social Care
Rahilly, Simon J. Lectr./Sr. Lectr.
Randall, Kathryn N. Lectr./Sr. Lectr.
Rawstorne, Shirley Lectr./Sr. Lectr.
Roskin, Diane Lectr./Sr. Lectr.
Salako, Soloman E. Lectr./Sr. Lectr.
Selfe, David W. Principal Lectr.
Selkridge, Earl R. J. Lectr./Sr. Lectr.
Sharkey, Peter Principal Lectr.
Sim, Joseph Prof., Criminology
Stevens, Robert K. Lectr./Sr. Lectr.

Swain, Martin R.   Lectr./Sr. Lectr.
Thomas, Huw G.   Lectr./Sr. Lectr.
Wardman, Kevin   Lectr./Sr. Lectr.
Other Staff: 1 Lectr.; 2 Sr. Lectrs.†

Liverpool Art School

Tel: (0151) 231 5095 Fax: (0151) 231 5096
Bailey, Peter C.   Lectr./Sr. Lectr.
Barraclough, John, BA CNAA   Asst. Dir.,
   Indust. Liaison; Head*
Byrne, John   Sr. Lectr.
Crighton, Cecilia   Head*
Crow, David J.   Principal Lectr.
Cuthbert, Vanessa J.   Lectr./Sr. Lectr.
Dawber, Carol   Lectr./Sr. Lectr.
Dawber, Martin   Principal Lectr.
Dossor, Di J.   Lectr./Sr. Lectr.
Fallows, Colin   Reader
Gant, Richard M.   Lectr./Sr. Lectr.
Godfrey, Julia K.   Reader
Hardstaff, Stephen W.   Lectr./Sr. Lectr.
Holden, John T.   Principal Lectr.
Holt, Roy B.   Reader
Lowy, Adrienne S.   Lectr./Sr. Lectr.
Mairs, Richard N.   Lectr./Sr. Lectr.
Morris, David B.   Lectr./Sr. Lectr.
Morris, Neil   Lectr./Sr. Lectr.
Newton, John   Reader
Oram, Scott R.   Lectr./Sr. Lectr.
Sheldon, Julie L.   Lectr./Sr. Lectr.
Smith, Merilyn M.   Prof., Fine Art
Wardle, Michelle M.   Sr. Lectr.
Weston, Philip J.   Sr. Lectr.
Williams, Richard J.   Lectr./Sr. Lectr.
Other Staff: 6 Lectrs.; 5 Sr. Lectrs.†

Liverpool Business School

Tel: (0151) 231 3401 Fax: (0151) 707 0423
Adams, Denis C.   Prof.
Addley, Pamela J.   Lectr./Sr. Lectr.
Ahmad, Bakri   Lectr./Sr. Lectr.
Allard, Gillian M.   Lectr./Sr. Lectr.
Ansell, Elaine   Lectr./Sr. Lectr.
Ashcroft, Linda S.   Lectr./Sr. Lectr.
Baines, Mitchell I.   Lectr./Sr. Lectr.
Beere, Alistair S.   Lectr./Sr. Lectr.
Bloor, Kelvin   Lectr./Sr. Lectr.
Bowdery, Angela   Lectr./Sr. Lectr.
Bryde, David J.   Lectr./Sr. Lectr.
Cailes, John E.   Lectr./Sr. Lectr.
Chandler, Helen E.   Lectr./Sr. Lectr.
Chaplin, Anthony G. L.   Lectr./Sr. Lectr.
Conaghan, Manus   Lectr./Sr. Lectr.
Cook, Anne M.   Lectr./Sr. Lectr.
Corley, Aileen   Lectr./Sr. Lectr.
Dawson, Anthony G.   Lectr./Sr. Lectr.
Dereli, Noyan   Lectr./Sr. Lectr.
Doig, R. Alan   Prof., Public Service
   Management
Eades, Elaine M.   Lectr./Sr. Lectr.
Eden, James A.   Lectr./Sr. Lectr.
Evans, John M.   Lectr./Sr. Lectr.
Farrow, Anne J.   Lectr./Sr. Lectr.
Fisher, Ian G.   Lectr./Sr. Lectr.
Foster, George   Lectr./Sr. Lectr.
Gardner, David N.   Principal Lectr.
Gill, Colin J.   Lectr./Sr. Lectr.
Grant, Sheila   Lectr./Sr. Lectr.
Hall, Anthony R.   Principal Lectr.
Harper, Karl P.   Lectr./Sr. Lectr.
Harvey, Peter J.   Lectr./Sr. Lectr.
Hawkins, James N.   Lectr./Sr. Lectr.
Haynes, Doug L.   Principal Lectr.
Hickie, Desmond J.   Principal Lectr.
Holden, Kenneth   Prof.
Hopkins, Robert N.   Lectr./Sr. Lectr.
Hutchinson, Keith F.   Lectr./Sr. Lectr.
Iles, Paul A., BA Oxf., MSc Manc.   Prof.
Kennedy, Michael J.   Lectr./Sr. Lectr.
Kershaw, George S.   Lectr./Sr. Lectr.
Laws, Jason P.   Lectr./Sr. Lectr.
Levy, Gerald M.   Principal Lectr.
Lisewski, Bernard   Principal Lectr.
Liston, Isobel M.   Lectr./Sr. Lectr.
Lovegrove, Ian W.   Lectr./Sr. Lectr.
Marsters, Stanley   Lectr./Sr. Lectr.†
Matthews, K. G. P., BSc Lond.., MSc Lond., PhD
   Liv.   Prof.

Mawdsley, David V.   Lectr./Sr. Lectr.
McClelland, Bob   Reader
McMahon, Chris   Lectr./Sr. Lectr.
Mearns, Albert F.   Lectr./Sr. Lectr.
Meehan, John P.   Lectr./Sr. Lectr.
Meehan, Karon M.   Lectr./Sr. Lectr.
Mulhaney, Ann   Lectr./Sr. Lectr.
Murray, Terence M.   Lectr./Sr. Lectr.
Naylor, John B.   Principal Lectr.
O'Farrell, Jack   Lectr./Sr. Lectr.
Padgett, Graham C.   Principal Lectr.
Parnell, Martin F.   Lectr./Sr. Lectr.
Paul, Colin S.   Lectr./Sr. Lectr.
Pegum, Roger H.   Principal Lectr.
Prendergast, Maurice   Lectr./Sr. Lectr.
Pyke, Chris J.   Lectr./Sr. Lectr.
Quirke, Brendan J.   Lectr./Sr. Lectr.
Read, Jonathon F.   Lectr./Sr. Lectr.
Reynolds, John G.   Principal Lectr.
Roberts, Brian D.   Lectr./Sr. Lectr.
Roper, V. P.   Lectr./Sr. Lectr.
Rose, Edward   Lectr./Sr. Lectr.
Rowland, Glyn   Lectr./Sr. Lectr.
Royce, Maureen   Lectr./Sr. Lectr.
Rudd, Leon   Lectr./Sr. Lectr.
Sanderson, Frank, BEd Leeds, PhD Leeds   Prof.;
   Acting Head*
Sargant, Christina M.   Lectr./Sr. Lectr.
Shannon, Beryl   Lectr./Sr. Lectr.
Sheehan, James F.   Lectr./Sr. Lectr.
Shoesmith, David E.   Lectr./Sr. Lectr.
Simcock, Peter J.   Lectr./Sr. Lectr.
Smith, Henry J.   Principal Lectr.
Sudbury, Lynn   Lectr./Sr. Lectr.
Swash, Gillian D.   Lectr./Sr. Lectr.
Thorne, E. Ann   Lectr./Sr. Lectr.
Tombs, Steven P.   Reader
Trickey, Keith V.   Lectr./Sr. Lectr.
Whorrall, Brian   Lectr./Sr. Lectr.
Williamson, Peter M.   Principal Lectr.
Wilson, Elizabeth M.   Lectr./Sr. Lectr.
Wilson, John E.   Prof.
Yolles, Maurice   Lectr./Sr. Lectr.
Other Staff: 4 Lectrs.; 2 Temp. Lectrs.

Media, Critical and Creative Arts

Tel: (0151) 231 5010 Fax: (0151) 231 5049
Ashplant, Timothy G.   Principal Lectr.
Buckland, Warren   Lectr./Sr. Lectr.
Callery, Dymphna M.   Lectr./Sr. Lectr.
Childs, Peter   Lectr./Sr. Lectr.
Clark, Jaden S.   Lectr./Sr. Lectr.
Croft, Joanne   Lectr./Sr. Lectr.
Cubitt, Sean, BA Camb., MA Camb., PhD
   Montr.   Reader
Cusick, Edmund   Lectr./Sr. Lectr.
Dawson, Ross   Lectr./Sr. Lectr.
Francombe, Benedict   Lectr./Sr. Lectr.
Freeman, John   Principal Lectr.
Friel, James   Lectr./Sr. Lectr.
Graham, Elspeth   Reader
Irobi, Esiaba A.   Lectr./Sr. Lectr.
Jones, Judith   Lectr./Sr. Lectr.
Jordan, Mathew   Lectr./Sr. Lectr.
Llewellyn, D. Llew J.   Principal Lectr.
Long, Trevor S.   Lectr./Sr. Lectr.
Machin, Brian   Lectr./Sr. Lectr.
Manoch, Claire   Lectr./Sr. Lectr.
Marshment, Margaret   Lectr./Sr. Lectr.
Matthews, Nichole D.   Lectr./Sr. Lectr.
McNeill, David   Lectr./Sr. Lectr.
Mellor, Adrian, BA York(UK), MA
   York(UK)   Reader
Merkin, Ros   Lectr./Sr. Lectr.
Millington, Bob J.   Lectr./Sr. Lectr.
Moody, Nickianne A.   Lectr./Sr. Lectr.
Morris, Pam   Reader
Moy, Ronald   Lectr./Sr. Lectr.
Newhan, Jenny   Lectr./Sr. Lectr.
Norquay, Glenda   Lectr./Sr. Lectr.
Pepp, Harry   Principal Lectr.
Price, Joanna H.   Lectr./Sr. Lectr.
Pudlo, Michael   Lectr./Sr. Lectr.
Rawlinson, Alan   Lectr./Sr. Lectr.
Rogers, Helen   Lectr./Sr. Lectr.
Rooney, Dick C.   Lectr./Sr. Lectr.
Ruddock, Andy   Lectr./Sr. Lectr.
Smith, Desmond A.   Lectr./Sr. Lectr.

Smith, Jeanette P.   Lectr./Sr. Lectr.
Smyth, Gerry A.   Lectr./Sr. Lectr.
Spargo, Tamsin E. M.   Lectr./Sr. Lectr.
Spiers, Judi   Lectr./Sr. Lectr.
Storry, Michael F.   Lectr./Sr. Lectr.
Webster, Roger J., BA Lond., MA Lond., PhD
   Lond.   Prof.; Head*
Wills, Colin C.   Lectr./Sr. Lectr.
Other Staff: 6 Lectrs.

Modern Languages

Tel: (0151) 231 3839 Fax: (0151) 707 2896
Allwood, W. Blair   Lectr./Sr. Lectr.
Archibald, Linda, BA Stir., PhD Stir.   Head*
Beaken, Michael   Principal Lectr.
Collins, John P.   Lectr./Sr. Lectr.
Dover, Rosa   Lectr./Sr. Lectr.
Foulkes, Christine   Lectr./Sr. Lectr.
Haeckel, Ursula R.   Lectr./Sr. Lectr.
Haworth, William J.   Lectr./Sr. Lectr.
Helluer, Rosemary   Lectr./Sr. Lectr.
Hickman, Jarmila   Lectr./Sr. Lectr.
Hughes, Bernadette   Lectr./Sr. Lectr.
Korsten, Franz-Josef   Lectr./Sr. Lectr.
Luukko-Vinchenzo, Leila   Lectr./Sr. Lectr.
Menacere, Mohamed K. M.   Lectr./Sr. Lectr.
Morris, Terry E.   Lectr./Sr. Lectr.
Oleinik, Olga A.   Lectr./Sr. Lectr.
Sansot, Evelyne   Lectr./Sr. Lectr.
Shepherd, Martine T.   Principal Lectr.
Sturani, Federica   Lectr./Sr. Lectr.
Teso, Elena   Lectr./Sr. Lectr.
Tufi, Stefania   Lectr./Sr. Lectr.
Wang, Yang Jing   Lectr./Sr. Lectr.
Ward, David S.   Lectr./Sr. Lectr.
Other Staff: 3 Lectrs.; 1 Sr. Lectr.†

EDUCATION, HEALTH AND SOCIAL SCIENCE, DIVISION OF

Education and Community Studies

Tel: (0151) 231 5240 Fax: (0151) 729 0136
Aeillo, Michael   Lectr./Sr. Lectr.
Akroyd, Sue   Lectr./Sr. Lectr.
Bainbridge, Roger   Lectr./Sr. Lectr.
Bell, Leslie, BA PhD   Prof.; Head*
Bell, Stephen   Lectr./Sr. Lectr.
Bowe, Stephen J.   Lectr./Sr. Lectr.
Brooks, Pauline   Lectr./Sr. Lectr.
Burns, Dennis J.   Lectr./Sr. Lectr.
Butters, Jonathan A.   Lectr./Sr. Lectr.
Chidlow, John W.   Lectr./Sr. Lectr.
Clemson, David   Reader
Cooper, Alison M.   Lectr./Sr. Lectr.
Dixon, Malcolm R.   Lectr./Sr. Lectr.
Downie, Martin   Lectr./Sr. Lectr.
Erskine, Brian   Lectr./Sr. Lectr.
Fairhurst, John   Lectr./Sr. Lectr.
Fenwick, Geoffrey   Lectr./Sr. Lectr.
Fowler, Alan   Principal Lectr.
Gatiss, Ian C.   Lectr./Sr. Lectr.
Gee, Brenda   Lectr./Sr. Lectr.
Griffiths, Thomas G. H.   Lectr./Sr. Lectr.
Hackett, Allan F., BSc Leeds, PhD
   Newcastle(UK)   Reader
Hall, Neil   Reader
Hardy, David P.   Lectr./Sr. Lectr.
Haskins, David   Lectr./Sr. Lectr.
Hatfield, Susan C.   Lectr./Sr. Lectr.
Heath, Ann W.   Lectr./Sr. Lectr.
Hepworth, Nicola   Lectr./Sr. Lectr.
Hopper, Matthew G.   Lectr./Sr. Lectr.
Huddart, David, BA Reading, PhD
   Reading   Reader
Jenkin, William E. D.   Lectr./Sr. Lectr.
Jepson, Margaret B.   Lectr./Sr. Lectr.
Jones, Russell J.   Lectr./Sr. Lectr.
Kalu, Clara   Lectr./Sr. Lectr.
Kassem, Derek   Lectr./Sr. Lectr.
Killen, Paul   Lectr./Sr. Lectr.
King, Patricia M.   Principal Lectr.
Latham, John R.   Principal Lectr.
Leaman, Oliver N.   Reader
Loy, Jennifer   Lectr./Sr. Lectr.
Mantle, Hugh I. P.   Lectr./Sr. Lectr.
Margham, Sarah   Lectr./Sr. Lectr.
Martin, Duncan J.   Lectr./Sr. Lectr.
Mason, Monica   Lectr./Sr. Lectr.
Meecham, Pamela J.   Lectr./Sr. Lectr.

Miller, Anne M.   Principal Lectr.
Miller, Jennifer M.   Lectr./Sr. Lectr.
Money, Julie   Lectr./Sr. Lectr.
Morton, Ian   Lectr./Sr. Lectr.
Mullins, Patricia   Lectr./Sr. Lectr.
Peel, Jennifer   Principal Lectr.
Phillips, C. Rosamund   Principal Lectr.
Pollard, Janet A.   Principal Lectr.
Porter, Joyce A.   Lectr./Sr. Lectr.
Richards, Jacqueline   Lectr./Sr. Lectr.
Roche, Denise   Lectr./Sr. Lectr.
Sarland, Charles   Lectr./Sr. Lectr.
Scholefield, Peter S.   Lectr./Sr. Lectr.
Sellers, Val T.   Lectr./Sr. Lectr.
Shenton, Patricia A.   Principal Lectr.
Singh-Raud, Harkirtan   Lectr./Sr. Lectr.
Smith, Judy E. A.   Lectr./Sr. Lectr.
Stanley, Neil R.   Lectr./Sr. Lectr.
Stott, Timothy A.   Lectr./Sr. Lectr.
Stratton, Gareth   Lectr./Sr. Lectr.
Tedder, John A.   Lectr./Sr. Lectr.
Thomson, Ann   Lectr./Sr. Lectr.
Vickerman, Philip B.   Lectr./Sr. Lectr.
Walker, Peter   Lectr./Sr. Lectr.
Walsh, Barbara   Lectr./Sr. Lectr.
Walsh, Catherine   Lectr./Sr. Lectr.
Whittle, Rhiannon M.   Principal Lectr.
Wyse, Dominic   Lectr./Sr. Lectr.
Other Staff: 7 Lectrs.

Health

Tel: (0151) 231 4087 Fax: (0151) 258 1593
Adams, Terry A.   Lectr./Sr. Lectr.
Ainscough, John   Lectr./Sr. Lectr.
Appleton, Carol   Lectr./Sr. Lectr.
Atherton, Margaret A.   Lectr./Sr. Lectr.
Banton, Robert   Lectr./Sr. Lectr.
Barton, Linda J.   Lectr./Sr. Lectr.
Bellis, Mark A.   Prof.
Boojawon, Rajman   Principal Lectr.
Bradley, David   Lectr./Sr. Lectr.
Bree-Williams, Frances J.   Lectr./Sr. Lectr.
Browne, Michael   Lectr./Sr. Lectr.
Busgeet, Toynarain   Lectr./Sr. Lectr.
Byatt, Kay   Principal Lectr.
Campbell, Margaret   Lectr./Sr. Lectr.
Carey, Lynda P.   Principal Lectr.
Clabby, Margaret   Lectr./Sr. Lectr.
Costello, John   Lectr./Sr. Lectr.
Crosby, Charles   Reader
Deane, Ann   Lectr./Sr. Lectr.
Dobson, Susan L.   Lectr./Sr. Lectr.
Dodds, Margaret M. B.   Lectr./Sr. Lectr.
Drummy, Gerrard   Lectr./Sr. Lectr.
Dunbar, Sheila F.   Lectr./Sr. Lectr.
Essay, Rosemarie   Lectr./Sr. Lectr.
Gibbon, Carolyn J.   Lectr./Sr. Lectr.
Giridharan, Madhavan   Lectr./Sr. Lectr.
Glenn, Sheila, BSc Lond.   PhD Lond.   Prof.,
   Applied Development Psychology
Goodlad, Susan   Lectr./Sr. Lectr.
Gopaul, Daneshean H.   Lectr./Sr. Lectr.
Grant, Madge   Lectr./Sr. Lectr.
Gray, Anne   Lectr./Sr. Lectr.
Green, Jean   Principal Lectr.
Griffiths, Anne E.   Lectr./Sr. Lectr.
Grimes, C.   Lectr./Sr. Lectr.
Hall, Patricia   Lectr./Sr. Lectr.
Harland, Menna W.   Lectr./Sr. Lectr.
Harrison, Marie R.   Lectr./Sr. Lectr.
Harrison, Mary R.   Lectr./Sr. Lectr.
Harrison, Nigel   Lectr./Sr. Lectr.
Hindley, Carol   Lectr./Sr. Lectr.
Horgan, Maureen   Lectr./Sr. Lectr.
Hurst, Barry   Lectr./Sr. Lectr.
Jacks, E. Jane, BEd Manc., MEd Manc.   Prof.;
   Head*
Jones, Colin   Lectr./Sr. Lectr.
Kilshaw, Linda J.   Lectr./Sr. Lectr.
King, Stanley J.   Lectr./Sr. Lectr.
Kinrade, Edward L.   Lectr./Sr. Lectr.
Kinsella, Mary   Lectr./Sr. Lectr.
Laghari, Sara   Lectr./Sr. Lectr.
Leach, Vivienne A.   Lectr./Sr. Lectr.
Leather, Nicola C.   Lectr./Sr. Lectr.
Lyons, Christina M.   Principal Lectr.
Mackay, Carol L.   Lectr./Sr. Lectr.
Male, Joyce B,   Lectr./Sr. Lectr.

Malin, Anitra M.   Lectr./Sr. Lectr.
Martin, Susan   Lectr./Sr. Lectr.
McCoy, Maureen A.   Lectr./Sr. Lectr.
McGhie, Ailsa   Lectr./Sr. Lectr.
McMurchie, Colin   Principal Lectr.
Medforth, Nick   Lectr./Sr. Lectr.
Melville, Dave   Lectr./Sr. Lectr.
Mitchenson, Susan   Lectr./Sr. Lectr.
Napier, Nell   Lectr./Sr. Lectr.
Nugent, Ansel B.   Principal Lectr.
O'Hara, Jane E.   Lectr./Sr. Lectr.
Ogden, Sheila   Lectr./Sr. Lectr.
Ollerton, Ian   Lectr./Sr. Lectr.
Owen, Beverley L.   Lectr./Sr. Lectr.
Painter, William K.   Lectr./Sr. Lectr.
Ramasawmy, Coo M.   Lectr./Sr. Lectr.
Rothwell, Susan   Lectr./Sr. Lectr.
Roulston, John   Principal Lectr.
Russell, Susan   Lectr./Sr. Lectr.
Salter, Paul W.   Lectr./Sr. Lectr.
Sargent, Rosemary A.   Lectr./Sr. Lectr.
Savage, Bryan   Lectr./Sr. Lectr.
Simpson, George   Lectr./Sr. Lectr.
Simpson, Margaret H.   Lectr./Sr. Lectr.
Sorofan, Kathleen   Lectr./Sr. Lectr.
Spyropoulos, Andrea   Lectr./Sr. Lectr.
Stitt, Pauline   Principal Lectr.
Tate, Sylvina   Lectr./Sr. Lectr.
Thompson, Peter   Principal Lectr.
Utley, Carole   Lectr./Sr. Lectr.
Wakefield, Shelagh   Lectr./Sr. Lectr.
Walker, Caroline   Lectr./Sr. Lectr.
Wall, Christine T.   Lectr./Sr. Lectr.
Wallymahmed, Akhtar H.   Principal Lectr.
Walton, Irene   Principal Lectr.
Welsh, Ian   Principal Lectr.
Wilkinson, Joan T.   Lectr./Sr. Lectr.
Woods, Susan   Lectr./Sr. Lectr.
Other Staff: 1 Visiting Prof.; 5 Lectrs.

Human Sciences

Tel: (0151) 231 4030 Fax: (0151) 258 1224
Atkinson, Gregory   Sr. Lectr.
Borrie, Andrew G.   Lectr./Sr. Lectr.
Brooks, Philip G.   Lectr./Sr. Lectr.
Buckley, Elizabeth A.   Lectr./Sr. Lectr.
Cable, Nigel T.   Reader
Collier, Henrietta E.   Lectr./Sr. Lectr.
Daniels, Michael I.   Lectr./Sr. Lectr.
De Viggiani, Nicholas P. A.   Lectr./Sr. Lectr.
Doran, Dominic A.   Lectr./Sr. Lectr.
Dugdill, Lindsey   Lectr./Sr. Lectr.
El Sayad, Mahmoud S.   Prof.
Gibson, B. Linda   Lectr./Sr. Lectr.
Gilbourne, David   Lectr./Sr. Lectr.
Graham-Smith, Philip   Lectr./Sr. Lectr.
Guppy, Andrew   Reader
Hare, Michael E. D.   Lectr./Sr. Lectr.
Hart, Norah I.   Lectr./Sr. Lectr.
James, Pamela E.   Dir.*
Lake, Mark J.   Lectr./Sr. Lectr.
Lancaster, Brian L.   Lectr./Sr. Lectr.
Leavey, Conan   Lectr./Sr. Lectr.
Lees, Adrian, BSc Leeds, PhD Leeds   Reader
Maclaren, Donald P. M.   Principal Lectr.
McNamara, Edward   Lectr./Sr. Lectr.
Money, Michael C.   Principal Lectr.
Murphy, Peter   Lectr./Sr. Lectr.
Nevill, A. M.   Reader, Sports Science
O'Carroll, Pierce J.   Lectr./Sr. Lectr.
Peiser, Benny   Lectr./Sr. Lectr.
Reid, Juliet M. V.   Sr. Lectr.
Richardson, David O. J.   Lectr./Sr. Lectr.
Sands, Rosemary J.   Lectr./Sr. Lectr.
Shelton, James A.   Lectr./Sr. Lectr.
Springett, Rosemary J., BA Leeds, MA Leeds, PhD
   Leeds   Reader
Williams, M.   Lectr./Sr. Lectr.
Woods, Sally C.   Lectr./Sr. Lectr.
Other Staff: 5 Lectrs.; 2 Hon. Lectrs.

Social Science

Tel: (0151) 231 4029 Fax: (0151) 258 1224
Baker, Clifford   Lectr./Sr. Lectr.
Barrett, Giles   Lectr./Sr. Lectr.
Binnie, Jon   Lectr./Sr. Lectr.
Boothby, John   Lectr./Sr. Lectr.
Bretherton, Charlotte A.   Lectr./Sr. Lectr.

Caslin, Terence J.   Principal Lectr.
Cook, Ian J.   Reader
Davies, Robert S. W.   Reader
Donnelly, Dennis M.   Lectr./Sr. Lectr.
Edwards, Margaret M.   Principal Lectr.
Francis, Andrew J.   Lectr./Sr. Lectr.
Hall, Gillian   Lectr./Sr. Lectr.
Herson, John D.   Principal Lectr.
Hull, Andrew P.   Principal Lectr.
Li, Rex Y. F.   Lectr./Sr. Lectr.
Mannin, Michael L.   Principal Lectr.
McDonough, Francis X.   Lectr./Sr. Lectr.
McEvoy, David, BA Manc., MA Manc.   Prof.;
   Dir.*
Morley, Robert E.   Lectr./Sr. Lectr.
Mulhearn, Christopher J.   Lectr./Sr. Lectr.
Newman, Janis   Lectr./Sr. Lectr.
Newton, Brian   Lectr./Sr. Lectr.
Nightingale, Martin   Principal Lectr.
Noon, Robert P.   Lectr./Sr. Lectr.
Owen, Mairead   Lectr./Sr. Lectr.
Parker, Sara   Lectr./Sr. Lectr.
Pasker, Pauline   Lectr./Sr. Lectr.
Price, Marion E.   Principal Lectr.
Routledge, Derek A.   Lectr./Sr. Lectr.
Scott, Bryan L.   Lectr./Sr. Lectr.
Smith, Stephen E.   Principal Lectr.
Sperling, Elizabeth   Lectr./Sr. Lectr.
Standing, Kay E.   Lectr./Sr. Lectr.
Vane, Howard R.   Reader
Vogler, John F., BA Reading, MSc Reading, PhD
   Reading   Prof., International Relations
Walsh, Linda   Lectr./Sr. Lectr.
White, Nicholas   Lectr./Sr. Lectr.
Williams, John A.   Lectr./Sr. Lectr.
Wright, Michael T.   Lectr./Sr. Lectr.

ENGINEERING AND SCIENCE, DIVISION OF

Biological and Earth Science

Tel: (0151) 231 2168 Fax: (0151) 298 1014
Argo, Caroline M.   Lectr./Sr. Lectr.
Bishop, Christopher D.   Lectr./Sr. Lectr.
Clare, Tom   Lectr./Sr. Lectr.
Crossley, Joseph D.   Principal Lectr.
Dickinson, Nicholas M.   Lectr./Sr. Lectr.
Dowell, Simon D.   Lectr./Sr. Lectr.
Feltham, Mark J.   Lectr./Sr. Lectr.
Gibson, Raymond, BSc Leeds, PhD Leeds   Prof.,
   Marine Biology
Glasser, Neil F.   Lectr./Sr. Lectr.
Gunn, Alan   Lectr./Sr. Lectr.
Haram, Owen J.   Principal Lectr.
Hodkinson, Ian D., BSc Newcastle(UK), PhD
   Lanc.   Prof., Entomology and Animal
   Ecology
Jones, Jennifer   Lectr./Sr. Lectr.
Lepp, Nicholas W., BSc Hull, PhD Hull   Prof.,
   Plant Sciences
Mislom, Clare   Lectr./Sr. Lectr.
Nicholson, Frank H.   Lectr./Sr. Lectr.
Oakland, Penny J.   Lectr./Sr. Lectr.
Olabrian, Yemisi   Lectr./Sr. Lectr.
Sambrook-Smith, Gregory H.   Lectr./Sr. Lectr.
Settle, Christopher G.   Lectr./Sr. Lectr.
Sherwood, Graham J.   Lectr./Sr. Lectr.
Small, Richard W.   Lectr./Sr. Lectr.
Sneddon, Jennifer C.   Lectr./Sr. Lectr.
Taylor, William P.   Lectr./Sr. Lectr.
Triggs, Graham S.   Lectr./Sr. Lectr.
Turner, Alan   Reader
Wheeler, Peter E., BSc Durh., PhD Durh.   Prof.;
   Dir.*
Wilkinson, David M.   Lectr./Sr. Lectr.
Willcox, Mark S.   Lectr./Sr. Lectr.
Young, Andrew J.   Reader

Biomolecular Sciences

Tel: (0151) 231 2168 Fax: (0151) 298 2821
Andrews, Margaret M.   Lectr./Sr. Lectr.
Billington, David, BSc Liv., PhD
   Newcastle(UK)   Reader
Bilton, Rodney F., BSc Durh., PhD
   Newcastle(UK)   Prof., Applied Biochemistry
Burke, Patricia A.   Lectr./Sr. Lectr.
Carter, John B.   Lectr./Sr. Lectr.
Crosby, Steven R.   Lectr./Sr. Lectr.
Evans, F. E. Hilary, BSc Brist., PhD Brist.   Prof.;
   Dir.*

Gadson, Derek R. Prof., Medical Cell Pathology
Gadson, Patricia A. Lectr./Sr. Lectr.
Gatherer, Derek Lectr./Sr. Lectr.
Harland, Janice C. Lectr./Sr. Lectr.
Hobbs, Glyn Lectr./Sr. Lectr.
Humphreys, Ann M. Lectr./Sr. Lectr.
Kilgour, Joanne Lectr./Sr. Lectr.
Korber, Fritjof C. Lectr./Sr. Lectr.
Lowe, Gordon M. Lectr./Sr. Lectr.
Manning, Frank E. C. R. Lectr./Sr. Lectr.
McColl, Suzanne M. Lectr./Sr. Lectr.
Muir, Michael J. Lectr./Sr. Lectr.
Olabiran, Yemisi Lectr./Sr. Lectr.
Phipps, David A., BSc Sheff., MSc Kent, PhD Kent Reader
Rahman, Khalid Lectr./Sr. Lectr.
Reed, Celia J. Lectr./Sr. Lectr.
Reid, Amanda J. Lectr./Sr. Lectr.
Reynolds, Colin D., BSc Lond., MSc Lond., PhD Liv. Prof., Molecular Biophysics
Sands, Richard L. Lectr./Sr. Lectr.
Saunders, Venetia A., BSc Brist., PhD Brist. Prof., Microbiology Genetics
Sharples, George P. Lectr./Sr. Lectr.
Whalley, Anthony J. Prof., Mycology
Zuzel, Katherine A. Lectr./Sr. Lectr.

Computing and Mathematical Sciences

Tel: (0151) 231 2168 Fax: (0151) 207 4594
Al Yasiri, Adil Lectr./Sr. Lectr.
Bamford, Carl Principal Lectr.
Brooke, Geoffrey A. Lectr./Sr. Lectr.
Brown, Richard P. Lectr./Sr. Lectr.
Clegg, David, BSc Nott., PhD Nott. Dir.*
Denton, Brian H. Lectr./Sr. Lectr.
Duffy, Sandra P. Lectr./Sr. Lectr.
England, David Lectr./Sr. Lectr.
Etchells, Terence Lectr./Sr. Lectr.
Ghaoui, Claude Lectr./Sr. Lectr.
Harris, Peter Lectr./Sr. Lectr.
James, Douglas Lectr./Sr. Lectr.
King, Melvyn J. Lectr./Sr. Lectr.
Kirby, Simon P. J. Principal Lectr.
Laws, Andrew Lectr./Sr. Lectr.
McClennan, Thomas J. Lectr./Sr. Lectr.
Merabti, Abdel M. Reader/Principal Lectr.
Moynihan, Edmund P., BSc Manc. Reader
Ng, Eng H. Lectr./Sr. Lectr.
Pereira, Rubem Lectr./Sr. Lectr.
Peters, John M. H. Lectr./Sr. Lectr.
Pountney, David C. Principal Lectr.
Ravindran, Somassundaram Lectr./Sr. Lectr.
Rimmer, Angela R. Lectr./Sr. Lectr.
Rogers, Athena A. Lectr./Sr. Lectr.
Shi, Qi Lectr./Sr. Lectr.
Strickland, Paul M. Lectr./Sr. Lectr.
Taylor, Mark J. Lectr./Sr. Lectr.
Vickers, Paul Lectr./Sr. Lectr.
Wade, Stuart J. Principal Lectr.
Wright, Lesley F. Lectr./Sr. Lectr.
Other Staff: 7 Lectrs.; 1 Sr. Lectr.†

Engineering

Tel: (0151) 231 2094 Fax: (0151) 298 1014
Alexander, Graham I. Principal Lectr.
Barclay, Ian Prof., Technology Management
Barlow, Neil Ford Prof., Engineering
Bartlett, Rebecca Lectr./Sr. Lectr.
Bettley, Alison Lectr./Sr. Lectr.
Bode, Michael F., BSc Leeds, PhD Keele Prof., Astrophysics
Bond, Peter L. Principal Lectr.
Bonsall, Stephen Lectr./Sr. Lectr.
Boyle, Alan Principal Lectr.
Burton, David R. Prof., Engineering Science; Head*
Carroll, Anthony G. Lectr./Sr. Lectr.
Chapman, Colin Lectr./Sr. Lectr.
Collins, Christina A. Reader
Colquhoun, Gary J. Reader
Davies, Clara Lectr./Sr. Lectr.
Deboux, Bruno J. C. Lectr./Sr. Lectr.
Donnan, Trevor M. Lectr./Sr. Lectr.
Douglas, Steven S. Lectr./Sr. Lectr.
Dumbell, Keith Lectr./Sr. Lectr.
Dutch, William R. Lectr./Sr. Lectr.
Ellis, David L. Lectr./Sr. Lectr.

English, Russell G. Lectr./Sr. Lectr.
Gilmartin, Michael J. Reader
Gomm, James B. Lectr./Sr. Lectr.
Goodier, Alan V. Principal Lectr.
Graham, Ian D. Principal Lectr.
Greenwood, Andrew R. Lectr./Sr. Lectr.
Griffiths, Denis Lectr./Sr. Lectr.
Harrison, Gilbert Lectr./Sr. Lectr.
Harvey, David M. Reader
Hough, Ronald R. Lectr./Sr. Lectr.
Hughes, Edward E. Lectr./Sr. Lectr.
Ives, David Lectr./Sr. Lectr.
James, Philip A. Lectr./Sr. Lectr.
Jenkinson, Ian D. Programme Leader
Jones, Hugh Lectr./Sr. Lectr.
Jones, Ian S. Lectr./Sr. Lectr.
Jones, Karl O. Principal Lectr.
Kaldos, Andrew Lectr./Sr. Lectr.
Kelly, Barbara Lectr./Sr. Lectr.
Kelly, Trevor Lectr./Sr. Lectr.
Lalor, Michael J., BSc Liv., PhD Liv. Prof., Engineering Optics
Levi, Emil Reader
Lyons, Andrew C. Lectr./Sr. Lectr.
McLean, John G. Lectr./Sr. Lectr.
McTavish, James P. Lectr./Sr. Lectr.
Metcalfe, Keith R. Lectr./Sr. Lectr.
Middleton, John Lectr./Sr. Lectr.
Montgomery, Paul A. Lectr./Sr. Lectr.
Moore, Timothy A. Lectr./Sr. Lectr.
Moore, Toby J. T. Lectr./Sr. Lectr.
Morgan, Roger, BA Camb., PhD Camb. Prof.
Nicholls, Charles E. Principal Lectr.
Otterson, Paul Lectr./Sr. Lectr.
Page, George F. Lectr./Sr. Lectr.
Pearson, Jeremy D. Lectr./Sr. Lectr.
Pettit, Joseph A. Lectr./Sr. Lectr.
Porter, John K. Lectr./Sr. Lectr.
Prosser, George E. D. Principal Lectr.
Raby, Paul S. Lectr./Sr. Lectr.
Roberts, Charles C. Lectr./Sr. Lectr.
Rothwell, Glynn Lectr./Sr. Lectr.
Scully, Patricia J. Lectr./Sr. Lectr.
Skiffington, John Lectr./Sr. Lectr.
Smith, Colin Principal Lectr.
Terry, Stephen R. Lectr./Sr. Lectr.
Tridimas, Yiannis D. Lectr./Sr. Lectr.
Utting, William S. Lectr./Sr. Lectr.
Wall, Alan D. Lectr./Sr. Lectr.
Wang, Jin Q. Lectr./Sr. Lectr.
Williams, David, BEng Liv., PhD Liv. Prof., Control Systems
Williams, Vincent J. Lectr./Sr. Lectr.
Wood, Christopher M. Lectr./Sr. Lectr.
Wood, Mark S. Lectr./Sr. Lectr.
Woolley, Neil H., BSc Manc., MSc Manc., PhD Manc. Reader
Zhang, Jiam F. Lectr./Sr. Lectr.
Other Staff: 4 Lectrs.

Pharmacy and Chemistry

Tel: (0151) 231 2259 Fax: (0151) 207 2620
Argomandkhah, Hassan Lectr./Sr. Lectr.
Armstrong, David J., BSc Brist., PhD Brist. Reader
Berry, Michael I. Lectr./Sr. Lectr.
Bradshaw, Ian J. Lectr./Sr. Lectr.
Bresnen, Gaynor Lectr./Sr. Lectr.
Bush, Nicola A. Lectr./Sr. Lectr.
Bux, Mumtaz Lectr./Sr. Lectr.
Chan, Kelvin Head of Res.
Cronin, Mark T. D. Lectr./Sr. Lectr.
Cubbin, Ian J. Lectr./Sr. Lectr.
Dearden, John Prof.
Edwards, Robert Lectr./Sr. Lectr.
Elliott, Peter N. C. Lectr./Sr. Lectr.
Fairbrother, Jean M. Sr. Lectr.
Ford, James L., BSc CNAA, PhD CNAA Prof.
George, Alan J., BSc S'ton., PhD Brad. Reader
Goldberg, Laurence A. Lectr./Sr. Lectr.
Hamilton, Richard J., BSc Glas., PhD Glas., FRSChem Prof.
Heaton, C. Alan, PhD Durh., FRSChem Reader, Industrial Chemistry
Jones, Pauline E. Lectr./Sr. Lectr.
Large, David O. G. Principal Lectr.
Malhi, Jaspal S. Lectr./Sr. Lectr.
Marriott, Paul H. Lectr./Sr. Lectr.

Morris, Harold M. Reader, Physical and Theoretical Chemistry
Mottram, David R., BSc Wales, PhD Prof., Pharmacy Practice
Moynihan, Humphrey A. Lectr./Sr. Lectr.
Nicholls, Barry S. Lectr./Sr. Lectr.
Nolan, Terence J. Principal Lectr.
Palit, Piali Lectr./Sr. Lectr.
Pearce, Jack Principal Lectr.
Rajabi-Siahboomi, Ali-Reza Lectr./Sr. Lectr.
Rhodes, Chris J. Prof., Chemistry
Rostron, Christopher Reader, Medicinal Chemistry
Rowe, Philip H. Lectr./Sr. Lectr.
Rubinstein, Michael H. Prof.; Head*
Wells, Jim Lectr./Sr. Lectr.
Wood, Alexander Lectr./Sr. Lectr.
Robertson, David J. Prof., Public Policy
Yorke, D. Mantz Prof., Higher Education

Other Appointments

Reilly, Thomas, BA Trinity(Dub), MSc Lond., PhD CNAA Head, Grad. Sch.
Robertson, David J. Prof., Public Policy
Yorke, D. Mantz Prof., Higher Education
Other Staff: 2 Lectrs.; 1 Sr. Lectr.†; 4 Hon. Lectrs.

SPECIAL CENTRES, ETC

Urban Affairs, European Institute of

Tel: (0151) 231 3428 Fax: (0151) 708 0650
Harding, Alan P. Prof., Urban Policy and Politics
Parkinson, Prof. Michael, BA Liv., MA(Econ) Manc. Dir.*

CONTACT OFFICERS

Academic affairs. Head, Programme Logistics: Margham, J. Phil, BSc Manc., PhD Manc.
Accommodation. Atkinson, Peter
Admissions (first degree). Gross, Natalie
Admissions (higher degree) (research). Ward, Sue
Admissions (higher degree) (taught courses). Gross, Natalie
Adult/continuing education. Head, Programme Logistics: Margham, J. Phil, BSc Manc., PhD Manc.
Alumni. Sharples, Lindsay, BSc CNAA
Archives. Head, Learning Services: Melling, Maxine, Mlib
Careers. James, Chris, BA Salf.
Computing services. Head, CIS: Wrightson, Jim, BSc Tor., BA Camb., MA Camb., PhD Camb.
Consultancy services. Ashton, Michael, BSc CNAA, MEd Liv.
Credit transfer. Head, Programme Logistics: Margham, J. Phil, BSc Manc., PhD Manc.
Development/fund-raising. Sharples, Lindsay, BA Liv.
Distance education. Associate Development Director: Jeves, Terry, BSc Hull, PhD Hull
Equal opportunities. Head: Anwar, Naseem, BA Essex
Estates and buildings/works and services. Head, Estate Management: Connell, Joe, FRICS
Finance. Head, Financial Services: Hyett, Peter
General enquiries. Assistant Secretary: Marsh, Cathy, BA CNAA, MSc Lond.
Health services. Jeffcott, Ian, BA CNAA
Industrial liaison. Ashton, Michael, BSc CNAA, MEd Liv.
International office. Assistant Provost, Logistics: Kenny, Steve, MA Manc., MSc Manc.
Library (chief librarian). Head, Learning Services: Melling, Maxine, MLib
Library (enquiries). Head, Learning Services: Melling, Maxine, MLib
Minorities/disadvantaged groups. Head: Anwar, Naseem, BA Essex
Personnel/human resources. Head: Jeffcott, Ian, BA CNAA

Public relations, information and marketing. Martin, Janet

Publications. Martin, Janet

Purchasing. McDonald, Shaun, BA *Manc.*

Quality assurance and accreditation. Head, Academic Standards: Marquet, Roma, BA *Newcastle(UK)*

Research. Assistant Provost (Research): Kelleher, Prof. Gerry, BSc *Lond.*

Safety. Duffy, Eamonn

Scholarships, awards, loans. Jeffcott, Ian, BA *CNAA*

Scholarships, awards, loans. Jeffcott, Ian, BA *CNAA*

Schools liaison. Gross, Natalie

Security. Shackleton, Steve

Sport and recreation. Nixon, Sarah

Staff development and training. Head: Box, Meriel

Student union. Akhtar, Tasleem

Student welfare/counselling. Jeffcott, Ian, BA *CNAA*

Students from other countries. International office: Hesketh, Isabella

Students with disabilities. Head: Anwar, Naseem, BA *Essex*

University press. Martin, Janet

Women. Head: Anwar, Naseem, BA *Essex*

CAMPUS/COLLEGE HEADS

Liverpool Institute of Performing Arts, Mount Street, Liverpool LI 9HF. (Tel: (0151) 330 3000; Fax: (0151) 330 3131.) Chief Executive: Featherstone-Witty, Mark

[Information supplied by the institution as at 2 March 1998, and edited by the ACU]

UNIVERSITY OF LONDON

Founded 1836

Member of the Association of Commonwealth Universities

Postal Address: Senate House, Malet Street, London, England WC1E 7HU
Telephone: (0171) 636 8000 **Fax**: (0171) 636 5841 **Cables**: University, London
Telex: (Library only) 269400 SENLIBG **E-mail formula**: Firstinitial.Surname@Department.lon.ac.uk

VISITOR—Elizabeth, H.M. The Queen

CHANCELLOR—Anne, H.R.H. The Princess Royal, GCVO

PRO-CHANCELLOR—Woolf, The Rt. Hon. Lord, LLD

VICE-CHANCELLOR*—Zellick, Prof. Graham J., MA *Camb.*, PhD *Camb.*

DEPUTY VICE-CHANCELLOR—Lucas, Prof. Arthur M., BSc *Melb.*, BEd *Melb.*, PhD *Ohio State*, FIBiol, FKC, FACE

CHAIRMAN OF CONVOCATION—Leslie, Drummond D. A., BA MA

DIRECTOR OF ADMINISTRATION‡—Davidson, J. R., BA

DIRECTOR OF FINANCE—Morgan, John E. A.

ACADEMIC REGISTRAR—Roberts, Gillian F., BA

GENERAL INFORMATION

History. The university was constituted by royal charter in 1836 as a body empowered to grant degrees to students of approved institutions after examination. In 1900 the university was reconstituted: institutions were admitted as schools of the university and it thus became a teaching as well as an examining university. It is a federation of colleges and institutes in which teaching for degrees of the university is carried out.

The university precinct is situated in Bloomsbury, central London. Apart from Royal Holloway (Surrey) and Wye (Kent), almost all the colleges and institutes are located within a 5km radius of Bloomsbury.

Admission to first degree courses (see also United Kingdom Introduction). Through Universities and Colleges Admissions Service (UCAS). Course requirements are set by the colleges themselves: see individual college entries, below.

First Degrees (see also University of London Directory to Subjects of Study). BA, BD, BDS, BEd, BEng, BMedSci, BMus, BPharm, BSc, BSc(Econ), BSc(Eng), BVetMed, LLB, MB BS, MEng, MPharm, MSci.

Most first degrees last 3 years full-time or equivalent part-time. MEng, MPharm, MSci: 4 years; BDS, BVetMed, MB BS: 56 months.

Higher Degrees (see also University of London Directory to Subjects of Study). LLM, MA, MArch, MBA, MClinDent, MEd, MFA, MMus, MRes, MSc, MTh, MVetMed, MD, MDS, MS, MPhil, PhD, DClinPsy, DD, DEdPsy, DLit, DLit(Ed), DMus, DrPH, DPsychotherapy, DSc, DSc(Econ), DSc(Eng), DSc(Med), DVetMed, EdD, LLD.

Taught degrees (LLM, MA, MArch, MBA, MClinDent, MEd, MFA, MMus, MRes, MSc, MTh, MVetMed): minimum 1 year full-time or equivalent part-time (MClinDent, MFA: 2 years full-time). Research degrees (DVetMed, MD, MDS, MS, MPhil, PhD): minimum 2 years full-time or equivalent part-time. Specialist doctorates (DClinPsy, DEdPsy, DPsychotherapy, DrPH): 2 years full-time or equivalent part-time. Higher doctorates (DD, DLit, DLit(Ed), DMus, DSc, DSc(Econ), DSc(Eng), DSc(Med), LLD: open only to graduates and professors, reader and teachers of this university; awarded on published work.

Libraries. University library, Senate House: 2,000,000 volumes; 5500 current periodical titles. Each college and institute has its own library: see individual entries, below.

Fees, Academic Awards, Academic Year, Income, Statistics. See individual college entries, below.

Directory to Subjects of Study. See p. 1586.

CONTACT OFFICERS

Academic affairs. Academic Registrar: Roberts, Gillian F., BA

Accommodation. Goble, Jennifer, BA

Archives. Vyse, Ruth F., BA

Careers. Director, Careers Advisory Service: Martin, Anne-Marie, BSc MSc

Computing services. Director, University of London Computer Centre and Management Information Services Division: Baker, R. W., BSc PhD

Credit transfer. Academic Registrar: Roberts, Gillian F., BA

Distance education. Director, External and Internal Student Administration: McConnell, J. A. R., MA *Brun.*

Estates and buildings/works and services. Director, Estates: Rous, P.

Examinations. Director, External and Internal Student Administration: McConnell, J. A. R., MA *Brun.*

Finance. Director of Finance: Morgan, John E. A.

General enquiries. Head, Information Centre: Harris, Jo

Health services. Anderson, Barbara, MB BS

Library (chief librarian). University of London Librarian: Robinson, Emma J., BSc

Personnel/human resources. Director of Staff and Student Services: Buckley, Dennis G., BSc PhD

Public relations, information and marketing. Anderson, Barbara M., BA

Publications. Anderson, Barbara M., BA

Quality assurance and accreditation. Academic Registrar: Roberts, Gillian F., BA

Scholarships, awards, loans. Head of Academic Office: Johnson, Susan E.

Schools liaison. Hurford, Susan

Staff development and training. Small, Susan A.

Student union. Director of Staff and Student Services: Buckley, Dennis G., BSc PhD

Student welfare/counselling. Director of Staff and Student Services: Buckley, Dennis G., BSc PhD

COLLEGES, INSTITUTES, ETC, OF THE UNIVERSITY OF LONDON

The teaching and research work of the University is carried out in (1) colleges of the University each controlled by its own governing body; (2) and (3) institutes established and controlled by the University; (4) associate institutions under teachers of the University.

(1) Colleges of the University
Birkbeck College, p 1521
Goldsmiths College, p 1524
Heythrop College, p 1526
Imperial College of Science, Technology and Medicine, p 1526
Institute of Education, p 1533
King's College London, p 1535
London Business School, p 1544

London School of Economics and Political Science, p 1545
London School of Hygiene and Tropical Medicine, p 1549
Queen Mary and Westfield College, p 1551
Royal Holloway, p 1557
Royal Veterinary College, p 1560
St George's Hospital Medical School, p 1561
School of Oriental and African Studies, p 1563
School of Pharmacy, p 1567
University College London, p 1568
Wye College, p 1578

(2) Institutes, p 1580
British Institute in Paris
Centre for Defence Studies
Courtauld Institute of Art
School of Slavonic and East European Studies

(3) School of Advanced Study, p 1581
Centre for English Studies

Institute of Advanced Legal Studies
Institute of Classical Studies
Institute of Commonwealth Studies
Institute of Germanic Studies
Institute of Historical Research
Institute of Latin American Studies
Institute of Romance Studies
Institute of United States Studies
Warburg Institute

(4) Associate Institutions, p 1583
Institute of Cancer Research
Jews' College
Royal Academy of Music
Royal College of Music
Trinity College of Music

[Information supplied by the institution as at 16 July 1998, and edited by the ACU]

COLLEGES OF THE UNIVERSITY

BIRKBECK COLLEGE

Incorporated 1926; previously established as the London Mechanics' Institution 1823

Postal Address: Malet Street, Bloomsbury, London, England WC1E 7HX
Telephone: (0171) 631 6000 **Fax**: (0171) 631 6270 **WWW**: http://www.bbk.ac.uk
E-mail formula: firstinitial.lastname@dept.bbk.ac.uk
(department names sometimes in full and sometimes abbreviated)

PATRON—Elizabeth, H.M. The Queen Mother
PRESIDENT—Smith of Gilmorehill, Baroness, MA
VICE-PRESIDENT—The Rt. Hon. the Lord Mayor of London (*ex officio*)
CHAIRMAN OF THE GOVERNORS—Gillmore of Thamesfield, Lord, KCMG
MASTER*—O'Shea, Prof. Timothy M. M., BSc *Sus.*, PhD *Leeds*
DEAN—Barnes, Prof. Paul, BSc PhD
SECRETARY AND CLERK TO THE GOVERNORS‡—Mabey, Christine, BA PhD
REGISTRAR—Harwood, B. A., BSc PhD
DIRECTOR OF FINANCE—Westley, Peter
LIBRARIAN—Dolphin, Philippa, MA

GENERAL INFORMATION

History. The college was established by George Birkbeck in 1823 as the London Mechanics' Institution, and incorporated as a college of the University of London in 1926. It is located in Bloomsbury, central London.

Admission to first degree courses (see also United Kingdom Introduction). Applicants under 21: recognised school-leaving or professional qualification. Applicants over 21 do not require formal qualifications. All applicants must show evidence of the right to work in the UK; international students living in the UK on a student or visitor's visa are not eligible to enrol as part-time students. Students whose first language is not English will be asked to demonstrate competence in the English language (eg IELTS score of 7.0; TOEFL (550); AEB test in English for educational purposes (4)).

First Degrees (of University of London) (see also University of London Directory to Subjects of Study). BA, BSc, BSc(Econ), LLB.

All courses are part-time and most last 4 years. Accelerated LLB: 3 years.

Higher Degrees (of University of London) (see also University of London Directory to Subjects of Study). MA, MRes, MSc, MPhil, PhD.
Applicants for admission to master's degrees should hold a good first degree in a relevant subject.
MA, MSc: 2 years part-time; MRes: 1 years full-time; MPhil, PhD: minimum 3 years full- or part-time.

Libraries. 250,000 volumes; about 900 periodicals subscribed to.

Fees (1998–99). Part-time students—BA, BSc: £624–765; BSc(Econ): £999; LLB: £744; accelerated LLB: £993. MA, MSc: £1254–2121. MPhil, PhD: £999. Full-time UK/EU postgraduates: £2610 (except MSc in finance, international business: £4242). Full-time international students: £7032 (arts); £8838 (science).

Academic Year (1998–99). 28 September–11 December; 11 January–26 March; 26 April–9 July.

Income (1996–97). Total, £33,056,000.

Statistics (1997–98). Staff: 524 (254 academic, 270 administrative). Students: full-time 423; part-time 4541; international 208; total 4964.

FACULTIES/SCHOOLS

Computing, Mathematical and Social Sciences, Centre for
Tel: (0171) 631 6700 Fax: (0171) 631 6727
Head: Johnson, Roger G., BSc *Wales*, PhD *Lond.*
Personal Assistant: Da Silva, Ana M.

Continuing Education, Faculty of
Tel: (0171) 631 6633 Fax: (0171) 631 6688
Dean: Schuller, Prof. Tom, MA *Oxf.*, DrPhil *Bremen*
Personal Assistant: ......

Humanities, Centre for Studies in the

Tel: (0171) 631 6196 Fax: (0171) 631 6107

Head: Vaughan, Prof. W. H. T., BA Lond., PhD Lond.

Personal Assistant: Beaver, Bonnie

Language and Literature, Centre for

Tel: (0171) 631 6122 Fax: (0171) 383 3729

Head: Wells, Prof. David A., MA Camb., PhD Camb.

Personal Assistant: McNally, Claire

Physical and Life Sciences, Centre for

Tel: (0171) 631 6215 Fax: (0171) 631 6206

Head: Walker, Stephen F., BSc Brist., PhD Lond.
Personal Assistant: Bray, Catherine, BSc

ACADEMIC UNITS

Art, see Hist. of Art

Biology

Tel: (0171) 631 6238 Fax: (0171) 631 6246

Blaney, W. M., MSc Lond., PhD Lond.   Emer. Prof.

Coast, G. M., BSc Lond., PhD Lond.   Reader, Comparative Endocrinology

Goldsworthy, G. J., BSc Sheff., PhD Sheff., FIBiol   Prof.; Chairman*

Milner, Andrew R., BSc Newcastle(UK), PhD Newcastle(UK)   Reader, Vertebrate Palaeontology

Simmonds, Monique S. J., BSc Leeds, PhD Lond.   Visiting Prof.

Other Staff: 6 Lectrs.; 3 Researchers

Research: avian development biology; insect science; microbiology; plant science; vertebrate palaeontology

Chemistry

Tel: (0171) 380 7466 Fax: (0171) 387 7464

Carless, H. A. J., MA Oxf., DPhil Oxf., FRSChem   Sr. Lectr.

Davies, David B., BSc Edin., PhD Essex   Reader, Biophysical Chemistry; Chairman*

Flint, Colin D., BSc Lond., PhD Lond., DSc Lond., FRSChem   Prof.

Thompson, Michael, BSc Lond., PhD Lond., DSc Lond., FRSChem   Reader, Analytical Chemistry

Wiedemann, Hans G., MSc Rostock, PhD Berne   Visiting Prof.

Other Staff: 4 Lectrs.; 4 Researchers

Research: analytical chemistry; computational chemistry; environmental analytical chemistry; environmental research for art conservation; inorganic/organometallic chemistry

Computer Science

Tel: (0171) 631 6700 Fax: (0171) 631 6727

Johnson, Roger G., BSc Wales, PhD Lond.   Reader

King, P. J. H., MSc Lond.   Emer. Prof.

Liu, X., BSc Nanjing, PhD H-W   Sr. Lectr.

Loizou, G., BA Lond., PhD Lond.   Prof., Mathematics of Computation; Chairman*

Sharman, G. C. H., BSc S'ton., PhD S'ton.   Visiting Prof.

Other Staff: 9 Lectrs.; 2 Researchers; 1 Lectr.†

Research: applied artificial intelligence (AI); data structures and algorithms (including genetic and probabilistic algorithms); database programming languages; databases; knowledge base processing

Continuing Education, Faculty of

Tel: (0171) 631 6633 Fax: (0171) 631 6688

Brah, Avtar, BSc Calif., MSc Wis., PhD Brist.   Sr. Lectr., Sociology

Brake, Laurel L., BA Brandeis, MPhil Lond., PhD Lond.   Sr. Lectr., Literature

Harris, Michael R. A., MA Trinity(Dub.), PhD Lond.   Sr. Lectr., History

Legge, A. J., MA Camb.   Reader, Environmental Archaeology

Schuller, Tom, MA Oxf., DrPhil Bremen   Prof., Lifelong Learning

Other Staff: 11 Lectrs.; 1 Sr. Lectr.†; 4 Lectrs.†; 5 Academic Advisers†

Crystallography

Tel: (0171) 631 6800 Fax: (0171) 631 6803

Barnes, Paul, BSc Brist., PhD Camb.   Prof., Applied Crystallography

Blundell, Sir Tom, BA Oxf., DPhil Oxf., Hon. DSc Edin., Hon. DSc E.Anglia, FRS   Visiting Prof.

Catlow, C. R. A., BA Oxf., DPhil Oxf.   Visiting Prof.

Cernik, R. J., BSc Wales, PhD Wales   Visiting Prof.

Cockcroft, J., MA Oxf., DPhil Oxf.   Sr. Lectr.

Creighton, Thomas, BSc Calif., PhD Calif.   Visiting Prof.

Goodfellow, Julia M., BSc Brist., PhD Open(UK)   Prof., Biomolecular Sciences; Chairman*

Goodfellow, Peter, BSc Brist., DPhil Oxf.   Visiting Prof.

Lindley, Peter F., BSc Brist., PhD Brist.   Visiting Prof.

Moss, David S., BSc Lond., PhD Lond.   Prof., Biomolecular Structure

Murray-Rust, P., MA Oxf., DPhil Oxf.   Visiting Prof.

Palmer, Rex A., BSc Lond., PhD Lond., FIP   Reader, Structural Crystallography

Pitts, J. E., BSc Sus., PhD Lond.   Sr. Lectr.

Saibil, Helen R., BSc McG., PhD Lond.   Prof., Structural Biology

Thornton, Janet M., BSc Nott., PhD Lond.   Bernal Prof.†, Biomolecular Structure

Wallace, Bonnie A., BS Rensselaer, MPhil Yale, PhD Yale, DSc Lond.   Reader

Other Staff: 2 Lectrs.; 21 Researchers; 1 Reader†

Research: bioinformatics; computer simulation and modelling of proteins and DNA; development of techniques and software for analysis of protein structures; structure and biochemistry of proteins involved in cell signalling and membrane channels; structure and dynamics of chaperones

Economics

Tel: (0171) 631 6403 Fax: (0171) 631 6416

Begg, David K. H., BA Camb., MPhil Oxf., PhD M.I.T.   Prof.; Chairman*

Blake, David P. C., MSc(Econ) Lond., PhD Lond.   Reader, Financial Economics

Perraudin, William, BA Oxf., MA Oxf., MSc Lond., MSc Harv., PhD Harv.   Prof., Financial Economics

Sibert, Anne, BA Carnegie-Mellon, MSc Carnegie-Mellon, PhD Carnegie-Mellon   Prof., International Finance

Smith, Ron P., BA Camb., PhD Camb.   Prof., Applied Economics

Snower, Dennis J., MA Oxf., PhD Prin.   Prof.

Sola, Martin, BSc Republic(Montevideo), MSc S'ton., PhD S'ton., MSc   Reader

Spencer, Peter, BSc Lond., MSc Lond.   Prof., Financial Economics

Other Staff: 9 Lectrs.; 1 Researcher

Research: applied economics; econometrics; financial econometrics; industrial organisation; international economics

English

Tel: (0171) 631 6070-1 Fax: (0171) 631 6072

Armstrong, Isobel, BA Leic., PhD Leic.   Prof. (on leave)

Clark, Sandra S., BA Lond., PhD Lond.   Reader, Renaissance Literature(on leave)

Connor, Steven K., BA Oxf., DPhil Oxf.   Prof., Modern Literature and Theory

Hardy, Barbara, MA Lond., DUniv Open(UK), FRSL   Emer. Prof.

Healy, Thomas F., BA Reading, PhD Lond.   Reader, Renaissance Studies

Inglesfield, Robert, MA Camb., PhD Camb.   Lectr.; Chairman*

McCabe, Colin, MA Camb., PhD Camb.   Visiting Prof.

McDonagh, Josephine, BA Wales, MA S'ton., PhD S'ton.   Sr. Lectr., Humanities

Mudford, P. G., MA Oxf., BLitt Oxf.   Reader, Modern English Literature

Slater, Michael D., MA Oxf., DPhil Oxf.   Prof., Victorian Literature

Other Staff: 10 Lectrs.

Research: literary and cultural theory and feminist criticism; mediaeval literature and culture; modern and post-modern periods; old English; old Norse

French

Tel: (0171) 631 6170 Fax: (0171) 383 3729

Howells, Robin J., BA Qld., PhD Lond.   Reader

Pollard, Patrick J., BA Lond., PhD Lond.   Reader

Renouard, Madeleine, LèsL Poitiers, MèsL Poitiers   Sr. Lectr.

Sewell, Penelope M., LèsL Aix-Marseilles, MA Essex   Sr. Lectr.; Chairman*

Short, Ian R., BA Lond., PhD Lond., FSA   Prof.

Other Staff: 4 Lectrs.

Research: Canadian studies; classicism; French cinema; French contemporary history; French linguistics

Geography

Tel: (0171) 631 6475 Fax: (0171) 631 6498

Callingham, Martin, BSc Sheff.   Visiting Prof.

Maguire, David J., BSc Exe., PhD Brist.   Visiting Prof.

Raper, Jonathan, BA Camb., PhD Lond.   Sr. Lectr.

Rhind, D. W., BSc Brist., PhD Edin., DSc Lond., DSc Lough., DSc Brist., FRICS   Visiting Prof.

Shepherd, John W., BSc(Econ) Lond., MSc Lond., PhD Lond., FRICS   Prof.; Chairman*

Unwin, David J., BSc Lond., MPhil Lond.   Prof.

Yelling, Jim A., BA Birm., PhD Birm.   Sr. Lectr.

Other Staff: 4 Lectrs.; 1 Prof. Res. Fellow; 5 Researchers

Research: coastal geomorphology and policy; economic geography; geographical information systems and geographical database development; historical geography; regional planning

Geology

Tel: (0171) 380 7333 Fax: (0171) 383 0008

Downes, Hilary, BSc Durh., MSc Calg., PhD Leeds   Reader, Geochemistry; Chairman*

Harbury, Neil A., BSc Lond., PhD Lond.   Sr. Lectr.

Morton, Nicol, BSc Glas., PhD Glas.   Sr. Lectr.

Price, G. David, MA Camb., PhD Camb.   Prof.†, Mineral Physics

Temple, John T., MA Camb., PhD Camb., ScD Camb.   Emer. Prof.

White, Roy E., BA Camb., MA Camb., PhD Adel.   Prof.

Other Staff: 3 Lectrs.; 2 Researchers

Research: igneous petrology and geochemistry; reservoir geophysics; sedimentology and environmental geology; seismic prospecting; stratigraphy and palaeontology

German

Tel: (0171) 631 6105 Fax: (0171) 383 3729

Walker, John, MA Camb., PhD Camb.   Lectr.; Chairman*

Wells, David A., MA Camb., PhD Camb.   Prof.

Other Staff: 4 Lectrs.; 1 Lektorin†

Research: German literature; German thought and cultural history

History

Tel: (0171) 631 6299 Fax: (0171) 631 6552

Bourke, Joanna, BA Auck., MA Auck., PhD ANU, FRHistS   Reader, Modern British Economic and Social History

Coward, Barry, BA Sheff., PhD Sheff., FRHistS   Reader

Dench, Emma, MA Oxf., DPhil Oxf.   Sr. Lectr., Ancient History

Feldman, D. M., MA *Camb.*, PhD *Camb.*, FRHistS   Sr. Lectr., Modern British History; Chairman*

Figes, Orlando, BA *Camb.*, PhD *Camb.*   Prof.

Harding, Vanessa A., MA *St And.*, PhD *St And.*, FRHistS   Sr. Lectr., London History (on leave)

Hobsbawm, E. J. E., CH, MA *Camb.*, PhD *Camb.*, Hon. PhilDr *Stockholm*, Hon. DHL *Chic.*, Hon. LittD *E.Anglia*, Hon. DLitt *Lond.*. Hon. PhD *Col.*, FBA   Emer. Prof.

Hunter, Michael C. W., MA *Camb.*, DPhil *Oxf.*, FRHistS, FSA   Prof.

Mason, E. Emma, BA *Lond.*, PhD *Lond.*, FRHistS, FSA   Reader, Mediaeval History

Porter, Dorothy, MA *Sus.*, PhD *Lond.*, FRHistS   Wellcome Reader, History of Medicine

Sturgis, J. L., BA *W.Ont.*, MA *Lond.*, PhD *Tor.*   Sr. Lectr., Imperial and Commonwealth History

Other Staff: 9 Lectrs.

Research: British social, cultural and political history from the late eighteenth century; classical Greek, Hellenistic and Roman Republican archaeology; cultural and social history of ancient Greece, the Hellenistic world, and ancient Italy and Rome; French history since 1400; German history since 1800

History of Art

Tel: (0171) 631 6110 Fax: (0171) 631 6107

Ames-Lewis, F. A., BSc *St And.*, MA *Lond.*, PhD *Lond.*   Reader

Coombes, A., BA *E.Anglia*, PhD *E.Anglia*, FRAI   Sr. Lectr.

Draper, P. J., MA *Camb.*, FSA   Sr. Lectr.

Nead, Lynda D., BA *Leeds*, PhD *Lond.*   Reader; Chairman*

Steer, J. R., BA *Lond.*, MA *Oxf.*, Hon. DLitt *St And.*, FSA   Emer. Prof.

Vaughan, W. H. T., BA *Lond.*, PhD *Lond.*   Prof.

Wainwright, Clive, PhD *Lond.*, FSA   Visiting Prof.

Other Staff: 2 Lectrs.; 2 Lectrs.†

Research: architecture and design in France and England; aspects of gender and visual culture; computer applications for art history; English and German art (c.1750–1880); ethnography, anthropology and cultural history in late nineteenth and twentieth centuries

Law

Tel: (0171) 631 6507 Fax: (0171) 631 6506

Douzinas, Constantine, BA *Athens*, LLB *Athens*, LLM *Lond.*, PhD *Lond.*   Prof.; Chairman*

Farmer, Lindsay, LLB *Edin.*, MPhil *Camb.*, PhD   Sr. Lectr

Goodrich, Peter, LLB *Sheff.*, PhD *Edin.*   Corp. of London Prof.

McAuslan, J. Patrick W., BA *Oxf.*, BCL *Oxf.*   Prof.†

Moran, Leslie, LLB *Sheff.*, MA *Sheff.*, PhD *Lanc.*   Reader

Robertson, Geoffrey, QC, BA LLB BCL   Visiting Prof.

Other Staff: 8 Lectrs.

Research: commercial law; company law; EC law; environmental and planning law; gender and the law

Linguistics, Applied

Tel: (0171) 631 6117 Fax: (0171) 383 3729

Edwards, Malcolm, BA *CNAA*, PhD *Lond.*   Lectr.; Chairman*

Sachdev, I., BSc *Brist.*, PhD *McM.*   Sr. Lectr.

Selinker, L., BA *Brandeis*, MA *American(D.C.)*, PhD *Georgetown*   Prof.

Other Staff: 1 Lectr.; 1 Lectr.†

Research: linguistic analysis; psycholinguistics; second language acquisition; social psychology of language; sociolinguistics

Management

Tel: (0171) 631 6772 Fax: (0171) 631 6769

Casson, Peter D., BTech *Brun.*, MSc *Lond.*, PhD *Brun.*, FCA   Sr. Lectr.

Michie, Jonathan, BA *Oxf.*, MSc *Lond.*, DPhil *Oxf.*   Salisbury Prof.; Chairman*

Oughton, Christine P., BA *E.Anglia*, PhD *Camb.*   Reader

Piesse, Jenifer, BA *Col.*, MA *Col.*, MSc(Econ) *Lond.*, PhD *Lond.*   Sr. Lectr.

Other Staff: 8 Lectrs.; 1 Researcher

Research: international business; managerial economics; marketing; strategic management

Mathematics and Statistics

Tel: (0171) 631 6308 Fax: (0171) 631 6344

Bingham, N. H., MA *Oxf.*, PhD *Camb.*, ScD *Camb.*   Prof.; Chairman*

Other Staff: 5 Lectrs.; 1 Lectr.†

Research: applied statistics and multivariate analysis; combinatorics, algebra and designs; mathematical finance; modelling of variability in space and/or time; probability and stochastic processes, pure and applied

Organizational Psychology

Tel: (0171) 631 6751-2 Fax: (0171) 631 6750

Guest, David E., BA *Birm.*, PhD *Lond.*   Prof., Occupational Psychology; Chairman*

Kidd, Jennifer M., BA *Keele*, PhD *CNAA*   Sr. Lectr.

Shipley, Pat, BA *S'ton.*, BA *Lond.*, PhD *Lond.*   Emer. Reader

Other Staff: 6 Lectrs.; 1 Teaching Fellow; 2 Researchers

Research: careers and innovation; employment and psychological contracts; human resource management; organizational communication; organization studies and organizational sociology

Philosophy

Tel: (0171) 631 6383 Fax: (0171) 631 6564

Dupré, John A., PhD *Camb.*, BA MA   Prof.†

Edgington, Dorothy, BA *Oxf.*, BPhil *Oxf.*   Sr. Lectr. (on leave)

Guttenplan, Samuel D., BA *C.C.N.Y.*, DPhil *Oxf.*   Sr. Lectr.

Hornsby, Jennifer, BA *Oxf.*, MPhil *Lond.*, PhD *Camb.*   Prof.

Janaway, Christopher, BA *Oxf.*, DPhil *Oxf.*   Reader

Price, Anthony, BA *Oxf.*, BPhil *Oxf.*   Reader; Chairman*

Scruton, Roger, BA *Camb.*, PhD *Camb.*   Visiting Prof.

Wiggins, David, MA *Oxf.*, FBA   Visiting Prof.

Other Staff: 5 Lectrs.; 1 Temp. Lectr.

Research: aesthetics; epistemology and methodology; empiricists; ethics; Greek philosophy

Politics and Sociology

Tel: (0171) 631 6780-9 Fax: (0171) 631 6787

Hirst, Paul Q., BA *Leic.*, MA *Sus.*   Prof., Social Theory

Khilnani, Sunil, BA *Camb.*, MA *Camb.*, PhD *Camb.*   Reader, Politics (on leave)

Pimlott, B. J., BA *Oxf.*, BPhil *Oxf.*, PhD *Newcastle(UK)*, FRHistS, FBA   Visiting Prof.

Solomos, John, BA *Sus.*, DPhil *Sus.*   Visiting Prof.

Taylor, Laurie, BA *Lond.*, MA *Leic.*   Visiting Prof.

Zubaida, Sami D., BA *Hull*, MA *Leic.*   Reader, Sociology; Chairman*

Other Staff: 7 Lectrs.

Research: civil society and the state; comparative public policy; European politics; gender and social relations; modern British politics and society

Psychology, see also Orgnl. Psychol.

Tel: (0171) 631 6207 Fax: (0171) 631 6312

Barber, Paul J., BSc *Brist.*, BSc *Lond.*, PhD *Lond.*   Reader, Cognitive Psychology

Dowling, Emilia, MSc   Visiting Prof.

Frosh, Stephen, BA *Sus.*, MPhil *Lond.*, PhD *Lond.*   Prof.†

Green, Simon E., BSc *Wales*, PhD *Lond.*   Sr. Lectr.; Chairman*

Gregg, Vernon H., BSc *Lond.*, PhD *Lond.*   Sr. Lectr.

Johnson, Mark, BSc *Edin.*, PhD *Camb.*   Prof.

Jones, David, BSc *Exe.*, PhD *Lond.*   Sr. Lectr.

Marslen-Wilson, William D., BA *Oxf.*, PhD *M.I.T.*, FBA   Visiting Prof.

Müller, Hermann J., MSc *Würzburg*, PhD *Durh.*   Reader, Cognitive Psychology (on leave)

Phoenix, Ann, MA *St And.*, PhD *Lond.*   Sr. Lectr.

Richards, Anne, BSc *Leic.*, PhD *Leic.*   Sr. Lectr.

Simon, J. Richard, BBA *Wis.*, MS *Wis.*, PhD *Wis.*   Visiting Prof.

van der Lely, Heather, BSc *Birm.*, MSc *Lond.*, PhD *Lond.*   Res. Fellow and Reader, Developmental Psycholinguistics

Walker, Stephen F., BSc *Brist.*, PhD *Lond.*   Sr. Lectr.

Other Staff: 5 Lectrs.; 12 Researchers; 1 Lectr.†

Research: child development and family studies; cognitive neuropsychology; cognitive psychology; cognitive science; psychoanalysis and psychotherapy

Sociology, see Pol. and Sociol.

Spanish

Tel: (0171) 631 6145 Fax: (0171) 383 3729

Hanlon, David, BA *Exe.*, PhD *Exe.*   Lectr.; Chairman*

Labanyi, Josephine M., MA *Oxf.*   Prof., Modern Spanish Literature and Cultural Studies

Walker, Roger M., BA *Manc.*, PhD *Lond.*, FRHistS, FSA   Prof.

Other Staff: 4 Lectrs.; 1 Lectr.†

Research: film; gender studies; Golden Age art; Hispano-Arabic studies; mediaeval studies

Statistics, see Maths. and Stats.

SPECIAL CENTRES, ETC

Analytical Science, Centre for

Thompson, Michael, BSc *Lond.*, PhD *Lond.*, DSc *Lond.*, FRSChem   Dir.*

Brain and Cognitive Development, Centre for

Johnson, Mark, BSc *Edin.*, PhD *Camb.*   Dir.*

Canadian Studies, Centre for

Sturgis, J. L., BA *W.Ont.*, MA *Lond.*, PhD *Tor.*   Dir.*

Child and Family Studies

Frosh, Stephen, BA *Sus.*, MPhil *Lond.*, PhD *Lond.*   Dir.*

Financial Research, Institute for

Perraudin, William, BA *Oxf.*, MA *Oxf.*, MSc *Lond.*, MSc *Harv.*, PhD *Harv.*   Dir.*

Human Performance Group

Gregg, Vernon H., BSc *Lond.*, PhD *Lond.*   Dir.*

Interdisciplinary Research in Culture and the Humanities, Centre for

Connor, Steven K., BA *Oxf.*, DPhil *Oxf.*   Dir.*

Interlanguage Studies, Centre for

Selinker, L., BA *Brandeis*, PhD *Georgetown*, MA   Dir.*

Nineteenth-Century Studies, Centre for

Armstrong, Isobel, BA *Leic.*, PhD *Leic.*   Dir.*

South East Regional Research Laboratory

Shepherd, John W., BSc(Econ) *Lond.*, MSc *Lond.*, PhD *Lond.*, FRICS   Dir.*

Theoretical Physics Research Unit
Tel: (0171) 631 6347, 631 6289

Hiley, Basil J., BSc Lond., PhD Lond.   Prof.†
Leader, Elliott, BSc Witw., MS Cal.Tech., PhD Camb.   Prof.†

CONTACT OFFICERS

Accommodation. Lettings Officer: ......
Admissions (first degree). (Contact the registry)
Admissions (higher degree). (Contact the registry)

Adult/continuing education. Acting Publicity and Liaison Officer: Cleaver, Christine, BA
Alumni. Events and Alumni Officer: Elias, Julie
Computing services. Director, Central Computing Services: Gill, Jasbir S., BSc MSc PhD
Development/fund-raising. Events and Alumni Officer: Elias, Julie
Estates and buildings/works and services. Director, Estates and Facilities: Sanders, David, BEng
Examinations. Examinations Officer: Barnes, Jacqueline A.

Finance. Director of Finance: Westley, Peter
General enquiries. Secretary and Clerk to the Governors: Mabey, Christine, BA PhD
Library. Librarian: Dolphin, Philippa, MA
Personnel/human resources. Director of Personnel: Moore, Michael, BA
Public relations, information and marketing. Director of External Relations: Charlton, Josie, BSc

[Information supplied by the institution as at 30 September 1998, and edited by the ACU]

GOLDSMITHS COLLEGE, UNIVERSITY OF LONDON

Founded 1891

Associate Member of the Association of Commonwealth Universities

Postal Address: New Cross, London, England SE14 6NW
Telephone: (0171) 919 7171 **Fax**: (0171) 919 7113 **Cables**: Goldsmiths College, London
WWW: http://www.gold.ac.uk **E-mail formula**: initialfirstname.surname@scorpio.gold.ac.uk

CHAIRMAN OF COUNCIL—Girolami, Sir Paul
WARDEN*—Pimlott, Prof. Ben J., BA Oxf., BPhil Oxf., PhD Newcastle(UK), FRHistS, FBA
PRO-WARDEN—Downie, Prof. J. Alan, BA Newcastle(UK), MLitt Newcastle(UK), PhD Newcastle(UK)
PRO-WARDEN—Jenks, Prof. Chris, BSc MSc
PRO-WARDEN—Aylett, Robert, BA Camb., MA Camb., PhD Camb.
SECRETARY‡—Guy, S., BA E.Anglia
DIRECTOR OF FINANCE‡—Tait, Barry W.
ACADEMIC REGISTRAR—Barrie, Mary A., BA Hull
DIRECTOR OF CONTINUING EDUCATION AND HEAD OF PROFESSIONAL AND COMMUNITY EDUCATION—Barry, Malcolm V., BMus MMus MA
DIRECTOR OF QUALITY AFFAIRS—Aylett, Robert, BA Camb., MA Camb., PhD Camb.
DIRECTOR OF INFORMATION SERVICES AND LIBRARIAN—Horrill, Ronald J. E., BA Exe.

GENERAL INFORMATION

History. The college was founded by the Worshipful Company of Goldsmiths in 1891, and was established as Goldsmiths College in 1904. In 1977 it amalgamated with the Rachel McMillan and St Gabriel's Colleges. It became a school (now college) of the University of London in 1988 and was granted its Royal Charter in 1990.

Admission (see also United Kingdom Introduction). Full-time degrees: through Universities and Colleges Admissions Service (UCAS). Part-time degrees: through the Registry Admissions Office. Home students: 2 passes at General Certificate of Education (GCE) A level, or 1 pass at A level and 2 at AS level, or 4 passes at AS level. Scottish Certificate of Education, Advanced GNVQ (Level 3) and BTEC National and Higher National Certificates and Diplomas also accepted. Overseas students: qualifications equivalent to those listed above, plus General Certificate of Secondary Education (GCSE) or GCE O level English language (grade C or above), or IELTS score 6.5, or TOEFL score 580.

First Degrees (of University of London) (see also United Kingdom Directory to Subjects of Study). BA, BAEd (extension degree), BMus, BMusEd (extension degree), BSc, BScEd (extension degree).
Courses normally last 3 years full-time.† Extension degree courses, courses incorporating design and/or a European

language: 4 years full-time. Some courses available part-time (minimum 4 years).

Higher Degrees (of University of London) (see also United Kingdom Directory to Subjects of Study). MA, MMus, MRes, MSc, MPhil, PhD.
Applicants for admission to master's degrees must normally hold an appropriate first degree with at least upper second class honours. PhD: appropriate master's degree or completion of an agreed part of MPhil research and training programme.
MA, MMus, MSc: 1 year full-time or 2 years part-time; MPhil: 2 years full-time or 3 years part-time; PhD: 4 years full-time or 6 years part-time.

Libraries. 200,000 monographs; 1500 journals subscribed to. Special collection: School Practice (teaching practice).

Fees (1998–99). UK/EU students: £1000 (undergraduate, annual); £1305 (part-time postgraduate); £2610 (full-time postgraduate). International students: £1000 (undergraduate); £6835–8695 (postgraduate).

Academic Year (1999–2000). Three semesters: 27 September–17 December; 17 January–31 March; 1 May–23 June.

Income (1997–98). Total, £34,000,000.

Statistics. Staff: 850 (310 academic, 540 non-academic). Students: full-time 4669 (1588 men, 3081 women); part-time 1716 (584 men, 1132 women); international (non-EU) 560; total 6385.

ACADEMIC UNITS

Anthropology

Tel: (0171) 919 7800 Fax: (0171) 919 7813

Besson, Jean, MA Edin., PhD Edin.   Sr. Lectr.
Caplan, A. Patricia, BA MA PhD   Prof.
Harris, Olivia J., BA Oxf.   Reader
Morris, Brian, BEd Sus., PhD   Prof.
Nelson, Nici M., MA Col., PhD, FRAI   Sr. Lectr.
Nugent, Stephen L., BA Reed, PhD   Reader; Head*
Shore, Crispin, BA DPhil

Cultural Studies, see Hist. and Cultural Studies

Design Studies

Tel: (0171) 919 7777 Fax: (0171) 919 7797

Kimbell, Richard A., BEd MPhil   Prof.
Stables, Kay, BEd MA   Reader; Head*
Wood, John B.   Sr. Lectr.
Woolley, Martin S., BA MDes PhD   Prof.

Drama

Tel: (0171) 919 7414 Fax: (0171) 919 7413

Gordon, Robert J., MA   Reader
Gottlieb, Vera, BA MLitt   Prof.
Shepherd, Simon, BA Nott., MA Nott., MLitt Nott., PhD Nott.   Prof.; Head*

Educational Studies, see also Professl. and Community Educn.

Tel: (0171) 919 7313 Fax: (0171) 919 7300

Chitty, Clyde, BA PhD   Prof.; Head*
Gregory, Evelyn E., BA PhD   Reader

Halpin, David, BEd Brist., MEd Brist., PhD
Lanc. Prof.
Harris, Jennifer Reader
Inman, Sally, BSc MA Sr. Lectr.
Jones, Lesley, BPhil Birm., MEd Sr. Lectr.
Mace, Jane S., BA Oxf. Sr. Lectr.
Modgil, Celia, MPhil Sur., PhD Sr. Lectr.
Tomlinson, Sally, BA Liv., PhD Warw. Prof.

English
Tel: (0171) 919 7436 Fax: (0171) 919 7453
Baldick, C. G., BA Oxf., DPhil Oxf. Prof.
Carr, Helen, BA MA PhD Reader
Downie, J. Alan, BA Newcastle(UK), MLitt
Newcastle(UK), PhD Newcastle(UK) Prof.
Margolies, David N., BA Chic., BLitt Oxf., PhD
Essex Reader
McCormack, William J., BA Trinity(Dub.), MA
Ulster, DPhil Ulster Prof.; Head*
Moore-Gilbert, Bart, MA DPhil Sr. Lectr.
Radford, Jean F., BA Manc., MA Manc., MPhil
Warw. Sr. Lectr.
Sokol, Jerry, BSc MA MPhil PhD Sr. Lectr.

European Languages
Tel: (0171) 919 7460 Fax: (0171) 919 7455
Aylett, Robert, BA Camb., MA Camb., PhD
Camb. Sr. Lectr., German
Castein-Strange, Hanne C., DrPhil
Freib. Reader, German
Dunwoodie, P., BA Edin., MA Edin., PhD
Edin. Reader, French
Garner, Paul, BA PhD Prof.; Head*

Fine Arts, see Visual Arts

French, see European Langs.

German, see European Langs.

Historical and Cultural Studies
Tel: (0171) 919 7490 Fax: (0171) 919 7398
Alexander, Sally, BA Lond. Prof.
Caygill, Howard, BSc MA DPhil Prof.; Head*
Fouracre, Paul, BA PhD Reader
Keown, Damien, BA DPhil Reader
Killingray, David, BSc(Econ) PhD,
FRHistS Prof.
Lowe, Katherine, BA PhD Sr. Lectr.
Maharaj, Sarat C., MA PhD Prof.
Rogoff, Irit, BA MA PhD Prof.
Ward, Jennifer C., MA PhD Sr. Lectr.

Mathematical Sciences
Tel: (0171) 919 7850 Fax: (0171) 919 7853
Brownrigg, David R. K., BSc Reading, MSc
Reading, PhD Reading Sr. Lectr.
Chu, Cho-Ho, BSc HK, PhD Wales Prof.
Donnison, J. Richard, BSc Sur., MSc PhD Sr.
Lectr.
Jackson, William, BSc MSc PhD Prof.
Pettit, Lawrence, BSc MSc PhD Reader
Stephens, Nelson M., PhD Prof.; Head*

Media and Communications
Tel: (0171) 919 7600 Fax: (0171) 919 7616
Beacham, John P. Sr. Lectr.
Curran, James P., BA Prof.
Gaber, Ivor H., MA Prof.†
Geraghty, Christine Sr. Lectr.; Head*
McRobbie, Angela, MA Prof.
Morley, David G., BSc Kent, PhD Kent Prof.
Phillips, Angela Sr. Lectr.
Schwarz, Bill, BA Reader

Music
Tel: (0171) 919 7640 Fax: (0171) 919 7644
Baily, John S., BA Oxf., DPhil Sus., PhD
Belf. Reader
Lawson, Colin, MA PhD Prof.

McVeigh, Simon W., MA Oxf., DPhil
Oxf. Prof.; Head*
Potter, Keith, BMus MA Sr. Lectr.

Professional and Community Education
Tel: (0171) 919 7200 Fax: (0171) 919 7223
Dryden, Windy, BSc MSc PhD, FBPsS Prof.
Mayo, Marjorie, BA Oxf., MSc Lond.,
PhD Reader
Pearson, G., BA Camb., MA Prof.
Simmonds, John A., BSc(Econ) PhD Sr. Lectr.
Waller, Diane E., MA RCA, DPhil Sus. Reader

Psychology
Tel: (0171) 919 7870 Fax: (0171) 919 7873
Anderson, Neil R., MSc Aston, PhD Aston Prof.
Blumberg, Herb H., MA Johns H., PhD Johns
H. Sr. Lectr.
Davidoff, Jules, BSc PhD DSc, FBPsS Prof.
Davies, Martin F., BA Camb., PhD Sr. Lectr.
Dryden, Windy, BSc MSc PhD, FBPsS Prof.
Fletcher, Clive A., BA Wales, PhD Wales,
FBPSS Prof.; Head*
French, Christopher C., BA PhD,
FBPsS Reader; Head*
Powell, Jane H., BA Oxf., MPhil Lond., PhD
Lond. Sr. Lectr.
Pring, Linda, BSc Newcastle(UK), PhD Reader
Rust, John N., BSc MA Sr. Lectr.
Smith, Peter, BA PhD, FBPsS Prof.
Valentine, Tim, BSc PhD Prof.
Velmans, Max L., BSc Syd., PhD, FBPsS Reader
Wells, Pamela A., BA Hull, BSc Hull, PhD Sr.
Lectr.

Social Politics and Policy
Tel: (0171) 919 7740 Fax: (0171) 919 7743
Butcher, Anthony M., MA(Econ) Manc. Lectr.;
Head*
Heidensohn, Frances M., BA Prof.
Levin, Mike M. J., PhD Leic., BA
MSc(Econ) Sr. Lectr.
Littlewood, Jane, BSc Brad., PhD Leic. Sr. Lectr.
Newburn, Tim Prof.
Rao, Nirmala, BA MA MPhil PhD Sr. Lectr.

Sociology
Tel: (0171) 919 7709 Fax: (0171) 919 7713
Back, Leslie, BSc PhD Sr. Lectr.
Filmer, Paul A., BA Nott. Sr. Lectr.
Gilroy, Paul, BA Sus., PhD Birm. Prof.
Jenks, Chris, BSc Sur., MSc(Econ) Prof.
Keith, Michael, BA Oxf., DPhil Oxf. Reader
Ramazanoglu, Caroline, BA MA PhD Reader
Rose, Nikolas S., BA Sus., MSc PhD Prof.
Seale, Clive, BEd MSc PhD Sr. Lectr.
Seidler, Vic J. J., BA Oxf., MPhil Kent Prof.
Silverman, David, BSc Calif., MA Calif.,
PhD Prof.
Thomas, Helen, BA PhD Sr. Lectr.; Head*
Walsh, Dave F., BA Leic., MSc(Econ) Sr. Lectr.

Visual Arts
Tel: (0171) 919 7671 Fax: (0171) 919 7403
Craig-Martin, Michael, BA Yale, BFA
MFA Millard Prof., Fine Art
De Ville, Nick, BA Prof.
Falconbridge, Brian Sr. Lectr.; Head*
Fisher, Chris, BA MA Sr. Lectr.
Hemsworth, Gerald Reader
Jefferies, Janis K., BA CNAA Reader
Plackman, Carl Sr. Lectr.

CONTACT OFFICERS

Academic affairs. Academic Registrar: Barrie,
Mary A., BA Hull
Accommodation. Accommodation Officer:
Dyer, June
Admissions (first degree). Administrative
Assistant (Undergraduate/PGCE): Fox,
Geraint, BA

Adult/continuing education. Director of
Continuing Education and Head of
Professional and Community Education:
Barry, Malcolm V., BMus MMus MA
Alumni. Alumni Relations Officer: Clarke,
Stephen
Careers. Senior Careers Adviser: Murdoch,
Linda
Computing services. Computer Services
Manager: Pateman, Joan G.
Credit transfer. Assistant Registrar
(Examinations): Beevers, Pamela M., BA
Open(UK), MA
Credit transfer. Administrative Assistant
(Undergraduate/PGCE): Fox, Geraint, BA
Development/fund-raising. (Contact the
Warden's Office)
Equal opportunities. Deputy Head of
Personnel: May, Johanna K., BA
Estates and buildings/works and services.
Facilities Manager: Gamble, Diana
Examinations. Assistant Registrar
(Examinations): Beevers, Pamela M., BA
Open(UK), MA
Finance. Director of Finance: Tait, Barry W.
General enquiries. Secretary: Guy, S., BA
E.Anglia
Health services. Medical Officer: MacFarlane,
A. E., MB BS
International office. Assistant Registrar
(International Office): Thorn, Jill
Library (chief librarian). Director of
Information Services and Librarian: Horrill,
Ronald J. E., BA Exe.
Library (enquiries). Assistant Librarian:
Houston, Sally
Minorities/disadvantaged groups. Deputy
Head of Personnel: May, Johanna K., BA
Personnel/human resources. Head of
Personnel: Letham, Robert, BA
Public relations, information and marketing.
(Contact the Warden's Office)
Publications. Assistant Registrar (Publications):
Annand, Vicky, BA
Purchasing. Purchasing Officer: Ishmael,
Kalam
Quality assurance and accreditation. Quality
Affairs Administrator: Cardell, Rosemary, BA
Research. Administrative Assistant
(Undergraduate/PGCE): Fox, Geraint, BA
Safety. Safety Officer: Robson, Gordon
Scholarships, awards, loans. Administrative
Assistant (Grants and Awards): Smith, John
H., BA
Schools liaison. (Responsibility of individual
departments)
Security. College Superintendent: Prendergast,
Des J.
Staff development and training. Director of
Professional Training and Staff Development
Co-ordinator: Halvorson, Mary-Claire
Student union. General Manager: Courtney,
Josie
Student welfare/counselling. Students' Union
Vice-President, Welfare and Academic Affairs:
(and Medical Centre Counsellors)
Students from other countries. Assistant
Registrar (International Office): Thorn, Jill
Students with disabilities. Administrative
Assistant (Accommodation/Timetabling):
Francis, Kay L.
Women. Deputy Head of Personnel: May,
Johanna K., BA

[Information supplied by the institution as at 6 November
1998, and edited by the ACU]

HEYTHROP COLLEGE

Founded 1926; originally established 1614

Postal Address: Kensington Square, London, England W8 5HQ
Telephone: (0171) 795 6600 **Fax**: (0171) 795 4200 **E-mail formula**: initial.surname@heythrop.ac.uk

PRINCIPAL*—......
SECRETARY/ACADEMIC REGISTRAR—Clarkson, Annabel
LIBRARIAN—Walsh, Michael J., MA Oxf., STL *Greg.*

ACADEMIC UNITS

Biblical Studies
Isaacs, Rev. Marie E., BD Oxf., MA Oxf., DPhil
    Oxf.   Lectr.; Head*

Church History
Price, Rev. Richard M., MA Oxf., DPhil Oxf., BD
    MTh   Lectr.; Head*

Pastoral Studies
Davey, Rev. Theodore P. O., DCL
    Pontif.Lateran   Lectr.; Head*

Philosophy
Carter, Alan B., BA Kent, MA Sus., DPhil
    Oxf.   Lectr.; Head*

Systematic Theology
McDade, Rev. John, MA Oxf., PhD Edin.,
    BD   Lectr.; Head*

CONTACT OFFICERS
Admissions (first degree). Secretary/Academic
    Registrar: Clarkson, Annabel
Admissions (higher degree). Dean of
    Postgraduate Studies: Price, Rev. Richard M.,
    MA Oxf., DPhil Oxf., BD MTh
Alumni. Alumni Secretary: Colliston, James,
    BA Greg., STL Greg.
General enquiries. Secretary/Academic
    Registrar: Clarkson, Annabel
Library (chief librarian). Librarian: Walsh,
    Michael J., MA Oxf., STL Greg.

Library (enquiries). Morgan, Michael, BA
    Warw., BA Lond.
Public relations, information and marketing.
    Head of Development: Hoose, B., STL Greg.,
    STD Greg.
Student union. Senior Treasurer: Gilfillan
    Upton, E. Bridget, BAgrSc Massey, BA Lond.

[Information supplied by the institution as at 8 June
1998, and edited by the ACU]

IMPERIAL COLLEGE OF SCIENCE, TECHNOLOGY AND MEDICINE

Founded 1907

Associate Member of the Association of Commonwealth Universities

Postal Address: South Kensington, London, England SW7 2AZ
Telephone: (0171) 589 5111 **Fax**: (0171) 584 7596 **Telex**: 929484 **WWW**: http://www.ic.ac.uk
E-mail formula: initial.surname@ic.ac.uk (Department of Computing: initial.surname@doc.ic.ac.uk)

VISITOR—Elizabeth, H.M. The Queen
CHAIRMAN OF THE GOVERNING BODY—Vincent, Field Marshal Lord Richard, GBE, KCB, DSO
RECTOR*—Oxburgh, Sir Ronald, KBE, MA Oxf., PhD Prin., Hon. DSc Paris, Hon. DSc Leic., Hon. DSc Lough., Hon.
    DSc Edin., Hon. DSc Birm., Hon. DSc Liv., FGSA, FRS, Hon. FIMechE
DEPUTY RECTOR AND PRO RECTOR (RESEARCH)—Wakeham, William A., BSc Exe., PhD Exe., FIEE, FIChemE
COLLEGE SECRETARY AND CLERK TO THE GOVERNORS‡—Mitcheson, K. Anthony, OBE, MA
PRO RECTOR (RESOURCES)—Davies, Prof. Glyn A. O., BEng Liv., PhD Syd., FRAeS
PRO RECTOR (EDUCATIONAL QUALITY)—Clark, Prof. Tim J. H., BSc Lond., MB BS MD, FRCP
PRO RECTOR (EXTERNAL RELATIONS)—Aleksander, Prof. Igor, BSc Witw., PhD Lond., FIEE
PRINCIPAL, IMPERIAL COLLEGE SCHOOL OF MEDICINE—Edwards, Prof. Christopher R. W., MA Camb., MD Camb.,
    FRCP, FRCPEd, FRSEd
DEAN (ROYAL COLLEGE OF SCIENCE)—Mingos, Prof. D. Michael P., BSc Manc., DPhil Sus., FRSChem, FRS
DEAN (CITY AND GUILDS COLLEGE)—Briscoe, Prof. Brian J., BSc Hull, MA Camb., PhD Hull, FRSChem, FIP, FIM
DEAN (ROYAL SCHOOL OF MINES)—Kilner, Prof. John A., MSc Birm., PhD Birm.

GENERAL INFORMATION

History. The college is made up of the
former Royal College of Science, City and
Guilds College, Royal School of Mines, St
Mary's Hospital Medical School, National Heart
and Lung Institute, Charing Cross and
Westminster Medical School, and Royal
Postgraduate Medical School.

It has five campuses in west London and a
field station in Berkshire.

Admission to first degree courses (see also
United Kingdom Introduction). Through
Universities and Colleges Admissions Service

(UCAS). International candidates are normally
required to take an English language test.

First Degrees (of University of London)
(see also University of London Directory to
Subjects of Study). BEng, BSc, MB BS, MEng,
MSci.

All courses are full-time and last for 3, 4, 5
or 6 years.

Higher Degrees (of University of London)
(see also University of London Directory to
Subjects of Study). MBA, MSc, MPhil, PhD.

Applicants for admission to higher degree
courses must normally possess the equivalent

of a University of London first or second class
honours degree.

Libraries. 1,047,000 volumes; 7950
periodicals.

Fees. Undergraduate (UK/EU students,
1998–99, annual): £1000. Postgraduate (UK/
EU students, 1997–98, per 3-term session):
£12,000 (MBA in management); £10,000
(MSc in finance); £8400 (petroleum
production management); £6400 (corrosion of
engineering materials); £2540 (all other
courses). Postgraduate research degrees
(international students, 1997–98): £6700
(mathematics, humanities); £17,320 (clinical

medicine); £8,500 (all other courses). Advanced postgraduate courses (international students, 1997–98): £7350 (mathematics, humanities); £8400 (petroleum production management); £6400 (corrosion of engineering materials); £12,000 (MBA in management); £11,250 (MBA in management, overseas programme); £10,000 (MSc in finance); £13,750 (clinical medicine).

Academic Year (1999–2000). Three terms: 2 October–17 December; 8 January–24 March; 29 April–30 June.

Income (1996–97) Total, £210,012,000.

Statistics. Staff: 2674 (1192 academic, 1482 administrative). Students: full-time 8824 (6042 men, 2782 women); part-time 894 (582 men, 312 women); international 3376; total 9718.

FACULTIES/SCHOOLS

City and Guilds College
Dean: Briscoe, Prof. Brian J., BSc Hull, MA Camb., PhD Hull, FRSChem, FIP, FIM

Imperial College School of Medicine
Principal: Edwards, Prof. C. R. W., MA MD, FRCP, FRCPEd, FRSEd

Royal College of Science
Dean: Mingos, Prof. D. Michael P., BSc Manc., DPhil Sus., FRSChem, FRS

Royal School of Mines
Dean: Kilner, Prof. John A., MSc Birm., PhD Birm.

ACADEMIC UNITS

Aeronautics
Tel: (0171) 594 5100 Fax: (0171) 584 8120

Bearman, Peter W., MA Camb., PhD Camb., FRAeS Prof., Experimental Aerodynamics; Head*
Crisfield, Michael A., BSc Belf., PhD Belf. Prof., Computational Mechanical
Davies, Glyn A. O., BEng Liv., PhD Syd., FRAeS Prof., Aeronautical Structures
Doorly, Denis J., DPhil Oxf. Reader, Fluid Dynamics
Graham, J. Michael R., BA Camb., PhD Lond. Prof., Unsteady Aerodynamics
Harvey, John K., BSc(Eng) Lond., PhD Lond. Prof., Gas Dynamics
Hillier, Richard, MA Camb., PhD Camb. Prof., Compressible Flow
Hitchings, Dennis, BSc(Eng) MSc Sr. Lectr.
Mathews, Ian C., BSc(Eng) Lond., MSc Lond., PhD Lond. Reader, Computational Acoustics
Matthews, Frank L., BSc(Eng), FRAeS Reader
Morrison, Jonathan F., BSc Durh., PhD Durh. Sr. Lectr.
Robinson, Paul, PhD Lond. Sr. Lectr.
Soutis, Costas, BSc(Eng) Lond., MSc(Eng) Lond., PhD Lond. Reader, Mechanics of Composites
Stevens, Kenneth A. Sr. Lectr.
Research: aerodynamics; aeronautical structures; aircraft aerodynamics; general structural analysis; structural mechanics

Biochemistry
Tel: (0171) 594 5297 Fax: (0171) 594 5207, 225 0960

Barber, James, BSc Wales, MSc E.Anglia, PhD E.Anglia, FRSChem, FIBiol Ernst Chain Prof.; Head*
Bradford, Henry F., PhD Lond., DSc Lond., FRCPath Prof., Neurochemistry
Cass, Anthony E. G., BSc York(UK), DPhil Oxf. Reader, Bioanalytical Chemistry
Dell, Anne, BSc W.Aust., PhD Camb. Prof., Carbohydrate Biochemistry
Dolly, J. Oliver, MSc N.U.I., PhD Wales Prof., Molecular Neurobiology
Dougan, Gordon, MA Sus., DPhil Sus. Rank Prof., Physiological Biochemistry
Fairweather, Neil F., BSc Edin., PhD Leic.

Leak, David J., BA Camb., MA Camb., MSc Newcastle(UK), PhD Warw.
Little, Peter F. R., BSc Brist., PhD Edin. Reader, Molecular Genetics
Mantle, Peter G., PhD Lond., DSc Lond. Prof., Microbial Biochemistry
Morris, Howard R., BSc Leeds, PhD Leeds, FRS Prof., Biological Chemistry
O'Hare, Kevin, BA Camb., PhD Edin.
Selkirk, Murray E., PhD Brun. Reader, Biochemical Parasitology
Smith, Deborah F., BSc S'ton., PhD S'ton. Reader, Molecular Parasitology
van Heel, Marin, Dr Gron. Prof., Structural Biology
Wilkin, Graham P., MSc CNAA, PhD CNAA Reader, Neurobiology
Vacant Posts: 1 Prof.
Research: biomolecular structure; molecular basis of infection; molecular genetics; molecular neurobiology; photobioenergetics and molecular dynamics

Biological and Medical Systems
Tel: (0171) 594 5176, 5179 Fax: (0171) 594 5177

Bailey, Anita J., BSc PhD Kodak Emer. Prof., Interface Science
Caro, Colin G., BSc BCh MD, FRCP, FRCPEd Emer. Prof., Physiological Mechanics
Kitney, Richard I., MSc Sur., PhD Lond., DSc(Eng) Lond., FIEE Prof., Biomedical Systems Engineering; Head*
Lever, Michael J., BA Oxf., DPhil Oxf. Reader, Physiological Mechanics
Parker, Kim H., BSc Prin., MA Prin., PhD Prin., BSc(Eng) Reader, Physiological Fluid Mechanics
Schroter, Robert C., PhD Lond., FIChemE Prof., Biological Mechanics
Winlove, C. Peter, BSc Lond., MSc Oxf., DPhil Oxf. Reader, Connective Tissue
Research: biophysics of connective tissues; circulatory mechanics and arterial disease; medical signal and image analysis and processing; respiratory mechanics; three-dimensional visualisation

Biology
Tel: (0171) 594 5385 Fax: (0171) 225 1234

Archer, Simon A., BSc Lond., PhD Brist. Sr. Lectr.
Beddington, John R., BSc Lond., PhD Edin. Prof., Applied Population Biology
Bell, J. Nigel B., BSc Manc., MSc Wat., PhD Manc. Prof., Environmental Pollution
Buck, Kenneth W., BSc Birm., Phd Birm. Prof., Plant Virology
Buck, Martin, BSc Lond., PhD Lond. Reader, Molecular Microbiology
Canning, Elizabeth U., PhD Lond., DSc Lond., FIBiol Emer. Prof., Protozoology
Coutts, Robert H. A., BSc Lond., PhD Nott. Sr. Lectr.
Crawley, Michael J., BSc Edin., PhD Lond. Prof., Plant Ecology
Crisanti, Andrea, PhD Basle Reader, Molecular Parasitology
Dallman, Margaret, BSc Brist., DPhil Oxf. Reader, Immunoregulation
Dickinson, David J., BSc Hull, PhD Hull Sr. Lectr.
Djamgoz, Mustafa B. A., BSc Lond., PhD Lond. Prof., Neurobiology
Foster, Russell G., PhD Brist. Reader, Zoology
Godfray, H. Charles J., PhD Lond. Prof., Evolutionary Biology
Hardie, Robert J., PhD Birm., DSc Lond. Reader, Insect Physiology
Hassell, Michael P., MA Camb., DPhil Oxf., DSc Oxf., FIBiol, FRS Prof., Insect Ecology; Head*
Isacke, Clare, DPhil Oxf. Reader, Molecular Cell Biology
Lamb, Bernard C., BSc Brist., PhD Brist., FIBiol Reader, Genetics

Langhorne, Jean, BSc Lond., MSc Lond., PhD Lond. Reader, Immunobiology
Lawton, John H., BSc Durh., PhD Durh., FRS Prof., Community Ecology
Leather, Simon, BSc Leeds, PhD E.Anglia Sr. Lectr.
Matthews, Graham A., BSc Lond., PhD Lond. Prof., Pest Management
Palmer, John M., BSc Reading, DPhil Oxf. Prof., Plant Biochemistry
Sinden, Robert E., BSc Newcastle(UK), PhD Edin., DSc Lond. Prof., Parasite Cell Biology
Williams, Huw D., PhD Lond. Sr. Lectr.
Wright, Denis J., BSc Newcastle(UK), PhD Newcastle(UK) Sr. Lectr.
Research: agricultural and environment management; animal physiology and neurobiology; ecology; immunology; microbiology

Chemical Technology, see Engin., Chem., and Chem. Technol.

Chemistry
Tel: (0171) 594 5817 Fax: (0171) 594 5804

Barrett, Antony G. M., BSc Lond., PhD Lond. Prof., Organic Chemistry
Craig, Donald, BSc Lond., PhD Lond. Reader, Organic Chemistry
Gibson, Susan, BA Camb., DPhil Oxf. Reader, Organic Chemistry
Gibson, Vernon, BSc Sheff., DPhil Oxf. Prof., Organic Chemistry
Goodgame, David M. L., BSc Oxf., MA Oxf., DPhil Oxf., DSc, FRSChem Prof., Inorganic Chemistry
Griffith, William P., PhD Lond., DSc Lond. Prof., Inorganic Chemistry
Hayward, David O., BA Camb., PhD Liv. Sr. Lectr.
Jones, Timothy S., BSc Liv., PhD Liv. Reader, Physical Chemistry
Manz, Andreas, PhD E.T.H.Zürich Prof., Analytical Chemistry
Mingos, D. Michael P., BSc Manc., DPhil Sus., FRSChem, FRS Prof., Organic Chemistry
Nicholson, David, BSc Hull, PhD Salf., FRSChem Reader, Physical Chemistry
O'Brien, Paul, BSc Liv., PhD Wales Prof., Inorganic Chemistry
Phillips, David, BSc Birm., PhD Birm., FRSChem Prof., Physical Chemistry; Head*
Rumbles, Garry, BSc S'ton., PhD Lond. Sr. Lectr.
Rzepa, Henry S., BSc Lond., PhD Lond., DSc Lond. Reader, Organic Chemistry
Seddon, John M., BSc Stir., PhD Lond. Reader, Physical Chemistry
Templer, Richard H., BSc Brist., DPhil Oxf. Reader, Physical Chemistry
Widdowson, David A., BSc Nott., PhD Lond., DSc Lond. Reader, Organic Chemistry
Williams, David J., BSc CNAA, PhD Prof., Structural Chemistry
Young, G. Brent, BSc Glas., PhD Glas. Sr. Lectr.
Research: biological chemistry; crystallography; surface chemistry; synthetic chemistry (organic and inorganic); theoretical and computational chemistry

Computing
Tel: (0171) 594 8298 Fax: (0171) 594 8282

Bailey, Roger, BSc Lond., MTech Brun. Sr. Lectr.
Broda, Krysia, BSc Lond., BA Lond., MSc Lond., PhD Lond. Sr. Lectr.
Brough, Derek R., BSc Lond. Sr. Lectr.
Burger, Peter, BE Tennessee, ME Stan., PhD Stan. Sr. Lectr.
Clark, Keith L., BA Durh., MA Camb., PhD Lond. Prof., Computational Logic
Cunningham, Margaret R., BSc Lond. Sr. Lectr.
Cunningham, R. James, BE Melb., MEngSc Melb. Sr. Lectr.
Darlington, J., BSc(Econ) Lond., PhD Edin. Prof., Programming Methodology

Edalat, Abbas, BSc Lond., MSc Warw., PhD Warw. Reader, Computer Science and Mathematics

Eisenbach, Susan, BA Vassar, MSc Lond. Sr. Lectr.

Field, Anthony J., BSc Reading, PhD Lond. Sr. Lectr.

Gabbay, Dov. M., BSc Jerusalem, MSc Jerusalem, PhD Jerusalem Prof., Computing Science

Gillies, Duncan F., MusB Camb., MA Camb., MSc Lond., PhD Lond. Reader, Computer Graphics and Vision

Hankin, Christopher L., BSc City(UK), PhD Lond. Prof., Computing Science

Harrison, Peter G., BA Camb., MSc Lond., PhD Lond. Prof., Computing Science

Hogger, Christopher J., BSc Lond., PhD Lond. Sr. Lectr.

Kelly, Paul H. J., BSc Lond., PhD Lond. Sr. Lectr.

Kowalski, Robert A., MSc Stan., PhD Edin. Prof., Computational Logic; Head*

Kramer, Jeffrey, BSc Natal, MSc Lond.,PhD Lond. Prof., Distributed Computing

Lehman, Meir M., BSc Lond., PhD Lond., DSc Lond. Emer. Prof., Computing Science

Magee, Jeffrey N., BSc Belf., MSc Lond., PhD Lond. Reader, Computing Science

Maibaum, Thomas S. E., BSc Tor., PhD Lond. Prof., Foundations of Software Engineering

Maros, Istvan, PhD Bud. Reader, Computational Methods in Operational Research

Rustem, Berc, BSc Istanbul, MSc Lond., PhD Lond. Prof., Computational Methods in Operational Research

Sergot, Marek J., MA Camb. Reader, Computational Logic

Sloman, Morris S., BSc Cape Town, PhD Essex Prof., Distributed Systems Management

Smyth, Michael B., BA Camb., MSc Lond., MPhil Lond., DPhil Oxf. Reader, Computing Science

Research: advanced languages and architectures; computer vision and graphics; decision support; distributed systems and software engineering; operations research and financial modelling

Engineering, Chemical, and Chemical Technology

Tel: (0171) 594 5575 Fax: (0171) 594 5604

Briscoe, Brian J., BSc Hull, MA Camb., PhD Hull, FRSChem, FIP, FIM Prof., Interface Engineering

Carabine, Michael D., BSc Edin., PhD Camb. Sr. Lectr.

Chadwick, David, BSc Lond., PhD Lond. Reader, Applied Catalysis

Clay, Peter G., BSc Durh., PhD Durh. Sr. Lectr.

Dugwell, Denis R., BSc Sheff., PhD Sheff., FIChemE Sr. Lectr.

Hewitt, Geoffrey F., BSc Manc., PhD Manc., DSc Louvain, FEng, FIChemE, FRSChem, FRS Prof.†

Higgins, Julia, CBE, MA Oxf., DPhil Oxf., FRSChem, FIM, FRS Prof., Polymer Science

Jones, Alan R., BSc Wales, PhD Wales, DSc Wales, FIP Prof., Combustion Physics

Jones, William P., BSc Wales, MSc PhD, FIP Prof., Combustion Engineering

Kandiyoti, Rafael, BSc Col., PhD Lond., FIChemE Prof., Chemical Engineering

Kershenbaum, Lester S., MS Mich., PhD Mich., FIChemE Prof., Chemical Engineering

Livingston, Andrew G., BEng Cant., PhD Camb. Reader, Chemical Engineering

Luckham, Paul F., BSc Brist. Reader, Particle Technology

Macchietto, Sandro, MS Conn., PhD Conn. Prof., Process Systems Engineering

Michels, Hans J., CandDrs Amst., PhD Lond. Sr. Lectr.

Ortiz, E. Susana, MSc Lond., PhD Lond. Reader, Chemical Engineering

Pantelides, Constantinos C., BSc(Eng) Lond., MS M.I.T., PhD Lond. Prof., Chemical Engineering

Perkins, J. D., BSc Lond., MA Camb., PhD Lond., FIChemE, FIMA, FEng Prof., Chemical Engineering; Head*

Pistikopoulos, Stratos N., DPhil Carnegie-Mellon Reader, Process Systems Engineering

Richardson, Stephen M., BSc Lond., PhD Lond., FIChemE, FEng Prof.

Sargent, Roger W. H., BSc Lond., PhD Lond. Emer. Prof.

Saville, Graham, MA Oxf., DPhil Oxf. Reader, Thermodynamics

Stuckey, David C., BE Melb., MEngSc Melb., PhD Stan. Sr. Lectr.

Trusler, J. P. Martin, BSc Lond., PhD Lond. Sr. Lectr.

Wakeham, William A., BSc Exe., PhD Exe., DSc, FIEE, FIChemE, FIP Prof., Chemical Physics of Fluids

Weinberg, Felix J., BSc Lond., PhD Lond. Emer. Prof.

White, David A., MA Camb., PhD Camb., FIChemE Reader, Process Engineering

Research: applied catalysis and reaction engineering; biotechnology; combustion; fluids; separations and their applications to the environment

Engineering, Civil

Tel: (0171) 594 6043 Fax: (0171) 594 6053

Anastasiou, Konstantinos, MSc Manc., PhD Liv. Reader

Burland, John B., PhD Camb., DSc(Eng) Witw., FICE, FIStructE, FEng, FGS, FRS Prof., Soil Mechanics

Butler, D., BSc(Eng) Lond., MSc Lond., PhD Lond. Sr. Lectr.

Chana, Palvinder, B., PhD Lond. Sr. Lectr.

Chandler, Richard J., MSc Birm., PhD Birm., DSc(Eng), FICE, FGS Prof., Geotechnical Engineering

Chryssanthopoulos, M. K., BSc Newcastle(UK), MSc Mass., PhD Lond. Reader, Engineering Structures

De Freitas, Michael H., BSc Lond., PhD Lond. Reader, Engineering Geology

Elnashai, Amr, MSc Lond., PhD Lond. Prof., Earthquake Engineering

England, George L., PhD Lond., DSc(Eng) Lond., FICE, FIStructE Prof., Mechanics and Structures

Evans, Andrew W., BA Birm., MSc Camb., PhD Birm. Prof., Transport Safety

Graham, Nigel J. D., BA Camb., MA MSc PhD Prof., Environmental Engineering

Hardwick, J. David, BASc Tor., PhD Sr. Lectr.

Hobbs, Roger E., BSc Lond., PhD Lond., DSc(Eng) Lond., FICE, FIStructE Prof., Structural Engineering

Holmes, Patrick, BSc Wales, PhD Wales Prof., Hydraulics

Jardine, Richard J., MSc PhD Reader, Soil Mechanics

Lloyd Smith, David, BEng Sheff., MSc Lond., PhD Lond. Sr. Lectr.

Newman, John B., BSc(Eng) Lond., PhD Lond. Reader, Concrete Structures

Pavlovic, Milija, BE Melb., MEngSc Melb., PhD Camb., PhD Lond. Prof., Structural Engineering

Polak, J., BSc Lond., MSc Birm., MA Oxf. Sr. Lectr.

Potts, David M., BSc Camb., PhD Camb., ScD Camb., FICE Prof., Analytical Soil Mechanics

Ridley, Tony M., CBE, MS Northwestern, PhD Calif., FEng, FICE Prof., Transport Engineering; Head*

Sarma, Surada K., BTech Kharagpur, PhD Lond. Reader, Engineering Seismology

Wheater, Howard S., MA Camb., PhD Brist. Prof., Engineering Hydrology

Wing, Robert D., BSc(Eng) Lond., MS Calif., PhD Lond. Sr. Lectr.

Research: civil engineering hydraulics; concrete and steel structures; earthquake engineering;

engineering geology, hydrology and seismology; hydrology and water resources

Engineering, Electrical

Tel: (0171) 594 6185 Fax: (0171) 823 8125

Aleksander, Igor, BSc Witw., PhD Lond., FIEE, FEng Prof., Neural Systems Engineering

Allwright, John C., BSc(Eng) Lond., PhD Lond. Prof.

Brookes, D. Michael, MA Camb. Sr. Lectr.

Bryant, Greyham F., BSc Reading, PhD Lond., FIEE, FIMA, FEng Emer. Prof., Control Engineering

Cheung, Peter Y. K., BSc HKUST Reader

Clark, J. Martin C., MA Camb., PhD Lond. Sr. Lectr.

Clarke, Richard H., PhD Lond., DSc(Eng) Lond., FIEE Reader, Electrical Engineering Analysis

Constantinides, Anthony G., BSc Lond., PhD Lond., FIEE Prof., Signal Processing

Freeman, Ernest M., BSc(Eng) Lond., PhD Lond., FIEE, FEng Prof., Applied Electromagnetics

Freris, Leon L., MSc(Eng) Lond., PhD Lond., FIEE Reader, Power Systems

Green, Mino, BSc Durh., PhD Durh., DSc, FIEE Emer. Prof., Electrical Device Science

Juhasz, Csaba, BSc(Eng) Lond., PhD Lond. Sr. Lectr.

Kitney, Richard I., MSc Sur., PhD DSc(Eng), FIEE Prof., Biomedical Systems Engineering

Leaver, Keith D., BA Oxf., PhD Lond. Sr. Lectr.

Limebeer, David J. N., MSc Natal, PhD Natal, FEng Prof., Control Engineering

Macdonald, D. C., BSc(Eng) Lond., PhD Lond., FIEE Sr. Lectr.

Mamdani, Ebrahim H., BSc Lond., PhD Lond., FIEE, FEng Prof., Intelligence in Communication Systems

Manikas, A., BEd Athens, BSc Essex, PhD Lond. Reader, Digital Communications

Spence, Robert, BSc(Eng) Lond., PhD Lond., DSc(Eng) Lond., DEng, FIEE, FEng Prof., Information Engineering; Head*

Syms, Richard R. A., MA Oxf., DPhil Oxf. Prof., Microsystems Technology

Thornton, Trevor, MA Camb., PhD Camb. Reader, Semiconductor Devices

Toumazou, Christofer, BSc PhD Prof., Analog Circuit Design

Turner, Laurence F., BSc Birm., PhD Birm., DSc(Eng) Lond., FIEE Prof., Digital Communication

Vickery, J. Colin, BSc(Eng) Lond., PhD Lond. Sr. Lectr.

Vinter, Richard B., BA Oxf., PhD Camb., ScD Camb. Prof., Control Theory

Yeatman, Eric M., BSc Dal., BEng Nova Scotia TC, MSc Nova Scotia TC, PhD Sr. Lectr.

Research: analogue and digital circuit design; biomedical systems engineering; control and instrumentation; digital communication; energy and electromagnetics

Engineering, Mechanical

Tel: (0171) 594 7006 Fax: (0171) 823 8845

Amis, Andrew A., BSc Leeds, PhD Leeds Reader, Orthopaedic Mechanics

Arcoumanis, Constantine, MSc(Eng) Salonika, PhD Lond. Prof., Internal Combustion Engines

Besant, Colin B., BSc(Eng) Lond., PhD Lond., FIMechE, FIEE, FEng Prof., Computer-Aided Manufacture

Cawley, Peter, BSc Brist., PhD Brist. Prof.

Crane, Robert I., DPhil Oxf. Sr. Lectr.

Crofton, P. Shaun J., MSc Lond., PhD Lond. Sr. Lectr.

Davies, Brian L., MPhil PhD Reader, Robotic Applications

Ewins, David J., BSc Lond., PhD Camb., FIMechE Prof., Vibration Engineering

Fenner, Roger T., BSc(Eng) Lond., PhD Lond. Prof., Engineering Computing

Gosman, A. David, BASc Br.Col., PhD Lond. Prof., Fluid Mechanics

Hibberd, Roger D., BSc Brist., PhD Lond. Sr. Lectr.

Imregun, Mehmet, BSc(Eng) *Istanbul*, MSc *Lond.*, PhD *Lond.* Reader, Structural Dynamics and Aeroelasticity

Isherwood, D. Paul, BSc *Lond.*, PhD *Lond.* Sr. Lectr.

Issa, Raad I., BA *Camb.*, MSc PhD Reader, Thermofluid Dynamics

Kinloch, Anthony J., PhD *Lond.*, DSc(Eng) *Lond.*, FRSChem Prof., Comparative Fluid Dynamics Adhesion

Leevers, Patrick S., BSc(Eng) *Lond.*, MSc *Lond.*, PhD *Lond.* Reader, Polymer Engineering

Lindstedt, R. Peter, MEng *Gothenburg*, PhD *Lond.* Reader, Thermofluids

Lockwood, Frederick C., BSc *Qu.*, PhD *Lond.* Prof., Combustion

Robb, David A., BTech *Lough.*, MSc *Lond.* Sr. Lectr.

Sayles, Richard S., BSc *CNAA*, PhD *CNAA* Reader

Spikes, Hugh A., BA *Camb.*, PhD *Lond.* Prof., Lubrication

Taylor, Alexander M. K. P., MA *Lond.*, PhD *Lond.* Reader, Fluid Mechanics

Turner, Cedric, CBE, PhD DSc(Eng), FEng, FIMechE Emer. Prof.

Walker, Siman P., BSc *Lond.*, PhD Reader

Webster, George A., BSc(Eng) *Lond.*, PhD *Lond.*, FIMechE, FIM Prof., Engineering Materials

Weightman, Barry O., PhD *Sur.*, BSc Sr. Lectr.

Whitelaw, James H., BSc *Glas.*, PhD *Glas.*, DSc(Eng) *Lond.* Prof., Convective Heat Transfer

Williams, J. Gordon, PhD DSc(Eng), FEng, FIMechE, FRS Prof., Mechanical Engineering; Head*

Research: biomechanics; CAD/CAM; flexible manufacturing systems; medical engineering; tribology

Environment, Earth Sciences and Engineering, T. H. Huxley School of

Tel: (0171) 594 7460 *Fax*: (0171) 594 7462

Apsimon, Helen M., MA *Oxf.*, PhD *St And.*, FRAS Reader, Air Pollution

Ashmore, Michael R., BSc *E.Anglia*, PhD *Leeds* Reader, Pollution Impacts

Beddington, John R., MSc *Lond.*, PhD *Edin.* Prof., Applied Population Biology; Head*

Bell, J. N. B., BSc *Manc.*, MSc *Wat.*, PhD *Manc.* Prof., Environmental Pollution

Buchanan, Dennis L., BSc *Rhodes*, MSc *Pret.*, PhD *Lond.* Mineral Industries Prof., Mining Geology

Cartwright, Joseph A., MA *Oxf.*, DPhil *Oxf.* Sr. Lectr.

Cosgrove, John W., BSc *Lond.*, MSc *Lond.*, PhD, FGS Sr. Lectr.

Coward, Michael P., BSc PhD, FGS H.H. Read Prof.

Cronan, David S., PhD DSc, FGS Prof., Marine Geochemistry

Dixon, Colin J., BSc *Lond.*, FGS Sr. Lectr.

Dudeney, A. William L., BSc *Leic.*, BSc *Birm.*, PhD *Birm.* Reader, Process Technology

Durucan, Sevket, BSc *Middle East Tech.*, PhD *Nott.* Reader, Environmental Engineering

Evans, Julian, BSc *Wales*, PhD *Wales* Prof., Tropical Forestry

Farago, Margaret, PhD *Lond.*, FRSChem Reader, Environmental Inorganic Chemistry

Garrard, Paul, BSc *Lond.*, PhD *Lond.*, FGS Sr. Lectr.

Gochin, Rodney J., BSc *Lond.*, PhD *Lond.* Sr. Lectr.

Goddard, Anthony J. H., BSc *Lond.*, PhD *Lond.*, FIP Prof., Environmental Science

Gringarten, Alain C., MSc *Calif.*, PhD *Calif.* Prof., Petroleum Engineering

Halls, Christopher, BSc PhD *Lond.* Sr. Lectr.

Harrison, John P., MSc *Lond.*, PhD *Lond.* Sr. Lectr.

Hatamian, A. Hamid, MSc *Lond.*, PhD *Lond.* Sr. Lectr.

Johnson, Howard D., BSc *Liv.*, DPhil *Oxf.*, FGS Enterprise Oil Prof., Petroleum Geology

Kazantzis, George, MB BS *Lond.*, PhD *Lond.*, FRCS, FRCP Prof.

Kelsall, Geoffrey H., MSc *Manc.*, PhD *S'ton.* Prof., Electrochemical Engineering

Kirkwood, Geoff P., BSc *Melb.*, PhD *NSW* Sr. Lectr., Resource Modelling

Lester, John N., BSc *Brad.*, MSc *Lond.*, PhD *Lond.* Prof.

Macrory, Richard, BA *Oxf.*, MA *Oxf.* Prof.

Monhemius, A. John, BSc *Birm.*, MASc *Br.Col.*, PhD *Lond.* Prof., Mineral and Environmental Engineering

Moore, John McM., BSc, FGS Sr. Lectr.

Mumford, John D., BSc *Purdue*, PhD *Lond.* Reader

Nolan, John, BSc *Manc.*, PhD *Manc.* Sr. Lectr.

Parry, Susan J., PhD *Lond.*, FRSChem Reader, Analytical Chemistry

Pearson, Peter J. G., BA *Keele*, MSc *Lond.*, PhD *Sur.* Reader, Energy and Environmental Geochemistry

Ramsey, Michael H., BSc *Hull*, MSc *Birm.*, PhD *Lond.*, FRS Sr. Lectr.

Rosenbaum, Michael S., BSc PhD, FGS Sr. Lectr.

Shaw, C. Timothy, MSc *McG.* Prof., Mining Engineering

Shaw, Graeme, BSc *Hull*, PhD *Sheff.* Reader, Industrial Ecology

Shaw, Howard F., MSc *Lond.*, PhD *Lond.*, FGS Reader, Sedimentology

Smith, Michael R., BSc *Leeds*, PhD *Leeds* Sr. Lectr.

Terezopoulos, Nicos G., BSc *Lond.*, PhD *Lond.* Sr. Lectr.

Thomas-Betts, Anna, BSc *Madr.*, MA *Madr.*, PhD *Keele* Sr. Lectr.

Thornton, Iain, PhD *Lond.*, DSc *Lond.*, FGS Prof., Environmental Geochemistry

Warner, Michael R., BA *York(UK)*, DPhil *York(UK)* Reader, Geophysics

Woods, John D., CBE, BSc *Lond.*, PhD *Lond.* Prof., Oceanography

Worthington, Michael H., MSc *Durh.*, PhD *ANU* Prof., Geophysics

Vacant Posts: G. H. H. Prof. of Geology; 2 Profs.

Research: evolution of the earth; human intervention in the environment; use of the earth's natural resources

Humanities Programme

Tel: (0171) 594 8751 *Fax*: (0171) 594 8759; (History of Science, Technology and Medicine) (0171) 594 9353

Brinson, Charmian E. J., MA *Lond.*, PhD *Lond.* Reader

Durant, John, MA *Camb.*, PhD *Camb.* Prof., Public Understanding of Science

Gillon, Raanan, BA *Lond.*, MB BS *Lond.*, FRCP Prof., Medical Ethics

Goodlad, J. Sinclair R., MA *Camb.*, PhD *Lond.* Prof.; Dir.*

Russell, Nicholas C., BSc *Exe.*, MSc *Lond.*, PhD *Lond.* Sr. Lectr.

Management School

Tel: (0171) 594 9152 *Fax*: (0171) 823 7685, 823 8134

Barnett, C., BSc *Hull*, PhD Reader, Pure Mathematics

Beasley, John E., MA *Camb.*, MSc *Lond.*, PhD *Lond.* Sr. Lectr.

Betts, Roger J., BA *Keele*, BLitt *Oxf.* Reader, Management Science

Birley, Sue, BSc *Lond.*, PhD *Lond.* Prof.

Christofides, Nicos, BSc *Lond.*, PhD *Lond.* Prof., Operational Research

Clubb, BA *Manc.*, MSc *Lond.*, PhD *Lond.*

Cox, Benita M., MA *S.Af.* Sr. Lectr.

Cuthbertson, K., BSc *Sus.*, PhD *Manc.* Prof.

Driver, Ciaran F., MA *Lanc.*, MSc *Camb.*, PhD *Camb.* Reader

Ferlie, E., BA *Oxf.*, MSc *Oxf.*

Griffiths, Dorothy S., MSc *Bath* Sr. Lectr.

Hall, Stephen, BSc(Econ) *Lond.*, MSc(Econ) *Lond.*, PhD *Lond.* Prof., Economics

Karakitsos, Elias, MSc *Sur.*, PhD *Sur.* Prof., Economics

Meade, Nigel, BSc *Sheff.*, MSc *Sheff.*, PhD *Lond.* Reader, Management Science

Miles, David, BA *Oxf.*, MPhil *Oxf.*, PhD *Lond.* Prof., Finance

Norburn, David, PhD *City(UK)*, BSc Prof.; Dir.*

Salkin, Gerald R., BSc *Lond.*, FCA Reader, Management Science

Shepherd, David, BSc *Hull*, MA *Manc.* Sr. Lectr.

Silberston, Z. Aubrey, CBE, MA Emer. Prof., Economics

Szymanski, Stefan A., BA *Lond.*, MSc *Lond.*, PhD *Lond.* Sr. Lectr.

Tidd, Joseph, BSc *Essex*, MSc *Sus.*, DPhil *Sus.* Sr. Lectr.

Vandermerwe, Sandra, BA *Cape Town*, MBA *Cape Town* Prof.

Vacant Posts: 1 Prof. (Orgnl. Behaviour)

Research: financial management and accounting; innovation, venturing and marketing; operational research and systems; organisational behaviour; strategic management and economics

Materials

Tel: (0171) 594 6733 *Fax*: (0171) 584 3194

Atkinson, Alan, BA *Camb.*, MA *Camb.*, PhD *Leeds*, FIP, FIM Prof., Materials Chemistry

Christodoulou, Leontios, BSc *Lond.*, PhD *Lond.* Reader, Materials Processing and Performance

Flower, Harvey M., MA *Camb.*, PhD *Lond.* Prof., Materials Science

Hench, Larry L., BCerE *Ohio*, PhD *Ohio*, FIP, FIM Prof., Ceramic Materials

Hocking, M. Gwyn, BSc *Lond.*, PhD *Lond.* Reader, Materials Chemistry

Kilner, John A., MSc *Birm.*, PhD *Birm.* Prof., Materials Science

McLean, Malcolm, PhD *Glas.*, FIM Prof.; Head*

McPhail, David S., BSc *Brist.*, PhD *Lond.* Sr. Lectr.

McShane, Henry B., BSc *Lond.*, PhD *Lond.* Sr. Lectr.

Rawlings, Rees D., BSc *Lond.*, PhD *Lond.* Prof., Materials Science

Shollock, Barbara A., BS *Lehigh*, MS *Lehigh*, DPhil *Oxf.* Sr. Lectr.

Staton-Bevan, Anne E., BSc *Lond.*, PhD *Lond.* Sr. Lectr., Physical Metallurgy

Williamson, James, BSc *Nott.*, MSc *Aberd.*, PhD *Aberd.* Reader, Materials Chemistry

Research: biomaterials; cement and concrete; ceramic matrix composites; chemical and electrochemical processing; corrosion and protection

Mathematics

Tel: (0171) 594 8481 *Fax*: (0171) 594 8517

Atkinson, Colin, BSc *Leeds*, PhD *Leeds* Prof., Applied Mathematics

Barnett, Chris, BSc *Hull*, PhD *Hull* Reader, Pure Mathematics (on leave)

Barrett, John W., BSc *S'ton.*, PhD *Reading* Reader, Numerical Analysis

Berkshire, Frank H., MA *Camb.*, PhD *Lond.*, FRMetS Sr. Lectr.

Cash, Jeff R., BSc *Lond.*, PhD *Camb.* Prof., Numerical Analysis

Chen, Yang, BSc *Sing.*, MSc *Ill.*, PhD *Mass.* Reader, Mathematical Physics (on leave)

Coleman, Rodney, BSc *Leeds*, PhD *Camb.* Sr. Lectr.

Edwards, David M., BSc *Lond.*, PhD *Lond.* Prof., Mathematical Physics

Elgin, John N., BSc *H.-W.*, PhD *Camb.* Prof., Applied Mathematics

Fokas, Thanasis S., BSc *Lond.*, MD *Miami(Fla.)*, PhD *Cal.Tech.* Prof.

Gibbon, John D., BSc *Birm.*, PhD *Manc.* Prof., Applied Mathematics (on leave)

Grigoryan, Sasha, PhD *Moscow* Reader, Pure Mathematics

Hall, Philip, BSc *Lond.* Prof.; Chair, Applied Mathematics

Haymen, Walter K., MA ScD, FRS Emer. Prof., Pure Mathematics

Herbert, David M., BSc *Manc.*, PhD *Manc.* Sr. Lectr.

Jacobs, Roy L., BSc *Witw.*, PhD *Camb.* Reader, Mathematical Physics

James, Gordon D., PhD *Camb.* Prof., Pure Mathematics

Jensen, Henrik J., MA *Aarhus*, PhD *Aarhus* Reader, Mathematical Physics

Leppington, Frank G., BSc *Manc.*, PhD *Manc.* Prof., Applied Mathematics

Liebeck, Martin W., MSc *Oxf.*, DPhil *Oxf.* Prof., Pure Mathematics

Lyons, Terry J., BA *Camb.*, DPhil *Oxf.*, FRSEd Prof., Materials

Moore, Dan R., AB *Prin.*, PhD *Camb.* Reader, Numerical Analysis

Moore, Derek W., MA *Camb.*, PhD *Camb.*, FRS Emer. Prof., Applied Mathematics

Moore, Gerald, BSc *Bath*, PhD *Bath* Reader, Numerical Analysis

Parry, Andrew O., BSc *Brist.*, PhD *Brist.* Reader, Statistical Mechanics

Pretzel, Oliver R. L., DrRerNat *F.U.Berlin* Sr. Lectr.

Smith, Adrian F. M., MA *Camb.*, MSc *Lond.*, PhD, FIMA Prof., Statistics; Head*

Stuart, J. Trevor, BSc *Lond.*, PhD *Lond.*, FRS Emer. Prof., Applied Mathematics

Walden, Andrew T., BSc *Wales*, MSc *S'ton.*, PhD *S'ton.* Prof., Statistics (on leave)

Zegarlinski, Boguslaw, MASc *Gliwice*, PhD *Wroclaw* Prof., Pure Mathematics

Research: applied mathematics; mathematical physics; numerical analysis; pure mathematics; statistics

Medicine, Imperial College School of,
see below

Physics

Tel: (0171) 594 7502-3 Fax: (0171) 594 7777

Albrecht, Andreas, PhD *Penn.* Reader

Bacon, Trevor C., BSc *Leeds*, PhD *Leeds* Sr. Lectr.

Balogh, Andre, MSc *Lond.* Prof., Space Physics

Barnham, Keith W. J., BSc *Birm.*, PhD *Birm.* Reader

Bell, Anthony R., MA *Camb.*, PhD *Camb.* Prof., Plasma Physics

Burns, Roy G., BSc *E.Anglia*, PhD *Edin.* Sr. Lectr.

Butterworth, Ian, CBE, BSc *Manc.*, PhD *Manc.*, FRS Emer. Prof.

Caplin, Antony D., MA *Camb.*, MSc *Yale*, PhD *Camb.* Prof., Solid State Physics

Cargill, Peter J., MSc *St.And.*, PhD *St.And.* Reader, Particle Physics

Connerade, Jean-Patrick, BSc *Lond.*, PhD *Lond.* Prof., Atomic and Molecular Physics

Dainty, J. Christopher, MSc *Lond.*, PhD *Lond.* Pilkington Prof., Applied Optics

Damzen, Michael J., BSc *Lond.*, PhD *Lond.* Reader

Dornan, Peter J., BA *Camb.*, PhD *Camb.* Prof., Experimental Particle Physics

Drew, Janet E., BSc *Durh.*, PhD *Lond.*, DPhil *Oxf.* Reader, Astrophysics

Engel, Andrew R., BSc *Lond.*, PhD *Wash.* Sr. Lectr.

Franks, Nicholas P., BSc *Brun.*, PhD *Lond.* Prof., Biophysics

French, Paul M. W., BSc *Lond.*, PhD *Lond.* Reader

Haigh, Joanna D., BA *Oxf.*, MSc *Lond.*, DPhil *Oxf.* Reader

Haines, Malcolm G., BSc *Lond.*, PhD *Lond.* Prof.

Halliwell, Jonathan J., BSc *Brist.*, MSc *Camb.*, PhD *Camb.* Reader

Harries, John E., BSc *Birm.*, PhD *Lond.* Prof., Earth Observation

Isham, Christopher J., BSc *Lond.*, PhD *Lond.* Prof., Theoretical Physics

Jones, Hugh F., BA *Camb.*, PhD *Lond.* Sr. Lectr.

Jones, William G., BSc *Lond.*, PhD *Lond.* Sr. Lectr.

Kibble, Tom W. B., MA *Edin.*, BSc *Edin.*, PhD *Edin.*, FRS Emer. Prof., Theoretical Physics

Knight, Peter L., BSc *Sus.*, DPhil *Sus.* Prof., Quantum Optics

Learner, Richard C. M., CBE, BSc *Lond.*, PhD *Lond.* Sr. Lectr.

Mackinnon, Angus, BSc *H.-W.*, PhD *Lond.* Prof.

Maxwell, Jonathan, MSc *Lond.* Sr. Lectr.

Meikle, W. Peter S., BSc *Glas.*, PhD *Glas.* Reader

Miller, Donald B., BSc *Glas.*, PhD *Glas.* Sr. Lectr.

Morgan, Brian L., BSc *Lond.*, PhD *Lond.* Prof.

New, Geoffrey H. C., MA *Oxf.*, DPhil *Oxf.* Prof., Nonlinear Optics

Parry, Gareth, BSc *Lond.*, PhD *Lond.* Prof., Applied Physics

Pendry, John B., MA *Camb.*, PhD *Camb.*, FRS Prof., Theoretical Solid State Physics; Head*

Phillips, Christopher C., BA *Camb.*, PhD *Lond.* Reader

Quenby, J. John, BSc *Lond.*, PhD *Lond.* Prof.

Rivers, Raymond J., BA *Camb.*, PhD *Lond.* Reader

Rowan-Robinson, Michael, BA *Camb.*, PhD *Lond.* Prof., Astrophysics

Smith, Robin W., BA *Camb.*, PhD *Lond.* Prof., Applied Optics

Southwood, David J., BA *Lond.*, PhD *Lond.* Prof. (on leave)

Speer, Robert J., BSc *Lond.*, PhD *Lond.* Sr. Lectr.

Squire, John M., BSc *Lond.*, PhD *Lond.* Prof., Biophysics

Stelle, Kellogg, PhD *Brandeis* Prof.

Stradling, Richard A., BA *Oxf.*, DPhil *Oxf.*, FIP, FRSEd Prof.

Sumner, Timothy J., BSc *Sus.*, DPhil *Sus.*, FRAS Sr. Lectr.

Thompson, Richard C., DPhil *Oxf.* Reader

Virdee, Tejinder S., BSc *Lond.*, PhD *Lond.* Prof., Physics (on leave)

Vvedensky, Dimitri D., SM *M.I.T.*, PhD *M.I.T.*, BSc Prof., Theoretical Solid State Physics

Websdale, David M., BSc *Lond.*, PhD *Lond.* Prof.

Willi, Oswald, BSc *Innsbruck*, MSc *Oxf.*, DPhil *Oxf.* Prof.

Research: applied optics; astrophysics; biophysics; condensed matter theory; experimental solid state physics

IMPERIAL COLLEGE SCHOOL OF MEDICINE

Hellewell, Paul G., BSc PhD Sr. Lectr., Inflammation Pharmacology

Biomedical Science

Tel: (0171) 594 3798

Allen, A. K., BSc PhD Sr. Lectr.

Archard, L. C., BSc PhD Prof.

Bulawela, L., BSc PhD Sr. Lectr.

Caldwell, John, BPharm *Lond.*, PhD *Lond.*, DSc Prof.; Head*

Canfield, S. Paul, BSc *Lond.*, PhD *Lond.* Sr. Lectr.

Coutelle, Charles, DrMed *Jena*, DrScMed *Humboldt* Prof.

Curtin, Nancy A., PhD *Penn.* Reader

Firth, J. Anthony, MA *Camb.*, PhD *Lond.* Prof.

Hirom, Paul C., BSc *Nott.*, PhD *Lond.* Sr. Lectr.

Jose, Peter J., BSc *Lond.*, PhD *Lond.* Sr. Lectr.

Lab, M. J., BSc *Witw.*, MB BCh *Witw.*, MD PhD Prof.

Lowrie, Margaret B., BSc *Lond.*, PhD *Lond.* Sr. Lectr.

Mason, R. M., MB BCh *Wales*, MD PhD Prof.

Michel, Charles C., BM BCh *Oxf.*, MA *Oxf.*, DPhil *Oxf.* Prof.

Millburn, Peter, BSc *Liv.*, PhD *Lond.* Sr. Lectr.

Nicholson, Jeromy K. Prof.

Rampling, Michael W., BSc *Lond.*, PhD *Lond.* Reader

Seabra, Miguel, MD *Lisbon*, PhD *Texas* Sr. Lectr.

Shirley, D. G., PhD *Sheff.* Sr. Lectr.

Walter, S. J., PhD Sr. Lectr.

Williams, Frances M., BSc *Bath*, PhD *Strath.* Sr. Lectr.

Williams, Timothy, BSc *Lond.*, PhD *Lond.* Prof.

Other Staff: 18 Lectrs.

Investigative Science

Tel: (0181) 383 8419

Abdalla, Saad H., MB BS *Khart.* Sr. Lectr.

Alaghband-Zadeh, J., PhD Reader

Alison, M. R., BSc *CNAA*, PhD *Newcastle(UK)* Reader

Allison, David J., BSc MD, FRCR Prof.

Apperley, Jane F., MB ChB *Birm.*, MD *Birm.* Sr. Lectr.

Arst, Herbert N., AB *Prin.*, PhD *Camb.*, ScD *Camb.* Prof., Microbiology (General)

Bain, Barbara J., MB BS *Qld.*, FRACP Sr. Lectr.

Ball, S. G., MB BS MSc Sr. Lectr.

Bangham, Charles R. M., BM BCh MA PhD Prof.

Bloom, Stephen R., MA *Oxf.*, MB BChir *Camb.*, MD *Camb.*, DSc *Lond.*, FRCP, FRCPath Prof.

Brown, Ivor N., BSc *Brist.*, PhD *Lond.* Sr. Lectr.

Casimir, Colin M., BSc *Lond.*, PhD *Glas.* Sr. Lectr.

Cattell, Victoria, MD *Lond.* Sr. Lectr.

Cohen, Hannah, MD *Manc.* Sr. Lectr.

Cohen, Jonathan, BSc *Lond.*, MB BS *Lond.*, MSc *Lond.*, FRCP Prof.

Coleman, Dulcie V., MD *Lond.* Prof.

Cook, H. Terence, BA *Oxf.*, MB BS *Lond.* Sr. Lectr.

Cosgrove, David O., BA *Oxf.*, BM BCh *Oxf.*, MSc Sr. Lectr.

Cox, Philip M., MB BS *Lond.*, PhD *Lond.* Sr. Lectr.

Cross, Nicholas C. P., BA *Camb.*, PhD *Camb.* Sr. Lectr.

Curati-Alasonatti, Walter, MD *Geneva* Sr. Lectr.

Dawson, Peter, BSc *Lond.*, MB BS *Lond.*, PhD, FRCR Prof.

De Souza, Nandita M., BSc *Newcastle(UK)*, MB BS *Newcastle(UK)* Sr. Lectr.

Dilworth, Stephen, MA *Camb.*, PhD Sr. Lectr.

Epstein, Richard J., MB BS *Syd.*, PhD *Camb.*, FRACP Sr. Lectr.

Evans, David J., MB BChir *Camb.*, MA *Camb.*, FRCPath Prof.

Evans, T. J., BA MB BChir PhD Sr. Lectr.

Farrell, Paul J. Prof.

Firmin, David, BSc MPhil PhD Reader, Physics of Cardiovascular Magnetic Resonance

Flanagan, Adrienne M., MB ChB *Leic.*, PhD *Lond.* Sr. Lectr.

Foadi, Minou D. Sr. Lectr.

Francis, N. D., MB BS Sr. Lectr.

Friedland, J. S., MA *Lond.*, MB BS *Lond.*, PhD Sr. Lectr.

Ghatei, Mohammad, BSc *Pahlavi*, MSc *Pahlavi*, PhD *Lond.* Sr. Lectr.

Girgis, Samia I., MB BS *Assiut*, PhD Sr. Lectr.

Goldin, Robert D., MB ChB *Z'bwe.*, MD *Z'bwe.* Sr. Lectr.

Goldman, John M., DM *Oxf.* Prof., Leukaemia Biology and Therapy

Gordon, Myrtle Y. A., DSc *Liv.*, FRCPath Prof.

Gotch, Frances, DPhil *Oxf.* Prof.

Hasserjian, Robert P., BS MD Sr. Lectr.

Henry, Diana K., MB BS, FRCPath Prof.

Holden, D. W., BSc *Durh.*, PhD Prof., Microbiology

Ison, Catherine A., MSc *Lond.*, PhD *Lond.* Sr. Lectr.

Jackson, James E., MB BS *Lond.*, FRCR Sr. Lectr.

Kanfer, Edward J., MB BS Sr. Lectr.

Karim, Q. Najma, MB BS *Dhaka* Sr. Lectr.

Krausz, Tomas, MD *Budapest* Prof.

Laffan, Michael A., BA *Oxf.*, BM BCh *Oxf.* Sr. Lectr.

Lalani, El-Nasir M. A., BSc *Dund.*, PhD *Lond.*, MB ChB Sr. Lectr.

Lane, D. A., BA *Essex*, PhD Prof.

Larsson-Solard, Eva-Lotte, BSc DMedSci Sr. Lectr.
Lortan, Jennifer E., MB ChB Natal, PhD Birm. Sr. Lectr.
Maitland, Jennifer, MB BS Sr. Lectr.
Mason, Philip J., BSc Edin., PhD Edin. Sr. Lectr.
Meeran, Mohammed K., BSc Lond., MB BS Lond. Sr. Lectr.
Moss, Jill, PhD Sr. Lectr.
Muller, Ingrid Sr. Lectr.
O'Shea, Donal B., MB BCh BAO N.U.I. Sr. Lectr.
Paradinas, F. J., LMS Madrid Sr. Lectr.
Pennell, Dudley, BA MB BChir MA MD Sr. Lectr.
Pereira, Raul S., MB BChir Camb., PhD, FRCPath Sr. Lectr.
Peters, A. M., MD Liv., BSc Prof., Nuclear Medicine
Pignatelli, Massimo N., MD Bologna, PhD Reader
Pillay, Tahir S., MB ChB Durban-W., PhD Camb. Sr. Lectr.
Polak, Julia M., MD DSc Prof., Endocrine Pathology
Reavely, D. A. Sr. Lectr.
Roberts, A. P., BSc PhD Sr. Lectr.
Roberts, Irene A. G., MD Glas., FRCP Sr. Lectr.
Rogers, T. R. F., MSc, FRCPath, FRCPI Prof.
Samson, Diana M., MB BS MD Sr. Lectr.
Shaunak, S., BSc MB BS Sr. Lectr.
Shousha, M. S. M., MD Cairo Sr. Lectr.
Skacel, Patricia O., BSc Lond., MB BS Lond., PhD Lond. Sr. Lectr.
Smith, David M., BSc Brist., PhD Sr. Lectr.
Stamp, Gordon H. W., MB ChB Liv. Prof.
Strickland, Nicola H., BA Oxf., BM BCh Oxf., FRCR Sr. Lectr.
Swirsky, David M., MB BS, FRCP Sr. Lectr.
Taylor-Robinson, David, MB ChB Liv., MD Liv., FRCPath Prof.
Townsley-Hughes, David, BSc Wales, PhD Wales Sr. Lectr.
Underwood, Stephen R., BM BCh Oxf., MA Oxf. Prof., Cardiac Imaging
Vaz de Melo, Junia, MD Minas Gerais, PhD Sr. Lectr.
Walker, Marjorie M., BMedSci Nott., BM BS Nott. Sr. Lectr.
Ward, Katherine N., BSc Camb., MB BChir Camb., PhD Sr. Lectr.
Watson, Roger J. Sr. Lectr.
Wharton, John, BSc Sur., PhD Sr. Lectr.
Wickramasinghe, S. N., MB BS Ceyl., PhD Camb., ScD Camb., FRCPath, FIBiol Prof.
Wigglesworth, Jonathan S., MA Camb., MD Camb., FRCPath Prof.†, Perinatal Pathology
Williamson, John D., BSc Liv., PhD Liv. Sr. Lectr.
Wright, D. J. M., MD Reader
Wright, Nick A. Prof.
Young, Douglas B., BSc Edin., DPhil Oxf. Prof.
Other Staff: 17 Lectrs.; 1 Reader†; 2 Sr. Lectrs.†; 5 Lectrs.†

Medicine

Tel: (0181) 383 2363

Boobis, Alan R., BSc Glas., PhD Glas. Prof., Biochemical Pharmacology
Bower, Mark, MB BChir Camb., MA Camb., PhD Lond. Sr. Lectr.
Bulpitt, Christopher J., MSc Lond., MD Lond., MB BS, FRCP Prof., Geriatric Medicine
Calam, John, BSc Liv., MD Liv. Reader, Gastroenterology
Chu, Anthony C., BSc MB BS Sr. Lectr.
Clutterbuck, Elaine J., BSc Leeds, MB ChB Leeds, PhD Brun. Sr. Lectr.
Coombes, R. C. D. S., MD PhD, FRCP Prof.
Davies, Donald S., BSc Wales, PhD Prof.
Davies, K. A. A., BA Camb., MB BS Sr. Lectr.
Easterbrook, Phillipa J., MB BChir Camb. Sr. Lectr.
Fairney, Angela, MD Lond., FRCP Sr. Lectr.
Feher, M. D., MB BS Sr. Lectr.
Feldmann, M., MB BS PhD, FRCPath Prof.

Foster, Graham R., MB BS Lond., PhD Lond. Sr. Lectr.
Gaskin, Gillian, MB BChir Camb., MA Sr. Lectr.
George, Andrew J. T., BA Camb., PhD S'ton. Sr. Lectr.
Godsland, Ian F., BA Oxf., PhD Lond. Sr. Lectr.
Gooderham, Nigel, BSc Liv., PhD Sr. Lectr.
Gray, David, BSc Birm., MSc Birm., PhD Birm. Reader
Hawkins, Philip N., MB BS Lond. Sr. Lectr.
Hodgson, Humphrey J. F., MA Oxf., DM Oxf., FRCP Prof., Gastroenterology
Johnston, Desmond G., MB ChB Edin., PhD S'ton. Prof.
Karayiannis, Peter Sr. Lectr.
Kitchen, Valerie S., MB ChB Leic. Sr. Lectr.
Lacey, Charles J. Sr. Lectr.
Lechler, Robert I., MB ChB Manc., PhD Prof.
Lightstone, Elizabeth B., MB BS Lond., MA Lond., PhD Lond. Sr. Lectr.
Livesley, B., MB ChB Leeds, MD, FRCP Prof.
Lombardi, Giovanna, BSc Rome, PhD Rome Sr. Lectr.
MacDermot, John, MSc Lond., MD Lond., PhD Lond. Prof.
Main, Janice, MB ChB Dund. Sr. Lectr.
Maini, R. N., BA Camb., MB BChir Camb., FRCP Prof.†
McCarthy, Mark, MB BChir Sr. Lectr.
McClure, Myra O., BSc PhD Sr. Lectr.
Miskelly, F. G., MB BCh BAO Belf., MSc Edin. Sr. Lectr.
Monjardino, Joao P. Prof.
Morgan, D. J. R., MB BS Sr. Lectr.
Morley, Bernard J., BSc Liv., DPhil Oxf. Sr. Lectr.
Newlands, E. S., BA Oxf., BM BCh Oxf., PhD Prof.
Nicholl, Claire G., BSc Lond., MB BS Lond. Sr. Lectr.
Nunez, Derek J. R., BA Camb., MB BS Sr. Lectr.
Pasvol, Geoffrey, MB ChB Cape Town, MA Oxf., DPhil Cape Town, FRCP Prof.
Pelly, M., MSc MB BS Sr. Lectr.
Pepys, Mark B., MA MD PhD, FRCP Prof., Immunology Medicine
Price, Patricia M., MA Camb., MB BS, FRCR Reader
Pusey, Charles D., MA Camb., MB BChir Camb. Prof.
Reed, Michael J., MSc PhD Prof.
Reiser, Hans, MD Heidel., PhD Prof.
Ritter, Mary A., MA Oxf., DPhil Oxf. Prof.
Saklatvala, Jeremy, MB BS Lond. Prof., Experimental Pathology
Saunders, Brian P., MB BS Lond., MD Lond. Sr. Lectr.
Sekl, M. J., MB BS Lond. Sr. Lectr.
Sikora, Karol, MB BChir Camb., MA Camb., PhD Camb., FRCR Prof.
Stauss, Hans G., MD Chic., DMSc Chic., PhD Chic. Sr. Lectr.
Stevenson, John C., MB BS Lond., FRCP Sr. Lectr.
Summerfield, John A., MD Lond., FRCP Prof.
Taylor, Graham W., BA Oxf., PhD Sr. Lectr.
Taylor, Peter C., BM BCh Oxf., PhD Sr. Lectr.
Taylor-Robinson, David, MB ChB Liv., MD Liv., FRCPath Prof.
Thomas, Howard C., BSc Newcastle(UK), MB BS Newcastle(UK), PhD Glas., FRCP Prof.
Thursz, Mark R. Sr. Lectr.
Venables, P. J. W., MB BChir Camb., MA Camb., MD Reader
Walport, Mark J., MA Camb., MB BChir Camb., PhD Camb., FRCP Prof.
Walters, Julian R. F., MA Camb., MB BChir Camb. Sr. Lectr.
Warrens, Anthony N., BSc Glas., BM BCh Oxf. Sr. Lectr.
Wasan, Harpreet S., MB BS Lond. Sr. Lectr.
Waxman, Jonathan N., BSc Lond., MB BS Reader, Oncology
Weber, Jonathan N., BA Camb., MB BChir Camb. Prof.
Wilkins, Martin R., MD Birm. Sr. Lectr.

Williams, Graham R., BSc Lond., MB BS Lond., PhD Birm. Sr. Lectr.
Wright, Geraldine M., BSc MB BS Sr. Lectr.
Other Staff: 20 Lectrs.; 3 Sr. Lectrs.†; 1 Lectr.†

National Heart and Lung Institute

Tel: (0171) 351 8190

Adams, L., BSc PhD Reader
Alton, Eric, BA Camb., MB BS Lond., MD Lond. Reader, Thoracic Medicine
Amrani, Mohamed, PhD Lond., MD Sr. Lectr.
Anderson, Robert H., BSc Manc., MD Manc. BHF Prof., Paediatric Cardiac Morphology
Bagger, Jens P., MD Aarhus, DrSci Sr. Lectr.
Barnes, Peter J., MA Camb., BM BCh Oxf., DM Oxf. Prof., Thoracic Medicine
Barton, Paul J. R., BSc PhD Reader, Molecular Biology
Bush, Andrew, BA CNAA, MB BS Lond., MD Camb. Reader, Paediatric Respirology
Child, Anne H. Sr. Lectr.
Chung, Kian F., MB BS Lond., MD Lond., FRCP Prof., Respiratory Medicine
Clague, Jonathan R., BSc MB BS MD Sr. Lectr.
Coats, Andrew J., MA MB BChir, FRACP Prof., Clinical Cardiology
Cole, Peter, MB BS Lond., BSc Lond., FRCP Prof., Respiratory Medicine
Collins, Peter, MB BChir Camb., MA Camb. Sr. Lectr.
Corrigan, Christopher J., MSc Oxf., MB BS PhD Sr. Lectr.
Corrin, Brian, MD, FRCPath Prof., Thoracic Pathology
Cullinan, Timothy P., MB BS Lond., MD Lond., MSc McG. Sr. Lectr.
Cummin, Andrew R. Sr. Lectr.
Davies, Graham J., MD Brist. Sr. Lectr.
Dunn, Michael J., BSc PhD Reader
Durham, Stephen R., MA Camb., MB BChir Camb., MD Camb. Reader
Evans, Timothy W., BSc MB ChB PhD Prof.†, Intensive Care Medicine
Gardiner, Helena, MB BCh Wales, MD Brist. Sr. Lectr.
Gibbs, John S., BA Cant., MB BChir Camb., MD Camb., MA Sr. Lectr.
Gorchein, Abel, MB ChB Glas., PhD, FRCPEd Sr. Lectr.
Grange, John M., MD MSc Reader
Hall, Roger J. C., BA Camb., MB BChir Camb., MD Camb. Prof., Cardiology
Hansel, Trevor, BSc Liv., MB BCh Wales, MSc Birm., PhD Lond. Sr. Lectr.
Harding, Sian E., BSc PhD Sr. Lectr.
Haskard, Dorian O., MA Oxf., DM Oxf. Prof., Rheumatology; Chair*
Haslam, Patricia L., BSc PhD Sr. Lectr.
Ho, Siew Y., BSc PhD Sr. Lectr.
Hodson, Margaret E., MSc MD Prof., Respiratory Medicine
Hughes, Alun D., BSc Lond., MB BS Lond., PhD Lond. Sr. Lectr.
Ind, Philip W., BA CNAA, MA CNAA, MB BChir, FRCP Sr. Lectr.
Jeffery, Peter K., MSc PhD Reader, Experimental Pathology
Kay, A. Barry, PhD, FRCPEd Prof., Clinical Immunology
Knight, Richard A., MB BS BSc PhD Sr. Lectr.
Kooner, Jaspal S., MB BS Sr. Lectr.
Lab, M. J., BSc Witw., MB BCh Witw., MD PhD Prof.
Lefroy, David C., BA Camb., MB BChir MA Sr. Lectr.
Macleod, Kenneth, BSc PhD Sr. Lectr.
Marston, Steven B., BA Oxf. Prof.
Newman Taylor, A. J., OBE, MB BS MSc, FRCP Prof.
Nihoyannopoulos, Petros, MD Athens Sr. Lectr.
Noble, M. I. M., MB BS PhD DSc Prof.
Nourshargh, Sussan, BSc Lond., PhD Lond. Sr. Lectr.
Pepper, John, MA MChir, FRCS Reader
Peters, Nicholas S., MD Lond. Sr. Lectr.
Poole-Wilson, Philip, BA MB BChir MD Prof.

Poulter, Neil R., MB BS Lond., MSc Lond., FRCP   Sr. Lectr.

Ratnatunga, Claudana P., BSc Lond., MB BS Lond., FRCS   Sr. Lectr.

Robinson, Douglas, BA MB BChir MD   Sr. Lectr.

Rogers, Duncan F., BSc PhD   Sr. Lectr.

Rose, Marlene L., MSc PhD   Reader

Rosen, Stuart D., BA Camb., MB BS Lond., MA Camb., MD Lond.   Sr. Lectr.

Schachter, Michael   Sr. Lectr.

Scott, James, MB BS MSc, FRCP   Prof.

Seed, W. A., BM BCh Oxf., MA Oxf., PhD, FRCP   Prof.

Sever, Peter S., MB BChir Camb., MA Camb., PhD Lond., FRCP   Prof.

Severs, Nicholas J., BSc PhD   Prof.

Shaw, Rory J. S., BSc Lond., MD Lond.   Sr. Lectr.

Sheridan, D. J., BA Trinity(Dub.), MB BCh BAO Trinity(Dub.), MD Trinity(Dub.), PhD Newcastle(UK), FRCP   Prof.

Smith, Peter L. C., MB BS, FRCS   Sr. Lectr.

Sugden, Peter H., MA Oxf., DPhil Oxf.   Reader

Tetley, Teresa D., BSc PhD   Sr. Lectr.

Thom, Simon A. M., MB BS Lond., MD Lond.   Sr. Lectr.

Venables, Katherine M., MB BS MSc, FRCP   Sr. Lectr.

Williams, Alan J., BSc PhD   Prof.

Wilson, Robert, MB BChir Camb., MA Camb., MD Camb.   Sr. Lectr.

Wood, David A., MB ChB MSc   Prof.

Yacoub, Magdi H., KBE, FRCS   BHF Prof., Cardiothoracic Surgery

Other Staff: 22 Lectrs.; 6 Sr. Lectrs.†; 1 Lectr.†

Neuroscience and Psychological Medicine

Tel: (0181) 846 7276

Barnes, T. R. E., MB BS   Prof.

Bench, C., MB BS   Sr. Lectr.

Blane, D. B.   Sr. Lectr.

Brooks, D. J., BA Oxf., DPhil Oxf., MD   Hartnett Prof., Clinical Neurology

Brooks, David, MB BS MD DPhil, FRCP   Prof.

Buckingham, Julia C., PhD DSc   Prof.; Head*

Catalan, J., LMS Valencia, MSc Oxf.   Reader

Collinge, John, BSc Brist., MD Lond., BA   Prof.

Croucher, Martin J.   Sr. Lectr.

de Belleroche, Jaqueline S., BA MSc PhD   Prof.

Eagger, Sarah A., MB BS   Sr. Lectr.

Ellaway, P. H., PhD   Prof.

Evans, Kevin, BSc Lond., MB BS MD, FRCS   Sr. Lectr.

Fielder, Alistair R., MB BS Lond., FRCS, FRCP   Prof.

Garey, L. J., BM BCh Oxf., MA Oxf., DPhil Oxf.   Prof.

Garralda Hualde, M. Elena, MD Navarra, MPhil Lond., FRCPsych   Prof., Child and Adolescent Psychiatry

Gillies, Glenda, PhD   Reader

Glickman, S., MB BS, FRCS   Sr. Lectr.

Grasby, P. M., BSc Lond., MB BS Lond., MD Lond.   Sr. Lectr.

Gruzelier, J., MA Auck., PhD Auck.   Prof., Psychology

Hawke, Simon   Sr. Lectr.

Hirsch, S. R., BA Amherst, MD Johns H., MPhil, FRCPsych   Prof.

Hodes, Matthew, MB BS Lond., MSc Lond.   Sr. Lectr.

Jen, L. S., PhD   Sr. Lectr.

Jenkins, Leuan   Sr. Lectr.

Joyce, Elizabeth M., MB BS   Sr. Lectr.

Kennard, C., BSc MB BS PhD, FRCP   Prof.

Legg, N. J., MB BS, FRCP   Sr. Lectr.

Maier, M., MB BS DPhil   Sr. Lectr.

Mathias, Christopher J., MB BS B'lore., DPhil Oxf., FRCP   Prof.

Moseley, Merrick J., PhD   Sr. Lectr.

Navarette, Roberto   Sr. Lectr.

Reynolds, Richard, BSc PhD   Sr. Lectr.

Sensky, T. E., BSc MB BS PhD   Reader

Shah, Ajit K.   Sr. Lectr.

Steiner, T. J., BSc MB BS PhD   Sr. Lectr.

Tyrer, Peter J., BA Camb., MB BChir Camb., MD, FRCPsych   Prof.

Watt, Diana J., BSc Aberd., PhD Aberd.   Reader

Wells, D. J., PhD Lond.   Sr. Lectr.

Other Staff: 31 Lectrs.; 1 Reader†; 3 Sr. Lectrs.†

Paediatrics, Obstetrics and Gynaecology

Tel: (0181) 383 1862

Azzopardi, Denis V., MD Malta   Sr. Lectr.

Barltrop, D., BSc MD, FRCP   Prof.

Bennett, Phillip R., BSc Lond., MB BS Lond., MD Lond., PhD Lond.   Prof.

Brueton, M. J., MSc MD, FRCP   Reader

Byrne, Micheline, MB ChB BAO   Sr. Lectr.

Edwards, Anthony D., MA Oxf., MB BS   Prof.

El-Refaey, Hazem, MB BCh Cairo, MD Aberd.   Sr. Lectr.

Elder, Murdoch G., MB ChB Edin., MD Edin., DSc, FRCS, FRCOG   Prof.

Fisk, Nicholas M., MB BS Syd., PhD   Prof.

Franks, Stephen, MD Lond.   Prof.

Fusi, Luca, MD Rome   Sr. Lectr.

Gardiner, Helena M., MB BCh Wales, MD Brist.   Sr. Lectr.

Goldmeier, David, MD Lond.   Sr. Lectr.

Habibi, Parviz, MB ChB Birm., BSc Aston, PhD Birm.   Sr. Lectr.

Halliday, David, BSc PhD   Prof.

Harris, J. William R., MB BCh BAO Belf., FRCP   Prof.

Harvey, David R., MB BS, FRCP   Prof.

Higham, Jennifer M., MB BS MD   Sr. Lectr.

Johnson, M. R., MB BS PhD   Sr. Lectr.

Johnson, Pamela V., MB BS Lond., MD Lond.   Sr. Lectr.

Knight, Stella C., BSc PhD, FIBiol   Prof.

Kroll, J. Simon, BM BCh Oxf., MA Oxf.   Prof.

Levin, Michael, MB BCh Witw., FRCP   Prof.

Margara, Raul A., MD Buenos Aires   Sr. Lectr.

Markiewicz, M., BSc MB BS   Sr. Lectr.

McManus, I. Christopher, BA Birm., MB ChB Birm., PhD Camb., MD   Prof.

Modi, Neena, MB ChB Edin.   Sr. Lectr.

Moore, Gudrun E., BA York(UK), PhD Hull   Sr. Lectr.

Muntoni, Francesco, MD Cagliari   Reader

Rees, Richard G., MB BS Wales   Prof.

Regan, Lesley, MD Lond.   Prof.

Rivers, Rodney P. A., MB BChir Camb., MA Camb., FRCP   Reader

Rossor, Martin N., MA Camb., MD Lond., FRCP   Sr. Lectr.

Seitert, Martin H., MB BS Lond., FRCP   Sr. Lectr.

Soutter, William P., MD ChB Glas., MSc Glas., FRCOG   Reader

Stanier, Phillip M., BSc Brist., PhD Lond.   Sr. Lectr.

Steer, P. J., BSc MB BS MD   Prof.

Thomas, David J., MA Camb., MD Birm., FRCP   Sr. Lectr.

Tolley, Neil S., MD Wales, FRCS, FRCSEd   Sr. Lectr.

Tudor-Williams, T. Gareth, MB BS Lond.   Sr. Lectr.

Walters, M. D. Samuel, MB BChir Camb., MA Camb.   Sr. Lectr.

White, John, BSc Portsmouth, MSc Lond., PhD Lond.   Sr. Lectr.

Winston of Hammersmith, Lord, MB BS Lond., FRCOG   Prof., Fertility Studies

Other Staff: 24 Lectrs.; 1 Reader†; 4 Sr. Lectrs.†

Primary Care and Population Health Sciences

Tel: (0171) 594 3375

Aylin, Paul, MB ChB   Sr. Lectr.

Beck, Eduard J.   Sr. Lectr.

Berlin, Anne, MB BS Newcastle(UK)   Sr. Lectr. (on leave)

Bosanquet, Nicholas, BA Camb., MA Yale, MSc Lond.   Prof.

Boulton, Mary G., BA Tor., PhD Tor.   Sr. Lectr.

Dickenson, Donna L., BA MSc PhD   Sr. Lectr.

Elliott, Paul, MB BS Lond., MA Camb., MSc Lond., PhD Lond.   Prof.

Farmer, R. D. T., PhD Ley., MB BS   Prof.; Head*

Freeman, G. K., MB BChir Camb., MA Camb., FRCGP   Prof.

Hooper, Shirley A.   Sr. Lectr.

Hurwitz, Brian, BA Camb., MD Lond., MA Lond.   Sr. Lectr.

Jacobs, Leonard   Sr. Lectr.

Jarman, Brian, OBE, MB BS Lond., MA Camb., PhD Lond., FRCGP   Prof.; Head*

Jarup, Lars, MSc Lond., MD Stockholm, PhD Stockholm   Sr. Lectr.

Jarvelin, Marso-Riitta, MScD Oslo, MSc Lond.   Sr. Lectr.

Joffe, Michael, MA Camb., MSc Lond., MD Lond., FRCP   Reader

Kessling, Anna M., BMSc Dund., MB ChB Dund., PhD Lond.   Prof.

Lausen, Berthold, PhD   Sr. Lectr.

MacRae, K. D., MA PhD   Reader, Medical Statistics

Renton, Adrian M., MB BS MSc   Sr. Lectr.

Royston, John P., BA Essex, MSc Warw.   Prof., Medical Statistics

Stimson, G. V., PhD   Prof., Sociology

Thompson, Simon G., MA   Prof., Medical Statistics and Epidemdiology

Wakefield, Jonathan C.   Sr. Lectr.

Ward, Helen, MB ChB Sheff., MSc Lond.   Sr. Lectr.

Other Staff: 19 Lectrs.; 5 Sr. Lectrs.†; 6 Lectrs.†

Surgery and Anaesthesia

Tel: (0181) 746 8303

Abel, Paul D., ChM Liv., FRCS   Reader

Allen-Mersh, T. G., BSc St And., MB ChB Dund., MD Dund., FRCS   Reader

Crowhurst, John, MB BS, FFARACS, FANZCA   Reader

Davies, Alun H., MB BS, FRCS   Sr. Lectr.

Forester, A. J., MB ChB Leic., BSc, FRCS   Sr. Lectr.

Greenhalgh, R. M., MB BChir Camb., MA Camb., MChir Camb., FRCS   Prof.

Habib, Nagy A., MB BCh Ain Shams, ChB Brist., FRCS   Sr. Lectr.

Harris, David N. F., MD Brist., FFARCS   Sr. Lectr.

Henry, John A., MB BS, FRCP   Prof.

Holdcroft, Anita, MD Sheff., FFARCS   Reader

Hughes, Sean, MS, FRCS   Prof.†, Orthopaedic Surgery

Jones, Ronald M., MD Liv., MB ChB, FRCA   Prof.

Lakhoo, Kokilakumari, MB Natal, PhD Witw., FRCSEd, FCS(SA)   Sr. Lectr.

Lockwood, G. G., BSc MB BS, FFARCS   Sr. Lectr.

Mansfield, Averil O., ChM Liv., FRCSEd, FRCS   Prof.

Massoud, Tarik, MB BCh BAO Trinity(Dub.)   Sr. Lectr.

Mathie, Robert T., BSc Glas., PhD Glas.   Sr. Lectr.

McCarthy, Ian D., BSc Brist., PhD Leeds   Sr. Lectr.

Morgan, M., MB BS, FFARCS   Reader, Anaesthesia Practice

Nanchahal, Jaydeep, MB BS, FRCS   Sr. Lectr.

Newton, Douglas E. F., MB BS Lond., FRCA   Sr. Lectr.

Nicolaides, Andrew N., MB BS Lond., FRCSEd, FRCS   Prof.

Palazzo, M., MB ChB Brist.   Sr. Lectr.

Pearse, Michael, MB ChB Leic., FRCP   Sr. Lectr.

Powell, Janet T., MD PhD   Prof., Surgery

Rice, Andrew S. C., MD Lond., FRCA   Sr. Lectr.

Robotham, James, BA MD   Prof.

Sellu, David, MB ChB Manc., ChM Manc., FRCS   Sr. Lectr.

Soni, N. C., MB ChB Brist., FFARCS   Sr. Lectr.

Spencer, J., MB BS MS, FRCS   Reader

Stansby, Gerald P., MB BChir Camb., MChir Camb., MA Camb., FRCS   Sr. Lectr.

Thomas, Rhidian   Sr. Lectr.

Thompson, Albert E., MB BS Lond., MS, FRCS   Sr. Lectr.

Williamson, Robin C. N., MA *Camb.*, MB BChir
Camb., MD *Camb.*, MChir *Camb.*, FRCS   Prof.
Moxham, John, BSc MB BS MD, FRCP   Sr.
Lectr.
O'Connor, Brian J., MB BCh BAO   Sr. Lectr.
Other Staff: 4 Lectrs.; 5 Sr. Lectrs.†

SPECIAL CENTRES, ETC

Computing Services, Centre for
Tel: (0171) 594 6901 Fax: (0171) 594 6958
Hynds, Robert J., BSc *Lond.*, PhD *Lond.*   Prof.;
Head*

History of Science, Medicine and Technology Group
Tel: (0171) 594 6351
Edgerton, David E., BA *Oxf.*, PhD
Lond.   Reader, History of Technology

Planning and Resource Control, Centre for (IC-PARC)
Richards, E. Barry, BA *Notre Dame(Ind.)*, PhD
Camb.   Prof., Computing Science; Head*

Semiconductor Materials, Interdisciplinary Research Centre for
Tel: (0171) 594 6666 Fax: (0171) 581 3817
Joyce, Bruce A., DSc *Birm.*, FIP   Prof.
Newman, Ronald C., BSc *Birm.*, BSc *Lond.*, PhD
Lond., FIP   Prof.

CONTACT OFFICERS

Academic affairs. Academic Registrar:
McClure, F. Vernon, BA *Lond.*
Accommodation. Brown, Sharine
Admissions (first degree). Atkins, David, BSc
Lond.
Admissions (higher degree). Atkins, David,
BSc *Lond.*
Adult/continuing education. Jones, Mervyn,
BSc *Lond.*, MSc *Lond.*, PhD *Lond.*
Alumni. Acting Head of Development: Oakley,
Clive
Archives. Barrett, Anne, BA *Middx.*, MA *Lond.*
Careers. Simpson, John, BSc(Eng) *Lond.*
Computing services. Hynds, Prof. Robert, BSc
Lond., PhD *Lond.*
Conferences/corporate hospitality. Foster,
John
Consultancy services. Docx, Paul, BA *Keele*,
MSc(Econ) *Lond.*
Development/fund-raising. Acting Head of
Development: Oakley, Clive
Equal opportunities. Employee Relations
Manager: Payne, John
Estates and buildings/works and services.
Director of Estates: Caldwell, Ian, BSc *Strath.*,
BArch *Strath.*
Examinations. Oldroyd, Soosan J., BSc *S'ton.*
Finance. Director of Finance: Hansen, Mike,
BA *Stir.*
Health services. Weinreb, Irene R., MB BS
Lond.
Industrial liaison. Wakeham, William A., BSc
Exe., PhD *Exe.*, FIEE, FIChemE, FIP
International office. Director, International
Office: Seller, Tim J., BSc *Lond.*, PhD *Lond.*

Language training for international students.
Co-ordinator, English Language Support
Programme: Hughes, John M., MA
Library (chief librarian). Director of Library
and Audio-Visual Services: Czigany, Magda
M., BA *Lond.*
Minorities/disadvantaged groups. Disabilities
Officer: O'Callaghan, Loretto
Personnel/human resources. Senior Personnel
Manager: Kimberley, Marion, BSc *Lond.*, MSc
Brun., PhD *Lond.*
Public relations, information and marketing.
Head of Press, Public Relations and
Publications: Davies, Lynda W., BA *E.Anglia*
Publications. Daniel, Saskia K., BA *Sus.*
Purchasing. Purchasing Manager: Greaves, Ian
B.
Research. Chadwick, Linda
Safety. Safety Director: Gillett, Ian, BSc *Lond.*
Scholarships, awards, loans. Atkins, David,
BSc *Lond.*
Schools liaison. Thody, Melanie A.
Security. Reynolds, Keith
Sport and recreation. Sports Centre Manager:
Murray, Frank, MBA *Brad.*
Staff development and training. Everitt, Kim,
BA *Warw.*
Student union. Hurford, Mandy
Student welfare/counselling. Thomson,
Martin
Students from other countries. Director,
International Office: Seller, Tim J., BSc *Lond.*,
PhD *Lond.*
Students with disabilities. Disabilities Officer:
O'Callaghan, Loretto

[Information supplied by the institution as at 31 March
1998, and edited by the ACU]

INSTITUTE OF EDUCATION

Founded 1902; incorporated as a constituent School of the University of London in 1987

Associate Member of the Association of Commonwealth Universities

Postal Address: 20 Bedford Way, London, England WC1H 0AL
Telephone: (0171) 580 1122 **Fax**: (0171) 612 6126 **Cables**: Institute of Education, London WC1
WWW: http://www.ioe.ac.uk/ **E-mail formula**: initial.surname@ioe.ac.uk

COUNCIL CHAIRMAN—Whitmore, Sir Clive, GCB, CVO, BA *Camb.*
DIRECTOR*—Mortimore, Prof. Peter J., OBE, BSc *Lond.*, MSc *Lond.*, PhD *Lond.*, Hon. DLitt
H-W, FBPsS
SECRETARY‡—Warren, D. J., BSc

GENERAL INFORMATION

History. The institute was founded in 1902
as the London Day Training College under the
control of London County Council. In 1932 it
came under control of the University of
London and took the title of University of
London Institute of Education. In 1987 the
institute became a separate school of the
university.

First Degrees (of University of London)
(see also University of London Directory to
Subjects of Study). BEd (for serving teachers):
normally 2 years full-time or 3 years part-
time.

Higher Degrees (of University of London)
(see also University of London Directory to
Subjects of Study). MA, MSc, MPhil, PhD, EdD.

Applicants for admission to courses should
hold a first degree with second class honours,
or equivalent qualification, and (for most
courses) relevant professional experience.
MPhil, PhD: first degree with second class
honours and either a teaching qualification or
2 years' relevant experience. EdD: good
master's degree plus 4 years' relevant
experience. Applicants whose native language
is not English must produce evidence of
proficiency in English.

Language of Instruction. English. A twelve-
week pre-sessional course is available during
summer vacation for those applicants whose
English does not meet normal entry
requirements.

Libraries. 300,000 volumes; 900 periodicals
subscribed to.

Fees (international students). MSc in
educational psychology (1997–98):
£14,000–15,000; all other courses:
£6500–7500.

Academic Year (1998–99). Three terms: 29
September–11 December; 11 January–19
March; 26 April–2 July.

Income (1996–97). Total, £23,614,139.

Statistics. Staff: 333 (256 academic, 77
administrative). Students: full-time 1663 (531
men, 1132 women); part-time 2695 (754
men, 1941 women); international 673 (204
men, 469 women); total 4358.

FACULTIES/SCHOOLS

Initial Teacher Education Programme Area

Tel: (0171) 612 6094 Fax: (0171) 612 6090

Dean of Initial Teacher Education:
MacGilchrist, Barbara A., BEd Lond., MA Lond., PhD Lond.
Secretary: Porch, Sarah

New Initiatives Programme Area

Tel: (0171) 612 6099 Fax: (0171) 612 6090

Dean of New Initiatives: Griffiths, Toni, BA Lond.
Secretary: ......

Professional Development Programme Area

Tel: (0171) 612 6092 Fax: (0171) 612 6090

Dean of Professional Development: Barnett, Prof. Ronald A., BA Durh., PhD Lond.
Secretary: Levingston, Nicole

Research Programme Area

Tel: (0171) 612 6033 Fax: (0171) 612 6090

Dean: Gipps, Prof. Caroline V., BSc Brist., MSc Lond., PhD Lond.
Secretary: Myronidis, Kate

ACADEMIC UNITS

Art and Design Education

Tel: (0171) 612 6192 Fax: (0171) 612 6202

Prentice, R. A., BEd MA Sr. Lectr.; Head*
Other Staff: 2 Lectrs.; 2 Lectrs.†; 1 Temp. Lectr.
Vacant Posts: 1 Lectr.
Research: contemporary art and artists in education; museums and galleries in education; nature of research in art and design; resource-based learning; teacher education and art and design

Assessment, Guidance and Effective Learning

Tel: (0171) 612 6156 Fax: (0171) 612 6157

Barber, Michael B., BA Oxf., MA Lond. Prof. (On leave)
Gipps, Caroline V., BSc Brist., MSc Lond., PhD Lond. Prof.
Stoll, Louise A., BSc Leic., PhD Lond. Sr. Lectr.
Watkins, Chris, BTech Brun. Sr. Lectr.; Head*
Other Staff: 1 Sr. Lectr.†; 4 Lectrs.†; 3 Temp. Lectrs.
Research: assessment at school and national level; personal and classroom learning; school effectiveness; use of outcome information in evaluating performance

Child Development and Learning

Tel: (0171) 612 6588 Fax: (0171) 612 6230

Cowan, Richard C. J., BA Oxf., PhD Lanc. Sr. Lectr.
Nunes, Terezinha, BS Minas Gerais, MA C.U.N.Y., PhD C.U.N.Y. Prof., Child Development; Head*
Sirag-Blatchford, Iram, BEd Herts., MA Essex, PhD Warw. Sr. Lectr.
Other Staff: 1 Lectr.; 1 Temp. Lectr.
Vacant Posts: 2 Sr. Lectrs.
Research: children's emotional and behavioural problems; developmental psychology; early childhood education and care; foundations for school learning

Culture, Communication and Societies

Tel: (0171) 612 6495 Fax: (0171) 612 6177

Buckingham, David D., BA Camb., MA CNAA Reader
Cowen, Robert, BSc(Econ) Lond., MA Lond., PhD Lond. Sr. Lectr.
Epstein, Deborah A., BA Sus., PhD Birm. Sr. Lectr.
Ferguson, Robert J. Sr. Lectr.
Gundara, Jagdish, BA Bowdoin, MA McG., PhD Edin. Reader

Jones, Crispin R. M., MA Camb., MA Lond. Sr. Lectr.
Kress, Gunther, BA Newcastle(NSW), DLitt Newcastle(NSW) Prof.; Head*
Leonard, Diana M., MA Camb., PhD Wales Reader
Reid, Evan C., MA Glas., MA Essex, MLitt Edin. Sr. Lectr.
Other Staff: 4 Lectrs.; 2 Lectrs.†
Research: cultural diversity and hybridity; ethnicity; forms and processes of representation and communication; gender; power in its various social forms

Curriculum Studies

Tel: (0171) 612 6313 Fax: (0171) 612 6330

Klenowski, Val, BA W.Aust., BEd W.Aust., MEd W.Aust., PhD Lond. Sr. Lectr.
Lawton, D., BA PhD Prof.†
Walsh, P. D., BA N.U.I., MA Sr. Lectr.; Head*
Other Staff: 1 Lectr.; 4 Sr. Lectrs.†; 4 Lectrs.†; 1 Temp. Lectr.
Research: children's thinking in history; curriculum policy and implementation; programme, policy and school level evaluation; religious education and church schools; school culture and ethos

Drama, see Music and Drama

Education and International Development

Tel: (0171) 612 6628 Fax: (0171) 612 6632

Carr-Hill, Roy A., BA Camb., MCrim Calif., DPhil Oxf. Visiting Prof.†, Education in Developing Countries
Little, Angela, BSc Sur., DPhil Sus. Prof., Education in Developing Countries; Head*
Other Staff: 1 Lectr.; 1 Lectr.†; 1 Temp. Lectr.
Research: methods of policy analysis, planning and evaluation; relations between learning and health

Education, Environment and Economy

Tel: (0171) 612 6436 Fax: (0171) 612 6450

Graves, Norman J., BSc(Econ) Lond., MA Lond., PhD Lond. Emer. Prof.
Kent, W. A., MA Camb. Sr. Lectr., Geography Education; Head*
Lambert, D. M., BA Newcastle(UK) Sr. Lectr., Geography Education
Other Staff: 1 Lectr.; 3 Lectrs.†; 1 Temp Lectr.
Research: curriculum development; values and environmental education; values in business and economics education

English

Tel: (0171) 612 6568 Fax: (0171) 612 6717

Burgess, A. M. K., BA Camb., PhD Reader, English; Head*
Other Staff: 1 Lectr.; 2 Lectrs.†; 1 Temp. Lectr.
Research: gender; multi-lingualism; reading; writing

Geography, see Educn., Environment and Economy

History and Philosophy

Tel: (0171) 612 6543 Fax: (0171) 612 6555

Aldrich, R. E., MA Camb., MPhil PhD Prof., History of Education
Gordon, Peter, BSc(Econ) Lond., MSc(Econ) Lond., PhD Lond. Emer. Prof.
White, J. P., BA Oxf., BA Lond. Prof., Philosophy; Head*
Other Staff: 2 Lectrs.
Research: history of education; philosophy of education

Languages in Education

Tel: (0171) 612 6531 Fax: (0171) 612 6534

Cook, G. W. D., MA Camb., MA Lond., PhD Leeds Reader; Head*
Widdowson, H. G., MA Camb., PhD Edin. Prof.†
Other Staff: 7 Lectrs.; 4 Lectrs.†
Research: applied linguistics; modern foreign language teaching; TESOL

Mathematical Sciences

Tel: (0171) 612 6653 Fax: (0171) 612 6686

Goldstein, H., BSc Manc. Prof., Statistical Methods
Hoyles, Celia M., BSc Manc., MEd PhD Prof., Mathematics Education; Head*
Noss, R. L., BSc Sus., MPhil Sus., PhD Prof., Mathematics Education
Wolf, Alison M., BA Oxf., MPhil Oxf. Prof.
Other Staff: 3 Lectrs.; 1 Sr. Lectr.†; 1 Lectr.†
Research: international assessment; mathematics education; multilevel modelling of statistical data

Music and Drama

Tel: (0171) 612 6740 Fax: (0171) 612 6741

Plummeridge, C. T., MA PhD Sr. Lectr.
Swanwick, K., MEd Leic., PhD Leic. Prof.; Head*
Other Staff: 1 Lectr.; 3 Lectrs.†
Research: curriculum evaluation and student assessment; gender and music education; musical development of children; music curriculum structure and content; psychology of music

Policy Studies

Tel: (0171) 612 6368 Fax: (0171) 612 6366

Barnett, Ronald A., BA Durh., PhD Lond. Prof., Higher Education Policy Studies
Bernstein, Basil B., BSc(Econ) Lond., PhD Lond., Hon. DLitt Leic., Hon. FilHDr Lund, Hon. DUniv Open(UK) Emer. Prof.
Earley, Peter, BA Kent, MA Essex Sr. Lectr.
Gillborn, D., BA Nott., PhD Nott. Reader, Sociology of Education
Green, A. D., BA Oxf., MA Birm., PhD Reader
Mace, J. D., BA Leic., MA Sr. Lectr., Economics of Education
Power, Sally A. R., BEd Brist., PhD Brist. Sr. Lectr.
Whitty, G. J., BA Camb., MA Karl Mannheim Prof., Sociology of Education
Williams, G. L., MA Camb. Prof., Educational Administration; Head*
Young, M. F. D., BA Camb., MA Essex, BSc PhD Sr. Lectr.
Other Staff: 4 Lectrs.; 1 Sr. Lectr.†; 6 Lectrs.†; 1 Temp. Lectr.
Research: policy and management issues in education; related areas of social policy

Primary Education

Tel: (0171) 612 6608 Fax: (0171) 612 6230

Riley, Jeni L., MA Lond., PhD Lond. Sr. Lectr.; Head*
Rowland, Timothy, BSc S'ton., MSc S'ton., PhD Open(UK) Sr. Lectr.
Other Staff: 2 Lectrs.; 9 Lectrs.†; 2 Temp. Lectrs.
Vacant Posts: 1 Sr. Lectr.; 1 Lectr.†
Research: effective teaching of literacy, mathematics and science

Psychology and Special Needs

Tel: (0171) 612 6265 Fax: (0171) 612 6304

Blatchford, P. J., BSc Sur., PhD Sur. Reader, Educational Psychology
Corbett, Jenny D., BA Open(UK), PhD Open(UK) Sr. Lectr.
Francis, Hazel, MA Camb., MA Leeds, PhD Leeds Emer. Prof., Educational Psychology
Henderson, Sheila E., BA Guelph, MA Wat., PhD Wat. Reader, Child Development
Ireson, Judith M., BSc Brist., PhD Sur. Sr. Lectr., Educational Psychology
Lunt, Ingrid C., BA Oxf., MSc Lond., PhD Lond. Reader, Educational Psychology
Norwich, B., MA Camb., MSc Brist., PhD Prof., Children with Special Needs; Head*
Stuart, K. Morag, BA Lond., BSc Lond., PhD Lond. Sr. Lectr.
Wedell, K. W., MA Camb., PhD Brist. Emer. Prof., Children with Special Needs
Other Staff: 2 Lectrs.; 1 Lectr.†

Research: curriculum access and differentiation; development of word recognition strategies; effects of class size differences in schools

Science and Technology

Tel: (0171) 612 6777 *Fax*: (0171) 612 6792

Frost, Jennifer, BSc *Manc.* Sr. Lectr., Integrated Science

Mellar, Harvey G., BA *Oxf.*, PhD *Lond.* Sr. Lectr.

Turner, Sheila A., BSc Sr. Lectr., Biology Science; Head*

Other Staff: 1 Lectr.; 1 Sr. Lectr.†; 1 Lectr.†; 1 Temp. Lectr.

Research: conceptions of technological literacy; explanation and reasoning in science; professional training of engineers

Social Science Research Unit

Tel: (0171) 612 6391 *Fax*: (0171) 612 6400

Mayall, M. Berry, BA *Camb.*, MSc *Lond.*, PhD *Lond.* Reader

Oakley, Ann, MA PhD Prof.; Head*

Research: civil rights in schools; evaluation of interventions; lay involvement in health research; prenatal screening services in Europe; sociology of childhood

Special Needs, see Psychol. and Spec. Needs

Statistics, see Mathl. Scis.

Thomas Coram Research Unit

Tel: (0171) 612 6957 *Fax*: (0171) 612 6927

Aggleton, Peter J., BA *Oxf.*, MEd *Aberd.*, MA *Oxf.*, PhD *Lond.* Prof.; Dir.*

Brannen, Julia, BA *Manc.*, MSc *Sur.*, PhD Reader

Smith, Marjorie, BSc *Sus.*, PhD Reader

St. James-Roberts, I., BA *Newcastle(UK)*, PhD *Newcastle(UK)* Sr. Lectr.

Research: development of children and young people; family life and employment; health-related issues

CONTACT OFFICERS

Accommodation. Student Welfare and Accomodation Officer: Cifuentes, Bernadette, BA *Chile*, MSc *Lond.*

Admissions (first degree). Academic Registrar: Loughran, Loreto G., BA *Brist.*, PhD *Brist.*

Admissions (higher degree). Academic Registrar: Loughran, Loreto G., BA *Brist.*, PhD *Brist.*

Alumni. Executive Officer: Rajagopalan, Rajee, BSc *Madr.*

Computing services. Director, Institute Computing Service: Pateman, Joan G., BSc *McG.*

Conferences/corporate hospitality. Head of External Relations and Conferences: Bird, Catherine I., BA *Durh.*, MPhil *Durh.*

Consultancy services. Dean of New Initiatives: Griffiths, Toni, BA *Lond.*

Credit transfer. Dean of Professional Development: Barnett, Prof. Ronald A., BA *Durh.*, PhD *Lond.*

Distance education. Flavell, Roger H., MA *Camb.*, MA *Manc.*, DU *Paris*

Equal opportunities. Dean of Initial Teacher Education: MacGilchrist, Barbara A., BEd *Lond.*, MA *Lond.*, PhD *Lond.*

Estates and buildings/works and services. Head of Building Services: Crane, David M.

Examinations. Examinations Officer: Rees, Yvonne, BSc *Lond.*, PhD *Lond.*

Finance. Finance Officer: McDonald, Marcus G., BSc *Leic.*

General enquiries. Secretary: Warren, D. J., BSc

International office. Head of International Development Unit: Breakell, John, BA *Lond.*, MSc *Lond.*

Language training for international students. Scott, Mary, BEd *Cape Town*

Library (chief librarian). Librarian: Peters, Anne, BA *Mich.State*

Personnel/human resources. Personnel Officer: Wood, Susan M., BA *Camb.*

Public relations, information and marketing. Head of External Relations and Conferences: Bird, Catherine I., BA *Durh.*, MPhil *Durh.*

Public relations, information and marketing. Press Officer: ......

Publications. Publications Officer: Spring, Deborah C. A., BA *Camb.*

Purchasing. Head, Purchasing Stores and Postal Services: Bush, Christopher N., BSc *Leeds*, MSc *Birm.*

Quality assurance and accreditation. Dean of Professional Development: Barnett, Prof. Ronald A., BA *Durh.*, PhD *Lond.*

Research. Research Administrator (Deputy Finance Officer): Palfreyman, Lucy, MSc *Lond.*

Safety. Safety Officer: Waldron, Thomas, BSc *N.U.I.*

Security. Head of Domestic Services: Easer-Thomas, Edward W. T.

Staff development and training. Staff Development Facilitator for Non-Teaching Staff: Thomas, Patricia

Student union. Permanent Secretary, Students Union: Donaghy, Rita M., BA *Durh.*

Student welfare/counselling. Student Welfare and Accommodation Officer: Cifuentes, Bernadette, BA *Chile*, MSc *Lond.*

[*Information supplied by the institution as at 4 March 1998, and edited by the ACU*]

KING'S COLLEGE LONDON

Founded 1829

Associate Member of the Association of Commonwealth Universities

Postal Address: Cornwall House, Waterloo Road, London, England SE1 8WA

Telephone: (0171) 836 5454 **Fax**: (0171) 836 1799 **Cables**: King's College, London **WWW**: http://www.kcl.ac.uk

CHAIRMAN OF THE COUNCIL—Spooner, Sir James, MA *Oxf.*, FCA, FKC
PRINCIPAL*—Lucas, Prof. Arthur M., BSc *Melb.*, BEd *Melb.*, PhD *Ohio State*, FIBiol, FKC, FACE
VICE-PRINCIPAL—Ife, Prof. Barry W., BA *Lond.*, PhD *Lond.*, FKC
DEAN—Burridge, Rev. R. A., MA *Oxf.*, PhD *Nott.*
COLLEGE SECRETARY‡—Slade, W. C., BSc *Wales*, FKC
DEPUTY COLLEGE SECRETARY (PLANNING AND RESOURCES)—Ball, D. O., FCA, FKC
ACADEMIC REGISTRAR—Salter, Brian E., BSc *Leeds*, FKC
DIRECTOR OF INFORMATION SERVICES AND SYSTEMS—Law, D. G., MA *Glas.*, FLA, FKC
DIRECTOR OF LIBRARY SERVICES—Bell, Anne, BA MA
DIRECTOR OF COMPUTING SERVICES—Byerley, Andrew J., BSc *S'ton.*, PhD *S'ton.*

GENERAL INFORMATION

History. The college, one of the two founding college of the University of London, was established in 1829 by King George IV and the Duke of Wellington. The college merged with Queen Elizabeth College and Chelsea College in 1985, the Institute of Psychiatry in 1997 and United Medical and Dental Schools of Guy's and St Thomas's (UMDS) in 1998.

Admission to first degree courses (see also United Kingdom Introduction). Through Universities and Colleges Admissions Service (UCAS).

First Degrees (of University of London) (see also University of London Directory to Subjects of Study). BA, BDS, BEng, BMus, BSc, LLB, MB BS, MEng, MSci.

All courses are full-time and usually last 3 years. MSci, MEng (1 year abroad): 4 years; MB BS, BDS: 5–6 years.

Higher Degrees (of University of London) (see also University of London Directory to Subjects of Study). LLM, MA, MMus, MSc, MPhil, PhD.

Applicants for research degrees should normally hold at least an upper second class honours degree. Taught master's degrees: a first degree from a recognised university. Equivalent qualifications are considered.

Language of Instruction. English. English language courses available.

Libraries. 800,000 volumes; 3500 journals subscribed to; over 60 networked CD-ROM titles.

Fees (1998–99). Undergraduate/postgraduate international students: £7500–8000 (arts); £9300–10,000 (sciences); £17,300–18,000 (clinical medicine and dentistry).

Academic Year (1998–99). 28 September–18 December; 11 January–31 March; 26 April–4 June.

Income (1996–97). Total, £168,874,000.

Statistics. Staff: 3517. Students: undergraduate 10,696; postgraduate 3419; total 14,115.

FACULTIES/SCHOOLS

Education, School of

Head: Wiliam, Dylan, BSc Durh., BA Open(UK), MSc Lond., PhD Lond.

Humanities, School of

Head: Newson, Prof. Linda A., BA PhD

Law, School of

Head: Morse, Prof. C., MA Oxf., BCL Oxf.

Life, Basic, Medical and Health Sciences, School of

Head: Hider, Prof. Robert, BSc Lond., PhD Lond., FRSChem, FKC

Medicine and Dentistry, School of

Head: Eddleston, Prof. Adrian A. W. F., DM, FRCP, FKC

Physical Sciences and Engineering, School of

Head: Bushnell, Prof. Colin, BSc PhD

Psychiatry, Institute of

Tel: (0171) 703 5411

Dean: Checkley, Prof. Stuart, BM, FRCP, FRCPsych

ACADEMIC UNITS

Anatomy, see under Biomed. Scis., Div. of

Biomedical Sciences, Division of

Tel: (0171) 333 4230 Fax: (0171) 333 4008
Howell, S., PhD DSc   Prof.; Head of Div.*

Anatomy Group

Tel: (0171) 873 2484 Fax: (0171) 873 2285
Berkovitz, B. K., PhD Lond., BDS MSc   Reader
Fraser, L. R., BA Colorado, MPhil Yale, PhD Yale   Prof.
Gordon-Weeks, P. R., PhD Lond., BSc   Reader
Jones, G. E., BSc Lond., PhD Glas.   Prof.
Maden, M., BSc Birm., PhD Birm.   Prof.
Mahadevan, L., BSc Lond., MSc Lond., PhD Lond.   Reader
Stolkin, C., BM BCh Oxf., MA Oxf.   Sr. Lectr.
Webster, K. E., BSc MB BS PhD   Prof.; Head*

Molecular Biology and Biophysics Group

Tel: (0171) 873 2484, 836 5454 Fax: (0171) 873 2285, 497 9078
Brown, P. R., PhD Lond., BSc   Sr. Lectr.
Cannon, M., MA Camb., MSc Manc., PhD Manc., ScD Camb.   Reader; Head*
Dudley, R. K., MA Camb., PhD Camb.
Eagles, P. A. M., BSc Sheff., DPhil Oxf.   Sr. Lectr.
Gould, H. J., MA Harv., PhD Harv.   Prof.
Hipkiss, A. R., BScTech Manc., PhD Manc.   Sr. Lectr.
Irving, M., MA Camb., MSc Lond., PhD Lond.   Reader
Patient, R. K., BSc Exe., PhD Birm.   Prof.
Simmons, R., MSc Lond., PhD Lond., FRS, FKC   Prof.
Sutton, B. J., MA Oxf., DPhil Oxf.   Reader

MRC Muscle and Cell Motility Unit

Tel: (0171) 836 8851 Fax: (0171) 497 9078
No staff at present

Pharmacology Group

Tel: (0171) 333 4739 Fax: (0171) 333 4739
Brain, S. D., PhD Lond., BSc MA   Reader
Curtis, M. J., BSc Lond., PhD Col.   Reader
Gibson, A., BSc Glas., PhD Glas.   Dean of Sch.
Haliwell, B., DPhil Oxf., DSc Lond.   Prof.
Hart, S. L., PhD Lond.   Sr. Lectr.
Hoult, J. R. S., BA Camb., PhD Camb.   Reader
Jenner, P. G., DSc Lond., BPharm PhD, FRPharmS   Prof.; Head*
Littleton, J. M., BSc MB BS PhD   Prof.
Moore, P. K., PhD Lond., BSc   Reader
Page, C., PhD Lond., BSc   Prof.
Tucker, J. F., PhD Lond., BSc   Sr. Lectr.

Physiology Group

Tel: (0171) 333 4230, 873 2475 Fax: (0171) 333 4008, 873 2286
Abbot, N. J., MA Camb., PhD Camb.   Reader
Begley, D. J., BSc Nott., PhD Nott.   Sr. Lectr.
Howell, S. L., DSc Lond., PhD, FKC   Prof.; Head of Div.*
Knight, D. E., MSc PhD Lond.   Reader
Mann, G. E., BSc George Washington, PhD Lond.   Prof.
McNaughton, P. A., BSc Auck., MA Camb., DPhil Oxf.   Prof.
Milligan, S. R., MA Oxf., DPhil Oxf.   Sr. Lectr.
Naftalin, R. J., MB ChB Glas., DSc Glas., PhD   Prof.
Robins, M. W., PhD Lond., BSc   Sr. Lectr.
Rowlands, S. D., PhD Lond., BSc   Sr. Lectr.
Simons, T. J. B., MA Camb., PhD Camb.   Sr. Lectr.
Smith, I., BSc Sus., MSc Lond., PhD Lond.   Sr. Lectr.
Tonge, D. A., BSc S'ton., MPhil Sus., PhD Lond.   Sr. Lectr.

Physiotherapy Group

Tel: (0171) 333 4030 Fax: (0171) 333 4032
Hilton, R., MSc Sur.   Sr. Lectr.
Newham, D., PhD Lond., MPhil   Prof.; Head*

Brazilian Studies, see Portuguese and Brazilian Studies

Byzantine and Modern Greek Studies

Tel: (0171) 873 2088 Fax: (0171) 873 2830
Beaton, R. McL., MA Camb., PhD Camb.   Koraes Prof., Modern Greek and Byzantine History, Language and Literature; Head*
Herrin, J., BA MA PhD   Prof.
Rouché, C. M., MA Camb.   Reader, Byzantine Language and Literature

Chemistry

Tel: (0171) 873 2810 Fax: (0171) 873 2810
Fielding, H., BA MA PhD   Reader
Green, N. J., DPhil Oxf., MA   Reader
Hall, C. D., PhD Lond., DSc Lond., FRSChem   Reader
Hibbert, F., PhD Lond., DSc Lond.   Prof.; Head*
Hughes, M. N., BSc Wales, PhD Wales, DSc Lond., FRSChem   Prof.
Malcolme-Lawes, D. J., PhD Lond., DSc Lond., FRSC   Reader
Nicholas, J., BSc Lond., PhD Camb.   Sr. Lectr.
Reese, C. B., MA Camb., PhD Camb., DSc, FRS FKC FRSC   Daniell Prof.
Rigby, M., MA Oxf., DPhil Oxf.   Sr. Lectr.
Robb, M. A., MSc Tor., PhD Tor., DSc   Prof.
Robinson, S. D., PhD Leeds, DSc Lond., FRSChem FRSC   Reader

Classics

Tel: (0171) 873 2343 Fax: (0171) 873 2545
Arafat, K., MA Oxf., DPhil Oxf.   Reader
Ganz, D., BA DPhil   Prof.
Herrin, J., BA MA PhD   Prof.
Mayer, R. G. M., BA Calif., MA Camb., PhD Camb.   Prof.

Rathbone, D. W., MA Camb., PhD Camb.   Reader
Rouché, C., MA Camb.   Reader
Schiesaro, A., MA Calif., PhD Pisa   Prof.
Silk, M. S., MA Camb., PhD Camb.   Prof.; Head*
Vessey, D., MA Camb., PhD Camb., FRHistS, FSA   Reader
Waywell, G. B., MA Camb., PhD Camb., FSA   Prof., Classical Archaeology

Computer Science

Tel: (0171) 873 2588 Fax: (0171) 873 2851
Gabbay, D., BSc MSc PhD   Prof.
Iliopoulos, C., BSc Athens, MSc Warw., PhD Warw.   Reader
Ohlbach, H., PhD Lond.   Sr. Lectr.
Overill, R., BSc Leic., PhD Leic., FIMA   Sr. Lectr.
Poulovassius, A., MA Camb., MSc Lond., PhD Lond.   Sr. Lectr.
Winder, R., BSc PhD   Prof.; Acting Head*

Construction Law and Management, Centre for

Tel: (0171) 873 2685 Fax: (0171) 872 0210
Uff, J. F., QC, BSc PhD, FICE, FEng   Prof.; Dir.*

Dentistry, see below

Education

Tel: (0171) 872 3167 Fax: (0171) 872 3182
Adey, Philip, BSc Lond., PhD Lond.   Reader
Ball, Stephen J., BA Essex, MA Sus., DPhil Sus.   Prof.
Brown, Margaret L., MA Camb., PhD Lond., FKC   Prof.
Cox, Margaret J., BSc Lond., PhD Lond.   Sr. Lectr.
Cribb, Alan, BA S'ton., PhD Manc.   Sr. Lectr.
Head, John O., BSc Nott., MA Sus., PhD   Sr. Lectr.
Holland, R., BA MSc   Sr. Lectr.
Johnson, David C., BA Colgate, PhD Minn., FIMA   Shell Prof., Mathematics Education
May, J., BSc Lond., MPhil Lond.   Sr. Lectr.
Osborne, J., BSc Brist., MSc Lond., PhD Lond.   Sr. Lectr.
Squires, David J., BSc Lond., PhD Lond.   Sr. Lectr.
Street, Brian V., DPhil Oxf., BA   Prof.
Walker, Andrew G., BA Hull, MSc Salf., PhD Lond.   Sr. Lectr.
Watson, Deryn M., MA Camb.   Sr. Lectr.
Wiliam, Dylan, BSc Durh., BA Open(UK), MSc Lond., PhD Lond.   Sr. Lectr.; Head*

Engineering, Division of

Yianneskis, M., BScTech Manc., PhD Lond., MSc, FIEE   Prof.; Head of Div.*

Engineering, Electronic and Electrical

Tel: (0171) 873 2369 Fax: (0171) 873 5071
Aghvami, H., BSc Teheran, PhD Lond., MSc, FIEE   Prof.
Clarkson, T., BSc Lond., PhD Lond.   Prof.
Davies, A. C., BSc S'ton., MPhil Lond., PhD City(UK), FIEE   Prof.
Hall, T. J., MA Camb., PhD Lond.   Prof.
Rezazadeh, A. H., BSc Teheran, DPhil Sus.   Reader
Robertson, I. D., BSc Lond., PhD Lond.   Reader
Rogers, A. J., MA Camb., PhD Lond., FIP, FIEE   Prof., Electronics
Sandler, M. B., BSc Essex, PhD Essex   Prof.; Head*
Swanson, J. G., BSc(Eng) Lond., PhD Lond.   Prof.
Turner, C. W., PhD Stan., BSc, FEng, FIEE   William Siemens Prof., Electrical Engineering

Engineering, Mechanical

Tel: (0171) 873 2437 Fax: (0171) 873 2437
Borrett, N. A., PhD Lond., BSc   Lectr.; Head*
Seneviratne, L., BSc Lond., PhD Lond.   Reader

Yianneskis, M., BScTech Manc., PhD Lond., MSc, FIMechE   Prof.

English Language and Literature

Tel: (0171) 873 2146 Fax: (0171) 873 2257
Bush, C. W., PhD Lond., MPhil   Prof.; Head*
Cowen, J., BA Birm., MA Birm.   Sr. Lectr.
Ganz, D., BA DPhil   Prof.
Myerson, G., BA Camb., PhD Camb.   Reader
Nokes, D. L., MA Camb., PhD Camb., FRSL   Reader
Ormond, L., BA Oxf., MA Birm.   Reader
Porter, J. C., BA Brist., MPhil Lond.   Sr. Lectr.
Rees, J., MA Edin., BLitt Oxf.   Sr. Lectr.
Roberts, J. A., MA Trinity(Dub.), MLitt Trinity(Dub.), DPhil Oxf.   Prof.
Saunders, M., BA Camb., AM Harv., PhD Camb.   Reader
Stokes, J., BA Reading, PhD Reading   Prof.
Woolford, J., MA Camb.   Reader

English Language Teaching Centre

Tel: (0171) 333 4075 Fax: (0171) 333 4066
Thorne, A., BA Kent   Dir.*

French, see also Lang. and Communicn. Centre

Tel: (0171) 873 2404 Fax: (0171) 873 2720
Clarke, D. R., MA Camb., PhD Camb.   Sr. Lectr.
Griffiths, R., MA Camb., MA Oxf., DPhil Oxf., PhD Camb., FKC   Prof.; Head*
Heath, M. J., MA Exe., PhD Wales   Prof.

Geography

In conjunction with staff of London School of Economics
Tel: (0171) 873 2612 Fax: (0171) 873 2287
Frost, M., BA Lond., MSc Lond., PhD Lond.   Sr. Lectr.
Hamnett, C., BSc   Prof.
Hoggart, K., MSc Salf., PhD Lond.   Sr. Lectr.; Head*
Newson, L. A., BA PhD Lond.   Prof.
Thornes, J., MSc McG., PhD   Prof.

German

Tel: (0171) 873 2124 Fax: (0171) 873 2089
Adler, J. D., PhD   Prof.; Head*
Jones, M., MA Oxf.   Sr. Lectr.
White, J. J., BA Leic., MA Alta., PhD Lond.   Prof.
Yeandle, A., MA Camb., PhD Camb.   Reader

Gerontology, see under Health Scis., Div. of

Greek, Modern, see Byzantine and Mod. Greek Studies

Health Sciences, Division of

Geissler, C., BDS Edin., MS Calif., PhD Calif.   Prof.; Head of Div.*

Gerontology, Age Concern Institute of

Tel: (0171) 872 3035 Fax: (0171) 872 3235
Askham, J., BA Lond., PhD Aberd.   Prof.
Tinker, A., BCom Birm., PhD City(UK)   Prof.; Dir.*

Nutrition and Dietetics

Tel: (0171) 333 4268 Fax: (0171) 333 4185
Emery, P. W., MA Camb., MSc Lond., PhD Lond.   Sr. Lectr.
Geissler, C., BDS Edin., MS Calif., PhD Calif.   Prof.
Judd, P. A., MSc Lond., PhD Lond.   Sr. Lectr.
Leeds, A. R., MSc Lond., MB BS   Sr. Lectr.
Nelson, M., BSc Montr., MSc Lond., PhD   Sr. Lectr.
Sanders, T. A., BSc Lond., PhD Lond., DSc Lond.   Prof.; Head*

Pharmacy

Tel: (0171) 333 4830 Fax: (0171) 351 5307
Barlow, D., BSc Lond., MSc Lond., PhD Lond.   Sr. Lectr.
Drake, A. F., MSc E.Anglia, PhD E.Anglia   Sr. Lectr.

Greene, R., BPharm Nott., MSc Bath, PhD Lond.   Sr. Lectr.
Hider, Robert, BSc Lond., PhD Lond., FRSChem   Prof.
Houghton, P. J., BPharm Lond., PhD Lond., FRPharms   Sr. Lectr.
Lawrence, M., BSc CNAA, PhD Manc.   Sr. Lectr.
Marriott, C., PhD CNAA, DSc CNAA, FRPharmS, FRSChem   Prof.; Head*
Martin, G., BPharm Nott., PhD Nott.   Reader
Theobald, A. E. E., BPharm Lond., PhD Lond., FRPharmS   Sr. Lectr.
Timbrell, J., BSc PhD DSc, FRSChem   Prof.

History

Tel: (0171) 873 1078 Fax: (0171) 836 1799
Carpenter, D., MA Oxf., DPhil Oxf., FRHistS   Reader
Duggan, A. J., PhD Lond., BA, FRHistS   Sr. Lectr.
Nelson, J. L., MA Camb., PhD Camb., FRHistS, FBA   Prof.
Overy, R. J., MA Camb., PhD Camb.   Prof.
Porter, A. N., MA Camb., PhD Camb., FRHistS   Rhodes Prof.
Roseveare, H. G., MA Camb., PhD Camb., FRHistS   Prof.
Russell, C. S., MA Oxf., FRHistS, FBA, FKC   Prof.
Webb, D., BA Lond., PhD Lond.   Dir., Combined Studies

Language and Communication Centre

Tel: (0171) 873 2485 Fax: (0171) 240 0035
Davies, V. L., BA Leic., PhD   Dir.*

Laws, see also Construcn. Law and Management, Centre for

Fax: (0171) 873 2465
Blackburn, R. W., BA Leeds, PhD Leeds, MSc, FRHistS   Reader
Eeckhout, P., Lic Ghent, PhD Ghent   Prof.
Ewing, K. D., LLB Edin., PhD Camb.   Prof., Public Law
Fortin, J. E. S., LLB Lond.   Sr. Lectr.
Gardner, J., BA Oxf., BCL Oxf., DPhil Oxf.   Reader
Gearty, C., LLB Camb., PhD Camb., BCL   Prof.
Glover, J., BA BPhil   Prof.
Guest, A. G., CBE, QC, MA Oxf., FBA   Emer. Prof., English Law
Hayton, D. J., MA Camb., LLB Newcastle(UK), LLD Newcastle(UK)   Prof.
Hughes, A. D., BCL Oxf., MA Oxf.   Sr. Lectr.
Kennedy, Ian McC., LLB Lond., LLM Calif., LLD Lond.   Prof., Medical Law and Ethics
Kerse, C. R., LLB Hull   Visiting Prof.
Kirafly, A. K., LLB Lond., LLM Lond., PhD Lond.   Emer. Prof.
Lomnicka, E. Z., LLB Camb., MA Camb.   Prof.
Martin, J. E., LLB Lond., LLM Lond., LLD Lond.   Prof.
Morse, C., MA Oxf., BCL Oxf.   Prof.; Head*
Mullerson, R., LLD Moscow   Prof.
Norrie, A., LLB MA PhD   Prof.
Phillips, J. C., BA Camb., MA Camb., LLM Camb., PhD Camb.   Prof., English Law
Player, E., BSc   Reader
Price, J. W., MA Oxf., BCL Oxf.   Sr. Lectr.
Whish, R., BA Oxf., BCL Oxf.   Prof.

Life Sciences, Division of

Fax: (0171) 333 4500
Bailey, R. G., BSc Nott., PhD Exe.   Sr. Lectr.
Bainbridge, B. W., BSc Manc., PhD Sheff.   Sr. Lectr.
Butterworth, P. J., PhD Lond., MSc   Sr. Lectr.
Cammack, R., MA Camb., PhD Camb.   Prof.
Ebringer, A. M. A., BSc Melb., MB BS Melb., MD Melb., FRACP, FRCP   Prof.
Emson, R. H., BSc Wales, PhD Wales   Sr. Lectr.
Gahan, P. B., PhD Lond., FIBiol   Prof.
Hall, D. O., BSc Natal, MS Calif., PhD Calif.   Prof.
Heale, J. B., BSc Exe., PhD Wales   Reader
Miles, R., PhD Lond., BSc   Sr. Lectr.
Moore, P. D., BSc Wales, PhD Wales   Reader
Price, R. G., PhD Wales, DSc Wales   Prof.

Quinn, P. J., BAgrSc Melb., MSc Syd., PhD Syd., DSc Lond.   Prof.
Ross-Murphy, S. B., BSc Manc., PhD Essex   Prof.
Sales, G. D., BSc PhD Lond.   Sr. Lectr.
Staines, N. A., BSc Edin., PhD Edin.   Prof.
Stirling, J. L., PhD Lond., BSc   Sr. Lectr.
Thurston, C. F., BSc PhD   Prof.
Turner, B., BSc Lond., PhD Leeds   Sr. Lectr.
Whitfield, P. J., MA Camb., PhD Camb.   Prof.; Head*
Williams, W. Patrick, BSc Nott., PhD Nott.   Sr. Lectr.
Williams, W. Peter, BSc Leic., PhD Reading   Sr. Lectr.
Wrigglesworth, J. M., MSc Birm., PhD Birm., DSc Lond.   Reader

Management Centre

Tel: (0171) 333 4254 Fax: (0171) 333 4254
Clark, T. A. B., BA Leic., PhD De Mont.   Reader
Gospel, H., BA Oxf., PhD Lond.   Prof.
Grant, D., BA Essex, PhD Lond.   Lectr.; Head*
Heath, C., BA MA PhD   Prof.
Keenoy, T., BSc Glas., DPhil Oxf.   Reader
Mark, J., MA Camb., MSc Lond.
Oswick, C., MSc   Sr. Lectr.
Strange, R. N., BSc Birm., BCom Birm., MSc Lond.   Sr. Lectr.

Mathematics

Tel: (0171) 873 2216 Fax: (0171) 873 2017
Bushnell, C. J., BSc Lond., PhD Lond.   Prof.; Head*
Coolen, A. C. C., MSc Utrecht, PhD Utrecht   Reader
Davies, E. B., MA Oxf., DPhil Oxf., FRS, FKC   Prof.
Erdos, J. A., MSc Well., PhD Camb.   Reader; Head*
Harvey, W. J., BSc Birm., PhD Birm.   Reader
Hodgkin, L. H., BA Oxf., DPhil Oxf.   Reader
Howe, P. S., BSc Manc., PhD Lanc.   Prof.
Laird, M. J., PhD Lond., BSc   Sr. Lectr.
Landau, L. J., BS Troy, MA Calif., PhD Calif.   Reader
Lavis, D. A., BSc Lond., PhD Manc., FIP, FIMA   Sr. Lectr.
Pressley, A. N., BA Oxf., MSc Oxf., DPhil Oxf.   Reader
Robinson, D. C., MSc Auck., PhD Syr.   Prof.
Rogers, F. A., MA Camb., PhD Lond.   Reader
Safarov, Y., BSc PhD DSc   Prof.
Saunders, P. T., BA Tor., PhD Lond.   Prof.
Streater, R. F., BSc Lond., PhD Lond.   Prof.
West, P. C., BSc Lond., PhD Lond.   Prof.
Wilde, I. F., BSc PhD   Reader

Medicine, see below

Music

Tel: (0171) 873 2029 Fax: (0171) 873 2326
Birtwistle, H.   Prof.
Deathridge, J., BA Oxf., MA Oxf., DPhil Oxf.   Prof.; Acting Head*
Dreyfus, L., MA Col., MPhil Col., PhD Col.   Prof.
Eisen, C., BA MA PhD   Reader
Leech-Wilkinson, D., BMus MMus PhD   Reader
Milstein, BMus Glas., MPhil Camb., PhD Camb.   Sr. Lectr.
Wintle, C. S., BA Oxf., BMus Oxf.   Sr. Lectr.

Nursing and Midwifery, Division of

Nightingale Institute: Biological Sciences

Tel: ((0171) 873 5133, 873 5141
Haynes, Sheila, BEd S.Bank   Principal Lectr.
Herbert, Ros, BSc Sur., MSc Lond.   Head*
O'Brien, Frances, BSc Open(UK), MBA S.Bank   Principal Lectr.

Nightingale Institute: Inter Personal Studies and Health Promotion

Tel: (0171) 873 5261, 873 5113
Benson, Anne, BEd S.Bank, MA Lond.   Principal Lectr.
Cooper, Serena, BSc Lond., MSc Lond.   Head*

Nightingale Institute: Midwifery and Women's Health Studies

Tel: (0171) 873 5207, 873 5208

Jamieson, Lea, BEd Lond., MSc Lond.   Head*
Pacanowski, Lynne, BSc Roehampton
IHE   Principal Lectr.

Nightingale Institute: Philosophy and Practice of Nursing

Tel: (0171) 873 5112, 873 5144

Chan, Wai Cheng, BEd S.Bank   Principal Lectr.
Mingay, Julia, BSc Cant., MSc City(UK)   Head*
Smith, Sue, BSc Manc.   Principal Lectr.; Head,
Child Branch

Nightingale Institute: Social Sciences

Tel: (0171) 955 4185

Anderson, John, BA Aberd., MA   Principal
Lectr.
MacAlister, Lyn, BA Open(UK), MA
Lond.   Principal Lectr.
Torkington, Sue, BSc Brighton   Head*

Nursing Studies

Tel: (0171) 872 3024 Fax: (0171) 872 3219

MacLeod Clark, J., PhD Lond., BSc   Prof.; Dir.,
Nightingale Inst.
Norman, I. J., BA Keele, MSc Edin., PhD
Lond.   Sr. Lectr.
While, A., BSc S'ton., MSc CNAA, PhD
Lond.   Prof.
Wilson-Barnett, J., BA Leic., MSc Edin., PhD
Lond., FKC   Prof.; Head*

Nutrition and Dietetics, see under Health
Scis., Div. of

Pharmacology, see under Biomed. Scis., Div.
of

Pharmacy, see under Health Scis., Div. of

Philosophy

Tel: (0171) 873 2231 Fax: (0171) 873 2270

Gillies, D., MA Camb., PhD Camb.   Prof.
Hopkins, G., AB Harv., BA Camb., PhD   Reader
Machover, M., MSc Jerusalem, PhD
Jerusalem   Reader
McCabe, M., MA Camb., PhD Camb.   Reader
Papineau, D., BSc Natal, PhD Camb.   Prof.;
Head*
Sainsbury, R. M., MA Oxf., DPhil Oxf.,
FKC   Prof.
Savile, A. B., MA Oxf., BPhil Oxf.   Reader
Segal, G., BA Lond., BPhil Oxf., PhD
M.I.T.   Reader
Sorabji, R. R. K., MA Oxf., BPhil Oxf.,
FBA   Prof., Ancient Philosophy

Physics

Tel: (0171) 873 2148 Fax: (0171) 873 2420

Boyce, J. F., BSc Lond., PhD Lond.   Reader
Burge, R. E., PhD Lond., DSc Lond., FKC,
FIP   Prof.
Collins, A. T., PhD Lond., DSc Lond., FIP   Prof.
Davies, G., PhD Lond., DSc Lond., FIP   Prof.;
Head*
Gaunt, D. S., PhD Lond., DSc Lond., FIP   Prof.
Hill, Robert M., PhD Glas., DSc Glas., FIEE, FIP,
FKC   Prof.
Holwill, M. E. J., BSc Lond., PhD Lond.   Reader
Jones, D. Ll., BSc Lond., PhD Lond.   Reader
Lightowlers, E. C., BSc Lond., PhD Lond.,
FIP   Prof.
Michette, A. G., BSc Lond., PhD Lond.,
FIP   Reader
Pike, E. R., BSc Wales, PhD Wales, FRS, FIMA,
FIP, FKC   Clerk Maxwell Prof., Theoretical
Physics
Sarkar, S., PhD Lond.   Prof.

Physiology, see under Biomed. Scis., Div. of

Physiotherapy, see under Biomed. Scis., Div.
of

Portuguese and Brazilian Studies

Tel: (0171) 873 3531 Fax: (0171) 873 2787

Cabral, M., LenLett Paris IV, Dr Paris   Prof.
Chabal, P. E., BA Harv., MPhil Col., PhD
Camb.   Prof.; Head*
Treece, D., BA Liv., PhD Liv.   Reader

Religious Studies, see Theol. and Religious
Studies

Spanish and Spanish American Studies

Tel: (0171) 873 2205 Fax: (0171) 873 2207

Butt, J. W., MA Camb., DPhil Oxf.,
PhD   Reader
Hook, D., MA Oxf., DPhil Oxf.   Prof.; Head*
Ife, Barry W., BA Lond., PhD Lond., FKC   Prof.
Rowe, W. W., MA Camb., PhD   Prof., Spanish
American Literature

Theology and Religious Studies

Tel: (0171) 873 2339 Fax: (0171) 873 2255

Baldick, R., MA Oxf., DPhil Oxf.   Reader
Banner, Rev. M., DPhil Oxf.   Frederick
Denison Maurice Prof., Moral and Social
Theology
Byrne, P. A., BA York(UK), BPhil Oxf.   Sr. Lectr.
Clarke, P. B., MA Oxf., MA Lond., PhD Lond.,
MPhil   Sr. Lectr.
Gunton, C. E., MA Oxf., DPhil Oxf., DD
Lond.   Prof., Christian Doctrine; Head*
Hardy, F. E., MA Oxf., DPhil Oxf.   Prof.
Helm, P., MA Oxf.   Prof.
Knibb, M. A., STM U.T.S.(N.Y.), BD PhD, FBA,
FKC   Prof., Old Testament Studies
Stanton, G. N., MA Otago, BD Otago, PhD
Camb.   Prof., New Testament Studies
Torrance, A., MA Edin., BD Aberd., DrTheol
Erlangen   Sr. Lectr.
Watson, F., MA Oxf., DPhil Oxf.   Reader

**United Medical and Dental Schools of
Guy's and St Thomas's**, see below

War Studies

Tel: (0171) 873 2178 Fax: (0171) 873 2026

Bond, B. J., BA Oxf., MA Lond., FKC   Prof.
Dandeker, C., PhD Leic.   Prof.
Dockrill, M. L., MA Ill., PhD Lond.   Reader
Dockrill, S., BA Kyoto, MA Sus., PhD Lond.   Sr.
Lectr.
Freedman, Lawrence D., CBE, BA(Econ) Manc.,
BPhil York(UK), DPhil Oxf., FKC   Prof.;
Head*
Gow, A., BA Lanc., PhD Lond.   Reader
Heuser, D., BA Lond., MA Lond., DPhil Oxf.   Sr.
Lectr.
Honig, J., Drs Amst., PhD Lond.   Sr. Lectr.
Karsh, E., BA Jerusalem, MA Tel-Aviv, PhD Tel-
Aviv   Prof.
Lambert, LLB Lond.Guild., MA Lond., PhD Lond.,
FRHistS   Sr. Lectr.
Paskins, B. A., MA Camb., PhD Camb.   Sr.
Lectr., Ethical Aspects of War
Sabin, P. A. G., MA Camb., PhD Lond.   Sr.
Lectr.

DENTISTRY

Conservation

Tel: (0171) 346 3585

Dunne, S. M., PhD Lond., BDS, FDSRCS   Sr.
Lectr.
Inglis, A. T., PhD Lond., BDS, FDSRCS   Sr.
Lectr.; Head*
Linden, R., PhD Brist., BDS   Prof.
Millar, B., BDS Dund., PhD Lond., FDSRCS   Sr.
Lectr.
Nicholson, J., BSc CNAA, PhD CNAA,
FRSChem   Reader
Robinson, P. B., BDS PhD Lond., MBA Lond.,
FDSRCS   Sr. Lectr.
Deb, S., BSc MSc PhD   Sr. Lectr.
Nicholson, J., BSc PhD, FRCS   Sr. Lectr.

Dental Public Health and Community Dentistry

Tel: (0171) 346 3481 Fax: (0171) 346 3494

Gelbier, S., MA PhD, FDRCS   Prof.; Head*
Robinson, P., BDS MSc PhD   Sr. Lectr.

Dental Radiology

Tel: (0171) 346 3053 Fax: (0171) 346 3494

Smith, N., BDS Lond., MSc Lond., PhD Lond.,
DUniv Open(UK), FRCR

Dental Sciences/Oral Medicine and Pathology

Royal College of Surgeons

Tel: (0171) 346 3608

Beighton, D., PhD Melb., BSc   Prof.
Harrison, J. D., PhD Lond., BDS,
FRCPath   Reader
Johnson, N. W., BDS Melb., MDSc Melb., PhD
Brist., FRACDS, FRCPath   Prof.; Head*
Pankhurst, C., BSc Lond., BDS Lond., MSc Lond.,
PhD Lond.   Sr. Lectr.
Proctor, G., BSc Brad., PhD Sheff.   Sr. Lectr.
Wamakulasuriya, K. A., BDS Ceyl., PhD Glas.,
FDSRCS   Sr. Lectr.

General Dental Practice

Tel: (0171) 346 3088

Weir, D. I., BDS NZ   Acting Dir.*

Oral and Maxillofacial Surgery

Tel: (0171) 346 3783 Fax: (0171) 346 3754

Langdon, J. D., MB BS BDS, FDSRCS,
FRCSEd   Prof.; Head*
Partridge, M., BDS Brist., MPhil Lond., PhD Lond.,
FDSRCS   Sr. Lectr.
Reynolds, P., MB BS Lond., BDS Lond.   Sr. Lectr.

Oral Medicine and Pathology, see Dental
Scis./Oral Med. and Pathol.

Orthodontics

Tel: (0171) 346 3552

Bhatia, S. N., BSc MDS, FDSRCS   Sr. Lectr.

Paedodontics

Tel: (0171) 346 3375

Seddon, R. P., BDS MSc, FDSRCS   Sr. Lectr.
Smith, P. B., BDS, FDSRCS   Sr. Lectr.; Head*

Periodontology

Tel: (0171) 346 3492

Eley, B. M., BDS PhD, FDSRCS   Reader; Head*
Soory, M., BDS S.Lanka, PhD, FDSRCS   Sr.
Lectr.

Prosthetics

Tel: (0171) 346 3584 Fax: (0171) 346 3775

Davis, D., PhD Lond., BDS, FDSRCS   Sr. Lectr.
Watson, R. M., MDS Lond., FDSRCS   Prof.;
Head*
Wright, S. M., MDS Lond., FDSRCS   Sr. Lectr.

MEDICINE

Accident and Emergency

Tel: (0171) 346 3235

Glucksman, E., MD Virginia, FRCP   Head*

Anaesthetics

Tel: (0171) 346 3358

Peat, S. J., BSc MB BS, FFARCS Lond.   Sr. Lectr.
Ponte, J. C., MD Lisbon, PhD Brist., FFARCS   Sr.
Lectr.; Head*

Analytical Pharmacology

Black, Sir James, MB ChB St And., FRCP,
FRS   Prof.; Head*

Biomedical Sciences, Division of, see
above

Cardiology

Tel: (0171) 737 4000

Jewitt, D. E., BSc MB BS, FRCP   Clin.
Teacher†; Head*

Child Health, see also Community Paed.

Tel: (0171) 346 3214

Buchanan, C., BSc Manc., MB ChB Manc.
Greenough, A., MD Camb., MA MB BS,
    FRCP   Prof.
Mieli Vergani, G., MD Milan, PhD Lond.,
    FRCP   Sr. Lectr.

Clinical Biochemistry

Tel: (0171) 737 4000

Marshall, W. J., MA Oxf., MSc MB BS PhD,
    FRCPEd, FRCPath   Sr. Lectr.
Peters, T. J., MB ChB St And., DSc St And., PhD,
    FRCP, FRCPath   Prof.; Head*
Preedy, V., PhD Lond., DSc Aston, BSc,
    FIBiol   Reader

Community Paediatrics

Ross, E. M., MB ChB Brist., MD Brist.,
    FRCP   Prof.; Head*

Dermatology

Tel: (0171) 737 4000
No staff at present

Diabetes

Tel: (0171) 346 3241 Fax: (0171) 346 3407
Watkins, P. J., MD, FRCP   Clin. Teacher†;
    Head*

Diagnostic Radiology

Tel: (0171) 346 3157 Fax: (0171) 346 3061
Vacant Posts: 1 Lectr.

Epidemiology, see Public Health and
    Epidemiol.

General Practice and Primary Care

Tel: (0171) 346 3016

Aitken, V., MSc Lond., PhD Herts.   Sr. Lectr.
Blache, G., MSc   Sr. Lectr.
Booton, P., BSc MB BS   Sr. Lectr.
Copperman, J., BA Sus., MSc Lond.   Sr. Lectr.
Graham, H., MB ChB Manc.   Sr. Lectr.
Higgs, R. H., MBE, MA Camb., MB BChir
    Camb., FRCP, FRCGP   Prof.; Head*
Morely, V., BA Newcastle(UK), MSc Sur.   Sr.
    Lectr.
Stephenson, A., MB ChB Otago, PhD Otago   Sr.
    Lectr.
White, P., MB BCh BAO   Sr. Lectr.

Haematology

Tel: (0171) 346 3080 Fax: (0171) 346 3514
Layton, D. M., MB BS   Sr. Lectr.
Mufti, G. J., MB BS J&K, DM S'ton.,
    FRCPath   Prof.

Health Care of the Elderly

Tel: (0171) 346 6083 Fax: (0171) 346 6476
Carpenter, G. I., BSc Edin., MB ChB Edin., MD,
    FRCP   Sr. Lectr.
Jackson, S. H. D., MB ChB MD, FRCP   Prof.
Pettingale, K. W., MD, FRCP   Sr. Lectr.
Swift, C. G., PhD Dund., MB BS   Prof.; Head*
Vacant Posts: 1 Lectr.

Health Sciences, Division of, see above

Histopathology

Tel: (0171) 346 3005
Nash, R., BSc Edin., MB BS   Sr. Lectr.
Salisbury, J. R., BSc MB BS, FRCPath   Reader
Vacant Posts: 1 Sr. Lectr.

Immunology

Tel: (0171) 346 3012
Kemeny, D. M., BSc PhD   Chair*
Peakman, M., BSc Lond., MB BS Lond., MSc Lond.,
    PhD Lond.   Reader
Vyakarnum, A.   Sr. Lectr.
Vacant Posts: 2 Lectrs.

Liver Studies, Institute of

Tel: (0171) 346 3254
Bomford, A., BSc MD, FRCP   Sr. Lectr.
Gibbs, P., MB BCh Wales, FRCSEd   Sr. Lectr.

Harrison, P. M., BSc MB BS MD PhD   Sr.
    Lectr.
Hughes, R. D., BSc Sus., PhD Lond.   Sr. Lectr.
Tredger, J., BSc Liv., PhD Sur.
Wendon, J. A., MB ChB Dund., FRCP   Sr. Lectr.

Medical Engineering and Physics

Tel: (0171) 346 3491 Fax: (0171) 346 3314
Leeman, S., MSc Cape Town, DPhil Oxf.   Sr.
    Lectr.
Lord, M., PhD Lond., BSc MA MPhil   Sr. Lectr.
Roberts, V. C., BSc Lond., MSc Sur., PhD Sur.,
    FIEE, FIP   Prof.; Head*
Turner-Smith, A. R., BSc Birm., DPhil Oxf.   Sr.
    Lectr.

Medical Microbiology

Tel: (0171) 346 3213 Fax: (0171) 346 3404
Philpott-Howard, J. N., MB ChB   Sr. Lectr.
Vacant Posts: 1 Lectr.

Medicine

Tel: (0171) 346 3013
Amiel, S. A., BSc MB BS, FRCP   Chair
Banga, J. P., PhD Lond., BSc   Sr. Lectr.
Harris, P. E., BSc Wales, MB BCh Wales, PhD
    Wales, FRCP   Sr. Lectr.
McGregor, A. M., MA Camb., MB BChir Camb.,
    MD Camb., FRCP, FKC   Prof.; Head*
Pozniak, A. L., MB ChB Brist.   Sr. Lectr.

Molecular Medicine

Tel: (0171) 737 4000
Farzaneh, F., BSc Aberd., MSc Aberd., DPhil Sus.,
    FRCPath   Prof.
Vacant Posts: 1 Lectr.

Neurology

Tel: (0171) 346 3877
Markus, H. S., BA Camb., BM BCh Oxf.   Sr.
    Lectr.
Polkey, C. E., BSc Brist., MB ChB Brist., MD,
    FRCS   Sr. Lectr.
Shaw, C., MB ChB Otago, MD Otago, FRACP

Neurosurgery

Tel: (0171) 737 4000
No staff at present

Nuclear Medicine

Tel: (0171) 346 3153
No staff at present

Obstetrics and Gynaecology

Tel: (0171) 346 3030
Bolton, V., MA Oxf., PhD Camb.   Sr. Lectr.
Collins, W., BSc S'ton., PhD Lond., DSc Lond.,
    FRSChem, FRCOG   Prof.
Nicolaides, K. H., MB BS BSc   Prof.; Head*
Parsons, J. H., MB ChB Dund.   Sr. Lectr.
Tan, S., MB BS MD   Sr. Lectr.
Whitehead, M. I., MB BS, FRCOG   Sr. Lectr.

Ophthalmology

Tel: (0171) 737 4000
Reynolds, P., MB BS Lond.   Sr. Lectr.

Orthopaedics

Tel: (0171) 737 4000
No staff at present

Oto-Rhino-Laryngology

Tel: (0171) 737 4000
No staff at present

Palliative Care Medicine

Tel: (0171) 737 4000
Addington-Hall, J., BA Durh., PhD Durh.   Sr.
    Lectr.
Edmonds, P., MB   Sr. Lectr.
Higginson, I., BMedSci BM BS PhD   Prof.

Pathology, School of, see Clin. Biochem.,
    Haematol., Histopathol., Immunol., and
    Med. Microbiol.

Plastic Surgery

Tel: (0171) 737 4000
No staff at present

Psychiatry

Tel: (0171) 737 4000
No staff at present

Psychiatry, Institute of

Anderton, B. H., BSc PhD   Prof.,
    Neuroscience; Head*
Asherson, P., MB BS Lond.   Sr. Lectr.
Ball, David, MA BM BCh   Sr. Lectr.
Banerjee, S., MB BS Lond.   Sr. Lectr.
Beecham, Jennifer, BA PhD   Sr. Lectr.
Bhugra, D., MB BS MPhil   Sr. Lectr.
Bolton, D., BA Camb., MPhil Camb., PhD
    Camb.   Sr. Lectr.
Brammer, M. J., BSc Leeds, PhD Leeds   Reader
Brindley, Miles S.   Prof.
Buchanan, Alexander, MD MPhil PhD   Sr.
    Lectr.
Campbell, I. C., PhD DSc   Prof.,
    Neurochemical Pharmacy
Carson, J. F. J., MSc   Sr. Lectr.
Chadwick, Oliver, MSc   Sr. Lectr.
Chapman, Astrid G., BSc PhD   Sr. Lectr.
Checkley, S. A., MB BS Lond.   Prof.
Collier, D. A., BSc PhD   Sr. Lectr.,
    Cytogenetics
Craig, Ian   Prof.
Dare, C., BA MB, FRCPsych   Reader
De Silva, W. P., MA MPhil   Sr. Lectr.
Dunn, Judith   Prof.
Eisler, I., PhD   Sr. Lectr.
Everall, I. J., MB ChB Leic., PhD   Sr. Lectr.
Everitt, B. S., MSc   Prof.; Head*
Fahy, Tom, MPhil MD   Sr. Lectr.
Farrell, M., MB BCh BAO Trinity(Dub.)   Sr.
    Lectr.
Fornbonne, E., MD   Reader
Frangou, S., MD Athens, MSc Lond.   Sr. Lectr.
Fulker, D. W., BSc Lond., MSc Birm., PhD
    Birm.   Prof., Statistical Genetics
Gallo, Jean, MSc PhD   Sr. Lectr.
Glover, Gyles, MSc   Sr. Lectr.
Goldberg, Sir David, MA Oxf., BM BCh
    Oxf.   Prof.; Head*
Goldstein, Laura H., BSc MPhil PhD   Sr. Lectr.
Goodman, R. N., MA Oxf., BM BCh
    Oxf.   Reader, Brain and Behavioural
    Medicine
Gournay, Kevin   Prof.
Gray, J. A., BA Oxf., PhD   Prof.; Head*
Gray, Susan, BA Oxf., MPhil   Sr. Lectr.
Gudjonsson, G. H., BSc Brun., MSc Sur., PhD
    Sur.   Reader, Forensic Psychology
Gunn, J. C., CBE, MD Birm., FRCPsych   Prof.,
    Forensic Psychiatry; Head*
Hemsley, D. R., MA MPhil PhD   Prof.,
    Abnormal Psychology
Hodges, Helen M. H., BA BSc PhD   Reader
Howard, R. J., MA MB   Sr. Lectr.
Jenkins, Hugh, BA BPhil   Sr. Lectr.
Johns, Andrew   Sr. Lectr.
Kerwin, R. W., MA Camb., MB BChir Camb.,
    PhD Brist.   Prof.
Knapp, M. R., MSc Kent, PhD Kent   Prof.,
    Clinical Neuropharmacology
Kuipers, Elizabeth A., BSc Brist., MSc Birm.,
    PhD   Prof.
Kumar, R., MD Camb., PhD MPhil   Prof.,
    Perinatal Psychiatry
Lader, Malcolm H., OBE, BSc MD PhD,
    FRCPsych   Prof., Clinical Psycho-Pharmacy
Lam, D., BSc MPhil   Sr. Lectr.
Lantos, P. L., MD PhD   Prof., Neuropathology;
    Head*
Leff, J. P., MD, FRCPsych   Prof., Social and
    Transcultural Psychiatry
Leigh, P. N., BSc MB BS PhD, FRCP   Prof.*
Lindsay, S. J. E., BA MSc PhD   Sr. Lectr.
Lovestone, Simon, BSc BM MPhil   Sr. Lectr.
Maden, A., BSc MB BS   Sr. Lectr.

Makoff, A., BA *Camb.*, PhD *Leeds*   Sr. Lectr.
Male, D. K., MA PhD   Sr. Lectr., Immunology
Mann, A. H., MA *Camb.*, MD BChir *Camb.*, MPhil, FRCPsych, FRCP   Prof., Epidemiology Psychiatry
Marks, I. M., MD *Cape Town*, FRCPsych   Prof., Experimental Psychopathology
Marks, Maureen N., BA *Well.*, DPhil *Sus.*   Sr. Lectr.
Marshall, Elizabeth, MB BCh   Sr. Lectr.
Maughan, Barbara, BA MSc   Sr. Lectr.
McGuire, Philip, BSc MB ChB   Sr. Lectr.
Meldrum, B. S., MA *Camb.*, MB BChir *Camb.*   Prof., Experimental Neurology
Meux, C. J., MB BS   Sr. Lectr.
Miller, C., BSc *Wales*, PhD   Sr. Lectr.
Morris, R. G., MA MSc PhD   Reader
Murphy, D., MB BS   Sr. Lectr.
Murray, R. M., MD MPhil   Prof., Psychology Medicine; Head*
Nikapota, Anula, MB BS   Sr. Lectr.
Parkes, J. D., MD   Prof.
Pickles, A., MA MSc PhD   Sr. Lectr.
Pilkington, G., BSc *CNAA*, PhD   Reader
Plomin, Robert   Prof.
Powell, J. F., MA *Oxf.*, DPhil *Oxf.*   Sr. Lectr.
Price, Jack, PhD   Sr. Lectr.
Prince, Martin, BA MB BChir MSc   Sr. Lectr.
Rushton, D. N., MA MD   Reader
Russell, M. A. H., MA *Oxf.*, BM BCh *Oxf.*, FRCPsych   Prof., Addiction
Rutter, Sir Michael, KBE, MD *Birm.*, FRCP, FRCPsych, FRS   Prof., Child Psychiatry; Head*
Scott, S. B. C., BSc   Sr. Lectr.
Sham, P. C., MA *Camb.*, BM BCh *Oxf.*   Sr. Lectr.
Sharma, Tonmoy   Sr. Lectr.
Sinden, J. D., MA *Syd.*, Dr3rdCy *Paris*   Reader, Neurobiology of Behaviour
Stephenson, J. D., BSc PhD   Sr. Lectr.
Stolerman, I. P., BPharm PhD   Prof., Behavioural Pharmacology
Strang, J., MB BS   Prof.
Taylor, E. A., MA *Camb.*, MB BChir *Camb.*, FRCP   Prof., Development Neuropsychiatry
Taylor, Pamela, MB BS   Prof., Special Hospital Psychiatry
Thornicroft, G., BA *Camb.*, MB   Prof., Community Psychiatry
Toone, Brian   Sr. Lectr.
Treasure, Janet L., BSc MB BS PhD   Sr. Lectr.
Wardle, F. Jane, BA *Oxf.*, MPhil PhD   Reader
Whatley, S. A., BSc PhD   Sr. Lectr.
Williams, Steven, BSc PhD   Sr. Lectr.
Wilson, G. D., MA *Cant.*, PhD   Reader
Wykes, T. I. R., BSc *Nott.*, DPhil *Sus.*   Reader
Yule, W., MA *Aberd.*, PhD   Prof.

Psychological Medicine

Tel: (0171) 346 3014

David, A. S., MB BCh *Glas.*, MSc *Glas.*, MPhil *Lond.*, FRCP   Reader
Mathew, V., MB BS MPhil   Sr. Lectr.
Olajide, O., MB BS PhD   Sr. Lectr.
Wessely, S., BM BCh *Oxf.*, MSc *Lond.*, MA *Camb.*   Prof.
Vacant Posts: 1 Lectr.

Public Health and Epidemiology

Tel: (0171) 346 3170

Noah, N. D., MB BS, FRCP   Prof.†; Head*
Vacant Posts: 1 Lectr.

Radiotherapy

Tel: (0171)737 4000
No staff at present

Renal Medicine

Tel: (0171) 737 4000

Hendry, B., BA MA BMBCH *Oxf.*, MD PhD *Camb.*, FRCP   Prof.

Respiratory Medicine

Tel: (0171) 346 3165

Gardner, W. N., MB BS *Syd.*, DPhil *Oxf.*, FRCP   Sr. Lectr.
Moxham, J., MB BS MD, FRCP   Prof.

O'Connor, B., MB BCh   Sr. Lectr.

Rheumatology and Rehabilitation

Tel: (0171) 737 4000

Choy, E., MB BCh MD   Sr. Lectr.
Scott, D., BSc *Leeds*, MB ChB *Leeds*, MD *Leeds*, FRCP   Prof.

Surgery

Tel: (0171) 346 3017

Benjamin, I. S., BSc MD, FRCSGlas, FRCS   Prof.
Coptcoat, M., MB ChB, FRCS   Sr. Lectr.
Rennie, J. A., MS, FRCS   Sr. Lectr.
Tavares, I. A. F., BSc *S'ton.*, PhD *S'ton.*   Sr. Lectr.
Vacant Posts: 1 Lectr.

Thoracic Surgery

Tel: (0171) 737 4000
No staff at present

Thrombosis Research Institute

Tel: (0171) 346 3015

Kakkar, V. V., MB BS *Vikram*, FRCS   Prof.; Head*

Urology

Tel: (0171) 737 4000
No staff at present

Other Appointments

Also 21 other Recognised Teachers of Clinical Teacher status in the teaching hospitals

UNITED MEDICAL AND DENTAL SCHOOLS OF GUY'S AND ST THOMAS'S

Anaesthetics

Adams, Anthony P., MB BS PhD, FRCA   Prof.; Chairman*
Hamann, Wolfgang C., MD PhD   Sr. Lectr.
Miller, Donald M., MB ChB PhD   Sr. Lectr.

Anatomy and Cell Biology

Bannister, Lawrence H., BSc PhD DSc   Reader
Berry, Martin, BSc MB ChB MD PhD, FRCPath   Prof.; Chairman*
Buckland-Wright, John C., BSc PhD DSc   Prof.
Cohen, James, BSc PhD   Reader
Dyson, Mary, BSc PhD   Reader
Ellis, Harold, DM MCh, FRSChem   Sr. Lectr.
Guthrie, Sarah C., BA MA PhD   Sr. Lectr.
Hutchinson, Michael C. E., BDS MB BS   Sr. Lectr.
Lumsden, Andrew G. S., MA *Oxf.*, BA PhD, FRS   Prof.
Mason, Ivor J., BA PhD   Sr. Lectr.
Parker, Roger J., MB BS MS, FRSChem   Sr. Lectr.
Perry, Marta E., MUDr *Palacky*, PhD   Sr. Lectr.
Standring, Susan M., BSc PhD DSc   Prof.
Wigley, Caroline B., BSc PhD   Sr. Lectr.

Biochemistry

Diplock, Anthony T., BSc PhD DSc   Prof.; Chairman*
Evans, Robert W., BA PhD   Reader
Faik, Pelin, BSc PhD   Sr. Lectr.
Francis, Paul T., BSc PhD   Sr. Lectr.
Garlick, Pamela B., BA *Oxf.*, DPhil *Oxf.*, MA   Sr. Lectr.
Hearse, David J., BSc PhD DSc   Prof.
Kelly, Francis J., BSc PhD   Reader
Moreland, Barbara H., BSc PhD   Sr. Lectr.
Murphy, Gerard M., BSc PhD, FRSChem   Reader
Papachristodoulou, Despina, MSc BSc PhD   Sr. Lectr.
Rattray, Marcus A. N., BSc PhD   Sr. Lectr.
Reed, Francis B., BSc PhD   Sr. Lectr.
Rice-Evans, Catherine, BSc PhD   Prof.
Thomas, John H., BSc PhD, FIBiol   Sr. Lectr.

Chemical Pathology

Crook, Martin A., BSc MB BS PhD   Sr. Lectr.
Hampson, Geeta N., MB ChB MSc MD   Sr. Lectr.
Pickup, John C., BM BCh *Oxf.*, MA *Oxf.*, DPhil *Oxf.*, BA, FRCPath   Reader
Swaminathan, Ramasamyiyer, MB BS MSc PhD, FRCPath, FRCP   Prof.; Chairman*
Wierzbicki, Anthony S., BM BCh MA   Sr. Lectr.

Dentistry

Ashley, Francis P., BDS PhD, FDSRCS   Prof.
Brown, David, MSc *Manc.*, PhD *Manc.*, BSc, FIM   Sr. Lectr.
Challacombe, Stephen J., BDS PhD, FRCPath   Prof.
Clark, Robert K. F., BDS PhD   Sr. Lectr.
Fiske, Janice, BDS MPhil, FDSRCS   Sr. Lectr.
Fortune, Farieda, MB BS BDS PhD   Sr. Lectr.
Gibbons, David E., BDS MA MSc   Prof.
Grenby, Trevor H., BSc PhD, FRSChem   Reader
Hill, Peter A., BSc BDS PhD, FDSRCS   Sr. Lectr.
Jupp, Susan D., BDS, FDSRCS   Sr. Lectr.
Kelly, Charles G., BSc PhD   Reader
Kidd, Edwina A. M., BDS PhD, FDSRCS   Prof.
Lax, Alistair J., BSc PhD   Sr. Lectr.
Likeman, Peter R., BDS PhD, FDSRCS   Sr. Lectr.
Longhurst, Peter, BDS, FDSRCS   Sr. Lectr.
Ma, Julian, BDS PhD   Sr. Lectr.
MacDonald, Fraser, BDS MSc PhD, FDSRCS, FFDRCSI   Sr. Lectr.
McGurk, Mark, MB ChB BDS MD, FRCS, FDSRCS   Prof.
Meikle, Murray C., BDS MSD PhD, FDSRCS   Prof.
Meredith Smith, Moya, BSc PhD DSc   Reader
Mordecai, Robert M., BDS, FDSRCS   Sr. Lectr.
Morgan, Peter R., BSc BDS PhD   Reader
Odell, Edward W., BDS MSc, FDSRCS   Sr. Lectr.
Palmer, Richard M., BDS PhD, FDSRCS   Prof.
Pitt Ford, Thomas R., BDS PhD, FDSRCS   Prof.
Pool, Deirdre M., BDS, FDSRCS   Sr. Lectr.
Preiskel, Harold W., BDS MDS MSc, FDSRCS   Sr. Lectr.
Radford, David R., BDS PhD, FDSRCS   Sr. Lectr.
Sharpe, Paul T., BA PhD   Prof.
Sherriff, Martin, BSc PhD   Sr. Lectr.
Skelly, Ann M., BDS MDS, FDSRCPSGlas   Sr. Lectr.
Smith, Bernard G. N., BDS MSc PhD, FDSRCS   Prof.
Wade, William G., BSc MSc PhD   Prof.
Walter, John D., DDS *Edin.*, BDS, FDSRCS   Reader
Watson, Timothy F., BSc BDS PhD, FDSRCS   Sr. Lectr.
Watts, Trevor L. P., BDS MDS PhD, FDSRCS   Sr. Lectr.
Whaites, Eric J., BDS MSc   Sr. Lectr.
Wilson, Ronald F., MPhil PhD   Sr. Lectr.
Woolford, Mark J., BDS PhD, FDSRCS   Sr. Lectr.

Dermatology

Barker, Jonathan N. W. N., BSc MB BS, FRCP   Sr. Lectr.
Barr, Robert M., BSc PhD   Sr. Lectr.
Breathnach, Stephen M., MA *Camb.*, MD *Camb.*, PhD *Camb.*, MB BS, FRCP   Sr. Lectr.
Eady, Robin A., MB BS BDSc, FRCP   Prof.
Greaves, Malcolm W., MB BS MD PhD, FRCP   Prof.
Hay, Roderick J., DM *Oxf.*, BA MA, FRCP, FRCPath   Prof.; Chairman*
Kobza Black, Aniko, MD MB BS, FRCP   Sr. Lectr.
MacDonald, Donald M., MB BCh MA, FRCPath, FRCP   Sr. Lectr.
Markey, Andrew C., MB ChB MD   Sr. Lectr.
McFadden, John P., BM   Sr. Lectr.
McGrath, John A., MB BS MD   Sr. Lectr.
Midgley, Gillian, BSc PhD   Sr. Lectr.

Smith, Catherine H., MB BS MD   Sr. Lectr.
Young, Anthony R., BSc MSc PhD   Sr. Lectr.

Haematology

Carr, Robert, BSc MB ChB   Sr. Lectr.
Pearson, Thomas C., MD, FRCPath   Prof.;
  Chairman*
Schey, Stephen A., MB BS, FRACP, FRCP   Sr.
  Lectr.

Histopathology

Antoniou, Michael, BA PhD   Sr. Lectr.
Chinyama, Catherine N., MB ChB   Sr. Lectr.
Derias, Nawal W., MB ChB MPhil PhD   Sr.
  Lectr.
Djurovic, Vesna, MD   Sr. Lectr.
Doherty, Patrick, BSc PhD   Prof.
Fagg, Nuala L., MB BS   Sr. Lectr.
Hanby, Andrew M., BM   Sr. Lectr.
Hartley, Richard B., MB BS, FRCPath   Sr.
  Lectr.
Hill, Ian R., MA PhD   Sr. Lectr.
Lucas, Sebastian B., BA BM BCh MA, FRCP,
  FRCPath   Prof.
Morris, Roger J., BSc PhD   Sr. Lectr.
Poston, Robert N. (Robin), MD Camb., MB
  BChir MA, FRCPath   Sr. Lectr.
Spencer, Jo M., BSc PhD   Sr. Lectr.
Sundaresan, Vasi, MB BS PhD   Sr. Lectr.
Tungekar, Muhammad F., MB BS MD,
  FRCPath   Sr. Lectr.
Van der Walt, Jon D., MB BCh, FRCPath   Sr.
  Lectr.
West, Ian E., MB ChB   Sr. Lectr.

Immunology

Brown, Kenneth A., BSc PhD   Sr. Lectr.
Klavinskis, Linda, PhD   Sr. Lectr.
Lehner, Thomas, Hon. PhD Stockholm, MB BS
  MD BDS, FRCPath, FDSRCS   Prof.;
  Chairman*
Mitchell, Graham H., BSc PhD   Sr. Lectr.
Shepherd, Philip S., MB ChB MSc, FRCP   Sr.
  Lectr.
Wolstencroft, Robert A., BSc MSc   Sr. Lectr.

Infection

Banatvala, Jehangir E., MB BChir MD,
  FRCPath   Prof.
Best, Jennifer M., BSc PhD, FRCPath   Reader
Cason, John W., BSc MPhil PhD   Sr. Lectr.
Eykyn, Susannah J., MB BS, FFARCS,
  FRCS   Prof.
French, Gary L., BSc MB BS MD, FRCP,
  FRCPath   Prof.
Gant, Vanya A., BSc MB BS MSc   Sr. Lectr.
Gransden, William R., MA MB BCh   Sr. Lectr.

Medical and Molecular Genetics

Bates, Gillian P., BSc MSc PhD   Sr. Lectr.
Daker, Michael G., BSc Wales, PhD Wales   Sr.
  Lectr.
Flinter, Frances A., MB BS MD   Sr. Lectr.
Giannelli, Francesco B., MD Rome, PhD
  DSc   Prof.
Hodgson, Shirley V., BCh Oxf. BSc DM,
  FRCP   Sr. Lectr.
Lewis, Catherine M., BA MSc PhD   Sr. Lectr.
Ragoussis, Ioannis, PhD   Sr. Lectr.
Seller, Rev. Mary J., BSc PhD DSc   Reader
Solomon, Ellen, BSc PhD   Prof.; Chairman*

Medicine

Allergy and Respiratory Medicine

Hawrylowicz, Catherine M., BSc PhD   Sr.
  Lectr.
Lee, Tak Hong, MA Camb., MD Camb., MB
  BChir, FRCP   Prof.; Head*
Santis, George, MB ChB MD   Sr. Lectr.
Staynov, Dontcho Z., MSc PhD   Sr. Lectr.
Twort, Charles H., MB BChir MA MD,
  FRCP   Sr. Lectr.
Ward, Jeremy P. T., BSc PhD   Reader

Cardiology

Chambers, John B., BA MB BChir MA MD   Sr.
  Lectr.; Head*
Marber, Michael S., BSc MB BS PhD   Sr. Lectr.

Clinical Science Laboratories

Rees, Peter J., MB BChir MD, FRCP   Sr. Lectr.

Diabetes, Endocrinology and Metabolic Medicine

Gnudi, Luigi   Sr. Lectr.
Grenfell, Anasuya, MD, FRCP   Sr. Lectr.
Hennessy, Thomas R., BSc MA MD MSc
  PhD   Sr. Lectr.
Jones, Richard H., MA Camb., MB BChir Camb.,
  PhD, FRCP   Sr. Lectr.
Lowy, Clara, MB BS MB BChir MD MSc,
  FRCP   Reader
Sönksen, Peter H., MB BS MD, FRCP   Prof.;
  Chairman*
Thomas, Christopher R., BSc MD PhD   Sr.
  Lectr.
Umpleby, Anne M., BA PhD   Sr. Lectr.
Viberti, Gian-Carlo, MD Milan, FRCP   Prof.

Gastroenterology

Dowling, Robert H., MB BChir MD,
  FRCP   Prof.; Head*
Murphy, Gerard M., PhD, FRSChem   Reader
Wilkinson, Mark L., BSc MB BS MD, FRCP   Sr.
  Lectr.

Haemophilia

Savidge, Geoffrey F., MA MB BS MD   Prof.

Lupus Arthritis Research Unit

Hughes, G. V. R., MD, FRCP   Head*
Khamashta, M. A., MD PhD   Sr. Lectr.

Molecular Immunogenetics

Lanchbury, Jerry S., BSc PhD   Reader; Head*

Neurology

Gregson, Norman A., BSc PhD   Sr. Lectr.
Hughes, Richard A. C., BA MD, FRCP   Prof.;
  Head*
Kapoor, Raju, BA BM BCh DM   Sr. Lectr.
Sharief, Mohammed, MB ChB MPhil PhD   Sr.
  Lectr.
Smith, Kenneth J., BSc PhD   Reader

Renal Medicine

Sacks, Steven H., BSc MB ChB PhD,
  FRCP   Prof.; Head*
Williams, Daniel G., MB BChir MD,
  FRCP   Prof.; Chairman*

Rheumatology

Khamashta, Munther A., MD PhD   Sr. Lectr.
Kingsley, Gabrielle H., BSc MB ChB, FRCP   Sr.
  Lectr.
MacGregor, Alexander J., BA MD MB BS
  MSc   Sr. Lectr.
Panayi, Gabriel S., ScD MD, FRCP   Prof.;
  Head*
Pitzalis, Costantino, MD PhD   Sr. Lectr.

Obstetrics and Gynaecology

Braude, Peter R., BSc MB ChB MA PhD,
  FRCOG   Prof.; Chairman*
Forsling, Mary L., BSc PhD DSc   Prof.
Handyside, Alan H., BSc MA PhD   Reader
Poston, Lucilla, BSc PhD   Prof.
Rymer, Janice M., BHB MB ChB MD   Sr.
  Lectr.
Shennan, Andrew H., MB BS MD   Sr. Lectr.
Taylor, Alison S., MB BS   Sr. Lectr.

Oncology
(including Palliative Medicine)

Beynon, Teresa A., MB ChB   Sr. Lectr.
Burman, Rachel E., MA MB BS   Sr. Lectr.
Camplejohn, Richard S., BSc MSc PhD   Sr.
  Lectr.
Fentiman, Ian S., MB BS MD, FRCS   Prof.
Hart, Ian R., BVSc PhD, FRCPath   Prof.
Miles, David W., MB BS MD   Sr. Lectr.
Rubens, Robert D., BSc MD, FRCP   Prof.;
  Chairman*
Richards, Michael A., MA MB BChir MD,
  FRCP   Prof.

Ophthalmology

Marshall, John, BSc PhD   Prof.
Stanford, Miles R., BChir MA MSc, FRCS   Sr.
  Lectr.

Paediatrics

Baker, Edward J., MB BChir Camb., MA Camb.,
  MD, FRCP   Sr. Lectr.
Chantler, Sir Cyril, MA Camb., MD Camb.,
  FRCP   Prof.
Clark, Arthur G. B., BA MA MB BS   Sr. Lectr.
Clayden, Graham S., MB BS MD,
  FRCP   Reader
Dalton, Raymond N., BSc MA PhD   Sr. Lectr.
Dykes, Evelyn H., MB ChB, FRCS   Sr. Lectr.
Garvie, Dorothy C., MB ChB BPharm,
  FRCP   Sr. Lectr.
Haycock, George B., MB BChir Camb., BA,
  FRCP   Prof.
Lynch, Margaret A., MB BS MD, FRCP   Reader
Milner, Anthony D., MB BChir Camb.,
  FRCP   Prof.; Chairman*
Robinson, Richard O., MA MB ChB,
  FRCP   Prof.
Sharland, Gurleen, BSc MB BS MD   Sr. Lectr.
Tynan, Michael J., MB BS MD, FRCP   Prof.

Palliative Medicine, see Oncol.

Pharmacology

Aaronson, Philip I., BA PhD   Sr. Lectr.
Ciclitira, Paul J., MB BS MD PhD, FRCP   Prof.
Cox, Helen M., BA BSc PhD   Sr. Lectr.
Docherty, Reginald J., BSc PhD   Sr. Lectr.
File, Sandra E., BSc PhD DSc   Prof.
Kentish, Jonathan C., MA PhD   Sr. Lectr.
Neal, Michael J., BPharm MA PhD DSc   Prof.;
  Chairman*
Robinson, Bryan V., PhD   Sr. Lectr.

Pharmacology and Toxicology (Clinical)

Chowienczyk, Philip J., BSc MB BS   Sr. Lectr.
Ferro, Albert, BSc MB BS PhD   Sr. Lectr.
Ritter, James M., MA Oxf., DPhil Oxf.,
  FRCP   Prof., Clinical Pharmacology

Physiology

Band, David M., MB BChir Camb., MA
  Camb.   Reader
Butt, Arthur, BSc MPhil PhD   Reader
Imms, Frederick J., BSc MB BS PhD   Sr. Lectr.
McMahon, Stephen B., BSc PhD   Prof.
Pini, Adrian P. J., BSc MSc PhD   Sr. Lectr.
Segal, Malcolm B., BSc PhD   Reader;
  Chairman*
Thexton, Allan J., BSc BDS PhD,
  FDSRCS   Reader
Ward, Jane, BSc MB ChB PhD   Sr. Lectr.
Ward, Jeremy P. T., BSc PhD   Reader

Primary Health Care

Armstrong, David, MB BS MSc PhD,
  FRCGP   Reader
Britten, Nicky, BA MA MSc PhD   Sr. Lectr.
Campbell, John L., BSc MB ChB   Sr. Lectr.
Jones, Roger H., BM BCh MA DM, FRCP,
  FRCGP   Prof.; Chairman*
Ogden, Jane E., BSc PhD   Sr. Lectr.
Peters, Barry S., MB BS MD   Sr. Lectr.
Phillips, Richard J. W., BA BM BCh MA   Sr.
  Lectr.
Ridsdale, Leone L., BA MD MSc PhD,
  FRCPCan, FRCGP   Reader
Wass, Valerie J., BSc MB BS, FRCGP   Sr. Lectr.
Zander, Lucas I., MB BCh, FRCGP   Sr. Lectr.

Psychiatry and Psychology

Abdel-Mawgoud, Mohamed, MB BCh MD,
  FRCPsych   Sr. Lectr.
Anderson, James S., MB BChir   Sr. Lectr.
Atakan, Zerrin, MD   Sr. Lectr.
Ball, Christopher J., MB BS   Sr. Lectr.
Barker, Ann F., MB BS   Sr. Lectr.
Beer, Michael D., MB BS MA MD   Sr. Lectr.
Besson, John A. O., BSc MB ChB   Sr. Lectr.
Boardman, Anthony P., MB BS PhD   Sr.
  Lectr.
Bouras, Nicandros, MD PhD, FRCPsych   Sr.
  Lectr.

Brooks, David S., MB BS Sr. Lectr.
Browning, Sally M., MB ChB Sr. Lectr.
Cope, Susan J., BA MA MB BChir Sr. Lectr.
Craig, Kenneth D., MB ChB Sr. Lectr.
Craig, Thomas K. J., MB BS PhD,
   FRCPsych Prof.
Davies, Teifion W., MB BS BSc PhD Sr. Lectr.
Davis, Hilton M., BA PhD, FBPsS Prof.
Dratcu, Luiz, MD MSc PhD Sr. Lectr.
Euba, Raphael Sr. Lectr.
Fitzpatrick, Declan, MB BCh BAO Sr. Lectr.
Fottrell, Eamonn M., MD, FRCPsych Sr. Lectr.
Garety, Philippa A., MA MPhil PhD Prof.
Gaughran, Fiona P., MB BCh BAO Sr. Lectr.
Goddard, Catherine A., MB BS Sr. Lectr.
Gupta, Kamal, MB BS MD Sr. Lectr.
Hindler, Charles G., MB BCh MPhil Sr. Lectr.
Holt, Geraldine M., BSc MB BS, FRCPsych Sr.
   Lectr.
Isaac, Michael T., BA MB BS MA Sr. Lectr.
Jeffers, A. M., MB BCh Sr. Lectr.
Jezzard, Robert G., MB BChir, FRCPsych Sr.
   Lectr.
Klemperer, Frances J., BA MA MB BS Sr.
   Lectr.
Kopelman, Michael D., BA MB BS PhD, FBPsS,
   FRCPsych Prof.
Loader, Peter J., MB BS Sr. Lectr.
Macdonald, Alastair J. D., MB ChB MD,
   FRCPsych Prof.
Malik, Shakil J., MB BS Sr. Lectr.
Marlowe, Martin J., MB BS Sr. Lectr.
Marteau, Theresa M., BSc MSc PhD Prof.
Master, Dinshaw R., MB BS, FRCP,
   FRCPsych Sr. Lectr.
McLaren, Paul M., BA BSc MB BS MA Sr.
   Lectr.
Morgan, Judith, MB ChB, FRCPsych Sr. Lectr.
Muijen, Matthijs F., MD MSc PhD Sr. Lectr.
O'Neill-Byrne, Katrina, MB BCh BAO Sr.
   Lectr.
Onyeama, Warwick P., MB DM, FRSPysch Sr.
   Lectr.
Parker, Elizabeth, MB BChir MA Sr. Lectr.
Parrott, Janet M., BSc MB ChB, FRCPsych Sr.
   Lectr.
Ramirez, Amanda-Jane, BSc MB BS Prof.
Richardson, Philip H., BSc Mphil PhD Sr.
   Lectr.
Roy, David H., MB, FRCPsych Sr. Lectr.
Shepherd, Eric W., BA MSc PhD Sr. Lectr.
Shepherd, Geoffrey W., BSc MPhil PhD Prof.
Shyam Ansari, Shakir U., MB BS Sr. Lectr.
Simonoff, Emily A., BA MD Prof.
Starke, Ian D., MB BS Sr. Lectr.
Timms, Philip W. Sr. Lectr.
Treloar, Adrian J., MB BS Sr. Lectr.
Watson, James P., MA Camb., MD Camb., FRCP,
   FRCPsych Prof.; Chairman*
Weinman, John A., BA PhD, FBPsS Prof.
White, Karen, MB ChB Sr. Lectr.
Wiseman, Malcolm, MB BChir Sr. Lectr.
Wood, Stephen, BSc MB BS, FRCPsych Sr.
   Lectr.

Public Health Sciences

Burney, Peter G. J., BA MB BS MA MD Prof.;
   Chairman*
Chinn, Susan, MA Camb. Reader
Gulliford, Martin C., MB BS MA Sr. Lectr.
Jarvis, Deborah L., MB BS Sr. Lectr.
Maryon Davis, Alan R., MB BChir MA
   MSc Sr. Lectr.
Morgan, Myfanwy A., BA MA PhD Reader
Peel, Michael, MB BS Sr. Lectr.
Rona, Roberto J., PhD Reader
Snashall, David C., MB ChB MSc, FRCP Sr.
   Lectr.
Sterne, Jonathan A. C., BA MSc PhD Sr. Lectr.
West, Peter A., BA DPhil Sr. Lectr.
Wolfe, Charles D. A., MB BS MD Sr. Lectr.

Radiological Sciences

Adam, Andreas, MB BS, FRCP, FRCR Prof.
Bingham, John B., MB BChir MA MSc, FRCP
   FRCR Prof.
Clarke, Susan E. M., MB BS Sr. Lectr.
Fogelman, Ignac, BSc MD MB ChB,
   FRCP Prof.

Garlick, Pamela B., BA Oxf., DPhil Oxf.,
   MA Sr. Lectr.
Hawkes, David J., BA MSc PhD Reader
Maisey, Michael N., BSc MD, FRCP,
   FRCR Prof.; Chairman*
O'Doherty, Michael J., BA MA MB BS MD
   MSc Sr. Lectr.
Padayachee, Thirupasundrie, BSc PhD Sr.
   Lectr.

SEIPH

O'Neill, Declan F., MB BCh BAO MPH Sr.
   Lectr.

Surgery

Brueton, Richard N., MB BS MD, FRCS Sr.
   Lectr.
Burnand, Kevin G., MB BS MS, FRCS Prof.;
   Chairman*
Gleeson, Michael J., MB BS MD BDS,
   FRCS Prof.
Heatley, Frederick W., MB BChir, FRCS Prof.
Jourdan, Martin H., BSc MS PhD,
   FRCS Reader
Mundy, Anthony R., MB BS MRCP MS,
   FRCS Prof.
Owen, William J., BSc MB BS MS, FRCS Sr.
   Lectr.
Smith, Alberto, BSc PhD Sr. Lectr.
Spencer, John D., MB BS MS, FRCS Reader

Toxicology, see Pharmacol. and Toxicol.
   (Clin.)

SPECIAL CENTRES, ETC

Advanced Biblical Studies, Centre for
Tel: (0171) 873 2335 Fax: (0171) 873 2255
Larkin, K. J. A., BSc Durh., BD Lond., PhD
   Lond. Dir.*

Advanced Musical Studies, Institute of
Tel: (0171) 873 2354 Fax: (0171) 873 2326
Wintle, C. S., BA Oxf., BMus Oxf. Dir.*

**Advanced Performance Studies, Centre
for**
Tel: (0171) 873 2392 Fax: (0171) 873 2326
Dreyfus, Prof. L., PhD Col. Dir.*

Advancement of Thinking, Centre for
Tel: (0171) 872 3079 Fax: (0171) 872 3182
Adey, P., BSc Lond., PhD Lond. Dir.*

Algorithm Design Group
Tel: (0171) 873 2809 Fax: (0171) 873 2851
Iliopoulos, C. S., BSc Athens, MSc Warw., PhD
   Warw. Dir.*

**Analytical Chemistry and
Instrumentation, Centre for Research
in**
Tel: (0171) 873 2039 Fax: (0171) 873 2810
Malcolme-Lawes, D. J., PhD DSc,
   FRSChem Dir.*

**British Constitutional Law and History,
Centre of**
Tel: (0171) 873 2516 Fax: (0171) 873 2465
Blackburn, R. W., BA MSc PhD,
   FRHistS Dir.*

Civil Liberties Research Unit
Tel: (0171) 873 2376 Fax: (0171)873 2465
Gearty, C. A., BCL N.U.I., LLB Camb., PhD
   Camb. Dir.*

**Computing in the Humanities, Centre
for**
Tel: (0171) 873 2739 Fax: (0171) 873 5081
McCarty, W., BA PhD Sr. Lectr.

**Data and Knowledge Engineering,
Centre for**
Tel: (0171) 873 2588 Fax: (0171) 873 2851
No staff at present

Defence Studies, Centre for
Tel: (0171) 873 2338 Fax: (0171) 873 2748
Freedman, Prof. Lawrence D., CBE, BA(Econ)
   Manc., BPhil York(UK), DPhil Oxf., FBA Dir.*

**Delinquency, Institute for the Study and
Treatment of**
Tel: (0171) 873 2822 Fax: (0171) 873 2823
Braggins, J., BA Dir.*

**Developmental Biology Research
Centre**
Tel: (0171) 836 8851 Fax: (0171) 497 9078
Holder, Prof. N., BSc PhD ; Dir.*

Drug Control Centre
Tel: (0171) 352 3838 Fax: (0171) 351 2591
Cowan, Prof. D. A., BPharm PhD ; Dir.*

Educational Computing Unit
Tel: (0171) 872 3107, 872 3189 Fax: (0171)
   872 3182
Squires, David, BSc Lond., PhD Lond. Dir.*

European Law, Centre of
Tel: (0171) 873 2387 Fax: (0171) 873 2387
Andenas, Mads, CandJur Oslo, PhD
   Camb. Dir.*

Gerontology, Age Concern Institute of
Tel: (0171) 872 3035 Fax: (0171) 872 3235
Tinker, Prof. Anthea, BCom Birm., PhD
   City(UK) Dir.*

Health, Institute of
Tel: (0171) 333 4646 Fax: (0171) 937 5690
Hider, Prof. Robert, BSc Lond., PhD Lond.,
   FRSChem Dir.*

**Heat Transfer and Fluid Flow
Measurement, Centre for**
Tel: (0171) 873 2428 Fax: (0171) 873 2437
Yianneskis, Prof. M., BSc MSc PhD,
   FIMechE ; Dir.*

Hellenic Studies, Centre for
Tel: (0171) 873 2330 Fax: (0171) 873 2830
Herrin, Prof. J. E., MA Camb., PhD Birm. Dir.*

Human Rights, British Institute of
Tel: (0171) 873 2352 Fax: (0171) 873 2048
Busuttil, James J., BA Harv., DPhil Oxf., JD
   N.Y. Dir.*

Humanities Research Centres
Tel: (0171) 873 2360 Fax: (0171) 873 2415
Nelson, Prof. J. L., BA Camb., PhD Camb.,
   FBA ; Dir.*

**International Antioxidant Research
Centre**
Tel: (0171) 333 4860 Fax: (0171) 333 4949
Halliwell, Prof. B. A., DPhil Oxf., DSc
   Lond. Dir.*

Japanese New Religions Project
Tel: (0171) 873 3792 Fax: (0171) 873 2292
Clarke, Prof. P. B., MA Oxf., MA Lond., MPhil
   PhD Dir.*

Kew–King's Phytochemical Group
Tel: (0171) 333 4775, 333 4298 Fax: (0171)
   351 5307, 351 4500
Houghton, Peter J., BPharm PhD, FRPharmS,
   FRSChem Dir.*

Late Antique and Medieval Studies, Centre for

Fax: (0171) 873 2052

Nelson, Prof. J. L., BA Camb., PhD Camb., FBA Dir.*

Latin American Cultural Studies, Centre for

Tel: (0171) 873 2067 Fax: (0171) 873 2207

Rowe, W. W., MA Camb., PhD Dir.*

Mechatronics and Manufacturing Systems Engineering, Centre for

Tel: (0171) 873 2236 Fax: (0171) 873 2437

Seneviratne, L. D., PhD Dir.*

Medical Law and Ethics, Centre of

Tel: (0171) 873 2382 Fax: (0171) 873 2575

Walsh, P., BA Lond. Lectr.; Acting Dir.*

Medieval Lexicology and Source Studies, Archive of

Tel: (0171) 873 1129 Fax: (0171) 873 2257

Bately, Prof. J. M., MA Oxf., FBA Dir.*
Roberts, Prof. J. R., DPhil Oxf. Dir.*

Mental Health Services Development, Centre for

Tel: (0171) 333 4194 Fax: (0171) 333 4089

Peck, E., MA PhD Dir.*

Metals in Biology and Medicine, Centre for

Tel: (0171) 333 4264 Fax: (0171) 333 4500

Cammack, Prof. R., BA Camb., PhD Camb., ScD Camb. Dir.*
Wrigglesworth, J. M., MSc Birm., PhD Birm. Dir.*

Military Archives, Liddell Hart Centre for

Tel: (0171) 873 2187, 873 2015 Fax: (0171) 873 2760

Methven, P. J., BA Dir.*

Molecular Cell Biology, Interdisciplinary Research Institute in

Tel: (0171) 380 7802 Fax: (0171) 380 7804

Hopkins, Prof. C. R., BSc Wales, PhD Wales Dir.*

Monitoring and Assessment Research Centre

Tel: (0171) 376 1577 Fax: (0171) 937 5396

Williams, W. Peter, BSc Leic., PhD Reading Dir.*

Muscle and Motility, Research Centre

Tel: (0171) 465 5031 Fax: (0171) 497 9078

Simmons, Prof. R. M., MSc PhD, FRS Dir.*

Neural Networks, Centre for

Tel: (0171) 873 2214 Fax: (0171) 873 2017

Taylor, Prof. J. G., MA Camb., PhD Camb. Dir.*

Neurodegenerative Diseases Research Centre

Tel: (0171) 333 4716 Fax: (0171) 376 4736

Halliwell, Prof. B. A., DPhil Oxf., DSc Lond. Dir.*
Jenner, P. G., BPharm PhD DSc, FRPharmS Dir.*

New Religious Movements, Centre for

Tel: (0171) 873 3796 Fax: (0171) 873 2255

Clarke, Prof. P. B., MA Oxf., MA Lond., MPhil PhD Dir.*

Nursing Research Unit

Tel: (0171) 872 3065, 872 3057 Fax: (0171) 872 3069

Redfern, Prof. S. J., BSc Aston, PhD Aston Dir.*

Optics and Electronics, Centre for

Tel: (0171) 873 2592 Fax: (0171) 836 4781

Rogers, Prof. A. J., MA Camb., PhD Lond. Dir.*

Philosophy Studies, Centre for

Tel: (0171) 873 2340 Fax: (0171) 873 2270

Milton, J. R., MA Camb., PhD Lond. Dir.*

Public Policy Research, Centre for

Tel: (0171) 872 3163 Fax: (0171) 872 3182

Ball, Prof. S. J. Dir.*

Randall Institute

Biomedical research

Tel: (0171) 465 5031 Fax: (0171) 497 9078

Simmons, Prof. R. M., MSc PhD, FRS Dir.*

Signals, Circuits and Systems Research Group

Tel: (0171) 873 2365 Fax: (0171) 836 4781

Sandler, Prof. Mark, BSc Essex, PhD Essex Dir.*

Systematic Theology, Research Institute in

Tel: (0171) 873 2398 Fax: (0171) 873 2255

Torrance, A. J., MA Edin., BD Aberd., , DrTheol Erlangen Dir.*

Theology and Culture Research Centre

Tel: (0171) 872 3154 Fax: (0171) 872 3182

Walker, A., BA Lond., MSc Lond., PhD Lond. Dir.*

Twentieth-Century Cultural Studies, Centre for

Tel: (0171) 873 2404 Fax: (0171) 873 2720

Griffiths, Prof. R. M., MA Camb., MA Oxf., PhD Camb. Dir.*

Vascular Biology Research Centre

Tel: (0171) 333 4083 Fax: (0171) 333 4083

Pearson, Prof. J. D., MA Oxf., MA Camb., PhD Camb. Dir.*

CONTACT OFFICERS

Academic affairs. Academic Registrar: Salter, Brian E., BSc Leeds, FKC
Accommodation. Accommodation Officer: Stringer, Susannah
Admissions (first degree) (School of Dentistry). Dental Faculty Administrator: ......
Admissions (first degree) (School of Humanities). Executive Officer, Admissions: Sacchetti, Stephen
Admissions (first degree) (School of Law). Gibbens, Wendy
Admissions (first degree) (School of Life Sciences). Hargreaves, Helen
Admissions (first degree) (School of Medicine). Admissions Co-ordinator: Smedley, Janine, BA Exe.
Admissions (first degree) (School of Physical Sciences). Undergraduate Admissions Officer: Osbourn, Chris
Admissions (higher degree) (School of Education). Admissions Secretary: Thorley, Lois
Admissions (higher degree) (School of Law). Postgraduate Administrative Officer: Layfield, Penny
Admissions (higher degree) (School of Life Sciences). Hargreaves, Helen
Admissions (higher degree) (School of Medicine and Dentistry). Registry Assistant, Postgraduate: Campbell, Venice

Admissions (higher degree) (School of Physical Sciences). Postgraduate Admissions Officer: Panayi, Barbara
Adult/continuing education. Murray, Robin, PhD
Alumni. KCLA Officer: McLoughlin, John, PhD Trinity(Dub.)
Archives. College Archivist: Methven, Patricia, BA Lond.
Careers. Head of Careers Advisory Service: Dirmikis, Susan, PhD
Computing services. Director of Computing Services: Byerley, Andrew J., BSc S'ton., PhD S'ton.
Consultancy services. Managing Director, KCL Enterprises Ltd: Sims, Malcolm, BSc PhD
Credit transfer. Deputy Academic Registrar: Wainwright, Virginia, BA Sus.
Development/fund-raising. Development Director: Agnew, Jo, BA W.Aust.
Equal opportunities. Personnel Manager: Rowlands, Keren
Estates and buildings/works and services. Estates Manager: McCarthy, Jeffrey, FRICS
Examinations. Assistant Registrar: Ironside, Kathryn
Finance. Deputy College Secretary (Planning and Resources): Ball, David, FCA, FKC
General enquiries. College Secretary: Slade, W. C., BSc Wales, FKC
Health services. Senior College Medical Officer: Pathmanathan, K., PhD
Industrial liaison. Managing Director, KCL Enterprises Ltd: Sims, Malcolm, BSc PhD
International office. International Liaison Officer: Anning, Jennifer, BA Lond.
Library (chief librarian). Director of Library Services: Bell, Anne, BA MA
Minorities/disadvantaged groups. Student Welfare and Information Officer: Cockburn, Celia, MA
Personnel/human resources. Director of Personnel and Training: Young, Marjorie, BA Liv.
Public relations, information and marketing. Director of Public Relations: Kenyon-Jones, Christine, MA Oxf.
Publications. Publications Officer: Fitzpatrick, Bridget
Purchasing. Purchasing Manager: Wrigg, James
Quality assurance and accreditation. Senior Assistant Registrar (Academic Standards): Placito, Hilary, BA
Research. Senior Administrative Assistant (Academic Standards): Clarke, Jason
Safety. College Safety Officer: Slade, Roger, BSc PhD
Scholarships, awards, loans. Senior Clerical Officer, Student Finance: Greene, Alison, BA Lond.
Schools liaison. Director of Student Recruitment: Claas, Richard, MA
Security. General Services Manager: Redmond, Robert
Staff development and training. Academic Training Officer: Mayhew, Roger, BSc Lond.
Staff development and training. Training Officer (non-teaching staff): Bromfield, Kenneth
Student welfare/counselling. Director of Student Services: Conlon, Ann, BEd Leeds
Students from other countries. International Liaison Officer: Anning, Jennifer, BA Lond.
Students with disabilities. Student Welfare and Information Officer: Cockburn, Celia, MA
Women. Student Welfare and Information Officer: Cockburn, Celia, MA

[Information supplied by the institution as at 22 June 1998, and edited by the ACU]

LONDON BUSINESS SCHOOL

Incorporated under Companies Act 1965; Royal Charter granted 1986

Associate Member of the Association of Commonwealth Universities

Postal Address: Sussex Place, Regent's Park, London, England NW1 4SA
Telephone: (0171) 262 5050 **Fax**: (0171) 724 7875 **Cables**: Lonbiskol **Telex**: 27461
WWW: http://www.lbs.ac.uk

DEAN*—Quelch, Prof. John A., BA Oxf., MBA Penn., MS Harv., DBA Harv.
DEPUTY PRINCIPAL—Earl, Prof. Michael J., BA Newcastle(UK), MSc Warw.
DEPUTY PRINCIPAL—Robertson, Prof. Tom S., MA Northwestern, PhD Northwestern
SECRETARY AND TREASURER‡—Quincey, Gerry
RESEARCH DEAN—Nicholson, Prof. Nigel, BA Wales, PhD Wales, FBPsS

GENERAL INFORMATION

History. The school was founded in 1965 and granted its Royal Charter in 1986.

First Degrees are not offered.

Higher Degrees (of University of London) (see also University of London Directory to Subjects of Study). MBA, MSc, PhD.
Entry requirements: good Graduate Management Aptitude Test (GMAT) score, work experience and management potential.

Academic Year. September–July.

Income (1996–97). Total, £34,000,000.

Statistics. Staff: 139. Students: 1100 (degree); 3000 (non-degree course participants).

FACULTIES/SCHOOLS

Executive Education
Director: Haskins, G., BA McG., MBA York(Can.)
Assistant: Dales, T.

Executive MBA Programme
Dean: McWilliam, Gil, BA Exe., MA Birm., MBA Manc., PhD Cran.
Director: Pederson, I.

Finance Programmes Office
Director (Part-Time): Marsh, Prof. P. R., BSc(Econ) Lond., PhD Lond.
Director: Neuberger, A. J., BA Camb., MSc Lond., PhD Lond.
Administrator: Dobson, J.

MBA Programme
Dean: Geroski, Prof. P. A., BA Bard, MA Warw., PhD Warw.
Director: Tyler, J.

Research
Dean: Nicholson, Prof. Nigel, BA Wales, PhD Wales, FBPsS
Director: Madden, R., BA E.Anglia, MSc York(UK), PhD City(UK)

Sloan Fellowship Masters Programme
Chairman: Westbrook, R. K., BA Lond., PhD Lond.
Director: Hoffman, L.

ACADEMIC UNITS
Arranged by Subject Areas

Accounting
Higson, Chris J., BA Lond., MSc Lond., PhD Lond.   Assoc. Prof.; Head*
Livne, Gilad, BA Tel-Aviv, MSc Calif., PhD Calif.   Asst. Prof.
Shivakumar, Lakshmanan, BCom Madr., MBA Vanderbilt, PhD Vanderbilt   Asst. Prof.
Zimmermann, J., MSc Mannheim, PhD Mannheim   Asst. Prof.

Decision Sciences
Bunn, Derek W., MA Camb., MSc Lond., PhD Lond.   Prof.; Head*
Jackson, Mary, MA Oxf., MSc Lond.   Asst. Prof.
Morecroft, J. D. W., BSc Brist., MSc Lond., PhD M.I.T.   Assoc. Prof.
van Ackere, Ann, LicTWE Antwerp, PhD Stan.   Assoc. Prof.
Vlahos, K., BSc Athens, PhD Lond.   Asst. Prof.

Economics
Barrett, S. A., BS Mass., MA Br.Col., PhD Lond.   Assoc. Prof.
Cabral, Luis, BA C.U.Portugal, MA Lisbon, PhD Stan.   Assoc. Prof.
Currie, D. A., BSc Manc., MSc Birm., PhD Lond.   Prof.
Estrin, Saul, BA Camb., MA Camb., DPhil Sus.   Prof.; Head*
Geroski, P. A., BA Bard, MA Warw., PhD Warw.   Prof.
Graddy, K., BA Tulane, MBA Col., PhD Prin.   Asst. Prof.
Portes, R., BA Yale, MA Oxf., DPhil Oxf.   Prof.
Scott, Andrew, MA Oxf., MSc Lond., DPhil Oxf.   Assoc. Prof.

Finance
Brealey, R. R., MA Oxf.   Tokai Bank Prof., Corporate Finance; Head*
Britten-Jones, M., BEc Adel., MA Calif.   Asst. Prof.
Buraschi, A., BA Bocconi, MA Chic., PhD Chic.   Asst. Prof.
Cooper, I. A., MA Camb., MBA N.Carolina, PhD N.Carolina   B.Z.W. Prof.
Cornelli, Francesca, BA Bocconi, PhD Harv.   Asst. Prof.
Dimson, E., BA Newcastle(UK), MCom Birm., PhD Lond.   Prof.; Prudential Res. Fellow
Dow, J. C. F., MA Camb., PhD Prin.   Assoc. Prof.
Franks, Julian R., BA Sheff., MBA Col., PhD Lond.   Prof.
Goldreich, David, BS Calif., MSIA Carnegie-Mellon, MS Carnegie-Mellon   Asst. Prof.
Habib, M., BEng McG., MEng McG., PhD Penn.   Asst. Prof.
Marsh, P. R., BSc(Econ) Lond., PhD Lond.   Prof.
Milbourn, Todd, BA Augustana, PhD Indiana   Asst. Prof.
Mussavian, M., BSc Lond., MPhil N.Y., PhD N.Y.   Asst. Prof.
Naik, N., BTech IIT Bombay, PhD Duke   Asst. Prof.
Neuberger, A. J., BA Camb., MSc Lond., PhD Lond.   Asst. Prof.
Nyborg, K. G., BS Chic., PhD Stan.   Asst. Prof.
Schaefer, S. M., MA Camb., PhD Lond.   Esmee Fairbairn Prof.
Torous, W., BMath Wat., PhD Penn.   Corporation of London Prof.

Marketing
Barwise, T. P., MA Oxf., MSc Lond., PhD Lond.   Prof., Management and Marketing
Grayson, K., BA Mich., MA Mich., PhD Northwestern   Asst. Prof.

Hardie, B. G. S., BCom Auck., MCom Auck., MA Penn., PhD Penn.   Asst. Prof.
McWilliam, Gil, BA Exe., MA Birm., MBA Manc., PhD Cran.   Assoc. Prof.
Putsis, W. P., BA N.Y., PhD Cornell   Assoc. Prof.
Robertson, Tom S., MA Northwestern, PhD Northwestern   Sainsbury Prof.; Head*
Sahay, Arvind, BTech Kanpur, PhD Texas   Asst. Prof.
Simmonds, K., MCom NZ, DBA Harv., PhD Lond., FCA(NZ), FCIS   Prof., Marketing and International Business
Swartz, G. S., BSc M.I.T., MBA Northeastern, DBA Harv.   Asst. Prof.

Operations Management
Frohlich, M., BA Mass., MBA Calif., DBA Boston   Asst. Prof.
Hill, Terry, BA Manc., MSc Manc., PhD Warw.   Prof.
Nicholson, T. A. J., BSc Lond., PhD Lond.   Prof.
Voss, C., MSc Lond., PhD Lond.   British Telecom Prof.; Head*
Westbrook, R. K., BA Lond., PhD Lond.   Assoc. Prof.

Organisational Behaviour
Audia, Giuseppe, BS Calabria, MBA Bocconi, PhD Maryland   Asst. Prof.
Earley, P. Chris, BA Knox(Ill.), MA Ill., PhD Ill.   Prof.
Goffee, R. E., BA Kent, PhD Kent   Prof.; Head*
Gratton, Lynda C., BA Liv., PhD Liv.   Assoc. Prof.
Mahoney, J., MA Glas., DTheol Greg.   Dixons Prof., Business Ethics and Social Responsibility
Morris, T. J., BA Camb., MSc Lond., PhD Lond.   Assoc. Prof.
Nicholson, Nigel, BA Wales, PhD Wales, FBPsS   Prof.
Peiperl, M., BSE Prin., MBA Harv., AM Harv., PhD Harv.   Asst. Prof.
Robertson, Diana, AB Northwestern, MA Calif., PhD Calif.   Asst. Prof., Organisational Behaviour and Business Ethics
Willman, P. W., MA Camb., DPhil Oxf.   Prof., Organisational Behaviour and Industrial Relations

Strategic and International Management
Chacar, A., BSc Lebanon, MBA Rensselaer, PhD Calif.   Asst. Prof.
Earl, Michael J., BA Newcastle(UK), MSc Warw.   Andersen Consulting Prof., Information Management
Ghoshal, S., MS M.I.T., PhD M.I.T., DBA Harv.   Robert P. Bauman Prof., Strategic Leadership
Hay, M., BA York(UK), DPhil York(UK)   Assoc. Prof.
Hayward, M. L. A., BCom Melb., PhD Col.   Asst. Prof.
Korine, H. D., BA Stan., BS Stan., MBA Calif., PhD Europ.Inst.Bus.Admin., BA   Asst. Prof.

Markides, C., MA *Boston*, MBA *Harv.* Assoc. Prof.

Sampler, J. L., BS *Texas*, MBA *Texas*, PhD *Pitt.* Asst. Prof.

Short, J. E., SM *M.I.T.*, PhD *M.I.T.* Assoc. Prof.

Stopford, J. M., BA *Oxf.*, SM *Mass.*, DBA *Harv.* Prof., International Business; Head*

Sull, Donald, BA *Harv.*, MBA *Harv.*, DBA *Harv.* Asst. Prof.

Other Staff: 1 Lectr.

SPECIAL CENTRES, ETC

CIS–Middle Europe Centre

Estrin, Saul, BA *Camb.*, MA *Camb.*, DPhil *Sus.* Prof.; Dir.*

Design Technology, Centre for

Bunn, D., MA *Camb.*, MSc *Lond.*, PhD *Lond.* Dir.*

Economic Forecasting, Centre for

Henry, Brian, BSc *Lond.*, MSc *Lond.* Res. Dir.; Prof. Fellow; Dir.*

Finance and Accounting, Institute of

Brealey, R. A., MA *Oxf.* Prof.; Dir.*

Foundation for Entrepreneurial Management

Bates, J., BSc *Nott.*, MBA *Harv.* Prof.; Exec. Dir.*

Information Management, Centre for Research in

Earl, Michael J., BA *Newcastle(UK)*, MSc *Warw.* Prof.; Dir.*

Marketing, Centre for

Barwise, T. P., MA *Oxf.*, MSc *Lond.*, PhD *Lond.* Prof.; Dir.*

Operations Management, Centre for

Voss, C. A., BSc *Lond.*, MSc *Lond.*, PhD *Lond.* British Telecom Prof.; Dir.*

Organisational Research, Centre for

Willman, P., MA *Camb.*, DPhil *Oxf.* Prof.; Dir.*

Regulation Initiative

Currie, David A., BSc *Manc.*, MSc *Birm.*, PhD *Lond.* Prof.; Dir.*

CONTACT OFFICERS

Academic affairs. Director of Academic Planning: Vipond, Rosemary, BA *Leeds*, PhD *Leeds*

Alumni. Director, London Business School Alumni Association: Caseley, Emma, MA *Oxf.*

Careers. Director, Career Management Centre: Aylward, Lesley, LLB *Glas.*, MA *Glas.*, MBA *Durh.*

Computing services. Director, Information Systems: Robiette, Alan, BA *Camb.*, MA *Camb.*, PhD *Camb.*

Development/fund-raising. Director, Development: Conner, W.

Finance. Deputy Treasurer: Rudkin, Adrienne

General enquiries. Secretary and Treasurer: Quincey, Gerry

Library (enquiries). Head of Library: Edwards, Helen

Personnel/human resources. Director, Personnel: Hoare, Lyndon, BSc(Econ) *Wales*

Public relations, information and marketing. Director, Communications and Corporate Marketing: Griffin, Gerry, BA *N.U.I.*, MA *N.U.I.*

Research. Director, Research Support: Madden, Raymond, BA *E.Anglia*, MSc *York(UK)*, PhD *City(UK)*

Security. Head of Management Services: Ramsden, David

Staff development and training. Faculty Development Advisor: Morrison, Philippa

[Information supplied by the institution as at 6 February 1998, and edited by the ACU]

LONDON SCHOOL OF ECONOMICS AND POLITICAL SCIENCE

Founded 1895

Associate Member of the Association of Commonwealth Universities

Postal Address: Houghton Street, London, England WC2A 2AE
Telephone: (0171) 405 7686 **Fax**: (0171) 242 0392 **Telex**: 24655 LSELON G **WWW**: http://www.lse.ac.uk
E-mail formula: Initial.Surname@lse.ac.uk

CHAIRMAN OF COURT OF GOVERNORS—......

DIRECTOR*—Giddens, Prof. Anthony, BA *Hull*, MA *Lond.*, PhD *Camb.*, Hon. DLitt *Salf.*, Hon. DLitt *Hull*, Hon. LittD *E.Anglia*, Hon. Dr *Brussels*, Hon. DLitt *Open(UK)*

PRO-DIRECTOR—Hill, Prof. S. R., BA *Oxf.*, MSc *Lond.*, PhD *Lond.*

SECRETARY‡—Challis, Christine, BA *Lond.*, PhD *Lond.*

ACADEMIC REGISTRAR—Kiloh, G., MA *Oxf.*

FINANCE OFFICER—Pearce, B.

LIBRARIAN—Sykes, J. M., MA *Glas.*, MLitt *Glas.*

GENERAL INFORMATION

History. The school was founded in 1895 by Sydney and Beatrice Webb following a bequest from Henry Hunt Hutchinson, a member of the Fabian Society. It is located in central London.

Admission to first degree courses (see also United Kingdom Introduction). Through Universities and Colleges Admissions Service (UCAS). General Certificate of Education (GCE) A level passes in 3 subjects with high grades. There are specific requirements for each degree course. Certain overseas qualifications are also accepted.

First Degrees (of University of London) (see also University of London Directory to Subjects of Study). BA, BSc, LLB.

All courses are full-time and normally last 3 years. LLB with French law: 3 years plus 1 year studying abroad.

Higher Degrees (of University of London) (see also University of London Directory to Subjects of Study). MA, MSc, LLM, MPhil, PhD.

Applicants for admission to master's degree courses must normally hold an appropriate first degree with at least second class honours. MPhil, PhD: appropriate master's degree or, exceptionally, a very good appropriate first degree.

MA, MSc, LLM: 1 year full-time or 2 years part-time; MPhil, PhD: 2–4 years full-or part-time.

Libraries. 4,000,000 bibliographic items; 10,000 periodicals subscribed to. Special

collections include; Beveridge (working papers); Gladstone (election addresses); liberal party (archives); pamphlets (rare political material); Shaw (personal collection); Webbs' Passfield papers (founders' personal collections); world-wide governments (official statistics).

Fees (1997–98). Undergraduate (annual): £750–8535. Postgraduate (annual): £1905-8535 (arts, UK students); £5900–10,573 (arts, international students).

Academic Awards (1997–98). 97 awards ranging in value from £15 to £7000.

Academic Year (1998–99). Three terms: 1 October–11 December; 11 January–19 March; 26 April–2 July.

Income (1996–97). Total, £73,830,000.

Statistics. Staff: 1649 (970 academic, 679 administrative). Students: international 3802; total 6389.

FACULTIES/SCHOOLS

Graduate School

Tel: (0171) 955 7152

Dean: Steuer, M. D., BSc Col., MA Col.

Undergraduate Studies

Tel: (0171) 955 7124

Dean: Noke, C. W., MA Oxf., MSc Lond., FCA

ACADEMIC UNITS

Accounting and Finance

Tel: (0171) 955 7324 Fax: (0171) 955 7420

Bhattacharya, S., BSc Delhi, PhD Mass. Prof., Finance

Bhimani, A., BSc Cornell, MBA Cornell, PhD Lond. Sr. Lectr.

Board, J. L. G., BA Newcastle(UK), PhD Newcastle(UK) Reader

Bromwich, M., BSc(Econ) Lond. Prof., Accounting and Financial Management

Day, Judith F. S., BSc(Econ) Lond., MSc Lond. Sr. Lectr., Accounting

Dent, J. F., BSc S'ton., PhD Lond. Reader, Accounting

Gietzmann, M. B., BA Newcastle(UK), PhD Durh. Sr. Lectr.

Macve, R. H., BA Oxf., MA Oxf., MSc Lond., FCA Prof., Accounting

Miller, P., BSc CNAA, PhD Lond. Prof., Management Accounting

Noke, C. W., MA Oxf., MSc Lond., FCA Sr. Lectr., Accounting

Power, M. K., MA Oxf., MPhil Camb., PhD Camb. Prof.; Convenor*

Webb, D. C., BA Manc., MA Manc., PhD Lond. Prof., Finance

Other Staff: 7 Lectrs.; 1 Res. Officer; 3 Temp. Lectrs.

Research: developments in accounting and financial practices; financial accounting innovations and security prices; international orientated accounting and finance; measurement and control of financial instruments; social/organisational context of accounting practices

Actuarial Science, see Stats.

Anthropology

Tel: (0171) 955 7202 Fax: (0171) 955 7603

Bloch, M. E. F., BA Camb., PhD Camb. Prof.

Fuller, C. J., MA Camb., PhD Camb. Prof.; Convenor*

Loizos, P., BA Camb., MA Penn., PhD Camb. Prof.

Moore, H. L., BA Durh., PhD Lond. Prof.

Parry, J. P., BA Camb., PhD Camb. Prof.

Woodburn, J. C., MA Camb., PhD Camb. Sr. Lectr.

Other Staff: 6 Lectrs.; 2 Temp. Lectrs.

Research: anthropological contributions to theories of cognition; anthropology of religion; combining ethnography and general theory; integration of anthropology and history; non-European field

Economics

Tel: (0171) 955 7545 Fax: (0171) 831 1840

Barr, N. A., PhD Calif., MSc(Econ) Lond. Sr. Lectr.

Bean, C. R., MA Camb., PhD M.I.T. Prof.

Besley, T., BA Oxf., MA Oxf., MPhil Oxf., DPhil Oxf. Prof.

Cowell, F. A., MA Camb., PhD Camb. Prof.

Desai of St Clement Danes, Lord, MA Bom., PhD Penn. Prof.

Dougherty, C. R. S., MA Camb., MA Harv., PhD Harv. Sr. Lectr.

Felli, L., PhD M.I.T. Reader

Gomulka, S., MSc Warsaw, DrEcon Warsaw Reader

Goodhart, Charles A. E., CBE, BA Camb., PhD Harv. Norman Sosnow Prof.†, Banking and Finance

Hajivassiliou, V. A., BSc Mass., MSc Mass., PhD Mass. Reader

Hardman Moore, J. H., BA Camb., MSc PhD Prof., Economic Theory

Hart, O. S. D. A., MA Camb., MA Warw., PhD Prin. Visiting Centennial Prof.

Hills, J., BA Camb., MSocSci Birm. Prof., Social Policy

Hindley, B. V., AB Chic., PhD Chic. Reader

Jackman, R. A., MA Camb. Prof.

Kiyotaki, N., BA Tokyo, PhD Harv. Prof.

Krugman, P., BA Yale, PhD M.I.T. Prof.

Kuska, E. A., BA Idaho State, PhD Lond. Sr. Lectr.

Layard, P. R. G., BA Camb., MSc(Econ) Prof.

Manning, A., BA Camb., DPhil Oxf. Prof.

Perlman, M., BBA C.C.N.Y., PhD Chic. Reader

Pissarides, C. A., MA Essex, PhD Prof.; Convenor*

Quah, D., PhD Harv. Prof.

Roberts, K. W. S., BSc Essex, BPhil Oxf., DPhil Oxf. Prof.

Robinson, P. M., BSc ANU, MSc ANU, PhD ANU Tooke Prof., Economic Science and Statistics

Schankerman, M., MA Harv., PhD Harv. Reader

Scott, Christopher D., BA York(UK), PhD E.Anglia Sr. Lectr.

Sutton, J., BSc Trinity(Dub.), MSc Trinity(Dub.), PhD Sheff. Prof.

Thomas, J. J., BSc(Econ) Lond. Sr. Lectr.

Venables, A. J., BPhil Oxf., MA Camb., DPhil Oxf. Prof., International Economics

Whitehead, Christine M. E., OBE, BSc(Econ) Lond., PhD Lond. Reader, Housing

Other Staff: 14 Lectrs.; 1 Res. Officer; 1 Reader†; 7 Temp. Lectrs.

Finance, see Acctg. and Finance

Geography and Environment

Tel: (0171) 955 7587 Fax: (0171) 955 7412

Chant, S. H., BA Camb., PhD Lond. Reader

Cheshire, Paul C., BA Camb. Prof.

Glaister, S., BA Essex, MSc Lond., PhD Lond. Cassel Reader, Economic Geography/Transport

Hamilton, F. E. I., BSc(Econ) Lond., PhD Lond. Sr. Lectr., Economic and Social Studies of East Europe

Jones, D. K. C., BSc, FGS Prof.

Rees, J., BSc Lond., MPhil Lond., PhD Lond. Prof., Environmental and Resources Management Geography; Convenor*

Rydin, Y. J., BA Camb., PhD Sr. Lectr.

Other Staff: 8 Lectrs.; 1 Res. Officer

Research: economic performance and regulation; economic transformation and environmental policy; geographical information systems; planning and regulation; urban and social geography

Government

Tel: (0171) 955 7204 Fax: (0171) 831 1707

Balfour, S., MA Lond., PhD Lond., BA Reader, Con Spanish Studies

Barker, R. S., BA Camb., PhD Lond. Reader

Barry, B., BA Oxf., MA Oxf., DPhil Oxf., FBA Prof.

Beattie, A. J., BSc(Econ) Lond. Sr. Lectr.

Charvet, J. C. R., MA Camb., BPhil Oxf. Prof.

Coleman, Janet, BA Yale, MPhil Yale, PhD Yale Prof., Ancient and Medieval Political Thought

Dowding, K. M., BA Keele, DPhil Oxf. Reader, Public Choice and Public Policy

Dunleavy, P. J., MA Oxf., DPhil Oxf. Prof.

Hood, C. C., BA York(UK), BLitt Glas., DLitt York(UK) Prof.; Convenor*

Jones, G. W., MA Oxf., DPhil Oxf., FRHistS Prof.

Leonardi, R., BA Calif., MA Johns H., PhD Ill. Jean Monnet Sr. Lectr.

Lieven, D. C. B., BA Camb. Prof., Russian Government

O'Leary, D. B., BA Oxf., PhD Lond. Prof., Public Administration

Philip, G. D. E., BA Oxf., DPhil Oxf. Reader, Comparative and Latin American Politics

Other Staff: 17 Lectrs.; 3 Res. Officers; 1 Temp. Lectr.

Research: ancient and mediaeval political thought; interaction of economics and politics; local government; politics of nationalism and ethnic conflicts; world-wide politics

History, Economic

Tel: (0171) 955 7084 Fax: (0171) 955 7730

Baines, D. E., BSc(Econ) Reader

Crafts, N. F. R., BA Camb. Prof.; Convenor*

Epstein, S., MA Siena, PhD Camb. Reader

Hunt, E. H., BSc(Econ) PhD Sr. Lectr.

Hunter, Janet E., BA Sheff., DPhil Oxf. Saji Res. Sr. Lectr., Japanese Economic and Social History

Johnson, P. A., MA Oxf., DPhil Oxf. Reader

Lewis, C. M., BA Exe., PhD Lond. Sr. Lectr., Latin American Economic History

Other Staff: 6 Lectrs.; 1 Res. Fellow; 1 Reader†; 1 Temp. Lectr.

Research: economic history of the developed world; international economic history of the twentieth century; performance and structure of modern business

History, International

Tel: (0171) 955 7126 Fax: (0171) 955 6880

Boyce, R. W. D., BA W.Laur., MA PhD Sr. Lectr.

Gillingham, J. B., BA Oxf., BPhil Oxf. Prof., International History

Hartley, Janet M., BA PhD Sr. Lectr.

Howe, A. C., BA Oxf., DPhil Oxf. Sr. Lectr.

Kent, C. J., MA Aberd., PhD Aberd. Reader

Knox, B. M. B., BA Harv., MA Yale, PhD Yale Stevenson Prof.; Convenor*

Meisner, M. J., MA Chic., PhD Chic. Prof.

Prazmowska, A.-J., BA Birm., PhD Lond. Sr. Lectr.

Preston, P., MA Oxf., MA Reading, DPhil Oxf., FRHistS Principle de Asturias Prof., Con Spanish Studies

Rodriguez-Salgado, Maria J., BA Durh., PhD Hull Prof.

Sked, A., MA Glas., DPhil Oxf. Sr. Lectr.

Stevenson, D., MA Camb., PhD Camb. Sr. Lectr.

Other Staff: 6 Lectrs.

Research: British political history; foreign policy/domestic history in Europe; international/European history from 1200 onwards; international politics of USA and Middle East; Russian and Soviet history

Industrial Relations

Tel: (0171) 955 7026 Fax: (0171) 955 7424

Kelly, J. E., BSc Sheff., PhD Lond. Sr. Lectr.

Marsden, D. W., BA Oxf., MA Leeds, DrScEc Aix-Marseilles Reader

Metcalf, D., MA Manc., PhD Prof.

Richardson, G. R. J., BSc(Econ) Pitt., MA Pitt., PhD Col. Reader; Convenor*

Wood, S. J., BSc Birm., PhD Manc. Reader

Other Staff: 5 Lectrs.; 1 Res. Officer; 1 Temp. Lectr.

Research: impact of unions on labour productivity; payment systems and performance; privatisation and industrial relations; profit related pay; role of union officials/shop stewards

Information Systems

Tel: (0171) 955 7655 Fax: (0171) 955 7385

Angell, I. O., BSc Wales, PhD Lond. Prof.

Cornford, A., BSc(Econ) Lond., MSc Lond., PhD Lond. Sr. Lectr.

Liebenau, J. M., BA Roch., MA Penn., PhD Penn. Sr. Lectr.

Smithson, S. C., BSc(Econ) Lond., MSc Lond., PhD Lond. Sr. Lectr.; Convenor*

Other Staff: 7 Lectrs.; 2 Res. Fellows; 1 Temp. Lectr.

Research: implementation of IS in organisations; information systems security; inter-organisational systems and electronic commerce; IS in developing countries; public sector computing

International Relations

Tel: (0171) 955 7404 Fax: (0171) 955 7446

Banks, M. H., BSc(Econ) *Lehigh*, MA *Lehigh* Reader

Coker, C., BA *Oxf.*, DPhil *Oxf.* Reader

Halliday, S. F. P., BA *Oxf.*, MSc *Lond.*, PhD *Lond.* Prof.

Hill, C. J., BA *Oxf.*, DPhil *Oxf.* Montague Burton Prof.

Hodges, Michael R., MA *Camb.*, PhD *Penn.* Sr. Lectr.

Light, M. M., BSc *Witw.*, BSc *Sur.*, PhD *Sur.* Reader

Mayall, James B. L., BA *Camb.* Prof.

Sims, N. R. A., BSc(Econ) *Lond.* Sr. Lectr.

Stern, G. H., BSc(Econ) *Lond.* Sr. Lectr.

Taylor, P. G., BA *Wales*, MScEcon *Wales*, PhD *Lond.* Prof.; Convenor*

Wallace, William, BA *Camb.*, PhD *Cornell* Reader

Wyatt-Walter, A. R., BA *W.Aust*, MPhil *Oxf.*, DPhil *Oxf.* Sr. Lectr.

Yahuda, M. B., BA MSc(Econ) Prof.

Other Staff: 9 Lectrs.; 1 Res. Officer; 1 Emer. Reader; 2 Temp. Lectrs.

Research: international institutions, revolutions, nationalism and modernity; international politics; issues of gender; methodology, conflict and foreign policy; strategic studies and arms control

Law

Tel: (0171) 955 7278 Fax: (0171) 955 7366

Baldwin, G. R., LLB *Edin.*, PhD *Edin.* Prof.

Bradley, D. C., LLB *Manc.* Reader

Chinkin, C. M., LLB *Lond.*, LLM *Lond.*, LLM *Yale*, PhD *Syd.* Prof., International Law

Collins, H. G., BA *Oxf.*, BCL *Oxf.*, LLM *Harv.* Prof.

Davies, P. L., MA *Oxf.*, LLM *Lond.*, LLM *Yale* Cassel Prof., Commercial Law

Finch, Vanessa M. I., BA *CNAA*, LLM *Lond.* Sr. Lectr.

Freedman, Judith, BA *Oxf.*, MA *Oxf.* Reader

Greenwood, C. J., BA *Camb.*, LLB *Camb.* Prof., International Law

Harlow, Carol R., LLM PhD Prof., Public Law

Hartley, T. C., BA *Cape Town*, LLB *Cape Town*, LLM *Lond.* Prof.

Jacob, J. M., LLB *Lond.* Sr. Lectr.

Lacey, N. M., LLB *Oxf.*, BCL *Oxf.* Prof., Criminal Law

Muchlinski, P. T., LLB *Lond.*, LLM *Camb.* Sr. Lectr.

Murphy, W. T., BA *Camb.*, MA *Camb.* Reader

Nobles, R. L., LLB *Warw.*, LLM *Yale* Sr. Lectr.

Peay, J. V., BSc *Lond.*, PhD *Lond.* Sr. Lectr.

Rawlings, R. W., BA *Oxf.*, BCL *Oxf.* Reader

Reiner, Robert, BA *Camb.*, MSc *Brist.*, PhD *Brist.* Prof., Criminology

Roberts, S. A., LLB *Lond.*, PhD *Lond.* Prof.

Schiff, D. N., LLB *S'ton.* Sr. Lectr.

Simpson, R. C., LLM *Lond.* Reader

Teubner, G., MA *Calif.*, DrJur *Tübingen* Otto Kahn-Freud Prof., Comparative Law and Social Theory

Worthington, S. E., BSc *ANU*, LLB *Qld.*, LLM *Melb.*, PhD *Cant.* Sr. Lectr.

Zander, M., BA *Camb.*, LLB *Camb.*, LLM *Harv.* Prof.; Convenor*

Other Staff: 13 Lectrs.; 1 Res. Fellow

Research: alternative dispute resolution; environmental, EC and EU law; law of defamation; reform of civil and criminal procedure; regulation of financial markets and utilities

Mathematics

Tel: (0171) 955 7732 Fax: (0171) 955 6877

Alpern, S. R., AB *Prin.*, PhD *N.Y.* Prof.

Anthony, M. H. G., BSc *Glas.*, PhD *Lond.* Reader

Biggs, Norman L., BA *Camb.*, DSc *Lond.* Prof.; Convenor*

Brightwell, G., BA *Camb.*, PhD *Camb.* Reader

Osotoja-Ostaszewski, A. J., BSc *Lond.*, PhD *Lond.* Sr. Lectr.

Other Staff: 1 Lectr.; 1 Instr.; 2 Res. Officers; 1 Temp. Lectr.

Research: applications of mathematics in social sciences; combinatorics; discrete and applicable mathematics; graph, game and computational learning theories; pure mathematics

Operational Research

Tel: (0171) 955 7653 Fax: (0171) 955 6885

Appa, G. M., BSc *Lond.*, MSc *Lond.*, PhD *Lond.* Sr. Lectr.; Convenor*

Howard, J. V., MA *Camb.*, MSc *Newcastle(UK)*, PhD *Brist.* Sr. Lectr.

Rosenhead, J. V., MA *Camb.*, MSc *Lond.* Prof.

Other Staff: 3 Lectrs.; 2 Res. Officers; 1 Temp. Lectr.

Research: combinatorial optimisation; data envelopment analysis; mathematical programming; problem structuring methods; visual interacitve simulation

Philosophy, Logic and Scientific Method

Tel: (0171) 955 7340 Fax: (0171) 955 6845

Cartwright, N. L. D., BSc *Pitt.*, PhD *Ill.* Prof.†

Howson, C., BSc(Econ) Prof., Logic

Ruben, D.-H., BA *Dartmouth*, PhD *Harv.* Prof.

Worrall, J., BSc(Econ) *Lond.*, PhD *Lond.* Prof.; Convenor*

Other Staff: 1 Lectr.; 1 Res. Fellow; 3 Temp. Lectrs.

Research: evidence/testing in science; free will and determinism; holism; nature of mind; reductionism

Population Studies, see Soc. Policy and Admin.

Psychology, Social

Tel: (0171) 955 7714 Fax: (0171) 955 7565

Collins, Richard E., BA *York(UK)*, MA *Warw.*, PhD *Strath.* Sr. Lectr., Media and Communications

Farr, R. M., MA *Belf.*, DSc *Belf.*, PhD *Lond.*, FBPsS Prof.; Convenor*

Gaskell, G. D., BSc *Lond.*, PhD *Lond.* Reader

Humphreys, P. C., BSc *Lond.*, PhD *Lond.* Prof.

Livingstone, Sonia M., BSc *Oxf.*, DPhil *Oxf.* Sr. Lectr.

Stockdale, J. E., BSc *Lond.*, PhD *Lond.* Sr. Lectr.

Other Staff: 7 Lectrs.; 2 Res. Fellows; 2 Res. Officers; 1 Temp. Lectr.

Research: history of psychology as social science; new media, audiences and children; psychology of gender; public understanding of science and technology; social representations of economic/political change

Social Policy and Administration

incorporating Population Studies

Tel: (0171) 955 7345 Fax: (0171) 955 7145

Carrier, J. W., BSc(Soc) *Lond.*, LLB *Lond.*, MPhil *Lond.*, PhD *Lond.* Sr. Lectr.

Downes, D. M., BA *Oxf.*, PhD Prof.

Dyson, T. P. G., BSc *Lond.*, MSc *Lond.* Prof.; Convenor*

Glennerster, H., BA *Oxf.* Prof.

Hall, A. L., BA *Sheff.*, MPhil *Glas.*, PhD *Glas.* Sr. Lectr., Social Planning in Developing Countries

Hills, J. R., BA *Camb.*, MA *Camb.*, MSocSc *Birm.* Reader

Hobcraft, John N., BSc *Lond.* Prof.

Kiernan, K. E., BA *Liv.*, MSc *Lond.*, PhD *Lond.* Reader

Kleinman, M., MA *Oxf.*, PhD *Lond.* Sr. Lectr.

Langford, C. M., BSc(Soc) Reader, Demography

Le Grand, Julian, BA *Sus.*, PhD *Penn.* Titmuss Prof., Health Policy

Murphy, M. J., BA *Camb.*, BPhil *York(UK)* Prof.

Piachaud, D. F. J., BA *Oxf.*, MPA *Mich.* Prof.

Power, Anne E., MBE, BA *Manc.*, MA *Wis.*, PhD Reader

Sainsbury, Sally B., BA *Lond.* Sr. Lectr.

Other Staff: 10 Lectrs.; 3 Res. Officers; 5 Temp. Lectrs.

Research: crime and deviance; de-institutionalisation and community care; economic impact of social security; finance and management of health care; population studies and management of housing

Sociology

Tel: (0171) 955 7305 Fax: (0171) 955 7405

Anderson, P., BA *Oxf.* Prof.

Badcock, C. R., BA *Lond.*, PhD *Lond.* Reader

Barker, Eileen V., BSc(Soc) *Lond.*, PhD *Lond.* Prof.; Convenor*

Beck, U., PhD *Munich* Prof.

Cohen, Stanley, BA *Witw.*, PhD *Lond.* Martin White Prof.†

Hill, S. R., BA *Oxf.*, MSc *Lond.*, PhD *Lond.* Prof.

Husbands, C. T., BA(Econ) *Manc.*, MA *Chic.*, PhD *Chic.* Reader

Mouzelis, N. P., LèsScComm *Geneva*, LèsSociol *Geneva*, PhD *Lond.* Prof.†

Rock, P. E., BSc(Soc) *Lond.*, DPhil *Oxf.* Prof.

Sennett, R., BA *Chic.*, PhD *Harv.* Visiting Centennial Prof.

Silverstone, R. S., MA *Oxf.*, PhD *Lond.* Prof., Media and Communications

Sklair, L. A., BA *Leeds*, MA *McM.*, PhD Reader

Swingewood, A. W., BSc(Soc) *Lond.*, PhD *Lond.* Sr. Lectr.

Other Staff: 7 Lectrs.; 1 Res. Fellow

Research: criminology, deviance and regulation; politics, ethnicity and racism; modern Darwinism and psychoanalysis; religion and contemporary 'cults'; sex and gender

Statistics

Tel: (0171) 955 7731 Fax: (0171) 955 7416

Atkinson, A. C., BA *Camb.*, MA *Camb.*, PhD *Lond.* Prof.

De Jong, Piet, BEc *Syd.*, PhD *La Trobe* Reader, Actuarial Science

Howard, J. V., MA *Camb.*, MSc *Newcastle(UK)*, PhD *Brist.* Sr. Lectr.

Knott, M., BSc(Econ) *Lond.*, PhD *Lond.* Sr. Lectr.; Convenor*

O'Muircheartaigh, Colin A., BA *N.U.I.*, MSc *Mich.*, LicPhil *Berne*, PhD *Lond.* Sr. Lectr.

Other Staff: 7 Lectrs.; 1 Stat. Consultant; 2 Temp. Lectrs.

Research: latent variable modelling and time series; regression diagnostics and optimal experimental design; robustness; stochastic processes in finance and insurance; survey sampling

Other Appointments

In addition to the above, a large number of fixed-term occasional research and teaching appointments are made from year to year.

SPECIAL CENTRES, ETC

Asia Research Centre

Tel: (0171) 405 7699

Hussain, S. A., BA *Karachi*, MA *Karachi*, BPhil *Oxf.*, BLitt *Oxf.* Dir. of Res.

Leifer, M., BA *Reading*, PhD *Lond.* Sir John Bremridge Dir.*

Research: social science research

Business History Unit

Tel: (0171) 955 7109 Fax: (0171) 955 6861

Gourvish, T. R., BA *Lond.*, PhD *Lond.*, FRHistS Dir.*

Other Staff: 1 Res. Fellow; 2 Res. Officers

Research: banking projects; genesis of business leaders; international bibliography of business history; multi-national corporations; pharmaceutical, chocolate and brewing industrial history

Computer Security Research Centre

Tel: (0171) 955 7641

Backhouse, James, BA Exe., MSc   Director*
Other Staff: 3 Res. Fellows
Research: analysis of responsibility; management
of information security; management policy
and security procedure analysis; risk to
computer systems; use of information in
organisations

Criminology and Criminal Justice, Mannheim Centre for the Study of

Tel: (0171) 955 7240

Downes, Prof. D. M., BA Oxf., PhD   Dir.*
Research: criminal justice process and policy;
media and crime; policing; sentencing and
penal policy; theories of crime/deviance/
social control

Development Studies Institute (DESTIN)

Tel: (0171) 955 7424 Fax: (0171) 955 6844

Harriss, J. C., MA Camb., PhD E.Anglia   Sr.
Lectr.
Saith, A., BA Delhi, MA Delhi, PhD Camb.   Prof.;
Dir.*

Discrete and Applicable Mathematics, Centre for

Tel: (0171) 955 7732 Fax: (0171) 955 6877

Biggs, Prof. Norman L., BA Camb., DSc   Dir.*
Research: artificial neural networks; discrete
probabilistic analysis; mathematical theories;
mathematics in finance; theory of economic
forecasting

Economic and Related Disciplines, Suntory and Toyota International Centres for (STICERD)

Tel: (0171) 955 6699 Fax: (0171) 242 2357

Besley, T. J., MA Oxf., MPhil Oxf., DPhil
Oxf.   Prof.
Glennerster, Prof. H., BA Oxf.   Chairman*
Other Staff: 3 Res. Fellows; 8 Res. Officers
Research: analysis of social exclusion;
distributional analysis; economic
organisation and public policy; economics
of industry; Japanese studies

Economic Performance, Centre for (CEP)

Tel: (0171) 955 7596 Fax: (0171) 955 7595

Freeman, R. B., BA Harv., PhD Harv.   Prof.
Layard, Prof. P. R. G., BA Camb., MSc(Econ)
Lond.   Dir.*
Metcalf, D., MA Manc., PhD   Prof.†
Other Staff: 2 Res. Fellows; 4 Res. Officers
Research: corporate performance and business
policy; economic reform; economics of
discontinuous change; human resources and
industrial relations; national and
international economic performance

Economics and Finance in South Africa, Centre for Research into (CREFSA)

Tel: (0171) 955 7280 Fax: (0171) 430 1769

Leape, J. I., BA Harv., BA Oxf., PhD
Harv.   Prof.; Dir.*
Other Staff: 3 Res. Officers
Research: foreign exchange policy;
macroeconomic and financial issues in South
Africa; regional economic integration in
Development Community; role of
international finance in South Africa;
structure of South African financial system

Educational Research, Centre for

Tel: (0171) 955 7809 Fax: (0171) 955 7733

West, A., BA Lond., PhD Lond.   Dir. of Res.*
Other Staff: 1 Res. Fellow; 3 Res. Officers
Research: choice of schools and parental
involvement; curricula and examinations in
Europe; educational performance; European
and international issues; funding of
education and schools admissions

European Institute

Tel: (0171) 955 6780 Fax: (0171) 955 7546

Balfour, S., BA Trinity(Dub.), MA Lond., PhD
Lond.   Reader, Contemporary Spanish Studies
Colley, L., BA Brist., MA Camb., PhD
Camb.   Sch. Prof., History
Gray, J. N., BA Oxf., MA Oxf., DPhil Oxf.   Sch.
Prof., European Thought
Leonardi, R., BA Calif., MA Johns H., PhD
Ill.   Sr. Lectr.
Machin, H., BA Newcastle(UK), PhD Lond.   Sr.
Lectr., European Integration; Dir.*
Preston, P., MA Oxf., MA Reading, DPhil Oxf.,
FRHistS   Prof.
Smith, A. D. S., BA Oxf., MSc Lond., PhD
Lond.   Prof.
Tsoukalis, L., BA Manc., MA Oxf., DPhil
Oxf.   Eleftherios Venizelos Prof.
Other Staff: 2 Lectrs.; 2 Res. Fellows; 2 Temp.
Lectrs.
Research: contemporary Greek studies;
contemporary Spanish studies; economic and
social cohesion laboratory; ethnicity and
nationalism; forum for European philosophy

Financial Markets Group

Tel: (0171) 955 7891 Fax: (0171) 242 1006

Webb, D. C., BA Manc., MA Manc., PhD
Lond.   Prof., Finance; Dir.*
Other Staff: 2 Res. Fellows; 3 Res. Officers
Research: corporate finance; efficiency of
financial markets/asset pricing; market
microstructure; regulation of financial
markets; sources of shocks to the economy

Gender Institute

Tel: (0171) 955 7602 Fax: (0171) 955 6408

Moore, Prof. H. L., BA Durh., PhD Lond.   Dir.*
Other Staff: 1 Lectr.; 1 Res. Fellow; 1 Res.
Officer
Research: analysis of gender in social sciences;
gender, violence and conflict; health and
social capital; households, family and work;
social identities and citizenship

Global Governance, Centre for the Study of

Tel: (0171) 955 7583 Fax: (0171) 955 7591

Desai of St Clement Danes, Prof. Lord, MA
Bom., PhD Penn.   Dir.*
Other Staff: 2 Res. Fellows
Research: global civil society; globalisation and
global governance; human rights;
peacekeeping and humanitarian assistance;
reform of the UN

Greater London Group

Tel: (0171) 955 7570

Jones, Prof. G. W., MA Oxf., DPhil Oxf.,
FRHistS   Chairman*
Travers, A. J., BA Lond.   Dir.*
Other Staff: 1 Res. Fellow
Research: government and economy of London

International Studies, Centre for

Tel: (0171) 955 7400 Fax: (0171) 955 7446

Mayall, Prof. James B. L., BA Camb.   Dir.*
Other Staff: 6 Visiting Fellows
Research: social science

Language Studies Centre

Tel: (0171) 955 7043 Fax: (0171) 955 6847

Gooch, A. L., MA Edin.   Emer. Reader, Spanish
Johnson, B. S., BA Nott., PhD Nott.   Dir.,
Russian*
Other Staff: 4 Lang. Instrs.
Research: general and historical linguistics and
stylistics; study of literature from
sociological viewpoint; usage of taught
languages

LSE Health

Tel: (0171) 955 7540 Fax: (0171) 955 6803

Le Grand, Prof. Julian, BA Sus., PhD
Penn.   Chairman
Mossialos, Elias, BSc Athens, MSc Athens, MD
Athens, PhD Athens   Exec. Dir.*†

Other Staff: 11 Res. Assocs.
Research: comparative health studies; health
economics; health technology assessment;
health services; public health

LSE Housing

Tel: (0171) 955 6722 Fax: (0171) 955 6144

Power, Anne E., MBE, MA Wis., PhD
Lond.   Co-ordinator*
Other Staff: 1 Lectr.
Research: development of local housing
companies; European difficult-to-let estates;
methods for improving low-income
communities; problems with urban housing
areas; riots in the 1990s

Management, Interdisciplinary Institute of

Tel: (0171) 955 7920 Fax: (0171) 955 6887

Abell, P. M., BSc Leeds, PhD Leeds   Eric Sosnow
Prof.; Dir.*
de Meza, D. E., BSc Lond., MSc Lond.   Prof.†
Hill, S. R., BA Oxf., MSc Lond., PhD Lond.   Prof.
Reyniers, D. J., BSc Antwerp, MSc Lond., PhD
Lond.   Reader
Other Staff: 2 Lectrs.; 5 Res. Fellows; 1 Temp.
Lectr.
Research: economic implications of profit
sharing; entrepreneurship; management in
the public sector; management of
international organisations; market for
corporate control

Methodology Institute

Tel: (0171) 955 7639 Fax: (0171) 955 7005

Gaskell, G. D., BSc Lond., PhD Lond.   Dir.*
O'Muircheartaigh, Colin A., BA N.U.I., MSc
Mich., LicPhil Berne, PhD Lond.   Assoc. Dir.
Other Staff: 5 Lectrs.
Research: cognitive survey laboratory;
judgement, decision making and theory;
multilevel modelling of family planning;
public understanding of science; quality
indicators for qualitative research

Personal Social Services Research Unit

Tel: (0171) 955 6238 Fax: (0171) 955 6131

Davies, B. P., MA Camb., DPhil Oxf.   Prof.
Fellow†; Dir.†*
Knapp, M. R. J., BA Sheff., MSc Kent, PhD
Kent   Dir.†*
Other Staff: 1 Res. Fellow; 5 Res. Officers
Research: 'community care'; criminal justice
services; in-patient health care; needs
resources and outcomes; social and health
care

Philosophy of the Natural and Social Sciences, Centre for the

Tel: (0171) 955 7573 Fax: (0171) 955 6869

Callender, C. A., BA Providence(R.I.), PhD
Rutgers   Co-Dir.
Cartwright, N. L. D., BSc Pitt., PhD Ill.   Prof.†;
Dir.*
Cronin, H., BA Manc.Met., MSc Lond., PhD
Lond.   Co-Dir.
Redhead, M. G., PhD Lond.   Acting Dir.*
Worrall, J., BSc(Econ) Lond., PhD
Lond.   Reader; Co-Dir.
Other Staff: 1 Res. Fellow; 1 Res. Officer
Research: Darwin at LSE; economics and human
values; German historical school in
economics; measurement in physics and
economics; methodology of experimental
economics

Population Investigation Committee

Tel: (0171) 955 7666 Fax: (0171) 955 6833

Hobcraft, Prof. John N.   Chairman*
Research: demographic questions

USA, Centre for Research on the (CRUSA)

Tel: (0171) 955 7325

Hodges, Michael, MA Camb., PhD Penn.   Dir.*
Research: American federal experience; Atlantic
relationship; future of American society

Voluntary Organisation, Centre for (CVO)

Tel: (0171) 955 7205 Fax: (0171 955 6039

Harris, M. E., BSocSc *Birm.*, MA *Brun.*, PhD *Lond.*   Acting Dir.*

Research: change in American non-profit management; improving effectiveness of small voluntary agencies; international comparisons of issues facing NGOs; models of organisation in housing associations; organisational issues in religious congregations

CONTACT OFFICERS

Academic affairs. Academic Registrar: Kiloh, G., MA *Oxf.*

Accommodation. Assistant Secretary: Segal, D., BA *CNAA*

Admissions (higher degree). Assistant Registrar: Manthorpe, C., BA *Leeds*, PhD *Leeds*

Adult/continuing education. Administrative Officer: Brown, Ann

Alumni. Alumni Relations Manager: Simpson, R., BA *Kent State*, MA *Kent State*

Archives. Sub-Librarian: Raspin, G. E. Angela, BA *Durh.*, PhD

Careers. Careers Adviser: Tiley, M., MA *Oxf.*, FCA

Computing services. Computer Services Manager: Dalby, D. P., BSc(Econ) MSc

Conferences/corporate hospitality. Conferences Manager: Hickson, C., BSc *Lond.*

Consultancy services. Head of Research Services: Gregory, N., BA *Lond.*, MA *Lond.*

Distance education. Programme Director (External Study): Gosling, R. A., BSc *Lond.*, MSc *Lond.*

Estates and buildings/works and services. Estates Officer: Kudliki, Christopher

Examinations. Administrative Officer, Examinations: Ashton, D., BA *Brist.*

Finance. Finance Officer: Pearce, B.

General enquiries. Secretary: Challis, Christine, BA *Lond.*, PhD *Lond.*

Health services. Director, LSE Health Service: Fender, E., BSc *Wales*, BM BCh *Oxf.*

Industrial liaison. Head of Research Services: Gregory, N., BA *Lond.*, MA *Lond.*

International office. Assistant Registrar: Wallace, P. J., BA *Camb.*

Library (chief librarian). Librarian: Sykes, J. M., MA *Glas.*, MLitt *Glas.*

Library (enquiries). Sub-Librarian, User Services: Wilkinson, Janet, BA

Public relations, information and marketing. Head of Public Relations: Annett, D., BA *CNAA*

Publications (academic). Publications Officer: Friedgood, B. S., BA *Lond.*, MA *Lond.*

Publications (institutional). Assistant Registrar: Wallace, P. J., BA *Camb.*

Purchasing. Site Development and Services Officer: Arthur, M., LLB

Quality assurance and accreditation. Assistant Registrar: Wallace, P. J., BA *Camb.*

Research. Head of Research Services: Gregory, N., BA *Lond.*, MA *Lond.*

Scholarships, awards and loans. Assistant Registrar: Wallace, P. J., BA *Camb.*

Scholarships, awards, loans. Administrative Officer: Brooks, S. M., BA *Lond.*

Schools liaison. Assistant Registrar: Wallace, P. J., BA *Camb.*

Security. Facilities Manager: Edwards, H.

Sport and recreation. Assistant Secretary: Segal, D., BA *CNAA*

Student welfare/counselling. Director, LSE Health Service: Fender, E., BSc *Wales*, BM BCh *Oxf.*

Students from other countries. Academic Registrar: Kiloh, G., MA *Oxf.*

[*Information supplied by the institution as at 4 March 1998, and edited by the ACU*]

LONDON SCHOOL OF HYGIENE AND TROPICAL MEDICINE

Founded 1899

Postal Address: Keppel Street, London, England WC1E 7HT
Telephone: (0171) 636 8636 **Fax**: (0171) 436 5389 **Telex**: 8953474 **WWW**: http://www.lshtm.ac.uk
E-mail formula: initial.surname@lshtm.ac.uk

PATRON—Edinburgh, H.R.H. The Duke of, KG, KT, OM, GBE, Hon. LLD *Lond.*, Hon. LLD *Wales*, Hon. LLD *Edin.*, Hon. LLD *Malta*, Hon. DSc *Delhi*, Hon. DSc *Salf.*, Hon. Dr *RCA*, FRS
CHAIRMAN OF THE COURT OF GOVERNORS—Crawford, I. P., GM
CHAIRMAN OF THE BOARD OF MANAGEMENT—Chalker of Wallasey, Baroness
DEAN*—Spencer, Prof. Harrison C., MD *Johns H.*, MPH *Calif.*, FACP
SECRETARY AND REGISTRAR‡—Surridge, Wendy S., BA *Reading*, MA *Lond.*

GENERAL INFORMATION

History. The school was originally established as the London School of Tropical Medicine in 1899. An institute of state medicine to be called the School of Hygiene was recommended in 1921 and a united school was established in 1924 and opened in 1929. The school is located in central London.

First Degrees are not offered.

Higher Degrees (of University of London) (see also University of London Directory to Subjects of Study). MSc, MPhil, PhD, DrPH.

Applicants for admission to higher degree courses should hold a first degree with at least second class honours of a UK university, or an overseas qualification of an equivalent standard in an appropriate subject, or another appropriate qualification (eg registrable qualification in medicine, dentistry or veterinary studies, master's degree, other professional qualification). Applicants whose first language is not English or whose university studies were not conducted in

English will be required to take an approved English language test.

MSc: 1 year full-time or 2 years part-time, or (some courses) by distance learning (2–5 years); MPhil, PhD, DrPH: 3 years full-time or 6 years part-time.

Libraries. 800 journals; over 50,000 monographs. Special collections: international public health; tropical medicine.

Fees. Postgraduate (annual): home/EC students £2610–3610; international students £7350–11,400 (community-based clinical), £10,000–14,950 (clinical laboratory sciences).

Academic Awards. Some scholarships available.

Academic Year (1998–99). 28 September–18 December; 11 January–26 March; 26 April–2 July. Calendar year courses terminate on 17 September 1999.

Income (1996–97). Total, £28,000,000.

Statistics. Staff: 593 (389 academic and academic-related, 204 other). Students: full-

time 489 (225 men, 264 women); part-time 129 (42 men, 87 women); international 224; total 618.

ACADEMIC UNITS

Epidemiology and Population Health

Tel: (0171) 927 2482 Fax: (0171) 436 4230

Ashworth-Hill, Ann, BSc PhD   Sr. Lectr.

Beral, Valerie, MB BS   Visiting Prof.

Campbell, Oona M. R., BS *Beirut*, MSc *Johns H.*, PhD *Johns H.*   Sr. Lectr.

Cleland, J. G., MA *Camb.*   Prof., Medical Demography

Coleman, M. P., BA *Oxf.*, BM BCh *Oxf.*, MSc *Lond.*   Prof., Epidemiology and Vital Statistics

DeStavola, B. L., MSc PhD   Sr. Lectr.

dos Santos Silva, Isobel M., MD *Lisbon*, MSc   Sr. Lectr.

Doyle, Patricia E., BSc *Sur.*, MSc PhD   Sr. Lectr.

Elbourne, D., BSc *Lond.*, MSc *Lond.*, PhD *Lond.*   Sr. Lectr.

Evans, S. J., BA *Keele*, MSc *Lond.*   Visiting Prof.

Feachem, R. G. A., CBE, BSc *Birm.*, PhD *NSW*, DScMed, FEng, FICE   Visiting Prof.

Feldman, R. A., MD *Penn.*, BA   Visiting Prof.

Fletcher, Astrid E., BA *Newcastle(UK)*, PhD   Reader
Fox, A. J., BSc PhD   Visiting Prof.
Grundy, E. M. D., MA MSc PhD   Reader
Huttly, Sharon R. A., BSc *Exe.*, MSc *Reading*   Sr. Lectr.
Ismail, Suraiya, BA *Camb.*, PhD *Cornell*   Sr. Lectr.
Juarez, F., BSc *Mexico*, MSc *Lond.*, PhD *Lond.*   Sr. Lectr.
Kirkwood, Betty R., MA *Camb.*, MSc   Prof., Epidemiology and International Health; Head*
Leon, D., BA *Camb.*, PhD   Sr. Lectr.
Marshall, T. F. de C., BA *Camb.*, MSc *Essex*   Sr. Lectr.
McKeigue, P. M., BA *Camb.*, MB BChir *Camb.*, MSc PhD   Reader
McMichael, A. J., MB BS *Adel.*, PhD *Monash*   Prof., Epidemiology
McPherson, K., MA *Camb.*, PhD   Prof., Public Health Epidemiology
Meilahn, Elaine, BS *Wis.*, DrPH *Minn.*   Sr. Lectr.
Pocock, S. J., BA *Camb.*, MSc PhD   Prof., Medical Statistics
Prince, M. J., BA *Lond.*, MSc *Lond.*   Sr. Lectr.
Shetty, P. S., MD *Madr.*, PhD *Camb.*   Prof., Human Nutrition
Swerdlow, A. J., MA *Camb.*, PhD *Glas.*, DM *Oxf.*   Prof.
Timaeus, I., MA *Camb.*, MSc(Econ) PhD   Sr. Lectr.
Victoria, C. G., PhD *Lond.*   Visiting Prof.
Zaba, B. W., BSc *Lond.*, MSc *Lond.*   Sr. Lectr.

Infectious and Tropical Diseases

Tel: (0171) 927 2256 Fax: (0171) 637 4314

Ackers, J. P., MA *Oxf.*, DPhil *Oxf.*   Sr. Lectr.
Bailey, R., BA *Oxf.*, BM *S'ton.*, PhD *Lond.*   Sr. Lectr.
Bancroft, G. J., BSc *W.Aust.*, PhD   Sr. Lectr.
Bartlett, C. L. R., MB BS MSc   Visiting Prof.
Bavoil, P. M., PhD *Calif.*   Sr. Lectr.
Bennett, S., MA *Oxf.*, MSc *Reading*, PhD   Sr. Lectr.
Bickle, Q. D., BA *Oxf.*, MSc PhD   Sr. Lectr.
Blumenthal, Ursula J., BA *York(UK)*, MSc *Liv.*, PhD *Liv.*   Sr. Lectr.
Borriello, S. P., BSc PhD   Visiting Prof.
Bradley, D. J., MB BChir *Camb.*, MA *Camb.*, DM *Oxf.*, FIBiol, FRCPath, FRCP   Prof., Tropical Hygiene
Bryceson, A. D. M., BA *Camb.*, MB BChir *Camb.*, MD *Camb.*, FRCP   Prof.
Cairncross, A. M., MA *Camb.*, PhD   Reader
Clark, C. G., BSc *Edin.*, PhD *N.Y.*   Sr. Lectr.
Cousens, S. N., MA *Camb.*   Sr. Lectr.
Croft, S. L., BSc *Durh.*, PhD *Liv.*   Sr. Lectr.
Cutts, Felicity T., MD *Manc.*, MSc   Sr. Lectr.
Davies, C. R., MA MSc DPhil   Sr. Lectr.
De Cock, K. M., MD *Brist.*   Visiting Prof.
Dockrell, Hazel M., BA *Trinity(Dub.)*, PhD   Reader

Drasar, B. S., DSc *Birm.*, PhD, FRCPath   Prof., Bacteriology
Dye, C. M., BA *York(UK)*, DPhil *Oxf.*   Reader
Elliott, A., BA *Camb.*, MB BS *Lond.*, MA *Camb.*, PhD *Camb.*   Sr. Lectr.
Fine, P. E. M., AB *Prin.*, MSc *Penn.*, PhD *Penn.*, VMD *Penn.*   Prof., Communicable Diseases Epidemiology
Godfrey-Faussett, P., BA *Oxf.*, MB BS   Sr. Lectr.
Gompels, Ursula A., BA *Rutgers*, MSc *Chic.*, PhD *Camb.*   Sr. Lectr.
Greenwood, B. M., BA *Lond.*, MB *Lond.*, MA *Lond.*   Prof.
Grosskurth, H.   Sr. Lectr.
Hall, A. J., PhD *S'ton.*, MB BS MSc   Reader
Hayes, R. J., MSc *Edin.*   Prof.
Kaye, P. M., BSc PhD   Reader
Kelly, J. M., BSc *Glas.*, PhD   Sr. Lectr.
Lambert, H., MA *Camb.*, MD *Camb.*, FRCP   Visiting Prof.
Lockwood, D. N. J., BSc *Birm.*, MB ChB *Birm.*   Sr. Lectr.
Mabey, D. C. W., BM BCh *Oxf.*, MA   Prof.
McAdam, K. P. W. J., MB BChir *Camb.*, MA *Camb.*, FRCP   Prof.
Meek, S. R., BA *Oxf.*, MSc *Wales*, PhD *Liv.*   Sr. Lectr.
Miles, M. A., PhD DSc   Prof., Medical Protozoology
Parry, E. H. O., BA MA   Visiting Prof.
Porter, J. D. H., MB BS MPH   Sr. Lectr.
Raynes, J. G., BSc PhD   Sr. Lectr.
Roberts, C., BSc *Liv.*, MD *Liv.*   Visiting Prof.
Rodrigues, Laura, MSc PhD   Sr. Lectr.
Ross, D. A., MB BCh *Wales*, MA *Wales*, MSc *Oxf.*   Sr. Lectr.
Smith, P. G., DSc *City(UK)*   Prof., Tropical Epidemiology; Head*
Steward, M. W., PhD *Leeds*, DSc, FRCPath   Prof., Immunology
Stoker, N. G., BSc *Leic.*, PhD   Sr. Lectr.
Sturrock, R. F., BSc PhD, FIBiol   Sr. Lectr.
Targett, G. A. T., BSc *Nott.*, PhD DSc   Prof., Immunology of Protozoal Diseases
Taylor, M. G., BSc *Brist.*, MSc *Brun.*, PhD DSc   Prof., Medical Helminthology
Thomas, J. Alero, MSc *Oxf.*, MB BS   Sr. Lectr.
Tsiquaye, K. N., BSc PhD   Sr. Lectr.
Warhurst, D. C., BSc *Leic.*, PhD *Leic.*, DSc *Lond.*, FRCPath   Reader
Webber, R. H., MSc MD   Sr. Lectr.
Whitworth, J. A. G., MD *Liv.*   Sr. Lectr.
Ziegler, J. L., MD *Cornell*   Visiting Prof.

Public Health and Policy

Tel: (0171) 927 2432 Fax: (0171) 436 3611

Acheson, Donald, KBE, MA *Oxf.*, DM *Oxf.*, FRCP, FRCS   Visiting Prof.
Armstrong, B., BSc *Lond.*, MSc *Lond.*, PhD *Lond.*   Sr. Lectr.
Berridge, Virginia, BA PhD, FRHistS   Prof., History
Black, N. A., MD *Birm.*   Prof., Health Services Research; Head*

Clarke, A. E., BA *Oxf.*, BM BCh *Oxf.*, MSc *Lond.*, MD *Lond.*   Sr. Lectr.
Cuzick, J., BSc *Calif.*, MSc *Lond.*, PhD *Calif.*   Visiting Prof.
Dolk, Helen, BA *Oxf.*, PhD *Louvain*   Sr. Lectr.
Fine, D. J., BA *Minn.*   Visiting Prof.
Fletcher, A. C., MA *Camb.*, MSc *Aston*, PhD *Aston*   Sr. Lectr.
Foster, Susan D., BA *Colorado*, MA *Ohio*, PhD   Sr. Lectr.
Fox-Rushby, J. A., BSc PhD   Sr. Lectr.
Fulop, N. J., PhD   Sr. Lectr.
Gilson, L. J., BA *Oxf.*, MA *E.Anglia*, PhD *Lond.*   Sr. Lectr.
Hagard, S., MB ChB *St And.*, MA *Camb.*, PhD *Glas.*   Visiting Prof.
Hundt, G., MA *Edin.*, MPhil *Edin.*, PhD *Warw.*   Sr. Lectr.
Lambert, H., DPhil   Sr. Lectr.
Lamping, Donna L., BA *Harv.*, PhD *Harv.*   Sr. Lectr.
Mays, N. B., BA *Oxf.*   Visiting Prof.
McKee, C. M., MB BCh BAO *Belf.*, MD *Belf.*, MSc   Prof.
McPake, B. I., PhD   Sr. Lectr.
Mills, Anne J., MA *Oxf.*, PhD   Prof., Health Economics and Policy
Normand, C. E. M., BA *Stir.*, DPhil *York(UK)*   Prof., Health Policy
Rafferty, A. M., BSc *Edin.*, MPhil *Nott.*, DPhil *Oxf.*   Sr. Lectr.
Reeves, B. C., MSc DPhil   Sr. Lectr.
Roberts, Jennifer A., MSc PhD   Reader
Sanderson, C. F. B., MA *Oxf.*, MSc *Camb.*, PhD *Camb.*   Sr. Lectr.
Smith, R. S. W., BSc *Edin.*   Visiting Prof.
Stephens, C., MSc PhD   Sr. Lectr.
Thorogood, M., BSc *Lond.*, PhD *Lond.*   Reader
Vaughan, J. P., MD, FRCPEd   Prof., Health Care Epidemiology
Walt, Gillian, BSc PhD   Reader
Wellings, K., BA *Lond.*, MA *Lond.*, MSc *Lond.*   Sr. Lectr.
Wilkinson, P., MSc   Sr. Lectr.
Zwi, A. B., MB BCh *Witw.*, MSc   Sr. Lectr.

CONTACT OFFICERS

Academic affairs. Dean: Spencer, Prof. Harrison C., MD *Johns H.*, MPH *Calif.*, FACP
Admissions (higher degree). Deputy Registrar: Targett, Julie
General enquiries. Secretary and Registrar: Surridge, Wendy S., BA *Reading*, MA *Lond.*
Library (chief librarian). Librarian and Director of Information Services: Furner, R. Brian, BA MSc
Research. Secretary and Registrar: Surridge, Wendy S., BA *Reading*, MA *Lond.*
Scholarships, awards, loans. Deputy Registrar: Targett, Julie
Students from other countries. Deputy Registrar: Targett, Julie

[*Information supplied by the institution as at 29 May 1998, and edited by the ACU*]

QUEEN MARY AND WESTFIELD COLLEGE

Founded 1989 from the merger of Queen Mary College (incorporated in 1934; previously established as East London College and originally founded as People's Palace Technical Schools, 1887) and Westfield College (incorporated in 1933; founded in 1882)

Associate Member of the Association of Commonwealth Universities

Postal Address: Mile End Road, London, England E1 4NS
Telephone: (0171) 975 5555 **Fax**: (0171) 975 5500 **Telex**: 893750 (Mercury Link: 19019285)
WWW: http://www.qmw.ac.uk **E-mail formula**: initial.surname@qmw.ac.uk

VISITOR—The Queen-in-Council
PATRON—Elizabeth, H.M. The Queen
CHAIRMAN OF COUNCIL—France, Sir Christopher, GCB
PRINCIPAL*—Smith, Prof. Adrian F. M., BA Camb., MSc Lond., PhD Lond., FIMA
SENIOR VICE-PRINCIPAL—Scopes, P. Molly, BSc Oxf., MA Oxf., DPhil Oxf.
VICE-PRINCIPAL—Young, Prof. K., PhD, FRHistS
VICE PRINCIPAL—Edgington, Prof. John A., MA Camb., PhD Camb.
VICE-PRINCIPAL AND WARDEN OF ST BARTHOLOMEW'S AND THE ROYAL LONDON SCHOOL OF MEDICINE AND
 DENTISTRY —McNeish, Prof. Alexander S., MB ChB Glas., MSc Birm., FRCP, FRCPGlas
SECRETARY AND REGISTRAR‡—Aldred, Keith, MA Camb., MA Lanc., PhD Lanc.
DIRECTOR OF ACADEMIC INFORMATION SERVICES—Murphy, Brian, BA

GENERAL INFORMATION

History. The college was formed in 1989 from the merger of Queen Mary College and Westfield College. In 1995 the London Hospital Medical College and St Bartholomew's Hospital Medical College merged to create St Bartholomew's and the Royal London School of Medicine and Dentistry within the college.

The campus is based in the East End of London (originally the site of Queen Mary College). Clinical students are based at hospital sites in Whitechapel and in the City at West Smithfield and Charterhouse Square.

Admission to first degree courses (see also United Kingdom Introduction). Through Universities and Colleges Admissions Service (UCAS). Two General Certificate of Education (GCE) A levels or 4 GCE AS levels, or a combination of the two, General Certificate of Secondary Education (GCSE) in English and mathematics may also be required; related BTEC diplomas and certificates with at least three merits; pass with merit in advanced General National Vocational Qualification (GNVQ); 'kitemarked' or 'validated' access and foundation courses. Scottish applicants: Scottish Certificate of Education (SCE) Higher level (minimum BCCCC) and/or CSYS; related Scottish Vocational Education Council (SCOTVEC) diploma or certificate. Irish applicants: Irish Leaving Certificate with five subjects at honours (minimum BCCCC); related NCEA certificates and diplomas. International applicants: French or European Baccalaureate (except for medicine and dentistry). For candidates whose first language is not English: GCSE in English, JMB University Entrance Test, Cambridge Certificate of Proficiency, Hong Kong Examination authority, International English Language Testing Service (IELTS), Test of English as a Foreign Language (TEFL).

First Degrees (of University of London) (see also University of London Directory to Subjects of Study). BA, BDS, BEng, BSc, BScEcon, BSc(Eng), LLB, MB BS, MEng, MSci.

All courses are full-time and normally last 3 years; BEng sandwich courses, joint language degree courses: 4 years. LLB (English and European Law), MEng, MSci: 4 years. BDS, MB BS: 5 years.

Higher Degrees (of University of London) (see also University of London Directory to Subjects of Study). LLM, MA, MSc, MPhil, PhD.

Applicants for admission to taught master's degrees (LLM, MA, MSc) must normally hold a good first degree with at least second class honours from a UK university, or recognised overseas equivalent, or equivalent professional qualification. MPhil, PhD: good first degree with at least second class honours or master's degree from UK university, or recognised overseas equivalent, or equivalent professional qualification.

LLM, MA, MSc: 1 year full-time or 2 years part-time. MPhil: 2 years full-time or 3 years part-time. PhD: 3 years full-time or 4 years part-time.

Libraries. 600,000 volumes; 2500 periodicals received annually. The library is a European Documentation Centre and receives publications from the European Union.

Fees. Undergraduate home students (1996–97, annual): £750 (arts, social studies and laws); £2800 (clinical medicine and dentistry); £1600 (engineering, sciences and pre-clinical medicine); £1600–2000 (pre-clinical dentistry). Undergraduate overseas students (1996–97, annual): £6900 (arts, social studies and laws); £15,400 (clinical medicine and dentistry); £8600 (engineering, sciences and pre-clinical medicine); £8600–10,866 (pre-clinical dentistry). Postgraduate home students (1997–98): £2540 (full-time), £1270 (part-time). Postgraduate overseas students (1997–98): £8250 (full-time), £4125 (part-time) (laboratory-based research degrees); £9200 (full-time), £4600 (part-time) (taught laboratory-based courses); £7100 (full-time), £3550 (part-time) (other taught courses).

Academic Awards (1996–97). 333 awards ranging in value from £15 to over £250.

Academic Year (1998–99). Three terms: 28 September–18 December; 18 January–16 April; 10 May–18 June.

Income. Total, £118,000,000.

Statistics (1996–97). Staff: 2718 (1527 academic/research etc, 1191 administrative and other). Students: 8178.

FACULTIES/SCHOOLS

Arts
Tel: (0171) 955 5003 Fax: (0181) 980 9142
Dean: Kuhn, R. J., MA Glas., MA Warw., PhD Warw.
Secretary: Salucideen, Jasmin

Basic Medical Sciences
Tel: (0171) 775 6301 Fax: (0181) 983 0502
Dean: Bird, Margaret M., BSc PhD

Secretary: Young, Nina

Clinical Dentistry
Dean: Williams, Prof. David M., BDS MSc PhD, FRCPath, FDSRCS
Secretary:......

Engineering
Tel: (0171) 975 5189 Fax: (0181) 983 1007
Dean: Crookes, Roy J., BSc Leeds, PhD Leeds
Secretary: Hefford, Jean

Informatics and Mathematical Sciences
Tel: (0171) 975 5455 Fax: (0181) 981 9587
Dean: MacCallum, Prof. M. A. H. M., MA Camb., PhD Camb., FIP, FRAS
Secretary: Wilkinson, Shirley

Laws
Tel: (0171) 775 3283 Fax: (0181) 981 8733
Dean: Richardson, Prof. Genevra M., LLM
Secretary: Oliver, S. C.

Natural Sciences
Tel: (0171) 775 3012 Fax: (0181) 983 0973
Dean: Heathcote, P., BSc PhD
Secretary: Moran, M.

Research
Tel: (0171) 975 5006
Dean for Research: Edgington, Prof. John A., MA Camb., PhD Camb.
Secretary: Cosford, D.

Social Sciences
Tel: (0171) 975 5400 Fax: (0181) 981 6276
Dean: Ogden, Prof. P. E., BA Durh., DPhil Oxf.
Secretary: Page, J.

ACADEMIC UNITS

§ = Faculty appointment

Astronomy Unit
Carr, B. J., BA Camb., PhD, FRAS   Prof., Mathematics and Astronomy
Ellis, G. F. R., BSc Cape Town, PhD Camb., FRSSAf, FRAS   Visiting Prof.
MacCallum, M. A. H. M., MA Camb., PhD Camb., FIP, FRAS   Hon. Prof.
Murray, C. D., BSc PhD, FRAS   Prof., Mathematics and Astronomy
Papaloizou, J. C. B., BSc Sus., DPhil Sus., FRAS   Prof.
Pringle, J., MA Camb., PhD, FRAS   Visiting Prof.
Roxburgh, I. W., BSc Nott., PhD Camb., FIP, FRAS   Prof., Mathematics and Astronomy; Dir.*
Schwartz, S. J., BSc Cornell, PhD Camb., FRAS   Prof., Space Plasma Physics

Tavakol, R. K., BSc PhD, FRAS Reader
Thompson, M., MA *Camb.*, PhD *Camb.*, FRAS Reader
Williams, Iwan P., BSc *Wales*, PhD *Lond.*, FRAS, FIP Prof., Mathematics and Astronomy
Research: cosmology; gravitation; plasmas; stellar physics and dynamics

Biological Sciences, School of

Tel: (0171) 775 3200 Fax: (0181) 983 0973
Bevan, E. A., BSc *Wales*, MA *Oxf.*, PhD *Glas.*, FLS, FIBiol Emer. Prof.
Bignell, D. E., BSc *Nott.*, PhD *Nott.*, MSc Sr. Lectr.
Boxshall, G. A., BSc *Leeds*, PhD *Leeds*, FRS Visiting Prof.
Campbell, A. C., BSc *St And.*, DPhil *Oxf.*, FLS Sr. Lectr.
Casselton, L. A., PhD DSc Visiting Prof.
Clymo, R. S., Hon. PhD *Lund*, BSc PhD Emer. Prof.†, Ecology
Duckett, J. G., BA *Camb.*, PhD *Camb.*, FLS Prof., Botany
Godward, MSc PhD, FLS Emer. Prof.
Goodman, L. J., MA *Camb.*, PhD *Liv.* Emer. Reader
Green, J., PhD DSc, FIBiol, FLS Emer. Prof.
Gurnell, J., BSc *Exe.*, PhD *Exe.* Reader, Ecology
Heathcote, P., BSc PhD Reader, Biochemistry
Hildrew, A. G., BSc *Wales*, PhD *Wales* Prof., Ecology
Lichtenstein, C. P., BSc *Sus.*, PhD *Camb.* Prof., Molecular Biology
McCarthy, D. A., BSc PhD Sr. Lectr.
Moses, V., MA *Camb.*, PhD DSc, FIBiol Emer. Prof.
Nichols, R. A., BSc *E.Anglia*, PhD *E.Anglia* Reader, Genetics
Pye, J. D., BSc *Wales*, PhD, FLS Emer. Prof.
Rainbow, P. S., MA *Camb.*, PhD *Wales*, DSc *Wales*, FLS Visiting Prof., Marine Biology
Smith, J., PhD, FRS Visiting Prof.
Swift, M. J., MA *Camb.*, PhD Visiting Prof.
Taylor, J. D., BSc PhD Visiting Prof.
Thorpe, A., BSc *Sheff.*, PhD *Nott.* Prof., Biology
Research: ecology (community ecology, forests, freshwater, marine, peat bogs); evolution (ENDOR, photosynthesis, protein structure, spectroscopy, X-ray crystallography); genetics and molecular biology (chromosome structure, pathogenesis, plant development); neuroscience (insect neurophysiology, neuronal signalling molecules)

Chemistry

Tel: (0171) 775 3252 Fax: (0181) 981 8745
Aylett, B. J., MA *Camb..*, PhD *Camb..*, FRSChem Emer. Prof., Inorganic Chemistry
Bonnett, R., PhD *Camb.*, DSc, FRSChem Scotia Res. Prof. Emer.
Bradley, D. C., PhD DSc, FRS, FRSChem Emer. Prof., Inorganic Chemistry
Griffiths, D. Vaughan, BSc *Nott.*, PhD *Nott.* Reader, Organic Chemistry
Hamilton, P. A., BSc PhD, FRSChem Reader, Physical Chemistry
Hawkes, G. E., BSc PhD, FRSChem Reader, Organic Chemistry
Marson, C. M., MA MSc PhD, FRSChem Reader, Organic Chemistry
Moss, G. P., BSc *Lond.*, PhD *Camb.* Sr. Lectr.
Pritchard, J., BSc PhD, FRSChem Emer. Prof., Physical Chemistry
Randall, E. W., BA *Oxf.*, DPhil *Oxf.*, FRSChem Emer. Prof., Inorganic Chemistry
Sullivan, A. C., BA PhD Reader, Inorganic Chemistry
Utley, J. H. P., BSc *Hull*, PhD *Hull*, DSc, FRSChem Prof., Organic Chemistry; Head*
Vlcek, A., CSc *Czech.Acad.Sc.*, RNDr *Prague*, PhD Prof., Inorganic Chemistry

Commercial Law Studies, Centre for

Blair, W., QC, BA *Oxf.* Visiting Prof.
Collins, L., BA *Camb.*, MA *Camb.*, LLM *Col.* Visiting Prof.§

Firth, A. M., MA *Oxf.*, MSc *CNAA* Sr. Lectr.
Fletcher, I., LLM *Camb.*, MA *Camb.*, MCL *Tulane*, PhD *Camb.*, LLD *Camb.* Prof., Commercial Law; Dir.*
Lahore, J. C., BCL *Oxf.*, MA *Oxf.*, LLM *Penn.*, LLD *Melb.* Herchel Smith Emer. Prof., Intellectual Property Law
Napier, B. W., LLB *Edinboro State*, MA *Edin.*, PhD *Camb.* Digital Visiting Prof., Information Technology Law
Norton, J. J., AB *Providence(R.I.)*, LLB *Edinboro State*, LLM *Texas*, SJD *Mich.* Sir John Lubbock Prof., Banking Law
Reed, C. M., BA *Keele*, LLM *Lond.* Reader, Information Technology Law; Acting Dir.*
Williams, D. W., LLM *Brist.*, PhD *Brist.* Prof., Tax Law
Wood, P. R., BA *Cape Town*, BA *Oxf.* Allen and Overy Visiting Prof.
Research: copyright and design (moral rights, trade mark and competition); emerging economics and international banking; international and comparative aspects of insolvency law; internet (telecommunications and IT law); tax in intellectual property

Computer Science

Tel: (0171) 975 5200 Fax: (0181) 980 6533
Beal, D. F., BSc MSc Sr. Lectr.
Bornat, Richard, BSc *Manc.*, MSc *Manc.* Prof., Computer Programming
Coulouris, G. F., BSc Emer. Prof., Computer Systems
Dollimore, J. B., MSc Sr. Lectr.
Gong, S., DPhil *Oxf.*, BSc Sr. Lectr.
Johnson, P., BSc *Salf.*, PhD *Warw.* Prof., Human Computer Interaction
Kinberg, T., BA *Camb.*, PhD *CNAA* Sr. Lectr.
Landin, P., MA *Camb.* Emer. Prof., Theoretical Computation
Liddell, Heather M., BSc PhD Emer. Prof., Parallel Computing Applications; Head*
O'Hearne, P. W., BSc *Dal.*, MSc *Qu.*, PhD *Qu.* Reader
Paker, Y., MSc *Col.*, PhD *Col.* Prof., Parallel Computing
Pym, D., MA *Camb.*, PhD *Edin.*, FIMA Reader
Ringwood, G., BSc *Birm.*, MSc *Durh.*, MSc *Lond..*, PhD *Birm.* Sr. Lectr.
Robinson, E., MA *Camb.*, PhD *Camb.* Prof., Computer Science
Wilbur, S., BA *Open(UK)*, MSc *Kent* Sr. Lectr.
Research: artificial intelligence; distributed systems; human computer interaction; logic and foundations of programming; parallel computing

Dentistry, see St Barthomomew's and the Royal London School of Medicine and Dentistry (Clinical Dentistry)

Economics

Fax: (0181) 983 3580
Allard, Richard J., BA *Camb.*, MSc(Econ) Sr. Lectr.
Baillie, R. T., BSc *Middx.*, MSc *Kent*, PhD Prof., International Finance
Corry, B. A., BSc(Econ) *Lond.*, PhD *Lond.* Emer. Prof.
Disney, R., BA *Camb.*, MA *Sus.* Prof.
Gilbert, C. L., MA *Oxf.*, DPhil *Oxf.*, MSc Prof., Applied Econometrics
Grahl, J. G., MA *Edin.*, MSc(Econ) Sr. Lectr.
Haskel, J., BSc *Brist.*, MSc(Econ) PhD Sr. Lectr., Industrial Economics
Mohun, S., BA *Oxf.*, BPhil *Oxf.*, PhD Sr. Lectr.; Head*
Peston, Lord, BSc(Econ) Emer. Prof.†
Pollock, D. S. G., BA *Sus.*, MSc *S'ton.*, PhD *Amst.* Reader
Vanags, A. H., MSc(Econ) Sr. Lectr.
Yarrow, G. K., BA *Camb.* Visiting Prof.; Dir., European Regulatory Res. Inst.

Engineering

Tel: (0171) 975 5190 Fax: (0181) 983 3052
Aliabadi, M. H., BSc PhD Prof., Computational Mechanics
Bernstein, L., BSc(Eng) PhD Sr. Lectr.
Collins, W. J. M. Visiting Prof.
Cooper, J. R., BSc(Eng) Sr. Lectr.
Crookes, Roy J., BSc *Leeds*, PhD *Leeds* Sr. Lectr.
French, W., BSc *Nott.*, DPhil *Oxf.* Sr. Lectr.
Gaster, M., BSc(Eng) PhD, FRS Res. Prof.
Horton, H. P., BSc *Brist.*, PhD Sr. Lectr.
Jones, J. G., BA *Camb.*, BSc *Lond.* Visiting Prof.
Kirk, G. E., FRAeS, FIMechE Visiting Prof.
Lawn, C. J., MA *Camb.*, PhD *Camb.* Prof.
Loxham, M., PhD *Delft*, BSc Visiting Prof.†
Lusher, J. K., BSc(Eng) PhD Sr. Lectr.
Parkinson, Robert, BSc *Nott.*, PhD *Nott.* Visiting Prof.
Poole, A., BSc *Nott.*, DPhil *Oxf.* Sr. Lectr.
Raichura, R. C., BSc(Eng) PhD Sr. Lectr.
Rigden, S. R., BSc *Leic.*, MSc *Warw.* Sr. Lectr.
Rose, J. W., PhD DSc(Eng), FIMechE Prof.
Samdham, N. D., BSc *Leeds*, MS *Stan.*, PhD *Stan.* Reader
Stark, J. P. W., BSc *Exe.*, MSc *Manc.*, PhD, FRAeS, FRAS Prof.; Head*
Sweeting, D., BSc(Eng) Sr. Lectr.
White, G. C., BSc *Strath.*, PhD *Strath.* Visiting Prof.
White, J. K., MA *Oxf.*, DPhil *Oxf.*, FICE Prof.
Wormleeton, P. R., BSc *Birm.*, PhD Sr. Lectr.

Engineering, Electronic

Fax: (0181) 981 0259
Adams, R. N., BSc(Eng) PhD Sr. Lectr.
Bigham, J., BSc *Edin.*, MSc PhD Sr. Lectr.
Clarricoats, Peter J. B., CBE, Hon. DSc *Kent*, Hon. DSc *Aston*, PhD DSc(Eng), FRS, FEng, FIP, Hon. FIEE Prof.
Cuthbert, L. G., BSc(Eng) PhD, FIEE Prof.
Jennings, N. R., BSc *Exe.*, PhD Prof., Intelligent Systems
Laughton, M. A., BASc *Tor.*, PhD DSc(Eng), FEng, FIEE Prof.
Olver, David, BSc *Leeds*, PhD *Leeds*, FIEE, FEng Prof.; Head*
Parini, C. G., BSc(Eng) PhD Reader
Pearmain, A. J., BSc(Eng) *S'ton.*, PhD *S'ton.* Sr. Lectr.

English and Drama

Tel: (0171) 775 3356 Fax: (0181) 980 6200
Allen, Rosamund S., MA Reader
Boffey, Julia, MA *Camb.*, DPhil *York(UK)* Sr. Lectr.
Cook, Cornelia, BA *Mt.Holyoke*, MA *Oxf.*, DPhil *Oxf.* Sr. Lectr.
Hamilton, P. W. A., MA *Glas.*, MA *Oxf.*, DPhil *Oxf.* Prof.; Head*
Heritage, P., BA *Manc.* Sr. Lectr.
Hutson, Lorna, MA *Oxf.*, DPhil *Oxf.* Reader
Jardine, Lisa A., MA *Camb.*, PhD *Camb.*, FRHistS Prof.
Lincoln, Andrew W. J., MA *Wales*, PhD *Wales* Sr. Lectr.
Maslen, Elizabeth J., BA *Oxf.* Sr. Lectr.
Nasta, Susheila, MA *Kent* Sr. Lectr.
Raitt, Suzanne, BA *Camb.*, MA *Yale*, PhD *Camb.* Sr. Lectr.
Redmond, James, MA *Glas.*, EdB *Glas.*, BA *Camb.*, BLitt *Oxf.* Sr. Lectr.
Reid, Christopher G. P., MA *Camb.*, PhD Sr. Lectr.
Rose, Jacqueline, MA *Oxf.*, PhD Prof.
Shiach, Morag, MA *Glas.*, MA *McG.*, PhD *Camb.* Reader
Research: cultural studies, literature and history; drama and performance; feminism (Renaissance, nineteenth and twentieth centuries); modern literature (including psychoanalysis); postcolonial studies and new literatures in English

French Language and Literature, see under Mod. Langs.

Geography

Tel: (0171) 975 5400 Fax: (0181) 981 6276

Atkinson, B. W., BSc PhD   Prof.

Butterfield, G. R., BSc Cant.   Sr. Lectr.

Curtis, Sarah E., BA Oxf., PhD Kent   Reader

Drewry, D., BSc Lond., PhD Camb., DSc Camb.   Visiting Prof.

Gardner, Rita A. M., BA Lond., DPhil Oxf.   Visiting Prof.; Res. Fellow

Gray, J. M., BSc Edin., PhD Edin.   Reader

Gregory, Kenneth J., PhD Lond., DSc Lond.   Visiting Prof. Fellow

Hall, Ray, BA Liv., PhD   Sr. Lectr.

Lee, R. K., BSc Nott.   Prof.

Ogden, P. E., BA Durh., DPhil Oxf.   Prof.

Smith, D. M., BA Nott., PhD Nott.   Prof.

Southall, H. R., BA Camb., PhD Camb.   Reader

Spence, N. A., BSc Wales, PhD Lond.   Prof.; Head*

Storrie, M. C., BSc Glas., PhD Glas.   Sr. Lectr.

Research: earth and atmospheric processes (aeolian sediment dynamics, environmental change, fluvial and hydrological processes, meso-scale meterology); historical GIS group (demographic change and the economy: Britain 1801–2001); population dynamics and health (processes affecting the spatial differentiation of demography and health); socio-economic change and geographies of inequality (intersection and mutual constitution of social, cultural, political and economic processes, social construction of relations of power and of responses to them)

German, see under Mod. Langs.

Hispanic Studies, see Hispanic Studies and Italian under Mod. Langs.

History

Bolton, Brenda M., MA Leeds, FRHistS, FSA   Sr. Lectr.

Crozier, A. J., MA PhD, FRHistS   Sr. Lectr.; Jean Monnet Lectr., History of Contemporary History

Denley, P. R., MA Oxf., DPhil Oxf., FRHistS   Sr. Lectr.

Hennessy, P. J., BA Camb., PhD Camb., DLitt W.England, FRHistS   Prof., Contemporary History

Mettam, R. C., MA Camb., PhD Camb., FRHistS   Reader

Miller, J. L., MA Camb., PhD Camb., FRHistS   Prof.

Pick, D. M., MA Camb., PhD Camb.   Reader

Ramsden, J. A., MA Oxf., DPhil Oxf., FRHistS   Prof., Modern History; Head*

Sassoon, D., MA Penn., BSc(Econ) PhD   Prof., Comparative European History

Williams, G., DLitt Nfld., BA PhD, FRHistS   Emer. Prof.

Italian, see Hispanic Studies and Italian under Mod. Langs.

Law, see also Comml. Law Studies, Centre for

Tel: (0171) 975 5146 Fax: (0181) 981 8733

Adams, J. E., LLB Brist.   Emer. Prof.

Barnett, H., BA CNAA, LLM Lond.   Sr. Lectr.

Birnie, Patricia, BA Oxf., PhD Edin.   Visiting Prof. Fellow

Collins, L., BA Camb., MA Camb., LLM Col., LLD Camb.   Visiting Prof.§

Cotterell, Roger, MSc(Soc) LLD   Prof., Legal Theory

Fitzmaurice, M., LLM Warsaw, PhD Warsaw   Sr. Lectr.

Fitzpatrick, P., LLB Qld., LLM   Prof.

Lane, Shelley M., BA Case W.Reserve, LLB   Sr. Lectr.

McConville, Sean D. M., BSc Bath, PhD Camb.   Prof. Fellow, Criminal Justice

Morrison, W., LLB Cant., LLM Lond., PhD Lond.   Sr. Lectr.

O'Donovan, K., BCL N.U.I., LLM Harv., PhD Kent   Prof.

Scott, J., LLB Aberd., LLM   Sr. Lectr.

Thomas, G., BA Wales, DPhil Oxf.   Sr. Lectr.

Tunkel, V., LLB Nott.   Sr. Lectr.

Van Bueren, Geraldine, LLB Wales, LLM   Prof., International Human Rights

Yeats, I. M., MA Aberd., MA Oxf., BCL Oxf.   Sr. Lectr.

Yelland, J. L., BA Oxf., BCL Oxf.   Prof.; Head*

Linguistics, see under Mod. Langs.

Materials

Tel: (0171) 975 5159 Fax: (0181) 981 9804

Andrews, E. H., PhD DSc, FIP, FIM   Prof.

Bader, D. L., BSc S'ton., PhD S'ton.   Reader

Behiri, J. C., BSc(Eng) PhD   Sr. Lectr.

Bonfield, William, CBE, BSc(Eng) PhD, FIM, FEng   Prof.

Davies, C. K. L., BSc Wales, PhD Wales, FIM   Prof.; Head*

Galiotis, C., BSc Athens, PhD   Reader

Hogg, P. J., BSc Liv., PhD Liv., FIM   Sr. Lectr.

Stevens, R. N., BSc Wales, PhD Wales   Sr. Lectr.

Tanner, K. Elizabeth, MA Oxf., DPhil Oxf., FIMechE   Prof., Biomedical Materials

Thomas, A. J., MA Oxf., FIP   Visiting Prof.†

Research: biomedical materials and biomechanics; fatigue, creep, and crack growth in metals and ceramics; ferroelectric and piezoelectric materials; powder manufacture of MMC's; processing and properties of polymer composites and elastomers

Mathematical Sciences, School of

Tel: (0171) 975 5440 Fax: (0181) 981 9587

Arrowsmith, D. K., BSc Leic., PhD Leic.   Prof.; Dir., Maths. Res. Centre

Bailey, R. A., MA Oxf., DPhil   Prof.

Beck, C. A., MSc T.H.Aachen, PhD T.H.Aachen   Reader

Bonnor, W. B., BSc PhD   Prof. Res. Fellow

Bullett, S. R., BA Camb., PhD Warw.   Reader

Cameron, P. J., BSc Qld., DPhil Oxf.   Prof.

Carr, B. J., BA Camb., PhD Camb., FRAS   Prof.

Chiswell, I. M., BA Oxf., MS Mich., PhD Mich.   Reader

Collins, D. J., BSc Dund., PhD Prin.   Reader; Head*

Donkin, S., MA Oxf., MSc Warw., PhD   Prof.

Ellis, G. F. R., BSc Cape Town, PhD Camb., FRSSAf, FRAS   Visiting Prof.

Glendinning, P. A., MA Camb., PhD Camb.   Prof.

Goldsheid, I., PhD Moscow   Prof.

Gruenberg, K. W., BA Camb., PhD Camb.   Emer. Prof.

Hodges, W. A., MA Oxf., DPhil Oxf.   Prof.

Hughes, D. R., BSc Maryland, MA Wis., PhD Wis.   Emer. Prof.

Hughes, J. W. B., BSc PhD   Reader

Kropholler, P., MA Camb., PhD   Reader

Leedham-Green, C. R., MA Oxf., DPhil Oxf.   Reader

MacCallum, M. A. H. M., MA Camb., PhD Camb., FIP, FRAS   Prof.

Macdonald, I. G., MA Camb., MA Oxf., FRS   Emer. Prof.

McCarthy, P. J., BA Oxf., PhD   Reader

Murray, C. D., BSc PhD, FRAS   Prof.

Papaloizou, J. C. B., BSc Sus., DPhil Sus., FRAS   Prof.

Pringle, J., MA Camb., PhD, FRAS   Visiting Prof.

Roxburgh, I. W., BSc Nott., PhD Camb., FIP, FRAS   Prof.

Schwartz, S. J., BSc Cornell, PhD Camb., FRAS   Prof.

Simons, S., MA Camb., PhD   Reader

Tavakol, R. K., BSc PhD, FRAS   Reader

Thompson, M. J., MA Camb., PhD Camb., FRAS   Reader

Tworkowski, A. S. S., PhD Camb., BSc   Computer Manager

Vivaldi, F., PhD Milan   Reader

Wehrfritz, B. A. F., PhD DSc   Prof.; Dir., Undergrad. Studies

Williams, I. P., BSc Wales, PhD, FRAS   Prof.

Wright, F. J., MA Camb., PhD Brist.   Reader

Research: applied mathematics (computer algebra, dynamical systems, epedemics); probability and statistics (design of experiments, statistical physics); pure mathematics (algebra, combinatorics, group theory logic, topology)

Medicine and Dentistry, St Bartholomew's and the Royal London School of, see below

Modern Languages

Tel: (0171) 775 3335 Fax: (0181) 980 5400

Penny, R. J., MA Edin., PhD Edin.   Prof., Romance Philology; Head*

French Language and Literature

Tel: (0171) 775 3372 Fax: (0181) 980 5400

Hobson Jeanneret, M. E., MA Camb., PhD Camb.   Prof.

Moriarty, M., MA Camb., PhD Camb.   Prof., French Literature and Thought; Head*

Slater, Maya, MA Oxf., DPhil Oxf.   Sr. Lectr.

Whitford, M. L., BA Sus., PhD Camb.   Prof., Modern French Thought

Whyte, A., MA Aberd.   Sr. Lectr.

Wise, M., MA PhD   Sr. Lectr.

Research: French linguistics; modern critical theory; seventeenth–twentieth-century French literature; seventeenth–twentieth-century French thought

German

Tel: (0171) 775 3374 Fax: (0181) 980 5400

Howe, P. A., BA PhD   Sr. Lectr.

Olschner, L. M., BA Virginia, DrPhil Freib.   Prof.; Head*

Ranawake, S. A. O. H., DrPhil Munich   Prof.

Hispanic Studies and Italian

Tel: (0171) 975 5061 Fax: (0181) 980 5400

Evans, P. W., MA St And., PhD Camb.   Prof., Hispanic Studies

Lee-Six, A. E., MA Camb., PhD Camb.   Sr. Lectr.; Head*

Penny, R. J., MA Edin., PhD Edin.   Prof., Romance Philology

Terry, A. H., MA Camb., PhD Camb.   Visiting Prof., Catalan

Linguistics

Tel: (0171) 775 3392 Fax: (0181) 980 5400

Cheshire, J. L., BA Lond., PhD Reading   Prof.; Head*

Research: dialect levelling; language and gender; language variation and change; spoken English grammar

Russian

Tel: (0171) 775 3392 Fax: (0181) 980 5400

Rayfield, P. D., MA Camb., PhD Camb.   Prof., Russian and Georgian; Head*

Research: Chekhov, Russian diaries 1870-1917; Georgian literature; Mandelstam; Russian literary relations with the West

Physics

Tel: (0171) 975 5051 Fax: (0181) 981 9465

Ade, P. A. R., BSc PhD, FRAS   Prof., Experimental Astrophysics

Bugg, D. V., BA Camb., PhD Camb., FIP   Prof., Nuclear Physics

Carter, A. A., MA Camb., PhD Camb.   Prof., Particle Physics

Charap, J. M., MA Camb., PhD Camb., FIP   Prof., Theoretical Physics

Clegg, P. E., MA Oxf., PhD Reading, FRAS   Prof., Astrophysics; Head*

Dunstan, D. J., BA Camb., PhD Hull, FIP   Prof., Experimental Physics

Edgington, John A., MA Camb., PhD Camb.   Prof.

Emerson, J. P., MA Camb., PhD, FRAS   Reader

Felderhof, B. U., PhD Utrecht   Visiting Prof.

Gibson, W. R., BSc Belf., PhD Belf. Sr. Lectr.
Green, M. B., PhD Camb., FIP, FRS Visiting Prof.
Griffin, M. J., BEng Trinity(Dub.), MSc PhD Reader, Astrophysics
Hull, C. M., BA Camb., PhD Camb. Prof., Theoretical Physics
Jones, R. B., BA Wabash, PhD Birm. Reader, Theoretical Physics
Kalmus, P. I. P., BSc PhD, FIP Emer. Prof.
Lloyd, S. L., BSc PhD Reader, Experimental Particle Physics
Martin, D. H., BSc Nott., PhD Nott., FIP Emer. Prof.
Michael, B. D., MSc PhD Visiting Prof.
Sewell, G. L., MA Oxf., PhD Emer. Prof., Mathematical Physics
Smith, F. A., BSc Wales, PhD Liv. Reader, Radiation Physics
Thompson, G., BSc PhD Prof.
White, G. J., BSc Kent, MSc Manc., PhD Kent, FRAS Prof., Physics and Astronomy
Williams, P. G., BSc Witw., PhD Birm. Sr. Lectr.
Wilson, E. G., MA Camb., PhD Camb., FIP Prof.
Yeung, W., BSc Birm., PhD Birm. Sr. Lectr.
Research: astrophysics; experimental particle physics; molecular and material physics; radiation physics; theoretical physics

Political Studies

Tel: (0171) 975 5003 Fax: (0181) 980 9142

Coole, D., BA Wales, PhD Tor., MSc Sr. Lectr.; Head*
Dunkerley, J., BA York(UK), DPhil Oxf. Prof.
Fishman, W. J., DSc(Econ) Visiting Prof.
Kershen, A. J., MPhil Warw. Res. Fellow; Dir. for Study of Migration
Kuhn, R. J., MA Glas., MA Warw., PhD Warw. Sr. Lectr.
Parsons, D. W., MScEcon Wales, PhD Prof.
Saggar, S., BA Essex, PhD Essex Sr. Lectr.
Solesbury, W., BA Camb., MCD Liv. Visiting Prof.
Vallance, E. M., MA St And., MSc PhD Visiting Prof.
Young, K., MSc(Econ) PhD, FRHistS Prof.
Research: African politics; Latin American studies; media studies; politics of race; postmodernism

Russian, see under Mod. Langs.

Spanish, see Hispanic Studies and Italian under Mod. Langs, Sch. of

SPECIAL CENTRES, ETC

Public Policy Research Unit

Parsons, D. W., MScEcon Wales, PhD Dir.*

ST BARTHOLOMEW'S AND THE ROYAL LONDON SCHOOL OF MEDICINE AND DENTISTRY

BASIC MEDICAL SCIENCES

Anatomy

Tel: (0171) 982 6311 Fax: (0181) 983 0613

Bird, Margaret M., BSc PhD Reader, Neurobiology; Head*
Bishop, Mark A., BDS Iowa, MSc Iowa, PhD Brist. Sr. Lectr.
Priestley, J. V., BScLond., MA Camb., DPhil Oxf., PhD Lond. Prof., Cell Biology
Research: distribution of neurotransmitter receptors in the nervous system (with particular emphasis on somatosensory systems); effects of neurotransmitters on developing nerve cells in culture, role of brain derived neurotrophic factor (BDNF) and neurotrophin-4 (NT-4), effect of amyloid pelides on cultured neurons; pulp,

dentine, permeability, sensitivity, mineralisation, development

Biochemistry

Tel: (0181) 982 6331 Fax: (0181) 983 0531

Brocklehurst, Keith, BSc Manc., PhD Manc., DSc Prof., Enzyme Biochemistry
Carroll, Mark, BSc PhD Sr. Lectr.
Hinson, J. P., BSc Lond., PhD Lond. Sr. Lectr.
Phillips, Ian R., BSc Rand Afrikaans, PhD Prof., Molecular Biology
Smith, Kelvin E., BSc Hull, PhD Sr. Lectr.
Sugden, Mary C., MA Oxf., DPhil Oxf., DSc Prof., Cellular Biochemistry
Vinson, Gavin P., PhD Sheff., DSc Sheff. Prof.; Head*
Welch, Simon G., PhD Sr. Lectr.
Williams, R. Anthony D., BSc PhD Sr. Lectr.
Research: biomolecular NMR spectroscopy and protein folding; microbial thermostable enzymes; molecular and cellular endocrinology and metabolism; molecule genetics; protein structure and function (particularly enzyme kinetics)

Pharmacology

Tel: (0171) 982 6351 Fax: (0181) 983 0470

Burleigh, David E., BSc PhD Sr. Lectr.
Tomlinson, David R., BSc CNAA, PhD Sheff., DSc Nott. Prof.; Head*
Whelpton, Robin, BSc Salf., PhD Sr. Lectr.
Research: drug analysis and pharmacokinetics; intestinal epithelial transport in man; metabolism, nervous systems, neuropeptides, neurotransmission, peptide, peptide receptors; peripheral neuropathies and neurotrophic factors; receptor mediated modulation of acetylcholine release

Physiology

Tel: (0171) 982 6366 Fax: (0181) 983 0467

Armstrong-James, Michael A., BSc Brist., PhD Brist. Prof., Neurophysiology
Bird, M., BSc PhD ; Acting Head*
Keatinge, William R., MB BChir Camb., MA Camb., PhD Camb., FRCP Emer. Prof.
Millar, Julian, MA Oxf., PhD Sr. Lectr.
Savage, George E., BSc Nott., PhD Sr. Lectr.
Research: neurophysiology (effects of heat and cold on man)

CLINICAL DENTISTRY

Research: biomaterials; community health care; development, function and ageing; hard tissues; mucocutaneous biology and infectious diseases

Biomaterials in Relation to Dentistry

Anseau, Michel R., DSc Mons Prof.; Head*
Braden, Michael, BSc PhD, FIM Prof. Res. Fellow; Emer. Prof.

Child Dental Health

Davenport, Elizabeth S., BDS MSc PhD Sr. Lectr.
Hector, Marc P., BDS PhD Sr. Lectr.; Acting Head*
Wong, Ferranti, BDS Dund., MSc, FDSRCSEd Sr. Lectr.

Conservative Dentistry

Dowker, Stephanie E. P., BDS PhD Sr. Lectr.
Leon, Adrianne R., MDS, FDSRCS Sr. Lectr.
Lynch, Edward R. J., BDentSc MA PhD, FDSRCSEd Sr. Lectr.
Morganstein, Stuart I., BDS, FDSRCS Sr. Lectr.
Osborne, David S., BDS MSc Sr. Lectr.
Samarawickrama, Dayananda Y. D., BDS Ceyl., PhD, FDSRCS Sr. Lectr.; Head*
Shukle, Neilesh, BDS Sr. Lectr.
Tay, Wey Ming, BDS NU Singapore, PhD, FDSRCS Reader

Dental Auxiliary School

Davenport, Elizabeth S., BDS MSc PhD Sr. Lectr.; Dir.*

Dental Biophysics

Elliott, James C., BA Camb., PhD Prof.; Head*

Dental Public Health

Croucher, Ray, BSc MA PhD Sr. Lectr.; Acting Head*

Oral and Maxillo-Facial Surgery

Aiken, Anne, BDS Sr. Lectr.
Bradley, Paul F., BDS MD, FRCS Prof., Oral Surgery; Head*
Cannell, Hugh, MD Reader, Oral Surgery
Richards, John M., BDS Sr. Lectr.

Oral Medicine

Zakrzewska, Joanna, MD Camb., FDSRCS, FFDRCSI Sr. Lectr.; Head*

Oral Microbiology

Curtis, Michael, BSc Brist., PhD Reader; Head, MRC Molecular Pathogenesis Group
Hardie, Jeremy M., BDS PhD, FRCPath Prof.; Head*

Oral Pathology

Farthing, Paula M., BSc Edin., BDS Edin., PhD, FDSRCSEd Sr. Lectr.
Howells, Gareth L., BDS Wales, MSc PhD Sr. Lectr.
Williams, David M., BDS MSc PhD, FRCPath, FDSRCS Prof.; Head*

Orthodontics

Battagel, Joanna, BDS PhD, FDSRCS Sr. Lectr.
Calvert, Mary, BDS, FDSRCS Sr. Lectr.
Moss, James P., BDS PhD, FDSRCS Prof.; Head*

Periodontology

Hughes, Francis J., BDS, FDSRCS Reader; Acting Head*

Prosthetic Dentistry

Barsby, Michael J., BSc Open(UK), BDS PhD, FDSRCS Sr. Lectr.
Heath, M. Robin, BDS PhD, FDSRCS Prof., Gerontology; Head*
Wright, Paul S., BDS PhD, FDSRCS Sr. Lectr.

CLINICAL MEDICINE

Anaesthetics

Flynn, Patricia J., MB NZ, FRCA Sr. Lectr.; Acting Head*
Goldhill, David R., MA Oxf., MB BS, FRCA Sr. Lectr.
Hinds, Charles J., MB BS, FRCA Sr. Lectr.
Langford, Richard M., MB BS, FRCA Sr. Lectr.
Samra, Gurdip, BSc MB BS, FRCA Sr. Lectr.
Stamford, Jonathan A., BSc PhD Sr. Lectr.
Strunin, Leo, MB BS Durh., MD Newcastle(UK), FRCA, FRCPCan BOC Prof.
Watson, BSc MB BS, FRCA
Withington, Peter S., MB BS, FRCA Sr. Lectr.

Biochemical Pharmacology

Flower, Roderick J., BSc Sheff., PhD DSc Prof.; Head*
Goulding, Nicholas, BSc S'ton., PhD S'ton. Sr. Lectr.
Whittle, Brendan J., BPharm PhD DSc Prof., Applied Pharmacology

Cardiology

Dymond, Duncan, MD, FRCP Sr. Lectr.
McDonald, Alastair H., FRCP Sr. Lectr.
Mills, Peter G., BSc Oxf., BM BCh Oxf., FRCP Sr. Lectr.; Head*
Nathan, Anthony, MD, FRCP Sr. Lectr.
Tunstall-Pedoe, Dan, MB BChir Camb., MA Camb., DPhil Oxf., FRCP Sr. Lectr.

Cardiovascular Biochemistry

Miller, Norman E., MD Manc., PhD ANU, DSc Manc., FRCP, FACP, FRCPath Prof.; Head*

Chemical Endocrinology

Clark, Adrian, BSc MB BS, FRCP Reader, Molecular Endocrinology
Medbak, Sami, MB ChB Basrah, PhD Sr. Lectr.
Rees, Lesley H., Hon. DSc Ulster, MD DSc, FRCP, FRCPath Prof.; Head*

Child Health, see also Paed. Endocrinol., Paed. Gastroenterol., and Paed. Oncol.

Costeloe, Kate, BA Camb., MB BChir Camb. Prof., Neonatal Paediatrics; Head*
Harris, Roger J., MD Brist., FRCP Sr. Lectr.
Husain, Shad, MB ChB Manc. Sr. Lectr.
Roper, Janice, BM BS Nott., BMedSci Nott. Sr. Lectr.
Savage, Martin O., MB BChir Camb., MA Camb., MD Camb., FRCP Reader, Paediatric Endocrinology
Snodgrass, Graeme J. A. I., MB ChB Edin., FRCP Sr. Lectr.

Clinical Biochemistry

Bulusu, S., MD S'ton, FRCPath Reader
Burrin, Jacky M., BSc CNAA, PhD Manc.Met. Prof., Experimental Endocrinology
Dawnay, Anne, BSc PhD, FRCPath Sr. Lectr.
Landon, John, MD, FRCP Emer. Prof.
Makin, Hugh L. J., MA Camb., PhD, FRSChem, FRCPath Prof., Analytical Biochemistry
Newman, David J., BSc Brist., MSc Sur., PhD Sr. Lectr.
Price, Chris P., BSc Birm., MA Camb., PhD Birm., FRSChem, FRCPath Prof.; Head*

Clinical Haematology

Amos, Roger J., MB BChir Camb., MA Camb., MD Camb. Sr. Lectr.
Colvin, Brian T., MA Camb., MB BChir Camb., MD Camb., FRCP, FRCPath Sr. Lectr.
Facer, Christine A., MSc PhD Reader, Tropical Haematology
Gutteridge, Charles N., MB BChir Camb., MA Camb. Sr. Lectr.
Kelsey, Stephen M., BSc Birm., MD Birm. Sr. Lectr.
Kovacs, Irene B., MD PhD, FRCPath Sr. Lectr.
MacCallum, Peter K., MB ChB Sheff., MD Sheff. Sr. Lectr.
Newland, Adrian C., MB BChir Camb., MA Camb., FRCP, FRCPath Prof.; Head*
Tillyer, M. Louise, MB ChB Edin., FRCPath Sr. Lectr.

Clinical Pharmacology

Abrams, S. M. Louise, BSc Lond., MB BS Lond. Sr. Lectr.
Benjamin, Nigel, DM Nott., FRCP Prof.; Head*
Caulfield, Mark, MB BS Reader
Chaput de Saintonge, D. Mark, PhD, FRCP Sr. Lectr.
Pearson, Richard M., MB BChir Camb., MA Camb., FRCP Sr. Lectr.

Dermatology

Bataille, Veronique A., MD Brussels, PhD Sr. Lectr.
Leigh, Irene M., MD, FRCP Prof.; Head*
McGregor, Jane, MB BChir Camb., MA Camb. Sr. Lectr.
McKay, Ian, MA Camb., PhD Camb. Sr. Lectr.
Proby, Charlotte M., MA Oxf. Sr. Lectr.
Quinn, Anthony G., PhD Newcastle(UK) Sr. Lectr.

Diabetes

Leslie, R. David G., MD, FRCP Prof., Diabetes and Autoimmunity

Diagnostic Radiology

Armstrong, Peter, MB BS, FRCR Prof.; Head*
Brooks, Alan P., BSc MB BS, FRCR Sr. Lectr.
Reznek, Rodney H., MB ChB Cape Town, FRCR, FRCP Prof., Medical Imaging

Environmental and Preventive Medicine

Ashby, D., BSc Exe., MSc PhD Prof., Medical Statistics
Law, Malcolm, MB BS Adel., MSc Adel., FRCP Reader, Epidemiology
Morris, J., MA Camb., MSc Oxf., PhD Sr. Lectr.
Wald, Nicholas J., MB BS DSc, FRCP, FRCOG Prof.; Head*

MRC Epidemiology and Medical Care Unit

Meade, Thomas W., CBE, DM Oxf., FRCP, FRS Prof., Epidemiology; Dir.*

Experimental Pathology

Willoughby, Derek A., PhD DSc, FRCPath, FIBiol Emer. Prof.

Gastroenterology

Alstead, Elspeth M., MD Liv., FRCP Sr. Lectr.
Evans, David F., BA PhD Reader, Gastrointestinal Science
Fairclough, Peter D., MD, FRCP Sr. Lectr.
Farthing, Michael J. G., BSc MD, FRCP Prof.
Kumar, Parveen J., BSc MD, FRCP Reader
Patchett, Stephen, MD Sr. Lectr.
Rampton, David S., BM BCh Oxf., MA Oxf., DPhil Oxf., FRCP Reader
Wingate, David L., MSc Oxf., MA Oxf., DM Oxf., FRCP Prof.; Head*

General Practice and Primary Care

Carter, Yvonne H., BSc MD, FRCGP Prof.; Head*
Derret, Chris, BSc Durh., MB BS MPhil Sr. Lectr.
Feder, Gene, BSc Sus., MB BS MD Sr. Lectr.
Gantley, M., BA MSc PhD Sr. Lectr.
Griffiths, Chris, BSc MB BS MPhil Sr. Lectr.
Harris, Brian, MB ChB Liv., FRCGP Sr. Lectr.
Hill, A., BSc MB BS Sr. Lectr.
Hull, Sally, MA Camb., MSc Camb., FRCGP Sr. Lectr.
Julian, Paul, MB BS Sr. Lectr.
Naish, Jenette, MB BS MSc Sr. Lectr.
Raiman, John, MB BS, FRCGP Sr. Lectr.
Robson, John P., MB BS MSc MD, FRCGP Sr. Lectr.
Savage, Wendy D., BA MB BCh, FRCOG Sr. Lectr.
Sheldon, Mike, BA Open(UK), MB BS, FRCGP Sr. Lectr.
Smith, Mike, BSc Wales, MA Calif., PhD Prof. Fellow
Underwood, Martin, MB ChB Manc., MSc Keele Sr. Lectr.

Health Care of the Elderly

Bennett, Gerald, MB ChB Wales, FRCP Reader; Head*

Histopathology, see Morbid Anat. and Histopathol.

Human Metabolism and Molecular Genetics

Galton, David J., MD DSc, FRCP Prof.; Head*

Human Nutrition

Powell-Tuck, Jeremy, MD Birm., FRCP Sr. Lectr.; Head*

Human Science and Medical Ethics

Cushing, Annie, BDS PhD, FDSRCS Sr. Lectr.
Doyal, Len, BA Atlanta, MSc Prof., Medical Ethics
Hajek, Peter, PhD Prague Sr. Lectr.
Hillier, Sheila M., MSc PhD Prof., Medical Sociology; Head*
King, Rev. Jenny, BDS Lond., PhD Lond. Sr. Lectr.

Immunology (Smithfield)

Anderson, Jane, BSc MB BS PhD, FRCP Sr. Lectr.
Morrow, W. John W., BSc Wales, PhD Plym. Sr. Lectr.
Parkin, Jackie M., MB BS PhD, FRCP Sr. Lectr.
Pinching, Anthony J., BM BCh Oxf., MA Oxf., DPhil Oxf., FRCP Louis Freedman Prof.; Head*

Immunology (Whitechapel)

Biro, P. Andrew, MA Oxf., PhD Edin. Sr. Lectr.
Bottazzo, Gian F., MD Padua, FRCP, FRCPath Prof.; Head*
Mirakian, Rita, MD Padua Sr. Lectr.
Rogers, Arpi M., MSc Beirut, PhD Sr. Lectr.

Sachs, John A., MB ChB Cape Town, PhD, FRCPath Reader
Schwarz, Gissele L., MD Sr. Lectr.
Yeatman, Nigel, BSc MB BS Sr. Lectr.

Intensive Care

Hinds, Charles J., MB BS, FRCA Sr. Lectr.; Head*
Watson, J. David, BSc MB BS, FRCA Sr. Lectr.

Medical and Dental Education

McCrorie, Peter, BSc Glas., PhD Sr. Lectr.; Dir., Curric. Devel.; Head*
McLennan, Eleanor, MSc Qld. Sr. Lectr.

Clinical Skills

Chaput de Saintonge, D. M., BSc MB BS PhD, FRCP Sr. Lectr.; Dir.*

Medical Electronics

Jones, Deric P., BSc PhD Reader, Medical Electronics and Physics; Jt. Head*
Roberts, John R., BSc Reading, PhD, FIEE Sr. Lectr.; Jt. Head*

Medical Ethics, see Human Sci. and Med. Ethics

Medical Microbiology

Hall, Lucinda M. C., BSc PhD Sr. Lectr.
Lessing, A., MB ChB Pret., MSc Pret.
Pallen, Mark J., MA MD Sr. Lectr.
Prentice, Michael B., MB ChB Birm. Sr. Lectr.
Sefton, Armine M., MSc MD, FRCPath Sr. Lectr.
Tabaqchali, Soad, MB ChB St And., FRCP, FRCPath Emer. Prof.; Head*
Wilson, Peter, MB BChir Camb., MA Camb. Sr. Lectr.
Wren, Brendan, BSc Leic., PhD Leic. Reader, Microbiology

Academic Virology Section

Breuer, Judith, MB BS Sr. Lectr.
Oxford, John, BSc PhD Prof.

Medical Oncology

Gallagher, Christopher J., MB ChB Auck., PhD Sr. Lectr.
Gupta, Rajnish K., BSc MB BS PhD Sr. Lectr.
Lister, T. Andrew, MB BChir Camb., MA Camb., MD Camb., FRCP ICRF Prof.; Head*
Oliver, R. Tim D., MA Camb., MD Camb., FRCP Sir Joseph Maxwell Prof.
Phillips, Clare F., BSc MB BS Sr. Lectr.
Rohatiner, Ama Z., MD, FRCP Reader, Molecular Oncology
Young, Brian, BSc Glas., PhD Glas. ICRF Prof., Molecular Oncology

Medical Unit/Diabetes and Metabolism
Whitechapel

Boucher, Barbara J., BSc MD, FRCP Sr. Lectr.
Cohen, Robert D., CBE, MB BChir Camb., MA Camb., MD Camb., FRCP Prof., Medicine; Head*
Gelding, Sue V., MD Sr. Lectr.
Hitman, Graham A., MD, FRCP Prof., Molecular Medicine; Asst. Dir. of Unit
Kopelman, Peter G., MD, FRCP Prof.
Wood, Diana F., MD Sr. Lectr.

Metabolism and Endocrinology Unit

Iles, Richard A., BSc Birm., PhD Prof., Biochemistry of Metabolic Disorders

Medical Unit/Endocrinology
Smithfield

Besser, G. Michael, MD Turin, DSc Turin, Hon. DSc Turin, FRCP Prof., Medicine; Head*
Camacho-Hubner, Cecilia, MD Col. Sr. Lectr.
Chew, Shern L., BSc Leeds, MB BChir Camb., MD Sr. Lectr.
Clark, Adrian J., BSc MB BS Prof., Molecular Endocrinology
Grossman, Ashley, BA BSc MD, FRCP Prof., Neuroendocrinology
Monson, John P., MD, FRCP Reader, Medicine

Perrett, David, PhD Sur., FRSChem   Prof.,
Analytical Biochemistry
Savage, Martin O., MA Camb., MD Camb.,
FRCP   Reader, Paediatric Endocrinology
Tate, Theresa A., MB BS, FRCR   Sr. Lectr.
Trainer, Peter, BSc Edin., MB ChB Edin.   Sr.
Lectr.

Morbid Anatomy and Histopathology

Baithun, Suhail I., MB ChB Baghdad,
FRCPath   Sr. Lectr.
Berry, Sir Colin, MD PhD DSc, FRCPath,
FRCP   Prof., Morbid Anatomy and
Histopathology; Head*
Brown, Chris L., MB BS, FRCPath   Sr. Lectr.
Cerio, Rino, BSc, FRCP, FRCPEd   Sr. Lectr.
Dodd, Susan M., BSc St And., MB ChB St And.,
FRCPath   Sr. Lectr.
Domizio, Paola, BSc MB BS   Sr. Lectr.
Feakins, Roger M., BA MB BCh BAO   Sr.
Lectr.
Geddes, Jennian, BA Reading, MB BS,
FRCPath   Sr. Lectr.
Greenwald, Steve E., BA Oxf., PhD   Reader,
Cardiovascular Biomechanics and
Biomaterials
Lowe, David G., MD, FRCS, FRCPath,
FIBiol   Prof., Surgical Pathology
Martin, Jo, MA Camb., MB BS   Prof.,
Neuropathology
Norton, Andrew, MB BS   Sr. Lectr.
Scheimberg, Irene, MD Madrid   Sr. Lectr.
Swash, Michael, MD, FRCP, FRCPath   Prof.,
Neurology

Nephrology

Cramp, H., MB BS   Sr. Lectr.
Marsh, Frank P., MA, FRCP   Sr. Lectr.; Head*

Neurology

Anand, Praveen, MA Oxf., PhD Camb.,
FRCP   Reader; Head*
Swash, Michael, MD, FRCP, FRCPath   Prof.

Neurosurgery

Koeze, Tom H., MD George Washington, DPhil
Oxf.   Sr. Lectr.; Head*

Nuclear Medicine

Britton, Keith E., MSc Camb., MD Camb., FRCR,
FRCP   Prof.; Head*
Granowska, Marie, MSc Warsaw, MD
Warsaw   ICRF Reader

Obstetrics and Gynaecology

Armstrong, N. Paul I., MB ChB Manc., MD   Sr.
Lectr.
Chard, Tim, MD, FRCOG   Prof.; Head*
Djahanbakhch, Ovrang, MD, FRCOG   Prof.
Grudzinskas, J. Gedis, BSc Syd., BS Syd., MD
Syd., FRACOG, FRCOG   Prof.
Gunnarsson, G., MD   Sr. Lectr.
Harrington, K., MD   Sr. Lectr.
Iles, R., MSc Brun., PhD Camb.   Sr. Lectr.
Jacob, I., MB   Sr. Lectr.
Silman, Robert, BSc MB BS PhD   Sr. Lectr.

Occupational Therapy, School of

Gannon, Kenneth, BA PhD   Sr. Lectr.
Roberts, Gwilym, MA   Sr. Lectr.
Summerfield-Mann, Lynn, MSc   Sr. Lectr.;
Dir.*

Paediatric Endocrinology

Savage, M. O., MB BChir Camb., MA Camb., MD
Camb., FRCP, FRCPCH   Prof.; Head*

Paediatric Gastroenterology

MacDonald, Tom T., PhD Glas.,
FRCPath   Prof., Mucosal Immunology;
Head*
Sanderson, I. R., MA Oxf., MSc Oxf., MD   Prof.

Paediatric Oncology

Kingston, Judith E., BSc Brist., MB BCh Brist.,
FRCP   Sr. Lectr.
Lilleyman, John S., MB BS, FRCP,
FRCPath   Mark Ridgwell Prof.; Head*
Saha, Vaskar, MD Madr.   Sr. Lectr.

Pathology, see Exper. Pathol., Morbid Anat.
and Histopathol.

Pathopharmacology

Born, Gustav V. R., MD Edin., MA Oxf., DPhil
Oxf., FRCP, FRS   Emer. Prof.; Head*
Gorog, Peter, PhD Semmelweis, DSc Semmelweiss,
FRCPath   Sr. Lectr.

Preventive Medicine, see Environmental
and Preventive Med.

Psychological Medicine

Akuffo, Emanuel, MB ChB Ghana,
FRCPsych   Sr. Lectr.
Caviston, Paul   Sr. Lectr.
Coid, Jeremy, MB ChB Sheff., MPhil,
FRCPsych   Prof., Forensic Psychiatry
Deahl, Martin, TD, BM BCh Oxf., MA Oxf.,
MPhil   Sr. Lectr.
Dinan, Ted G., MA N.Y., MD Lond., PhD Lond.,
DSc N.U.I., FRCPI, FRCPsych   Prof.; Head*
Evans, Sandra I. R., MB BS   Sr. Lectr.
Kelly, Cornelious A., MB BCh BAO   Sr. Lectr.
Lucey, Jim V., MD   Sr. Lectr.
Murphy, Siobhan, BMedSci Nott., BM BS Nott.,
DM   Sr. Lectr.
Ndegwa, David, MB ChB   Sr. Lectr.
Nias, David, BA Leic., MPhil PhD   Sr. Lectr.
Priebe, S., MD Hamburg   Prof., Community and
Social Psychiatry
Ring, Howard, MD   Sr. Lectr.
Thakore, J., PhD   Sr. Lectr.
White, Peter, BSc MD, FRCP, FRCPsych   Sr.
Lectr.

Radiation Biology

Bowlt, Colin, BSc PhD   Sr. Lectr.
Coggle, John E., BSc Leic., PhD   Reader
Lambert, Barrie E., MSc PhD   Sr. Lectr.
Trott, Klaus R., MD Munich, FRCR   Prof.;
Head*

Radiology, see Diagnostic Radiol.

Rehabilitation

Rushton, David N., MD Camb., FRCP   Prof.;
Head*

Respiratory Medicine

Davies, Robert J., MA Camb., MD Camb.,
FRCP   Prof.; Head*
Wedzicha, J. A., MA Camb., MD Camb.,
FRCP   Reader

Rheumatology

Archer, James, BSc Edin., PhD Adel.   Sr. Lectr.
D'Cruz, David, MB BS   Sr. Lectr.
Grootveld, Martin, BSc PhD   Sr. Lectr.
Kidd, Bruce L., BSc Auck., MB ChB Auck., MD
S'ton., FRACP   Reader, Rheumatology and
Musculoskeletal Medicine
Winyard, Paul E., MSc Gothenburg, PhD
Birm.   Reader, Experimental Medicine

Sports Medicine

King, John B., MB BS, FRCS   Sr. Lectr.; Head*
Wade, Andrew, BSc BVSc PhD   Sr. Lectr.

Surgery

Bustin, Stephen A., MA PhD   Sr. Lectr.
Goode, Anthony W., MD Newcastle(UK),
FRCS   Prof., Endocrine and Metabolic
Surgery
Grahl, M., BSc Wales, PhD   Sr. Lectr.
Meleagras, L., MB BS   Sr. Lectr.
Purkiss, Shaun F., MD, FRCS   Sr. Lectr.
Rogers, John, FRCS   Sr. Lectr.
Williams, Norman S., MS, FRCS   Prof.; Head*

Urology

Badenoch, David F., DM Oxf., MCh Oxf.,
FRCS   Sr. Lectr.
Fowler, Christopher G., BSc, FRCS   Sr. Lectr.

Vascular Surgery

Lumley, John S. P., MB BS MS, FRCS   Prof.

Toxicology

Dayan, Anthony D., BSc MD, FRCP, FRCPath,
FIBiol   Prof.; Head*
Paine, Alan J., BSc PhD, FIBiol   Prof.,
Biochemical Toxicology
Powell, Christopher J., BSc Wales, MSc Sur.,
PhD Sur., FRCPath   Reader, Chemical and
Pharmaceutical Safety

Urology, see under Surg.

Virology, see also under Med. Microbiol.
Aitken, Cecilia, MB BS   Sr. Lectr.
Chan, Woon Ling, PhD Malaya   Reader
Jeffries, Don J., MB BS, FRCPath   Prof.; Head*

SPECIAL CENTRES, ETC

William Harvey Research Institute

Vane, Prof. Sir John, BSc Birm., DPhil Oxf., DSc
Oxf., FRCS, FRS   Prof.; Dir.-Gen.*

CONTACT OFFICERS

Academic affairs. Secretary and Registrar:
Aldred, Keith, MA Camb., MA Lanc., PhD Lanc.
Accommodation. Residences Manager: Barber,
Ron
Admissions (first degree). Undergraduate
Admissions Officer: Gosling, June
Admissions (higher degree). Graduate
Admissions Officer: Harris, Arnold, BSc
City(UK)
Adult/continuing education. Head of
Continuing Education: Brennan, Michael,
BSc Wales, MA Warw.
Alumni. Head of Alumni Relations: Boswell,
Sue, BA
Archives. Assistant Librarian: Nye, Anselm
Careers. Senior Careers Adviser: Hughes,
Roger D., BA Well., DPhil Oxf.
Computing services. Director of Academic
Information Services: Murphy, Brian, BA
Consultancy services. Dean for Research:
Williams, Prof. Iwan P., BSc Wales, PhD
Lond., FRAS
Estates and buildings/works and services.
Buildings Officer: Wilson, Paul, MA Camb.
Examinations. Records and Examinations
Officer: McLennan, Diane E., MA Aberd.
Finance. Director of Finance: ......
General enquiries. Secretary and Registrar:
Aldred, Keith, MA Camb., MA Lanc., PhD Lanc.
Health services. Senior Nursing Officer:
Murray, Jenny
Industrial liaison. Secretary and Registrar:
Aldred, Keith, MA Camb., MA Lanc., PhD Lanc.
International office. International Officer:
Halley, Robin, BA Sund.
Library (chief librarian). Director of
Academic Information Services: Murphy,
Brian, BA
Personnel/human resources. Senior Personnel
Officer: Barnes, Claire, MA
Public relations, information and marketing.
Head of Press and Publications: Ray, Delia
E., BA Warw.
Publications. Publications Officer: Cooper,
Mari
Purchasing. Purchasing Officer: Brett, John D.,
MA Camb.
Quality assurance and accreditation. Senior
Assistant Registrar: Wagstaffe, Mary
Research. Dean for Research: Williams, Prof.
Iwan P., BSc Wales, PhD Lond., FRAS
Safety. Health and Safety Adviser: Robinson,
John P., BAgrSc Melb., PhD Calif.
Scholarships, awards, loans. Academic
Registrar: Holiday, Peter G., BA Leeds, PhD
Leeds
Security. Security Officer: Anacoura, Lovett
Sport and recreation. Sports Officer: Lane,
Michael, BSc
Staff development and training. Staff
Development and Training Officer:
Ketteridge, Steven W., BSc PhD
Student welfare/counselling. Welfare Officer:
Holloway, Louise A. E., BA Brist., MA

Students from other countries. International Officer: Halley, Robin, BA *Sund.*
Students with disabilities. Welfare Officer: Holloway, Louise A. E., BA *Brist.*, MA

CAMPUS/COLLEGE HEADS

St Bartholomew's and the Royal London School of Medicine and Dentistry. Warden: McNeish, Prof. Alexander S., MB ChB *Glas.*, MSc *Birm.*, FRCP, FRCPGlas

[Information supplied by the institution as at March 1998, and edited by the ACU]

ROYAL HOLLOWAY, UNIVERSITY OF LONDON

Founded 1985 by merger of Bedford College (1849) and Royal Holloway College (1886) (Royal Holloway and Bedford New College)

Postal Address: Egham, Surrey, England TW20 0EX
Telephone: (01784) 434455 **Fax**: (01784) 437520 **Cables**: Royal Holloway, University of London, Egham
Telex: (Library) 935504 **WWW**: http://www.rhbnc.ac.uk **E-mail formula**: Initial.surname@rhbnc.ac.uk

PATRON—Elizabeth, H.M. the Queen Mother
VISITOR—Warnock of Weeke, Baroness
CHAIRMAN OF COUNCIL—Andrew, Sir Robert, KCB
PRINCIPAL*—Gowar, Prof. Norman W., BSc *City(UK)*, MPhil *City(UK)*, FIMA
VICE-PRINCIPAL—Miller, Roy F., BSc *Lond.*, PhD *Lond.*, FIP
VICE-PRINCIPAL—Lethbridge, Robert, BA *Kent*, MA *McM.*, MA *Camb.*, PhD *Camb.*
VICE-PRINCIPAL—Robinson, Prof. Francis, MA *Camb.*, PhD *Camb.*, FRHistS
VICE-PRINCIPAL—Turner, Prof. John, MA *Oxf.*, DPhil *Oxf.*, FRHistS
SECRETARY TO COUNCIL‡—Miller, Michael A., BA *Lond.*
ACADEMIC REGISTRAR—Price, Alison
BURSAR—Allen, Clive M., BSc *Durh.*
DIRECTOR OF FINANCE—Ross, J. Jane, BSc *S'ton.*
DIRECTOR OF INFORMATION SERVICES—Sweeney, David G., BSc *Aberd.*

GENERAL INFORMATION

History. The college was established in 1985 by the merger of Royal Holloway College (1886) and Bedford College (1849). It is located in Egham, Surrey.

Admission to first degree courses (see also United Kingdom Introduction). Through Universities and Colleges Admissions Service (UCAS). Minimum requirements: passes in 2 subjects at General Certificate of Education (GCE) A level or 1 A level and 2 AS levels or equivalent. Equivalent international qualifications are also accepted.

First Degrees (of University of London) (see also University of London Directory to Subjects of Study). BA, BMus, BSc, MSci.
All courses are full-time and normally last 3 years. MSci: 4 years.

Higher Degrees (of University of London) (see also University of London Directory to Subjects of Study). MA, MBA, MMus, MSc, MPhil, PhD.

Fees. Undergraduate UK students: £750 (arts and social sciences), £1600 (science, drama and media, music). Postgraduate UK students: full-time £2500–3300; MBA international management £6600. International students: £6700–9300 (reduced for part-time or higher degrees).

Academic Awards (1996). 86 awards.

Academic Year (1999–2000). Three terms: 27 September–17 December; 10 January–24 March; 1 May–16 June.

Income (1996–97). Total, £48,638,000.

Statistics. Staff: academic, research and related 471; technical 82; administrative 89; clerical 206; manual and ancillary 133; student union 32; total 1013.

FACULTIES/SCHOOLS

Arts and Music
Tel: (01784) 443308
Dean: Stockwell, Prof. Anthony J., MA *Camb.*, PhD *Lond.*, FRHistS

Graduate School
Tel: (01784) 443806
Dean: Wathey, Andrew, MA *Oxf.*, DPhil *Oxf.*, FSA, FRHistS

Research and Enterprise
Tel: (01784) 443811
Dean: Blundell, Prof. Derek J., BSc *Birm.*, PhD *Lond.*

Science
Dean: Lowe, Prof. John J., MA *St.And.*, PhD *Edin.*

Students
Tel: (01784) 443395
Dean: Hancock, Richard A., BSc *Lond.*, PhD *Lond.*, FRSChem

ACADEMIC UNITS

Biological Sciences, School of
Tel: (01784) 443559 Fax: (01784) 434326
Andrews, Elizabeth B., BSc *Reading*, PhD *Reading* Sr. Lectr.
Angus, Robert B., MA *Oxf.*, DPhil *Oxf.* Sr. Lectr.
Beesley, Philip W., BSc *S'ton.*, PhD *S'ton.* Sr. Lectr.
Bolwell, G. Paul, BA *Oxf.*, DPhil *Oxf.* Reader

Bowyer, John R., MA *Camb.*, PhD *Brist.* Prof.; Head*
Bramley, Peter M., BSc *Wales*, PhD *Wales* Prof.; Head, Biochem. Div.
Brown, Valerie, PhD Hon. Prof.
Catchpole, Clive K., BSc *Nott.*, PhD *Nott.* Prof.
Credland, Peter F., BSc *Nott.*, PhD *Nott.* Sr. Lectr.; Head, Biol. Div.
Dey, Prakash M., MSc *Ban.*, PhD *Ban.*, PhD *Lond.* Reader
Dixon, J. George, BSc *Glas.*, PhD Prof.
Dodge, John D., PhD DSc Prof.†, Botany
Hawksworth, David Hon. Prof.
Hussey, Patrick J., BSc *Liv.*, PhD *Kent* Sr. Lectr.
Lewis, John W., BSc *Wales*, PhD *Wales* Prof.
Morris, Patrick A., BSc PhD Sr. Lectr.
Rider, Christopher C., BSc *Sheff.*, PhD *Sheff.* Sr. Lectr.
Schuch, Wolfgang, MSc *Edin.*, PhD *Edin.* Hon. Prof.
Thorndyke, Michael C., BSc PhD Prof.
Zagalsky, Peter F., MA *Camb.*, PhD *Lond.* Sr. Lectr.

Chemical Sciences, Centre for
Tel: (01784) 443415 Fax: (01784) 443386
Cooke, Michael, BSc *Brist.*, PhD *Brist.*, FRSChem Dir.*
Gardner, Peter J., BSc *Lond.*, PhD *Lond.* Sr. Lectr.
Gates, Peter N., BSc *Lond.*, PhD *Lond.* Sr. Lectr.
Hancock, Richard A., BSc *Lond.*, PhD *Lond.*, FRSChem Sr. Lectr.

Classics
Tel: (01784) 443417 Fax: (01784) 439855
Braund, Susanna, BA *Camb.*, PhD *Camb.* Prof.
Carey, Christopher, MA *Camb.*, PhD *Camb.* Prof.
Hall, J. Barrie, MA *Camb.*, PhD *Camb.* Hildred Carlile Res. Prof.†, Latin

Howell, Peter A., MA Oxf., MPhil Oxf. Sr. Lectr.

Papadakis, A., PhD Hon. Prof.

Sheppard, Anne D. R., MA Glas., DPhil Oxf. Sr. Lectr.; Head*

Computer Science

Tel: (01784) 443421 Fax: (01784) 439786

Cohen, D. A., BA Oxf., DPhil Oxf. Sr. Lectr.

Davies, Alan R., MSc Sr. Lectr.

Gammerman, Alex, BSc St.Petersburg, PhD St.Petersburg Prof.; Head*

Johnstone, A. I. C., BSc Lond., PhD Lond. Sr. Lectr.

Mitchell, Christopher J., BSc PhD Prof.

Shawe-Taylor, John S., PhD Reader

Vapnik, V. N., BSc Moscow, DSc Moscow Prof.

Drama, Theatre and Media Arts

Tel: (01784) 443943 Fax: (01784) 431018

Bradby, David H., MA Oxf., PhD Glas. Prof.

Bratton, Jacqueline S., MA Oxf., DPhil Oxf. Prof.; Head*

Cave, Richard A., MA Camb., PhD Camb. Prof.

Dench, Dame Judi, DBE Hon. Prof.

Dymkowski, Christine, MA Oxf., AB Bryn Mawr, PhD Virginia Sr. Lectr.

Forgacs, David, BA Oxf., MA Oxf., DPhil Pisa Reader

Lorac, Carol, MPhil Open(UK) Sr. Lectr.

Wiles, David, BA Camb., PhD Brist. Reader

Economics

Tel: (01784) 443383 Fax: (01784) 439534

Frank, Jeff, BA Reed, PhD Yale Prof.; Head*

Heyes, Anthony, MA Camb., PhD McG. Sr. Lectr.

Knoblauch, Vicki, BA Wis., PhD Wis. Sr. Lectr.

Mariotti, Marco, PhD Camb. Sr. Lectr.

Spagat, Michael, BA Northwestern, PhD Harv. Sr. Lectr.

Wadsworth, Jonathan, BSc Hull, PhD Lond. Sr. Lectr.

English

Tel: (01784) 443214 Fax: (01784) 439196

Caracciolo, Peter L., BA Sr. Lectr.

Creaser, John, MA Oxf. Hildred Carlile Prof.†

Davenport, W. Anthony, MA Prof.†

Davies, Eirian C., BA PhD Sr. Lectr.

Dodsworth, J. Martin, MA Oxf. Prof.

Dzelzainis, Martin, MA Camb., PhD Camb. Sr. Lectr.

Field, Rosalind, MA Camb., DPhil York(UK) Sr. Lectr.

Gibson, Andrew W., MA Oxf., BPhil Oxf. Reader

Gould, Warwick L., BA Qld. Prof.

Hampson, Robert G., MA Tor., BA Reader

Ryan, Kiernan, MA Camb., PhD Amst. Prof.; Head*

French

Tel: (01784) 443254 Fax: (01784) 470180

Bloch, Jean H., MA Sr. Lectr.

Cockerham, Harry, MA Manc. Sr. Lectr.

Harvey, Ruth, BA Lond., PhD Lond. Sr. Lectr.

Hughes, Edward J., BA Belf., PhD Belf. Sr. Lectr.

L'Huiller, Monique, MèsL Paris, MSc CNAA Sr. Lectr.

Lethbridge, Robert D., BA Kent, PhD Camb. Prof.

O'Brien, John P., BA Camb., MA Camb., DPhil Oxf. Reader

Routledge, Michael J., BA Birm., PhD Birm. Sr. Lectr.

Sheringham, Michael, BA Kent, PhD Kent Prof.; Head*

Geography

Tel: (01784) 443563 Fax: (01784) 472836

Coope, Russell Hon. Prof.

Cosgrove, Denis E., BA Oxf., MA Tor., DPhil Oxf. Prof.

Derbyshire, Edward, BA Keele, MSc McG., PhD Monash Hon. Prof.

Driver, Felix, MA Camb., PhD Camb. Reader

Green, Christopher P., BA Oxf., DPhil Oxf. Sr. Lectr.

Imrie, Rob F., BA Sus., MPhil Reading, PhD Wales Reader

Kemp, Rob A., BSc Reading, PhD Lond., MSc Reader

Lowe, J. John, MA St And., PhD Edin. Prof.

Maltby, Edward, BSc Sheff., PhD Brist. Prof.

McGregor, Duncan F. M., BSc Edin., PhD Edin. Sr. Lectr.

Potter, Robert B., BSc PhD Prof.; Head*

Rose, James, BA Leic. Prof.

Simon, David, BA Reading, BA Cape Town, DPhil Oxf. Reader

Stringer, Chris, BSc Lond., PhD Brist. Hon. Prof.

Unwin, P. Timothy H., MA Camb., PhD Durh. Reader

Worsley, Peter, BA Keele, PhD Manc. Hon. Prof.

Geology

Tel: (01784) 443581 Fax: (01784) 471780

Blundell, Derek J., BSc Birm., PhD Lond., FGS Prof., Environmental Geology

Bosence, Daniel W. J., BSc Reading, PhD Reading Prof.

Collinson, Margaret, BSc Wales, PhD Lond. Reader

Coney, Peter Hon. Prof.

Cox, C. Barry, MA Oxf., PhD Camb., DSc Lond. Hon. Prof.

Davison, Ian, BSc Leeds, PhD Leeds Sr. Lectr.

Foster, Stephen Hon. Prof.

Gibbs, Andrew, MSc Lond.., PhD Exe. Hon. Prof.

Gill, Robin C. O., BSc Manc., PhD Durh. Sr. Lectr.

Hall, Robert, BSc Lond., PhD Lond. Prof.

Joseph, Jeremy, BSc Durh. Hon. Prof.

Knill, Sir John, BSc Lond., PhD Lond., DSc Lond. Hon. Prof.

Mather, John D., PhD Liv., DSc Liv. Lyell Prof.

Mattey, David P., BA Camb., PhD Reader

McClay, Kenneth R., BSc Adel., MSc PhD Prof.

Menzies, Martin A., BSc Aberd., PhD Camb. Prof.; Head*

Muir, Richard O., MA Edin., PhD Edin. Sr. Lectr.

Nichols, Gary J., BSc Camb., PhD Camb. Sr. Lectr.

Nisbet, Euan G., MSc Camb., PhD Camb. Foundation Prof.

Roberts, David, BSc Manc. Hon. Prof.

Rose, Edward P. F., TD, MA Oxf., DPhil Oxf. Sr. Lectr.

Scott, Andrew C., BSc PhD, FGS Prof.

Thirlwall, Mathew F., MA Oxf., PhD Edin. Sr. Lectr.

Walsh, J. Nicholas, BSc PhD Sr. Lectr.

Waltham, David, BSc Leic., PhD Lond. Sr. Lectr.

German

Tel: (01784) 443201 Fax: (01784) 439196

Davies, Máire, BA Lond. Head*

Gibbs, Marion E., MA PhD Reader

Jones, William J., MA Oxf., DPhil Oxf. Prof.

Longerich, Peter, MA Munich, DPhil Munich Reader

History

Tel: (01784) 443314 Fax: (01784) 433032

Ansari, Humayan K., MA Lond., MPhil Lond. Sr. Lectr.

Barron, Caroline M., MA Oxf., PhD, FSA, FRHistS Reader

Blake, Hugo McK., MA Camb., PhD Lanc. Reader

Brown, Alison M., MA, FRHistS Reader

Brown, Peter, MA Oxf. Hon. Prof.

Claeys, Gregory R., MA PhD Prof.

Corfield, Penelope J., MA Oxf., PhD, FRHistS Prof.

Crimmin, Patricia K., BA Wales, MPhil, FRHistS Sr. Lectr.

Croft, J. Pauline, MA Oxf., DPhil Oxf., FSA, FRHistS Sr. Lectr.

Crook, J. Mordaunt, MA Oxf., DPhil Oxf., FSA, FBA Prof.†, Architecture History

Dewey, Peter E., BA Exe., PhD Reading, FRHistS Sr. Lectr.

Hamilton, Nigel, BA Camb. Hon. Prof.

Pilbeam, Pamela M., BA PhD Prof.

Robinson, Francis C. R., MA Camb., PhD Camb., FRHistS Prof.

Roper, Lyndal A., BA Melb., PhD Reader

Saul, Nigel E., MA Oxf., DPhil Oxf. Prof.

Stockwell, Anthony J., MA Camb., PhD Lond., FRHistS Prof.; Head*

Thompson, Francis, MA Oxf., DPhil Oxf. Hon. Prof.

Turner, John A., MA Oxf., DPhil Oxf. Prof.

Italian

Tel: (01784) 443238 Fax: (01784) 439196

Armour, Peter J., BA Manc., PhL Greg., PhD Leic. Prof.

Oundle, Stephen, BA Liv., MA N.Y.State, PhD Camb. Sr. Lectr.

Tosi, Arturo F., DottLitt Padua, PhD Prof.; Head*

Management, School of

Tel: (01784) 443780 Fax: (01784) 439854

Baillie, T. W. T., MSc Belf., PhD Belf. Visiting Prof.

Broadbent, Jane, BA York, MA Sheff., PhD Sheff. Prof.

Cox, George Hon. Prof.

Fitzgerald, Robert, BA PhD Sr. Lectr.

Harvey, Charles E., PhD Brist. Prof.; Head*

Haslam, Colin, BSc Wales, PhD Wales Reader

King, J. R., BSc(Eng) Visiting Prof.

King, John, BSc Durh. Hon. Prof.

McLean, K. Mairi, MA St And., MBA Bath, PhD St And. Sr. Lectr.

Reed, Alec Hon. Prof.

Sillince, John, BA Manc., MSc Birm., PhD Lond. Sr. Lectr.

Smith, Chris, PhD Brist., BA Prof.

Triggs, Jon, BA Bath, MSc Bath Sr. Lectr.

Mathematics

Tel: (01784) 443093 Fax: (01784) 430766

Beker, Henry, BA Open(UK), BSc Lond., PhD Lond. Hon. Prof.

Bowen, Kenneth C., BA Oxf., PhD Lond. Visiting Prof.

Burmester, Michael V. D., BSc Athens, PhD Rome Reader

Cohn, John H. E., MA Oxf., DPhil Oxf. Reader

De Barra, Gearoid, MSc N.U.I., PhD Sr. Lectr.

Essam, John W., BSc PhD Prof.

Godolphin, Edward J., MSc Wales Reader

Hebborn, John E., BSc PhD, FIMA Sr. Lectr.

Knowles, J. David, BA Camb., PhD Camb. Sr. Lectr.

Mannion, David, MA Oxf., PhD Camb. Reader

O'Mahony, Patrick F., BSc N.U.I., MS Chic., PhD Chic. Reader

Piper, Fred C., BSc PhD, FIMA Prof.; Head*

Scourfield, Eira J., MSc Exe., PhD Glas., BSc Sr. Lectr.

Wild, Peter R., BSc Adel., PhD Prof.

Wilson, Brian J., MSc PhD Sr. Lectr.

Media Arts, see Drama, Theatre and Media Arts

Music

Tel: (01784) 443532 Fax: (01784) 439441

Carter, Timothy A., BA Durh., PhD Birm. Prof.; Head*

Charlton, David, BA Nott., DPhil Camb. Reader

Chew, Geoffrey A., MusB Camb., PhD Manc., BMus, FRCO Sr. Lectr.

Ehrlich, Cyril, BSc Lond., PhD Lond. Hon. Prof.

Levi, Erik W., BA Camb., BPhil York(UK) Sr. Lectr.

McGuinness, Rosamond, BA Vassar, MA Smith, MA Oxf., DPhil Oxf. Emer. Prof.

Pike, Lionel J., BMus Oxf., MA Oxf., DPhil Oxf., FRCO Sr. Lectr.

Rink, John, MMus Lond., PhD Camb. Sr. Lectr.

Wathey, Andrew, MA Oxf., DPhil Oxf. Reader

Physics

Tel: (01784) 443448 Fax: (01784) 472794

Cowan, Brian P., BSc Sus., DPhil Sus.　Reader
Davies, E. Roy, MA Oxf., DPhil Oxf., DSc
　Lond.　Prof.
Flockton, Stuart, BSc Liv., PhD Liv.　Sr. Lectr.
Gledhill, Gary A., BSc PhD　Sr. Lectr.
Green, Michael G., BSc Nott., PhD　Prof.
Jonsher, Andrzej, BSc(Eng) Lond., PhD
　Lond.　Emer. Prof.
Lea, Michael J., BA Oxf., PhD Lanc.　Prof.
Love, Alexander, BSc Glas., PhD Glas.　Reader
Mikheer, Vladimir, PhD　Hon. Prof.
Miller, Roy F., BSc Lond., PhD Lond.　Sr. Lectr.
Moore, A. Moreton, MA Camb., MSc Brist., PhD
　Brist.　Reader
Petrashov, Victor, MSc Moscow, PhD
　U.S.S.R.Acad.Sc.　Prof.
Rice-Evans, Peter, BSc Exe., MBA Col., PhD
　DSc　Prof., Experimental Physics
Saunders, John, BA Oxf., DPhil Sus.　Prof.
Stewart, Noel M., BSc Belf., PhD　Sr. Lectr.;
　Head*
Strong, John A., BSc PhD　Prof.
Vacant Posts: Hildred Carlile Prof.

Psychology

Tel: (01784) 443526 Fax: (01784) 434347

Anderson, Stephen, BOptom NSW, BSc W.Aust.,
　PhD W.Aust.　Reader
Andrews, Bernice, PhD Lond.
Bradley, Claire, BSc Nott., PhD Nott.　Reader
Brewin, Christopher R., BA Oxf., MSc Oxf., PhD
　Sheff.　Prof.
Christie, Margaret, BA PhD　Emer. Prof.
Eysenck, Michael W., BA PhD　Prof.; Head*
Funnell, Elaine, BSc Reading, PhD Reading　Prof.
Harris, Margaret, BSc PhD　Reader
Loewenthal, Catherine M., BSc PhD　Sr. Lectr.
Smith, Andrew T., BSc Durh., MSc Qld., PhD
　Keele　Prof.
Valentine, Elizabeth R., BA PhD　Reader
Waller, Glenn, BA Reading, MClinPsychol Liv.,
　PhD Lond.　Reader
Wilding, John, MA Oxf., PhD Lond.　Reader

Social Policy and Social Science

Tel: (01784) 443149 Fax: (01784) 434375

Brown, George W., OBE, BA PhD　Hon. Prof.,
　Sociology
Bury, Michael R., BA Sus., MSc Brist.　Prof.;
　Head*
Drewry, Gavin R., BSc(SocialSciences)
　S'ton.　Prof.
Edwards, John R., BSc Bath　Prof.
Elston, Mary A. C., BSc Brist., MA Essex,
　PhD　Sr. Lectr.
Gordon, Alan G., BA Exe., PhD Brist.　Sr. Lectr.
Lee, Raymond, BEd Leeds, PhD Edin.　Reader
Macnicol, John S., MA Edin., PhD Edin.　Reader
Saward, Michael, BA ANU, PhD Essex　Sr. Lectr.
Sheldon, M. Brian, MPhil Birm.　Prof.; Dir.,
　Appl. Soc. Study Courses
Tunstill, Jane, BA Hull, MA Brun.　Prof.

Theatre, see Drama, Theatre and Media Arts

SPECIAL CENTRES, ETC

Environmental Research, Royal Holloway Institute for

Tel: (01784) 477404 Fax: (01784) 477427

Gardner, Peter, PhD Lond.　Sr. Lectr.
Maltby, Edward, BSc Sheff., PhD Brist.　Prof.;
　Dir.*
Other Staff: 1 Emer. Reader

Ethnic Minority Studies, Centre for

Tel: (01784) 443815 Fax: (01784) 437520

Ansari, K. Humayun, BSc Exe., PhD Lond.　Sr.
　Lectr.; Dir.*

Victorian Art and Architecture, Centre for

Tel: (01784) 443663 Fax: (01784) 437520

Crook, J. Mordaunt, MA Oxf., DPhil Oxf., FSA,
　FBA　Prof.; Dir.*

CONTACT OFFICERS

Academic Affairs. Academic Registrar: Price,
　Alison
Accommodation. Accommodation Officer:
　Johnson, Trevor
Admissions (first degree). Admissions Officer:
　Cox, Fiona, BA Lond.†
Admissions (first degree). Admissions Officer:
　Wilkinson, Alison, BA Lond.†
Admissions (higher degree). Postgraduate
　Officer: Smith, Penelope J., BSc Bath, PhD
　Lond.†
Adult/continuing education. Educational and
　International Liaison Officer: Walls, Robert
　J., BA Belf.
Alumni. Alumni Relations and Events Officer:
　Baker, Marta
Archives. Archivist: Badham, Sophie H., BA
　Birm., MA Lond.
Careers. Head of Careers Service: Langley,
　Dinah, MA Oxf.
Computing services. Director of Information
　Services: Sweeney, David G., BSc Aberd.
Conferences/corporate hospitality. Residence
　and Catering Services Manager: Bland,
　Steven
Consultancy services. Head of Research and
　Enterprise Services: Thirunamachandran,
　Rama, MA Camb.
Credit transfer. Admissions Officer: Cox,
　Fiona, BA Lond.†
Credit transfer. Admissions Officer:
　Wilkinson, Alison, BA Lond.†
Equal opportunities. Head of Personnel:
　Hughes, Lynne, BA
Estates and buildings/works and services.
　Estates Manager: Taylor, Frank P., BSc S.Bank,
　FRICS

Examinations. Administrative Officer: Davie,
　Kate, BA Oxf., MA Oxf.
Finance. Director of Finance: Ross, J. Jane, BSc
　S'ton.
General enquiries. Press and Public Relations
　Manager: Uttley, Anne C., BA Lond.
Health services. Sister in Charge: Jackson, Jean
Industrial liaison. Head of Research and
　Enterprise Services: Thirunamachandran,
　Rama, MA Camb.
International office. Educational and
　International Liaison Officer: Walls, Robert
　J., BA Belf.
Language training for international students.
　Director of Language Centre: Simon, Sheryl
Library (enquiries). Director of Information
　Services: Sweeney, David G., BSc Aberd.
Minorities/disadvantaged groups. Training
　and Consultancy Manager, Centre for Ethnic
　Minority Studies: Jackson, June, BA Portsmouth
Personnel/human resources. Head of
　Personnel: Hughes, Lynne, BA
Public relations, information and marketing.
　Press and Public Relations Manager: Uttley,
　Anne C., BA Lond.
Publications. Roddy, Sarah, BA Camb.
Purchasing. Bursar: Allen, Clive M., BSc Durh.
Quality assurance and accreditation. Deputy
　Registrar: Boylan, Maureen F., MA Birm.
Research. Head of Research and Enterprise
　Services: Thirunamachandran, Rama, MA
　Camb.
Safety. Safety Officer: Timson, Ben J.
Scholarships, awards, loans (LEA awards).
　Administrative Officer: Smalls, Julie E.,
　BCom Nott.
Scholarships, awards, loans (loans). Student
　Loans Officer: Lavender, Diane
Scholarships, awards, loans (scholarships).
　Administrative Officer: Hammond, Elizabeth
　H. R., BSc Durh.
Schools liaison. Educational and International
　Liaison Officer: Walls, Robert J., BA Belf.
Security. Bathews, Tony
Sport and recreation. Sports Officer: Ross,
　Stuart M., BA Reading
Staff development and training. Staff
　Development Officer: Hunt, David
Student union. General Secretary: Lloyd
　Davies, Mark
Student welfare/counselling. Dean of
　Students/Dean: Hancock, Richard A., BSc
　Lond., PhD Lond., FRSChem
Students from other countries. Administrative
　Officer: Macbeth, Moira, BA Reading
Students with disabilities. Dean of Students/
　Dean: Hancock, Richard A., BSc Lond., PhD
　Lond., FRSChem

[Information supplied by the institution as at 12 March
1998, and edited by the ACU]

ROYAL VETERINARY COLLEGE

Founded 1791

Postal Address: Royal College Street, Camden Town, London, England NW1 0TU
Telephone: (0171) 468 5000 **Fax**: (0171) 388 2342 **E-mail formula**: Initialsurname@rvc.ac.uk

PATRON—Edinburgh, H.R.H. The Duke of, KG, KT, OM, GBE, Hon. LLD *Edin.*, Hon. LLD *Malta*, Hon. LLD *Wales*, Hon. DSc *Delhi*, Hon. DSc *Salf.*, Hon. Dr *RCA*, FRS
CHAIRMAN OF THE COUNCIL—Prior, The Rt. Hon. Lord
PRINCIPAL AND DEAN*—Lanyon, Prof. L. E., BVSc *Brist.*, PhD *Brist.*, DSc *Brist.*
DEPUTY-PRINCIPAL—Lees, Prof. P., CBE, BPharm *Lond.*, PhD *Lond.*, Hon. Dr *Ghent*
VICE-PRINCIPAL (TEACHING)—Lees, Prof. P., CBE, BPharm *Lond.*, PhD *Lond.*, Hon. Dr *Ghent*
VICE-PRINCIPAL (RESEARCH)—Howard, Prof. C. R., BSc *Durh.*, MSc *Birm.*, PhD, FRCPath, FIBiol
SECRETARY‡—Smith, A. N., MA *Oxf.*, BPhil *Newcastle(UK)*

GENERAL INFORMATION

History. The college was founded in 1791 and became a college of the University of London in 1949. It is located on two campuses, in central London and in Hertfordshire.

Admission to first degree courses (see also United Kingdom Introduction). Through Universities and Colleges Admissions Service (UCAS). Good General Certificate of Education (GCE) A level passes in 3 subjects including biology and chemistry, or equivalent qualifications.

First Degrees (of University of London) (see also University of London Directory to Subjects of Study). BSc, BVetMed.
BSc (in veterinary nursing): 4 years; BVetMed: 5 years.

Higher Degrees (of University of London) (see also University of London Directory to Subjects of Study). MSc, MVetMed, MPhil, PhD, DVetMed.
Applicants for admission to higher degrees should possess a good first degree in a relevant subject.
MSc, MVetMed: 1 year; MPhil, PhD, DVetMed: 3 years.

Libraries. 13,000 volumes; 400 periodicals subscribed to. Special collection: historical (veterinary medicine and surgery).

Fees. Undergraduate: £1000 (home students); £11,515 (international students). Postgraduate (home students): £3000–4950 (MSc); £8240 (MVetMed); £2610 (MPhil, PhD). Postgraduate (international students): £11,500–13,980 (MSc); £14,708 (MVetMed); £7825 (MPhil, PhD, pre-clinical); £14,400 (MPhil, PhD, clinical).

Academic Year (1998–99). Three terms: 28 September–11 December; 4 January–5 March; 19 April–25 June.

Income (1997–98). Total, £18,000,000.

Statistics. Staff: 390 (130 academic, 260 technical and support). Students: full-time 631 (218 men, 413 women); part-time 23 (13 men, 10 women); international 118 (47 men, 71 women).

ACADEMIC UNITS

Farm Animal and Equine Medicine and Surgery

Tel: (01707) 666333 Fax: (01707) 660671, 647085

Clarke, Kathleen W., MA *Camb.*, VetMB *Camb.*, DVetMed *Lond.* Sr. Lectr.
England, G. C. W., BVetMed *Lond.*, PhD *Lond.*, FRCVS Sr. Lectr.
Gilbert, R. J., BPharm *Lond.*, MPharm *Lond.*, PhD *Lond.*, FRPharmS, FRCPath, FIBiol Visiting Prof.
Goodship, A. E., BVSc *Brist.*, PhD *Brist.* Prof., Orthopaedic Sciences
Johnston, A. M., BVMS *Edin.*, DVetMed *Lond.*, FRCVS Sr. Lectr.
Madel, A. J., BA *Camb.*, VetMB *Camb.* Sr. Lectr.
May, S. A., VetMB *Camb.*, MA *Camb*, PhD Prof., Equine Medicine and Surgery; Head*
Mead, G. C., BSc *Lond.*, PhD *Lond.* Vestey Prof., Food Safety and Veterinary Public Health
Newell, D. G., PhD Visiting Prof.
Noakes, D. E., BVetMed *Lond.*, PhD *Lond.*, FRCVS Prof., Veterinary Obstetrics and Diseases of Reproduction
Schulster, Dennis, MA *Camb.*, PhD *Lond.*, DSc Visiting Prof., Endocrinology
Varma, M. G. R., DSc *Lond.*, FIBiol Visiting Prof., Entomology
Other Staff: 9 Lectrs.; 1 Hon. Sr. Lectr.; 3 Hon. Lectrs.
Vacant Posts: 1 Prof.; 2 Sr. Lectrs.

Pathology and Infectious Diseases

Immunology

Hamblin, Anne S., BSc *E.Anglia*, PhD *Lond.* Reader

Laboratory Animal Science

Stewart, J. D., BVMS *Glas.*, MSc *Lond.* Head, NVS Services*

Microbiology

Biggs, P. M., CBE, PhD *Brist.*, Hon. DVM *Munich*, DSc, FRCPath, FIBiol, FRCVS, FRS Visiting Prof.
Bridger, Janice C., BSc *Brist.*, PhD *Reading* Sr. Lectr.
Edington, N., BVSc *Liv.*, PhD *Liv.*, FRCVS, FRCPath Prof., Veterinary Virology
Howard, C. R., BSc *Durh.*, MSc *Birm.*, DSc *Birm.*, PhD, FRCPath, FIBiol Prof., Microbiology and Parasitology
Russell, P. H., BVSc *Brist.*, MSc *Stir.*, PhD *Glas.* Reader
Rycroft, A. N., BSc *Leeds*, PhD *Leeds* Sr. Lectr.
Other Staff: 1 Temp. Lectr.

Parasitology

Fox, M. T., BVetMed *Lond.*, PhD *Lond.* Sr. Lectr.
Jacobs, D. E., BVMS *Glas.*, PhD *Glas.*, FRCVS, FRCPath Prof., Veterinary Parasitology
Kirkwood, J., BVSc *Birst.*, PhD Visiting Prof.
Other Staff: 1 Hon. Lectr.

Pathology

Tel: (01707) 666333 Fax: (01707) 652090

Archer, F. J., VMD *Penn.*, PhD *Lond.* Sr. Lectr.
Baskerville, A., BVSc *Liv.*, PhD, FRCVS Visiting Prof.
Brownlie, J., BVSc *Brist.*, PhD *Reading* Prof., Veterinary Pathology; Head*
Other Staff: 2 Lectrs.; 2 Temp. Lectrs.
Vacant Posts: 2 Sr. Lectrs.

Small Animal Medicine and Surgery

Tel: (01707) 666333 Fax: (01707) 652090

Batt, R. M., BVSc *Brist.*, MSc *Lond.*, PhD *Lond.* Prof., Veterinary Medicine
Bedford, P. G. C., BVetMed *Lond.*, PhD *Lond.*, FRCVS Guide Dog Prof., Canine Medicine and Surgery; Head*
Lloyd, D. H., BVetMed *Lond.*, PhD *Lond.*, FRCVS Reader
Wheeler, S. J., BVSc *Brist.*, PhD *Lond.* Sr. Lectr.
Other Staff: 10 Lectrs.; 3 Sr. Res. Fellows
Vacant Posts: 1 Lectr.

Veterinary Basic Sciences

2 Sr. Res. Fellows

Anatomy

Dhoot, G. J., BSc *Birm.*, PhD *Birm.*, DSc *Birm.* Sr. Lectr.
Dyce, K. M., BSc *Edin.*, DVM&S *Edin.* Visiting Prof.
Goodship, A. E., BVSc *Brist.*, PhD *Brist.* Prof., Orthopaedic Sciences
Loughna, P. T., BSc *Liv.*, PhD *Hull* Sr. Lectr.
Stickland, N. C., BSc *Lond.*, PhD *Hull* Prof., Veterinary Anatomy; Head*
Other Staff: 2 Lectrs.; 1 Temp. Lectr.

Biochemistry

Bayliss, M. T., BSc *Brist.*, PhD *Lond.* Prof., Connective Tissue Biochemistry
Botham, Kathleen M., BSc *Liv.*, PhD *Liv.* Sr. Lectr.
Other Staff: 1 Lectr.

Molecular and Cellular Biology

Chantler, P. D., BSc *Lond.*, PhD *Lond.* Prof.

Pharmacology

Cunningham, Fiona M., BSc *Lond.*, PhD *Lond.* Sr. Lectr.
Elliott, J., MA *Camb.*, VetMB *Camb.*, PhD *Camb.* Sr. Lectr.
Lees, P., CBE, BPharm *Lond.*, PhD *Lond.*, Hon. Dr *Ghent*, FIBiol Prof.
Other Staff: 1 Lectr.

Physiology

Lodge, D., BVSc *Brist.*, PhD *Brist.* Visiting Prof.
Michell, R., BSc *Lond.*, BVetMed *Lond.*, PhD *Lond.* Visiting Prof.
Plummer, Jenifer M., BSc *Sheff.*, PhD *Lond.* Sr. Lectr.
Scaramuzzi, R. J., BSc *Syd.*, PhD *Syd.* Prof., Veterinary Physiology
Wathes, D. Claire, BSc *Birm.*, PhD *Nott.*, DSc *Brist.* Prof., Veterinary Reproduction
Watson, P. F., BSc *Lond.*, BVetMed *Lond.*, PhD *Syd.* Prof., Reproductive Cryobiology
Other Staff: 2 Lectrs.

CONTACT OFFICERS

Academic affairs. Principal and Dean: Lanyon, Prof. L. E., BVSc *Brist.*, PhD *Brist.*, DSc *Brist.*
Accommodation. Registrar: Tribble, Ann R., MA *Oxf.*
Admissions (first degree). Registrar: Tribble, Ann R., MA *Oxf.*

Admissions (higher degree). Registrar: Tribble, Ann R., MA Oxf.

Adult/continuing education. Head of Learning Resources and Continuing Professional Development: Taylor, John S., BSc Wales

Alumni. Head of Public Relations and Fundraising: Blake, Marjorie, BA CNAA, MA Vic.(BC)

Archives. Walker, Deborah, BSc Birm.

Careers. Registrar: Tribble, Ann R., MA Oxf.

Computing services. Computer Network and Database Manager: Hayward, Alan, BA CNAA, MSc CNAA

Consultancy services. Principal and Dean: Lanyon, Prof. L. E., BVSc Brist., PhD Brist., DSc Brist.

Credit transfer. Registrar: Tribble, Ann R., MA Oxf.

Development/fund-raising. Head of Public Relations and Fundraising: Blake, Marjorie, BA CNAA, MA Vic.(BC)

Distance education. Head of Learning Resources and Continuing Professional Development: Taylor, John S., BSc Wales

Equal opportunities. Personnel Officer: Glover, Pam

Estates and buildings/works and services. Assistant Secretary (General): Fisher, G. J., BA Reading

Examinations. Registrar: Tribble, Ann R., MA Oxf.

Finance. Finance Officer and Accountant: Mobley, L. F. F., BA Open(UK)

General enquiries. Secretary: Smith, A. N., MA Oxf., BPhil Newcastle(UK)

Health services. Safety Officer: Tyler, David D., MA Camb., PhD Lond.

Industrial liaison. Personnel Officer: Glover, Pam

International office. Registrar: Tribble, Ann R., MA Oxf.

Library (chief librarian). Acting Librarian: Pridmore, Jane C., BA Hull

Minorities/disadvantaged groups. Personnel Officer: Glover, Pam

Personnel/human resources. Personnel Officer: Glover, Pam

Public relations, information and marketing. Head of Public Relations and Fundraising: Blake, Marjorie, BA CNAA, MA Vic.(BC)

Publications. Head of Public Relations and Fundraising: Blake, Marjorie, BA CNAA, MA Vic.(BC)

Purchasing. Assistant Secretary (General): Fisher, G. J., BA Reading

Quality assurance and accreditation. Academic Registrar: Probyn, Paul A., BSc Lond.

Research. Principal and Dean: Lanyon, Prof. L. E., BVSc Brist., PhD Brist., DSc Brist.

Safety. Safety Officer: Tyler, David D., MA Camb., PhD Lond.

Scholarships, awards, loans. Registrar: Tribble, Ann R., MA Oxf.

Schools liaison. Registrar: Tribble, Ann R., MA Oxf.

Security. Assistant Secretary (General): Fisher, G. J., BA Reading

Sport and recreation. Hawkshead Campus Administrator: Pinchard, Geraldine, BSc Lond.

Staff development and training. Personnel Officer: Glover, Pam

Student union. Schroeder, Sally

Student welfare/counselling. Registrar: Tribble, Ann R., MA Oxf.

Students from other countries. Registrar: Tribble, Ann R., MA Oxf.

Students with disabilities. Academic Registrar: Probyn, Paul A., BSc Lond.

University press. Head of Public Relations and Fundraising: Blake, Marjorie, BA CNAA, MA Vic.(BC)

Women. Personnel Officer: Glover, Pam

CAMPUS/COLLEGE HEADS

Hawkshead Campus, Hawkshead House, Hawkshead Lane, North Mymms, Hatfield, Herts., England AL9 7TA. (Tel: (01707) 662255; Fax: (01707) 652090.) Administrator: Pinchard, Geraldine, BSc Lond.

[Information supplied by the institution as at March 1998, and edited by the ACU]

ST GEORGE'S HOSPITAL MEDICAL SCHOOL

Founded 1751

Postal Address: Cranmer Terrace, London, England SW17 0RE
Telephone: (0181) 725 5000 **Fax**: (0181) 725 3426

CHAIRMAN OF THE MEDICAL SCHOOL COUNCIL—Heron, Sir Michael G.
PRINCIPAL*—Boyd, Prof. Robert D. H., MB BChir Camb., MA Camb., MSc, FRCP
SECRETARY‡—......
FINANCE OFFICER—Turner, Ian C., BA CNAA
ACADEMIC SECRETARY—Jones, Gareth, MA Oxf., DPhil Oxf.
ACADEMIC REGISTRAR—Brown, Philip J., BA Leeds
LIBRARIAN—Gove, Susan, BSc

GENERAL INFORMATION

History. The school was founded in 1751.

Admission to first degree courses (see also United Kingdom Introduction). Through Universities and Colleges Admissions Service (UCAS).

First Degrees (of University of London) (see also University of London Directory to Subjects of Study). MB BS.

Higher Degrees (of University of London) (see also University of London Directory to Subjects of Study). MPhil, PhD.

Fees (1998–99, annual). Undergraduate: LEA-supported students £1000; self-supporting students £1650 (years 1 and 2), £2880 (years 3, 4 and 5). Postgraduate: home students £2610 full-time, £1305 part-time; international students £8560 full-time or £4280 part-time (science, pre-clinical), £15,750 full-time or £7875 part-time (clinical).

Academic Year (1998–99). Three terms: 6 October–16 December; 13 January–24 March; 28 April–11 July.

Income. Total, £42,362,425.

ACADEMIC UNITS

Accident and Emergency

No staff at present

Anaesthetics

Desborough, Jane P., MB ChB Leeds, FRCA   Sr. Lectr.
Hall, George M., MB BS PhD, FIBiol, FRCA   Prof.; Head*
Vacant Posts: 1 Lectr.

Anatomy

Bennett, Dorothy C., MA Camb., PhD   Reader
Davies, D. Ceri, BSc Wales, PhD   Sr. Lectr.
Dilly, P. Noël, GM, RD, BSc MB BS PhD   Prof.; Head*

Biochemistry

Bashford, C. Lindsay, MA Oxf., DPhil Oxf.   Reader

Clemens, Michael J., BSc Brist., DPhil Sus.   Prof.; Head*
Fisher, L. Mark, MA Oxf., PhD   Prof.
Goodbourn, Stephen E. Y., BA Oxf., DPhil Oxf.   Sr. Lectr.
Griffiths, John R., DPhil Oxf., MB BS   Prof.
Whitley, Guy S. J., PhD   Sr. Lectr.

Cardiothoracic Surgery

No staff at present

Child Health

Bain, Murray D., BSc Edin., MB ChB Edin.   Sr. Lectr.
Calvert, Sandra A., MB BChir Camb., MA Camb.   Sr. Lectr.
Carter, Nicholas D., BSc PhD   Prof.
Chalmers, Ronald A., PhD CNAA, DSc CNAA   Prof.
De Souza, Carlos M. R., MD   Sr. Lectr.
Hamilton, Patricia A., BSc Brist., MB ChB Brist., FRCP   Sr. Lectr.
Haque, Khalid N., MB BS Karachi, FRCP   Sr. Lectr.
Jeffery, Stephen, PhD   Sr. Lectr.
Mitton, Sally, MD   Sr. Lectr.

Patton, Michael A., MB ChB Edin., MSc Edin.,
MA Camb., FRCP   Reader
Walters, Dafydd V., BSc MB BS, FRCP   Prof.;
Head*
Williams, Anthony F., DPhil Oxf., BSc MB BS,
FRCP   Sr. Lectr.

Dermatology

Harland, Christopher C., MB BS   Sr. Lectr.
Mortimer, Peter S., MB BS MD, FRCP   Sr.
Lectr.

Ear, Nose and Throat

No staff at present

Forensic Medicine

Shepherd, Richard T., MB BS   Sr. Lectr.

Haematology

Ball, Sarah E., BA Oxf., DM Oxf.   Sr. Lectr.
Bevan, David H., MB BS Newcastle(UK), FRCP,
FRCPath   Sr. Lectr.
Gordon-Smith, E. C., BSc Oxf., BM BCh Oxf.,
MA Oxf., MSc, FRCP, FRCPath   Prof.; Head*
Marsh, Judith C. W., BSc Birm., MD Birm.   Sr.
Lectr.
Parker-Williams, E. J., MB BS, FRCPath   Sr.
Lectr.
Pettengell, Ruth, BSc Well., MB ChB Otago, PhD
Manc., FRACP   Sr. Lectr.
Rutherford, Timothy R., MA Camb., PhD
Glas.   Sr. Lectr.

Histopathology

Chambers, Timothy J., BSc MB BS PhD   Prof.;
Head*
Chow, Jade W. M., BA Trinity(Dub.), MB BCh
BAO Trinity(Dub.), PhD   Sr. Lectr.
Corbishley, Catherine M., BSc Brist., MB ChB
Brist.   Sr. Lectr.
Davies, Michael J., MD, FRCPath,
FRCP   British Heart Foundation Prof.,
Cardiovascular Pathology
Dilly, Susan A., BSc MB BS   Sr. Lectr.
Finlayson, Caroline J., MB BS   Sr. Lectr.
Warburton, Michael J., BSc Wales, PhD
Manc.   Sr. Lectr.

Immunology

Axford, John S., BSc CNAA, MD   Sr. Lectr.
Hay, Frank C., BTech Brun., PhD   Prof.
Johnstone, Alan P., BSc Manc., DPhil
Oxf.   Prof.; Head*
Poulton, Terence A., PhD   Sr. Lectr.

Medical Microbiology

Banerjee, Dilip K., MD Delhi, PhD,
FRCPath   Reader
Butcher, Philip D., PhD CNAA   Sr. Lectr.
Carrington, David, BSc MB BS   Sr. Lectr.
Coates, Anthony R. M., BSc MD   Prof.; Head*
Holliman, Richard E., MB BS MSc   Reader
Roberts, Michael M., BSc Sur., PhD Warw.   Sr.
Lectr.

Medicine

Cardiology

Baboonian, Christina, PhD   Sr. Lectr.
Camm, A. John, MB BS, FRCP   British Heart
Foundation Prudential Prof., Clinical
Cardiology; Head*
Kaski Fullone, Juan C. C., MD Buenos Aires   Sr.
Lectr.
McKenna, William J., BA Yale, MD CM McG.,
FRCP   Prof.
Rowland, Edward, MD   Sr. Lectr.
Seymour, Carol A., BM BCh Oxf., MA Camb.,
MSc PhD, FRCP   Prof.
Treasure, Thomas, MD MS, FRCS   Prof.

Clinical Neuroscience

Bell, Brian A., MD Newcastle(UK), FRCS   Prof.;
Head*
Brown, Martin M., MA Camb., MD Camb.,
FRCP   Reader

Gastroenterology, Endocrinology and Metabolism

Colston, Kay W., BSc PhD   Sr. Lectr.
Howard, Philip J., MA Oxf., MD   Sr. Lectr.
Hyer, Stephen L., MB BS   Sr. Lectr.
Levin, Gerald E., MB BS MSc, FRCPath   Sr.
Lectr.
Maxwell, J. Douglas, BSc Glas., MD Glas.,
FRCP   Reader
Mendall, Michael A.   Sr. Lectr.
Northfield, Timothy C., MA Camb., MD Camb.,
FRCP   Prof.; Head*
Nussey, Stephen S., BM BCh Oxf., MA Oxf.,
DPhil Oxf.   Reader

General Practice

Hilton, Sean R., MD   Prof.; Head*
McCoubrie, Malcolm, MB BS, FRCGP   Sr.
Lectr.

Geriatric Medicine

Colgan, John, BSc MB BS   Sr. Lectr.
Hastie, Ian R., MB BS, FRCP   Sr. Lectr.
Millard, Peter H., MD PhD, FRCP   Eleanor
Peel Prof.; Head*

Infectious Diseases

Griffin, George E., PhD Hull, BSc MB BS,
FRCP   Prof.; Head*
Lewis, David J. M., MB BCh Wales   Sr. Lectr.
Wansbrough-Jones, Mark H., MSc MB BS,
FRCP   Sr. Lectr.

Physiological Medicine

Bennett, E. David, MB BS, FRCP   Reader
Cappuccio, Francisco P., MD Naples   Sr. Lectr.
Jones, Paul W., MB BS PhD, FRCP   Prof.
MacGregor, Graham A., MB BChir Camb., MA
Camb., FRCP   Prof.; Head*
Sagnella, Guiseppe A., BSc CNAA, PhD
DSc   Reader

Renal Medicine

Eastwood, John B., MD, FRCP   Sr. Lectr.
Oliveira, David B. J., MB BChir Camb., MA
Camb., PhD, FRCP   Prof.; Head*

Obstetrics and Gynaecology

Bourne, Thomas H., PhD Gothenburg, MB
BS   Sr. Lectr.
Campbell, Stuart, MB ChB Glas., FRCS,
FRCOG   Prof.; Head*
Hay, Philip E., MB BS   Sr. Lectr.
Wilson, Catherine A. J., BPharm PhD
DSc   Prof.

Oncology

Dalgleish, Angus G., BSc MD, FRACP, FRCPath,
FRCP   Prof.

Ophthalmology

No staff at present

Orthopaedics

No staff at present

Paediatric Surgery

No staff at present

Pharmacology

Bolton, Thomas B., MA Oxf., BSc BVetMed
PhD   Prof.; Head*
Horton, Roger W., BSc Birm., PhD
DSc   Reader
Large, William A., BPharm PhD   Prof.
Robinson, Clive, PhD   Sr. Lectr.

Pharmacology, Clinical

Collier, Joseph G., MA Camb., MD Camb.,
FRCP   Reader
Singer, Donald R. J., MD Aberd., BMedBiol
Aberd.   Sr. Lectr.

Physiology

Andrews, Paul L. R., PhD Sheff.   Reader
Levick, J. Rodney, BM BCh Oxf., MA Oxf.,
DPhil Oxf., DSc Oxf.   Prof.
Richardson, Paul S., BSc Oxf., MA Oxf., DM
Oxf.   Reader
Stock, Michael J., BSc Sheff., PhD   Prof.; Head*

Whitehead, Saffron A., PhD McM., BSc   Sr.
Lectr.
Williams, Thelma L., BSc Pitt., PhD Case
W.Reserve   Reader

Plastic Surgery

No staff at present

Psychiatry

Child Psychiatry

Hill, Peter D., MB BChir Camb., MA Camb.,
FRCP, FRCPsych   Prof.; Head*
Hindley, Peter A., BSc MB BS   Sr. Lectr.
Spender, Quentin W., MB BS   Sr. Lectr.
Turk, Jeremy, BSc MD   Sr. Lectr.

Forensic Psychiatry

Bartlett, Ann E. A., MB BChir Camb., MA Camb.,
MPhil Camb.   Sr. Lectr.
Eastman, Nigel G. L., MB ChB Brist.,
BSc(Econ)   Sr. Lectr.; Head*
McGauley, Gillian A., BSc MB BS   Sr. Lectr.
Mezey, Gillian C., MB BS   Sr. Lectr.

Liaison and Psychosomatic Medicine

Bristow, Michael F., BA Oxf., MB BS   Sr. Lectr.
Burke, Aggrey W., BSc Birm., MB ChB
Birm.   Sr. Lectr.
Burns, Tom P., MA Camb., MD Camb.   Prof.
Evans, Christopher D. H., BA Camb., MB
BS   Sr. Lectr.
Jacobson, Robin R., BA Camb., MB BChir
Camb.   Sr. Lectr.
Kent, Andrew J., MB BS   Sr. Lectr.
Lacey, J. Hubert, MD St And., MPhil,
FRCPsych   Prof.; Head*

Addictive Behaviour and Psychological Medicine

Checinski, Kenneth M., MA Camb., MB BS   Sr.
Lectr.
Drummond, David C., MD Glas.   Sr. Lectr.
Edeh, James C. T., MB BS Ib., PhD   Sr. Lectr.
Farmer, Roger, MSc Manc., MD Belf.,
FRCPsych   Sr. Lectr.
Ghodse, A. Hamid, MD Tabriz, PhD, FRCP,
FRCPsych   Prof.; Head*
Porter, Sally-Anne M., MB BS   Sr. Lectr.

Psychiatry of Disability

Bernal, Susanna J., MB ChB Birm.   Sr. Lectr.
Drummond, Catherine R., MB BS   Sr. Lectr.
Hollins, Sheila C., MB BS, FRCPsych   Prof.;
Head*
Matthews, Sara H. M., MB BCh Wales   Sr.
Lectr.

Psychotherapy

Drummond, Lindsay M., MB ChB Glas.   Sr.
Lectr.
Warwick, Hilary M. C., MB ChB Leeds, MMedSc
Leeds   Sr. Lectr.

Psychology

Pickering, Alan D., BA Camb., PhD Manc.   Sr.
Lectr.
Steptoe, Andrew P. A., MA Camb., MA Oxf.,
DPhil Oxf., DSc, FBPsS   Prof.; Head*
West, Robert J., BSc PhD   Prof.

Public Health Sciences

Anderson, H. Ross, MD Melb., MSc   Prof.;
Head*
Bland, J. Martin, MSc PhD   Prof.
Cook, Derek G., PhD   Reader
Littlejohns, Peter, BSc MB BS MD   Prof.
Pollock, Allyson M., BSc Dund., MB ChB Dund.,
MSc   Sr. Lectr.
Strachan, David P., MB ChB Edin., MSc   Prof.
Victor, Christina R., PhD Wales, MPhil   Reader

Radiology, Diagnostic

Grundy, Alan, MB ChB Dund., FRCR   Sr. Lectr.

Radiotherapy

No staff at present

Rheumatology and Rehabilitation

No staff at present

Surgery, General

Austen, Brian M., MA Oxf., PhD   Prof.
Dormandy, John A., MB BS DSc(Med),
    FRCS   Prof.
Hermon-Taylor, John, MChir Camb., BA,
    FRCS   Prof.; Head*
Treasure, Thomas, MD MS, FRCS   Prof.
Twistleton-Wykeham-Fiennes, Alberic G., BSc
    MS, FRCS   Sr. Lectr.
Winterbourne, David J., BSc Manc., DPhil
    Oxf.   Sr. Lectr.

Urology

No staff at present

Venereology

No staff at present

CONTACT OFFICERS

Accommodation. Accommodation Officer:
    Walton, Diana

Admissions (first degree). Admissions Officer:
    Evans, William B., LLB Wales
Admissions (higher degree). Admissions
    Officer: Evans, William B., LLB Wales
Adult/continuing education. Dean for Pre-
    Registration Studies: Parker-Williams, John,
    MB BS, FRCPath
Alumni. Admissions Officer: Evans, William
    B., LLB Wales
Archives. Librarian: Gove, Susan, BSc
Computing services. Director of Computing:
    Morris, Stephen G., MSc
Estates and buildings/works and services.
    Building Officer: Varney, John M.
Examinations. Deputy Academic Registrar:
    Staniforth, Kay, BA Hull
Finance. Finance Officer: Turner, Ian C., BA
    CNAA
General enquiries. Secretary: ......
Health services. Director, Staff and Student
    Health Service: Mitchell-Heggs, Nita, MB BS,
    FRCP

Library (chief librarian). Librarian: Gove,
    Susan, BSc
Personnel/human resources. Personnel
    Officer: Ball, Frank C., MA Oxf.
Purchasing. Supplies Officer: Umaria Gomez,
    Hasmita
Quality assurance and accreditation.
    Academic Secretary: Jones, Gareth, MA Oxf.,
    DPhil Oxf.
Safety. Safety Officer: Warburton, Dennis, PhD
    Liv.
Schools liaison. Admissions Officer: Evans,
    William B., LLB Wales
Security. Bursar: ......
Staff development and training. Personnel
    Officer: Ball, Frank C., MA Oxf.
Student welfare/counselling. Student
    Counsellor: Curra, Jenni

[Information supplied by the institution as at 13 July
1998, and edited by the ACU]

SCHOOL OF ORIENTAL AND AFRICAN STUDIES

Founded 1916

Associate Member of the Association of Commonwealth Universities

Postal Address: Thornhaugh Street, Russell Square, London, England WC1H 0XG
Telephone: (0171) 637 2388 **Fax**: (0171) 436 3844 **Telex**: 262433 W6876 **WWW**: http://www.soas.ac.uk

PATRON—Elizabeth, H.M. The Queen
VISITOR—Howe of Aberavon, The Rt. Hon. Lord, CH, QC
CHAIRMAN OF THE GOVERNING BODY—Taylor, Jonathan F., MA Oxf.
DIRECTOR*—Lankester, Sir Tim, KCB, BA Camb., MA Yale
SCHOOL SECRETARY‡—Dabell, Frank L., BA York(UK)
REGISTRAR—Harvey, Terry, BSc CNAA
DIRECTOR OF RESOURCES AND PLANNING—Morley, John, BSc Leeds, MSc Lond.
DIRECTOR OF EXTERNAL RELATIONS—Coe, Jim
LIBRARIAN—......

GENERAL INFORMATION

History. The school was founded in 1916 as
the School of Oriental Studies and adopted its
present name in 1938. It is located in
Bloomsbury, central London.

Admission to first degree courses (see also
United Kingdom Introduction). Through
Universities and Colleges Admissions Service
(UCAS).

First Degrees (of University of London)
(see also University of London Directory to
Subjects of Study). BA, BSc, LLB.
    All courses are full-time and last 3–4 years.

Higher Degrees (of University of London)
(see also University of London Directory to
Subjects of Study). LLM, MA, MMus, MSc,
MPhil, PhD.
    LLM, MA, MMus, MSc: 1 year full-time or
2–3 years part-time; MPhil, PhD: minimum 3
years full-time.

Libraries. 890,000 volumes; 4400 periodicals
subscribed to.

Fees (1998–99, annual). Undergraduate:
£1000. Postgraduate: UK students £2610;
international students £7730.

Academic Awards. 47 awards ranging in
value from £600 to £6720.

Academic Year (1998–99). Three terms: 23
September–11 December; 11 January–26
March; 26 April–18 June.

Income (1996–97). Total, £28,822,000.

Statistics. Staff: 540 (290 academic, 250
administrative). Students: full-time 2584; part-
time 455; total 3039.

FACULTIES/SCHOOLS

Academic Affairs

Tel: (0171) 323 6243 Fax: (0171) 691 3393
Pro-Director: Shackle, Prof. Christopher, BA
    Oxf., BLitt Oxf., PhD Lond., FBA

Research

Tel: (0171) 323 6398 Fax: (0171) 691 3393
Pro-Director: Harris, Prof. Laurence,
    MSc(Econ) Lond.

Taught Courses

Pro-Director: Taylor, David D., BA Camb., MA
    Lond., PhD Lond.

ACADEMIC UNITS

Africa, Languages and Cultures of

Tel: (0171) 323 6255 Fax: (0171) 323 0174
Appleyard, David L., BA Lond., PhD
    Lond.   Reader, Ethiopian Semitic and
    Cushitic Languages; Head*

Brenner, Louis, BS Wis., MA Col., PhD
    Col.   Prof., Religions of Africa
Furniss, Graham L., BA Lond., PhD
    Lond.   Reader, Hausa
Hayward, Richard J., BSc Lond., PhD Lond.,
    FBA   Prof., Ethiopian Linguistics
Jaggar, Philip J., BA Lond., MA Calif., MPhil
    Lond., PhD Calif.   Sr. Lectr., Hausa
Mann, W. Michael, BA Oxf.   Sr. Lectr., Bantu
    Languages
Topan, Farouk M. T., BA Lond., PhD Lond.   Sr.
    Lectr., Swahili
Other Staff: 6 Lectrs.; 1 Res. Fellow
Research: African Islamic culture and tradition;
    broadcast culture in contemporary Africa;
    descriptive and comparative linguistics of
    African languages; gender and history in the
    African novel; media for development in
    contemporary Africa

Anthropology and Sociology

Tel: (0171) 323 6331 Fax: (0171) 323 6363
Bernstein, Henry, MA Camb., MSc Lond.   Prof.,
    Africa
Cantlie, Audrey, South Asia
Croll, Elisabeth J., MA Cant., MA Lond., PhD
    Lond.   Prof., China
Fardon, Richard O., BSc(Econ) Lond., PhD
    Lond.   Prof., Nigeria and Cameroon
Hobart, P. Mark, MA Camb., PhD Lond.   Sr.
    Lectr., South East Asia
Hughes, David W., MA Camb., MPhil Yale, PhD
    Mich.   Sr. Lectr., Ethnomusicology

Kandiyoti, Deniz, BA *Paris*, MSc *Lond.*, PhD *Lond.* Sr. Lectr., Middle East and Central Asia

Lindisfarne, Nancy, BA *Wash.(Mo.)*, MPhil *Lond.*, PhD *Lond.* Sr. Lectr., Middle East

Peel, John D. Y., MA *Oxf.*, PhD *Lond.*, DLit *Lond.*, FBA Prof., West Africa

Pottier, Johan P. J., BA *Sus.*, DPhil *Sus.* Sr. Lectr., Africa

Tapper, Richard L., MA *Camb.*, PhD *Lond.* Reader, Middle East

Turton, Andrew G. W., MA *Camb.*, PhD *Lond.* Reader, South East Asia; Head*

Other Staff: 8 Lectrs.; 1 Visiting Reader†; 2 Hon. Prof. Res. Assocs.; 4 Hon. Sr. Res. Assocs.

Research: anthropology and history; anthropology of development; anthropology of religion; theory in anthropology; visual anthropology and anthropology of media

Art and Archaeology

Tel: (0171) 323 6259 Fax: (0171) 323 6241

Khalili, Nasser D., BA *Lond.*, PhD *Lond.* Visiting Prof.†, Islamic Art

King, Geoffrey R. D., MPhil *Lond.*, PhD *Lond.*, FSA Reader, Islamic Middle East

Moore, Elizabeth H., BA *Pomona*, PhD *Lond.* Sr. Lectr., South East Asia; Head*

Picton, John W., BSc *Lond.* Reader, Africa

Rogers, J. Michael, MA *Oxf.*, DPhil *Oxf.*, FSA, FBA Khalili Prof., Islamic Middle East

Screech, Timon, MA *Oxf.*, AM *Harv.*, PhD *Harv.* Sr. Lectr., Japanese Art

Tillotson, Giles H. R., MA *Camb.*, PhD *Camb.* Sr. Lectr., South Asia

Whitfield, Roderick, BA *Camb.*, MA *Prin.*, PhD *Prin.* Percival David Prof., China and East Asia

Other Staff: 6 Lectrs.

Research: architecture in religious and court contexts; arts of Africa and the African diaspora; Buddhist and Hindu art and archaeology; Islamic art and pre-Islamic architecture; ritual practice and material culture

Development Studies

Fax: (0171) 323 6605

Bernstein, Henry, MA *Camb.*, MSc *Lond.* Prof., East and South Africa

Croll, Elisabeth J., MA *Cant.*, MA *Lond.*, PhD *Lond.* Prof., China; Head*

Kandiyoti, Deniz, BA *Paris*, MSc *Lond.*, PhD *Lond.* Sr. Lectr., Middle East and Central Asia

Weeks, John, BSc(Econ) *Texas*, MSc(Econ) *Mich.*, PhD *Mich.* Prof., Africa

Other Staff: 3 Lectrs.

Research: development discourses and institutions; East, South and Central Asia; gender and children's issues; rural development and agrarian reform; structural adjustment; transitional market economies in Africa

East Asia, Languages and Cultures of

Tel: (0171) 323 6193 Fax: (0171) 323 6234

Baker, Hugh D. R., BA *Lond.*, PhD *Lond.* Prof., Chinese; Head*

Breen, John L., MA *Camb.*, PhD *Camb.* Sr. Lectr., Japanese

Deuchler, Martina, BA *Ley.*, PhD *Harv.* Prof., Korean Studies

Gerstle, C. Andrew, BA *Col.*, MA *Waseda*, PhD *Harv.* Prof., Japanese

Howard, Keith D., BA *CNAA*, MA *Durh.*, PhD *Belf.* Sr. Lectr., Korean Studies and Music

Lo, Andrew H.-B., MA *Prin.*, PhD *Prin.* Sr. Lectr., Chinese

T'ung, P. C., BA *Taiwan Normal* Sr. Lectr., Chinese

Zhao, Y. Henry, BA *Nanking*, MA *Peking*, PhD *Calif.* Sr. Lectr., Chinese

Other Staff: 10 Lectrs.; 1 Hon. Sr. Res. Assoc.

Research: classical Chinese (aesthetics, games, literature, philosophy, poetry); Japanese (drama, linguistics, literature, pedagogy, religion); modern Chinese (fiction, languages, literary criticism, poetry, society); Tibetan architecture and language

Economics

Tel: (0171) 323 6180 Fax: (0171) 323 6277

Ash, Robert F., BA *Lond.*, MSc(Econ) *Lond.*, PhD *Lond.* Sr. Lectr., China, Korea

Booth, Anne, BA *Well.*, PhD *ANU* Prof., South East Asia; Head*

Byres, Terence J., BLitt *Glas.*, MA *Aberd.* Prof., South Asia

Fine, Ben J., BA *Oxf.*, BPhil *Oxf.*, PhD *Lond.* Prof., Southern Africa

Hakimian, Hassan, BSc(Econ) *Lond.*, DPhil *Sus.* Sr. Lectr., Middle East

Harris, Laurence, MSc(Econ) *Lond.* Prof., Southern Africa

Howe, Christopher B., MA *Camb.*, PhD *Lond.* Prof., Japan

Karshenas, Massoud, MSc(Econ) *Lond.*, PhD *Camb.* Reader, Middle East

Nissanke, Machiko K., MSc *Moscow*, MSc(Econ) *Lond.*, PhD *Lond.* Sr. Lectr., Africa and Japan

Scaramozzino, Pasquale, BSc(Econ) *Rome*, MSc(Econ) *Lond.*, PhD *Lond.* Sr. Lectr., Fiscal Policy

Sender, John, MA *Oxf.*, MSc(Econ) *Lond.*, PhD *Lond.* Prof., East and Southern Africa

Smith, Graham, BA *Durh.*, MA *Warw.*, PhD *Manc.* Sr. Lectr., Econometrics

Wall, David, BSc(Econ) *Lond.* Visiting Prof.†, China

Weeks, John, BSc(Econ) *Texas*, MSc(Econ) *Mich.*, PhD *Mich.* Prof., Africa

Other Staff: 10 Lectrs.; 2 Hon. Prof. Res. Assocs.

Research: agricultural economics; economic history; financial economics; human resource development; industrial economics

Geography

Tel: (0171) 323 6134 Fax: (0171) 691 3432

Allan, J. Anthony, BA *Durh.*, PhD *Lond.* Prof., Middle East and North Africa

Bradnock, Robert W., MA *Camb.*, PhD *Lond.* Sr. Lectr., South Asia; Head*

Edmonds, Richard L., MA *Seton Hall*, MA *Pitt.*, PhD *Chic.* Sr. Lectr., China

Sargent, John, BA *Leeds* Reader, Japan

Stott, Philip A., BA *Lond.* Prof., South East Asia

Wiltshire, Richard J., BSc *Lond.*, MA *York(Can.)*, PhD *Lond.* Sr. Lectr., Japan

Other Staff: 6 Lectrs.; 1 Hon. Sr. Res. Assoc.†

Research: forest management in South Asia (society and sustainable resource use in India); historical geography of East Asia; man and environment in Africa (agricultural and urban geography of Africa); political ecology; political geography and border studies (environment, international relations, law, territory)

History

Tel: (0171) 323 6137 Fax: (0171) 323 6046

Anderson, David M., BA *Sus.*, PhD *Camb.* Sr. Lectr., Africa

Arnold, David J., BA *Exe.*, DPhil *Sus.* Prof., South Asia

Brett, Michael, BA *Camb.*, PhD *Lond.* Reader, North Africa

Brown, Ian G., BA *Brist.*, MA *Lond.*, PhD *Lond.* Reader, South East Asian Economic History

Clarence-Smith, William G., MA *Camb.*, PhD *Lond.* Reader, Asian and African Economic History

Cullen, Christopher, MA *Oxf.*, MA *Camb.*, PhD *Lond.* Sr. Lectr., Chinese Science and Medicine

Deuchler, Martina, BA *Ley.*, PhD *Harv.* Prof., Korea

Dikötter, Frank, BA *Geneva*, MA *Geneva*, PhD *Lond.* Sr. Lectr., Chinese Medicine

Hawting, Gerald R., BA *Lond.*, PhD *Lond.* Sr. Lectr., Middle East

Marks, Shula, OBE, BA *Cape Town*, PhD *Lond.*, DLitt *Cape Town*, FBA Prof., South Africa

Morgan, David O., BA *Oxf.*, PhD *Lond.* Reader, Middle East

Powell, Avril A., BA *Camb.*, PhD *Lond.* Sr. Lectr., South Asia

Rathbone, Richard J. A. R., BA *Lond.*, PhD *Lond.* Prof., Africa

Robb, Peter G., BA *Well.*, PhD *Lond.* Prof., South Asia; Head*

Roberts, Andrew D., BA *Camb.*, PhD *Wis.* Prof., Africa

Sims, Richard L., BA *Lond.*, PhD *Lond.* Sr. Lectr., Far East

Smith, Ralph B., BA *Leeds*, PhD *Leeds* Prof., South East Asia

Other Staff: 6 Lectrs.; 2 Res. Fellows; 1 Hon. Prof. Res. Assoc.; 1 Hon. Sr. Res. Assoc.

Research: economic history; gender history; history of empire, colonialism and decolonisation; history of ideas; history of medicine and science; religious and cultural history

Law

Tel: (0171) 323 6333 Fax: (0171) 636 5615

Ballantyne, William M., MA *Camb.* Visiting Prof.†, Arab Law

Coldham, Simon F. R., BA *Oxf.*, MA *Lond.*, PhD *Lond.* Sr. Lectr., Africa

Cotran, His Honour Judge Eugene, LLM *Leeds*, LLD *Lond.* Visiting Prof.†, Africa and Middle East

Craven, Matthew, BA *Nott.*, LLM *Nott.*, PhD *Nott.* Sr. Lectr., Public International Law

Dicks, Anthony R., QC, LLB *Camb.*, MA *Camb.* Prof., China

Harding, Andrew J., MA *Oxf.*, LLM *Sing.*, PhD *Monash* Prof., South East Asia; Head*

Hatchard, John, LLB *Lond.*, LLM *Lond.* Sr. Lectr., Southern Africa

Lauterpacht, Elihus, CBE, QC, LLB *Camb.*, MA *Camb.* Visiting Prof.†, International Law

Menski, Werner F., MA *Kiel*, PhD *Lond.* Sr. Lectr., South Asia

Palmer, Michael J. E., LLB *Camb.*, BSc(Econ) *Lond.*, MA *Lond.* Sr. Lectr., China

Sands, Philippe J., BA *Camb.*, LLM *Camb.* Reader, Environmental Law

Slinn, Peter E., MA *Oxf.*, PhD *Lond.* Sr. Lectr., Africa

Other Staff: 10 Lectrs.; 5 Visiting Lectrs.†; 1 Hon. Sr. Res. Assoc.

Research: comparative law (commercial, ethnic minorities, immigration); environmental law (EC, international, natural resources); human rights law (developing world, protection, women); regional law (China, Commonwealth Africa, Middle East, South Asia)

Linguistics

Tel: (0171) 323 6332 Fax: (0171) 323 6211

Bennett, David C., MA *Lond.*, PhD *Yale* Sr. Lectr., Phonetics and Linguistics

Ingham, Bruce, BA *Lond.*, PhD *Lond.* Reader, Arabic Dialectology; Head*

Kaye, Jonathan D., BA *C.C.N.Y.*, MA *Col.*, PhD *Col.* Prof., General Linguistics

Kempson, Ruth M., BA *Birm.*, MA *Lond.*, PhD *Lond.*, FBA Prof., General Linguistics

Lappin, Shalom, BA *York(Can.)*, MA *Brandeis*, PhD *Brandeis* Prof., Semantics

Other Staff: 4 Lectrs.

Research: automatic multi-lingual speech recognition; computational linguistics; formal semantics and formal syntax; cross linguistic vowel perception; English Lakota dictionary project; phonology and morphology of Altaic languages

Near and Middle East, Languages and Cultures of

Tel: (0171) 323 6252 Fax: (0171) 691 3424

Abdel-Haleem, Muhammad A. S., BA *Cairo*, PhD *Camb.* King Fahd Prof., Islamic Studies

Abu-Deeb, Kamel M., LèsL *Damascus*, DPhil *Oxf.* Prof., Arabic

George, Andrew R., BA *Birm.*, PhD *Birm.* Reader, Assyriology

Günay, Umay, PhD *Ankara* Visiting Prof.†, Turkish

Hafez, Sabry, MA *Cairo*, PhD *Lond.* Prof., Arabic

Hawkins, J. David, MA *Oxf.*, FBA Prof., Ancient Anatolian Languages

Hewitt, B. George, MA *Camb.*, PhD *Camb.*, FBA Reader, Caucasian Languages

Ingham, Bruce, BA *Lond.*, PhD *Lond.* Reader, Arabic Dialectology

Morton, Alexander H., MA *Oxf.* Sr. Lectr., Persian

Parfitt, Tudor V., MA *Oxf.*, DPhil *Oxf.* Reader, Jewish Studies

Sims-Williams, Nicholas J., MA *Camb.*, PhD *Camb.*, FBA Prof., Iranian Studies; Head*

Sperl, Stefan, BA *Oxf.*, PhD *Lond.* Sr. Lectr., Arabic

Wright, Owen, BA *Leic.*, BA *Lond.*, PhD *Lond.* Prof., Middle East Musicology

Other Staff: 6 Lectrs.; 2 Res. Fellows; 1 Visiting Reader†

Research: Arabic and Persian language, literature and culture; classical and modern Islamic studies; decipherment of Bactrian documents (pre-Islamic Afghanistan); modern Hebrew, Israeli culture and Yiddish language; Ottoman and modern Turkish language and literature

Phonetics, see Linguistics

Political Studies

Tel: (0171) 323 6135 *Fax:* (0171) 323 6020

Cruise O'Brien, Donal B., BA *Camb.*, MA *Calif.*, PhD *Lond.* Prof., West Africa

Hale, William M., MA *Oxf.*, PhD *ANU* Reader, Turkey

Kaviraj, Sudipta, MA *Calc.*, PhD *J. Nehru U.* Reader, South Asia

Taylor, David D., BA *Camb.*, MA *Lond.*, PhD *Lond.* Sr. Lectr., South Asia

Tripp, Charles R. H., BA *Oxf.*, MSc *Lond.*, PhD *Lond.* Sr. Lectr., Middle East; Head*

Young, Tom, BSc(Soc) *Lond.*, MA *Lond.*, PhD *Lond.* Sr. Lectr., Southern Africa

Other Staff: 11 Lectrs.

Research: development; ethnicity; human rights; international relations; nationalism; structural adjustment

Religions, Study of

Tel: (0171) 323 6137

Barrett, Timothy H., MA *Camb.*, PhD *Yale* Prof., Taoism and Buddhism

Brenner, Louis, BS *Wis.*, MA *Col.*, PhD *Col.* Prof., Islam in Africa

Hawting, Gerald R., BA *Lond.*, PhD *Lond.* Sr. Lectr., Islam in Middle East

Leslie, Julia, BA *Sus.*, DPhil *Oxf.* Sr. Lectr., Hindu Studies

Piatigorsky, Alexander, BA *Moscow* Emer. Prof.†, Buddhism

Shackle, Christopher, BA *Oxf.*, BLitt *Oxf.*, PhD *Lond.*, FBA Prof., Sikhism

Skorupski, Tadeusz, LTh *Pontif.U.S.Th.Aq.*, PhD *Lond.* Sr. Lectr., Buddhism

Weightman, Simon, MA *Oxf.* Sr. Lectr., Hinduism; Head*

Other Staff: 4 Lectrs.; 1 Res. Fellow; 1 Emer. Reader.†; 4 Hon. Prof. Res. Assocs.

Research: contemporary religions from Asia/Africa; gender and religion in Asia/Africa; media of Asian/African religions; religious texts of Asia/Africa

Sociology, see Anthropol. and Sociol.

South Asia, Languages and Cultures of

Tel: (0171) 323 6251 *Fax:* (0171) 436 2664

Blackburn, Stuart H., BA *Wesleyan*, MA *Calif.*, PhD *Calif.* Sr. Lectr., Tamil

Hutt, Michael J., BA *Lond.*, PhD *Lond.* Sr. Lectr., Nepali; Head*

Kalsi, Amrik S., BA *Panjab.*, MA *Alld.*, PhD *Camb.* Sr. Lectr., Hindi and Urdu

Matthews, David J., BA *Lond.*, PhD *Lond.* Sr. Lectr., Urdu and Nepali

Shackle, Christopher, BA *Oxf.*, BLitt *Oxf.*, PhD *Lond.*, FBA Prof., Punjabi and Urdu

Snell, Rupert, BA *Lond.*, PhD *Lond.* Reader, Hindi

Söhnen-Thieme, Renate, DrPhil *Mainz* Sr. Lectr., Sanskrit

Widdess, D. Richard, MusB *Camb.*, PhD *Camb.*, MA *Camb.*, MA *Lond.* Sr. Lectr., Ethnomusicology

Other Staff: 4 Lectrs.; 2 Res. Fellows; 2 Hon. Prof. Res. Assocs.; 1 Hon. Sr. Res. Assoc.

Research: film and popular culture; oral folk literature and performance; text-based research on religion; translations of South Asian literature

South East Asia and the Islands, Languages and Cultures of

Tel: (0171) 323 6008 *Fax:* (0171) 323 6074

Braginsky, Vladimir I., PhD *Moscow*, DLit *Moscow* Prof., Indonesian and Malay

Chitakasem, Manas, BS(Ed) *Coll.of Educn.*, *Prasarnmitr*, MA *Mich.*, MA *Hawaii*, PhD *Lond.* Sr. Lectr., Tai

Kratz, E. Ulrich, DrPhil *Fran.* Reader, Indonesian and Malay; Head*

Okell, John W. A., MA *Oxf.* Sr. Lectr., Burmese

Phillips, Nigel G., MA *Camb.*, PhD *Lond.* Sr. Lectr., Austronesian Languages

Other Staff: 4 Lectrs.

Research: South East Asian languages and literatures in their traditional, modern, written and oral forms (Burmese, Cambodian, Indonesian, Malay, Tagalog, Thai, Vietnamese)

SPECIAL CENTRES, ETC

African Studies, Centre of

Tel: (0171) 323 6395 *Fax:* (0171) 323 6254

Bowyer-Bower, Tanya A. S., BA *Lond.*, MSc *Tor.*, DPhil *Oxf.* Lectr.; Chair*

Other Staff: 3 Hon. Prof. Res. Assocs.; 2 Hon. Sr. Res. Assocs.

Research: environmental and farming systems (management and impact); ethnography, anthropology, social and economic history; language and the arts in Africa; political economy, law and the state; rural and urban systems and development

Brunei Gallery

Tel: (0171) 323 6036 *Fax:* (0171) 323 6010

Hollingworth, John, BA *Brighton* Exhibitions Officer

Central Asia Research Forum

Tel: (0171) 323 6200

Akiner, Shirin, BA *Lond.*, PhD *Lond.* Lectr.; Dir.*

Research: political and social change in newly independent Central Asian states; sustainable development

Chinese Art, Percival David Foundation of

Tel: (0171) 387 3909 *Fax:* (0171) 383 5163

Pierson, Stacey, BA *Loyola*, MA *Lond.* Acting Curator

Chinese Studies, Centre of

Tel: (0171) 323 6190

Palmer, Michael J. E., LLB *Camb.*, BSc *Lond.*, MA *Lond.* Sr. Lectr.; Chair*

Research: contemporary economic, political and social issues; law and foreign relations

Contemporary China Institute

Tel: (0171) 323 6382 *Fax:* (0171) 323 6046

Dikkötter, Frank, BA *Geneva*, MA *Geneva*, PhD *Lond.* Sr. Lectr.; Dir.*

Research: twentieth-century China (economics, history, law, literature, politics, sociology)

Development Policy and Research, Centre of

Tel: (0171) 436 6295 *Fax:* (0171) 323 6605

Weeks, John, BSc(Econ) *Texas*, MSc(Econ) *Mich.*, PhD *Mich.* Prof.; Dir.*

Research: economic and social effects of drugs in the sub-Saharan region; labour standards and trade union rights in the world trading system; post-apartheid NGO work in southern Africa; problems of conflict-affected countries; social impact of structural adjustment

East Asian Law, Centre of

Tel: (0171) 323 6333 *Fax:* (0171) 636 5615

Vacant Posts: 1 Dir.

Research: administrative law; civil law and civil procedure; family mediation; foreign trade law

Economic Policy for Southern Africa, Centre for

Tel: (0171) 323 6169 *Fax:* (0171) 323 6277

Fine, Ben J., BA *Oxf.*, BPhil *Oxf.*, PhD *Lond.* Prof.; Dir.*

Research: economic policy-making for Southern Africa; political economy of Southern Africa

Geopolitics and International Boundaries Research Centre

Tel: (0171) 323 6308 *Fax:* (0171) 323 6274

Bradnock, Robert W., MA *Camb.*, PhD *Lond.* Sr. Lectr.; Dir.*

Other Staff: 1 Res. Fellow

Research: Arab/Iranian rivalry across Gulf waters; history of partition as means of settling inter-state disputes; legal settlements of territorial questions and regional dynamics; origins of territorial disputes in Persian Gulf and Arabian Peninsula; problems associated with boundaries in deltaic regions

International Education in Economics, Centre for

Tel: (0171) 323 6068 *Fax:* (0171) 637 7075

Johnson, Alison, BA *Qu.*, MSc(Econ) *Lond.* Lectr.; Acting Dir.*

Other Staff: 2 Lectrs.

Islamic and Middle Eastern Law, Centre of

Tel: (0171) 323 6348 *Fax:* (0171) 636 5615

Welchman, Lynn, BA *Camb.*, PhD *Lond.* Dir.*

Research: comparative developments in Islamic personal status law; constitutional law and courts; human rights and law; rule of law in the Arab and Islamic world; Shari'a and legislation

Islamic Studies, Centre of

Tel: (0171) 637 6297 *Fax:* (0171) 436 9391

Abdel Haleem, Muhammad A. S., BA *Cairo*, PhD *Camb.* Prof.; Dir.*

Other Staff: 1 Res. Fellow; 1 Hon. Sr. Res. Assoc.

Research: classical and contemporary Islamic moral and political thought; Islamic legal and theological texts; prophetic Hadith (contents, style, translation); the Qu'ran (contents, language, style); translations and interpretations

Japan Research Centre

Tel: (0171) 323 6278

Screech, Timon, MA *Oxf.*, AM *Harv.*, PhD *Harv.* Sr. Lectr.; Chair*

Other Staff: 1 Hon. Prof. Res. Assoc.

Research: humanities (art history, history, linguistics, literature, music, religion); social science (anthropology, economics, geography, law, politics)

Jewish Studies, Centre for

Tel: (0171) 323 6275 *Fax:* (0171) 691 3424

Parfitt, Tudor V., MA *Oxf.*, DPhil *Oxf.* Reader; Chair*

Other Staff: 2 Hon. Prof. Res. Assocs.†
Research: history, languages and literatures of Jews of Asia and Africa; the State of Israel; Yiddish language and literature

Korean Studies, Centre of

Tel: (0171) 323 6065 Fax: (0171) 323 6179
Pak, Youngsook, BA Ewha, PhD Heidel.   Lectr.; Chair*
Research: art history; economics; ethnomusicology; history; linguistics; politics

Language Centre

Tel: (0171) 323 6379 Fax: (0171) 637 7355
Kratz, E. Ulrich, DrPhil Fran.   Head*
Other Staff: 4 Engl. Teachers

Music Studies, Centre of

Tel: (0171) 323 6188
Howard, Keith D., BA CNAA, MA Durh., PhD Belf.   Sr. Lectr.; Chair*
Research: Afro-Caribbean music; composition, creativity and cognitive analysis; ethnomusicology (music of non-Western world); historical musicology of the Middle East and Asia; music grammars, music and linguistics

Near and Middle Eastern Studies, Centre of

Tel: (0171) 323 6239 Fax: (0171) 637 4248
Parfitt, Tudor V., MA Oxf., DPhil Oxf.   Chair*
Other Staff: 2 Hon. Prof. Res. Assocs.
Research: Caucasus, Central Asia, Middle East and North Africa (archaeology, anthropology, economics, geography including water issues, history, law, linguistics, literature, music, politics)

Overseas Students, International Foundation Courses for

Tel: (0171) 323 6028 Fax: (0171) 637 1006
Yates, Susan E., BA Lond.   Head*
Other Staff: 22 Engl. Teachers; 18 Subj. Teachers†

SOAS/Sotheby's Asian Arts Programme

Tel: (0171) 637 6129 Fax: (0171) 637 0406
King, Geoffrey R. D., MPhil Lond., PhD Lond., FSA   Academic Dir.*

South Asian Studies, Centre of

Tel: (0171) 323 6353
Blackburn, Stuart H., BA Wesleyan, MA Calif., PhD Calif.   Sr. Lectr.; Chair*
Other Staff: 2 Hon. Prof. Res. Assocs.†
Research: life histories in South Asia and the South Asian diaspora; literary criticism in South Asian languages; modern South Asian history; modern South Asian societies

South East Asian Studies, Centre of

Tel: (0171) 323 6190 Fax: (0171) 323 6190
Phillips, Nigel G., MA Camb., PhD Lond.   Sr. Lectr.; Chair*
Other Staff: 1 Hon. Prof. Res. Assoc.; 1 Hon. Sr. Res. Assoc.
Research: Buddhism; economics and geography (agriculture, biogeography, poverty measurement, sustainable development); history (Burmese and Indonesian economies, Vietnam war); linguistics and traditional and modern literatures; music, art and archaeology (Buddhist art, Javanese music, remote sensing)

CONTACT OFFICERS

Academic affairs. School Secretary: Dabell, Frank L., BA York(UK)
Accommodation. Student Welfare Officer: Norman, Denise A., BA CNAA
Admissions (first degree). Deputy Registrar: Page, Nicholas J., BA S'ton.
Admissions (higher degree). Deputy Registrar: Radford, Pam, BA Lond.
Adult/continuing education. Pro-Director, Postgraduate Studies: King, Geoffrey R. D., MPhil Lond., PhD Lond.
Alumni. Alumni Relations Officer: Sexton, Maureen
Archives. Archivist: Seton, Rosemary E., BA Wales, MA Lond.
Careers. Careers Adviser: Smith, Fiona, MA Glas.
Computing services. Information Technology Manager: Villars, Chris, BA Birm.
Conferences/corporate hospitality. Conference Manager: Jones, Siân
Consultancy services. Head of Briefing Office: Thomas, Graham, MA Cant., MA Lond., MEd Wales
Credit transfer. Registrar: Harvey, Terry, BSc CNAA
Development/fund-raising. Head of Development Office: Brow, Richard, BA C'dia., MA Lond.

Distance education. Programme Manager, Centre for International Education in Economics: Davies, Julie A., BA Birm., MA Open(UK), MBA Kingston(UK)
Equal opportunities. Personnel Manager: Lee, Paul T., BA Open(UK)
Estates and buildings/works and services. Head of Estates and Services: Martin, Kenneth, MSc Sur.
Examinations. Assistant Registrar (Examinations): Dunn, Caroline, BA Wales
Finance. Director of Resources and Planning: Morley, John, BSc Leeds, MSc Lond.
General enquiries. School Secretary: Dabell, Frank L., BA York(UK)
Industrial liaison. Personnel Manager: Lee, Paul T., BA Open(UK)
International office. Registrar: Harvey, Terry, BSc CNAA
Language training for international students. Head, International Foundation Courses for Overseas Students: Yates, Susan E., BA Lond.
Ombudsperson. School Secretary: Dabell, Frank L., BA York(UK)
Personnel/human resources. Personnel Manager: Lee, Paul T., BA Open(UK)
Public relations, information and marketing. Director of External Relations: Coe, Jim
Publications. Research and Publications Manager: Daly, Martin J., MA Oxf.
Purchasing. Purchasing Manager: Spooner, Matthew C.
Quality assurance and accreditation. Registrar: Harvey, Terry, BSc CNAA
Research. Research and Publications: Daly, Martin J., MA Oxf.
Safety. Safety Officer: Timson, Ben†
Scholarships, awards, loans. Assistant Registrar: Goodman, Deirdre, BA Lond.
Schools liaison. Educational Liaison Officer: ......
Security. Head of Estates and Services: Martin, Kenneth, MSc Sur.
Staff development and training. Personnel Manager: Lee, Paul T., BA Open(UK)
Student welfare/counselling. Student Welfare Officer: Norman, Denise A., BA CNAA
Students from other countries. Registrar: Harvey, Terry, BSc CNAA
Students with disabilities. Student Welfare Officer: Norman, Denise A., BA CNAA
Women. Personnel Manager: Lee, Paul T., BA Open(UK)

[Information supplied by the institution as at 12 March 1998, and edited by the ACU]

SCHOOL OF PHARMACY

Founded 1842; incorporated by Royal Charter 1952

Postal Address: 29-39 Brunswick Square, London, England WC1N 1AX
Telephone: (0171) 753 5800 **Fax**: (0171) 278 0622 **E-mail**: postmaster@cua.ulsop.ac.uk
WWW: http://pck.ulsop.ac.uk

CHAIRMAN OF COUNCIL—Wilkins, Sir Graham, BSc, Hon. FRCP
DEAN*‡—Florence, Prof. A. T., CBE, BSc *Glas.*, PhD *Glas.*, DSc *Strath.*, FRSChem, FRSEd, FRPharmS
CLERK TO THE COUNCIL AND SECRETARY—Roberts, B. D., BA *Oxf.*
REGISTRAR—Stone, Margaret, BSc *Georgetown*, JD *Georgetown*
SCHOOL LIBRARIAN—Lisgarten, Linda, BA

GENERAL INFORMATION

History. The school was founded in 1842 by the Royal Pharmaceutical Society of Great Britain, and remained a college of the society until 1949. In 1925 it was admitted as a school of the University of London; in 1949 it became an independent grant-aided institution of the university and in 1952 it was granted a Royal Charter. It moved into its present building, in central London, in 1960.

Admission to first degree courses (see also United Kingdom Introduction). Through Universities and Colleges Admissions Service (UCAS). Entrance requirements: 3 General Certificate of Education (GCE) A levels, including chemistry and at least 1 further science subject. Other equivalent qualifications may be accepted. All applicants must demonstrate proficiency in the English language.

First Degrees (of University of London). MPharm: 4 years full-time.

Higher Degrees (of University of London). MSc, MPhil, PhD.

Applicants for admission to MSc must normally hold a first degree in pharmacy with at least second class honours. MPhil, PhD: a first degree in a relevant subject (not necessarily pharmacy) with at least second class honours.

MSc: 1 year full-time or 2 years part-time; MPhil, PhD: 3 years full-time or 5 years part-time.

Libraries. 500,000 volumes; 220 periodicals subscribed to.

Fees (annual). Undergraduate: £1000 (UK/EU students); £8970 (international students). Postgraduate: £2620 (UK/EU students); £8970 (international students).

Academic Awards (1997–98). Twenty awards to a total value of £9500.

Academic Year (1998–99). Three terms: 5 October–11 December; 11 January–19 March; 19 April–25 June.

Income (1996–97). Total, £8,700,000.

Statistics. Staff: 193 (131 academic, 62 administrative). Students: full-time 535 (203 men, 332 women); part-time 350 (87 men,

263 women); international 142 (41 men, 101 women); total 885.

ACADEMIC UNITS

Pharmaceutical and Biological Chemistry

Tel: (0171) 753 5883 *Fax*: (0171) 753 5909
Gibbons, W. A., BSc *Alta.*, MSc *Alta.*, PhD *Sheff.*   Prof.; Head*
Munday, M. R., MSc *Oxf.*, DPhil *Oxf.*   Sr. Lectr.
Nizetic, D., MD *Zagreb*, PhD *Belgrade*   Sr. Lectr.
Stephenson, F. Anne, MA MSc PhD   Prof.
Toth, I., CandSc *Bud.*, MSc PhD DSc   Reader

Pharmaceutics

Tel: (0171) 753 5870 *Fax*: (0171) 753 5942
Barber, N. D., BPharm PhD   Prof.
Bates, I. P., BPharm MSc   Sr. Lectr.
Buckton, G., BPharm PhD DSc, FRPharmS   Reader
Craig, D. Q. M., BPharm *Bath*, PhD   Sr. Lectr.
Newton, J. M., BPharm *Nott.*, PhD *Nott.*, DSc, FRPharmS   Prof.; Head*
Pinney, R. J., BPharm PhD, FRPharmS   Sr. Lectr.
Smith, Felicity J., BPharm MA PhD   Sr. Lectr.
Taylor, K. M. G., BPharm *Wales*, PhD *Wales*   Sr. Lectr.

Pharmacology

Tel: (0171) 753 5900 *Fax*: (0171) 753 5902
Constanti, A., BSc *CNAA*, PhD   Reader
Fowler, L. J., BSc *Wales*, PhD *Wales*   Sr. Lectr.
Main, I. H. M., MSc *Edin.*, PhD   Sr. Lectr.
Pearce, B., BSc *Open(UK)*, PhD *Open(UK)*   Sr. Lectr.
Simmonds, M. A., BPharm PhD DSc   Prof.
Smart, T. G., BPharm PhD   Wellcome Prof.; Head*
Starr, M. S., BPharm MSc PhD   Reader

SPECIAL CENTRES, ETC

Drug Delivery Research, Centre for

Tel: (0171) 753 5820 *Fax*: (0171) 753 5820
Gregoriadis, Prof. G., BSc PhD   Head*

Pharmacognosy, Centre for

Tel: (0171) 753 5846
Evans, F. J., BPharm PhD DSc, FRPharmS, FLS   Prof.; Head*

Polymer Therapeutics, Centre for

Tel: (0171) 753 5932
Duncan, Ruth, BSc *Liv.*, PhD *Keele*   Prof.

Toxicology, Centre for

Tel: (0171) 753 5811 *Fax*: (0171) 753 5811
Turton, J. A., BSc PhD   Sr. Lectr.

CONTACT OFFICERS

Academic affairs. Registrar: Stone, Margaret, BSc *Georgetown*, JD *Georgetown*
Academic affairs. Dean: Florence, Prof. A. T., CBE, BSc *Glas.*, PhD *Glas.*, DSc *Strath.*, FRSChem, FRSEd, FRPharmS
Accommodation. Registrar: Stone, Margaret, BSc *Georgetown*, JD *Georgetown*
Accommodation. Assistant Secretary: Gair, Nicholas P., BEd *CNAA*, MA
Admissions (first degree). Registrar: Stone, Margaret, BSc *Georgetown*, JD *Georgetown*
Admissions (higher degree). Registrar: Stone, Margaret, BSc *Georgetown*, JD *Georgetown*
Alumni. Clerk to the Council and Secretary: Roberts, B. D., BA *Oxf.*
Computing services. School Librarian: Lisgarten, Linda, BA
Consultancy services. Dean: Florence, Prof. A. T., CBE, BSc *Glas.*, PhD *Glas.*, DSc *Strath.*, FRSChem, FRSEd, FRPharmS
General enquiries. Clerk to the Council and Secretary: Roberts, B. D., BA *Oxf.*
Library (chief librarian). School Librarian: Lisgarten, Linda, BA
Safety. School Safety Officer: Marley, Derek
Scholarships, awards, loans. Registrar: Stone, Margaret, BSc *Georgetown*, JD *Georgetown*
Schools liaison. Briggs, Alan, BPharm PhD
Security. Assistant Secretary: Gair, Nicholas P., BEd *CNAA*, MA
Sport and recreation. Assistant Secretary: Gair, Nicholas P., BEd *CNAA*, MA
Staff development and training. Assistant Secretary: Gair, Nicholas P., BEd *CNAA*, MA
Student welfare/counselling. Assistant Secretary: Gair, Nicholas P., BEd *CNAA*, MA
Students from other countries. Registrar: Stone, Margaret, BSc *Georgetown*, JD *Georgetown*
Students with disabilities. Registrar: Stone, Margaret, BSc *Georgetown*, JD *Georgetown*
University press. Assistant Secretary: Gair, Nicholas P., BEd *CNAA*, MA

[*Information supplied by the institution as at 25 March 1998, and edited by the ACU*]

UNIVERSITY COLLEGE LONDON

Founded 1826; incorporated in the University of London 1907; a constituent college of the University from 1977

Associate Member of the Association of Commonwealth Universities

Postal Address: Gower Street, London, England WC1E 6BT
Telephone: (0171) 387 7050 **Fax**: (0171) 387 8057 **Cables**: University College London
WWW: http://www.ucl.ac.uk **E-mail formula**: initial.surname@ucl.ac.uk or firstname.surname@ucl.ac.uk

VISITOR—The Master of the Rolls (*ex officio*)
CHAIRMAN OF THE COLLEGE COUNCIL—Young of Graffham, Lord, LLB
VICE-CHAIRMAN OF THE COLLEGE COUNCIL—Hamilton, Sir James, KCB, MBE
TREASURER—Priestley, H. M., MA
PROVOST*—(until 31 March 1999) Roberts, Sir Derek, CBE, BSc *Manc.*, Hon. DSc *Bath*, Hon. DSc *Lough.*, Hon. DSc
   City(UK), Hon. DSc *Lanc.*, Hon. DSc *Manc.*, Hon. DSc *Salf.*, Hon. DSc *Essex*, Hon. DSc *Lond.*, Hon. DUniv *Open(UK)*,
   FIEE, FEng, FIP, FRS
PROVOST*—(from 1 April 1999) Llewellyn Smith, Prof. Christopher H., BA DPhil, Hon. DSc *Brist.*, Hon. DCien
   Granada, Hon. DSc *Shandong*, FRS, FAPS
VICE-PROVOST—Midwinter, Prof. John E., OBE, BSc PhD, FIEE, FEng, FRS
VICE-PROVOST (HEAD OF GRADUATE SCHOOL)—Jowell, Prof. Jeffrey L., QC, MA *Oxf.*, LLM *Harv.*, SJD *Harv.*
VICE-PROVOST—Bowles, David V., BA, FCA
VICE-PROVOST—Worton, Prof. Michael J., MA *Edin.*, PhD *Lond.*
VICE-PROVOST—Gallyer, Marilyn J., BA
VICE-PROVOST—Pattison, Prof. Sir John, BSc MA DM, FRCPath
PRO-PROVOST—Davies, Prof. Wendy, BA PhD, FBA, FSA, FRHistS
PRO-PROVOST—Treleaven, Prof. Philip C., BTech MSc PhD
PRO-PROVOST—Biscoe, Prof. Timothy J., MB BS BSc DSc, FRCP
PRO-PROVOST—Huggins, Alan K., MSc PhD
REGISTRAR—Butcher, Martin H., MA *Oxf.*, MLitt *Oxf.*
DIRECTOR OF LIBRARY SERVICES—Ayris, Paul, BA MA PhD

GENERAL INFORMATION

History. The college was founded in 1826, incorporated in the University of London in 1907, and became a constituent college of the university in 1977. The Institutes of Child Health, Neurology and Ophthalmology, and Royal Free Hospital School of Medicine (founded 1874) have all merged with the college. It is located in central London.

Admission to first degree courses (see also United Kingdom Introduction). Through Universities and Colleges Admissions Service (UCAS). Minimum requirements: passes in 2 subjects at General Certificate of Education (GCE) A level, or passes in 1 subject at A level and 2 at GCE advanced supplementary (AS) level, or passes in 4 subjects at GCE AS level. In addition all degree programmes require General Certificate of Secondary Education (GCSE) passes at grade C or above in mathematics and English language, and candidates need to show evidence of a broad general education. A range of international qualifications is accepted as equivalent to the qualifications listed above. International students must also satisfy the college's English language proficiency requirement.

First Degrees (of University of London).
BA, BEng, BSc, BSc(Econ), LLB, MB BS, MEng, MSci.

Most degrees are full-time and last 3 years. MEng, MSci, modern language degrees: 4 years; MB BS: 5 years. Part-time degree courses are at least twice as long as the corresponding full-time degree programmes.

Higher Degrees (of University of London). LLM, MA, MArch, MFA, MRes, MS, MSc, MPhil, PhD, DClinPsy, DEdPsy, DSc, DLit, LLD, MD.

Applicants for admission to taught master's degree courses should hold a first degree with first or second class honours from a UK university or an overseas qualification of an equivalent standard. Research degrees (MRes, MPhil, PhD, DClinPsy, DEdPsy): first degree with first or upper second class honours from a UK university, or master's degree, or an overseas qualification of an equivalent

standard. DSc, DLit, LLD: awarded on published work.

LLM, MA, MRes, MSc: normally 1 year full-time or 2 years part-time; MArch: 1 year full-time; MD, MPhil, MS, PhD: minimum 2 years full-time or equivalent part-time; DClinPsy, DEdPsy: 3 years full-time.

Libraries. Over 13,000,000 volumes; 6000 periodicals subscribed to. Special collections include: Barlow (Dante); Jeremy Bentham manuscripts; Graves (early science); James Joyce; Johnston Lavis (vulcanology); C. K. Ogden (language, linguistics, literature); George Orwell archive; Sir John Rotton (eighteenth-century literature, economics, politics, French, Italian); Whitley Stokes (Celtic).

Fees (1998–99, annual). Undergraduate (UK/EU): £1000. Postgraduate: (UK/EU) £2610; international students £8395–8795 (arts), £10,125–11,435 (sciences), £18,125 (clinical).

Academic Awards (1997–98). 65 awards for new students ranging in value from £200 to £18,000.

Academic Year (1998–99). Three terms: 28 September–18 December; 11 January–26 March; 26 April–11 June.

Income (1997–98). Total, £278,600,000.

Statistics. Staff: approximately 8000. Students: full-time 13,393 (6660 men, 6733 women); part-time 1622 (901 men, 721 women); international (non-EU) 2368; total 15,015.

FACULTIES/SCHOOLS

Arts
Dean: Worton, Prof. Michael J., MA *Edin.*, PhD *Lond.*

Built Environment
Dean: O'Sullivan, Prof. Patrick E., OBE, BSc *Leeds*, PhD *Durh.*, Hon. FRIBA

Clinical Sciences
Dean: Souhami, Prof. Robert L., MD, FRCP, FRCR

Engineering
Dean: Dowman, Prof. Ian, BSc PhD, FRICS

Laws
Dean: Oliver, Prof. A. Dawn H., MA *Camb.*, PhD *Camb.*

Life Sciences
Dean: Lieberman, Prof. A. Robert, BSc PhD DSc

Mathematical and Physical Sciences
Dean: Lord, Prof. Alan R., BSc *Hull*, PhD *Hull*, FGS

Social and Historical Sciences
Dean: Clout, Prof. Hugh D., DU *Paris*, BA MPhil PhD

ACADEMIC UNITS

Anatomy and Developmental Biology, see Medicine; and Royal Free Hospital School of Medicine

Ancient History, see Hist.

Anthropology
Aiello, Leslie C., MA *Calif.*, PhD   Prof.; Head*
Bender, M. Barbara, BA PhD   Reader
Burnham, Philip C., BA *Cornell*, MA *Calif.*, PhD   Prof.
Dunbar, Robin I. M., BA *Oxf.*, PhD *Brist.*   Visiting Prof.
Gledhill, John E., BA *Oxf.*, BLitt *Oxf.*   Reader
Harris, Rosemary L., BA *Belf.*, MA PhD   Reader
Homewood, Katherine, MA *Oxf.*, PhD   Prof.
Kapferer, Bruce, BA *Syd.*, PhD *Manc.*   Prof.
Last, D. Murray, BA *Camb.*, MA *Yale*, PhD *Nigeria*   Prof.
Littlewood, Roland M., BSc MB BS DPhil   Prof., Anthropology as Applied to Psychiatry
Miller, Daniel M. S., BA *Camb.*, PhD   Prof.
Morphy, Howard, BSc MPhil PhD   Prof.
Pinney, Christopher, BSc PhD   Sr. Lectr.
Redclift, E. S. Nanneke, BA *Sus.*, DPhil *Sus.*   Sr. Lectr.
Richards, Paul, BSc MA PhD   Prof.
Rowlands, Michael J. J., MB PhD   Prof.
Schieffelin, Edward L., PhD   Reader
Sommer, Volker, BSc PhD   Sr. Lectr.

Strickland, Simon S., PhD   Sr. Lectr.
Wallman, Sandra S., BSc PhD   Prof., Urban Change

Archaeology, Institute of

Ucko, Peter J., BA PhD   Prof.; Dir.*

Archaeo-Metallurgical Studies, Institute of

Bachmann, Hans G.-G., PhD   Visiting Prof.
Charles, James A., BSc MA ScD, FIM, FEng   Visiting Prof.
Rothenberg, Beno, MA PhD   Visiting Prof.

Conservation and Museum Science

Price, Clifford A., MA PhD, FRCS, FSA   Reader; Tutor
Pye, Elizabeth M., MA   Sr. Lectr.

Egyptology

Hassan, Fekri A., BSc MSc MA PhD   Petrie Prof.
Tait, W. John, MA PhD DPhil   Edwards Prof.

Greek and Roman Archaeology

Coldstream, J. N., MA, FBA, FSA   Visiting Prof.
Hassall, Mark W. C., MA Oxf., FSA   Reader, Roman Archaeology; Tutor
Johnston, Alan W., MA Oxf., DPhil Oxf., FSA   Reader
Reece, Richard M., DPhil Oxf., BSc, FSA   Reader
Wilkes, John J., PhD, FSA   Yates Prof., Greek and Roman Archaeology

Human Environment

Hillman, Gordon C., BSc   Reader
Hillson, Simon W., BSc Birm., PhD   Reader
Thomas, Ken D., PhD Liv., BSc   Reader

Materials and Data Science

Bachman, Hans G.-G., PhD   Visiting Prof.
Charles, James A., BSc MA ScD, FIM, FEng   Visiting Prof.
Orton, Clive R., MA Camb., FSA   Reader
Rothenberg, Beno, MA PhD   Visiting Prof.

Medieval Archaeology

Graham-Campbell, James A., MA PhD, FSA   Prof.
Welch, Martin G., MA DPhil, FSA   Sr. Lectr.
Wilson, Sir David, MA LittD DrPhil, FBA, FSA, FRHistS   Visiting Prof.

Prehistoric Archaeology

Bray, Warwick M., MA Camb., PhD Camb., FSA   Prof., Latin American Archaeology
Drewett, Peter L., BSc PhD, FSA   Reader
Glover, Ian C., BA PhD   Reader
Nandris, John G., MA Camb., PhD Camb., FSA   Sr. Lectr.
Tilley, Christopher Y., MA PhD   Prof.
Whitehouse, Ruth D., MA PhD, FSA   Reader; Tutor

Western Asiatic Archaeology

Crawford, Harriet, PhD, FSA   Sr. Lectr.
Herrman, Georgina, DPhil, FSA   Reader

Architecture, Building, Environmental Design and Planning, Bartlett School of

Atkinson, Adrian, MA PhD   Sr. Lectr., Devel. Planning Unit
Banister, David J., BA Nott., PhD Leeds   Prof., Transport Planning
Batty, Susan E., BA MSc PhD   Sr. Lectr.
Borden, Iain, BA MSc MA   Sr. Lectr.
Collins, Michael P., BA Nott., FRTPI   Sr. Lectr.
Cook, Peter F. C., BDA   Prof., Architecture
Edwards, Michael, MA Oxf., MPhil   Sr. Lectr.
Ellison, Michael   Visiting Prof.
Fiori, Jorge, BA MSc   Sr. Lectr.
Forty, J. Adrian, MA PhD   Sr. Lectr.; Res. Tutor
Gage, Stephen A.   Sr. Lectr.
Gyford, John E. B., MA Oxf., MSc(Econ)   Reader
Hall, Peter G., MA PhD   Prof., Planning
Hanson, Julienne M., MSc PhD   Reader

Harris, Nigel, BA Oxf., MPhil PhD   Prof., Development Planning
Hawley, Christine E.   Prof., Architecture Studies; Dir., Archit. Studies
Hillier, Bill R. G., MA Camb.   Prof., Architecture and Urban Morphology
Howes, Christopher K., MPhil Reading, BSc, FRICS   Visiting Prof.
Ive, Graham J., BA MA   Sr. Lectr.
Kincaid, David, BASc   Sr. Lectr.
Levy, Caren, MA   Sr. Lectr.
Malby, Clyde C., FRICS   Visiting Prof.
Mattingly, Michael J., BS Duke, AM Penn., MA   Sr. Lectr.
McAuslan, J. Patrick W. B.   Prof., Urban Management
Meikle, Sheilah F., BA MCD PhD   Sr. Lectr.
Mumtaz, Babar K., BSc Kumasi   Reader
Nazir, Pervaiz, BA MA   Sr. Lectr., Devel. Planning Unit
Nutt, Bev B., BA   Prof., Facility and Environment Management
O'Sullivan, Patrick E., OBE, BSc Leeds, PhD Durh., Hon. FRIBA   Haden-Pilkington Prof., Environmental Design and Engineering; Head*
Oreszczyn, Tadeusz, BSc PhD   Sr. Lectr.; Dir., Energy Des. Advice Scheme Centre
Penn, Alan, BSc MSc   Sr. Lectr.; Dir., Virtual Reality Centre
Pimenides, Frosso, BA MPhil   Sr. Lectr.
Ramirez, Ronaldo R.   Sr. Lectr.
Safier, Michael S., BSc(Econ)   Sr. Lectr.
Simmie, James M, MPhil S'ton., BSc(Econ) MPhil PhD   Reader
Sugden, Derek G., Hon. FRIBA   Visiting Prof.
Tabor, O. Philip, MA Camb., PhD Camb.   Sr. Lectr.
Tomalin, Christina, BSc MPhil   Sr. Lectr.
Wakely, Patrick I.   Prof., Urban Development; Dir., Devel. Planning Unit
Ware, Susan   Sr. Lectr.; Dir., Professl. Educnl. Services
Winch, Graham M., MA MSc   Sr. Lectr.
Woodward, Christopher H.   Banister Fletcher Sr. Lectr.
Young, Alan M., BSc Belf., PhD Camb.   Sr. Lectr.
Young, Barbara A., BA PhD   Dir., Development Planning

Archives, see Library, Archive, and Information Studies, Sch. of

Art

(Slade School of Fine Art)

Aiken, John C., BA   Prof.
Barlow, Phyllida   Reader
Bowen, James R., MFA   Sr. Lectr.
Brisley, Stuart, MA   Prof.
Cohen, Bernard   Slade Prof.; Head*
dos Santos, Bartolomeu   Prof.
Hepher, David, DFA   Prof.
Hilliard, John   Sr. Lectr.
Jaray, Tess   Reader
McLean, P. Bruce   Sr. Lectr.
Morris, Sharon M., MA   Sr. Lectr.
Newman, Michael O. J., MA PhD   Sr. Lectr.
Proud, David R., BA   Sr. Lectr.
Prowse, Philip, DFA   Sr. Lectr.
Volley, Jo   Sr. Lectr.

Art, History of

Bindman, David, MA PhD   Durning Lawrence Prof.; Head*
Boucher, Bruce A., AB Harv., BA Oxf., MA PhD   Reader
Davies, David B., BA   Reader
Fer, Briony A., BA PhD   Reader
Garb, Tamar, MA PhD   Reader
Gretton, Tom H., BA E.Anglia, PhD   Sr. Lectr.
Hemingway, Andrew F., BA Hull, MA E.Anglia, PhD   Reader
Weston, Helen D., BA Reading, MA   Sr. Lectr.
Wilson, Christopher, BA PhD   Reader

Astronomy, see Phys. and Astron.

Biochemistry, see Medicine; and Royal Free Hospital School of Medicine

Bioengineering, see Medicine (Med. Phys. and Bioengin.)

Biology

Berry, Robert J., MA PhD DSc, FRSEd, FLS   Prof., Genetics
Bodmer, Sir Walter, BA PhD, FRS   Visiting Prof.
Danpure, Christopher, BSc PhD   Prof.
Delhanty, Joy D. A., BSc PhD   Prof.
Edwards, Yvonne H., PhD   Prof.
Evans, Michael C. W., BSc Sheff., PhD Sheff.   Prof., Plant Chemistry
Fisher, Roderick C., MA Camb., PhD Camb., FLS   Sr. Lectr.
Flint, Anthony P. F., PhD DSc   Visiting Prof.
Goldsmith, F. Barrie, BSc Wales, PhD Wales   Sr. Lectr.
Hearn, John P., MSc PhD   Visiting Prof.
Hopkins, Colin R., BSc PhD   Prof., Molecular Cell Biology; Dir., MRC Lab.
Hyams, Jeremy S., BSc E.Anglia, PhD E.Anglia   Prof., Cell Biology; Head*
Jones, J. Steve, BSc Edin., PhD Edin.   Prof., Genetics
King, Conrad A., MSc PhD   Sr. Lectr.
Lister, Adrian M., MA PhD   Reader
Mallett, James, BA MSc PhD   Reader
Mole, Sara E., BA MA PhD   Sr. Lectr.
Mudge, Anne P., BSc AM PhD   Sr. Lectr.
Nugent, Jonathan H. A., BSc Liv., PhD Camb.   Reader; Tutor
Partridge, Linda, DPhil   Weldon Prof.
Preston, Terence M., BSc Exe.   Sr. Lectr.
Purton, Saul, BSc PhD   Sr. Lectr.
Raff, Martin C., MD CM McG., FRS   Prof.
Rich, Peter R., BSc PhD   Prof.
Richardson, William D., BSc Manc., PhD   Prof.
Robson, Elizabeth B., BSc Durh., PhD   Emer. Prof.
Roscoe, David H., MA Oxf., DPhil Oxf.   Sr. Lectr.; Tutor
Rowbury, Robin J., MA Oxf., DPhil Oxf., DSc, FIBiol   Prof., Microbiology
Smith, David G., BSc Reading, PhD Reading   Sr. Lectr.
Strange, Richard N., BSc PhD   Sr. Lectr.
Swallow, Dallas M., PhD   Prof.
Williams, Jeffrey G., BSc PhD   Jodrell Prof.
Wolfe, Jonathan, BA Camb., DPhil Oxf.   Reader
Wood, J. Brian, BSc Wales, MSc Durh., PhD Aberd.   Sr. Lectr.
Wood, John N., MSc PhD   Reader
Wotton, Roger S., MSc PhD   Sr. Lectr.

Chemistry

Anderson, J. Edgar, BSc Glas., PhD Glas., DSc   Sr. Lectr.
Bloodworth, A. John, PhD DSc   Reader
Bramwell, Steven T., BA DPhil   Sr. Lectr.
Clark, Robin J. H., MSc NZ, PhD DSc, FRSChem, FRS   Sir William Ramsay Prof.; Head*
Clary, David C., BSc PhD   Prof.
Craig, David P., MSc Syd., DSc, FRSChem, FRS   Visiting Prof.
Day, Peter, MA DPhil, FRS   Royal Institute Prof. Res. Fellow
Deeming, Anthony J., BSc Leeds, PhD Leeds, DSc, FRSChem   Prof.
Ewing, Michael B., BSc NE, PhD NE   Reader
Ganellin, C. Robin, PhD DSc, FRSChem, FRS   Smith Kline and French Prof.
Garratt, Peter J., BSc Brist., MA Camb., PhD Col., DSc   Prof.
Hale, Karl J., BSc PhD, FRSChem   Prof.
Hogart, Graeme, BSc PhD   Sr. Lectr.
Motherwell, William B., BSc PhD   Alexander Williamson Prof.
Parkin, Jim E., BSc PhD, FRSChem   Sr. Lectr.
Pearce, Frederick L., BSc PhD, FRSChem   Prof., Biology Chemistry
Price, Sally L., MA PhD, FRSChem   Reader
Price, Stephen D., MA DPhil   Sr. Lectr.
Roberts, Brian P., PhD DSc, FRSChem   Reader

Sella, Andrea, MSc DPhil   Sr. Lectr.
Thirunamachandran, Thuraiappah, BSc Ceyl., PhD, FRSChem   Reader
Tocher, Derek A., BSc Edin., PhD Edin.   Reader
Truter, Mary R., PhD DSc, FRSChem   Visiting Prof.
Walmsley, Stuart H., BSc PhD, FRSChem   Reader
Williams, David E., MSc PhD, FRSChem   Thomas Graham Prof.
Wrigglesworth, Roger, DPhil Sus.   Visiting Prof.

Computer Science

Arridge, Simon R., BA MA PhD   Reader
Buxton, Bernard F., BA MA PhD   Prof., Information Processing
Campbell, John A., MSc Adel., MA Camb., SM M.I.T., DPhil Oxf.   Prof.
Clack, Chris D., MA MSc   Sr. Lectr.
Crowcroft, John A., BA Camb., MSc PhD   Prof.
Finkelstein, Anthony C. W., BEng MSc PhD   Prof.
Knight, Graham J., BSc S'ton., MSc   Sr. Lectr.
Lesk, Michael, BA PhD   Visiting Prof.
Levene, Mark, PhD   Sr. Lectr.
McDonnell, Janet T., BSc MSc PhD   Sr. Lectr.
Rounce, Peter A., BSc Sus., PhD   Sr. Lectr.
Samet, Paul A., BSc Manc., PhD Camb., FIMA   Prof.
Sasse, Martina-Angela, MSc   Sr. Lectr.
Slater, Melvyn, BSc MA MSc   Prof.
Sorensen, Soren-Aksel, CandSc PhD   Sr. Lectr.
Treleaven, Philip C., BTech Brun., MSc Manc., PhD Manc.   Prof.
Washbrook, John, BSc Durh., MSc   Sr. Lectr.
Wilbur, Steve R., MSc, FIEE   Prof., Distributed Systems; Head*
Winder, Russel L., BSc Sus., PhD Liv.   Reader

Danish, see Scandinavian Studies

Dutch, see also Hist.

Fenoulhet, Jane K., BA MPhil   Sr. Lectr.; Head*
Hermans, Theo J., LicLett Ghent, MA Essex, PhD Warw.   Prof.
Salverda, Reinier, MA PhD   Prof., Dutch Language and Literature

Economic History, see Hist.

Economics

Aghion, Philippe, PhD   Prof.
Attanasio, Orazio, PhD   Prof.
Binmore, Ken, MSc PhD, FBA   Prof.
Blundell, Richard, BSc Brist., MSc   Prof.
Borgers, Tilman, PhD   Prof.
Carlin, Wendy J., BA(Econ) MPhil   Sr. Lectr.
Catephores, G., LLB Athens, MSc   Sr. Lectr.
Chick, Victoria, BS Calif., MA Calif.   Prof.
Machin, Stephen J., BA PhD   Prof.
Meghir, Costas H., MA Manc., PhD Manc.   Prof.
Pearce, D. W., MA Oxf.   Prof.
Pemberton, Malcolm, MA Camb., PhD Camb., MSc   Sr. Lectr.
Rau, Nicholas J., BA Oxf., BPhil Oxf.   Sr. Lectr.
Smith, Stephen, MA   Prof.; Head*
Swierzbwski, Joseph, PhD   Sr. Lectr.
Symons, James S. V., MSc Monash, PhD W.Aust.   Reader
Szroeter, Jerzy, BSc(Econ) MSc PhD   Sr. Lectr.
Ulph, David, MA BLitt   Prof.
Van Reenan, John, MA MSc PhD   Reader
Vaughan, Richard N., MSc PhD   Sr. Lectr.
Verry, Donald W., BA Well., MSc PhD   Sr. Lectr.

Egyptology, see under Archaeol., Inst. of

Engineering, Biochemical

Dunnill, Peter, PhD DSc, FIChemE, FRSChem, FEng   Prof.
Hoare, Michael, BSc(Eng) MSc PhD, FIChemE   Prof.; Head*
Lilly, Malcolm D., PhD DSc, FEng, FIChemE, FRS   Prof.
Shamlou, Parviz A., PhD   Sr. Lectr.

Titchener-Hooker, Nigel J., BSc Manc., PhD   Sr. Lectr.
Turner, Michael K., PhD   Prof.

Engineering, Chemical

Bogle, I. David L., PhD   Sr. Lectr.
Burgess, Anthony R., BSc PhD, FRSChem   Visiting Prof.; Sr. Lectr.
Elson, Tim P., BSc(Eng) PhD   Sr. Lectr.
Jones, Alan G., BSc Manc., PhD DSc(Eng), FIChemE   Prof.
Mahgerefteh, Haroun, BSc Leeds, MSc PhD   Sr. Lectr.
Norton, Christopher E., BEng McG., MSc Birm.   Sr. Lectr.
Yates, John G., BSc PhD DSc(Eng), FRSChem   Prof.; Head*

Engineering, Civil and Environmental

Allsop, Richard E., OBE, MA Camb., PhD DSc(Eng), FICE   Prof., Transport Studies
Bassett, Richard H., BSc PhD   Reader, Geomechanics
Bishop, Steven, MSc PhD   Reader
Chandler, Adrian M., BSc(Eng) PhD   Reader
Croll, James G. A., BE Cant., PhD Cant., FIStructE, FIMA   Chadwick Prof.; Head*
Domone, Peter L. J., BSc(Eng) PhD   Sr. Lectr.
Dunstan, Treve, BSc(Eng) PhD   Sr. Lectr.; Tutor
Evans, Andrew W., BA MSc PhD   Prof., Transport Safety
Eyre, John R., BA Brist., BSc Brist., PhD   Sr. Lectr.
Fitzpatrick, Caroline, PhD   Sr. Lectr.
Goodwin, Phillip B., PhD   Prof., Transport Policy
Grass, Anthony J., BSc(Eng) PhD   Prof., Fluid Mechanics
Gregory, John, BSc PhD, FRSChem   Prof., Water Chemistry
Heydecker, Benjamin G., BA Camb., PhD   Reader
Mackett, Roger L., BA Lanc., MSc Reading, PhD Leeds   Prof., Transport Studies
Morreau, Patrick   Visiting Prof.
Rainey, Rod C. T., MA MSc   Visiting Prof.
Simons, Richard R., BSc Manc., PhD   Sr. Lectr.
Stark, Jaroslav, BA PhD   Reader
Stevenson, David G., BSc PhD   Visiting Prof.
Thompson, J. Mike T., MA Camb., PhD Camb., ScD Camb., FIMA, FRS   Prof., Nonlinear Dynamics
Tyler, Nicholas A., MSc PhD   Sr. Lectr.
Yarimer, Errol, MSc Georgia I. T., PhD Lehigh   Sr. Lectr.

Engineering, Electronic and Electrical

Boyd, Ian W., BSc H.-W., PhD H.-W., FIEE, FIP   Prof.
Cole, Roy S., BSc PhD   Emer. Prof.
Davies, J. Brian, MA Camb., MSc PhD DSc(Eng), FEng, FIEE   Emer. Prof., Electrical Engineering
Fernandez, Frederico A., BSc Chile, PhD   Sr. Lectr.
Flanagan, Michael, PhD   Sr. Lectr.; STC Res. Fellow
French, Herbert A., BSc(Eng) PhD, FIEE, FIP, FEng   Visiting Prof.
Giblin, Roger A., BSc(Eng) PhD   Sr. Lectr.
Griffiths, Hugh D., MA Oxf., PhD   Prof.
Haigh, David, BSc Brist., PhD   Reader
Harris, Jeffrey, BA PhD, FIP   Reader; Dir., Device Res.
Jackman, Richard B., BSc PhD   Reader
Kirkby, Paul   Visiting Prof.
Mackintosh, Ian, BSc PhD, FIEE, FIP   Visiting Prof.
Midwinter, John E., OBE, BSc PhD, FIEE, FEng, FRS   Pender Prof.
Milne, K., OBE, BSc(Eng) PhD, FIEE, FEng   Visiting Prof.
O'Reilly, John J., PhD DSc, FEng, FIEE   Prof.; Head*
Pitt, Christopher W., MSc, FIEE, FIP   Prof., Electronic Engineering
Radmore, Paul M., BSc PhD   Sr. Lectr.
Seeds, Alwyn J., BSc PhD   Prof.

Stewart, William J., MA MSc, FEng, FIEE   Visiting Prof.
Taylor, John T., BSc PhD, FCA   Reader
Thornhill, Nina F., BA Oxf., MSc Oxf.   Sr. Lectr.
Todd, Christopher J., PhD   British Telecom Prof.
Voles, Roger   Visiting Prof.
Ward, Keith, FIEE   Visiting Prof.
Wilson, Michael G. F., BSc(Eng) PhD, FIEE   Emer. Prof.

Engineering, Environmental, see Engin., Civil and Environmental

Engineering, Geomatic

Atkinson, Keith B., BSc   Sr. Lectr.
Chapman, D. P., BSc   Sr. Lectr.
Cross, Paul A., BSc PhD, FRICS, FIMA, FRAS   Prof.; Head*
Dale, Peter F., MA PhD, FRICS   Prof.
Dowman, Ian J., BSc PhD, FRICS   Prof., Photogrammetry and Remote Sensing
Gates, John W. C., BSc MSc DSc, FIP   Visiting Prof.
Harley, Ian A., BSurv Qld., PhD, FRICS   Emer. Prof.
Iliffe, Jonathan C., BSc PhD   Sr. Lectr.
Muller, Jan-Peter A., BSc Sheff., MSc PhD   Prof., Image Understanding and Remote Sensing

Engineering, Mechanical

Andrews, David, BSc(Eng) MSc PhD   RCNC Prof., Naval Architecture
Broome, David R., BSc(Eng) PhD, FIMechE, FIMarE   Prof.
Brown, David T., BSc PhD
Collins, Roy, BSc Brist., PhD   Prof.
Corbishley, Terry J., MSc(Eng)   Visiting Prof.
Dewar, Mike E., BSc PhD   Sr. Lectr.
Dover, William D., PhD, FIMechE   Shell Prof.
Friedman, Norman, AB Col., PhD Col.   Visiting Prof.
Hambleton, Ken G., MA, FEng, FIEE, FRAeS   Prof.
Kirkpatrick, David, BSc MSc PhD   Sr. Lectr.
Lipman, Norman H., BSc Liv., PhD Liv.   Visiting Prof.
Lyons, Geoffrey J., BSc Nott., PhD, FIMechE   Sr. Lectr.; Tutor
Nightingale, Christopher J. E., MA Camb., PhD Wales, FIMarE   Sr. Lectr.; Tutor
Patel, Minoo H., BSc(Eng) PhD, FIMechE   Prof.; Head*
Patten, Thomas D., CBE, PhD DEng, FEng, FIMechE, FRSEd   Visiting Prof.
Suen, Kwok O., BSc(Eng) MSc PhD   Sr. Lectr.
Witz, Joel, BSc(Eng) PhD   Reader
Wu, Guoxiong, BSc(Eng) MSc PhD   Reader

English Language and Literature

Aarts, Bas, MA PhD Drs   Sr. Lectr.
Ashton, Rosemary D., MA Aberd., PhD Camb.   Prof.
Daniell, David J., MA Oxf., PhD   Emer. Prof.
Horne, F. Philip, BA Camb., PhD Camb.   Reader
Irvine, Susan E., DPhil   Sr. Lectr.
Jacobson, Dan, BA, FRSL   Emer. Prof.
Karlin, Danny R., BA Camb., PhD   Prof.
Mason, Michael Y., MA Oxf., BLitt Oxf.   Prof.
Miller, Karl, MA, FRSL   Emer. Prof.
Rennie, Neil, PhD   Reader
Sutherland, John A., MA PhD   Lord Northcliffe Prof.
Trotter, W. David, BA PhD   Quain Prof.; Head*
Walker, Keith, MA Well., PhD Camb.   Sr. Lectr.
Weis, Rene, BA PhD   Reader
Wintle, Sarah E., MPhil   Sr. Lectr.
Woudhuysen, Henry, BA Oxf., DPhil Oxf.   Prof.

French

Baker, Felicity R., BA Syd.   Reader; Tutor
Calder, Andrew, BA PhD   Reader
Hannoosh, Michele, PhD   Prof.
Leak, Andrew, BA PhD   Sr. Lectr.
Matthews, Timothy, PhD   Prof.; Head*

Mercer, Wendy S., MA PhD   Sr. Lectr.
Worton, Michael J., MA Edin., PhD Lond.   Prof.

Geography

Adams, John G. U., MA W.Ont., PhD   Prof.
Agnew, Clive T., BSc Newcastle(UK), PhD
  E.Anglia   Sr. Lectr.
Battarbee, Richard W., BA Ulster, DPhil
  Ulster   Prof.
Batty, J. Michael, BA PhD, FRTPI   Prof.
Burgess, Jacquelin A., BA Hull, PhD
  Hull   Reader
Clout, Hugh D., DU Paris, BA MPhil
  PhD   Prof.
Dennis, Richard J., MA Camb., PhD
  Camb.   Reader
Densham, Paul J., BA MSc PhD   Reader
Gilbert, Alan G., BSocSc Birm., PhD   Prof.
Harris, Raymond, BA PhD   Prof.; Dir., Remote
  Sensing
Harrison, Carolyn M., BSc PhD   Sr. Lectr.
Munton, Richard J. C., BA Birm., PhD
  Birm.   Prof.
O'Connor, Anthony M., MA Camb., PhD
  Camb.   Reader
Parry, Martin L., BA BSc PhD   Prof.
Salt, John, BA Liv., PhD Liv.   Prof.
Warren, Andrew, BSc Aberd., PhD Camb.   Prof.
Wood, Peter A., BSc Birm., PhD Birm.   Prof.;
  Head*

Geological Sciences

Audley-Charles, Michael, PhD   Emer. Prof.
Banner, Frederick T., PhD DSc   Visiting Prof.
Barker, John A., BSc PhD, FIMA   Prof.
Barnard, Tom, PhD DSc   Emer. Prof.
Bown, Paul R., BSc PhD   Sr. Lectr.
Burgess, William G., BA MSc PhD   Sr. Lectr.
Catlow, C. Richard A., DPhil   Royal Institution
  Prof. Res. Fellow
David, William J. F., MA DPhil   Visiting Prof.
Dottridge, N. Jane, BA MSc MA   Sr. Lectr.
Henderson, Paul, BSc DPhil   Visiting Prof.
Howarth, Richard J., PhD   Visiting Prof.
Hurford, Anthony J., BSc PhD   Reader; Tutor
Jones, E. J. W., PhD Camb., BSc   Reader
Jones, Glyn P., MSc   Visiting Prof.
Lord, Alan R., BSc Hull, PhD Hull, FGS   Prof.,
  Micropalaeontology
Martin, A. John, BSc PhD   Visiting Prof.
McArthur, John M., BSc PhD   Reader
McGuire, William J., BSc PhD   Visiting Prof.
Meredith, Philip G., BSc PhD   Prof.
Milsom, John, BSc PhD   Sr. Lectr.
Murrell, Stanley A. F., MA Camb., PhD
  Sheff.   Emer. Prof.
Pickering, Kevin T., BSc DPhil   Reader
Platt, John, BA PhD   Yates Goldsmid Prof.
Price, G. David, MA Camb., PhD Camb.   Prof.,
  Mineral Physics; Head*
Price, Neville J., PhD DSc, FGS   Visiting Prof.
Rawson, Peter F., BSc Hull, PhD Hull   Prof.
Ross, Nancy L., BS Virginia, MSc Br.Col.,
  PhD   Reader
Starmer, Ian C., BSc Nott., PhD Nott.   Sr. Lectr.;
  Tutor
Summerhayes, Colin P., DSc Well., BSc
  PhD   Visiting Prof.
Thurow, Jurgen W., PhD   Reader
Vita-Finzi, Claudio, MA Camb., PhD
  Camb.   Prof., Geography
Wood, Ian G., MA PhD   Sr. Lectr.

German

Fulbrook, Mary J. A., MA Camb., AM Harv.,
  PhD Harv.   Prof.; Head*
Larrett, William H. A., BA   Sr. Lectr.
McFarland, Timothy D., MA NZ   Sr. Lectr.
Stevens, Adrian K., MA Camb., PhD Camb.   Sr.
  Lectr.
Stillmark, Alexander, BA Camb., MA
  Camb.   Reader
Swales, Martin W., MA Camb., PhD
  Birm.   Prof.

Greek and Latin

Griffiths, Alan H., BA Camb.   Sr. Lectr.; Tutor
Hornblower, Simon, BA MA PhD   Sr. Lectr.
Ireland, Robert I., BA   Sr. Lectr.

Janko, Richard C. M., MA PhD   Prof., Greek
Maehler, Hernig G. T., PhD Hamburg,
  FBA   Prof., Papyrology
O'Daly, Gerard J. P., MA DPhil   Prof., Latin
Sharples, Robert W., MA Camb., PhD   Prof.;
  Head*

Hebrew and Jewish Studies

Berkowitz, Michael, PhD   Prof.
Geller, Markham J., AB Prin., MA Brandeis, PhD
  Brandeis   Prof.
Klier, John, MA PhD   Corob Reader; Head*
Rapoport Albert, Ada, BA PhD   Reader; Tutor
Weitzman, Michael P., BSc MA PhD   Reader

History

Abel, Christopher G., BA Oxf., DPhil Oxf.,
  MA   Sr. Lectr., Latin-American History
Burk, Kathleen, DPhil, FRHistS   Prof., Modern
  Contemporary History
Conway, Stephen R., BA PhD   Reader
Crawford, Michael H., MA Oxf., FBA   Prof.,
  Ancient History
d'Avray, David L., MA Camb., DPhil Oxf.   Prof.
Davies, Wendy E., BA Lond., PhD Lond., FBA,
  FSA, FRHistS   Prof.
French, David W., BA York(UK), PhD   Prof.;
  Head*
Harte, Negley B., BSc(Econ)   Sr. Lectr.,
  Economic History
Heather, Peter J., BA DPhil   Reader
Hoppit, Julian, MA Camb., PhD Camb.   Reader
Israel, Jonathan I., MA Camb., DPhil Oxf.,
  FBA   Prof., Dutch History and Institutions
Kuhrt, Amelie T. L., BA   Prof., Ancient
  History
Morgan, David A. L., MA Oxf.   Sr. Lectr.
North, John A., MA Oxf., DPhil Oxf.   Prof.
Rosen, Frederick, MA Syr., DPhil   Prof.
Tyacke, Nicholas R. N., MA Oxf., DPhil
  Oxf.   Reader
Van Bremen, Henrietta C., DrsLitt   Sr. Lectr.

Information Studies, see Library, Archive, and Information Studies, Sch. of

Italian

James, Prudence A., BA Syd., BPhil Oxf.,
  DottLett&Fil Florence   Sr. Lectr.
Lepschy, A. Laura M., MA Oxf., BLitt
  Oxf.   Prof.; Head*
Lindon, John M. A., MA Oxf.   Prof.
Tandello, Emmanuela, MPhil DottLing
  DPhil   Sr. Lectr.
Took, John F., BA Leeds, PhD Leeds   Reader

Jewish Studies, see Hebrew and Jewish Studies

Latin, see Greek and Latin

Latin-American Studies, see Spanish and Latin-American Studies

Laws

Austin, Rodney C., LLB Auck.   Sr. Lectr.
Barendt, Eric M., MA BCL   Goodman Prof.
Bindman, Geoffrey L., MA   Visiting Prof.
Burrows, Andrew S., BCL MA LLM   Prof.
Butler, William E., MA Johns H., PhD Johns H.,
  JD Harv., LLD   Prof., Comparative Law
Clarke, Alison C., BA Oxf.   Sr. Lectr.
Dennis, Ian H., MA Camb.   Prof., English Law
Dworkin, Ronald M., MA, FBA   Visiting Prof.,
  Legal Philosophy
Farrand, Julian T., LLM LLD   Visiting Prof.
Freeman, Michael D. A., LLM   Prof., English
  Law
Genders, Elaine, BSocSc MPhil   Reader,
  Criminology
Genn, Hazel G., BA LLB LLM   Prof.
Glasser, Cyril, LLM   Visiting Prof.
Gormley, Laurence W., MA MSc LLD   Visiting
  Prof.
Guest, Stephen F. D., BA Otago, LLB Otago, BLitt
  Oxf., PhD   Reader
Halson, D. Roger, LLB MLitt   Sr. Lectr.

Hepple, Bob A., QC, BA Witw., LLB Witw., LLB
  Camb., MA Camb., LLD Camb.   Visiting Prof.,
  English Law
Horspool, Margot, LLM   Sr. Lectr., European
  Legal Studies; Dir.
Jowell, Jeffrey L., MA Oxf., LLM Harv., SJD
  Harv.   Prof., Public Law
Kallaugher, John, BA JD   Visiting Prof.
Kohler, Paul, BA   Sr. Lectr.
Korah, Valentine, PhD   Emer. Prof.,
  Competition Law
Lester of Herne Hill, Lord, QC, BA
  LLM   Visiting Prof., Public Law
Lewis, Andrew D. E., MA Camb., LLB
  Camb.   Sr. Lectr.
Mandaraka-Sheppard, Aleka, LLB LLM PhD   Sr.
  Lectr.
Martin, Peter, LLB, FRAeS   Visiting Prof.,
  Aerospace Law
McKendrick, Ewan, LLB BCL MA   Prof.,
  English Law
Mendelson, Maurice H., MA Oxf., DPhil
  Oxf.   Prof., International Law
Michael, James R., BSc Ill., JD Wash., LLM   Sr.
  Lectr.
Nelken, David, MA Camb., PhD Camb.   Visiting
  Prof.
O'Keefe, David, BCL LLM DL   Prof., European
  Law
Oda, Hiroshi, LLD   Sir Ernest Satow Prof.
Oliver, A. Dawn H., MA Camb., PhD
  Camb.   Prof.; Head*
Palmer, Norman, BCL MA   Rowe and Maw
  Prof.
Penn, Graham A., LLB   Visiting Prof.
Pettet, Ben G., LLB   Sr. Lectr.
Rideout, Roger W., LLB PhD   Prof., Labour
  Law
Schofield, T. Philip, BA LLM PhD   Reader,
  History of Legal and Political Thought
Snyder, Francis F., BA Yale, JD Harv.   Visiting
  Prof.
Twining, William L., MA LLD JD   Quain
  Prof., Jurisprudence

Library, Archive, and Information Studies, School of

Alston, Robin C., MA PhD, Hon. FLA,
  FSA   Prof.
Danbury, Elizabeth A., BA   Sr. Lectr.
McIlwaine, John H. St. J., BA Oxf.   Sr. Lectr.;
  Tutor
McIlwaine, la C., BA PhD, FLA   Reader,
  Classification; Dir.*
Sayers, Jane E., BA Camb., MA Oxf., BLitt Oxf.,
  DPhil Oxf., LittD, FSA   Prof., Archive Studies
Thurston, Anne, BA Wash., PhD Cinc.   Reader

Linguistics, see Phonetics and Linguistics

Mathematics

Anderson, J. M., BSc Glas., PhD DSc   Prof.,
  Pure Mathematics
Ball, Keith, BA PhD   Prof.
Berger, Mitchell A., MA PhD   Reader
Bowles, Robert I., BSc PhD   Sr. Lectr.
Brown, Susan N., MA Oxf., DPhil Oxf.   Prof.
Haight, John A., BA PhD   Sr. Lectr.
Jansons, Kalvis M., MA Camb., PhD
  Camb.   Reader
Jayne, John E., AB Calif., MA Col., PhD Col.,
  DSc   Prof.
Johnson, Edward R., MSc Monash, PhD Monash,
  PhD Camb.   Prof.
Johnson, Francis E. A., BA Liv., PhD   Reader
Larman, David G., PhD DSc   Prof.; Head*
Leader, Imre, PhD   Reader
McMullen, Peter, MA Camb., PhD Birm.,
  DSc   Prof.
O'Neill, Michael E., MSc PhD   Prof.
Preiss, David, CSc RNDr   Astor Prof.
Seymour, Rob M., BA Camb., MSc Warw., PhD
  Warw.   Reader
Smith, Frank T., DPhil, FRS   Goldsmid Prof.
Stephenson, William, MA Camb., PhD   Sr.
  Lectr.; Tutor
Timoshin, Sergei N., PhD   Prof.

Medicine, see below

Medicine, Royal Free Hospital School of, see below

Microbiology, see Biol.

Norwegian, see Scandinavian Studies

Pharmacology, see Medicine, and Royal Free Hospital School of Medicine, below

Philosophy

Budd, Malcolm J., MA Camb., PhD Camb.   Prof.
Crane, Tim M., BA MA PhD   Reader; Tutor
Heinaman, Robert E., BA BPhil PhD   Reader
Horwich, Paul G., BA MA PhD   Prof.
Valberg, Jerry J., MA Chic., PhD Chic.   Sr. Lectr.; Tutor
Wolff, Jonathan, BA   Sr. Lectr.; Head*

Phonetics and Linguistics

Abberton, Evelyn R. M., BA PhD   Sr. Lectr.
Ashby, Michael G., BA MA   Sr. Lectr.
Black, Maria, BA   Sr. Lectr.
Brody, Michael, LèsL Paris VI, PhD   Reader
Fourcin, Adrian J., BSc(Eng) PhD   Emer. Prof.
Harris, John M., MA Edin., PhD Edin.   Reader
Hazan, Valerie, BSc MA PhD   Sr. Lectr.
Huckvale, Mark A., BSc PhD   Sr. Lectr.
Hudson, Richard A., BA Camb., PhD   Prof., Linguistics
Rosen, Stuart, MS PhD   Prof.
Smith, Neil V., MA Camb., PhD   Prof., Linguistics; Tutor
Wells, John C., BA Camb., MA PhD   Prof., Phonetics; Head*
Wilson, Deirdre S. M., BPhil PhD, FBA   Prof., Linguistics

Photogrammetry, see Engin., Geomatic

Physics and Astronomy, see also Space and Climate Phys.

Aylward, Alan, PhD   Sr. Lectr.
Barlow, Michael J., BSc PhD   Prof.
Bartley, John H., BSc Liv., PhD Liv.   Sr. Lectr.
Boksenberg, Alexander, CBE, BSc PhD, FRS   Visiting Prof.
Buckley-Golder, Ian M., DPhil   Visiting Prof.
Bullock, Fred W., BSc PhD, FIP   Prof., Physics; Tutor
Charlton, Michael, PhD   Reader
Coupland, Malcolm, BSc PhD   Sr. Lectr.
Cox, Stephen F. J., PhD   Visiting Prof.
Davis, Donald H., BSc PhD, FIP   Prof., Physics; Tutor
Drinkwater, Gaetana, PhD   Reader
Dworetsky, Michael M., BS Harv., MA Calif., PhD Calif.   Sr. Lectr.
Esten, Michael J., BSc PhD   Reader
Eyre, Brian L., CBE, FIM, FIP   Visiting Prof.
Finney, John L., PhD, FIP, FRSChem   Quain Prof.
Fountain, Terence J., BSc MPhil PhD   Reader
Furniss, Ian, PhD   Sr. Lectr.
Glencross, William M., BSc PhD   Reader
Guest, John E., MSc PhD   Prof., Planetary Science
Harries, John E., BSc Birm., PhD, FIP   Visiting Prof.
Hayns, Michael R., PhD, FIP, FIMechE   Visiting Prof.
Hilsum, Cyril, CBE, PhD, FRS   Visiting Prof.
Howarth, Ian D., BSc PhD   Prof.
Humberston, John W., BSc Manc., PhD   Reader
Imrie, Derek C., PhD, FIP   Visiting Prof.
Jones, Tegid W., BSc Birm., PhD Birm.   Prof.
Kalmus, George E., BSc PhD, FRS   Visiting Prof.
Manning, Geoffrey, CBE, PhD, FIP   Visiting Prof.
Martin, Brian R. C., BSc Birm., PhD, FIP   Prof., Physics; Head*
McEwen, Keith A., MA PhD   Prof.
McKenzie, John, MA Camb., PhD Camb.   Sr. Lectr.
McNally, Derek, MSc Belf., PhD   Sr. Lectr.

Miller, David J., MSc Manc., BSc PhD, FIP   Prof., Physics
Miller, Steven, MSc PhD   Sr. Lectr.
Moores, David L., BSc PhD   Reader
Newell, W. R., BSc Belf., PhD Belf., FIP   Reader, Physics
Peach, Gillian, BSc PhD, FIP   Reader
Smith, Anthony C. H., BSc PhD, FIP   Reader; Tutor
Somerville, William B., BSc Belf., PhD Belf.   Sr. Lectr.
Soper, Alan K., BSc PhD   Visiting Prof.
Stoneham, Arthur, PhD, FIP, FRS   Prof.
Storey, Peter J., BSc PhD   Reader
Tennyson, Jonathan, BA Camb., DPhil Sus.   Prof.
Tovee, David M., BSc PhD, FIP   Reader
Walker, David D., BSc PhD   Reader
Wilkin, Colin, MSc Birm., PhD Birm., FIP   Prof., Physics
Williams, David A., PhD DSc, FIP   Perren Prof.
Willis, Allan J., PhD   Prof.
Wilson, Sir Robert, CBE, BSc Newcastle(UK), PhD Edin., FIP, FRS   Emer. Prof.

Physiology, see Medicine, and Royal Free Hospital School of Medicine, below

Psychology

Atkinson, Janette, BSc PhD   Prof.
Audley, Robert J., BSc PhD, FBPsS   Emer. Prof.; Co-Dir., Psychoanalysis Unit
Barker, Christopher B., MA MSc PhD   Sr. Lectr., Clinical Pyschology
Braddick, Oliver, BSc PhD   Prof.; Head*
Bucci, Wilma S.   Visiting Prof.
Butterworth, Brian L., BA Oxf., MA Sus., PhD   Prof.
Curran, Helen, PhD   Sr. Lectr., Clinical Psychology
Einon, Dorothy F., PhD   Sr. Lectr.
Emde, Robert N.   Visiting Prof.
Fonagy, Peter, BSc PhD   Freud Memorial Prof.; Co-Dir., Psychoanalysis Unit
Fox, John P., BSc PhD   Visiting Prof.
Frederickson, Norah, MSc PhD   Sr. Lectr.
Frith, Chris, PhD   Visiting Prof.
Frith, Uta, PhD   Prof., Cognitive Development
Furnham, Adrian F., BA Natal, MA Oxf., DPhil Oxf., MSc(Econ) DSc DLitt   Prof.
Graham   Sr. Lectr.
Green, David W., BScEcon Wales, PhD   Sr. Lectr.
Gunter, Barrie, BSc MSc PhD   Visiting Prof.
Harvey, Nigel J. W., BSc Hull, DPhil Oxf.   Reader
Heyes, Cecilia M., BSc PhD   Reader
Howell, Peter, BSc Brad., PhD   Prof.
Jerison, Harry, PhD   Visiting Prof.
Johnston, Alan, BSc Aberd., DPhil York(UK)   Reader
Kachele, H.   Visiting Prof.
Karmiloff-Smith, Annette, PhD   Visiting Prof.
Long, John B., BA Camb., PhD Camb., BSc Hull   Prof., Cognitive Ergonomics
Lunt, Peter K., BSc DPhil   Sr. Lectr.
Mandler, George, PhD   Visiting Prof.
Mandler, Jean H., PhD   Visiting Prof.
McManus, I. Christopher, BA Birm., MB ChB Birm., PhD Camb., MD   Prof.
Monsen, J.   Sr. Lectr.
Morton, John, MA PhD   Visiting Prof.
Oakley, David A., PhD, FAPA, FBPsS   Sr. Lectr.
Pitstrang, Nancy E., MA PhD   Sr. Lectr., Clinical Psychology
Plotkin, Henry C., BSc Witw., PhD   Prof.
Rawles, Richard E., BSc   Sr. Lectr.
Reed, Phil, BSc DPhil PhD   Sr. Lectr.
Sandler, J., MA Cape Town, DSc Cape Town, MD Ley., Hon. FilDr Lund, PhD   Emer. Prof., Psychoanalysis
Shallice, Timothy J., BSc PhD   Prof.; Dir., Inst. of Cognitive Neurosci.
Shanks, David R., MA PhD   Reader
Ussher, Jane M., PhD   Sr. Lectr.
Vincent, Charles, BA Oxf., MPhil PhD   Sr. Lectr.

Waller, Glenn C., BA MClinPsychol DPhil   Sr. Lectr., Clinical Psychology
Woods, Robert, MSc   Prof., Clinical Psychology
Yardley, Lucy, MSc PhD   Sr. Lectr.

Public Policy, School of

Kennedy, Ian M., LLB LLM LLD   Prof., Health Law, Ethics and Policy
Peckham, Michael J.   Dir., Forum for Sci. and Health
Swanson, Timothy M., PhD   Prof., Environmental Policy
Wyatt, Jeremy C., BA MB BS DM   Sr. Lectr.

Royal Free Hospital School of Medicine, see below

Scandinavian Studies

Allan, Robert D. S., BA MLitt   Queen Alexandra Sr. Lectr., Danish; Tutor
Barnes, Michael P., MA   Prof.; Head*
Meulengracht Sorensen, Preben   Visiting Prof.
Munch-Petersen, Thomas, BA PhD   Sr. Lectr.
Perkins, Richard M., MA Oxf., DPhil Oxf.   Sr. Lectr., Norse Studies; Tutor
Walton, Stephen J., BA Glas., PhD   Reader, Norwegian

Science and Technology Studies

Miller, Arthur I., BS PhD   Prof.; Head*
Rattansi, Piyo M., MA Camb., BSc PhD   Emer. Prof.
Turney, Jon W., BSc MSc PhD   Sr. Lectr.

Space and Climate Physics

Branduardi-Raymont, Graziella, PhD   Reader
Coates, Andrew J., MSc DPhil   Reader; Royal Soc. Res. Fellow
Culhane, J. Leonard, MSc Trinity(Dub.), PhD, FIP, FRS   Prof., Physics; Head*; Dir., Mullard Space Sci. Lab.
Johnstone, Alan D., BA Oxf., PhD Alaska, MSc   Prof.
Mason, Keith O., PhD   Prof.
Norman, Keith, BSc   Sr. Lectr.
Wingham, Duncan, BSc PhD

Spanish and Latin-American Studies, see also Hist.

Garcia, Angel M., LicFil Madrid, BA BD PhD   Prof.; Head*
Henn, David F., MA PhD   Sr. Lectr.; Tutor
Wilson, E. Jason, BA   Reader; Tutor

Statistical Science

Brooks, Rodney J., BSc Brist., PhD   Sr. Lectr.
Dawid, A. Philip, MA Camb., ScD Camb.   Prof., Statistics
Farewell, Vern, PhD   Prof.
Fearn, Tom, BA MSc PhD   Reader
Galbraith, Rex F., MSc Otago   Reader
Isham, Valerie S., BSc PhD   Prof., Probability and Statistics; Head*
Senn, Stephen, BA MSc PhD   Prof.

Town Planning, see Archit., etc.

MEDICINE

University College London Medical School

Anatomy and Developmental Biology

Anderson, Patrick N., BSc PhD   Reader
Arnett, Timothy R., BSc PhD   Sr. Lectr.
Boyde, Alan, BDS PhD   Prof., Mineralised Tissue Biology
Browne, E. Janet, MSc PhD   Reader
Burnstock, Geoffrey, DSc Melb., PhD, FAA, FRS   Prof., Anatomy
Cook, Heremy E., BM BCh MA DPhil   Sr. Lectr.
Dean, M. Christopher, BDS PhD   Prof., Anatomy
Evans, Susan E., BSc PhD   Reader
Fitzgerald, Maria, PhD   Prof., Development Neurobiology
Frackowiak, Richard S. J., MA MD   Visiting Prof.
Fulton, Barbara P., PhD   Sr. Lectr.

Gabella, Giorgio, MD Turin, DSc   Prof.,
   Cytology
Gilula, N. B., MA Ill., PhD Calif.   Visiting Prof.
Glickstein, Mitchell, MA Chic., PhD
   Chic.   Emer. Prof., Neuroscience
Hall, James E., BSc PhD   Visiting Prof.
Holder, Nigel H. K., BSc PhD   Prof.; Head*
Jessen, Kristjan, MSc PhD   Prof.,
   Neurobiology
Jones, Sheila J., BDS PhD   Prof., Anatomy
Keating, Michael J., BSc MB BS PhD   Visiting
   Prof.
Lefford, Frances, MB BS PhD   Sr. Lectr.
Lieberman, A. Robert, BSc PhD DSc   Prof.,
   Anatomy
Martin, Paul, BSc PhD   Reader
Mirsky, Rhona, BA Camb., PhD   Prof.,
   Neurobiology
Morgan, Michael, MA PhD   Prof.
O'Higgins, Paul, BSc MB ChB PhD   Reader
O'Keefe, John, MA PhD, FRS   Prof., Cognitive
   Neuroscience
Parnavelas, John G., PhD Roch.   Prof.,
   Neuroanatomy
Raisman, G., DM Oxf., DPhil Oxf.   Visiting
   Prof.
Rosendaal, Martin, BA Oxf., BM BCh Oxf., MD
   Oxf., PhD   Sr. Lectr.
Rubin, Lee, BA PhD   Prof.; Dir., Eisai London
   Res. Lab.
Swann, Karl, BSc PhD   Reader
Tickle, Cheryll, MA PhD   Prof., Cellular
   Biology
Warner, Anne E., PhD, FRS   Royal Soc.
   Foulerton Res. Prof., Development Biology
Wolpert, Lewis, CBE, BSc PhD Hon. DSc,
   FIBiol, FRS   Prof., Biology as Applied to
   Medicine
Wood, John N., MSc PhD   Sr. Lectr.,
   Neurobiology
Yeo, Christopher, BSc PhD   Reader
Zeki, Semir M., BSc PhD, FRS   Prof.,
   Neurobiology

History of Medicine

Bynum, William F., MD PhD, FRCP   Prof.
Lawrence, Christopher, MB ChB MSc
   PhD   Reader
Neve, Michael, MA PhD   Sr. Lectr.
Nutton, Vivian, MA PhD   Prof.
Porter, Roy S., MA PhD   Prof.
Tansey, Tilly, BSc PhD   Sr. Lectr.
Wear, Andrew, BA MSc PhD   Sr. Lectr.

Bacteriology, see under Pathol., Div. of

Biochemistry and Molecular Biology

Bender, David A., BSc Birm., PhD   Sr. Lectr.
Brockes, Jeremy P., MA PhD, FRS   Prof.
Burlingme, Alma L., PhD   Prof.
Clark, John B., PhD DSc   Visiting Prof.
Coulson, William, BSc PhD, FRSChem   Sr.
   Lectr.
Cowan, Donald A., MSc Waik., DPhil
   Waik.   Sr. Lectr.; Tutor
Crompton, Martin, BSc PhD   Reader,
   Biochemistry
Cutler, Daniel F., PhD   Reader
Evan, Gerard I., BA PhD   Royal Society Napier
   Prof.
Garland, Peter B., MB BChir Camb., PhD
   Camb.   Visiting Prof.
Hall, Alan, BA PhD   Prof.
Hounsell, Elizabeth F., BSc PhD,
   FRSChem   Reader
Jat, Parmjit, BSc PhD   Reader
Marsh, Mark C. P., BSc PhD   Reader
Mowbray, John, BSc Edin., PhD Edin.   Reader;
   Tutor
Pearl, Laurence H., MSc PhD   Prof.
Piper, Peter W., BSc Brist., PhD Camb.   Reader
Saggerson, E. David, PhD DSc   Prof.,
   Biochemistry
Shephard, Elizabeth, MSc S.Af., PhD   Prof.,
   Molecular Biology
Swann, Peter F., MSc Birm., PhD   Prof.,
   Molecular Oncology
Thornton, Janet M., BSc PhD   Prof.,
   Biomolecular Structure

Ward, John M., BSc Brist., PhD Brist.   Sr. Lectr.
Waterfield, Mike D., BSc PhD, FRS, Hon.
   FRCPath   Courtauld Prof.; Head*

Bioengineering, see Med. Phys. and
Bioengin.

Child Health, Institute of

Tel: (0171) 242 9789 Fax: (0171) 831 0488

Ades, Anthony E., BSc Sus., MSc M.I.T., PhD
   M.I.T.   Reader
Atherton, David, MB MA, FRCP   Sr. Lectr.
Aynsley-Green, Al, MA Oxf., DPhil Oxf., MB BS,
   FRCP   Nuffield Prof.
Beach, David, BA MA PhD   Prof., Cancer
   Biology
Brickell, Paul, BA MA PhD   Prof.
Bull, Catherine, MB BChir Camb., FRCP   Sr.
   Lectr.
Callard, Robin E., MSc Auck., PhD Syd.   Prof.
Chessells, Judith M., MD, FRCP,
   FRCPath   Prof., Haematology and Oncology
Chitty, Lynn, MB BS BSc PhD   Sr. Lectr.
Clayton, Peter T., MA Camb., MB BChir
   Camb.   Reader
Connelly, Alan, BSc Glas., PhD   Sr. Lectr.
Copp, Andrew J., MA Oxf., DPhil Oxf., MB
   BS   Prof.
Costello, Anthony M. de L., MB BChir Camb.,
   MA Camb.   Reader
Cotter, Finbarr E., MB BS PhD   Reader
Deanfield, John, MB BChir MD, FRCP   Prof.
Dezateux, Carol A., MB BS   Sr. Lectr.
Dillon, Michael, FRCP   Sr. Lectr.
Fabre, John W., MB BS MMedSc PhD   Prof.,
   Paediatric Cardiology
Ferretti, Patrizia, DottBiol Pisa   Sr. Lectr.,
   Development Biology
Filteau, Suzanne M., BSc MSc PhD   Sr. Lectr.,
   CICH
Gadian, David G., BA Oxf., DPhil Oxf.   Rank
   Prof.
Gilbert, Ruth, MB ChB   Sr. Lectr.
Goldblatt, David, MB ChB Trinity(Dub.)   Sr.
   Lectr.
Goswami, Usha C., BA Oxf., DPhil   Prof.,
   Behavioural Sciences
Gustafsson, Kenth T., BSc PhD   Reader
Harris, Christopher M., MSc PhD   Sr. Lectr.
Hatch, David J., MB BS, FFARCS   Prof.
Haworth, S. Glennis, MB BS MD, FRCPath,
   FRCP   Prof.
Hislop, Alison A., BSc PhD   Sr. Lectr.
Johnson, Andrew W., BSc Nott., PhD   Sr.
   Lectr.
Jones, Richard W., BSc Edin., MB ChB Edin.,
   DPhil   Sr. Lectr.
Kinnon, Christine T., BSc Newcastle(UK),
   PhD   Reader
Kirkham, Fenella J., MB BChir MA   Sr. Lectr.,
   Neurosciences
Klein, Nigel J., BSc MB BS PhD   Sr. Lectr.,
   Immunobiology
Lawson, Margaret S. L., MSc PhD   Sr. Lectr.
Leonard, James V., MB BChir Camb., PhD,
   FRCP   Prof.
Levinsky, Roland J., BSc MD, FRCP   Hugh
   Greenwood Prof.; Dean*
Logan, G. Stuart, MB ChB Cape Town, MSc   Sr.
   Lectr.
Lucas, Alan, MB BChir MA MD, FRCP   Prof.,
   Nutrition
Malcolm, Susan, BA Oxf., PhD   Prof.
McGregor, Sally M., MB BS MD   Prof., CICH
Milla, Peter J., MB BS MSc, FRCP   Reader
Monk, Marilyn, MSc PhD   Prof.
Muller, David P. R., BSc PhD   Reader
Neville, Brian G. R., MB BS, FRCP   Prof.
Newell, Marie-Louise H. F., MSc PhD   Sr.
   Lectr.
Peckham, Catherine S., MD, FRCPath,
   FRCOG   Prof.
Pembrey, Marcus E., BSc MD BS, FRCP   Prof.
Pierro, Agostino, MD   Reader
Power, Christine, BA MSc PhD   Reader
Preece, Michael A., MD MSc, FRCP   Prof.,
   Child Health and Growth

Ransley, Philip G., MA Camb., MB BChir Camb.,
   FRCS   Sr. Lectr.
Reardon, William, MD   Sr. Lectr., Clinical
   Genetics
Risdon, R. Anthony, MD, FRCPath   Prof.,
   Histopathology
Roberts, Graham J., BDS MDS PhD,
   FDSRCS   Prof.
Roberts, Ian, MB BCh PhD   Sr. Lectr.
Scambler, Peter J., BSc Manc., MB ChB Manc.,
   MD Manc.   Prof.
Scrutton, David R., MSc   Sr. Lectr.
Skuse, David H., MB ChB Manc., FRCP,
   FRCPsych   Prof.
Smith, Isabel, FRCP   Sr. Lectr.
Sonksen, Patricia M., MB BS MD   Sr. Lectr.
Spitz, Lewis, MB ChB Pret., PhD Witw., FRCSEd,
   FRCS   Nuffield Prof., Paediatrics
Stocks, Janet, BSc PhD   Reader
Strobel, Stephan, MD Fran., PhD Edin.   Prof.
Sullivan, Keith R., MSc CNAA, BA PhD   Sr.
   Lectr.
Surtees, Robert A., BM BCh Oxf., MA Oxf.,
   PhD   Sr. Lectr.
Thorogood, Peter V., BSc PhD   Prof.,
   Development Biology
Todd-Pokropek, Andrew, PhD   Prof.
Tomkins, Andrew, MB BS, FRCP   Prof.,
   International Child Health
Turner, Malcolm W., BSc Birm., PhD Birm.,
   DSc(Med), FRSChem, FRCPath   Prof.,
   Molecular Immunology
Vargha-Khadem, Faraneh, MA PhD   Reader
Williams, Steve R., BA Oxf., DPhil Oxf.,
   MA   Reader
Winchester, Bryan G., BA Camb., MSc
   PhD   Prof.
Winter, Robin M., BSc MB BS, FRCP   Prof.
Wirz, Sheila, MEd PhD   Sr. Lectr.
Woo, Patricia, BSc MB BS PhD, FRCP   Prof.
Woolf, Adrian S., MA Camb., MB BS
   MD   Reader

Computerised Tomography

Shaw, Penelope J., MB BS, FRCR   Dir.*

Epidemiology and Public Health

Acheson, Sir Donald, MBE, MA DM, FRCP,
   FRCS, FRCOG   Chairman, International
   Centre for Health and Society
Brunner, Eric J., BSc MSc PhD   Sr. Lectr.
Bunker, John P., BA MD   Visiting Prof.
Chaturvedi, Nishi, MB BS MD MSc   Sr. Lectr.
Fuller, John H., MA Oxf., MB BS   Prof.
Gillespie, George M., BDS DDS MPH   Visiting
   Prof.
Jarvis, Martin J., BA MA MPhil   Reader,
   Health Psychology
Marcenes, Wagner S., BDS MSc PhD   Sr. Lectr.
Marmot, Michael G., BSc Syd., MB BS Syd., PhD
   Calif.   Prof.; Head*
McCarthy, Mark, MB BChir MA MSc PhD,
   FRCP   Prof., Public Health
Russell, Michael A., BM BCh MA, FRCP   Prof.,
   Addiction
Sheiham, Aubrey, BDS Witw., PhD   Prof.,
   Dental Public Health
Shipley, Martin, BA MSc   Sr. Lectr.
Stansfeld, Stephen, MB BS PhD   Reader
Sutton, Stephen R., BA BSc PhD   Reader,
   Social/Health Psychology
Wadsworth, Michael, BA MPhil PhD   Visiting
   Prof.
Wardle, Jane F., BA MPhil PhD   Prof.
Watt, Richard G., BDS MSc PhD   Sr. Lectr.

Haematology

Cline, Martin, MD   Visiting Prof.
Devereux, Stephen, PhD   Sr. Lectr.
Khwaja, Asim, MB BS MD   Sr. Lectr.
Linch, David C., BA Camb., MB BChir Camb.,
   FRCP   Prof., Clinical Haematology; Head*
Machin, Samuel J., MB ChB Sheff., FRCP,
   FRCPath   Prof.
Mackie, Ian J., BSc PhD   Sr. Lectr.
Mackinnon, Stephen, MB ChB MD   Sr. Lectr.
Porter, John B., BA Camb., MB BChir
   Camb.   Reader
Thomas, N. Shaun, BSc PhD   Sr. Lectr.

Hepatology, Institute of

Bertoletti, Antonio   Sr. Lectr.
Naoumov, Nikolai V., MD DSc   Sr. Lectr.
Skouteris, George   Sr. Lectr.
Vergani, Diego, MD PhD, FRCP   Richard Cristin Prof.
Williams, Roger S., MD, FRCP, FRCS, FRCPEd, FRACP, FACP   Prof.; Dir.*

History of Medicine, see under Anat. and Devel. Biol.

HIV Clinical Trials Centre

Medical Research Council

Darbyshire, Janet H., OBE, MB ChB MSc, FRCP   Prof.; Head*
Gibb, Diana M., MB ChB MD MSc   Sr. Lectr.
McCormack, Sheena M. G., MB BS   Sr. Lectr.

Human Communication Science

Bryan, Karen L., BSc PhD   Sr. Lectr.
Campbell, Ruth, BA PhD   Prof.
Donlan, Christopher, BA MSc PhD   Sr. Lectr.
Kersner, Myra, MSc   Sr. Lectr.
Maxim, Jane E., MA PhD   Sr. Lectr.
Parker, Ann C.   Sr. Lectr.
Stackhouse, R. Joy, BSc PhD   Reader
Well, William H. G., BA DPhil   Prof.; Head*
Wright, Jannet A., MA PhD

Immunology, see under Pathol., Div. of

Laryngology and Otology, Institute of, see also Oto-Laryngol., Ferens Inst. of

Dodson, Hilary C., BSc PhD   Sr. Lectr.
Forge, Andrew, MSc PhD   Reader
Hazell, Jonathan, MB BChir, FRCS   Sr. Lectr.
Howard, David J., BSc MB BS, FRCS, FRCSEd   Sr. Lectr.
Kemp, David T., BSc PhD   Prof., Biophysics
Lund, Valerie J., MB BS MS, FRCS, FRCSEd   Prof., Rhinology
Luxon, Linda, MB BS, FRCP   Duphar Prof., Audiological Medicine
Prasher, Deepak, PhD   Reader
Pye, Ade, BSc PhD   Sr. Lectr.
Raglan, Ewa, FRCS   Sr. Lectr.
Wright, Anthony, BA Camb., DM Oxf., FRCSEd   Prof.; Dir.*

Medical Physics and Bioengineering

Blackwell, Roland, BSc MSc, FIP, FIEE   Visiting Prof.
Cope, Mark, BSc(Eng) PhD   Sr. Lectr.
Delpy, David T., BSc DSc   Hamamatsu Prof.; Head*
Gadian, David, BA DPhil   Visiting Prof.
Linney, Alf, BSc PhD   Reader
Moss, James, BDS PhD   Visiting Prof.
Ordidge, Roger J., BSc PhD   Joel Prof.
Speller, Robert D., BSc PhD   Reader
Todd-Pokropek, Andrew, BA MPhil   Prof.

Medicine

Betteridge, D. John, BSc MD PhD, FRCP   Prof.
Brenton, David, MD, FRCP   Reader
Brook, Charles G. D., MA Camb., MD Camb., FRCP   Prof., Paediatric Endocrinology
Conway, Gerard S., MB BS   Sr. Lectr.
Coppack, Simon W., MB BS, FRCP   Reader
Dowd, Pauline, BSc MD, FRCP   Prof.
Earle, Kenneth, MB BS   Sr. Lectr.
Edwards, Jonathan, MD, FRCP   Prof.
Fine, Leon G., MB ChB, FRCP, FACP, FRCPGlas   Prof.; Head*
Gillams, Alison R., MB ChB, FRCP   Sr. Lectr.
Groves, Richard W.   Sr. Lectr.
Hindmarsh, Peter C., MB BS, FRCP   Reader
Horton, Michael A., BSc MB BS, FRCPath   Prof.
Humphries, Steve E., BSc PhD   Prof.
Isenberg, David A., MD, FRCP   ARC Diamond Jubilee Prof.
Jacobs, Howard S., MD Camb., FRCP, FRCOG   Prof., Reproductive Endocrinology
Kitamura, Masanori, MD PhD   Reader
Laurent, Geoff, BSc PhD   Prof.
Lees, William R., MB BS, FRCR, FRACR   Prof.

MacAllister, Raymond J., BA MB BS MD   Sr. Lectr.
Malone-Lee, James G., MB BS MD, FRCP   Barlow Prof.
McAnulty, Robin J., BSc PhD   Sr. Lectr.
McEwan, Jean R., BSc MB ChB PhD, FRCP   Sr. Lectr.
McLean, Andre E. M., BM BCh Oxf., PhD, FRCPath   Emer. Prof.
Norman, Jill T., BSc PhD   Sr. Lectr.
O'Riordan, Jeffrey L. H., MA Oxf., BSc Oxf., DM Oxf., DSc, FRCP   Emer. Prof., Metabolic Medicine
Owens, Christopher W. I., BSc Wales, MB BS PhD, FRCP   Sr. Lectr.
Peck, Anthony W., BSc MB BS PhD, FRCP   Sr. Lectr.
Prelevic, Gordana, MD MSc DSc   Sr. Lectr.
Prichard, Brian N. C., CBE, MSc MB BS, FRCP   Emer. Prof.
Segal, Anthony W., MB ChB Cape Town, MD Cape Town, PhD DSc, FRCP   Charles Dent Prof.
Singer, Mervyn, MB BS MD   Sr. Lectr.
Spiro, Stephen, BSc MB ChB MD, FRCP   Prof., Respiratory Medicine
Stewart, Gordon W., BSc MB ChB MD   Sr. Lectr.
Taggart, Peter, MD, FRCP   Reader
Talmud, Philippa, BSc PhD   Reader
Unwin, Robert, BM PhD, FRCP   Reader
Vallance, Patrick, BSc MB BS MD   Prof., Clinical Pharmacology
Winska-Wiloch, Halina, MB BS   Sr. Lectr.
Yellon, Derek M., PhD DSc   Prof.
Yudkin, John S., BA Camb., MB BChir Camb., FRCP   Prof.
Zumla, Ali, MB ChB PhD   Reader

Molecular Cell Biology, Laboratory in

Medical Research Council

Hopkins, Colin R., BSc PhD   Prof.; Dir.*
Moss, Stephen J., PhD   Reader, Pharmacology and Molecular Cell Biology

Molecular Endocrinology

Ekins, Roger P., MA Camb., PhD   Prof.; Head*

Neurological Studies, Reta Lila Weston Institute of

Allt, Gerry, PhD, FRCPath   Sr. Lectr.
Harrison, Michael J. G., MA Oxf., DM Oxf., FRCP   Prof., Clinical Neurology; Francis and Renee Hock Dir.*
Lees, Andrew J., MD, FRCP   Sr. Lectr.
Paley, Martyn N., BSc PhD   Sr. Lectr.

Neurology, Institute of

Tel: (0171) 837 3611 Fax: (0171) 278 5069

Bhatia, K. P., MB BS Bom., MD Bom., DM Bom.   Sr. Lectr.
Bostock, H., BA MSc PhD   Prof., Neurophysiology
Branston, N. M., BSc Edin., MS Cornell, PhD Case W.Reserve   Reader, Neurophysiology
Brooks, D. J., BA Oxf., DPhil Oxf., MD   Prof.
Clark, J. B., PhD DSc   Prof., Neurochemistry
Cuzner, M. Louise, PhD DSc   Prof., Neurochemistry
Daniel, S. E., BSc MD   Sr. Lectr.
Darling, J. L., BSc Kent, MSc Reading, PhD   Sr. Lectr., Neuro-Oncology
Dolan, R. J., MD, FRCPsych   Prof.
Duncan, John S., MA Oxf., DM Oxf.   Reader
Fish, D. R., MA Camb., MD   Reader
Fowler, Clare J., MB BS MSc   Sr. Lectr.
Frackowiak, Richard S., MA Camb., MD Camb., BChir, FRCP   Prof.
Friston, K. J., MB BS MA   Reader
Frith, C. D., MA Camb., PhD   Prof., Neuropsychology
Goadsby, D. J., BMedSc MD PhD, FRACP   Reader
Hall, Christine, BSc PhD   Sr. Lectr.
Hanna, M. G., BSc Manc., MB ChB Manc.   Sr. Lectr.
Jaeger, H.-R., MD Freib., FRCR   Sr. Lectr.

Kirkwood, P. A., BSc(Eng) MSc PhD   Sr. Lectr., Neurophysiology
Kitchen, N. D., BSc MB BChir, FRCS   Sr. Lectr.
Kullmann, D. M., MA Oxf., DPhil Oxf., MB BS   Sr. Lectr.
Land, J. M., BSc BM BCh PhD   Sr. Lectr.
Landon, D. N., BSc MB BS   Prof., Neurocytology
Lemon, R. N., BSc Sheff., PhD Sheff.   Prof., Neurophysiology
Lim, L., BSc Sing., PhD DSc   Prof., Neurochemistry
Marsden, C. D., MB BS DSc, FRCP, FRS   Prof.; Dean*
Mathias, C. J., MB BS B'lore., DPhil Oxf., FRCP   Prof.†
Miller, D. H., MD, FRACP   Prof.
Palmer, J. D., MB BS, FRCS   Sr. Lectr., Surgical Neurology
Patsalos, P. N., BSc Reading, MSc PhD   Sr. Lectr.
Price, Catherine J., BSc PhD   Sr. Lectr.
Pullen, A., BSc PhD   Sr. Lectr., Neurophysiology
Quinn, N. P., MA Camb., MD Camb.   Prof.
Revesz, T., MD Semmelweis   Sr. Lectr.
Ron, Maria, MPhil PhD, FRCPsych   Prof., Neuropsychiatry
Rossor, M. N., MA MD   Sr. Lectr.
Scaravilli, F., MD Padua, PhD, FRCPath   Prof., Neuropathology
Schapira, A. H. V., MD DSc, FRCP   Prof.†
Shorvon, S., MA MD, FRCP   Prof.
Thom, Maria, BSc MB BS   Sr. Lectr.
Thomas, D. G. T., MA Camb., MB BChir Camb., FRCSEd, FRCPGlas   Prof., Neurosurgery
Thomas, D. J., MA MD, FRCP   Sr. Lectr.
Thompson, A. J., MD, FRCP   Prof., Neurorehabilitation
Thompson, E. J., BS Buffalo, MD Roch., PhD Roch., FRCPath   Prof., Clinical Neurochemistry
Tofts, P. S., BA Oxf., DPhil Sus.   Reader
Trimble, M. R., BSc Birm., MD, FRCP, FRCPsych   Prof., Behavioural Neurology
Turner, R., BA Cornell, PhD S.Fraser   Prof., Physics related to Imaging
Wood, N. W., MB ChB PhD   Sr. Lectr.

Nuclear Medicine

Bomanji, Jamshed B., MB BS MSc PhD   Sr. Lectr.
Campos-Costa, Durval, MD MSc PhD   Sr. Lectr.; Hon. Consultant Physician
Ell, Peter J., MSc MD PhD, FRCR   Prof.; Head*
Jarritt, Peter H., BSc PhD   Sr. Lectr.

Obstetrics and Gynaecology

Adinolfi, Matteo   Visiting Prof.
Craft, Ian, MB BS, FRCS   Visiting Prof.
Dawes, Geoffrey, BM BCh   Visiting Prof.
Guillebaud, John, MA Camb., MB BChir Camb., FRCS, FRCOG   Prof.
Hanson, Mark, MA DPhil   Prof., Fetal and Neonatal Physiology
Jauniaux, Eric, MD PhD   Sr. Lectr.
Katz, Maurice, MB ChB CapeT., FRCP   Sr. Lectr.
Kingdom, John C. P., MB BCh MD   Sr. Lectr.
Lachelin, Gillian C. L., MA Camb., MD BChir Camb., FRCOG   Reader
Morgan, Heulwen, MB BCh Wales, FRCOG   Sr. Lectr.
Noble, Ray, BSc PhD   Sr. Lectr.
Rodeck, Charles H., BSc MB BS, FRCOG, FRCPath   Prof.; Head*
Singer, Albert, MB BS Syd., PhD Syd., DPhil Oxf., FRCOG   Prof.
Ward, Richard H. T., MB BChir Camb., FRCOG   Sr. Lectr.

Oncology

Begent, Richard H., MB BS MD, FRCP   Ronald Raven Prof.; Head*
Berry, Roger E., DPhil, FRCP, Hon. FRCR   Visiting Prof.
Beverley, Peter C. L., BSc MB BS DSc   Prof., Tumour Immunology; Head, ICRF Tumour Immunol. Unit

Cassoni, Anna M., FRCR   Sr. Lectr.
Denekamp, Juliana, PhD DSc   Visiting Prof.
Dische, Stanley, MD, FRCR   Visiting Prof.
Fallowfield, Lesley, BSc DPhil   Prof.
Hartley, John A., BSc PhD   Prof.
Ledermann, Jonathan A., BSc MB BS,
   FRCP   Reader
Nicholson, Paul W., BSc PhD   Sr. Lectr.,
   Medical Physics
Saunders, Michele, MB BS MD, FRCR   Prof.
Souhami, Robert L., MD, FRCP, FRCR   Prof.
Vaughan Hudson, Gillian N., MB BS   Sr. Lectr.
Waterfield, Mike D., PhD, FRS,
   FRCPath   Visiting Prof.

Ophthalmology, Institute of

Arden, G. B., BSc PhD MB BS   Prof.,
   Neurophysiology
Bhattacharya, Shom S., BSc Bom., MSc
   Newcastle(UK), PhD Newcastle(UK)   Sembal
   Prof., Experimental Ophthalmology
Bird, Alan C., MD, FRCS   Prof., Clinical
   Ophthalmology
Bowmaker, J. K., BSc PhD   Prof., Visual
   Science
Cree, Ian A., PhD   Sr. Lectr.
Foster, Allen, MB BS Birm., FRCS   Sr. Lectr.
Greenwood, John, BSc PhD   Sr. Lectr.
Hunt, David M., BSc Sheff., PhD Sheff.   Reader
Jay, Marcelle R., BSc MPhil PhD   Sr. Lectr.
Jeffery, Glen, BSc Oxf., DPhil Oxf.   Sr. Lectr.
Johnson, Gordon J., MA Camb., MD Camb.,
   FRCSCan   Rothes Prof., Preventative
   Ophthalmology
Lightman, Susan L., MB BS PhD   Prof.,
   Clinical Ophthalmology
Lund, Jennifer S., BSc PhD   Prof., Visual
   Neurobiology
Lund, Raymond D., BSc PhD   Duke Elder Prof.
Luthert, Philip J., BSc MB BS   Prof.,
   Neuropathology
McDonald, M. I., MB ChB NZ, BMedSc NZ,
   PhD NZ, FRCP, FRACP   Prof.†, Clinical
   Neurology
Minassian, D., MB BS, FRCS   Sr. Lectr.
Minassian, Darwin, MB BS MSc, FRCS   Sr.
   Lectr.
Morgan, Michael J., MA PhD   Prof.
Salt, T. E., BSc Birm., PhD Birm.   Reader
Sillito, Adam M., BSc Birm., PhD Birm.   Prof.;
   Head*
Warren, Martin J., BSc PhD   Sr. Lectr.
Wormald, Richard P.   Sr. Lectr.

Orthopaedics, Institute of

Ali, Syed Y., PhD   Emer. Prof., Biochemistry
   of Connective Tissues
Bentley, Prof. George, ChM Sheff.,
   FRCS   Tutor; Dir.*
Blunn, Gordon, PhD   Sr. Lectr.
Ferguson-Pell, Martin W., BSc PhD   ASPIRE
   Prof., Neuromuscular Restoration and
   Rehabilitation
Goodship, Allen W., BVSc PhD   Prof.,
   Orthopaedic Sciences
Pringle, Jean A. S., MB ChB Glas.   Sr. Lectr.
Seetulsingh, Dishan, MB ChB, FRCS   Sr. Lectr.
Stamp, Trevor C. B., MD MSc, FRCP   Sr. Lectr.
Walker, Peter S., PhD Leeds   Prof.
Williams, Andrew M., BM MS, FRCS   Sr.
   Lectr.

Oto-Laryngology, Ferens Institute of, see
also Laryngol. and Otol., Inst. of
Vacant Posts: Dir.*

Paediatrics

Bantock, Helen M. E., MB BS   Sr. Lectr.
Brook, Charles G. D., MA Camb., MD Camb.,
   FRCP   Prof., Paediatric Endocrinology
Chung, Eddie M. K., MB ChB   Sr. Lectr.
Gardiner, R. Mark, MB BChir MD,
   FRCP   Prof.; Head*
Hindmarsh, P. R. C., MB BS, FRCP   Sr. Lectr.;
   Dir., Kabivitrum Growth Unit
O'Rawe, Angela, MB BS MD   Reader
Reynolds, E. Osmund R., CBE, BSc MD, FRCP,
   FRCOG, FRS   Emer. Prof., Neonatal
   Paediatrics

Wyatt, John S., BSc MB BS   Prof.

Pathology

Bacteriology

Donoghue, Helen D., BSc PhD   Sr. Lectr.
Holton, John M., BSc Edin., MB ChB Edin., PhD
   Kent   Sr. Lectr.
Pattison, John R., BSc Oxf., MA Oxf., DM Oxf.,
   FRCPath   Prof.
Rook, Graham A. W., BA MD   Prof.,
   Microbiology
Stanford, John L., MD   Prof.; Head*

Histopathology

Benjamin, Elizabeth, MB BS, FRCPath   Sr.
   Lectr.
Gallimore, Andrew P., BSc MB BS   Sr. Lectr.
Griffiths, Meryl, MB BS, FRCPath, FRCPA   Sr.
   Lectr.
Isaacson, Peter G., MB ChB CapeT., DM S'ton.,
   DSc, FRCPath   Prof., Morbid Anatomy;
   Head*
Kocjan, Gabriela, MB BS   Sr. Lectr.
Lakhani, Suni, MB BS   Sr. Lectr.
Pan, Lang-Xing X., MB PhD   Sr. Lectr.
Pezzella, Francesco, MD   Sr. Lectr.

Immunology

Brostoff, Jonathan, MA Oxf., DM Oxf., DSc,
   FRCP, FRCPath   Prof., Allergy and
   Environmental Health
Chain, Benjamin M., BA PhD   Prof.; Head*
Collins, Mary K. L., MA PhD   Prof.,
   Immunology
Delves, Peter J., MSc PhD   Sr. Lectr.
Katz, David R., MB ChB PhD, FRCPath   Prof.
Lund, Torben, MSc PhD   Reader, Immunology
Lydyard, Peter M., BSc PhD   Prof.
Playfair, John H. L., MB BChir Camb., PhD
   DSc   Emer. Prof.

Molecular Pathology

Batle, A. M., PhD   Visiting Prof.
Brickell, Paul M., MA PhD   Visiting Prof.
Honour, John W., BSc PhD, FRCPath   Reader,
   Steroid Endocrinology
Latchman, David S., MA PhD DSc   Prof.,
   Molecular Pathology; Head*
Lawson, Durward, BSc PhD   Reader
Marshall, Nicholas J., MSc PhD   Reader
Rademacher, Thomas M., MD MA PhD   Prof.
Riley, Patrick A., MB BS PhD, FRCPath,
   FIBiol   Prof., Cell Pathology
Stier, A., MD PhD   Visiting Prof.
Woo, Patricia, BSc MB BS PhD, FRCP   Prof.

Sexually Transmitted Diseases

Adler, Michael W., MD, FRCP   Duncan
   Guthrie Prof.
Cowan, Frances M., MB BS MSc   Sr. Lectr.
Darbyshire, Janet H., OBE, MB ChB MSc,
   FRCP   Prof., Epidemiology
Gilson, Richard J. C., MB BChir Camb.   Sr.
   Lectr.
Johnson, Anne M., MA MB BS MSc   Prof.
Mercey, Danielle E., MB ChB   Sr. Lectr.
Miller, Rob, MB BS   Sr. Lectr.
Power, Robert, PhD   Sr. Lectr.
Stephenson, Judith, MA MSc MD   Sr. Lectr.
Weller, Ian V. D., BSc MD, FRCP   Prof.;
   Head*
Williams, Ian G., MB ChB   Sr. Lectr.

Virology

Garson, Jeremy A., MB ChB MD   Sr. Lectr.
Tedder, Richard S., MB BChir Camb., MA
   Camb.   Prof., Medical Virology; Head*

Pharmacology

Bevan, Stuart J., BSc PhD   Prof.
Brown, David A., PhD, FIBiol, FRS   Prof.;
   Head*
Buckley, Noel J., BSc PhD   Reader
Colquhoun, David, BSc Leeds, PhD Leeds,
   FRS   Prof.
Cull-Candy, Stuart G., PhD   Prof.
Dickenson, Anthony H., BSc Reading,
   PhD   Prof., Neuropharmacology

Foreman, John C., MB BS BSc PhD DSc,
   FIBiol   Prof., Immunopharmacology
Gibb, Alasdair J., BSc PhD   Reader
Haylett, Dennis G., BSc PhD   Reader
Jenkinson, Donald H., BA Trinity(Dub.), MSc
   Trinity(Dub.), PhD   Emer. Prof.
Marshall, Ian, BSc Wales, PhD   Sr. Lectr.
Rang, Humphrey P., MA Oxf., DPhil Oxf., MSc
   MB BS, FRS   Prof.; Dir., Sandoz Inst.
Schoepfer, Ralaf, MD   Reader
Stanford, S. Clare, DPhil   Sr. Lectr.
Other Staff: 1 Emer. Reader

Physiology

Allen, David G., BSc MB BS PhD   Reader
Ashmore, Jonathan F., BSc MSc PhD   Sir
   Bernard Katz Prof.
Attwell, David I., BA Oxf., DPhil Oxf.   Prof.
Banks, Barbara E. C., PhD DSc,
   FRSChem   Prof., Chemical Physiology;
   Tutor
Bindman, Lynn J., BSc PhD   Reader
Bliss, Timothy V., BSc PhD, FRS   Visiting Prof.
Bolsover, Stephen, MA Camb., PhD Brist.   Prof.
Caddy, Keith W. T., PhD Brist.   Sr. Lectr.;
   Tutor
Cockcroft, Shamshad, BSc PhD   Prof.
Duchen, Michael R., BA MB BS PhD   Reader
Edwards, Frances A., BSc MSc PhD   Sr. Lectr.
Fry, Jonathan P., MA Camb., PhD Camb.   Sr.
   Lectr.
Gardner-Medwin, Anthony R., BA Camb., PhD
   Camb.   Reader, Neurobiology
Gomperts, Bastien D., PhD   Prof.,
   Biochemistry
Harrison, Philip J., BSc PhD   Sr. Lectr.
Holder, David S., BSc MSc MB BS   Sr. Lectr.
Koffer, Anna, PhD   Sr. Lectr.
Lynn, Bruce, BSc PhD   Reader
Mobbs, Peter G., BSc PhD   Reader
Moss, Stephen E., PhD   Reader
Page, Sally G., MSc NZ, PhD   Sr. Lectr.; Tutor
Quinn, Paul S., BSc PhD   Sr. Lectr.
Spyer, K. Michael, BSc MD PhD DSc   Prof.;
   Head*
Stephens, John A., PhD DSc   John Astor Prof.
Sutton, Peter M. I., BSc PhD   Sr. Lectr.
Tatham, Peter E. R., BSc PhD   Reader
Unwin, Robert J., BM PhD   Prof.
Whitaker, Michael J., BA Camb., MA
   PhD   Visiting Prof.
Woledge, Roger C., BSc PhD   Prof.; Dir., IHP

Podiatry, School of

Wilson, Anne

Primary Care and Population Sciences

Buszewicz, Marta J., BA MB BS   Sr. Lectr.
Cohen, John, MSc MB BS, FRCGP   Sr. Lectr.
Drennan, Vari M., BSc MSc   Sr. Lectr.
Evans, David J.   Sr. Lectr.
Haines, Andrew P., MB BS MD, FRCP,
   FRCGP   Prof.
Helman, Cecil G., MB ChB Cape Town   Sr.
   Lectr.
Iliffe, Stephen R., BSc MB BS   Reader
Modell, C. Bernadette, BSc MB BChir PhD,
   FRCP, FRCOG   Prof., Community Genetics
Modell, Michael, FRCP, FRCGP   Prof.
Murray, Elizabeth, BA MB BS MSc   Sr. Lectr.
Nazareth, Irwin, MB BS   Sr. Lectr.
Rogers, Stephen   Sr. Lectr.
Wallace, Paul, BSc MB BS MSc   Prof.; Head*

Psychiatry and Behavioural Sciences

Fax: (0171) 323 1459

Bebbington, Paul E., BA MB BChir MA MPhil
   PhD   Prof., Social and Community
   Psychiatry
Dein, Simon, BSc MB BS MSc   Sr. Lectr.
Feinmann, Charlotte, MB ChB Manc., MSc
   Manc., MD Manc.   Sr. Lectr.
Frost, David P., BSc MB BS PhD   Sr. Lectr.
George, Robert J. D., MA MD   Sr. Lectr.
Gurling, Hugh M. D., MB BS MPhil   Prof.,
   Molecular Psychiatry
Hobson, Robert P., MA MB BChir PhD,
   FRCPsych   Tavistock Prof.
Houlihan, Brian, BL MB   Sr. Lectr.

Johnson, Sonia I. Sr. Lectr.
Katona, Cornelius L. E., MA *Camb.*, MB BChir *Camb.*, MD, FRCPsych Prof., Psychiatry of the Elderly
Littlewood, Roland M., BSc MB BS Prof., Anthropology as Applied to Psychiatry
Livingstone, Gillian A., MB ChB MD Sr. Lectr.
Newman, Stanton P., BSocSci *Natal*, DPhil Prof.; Head*
Orrell, Martin, BSc BM BS PhD Sr. Lectr.
Patrick, Matthew P. H., BSc MB BS Sr. Lectr.
Robertson, Mary M., MB ChB *CapeT.*, MD *Cape Town*, FRCPsych Reader
Rosser, Rachel, MA *Camb.*, MB BChir *Camb.*, PhD, FRCP, FRCPsych Emer. Prof.
Scambler, Graham, BSc PhD Reader, Medical Sociology
Thompson, James A., BA *Keele*, PhD Sr. Lectr.
Walker, Zuzana Sr. Lectr.
Zeitlin, Harry, BSc MB BS MD MPhil, FRCPsych, FRCP Prof., Child, Adolescent and Family Psychiatry

Rheumatology Research

Edwards, Jo C. W., MD Sr. Lectr.
Lydard, P. M., MSc PhD Prof.

Sexually Transmitted Diseases, see under Pathol., Div. of

Surgery

Baum, Michael, ChM, FRCS Prof.
Boulos, Paul B., MS, FRCS, FRCSEd Prof.
Bown, Stephen G., AM MD, FRCP Prof., Laser Medicine
Bromley, Lesley M., BSc MB BS, FFARCS Sr. Lectr.
Brown, Robert A., BSc PhD Reader
Coleridge-Smith, Philip D., BA *Oxf.*, BM BCh *Oxf.*, FRCS Reader
Davidson, Timothy, MS ChM, FRCS Sr. Lectr.
Edgar, M. A., MChir, FRCS Reader
Goldstone, John, MB BS MD, FFARCS Sr. Lectr.
Green, Colin J., BVetMed PhD DSc, FRCVS, FRCS, FRCPath Prof.
Hopper, Colin, BDS MB BS, FRCS, FDSRCS Prof.
Hulf, Judith A., MB BS, FFARCS Sr. Lectr.
Leathem, Anthony, MB ChB MD PhD Sr. Lectr.
MacRobert, Alexander J., BA PhD Sr. Lectr.
McGrouther, Duncan A., MSc *Strath.*, MD ChB *Glas.*, FRCSGlas Prof., Plastic and Reconstructive Surgery
O'Hare, Michael J., PhD Sr. Lectr.
Ryan, James M., MB BCh BAO *N.U.I.*, FRCS Leonard Cheshire Prof.
Safaei-Keshtgar, Mohammad R., BSc MB BS, FRCSI, FRCS Sr. Lectr.
Taylor, Irvine, MD ChM, FRCS David Patey Prof.; Head*
Witt, John D., MB BS, FRCS Sr. Lectr.
Wyllie, John H., MSc *Aberd.*, MD *Aberd.*, FRCS, FRCSEd Emer. Prof., Surgical Studies
Yiu, Cu-Yiu, BSc MS, FRCS Sr. Lectr.

Urology and Nephrology, Institute of

Bartholomew, R. E. Sr. Lectr.
Craggs, Michael D., BSc PhD Reader, Neurophysiology; Dir., Neuroprosthesis Research Centre
Duffy, Patrick G., MB BCh BAO *Belf.*, FRCSI Sr. Lectr.
Fry, Christopher H., BSc BA PhD Prof.
Harland, Stephen J., MD MSc, FRCP Sr. Lectr.
Masters, John R. W., BSc PhD Reader
Mundy, Anthony R., MS, FRCS Prof.; Dir.; Head*
Neild, Guy H., MD, FRCP Prof.
Parkinson, M. Constance, BSc MD, FRCPath Sr. Lectr.
Pryor, John P., MB BS, FRCS Reader
Shah, P. Julian, MB BS ChB, FRCR, FRCS Sr. Lectr.
Thompson, F. Derek, MB BChir *Camb.*, FRCP Dean
Unwin, Robert J., BM PhD, FRCP Reader

Whitfield, Hugh, MA MCh, FRCS Sr. Lectr.
Woodhouse, Christopher R. J., FRCS Reader

Virology, see under Pathol., Div. of

SPECIAL CENTRES, ETC

Biochemical Engineering and Biotechnology, Interdisciplinary Research Centre for

Dunnill, Peter, PhD DSc, FIChemE, FEng, FRSChem, FRS Dir.*

Biomedical Research, Wolfson Institute for

Barker, Stephen G. E., BSc MS, FRCS Sr. Lectr.
Charles, Ian G., BSc PhD Prof., Molecular Biology
Erusalimsky, Jorge D., BSc PhD Sr. Lectr.
Garthwaite, Giti, DVM PhD Sr. Lectr.
Garthwaite, John, BSc PhD Prof.
Martin, John F., MA MB ChB MD, FRCP Prof.
Moncada, Salvador, MD PhD DSc Prof.; Dir.*
Powell, Ken, BSc PhD Prof.
Tinker, Andrew, BA MB BS PhD Sr. Lectr.
Zachary, Ian C., PhD Sr. Lectr.

Health Informatics and Professional Education, Centre for (CHIME)

Bowling, Ann, BSc MSc PhD Prof.
Collins, Brian, MA DPhil, FIP
Dacre, Jane, BSc MB BS MD Reader
Ingram, David, PhD Prof.; Dir.*
Kalra, Dipak, MB BS, FRCGP Sr. Lectr.
McLennan, Eleanor R., MSc Sr. Lectr.
McManus, I. Christopher, MB ChB MA MD PhD Prof., Psychology and Medical Education
Murphy, Jeanette, BA Sr. Lectr.
Southgate, Lesley, MB ChB Prof.
Worrall, Jennifer G., MD Sr. Lectr.

EASTMAN DENTAL INSTITUTE

in academic association with University College London

Tel: (0171) 915 1000 Fax: (0171) 915 1012
Banks, P., MB BS, FDSRCS, FRCS Sr. Lectr.
Brown, J., MB BCh Sr. Lectr.
Bulman, J. J., BDS PhD Reader, Community Dental Health
Carr, C., MB BS Sr. Lectr.
Cawson, R. A., MD, FDSRCPSGlas, FDSRCS, FRCPath Sr. Lectr.
Coonar, H., FDSRCS Sr. Lectr.
Coventry, J., BDS MSc Sr. Lectr.
Croysdill, A., BDS MSc, FDSRCS Sr. Lectr.
Downer, M. C., PhD DDS Prof., Dental Health Policy
Evans, R., BDS, FDSRCS Sr. Lectr.
Farthing, P., BSc BDS PhD, FDSRCS Sr. Lectr.
Feinmann, C., MD MSc Sr. Lectr.
Goodman, J., BDS, FDSRCSEd Sr. Lectr.
Griffiths, B., BDS, FDSRCS Sr. Lectr.
Harley, K., BDS MSc, FDSRCSEd Sr. Lectr.
Harris, M., BChD *Leeds*, MD, FFDRCSI, FDSRCS Prof., Oral Surgery
Henderson, B., BSc *Brun.*, PhD *Brun.* Prof., Oral Biochemistry
Hobkirk, J. A., BDS *Newcastle(UK)*, PhD *Newcastle(UK)*, FDSRCS, FDSRCSEd Prof., Prosthodontistry
Holt, Ruth D., BChD *Leeds*, MSc PhD Sr. Lectr., Children's Dentistry
Hopper, C., MB BS BDS, FRCS, FDSRCS Sr. Lectr., Oral Surgery
Hopps, R., BSc PhD Sr. Lectr.
Horrocks, E. N., FDSRCS Sr. Lectr.
Hoskinson, A., BDS MSc Sr. Lectr.
Howlett, Julie, BDS MSc PhD, FDSRCPSGlas Sr. Lectr., Prosthodontistry
Hunt, N., MSc PhD, FDSRCS Sr. Lectr.
Ibbetson, R. J., BDS MSc, FDSRCS Sr. Lectr.
Jacobs, J., BDS Sr. Lectr.

Jones, S., MSc, FDSRCS Sr. Lectr.
Lynch, M., MB BS Sr. Lectr.
Marsh, P., BSc PhD Sr. Lectr.
McEwan, T., MB BS Sr. Lectr.
McIvor, J., MB ChB, FRCR Sr. Lectr.
Murray, A., BDS MSc, FDSRCPS Sr. Lectr.
Naylor, M., BSc BDS PhD, FDSRCS Prof.
Newman, H. N., MA Trinity(*Dub.*), BDSc Trinity(*Dub.*), MDS *Brist.*, PhD *Brist.* Prof., Periodontistry and Preventative Dentistry
Noar, J., BDS MSc, FDSRCS Sr. Lectr.
Olsen, I., BS PhD Sr. Lectr.
Pearson, G. J., BDS PhD Sr. Lectr., Biomaterials Science
Petrie, A., BSc MSc Sr. Lectr.
Porter, S., MB ChB BDS PhD, FDSRCS Sr. Lectr., Oral Medicine
Rodesano, A., BDS, FDSRCS Sr. Lectr.
Rule, D., BDS, FDSRCS Sr. Lectr.
Scully, C., MD MDS PhD, FDSRCS, FFDRCSI, FRCPath Prof., Oral Medicine; Dean*
Searson, L., BDS MS, FDSRCS Sr. Lectr.
Setchell, D. J., MS *Mich.*, BDS, FDSRCSEd Sr. Lectr., Conservative Dentistry
Shah, H. N., BSc PhD Sr. Lectr.
Speight, P. M., PhD *Dund.*, BDS, FDSRCS Sr. Lectr., Oral Pathology
Ward, V. J., BDS, FDSRCPSGlas Sr. Lectr.
Welfare, R. D., BDS, FDSRCS Sr. Lectr.
Wickens, J., BDS MSc, FDSRCS Sr. Lectr.
Williams, B., BDS MPhil PhD, FDSRCS Sr. Lectr.
Wilson, M., MSc PhD Reader
Zakrzewska, J., MD, FDSRCS Sr. Lectr.
Kirkham, Fenella J., MB BChir *Camb.*, FRCP Sr. Lectr.

ROYAL FREE HOSPITAL SCHOOL OF MEDICINE

Tel: (0171) 794 0500
Accident and Emergency
1 Clin. Teacher†

Anaesthetics
13 Clin. Teachers†

Anatomy and Developmental Biology
Barnard, E., PhD, FRS Prof.
Cowen, T., BSc *Brist.*, PhD Sr. Lectr.
Goldspink, G. E., PhD ScD, FRSChem Prof.; Head*
Piasecki, K. K. W., MB BS PhD Sr. Lectr.

Biochemistry and Molecular Biology
Bruckdorfer, K. R., BSc *Liv.*, PhD *Liv.* Prof.
Cooke, B. A., BSc *Newcastle(UK)*, PhD *Newcastle(UK)* Prof., Endocrine Biochemistry; Head*
Fisher, D., MSc *Birm.*, MA *Oxf.*, DPhil *Oxf.*, FRSChem Reader
Hallinan, T., MSc *Syd.*, PhD *Syd.* Sr. Lectr.
Perkins, S. J., BA *Oxf.*, DPhil *Oxf.* Reader
Srai, S. K. B., MSc PhD Sr. Lectr.

Cardiology
2 Clin. Teachers†

Child and Family Mental Health, Leopold Muller Department of
Barnes, Jacqueline, BSc MSc PhD Sr. Lectr.
McFadyen, Anne, MB ChB MSc Sr. Lectr.
Stein, A., MB ChB Prof.; Head*

Clinical Genetics
MacDermot, Kay D., MB BS Sr. Lectr.

Clinical Immunology
Akbar, A., BSc PhD Sr. Lectr.
Farrant, J., PhD Sr. Lectr.
Grundy, Jane E., BSc *W.Aust.*, PhD *W.Aust.* Sr. Lectr.
Janossy, G., MD *Bud.*, PhD Prof.
Poulter, L. W., MPhil PhD Prof.; Head*
Webster, A. D. B., MD, FRCP Sr. Lectr.

Clinical Neurosciences

Cooper, J. M., BSc PhD   Sr. Lectr.
Ginsberg, L., PhD   Sr. Lectr.
Schapira, A. H. V., MB BS   Prof.†; Head*
Wise, R. S. J., MA MD, FRCP   Sr. Lectr.

Clinical Oncology

Begent, R. H. J., MB BS, FRCP   Ronald Raven Prof.; Head*
Chester, Kerry, BSc PhD   Sr. Lectr.
Hockhauser, D., BA MA MB BS DPhil   Sr. Lectr.

Community Child Health, see also Paed.

Flynn, D. M., MD, FRCP   Sr. Lectr.
Lloyd, B., MD, FRCP   Sr. Lectr.
Lloyd Evans, A., MA MD, FRCP   Sr. Lectr.
Taylor, B., MB ChB Otago, PhD Brist., FRCP, FRACP   Prof.; Head*
Van Someren, V., BSc MD, FRCP   Sr. Lectr.

Dental Surgery

No staff at present

Dermatology

No staff at present

Endocrinology

Al-Damluji, S., BSc MB BS, FRCP   Sr. Lectr.
Bouloux, P., BSc MD, FRCP   Reader

Geriatric Medicine

Stone, S. P., BSc MB BS   Sr. Lectr.

Haematology

Foroni, L., MD PhD   Sr. Lectr.
Harrison, C., BSc PhD   Sr. Lectr.
Lee, C. A., MA MD DSc, FRCP, FRCPath   Prof.
Madrigal, J. A., BS MD PhD   Prof.
Perry, D. J., BSc MB ChB   Sr. Lectr.
Potter, M. M., MB BS MA   Sr. Lectr.
Prentice, H. G., MB BS, FRCP, FRCPath   Prof.; Head*
Secker-Walker, Lorna, MA PhD   Prof.
Wickremasinghe, R. G., BSc PhD   Sr. Lectr.
Yong, K., MA PhD   Sr. Lectr.

Histopathology

Crow, Julie C., BSc MB BS   Sr. Lectr.
Dhillon, A. P., MA Camb., MB BChir Camb.   Sr. Lectr.
Francis, Gillian, MB BS MSc   Sr. Lectr.
Revell, P. A., BSc MB BS PhD, FRCPath   Prof.; Head*

Medical Microbiology

Gillespie, S. H., MB BCh Belf.   Reader
Hamilton-Miller, J. M. T., MA Camb., MA Oxf., PhD DSc, FRCPath   Prof.
Zuckerman, A. J., DSc Birm., MD, FRCP, FRCPath   Prof.; Head*

Medicine

Dooley, J. S., BSc MB BS MD   Sr. Lectr.
Dusheiko, G. M., MB BCh Witw.   Prof.
Fine, L. G., MD, FRCP, FACP   Prof.; Head*
Harrison, T. J., BSc PhD   Reader
James, I. M., MB BS PhD, FRCP   Reader
Johnson, M. A., MD, FRCP   Sr. Lectr.
McIntyre, N., BSc MD, FRCP   Prof.
Mistry, P., BSc MB BS PhD   Sr. Lectr.
Moore, K., BSc PhD   Sr. Lectr.
Morgan, Marsha Y., MB ChB Manc.   Sr. Lectr.
Owen, J. S., BSc Nott., PhD   Sr. Lectr.
Pounder, R. E., MA Camb., MD Camb., FRCP   Prof.
Wakefield, Andrew G., MB BS, FRCS   Sr. Lectr.

Nephrology and Renal Transplantation

Moorhead, J. F., MB ChB, FRCP   Prof.
Powis, S., BSc BM BCh PhD   Prof.; Head*

Neurosurgery

Tel: (0171) 794 0500
No staff at present

Nuclear Medicine

No staff at present

Obstetrics and Gynaecology

de Swiet, M., MA MD, FRCP, FRCOG   Sr. Lectr.
Economides, D. L., MB BS MD   Sr. Lectr.
Hardiman, P., MD   Sr. Lectr.
Maclean, A. B., MB ChB   Prof.; Head*
Okolo, S., PhD   Sr. Lectr.
Other Staff: 1 Sr. Lectr.†

Ophthalmology

No staff at present

Orthopaedic Surgery

No staff at present

Oto-Rhino-Laryngology

No staff at present

Paediatric Gastroenterology

Murch, Simon, BSc MB BS PhD   Sr. Lectr.
Phillips, A., PhD   Sr. Lectr.
Walker-Smith, John, MB BS, FRCP   Prof.; Head*

Paediatrics, see also Community Child Health

No staff at present

Pathology, Chemical

Mikhailidis, D. P., MSc MD   Sr. Lectr.
Winder, A. F., MSc Oxf., MA Oxf., DM Oxf., PhD, FRCPath   Prof.; Head*

Pharmacology

Dolphin, Annette C., BSc PhD   Prof.; Head*
Jacobs, A., BSc PhD   Sr. Lectr.
Mathie, A., BSc PhD   Sr. Lectr.
Ramage, A., BSc S'ton., MPhil S'ton., PhD Manc.   Sr. Lectr.

Physiology

Bradley, D. J., PhD Brist., BSc   Sr. Lectr.
Debnam, E. S., BSc Sheff., PhD Sheff.   Reader
Gilbey, M. P., BSc PhD   Sr. Lectr.
Halliwell, J. V., BSc PhD   Reader
Jordan, D., BSc Birm., PhD Birm.   Reader
Richards, C. D., BSc Brist., PhD Brist.   Reader
Spyer, K. M., BSc Sheff., PhD Birm., DSc Birm.   Sophia Jex-Blake Prof.; Head*
Thomson, Alexandra M., BSc Brist., PhD Brist.   Reader

Primary Care and Population Sciences

Ebrahim, S. B. J., BMedSci MSc DM   Prof.
Elford, J., BSocSci Birm., MSc PhD   Sr. Lectr.
Humphreys, C., BA MSc PhD   Sr. Lectr.
Lloyd, Margaret H., BSc MD   Reader
Morris, R., MSc PhD   Sr. Lectr.
Perry, I., MD BCh MSc   Sr. Lectr.
Philips, Andrew, BSc PhD   Prof.
Rosenthal, J. J., BSc MB BS   Sr. Lectr.
Sherr, L., BA PhD   Sr. Lectr.
Wallace, P., MB MSc   Prof.; Head*
Whincup, P. H., BA Camb., MB BChir Camb., MSc Camb.   Reader
Other Staff: 1 Sr. Lectr.†

Psychiatry

Blanchard, M., BSc MD   Sr. Lectr.
Dolan, R., MD   Prof.
James, D., MB BS MA   Sr. Lectr.
King, M. B., BSc Auck., MD Auck.   Reader; Head*
Leff, J., BSc MD, FRCPsych   Prof.
Mann, A., MD, FRCP, FRCPsych   Prof.
Raven, P., BSc MB BS PhD   MRC Sr. Lectr.
Serfaty, M., BSc MB ChB MPhil   Sr. Lectr.
Weich, S., BA MA MSc   Sr. Lectr.

Radiology

No staff at present

Radiotherapy

No staff at present

Retrovirology

Loveday, C.   Prof.; Head*

Rheumatology

Black, Carol, BA MD, FRCP   Prof.

Surgery

Bradford, R., BSc MD, FRCS   Sr. Lectr.
Davidson, B. R., MB ChB Glas., FRCS   Sr. Lectr.
Fuller, B. J., BSc CNAA, PhD CNAA   Sr. Lectr.
Hobbs, K. E. F., ChM Brist., MB BS, FRCS   Prof.; Head*
Rolles, K., MS, FRCS   Sr. Lectr.
Winslet, M. C., MS, FRCS   Prof.

Travel Medicine and Vaccines

Zuckerman, Jane, MB BS MD   Head*

Urology

No staff at present

Venereal Diseases

No staff at present

Virology

Emery, V. C., BSc S'ton., PhD S'ton.   Reader
Griffiths, P. D., BSc MD   Prof.; Head*

CONTACT OFFICERS

Admissions (first and higher degree). Assistant Registrar (Admissions and Statistics): Percival, Nigel, BSc
Adult/continuing education. Director, Continuing Education: Cross, Susan M., BEd MEd
Alumni. Director, Alumni Relations: Freeman, Michael L., BA
Archives. Records and Administration Manager: Cummings, Rosamund
Careers. Senior Careers Advisor: Harris, Neil, BSc PhD
Credit transfer. Senior Administrative Assistant (Administration): Saffery, Andy K., BA
Development/fund-raising. Director of Development: Hall, Rachel, BA
Equal opportunities. Senior Personnel Officer: Moss, Julia, MA
Estates and buildings/works and services. Director: Furter, J. Richard
Examinations. Assistant Registrar (Examinations): Baxter, Lynne, BA
Finance. Director: Foster, Jack W., FCA
General enquiries. Registrar: Butcher, Martin H., MA Oxf., MLitt Oxf.
Health services. Manager and Psychiatric Adviser, Student Counselling Service: Greenberg, Maurice, MB MPhil
International office. Director, Educational Liaison and International Relations: Craggs, Peter, BA MPhil
International office. Assistant Director (Europe): Duncan, Lesley J. R., BA
International office. Assistant Director (International Office): Hibbert, Sara J., BSc
Language training for international students. Director, Language Centre: Ditner, Dolores
Library (chief librarian). Director of Library Services: Ayris, Paul, BA MA PhD
Minorities/disadvantaged groups. Senior Personnel Officer: Moss, Julia, MA
Personnel/human resources. Personnel Director: Deer, Peter J., BA
Purchasing. Purchasing Co-ordinator: Mee, Michael S. R.
Research. Vice-Provost (Head of Graduate School): Jowell, Prof. Jeffrey L., QC, MA Oxf., LLM Harv., SJD Harv.
Safety. Safety Officer: Layton, Alfred J., BSc PhD
Schools liaison. Assistant Director: Clewley, Nicholas, BA
Security. College Security Manager: Ford, Bill L.
Sport and recreation. Sports/Recreation Manager: Squires, David
Staff development and training. Head of Staff Development and Training: Taylor, Judith A., BA
Staff development and training. Training Officer: Taylor, Andrew G. S., BA
Student union. General Manager: McLeod, Mike

Students with disabilities. Administrative Assistant (Academic Services): Mulcahy, Patrick M., BA

CAMPUS/COLLEGE HEADS

Eastman Dental Institute, Eastman Dental Hospital, Gray's Inn Road, London, England WC1X 8LD. (Tel: (0171) 915 1000; Fax: (0171) 915 1012.) Dean and Director of Studies: Scully, Prof. C., MD MDS PhD, FDSRCS, FFDRCSI, FRCPath

Royal Free Hospital School of Medicine, Rowland Hill Street, London, England NW3 2PF. (Tel: (0171) 794 0500; Fax: (0171) 794 3505.) Dean: Zuckerman, Prof. Arie J., DSc Birm., MD, FRCP, FRCPath

[Information supplied by the institution as at April 1998, and edited by the ACU]

WYE COLLEGE, UNIVERSITY OF LONDON

Founded 1894; previously established 1447; incorporated by Royal Charter 1948 (College of St Gregory and St Martin at Wye)

Postal Address: Wye, Ashford, Kent, England TN25 5AH
Telephone: (01233) 812401 **Fax**: (01233) 813320 **Cables**: College, Wye **WWW**: http://www.wye.ac.uk
E-mail formula: initial.surname@wye.ac.uk

VISITOR—Canterbury, His Grace The Lord Archbishop of
CHAIRMAN OF GOVERNING BODY—Brabourne, The Rt. Hon. the Lord, CBE
PRINCIPAL*—Prescott, Prof. John H. D., BSc Nott., PhD Nott., FIBiol
VICE-PRINCIPAL—Webster, Prof. J. Paul G., BSc Reading, PhD Lond.
DEAN OF GRADUATE SCHOOL FOR POSTGRADUATE STUDIES—Leaver, Prof. J. David, BSc Durh., PhD Lond., FIBiol
DEAN OF HONOURS SCHOOL FOR UNDERGRADUATE STUDIES—Hill, G. Paul, BSc Lond., MSc Reading
DIRECTOR OF FINANCE AND ADMINISTRATION‡—Quirke, Terence M., BA Sus.

GENERAL INFORMATION

History. The college was originally founded in 1447 by Cardinal John Kempe. In 1894 it became South-Eastern Agricultural College; it amalgamated with Swanley Horticultural College in 1945, when its present name was adopted. It has been part of the University of London since 1900 and received a Royal Charter in 1948.

Admission to first degree courses (see also United Kingdom Introduction). Through Universities and Colleges Admissions Service (UCAS). Applicants may be asked to achieve specific grades in named subjects in General Certificate of Education (GCE) A or AS levels, Business and Technology Education Council (BTEC) or General National Vocational Qualifications (GNVQ) examinations, or good grades in Scottish or Irish Highers, in Access courses, in the International Baccalaureate, or in other comparable examinations. In addition, candidates should normally hold General Certificate of Secondary Education (GCSE) grade C or higher in English and mathematics.

First Degrees (of University of London) (see also University of London Directory to Subjects of Study). BSc (honours).
All courses are full-time and normally last 3 years. Programmes that include industrial placements: 4 years.

Higher Degrees (of University of London) (see also University of London Directory to Subjects of Study). MSc, MPhil, PhD.
Applicants for admission to postgraduate courses should normally hold an appropriate first degree with first-or second-class honours. Applicants who are not eligible for direct entry to MSc courses may register for a college diploma course, with the possibility of transfer to an MSc programme. Applicants whose first language is not English are required to demonstrate proficiency in the English language.
MSc: 1 year full-time, 2–5 years by distance learning, or 15 months–4 years by mixed

mode; MPhil: normally 2 years full-time; PhD: normally 3 years full-time. MPhil, PhD: part-time or split programme options available.

Libraries. 35,000 books; 600 periodical titles; specialised databases on CD-ROM and networked information sources with access to electronic journals. Special collection: agricultural and horticultural books pre-1918.

Fees (annual). Undergraduate (1998–99): £1000. Postgraduate: home students, 1998–99, £2610; international students, 1997–98, £6600–£8790.

Academic Awards (1997–98). 21 awards ranging in value from £1300 to £4600.

Academic Year (1999–2000). Three terms: 4 October–17 December; 10 January–18 March; 25 April–1 July.

Income (1996–97). Total, £12,404,000.

Statistics. Staff: 180 (120 academic, 60 administrative). Students: full-time (1996–97) 852 (509 men, 343 women); international (non-EU) 205; part-time (distance learning) (as at October 1997) 893 (623 men, 270 women).

ACADEMIC UNITS

Agricultural Economics and Business Management

Agrarian Development Unit

Fax: (01233) 813126

Duncan, Alex, MA Oxf., MSc Reading   Visiting Prof.
Kydd, Jonathan G., BA Keele, MSc Lond., DPhil Sus.   Sr. Lectr.; Head*
Pearce, Richard W., BSc Reading, MSc Lond.   Sr. Lectr.
Other Staff: 4 Lectrs.; 2 Res. Officers; 3 Hon. Res. Fellows
Research: economics of irrigation and drainage; macro trade and sector policy; peasant agriculture; rural markets

Agricultural Policy Unit

Fax: (01233) 813126

Buckwell, Allan E., BSc Lond., MA(Econ) Manc.   Prof., Agricultural Economics; Head*
Hill, N. W. F. Berkeley, BSc Nott., PhD Reading   Reader
Other Staff: 2 Lectrs.; 1 Sr. Res. Fellow†
Research: biotechnology and agriculture; European agricultural policy; European economies in transition; total incomes of agricultural households

Farm Business Unit

Fax: (01233) 813126

Coward, Norman, BSc Lond., MS Ill.   Visiting Prof.
Hill, G. Paul, BSc Lond., MSc Reading   Sr. Lectr.
Nix, John S., BSc(Econ) Lond., MA Camb.   Emer. Prof.
Scase, Richard, BA Leic., MA Leic., PhD Kent   Visiting Prof.
Webster, J. Paul G., BSc Reading, PhD Lond.   Prof., Agricultural Business Management; Head*
Williams, Nigel T., BSc Wales, MA(Econ) Manc.   Sr. Lectr.
Other Staff: 4 Lectrs.; 1 Sr. Investigational Officer; 2 Investigational Officers; 3 Lectrs.†
Research: cost benefit analysis of pesticide usage; dairy sector changes; impacts of changes in policy and technology on farm businesses

Food Industry Management Unit

Fax: (01233) 813126

Fearne, Andrew, BSc Newcastle(UK), PhD Newcastle(UK)   Sr. Lectr.
Hughes, David R., BSc Reading, MSc Newcastle(UK), PhD Newcastle(UK)   Sainsbury Prof., Agribusiness and Food Marketing; Head*
Morris, John, BAgrSc NZ, MAgrSc NZ, MBA Cran., PhD Cornell   Visiting Prof.
Ray, Derek, BSc(Econ) Lond., MPhil Edin.   Sr. Lectr.
Other Staff: 4 Lectrs.; 2 Res. Officers; 1 Placement Officer; 2 Lectrs.†

Research: analysis of strategic alliances and transaction costs; market pricing mechanisms; supply chain management issues

Agriculture and Horticulture

Fax: (Agriculture) (01233) 812855, (Horticulture) (01233) 813017

Anderson, Simon, BSc *Wales*, MSc *Edin.*, PhD *Lond.* Sr. Lectr.
Fordham, Ray, BSc *Nott.*, PhD *Brist.* Sr. Lectr.
Gill, Margaret, BSc *Edin.*, BA *Open(UK)*, PhD *Massey* Visiting Prof.
Lean, Ian J., BSc *Wales*, PhD *Wales* Sr. Lectr.
Leaver, J. David, BSc *Durh.*, PhD *Lond.*, FIBiol Prof., Agriculture; Head*
Lee, Howard C., MSc *Durh.*, PhD *CNAA* Sr. Lectr.
Moorby, Jeffrey, BSc *Manc.*, PhD *Manc.* Emer. Prof.
Pollott, Geoffrey E., BSc *Reading*, PhD *Newcastle(UK)* Sr. Lectr.
Scarisbrick, David H., BSc *Wales*, MA *Camb.*, PhD *Nott.* Sr. Lectr.
Other Staff: 1 Sr. Lectr.†; 5 Lectrs.; 1 Res. Officer; 2 Lectrs.†; 1 Hon. Sr. Res. Fellow; 5 Hon. Res. Fellows; 1 Hon. Res. Assoc.
Vacant Posts: 1 Lectr.
Research: animal genetic resources; horticultural crops; livestock systems and animal nutrition; plant propagation and tissue culture; sustainable agriculture

Biological Sciences

Fax: (01233) 813140

Ainsworth, Charles C., BSc *Lond.*, PhD *Lond.* Sr. Lectr.
Baker, Dennis A., BSc *Aberd.*, PhD *Aberd.*, FIBiol Prof., Biology; Head*
Blatt, Michael R., BSc *Wis.*, PhD *Stan.* Prof., Plant Physiology and Biophysics
Davis, Raymond H., BSc *Nott.*, PhD *Nott.* Sr. Lectr.
Giller, Kenneth E., BSc *Sheff.*, PhD *Sheff.* Prof., Tropical Soil Microbiology
Lopez-Real, Joseph M., BSc *Sur.*, PhD *Lond.* Sr. Lectr.
Mansfield, John W., BSc *Wales*, PhD *Lond.* Prof., Plant Pathology
Mantell, Sinclair H., BSc *Brist.*, MSc *Lond.*, PhD *WI* Reader
Peat, Edward, BSc *Nott.*, PhD *Nott.* Sr. Lectr.
Rossiter, John T., BSc *Lond.*, PhD *Lond.* Sr. Lectr.
Russell, Nicholas J., MA *Camb.*, PhD *Camb.* Bridge Wardens' Prof., Food Microbiology
Scofield, Anthony M., BSc *Brist.*, MSc *Wales*, PhD *Nott.* Sr. Lectr.
Swinburne, Terence R., PhD *Lond.*, DSc *Lond.* Emer. Prof.
Thomas, Tudor, BSc *Wales*, PhD *Wales*, DSc *Wales* Visiting Prof.
Wain, R. Louis, CBE, PhD *Sheff.*, DSc *Lond.*, Hon. DAgricSci *Ghent*, Hon. DSc *Kent*, Hon. DSc *Sheff.*, Hon. DSc *Lausanne*, FRS Emer. Prof.
Other Staff: 6 Lectrs.; 1 Sr. Res. Fellow; 1 Scientific Curator; 14 Res. Fellows; 6 Res. Officers; 1 Res. Assoc.; 1 Sr. Lectr.†; 4 Hon. Sr. Res. Fellows; 6 Hon. Res. Fellows; 1 Hon. Res. Assoc.
Research: animal physiology and biochemistry; biochemistry and biophysics; plant molecular biology and biotechnology; plant physiology and genetics; soils and environmental microbiology

Environment

Fax: (01233) 812855

Buckley, G. Peter, BSc *Aberd.*, MSc *Wales*, PhD *Leeds* Sr. Lectr.
Copland, Michael J. W., BSc *Wales*, PhD *Wales* Sr. Lectr.
Green, Brynmor H., OBE, BSc *Nott.*, PhD *Nott.* Emer. Prof.
Hodgson, Christopher J., BSc *Lond.*, PhD *Lond.* Sr. Lectr.
Redclift, Michael R., BA *Sus.*, DPhil *Sus.* Visiting Prof.
Rogers, Alan W., MA *Oxf.*, MPhil *Lond.*, PhD *Lond.* Sr. Lectr.
Watt, Trudy A., BA *Open(UK)*, MA *Oxf.*, MSc *Sheff.Hallam*, DPhil *Oxf.* Sr. Lectr.; Head*
Other Staff: 5 Lectrs.; 1 Res. Officer; 2 Res. Assocs.; 2 Sr. Lectrs.†; 1 Lectr.†; 1 Hon. Sr. Res. Fellow; 1 Hon. Res. Fellow
Vacant Posts: 1 Lectr.
Research: biological control of insect pests; land evaluation, restoration and habitat management; rural policy and countryside change; sustainable development; woodland management

SPECIAL CENTRES, ETC

Continuing Professional Development

Fax: (01233) 813006

Kydd, Jonathan G., BA *Keele*, MSc *Lond.*, DPhil *Sus.* Sr. Lectr.; Head*
Other Staff: 1 Tutor; 1 Administrator

European Agricultural Studies, Centre for

Fax: (01233) 813498

Buckwell, Prof. Allan E., BSc *Lond.*, MA(Econ) *Manc.* Hon. Dir.*

External Programme

Fax: (01233) 812138

Bryson, Jane E., BSc *Wales*, PhD *Lond.* Deputy Dir.*
Pearce, Richard W., BSc *Reading*, MSc *Lond.* Sr. Lectr.
Ray, Derek, BSc(Econ) *Lond.*, MPhil *Edin.* Sr. Lectr.
Other Staff: 1 Lectr.; 1 Res. Officer; 1 Sr. Lectr.†

Horticulture Research International, Hop Research

Fax: (01233) 813126

Darby, Peter, BSc *E.Anglia*, PhD *E.Anglia* Hon. Res. Fellow; Head*
Other Staff: 1 Hon. Res. Fellow

CONTACT OFFICERS

Accommodation. General Manager, Residential, Catering and Conference Services: Traske, David L., BA *Strath.*
Admissions (first degree). Head of Registry: Wilkes, J. Malcolm, BSc *Reading*, MPhil *Lond.*
Admissions (higher degree). Head of Registry: Wilkes, J. Malcolm, BSc *Reading*, MPhil *Lond.*
Adult/continuing education. Deputy Director of External Programme: Bryson, Jane E., BSc *Wales*, PhD *Lond.*
Alumni. Assistant to Dean: Festing, Harriet, BSc *Lond.*, MPhil *Lond.*
Archives. Librarian: Lucas, E. Mary, JP, BSc *S'ton.*

Careers. Careers Adviser: Hunt, Alan R., BSc *Lond.*, MSc *Lond.*
Computing services. Head of IT Services: Kentish, Paul A., BSc *Newcastle(UK)*, MSc *Newcastle(UK)*
Conferences/corporate hospitality. General Manager, Residential, Catering and Conference Services: Traske, David L., BA *Strath.*
Consultancy services. Director of Finance and Administration: Quirke, Terence M., BA *Sus.*
Credit transfer. Head of Registry: Wilkes, J. Malcolm, BSc *Reading*, MPhil *Lond.*
Development/fund-raising. Principal: Prescott, Prof. John H. D., BSc *Nott.*, PhD *Nott.*, FIBiol
Distance education. Deputy Director of External Programme: Bryson, Jane E., BSc *Wales*, PhD *Lond.*
Estates and buildings/works and services. Director of Finance and Administration: Quirke, Terence M., BA *Sus.*
Examinations. Head of Registry: Wilkes, J. Malcolm, BSc *Reading*, MPhil *Lond.*
Finance. Finance Officer: McCrow, Roger
General enquiries. Head of Registry: Wilkes, J. Malcolm, BSc *Reading*, MPhil *Lond.*
Industrial liaison. Director of Finance and Administration: Quirke, Terence M., BA *Sus.*
International office. Head of Registry: Wilkes, J. Malcolm, BSc *Reading*, MPhil *Lond.*
Language training for international students. Head of Registry: Wilkes, J. Malcolm, BSc *Reading*, MPhil *Lond.*
Library (chief librarian). Librarian: Lucas, E. Mary, JP, BSc *S'ton.*
Ombudsperson. Assistant Director of Administration: Hill, Thomas A., MA *Camb.*, PhD *Lond.*
Personnel/human resources. Assistant Director of Administration: Hill, Thomas A., MA *Camb.*, PhD *Lond.*
Public relations, information and marketing. Public Relations and Press Officer: Raeside, Wendy
Publications. Publication Sales: Jones, Hazel
Quality assurance and accreditation. Academic Registrar: Evans, Ninette, JP, BA *Kent*
Research. Dean of Graduate School for Postgraduate Studies: Leaver, Prof. J. David, BSc *Durh.*, PhD *Lond.*, FIBiol
Safety. Safety Officer: Price, R., BSc *Birm.*, PhD *Lond.*
Scholarships, awards, loans. Head of Registry: Wilkes, J. Malcolm, BSc *Reading*, MPhil *Lond.*
Schools liaison. Assistant to Dean: Festing, Harriet, BSc *Lond.*, MPhil *Lond.*
Security. General Manager, Residential, Catering and Conference Services: Traske, David L., BA *Strath.*
Sport and recreation. Director of Finance and Administration: Quirke, Terence M., BA *Sus.*
Staff development and training. Assistant Director of Administration: Hill, Thomas A., MA *Camb.*, PhD *Lond.*
Student welfare/counselling. Welfare Adviser: King, Janet
Students from other countries. Assistant to Dean: Lohmann, Susanne
Students with disabilities. Head of Registry: Wilkes, J. Malcolm, BSc *Reading*, MPhil *Lond.*
University press. Hill, N. W. F. Berkeley, BSc *Nott.*, PhD *Reading*

[Information supplied by the institution as at 10 March 1998, and edited by the ACU]

INSTITUTES

BRITISH INSTITUTE IN PARIS

Institut Britannique

Postal Address: 11 rue de Constantine, 75340-Paris Cedex 07, France; (London address: Senate House, Room 359, Malet Street, London, England WC1E 7HU)

Telephone: (Paris) (1) 44 11 73 73; (London) (0171) 862 8656 *Fax:* (Paris) (1) 45 50 31 55; (London) (0171) 862 8655

Chairman of Board—James, Sir Kenneth, KCMG

Chairman of Paris Consultative Board—H.E. The British Ambassador to France (*ex officio*)

Director*—Campos, Prof. C. L., OBE, LèsL *Paris*, PhD *Camb.*

London Secretary—Buchanan, Christine, BA *Lond.*, MA *Lond.*

General Secretary (Paris)‡—Stone, Simon

GENERAL INFORMATION

History. The institute was founded in 1894 as 'La Guilde Franco-Anglaise'. In 1927, it was attached to the University of Paris and became known under its present name. It was incorporated into the University of London in 1969.

Admission to first degree courses (see also United Kingdom introduction). By interview and qualifying test.

First Degrees (of University of London). BA in French studies.

Higher Degrees (of University of London). MA in: contemporary French studies; French theatre studies; translation (French and English).

Language of Instruction. French and English.

Libraries. 15,000 volumes.

Fees (annual). BA: £2600; MA: £2850.

Academic Awards. Eight awards ranging in value from £600 to £1800.

Academic Year (1998–99). Three terms: October–June (11 weeks each).

Income (1996–97). Total, £2,300,000.

Statistics. 2132 part-time students; 680 distance course students; 32 undergraduates; 24 postgraduates.

ACADEMIC UNITS

English as a Foreign Language

Tel: (1) 44 11 73 71

Foster-Cohen, Susan, BA *Lanc.*, PhD *Lanc.* Sr. Lectr.; Head*

Oliver, Douglas, BA *Essex*, MA *Essex* Sr. Lectr.

Other Staff: 16 Lectrs.; 11 Tutors†

French Language, Literature and Civilisation

Tel: (1) 44 11 73 83

Sadler, M., MA *Oxf.*, DPhil *Oxf.* Sr. Lectr.

Williamson, Elaine, BA *Birm.*, MèsL *Paris*, PhD *Birm.* Sr. Lectr.; Head*

Other Staff: 3 Lectrs.; 5 Assoc. Lectrs.; 9 Tutors

[*Information supplied by the institution as at 12 March 1998, and edited by the ACU*]

CENTRE FOR DEFENCE STUDIES

Postal Address: King's College London, Strand, London, England WC2R 2LS

Telephone: (0171) 873 2338 *Fax:* (0171) 873 2748 *E-mail:* jen.smith@kcl.ac.uk

Honorary Director—Freedman, Prof. L. D., BA(Econ) *Manc.*, BPhil *York(UK)*, DPhil *Oxf.*

Executive Director*‡—Clarke, Prof. Michael, MScEcon *Wales*

[*Information supplied by the institution as at 17 February 1998, and edited by the ACU*]

COURTAULD INSTITUTE OF ART

Founded 1932

Postal Address: Somerset House, Strand, London, England WC2R 0RN

Telephone: (0171) 873 2777 *Fax:* (0171) 873 2410

Chairman of the Board of the Institute—Goodison, Sir Nicholas, MA *Camb.*, FSA

Director*—Fernie, Prof. Eric C., CBE, BA(FineArts) *Witw.*, FSA, FRSEd

Deputy Director—House, Prof. John P. H., MA PhD

Secretary and Registrar‡—Hearnshaw, J. A., BA

Academic Registrar—Walker, Rose J., MA PhD

GENERAL INFORMATION

History. The institute was founded in 1932.

Admission to first degree courses (see also United Kingdom Introduction). Through Universities and Colleges Admissions Service (UCAS).

First Degrees. BA in history of art.

Higher Degrees. MA in history of art, MPhil, PhD.

Fees. Postgraduate: (UK/EU students) £2610; (international students) £6950.

Academic Year. (1998–99). Three terms: 5 October–16 December; 13 January–24 March; 21 April–30 June.

Statistics. Staff: 26 academic. Students: full-time 318; part-time 78; international 59; total 396.

ACADEMIC UNITS

Art, History of

Tel: (0171) 873 2636

Cormack, Robin S., MA *Oxf.*, PhD, FSA Prof.

Crossley, B. Paul, MA *Camb.*, PhD, FSA Sr. Lectr.

Fletcher, Jennifer M., BA Sr. Lectr.

Green, Christopher K., MA *Camb.*, MA *Lond.*, PhD Prof.

House, John P. H., MA PhD Prof.

Lowden, John H., MA PhD Reader

Newman, John A., MA *Oxf.*, FSA Reader

Rubin, Pat L., MA PhD Reader

Solkin, David H., MA PhD Reader

Conservation of Paintings

Tel: (0171) 873 2191 *Fax:* (0171) 873 2878

Bruce-Gardner, Robert H., BA Dir.*

Conservation of Textiles

Tel: (0181) 977 4943 *Fax:* (0181) 977 9081

Brooks, Mary, MA *Camb.* Head of Studies

Hoare, Nell, BA Dir.*

Conservation of Wall Paintings

Tel: (0171) 873 2848

Park, David, MA, FSA Dir.*

Dress, History of

Tel: (0171) 873 2636

Ribeiro, Aileen E., MA PhD Reader

[*Information supplied by the institution as at 30 March 1998, and edited by the ACU*]

SCHOOL OF SLAVONIC AND EAST EUROPEAN STUDIES

Postal Address: Senate House, Malet Street, London, England WC1E 7HU

Telephone: (0171) 636 8000 *Fax:* (0171) 862 8641 *Cables:* University London Slavonic *WWW:* http://www.ssees.ac.uk *E-mail formula:* initial.surname@ssees.ac.uk

Chairman of Council—Wooding, Sir Norman, CBE, PhD

Director*—Branch, Prof. Michael A., BA *Lond.*, PhD *Lond.*, Hon. PhD *Oulu*, FRAI

Clerk to the Council‡—Widdowson, Maria D. C., BA *Open(UK)*, MA *Lond.*

Academic Registrar—Pearce, Carol G., MA *Oxf.*

Librarian—Pitman, Lesley, BA *Leeds*

GENERAL INFORMATION

History. The school was founded in 1915 as a department of King's College and has been a central institute of the University of London since 1932.

Admission to first degree courses (see also United Kingdom Introduction). Through Universities and Colleges Admissions Service (UCAS).

First Degrees. BA: normally 3 years full-time or (for some language-based courses) 4 years full-time.

Higher Degrees. MA, MPhil, PhD.

Applicants for admission to higher degrees must normally hold an appropriate first degree with at least second class honours, or equivalent qualification.

MA: 1 year full-time or 2 years part-time. MPhil, PhD: minimum 2 years full-time or 4 years part-time.

Language of Instruction. English, though special lectures and seminars may be conducted in the language of the region concerned.

Libraries. 340,000 items; 1000 current periodicals; 800 videotapes; extensive microform collection. Special collections include: papers of R. W. Seton-Watson; topographical maps (some from fifteenth century).

Fees (1998–99, annual). Undergraduate: £1000. Postgraduate: £2620 (EU); £7400 (non-EU).

Academic Awards (1997–98). Eight awards ranging in value from £30 to £14,000.

Academic Year (1998–99). Three terms: 28 September–18 December; 11 January–26 March; 26 April–11 June.

Income (1997-98). Total, £4,085,000.

Statistics. Staff: 103 (72 academic, 31 library and administrative). Students: full-time 417; part-time 52; non-EU 47; total 469.

ACADEMIC UNITS

East European Languages and Culture

Tel: (0171) 862 8557

Deletant, Dennis J., OBE, BA Lond., PhD Lond., Hon. PhD Prof., Romanian; Head*
Eile, S., MA Cracow, PhD Cracow Sr. Lectr., Polish
Hawkesworth, E. Celia, BA Camb., MPhil Sr. Lectr., Serbo-Croat
Pynsent, R. B., MA Camb., PhD Camb. Prof., Czech and Slovak
Other Staff: 7 Lectrs.; 5 Res. Fellows; 5 Hon. Res. Fellows
Research: culture and ideas of Central and Eastern Europe; language; literature; oral tradition

History

Tel: (0171) 862 8575 Fax: (0171) 862 8643

Bartlett, R. P., MA Camb., DPhil Oxf. Reader, Russian History
Bracewell, C. Wendy, MA Stan., PhD Stan. Sr. Lectr., South East Europe

Hosking, G. A., MA Camb., PhD Camb., FBA Prof., Russian History
Hughes, Lindsey A. J., BA Sus., PhD Camb. Reader, Russian History
Kirby, D. G., BA PhD Prof.; Head*
Other Staff: 4 Lectrs.; 12 Hon. Res. Fellows
Research: history of Central and Eastern Europe, particularly nation-building and nationalism

Russian

Tel: (0171) 862 8586 Fax: (0171) 862 8643

Aizlewood, R., MA Oxf., DPhil Oxf. Sr. Lectr.
Brown, N. J., BA Birm. Sr. Lectr.
Davidson, P., MA Camb., DPhil Oxf. Sr. Lectr.
Graffy, J. J., BA Oxf. Sr. Lectr.
McMillin, A. B., BA PhD Prof.
Wigzell, Faith C. M., BA PhD Reader; Head*
Other Staff: 3 Lectrs.; 2 Lectors; 4 Hon. Res. Fellows
Research: culture and ideas; literature; oral tradition

Social Sciences

Tel: (0171) 862 8595 Fax: (0171) 862 8642

Carter, F. W., BA Sheff., MA Lond., PhD Lond., DrNatSc Prague, DPhil Cracow Reader, Geography of Eastern Europe
Duncan, P. J. S., BCom Birm., MA Ott., PhD Glas. Sr. Lectr., Contemporary Russian Economic and Social Policy
Hamilton, F. E. I., BSc(Econ) Lond., PhD Lond. Sr. Lectr., Economic Social Studies; Head*
Schöpflin, G. A., LLB Glas., MA Glas. Jean Monnet Prof., Central and East European Integration
Smith, A. H., BSocSc Birm. Reader, Economic and Social Studies of East Europe

Other Staff: 4 Lectrs.; 3 Res. Fellows; 3 Instructors†; 11 Hon. Res. Fellows; 2 Temp. Lectrs.†
Research: migration; nationalism; political, economic, security developments

SPECIAL CENTRES, ETC

Albanian Studies, Centre for

Schwandner-Sievers, S., MA Berlin Convenor*

Central European Studies, Centre for

Pynsent, R. B., MA Camb., PhD Camb. Convenor*

Language Unit

Dingley, J., MA Camb. Manager†*
Other Staff: 5 Lectors; 1 Sr. Lectr. (Czech and Slovak)†; 5 Instructors†

Nationalism in Europe, Centre for the Study of

Schöpflin, G. A., LLB Glas., MA Glas. Convenor*

Polish Migration Studies, Centre for

Hamilton, F. E. I., BSc(Econ) Lond., PhD Lond. Acting Convenor*
Other Staff: 1 Res. Fellow

South-East European Studies, Centre for

Bracewell, C. Wendy, MA Stan., PhD Stan. Convenor*

[Information supplied by the institution as at June 1998, and edited by the ACU]

SCHOOL OF ADVANCED STUDY

SCHOOL OF ADVANCED STUDY

Postal Address: Senate House, Malet Street, London WC1E 7HU
Telephone: (0171) 636 8000, extn 3450
Fax: (0171) 436 2301 *E-mail:* dean@sas.ac.uk
WWW: http://www@sas.ac.uk
Chairman of Curators—Zellick, Prof. Graham
Dean*‡—Daintith, Prof. Terence C., MA Oxf.
Personal Assistant to the Dean—Dinning, Isabel, BA Manc.

GENERAL INFORMATION

History. The school was created in 1994 to support, develop and extend the work of the nine research institutes in humanities and social sciences that were its founding members. It is located in Bloomsbury, central London.

[Information supplied by the institution as at 9 March 1998, and edited by the ACU]

The School is an administrative grouping of the following institutes.

CENTRE FOR ENGLISH STUDIES

Postal Address: Room 307 Senate House, Malet Street, London, England WC1E 7HU
Telephone: (0171) 862 8675 *Fax:* (0171) 862 8672 *E-mail:* ces@sas.ac.uk *E-mail formula:* initialsurname@sas.ac.uk

Programme Director*—Gould, Prof. Warwick L., BA Qld.
Administrative Secretary‡—Buckle, Anne C., BA Lond., MA Lond.

GENERAL INFORMATION

History. Established in 1991, the centre is a programme of the School of Advanced Studies. It is located in central London.

First Degrees are not offered.

Higher Degrees (of University of London). MA, MPhil, PhD.
Applicants for admission should hold a first degree or equivalent and have a good command of written and spoken English.

Fees (1997–98, annual). Home/EU students: £2490 (full-time); £1245 (part-time). International students (full-time): £6610.

Academic Year. Two semesters.

Statistics. Staff: 5 (2 academic, 3 administrative).

[Information supplied by the institution as at May 1998, and edited by the ACU]

INSTITUTE OF ADVANCED LEGAL STUDIES

Postal Address: Charles Clore House, 17 Russell Square, London, England WC1B 5DR
Telephone: (0171) 637 1731 *Fax:* (0171) 580 9613 *E-mail:* dphillip@sas.ac.uk

Chairman of the Institute Board—Nolan, The Rt. Hon. Lord, MA Oxf.
Director*—Rider, Prof. B. A. K., LLB Lond., MA Camb., PhD Lond., PhD Camb., Hon. LLD Dickinson Sch.Law
Librarian—Winterton, J. R., BA Kent, LLB Lond.

Administrative Secretary—Phillips, D. E., BA Leeds

GENERAL INFORMATION

History. The institute was established in 1947. It is located in central London.

First Degrees are not offered.

Higher Degrees (of University of London). MPhil, PhD: by research.

Libraries. Over 226,000 volumes; 2800 serials subscribed to. Special collections: Commonwealth law (including Commonwealth Law Library of the Foreign and Commonwealth Office); public and private law; UK and European law.

Academic Year (1997–98). 28 September–10 September.

Income (1996–97). Total, £2,273,900.

Statistics. Staff: 69 (15 academic; 54 library/administrative/domestic). Students: full-time 19 (10 men, 9 women); part-time 27 (19 men, 8 women).

ACADEMIC UNITS

Daintith, Terence C., MA Oxf. Prof.†
Sherr, Avrom, LLB Lond., PhD Warw. Woolf Prof., Legal Education

[Information supplied by the institution as at 21 March 1998, and edited by the ACU]

INSTITUTE OF CLASSICAL STUDIES

Postal Address: Senate House, Malet Street, London, England WC1E 7HU
Telephone: (0171) 862 8700 Fax: (0171) 862 8722

Chairman of the Board—Miller, R. F., BSc PhD, FIP
Director*—Waywell, Prof. G. B., MA Camb., PhD Camb., FSA
Secretary‡—Packer, Margaret M., BA
Librarian—Annis, C. H., BA

[Information supplied by the institution as at March 1998, and edited by the ACU]

INSTITUTE OF COMMONWEALTH STUDIES

Postal Address: 28 Russell Square, London, England WC1B 5DS
Telephone: (0171) 580 5876 Fax: (0171) 255 2160 E-mail: rowenak@sas.ac.uk E-mail formula: initial.surname@sas.ac.uk

Chairman of Board—Porter, Prof. Andrew N., MA Camb., PhD Camb.
Director*—Caplan, Prof. A. Patricia, MA PhD
Head, Sir Robert Menzies Centre for Australian Studies—Bridge, Prof. Carl R., BA Syd., PhD Flin.
Pro Director—Holland, Robert F., MA Oxf., DPhil Oxf.
Administrative Secretary‡—Kochanowska, Rowena M., BA Wales, BA Lond.
Librarian—Blake, David S., BA Reading, MSc

GENERAL INFORMATION

History. The institute was established by the University of London in 1949. It is located in central London.

First Degrees are not offered.

Higher Degrees (of University of London). MA, MPhil, PhD.

Applicants for admission to master's degree courses must normally hold a first degree with at least upper second class honours or equivalent qualification.

Libraries. 160,000 volumes; 900 periodicals subscribed to. Special collections include: archival collections; political party, trades union and pressure group materials; West India Committee.

Fees. Postgraduate (annual): £2560 (UK/EU students, 1997–98); £7000 (international students).

Academic Year (1998–99). Three terms: 28 September–18 December; 18 January–16 April; 10 May–18 June.

Income (1997–98). Total, £851,493.

Statistics. Staff: 21 (9 academic, 12 library/administrative). Students: full-time 21 (8 men, 13 women); part-time 10 (3 men, 7 women); international 14 (5 men, 9 women); total 31.

ACADEMIC UNITS

Caplan, A. Patricia, MA Lond., PhD Lond. Prof., Social Anthropology
Fottrell, Deirdre, BA N.U.I., LLB N.U.I., MA Dublin City, LLM Programme Dir., MA in Understanding and Securing Human Rights
Holland, Robert F., MA Oxf., DPhil Oxf. Reader, Imperial and Commonwealth History
Lyon, Peter H., BSc(Econ) PhD Reader, International Relations
Twaddle, Michael J., BA Camb., PhD Reader
Other Staff: 1 Res. Fellow; 1 Lectr.†
Research: colonial/imperial history including decolonisation, modern African and Caribbean history; politics and international affairs (conflict and accommodation in the new states of the Commonwealth, migration and ethnicity, nationalism); social anthropology (food and food security, gender and development, sexuality); specialist areas (Australia, East Africa, English-speaking Caribbean, Mediterranean (especially Cyprus), South Asia)

Australian Studies, Sir Robert Menzies Centre for

Fax: (0171) 580 9627

Bridge, Carl R., BA Syd., PhD Flin. Prof.; Head*
Other Staff: 1 Lectr.
Research: Australia in the international economy; Australian cultural, economic, diplomatic and military history since 1900

[Information supplied by the institution as at 1 April 1998, and edited by the ACU]

INSTITUTE OF GERMANIC STUDIES

Postal Address: 29 Russell Square, London, England WC1B 5DP
Telephone: (0171) 580 2711 Fax: (0171) 436 3497 E-mail: igs@sas.ac.uk Cables: Germanic Institute, Russell Square, London

Chairman of Board—Balzer, K.
Honorary Director*—......
Deputy Director—Flood, Prof. J. L., MA Nott., PhD Lond.
Administrative Secretary—Hellmer, Karin
Librarian—Abbey, W., BA Leeds

ACADEMIC UNITS

Flood, J. L., MA Nott., PhD Lond. Prof., German

[Information supplied by the institution as at 12 February 1998, and edited by the ACU]

INSTITUTE OF HISTORICAL RESEARCH

Postal Address: Senate House, Malet Street, London, England WC1E 7HU
Telephone: (0171) 862 8740 Fax: (0171) 436 2183 E-mail: ihr@sas.ac.uk WWW: http://www.ihrinfo.ac.uk E-mail formula: initial.surname@sas.ac.uk

Director*—Cannadine, Prof. D. N., MA Camb., LittD Camb., DPhil Oxf., FRHistS
Academic Secretary‡—Smith, S. R. B., BA Lond., PhD Lond., FRHistS
Editor, Victoria History of the Counties of England—Currie, C. R. J., MA Oxf., DPhil Oxf., FSA
Librarian—Lyons, R., BA York(UK)

ACADEMIC UNITS

Cannadine, D. N., MA Camb., LittD Camb., DPhil Oxf., FRHistS Prof.
Greenway, Diana E., MA Camb., PhD Camb., FSA Prof., Mediaeval History

Metropolitan History, Centre for

Tel: (0171) 862 8790

Keene, D. J., MA Oxf., DPhil Oxf., FRHistS Dir.*

Victoria County History

No staff at present

[Information supplied by the institution as at 1 June 1998, and edited by the ACU]

INSTITUTE OF LATIN AMERICAN STUDIES

Postal Address: 31 Tavistock Square, London, England WC1H 9HA
Telephone: (0171) 387 5671 Fax: (0171) 388 5024 E-mail: ilas@sas.ac.uk

Chairman of Board—James, Sir Kenneth, KCMG
Director*—Dunkerley, Prof. James, BA York(UK), DPhil Oxf.
Administrative Secretary‡—Bell, A., MA St And., MPhil CNAA
Librarian—Biggins, A., BSc Salf.

GENERAL INFORMATION

History. The institute was established in 1965 as a Senate Institute of the University of London. It is a member institute of the university's School of Advanced Study.

Higher Degrees (of University of London). MA, MSc, MPhil, PhD.

ACADEMIC UNITS

Bulmer-Thomas, Victor G., OBE, MA Oxf., DPhil Oxf. Prof.
Dunkerley, James, BA York(UK), DPhil Oxf. Prof.
Molyneux, Maxine, BA Essex, PhD Essex Sr. Lectr.
Posada-Carbó, Eduardo, BA(Law) Pontif.Bogotá, MPhil Oxf., DPhil Oxf. Sr. Lectr.

[Information supplied by the institution as at 17 March 1998, and edited by the ACU]

INSTITUTE OF ROMANCE STUDIES

Postal Address: Room 307 Senate House, Malet Street, London, England WC1E 7HU
Telephone: (0171) 862 8676 *Fax:* (0171) 862 8672 *E-mail:* irs@sas.ac.uk E-mail formula: initialsurname@sas.ac.uk

Chairman of Advisory Board—Robey, Prof. David, BA PhD
Honorary Director*—Labanyi, Prof. Josephine M., MA *Oxf.*
Administrative Secretary‡—Buckle, Anne C., BA *Lond.*, MA *Lond.*

GENERAL INFORMATION

History. The institute was founded by the Senate of the University of London in 1989 and has been part of the School of Advanced Study since 1994. It is located in central London.
   Currently no degree courses are offered: the institute focuses on conferences and seminar programmes.

Academic Year (1998–99). Three terms: September–December; January–Easter; Easter–June/July.

Statistics. Staff (shared with Centre for English Studies): 8 (5 academic, 3 administrative).

ACADEMIC UNITS

Armour, Prof. Peter J., BA *Manc.*, PhD *Leic.* Hon. Assoc. Dir., Italian
Garcia Gomez, Prof. Angel M., LicFil *Madrid*, BA BD PhD Hon. Assoc. Dir., Spanish
Macedo, Prof. Helder M., BA *Lond.*, PhD *Lond.* Hon. Assoc. Dir., Portuguese
Worton, Prof. Michael J., MA *Edin.*, PhD *Lond.* Hon. Assoc. Dir., French

[Information supplied by the institution as at May 1998, and edited by the ACU]

INSTITUTE OF UNITED STATES STUDIES

Founded 1965

Postal Address: Senate House, Malet Street, London, England WC1E 7HU
Telephone: (0171) 862 8693 *Fax:* (0171) 862 8696 *E-mail:* iuss@sas.ac.uk

Director*‡—McDowell, Prof. Gary L., AM *Chic.*, PhD *Virginia*, MA
Assistant Director—McGeehan, R., PhD *Col.*
Programme Officer—Brooke, Anna, BA *Wales*

GENERAL INFORMATION

History. The institute was founded in 1965.

First Degrees are not offered.

Higher Degrees (of University of London). MA, MPhil, PhD.
   Admission to postgraduate degree programmes is based on prior academic record, letters of reference, possible interview and (for PhD) proposed research project.

Fees. UK/EU students: £2610; international students: £6500.

[Information supplied by the institution as at 10 June 1998, and edited by the ACU]

WARBURG INSTITUTE

Postal Address: Woburn Square, London, England WC1H 0AB
Telephone: (0171) 580 9663 *Fax:* (0171) 436 2852 *WWW:* http://www.sas.ac.uk/warburg E-mail formula: initial.surname@sas.ac.uk

Chairman of Board—Kenny, Sir Anthony, MA *Oxf.*, DPhil *Oxf.*, Hon. DLitt *Brist.*, Hon. DLitt *Glas.*, Hon. DLitt *Liv.*, Hon. DLitt *Lafayette*, Hon. DHumLitt *Dennison*, Hon. DCL *Oxf.*, FBA
Director*—Mann, Prof. Nicholas, MA *Camb.*, PhD *Camb.*, FBA
Secretary and Registrar‡—Pollard, Anita C., BA
Librarian—Ryan, W. F., MA *Oxf.*, DPhil *Oxf.*
Curator of Photographic Collection—McGrath, Elizabeth, MA *Glas.*, PhD

GENERAL INFORMATION

History. The institute was developed from the library of Professor A. M. Warburg

(1866–1929) of Hamburg. It was transferred to England in 1933 and incorporated in the University of London in 1944.

First Degrees are not offered.

Higher Degrees (of University of London). MA, MPhil, PhD.
   Applicants for admission must normally hold an appropriate first degree with at least upper second class honours. MA: knowledge of Latin essential.
   MA: 1 year full-time; MPhil, PhD: 3 years full-time or 4–5 years part-time.

Libraries. 340,000 volumes and offprints; 3000 journal titles; photographic collection (300,000 items).

Fees (1998–99, annual). Postgraduate: £2610 (UK/EU students); £6950 (international students).

Academic Awards. One–two long-term and about 12 short-term research fellowships offered annually.

Academic Year (1998–99). Three terms: 5 October–11 December; 11 January–19 March; 19 April–25 June.

Statistics. Staff: 19. Students: full-time 21 (8 men, 13 women); part-time 10 (3 men, 7 women); international 4 (3 men, 1 woman); total 31.

ACADEMIC UNITS

Chambers, D. S., MA *Oxf.*, DPhil *Oxf.* Reader, Renaissance Studies
Hope, Charles, DPhil *Oxf.*, MA Sr. Lectr., Renaissance Studies
Kraye, Jill, BA *Calif.*, MA *Col.*, MPhil *Col.*, PhD *Col.* Sr. Lectr., History of Philosophy
Mann, Nicholas, MA *Camb.*, PhD *Camb.*, FBA Prof., History of the Classical Tradition
Other Staff: 1 Lectr.
Research: interdisciplinary study of the classical tradition (influence of the ancient world on all aspects of European culture and intellectual history, especially the Renaissance)

[Information supplied by the institution as at 17 March 1998, and edited by the ACU]

ASSOCIATE INSTITUTIONS

These are public educational institutions not in receipt of HEFC grants at which the university recognises certain staff members giving courses for students studying for degrees or diplomas of the university as internal students, as teachers of the university.

INSTITUTE OF CANCER RESEARCH

Tel: (0171) 352 8133 *Fax:* (0171) 225 2574

Aherne, G. Wynne, BSc *Wales*, PhD Sr. Lectr., Biochemical Pharmacology
Ashworth, A., BSc PhD Prof., Molecular Biology
Brada, M., BSc *Brist.*, MB ChB *Brist.*, FRCR Sr. Lectr., Radiotherapy
Catovsky, D., MD DSc(Med) Prof., Haematology
Cooper, C. S., PhD *Birm.*, DSc *Warw.* Prof., Molecular Biology

Corner, Jessica L., BSc PhD Prof., Cancer Nursing
Dean, C. J., PhD Sr. Lectr., Microbiology
Dearnaley, D. P., MA *Camb.*, MB BChir *Camb.*, MD *Camb.*, FRCP, FRCR Sr. Lectr., Radiotherapy
Dowsett, M., BSc PhD Prof., Biochemical Endocrinology
Dyer, M. J. S., MB BChir *Camb.*, MA *Oxf.*, DPhil *Oxf.* Sr. Lectr., Haematology
Eccles, Suzanne A., BSc *Manc.*, MSc PhD Sr. Lectr., Experimental Oncology
Enver, T., BSc PhD Sr. Lectr., Molecular Biology

Garland, P. B., MB BChir *Camb.*, MA *Camb.*, PhD *Camb.*, Hon. LLD *Dund.*, FRSEd Prof., Biochemistry
Goodwin, G. H., MSc PhD Reader, Biochemistry
Greaves, M. F., BSc PhD Prof., Cell Biology
Gusterson, B. A., BSc BDS MB BS PhD Prof., Histopathology
Horwich, A., PhD *CNAA*, MB BS, FRCP, FRCR Prof., Radiotherapy
Husband, Janet E., MB BS, FRCP, FRCR Prof., Diagnostic Radiology
Jackman, Ann L., PhD Reader, Biochemistry
Jarman, M., MA *Camb.*, PhD *Camb.*, DSc, FRSChem Prof., Chemistry

Judson, I. R., MA Camb., MD Camb., FRCP Reader, Clinical Pharmacology

Kelland, L. R., BPharm Bath, PhD Bath Reader, Pharmacology

Lanceley, Anne, BA Lond. Sr. Lectr., Nursing Studies

Leach, M. O., BSc Sur., MSc Birm., PhD Birm. Prof., Physics applied to Medicine

Marshall, C. J., MA Camb., DPhil Oxf., FRS Prof., Cell Biology

Matutes, Estela, MD Barcelona, PhD Sr. Lectr., Haematology

McCready, V. R., MB BCh BAO Belf., DSc Belf., MSc, FRCP, FRCR Prof., Radiological Sciences

Millar, Barbara C., BSc PhD Sr. Lectr., Cell Biology

Millar, J. L., BSc Witw., MSc E.Anglia, PhD Sr. Lectr., Cell Biology and Experimental Pathology

Moss, Susan M., BSc Brist., MSc Exe., PhD Sr. Lectr., Epidemiology

Nahum, A. E., BA Oxf., PhD Edin. Reader, Medical Physics

Neidle, S., BSc PhD Prof., Biophysics

Ott, R. J., BSc S'ton., PhD S'ton. Prof., Radiation Physics

Peto, J., MA Oxf., MSc CRC Prof., Epidemiology

Phillips, D. H., BA Oxf., PhD Reader, Molecular Carcinogenesis

Pinkerton, C. R., MD Belf., FRCPI CRC Prof., Paediatric Oncology

Powles, R. L., MD, FRCP Prof., Haematological Oncology

Serafinowski, P., MPhil Warsaw, PhD Poznan, FRSChem Sr. Lectr., Organic Chemistry

Snell, K., BSc Manc., PhD Manc. Reader, Biochemistry

Springer, Caroline J., PhD Lond. Reader, Molecular Pharmacology

Steel, G. G., BSc Birm., PhD DSc Prof., Radiation Biology applied to Radiotherapy

Stratton, M. R., BA Oxf., MB BS PhD Prof., Cancer Genetics

Venitt, S., BSc S'ton., PhD S'ton. Reader, Cancer Studies

Webb, S., BSc PhD DSc Prof., Radiological Physics

Weiss, R. A., BSc PhD, FRCPath Prof., Viral Oncology

Wiedemann, Leanne M., BS St.Norbert, PhD Ohio Reader, Cellular and Molecular Biology

Willison, K. R., BSc Sus., PhD Camb. Prof., Molecular Cell Biology

Yarnold, J. R., BSc MB BS, FRCR Reader, Radiotherapy

Zelent, A. Z., PhD Mt. Sinai Sr. Lectr., Molecular Biology/Biochemistry

JEWS' COLLEGE

Tel: (0181) 203 6427 Fax: (0181) 203 6420

Fierstone, C. A., MA Teacher, Jewish Studies

Stern, Rabbi S. D., MA DrPhil Jewish Studies

ROYAL ACADEMY OF MUSIC

Tel: (0171) 873 7373 Fax: (0171) 873 7374

Biddlecombe, G. C., MA PhD Teacher, Music

Daiken, Melanie R., MMus Composition and Contemporary Music

Dreyfus, L., MA PhD Prof., Performance Studies in Music

Patterson, P. L., FRAM Teacher, Composition

ROYAL COLLEGE OF MUSIC

Tel: (0171) 589 3643 Fax: (0171) 589 7740

Burnand, D. G., BMus MA Teacher, Music

Roxburgh, E., BMus Durh., BA Camb., FRCM Teacher, Music

Salter, T. J., MA Camb., FRCM Teacher, Music

Swanston, R. B., MA Camb., MusB Camb., FRCO Teacher, Music

TRINITY COLLEGE OF MUSIC

Tel: (0171) 935 5773 Fax: (0171) 224 6278

Pipe, M., BMus Teacher, Music (History and Musical Techniques)

Wright, D. C. H., MMus, FTCL Teacher, Music

Young, Felicity, BMus, Hon. FTCL Teacher, Music

CAMPUS/COLLEGE HEADS

Institute of Cancer Research, 17a Onslow Gardens, London, England SW7 3AL. (Tel: (0171) 352 8133; Fax: (0171) 225 2574.) Chief Executive: Garland, Prof. P. B., MB BChir Camb., MA Camb., PhD Camb., Hon. LLD Dund., FRSEd

Jews' College, 44a Albert Road, London, England NW4 2SJ. (Tel: (0181) 203 6427; Fax: (0181) 203 6420.) Director: Ruben, Prof. D. H., BA Dartmouth, PhD Harv.

Royal Academy of Music, Marylebone Road, London, England NW1 5HT. (Tel: (0171) 873 7373; Fax: (0171) 873 7374.) Principal: Price, C. A., AM Harv., PhD Harv.

Royal College of Music, Prince Consort Road, London, England SW7 2BS. (Tel: (0171) 589 3643; Fax: (0171) 589 7740.) Director: Ritterman, Janet, BMus PhD, FTCL

Trinity College of Music, Mandeville Place, London, England W1M 6AQ. (Tel: (0171) 935 5773; Fax: (0171) 224 6278.) Principal: Henderson, G. D., BFA Hon. MA

[Information supplied as at 16 July 1998, and edited by the ACU]

The University of London Directory to Subjects of Study follows on p. 1586

UNIVERSITY OF LONDON : DIRECTORY

The table below shows which of the institutions indicated provide facilities for study and/or research in the subjects named. The table covers *broad subject areas* only: ie the individual subjects of specialisation in certain professional fields, such as education, law, medicine or verterinary science, are not included. In the case of related subject areas which have been grouped together (eg Botany/Plant Science), it should be borne in mind that one of more of the subjects may be offered by the institution concerned.

	Birkbeck Coll.	Goldsmiths Coll.	Heythrop Coll.	Imperial Coll. of Sci., Technol. and Med.	Institute of Education	King's Coll. London	London Business Sch.	London Sch. of Econ. and Pol. Sci.	London Sch. of Hyg. and Trop. Med.	Queen Mary and Westfield Coll.	Royal Holloway, U. of London	Royal Veterinary Coll.	St George's Hosp. Med. Sch.	School of Oriental and African Studies	School of Pharmacy	University Coll. London	Wye Coll., U. of London
Accountancy/Accounting	U							X									
Agriculture/Agricultural Science																	X
American Studies								X									
Animal Science											UD	X					UD
Anthropology		X						X						X		X	
Arabic														X			
Archaeology	X										D			X		X	
Architecture								UM								X	
Art, History of	X	X												X		X	
Asian Studies								X						X			
Astronomy											X					X	
Behavioural Sciences	U							X					X			MD	
Biochemistry	UM			X		X			MD	X	UD		UD			X	UD
Biology	X			X		X			MD	X	UD					X	X
Botany/Plant Science				X							UD					D	X
Building/Built Environment/Construction																X	
Business/Commerce	M						MD	X			X						X
Chemistry	X			X		X				X	MD				D	X	
Chinese														X			
Classics/Greek/Latin/Ancient History	X					X				X						X	
Computer Science	MD	X		X		X		X		X	X					X	
Dentistry						X				X							
Design		X															
Development Studies								X			MD			X			MD
Drama/Theatre/Dance		X								X	X						
Economics	X							X	MD	X	X			X		X	MD
Education		X			MD	X											
Engineering											X					X	
aeronautical/aerospace				X							X						
chemical/process				X												X	
civil/environmental/structural				X							X					X	
computer				X													
electrical/electronic				X		X				X	UD					X	
manufacturing				X													
mechanical				X		X				X						X	
English	X	X				X				X	X					X	
Environmental Science/Studies	X			X		X		X	MD	X	X						X
European Studies	M	X				U		X			X					X	
Fashion/Textiles		X															
Finance/Banking	X						M	X									
Film Studies/Television	M							U			X						
Fine Art		X														X	
Food Science/Nutrition						X			MD								
French	X	U				X				X	X					X	
Geography	X					X		X		X	X			X		X	
Geology/Earth Sciences	UD			X						X	X					X	

TO SUBJECTS OF STUDY

For further information about the individual subjects taught at each institution, please refer to the *Index to Department Names* at the end of the Yearbook, but for full details about subjects/courses offered at universities and university colleges in the Commonwealth each institution's own official publications must be consulted. U = may be studied for first degree course; M = may be studied for master's degree course; D = research facilities to doctoral level; X = all three levels (UMD).

	Birkbeck Coll.	Goldsmiths Coll.	Heythrop Coll.	Imperial Coll. of Sci., Technol. and Med.	Institute of Education	King's Coll. London	London Business Sch.	London Sch. of Econ. and Pol. Sci	London Sch. of Hyg. and Trop. Med.	Queen Mary and Westfield Coll.	Royal Holloway, U. of London	Royal Veterinary Coll.	St George's Hosp. Med. Sch.	School of Oriental and African Studies	School of Pharmacy	University Coll. London	Wye Coll., U. of London
Health Sciences/Studies						X			MD				MD			MD	
Hebrew/Semitic Studies														X		X	
History	X			MD		X		X		X	X			X		X	
Horticulture																	X
Industrial Relations/Human Resource Management				MD				X									
Information Science/Systems/Technology	X			X		X				M	MD					X	
International Relations/Studies						X		MD									
Islamic/Middle Eastern Studies														X			
Italian										U	X					X	
Japanese											U			X			
Journalism/Communication/Media Studies		X		M				U			U						
Law/Legal Studies	UD					X		X		X				X		X	
Library/Information Science																X	
Linguistics	X									X				X		X	
Management	X			MD		X		X			X						X
Marketing																	X
Materials Science	MD			X						X					D	D	
Mathematics	U	X				X		X		X	X					X	
Medicine/Surgery				X		X			MD	X			X			X	
Microbiology	M			X		X			MD	X			UD			X	MD
Music		X				X					X			X			
Nursing/Midwifery						X							UD				
Optometry																MD	
Pharmacology						X			MD	X			UD		X	X	
Pharmacy						X				X					X		
Philosophy	X	MD	X			X		X		X						X	
Physical Education/Sports Science										X							
Physics				X		X				X	X					X	
Physiology	M					X				X			UD			X	
Physiotherapy						X							UD			MD	
Planning, Urban/Regional		M						X								X	
Politics/Political Science/Government	X	X						X		X	X			X			
Portuguese						X										X	
Psychology	X	X						X			X		X			X	
Religion/Theology		MD				X		X						X			
Russian										X							
Sanskrit														X			
Scandinavian Studies																X	
Social Work/Policy/Studies	U	MD						X	MD		X						
Sociology	MD	X						X		X	X						
Spanish/Hispanic/Latin American Studies	X					X				X	UM					X	
Statistics	X	X						X	MD							X	
Surveying																MD	
Teacher Training		UM			MD												
Veterinary Science												X					
Zoology				X						UD						UD	

LONDON GUILDHALL UNIVERSITY

Established 1992; founded as City of London Polytechnic 1970

Postal Address: 31 Jewry Street, London, England EC3N 2EY
Telephone: (0171) 320 1000 **Fax**: (0171) 320 1315 **E-mail**: postmaster@lgu.ac.uk **WWW**: http://www.lgu.ac.uk

PROVOST*—Floud, Prof. Roderick C., MA Oxf., DPhil Oxf., FRHistS
ACADEMIC REGISTRAR‡—Grinstead, Jill, BA Brist., MPhil Lond.

LONDON INSTITUTE

Incorporated 1989; degree-awarding powers 1993

Postal Address: 65 Davies Street, London, England W1Y 2DA
Telephone: (0171) 514 6113 **Fax**: (0171) 514 6131 **E-mail**: m.jama@linst.ac.uk **WWW**: http://www.linst.ac.uk
E-mail formula: initial.surname@linst.ac.uk

RECTOR*—Stubbs, Sir William, BSc Glas., PhD Glas.
INSTITUTE SECRETARY‡—Prince, Martin H., BA York(UK), MA Reading

---

LOUGHBOROUGH UNIVERSITY

Incorporated by Royal Charter 1966; previously established as Loughborough College of Technology 1952

Member of the Association of Commonwealth Universities

Postal Address: Loughborough, England LE11 3TU
Telephone: (01509) 263171 **Fax**: (01509) 610813 **Cables**: Technology, Loughborough
WWW: http://www.lboro.ac.uk **E-mail formula**: initials.surname@lboro.ac.uk

VISITOR—Cooper, The Rt. Hon. Sir Frank, GCB, CMG
CHANCELLOR—Rooke, Sir Denis, CBE, OM, BSc(Eng) Lond., Hon. DSc Salf., Hon. DSc Leeds, Hon. DSc City(UK), Hon. DSc Durh., Hon. DSc Cran.IT, Hon. DSc Lond., Hon. DTech CNAA, Hon. DEng Brad., Hon. LLD Bath, Hon. DUniv Sur., Hon. DSc Lough., FEng, FRS
SENIOR PRO-CHANCELLOR—Miller, Stewart C., CBE, BSc Edin., Hon. DTech Lough., FEng, FIMechE, FRAeS, FRS
PRO-CHANCELLOR—Green, J. K., BSc Nott., Hon. DTech Lough., FICE
VICE-CHANCELLOR*—Wallace, Prof. David J., CBE, BSc Edin., PhD Edin., FRS, FRSEd, FIP
TREASURER—Higgins, Terence, OBE, JP, FCIS
SENIOR PRO-VICE-CHANCELLOR—McCaffer, Prof. Ronald, BSc Strath., PhD Lough., FEng, FICE
PRO-VICE-CHANCELLOR (TEACHING)—Feather, Prof. John P., BLitt Oxf., MA Oxf., MA Camb., PhD Lough., FLA
PRO-VICE-CHANCELLOR (RESEARCH)—Williams, Prof. Clyde, BSc Wales, MSc Wash., PhD Aberd.
PRO-VICE-CHANCELLOR (EXTERNAL RELATIONS)—Thomason, Prof. Harry, MSc Salf., PhD Lough.
REGISTRAR‡—Fletcher, David E., BA Sheff., PhD Sheff.
LIBRARIAN—Morley, Mary D., BA Nott.

GENERAL INFORMATION

History. The university was established as Loughborough College of Technology in 1952 and incorporated as a university in 1966. In 1998 Loughborough College of Art and Design merged with the university. The university is located in the East Midlands.

Admission to first degree courses (see also United Kingdom Introduction). For the purpose of its general entrance requirements the university recognises all General Certificate of Education (GCE) A level and AS level subjects. Many overseas qualifications also accepted.

First Degrees (see also United Kingdom Directory to Subjects of Study). BA, BEd, BEng, BLS, BSc, BTech, MChem, MComp, MEng, MMath, MPhys.

Higher Degrees (see also United Kingdom Directory to Subjects of Study). MA, MBA, MSc, MPhil, PhD, DLitt, DSc, DTech.

Language of Instruction. English (except for courses in modern European studies: French, German and Spanish). Four-week intensive English language course at the start of each semester; two-week study skills course and a one-week pre-sessional course.

Libraries. 550,000 volumes; about 4000 periodicals subscribed to. Special collection: European Union.

Fees (1998–99). Undergraduate: (UK/EU students) up to £1000; (international students) £6248 (arts), £8177 (sciences). Postgraduate: (UK/EU students) £2610; (international) £6248 (arts), £8177 (sciences).

Academic Awards (1997–98). 234 awards ranging in value from £25 to £1000.

Academic Year (1998–99). Two semesters: 28 September- 5 February; 8 February–11 June.

Income (1996–97). Total, £92,477,000.

Statistics (1996–97). Staff: 2551 (1331 academic/academic-related/research, 1220 clerical/secretarial/ancillary). Students: full-time 8789; part-time 1717; international 1048; total 10,506 (7105 men, 3401 women).

FACULTIES/SCHOOLS

Engineering
Tel: (01509) 223210 Fax: (01509) 223934
Dean: Halliwell, Prof. Neil A., BSc Liv., PhD Liv., DSc S'ton., FEng, FIMechE, FIP

Science
Tel: (01509) 222552 Fax: (01509) 223925
Dean: Dawkins, Prof. John V., BSc Birm., PhD Birm., DSc Birm., FRSChem

Social Sciences and Humanities
Tel: (01509) 222720 Fax: (01509) 223962
Dean: Morison, Prof. Ian C., MA Oxf.

ACADEMIC UNITS

Art and Design, School of
Tel: (01509) 261515 Fax: (01509) 265515
Bunkum, Alan, BA CNAA   Head, Introductory Studies
Kavanagh, Terence, MDes RCA, FTI   Dir.*
Minichiello, Mario A., BA CNAA   Sr. Lectr.
Rhodes, Colin, BA CNAA, MA Essex, PhD Essex   Head, Research
Wheeler, Peter J. H., MA Edin.   Head, Academic Affairs
Other Staff: 22 Lectrs.; 12 Lectrs.†; 28 Temp. Lectrs.
Research: art, craft and design practice; Loughborough drawing project and festival; theorisation of art and design practice; virtual reality gallery

Business School
Tel: (01509) 223393 Fax: (01509) 223960-1, 223963
Allen, David, CBE, MPhil, FCIS   CIMA Indust. Prof.†
Arnold, John, BSc Nott., PhD Sheff.   Sr. Lectr.
Calvert, John R., BSc Durh., MSc Warw., MSc Hull, PhD   Sr. Lectr.
Cox, Susan, MPhil Nott.   Prof., Health and Safety Management; Dir.*
Diamantopoulos, Adamantios, BA H-W, MSc H-W, PhD Strath.   Prof., Marketing and Business Research
Drake, Leigh, BA Essex, MA Essex   Dir., Banking Centre
Finlay, Paul N., BSc Manc., PhD Nott.   Prof., Strategic Information Systems
Hill, Malcolm R., BSc CNAA, MSc Birm., PhD Birm.   Prof., Russian and East European Industrial Studies
Howcroft, J. Barry, BA Wales, MSc Wales   Reader, Retail Banking; Dir., Banking Centre
Johnson, David G., BSc Leeds, FIMA   Sr. Lectr.
King, Michael, MA Oxf., DPhil Oxf.   Prof., Management Sciences
Lawrence, Peter A., BA Lond., MA Essex   Prof., Comparative Management
Morison, Ian C., MA Oxf.   Midland Group Prof., Banking and Finance
Saker, James, BSc Wales, MSc Manc.   Sr. Lectr.
Sizer, John, CBE, BA Nott., DLitt   Visiting Prof.
Smith, Gareth, BA Essex, MSc Warw.   Sr. Lectr.
Wilson, John M., BSc Glas., MSc Sus., DPhil Sus.   Reader, Operational Research
Wilson, Richard M. S., BA Open(UK), BPhil Open(UK), MSc Brad.   Prof., Business Administration and Financial Management

Other Staff: 26 Lectrs.; 3 Res. Fellows
Research: accounting and finance management; banking and finance; European business; management sciences; retail management

Hazard and Risk Management, Centre for
Tel: (01509) 222158 Fax: (01509) 223991
Petts, Judith I., BA Exe.   Dir.*
Other Staff: 6 Lectrs.
Research: hazardous waste management; healthcare risk management; investigatory management; occupational health and safety; security management

Chemistry
Tel: (01509) 222592 Fax: (01509) 223925
Bowman, W. Russel, BSc Cape Town, PhD Alta., FRSChem   Sr. Lectr.
Dart, R. Kinsey, BSc Wales, PhD Wales, FRSChem   Sr. Lectr.
Dawkins, John V., BSc Birm., PhD Birm., DSc Birm., FRSChem   Prof., Polymer Chemistry
Edmonds, Tony E., BSc Lond., MSc Lond., PhD Lond., FRSChem   Sr. Lectr.
Marples, Brian A., PhD Leeds, DSc Leeds, FRSChem   Prof., Organic and Medicine Chemistry
Miller, James N., MA Camb., PhD Camb., FRSChem   Prof., Analytical Chemistry
Page, Philip, CB, BSc Lond., PhD Lond., FRSChem   Prof., Organic Chemistry
Sharp, Barry L., BSc Lond., PhD Lond., FRSChem   Sr. Lectr.
Smith, Roger M., BSc Manc., MSc Manc., PhD ANU, FRSChem   Prof., Analytical Chemistry
Sutherland, Ian, BSc Brist., MSc Brist., PhD Brist.   Sr. Lectr.
Traynor, John R., BSc Aston, PhD Aston   Sr. Lectr.
Warwick, Peter, BA Open(UK), MSc Lough., PhD Lough., FRSChem   Sr. Lectr.
Wetton, Raymond E., BSc Brist., MSc Brist., PhD Manc.   Visiting Prof.†
Wilkinson, Francis, BSc Sheff., MA Oxf., PhD Sheff., FRSChem   Prof., Physical Chemistry; Head*
Woollins, J. Derek, BSc E.Anglia, PhD E.Anglia, FRSChem   Prof., Inorganic Chemistry
Other Staff: 9 Lectrs.; 4 Res. Fellows; 2 Temp. Lectrs.
Research: analytical; environmental; inorganic and structural; organic and biomedical; physical

Computer Studies
Tel: (01509) 222681 Fax: (01509) 211586
Alty, James L., BSc Liv., PhD Liv., FIEE   Prof.; Dir., Computer-Human Interface Res. Centre
Bedi, Satish, BSc Salf., MSc Manc.   Systems Manager
Bez, Helmut E., BSc Wales, MSc Oxf., DPhil Oxf.   Reader
Clarke, Anthony A., BSc(Tech) Wales   Sr. Lectr.
Connolly, John H., MA Camb., PhD Reading   Sr. Lectr.
Edmonds, Ernest A., BSc Leic., MSc Nott., PhD Nott., FIEE   Prof.; Exec. Dir., Computer-Human Interface Res. Centre
Evans, David J., MSc S'ton., PhD Manc., DSc Wales, FIMA   Emer. Prof.
Grant, Gordon, BSc Lond., FIMA   Sr. Lectr.
Hinde, Chris J., BSc Brist., PhD Brun.   Sr. Lectr.
Humrich, Al, BSc Lanc., MSc Leic., PhD Durh.   RAE Visiting Prof.
Lawson, Philip A., BSc Leic., PhD Leic.   Sr. Lectr.
Maller, Victor A. J., MA Camb., FIEE   ICL Visiting Prof., Computer Systems
Newman, Ian A., BSc Nott., PhD Nott.   Reader
Schröder, Heiko, PhD Kiel   Prof., Computing; Dir., Parallel Algorithm and Archits. Res. Centre; Head*
Other Staff: 10 Lectrs.; 1 Res. Fellow; 5 Programmers; 3 System Managers
Vacant Posts: 3 Lectrs.
Research: computer-human interaction(HCI); graphics design and intelligent systems;

information systems engineering; parallel computing

Design and Technology
Tel: (01509) 222652 Fax: (01509) 223999
Baynes, Ken   Visiting Prof.
Brittan, Ken W., BSc Nott., PhD Lond.   Emer. Prof.
Norman, Edwin, MA Oxf., MSc Cran.IT.   Sr. Lectr.
Porter, J. Mark, BSc Lough., PhD Lough.   Prof., Design Ergonomics; Dir., Vehicle Ergonomics Res. Group
Roberts, Phil H., MA(Ed) S'ton., PhD S'ton.   Prof.; Head*
Smith, John S., BSc(Eng) S'ton., MEd Nott.   Sr. Lectr.
Other Staff: 11 Lectrs.; 1 Res. Fellow
Research: design education; design ergonomics; hand performance; vehicle ergonomics

Drama, see Engl. and Drama

Economics
Tel: (01509) 222729 Fax: (01509) 223910
Drake, Leigh M., BA Essex, MA Essex   Reader
Green, Christopher J., BA Oxf., MSc Yale, BPhil Oxf., MPhil Yale, PhD Yale   Prof., Economics and Finance
Hall, Maximilian J. B., BA Nott., PhD Nott.   Sr. Lectr.
Llewellyn, David T., BSc Lond.   Prof., Money and Banking
Maunder, W. Peter J., BA Exe., MSc Nott.   Sr. Lectr.
Mills, Terence C., BA Essex, MA Warw., PhD Warw.   Prof.
Owen Smith, Eric, BA(Econ) Sheff., PhD   Sr. Lectr.
Pentecost, Eric J., BA CNAA, MA Warw., PhD Lond.   Reader
Presley, John R., BA Lanc., PhD Lough.   Prof.
Tew, J. H. Brian, OBE, BSc(Econ) Lond., PhD Camb.   External Prof., Banking Centre†
Westaway, Anthony J., BA Durh., MSc Lond.   Sr. Lectr.
Weyman-Jones, Thomas G., BSc Lond., MSc(Econ) Lond., PhD Melb.   Prof., Industrial Economics; Head*
Other Staff: 5 Lectrs.; 3 Res. Fellows
Vacant Posts: 1 Lectr.
Research: economics of law and regulation; finance, money and international banking; labour markets and industrial organisation; macroeconomics and exchange rates; time series and financial econometrics

Education
Tel: (01509) 222775 Fax: (01509) 223912
Blease, Derek, BA Lond., MPhil   Sr. Lectr.
Demaine, Jack, BA Liv., PhD Liv.   Sr. Lectr.
Hodgkinson, Keith, BA Lond., MEd Nott.   Sr. Lectr.
King, Peter R., BA Nott., MEd Nott.   Sr. Lectr.
Reid, Ivan, BA Leic., MA Liv., PhD Brad.   Schofield Prof.
Stratford, Brian, MA Leeds, DPhil, FBPsS   Sr. Visiting Prof.
Thomas, John B., BA Nott., MEd Wales, PhD Lough., FBPsS   Prof., Educational Studies
Wild, Phil, BSc Nott., PhD Leeds   Head*
Other Staff: 7 Lectrs.; 1 Res. Fellow; 8 Lectrs.†
Research: history of education; human resources management in education; inequality and policy issues; language and learning; school curriculum

Engineering, Aeronautical and Automotive, and Transport Studies
Tel: (01509) 223413 Fax: (01509) 223947
Callow, Geoff, BSc(Eng) S'ton., MSc S'ton., MBA Aston   Indust. Prof.
Caves, Robert, BSc Lond., MSc Cran., PhD Lough.   Sr. Lectr.
Gardner, David, BTech Lough., FRAeS   Visiting Prof.†
Gillingwater, David, MSc(Econ) Lond., PhD Lond.   Sr. Lectr.

Gordon, Tim J., BA Camb., PhD Camb. Ford Prof., Automotive Engineering

Jenkinson, Lloyd R., MSc Cran.IT, PhD Lough. Sr. Lectr.

Lucas, Gordon G., MSc Cran.IT, PhD Lough., FIMechE Ford Prof., Automotive Engineering

McGuirk, James J., BSc Lond., MSc Lond., PhD Lond. Prof., Aerodynamics; Head*

Petersson, Bj(um)orn A. T., MSc Chalmers U.T., PhD Chalmers U.T., DTech Lund, DSc Stockholm Prof., Structural Dynamics

Pitfield, David E., BSc Brist., PhD Stir. Sr. Lectr.

Pratt, Roger W., BSc S'ton., MEng Sheff. Sr. Lectr.

Stevens, Stanley J., MSc Nott., PhD Lough. Emer. Prof.†, Aeronautical Propulsion

Wilde, Geoffrey L., OBE, FRAeS, FIMechE Visiting Prof.†

Other Staff: 16 Lectrs.; 4 Sr. Visiting Fellows; 3 Res. Fellows; 2 Lectrs.†

Research: aeronautical engineering; airport planning; automotive engineering; systems engineering; transport management and planning

Engineering, Chemical

Tel: (01509) 222532 Fax: (01509) 223923

Akers, Richard, BSc Lond., PhD Lond. Sr. Lectr.

Brooks, Brian W., PhD Leeds, DSc Leeds, FIChemE Prof.

Buffham, Bryan A., MEng Yale, DSc(Eng) Lond., PhD, FIChemE Prof.

Carpenter, Keith J., BSc Leeds, PhD Leeds, FIChemE Indust. Prof.

Edwards, David, BSc Lond., PhD Lond., FIChemE Sr Lectr.

Hall, George M., BSc Leeds, PhD Nott. Sr. Lectr.

Holdich, Richard, BSc Birm., PhD Exe. Sr Lectr.

Mason, Geoff, PhD CNAA, DSc Brist. Reader

Nassehi, Vahid, MSc Teheran, MSc Wales, PhD Wales Sr. Lectr.

Patrick, John W., BSc Leic., PhD Lond., FRSChem Prof., Carbon Science

Stenhouse, J. Ian T., BSc Edin., PhD Lough., FIChemE Sr. Lectr.

Streat, Michael, BScTech UMIST., PhD Lond., FIChemE Prof.; Head*

Wakeman, Richard, BSc Manc., MSc Manc., PhD UMIST, FEng, FIChemE Prof.

Ward, Anthony S., BScTech Manc., PhD Lough., FIChemE Sr. Lectr.

Other Staff: 8 Lectrs.; 3 Res. Fellows; 1 Sr. Lectr.†

Research: environmental process engineering; food engineering and biotechnology; particle technology; plant engineering; reaction engineering and transfer processes

Engineering, Civil and Building

Tel: (01509) 222884 Fax: (01509) 223980

Austin, Simon, BSc Lough., PhD Lough. Sr. Lectr.

Baldwin, Andrew N., BSc City(UK), MSc Lough., PhD Lough. Sr. Lectr.

Chandler, James, BSc Newcastle(UK), PhD Lond. Sr. Lectr.

Coad, Adrian, MA Camb., MS Shiraz, PhD Lond. Programme/Project Manager

Dickens, John G., BSc Manc. Sr. Lectr.

Franceys, Richard W. A., BSc Birm., MBA Lough., PhD Lough. Sr. Programme/Project Manager

Hanby, Victor I., BSc Brist., PhD Sheff. Prof.; Head*

Haves, Philip, BA Oxf., PhD Manc. Sr. Lectr.

Holmes, Michael, BSc Visiting Prof.

Howlett, Barbara H., BA Essex Systems Manager

Ince, Margaret E., BSc Birm., PhD Birm. Programme/Project Manager

Loveday, Denis L., BSc Aston, PhD Aston Reader

McCaffer, Ronald, BSc Strath., PhD, FEng, FICE Prof., Construction Management; Dir., European Construcn. Inst.

Miles, Derek W. J., BSc Brist. Dir., Overseas Activities; Dir., Inst. of Devel. Engin.

Parr, Jeremy, BEng Leeds, PhD Leeds Programme/Project Manager

Price, Andrew D. F., BSc CNAA, PhD Lough. Reader

Raoof, Mohammed, BSc Lond., MSc Lond., PhD Lond. Prof., Structural Engineering

Reed, Robert A., BSc CNAA, MSc Lough. Programme/Project Manager

Robins, Peter J., BSc Nott., PhD Nott. Sr. Lectr.

Rogers, Christopher D. F., BSc Leeds, PhD Nott. Reader

Shiono, Koji, BSc Lond., MSc Salf., PhD Birm. Sr. Lectr.

Skinner, Brian H., BSc CNAA, MSc Lough. Programme/Project Manager

Smith, Michael D., MA Camb., MSc Lough. Programme/Project Manager

Smout, Ian K., BA Camb., MSc Reading Sr. Programme/Project Manager

Thorpe, Anthony, BSc Nott., MSc Lough., PhD Lough. Prof., Construction Information Technology

Twigg, David, BSc CNAA, MSc Oxf., PhD Newcastle(UK) Sr. Lectr.

Tyler, Alan H., FRICS Sr. Lectr.

Wheatley, Andrew D., BSc Aston, PhD Aston Prof., Water Technology

Other Staff: 16 Lectrs.

Research: building services; commercial management and quantity surveying; construction engineering management; European construction; water and waste engineering

Engineering, Electronic and Electrical

Tel: (01509) 228100 Fax: (01509) 222854

Cooling, Jim E., BSc Lough., PhD Lough. Sr. Lectr.

Cowan, Colin, BSc Edin., PhD Edin., FIEE Visiting Prof.

Curtis, Tom E., MSc S'ton., PhD S'ton. Visiting Prof.

Dwyer, Vincent M., BA Camb., DPhil York(UK) Sr. Lectr.

Forsythe, Bill, BSc Belf., MSc Cran.IT, PhD Lough. Sr. Lectr.

Freris, Leon L., BSc Lond., MSc Lond., PhD Lond., FIEE Visiting Prof., Centre for Renewable Energy Systems Technol.

Gabb, Bill C., BSc Aston Chief Exper. Officer

Gharavi, Hamid, BSc Teheran, MSc Lough., PhD Lough. Prof., Communications Engineering

Goodall, Roger M., MA Camb., FIEE, FIMechE Prof., Control Systems Engineering

Goodson, Dave, MPhil Chief Exper. Officer

Hackett, David Chief Exper. Officer

Harry, John E., BSc(Eng) Lond., PhD Aston, DSc, FIEE Reader, Electrical Discharges

Infield, David G., BA Lanc., PhD Kent Sr. Lectr.; Dir., Centre for Renewable Energy Systems Technol.

Jones, Simon H., BSc Brun., MSc Brun., PhD Brun., FIEE Prof., Electronic Design

Kearney, Michael, MA Oxf., PhD Warw. Prof., Electronic Device Engineering; Head*

Kettleborough, John G., BSc CNAA, MSc Aston Sr. Lectr.

Lindley, David, OBE, BSc Salf., PhD Wales, FEng, FIMechE Visiting Prof., Centre for Renewable Energy Systems Technol.

Manning, Carl D., BSc Aston, MSc Birm., PhD Birm. Sr. Lectr.

Murgatroyd, Paul N., BSc Brist., PhD Brist., FIP, FIEE Reader

Parish, Dave J., BSc Liv., PhD Liv. Sr. Lectr.

Rodgers, Tim, BSc Lough., MPhil Lough. Chief Exper. Officer

Schwarzenberger, Alan, MA Camb. Network Manager

Sinnadurai, Nihal, BSc Lond., MSc Lond., PhD S'ton. Visiting Prof.

Smith, Ivor A., BSc Brist., PhD Brist., DSc Brist., FIEE, FEng Prof., Electrical Power Engineering

Smith, Peter R., BSc Lond., PhD Lond. Prof., Photonic Engineering

Tomlinson, Roger, BSc Brad. Sr. Exper. Officer

Vadher, Von V., BSc Aston, MPhil Lond., MBA Lough., PhD Sr. Lectr.

Vardaxoglou, Yiannis C., BSc Kent, PhD Kent Prof., Wireless Communications

Withers, Michael J., MSc Birm., FIEE, FEng Royal Academy of Engin. Visiting Prof.

Woodward, Bryan, BSc Lond., MSc Lond., PhD Lond., FIEE Prof., Underwater Acoustics

Other Staff: 13 Lectrs.; 2 Sr. Res. Fellows; 2 Sr. Visiting Fellows; 2 Res. Fellows; 1 Temp. Lectr.

Research: communications and signal processing; electrical power and renewable energy; electronic devices and circuit design; photonics and microwave systems; systems and control

Engineering, Manufacturing

Tel: (01509) 222913 Fax: (01509) 223979

Backhouse, Chris J., BSc Durh., MSc CNAA, PhD CNAA, FIEE Sr. Lectr.; Head*

Bell, Robert, MSc(Tech) Manc., PhD Manc., DSc Manc., FIEE Prof., Manufacturing Technology

Burns, Neil D., BSc Brun., PhD Lough., FIMechE Davy Prof., Manufacturing Systems

Case, Keith, BSc Nott., PhD Nott. Prof., Computer Aided Engineering

Clegg, Allen J., MSc Lough., PhD Lough., FIM Sr. Lectr.

Doyle, Robert, BEng Hull, MSc Hull Systems Devel. Officer

Hodgson, Allan, BTech Lough., MSc Lough. Sr. Lectr.

Jones, Roy, BTech Lough., PhD CNAA Sr. Lectr.

Middle, John E., BTech MSc, FIEE Sr. Lectr.

Newman, Stephen, BSc Aston, PhD Lough. Sr. Lectr.

Popplewell, Keith, BSc Warw., PhD Nott. Sr. Lectr.

Stevens, Anthony, BSc Lond. RAE Visiting Prof.

Walters, David, BSc Wales Systems Manager

Weston, Richard H., BSc Lond., PhD S'ton., FIEE ICL Prof., Flexible Automation

Williams, David J., BSc Manc., PhD Camb., FIMechE, FIEE Prof., Manufacturing Processes

Young, Robert, BSc Dund., PhD Lough. Sr. Lectr.

Other Staff: 12 Lectrs.; 2 Res. Fellows

Research: information and simultaneous engineering; manufacturing organisation; manufacturing processes; manufacturing systems integration

Engineering, Materials, see Polymer Technol. and Materials Engin., Inst. of

Engineering, Mechanical

Tel: (01509) 223231 Fax: (01509) 223934

Acar, Memis, BS Middle East Tech., MSc Manc., PhD Lough., FTI, FIMechE Sr. Lectr.

Babitsky, Vladimir, PhD Moscow, DSc Moscow Prof., Dynamics

Chung, Thiam E., BTech Lough., MSc Lough., PhD Manc. Sr. Lectr.

Coupland, Jeremy M., BSc Exe., PhD S'ton. Lectr.; Co-ordinator, Inst. of Optical Engin.

Dent, John C., MS Mich., PhD Lough. Emer. Prof.

Fisher, Barry C., BScTech Manc., PhD Warw. Sr. Lectr.

Garner, Colin, BTech Lough., BEng Lough., PhD Lough. Reader

Halliwell, Neil A., BSc Liv., PhD Liv., DSc S'ton., FEng, FIMechE, FIP Prof., Optical Engineering; Dir., Inst. of Optical Engin.; Head*

Huntley, John, BA Camb., MA Camb., PhD Camb. Reader

James, E. Hedley, BTech Lough., MSc Lough., PhD Lough. Sr. Lectr.

Malalasekera, Weeratunge, BSc *Lough.* Sr. Lectr.

Parkin, Robert M., BSc *Leic.*, PhD *CNAA*, FIMechE, FIEE Prof., Mechatronics

Pendlebury, Robert M., BSc *Leeds*, FIMechE RAE Visiting Prof.

Rothberg, Steve J., BSc *S'ton.*, PhD *Lough.* Sr. Lectr.

Tyrer, John R., MSc *Cran.IT*, PhD *Lough.* Sr. Lectr.

Wickens, Alan H., OBE, BSc(Eng) *Lond.*, DSc *Lough.*, FIMechE, FEng Prof.†, Dynamics

Other Staff: 13 Lectrs; 2 Sr. Exper. Officers; 2 Sr. Tech. Tutors; 1 Tech. Tutor; 1 Sr. Lectr.†

Research: dynamics; mechatronics; optical engineering; structural integrity; thermofluids

English and Drama

Tel: (01509) 222969 *Fax:* (01509) 269994

Aston, Elaine F., BA *Warw.*, PhD *Warw.* Sr. Lectr.

Clarke, Ian R., BA *Hull*, PhD *Hull* Sr. Lectr.; Dir., Drama

Hanson, Claire, MA *Reading*, PhD *Reading* Sr. Lectr.

Hobby, Elaine A., BA *Birm.*, MA *Essex*, PhD *Birm.* Reader, Women's Studies

Lucas, John, BA *Reading*, PhD *Reading* Emer. Prof.

Mangan, Michael D. W., BA *Camb.*, PhD *Camb.* Sr. Lectr.

Overton, William J., MA *Camb.*, MA *Johns H.*, PhD *Camb.* Sr. Lectr.

Peach, Linden D., BA *Wales*, PhD *Wales*, MA Reader, English

Shaw, Marion, BA *Hull*, PhD *Hull* Prof., English; Head*

Other Staff: 7 Lectrs.

Research: contemporary women's drama; creative writing; semiotics of drama; seventeenth-century women's writing; twentieth-century women's writing

European Studies

Tel: (01509) 222991 *Fax:* (01509) 223917

Allen, Dave J., MSc *S'ton.* Sr. Lectr.

Byrne, Paul L., BA *Essex*, MA *Sheff.*, PhD *Lough.* Sr. Lectr.

Dine, Philip, MA *Dund.*, PhD *Stir.* Sr. Lectr.

Hantrais, Linda, BA *Lond.*, PhD *Flin.* Prof., Modern Languages

Hargreaves, Alec G., BA *Sus.*, DPhil *Sus.* Prof.; Head*

Leaman, Jeremy, BA *Liv.*, PhD *Liv.* Sr. Lectr.

Smith, Michael, MA *Camb.*, MA *Sus.* Prof., European Politics

Threlfall, Monica, BA *Oxf.*, MA *Leeds* Sr. Lectr.

Other Staff: 10 Lectrs.; 1 Res. Fellow; 4 Lectrs.†

Research: contemporary European politics and political thought; European society and culture; European Union international policies; European Union policymaking; recent European history

Geography

Tel: (01509) 222794 *Fax:* (01509) 223930

Armstrong, Adrian C., BSc *Lond.*, PhD *Lond.* Visiting Prof.

Bell, Morag, BA *Nott.*, DPhil *Oxf.* Reader

Black, Valerie J., BSc *Aberd.*, PhD *Aberd.* Sr. Lectr.

Calder, Ian R., BSc *Leeds*, PhD *Leeds* Visiting Prof.

Heffernan, Michael J., BSc *Wales*, PhD *Camb.* Reader

Reid, Ian, BA *Hull*, PhD *Hull* Prof., Physical Geography; Head*

Roberts, C. Neil, BA *Oxf.*, PhD *Lond.* Reader, Physical Geography

Sheail, John, BA *Lond.*, PhD *Lond.*, DLitt *Lond.* Visiting Prof.

Slater, David, BA *Durh.*, PhD *Lond.* Prof., Human Geography

Taylor, Peter, BA *Liv.*, PhD *Liv.* Prof., Geography

Wade, P. Max, BSc *CNAA*, PhD *Wales* Sr. Lectr.

Walker, David R. F., MA *Oxf.*, MSc(Econ) *Lond.* Sr. Lectr.

Other Staff: 8 Lectrs.

Research: development studies; global, social and economic geography; historical, political and cultural geography; palaeo and freshwater ecology; river sedimentology

Human Sciences, see also Special Centres, etc.

Tel: (01509) 223036 *Fax:* (01509) 223940-1

Bailey, Adrian D., BSc *Lough.* Systems Manager

Cameron, Noel, BEd *Nott.*, MSc *Lough.*, PhD *Lond.* Prof., Human Biology

Crook, Charles, BSc *Wales*, PhD *Camb.* Reader, Psychology

Eason, Kenneth D., BTech *Brun.*, PhD *Lough.*, DSc Prof., Cognitive Ergonomics

Galer Flyte, Margaret D., BSc *S'ton.*, MSc *Lough.*, PhD *Lough.* Prof., Vehicle Safety

Harker, Susan D. P., BA *Leic.*, MSc *Lough.* Sr. Lectr.

Havenith, George, BSc *Utrecht*, MSc *Utrecht*, PhD *Nijmegen* Sr. Lectr.

Horne, James A., BSc *Lond.*, MSc *Aston*, PhD *Aston*, DSc, FBPsS, FIBiol Prof., Psychophysiology

Jones, Peter R. M., MSc *Lough.*, PhD *Lough.* Emer. Prof.†, Human Functional Anatomy

Kalawsky, Roy, BSc *Hull*, MSc *Hull*, PhD *Hull* Prof., Human Computer Integration

Lansdale, Mark W., MA *Camb.*, PhD *Camb.* Sr. Lectr.

Middleton, David J., BSc *Wales*, PhD *Nott.* Sr. Lectr.

Norgan, Nick G., BSc *Lond.*, PhD *Glas.* Sr. Lectr.

Parsons, Ken C., BSc *Lough.*, PhD *S'ton.* Prof., Environmental Ergonomics; Head*

Shepherd, Andrew, BSc *Hull*, PhD *Hull* Sr. Lectr.

Sinclair, Murray A., BSc *Belf.*, MSc *Lough.* Sr. Lectr.

Other Staff: 9 Lectrs.; 2 Res. Fellows; 3 Res. Assocs.

Research: ergonomics; human biology; human psychology

Information and Library Studies

Tel: (01509) 223052 *Fax:* (01509) 223053

Borgman, Christine L., BA *Mich.*, PhD *Stan.* External Prof.

Evans, Margaret, BA *CNAA*, MBA *CNAA*, PhD *Lough.*, FLA, FIInfSc Prof.

Feather, John P., BLitt *Oxf.*, MA *Oxf.*, MA *Camb.*, PhD, FLA Prof.

McKnight, Cliff, BTech *Brun.*, PhD *Brun.* Head*

Meadows, A. Jack, MA *Oxf.*, MSc *Lond.*, DPhil *Oxf.*, FLA, FIInfSc Prof.

Morris, Anne, BSc *Lough.*, MSc *Lough.*, PhD *Lough.* Sr. Lectr.

Oppenheim, Charles, BSc *Manc.*, PhD *UMIST* Prof.

Reed, Michael A., MA *Birm.*, PhD *Leic.* Emer. Prof.

Sturges, R. Paul, BA *Leic.*, MA PhD, FLA Sr. Lectr.

Summers, Ronald, BSc *CNAA*, MSc *City(UK)*, PhD *City(UK)* Prof.

Tseng, Gwyneth M., BSc *Nott.*, MSc Sr. Lectr.

Other Staff: 18 Lectrs.; 1 Res. Fellow; 1 Visiting Fellow

Research: information handling; information management; information technology; library systems

Library and Information Statistics Unit

Tel: (01509) 223070 *Fax:* (01509) 223053

Spiller, David, OBE Dir.*

Other Staff: 1 Statistician

Research: collection and analysis of library statistics; public, academic and special libraries

Management Sciences, see Bus. Sch.

Mathematical Sciences

Tel: (01509) 222880 *Fax:* (01509) 223969

Andrews, John, BSc *Birm.*, PhD *CNAA* Sr. Lectr.

Bressloff, Paul, BA *Oxf.*, PhD *Lond.* Prof., Non-Linear and Complex Systems

Green, David R., BSc *Manc.*, MSc *Manc.*, MEd *Lond.*, PhD Reader

Griffiths, Jerry B., BSc *Wales*, PhD *Wales*, FIMA Prof., Applied Mathematics

Harrison, Martin C., BSc *Sheff.*, MSc *Sheff.*, PhD *Sheff.* Sr. Lectr.

Hoenselaers, Cornelius A., DSc *Hiroshima*, Dr *Munich* Reader, Relativity Theory

Kurylev, Slava, PhD *Russian Acad. Sc.* Reader

Linton, Christopher, BA *Oxf.*, PhD *Brist.* Sr. Lectr.

McIver, Maureen, BSc *Brist.*, PhD *Brist.* Reader

McIver, Philip, BSc *Liv.*, PhD *Liv.* Reader

Mustoe, Les R., BSc *Birm.*, MSc *Essex*, PhD, FIMA Sr. Lectr.

Peat, Keith S., MSc *Manc.*, PhD *Manc.* Sr. Lectr.

Pugh, A. Clive, BSc *Wales*, PhD Reader, Linear Systems Theory; Head*

Rossiter, Anthony, MA *Oxf.*, DPhil *Oxf.* Sr. Lectr.

Shiu, Peter M. K., BSc *Lond.*, PhD *Nott.* Reader

Smith, Roger, BSc *Manc.*, PhD *Manc.* Prof., Physical Modelling

Smith, Ron W., BSc *Brist.*, PhD *Brist.*, ScD *Camb.*, FIMA Prof., Applied Mathematics

Veselov, Sasha, PhD *Moscow*, DSc *Moscow* Prof., Mathematics

Watling, Keith D., BSc *Warw.*, MSc *Warw.*, PhD *Warw.* Computer Systems and Network Manager

Other Staff: 11 Lectrs.; 3 Res. Fellows

Vacant Posts: 1 Chair; 1 Reader; 2 Lectrs.

Research: computational PDE's and mathematical modelling; control theory, reliability and optimisation; integrable systems, inverse problems and relativity; non-linear dynamics and mathematical biology; waves and environmental fluid dynamics

Modern Languages, see European Studies

Physical Education, Sports Science and Recreation Management

Tel: (01509) 223283 *Fax:* (01509) 223971

Almond, Len, MEd *Manc.* Sr. Lectr.

Biddle, Stuart H., MSc *Penn.*, PhD *Keele* Prof., Exercise and Sport Psychology

Bunker, David J. Sr. Lectr.

Collins, Michael F., BA *Oxf.*, BLitt *Oxf.* Sr. Lectr.

Evans, John, BEd *Reading*, MA *Lond.*, PhD *Lond.* Prof., Physical Education

Hardman, Adrianne E., MSc *Salf.*, PhD Reader

Hardy, Colin A., MEd *Leic.*, PhD Sr. Lectr.

Henry, Ian P., BA *Stir.*, MSc PhD Prof., Recreation Management

Holliday, F. Michael, MA *Ohio* Sr. Lectr.

Jones, Thomas P., MSc *Lough.* Sr. Lectr.; Head*

Kerwin, David G., BEd *Keele*, MA *Leeds*, PhD *Leeds* Sr. Lectr.

Maguire, Joseph A., BEd *Lond.*, PhD *Leic.* Reader

Nevill, Mary, BSc *Lough.*, MSc *Lough.*, PhD *Lough.* Sr. Lectr.

Thomason, Harry, MSc *Salf.*, PhD *Lough.* Prof., Physical Education and Recreation Science

Thorpe, Rod D., MSc *Lough.* Dir., Sports Devel. Centre

Williams, Clyde, BSc *Wales*, MSc *Wash.*, PhD *Aberd.* Prof., Sports Science

Yeadon, Fred, MA *Camb.*, PhD Reader

Other Staff: 15 Lectrs.; 2 Res. Fellows

Research: health science; recreation and leisure studies; sport and human performance; sports science; teacher education

Physics

Tel: (01509) 228409 Fax: (01509) 223986

Alexandrov, Alexandre, BSc *Moscow*, PhD *Moscow*, ScD *Moscow* Prof., Theoretical Physics; Head*

Brown, P. Jane, MA *Camb.*, PhD *Camb.*, FIP Visiting Prof.

Crapper, Mike, BSc *York(UK)*, PhD *Warw.* Sr. Lectr.

Emmony, David C., BSc *Leic.*, PhD *Strath.* Prof., Applied Optics

Howson, Ron P., BSc *Sheff.*, PhD *Exe.* Prof., Applied Physics†

Kusmartsev, Feodor V., MS *Moscow*, PhD Prof., Condensed Matter Theory

Neumann, Klaus U., DrRerNat *Aachen* Sr. Lectr.

Parry, David J., BSc *Wales*, PhD *Wales* Sr. Lectr.

Walls, J. Mike, BSc *Aston*, PhD *Aston* Visiting Prof.

Williams, David E. G., BSc *Sheff.*, PhD *Sheff.* Sr. Lectr.

Ziebeck, Kurt R. A., BSc *Salf.*, PhD *Salf.*, FIP Prof.

Other Staff: 3 Lectrs.; 4 Res. Fellows

Research: electromagnetism; environmental science; laser technology; optics and thermal physics

Politics, see European Studies

Polymer Technology and Materials Engineering, Institute of

Tel: (01509) 222231 Fax: (01509) 223949

Edirisinghe, Mo J., BSc MSc PhD Reader

Faulkner, Roy G., BSc *Camb.*, PhD *Camb.*, DSc *Leeds*, FIM Prof., Physical Metallurgy

Gabe, David R., BSc *Wales*, PhD *Sheff.*, DMet *Sheff.*, FIM Prof., Materials Engineering

Gilbert, Marianne, BSc *Aston*, PhD *Aston*, FRSChem, FIM Reader; Dir.*

Harper, John F., BSc(Eng) *S'ton.*, MSc *Leeds* Sr. Lectr.

Haworth, Barry, BSc *Newcastle(UK)*, MSc *Newcastle(UK)* Sr. Lectr.

Heath, Richard J., MSc PhD Sr. Lectr.

Hourston, Douglas J., BSc *Leeds*, PhD *Leeds*, FRSChem Prof., Polymer Technology

Mascia, Leno, BSc *CNAA*, PhD *Aston*, FIM Reader

Menzies, Ian A., BSc *St And.*, MBA *CNAA*, PhD *Lond.*, DSc *Manc.*, FRSChem, FIM Emer. Prof.†

Richardson, Mel O. W., BTech *Brun.*, PhD *Brun.*, FRSChem, FIM Sr. Lectr.

Other Staff: 4 Lectrs.; 2 Sr. Res. Fellows; 2 Res. Fellows; 1 Reader†

Research: polymer science and technology; power and aerospace materials; rubber processing; surface and interface engineering

Recreation Management, see Phys. Educn., Sports Sci. and Recreation Management

Social Sciences

Tel: (01509) 223365 Fax: (01509) 223944

Antaki, Charles, BA *Newcastle(UK)*, PhD *Sheff.* Reader

Bagihole, Barbara, BA *Nott.*, PhD *Nott.* Sr. Lectr.

Bean, Philip T., MSc(Econ) *Lond.*, PhD *Nott.* Prof., Criminology; Dir., Midlands Centre for Criminol. and Criminal Justice

Becker, Saul, MA *Nott.*, PhD *Nott.* Sr. Lectr.

Billig, Michael G., BA *Brist.*, PhD *Brist.* Prof.

Blom-Cooper, Sir Louis, QC, LLB *Lond.*, DrJur *Amst.*, Hon. DLitt *Lough.* External Prof.

Bryman, Alan E., MA *Kent* Prof., Social Research

Cramer, Duncan, BSc *Lond.*, PhD *Lond.* Reader

Edwards, Derek, BA *Sus.*, DPhil *Sus.* Reader

Gane, Michael J., BA *Leic.*, PhD *Lond.* Sr. Lectr.

Golding, Peter, BSc *Lond.*, MA *Essex* Prof., Sociology; Head*

Gould, Arthur R., BSc(Soc) *Lond.*, PhD *Lough.* Sr. Lectr.

Howitt, Dennis L., BTech *Brun.*, DPhil *Sus.* Sr. Lectr.

Kitzinger, Celia C., BA *Oxf.*, PhD *Reading* Sr. Lectr.

Kniveton, Bromley H., BA *Belf.*, PhD *Nott.* Sr. Lectr.

Lister, M. Ruth A., BA *Essex*, MA *Sus.*, Hon. LLD *Manc.* Prof., Social Policy

Murdock, Graham, BSc(Soc) *Lond.*, MA *Sus.* Reader

Potter, Jonathan A., BA *Liv.*, MA *Sur.*, DPhil *York(UK)* Prof., Discourse Analysis

Prins, Herschel A., MPhil *Leic.* External Prof., Midlands Centre for Criminol. and Criminal Justice

Radley, Alan R., BTech *Brun.*, PhD *Lond.* Reader

Stephens, Michael, BSc *Wales*, DPhil *Oxf.* Sr. Lectr.

Vagg, John, BA *York(UK)*, MA *Sus.*, PhD *Lond.* Sr. Lectr.

Walker, Robert L., BSocSci *Brist.*, MSc(Econ) *Lond.*, PhD *Lond.* Prof., Social Policy Research; Dir., Centre for Res. in Soc. Policy

Wilkinson, Susan, BSc *Leic.* Sr. Lectr.

Other Staff: 7 Lectrs.; 5 Res. Fellows

Research: communication and media studies; social policy; social psychology; sociology

Sports Science, see Phys. Educn., Sports Sci. and Recreation Management

Transport Studies, see Engin., Aeronautical and Automotive, and Transport Studies

Women's Studies, see Engl. and Drama

SPECIAL CENTRES, ETC

Consumer Ergonomics, Research Institute for, and ICE Ergonomics Ltd

Tel: (01509) 283300 Fax: (01509) 283360

Page, Magdalen, BSc *CNAA*, MSc *Lough.* Sr. Res. Fellow; Dir.*

Other Staff: 19 Res.; 1 Res.†

Research: consumer products; occupational ergonomics; transport ergonomics; vehicle safety

Human Sciences and Advanced Technology Research Institute

Tel: (01509) 611088 Fax: (01509) 234651

Damodaran, Leela, BTech *Brun.* Prof.; Dir.*

Other Staff: 6 Sr. Res. Fellows; 6 Res. Fellows; 5 Assoc. Scientists

Research: assistive technology and people with special needs; human factors; user-centred design into practice; vehicle telematics and behaviour

CONTACT OFFICERS

Academic affairs. Academic Secretary: ......

Accommodation. Student Accommodation Officer: Green, Steven, BA *CNAA*

Admissions (first degree). Senior Assistant Registrar: Jones, Howard, JP, BA *Exe.*

Admissions (higher degree). Assistant Registrar: Vale, Brigette, BA *Lond.*, DPhil *York(UK)*

Adult/continuing education. Continuing Education Coordinator: Hunt, Steve, BA *Nott.*

Alumni. Clift, Catherine, BA *Leeds*

Archives. Archivist: Clark, Jenny, BA *Brist.*†

Careers. Director: Llewellyn, Wendy, BSc *Wales*, MEd *American(D.C.)*

Computing services. Director: Negus, Brian, BSc *Liv.*, PhD *Lanc.*

Conferences/corporate hospitality. Director: Brown, Malcolm

Consultancy services. Director, Loughborough Consultants Ltd: Jones, Claire, BSc *Wales*, PhD *Wales*

Credit transfer. (Contact relevant department)

Development/fund-raising. Walker, Jon, BSc *Lough.*

Equal opportunities. Jasper, Sandra, BA *Warw.*

Estates and buildings/works and services. Director, Estates Organisation: King, Murray, FRICS

Examinations. Assistant Registrar: Easton, Jane, BA *Durh.*

Finance. Bursar and Finance Officer: Pearson, Michael, BA *Manc.*, LLB *Lond.*

General enquiries. Registrar: Fletcher, David E., BA *Sheff.*, PhD *Sheff.*

Health services. University Medical Officer: Bhojani, Asghar, MB BS *Newcastle(UK)*

Industrial liaison. Pro-Vice-Chancellor (External Relations): Thomason, Prof. Harry, MSc *Salf.*, PhD *Lough.*

International office. Senior Assistant Registrar: Jones, Howard, JP, BA *Exe.*

Language training for international students. Mee, Jane, DSc *Birm.*

Library (chief librarian). Librarian: Morley, Mary D., BA *Nott.*

Minorities/disadvantaged groups. Jasper, Sandra, BA *Warw.*

Ombudsperson. Visitor: Cooper, The Rt. Hon. Sir Frank, GCB, CMG

Personnel/human resources. Personnel Officer: Cole, Patrick, BSc *Lond.*

Public relations, information and marketing. Communications and Publicity Officer: Howarth, Elizabeth, BA *Newcastle(UK)*

Publications. Assistant Publicity Officer: Price, Pamela, BA *Nott.*

Publications. Assistant Publicity Officer: Baldwin, Hannah, BA *Lond.*

Purchasing. Burton, Tim

Quality assurance and accreditation. Director, Quality Assessment Unit: Blease, Derek, BA *Lough.*, MA *Lough.*†

Research. Assistant Registrar: Hannah, Fidelma, BA *York(UK)*†

Safety. Health and Safety Officer: Ellis, Mike

Scholarships, awards, loans. Assistant Registrar: ......

Schools liaison. Senior Assistant Registrar: Jones, Howard, JP, BA *Exe.*

Security. Security Manager: Jones, Trevor, BA *CNAA*

Staff development. Director: Wilson, Andrew, BSc *Brist.*, MA *Sask.*, PhD *Brist.*

Student union. President: Moore, Will

Student welfare/counselling. Director, University Counselling Service: Bell, Jennifer, BA *Manc.*

Students from other countries. International Recruitment Officer: Prendergast, Claire, BA *Brad.*, MA *Brad.*

Students with disabilities. Tutor to Students with Special Needs: Hinton, Ron, BSc *Reading*, MA *Lough.*, PhD *Lough.*

University press. Director, Audio Visual Services: ......

[Information supplied by the institution as at 18 March 1998, and edited by the ACU]

UNIVERSITY OF LUTON

Member of the Association of Commonwealth Universities

Postal Address: Park Square, Luton, Bedfordshire, England LU1 3JU
Telephone: (01582) 734111 **Fax**: (01582) 743400 **WWW**: http://www.luton.ac.uk
E-mail formula: firstname.surname@luton.ac.uk

CHANCELLOR—Plastow, Sir David
PRO-CHANCELLOR AND CHAIRMAN OF THE BOARD OF GOVERNORS—Dixon, Sir Ian, CBE, Hon. PhD
VICE-CHANCELLOR*—John, David T. (Dai), BSc *Lond.*, PhD *Lond.*
PRO-VICE-CHANCELLOR—Robinson, Prof. Kate, BA PhD
PRO VICE-CHANCELLOR—Birch, Prof. Paul, BSc MBA PhD, FIBiol
CLERK TO THE BOARD OF GOVERNORS—Harris, Richard W., BA MSc MBA

GENERAL INFORMATION

History. Formerly Luton College of Higher Education, the university obtained degree-awarding powers from the Privy Council in 1993.

It is located about 60km north of London.

Admission to first degree courses (see also United Kingdom Introduction). Through the Universities and Colleges Admissions Service (UCAS).

First Degrees (see also United Kingdom Directory to Subjects of Study). BA, BSc, LLB.

Higher Degrees (see also United Kingdom Directory to Subjects of Study). MA, MBA, MSc, PhD.

Libraries. 200,000 volumes; 1700 periodicals subscribed to. Special collections: Bourne (nineteenth-century British diplomacy).

Fees. UK students: £1000. Overseas students: £5300 (band 1); £5900 (band 2 and above).

Academic Awards. Fifty awards of £500 each per annum.

Academic Year (1998–1999). Two semesters: 5 October–29 January; 15 February–11 June.

Income. Total, £43,500,000.

Statistics. Staff: 1062 (504 academic, 558 administrative/manual).

FACULTIES/SCHOOLS

Health Care and Social Studies
Tel: (01582) 489267 Fax: (01582) 489358
Dean: Robinson, Prof. Kate, BA PhD

Humanities
Tel: (01582) 489018 Fax: (01582) 489014
Dean: Boatswain, Tim, BA MSc

Luton Business School
Tel: (01582) 743121 Fax: (01582) 743143
Dean: Pettitt, Stephen, BSc MBA PhD

Science, Design and Technology
Tel: (01582) 489265 Fax: (01582) 489212
Dean: Mortimer, Stephen, MBA, FRICS

ACADEMIC UNITS

Accounting and Finance
Tel: (01582) 743137 Fax: (01582) 743143
Canny, Mary, BBS Sr. Lectr.
Carman, Rob, MBA Principal Lectr.; Acting Head*
Kelly, Martin, BA Sr. Lectr.
Pain, Brian, FCA Sr. Lectr.
Reynolds, Patrick, BA Sr. Lectr.
Tauringana, Venancio, BA MSc PhD Sr. Lectr.
Other Staff: 1 Teaching Asst.
Research: corporate and public sector financial reporting; development of cash flow ratio; efficiency of alternative investment markets; small business finance; strategic management and accounting

Acute and Critical Care, see also under Nursing, Pre-Registration
Luton and Dunstable Hospital
Tel: (01582) 497168 Fax: (01582) 497364
Bottoms, Rosemary, BSc Sr. Lectr.
Burden, Barbara, MSc Principal Lectr.
Da Roza, Annabelle, BA Sr. Lectr.
Hanks, Christine, BSc MSc Sr. Lectr.
Havill, Catherine, BSc MSc Head*
Henderson, Bernadette, MBA Sr. Lectr.
Hide, Elaine, BA Open(UK), MSc Sr. Lectr.
Igbolekwu, Pauline, BEd Sr. Lectr.
Jugessur, Devametra Sr. Lectr.
Laubeluck, Lali, BSc MSc Sr. Lectr.
Ogunji, Marcia, BA Sr. Lectr.
Rankin, Sarah, BA Sr. Lectr.
Sargent, Roy, BA Sr. Lectr.
Walker, Jacqueline, BA Sr. Lectr.
Wilson, Ann, BA MPhil Principal Lectr.
Other Staff: 1 Lectr.; 3 Sr. Lectrs.†
Research: evaluation of an emergency nurse practitioner development in a community hospital; evaluation of site practitioner service; pain management

Biology and Health Science
Tel: (01582) 489384 Fax: (01582) 489212
Harper, Ray, BSc MSc PhD Sr. Lectr.
Ladley, Phil, BSc PhD Sr. Lectr.
Punchard, Neville, PhD Sr. Lectr.
Seddon, Caroline, BSc PhD Sr. Lectr.
Steele, Graham, BSc PhD Head*
Other Staff: 5 Staff Members

Business, International, see Marketing and Internat. Business

Computing and Information Systems
Fax: (01582) 489212
Adjei, Osei, PhD Sr. Lectr.
Allum, Derek, BSc MSc Sr. Lectr.
Atkinson, Simon, BSc Principal Lectr.
Aybet, Jahid, BSc MSc PhD Sr. Lectr.
Burkhardt, Diana, BA MA Sr. Lectr.
Dunckley, Lynne, BSc PhD Sr. Lectr.
Olney, Penny Sr. Lectr.
Phillips, Paul, BSc MSc Sr. Lectr.
Slater, Paul, BA Open(UK), MSc Principal Lectr.
Smith, Andy, BSc MSc Principal Lectr.
Steven, Christine, BSc MSc Sr. Lectr.
Tinson, Andrew, BA BSc MSc Sr. Lectr.
Vella, Alfred, BA BSc MSc PhD, FIMA Head*

Design
Tel: (01582) 489372 Fax: (01582) 489212
Evans, Chris, BA Principal Lectr.
Glew, William, BSc Sr. Lectr.
Hughes, Ian, BSc Sr. Lectr.
Milner, Kate Sr. Lectr.
Painter, John, BSc MSc Sr. Lectr.
Philips, David, MA RCA, BA Sr. Lectr.
Raine, Michael, BSc MSc Sr. Lectr.
Stonnell, Michael, MSc Sr. Lectr.
Walsh, Elaine, BA MSc Head*
Walters, Mick, MSc Sr. Lectr.
Westwood, Carl, BEng Sr. Lectr.

Electronics and Mathematics
Tel: (01582) 489288 Fax: (01582) 489224
Allen, Richard, BSc Sr. Lectr.
Beveridge, Ian Sr. Lectr.
Davis, Paul, BA MSc Sr. Lectr.
Dent, Don Sr. Lectr.
Fahr, Fatima, BSc PhD, FIMA Principal Lectr.
Hearing, Rob, BSc MSc PhD Head*
Heath, David Sr. Lectr.
Kelly, Patrick, BSc Sr. Lectr.
Wilkinson, David, BA MSc Sr. Lectr.

Environment, Geography and Geology
Tel: (01582) 489264 Fax: (01582) 489212
Batham, Mike, BSc MSc PhD Sr. Lectr.
Davies, Frances, BSc MPhil Sr. Lectr.
Hunt, Brian, BSc MSc Sr. Lectr.
Mitchell, Wishart, MA PhD Sr. Lectr.
Orwin, David, BSc MSc Principal Lectr.
Rees, Christine, BSc MSc Sr. Lectr.
Salmon, Keith, BA MA PhD Sr. Lectr.
Shaw, Paul, BA MSc PhD Reader; Head*
Skipp, Ray Sr. Lectr.
Weedon, Graham, BSc DPhil Sr. Lectr.

Foreign Languages
Tel: (01582) 489033 Fax: (01582) 489014
Larrea, Carlota, MA PhD Sr. Lectr.
Lewis-Villien, Chantal, BA Sr. Lectr.
Page, Alan, BA Principal Lectr.
Ruthe, Monika, BA PhD Head*
Wendeler, Catherine, BA MA Sr. Lectr.
Other Staff: 6 Lectrs; 7 Visiting Lectrs.; 1 Sr. Lectr.†
Research: comparative literature; European studies (French, German, Italian, Spanish); machine translation

Geography, see Environment, Geog. and Geol.

Geology, see Environment, Geog. and Geol.

Health Science, see Biol. and Health Sci., and Nursing, Pre-Registration

History
Tel: (01582) 489033 Fax: (01582) 489014
Aston, Nigel, BA MPhil Sr. Lectr.
Beckett, Ian, BA PhD Prof.; Head*
Bridgeman, Ian, BA PhD Sr. Lectr.
Bunker, Stephen, BA PhD Sr. Lectr.
Clapson, Mark, BA MA PhD Sr. Lectr.
Jones, Harriet, BA MSc PhD Sr. Lectr.
Other Staff: 1 Lectr.; 1 Sr. Res. Fellow
Research: British and Japanese management styles; command in the late Victorian army; comparative suburbanisation in Britain and America; conservative politics and the welfare state; religion and revolution 1750–1830

Human Resource Management
Tel: (01582) 489074 Fax: (01582) 489076
Bedward, Diana Head*
Burnage, Andrea, BSc MA Principal Lectr.
Carr, Frank, BA MA PhD Sr. Lectr.
Churcher, John, BA MA Principal Lectr.
Cross, Ray Sr. Lectr.

Ellis, Steve, BA MBA MPhil   Sr. Lectr.
Foulkes, Pat, BA MA   Sr. Lectr.
Gammell, Martin, BSc MSc   Sr. Lectr.
Greenwood, Irene, MA   Sr. Lectr.
Hall, Dave, BA MEd   Sr. Lectr.
Kingsbury, Peter, BA   Sr. Lectr.
O'Neill, Mo, BSc   Sr. Lectr.
Punter, Anne, MEd   Sr. Lectr.
Smith, Alan, BA MEd   Sr. Lectr.
Smith, Paul, BSc MA   Sr. Lectr.
Stredwick, John, BCom   Sr. Lectr.

Information Systems, see Computing and Information Systems

Health Services Research, Institute for
Tel: (01582) 743770 Fax: (01582) 743771
1 Principal Res. Fellow; 4 Res. Fellows; 1 Sr. Researcher; 10 Res. Assocs.†

Law
Tel: (01582) 489033 Fax: (01582) 489014
Arthur, Nigel, LLB   Sr. Lectr.
Clutterbuck, Richard, BA LLB   Principal Lectr.
Dixon, Chris, BA LLM   Sr. Lectr.
Elwes, Sylvia, LLB   Sr. Lectr.
Hamer, John, LLB   Sr. Lectr.
Holroyd, Jessica, BA LLM   Sr. Lectr.
Lodge, John, LLB LLM   Sr. Lectr.
Olaseinde, Michael, BA LLM   Sr. Lectr.
Sanders, Chris, LLB   Principal Lectr.
Warfield, Sandra, LLB LLM   Sr. Lectr.
Young, Max, BA MA MPhil   Head*
Other Staff: 3 Lectrs.
Research: education law, especially education in schools; IT, innovation delivery of law studies; law for legal and other professions; law relating to the arts; recent developments in taxation law

Linguistics
Tel: (01582) 489033 Fax: (01582) 489014
Chandramohan, Balasubramanyam, BSc MA PhD   Sr. Lectr.
Halstead, Ildi, BA MA   Sr. Lectr.
Hounslow, Ed, BA MA   Head*
Melrose, Robin, BA MA PhD   Principal Lectr.
Spencer-Oatey, Helen, BA MEd PhD   Sr. Lectr.
Other Staff: 8 Lectrs.; 10 Visiting Lectrs.
Research: cross-cultural communication; language acquisition; literary stylistics; pragmatics and cognition; stylistics, systemic-functional grammar

Literary Studies
Tel: (01582) 489033 Fax: (01582) 489014
Cowley, Julian, BA MA PhD   Sr. Lectr.
Gray, Martin, MA MPhil   Head*
Titterington, Peter, BA MA   Sr. Lectr.
Other Staff: 7 Lectrs.
Research: American literature; critical theory; late Victorian literature; eighteenth-century literature; romanticism

Management, General, see Strategic and Gen. Management

Marketing and International Business
Tel: (01582) 743133 Fax: (01582) 743143
Burnley, Rosemary, BA MBA PhD   Sr. Lectr.
De Vita Carmine, Franco, MSc PhD   Sr. Lectr.
Hadland, Robert, MSc   Sr. Lectr.
Kerridge, John, BSc MA   Sr. Lectr.
Mathews, Ann, BA MSc   Head*
Mathews, Brian, BTech MBA PhD   Reader
Mortimer, Kathleen, BA MBA   Sr. Lectr.
Pyne, Anthony, BSc   Sr. Lectr.
Scott, Michael, MBA   Sr. Lectr.
Selassie, Habte, BBA MSc PhD   Sr. Lectr.
Townsend, Rob, BA MBA   Principal Lectr.
Other Staff: 8 staff members
Research: design/marketing interface; diffusion of innovations/word-of-mouth influences in the adoption process; international marketing; relationship marketing; services marketing

Mathematics and Statistics, see also Electronics and Maths.

Fax: (01582) 489212
Fahr, Fatima, BSc Lond., PhD Brun.   Sr. Lectr.
Heath, David, MSc CNAA, PhD CNAA   Sr. Lectr.
Matthews, Dewi, BSc   Sr. Lectr.
Nichol, John, BSc St And., MA Open(UK)   Sr. Lectr.
Shoostarian, Chris, BSc Lond.Guild.   Principal Lectr.
Thomas, Glan, MA Oxf., PhD Wales   Head*

Media Arts
Tel: (01582) 489033 Fax: (01582) 489014
Alvarado, Manuel, BA   Prof.; Ed. Dir., John Libbey Media
Darling, Peter, BA MA   Sr. Lectr.
Dean, Peter, BSc MSc   Sr. Lectr.
Dudley-Gurth, Jane, BA MA   Sr. Lectr.
Gordon, Janey, BA MA   Sr. Lectr.
Hockley, Luke, BA PhD   Head*
Knight, Julia, BA MA   Sr. Lectr.
Pines, James, BSc   Sr. Lectr.
Spring, Ian, BA PhD   Sr. Lectr.
Steemers, Jeanette, BA PhD   Sr. Lectr.
Wise, Richard, BSc   Sr. Lectr.
Other Staff: 12 Lectrs.
Research: broadcasting (television drama, semiotics, cable/digital broadcasting, economies); film/cinema (Hollywood, film policy, psychoanalysis, Third cinema, German cinema); new media techologies (multimedia, educational uses, internet/web, critical analysis); publishing (electronic publishing, history of publishing); video (video production, video and electronic art)

Nursing, Pre-Registration
§ = at Buckinghamshire; ¶ = at High Wycombe
Tel: (01296) 315554 Fax: (01296) 315567

Acute and Critical Care
Allen, Rodney, BSc MA(Ed)   Principal Lectr.§
Baille, Lesley, MSc   Sr. Lectr.§
Burrows, Denise, BSc   Sr. Lectr.¶
Cashin, Deirdre, BA   Sr. Lectr.¶
Child, Kay, BA   Sr. Lectr.¶
Corben, Veronica, BSc   Sr. Lectr.§
Grenside, Sara, BA   Sr. Lectr.¶
Neale, Nicky, MA(Ed)   Sr. Lectr.§
Other Staff: 1 Lectr.

Mental Health and Learning Disabilities
Bailey, Jan, BA   Sr. Lectr.§
Bromley, Barbara, MSc   Sr. Lectr.§
Hedges, Ann, MA   Sr. Lectr.§
Lockhart, Sonia, BA   Sr. Lectr.¶
MacDonald, Iain, MA   Head*¶
Matai, Chris, MSc   Principal Lectr.¶
Mooneeapen, Dharma, MSc   Principal Lectr.¶
O'Shaughnessy, John, BSc   Sr. Lectr.§
Stewart, David, MSc   Sr. Lectr.§
Other Staff: 1 Lectr.

Primary and Continuing Care
Chadwick, Sandra, BSc   Sr. Lectr.§
Fanning, Agnes, BSc   Sr. Lectr.§
Green, Christine, BSc   Sr. Lectr.¶
Merritt, Jane, MSc   Principal Lectr.¶
Nicoll, Lynne, MSc   Sr. Lectr.¶
Scott, Frances, BSc   Sr. Lectr.§
Watkins, Deidre, BSc   Sr. Lectr.¶
Young, Valerie   Sr. Lectr.§

Women's and Children's Health
Barron, Jan, BA   Sr. Lectr.§
Colson, Jan, MA   Principal Lectr.§
Simons, Joan, BA   Sr. Lectr.§
Spurling, Sue, MSc   Sr. Lectr.¶
Other Staff: 1 Lectr.

Operations Management, see Systems and Operations Management

Politics and Public Policy
Tel: (01582) 489033 Fax: (01582) 489014
Bharmal, Nashir, BSc MA MSc   Principal Lectr.
Dennis, Tony, BA BSc MSc   Sr. Lectr.
Dickens, John, BA MA   Head*
Fitch, Jerry, BA PhD   Sr. Lectr.
Fribbance, Ian, BA MA   Sr. Lectr.
Gray, Pat, BA MSc   Sr. Lectr.
Khan, Usman, BA PhD   Principal Lectr.
Rich, Paul, BA MPhil PhD   Principal Lectr.
Other Staff: 7 Lectrs.
Research: comparative perspectives; leadership in local government; policy disasters; public service ethics; urban democracy and community governance

Professional Social Studies
Tel: (01582) 732886 Fax: (01582) 734265
Ayre, Patrick, BA   Sr. Lectr.
Barrett, David, PhD   Head*
Berridge, David, PhD   Prof.
Burroughs, Lana, BA   Sr. Lectr.
Marlow, Alan, BSc   Principal Lectr.
Pitts, John, PhD   Prof.
Schild, Lis, BA   Principal Lectr.
Wenman, Helen, BA   Sr. Lectr.
Other Staff: 2 Lectrs.; 1 Res. Fellow

Psychology
Fax: (01582) 486260
Cline, Tony, BA, FBPsS   Prof., Educational Psychology; Head*
de Abreu, Guida, BSc MSc PhD   Sr. Lectr.
Hinton, Penny, BA BSc DPhil   Principal Lectr.
Ward, Tony, BSc PhD   Sr. Lectr.

Social Studies, see also Professl. Soc. Studies
Tel: (01582) 743226 Fax: (01582) 489358
Assiter, Alison, BA BPhil DPhil   Prof., Feminist Philosophy; Head*
Brindle, Steve, BA MSc PhD   Sr. Lectr.
Cooke, Veronica, BA MA   Sr. Lectr.
Davis, Sonia   Sr. Lectr.
Dean, Hartley, BTech MA PhD   Reader
Ellis, Kathryn, BA MA   Sr. Lectr.
Ferguson, Jessie, BA MSc   Sr. Lectr.
Fitches, Raheela, MSc   Sr. Lectr.
Khan, Zafar, MA   Sr. Lectr.
Melrose, Margaret, BSc MA   Researcher/Sr. Lectr.
Parry, Jose, BA   Sr. Lectr.
Stott, Dave, MA MSc DPhil   Sr. Lectr.
Wilson, Amrit, BSc PhD   Sr. Lectr.
Woodhams, Steve, BA MA PhD   Sr. Lectr.
Woods, Roger, BA MA   Sr. Lectr.

Sport and Exercise Science
Fax: (01582) 489212
Burrows, Carol, BA MSc   Sr. Lectr.
Doherty, Mike, BSc MSc   Sr. Lectr.
Forrester, Auriel, BSc PhD   Head*
Korkia, Pirkko, BA MSc   Sr. Lectr.
Other Staff: 7 Staff Members

Statistics, see Maths. and Stats.

Strategic and General Management
Tel: (01582) 489056 Fax: (01582) 489076
Anderson, Pamela   Sr. Lectr.
Brown, Christopher, MBA   Sr. Lectr.
Connor, Tom, BSc(Econ) MBA   Sr. Lectr.
Moore, Andrew, BA MA   Head*
Morris, Ron, MPhil   Sr. Lectr.
Osborne, Anthony, MA   Sr. Lectr.
Patrick, Peter, MSc   Sr. Lectr.
Punter, Anne, BA MEd   Sr. Lectr.
Rawson, Michael, MA MAB   Sr. Lectr.
Wymark, Kathryn, MBA   Sr. Lectr.

Strategy and Entrepreneurship
Tel: (01582) 743131 Fax: (01582) 743143
Brown, Chris, MBA   Sr. Lectr.
Connor, Tom, BScEcon MBA   Sr. Lectr.
Kalantaridis, Christos, BA MA PhD   Sr. Lectr.

Morris, Ron, MPhil   Sr. Lectr.
Pheby, John, BA MA   Prof.; Head*
Rawson, Mike, BEng MA   Sr. Lectr.
Souster, Colin, MBA   Principal Lectr.
Stewart, Alastair   Sr. Lectr.
Wakeley, Anthony, MBA   Sr. Lectr.
Whymark, Kathryn, MBA   Sr. Lectr.
Wright, David, MSc   Sr. Lectr.
Other Staff: 1 Lectr.†
Research: innovation hi-tech SMEs; language and culture in SMEs; managerial economics; quality in retailing; TQM as a strategy for SMEs

Systems and Operations Management

Tel: (01582) 743136 Fax: (01582) 743143
Clarke, Steve, BSc(Econ) MBA   Principal Lectr.
Hamblin, David   Prof.; Acting Head*
Platt, Avril   Sr. Lectr.
Warwick, Shamim, BSc MSc PhD   Sr. Lectr.
Xu, Mark   Sr. Lectr.
Other Staff: 1 Principal Res. Fellow; 2 Sr. Res. Fellows; 1 Sr Teaching Fellow
Research: concurrent engineering and supply chain management; innovation; systems; technology management

Technology

Tel: (01582) 489233 Fax: (01582) 489224
Baker, Martyn   Sr. Lectr.
Balfour-Layden, Gary, BA   Sr. Lectr.
Ball, Martin, MSc   Sr. Lectr.
Brown, David, MSc   Head*
Burgess, Graham, BSc   Sr. Lectr.
Burke, Tony, BSc   Sr. Lectr.
Clarke, Keith, BA   Sr. Lectr.
Dobson, Adrian, BA BArch   Sr. Lectr.
Evans, Charlie, MSc   Sr. Lectr.
Fletcher, Matthew, LLB BSc, FRICS   Sr. Lectr.
Geraint, John   Sr. Lectr.
Gibson, David, BA MSc, FRICS   Sr. Lectr.
Hassall, John   Principal Lectr.
Hill, Rob   Sr. Lectr.
Monk, Tony, MArch   Prof.; Principal Lectr.
O'Riordan, Kevin, BSc MSc   Sr. Lectr.
Samuels, Martin   Sr. Lectr.
Turner, Valerie   Sr. Lectr.
Other Staff: 1 Teaching Fellow

Tourism and Leisure

Tel: (01582) 743139 Fax: (01582) 743143
Alford, Philip, BA MSc   Sr. Lectr.
Augustyn, Marcjanna, MEcon PhD   Sr. Lectr.
Badmin, Pat, MSc   Sr. Lectr.
Burke, Veronica, BA MA   Sr. Lectr.
Burns, Peter, PhD   Head*

Dalley, Simon, BA MMedSci   Sr. Lectr.
Dann, Graham, PhL STL PhD   Prof.
David, Ian, BSc MSc   Sr. Lectr.
Gammon, Sean, BA   Sr. Lectr.
Girginov, Vassil, BA MA MSc   Sr. Lectr.
Grabowski, C. Peter, BA MPhil   Principal Lectr.
Hashimoto, Atsuko, BA MSc PhD   Sr. Lectr.
Knowles, Timothy, BSc   Sr. Lectr.
Lawrence, Lesley, BEd MSc PhD   Principal Lectr.
Lloyd, Eliot, BA MSc   Sr. Lectr.
Robinson, Tom, BSc MSc   Sr. Lectr.
Other Staff: 4 Staff Members
Research: hospitality; sociolinguistics of tourism; sociology of tourism; tourism motivation; tourism promotion

CONTACT OFFICERS

Academic affairs. Vice-Chancellor: John, David T. (Dai), BSc Lond., PhD Lond.
Accommodation. Director of Campus Services: Andrew, Reece
Admissions (first degree). Head of Access and Admissions: Kendall, Steve
Admissions (higher degree). Head of Access and Admissions: Kendall, Steve
Adult/continuing education. Head of Access and Admissions: Kendall, Steve
Alumni. Director of Marketing: Mathieson, C., BEd MA
Careers. Head of Careers: Scott, Eileen
Computing services. Director of Information Services: Bramwell, John
Conferences/corporate hospitality. Dean, Humanities: Boatswain, Tim, BA MSc
Consultancy services. Director of Research and External Affairs: Rawson, Prof. David, BSc
Credit transfer. Head of Modular Credit Scheme: Eccles, Charles, PhD
Development/fund-raising. Vice-Chancellor: John, David T. (Dai), BSc Lond., PhD Lond.
Distance education. Head of Access and Admissions: Kendall, Steve
Equal opportunities. Dean, Quality Assurance: Harris, Richard W., BA MSc MBA
Estates and buildings/works and services. Head, Property Services: Somerville, Brian
Examinations. Head of Modular Credit Scheme: Eccles, Charles, PhD
Finance. Director of Finance: Harding, Philip
General enquiries. Clerk to the Board of Governors: Harris, Richard W., BA MSc MBA

Health services. Pro Vice-Chancellor: Birch, Prof. Paul, BSc PhD MBA, FIBiol
Industrial liaison. Director of Commercial Affairs: Moore, Andy
International office. Director of Marketing: Mathieson, C., BEd MA
Language training for international students. Head of Linguistics: Hounslow, Ed, BA MA
Library (chief librarian). Director of Learning Resources: Stone, Tim
Minorities/disadvantaged groups. Head, Student Services: Jack, Gillian, BA
Personnel/human resources. Head of Personnel: Alleyne, Patrick
Public relations, information and marketing. Dean, Luton Business School: Pettitt, Stephen, BSc MBA PhD
Publications. Director of Marketing: Mathieson, C., BEd MA
Purchasing. Director of Finance: Harding, Philip
Quality assurance and accreditation. Dean, Quality Assurance: Harris, Richard W., BA MSc MBA
Research. Director of Research and External Affairs: Rawson, Prof. David, BSc
Safety. Pro Vice-Chancellor: Birch, Prof. Paul, BSc PhD MBA, FIBiol
Scholarships, awards, loans. Director of Finance: Harding, Philip
Schools liaison. Director of Marketing: Mathieson, C., BEd MA
Security. Director of Campus Services: Andrew, Reece
Sport and recreation. Pro Vice-Chancellor: Birch, Prof. Paul, BSc PhD MBA, FIBiol
Staff development and training. Head of Staff Development and Quality Enhancement: Atlay, Mark
Student union. Pro Vice-Chancellor: Birch, Prof. Paul, BSc PhD MBA, FIBiol
Student welfare/counselling. Head, Student Services: Jack, Gillian, BA
Students from other countries. Director of Marketing: Mathieson, C., BEd MA
Students from other countries. Head of International Office: Crick, Tim
Students with disabilities. Head, Student Services: Jack, Gillian, BA
University press. Dean, Humanities: Boatswain, Tim, BA MSc

[Information supplied by the institution as at 22 July 1998, and edited by the ACU]

UNIVERSITY OF MANCHESTER

Founded 1880; previously established as Owens College 1851

Member of the Association of Commonwealth Universities

Postal Address: Oxford Road, Manchester, England M13 9PL
Telephone: (0161) 275 2000 **Fax**: (0161) 275 3000 **Telex**: 668 932 **WWW**: http://www.man.ac.uk

VISITOR—Elizabeth, H.M. The Queen in Council
CHANCELLOR—Flowers, The Lord, MA Camb., MA Oxf., DSc Birm., FIP, FRS
VICE-CHANCELLOR*—Harris, Prof. Martin B., CBE, BA Camb., MA Camb., PhD Lond., Hon. LLD Belf., Hon. DU Essex, Hon. DLitt Salf.
PRO-VICE-CHANCELLOR—Trinci, Prof. A. P. J., MSc Manc., PhD Durh., DSc Durh., FIBiol
PRO-VICE-CHANCELLOR—Gummett, Prof. Philip J., BSc Birm., MSc Manc., PhD Manc.
PRO-VICE-CHANCELLOR—Barringer, Prof. Howard, MSc Manc., PhD Manc.
PRO-VICE-CHANCELLOR—Wilson, Prof. Nairn H. F., BDS Edin., MSc Manc., PhD Manc., FDSRCSEd, FDSRCS
PRO-VICE-CHANCELLOR—Perera, Prof. Katharine M., BA Lond., PhD Manc., MA
CHAIRMAN OF COUNCIL—Kenyon, C. G., MA Oxf.
TREASURER—Slade, D. H., JP, FCA
DEPUTY TREASURER (ESTATES)—Armstrong, R. G., BA
REGISTRAR AND SECRETARY‡—Newcomb, Eddie, BA Durh.
ACADEMIC REGISTRAR—McMenemy, Albert H., LLB CNAA, BA
DIRECTOR OF FINANCE—Thompson, Ian G.
DIRECTOR OF ESTATES—Hampson, Diana, BSc CNAA
DIRECTOR OF PERSONNEL—Kellett, Bernard, BA Open(UK)
DIRECTOR OF THE JOHN RYLANDS UNIVERSITY LIBRARY AND UNIVERSITY LIBRARIAN—Hunt, C. J., BA Exe., MLitt Durh.

GENERAL INFORMATION

History. The university was founded in 1851 after a bequest from John Owens, a Manchester merchant.. Since 1873 it has been located 3km south of Manchester city centre.

Admission to first degree courses (see also United Kingdom Introduction). Through Universities and Colleges Admissions Service (UCAS).

First Degrees († = available with honours only). BA, BA(Accg&Law), BA(Econ), BA(Govt&Law), BAPS(ECS) (professional studies, early childhood studies), BAPS(Educ)†, BAPS(SW)†, BAppLing, BArch, BD, BDS, BEconSc, BEd, BEng, BLang, BLing, BLD (landscape design), BMedSc, BNurs, BPharm, BPl (planning), BSc, BSc Pharm Sc, BScHCE (science in health care ethics), BSocSc, BTP (town and country planning), LLB, MB ChB, MusB, BPhil.

Higher Degrees. ChM, LLM, MA, MA(ArtGall&MusStud), MA(Econ), MA(Econ)Soc, MA(EnvirImpAssMan), MA(Theol), MA(UrbDesReg), MA(UrbPlanDev), MAppLing, MArch, MBA, MBIS, MBSc, MChem, MChem&MPhys, MDSc, MEarthSci, MEd, MEng, MHSc, MInf, MLang, MLing, MMath, MMath&MPhys, MMatSc, MPharm, MPhys, MPsy, MRes, MSc, MSc(Acc&Fin), MTP (planning), MTPl (town planning), MusM, MusM(Perf), MPhil, ClinPsyD, DBA, DD, DDSc, DMedSc, DSc, DSocSc, EngD, LittD, LLD, MD, MusD.

Language of Instruction. English. Remedial English language classes available in English Language Teaching Unit.

Libraries. 3,600,000 volumes; over 1,000,000 manuscripts or archival items.

Fees (1998–1999). UK/EU students: undergraduates £1000; postgraduates £2610. International students (undergraduate and postgraduate): £6600 (arts); £8750 (sciences); £16,800 (clinical).

Academic Awards. 100 awards annually, ranging in value from £200 to £1500.

Academic Year (1999–2000). Two semesters: 20 September–30 January; 31 January–9 June.

Income (1996–97). Total, £2,089,000.

Statistics. Staff: 6377 (2430 academic and research, 913 administrative, 3034 other). Students: full-time 18,631 (9160 men, 9471 women); part-time 4713 (1861 men, 2852 women); total 23,344.

FACULTIES/SCHOOLS

Arts
Tel: (0161) 275 3429 Fax: (0161) 275 3005
Dean: Elsworth, Prof. J. D., MA Camb., PhD Camb.
Secretary: Ferguson, Neil, MA Aberd., MA Leeds

Biological Sciences
Tel: (0161) 275 5632 Fax: (0161) 275 5586
Dean: Trinci, Prof. A. P. J., MSc Manc., PhD Durh., DSc Durh., FIBiol
Secretary: Callan, Andrew J., BA Lanc., MA Lanc.

Business Administration
Tel: (0161) 275 7149
Dean: Harvey, Prof. Brian, BA Sheff., MA(Econ) Sheff., PhD Nott.
Secretary: Wilson, J. R., BA Leeds

Economic and Social Studies
Tel: (0161) 275 4567 Fax: (0161) 275 4925
Dean: Moran, Prof. M. J., BA Lanc., MA Essex, PhD Essex
Secretary: Knox, Laurie, BA Belf.

Education
Tel: (0161) 275 3518 Fax: (0161) 275 3528
Dean: Ainscow, Prof. Mel, MEd Birm., PhD E.Anglia
Secretary: Evans, Gareth A., BA York(UK)

Law
Tel: (0161) 275 3561 Fax: (0161) 275 3579
Dean: Loughlin, Prof. Martin, LLB Lond., LLM Warw., LLM Harv.
Secretary: Hicks, Ruth H., BSc Brist., MSc Manc.

Medicine, Dentistry and Nursing
Tel: (0161) 275 5026 Fax: (0161) 275 5584
Dean: Tomlinson, Prof. Stephen, MD Sheff., FRCP

Science
Tel: (0161) 275 4041 Fax: (0161) 275 4042
Dean: Meudell, Prof. P. R., BSc Hull, MSc Manc., PhD Manc.
Secretary: Dawson, Brian A., BA Lond.

ACADEMIC UNITS

Accounting and Finance, see also Business Administration

Tel: (0161) 275 4028 Fax: (0161) 275 4023
Ezzamel, Mahmoud, BCom S'ton., MA S'ton., PhD S'ton. Prof.
Hopper, T. M., BSc Brad., MPhil Aston KPMG Peat Marwick Prof., Management Accounting
Kirkham, Linda M., BA Liv., MA(Econ) Manc. Sr. Lectr.
Newman, Michael, MSc Lond., PhD Br.Col. Reader
Scapens, R. W., MA(Econ) PhD, FCA Prof., Accounting
Skerratt, L. C. L., BSc(Econ) Lond. Emer. Prof.
Southworth, A. J., BSc(Econ) Lond., MA(Econ) Manc., FCA Sr. Lectr.
Strong, N. C., BA Newcastle(UK), MA Newcastle(UK) Prof.
Taylor, P. J., BA(Econ) Sheff. KPMG Peat Marwick Sr. Lectr.
Turley, W. S., MA(Econ) Manc. Prof.; Head*
Walker, Martin, BA Newcastle(UK), PhD Newcastle(UK) Prof.
Williams, K. H., BSc(Econ) Lond. Reader
Xu, Xinhong, BSc Beijing, MBA Aston, PhD Lanc. Sr. Lectr.
Other Staff: 10 Lectrs.; 2 Res. Staff; 3 Temp. Lectrs.
Research: financial reporting, corporate disclosure of financial markets; international accounting and finance; management accounting, information systems and technology; public policy aspects of accounting and finance; research methodology

Agricultural Economics, see Econ. Studies, Sch. of

American Studies, see Engl. and American Studies

Anatomy, see Biol. Scis., Sch. of

Anthropology, see Soc. Anthropol.

Anglo-Saxon, see under Engl. and American Studies

Arabic, see Middle Eastern Studies

Archaeology, see Art Hist. and Archaeol.; Engl. and American Studies

Architecture, Manchester School of

Joint School with Manchester Metropolitan University

Tel: (0161) 275 6934 Fax: (0161) 275 6935

Allen, P. C., BA(Arch) Manc. Sr. Lectr.
Allsopp, C. J. Prof.
Bell, J. A. M., BArch Liv., MCD Liv., PhD Manc. Emer. Prof.
Dovell, P., BArch Liv., MCD Liv., MA Liv. Emer. Prof.
Jessop, M. R., BA Manc. Head, Architecture
Lim, Datuk Chong Keat, BA Manc., MArch MIT Hon. Visiting Prof.
Starling, M. Head; Dir.*
Stonehouse, R. J., MA Camb. Prof.
Symes, M. S., MA Camb., PhD Lond. British Gas Prof., Urban Renewal
Yeomans, D. T., BSc(Eng) Lond., PhD Liv. Sr. Lectr.
Other Staff: 18 Lectrs.; 3 Hon. Fellows; 10 Tutors†; 3 Temp. Lectrs.

Art History and Archaeology

Tel: (0161) 275 3310 Fax: (0161) 275 3331

Buttes, Suzanne B., BA Mass., MA Rosary, PhD Lond. Sr. Lectr., History of Art
Causey, A. G., BA Camb., PhD Lond. Prof., Modern Art History; Head*
Coombs, D. G., MA Camb., PhD Camb., FSA Sr. Lectr., Archaeology
Jones, G. D. B., MA Oxf., MA Manc., DPhil Oxf., FSA Prof., Archaeology
Ling, R. J., MA Camb., PhD Camb., FSA Prof., Classical Art and Archaeology
Pointon, Marcia R., MA PhD Pilkington Prof., Art History
Rasmussen, T. C. B., BA Camb., PhD Camb., FSA Sr. Lectr., History of Art
Wild, J. P., MA Camb., PhD Camb., FSA Reader, Archaeology
Wolfenden, I. G., MA Camb. Sr. Lectr., History of Art
Other Staff: 7 Lectrs.; 3 Hon. Lectrs.; 1 Hon. Sr. Lectr.; 1 Simon Res. Fellow; 1 Hon. Fellow
Research: archaeological history and theory (fourteenth–twentieth centuries); archaeological theory, including ethnicity and historiography; art history: Britain and Europe since 1400; museology; visual culture and cultural theory; Roman, Mediterranean and Near Eastern archaeology

Astronomy, see Phys. and Astron.

Audiology, see Educn., Sch. of

Biochemistry, see Biol. Scis., Sch. of

Biological Sciences, School of

Tel: (0161) 275 5587 Fax: (0161) 275 5657

Research: basic aspects of molecular/cellular biology; cell death, apoptosis, ageing, and degeneration; extracellular matrix and adhesion molecules; integrative/systems biology in health and disease; tissue injury and repair

Biochemistry, Research Division of

Tel: (0161) 275 5072 Fax: (0161) 275 5082

Anderson, J. C., MA Camb., PhD Camb. Sr. Lectr., Medical Biochemistry
Boot-Handford, R. P., BSc Wales, PhD Lond. Sr. Lectr., Molecular Biology
Brass, A., BSc Nott., PhD Edin. Sr. Lectr.
Burdett, Keith, BSc Birm., PhD Birm., FRSChem Sr. Lectr., Medical Biochemistry
Dickson, A. J., BSc Edin., PhD Edin. Sr. Lectr.
Elliott, K. R. F., MA Camb., PhD Camb. Sr. Lectr.

Franklin, T., BSc Birm., PhD Birm. Hon. Prof. Fellow
Grant, M. E., BScTech Manc., DPhil Oxf. Prof., Medical Biochemistry
Gull, Keith, BSc Lond., PhD Lond. Prof., Molecular Biology
Hardingham, T. E., BSc Brist., PhD Brist., DSc Brist. Prof., Wellcome Trust Centre for Cell Matrix Res.
Humphries, M. J., BSc Manc., PhD Manc. Prof.; Res. Fellow; Chair*
Jacob, A. E., BSc Manc., PhD Manc. Sr. Lectr., Bacteriology
Jones, M. N., PhD Manc., DSc Manc., FRSChem Reader, Physical Biochemistry
Muir, Helen Hon. Visiting Prof.
Rosamond, John, MA Oxf., DPhil Oxf. Reader, Molecular Genetics
Sheehan, J. K., BSc Leic., MSc Brist., PhD Brist. Wellcome Reader, Physiological Biochemistry
Shuttleworth, C. A., BSc Liv., PhD Liv. Reader, Medical Biochemistry
Stirling, C. J., BSc Edin., PhD Glas. Reader, Molecular Biology
Wood, R. J., BSc Lond., PhD Lond. Reader, Genetics
Other Staff: 7 Lectrs.; 1 Clin. Training Fellow; 15 Res. Fellows; 52 Res. Assocs.; 1 Hon. Fellow; 1 Hon. Res. Fellow; 2 Temp. Lectrs.

Biological Sciences Education Research Centre

Tel: (0161) 275 5241 Fax: (0161) 275 5661

Evans, M. E. G., BSc Lond., PhD Lond. Sr. Lectr., Zoology
Ferguson, D. B., BDS Lond., PhD Lond. Sr. Lectr., Physiology for Dental Students; Chairman*
Humpherson, J. R., MB ChB St And. Sr. Lectr., Anatomy
Neave, Richard Dir., Unit of Art in Med. and Life Scis.
Other Staff: 4 Lectrs.

Cells, Immunology and Development, Research Division of

Tel: (0161) 275 5178 Fax: (0161) 275 5640

Allen, Terence, BSc Manc., PhD Manc., DSc Manc. Hon. Reader, Cellular Ultrastructure
Aplin, J. D., MA Oxf., PhD Br.Col. Sr. Lectr., Biochemistry
Bardsley, W. G., PhD Manc., DSc Manc. Reader, Biochemistry
Bell, E. B., BA Oberlin, VMD Penn., PhD Edin. Reader, Immunology
Boulton, M. E., BSc Reading, PhD CNAA Reader, Ophthalmology
Dixon, M. J., BDS Manc., PhD Manc. Prof., Dental Genetics
Ferguson, Mark W. J., BDS Belf., BSc Belf., PhD Belf., FFDRCSI Prof., Basic Dental Sciences
Garrod, D. R., MA Camb., PhD Lond. Prof., Development Biology
Grencis, R. K., BSc Nott., PhD Glas. Reader, Immunology
Hewitt, Jane, BA Oxf., PhD Camb. Sr. Lectr., Molecular Embryology
Hutchinson, I. V., BSc Sur., PhD Lond. Prof., Immunology
Kimber, Susan J., MA Camb., PhD Camb. Sr. Lectr., Basic Dental Sciences
Scott, J. E., PhD Manc., DSc Manc. Hon. Emer. Prof., Chemical Morphology
White, Anne, BSc Manc., PhD Manc. Reader, Clinical Biochemistry; Chair*
Yalden, Derek W., BSc Lond., PhD Lond. Sr. Lectr., Zoology
Other Staff: 8 Lectrs.; 11 Res. Fellows; 19 Res. Assocs.; 5 Hon. Lectrs.

Neuroscience, Research Division of

Tel: (0161) 275 5242 Fax: (0161) 275 5363

Brotchie, J. M., BSc Manc., PhD Manc. Sr. Lectr., Anatomy
Cody, F. W. J., BSc Lond., PhD Lond. Sr. Lectr., Physiology

Crossman, A. R., BSc S'ton., PhD S'ton., DSc Manc. Prof., Anatomy; Chairman*
Luheshi, G., BSc Manc., PhD Newcastle(UK) Jean Feger Hon. Visiting Prof.
McCrohan, Catherine R., BA Camb., DPhil Sus. Sr. Lectr., Zoology
Owen, Frank, BSc Sur., PhD Liv. Glaxo Prof., Neuroscience
Pleuvry, Barbara J., BPharm Lond., MSc Manc., PhD Manc. Sr. Lectr., Anaesthesia and Pharmacology
Rothwell, Nancy J., BSc Lond., PhD Lond., DSc Lond. Prof., Physiology
Slater, Paul, BPharm Nott., PhD Nott. Reader, Physiology
Wareham, A. C., BSc Durh., PhD Durh. Sr. Lectr., Physiology
Other Staff: 6 Lectrs.; 1 Clin. Res. Fellow; 1 Res. Fellow; 11 Res. Assocs.; 1 Hon. Lectr.

Physiology, Pharmacology and Toxicology, Research Division of

Tel: (0161) 275 5617 Fax: (0161) 275 5600

Atherton, J. C., BSc Newcastle(UK), PhD Manc. Sr. Lectr., Physiology
Balment, R. J., BSc Sheff., PhD Sheff. Prof., Zoology
Brown, P. D., BSc Brad., PhD Camb. Sr. Lectr., Physiology
Case, R. M., BSc Durh., PhD Newcastle(UK) Brackenbury Prof., Physiology
Duxbury, A. J., MSc Manc., PhD Manc., DDS Manc., FDSRCPSGlas Sr. Lectr., Dental Pharmacology and Therapy and Oral Medicine
Foster, R. W., BSc Lond., MB BS Lond., PhD Lond. Reader, Pharmacology
Green, Roger, MB ChB Sheff., MSc Manc. Prof., Physiology
Hickman, J. A., BSc Aston, MSc Lond., PhD Aston, DSc Aston Zeneca Prof., Molecular Pharmacology
Hollingsworth, Michael, MSc Manc., PhD Manc., DSc Manc. Sr. Lectr., Pharmacology
Little, R. A., BSc Lond., PhD Lond., FRCPath Hon. Prof., Surgical Science
Lowe, A. G., BSc Brist., PhD Brist. Sr. Lectr., Biochemistry
Minors, D. S., BSc Lond., PhD Manc. Sr. Lectr., Physiology
Morris, I. D., BPharm Lond., PhD Lond., DSc Manc. Reader, Pharmacology
Sibley, C. P., BSc Lond., PhD Lond. Sr. Lectr., Child Health and Physiology
Small, R. C., MSc Manc., PhD Manc., DSc Manc. Reader, Pharmacology
Weston, A. H., MSc Manc., PhD Manc., DSc Manc. Leech Prof., Pharmacology; Chairman*
Other Staff: 6 Lectrs.; 11 Res. Fellows; 29 Res. Assocs.; 1 Hon. Lectr.

Plants, Microbes and Environmental Biology, Research Division of

Tel: (0161) 275 3891 Fax: (0161) 275 3954, 275 3938

Bailey, S. E. R., BSc Birm., PhD Birm. Sr. Lectr., Zoology
Bray, Cliff M., BSc Sheff., PhD Manc. Sr. Lectr., Biochemistry
Butler, R. D., BSc Durh., PhD S'ton. Reader, Cytology
Cutter, Elizabeth G., PhD Manc., DSc St And. Emer. Prof., Botany; Hon. Fellow
Drucker, D. B., BSc Liv., PhD Liv., DSc Manc. Reader, Microbiology
Dunn-Coleman, N. Visiting Prof.
Emes, M. J., BSc Sheff., PhD Sheff. Prof., Plant Sciences; Chairman*
Ennos, A. R., MA Camb., PhD Exe. Sr. Lectr., Environmental Biology
Epton, H. A. S., BSc Lond., PhD Lond. Sr. Lectr., Botany
Handley, Pauline S., BSc Lond., PhD Lond. Sr. Lectr., Bacteriology and Virology
Loudon, Andrew S. I., BA Oxf., PhD Edin. Prof., Animal Biology

Moore, David, BSc Hull, PhD Hull, DSc Manc. Reader, Genetics

Roberts, I. S., BSc Leic., PhD Birm. Prof., Microbiology

Sheffield, Elizabeth, BSc Lond., PhD Lond. Sr. Lectr., Botany

Sigee, D. C., BA Camb., PhD Lond. Sr. Lectr., Cell Biology

Tallis, J. H., BSc Lond., PhD Wales Sr. Lectr., Botany

Trinci, A. P. J., MSc Manc., PhD Durh., DSc Durh., FIBiol Barker Prof., Cryptogamic Botany

Wood, D. A. W., BSc Lond., PhD Lond. Visiting Prof.

Other Staff: 14 Lectrs.; 3 Res. Fellows; 20 Res. Assocs.; 2 Hon. Lectrs.; 1 Hon. Fellow

Business Administration, see below

Chemistry

Tel: (0161) 275 4653 Fax: (0161) 275 4616

Allen, Sir Geoffrey, BSc Leeds, MSc Manc., PhD Leeds, FRS Hon. Visiting Prof.

Ashton, M. J., BSc CNAA, DPhil Oxf. Hon. Visiting Prof.

Booth, Colin, BSc Manc., PhD Manc., FRSChem Reader

Brown, R. T., BA Oxf., BSc Oxf., PhD Br.Col., FRSChem Sr. Lectr.

Budd, P. M., BSc PhD Sr. Lectr.

Byers-Brown, W., DSc, FRSChem Prof. Emer.

Collison, D., BSc Manc., PhD Manc. Sr. Lectr.

Connor, J. N. L., MA Oxf., BSc Oxf., DPhil Oxf. Prof., Theoretical Chemistry

Day, J. P., MA Oxf., DPhil Oxf., FRSChem Reader

Garner, C. D., BSc Nott., PhD Nott., FRSChem Prof., Inorganic Chemistry

Gorman, A. A., MSc Manc., PhD Manc. Reader

Grice, Roger, MA Camb., PhD Harv., MSc Prof., Physical Chemistry

Heatley, Frank, BSc PhD Sr. Lectr.

Helliwell, J. R., BSc York(UK), DPhil Oxf., DSc York(UK), FRSChem Prof., Structural Chemistry

Hillier, I. H., BSc Lond., PhD Lond., MSc Prof., Theoretical Chemistry

Hodge, Philip, MSc PhD, FRSChem Prof., Polymer Chemistry

Joule, J. A., MSc PhD, FRSChem Reader

Mabbs, F. E., BSc Lond., PhD Lond., DSc Lond. Reader

Masters, A. J., MA Camb., PhD Camb. Sr. Lectr.

Morris, G. A., BA Oxf., MA Oxf., DPhil Oxf. Reader

Oldham, R. J., MA Camb., PhD Camb. Hon. Visiting Prof.

Padget, J. C., BSc Manc., PhD Manc. Hon. Visiting Prof.

Price, Colin, MSc PhD Prof., Polymer Chemistry; Head*

Quayle, P., BSc Lond., PhD Lond. Sr. Lectr.

Sutherland, J. K., PhD Glas., DSc Glas., FRSChem Prof. Emer.

Thomas, E. J., MA Camb., PhD Camb., FRSChem Prof., Organic Chemistry

Thornton, Geoffrey, BSc Sus., DPhil Oxf. Prof., Surface Sciences

Tredgold, R. H., PhD Nott., DSc Nott. Hon. Visiting Prof.

Watt, C. I. F., BSc Edin., PhD Carnegie-Mellon Sr. Lectr.

Whitehead, J. C., BSc Edin., PhD Camb. Reader

Other Staff: 11 Lectrs.; 50 Res. Staff; 2 Hon. Readers; 8 Hon. Fellows; 2 Hon. Res. Fellows; 1 Temp. Lectr.

Computer Science

Tel: (0161) 275 6124, 275 6125 Fax: (0161) 275 6236

Aczel, P. H. G., BA Oxf., DPhil Oxf. Prof., Mathematical Logic and Computing Science

Banach, R. H., BSc Liv., PhD Manc. Sr. Lectr.

Barringer, Howard, MSc Manc., PhD Manc. Prof.

Bree, D. S., MA Camb., PhD Pitt. Prof., Artificial Intelligence

Capon, P. C., BSc S'ton., PhD Sr. Lectr.

Edwards, D. A., MSc PhD Sr. Lectr.

Furber, Steve B., MA Camb., PhD Camb. ICL Prof., Computer Engineering

Goble, Carole A., BSc Sr. Lectr.

Gurd, J. R., BSc Reading, PhD Reading Prof.

Hinchliffe, T. A., BSc Manc. Hon. Visiting Prof.

Hubbold, R. J., BSc Leic., PhD Leic. Sr. Lectr.

Jones, Cliff, MSc Manc., DPhil Oxf. Hon. Prof.

Kahn, Hilary J., BA Lond. Prof.

Kay, Stephen, BA CNAA, PhD Wales Sr. Lectr.

Kirkham, C. C., BA Camb., PhD Camb. Sr. Lectr.

Knowles, A. E., BSc Leeds, PhD Sr. Lectr.

Paton, N. W., BSc Aberd., PhD Aberd. Sr. Lectr., Information Systems

Rector, A. L., BA Calif., MD Minn., PhD Manc. Prof., Medical Informatics

Rydeheard, D. E., BA Camb., PhD Edin. Sr. Lectr.

Shapiro, J. L., BA Portland, MSc Calif., PhD Calif. Sr. Lectr.

Spink, M. A., BSc PhD Dir., PEVEit Unit

Sumner, Frank, BSc Manc., PhD Manc. Prof.†

Warboys, Brian C., BSc S'ton. Prof.†, Software Engineering; Head*

Wastell, D. G., BSc Durh., PhD Durh. Sr. Lectr., Information Systems

Watson, Ian, BSc PhD Prof.

Woods, J. V., MScTech PhD Sr. Lectr.

Zobel, R. N., BSc(Eng) Lond., PhD Sr. Lectr.

Other Staff: 22 Lectrs.; 50 Res. Staff; 1 Lectr.†; 1 Hon. Sr. Lectr.; 8 Hon. Lectrs.; 13 Hon. Fellows

Research: applications (medical and biological informatics, business processing engineering); computer hardware engineering (self-timed systems, ECAD, low power architecture); computer systems architecture (parallel computers, compilation and run-time libraries); formal system design and validation, foundational theory; information systems (information management, artificial intelligence, advanced interfaces)

Decision Theory

White, D. J., MA Oxf., MSc Birm., PhD Birm., DSc Birm., MA(Econ) Prof.

Dentistry, see Dental School, below

Development Policy and Management, Institute for

Tel: (0161) 275 2812

Clarke, R. F., MA Camb., MEd E.Af., PhD Sr. Lectr.

Cook, P. C., MSc(Econ) Lond., MPhil Lond. Reader

Fuller, Colin, MA Oxf. Sr. Lectr.

Hulme, David, BA Camb., PhD Qld. Prof., Development Studies

Kirkpatrick, Colin, PhD Manc. Prof., Development Economics; Dir.*

Mullen, Joseph, PhD Edin. Sr. Lectr.

Other Staff: 12 Lectrs.; 1 Sr. Res. Fellow; 1 Lectr.†; 1 Hon. Visiting Fellow

Research: development administration; economic development policy; human resource development; public sector management; social development; sustainable development

Drama

Tel: (0161) 275 3347 Fax: (0161) 275 3349

Gardner, Vivien A., BA Sr. Lectr.

Holt, Michael Sr. Lectr., Stage Design

Jackson, Anthony R., MA Wis., BA Sr. Lectr.

Richards, K. R., MA Oxf., MA Manc. Prof.; Head*; Dir., Univ. Theatre

Taylor, G. W., MA PhD Sr. Lectr.

Other Staff: 2 Lectrs.; 2 Sp. Lectrs.†; 1 Hon. Lectr.

Earth Sciences

Tel: (0161) 275 3804 Fax: (0161) 275 3947

Adams, A. E., BA Oxf., PhD Wales Sr. Lectr.

Anketell, J. M., BSc Belf., PhD Belf. Sr. Lectr.

Brodie, Katherine H., BSc Leeds, PhD Lond., FGS Sr. Lectr.

Curtis, C. D., BSc Sheff., PhD Sheff., FGS Prof., Geochemistry

Droop, G. T. R., BSc Edin., DPhil Oxf. Sr. Lectr.

Gawthorpe, R. L., BSc Leeds, PhD Leeds, FGS Sr. Lectr.

Gize, A. P., BSc St And., MSc Newcastle(UK), PhD Penn. Sr. Lectr.

Greaves, G. N., BSc St And., PhD Camb., FIP Hon. Visiting Prof.

Henderson, Colin M. B., PhD Lond., DSc Durh. Res. Prof., Petrology

Lyon, I. C., BSc Newcastle(UK), PhD Newcastle(UK) Sr. Lectr., Isotope Geochemistry

Manning, D. A. C., BSc Durh., PhD, FGS Reader, Geology

Pattrick, R. A. D., BSc St And., PhD Strath. Sr. Lectr.

Pollard, J. E., MA Oxf., PhD Durh., FGS Sr. Lectr.

Rutter, E. H., BSc Lond., PhD Lond. Prof., Structural Geology; Head*

Selden, P. A., PhD Camb., BSc Sr. Lectr.

Sowerbutts, W. T. C., BSc Leic., PhD Newcastle(UK) Sr. Lectr., Geophysics

Turner, Grenville, MA Camb., DPhil Oxf., FRS, FIP Prof., Isotope Geochemistry

Vaughan, D. J., MSc Lond., DPhil Oxf., DSc Oxf. Prof., Mineralogy

Other Staff: 6 Lectrs.; 4 Teaching Fellows; 3 Sr. Res. Fellows; 5 Res. Fellows; 9 Res. Assocs.; 4 Hon. Lectrs.

Economic Studies, School of

Tel: (0161) 275 3347 Fax: (0161) 275 3349

Andrews, M. J., BA Reading, MSc Lond., PhD Lond. Sr. Lectr.

Antonelli, C., LaurEcon Turin Hon. Visiting Prof., Economics

Artis, M. J., BA Oxf., MA(Econ) Manc., FBA Prof., Economics (on leave)

Birchenhall, C. R., BA Camb. Sr. Lectr.

Blackburn, Keith, BA Liv., MSc Lond., PhD Lond. Prof., Macroeconomics

Burton, M. P., BSc Bath, MA(Econ) Manc., PhD Manc. Sr. Lectr.

Colman, D. R., BSc Lond., MA Ill., PhD Manc. Prof., Agricultural Economics

Currie, J. M., MA(Econ) Manc., PhD Calif. Sr. Lectr.

Devine, P. J., BA Oxf., MA(Econ) Manc. Sr. Lectr.

Elson, Diane R., BA Oxf., PhD Manc. Prof.; Grad. Dean

Furness, G. W., MSc Leeds Hon. Visiting Prof., Agricultural Economics

Harrington, R. L., BScEcon Wales, MSc(Econ) Lond. Sr. Lectr.

Joseph, G., BA Leic., MA(Econ) Manc., PhD Manc. Reader, Social Statistics

Madden, P. J., BSocSc Birm., MA Essex Prof., Mathematical Economics

Metcalfe, J. S., CBE, BA(Econ) Manc., MSc Manc. Stanley Jevons Prof., Political Economy; Cobden Lectr.

Moore, S. A., MA(Econ) Manc. Hon. Prof. Fellow, Economics

Nixson, F. I., BA Leeds, PhD Leeds Prof.

Orme, C. D., BSc York(UK), MSc Lond., DPhil York(UK) Prof., Econometrics

Osborn, Denise R., MEc Syd., PhD Lond. Robert Ottley Prof., Econometrics; Head*; Dir. of Res.

Parrinello, S., LEcon Trieste Hon. Prof., Economics

Peach, T., BA Oxf., DPhil Oxf. Sr. Lectr.

Stubbs, P. C., MA Camb., PhD Melb. Emer. Prof., Economics

Young, T., BA Nott., MA(Econ) Manc., PhD Calif. Reader, Agricultural Economics

Other Staff: 19 Lectrs.; 6 Res. Staff; 2 Simon Res. Fellows; 1 Hailsworn Res. Fellow; 1 Hon. Reader; 1 Hon. Sr. Res. Fellow

Research: agricultural economics (agricultural markets, food demand, waste management); development economics (transitional economics, aid and growth); econometrics (applied labour economics, theory, time series); economic theory (inequality, general equilibrium theory, games, crime); history and methodology (Ricardo, justice, property rights, asymmetric information)

Cathie Marsh Centre for Census and Survey Research

Dale, Prof. Angela, BSc Lond., MPhil Lond., MSc Sur., PhD Sur. Dir.*

Research: census under-enumeration and statistical disclosure control; employment, labour markets and occupational attainment; household and family dynamics; social, ethnic and geographical inequalities

Farm Business Unit

Colman, D. R., BSc Lond., MA Ill., PhD Manc. Dir.*

Other Staff: 1 Managing Officer; 4 Investigational Officers

Education, School of

Tel: (0161) 275 3518 Fax: (0161) 275 3519

Ainscow, Mel, MEd Birm., PhD E.Anglia Prof., Special Needs and Educational Psychology

Aplin, D. Yvonne, BA Manc., MEd Manc., MSc Manc., PhD Manc. Sr. Lectr., Education of the Deaf

Bamford, J. M., BA Reading, PhD Reading Ellis Llwyd Jones Prof., Audiology and Education of the Deaf

Boreham, N. C., MA Nott., MPhil Nott., PhD Prof.

Brown, Marie, BA N.U.I., MSc Sheff. Sr. Lectr.

Carroll, Robert, MA(Econ) Manc., MEd Manc., PhD Manc. Sr. Lectr., Physical Education

Christie, Thomas, MA Edin., BEd Edin. Prof., Educational Assessment and Evaluation; Dir.*

Conti-Ramsden, Gina M., BA N.Y., MPhil Camb., PhD Texas Prof., Child Language and Learning

Farrell, P. T., BA Liv., MEd Birm., PhD Manc. Sr. Lectr., Education

Graham, D. G., CBE, MA Glas. Hon. Visiting Prof.

Hardman, K., MEd Liv., MSc Strath., BA Sr. Lectr., Physical Education

Harris, John M., BA Kent, DPhil Oxf. Sir David Alliance Prof., Clinical Bioethics

Harrison, M. A., BSc MEd Sr. Lectr., Primary Education

Lynas, Wendy A., BEd PhD Sr. Lectr., Education of the Deaf

Mittler, P. J., CBE, MA Camb., MEd Manc., PhD Lond. Prof.†, Special Education

Newton, Valerie E., MD Sheff., MSc Prof., Audiology Medicine

O'Brien, Teresa A., BA Lond., MA Manc., PhD Manc. Sr. Lectr., Teaching of English Overseas

Reason, Rea, MSc Manc., PhD Manc. Sr. Lectr.†

Price, G. W., MA Manc., PhD Manc. Sr. Lectr.

Reid, D. J., JP, BSc Sheff., MA(Ed) S'ton., PhD Prof.

Robertson, A. B., MA Durh., MEd Newcastle(UK), PhD Newcastle(UK) Sr. Lectr.

Shaw, C. D., CBE, MA Oxf. Hon. Visiting Prof.

Taylor, D. C., MA Camb., MEd Brist., PhD Sr. Lectr., International Education

Verma, G. K., BA Bihar, MA Patna, MA Lond., PhD Lond. Sarah Fielden Prof.

Warner, Jennifer A. W., MSc Lond. Sr. Lectr., Speech Pathology and Therapy

West, R. I., BA Brist., MA Lanc. Sr. Lectr., Teaching of English Overseas

Williams, J. S., BA Oxf., MSc Leeds Sr. Lectr.

Other Staff: 55 Lectrs.; 4 Lectrs.†; 10 Hon. Lectrs.; 78 Hon. Tutors

Engineering, Manchester School of

Tel: (0161) 275 4300 Fax: (0161) 257 4512

Evans, T. D. Lab. Supt.

Harris, S. J., BA Oxf., DPhil Oxf. Manager, Indust. Liaison

Ruban, A. I., PhD DSc Prof., Computational Fluid Dynamics

Research: heat transfer; nuclear engineering; reactor modelling; thermal hydraulics

Aerospace Engineering Division

Tel: (0161) 275 4261 Fax: (0161) 275 4261

Cooper, J. E., BSc Lond., PhD Lond. Sr. Lectr.

Lewis, S. J., BSc City(UK) Royal Academy Visiting Prof., Engineering Design

Mansell, Michael, MSc Sur., FRAeS, FIEE, FEng Hon. Visiting Prof.

Scott-Wilson, J. B., OBE, MA, FEng, FRAeS Hon. Visiting Prof.

Wood, N. J., BSc Bath, PhD Bath Beyer Prof.; Chairman*

Other Staff: 4 Lectrs.; 5 External Lectrs.

Research: experimental aerodynamics; flow control; flow diagnostics

Civil Engineering Division

Tel: (0161) 275 4406 Fax: (0161) 275 3844

Ball, D. J., BSc Leeds, PhD Leeds Sr. Lectr.

Craig, W. H., MSc Manc., PhD Manc. Reader

Davies, J. M., PhD DSc, FICE, FIStructE Prof., Structural Engineering

Merrifield, C. M., BSc Cape Town, PhD Sur. Sr. Lectr.

Mills, J. H., BSc Liv., PhD Liv. Royal Academy of Engin. Visiting Prof., Engineering Design

Procter, David C., MSc Manc. Sr. Lectr.

Smith, I. M., BSc Glas., MS Calif., PhD Glas., DSc Manc., FICE Prof., Geotechnical Engineering

Stansby, P. K., BA Camb., PhD Camb., DSc Manc. Prof., Engineering Hydrodynamics; Chairman*

Other Staff: 5 Lectrs.; 8 Res. Staff; 1 Hon. Reader; 1 Hon. Fellow

Research: geotechnics; hydrodynamics; structures

Electrical Engineering Division

Tel: (0161) 275 4524 Fax: (0161) 275 4512

Auckland, D. W., MSc Manc., PhD Manc. Prof.

Birchby, G., BSc Royal Academy of Engin. Visiting Prof., Engineering Design

Cunningham, Michael J., MSc Wales, PhD Wales Chairman*

Farrell, P. G., BSc City(UK), MSc Manc., PhD Camb., FEng, FIEE, FIMA Prof., Electrical Engineering; Head of Sch.*

Hill, E. W., BSc Nott., PhD Nott. Sr. Lectr.

Middleton, B. K., BSc Sheff., PhD Salf., FIEE Prof.

Miles, J. J., BSc Liv., MSc Salf., PhD Manc. Sr. Lectr.

Quayle, R. S., MSc Manc., PhD Manc. Sr. Lectr.

Varlow, B. R., BSc Manc., PhD Manc. Reader

Wright, C. D., BSc Lond., MSc Sheff., PhD CNAA Sr. Lectr.

Xydeas, Costas, MSc Lough., PhD Lough. Prof., Electrical Engineering

Other Staff: 8 Lectrs.; 20 Res. Staff; 4 Hon. Fellows; 2 Hon. Visiting Lectrs.; 3 External Lectrs.

Research: energy systems; information storage; signal processing

Mechanical Engineering Division

Tel: (0161) 275 4302 Fax: (0161) 275 3844

Day, B. V., BSc Nott., PhD Nott. Royal Academy of Engin. Visiting Prof., Engineering Design

Dye, R. C. F., MSc Manc., PhD Manc., FIMechE Clifton Sr. Lectr.

Jackson, J. D., BSc Manc. Prof., Mechanical and Nuclear Engineering

Leung, A. Y. T., MSc Manc., PhD Manc., DSc Manc. Prof., Engineering

Sandoz, David J., BEng Liv., PhD Liv. Prof.†, Industrial Control Engineering

Smart, John, BSc(Eng) Lond., PhD Lond. Sr. Lectr.

Stanley, Peter, MA Camb., MSc Manc., PhD Nott., DSc Manc., FIMechE, FIP Emer. Prof.

Turner, J. T., MSc Manc., PhD Manc., FIMechE Reader

Wright, J. R., BSc Brist., PhD Brist. Prof.; Chairman*

Other Staff: 8 Lectrs.; 8 Res. Staff; 1 Hon. Sr. Lectr.; 2 Hon. Lectrs.; 3 Hon. Fellows; 1 Hon. Visiting Lectr.; 3 External Lectrs.; 3 Temp. Lectrs.

Research: dynamics; dynamics and control; fracture; maintenance engineering; process control

English and American Studies

Tel: (0161) 275 3145 Fax: (0161) 275 3256

Anderson, C. Joy, BA Lond., MPhil Lond. Sr. Lectr., English Language

Anderson, J. J., MA Otago, PhD Adel. Sr. Lectr., English Language

Crowley, Tony E., BA Oxf., DPhil Oxf. Prof., Modern English Literature; Head*

Denison, D. M. B., MA Camb., DPhil Oxf. Prof., English Linguistics

Evans, Emrys, MA Wales, PhD Belf. Hon. Visiting Prof., Irish

Francis, Richard, MA Camb., PhD Exe. Sr. Lectr., American Literature and Creative Writing

Grant, D. J., MA Lond. Sr. Lectr., English Literature

Hammond, Gerald, BA Lond., PhD Lond. John Edward Taylor Prof., English Literature

Hicks, M. A., BA Leic., MA Sr. Lectr., English Literature

Hill, D. H., PhD S'ton., FSA Sr. Lectr., Archaeology

Hogg, Richard M., MA Edin., MA Manc., PhD Edin. Smith Prof., English Language and Mediaeval English Literature

Hutchings, W. B., BA S'ton., PhD S'ton. Sr. Lectr., English Literature

Lindop, G. C. G., MA Oxf., BLitt Oxf. Prof., Romantic and Early Victorian Studies

McCully, C. B., BA Newcastle(UK), PhD Sr. Lectr., English Language and Literature

Pearson, Jacqueline, BA Lond., PhD Lond. Sr. Lectr.

Pirie, D. B., BA Oxf., BPhil Oxf. Sr. Lectr., English Literature

Rumble, A. R., BA Leeds, PhD Lond., FRHistS Sr. Lectr., Palaeography; Dir., Centre for Anglo-Saxon Studies

Schmidt, M. N., MA Oxf. Sr. Lectr., Poetry; Dir., Poetry Centre

Scragg, D. G., BA Liv., PhD Prof., Anglo-Saxon Studies

Scragg, Leah, MA Liv. Sr. Lectr., English Literature

Shelston, A. J., MA Lond. Sr. Lectr., English Literature

Swinden, Patrick, BA Hull, PhD Camb. Sr. Lectr., English Literature

Walker, I. M., BA Nott., PhD Nott. Sr. Lectr., American Literature

Weinberg, Carole, MA Edin., MPhil Lond. Sr. Lectr.

Other Staff: 12 Lectrs.; 8 Res. Staff; 1 Hon. Lectr.; 1 British Academy HRB Instn. Fellow

Finance, see Acctg. and Finance

French Studies

Tel: (0161) 275 3208 Fax: (0161) 275 3031

Adams, D. J., MA PhD Reader

Brown, P. E., MA Manc. Sr. Lectr., Comparative Literary Studies

Flynn, J. W., MA Glas., PhD Sr. Lectr.; Head*

Phillips, J. Henry, BA Oxf., DPhil Oxf. Prof.

Wetherill, P. M., MA Birm., DU Stras. Prof.

Other Staff: 6 Lectrs.; 2 Hon. Fellows; 2 Temp. Lectrs.†

Research: contemporary French fiction; early modern French literature; literature and visual and performing arts; mediaeval literature, especially text and image; modern poetry

Geography

Tel: (0161) 275 3638

Bradford, Michael G., MA Camb., PhD Camb. Sr. Lectr.; Head*
Braithwaite, R. J., BSc Reading, MSc Reading, PhD McG Reader
Dicken, Peter, MA Prof.
Douglas, Ian, MA Oxf., MA Manc., BLitt Oxf., PhD ANU Prof., Physical Geography
Huggett, R. J., BSc Lond., PhD Lond. Sr. Lectr.
Peck, J. A., BA PhD Reader
Robinson, M. E., BA Leic., PhD ANU Sr. Lectr.
Robson, B. T., MA Camb., MA Manc., PhD Camb. Prof.
Shimwell, D. W., BSc Durh., PhD Durh. Sr. Lectr.
Sutton, K., MA Lond. Sr. Lectr.
Theakstone, W. H., MA Camb. Hon. Res. Fellow
Thomas, R. W., BA Nott., PhD Nott. Reader
Other Staff: 10 Lectrs.; 16 Res. Staff; 1 Simon Res. Fellow; 1 Hon. Lectr.

Geology, see Earth Scis.

German Language and Literature

Tel: (0161) 275 3182 Fax: (0161) 275 3031

Bell, David, MA Camb., PhD Camb. Sr. Lectr.; Head*
Blamires, David M., MA Camb., PhD Camb. Reader
Durrell, Martin, MA Camb., DrPhil Marburg Henry Simon Prof.
Parker, Stephen R., BA Leeds, PhD Sr. Lectr.
Purver, Judith O., MA Camb., PhD Camb. Sr. Lectr.
Other Staff: 3 Lectrs.; 1 Res. Fellow; 1 Hon. Lectr.

Government

Tel: (0161) 275 4885 Fax: (0161) 275 4925

Bulmer, S. J., BA Lough., MA Hull, PhD Lond. Prof.
Burch, M. S., BA Hull, PhD Glas. Sr. Lectr.
Cammack, P. A., BA Oxf., DPhil Oxf. Sr. Lectr.
Coates, David, BA York(UK), DPhil Oxf. Prof.
D'Entreves, M. P., BA Lond., MA Boston, PhD Boston Sr. Lectr. (on leave)
Farrell, D. M., BA Trinity(Dub.), MA Trinity(Dub.), PhD Florence Jean Monnet Sr. Lectr.
Geras, Norman M., BA Oxf. Prof.; Head*
Gummett, Philip J., BSc Birm., MSc Manc., PhD Manc. Prof., Government and Technology Policy
Holliday, I. M., MA Camb., DPhil Oxf. Sr. Lectr.
Humphreys, P. J., BA CNAA, MSc(Econ) Lond., PhD Brad. Reader
Moran, M. J., BA Lanc., MA Essex, PhD Essex Prof.
Parry, Geraint B., BSc(Econ) Lond., PhD Lond., MA(Econ) W. J. M. Mackenzie Prof.
Roberts, G. K., BSc(Econ) Lond., PhD Lond. Reader, German Politics
Steiner, Hillel I., BA Tor., MA Car., PhD Prof., Political Philosophy (on leave)
Vogel, Ursula, DrPhil Berl. Sr. Lectr.
Wokler, R. L., BA Chic., MSc(Econ) Lond., MA Camb., DPhil Oxf., FRHistS Reader, History of Political Thought
Wood, Bruce, BSc(Econ) Lond. Sr. Lectr. (on leave)
Wright, M. W., BA Nott., DPhil Oxf., MA(Econ), FRHistS Prof. (on leave)
Young, S. C., BA Sr. Lectr.
Other Staff: 13 Lectrs.; 2 Res. Fellows; 3 Hon. Res. Fellows; 3 Temp. Lectrs.
Research: British and American politics; comparative Third World politics; European politics and policy; international relations and international political economy; philosophy

Greek, see History

Health Services Management Unit

Tel: (0161) 275 2908 Fax: (0161) 273 5245

Forsyth, Gordon, BA(Econ) Manc. Emer. Prof., Health Service Studies
Girling, J. R., BA Kent, MA(Econ) Manc. Sr. Fellow; Head, Primary and Community Care
Glascott, F. Sr. Fellow; Head, Human Resource Management
Higgins, Joan, BA PhD Prof., Health Policy; Deputy Dir.
Martin, John, BA PhD Visiting Prof.
Nichol, Sir Duncan, CBE, MA St And. Dir.*; Head, Internat. Healthcare Management
Peel, V. J. Sr. Fellow; Head, Health Informatics
Schofield, Angela, BA York Sr. Fellow; Head, Integrated Care and Quality
Tinston, Robert S. Hon. Visiting Prof.
Other Staff: 9 Fellows, Health Service Management; 24 Hon. Fellows
Research: future of the NHS workforce; new organisations in NHS primary care; NHS/university relations; supporting the NHS to develop R&D culture; telemedicine and electronic patient records

History

Tel: (0161) 275 3106 Fax: (0161) 275 3098

Bain, D. M., MA St.And., PhD Camb. Prof., Greek
Balderston, Theodore, MA Edin., PhD Edin. Sr. Lectr., Economic History
Bergin, Joseph, MA N.U.I., PhD Camb. Prof.
Cornell, T. J., BA Lond., MA Camb., PhD Lond. Prof., Ancient History
Davies, R. G., MA PhD Sr. Lectr.
Denton, J. H., BA Hull, PhD Camb. Prof., Mediaeval History
Gatrell, P. W., MA Camb., PhD Camb. Prof., Economic History; Head*
Harrison, R. J., BA(Econ) Sheff., PhD Sheff. Sr. Lectr., Economic History
Haslam, Michael, BA Lond., PhD Lond. Prof., Greek
Higham, N. J., BA PhD Reader
Joyce, Patrick, BA Keele, DPhil Oxf. Prof.
Katzenellenbogen, S. E., BA Mich., DPhil Oxf. Sr. Lectr., Economic History
Lowe, P. C., BA Wales, PhD Wales Reader (on leave)
Millward, R., BSc(Econ) Hull, PhD Prof., Economic History (on leave)
Morris, Rosemary, MA Oxf., DPhil Oxf. Sr. Lectr.
Morrison, Andy, BSc(Econ) Hull, PhD Hull Sr. Lectr., Economic History
O'Gorman, Francis, BA Leeds, PhD Camb. Prof.
Phillips, C. B., BA Wales, PhD Lanc. Sr. Lectr., Economics and Social History
Prothero, I. J., PhD Camb., BA Sr. Lectr.
Pullan, B. S., MA Camb., MA Manc., PhD Camb., FBA Prof., Modern History
Rigby, S. H., BA Sheff., PhD Lond. Reader
Rose, Michael E., BA Oxf., DPhil Oxf. Prof., Modern Social History
Other Staff: 14 Lectrs. (Greek and Latin 3, History 11); 1 Res. Fellow; 1 Hon. Spec. Lectr.; 1 Hon. Lectr.; 1 Hon. Fellow
Research: ancient world studies (Byzantine, Greek and Roman history, language and literature); British and European economic and social history; early modern history (political, social and economic history of England and Europe); mediaeval history (early mediaeval to Renaissance, England and Europe); modern African, Asian and American history (Far East, southern Africa and US history)

Italian

Tel: (0161) 275 3124 Fax: (0161) 275 3031

Griffiths, Clive E. J., MA Birm. Sr. Lectr.; Head*
Robey, D. J. B., MA Oxf. Serena Prof.
Other Staff: 3 Lectrs.; 3 Hon. Fellows

Law

Tel: (0161) 275 3566 Fax: (0161) 275 3579

Bell, A. P., MA Camb. Sr. Lectr.
Bercusson, Brian, LLB Lond., LLM McG., PhD Camb. Prof.
Bragg, R. J., LLM Hull Sr. Lectr.
Brazier, Margaret R., OBE, LLB Prof.
Brazier, Rodney J., LLB S'ton., FRHistS Prof., Constitutional Law
Carty, Hazel F., MA Oxf. Sr. Lectr.
Davey, Martin, LLB Sr. Lectr.
Duxbury, N. T., LLB Hull, PhD Lond. Prof.
Gibbons, T. C., BA CNAA, LLB Camb. Sr. Lectr.
Jaconelli, J., MA Camb., LLB Camb., PhD Reader
Jones, T. H., LLB Birm., MPhil Camb., PhD Brun. Sr. Lectr.
Kloss, Diana M., JP, LLB Lond., LLM Tulane Sr. Lectr.
Loughlin, Martin, LLB Lond., LLM Warw., LLM Harv. Prof.; Head*
Milman, David, LLB Birm., PhD Birm. Herbert Smith Prof., Corporate and Commercial Law
Ogus, A. I., BCL Oxf., MA Oxf. Prof.
Robinson, Mary, BA Trinity(Dub.), MA Trinity(Dub.), LLB Trinity(Dub.), LLM Harv. Hon. Prof.
Wasik, M., MA Keele, LLB Prof.
Other Staff: 16 Lectrs.; 5 Res. Staff; 2 Hon. Lectrs.; 1 Temp. Lectr.
Research: business and commercial law; European and international law; health care law and ethics; legal method and thought; public law (criminal law and justice, gender and family law, obligations, property)

Linguistics

Tel: (0161) 275 3187 Fax: (0161) 275 3187

Croft, W. A., AM Chic., PhD Stan. Reader
Cruse, D. A., BSc Lond., MA Sr. Lectr.
Cruttenden, Alan, MA Oxf., PhD Prof., Phonetics
Durand, Jacques Hon. Prof.
Payne, J. R., MA Camb. Lectr.; Head*
Perera, Katharine M., BA Lond., PhD Manc., MA Prof., Educational Linguistics
Vincent, N. B., MA Camb. Mont. Follick Prof., Comparative Philology
Other Staff: 4 Lectrs.; 1 Sr. Res. Fellow

Materials Science

Manchester Materials Science Centre (joint centre with UMIST)

Tel: (0161) 801 3578 Fax: (0161) 801 3586

Berry, J. P., BScTech PhD Visiting Sr. Lectr., Polymer Science and Technology
Cuvenka, A. J., MSc Pardubice C.C.T., PhD Prague Hon. Prof. Fellow
Davies, T. J., BSc Wales, MScTech PhD Visiting Reader
Elliott, Roy, BSc PhD Reader, Metallurgy
Entwistle, K. M., MSc Manc., PhD Manc., FIM Emer. Prof.
Freer, Robert, MSc Newcastle(UK), PhD Newcastle(UK) Reader, Materials Science (Ceramics)
Hayes, F. H., BSc Liv., PhD Liv. Reader, Metallurgy
Humphreys, F. J., MA Oxf., DPhil Oxf., FIM Prof.
Leach, Colin A., MA Camb., PhD Lond. Sr. Lectr.
Lorimer, G. W., BASc Br.Col., PhD Camb. Prof., Physical Metallurgy and Materials Science
Lovell, P. A., BSc PhD Reader, Polymer Science and Technology
Morrell, Roger, PhD Brist., FIM Hon. Prof. Fellow
Pilkington, Richard, BSc Liv., PhD Liv., FIM Sr. Lectr., Metallurgy
Priestner, Ronald, BSc Birm., PhD Birm. Visiting Reader
Sale, F. R., MSc PhD, FIM Prof., Chemical Metallurgy and Materials Science; Head*
Smith, Edwin, MSc Manc., PhD Sheff., FIM, FRS Emer. Prof.

Speakman, S. P., PhD *Salf.*, FIEE, FIM   Hon. Prof. Fellow
Stanford, J. L., BSc PhD   Reader, Polymer Science and Technology
Stepto, R. F. T., BSc *Brist.*, PhD *Brist.*, DSc, FRSChem   Prof., Polymer Science
Stowell, M. J., PhD *Brist.*, FRS, FIM   Hon. Prof. Fellow
Taylor, R., MSc PhD DSc   Prof., Thermonuclear Properties of Materials
Young, R. J., MA *Camb.*, PhD *Camb.*, FIM   Royal Soc. Wolfson Prof., Polymer Science and Technology

Mathematics
Tel: (0161) 275 5801 *Fax:* (0161) 275 5819
Abrahams, I. D., BSc *Lond.*, PhD *Lond.*   Beyer Prof., Applied Mathematics
Aczel, P. H. G., BA *Oxf.*, DPhil *Oxf.*   Prof., Mathematical Logic and Computing Science
Baker, Christopher T. H., MA *Oxf.*, DPhil *Oxf.*   Prof.; Head*
Blackburn, N., BA *Camb.*, MSc *Manc.*, PhD *Camb.*   Emer. Prof.
Doney, R. A., BSc *Durh.*, PhD *Durh.*   Prof., Probability Theory
Duck, P. W., BSc *S'ton.*, PhD *S'ton.*   Reader
Eccles, P. J., BA *Camb.*, PhD   Sr. Lectr.
Freeman, T. L., MSc *Liv.*, PhD *Liv.*   Sr. Lectr.
Gajjar, J. S. B., BSc *Lond.*, PhD *Lond.*   Sr. Lectr.
Gani, J. M., DSc *Lond.*, PhD *ANU*   Hon. Visiting Prof., Mathematical Statistics
Gregory, R. D., BA *Camb.*, PhD   Prof.
Higham, Nicholas J., MSc PhD   Prof., Applied Mathematics
King-Hele, J. A., BSc *Lond.*, PhD *Lond.*   Sr. Lectr.
Martin, P. A., BSc *Brist.*, MSc PhD   Reader
McCrudden, Michael, MSc *Belf.*, PhD *Birm.*   Reader
Moss, D. L., BA *Camb.*, DPhil *Sus.*, DSc   Reader
Papangelou, F., MSc *Manc.*, PhD *Athens*   Emer. Prof.
Paris, J. B., BSc *Manc.*, PhD *Manc.*   Prof., Mathematical Logic
Plymen, R. J., MA *Oxf.*, DPhil *Oxf.*   Prof.
Pollicott, M., BSc *Warw.*, MSc *Warw.*, PhD *Warw.*   Fielding Prof., Pure Mathematics
Premer, A. A., MA PhD   Reader
Prest, M. Y., BSc *Aberd.*, PhD *Manc.*   Reader
Ray, J. N., BSc *Birm.*, PhD   Prof., Pure Mathematics
Ruban, A. I., PhD DSc   Prof., Computational Fluid Dynamics
Sandling, R., MS *Chic.*, PhD *Chic.*   Res. Teaching Fellow
Stewart, P., BSc *Aston*, PhD   Sr. Lectr.
Ursell, F. J., MA *Camb.*, MSc *Manc.*, ScD *Camb.*, FRS   Emer. Prof.
Walker, G., BSc *St And.*, PhD *Lond.*   Sr. Lectr.
Walsh, Joan E., MA *Oxf.*, DPhil *Oxf.*, MSc   Emer. Prof.
Williams, J., BTech *Brun.*, DPhil *Oxf.*   Sr. Lectr., Numerical Analysis
Wilson, S. D. R., BA *Camb.*, MSc *Sheff.*, PhD *Lond.*   Sr. Lectr.
Wood, R. M. W., BA *Oxf.*, DPhil *Oxf.*   Sr. Lectr.
Other Staff: 11 Lectrs.; 4 Res. and Teaching Fellows; 11 Res. Staff; 4 Hon. Fellows
Research: applied mathematics (continuum and fluid mechanics, modelling astronomy, numerics); pure mathematics (algebra, analysis, combinatorics, dynamical systems, logic); statistics (applications, mathematical statistics, probability, stochastic theory)

Medicine, see below

Microbiology, see Biol. Scis., Sch. of

Middle Eastern Studies
Tel: (0161) 275 3073 *Fax:* (0161) 275 3264
Calder, Norman, BA *Oxf.*, PhD *Lond.*   Sr. Lectr., Arabic Language and Literature (on leave)
Healey, J. F., MA *Trinity(Dub.)*, PhD *Lond.*   Prof., Semitic Studies (on leave)

Imber, Colin H., MA *Camb.*, PhD *Camb.*   Sr. Lectr., Turkish Studies; Head*
Luft, J. P., PhD *Gött.*   Sr. Lectr., Persian Studies (on leave)
Smith, G. R., BA *Lond.*, MA *Camb.*, PhD *Camb.*   Emer. Prof., Arabic Studies
Other Staff: 5 Lectrs.; 1 Hon. Lectr.; 2 Hon. Fellows; 1 Hon. Visiting Fellow; 2 Hon. Res. Fellows; 2 Hon. Visiting Res. Fellows; 5 Temp. Lectrs.
Research: Arabic, Persian and Turkish language and literature; Central Asia and the Caucasus; Islamic and Jewish studies; Middle Eastern and Balkan history; Semitic and Hebrew language and literature

Music
Tel: (0161) 275 4987 *Fax:* (0161) 275 4994
Casken, J., BMus *Birm.*, MA *Birm.*, DMus *Durh.*   Prof.
Cooper, B. A. R., MA *Oxf.*, DPhil *Oxf.*   Sr. Lectr.
Elcombe, D. Keith, MA *Camb.*, MusB *Camb.*, FRCO   Sr. Lectr.; Head*
Fallows, David N., BA *Camb.*, MMus *Lond.*, PhD *Calif.*   Reader
Fanning, D. J., MusB *Manc.*, PhD *Manc.*   Sr. Lectr.
Gregson, Edward, BMus *Lond.*, FRAM   Hon. Visiting Prof.
Poole, G. R., BA *E.Anglia*, BMus *S'ton.*, DMus *S'ton.*   Sr. Lectr.
Other Staff: 1 Lectr.; 5 Lectrs.†
Research: Austrian music from Beethoven to Bruckner; composition and contemporary music; English Baroque and early keyboard music; mediaeval/Renaissance song, polyphony, 1300–1520; Shostakovich, Nielsen, Berg, twentieth-century symphony

Neuroscience, see under Biol. Scis., Sch. of

Palaeography, see Engl. and American Studies

Persian Studies, see Middle Eastern Studies

Pharmacy
Tel: (0161) 275 2343 *Fax:* (0161) 275 2396
Aarons, L. J., BSc *Syd.*, MSc *Calg.*, PhD   Sr. Lectr.
Adams, G. E., BSc *Salf.*, PhD *Manc.*, DSc *Manc.*   Hon. Visiting Prof.
Attwood, D., BPharm *Lond.*, PhD *Lond.*   Reader
Barber, Jill A., MA *Camb.*, MA *Oxf.*, PhD *Camb.*, DPhil *Oxf.*   Sr. Lectr.
Cantrill, Judith A., MSc *Manc.*   Clin. Sr. Lectr.
Clarke, D. J., BSc *Wales*, PhD *Wales*   Prof., Drug Delivery
Collett, J. H., PhD DSc, FRPharmS   Reader
Douglas, K. T., MA *Oxf.*, PhD *Kent*   Prof.
Fell, J. T., BSc PhD   Sr. Lectr.
Freeman, Sally, BSc *Leic.*, PhD *Leic.*   Sr. Lectr.
Gifford, L. A., BSc *Lough.*, PhD *Lough.*, FRSChem   Sr. Lectr.
Gilbert, P., BSc *Newcastle(UK)*, PhD *CNAA*   Sr. Lectr.
Houston, J. B., BSc *Lond.*, PhD *Sur.*   Reader
Noyce, P. R., BPharm *Wales*, PhD *Wales*   Boots Prof., Pharmacy Practice; Head*
Rees, Judith A., BPharm *Lond.*, MSc PhD   Sr. Lectr.
Rowland, M., BPharm *Lond.*, MSc *Manc.*, PhD *Lond.*, DSc *Lond.*, DSc *Poitiers*, DPh *Uppsala*, FRPharmS, FIM   Prof.
Stratford, I. J., BSc *Exe.*, MSc *Warw.*, PhD *Manc.*   Prof.
Tozer, T., BSc *Calif.*, PhD *Calif.*   Hon. Visiting Prof.
Other Staff: 6 Lectrs.; 14 Res. Staff; 10 Univ. Teachers†; 1 Clin. Lectr.; 2 Hon. Lectrs.; 3 Hon. Res. Staff; .7 Hon. Clin. Lectrs.

Philosophy
Tel: (0161) 275 3204 *Fax:* (0161) 275 3613
Chidgey, J. R., BSc MA PhD   Sr. Lectr.

Lee, Kee-Kok, BA *Sing.*, BPhil *Oxf.*, PhD *Manc.*   Reader; Dir., Centre for Philos. and the Environment
Lesser, A. H., BA *Oxf.*, BPhil *Oxf.*   Sr. Lectr.
Macdonald, Cynthia A., BA *Wayne*, DPhil *Oxf.*   Sr. Lectr.
Parry, Geraint, BSc(Econ) *Lond.*, MA(Econ) *Manc.*, PhD *Lond.*   WJM Mackenzie Prof., Govt.; Head*

Physical Education, see Educn., Sch. of

Physics and Astronomy
Tel: (0161) 275 4101 *Fax:* (0161) 273 5867
Allison, John, MA *Oxf.*, DPhil *Oxf.*   Sr. Lectr.
Anderson, Bryan, BSc PhD   Sr. Lectr., Radio-Astronomy
Axon, D. J., BSc *Durh.*, PhD *Durh.*   Sr. Lectr., Radio-Astronomy ((on leave))
Baker, J. G., BA *Camb.*, PhD *Camb.*   Reader
Barlow, R. J., MA *Oxf.*, PhD *Camb.*   Reader
Billowes, Jonathan, BA *Oxf.*, DPhil *Oxf.*   Sr. Lectr.
Birse, M. C., BA *Oxf.*, PhD *Sur.*   Sr. Lectr., Theoretical Physics
Bray, A. J., BA *Camb.*, PhD *Kent*   Prof., Theoretical Physics
Browne, I. W. A., BSc *Wales*, MSc PhD   Reader, Radio-Astronomy
Cohen, R. J., MSc *Qld.*, BSc PhD   Reader, Radio-Astronomy (on leave)
Davis, R. J., BA *Camb.*, PhD   Sr. Lectr., Radio-Astronomy
Donnachie, Alexander, BSc *Glas.*, MSc *Manc.*, PhD *Glas.*   Res. and Emer. Prof., Theoretical Physics
Dowker, J. S., BSc *Nott.*, PhD *Birm.*   Reader, Theoretical Physics
Duerdoth, I. P., PhD *Birm.*, BSc   Sr. Lectr.
Durell, J. L., BSc *Liv.*, PhD *Liv.*   Reader
Gleeson, Helen F., BSc PhD   Sr. Lectr. (on leave)
Grant, I. S., MA *Camb.*, PhD *Camb.*   Reader
Hammond, Peter, BSc *Manc.*, PhD *Manc.*   Sr. Lectr.
Hook, J. R., MA *Camb.*, PhD *Camb.*   Reader
Ibbotson, Michael, BSc *Lond.*, PhD *Lond.*   Reader
James, M. G., BSc *Birm.*   Sr. Lectr., Theoretical Physics
King, G. C. M., BSc PhD   Reader
King, T. A., BSc PhD, FIP   Prof., Applied Physics
Lafferty, G. D., BSc *Glas.*, PhD *Glas.*   Sr. Lectr.
Lisle, J. C., BA *Oxf.*, DPhil *Oxf.*   Reader
Loebinger, F. K., BSc PhD   Sr. Lectr.
Lucas, P. G. J., BSc *Liv.*, PhD   Sr. Lectr.
Lyne, Andrew G., MA *Camb.*, PhD, FRAS, FRS   Prof., Radio-Astronomy
Marshall, Robin, BSc *Manc.*, PhD *Manc.*, FRS   Prof., Experimental Particle Physics
McKane, A. J., BSc *S'ton.*, PhD *S'ton.*   Sr. Lectr., Theoretical Physics
Meaburn, J., DSc PhD   Prof., Astronomy
Moore, M. A., BA *Oxf.*, DPhil *Oxf.*, MSc, FRS   Prof., Theoretical Physics; Dir., Phys. Labs.; Head*
Mullin, Thomas, PhD *Edin.*   Prof., Condensed Matter Physics
Pedlar, Alan, MSc PhD   Reader, Radio-Astronomy
Phillips, A. C., BSc *Lond.*, PhD *Lond.*   Sr. Lectr., Theoretical Physics
Phillips, W. R., BSc *Lond.*, PhD *Camb.*, MSc   Res. Prof.
Read, F. H., BSc *Lond.*, PhD DSc, FRS, FIP   Prof.
Shaw, Graham, BSc *Lond.*, PhD *Lond.*   Sr. Lectr.
Spencer, R. E., BSc *Birm.*, MSc PhD   Sr. Lectr., Radio-Astronomy
Wilkinson, P. N., BSc *Durh.*, PhD *Manc.*   Reader, Radio-Astronomy
Other Staff: 13 Lectrs. (Astronomy 2, Physics 9, Radio-Astronomy 2); 59 Res. Staff; 2 Univ. Res. Fellows; 7 Hon. Fellows; 1 Temp. Lectr.
Research: astronomy and radio-astronomy; atomic, molecular and optical physics;

condensed matter and non-linear dynamics; laser photonics; nuclear physics

Physiology, see under Biol. Scis., Sch. of

Planning and Landscape, School of

Tel: (0161) 275 6904 Fax: (0161) 275 6893

Banister, C. E., BSc *Warw.*, MSc *Leeds* Sr. Lectr., Town and Country Planning; Head*
Beaumont, R. D. Hon. Visiting Prof.
Bristow, M. R., MA *Camb.* Sr. Lectr., Urban Studies
Handley, J. F., BSc *Leeds*, MSc *Lond.*, PhD *Liv.* Groundwork Prof., Land Restoration and Management; Dir., Landscape Studies*
Hebbert, M. J., MA *Oxf.*, PhD *Reading* Prof., Town Planning
Williams, W. G. P., BA *Wales*, MSocSc *Birm.* Reader, Urban Planning and Development
Wood, C. M., BSc *Lond.*, MA PhD Prof., Environmental Planning
Other Staff: 6 Lectrs.; 4 Res. Staff; 2 Teaching Fellows†; 8 Hon. Lectrs.; 2 Hon. Sr. Res. Fellows; 1 Hon. Sr. Fellow; 4 Hon. Fellows; 2 Temp. Lectrs.

Portuguese Studies, see Spanish and Portuguese Studies

Psychology

Tel: (0161) 275 2553 Fax: (0161) 275 2588

Beattie, Geoffrey W., BSc *Birm.*, PhD *Camb.*, FBPsS Prof.
Bowers, John, MA *Oxf.*, PhD *Camb.* Sr. Lectr.
Cooper, C. L., BS *Calif.*, MBA *Calif.*, PhD *Leeds*, MSc Hon. Prof., Organisational Psychology
Gregory, A. H., BA *Camb.*, PhD *Hull* Sr. Lectr.
Hollnagel, Erik, MSc PhD Hon. Visiting Prof.
Leudar, Ivan, BSc *Lond.*, PhD *Lond.* Sr. Lectr.
Lieven, Elena V. M., BA *Camb.*, PhD *Camb.* Sr. Lectr. (on leave)
Manstead, A. S. R., BSc *Brist.*, DPhil*Sus.* Hon. Prof.
Meudell, P. R., BSc *Hull*, MSc PhD Prof., Neuropsychology
Reason, J. T., PhD *Leic.*, BSc Prof. (on leave)
Stradling, Steve G., BA *Newcastle(UK)*, PhD *Newcastle(UK)* Sr. Lectr.
Wearden, J. H., DSc *Manc.*, BSc Prof.; Head*
Other Staff: 12 Lectrs.; 11 Res. Staff

Radio-Astronomy, see Phys. and Astron.

Radiological Protection

Tel: (0161) 275 6980 Fax: (0161) 275 6984
No staff at present

Religions and Theology

Tel: (0161) 275 3602 Fax: (0161) 275 3613

Alexander, P. S., BA *Oxf.*, DPhil *Oxf.* Prof., Post-Biblical Jewish Literature
Brooke, George J., MA *Oxf.*, PhD *Claremont.* Prof., Biblical Studies; Head*
Curtis, A. H. W., JP, BA *Manc.*, PhD *Manc.* Sr. Lectr., Old Testament Studies
De Boer, M. C., AB *Brown*, MDiv *U.T.S.(N.Y.)*, PhD *U.T.S.(N.Y.)* Sr. Lectr., Biblical Studies
Dyson, A. O., MA *Camb.*, BD *Oxf.*, MA(Theol) *Manc.*, DPhil *Oxf.* Samuel Ferguson Prof., Social and Pastoral Theology
Jackson, Bernard, LLB *Liv.*, DPhil *Oxf.* Alliance Family Prof.†, Modern Jewish Studies
Jantzen, Grace, BA *Sask.*, MA *Calg.*, PhD *Calg.*, DPhil *Oxf.* John Rylands Prof. Res. Fellow
Pailin, D. A., MA *Camb.*, MA *Manc.*, PhD *Manc.*, DD *Camb.* Prof., Philosophy of Religion
Price, G. L., MA *Camb.*, MSc *Manc.*, PhD *Lond.* Hon. Res. Fellow; Dir., Centre for Voeglin Studies
Other Staff: 6 Lectrs.; 8 Lectrs.†; 7 Hon. Lectrs.; 4 Hon. Res. Fellows; 2 Hon. Fellows; 1 Hon. Tutor
Research: Bible (Canaanite religion, Dead Sea scrolls); Jewish studies: (Bible interpretation, law); practical theology (social policy, technology, urban environment); religion, culture and gender (continental philosophy,

post-modernism); South-East Asian studies (Hindu philosophy, Punjab)

Russian Studies

Tel: (0161) 275 3139 Fax: (0161) 275 3031

Elsworth, J. D., MA *Camb.*, PhD *Camb.* Sir William Mather Prof.
Young, Jekaterina, MA *Glas.* Lectr.; Head*
Other Staff: 2 Lectrs.; 2 Hon. Fellows; 1 Temp. Lectr.
Research: contemporary; Russian society, women's studies and film; twentieth-century Russian literature

Semitic Studies, see Middle Eastern Studies

Social Anthropology

Tel: (0161) 275 4000 Fax: (0161) 275 4023

Gledhill, John, BLitt *Oxf.* Prof.; Head*
Harvey, Penelope M., BSc *Lond.*, PhD *Lond.* Sr. Lectr.
Henley, Paul S., MA *Camb.*, PhD *Camb.* Sr. Lectr., Visual Anthropology; Dir., Granada Centre for Visual Anthropol.
Ingold, Timothy, MA *Camb.*, PhD *Camb.* Prof.
Wade, Peter, BA *Camb.*, PhD *Camb.* Sr. Lectr.
Werbner, Richard P., BA *Brandeis*, PhD Prof., African Anthropology
Other Staff: 5 Lectrs.; 6 Res. Fellows; 1 Visiting Fellow; 4 Hon. Lectrs.; 10 Hon. Res. Fellows; 3 Temp. Lectrs.

Social Policy and Social Work

includes School of Social Work

Tel: (0161) 275 4764 Fax: (0161) 275 4724

Chatterton, M. R., BA *Leeds*, PhD Sr. Lectr., Social Policy; Dir., Henry Fielding Centre for Police Studies and Crime Risk Management
Dobash, Rebecca E., BA *Arizona*, MS *Arizona*, PhD *Wash.* Prof., Social Research
Dobash, Russell P., MA *Arizona*, PhD *Wash.* Prof., Criminology and Social Policy
Foster, Margaret D., BA *Liv.*, MA(Econ) *Manc.*, PhD *Manc.* Sr. Lectr., Social Policy
Hearn, J. R., BA *Oxf.*, MA *Oxf.*, PhD *Brad.* Prof. Res. Fellow
Karn, Valerie A., BA *Oxf.*, PhD *Birm.* Prof., Housing Studies
Parker, Howard, MA *Liv.*, PhD *Liv.* Prof.
Purdy, David L., BA *Oxf.*, MSc(Econ) *Lond.* Head of Dept.*
Scott, Duncan W., BA *Durh.*, PhD *Brist.* Sr. Lectr., Social Policy
Smith, Carole R., BSc *CNAA*, LLB *CNAA*, MPhil *York(UK)*, PhD *Leeds* Sr. Lectr., Social Work; Head, Sch. of Soc. Work
Wilding, P. R., BA *Oxf.*, MA *Manc.*, PhD Emer. Prof.
Other Staff: 10 Lectrs.; 1 Sr. Res. Fellow; 8 Res. Staff; 1 Temp. Lectr.
Research: crime, drugs and violence; gender relations; health, community care and children; welfare theory and policy implementation

Sociology

Tel: (0161) 275 2626 Fax: (0161) 275 2514

Beynon, H., BA *Wales* Prof. (on leave)
Dale, Angela, BSc *Lond.*, MPhil *Lond.*, MSc *Sur.*, PhD *Sur.* Prof., Quantitative Social Research
Devine, Fiona, BA *Essex*, PhD *Essex* Sr. Lectr.
Glavanis, Pandeli M., BA *Prin.*, PhD *Hull* Sr. Lectr.
Halfpenny, Peter J., MA *Oxf.*, MA *Essex*, PhD *Essex* Prof.
Kushnick, Lou, AB *Col.*, MA *Yale* Sr. Lectr.
Martin, P. J., MA *Edin.*, MA(Econ) PhD Sr. Lectr.; Head*
McIlroy, John, LLB *Lond.*, LLM *Lond.*, MA *Warw.* Reader
Mellor, J. Rosemary, BA *Oxf.* Sr. Lectr.
Miller, Simon, BA *Sus.*, PhD *Durh.* Sr. Lectr.
Morgan, D. H. J., BSc(Econ) *Hull*, MA *Hull*, PhD Prof.
Savage, Michael, BA *York(UK)*, MA *Lanc.*, PhD *Lanc.* Prof.
Shanin, T., BA *Jerusalem*, PhD *Birm.*, MA(Econ) Prof. (on leave)
Sharrock, W. W., BA *Leic.*, PhD *Manc.* Prof.

Stanley, Lizbeth, BSc(Econ) *Lond.*, MSc *Salf.*, PhD *Salf.* Prof., Sociology and Women's Studies
Watson, D. R., MA *Leic.*, PhD *Warw.* Reader
Other Staff: 5 Lectrs.; 8 Res. Staff; 3 Sr. Res. Fellows; 2 Res. Fellows; 5 Hon. Fellows; 3 Temp. Lectrs.

Spanish and Portuguese Studies

Tel: (0161) 275 3040 Fax: (0161) 275 3031

Davis, Catherine, LicFilletr *Madrid*, PhD *Glas.* Prof., Spanish Studies; Head*
Lawrance, J. N. H., MA *Oxf.*, DPhil *Oxf.* Prof.
Other Staff: 4 Lectrs.; 1 Hon. Res. Fellow; 1 Hon. Tutor

Statistics, see Econ. Studies, Sch. of, and Maths.

Theology, see Religions and Theol.

Turkish, see Middle Eastern Studies

BUSINESS ADMINISTRATION

At the Manchester Business School

Tel: (0161) 275 6461 Fax: (0161) 275 6489

Arnold, J. A., MSc *Lond.*, MA(Econ), FCA KPMG Prof., Accounting and Financial Management; Dir.*
Ashton, David Visiting Prof., Managerial Leading
Barrar, P. R. N., BSc *CNAA*, MSc *Cran.IT* Prof., Operations Management
Bootle, Roger, BA *Oxf.*, MPhil *Oxf.* Visiting Prof.
Buttle, F. A., BSc *Manc.*, MA *Lanc.*, PhD *Mass.* Sr. Lectr., Service Management
Campbell, N. C. G., MA *Oxf.*, BSc *Oxf.*, MBA *Harv.*, PhD Sr. Lectr., Strategic Management
Carr, C. H., MA *Camb.*, PhD *Warw.* Sr. Lectr., Strategic Management
Channon, D. F., BSc *Lond.*, DBA *Harv.*, MBA Visiting Prof., Strategic Management and Marketing
Cooper, Robin, BSc *Manc.*, MBA *Harv.*, DBA *Harv.* Hon. Visiting Prof., Strategic Cost Management
Davies, Gary, BSc *Lond.*, PhD *Lond.* Post Office Counters Prof., Retailing
Easingwood, C. J., BSc *Lond.*, PhD *Penn.* Prof., Marketing
Hague, Sir Douglas, CBE, MCom *Birm.*, MBA *Manc.* Hon. Visiting Prof., Managerial Economics
Harvey, Brian, BA *Sheff.*, MA(Econ) *Sheff.*, PhD *Nott.* Co-op Bank Prof., Corporate Responsibility
Henderson, J. W., MSocSc *Birm.*, PhD *Warw.* Prof., International Economic Sociology
Hewitt, Gordon, MA *Glas.* Visiting Prof.
Holland, C. P., BSc *Warw.*, PhD *Manc.* Sr. Lectr., Information Management
Hutton, Will Visiting Prof., Economics
McGoldrick, P. J., BSc PhD Littlewoods Prof., Retailing(Joint with UMIST Manchester Sch. of Management)
Murphy, John Visiting Prof., Service Quality
Nandé, Peter, BSc *S.Af.*, BBusSc *Cape Town*, MSc *Sus.*, PhD *Manc.* Sr. Lectr., Marketing
Neville-Rolfe, Marianne, BA *Oxf.* Visiting Prof.
Oakey, R. P., BA *CNAA*, MSc *Lond.*, PhD *Lond.* ASL Prof., Business Development
Paxson, D. A., MA *Oxf.*, DBA *Harv.* Prof., Finance
Pearson, A. W., BSc *Lond.* Prof., Research and Development Management
Pitcher, Sir Desmond, FIEE Visiting Prof., Business Policy
Redding, S. G., MA *Camb.*, PhD *Manc.* Visiting Prof., Comparative Management
Rickards, Tudor, BSc *Wales*, PhD *Wales* Prof., Creativity and Organisational Change
Stark, A. W., BA *Camb.*, MBA *Manc.*, PhD *Manc.* Prof., Accounting

Swann, G. M. P., MA *St And.*, MSc *Brist.*, PhD *Lond.* Prof., Economics and Management of Innovation (Joint with PREST)

Vandermerwe, André Visiting Prof.

Westwood, J. B., BA *Oxf.*, PhD Sr. Lectr., Operational Research

Whitley, R. D., BA *Leeds*, MA *Penn.* Prof., Organisational Sociology

Wood, Douglas, MCom *Birm.*, PhD National Westminster Bank Prof., Banking and Corporate Finance

Other Staff: 10 Lectrs.; 6 Res. Staff; 8 Sr. Fellows; 9 Fellows; 1 Tutor

Research: comparative business systems, cultures and environments; finance and accounting; innovation, creativity and entrepreneurship; marketing, retailing and strategy; operations and information management

DENTAL SCHOOL

Tel: (0161) 275 6796

Research: clinical biosciences (molecular genetics, experimental oral pathology/ medicine, neurosciences); oral health services research (health services research, oral heatlh promotion, preventive dentistry); orthodontics/craniofacial research (orthodontic research, craniofacial research, evidence-based practice); primary dental care research (biomaterials, clinical evaluation of technological systems, maxillofacial rehabilitation)

Oral and Maxillofacial Surgery, see also
Oral Med. and Dent. Diagnostic Sci.

Tel: (0161) 275 6640 Fax: (0161) 275 6840

Hindle, Ian, BDS *Lond.*, MSc *Lond.*, PhD *Lond.*, FDSRCS, FFDRCSI Sr. Lectr., Oral Surgery

Rood, J. P., BDS *Durh.*, MB BS *Newcastle(UK)*, MDS *Newcastle(UK)*, MSc *Manc.*, FDSRCS, FRCS Prof.; Head*

Other Staff: 3 Lectrs.; 2 Clin. Lectrs.; 1 Clin. Teacher; 1 Lectr.†; 3 Clin. Teachers†; 4 Hon. Univ. Clin. Lectrs.; 1 Hon. Clin. Lectr.

Oral Health and Development

Tel: (0161) 275 6610 Fax: (0161) 275 6610

O'Brien, K. D., BDS *Manc.*, MSc *Manc.*, PhD *Manc.* Prof., Orthodontics; Head*

Dental Public Health, Unit of

Tel: (0161) 275 6746 Fax: (0161) 275 6746

Other Staff: 3 Lectrs.; 3 Clin. Res. Fellows; 9 Hon. Clin. Lectrs.

Orthodontics, Unit of

Tel: (0161) 275 6620 Fax: (0161) 275 6620

Semb, G., DDS *Oslo*, PhD *Oslo* Sr. Lectr., Craniofacial Anomatics

Shaw, W. C., BDS *Glas.*, MScD *Wales*, PhD *Wales*, FDSRCS Prof., Orthodontics and Dentofacial Development; Dean, Dental Sch.; Head*

Other Staff: 1 Lectr.; 4 Res. Staff; 4 Hon. Clin. Lectrs.

Paediatric Dentistry, Unit of

Tel: (0161) 275 6610 Fax: (0161) 275 6610

Blinkhorn, A. S., BDS *Lond.*, MSc *Manc.*, PhD *Manc.* Prof., Oral Health

Davies, R. M., BDS *Manc.*, PhD *Manc.* Hon. Prof., Clinical Dental Research

Mackie, I. C., BDS *Manc.*, MSc *Manc.*, PhD *Manc.*, FDSRCPGlas Sr. Lectr., Child Dental Health

Other Staff: 3 Lectrs.†; 1 Hon. Clin. Sr. Lectr.; 8 Hon. Clin. Lectrs. (Child Dental Health)

Primary Dental Care, Unit of

Kay, Elizabeth J., BDS *Edin.*, PhD *Glas.* Sr. Lectr., Health Services Research

Mellor, A. C., PhD *Manc.*, FRCS Sr. Lectr.

Other Staff: 2 Lectrs.; 1 Clin. Teacher†; 1 Hon. Clin. Teacher†

Oral Medicine and Dental Diagnostic Science

Tel: (0161) 275 6640 Fax: (0161) 275 6840

Duxbury, A. J., MSc *Manc.*, PhD *Manc.*, DDS *Manc.*, FDSRCPSGlas Sr. Lectr., Oral Medicine and Dental Pharmacology and Therapeutics

Horner, Keith, BChD *Leeds*, MSc *Lond.*, FDSRCPSGlas Sr. Lectr., Dental and Maxillofacial Radiology; Head, Clin. Academic Group

Sloan, Philip, BDS *Newcastle(UK)*, PhD *Brist.* Prof., Experimental Oral Pathology

Thakkar, N. S., BDS *Manc.*, MSc *Manc.*, PhD *Manc.* Sr. Lectr., Medical Genetics and Oral Pathology

Thornhill, M. H., MB BS *Lond.*, BDS *Lond.*, MSc *Lond.*, PhD *Lond.*, FDSRCSEd, FFDRCSI Prof., Medicine in Dentistry; Head*

Other Staff: 5 Lectrs.; 1 Lectr.†; 2 Hon. Clin. Lectrs.; 1 Hon. Consultant

Orthodontics, Paediatric Dentistry, Primary Dental Care, see under Oral
Health and Devel.

Periodontics, Prosthodontics,, see under
Restorative Dent.

Restorative Dentistry

Operative Dentistry and Endodentistry, Unit of

Tel: (0161) 275 6660 Fax: (0161) 275 6710

Qualtrough, Alison J. E., BChD *Leeds*, MSc *Manc.*, PhD *Manc.*, FDSRCSEd Sr. Lectr., Endodontology

Wilson, Nairn H. F., BDS *Edin.*, MSc *Manc.*, PhD *Manc.*, FDSRCSEd, FDSRCS Prof., Restorative Dentistry

Other Staff: 2 Lectrs.; 2 Res. Staff; 1 Sr. Lectr.†; 4 Lectrs.†; 3 Univ. Clin. Teachers†; 1 Hon. Sr. Lectr.; 1 Hon. Univ. Clin. Teacher

Periodontics, Unit of

Tel: (0161) 275 6715 Fax: (0161) 275 6710

Hull, P. S., BDS *Belf.*, MDS *Manc.*, FDSRCS, FDSRCSEd Sr. Lectr.

Other Staff: 1 Lectr.; 1 Hon. Assoc. Lectr.

Prosthodontics, Unit of

Tel: (0161) 275 6670 Fax: (0161) 275 6670

Devlin, H., BSc *Brist.*, BDS *Brist.*, MSc *Manc.*, PhD *Manc.* Sr. Lectr., Restorative Dentistry

McCord, J. F., BDS *Edin.*, DDS *Edin.*, FDSRCS, FDSRCSEd Prof., Restorative Care of the Elderly

Other Staff: 2 Lectrs.; 1 Sr. Lectr.†; 2 Lectrs.†; 2 Clin. Teachers; 1 Hon. Sr. Lectr.; 1 Hon. Fellow

MEDICINE

For subjects of first 2 years—Anatomy, Biochemistry, etc—see above

Anaesthesia

Tel: (0161) 275 4558 Fax: (0161) 273 5685

Beatty, P. C. W., BSc *Lond.*, MSc *Exe.*, PhD *Manc.* Sr. Lectr., Physics of Anaesthesia

Campbell, I. T., MD *Lond.*, FRCA Reader

Healy, T. E. J., BSc *Lond.*, MD *Lond.*, MSc, FRCA Emer. Prof.

Meakin, George H., MB ChB, FRCA Sr. Lectr., Paediatric Anaesthesia

Pleuvry, Barbara J., BPharm *Lond.*, MSc PhD Sr. Lectr., Anaesthesia and Pharmacology

Pollard, B. J., BPharm *Lond.*, MD, FRCA Prof.; Head*

Other Staff: 4 Lectrs.; 1 Sr. Res. Fellow; 50 Hon. Clin. Lectrs.; 1 Hon. Sr. Fellow; 1 Hon. Fellow

Audiology, see Educn., Sch. of, above

Biophysics, Medical, see Med. Biophys.

Child Health

Tel: (0161) 805 5536 Fax: (0151) 795 7542

Birch, Jillian M., BSc *S'ton.*, PhD *Lond.*, DSc *Manc.* Reader, Paediatric Oncology

Boyd, R. D. H. Hon. Visiting Prof.

Chiswick, M. L., MB BS *Newcastle(UK)* Visiting Prof.

Clayton, P. E., BSc MD Sr. Lectr.

D'Souza, S. W., MB ChB *E.Af.*, PhD, FRCP Reader

David, T. J., MD *Brist.*, PhD *Brist.* Prof.; Head*

Eden, O. B., MB BS *Lond.*, FRCP Prof., Paediatric Oncology

Lashford, Linda S., BMedSci *Nott.*, BS *Nott.*, PhD *Lond.* Sr. Lectr., Paediatric Oncology

McKinlay, I. A., BSc *Edin.*, MB ChB *Edin.* Sr. Lectr.

Patel, Leena, MB BS *Gujar.*, MD *Gujar.* Sr. Lectr.

Price, D. A., BA *Oxf.*, BM BCh *Oxf.* Sr. Lectr.

Sibley, C. P., BSc *Lond.*, PhD *Lond.* Prof., Child Health and Physiology

Other Staff: 16 Res. Staff; 5 Clin. Lectrs.; 1 Hon. Clin. Sr. Lectr.; 53 Hon. Clin. Lectrs.; 16 Hon. Univ. Clin. Teachers; 2 Hon. Clin. Teachers

Diagnostic Radiology

Tel: (0161) 275 5116 Fax: (0161) 275 5594

Adams, Judith E., MB BS *Lond.*, FRCR Prof.; Head*

Hawnaur, Jane M., MB ChB, FRCR Sr. Lectr.

Hounsfield, Sir Godfrey, CBE, MD *Basle*, DSc *City(UK)*, DSc *CNAA*, DSc *Lond.*, DSc *Manc.*, DTech *Lough.*, Hon. FUMIST, FRS Prof. Fellow, Imaging Science

Hutchinson, Charles E., BSc *Birm.*, MB ChB *Birm.*, FRCR, FFARCSI Sr. Lectr.

Isherwood, I., MD *Saragossa*, MB ChB, FRCR, FRCP Emer. Prof.

Jackson, Alan, BSc *Manc.*, MB ChB *Manc.*, PhD *Manc.*, FRCR Prof., Neuroradiology

Other Staff: 2 Lectrs.; 6 Univ. Teachers; 2 Univ. Clin. Teachers; 1 Res. Fellow; 27 Lectrs.†; 3 Hon. Clin. Sr. Lectrs.

Epidemiology and Health Sciences

Tel: (0161) 275 5200 Fax: (0161) 275 5219

Charlton, Ann, BA *Keele*, MEd *Manc.*, PhD *Manc.* Cancer Research Campaign Prof., Cancer Health Education

Cherry, Nicola M., MSc *McG.*, MD *McG.*, BSc *Wales*, PhD *Lond.* Prof., Occupational Health; Head*

Cruickshank, J. K., BSc *Birm.*, MD *Birm.*, MSc *Lond.* Sr. Lectr., Clinical Epidemiology

Donnan, S. P. B., MD *Syd.*, MSc *Lond.*, MPhil *S'ton.*, FRCS Prof., Epidemiology and Public Health

Dunn, G., MA *Camb.*, MSc *Oxf.*, PhD *Edin.* Prof., Biomedical Statistics

MacFarlane, Gary F., BSc *Glas.*, PhD *Brist.* Sr. Lectr., Clinical Epidemiology

McNamee, R., MSc *Manc.*, PhD *Manc.* Sr. Lectr., Medical Statistics

O'Neill, T. W., BSc *Trinity(Dub.)*, MB BCh *Trinity(Dub.)*, MA *Trinity(Dub.)*, MSc *Manc.* Sr. Lectr., Epidemiology and Rheumatology

Ollier, Prof. W. E. R., BSc *Wales*, PhD *Lond.* Prof., Immunogenetics

Pickering, C. A. C., MB BS *Lond.*, FRCP Hon. Visiting Prof., Occupational Medicine

Povey, A. C., BSc *Brist.*, MSc *Sur.*, PhD *Lond.* Sr. Lectr., Molecular Epidemiology

Silman, Alan J., MB ChB *Leeds*, MSc *Lond.*, MD *Lond.*, FRCP A.R.C. Prof., Rheumatic Diseases Epidemiology

Symmons, D. P. M., MD *Birm.* Reader, Rheumatic Diseases Epidemiology

Woodman, C. B. J., MD *N.U.I.* Prof., Cancer Epidemiology and Public Health

Other Staff: 20 Lectrs.; 37 Res. Staff; 1 Clin. Lectr.; 1 Sr. Res. Fellow; 3 Univ. Teachers; 2 Sr. Lectrs.† (public health management 1, occupational medicine 1); 17 Hon. Clin. Lectrs.; 4 Hon. Univ. Clin. Teachers; 1 Sr.

Hon. Res. Fellow; 2 Hon. Fellows; 3 Hon. Univ. Teachers

Research: arthritis and rheumatism; biostatistics; cancer; occupational health

General Practice

Tel: (0161) 225 6699

Chew, Carolyn A., BSc MB ChB   Sr. Lectr.
Esmail, Aneez, MB ChB *Sheff.*   Sr. Lectr.
Lovell, Hermione J., BSc *Sus.*, MPhil *Sus.*   Sr. Lectr.
Roland, M. O., MA *Oxf.*, DM *Oxf.*   Prof.
Whitehouse, C. R., MB BChir *Camb.*, MA *Camb.*   Prof., Teaching Medicine in the Community; Head*
Other Staff: 8 Lectrs.; 4 Res. Staff; 1 Clin. Res. Fellow; 2 Clin. Assocs.; 1 Sr. Res. Fellow

Geriatric Medicine

Tel: (0161) 447 4516 Fax: (0161) 447 3785

Connolly, M. J., MB BS *Newcastle(UK)*, MD *Newcastle(UK)*   Sr. Lectr.
Horan, M. A., MB BChir *Camb.*, MA *Camb.*, PhD *Utrecht*, FRCP   Prof.; Head*
Kirkwood, T. B. L., BA *Camb.*, MSc *Oxf.*, PhD *Camb.*   Prof., Biology Gerontology
O'Neill, P. A., BSc MB ChB MD   Sr. Lectr.
Pendleton, N., MB ChB *Liv.*   Sr. Lectr.
Pomeroy, V., BA *Open(UK)*, PhD *S'ton.*
Scott, A. K., BMedBiol *Aberd.*, MB ChB *Aberd.*, MD *Aberd.*   Sr. Lectr.
Tallis, Raymond C., BM BCh *Oxf.*, MA *Oxf.*, FRCP   Prof.
Other Staff: 2 Lectrs.; 10 Res. Staff; 3 Clin. Lectrs.; 6 Hon. Clin. Lectrs.; 2 Hon. Clin. Lectrs.†

Health Sciences, see Epidemiol. and Health Scis.

Medical Biophysics

Tel: (0161) 275 5130 Fax: (0161) 275 5145

Beatty, P. C. W., BSc *Lond.*, MSc *Exe.*, PhD *Manc.*   Sr. Lectr., Physics of Anaesthesia
Graham, J., BSc *Edin.*, PhD *Camb.*   Sr. Lectr.
Hillier, V. F., BSc *Lond.*, MSc *Manc.*, PhD *Manc.*   Sr. Lectr.
Hounsfield, Sir Godfrey, CBE, MD *Basle*, Hon. DSc *City(UK)*, Hon. DSc *CNAA*, Hon. DSc *Lond.*, Hon. DSc *Manc.*, DTech *Lough.*, FRS, Hon. FUMIST   Prof. Fellow, Imaging Sciences
Sharma, H. L., BSc *Punjab*, PhD *Minn.*, DSc *Manc.*   Sr. Lectr.
Taylor, C. J., BSc PhD   Prof.; Head*
Other Staff: 3 Lectrs.; 4 Res. Fellows; 8 Res. Assocs.; 1 Univ. Teacher; 4 Hon. Lectrs.; 7 Hon. Res. Fellows; 16 Hon. Res. Assocs.

Medical Informatics, see Computer Sci., above

Medical Microbiology, see Pathol. Scis.

Medicine

Tel: (0161) 803 4684 Fax: (0161) 803 4684

Ballardie, F. W., BSc *Glas.*, PhD *Glas.*, MB ChB, FRCP   Sr. Lectr.
Best, L. C., BSc *Sheff.*, PhD *Aston*   Sr. Lectr., Physiology Sciences
Boulton, A. J. M., MD *Newcastle(UK)*, FRCP   Prof.
Braganza, Joan M., MB BS *Bom.*, DSc *Manc.*, MSc, FRCP   Reader, Gastroenterology
Castro, Maria G., BSc *Buenos Aires*, MSc *Buenos Aires*, PhD *Buenos Aires*   Sr. Lectr.
Craufurd, D. I. O., MB BS *Lond.*, MSc   Sr. Lectr., Clinical Genetics
Davies, Michael, MB BS *Durh.*, FRCP   Sr. Lectr.
Davis, J. R. E., BSc *Edin.*, MD *Edin.*, PhD *Birm.*, FRCP   Reader
Denning, D. W., MB BS *Lond.*, FRCP   Sr. Lectr., Infectious Diseases
Donnai, Dian, MB ChB *Lond.*, FRCP   Hon. Visiting Prof.

Durrington, P. N., BSc *Brist.*, MD *Brist.*, FRCP, FRCPath   Prof.
Freemont, A. J., BSc *Lond.*, MB BS *Lond.*, MD *Lond.*   Prof., Osteoarticular Pathology
Griffiths, C. E. M., BSc *Lond.*, MB BS *Lond.*, MD *Lond.*   Prof., Dermatology
Heagerty, A. M., MB BS *Lond.*, MD *Leic.*, FRCP   Head, Dept. of Med. (South and Central)*
Hendry, J. H., BSc *St And.*, PhD *Lond.*, DSc *Lond.*   Hon. Prof.
Herrick, Ariane L., MD *Aberd.*   Sr. Lectr., Rheumatology
Hillier, Valerie F., BSc *Lond.*, PhD   Sr. Lectr., Computational Methods in Medical Science
Jones, A. K. P., BA *Oxf.*, MD *Lond.*   Sr. Lectr., Rheumatology
Kielty, Catherine M., BSc *Lond.*, PhD *Lond.*   Sr. Lectr.
Lowenstein, P. R., MD *Buenos Aires*, PhD *Buenos Aires*   Prof., Molecular Medicine and Gene Therapy
Mallick, N. P., BSc *Manc.*, MB ChB *Manc.*, FRCP, FRCPEd   Prof., Renal Medicine
Marsh, M. N., DM *Oxf.*, DSc *Leeds*, FRCP   Reader
Mawer, E. Barbara, BSc *Edin.*, PhD *Edin.*   Prof., Bone and Mineral Metabolism
Moulton, Christopher, MB ChB *Manc.*, FRCA   Sr. Lectr., Accident and Emergency Medicine
Neary, David, MD *Manc.*, FRCP   Hon. Visiting Prof., Neurology
O'Neill, T. W., BSc *Trinity(Dub.)*, MA *Trinity(Dub.)*, MB BCh *Manc.*. MSc *Manc.*   Sr. Lectr., Epidemiology and Rheumatology
Orme, Michael, MD BChir *Camb.*, MB *Lond.*, MA *Lond.*, FRCP   Hon. Visiting Prof.
Pickering, C. A. C., MB BS *Lond.*, MS *Lond.*, FRCP   Hon. Visiting Prof., Occupational Medicine
Read, A. P., MA *Camb.*, PhD *Camb.*   Prof., Human Genetics
Roberts, Trudie E., BSc *Manc.*, MB ChB *Manc.*, PhD *Manc.*   Sr. Lectr., Transplant Immunology
Sandle, G. I., BSc *Leeds*, MD *Leeds*, PhD, FRCP   Sr. Lectr.
Schady, Wolfgang, LMS *Madrid*, MD *Uppsala*, FRCP   Sr. Lectr., Neurology
Thakker, Nalin, BDS *Manc.*, MSc *Manc.*, PhD *Manc.*   Sr. Lectr., Human Genetics
Thompson, David G., BSc *Lond.*, MD *Lond.*, FRCP   Prof., Gastroenterology
Tomlinson, Stephen, MD *Sheff.*, FRCP   Prof., Dentistry and Nursing
Tunbridge, R. D. G., MD *Lond.*, FRCP   Sr. Lectr.
Turnberg, Sir Leslie, MD, FRCP   Prof.
Vadgama, P., MB BS *Newcastle(UK)*, BSc *Newcastle(UK)*, PhD *Newcastle(UK)*, FRCPath   Prof., Clinical Biochemistry; Head, Dept. of Med. (Salford)*
Waddell, Gordon   Hon. Visiting Prof., Rheumatology
Watson, Alastair, BA *Camb.*, MD *Camb.*   Sr. Lectr.
Weinkove, Cyril, BSc *Cape Town*, MB ChB *Cape Town*, PhD *Cape Town*   Sr. Lectr., Clinical Biochemistry
White, Anne, BSc PhD   Reader, Clinical Biochemistry
Whorwell, P. J., BSc *Lond.*, MD *Lond.*   Sr. Lectr.
Woolley, D. E., BSc *Wales*, PhD *Wales*, DSc, FRCPath   Reader
Wu, Fred C. W., BSc *Edin.*, MB ChB *Edin.*, FRCPEd   Sr. Lectr., Endocrinology
Other Staff: 16 Lectrs.; 116 Res. Staff; 13 Clin. Lectrs.; 1 Reader†; 2 Hon. Readers; 2 Hon. Sr. Lectrs.; 15 Hon. Lectrs.; 4 Hon. Clin. Sr. Lectrs.; 59 Hon. Clin. Lectrs.; 17 Hon. Clin. Teachers

National Primary Care Research and Development Centre

Guavelle, Hugh   Hon. Prof.
Howie, John   Hon. Visiting Prof.
Light, Donald W.   Visiting Prof.

Popay, Jennifer   Hon. Prof.
Rogers, Anne, BA *Lond.*, MSc *Lond.*, PhD *Nott.*   Reader, Sociology
Roland, Martin O., MA *Oxf.*, DM *Oxf.*, FRCGP   Prof., General Practice; Dir., Res. and Devel.
Sibbald, Bonnie S., BSc *McG.*, MSc *Qu.*, PhD *Lond.*   Reader, Health Services Research
Wilkin, David, BSc *Lond.*, MSc *Salf.*, PhD *Manc.*   Prof., Health Services Research; Head; Chief Exec.*
Other Staff: 1 Sr. Fellow; 2 Sr. Res. Fellows; 6 Res. Fellows; 20 Res. Assocs.

Neurology, see Med.

Neuroscience, see under Biol. Scis., Sch. of, above

Neurosurgery, see Surg.

Nursing

Tel: (0161) 275 5578 Fax: (0161) 275 5578

Brooker, Charles, BA MSc PhD   Prof.
Butterworth, C. Anthony, CBE, MSc *Birm.*, PhD *Birm.*   Queen's Nursing Inst. Prof., Community Nursing; Dean, Sch. of Nursing
Luker, Karen, BN PhD   Prof.
Oldham, Jacqueline A., BSc *Liv.*, PhD *Liv.*   Prof.
Waters, Karen R., BSc *CNAA*, PhD *Manc.*   Prof.
Williams, Anne M., MA PhD   Sr. Lectr.
Other Staff: 17 Lectrs.; 4 Res. Fellows; 2 Sr. Nurse Teachers; 67 Nurse Teachers; 16 Midwife Teachers
Research: acute care and rehabilitation; mental health nursing; primary healthcare nursing

Obstetrics and Gynaecology and Reproductive Health Care

Tel: (0161) 276 6446 Fax: (0161) 273 3958

Aplin, J. D., MA *Oxf.*, PhD *Br.Col.*   Reader, Biochemistry
Bajoria, Rekha, PhD *Manc.*, MB BS   Sr. Lectr., Obstetrics
Bardsley, W. G., PhD *Manc.*, DSc *Manc.*   Reader, Biochemistry
Buck, Pamela, MB BS *Newcastle(UK)*, FRCOG   Sr. Lectr.
Chantler, E. N., BSc *Lond.*, PhD *Lond.*   Sr. Lectr., Biochemistry
Hampson, Ian, BSc *Manc.*, PhD *Manc.*   Sr. Lectr., Gynaecological Oncology
Kirkman, Rosemary J. E., MB ChB *Leeds*, FRCOG   Sr. Lectr., Reproductive Health and Family Planning
Kitchener, H. C., MD *Glas.*, MB ChB, FRCSGLas, FRCOG   Prof., Gynaecological Oncology; Head*
Reynolds, Karina M. M., BA *Trinity(Dub.)*, MB ChB BAO*Trinity(Dub.)*   Sr. Lectr., Gynaecological Oncology
Seif, M. W., MB ChB *Ain Shams*, MSc *Ain Shams*, PhD *Manc.*   Sr. Lectr.
Other Staff: 2 Lectrs.; 10 Res. Staff; 3 Clin. Lectrs.; 2 Hon. Lectrs.; 21 Hon. Clin. Lectrs.; 54 Hon. Univ. Clin. Teachers
Research: cervical intrapithelial neoplasia; early placental development; endometrial development and embryo implantation; novel therapies in gynaecological oncology; placental function in multiple pregnancy

Occupational Health, see Epidemiol. and Health Scis.

Oncology, see also Child Health

Tel: (0161) 446 3595 Fax: (0161) 446 3401

Dexter, T. M., BSc *Salf.*, PhD DSc   Hon. Prof., Experimental Haematology
Gallagher, J. T., BTech *Brun.*, DPhil *York(UK)*   Prof.
Howell, A., MB BS *Lond.*, MSc *Lond.*   Sr. Lectr., Medical Oncology
McClure, John, BSc *Belf.*, MD *Belf.*, FRCPath   Procter Prof., Pathology
Potten, C. S., MSc *Lond.*, PhD *Lond.*, DSc *Manc.*   Hon. Prof., Epithelial Biology

Radford, J. A., MB MD   Sr. Lectr., Medical
  Oncology
Ranson, M. R., BSc *Manc.*, MB ChB *Manc.*, PhD
  Manc.   Sr. Lectr., Medical Oncology
Scarffe, J. H., MB BS *Lond.*, MD, FRCP   Prof.,
  Medical Oncology
Thatcher, Nicholas, BA *Camb.*, MB BChir *Camb.*,
  PhD, FRCP   Reader, Medical Oncology
Other Staff: 1 Lectr.; 2 Res. Staff; 2 Lectrs.†; 8
  Univ. Teachers†; 10 Clin. Lectrs.; 2 Hon.
  Readers; 9 Hon. Univ. Readers; 2 Hon. Sr.
  Clin. Lectrs.; 19 Hon. Clin. Lectrs.; 5 Hon.
  Sr. Lectrs.; 12 Hon. Lectrs.
Research: clinical trials (chemotherapeutic
  agents, endocrine, new biological)

Ophthalmology

Tel: (0161) 276 5620 Fax: (0161) 273 6354
Boulton, M. E., BSc *Reading*, PhD *CNAA*   Reader
Efron, Nathan, BSc *Melb.*, PhD *Melb.*, DSc
  UMIST   Hon. Prof., Ophthalmology
Henson, D. B., BSc *City(UK)*, MSc *Aston*, PhD
  Indiana   Sr. Lectr.
Jones, N. P., BSc *St And.*, MB ChB, FRCS   Sr.
  Lectr., Ophthalmology
McLeod, David, BSc *Edin.*, MB ChB *Edin.*,
  FRCS   Prof.; Head*
Other Staff: 3 Lectrs.; 10 Res. Staff; 1 Hon. Sr.
  Lectr.; 3 Hon. Lectrs.; 12 Hon. Clin. Lectrs.;
  1 Hon. Sr. Res. Fellow; 3 Hon. Res. Fellows
Research: biochemistry and molecular
  organisation; detection and monitoring of
  ophthalmic disease; ocular cell biology,
  physiology and pathology

Orthopaedic Surgery

Tel: (0161) 787 4211 Fax: (0161) 787 4706
Andrew, J. G., BA *Camb.*, MB ChB *Sheff.*,
  FRCS   Sr. Lectr.
Galasko, Charles S. B., ChM *Witw.*, MSc,
  FRCS   Prof.; Head*
Kay, P. R., BA *Open(UK)*, MB ChB *Manc.*,
  FRCSGlas   Sr. Lectr.
Stanley, J. K., MB ChB *Liv.*, MChOrth *Liv.*,
  FCRS, FCRSEd   Prof.†, Hand Surgery
Other Staff: 6 Lectrs.; 9 Res. Staff; 1 Hon. Clin.
  Sr. Lectr.; 8 Hon. Clin. Lectrs.; 4 Hon. Univ.
  Clin. Teachers; 1 Hon. Sr. Lectr.; 1 Hon.
  Lectr.; 6 Hon. Assoc. Lectrs.
Research: bone biology, including intracellular
  signalling, cell adhesion, bone resorption;
  evaluating disability following road traffic
  accidents; examination of neuromuscular
  disorders in children; fracture healing;
  skeletal metastases

Pathological Sciences

Tel: (0161) 275 5300 Fax: (0161) 275 5289
Barson, A. J., MD   Reader, Paediatric
  Pathology
Benbow, E. W., BSc MB ChB   Sr. Lectr.,
  Pathology
Buckley, Cathryn H., MB ChB MD,
  FRCPath   Reader, Pathology
Burnie, John P., MA *Camb.*, MD *Camb.*, MSc
  Lond., PhD   Prof., Medical Microbiology;
  Head*
Cleator, G. M., MSc PhD   Reader, Medical
  Virology
Freemont, A. J., BSc *Lond.*, MD *Lond.*   Prof.,
  Osteo-articular Pathology
Kumar, Shant, BVetSci *Indore*, MVetSci *Indore*,
  PhD *Manc.*   Hon. Prof., Pathology
Mann, D. M. A., BSc *Durh.*, PhD   Reader,
  Pathology
Matthews, Ruth C., MSc *Lond.*, MD *Lond.*, PhD
  Lond.   Reader, Medical Microbiology
McClure, J., BSc *Belf.*, MD *Belf.*,
  FRCPath   Procter Prof., Pathology
McMahon, R. F. T., BSc *N.U.I.*, MB BCh BAO
  N.U.I., MD *N.U.I.*   Sr. Lectr., Pathology
Ollier, W. E. R., BSc *Wales*, PhD *Lond.*   Prof.,
  Immunogenetics
Poller, L., MD *Manc.*,DSc *Manc.*   Hon. Prof.,
  Pathology
Stoddart, R. W., MA *Camb.*, PhD *Camb.*   Sr.
  Lectr., Pathology

Struthers, J. K., MB ChB *Witw.*, MSc *Rhodes*,
  DPhil *Oxf.*   Sr. Lectr., Medical Microbiology
Other Staff: 10 Lectrs.; 31 Res. Staff; 4 Clin.
  Lectrs.; 2 Lectrs.†; 34 Hon. Clin. Lectrs.; 5
  Hon. Univ. Clin. Teachers; 2 Hon. Readers;
  6 Hon. Lectrs.; 1 Temp. Lectr.

Pharmacology, see Biol. Scis., Sch. of, above

Physiology, see Biol. Scis., Sch. of, above

Psychiatry

Tel: (0161) 275 5220 Fax: (0161) 275 3924
Anderson, I. M., MB BS *Lond.*, MA *Camb.*   Sr.
  Lectr.
Appleby, Louis, BSc *Edin.*, MB ChB *Edin.*,
  FRCP   Prof.
Barrowclough, Christine, BA *Liv.*, MSc *Manc.*,
  PhD *Lond.*   Reader, Clinical Psychology
Benjamin, Sidney, MD *Lond.*, MPhil *Lond.*   Sr.
  Lectr.
Burns, A. S., MD *Glas.*, MPhil *Lond.*   Ben and
  Marianne Porges Prof., Psychiatry of Old
  Age
Byrne, Eleanor J., MB ChB   Sr. Lectr.,
  Psychiatry of Old Age
Challis, D., BA *York(UK)*, PhD *Manc.*   Prof.,
  Personal Social Services Research Unit
Clark, A. F., MA *Camb.*, MB BS
  Newcastle(UK)   Sr. Lectr., Adolescent
  Psychiatry
Creed, H., MA *Camb.*, MD *Camb.*   Prof.,
  Community Psychiatry
Deakin, J. F. W., BSc *Leeds*, MB ChB *Leeds*, PhD
  Lond., FRCPsych   Prof.
Dolan, Margaret C., MB BCh BAO *Trinity(Dub.)*;
  MSc *Manc.*   Sr. Lectr., Forensic Psychiatry
Emerson, E., BSc *S'ton*, MSc *Manc.*   Prof.,
  Learning Difficulties
Gask, Linda, MB ChB *Edin.*, MSc *Manc.*, MD
  Lond., PhD *Manc.*   Sr. Lectr.
Gater, R. A., MB ChB *Manc.*, MSc *Manc.*, MD
  Manc.   Sr. Lectr.
Green, J. M., MA *Camb.*, MB BS *Lond.*   Sr.
  Lectr., Child and Adolescent Psychiatry
Guthrie, Elspeth A., MB ChB *Manc.*, MSc
  MD   Sr. Lectr.
Haddock, Gillian, BSc *York(UK)*, MClinPsychol
  Liv., PhD *Manc.*   Sr. Lectr., Clinical
  Psychology
Harrington, R. C., MD *Birm.*, MPhil
  Lond.   Prof., Child and Adolescent Psychiatry
Huxley, P. J., BA *Reading*, MSc PhD   Prof.,
  Psychiatric Social Work; Head*
Kerfoot, M. J., MSc *Leeds*, PhD *Manc.*   Prof.,
  Psychiatric Social Work
Kiernan, C.   Prof., Learning Disabilities
Lewis, S. W., BSc *Lond.*, MB BS *Lond.*, MPhil
  Lond., MD *Lond.*   Prof., Adult Psychiatry
Maguire, G. P., BA *Camb.*, MB BChir *Camb.*   Sr.
  Lectr.
Marshall, Matthew, BSc *Brist.*, MB ChB *Brist.*,
  MD *Brist.*   Sr. Lectr.
Morriss, R. K., MB ChB *Leeds*, MSc *Leeds*,
  MMedSc *Leeds*   Sr. Lectr.
Oliver, J. P. J., BA *St.Bonaventure*, MSc *Leeds*, MSc
  Oxf.   Sr. Lectr., Psychiatric Social Work
Shaw, Jennifer J., MB ChB *Manc.*, MSc
  Manc.   Sr. Lectr., Forensic Psychiatry
Tarrier, N., BSc *Nott.*, MSc *Sus.*, MSc *Manc.*, PhD
  Lond., FBPsS   Prof., Clinical Psychology
Thapar, Anita, MB ChB *Manc.*, PhD *Manc.*   Sr.
  Lectr.
Wells, Adrian, BSc *Aston*, MSc *Leeds*, PhD
  Aston   Sr. Lectr., Clinical Psychology
Wieck, Angelika, MD *Bonn*   Sr. Lectr.
Woodruff, P. W. R., MB BS *Newcastle(UK)*   Sr.
  Lectr., Adult Psychiatry
Other Staff: 12 Lectrs.; 99 Res. Staff; 1 Sr. Res.
  Fellow; 7 Tutors; 1 Sr. Clin. Tutor; 1 Clin.
  Lectr.; 1 Reader†; 1 Sr. Lectr.†; 2 Sr.
  Tutors†; 1 Hon. Clin. Sr. Lectr.; 32 Hon.
  Clin. Lectrs.; 2 Hon. Clin. Teachers; 2 Hon.
  Readers; 5 Univ. Readers; 4 Hon. Lectrs.; 2
  Temp. Lectrs.
Research: cross-cultural comparisons in
  psychiatric services; evaluating new
  psychosocial treatments for schizophrenia;
  investigating brain mechanisms in

psychiatry; psychiatric disorders in
  childhood and adolescence; psychological
  disorder in medical illness

Public Health, see Epidemiol. and Health
  Scis.

Renal Medicine, see Med.

Rheumatology, see Med.

Surgery

Tel: (0161) 276 4534
Anderson, I., MD *Manc.*, BSc MB ChB,
  FRCS   Sr. Lectr.
Baildam, A. D., BSc MD, FRCS   Sr. Lectr.
Bancewicz, John, BSc *Glas.*, MB ChB *Glas.*, ChM,
  FRCSGlas   Reader
Bundred, N. J., MD *Newcastle(UK)*, FRCS,
  FRCSEd, FRCSGlas   Reader, Oncology
  Surgery
Charlesworth, David   Hon. Prof.
Doig, Caroline M., MB ChB *St And.*, ChM *Dund.*,
  FRCS   Sr. Lectr., Paediatric Surgery
Driscoll, P. A., BSc *Leeds*, MB ChB *Leeds*,
  FRCSEd   Sr. Lectr., Accident and Emergency
  Medicine
George, N. J. R., MB BS *Lond.*, MD *Brist.*,
  FRCS   Sr. Lectr., Urology Surgery
Hooper, T. L., BSc MD, FRCS   Sr. Lectr.,
  Cardiothoracic Surgery
Irving, Sir Miles, MD *Liv.*, ChM *Liv.*, MSc,
  FRCS   Prof.
Kitchener, H. C., MB ChB *Manc.*, MD *Glas.*,
  FRCSGlas, FRCOG   Prof., Gynaecological
  Oncology; Head of Dept. (Central)*
Little, R. A., BSc *Lond.*, PhD *Lond.*,
  FRCPath   Hon. Prof., Surgical Science
Lye, R. H., MB ChB *Manc.*, MSc *Manc.*, PhD
  Manc., FRCS   Reader, Neurosurgery
McCloy, R. F., BSc *Lond.*, MD *Lond.*, FRCS   Sr.
  Lectr.
McCollum, C. N., MD *Birm.*, FRCS   Prof.;
  Head of Dept. (South)*
Parrott, N. R., MB BS *Newcastle(UK)*, FRCS,
  FRSCEd   Sr. Lectr.
Walker, M. G.   Hon. Prof.
Whitlham, James G.   Hon. Visiting Prof.
Yates, D. W., MA *Camb.*, MB BChir *Camb.*,
  MChOrth *Liv.*, MD *Camb.*, FRCSGlas,
  FRCS   Prof.; Head of Dept. (Salford)*
Other Staff: 5 Lectrs.; 20 Res. Staff; 8 Clin.
  Lectrs.; 44 Hon. Clin. Lectrs.; 5 Hon. Univ.
  Clin. Teachers; 8 Hon. Clin. Teachers; 1
  Hon. Reader; 2 Hon. Fellows; 2 Hon. Res.
  Fellows
Research: measurement and analysis of
  oesophageal function; responses to trauma
  and critical illness; virtual reality surgical
  simulation, telemedicine and remote surgical
  teaching

SPECIAL CENTRES, ETC

Age and Cognitive Performance Research Centre

Tel: (0161) 275 2873 Fax: (0161) 275 2873
Rabbitt, Prof. P. M., MA *Oxf.*, MA *Camb.*, PhD
  Camb., MSc   Dir.*

Anglo-Saxon Studies, Centre for

Tel: (0161) 275 3145 Fax: (0161) 275 3256
Scragg, D. G., BA *Liv.*, PhD   Prof.; Dir.*

Business Research, Centre for

Tel: (0161) 275 6399 Fax: (0161) 275 6489
Sanghavi, Nitin, BSc *Saur.*, MSc   Dir.*

Chronic Rheumatism, Centre for the Study of

Tel: (0161) 807 4369
No staff at present

Continuing Education, Centre for the Development of

Tel: (0161) 275 3271 Fax: (0161) 275 3300

Hostler, John M., MA *Camb.*, PhD *Camb.*, MEd   Dir.*

Hester Adrian Research Centre

Psychiatry and behavioural science

Tel: (0161) 275 3339 Fax: (0161) 275 3333

Emerson, E. B., MSc *Manc.*, PhD *Manc.*   Prof.
Kiernan, Prof. C. C., BA *Nott.*, PhD *Lond.*   Dir.*
Other Staff: 1 Sr. Res. Fellow; 4 Res. Fellows;
  2 Res. Assocs.; 1 Hon. Res. Fellow

Manchester Computing Centre

Tel: (0161) 275 6124 Fax: (0161) 275 6236

McDonough, Robin, BSc *Belf.*, PhD *Belf.*   Dir.,
  Information Systems

Manchester Visualisation Centre

Tel: (0161) 275 6095

Hewitt, W. Terry, BSc *Wales*, FIMA   Dir.*

Robert Darbishire Practice

Clinical base of the University Department of
General Practice

Tel: (0161) 225 6699

Roland, Prof. M. O., MA MB BCh   Dir.*

Training and Development Unit

Tel: (0161) 275 2521 Fax: (0161) 275 2529

Littlewood, Mike, MA *Lanc.*   Trg. and Devel.
  Manager

Visual Anthropology, Granada Centre for

Tel: (0161) 275 3999 Fax: (0161) 275 3970

Henley, Paul S., MA *Camb.*, PhD *Camb.*   Dir.*

CONTACT OFFICERS

Academic affairs. Deputy Academic Secretary:
  Sponder, Patricia M., BSc *Hull*, PhD *Hull*
Accommodation. Senior Administrative
  Assistant: Bogg, Angela, BA *Leeds*.
Admissions (first degree). Senior
  Administrative Assistant: Henshaw,
  Jacqueline, BSc *Manc.*, MSc *Manc.*, PhD *Keele*
Adult/continuing education. Hostler, J. M.,
  MA *Camb.*, MEd *Manc.*, PhD *Camb.*
Alumni. Director of Development: Eades,
  William, LLB *S'ton.*
Careers. Director, Careers Service: Dugdale,
  Keith, MA
Computing services. McDonough, Robin, BSc
  Belf., PhD *Belf.*
Conference/corporate hospitality. Bolton,
  Christine S., BSc *Lond.*
Development/fund-raising. Director of
  Development: Eades, William, LLB *S'ton.*
Estates and buildings/works and services.
  Director of Estates: Hampson, Diana L., BSc
  CNAA
Examinations. Harris, P. W. V., BSc *Wales*,
  PhD *E.Anglia*
Finance. Director of Finance: Thompson, Ian
  G.
General enquiries. Registrar and Secretary:
  Newcomb, Eddie, BA *Durh.*
International office. Burge, W. C., BA *Nott.*,
  MPhil *Lond.*
Language training for international students.
  Morley, John C., BA *CNAA*, MEd *NE*

Library. Director of the John Rylands
  University Library and University Librarian:
  Hunt, C. J., BA *Exe.*, MLitt *Durh.*
Personnel/human resources. Kellett, Bernard,
  BA *Open(UK)*
Public relations, information and marketing.
  Burge, W. C., BA *Nott.*, MPhil *Lond.*
Publications. Ferns, A., BA *Lanc.*
Purchasing. Purchasing Consultant: McGeehan,
  R. F.
Research. Head of Research Support: Jenkins,
  Helen, BSc *CNAA*, PhD *Wales*
Safety. Nicholson, P. J., MSc *Manc.*
Scholarships, awards, loans. Harris, P. W. V.,
  BSc *Wales*, PhD *E.Anglia*
Schools liaison. Bedigan, Julie, BA *Sus.*
Security. Deputy Director of Estates and
  Services: Wilson, John G.
Sport and recreation. Director of Sport:
  Sainsbury, A. J., OBE, BEd
Staff development and training. Training and
  Development Manager: Littlewood, Mike,
  MA *Lanc.*
Student union. General Manager, Student
  Union: Silcock, V. W.
Student welfare/counselling (counselling).
  Director, Counselling Service: Potter,
  Stephen, BSocSc *Trinity(Dub.)*, MEd *Manc.*
Students with disabilities. Argust, Janet E.,
  BSc *Manc.*, MSc *Sheff.*
University press. Chief Executive and
  Production Director: Rogers, David
Women. Stanley, Liz, BSc(Econ) *Lond.*, MSc
  Salf., PhD *Salf.*

[*Information supplied by the institution as at July 1998,
and edited by the ACU*]

UNIVERSITY OF MANCHESTER INSTITUTE OF SCIENCE AND TECHNOLOGY

Incorporated 1956 as Manchester College of Science and Technology; previously established as the Manchester
Mechanics' Institution

Member of the Association of Commonwealth Universities

Postal Address: PO Box 88, Manchester, England M60 1QD
Telephone: (0161) 236 3311 **Fax**: (0161) 228 7040, 200 4019 **Cables**: Technology Manchester **Telex**: 666 094
WWW: http://www.umist.ac.uk **E-mail formula**: initial or first name.surname@umist.ac.uk

VISITOR—Edinburgh, H.R.H. The Duke of, KG, KT, OM, GBE, Hon. LLD *Edin.*, Hon. LLD *Wales*, Hon. LLD *Malta*,
  Hon. DSc *Delhi*, Hon. DSc *Salf.*, Hon. Dr *RCA*, FRS
CHANCELLOR—Smith, Sir Rowland, BA *Birm.*, MSc *Birm.*, PhD *Birm.*, Hon. DSc *UMIST*
PRO-CHANCELLOR AND CHAIRMAN OF COUNCIL—Pitt, Margo H. C., MA *Glas.*, LLB *Glas.*
PRO-CHANCELLOR—Horlock, J., MA PhD ScD, FIMechE, FEng, FRS
TREASURER—Carter, R. M. G., MA, FCA
PRINCIPAL AND VICE-CHANCELLOR*—Boucher, Prof. Robert F., PhD *Nott.*, FEng, FIMechE
PRO-VICE-CHANCELLOR—Cooper, Prof. C. L., BS *Calif.*, MBA *Calif.*, MSc *Manc.*, PhD *Leeds*, FBPsS
PRO-VICE-CHANCELLOR—Procter, R. P. M., MA *Camb.*, PhD *Camb.*, FIM
PRO-VICE-CHANCELLOR—Winterbone, Prof. D. E., BSc *CNAA*, PhD *Bath*, DSc, FEng
PRO-VICE-CHANCELLOR—Garside, J., BSc *Lond.*, PhD *Lond.*, DSc, FEng, FIChemE
SECRETARY AND REGISTRAR‡—Stephenson, P. C. C., MA *Camb.*
BURSAR—Lillis, B. J., BA *Manc.Met.*
LIBRARIAN—Day, M. P., BSc *Wales*, MSc *Sheff.*

GENERAL INFORMATION

History. Originally established as the
Manchester Mechanics' Institution, the
university was incorporated as Manchester

College of Science and Technology in 1956. It
is located very close to the city centre of
Manchester.

Admission to first degree courses (see also
United Kingdom Introduction). Through the
Universities and Colleges Admissions Service
(UCAS). Minimum entry requirements: 2
General Certificate of Education (GCE) A level

passes, competence in English language and a wider study at General Certificate of Secondary Education (GCSE) level, normally including maths. A level grades above the minimum pass are needed, AS level qualifications are also considered. National Diplomas and General National Vocational Qualifications are welcomed, in addition to Scottish Highers or the Irish Leaving Certificate. Students with the International Baccalaureate are accepted on the basis of total points score, but specific grades in science or mathematics are normally required.

First Degrees (of University of Manchester) (see also United Kingdom Directory to Subjects of Study). BEng, BSc, MChem, MChemPST (chemistry and polymer science and technology), MEng, MLangEng (language engineering), MLangTrans, MMatSci, MOptom, MPhys.

All courses are full-time and last 3 or 4 years.

Higher Degrees (see also United Kingdom Directory to Subjects of Study). MBA, MMath, MRes, MSc, MPhil, PhD, DSc, DEng, EngD.

Applicants for admission to master's degrees must normally hold an appropriate first degree with at least second class honours. PhD, EngD: first or second class honours degree and a master's degree which has involved some research. DSc, EngD: awarded on published work; candidates must be either graduates of UMIST or members of staff who have been employed continuously for 4 years.

MRes: 1 year; MSc: 1 year full-time or 2–3 years part-time; MBA (offered jointly with the University of Manchester): 3 years part-time; MPhil: 1–2 years full-time or 2 years part-time; PhD: 2–3 years full-time or minimum of 4 years part-time; EngD: 3–4 years full-time.

Libraries. 270,294 items; 1066 periodicals currently subscribed to . Special collections include: Joule (library of the Manchester scientist James Prescott Joule); Shirley (textiles).

Fees (1998–99, annual). Undergraduate: UK students £1000; international students £6800 (arts), £8800 (science, engineering, technology). Postgraduate: UK students £2610; international students £6800 (arts), £8800 (science, engineering and technology).

Academic Year (1998–99). Two semesters: 21 September–31 January; 1 February–11 June.

Income (1996–97). Total, £83,804,000.

Statistics. Staff: 477 academic; 492 administrative. Students: full-time 4730 (3252 men, 1478 women); part-time 183 (129 men, 54 women); international 1467 (1101 men, 366 women); total 6380.

FACULTIES/SCHOOLS

Management
Dean: Marchington, Prof. M. P., BSc Manc., MSc Manc., PhD Manc.

Postgraduate
Dean: Davies, Prof. G. A., BSc Birm., PhD Birm., DSc Manc., FEng, FIChemE

UMIST
Dean: Munn, Prof. R. W., BSc Brist., PhD Brist., FRSChem

Undergraduate
Dean: McDougall, A. O., MA Oxf., DPhil Oxf., FRSChem

ACADEMIC UNITS

Analytical Science, see Instrumentation and Analyt. Sci.

Biomolecular Sciences
Tel: (0161) 200 4200 Fax: (0161) 236 0409
Beynon, R. J., BSc Wales, PhD Wales   Prof.; Head*
Broda, P. M. A., BA Camb., PhD Lond.   Visiting Prof.
Brown, T. A., BSc Lond., PhD Lond.   Reader
Dexter, T. M., BSc Salf., PhD Manc., DSc Salf.   Visiting Prof. Fellow
Ford, R. C., BSc Lond., PhD Lond.   Sr. Lectr.
Hyde, J. E., MA Oxf., DPhil Oxf.   Sr. Lectr.
McCarthy, J. E. G., BSc Oxf., PhD Birm.   Prof.
Oliver, S. G., BSc Brist., PhD CNAA   Prof.; Dir., Biotechnol. Centre
Sims, P. F. G., BSc Sus., PhD Kent   Sr. Lectr.
Spooncer, Elaine, BSc Reading, PhD Manc.   Sr. Lectr.
Tyrer, N. M., MA Camb., PhD Camb.   Sr. Lectr., Physiology
Walmsley, R. M., BSc Kent, PhD Kent   Sr. Lectr.
Whetton, A. D., MSc PhD   Prof.
Other Staff: 9 Lectrs.; 2 Visiting Lectrs.; 1 Hon. Lectr.
Research: biochemistry; biotechnology; cell biology; genetics; molecular biology

Chemistry
Tel: (0161) 200 4416 Fax: (0161) 236 7677
Anderson, M. W., BSc Edin., PhD Camb.   Reader
Banks, R. E., BSc Durh., PhD Durh., FRSChem   Visiting Prof. Fellow
Barlow, M. G., MA Camb., PhD DSc, FRSChem   Sr. Lectr.
Booth, B. L., BScTech PhD   Reader
Briggs, D., BSc Durh., PhD Durh., DSc Durh.   Visiting Prof.
Clarke, J. H. R., MA Oxf., DPhil Oxf.   Prof.
Gaskell, S. J., BSc Brist., PhD Brist., FRSChem   Prof.
Hinchliffe, A., PhD Sheff., DSc Sheff.   Reader
Jennings, K. R., BA Oxf., MA Oxf., DPhil Oxf.   Visiting Prof.
Jones, K., PhD, FRSChem   Sr. Lectr.
Lawrence, N. J., BA Camb., MA Camb., PhD Camb.   Sr. Lectr.
Leigh, D. A., MSc Sheff., PhD Sheff.   Reader
McAuliffe, C. A., MS Flor., DPhil Oxf., BScTech DSc   Prof.
McDougall, A. O., MA Oxf., DPhil Oxf., FRSChem   Sr. Lectr.
Munn, R. W., BSc Brist., PhD Brist., FRSChem   Prof.
O'Malley, P. J., BSc N.U.I., PhD N.U.I.   Sr. Lectr.
Parish, R. V., BSc Lond., PhD Lond.   Prof.
Stoodley, R. J., BSc Brist., PhD Qu.   Prof.
Tait, P. J. T., BSc Aberd., PhD Aberd.   Reader
Taylor, D. R., BA Camb., PhD Camb.   Sr. Lectr.
Tipping, A. E., PhD DSc, FRSChem   Reader
Vickerman, J. C., BSc Edin., PhD Brist.   Prof.
Waugh, K. C., BSc H.-W., PhD Edin.   Prof.; Head*
Whiting, A., BSc Newcastle(UK), PhD Newcastle(UK)   Sr. Lectr.
Other Staff: 2 Visiting Sr. Lectrs.; 11 Lectrs.; 5 Visiting Lectrs.; 1 Hon. Reader; 5 Hon. Lectrs.
Research: inorganic chemistry; organic chemistry; physical chemistry

Computation
Tel: (0161) 200 3329 Fax: (0161) 200 3324
Conroy, G. V., BA Lanc., BSc   Sr. Lectr.
Edwards, M. D., BSc Reading, MSc Wales, PhD Wales   Sr. Lectr.
Flynn, D. J., BSc Kent, MSc Lond., PhD E.Anglia   Sr. Lectr.
Layzell, P. J., BA(Econ) MSc PhD   Prof.; Head*
Loucopoulos, P., BSc Brad., MSc CNAA, PhD   Prof.
Macaulay, Linda A., BSc Sheff., MSc St And.   Sr. Lectr.
Richards, B., MSc PhD   Prof.

Ritchings, R. T., BSc PhD   Sr. Lectr.
Singh, M. G., BSc Exe., MSc Camb., PhD Camb., DèsSc Toulouse   Prof., Information Engineering
Theodoulidis, C. I., MSc Glas., PhD UMIST   Sr. Lectr.
Other Staff: 1 Visiting Sr. Lectr.; 17 Lectrs.; 1 Visiting Lectr.; 1 Hon. Lectr.
Research: computer systems design; decision technology; healthcare systems; information systems engineering; software management

Corrosion and Protection Centre
Fax: (0161) 200 4865
Cottis, R. A., MA Camb., PhD Camb.   Sr. Lectr.
Graham, M. J., BSc Liv., PhD Liv.   Visiting Prof.
Lyon, S. B., MA Camb., PhD Camb., MA   Sr. Lectr.
Newman, R. C., MA Camb., PhD Camb., MA   Prof.
Procter, R. P. M., MA Camb., PhD Camb., FIM   Prof.
Scantlebury, J. D., MA Camb., PhD Camb.   Sr. Lectr.
Skeldon, P., MSc PhD   Sr. Lectr.
Stott, F. H., MA Camb., PhD DSc, FIM   Prof.
Thompson, G. E., BSc Nott., PhD Nott., DSc   Prof.; Head*
Wood, G. C., MA Camb., PhD Camb., ScD Camb., MSc, FIM, FRSChem, FEng   Visiting Prof., Corrosion Science
Other Staff: 2 Lectrs.

Electronics, see Engin., Electr., and Electronics

Engineering, Building
Tel: (0161) 200 4241 Fax: (0161) 200 4252
Birtles, A. B.   Visiting Prof.
Duff, A. R., BSc Birm., MSc Lough., PhD   Sr. Lectr.
Gale, A. W., BSc Brun., PhD Bath   Sr. Lectr.
Hall, C., BA Oxf., MA Oxf., DPhil Oxf.   Visiting Prof.
Hoff, W. D., BSc Liv., PhD   Prof.
Letherman, K. M., BScTech MSc PhD   Prof.; Head*
Levermore, G. J., BSc Lond., PhD Lond.   Sr. Lectr.
Other Staff: 5 Visiting Sr. Lectrs.; 12 Lectrs.; 17 Visiting Lectrs.; 1 Hon. Lectr.
Research: building environment and services; building science and technology; construction management and law; quantity surveying

Engineering, Chemical
Tel: (0161) 200 4340 Fax: (0161) 200 4399
Bos, A.   Visiting Prof.
Carpenter, K. J.   Visiting Prof.
Clegg, G. T., MScTech PhD   Sr. Lectr.
Davey, R. J., BSc Brist., PhD Lond.   Prof.
Davies, G. A., BSc Birm., PhD Birm., DSc Manc., FEng, FIChemE   Prof.
Garside, J., BSc(Eng) Lond., PhD Lond.   Prof.
Griffiths, R. F., BSc PhD   Prof.; Dir., Environmental Technol. Centre
Heggs, P. J., BSc PhD   Prof.; Head*
Korchinsky, W. J., BSc Alta., MS Purdue, PhD Purdue   Sr. Lectr.
Mann, R., MSc PhD   Prof.
Mavituna, Ferda, BSc Ankara, MSc PhD   Prof.
Pickett, D. J., BSc Durh., PhD Leeds   Sr. Lectr.
Rushton, E., MSc PhD   Sr. Lectr.
Senior, P. R., MSc Lough.   Sr. Lectr.
Sharratt, P. N., MA Camb., MSc Manc., PhD UMIST   Sr. Lectr.
Tiddy, G. J. T.   Visiting Prof.
Webb, C., MSc Aston, PhD Aston   Satake Prof., Grain Processing
Webb, D. R., BSc Cape Town, PhD Camb.   Reader
Other Staff: 1 Visiting Sr. Lectr.; 13 Lectrs.; 3 Visiting Lectrs.; 1 Hon. Lectr.
Research: biochemical engineering; environmental technology; fluid dynamics; grain process engineering

Engineering, Civil and Structural

Tel: (0161) 200 4637 *Fax:* (0161) 200 4646

Bell, A. J., BEng *Liv.*, MSc PhD Sr. Lectr.

Burdekin, F. M., MA *Camb.*, PhD *Camb.*, FRS, FEng Prof.

McCarthy, T. J., MSc *Cran.*, PhD *N.U.I.* Sr. Lectr.

Millar, M. A., MSc *Manc.* Sr. Lectr.

Molenkamp, F., PhD Prof.

Morris, P. W. G. Visiting Prof.

Narayanan, R., BE *Madr.*, MSc *B'lore.*, MEng *McG.*, PhD *Brun.* Sr. Lectr.

Phipps, M. E., PhD *Sheff.*, BScTech Prof.; Head*

Roberts, J. M. Visiting Prof.

Thompson, P. A. Visiting Prof.

Vickridge, I. G., BSc *Lond.*, MSc *Strath.* Sr. Lectr.

Whyte, I. L., BScTech Sr. Lectr.

Other Staff: 2 Visiting Sr. Lectrs.; 11 Lectrs.; 6 Visiting Lectrs.

Research: computation and project management; geotechnics; knowledge-based systems; masonry structures

Engineering, Electrical, and Electronics

Tel: (0161) 200 4703 *Fax:* (0161) 200 4782

Allan, D. A., FEng Visiting Prof.

Allan, R. N., MScTech PhD Visiting Prof.

Allinson, N. M., BEng *Brad.*, MSc *Camb.*, FIEE Prof.

Bowler, P., BSc(Eng) *Lond.*, FIEE Sr. Lectr.

Brozel, M. R., MSc PhD Sr. Lectr.

Chalmers, B. J., BSc *Brist.*, PhD *Brist.*, DSc, FIEE Prof.; Head*

Cook, P. A., MA *Camb.*, PhD Sr. Lectr., Control Engineering

Crossley, P. A., BSc *Manc.*, PhD *Camb.* Sr. Lectr.

Darwazeh, I. Z., BSc *Jordan*, MSc *Manc.*, PhD *UMIST* Sr. Lectr.

Davis, L. E., BSc *Nott.*, PhD *Lond.* Prof., Communication Engineering

Drury, W., BSc *Newcastle(UK)*, PhD *Newcastle(UK)* Visiting Prof.

Duncan, S. R., MA *Camb.*, MSc *Lond.*, PhD *Lond.* Sr. Lectr.

Edmunds, J. M., MA *Camb.*, MSc *Manc.*, PhD *UMIST* Sr. Lectr.

Efthymiadis, A. E., BSc *Durh.*, MScTech PhD Sr. Lectr., Electrical Power Systems

Evans-Freeman, Janette H., BSc PhD Sr. Lectr.

Extance, P. Visiting Prof.

Gibson, A. A. P., MEng *H.-W.*, PhD *H.-W.* Sr. Lectr.

Gott, G. F., BSc *Nott.*, PhD *Nott.* Prof.

Green, D. H., MScTech PhD DSc Reader, Electronics

Grundy, D. L., FEng Visiting Prof.

Harrold, S. J., BSc *Durh.*, PhD *Exe.* Sr. Lectr.

Hatfield, J. V., BSc *Leeds*, MSc *Manc.*, PhD *Manc.* Reader

Hicks, P. J., BSc PhD Prof., Microelectronics Circuit Design

Hill, C. Visiting Prof.

Hughes, F. M., MEng *Liv.*, PhD Sr. Lectr.

Hughes, M. A. Visiting Prof.

Hunt, A. Visiting Prof.

Jenkins, N., BSc *S'ton.*, MSc *Reading*, PhD *Lond.* Sr. Lectr.

McCann, Hugh, BSc *Glas.*, PhD *Glas.* Prof.

McKell, H. D., BA *Camb.* Sr. Lectr.

Missous, M., BSc *Salf.*, MSc PhD Reader

Munro, N., BSc *Strath.*, MSc PhD Prof., Applied Control Engineering

Oakley, J. P., BSc *Warw.*, MSc *Brun.*, PhD *Manc.* Sr. Lectr.

Paul, D. K., BSc *Calc.*, MTech *Calc.*, MScTech PhD Sr. Lectr.

Peaker, A. R., MScTech PhD Prof., Solid State Electronics

Renfrew, A. C., BSc *Edin.*, PhD *Edin.* Sr. Lectr.

Rosenbrock, H. H. Hon. Prof.

Singer, K. E., PhD *Camb.*, BSc GEC Prof., Solid State Electronics

Truscott, W. S., BA *Oxf.*, DPhil *Oxf.* Sr. Lectr.

Waterfall, R. C., BSc *Birm.*, MSc PhD Reader

Wellstead, P. E., BSc *CNAA*, MSc PhD Prof., Control Engineering

Williamson, A. C., BSc *Brist.*, PhD Sr. Lectr.

Wilson, B., BSc PhD Reader

York, T. A., BSc PhD Sr. Lectr.

Zarrop, M. B., MA *Lond.*, MSc *Lond.*, PhD *Lond.* Sr. Lectr.

Other Staff: 2 Visiting Sr. Lectrs.; 22 Lectrs.; 7 Visiting Lectrs.; 1 Hon. Reader; 1 Hon. Lectr.

Research: communications and electronics; control and instrumentation systems; electrical energy; microelectronic materials and devices

Engineering, Mechanical

Tel: (0161) 200 3750

Al-Hassani, S. T. S., MSc PhD Prof.

Ashton, J. N., BSc *Leeds*, PhD *Leeds* Sr. Lectr.

Atkinson, J., MSc PhD Sr. Lectr.

Barrow, G., MScTech PhD Sr. Lectr.

Betts, P. L., MA *Camb.*, PhD *Camb.* Sr. Lectr.

Burdekin, M., MSc PhD Sr. Lectr.

Bush, S. F., MA *Camb.*, PhD *Camb.* Prof., Polymer Engineering

Chitkara, N. R., BSc(Eng) *Bihar*, PhD Sr. Lectr.

Hannam, R. G., BSc *Brist.*, PhD *Brist.* Sr. Lectr.

Hayhurst, D. R., BSc *Manc.*, PhD *Camb.* Prof., Design and Manufacture

Hinduja, S., BE *Madr.*, MSc PhD Sr. Lectr.

Hinton, M. J. Visiting Prof.

Iacovides, H., BSc *Lond.*, MSc *Manc.*, PhD *Manc.* Sr. Lectr.

James, D. D., BSc *Wales*, PhD *Lond.* Sr. Lectr.

Kochhar, A. K., BSc(Eng) *Lond.*, PhD Lucas Prof., Manufacturing Engineering; Head*

Launder, B. E., DSc(Eng) *Lond.*, ScD *M.I.T.*, FRS, FEng Prof.

Leech, C. M., BSc *Lond.*, MEng *Tor.*, PhD *Tor.*, DSc(Eng) *Lond.* Reader

Leschziner, M. A., MSc *Lond.*, PhD *Lond.* Prof.

Methven, J., BSc *Lond.*, PhD *Dund.* Sr. Lectr.

Reddy, T. Y., ME *B'lore.*, PhD *Camb.* Sr. Lectr.

Reid, S. R., MA *Camb.*, ScD *Camb.*, BSc PhD, FEng Conoco Prof.

Soden, P. D. W., MSc Sr. Lectr.

Thompson, G., MSc Sr. Lectr.

Watkins, A. P., BA *Camb.*, MSc *Lond.*, PhD *Lond.* Sr. Lectr.

Winterbone, D. E., BSc *CNAA*, PhD *Bath*, DSc, FEng Prof.

Yu, T. X. Visiting Prof.

Yule, A. J., MSc *Lond.*, PhD *Lond.* Reader

Other Staff: 1 Visiting Sr. Lectr.; 13 Lectrs.; 1 Visiting Lectr.; 2 Hon. Lectrs.

Research: applied mechanics; manufacturing and machine tools; polymer engineering; thermodynamics and fluid mechanics

Engineering, Structural, see Engin., Civil and Struct.

Instrumentation and Analytical Science

Tel: (0161) 200 4887 *Fax:* (0161) 200 4911, 200 4879

Alder, J. F., BSc *Lond.*, PhD *Lond.*, DSc, FRSChem Prof.

Clarke, J. R. P. Visiting Prof.

Dewhurst, R. J., BSc *Leeds*, PhD *Hull*, FIP Prof.

Fielden, P. R., BSc *Lond.*, PhD Sr. Lectr.

Gaydecki, P. A., BSc *CNAA*, PhD *Cran.IT* Sr. Lectr.

Kvasnik, F., BSc PhD Sr. Lectr.

Lewis, C., OBE Visiting Prof.

Narayanaswamy, R., BSc *S.Lanka*, PhD *Lond.*, FRSChem Reader

Payne, P. A., MSc *Wales*, PhD *Wales*, FIEE, FIP Prof.

Persaud, K. C., BSc *Newcastle(UK)*, MSc *Warw.*, PhD *Warw.* Sr. Lectr.

Snook, R. D., MSc *Lond.*, PhD *Lond.* Prof.; Head*

Thomas, C. L., BSc *Manc.*, PhD *UMIST* Sr. Lectr.

Zweit, J., BSc *Kansas*, MSc *Manc.* Sr. Lectr.

Other Staff: 1 Lectr.

Research: laser ultrasound and laser spectroscopy; measurement in physical, chemical and biochemical systems; miniaturisation of analytical instrumentation; odour and array sensing; vapour and gas monitoring

Language Engineering

Tel: (0161) 200 3100 *Fax:* (0161) 200 3099

Baker, Mona, BA *Cairo*, MA *Birm.* Reader

Bennett, P. A., BA *Lond.*, PhD *Lond.* Sr. Lectr.

Black, W. J., MA *Leeds* Sr. Lectr.

Ramsay, A. M., BSc *Sus.*, MSc *Lond.*, DPhil *Sus.* Prof.; Head*

Somers, H. L., BA *Wales*, MA PhD Sr. Lectr.

Tsujii, J.-I., MA *Kyoto*, PhD *Kyoto* Prof.†, Computational Linguistics

Other Staff: 11 Lectrs.; 1 Visiting Lectr.

Research: computer-aided language learning; language engineering; theoretical linguistics; translation

Linguistics, see Lang. Engin.

Management, Manchester School of, see

also Property Devel. and Management, Centre for

Tel: (0161) 200 3500 *Fax:* (0161) 200 3505

Berridge, J. R. K., BA *S'ton.*, MSc *Lond.* Sr. Lectr.

Bloomfield, B. P., BSc *Lanc.*, PhD *Open(UK)* Visiting Prof.

Bosworth, D. R., BA *CNAA*, MSc *Warw.*, PhD *Warw.* Prof., Economics

Bowe, M. A., BA *Oxf.*, MA *Manc.*, PhD *Car.* Sr. Lectr.

Burton, F. N., BSc(Econ) *Hull* Sr. Lectr.

Carew, A. B., BSc(Econ) *Hull*, MPhil *Sus.*, DPhil *Sus.* Sr. Lectr.

Coombs, R. W., BSc *Kent*, MSc PhD Prof.

Cooper, C. L., BS *Calif.*, MBA *Calif.*, PhD *Leeds*, MSc Prof., Organisational Psychology

Dale, B. G., PhD *Nott.*, MSc Prof.

Duffy, M. H., BSc(Econ) *Lond.*, MSc *Brist.*, PhD Sr. Lectr.

Earnshaw, Jill M., BSc *Manc.*, MSc *Manc.* Sr. Lectr.

Edwards, P., BSc *Manc.*, MSc *Manc.* Sr. Lectr.

Eyre-Morgan, M. J., BA *Lond.*, MA *Qld.*, PhD *Manc.* Sr. Lectr.

Foxhall, G. R. Visiting Prof.

Goodman, J. F. B., BSc(Econ) *Lond.*, PhD *Nott.*, MSc Frank Thomas Prof., Industrial Relations

Green, K., BSc PhD Sr. Lectr.

Hollier, R. H., MSc *Birm.*, PhD *Birm.* Visiting Prof., Operations Management

Hoskin, K. W., BA *Oxf.*, MSc *Penn.*, PhD *Penn.* Prof.

Leahy, T. Visiting Prof.

Levicki, C. J. Visiting Prof. Fellow

Lewis, Barbara R., SM *M.I.T.*, BSc PhD Sr. Lectr.

Littler, D. A., BSc PhD Prof., Marketing; Head*

Marchington, M. P., BSc *Manc.*, MSc *Manc.*, PhD *Manc.* Prof.

McGoldrick, P. J., BSc Littlewoods Prof., Retailing

Michell, L. N. Visiting Prof.

Mitchell, V., BSc *Manc.*, MSc *Manc.*, PhD *UMIST* Sr. Lectr.

Monks, J. Visiting Prof.

Murphy, D., MSc *Salf.*, PhD Sr. Lectr.

Nicholson, R. Visiting Prof.

Oakland, J. S. Visiting Prof.

Robertson, I. T., BSc *Exe.*, PhD *Open(UK)* Prof.

Robson, K., MA PhD Sr. Lectr.

Rubery, Jill C., MA *Camb.*, PhD *Camb.* Prof.

Smith, J. M., BA *Liv.*, PhD *Liv.* Sr. Lectr.

Smith, Sir Roland Visiting Prof.

Sweeting, R. C., BSc *Lond.*, PhD *Keele* Sr. Lectr.

Torrington, D. P. Visiting Prof.

Turnbull, P. W., BSc Hepworth Prof., Marketing

Walsh, Vivian M., BSc *Sus.*, MSc PhD Sr. Lectr.

Wilkinson, A. J., BSc *Lond.*, MSc *Lond.*, PhD *Durh.* Sr. Lectr.

Willmott, H. S., BSc PhD Prof.

Yorke, D. A., BCom *Liv.*, MSc Sr. Lectr.

Other Staff: 1 Visiting Sr. Lectr.; 33 Lectrs.; 16 Visiting Lectrs.; 6 Hon. Lectrs.

Research: accounting and finance and business economics; marketing; occupational and organisational psychology; operations and technology management; organisation and employment studies

Materials Science Centre

Tel: (0161) 200 3617 Fax: (0161) 200 3586

Berry, J. P., BSc Manc., PhD UMIST   Sr. Lectr.
Davies, T. J., BSc Wales, MSc Manc., PhD UMIST   Reader
Freer, R., MSc Newcastle(UK), PhD Newcastle(UK)   Reader
Hayes, F. H., BSc Liv., PhD Liv.   Reader
Humphreys, F. J., MA Oxf., DPhil Oxf., FIM   Prof.
Lovell, P. A., BSc Manc., PhD UMIST   Reader
Morrell, R.   Visiting Prof.
Priestner, R., BSc Birm., PhD Birm., FIM   Reader, Physical Metallurgy
Stanford, J. L., BSc PhD   Reader
Stepto, R. F. T., BSc Brist., PhD Brist., DSc   Prof.; Head*
Stowell, M. J.   Visiting Prof.
Taylor, R., MSc PhD   Visiting Prof.
Young, R. J., MA Camb., PhD Camb., FIP   Royal Society Wolfson Prof.
Other Staff: 1 Visiting Reader; 2 Visiting Sr. Lectrs.; 6 Lectrs.; 3 Visiting Lectrs.; 1 Hon. Lectr.

Research: biomedical materials; ceramic materials; composite materials; metallic materials; polymeric materials

Mathematics

Tel: (0161) 200 3690 Fax: (0161) 200 3669

Bell, D. J., BSc Lond., MSc Lond., PhD Lond., DSc   Prof.
Borovik, A. V., BSc Novosibirsk, PhD Minsk   Reader
Broomhead, D. S., BA Oxf., DPhil Oxf.   Prof.
Bryant, R. M., MA Oxf., DPhil Oxf.   Prof.
Bullough, R. K., MA Camb., PhD Leeds, MSc, FIP   Visiting Prof. Fellow
Caudrey, P. J., MSc S'ton., PhD S'ton.   Sr. Lectr.
Clarke, J. F.   Visiting Prof.
Dold, J. W., BSc Z'bwe., MA Lond., PhD Cran.   Prof.
Laycock, P. J., BSc PhD   Sr. Lectr.
Rowley, P. J., BA Essex, MSc Warw., PhD Warw.   Reader
Sharma, C. B., MSc Agra, PhD Kanpur, PhD Lough.   Sr. Lectr.
Silvester, D. J., BSc PhD   Sr. Lectr.
Stöhr, R., MSc Moscow, PhD Moscow, DSc Rostock   Sr. Lectr.
Subba Rao, T., MA Karn., PhD Gauh., MSc   Prof.
Taylor, M. J., MA Oxf., MA Camb., PhD Lond., FRS   Prof., Pure Mathematics
Thatcher, R. W., BSc Durh., PhD Lond.   Sr. Lectr.; Head*
Thomas, Ruth M., BA Oxf., MSc PhD   Sr. Lectr.
Other Staff: 13 Lectrs.; 4 Visiting Lectrs.; 1 Hon. Sr. Lectr.; 3 Hon. Lectrs.

Research: applied mathematics; pure mathematics; statistics

Optometry and Vision Sciences

Tel: (0161) 200 3870 Fax: (0161) 200 3887

Abadi, R. V., BSc Aston, MSc PhD   Reader
Bannister, C. M., MB BS Lond., BSc Oxf., FRCSEd   Visiting Prof.
Butler, S. R., BA Camb., MA Camb., PhD Lond.   Visiting Prof.
Charman, W. N., BSc Lond., PhD Lond.   Prof.; Head*
Cronly-Dillon, J. R., MA Camb., PhD Prin., MSc   Prof.
Dickson, Christine M.   Sr. Lectr.
Efron, N., BScOptom Melb., PhD Melb.   Bausch and Lomb Prof.
Gregory, R.   Visiting Prof.
Hirj, N. K.   Visiting Prof.
Howland, H. C.   Visiting Prof.

Itzhaki, R. F.   Visiting Prof. Fellow
Jennings, J. A. M., BSc Wales, MSc Aston, PhD   Sr. Lectr.
Kulikowski, J. J., MSc(Eng) T.U.Warsaw, PhD Polish Acad.Sc.   Prof.
McLeod, M.   Visiting Prof.
Norman, R. A.   Visiting Prof.
Rosen, E.   Visiting Prof.
Tullo, A. B.   Visiting Prof.
Other Staff: 1 Visiting Reader; 4 Visiting Sr. Lectrs.; 5 Lectrs.; 4 Visiting Lectrs.; 1 Hon. Lectr.

Research: cell and molecular biology of the brain and visual system; contact lenses and clinical optometry; vision sciences and visual neurophysiology; visual optics and instrumentation

Paper Science

Tel: (0161) 200 3891 Fax: (0161) 200 3858

Dodson, C. T. J.   Prof.
Jaycock, M. J.   Visiting Prof.
Roberts, J. C.   Visiting Prof.
Sinnott, M. L., PhD Brist.   Prof.; Head*
Wang, H., MEng Huazhong, PhD Huazhong   Sr. Lectr.
Wiseman, N., BE Cant., PhD McG.   Prof.
Other Staff: 5 Lectrs.; 1 Visiting Lectr.; 1 Hon. Lectr.

Research: paper chemistry and conservation; paper physics and microscopy; process engineering and control; raw materials and environment

Physics

Tel: (0161) 200 3940 Fax: (0161) 200 3941

Bishop, R. F., BA Oxf., PhD Stan.   Prof.
Browning, Philippa K., MA Camb., PhD St And.   Sr. Lectr.
Choularton, T. W., PhD DSc, FRMetS   Prof.
Dawson, P., BSc Hull, PhD Hull   Sr. Lectr.
Elliott, J. A., BSc PhD   Sr. Lectr.
Flavell, Wendy R., BA Oxf., MA Oxf., DPhil Oxf.   Reader
Hamilton, B., MSc PhD DSc   Prof., Solid State Physics
Hugill, J., BA Camb., PhD Camb.   Prof.
Jonas, P. R., BSc Brist., PhD Lond., FRMetS   Prof.
Millar, T. J., BSc PhD   Prof.; Head*
Munro, I. H.   Prof.
Nagarajan, M. A., BSc Hyd., MSc Hyd., PhD Calc.   Visiting Prof.
Parkinson, J. B., BA Oxf., MA Oxf., DPhil Oxf.   Sr. Lectr.
Rusbridge, M. G.   Visiting Prof.
Saunders, C. P. R., BScTech PhD DSc, FRMetS   Sr. Lectr.
Walker, G., BSc Glas., MSc Manc., PhD Manc.   Sr. Lectr.
Other Staff: 1 Visiting Sr. Lectr.; 19 Lectrs.; 1 Hon. Lectr.

Research: astrophysics; atmospheric physics; condensed matter physics; plasma physics; theoretical physics

Process Integration, Centre for

Tel: (0161) 200 4393 Fax: (0161) 200 4392

Lazenby, M.   Visiting Prof.
Smith, R., BTech Brad., MSc Brad., PhD Brad.   Prof.; Head*
Other Staff: 3 Lectrs.; 2 Visiting Lectrs.; 1 Hon. Lectr.

Research: efficient use of raw materials; emission reduction; energy efficiency; process design and integration

Property Development and Management, Centre for

Tel: (0161) 200 4218 Fax: (0161) 200 4217

Birrell, G. S., MSc Ill., PhD Mich.   Dares Estates plc Prof.
Other Staff: 1 Lectr.

Textiles

Tel: (0161) 200 4114 Fax: (0161) 4019

Amirbayat, J.   Reader

Bruce, Margaret A., BSc Salf., PhD CNAA   Sr. Lectr.
Carr, C. M., BSc PhD   Sr. Lectr.
Cooke, W. D., MSc PhD   Sr. Lectr.
Phillips, D. A. S., BSc Wales, PhD Wales   Prof.; Head*
Porat, I., BTech Shenkar, PhD Leeds   Coats Viyella plc Prof., Clothing Engineering
Rigby, D. A., BSc Lond., MSc Lond.   Visiting Prof.
Taylor, J. A., BSc Wales, PhD Wales   Sr. Lectr.
Other Staff: 1 Visiting Sr. Lectr.; 13 Lectrs.; 1 Visiting Lectr.; 5 Hon. Lectrs.

Research: colour communication and computer-aided design; mechanical processing and automation; physics of fibres and fibre assemblies; textile chemistry; textile design and management

Total Technology

Tel: (0161) 200 4155 Fax: (0161) 200 4163

Barber, K. D., MSc PhD   Sr. Lectr.
Leonard, R., BSc Salf., PhD Salf., DSc   Visiting Prof.

Research: production engineering and management

Vision Sciences, see Optom. and Vision Scis.

CONTACT OFFICERS

Academic affairs. Deputy Registrar and Academic Secretary: Halstead, Renata J., BA York(UK), MA York(UK)

Accommodation. Accommodation Officer: Bogg, A. J.

Admissions (first degree). Senior Administrative Officer: Conway, M. F., BSc Aston

Admissions (higher degree). Assistant Registrar: Beresford, A. J., MA Oxf., BLitt Oxf.

Adult/continuing education. Acting Director: Fortune, Jacqueline D.

Alumni. Babczuk, Annette A., BSc Open(UK)

Archives. Assistant Registrar: Partington, J., BA Manc., MSc Lond.

Careers. Head of UMIST Careers Service: Phillips, C. J.

Computing services. Director, Academic Computing: Swindells, W., MPhil

Conferences/corporate hospitality. Director of Trading Services: Yates, A. F., BA Keele

Consultancy services. Managing Director, UMIST Ventures: Rowland, C. G.

Credit transfer. Deputy Registrar and Academic Secretary: Halstead, Renata J., BA York(UK), MA York(UK)

Development/fund-raising. Director of Management Services: McGlennan, S.

Equal opportunities. Director of Personnel: Clayton, Judith M., BA Open(UK)

Estates and buildings/works and services. Director: Slater, V., BSc Salf.

Examinations. Deputy Registrar and Academic Secretary: Halstead, Renata J., BA York(UK), MA York(UK)

Finance. Bursar: Lillis, B. J., BA Manc.Met.

General enquiries. Secretary and Registrar: Stephenson, P. C. C., MA Camb.

Health services. Safety Officer: Gerrard, P. M., MA Camb.

Industrial liaison. Managing Director, UMIST Ventures: Rowland, C. G.

International office. Director, International Relations: Bride, I. M., MA Edin., MScTech PhD

Language training for international students. Director of ELTC: Hinton-Lever, Justine M. L., MA Lanc.

Library (chief librarian). Librarian: Day, M. P., BSc Wales, MSc Sheff.

Minorities/disadvantaged groups. Tutor for Special Needs: Conroy, G. V., BA Lanc., BSc Manc.

Personnel/human resources. Director of Personnel: Clayton, Judith M., BA Open(UK)

Public relations, information and marketing. Director of Information: Yates, T., BA Manc., MA Manc.

Purchasing. Purchasing and Insurance Officer: Walker, N., BA Lond.

Quality assurance and accreditation. Deputy Registrar and Academic Secretary: Halstead, Renata J., BA York(UK), MA York(UK)

Research. Director, UMIST Ventures: Charlton, P.

Safety. Safety Officer: Gerrard, P. M., MA Camb.

Scholarships, awards, loans. Deputy Registrar and Academic Secretary: Halstead, Renata J., BA York(UK), MA York(UK)

Schools liaison. Director, Student Recruitment: Lumb, M. D., BScTech PhD

Security. Security Officer: Smith, R. K.

Sport and recreation. Physical Recreation Officer: Cox, R., BEd Durh., MA Leeds, MSc Sheff., PhD

Staff development and training. Director: Tomkinson, C. B., BA Open(UK), BSc

Student union. Manager of Student Union: Hammond, C. W.

Student welfare/counselling. Director of Counselling: Potter, S.

Students from other countries. External Relations Officer: Carver, Katherine, BSc Sheff., PhD Sheff.

Students with disabilities. Tutor for Special Needs: Conroy, G. V., BA Lanc., BSc Manc.

University Press. Director of Information: Yates, T., BA Manc., MA Manc.

Women. Director of Personnel: Clayton, Judith M., BA Open(UK)

[Information supplied by the institution as at 2 April 1998, and edited by the ACU]

MANCHESTER METROPOLITAN UNIVERSITY

Founded 1992; previously established as Manchester Polytechnic 1970

Member of the Association of Commonwealth Universities

Postal Address: All Saints, Manchester, England M15 6BH
Telephone: (0161) 247 2000 **Fax**: (0161) 247 6390 **WWW**: http://www.mmu.ac.uk

CHANCELLOR—Westminster, His Grace the Duke of, OBE, TD, Hon. DLitt
PRO-CHANCELLOR—Booth, A. T., CBE
VICE-CHANCELLOR*—Burslem, Alexandra V., OBE, JP, BA Manc.
ACADEMIC DIRECTOR—Plumb, Prof. B., MSc
FINANCIAL DIRECTOR—Grant, L., MBA
PERSONNEL DIRECTOR—Hallam, I. W., BA Manc., MA Nott., MSc Salf.
UNIVERSITY SECRETARY AND CLERK TO THE BOARD OF GOVERNORS—Hendley, T., LLB, FCIS
ACADEMIC REGISTRAR—Karczewski-Slowikowski, J. D. M., BEd Manc., MSc CNAA
LIBRARIAN—Harris, Prof. C. G. S., BA BPhil MA MLS PhD, FLA, FIInfSc

GENERAL INFORMATION

History. The university was originally established as Manchester Polytechnic in 1970 and became an independent corporate body in 1989. It obtained university status in 1992 and amalgamated with Crewe and Alsager College of Higher Education in the same year.

Admission to first degree courses (see also United Kingdom Introduction). Through Universities and Colleges Admissions Service (UCAS).

First Degrees (see also United Kingdom Directory to Subjects of Study). BA, BEd, BEng, BSc, LLB.

Higher Degrees (see also United Kingdom Directory to Subjects of Study). MA, MBA, MChem, MEd, MEng, MSc, MSci, MPhil, PhD.

Libraries. Over 1,000,000 volumes; over 4000 periodical titles.

Fees (1998–99). Home students: £1000 (undergraduate); £2610 (postgraduate). International students: £6500–7200 (postgraduate).

Academic Year (1998–99). Three terms: 20 September–18 December; 11 January–7 April; 19 April–25 June.

Statistics. Students: full-time 20,747 (9210 men, 11,537 women); part-time 8313 (3489 men, 4824 women); international (Ireland, EC, non-EC) 1807 (948 men, 859 women); total 29,060.

FACULTIES/SCHOOLS

Art and Design
Tel: (0161) 247 1713 Fax: (0161) 247 6361
Dean: Wilson, Prof. R., MA

Secretary: Sherratt, Marie

Community Studies, Law and Education
Tel: (0161) 247 2001 Fax: (0161) 247 6327
Dean: ......
Secretary: McLean, Cheri

Crewe and Alsager
Tel: (0161) 247 5182 Fax: (0161) 247 6371
Dean: Wilson, G., BEng PhD
Secretary: Payne, Pat L.

Hollings
Tel: (0161) 247 2616 Fax: (0161) 247 6395
Dean: Murray, Prof. R., BSc PhD
Secretary: Lilley, Paula

Humanities and Social Science
Tel: (0161) 247 1749 Fax: (0161) 247 6308
Dean: Kirby, S., BA MSc PhD
Secretary: Egan, Teresa

Management and Business
Tel: (0161) 247 3703 Fax: (0161) 247 6350
Dean: Lock, Prof. A. R., BA MSc MSc(Econ) PhD
Secretary: Blackmore, Alice

Science and Engineering
Tel: (0161) 247 1783 Fax: (0161) 247 6315
Dean: Gacesa, P., BSc(Hons), PhD, CBiol, SIBiol F
Secretary: Howarth, Margaret A.

ACADEMIC UNITS

Accounting and Finance
Tel: (0161) 247 3759 Fax: (0161) 247 6303
Alali, J.   Sr. Lectr.
Arkwright, A.   Sr. Lectr.
Barrow, N.   Sr. Lectr.
Bishop, C.   Sr. Lectr.

Brander Brown, Jacqueline C.   Sr. Lectr.
Broadbent, J. M.   Head*
Brosnan, K. D.   Sr. Lectr.
Colin, M.   Sr. Lectr.
Helps, Lynda C.   Sr. Lectr.
Holt, G. J.   Principal Lectr.
Hughes, R.   Sr. Lectr.
Lee-Faulkner, R.   Sr. Lectr.
Leigh, B.   Sr. Lectr.
Marland, P.   Sr. Lectr.
McKeon, Pamela   Sr. Lectr.
Molyneux, S. R.   Sr. Lectr.
Murphy, D.   Principal Lectr.
Rodda, N. G.   Sr. Lectr.
Scott, S.   Sr. Lectr.
Somerfield, A.   Sr. Lectr.
Watson, M. H.   Sr. Lectr.
Wayte, K.   Sr. Lectr.
Williamson, T. C.   Principal Lectr.
Wilson, R.   Sr. Lectr.
Woods, C. M.   Sr. Lectr.
Worsick, A. C.   Principal Lectr.

Applied Community Studies
Tel: (0161) 247 2098 Fax: (0161) 247 6392
Batsleer, Janet R.   Sr. Lectr.
Boulton, D. K.   Principal Lectr.
Campbell, W. H.   Principal Lectr.
Chatterjee, M.   Sr. Lectr.
Done, Judith M.   Principal Lectr.
Goodwin, S. C.   Sr. Lectr.
Gutfreund, R.   Sr. Lectr.
Hayes, D.   Sr. Lectr.
Hodgkiss, P.   Sr. Lectr.
Humphries, Elizabeth M.   Principal Lectr.
John, Jill V.   Sr. Lectr.
Jones, A. D.   Sr. Lectr.
Jones, Susan G.   Sr. Lectr.
Keetch, Dianne   Sr. Lectr.
Kenny, Stephanie E.   Sr. Lectr.
Kirk, Katherine   Sr. Lectr.
Lines, S. M.   Sr. Lectr.

Lund, B.   Principal Lectr.
Manson, Doreen E.   Sr. Lectr.
Martin, D. I.   Sr. Lectr.
Meryll, Lydia   Principal Lectr.
Morgan, R. S.   Sr. Lectr.
Myers, J. S.   Sr. Lectr.
Nesbitt, S. M.   Sr. Lectr.
Packham, Carol   Sr. Lectr.
Patterson
Payne, M. S., BA   Prof.; Head*
Sargeant, A. V.   Sr. Lectr.
Webb, M.   Sr. Lectr.
Wilkins, P.   Sr. Lectr.

Applied Social Studies, see Humanities and
   Appl. Soc. Studies

**Architecture, Landscape and Three
   Dimensional Design**
Tel: (0161) 247 1103 Fax: (0161) 247 6393
Allen, P. C.   Principal Lectr.
Barham, D. G.   Sr. Lectr.
Bennis, E. M.   Principal Lectr.
Blakey, S.   Sr. Lectr.
Brinton, T. J.   Sr. Lectr.
Brown, M. R.   Sr. Lectr.
Campion, J.   Sr. Lectr.
Chadwick, A. P.   Sr. Lectr.
Cooper, H. J.   Sr. Lectr.
Cowland, T.   Sr. Lectr.
Dargavel, R.   Sr. Lectr.
Doyle, J. P.   Sr. Lectr.
Dyke, J.   Sr. Lectr.
Dyter, A.   Sr. Lectr.
Ellis, D. M.   Sr. Lectr.
Finlay, R. J.   Sr. Lectr.
Fisher, I.   Sr. Lectr.
Frost, D. B.   Sr. Lectr.
Gittoes, M. S.   Sr. Lectr.
Grimshaw, D.   Sr. Lectr.
Islam, M. A.   Sr. Lectr.
Jackson, R. L.   Sr. Lectr.
Jeffries, T. E.   Sr. Lectr.
Jessop, M. R.   Principal Lectr.
Keeffe, G.   Sr. Lectr.
McErlain, A. J.   Sr. Lectr.
McFadyen, J.   Principal Lectr.
McKennan, G. T.   Sr. Lectr.
Pinder, J. M.   Sr. Lectr.
Pope, D. J.   Sr. Lectr.
Pugh, C. L.   Sr. Lectr.
Roberts, I. D.   Principal Lectr.
Sheldon, M. M.   Sr. Lectr.
Staines, D. A.   Principal Lectr.
Starling, M. J.   Head*
Stone, Sally H.   Sr. Lectr.
Swanson, N. C.   Sr. Lectr.
Wonnacott, B. J.   Sr. Lectr.

Art, see Arts, Des. and Performance; Fine Art;
   and Hist. of Art and Des.

Arts and Humanities Education
Tel: (0161) 247 2347 Fax: (0161) 247 6368
Archer, M. F.   Principal Lectr.
Campbell, A. J.   Principal Lectr.
Cox, J. A.   Sr. Lectr.
Coxon, A. B.   Sr. Lectr.
Frank Keyes, G. V.   Sr. Lectr.
Gatti, K.   Sr. Lectr.
Goodwin, A. J.   Head*
Grinter, R. E.   Sr. Lectr.
Halsall, R.   Principal Lectr.
Hogbin, J. W.   Principal Lectr.
Hoodless, Patricia A.   Sr. Lectr.
Jarmany, Ann K.   Sr. Lectr.
Jones, P. S. G.   Sr. Lectr.
Kane, I. S., BA   Head*
Macrory, Geraldine F.   Sr. Lectr.
Matson, P.   Sr. Lectr.
Palmer, D. H.   Sr. Lectr.
Palmer, J.   Sr. Lectr.
Palmer, Sandra   Sr. Lectr.
Payne, Gillian M.   Sr. Lectr.
Peplow, T. A.   Principal Lectr.
Rainer, J. A.   Sr. Lectr.
Robson, C.   Sr. Lectr.
Sinclair, Yvonne   Sr. Lectr.

Smith, Elizabeth M.   Sr. Lectr.
Stone, Valerie A.   Sr. Lectr.
Sweasey, Penny   Sr. Lectr.
Turner, C. C.   Sr. Lectr.
Turton, D. J.   Sr. Lectr.
Voiels, Veronica M.   Sr. Lectr.
Walker, K.   Sr. Lectr.
Wallace, J. C.   Sr. Lectr.
Waring, S. M.   Sr. Lectr.
Whitley, Barbara M.   Sr. Lectr.
Whitley, Margaret J.   Principal Lectr.
Willcock, Pamela H.   Sr. Lectr.

Arts, Design and Performance, see also
   Hist. of Art and Des.
Tel: (0161) 247 5305 Fax: (0161) 247 6377
Brodie, D.   Sr. Lectr.
Chatwin, P.   Sr. Lectr.
Dobson, C.   Sr. Lectr.
Fisher, N.   Sr. Lectr.
Heaton, D.   Sr. Lectr.
Landy, L.   Prof.; Head*
Lawson, Susan M.   Sr. Lectr.
Mackenzie, N. K.   Sr. Lectr.
Malone, K.   Sr. Lectr.
Maxfield, A.   Sr. Lectr.
McVittie, F. E.   Sr. Lectr.
Mitchison, L.   Sr. Lectr.
Morley, J. W.   Principal Lectr.
Nelson, R. A.   Principal Lectr.
Nowakowski, O.   Sr. Lectr.
O'Shea, D.   Sr. Lectr.
Pickering, Dorothy   Sr. Lectr.
Purcell, S. P.   Sr. Lectr.
Reilly McVittie, N. O.   Sr. Lectr.
Richardson, Rachel S.   Sr. Lectr.
Saddington, R. J.   Sr. Lectr.
Shrubsole, A. G.   Sr. Lectr.
Singleton, C. J.   Principal Lectr.
Smith, D. W.   Sr. Lectr.
Stevens, B.A.   Sr. Lectr.
Turner, Jane C.   Sr. Lectr.
Whitehead, A. G.   Sr. Lectr.
Wilkinson, R. J.   Principal Lectr.
Wood, P.   Sr. Lectr.

Biological Sciences
Tel: (0161) 247 1234 Fax: (0161) 247 6325
Attwell, R. W.   Principal Lectr.
Backen, K. E.   Principal Lectr.
Barnett, Ann   Sr. Lectr.
Bingham, Enid   Sr. Lectr.
Bohme, K. T.   Sr. Lectr.
Brough, Denise E.   Principal Lectr.
Craig, G. D.   Sr. Lectr.
Dawson, Maureen M.   Sr. Lectr.
Dempsey, M. J.   Sr. Lectr.
Edwards Jones, Valerie   Sr. Lectr.
Fielding, A.   Sr. Lectr.
Gaffney, J. J.   Sr. Lectr.
Goldspink, C. R.   Sr. Lectr.
Gordon, D. B.   Prof.
Graham, I.   Principal Lectr.
Gregson, Olga   Sr. Lectr.
Gross, T. S.   Principal Lectr.
Hayes, M.   Sr. Lectr.
Hibbert, J. R.   Sr. Lectr.
Hick, V.   Sr. Lectr.
Hughes, H.   Sr. Lectr.
Hume, K. I.   Principal Lectr.
Jones, M. J.   Sr. Lectr.
Kay, I. S.   Sr. Lectr.
Kumar, Patricia M.   Reader
Looker, T., BSc PhD   Prof.; Head*
McLaughlin, N. J.   Sr. Lectr.
Morris, G. F.   Sr. Lectr.
Morris, June   Sr. Lectr.
Navagam, S.   Sr. Lectr.
Overfield, Joyce A.   Sr. Lectr.
Powell, Susan C.   Sr. Lectr.
Ralphs, N.   Sr. Lectr.
Seal, L. H.   Sr. Lectr.
Smith, C. A.   Sr. Lectr.
Sullivan, M.   Sr. Lectr.
Taylor, I. G.   Sr. Lectr.
Verran, Joanna   Sr. Lectr.
Whalley, W. M.   Sr. Lectr.
Willcox, J.   Sr. Lectr.

Business and Management Studies, see
   also Bus. Studies, and Internat. Bus. Unit
Tel: (0161) 247 5256 Fax: (0161) 247 6378
Brindley, C. S.   Sr. Lectr.
Broomfield, Christina J.   Sr. Lectr.
Cox, W. P.   Sr. Lectr.
Cuthbert, P. F.   Sr. Lectr.
Farmer, D. W.   Sr. Lectr.
Fisher, R. A.   Principal Lectr.
Hannigan, T. T.   Principal Lectr.
Knibbs, A. P.   Sr. Lectr.
Lovatt, L. C.   Sr. Lectr.
O'Leary, Barbara J.   Sr. Lectr.
Owen, A. S.   Sr. Lectr.
Pratten, J. D.   Principal Lectr.
Roberts, A.   Sr. Lectr.
Roper, J.   Sr. Lectr.
Slack, F. E.   Sr. Lectr.
Spowage, R.   Sr. Lectr.
Towers, N. S.   Sr. Lectr.
Williams, J. A.   Sr. Lectr.
Williams-Slaven, N.   Sr. Lectr.

Business Information Technology
Tel: (0161) 247 3810 Fax: (0161) 247 6317
Batho, P. G.   Sr. Lectr.
Brady, R.   Sr. Lectr.
Clark, Janet   Sr. Lectr.
Davidson, C. R.   Sr. Lectr.
Dunn, D., JP, BA   Head*
Endlar, L. D.   Sr. Lectr.
Griffiths, G. H.   Sr. Lectr.
Hackney, R. A.   Principal Lectr.
Jones, L.   Sr. Lectr.
Lester, G. C.   Sr. Lectr.
Little, S. E.   Sr. Lectr.
Lockley, B. J.   Sr. Lectr.
Meldrum, Mary C.   Sr. Lectr.
Mole, G.   Principal Lectr.
Morris, M.   Sr. Lectr.
Rose, J.   Sr. Lectr.
Scown, P. J.   Sr. Lectr.
Sheard, V.   Sr. Lectr.
Stubbs, M. A.   Sr. Lectr.
Tucker, D. E.   Sr. Lectr.
Weaver, C. R.   Sr. Lectr.

Business Studies, see also Bus. and
   Management Studies, and Internat. Bus. Unit
Tel: (0161) 247 3821 Fax: (0161) 247 6307
Avery, J. D.   Sr. Lectr.
Bainbridge, S. F.   Sr. Lectr.
Bundy, F. J.   Sr. Lectr.
Doyle, A. J.   Sr. Lectr.
Elphick, S.   Sr. Lectr.
Forbes, Carole A.   Sr. Lectr.
Freeman, Susan   Sr. Lectr.
Gardner, H.   Sr. Lectr.
Gibson-Sweet, Monica F.   Sr. Lectr.
Harris, C. P.   Sr. Lectr.
Harris, W. J.   Sr. Lectr.
Healey, N. M.   Prof.; Head*
Howe, Susan A.   Sr. Lectr.
Hunt, W. J.   Sr. Lectr.
Hurt, D.   Principal Lectr.
Hynes, M.   Sr. Lectr.
Jackson, A. B.   Sr. Lectr.
Jackson, M.   Sr. Lectr.
Jones, D.   Sr. Lectr.
Killeya, J. C.   Principal Lectr.
Lyon, P. S.   Principal Lectr.
Marsden, A.   Sr. Lectr.
Mead, P.   Sr. Lectr.
Miller, F.   Sr. Lectr.
Mitton, A. E.   Sr. Lectr.
Parry, E.   Sr. Lectr.
Paucar-Caceres, A. L.   Sr. Lectr.
Roddy, Eileen M.   Sr. Lectr.
Skidmore, D.   Sr. Lectr.
Sorah, I.   Sr. Lectr.
Springthorpe, Valerie A.   Sr. Lectr.
Stone, B. W.   Sr. Lectr.
Taylor, M.   Sr. Lectr.
Taylor, Tony G.   Principal Lectr.
Walley, E. E.   Sr. Lectr.
Warren, R. C.   Principal Lectr.

Chemistry and Materials
Tel: (0161) 247 1437 Fax: (0161) 247 6357

Allen, N. S. Prof.
Allock, S. Sr. Lectr.
Anderson, G. J. Sr. Lectr.
Anderton, G. E. Sr. Lectr.
Bannister, W. D. Sr. Lectr.
Clements, M. Sr. Lectr.
Cole, D. Sr. Lectr.
Cole, M. Sr. Lectr.
D'Silva, C. Sr. Lectr.
Dolphin, G. P. Sr. Lectr.
Duffield, J. R. Principal Lectr.
Edge, M. Sr. Lectr.
Harrison, D. Sr. Lectr.
Hopkinson, A. Sr. Lectr.
Horne, S. Sr. Lectr.
Hughes, A. Sr. Lectr.
Kelly, D. G. Sr. Lectr.
Leach, J., MSc PhD Prof.; Head*
Mclean, Megan M. Sr. Lectr.
McMahon, A. W. Sr. Lectr.
Monk, P. M. Sr. Lectr.
Murphy, B. P. Sr. Lectr.
Nicholas, G. A. Sr. Lectr.
Porgess, P. V. Sr. Lectr.
Shaw, J. B. Sr. Lectr.
Taylor, H. Sr. Lectr.
Wilkinson, A. N. Sr. Lectr.
Williams, K. Principal Lectr.
Williamson, K. Principal Lectr.

Clothing Design and Technology, see also
Textiles/Fashion

Tel: (0161) 247 2645 Fax: (0161) 247 6329

Ball, Christina S. Sr. Lectr.
Bond, T. D. Sr. Lectr.
Cadman, Barbara A. Sr. Lectr.
Davies, J. H. Principal Lectr.
Fairclough, Dorothy Sr. Lectr.
Fairhurst, Catherine L. Sr. Lectr.
Harrow, Christine Sr. Lectr.
Hughes, C. J. Sr. Lectr.
Jeffrey, M. Sr. Lectr.
Jones, Jacqueline L. Sr. Lectr.
Jones, R. M. Principal Lectr.
Lea Greenwood, Jacquetta G. Sr. Lectr.
McAdam, Anita L. Sr. Lectr.
Mee, Christine Sr. Lectr.
Norman, Debra L. Sr. Lectr.
Payne, Veronica E. Sr. Lectr.
Peers, Angela C. Sr. Lectr.
Robinson, Kathleen Sr. Lectr.
Rowe, Helen D. Sr. Lectr.
Sinclair, D. S., MSc Head*
Tate, Muriel A. Sr. Lectr.
Turner, J. P. Principal Lectr.
Twine, C. Sr. Lectr.
Tyler, D. J. Sr. Lectr.
Vowles, Karen L. Sr. Lectr.
Wallace, Thomasina D. Sr. Lectr.

Combined Studies Scheme
Tel: (0161) 247 1460 Fax: (0161) 247 6336

Barnett, A. Sr. Lectr.
Brough, B. J. Principal Lectr.
Hubert, E. G. Head*
Ryan, J. Sr. Lectr.
Williamson, R. Sr. Lectr.

Communication Media
Tel: (0161) 247 1284 Fax: (0161) 247 6805

Alexander, D. J. Sr. Lectr.
Blatchford, P. R. Sr. Lectr.
Clements, A. F. Sr. Lectr.
Cox, S. Sr. Lectr.
Cuthbert, Vanessa J. Sr. Lectr.
Dowling, Niamh C. Principal Lectr.
East, H. Sr. Lectr.
Gorman, M. D. Sr. Lectr.
Grant, N. O. Sr. Lectr.
Green, C. S. Sr. Lectr.
Green, R. L. Sr. Lectr.
Gristwood, E. Sr. Lectr.
Gristwood, Lenore Sr. Lectr.
Hutson, P. E. Sr. Lectr.
Lichtenfels, P. K. Sr. Lectr.

Limon, D. F. Sr. Lectr.
Mills, D. W. Sr. Lectr.
Moritz, C. Sr. Lectr.
Nestor, M. E. Sr. Lectr.
Northey, E. Sr. Lectr.
Robb, W. A. Sr. Lectr.
Scholey, Sharon E. Sr. Lectr.
Sherfield, J. Sr. Lectr.
Spencer, B. R. Sr. Lectr.
Taylor, M. J. Sr. Lectr.
Tebbit, J. Sr. Lectr.
Wood, Amanda Head*

Community Studies, see Appl. Community
Studies

Computing and Mathematics
Tel: (0161) 247 1500 Fax: (0161) 247 6337

Ananiadou, Sophia Sr. Lectr.
Bandar, Z. Sr. Lectr.
Boyle, T. H. Principal Lectr.
Brindle, G. J. Sr. Lectr.
Fisher, M. D. Principal Lectr.
Gray, J. R. Sr. Lectr.
Hancox, M. P. Principal Lectr.
Heathfield, Heather A. Sr. Lectr.
Hicks, Helen C. Sr. Lectr.
Hoad, J. E. Sr. Lectr.
Hurt, J. Sr. Lectr.
Ingham, D. M. Sr. Lectr.
Lynch, S. Sr. Lectr.
Marsden, P. J. Sr. Lectr.
Miller, R. K. Sr. Lectr.
Mingham, C. G. Sr. Lectr.
Moore, Karen J. Sr. Lectr.
Oakey, S., BSc Head*
Petrounias, I. Sr. Lectr.
Quick, Pamela Sr. Lectr.
Quigley, P. Sr. Lectr.
Rolland, F. D. Sr. Lectr.
Ryan, J. D. Sr. Lectr.
Saberton, R. Sr. Lectr.
Scallan, Anthony J. Sr. Lectr.
Shea, B. L. Sr. Lectr.
Slack, R. S. Sr. Lectr.
Strom, J. H. Sr. Lectr.
Thorpe, J. C. Sr. Lectr.
Toro, J. C. Prof.
Tyrrell, A. J. Principal Lectr.
Wagenblast, L. Sr. Lectr.
Wendl, B. A. Sr. Lectr.
Whiteley, D. Sr. Lectr.
Williamson, R. J. Sr. Lectr.
Wiseman, A. N. Sr. Lectr.

Consumer Technology, see Food and
Consumer Technol.

Design, see Arts, Des. and Performance

Economics
Tel: (0161) 247 3892 Fax: (0161) 247 6302

Askew, R. P. Sr. Lectr.
Carline, D. W. Sr. Lectr.
Dearden, S. J. Sr. Lectr.
Evans, Susan T. Sr. Lectr.
Gibbard, K. M. Sr. Lectr.
Hurst, P. Sr. Lectr.
Kemp, J. R. Sr. Lectr.
Khan, J. Sr. Lectr.
Leslie, D. Res. Prof.
Milner, A. E. Principal Lectr.
Ndhlovu, T. P. Sr. Lectr.
Steedman, Ian Res. Prof.
Thomas, R. L. Principal Lectr.
Tinsdale, K. P. Sr. Lectr.
Tomkins, Judith M. Sr. Lectr.
Triantafillou, P. Sr. Lectr.
Vint, John Head*
Zang, W. Sr. Lectr.
Zis, G. Res. Prof.

Education, see also Arts and Humanities
Educn., and Scis. Educn.

Tel: (0161) 247 5057 Fax: (0161) 247 6370

Anthony, Sheila A. Sr. Lectr.
Artess, J. K. Sr. Lectr.
Bailey, S. S. C. Sr. Lectr.

Barnes, Elaine M. Principal Lectr.
Boardman, S. Sr. Lectr.
Bowen, P. Sr. Lectr.
Burton, Diana M. Principal Lectr.
Cooper, W. J. Sr. Lectr.
Cubillo, L. Sr. Lectr.
Devlin, A. Sr. Lectr.
Devlin, L. M. Sr. Lectr.
Ellis, S. W. Sr. Lectr.
Fabian, Hilary Sr. Lectr.
Forrester, R. Sr. Lectr.
Foster, P. Sr. Lectr.
Goggin, P. F. J. Sr. Lectr.
Haldane, M. J. Sr. Lectr.
Harrison, G. O. Sr. Lectr.
Haworth, Avril Sr. Lectr.
Hitchman, A. M. Sr. Lectr.
Hodkinson, P. Prof.
Hollis, M. J. Sr. Lectr.
Jordan, P. D. Sr. Lectr.
Keating, Iris Sr. Lectr.
Kelly, B. Sr. Lectr.
Keogh, Brenda Sr. Lectr.
Lancaster, L. G. Sr. Lectr.
Leigh, Elisabeth L. Sr. Lectr.
Lewis, S. E. Sr. Lectr.
Mattinson, K. G. Sr. Lectr.
Mavers, D. E. Sr. Lectr.
Mills, B. A. Sr. Lectr.
Mindham, Carol E. Sr. Lectr.
Moorcroft, R. Sr. Lectr.
Redfern, A. R. Sr. Lectr.
Roberts, Ivy M. Sr. Lectr.
Roberts, J. Sr. Lectr.
Robertson, Christine D. Principal Lectr.
Robinson, J. F. Principal Lectr.
Robinson, R. S. Sr. Lectr.
Ryan, J. T. Sr. Lectr.
Sayers, S. Sr. Lectr.
Selby, D. B. Sr. Lectr.
Shenton, Lesley L. Sr. Lectr.
Smith, Kim E. Sr. Lectr.
Smith, Pauline V. Principal Lectr.
Smith, W. N. Sr. Lectr.
Spink, E. Sr. Lectr.
Sugarman, I. Sr. Lectr.
Welch, J. Sr. Lectr.
Wood, D. Sr. Lectr.
Woodrow, D., BSc PhD Prof.; Head*

Educational Studies
Tel: (0161) 247 2052

Ackers, Janet D. Sr. Lectr.
Cordwell, N. J. Sr. Lectr.
Goodwin, J. Sr. Lectr.
Griffin, B. M. Sr. Lectr.
Hadrill, Romla V. Sr. Lectr.
Hall, N. Sr. Lectr.
Harnor, M. J. Sr. Lectr.
Heron, R. Sr. Lectr.
Johnson, M. Sr. Lectr.
Kelly, M. J. Sr. Lectr.
Leigh-Baker, P. Sr. Lectr.
Loftus, E. Sr. Lectr.
Mallik, Kank Sr. Lectr.
Marsh, C. Sr. Lectr.
Moylett, H. R. Sr. Lectr.
Mulligan, A. Sr. Lectr.
Naftalin, I. H. Sr. Lectr.
Phillips, Sylvia M. Principal Lectr.
Pickard, A. J. Principal Lectr.
Rigby, K. Sr. Lectr.
Roberts, P. Sr. Lectr.
Robertson, J. Sr. Lectr.
Robinson, Anne Sr. Lectr.
Rodger, R. Sr. Lectr.

Engineering, Electrical and Electronic
Tel: (0161) 247 1632 Fax: (0161) 247 1633

Ainscough, J. Principal Lectr.
Al-raweshidy, H. Sr. Lectr.
Allwork, J. B. Sr. Lectr.
Anani, Nader Sr. Lectr.
Cusworth, S. Sr. Lectr.
Deloughry, R. J. Sr. Lectr.
Green, H. Sr. Lectr.
Halliwell, B. Sr. Lectr.
Hartley, T. Sr. Lectr.

Hewitt, D.   Sr. Lectr.
Nixon, S. A.   Sr. Lectr.
Ponnapalli, P. V. S.   Sr. Lectr.
Ross, Fiona A.   Sr. Lectr.
Ross, J. S.   Sr. Lectr.
Samosa, M. D.   Sr. Lectr.
Senior, J. M., MSc   Prof.; Head*
South, G. E.   Principal Lectr.
Steele, A. L.   Sr. Lectr.
Swift, F. J.   Principal Lectr.
Thompson, C. M.   Sr. Lectr.
Thomson, M.   Principal Lectr.
Vosper, J. V.   Sr. Lectr.
Watson, R.   Sr. Lectr.
Wormald, P.   Sr. Lectr.

Engineering, Mechanical, Design and Manufacture

Tel: (0161) 247 6255 Fax: (0161) 247 6326
Austin, N. M.   Sr. Lectr.
Barker, S. J.   Sr. Lectr.
Briggs, D.   Sr. Lectr.
Brookes, D. S.   Sr. Lectr.
Golten, J. W.   Principal Lectr.
Iwnicki, S. D.   Sr. Lectr.
Lo, Hong R.   Sr. Lectr.
Mather, J., BSc PhD   Prof.; Head*
McCann, W. J.   Sr. Lectr.
Parkinson, H. J.   Sr. Lectr.
Read, A. G.   Sr. Lectr.
Saul, G.   Sr. Lectr.
Simon, M.   Sr. Lectr.
Slaouti, A.   Sr. Lectr.
Soufian, M.   Sr. Lectr.
Verwer, A. A.   Principal Lectr.
Ward, A. J.   Sr. Lectr.

English

Beer, J.   Head*
Beetham, Margaret R.   Sr. Lectr.
Birch, Eva   Sr. Lectr.
Easthope, A. K.   Prof.
Harker, D. I.   Sr. Lectr.
Louvre, A.   Sr. Lectr.
McGowan, K. A.   Sr. Lectr.
Olive, D. C.   Sr. Lectr.
Roy, J.   Sr. Lectr.
Wainwright, J. P.   Sr. Lectr.
Walsh, T. J.   Principal Lectr.

Environmental and Geographical Sciences, see also Sports and Environmental Sci.

Tel: (0161) 247 1600 Fax: (0161) 247 6318
Allman, W. R.   Sr. Lectr.
Appleyard, J. H.   Sr. Lectr.
Cornelius, Sarah C.   Sr. Lectr.
Dalton, S. A., JP, MSc PhD   Prof.; Head*
Dobson, M. K.   Sr. Lectr.
Dunleavy, P. J.   Principal Lectr.
Gibson, Christine S.   Sr. Lectr.
Hardman, D. B.   Principal Lectr.
Heywood, D. I.   Sr. Lectr.
Lambrick, D. B.   Sr. Lectr.
Paget, G. E.   Sr. Lectr.
Ratcliffe, G.   Principal Lectr.
Watson, A. F. R.   Sr. Lectr.
Wheater, C. P.   Principal Lectr.
Young, C.   Sr. Lectr.

Fashion, see Textiles/Fashion, and Clothing Des. and Technol.

Finance, see Acctg. and Finance

Fine Art

Tel: (0161) 247 1901 Fax: (0161) 247 6347
Billany, K. D.   Head of Sch.
Brown, J. K.   Principal Lectr.
Chantrey, M.   Sr. Lectr.
Crabtree, T.   Sr. Lectr.
Dolphin, T. F.   Sr. Lectr.
Eve, A.   Sr. Lectr.
Fleming, C. N.   Sr. Lectr.
Hall, Sharon J.   Sr. Lectr.
Hyatt, J., BA   Head*
Johnson, B.   Sr. Lectr.
Jones, C. J.   Sr. Lectr.

Kirby, P. C.   Sr. Lectr.
Morley, B. M.   Principal Lectr.
Oliver, Mary L.   Sr. Lectr.
Orobiej, W. M.   Sr. Lectr.
Peake, F.   Sr. Lectr.
Pearson, D. S.   Sr. Lectr.
Ratcliffe, A.   Sr. Lectr.
Smith, D.   Sr. Lectr.
Sweet, D. F.   Principal Lectr.

Food and Consumer Technology

Tel: (0161) 247 2682 Fax: (0161) 247 6331
Ainsworth, P. A.   Principal Lectr.
Barron, J. B.   Sr. Lectr.
Bayliss, P. A.   Sr. Lectr.
Burnett, S.   Sr. Lectr.
Carton, Janet   Sr. Lectr.
Densem, Barbara J.   Sr. Lectr.
Farmer, N. C.   Principal Lectr.; Acting Head*
Fuller, D. B.   Sr. Lectr.
Glover, A. D.   Sr. Lectr.
Gomes, F. H.   Sr. Lectr.
Hall, A. Haulwen, BSc PhD   Prof.; Head*
Hayes, G.   Sr. Lectr.
Holgate, D. J.   Sr. Lectr.
Peel, R. J.   Sr. Lectr.
Ramsden, R.   Sr. Lectr.
Roberts, D. G.   Principal Lectr.
Shelton, D. R.   Sr. Lectr.
Simms, I. D.   Principal Lectr.
Smith, C.   Sr. Lectr.

Geography, see Environmental and Geog. Scis.

Health Care Studies

Tel: (0161) 247 2524 Fax: (0161) 247 6328
Canham, J. C.   Sr. Lectr.
Carter, Mary B.   Sr. Lectr.
Deacon, M.   Sr. Lectr.
Fairhurst, E.   Sr. Lectr.
Garvey, J. P.   Sr. Lectr.
Groves, Margaret E.   Sr. Lectr.
Hoare, T.   Sr. Lectr.
Humphries, Jennifer L.   Sr. Lectr.
King, M.   Sr. Lectr.
Lord, J. W.   Principal Lectr.
Moore, Susan   Sr. Lectr.
Sbaih, L. C.   Sr. Lectr.
Skidmore, D.   Acting Head*
Street, C.   Sr. Lectr.
Warne, A.   Sr. Lectr.
Wibberley, C.   Principal Lectr.

History and Economic History

Tel: (0161) 247 1732
Adams, A. J.   Sr. Lectr.
Aldcroft, D. H.   Res. Prof.
Ayres, P.   Sr. Lectr.
Barlow, Dorothy W.   Sr. Lectr.
Danks, Catherine J.   Sr. Lectr.
Davies, S. J.   Sr. Lectr.
Fowler, A.   Principal Lectr.
Hassan, J. A.   Sr. Lectr.
Hunt, K.   Sr. Lectr.
Kidd, A. J.   Sr. Lectr.
Kirk, N.   Prof.
Ling, Lesley A.   Sr. Lectr.
Lloyd, P.   Sr. Lectr.
Mason, J. J.   Sr. Lectr.
Moore, R.   Sr. Lectr.
Mosley, J. V.   Principal Lectr.
Nicholls, D.   Head*
Turner, B. C.   Sr. Lectr.
Wilson, E. R.   Sr. Lectr.
Wyke, T. J.   Sr. Lectr.

History of Art and Design

Tel: (0161) 247 1931
Aulich, J.   Sr. Lectr.
Barber, F. C.   Sr. Lectr.
Christie, C. J.   Sr. Lectr.
Coatsworth, Elizabeth   Sr. Lectr.
Donald, Diana, BA   Prof.; Head*
Hamilton, R. A.   Sr. Lectr.
Hewitt, J. H.   Principal Lectr.
Howard, M. J.   Sr. Lectr.
Huxley, D. W.   Sr. Lectr.

Parkinson-Bailey, J. J.   Sr. Lectr.
Sharp, Mary E.   Sr. Lectr.
Taylor, J. S.   Sr. Lectr.
Tilston, R. P.   Sr. Lectr.
Young, D. W.   Sr. Lectr.

Hotel Catering and Tourism Management

Tel: (0161) 247 2721 Fax: (0161) 247 6334
Abbott, P. R.   Principal Lectr.
Adams, F. A.   Sr. Lectr.
Askew, K.   Sr. Lectr.
Beckett, J. E.   Principal Lectr.
Briggs, D. J.   Sr. Lectr.
Brown, S. H.   Principal Lectr.
Callan, R. J.   Principal Lectr.
Cook, K. P.   Sr. Lectr.
Ellis, W. A.   Sr. Lectr.
Feeny, Catherine   Sr. Lectr.
Fenby, J.   Sr. Lectr.
Gilpin, Suzanne C.   Sr. Lectr.
Hall, P. W.   Sr. Lectr.
Harris, A. D.   Principal Lectr.
Hill, D. J.   Sr. Lectr.
Hill, Elizabeth   Sr. Lectr.
Hobson, J. R.   Sr. Lectr.
Hughes, H. L.   Principal Lectr.
Ineson, Elizabeth M.   Sr. Lectr.
Johnson, P. A.   Sr. Lectr.
Lewry, Mary S.   Sr. Lectr.
Lowe, M.   Sr. Lectr.
Lucas, Rosemary E.   Sr. Lectr.
McDowall, F. W.   Sr. Lectr.
McKinlay, Joanne   Sr. Lectr.
Mock, Janet M.   Sr. Lectr.
Nevett, W., BSc BA MEd   Head*
Palin, M. G.   Sr. Lectr.
Parkin, N. E.   Sr. Lectr.
Ralston, Rita B.   Sr. Lectr.
Scallan, Heather M.   Sr. Lectr.
Stone, G. J.   Principal Lectr.
Theodore, J. A.   Sr. Lectr.
Thomas, A. S.   Sr. Lectr.
Warren, T.   Sr. Lectr.
Wong, J. H.   Sr. Lectr.
Wynne, Jennifer L.   Sr. Lectr.

Humanities and Applied Social Studies

Tel: (0161) 247 5571 Fax: (0161) 247 6374
Anderson, J. A. H.   Sr. Lectr.
Beavan, G. N. D.   Sr. Lectr.
Bolland, W. J.   Sr. Lectr.
Bottomley, M. A.   Sr. Lectr.
Churchill, H. L.   Sr. Lectr.
Cuthbert, Katherine   Sr. Lectr.
D'Cruze, Shani   Sr. Lectr.
Doughty, P. F.   Principal Lectr.
Fair, A.   Sr. Lectr.
Hamilton, Cynthia A.   Sr. Lectr.
Heathcote, Gaye M., BA PhD   Head*
Issitt, Mary A.   Sr. Lectr.
Morris, Mary   Sr. Lectr.
Parsons, K.   Sr. Lectr.
Singleton, M. H.   Principal Lectr.
Webster, D. C. H.   Principal Lectr.
West-Burnham, Jocelyn M.   Sr. Lectr.

Information and Communications

Tel: (0161) 247 6144 Fax: (0161) 247 6351
Burke, Maria   Sr. Lectr.
Cawood, J.   Principal Lectr.
Farrow, J. F.   Sr. Lectr.
Geekie, G.   Sr. Lectr.
Hartley, Dick J.   Head*
Johnson, F. C.   Sr. Lectr.
Kendall, Margaret   Sr. Lectr.
Lambert, J. S.   Sr. Lectr.
Lea, P. W.   Sr. Lectr.
Lett, Brenda M.   Sr. Lectr.
Lund, K.   Sr. Lectr.
Meakin, B.   Sr. Lectr.
Stephen, P.   Sr. Lectr.
Willson, J. P.   Sr. Lectr.

Information Technology, see Bus.
Information Technol.

International Business Unit

Tel: (0161) 247 3709 Fax: (0161) 247 6313

Jeremy, D. J. Principal Lectr.
Kuznetson, A. Sr. Lectr.
McDonald, F. E. Head*
Took, L. J. Sr. Lectr.
Tuselmann, H. J. Sr. Lectr.

Landscape, see Archit., Landscape and Three
Dimensional Des.

Languages

Tel: (0161) 247 3945 Fax: (0161) 247 6323

Belkacemi, C. Sr. Lectr.
Cairns, W. J. Sr. Lectr.
Corkill, D. Reader
Crompton, P. M. Sr. Lectr.
Fieldhouse, Liliane S. Sr. Lectr.
Hand, D. Sr. Lectr.
Handley, Sharon Sr. Lectr.
Herhoffer, B. L. Principal Lectr.
Jeutter, R. Sr. Lectr.
Johnson, R. J. Sr. Lectr.
Jones, C. Sr. Lectr.
Morey, P. G., MA Prof.; Head*
Samely, U. Sr. Lectr.
Sheppard, G. A. Sr. Lectr.
Smythe, E. Reader

Law

Tel: (0161) 247 3049 Fax: (0161) 247 6309

Brinkworth, K. J. Principal Lectr.
Broadbent, Lorraine Sr. Lectr.
Broadbent, P. J. Sr. Lectr.
Carroll, A. J. Sr. Lectr.
Deehan, Siobhan M. Sr. Lectr.
Delany, Linda M. Sr. Lectr.
Doyle, Kathleen M. Sr. Lectr.
Fairhurst, Joy M. Sr. Lectr.
Farrell, R. Sr. Lectr.
Gibb, T. A. Sr. Lectr.
Gill, M. Sr. Lectr.
Gorman, H. Sr. Lectr.
Grout, T. J. Sr. Lectr.
Higgins, Catherine A. Sr. Lectr.
Horton, B. Sr. Lectr.
Hoyle, C. Sr. Lectr.
Hughes, Diane B. Sr. Lectr.
Jones, I. J. Sr. Lectr.
Jones, Lynda A. Sr. Lectr.
Kay, D. V. Sr. Lectr.
Kemble, M. J. Sr. Lectr.
Leighton, P. E. Prof.; Head*
Links, A. C. Sr. Lectr.
Lipkin, H. Sr. Lectr.
Little, C. Sr. Lectr.
Lunn, J. Sr. Lectr.
Makepeace, R. W. Principal Lectr.
Maynard, Fiona Sr. Lectr.
McKeon, R. C. Sr. Lectr.
Okojie, P. D. Sr. Lectr.
Rayburn, P. A. Principal Lectr.
Redhead, S. C. Prof.
Singleton, R. J. Sr. Lectr.
Vickers, Susan E. Sr. Lectr.
Walker, D. I. Sr. Lectr.
Whittle, S. T. Sr. Lectr.

Management, see also Business and
Management Studies, and Hotel Catering and
Tourism Management

Tel: (0161) 247 3959 Fax: (0161) 247 6304

Clark, B. Sr. Lectr.
Copping, P. S. Principal Lectr.
Corby, Susan R. Sr. Lectr.
Elliott, Margaret Sr. Lectr.
Hawley, R. S. Sr. Lectr.
Herald, S. R. Sr. Lectr.
Homan, G. Sr. Lectr.
Horsburgh, S. Sr. Lectr.
Jump, P. Sr. Lectr.
Mathieson, A. H. Sr. Lectr.
McGoldrick, Ann E. Sr. Lectr.
Nicholls, Patricia L. Sr. Lectr.

Orgee, L. Sr. Lectr.
Palowski, H. T. Sr. Lectr.
Thorpe, R. Principal Lectr.
Wales, J. D. Sr. Lectr.

Manufacture, see Engin., Mech., Des. and
Manufacture

Marketing, see Retailing and Marketing

Mathematics, see Computing and Maths.

Media, see Communicn. Media

Performance, see Arts, Des. and
Performance

Politics and Philosophy

Archer, T. A. Res. Prof.
Barberis, J. P. Sr. Lectr.
Bell, M. Prof.; Head*
Bennett, R. J. Sr. Lectr.
Carr, F. T. Sr. Lectr.
Chilton, Patricia A. Sr. Lectr.
Garfield, M. J. Principal Lectr.
Gibbons, J. P. Sr. Lectr.
Hodge, Joanna Sr. Lectr.
Joyce, N. P. Sr. Lectr.
Lee, D. Sr. Lectr.
May, T. C. Principal Lectr.
McHugh, J. Principal Lectr.
Nugent, N. Prof.
Townshend, J. Sr. Lectr.
Tyldesley, M. G. Sr. Lectr.

Psychology and Speech Pathology

Tel: (0161) 247 2555

Banister, P. A., BA PhD Head*
Bell, A. J. Sr. Lectr.
Burman, Erica Sr. Lectr.
Cavill, J. Sr. Lectr.
Clokie, Anita Sr. Lectr.
Foster, J. J. Principal Lectr.
French, Ann Sr. Lectr.
Godwin, Rowena A. Sr. Lectr.
Goldbart, Juliet L. Sr. Lectr.
Grogan, Sarah C. Sr. Lectr.
Holmes, D. A. Sr. Lectr.
Kagan, Carolyn M. Principal Lectr.
Klee, Hilary A. Prof.
Knowles, K. B. Sr. Lectr.
Lawthom, R. Sr. Lectr.
Lewis, Suzan N. Sr. Lectr.
Moore, Michele P. Sr. Lectr.
Munley, G. A. Sr. Lectr.
Murray, J. Sr. Lectr.
Robertson, Sandra J. Principal Lectr.
Rout, U. Sr. Lectr.
Rowley, K. Sr. Lectr.
Sixsmith, J. Sr. Lectr.
Stirling, J. D. Sr. Lectr.
Taylor, Maye Sr. Lectr.
Tindall, Carol M. Sr. Lectr.
Wilkie, D. T. Principal Lectr.
Wright, Victoria L. P. Sr. Lectr.

Recreational Services

Watson, F. J. Sr. Lectr.

Retailing and Marketing

Tel: (0161) 247 3981 Fax: (0161) 247 6305

Alexander, A. F. Sr. Lectr.
Baron, J. S. Principal Lectr.
Bennison, D. J. Sr. Lectr.
Betts, P. B. Sr. Lectr.
Cassidy, K. J. Sr. Lectr.
Gardner, Hanne T. Sr. Lectr.
Holman, S. J. Sr. Lectr.
Huntington, Susan M. Sr. Lectr.
Jones, K. Sr. Lectr.
Leaver, D. Sr. Lectr.
Pal, J. W. Sr. Lectr.
Pedley, M. C. Sr. Lectr.
Schmidt, Ruth A. Principal Lectr.
Vignali, C. Sr. Lectr.
Warnaby, G. C. Sr. Lectr.
Whitehead, Maureen B. Sr. Lectr.
Wright, H. E. Sr. Lectr.

Sciences Education

Tel: (0161) 247 2289 Fax: (0161) 247 6801

Andrews, P. R. Sr. Lectr.
Binns, B. Sr. Lectr.
Brown, A. M. Principal Lectr.
Cleall-Hill, M. J. Sr. Lectr.
Cockett, Patricia M. Principal Lectr.
Craig, Barbara Sr. Lectr.
Eade, F. Sr. Lectr.
Eastwood, Margaret Sr. Lectr.
Ensor, Karen A. Sr. Lectr.
Fasciato, Melanie Sr. Lectr.
Gibson, F. Sr. Lectr.
Goodwin, A. J., BSc MPhil, FRSChem Head*
Green, Janet Sr. Lectr.
Hanley, Una M. Sr. Lectr.
Hatch, Gillian M. Principal Lectr.
Heywood, D. S. Sr. Lectr.
McPeake, J. C. Sr. Lectr.
Naylor, S. Principal Lectr.
Palmerone, Wendy A. Sr. Lectr.
Parker, J. Sr. Lectr.
Peckett, Janet A. Principal Lectr.
Price, J. M. Sr. Lectr.
Rowlands, M. A. Sr. Lectr.
Savin, J. R. Principal Lectr.
Wilson, E. D. Sr. Lectr.
Wood, D. J. Sr. Lectr.

Social Studies, see Humanities and Appl.
Soc. Studies

Sociology

Tel: (0161) 247 3021 Fax: (0161) 247 6321

Allsop, G. A. Sr. Lectr.
Barker, C. G. Sr. Lectr.
Bennett, D. J. Sr. Lectr.
Berry, I. J. Sr. Lectr.
Clarke, J. Principal Lectr.
Dant, T. C. Sr. Lectr.
Francis, D. W. Sr. Lectr.
Hawkes, Gail Sr. Lectr.
Hepworth, Frances A. Sr. Lectr.
Hodgkinson, D. L. Sr. Lectr.
Jacobs, Susie M. Sr. Lectr.
Johnson, W. Sr. Lectr.
Kennedy, P. T. Sr. Lectr.
Leach, B. T., BA(Econ) MSc Head*
Marr, E. A. Sr. Lectr.
Mole, P. J. Sr. Lectr.
Phillips, Dianne Sr. Lectr.
Powell, Carolyn A. Sr. Lectr.
Randall, D. Sr. Lectr.
Ryan, Jennifer M. Sr. Lectr.
Stott, D. J. Sr. Lectr.
Taylor, J. M. D. Sr. Lectr.
Turvey, Peta M. Sr. Lectr.
Walklate, S. Prof.
Wowk, Maria T. Sr. Lectr.
Wright, Rachel M. Sr. Lectr.
Wynne, D. F. Sr. Lectr.

Speech Pathology, see Psychol. and Speech
Pathol.

Sports and Environmental Science

Environmental and Leisure Studies

Tel: (0161) 247 5251 Fax: (0161) 247 6372

Bates, J. E. Sr. Lectr.
Caporn, S. J. M. Sr. Lectr.
Cresswell, N. Sr. Lectr.
Dare, D. J. Sr. Lectr.
Eastwood, I. W. Head*
Gee, Kathleen Sr. Lectr.
Heath, B. A. Sr. Lectr.
Lageard, J. G. A. Sr. Lectr.
Lilly, T. Sr. Lectr.
Lofkin, M. Sr. Lectr.
Morrison, A. A. Principal Lectr.
Peart, J. R. Sr. Lectr.
Taylor, W. Sr. Lectr.

Exercise and Sport Science

Tel: (0161) 247 5472 Fax: (0161) 247 6375

Ball, D. Sr. Lectr.
Baltzopoulos, V. Reader
Bartlett, R. M. Prof.; Dir.of Res.

Bell, T. C.   Sr. Lectr.
Bradbeer, P. A.   Principal Lectr.
Burwitz, L.   Prof.; Head*
Chadwick, D. L.   Sr. Lectr.
Collins, D. J.   Reader
Davids, K. W.   Reader
Day, D.   Sr. Lectr.
Dimond, D. H.   Sr. Lectr.
Dulla, J. R.   Sr. Lectr.
Fernogolio, R. A.   Sr. Lectr.
Fowler, N. E.   Sr. Lectr.
George, K. P.   Sr. Lectr.
Gorman, J. K.   Sr. Lectr.
Herrington, L.   Sr. Lectr.
Holmes, P.   Sr. Lectr.
Jess, M. C.   Sr. Lectr.
Jones, A. M.   Sr. Lectr.
Jones, S.   Sr. Lectr.
Laycock, D. C.   Sr. Lectr.
Lee, P. H.   Principal Lectr.
McGuire, B. H.   Sr. Lectr.
Moore, P.   Sr. Lectr.
Mullan, N. F.   Sr. Lectr.
Payton, C.   Sr. Lectr.
Richards, H. D.   Sr. Lectr.
Roach, N. K.   Sr. Lectr.
Sargeant, A. J.   Prof.
Slattery, M.   Sr. Lectr.
Smith, N. C.   Principal Lectr.
Williams, P. J.   Sr. Lectr.
Williams, S.   Sr. Lectr.

Textiles/Fashion, see also Clothing Des. and Technol.

Tel: (0161) 247 3525 Fax: (0161) 247 6341

Barlow, Delma   Sr. Lectr.
Bezzant, J.   Sr. Lectr.
Callaghan, Judy   Sr. Lectr.
Canning-Smith, Hazel E.   Principal Lectr.
Coughlin, Vivienne H.   Sr. Lectr.
Hargreaves, Janet B.   Sr. Lectr.
Holmes, A. M.   Sr. Lectr.
Holtom, Teresa   Sr. Lectr.

McKeating, J. E.   Sr. Lectr.
Parkinson-Bailey, Susan M.   Principal Lectr.
Setterington, L.   Sr. Lectr.
Shaw, Ann M.   Sr. Lectr.
Squires, Therese M.   Principal Lectr.
Wayman, Maureen   Head*
Welsh, Alison   Sr. Lectr.
Worth, S. G.   Sr. Lectr.
Wright, Isabel M.   Sr. Lectr.

Three Dimensional Design, see Archit., Landscape and Three Dimensional Des.

Tourism, see Hotel Catering and Tourism Management

Other Appointments

Faculty Appointments

Mawdsley, H. P.   Principal Lectr.

SPECIAL CENTRES, ETC

Centre for Policy Modelling

Moss, S.   Head*

Modular Office

Tel: (0161) 247 5310

Jordan, J.   Principal Lectr.
Piper, J. S.   Head*
Price, B. E.   Sr. Lectr.
Purchase, I. C.   Principal Lectr.

CONTACT OFFICERS

Academic affairs. Academic Registrar: Karczewski-Slowikowski, J. D. M., BEd Manc., MSc CNAA
Accommodation. Head of Student Services: Aynsley Smith, S.
Careers. Head of Student Services: Aynsley Smith, S.

Computing services. Head of Information Systems: Niman, J. N.
Consultancy services. Head of Research: Roberts, I.
Development/fund-raising. Head of Research: Roberts, I.
Estates and buildings/works and services. Head of Buildings and Estates: Jones, E.
Finance. Financial Director: Grant, L., MBA
General enquiries. University Secretary and Clerk to the Board of Governors: Hendley, T., LLB, FCIS
Library (chief librarian). Librarian: Harris, Prof. C. G. S., BA BPhil MA MLS PhD, FLA, FIInfSc
Minorities/disadvantaged groups. Principal Lectr.: Avari, B.
Minorities/disadvantaged groups. Head of Research: Roberts, I.
Personnel/human resources. Personnel Director: Hallam, I. W., BA Manc., MA Nott., MSc Salf.
Quality assurance and accreditation. Head of Academic Standards: Turner, R.
Research. Head of Research: Roberts, I.
Safety. Health and Safety Advisor: Gibb, A.
Schools liaison. External Liaison Co-ordinator: Baker, G.
Sport and recreation. Head of Student Services: Aynsley Smith, S.
Staff development and training. Development and Training Manager: Simpson, B. N.
Student welfare/counselling. Head of Student Services: Aynsley Smith, S.
Students from other countries. Head of Student Services: Aynsley Smith, S.
Students with disabilities. Head of Student Services: Aynsley Smith, S.

[Information supplied by the institution as at February 1998, and edited by the ACU]

MIDDLESEX UNIVERSITY

Founded 1973 as Middlesex Polytechnic; university title achieved 1992

Member of the Association of Commonwealth Universities

Postal Address: Bramley Road, Southgate, London, England N14 4YZ
Telephone: (0181) 362 5000 **Fax**: (0181) 449 0798 **E-mail**: admissions@mdx.ac.uk **Telex**: 8954762
WWW: http://www.mdx.ac.uk **E-mail formula**: initial.surname@mdx.ac.uk

CHANCELLOR—Platt of Writtle, The Baroness
CHAIR OF THE BOARD OF GOVERNORS—Partridge, Sir Michael, KCB
VICE-CHANCELLOR*—Driscoll, Prof. Michael, BA
DEPUTY VICE-CHANCELLOR—Goulding, Prof. Ken, BSc PhD Hon. DSc
ASSISTANT VICE-CHANCELLOR AND DIRECTOR OF FINANCE—Horne, Annie
ASSISTANT VICE-CHANCELLOR AND DIRECTOR OF CORPORATE SERVICES—Butland, Terry, BA MA PhD
PRO VICE-CHANCELLOR (STUDENTS)—Hardy, Prof. Dennis, PhD
PRO VICE-CHANCELLOR (RESEARCH)—Penning-Rowsell, Prof. Edmund, BSc MA PhD
PRO VICE-CHANCELLOR (QUALITY AND STANDARDS)—Alderman, Prof. Geoffrey, MA DPhil
PRO VICE-CHANCELLOR (ACADEMIC REGISTRAR AND CLERK TO THE BOARD OF GOVERNORS)‡—Jones, Gareth W., BA Lond., BA Open(UK), MA Lond.

FACULTIES/SCHOOLS

Art, Design and Performing Arts, School of
Dean: Pitts, Prof. Martin*

Business School
Dean: Kirby, Prof. David, BA PhD

Computing Science, School of
Dean: Revell, Prof. Norman, MA

Engineering Systems, School of
Dean: White, Anthony, BSc PhD

Health, Biological and Environmental Sciences, School of
Dean: Hamilton, Prof. Ron, BSc DPhil

Humanities and Cultural Studies, School of
Dean: Parker, Prof. Gabrielle, LèsL MèsL

Lifelong Learning and Education, School of

Dean: Tufnell, Prof. Richard, BSc PhD

Social Science, School of

Dean: Parker, Prof. Dennis, BA PhD

ACADEMIC UNITS

Arranged by Schools

Art, Design and Performing Arts

Curtis, Barry   Dir., Res. and Postgrad. Studies
Guille, Jackie   Prof.; Dir., Curric., Learning and Quality
Kevill, Paul   Dir., Resources and Admin.
Pitts, Martin   Prof.; Dean*

Business School

Ghobadian, Abby   Prof.; Dir., Res. and Postgrad. Studies
Kirby, David, BA PhD   Prof.; Dean*
Morrice, Lynn   Dir., Resources and Admin.
Simpson, Mary   Dir., Curric., Learning and Quality

Computing Science

Murphy, Alan   Dir., Curric., Learning and Quality
Revell, Norman, MA   Prof.; Dean*

Thimbleby, Harold   Prof.; Dir., Res. and Postgrad. Studies
Worrall, Peter   Dir., Resources and Admin.

Engineering Systems

Gill, Raj   Dir., Res. and Postgrad. Studies
Lewis, John   Dir., Curric., Learning and Quality
Malpas, David   Dir., Resources and Admin.
White, Anthony, BSc PhD   Dean*

Health, Biological and Environmental Sciences

Beaumont, Richard   Dir., Curric., Learning and Quality
Frome, David   Dir., Resources and Admin.
Hamilton, Ron, BSc DPhil   Prof.; Dean*
Revitt, Mike   Prof.; Dir., Res. and Postgrad. Studies

Humanities and Cultural Studies

Giles, Steve   Prof.; Dir., Res. and Postgrad. Studies
Hannan, Marie   Dir., Resources and Admin.
Parker, Gabrielle, LèsL MèsL   Prof.; Dean*
Wend, Petra   Dir., Curric., Learning and Quality

Lifelong Learning and Education

Andrews, Richard   Prof.; Dir., Res. and Postgrad. Studies

Bull, Roger   Dir., Curric., Learning and Quality
Bunce, Richard   Dir., Resources and Admin.
Tufnell, Richard, BSc PhD   Prof.; Dean*

Social Science

Annette, John   Prof.; Dir., Curric., Learning and Quality
Bailey, Sue   Dir., Resources and Admin.
MacGregor, Susanne   Prof.; Dir., Res. and Postgrad. Studies
Parker, Dennis, BA PhD   Prof.; Dean*

CONTACT OFFICERS

Admissions (first degree). Read, Jenny
Alumni. Aristidou, Maria
Computing services. Vickers, Paula
International office. Gladstone, Joel
Library (enquiries). Marsterson, William
Public relations, information and marketing (marketing). Ormerod, Joe
Publications. Ormerod, Joe
Purchasing. Parsons, Richard
Quality assurance and accreditation. Pro Vice-Chancellor (Quality and Standards): Alderman, Prof. Geoffrey, MA DPhil
Research. Mayor, Jennifer

[*Information supplied by the institution as at 5 November 1998, and edited by the ACU*]

NAPIER UNIVERSITY

Founded 1992; previously Napier Polytechnic of Edinburgh 1988; originally established as Napier Technical College 1964

Member of the Association of Commonwealth Universities

Postal Address: 219 Colinton Road, Edinburgh, Scotland EH14 1DJ
Telephone: (0131) 444 2266 **Fax**: (0131) 455 4666 **E-mail**: info@napier.ac.uk **WWW**: http://www.napier.ac.uk/
E-mail formula: initial.surname@napier.ac.uk

CHAIRMAN OF THE COURT—Stewart, A. Lindsay, OBE, Hon. FRCSEd, Hon. FRCSI
PRINCIPAL AND VICE-CHANCELLOR*—Mavor, Prof. John, BSc *City(UK)*, PhD *Lond.*, DSc(Eng) *Lond.*, FRSEd, FIEE, FIP, FEng
VICE-PRINCIPAL—Thorne, Prof. Michael, BSc *Lond.*, PhD *Birm.*, FIMA, FBCS
ASSISTANT PRINCIPAL/HEAD OF ACADEMIC DEVELOPMENT—Dickinson, Prof. Keith W., BSc *Sheff.*, MEng *Sheff.*, PhD *Sheff.*
DIRECTOR OF STRATEGIC PLANNING—Webber, Gerry, BA *Wales*, MBA *Open(UK)*, DPhil *Oxf.*
BUSINESS DIRECTOR—Angus, Edward, MBE
ASSISTANT PRINCIPAL/HEAD OF LEARNING RESOURCES—Peattie, Prof. P., BSc *Edin.*
SECRETARY AND ACADEMIC REGISTRAR‡—Miller, I. J., LLB *Edin.*, MA *Aberd.*
CHIEF LIBRARIAN—McElroy, Prof. A. R., MA *Edin.*, MBA *Glas.*, FLA

GENERAL INFORMATION

History. The university was originally established as Napier Technical College in 1964 and merged with Edinburgh College of Commerce in 1974 to become Napier College of Commerce and Technology. It became a polytechnic in 1987 and a university in 1992. It is located in the city of Edinburgh.

Admission to first degree courses (see also United Kingdom Introduction). Through Universities and Colleges Admissions Service (UCAS).

First Degrees. (see also United Kingdom Directory to Subjects of Study). BA, BDes, BEd, BEng, BMus, BSc, BScNurs.

Courses normally last 3 years for an ordinary degree and 4 years for honours.

Some sandwich courses last 6–12 months longer.

Higher Degrees (see also United Kingdom Directory to Subjects of Study). LLM, MA, MBA, MSc, MPhil, PhD, DDes, DEng, DLitt, DSc, DTech.

Libraries. 250,000 volumes; 2500 periodicals subscribed to. Special collections include: Edward Clark (printing from fifteenth century); war poets (Sassoon and Owen).

Fees (1998–99, annual). Undergraduate: £1000 (arts, new students); £750 (arts, continuing students); £1000 (sciences, new and continuing students). Postgraduate: £1350–2610 (arts, UK students); £4500–7300 (arts, international students); £1350 (science and engineering, UK students); £6750 (science and engineering, international students).

Academic Awards (1997–98). Seventeen awards ranging in value from £1000 to £10,000.

Academic Year (1998–99). Two semesters: 5 October–29 January; 8 February–4 June.

Income (1996–97). Total, £55,561,000.

Statistics. Staff: 1409 (577 academic, 832 administrative and other). Students: full-time 8650 (4457 men, 4193 women); part-time 2762 (1352 men, 1410 women); international 1019; total 11,412.

FACULTIES/SCHOOLS

Arts and Social Sciences

Tel: (0131) 455 2216 Fax: (0131) 455 2293
Dean: Bryce, Colin
Secretary: ......

Engineering

Tel: (0131) 455 2401 *Fax:* (0131) 455 2400

Dean: Sibbald, Prof. A., BSc *Edin.*, MSc *H-W*, PhD *Edin.*

Secretary: Jack, I., BA *Edin.*

Health Studies

Tel: (0131) 536 5602 *Fax:* (0131) 536 5624

Dean: Ross, J., MN *Glas.*

Secretary: Cruikshank, J.

Napier Business School

Tel: (0131) 455 3382 *Fax:* (0131) 455 3666

Dean: Worden, J., MA *Dund.*

Secretary: Timpson, J.

Science

Tel: (0131) 455 2525 *Fax:* (0131) 455 2291

Dean: Bryce, Prof. Charles F. A., BSc *Glas.*, PhD *Glas.*, FRSChem, FIBiol

Secretary: Robson, C.

ACADEMIC UNITS

Accounting and Finance

Tel: (0131) 455 3356 *Fax:* (0131) 455 3575

Bate, J. B., MA *Edin.*   Sr. Lectr.

Gardner, P.   Sr. Lectr.

McKay, T., BSc *St And.*   Sr. Lectr.

Sievewright, D. J. A.   Sr. Lectr.

Wright, I. A., MA   Sr. Lectr.

Young, D. O., MA *Aberd.*   Head*

Other Staff: 17 Lectrs.

Vacant Posts: 1 Prof.

Research: accounting for quality; auditing; corporate governance

Biological Sciences

Tel: (0131) 455 2526 *Fax:* (0131) 455 2291

Andrews, C. J. A., MSc *Lough.*   Sr. Lectr.

Beswick, P. H., BSc *Brun.*, PhD *Brun.*   Sr. Lectr.

Christofi, Prof. N., BSc *Dund.*, PhD *Dund.*   Reader

Donaldson, Prof. K., BSc *Stir.*, PhD *Edin.*, DSc *Edin.*, FIBiol   Reader

Guy, K., PhD *CNAA*   Sr. Lectr.

Houghton, C., BSc *Newcastle(UK)*, PhD *Newcastle(UK)*   Head*

Maitland, D. P., BSc *St And.*, PhD *NSW*   Sr. Lectr.

Tett, P., MA *Camb.*, PhD *Glas.*   Reader

Thomson, I., BSc *Glas.*, PhD *Glas.*   Sr. Lectr.

Other Staff: 21 Lectrs.

Research: applied microbiology and biotechnology: bioremediation and biosensor development, exploitation of metabolic diversity of rhodococci; aquatic environmental biology: aquatic environmental biology of organisms/ ecosystems; biomedicine: effect of toxin on the lungs, occupational and environmental air pollution

Building and Surveying

Tel: (0131) 455 2533 *Fax:* (0131) 455 2267

Deakin, I. M.   Sr. Lectr.

Fraser, L. G., BSc *H-W*   Sr. Lectr.

Mackenzie, Prof. R. K., BSc *H-W*, MSc *H-W*, PhD *H-W*   Head*

Sloan, Prof. B., MPhil *Salf.*, FRICS   Sr. Lectr.

Smith, R. M., MSc *H-W*   Sr. Lectr.

Other Staff: 11 Lectrs.; 3 Res. Fellows; 16 Lectrs.†

Vacant Posts: 1 Prof.

Research: air quality and thermal performance; building acoustics and sound insulation; building product design; property and construction IT; property and urban planning

Business Operations Management

Tel: (0131) 455 5004 *Fax:* (0131) 455 5040-1

Fernie, J. M., BSc *Edin.*, PhD *Edin.*   Sr. Lectr.

MacIntosh, H.   Sr. Lectr.

Stobie, D. H., MSc *H-W*

Tan, H.   Sr. Lectr.

Taylor, M., BSc *St And.*, MSc *Birm.*   Sr. Lectr.

Thomas, G., BSc *CNAA*   Sr. Lectr.

Thomson, J. S.   Sr. Lectr.

Tully, L. B., MSc *City(UK)*   Head*

Wilkinson, R.   Sr. Lectr.

Research: global operations; quality of service; supply chain management

Chemical and Physical Sciences, Applied

Tel: (0131) 455 2474 *Fax:* (0131) 455 2290

Allan, D. D. M., BSc *Edin.*, PhD *Edin.*   Sr. Lectr.

Barker, M. B., BSc *Liv.*, MBA *Edin.*, PhD *Brun.*   Reader

Barrow, M. J., BSc *Oxf.*, PhD *Manc.*   Acting Head*

Broadfoot, A. W., BSc *Glas.*   Sr. Lectr.

Hajto, J. P., BSc *Debrecen*, MSc *Debrecen*, PhD *Debrecen*, DSc *Edin.*   Sr. Lectr.

Higinbotham, J., BSc *NSW*, MSc *NSW*, PhD *Tor.*   Sr. Lectr.

McRoberts, A. M. M., BSc *St And.*, PhD *St And.*   Sr. Lectr.

Werninck, A. R., BSc *St And.*, PhD *St And.*   Reader

Other Staff: 13 Lectrs.; 2 Lectrs.†

Research: anti-cancer drugs and model membrane systems for drug delivery; optical device physics: LEDs, biosensors, liquid crystals; simulation of polymer processes; synthesis of optoelectronic materials; thermal analysis of metal complexes

Communication, see Print Media, Publishing and Communicn.

Computer Studies

Tel: (0131) 455 4675 *Fax:* (0131) 455 4552

Barclay, K. A., BSc *H-W*, MSc   Sr. Lectr.

Beddie, Prof. L. A., BSc *Edin.*   Head*

Benyon, Prof. D., BSc *Essex*, MSc *Warw.*, PhD *Open(UK)*   Sr. Lectr.

Crerar, A., BA *Liv.*, MSc *H-W*, PhD *CNAA*   Sr. Lectr.

Fogarty, T., BA *Open(UK)*, PhD *CNAA*   Prof.

Kennedy, J. B., BSc *CNAA*, MPhil *CNAA*   Sr. Lectr.

Kerridge, Prof. J.   Sr. Lectr.

Munoz, J. M., BSc *Santiago(Chile)*, PhD *Stir.*   Sr. Lectr.

Rankin, R. C., BSc *Glas.*   Sr. Lectr.

Research: analysis and design of human computer systems; database and object systems; evolutionary computing

Design

Tel: (0131) 455 2678 *Fax:* (0131) 455 2292

Maden, Leslie, BA *Leic.*   Sr. Lectr.

Rodnes, B.   Sr. Lectr.

Turner, Matthew, PhD *RCA*   Head*

Other Staff: 8 Lectrs.; 8 Lectrs.†

Vacant Posts: 1 Lectr.

Economics

Tel: (0131) 455 3374 *Fax:* (0131) 455 3475

Adams, J., BA *CNAA*, PhD *CNAA*   Sr. Lectr.

Fowdar, N., BA *CNAA*, PhD *CNAA*   Sr. Lectr.

Fyfe, J., BA *Wales*, MBA   Sr. Lectr.

Kerevan, G., MA *Glas.*   Sr. Lectr.

Marek, S. A., MSc *Napier*, FCIS   Sr. Lectr.

McQuaid, R., BA *Lanc.*, MSc *Lond.*, PhD *Harv.*   Sr. Lectr.

Ritchie, M., MA *Edin.*   Sr. Lectr.

Troy, John, BA *Strath.*, MSc *Wales*   Head*

Other Staff: 15 Lectrs.; 6 Lectrs.†

Research: development economics, Mauritius; entrepreneurship and small firms; financial systems in eastern Europe; local labour markets; regional and local economic development

Engineering, Civil and Transportation

Tel: (0131) 455 2477, 455 2274 *Fax:* (0131) 455 2239

Barker, D., BTech *Brad.*, MSc *Salf.*   Reader

Maher, M. J., BA *Camb.*, PhD *Camb.*   Prof.; Head*

McNeil, J. B., BSc *Edin.*   Sr. Lectr.

Pyrah, I., BSc(Eng) *Lond.*, PhD *Lond.*   Prof.

Reid, D. B., BSc *Edin.*, MSc *H-W*   Sr. Lectr.

Wan, C., BSc *Glas.*, MSc   Sr. Lectr.

Other Staff: 13 Lectrs.

Research: fluid dynamics; geotechnics; structures; transport planning/engineering

Engineering, Electrical, Electronic and Computer

Tel: (0131) 455 4361 *Fax:* (0131) 455 4231

Almaini, Prof. A. E.   Sr. Lectr.

Binnie, D., BSc *H-W*, PhD *H-W*   Reader

Buchanan, W., BSc *CNAA*   Sr. Lectr.

Gair, Prof. S., MSc *Strath.*, PhD, FIEE   Sr. Lectr.

Hunt, Prof. I.   Sr. Lectr.

Lidgate, Prof. David, BEng *Liv.*, PhD *Liv.*   Head*

Rae, G. D.   Sr. Lectr.

Sharp, J., MSc *H-W*, FIEE   Reader

South, R. B., BSc *Edin.*, PhD *Edin.*   Sr. Lectr.

Sutherland, D., BSc *CNAA*, MSc *H-W*   Sr. Lectr.

Other Staff: 16 Lectrs.

Vacant Posts: 1 Sr. Lectr.

Research: electric vehicles; electronics manufacturing; signals and instrumentation

Engineering, Mechanical, Manufacturing and Software

Tel: (0131) 455 2461 *Fax:* (0131) 455 2264

Cameron-MacDonald, P., BSc *CNAA*   Sr. Lectr.

Goh, T. N., MSc *Glas.*   Sr. Lectr.

Hay, N. C., BSc *H-W*, PhD *CNAA*   Sr. Lectr.

Kubie, Prof. J., BSc *Lond.*, PhD *Aston*, FIMechE   Head*

Lindsay, T. G., BSc *Strath.*, PhD *Strath.*   Reader

Mannion, M. A. G., BSc *Brun.*, PhD *Brist.*   Sr. Lectr.

McGregor, A. W. K., BSc *Edin.*, MSc *Strath.*   Sr. Lectr.

McLeod, I. C., MPhil *Napier*   Sr. Lectr.

Smith, G. J., BSc *Edin.*   Sr. Lectr.

Other Staff: 22 Lectrs.

Vacant Posts: 1 Lectr.

Research: daylight illuminance modelling; domain architecture and embedded systems; frequency of condensation on windows; life-cycle analysis of double glazed windows; outsourcing and the selection of outsourcers

Film, see Photog., Film and TV

Health Studies, see below

Hospitality and Tourism Management

Tel: (0131) 455 6234 *Fax:* (0131) 455 6269

Allardyce, Myrtle, MBA   Head*

Frew, A. J., PhD *Strath.*   Reader

Shill, P., BSc *Strath.*, MBA   Sr. Lectr.

Other Staff: 10 Lectrs.; 1 Lectr.†

Information Management

Tel: (0131) 455 3337 *Fax:* (0131) 455 3486

Finch, E., BA *Birm.*, BA *Open(UK)*   Sr. Lectr.; CATS Adviser to NUBS (on leave)

Moar, S. A., BA   Sr. Lectr.

Raeburn, S., BSc *Glas.*, BA *Open(UK)*, MBA *Glas.*   Head*

Ritchie, B. D., BSc *Manc.*, MSc *Cran.IT*   Sr. Lectr.

Other Staff: 9 Lectrs.; 2 Lectrs.†

Vacant Posts: 1 Prof.; 1 Sr. Lectr.; 1 Lectr.

Research: complexity studies; E-commerce; strategic information systems

Languages

Tel: (0131) 455 3514 *Fax:* (0131) 455 3477

Wight, T. W., BA *Open(UK)*, MA *Edin.*, MBA *Strath.*   Acting Head*

Law

Tel: (0131) 455 3488 *Fax:* (0131) 455 3500

Bayne, D. J., BL *Edin.*   Sr. Lectr.

Bisacre, J., LLB   Sr. Lectr.

Finch, V.   Sr. Lectr.

Ross, H.   Sr. Lectr.

Shepherd, J., BSc *Glas.*, PhD *Glas.*, LLB   Sr. Lectr.

Wallace, Prof. R., LLB Dund., MA Aberd, PhD Glas. Head*
Other Staff: 14 Lectrs.
Research: criminal justice; international, European and environmental law

Management Studies
Tel: (0131) 455 5004 Fax: (0131) 455 5040-1
MacPherson, N. C., BSc H-W, MSc Strath. Sr. Lectr.
Ryan, J., MA Glas., MBA Glas. Sr. Lectr.
Stobie, D. H., MSc H-W Head*
Thomson, John R., BA S'ton., MBA Strath. Sr. Lectr.
Wallace, M., BA Sheff. Sr. Lectr.

Marketing
Tel: (0131) 455 5038 Fax: (0131) 455 5046
Ensor, J. G., BA Staffs., MBA Cran. Head*
MacPherson, N. C., BSc H-W, MSc Strath. Sr. Lectr.
Thomson, J. R., BA S'ton., MBA Strath. Sr. Lectr.
Other Staff: 10 Lectrs.; 5 Lectrs.†
Vacant Posts: 1 Prof.
Research: consumer behaviour; international marketing; services marketing

Mathematics
Tel: (0131) 455 4634 Fax: (0131) 455 4232
Dodgson, J. H., MSc Nott., PhD Lough. Sr. Lectr.
Goldfinch, J. M., MA Oxf., PhD Strath. Sr. Lectr.
Henderson, G. R., MA Edin. Sr. Lectr.
Raab, Gillian, BSc Edin., PhD Edin. Prof., Applied Statistics
Raeside, R., BSc CNAA, MSc Strath., PhD CNAA Sr. Lectr.
Roberts, D. E., BSc Glas., PhD Durh. Sr. Lectr.
Scott, T. D., BA Essex, MSc Edin. Sr. Lectr.
Wise, J. T., BSc Sheff., MSc Sheff., PhD Sheff. Head*
Other Staff: 19 Lectrs.; 5 Lectrs.†
Research: applied statistics; computational applied mathematics; mathematics education

Music
Tel: (0131) 455 6200 Fax: (0131) 455 6211
Butterworth, A. M., BMus Nott., MA Nott. Sr. Lectr.
Sawyer, P., MA Camb., MMus Edin. Head*
Other Staff: 4 Lectrs.; 1 Res. Fellow; 21 Lectrs.†
Vacant Posts: 1 Sr. Lectr.

Nursing, see Health Studies, below

Photography, Film and Television
Tel: (0131) 538 7301, 538 7615 Fax: (0131) 538 7629
Bell, Prof. D., BA Warw., PhD Warw. Head*
Davies, Huw, BA Nott.Trent, MA Manc. Reader
MacLeod, C. Sr. Lectr.
Willemen, Prof. P., PhD Middx. Sr. Lectr.
Other Staff: 3 Lectrs.; 5 Lectrs.†
Research: digital media; film studies; photographic and imaging art

Physical Sciences, Applied, see Chem. and Phys. Scis., Appl.

Print Media, Publishing and Communication
Tel: (0131) 455 6150 Fax: (0131) 455 6193
Brand, D., BA E.Anglia Sr. Lectr.
Lodge, S. G., MA Edin., PhD Edin. Sr. Lectr.
McCleery, Prof. A. M., MA St And., MLitt Stir., PhD St And. Head*
Other Staff: 15 Lectrs.; 1 Res. Fellow
Vacant Posts: 2 Sr. Lectrs.; 2 Lectrs.
Research: communication research unit; information society studies; Scottish centre for the book; Scottish colour centre

Psychology and Sociology
Tel: (0131) 455 2522 Fax: (0131) 455 2295
Bonney, Prof. Norman, BSc Lond., MA Chic., PhD Chic. Head*
Brennan, M., PhD Edin. Sr. Lectr.
Falchikov, N., PhD Edin. Sr. Lectr.
Marshall, I. S., BA Keele Sr. Lectr.
McCleery, A., PhD Glas. Sr. Lectr.
Wollman, H., BPhil Oxf. Sr. Lectr.
Other Staff: 15 Lectrs.
Vacant Posts: 1 Prof. (Soc. Aspects of Transport)
Research: employment and social trends; nationalism; population geography and migration; teaching and learning in higher education

Strategic Management
Tel: (0131) 455 3337 Fax: (0131) 455 3486
Bryans, P., BA Lanc., MSc Lond. Head*
Cowe, A., BA H-W, MBA Glas., FCIS Sr. Lectr.
Hamilton, R. Corporate Head, Undergrad. Programmes
Morrison, A. Corporate Head, Comml. Activities
Sharkey, G., MA Dund., MBA Strath. Sr. Lectr.
Other Staff: 6 Lectrs.
Research: bus industry (strategy, developments, industry groups); call centres (strategy, benchmarking, customer satisfaction); maritime transport (shipping lines, vessels, ports)

Surveying, see Bldg. and Surv.

Television, see Photog., Film and TV

Tourism Management, see Hospitality and Tourism Management

HEALTH STUDIES

Adult Physical Health
Tel: (01506) 422800 Fax: (01506) 462535
Collingwood, M. P., TD, MBA H-W, PhD H-W Sr. Lectr.
Lockhart, K., MSc Glas. Sr. Lectr.
McIntosh, I., BA Open(UK), MSc Edin. Head*
Sheard, H., MSc Edin. Sr. Lectr.
Other Staff: 21 Lectrs.; 7 Lectrs.†
Vacant Posts: 1 Prof.

Advanced Nursing and Midwifery Studies
Tel: (0131) 536 5649 Fax: (0131) 536 5623
Brieditis, S. Head*

Foundation Studies
Tel: (0131) 536 5674 Fax: (0131) 536 5621
Jones, J., BA Open(UK) Head*
Leadbetter, V., BA E.Anglia, MSc Edin. Sr. Lectr.
Mitchell, R. Sr. Lectr.
Stratford, J. Sr. Lectr.
Waugh, A., BSc Edin., MSc Edin. Sr. Lectr.
Other Staff: 32 Lectrs.

Maternal and Child Health, Mental Health and Handicap
Tel: (0131) 343 7900 Fax: (0131) 343 7959
Davidson, J., BEd Hudd. Sr. Lectr.
Forrest, S., MPhil Edin. Sr. Lectr.
Gibbs, A., BA Manc. Head*
Mackenzie, H., BSc Edin., MSc Edin. Sr. Lectr.
Maclean, D., BA Open(UK) Sr. Lectr.
McFarlane, W. C., BEd Thames V., MA Reading Sr. Lectr.
Other Staff: 34 Lectrs.
Research: domestic abuse in pregnancy; neonatal nursing; user involvement in curriculum design and delivery

SPECIAL CENTRES, ETC

Advanced Materials Centre
Tel: (0131) 455 2600 Fax: (0131) 455 2264
Lindsay, T. G., BSc Strath., PhD Strath. Dir.*

Advanced Technology Centre
Tel: (0131) 455 2672 Fax: (0131) 455 2264
Masson, R. J., BSc Glas. Dir.*
Research: new technology management and outsourcing; quality management

Computer Aided Engineering Centre
Tel: (0131) 455 2612 Fax: (0131) 455 2264
Summers, T. W., BSc CNAA, MBA Napier Dir.*

Language School
Tel: (0131) 455 2209 Fax: (0131) 455 2345
McFarlane, I. Lang. Sch. Co-ordinator*

Real Time Technologies
Tel: (0131) 455 4636 Fax: (0131) 455 4231
Buchanan, W. J. Sr. Lectr.
Mowbray, R. S. Dir.*

Scottish Energy Centre
Tel: (0131) 455 2612 Fax: (0131) 455 2264
Summers, T. W., BSc CNAA, MBA Napier Dir.*

Technology and Management Development Unit
Tel: (0131) 455 2315 Fax: (0131) 455 2264
Cameron-MacDonald, P., BSc CNAA Dir.*

CONTACT OFFICERS
Academic affairs. Depute Academic Registrar: Fraser, L. E., MA Aberd.
Accommodation. Head of Residential Accommodation Service: McNicholl, William, MA
Admissions (first degree). Admissions Officer: MacLeod, J. Gus, MA Edin.
Admissions (higher degree). Admissions Officer: MacLeod, J. Gus, MA Edin.
Adult/continuing education. Head of Department, Continuing Professional Development: Haddow, Maureen, BA Strath., MSc Strath.
Adult/continuing education. Director, Educational Development Unit: Percival, Fred, BSc Glas., PhD Glas.
Alumni. Alumni Officer: MacLean, L., BSc Edin.
Archives. Morgan, C.
Careers. Senior Careers Adviser: Barbour, K., MA Aberd.
Computing services. Director: Dean, Paul, BSc Birm., MSc Birm.
Conferences/corporate hospitality. Conference Co-ordinator: Crocker, H., MA St And.
Consultancy services. Managing Director, Napier University Ventures Ltd: Angus, Edward, MBE
Credit transfer. CATS Co-ordinator: McDonagh, Mike
Development/fund-raising. Development Manager: Macgregor, K.
Distance education. Flexible Learning Co-ordinator: Campbell, F., BA York(UK)
Estates and buildings/works and services. Head of Buildings and Estates: Brown, T. Sandy, BSc H-W
Examinations. Examinations Officer: Holland, Paul A., BA CNAA
Finance. Director of Finance: Anderson, Alastair
General enquiries. Secretary and Academic Registrar: Miller, I. J., LLB Edin., MA Aberd.
Health services. Physician: Brown, K. S. A.
Industrial liaison. Managing Director, Napier University Ventures Ltd: Angus, Edward, MBE
International office. Overseas Student Recruitment Officer: Lewis, Vicky
Library (enquiries). Depute Librarian: Pinder, C. J., BA CNAA
Ombudsperson. Secretary and Academic Registrar: Miller, I. J., LLB Edin., MA Aberd.
Personnel/human resources. Head of Personnel Services: Macintosh, Neil, MA Glas., MSc Strath.
Public relations, information and marketing. Public Relations Officer: Pate, Marion-Jane

Publications. Publications Officer: Manson, Elayne P., BA *CNAA*

Purchasing. Purchasing and Supplies Officer: Dunlop, J.

Quality assurance and accreditation. Head, Quality Assurance Unit: Pollock, Ann, BSc *Glas.*

Research. Research Officer: Pemberton, Colette M., LLB *Edin.*

Safety. Safety Adviser: Young, Liz, BSc *Napier*

Schools liaison. Schools Liaison Officer: McLaughlin, Gerry

Security. Security Service Manager: Naylor, A.

Sport and recreation. Director: Davidson, D. C.

Staff development and training. Staff Development Officer: Moyes, Barbara, MA *Edin.*, MSc *Lond.*, PhD *Edin.*

Student union. President: McDonald, Bill

Student welfare/counselling. University Chaplain/Manager of Student Services: Brown, Rev. A.

Students from other countries (Europe). Overseas Student Recruitment Officer: Lewis, Vicky

Students with disabilities. Collingwood, Rev. D., BA *Camb.*, BD *Edin.*†

CAMPUS/COLLEGE HEADS

Craighouse Campus, Craighouse Road, Edinburgh EH10 5LG. (Tel: (0131) 455 6000; Fax: (0131) 455 6195.) Campus Principal: Dickinson, Prof. Keith W., BSc *Sheff.*, MEng *Sheff.*, PhD *Sheff.*

Craiglockhart Campus. (Tel: (0131) 455 4607; Fax: (0131) 455 4238.) Campus Principal: Thorne, Prof. Michael, BSc *Lond.*, PhD *Birm.*, FIMA, FBCS

Merchiston Campus, 10 Colinton Road, Edinburgh EH10 5DT. (Tel: (0131) 455 2250; Fax: (0131) 455 2294.) Campus Principal: Angus, Edward, MBE

Sighthill Campus, Sighthill Court, Edinburgh EH11 4BN. (Tel: (0131) 455 3383; Fax: (0131) 455 3526.) Campus Principal: Peattie, Prof. P., BSc *Edin.*

[Information supplied by the institution as at 5 March 1998, and edited by the ACU]

UNIVERSITY OF NEWCASTLE UPON TYNE

Early foundations in nineteenth century; reconstituted with present title of University 1963

Member of the Association of Commonwealth Universities

Postal Address: Newcastle upon Tyne, England NE1 7RU
Telephone: (0191) 222 6000 **Fax**: (0191) 222 6229 **E-mail**: postmaster@ncl.ac.uk
Cables: University, Newcastle upon Tyne, England **WWW**: http://www.ncl.ac.uk

VISITOR—The Lord Chancellor
CHANCELLOR—Ridley, Viscount, KG, GCVO, TD, Hon. DCL
VICE-CHANCELLOR*—Wright, James R. G., BA *Camb.*, MA *Edin.*, MA *Camb.*
PRO-VICE-CHANCELLOR—Goddard, Prof. John B., OBE, BA *Lond.*, PhD *Lond.*
PRO-VICE-CHANCELLOR—Archibald, Prof. A. R., BSc *Edin.*, PhD *Edin.*
PRO-VICE-CHANCELLOR—Hamnett, Prof. A., MA *Oxf.*, DPhil *Oxf.*
REGISTRAR‡—Nicholson, D. E. T., MA *Birm.*
BURSAR—Farnhill, H. B., FCA
DIRECTOR OF FINANCE—Ranson, M. L., JP, FCA
LIBRARIAN AND KEEPER OF THE PYBUS COLLECTION—Graham, Thomas W., MA *Glas.*, PhD *Glas.*

GENERAL INFORMATION

History. The university was established in 1963. It is located in the north-east of England.

Admission to first degree courses (see also United Kingdom Introduction). Through Universities and Colleges Admissions Service (UCAS). The university recognises a wide range of qualifications, including Business and Technology Education Council (BTEC) certificates and diplomas, advanced level General National Vocational Qualifications (GNVQ), Open University credits, International Baccalaureate, and certain access courses.

First Degrees (see also United Kingdom Directory to Subjects of Study). BA, BArch, BDS, BMedSci, BSc, LLB, MB BS, MChem, MEng, MMath, MPhys.

All courses are full-time and normally last 3 or 4 years. BArch, MEng: 5 years; BDS, MB BS: 5 years (main entry) or 6 years (including pre-dental/pre-medical year).

Higher Degrees (see also United Kingdom Directory to Subjects of Study). BPhil, LLM, MA, MArch, MBA, MD, MEd, MFA, MIHSc (international housing science), MLitt, MMedSci, MMus, MRes, Msc, MTP, MPhil, PhD, DBA, DClinPsychol, DDS, DEng, DLitt, DSc, EdD, LLD.

Applicants for admission to higher degrees must normally hold a good first degree in a relevant subject. Other qualifications and relevant professional experience are considered.

Most master's degrees: 12 months full-time or 24 months part-time. MRes: 12 months full-time; MArch: 21 months after RIBA Part II or 9 months full-time plus 21 months part-time; MFA, MIHSc: 24 months full-time; MTP: 24 months full-time or 12 months full-time plus 24 months part-time; EdD: 24 months full-time or minimum 48 months part-time; DDS, MD: 2–3 years full-time or 4 years part-time; PhD: 3 or 4 years full-time or 5 years part-time; DBA: 30 months full-time or 60 months part-time; DClinPsychol: 48 months part-time; DEng, DLitt, DSc, LLD: awarded on published work.

Libraries. Over 1,000,000 volumes; 4500 periodicals. Special collections: Pybus collection; Walton library (medical and dental).

Academic Year (1998–99). Two semesters: 22 September–22 January; 25 January–11 June.

Income (year ended 31 July 1997). Total, £152,728,000.

Statistics. Staff: 2171 (1968 academic, 203 administrative). Students: full-time 11,922 (6350 men, 5572 women); part-time 1333 (632 men, 701 women); international 1183; total 13, 255.

FACULTIES/SCHOOLS

Agriculture and Biological Sciences

Dean: Ritson, Prof. Christopher, BA *Nott.*, MAgrSc *Reading*

Arts

Dean: Cross, Eric G. N., BMus *Birm.*, PhD *Birm.*

Dentistry

Dean: Murray, Prof. John J., CBE, MChD *Leeds*, PhD *Leeds*, FDSRCS

Education

Dean: Atkins, Madeleine J., BA *Camb.*, PhD *Nott.*

Engineering

Dean: Hills, Prof. Peter J., OBE, BSc(Eng) *Lond.*, MSc *Birm.*

Law, Environment and Social Sciences

Acting Dean: Stevenson, Prof. Anthony C., BSc *Lond.*, PhD *Lond.*

Medicine

Dean: Baylis, Prof. Peter H., BSc *Brist.*, MB ChB *Brist.*, MD *Birm.*, FRCP

Science

Dean: Straughan, Brian P., BSc *Nott.*, PhD *Nott.*, FRSChem

ACADEMIC UNITS

Accounting and Finance

Appleyard, A. R., BSc(Econ) Hull, MA Hull Northern Soc. Prof., Accounting and Finance; Head*

Dobbs, I. M., MA Camb., MSc City(UK), PhD Reader, Business Economics and Finance

Other Staff: 11 Lectrs.

Research: accounting history; business; financial markets; interest rates and the stock market; international accounting and finance

Agricultural and Environmental

Science, see also Marine Scis. and Coastal Management

Fax: (0191) 222 5228

Adey, Michael A., MA Oxf., PhD Birm. Sr. Lectr.

Davison, A. W., BSc Durh., PhD Sheff. Prof., Environmental Biology

Fowler, Peter J., MA Oxf., PhD Brist., FSA Emer. Prof.

Goodfellow, M., BSc Liv., PhD Liv., DSc Liv., FIBiol Prof., Microbial Systematics

Gowing, J. W., BSc Durh., MSc Cran.IT Sr. Lectr., Agricultural Engineering

Griffiths, H., BSc Dund., PhD Dund. Prof., Plant Ecophysiology

O'Donnell, A. G., BSc Glas., PhD Brist. Reader, Soil Microbiology and Molecular Ecology

Ollerenshaw, J. H., BSc Leeds, PhD Leeds Sr. Lectr., Agricultural Biology; Head*

Port, G. R., BA Lanc., PhD Lond. Sr. Lectr., Agricultural Biology

Richards, A. J., BSc Durh., PhD Durh. Reader, Plant Biology

Selman, B. J., BSc Brist., PhD Brist. Sr. Lectr., Agricultural Biology

Syers, J. K., BSc Durh., PhD Durh., DSc Cant., FRSChem, FRSNZ, FNZIC Prof., Soil Science

Ward, Alan C., BSc Leeds, PhD Leeds Sr. Lectr.

Wilkins, R. M., BSc Exe., MSF Wash., PhD Wash. Sr. Lectr., Agricultural Biology

Woods, J. L., BEng Liv., DPhil Sus. Sr. Lectr., Agricultural Engineering

Other Staff: 12 Lectrs.; 2 Royal Society Res. Fellows

Vacant Posts: 1 Prof.

Research: agricultural and environmental processes; conservation policy and practice; ecological modelling; engineering design and control; plant and crop ecology

Agricultural Economics and Food Marketing

Including Centre for Rural Economy (CRE)

Tel: (0191) 222 6900 Fax: (0191) 222 6720

Dawson, P. J., BA CNAA, MA(Econ) Manc., PhD Manc. Sr. Lectr., Agricultural Economics

Harvey, D. R., MA(Econ) Manc., PhD Manc., BSc Prof., Agricultural Economics

Hubbard, L. J., BSc Lond., MApplSc Cant. Sr. Lectr., Agricultural Economics; Head*

Lingard, J., BSc Reading, MA(Econ) Manc., PhD Sr. Lectr., Agricultural Economics

Lowe, P. D., MA Oxf., MSc Manc., MPhil Sus. Duke of Northumberland Prof., Rural Economics; Dir., CRE

Ritson, Christopher, BA Nott., MAgrSc Reading Prof., Agricultural Marketing

Other Staff: 10 Lectrs.; 1 Lord Richard Percy Fellow; 1 Lectr.†

Vacant Posts: 1 Prof.

Research: areas of social science applied to the analysis of agricultural, food and rural issues

Agriculture

Fax: (0191) 222 7811

Evans, E. J., BSc Wales, PhD Sr. Lectr., Crop Production

Rowlinson, P., BSc Nott., PhD Reading Sr. Lectr., Animal Production

Willis, M. B., BSc Durh., PhD Edin. Sr. Lectr., Animal Breeding and Genetics

Younger, A., BSc Leeds, PhD Nott. Sr. Lectr., Crop Production; Head*

Other Staff: 3 Lectrs.; 1 Royal Society Res. Fellow; 1 TMR Fellow

Vacant Posts: 1 Prof.

Research: animal production; crop production; farm management

Archaeology

Fax: (0191) 222 8561

Bailey, Geoffrey N., BA Camb., PhD Camb., FSA Prof.; Head*

Davis, P. S., BSc Wales, MSc Durh., FLS Sr. Lectr.

Dolukhanov, P. M., MA Leningrad, PhD Leningrad Reader, Eastern European Archaeology

Greene, K. T., BA Wales, PhD Wales, FSA Sr. Lectr.

Other Staff: 5 Lectrs.; 1 Sir James Knott Res. Fellow; 7 Hon. Lectrs.

Research: archaeology of central and eastern Europe; heritage resource management; prehistoric archaeology; Roman and early medieval archaeology

Architecture

Including Centre for Architectural Research and Development Overseas

Fax: (0191) 222 6115

Leitch, Diana M., BA BArch Head*

Louw, H. J., BArch Pret., DPhil Oxf., MPhil Sr. Lectr.

Richards, Ivor J., MA Wales Prof.

Tipple, A. G., MA Sheff., PhD Reader, Housing Policy and Development

Wiltshire, T. J., BEng(Tech) Wales, PhD Prof., Architecture Science

Other Staff: 11 Lectrs.

Vacant Posts: 1 Prof.

Research: architectural science; computing; history and theory; housing and international development; urban design

Biochemistry, see Medicine

Biological and Nutritional Sciences, see

also Agric. and Environmental Sci., and Marine Scis. and Coastal Management

Including Human Nutrition Research Centre

Fax: (0191) 222 8684

Cain, R. B., PhD Birm., DSc Birm. Prof., Environmental Microbiology

Cram, W. J., MA Camb., PhD Camb. Prof., Plant Biology

Dickinson, C. H., BSc Nott., MA Trinity(Dub.), PhD Nott. Sr. Lectr.

Finlayson, Heather J., BSc PhD Sr. Lectr.

Gilbert, H. J., BSc S'ton., PhD S'ton. Prof., Agricultural Biochemistry and Nutrition

Mathers, J. C., BSc PhD Prof., Human Nutrition

Parker, D. S., BSc Nott., PhD Leeds Sr. Lectr.; Head*

Pearce, R. S., BSc Brist., MSc Birm., PhD Nott. Sr. Lectr.

Smithard, R. R., MSc NSW Sr. Lectr.

Weekes, T. E. C., PhD Aberd., BSc Sr. Lectr.

Other Staff: 5 Lectrs.

Research: animal nutrition; human nutrition; pure and applied biological sciences

Chemistry

Fax: (0191) 222 6929

Christensen, P. A., MA Oxf., PhD Lond. Sr. Lectr.

Clegg, W., MA Camb., PhD Camb., ScD Camb., FRSChem Prof., Structural Crystallography

Cooper, I. L., BSc Edin., PhD Edin. Sr. Lectr.

Errington, R. J., BSc Leeds, PhD Leeds Reader, Metallorganic Chemistry

Golding, B. T., MSc Manc., PhD Manc., FRSChem Prof., Organic Chemistry

Griffin, R. J., BSc CNAA, PhD Aston Sr. Lectr.

Hamnett, A., MA Oxf., DPhil Oxf., FRSChem Prof., Physical Chemistry

Jackson, R. F. W., BA Camb., PhD Camb. Prof., Synthetic Organic Chemistry

Maskill, H., BA Oxf., PhD Brist., DSc Brist., FRSChem Sr. Lectr.

McFarlane, W., MA Camb., PhD Lond., DSc Lond. Prof., Magnetic Resonance

Minnikin, D. E., MA Oxf., DPhil Oxf., FRSChem Prof., Microbial Chemistry

Straughan, Brian P., BSc Nott., PhD Nott., FRSChem Sr. Lectr.

Sykes, A. G., PhD Manc., DSc Manc., FRSChem Prof., Inorganic Chemistry

Thomas, K. M., BSc Brist., PhD Camb., FRSChem Reader, Carbon Science; Head*

Other Staff: 11 Lectrs.; 1 Royal Society Res. Fellow; 1 Training and Mobility Res. Fellow

Research: biological chemistry; electrochemistry; environmental chemistry; structural chemistry; synthetic chemistry

Classics

Fax: (0191) 222 5432

Hill, D. E., JP, MA Camb., MA Wash. Sr. Lectr.; Head*

Lazenby, J. F., MA Oxf. Prof., Ancient History

Longrigg, J., BA Durh., MLitt Oxf. Reader, Ancient Philosophy and Science

Paterson, J. J., MA Oxf. Sr. Lectr., Ancient History

Powell, J. G. F., MA Oxf., DPhil Oxf. Prof., Latin

Saunders, T. J., BA Lond., PhD Camb. Prof., Greek

Spawforth, A. J. S., BA Birm., PhD Birm. Sr. Lectr., Ancient History/Greek Archaeology

Other Staff: 4 Lectrs.; 1 Wellcome Trust Res. Fellow

Research: Greek social and political theory and practice, especially penology; Homeric archaeology; Latin language and literature, especially Cicero; social and cultural history of the Roman Empire

Computing Science

Fax: (0191) 222 8232

Anderson, T., BSc PhD Prof.

Dobson, John E., MA Camb. Prof., Information Management

Koutny, M., MSc Warsaw, PhD Warsaw Reader

Lee, P. A., MSc Manc., PhD Manc. Prof.

Lloyd, J. L., BSc Manc., PhD Sr. Lectr.; Head*

Mitrani, I., BSc Sofia, MSc Haifa, PhD Prof.

Phillips, Christopher, MSc Liv., PhD Liv. Sr. Lectr.

Randell, B., DSc Lond. Prof.

Shrivastava, S. K., ME Poona, PhD Camb. Prof.

Whitfield, H., BSc Lond. Prof., Computing and Data Processing

Yakovlev, Alexandre V., MSc Leningrad, PhD Leningrad Reader, Computing System Design

Other Staff: 15 Lectrs.

Research: dependability; distributed systems; parallelism; software reliability; theoretical computing science

Dentistry, see Medicine

Economics

Fax: (0191) 222 6548

Barmby, T. A., BSc(Econ) Hull, MSocSc Birm. Reader, Labour Economics

Dolton, P. J., BA Essex, MA Warw., PhD Camb. David Dale Prof.; Head*

Jones-Lee, M. W., BEng Sheff., DPhil York(UK) Prof.

Loomes, Graham C., BA(Econ) Essex, MSc(Econ) Lond. Res. Devel. Prof.

Molho, I., BA Manc., MA Warw., PhD Kent Reader, Microeconomics

Seidmann, D. J., BA Oxf., PhD Lond. Prof., Economic Theory

Other Staff: 11 Lectrs.; 1 Lectr.†

Vacant Posts: 1 Prof.

Research: game theory and experiments; industry and environment; macroeconomics; money and finance; safety, health and risk

Education

Including Centre for Higher Education Research (CHER) and Centre for International Studies in Education (CISE)

Fax: (0191) 222 8170

Ackers, William J., BSc(Econ) Lond., MA Leic.   Lectr.; Dir., CISE

Atkins, Madeleine J., BA Camb., PhD Nott.   Sr. Lectr.

Carrington, L. B., BA CNAA, MSc(Econ) Lond.   Sr. Lectr.

Coffield, Francis J., MEd Glas., MA Glas.   Res. Devel. Prof.

Dennison, W. F., BSc Durh., PhD   Sr. Lectr.; Head*

Dyson, David A., BA Sus., MA Durh.   Prof., Special Needs Education

Easen, P. R., BEd Lond., PhD   Sr. Lectr.

Leat, David J. K., BA Exe., PhD Exe.   Sr. Lectr.

Millward, A. J., BSc Lond., MEd Brist.   Sr. Lectr.

Moseley, D. V., MA Oxf.   Reader, Applied Psychology

Newton, D. P., MEd Durh., BSc   Reader

Reynolds, D., BA Essex   Prof.

Tomlin, Richard I., MBA   Dir., CHER

Westgate, D. P. G., BA Oxf., MA Lond.   Sr. Lectr.

Other Staff: 23 Lectrs.; 3 Hon. Lectrs.

Vacant Posts: 3 Profs.

Research: development of learning and understanding; educational management, school effectiveness and school improvement; policy studies; special educational needs; teacher education and professional development

Engineering, Agricultural, see Agric. and Environmental Sci.

Engineering, Chemical and Process

Fax: (0191) 222 5292

Akay, Galip, MSc Manc., PhD UMIST   Prof.

Backhurst, J. R., BSc PhD   Sr. Lectr.; Head*

Howarth, C. R., BSc Sheff., PhD Sheff.   Sr. Lectr.

Montague, G. A., MEng Sheff., BSc PhD   Prof., Bioprocess Control

Morris, A. J., BSc Durh., PhD   Prof., Process Control

Norman, Peter W., BSc PhD   Sr. Lectr.

Ramshaw, C., BSc Durh., PhD, FEng, FIChemE   IMI/Royal Academy of Engineering Prof., Responsive Processing

Scott, K., BSc PhD, FIChemE   Prof., Electrochemical Engineering

Other Staff: 6 Lectrs.

Engineering, Civil

Fax: (0191) 222 6502

Anderson, G. K., BSc Durh., PhD   Prof., Environmental Engineering

Bathurst, James C., BSc(Eng) Lond., MSc Lond., PhD E.Anglia   Reader, Erosion and Sediment Transport

Bell, Michael G. H., BA Camb., MSc Leeds, PhD Leeds   Prof., Transport Operations; Dir., Transport Operations Res. Group

Clarke, B. G., PhD Camb., BSc, FGS   Sr. Lectr., Geotechnical Engineering

Ewen, John, BSc Aberd., PhD Wales   Sr. Lectr.

Hills, Peter J., OBE, BSc(Eng) Lond., MSc Birm.   Prof., Civil and Transport Engineering

Jamieson, Derek G., BSc Durh., PhD   Royal Academy of Engin. Thames Water plc Prof., River Basin Management

Jones, C. J. F. P., BSc Durh., PhD Leeds, MSc, FICE   Prof., Geotechnical Engineering

Knapton, J., BSc PhD, FICE, FIStructE   Prof., Structural Engineering

Moffat, A. I. B., RD, BSc Edin., FGS   Sr. Lectr., Dam Engineering

Nalluri, C., BE Madr., DU Toulouse   Reader, Hydraulic Engineering

O'Connell, P. E., BE N.U.I., PhD Lond.   Prof., Water Resources Engineering

Pescod, M. B., OBE, BSc Durh., SM M.I.T., FICE   Tyne and Wear Prof., Environmental Control Engineering

Other Staff: 18 Lectrs.

Research: environmental engineering; structural engineering; transport engineering; water resources engineering

Engineering, Electrical and Electronic

Tel: (0191) 222 7340 Fax: (0191) 222 8180

Acarnley, P. P., MA Camb., PhD Leeds   Prof., Electric Drives

Adams, A. E., BSc CNAA, MSc Durh.   Sr. Lectr.

Allen, Charles R., BSc Lond., DPhil Oxf.   Sr. Lectr.

Farsi, M., BSc Idaho, PhD   Sr. Lectr.

Finch, J. W., BSc(Eng) Lond., PhD Leeds   Reader, Electrical Control Engineering

Hinton, O. R., BSc(Eng) Lond., PhD Lond.   Prof., Signal Processing; Head*

Jack, A. G., BSc CNAA, PhD S'ton.   Prof., Electrical Engineering

Kinniment, D. J., MSc Manc., PhD Manc.   Prof., Electronic Engineering

Mecrow, B. C., BSc PhD   Reader, Electrical Power Engineering

O'Neill, A. G., BSc Nott., PhD St And.   Siemens Prof., Microelectronics

Other Staff: 12 Lectrs.; 1 Sr. Lectr.†

Vacant Posts: 1 Prof.; 1 Reader

Research: digital signal processing; electric drives and machines; microelectronics system design; physical electronics; robotics and automation

Engineering Mathematics

Fax: (0191) 222 5498

Firth, Jean M., BA Oxf., PhD Sheff.   Sr. Lectr.

Metcalfe, A. V., BSc PhD   Sr. Lectr.

Petrie, C. J. S., MA Camb., PhD Camb., FIM   Reader, Theoretical and Applied Rheology

Sergeev, Yuri A., MSc Moscow, PhD Russian Acad.Sc., DSc Russian Acad.Sc., FIMA   Prof.; Head*

Other Staff: 5 Lectrs.; 1 Temp. Lectr.

Research: applied statistics; computer-aided learning; control engineering; electrical impedance tomography; two-phase flows/ turbulent flows

Engineering, Mechanical, Materials and Manufacturing

Including Design Unit and Industrial Statistics Research Unit

Fax: (0191) 222 8600

Anderson, A., BSc(Eng) Aberd., PhD Aberd.   Sr. Lectr.

Braiden, P. M., MEng Sheff., PhD Sheff., FEng, FIMechE, FIEE   Sir James Woodeson Prof., Manufacturing Engineering

Bull, Stephen J., MA Cam., PhD Camb.   Reader, Surface Engineering

Burdess, J. S., BSc PhD, FIMechE   Prof., Engineering Dynamics

Evans, J. T., BSc Wales, PhD Wales   Reader, Materials Engineering; Head*

Fawcett, J. N., BSc Nott., PhD Nott., FIMechE   Prof., Machine Dynamics

Fisher, E. H., BSc PhD   Sr. Lectr.

Gibson, A. G., BSc Manc., MSc Lough., PhD Leeds   Roland Cookson Prof., Composite Materials Engineering

Hofmann, D. A., BSc Durh.   Dir., Design Unit

Johnson, G. R., BSc Leeds, PhD Leeds, FIMechE   Prof., Rehabilitation Engineering

Page, T. F., MA Camb., PhD Camb., FIM   Cookson Group Prof., Engineering Materials

Smith, M. R., BSc Durh., PhD, FIP   Sr. Lectr.

Taylor, Paul M., MA Camb., MSc Manc., PhD UMIST, FIEE   Prof., Mechanical Engineering

Thompson, D. P., MA Camb., PhD Camb.   Prof., Engineering Ceramics

White, J. R., BSc Lond., PhD Lond., FIM, FIP   Reader, Polymer Science Engineering

Other Staff: 12 Lectrs.

Vacant Posts: 1 Prof.

Research: biomedical engineering; dynamics and control; manufacturing; materials; mechanical power transmissions

Engineering, Process, see Engin., Chem. and Process

English Literary and Linguistic Studies

Fax: (0191) 222 8708

Anderson, Linda R., MA Aberd., PhD Aberd.   Reader, Modern English Literature and Women's Studies

Babington, B. F., BA Auck., MA Well., BLitt Oxf.   Reader, Film Studies

Bailey, R. N., MA Durh., PhD Durh., FSA   Prof., Anglo-Saxon Civilization

Batchelor, J. B., BA Camb., MA New Br., PhD Camb.   Joseph Cowen Prof., English Literature

Burton-Roberts, N. C., BA Kent, MA Lond., PhD   Prof., English Language and Linguistics

Cain, T. G. S., MA Camb., PhD Camb.   Sr. Lectr.; Head*

Carr, P., MA Edin., PhD Edin.   Sr. Lectr.

Graham, D. F., BA Leeds, PhD Leeds   Reader, Modern English Poetry

Lamont, Claire, MA Edin., BLitt Oxf.   Sr. Lectr.

Moisl, H. L., BA McG., MPhil N.U.I., DPhil Oxf., MSc   Sr. Lectr.

Newman, Judith A., MA Edin., PhD Camb.   Prof., American and Post-Colonial Literature

Saunders, J. N. R., MA Camb., BPhil Oxf.   Sr. Lectr.

Whaley, Diana C., BA Durh., DPhil Oxf.   Sr. Lectr.

Wright, T., BA Lond., MPhil Lond.   Sr. Lectr.

Wright, T. R., MA Oxf., DPhil Oxf.   Prof., English Lit

Other Staff: 9 Lectrs.; 1 Earl Grey Memorial Fellow; 1 Northern Arts Literary Fellow; 1 Lectr.†

Research: linguistic studies: semantics, pragmatics, historical linguistics, neural networks; mediaeval studies: mediaeval English, Old Icelandic and Icelandic literature; post-mediaeval literary studies (sixteenth to twentieth centuries)

Environmental Geochemistry, see Fossil Fuels and Environmental Geochem.

Environmental Science, see Agric. and Environmental Sci.

Film Studies, see Engl. Literary and Linguistic Studies

Fine Art

Fax: (0191) 222 6057

Burton, Andrew G. C., BA Newcastle(UK), MFA Newcastle(UK)   Lectr., Sculpture; Head*

Milner, J., BA Lond., PhD Lond.   Prof., History of Art

Varley, E. W., BA Durh.   Lectr.; Dir., Foundation Studies

Other Staff: 4 Lectrs.; 1 Sr. Lectr.†; 4 Lectrs.†

Vacant Posts: 1 Prof.

Research: aesthetic theory and innovative technologies of painting, sculpture and printmaking; art history

Fossil Fuels and Environmental Geochemistry

(Postgraduate Institute)

Fax: (0191) 222 5431

Aplin, A. C., BSc E.Anglia, PhD Lond.   Sr. Lectr.

Larter, S. R., BA Camb., MSc PhD   J. B. Simpson Prof., Geology; Head*

Other Staff: 5 Lectrs.; 1 NERC Res. Fellow

Research: archaeological geochemistry; hopanoid geochemistry; microbial geochemistry; molecular characterisation of early land plant fossil remains; petroleum reservoir and basin modelling

French Studies, see under Mod. Langs., Sch. of

Genetics, see Medicine (Biochem. and Genetics)

Geography

Including Centre for Urban and Regional Development Studies (CURDS)

Fax: (0191) 222 5421

Anderson, James, BA Belf., MA Alta.   Prof., International Development

Champion, A. G., MA Oxf., MPhil Lond., DPhil Oxf.   Prof., Population Geography; Acting Head*

Fotheringham, S. A., BSc Aberd., MA McM., PhD McM.   Prof., Quantitative Geography

Gillespie, A. E., BA Lond.   Prof., Communications Geography; Exec. Dir., CURDS

Goddard, John B., OBE, BA Lond., PhD Lond.   Henry Daysh Prof., Regional Development Studies

Hellen, J. A., MA Oxf., DrPhil Bonn   Sr. Lectr.

Marshall, J. N., BA Durh., MPhil Durh., PhD Birm.   Reader, Industrial Geography

Newson, M. D., BSc Exe., PhD Brist.   Prof., Physical Geography

Robins, K., BA Sus., BPhil York(UK)   Prof., Cultural Geography

Stevenson, Anthony C., BSc Lond., PhD Lond.   Prof., Environmental Geography

Thwaites, A. T., MA Durh.   Sr. Lectr.

Other Staff: 11 Lectrs.; 1 Fellow

Research: environmental change; information and communications technologies in cities and regions; political geography; spatial analysis and GIS; urban and regional development in Britain and Europe

Geomatics

Fax: (0191) 222 8691

Blewitt, Geoffrey, BSc Lond., PhD Cal.Tech.   Prof., Space Geodesy

Cross, Paul A., BSc Nott., PhD Nott., FRAS, FRICS, FIMA   Prof.

Newton, I., MSc Lond.   Sr. Lectr.

Parker, D., BSc Nott., PhD Nott.   Sr. Lectr.; Head*

Other Staff: 5 Lectrs.

Vacant Posts: 1 Prof.

Research: geographic information; photogrammetry; satellite geodesy

German Studies, see under Mod. Langs., Sch. of

History

Fax: (0191) 222 6484

Boulton, Jeremy P., MA St And., PhD Camb.   Sr. Lectr.

Cameron, E. K., MA Oxf., DPhil Oxf., FRHistS   Prof., Early Modern History

Derry, J. W., MA Camb., PhD Camb.   Prof., Modern British History

Lloyd, S. D., BA Oxf., DPhil Oxf.   Sr. Lectr.

Moon, David G., BA Newcastle(UK), PhD Birm.   Sr. Lectr.

Moore, R. I., MA Oxf., FRHistS   Prof., Medieval History

Porter, B. J., MA Camb., PhD Camb., FRHistS   Prof., Modern History; Head*

Pugh, M. D., BA S'ton., PhD Brist., FRHistS   Prof., Modern British History

Salmon, P. J. K., MA Camb., PhD Camb.   Sr. Lectr.

Saunders, D. B., MA Oxf., DPhil Oxf., FRHistS   Reader, History of the Russian Empire

Other Staff: 4 Lectrs.; 1 Res. Fellow

Research: heresy and dissent; mediaeval European history; modern British history; nineteenth-century Russian and Ukrainian history; twnetieth-century African-American history and culture

Japanese Studies, see Pol.

Latin American Studies, see Spanish, Portuguese and Latin American Studies under Mod. Langs., Sch. of

Law

Fax: (0191) 212 0064

Alder, John E., LLB Exe., BCL Durh.   Prof.

Allen, M. J., LLM Belf.   Prof.; Head*

Cheyne, Ilona C., LLB Edin., LLM Lond.   Sr. Lectr.

Collier, R. S., LLB Sheff., MA Sheff., PhD Leic.   Reader

Frazer, T. J., LLB Nott., LLM Exe.   Visiting Prof.

Harte, J. D. C., MA Camb.   Sr. Lectr.

Ingman, T., LLB Durh., PhD CNAA, LLM   Sr. Lectr.

Wilton, A. M., LLB   Sr. Lectr.

Other Staff: 10 Lectrs.; 1 Lectr.†

Research: commercial and trade law; environmental law; international, comparative and European law

Management Studies

Fax: (0191) 222 6929

Chell, Elizabeth, BA Keele, MPhil Edin., PhD Nott.   Alcan Prof.

Fowler, A., BSc Edin., MBA Durh., MSc PhD   Sr. Lectr.

Jackson, Norman V., MA Lanc., PhD Aston   Sr. Lectr.

Vaughan, Roger, BSc Newcastle(UK), PhD Newcastle(UK), FEng   Exec. Dir., Newcastle Sch. of Management; Head*

Other Staff: 7 Lectrs.; 1 Programme Manager

Research: entrepreneurship and small business management

Marine Sciences and Coastal Management

Including Dove Marine Laboratory

Tel: (0191) 222 6661 Fax: (0191) 222 7891

Burbridge, Peter R., BA Conn., MPS Cornell, PhD Cornell   Res. Devel. Prof.

Edwards, Alasdair J., MSc Newcastle(UK), MSc Camb., PhD Camb.   Sr. Lectr.

Evans, S. M., BSc Brist., PhD Brist.   Sr. Lectr.

Frid, Christopher L. J., BSc Wales, MSc S'ton., PhD E.Anglia   Sr. Lectr.

Olive, P. J. W., BSc PhD   Reader, Marine Biology

Owens, N. J. P., BSc Liv., PhD Dund.   Prof., Marine Science; Head*

Pethick, John, MA Camb., MSc Lond., PhD Camb.   Res. Devel. Prof., Coastal Sciences

Other Staff: 5 Lectrs.

Research: temperate and polar marine science; tropical marine science

Marine Technology

Buxton, I. L., BSc Glas., PhD Glas.   Reader, Marine Transport

Downie, M. J., BSc CNAA, MPhil CNAA, PhD CNAA   Sr. Lectr.

Hearn, G. E., BSc Bath, MSc Sheff., FIMA   Prof., Hydrodynamics

Incecik, Atilla, BEng Istanbul, PhD Glas.   Lloyds Register Prof., Offshore Engineering

Roskilly, Anthony P., BSc Salf., PhD Lanc., FIMarE   Sr. Lectr.

Sen, P., BTech Kharagpur, DrIng Trondheim   Prof., Marine Design and Construction; Head*

Thorp, Ian, BSc Lond., MPhil Lond., FIMarE   Sr. Lectr.

Other Staff: 9 Lectrs.

Vacant Posts: 1 Prof.

Research: computational fluid dynamics; design; marine engineering; offshore structures and materials; robotics and control

Mathematics and Statistics, School of,

see also Engin. Maths.

Fax: (0191) 222 8020

Glazebrook, Kevin D., MA Camb., PhD Camb.   Prof., Applied Probability; Head*

Mathematics

Fax: (0191) 222 8020

Barenghi, C. F., Laur Milan, MA Oregon, PhD Oregon   Prof., Fluid Dynamics

Brandenburg, Axel, DrPhil Helsinki   Prof., Applied Mathematics

Dye, R. H., MA Camb., PhD Camb., ScD Camb.   Prof., Pure Mathematics

Horrocks, G., MA Camb., PhD Camb.   Prof., Pure Mathematics

Johnson, B. E., BSc Tas., PhD Camb., FRS   Prof., Pure Mathematics

Johnson, R. S., BSc(Eng) Lond., MSc Lond., PhD Lond., FIMA   Reader, Applied Mathematics

Young, Nicholas J., MA Oxf., DPhil Oxf.   Prof., Pure Mathematics; Acting Head*

Other Staff: 10 Lectrs.

Research: applied mathematics: modern fluid mechanics and related topics; pure mathematics: group theory and analysis

Statistics

Fax: (0191) 222 8020

Aitken, Murray, BSc Syd., PhD Syd.   Prof.

Boys, R. J., MSc Sheff., BSc PhD   Sr. Lectr.

Cox, T. F., BSc Brist., MSc Sheff., PhD Hull   Sr. Lectr.

Glazebrook, Kevin D., MA Camb., PhD Camb.   Prof., Applied Probability; Head*

Howel, Denise M., MSc Lond.   Sr. Lectr.

Hutton, Jane L., BSc Edin., PhD Lond.   Sr. Lectr.

Matthews, J. N. S., MA Camb., PhD Lond.   Sr. Lectr.

Other Staff: 1 TMR Fellow; 1 Hon. Sr. Lectr.

Research: applied statistics; mathematics of operational research/applied probability; medical statistics

Medicine, see below

Microbiology, see Medicine, below

Modern Languages, School of

Fax: (0191) 222 5442

Powrie, Prof. Philip P., BA Oxf., DPhil Oxf.   Head of Sch.*

French Studies

Fax: (0191) 222 5442

Hare, G. E., BA Hull, PhD Hull   Sr. Lectr.

Powrie, Philip P., BA Oxf., DPhil Oxf.   Prof., French Cultural Studies

Reader, Keith A., BA Camb., DPhil Oxf.   Prof.; Head*

Other Staff: 5 Lectrs.; 1 Sr. Lectr.†

Research: contemporary French politics; French film; French language acquisition; modern French language and sociolinguistics; sixteenth-century French prose literature

German Studies

Fax: (0191) 222 5442

Andersen, Elizabeth A., MA St And., PhD Edin.   Lectr.; Head*

Menhennet, A., MA Oxf., DPhil Oxf.   Emer. Prof.†

West, J., MA Manc., MA Trinity(Dub.), PhD Trinity(Dub.)   Sr. Lectr.

Other Staff: 3 Lectrs.

Research: German and Germanic philology; German mediaeval literature; modern Germanic literature; seventeenth-century German novel, especially Grimmelshausen; theoretical phonology and morphology

Spanish, Portuguese and Latin American Studies

Fax: (0191) 222 5442

Bradley, P. T., BA Leeds, PhD Leeds   Reader, Latin American Studies

Perriam, Christopher G., MA Oxf., DPhil Oxf.   Prof., Hispanic Studies; Head*

Other Staff: 3 Lectrs.; 1 Lectr.†

Research: avant-garde and contemporary Spanish poetry; colonial history of Latin America (especially Peru); lesbian and gay studies in Hispanic context; modern Portuguese literature; women's writing in Spain in the twentieth century

Music

Clarke, David I., BMus *Lond.*, PhD *Exe.* Sr. Lectr.
Cross, Eric G. N., BMus *Birm.*, PhD *Birm.* Sr. Lectr.
Middleton, Richard, MA *Camb.*, DPhil *York(UK)* Prof.; Head*
Other Staff: 4 Lectrs.
Research: aesthetics and theory; Baroque opera; music analysis; music of the eighteenth century; twentieth-century music, especially English music

Nutrition, see Biol. and Nutr. Scis.

Physics

Fax: (0191) 222 7361
Crowe, A., BSc *Belf.*, PhD *Belf.*, FIP Prof.; Head*
de Sa, A., MSc *Bom.*, PhD *Durh.*, FIP Sr. Lectr.
Dickinson, A. S., BSc *Belf.*, PhD *Belf.* Prof., Theoretical Atomic Physics
Jaros, M., MSc *T.U. Prague*, PhD *T.U. Prague* Prof., Theoretical Physics
Lewis, E. L., MA *Oxf.*, DPhil *Oxf.* Sr. Lectr.
Moss, I. G., BA *Camb.*, PhD *Camb.* Reader, Theoretical Cosmology
Snowdon, Kenneth J., BSc *ANU*, PhD *Salf.* Res. Devel. Prof.
Toms, D. J., MSc *Tor.*, PhD *Tor.* Reader, Mathematical Physics
Tozer, D. C., BSc *Brist.*, PhD *Camb.* Reader, Theoretical Geophysics
Other Staff: 8 Lectrs.; 1 Sir James Knott Fellow; 1 Sr. Lectr.†; 1 Lectr.†
Research: atomic, molecular and optical physics; relativity and quantum fields; surface physics; theory of condensed matter

Politics

Fax: (0191) 222 5069
Campbell, David, BA *Melb.*, PhD *ANU* Prof., International Politics
Drifte, R., DrPhil *Bochum* Prof., Japanese Studies
Gray, T. S., BA *Durh.*, PhD Prof., Political Thought; Head*
Hague, R. A., BA *Oxf.* Sr. Lectr.
Harrop, M. W., BA *Oxf.*, MSc *Strath.*, PhD *Yale* Sr. Lectr.
Jones, P. N., BSc(Econ) *Lond.*, MSc *Lond.* Prof., Political Philosophy
Rhodes, Roderick A. W., BSc *Brad.*, BLitt *Oxf.*, PhD *Essex* Prof.
Ritchie, Ella, BA *Lanc.*, PhD *Lond.* Sr. Lectr.
Wiseman, J. A., BA *Manc.*, PhD *Manc.* Sr. Lectr.
Other Staff: 10 Lectrs.; 1 Sir James Knott Fellow
Research: British politics; East Asian politics; European politics; international politics; political theory

Portuguese, see Spanish, Portuguese and Latin American Studies under Mod. Langs., Sch. of

Religious Studies

Fax: (0191) 261 1182
Killingley, D. H., MA *Oxf.*, PhD *Lond.* Sr. Lectr.
Loughlin, G. P., MA *Wales*, PhD *Camb.* Sr. Lectr.; Head*
Sagovsky, Nicholas, BA *Oxf.*, BA *Nott.*, PhD *Camb.* William Leech Prof. Fellow, Applied Christian Theology
Other Staff: 1 Dir. of Islamic Studies; 2 Lectrs.
Research: anthropology of religion; contemporary Christian theology and philosophy of religion; Hindu studies; new religious movements; New Testament studies

Social Policy

Fax: (0191) 222 7497
Haimes, Erica V., BA *Durh.*, PhD *Newcastle(UK)* Sr. Lectr.
Hill, M. J., BSc *Lond.* Prof.
Phillimore, P. R., MA *Edin.*, PhD *Durh.* Sr. Lectr.
Selman, P. F., BA *Oxf.*, PhD Sr. Lectr.; Head*
Walker, Janet A., BA *York(UK)*, BPhil *York(UK)* Prof., Family Policy
Wheelock, J., BA *Brist.*, PhD *Glas.* Reader
Other Staff: 8 Lectrs.; 1 Lectr.†
Research: family studies; health studies; political economy; youth and student lives

Family Studies, Newcastle Centre for

Fax: (0191) 222 7871
Walker, Janet A., BA *York(UK)*, BPhil *York(UK)* Prof.; Dir.*
Research: families in society; family communication; family justice

Soil Science, see Agric. and Environmental Sci.

Spanish, see under Mod. Langs., Sch. of

Speech

Tel: (0191) 222 7388, 222 7385 Fax: (0191) 222 6518
Docherty, G. J., BA *Salf.*, PhD *Edin.* Sr. Lectr.; Head*
Dodd, Barbara, PhD *Lond.* Prof., Speech and Language Pathology
Franklin, Susan E., MSc *Lond.*, PhD *City(UK)* Sr. Lectr.
Howard, David, MA *Camb.*, PhD *Lond.* Res. Devel. Prof.
Klee, Thomas, BS *Indiana*, MA *Indiana*, PhD *Wis.* Sr. Lectr.
Li, Wei, MA *Newcastle(UK)*, PhD *Newcastle(UK)* Sr. Lectr.
Milroy, Ann L., MA *Manc.*, PhD *Belf.* Prof., Sociolinguistics
Mogford-Bevan, Katherine P., BSc *Brist.*, PhD *Nott.* Sr. Lectr.
Other Staff: 3 Lectrs.
Research: applied linguistics; bilingualism; clinical linguistics and phonetics; speech and language pathology

Statistics, see Maths. and Stats., Sch. of

Town and Country Planning

Including Centre for Research in European Urban Environments (CREUE)
Fax: (0191) 222 8811
Benson, J. F., BTech *Brad.*, DPhil *Oxf.* Sr. Lectr., Landscape Design
Cameron, S. J., BA *Exe.* Sr. Lectr.
Downing, M. F., MSc Reader, Landscape Design
Gillard, A. A., BA *Sheff.*, MCD *Liv.* Sr. Lectr.; Head*
Graham, Stephen D. N., BSc *S'ton.*, MPhil *Newcastle(UK)*, PhD *Manc.*
Healey, Patsy, BA *Lond.*, PhD *Lond.* Prof.; Dir., CREUE
Marvin, S. J., BA *Hull*, MA *Sheff.*, PhD *Open(UK)* Sr. Lectr.
Shaw, T., MA *Edin.* Sr. Lectr.
Williams, R. H., BA *Nott.* Sr. Lectr.
Willis, K. G., BSc(Econ) *Lond.*, PhD Prof., Economics of the Environment
Other Staff: 10 Lectrs.; 1 Lectr.†
Research: environmental appraisal and management; European urban environments; housing and society; urban technology

MEDICINE

§ = Joint University/NHS Appointment

Biochemistry and Genetics

Fax: (0191) 222 7424
Connolly, B. A., BSc *Sheff.*, PhD *Birm.* Prof., Biochemistry
Emmerson, P. T., BSc *Durh.*, PhD *Durh.* Prof., Molecular Biology
Hawkins, A. R., BSc *Leeds*, PhD *Leeds* Prof., Molecular Genetics
Hughes, Monica A., BSc *Reading*, PhD Prof., Plant Molecular Genetics
Lakey, Jeremy H., BSc *Liv.*, PhD *E.Anglia* Reader, Structural Biochemistry
Robinson, Nigel J., BSc *Liv.*, PhD *Liv.* Prof., Molecular Genetics
Rogers, Margaret P., MA *Oxf.*, DPhil *Oxf.* Sr. Lectr.
Samson, A. C. R., BSc *Lond.*, PhD *Leic.* Sr. Lectr., Genetics
Shaw, N., BSc *Nott.*, PhD *Nott.* Sr. Lectr.
Virden, Richard, MSc *Lond.*, PhD *Lond.* Sr. Lectr.
Yeaman, S. J., BSc *Dund.*, PhD *Dund.*, FRSEd Prof., Molecular Enzymology; Head*
Other Staff: 5 Lectrs.; 1 Leukaemia Society of America Fellow
Vacant Posts: 1 Prof.
Research: eukaryotic gene regulation; hormonal control of metabolism; membranes and proteins; plant molecular biology; protein-DNA interactions

Cardiology, see under Clin. Med. Scis., Sch. of

Child Health

Tel: (0191) 202 3033 Fax: (0191) 202 3022
Bartlett, K., BSc *Wales*, PhD *Wales* Prof., Paediatric Biochemistry
Bhate, Surya R., MB BS *Nag.*, FRCPsych Sr. Lectr.§
Cheetham, Timothy D., MB ChB *Leic.*, BSc *Leic.*, MD *Leic.* Sr. Lectr.§
Colver, Allan F., MB BS *Lond.*, MA *Camb.*, MD, FRCP, FRCPEd Sr. Lectr., Community Child Health§
Craft, A. W., MB BS MD, FRCP Sir James Spence Prof., Paediatric Oncology
De San Lazaro, Camille M., MB BS *B'lore.*, FRCP Sr. Lectr., Forensic Paediatrics
Eyre, Janet A., MB ChB *Auck.*, BSc *Auck.*, DPhil *Oxf.*, FRCP Prof., Paediatric Neuroscience
Forsyth, Robert J., MB BChir *Camb.*, MA *Camb.*, PhD Sr. Lectr.§
Jaffray, Bruce, BMedBiol *Aberd.*, MB ChB *Aberd.*, ChM *Aberd.*, FRCSGlas Sr. Lectr.§
Jarvis, S. N., MB BS *Lond.*, MD *Lond.* Donald Court Prof., Community Child Health
Kaplan, Carole A., MB ChB *Cape Town*, FRCPsych Sr. Lectr., Child and Adolescent Psychiatry§
Le Couteur, Ann S., BSc *Lond.*, MB BS *Lond.*, FRCPsych Prof., Child Psychiatry
McArdle, P., MB BCh BAO *Trinity(Dub.)*, FRCPsych Sr. Lectr., Child and Adolescent Psychiatry§
Miller, John S. G., BM BCh *Oxf.*, MA *Oxf.*, DPhil *Oxf.* Emer. Prof.†, Anatomy
Morris, Andrew A. M., BM BCh *Oxf.*, BA *Camb.*, PhD Sr. Lectr.
Parker, Louise, BSc *Newcastle(UK)*, PhD *Newcastle(UK)* Sr. Lectr., Epidemiology
Pearson, A. D. J., MB BS MD, FRCP Prof., Paediatric Oncology
Sein, E. P., MB BS *Rangoon* Sr. Lectr., Child and Adolescent Psychiatry§
Sernagor, Evelyne, BSc *Jerusalem*, MSc *Jerusalem*, PhD *Jerusalem* Sr. Lectr., Paediatric Neuroscience
Skinner, R., BSc *Birm.*, MB ChB *Birm.* Sr. Lectr., Paediatric Oncology
Towner, Elizabeth M. L., BSc *Durh.*, MA *York(Can.)*, PhD *Birm.* Sr. Lectr., Community Child Health
Windebank, K. P., BM BCh *Oxf.*, FRCP Sr. Lectr., Paediatric Oncology
Other Staff: 6 Lectrs.; 4 Hon. Sr. Lectrs.; 1 Hon. Lectr.
Vacant Posts: 1 Sr. Lectr.
Research: child and adolescent psychiatry; community child health; metabolism; neuroscience; paediatric oncology

Clinical Biochemistry and Metabolic Medicine

Tel: (0191) 222 7135 Fax: (0191) 222 6227

Bartlett, K., BSc *Wales*, PhD *Wales* Prof., Paediatric Biochemistry

Datta, H. K., BSc *Sur.*, MB BS PhD Sr. Lectr.

Laker, M. F., MB BS *Lond.*, MD *Lond.*, FRCPath Reader§

McNeil, C. J., BSc *Strath.*, PhD *Strath.* Reader, Bioelectrochemistry and Biosensors

Self, C. H., MB BChir *Camb.*, BSc *Leic.*, PhD *Leic.*, FRSChem Prof.; Head*

Skillen, A. W., BSc *Durh.*, PhD *Durh.* Sr. Lectr.

Thomas, T. H., BSc *Lond.*, PhD *CNAA* Sr. Lectr.

Turner, G. A., BSc *Durh.*, PhD *Lond.* Sr. Lectr.

Other Staff: 1 Lectr.; 3 Hon. Lectrs.

Vacant Posts: 1 Sr. Lectr.

Research: biosensors; development of novel drugs based on photoactivation; glycosylation and glycation; high performance immunoassay technology; metabolic disorders

Clinical Medical Sciences, School of

James, Prof. Oliver F. W., BM BCh *Oxf.*, MA *Oxf.*, FRCP Head of Sch.*

Cardiology

Fax: (0191) 261 5801

Bourke, John P., MB BCh BAO *N.U.I.*, MD *N.U.I.* Sr. Lectr.

Campbell, R. W. F., BSc *Edin.*, MB ChB *Edin.*, FRCP, FRCPEd, FRCPGlas British Heart Foundation Prof.; Head*

Furniss, S. S., MB BS *Lond.*, MA *Lond.*, FRCP Sr. Lectr.

Other Staff: 1 Lectr.

Research: arrhythmia mapping; arrhythmology; ECG and signal analysis; lipid research; post MI risk prediction

Environmental and Occupational Medicine

Fax: (0191) 222 6442

Blain, P. G., BMedSci MB BS PhD, FIBiol, FRCP, FRCPEd Prof., Environmental Medicine; Head*

Harrison, J., MB ChB *Manc.*, BSc *St And.* Sr. Lectr., Occupational Medicine

Williams, Faith M., MA *Camb.*, PhD *Lond.* Reader, Biochemical Toxicology

Other Staff: 3 Lectrs.; 1 Hon. Lectr.

Research: biochemical mechanisms of toxicity; health effects of toxic chemicals; molecular epidemiology; monitoring genotoxicity; neurotoxicology

Medical Physics

Tel: (0191) 222 8261 Fax: (0191) 222 6442

Boddy, K., OBE, BSc *Liv.*, MSc *Lond.*, PhD *Glas.*, DSc *Strath.*, FIP Hon. Prof.†

Diffey, Brian L., BSc *Lond.*, PhD *Lond.* Hon. Prof., Photobiology; Head*

Murray, Alan, BSc *Strath.*, PhD *Edin.*, FIEE Prof., Cardiovascular Physics

Other Staff: 5 Hon. Lectrs.

Research: clinical applications of radioactivity; clinical instrumentation and physiological measurements; medical use of lasers; radiation protection; ultrasonic imaging

Medicine

Fax: (0191) 222 0723

Agius, Loranne, MSc *Malta*, DPhil *Oxf.* Reader, Metabolism

Alberti, Kurt G. M. M., BM BCh *Oxf.*, MA *Oxf.*, DPhil *Oxf.*, FRCP, FRCPEd, FRCPath Prof.

Barer, D. H., BM BS DM MA MSc, FRCP Prof., Stroke Medicine

Barton, John R., PhD *Edin.*, MB BS Addison Reader

Bassendine, Margaret F., BSc *Lond.*, MB BS *Lond.*, FRCP, FRCPEd Prof., Hepatology

Baylis, Peter H., BSc *Brist.*, MB ChB *Brist.*, MD *Birm.*, FRCP Prof., Experimental Medicine§

Bilous, Rudolf W., MB BS *Lond.*, MD *Lond*, BSc *Lond.*, FRCP Reader, Diabet. and Endocrinology

Bourke, John P., MB BCh BAO *N.U.I.*, MB *N.U.I.* Sr. Lectr., General Medicine§

Brewis, R. A. L., MB BS *Durh.*, MD, FRCP Sr. Lectr.§

Cawston, Timothy E., BSc *Leeds*, PhD *Reading* William Leech Prof., Rheumatology

Corris, Paul A., MB BS *Lond.*, FRCP Reader, Thoracic Medicine

Davis, Michelle, MB BS *Lond.* Sr. Lectr., Stroke Medicine and Elderly Care

Ford, G. A., MB BChir *Camb.*, MA *Camb.* Sr. Lectr., Clinical Pharmacology§

Francis, R. M., MB ChB *Leeds* William Leech Sr. Lectr., Geriatrics

Gibson, Gerald J., BSc *Lond.*, MB BS *Lond.*, MD *Lond.*, FRCP Hon. Prof., Respiratory Medicine

Goodship, T. H. J., MB BS *Lond.*, BSc *Lond.*, FRCP Sr. Lectr., Nephrology

Gray, Christopher S., MD BS, FRCP Prof., Stroke Medicine

Hendrick, David J., MB BS *Lond.*, MD, FRCP Sr. Lectr.§

Home, P. D., BM BCh *Oxf.*, MA *Oxf.*, DPhil *Oxf.*, FRCP Prof., Diabetes Medicine

James, Oliver F. W., BM BCh *Oxf.*, MA *Oxf.*, FRCP Hon. Prof.†, Geriatric Medicine; Head*

James, Robert A., BSc *Wales*, MB BCh *Wales*, MD Sr. Lectr.

Kendall-Taylor, Patricia A., MB BS *Lond.*, MD *Lond.*, FRCP Prof., Endocrinology§

Kenny, Rose A., MB BCh BAO *Trinity(Dub.)*, MD *Trinity(Dub.)*, FRCP, FRCPI Prof., Cardiovascular Research

Lendrum, R., MA *Camb.*, MB BChir *Camb.*, FRCP Sr. Lectr.§

Marshall, Sally M., BSc *Glas.*, MB ChB *Glas.*, FRCP, FRCPGlas Reader, Diabetes

O'Connell, Janice E., BSc *Glas.*, MB ChB *Glas.* Sr. Lectr., Clinical Geriatric Medicine§

Ong, E. L. C., MSc *Lond.*, MB BS, MD, FRCP Sr. Lectr.§

Proctor, S. J., MB BS, FRCP, FRCPath Prof., Haematological Oncology

Record, C. O., MB BS *Lond.*, DPhil *Oxf.*, FRCP Sr. Lectr.§

Rodgers, Helen, MB ChB *Leeds* Sr. Lectr., Stroke Medicine and Services

Snashall, P. D., MB BS *Lond.*, BSc *Lond.*, MD *Lond.*, FRCP Harold Macmillan Prof.

Snow, M. H., MB BS, FRCP Sr. Lectr.§

Stenton, Samuel C., MB BCh Sr. Lectr.§

Taylor, R., BSc(MedSci) *Edin.*, MB ChB *Edin.*, MD *Edin.*, FRCP Prof., Medicine and Metabolism

Thomas, T. H., BSc *Lond.*, PhD *CNAA* Sr. Lectr.

Unwin, Nigel C., BM BCh *Oxf.*, BA *Oxf.*, MSc *Manc.* Sr. Lectr., Epidemiology (Non-Communicable Diseases)

Walker, M., MB BS BMedSci Sr. Lectr.

Ward, M. K., MB BS, FRCP Sr. Lectr.§

Weaver, Jolanta U., PhD *Lond.* Sr. Lectr., Diabetes Medicine

Wilkinson, R., BSc *Durh.*, MB BS *Durh.*, MD, FRCP Prof., Renal Medicine§

Wynne, Hilary A., MB BS *Lond.*, MA *Camb.*, MD *Lond.*, FRCP Sr. Lectr.§

Other Staff: 9 Lectrs.; 1 Principal Clin. Res. Assoc.; 2 Sr. Lectrs.†

Research: diabetes and metabolism; endocrinology; gastroenterology; geriatric medicine; hepatology

Radiology

Fax: (0191) 233 0853

Owen, J. P., MB BS, FRCR Sr. Lectr.

Other Staff: 1 Lectr.§

Research: image processing and development of expert systems; imaging and primary health care; renal diseases including lymphomas and breast screening

Dentistry, School of

Murray, Prof. John J., CBE, MChD *Leeds*, PhD *Leeds*, FDSRCS Head of Sch.*

Research: biomaterials; clinical pharmacology; epidemiology; oral biology

Child Dental Health

Gordon, P. H., BDS *St And.*, PhD *Birm.*, FDSRCS Sr. Lectr.

Lowry, Raymond J., BDS *Birm.*, MB ChB *Leic.* Sr. Lectr., Public Health Medicine

Murray, John J., CBE, MChD *Leeds*, PhD *Leeds*, FDSRCS Prof.

Nunn, June H., BDS *Dund.*, PhD, FDSRCSEd Sr. Lectr.

Rugg-Gunn, A. J., RD, BDS *Lond.*, PhD *Manc.*, FDSRCSEd Prof., Preventive Dentistry

Other Staff: 4 Lectrs.; 1 Lectr.†; 1 Hon. Sr. Lectr.; 1 Hon. Lectr.

Dental Radiology

1 Lectr.; 1 Hon. Lectr.

Oral and Maxillofacial Surgery

Fanibunda, K. B., BDS *Bom.*, MDS, FDSRCS Sr. Lectr.

Martin, Ian C., BDS *Lond.*, MB BS *Lond.*, FDSRCS, FRCS, FRCSEd Sr. Lectr.§

Meechan, J. G., BSc *Glas.*, BDS *Glas.*, PhD, FDSRCPSGlas Sr. Lectr.

Thomson, Peter J., BDS *Manc.*, MSc *Manc.*, MB BS, FDSRCS, FFDRCSI, FRCSEd Prof.; Head*

Other Staff: 1 Lectr.

Oral Biology

Fax: (0191) 222 6137

Russell, R. R. B., BA *Trinity(Dub.)*, PhD *Melb.*, FDSRCS Prof.

Other Staff: 4 Lectrs.

Oral Pathology

Fax: (0191) 222 6137

Nolan, Anita, BDentSc *Trinity(Dub.)*, MB BCh BAO *N.U.I.*, FFDRCSI Sr. Lectr.

Soames, J. V., BDS *Manc.*, PhD *Manc.*, FDSRCPSGlas, FRCPath Prof.

Other Staff: 2 Lectrs.

Restorative Dentistry

Fax: (0191) 222 6137

Girdler, Nicholas M., JP, BDS *Brist.*, BSc *Nott.*, PhD *Lond.*, FDSRCS, FFDRCSI Sr. Lectr., Dental Sedation

Heasman, P. A., MDS PhD, FDSRCPSGlas Sr. Lectr., Periodontistry

Macgregor, I. D. M., BDS *Brist.*, PhD, FDSRCS Sr. Lectr.

McCabe, J. F., BSc *Birm.*, PhD *Birm.* Prof., Dental Materials Science

McMillan, Anne S., BDS *Dund.*, PhD *Br.Col.*, FDSRCPSGlas Sr. Lectr.

Seymour, R. A., BDS *Lond.*, PhD, FDSRCSEd Prof.; Head*

Walls, A. W. G., BDS PhD, FDSRCS Prof.

Wassell, R. W., BDS *Lond.*, MSc *Lond.*, FDSRCS Sr. Lectr., Conservation

Other Staff: 8 Lectrs.; 1 Lectr.†

Dermatology

Fax: (0191) 222 7094

Rees, J. L., MB BS BMedSci, FRCP Prof.; Head*

Reynolds, Nicholas J., MB BS *Lond.*, BSc *Lond.* Sr. Lectr.§

Thody, A. J., BSc *Lond.*, PhD *Lond.*, DSc *Lond.* Prof., Experimental Dermatology

Other Staff: 1 Lectr.; 1 Hon. Sr. Lectr.

Research: clinical photobiology; computer studies; keratinocyte cell biology; molecular studies; pigment cell biology

Environmental and Occupational Medicine, see under Clin. Med. Scis., Sch. of

Epidemiology and Public Health, see under Health Scis., Sch. of

Health Sciences, School of

McAvoy, Prof. Brian R., BSc *Glas.*, MB ChB *Glas.*, MD *Leic.*, FRCGP, FRCP Head of Sch.*

Epidemiology and Public Health

Fax: (0191) 222 8211, 222 6746

Bhopal, R. S., MB ChB Edin., BSc Edin. Prof.;
Head*
Donaldson, L. J., MB ChB Brist., MD Leic., MSc
Birm., FRCSEd Hon. Prof., Applied
Epidemiology
Howel, Denise M., MSc Lond. Sr. Lectr.,
Epidemiological Statistics
Kirkup, W., BM BCh Oxf., MA Oxf. Sr. Lectr.§
Parkin, D. W., BA Leeds, DPhil York(UK) Sr.
Lectr., Health Economics
Pledger, H. G., MB BS Durh., MD Durh.,
FCAnaesth Sr. Lectr.§
Rodgers, Helen, MB ChB Leeds Sr. Lectr.,
Stroke Medicine and Services
Sanders, Gillian L., MB BS Sr. Lectr.§
Thomson, R. G., BA Oxf., MD Sr. Lectr.§
Unwin, Nigel C., BM BCh Oxf., BA Oxf., MSc
Manc. Sr. Lectr., Epidemiology (Non-
Communicable Diseases)
White, M., MB ChB Birm., MSc Sr. Lectr.§
Other Staff: 4 Lectrs.; 1 Lectr.†; 7 Hon. Lectrs.
Research: cardiovascular diseases (coronary heart
disease and stroke); environmental
epidemiology; health economics; health
promotion

Health Services Research, Centre for

Fax: (0191) 222 6043

Bond, J., BA Essex Prof.
Bond, Senga, BA Strath., MSc Strath., PhD
Edin. Prof., Nursing Research; Head*
Eccles, Martin P., FRCP Prof., Clinical
Effectiveness
Research: care for chronic illness; health
informatics; health services for older people;
nursing care; primary health care

Primary Health Care

Fax: (0191) 222 7892

Drinkwater, C. J., BA Camb., MB BChir Camb.,
FRCGP Sr. Lectr., Family Medicine
Jones, Kevin P., MB BS Lond., MA Camb., DM
S'ton. Sr. Lectr.
McAvoy, Brian R., BSc Glas., MB ChB Glas., MD
Leic., FRCGP, FRCP William Leech Prof.
Pearson, Pauline H., BA CNAA, PhD CNAA Sr.
Lectr., Primary Care Nursing
Spencer, J. A., MB ChB Edin., FRCGP Sr.
Lectr., Family Medicine
Other Staff: 10 Lectrs.; 1 Res. Fellow; 8
Lectrs.†; 1 Hon. Lectr.
Research: evidence-based practice; inequalities in
health; prescribing strategies; research into
education; service development in primary
care

Human Genetics

Burn, J., BMedSci MB BS, FRCP Prof., Clinical
Genetics; Head*
Goodship, J. A., MB ChB Edin., BSc Edin., MD
Edin. Sr. Lectr.§
Papiha, S. S., MSc Panjab, PhD, FIBiol Sr.
Lectr.
Strachan, T., BSc ABerd., PhD Glas. Prof.,
Human Molecular Genetics
Other Staff: 3 Lectrs.; 1 Sr. Lectr.†; 4 Hon.
Lectrs.
Research: gene expression during human
embryonic development; human cancer
genetics; human genome evolution;
molecular genetics of developmental
disorders; molecular genetics of other
inherited disorders

Immunology, see under Microbiol.,
Immunol. and Virol. Scis., Sch. of

Microbiological, Immunological and Virological Sciences, School of

Hormaeche, Prof. Carlos E., PhD Camb.,
MD Head of Sch.*
Research: immune mechanisms of disease;
lymphocyte cell biology; medical
microbiology; microbial pathogenicity and
immunity; microbial physiology

Immunology

Fax: (0191) 222 8803

Brooks, C. G., MA Camb., PhD Lond. Sr. Lectr.
Calvert, Jane E., MSc Birm., PhD Birm. Sr.
Lectr.
Diamond, A. G., BA Oxf., DPhil Oxf. Sr. Lectr.
Fay, Anne C., BSc Belf., MB BCh Belf., MD
Belf. Sr. Lectr.§
Robinson, J. H., BSc Brist., PhD Sr. Lectr.
Searle, R. F., BSc Brist., PhD Brist. Sr. Lectr.
Spickett, G. P., BM BCh Oxf., MA Oxf., DPhil
Oxf., FRCP Sr. Lectr.§
Other Staff: 1 Lectr.†; 1 Hon. Lectr.

Microbiology

Archibald, A. R., BSc Edin., PhD Edin. Prof.,
Microbiological Chemistry
Barer, M. R., MB BS Lond., MSc Lond., PhD
Lond. Reader
Demarco de Hormaeche, R., PhD Camb. Sr.
Lectr.
Hancock, I. C., BSc Lond., PhD Lond. Sr. Lectr.
Harwood, C. R., BSc Lond., PhD Leeds Sr. Lectr.
Hormaeche, Carlos E., PhD Camb., MD Prof.
Kehoe, M. A., BSc N.U.I., PhD
Trinity(Dub.) Prof.
Williams, E., BSc Lond., PhD Lond. Sr. Lectr.
Other Staff: 1 Lectr.; 1 Hon. Sr. Lectr.; 1 Hon.
Lectr.

Virology

Scott, R., BSc PhD Sr. Lectr.
Toms, G. L., PhD Manc., BSc Sr. Lectr.
Turner, Andrew J. L., MB ChB Manc.,
FRCPath Sr. Lectr.§
Other Staff: 1 Lectr.

Neurosciences and Psychiatry, School of

Harris, J. B., BPharm Lond., PhD Brad.,
FIBiol Head of Sch.*

MRC Neurochemical Pathology Unit

Tel: (0191) 273 5251 Fax: (0191) 272 5291

Edwardson, J. A., BSc Nott., PhD Lond. Hon.
Prof.†, Neuroendocrinology
Ince, P. G., MB BS BSc MD Sr. Lectr.,
Neuropathology§
Perry, Elaine K., BSc St And., PhD Camb. Prof.,
Neurochemical Pathology
Perry, Robert H., MB ChB St And., FRCP,
FRCPath Reader, Neurochemical
Pathology§
Other Staff: 1 Hon. Reader; 1 Hon. Sr. Lectr.;
3 Hon. Lectrs.
Research: Alzheimer's disease and other
neurodegenerative disorders

Neurobiology

Fax: (0191) 222 5227

Bradley, P. M., BSc Birm., PhD Birm. Sr. Lectr.;
Head*
Hammond, G. R., BSc Brist., PhD Brist. Sr.
Lectr.
Harris, J. B., BPharm Lond., PhD Brad.,
FIBiol Action Res. Fund Prof., Experimental
Neurobiology
Murphy, P. R., BSc Glas., PhD Lond. Sr. Lectr.
Slater, C. R., AB Harv., PhD Lond. William
Leech Sr. Lectr., Clinical Science
Webb, Alison C., BA Lond., PhD Lond. Sr.
Lectr.
Other Staff: 4 Lectrs.; 1 Royal Society Res.
Fellow
Research: cellular and molecular pathology of
diseases of nerve and muscle; development
and plasticity in the nervous system;
information processing

Neurology

Fax: (0191) 222 8553

Barnes, M. P., MB ChB Brist., MD Brist.,
FRCP Prof., Neurological Rehabilitation
Bates, D., MA Camb., MB BChir Camb.,
FRCP Sr. Lectr.§
Burn, David J., MB BS Newcastle(UK), MD
Newcastle(UK), MA Oxf. Sr. Lectr.§
Cartlidge, N. E. F., MB BS, FRCP Sr. Lectr.§

Field, Anthony B., MB BS William and Dick
Leech Sr. Lectr., Neurological Rehabilitation
Goonetilleke, Ajith, MB BS Lond. Sr. Lectr.§
Hudgson, P., MB BS Melb., FRACP, FRCP Sr.
Lectr.§
Shaw, Pamela J., MD BS Prof., Neurological
Medicine
Turnbull, D. M., MB BS MD PhD, FRCP Prof.,
Neurology
Other Staff: 2 Lectrs.
Research: motor neurone disease and metabolic
diseases of the central nervous system;
pathogenesis of multiple sclerosis; peripheral
nervous system and muscle, including
development of appropriate forms of
rehabilitation for patients with severe
chronic neurological disease

Ophthalmology

Fax: (0191) 227 5165

Other Staff: 1 Lectr.; 1 Hon. Lectr.
Vacant Posts: 1 Prof.
Research: electrophysiological studies of retinal
disease and other diseases of the visual
system resulting from mitochondrial
abnormality

Psychiatry

Fax: (0191) 227 5108

Barker, P. J., PhD CNAA Prof., Psychiatric
Nursing Practice
Britton, P. G., BSc Durh., PhD, FBPsS Sr.
Lectr., Applied Psychology
Ferrier, I. N., BSc Glas., MB ChB Glas., MD Glas.,
FRCPsych, FRCP Prof.
Grubin, Donald, MB BS Lond., MA Oxf., MD
Lond. Prof., Forensic Psychiatry
Kalaria, Rajesh N., PhD Lond., FRCPath Prof.
Res. Fellow
McKeith, I. G., MB BS MD, FRCPsych Prof.,
Old Age Psychiatry
Moore, P. B., PhD Liv., MB BS Sr. Lectr.§
O'Brien, Gregory P., MB ChB Aberd., MA Camb.,
FRCPsych Sr. Lectr., Learning Disabilities§
O'Brien, John T., BM BCh DM Sr. Lectr.§
Scott, Janine L., MB BS MD, FRCPsych Prof.,
Community Psychiatry
Young, Alan H., MB ChB Edin., MPhil Edin.,
PhD Edin. Sr. Lectr.
Other Staff: 10 Lectrs.; 3 Hon. Sr. Lectrs.; 1
Hon. Lectr.
Vacant Posts: 1 Prof.; 1 Sr. Lectr.§
Research: clinical psychology and mental
handicap, and in-service evaluation and
epidemiology; neurobiology and treatment
of affective disorders and dementia;
psychiatric morbidity in prisons and the
treatment of sex offenders

Obstetrics and Gynaecology

Fax: (0191) 222 5066

Davison, J. M., BSc Durh., MSc Wales, MD BS,
FRCOG Hon. Prof., Obstetric Medicine
Dunlop, W., MB ChB Glas., PhD, FRCSEd,
FRCOG Prof.; Head*
Macphail, Sheila, BM S'ton., PhD Sr. Lectr.
Michael, Enid M., BM BCh Oxf., MA Oxf., DPhil
Oxf. Sr. Lectr.§
Robson, S. C., MB BS MD Prof., Fetal
Medicine
Singh, M. M., MB ChB Aberd., DM S'ton.,
FRCOG Sr. Lectr., Family Planning§
Other Staff: 2 Lectrs.; 2 Hon. Sr. Lectrs.
Vacant Posts: 1 Prof. Res. Fellow
Research: foetal medicine; gynaecological
urology; maternal medicine; reproductive
medicine

Oncology

Including North of England Cancer Research
Campaign -Cancer Research Unit

Calvert, A. H., MB BChir Camb., BA Camb., MSc
Lond., FRCP Prof.; Head*
Durcakz, Barbara W., BSc Edin., DPhil
Sus. Reader
Griffin, R. J., BSc CNAA, PhD Aston Sr. Lectr.
Lind, M. J., MB BS Lond., BSc Lond. Sr. Lectr.
Lunec, J., BSc Lond., PhD Lond. Sr. Lectr.

Newell, D. R., PhD *Lond.* Prof., Cancer
  Therapeutics
Sherbet, G. V., MSc *Poona*, PhD *Poona*, DSc *Lond.*,
  FIBiol, FRSChem, FRCPath Reader,
  Experimental Oncology
Other Staff: 6 Lectrs.
Research: cancer metastasis; clinical oncology;
  DNA damage and repair in cancer
  chemotherapy; molecular biology of cancer;
  pre-clinical and clinical pharmacology of
  anti-cancer drugs

Pathology

Fax: (0191) 222 8100

Angus, B., MB ChB *Aberd.*, BMedBiol *Aberd.*,
  PhD, FRCPath Sr. Lectr.
Bulmer, Judith N., MB ChB *Manc.*, PhD *Brist.*,
  FRCPath Sr. Lectr.
Burt, A. D., MB ChB *Glas.*, BSc *Glas.*, MD *Glas.*,
  FIBiol, FRCPath Prof., Hepatopathology;
  Head*
Cooper, Peter N., MB BS *Lond.*, BA *Camb.* Sr.
  Lectr., Forensic Pathology
Malcolm, A. J., MB ChB *Glas.*, FRCPath Prof.,
  Clinical Pathology
May, Felicity E. B., BSc *Glas.*, DPhil *Oxf.* Sr.
  Lectr.
Morley, A. R., MB BS *Durh.*, MD,
  FRCPath Reader, Renal Pathology
Westley, B. R., BSc *Brist.*, PhD *Brist.* Prof.,
  Molecular Pathology
Wright, C., BMedSci MB BS PhD Sr. Lectr.,
  Perinatal Pathology
Other Staff: 3 Lectrs.; 5 Hon. Lectrs.
Vacant Posts: 1 Prof.
Research: diagnostic dermatology; forensic
  pathology; molecular and cell biology of
  cancer; pathogenesis of immune mediated,
  metabolic and inflammatory disorders;
  perinatal pathology

Pharmacological Sciences

Including Northern Regional Drug and
  Therapeutic Centre

Fax: (0191) 222 7230

Bateman, D. N., BSc *Lond.*, MB BS *Lond.*, MD
  Lond., FRCP Reader, Therapeutics§
Ford, G. A., MB BChir *Camb.*, MA *Camb.*,
  FRCP Sr. Lectr., Clinical Pharmacology§
Rawlins, M. D., BSc *Lond.*, MD *Lond.*,
  FRCPEd Ruth and Lionel Jacobson Prof.,
  Clinical Pharmacology; Head*
Thomas, Simon H. L., MB BS *Lond.*, BSc *Lond.*,
  MD *Lond.* Sr. Lectr., Clinical Pharmacology§
Other Staff: 5 Lectrs.; 4 Hon. Lectrs.
Research: mechanisms of adverse drug reactions;
  pharmacoepidemiology; pharmacogenetics
  including zenobiotic metabolism;
  pharmacology of the elderly

Physiological Sciences

Fax: (0191) 222 6706

Allen, A., MA *Oxf.*, DPhil *Oxf.* Prof.,
  Physiological Biochemistry
Argent, B. E., PhD *Edin.*, BSc Prof., Cell
  Physiology
Gillespie, J. I., BSc *Glas.*, PhD *Glas.* Reader,
  Cellular Physiology
Gray, Michael A., BSc *Leeds*, PhD *Lond.* Sr.
  Lectr.
Green, G. R. G., MA *Oxf.*, BM BCh *Oxf.*, DPhil
  Oxf. Reader, Neurophysiology
Hirst, B. H., BSc PhD Prof., Cellular
  Physiology
Hurlbert, Anya G., MD *Harv.*, PhD *Harv.*, MA
  Camb. Reader, Visual Neuroscience
Pearson, J. P., BSc *Essex*, PhD *Lond.* Reader,
  Molecular Physiology
Reed, J. W., BSc *St And.*, PhD *Wales* Sr. Lectr.
Rees, Adrian, MA *Oxf.*, DPhil *Oxf.* Sr. Lectr.
Robinson, C. J., CBE, BSc *Sheff.*, PhD *Lond.* Sr.
  Lectr.
Sanders, D. J., BSc PhD Sr. Lectr.
Simmons, Nicholas L., BSc *Leic.*, PhD
  Leic. Prof., Epithelial Physiology
Whitaker, Michael J., MA *Camb.*, PhD
  Lond. Prof.; Head*
Other Staff: 4 Lectrs.; 1 Wellcome Res. Fellow

Research: cell signalling; epithelial physiology;
  mucous glycoproteins; respiratory function
  and exercise physiology; sensory and
  computational neuroscience

Psychiatry, see under Neuroscis. and
  Psychiat., Sch. of

Psychology

Fax: (0191) 222 5622

Lazarus, J., BSc *Lond.*, PhD *Wales* Reader,
  Animal Behaviour
Petrie, Marion, BSc *Sus.*, PhD *E.Anglia* Sr. Lectr.
Young, Malcolm P., BSc *Brist.*, PhD *St
  And.* Prof.; Head*
Other Staff: 10 Lectrs.; 1 Lectr.†
Research: behavioural ecology; brain and
  behaviour; health and applied psychology

Radiology, see under Clin. Med. Scis., Sch. of

Surgical Sciences, School of

Neal, Prof. David E., MB BS *Lond.*, BSc *Lond.*, MS
  Lond., FRCS, Hon. FRCSEd Head of Sch.*
Research: epithelial proliferation; smooth muscle
  research; surgical immunobiology

Anaesthesia

Fax: (0191) 222 8988

Baudouin, Simon V., BSc *Oxf.*, MB BS *Lond.*,
  MD *Lond.* Sr. Lectr.
Graham, Stephen G., MB ChB *Leeds*, FRCA Sr.
  Lectr.
Hull, C. J., MB BS *Lond.*, FRCA Prof.; Head*
Wright, Peter M. C., MB BCh BAO *Belf.*, MD
  Belf., FFARCSI Sr. Lectr.
Other Staff: 1 Lectr.

Anatomy and Clinical Skills Centre

Fax: (0191) 222 8803

Bradley, P. M., BSc *Birm.*, PhD *Birm.* Sr. Lectr.
Hammond, G. R., BSc *Brist.*, PhD *Brist.* Sr.
  Lectr.
Jordan, R. K., BSc PhD Prof., Medical
  Education; Dir.*
Miller, J. S. G., BM BCh *Oxf.*, MA *Oxf.*, DPhil
  Oxf. Emer. Prof.†
Murphy, P. R., BSc *Glas.*, PhD *Lond.* Sr. Lectr.
Searle, R. F., BSc *Brist.*, PhD *Brist.* Sr. Lectr.
Webb, Alison C., BA *Lond.*, PhD *Lond.* Sr.
  Lectr.
Other Staff: 2 Lectrs.

Surgery

Fax: (0191) 222 8514

Campbell, Frederick C., MB ChB *Glas.*, MD
  Glas., FRCSGlas, FRCSEd Prof.,
  Gastroenterological Surgery
Carding, Paul N., BA *Hull*, PhD Sr. Lectr.,
  Voice Pathology§
Dark, J. H., MB BS, FRCS, FRCSEd Reader,
  Cardiothoracic Surgery
Forty, J., MB BS BA MA, FRCSEd, FRCS Sr.
  Lectr.
Hamdy, F. C., MB ChB *Alexandria*, MD *Sheff.*,
  FRCSEd Sr. Lectr.
Jaffray, Bruce, BMedBiol *Aberd.*, MB ChB *Aberd.*,
  ChM *Aberd.*, FRCSGlas, FRCS Sr. Lectr.§
Jenkins, A. J., MB ChB *Glas.*, MD *Glas.*,
  FRCS Sr. Lectr., Neurosurgery
Kelly, Seamus B., MB BCh BAO *Belf.*, MD *Belf.*,
  FCRS Sr. Lectr.
Kirby, J. A., BA *York(UK)*, DPhil *York(UK)* Sr.
  Lectr., Transplantation Immunology
Leaper, David J., MB ChB *Leeds*, MD *Leeds*, ChM
  Leeds, FRCS, FRCSEd Prof.
Lennard, T. W. J., MB BS MD, FRCS Reader,
  Breast Surgery
Mellon, John K., MB BCh BAO *Belf.*, FRCSEd,
  FRCSI Sr. Lectr.
Mendelow, A. D., MB BCh *Witw.*,
  FRCSEd William Leech Prof.
Milner, R. H., MB ChB *Manc.*, BSc *Manc.*, MD
  Manc., FRCS Sr. Lectr., Plastic
  Reconstructive Surgery§
Neal, D. E., BSc *Lond.*, MB BS *Lond.*, MS *Lond.*,
  FRCS, Hon. FRCSEd Prof.; Head*

Proud, G., BDS *Durh.*, MB BS MD, FRCS Sr.
  Lectr.§
Varma, J. S., BSc *Edin.*, MB ChB *Edin.*, MD *Edin.*,
  FRCSEd Sr. Lectr.
Wilson, Janet A., MB ChB *Edin.*, MD
  Edin. Prof., Otolaryngology and Head and
  Neck Surgery
Wilson, Robert G., MD BS, FRCS, FRCSEd Sr.
  Lectr.§
Wright, P. D., MB BS MD, FRCS Sr. Lectr.§
Other Staff: 5 Lectrs.; 1 Hon. Lectr.
Vacant Posts: 1 Lectr.

Trauma and Orthopaedic Surgery

Fax: (0191) 222 8943

Gregg, Paul J., MD BS, FRCS Prof.,
  Orthopaedic Surgery; Head*§
Other Staff: 3 Lectrs.
Vacant Posts: 1 Sr. Lectr.

Virology, see under Microbiol., Immunol.
  and Virol. Scis., Sch. of

Other Appointments

Postgraduate Institute for Medicine and
  Dentistry

Fax: (0191) 221 1049

Anderson, Prof. J., MB BS *Durh.*, FRCP,
  FRCOG Postgrad. Dean; Dir.*
Smith, David G., BDS *Liv.*, FDSRCSEd Dent.
  Postgrad. Dean
van Zwanenberg, Timothy D., MB BChir *Camb.*,
  MA *Camb.*, FRCGP Prof., Postgraduate
  General Practice; Dir., Postgrad. Gen.
  Practice Educn.
Other Staff: 1 Lectr.

SPECIAL CENTRES, ETC

Audio Visual Centre

Down, Paul H. Dir.*

Computing Service

Salotti, Paul S., MA *St And.* Dir.*

Continuing Education, Centre for

Fax: (0191) 222 7090

Bavidge, M. C., BA *N.U.I.*, BD *Greg.* Sr. Lectr.,
  Philosophy; Head, Adult Educn. Programme.
Forster, I. H., OBE, BA *Durh.* Dir.*
Other Staff: 3 Lectrs.; 1 Course Devel. Officer

Engineering Design Centre

Hills, William, BSc *CNAA*, MPhil *CNAA* Prof.;
  Dir.*

Health of the Elderly, Institute for the

Edwardson, Prof. James A., BSc *Nott.*, PhD
  Lond. Dir.*

Language Centre

Including Business Language School

Fax: (0191) 222 5239

Green, B. D., MA *Birm.* Lectr.; Dir.*
Ogden, Mark R., BA *Camb.*, PhD *Camb.* Dir.,
  Bus. Lang. Sch.
Other Staff: 12 Lectrs.

Management, Newcastle School of

Vaughan, Roger, BSc PhD, FEng Exec. Dir.*

Physical Recreation and Sport, Centre for

Mayne, Vincent P., BSc *Sur.* Head of Fitness
  and Performance
Rayner, Graham S., BSc *Lond.* Dir.*

Urban and Rural Research, Institute for

Goddard, Prof. John B., OBE, BA *Lond.*, PhD
  Lond. Hon. Dir.*

CONTACT OFFICERS

Academic affairs. Senior Assistant Registrar: Draper, Ruth, BA *CNAA*, MBA

Accommodation. Head of Accommodation: Chabrzyk, Gillian I., BA *Durh.*

Admissions (first degree). Admissions Officer: Young, Kenneth J., MA *Oxf.*

Admissions (higher degree). Admissions Officer: Young, Kenneth J., MA *Oxf.*

Adult/continuing education. Director, Continuing Education: Forster, Ian H., OBE, BA *Durh.*

Alumni. Alumni Relations Officer: Cox, Christopher J., BA *Lond.*

Careers. Director, Careers Advisory Service: Firth, Richard A., MA *Oxf.*, DPhil *Oxf.*

Computing services. Director, Computing Service: Salotti, Paul S., MA *St And.*

Consultancy services. Director, Research Services: Wallen, Judith, BSc *Birm.*, MSc *Sheff.*

Credit transfer. Assistant Registrar: Braiden, Lesley, BA *Manc.*

Development/fund-raising. Secretary, University Development Trust: Thurgar-Dawson, C. J.

Estates and buildings/works and services. Director of Estates: Henderson, Stanley F.

Examinations. Examinations Officer: Minto, David C., BA *CNAA*

Finance. Director of Finance: Ranson, M. L., JP, FCA

General enquiries. Registrar: Nicholson, D. E. T., MA *Birm.*

Industrial liaison. Director, Research Services: Wallen, Judith, BSc *Birm.*, MSc *Sheff.*

International office. Director, International Office: McCarthy, Terence T., BE *N.U.I.*, MEngSc *N.U.I.*

Library (chief librarian). Librarian and Keeper of the Pybus Collection: Graham, Thomas W., MA *Glas.*, PhD *Glas.*

Personnel/human resources. Director of Human Resources: Johnston, Veryan S., BA *Durh.*, MBA *Durh.*

Public relations, information and marketing. Communications and Public Affairs Director: Harris, Christopher J., MA *Oxf.*

Publications. Publications Officer: Michie, Dinah A., BA *York(UK)*

Purchasing. Head of Procurement: Smith, Michael K.

Quality assurance and accreditation. Deputy Registrar: Mitchell, Paul S., BA *Liv.*, MA *Brist.*

Research. Director, Research Services: Wallen, Judith, BSc *Birm.*, MSc *Sheff.*

Safety. Safety Officer: Weston, Michael E., BSc(Eng) *S'ton.*

Scholarships, awards, loans. Deputy Registrar: Kidd, Jessica M., MA *Edin.*

Schools liaison. Assistant Registrar: Braiden, Lesley, BA *Manc.*

Student union. Union Society President: ......

Student welfare/counselling. Deputy Registrar: Kidd, Jessica M., MA *Edin.*

Students from other countries. Director, International Office: McCarthy, Terence T., BE *N.U.I.*, MEngSc *N.U.I.*

Students with disabilities. Deputy Registrar: Kidd, Jessica M., MA *Edin.*

[Information supplied by the institution as at March 1998, and edited by the ACU]

UNIVERSITY OF NORTH LONDON

Founded 1992; previously established as the Polytechnic of North London 1971

Member of the Association of Commonwealth Universities

Postal Address: 166-220 Holloway Road, London, England N7 8DB
Telephone: (0171) 607 2789 **Fax**: (0171) 753 5166 **Telex**: 25228 **WWW**: http://www.unl.ac.uk
E-mail formula: name@unl.ac.uk

CHAIR OF THE BOARD OF GOVERNORS—Coldwell, R., BA *Sus.*
VICE-CHANCELLOR AND CHIEF EXECUTIVE*—Roper, Brian A., BScEcon *Wales*, MA(Econ) *Manc.*
DEPUTY VICE-CHANCELLOR (ACADEMIC)—Ashman, Sandra, BA *Lond.*, MA *Sus.*
DEPUTY VICE-CHANCELLOR (FINANCE AND RESOURCES)—Atchison, M., BA *CNAA*, MSc *Lond.*
SECRETARY AND CLERK TO THE BOARD OF GOVERNORS—McParland, John, BA *Lond.*
ACADEMIC REGISTRAR‡—Storey, Moira, BSc *Nott.*, PhD *CNAA*

FACULTIES/SCHOOLS

Business School

Dean: Fawcett, Jean, BA *Leic.*, MSc(Econ) *Lond.*

Environmental and Social Studies

Dean: Somerville, Jennifer, BA *Lond.*, MSc *Lond.*, PhD *Lond.*

Humanities and Teacher Education

Dean: Condry, Gregory, BSc *Lond.*, PhD *Sur.*

Science, Computing and Engineering

Dean: Haines, Prof. L. Ian B., BSc PhD

ACADEMIC UNITS

Accounting

Tel: (0171) 753 5064 Fax: (0171) 753 5051

Allan, Stuart J., MA *Dund.* Sr. Lectr.
Archbold, J. Stuart, BA *CNAA*, MSc *Lond.* Principal Lectr.
Blewett, Frank, BA *Oxf.*, MA *Lanc.* Head*
Dawes, N. Sr. Lectr.
Filmer, Angela S., MA *Kent*, FCA Principal Lectr.
Naylor, Denise J., BSc *Durh.*, FCA Sr. Lectr.
Odedra, Sau, BSc MA Sr. Lectr.
Rajalingam, Nallathamby, MSc *Brun.* Sr. Lectr.
Reid, Ken C., BA *Strath.*, MBA Sr. Lectr.
Shaw, Humphrey R., MA *CNAA*, MSc *CNAA*, PhD *Wales* Sr. Lectr.

Architecture and Interior Design

Tel: (0171) 753 7006 Fax: (0171) 753 5764

Barnes, Robert, BA *Lond.*, MA Sr. Lectr.
Beigel, Florian, MSc Prof.
Caruso, Adam, BSc Sr. Lectr.
Chard, Nat, BA Sr. Lectr.
Clews, David Sr. Lectr.
Davies, Colin, MSc Sr. Lectr.
Harbison, Robert, BA PhD Prof.
Henry, Rex Sr. Lectr.
Hewitt, Mark, MA Sr. Lectr.
Holliss, Frances, BSc Sr. Lectr.
Kerr, Joe, BA MSc Sr. Lectr.
Lane, Andrew Sr. Lectr.
Lim, C. J. Sr. Lectr.
MacLaren, Gordon, BSc *Lond.* Sr. Lectr.
Mallinson, Helen, MA Head*
Mitchell, Maurice Sr. Lectr.
Montgomerie, Ian Sr. Lectr.
Nag, Rose, BA Sr. Lectr.
Nys, Rik Sr. Lectr.
Pascoe, Angie Principal Lectr.
Roberts, Chianna, BA Sr. Lectr.
St John, Peter, BSc Sr. Lectr.
Stone, Andrew Sr. Lectr.
Wilson, Michael, MA MSc Sr. Lectr.

Caribbean Studies

Seecharan, Clem, BA *McM.*, MA *McM.*, PhD *Warw.* Sr. Lectr.
Stubbs, Jean, BA *Essex*, PhD *Lond.* Prof.

Chemistry, Applied

Tel: (0171) 753 5152 Fax: (0171) 753 5402

Adatia, Trusha, BSc *CNAA*, PhD *CNAA* Sr. Lectr.
Anderson, P. N., BSc *Edin.*, PhD *Edin.* Sr. Lectr.
Bligh, S. W. Annie, BSc *Essex*, PhD *Essex* Sr. Lectr.
Charalambous, John, BSc *Lond.*, PhD *Lond.*, FRSChem Prof.
Conole, Grainne, BSc *Sheff.*, PhD *CNAA* Principal Lectr.
Hyatt, D., BSc *Leeds*, PhD *Leeds* Sr. Lectr.
Matthews, Ray W., BSc *S'ton.*, PhD *Reading*, FRSChem Head*
McPartlin, E. Mary, MSc *Lond.*, PhD *NSW* Prof.
Rees, R. G., BSc *Wales*, PhD *Lond.* Sr. Lectr.
Shepherd, Mike K., BSc *Brist.*, PhD *Brist.* Sr. Lectr.
Spillane, Dominic E. M., BSc *Lond.*, PhD *Lond.* Sr. Lectr.
Turner, D., BSc *Liv.*, PhD *Liv.* Sr. Lectr.
Watts, A. T., BSc *Lond.*, PhD *Lond.* Sr. Lectr.

Classics

Tel: (0171) 753 5109 Fax: (0171) 753 5090
Butterworth, John A., PhD *Lond.* Sr. Lectr.

Communication Studies, see Information and Communication Studies

Computing

Tel: (0171) 753 5127 Fax: (0171) 753 7009

Bavan, A. Siri, MSc Lond. Sr. Lectr.
Burton, Ronnie E., BA Trinity(Dub.), PhD Trinity(Dub.) Sr. Lectr.
Currie, Ed, BSc Salf., MSc Lond. Sr. Lectr.
Danicic, Seb, BSc Lond., MSc Oxf. Sr. Lectr.
Datta, Ashesh, MSc Lond Sr. Lectr.
Davidson, Keith V., BA Sr. Lectr.
Fairney, Paul T., BSc Wales, PhD Wales Sr. Lectr.
Feather, Howard N., BA Lond., MSc Lond. Sr. Lectr.
Georgiadou, Elli G., BA Lond. Sr. Lectr.
Harman, Mark, MSc Lond. Sr. Lectr.
Jones, Ray A. Sr. Lectr.
Milankovic-Atkinson, Maja, BSc Belgrade, MSc Sr. Lectr.
Mulholland, Mike, BA Kent, MSc Essex Sr. Lectr.
Paterson, Ross, PhD Qld. Sr. Lectr.
Sadler, Chris, MSc Rhodes, MSc Lond. Head*
Ward, Patricia, BSc Edin., MSc Sr. Lectr.

Economics

Tel: (0171) 753 5064 Fax: (0171) 753 5051

Cole, Stuart, BA E.Anglia, MSc Salf. Prof.
Curran, John G. M., BA CNAA, MA Lond. Principal Lectr.
Lysandrou, Photis, MSc(Econ) Lond., PhD Lond. Sr. Lectr.
Mananyi, Anthony, BA H.-W., MSc H.-W., PhD Paisley Sr. Lectr.
Morgan, Robert J., BA Lond., MSc(Econ) Lond. Head*
Sedgwick, John D., BSc(Econ) Lond., MA Lond., PhD Lond.Guild. Principal Lectr.
Simpson, Ruth C., MA Brun., BSc Sr. Lectr.
Smith, Steve W., MA Sus. Sr. Lectr.
Stang, Norman, BSc(Econ) Lond. Principal Lectr.

Engineering, Electronic and Communications

Tel: (0171) 753 5126 Fax: (0171) 753 7002

Bishop, Peter, BA Lond., MSc Sur. Principal Lectr.
Brinson, Michael E., BSc PhD, FIEE Principal Lectr.
Burnett, Stella J., BA Oxf., MA Sr. Lectr.
Chapman, Peter E., MSc PhD Sr. Lectr.
Cullinan, Michael, MSc Sr. Lectr.
Drake, Anthony J., MSc Sr. Lectr.
Duck, Michael, BSc Sr. Lectr.
Faulkner, David J., BSc Lond., PhD Lond. Sr. Lectr.
Hassan, Hoda, MSc Lond. Sr. Lectr.
Holmes, George E., BSc Hull, MSc Lond., PhD Lond. Sr. Lectr.
Kalymnios, Demetri, BSc PhD Sr. Lectr.
McFarlane, Craig, BSc Glas., PhD Stir. Sr. Lectr.
Meadows, Richard G., MSc Lond., PhD Lond., FIEE Prof.; Head*
Outred, Michael, BSc Lond., PhD Lond. Sr. Lectr.
Parsons, Alan J., BSc PhD Principal Lectr.
Ramnarine, Ray, MSc Lond., PhD Lond. Sr. Lectr.
Read, Richard J., BSc MSc Sr. Lectr.
Rogers, Ian W., BSc Durh., PhD Durh. Sr. Lectr.
Taghizadeh, Saeed, BSc Essex, MSc Lond. Sr. Lectr.
Virdee, Bal, BSc Leeds, MPhil Sr. Lectr.
Wilkins, Philip R., BSc Sr. Lectr.

European Studies, see Langs. and European Studies

Geography

Tel: (0171) 753 5133 Fax: (0171) 753 7014

Faulkner, Hazel, BSc Newcastle(UK), MSc Alta., PhD CNAA Sr. Lectr.
Foord, Joanna, BA Lond., PhD Kent Sr. Lectr.

Harris, Martin J., MA Oxf., MSc Oxf. Sr. Lectr.
Jennings, Simon C., BSc CNAA, PhD CNAA Sr. Lectr.
Knowles, Richard, MA Camb., MA Nott. Sr. Lectr.
Lewis, Jane, BA Sus., PhD Lond. Sr. Lectr.
Lindsay, J. M., PhD Edin. Sr. Lectr.
Millman, Roger N., BSc Lond., PhD Aberd. Sr. Lectr.
O'Reilly, Kevin J., BSc Hull, PhD Lond. Sr. Lectr.
Riley, David, BSc Reading, MSc Birm. Sr. Lectr.
Walters, Graham, BSc Lond., PhD Lond. Sr. Lectr.
Wareing, John, BA Leeds, MSc Lond. Head*

Health Studies

Tel: (0171) 753 5030 Fax: (0171) 753 5763

Bola, Manjit, BSc Manc.Met., MSc Manc. Sr. Lectr.
Borgeaud, Michael A., MA MSc Sr. Lectr.
Browne, Carina O., BEd MSc Sr. Lectr.
Goodman, Lesley Sr. Lectr.
Hendry, Joy M., BA Sr. Lectr.
Hosin, Amer, DPhil Ulster Sr. Lectr.
Moore, Simon, BSc Plym., PhD Middx. Sr. Lectr.
O'Keefe, Eileen, BA N.Y. Sr. Lectr.
Pfeffer, Naomi, BSc Lond., MSc Lond., PhD Essex Sr. Lectr.
Pike, Susan, BA MSc Head*
Skinner, Catherine J., MA N.Lond. Sr. Lectr.
Walpole, Tim, BSc Manc.Met., MSc Brun. Sr. Lectr.

History

Tel: (0171) 753 5109 Fax: (0171) 753 5090

Broad, John P. F., MA Oxf., DPhil Oxf., FRHistS Principal Lectr.
Castle, Kathryn A., MA Lond CNAA Lectr.
Fowkes, F. Ben M., BA Oxf., PhD Lond. Sr. Lectr.
Hitchcock, Tim V., DPhil Oxf. Sr. Lectr.
Holmes, Peter I., MA Lond., PhD Leic. Head*
Judd, Denis, BA Oxf., PhD Lond. Prof.
Lerman, Katherine A., BA Sus., DPhil Sus. Sr. Lectr.
Mercer, Patricia A., MA Oxf., PhD Lond. Sr. Lectr.
Murshid, Tazeen M., DPhil Oxf. Sr. Lectr.
Nicolson, Colin, BA Birm. Sr. Lectr.
O'Day, Alan E., BA Mich., MA Lond., PhD Lond. Sr. Lectr.
Quinault, Roland E., BA Oxf., MPhil Oxf. Sr. Lectr.
Scott, Catherine, MSc Lond. Sr. Lectr.
Soper, Catherine F., BA Oxf. Sr. Lectr.
Szondi, Juliet O., BSc York, MSc Lond. Sr. Lectr.
Tosh, John A., BA Oxf., MA Kent, PhD Lond. Prof.

HITECC

Tel: (0171) 753 5117 Fax: (0171) 753 5047

Pickard, M., BSc Newcastle(UK) Sr. Lectr.

Information and Communication Studies

Tel: (0171) 753 5031 Fax: (0171) 753 5763

Andretta, Susan, BA CNAA, MA N.Lond. Sr. Lectr.
Banks, Marion, BSc CNAA, MA City(UK) Sr. Lectr.
Beard, Anthony J., BA Exe. Sr. Lectr.
Beck, Terry J., MSc Lond. Sr. Lectr.
Datta, Suman, BSc Delhi, PhD City(UK) Sr. Lectr.
Entwistle, Joanne, BA Lond. Sr. Lectr.
Freedman, Des, BA Col., MA Lond. Sr. Lectr.
Lievesley, Geoffrey, MSc Lond. Sr. Lectr.
Milner, Eileen, BA Wales Sr. Lectr.
Skues, Richard, BA Wales, MSc Lond. Principal Lectr.
Vaughan, Anthony H., BA Hull, MA Hull Sr. Lectr.
Webb, Stephen, MSc Oxf. Head*
Wilson, Elizabeth, BA Oxf. Prof.

Information Science, see Quantitative Methods and Information Sci.

Interior Design, see Archit. and Interior Des.

Languages and European Studies

Tel: (0171) 753 5108 Fax: (0171) 753 7069

Bissar, Dounia, Lic Bruxelles, MA Lond. Sr. Lectr.
Bojcun, Marko, BA Tor., MLitt Glas., PhD Tor. Sr. Lectr.
Brouwer, Frank W., BA Essex, MPhil Camb. Sr. Lectr.
Carlisle, Ann, BA Nott., MA Lond. Principal Lectr.
Cottis, Eileen, BLitt Oxf., MA Oxf. Sr. Lectr.
Davies, Howard, PhD Lond. Principal Lectr.
Desblache, Lucile, Lic Aix-Marseilles, Dr Paris Sr. Lectr.
Duenas-Tancred, Marta, BA Lond. Sr. Lectr.
Edye, David W. M., BA Kent, MPhil Bath Sr. Lectr.
Farrell, Mary, BComm N.U.I., MA N.U.I. Sr. Lectr.
Fishburn, Evelyn, BA Lond., PhD Lond. Prof.
Gowan, Peter, BA S'ton., MA Birm. Principal Lectr.
Hickman, Mary, BA Liv., MSc Liv., PhD Liv. Principal Lectr.
Hinrichsen, P. Alberto, BSc Concepción Sr. Lectr.
Jones, Monique Sr. Lectr.
Kemp, Patricia, BA Brist., MA Cran. Sr. Lectr.
Ketteringham, Graham, BA Coventry Sr. Lectr.
Kidman, John, BA Adel., DU Paris Head*
McBride, Nicole, Lic Paris Principal Lectr.
Moore, Jonathan, BA Leeds, MA Essex Principal Lectr.
Newman, Michael D., DPhil Oxf. Prof.
Oppenheimer, Helen, BA Lond., PhD Lond. Sr. Lectr.
Palmer, Yvette, Lic Caen, MA Reading Sr. Lectr.
Phillips, Helen, BA Sheff.Hallam, MA Lond. Sr. Lectr.
Russell, Susan, BA Lanc. Sr. Lectr.
Seago, Karen, MA Manc. Sr. Lectr.
Souto, Carmen, BA N.Lond., MA Lond. Sr. Lectr.
Stang, Hilary, BA Lond., MA Lond. Sr. Lectr.
Swithinbank, Ron, BA Sheff., MA Lond. Principal Lectr.
Thomas, Lyn, BA Oxf., MA Lond. Sr. Lectr.
Weber-Newth, Ingelore, MPhil Cran. Sr. Lectr.

Law

Tel: (0171) 753 5032 Fax: (0171) 753 5403

Barrow, Charles J., BSc Wales Sr. Lectr.
Barter, Caron Sr. Lectr.
Carr, Helen Sr. Lectr.
Conway, Margaret Sr. Lectr.
Davidson, Tom Sr. Lectr.
Goonewardene, Anil D., LLM S.Lanka Sr. Lectr.
Harden, Janetta H., LLB Principal Lectr.
Leyland, Peter J., MA Sr. Lectr.
Loveless, Janet Sr. Lectr.
Martin, Patricia Sr. Lectr.
Mulcahey, Linda, LLM Lond. Reader
Rich, Anthony, BA Sr. Lectr.
Sheinman, Leslie, LLB MA Head*
Snaith, Clifton V., PhD Hull, LLB Sr. Lectr.
Sutters, Mark, LLB MA Sr. Lectr.
Weyland, Rene I., PhD Sr. Lectr.
Woods, Terry Sr. Lectr.

Leisure and Tourism

Tel: (0171) 753 5064 Fax: (0171) 753 5051

Aitchison, Cara, MA Edin. Principal Lectr.
Burns, Peter M., MA CNAA Sr. Lectr.
Cleverdon, Robert Sr. Lectr.; Sloan Fellow
Coghlan, Patrick, MA Exe. Sr. Lectr.
Curson, Anthony, BA Leic., MA CNAA Sr. Lectr.
Evans, Graham L., PhD City(UK) Reader
Fitzgerald, Kevin P., BSc Sur., MSc Lond. Head*
Flagg, Michael J., MA CNAA Sr. Lectr.
Hitchcock, Michael, BA Belf., DPhil Oxf. Prof.
Holden, Andrew, BSc E.Anglia Sr. Lectr.
Kitts, Clare, BA CNAA, MA CNAA Sr. Lectr.

Lentell, Robert N., BA Camb. Sr. Lectr.
McFarlane-Smith, Melanie Sr. Lectr.
Peacock, Martin J., BSc(Econ) Lond. Sr. Lectr.
White, Judy, BA Birm., PhD Camb. Reader
Wood, Patricia A., MA Principal Lectr.

Life Sciences

Tel: (0171) 753 7023 Fax: (0171) 753 5081
Ahluwalia, Kathleen P., BSc Sheff., PhD
Sheff. Sr. Lectr.
Bailey, Susan E. K., BEd Brist., MSc Lond. Sr.
Lectr.
Bointon, Brian, BSc Reading, PhD Reading Head*
Boothby, Derek, BSc Hull, PhD Lond. Sr. Lectr.
Bowden, Christopher, BSc Leeds Sr. Lectr.
Brownson, Carol, BSc Adel., PhD
Lond. Principal Lectr.
Cragg, Paul, BSc Lond., PhD Lond. Sr. Lectr.
Giles, Barry, BSc Lond., PhD Lond. Sr. Lectr.
Harrison, Maureen A., MSc Lond. Sr. Lectr.
Heydecker, Jane, BSc E.Anglia, PhD Lond. Sr.
Lectr.
Kitson, Michael, MSc Lond. Sr. Lectr.
Marlow, Nigel, BA Leeds, BSc Lond., MSc
Lond. Sr. Lectr.
Marshall, Richard J. Sr. Lectr.
Matewele, Paul, MSc S'ton., PhD S'ton. Sr.
Lectr.
McAthey, Pamela, BSc Newcastle(UK), PhD
Newcastle(UK) Principal Lectr.
McCarthy, H. David, BSc Lond., PhD Manc. Sr.
Lectr.
Mooney, Catherine A., MSc Trinity(Dub.) Sr.
Lectr.
Roberts, Michael, BSc Lond., PhD Lond. Sr.
Lectr.
Sanderson, Margaret E., MSc Cran.IT Principal
Lectr.
Searle, Andrew J., PhD Sr. Lectr.
Shaw, P. Graham, BSc Brist., PhD Sr. Lectr.
Woodward, Christopher, BA Oxf., MSc Lond.,
PhD Camb. Sr. Lectr.

Literary and Media Studies

Tel: (0171) 753 5019 Fax: (0171) 753 5090
Barker, Robert I., MA Sr. Lectr.
Bland, Lucy S., MA Manc. Sr. Lectr.
Breen, Jennifer M., BA Lond., PhD Lond. Sr.
Lectr.
Buck, Claire E., PhD Kent Principal Lectr.
Carson, Bruce J., BA Kent, MA CNAA Sr. Lectr.
Cooper, Caroline M., PhD Lond. Sr. Lectr.
Crowley, Helen C., PhD Syd. Sr. Lectr.
Griffiths, Trevor R., MA Warw., PhD
Warw. Prof.
Jackson, Patricia M., BA Sr. Lectr.
Jaeger, Joan, BA Lond., MSc Kent Head*
Lees, Sue, BA Lond., MA Lond. Prof.
Llewellyn-Jones, Margaret, BA Brist., MA CNAA,
MPhil Essex Principal Lectr.
MacKinnon, J. Kenneth, MA Edin., BLitt
Oxf. Prof.
McMurtrie, Alan M. Sr. Lectr.
McSorley, Paul, MA Leeds Sr. Lectr.
Metcalf, Margaret, BA Leic., MA Leic. Sr. Lectr.
Murray, Patricia, BA Oxf., MA Warw., PhD Sr.
Lectr.
Rolfe, Chris J., BA BPhil Principal Lectr.
Smith, Suzanne H. H., BA Reading Sr. Lectr.
Wheeler, Wendy J., BA CNAA, DPhil Sus. Sr.
Lectr.
White, Fiona W., MA Sus. Principal Lectr.
Wilson, Peter, PhD Essex Principal Lectr.
Wood, Briar, DPhil Sus. Sr. Lectr.

Mathematical Sciences

Tel: (0171) 753 5119 Fax: (0171) 753 7009
Alexandrou, Nick, BSc Lond., PhD Lond. Head*
Atkinson, J. B., MSc Hull, MA Oxf. Sr. Lectr.
Bowles, J. G., MSc S'ton. Sr. Lectr.
Carling, J., BSc S'ton., PhD Brist. Sr. Lectr.
Comley, W. J., MSc Lond., PhD Lond. Sr. Lectr.
Cooper, Colin D., BSc Sus., MSc Lond., PhD
Lond. Sr. Lectr.
Kennard, K. C. V., BA MSc Sr. Lectr.
Kissin, Edward, BSc Moscow, PhD Moscow Prof.
O'Gorman, Sue, MSc Lond., PhD
Lond. Principal Lectr.

Pegg, P. A., BSc Sheff., PhD Sheff. Sr. Lectr.
Rigby, R. A., MSc Lond., PhD Lond. Sr. Lectr.
Robert, Helen R., BSc Manc. Principal Lectr.
Shapiro, Janet R. M., BSc Lond. Sr. Lectr.
Singh, Pinder, MSc Reading, PhD CNAA Sr.
Lectr.
Smallwood, Catherine V., MSc Sheff., MSc
Lond. Principal Lectr.
Stasinopoulos, D. M., BA Athens, PhD Exe. Sr.
Lectr.
Tan, Hwee Y., MSc Lond. Sr. Lectr.

Media Studies, see Literary and Media
Studies

Operational Management

Tel: (0171) 753 5064 Fax: (0171) 753 5051
Bamford, Janet, BA Lond., LLM Lond. Sr. Lectr.
Dutta, Robene, BSc Manc., MSc Lough.,
MBA Sr. Lectr.
Goodfellow, John H., BA CNAA, MSc
City(UK) Principal Lectr.
Johnson, Linda R., LLB Lond., LLM
Lond. Principal Lectr.
Johnstone, Susan, BA Lond., LLM Lond. Sr.
Lectr.
Loncke, Vernon, LLB Lond., MA Sr. Lectr.
Ludlow, Stephen, BSc Brun., MBA Sr. Lectr.
Moore, Mark, BA Sr. Lectr.
Shaw, Steve J., BA Lond. Sr. Lectr.
Shoderu, Ronke, BA Sr. Lectr.
Winstanley, Nick C., BA Oxf., MBA Sr. Lectr.
Woolrich, Rod G., BA Wales, MSc
Salf. Principal Lectr.

Organisation and Employment Studies

Tel: (0171) 753 5064 Fax: (0171) 753 5051
Andrew, David J., BA Sus., MSc Lond. Principal
Lectr.
Bhopal, Mhinder, BA Abertay, MSc Lond. Sr.
Lectr.
Clark, John T., BA Warw. Sr. Lectr.
Clarke, Adrienne, BA CNAA, MA Principal
Lectr.
Colgan, Fiona B., BA Sheff., MA Sr. Lectr.
Fisk, Barbara, MSc City(UK), PhD City(UK) Sr.
Lectr.
Green, Miriam R., BA Cape Town, MA Lond. Sr.
Lectr.
Holmes, Len M., BA Nott., MPhil
Lanc. Principal Lectr.
Joyce, Paul C., BSc City(UK), PhD Lond. Prof.
Kalsi, Kiran, BA Brad., MA Lond., MBA Sr.
Lectr.
McNulty, Anthony J., BA Liv., MA Principal
Lectr.
Tomlinson, Frances D., BSc Brist. Principal
Lectr.
Upchurch, Martin, BSc(Econ) Hull, MSc
Reading Sr. Lectr.

Philosophy

Tel: (0171) 753 5109 Fax: (0171) 753 5090
Grant, James P. C., BA E.Anglia, BPhil Oxf. Sr.
Lectr.
Haworth, Alan E., BA Keele, PhD Lond. Sr.
Lectr.
Pickering, Rodney, MA Oxf., PhD
Lond. Principal Lectr.
Wright, Andrew C. H., BA MPhil Principal
Lectr.

**Policy Studies, Politics, and Social
Research**

Tel: (0171) 753 5033 Fax: (0171) 753 5763
Castle, Mita, BSc Liv., MLitt Lond. Sr. Lectr.
Gallacher, Roddy, BA Paisley Principal Lectr.
Ginsburg, Norman, BA Camb. Prof.
Hallam, Roger, BA Leic., MPhil Lond. Principal
Lectr.
Hodgkinson, Peter, BA CNAA, PhD Lond. Sr.
Lectr.
Kellaher, Leonie, BA Lond. Sr. Lectr.
Knight, Kelvin, BA York(UK), PhD Lond. Sr.
Lectr.
Nafissi, Mohammad, MA Principal Lectr.
Parry-Crooke, Georgie, BA CNAA Sr. Lectr.

Phillips, David R., BA York(UK), MSc
Lond. Head*
Rose, Aidan, BA Brad., PhD Principal Lectr.
Sefton-Green, Dorothy B., MA Oxf., MSc(Econ)
Lond. Sr. Lectr.
Sharp, Cathy, BA Sheff., PhD Sheff. Sr. Lectr.
Storey, Angele, BA Keele Sr. Lectr.
Sullivan, Cathy, BA E.Anglia Sr. Lectr.
Taylor, David, BSc Bath, MA(Econ) Manc. Sr.
Lectr.
Watts, Nicholas, BA Keele, MSc Sur.,
PhD Principal Lectr.

Polymer Technology

Tel: (0171) 753 5128 Fax: (0171) 753 5081
Alger, Mark S. M., BSc Lond., PhD Lond. Sr.
Lectr.
Cracknell, Peter S. Sr. Lectr.
Dunning, David J., MSc Lond. Sr. Lectr.
Dyson, Robert W., BSc Liv., PhD Liv.,
FRSChem Sr. Lectr.
Farid, A. S., BSc Lond., PhD Lond. Sr. Lectr.
Hashemi, S., MSc PhD Sr. Lectr.
O'Brien, Michael G., BSc Sur., PhD Sur. Head*
Read, Robin T., MSc Lond., PhD Lond. Sr.
Lectr.
Stanworth, Ben Sr. Lectr.

**Quantitative Methods and Information
Science**

Tel: (0171) 753 5064 Fax: (0171) 753 5051
Broadbent, Michael A., BSc Lond., MA Sr.
Lectr.
Charlesworth, Richard, BSc Manc., MSc
Manc. Principal Lectr.
Coshall, John T., BSc Lond., PhD Lond. Sr.
Lectr.
Geary, Janet C. Sr. Lectr.
Musa, Ghulam M., MA Punjab Sr. Lectr.
Pokorny, Michael, BSc Syd., MSc
Lond. Principal Lectr.
Rauchwerger, John V., BSc Lond. Sr. Lectr.
Slack, Robert, BSc Lanc. Sr. Lectr.
Tootoonchian, Soodabeh, BA Lond., MSc
Lond. Sr. Lectr.
Topple, Martin S., BA CNAA, MSc
Lond. Principal Lectr.

Social Work

Tel: (0171) 753 5034 Fax: (0171) 753 5763
Daulphin, Jaye, MA CNAA Sr. Lectr.
Dustin, Donna, BSc Brad., MSc Lond. Sr. Lectr.
Einhorn, Susan J., BA Sr. Lectr.
Goosey, David J. P., BA Birm., MSc
Birm. Principal Lectr.
Keating, F., BSc Cape Town, MEd Manc., PhD
Wash. Sr. Lectr.
Kirkwood, Richard J., BA Oxf. Sr. Lectr.
Lawrence, Susan, MA CNAA Sr. Lectr.
Liverpool, Verrol, MSc Sr. Lectr.
Madge, Gillian R., BA Lond., MSc Lond. Sr.
Lectr.
Onslow, Vivien, BSc Sr. Lectr.
Sobers, Anthony A., BA Lond., MSc Lond. Sr.
Lectr.

Teaching Studies

Tel: (0171) 753 5104 Fax: (0171) 753 5400
Adams, Julie, MA Lond. Sr. Lectr.
Brown, Maureen, BEd Lond. Sr. Lectr.
Burn, Elizabeth, BA Open(UK) Sr. Lectr.
Collison, Helen, MEd Lond. Sr. Lectr.
Cunningham, Peter, BSc CNAA Sr. Lectr.
Datta, Manjula, BA Calc., MA Lond. Sr. Lectr.
Dyton, Philip E., MPhil Nott. Principal Lectr.
East, Patricia A., BSc Lond., MA Lond. Principal
Lectr.
Emblen, Valerie, MPhil Sr. Lectr.
Eve, Patrick, MEd Lond. Sr. Lectr.
Faust, Hilary, BA Manc. Sr. Lectr.
Fine, Carol A., MEd Liv. Sr. Lectr.
Goymer, Clare R., BA Lond., MA
Lond. Principal Lectr.
Holmes, Angela M., MSc Reading Sr. Lectr.
Hutchings, Merryn, MA Camb. Reader
Kendrick, Tony P., MA Lond. Sr. Lectr.
Mann, Alan J., MA Lond. Principal Lectr.
Menter, Ian, MEd CNAA Head*

Merttens, Ruth P., MEd Lond.   Prof.
Moger, Rosalind, MEd Exe.   Sr. Lectr.
Neophytou, Maria, MA Lond.   Sr. Lectr.
Northcote, Anny, MA Lond.   Sr. Lectr.
O'Keeffe, Dennis J., BA Durh., BSc(Econ) Lond.,
   PhD Lond.   Sr. Lectr.
Patel, Lina, MSc Lond.   Sr. Lectr.
Pomphrey, Catherine, MA Reading   Sr. Lectr.
Richards, Christopher, MA Lond.   Sr. Lectr.
Ross, Alistair G., PhD Lond.   Prof.
Sanders, Peter   Sr. Lectr.
Singh, Bhupinder K.   Sr. Lectr.
Smidt, Sandra, MEd Manc.   Sr. Lectr.
Staley, Jill, MA Open(UK)   Principal Lectr.
Taylor, Lindsay J., BSc Birm.   Sr. Lectr.
Thornbury, Mary-Lou, MA NZ   Sr. Lectr.
Wadsworth, Pamela A., MA Lond.   Sr. Lectr.
Williams, Claudette C., MA Lond.   Sr. Lectr.
Wright, Susan, MA Lond., BEd   Sr. Lectr.
Wyvill, Barbara, MSc Lond.   Sr. Lectr.

Tourism, see Leisure and Tourism

SPECIAL CENTRES, ETC

Applied Social Research Unit
Tel: (0171) 753 5379 Fax: (0171) 753 5421
Hayes, Michael, BA Leic.   Dir.*

Architecture Research Unit
Tel: (0171) 753 5036 Fax: (0171) 753 7034
Beigel, Florian, MSc   Dir.*

Child and Women Abuse Studies Unit
Tel: (0171) 753 5037 Fax: (0171) 753 5763
Burton, Sheila   Dir.*
Kelly, Elizabeth   Dir.*
Regan, Linda, BA CNAA   Dir.*

Environmental and Social Studies in Ageing, Centre for
Tel: (0171) 753 5038 Fax: (0171) 753 7018
Kellaher, Leonie, BSc Lond.   Dir.*

Environmental Resource Management, Centre for
Tel: (0171) 753 5133 Fax: (0171) 753 5763
Jennings, Simon, BA CNAA, PhD CNAA   Dir.*

Equality Research in Business, Centre for
Tel: (0171) 753 7063 Fax: (0171) 753 5051
Colgan, Fiona, BA Sheff., MA McG.   Dir.*

Ethnicity and Gender, Centre for Research in
Fax: (0171) 753 5420
Lees, Sue, BSc Lond., MA Lond.   Dir.*

Higher Education and Access Development Centre
Tel: (0171) 753 7045 Fax: (0171) 753 5012
Joscelyne, Trevor, MA Camb., DPhil York(UK)   Dir.*

Irish Studies Centre
Tel: (0171) 753 5018 Fax: (0171) 753 7069
Hickman, Mary, BA Liv., MSc CNAA, PhD Lond.   Dir.*

Leisure and Tourism Studies, Centre for
Tel: (0171) 753 5065 Fax: (0171) 753 5051
Evans, Graham, MA City(UK)   Dir.*

Local Enterprise Research Unit
Tel: (0171) 753 5184 Fax: (0171) 753 5051
McNulty, Tony, BA Liv., MA   Dir.*

London European Research Centre
Tel: (0171) 753 5104 Fax: (0171) 753 5420
Newman, Michael, BA Oxf., DPhil Oxf.   Dir.*

Low Energy Architecture Research Unit
Tel: (0171) 753 7006 Fax: (0171) 753 5786
Wilson, Michael, MA MSc   Dir.*

Management Research Centre
Tel: (0171) 753 3219 Fax: (0171) 753 5051
Joyce, Paul C., BSc City(UK), PhD Lond.   Dir.*

Parents and Teachers in Maths Teaching Unit
Tel: (0171) 753 5104 Fax: (0171) 753 5400
Merttens, Ruth, BA MEd   Dir.*

Primary Schools and Industry Centre
Tel: (0171) 753 5104 Fax: (0171) 753 5400
Ross, Alistair, BScEcon Lond., MA Lond., PhD Lond.   Dir.*

Statistics, OR and Probability Methods Research Centre
Tel: (0171) 753 5792 Fax: (0171) 753 5793
Gilchrist, Robert, BPhil Oxf., MA Oxf., PhD Lond.   Dir.*

Transport Research and Consultancy
Tel: (0171) 753 5080 Fax: (0171) 753 5051
Cole, Stuart, BA E.Anglia, MSc Salf.   Dir.*

University of North London Microwaves
Tel: (0171) 753 5372 Fax: (0171) 753 7002
Meadows, Richard, BSc MSc PhD, FIEE   Dir.*

Urban Research Centre
Tel: (0171) 753 5133 Fax: (0171) 753 5763
Foord, Joanna, BA Lond., PhD Kent   Dir.*

CONTACT OFFICERS

Academic affairs. Academic Registrar: Storey, Moira, BSc Nott., PhD CNAA
Accommodation. Accommodation Officer: Furey, Mary
Admissions (first degree). Head of Admissions Office: Watt, Stephanie, BA Liv.
Admissions (higher degree). Head of Admissions Office: Watt, Stephanie, BA Liv.
Adult/continuing education. Director of Higher Education Access Development: Joscelyne, Trevor, MA Camb., DPhil York(UK)
Alumni. Alumni/Direct Marketing Officer: ......
Careers. Senior Careers Advisory Manager: Jones, Terry, BA Brist.
Computing services. Head of Computing, Library and Media Services: Harrigan, Kevin
Credit transfer. Head of Interfaculty Studies: Payne, Helen, BSc CNAA, MBA
Development/fund-raising. Secretary and Clerk to the Board of Governors: McParland, John, BA Lond.
Equal opportunities. Secretary and Clerk to the Board of Governors: McParland, John, BA Lond.
Estates and buildings/works and services. Head of Property Planning and Estates Development: Elderton, Richard
Examinations. James, Nicola
Finance. Head of Finance: Dryden, Peter
General enquiries. Secretary and Clerk to the Board of Governors: McParland, John, BA Lond.

Health services. Director of Student Services: Dedman, Steven
International office. Director of International Office: Harvey, Stephen, BA Kent
Library (enquiries). Associate Head of Computing, Library and Media Services: Williams, Roy, BA
Minorities/disadvantaged groups. Director of Personnel Services: Link, Lyn, BA Leic.
Ombudsperson. Secretary and Clerk to the Board of Governors: McParland, John, BA Lond.
Personnel/human resources. Director of Personnel Services: Link, Lyn, BA Leic.
Public relations, information and marketing. Head of Marketing and Communications: Callen, John
Publications. Head of Marketing and Communications: Callen, John
Purchasing. Head of Purchasing: Foss, Jenny
Quality assurance and accreditation. Assistant Academic Registrar (Quality): Stead, Christina, BA Durh.
Research. Assistant Academic Registrar (Research): Jones, Sharon, BSc CNAA, MSc Sus.
Safety. Facilities Manager: Friary, John
Scholarships, awards, loans. Administrative Officer: Smith, Adrian, BA Leic.
Schools liaison. Head of Marketing and Communications: Callen, John
Sport and recreation. Sports and Recreation Organiser: Jennings, Ian, BA CNAA
Staff development and training. Personnel Officer: Winder, Marjorie, BA Sus.
Student union. President of Student Union: ......
Student welfare/counselling. Assistant Director of Student Services: Nelson, Ian, PhD
Students from other countries. Director of International Office: Harvey, Stephen, BA Kent
Students with disabilities. Disabilities Co-ordinator: Davies, Caroline, BA York(UK), PhD Lond.
University press. Publications Officer: Powell, Susan, BA Leic.
Women. Director of Personnel Services: Link, Lyn, BA Leic.

CAMPUS/COLLEGE HEADS

City and Islington College, City Campus, Bunhill Row, London EC1Y 8LQ. Principal: Jupp, Thomas
College of North East London, Park Road, Bounds Green, London N11 2QF. Principal: Macwhinnie, Ian
Kingsway College, Regents Park Centre, Longford Street, London NW1 3HB. Principal: Haikin, Patricia
Lambeth College, 45 Clapham Common, Southside, London SW4 9BL. Principal: Perry, Adrian
London International College, 7-9 Palace Gate, London W8 5LS. Director: Theodorou, Theo P.
South-East Essex College of Arts and Technology, Carnarvon Road, Southend-on-Sea, Essex SS2 6LS. Director and Chief Executive: Pritchard, Anthony
Waltham Forest College, Forest Road, London E17 4JB. Chief Executive: Bourke, Michael

[Information supplied by the institution as at 17 December 1996, and edited by the ACU]

UNIVERSITY OF NORTHUMBRIA AT NEWCASTLE

Founded 1992; previously Newcastle Polytechnic 1969

Member of the Association of Commonwealth Universities

Postal Address: Ellison Building, Ellison Place, Newcastle upon Tyne, England NE1 8ST
Telephone: (0191) 232 6002 **Fax**: (0191) 227 4017 **Telex**: 53519

VICE-CHANCELLOR AND CHIEF EXECUTIVE*—Smith, Prof. Gilbert, BA *Leeds*, MA *Essex*, PhD *Aberd*.
UNIVERSITY SECRETARY—Bott, Richard A., BSc(Econ) MSc, FCIS
ACADEMIC REGISTRAR‡—Penna, Cheryl, BA

GENERAL INFORMATION

History. The university was originally established as Newcastle upon Tyne Polytechnic by the amalgamation in 1969 of the College of Art and Industrial Design, Municipal College of Commerce, and Rutherford College of Technology. It was later amalgamated with City College of Education (1974), Northern Counties College of Education (1976), and with Bede, Newcastle and Northumbria College of Health Studies (1995). University status was achieved under its present name in 1992.

Admission to first degree courses (see also United Kingdom Introduction). Through Universities and Colleges Admissions Service (UCAS).

First Degrees (see also United Kingdom Directory to Subjects of Study). BA, BEng, BSc, LLB, MChem, MEng, MMath.

Higher Degrees (see also United Kingdom Directory to Subjects of Study). MA, MEd, MSc, MPhil, PhD.

Libraries. 500,000 volumes. Special collection: European Documentation Centre, which receives one copy of all official EC documents direct from Brussels or Luxembourg.

Fees (1998–99, annual). Undergraduate (international students): £4700 (foundation years); £5600 (classroom-based courses); £6100 (laboratory-based courses).

Academic Year. Two semesters.

Income (year ending July 1997). Total, £89,245,000.

Statistics. Staff: 792 academic, 1202 administrative. Students: full-time 14,043; part time 9,621; international 1319; total 23,664.

FACULTIES/SCHOOLS

Arts and Design
Tel: (0191) 227 4413 Fax: (0191) 227 4559
Dean: McConkey, Prof. Kenneth, MA
Secretary: Sweet, Barbara

Engineeering, Science and Technology
Tel: (0191) 227 4453 Fax: (0191) 227 4561
Dean: Wilson, Prof. John, BSc PhD
Secretary: Plumridge, Jackie

Health, Social Work and Education
Tel: (0191) 227 4431 Fax: (0191) 227 4419
Dean: Stephens, Prof. Royston, BA MA PhD
Secretary: Anderson, Julie

Newcastle Business School
Tel: (0191) 227 4433 Fax: (0191) 227 3893
Director: Weir, Prof. David, MA
Secretary: Alexander, Lisa

Social Sciences
Tel: (0191) 227 4444 Fax: (0191) 227 4558
Dean: Shaw, Prof. Monica, BA MPhil PhD
Secretary: Howe, Linda

ACADEMIC UNITS

Behavioural and Environmental Sciences, School of
Tel: (0191) 227 4444 Fax: (0191) 227 4715
Buswell, Dick, BA Prof.; Head*
Research: applied cognition; applied psychology; geography and environmental management; housing; social cognition

Built Environment
Tel: (0191) 227 4722 Fax: (0191) 227 3167
Newall, Alan, BSc PhD Prof.; Head*
Research: building design and conservation; building management; energy systems and photovoltaics; urban design; urban property analysis

Business, see Newcastle Bus. Sch.

Chemical and Life Sciences
Tel: (0191) 227 4721 Fax: (0191) 227 3519
Gardiner, Derek, BSc PhD Prof.; Head*
Research: analytical chemistry; biomedical science; chemical reaction mechanisms and dynamics; environmental chemistry; synthetic and structural chemistry

Computing and Mathematics
Tel: (0191) 227 4740 Fax: (0191) 227 3662
Burgess, Rodney, BSc MSc Prof.; Head*
Research: applied statistics; computing (applied image analysis; contextual analysis, design and evaluation of novel computing environments; high-integrity embedded systems); mathematical modelling in science and engineering

Design
Tel: (0191) 227 4913 Fax: (0191) 227 4655
More, James, BA Prof.; Head*
Research: fashion design; fashion marketing; graphic design; industrial and three-dimensional craft design; product design

Economic Sciences, see Soc., Pol. and Econ. Scis., Sch. of

Education, see Health, Soc. Work and Educn., Fac. of

Engineering, School of
Tel: (0191) 227 4620 Fax: (0191) 227 3684
Cryan, Bob, BSc PhD Prof.; Head*
Research: applied physics and optoelectronics; design and manufacture; electrical and electronic engineering; mechanical engineering and materials

Environmental Sciences, see Behavioural and Environmental Scis., Sch. of

Health, Social Work and Education, Faculty of
Tel: (0191) 227 4431 Fax: (0191) 227 4419
Bines, Hazel, BSc MA DPhil Prof.
Dunning, Mary, MA Prof.
Firth, Ralph, BA Prof.
Potts, Jean, BA PhD Prof.
Ramprogus, Vince, BA MSc PhD Prof.
Stephens, Royston, BA MA PhD Prof.; Dean*

Research: health research: policy and practice

Historical and Critical Studies
Tel: (0191) 227 4925 Fax: (0191) 227 4630
Bailey, Christopher, BA Prof.; Head*
Research: conservation of fine art; film studies; history of art; history of design; history of ideas

Information and Library Management
Tel: (0191) 227 4917 Fax: (0191) 227 3671
Day, Joan, BA MA Prof.; Head*
Research: human impact of IT; users' information needs

Law, School of
Tel: (0191) 227 3490 Fax: (0191) 227 4557
Kenny, Philip, LLB LLM Prof.; Head*
Research: company law; employment law; environmental and planning law; legal information; property law

Library Management, see Information and Library Management

Life Sciences, see Chem. and Life Scis.

Mathematics, see Computing and Maths.

Modern Languages
Tel: (0191) 227 4919 Fax: (0191) 227 4439
Head, David, MA MPhil Prof.; Head*
Research: European languages; nation studies

Newcastle Business School
Prabhu, Vas, BE PhD Prof.
Weir, David, MA Prof.; Dir.*
Research: capacity dynamics; corporate reporting and financial disclosure; ethics and environmental issues in business; health information management; market intelligence and strategy

Performing Arts, see Visual and Performing Arts

Social, Political and Economic Sciences, School of
Tel: (0191) 227 4444 Fax: (0191) 227 4558
Garrahan, Philip, BA MSc PhD Prof.; Head*
Research: economics; employment studies; government and politics; sociology

Social Work, see Health, Soc. Work and Educn., Fac. of

Visual and Performing Arts
Tel: (0191) 227 4936 Fax: (0191) 227 3632
Roper, Gerda, BA MFA Prof.; Head*

CONTACT OFFICERS

Academic affairs. Academic Registrar: Penna, Cheryl, BA
Accommodation. Accommodation Officer: Warman, Dave
Admissions (first degree). Head of Student Administration: Carr, John
Admissions (higher degree). (Contact the registrar of the relevant faculty)
Adult/continuing education. Head of Student Services: Rolfe, John
Alumni. Alumni Officer: ......

Archives. University Secretary: Bott, Richard A., BSc(Econ) MSc, FCIS

Careers. Principal Careers Adviser: Riddick, Ed

Computing services. Director of Information Services: Winkworth, Ian

Consultancy services. Director of UNN Commercial Enterprises: Hackney, Tony

Credit transfer. CATS Officer: ......

Equal opportunities. Equal Opportunities Officer: Bell, Ranjana

Estates and buildings/works and services. Director of Estate Services Department: Purdie, Nick

Examinations. Academic Registrar: Penna, Cheryl, BA

Finance. Director of Finance Department: Leslie, David

General enquiries. Academic Registrar: Penna, Cheryl, BA

Health services. Head of Student Services: Rolfe, John

International office. Head of International Office: Dimmock, Maurice

Library (chief librarian). Director of Information Services: Winkworth, Ian

Library (enquiries). Library Customer Services Manager: Moreland, Carole

Minorities/disadvantaged groups. Equal Opportunities Officer: Bell, Ranjana

Personnel/human resources. Director of Personnel: Paton, Bernard

Public relations, information and marketing. Head of Press, PR and Publications: Figgis, Sean

Publications. Head of Press, PR and Publications: Figgis, Sean

Purchasing. Head of Purchasing and Supplies: Hayhoe, Mike

Quality assurance and accreditation. Academic Registrar: Penna, Cheryl, BA

Research. Assistant Registrar (Research): Siddalls, Dr. Ruth

Safety. Health and Safety Officer: Robson, Terry

Scholarships, awards, loans. Welfare Officer: Wooden, Barbara

Schools liaison. Education Liaison Manager: Urquhart, Norma

Security. Security and Services Manager: Fox, Keith

Sport and recreation. Director of Sport: Elvin, Ian

Staff development and training. Staff Development Manager: Harden, Louise

Student union. President: Reid, Colin

Student welfare/counselling. Head of Student Services: Rolfe, John

Students from other countries. Head of International Office: Dimmock, Maurice

Students with disabilities. Student Adviser (Disabilities): Chilton, Sandra

University press. Press Officer: ......

CAMPUS/COLLEGE HEADS

Carlisle Campus, 4-5 Paternoster Row, Carlisle, Cumbria, England CA3 8TB. (Tel: (0191) 227 4550; Fax: (0191) 227 4820.) Head: Smith, Prof. Robin, BScSoc MScEcon DPhil

[Information supplied by the institution as at 4 March 1998, and edited by the ACU]

UNIVERSITY OF NOTTINGHAM

Founded 1948; previously established as University College, Nottingham 1881

Member of the Association of Commonwealth Universities

Postal Address: University Park, Nottingham, England NG7 2RD
Telephone: (0115) 951 5151 **Fax**: (0115) 951 3666 **WWW**: http://www.nottingham.ac.uk
E-mail formula: firstname.familyname@nottingham.ac.uk

VISITOR—Elizabeth, H.M. The Queen
CHANCELLOR—Dearing, Lord, CB, BSc
PRO-CHANCELLOR—Hawksworth, A. H., TD, MA
PRO-CHANCELLOR—Haylor, J. R., BSc
VICE-CHANCELLOR*—Campbell, Prof. Sir Colin, LLB Aberd.
PRESIDENT OF COUNCIL—Haylock, J. R., BSc
TREASURER—Hamill, K., BA, FCA
PRO-VICE-CHANCELLOR—Bailey, Prof. S. H., LLB Camb., MA Camb.
PRO-VICE-CHANCELLOR—Clayton, Prof. B. R., BSc(Eng) Lond., PhD Lond., DSc, FIMechE
PRO-VICE-CHANCELLOR—Pattenden, Prof. G., PhD Lond., DSc Lond., FRSChem, FRS
PRO-VICE-CHANCELLOR—Greenaway, Prof. D., BSc Lond., MCom Liv.
REGISTRAR‡—Jones, Keith H., MA Camb.
DIRECTOR OF LIBRARY SERVICES—Oldroyd, R. E., BA Hull
BURSAR—Beeby, D. A., BA Manc.

GENERAL INFORMATION

History. The university was established as University College, Nottingham in 1881. It moved to its present site on the outskirts of Nottingham in the 1920s and received its Royal Charter in 1948.

Admission to first degree courses (see also United Kingdom Introduction). Through Universities and Colleges Admissions Service (UCAS).

First Degrees (see also United Kingdom Directory to Subjects of Study). BA, BArch, BEd, BEng, BM BS, BMedSci, BMus, BN, BPharm, BPhil(Ed), BSc, BTh, LLB, MEng, MMath, MNurse, MPharm, MSci.

Higher Degrees (see also United Kingdom Directory to Subjects of Study). AMusM, DM, LLM, MA, MArch, MBA, MDiv, MEd, MMedSci, MPH, MRes, MSc, MSW, MTh, MPhil, PhD, AMusD, DArch, DBA, DD, DLitt, DMus, EdD, LLD.

Applications for postgraduate courses should be made through university's Graduate School.

Libraries. Over 1,000,000 volumes; over 5000 current periodicals.

Fees (1998–99, full-time). Undergraduate: £1000. Postgraduate: home students £2610; international students £6795, £8977, or £16,444 (depending on course).

Academic Year (1998–99). Three terms: 28 September–16 December; 1 January–19 March; 19 April–25 June.

Income (1997–98). Total, £188,000,000.

Statistics. Staff: 4900 (2400 academic/research, academic-related; 2500 clerical, technical, manual). Students: full-time 14,450; part-time 7950; international (non-EU) 1840; total 22,400.

FACULTIES/SCHOOLS

Arts
Dean: Hewitt, Prof. Nicholas, BA Hull, PhD Hull

Education
Dean: Murphy, Prof. Roger J. L., BSc St And., PhD St And.

Engineering
Dean: Clayton, Prof. Brian R., BSc(Eng) Lond., PhD Lond., FIMechE

Law and Social Sciences
Dean: Bailey, Prof. Steven H., MA Camb., LLB Camb.

Medicine and Health Sciences
Dean: Rubin, Prof. Peter C., MA Camb., DM Oxf., FRCP

Science
Dean: Bates, Prof. Colin A., BSc PhD, FIP

ACADEMIC UNITS

Accounting, see Management and Finance, Sch. of

Agriculture, see under Biol. Scis., Sch. of

American and Canadian Studies

Tel: (0115) 951 4261 Fax: (0115) 951 4270

Boyle, P. G., MA *Glas.*, PhD *Calif.* Sr. Lectr.
Giles, P. D., MA *Oxf.*, DPhil *Oxf.* Reader
King, R. H., BA *N.Carolina*, MA *Yale*, PhD *Virginia* Prof.
Ling, P. J., BA *Lond.*, PhD *Keele* Sr. Lectr.
Messent, P. B., MA *Manc.*, PhD Reader
Murray, D. J., BA *Lond.*, PhD *Lond.* Sr. Lectr.
Tallack, D. G., MA *Sus.*, DPhil *Sus.* Prof.; Head*
Walsh, M., MA *St And.*, AM *Smith*, PhD *Wis.* Reader
Other Staff: 3 Lectrs.
Research: Canadian women writers; civil rights movement and race theories; literary/visual representation of US cities; native peoples of US and Canada; nineteenth-and twentieth-century American literature

Archaeology

Tel: (0115) 951 4820

Cavanagh, W. G., MA *Edin.*, PhD *Lond.*, FSA Sr. Lectr.
Dixon, P. W., MA *Oxf.*, DPhil *Oxf.*, FSA Reader
Henderson, J., BA *Belf.*, PhD *Brad.*, FSA Reader
Laing, L., MA *Edin.*, PhD *Liv.* Sr. Lectr.
Poulter, A. G., MA *Birm.*, PhD *Lond.* Sr. Lectr.
Wilson, R. J. A., MA *Oxf.*, DPhil *Oxf.* Prof.; Head*
Other Staff: 2 Lectrs.; 1 Temp. Assoc. Sr. Lectr.†
Research: early copper mining in Italy; glass production in Islamic Syria; mediaeval construction techniques; prehistoric burial practices in Greece; transition from late antiquity (Bulgaria)

Architecture, see Built Environment, Sch. of

Art History

Tel: (0115) 951 3185 Fax: (0115) 951 3194

Alfrey, N., MA *Edin.*, MA *Lond.* Lectr.; Acting Head*
Other Staff: 2 Lectrs.; 1 Temp. Lectr.

Biochemistry, see Nutritional Biochem., Div. of under Biol. Scis., Sch. of

Biological Sciences, School of

Tel: (0115) 951 3229 (University Park); 951 6121 (Sutton Bonington) Fax: (0115) 951 3251 (University Park); 951 6122 (Sutton Bonington)

Agriculture and Horticulture, Division of

Tel: (0115) 951 6100 Fax: (0115) 951 6060

Atherton, J. G., BSc *Durh.*, PhD *Reading* Sr. Lectr.
Azam-Ali, S. N., BSc *Wales*, MSc *Nott.*, PhD Sr. Lectr.
Garnsworthy, P. C., BSc *Aberd.*, PhD *Aberd.* Sr. Lectr.
Scott, R. K., BSc *Nott.*, PhD *Nott.*, FIBiol Prof.
Seabrook, M. F., BSc *Reading*, PhD *Reading* Sr. Lectr.
Webb, Robert, BSc *Nott.*, PhD *Nott.* Prof., Animal Production
Wiseman, J., BSc *Wales*, PhD *Nott.* Sr. Lectr.
Other Staff: 1 Lectr.; 1 Temp. Lectr.

Animal Physiology, Division of

Clarke, R. W., BSc *Manc.*, PhD *Lond.* Sr. Lectr.
Flint, A. P. F., BSc *St And.*, PhD *Brist.*, DSc *Brist.*, FIBiol Prof., Animal Physiology
Hunter, M. G., BSc *Strath.*, PhD *Edin.* Reader
Other Staff: 1 Lectr.; 1 Temp. Lectr.†

Behaviour/Infection and Immunity, Division of

Barnard, C. J., BSc *Liv.*, DPhil *Oxf.* Prof.
Behnke, J. M., BSc *S'ton.*, PhD *Lond.* Reader
Gilbert, F. S., BA *Camb.*, PhD *Camb.* Sr. Lectr.
Lowe, K. C., BSc *Leeds*, MA *Camb.*, PhD *Camb.* Sr. Lectr.
Pritchard, D. I., BSc *Wales*, MSc *Birm.*, PhD *Birm.* Prof.
Wakelin, Derek, BSc *Lond.*, PhD *Lond.*, DSc *Lond.*, FIBiol, FRCPath Prof.

Environmental Science, Division of

Colls, J. J., BSc *Lond.*, PhD *Camb.* Sr. Lectr.
Gregson, K., BTech *Brad.*, PhD *Nott.* Sr. Lectr.
Laybourn-Parry, Johanna E. M., BSc *Reading*, MSc *Wales*, PhD *Stir.*, DSc *Reading* Prof., Environmental Biology
Other Staff: 5 Lectrs.

Food Sciences, Division of

Harding, S. E., MA *Oxf.*, PhD *Leic.* Reader, Physical Biochemistry
Mitchell, J. R., BSc *Newcastle(UK)*, PhD *Nott.* Prof., Food Technology
Taylor, A. J., BSc *Wales*, PhD *Wales* Prof., Flavour Technology
Waites, W. M., BSc *Newcastle(UK)*, PhD *Sheff.* Prof., Food Microbiology
Other Staff: 5 Lectrs.; 1 Temp. Lectr.

Microbiology, Division of

Peberdy, J. F., BSc *Durh.*, PhD *Nott.*, DrNatSci, FIBiol Prof.
Other Staff: 2 Lectrs.

Molecular and Immunotoxicology, Division of

De Pomerai, D. I. M., BSc *Edin.*, PhD *Lond.* Sr. Lectr.
Duce, I. R., BSc *Wales*, PhD *Wales* Sr. Lectr.
Usherwood, P. N. R., BSc *Wales*, PhD *Glas.*, FIBiol, FRSEd Prof.
Other Staff: 1 Lectr.

Nutritional Biochemistry, Division of

Boorman, K. N., BSc *Nott.*, MS *Rutgers*, PhD *Nott.* Sr. Lectr.
Buttery, P. J., BSc *Manc.*, PhD *Manc.*, DSc Prof.; Head of Sch.*
Neale, R. J., BSc *Sheff.*, PhD *Sheff.* Sr. Lectr.
Norton, G., BSc *Nott.*, PhD *Nott.* Sr. Lectr.
Salter, A. M., BSc *Leic.*, PhD *Lond.* Sr. Lectr.
Tucker, G. A., BSc *E.Anglia*, PhD *E.Anglia* Reader, Plant Biochemistry
Other Staff: 2 Lectrs.

Plant Science/Biology, Division of

Tel: (0115) 951 6301 Fax: (0115) 951 6261

Black, C. R., BSc *Aberd.*, PhD *Aberd.* Reader
Grierson, D., BSc *E.Anglia*, PhD *Edin.*, FIBiol Prof., Plant Physiology
Power, J. B., BSc PhD Reader
Roberts, J. A., MA *Oxf.*, PhD *Camb.* Reader
Other Staff: 5 Lectrs.; 1 Temp. Lectr.

Built Environment, School of

Tel: (0115) 951 3155 Fax: (0115) 951 3159

Eames, I. W., MSc *Cran.IT*, PhD *Cran.IT* Sr. Lectr.
Fawcett, A. P., BA *Manc.* Prof.
Jackson, N. M. T., MA *Lond.*, PhD *CNAA* Sr. Lectr.
Oc, T., BArch *Middle East Tech.*, MCP *Middle East Tech.*, MA *Chic.*, PhD *Penn.* Sr.Lectr.
Riffat, S. B., MSc DPhil British Gas Prof., Architecture Technology and Energy; Head*
Scoffham, E. R., BArch *Durh.*, PhD, FRIBA Reader
Other Staff: 11 Lectrs.; 2 Temp. Lectrs.; 1 Temp. Assoc. Sr. Lectr.†; 2 Temp. Assoc. Lectrs.†
Research: building and environmental services; history of architecture, architectural/critical theory; renewable energy and heat powered cycles; sustainable cities and building re-use; urban revitalisation and urban design

Canadian Studies, see American and Canadian Studies

Chemistry

Tel: (0115) 951 3500, 951 3499 Fax: (0115) 951 3555

Barker, M. G., BSc PhD Sr. Lectr.
Chesters, M. A., BSc PhD, FRSChem Prof.; Head*
Davidson, G., BA *Oxf.*, DPhil *Oxf.*, FRSChem Sr. Lectr.
Gill, G. B., BSc *Lond.*, PhD *Lond.* Sr. Lectr.
Harrison, P. G., PhD *Lond.*, DSc *Lond.* Reader, Inorganic Chemistry
Hey, M. J., MSc *Leeds*, PhD Sr. Lectr.
Hubberstey, P., BSc PhD, FRSChem Sr. Lectr.
Jones, R. G., BSc *E.Anglia*, PhD *Camb.*, FIP Reader, Surface Science
Packer, K. J., BSc PhD, FRSChem, FRS Prof.
Pattenden, G., PhD *Lond.*, DSc *Lond.*, FRS, FRSChem Sir Jesse Boot Prof.
Poliakoff, M., MA *Camb.*, PhD *Camb.* Prof.
Powis, I., BA *Oxf.*, DPhil *Oxf.* Reader
Pulham, R. J., BSc PhD Reader, Inorganic Chemistry
Sarre, P. J., BSc *Sus.*, PhD *S'ton.*, FRSChem, FRAS Prof., Chemical Physics
Schröder, M., BSc *Sheff.*, PhD *Lond.*, FRSChem, FRSEd Prof., Inorganic Chemistry
Simpkins, N. S., BSc *Lond.*, PhD *Lond.* Prof.
Sowerby, D. B., BSc *Sheff.*, PhD *Sheff.* Sr. Lectr.
Whiting, D. A., PhD *Lond.*, DSc *Lond.*, FRSChem Reader, Organic Chemistry
Willis, M. R., BSc PhD, FRSChem Reader, Physical Chemistry
Other Staff: 10 Lectrs.

Classics

Tel: (0115) 951 4800

Drinkwater, J. F., MA *Camb.*, DPhil *Oxf.* Prof., Roman Provincial History
Drummond, A., MA *Oxf.*, DPhil *Oxf.* Sr. Lectr.
Rich, J. W., MA *Oxf.*, MPhil *Oxf.* Sr. Lectr.
Roy, J., MA *Edin.*, MA *Camb.*, PhD *Camb.* Sr. Lectr.
Salmon, J. B., DPhil *Oxf.* Sr. Lectr.
Sommerstein, A. H., MA *Camb.*, PhD *Camb.* Prof., Greek
Wiedemann, T. E. J., MA *Oxf.*, PhD *Brist.* Prof., Latin; Head*
Other Staff: 2 Lectrs.
Research: Greek and Roman historiography; Greek and Roman social history; Greek drama; history of slavery; late antiquity

Computer Science

Tel: (0115) 951 4251 Fax: (0115) 951 4254

Benford, S. D., BSc PhD Reader
Brailsford, D. F., BSc *Lond.*, PhD *Lond.* Prof.
Elliman, D. G., BSc *Nott.*, PhD *Nott.* Prof.
Ford, P. H., MA *Camb.* Prof.; Head*
Jones, M. P., BA *Oxf.*, MSc *Oxf.*, DPhil *Oxf.* Reader
Other Staff: 7 Lectrs.; 1 Temp. Lectr.

Information, ICL Institute of

Ford, P. H., MA *Camb.* Prof.; Dir.*
Other Staff: 1 Lectr.

Critical Theory, Postgraduate School of

1 Lectr.

Economics

Tel: (0115) 951 5469 Fax: (0115) 951 4159

Bleaney, M. F., BA *Camb.*, PhD *Camb.* Prof.
Bossert, W., MA *Br.Col.*, DrRerPl *Karlsruhe* Prof., Economic Theory
Falvey, R. E., BA *Cant.*, MA *Cant.*, MA *Roch.*, PhD *Roch.* Prof.
Gemmell, N., BA *Durh.*, PhD *Durh.* Prof.
Greenaway, D., BSc(Econ) *Lond.*, MCom *Liv.* Prof.
Hine, R. C., BA *Lond.*, MSc Sr. Lectr.
Leybourne, S., BSc *Leeds*, MSc *Lond.*, PhD *Leeds* Reader
Milner, C. R. Prof.; Head*
Morrisey, W. O., BA *Trinity(Dub.)*, MSc *Bath*, PhD *Bath* Sr. Lectr.

Newbold, P., BSc(Econ) Lond., PhD Wis.   Prof.
Rayner, A. J., BA Camb., MA Manc., PhD
Manc.   Prof., Agricultural Economics
Reed, G. V., BSc   Sr. Lectr.
Whynes, D. K., BA York(UK), BPhil York(UK),
MLitt St And.   Prof.
Other Staff: 12 Lectrs.; 2 Temp. Lectrs.
Research: econometrics (time series analysis and
forecasting); economic development
(infrastructure and institutions in export
promotion); international trade (impact of
globalisation on labour markets);
macroeconomics (exchange rate and interest
rate policies); microeconomics (social
choice, ethics and welfare economics)

Economics, Industrial, see Management
and Finance, Sch. of

Education, School of
Tel: (0115) 951 4423 Fax: (0115) 951 4435
Coles, M. J., BEd Oxf., MA Lond.   Sr. Lectr.
Day, C. W., MA Sus., DPhil Sus.   Prof.
Hall, E., BSc Hull, BA Lond., PhD   Sr. Lectr.
Harrison, C., BA Leeds, MPhil PhD   Prof.
Hay, J. D. L., BSc Aberd., MSc PhD   Reader
Hopkins, D. W. R., BA Reading, MEd Sheff., PhD
S.Fraser   Prof.; Head*
Murphy, Roger J. L., BSc St And., PhD St
And.   Prof.
Phillips, R. J., BSc Sus., PhD Lond.   Reader
Youngman, B. M., BA York(UK), MA Lanc.,
PhD   Reader
Other Staff: 20 Lectrs.; 1 Temp. Lectr.; 4
Temp. Lectrs.†; 2 Temp. Assoc. Sr. Lectrs.†;
3 Temp. Assoc. Lectrs.†

**Engineering, Chemical, Environmental
and Mining, School of**
Tel: (0115) 951 4163 Fax: (0115) 951 4181
Atkin, B. P., BSc Liv., PhD Liv., FGS   Sr. Lectr.
Azzopardi, B. J., BTech Brad., PhD Exe.,
FIChemE   Lady Trent Prof.
Biddulph, M. W., BSc Birm., PhD Birm., DEng
Birm.   Reader
Cloke, M., BSc Nott., PhD Nott., FIChemE   Sr.
Lectr.
Denby, B., BSc Nott., PhD Nott.   Prof., Minerals
Computing; Head*
Dunham, R. K., BSc PhD   Prof.†
Edwards, J. S., BSc Nott., PhD Nott.   Sr. Lectr.
Miles, N. J., BSc Leeds, PhD Nott.   Sr. Lectr.
Ocone, Raffaella, Laur Naples, MA Prin., PhD
Prin.   Reader
Reddish, D. J., BSc Nott., PhD Nott.   Sr. Lectr.
Walters, J. K., MA Camb., PhD Camb.,
FIChemE   Sr. Lectr.
Wilson, J. A., BSc Nott., PhD Nott.   Sr. Lectr.
Other Staff: 12 Lectrs.; 1 Teaching Fellow
Research: mining technology (after-use, design,
environmental, geotechnics, safety);
multiphase flow (gas-solid, solid-liquid, gas-
liquid); process engineering (minerals,
chemical and environmental engineering
processes)

Engineering, Civil
Tel: (0115) 951 3907 Fax: (0115) 951 3898
Ashkenazi, V., MSc Haifa(Technion), DPhil Oxf.,
DSc Oxf., FICE, FIMA, FRICS, FRAS   Prof.,
Engineering Surveying
Baker, C. J., MA Camb., PhD Camb.   Prof.
Brown, S. F., PhD Nott., DSc Nott., FICE   Prof.
Choo, B. S., BSc Strath., PhD Glas.   Sr. Lectr.
Dawson, A. R., BA Lanc., MSc Lond., FGS   Sr.
Lectr.
Dodson, A. H., BSc Nott., PhD Nott.,
FRAS   Prof., Geodesy
Elliot, K. S., BTech Brad., PhD Nott.   Sr. Lectr.
Mawdesley, M. J., BSc Nott., PhD Nott.   Sr.
Lectr.
Moon, T., BSc Nott., PhD Nott., FRAS   Reader
Nethercot, D. A., BSc Wales, PhD Wales, DSc
Wales, FICE, FIStructE   Prof.; Head*
Wood, R. C., BSc Nott., PhD Nott.   Sr. Lectr.
Other Staff: 15 Lectrs.; 1 Sr. Lectr.†

Research: construction management; information
technology; pavements/geotechnics;
structural engineering; surveying

Engineering, Electrical and Electronic
Tel: (0115) 951 5600 Fax: (0115) 951 5616
Asher, G. M., BSc Bath, PhD Bath   Reader
Benson, T. M., BSc Sheff., PhD Sheff.   Prof.,
Opto-Electronics
Bradley, K. J., BEng Sheff., PhD Sheff.   Sr. Lectr.
Christopoulos, C., MSc Sus., DPhil Sus.   Prof.
Cross, T. E., BSc Wales, PhD Wales   Sr. Lectr.
Jakeman, Eric, BSc Birm., PhD Birm.,
FIP   Prof.†
Somekh, M. G., MA Oxf., PhD Lanc.   Prof.,
Optical Engineering
Tuck, B., PhD Lond., DSc Lond., FIP, FIEE   Prof.;
Head*
Walker, J. G., BSc Lond., PhD Lond.   Reader
Other Staff: 13 Lectrs.
Research: electromagnetic modelling; optical
engineering for materials characterisation;
optoelectronic devices; power electronics;
statistical electromagnetic scattering

**Engineering, Manufacturing, and
Operations Management**
Tel: (0115) 951 4008 Fax: (0115) 951 4000
Gindy, N. N. Z., BSc Mansourah, MSc Aston, PhD
Aston   Prof., Advanced Manufacturing
Technology
Haslegrave, Christine M., BSc Brist., MSc Birm.,
PhD Nott.   Sr. Lectr.
MacCarthy, B. L., BA Open(UK), PhD Brad.   Sr.
Lectr.
O'Brien, C., BSc Leeds   Cripps Prof.; Head*
Pawar, K. S., BSc CNAA, MSc Aston, PhD
Aston   Sr. Lectr.
Standring, P. M., BSc Nott., PhD Nott.   Sr.
Lectr.
Wilson, J. R., BTech Lough., MSc Lough., PhD
Birm.   Prof., Occupational Ergonomics
Wykes, Catherine, BSc N.U.I., PhD Edin.   Sr.
Lectr.
Other Staff: 11 Lectrs.

**Engineering, Materials, and Materials
Design**
Tel: (0115) 951 3756 Fax: (0115) 951 3741
Binner, J. G. P., BSc Leeds, PhD Leeds   Sr. Lectr.
Grant, D. M., BSc York(UK), PhD Open(UK)   Sr.
Lectr.
Harris, S. J., MScTech Manc., PhD Nott.,
FIM   Prof., Metallurgy
McCartney, D. G., MA Oxf., DPhil Oxf.   Reader
McColl, I. R., BSc Hull, PhD Nott.   Sr. Lectr.
Moon, J. R., BSc Wales, PhD Wales, FIM,
FIP   Reader
Noble, B., BSc Nott., PhD Nott., FIM   Reader
Wood, J. V., BMet Sheff., PhD Camb.,
FIM   Cripps Prof.; Head*
Other Staff: 4 Lectrs.

Engineering, Mechanical
Tel: (0115) 951 3777 Fax: (0115) 951 3800
Aroussi, A., BSc CNAA, PhD CNAA   Sr. Lectr.
Becker, A. A., BSc(Eng) Lond., PhD
Lond.   Reader
Choi, K.-S., MSc Cornell, PhD Cornell   Sr. Lectr.
Clayton, Brian R., BSc(Eng) Lond., PhD Lond.,
FIMechE   Hives Prof.; Head*
Fox, C. H. J., BSc Newcastle(UK), PhD
Newcastle(UK)   Sr. Lectr.
Hyde, T. H., MSc Aston, PhD Nott., DSc Nott.,
FIM, FIMechE   Prof.
Mather, J. S. B., BSc Manc., PhD Manc.   Sr.
Lectr.
Middleton, V., BSc Nott., PhD Nott.   Prof.,
Engineering Design
Pickering, S. J., BSc Nott., PhD Nott.   Sr. Lectr.
Rudd, C. D., BSc CNAA, PhD Nott., FIM,
FIMechE   Prof.
Shayler, P. J., MSc Birm., PhD Birm.,
FIMechE   Ford Prof.
Williams, E. J., BSc(Eng) Lond., PhD Lond.   Sr.
Lectr.
Other Staff: 9 Lectrs.

Research: component design and integrity;
experimental/computational fluid
mechanics; internal combustion engine;
Rolls-Royce technology centre

English Studies
Tel: (0115) 951 5900 Fax: (0115) 951 5924
Carter, R. A., BA Leeds, MA Birm., PhD
Birm.   Prof., Modern English Language
Dillon, J., BA Oxf., DPhil Oxf.   Sr. Lectr.
Herman, Vimala V., BA Madr., MA Madr., PhD
Exe.   Sr. Lectr.
Jesch, Judith, BA Durh., PhD Lond.   Sr. Lectr.
McCarthy, M. J., MA Camb., PhD Camb.   Prof.,
Applied Linguistics
Phillips, Helen, BA Oxf., BPhil Oxf., MA
Warw.   Sr. Lectr.
Smallwood, Angela J., BA Oxf., BPhil Oxf.,
DPhil Oxf.   Sr. Lectr.
Turville-Petre, T. S. F., MA Oxf., BLitt
Oxf.   Prof., Medieval Literature; Head*
Worthen, J., MA Kent, PhD Kent   Prof.
Other Staff: 6 Lectrs.
Research: applied linguistics; literature post-1500
(D H Lawrence, literature and culture);
mediaeval language and literature (Old and
Middle English, Old Norse); modern English
language (language, culture and discourse)

English Language Education, Centre for
2 Lectrs.; 1 Temp. Lectr.

Environmental Science, see under Biol.
Scis., Sch. of

Finance, see Management and Finance, Sch.
of

Food Sciences, see under Biol. Scis., Sch. of

French
Tel: (0115) 951 5873 Fax: (0115) 951 4998
Bamforth, S. J., BA Durh., PhD Durh.   Reader
Chapman, Rosemary A., MA Reading, PhD
Exe.   Sr. Lectr.
Francis, R. A., MA Oxf., BLitt Oxf.,
PhD   Reader
Hewitt, Nicholas, BA Hull, PhD Hull   Prof.
King, R. S., MA Otago, DU Dijon   Sr. Lectr.
Knight, Diana M., MA Warw., PhD
Warw.   Prof.; Head*
Offord, M. H., BA Leeds, MPhil Leeds   Reader
Rossello, M., PhD Mich.   Reader
Still, Judith M., BA Lond., MSc Lond., PhD
Lond.   Prof.
Other Staff: 6 Lectrs.
Research: critical theory; French and
Francophone literature (middle ages to
present)

Geography
Tel: (0115) 951 5428 Fax: (0115) 951 5249
Bradshaw, R. P., BA Keele, PhD Keele   Sr. Lectr.
Daniels, S. J., MA St And., MSc Wis., PhD
Lond.   Reader
Haines-Young, R. H., BSc Sus., PhD
Lond.   Reader
Mather, P. M., MA Camb., PhD Nott.   Prof.,
Geographical Information Systems
McGowan-Crewe, Louise J., BA Leeds, PhD
Leeds   Sr. Lectr.
Phillips, D. R., BSc Wales, PhD Wales   Prof.,
Human Geography; Head*
Steven, M. D., BSc McG., MSc Reading, PhD   Sr.
Lectr.
Thorne, C. R., BSc E.Anglia, PhD E.Anglia   Prof.,
Physical Geography
Watkins, C., BSc Lond., PhD Nott.   Sr. Lectr.
Other Staff: 8 Lectrs.; 5 Temp. Lectrs.; 1
Temp. Assoc. Lectr.†
Research: environmental management; health
and economic development; landscape and
culture; process and applied geomorphology

German
Tel: (0115) 951 5815 Fax: (0115) 951 5814
Boa, E. J., MA Glas., PhD Nott.   Prof.; Head*
Duckworth, D., MA Manc., PhD Nott.   Sr. Lectr.

Woods, R. A., MA Lond., DPhil Oxf. Prof.
Other Staff: 3 Lectrs.
Research: mediaeval German literature; minority stereotyping in German literature; national identity in modern Germany; the new right in Germany; recent women's writing in Germany

Hispanic and Latin American Studies

Tel: (0115) 951 5800 Fax: (0115) 951 5814
Cardwell, R. A., BA S'ton., PhD Prof., Modern Spanish Literature
McGuirk, B. J., MA Glas., DPhil Oxf. Prof., Romance Literatures
Millington, M. I., MA Camb., PhD Camb. Prof., Hispanic Studies; Head*
Other Staff: 4 Lectrs.

History

Tel: (0115) 951 5928 Fax: (0115) 951 5948
Beckett, J. V., BA Lanc., PhD Lanc., FRHistS Prof., English Regional History
Booth, A., BA Lanc., PhD Lanc. Sr. Lectr.
Ellis, Joyce M., MA Oxf., DPhil Oxf. Sr. Lectr.
Geary, R. J., MA Camb., PhD Camb. Prof., Modern History; Head*
Heywood, C. M., BA Reading, PhD Reading Sr. Lectr.
Jones, M. C. E., MA Oxf., DPhil Oxf., FRHistS, FSA Prof., Mediaeval French History
McHardy, Alison K., MA Oxf., DPhil Oxf., FRHistS Sr. Lectr.
Meller, Helen E., BA Brist., PhD Brist., FRHistS Prof., Urban History
Spring, D. W., BA Lond., PhD Lond. Sr. Lectr.
Watts, M. R., BA Oxf., DPhil Oxf., FRHistS Reader, Modern History
Wrigley, C. J., BA E.Anglia, PhD Lond., FRHistS Prof., Modern British History
Other Staff: 4 Lectrs.
Research: European middle ages; international labour history; medical history; modern British and Russian history; urban history

Horticulture, see Agric. and Hort., Div. of, under Biol. Scis., Sch. of

Immunotoxicology, see Molecular and Immunotoxicol., Div. of, under Biol. Scis., Sch. of

Insurance Studies, see Management and Finance, Sch. of

Latin American Studies, see Hispanic and Latin American Studies

Law

Tel: (0115) 951 5699, 951 5700 Fax: (0115) 951 5696
Bailey, Steven H., MA Camb., LLB Camb. Prof., Public Law
Bennett, H. N., LLM Lond., MenD Paris Sr. Lectr.
Birch, Diane J., LLB Prof., Criminal Justice and Evidence
Bowman, M. J., LLB Sr. Lectr.
Bridge, M. J., LLM Lond. Prof., Commercial Law
Fawcett, J. J., LLB Nott., PhD Brist. Prof.
Girvin, S. D., BA Natal, LLM Natal, PhD Aberd. Sr. Lectr.
Gravells, N. P., MA Oxf. Prof., English Law
Harris, D. J., LLM Lond., PhD Lond. Prof., Public International Law
Hervey, T. K., LLB Glas., PhD Sheff.
Livingstone, S. W. S., BA Camb., LLM Harv. Reader
Morse, G. K., LLB Newcastle(UK) Herbert Smith Prof., Company Law; Head*
Mowbray, A., LLB Warw., PhD Edin. Sr. Lectr.
Redgwell, Catherine J., BA Winn., LLB Br.Col., MSc Lond. Sr. Lectr.
White, N. D., MA Oxf., PhD Sr. Lectr.
Other Staff: 19 Lectrs.; 1 Lectr.†
Research: commercial law; criminal law and evidence; human rights; international law; public law

Management and Finance, School of

Tel: (0115) 951 5252 Fax: (0115) 951 5503
Barnes, P. A., MSc Brad., PhD Sheff., MA Touche Ross Reader, Accounting and Corporate Finance
Berry, R. H., BSc(Econ) Lond., MSc Lond., PhD Warw. Prof.; Head*
Binks, M. R., BA Durh., PhD Sr. Lectr.
Bruce, A. C., MA St And., PhD H.-W. Sr. Lectr.
Buck, T. W., BCom Liv., MA Liv. Sr. Lectr.
Chiplin, B., BA Prof., Industrial Economics
Diacon, S. R., BSc PhD Sr. Lectr.
Dobson, P. W., BA CNAA, MSc Lond., PhD Lond. Sr. Lectr.
Ennew, Christine T., BA Camb., PhD Nott. Prof., Marketing
Fenn, P. T., BA Lanc., BPhil York(UK) Norwich Union Prof., Insurance Studies
Goddard, S., BA Reading, MCom Birm. Sr. Lectr.
Knights, D., BSc Salf., MSc Manc., PhD Manc. Midland Bank Prof., Management of Financial Services
Rowlinson, M. C., BSc Brist., PhD Aston Sr. Lectr.
Scullion, H. G., MA Glas., PhD Newcastle(UK) Reader
Starkey, K. P., BA Sheff., BSc Lond., PhD Aston Prof., Strategic Management
Thompson, R. S., BSc Hull, MA Durh., PhD Prof., Managerial Economics
Wright, D. M., BA CNAA, MA Durh., PhD Prof., Financial Studies
Other Staff: 12 Lectrs.; 5 Temp. Lectrs.
Research: corporate governance and strategy; enterprise in emerging markets; financial services marketing; human resource management; insurance and risk management

Materials Design, see Engin., Materials, and Materials Des.

Mathematics

Tel: (0115) 951 4949 Fax: (0115) 951 4951
Anderson, J. A., BA Belf., PhD Belf. Sr. Lectr.
Armour, E. A. G., BSc Edin., PhD Camb. Reader
Ball, F. G., BSc Manc., DPhil Oxf. Prof., Applied Probability; Head*
Barnett, V., BSc Manc., MSc Manc., PhD Manc., DSc Birm. Prof., Environmental Statistics
Belavkin, V. P., MSc Moscow, PhD Moscow, DSc Moscow Prof.
Burgess, D. A., BSc Lond., PhD Lond. Prof., Pure Mathematics
Fesenko, J. B., PhD St.Petersburg Prof., Pure Maths
Langley, J. K., BA Leeds, MSc Lond., PhD Lond. Reader
Lindsay, J. M., BSc Lond., PhD Reader
Litton, C. D., BSc Birm., PhD Lanc. Sr. Lectr.
O'Hagan, A., BSc Lond., PhD Lond. Prof., Statistics
Skene, A. M., BSc Otago, PhD Lond. Sr. Lectr.
Woodall, D. R., MA Camb., PhD Reader, Pure Mathematics
Other Staff: 8 Lectrs.; 1 Temp. Lectr.
Research: mathematical physics and related applied mathematics (traditional areas); pure mathematics; quantum gravity; quantum probability

Mechanics, see Theoret. Mech.

Medicine, see below

Microbiology, see under Biol. Scis., Sch. of, and Medicine (under Clin. Lab. Scis., Sch. of)

Music

Morehen, J. M., MA Oxf., PhD Camb., FRCO Prof.
Pascall, R. J., MA Oxf., DPhil Oxf., FRCO Prof.; Head*
Sackman, N., MA Leeds, DMus Nott.
Other Staff: 3 Lectrs.

Operations Management, see Engin., Manufacturing, and Operations Management

Pharmaceutical Sciences

Tel: (0115) 951 5100 Fax: (0115) 951 5102, 951 5122
Aslam, M., MSc Aston, LLM Wales, PhD, FRPharmS Sr. Lectr.
Bycroft, B. W., BSc PhD, FRSChem Prof., Pharmaceutical Chemistry; Head*
Davies, M. C., BSc CNAA, BPharm CNAA, PhD Lond. Prof.
Davis, S. S., BPharm Lond., PhD Lond., DSc Lond., FRSChem, FRPharmS Lord Trent Prof.
Li Wan Po, A., BPharm Brad., PhD Lond., BA, FRSChem Prof.
Melia, C. D., BSc CNAA, PhD Nott. Sr. Lectr.
Murray-Rust, P., BA Oxf., MA Oxf., DPhil Oxf. Prof., Molecular Sciences
Price, M. R., BSc PhD DSc Reader
Shaw, P. N., BSc Manc., PhD Manc., FRSChem Sr. Lectr.
Stevens, M. F. G., BPharm PhD DSc, FRSChem Prof., Experimental Cancer Chemotherapy
Stewart, G. S. A. B., BSc St And., PhD Camb. Prof., Applied Molecular Biochemistry
Tendler, S. J. B., BSc Manc., PhD Aston, FRSChem Reader
Williams, P., PhD Aston, BPharm Prof.
Other Staff: 7 Lectrs.; 6 Temp. Lectrs.
Research: advanced drug delivery; biophysics and surface analysis; cancer research (novel chemistry and molecular evaluation); medicinal chemistry; molecular microbiology

Philosophy

Tel: (0115) 951 5850 Fax: (0115) 951 5840
Carr, B., BA Lond., MPhil Lond., PhD Exe. Sr. Lectr.
Clark, M., MA Oxf. Reader; Head*
Kirk, Robert, BA Camb., PhD Lond. Prof.
Wilkerson, T. E., MA Oxf., BPhil Oxf. Reader
Other Staff: 5 Lectrs.; 1 Temp. Assoc. Lectr.†
Research: Indian philosophy of language and epistemology; metaphysics (causation, laws and dispositions); mind (consciousness, intentionality and mental causation); moral psychology (irrationality, compassion and friendship); philosophy of law (punishment, self-defence and responsibility)

Physics

Tel: (0115) 951 5164, 951 5165 Fax: (0115) 951 5180
Bates, Colin A., BSc PhD, FIP Prof., Theoretical Physics; Head*
Beton, P. H., BA Camb., PhD Manc. Reader
Blake, P. R., BSc Lond., PhD Lond. Sr. Lectr.
Bowley, R. M., BA Camb., PhD Camb. Prof.
Bowtell, R. W., BA Camb., PhD Reader
Challis, L. J., OBE, MA Oxf., DPhil Oxf., FIP Prof., Low Temperature Physics
Chamberlain, J. M., MA Oxf., DPhil Oxf. Reader
Dunn, J. L., BSc Liv., PhD Nott. Reader
Eaves, L., MA Oxf., DPhil Oxf. Prof.
Foxon, C. T., BSc Lond., PhD Lond. Prof.
Gallagher, B. L., BSc Leeds, PhD Leeds Sr. Lectr.
Heath, M., MA Oxf., DPhil Oxf. Sr. Lectr.
Horsewill, A. J., BSc Sheff., PhD Sheff. Sr. Lectr.
Hughes, O. H., BSc Wales, PhD Wales Sr. Lectr.
Kent, A. J., BSc Lond., PhD Lond. Sr. Lectr.
King, P. J., MA Oxf., DPhil Oxf. Reader
Main, P. C., BSc Birm., PhD Manc. Prof.
Maxwell, K. J., BSc Belf., DPhil Oxf. Reader
Mellor, C. J., BSc Birm., PhD Birm. Sr. Lectr.
Morris, P. G., MA Camb., PhD Prof.
Owers-Bradley, J. R., BSc Sus., DPhil Sus. Reader
Rampton, V. W., MA Camb., PhD Reader
Sheard, F. W., BSc Durh., PhD Camb. Prof., Theoretical Physics
Other Staff: 3 Lectrs.; 2 Temp. Lectrs.

Research: condensed matter theory; low-dimensional semiconductor structures; nanoscience and technology; nitride semiconductors (growth and properties); nuclear magnetic resonance (imaging, spectroscopy and microscopy)

Physiology, see Animal Physiol., Div. of, under Biol. Scis., Sch. of, and Medicine (Biomed. Scis., Sch. of)

Plant Science, see under Biol. Scis., Sch. of

Politics

Tel: (0115) 951 4862 Fax: (0115) 951 4859

Aldrich, R. J., BA *Manc.*, MLitt *Aberd.*, PhD *Camb.*   Sr. Lectr.
Forbes, I., MA *Adel.*, PhD *E.Anglia*   Prof.
Heywood, P. M., BA *Edin.*, MA *Edin.*, MSc *Lond.*   Prof.; Head*
Pierson, C. C., MA *Camb.*, PhD *Camb.*   Prof.
Other Staff: 9 Lectrs.
Research: Asia-Pacific (civil society, politics and media); comparative politics; Europe (defence, economic and monetary union, integration); international relations; political theory

Psychology

Tel: (0115) 951 8363 Fax: (0115) 951 5324

Clarke, D. D., MA *Camb.*, MA *Oxf.*, PhD *Camb.*, DPhil *Oxf.*, FBPsS   Reader
Cox, T. R., BSc PhD   Prof., Organisational Psychology; Head*
Derrington, A. M., BA *Oxf.*, PhD *Camb.*   Prof.
Ferguson, E., BSc *York(UK)*, PhD *Nott.*
Lincoln, N. B., BSc *Wales*, MSc *Leeds*, PhD *Lond.*   Reader
O'Malley, Clair E., BA *Leeds*, PhD *Leeds*   Sr. Lectr.
Pine, J. M., BA *Liv.*, PhD *Manc.*   Reader
Shadbolt, N. R., BA *Newcastle(UK)*, PhD *Edin.*   Prof., Intelligent Systems
Stevens, R. G., BTech *Brun.*, DPhil *Oxf.*   Sr. Lectr.
Underwood, G., BSc *Lond.*, PhD *Sheff.*, DSc *Lond.*   Prof., Cognitive Psychology
Wood, D. J., BA PhD   Prof.
Other Staff: 9 Lectrs.; 2 Temp. Teaching Fellows; 1 Temp. Lectr.†
Research: artificial intelligence and neuroscience; cognitive psychology; developmental and educational psychology; occupational and health psychology

Slavonic Studies

Tel: (0115) 951 5824 Fax: (0115) 951 5814

Herrity, P., BA *Lond.*, PhD *Lond.*   Reader; Head*
Luker, N. J. L., MA *Oxf.*, PhD   Sr. Lectr.
Marsh, Cynthia E. A., MA *Lond.*, PhD *Lond.*, BA   Sr. Lectr.
Milne, Lesley, BA *Camb.*, PhD *Camb.*   Reader
Rosslyn, Wendy A., BA *Lond.*, MPhil *Lond.*   Reader
Other Staff: 1 Lectr.
Research: identity and modernity in the Balkans; Maxim Gorky; Russian women poets and translators; Slovene language: a comprehensive reference grammar; Soviet prose (including Bukhov, Kharms, Zoschenko)

Sociology and Social Policy, School of

Tel: (0115) 951 5234 Fax: (0115) 951 5232

Aldridge, A. E., BA *Oxf.*, BPhil *Oxf.*   Sr. Lectr.
Aldridge, Meryl E., BScEcon *Wales*, MA *Essex*, PhD   Sr. Lectr.
Butler, Sandra, BA *Lanc.*, MA *Leic.*   Sr. Lectr.; Dir., Soc. Work
Dingwall, R. W. J., MA *Camb.*, PhD *Aberd.*   Prof., Social Work Studies
Evetts, Julia A., BA *Sheff.*   Prof.
Lomax, W. A., BA *Keele*, MA *Sus.*, DPhil *Sus.*   Sr. Lectr.
Manning, N. P., MA *Camb.*, MPhil *York(UK)*, PhD *Kent*   Prof., Social Policy and Sociology; Head*

Murphy, E. A., MA *St And.*, MSc *S'ton.*, PhD *S'ton.*
Pascall, G., MA *Oxf.*, PhD
Other Staff: 7 Lectrs.; 1 Temp. Lectr.†; 2 Temp. Assoc. Sr. Lectrs.†; 4 Temp. Assoc. Lectrs.†
Research: counselling and mental health; gender issues (domestic violence, family policy, housing, welfare theory); health policy (health services); international social policy; professions (international regulation, occupations, professional work)

Spanish, see Hispanic and Latin American Studies

Statistics, see Maths.

Theology

Tel: (0115) 951 5852 Fax: (0115) 951 5887

Bell, Rev. R. H., BSc *Lond.*, MA *Oxf.*, PhD *Lond.*   Sr. Lectr.
Casey, P. M., BA *Durh.*, PhD *Durh.*   Reader
Goddard, H. P., MA *Oxf.*, PhD *Birm.*   Sr. Lectr.
Thiselton, Rev. A. C., BD MTh PhD   Prof., Christian Theology; Head*
Other Staff: 3 Lectrs.
Research: biblical theology (Jesus, Paul, Old Testament); hermeneutics (biblical, literary, philosophical, theological); historical theology (modern, puritan, Reformation); languages; religions (ancient and modern Judaism/Islam)

Theoretical Mechanics

Tel: (0115) 951 3838 Fax: (0115) 951 3837

England, A. H., BSc *Durh.*, PhD *Durh.*, FIMA   Sr. Lectr.
Faulkner, T. R., BSc *Liv.*, PhD *Liv.*, FIMA   Sr. Lectr.
Hibberd, S., BSc *Brist.*, MSc *Manc.*, PhD *Brist.*, FIMA   Sr. Lectr.
Hopcraft, K. I., BSc *Sus.*, PhD *Lond.*   Sr. Lectr.
King, J. R., MA *Camb.*, DPhil *Oxf.*   Prof.
Parry, Gareth P., BSc *Wales*, PhD *Camb.*   Reader
Riley, D. S., BSc *Hull*, PhD *Hull*   Prof.; Head*
Other Staff: 7 Lectrs.

MEDICINE

Biomedical Sciences, School of

Bennett, G. W., MSc *Lond.*, PhD *Lond.*   Reader
Bennett, T., PhD *Melb.*, BSc   Prof.
Birmingham, A. T., BSc *Lond.*, MB BS *Lond.*   Emer. Prof., Pharmacology
Clothier, R. H., BSc *Lond.*, PhD *E.Anglia*   Reader
Downes, Sandra, BSc *Sheff.*, MSc *Tees.*, PhD *Lond.*   Prof., Biomaterials
Fone, K. C., BSc *Liv.*, PhD *Liv.*   Sr. Lectr.
Fry, J. R., BSc *Sur.*, PhD *Sur.*   Reader
Gardiner, Sheila M., BSc PhD   Prof., Cardiovascular Physiology
Glass, R. E., BSc *Lond.*, PhD *Lond.*   Prof., Molecular Biology
Greenhaff, P. L., BSc *Salf.*, PhD *Aberd.*   Reader
Gregory, C. D., BSc *Sheff.*, PhD *Sheff.*   Res. Prof., Cell Death and Survival
Hemming, F. W., BSc *Liv.*, PhD *Liv.*   Emer. Prof.
Hill, S. J., BSc *Brist.*, PhD *Camb.*   Prof., Molecular Biology
Kendall, D. A., PhD *CNAA*, BPharm   Reader
Landon, M., BSc *Birm.*, PhD *Birm.*   Reader
Macdonald, I. A., BSc *Lond.*, PhD *Lond.*   Prof., Physiology; Head*
Marsden, C. A., PhD *S'ton.*, DSc *Lond.*, DSc *S'ton.*   Prof., Neuropharmacology
Mason, R., BSc *S'ton.*, PhD *Keele*   Sr. Lectr.
Mayer, R. J., BSc *Birm.*, PhD *Birm.*, DSc *Nott.*, FRCPath   Prof., Molecular Cell Biology
Mayhew, T. M., BA *Oxf.*, PhD *Sheff.*   Prof.
Middleton, B., MA *Camb.*, PhD *Camb.*   Sr. Lectr.
Parker, T. L., PhD *Wales*   Sr. Lectr.
Pratten, M. K., BSc *Sheff.*, PhD *Sheff.*   Sr. Lectr.
Shaw, P. E., BSc *Heidel.*, PhD *Heidel*   Prof.
Short, A. H., BSc *Liv.*, MD *Liv.*   Sr. Lectr.
Sparrow, R. A., BSc *Lond.*, BMedSci BM BS   Sr. Lectr.

White, D. A., BSc *Birm.*, PhD *Birm.*, DSc *Nott.*   Reader
Wilson, V. G., BSc *Aston*, PhD *Aston*   Sr. Lectr.
Other Staff: 10 Lectrs.; 1 Lectr.†; 2 Temp. Lectrs.
Research: from molecules to man (apoptosis, biomaterials, G-protein coupled receptors, gene expression, neuropharmacology and integrated cardiovascular and metabolic control, protein degradation, vascular smooth muscle and endothelial structure and function)

Clinical Laboratory Sciences, School of

Clinical Chemistry, Division of

Kalshekar, N., MSc *Birm.*, MD *Birm.*, FRCPath   Prof., Chemical Pathology and Human Metabolism; Head*
Morgan, L. J., MB ChB *Sheff.*, DM   Sr. Lectr.
Other Staff: 1 Lectr.

Clinical Oncology, Division of

Carmichael, J., MSc *Edin.*   Prof.
Murray, John C., BSc *St And.*, PhD *Camb.*   Reader
Wilcock, A., MB ChB *Birm.*   Sr. Lectr.
Woll, P. J., BMedSci *Newcastle(UK)*, MB BS *Newcastle(UK)*, PhD *Lond.*   Sr. Lectr.
Other Staff: 1 Lectr.; 1 Temp. Lectr.
Research: allergy (dust mite allergens, immunomodulation); bacterial pathogenicity (communication and signalling, methicillin resistance, staphlococcal and E. coli infections); genetics (bacterial, human/enkaryotic, population/evolutionary); oncolocy (angiogenesis, stem cell transplantation)

Genetics

Tel: (0115) 970 9398 Fax: (0115) 970 3906

Armour, J. A., MA *Camb.*, BM BCh *Oxf.*, PhD *Leic.*   Reader
Brook, J. D., BSc *Manc.*, PhD *Edin.*   Prof.
Brookfield, J. F., BA *Oxf.*, PhD *Lond.*   Reader
Day, T. H., BSc *Edin.*, PhD *Edin.*   Sr. Lectr.
Lloyd, R. G., BSc *Brist.*, DPhil *Sus.*   Prof.
Parkin, D. T., BSc *Durh.*, PhD *Manc.*   Prof.
Raeburn, J. A., MB ChB *Edin.*, PhD *Edin.*, FRCPEd   Prof., Medical Genetics
Sharp, P. M., BSc *Edin.*, PhD *Edin.*   Prof.
Other Staff: 3 Lectrs.

Immunology, Division of

Tel: (0115) 970 9123 Fax: (0115) 970 9919

Robins, R. A., BPharm *Nott.*, PhD *Nott.*   Reader
Sewell, H. F., MB ChB *Leic.*, BDS *Birm.*, MSc *Birm.*, PhD *Birm.*, FRCP, FRCPath   Prof.
Todd, I., MA *Oxf.*, PhD *Lond.*   Sr. Lectr.
Other Staff: 2 Lectrs.; 1 Temp. Lectr.

Microbiology, Division of

Tel: (0115) 970 9162 Fax: (0115) 970 9233

Emmerson, A. M., BSc *Lond.*, MB BS *Lond.*, FRCPath, FRCPGlas   Prof.
Finch, R. G., MB ChB *Birm.*, FRCP, FRCPath   Prof., Infectious Diseases
Greenwood, D., BSc *Lond.*, PhD *Lond.*, DSc *Nott.*, FRCPath   Prof., Antimicrobial Science
Grundmann, H., MSc *Lond.*, MD *Freib.*   Sr. Lectr.
Irving, W. L., MA *Camb.*, MB BChir *Camb.*, PhD *Lond.*   Reader, Virology
Slack, R. C. B., MA *Camb.*, MB BChir *Camb.*   Sr. Lectr., Communicable Diseases Control
Thomson, B., MB ChB *Edin.*, PhD *Lond.*   Sr. Lectr., Infectious Diseases
Other Staff: 1 Lectr.; 3 Temp. Lectrs.

Pathology, Division of

Tel: (0115) 970 9169 Fax: (0115) 970 4852

Anderson, M. C., MA *Camb.*, MB BChir *Camb.*, FRCPath, FRCOG   Reader
Cowley, G. P., BSc *Wales*, MB BS *Lond.*, PhD   Sr. Lectr.
Ellis, I. O., BMedSci *Nott.*, BM BS *Nott.*   Reader
Fagan, D. C., MA *Camb.*, MD *Camb.*, FRCPath   Sr. Lectr.
Haynes, A. P., BA *Camb.*, DM *Nott.*   Sr. Lectr.

Jenkins, D., MA *Camb.*, MD *Camb.*, FRCPath   Reader

Lowe, J., BMedSci BM BS   Prof., Neuropathology

Pinder, S. E., MB ChB *Manc.*   Sr. Lectr.

Russell, N. H., MD *Liv.*   Reader, Haematology

Stevens, A., MB BS *Lond.*, FRCPath   Sr. Lectr.

Other Staff: 3 Lectrs.

Community Health Sciences, School of

Child and Adolescent Psychiatry Unit

Tel: (0115) 952 9455 *Fax:* (0115) 952 9455

Bramble, David J., MB ChB *Leic.*, MD   Sr. Lectr.

Hollis, Chris P., BSc *Lond.*, MB BS *Lond.*   Sr. Lectr.

Pearce, J. B., MB BS *Lond.*, MPhil *Lond.*, FRCP, FRCPsych   Prof.

Other Staff: 1 Lectr.

Research: analysis of cohorts; epidemiology of influenza and meningitis; epidemiology of schizophrenia; referral to hospital from primary care; social capital and health inequalities

General Practice

Tel: (0115) 970 9387

Avery, A. J., BMedSci *Sheff.*, MB ChB *Sheff.*   Sr. Lectr.

Jones, J. A., MB ChB *Leic.*, MSc   Sr. Lectr.

Kendrick, D., BM   Sr. Lectr

Pringle, M. A. L., MD *Lond.*   Prof.

Williams, Edward I., OBE, MD *Manc.*, FRCGP   Emer. Prof.

Other Staff: 1 Lectr.; 2 Lectrs.†; 2 Temp. Lectrs.; 13 Temp. Lectrs.†

Health Care of the Elderly

Tel: (0115) 970 9408 *Fax:* (0115) 942 3618

Gladman, J. R. F., BSc *Birm.*, MB ChB *Birm.*   Sr. Lectr.

Jones, R. G., MB ChB *Manc.*   Sr. Lectr.

Pinner, G. T., MB BS *Lond.*, MSc *Lond.*   Sr. Lectr.

Other Staff: 2 Lectrs.

Vacant Posts: 1 Prof.

Learning Disabilities

Tel: (0115) 970 9247 *Fax:* (0115) 978 1598

Standen, J., BSc *Lond.*, PhD *Leic.*   Reader

Wilson, D. N., MB BS *Lond.*   Sr. Lectr.

Physiotherapy

Tel: (0115) 962 7681 *Fax:* (0115) 960 6993

Kerr, K. M., BA PhD   Sr. Lectr.

Rutherford, I. C., BA MPhil   Sr. Lectr.

Other Staff: 4 Lectrs.; 3 Lectrs.†; 1 Temp. Lectr.†

Psychiatry

Tel: (0115) 970 9336 *Fax:* (0115) 970 9495

Bradshaw, C. M., BSc PhD   Prof.

Garrud, P., MA *Oxf.*, DPhil *Oxf.*   Sr. Lectr.

Jones, Peter, BSc *Lond.*, MB BS *Lond.*, MSc *Lond.*   Prof.

Middleton, H. C., BA *Camb.*, MD *Camb.*   Sr. Lectr.

Oates, Margaret R., MB ChB *Liv.*   Sr. Lectr.

Park, S. B. G., BA *Camb.*, BM BCh *Oxf.*   Sr. Lectr.

Szabadi, E., MD *Semmelweis*, PhD *Edin.*, DSc *Manc.*, FRCPsych   Prof.

Other Staff: 5 Lectrs.; 1 Temp. Lectr.

Public Health Medicine and Epidemiology

Tel: (0115) 970 9306 *Fax:* (0115) 970 9316

Chilvers, Clair E. D., MSc *Lond.*   Prof.

Dewey, M. E., BA *Hull*   Sr. Lectr.

Gillies, Pamela A., BSc *Aberd.*, MEd *Aberd.*, MMedSci PhD   Prof., Public Health

Logan, Richard F. A., BSc *Edin.*, MB ChB *Edin.*, MSc *Lond.*, FRCP   Reader

Madeley, R. J., MB BS *Lond.*, MSc *Lond.*, DM   Prof.; Head*

Muir, K. R., BSc *CNAA*, PhD *Birm.*   Sr. Lectr.

Neal, Keith R., BMed *S'ton.*   Sr. Lectr.

Nguyen-Van-Tam, J. S., BMedSci *Nott.*, BM BS *Nott.*   Sr. Lectr.

Pearson, J. C. G., BSc *St And.*, MSc *Harv.*, PhD *Dund.*   Sr. Lectr.

Silcocks, P. B., BSc *Brist.*, BM BCh *Oxf.*, MSc *Sheff.*   Sr. Lectr.

White, J. A., MSc *Purdue*, PhD *Purdue*   Sr. Lectr.

Williams, Brian T., MB BS *Lond.*, MD *Sheff.*, FRCP   Prof., Public Health Medicine

Other Staff: 5 Temp. Lectrs.; 2 Temp. Lectrs.†

Rehabilitation Medicine

Playford, Edith, MB BS *Lond.*, MD *Lond.*   Sr. Lectr.

Ward, Christopher O., MB BChir *Camb.*, MD *Camb.*   Prof.

Other Staff: 2 Lectrs.

Human Development, School of

Child Health

Tel: (0115) 970 9255 *Fax:* (0115) 970 9382

Blair, M. E., BSc *Lond.*, MB BS *Lond.*   Sr. Lectr., Paediatric Oncology

Choonara, I. A., MB ChB *Liv.*   Prof.

Marlow, N., BA *Oxf.*, MB BS *Lond.*, MA *Oxf.*, DM *Oxf.*   Prof., Neonatal Medicine

McIntyre, J. W., BSc *Liv.*, MB ChB *Nott.*, DM *Nott.*   Sr. Lectr.

Polnay, L., BSc *Lond.*, MB BS *Lond.*, FRCP   Reader

Punt, J. A., MB BS *Lond.*, FRCS   Sr. Lectr.

Rutter, N., BA *Camb.*, MB BChir *Camb.*, FRCP   Prof., Paediatric Medicine

Stephenson, T. J., BSc *Brist.*, BM BCh *Oxf.*, DM *Nott.*, FRCP   Reader

Vloeberghs, M. H., MD *Brussels*   Sr. Lectr.

Walker, D. A., BMedSci *Nott.*, BM BS *Nott.*   Sr. Lectr., Paediatric Oncology

Other Staff: 3 Lectrs.; 4 Temp. Lectrs.

Obstetrics and Gynaecology

Tel: (0115) 970 9240 *Fax:* (0115) 970 9034

Arulkumaran, S., MB BS *Ceyl.*, PhD *Sing.*, FRCSEd, FRCOG   Prof.

Baker, P. N., BMedSci BM BS   Prof.

Brincat, M. P., PhD *Lond.*   Prof., Reproductive Medicine

Broughton Pipkin, Fiona, MA *Oxf.*, DPhil *Oxf.*   Prof., Perinatal Physiology

Filshie, G. M., MB BS *Lond.*, FRCOG   Reader

Fraser, D. M., BEd *Nott.*, MPhil *Nott.*   Sr. Lectr., Midwifery

Gardosi, J. O., MB BS *W.Aust.*, FRCSEd   Sr. Lectr.

James, D. K., MA *Camb.*, MD *Camb.*   Prof., Feto-Maternal Medicine

Johnson, I. R., BSc *Lond.*, MB BS *Lond.*, DM   Prof.; Head*

Maynard, P. V., BSc *Wales*, PhD *Wales*   Sr. Lectr.

Perkins, Alan C., BSc *Coventry*, MSc *Leeds*, PhD *Nott.*   Reader, Medical Physics

Ramsay, M. M., BA *Camb.*, MB BCh *Camb.*, MA *Camb.*, MD *Camb.*   Sr. Lectr.

Robinson, G., BSc *Belf.*, PhD *Belf.*   Sr. Lectr.

Symonds, I. M., BMedSci *Nott.*, DM *Nott.*   Sr. Lectr.

Thornton, Simon J., MB BChir *Camb.*, MA *Camb.*, MD *Melb.*   Sr. Lectr.

Other Staff: 2 Lectrs.

Medical and Surgical Sciences, School of

Anaesthesia

Aitkenhead, A. R., BSc *Edin.*, MD *Edin.*, FRCA   Prof.

Hobbs, G. J., BM BS *Flin.*, FRCA   Sr. Lectr.

Mahajan, R. P., MB BS *Meerut*, MD *Panjab*, FFARCSI   Sr. Lectr.

Other Staff: 2 Lectrs.

Diagnostic Radiology

Ludman, C. N., MB BS *Lond.*, FRCP   Sr. Lectr.

Moody, Alan R., BA *Oxf.*, MB BS *Lond.*, MA *Oxf.*, FRCR   Sr. Lectr.

Medicine

Bath, P. M. W., BSc *Lond.*, MB BS *Lond.*, MD *Lond.*   Stroke Assocn. Prof., Stroke Medicine

Blumhardt, L. D., MD *Otago*, BSc   Prof., Clinical Neurology

Britton, J. R., MD *Lond.*, MSc *Lond.*   Reader

Cowley, A. J., MB BS *Lond.*   Sr. Lectr.

Doherty, M., MA *Camb.*, MD *Camb.*   Prof., Rheumatology

Donnelly, R., MB ChB *Birm.*, MD *Birm.*, PhD *Glas.*, FRACP   Prof., Vascular Medicine

Gray, D., BMedSci BM BS   Reader

Hall, I. P., BA *Oxf.*, BM BCh *Oxf.*, MD   Reader

Hampton, J. R., MA *Oxf.*, DM *Oxf.*, DPhil *Oxf.*, FRCP   Prof., Cardiology

Hawkey, C. J., BA *Oxf.*, DM *Oxf.*, FRCP   Prof., Gastroenterology

Heptinstall, S., BSc *Newcastle(UK)*, PhD *Newcastle(UK)*   Prof.

Horn, Elizabeth H., MB ChB *Glas.*   Sr. Lectr.

Knox, A. J., MB ChB *Edin.*, DM   Reader

Lennox, G. G., BA *Oxf.*, BM BCh *Oxf.*   Sr. Lectr.

Logan, R. P., MB BS *Lond.*   Sr. Lectr.

Mahida, Yashwant, MB ChB *Liv.*   Sr. Lectr.

Rubin, Peter C., MA *Camb.*, DM *Oxf.*, FRCP   Boots Prof.

Savill, J. S., BA MB ChB PhD   Prof., Renal and Inflammatory Diseases

Sawle, G. V., DM *Nott.*   Sr. Lectr.

Sunderland, A., BSc *Aberd.*, MPhil *Glas.*, PhD *Brun.*   Sr. Lectr.

Tattersfield, Anne E., MD *Newcastle(UK)*, FRCP   Prof., Respiratory Medicine; Head*

Wilcox, R. G., BSc *Lond.*, MB BS *Lond.*, DM, FRCP   Prof., Cardiovascular Medicine

Williams, H. C., BSc *Lond.*, MB BS *Lond.*   Sr. Lectr.

Other Staff: 1 Lectr.; 3 Temp. Lectrs.; 2 Temp. Lectrs.†

Orthopaedic and Accident Surgery

Tel: (0115) 970 9630 *Fax:* (0115) 942 3656

Batt, Mark E., BSc *St And.*, MB BChir *Camb.*   Sr. Lectr.

Korngreen, A., MD   Sr. Lectr.

Scammell, Bridget E., MB ChB *Birm.*, DM *S'ton.*, FRCS, FRCSEd   Sr. Lectr.

Wallace, W. A., MB ChB *St And.*, FRCSEd   Prof.

Other Staff: 1 Temp. Lectr.; 1 Temp. Lectr.†

Surgery

Tel: (0115) 962 5707 *Fax:* (0115) 962 7765

Amoaku, Wilfred M., MB ChB *Ghana*, PhD *Belf.*, FRCSEd   Sr. Lectr.

Balfour, T. W., MB ChB *Edin.*, FRCSEd   Sr. Lectr.

Birchall, J. P., MD *Newcastle(UK)*   Prof., Otorhinolaryngology

Blamey, R. W., MA *Camb.*, MD *Camb.*, FRCS   Prof., Surgical Science

Dua, H. S., PhD *Nag.*   Prof., Ophthalmology

Durrant, L. G., BSc *Manc.*, PhD *Manc.*   Sr. Lectr.

Hardcastle, J. D., MA *Camb.*, MChir *Camb.*, FRCP, FRCS   Prof.

Hopkinson, B. R., MB ChB *Birm.*, ChM, FRCS   Prof., Vascular Surgery

McGlashan, J. A., MB BS *Lond.*, FRCS   Sr. Lectr.

O'Donoghue, Gerald M., MB BCh BAO *N.U.I.*, MCh, FRCSI, FRCS   Sr. Lectr.

Robertson, J. F. R., BSc *Glas.*, MB ChB *Glas.*, FRCSGlas   Reader

Rowlands, B. J., MB BS *Lond.*, MD *Sheff.*, FRCS, FACS, FRCSI   Prof., Gastroenterological Surgery

Scholefield, J. H., ChM *Liv.*   Reader

Watson, S. A., BSc *Leeds*, PhD *Nott.*   Sr. Lectr.

Other Staff: 3 Lectrs.; 1 Lectr.†; 1 Temp. Lectr.

Nursing, School of

Tel: (0115) 970 9265 *Fax:* (0115) 970 9955

Fletcher, J., BA *Hull*, MSc *Oxf.*, PhD *Brist.*, MPhil   Sr. Lectr.

Hart, Elizabeth A., BA *Keele*, PhD *Lond.*   Sr. Lectr.

James, V. C., MA *Aberd.*, PhD *Aberd.*   Prof.; Head*

Noon, J. P., BA *Edin.*, PhD *Edin.*   Reader
Other Staff: 22 Lectrs.; 1 Lectr.†; 1 Temp.
   Lectr.; 2 Temp. Lectrs.†

Postgraduate Medical Education, Centre for

Batstone, G. F., BSc *Brist.*, MSc *Wales*, MB BS
   Lond., FRCPath   Prof.
Brown, G. A., BSc *Lond.*, DPhil *Ulster*   Sr. Lectr.
Challis, M., BA *Oxf.*, MA *Oxf.*   Sr. Lectr.

SPECIAL CENTRES, ETC

Cancer Campaign Research Laboratory

Tel: (0115) 951 3406 Fax: (0115) 951 3412

Price, M. R., BSc PhD DSc   Reader
Robins, R. A., BPharm PhD   Reader
Stevens, Prof. M. F. G., BPharm PhD DSc,
   FRSChem   Dir.*

Continuing Education

Tel: (0115) 951 4398 Fax: (0115) 951 4397

Jones, D. J., MEd *Manc.*, PhD   Sr. Lectr.
Markham, D., BA *York(UK)*, PhD *Durh.*   Sr.
   Lectr.
Morgan, W. J., BA *Wales*, MEd *Wales*   Prof.,
   Politics and International Studies(Derby, S.
   Derbyshire)
Parker, S., BSc *Lond.*, MSc *Lond.*, PhD
   Lond.   Robert Peers Prof., Adult Education;
   Head*
Preston, P. J. D., MA   Sr. Lectr., Literature
Sutton, I. D., BSc PhD   Sr. Lectr., Geology;
   Dir. of Extra-mural Studies
Wallis, J. V., MA *Birm.*, PhD   Sr. Lectr.
Other Staff: 7 Lectrs.; 1 Temp. Lectr.
Research: adult education and social exclusion;
   comparative education and international
   development; continuing education and
   professional development; lifelong learning
   and the adult curriculum

Hearing Research, Medical Research Council Institute of

Haggard, Prof. M. P., MA *Edin.*, PhD
   Camb.   Dir.*

Language Centre

No staff at present

Mathematical Education, Shell Centre for

Tel: (0115) 951 4410 Fax: (0115) 979 1813

Phillips, R. J., BSc *Sus.*, PhD *Lond.*   Reader

CONTACT OFFICERS

Academic affairs. Deputy Registrar and Head
   of Policy Development: Smith, Margaret S.,
   BSc *Glas.*, DPhil *Oxf.*
Academic affairs. Academic Secretary: Hart,
   Alan, BA *Keele*
Accommodation. Assistant Registrar: Adams,
   Hamish, BA *CNAA*
Admissions (first degree). Assistant Registrar:
   Baker, Lucy, BA *Nott.*
Admissions (higher degree). Assistant
   Registrar: Watson, C. Jane, BA *Liv.*
Adult/continuing education. Head,
   Continuing Education: Parker, Prof. S., BSc
   Lond., MSc *Lond.*, PhD *Lond.*
Alumni. Graduate Liaison Officer: Cowling,
   Helen, BA *CNAA*
Archives. Keeper of the Manuscripts and
   Special Collections: Johnston, D. B., BA PhD
Careers. Director, Careers Advisory Service:
   Thorne, Martin E., MA *Edin.*
Computing services. Director, Information
   Services: Ford, Peter H., MA *Camb.*
Consultancy services. Director, Office of
   Research and Business Services: Robertson,
   Douglas W., MA *Aberd.*, PhD *Wales*
Credit transfer. Administrative Assistant:
   Brimble, Marc, BA *Wales*, MSc *Wales*
Development/fund-raising. Development
   Officer: Smith, Elizabeth A., BA *Reading*
Distance education. Head, Continuing
   Education: Parker, Prof. S., BSc *Lond.*, MSc
   Lond., PhD *Lond.*
Equal opportunities. Director of Personnel:
   Morehen, Marie, BA *Wash.*, MA *De Mont.*
Estates and buildings/works and services.
   Director of Estate Management: Jagger, C.
   H., BSc *Warw.*
Examinations. Assistant Registrar: Baker, Lucy,
   BA *Nott.*
Finance. Finance Director: Hedges, M. S., MA
   Oxf., FCA
General enquiries. Registrar: Jones, Keith H.,
   MA *Camb.*
Industrial liaison. Director, Office of Research
   and Business Services: Robertson, Douglas
   W., MA *Aberd.*, PhD *Wales*

International office. Director: Humfrey,
   Christine H., BA *Reading*, MEd *Nott.*, PhD *Nott.*
Library (chief librarian). Director of Library
   Services: Oldroyd, R. E., BA *Hull*
Library (enquiries). Director of Library
   Services: Oldroyd, R. E., BA *Hull*
Minorities/disadvantaged groups. Director of
   Personnel: Morehen, Marie, BA *Wash.*, MA
   De Mont.
Ombudsperson. Registrar: Jones, Keith H., MA
   Camb.
Personnel/human resources. Director of
   Personnel: Morehen, Marie, BA *Wash.*, MA
   De Mont.
Public relations, information and marketing.
   Public Affairs Manager: Dalling, Philip J.
Publications. Public Affairs Manager: Dalling,
   Philip J.
Purchasing. Director of Procurement:
   Simmonds, Peter
Quality assurance and accreditation.
   Academic Secretary: Hart, Alan, BA *Keele*
Research. Deputy Registrar and Head of Policy
   Development: Smith, Margaret S., BSc *Glas.*,
   DPhil *Oxf.*
Safety. Safety and Radiation Protection Officer:
   Sutherland, J. A., BSc *Nott.*, PhD *E.Anglia*
Scholarships, awards, loans. Registrar: Jones,
   Keith H., MA *Camb.*
Schools liaison. Assistant Registrar: Baker,
   Lucy, BA *Nott.*
Security. Security Officer: Lowe, R. A.
Sport and recreation. Director of Physical
   Recreation: Williams, V. P., BEd *Nott.*
Staff development and training. Head of
   Training and Staff Development Unit:
   Blackwell, Richard J., BA *Exe.*, MA *Warw.*
Student union. President of the Students'
   Union: ......
Student welfare/counselling. Senior
   Counsellor: Henry, Helen M., BA *Nott.*
Students from other countries. Administrative
   Assistant: Ward, Christine, BA *Nott.*
Students with disabilities. Officer for
   Disability Issues: Foley, Mary, MA *Oxf.*
Women. Director of Personnel: Morehen,
   Marie, BA *Wash.*, MA *De Mont.*

*[Information supplied by the institution as at 1 April
1998, and edited by the ACU]*

NOTTINGHAM TRENT UNIVERSITY

Founded 1992; previously established as Nottingham and District Technical College 1945, Trent Polytechnic 1970, and Nottingham Polytechnic 1989

Member of the Association of Commonwealth Universities

Postal Address: Burton Street, Nottingham, England NG1 4BU
Telephone: (0115) 941 8418 **Fax**: (0115) 948 4266 **Telex**: 377534 Polnot G **WWW**: http://www.ntu.ac.uk

VICE-CHANCELLOR*—Cowell, Prof. R., BA Brist., PhD Brist.
DEPUTY VICE-CHANCELLOR—Short, Prof. K., BSc Wales, MEd Lond., PhD Wales, FIBiol
PRO-VICE-CHANCELLOR—Thompson, Prof. G. H., BSc(Eng) Lond., MSc Brad., FIEE
PRO-VICE-CHANCELLOR—Stancer, Prof. J. D., BSc Lond., MSc(Econ) Lond., PhD Lond.
DIRECTOR OF FINANCE—Morgan, E., MA Oxf., FCA
REGISTRAR—Samson, D., BA MBA
HEAD OF LIBRARY AND INFORMATION SERVICES—Lines, Elizabeth, BSc Sus.

FACULTIES/SCHOOLS

Art and Design
Tel: (0115) 948 6404 Fax: (0115) 948 6403
Dean: Newton, Prof. E. W., FTI
Secretary: Purssord, Lindsey

Construction and the Environment
Tel: (0115) 948 6501 Fax: (0115) 948 6064
Dean: Hawkins, Prof. R. K., MSc Sur., PhD Nott., FICE
Faculty Administrator: Gresson, Marvin

Economic and Social Sciences
Tel: (0115) 948 6817 Fax: (0115) 948 6808
Dean: Webb, Prof. D., BA MA
Faculty Administrator: Rees Childs, Rosemary

Education
Tel: (0115) 948 6711
Dean: Hastings, Prof. Nigel, BTech Lond., MSc Lond.
Secretary: Ridgley, Cynthia

Engineering and Computing
Tel: (0115) 948 6482 Fax: (0115) 948 6518
Dean: Whitrow, Prof. R. J., BSc Lond., PhD Essex
Secretary: Himsworth, K.

Humanities
Dean: Chan, Prof. S., MA PhD

Nottingham Business School
Dean: Reynolds, Prof. M. L., BA Sheff., DPhil York(UK)

Nottingham Law School
Tel: (0115) 948 6871 Fax: (0115) 948 6878
Dean: Jones, Prof. P.

Science and Mathematics
Dean: Palmer, Prof. T., BA Camb., PhD Lond.

ACADEMIC UNITS

Accounting
Ball, G. Sr. Lectr.
Barker, I., BA Oxf. Sr. Lectr.
Blackwell, G., BSc Open(UK), MBA Sr. Lectr.
Boot, L., BSc Nott. Sr. Lectr.
Bowler, I. Sr. Lectr.
Cobb, C. P., BA Birm. Sr. Lectr.
Cosserat, G. W. P., MA Camb.., MSc Lond. Principal Lectr.
Hancox, S., BA Nott. Sr. Lectr.
Hand, L. F., BA CNAA Principal Lectr.
Harradine, D. Sr. Lectr.
Hawley, M. B., MPhil Sheff. Principal Lectr.
Hunt, S. P., BSc(Econ) Sr. Lectr.
Isaaks, C. M., BSc(Econ) Lond. Sr. Lectr.
Kellett, S., BA CNAA Sr. Lectr.
Knight, C., BA Nott. Sr. Lectr.
Lovejoy, P. D., MA Oxf. Sr. Lectr.
Lovell, A. T. A., MSc Birm. Principal Lectr.; Head*

Oakes, R. J., FCA Sr. Lectr.
Potter, J. Sr. Lectr.
Rees-Jones, M. Sr. Lectr.
Sanderson, P. Principal Lectr.
Slaich, V., BA N.Lond. Sr. Lectr.
Welch, D. J. Sr. Lectr.
Widdowson, G. W., MA Lanc. Sr. Lectr.

Art, see Visual and Performing Arts

Building and Environmental Health
Tel: (0115) 948 6438
Blake, R. N. E., PhD Lond. Sr. Lectr.
Carter, W. G., MSc Manc. Principal Lectr.
Charlett, A. J., BA MPhil Principal Lectr.
Darkwa, K., MSc Cran.IT, BEng PhD Sr. Lectr.
Fewkes, A., BSc CNAA, MSc CNAA, MPhil CNAA Sr. Lectr.
Frampton, D. I., BA Open(UK), MSc CNAA Principal Lectr.
George, B. W., BSc Aston, MSc Lond. Principal Lectr.
Gregg, T. R., MPhil Sr. Lectr.
Hardy, P. A. Sr. Lectr.
Hooper, A. J., BSc(Econ) Lond., MSc Wales Cala Homes Residential Devel. Prof.
Houldsworth, H. K., BA MPhil Principal Lectr.
Hurst, A. G., MSc Reading, MBA Sr. Lectr.
Lane, T. J., MSc Aston Prof.; Head*
Lyons, P. E., BEd Hull Sr. Lectr.
Maguire, K. J. P., BA Open(UK), BSc E.Anglia, MSc CNAA Sr. Lectr.
Marchant, D. R. Sr. Lectr.
McCarthy, A., MA Lough. Sr. Lectr.
McGrath, P. T., BSc Manc., MSc Manc. Sr. Lectr.
O'Rourke, A., BSc Leeds, PhD Sr. Lectr.
Orchard, K. J., BSc CNAA, MSc Lough. Sr. Lectr.
Paddock, P. B., BSc Nott., MPhil CNAA, MBA Principal Lectr.
Pritchard, C., BA Sr. Lectr.
Ramsay-Dawber, P. J., BSc CNAA, MBA CNAA Sr. Lectr.
Trevorrow, A., MPhil Sr. Lectr.
Woollard, A., BEng Liv., MA S'ton. Sr. Lectr.
Research: construction companies: water recycling, corporate performance; housebuilding: structural defects, rectification, warranties, standardisation; thermal energy technology for sustainable development; urban regeneration: land use change, airfields; water management: rain water, grey water

Business, see Nottingham Bus. Sch.

Business Information Systems, see
Finance and Bus. Information Systems

Chemistry and Physics
Bottrill, S. J., BSc MEd Sr. Lectr.
Braithwaite, A., BSc Lough., PhD Manc. Sr. Lectr.

Coutts, I. G. C., BSc Aberd., PhD Aberd. Sr. Lectr.
Creaser, C. S., BSc Kent, PhD Kent Prof.; Head*
Crookes, J. N., BSc Birm., PhD Nott. Principal Lectr.
Fowell, J. C. T., BSc Nott., PhD Nott. Sr. Lectr.
Halfpenny, J. C., BSc Lanc., PhD Lanc. Principal Lectr.
Harrison, C. C., MA Oxf., DPhil Oxf. Sr. Lectr.
Hearn, J., BSc Edin., MSc Brist., PhD Brist. Reader
Hill, R., BSc Lond., PhD Lond. Principal Lectr.
Hills, C. C., BSc CNAA Sr. Lectr.
Jackson, E., BSc Durh., PhD Durh. Sr. Lectr.
Matharu, A. S., BSc CNAA, PhD CNAA Sr. Lectr.
McHale, G., BSc Nott., PhD Nott. Sr. Lectr.
McKenzie, N. L., BSc Lond. Sr. Lectr.
Moss, K., BSc Manc., PhD Manc. Sr. Lectr.
Murray, R., BSc Lond., PhD Lond. Principal Lectr.
Neal, D. B., BSc PhD Sr. Lectr.
Newton, M. I., BSc MSc PhD Sr. Lectr.
Richards, J., MSc Manc., PhD Manc. Sr. Lectr.
Rowan, S. M., BSc Sheff., MSc Durh. Principal Lectr.
Turner, R. J., BSc Sur., PhD Nott. Sr. Lectr.
Wallace, R. G., BSc S'ton., PhD CNAA Sr. Lectr.
Wilson, R. C., BSc Hull, PhD Hull, FRSChem Principal Lectr.
Woolley, R. G., MA Oxf., DPhil Oxf., ScD Camb. Prof.

Computing
Tel: (0115) 948 6482 Fax: (0115) 948 6518
Al-Dabass, D., BSc Lond., PhD CNAA Principal Lectr.
Allison, I. K., BSc CNAA Sr. Lectr.
Bai, L., BSc Siping, MSc Lanzhou, PhD Nott. Sr. Lectr.
Bargiela, A., MSc Silesia, PhD Durh. Prof.
Battersby, A., BSc Salf. Sr. Lectr.
Bidwell, L. M., BSc Sus., MSc Sheff. Sr. Lectr.
Cant, R. J., BSc Manc., PhD Lond. Sr. Lectr.
Claramand, C., MSc Lausanne, PhD
Cuming, C. B., MA Oxf. Principal Lectr.
Evett, L. J., BSc CNAA, PhD Brist. Sr. Lectr.
Fazackerley, P. L., BSc Liv., MSc Oxf. Principal Lectr.
Halstead, P., BSc Manc., MPhil CNAA Sr. Lectr.
Hibberd, R. B., BEd Sheff., MSc CNAA Sr. Lectr.
King, S. J., MSc CNAA Sr. Lectr.
Langenseipen, C., BSc Manc., PhD Manc. Sr. Lectr.
McDonald, P. W., BSc CNAA, MSc CNAA Sr. Lectr.
Newman, F. T., BSc Leic., BA Leic., DPhil Oxf. Principal Lectr.
O'Sullivan, S. D., BA Lond. Sr. Lectr.
Orton, P. A., BSc Sus. Sr. Lectr.
Palmer-Brown, D. P., BSc Leeds, MSc CNAA, PhD Nott. Sr. Lectr.
Poliakoff, J., MA Nott.Trent, PhD Nott.Trent Sr. Lectr.

Powell, H. M., BEng Sheff., PhD Sheff. Sr. Lectr.

Sherkat, N., BEng Nott., PhD CNAA Sr. Lectr.

Smith, J. R., BSc Wales Sr. Lectr.

Smith, P. A., BSc Nott., PhD Nott. Sr. Lectr.

Thomas, P. D., BSc Wales, MSc Lough., PhD Lough. Principal Lectr.

Whitrow, R. J., BSc Lond.., PhD Essex Prof.; Head*

Research: network simulation and modelling; pattern and handwriting recognition; real time machine control

Design

Arthur, Les, MA CNAA Sr. Lectr.

Barnes, A., BA Nott.Trent Sr. Lectr.

Bowkett, J. A., MA Lond. Principal Lectr.

Briggs, P. M., BA CNAA Sr. Lectr.

Bull, Karen, BA CNAA, MA C.England Sr. Lectr.

Clarke, J. T., BSc CNAA Principal Lectr.

Colwell, A., BA CNAA, MA C.England Sr. Lectr.

Crabbe, A., MA Essex Sr. Lectr.

Cross, D., BA CNAA, MA RCA Sr. Lectr.

Hardy, C., BSc Nott., MBA Brighton Sr. Lectr.

Hebbditch, N., BA CNAA, MA Nott.Trent Sr. Lectr.

Higgins, I. K., BA CNAA Sr. Lectr.

Hope, M., MA Leic. Principal Lectr.

Johnson, P., MA CNAA Sr. Lectr.

Kennedy, G. M., MA CNAA Prof.; Head*

Lester, P., BA CNAA Sr. Lectr.

Lloyd-Thomas, K., BA Camb. Sr. Lectr.

Oldfield, J. A., MA CNAA Principal Lectr.

Reavley, G., BA CNAA, MA Nott. Sr. Lectr.

Saunders, B. J., MA RCA Sr. Lectr.

Senter, T. A., BA Newcastle(UK), MPhil Nott. Sr. Lectr.

Simpson, K., BA CNAA Sr. Lectr.

Taylor, B. M., MA CNAA Principal Lectr.

Tomlinson, J., MA RCA Sr. Lectr.

Varley, T., MA CNAA Sr. Lectr.

Vickers, P. A., MA RCA Principal Lectr.

Walker, S., BA Nott., MA Nott. Sr. Lectr.

Ward, K. A. Sr. Lectr.

Research: designed environment; digital imagery; history of design; product design and evaluation

Economics and Public Administration

Fax: (0115) 948 6808

Armstrong, J., BSc Lough., MPhil CNAA Principal Lectr.

Baker, D., PhD Sheff. Sr. Lectr.

Bellamy, C. A., BA Nott., PhD Nott. Prof.; Principal Lectr.

Burns, A., BA Sheff.

Cameron, D. J., BA Strath., MA(Econ) Manc. Principal Lectr.

Cooke, A. J., BA Nott., PhD Nott., MSc York(UK) Sr. Lectr.

Fraser, I., MA Edin., MA York(UK), PhD Warw. Sr. Lectr.

Fraser, S., LLB Glas., MSc Brist., PhD Warw. Sr. Lectr.

Galt, A. V., MA Wales Principal Lectr.

Harrison, B., BA Nott., MA Sheff. Sr. Lectr.

Haselden, K., BA CNAA, MA CNAA Sr. Lectr.

Heasell, S. L., BA CNAA Sr. Lectr.

Henn, M. C., BA Kingston(UK) Sr. Lectr.

Hunter, J., BA Glam., PhD Glam. Sr. Lectr.

Jahn, Detlef G., BA Duisburg, PhD European Univ.Inst. Prof.

Jones, R. H., BA CNAA, MSc(Econ) Lond. Sr. Lectr.

O'Neill, M. P., MA PhD Sr. Lectr.

Paton, D., BSc Lond., MA Warw., PhD Lond. Sr. Lectr.

Pearson, J. M., BSc Manc., MA(Econ) Manc. Principal Lectr.

Peppard, R. S., BSc Lond., MPhil Leeds Sr. Lectr.

Periton, P. D., BLitt Oxf., MA Camb. Head*

Quinn, P. A., MA Essex Sr. Lectr.

Sanderson, B., BA York(UK), MA Liv. Sr. Lectr.

Simon, R., BA Nott., MA CNAA, PhD Birm. Sr. Lectr.

Swift, S. B., MA Leic. Sr. Lectr.

Vaughan Williams, L., BSc Wales, PhD Nott.Trent Sr. Lectr.

Wallis, D., BSc Lond. Sr. Lectr.

Webb, J. J., BSc(Econ) Lond. Principal Lectr.

Wilde, L., BA Liv., PhD Liv. Reader

Young, M. A., BA Essex, MA Kent Principal Lectr.

Other Staff: 1 Res. Fellow

Research: British politics and administration: Conservative Party, information and government; comparative politics: environmental politics, election rhetoric; effects of advertising on firm performance; efficiency of financial and betting markets; political theory: Hegel and Marx studies, needs and ethics

Education, Primary

Tel: (0115) 948 6711

Baker, T. C., MA Lough. Sr. Lectr.

Bindon, A. E., BEd Sheff. Sr. Lectr.

Bloomfield, A., PhD Hull Reader

Bowen, R., MEd Wales Sr. Lectr.

Cooper, A. S., BSc Lond., MEd CNAA Sr. Lectr.

Corden, R. E., PhD Keele Sr. Lectr.

Cox, S. P., MA Lond. Sr. Lectr.

Delaney, K. C., BSc Brist., MPhil S'ton. Sr. Lectr.

Disney, A. C., BA Open(UK), MPhil Nott. Sr. Lectr.

Eland, S. E., BSc Wales, MEd Leic. Sr. Lectr.

Gibbons, I. B., BA Newcastle(UK), MA Nott.Trent Sr. Lectr.

Green, K. L., MA Open(UK) Sr. Lectr.

Griffiths, Morwenna, BSc Brist., MEd Brist., PhD Brist. Res. Co-ordinator

Hastings, Nigel, BTech Lond., MSc Lond. Prof.; Head*

Hayes, S. A., MA Lond. Sr. Lectr.

Hilditch, F. A., MA Leic. Sr. Lectr.

Hunt, K. M., MEd Nott.Trent Principal Lectr.

Impey, G. N., BA Reading, MA Leic. Principal Lectr.

Lee, Judith B., BEd Nott., MPhil Nott.Trent Sr. Lectr.

Moore, J. D., MSc Brad. Principal Lectr.

Ovens, P. J., BSc Leeds, MEd Manc., PhD E.Anglia Principal Lectr.

Pawluch, D. C. T., BA Leic. Sr. Lectr.

Robinson, Pauline J., MA Dund. Sr. Lectr.

Spavin, S., BEd Hull, MEd Leic. Principal Lectr.; Schs. Partnership Co-ordinator

Walton, A., MA Leeds, MEd Leic. Sr. Lectr.

Williamson, D. C., BSc Oregon, MEd Missouri Principal Lectr.

Other Staff: 3 Lectrs.

Education, Secondary and Tertiary

Anderson, J., BEd CNAA Sr. Lectr.

Antonouris, G., PhD Sr. Lectr.

Archer, J. C. Sr. Lectr.

Bostock, P. F., MEd CNAA Sr. Lectr.

Browne, A. J., BEd CNAA Sr. Lectr.

Bushnell, R. C., BSc Durh. Sr. Lectr.

Dransfield, R. B. W., BSc Wales Sr. Lectr.

Ghee, P. W., BSc Bath Sr. Lectr.

Howkins, S., MEd Nott. Sr. Lectr.

Kicks, M. Sr. Lectr.

Kidner, D. W., PhD Lond. Sr. Lectr.

Lesquereux, J. P., MEd Nott. Head*

Mills, R. J., MA Leic. Sr. Lectr.

Mitchell, D. R., MEd Nott. Sr. Lectr.

Morris, A., PhD Nott. Acting Head*

O'Neil, M., MEd Alta. Principal Lectr.

Onion, K. H., MA Nott. Sr. Lectr.

Paul, A., BEd CNAA Sr. Lectr.

Plant, M., MSc Leic. Principal Lectr.

Richards, J. K., MEd Brist. Sr. Lectr.

Shaw, P. A., MSc Lough. Sr. Lectr.

Smith, H. B., BA Sr. Lectr.

Sutcliffe-Binns, S. A., MEd Liv. Sr. Lectr.

Vaughan, S., MEd CNAA Sr. Lectr.

Weston, V. C. H., MEd Manc. Principal Lectr.

Engineering, Civil and Structural

Tel: (0115) 948 6440 Fax: (0115) 948 6450

Abbiss, J. C., BSc Nott., MSc Newcastle(UK) Sr. Lectr.

Braithwaite, R. P., BSc Leeds Sr. Lectr.

Breach, M. C., MA Camb., MSc Oxf., FRAS, FRICS Principal Lectr.

Cowley, J. A., BSc Birm. Sr. Lectr.

Daffern, C., BSc Nott., MPhil Nott. Sr. Lectr.

Davison, M., BSc Nott., PhD Nott. Sr. Lectr.

Dixon, N., BSc CNAA, PhD CNAA, FGS Principal Lectr.

Djerbib, Y., BEng Sheff., MEng Sheff., PhD Sheff. Sr. Lectr.

Goodall, G., MSc Birm. Sr. Lectr.

Greenwood, J., BSc(Eng) Lond., MEng McM., FGS Sr. Lectr.

Hawkins, R. K., MSc Sur., PhD Nott., FICE Prof.; Head*

Hoppitt, J. W., BSc Nott. Principal Lectr.

Jefferson, I., BEng Lough., PhD Lough. Sr. Lectr.

Johnson, D., BSc Lond., MSc Manc., PhD CNAA, FIStructE Principal Lectr.

Joynes, H. W., BSc Leeds, PhD Leeds Sr. Lectr.

Krylov, V. V., MSc Moscow, PhD Moscow, DSc Moscow Prof.

Roodbaraky, K., BSc CNAA, PhD Nott. Sr. Lectr.

Rosenbaum, M. S., BSc Lond., PhD Lond., FGS Prof.

Sane, K. A., BSc CNAA Sr. Lectr.

Sargent, P. T. H., BEng Sheff. Sr. Lectr.

Shapley, M. J., BSc Wales, BA Open(UK), MSc Birm. Sr. Lectr.

Sholji, I. H., BSc Lond., PhD Lond. Sr. Lectr.

Waltham, A. C., BSc Lond., PhD Lond. Sr. Lectr.

Wright, D. Sr. Lectr.

Wright, S., BSc CNAA Sr. Lectr.

Other Staff: 7 Lectrs.†

Research: acoustics: train generated ground vibrations; environmental engineering: water treatment and small scale hydropower; geohazards; structures: finite element analysis, structural defects; surveying: gyrotheodolite azimuth deterioration

Engineering, Electrical and Electronic

Fax: (0115) 948 6567

Clark, S., MA Camb., PhD CNAA Sr. Lectr.

Cranton, W. M., BSc Sur., PhD Brad. Sr. Lectr.

Germon, R. K., BSc Sheff., PhD Nott.Trent Sr. Lectr.

Kansara, M., BSc Lond., MPhil Lond. Sr. Lectr.

Mendenhall, P. C., BSc CNAA, MSc Aston Sr. Lectr.

Mias, C., BEng Bath, PhD Camb. Sr. Lectr.

Moore, P. W., BSc CNAA, MSc Nott. Sr. Lectr.

Morley, D., BSc Wales, MSc Wales, PhD Wales Principal Lectr.

Moss, P. B., BSc Manc., MEng Sheff. Sr. Lectr.

O'Neill, B. C., BA Trinity(Dub.), BAI Trinity(Dub.), PhD Liv. Reader

Patterson, E. B., PhD CNAA Principal Lectr.

Powell, R. G., BSc Nott., MSc Nott. Principal Lectr.

Redgate, J. S., BSc CNAA Sr. Lectr.

Robinson, M., BSc Salf., MSc Manc., PhD Leeds Prof.

Stevens, R., BEng Brad., PhD Brad. Sr. Lectr.

Teague, B. R., BSc Manc., PhD Nott. Principal Lectr.

Thomas, C. B., BSc Wales, MSc Wales, PhD Bath Prof.; Head*

Ward, E. S., BSc Wales, MPhil Nott., PhD Nott. Sr. Lectr.

Waters, A., BSc Aston, MPhil Nott. Sr. Lectr.

Other Staff: 1 Sr. Res. Fellow; 2 Res. Fellows; 2 Principal Lectrs.†; 3 Sr. Lectrs.†

Research: display technology: electroluminescent for flat-screen displays; electronic systems: networking hardware solutions for parallel systems; renewable energy: microhydropower for developing countries; three-dimensional imaging: stereoscopic imaging and metrology systems

Engineering, Manufacturing

Ashworth, D. W. C., BA Open(UK), MSc CNAA Sr. Lectr.

Drysdale, J. S., BSc CNAA Sr. Lectr.

Gildersleeve, M. J., MPhil CNAA, PhD Leeds Sr. Lectr.

Hague, A. G., BSc Durh., FIMechE, FIEE   Head*

Harvey, E. D., BSc Lond., MSc Aston, PhD Aston   Principal Lectr.

Hewitt, I. E., BSc CNAA, MSc CNAA   Sr. Lectr.

Hicking, P. R., BSc CNAA   Sr. Lectr.

Higginson, M., MSc Lough.   Sr. Lectr.

Howarth, M., BSc CNAA   Sr. Lectr.

Huddleston, J., MMet Sheff., PhD Leic.   Principal Lectr.

Kennedy, S. J., BSc Brad., MSc Lough., PhD Lough.   Sr. Lectr.

McGraw, K. L.   Sr. Lectr.

Parrish, J., MSc Sur.   Principal Lectr.

Prentice, P., DPhil Sus., FIM   Sr. Lectr.

Scott-Howes, P., MSc Manc., FIEE, FIMechE   Principal Lectr.

Sivayoganathan, K., PhD Birm.   Sr. Lectr.

Starkey, P.   Sr. Lectr.

Stratton, R., BSc Nott., MSc Warw.   Sr. Lectr.

Swetnam, D., BSc Wales, MSc Cran.IT, PhD Cran.IT   Sr. Lectr.

Tranfield, G., BSc Birm., PhD Warw.   Sr. Lectr.

Turner, M., BSc Nott., PhD Nott.   Sr. Lectr.

Turner, T. S., BSc Manc., PhD Nott.   Sr. Lectr.

Engineering, Mechanical

Ashforth-Frost, S. A., BEng CNAA, PhD CNAA   Sr. Lectr.

Charyszyn, S. M., BSc Lough., MSc   Sr. Lectr.

Codman, A. C., BEng Manc.   Sr. Lectr.

Crisp, A. R.   Sr. Lectr.

Dobbins, B. N., BSc CNAA, MPhil CNAA   Sr. Lectr.

Douglas, P., BSc Strath.   Sr. Lectr.

Eastwood, D., BSc Leeds, MPhil Leeds   Sr. Lectr.

Gentle, C. R., PhD Lond.   Prof.

Goodson, R., MEng CNAA   Sr. Lectr.

Hartle, S. L., BEng CNAA, PhD Nott.Trent   Sr. Lectr.

Henthorn, K. S., BSc Salf., MSc Manc., PhD Manc.   Principal Lectr.

Hughes, A., MPhil   Sr. Lectr.

Hull, J. B., BEng Liv., MMet PhD   Head*

Jambunathan, K., BSc Wales, PhD CNAA, FIMechE   Principal Lectr.

Jeffery, G. S. B., BSc Lond., MPhil Nott.   Sr. Lectr.

Jones, A. R., BEng Sheff., PhD Sheff.   Sr. Lectr.

Keysell, M., MSc Leeds   Sr. Lectr.

Lacey, M. R., BSc CNAA, PhD CNAA   Sr. Lectr.

Lai, E., BSc Lond., PhD Camb.   Sr. Lectr.

Laing, F. A., BSc Coventry   Sr. Lectr.

Loughton, E. W., BA   Sr. Lectr.

Montgomery, J., BSc Glas., PhD Nott., FIMechE   Principal Lectr.

Newton, E. A. A., BSc Nott., PhD Nott.   Sr. Lectr.

Sims, R., BSc Leeds   Sr. Lectr.

Skellern, P., BSc Nott., PhD Nott.   Principal Lectr.

Solomonides, I. P., BEd   Sr. Lectr.

Su, D., MSc Strath., PhD Strath.   Sr. Lectr.

Swannell, M. J., BSc CNAA, PhD CNAA   Sr. Lectr.

Engineering, Structural, see Engin., Civil and Struct.

English and Media Studies

Fax: (0115) 948 6632

Ashley, R. B., BA Nott., MPhil Nott.   Principal Lectr.

Bromley, R., BA Wales, MA Ill., DPhil Sus.   Prof.

Chadder, V. A. M., BA Reading, MA Brun.   Sr. Lectr.

Chambers, Deborah, BA Essex, MA Kent, PhD Kent   Reader

Clarke, E. R., BA Lond., DPhil Oxf.   Sr. Lectr.

Conolly, I., BA Oxf., MA Sus.   Principal Lectr.

de Burgh, Hugo, BA Lond., MA Lond.   Sr. Lectr.

Edley, N., PhD Lough.   Sr. Lectr.

Ellis, R. J., PhD Exe.   Reader

Featherstone, Mike, BA Durh., MA Durh., PhD Utrecht   Prof.

Fleming, C., BA Nott.   Sr. Lectr.

Fulford, Tim, MA Camb., PhD Camb.   Reader

Goodrich, J., BA Newcastle(UK), PhD Newcastle(UK)   Sr. Lectr.

Hapgood, E. L., BA Brist., MA Warw., PhD Warw.   Principal Lectr.

Harris, Sandra J., BA Iowa, MA Mich., PhD Nott.   Prof.; Head*

Hollows, J., BSc Salf., MA Lond.   Sr. Lectr.

Ives, J., BA Essex, MSc Lond.   Principal Lectr.

Johnson, R., PhD Camb.   Prof.

Lodziak, C. M. J., MEd N.Carolina, PhD N.Carolina   Sr. Lectr.

Lucas, John, BA Reading, PhD Reading   Prof.

MacDonald-Shaw, W. C., MA Oxf., MA Nott.   Sr. Lectr.

Morrish, E. C. E., BA Leeds, PhD Leeds   Sr. Lectr.

Nattrass, L., BA CNAA, MA York(UK), PhD Sheff.   Sr. Lectr.

Ouditt, S., BA Warw., MA York, PhD Leic.   Sr. Lectr.

Polkey, P., BA Lough., PhD Lough.   Sr. Lectr.

Rojek, Chris, BA Leic., MPhil Leic., PhD Glas.   Prof.

Shepherd, V., BA Lough., PhD Lough.   Reader

Smith, Peter, BA Lanc., MA Lanc., PhD Leic.   Sr. Lectr.

Stainton, C. E., BA CNAA, MA Nott., PhD Manc.   Sr. Lectr.

Stone, G., BA CNAA   Sr. Lectr.

Thomas, S. J., BA CNAA   Sr. Lectr.

Tincknell, Estella, BA CNAA, MA Birm.   Sr. Lectr.

Tomlinson, J. B., BEd CNAA, PhD Brad.   Principal Lectr.

Turnbull, N., BA Sheff., MSc CNAA   Sr. Lectr.

van Loon, J., BA Rotterdam, MA Car., PhD Lanc.   Sr. Lectr.

Williams, R. J. P., BA Nott., MPhil Nott., PhD Nott.   Reader

Woods, D. J., BA Manc., PhD Nott.   Sr. Lectr.

Woods, G. K. W., BA E.Anglia, MA E.Anglia, PhD E.Anglia   Sr. Lectr.

Youngs, T. D., BA CNAA, MA Nott., PhD CNAA   Sr. Lectr.

Other Staff: 4 Lectrs.; 1 Reader†; 3 Sr. Lectrs.†; 4 Lectrs.†; 1 Res. Fellow†

Research: critical social theory; inter-cultural pragmatics relating to business discourse; literary recovery research and radical texts; media and cultural studies; post-colonial studies; technology

Environmental Health, see Bldg. and Environmental Health

Fashion and Textiles

Aldrich, W. M., MEd PhD   Prof.; Sr. Res. Fellow

Allen, D. P.   Sr. Lectr.

Backhouse, S., BA   Sr. Lectr.

Brown, D. H. G.   Sr. Lectr.

Byrne, K.   Sr. Lectr.

Carpenter, M. F.   Sr. Lectr.

Challendar, C., MA   Sr. Lectr.

Danjoux, M., BA   Sr. Lectr.

Elson, D. M., FTI   Principal Lectr.

Goulding, R., BA   Sr. Lectr.

Gray, S., BSc MSc   Prof.; Sr. Res. Fellow

Haynes, L. G.   Sr. Lectr.

Hillier, E. P.   Sr. Lectr.

Jones, C. A., BA CNAA, MDes RCA   Sr. Lectr.

Keen, S. P.   Principal Lectr.

Newton, E. W., FTI   Prof.; Head*

O'Connor, C.   Sr. Lectr.

Phillips, P., MA RCA   Principal Lectr.

Pinches, J. L., BA CNAA, MDes RCA   Principal Lectr.

Richardson, R., BA CNAA   Sr. Lectr.

Robinson, J.   Sr. Lectr.

Smith, B.   Sr. Lectr.

Sonnet, E. J., BA CNAA, MA Nott., PhD Nott.   Sr. Lectr.

Sparkes, B. M., MA RCA   Principal Lectr.

Stafford, M., BA   Sr. Lectr.

Walton, M.   Sr. Lectr.

Williamson, M. J.   Principal Lectr.

Research: computer clothing research; design culture and technology; design of materials; structure, pattern and colour

Finance and Business Information Systems

Fax: (0115) 948 6512

Binner, J. M., BA Leeds, MSc Leeds, PhD Leeds   Sr. Lectr.

Bowker, P., BA CNAA, MSc Cran.   Principal Lectr.

Edwards, K., BSc CNAA   Sr. Lectr.

Gazely, A. M., BSc Open(UK), BA Manc., PhD Lough.   Sr. Lectr.

Hunt, C., BSc E.Anglia   Sr. Lectr.

Keady, H., BA CNAA   Sr. Lectr.

Mallin, C. A., BSc Aston, PhD Nott., FCA, FRS   Prof.

McAdam, D. R., BA Essex, MSc Sus., MSc CNAA   Sr. Lectr.

McCaughey, G. P., BA CNAA   Sr. Lectr.

Mutch, A. F., LLB Dund., MA Manc., PhD Manc.   Sr. Lectr.

Ow-Yong, K. H., MA CNAA   Sr. Lectr.

Pybus, Elizabeth J., BA Lond., MA Nott.   Sr. Lectr.

Reynolds, M. L., BA Sheff., DPhil York(UK)   Prof.; Head*

Sargent, B. A., BA CNAA   Sr. Lectr.

Scivier, J. E., MSc Lough.   Sr. Lectr.

Shirole, R. S., MS Chic.   Sr. Lectr.

Wattam, S. I., BSc Sheff., MSc CNAA   Sr. Lectr.

Whiston, I. C.   Sr. Lectr.

Williams, V. A., BSc Newcastle(UK), MA   Sr. Lectr.

Other Staff: 1 Lectr.

Health and Human Services

Fax: (0115) 948 6813

Allen, Ann, BA Sheff.   Sr. Lectr.

Baugh, A. F., BSc Bath, MPhil York(UK)   Sr. Lectr.

Broadley, C. R.   Principal Lectr.

Davies, D.   Sr. Lectr.

Frankland, A. M., BA Sus., MA Nott.   Principal Lectr.

Hambly, Liane, BA Nott.   Sr. Lectr.

Henderson, Alison, BSc   Sr. Lectr.

Higham, Patricia, BA Wellesley, PhD Cran.   Head*

Hodgkinson, C., MA Nott.   Acting Principal Lectr.

Horner, Nigel, BA Durh.   Sr. Lectr.

Howe, D. E., BA Camb.   Sr. Lectr.

Jenkins, A., BSc Lond.   Principal Lectr.

Liggett, Ann, BA MBA   Sr. Lectr.

Malkin, J. G.   Principal Lectr.

Mott, E., MA CNAA   Sr. Lectr.

Purdie, Fiona   Sr. Lectr.

Raithby, Michele, BSc Lond., MSc Oxf.   Sr. Lectr.

Regel, Stephen, MA Lough.   Sr. Lectr.

Other Staff: 5 Sr. Lectrs.†

Research: community care; head injury; residential childcare; trauma

Human Resource Management

Tel: (0115) 948 6165 Fax: (0115) 948 6175

Amans, J. A., MSc Birm., MEd Nott.   Sr. Lectr.

Bott, D., BSc Lond.   Sr. Lectr.

Bryson, C., MSc Stir.   Sr. Lectr.

Clark, E. D., BSc S'ton., PhD Glas.   Principal Lectr.

Crow, Mary, BA Coventry, MA Warw.   Sr. Lectr.

Doughty, D. A., BA CNAA   Sr. Lectr.

Fisher, C. M., BA Camb., MA Camb., PhD Camb.   Principal Lectr.

Fredericks, J. R., BA CNAA   Sr. Lectr.

Hall, R., BA Leeds, MSc Nott.Trent   Sr. Lectr.

Harris, L. M., MA Lough.   Sr. Lectr.

Hawkins, E. R., BA Lond., MSc   Sr. Lectr.

Jukes, B.   Sr. Lectr.

Kirk, S., Nott.Trent, MA Nott.Trent   Sr. Lectr.

Lashley, C. W., BA Open(UK), MA Warw.   Principal Lectr.

Leopold, J. W., MA Edin., MPhil Glas.   Prof.; Head*

Love, C. D., BA Kent, MPhil Nott.   Principal Lectr.

Lyon, U. M.   Sr. Lectr.

Manhire, E. M., BA MEd   Sr. Lectr.

Newsome, K., BA Liv., MA Warw. Sr. Lectr.
Rice, C. A. Sr. Lectr.
Royle, T., BA Nott.Trent, PhD Nott.Trent Sr. Lectr.
Soulsby, A. M., BA CNAA Sr. Lectr.
Stephens, J., BA Open(UK), MBA Lough. Sr. Lectr.
Stewart, J. D., BA Open(UK) Sr. Lectr.
Tansley, C., MA CNAA Sr. Lectr.
Taylor, B., BA N.Y., MScEd N.Y. Sr. Lectr.
Towers, B., BA Manc., BSc Lond., PhD Nott. Prof.
Tuckman, A., BA Hull, PhD Hull Sr. Lectr.
Walsh, D. A., BA Nott.. Principal Lectr.
Watson, T. J., BA Lond., MSc Lough., PhD Nott. Prof.
Other Staff: 1 Res. Fellow
Research: changing employment policies and practices; international and comparative industrial relations; managerial behaviour and strategic direction; models and concepts of human resource development: academic and practitioner perspectives; organisation and management in post-communist society

International Studies

Bennett, M., BA Lough., PhD Lough. Sr. Lectr.
Brown, A., BA Wales Sr. Lectr.
Dingsdale, A., BA Durh. Principal Lectr.
Dittmer, B. R., MA Lond. Sr. Lectr.
Farrands, C. E. H., MSc Wales Principal Lectr.
George, P. K., BSc Liv., PhD Liv. Sr. Lectr.
Graham, D., BA MSc PhD Sr. Lectr.
Griffin, C. P., BA Nott., PhD Nott. Sr. Lectr.
Hayes, Nick, BA Open(UK), PhD Open(UK) Sr. Lectr.
Hill, J., BA Oxf., PhD Keele Principal Lectr.
Hope, A. M. L., BA Nott., PhD Nott. Sr. Lectr.
Kofman, E., BA Syd., DPhil Oxf. Prof.
Law, Margaret, BA CNAA Sr. Lectr.
Lomas, Heather, BA Leic. Sr. Lectr.
MacKay, R. I., BA Manc. Sr. Lectr.
Mitson, Anne, BA CNAA, MA Leic., PhD Leic. Sr. Lectr.
Moses, G. W., BA CNAA Sr. Lectr.
Pettifer, L., PhD S'ton. Sr. Lectr.
Phelps, A., BA Hull, MSocSc Birm., PhD Hull Sr. Lectr.
Renwick, N., BA PhD Sr. Lectr.
Rowbotham, J. D., BA Wales, PhD Wales Sr. Lectr.
Simon, R. E., BA Nott., MA CNAA Sr. Lectr.
Skelton, T. L., MA Oxf., PhD Newcastle(UK) Sr. Lectr.
Smith, R., BA CNAA, MSc S'ton., PhD S'ton. Sr. Lectr.
Strange, A. N., BA Lond. Sr. Lectr.
Young, J. R., BA Nott., PhD Nott. Sr. Lectr.
Youngs, G. M., MA Sus. Sr. Lectr.

Law, see Nottingham Law Sch.

Life Sciences

Ahmad, S. I., PhD Leic. Sr. Lectr.
Barnett, A., MA Ball Sr. Lectr.
Bates, R. F. L., PhD Leeds Sr. Lectr.
Beattie, R. C., PhD Durh. Sr. Lectr.
Billett, E. E., BSc Wales, DPhil Oxf. Sr. Lectr.
Bonner, P. L. R., BSc Sur., PhD CNAA Sr. Lectr.
Buckley, G. A., PhD Liv. Principal Lectr.
Carlile, W. R., BSc Lond., PhD CNAA Principal Lectr.
Cartledge, T. G., BSc Wales, PhD Lond. Principal Lectr.
Cobb, A. H., BSc CNAA, PhD Lanc. Prof.
Compton, G. J., BSc E.Anglia, PhD Birm. Sr. Lectr.
Davies, L. G., PhD Wales Principal Lectr.
Forsythe, S. J., BSc CNAA, PhD Newcastle(UK) Sr. Lectr.
Godden, D. H., DPhil Oxf. Sr. Lectr.
Griffin, M., BSc Salf., PhD Wales Prof.
Hammonds, S. J., BSc Reading, PhD Lond. Sr. Lectr.
Hargreaves, A., PhD CNAA Sr. Lectr.
Hughes, C. E., PhD Nott. Sr. Lectr.
Kirk, S. H., BSc Birm., PhD Nott. Sr. Lectr.

MacFarlane, N. A. A., BSc Aberd., PhD Stir. Principal Lectr.
Mills, G. E., BSc Nott., PhD CNAA Sr. Lectr.
Mireylees, S. E., BSc Sheff., PhD Manc. Sr. Lectr.
Olsson, R. N. S., PhD Liv. Sr. Lectr.
Palmer, T., BA Camb., PhD Lond. Prof.; Head*
Priestland, R. N., PhD Manc. Principal Lectr.
Pyatt, F. B., BSc Wales, PhD Lond. Reader
Pye, R. G., BSc Hull, PhD Birm. Sr. Lectr.
Redfern, P., PhD Wales Sr. Lectr.
Rees, Robert C., BSc Sur., PhD Sheff. Prof.
Scanlon, B. F., PhD Lough. Principal Lectr.
Smith, A., MSc Manc., PhD Nott. Principal Lectr.
Terrell-Nield, C. E., PhD Manc. Sr. Lectr.
Whetton, J., BPhil Manc. Principal Lectr.
Williams, C. R., BSc Wales, PhD Lough. Sr. Lectr.
Other Staff: 1 Principal Lectr. (seconded); 4 Lectrs.; 4 Principal Lectrs.†; 1 Sr. Lectr.†
Research: Bayesian statistics; discrete optimisation; engineering mathematics; statistical archaeology; theoretical probability

Marketing, see Strategic Management and Marketing

Mathematics, Statistics and Operational Research

Applebaum, D. B., MSc St And., PhD Nott. Reader
Baxter, M. J., BSc Birm., PhD Edin. Reader
Baylis, D. J., BSc Lond., DPhil Sus. Sr. Lectr.
Bland, J. A., BSc Reading, PhD E.Anglia Principal Lectr.
Bootyman, D. J., BSc Hull, MSc Warw., MSc Brad., PhD Leeds Sr. Lectr.
Brindley, G., BSc Wales, PhD Sr. Lectr.
Buglear, J., BA CNAA, MSc Hull Sr. Lectr.
Davies, N., PhD Nott. Reader/Prof.
Disney, J., BSc Nott., PhD Nott.Trent Sr. Lectr.
Dixon, P. B., BSc St And., MSc Lond. Principal Lectr.
Frost, M. G., BSc Nott. Principal Lectr.
Hood, D. J., BSc Leic., PhD Lough. Sr. Lectr.
Hudson, R. L., BA Oxf., DPhil Oxf. Prof.; Sr. Res. Fellow
Kolokoltsov, V., PhD Moscow Reader
Lightfoot, J. B., MSc Nott. Sr. Lectr.
Lincoln, J. A. P., BSc Brad. Sr. Lectr.
Marriott, J. M., BSc Sus., MSc Lond., PhD Nott. Principal Lectr.
McCollin, C., BSc Birm., MSc Brad., PhD CNAA Sr. Lectr.
Naylor, J. C., BSc Lond., PhD Nott. Principal Lectr.
Sackfield, A., PhD Lond. Reader
Shaw, J. L., BSc Nott.Trent Sr. Lectr.
Short, K. M., BSc Manc. Principal Lectr.
Spooner, B. F., BSc Lond. Sr. Lectr.
Tew, R. E., BSc CNAA, MA Lanc. Sr. Lectr.
Williams, H. C., MA Oxf., MSc Nott. Sr. Lectr.

Media Studies, see Engl. and Media Studies

Modern Languages

Tel: (0115) 948 6686 Fax: (0115) 948 6513
Boulé, J. P., PhD Nott. Principal Lectr./Reader
Fysh, P. M., PhD CNAA Sr. Lectr.
Grzegorzewski, M. L., BA Nott. Sr. Lectr.
Howarth, M. S., BA Hull, MPhil Nott. Prof.; Head*
Humphrey, D. L. C., BA Leeds Sr. Lectr.
Jones, A. E., BA Wales, PhD Nott. Sr. Lectr.
Leahy, C., MA Sr. Lectr.
McCaffrey, E., PhD Col., MA Sr. Lectr.
O'Shaughnessy, M. P., BA Birm., MA Queb., PhD CNAA Sr. Lectr.
Stewart, R. E., MA Edin., MA Lough. Sr. Lectr.
Taylor, L., MA Birm. Sr. Lectr.
Willis, L. L., BA Sheff. Sr. Lectr.
Other Staff: 8 Lectrs.
Research: applied language learning: learner autonomy, second language acquisition, technology in language learning; French: contemporary French cultural studies and politics; German: Migrantenliteratur, political

and cultural relations between Britain and Germany; Spanish: hispanic cultures and societies, gender and critical theory

Nottingham Law School

Allen, N. F., BA CNAA, MPhil Sr. Lectr.
Atkins, C. W. T., LLB Kingston(UK), BCL Oxf. Principal Lectr.
Bamforth, S. J., BA Exe. Sr. Lectr.
Bell-Boulé, E. A., BA CNAA, LLM Exe. Sr. Lectr.
Bielby, E., LLB Manc. Sr. Lectr.
Booth, P., LLB S'ton. Sr. Lectr.
Brealey, A. C., LLB S'ton. Sr. Lectr.
Chapman, J. A., LLB Nott. Sr. Lectr.
Ching, J. P. L., MA Camb. Sr. Lectr.
Clarke, S. C., BA Nott. Sr. Lectr.
Collins, V. S., BA Nott., MPhil Nott. Sr. Lectr.
Costello, G., LLB Liv. Sr. Lectr.
Craven-Griffiths, J. A., LLB Leeds, LLM Lond. Principal Lectr.
Cumper, P., LLB Belf., LLM Essex Sr. Lectr.
Dumbill, E. A., LLB Sr. Lectr.
Duxbury, R. M. C., LLB Leeds Principal Lectr.
Elkins, K., BSocSc Keele Sr. Lectr.
Ellis, J., BA Oxf. Sr. Lectr.
Fay, S. J., BA CNAA, MA Warw., MA Nott., LLM Warw. Sr. Lectr.
Fazal, M. A., MA Dhaka, LLB Dhaka, DPhil Oxf. Principal Lectr.
Field, J. R., LLB Hull Principal Lectr.
Firth, N. J., LLB Sheff. Sr. Lectr.
Hamilton, N., BA CNAA Principal Lectr.
Hargreaves, S., PhD Sr. Lectr.
Harrison, N. J., LLB Liv. Sr. Lectr.
Heaton, R., LLB Lond. Principal Lectr.
Henham, R. J., LLB Keele, MA Keele, MPhil Nott. Sr. Lectr.
Hodgson, J. S., MA Camb., LLM Camb. Principal Lectr.
Hooper, J. M., LLB Leeds Sr. Lectr.
Hudson, N., LLB Leic. Sr. Lectr.
Huxley, P. H. J., LLB Leeds, LLM Keele Principal Lectr.
Jacobs, A., LLB Wales Sr. Lectr.
Jones, A. T. P., LLB Brist. Prof.
Kimpton, H., LLB CNAA Sr. Lectr.
Kirk, E. C., LLB Nott. Principal Lectr.
Knott, P. M., LLB Newcastle(UK) Principal Lectr.
Kunzlik, P. F., MA Camb., LLM Camb. Prof.
Latham, A. J., LLB Brist. Sr. Lectr.
Lewthwaite, T. J., LLB Lond., LLM Leic. Sr. Lectr.
Lloyd-Davies, P. J., LLM Lond. Sr. Lectr.
Lucas, N., LLB Sheff., LLM Leic. Sr. Lectr.
Luke, S. E., LLB Warw. Sr. Lectr.
Lyons, P., BA LLB Course Leader
McLachlan, I., BSc Glas. Sr. Lectr.
Miers, L., BA CNAA Sr. Lectr.
Miller, S. E., LLB Manc. Principal Lectr.
Millward, M. R., BA Oxf. Sr. Lectr.
Morton, S. G. C., LLB Lond. Sr. Lectr.
Peysner, J. C., MA Camb. Sr. Lectr.
Poole, A., LLB Leic. Sr. Lectr.
Pugh, C., BA CNAA Sr. Lectr.
Rawley, R. E., BA Keele Sr. Lectr.
Russell, S., LLB Sr. Lectr.
Savage, R. N., BA CNAA, LLM Sheff., PhD Sheff. Prof.; Head*
Sexton, R. N., LLB Exe., LLM Birm., PhD Birm. Sr. Lectr.
Slorach, J. S., MA Oxf. Principal Lectr.
Smith, J. D., LLB CNAA Sr. Lectr.
Snape, E. J., MA Oxf. Sr. Lectr.
Sood, U. R., LLB Nott., MPhil Nott. Sr. Lectr.
Spearing, F. E., LLB Birm. Sr. Lectr.
Stevenson, K. A., LLB Nott. Sr. Lectr.
Stone, R. T. H., LLB S'ton., LLM Hull Prof.
Storey, I. R., MA Camb. Prof.
Taylor, M., BSc Kent Course Leader
Thornton, M. A. L., LLB Manc. Principal Lectr.
Tingle, J. H., BA CNAA, MEd Birm. Sr. Lectr.
Toporowski, T., LLB CNAA Sr. Lectr.
Twycross, H. C., BA CNAA Sr. Lectr.
Ulph, J. S., LLB Nott., LLM Harv., LLM Camb. Sr. Lectr.
Wainwright, J. A., BA Nott. Sr. Lectr.
Ward, B. S., BA Lond. Sr. Lectr.
Wheat, V. K., BA Reading Sr. Lectr.

White, R. D., BA *CNAA* Principal Lectr.
Wilcockson, A. C., LLB *Birm.* Principal Lectr.

Nottingham Technology Education Development Group

Batchelor, M. C., BEd *Lough.* Head*
Harrison, G. B., MA *Camb.* Prof.

Operational Research, see Maths., Stats. and Operational Res.

Performing Arts, see Visual and Performing Arts

Physics, see Chem. and Phys.

Public Administration, see Econ. and Public Admin.

Statistics, see Maths., Stats. and Operational Res.

Strategic Management and Marketing

Fax: (0115) 948 6512
Barley, G., MBA *Brad.* Sr. Lectr.
Beaver, G., BSc *Leic.*, MSc *Warw.* Prof.
Bedrock, R. M., BA *Liv.*, MBSc *Manc.* Principal Lectr.
Bird, M. G., BA *Open(UK)*, MA *Lanc.* Sr. Lectr.
Brittain, J. P. R., BSc *CNAA*, MA *Lanc.* Sr. Lectr.
Brown, D. M., MBA *Lough.* Sr. Lectr.
Clewes, D. L., BA *CNAA* Sr. Lectr.
Driver, F. E., BA *Nott.* Sr. Lectr.
Fletcher, D. E., BA *CNAA* Sr. Lectr.
Franklin, P. J., MA *Sus.* Prof.; Head*
Griffiths, C. T., MA *Lough.* Sr. Lectr.
Horsley, P. D., MBA Sr. Lectr.
Jennings, D. R., BSc *Hull*, PhD *City(UK)* Principal Lectr.
Lewis, C. I., MA *Camb.*, PhD *CNAA* Sr. Lectr.
Llewelyn, A. E., BSc *Lond.* Sr. Lectr.
Melton, K. M., BSc *Manc.* Sr. Lectr.
Mercado, S. A., BA MA Sr. Lectr.
Murphy, M. J., MPhil *Nott.* Sr. Lectr.
Pick, P. A. Sr. Lectr.
Prince, C. W., BA *Warw.*, MBA *Warw.* Principal Lectr.
Rhodes, J., MA *Brun.* Sr. Lectr.
Shackley, Myra L., PhD *S'ton.* Prof.
Slater, K., MPhil *Nott.* Sr. Lectr.
Stewart, J., BA *Open(UK)*, MA *Lanc.* Principal Lectr.
Tynan, Caroline Prof.
Vickerstaff, A., BA Sr. Lectr.
Vyakarnam, Shai Prof.
Whysall, P. T., PhD *Nott.* Prof.

Winfield, F. M., BA *CNAA* Sr. Lectr.
Wood, C. J., BA *Nott.* Sr. Lectr.

Surveying

Tel: (0115) 948 6182 Fax: (0115) 948 6507
Beynon, N. J., BA *Nott.*, MA *Lond.* Principal Lectr.
Butler, I., BSc MA Sr. Lectr.
Collins, P. R., MSc Principal Lectr.
Corner, R. B. Sr. Lectr.
Cudworth, A. L., MPhil, FRICS Sr. Lectr.
Fleming, D. N., BSc *CNAA* Sr. Lectr.
Gallimore, P., MA PhD, FRICS Prof.; Head*
Griffiths, P. A. Sr. Lectr.
Hawkins, P. R., MSc *Sheff.Hallam* Sr. Lectr.
Hogg, K. I., BSc *CNAA*, FRICS Sr. Lectr.
Holden, P. Sr. Lectr.
Mansfield, John, BSc MSc Sr. Lectr.
Massey, R., MSc *Aston* Sr. Lectr.
Moohan, J. A. J., MA Prof.
Morledge, R., MSc *H-W*, FRICS Prof.
Noor-Mohamed, B., BSc *CNAA*, MBA Sr. Lectr.
Reyers, John, BSc Sr. Lectr.
Rowe, D. G. Sr. Lectr.
Royston, P. J., BSc *City(UK)*, MBA *City(UK)* Sr. Lectr.
Shaw, S. B., BA, FRICS Sr. Lectr.
Simcock, J. E., FRICS Sr. Lectr.
Stafford, K. D., FRICS Principal Lectr.
Stone, K., BSc MA Sr. Lectr.
Trow, P. S. Sr. Lectr.
Tyler, S. B., BSc *Lough.*, MBA *Lough.*, FRICS Principal Lectr.
Wetton, B. W., BA *S'ton.*, MA *S'ton.* Principal Lectr.
Wiltshaw, D. G., BSc MSc Reader
Winfield, R., FRICS Principal Lectr.
Yarwood, C. P. D., FRICS Sr. Lectr.
Other Staff: 16 Lectrs.†
Research: construction procurement: appropriate strategies for clients; contaminated land: economics and policy evaluation; real estate decision-making behaviour

Textiles, see Fashion and Textiles

Visual and Performing Arts

Tel: (0115) 948 6088 Fax: (0115) 948 6403
Abbott, F. J., BA *Hull* Sr. Lectr.
Ayers, A. R., BA *Exe.*, MA *Birm.* Sr. Lectr.
Ayers, R., BA *Leeds* Artistic Dir.
Bannister, A., BA *CNAA*, MA *Lond.Inst.* Sr. Lectr.
Beecroft, R. A., MA *CNAA* Sr. Lectr.
Cantouris, Andrew, BA *Westminster* Sr. Lectr.
Carradice, M. G. Comml. Manager

Chandler, D. Sr. Lectr.
Chapman, J. Sr. Lectr.
Gale, D., BA *Camb.*, MA *RCA* Sr. Lectr.
Griffiths, M., MA *Camb.* Principal Lectr./Prof.
Horn, D. G. Principal Lectr.
Kandhola, P. M., BA *Wolv.*
Lewis, S., MFA *Reading* Prof.; Head*
Linklater, R. V. Sr. Lectr.
Love, K., BA *Lond.*, MA *Lond.* Sr. Lectr.
Lycouris, S., PhD *Sur.*
Lydiat, A., BA *CNAA*, MA *CNAA* Sr. Lectr.
McWilliam, S.
Newling, J. B., BA *CNAA*, MA *CNAA*, MPhil *CNAA* Prof.
Park, J. E., BA *Leeds*, MA *Brist.* Sr. Lectr.
Sayers, C. E., BA *Manit.*, MFA *Wash.* Sr. Lectr.
Scriven, A. M., MA Sr. Lectr.
Smith, B. C., PhD *E.Anglia* Principal Lectr.
Smith, N. E. Sr. Lectr.
Sprawson, D. H., BA *CNAA*, MFA *Reading* Sr. Lectr.
Stokes, P. G., BEd *Exe.*, PhD *Exe.* Sr. Lectr.
Welling, C. A. Principal Lectr.
Wilson, R., MA *CNAA* Sr. Lectr.
Woodfield, R. A., BA *Hull*, MA *Hull* Sr. Lectr.
Research: digital imaging photography; film and video; fine art and documentary photography; live art and live art archiving; performance

SPECIAL CENTRES, ETC

Built Environment, Centre for Research into the

Ferguson, C. C., BSc *Nott.*, PhD *Nott.* Prof.; Head*
Krylov, V. V., MSc *Moscow*, PhD *Moscow*, DSc *Moscow* Prof.

Training Development, Centre for

Standish, S. Carol Manager; Head, Dept. of Comml. Services*

CONTACT OFFICERS

Computing services. Head, Computing Services: Griffiths, I. D., BSc *Wales*
General enquiries. Registrar: Samson, D., BA MBA
Research. Director of Research: Joyner, Prof. R. W., BSc PhD DSc, FRSChem

[*Information supplied by the institution as at 26 March 1998, and edited by the ACU*]

OPEN UNIVERSITY

Founded 1969

Member of the Association of Commonwealth Universities

Postal Address: Walton Hall, Milton Keynes, England MK7 6AA
Telephone: (01908) 274066 **Fax**: (01908) 653744 **E-mail**: name@open.ac.uk **Cables**: Openuniv Walton
Telex: 825061 **WWW**: http://open.ac.uk **E-mail formula**: name@open.ac.uk

CHANCELLOR—Boothroyd, Rt. Hon. Betty
PRO-CHANCELLOR—Nicholson, Sir Bryan, BA DEd
VICE-CHANCELLOR*—Daniel, Sir John, BA Oxf., MA Oxf., MA C'dia.IT, DèsSc Paris, Hon. DLitt Deakin, Hon. DLitt
    Thomas A. Edison State, Hon. DLitt Richmond Coll., Hon. DLitt L&H, Hon. DèsScC.M.R.St.-Jean, Hon. DEd CNAA, Hon.
    LLD Wat., Hon. DSc Open S.Lanka, Hon. DUniv Lisbon Open.
TREASURER—Young, D. A.
SECRETARY‡—Woodburn, A. Fraser, BSc Edin.
PRO-VICE-CHANCELLOR (CURRICULUM DEVELOPMENT)—Floyd, Ann R., MA Camb., MA Br.Col., PhD Brun.
PRO-VICE-CHANCELLOR (TECHNOLOGY DEVELOPMENT)—Laurillard, Prof. Diana, BSc Sus., PhD Sur.
PRO-VICE-CHANCELLOR (STRATEGY AND PLANNING)—Peters, Geoff, BSc Lough., MSc Sus.
PRO-VICE-CHANCELLOR (STUDENT TUTORIAL AND REGIONAL SERVICES)—Lewis, Richard, MSc Lond., FCA
PRO-VICE-CHANCELLOR (QUALITY ASSURANCE AND RESEARCH)—......
DIRECTOR, ACADEMIC COMPUTING SERVICES—Burrows, D. Jim A., MSc Belf.

GENERAL INFORMATION

History. The university was established in 1969. It is an international university providing part-time higher education to the United Kingdom, the European Union and elsewhere overseas. Its central offices are located in Milton Keynes, 80km north-west of London.

Admission. to first degree courses (see also United Kingdom Introduction). Those resident in the UK/other parts of the EU/other areas where the university has agreed to register students are eligible for admission. There are no formal academic entry requirements. Students must normally be aged 18 or over.

First Degrees (see also United Kingdom Directory to Subjects of Study) (* = also available with honours). BA*, BSc*, MEng, MMaths.

Degrees are awarded on the basis of successful completion of courses which are assigned a credit points rating. All courses are part-time and usually require 60 or 30 credit points. Minimum credit point requirements for a first degree are 360 credit points at specific levels. First degree master's: minimum 480 credit points. Most students study at the rate of 60 credit points a year.

Higher Degrees. (see also United Kingdom Directory to Subjects of Study). MA, MBA, MSc, BPhil, MPhil, PhD, DLitt, DSc.

Direct applicants for admission to master's degree courses should normally hold a good first degree with honours; entry to master's degrees by coursework is also possible via a relevant diploma of the university. Master's degrees normally require 180 credit points; entrants with university diploma (certain courses): 120 credit points. BPhil: 9 months–2 years full-time or 1–4 years part-time; MPhil: 1 year 3 months–4 years full-time or 2–6 years part-time; PhD: 2–4 years full-time or 3–8 years part-time. DLitt, DSc: by published work.

Libraries. 180,000 books and microforms; 150,000 non-book materials; 2400 periodicals subscribed to. Students following courses for a taught award are provided with printed course materials and other appropriate learning materials as an integral part of the course.

Fees. First degrees (60 credit point courses), UK students: £380– 650. Taught higher degrees (60 credit point courses), UK students: £535– 2550. Research degrees, full-time (1998–99): EU students £2610; overseas students £6524 (arts), £8732 (sciences).

Research degrees, part-time (1999): £376 (all students).

Academic Awards. Financial awards are available to new students resident in the UK. The amount of the award covers the fee for the course (less a personal contribution of £50) and may also assist with access to other student materials or facilities.

Academic Year. 60 credit point and 30 credit point undergraduate courses: February–October. Some 30 and 15 credit point courses are taught over a shorter period with courses starting in November or May.

Income. (1996–97). Total, £216,000,000.

Statistics. Staff: 3700 (920 academic, 1046 academic-related). Students: full-time 213; part-time 155,930.

FACULTIES/SCHOOLS

Arts
Tel: (01908) 652479 Fax: (01908) 653750
Dean: Benton, Prof. T. J., BA Camb., MA Lond., PhD Lond.
Senior Assistant Secretary: Robertson, Hilary

Education, School of
Tel: (01908) 653299 Fax: (01908) 654111
Dean: Glaister, Robert T. D., MA St And., MEd St And., PhD
Senior Assistant Secretary: Roberts, Ann

Educational Technology
Tel: (01908) 653536 Fax: (01908) 654173
Dean: Thorpe, Mary, MA Camb.
Senior Assistant Secretary: Bearman, Sandra

Health and Social Welfare
Tel: (01908) 653743 Fax: (01908) 654124
Dean: Jones, Linda J., BA Camb., PhD Birm.
Senior Assistant Secretary: Walton, Tony

Management, School of
Tel: (01908) 655888 Fax: (01908) 655898
Dean: Asch, D., MSc Brad., FCA
Secretary: Taylor, Lee

Mathematics and Computing
Tel: (01908) 653241 Fax: (01908) 652140
Dean: Brannan, Prof. David A., BSc Glas., PhD Lond.
Senior Assistant Secretary: Kirby, Mary

Science
Tel: (01908) 653485 Fax: (01908) 652559
Dean: Bassindale, Prof. Alan R., MSc Sus., DPhil Sus.

Senior Assistant Secretary: Dean, Sarah

Social Sciences
Tel: (01908) 654431 Fax: (01908) 684488
Dean: Sarre, Philip K.D., BSc S'ton., MA Calif., PhD Brist.
Senior Assistant Secretary: Hargreaves, John

Technology
Tel: (01908) 653062 Fax: (01908) 654355
Dean: Meade, M. L., BScTech Manc., PhD Reading
Senior Assistant Secretary: Creek, Hilary

ACADEMIC UNITS

Note—The academic staff of the university are organised into faculties but not into departments. The disciplines listed below represent the general subject interest of the staff concerned.

Art History
Tel: (01908) 652479 Fax: (01908) 653750
Benton, Tim J., BA Camb., MA Lond. Prof.; Head*
Cunningham, Colin J. K., MA Oxf., PhD Leeds, FSA Reader, Architectural History
King, Catherine E., BA Lond., MPhil Lond., PhD E.Anglia Sr. Lectr.
Norman, Diana, BA Lond., MA Lond., PhD Open(UK) Sr. Lectr.
Perry, Gillian M., BA Sus., DPhil Sus. Sr. Lectr.
Other Staff: 5 Lectrs.; 3 Staff Tutors

Biology
Tel: (01908) 653485 Fax: (01908) 654167
Burnett, John, BA Oxf., MA Oxf., DPhil Oxf. Visiting Prof.
Davey, Basior C., BSc Lond., PhD Lond. Sr. Lectr.
Halliday, Tim R., MA Oxf., DPhil Oxf. Prof.
Ho, Mae Wan, BSc HK, PhD HK Reader
Osborne, Daphne J., BSc Lond., MSc Lond., MA Camb., PhD Lond., DSc Lond. Visiting Prof.
Pond, Caroline, MA Oxf., DPhil Oxf. Reader
Ridge, Irene, MA Oxf., DPhil Oxf. Sr. Lectr.
Robinson, David J., BSc Newcastle(UK), PhD Nott. Sr. Lectr.
Rose, Steven P. R., BA Camb., PhD Lond., FIBiol Prof.
Silvertown, Jonathan W., BSc Sus., DPhil Sus. Reader
Stewart, Mike G., BSc Belf., PhD Belf. Reader; Head*
Toates, Fred M., DSc City(UK), DPhil Sus. Sr. Lectr.
Other Staff: 8 Lectrs.

Chemistry

Tel: (01908) 653485 Fax: (01908) 658327
Bassindale, Alan R., MSc Sus., DPhil Sus. Prof.
Bennett, Stuart W., BSc Sus., DPhil Sus. Sr. Lectr.
Berry, Frank, BSc Lond., PhD Lond. Prof.
Bolton, Keith A., BSc Wales, PhD Wales Sr. Lectr.
Harding, Charlie J., BSc Lond., PhD Lond. Sr. Lectr.
Hill, Roger R., BSc Lond., PhD S'ton. Reader
Iley, Jim, BSc Lond., PhD Lond. Sr. Lectr.
Johnson, David A., MA Camb., PhD Camb. Sr. Lectr.
Jones, R. C. F., MA Camb., PhD Camb. Head*
Mortimer, Michael, BSc Lond., PhD Leeds Sr. Lectr.
Roberts, David R., MSc E.Anglia, MA Camb., PhD E.Anglia Sr. Lectr.
Taylor, Peter G., BSc E.Anglia, PhD E.Anglia
Other Staff: 4 Lectrs.

Classics

Tel: (01908) 653247 Fax: (01908) 653750
Emlyn-Jones, C., BA Birm., PhD Birm. Sr. Lectr.; Head*
Other Staff: 4 Lectrs.; 2 Staff Tutors; 1 Res. Fellow; 2 Res. Assocs.

Complexity and Change, Centre for

Development Policy and Practice Discipline

Tel: (01908) 652103, 653462 Fax: (01908) 652175
Hewitt, Tom, BA Essex, MPhil Sus., DPhil Sus. Sr. Lectr.
Thomas, Alan, BA Camb., MA Lanc. Sr. Lectr.
Wield, David V., BSc Lond., PhD Lond. Sr. Lectr.
Wilson, Gordon, BSc Leeds, PhD Leeds Sr. Lectr.
Other Staff: 2 Lectrs.

Systems Discipline

Tel: (01908) 652918 Fax: (01908) 652175
Chapman, P. F., MA Camb., PhD Camb. Prof.
Ison, Ray L., BScAgr Qld., PhD Qld. Prof.
Lane, Andrew, BSc Lond., PhD Lond. Sr. Lectr.; Head*
Martin, John N. T., BSc Edin., MA Edin., PhD Lond. Sr. Lectr.
Morris, R. M., MA Oxf., PhD Reading Sr. Lectr.
Naughton, John J., BE N.U.I. Sr. Lectr.
Other Staff: 5 Lectrs.

Technology Management and Manufacturing Discipline

Tel: (01908) 652105 Fax: (01908) 653718
Fortune, Joyce, BSc Lough., PhD Nott. Sr. Lectr.
Hughes, John, BA S'ton., DPhil Oxf. Sr. Lectr.; Head*
Martin, Glyn, BSc Lond. Sr. Lectr.
Other Staff: 3 Lectrs.

Computing

Davies, Gordon, BSc Liv., MSc Lond. Sr. Lectr.; Head*
Hall, Patrick A. V., BSc Cape Town, MA Camb., PhD Lond. Prof.
Ince, Darrel C., BSc Wales, PhD Wales Prof.
Keller, Laurie S., BA S.Calif., MSc Lond. Sr. Lectr.
Newton, Mike A., BSc Lond., MSc Camb. Sr. Lectr.
Robinson, Hugh M., BA Keele, MSc Lond., PhD CNAA Sr. Lectr.
Thomas, Peter G., BSc Leic., MSc Dund., PhD Dund. Sr. Lectr.
Other Staff: 11 Lectrs.

Design and Innovation (Technology)

Tel: (01908) 652944 Fax: (01908) 654052
Boyle, G. Sr. Lectr.
Cross, N. G., BSc Bath, MSc Manc., PhD Manc. Prof.
Demaid, A., BSc Aston, MPhil Sr. Lectr.
Elliott, D. A., BSc Lond., PhD Lond. Sr. Lectr.
Everett, R. C., MA Camb., PhD Open(UK)
Roy, R., MSc Manc., PhD Manc. Sr. Lectr.

Rzevski, G. Prof.
Steadman, J. P., MA Camb., ScD Camb. Prof.
Wiese, P., BA BEng, FIMechE Visiting Prof.
Other Staff: 5 Lectrs.; 2 Sr. Res. Fellows; 1 Res. Fellow

Development Studies

Tel: (01908) 653062
Wield, David, BSc Lond., PhD Lond. Sr. Lectr.

Earth Sciences

Tel: (01908) 653485 Fax: (01908) 655151
Francis, Peter W., BSc Lond., PhD Lond., FGS Reader
Harris, Nigel B. W., MA Camb., PhD Camb., FGS Sr. Lectr.
Hawkesworth, Chris J., BA Trinity(Dub.), DPhil Oxf. Prof.; Head of Discipline*
Pillinger, Colin T., BSc Wales, PhD Wales, DSc Brist., FRAS, FRS Prof.
Rothery, David A., MA Camb., PhD, FGS Sr. Lectr.
Skelton, Peter W., BSc Brist., DPhil Oxf., FGS Sr. Lectr.
Smith, Peter J., BSc Lond., PhD Lond., FGS Reader
Spicer, Robert, BSc Lond., MA Oxf., PhD Lond. Prof.
Williams, David W., BSc Leeds, PhD Leeds, FGS Sr. Lectr.
Wilson, R. Chris L., MBE, BSc Sheff., PhD Sheff. Prof.
Wright, John B., MA Oxf., MSc Oxf. Reader
Other Staff: 11 Lectrs.; 2 Sr. Res. Fellows

Economics

Tel: (01908) 654431 Fax: (01908) 654488
Brown, Vivienne, BSc(Econ) Lond., PhD Lond. Sr. Lectr.
Himmelweit, Susan, BA Sr. Lectr.
Mackintosh, Maureen, BA Oxf., DPhil Sus. Prof.; Head of Discipline*

Education, School of

Tel: (01908) 652896 Fax: (01908) 654411
Banks, Frank, BA York(UK), MA Open(UK) Sr. Lectr.
Barnes, Peter R. W., BA Nott., MPhil Nott. Sr. Lectr.
Booth, A. J., BA Oxf. Sr. Lectr.
Bourdillon, Hilary, BA S'ton., MA CNAA Sr. Lectr.
Craft, Anna, MA Camb., MA Lond. Sr. Lectr.
Edwards, Richard, BA CNAA, PhD Kent Sr. Lectr.
Esland, G. M., MA Lond. Sr. Lectr.
Glaister, Robert T. D., MA St And., MEd St And., PhD Dean*
Glatter, Ron, MA Oxf. Prof.
Hammersley, Martin, BSc Lond., MA(Econ) Manc., PhD Manc. Prof.
Leach, Jenny, BA Exe., MA Lond. Sr. Lectr.
Levacic, Ros, MSc(Econ) Lond. Reader
Lewis, Vicky, BA Oxf., MA Oxf., DPhil Oxf. Prof.
McCormick, Robert, BSc Leeds, MA Leeds, PhD Open(UK) Prof.
Mercer, Neil, BSc Manc., PhD Leic. Prof.
Moon, Robert E., MA Warw., DPhil Sus. Prof.
Murphy, Patricia F., BSc Manc. Sr. Lectr.
Potts, Patricia, BA Oxf., BA Lond. Sr. Lectr.
Prescott, William, MA Oxf. Prof.
Raggatt, Peter, BSc Brist., MPhil Lond. Sr. Lectr.
Richardson, Ken, BEd Manc., PhD Open(UK) Sr. Lectr.
Scrimshaw, Peter, BA Wales Sr. Lectr.
Shelton-Mayes, Anne, BSc Sus., MSc Aberd. Sr. Lectr.
Swann, Joan, BA Manc., MA Reading Sr. Lectr.
Swann, Will S., BA Manc. Sr. Lectr.
Woodhead, Martin, MA Manc., MA(Ed) Leic., PhD Sr. Lectr.
Woods, Peter E., BA Lond., MSc Brad., PhD Open(UK) Prof.

Educational Technology, Institute of, see
Special Centres, etc

Engineering Mechanics

Tel: (01908) 653944 Fax: (01908) 652192
Attenborough, Keith, BSc Lond., PhD Leeds Prof.
Barratt, R. S., BSc Birm., PhD Birm., FRSChem Sr. Lectr.
Dixon, J. C., MA Oxf., PhD Reading Sr. Lectr.
Parkinson, A. G., MSc Lond., PhD Lond., FIMechE Prof.
Porteous, Andrew, BSc H.-W., MEng Dartmouth, DEng Dartmouth, FIMechE Prof.
Other Staff: 6 Lectrs.

Geography

Tel: (01908) 654431 Fax: (01908) 654488
Allen, J., BA Kent Sr. Lectr., Economic Geography; Head*
Blowers, Andy T., BA Durh., MLitt Durh. Prof., Planning
Blunden, John R., BA Exe., PhD Exe. Reader
Massey, Doreen B., BA Oxf., MA Penn. Prof.
Sarre, Philip K., BSc S'ton., MA Calif., PhD Brist. Sr. Lectr., Applied Regional Studies

Government

Tel: (01908) 654431 Fax: (01908) 654488
Held, David, BSc Manc., MSc Mass., PhD Mass. Prof.
Lewis, Paul G., BSocSc Birm., PhD Birm. Sr. Lectr.
Maidment, Richard, BSc Lond., MA Kent, PhD Kent Prof.; Head of Discipline*
McGrew, Tony, BSc S'ton., PhD S'ton. Sr. Lectr.
Murray, David J., MA Oxf., DPhil Oxf. Prof.

History and European Humanities

Tel: (01908) 653266 Fax: (01908) 653750
Aldgate, A., MA Edin., PhD Edin. Sr. Lectr.
Bessel, R. J., BA Antioch, DPhil Oxf. Sr. Lectr.
Emsley, C., BA York(UK), MLitt Camb., FRHistS Prof.
Englander, David, BA Warw., MA Warw., PhD Warw. Reader
Laurence, Anne, BA York(UK), DPhil Oxf. Sr. Lectr.
Lentin, A., MA Camb., PhD Camb., LLB, FRHistS Reader
Marwick, Arthur J. B., MA Edin., BLitt Oxf., DLitt Edin., FRHistS Prof.; Head of Discipline*
O'Day, M. Rosemary, BA York(UK), PhD Lond., FRHistS Sr. Lectr.
Other Staff: 2 Lectrs.; 5 Staff Tutors

History of Science and Technology

Tel: (01908) 653547 Fax: (01908) 653750
Goodman, D. C., MA Oxf., DPhil Oxf. Sr. Lectr.; Head of Discipline*
Moore, Jim S., MDiv Trinity Evang.Div.Sch.(Ill.), PhD Manc. Sr. Lectr.
Roberts, Gerrylynn, BA Vassar, PhD Johns H. Reader
Other Staff: 1 Lectr.; 1 Staff Tutor

Literature

Tel: (01908) 652092 Fax: (01908) 653750
Havely, Cicely A., MA Oxf., BPhil Oxf. Sr. Lectr.
Walder, D. J., BA Cape Town, BCom Cape Town, MA Edin., MLitt Edin., PhD Edin. Sr. Lectr.; Head of Discipline*
Other Staff: 3 Lectrs.; 6 Staff Tutors

Management, School of

Tel: (01908) 655888 Fax: (01908) 655898
Alderman, J., MBA Open(UK) Regional Manager
Armitt, J., BSc City(UK) Regional Manager
Asch, D., MSc Brad., FCA Prof.; Dir. of Studies; Dean*
Batsleer, J., MA Camb., MPhil Nott. Lectr., Management Development; Cert. and Dip. Programme Dir.

Bolleurs, N., BSocSc *Cape Town*, MBA *Stell.* Regional Manager

Cameron, Sheila, BSc *Exe.*, MPhil *Lond.* Regional Manager

Cooper, D., BSc(Econ) *Lond.*, MSc(Econ) *Lond.* Regional Manager

Goodey, J., BA *Kent*, MA *Leic.* Regional Manager

Graham, R., BSc(Econ) MSc Regional Manager

Gray, C., BA *Syd.*, MSc(Econ) *Lond.*, PhD *Lond.Guild.* Lectr., Small Business Management; Dir., External Affairs

Green, M., BA *Oxf.*, MBA *Open(UK)* Regional Manager

Hooker, C., BA *Exe.*, MPhil *Brun.* Regional Manager

Hunt, J., BA *Duke*, MBA *Lond.* Regional Manager

Kassier, H., BCom *Natal*, MBA *Boston* Regional Manager

Leonetti, A., Lic *Lille*, MBA *Open(UK)* Group Regional Manager

Lewis, J., BSc *City(UK)*, PhD *Open(UK)* Sr. Lectr., Management; MBA Programme Dir.

Lucus, M., BSc *Salf.*, MA *Keele* Regional Manager

MacMillan, A., BA *Open(UK)*, MA *Open(UK)* Regional Manager

McMahon, C., BSSc *Belf.*, MBA *Open(UK)* Regional Manager

Mole, R., BSc *S'ton.*, MSc *Birm.*, PhD *UMIST* Sr. Lectr., Operations Management; Dir. of Prodn.

Morant, Ruth A., BSc *Lond.*, BA *Open(UK)*, MSc *Durh.* Regional Manager

Muller, P., BSc *Manc.*, MSc *Lond.* Regional Manager

Nelson, R. T., BSc(Econ) *Lond.*, MA(Econ) *Manc.* Group Regional Manager

Pearce, S., BA *Lond.*, MSc *Aston* Regional Manager

Power, B., BSc *Belf.*, MBA *Belf.* Regional Manager

Quintas, P., BSc *Brad.*, MSc *Sus.* Sr. Lectr., Information Management; Dir. of Res.

Salmon, G., BA *Open(UK)*, MPhil *Cran.* Dir., Presentation

Sheppard, A., BA *Open(UK)* Regional Manager

Slade, J., BA *Reading*, MBA *Open(UK)* Regional Manager

Slapper, G., LLB *Lond.*, LLM *Lond.*, PhD *Lond.* Sr. Lectr., Law; Law Programme Dir.

Smith, J., MA *Glas.* Regional Manager

Smith, L., BA *Sheff.* Regional Manager

Street, A., MBA *Wales* Regional Manager

Thomas, D., BA *Wales*, MA *Warw.*, MEd *Wales* Regional Manager

Virdee, H., BSc(Econ) *Lond.*, MBA *Birm.* Regional Manager

Windy, N., BA *Open(UK)* Regional Manager

Other Staff: 1 Lectrs

Comparative Management, Centre for

Cornforth, C. J., BSc *Exe.*, MA *RCA* Sr. Lectr.*

Henderson, E., MA *Oxf.*, PhD *Reading* Prof.

Paton, R., BA *Oxf.*, MA *Penn.* Sr. Lectr.

Thomson, A., OBE, BA *Oxf.*, MSc *Cornell*, PhD *Cornell* Prof.

Other Staff: 4 Lectrs.

Development and Financial Management of Organisations, Centre for

Parkinson, A., MSc *City(UK)* Hill Samuel Sr. Lectr., Accounting and Finance

Rutterford, J., BSc *Lond.*, MSc *Oxf.*, MBA *Lond.*, PhD *Lond.* Prof.

Other Staff: 4 Lectrs.

Human Resource and Change Management, Centre for

Mabey, C., BA *Reading*, PhD *Brun.* Sr. Lectr.

Storey, J., BA *Hull*, MSc(Econ) *Lond.*, PhD *Lanc.* Prof.

Other Staff: 5 Lectrs.

Information and Innovation, Centre for

Bradley, K., BA *Essex*, MA *Essex*, PhD *Essex* Prof.

Kaye, G. R., BA MSc Prof.

Other Staff: 5 Lectrs.

Strategy and Policy, Centre for

de Chernatony, L., BSc *Kent*, PhD *City(UK)* Prof.

Lawton, A., BA *York(UK)*, MA *Durh.*, PhD *Leic.* Sr. Lectr.

Mercer, D., BSc *Lond.*, BA *Open(UK)* Sr. Lectr.

Segal-Horn, S., BA *Essex*, MA *Sus.* Sr. Lectr.

Simintiras, A. C., BA *Macedonia*, MBA *New Haven*, PhD *CNAA* Reader

Stapleton, A., BA *Camb.*, PhD *Camb.* Sr. Lectr.

Other Staff: 4 Lectrs.

Materials and Engineering (Technology)

Tel: (01908) 653271 Fax: (01908) 653858

Braithwaite, N. St. J., BSc *Manc.*, MA *Oxf.*, MSc *Oxf.*, DPhil *Oxf.* Sr. Lectr.

Edwards, L., MA *Oxf.*, DPhil *Oxf.* Sr. Lectr.

Hopgood, A., BSc *Brist.*, DPhil *Oxf.* Sr. Lectr.

Lewis, P. R., BSc *Manc.*, PhD *Manc.* Sr. Lectr.

Plumbridge, W. J., MSc MA PhD, FIM, FIEAust Prof.

Reynolds, K. A., MSc *Lond.*, FIM Sr. Lectr.

Weaver, G. H., MSc *Oxf.*, MA *Oxf.* Sr. Lectr.

Williams, K., MA *Camb.*, PhD *Camb.* Sr. Lectr.

Other Staff: 4 Staff Lectrs.

Mathematics, Applied

Bromilow, T. Mick, BA *Oxf.*, MA *Oxf.*, MSc *Oxf.*, DPhil *Oxf.* Sr. Lectr.

Crampin, Mike, BA *Oxf.*, PhD *Lond.* Prof.

Graham, Alex, MA *Trinity(Dub.)*, MSc *Lond.*, PhD *Lond.* Sr. Lectr.

Read, Graham A., MSc *Lond.*, PhD *Lond.*, FIMA Sr. Lectr.

Richards, Derek, BSc *Lond.*, PhD *Lond.* Reader

Solomon, Allan I., BA *Trinity(Dub.)*, PhD *Paris*, FIP Prof., Mathematical Physics

Thorpe, Mike A., MA *Camb.*, PhD *Birm.* Staff Tutor; Head*

Other Staff: 6 Lectrs.

Mathematics Education, Centre for

Mason, John H., MSc *Tor.*, PhD *Wis.* Prof.; Head*

Shiu, Christine M., BSc *Lond.*, PhD *Nott.* Sr. Lectr.

Other Staff: 4 Lectrs.

Mathematics, Pure

Aldous, Joan M., BSc *Reading*, PhD *Reading* Sr. Lectr.

Fauvel, John, BA *Essex*, MSc *Warw.*, MPhil *Warw.* Sr. Lectr.

Gray, Jeremy J., MSc *Warw.*, MA *Oxf.*, PhD *Warw.* Sr. Lectr.

Holroyd, Fred C., MA *Oxf.*, DPhil *Oxf.* Sr. Lectr.

Knight, Roy J., BSc *S'ton.* Sr. Lectr.

Rippon, Phil J., MA *Camb.*, MSc *Lond.*, PhD *Lond.* Sr. Lectr.; Head*

Wilson, Robin J., MA *Oxf.*, PhD *Penn.* Sr. Lectr.

Other Staff: 4 Lectrs.

Modern Languages, Centre for

Tel: (01908) 653834 Fax: (01908) 652187

Garrido, Cecilia, BA MA

Lamy, Marie-Noëlle, LèsL *Paris*, Maîtrise *Paris* Sr. Lectr.

Sidwell, Duncan, BA *Brist.*, MA *Warw.*

Stevens, Anne E., BA *Lond.*, MSc *Aston* Sr. Lectr.; Dir.*

Music

Tel: (01908) 653280 Fax: (01908) 653750

Burrows, Donald J., MA *Camb.*, PhD Prof.; Head of Discipline*

Other Staff: 6 Lectrs.; 2 Staff Tutors

Philosophy

Tel: (01908) 652032 Fax: (10908) 653750

Brown, Stewart C., MA *St And.*, PhD *Lond.* Prof.; Head of Discipline*

Hursthouse, Rosalind M., MA *Auck.*, DPhil *Oxf.* Sr. Lectr.

Other Staff: 3 Lectrs.; 2 Staff Tutors

Physics

Tel: (01908) 653485 Fax: (01908) 654192

Bell-Burnell, S. Jocelyn, BSc *Glas.*, PhD *Camb.* Prof.; Head*

Bolton, John P. R., BSc *Leeds*, DPhil *Sus.*

Broadhurst, David J., MA *Oxf.*, DPhil *Sus.* Reader

Clark, Paul M., BEng *McG.*, PhD *Lond.* Sr. Lectr.

Durrant, Alan V., MA *Camb.*, PhD *Otago* Sr. Lectr.

Elliott, Gerald F., MA *Oxf.*, PhD *Lond.*, DSc *Oxf.* Visiting Prof.

Freake, Studart M., MA *Camb.*, PhD *Camb.*

Jones, Barrie W., BSc *Brist.*, PhD *Brist.* Sr. Lectr.

Lambourne, R. J. A., BSc *Lond.*, PhD *Lond.* Sr. Lectr.

Mackintosh, Raymond S., MSc *Auck.*, PhD *Calif.* Sr. Lectr.

Meek, Keith M. A., BSc *Manc.*, PhD *Manc.* Sr. Lectr.

Swithenby, Stephen J., MA *Oxf.*, DPhil *Oxf.* Sr. Lectr.

Other Staff: 4 Lectrs.

Psychology

Tel: (01908) 654431 Fax: (01908) 654488

Cohen, Gillian M., BA *Oxf.*, MA *Edin.*, DPhil *Oxf.* Prof.

Eisenstadt, M., BA *Wash.*, PhD *San Diego* Prof., Knowledge Media Institute

Greene, Judith M., BA *Lond.*, MA *Oxf.*, PhD *Lond.* Prof.

Miell, Dorothy, BSc *Lanc.*, PhD *Lanc.* Sr. Lectr.

Stevens, Richard J., MA *Edin.*, MA *Trinity(Dub.)* Sr. Lectr.; Head of Discipline*

Thomas, Kerry, BSc *Birm.*, MSc(Econ) *Lond.*, PhD *Lond.* Sr. Lectr.

Wetherell, Margaret, BA *Auck.*, PhD *Auck.* Sr. Lectr.

Religious Studies

Tel: (01908) 652032 Fax: (01908) 653750

Parsons, G. A., BA *Wales* Sr. Lectr.; Head*

Wolffe, John R., BA *Oxf.*, MA *Oxf.*, DPhil *Oxf.* Sr. Lectr.

Other Staff: 2 Lectrs.; 2 Staff Tutors

Science Education, Centre for

Tel: (01908) 653485 Fax: (01908) 654619

Solomon, Joan, BA *Camb.*, PhD *Lond.* Visiting Prof.

Thomas, J. N., BSc *Birm.*, PhD *Birm.* Sr. Lectr.; Head*

West, Dick W., AC, DPhil *Sus.* Hon. Prof.

Other Staff: 2 Lectrs.

Social Sciences, Applied

Tel: (01908) 654431 Fax: (01908) 684488

Clarke, John, BSc *Aston*, MA *Birm.* Prof.; Head of Discipline*

Cochrane, Allan D., BA *Oxf.*, PhD Prof., Urban Studies

Dowie, Jack A., MA *NZ*, PhD *ANU* Sr. Lectr.

Drake, Michael, MA *Camb.*, PhD *Camb.* Emer. Prof.

Langan, Mary, MA *Essex* Sr. Lectr.

McLaughlin, J. Eugene, BA *Manc.*, MPhil *Camb.*, PhD *Sheff.* Sr. Lectr.

Muncie, John, BSc *Leic.*, PhD *Leic.* Sr. Lectr., Social Administration and Social Policy

Thompson, Graeme F., MA *Leic.*, PhD *Birm.* Sr. Lectr.

Sociology

Tel: (01908) 654431 Fax: (01908) 654488

Bennett, Tony, MA *Oxf.*, PhD *Sus.* Prof.; Head of Discipline*

Boswell, David M., MA *Camb.*, MPhil *Lond.*, PhD *Manc.* Sr. Lectr.

Finnegan, Ruth H., MA *Oxf.*, BLitt *Oxf.*, DPhil *Oxf.* Prof., Comparative Social Institutions and Social Anthropology

Held, David J. A., BSc *Manc.*, MSc *M.I.T.*, PhD *M.I.T.* Prof.

Salaman, J. Graeme, BA *Leic.*, PhD *Camb.* Sr. Lectr.
Thompson, Ken A., BA *Leic.*, DPhil *Oxf.* Prof.

Statistics

Hand, David J., MA *Oxf.*, MSc *S'ton.*, PhD *S'ton.* Prof.; Head*
Jones, M. Chris, BSc *Bath*, PhD *Bath* Reader
McConway, Kevin J., BA *Open(UK)*, MA *Camb.*, MSc *Lond.*, PhD *Lond.* Sr. Lectr.
Other Staff: 3 Lectrs.

Telematics

Tel: (01908) 652854 Fax: (01908) 653658
Alexander, G. R., BS *Col.*, PhD *Purdue* Sr. Lectr.
Bissell, C., MA *Camb.*, PhD *Open(UK)* Sr. Lectr.
Crecraft, D. I., BSc *Nott.*, MS *Tennessee*, PhD *Birm.*, FIEE Reader
Gorham, D. A., MA *Camb.*, PhD, FIP Sr. Lectr.
Hasemer, T., PhD *Open(UK)*, BA *Open*
Heap, N. W., BSc *CNAA*, PhD Sr. Lectr.
Meade, M. L., BScTech *Manc.*, PhD *Reading* Sr. Lectr.
Monk, John, BSc(Eng) *Lond.*, PhD *Warw.*, FIEE Prof.
Other Staff: 12 Lectrs.; 2 Res. Fellows

Other Appointments

Staff Tutors and Research Fellows
Harrison, C., MA *Camb.*, PhD *Lond.* Staff Tutor, Art History; Prof.

SPECIAL CENTRES, ETC

Educational Technology, Institute of

Tel: (01908) 653216 Fax: (01908) 654173
Calder, Judith A., BA *Wales*, DPhil *Oxf.* Sr. Lectr.
Chambers, Eleanor A., BA *Leic.*, MA *Lond.* Sr. Lectr.
Grant, Janet, BA *Sus.*, MSc *Lond.*, PhD *Lond.* Prof., Education in Medicine
Harry, Keith W., MA *Aberd.*, PhD *Aberd.* Dir., ICDL
Hawkridge, David G., BEd *Cape Town*, MA *Cape Town*, PhD *Lond.* Prof., Applied Educational Sciences
Henry, Jane, BA *Manc.* Sr. Lectr.
Kaye, A. R., MA *Camb.* Sr. Lectr.
Kirkup, Gillian, BEd *Lond.*, BA *CNAA*, MPhil *CNAA* Sr. Lectr.
Lawless, Clive J., MA *Oxf.*, PhD *Reading* Prof.
Lockwood, Fred G., MA *Malawi*, MPhil *Reading*, PhD Sr. Lectr.
Macdonald-Ross, M., BSc *Lond.* Reader
Melton, R. F., MA *Camb.*, PhD Sr. Lectr.
Morgan, A. R., MSc *Manc.*, PhD *Strath.* Sr. Lectr.
Rowntree, Derek G. F., BSc(Econ) *Hull*, DTech *CNAA* Prof., Educational Development
Scanlon, Eileen, BSc *Glas.*, PhD Reader
Thorpe, Mary, MA *Camb.* Dir.*

Health and Social Welfare, School of

Tel: (01908) 653743 Fax: (01908) 654124
Atkinson, Dorothy, BA *Leeds*, MPhil *S'ton.* Sr. Lectr.
Bailey, Lorna, BSc *Lond.* Sr. Lectr.
Brown, Hilary, BA *Birm.*, MSc *Lond.*, PhD *Kent.* Prof.
Cornwell, A., BA *Liv.*, MA *Sus.* Sr. Lectr.
Davies, Celia, BA MA PhD Prof.
Dickenson, Donna, BA *Mass.*, MSc *Lond.*, PhD Sr. Lectr.
Finkelstein, V., BA *Natal*, MA *Witw.* Sr. Lectr.
Gearing, Brian, MSocSc *Birm.*, BA Sr. Lectr.
Heller, T. D., MB BS *Lond.* Sr. Lectr.
Jones, Linda J., BA *Camb.*, PhD *Birm.* Dean*
Northedge, Andrew, BSc *Durh.* Sr. Lectr.
Pattison, S., MA *Camb.*, MSocSc *Birm.*, PhD *Edin.* Sr. Lectr.
Peace, Sheila M., BA *Wales*, PhD *Wales* Sr. Lectr.
Shakespeare, Pam, MA *Sus.* Sr. Lectr.

Stainton-Rogers, Wendy, BSc *Brist.*, MPhil *Reading*, PhD Sr. Lectr.

Knowledge Media Institute

Tel: (01908) 653800 Fax: (01908) 653169
Eisenstadt, Marc, BA *Wash.*, PhD *San Diego* Prof.; Dir.*

Planetary Sciences Research Institute

Fax: (01908) 655151
Pillinger, Colin T., BSc *Wales*, PhD, FGS Sr. Lectr.
Other Staff: 1 Sr. Res. Fellow

Vice-Chancellor's Office

Tel: (01908) 653631 Fax: (01908) 655093
Grugeon, D. A., MA *Camb.* Dir., Univ. Relns. Projects*

REGION 01: LONDON

Tel: (0171) 794 0575 Fax: (0171) 556 6196
Fage, Judith, MA *Camb.* Regional Dir.*

REGION 02: SOUTH

Tel: (01865) 327000 Fax: (01865) 736288
Watts, Sheelagh, BSc *Birm.* Regional Dir.*

REGION 03: SOUTH WEST

Tel: (0117) 929 9641 Fax: (0117) 925 5215
Emms, Judy, BSc *Sus.*, MSc *CNAA* Regional Dir.*

REGION 04: WEST MIDLANDS

Tel: (0121) 426 1661 Fax: (0121) 427 9484
Hancock, G. F., MSc *Manc.*, PhD *Manc.* Regional Dir.*

REGION 05: EAST MIDLANDS

Tel: (0115) 947 3072 Fax: (0115) 941 1750
Lammie, Gordon A., MA *Camb.* Regional Dir.*

REGION 06: EAST ANGLIA

Tel: (01223) 364721 Fax: (01223) 355207
Mills, A. Roger, BSc *Durh.*, MSc *Liv.* Regional Dir.*

REGION 07: YORKSHIRE

Tel: (0113) 244 4431 Fax: (0113) 234 1862
Smith, Peter H. K., DPhil *York(UK).* Regional Dir.*

REGION 08: NORTH WEST

Tel: (0161) 861 9823 Fax: (0161) 956 6811
Horner, Howard, BA *Open(UK)*, BSc *Sus.*, MSc *Aston* Regional Dir.*

REGION 09: NORTH

Tel: (0191) 284 1611 Fax: (0191) 284 6592
Shipley, John W., OBE, BA *Lond.* Regional Dir.*

REGION 10: WALES

Tel: (01222) 397911 Fax: (01222) 227930
McGrath, J., BSc *Wales*, PhD *Wales*, MSc *CNAA* Welsh Dir.*

REGION 11: SCOTLAND

Tel: (0131) 226 3851 Fax: (0131) 220 6730
Syme, P. W., MA *Camb.* Regional Dir.*

REGION 12: NORTHERN IRELAND

Tel: (01232) 245025 Fax: (01232) 230565
Hamilton, Rosemary K., BSc *Belf.*, PhD *Belf.* Regional Dir.*

REGION 13: SOUTH EAST

Tel: (01342) 327821 Fax: (01342) 317411
Rumble, Greville, BA *Kent*, MA *Kent* Regional Dir.*

CONTACT OFFICERS

Estates and buildings/works and services. Director: Baily, R.
Finance. Director: Chicken, S. W.
General enquiries. Secretary: Woodburn, A. Fraser, BSc *Edin.*
Personnel/human resources. Director: Marsh, P., BA *Open(UK)*, MBA *Open(UK)*, MPhil *Warw.*
Public relations, information and marketing (public relations). Director: Prior, D.
Student union. Permanent Secretary, Open University Students' Association: Needham, J., BA *Lanc.*

CAMPUS/COLLEGE HEADS

Region 01: London, Parsifal College, 527 Finchley Road, Hampstead, London, England NW3 7BG. (Tel: (0171) 794 0575; Fax: (0171) 556 6196.) Regional Director: Fage, Judith, MA *Camb.*
Region 02: South, Foxcombe Hall, Boar's Hill, Oxford, England OX1 5HR. (Tel: (01865) 327000; Fax: (01865) 736288.) Regional Director: Watts, Sheelagh, BSc *Birm.*
Region 03: South West, 4 Portwall Lane, Bristol, England BS1 6ND. (Tel: (0117) 929 9641; Fax: (0117) 925 5215.) Regional Director: Emms, Judy, BSc *Sus.*, MSc *CNAA*
Region 04: West Midlands, 66-68 High Street, Harborne, Birmingham, West Midlands, England B17 9NB. (Tel: (0121) 426 1661; Fax: (0121) 427 9484.) Regional Director: Hancock, G. F., MSc *Manc.*, PhD *Manc.*
Region 05: East Midlands, The Octagon, 143 Derby Road, Nottingham, England NG7 1PH. (Tel: (0115) 947 3072; Fax: (0115) 941 1750.) Regional Director: Lammie, Gordon A., MA *Camb.*
Region 06: East Anglia, Cintra House, 12 Hills Road, Cambridge, England CB2 1PF. (Tel: (01223) 364721; Fax: (01223) 355207.) Regional Director: Mills, A. R., BSc *Durh.*, MSc *Liv.*
Region 07: Yorkshire, Fairfax House, Merrion Street, Leeds, England LS2 8JU. (Tel: (0113) 244 4431; Fax: (0113) 234 1862.) Regional Director: Smith, P. H. K., DPhil *York(UK)*
Region 08: North West, Chorlton House, 70 Manchester Road, Chorlton cum Hardy,

Manchester, England M21 1PQ. (Tel: (0161) 861 9823; Fax: (0161) 956 6811.) Regional Director: Horner, Howard, BA Open(UK), BSc Sus., MSc Aston

Region 09: North, Eldon House, Regent Centre, Gosforth, Newcastle upon Tyne, England NE3 3PW. (Tel: (0191) 284 1611; Fax: (0191) 284 6592.) Regional Director: Shipley, John W., OBE, BA Lond.

Region 10: Wales, 24 Cathedral Road, Cardiff, Wales CF1 9SA. (Tel: (01222) 397911; Fax:

(01222) 397911.) Welsh Director: McGrath, J., BSc Wales, MSc CNAA, PhD Wales

Region 11: Scotland, 10 Drumsheugh Gardens, Edinburgh, Scotland EH3 7QJ. (Tel: (0131) 226 3851; Fax: (0131) 220 6730.) Regional Director: Syme, P. W., MA Camb.

Region 12: Northern Ireland, 40 University Road, Belfast, Northern Ireland BT7 1SU. (Tel: (01232) 245025; Fax: (01232) 230565.) Regional Director: Hamilton, Rosemary K., BSc Belf., PhD Belf.

Region 13: South East, St James's House, 150 London Road, East Grinstead, West Sussex, England RH19 1ES. (Tel: (01342) 327821; Fax: (01342) 317411.) Regional Director: Rumble, G., BA Kent, MA Kent

[Information supplied by the institution as at 2 June 1998, and edited by the ACU]

UNIVERSITY OF OXFORD

Founded in the 12th century

Member of the Association of Commonwealth Universities

Postal Address: University Offices, Wellington Square, Oxford, England OX1 2JD
Telephone: (01865) 270000 **Fax**: (01865) 270708 **E-mail**: exrel@admin.ox.ac.uk **WWW**: http://www.ox.ac.uk

CHANCELLOR—Jenkins, The Rt. Hon. the Lord, OM, DCL Oxf., Hon. LLD Leeds, Hon. LLD Harv., Hon. LLD Penn., Hon. LLD Dund., Hon. LLD Lough., Hon. DLitt Glas., Hon. DLitt City(UK), Hon. DSc Aston, Hon. Fellow of Balliol and St Antony's Colleges

HIGH STEWARD—Goff of Chieveley, The Rt. Hon. the Lord, DCL Oxf., FBA, Hon. Fellow of Lincoln and New Colleges

VICE-CHANCELLOR*—Lucas, Colin R., MA Oxf., DPhil Oxf., Hon. Dr Lyons II, FRHistS (Ball.)

PROCTOR, SENIOR—(1998–99) Ainsworth, R. W., MA Oxf., DPhil Oxf. (S.Cat.)

PROCTOR—(1998–99) Hart, M. W., MA Oxf., MA Camb., DPhil Oxf. (Exet.)

ASSESSOR—(1998–99) Bowie, A. M., MA Camb., MA Oxf., PhD Camb., DPhil Oxf. (Qu.)

PUBLIC ORATOR—Griffin, Prof. J., MA Oxf., FBA (Ball.)

DIRECTOR OF UNIVERSITY LIBRARY SERVICES AND BODLEY'S LIBRARIAN—Carr, R. P., BA Leeds, MA Manc., MA Camb. (Ball.)

KEEPER OF THE ARCHIVES—Vaisey, David G., CBE, MA Oxf., FSA, FRHistS, Hon. Fellow of Kellogg College (Exet.)

REGISTRAR‡—Holmes, D. R., MA Oxf.

CHAIRMAN OF THE GENERAL BOARD OF THE FACULTIES—Black, L. G., BA Cape Town, MA Oxf., DPhil Oxf. (Oriel)

SECRETARY OF THE CHEST—Clements, J. R., BA Manc., FCA (Mert.)

SECRETARY OF FACULTIES—Weale, A. P., MA Oxf. (Worc.)

GENERAL INFORMATION

History. There is no clear date of foundation for the university, but teaching existed at Oxford in some form in 1096 and developed rapidly from 1167, when Henry II banned English students from attending the University of Paris. The oldest colleges—University, Balliol and Merton—were founded between 1249 and 1264.

The university is located in the city of Oxford, about 90km north-west of London.

Admission to first degree courses (see also United Kingdom Introduction). Through Universities and Colleges Admissions Service (UCAS) and the university's individual colleges and halls. Enquiries should be directed to Oxford Colleges Admissions Office and not to the university.

First Degrees (see also United Kingdom Directory to Subjects of Study). BA, BFA, BTh, MBiochem, MChem, MEarthSc, MEng, MMath, MPhys.

All courses are full-time and most last 3 years. BA (certain courses), MBiochem, MChem, MEarthSc, MEng, MMath, MPhys: 4 years.

Higher Degrees (see also United Kingdom Directory to Subjects of Study). BCL, BD, BM BCh, BMus, BPhil, MBA, MJur, MLitt, MSc, MSt, MTheol, MPhil, DPhil.

Applicants for admission to higher degrees must normally hold a first degree with upper second class honours, or equivalent.

MBA, MJur, MSc, MSt: 1 year full-time; BCL: 1–2 years full-time; BD, BPhil, MPhil: 2 years full-time; MLitt: minimum 2 years full-time; MTheol: 2 years full-time or 3–4 years part-time; DPhil: 3–4 years full-time.

Libraries. Bodleian and dependent libraries: 6,333,000 volumes; 57,250 serial titles; many special collections. Taylor Institution Library: 500,000 volumes and many special collections. Ashmolean Library: 220,000 volumes. Many faculty, departmental and college libraries.

Fees (1998–99, annual). Undergraduate: UK/EU students £1000; international students £6489 (arts), £8652 (fine art, music, sciences), £15,861 (clinical medicine); college fees £3235 (average). Postgraduate: UK/EU students £1000–2610; international students £6489–15,861; MBA (all students) £15,000; college fees £1399–1846.

Academic Year (1999–2000). Three terms: 10 October–4 December; 16 January–11 March; 30 April–24 June.

Income (1996–97). Total, £284,916,000.

Statistics (1997–98). Staff: 6771 (3382 academic, 3389 administrative). Students: full-time 15,744 (9173 men, 6571 women); part-time 201 (127 men, 74 women); international 3830 (2217 men, 1613 women); total 15,945.

ACADEMIC UNITS

CUF Lectr. = Common University Fund Lectr.

Accounting, see Management Studies

Agricultural Economics, see Special Centres, etc (Queen Elizabeth House)

Akkadian

Tel: (01865) 278200 Fax: (01865) 278190

Black, J. A., BPhil Oxf., MA Oxf., DPhil Oxf. Lectr. (Wolfs.)

Anglo-Saxon, see Engl.

Anthropology, Biological

Tel: (01865) 274700 Fax: (01865) 274699

Boyce, A. J., MA Oxf., DPhil Oxf. Reader, Human Population Biology (S.Joh.)

Reynolds, V., MA Lond., PhD Lond. Prof., Physical Anthropology (Magd.)

Ulijasek, S. J., BSc Manc., MSc Lond., PhD Lond. Lectr., Human Ecology (S.Cross)

Ward, R. H., BA Auck., BSc Auck., MA Auck., MA Oxf., MSc Mich., PhD Mich. Prof.; Head* (Linac.)

Other Staff: 1 Lectr.

Anthropology, Social and Cultural

Tel: (01865) 274687 Fax: (01865) 274630

Allen, N. J., BM Oxf., BLitt Oxf., BSc Oxf., MA Oxf., DPhil Oxf. Reader, Social Anthropology of South Asia (Wolfs.)

The abbreviation in brackets after a teacher's name denotes the college of which the teacher is a present member or fellow. The names of the colleges are indicated by abbreviations as follows:

All S.	All Souls College	Oriel	Oriel College
Ball.	Balliol College	Pemb.	Pembroke College
Bras.	Brasenose College	Qu.	Queen's College
Camp.	Campion Hall	Reg.P.	Regent's Park College
Ch.Ch.	Christ Church	S.Ann.	St Anne's College
Corp.	Corpus Christi College	S.Ant.	St Antony's College
Exet.	Exeter College	S.Ben.	St Bent's Hall
Gre.	Green College	S.Cat.	St Catherine's College
Greyf.	Greyfriars	S.Cross	St Cross College
Harris	Harris Manchester College	S.Edm.	St Edmund Hall
Hert.	Hertford College	S.Hil.	St Hilda's College
Jes.	Jesus College	S.Hug.	St Hugh's College
Keb.	Keble College	S.Joh.	St John's College
Kell.	Kellogg College	S.Pet.	St Peter's College
Linac.	Linacre College	Som.	Somerville College
Linc.	Lincoln College	Templ.	Templeton College
Magd.	Magdalen College	Trin.	Trinity College
Mansf.	Mansfield College	Univ.	University College
Mert.	Merton College	Wadh.	Wadham College
New	New College	Wolfs.	Wolfson College
Nuff.	Nuffield College	Worc.	Worcester College
		Wycl.H.	Wycliffe Hall

Banks, M. J., BA Camb., MA Oxf., PhD Camb. Lectr. (Wolfs.)

Barnes, R. H., BLitt DPhil Prof., Social Anthropology (S.Ant.)

Dresch, P. K., MA Oxf., DPhil Oxf. Lectr. (S.Joh.)

Gosden, C., BA Sheff., MA Oxf., PhD Sheff. Lectr., Prehistory; Curator (S.Cross)

Harris, Clare, BA Camb., MA Lond., PhD Lond. Lectr., Ethnology; Curator (Linac.)

James, Wendy R., BLitt Oxf., MA Oxf., DPhil Oxf. Prof., Social Anthropology (S.Cross)

La Rue, Helena, MA Oxf., DPhil Oxf. Lectr., Musicological Collection; Curator (S.Cross)

Mitchell, P. J., MA Camb., MA Oxf., DPhil Oxf. Lectr., Prehistoric Archaeology; Curator (S.Hug.)

Parkin, D. J., BA Lond., MA Oxf., PhD Lond., DPhil Oxf., FBA Prof.; Head* (All S.)

Peers, Laura L., BA Trent, MA Winn., MA Manit., MA Oxf., PhD McM. Lectr., Ethnology; Curator (Linac.)

Pieke, F. N., BA Amst., MA Amst., MA Oxf., PhD Calif. Lectr., Modern Politics and Society of China (S.Cross)

Rivière, P. G., BLitt Oxf., MA Camb., MA Oxf., DPhil Oxf. Prof., Social Anthropology (Linac.)

Roe, D. A., PhD Camb., MA Camb., MA Oxf., DLitt Oxf. Prof., Prehistoric Archaeology (S.Cross)

Arabic

Tel: (01865) 278200 Fax: (01865) 278190

Allan, J. W., MA Oxf., DPhil Oxf. Prof., Eastern Art (S.Cross)

Johns, J., MA Oxf., DPhil Oxf. Lectr., Islamic Archaeology (Wolfs.)

Jones, A., MA Camb., MA Oxf. Prof., Classical Arabic (Pemb.)

Ostle, R. C., MA Oxf., DPhil Oxf. Lectr., Modern Arabic Language and Literature (S.Joh.)

Raby, J. A. J., MA Oxf., DPhil Oxf. Lectr., Islamic Art and Architecture (S.Hug.)

Richards, D. S., MA Oxf. Lectr. (S.Cross)

Robinson, C. F., BA Brown, MA Oxf., PhD Harv. Lectr., Islamic History (Wolfs.)

S'Hiri, S., BA Tunis

Treadwell, W. L., BA Camb., BA Oxf., DPhil Lectr., Islamic Numismatics (S.Cross)

Van Gelder, G. J. H., MA Oxf. Laudian Prof. (S.Joh.)

Zimmermann, F. W., MA Erlangen, MA Oxf., DPhil Oxf. Lectr., Islamic Philosophy (S.Cross)

Archaeology, see also Anthropol, Social and Cultural, and Hist., Mod.

Tel: (01865) 278240 Fax: (01865) 278254

Bennet, J., MA Camb., PhD Camb. Sinclair and Rachel Hood Lectr., Aegean Prehistory (Keb.)

Coulton, J. J., MA Camb., MA Oxf., PhD Camb. Reader, Classical Archaeology (Mert.)

Cunliffe, B. W., CBE, MA Camb., MA Oxf., PhD Camb., DPhil Oxf., FBA, FSA Prof., European Archaeology; Head* (Keb.)

Gale, N. H., MA Oxf. Prof.; Dir., Isotrace Lab. (Nuff.)

Hawkes, Sonia E. C., BA Lond., MA Lectr., European Archaeology (S.Cross)

Hedges, R. E. M., MA Camb., MA Oxf., PhD Camb., DPhil Oxf. Prof. (S.Cross)

Kurtz, Donna C., BA Cinc., MA Yale, MA Oxf., DPhil Oxf. Reader, Clinical Archaeology (Wolfs.)

Lloyd, J. A., BA Manc., MA Oxf., PhD Manc. Lectr., Roman Archaeology (Wolfs.)

Lock, G. R., BA Leic., MA Oxf., PhD Leic., PhD CNAA Lectr., Computing and Statistical Methods and Continuing Education (Kell.)

Roe, D. A., MA Oxf., MA Camb., PhD Camb., DLitt Oxf. Lectr., Prehistoric Archaeology (S.Cross)

Sherratt, A. G., MA Oxf., DPhil Oxf. Reader, Antiquities (Linac.)

Smith, R. R. R., CBE, MA Oxf., MPhil Oxf., DPhil Oxf., FBA Lincoln Prof., Classical Archaeology and Art (Linc.)

Steinby, Eva M., MA Oxf., MA Helsinki, PhD Helsinki Prof., Archaeology of the Roman Empire (All S.)

Tite, M. S., MA Oxf., DPhil Oxf. Edward Hall Prof., Archaeology Science; Dir., Res. Lab. for Archaeol. and the Hist. of Art (Linac.)

Armenian Studies

Tel: (01865) 278200 Fax: (01865) 278190

Thomson, R. W., MA Camb., MA Oxf., PhD Camb. Calouste Gulbenkian Prof. (Pemb.)

Art, see also Arabic, Archaeol., and Chinese

Tel: (01865) 276940 Fax: (01865) 276949

Bull, M. G., MA Oxf., MA Lond. Lectr., Art History (Wolfs.)

Catling, B. D., MA RCA, MA Oxf. Lectr., Fine Art (Linac.)

Chevska, Maria, MA Oxf. Lectr., Fine Art (Bras.)

Davis, K., MA Oxf. Tutor

Dennis, J., MA Oxf. Tutor

Farthing, S., MA RCA, MA Oxf. Ruskin Master, Drawing; Head* (S.Edm.)

Furneaux, S. H., BA Tutor

Haskell, F. J. H., MA Camb., MA Oxf. Prof., History of Art (Trin.)

Morgan, S., MA Oxf. Tutor

Payne, A., MA Oxf. Tutor

Other Staff: 5 Tutors†

Vacant Posts: 1 Lectr.

Astrophysics

Tel: (01865) 273303 Fax: (01865) 273390

Charles, P. A., BSc Lond., MA Oxf., PhD Lond. Prof., Astronomy; Head* (S.Hug.)

Efstathiou, G. P., PhD Durh., MA Savilian Prof., Astronomy (New)

Miller, L., BSc Leic., MA Oxf., PhD Camb. Lectr. (S.Cat.)

Peach, J. V., MA Oxf., DPhil Oxf. Lectr. (Bras.)

Podsiadlowski, P., MA Oxf., PhD MIT Lectr. (S.Edm.)

Rawlings, S. G., MA Oxf., MA Camb., DPhil Oxf., PhD Camb. Lectr. (S.Pet.)

Roche, P. F., BSc Lond., MA Oxf., PhD Lond. Lectr. (Hert.)

Silk, J. I., BA Camb., PhD Harv. Savilian Prof., Astronomy (New)

Smith, G., MA Oxf., DPhil Oxf. Lectr. (S.Cross)

Ward, M. J., BSc Lond., MA Camb., MA Oxf., DPhil Sus. Lectr.

Other Staff: 2 Temp. Lectrs.

Biochemistry

Tel: (01865) 275263 Fax: (01865) 275259

Armitage, Judith P., BSc Lond., MA Oxf., PhD Lond. Prof. (S.Hil.)

Barford, D., BSc Brist., MA Oxf., DPhil Oxf. Lectr., Molecular Biophysics (Som.)

Brown, G. K., MB BS Syd., BSc(Med) Syd., MA Oxf., PhD Syd. Lectr. (L.M.H.)

Campbell, I. D., BSc St And., MA Oxf., PhD St And. Prof., Structural Biology (S.Joh.)

Cox, Lynne S., MA Oxf., PhD Camb., DPhil Oxf. Lectr. (Oriel)

Craig, I. W., BSc Liv., MA Oxf., PhD Liv. Prof., Genetics (S.Cat.)

Dwek, R. A., BSc Manc., MSc Manc., MA Oxf., DPhil Oxf., DSc Oxf., FRS Prof., Glycobiology; Dir., Glycobiol. Inst. (Exet.)

Dyke, K. G. H., MA Camb., MA Oxf., PhD Camb. Reader, Microbiology (Wadh.)

Endicott, Jane A., BA Oxf., PhD Tor. Lectr., Molecular Biophysics (S.Cross)

Ferguson, S. J., MA Oxf., DPhil Oxf. Prof. (S.Edm.)

Handford, Penelope A., BSc S'ton., MA Oxf., PhD S'ton. Lectr. (S.Cat.)

Harris, D. A., MA Oxf., DPhil Oxf. Lectr. (S.Ann.)

Johnson, Louise N., BSc Lond., MA Oxf., PhD Lond., Hon. DSc St And., FRS David Phillips Prof., Molecular Biophysics (Corp.)

Kingsman, A. J., BSc Birm., MA Oxf., PhD Birm. Prof. (S.Cat.)

Kingsman, Sue M., BSc Birm., MA Oxf., PhD Birm. Prof. (Trin.)

Knowland, J. S., MA Oxf., DPhil Oxf. Lectr. (Pemb.)

Louis, E. J., BS Clarkson, MA Oxf., PhD Calif. Lectr., Microbiology (Corp.)

Mellor, E. Jane C., BSc Manc., MA Oxf., PhD Reading Lectr. (Qu.)

Newell, P. C., MA Oxf., DPhil Oxf., DSc Oxf. Prof.; Head* (S.Pet.)

Newsholme, E. A., MA Camb., MA Oxf., PhD Camb., ScD Camb., DPhil Reader, Cellular Nutrition (Mert.)

Pears, Catherine J., BA Camb., MA Oxf., PhD Lond. Lectr. (Univ.)

Radda, G. K., CBE, MA Oxf., DPhil Oxf., FRS British Heart Foundation Prof., Molecular Cardiology (Mert.)

Roberts, D. B., MA Camb., MA Oxf., PhD Camb. Reader, Genetics (Magd.)

Sansom, M. S. P., MA Oxf., DPhil Oxf. Reader, Molecular Biophysics (Ch.Ch.)

Sherratt, D. J., BSc Edin., MA Oxf., PhD Edin., FRS Iveagh Prof., Microbiology (Linac.)

Southern, E. M., BSc Manc., MA Oxf., PhD Glas. Whitley Prof. (Trin.)

Stuart, D. I., BSc Lond., MA Oxf., PhD Brist. Lectr., Structural Molecular Biology; MRC Prof. (Hert.)

Watts, A., BSc Leeds, MA Oxf., PhD Leeds, DSc Prof. (S.Hug.)

Wigley, D. B., BSc York(UK), PhD Brist. Lectr., Molecular Biophysics (Linc.)

Wild, D. G., MA DPhil Lectr., Microbiology (Corp.)

Yudkin, M. D., MA Camb., MA Oxf., PhD Camb., DPhil Oxf. Prof. (Kell.)

Other Staff: 1 Temp. Lectr.

Vacant Posts: 1 Prof.; 3 Lectrs.

Botany, see Plant Scis.

Brazilian Studies, Centre for, see also Portuguese Studies

Tel: (01865) 554026 Fax: (01865) 554030

Bethell, L. M., MA Oxf. Dir.* (S.Ant.)

Byzantine Studies, see Greek Lang. and Lit., Byzantine and Mod., and Hist. Mod.

Celtic

Tel: (01865) 270750 Fax: (01865) 270757

Charles-Edwards, T. M. O., MA Oxf., DPhil Oxf. Jesus Prof. (Jes.)

Chemistry, Inorganic

Tel: (01865) 272600 Fax: (01865) 272690

Armstrong, F. A., BSc Leeds, MA Oxf., PhD Leeds Reader (S.Joh.)

Battle, P. D., BSc Brist., MA Oxf., DPhil Oxf. Lectr. (S.Cat.)

Beer, P. D., BSc Lond., MA Oxf., PhD Lond. Prof. (Wadh.)

Cox, P. A., MA Oxf., DPhil Oxf. Lectr. (New)

Denning, R. G., MA Oxf., DPhil Oxf. Prof. (Magd.)

Dilworth, J. R., MA Oxf., DPhil Sus., DSc Sus. Prof. (S.Ann.)

Dobson, C. M., MA Oxf., DPhil Oxf. Prof.; Aldrichian Praelector; Dir., Oxford Centre for Molecular Scis. (L.M.H.)

Downs, A. J., MA Camb., MA Oxf., PhD Camb., DPhil Oxf. Prof. (Jes.)

Egdell, R. G., MA Oxf., DPhil Oxf. Reader (Trin.)

Green, M. L. H., BSc Lond., MA Oxf., PhD Lond., FRS Prof.; Head* (S.Cat.)

Heyes, S. J., MA Oxf., DPhil Oxf. Lectr. (Keb.)

Hill, H. A. O., BSc Belf., MA Oxf., PhD Belf., DSc Oxf., FRS Prof., Bio-inorganic Chemistry (Qu.)

Mountford, P., BSc CNAA, MA Oxf., DPhil Oxf. Lectr. (S.Edm.)

O'Hare, D. M., MA Oxf., DPhil Oxf. Prof. (Ball.)

Orchard, A. F., MA Oxf. Lectr. (Univ.)

Prout, C. K., MA Oxf., DPhil Oxf., FRSChem Prof., Chemical Crystallography (Oriel)

Rosseinsky, M. J., MA Oxf., DPhil Oxf. Lectr. (Ch.Ch.)

Wong, L. L., MA Oxf., DPhil Oxf. Lectr. (S.Hug.)

Vacant Posts: 1 Lectr.

Chemistry, Organic

Tel: (01865) 275680 Fax: (01865) 275674

Adlington, R. M., BSc Lond., MA Oxf., PhD Lond. Lectr. (L.M.H.)

Anderson, H. L., MA Oxf., PhD Camb. Lectr. (Keb.)

Baldwin, Sir Jack, BSc Lond., MA Oxf., PhD Lond., FRS Waynflete Prof.; Head* (Magd.)

Brown, J. M., BSc Manc., MA Oxf., PhD Manc. Lectr. (Wadh.)

Burn, P. L., BSc Syd., MA Oxf., PhD Syd. Lectr. (Univ.)

Davies, S. G., MA Oxf., DPhil Oxf. Prof. (New)

Fairbanks, A. J., MA Oxf., DPhil Oxf. Lectr. (Jes.)

Gouverneur, Veronique, PhD Louvain Lectr. (Mert.)

Hodgson, D. M., BSc Bath, MA Oxf., PhD S'ton. Lectr. (Oriel)

Jones, J. H., MA Oxf., DPhil Oxf., FRSChem, FRHistS Lectr. (Ball.)

Lowe, G., MA Oxf., PhD Lond., DSc Oxf., FRS Prof., Biological Chemistry (Linc.)

Moloney, M. G., BSc Syd., MA Oxf., PhD Syd. Lectr. (S.Pet.)

Robertson, J., MA Oxf., DPhil Oxf. Lectr. (Bras.)

Schofield, C. J., BSc Manc., MA Oxf., DPhil Oxf. Prof. (Hert.)

Vacant Posts: 4 Lectrs.

Chemistry, Physical and Theoretical

Tel: (01865) 275400 Fax: (01865) 275410

Abraham, D. B., MA Camb., MA Oxf., PhD Camb., DSc Reader, Statistical Mechanics (Wolfs.)

Atkins, P. W., MA Oxf., PhD Leic. Prof. (Linc.)

Bain, C. D., MA Camb., MA Oxf., PhD Harv. Lectr. (Magd.)

Brouard, M., BA Oxf., MA Oxf., DPhil Oxf. Lectr. (Jes.)

Brown, J. M., BA Camb., MA Oxf., PhD Camb., DPhil Oxf. Prof. (Exet.)

Child, M. S., MA Camb., MA Oxf., PhD Camb., FRS Coulson Prof., Theoretical Chemistry (Univ.)

Coles, B. A., MA Oxf., DPhil Oxf. Sr. Res. Officer (S.Cross)

Compton, R. G., MA Oxf., DPhil Oxf. Prof. (S.Joh.)

Eland, J. H. D., MA Oxf., DPhil Oxf. Prof. (Worc.)

Foord, J. S., MA Camb., MA Oxf., PhD Camb. Reader (S.Cat.)

Hancock, G., MA Trinity(Dub.), MA Camb., MA Oxf., PhD Camb. Prof. (Trin.)

Hore, P. J., MA Oxf., DPhil Oxf. Reader (Corp.)

Howard, B. J., MA Camb., MA Oxf., PhD S'ton., DPhil Prof. (Pemb.)

Logan, D. E., MA Camb., MA Oxf., PhD Camb., DPhil Oxf. Prof. (Ball.)

Madden, P. A., BSc Sus., MA Oxf., DPhil Sus. Prof. (Qu.)

Manolopoulos, D. E., BA Camb., MA Oxf., PhD Camb. Lectr. (S.Edm.)

McLauchlan, K. A., BSc Brist., MA Oxf., PhD Brist., FRS Prof., Physical Chemistry (Hert.)

Richards, W. G., MA Oxf., DPhil Oxf., DSc Oxf. Prof., Computational Chemistry; Chairman of Chemistry (Bras.)

Simons, J. P., BA Camb., MA Oxf., PhD Camb., DPhil Oxf., ScD Camb., DSc Oxf., FRS Dr. Lee's Prof.; Head* (Exet.)

Simpson, C. J. S. M., MA DPhil Lectr. (Wadh.)

Softley, T. P., MA Oxf., PhD S'ton. Reader (Mert.)

Thomas, R. K., MA Oxf., DPhil Oxf. Lectr. (Univ.)

Wayne, R. P., MA Oxf., PhD Camb. Prof. (Ch.Ch.)

Vacant Posts: 1 Lectr.

Chinese

Tel: (01865) 280387 Fax: (01865) 280431

Chard, R. L., MA Calif., MA Oxf., PhD Calif. Lectr., Classical Chinese (S.Ann.)

Dudbridge, G., MA Camb., MA Oxf., PhD Camb., DPhil Oxf., FBA Shaw Prof.; Dir., Inst. for Chinese Studies (Univ.)

Fauré, D. W., BA HK, MA Oxf., PhD Prin. Lectr., Modern Chinese History (S.Ant.)

Kan, S.-Y. Instr., Modern Chinese

Liu, Tao Tao, MA Oxf., DPhil Oxf. Lectr., Modern Chinese (Wadh.)

Newby, Laura J., BA Lond., MA Oxf., MPhil Oxf., DPhil Oxf. Lectr. (S.Hil.)

Vainker, Shelagh J., BA Lond., MA Oxf. Lectr., Chinese Art

Yang, S., BA Liaoning Shaw Instr.

Other Staff: 2 Instrs.

Classical Languages and Literature

Tel: (01865) 270545 Fax: (01865) 270548

Bowie, A. M., MA Camb., MA Oxf., PhD Camb., DPhil Oxf. CUF Lectr. (Qu.)

Bowie, E. L., MA Oxf. Reader (Corp.)

Brown, P. G. M., MA Oxf. CUF Lectr. (Trin.)

Davies, Anna E., MA Oxf., FBA Prof., Comparative Philology (Som.)

Davies, M., MA Oxf., DPhil Oxf. CUF Lectr. (S.Joh.)

Edwards, Laetitia P. E., MA Camb., MA Oxf., PhD Lond. CUF Lectr. (S.Hug.)

Feeney, D. C., MA Auck., MA Oxf., DPhil Oxf. CUF Lectr. (New)

Fowler, D. P., MA Oxf., DPhil Oxf. CUF Lectr. (Jes.)

Griffin, J., MA Oxf., FBA Prof., Classical Literature (Ball.)

Hall, Edith M., BPhil Oxf., MA Oxf., DPhil Oxf. CUF Lectr. (Som.)

Heyworth, S. J., MA Camb., MA Oxf., PhD Camb., DPhil CUF Lectr. (Wadh.)

Hollis, A. S., BPhil Oxf., MA Oxf. CUF Lectr. (Keb.)

Hutchinson, G. O., MA Oxf., DPhil Oxf. Prof. (Exet.)

Innes, Doreen C., MA Aberd., MA Oxf., DPhil Oxf. CUF Lectr. (S.Hil.)

Jenkyns, R. H. A., MA Oxf., MLitt Oxf. Reader (L.M.H.)

Kerkhecker, A., MA Oxf., MA Tübingen CUF Lectr. (Worc.)

Kraus, Christina S., BA Prin., MA Oxf., PhD Harv. CUF Lectr. (Oriel)

Langslow, D. R., MA Oxf., MPhil Oxf. Lectr., Latin Philology and Linguistics (Wolfs.)

Leigh, M. G. L., BA Oxf., MA Oxf., DPhil Oxf. CUF Lectr. (S.Ann.)

Lyne, R. O. A. M., MA Camb., MA Oxf., PhD Camb., DPhil Oxf. Reader (Ball.)

Obbink, D., MA Stan., MA Oxf., PhD Stan. Lectr., Papyrology and Greek Literature (Ch.Ch.)

Parsons, P. J., MA Oxf., Hon. DPhil Berne, FBA Regius Prof., Greek (Ch.Ch.)

Pelling, C. B. R., MA Oxf., DPhil Oxf. CUF Lectr. (Univ.)

Penney, J. H. W., MA Penn., MA Oxf., DPhil Oxf. Lectr., Classical Philology (Wolfs.)

Rea, J. R., BA Belf., PhD Lond., MA, FBA Lectr., Documentary Papyrology (Ball.)

Reynolds, L. D., BA Wales, MA Camb., MA Oxf., FBA Prof. (Bras.)

Richardson, N. J., BPhil Oxf., MA Oxf., DPhil Oxf. CUF Lectr. (Mert.)

Rutherford, R. B., MA Oxf., DPhil Oxf. CUF Lectr. (Ch.Ch.)

Taplin, O. P., MA Oxf., DPhil Prof., Greek Literature (Magd.)

Wilson, N. G., MA Oxf., FBA CUF Lectr. (Linc.)

Winterbottom, M., MA Oxf., DPhil Oxf., FBA Corpus Christi Prof., Latin (Corp.)

Other Staff: 1 Lectr.; 1 Lector

Vacant Posts: 1 Lectr.; 1 CUF Lectr.

Commonwealth Studies, see also Special Centres, etc (Queen Elizabeth House)

Tel: (01865) 273600 Fax: (01865) 273607

Gooptu, Nandini, MA Calc., MA Oxf., PhD Camb. Lectr., South Asian Studies (S.Ant.)

Stewart, Frances J., MA DPhil Sr. Res. Officer; Dir. (Som.)

Vaughan, Megan A., BA Kent, PhD Lond., MA Rhodes Prof. (Nuff.)

Comparative Literature

Oz, A. Weidenfeld Visiting Prof., European Comparative Literature (1998-99) (Qu.)

Computing Laboratory

Tel: (01865) 273838 Fax: (01865) 273839

Bird, R. S., MA Camb., MA Oxf., PhD Lond. Prof., Computation; Dir.* (Linc.)

Brent, R. P., BSc Monash, MA Oxf., MS Stan., PhD Stan., DSc Monash Prof. (S.Hug.)

Cameron, S. A., BA Edin., MA Oxf., PhD Edin. Reader (Keb.)

Davies, J. W. M., MA Oxf. Lectr., Computation and Continuing Education (Kell.)

de Moor, O., MA Oxf., DPhil Lectr. (Magd.)

Donnelly, J. D. P., MA Oxf., DPhil Oxf. Lectr., Numerical Mathematics (Exet.)

Giles, M., MA Camb., MA Oxf., PhD M.I.T. Rolls Royce Prof., Computational Fluid Dynamics (S.Hug.)

Hoare, C. A. R., BA Oxf., Hon. DSc S. Calif., Hon. DSc Warw., FRS James Martin Prof. (Wolfs.)

Jones, G., MA Oxf., DPhil Oxf. Lectr. (Wolfs.)

Mayers, D. F., PhD Camb., MA Lectr., Numerical Mathematics (New)

McColl, W. F., BSc Strath., MA Oxf., PhD Warw. Prof. (Wadh.)

Morgan, C. C., BSc NSW, MA Oxf., PhD Syd. Reader (Pemb.)

Morton, K. W., BA N.Y., PhD N.Y., MA Prof., Numerical Analysis; Dir.* (Ball.)

Ong, C. H. L., MA Camb., MA Oxf., PhD Lond. Lectr. (Mert.)

Page, I., BSc Lond., MSc City(UK), MA Oxf. Reader (S.Cross)

Reed, G. M., MS Auburn, MA Oxf., PhD Auburn, DPhil Lectr. (S.Edm.)

Roscoe, A. W., MA Oxf., DPhil Oxf. Prof. (Univ.)

Sanders, J. W., BSc Monash, MA Oxf., PhD ANU Lectr. (L.M.H.)

Sobey, I. J., BSc Adel., MA Oxf., PhD Camb. Lectr., Numerical Analysis (S.Joh.)

Spivey, J. M., BA Camb., MA Oxf., DPhil Oxf. Lectr. (Oriel)

Stoy, J. E., MA Oxf. Lectr. (Ball.)

Sufrin, B. A., BSc Sheff., MSc Essex, MA Oxf. Lectr. (Worc.)

Süli, E. E., MSc Belgrade, MA Oxf., PhD Belgrade Reader, Numerical Mathematics (Linac.)

Trefethen, L. N., AB Harv., MS Stan., MA Oxf., PhD Stan. Prof., Numerical Analysis (Ball.)

Walker, D. J., BSc Glas., MA Oxf., MSc Oxf., DPhil Oxf. Lectr. (S.Hug.)

Wallen, L. A., BSc Durh., MA Oxf., PhD Edin. Reader (S.Cat.)

Wathen, A. J., MA Oxf., PhD Reading Reader (New)

Vacant Posts: 1 Lectr.

Continuing Education

Tel: (01865) 270360 Fax: (01865) 270309

Airs, M. R., MA Oxf., DPhil Oxf. Reader, Conservation and the Historic Environment (Kell.)

Buchanan, T. C., MA Oxf., DPhil Oxf. Lectr., Modern History and Politics (Kell.)

Davies, J. W. M., MA Oxf. Lectr., Computation and Continuing Education (Kell.)

Davies, P. T., BA Lond., MA Calif., MA Oxf., MLitt Oxf., PhD Calif. Lectr., Social Studies (Kell.)

Dawkins, C. R., MA Oxf., DPhil Oxf., DSc Oxf. Charles Simonyi Prof., Public Understanding of Science (New)

Flood, R. G., BSc Belf., MSc Oxf., MA Oxf., PhD Trinity(Dub.) Lectr., Computing Studies and Mathematics (Kell.)

Gray, M. A., MA Oxf., PhD Camb., DPhil Oxf. Dep. Dir., Continuing Professional Development (Kell.)

Grylls, D. S., BA Lond., MA Oxf., PhD Lond. Lectr., Literature (Kell.)

Hawkins, A. B., BA Reading, MA Oxf., PhD Lond. Dep. Dir., Internat. Programmes (Kell.)

Lock, G. R., BA Leic., MA Oxf., PhD Leic., PhD CNAA Lectr., Archaeology (Computing and Statistical Methods and Continuing Education) (Kell.)

Lockwood, M. J., MA Oxf., DPhil Oxf. Reader, Philosophy (Gre.)

Rowley, R. T., BA Lond., MLitt Oxf., MA Oxf. Dep. Dir., Public Programmes (Kell.)

Shacknove, A., BA Lond., MA Oxf., PhD Lond., JD Harv. Lectr., Law (Kell.)

Thomas, G. P., BSc Wales, MA Oxf., PhD Camb. Dir.* (Kell.)

Tiller, Kathleen, BA Birm., MA Oxf., PhD Birm. Lectr., Local History (Kell.)

Woodcock, J. C. P., BSc Liv., MSc Liv., MA Oxf., PhD Liv. Reader, Education (Kell.)

Wyatt, T. D., MA Camb., MA Oxf., PhD Camb. Lectr., Biological Sciences (Kell.)

Other Staff: 1 Lectr.; 1 Staff Tutor; 2 Lectrs.†; 1 Staff Tutor†

Vacant Posts: 3 Lectrs.; 2 Lectrs.†

Czech, see Slavonic and East European Studies

Divinity, see Theol.

Earth Sciences

Tel: (01865) 272000 Fax: (01865) 272072

Atkins, F. B., MA DPhil Lectr., Mineralogy (S.Cross)

Bell, J. D., MA Oxf., DPhil Oxf. Lectr., Petrology (Univ.)

Brasier, M. D., BSc Lond., MA Oxf., PhD Lond. Reader, Geology (S.Edm.)

Das, Shamita, MS Boston, MSc Calc., MA Oxf., ScD M.I.T. Lectr., Geology (Gre.)

Dewey, J. F., BSc Lond., MA Camb., MA Oxf., PhD Lond., ScD Camb., DSc Oxf. Prof., Geology (Univ.)

England, P. C., BSc Brist., MA Oxf., DPhil Oxf. Lectr., Geophysics (Exet.)

Fraser, D. G., BSc Edin., MA Oxf., DPhil Oxf. Prof., Geochemistry (Worc.)

Henderson, G. M., BA Oxf., PhD Camb. Lectr., Environmental Earth Sciences (Linac.)

Hesselbo, S. P., BSc Aberd., MA Oxf., PhD Brist. Lectr., Stratigraphy (S.Pet.)

Jenkyns, H. C., BSc S'ton., MA Camb., MA Oxf., PhD Leic. Lectr., Geology (S.Edm.)

Kennedy, W. J., BSc Lond., MA Oxf., PhD Lond., DSc Oxf. Prof., Palaeontology (Wolfs.)

Lamb, S. H., MA Oxf., MA Camb., PhD Camb., DPhil Oxf. Lectr., Structural Geology and Tectonics (S.Ann.)

McClelland, Elizabeth A., BSc Liv., MSc Leeds, MA Oxf., PhD Leeds Lectr., Environmental Earth Sciences (Jes.)

O'Nions, R. K., BSc Nott., MA Oxf., PhD Alta., FRS Prof., Physics and Chemistry of Minerals; Head* (S.Hug.)

Parsons, B. E., MA Camb., MA Oxf., PhD Camb., DPhil Oxf. Reader, Geodesy (S.Cross)

Waters, D. J., MA Oxf., DPhil Oxf. Lectr., Metamorphic Petrology (S.Cross)

Watts, A. B., BSc Lond., MA Oxf., PhD Durh. Prof., Marine Geology and Geophysics (Wolfs.)

Woodhouse, J. H., BSc Brist., MA Camb., MA Oxf., PhD Camb., DPhil Oxf. Prof., Geophysics (Worc.)

Young, E. D., MA Oxf., MS Vanderbilt, PhD S.Calif. Lectr., Geochemistry (Linac.)

Vacant Posts: 3 Lectrs.

East European Studies, see Slavonic and East European Studies

Eastern Religions and Ethics, see Theol.

Economics, see also Econ. and Stats., Inst. of; Japanese; and Special Centres, etc (Queen Elizabeth House)

Tel: (01865) 271073 Fax: (01865) 271094

Allsopp, C. J., BPhil Oxf., MA Oxf. Reader (New)

Anand, S., BPhil Oxf., MA Oxf., DPhil Oxf. Prof., Quantitative Economic Analysis (S.Cat.)

Bacharach, M. O. L., BA Camb., MA Oxf., PhD Camb., DPhil Oxf. Prof. (Ch.Ch.)

Bacon, R. W., BA Brist., MA Oxf., DPhil Fac. Lectr., Econometrics (Linc.) Bevan, D. L., MA Camb., MA Oxf. CUF Lectr. (S.Joh.)

Bliss, C. J., MA Camb., MA Oxf., PhD Camb., FBA Nuffield Prof., International Economics (Nuff.)

Boltho Von Hohenbach, A. G. A., BSc Lond., BLitt Oxf., MA Oxf. Reader (Magd.)

Chawluk, A., MA Warsaw, MA Oxf., PhD Lond. Fac. Lectr., Soviet-type Economics and their Transformation (Mansf.)

Courakis, A. S., BA(Econ) Manc., MA Oxf. CUF Lectr. (Bras.)

Cowan, S. G. B., MA Oxf., MPhil CUF Lectr. (Worc.)

Davis, C. M., BA Harv., MA Oxf., MSA George Washington, PhD Camb., DPhil Oxf. Lectr., Russian and East European Political Economy (Wolfs.)

Dimsdale, N. H., MA Oxf. CUF Lectr. (Qu.)

Fafchamps, M., PhD Calif. Reader (Mansf.)

Foreman-Peck, J. S., BA Essex, MSc(Econ) Lond., MA Oxf., PhD Lond. Lectr., Economic History (S.Ant.)

Glyn, A. J., MA Oxf. CUF Lectr. (Corp.)

Graham, A. W. M., MA Oxf. CUF Lectr. (Ball.)

Greenhalgh, Christine A., MSc Lond., MA Oxf., PhD Prin. Reader (S.Pet.)

Gregory, Mary B., MA Glas., MA Oxf., DPhil Oxf. CUF Lectr. (S.Hil.)

Hall, Bronwyn H., BA Wellesley, PhD Stan. Prof. (Nuff.)

Hay, D. A., MA Camb., MA Oxf., MPhil Oxf. CUF Lectr. (Jes.)

Hendry, D. F., MA Aberd., MA Oxf., MSc Lond., PhD Lond. Prof. (Nuff.)

Heyer, Judith U., MA Oxf., PhD Lond. CUF Lectr. (Som.)

Hoddinott, J. F. A., BA Tor., MA York(Can.), MA Oxf., DPhil CUF Lectr. (L.M.H.)

Jenkinson, T. J., AM Penn., MA Camb., MA Oxf., DPhil CUF Lectr. (Keb.)

Joshi, V. R., MA Oxf. Reader (Mert.)

Klemperer, P. D., MBA Stan., MA Camb., MA Oxf., PhD Stan. Edgeworth Prof. (Nuff.)

Leonard, Carol S., MA Oxf. Lectr., Regional Studies in Post-Communist States (S.Ant.)

Lin, C. Z., BSc M.I.T., MA Harv., MA Oxf., DPhil Oxf. Lectr., Economy of China (S.Ant.)

Malcolmson, J. M., BA Camb., MA Harv., PhD Harv. Prof. (All S.)

Maldoom, D. J. P., MA Oxf., DPhil Oxf. Lectr. (Univ.)

Mayhew, K., MSc(Econ) Lond., MA Oxf. Reader (Pemb.)

McDiarmid, C. J. H., BSc Edin., MA Oxf., MSc Oxf., DPhil Oxf. Prof., Operations Research (Corp.)

Myatt, D. P., BSc Lond., PhD Camb., DPhil Oxf. Lectr. (S.Cat.)

O'Shaughnessy, T. J., BSc Adel., BE Adel., MA Oxf., MPhil Camb., PhD Camb. CUF Lectr. (S.Ann.)

Offer, A., MA Oxf., DPhil Oxf. Reader, Recent Social and Economic History (Nuff.)

Oppenheimer, P. M., MA Oxf. CUF Lectr. (Ch.Ch.)

Quah, J. K. H., BSc Sing., MA Oxf., PhD Calif. CUF Lectr. (S.Hug.)

Shin, H. S., MA Oxf., MPhil Oxf., DPhil Oxf. Lectr., Public Economics (Nuff.)

Slater, M. D. E., MA Oxf., MPhil Oxf. CUF Lectr. (S.Edm.)

Stevens, Margaret J., MA MSc DPhil CUF Lectr. (Trin.)

Taylor, M. P., MSc Lond., MA Oxf., PhD Lond. CUF Lectr. (Univ.)

Thorp, T. Rosemary, MA Oxf. Reader, Economics of Latin America (S.Ant.)

Van Noorden, R. J., MA Oxf. CUF Lectr. (Hert.)

Vickers, J. S., MA Oxf., MPhil Oxf., DPhil Oxf. Drummond Prof., Political Economy (All S.)

Vines, D. A., BA Melb., MA Camb., MA Oxf., PhD Camb., DPhil Reader (Ball.)

Other Staff: 1 Temp. CUF Lectr.

Vacant Posts: 3 Lectrs.; 4 CUF Lectrs.

Economics and Statistics, Institute of,

see also Stats.

Tel: (01865) 271073 Fax: (01865) 271094

Banerjee, Anindya, BSc Lond., MA Oxf., MPhil Oxf., DPhil Oxf. Lectr., Economic Statistics and Econometrics (Wadh.)

Beggs, A. W., BA Camb., MA Oxf., DPhil Lectr. (Wadh.)

Bond, S. R., MA Camb., MA Oxf., DPhil Res. Officer (Nuff.)

Collier, P., MA Oxf., DPhil Oxf. Prof. (S.Ant.)

Knight, J. B., MA Camb., MA Oxf. Prof.; Dir.* (S.Edm.)

Lall, S., BPhil Oxf., MA Oxf. Lectr., Development Economics (Gre.)

Mabro, R. E., CBE, MSc(Econ) Lond., MA Oxf. Sr. Res. Officer, Economics of Middle East (S.Ant.)

Maldoom, D. J. P., MA Oxf., DPhil Oxf. (Univ.)

Roberts, K. W. S., BA Essex, MA Oxf., DPhil Oxf. Sir John Hicks Prof., Economics (Nuff.)

Robinson, D., MA Oxf. Sr. Res. Officer (Magd.)

Other Staff: 1 Lectr.; 2 Res. Officers

Educational Studies

Tel: (01865) 274024 Fax: (01865) 274027

Benton, P., MA Camb., MA Oxf. Lectr., English (S.Cross)

Childs, Ann C., BSc Birm., MA Oxf., PhD Birm. Lectr., Science Education (L.M.H.)

Corney, G. J., BA Durh., MA Oxf. Lectr., Geography (S.Ann.)

Davies, C. W. R., BA Camb., MA Oxf., MSc Oxf., DPhil Oxf. Lectr., English (Kell.)

Hacking, Elizabeth C., BA Liv. Tutor

Hagger, Hazel R., BA Leeds, MA Oxf. Lectr., Professional Education (S.Cross)

Hayward, G. F., MA Oxf., DPhil Lectr., Biology (Kell.)

Jaworski, Barbara, BSc Hull, BA Open(UK), MA Oxf., PhD Open(UK) Lectr., Mathematics (Worc.)

Lawson, C., BA Newcastle(UK), MSc Oxf. (Kell.)

McIntyre, D. I., MA Edin., MA Oxf., MEd Edin. Reader

Pendry, Anna E., BEd Camb., MA Lond., MA Oxf., DPhil Oxf. Lectr., History (S.Cross)

Phillips, D. G., BA Lond., MA Oxf., DPhil Oxf. Reader, German (S.Edm.)

Pirie, Susan E. B., PhD Nott., MA Lectr. (Linac.)

Pring, R. A., PhL Rome, BA Lond., MA Oxf., PhD Lond. Prof.; Dir.* (Gre.)

Sylva, K. D., BA Harv., MA Oxf., MA Harv., PhD Harv. Prof. (Jes.)

Walford, G., BSc Kent, BSc Open(UK), MA Oxf., MA Lond., MSc Open(UK), MPhil Oxf., PhD Kent Reader, Sociology (Gre.)

Watson, Anne, MA Oxf. Lectr., Mathematics (Linac.)

Williams, V., BA Wales, PhD Lond. Lectr. (S.Pet.)

Woolnough, B. E., BSc Reading, MA Oxf. Lectr., Physics (S.Cross)

Other Staff: 1 Temp. Lectr.; 4 Temp. Tutors†

Vacant Posts: 1 Lectr.; 3 Temp. Tutors; 2 Temp. Tutors†

Egyptology

Tel: (01865) 278200 Fax: (01865) 278190

Baines, J. R., MA Oxf., DPhil Oxf. Prof. (Qu.)

Smith, M. J., BA Chic., MA Oxf., PhD Chic. Reader, Egyptology and Coptic (Univ.)

Engineering Science

Tel: (01865) 273000 Fax: (01865) 273010

Ainsworth, R. W., MA Oxf., DPhil Oxf. Prof. (S.Cat.)

Allen, J. E., DEng Liv., MA Camb., MA Oxf., DSc, FIP, FIEE Reader

Bellhouse, B. J., MA Oxf., DPhil Oxf. Prof. (Magd.)

Blake, J. A., MA Camb., MA Oxf., PhD Edin. Prof., Information Engineering (Exet.)

Blakeborough, A., MA Oxf., PhD Camb., DPhil Oxf. Lectr. (Worc.)

Borthwick, A. G. L., BEng Liv., MA Oxf., PhD Liv. Reader (S.Edm.)

Brady, J. M., MA Manc., MA Oxf., PhD ANU, FEng BP Prof., Information Engineering (Keb.)

Buckley, C. P., MA Oxf., DPhil Oxf. Lectr. (Ball.)

Burd, H. J., MA Oxf., DPhil Oxf. Lectr. (Bras.)

Clarke, D. W., MA Oxf., DPhil Oxf., FRS, FEng Prof., Control Engineering; Head* (New)

Collins, S., BSc Warw., PhD Warw. Lectr. (Univ.)

Cui, Z., MA Oxf., MSc Dalian, PhD Dalian, BSc Lectr. (Keb.)

Daniel, R. W., BSc Brun., MA Oxf., MA Camb., PhD Camb. Lectr. (Bras.)

Dew-Hughes, D., BSc Birm., MA Camb., MA Oxf., DEng Yale, DSc Oxf. Prof. (Univ.)

Dexter, A. L., MA Oxf., DPhil Oxf. Reader (Worc.)

Dobson, P. J., BSc S'ton., PhD S'ton., MA Oxf. Prof. (Qu.)

Duncan, S. R., MA Camb., MSc Lond., PhD Lond. Lectr. (S.Hug.)

Dunne, F. P. E., BSc Brist., MA Oxf., PhD Sheff. Lectr. (Hert.)

Eatock Taylor, W. R., MS Stan., PhD Stan., MA Camb., MA Oxf. Prof., Mechanical Engineering (S.Hug.)

Edwards, D. J., MA Oxf., MSc Brist., PhD Brist. Prof. (Wadh.)

Efstathiou, H. Janet, MA Oxf., PhD Durh. Lectr. (Pemb.)

Elston, S. J., BSc Exe., MA Oxf., PhD Exe. Lectr. (S.Joh.)

Harding, J., MA Oxf., DPhil Oxf. Lectr. (Mansf.)

Hills, D. A., MA Oxf., PhD CNAA Prof. (Linc.)

Houlsby, G. T., MA Camb., MA Oxf., PhD Camb., DPhil Oxf. Prof., Civil Engineering (Bras.)

Jacobs, O. L. R., MA Camb., MA Oxf., PhD Camb., DPhil Oxf. Lectr. (S.Joh.)

Jones, T. V., MA Oxf., DPhil Oxf. Donald Schultz Prof., Turbomachinery (S.Cat.)

Kenning, D. B. R., MA Camb., MA Oxf., PhD Camb. Lectr. (Linc.)

Kouvaritakis, B., MA Oxf., MSc Manc., PhD Manc. Reader (S.Edm.)

Lord, R. G., MA Camb., MA Oxf., PhD Camb., DPhil Oxf. Lectr. (L.M.H.)

McCulloch, M. D., BSc Witw., MA Oxf., PhD Witw. Lectr. (Ch.Ch.)

McFadden, P. D., BE Melb., MA Oxf., PhD Melb. Reader (Jes.)

Milligan, G. W. E., MEng Glas., PhD Camb., MA Lectr. (Magd.)

Moore, W. R., BSc Brist., MA Oxf., PhD Camb., DPhil Oxf. Lectr. (Jes.)

Murray, D. W., MA Oxf., DPhil Oxf. Prof. (S.Ann.)

Noble, J. Alison, MA Oxf., DPhil Oxf. Lectr. (Oriel)

Nowell, D., BA Camb., MA Oxf., DPhil Oxf. Lectr. (Ch.Ch.)

O'Brien, D. C., MA Oxf., MA Camb., PhD Camb. Lectr. (Ball.)

O'Connor, J. J., BE N.U.I., MA Oxf., PhD Camb., DPhil Oxf. Prof. (S.Pet.)

Oldfield, M. L. G., BSc Syd., BE Syd., MA Oxf., DPhil Oxf. Reader (Keb.)

Parry, G., BSc Lond., PhD Lond., MA Prof., Electro-optic Engineering (S.Cross)

Probert, Penelope J., MA Camb., MA Oxf., PhD Camb., DPhil Oxf. Reader (L.M.H.)

Raynes, E. P., MA Camb., PhD Camb. Prof., Opto-electronic Engineering (S.Cross)

Renton, J. D., MA DPhil Lectr. (S.Cat.)

Ruiz, C., DrIng Madrid, MA Oxf. Prof., Materials Engineering (Exet.)

Sheard, S. J., BSc Lond., MA Oxf., PhD Lond. Lectr. (Trin.)

Sills, Gillian C., MA Lond., MA Oxf., PhD Lond. Lectr. (S.Cat.)

Smith, P. W., MSc S'ton., MA Oxf., PhD Lond. Lectr. (Pemb.)

Solymar, L., PhD Bud., MA Prof., Applied Electromagnetism (Hert.)

Stone, C. R., MA Camb., MA Oxf., DPhil Oxf. Lectr. (Som.)

Tarassenko, L., MA Oxf., DPhil Oxf. Prof., Electrical and Electronic Engineering (S.Joh.)

Taylor, P. H., MA Oxf., MA Camb., PhD Camb. Lectr. (Keb.)

Turnbull, S. R., BA Newcastle(UK), MA Oxf., PhD Newcastle(UK) Lectr. (S.Pet.)

Whalley, P. B., MA Camb., MA Oxf., PhD Camb. Reader (Ball.)

Williams, M. S., BSc Brist., MA Oxf., PhD Brist. Lectr. (New)

Wilson, T., MA Oxf., DPhil Oxf. Prof. (Hert.)

Witt, D. C., MA Oxf. Lectr. (Mert.)

Wood, C. J., MA Oxf., PhD Lond. Lectr. (Wadh.)

You, Z., BS Shanghai Jiaotong, MS Dalian, PhD Camb. Lectr. (Magd.)

Zavatsky, Amy B., BSc Penn., MA Oxf., DPhil Oxf. Lectr. (S.Edm.)

Vacant Posts: 1 Reader; 2 Lectrs.

English

Tel: (01865) 271055 Fax: (01865) 271054

Aitchison, Jean M., AM Harv., MA Camb., MA Oxf. Rupert Murdoch Prof., Language and Communication (Worc.)

Ballaster, Rosalind M., MA Oxf., DPhil Oxf. CUF Lectr. (Mansf.)

Barr, Helen, MA Oxf., MPhil Oxf., DPhil Oxf. CUF Lectr. (L.M.H.)

Birch, Dinah L., MA Oxf., DPhil Oxf. CUF Lectr. (Trin.)

Black, L. G., BA Cape Town, MA Oxf., DPhil Oxf. CUF Lectr. (Oriel)

Bradshaw, J. D., BA Newcastle(UK), MA Oxf., DPhil Oxf. CUF Lectr. (Worc.)

Brewer, Charlotte D., MA Oxf., DPhil Oxf. CUF Lectr. (Hert.)

Bruten, Avril G., BA Birm., MA Oxf., PhD Camb. CUF Lectr. (S.Hug.)

Bush, R. B., MA Oxf. Drue Heinz Prof., American Literature (S.Joh.)

Butler, I. C., MA Oxf. Prof. (Ch.Ch.)

Cannon, C. D., BA Oxf., MA Oxf., PhD Harv. CUF Lectr. (S.Edm.)

Carey, J., MA Oxf., DPhil Oxf. Merton Prof., English Literature (Mert.)

Coleman, J. S., BA York(UK), MA Oxf., DPhil York(UK) Reader, Phonetics (Wolfs.)

Conrad, P. J., BA Tas., MA Oxf., FRSL CUF Lectr. (Ch.Ch.)

Cooper, E. Helen, MA Camb., MA Oxf., PhD Camb. Prof. (Univ.)

Cunningham, V. D., MA Oxf., DPhil Oxf. Prof. (Corp.)

Duncan-Jones, Katherine D., BLitt Oxf., MA Oxf. Prof. (Som.)

Eagleton, T. F., MA Oxf., PhD Camb. Thomas Warton Prof., English Literature (S.Cat.)

Eltis, Sarah A., MA Oxf., MPhil Oxf., DPhil Oxf. CUF Lectr. (Bras.)

Everett, Barbara M., MA Oxf. CUF Lectr. (Som.)

Fenton, J. M., MA Oxf. Prof., Poetry (Magd.)

Flint, Kate, MA Lond., MA Oxf., DPhil Oxf. Reader, Victorian and Modern English Literature (Linac.)

Fuller, J. L., BLitt Oxf., MA Oxf. CUF Lectr. (Magd.)

Gearin-Tosh, M. B., MA Oxf. CUF Lectr. (S.Cat.)

Gerrard, Christine H., MA Oxf., DPhil Oxf. CUF Lectr. (L.M.H.)

Gill, S. C., BPhil Oxf., MA Oxf., PhD Edin. Prof., English Literature (Linc.)

Gillespie, V. A., MA Oxf., DPhil Oxf. Reader (S.Ann.)

Godden, M. R., MA Camb., MA Oxf., PhD Camb., DPhil Oxf. Rawlinson and Bosworth Prof., Anglo-Saxon (Pemb.)

Hamer, R. F. S., MA Oxf. CUF Lectr. (Ch.Ch.)

Hanna, R., AB Amherst, MA Oxf., PhD Yale Lectr., Palaeography (Keb.)

Hoad, T. F., MA Oxf. CUF Lectr. (S.Pet.)

Hudson, Anne M., MA Oxf., DPhil Oxf., FBA Prof., Medieval English (L.M.H.)

Jacobs, J. N., MA Oxf. CUF Lectr. (Jes.)

Johnson, Jeri L., BA Brigham Young, MA Oxf., MPhil Oxf. CUF Lectr. (Exet.)

Kelly, J. S., MA Trinity(Dub.), MA Oxf., PhD Camb., DPhil Oxf. Prof. (S.Joh.)

Keymer, T. E., BA *Camb.*, MA *Oxf.*, MA *Camb.*, PhD *Camb.* CUF Lectr. (S.Ann.)

Lee, Hermione, MA *Oxf.*, MPhil *Oxf.* Goldsmiths' Prof., English Literature (New)

Lonsdale, R. H., MA *Oxf.*, DPhil *Oxf.*, FRSL Prof., English Literature (Ball.)

Mapstone, Sally, MA *Oxf.*, DPhil *Oxf.* CUF Lectr. (S.Hil.)

McCabe, R. A., BA *Trinity(Dub.)*, MA *Oxf.*, MA *Camb.*, PhD *Camb.* Reader (Mert.)

McCullough, P. E., BA *Calif.*, MA *Oxf.*, PhD *Prin.* CUF Lectr. (Linc.)

McDonald, P. D., BA *Rhodes*, MA *Rhodes*, MA *Oxf.*, DPhil *Oxf.* CUF Lectr. (S.Hug.)

Moore, Helen D., MA *Oxf.*, DPhil *Oxf.* CUF Lectr. (Corp.)

Mugglestone, Lynda C., MA *Oxf.*, DPhil *Oxf.* CUF Lectr. (Pemb.)

Newlyn, Lucy A., MA *Oxf.*, DPhil *Oxf.* CUF Lectr. (S.Edm.)

Norbrook, D. G. E., MA *Oxf.*, DPhil *Oxf.* CUF Lectr. (Magd.)

Nuttall, A. D., BLitt *Oxf.*, MA *Oxf.* Prof., English Literature (New)

O'Donoghue, Heather, MA *Oxf.*, MPhil *Oxf.*, DPhil *Oxf.* Vigfusson-Rausing Reader, Ancient Icelandic Literature and Antiquities (Linac.)

O'Donoghue, J. B., BPhil *Oxf.*, MA *Oxf.* CUF Lectr. (Wadh.)

Pasternak-Slater, Ann, MA *Oxf.*, DPhil *Oxf.* CUF Lectr. (S.Ann.)

Paulin, T., MA *Oxf.* All Souls (G. M. Young) Lectr., 19th and 20th Century English Literature (Hert.)

Pitcher, J. C. G., MA *Oxf.*, DPhil *Oxf.* CUF Lectr. (S.Joh.)

Raine, C., BPhil *Oxf.*, MA *Oxf.* CUF Lectr. (New)

Reynolds, M. O. R., MA *Oxf.* CUF Lectr. (S.Ann.)

Rivers, Isabel, BA *Camb.*, BSc *Col.*, MA *Oxf.*, PhD *Col.* Reader (S.Hug.)

Robbins, R. H., MA *Oxf.*, DPhil *Oxf.* Lectr., English Literature (Wadh.)

Romaine, Suzanne, AB *Bryn Mawr*, MA *Oxf.*, MLitt *Edin.*, PhD *Birm.* Merton Prof., English Language (Mert.)

Schmidt, A. V. C., MA *Oxf.* CUF Lectr. (Ball.)

Shrimpton, N. G., MA *Oxf.*, DPhil *Oxf.* CUF Lectr. (L.M.H.)

Sloan, J., MA *Oxf.* CUF Lectr. (Harris)

Small, Helen W., MA *Oxf.*, DPhil CUF Lectr. (Pemb.)

Smith, Emma J., MA *Oxf.*, DPhil *Oxf.* CUF Lectr. (Hert.)

Smith, N. S., MA *Hull*, MA *McG.*, MA *Oxf.*, DPhil *Oxf.* Reader (Keb.)

Spencer, Helen L., BA *Newcastle(UK)*, MA *Oxf.*, DPhil *Oxf.* CUF Lectr. (Exet.)

Stafford, Fiona J., BA *Leic.*, MA *Oxf.*, MPhil *Oxf.*, DPhil *Oxf.* CUF Lectr. (Som.)

Stallworthy, J. H., BLitt *Oxf.*, MA *Oxf.* Prof., English Literature (Wolfs.)

Strohm, P. H., MA *Oxf.* J. R. R. Tolkien Prof., English Literature and Language (S.Ann.)

Sutherland, Kathryn, BA *Lond.*, MA *Oxf.*, DPhil Reader, Bibliography and Textual Criticism (S.Ann.)

Turner, M. L., BLitt *Oxf.*, MA *Oxf.*, MLitt *Oxf.* Lectr., History of Printing (Keb.)

Warner, F. R. Le P., MA *Camb.*, MA *Oxf.* CUF Lectr. (S.Pet.)

White, H. R. B., MA *Oxf.*, DPhil CUF Lectr. (S.Cat.)

Wilson, E. P., BA *Hull*, BLitt *Oxf.*, MA *Oxf.* CUF Lectr. (Worc.)

Womersley, D. J., MA *Camb.*, MA *Oxf.*, PhD *Camb.*, DPhil *Oxf.* CUF Lectr. (Jes.)

Wordsworth, J. F., MA *Oxf.* Prof., English Literature (S.Cat.)

Young, R. J. C., MA *Oxf.*, DPhil *Oxf.* Reader (Wadh.)

Vacant Posts: 1 Reader; 2 CUF Lectrs.

Entomology, see Zool.

Ethics, see Theol.

Fine Art, see Art, and Hist. Mod.

Forestry, see Plant Scis.

French

Tel: (01865) 270750 Fax: (01865) 270757

Bowie, M. M., MA *Oxf.*, DPhil *Sus.*, FBA Marshal Foch Prof., French Literature (All S.)

Cave, T. C., MA *Camb.*, MA *Oxf.*, PhD *Camb.*, DPhil *Oxf.* Prof., French Literature (S.Joh.)

Clark, Carol E., BA *Lond.*, MA *Oxf.*, PhD *Lond.* CUF Lectr. (Ball.)

Cooper, R. A., MA *Oxf.*, DPhil *Oxf.* Prof. (Bras.)

Cronk, N. E., MA *Oxf.*, DPhil *Oxf.* Fac. Lectr. (S.Edm.)

Davis, C. J., MA *Oxf.*, DPhil *Oxf.* Reader (L.M.H.)

Farrant, T. J., MA *Oxf.*, DPhil *Oxf.* CUF Lectr. (Pemb.)

Finch, Alison M., MA *Oxf.*, MA *Camb.*, DPhil *Oxf.*, PhD *Camb.* Reader (Mert.)

Garfitt, J. S. T., MA *Oxf.*, DPhil *Oxf.* CUF Lectr. (Magd.)

Goodden, Angelica R., MA *Oxf.* CUF Lectr. (S.Hil.)

Hawcroft, M. N., MA *Oxf.*, DPhil *Oxf.* CUF Lectr. (Keb.)

Hiddleston, J. A., MA *Edin.*, MA *Oxf.*, PhD *Edin.* Prof. (Exet.)

Holland, M. B., MA *Oxf.*, DPhil *Oxf.* CUF Lectr. (S.Hug.)

Howells, Christina M., BA *Lond.*, MA *Oxf.*, PhD *Lond.* Reader (Wadh.)

Hunt, A. B., BLitt *Oxf.*, MA *Oxf.*, DLitt *St And.* Fac. Lectr. (S.Pet.)

Jefferson, Ann M., MA *Oxf.*, DPhil *Oxf.* CUF Lectr. (New)

Mallinson, G. J., MA *Camb.*, MA *Oxf.*, PhD *Camb.* CUF Lectr. (Trin.)

Maskell, D. W., MA *Oxf.*, DPhil *Oxf.* CUF Lectr. (Oriel)

McGuinness, P., BA *Camb.*, MA *York(UK)*, MA *Oxf.*, DPhil *Oxf.* CUF Lectr. (S.Ann.)

Nye, E. M. J., MA *Oxf.*, DPhil *Oxf.* CUF Lectr. (Linc.)

Parish, R. J., BA *Newcastle(UK)*, MA *Oxf.*, DPhil *Oxf.* Prof. (S.Cat.)

Pearson, R. A. G., MA *Oxf.*, DPhil *Oxf.* Prof. (Qu.)

Pensom, R. M., MA *Oxf.*, MA *Manc.*, PhD *Exe.* Lectr., French Philology and Old French Literature (Hert.)

Pilkington, A. E., MA *Oxf.*, DPhil *Oxf.* CUF Lectr. (Jes.)

Robinson, C. F., MA *Oxf.* Prof. (Ch.Ch.)

Rutson, Elizabeth M., BLitt *Oxf.*, MA *Oxf.* CUF Lectr. (S.Ann.)

Smith, J. C., MA *Oxf.* Fac. Lectr., French Linguistics (S.Cat.)

Taylor, Jane H. M., MA *Oxf.*, DPhil *Oxf.* CUF Lectr. (S.Hil.)

Tooke, Adrianne J., BA *Lond.*, MA *Oxf.*, PhD *Camb.* CUF Lectr. (Som.)

Viala, A. B. J., MA *Oxf.* Prof. (Wadh.)

Watson, I. M. C., MA *Camb.*, MA *Oxf.* Lectr., French Language and Linguistics (Ch.Ch.)

Other Staff: 1 Instr.

Vacant Posts: 1 Prof.; 1 CUF Lectr.; 1 Lectr.†

Geography

Tel: (01865) 271919 Fax: (01865) 271929

Briden, J. C., MA *Oxf.*, PhD *ANU*, DSc *ANU* Prof.; Dir., Environmental Change Unit (Linac.)

Bull, P. A., MA *Oxf.*, MSc *Wales*, PhD *Wales* Lectr. (Hert.)

Clark, G. L., BEc *Monash*, MA *Monash*, MA *Oxf.*, PhD *McM.* Halford Mackinder Prof. (S.Pet.)

Clarke, C. G., MA *Oxf.*, DPhil *Oxf.* Prof., Urban/Social Geography; Head* (Jes.)

Collins, D. N., MA *Camb.*, MA *Oxf.*, PhD *Nott.* Lectr. (Keb.)

Daley, Patricia O., BA *CNAA*, MA *Lond.*, MA *Oxf.*, DPhil *Oxf.* Lectr., Human Geography (Jes.)

Goudie, A. S., MA *Camb.*, MA *Oxf.*, PhD *Camb.* Prof. (Hert.)

Kennedy, Barbara A., MA *Br.Col.*, MA *Camb.*, MA *Oxf.*, PhD *Camb.* CUF Lectr. (S.Hug.)

Langton, J., MA *Wales*, MA *Oxf.*, PhD *Camb.* Lectr., Human Geography (S.Joh.)

Lemon, A., MA *Oxf.*, DPhil CUF Lectr. (Mansf.)

MacMillan, W. D., BSc *Brist.*, MA *Oxf.*, PhD *Brist.* Reader, Human Geography (Hert.)

Pallot, Judith, BA *Leeds*, MA *Oxf.*, PhD *Lond.* Lectr., Geography of USSR (Ch.Ch.)

Peach, G. C. K., MA *Oxf.*, DPhil *Oxf.* Prof., Social Geography (S.Cat.)

Preston, J. M., BA *Nott.*, MA *Oxf.*, PhD *Leeds* Reader, Transport Studies; Dir., Transport Studies Unit (S.Ann.)

Scargill, D. I., MA *Oxf.*, DPhil *Oxf.* Lectr. (S.Edm.)

Stokes, S., MA *Oxf.*, MPhil *Oxf.* Lectr. (S.Cat.)

Swyngedouw, E. A. M., MA *Leuven*, MA *Oxf.*, PhD *Johns H.* Reader, Human Geography (S.Pet.)

Viles, Heather A., MA *Oxf.*, DPhil *Oxf.* Lectr., Physical Geography (Worc.)

Whittaker, R. J., BSc *Hull*, MSc *Wales*, MA *Oxf.*, PhD *Wales* Lectr. (S.Edm.)

Williams, M., BA *Wales*, MA *Oxf.*, PhD *Wales* Prof. (Oriel)

Willis, Katherine J., BSc *S'ton.*, PhD *Camb.* Lectr., Middle Eastern Geography (S.Hug.)

Geology, see Earth Scis.

German

Tel: (01865) 270750 Fax: (01865) 270757

Brown, Hilda M., BA *W.Aust.*, BLitt *Oxf.*, MA *Oxf.* Reader (S.Hil.)

Constantine, D. J., MA *Oxf.*, DPhil *Oxf.* CUF Lectr. (Qu.)

Currie, Pamela, MA *Oxf.* CUF Lectr. (L.M.H.)

Hilliard, K. F., MA *Oxf.*, DPhil *Oxf.* Lectr. (S.Pet.)

Kohl, Katrin M., MA *Lond.*, MA *Oxf.*, PhD *Lond.* Fac. Lectr. (Jes.)

Kuhn, T. M., MA *Oxf.*, DPhil *Oxf.* Fac. Lectr. (S.Hug.)

Lamport, F. J., MA *Oxf.* Fac. Lectr. (Worc.)

Leeder, Karen J., MA *Oxf.*, DPhil *Oxf.* Fac. Lectr. (New)

Martin, Victoria C., BA *Exe.*, MA *Oxf.*, MPhil *Camb.* Lectr., German Language and Linguistics (S.Ann.)

Ockenden, R. C., MA *Oxf.*, DPhil *Oxf.* Lectr. (Wadh.)

Palmer, N. F., MA *Oxf.*, DPhil *Oxf.* Prof., German Medieval and Linguistic Studies (S.Edm.)

Phelan, A., BA *Camb.*, PhD *Camb.* Fac. Lectr. (Keb.)

Reed, T. J., MA *Oxf.*, FBA Taylor Prof., German Language and Literature (Qu.)

Robertson, R. N. N., MA *Edin.*, MA *Oxf.*, DPhil *Oxf.* Reader (S.Joh.)

Sheppard, R. W., BA *Camb.*, MA *Oxf.*, PhD *E.Anglia* Prof. (Magd.)

Suerbaum, Almut M. V., MA *Oxf.* CUF Lectr. (Som.)

Volfing, Annette M., MA *Oxf.*, DPhil *Oxf.* Lectr., Medieval German (Oriel)

Watanabe-O'Kelly, Helen, MA *N.U.I.*, DPhil *Basle*, MA *Oxf.*, DPhil *Oxf.* Fac. Lectr., German Literature (Exet.)

Wells, C. J., MA *Oxf.* Lectr., Germanic Philology and Medieval German Literature (S.Edm.)

Other Staff: 1 Instr.

Vacant Posts: 1 CUF Lectr.

Greek Language and Literature, Byzantine and Modern, see also Classical Langs. and Lit.

Tel: (01865) 270750 Fax: (01865) 270757

Jeffreys, Elizabeth M., BLitt *Oxf.*, MA *Oxf.*, MA *Camb.* Bywater and Sotheby Prof. (Exet.)

MacKridge, P. A., MA Oxf., DPhil Oxf.   Prof.,
  Modern Greek (S.Cross)
Other Staff: 1 Instr.

Hebrew and Jewish Studies, see also
  Special Centres, etc

Tel: (01865) 377946 Fax: (01865) 375079

Goodman, M. D., MA Oxf., DPhil Oxf.   Prof.,
  Jewish Studies (Wolfs.)
Williamson, H. G. M., MA Camb., PhD Camb.,
  DD Camb., DD Oxf.   Regius Prof., Hebrew
  (Ch.Ch.)

History, Ancient

Tel: (01865) 270545 Fax: (01865) 270548

Bennet, J., MA Camb., PhD Camb.   Sinclair and
  Rachel Hood Lectr., Aegean Prehistory
  (Keb.)
Bowman, A. K., MA Tor., MA Oxf., PhD
  Tor.   CUF Lectr. (Ch.Ch.)
Braun, T. F. R. G., MA Oxf.   CUF Lectr.
  (Mert.)
Derow, P. S., BA Amherst, MA Oxf., PhD
  Prin.   CUF Lectr. (Wadh.)
Griffin, Miriam T., MA Oxf., DPhil Oxf.   CUF
  Lectr. (Som.)
Lane Fox, R. J., MA Oxf.   Reader (New)
Lintott, A. W., MA Oxf., PhD Lond., DLitt
  Oxf.   Reader (Worc.)
Millar, F. G. B., MA Oxf., DPhil Oxf., DLitt Oxf.,
  FBA   Camden Prof. (Bras.)
Murray, O., MA Oxf., DPhil Oxf.   CUF Lectr.
  (Ball.)
Osborne, R. G., MA Camb., MA Oxf., PhD
  Camb., DPhil Oxf.   Prof. (Corp.)
Parker, R. C. T., MA Oxf., DPhil
  Oxf.   Wykeham Prof. (New)
Price, S. R. F., MA Camb., MA Oxf., PhD Camb.,
  DPhil Oxf.   CUF Lectr. (L.M.H.)
Purcell, N., MA Oxf.   CUF Lectr. (S.Joh.)
Vacant Posts: 1 Lectr.; 2 CUF Lectrs.

History, Modern, see also Econ., Japanese,
  and Pol.

Tel: (01865) 277256 Fax: (01865) 250704

Andreyev, Constance C. L., MA Camb., MA Oxf.,
  PhD Camb., DPhil Oxf.   CUF Lectr. (Ch.Ch.)
Archer, I. W., MA Oxf., DPhil Oxf.   CUF Lectr.
  (Keb.)
Barnard, T. C., MA Oxf., DPhil Oxf.   CUF
  Lectr. (Hert.)
Beddard, R. A., BA Lond., MA Camb., MA Oxf.,
  DPhil Oxf., FRHistS   CUF Lectr. (Oriel)
Blair, W. J., MA Oxf., DPhil   CUF Lectr. (Qu.)
Brigden, Susan E., BA Manc., MA Oxf.   Reader
  (Linc.)
Briggs, R., MA Oxf., FRHistS   Sp. Lectr. (All
  S.)
Brinkley, A., MA Oxf.   Harmsworth Visiting
  Prof. (Qu.)(1998-99)
Brockliss, L. W. B., MA Camb., MA Oxf., PhD
  Camb., DPhil Oxf.   Reader (Magd.)
Brown, Judith M., MA Camb., MA Oxf., PhD
  Camb., DPhil Oxf., FRHistS   Beit Prof.,
  History of British Commonwealth (Ball.)
Burrow, J. W., MA Oxf., MA Camb., DPhil Oxf.,
  PhD Camb., FBA, FRHistS   Prof., European
  Thought (Ball.)
Campbell, J., MA Oxf., FBA   Prof., Medieval
  History (Worc.)
Carey, P. B. R., MA Oxf., DPhil Oxf.   CUF
  Lectr. (Trin.)
Catto, R. J. A. I., MA Oxf., DPhil Oxf.   CUF
  Lectr. (Oriel)
Charles-Edwards, T. M. O., MA DPhil,
  FRHistS   CUF Lectr.
Christiansen, E., MA Oxf.   CUF Lectr. (New)
Connors, J., AB Boston, BA Camb., PhD
  Harv.   Slade Prof., Fine Art (1998-99)
Conway, M. H., BA Oxf., MA Oxf., DPhil
  Oxf.   CUF Lectr. (Ball.)
Dabhoiwala, F. N., BA York(UK), MA Oxf., DPhil
  Oxf.   CUF Lectr. (Exet.)
Darwin, J. G., MA Oxf., DPhil Oxf.   Beit Lectr.,
  History of British Commonwealth (Nuff.)

Davidson, N. S., MA Camb.   Lectr., History of
  the European Renaissance and Reformation
  (S.Edm.)
Davies, C. S. L., MA Oxf.   CUF Lectr. (Wadh.)
Davies, R. R. R., CBE, BA Lond., MA Oxf., DPhil
  Oxf., FBA, FRHistS   Chichele Prof., Medieval
  History (All S.)
Davis, J. H., MA Oxf., DPhil Oxf.   CUF Lectr.
  (Qu.)
Dunbabin, Jean H., MA Oxf., DPhil
  Oxf.   Reader (S.Ann.)
Ellis, G. J., MA Oxf., DPhil Oxf.   CUF Lectr.
  (Hert.)
Evans, R. J. W., MA Camb., MA Oxf., PhD
  Camb., DPhil Oxf., FBA   Regius Prof. (Oriel)
Feinstein, C. H., MA Oxf., PhD Camb.,
  FBA   Chichele Prof., Economic History (All
  S.)
Ferguson, N. C., MA Oxf., DPhil Oxf.   CUF
  Lectr. (Jes.)
Foster, R. F., MA Trinity(Dub.), MA Oxf., PhD
  Trinity(Dub.), DPhil Oxf., FRHistS,
  FBA   Carroll Prof., Irish History (Hert.)
Fox, R., MA Oxf., DPhil Oxf.   Prof., History of
  Science (Linac.)
Garnett, E. Jane, MA Oxf., DPhil Oxf.   CUF
  Lectr. (Wadh.)
Garnett, G. S., MA Camb., MA Oxf., PhD
  Camb.   CUF Lectr. (S.Hug.)
Ghosh, P. R., MA Oxf.   CUF Lectr. (S.Ann.)
Gildea, R. N., MA Oxf., DPhil Oxf.   Reader
  (Mert.)
Goldman, L. N., MA Camb., MA Oxf.   CUF
  Lectr. (S.Pet.)
Green, E. H. H., BA Lond., MA Oxf., PhD
  Camb.   CUF Lectr. (Magd.)
Gregory, A. M., MA Camb., PhD Camb.   CUF
  Lectr. (Pemb.)
Gunn, S. J., MA Oxf., DPhil Oxf.   CUF Lectr.
  (Mert.)
Haigh, C. A., MA Camb., MA Oxf., PhD Manc.,
  FRHistS   CUF Lectr. (Ch.Ch.)
Hamerow, Helena F., BA Wis., MA Oxf., DPhil
  Oxf.   Lectr., European Archaeology (S.Cross)
Harris, José F., MA Camb., MA Oxf., PhD Camb.,
  FBA   Prof. (S.Cat.)
Harris, Ruth, MA Penn., MA Oxf., DPhil
  Oxf.   CUF Lectr. (New)
Heal, Felicity M., MA Camb., MA Oxf., PhD
  Camb., DPhil Oxf.   CUF Lectr. (Jes.)
Holmes, C. A., MA Camb., MA Oxf., PhD Camb.,
  DPhil Oxf.   CUF Lectr. (L.M.H.)
Howard-Johnston, J. D., MA Oxf., DPhil
  Oxf.   Lectr., Byzantine Studies (Corp.)
Howarth, Janet H., MA Oxf., FRHistS   CUF
  Lectr. (S.Hil.)
Howe, D. W., AB Harv., MA Rhodes, MA Oxf.,
  PhD Calif.   Rhodes Prof., American History
  (S.Cat.)
Hufton-Murphy, Olwen, BA Lond., PhD
  Lond.   Prof. (Mert.)
Humphries, Katherine J., BA Camb., MA Cornell,
  PhD Cornell   Reader, Economic History (All
  S.)
Ingram, M. J., MA Oxf., DPhil Oxf.   CUF Lectr.
  (Bras.)
Innes, Joanna M., MA Camb., MA Oxf.   CUF
  Lectr. (Som.)
Keen, M. H., MA Oxf., DPhil Oxf., FRHistS,
  FSA, FBA   CUF Lectr. (Ball.)
Kemp, M. J., MA Oxf., MA Camb., FBA   Prof.,
  History of Art; Head, Hist. of Art and Centre
  for Visual Studies (Trin.)
Knight, A., MA Oxf., DPhil Oxf.   Prof., History
  of Latin America (S.Ant.)
Landers, J. M., MA Oxf., PhD Camb.   Lectr.,
  Historical Demography (All S.)
Langford, P., MA Oxf., DPhil Oxf.   Prof. (Linc.)
Lannon, Frances, MA Oxf., DPhil Oxf.   CUF
  Lectr. (L.M.H.)
Lewis, R. Gillian, MA Oxf., DPhil Oxf.   CUF
  Lectr. (S.Ann.)
MacLeod, D. J., BA Lond., MA Camb., MA Oxf.,
  PhD Camb.   Lectr., American History (S.Cat.)
Maddicott, J. R. L., MA Oxf., DPhil Oxf.   CUF
  Lectr. (Exet.)

Mango, Marlia C. M., BA Newton., MA Oxf., MA
  Lond., DPhil Oxf.   Lectr., Byzantine Studies
  (S.Joh.)
Matthew, H. C. G., MA Oxf., DPhil Oxf.,
  FBA   Prof. (S.Hug.)
McKibbin, R. I., MA Syd., MA Oxf., DPhil
  Oxf.   CUF Lectr. (S.Joh.)
Misra, Anna-Maria S., MA Oxf., DPhil   CUF
  Lectr. (Keb.)
Mitchell, L. G., MA Oxf., DPhil Oxf.   CUF
  Lectr. (Univ.)
Murray, A., BPhil Oxf., MA Oxf.   CUF Lectr.
  (Univ.)
Nicholls, A. J., BPhil Oxf., MA Oxf.   Sp. Lectr.
  (S.Ant.)
Nightingale, J. B. W., MA Oxf., DPhil   CUF
  Lectr. (Magd.)
O'Neill, R. J., AO, BEngSc Melb., MA Oxf.,
  DPhil Oxf., FASSA   Chichele Prof., History
  of War (All S.)
Parrott, D. A., MA Oxf., DPhil Oxf.   CUF Lectr.
  (New)
Phimister, I. R., MA Oxf.   Lectr.,
  Commonwealth History (S.Cross)
Pogge Von Strandmann, H. J. O., MA Oxf.,
  DPhil Oxf.   Prof. (Univ.)
Pollmann, Judith S., MA Amst., MA Lond., MA
  Oxf.   CUF Lectr. (Som.)
Powis, J. K., MA Oxf., DPhil Oxf.   CUF Lectr.
  (Ball.)
Priestland, D. R., MA Oxf., DPhil   CUF Lectr.
  (S.Edm.)
Rauchway, E. A., MA Oxf.   Lectr., History of
  the USA since 1875 (Mansf.)
Raven, J. R., MA Oxf., DPhil Oxf.   CUF Lectr.
  (Mansf.)
Robertson, J. C., MA Oxf., DPhil Oxf.   CUF
  Lectr. (S.Hug.)
Rogan, E. L., BA Col., MA Harv., MA Oxf., PhD
  Harv.   Lectr., Modern History of the Middle
  East (S.Ant.)
Rosser, A. G., MA Lond., MA Oxf., PhD
  Lond.   CUF Lectr. (S.Cat.)
Rowett, J. S., MA Oxf., DPhil Oxf.   CUF Lectr.
  (Bras.)
Rubin, Miri, MA Jerusalem, MA Oxf., PhD Camb.,
  DPhil   Reader (Pemb.)
Service, R. J., BA Camb., MA Camb., MA Essex,
  PhD Essex   Lectr., Modern Russian History
  (S.Ant.)
Sharpe, R., MA Camb., MA Oxf., PhD
  Camb.   Prof., Diplomatic (Wadh.)
Skinner, S. A., MA Oxf., MPhil Oxf., DPhil
  Oxf.   CUF Lectr. (Ball.)
Stevenson, J., MA Oxf., DPhil Oxf.   Reader
  (Worc.)
Thomas, W. E. S., MA Oxf., FRHistS   CUF
  Lectr. (Ch.Ch.)
Thompson, B. J., MA Oxf., DPhil Oxf.   CUF
  Lectr. (Som.)
Thompson, P. J., MA Oxf.   Sydney L. Mayer
  Lectr., American History (S.Cross)
Tomlin, R. S. O., MA Oxf., DPhil Oxf.,
  FSA   Lectr., Late Roman History (Wolfs.)
Vale, M. G. A., MA Oxf., DPhil Oxf.,
  FRHistS   CUF Lectr. (S.Joh.)
Waller, P. J., MA Oxf.   CUF Lectr. (Mert.)
Ward-Perkins, B. R., MA Oxf.   CUF Lectr.
  (Trin.)
Washbrook, D. A., MA Camb., MA Oxf., PhD
  Camb., DPhil Oxf.   Reader, Modern South
  Asian History (S.Ant.)
Watts, J. L., MA Oxf.   CUF Lectr. (Corp.)
Whittow, M., MA Oxf.   CUF Lectr. (S.Pet.)
Wormald, C. P., MA Oxf., FRHistS, FSA   CUF
  Lectr. (Ch.Ch.)
Wormald, Jenny M., MA Glas., MA Oxf., PhD
  Glas., FRHistS   CUF Lectr. (S.Hil.)
Vacant Posts: 1 Prof.; 1 Reader; 2 Lectrs.; 3
  CUF Lectrs.

Icelandic, Ancient, see Engl.

Islamic Studies, see Arabic, and Special Centres, etc

Italian

Tel: (01865) 270750 Fax: (01865) 270757
Hainsworth, P. R. J., MA Oxf. Prof. (L.M.H.)
McLaughlin, M. L., MA Glas., MA Oxf., PhD Glas., DPhil Oxf. Lectr. (Ch.Ch.)
Stellardi, G. A., MA Oxf. Fac. Lectr. (S.Hug.)
Woodhouse, J. R., MA Oxf., PhDWales, DLitt Oxf. Fiat-Serena Prof., Italian Studies (Magd.)
Zancani, O., MA Oxf. Lectr. (Ball.)
Other Staff: 1 Lector; 1 Instr.
Vacant Posts: 1 Lectr.

Japanese

Tel: (01865) 274570 Fax: (01865) 274574
Corbett, Jennifer M., BA ANU, MA Oxf. Nissan Lectr., Economics and Social Development of Modern Japan (S.Ant.)
Goodman, R. J., BA Durh., MA Oxf., DPhil Oxf. Lectr., Social Anthropology of Japan (S.Ant.)
Harries, P. T., MA Oxf., DPhil Oxf. Lectr. (Qu.)
McMullen, I. J., MA Camb., MA Oxf., PhD Camb., DPhil Oxf. Lectr. (S.Ant.)
Powell, B. W. F., MA Oxf., DPhil Oxf. Lectr. (Keb.)
Rebick, M. E., AB Harv., MA Tor., PhD Harv. Lectr., Economy of Japan (S.Ant.)
Stockwin, J. A. A., MA Oxf., PhD ANU Nissan Prof., Modern Japanese Studies (S.Ant.)
Waswo, Ann, MA Stan., MA Oxf., PhD Stan. Nissan Lectr., Modern Japanese History (S.Ant.)
Other Staff: 3 Instrs.
Vacant Posts: 1 Lectr.

Jewish Studies, see Hebrew and Jewish Studies

Law

Tel: (01865) 271490 Fax: (01865) 271560
Ashworth, A. J., BCL Oxf., LLB Lond., DCL Oxf., PhD Manc., FBA Vinerian Prof., English Law (All S.)
Bagshaw, R. M., BCL Oxf., MA Oxf. CUF Lectr. (Mansf.)
Birks, P. B. H., LLM Lond., MA Oxf., LLD Edin., DCL Oxf., FBA Regius Prof., Civil Law (All S.)
Briggs, A., BCL Oxf., MA Oxf. CUF Lectr. (S.Edm.)
Bright, Susan, BCL Oxf., MA Oxf. CUF Lectr. (S.Hil.)
Brownlie, I., CBE, QC, MA Oxf., DPhil Oxf., DCL Oxf., FBA Chichele Prof., Public International Law (All S.)
Cartwright, J., BCL Oxf., MA Oxf. CUF Lectr. (Ch.Ch.)
Chen-Wishart, Mindy, BA Otago, LLB Otago, MA Oxf., LLM Otago CUF Lectr. (Mert.)
Clarke, P. J., BCL Oxf., MA Oxf. CUF Lectr. (Jes.)
Craig, P. P., BCL Oxf., MA Oxf. Prof. (S.Joh.)
Critchley, Patricia R., MA Oxf. CUF Lectr. (Hert.)
Dannemann, G., MA Oxf., DrJur Freib. Erich Brost Lectr., German Civil and Commercial Law (Worc.)
Davies, J. W., LLB Birm., BCL Oxf., MA Oxf. CUF Lectr. (Bras.)
de Búrca, Gráinne, BCL Trinity(Dub.), LLM Mich., MA Oxf. CUF Lectr. (Som.)
de Moor, Anne, MA Oxf. CUF Lectr. (Som.)
Eekelaar, J. M., LLB Lond., BCL Oxf., MA Oxf. Reader (Pemb.)
Finnis, J. M., LLB Adel., MA Oxf., DPhil Oxf. Prof., Law and Legal Philosophy (Univ.)
Fredman, Sandra D., BCL Oxf., MA Oxf. Reader (Exet.)
Freedland, M. R., LLB Lond., MA Oxf., DPhil Oxf. Prof. (S.Joh.)

Galligan, D. J., LLB Qld., BCL Oxf., MA Oxf. Prof., Socio-Legal Studies (Wolfs.)
Gardner, S., BCL Oxf., MA Oxf. CUF Lectr. (Linc.)
Getzler, J. S., BA ANU, LLB ANU, MA Oxf. CUF Lectr. (S.Hug.)
Goldstein, S., BA Penn., JD Penn. Heather Grierson Visiting Prof., European Comparative Law (Kell.)(1998-99)
Hackney, J., BCL Oxf., MA Oxf. CUF Lectr. (Wadh.)
Harris, J. W., BCL Oxf., MA Oxf., PhD Lond. Prof. (Keb.)
Hayward, P. A., MA Camb., MA Oxf. CUF Lectr. (S.Pet.)
Hood, R. G., CBE, BSc Lond., MA Camb., MA Oxf., PhD Camb., DPhil Oxf., FBA Prof., Criminology; Dir., Centre for Criminol. Res. and Probation (All S.)
Horder, J. C. N., LLB Hull, BCL Oxf., MA Oxf., DPhil Oxf. CUF Lectr. (Worc.)
Ibbetson, D. J., MA Camb., MA Oxf., DPhil Oxf. CUF Lectr. (Magd.)
Kaye, J. M., BCL Oxf., MA Oxf. CUF Lectr. (Qu.)
Kennedy, Ann S., MA Oxf. CUF Lectr. (L.M.H.)
Markesinis, B. S., MA Camb., PhD Camb., DPhil Oxf., LLD Camb., DCL Oxf., DJur Athens Clifford Chance Prof., European Law (L.M.H.)
Matthews, M. H., LLB Camb., LLB Nott., BCL Oxf., MA Oxf. CUF Lectr. (Univ.)
McCrudden, J. C., LLB Belf., LLM Yale, MA Oxf., DPhil Oxf. Reader (Linc.)
Mirfield, P. N., BCL Oxf., MA Oxf. CUF Lectr. (Jes.)
Payne, Jennifer S., BA Camb., MA Camb. CUF Lectr., Corporate Finance Law (Mert.)
Peel, W. E., BCL Oxf., MA Oxf. CUF Lectr. (Keb.)
Prentice, D. D., LLB Belf., MA Oxf., JD Chic. Allen and Overy Prof., Corporate Law (Pemb.)
Raz, J., MJur Jerusalem, MA Oxf., DPhil Oxf., FBA Prof., Philosophy of Law (Ball.)
Reynolds, F. M. B., BCL Oxf., MA Oxf., DCL Oxf., FBA Prof. (Worc.)
Rudden, B. A., MA Camb., MA Oxf., PhD Wales, LLD Camb., DCL Oxf. Prof., Comparative Law (Bras.)
Seymour, Jillaine K., MA Oxf. CUF Lectr. (Trin.)
Shale, Suzanne J., BA Kent, MA Oxf. CUF Lectr. (New)
Simpson, E. J. F., BCL Oxf., MA Oxf. Barclays Bank CUF Lectr. (Ch.Ch.)
Smith, L. D., MA Oxf., DPhil Oxf. CUF Lectr. (S.Hug.)
Smith, R. J., MA Camb., MA Oxf. CUF Lectr. (Magd.)
Spence, M. J., BA Syd., LLB Syd., MA Oxf. CUF Lectr. (S.Cat.)
Stevens, R. H., BCL Oxf., MA Oxf. CUF Lectr. (L.M.H.)
Stuart, R. R., BA Alta., LLB Alta., BCL Oxf., MA Oxf. CUF Lectr. (Hert.)
Swadling, W. J., MA Oxf. CUF Lectr. (Bras.)
Tapper, C. F. H., BCL Oxf., MA Oxf. Prof. (Magd.)
Tur, R. H. S., LLB Dund. CUF Lectr. (Oriel)
Vaver, D., MA Oxf. Reuters Prof., Intellectual Property and Information Technology (S.Pet.)
Weatherill, S. R., MA Camb., MSc Edin., MA Oxf. Jacques Delors Prof., European Community Law (Som.)
Whittaker, S. J., BCL Oxf., MA Oxf., DPhil Oxf. CUF Lectr. (S.Joh.)
Wyatt, D. A., LLB Camb., BCL Oxf., MA Camb., MA Oxf., JD Chic. Prof. (S.Edm.)
Yeung, Karen, BComm Melb., LLB Melb., BCL Oxf., MA Oxf. Linnells CUF Lectr. (S.Ann.)
Young, R. P., MA Oxf. Lectr., Criminology (Pemb.)

Zuckerman, A. A. S., MA Oxf. CUF Lectr. (Univ.)
Vacant Posts: 1 Prof.; 8 CUF Lectrs.

Linguistics, General, see also Classical Langs. and Lit., French, German, Portuguese Studies, and Spanish

Tel: (01865) 280400 Fax: (01865) 280412
Cram, D. F., MA Oxf., PhD Cornell Lectr. (Jes.)
Higginbotham, J. T., BSc Col., MA Oxf., PhD Col., FBA Prof. (Som.)
Ramchand, Gillian C., BS M.I.T., MA Oxf., MA Stan., PhD Stan. Lectr. (Linac.)

Management Studies

Tel: (01865) 228470 Fax: (01865) 228471
Barron, D. N., BA Camb., MA Oxf., MA Cornell, PhD Cornell Lectr., Business Organisation (Jes.)
Blois, K. J., BA Brist., MA Oxf., PhD Lough. Lectr. (Templ.)
Chapman, C. S., BSc Lond., MA Oxf., MSc Lond., PhD Lond. Lectr., Accounting (Linac.)
Darbishire, O. R., MS Cornell, MA Oxf. Lectr., Organisational Behaviour (Industrial Relations) (Pemb.)
Davies, R. L., MA Oxf., MA Leeds, MSc Northwestern, PhD Reading Lectr. (Templ.)
Dopson, Sue E., BSc Leic., MA Oxf., MSc Lond., PhD Birm. Lectr. (Templ.)
Elliott, R., BSc Lond., MA Oxf., PhD Brad. Reader (S.Ann.)
Faulkner, D. O., MA Oxf., DPhil Oxf. Lectr., Strategic Management (Ch.Ch.)
Grint, K., BA Open(UK), BA York, MA Oxf., DPhil Oxf. Reader (Templ.)
Hopwood, A. G., BSc Lond., MA Oxf., MBA Chic., PhD Chic., Hon. DEcon Gothenburg, Hon. DE American Standard Companies Prof., Operations Management (Ch.Ch.)
Howard, Elizabeth B., BA Durh., MA Oxf., MA Sheff. Lectr., Business Projects (Templ.)
Islei, G., MA Oxf. Lectr. (Templ.)
Jones, G., BA Open(UK), MSc Open(UK) Lectr. (Keb.)
Kay, J. A., MA Edin., MA Oxf., FBA Prof.; Peter Moores Dir.* (S.Edm.)
Kessler, I., BA Manc., MA Oxf., MA Warw., PhD Warw. Lectr. (Templ.)
Ljungqvist, A. P., MA Oxf., MSc Lund, MPhil Oxf., DPhil Oxf. Lectr., Finance (Mert.)
Mayer, C. P., BPhil Oxf., MA Oxf., DPhil Oxf. Peter Moores Prof. (Wadh.)
Murray, Fiona E., MA Oxf., MSc Harv., PhD Harv. Lectr., Management of Technology (S.Cat.)
New, S. J., BSc S'ton., MA Oxf., PhD Manc. Lectr., Operations Management (Hert.)
Raposo, Clara C., MA Lond. Lectr. (S.Edm.)
Reynolds, J., MA Oxf., MA Nott., PhD Newcastle(UK), DPhil Oxf. Lectr. (Templ.)
Sako, Mari, MSc Lond., MA Johns H., PhD Lond. Peninsular and Oriental Steam Navigation Company Prof. (Templ.)
Undy, R., MA Oxf. Reader (Templ.)
Whittington, R. C., MA Oxf., MBA Aston, PhD Manc. Reader, Strategic Management (New)
Willcocks, L. P., MA Oxf., MA Camb. Lectr. (Templ.)
Other Staff: 1 Lectr.; 1 Temp. Lectr.
Vacant Posts: 1 Prof.; 2 Lectrs.

Materials

Tel: (01865) 273700 Fax: (01865) 273789
Assender, Hazel E., MA Oxf., PhD Camb. Lectr., Mechanical Behaviour of Materials (Linac.)
Briggs, G. A. D., MA Oxf., PhD Camb. Reader, Metallurgy and Science of Materials (Wolfs.)
Brook, R. J., OBE, BSc Leeds, MA Oxf., ScD M.I.T. Prof. (S.Cross)
Cantor, B., MA Oxf.., MA Camb., PhD Camb., FIM Cookson Prof.; Head* (S.Cat.)
Cerezo, A., MA Oxf., DPhil Oxf. Lectr. (Wolfs.)
Czernuszka, J. T., BSc Lond., MA Oxf., PhD Camb., DPhil Oxf. Lectr. (Trin.)

Derby, B., MA *Camb.*, MA *Oxf.*, PhD *Camb.* Reader, Materials Science (Corp.)

Grovenor, C. R. M., MA *Oxf.*, DPhil *Oxf.* Reader, Metallurgy (S.Ann.)

Hunt, J. D., MA *Camb.*, MA *Oxf.*, PhD *Camb.*, DPhil *Oxf.* Prof., Physical Metallurgy (S.Edm.)

Pethica, J. B., MA *Camb.*, MA *Oxf.*, PhD *Camb.* Prof. (S.Cross)

Pettifor, D. G., BSc *Witw.*, MA *Oxf.*, PhD *Camb.* Isaac Wolfson Prof., Metallurgy (S.Edm.)

Roberts, S. G., BA *Camb.*, MA *Oxf.*, PhD *Camb.* Lectr. (S.Cross)

Smith, G. D. W., MA *Oxf.*, DPhil *Oxf.* George Kelley Prof., Physical Metallurgy (Trin.)

Sutton, A. P., MA *Oxf.*, PhD *Penn.* Prof. (Linac.)

Sykes, J. M., MA *Camb.*, MA *Oxf.*, PhD *Camb.* Lectr. (Mansf.)

Titchmarsh, J. M., BA *Camb.*, DPhil *Oxf.* AEA INSS Prof., Microanalytical Techniques (S.Ann.)

Viney, C., MA *Oxf.*, PhD *Camb.*, DPhil *Oxf.* Lectr. (S.Cat.)

Wilshaw, P. R., MA *Oxf.*, DPhil *Oxf.* Lectr., Electrical and Magnetic Properties of Materials (S.Ann.)

Other Staff: 1 Temp. Lectr.

Vacant Posts: 1 Prof.; 2 Lectrs.

Mathematical Sciences

Tel: (01865) 273525 Fax: (01865) 273583

Acheson, D. J., BSc *Lond.*, MSc *E.Anglia*, MA *Oxf.*, PhD *E.Anglia* CUF Lectr. (Jes.)

Ault, Irene A., BSc *Lond.*, MA *Oxf.*, PhD *Lond.* CUF Lectr. (S.Hil.)

Ball, J. M., MA *Oxf.*, MA *Camb.*, DPhil *Sus.*, FRS Sedleian Prof., Natural Philosophy (Qu.)

Batty, C. J. K., MA *Oxf.*, MSc *Oxf.*, DPhil *Oxf.* Reader, Pure Mathematics (S.Joh.)

Bridson, M. R., MA *Oxf.*, MSc *Cornell*, PhD *Cornell* Reader, Pure Mathematics (Pemb.)

Collins, M. J., MA *Oxf.*, DPhil *Oxf.* CUF Lectr. (Univ.)

Collins, P. J., MA *Oxf.*, DPhil *Oxf.* CUF Lectr. (S.Edm.)

Corner, A. L. S., MA *Camb.*, MA *Oxf.*, PhD *Camb.* Fac. Lectr. (Worc.)

Day, W. A., BA *Camb.*, MA *Oxf.*, PhD *Pitt.* Fac. Lectr. (Hert.)

Dyson, Janet, MA *Oxf.*, MSc *Oxf.*, DPhil *Oxf.* CUF Lectr. (Mansf.)

Edwards, C. M., MA *Oxf.*, DPhil *Oxf.* CUF Lectr. (Qu.)

Erdmann, Karin, MA *Oxf.*, DrRerNat *Giessen* CUF Lectr. (Som.)

Etheridge, Alison M., MA *Oxf.*, DPhil *Oxf.* CUF Lectr. (Magd.)

Fowler, A. C., MA *Oxf.*, MSc *Oxf.*, DPhil *Oxf.* Lectr. (Corp.)

Friesecke, G., MSc *H–W*, MA *Oxf.*, PhD *H–W* Prof., Applied Mathematics (S.Cat.)

Hannabuss, K. C., MA *Oxf.*, DPhil *Oxf.* CUF Lectr. (Ball.)

Haydon, R. G., MA *Camb.*, MA *Oxf.*, PhD *Camb.* Prof. (Bras.)

Heath-Brown, D. R., MA *Camb.*, MA *Oxf.*, PhD *Camb.*, DPhil *Oxf.*, FRS Reader (Magd.)

Hitchin, N. J., MA *Oxf.*, DPhil *Oxf.*, FRS Savilian Prof., Geometry (New)

Howison, S. D., MSc *Oxf.*, MA *Oxf.*, DPhil *Oxf.* CUF Lectr. (Ch.Ch.)

Joyce, D. D., MA *Oxf.*, DPhil *Oxf.* Lectr. (Linc.)

Kirwan, Frances C., MA *Camb.*, MA *Oxf.*, DPhil *Oxf.* Prof. (Ball.)

Luke, Glenys L., BA *W.Aust.*, MA *Oxf.*, DPhil *Oxf.* CUF Lectr. (S.Hug.)

Lunn, Mary, MA *Oxf.*, DPhil *Oxf.* CUF Lectr. (S.Hug.)

Maini, P. K., MA *Oxf.*, DPhil *Oxf.* Prof., Mathematical Biology (Bras.)

Martineau, R. P., MA *Oxf.*, DPhil *Oxf.* CUF Lectr. (Wadh.)

Mason, L. J., MA *Oxf.*, DPhil *Oxf.* CUF Lectr. (S.Pet.)

Moroz, Irene M., MA *Oxf.*, PhD *Leeds* CUF Lectr. (S.Hil.)

Neumann, P. M., MA *Oxf.*, DPhil *Oxf.*, DSc *Oxf.* CUF Lectr. (Qu.)

Norbury, J., BSc *Qld.*, MA *Oxf.*, PhD *Camb.* Lectr. (Linc.)

Ockendon, Hilary, MA *Oxf.*, DPhil *Oxf.* CUF Lectr. (Som.)

Ockendon, J. R., MA *Oxf.*, DPhil *Oxf.* Lectr., Applicable Mathematics (S.Cat.)

Powell, M. B., MA *Oxf.*, DPhil *Oxf.* Fac. Lectr. (S.Pet.)

Priestley, Hilary A., MA *Oxf.*, DPhil *Oxf.* Reader (S.Ann.)

Quillen, D. G., MA *Oxf.*, PhD *Harv.* Waynflete Prof., Pure Mathematics (Magd.)

Salamon, S. M., MA *Oxf.*, MSc *Oxf.*, DPhil *Oxf.* Reader (Trin.)

Screaton, G. R., MA *Camb.*, MA *Oxf.*, PhD *Camb.* Fac. Lectr. (Univ.)

Steer, B. F., MA *Oxf.*, DPhil *Oxf.* Fac. Lectr. (Hert.)

Stewart, W. B., MA *St And.*, MA *Oxf.*, DPhil *Oxf.* CUF Lectr. (Exet.)

Stirzaker, D. R., MA *Oxf.*, DPhil *Oxf.* CUF Lectr. (S.Joh.)

Stoy, Gabrielle A., BSc *Manc.*, MA *Oxf.*, DPhil *Oxf.* CUF Lectr. (L.M.H.)

Sutherland, W. A., MA *St And.*, MA *Oxf.*, DPhil *Oxf.* CUF Lectr. (New)

Tod, K. P., MA *Oxf.*, MSc *Oxf.*, DPhil *Oxf.* Reader (S.Joh.)

Vaughan-Lee, M. R., MA *Oxf.*, DPhil *Oxf.* Prof. (Ch.Ch.)

Vincent-Smith, G. F., MA *Oxf.*, DPhil *Oxf.* Fac. Lectr., Pure Mathematics (Oriel)

Welsh, J. A. D., MA *Oxf.*, DPhil *Oxf.* Prof.; Chairman* (Mert.)

Wilkie, A. J., MSc *Lond.*, MA *Oxf.*, PhD *Lond.* Prof., Mathematical Logic (Wolfs.)

Woodhouse, N. M. J., MSc *Lond.*, MA *Oxf.*, PhD *Lond.* Reader (Wadh.)

Other Staff: 1 Temp. CUF Lectr.

Vacant Posts: 3 Profs.; 1 Lectr.; 3 CUF Lectrs.

Medicine, see below

Metallurgy, see Materials

Microbiology, see Biochem.

Mineralogy, see Earth Scis.

Modern Middle Eastern Studies

Tel: (01865) 278200 Fax: (01865) 278190

Holes, C. D., MA *Oxf.*, MA *Birm.*, PhD *Camb.*, DPhil *Oxf.* Khalid bin Abdullah Al Saud Prof., Contemporary Arab World (Magd.)

Hopwood, D., MA *Oxf.*, DPhil *Oxf.* Reader (S.Ant.)

Music

Tel: (01865) 276125 Fax: (01865) 276128

Bujić, B., MA *Oxf.*, DPhil *Oxf.* Reader (Magd.)

Caldwell, J. A., BMus *Oxf.*, MA *Oxf.*, DPhil *Oxf.*, FRCO Reader (Jes.)

Darlington, S. M., MA *Oxf.*, FRCO CUF Lectr. (Ch.Ch.)

Franklin, P. R., BA *York(UK)*, MA *Oxf.*, DPhil *York(UK)* Reader (S.Cat.)

Higginbottom, E., MusB *Camb.*, MA *Camb.*, MA *Oxf.*, PhD *Camb.*, DPhil *Oxf.*, FRCO CUF Lectr. (New)

Johnstone, H. D., BMus *Trinity(Dub.)*, MA *Oxf.*, DPhil *Oxf.* Reader (S.Ann.)

Marston, N. J., MA *Oxf.*, DPhil *Oxf.* Reader (S.Pet.)

Olleson, D. E., MA *Oxf.*, DPhil *Oxf.* Lectr. (Mert.)

Parker, R., MA *Oxf.*, MMus *Lond.*, PhD *Lond.* Prof. (S.Hug.)

Rees, O. L., BA *Camb.*, MPhil *Camb.*, MA *Oxf.*, PhD *Camb.* CUF Lectr. (Qu.)

Sherlaw-Johnson, R., BA *Durh.*, BMus *Durh.*, MA *Leeds*, MA *Oxf.*, DMus *Leeds*, DMus *Oxf.* Reader (Worc.)

Strohm, R., MA *Oxf.*, PhD *Berlin* Heather Prof.; Head* (Wadh.)

Wollenberg, Susan L. F., MA *Oxf.*, DPhil *Oxf.* Lectr. (L.M.H.)

Numismatics

Tel: (01865) 278200 Fax: (01865) 278190

Kim, H. S., AB *Harv.*, MA *Oxf.*, MPhil *Oxf.* Lectr., Greek

Treadwell, W. L., MA *Oxf.*, DPhil *Oxf.* Lectr., Islamic Numismatics (S.Cross)

Palaeography, see Engl.

Papyrology, see Classical Langs. and Lit.

Persian

Tel: (01865) 278200 Fax: (01865) 278190

Gurney, J. D., MA *Oxf.*, DPhil *Oxf.* Lectr., Persian History (Wadh.)

Meisami, Julie S., MA *Calif.*, MA *Oxf.*, PhD *Calif.* Lectr. (Wolfs.)

Sheikholeslami, A. R., MA *Northwestern*, MA *Oxf.*, PhD *Calif.* Masoumeh and Fereydoun Soudavar Prof., Persian Studies (Wadh.)

Philology, see Classical Langs. and Lit., French, German, Russian, and Spanish

Philosophy

Tel: (01865) 276926 Fax: (01865) 276932

Atherton, Catherine, MA *Oxf.*, MA *Camb.*, PhD *Camb.*, DPhil *Oxf.* CUF Lectr. (New)

Avramides, Anita, BA *Oberlin*, MA *Oxf.*, MPhil *Lond.*, DPhil *Oxf.* CUF Lectr. (S.Hil.)

Ayers, M. R., MA *Oxf.*, PhD *Camb.* Prof. (Wadh.)

Baker, G. P., MA *Oxf.*, DPhil *Oxf.* CUF Lectr. (S.Joh.)

Bostock, D., BPhil *Oxf.*, MA *Oxf.* CUF Lectr. (Mert.)

Brewer, M. W., BPhil *Oxf.*, MA *Oxf.*, DPhil *Oxf.* CUF Lectr. (S.Cat.)

Brown, H. R., BSc *Cant.*, MA *Oxf.*, PhD *Lond.* Reader, Philosophy of Physics (Wolfs.)

Brown, Lesley, BPhil *Oxf.*, MA *Oxf.* CUF Lectr. (Som.)

Campbell, J. J., BA *Stir.*, BPhil *Oxf.*, MA *Calg.*, MA *Oxf.*, DPhil *Oxf.* Reader (New)

Cassam, A.-Q. A., BPhil *Oxf.*, MA *Oxf.*, DPhil *Oxf.* CUF Lectr. (Wadh.)

Charles, D. O. M., BPhil *Oxf.*, MA *Oxf.*, DPhil *Oxf.* CUF Lectr. (Oriel)

Child, T. W., BA *Oxf.*, BPhil *Oxf.*, MA *Oxf.*, DPhil *Oxf.* CUF Lectr. (Univ.)

Crisp, R. S., BPhil *Oxf.*, MA *Oxf.*, DPhil *Oxf.* CUF Lectr. (S.Ann.)

Davies, M. K., BA *Monash*, BPhil *Oxf.*, MA *Oxf.*, DPhil *Oxf.* Prof., Mental Philosophy; Wilde Reader (Corp.)

Day, Jane M., BPhil *Oxf.*, MA *Oxf.* CUF Lectr. (L.M.H.)

Denham, Alison E., BA *Calif.*, BPhil *Oxf.*, MA *Oxf.*, DPhil *Oxf.* CUF Lectr. (S.Ann.)

Edgington, Dorothy M., BPhil *Oxf.*, MA *Oxf.* Prof. (Univ.)

Foster, J. A., MA *Oxf.* CUF Lectr. (Bras.)

Frede, M., DrPhil *Gött.*, MA *Oxf.* Prof., History of Philosophy (Keb.)

Fricker, Elizabeth M., BPhil *Oxf.*, MA *Oxf.*, DPhil *Oxf.* CUF Lectr. (Magd.)

Griffin, J. P., BA *Yale*, MA *Oxf.*, DPhil *Oxf.* White's Prof., Moral Philosophy (Corp.)

Hacker, P. M. S., MA *Oxf.*, DPhil *Oxf.* CUF Lectr. (S.Joh.)

Hawkins, R. J., BPhil *Oxf.*, MA *Oxf.* CUF Lectr. (Keb.)

Hoekstra, S. J., BA *Brown*, MA *Oxf.* CUF Lectr. (Ball.)

Hussey, E. L., MA *Oxf.* Lectr., Ancient Philosophy (All S.)

Hyman, J., BPhil *Oxf.*, MA *Oxf.*, DPhil *Oxf.* CUF Lectr. (Qu.)

Inwood, M. J., MA *Oxf.* CUF Lectr. (Trin.)

Isaacson, D. R., AB *Harv.*, MA *Oxf.*, DPhil *Oxf.* Lectr., Philosophy of Mathematics (Wolfs.)

Judson, R. L., MA Oxf., DPhil Oxf. CUF Lectr. (Ch.Ch.)

Kenyon, J. D., MA Camb., MA Oxf., PhD Camb., DPhil Oxf. CUF Lectr. (S.Pet.)

Kirwan, C. A., MA Oxf. CUF Lectr. (Exet.)

Klein, Martha, BA Reading, BPhil Oxf., MA Oxf., DPhil Oxf. CUF Lectr. (Pemb.)

Logue, J., BA Keele, BPhil Oxf., MPhil CNAA, MA Oxf., DPhil Oxf. CUF Lectr. (Som.)

Lovibond, Sabina M., MA Oxf., DPhil Oxf., PhD Lond. CUF Lectr. (Worc.)

Malpas, R. M. P., BPhil Oxf., MA Oxf. CUF Lectr. (Hert.)

Mander, W. J., BA Lond., BPhil Oxf., MA Oxf., DPhil Oxf. CUF Lectr. (Harris)

Moore, A. W., BPhil Oxf., MA Camb., MA Oxf., DPhil Oxf. CUF Lectr. (S.Hug.)

Mulhall, S. J., BA Oxf., MA Oxf., DPhil Oxf. CUF Lectr. (New)

Newton-Smith, W. H., BA Qu., MA Cornell, MA Oxf., DPhil Oxf. CUF Lectr. (Ball.)

Peacocke, C. A. B., BPhil Oxf., MA Oxf., DPhil Oxf., FBA Waynflete Prof., Metaphysical Philosophy (Magd.)

Rice, D. H., BPhil Oxf., MA Oxf. CUF Lectr. (Ch.Ch.)

Rosen, M. E., MA Oxf., DPhil Oxf. CUF Lectr. (Linc.)

Rumfitt, I. P., MA Oxf., DPhil Oxf. CUF Lectr. (Univ.)

Rundle, B. B., BPhil Oxf., MA Oxf. CUF Lectr. (Trin.)

Saunders, S., MA Oxf., PhD Lond. Lectr., Philosophy of Science (Linac.)

Snowdon, P. F., BPhil Oxf., MA Oxf. CUF Lectr. (Exet.)

Strawson, G. J., BPhil Oxf., BA Camb., MA Oxf., DPhil Oxf. CUF Lectr. (Jes.)

Tasioulas, J., BA Melb., LLB Melb., MA Oxf. CUF Lectr. (Corp.)

Taylor, C. C. W., MA Edin., BPhil Oxf., MA Oxf. Reader (Corp.)

Walker, R. C. S., BA McG., BPhil Oxf., MA Oxf., DPhil Oxf. CUF Lectr. (Magd.)

Wiggins, D. R. P., MA Oxf. Wykeham Prof., Logic (New)

Wilkes, Kathleen V., MA Prin., MA Oxf., PhD Prin. CUF Lectr. (S.Hil.)

Other Staff: 1 Lectr.

Vacant Posts: 1 Prof.; 1 Lectr.; 2 CUF Lectrs.

Physics, Atmospheric, Oceanic, and Planetary

Tel: (01865) 272933 Fax: (01865) 272923

Andrews, D. G., MA Camb., MA Oxf., PhD Camb., DPhil Oxf. Reader (L.M.H.)

Irwin, P. G. J., MA Oxf., DPhil Oxf. Lectr. (S.Ann.)

Read, P. L., BSc Birm., MA Oxf., PhD Camb. Lectr. (Trin.)

Rodgers, C. D., MA Camb., MA Oxf., PhD Camb. Reader (Jes.)

Taylor, F. W., BSc Liv., MA Oxf., DPhil Oxf. Prof., Atmospheric Physics; Head* (Jes.)

Williamson, E. J., MA Oxf., DPhil Oxf. Lectr. (S.Cross)

Other Staff: 1 Temp. Lectr.

Vacant Posts: 1 Lectr.

Physics, Atomic and Laser

Tel: (01865) 272200 Fax: (01865) 272375

Brooker, G. A., MA Oxf., DPhil Oxf. Lectr. (Wadh.)

Burnett, K., MA Oxf., DPhil Oxf. Prof. (S.Joh.)

Ewart, P., MA Oxf. Prof. (Worc.)

Foot, C. J., MA Oxf., DPhil Oxf. Lectr. (S.Pet.)

Sandars, P. G. H., MA Oxf., DPhil Oxf. Prof., Experimental Physics (Ch.Ch.)

Silver, J. D., MA Oxf., DPhil Oxf. Prof. (New)

Stacey, D. N., MA Oxf., DPhil Oxf. Prof. (Ch.Ch.)

Wark, J. S., MA Oxf. Lectr. (Trin.)

Webb, C. E., BSc Nott., MA Oxf., DPhil Oxf., FRS Prof., Laser Physics; Head* (Jes.)

Vacant Posts: 1 Lectr.

Physics, Condensed Matter

Tel: (01865) 272200 Fax: (01865) 272400

Blundell, S. J., MA Oxf., PhD Camb., DPhil Oxf. Lectr. (Mansf.)

Boothroyd, A. T., BA Camb., MA Oxf., PhD Camb. Lectr. (Oriel)

Cowley, R. A., MA Oxf. Dr Lee's Prof., Experimental Philosophy; Head* (Wadh.)

Edmonds, D. T., MA Oxf., DPhil Oxf. Prof. (Wadh.)

Glazer, A. M., BSc Dund., MA Camb., MA Oxf., PhD Lond. Prof. (Jes.)

Hodby, J. W., MA Oxf., DPhil Oxf. Lectr. (Ball.)

Johnson, N. F., BA Camb., MA Harv., PhD Harv. Lectr. (Linc.)

Klipstein, P. C., MA Camb., MA Oxf., PhD Camb. Lectr. (Pemb.)

Leask, M. J. M., MSc Natal, MA Oxf., DPhil Oxf. Lectr. (S.Cat.)

Nicholas, R. J., MA Oxf., DPhil Oxf. Prof. (Univ.)

Ryan, J. F., BSc Edin., MA Oxf., PhD Edin. Prof. (Ch.Ch.)

Singleton, J., MA Oxf., DPhil Oxf. Reader (Corp.)

Stone, N. J., MA Oxf., DPhil Oxf. Prof. (S.Edm.)

Taylor, R. A., MA Oxf., DPhil Oxf. Lectr. (Qu.)

Turberfield, A. J., MA Oxf., DPhil Oxf. Reader (Magd.)

Vacant Posts: 1 Lectr.; 1 Sr. Res. Officer

Physics, Particle and Nuclear

Tel: (01865) 273333 Fax: (01865) 273418

Allison, W. W. M., MA Camb., MA Oxf., DPhil Oxf. Prof. (Keb.)

Bowler, M. G., BSc Brist., MAOxf., PhD Brist. Lectr. (Mert.)

Cashmore, R. J., MA Oxf., DPhil Oxf., FRS Prof., Experimental Physics; Chairman, Phys. (Ball.)

Cooper, Susan, BA Colby, MA Oxf., PhD Calif. Prof., Experimental Physics; Head* (S.Cat.)

Devenish, R. C. E., MA Camb., MA Oxf., PhD Camb., DPhil Oxf. Prof. (Hert.)

Harnew, N., BSc Sheff., MA Oxf., PhD Lond. Reader (S.Ann.)

Huffman, B. T., BS Nebraska, MS Purdue, PhD Purdue Lectr. (L.M.H.)

Jelley, N. A., MA Oxf., DPhil Oxf. Reader (Linc.)

Jones, P. B., MA Camb., MA Oxf., PhD Camb., DPhil Oxf. Lectr. (Exet.)

Kraus, H., MA Oxf., DrRerNatTech Munich Lectr. (Corp.)

Lyons, L., MA Oxf., DPhil Oxf. Lectr., Nuclear Physics (Jes.)

Myatt, G., BSc Birm., MA Oxf., PhD Liv. Reader (Gre.)

Nickerson, R. B., BSc Edin., MA Oxf., DPhil Oxf. Lectr. (Qu.)

Radojicic, D., MA Oxf., PhD Camb. Lectr. (Magd.)

Rae, W. D. M., BSc Edin., MA Oxf., DPhil Oxf. Lectr., Nuclear Physics (S.Cross)

Rook, J. R., BSc Manc., MA Oxf., PhD Manc. Lectr., Nuclear Physics (Computing Group) (Pemb.)

Salmon, G. L., BSc Tas., MA Oxf., DPhil Oxf. Lectr., Nuclear Physics (Qu.)

Segar, A. M., MSc Melb., MA Oxf., PhD Birm. Reader (Oriel)

Walczak, R., MSc Warsaw, MA Oxf. Lectr. (Som.)

Wark, D. L., BSc Indiana, MA Oxf., MS Cal.Tech., PhD Cal.Tech. Lectr. (Ball.)

Weidberg, A. R., BSc Lond., MA Oxf., PhD Camb., DPhil Oxf. Lectr. (S.Joh.)

Other Staff: 1 Res. Officer; 1 Temp. Lectr.

Vacant Posts: 2 Res. Officers

Physics, Theoretical

Tel: (01865) 273999 Fax: (01865) 273947

Abraham, D. B., MA Camb., MA Oxf., PhD Camb., DSc Prof., Statistical Mechanics (Wolfs.)

Aitchison, I. J. R., MA Camb., MA Oxf., PhD Camb., DPhil Oxf. Prof. (Worc.)

Binney, J. J., MA Oxf., DPhil Oxf. Prof. (Mert.)

Buck, B., MA Oxf., DPhil Oxf. Lectr. (Wolfs.)

Chalker, J. T., MA Camb., MA Oxf., DPhil Oxf. Lectr. (S.Hug.)

Jordan, Carole, MA Oxf., PhD Lond., FRS Prof. (Som.)

Kogan, I. I., MA Oxf. Lectr. (Ball.)

Llewellyn-Smith, C. H., MA Oxf., DPhil Oxf., FRS Prof. (S.Joh.)

Paton, J. E., BSc St And., MA Oxf., PhD Birm. Fac. Lectr. (Ch.Ch.)

Roaf, D. J., MA Oxf., PhD Camb. CUF Lectr. (Exet.)

Ross, G. G., BSc Aberd., MA Oxf., PhD Durh., FRS Prof. (Wadh.)

Sarkar, S., BSc Kharagpur, MSc Kharagpur, MA Oxf., PhD Bom. Lectr. (Linac.)

Sherrington, D., BSc Manc., MA Oxf., PhD Manc., FRS Wykeham Prof.; Head* (New)

Stinchcombe, R. B., BSc Birm., MA Oxf., PhD Birm. Reader (New)

Tsvelik, A. M., MA Oxf., PhD Moscow Prof. (Bras.)

Wheater, J. F., MA Oxf., DPhil Oxf. Reader (Univ.)

Vacant Posts: 3 CUF Lectrs.

Physiology

Tel: (01865) 272500 Fax: (01865) 272469

Ashcroft, Frances M., MA Oxf. Prof. (Trin.)

Ashley, C. C., BSc Brist., MA Oxf., PhD Brist., DSc Oxf. Prof. (Corp.)

Blakemore, C. B., MA Camb., MA Oxf., PhD Calif., ScD Camb., DSc Oxf., FRS Waynflete Prof. (Magd.)

Dorrington, K. L., BM Oxf., MA Oxf., DM Oxf., DPhil Oxf. Lectr. (Univ.)

Ellory, J. C., BSc Brist., MA Camb., MA Oxf., PhD Brist. Prof., Human Physiology; Head* (Corp.)

Jack, J. J. B., BM Oxf., MA Oxf., MMedSc Otago, PhD Otago Prof., Cellular Neuroscience (Univ.)

Judge, S. J., BA Keele, MA Oxf., PhD Keele Lectr. (S.Ann.)

Korbmacher, C., MA Oxf., DrMed F.U.Berlin Lectr. (S.Edm.)

Larkman, A. U., MA Oxf., PhD Open(UK) Lectr. (Keb.)

Noble, D., BSc Lond., MA Oxf., PhD Lond., FRS Burdon Sanderson Prof., Cardiovascular Physiology (Ball.)

Nye, P. C. G., MA Oxf., PhD Calif. Lectr. (Ball.)

Parker, A. J., BA Camb., MA Oxf., PhD Camb., DPhil Oxf. Prof. (S.Joh.)

Paterson, D. J., MA Oxf., DPhil Oxf. Reader (Mert.)

Powell, T., BSc Lond., MA Oxf., PhD Lond., PhD Houston, DSc Oxf. Prof., Cellular Cardiology; British Heart Foundation Winstone Reader (New)

Robbins, P. A., BM BCh Oxf., MA Oxf., DPhil Oxf. Prof. (Qu.)

Stein, J. F., BSc Oxf., BM BCh Oxf., MA Oxf. Prof. (Magd.)

Thompson, I. D., MA Camb., MA Oxf., PhD Camb. Lectr. (Ch.Ch.)

Vaughan-Jones, R. D., BSc Brist., MA Oxf., PhD Brist. Prof. (Exet.)

Wolfensohn, Sarah E., MA Oxf. Supervisor, Veterinary Services

Plant Sciences

Tel: (01865) 275000 Fax: (01865) 275074

Brown, N. D., BA Camb., MA Oxf., MSc Aberd., DPhil Oxf. Lectr. (Linac.)

Burley, J., CBE, MF Yale, MA Oxf., PhD Yale Prof., Forestry; Dir., Forestry Inst. (Gre.)

Campbell, M. M., BSc *Guelph*, MA *Oxf.*, PhD
Guelph Lectr., Forestry (Wolfs.)
Darrah, P. R., BSc *Liv.*, MA *Oxf.*, PhD
Reading Lectr. (Worc.)
Dickinson, H. G., MA *Oxf.*, PhD *Birm.*, DSc
Birm. Sherardian Prof., Botany (Magd.)
Fricker, M. D., MA *Oxf.*, PhD *Stir.* Lectr.
(Pemb.)
Grafen, A., MA *Oxf.*, MPhil *Oxf.*, DPhil
Oxf. Lectr., Quantitative Methods in Plant
Biology (S.Joh.)
Gurr, Sarah J., BSc *Lond.*, MA *Oxf.*, PhD
Lond. Lectr. (Som.)
Hall, R. L., BSc *Nott.*, MA *Oxf.*, PhD
Nott. Lectr. (Wolfs.)
Hill, S. A., MA *Camb.*, MA *Oxf.*, PhD
Edin. Lectr. (S.Hug.)
Juniper, B. E., MA *Oxf.*, DPhil *Oxf.* Reader
(S.Cat.)
Kruger, N. J., MA *Camb.*, MAOxf., PhD
Camb. Lectr. (S.Cross)
Langdale, Jane A., BSc *Bath*, MA *Oxf.*, PhD
Lond. Lectr. (Qu.)
Leaver, C. J., BSc *Lond.*, MA *Oxf.*, PhD *Lond.*,
FRS, FRSEd Sibthorpian Prof.; Head*
(S.Joh.)
Rainey, P. B., MA *Oxf.* Lectr., Microbial
Ecology and Population Biology (S.Cross)
Ratcliffe, R. G., MA *Oxf.*, DPhil *Oxf.* Reader
(New)
Savill, P. S., MSc *Wales*, MA *Oxf.*, PhD
Belf. Reader (Linac.)
Scotland, R. W., BSc *Lond.*, MA *Oxf.*, PhD
Lond. Lectr., Plant Systematics and
Biochemistry (Linac.)
Smith, J. A. C., MA *Camb.*, MA *Oxf.*, PhD
Glas. Prof. (Magd.)
Speedy, A. W., MA *Camb.*, MA *Oxf.*, PhD
Camb. Lectr. (Ch.Ch.)
Stewart, P. J., MA *Oxf.* Lectr. (S.Cross)
Thompson, F. B., BSc *Lond.*, MA *Oxf.* Lectr.
(Trin.)
Other Staff: 1 Temp. Lectr.

Politics

Tel: (01865) 278700 Fax: (01865) 278725

Angell, A. E., BSc(Econ) *Lond.*, MA *Oxf.* Lectr.,
Latin American Politics (S.Ant.)
Bogdanor, V. B., MA *Oxf.* Prof., Government
(Bras.)
Bowles, N., BA *Sus.*, MA *Oxf.*, DPhil *Oxf.* CUF
Lectr. (S.Ann.)
Brown, A. H., BSc(Econ) *Lond.*, MA *Oxf.*,
FBA Prof. (S.Ant.)
Ceadel, M. E., MA *Oxf.*, DPhil *Oxf.* CUF Lectr.
(New)
Cohen, G. A., BA *McG.*, BPhil *Oxf.*, MA *Oxf.*,
FBA Chichele Prof., Social and Political
Theory (All S.)
Crampton, R. J., BA *Trinity(Dub.)*, MA *Oxf.*, PhD
Lond. Prof., East European History (S.Edm.)
Currie, R., MA *Oxf.*, DPhil *Oxf.* CUF Lectr.
(Wadh.)
Deas, M. D., MA *Oxf.* Lectr., Politics and
Government of Latin America (S.Ant.)
Deighton, Anne F., MA *Oxf.*, PhD
Reading Lectr., European Politics (Wolfs.)
Dunbabin, J. P. D., MA *Oxf.* Reader (S.Edm.)
Frazer, Elizabeth J., MA *Oxf.*, DPhil *Oxf.* CUF
Lectr. (New)
Freeden, M. S., BA *Jerusalem*, MA *Oxf.*, DPhil
Oxf. Prof. (Mansf.)
Goldey, D. B., BA *Cornell*, MA *Oxf.*, DPhil
Oxf. CUF Lectr. (Linc.)
Harrison, B. H., MA *Oxf.*, DPhil *Oxf.* Prof.,
Modern British History (Corp.)
Hart, M. W., MA *Camb.*, MA *Oxf.*, DPhil CUF
Lectr. (Exet.)
Hazareesingh, S. K., MA *Oxf.*, DPhil *Oxf.* CUF
Lectr. (Ball.)
Hine, D. J., MA *Oxf.*, DPhil *Oxf.* CUF Lectr.
(Ch.Ch.)
Hurrell, A. J., BA *Oxf.*, MA *Oxf.*, MPhil *Oxf.*,
DPhil *Oxf.* Lectr., International Relations
(Nuff.)
Jones, C. O., MA *Oxf.* John M. Olin Visiting
Prof., American Government (1998-99)
(Nuff.)

Khong, Y. F., MA *Oxf.* Lectr., American
Foreign Policy (Nuff.)
King, D. S., BA *Trinity(Dub.)*, MA *Northwestern*,
MA *Oxf.*, PhD *Northwestern* Prof. (S.Joh.)
L'Estrange Fawcett, Louise, BA *Lond.*, MA *Oxf.*,
MPhil *Oxf.*, DPhil *Oxf.* CUF Lectr. (S.Cat.)
MacFarlane, S. N., AB *Dartmouth*, MA *Oxf.*,
MPhil *Oxf.*, DPhil *Oxf.* Lester B. Pearson
Prof., International Relations (S.Ann.)
McNay, Lois, MA *Sus.*, MA *Oxf.*, PhD *Camb.*,
DPhil *Oxf.* CUF Lectr. (Som.)
Menon, A., MA *Oxf.*, MPhil *Oxf.* Lectr.,
European Politics (S.Ant.)
Nicolaïdes, Kalypso A., MPA *Harv.*, PhD
Harv. Lectr., International Relations (S.Ant.)
Owen, N. J., MA *Oxf.*, DPhil *Oxf.* CUF Lectr.
(Qu.)
Peele, Gillian R., BA *Durh.*, BPhil *Oxf.*, MA *Oxf.*,
MPhil *Oxf.* CUF Lectr. (L.M.H.)
Philp, M. F. E., BA *Brad.*, MSc *Leeds*, MA *Oxf.*,
MPhil *Oxf.*, DPhil *Oxf.* CUF Lectr. (Oriel)
Pravda, A., MA *Oxf.*, DPhil *Oxf.* Lectr., Russian
and East European Politics (S.Ant.)
Richardson, J. J., MA *Oxf.* Nuffield Prof.,
Comparative European Politics (Nuff.)
Roberts, E. A., MA *Oxf.*, FBA Montague
Burton Prof., International Relations (Ball.)
Robertson, D. B., MA *Oxf.*, PhD *Essex* CUF
Lectr. (S.Hug.)
Robins, P. J., MA *Oxf.* Lectr., Middle East
Politics (S.Ant.)
Schleiter, Petra, BSc *Lond.*, MPhil *Oxf.*, DPhil
Oxf. CUF Lectr. (S.Hil.)
Shafer, B. E., BA *Yale*, MA *Oxf.*, PhD
Calif. Andrew W. Mellon Prof., American
Government (Nuff.)
Shlaim, A., BA *Camb.*, MSc(Econ) *Lond.*, MA
Oxf., PhD *Reading* Alastair Buchan Reader,
International Relations; Prof. (S.Ant.)
Siedentop, L. A., MA *Harv.*, MA *Oxf.*, DPhil
Oxf. Fac. Lectr. (Keb.)
Stepan, A., MA *Oxf.*, PhD *Col.* Gladstone Prof.,
Government (All S.)
Swift, A. R. G., MA *Oxf.*, MPhil *Oxf.*, DPhil
Oxf. CUF Lectr. (Ball.)
Trapido, S., BA *Witw.*, MA *Oxf.*, PhD
Lond. Lectr., Government of New States
(Linc.)
Ware, A. J., MA *Oxf.*, DPhil *Oxf.* Prof.
(Worc.)
Whitefield, S. D., BA *Oxf.*, MA *Oxf.*, DPhil
Oxf. CUF Lectr. (Pemb.)
Williams, G. P., BA *Stell.*, BPhil *Oxf.*, MA *Oxf.*,
MPhil *Oxf.* CUF Lectr. (S.Pet.)
Woods, Ngaire, BA *Auck.*, LLB *Auck.*, MA *Oxf.*,
MPhil *Oxf.*, DPhil *Oxf.* CUF Lectr. (Univ.)
Wright, J. R. C., MA *Oxf.*, DPhil *Oxf.* CUF
Lectr. (Ch.Ch.)
Vacant Posts: 1 Lectr.; 1 Fac. Lectr.; 2 CUF
Lectrs.

Portuguese Studies
Tel: (01865) 270750 Fax: (01865) 270757

Earle, T. F., MA *Oxf.*, DPhil *Oxf.* King John II
Prof. (S.Pet.)
Parkinson, S. R., MA *Camb.*, MA *Oxf.*, PhD
Camb. Lectr., Portuguese Language and
Linguistics (Linac.)
Pazos Alonso, Claudia, MA *Oxf.*, DPhil
Oxf. Lectr., Portuguese and Brazilian Studies
(Wadh.)
Other Staff: 1 Lector

Psychology, Experimental
Tel: (01865) 271410 Fax: (01865) 310447

Bryant, P. E., MA *Camb.*, MA *Oxf.*, PhD *Lond.*,
FRS Watts Prof. (Wolfs.)
Claridge, G. S., MA *Oxf.*, PhD *Lond.*, DSc
Glas. Prof., Abnormal Psychology (Magd.)
Cowey, A., MA *Camb.*, MA *Oxf.*, PhD *Camb.*,
DPhil *Oxf.*, FRS Prof., Physiological
Psychology (Linc.)
Emler, N. P., MA *Oxf.* Prof., Social
Psychology (Wolfs.)
Harris, P. L., MA *Oxf.*, DPhil *Oxf.* Prof.
(S.Joh.)
Harvey, Alison G., BSc *Syd.*, MA *Oxf.*, PhD
Syd. Lectr. (S.Ann.)

Henning, G. B., BA *Tor.*, MA *Oxf.*, PhD
Penn. Lectr. (S.Cat.)
Iversen, Susan D., MA *Camb.*, MA *Oxf.*, PhD
Camb., DPhil *Oxf.* Prof.; Head* (Magd.)
Martin, Rose M. A., MA *Oxf.*, DPhil *Oxf.* Lectr.
(S.Edm.)
Mcleod, P. D., MA *Camb.*, MA *Oxf.*, PhD *Camb.*,
DPhil *Oxf.* Lectr. (Qu.)
Nobre, Anna C. de O., BA *Mass.*, MS *Yale*,
MPhil *Yale*, MA *Oxf.*, PhD *Yale* Lectr. (New)
Passingham, R. E., MSc *Lond.*, MA *Oxf.*, PhD
Lond. Prof. (Wadh.)
Plunkett, K. R., BSc *Lond.*, MSc *Sus.*, MA *Oxf.*,
DPhil *Sus.* Prof. (S.Hug.)
Rawlins, J. N. P., MA *Oxf.*, DPhil *Oxf.* Prof.
(Univ.)
Rogers, B. J., BSc *Brist.*, MA *Oxf.*, PhD
Brist. Prof. (L.M.H.)
Rolls, E. T., MA *Oxf.*, DPhil *Oxf.*, DSc Prof.
(Corp.)
Spence, C. J., MA *Oxf.* Lectr. (Som.)

Romance Languages
Tel: (01865) 270570 Fax: (01865) 270757

Maiden, M. D., MA *Oxf.*, DPhil Prof. (Trin.)

Russian, see also Slavonic and East European
Studies, and Slavonic Langs.

Tel: (01865) 270570 Fax: (01865) 270757

Binyon, T. J., MA *Oxf.*, DPhil *Oxf.* Lectr.
(Wadh.)
Curtis, Julie A. E., MA *Oxf.*, DPhil *Oxf.* Lectr.
(Wolfs.)
Everitt, Rev. M., MA *Oxf.* CUF Lectr. (Mert.)
Kahn, A. S., BA *Amherst*, MA *Harv.*, MA *Oxf.*,
DPhil *Oxf.* Lectr. (S.Edm.)
Kelly, Catriona H. M., MA *Oxf.*, DPhil
Oxf. Reader (New)
MacRobert, C. Mary, MA *Oxf.*, DPhil
Oxf. Lectr., Russian and Comparative
Slavonic Philology (L.M.H.)
Smith, G. S., BA *Lond.*, MA *Oxf.*, PhD
Lond. Prof. (New)
Other Staff: 1 Lectr.
Vacant Posts: 1 Instr.

Sanskrit
Tel: (01865) 278200 Fax: (01865) 278190

Benson, J. W., MA *Oxf.* Lectr. (Wolfs.)
Gombrich, R. F., AM *Harv.*, MA *Oxf.*, DPhil
Oxf. Boden Prof. (Ball.)

Slavonic and East European Studies, see
also Russian

Tel: (01865) 276220

Naughton, J. D., MA *Camb.*, MA *Oxf.*, PhD
Camb. Lectr., Czech and Slovak (S.Edm.)
Nicholson, M. A., MA *Oxf.*, DPhil *Oxf.* Lectr.,
Russian (Univ.)

Slavonic Languages, see also Russian

Tel: (01865) 270570 Fax: (01865) 270757

Stone, G. C., BA *Lond.*, MA *Oxf.*, PhD *Lond.*,
FBA Lectr., Non-Russian Slavonic
Languages (Hert.)

Social Studies
Tel: (01865) 278700 Fax: (01865) 278725

Beinart, W., BA *Cape Town*, MA *Lond.*, MA *Oxf.*,
PhD *Lond.* Rhodes Prof., Race Relations
(S.Ant.)

Social Studies and Social Research,
Applied

Tel: (01865) 270325 Fax: (01865) 270324

Buchanan, Ann H., MA *Oxf.*, MSc *Bath*, PhD
S'ton. Lectr. (S.Hil.)
Coleman, D. A., MA *Lond.*, MA *Oxf.*, PhD
Lond. Reader, Demography (Qu.)
Evans, G. A., BA *Sus.*, MA *Oxf.*, MPhil *Oxf.*,
DPhil *Oxf.* Lectr., Sociology (Nuff.)
Hudson, Barbara L., MA *Camb.*, MA
Oxf. Lectr. (Gre.)
Lalljee, M. G., BA *Bom.*, MA *Oxf.*, DPhil
Oxf. Lectr., Social Psychology (Jes.)

MacDonald, K. I., BPhil Oxf., MA Aberd., MA Oxf. Lectr. (Nuff.)

Noble, M. W. J., MSc Oxf., MA Oxf. Lectr., Social Work (Gre.)

Ringen, S., MA Oslo, MA Oxf., DPhil Oslo Prof., Sociology and Social Policy (Gre.)

Roberts, C. H., BSc Bath, MA Oxf. Lectr. (Gre.)

Smith, Teresa, MA Oxf. Lectr.; Dir.* (S.Hil.)

Vacant Posts: 2 Lectrs.

Sociology, see also Soc. Studies and Soc. Res., Appl.

Tel: (01865) 278700 Fax: (01865) 278725

Gambetta, D., MA Oxf., PhD Camb. Reader (All S.)

Martins, H. G., BSc(Econ) Lond., MA Oxf. Lectr., Sociology of Latin America (S.Ant.)

Other Staff: 1 Temp. Fac. Lectr.

Spanish

Tel: (01865) 270570 Fax: (01865) 270757

Fiddian, R. W., MA Edin., MA Oxf., PhD Edin. Reader (Wadh.)

Garcia-Bellido, E. Paloma, MA Madrid, MA Oxf. Lectr., Spanish Linguistics and Philology (S.Cross)

Griffin, C. H., MA Oxf., DPhil Oxf. Lectr., Latin American Literature (Trin.)

Michael, I. D. L., BA Lond., MA Oxf., PhD Manc. King Alfonso XIII Prof., Spanish Studies (Exet.)

Pattison, D. G., MA Oxf., DPhil Oxf. Reader (Magd.)

Rutherford, J. D., MA Oxf., DPhil Oxf. Fac. Lectr. (Qu.)

Southworth, E. A., MA Camb., MA Oxf. Lectr. (S.Pet.)

Thompson, C. P., MA Oxf., DPhil Oxf. Fac. Lectr. (S.Cat.)

Truman, R. W., MA Oxf., DPhil Oxf. Lectr. (Ch.Ch.)

Other Staff: 2 Lectors; 1 Instr.

Statistics, see also Econ. and Stats., Inst. of

Tel: (01865) 272860 Fax: (01865) 272595

Bithell, J. F., MA Oxf., DPhil Oxf. Lectr. (S.Pet.)

Clifford, P., BSc Lond., MA Oxf., PhD Calif. Reader, Mathematical Statistics (Jes.)

Donnelly, P. J., BSc Qld., MA Oxf., DPhil Oxf. Prof., Statistical Science; Head* (S.Ann.)

Gittins, J. C., MA Camb., MA Oxf., PhD Wales, DSc Oxf. Prof., Mathematics (Keb.)

Griffiths, R. C., MA Oxf., PhD Syd. Lectr., Mathematical Statistics (L.M.H.)

Hiorns, R. W., MA Edin., MA Oxf., PhD Edin. Lectr. (Linac.)

Laws, C. N., MA Camb., MA Oxf., PhD Camb. Lectr. (Wolfs.)

Ripley, B. D., MA Camb., MA Oxf., PhD Camb. Prof., Applied Statistics (S.Pet.)

Syriac

Tel: (01865) 278200 Fax: (01865) 278190

Brock, S. P., MA Camb., MA Oxf., DPhil Oxf., FBA Reader (Wolfs.)

Theology

Tel: (01865) 270790 Fax: (01865) 270795

Barton, J., MA Oxf., DPhil Oxf., DLitt Oxf. Oriel and Laing Prof., Interpretation of Holy Scripture (Oriel)

Cross, R. A., MA Oxf., DPhil Oxf. CUF Lectr. (Oriel)

Day, J., MA Oxf., DPhil Oxf. Reader (L.M.H.)

Edwards, M. J., MA Oxf., DPhil Oxf. Lectr., Patristics (Ch.Ch.)

Gillingham, Susan E., MA Oxf., DPhil Oxf. CUF Lectr. (Worc.)

Joyce, P. M., MA Oxf., DPhil Oxf. Lectr., Old Testament (S.Pet.)

MacCulloch, D. N. J., MA Oxf., PhD Camb., DPhil Oxf. Prof., Reformation Church History and Theology (S.Cross)

Mayr-Harting, H. M. R. E., MA Oxf., DPhil Oxf., FBA Regius Prof., Ecclesiastical History (Ch.Ch.)

Morgan, Rev. R. C., MA Camb., MA Oxf. Reader, New Testament Theology (Linac.)

Muddiman, J. B., MA Oxf., DPhil Oxf. CUF Lectr. (Mansf.)

O'Donovan, Rev. O. M. T., MA Oxf., DPhil Oxf. Regius Prof., Moral and Pastoral Theology (Ch.Ch.)

Rowland, C. C., MA Camb., MA Oxf., PhD Camb., DPhil Oxf. Dean Ireland's Prof., Exegesis of Holy Scripture (Qu.)

Swinburne, R. G., BPhil Oxf., MA Oxf. Nolloth Prof., Philosophy of Christian Religion (Oriel)

Sanderson, A. G. J. S., MA Oxf. Spalding Prof., Eastern Religions and Ethics (All S.)

Tuckett, C. M., MA Oxf., MA Camb., PhD Lanc. Lectr., New Testament (Wolfs.)

Ward, Rev. J. S. K., BA Wales, BLitt Oxf., MA Camb., MA Oxf. Regius Prof., Divinity (Ch.Ch.)

Ware, Rt. Rev. K. T., MA Oxf., DPhil Oxf. Spalding Lectr., Eastern Orthodox Studies (Pemb.)

Webster, J. B., MA Oxf., MA Camb., PhD Camb., DPhil Oxf. Lady Margaret Prof., Divinity (Ch.Ch.)

Williams, Rev. T. S. M., MA Oxf. CUF Lectr. (Trin.)

Transport Studies, see Geog.

Turkish

Tel: (01865) 278200 Fax: (01865) 278190

Kerslake, Celia J., BA Camb., MA Oxf., DPhil Oxf. Lectr. (S.Ant.)

Repp, R. C., BA Williams(Mass.), MA Oxf., DPhil Oxf. Lectr., Turkish History (S.Cross)

Other Staff: 1 Instr.

Zoology

Tel: (01865) 271234 Fax: (01865) 310447

Anderson, R. M., BSc Lond., MA Oxf., PhD Lond., FRS Linacre Prof.; Dir., WT Centre for the Epidemiol. of Infectious Diseases (Mert.)

Axton, J. M., BA M.I.T., MA Oxf., PhD Stan. Lectr. (Ball.)

Bennet-Clark, H. C., BSc Lond., MA Oxf., PhD Camb., DPhil Oxf. Reader, Invertebrate Zoology (S.Cat.)

Bundy, D. A. P., BSc Lond., MA Oxf., PhD Lond. Prof., Parasite Epidemiology (Linac.)

Day, Karen P., BSc Melb., MA Oxf., PhD Melb. Reader, Molecular Epidemiology (Hert.)

Gardner, R. L., MA Camb., MA Oxf., PhD Camb., FRS Henry Dale Royal Soc. Res. Prof. (Ch.Ch.)

Goldstein, D. B., BS Calif., MA Oxf., MS Conn., PhD Stan. Lectr., Evolutionary Biology (New)

Graham, C. F., MA Oxf., DPhil Oxf., FRS Prof., Animal Development (S.Cat.)

Guilford, T. C., MA Oxf., DPhil Oxf. Lectr., Animal Behaviour/Ecology (Mert.)

Hamilton, W. D., MA Oxf. Royal Soc. Res. Prof. (New)

Harvey, P., BA York(UK), MA Oxf., DPhil York(UK), DSc Oxf., FRS Prof.; Head* (Jes.)

Iles, J. F., MA Oxf., DPhil Oxf. Lectr., Comparative Physiology (S.Hug.)

Kacelnik, A., LicCienBiol Buenos Aires, MA Oxf., DPhil Oxf. Prof. (Pemb.)

Kearsey, S. E., MA Oxf., DPhil Oxf. Lectr. (Keb.)

Kemp, T. S., MA Camb., MA Oxf., PhD Camb., DPhil Oxf. Lectr. (S.Joh.)

Krebs, J. R., MA Oxf., DPhil Oxf. Royal Soc. Res. Prof. (Pemb.)

May, Sir Robert, MA Oxf. Royal Soc. Res. Prof. (Mert.)

McFarland, D. J., BSc Liv., MA Oxf., DPhil Oxf. Reader, Animal Behaviour (Ball.)

Nee, S. P., BA Tor., MA W.Ont., MA Oxf., DPhil Sus. Lectr., Ecology (L.M.H.)

Newman, J. A., BA N.Y.State, PhD N.Y.State Lectr., Ecology (S.Pet.)

Perrins, C. M., BSc Lond., MB BChir Camb., MA Oxf., DPhil Oxf. Prof., Ornithology; Dir., Edward Grey Inst. of Field Ornithol. (Wolfs.)

Rogers, D. J., MA Oxf., DPhil Oxf. Lectr., Entomology (Gre.)

Shotton, D. M., MA Camb., MA Oxf., PhD Camb., DPhil Oxf. Lectr. (Wolfs.)

Simpson, S. J., BSc Qld., MA Oxf., PhD Lond. Prof., Entomology; Curator (Jes.)

Speight, M. R., BSc Wales, MA Oxf., DPhil York(UK) Lectr., Agricultural and Forest Entomology (S.Ann.)

MEDICINE

Tel: (01865) 221689 Fax: (01865) 750750

Chapel, Helen M., MB BChir Camb., MA Oxf. Sr. Clin. Lectr., Clinical Immunology (Som.)

Dunger, D. B., MD Lond., MA Oxf. Reader, Paediatrics

Hawton, K. E., MB BChir Camb., MA Camb., MA Oxf., DM Oxf. Prof., Psychiatry (Gre.)

Hopkin, J. M., MD Wales, MSc Edin., MA Oxf. Sr. Clin. Lectr., Chest Medicine (Bras.)

Jewell, D. P., BM Oxf., MA Oxf., DPhil Oxf. Reader, Gastroenterology (Gre.)

Matthews, D. R., BM Oxf., MA Oxf., DPhil Oxf. Sr. Clin. Lectr., Clinical Medicine (Harris)

Mayon-White, R. T., MB BS Lond., BA Open(UK), MA Oxf. Sr. Clin. Lectr., Public Health Medicine

Robson, P. J., MB BS Lond., MA Oxf. Sr. Clin. Lectr., Psychiatry

Stradling, J. R., BSc Lond., MB BS Lond., MA Oxf. Sr. Clin. Lectr., Chest Medicine

Tunbridge, W. M. G., MA Oxf., DM Oxf. Dir., Postgraduate Medical Studies (Wadh.)

Weatherall, Sir David, MD Liv., MA Oxf., DM Oxf., FRCP, FRS Regius Prof.; Hon. Dir., Inst. of Molecular Med. (Ch.Ch.)

Wojnarowska, Fenella, BM BCh Oxf., MSc Oxf., MA Oxf. Reader, Dermatology (Som.)

Anaesthetics

Tel: (01865) 224892 Fax: (01865) 794191

Foëx, P., MA Oxf., DPhil Oxf., DM Geneva Nuffield Prof.; Head* (Pemb.)

Hahn, C. E. W., MA Oxf., MSc Sheff., DPhil Oxf. Prof. (Gre.)

McQuay, H. J., MA Oxf., BM Oxf. Clin. Reader, Pain Relief (Ball.)

Sear, J. W., BSc Lond., MA Oxf., MB BS Lond., PhD Lond., FFARCS Clin. Reader; Dir., Clin. Studies (Gre.)

Young, J. D., MA Oxf., DM S'ton., FFARCS Clin. Reader (Worc.)

Bacteriology, see Pathol. and Bacteriol.

Biochemistry, Clinical, and Cellular Science

Tel: (01865) 220481 Fax: (01865) 221834

Ashcroft, S. J. H., BA Camb., MA Oxf., PhD Brist. Reader, Clinical Biochemistry (Magd.)

Callaghan, R., BSc Oxf., MA Oxf., PhD Melb. Lectr., Clinical Biochemistry (Mert.)

Gatter, K. C., BM Oxf., MA Oxf., DPhil Oxf. Prof., Pathology; Head* (S.Joh.)

Gibbons, R. J., BM Oxf., MA Oxf., DPhil Oxf. Lectr., Clinical Biochemistry (Gre.)

Mason, D. Y., MA Oxf., BM BCh Oxf., DM Oxf., FRCPath Prof., Cellular Pathology (Pemb.)

Sykes, B. C., BSc Liv., MA Oxf., PhD Brist. Prof., Molecular Pathology (Wolfs.)

Other Staff: 1 Clin. Lectr.

Vacant Posts: 1 Prof.; 1 Clin. Lectr.

Cardiovascular Medicine

Tel: (01865) 220257 Fax: (01865) 768844

Watkins, H. C., BSc Lond., MB BS Lond., MA Oxf., PhD Lond.   Field Marshal Alexander Prof.; Head* (Exet.)

Other Staff: 2 Clin. Lectrs.

Cellular Science, see Biochem., Clin., and Cellular Sci.

Human Anatomy and Genetics

Tel: (01865) 272169 Fax: (01865) 272420

Boyd, C. A. R., MB Lond., BSc Oxf., BM Oxf., MA Oxf., DPhil Oxf.   Lectr., Anatomy (Bras.)

Charlton, H. M., MA Oxf., DPhil Oxf.   Reader, Neuroendocrinology (Linac.)

Davies, Kay E., CBE, MA Oxf., DPhil Oxf.   Dr Lee's Prof., Anatomy; Head* (Hert.)

Horder, T. J., MA Oxf., PhD Edin.   Lectr., Human Anatomy (Jes.)

Matthews, Margaret R., BSc Oxf., MA Oxf., DM Oxf.   Prof., Human Anatomy (L.M.H.)

Morris, J. F., BSc Brist., MB ChB Brist., MD Brist., MA Oxf.   Prof., Human Anatomy (S.Hug.)

Morriss-Kay, Gillian M., BA Durh., MA Oxf., PhD Camb.   Prof., Human Anatomy (Ball.)

Storey, Kate G., BSc Sus., MA Oxf., PhD Camb.   Lectr. (Ch.Ch.)

Taylor, J. S. H., BSc Brist., MA Oxf., PhD Lond.   Lectr. (Pemb.)

Vacant Posts: 1 Lectr.

Medical Illustration

Tel: (01865) 220900 Fax: (01865) 741370

Dove, P. L. C., MA Oxf.   Dir.*

Medical School Administration

Tel: (01865) 221689 Fax: (01865) 750750

Fleming, K. A., MB ChB Glas., MA Oxf., DPhil Oxf.   Clin. Reader, Pathology (Gre.)

Goss, S. J., MA Oxf., DPhil Oxf.   Lectr., Pathology; Dir., Pre-Clin Studies (Wadh.)

Sear, J. W., BSc Lond., MA Oxf., MB BS Lond., PhD Lond., FFARCS   Clin. Reader, Anaesthetics; Dir., Clin. Studies (Gre.)

Weatherall, Sir David, MA Oxf., MD Liv., DM Oxf.,, FRCP, FRS   Regius Prof., Medicine; Hon. Dir., Inst. of Molecular Med. (Ch.Ch.)

Medicine, Clinical

Tel: (01865) 220558 Fax: (01865) 222901

Bell, Sir Jack, BSc Alta., MA Oxf., DM Oxf.   Nuffield Prof.; Head* (Magd.)

Fairweather, D. S., MB BChir Camb., MA Oxf.   Lectr., Geriatric Medicine (Corp.)

Grimley Evans, Sir John, MA Camb., MD Camb., DM Oxf., FRCP   Prof., Geriatric Medicine (Gre.)

Newbold, C. I., MA Camb., MA Oxf., PhD Camb., DPhil Oxf.   Prof. (Gre.)

Peto, R., MSc Lond., MA Camb., MA Oxf., FRS   ICRF Prof., Medical Statistics and Epidemiology; Co-Dir., Clinical Trials Service Unit and Epidemiological Studies Unit (Gre.)

Phillips, R. E., MA Oxf., MD Melb., MB BS, FRACP   Prof. (Wolfs.)

Ratcliffe, P. J., BA Camb., MB BChir Camb., MA Oxf., MD Camb.   Prof., Clinical Medicine and Immunology (Jes.)

Thakker, R. V., MA Camb., MB BChir Camb., MD Camb.   May Prof. (New)

Townsend, A. R. M., MB BS Lond., MA Oxf., PhD Lond.   Prof., Molecular Immunology (Linac.)

Turner, R. C., MA Oxf., MD Camb.   Prof.; Head, Diabetes Res. Labs. (Gre.)

Twycross, R. G., MB BS Lond., DM Oxf.   CRMF Clin. Reader, Palliative Medicine (S.Pet.)

Warrell, D. A., MA Oxf., DSc Oxf., DM Oxf.,, FRCP   Prof. (S.Cross)

Wordsworth, B. P., MA Oxf., MB BS Lond., MA Oxf.   Prof., Rheumatology (Gre.)

Other Staff: 1 Lectr.; 4 Clin. Lectrs.; 1 Clin. Tutor

Neurology, Clinical

Tel: (01865) 224205 Fax: (01865) 790493

Donaghy, M. J., BSc Lond., MB BS Lond., MA Oxf., PhD Camb., DPhil Oxf., FRCP   Clin. Reader; Acting Head* (Gre.)

Esiri, Margaret M., DM Oxf., MA   Prof., Neuropathology (S.Hug.)

Mills, K. R., MB BS Lond., BSc Lond., MA Oxf., PhD Lond.   Prof., Clinical Neurophysiology (Gre.)

Vincent, Angela C., MB BS Lond., MA Oxf., MSc Lond., MSt   Prof., Clinical Neuroimmunology (Som.)

Other Staff: 1 Clin. Lectr.

Vacant Posts: 1 Prof.

Obstetrics and Gynaecology

Tel: (01865) 221023 Fax: (01865) 769141

Barlow, D. H., BSc Glas., MA Oxf., MD Glas.   Nuffield Prof.; Head* (Oriel)

Bassett, J. M., BSc Reading, MA Oxf., PhD Reading   Lectr., Endocrinology (Ch.Ch.)

Chamberlain, P. F., BA Trinity(Dub.), MB BCh BAO Trinity(Dub.), MA Oxf., MD Trinity(Dub.)   NHS Lectr. (Mert.)

Ledger, W. L., BM Oxf., MA Oxf., DPhil Oxf.   Clin. Reader (Gre.)

MacKenzie, I. Z., MB ChB Brist., MA Oxf., MD Brist., DSc Oxf.   Clin. Reader (S.Hug.)

Mardon, Helen J., MA Oxf., DPhil Oxf.   Lectr. (S.Cat.)

Redman, C. W. G., MB BChir Camb., BM Oxf., MA Oxf., MA Camb.   Clin. Prof., Obstetric Medicine (L.M.H.)

Sargent, I. L., BSc Wales, MA Oxf., PhD Lond.   Lectr. (Mansf.)

Other Staff: 2 Clin. Lectrs.

Oncology, Medical

Tel: (01865) 226184 Fax: (01865) 226179

Harris, A. L., BSc Liv., MB ChB Liv., MA Oxf., DPhil Oxf., FRCP   ICRF Prof.; Dir.* (S.Hug.)

Ophthalmology

Tel: (01865) 248996 Fax: (01865) 794508

Bron, A. J., BSc Lond., MB BS Lond., MA Oxf., FRCS   Clin. Prof.; Margaret Ogilvie's Reader; Head* (Linac.)

Osborne, N. N., BSc Lond., MA Oxf., PhD St And.   Prof. (Gre.)

Tiffany, J. M., MA Camb., MA Oxf., PhD Camb.   Lectr., Ophthalmological Biochemistry (S.Cross)

Other Staff: 1 Clin. Lectr.

Orthopaedic Surgery

Tel: (01865) 741155 Fax: (01865) 227354

Bulstrode, C. J. K., BM Oxf., MA Oxf., FRCS   Prof. (Gre.)

Francis, M. J. O., MA Oxf., DPhil Oxf.   Lectr. (Wolfs.)

Kenwright, J., BM Oxf., MA Oxf., FRCS   Nuffield Prof.; Head* (Worc.)

Simpson, A. H. R. W., BM Oxf., MA Camb., MA Oxf., DM Oxf., FRCS, FRCSEd   Clin. Reader (S.Pet.)

Other Staff: 2 Clin. Lectrs.

Paediatrics

Tel: (01865) 221077 Fax: (01865) 220479

Harris, Ann, MA Oxf., PhD Lond.   Lectr. (S.Cross)

Moxon, E. R., BA Camb., MB BChir Camb., MA Camb., MA Oxf.   Action Res. Prof.; Head* (Jes.)

Sullivan, P. B., BSc Manc., MB ChB Manc., MA Oxf.   Lectr. (Magd.)

Wilkinson, A. R., MB ChB Birm., MA Oxf., FRCP   Prof. (All S.)

Other Staff: 2 Clin. Lectrs.

Pathology, see also Biochem., Clin., and Cellular Sci.

Tel: (01865) 275500 Fax: (01865) 275501

Brownlee, G. G., MA Camb., MA Oxf., PhD Camb., DPhil Oxf., FRS   E. P. Abraham Prof., Chemical Pathology (Linc.)

Cook, P. R., MA Oxf., DPhil Oxf.   Prof., Cell Biology (Bras.)

Errington, J., BSc Newcastle(UK), MA Oxf., PhD CNAA   Prof., Chemical Pathology (Magd.)

Gordon, S., MB ChB Cape Town, MA Oxf., PhD Rockefeller   Glaxo Prof., Cellular Pathology (Exet.)

Goss, S. J., MA Oxf., DPhil Oxf.   Lectr., Pathology; Dir., Pre-Clin. Studies (Wadh.)

Hunt, S. V., MA Oxf., DPhil Oxf.   Lectr., Immunology (Keb.)

MacPherson, G. G., BM Oxf., MA Oxf., DPhil Oxf.   Reader, Experimental Pathology (Oriel)

Mellman, I., AB Oberlin, PhD Yale   Newton Abraham Visiting Prof. (Linc.) (1998–99)

Proudfoot, N. J., BSc Lond., MA Oxf., PhD Camb.   Prof., Chemical Pathology (Bras.)

Smith, G. L., BSc Leeds, MA Camb., MA Oxf., PhD CNAA   Prof., Bacteriology (Wadh.)

Vaux, D. J. T., BM Oxf., MA Oxf., DPhil Oxf.   Lectr., Experimental Pathology (Linc.)

Waldmann, H., MB Camb., BM Oxf., MA Camb., MA Oxf., PhD Camb., DPhil Oxf., FRS   Prof.; Head* (Linc.)

Wigley, D. B., MA Oxf.   Reader, Experimental Pathology (Linc.)

Other Staff: 1 Temp. Lectr.

Pathology and Bacteriology

Tel: (01865) 220550 Fax: (01865) 220524

Fleming, K. A., MB ChB Glas., MA Oxf., DPhil Oxf.   Clin. Reader, Pathology; Dean, Fac. of Clin. Med. (Gre.)

McGee, J. O'D., MB ChB Glas., MD Glas., MA Oxf., PhD Glas.   Prof., Morbid Anatomy; Head* (Linac.)

Slack, Mary P. E., MB BChir Camb., BM Oxf., MA Camb., MA Oxf.   Lectr., Bacteriology (Gre.)

Other Staff: 1 Lectr.; 3 Clin. Lectrs.; 1 Clin. Tutor; 1 Temp. Clin. Reader

Vacant Posts: 1 Prof.

Pharmacology

Tel: (01865) 271850 Fax: (01865) 271853

Brading, Alison F., BSc Brist., MA Oxf., PhD Brist.   Prof. (L.M.H.)

Cunnane, T. C., BSc Bath, MA Oxf., PhD Glas.   Lectr. (Hert.)

Gill, E. W., MA Oxf., DPhil Oxf.   Lectr. (Worc.)

Greenfield, Susan A., MA Oxf., DPhil Oxf.   Prof., Synaptic Pharmacology (Linc.)

Sim, Edith, BSc Edin., MA Oxf., DPhil Oxf.   Prof. (S.Pet.)

Smith, A. D., MA Oxf., DPhil Oxf.   Prof.; Head* (L.M.H.)

Terrar, D. A., MA Oxf.   Reader (Worc.)

Pharmacology, Clinical

Tel: (01865) 224524 Fax: (01865) 791712

Aronson, J. K., MA Oxf., MB ChB Glas., DPhil Oxf., FRCP   NHS Clin. Reader (Gre.)

Grahame-Smith, D. G., CBE, MA Oxf., MB BS Lond., PhD Lond., FRCP   Rhodes Prof.; Head* (Corp.)

Other Staff: 2 Clin. Lectrs.

Physiology, see above

Postgraduate Medical Education and Training

Tel: (01865) 240600 Fax: (01865) 240699

Tunbridge, W. M. G., MA Oxf., DM Oxf.   Dir.* (Wadh.)

Psychiatry

Tel: (01865) 741717 Fax: (01865) 793101

Goodwin, G. M., BM Oxf., MA Oxf., DPhil Oxf.   Prof.; Head* (Mert.)

Harrison, P. J., BM Oxf., MA Oxf., DM Oxf.   Clin. Reader (Wolfs.)

Jacoby, R., MA Oxf., DM Oxf., FRCP, FRCPsych   Prof., Psychiatry of Old Age (Linac.)

Mayou, R. A., BSc Oxf., BM BCh Oxf., MA Oxf., MSc Oxf., MPhil Lond.   Prof. (Nuff.)

Stores, G., BA *Manc.*, MA *Oxf.*, DM *Manc.*, FRCP, FRCPsych Clin. Reader, Child and Adolescent Psychiatry (Linac.)
Other Staff: 1 Lectr.; 2 Clin. Lectrs.; 1 Clin. Tutor
Vacant Posts: 1 Clin. Lectr.

Public Health and Primary Health Care

Tel: (01865) 742277 Fax: (01865) 226720

Carpenter, Lucy M., BSc *Exe.*, MSc *Lond.*, MA *Oxf.*, PhD *Lond.* Lectr., Statistical Epidemiology (Nuff.)
Fitzpatrick, R. M., BA *Oxf.*, MSc *Lond.*, MA *Oxf.* Prof., Medical Sociology (Nuff.)
Graham-Jones, S., MB BS *Lond.*, MA *Oxf.*, DPhil *Oxf.* NHS Lectr., General Practice (Som.)
Hope, R. A., BA *Oxf.*, BM BCh *Oxf.*, MA *Oxf.* Reader, Practice Skills (S.Cross)
Lawrence, M. S. T. A., BM *Oxf.*, MA *Oxf.* NHS Lectr., General Practice (Gre.)
Mant, D., MB ChB *Birm.*, MA *Camb.*, MSc *Lond.* Prof., General Practice; Head, Primary Health Care (Kell.)
Neil, H. A. W., MB BS *Lond.*, MA *Oxf.*, MSc *Lond.* Lectr., Clinical Epidemiology (Wolfs.)
Venables, Katherine M., BSc *Lond.*, MB BS *Lond.*, MSc *Lond.*, MD *Lond.*, FRCP Lectr., Occupational Medicine
Vessey, M. P., CBE, MB BS *Lond.*, MD *Lond.*, MA *Oxf.* Prof., Public Health; Head* (S.Cross)
Other Staff: 2 Clin. Lectrs.
Vacant Posts: 1 Clin. Reader

Radiology

Tel: (01865) 224285 Fax: (01865) 721588

Golding, S. J., MB BS *Lond.*, MA *Oxf.* NHS Lectr. (Univ.)
Moore, N. R., MB BChir *Camb.*, MA *Camb.*, MA *Oxf.*, FRCR NHS Lectr. (Gre.)
Shepstone, B. J., BM BCh *Oxf.*, MA *Oxf.*, MD *Cape Town*, DPhil *Oxf.*, DSc *O.F.S.*, FIP, FRCR Reader; Head* (Wolfs.)

Surgery

Tel: (01865) 220532 Fax: (01865) 768876

Austyn, J. M., MA *Oxf.*, DPhil *Oxf.* Reader (Wolfs.)
Collin, J., MA *Oxf.*, MD *Newcastle(UK)*, FRCS Clin. Reader (Trin.)
Gray, D. W. R., BSc *Leeds*, MB ChB *Leeds*, MA *Oxf.*, DPhil *Oxf.* Lectr. (Oriel)
Hands, Linda J., BSc *Lond.*, MB BS *Lond.*, MS *Lond.*, MA *Oxf.*, FRCS Clin. Reader (Gre.)
Morris, Sir Peter, MB BS *Melb.*, MA *Oxf.*, PhD *Melb.*, FRS, FRCS, FRACS, FACS Nuffield Prof.; Head* (Ball.)
Wood, Kathryn J., BSc *Oxf.*, MA *Oxf.*, DPhil *Oxf.* Prof., Immunology (Univ.)
Other Staff: 1 Clin. Reader; 6 Clin. Lectrs.; 1 Clin. Tutor; 1 Temp. Clin. Reader
Vacant Posts: 1 Prof.; 1 Clin. Lectr. (ICRF)

SPECIAL CENTRES, ETC

Ashmolean Museum of Art and Archaeology

Tel: (01865) 278000 Fax: (01865) 278018

Brown, C. P. H., MA *Oxf.* Dir.* (Worc.)

Hebrew and Jewish Studies, Oxford Centre for

Tel: (01865) 377946 Fax: (01865) 375079

Wasserstein, B. M. J., MA *Oxf.*, DPhil *Oxf.* President* (S.Cross)

History of Science, Museum of the

Tel: (01865) 277280 Fax: (01865) 277288

Bennett, J. A., MA *Oxf.*, PhD *Camb.* Keeper* (Linac.)
Other Staff: 2 Asst. Keepers

Islamic Studies, Oxford Centre for

Tel: (01865) 278730 Fax: (01865) 248942

Nizami, F. A., MA *Alig.*, MA *Oxf.*, DPhil *Oxf.* Dir.* (Magd.)

Maison Française

Tel: (01865) 274220 Fax: (01865) 274225

Vatin, J. C., BLitt *Oxf.*, MA *Oxf.* Dir.* (S.Ant.)

Natural History, Museum of

Tel: (01865) 272959 Fax: (01865) 272970

Thomson, K. S., BSc *Birm.*, AM *Harv.*, PhD *Harv.* Dir.* (Kell.)

Pitt Rivers Museum

Tel: (01865) 270927 Fax: (01865) 270943

Gosden, C., BA *Sheff.*, MA *Oxf.*, PhD *Sheff.* Lectr.; Curator (S.Cross)
Harris, Clare, BA *Camb.*, MA *Oxf.*, PhD *Lond.* Curator; Lectr. (Linac.)
La Rue, Helena, MA *Oxf.*, DPhil *Oxf.* Lectr.; Curator, Bate Collection (S.Cross)
Mitchell, P. J., MA *Camb.*, MA *Oxf.*, DPhil *Oxf.* Lectr.; Curator (S.Hug.)
O'Hanlon, M. D. P., MA *Oxf.* Dir.* (Linac.)
Peers, Laura L., BA *Trent*, MA *Winn.*, MA *Manit.*, MA *Oxf.*, PhD *McM.* Curator; Lectr. (Linac.)

Queen Elizabeth House (International Development Centre)

Tel: (01865) 273600 Fax: (01865) 273607

Adam, C. S., MA *Oxf.*, MA *St And.*, MPhil *Oxf.*, DPhil *Oxf.* Lectr., Development Economics (S.Cross)
Cassen, R. H., PhD *Harv.*, MA Prof., Development Economics (S.Ant.)
Fennell, Rosemary, MA *N.U.I.*, MA *Oxf.*, PhD *Lond.* Lectr., Agricultural Economics (Linac.)
Gibney, M. J., BEc *Monash*, MA *Oxf.*, MPhil *Camb.*, PhD *Camb.* Lectr., Forced Migration (Linac.)
Gooptu, Nandini, MA *Calc.*, MA *Oxf.*, PhD *Camb.* Lectr., South Asian Studies (S.Ant.)
Harriss-White, Barbara, MA *Camb.*, MA *Oxf.*, PhD *E.Anglia* Prof., Development Studies (Wolfs.)
Peters, G. H., MSc(Econ) *Wales*, MA *Oxf.* Res. Prof.; Head, Agric. Econ. Unit (Wolfs.)
Sneath, D. A., BSc *Ulster*, MA *Oxf.*, PhD *Camb.*, DPhil *Oxf.* Lectr., Agricultural Economics (S.Cross)
Stewart, Frances J., DPhil *Oxf.* Prof., Development Economics; Dir.* (Som.)
Turton, D. A., MA *Oxf.* Res. Prof.; Dir., Refugee Studies Programme (Gre.)
Vaughan, Megan A., BA *Kent*, MA *Oxf.*, PhD *Lond.* Rhodes Lectr., Commonwealth Studies (Nuff.)
Other Staff: 1 Lectr.
Vacant Posts: 1 Prof.

ALL SOULS COLLEGE

Tel: (01865) 279379 Fax: (01865) 279299

Davis, John H. R., PhD *Lond.*, MA, FBA Warden*
Lever, J. F., QC, MA Sr. Dean
Seaman, T. W., MA Bursar

BALLIOL COLLEGE

Tel: (01865) 277777 Fax: (01865) 277803

Campbell-Lamerton, M. J., OBE, MA Domestic Bursar
Davies, P. L., LLM *Lond.*, LLM *Yale*, MA DPhil Estates Bursar
Graham, A. W. M., MA Acting Master
Hazareesingh, S. K., MA DPhil Sr. Tutor
Lucas, Colin R., MA *Oxf.*, DPhil *Oxf.*, Hon. Dr *Lyons II*, FRHistS Vice-Chancellor; Master*

BLACKFRIARS

Permanent Private Hall

Tel: (01865) 278441 Fax: (01865) 278403, 278441

Edney, Rev. R. M. W., MPhil Bursar
Ombres, Rev. R. Secretary of Studies
Parvis, Rev. P. M., BA *Emory*, BD *Emory*, MA *Oxf.*, DPhil *Oxf.*, STL Regent*

BRASENOSE COLLEGE

Tel: (01865) 277830 Fax: (01865) 277822

Ewens, M. Domestic Bursar
Gasser, R. P. H., MA DPhil Bursar
Ingram, M. J., MA DPhil Sr. Tutor
Windlesham, The Rt. Hon. Lord, CVO, MA DLitt Principal*

CAMPION HALL

Permanent Private Hall

Tel: (01865) 286100 Fax: (01865) 286148

Hughes, Rev. G. J., MA PhD Master*
Murphy, T., MA PhD Bursar
Rafferty, Rev. O., MSc DPhil Sr. Tutor

CHRIST CHURCH

Tel: (01865) 276150 Fax: (01865) 276276

Benthall, R. P., MA Treasurer
Cartwright, J., BCL MA Sr. Censor
Drury, Very Rev. J. H., MA *Camb.*, MA *Oxf.* Dean*
Harris, J. G., MA Steward

CORPUS CHRISTI COLLEGE

Tel: (01865) 276700 Fax: (01865) 793111

Harrison, S. J., MA DPhil Sr. Tutor
Holmes, C. P. H., BSc *Sur.*, MA Domestic Bursar
Ruck Keene, B. C., JP, BA *York(UK)*, MA Bursar
Taylor, C. C. W., MA *Edin.*, MA *Oxf.*, BPhil Acting President
Thomas, Sir Keith, Hon. DLitt *Kent*, Hon. DLitt *Wales*, Hon. LittD *Sheff.*, Hon. LLD *Williams(Mass.)*, MA, FBA President*

EXETER COLLEGE

Tel: (01865) 279600 Fax: (01865) 279630

Butler, Marilyn S., MA *Oxf.*, DPhil *Oxf.* Rector*
Kirwan, C. A., MA Sr. Tutor
Marshall, Susan E., MA Home Bursar
Stewart, W. B., MA *St And.*, MA *Oxf.*, DPhil Finance and Estates Bursar

GREEN COLLEGE

Tel: (01865) 274770 Fax: (01865) 274796

Hanson, Sir John, KCMG, CBE, MA Warden*
Kerr, J. H., MA DM, FFARCS Sr. Bursar
Wordsworth, B. P., MB BS *Lond.*, MA Sr. Tutor

GREYFRIARS

Permanent Private Hall

Tel: (01865) 243694 Fax: (01865) 727027

Barrie, C. W. Bursar

Innes, Rev. S., MA   Sr. Tutor
Weinandy, Rev. T. G., MA PhD   Warden*

HARRIS MANCHESTER COLLEGE

Tel: (01865) 271006 Fax: (01865) 271012
Carey, G. M. F., MA   Sr. Tutor
Smith, L. J., MSc DPhil   Academic Bursar
Waller, Rev. R., BD Lond., MTh Nott., PhD Lond.,
   MA   Principal*

HERTFORD COLLEGE

Tel: (01865) 279400 Fax: (01865) 279437
Baker, P. R., MA Reading, MA Oxf.   Bursar
Bodmer, Sir Walter, MA PhD Hon. DSc,
   FRS   Principal*
Tanner, N. W., MSc Melb., PhD Camb., MA   Sr.
   Tutor

JESUS COLLEGE

Tel: (01865) 279700 Fax: (01865) 279687
Beer, P. G., CB, CBE   Home Bursar
Clarke, P. J., BCL MA   Estates Bursar
North, Sir Peter, CBE, QC, MA DCL,
   FBA   Principal*
Wormersley, D. J., MA DPhil   Sr. Tutor

KEBLE COLLEGE

Tel: (01865) 272727 Fax: (01865) 272705
Cameron, Averil M., MA Oxf., PhD Lond., FBA,
   FSA   Warden*
Jenkinson, T. J., AM Penn., MA Camb., MA Oxf.,
   DPhil   Sr. Tutor
Lovett, K. J., CBE, MA   Bursar

KELLOGG COLLEGE

Tel: (01865) 270383 Fax: (01865) 270314
Flood, R. G., BSc Belf., PhD Trinity(Dub.), MSc
   MA   Sr. Tutor
Hawkins, A. B., BA Reading, PhD Lond.,
   MA   Bursar
Thomas, G. P., BSc Wales, PhD Camb.,
   MA   President*

LADY MARGARET HALL

Tel: (01865) 274300 Fax: (01865) 511069
Bailey, J. D., DPhil   Treasurer
Fall, Sir Brian, GCVO, KCMG, MA Oxf., LLM
   Mich., MA   Principal*
MacRobert, C. Mary, MA DPhil   Sr. Tutor

LINACRE COLLEGE

Tel: (01865) 271650 Fax: (01865) 271668
Flint, Kate, MA Lond., MA Oxf., DPhil   Sr.
   Tutor
Read, W. R., BSc Leeds, MA   Domestic Bursar
Reid, Alison A., MA   Finance Bursar
Slack, Paul A., MA DPhil, FBA   Principal*

LINCOLN COLLEGE

Tel: (01865) 279800 Fax: (01865) 279802
Anderson, W. E. K., MA Oxf., MLitt Oxf., DLitt,
   FRSEd   Rector*
Bacon, R. W., BA Brist., MA DPhil   Sr. Tutor

Norbury, J., BSc Qld., PhD Camb., MA   Bursar

MAGDALEN COLLEGE

Tel: (01865) 276000 Fax: (01865) 276103
Ibbetson, D. J., MA Camb., MA Oxf., DPhil   Sr.
   Tutor
Smith, A. D., CBE, MA   President*
Wills, K. P., MA   Estates Bursar
Woodford, A. A. G., CB, MA   Home Bursar

MANSFIELD COLLEGE

Tel: (01865) 270999 Fax: (01865) 270970
Forbes, D. A., MA   Bursar
Marquand, David I., MA, FBA,
   FRHistS   Principal*
Muddiman, Rev. J. B., MA Camb., MA Oxf.,
   DPhil   Sr. Tutor

MERTON COLLEGE

Tel: (01865) 276310 Fax: (01865) 276361
Gildea, R. N., MA DPhil   Sr. Tutor
Rawson, Jessica M., CBE, MA Oxf., MA Camb.,
   DLitt Oxf., LittD Camb., FBA   Warden*
Webb, C. R., BA MA MLitt, FCA   Bursar

NEW COLLEGE

Tel: (01865) 279555 Fax: (01865) 279590
Palfreyman, D., MBA Aston, MA   Bursar
Ryan, Prof. Alan J., MA DLitt, FBA   Warden*
Thomas, C. M., MA MLitt   Domestic Bursar
Williams, M. S., BSc Brist., PhD Brist., MA   Sr.
   Tutor

NUFFIELD COLLEGE

Tel: (01865) 278500 Fax: (01865) 278621
Atkinson, A. B., MA Camb., FBA   Warden*
Hughes, G. F., MDA MA   Bursar
Payne, C. D., BSc S'ton., MA   Sr. Tutor

ORIEL COLLEGE

Tel: (01865) 276555 Fax: (01865) 791823
Barratt, E. G., MA, FCA   Treasurer
Cross, R. A., MA DPhil   Sr. Tutor
Nicholson, Rev. E. W., MA Trinity(Dub.), MA
   Camb., MA Oxf., PhD Glas., DD Camb., DD
   Oxf., FBA   Provost*
Offen, J. F., MA   Estates Bursar
Stephens, Brig. M. J. F., MA Camb., MA
   Oxf.   Domestic Bursar

PEMBROKE COLLEGE

Tel: (01865) 276444 Fax: (01865) 276418
Rook, J. R., BSc Manc., PhD Manc.,
   MA   Academic Bursar
Stevens, R. B., MA DCL   Master*
Whitefield, S. D., MA DPhil   Sr. Tutor
Wyndham Lewis, T. A., BA Wales, MA Dal., MA
   Oxf.   Bursar

QUEEN'S COLLEGE

Tel: (01865) 279120 Fax: (01865) 790819
Bowie, A. M., MA Camb., MA Oxf., PhD Camb.,
   DPhil   Sr. Tutor
Gautrey, M. S., MA   Home Bursar

Marshall, G., MA Manc., MA Oxf., PhD Glas.,
   FBA   Provost*
Pearson, R. A. G., MA DPhil   Estates Bursar

REGENT'S PARK COLLEGE

Permanent Private Hall
Tel: (01865) 288120 Fax: (01865) 288121
Bradshaw, Rev. T., MA PhD   Sr. Tutor
Fiddes, Rev. P. S., MA DPhil   Principal*
Greenwood, E. J.   Bursar

RIPON COLLEGE, CUDDESDON

Theological College
Tel: (01865) 874404 Fax: (01865) 875431
Cambley, J.   Bursar
Clarke, Rev. J., BD MA   Principal*

SOMERVILLE COLLEGE

Tel: (01865) 270600 Fax: (01865) 270620
Caldicott, Dame Fiona, BM BCh MA,
   FRCPsych   Principal*
Cashman, S. E.   Domestic Bursar
Dawkins, Prof. Marian E. S., MA DPhil   Sr.
   Tutor
Younie, P., BA Camb., MA Camb., MA
   Oxf.   Treasurer

ST ANNE'S COLLEGE

Tel: (01865) 274800 Fax: (01865) 274899
Bennett, E. M., MA Glas.   Domestic Bursar
Chard, R. L., MA Calif., PhD Calif.   Sr. Tutor
Deech, Ruth L., MA Brandeis, MA
   Oxf.   Principal*
Saunders, R. S., MA   Treasurer

ST ANTONY'S COLLEGE

Tel: (01865) 284700 Fax: (01865) 310518
Daniels, G.   Domestic Bursar
Goulding, Sir Marrack, KCMG, MA   Warden*
Kaye, A., MA   Bursar
Nicholls, A. J., BPhil MA   Sr. Tutor

ST BENET'S HALL

Permanent Private Hall
Tel: (01865) 513917 Fax: (01865) 513917
Wansbrough, Rev. Dom J. H., STL Frib., LSS
   Rome, MA   Master*

ST CATHERINE'S COLLEGE

Tel: (01865) 271700 Fax: (01865) 271768
Dinshaw, F. E., MA DPhil   Investment Bursar
Franklin, P. R., BA York(UK), MA Oxf., DPhil
   York(UK)   Sr. Tutor
Jackson, M. L., OBE, MA   Bursar
Plant of Highfield, The Rt. Hon. Lord, MA
   Oxf., PhD Hull, Hon. DLit Lond.   Master*

ST CROSS COLLEGE

Tel: (01865) 278490 Fax: (01865) 278484
Doherty, M., MA   Bursar
MacCulloch, D. N. J., MA Oxf., MA Camb., PhD
   Camb.   Sr. Tutor

Repp, R. C., BA *Williams(Mass.)*, MA *Oxf.*,
DPhil   Master*

ST EDMUND HALL

Tel: (01865) 279000 Fax: (01865) 279090
Bourne-Taylor, G., MA   Domestic Bursar
Dunbabin, J. P. D., MA   Vice-Principal*
Jenkyns, H. C., BSc *S'ton.*, PhD *Leic.*, MA *Camb.*,
MA *Oxf.*   Sr. Tutor
Slater, M. D. E., MA MPhil   Investment Bursar

ST HILDA'S COLLEGE

Tel: (01865) 276884 Fax: (01865) 276816
Ault, Irene A., BSc *Lond.*, PhD *Lond.*, MA   Sr.
Tutor
Frost, D. T., MA   Bursar
Llewellyn-Smith, Elizabeth M., CB, MA *Camb.*,
MA *Oxf.*   Principal*

ST HUGH'S COLLEGE

Tel: (01865) 274900 Fax: (01865) 274912
Goodfellow, B. H.   Domestic Administrator
Honeyman, I., MA *Aberd.*, MA *Oxf.*   Sr. Bursar
Kennedy, Barbara A., MA *Br.Col.*, MA *Camb.*,
MA *Oxf.*, PhD *Camb.*   Sr. Tutor
Watson, N. M.   Domestic Bursar
Wood, D., CBE, QC, BCL MA   Principal*

ST JOHN'S COLLEGE

Tel: (01865) 277300 Fax: (01865) 277435
Boyce, A. J., MA DPhil   Principal Bursar
Campbell, I. D., BSc *St And.*, PhD *St And.*, MA,
FRS   Domestic Bursar
Fleet, G. W. J., MA *Camb.*, MA *Oxf.*, PhD *Camb.*,
DPhil   Estates Bursar
Hayes, W., MA DPhil   President*
Montgomery, J. A., FCA   Finance Bursar
Pitcher, J. C. G., MA DPhil   Sr. Tutor

ST PETER'S COLLEGE

Tel: (01865) 278900 Fax: (01865) 278855
Barron, J. P., MA DPhil, FSA, FKC   Master*
Bithell, J. F., MA DPhil   Sr. Tutor
Daukes, C. D., MA   Bursar

ST STEPHEN'S HOUSE

Theological College
Tel: (01865) 247874 Fax: (01865) 794338
Hague, H.   Bursar
Moss, Rev. D. G., MA   Dir. of Studies
Sheehy, Rev. J. P., MA *Oxf.*, DPhil
Oxf.   Principal*

TEMPLETON COLLEGE

Tel: (01865) 422500 Fax: (01865) 422501
Pritchard, G., MA *Oxf.*, FCA   Treasurer and
Chief Financial Officer
Reynolds, J., MA *Oxf.*, MA *Nott.*, PhD
Newcastle   Sr. Tutor
Rowland, Sir David, MA   President*

TRINITY COLLEGE

Tel: (01865) 279900 Fax: (01865) 279911
Beloff, The Hon. Michael J., QC,
MA   President*
Martyn, J. R., MA   Estates Bursar
Poyntz, J. M., MA   Domestic Bursar
Ward-Perkins, B. R., MA   Sr. Tutor

UNIVERSITY COLLEGE

Tel: (01865) 276602 Fax: (01865) 276790
Butler of Brockwell, The Rt. Hon. Lord, GCB,
KCB, CVO, MA   Master*
Cooper, Prof. E. H., MA *Camb.*, MA *Oxf.*, PhD
Camb., DLitt   Sr. Tutor
Crawford, Elizabeth J., BA *CNAA*,
MA   Domestic Bursar
Screaton, G. R., MA *Oxf.*, MA *Camb.*, PhD
Camb.   Estates Bursar

WADHAM COLLEGE

Tel: (01865) 277900 Fax: (01865) 277937
Flemming, J. S., MA, FBA   Warden*
Martineau, R. P., MA DPhil   Estates Bursar
Sauvage, Capt. M. P., MA   Domestic Bursar
Sharpe, R., MA *Camb.*, MA *Oxf.*, PhD *Camb.*   Sr.
Tutor

WOLFSON COLLEGE

Tel: (01865) 274100 Fax: (01865) 274125
Ashton, J. F., MA DLitt   Sr. Tutor
Gordon, A. F., CBE, MA *Oxf.*   Bursar
Rice, E. E., BA *Mt. Holyoke*, MA *Camb.*, MA *Oxf.*,
DPhil   Domestic Bursar
Smith, Sir David, MA DPhil, FRS,
FRSEd   President*

WORCESTER COLLEGE

Tel: (01865) 278300 Fax: (01865) 278387
King, Col. D. E., OBE, BSc(Eng) *Lond.*, MPhil
Camb., MA   Bursar
Smethurst, R. G., MA   Provost*
Ware, Prof. A. J., MA DPhil   Sr. Tutor

WYCLIFFE HALL

Theological College
Tel: (01865) 274200 Fax: (01865) 274215
McGrath, Rev. A. E., BD *Oxf.*, MA *Oxf.*, DPhil
Oxf.   Principal*
Nutman, C. A.   Bursar
Southwell, Rev. P. J. M., MA   Sr. Tutor

CONTACT OFFICERS

Academic affairs. Registrar: Holmes, D. R.,
MA *Oxf.*
Accommodation. Accommodation Officer:
Davenport, K. J., BA *Durh.*, MPhil *Reading*
Admissions (first degree). Secretary to the
Oxford Colleges Admissions Office: Minto, J.
A., MA *Camb.*
Admissions (higher degree). Graduate
Admissions Officer: Hughes, R. O., MA
Camb.
Adult/continuing education. Director:
Thomas, G. P., BSc *Wales*, PhD *Camb.*, MA
Alumni. Alumni Officer: Buckton, R. G., MA
Archives. Keeper of the Archives: Vaisey,
David G., CBE, MA *Oxf.*, FSA, FRHistS
Careers. Director, Careers Service: Butler, A. J.,
MA
Computing services. Director: Reid, T. A., BSc
W.Aust.

Consultancy services. Director, Research and
Commercial Services: ......
Development/fund-raising. Director,
Development Office: Pellew, J., MA *Lond.*,
PhD *Lond.*
Estates and buildings/works and services.
Surveyor to the University: Hill, P. M. R.,
MA *Camb.*
Examinations. (Contact the University
Proctors)
Finance. Secretary of the Chest: Clements, J.
R., BA *Manc.*, FCA
General enquiries. Information Officer:
Woodcock, Clare, BA *Hull*, MA *Sheff.*
Health services. Senior Occupational Health
Physician: ......
Industrial liaison. Industrial and European
Liaison: Espinasse, P-M. J., BA *CNAA*
International office. International Officer:
Potts, B. A., MSc *Wales*
Library (chief librarian). Director of
University Library Services and Bodley's
Librarian: Carr, R. P., BA *Leeds*, MA *Manc.*,
MA *Camb.*
Personnel/human resources. Director,
Personnel Services: Owen, D. C., MA *Camb.*,
PhD *Camb.*, MA DPhil
Public relations, information and marketing.
Director, External Relations: Flather, P. C. R.,
MA DPhil
Publications. Head of Publications: Brunner-
Ellis, A., BA *E.Anglia*
Purchasing. Purchasing Officer: Whitehead, P.
A.
Research. Director, Research and Commercial
Services: ......
Safety. Safety Officer: Bowker, K. W., PhD
Leic., MA
Schools liaison. Schools Liaison Officer: Pope,
S., MA
Security. The University Marshal: Roberts, E.
A., MA
Staff development and training. Nestor, R. J.,
MA *Camb.*
Student union. Bell, J.
Student welfare/counselling. Head of
Counselling: Bell, E. I., MA
Students from other countries. International
Officer: Potts, B. A., MSc *Wales*
Students with disabilities. Popham, D.
University press. Secretary and Chief Executive:
Reece, H., BA *Brist.*, MA DPhil

CAMPUS/COLLEGE HEADS

All Souls College, Oxford, England OX1 4AL.
(Tel: (01865) 279379; Fax: (01865)
279299.) Warden: Davis, John H. R., PhD
Lond., MA, FBA
Balliol College, Oxford, England OX1 3BJ.
(Tel: (01865) 277777; Fax: (01865)
277803.) Master: Lucas, Colin R., MA *Oxf.*,
DPhil *Oxf.*, Hon. Dr *Lyons II*, FRHistS
Blackfriars, 64 St Giles, Oxford, England OX1
3LY. (Tel: (01865) 278441; Fax: (01865)
278403, 278441.) Regent: Parvis, Rev. P.
M., BA *Emory*, BD *Emory*, MA *Oxf.*, DPhil *Oxf.*,
STL
Brasenose College, Oxford, England OX1 4AJ.
(Tel: (01865) 277830; Fax: (01865)
277822.) Principal: Windlesham, The Rt.
Hon. Lord, CVO, MA, DLitt
Campion Hall, Oxford, England OX1 1QS.
(Tel: (01865) 286100; Fax: (01865)
286148.) Master: Hughes, Rev. G. J., MA
PhD
Christ Church, Oxford, England OX1 1DP.
(Tel: (01865) 276150; Fax: (01865)
276276.) Dean: Drury, Very Rev. J. H., MA
Camb., MA *Oxf.*
Corpus Christi College, Oxford, England OX1
4JF. (Tel: (01865) 276700; Fax: (01865)
793121.) President: Thomas, Sir Keith, Hon.
DLitt *Kent*, Hon. DLitt *Wales*, Hon. LittD *Sheff.*,
Hon. LLD *Williams(Mass.)*, MA, FBA

Exeter College, Oxford, England OX1 3DP. (Tel: (01865) 279600; Fax: (01865) 279630.) Rector: Butler, Marilyn S., MA Oxf., DPhil Oxf.

Green College, Oxford, England OX2 6HG. (Tel: (01865) 274770; Fax: (01865) 274796.) Warden: Hanson, Sir John, KCMG, CBE, MA

Greyfriars, Oxford, England OX4 1SB. (Tel: (01865) 243694; Fax: (01865) 727027.) Warden: Weinandy, Rev. T. G., MA PhD

Harris Manchester College, Oxford, England OX1 3TD. (Tel: (01865) 271006; Fax: (01865) 271012.) Principal: Waller, Rev. R., BD Lond., MTh Nott., PhD Lond., MA

Hertford College, Oxford, England OX1 3BW. (Tel: (01865) 279400; Fax: (01865) 279437.) Principal: Bodmer, Sir Walter, MA PhD Hon. DSc, FRS

Jesus College, Oxford, England OX1 3DW. (Tel: (01865) 279700; Fax: (01865) 279687.) Principal: North, Sir Peter, CBE, QC, MA DCL, FBA

Keble College, Oxford, England OX1 3PG. (Tel: (01865) 272727; Fax: (01865) 272705.) Warden: Cameron, Averil M., MA Oxf., PhD Lond., FBA, FSA

Kellogg College, 1 Wellington Square, Oxford, England OX1 2JA. (Tel: (01865) 270383; Fax: (01865) 270314.) President: Thomas, G. P., BSc *Wales*, PhD *Camb.*, MA

Lady Margaret Hall, Oxford, England OX2 6QA. (Tel: (01865) 274300; Fax: (01865) 511069.) Principal: Fall, Sir Brian, GCVO, KCMG, MA Oxf., LLM *Mich.*, MA

Linacre College, Oxford, England OX1 3JA. (Tel: (01865) 271650; Fax: (01865) 271668.) Principal: Slack, Paul A., MA DPhil, FBA

Lincoln College, Oxford, England OX1 3DR. (Tel: (01865) 279800; Fax: (01865) 279802.) Rector: Anderson, W. E. K., MA Oxf., MLitt Oxf., DLitt, FRSEd

Magdalen College, Oxford, England OX1 4AU. (Tel: (01865) 276000; Fax: (01865) 276103, 276094.) President: Smith, A. D., CBE, MA

Mansfield College, Oxford, England OX1 3TF. (Tel: (01865) 270999; Fax: (01865) 270970.) Principal: Marquand, David I., MA, FBA, FRHistS

Merton College, Oxford, England OX1 4JD. (Tel: (01865) 276310; Fax: (01865) 276361.) Warden: Rawson, Jessica M., CBE, MA Oxf., MA Camb., DLitt Oxf., LittD Camb., FBA

New College, Oxford, England OX1 3BN. (Tel: (01865) 279555; Fax: (01865) 279590.) Warden: Ryan, Prof. Alan J., MA DLitt, FBA

Nuffield College, Oxford, England OX1 1NF. (Tel: (01865) 278500; Fax: (01865) 278621.) Warden: Atkinson, A. B., MA Camb., FBA

Oriel College, Oxford, England OX1 4EW. (Tel: (01865) 276555; Fax: (01865) 791823.) Provost: Nicholson, Rev. E. W., MA Trinity(Dub.), MA Camb., MA Oxf., PhD Glas., DD Camb., DD Oxf., FBA

Pembroke College, Oxford, England OX1 1DW. (Tel: (01865) 276444; Fax: (01865) 276418.) Master: Stevens, R. B., MA DCL

Queen's College, Oxford, England OX1 4AW. (Tel: (01865) 279120; Fax: (01865) 790819.) Provost: Marshall, G., MA *Manc.*, MA Oxf., PhD Glas., FBA

Regent's Park College, Oxford, England OX1 2LB. (Tel: (01865) 288120; Fax: (01865) 288121.) Principal: Fiddes, Rev. P. S., MA DPhil

Ripon College, Cuddesdon, Oxford, England OX44 9EX. (Tel: (01865) 874404; Fax: (01865) 875431.) Principal: Clarke, Rev. J., BD MA

Somerville College, Oxford, England OX2 6HD. (Tel: (01865) 270600; Fax: (01865) 270620.) Principal: Caldicott, Dame Fiona, BM MA, FRCPsych

St Anne's College, Oxford, England OX2 6HS. (Tel: (01865) 274800; Fax: (01865) 274899.) Principal: Deech, Ruth L., MA *Brandeis*, MA Oxf.

St Antony's College, Oxford, England OX2 6JF. (Tel: (01865) 284700; Fax: (01865) 310518.) Warden: Goulding, Sir Marrack, KCMG, MA

St Benet's Hall, 38 St Giles, Oxford, England OX1 3LN. (Tel: (01865) 513917; Fax: (01865) 513917.) Master: Wansbrough, Rev. Dom J. H., STL Frib., LSS Rome, MA

St Catherine's College, Oxford, England OX1 3UJ. (Tel: (01865) 271700; Fax: (01865) 271768.) Master: Plant of Highfield, The Rt. Hon. Lord, MA Oxf., PhD Hull, Hon. DLit Lond.

St Cross College, Oxford, England OX1 3LZ. (Tel: (01865) 278490; Fax: (01865) 278484.) Master: Repp, R. C., BA Williams(Mass.), MA Oxf., DPhil

St Edmund Hall, Oxford, England OX1 4AR. (Tel: (01865) 279000; Fax: (01865) 279090.) Vice-Principal: Dunbabin, J. P. D., MA

St Hilda's College, Oxford, England OX4 1DY. (Tel: (01865) 276884; Fax: (01865) 276816.) Principal: Llewellyn-Smith, Elizabeth M., CB, MA Camb., MA Oxf.

St Hugh's College, Oxford, England OX2 6LE. (Tel: (01865) 274900; Fax: (01865) 274912.) Principal: Wood, D., CBE, QC, BCL MA

St John's College, Oxford, England OX1 3JP. (Tel: (01865) 277300; Fax: (01865) 277435.) President: Hayes, W., MA DPhil

St Peter's College, Oxford, England OX1 2DL. (Tel: (01865) 278900; Fax: (01865) 278855.) Master: Barron, J. P., MA DPhil, FSA, FKC

St Stephen's House, Oxford, England OX4 1JX. (Tel: (01865) 247874; Fax: (01865) 794338.) Principal: Sheehy, Rev. J. P., MA Oxf., DPhil Oxf.

Templeton College, Oxford, England OX1 5NY. (Tel: (01865) 422500; Fax: (01865) 422501.) President: Rowland, Sir David, MA

Trinity College, Oxford, England OX1 3BH. (Tel: (01865) 279900; Fax: (01865) 279911.) President: Beloff, The Hon. Michael J., QC, MA

University College, Oxford, England OX1 4BH. (Tel: (01865) 276602; Fax: (01865) 276790.) Master: Butler of Brockwell, The Rt. Hon. Lord, GCB, KCB, CVO, MA

Wadham College, Oxford, England OX1 3PN. (Tel: (01865) 277900; Fax: (01865) 277937.) Warden: Flemming, J. S., MA, FBA

Wolfson College, Oxford, England OX2 6UD. (Tel: (01865) 274100; Fax: (01865) 274125.) President: Smith, Sir David, MA DPhil, FRS, FRSEd

Worcester College, Oxford, England OX1 2HB. (Tel: (01865) 278300; Fax: (01865) 278387.) Provost: Smethurst, R. G., MA

Wycliffe Hall, Oxford, England OX2 6PW. (Tel: (01865) 274200; Fax: (01865) 274215.) Principal: McGrath, Rev. A. E., BD Oxf., MA Oxf., DPhil Oxf.

[*Information supplied by the institution as at 13 November 1998, and edited by the ACU*]

OXFORD BROOKES UNIVERSITY

Founded 1992; previously established as Oxford School of Art (1865) and Oxford Polytechnic (1970)

Member of the Association of Commonwealth Universities

Postal Address: Gipsy Lane, Headington, Oxford, England OX3 0BP
Telephone: (01865) 741111 **Fax**: (01865) 483073 **Telex**: 83147 VIA or G **WWW**: http://www.brookes.ac.uk
E-mail formula: initialsurname@brookes.ac.uk

CHANCELLOR—Kennedy, H., QC
CHAIR OF GOVERNORS—Bagnall, P., MA *Oxf.*
VICE-CHANCELLOR*—Upton, Prof. Graham, BA *Syd.*, MA *Syd.*, MEd *NSW*, PhD *Wales*,
    FBPsS
DEPUTY VICE-CHANCELLOR, FINANCE AND MARKETING—Bradshaw, J.
DEPUTY VICE-CHANCELLOR—Fidler, Prof. Peter, MBE, MSc *Salf.*
SECRETARY‡—Summers, B., BSc *Exe.*
ACADEMIC SECRETARY—Winders, Elizabeth N., BA *Lond.*
LIBRARIAN—Workman, Helen M., BSc *Birm.*, MA *Sheff.*, PhD *Open(UK)*

GENERAL INFORMATION

History. The university was established in 1992 when Oxford Polytechnic achieved university status and is named in honour of John Brookes, a former principal. It is located on three campuses: Headington Hill and Gipsy Lane, 1.5km east of Oxford city centre, and Wheatley Campus, 8km from the outskirts of Oxford.

Admission to first degree courses (see also United Kingdom Introduction). Through Universities and Colleges Admissions service (UCAS). General academic requirements: acceptable passes in 5 subjects in Gerernal Certificate of Secondary Education (GCSE) or General Certificate of Education (GCE) including 2 at A level, or 4 subjects at GCSE or GCE including 3 at A level.

First Degrees (see also United Kingdom Directory to Subjects of Study). BA, BEng, BSc, LLB, MEng.

Programmes are taught on a modular basis, and most courses last 3–4 years full-time or up to a maximum of 8 years part-time.

Higher Degrees (see also United Kingdom Directory to Subjects of Study). LLM, MA, MBA, MSc, MPhil, PhD, EdD.

Normal entry requirement for master's degrees: honours degree, postgraduate diploma or equivalent professional qualification. MPhil: first or second class UK honours degree or equivalent; PhD: appropriate master's degree (including research training and research project); PhD by published work: at least 5 years' relevant postgraduate experience.

Master's degrees: 1 year full-time or 2 years part-time; MPhil: 2 years full-time or 3 years part-time; PhD: 3 years full-time or 4 years part-time.

Language of Instruction. English. The International Centre for English Language Studies (ICELS) provides a range of support and preparation classes for students whose first language is not English.

Libraries. 300,000 volumes; 2400 periodicals subscribed to.

Fees (annual). Undergraduate: UK students in their first year £1000; continuing students, LEA funded £1000, self-funded £1494 (arts) and £3183 (sciences); international students £6600. Postgraduate: UK students £2600–11,500; international students £6600–15,500.

Academic Awards (1996-97). 74 awards ranging in value from £10 to £500.

Income (1996-7). Total, £65,208,000.

Statistics. Staff: 1688 (656 academic, 783 administrative, 249 manual). Students: full-time 6700 (2914 men, 3786 women); part-time 4275 (1748 men, 2527 women); international 2755 (1432 men, 1323 women).

ACADEMIC UNITS

Arranged by Schools

Architecture

Tel: (01865) 483200 Fax: (01865) 483298
Ahmad, Taseer, BSc *Lond.*, MA *RCA* Sr. Lectr.
Allinson, Kenneth Sr. Lectr.
Allison, Julian P., MSc *Strath.* Principal Lectr.
Avis, Martin, MSc *Reading* Emer. Prof.
Bentley, Ian Principal Lectr.
Boddington, Anne D. M., BA *CNAA* Sr. Lectr.
Braham, Robert, MBA *Westminster* Sr. Lectr.
Burgess, Rob, BA *Lond.*, MSc *Lond.*, PhD *Lond.* Sr. Lectr.
Burton, Elizabeth J., BA *Camb.*, MA *Camb.*, PhD *Oxf.Brookes* Sr. Lectr.
Christie, Folla, BA *Oxf.*, MA *Oxf.* Principal Lectr.
Cross, Christopher Head*
Dent, Peter R., BA *Open(UK)*, MSocSci *Birm.* Principal Lectr.
Fraser, Murray, BSc *Lond.*, MSc *Lond.*, PhD *Lond.* Sr. Lectr.
Gaskin, Matthew N., BSc *CNAA* Sr. Lectr.
Glass, Jacqueline, BA *Oxf.Brookes*, PhD *Oxf.Brookes* Sr. Lectr.
Grindley, David, BA *Leeds* Sr. Lectr.
Grover, Richard, BA *Kent*, MPhil *Kent* Head, Centre of Real Estate Management
Hamdi, Nabeel K. Sr. Lectr.
Hancock, Mary, BA *Reading*, BSc *Brist.* Sr. Lectr.
Hartley-Gallagher, Angela, BA Sr. Lectr.
Hiscock, Nigel L., PhD *CNAA* Sr. Lectr.
Jenks, Mike, PhD *CNAA* Prof.
Keeping, Miles, BSc *Oxf.Brookes*, MSc Sr. Lectr.
Latter, Rosemary K., BA *Oxf.Brookes* Sr. Lectr.
Lavers, Anthony, LLB *Lond.*, MPhil *S'ton.*, PhD *Sing.* Reader, Law
MacAllister, Jane, BA *Lond.* Sr. Lectr.
McGlynn, Susan E., BSc *Lond.*, MA *Oxf.Brookes* Sr. Lectr.
McNamara, Paul, BSc PhD Visting Prof.
Mikellides, Byron, BA *Lond.*, PhD *Oxf.Brookes* Sr. Lectr.
Nicol, Fergus, BSc *Lond.* Sr. Lectr.
Nicolaou, Lora, MA *Oxf.Brookes*, MSc Sr. Lectr.
Ogden, Raymond G., BA *CNAA*, PhD *Bath* Reader
Porter, Tom Sr. Lectr.
Proudman, Paul Sr. Lectr.
Randell, Geoffrey Sr. Lectr.
Roach, Paul V., BA *Sheff.*, BSc Sr. Lectr.
Roaf, Susan, BA *Manc.*, PhD *CNAA* Principal Lectr.
Samuels, Ivor, MSc *Glas.* Principal Lectr.
Shamash, Layla Sr. Lectr.
Shiers, David E., BA *Kent*, BA *Liv.* Sr. Lectr.
Slim, Hugo, BA *Oxf.*, MA *Oxf.* Sr. Lectr.
Smith, Graham P., MA *RCA*, MA *CNAA* Sr. Lectr.
Soloviev, Mikhail Visiting Prof.
Stevenson, John Principal Lectr.
Stringer, Benedict N., BA *Lond.*, MSc *Lond.* Sr. Lectr.
Stubbs, Michael, BA *Oxf.Brookes*, MSc *Oxf.Brookes* Sr. Lectr.
Tankard, Jane N., BA *S.Bank* Sr. Lectr.
Taylor, Kenneth S., BA *Lond.* Sr. Lectr.
Temple, Marion, BA *Camb.*, MA *Camb.*, MA *Lanc.* Principal Lectr.
Tonge, Nigel, MSc, FRICS Sr. Lectr.
Webster, Helena M., BA *Sheff.* Sr. Lectr.
Whitman, Alexandra, BA *Hull*, MA *Durh.* Sr. Lectr.
Williams, Katie, BA *Sus.*, MSc *Oxf.Brookes*, PhD *Oxf.Brookes* Sr. Lectr.
Research: development and emergency practice (action and emergency planning); sustainable architecture (human thermal comfort standards, photovoltaics); sustainable cities (design, policy and culture, urban form); sustainable technology (innovative steel, facade and thermal design); vernacular architecture (design and forms, worldwide vernacular culture)

Art, Publishing and Music

Tel: (01865) 484951 Fax: (01865) 484952
Atherton, Catherine Sr. Lectr.
Bashford, Christina M., BA *Oxf.*, MMus *Lond.*, PhD *Lond.* Sr. Lectr.
Bullock, Adrian, BA *Oxf.*, MA *Oxf.* Sr. Lectr.
Corris, Michael, BA *C.U.N.Y.*, MFA *Maryland Inst.*, PhD *Lond.* Sr. Lectr., Reader of Art
Davis, Caroline, BA *Birm.*, MA *York(UK)* Sr. Lectr.
Ellard, Graham, BA *CNAA*, MA *RCA*, MA *CNAA* Sr. Lectr.
Fisher, Clare, BA *Sheff.* Sr. Lectr.
Goto, John, BA *CNAA* Sr. Lectr.
Green, Thomas M., MA *Lanc.* Sr. Lectr.
Griffiths, David M., MA *Camb.*, MMus *Lond.*, PhD *Lond.* Principal Lectr.; Head of Music
Howle, Timothy J., BA *Keele* Sr. Lectr.
Jennings, Christopher J. Sr. Lectr.
Miles, Malcolm, PhD Sr. Lectr.
Olsen, Geoff, BA *CNAA* Principal Lectr.
Richardson, Paul T., MA *Camb.* Principal Lectr.; Acting Head*
Sacks, Shelley Principal Lectr.
Sellars, David Sr. Lectr.
Timbrell, Nicola, BSc *Oxf.Brookes* Sr. Lectr.
Tucker, Gill, BMus *Lond.*, BA *Open(UK)*, MMus *Lond.* Head*
Young, Michael W., BA *Oxf.*, MA *Durh.*, PhD *Durh.* Sr. Lectr.
Research: American art since 1935; art and politics since the 1970s; art and postmodernism; contemporary art theory; contemporary typographic design

Biological and Molecular Sciences

Tel: (01865) 483240 Fax: (01865) 483242

Beadle, David J., BSc Brist., PhD Lond., FIBiol Prof.; Head*

Bermudez, Isabel, BSc Greenwich, PhD Greenwich Sr. Lectr.

Betteridge, Alan, BSc Sus., DPhil Sus. Sr. Lectr.

Blythe, G. Max, BSc Sheff., MA Oxf., MLitt Oxf. Reader

Bradshaw, Tony K., BSc Adel., PhD Flin. Sr. Lectr.

Brooks, Susan A., BSc Nott., PhD Lond. Reader

Butler, Michele A., BSc Lond. Sr. Lectr.

Craven, Richard P., BSc Sheff., PhD Sheff. Sr. Lectr.

Fell, David A., MA Oxf., DPhil Oxf. Principal Lectr.

Grebenik, Peter D., MA Oxf., DPhil Oxf. Sr. Lectr.

Griffiths, Alwyn, BSc Wales, PhD Wales Sr. Lectr.

Groome, Prof. Nigel P., BSc Birm., MSc Lond., PhD Lond. Reader

Hawes, Christopher R., BSc Brist., PhD Brist. RMC Reader

Henry, Jeya C. J. K., BSc Madr., BSc(Tech) Bom., MSc Lond., PhD Lond. Principal Lectr.

Heppell, Neil J., BSc Birm., MSc Birm., PhD Birm. Sr. Lectr.

Hodson, Martin, BSc Wales, PhD Wales Sr. Lectr.

Howells, Kenneth F., BSc Hull, PhD Hull Principal Lectr.

Johnston, Robert T., BSc Wales, MSc Wales, MA Lond. Sr. Lectr.

Kinch, Rhodri F. T., BSc Oxf.Brookes, PhD Oxf.Brookes Sr. Lectr.

King, Linda A., BSc Liv., DPhil Oxf. Principal Lectr.

Lack, Andrew J., BSc Aberd., PhD Camb. Sr. Lectr.

Miller, Anne, BSc Oxf.Brookes, PhD Oxf.Brookes Sr. Lectr.

Pearce, Deborah M. E., PhD Brist. Sr. Lectr.

Ramsbottom, Roger, BSc E.Anglia, PhD E.Anglia Sr. Lectr.

Ray, Steve, BSc Plym., PhD Plym. Sr. Lectr.

Rendell, Andrew R., BSc E.Anglia, MPhil Lough., PhD Lough. Sr. Lectr.

Robbins, Susan K. Sr. Lectr.

Rosenthal, Andrew J., BSc Brad., MSc Leeds, PhD Lond. Sr. Lectr.

Shreeve, Tim, MSc Oxf.Brookes, PhD Oxf.Brookes Sr. Lectr.

Smart, Katherine A., BSc Nott., PhD Nott. Sr. Lectr.

Smith, Allister G., BSc Exe., PhD Liv. Sr. Lectr.

Thompson, Stewart, BSc CNAA Sr. Lectr.

Thorn, Janet, BSc Lond. Sr. Lectr.

Thurling, David J., BA Camb., MA Camb., MSc Wales, PhD Leic. Principal Lectr.

Walters, Jean, BSc MPhil Sr. Lectr.

Watts, Simon F., BSc Brad., PhD Lond. Sr. Lectr.

Other Staff: 1 Lectr.

Research: biochemical regulation; cell biology; insect molecular virology; insect neuropharmacology; microbiology

Business

Tel: (01865) 485908 Fax: (01865) 485830

Amos-Wilson, Pauline M., BSc Lond., MSc Lond. Principal Lectr.

Bassett-Jones, Nigel, BA Leeds Sr. Lectr.

Bath, Geoff, BA Lanc., MSc Brun. Sr. Lectr.

Bee, Malcolm, BSc Hull, MA Hull Principal Lectr.

Benwell, Mary, BA Nott., PhD Cran. Prof.; Head*

Bibbings, Lyn, BA CNAA, BTP CNAA Sr. Lectr.

Blackburn, Alan, BA CNAA, MA Warw. Sr. Lectr.

Blackburn, Chris, BA Oxf., MA Oxf. Sr. Lectr.

Blanchard, Paul, BSc Leic., MSc CNAA Principal Lectr.

Bowen, David, BA Oxf. Sr. Lectr.

Brown, Howard N., BA Oxf., MA Oxf. Sr. Lectr.

Cammack, John Sr. Lectr.

Carey, Mary, BSc S'ton. Sr. Lectr.

Case, Peter, BSc Bath, MA Oxf., MA Mass., PhD Bath Sr. Lectr.

Champion, Christine K. Sr. Lectr.

Chantry, Len, LLB Lond., LLM Lond., PhD CNAA Sr. Lectr.

Clarke, Jackie, MSc Sur., BA Sr. Lectr.

Collins, Mike, BSc(Econ) Lond. Sr. Lectr.

Cracknell, Tim, BA Camb., MA Camb. Sr. Lectr.

Dennis, Ian, MA Oxf., BPhil Oxf. Sr. Lectr.

Diggle, Graham, BA Reading Sr. Lectr.

Duckett, Hilary R., BA Staffs., MA Thames V. Sr. Lectr.

Eastham, Albert, BA Manc., MA Kent, MSc Brun. Sr. Lectr.

Evans, David, BA Reading, PhD Sur. Sr. Lectr.

Gaffney, Paul, BSc MBA Sr. Lectr.

Ganley, Daniel W. F., BA Brist., MBA Bourne. Sr. Lectr.

Gardiner, Peter J. E., BA Lanc. Sr. Lectr.

Gibbs, Tony, BA Kent, MA Reading Sr. Lectr.

Gilliam, Paul, BSc(Econ) Lond., MA Lanc. Sr. Lectr.

Gooch, Larraine, BA Sheff., MA Thames V. Sr. Lectr.

Hackley, Christopher E., BA Staffs., MSc Salf., PhD Strath. Sr. Lectr.

Haffey, Mike, BA Camb., MA Camb. Sr. Lectr.

Harrison, Aileen, BA Birm., MSc Manc. Sr. Lectr.

Hoffen, Martin Sr. Lectr.

Holmberg, Geoffery P., BSc Sus. Principal Lectr.

Jarman, Alan, BA Wales, LLB Wales, MA McM. Sr. Lectr.

Jeffs, Richard Sr. Lectr.

Kilminster, Andy, BSc Brist., MPhil Oxf. Sr. Lectr.

King, Jane, BSocSc Birm. Sr. Lectr.

Larsson, Philip, MA Edin. Sr. Lectr.

Ledwith, Suzzanne, MBA City(UK) Sr. Lectr.

MacNeil, Christina M., BA Lond., MBA Lond. Sr. Lectr.

Matkin, Derek, BSc City(UK) Sr. Lectr.

Morgan, Philip, BA Leeds Sr. Lectr.

Mumby-Croft, Roger K. H. Sr. Lectr.

Netting, John, BSc Aston Sr. Lectr.

Percy, Chris, BSc St And. Sr. Lectr.

Pfunder, Sue, BSc CNAA Principal Lectr.

Piggott, Judith, BA Camb., MPhil Camb., MA Camb. Sr. Lectr.

Pike, Maureen, BA Kingston(UK), MSc Lond., PhD Lond. Principal Lectr.

Price, Margaret, BA CNAA, MSc Bath Principal Lectr.

Reddy, Hazel, BA CNAA, MPhil CNAA Principal Lectr.

Reynier, Paul, BEng Liv. Sr. Lectr.

Rooks, Stuart, BSc CNAA, MBA Brun. Sr. Lectr.

Rosamond, Ben, BA Manc., MA Manc., PhD Sheff. Sr. Lectr.

Ross, F. Don, MSc Lough., FCA Sr. Lectr.

Selzer, Haluk, BSc Ankara, MA Lanc. Sr. Lectr.

Shaw, Brian, BSc(Econ) Lond., MSc City(UK), DPhil Sus. Reader

Singh, Pritam, BA Panjab, MA Panjab, MPhil J.Nehru U., DPhil Oxf. Sr. Lectr.

Slinn, Judy, BA Oxf. Sr. Lectr.

Smallbone, Teresa, MA Camb., MA Lond. Sr. Lectr.

Spira, Laura, BA Manc., FCA Sr. Lectr.

Traves, Joanne, MA Oxf.Brookes, MBA Oxf.Brookes Sr. Lectr.

Turner, John, BA Essex, MSc Lond., PhD Lond. Principal Lectr.

Watts, Bill, MPhil Westminster, PhD S.Pac. Sr. Lectr.

Wildish, Clive C. W., BA Warw. Sr. Lectr.

Wychereley, Ian, BA Camb., MA Camb., MPhil Oxf. Sr. Lectr.

Research: cross-cultural learning; ethical/ sustainable business practice; organisational development and change; tourism management; transferability of models of management

Computing and Mathematical Sciences

Tel: (01865) 483652 Fax: (01865) 483666

Bala, Pon, BA Open(UK), MSc Lond., PhD Lond. Sr. Lectr.

Ball, Frank, BSc Lanc., PhD Lanc. Sr. Lectr.

Bertrand, Philip V., BSc Birm., PhD Birm. Sr. Lectr.

Brownsey, Ken W., BA Essex, MSc Manc. Sr. Lectr.

Champion, Ralph E. M., BSc Bath, MSc Kingston(UK), PhD Manc. Sr. Lectr.

Crook, Nigel T., BSc Lanc., PhD CNAA Sr. Lectr.

Dobbyn, Chris H., BA Keele, MSc Manc. Sr. Lectr.

Donaldson, A. Nora, BSc Valle, MSc Virginia Polytech., PhD Maryland Sr. Lectr.

Gethins, Trevor, BSc Birm., PhD McM. Principal Lectr.

Gibbons, Jeremy, BSc Edin., DPhil Oxf. Sr. Lectr.

Greenwood, Sue, BSc Open(UK), MSc Brun. Sr. Lectr.

Haggarty, Rod J., BSc Liv., PhD Liv. Principal Lectr.

Hobbs, Catherine A., BSc Warw., PhD Liv. Sr. Lectr.

Lightfoot, David E., BA Essex, MSc Oxf. Sr. Lectr.

Lionheart, Bill R. B., BSc Warw., PhD CNAA Sr. Lectr.

Long, John W., BSc Lond., MSc Lond. Principal Lectr.

Nealon, John L., BSc Sus., BA Open(UK), MTech Brun. Head, Knowledge Engin. Res. Group; Head*

Osborne, D. Richard, BA Birm., MSc Lond. Sr. Lectr.

Paulson, Kevin, MSc Auck., PhD Oxf.Brookes, BSc Sr. Lectr.

Peperell, Hazel Y. Sr. Lectr.

Phillimore, Rosemary Sr. Lectr.

Pidcock, Prof. Michael K., BSc Nott., PhD Kent Reader; Head, Appl. Analysis Res. Group

Priest, Tony G., BA Camb., MA Camb., PhD Open(UK) Sr. Lectr.

Reed, Joylyn N., BSc Auburn, MSc Auburn, MSc Maryland, PhD Auburn Sr. Lectr.

Rees, David G., MA Oxf., MSc City(UK) Principal Lectr.

Shrimpton, David H., BSc CNAA, PhD Oxf.Brookes Sr. Lectr.

Simonite, Vanessa, BSc Birm., MSc Lond. Sr. Lectr.

Simpkins, Neil K., BSc Birm., PhD Birm. Sr. Lectr.

Smith, Peter, MSc CNAA Sr. Lectr.

Stanczyk, Stefan, BSc Warsaw U.T., MSc(Eng) Warsaw U.T., MSc Lond., PhD Open(UK) Principal Lectr.

Tagg, A. Geoff, MSc Lanc. Reader; Head, Distributed Systems Res. Group

Turner, William M. D., BSc Lond., BA Open(UK), MSc Lond., MPhil Lond. Principal Lectr.

Zajicek, Mary P., BSc Nott., MSc CNAA Sr. Lectr.

Research: applied analysis (applied singularity theory, inverse problems); distributed systems (transmission of multimedia information over high-speed multi-service networks); intelligent systems (cognitive science, constraint-based reasoning, intelligent agents, intelligent user interfaces, knowledge-based systems, medical informatics, neural networks); software engineering (computer-aided software construction, databases, formal methods and data/systems)

Construction and Earth Sciences

Tel: (01865) 483901 Fax: (01865) 483387

Anson, Roger W., BA Oxf., MA Oxf. Principal Lectr.

Banks, Nigel, BA Oxf., MPhil Oxf. Visting Prof.†

Beale, Robert G., BSc S'ton. Sr. Lectr.

Branch, Robert F., MSc Lond. Sr. Lectr.

Childs, Alan, BSc Nott., PhD Lond., FGS Principal Lectr.
Colley, Howard, BSc Sheff., PhD Sheff. Prof.
d'Lemos, Richard S., BSc Plym., PhD CNAA Sr. Lectr.
Darkes, Giles T., BSc Oxf.Brookes, MPhil Camb. Sr. Lectr.
Davey-Wilson, Ian E. G., BTech Brad., MSc Wales, PhD Brad. Sr. Lectr.
Dennis, John M., BSc Leic., MPhil CNAA Principal Lectr.
Ellett, Brian G. S., BSc Leeds, MSc Lond. Sr. Lectr.
Fowler, Michael B., BSc Brist., MSc Birm., PhD Lond. Sr. Lectr.
Friend, Clark R. L., BSc Lond., PhD Lond. Principal Lectr.
Glassock, Terence I. G., BSc S.Bank Sr. Lectr.
Godley, Michael H. R., BSc Lond., PhD Lond. Head*
Gover, M. B. Sr. Lectr.
Guion, Paul D., BSc Liv., MSc Keele, PhD CNAA Principal Lectr.
Haile, Neville Visiting Prof.†
Jacob, Richard P., BSc Salf., PhD Salf. Sr. Lectr.
Jenkins, Paul L., BSc Manc., PhD Manc., FGS Sr. Lectr.
Jones, Kevin, BSc Keele, PhD Kingston(UK) Sr. Lectr.
Kearsley, Anthony T., BA Camb. Sr. Lectr.
McIlveen, Albert, BA Manc. Sr. Lectr.
Quirk, David G., BSc Liv., PhD Leic. Sr. Lectr.
Smyth, Hedley, BA Sus., PhD Brist. Sr. Lectr.
Spencer Chapman, Nicholas F., BA Camb., MA Camb., MSc Reading Sr. Lectr.
Strachan, Robin A., BSc Wales, PhD Keele Reader
Street, Marstan, BSc Aston, MSc Lough., MSc Sur. Sr. Lectr.
Suthren, Roger J., BA Oxf., MA Oxf., PhD Keele Sr. Lectr.
Walker, Paul R., BSc(Eng) S'ton., PhD CNAA Principal Lectr.
Washbourne, James, BSc(Eng) Lond., MSc Birm. Principal Lectr.
Wood, Brian R., BA Sheff. Sr. Lectr.
Woodhead, Roy M., BSc Sheff.Hallam Sr. Lectr.
Research: construction and value management; crustal evolution in the North Atlantic region; estuary morphology and coastal wave dynamics; hydrocarbon deposition in geological environments; post-buckling behaviour of cold-formed steel sections

Education

Tel: (01865) 485930 Fax: (01865) 485838
Allen, Jonathan R., MA Reading, MA Camb. Sr. Lectr.
Anderson, Lesley, BA Essex, MSc Warw. Sr. Lectr.; Educn. Services Manager
Arthur, Linet S., BA Sus., MA Lanc. Sr. Lectr.
Bainbridge, Richard, BA Durh., MA Lond., MPhil Lond. Principal Lectr.
Bell, Jocelyn, BA Keele, MEd Birm. Sr. Lectr.
Bentley, Diana, BA Nott., MA Oxf.Brookes Sr. Lectr.
Blandford, Sonia, BEd Leeds, MA Reading, MPhil Bath, EdD Brist. Sr. Lectr.
Brown, Michael P., BSc Lond., MEd Manc. Sr. Lectr.
Burman, Christine A., MEd Birm. Sr. Lectr.
Catling, Simon J., BEd Exe., MA Lond. Principal Lectr.
Chamberlin, Rosemary P., BEd Brist., MEd W.England, PhD W.England Sr. Lectr.
Clark, Jean A. Sr. Lectr.
Clipson-Boyles, Susan, BEd Warw., MEd CNAA Sr. Lectr.; Catch-Up Project Manager
Clow, Rosalind A., BSc Lond., MA S'ton. Sr. Lectr.
Davidson, Wendy G., BEd Reading, MA Lond. Sr. Lectr.
Domoney, William, BA Sheff., MSc York(UK) Sr. Lectr.
Fowler, Penny, MA Birm. Principal Lectr.
Fussell, Anne Sr. Lectr.
Gaunt, Diane E., BSc Wales, MA Lond., MSc Oxf. Principal Lectr.

Glenny, Georgina, BA Warw., MSc Sheff. Sr. Lectr.
Harkin, Joseph, BA(Econ) CNAA, MA Sus., DPhil Sus. Reader
Hickling, Elizabeth, BEd Lond., MA Lond. Sr. Lectr.
Holderness, Jackie, BA Wales, MA Lond. Sr. Lectr.
Holmes, Gary, BA Lond., MSc Oxf. Principal Lectr.; Head, Oxford Centre for Educn. Management
Kumsang, Margaret Sr. Lectr., Hearing Impairment
Lalljee, Barbara, BA Reading, MA Reading Sr. Lectr.
Lenton, Graham M., BSc Reading, MSc Durh., PhD Malaya Sr. Lectr.
Longshaw, Linda, BA CNAA Sr. Lectr.
Maidlow, Sarah, BA Liv., MA Reading, PhD Reading Sr. Lectr.
Mancey, David, BSc S'ton., MSc Durh., MA Lond. Sr. Lectr.
Mant, Jenny A., BA Camb., MA Camb. Sr. Lectr.
McClelland, Robin, BEd CNAA, MA Reading Sr. Lectr.
Nind, Melanie A. E., BEd Herts., PhD Camb. Sr. Lectr.
Ormston, Michael, BA Lond., MA Leic. Principal Lectr.; OXCEMS Manager
Parkin, Alison, MA Leic. Sr. Lectr.
Porter, John F., MA Sr. Lectr.
Price, Alison J., BSc Manc., MA Open(UK) Sr. Lectr.
Reid, Dee, BA Birm., MA Reading Sr. Lectr.
Scott, Irene P., MA Aberd. Sr. Lectr.
Shaw, Marian, BSc Lond., MA CNAA Sr. Lectr.
Speed, Richard R. J., BA Open(UK), MA Reading, MA Nott. Sr. Lectr.
Squire, Linda M. H. Sr. Lectr.
Stevens, Brenda J., BSc Reading Principal Lectr.
Vass, Peter, MA Exe., MEd Exe. Sr. Lectr.
Waugh, Robert D., MA St And. Sr. Lectr.
Welton, John M., BA Brist., PhD Brist. Prof.; Head*
Williams, Aled, BSc Brad. Sr. Lectr.
Wilson, Maggie, BA Durh., MA Lond. Principal Lectr.
Research: education administration; education development; education policy and management; primary, secondary and vocational education; special education

Engineering

Tel: (01865) 483500 Fax: (01865) 483637
Balkwill, James S., BEng Birm., PhD Oxf.Brookes Principal Lectr.
Bremble, Geoffrey R., BEng Liv., MEng Liv., PhD CNAA Head*
Bromley, Jonathan S. E., MA Oxf. Sr. Lectr.
Childs, Geoffrey N., BSc E.Anglia, PhD Durh. Sr. Lectr.
Cordery, Alla, BSc Col., PhD Sofia Principal Lectr.
Durodola, John, BSc Ib., MSc Ib., PhD Lond. Sr. Lectr.
Freeman-Bell, Gail, BSc Oxf.Brookes, MSc Cran.IT Sr. Lectr.
Green, Ashley A., BA Oxf., MA Oxf., PhD Wales Sr. Lectr.
Hern, Anthony, BEng Wales, MSc City(UK) Sr. Lectr.
Higgison, George D., BSc CNAA, MSc E.Anglia Sr. Lectr.
Hutchings, Mick G., BSc Nott., PhD Nott. Prof., Optical Materials; Head, Res. and Indust. Links
Hutchinson, Allan K., BSc Portsmouth, PhD Dund. Principal Lectr.; Head, Joining Technol. Res. Centre
Kalinin, Victor A., MSc Moscow, PhD Moscow Sr. Lectr.
Larminie, James, BSc S'ton. Sr. Lectr.
Lidgey, Prof. Francis J., BSc CNAA, PhD Sur., FIEE Prof., Electronics; Head, Dept. of Electronic Engin.
Lowry, John P. A., BSc Lond., MSc Sur., PhD Lond., FIMechE, FIEE Principal Lectr.

Martin, Kenneth G., BSc CNAA Sr. Lectr.
McLeod, Christopher N., MA Camb., MSc Strath., DPhil Oxf. Principal Lectr.
Morrey, Denise B., BSc Camb., MA Camb., PhD Oxf.Brookes Head, Dept. of Mech. Engin.
Pickering, David, BEng Sheff. Sr. Lectr.
Purbrick, Keith J., BSc Lond., MSc Lond., MSc CNAA Sr. Lectr.
Sehati, Sepehr, BSc Oxf.Brookes, MSc Lond., DPhil Oxf. Sr. Lectr.
Turner, David C., BTech Brun., MSc Birm. Principal Lectr.
Other Staff: 1 Lectr.
Research: advanced glazings and solar energy materials; analog and digital integrated circuit design; joining technology; medical instrumentation; properties and strengths of materials

Health Care

Tel: (01865) 221576 Fax: (01865) 220188
Adams, Gwyneth Sr. Lectr.
Appleton, Jane M., BA Oxf.Brookes Sr. Lectr.
Atkins, Jo M., BA MPhil Principal Lectr.
Atkins, Sue M., MSc Principal Lectr.
Bentley, Theresa, MA Sr. Lectr.
Bower, Nicola J., MSc Sr. Lectr.
Bulman, Chris A., BSc Sr. Lectr.†
Burrows, Elizabeth M., BSc Lond. Sr. Lectr.
Butler, Jennifer, BSc Wales Principal Lectr.
Challis, Linda, BA Oxf., MSc Prof.; Head*
Chambers, Claire, MSc Sr. Lectr.
Coombes, Elwyn, BA MA Sr. Lectr.
Couling, David, BEd Oxf.Brookes, MA Oxf.Brookes Sr. Lectr.
Dale, Susan, BA Sr. Lectr.
Dancer, Jane M., BA Manc., MA Reading Sr. Lectr.
Ersser, Steven J., BSc Lond., PhD Lond. Principal Lectr.
Feaver, Sally A., BA Oxf.Brookes, MA Oxf.Brookes Sr. Lectr.
Freston, Jill Principal Lectr.
Gillings, Beverley C., BSc Bath, MSc S.Bank Sr. Lectr.
Gottwald, Mary, BA Oxf.Brookes Sr. Lectr.
Hallworth, Sarah W., BSc C.England Sr. Lectr.
Hammick, Marilyn R., MSc S'ton. Principal Lectr.; Group Head
Healey, Elaine, BA Sr. Lectr.
Hobson, Stephanie, BA Open(UK), MA Oxf.Brookes Principal Lectr.
Hutchings, Sue E., BA Open(UK) Sr. Lectr.
List, Lynne, MA Nene Sr. Lectr.
Lloyd-Jones, Netta B. Principal Lectr.; Group Head
Marks, Julie A., BSc Lond., MSc Exe. Sr. Lectr.
McBride, John J., MA Sr. Lectr.
McIntyre, Margaret J., MSc Brist. Principal Lectr.; Group Head
McKenna, Clare, MA Oxf.Brookes Sr. Lectr.
Morgan, Michael G., MSc Lond. Sr. Lectr.
Muir, Julia B., BA Oxf.Brookes Sr. Lectr.
Newell-Jones, Kathryn, PhD Sr. Lectr.
Norman, Patricia A., BA Open(UK), MSc Oxf. Sr. Lectr.
Oldfield, Sandra J., BSc Sr. Lectr.
Peto, Joanna M., BA S'ton. Sr. Lectr.
Ryder, Elaine, BA MSc Sr. Lectr.
Sallussolia, Margie I., BSc Sr. Lectr.
Spouse, Jenny F., MSc PhD Sr. Lectr.
Taylor, Bridget Sr. Lectr.
Taylor, Mary-Clare, BA Open(UK), MA Warw. Principal Lectr.; Group Head
Thompson Lynch, Annie M., MSc Hull Principal Lectr.; Group Head
Wade, Mary S., BSc Birm., MA Keele Sr. Lectr.
Walsh, Rosemary, BSc Edin., MSc Lond. Sr. Lectr.
Warneford, Anita, BA Leeds, MA Exe., MLitt Oxf. Sr. Lectr.
Welham, Margaret, MSc Sr. Lectr.
Westcott, Liz Sr. Lectr.
Wheeler, Neil, MBA Keele Principal Lectr.
Wiles, Di-Anne M. Sr. Lectr.
Willmore, Esther, BA N.Lond., MSc City(UK) Sr. Lectr.
Wiltshire, Ursula H., BA Oxf.Brookes Sr. Lectr.

Wondrak, Rob F., BA MSc Principal Lectr.;
Group Head
Zaagman, Peter, MSc Sr. Lectr.
Other Staff: 1 Sr. Lectr.†
Research: advanced nursing practice; dementia;
gerontology; learning disabilities; mental
health care

Hotel and Restaurant Management

Tel: (01865) 483800 Fax: (01865) 483878
Bowie, David E. C., MBA *Manc.* Sr. Lectr.
Burgess, Cathy, MPhil *Oxf.Brookes* Sr. Lectr.
Clendining, Grant, BA *CNAA* Principal Lectr.
Doherty, Liz, BA *Exe.*, MA *Warw.* Principal
Lectr.
Downie, Nina J., BSc *CNAA*, MPhil
Oxf.Brookes Sr. Lectr.
Harris, Peter, MSc *Strath.* Principal Lectr.
Hemmington, Nigel R., BSc *Sur.*, PhD
Sur. Reader
Hodges, Richard, BA *Wales*, MBA *Brun.* Sr.
Lectr.
Jauncey, Stuart, BSc *CNAA*, MSc *Sur.* Sr. Lectr.
Maher, Angela, BA *Oxf.Brookes* Sr. Lectr.
Mitchell, Ian, BA *Strath.*, MSc
City(UK) Principal Lectr.
Mitchell, Kathy, BA *Strath.* Sr. Lectr.
Robertson, Clive, BSc *CNAA*, MSc
Reading Head*
Roper, Angela, BA *CNAA*, PhD *Hudd.* Principal
Lectr.
Seymour, Diane, BSc *Lond.*, MA *Kent* Sr. Lectr.
Sloan, Donald, BSc *Strath.* Sr. Lectr.
Soames, Stuart Sr. Lectr.
Teare, Richard E., BSc *Sur.*, PhD
City(UK) Granada Prof.
Other Staff: 1 Visiting Prof.; 1 Lectr.; 8
Visiting Fellows; 2 Sr. Lectrs†; 2 Temp.
Lectrs.; 1 Emer. Prof.
Research: hospitality management (education,
training and employment); hospitality
organisations (performance, policy, strategy)

Humanities

Tel: (01865) 483570 Fax: (01865) 484082
Andrews, Jonathan, BA *Lond.*, PhD *Lond.* Sr.
Lectr.
Bertram, Vicki, BA *Oxf.*, DPhil *York(UK)* Sr.
Lectr.
Burnett, Archie, MA *Edin.*, DPhil *Oxf.* Principal
Lectr.
Chamberlain, Mary, MA *Edin.*, MSc *Lond.* Prof.
Digby, Prof. Anne, BA *Camb.*, PhD
E.Anglia Reader; Dir., Humanities Res.
Centre
Durning, Louise, MA *St And.*, PhD *Essex* Sr.
Lectr.
Griffin, Roger D., MA *Oxf.*, DPhil *Oxf.* Prof.
Hammond, Ronald W., MA *Oxf.* Principal
Lectr.
Jackson-Houlston, Caroline M., MA *Oxf.*, MPhil
Oxf. Sr. Lectr.
King, Steven, BA *Kent*, PhD *Liv.* Sr. Lectr.
Lowry, Donal, BA *N.U.I.*, PhD *Rhodes* Sr. Lectr.
Matthews, Steven J., MA *York(UK)*, DPhil
York(UK) Sr. Lectr.
Messenger, Nigel P., BA *Leic.* Sr. Lectr.
Mühlberger, Detlef, BA *Lond.*, PhD *Lond.* Sr.
Lectr.
Nash, David S., BA *E.Anglia*, DPhil *York(UK)* Sr.
Lectr.
O'Flinn, Paul, BA *Oxf.*, BLitt *Oxf.*, MA
Essex Principal Lectr.
Perkins, John B., BA *Camb.*, MSc *Sus.* Head*
Pope, Robert, BA *Wales*, BPhil *York(UK)*, PhD
Wales Principal Lectr.
Sheehy, Jeanne I., BA *N.U.I.*, MLitt
Trinity(Dub.) Principal Lectr.
Stewart, John W., BA *CNAA*, MPhil *Lond.* Sr.
Lectr.
Tilbury, Clare, BA *Lond.* Sr. Lectr.
Wrigley, Richard B., BA *Reading*, DPhil *Oxf.* Sr.
Lectr.
Young, Stewart J., BA *E.Anglia*, MA *Essex* Sr.
Lectr.
Other Staff: 4 Lectrs.; 1 Res. Fellow; 3 Sr.
Lectrs.†; 3 Temp. Lectrs.

Research: history of British and French art;
history of medicine; modern and
contemporary poetry; modern socio-cultural
history (Britain and Europe); post-colonial
literature and 'new' Englishes

Languages

Tel: (01865) 483720 Fax: (01865) 483791
Ansell, Mary A., BA *Sus.*, MA *Lond.* Principal
Lectr.; Head, Internat. Centre for Engl. Lang.
Studies
Berghahn, Daniela, DrPhil *Cologne* Principal
Lectr.
Carter, John, BA *Lond.*, MA *Lond.* Principal
Lectr.; Chair, French Lit.
Errey, Lyn, BA *Syd.* Sr. Lectr.
Farr, Marilyn, BA *Birm.*, MSc *Aston* Principal
Lectr.; Chair, Langs. for Business
Hahn, Hans, DrPhil *Tübingen* Principal Lectr.;
Head, German Section; Chair, German Lit.
Haill, Richard, BA *Kent*, MA *Kent*, MA
Reading Sr. Lectr.
Hand, Sean, MA *Oxf.*, DPhil *Oxf.* Prof.; Head*
Headlam, Allan, MA *Edin.*, Dr3rdCy
Nice Principal Lectr.; Head, French Section
Helliwell, Kumiko, BA *Kyoritsu* Sr. Lectr.
Hewlett, Nick, BA *Sus.*, MA *Essex* Reader
Hill, Irène, BA *Oxf.Brookes*, MèsL *Orléans* Sr.
Lectr.
Hutchings, Ian, MSc *Lond.* Sr. Lectr.; Chair,
German Contemp. Studies
Jones, Norman, MA *Oxf.*, MA *Reading* Sr.
Lectr.; Head, Spanish Section
Jordan, Shirley A., BA *Hull*, PhD *Hull* Sr. Lectr.
Levy, Jonathan, BA *Liv.*, MA *Reading* Sr. Lectr.
Lunow Collins, Ingrid, BA *Lond.*, MA *Lond.* Sr.
Lectr.
MacLennan, Manuel, Lic *Madrid*, MA *Col.* Sr.
Lectr.
Manfredi, Simonetta, Laur *Urbino* Sr. Lectr.
Millar, Martin, MA *Edin.*, MSc *Edin.* Sr. Lectr.
Moreton, Monique J. Sr. Lectr.
Proudfoot, Anna, BA *Lond.* Sr. Lectr.; Head,
Italian Section
Rollin, Hilary, BA *Lond.*, MA *Oregon* Sr. Lectr.
Sayigh, Elizabeth A. Sr. Lectr.
Walker, Patricia, BA *Open(UK)*, MEd
Newcastle(UK) Sr. Lectr.
Woodbridge, Teresa Sr. Lectr.
Other Staff: 1 Sr. Lectr.†
Research: French literature since 1600 (including
interaction between literature and ideology);
French twentieth-century politics; history of
education in France since 1882; mass media
in France; modern German novel since 1900

Law, see Soc. Scis. and Law

Mathematical Sciences, see Computing
and Mathl. Scis.

Molecular Sciences, see Biol. and Molecular
Scis.

Music, see Art, Publishing and Music

Planning

Tel: (01865) 483450 Fax: (01865) 483559
Bixby, Bob, BSc *Nott.*, MSc *Birm.* Principal
Lectr.
Bourdillon, Nicola, BA *Sheff.*, MSc
Oxf.Brookes Sr. Lectr.
Breakell, Mike, BA *Durh.*, MA *Wis.* Sr. Lectr.
Brownill, Sue, BA *Hull*, PhD *Birm.* Sr. Lectr.
Butina, Prof. Georgia, BA *Zagreb*, DPhil *Oxf.*,
MA Principal Lectr.
Cooper, John, BA *Sund.*, MA *Sheff.* Sr. Lectr.
Darke, Jane, BSc *Lond.*, MA *Essex*, PhD *Sheff.* Sr.
Lectr.
Darke, Roy A., BSc *Lond.*, MSc *Lond.*, MSc(Econ)
Lond., PhD *Sheff.* Sr. Lectr.
Dimitriou, Basil, BSc *Leeds* Sr. Lectr.
Edwards, Peter, MA *Sus.* Sr. Lectr.
Elson, Prof. Martin, BA *Newcastle(UK)* Reader
Elwin, James, BA *Manc.*, MSc *Reading* Sr. Lectr.
France, Roger, MA *York(UK)*, MSc *Oxf.* Sr.
Lectr.

Glasson, Prof. John, BSc *Lond.*, MA
Lanc. Head*
Godfrey, Kerry B., BSc *Vic.(Tor.)*, MSc *Sur.*, PhD
Oxf.Brookes Sr. Lectr.
Goodey, Brian, BA *Nott.*, MA *Indiana* Prof.
Grover, Philip R., BA *Oxf.Brookes* Sr. Lectr.
Headicar, Peter, BA *Newcastle(UK)*, MSc *Lond.*,
MSc *Brist* Halcrow Fox Reader, Transport
Planning
Langridge, Bob, BA *Reading*, MA *Warw.*, PhD
Reading Sr. Lectr.
Marshall, Tim, BA *Oxf.*, PhD *Oxf.Brookes* Sr.
Lectr.
Mason, Roger, BA *Oxf.*, MA *Oxf.*, MPhil
Lond. Sr. Lectr.
McGlynn, Sue, BSc *Lond.*, MA *Oxf.Brookes* Sr.
Lectr.
Pearl, Martyn, BA *CNAA*, MSc *Lond.* Principal
Lectr.
Reeve, Alan Sr. Lectr.
Reynolds, Georgina, BA *Brad.* Sr. Lectr.
Rodriguez-Bachiller, Austin, BA *Madrid*, MSc
Reading, PhD *Reading* Sr. Lectr.
Simmonds, Roger, MSc *Yale*, PhD *M.I.T.* Sr.
Lectr.
Smith, Peter, BSc *Aston*, MSc *Reading* Sr. Lectr.
Therivel, Riki, BA *N.Y.*, BSc *N.Y.*, BA Sr. Lectr.
Thomas, Keith, BSc *Lond.*, MSc *Lond.*, PhD
Lond. Principal Lectr.
Thomas, Michael, BSc *Lond.*, MA *Kent* Principal
Lectr.
Walker, Stephen R., BA *CNAA*, MPhil
CNAA Sr. Lectr.
Ward, Prof. Stephen V., BA *Birm.*, PhD
Birm. Principal Lectr.
Weston, Joe, BA *Oxf.Brookes*, MSc *Oxf.Brookes* Sr.
Lectr.
Wilson, Elizabeth, BA *Oxf.*, MPhil *Lond.* Sr.
Lectr.
Zetter, Prof. Roger, BA *Camb.*, MA *Camb.*, MA
Nott. Principal Lectr.
Research: impact assessment (environmental
impact assessment and decision-making,
socio-economic impacts, strategic
environmental assessment, sustainable
development); planning policy (countryside
planning, green belt policy, sport, recreation
and leisure, urban growth management);
planning theory and history (social policy
and planning, urban management); urban
design and conservation (heritage and
conservation, landscape planning, quality in
the built environment, urban regeneration
and community development); urban policy
and management (housing management,
regeneration/economic development)

Publishing, see Art, Publishing and Music

Social Sciences and Law

Tel: (01865) 483750 Fax: (01865) 483937
Argyle, M., MA *Camb.*, DSc *Camb.*, DLitt *Camb.*
Axford, Barrie, BA *Reading*, MA
Reading Principal Lectr.
Barton, Roger N. E., BSc *Birm.*, DPhil *Oxf.* Sr.
Lectr.
Baxter, John, LLB *Wales* Sr. Lectr.
Bradley, Peter, BA *E.Anglia* Sr. Lectr.
Brennan, Carol, LLB *Lond.*, MA *Brun.*, PhD
Brun. Principal Lectr.
Brooker, Penny, BA *Belf.*, LLB *CNAA* Sr. Lectr.
Browning, Gary, BA *Reading*, MSc *Lond.*, MSc
S'ton., PhD *Lond.* Prof.
Carnibella, Giovanni, BA *Pontif.Athen.Sal.*, MA
Pontif.Athen.Sal., PhD *Pontif.Athen.Sal.* Sr. Lectr.
Catley, Paul, BA *Camb.*, MA *Camb.* Principal
Lectr.
Chance, Margaret J., BA *Oxf.* Sr. Lectr.
Daly, Mike, LLB *Lond.*, MA *Brun.* Sr. Lectr.
Elgar, Marian P. Sr. Lectr.
Elsom, Derek M., BSc *Birm.*, MSc *Birm.*, PhD
CNAA Prof.
Fearnley, Stephen, BSc *Wales*, DPhil
Oxf. Principal Lectr.
Gold, John R., BSc *Lond.*, MSc *Birm.*, PhD
Birm. Prof.
Grant, Alan, BA *Leeds*, MA *Warw.* Sr. Lectr.
Grant, Beryl, LLB *Lond.* Sr. Lectr.

Grant, Evadne, BA *Stell.*, LLB *Stell.*, LLM *Cape Town*, MPhil *Camb.* Sr. Lectr.

Haigh, Martin J., BSc *Birm.*, PhD *Birm.* Prof., Physical Geography

Hendrick, Judith, BA *Lond.*, LLM *Lond.* Sr. Lectr.

Hendry, Joy, BSc *Lond.*, BLitt *Oxf.*, DPhil *Oxf.* Prof.

Henshaw, Lindsay, BA *Brist.*, MA *Camb.* Sr. Lectr.

Huggins, Richard I., BA *Oxf.Brookes* Sr. Lectr.

Jordan, Tim, BSc *Oregon*, MA *Col.*, PhD *Stan.* Reader

Keene, Peter, BA *Hull* Sr. Lectr.

Lamb, Roger M., BA *Oxf.*, BPhil *Oxf.* Sr. Lectr.

Lewis-Anthony, Sian, BA *Durh.*, LLM *Lond.* Sr. Lectr.

Lindsay, Roger, BA *Keele*, BPhil *Oxf.*, DPhil *Oxf.* Principal Lectr.

Macbeth, Helen, BA *Lond.*, DPhil *Oxf.* Principal Lectr.

MacClancy, Jeremy V., MA *Oxf.*, MLitt *Oxf.*, DPhil *Oxf.* Sr. Lectr.

MacLean, Morag E. N., BA *Lond.*, MSc *Open(UK)* Sr. Lectr.

MacRae, Susan, BA *S.Fraser*, MA *Tor.*, DPhil *Oxf.* Prof.; Head*

McDonaugh, Christian E., BA *Oxf.*, MLitt *Oxf.*, DPhil *Oxf.* Sr. Lectr.

Miller, Tina A., BA *Wales*, MSc *Open(UK)* Sr. Lectr.

Nielsen, Helena, BA *Lond.*, MPhil *Glas.*, MA *Warw.* Sr. Lectr.

Palmer, Amanda M., BA *Oxf.*, MA *Oxf.*, PhD *Warw.* Sr. Lectr.

Paroussis, Evangelos, MA *Durh.*, BA Sr. Lectr.

Parsons, Maria S., BA *Sheff.* Sr. Lectr.

Paton, Renée, BA *C.U.N.Y.*, MA *C.U.N.Y.*, PhD *C.U.N.Y.* Sr. Lectr.; Sr. Tutor

Pepper, David M., MA *Oxf.*, BA PhD Prof.

Quoroll, Gillian, LLB *Wales*, MA *Brun.* Sr. Lectr.

Ramsey, Richard, BA *Birm.*, BA *Camb.*, LLB *Lond.*, MA *Camb.*,MSc *Oxf.*, MA *Lond.* Sr. Lectr.

Revill, George E., BSc *Lond.*, MA *Syr.*, DPhil *Oxf.* Sr. Lectr.

Ribbens, Jane, BA MSc PhD Sr. Lectr.

Robb, Bridget N., BA *Nott.*, MA *Nott.* Principal Lectr.

Sissons Joshi, Mary, BA *Sheff.*, DPhil *Oxf.* Sr. Lectr.

Turner, John, BA *Essex*, MSc *Lond.*, PhD *Lond.* Principal Lectr.

Vickers, Lucy, BA *Camb.* Sr. Lectr.

Webster, Frank, BA *Durh.*, MA *Durh.*, PhD *Lond.* Prof.

Woodhouse, Diana, BA *CNAA*, PhD *CNAA* Sr. Lectr.

Woolley, Thomas P., BA *Middx.*, MA *Essex* Sr. Lectr.

Young, Jeffrey, BA *Oxf.*, MA *Lond.*, LLM *Lond.* Sr. Lectr.

Other Staff: 6 Lectrs.

Research: human and physical geography (environmentalism); law and public policy (citizenship); politics (globalisation, Europe, theory); social and cognitive psychology; social and physical anthropology

CONTACT OFFICERS

Academic affairs. Academic Secretary: Winders, Elizabeth N., BA *Lond.*

Accommodation. Accommodation Officer: Eadie, Helen

Admissions (first degree). Admissions Officer (Institutional): Daniels, Helena K.

Adult/continuing education. Marketing Manager: Bibby, Darryl, BSc *E.Anglia*, PhD *E.Anglia*

Alumni. Alumni and Events Officer: Peacock, Felicity B., BA *Sus.*

Archives. Vice-Chancellor's Personal Assistant and Office Co-ordinator: Fox, Clare

Careers. Head of Careers: McCarthy, Mary A., BSc *Hull*, LLB *Hull*, MA *Liv.*

Computing services. Librarian: Workman, Helen M., BSc *Birm.*, MA *Sheff.*, PhD *Open(UK)*

Conferences/corporate hospitality. Head of Conferences: Moore, Eleanor

Consultancy services. Head of Contracts and Consultancy Services: Wheatley, Barry I., BSc *Brad.*, MSc *Brad.*

Credit transfer. Admissions Officer (Institutional): Daniels, Helena K.

Development/fund-raising. Director of Development: Wilson, Jacky B., BA *E.Anglia*

Equal opportunities. Head of Equal Opportunities: Priest, Judy R., BA *Syr.*

Estates and buildings/works and services. Head of Buildings and Estates: Longworth, Carl A. R., BSc *Leic.*, MSc *Strath.*

Examinations. Head of Examination and Conferment Unit: Ultsch, Frank C., BA *Maine(USA)*, MDiv *Maine(USA)*

Finance. Head of Finance: Large, Paul

General enquiries. Academic Secretary: Winders, Elizabeth N., BA *Lond.*

Health services. Head of Student Services: Cooper, Keith H., BA *Oxf.*

Industrial liaison. Head of Contracts and Consultancy Services: Wheatley, Barry I., BSc *Brad.*, MSc *Brad.*

International office. Director of International Admissions: Piggott, Susan M.

International office (European office). Officer: Michalski, Karla

Library (chief librarian). Librarian: Workman, Helen M., BSc *Birm.*, MA *Sheff.*, PhD *Open(UK)*

Minorities/disadvantaged groups. Head of Equal Opportunities: Priest, Judy R., BA *Syr.*

Personnel/human resources. Head of Personnel: Perlin, Phillip S., BA *Kent*

Public relations, information and marketing (information and marketing). Director of Recruitment and Marketing: Bright, Angela P., BA *CNAA*, MA *CNAA*

Public relations, information and marketing (public relations). Evans, Helen C., BA *Camb.*

Publications. Publications Officer: Brown, Pauline

Purchasing. Purchasing Manager: Horne, Andrew P., BA *Lanc.*

Quality assurance and accreditation. Deputy Vice-Chancellor: Fidler, Prof. Peter, MBE, MSc *Salf.*

Research. Head, School of Construction and Earth Sciences: Topley, Chris G., BSc *Wales*, DPhil *Oxf.*

Safety. Safety Officer: Pigott, John E., BSc *CNAA*

Scholarships, awards, loans. Student Support Officer: Davies, Hilary R.

Schools liaison. School and College Liaison Officer: Brierley, Sarah J., BA *Oxf.Brookes*

Security. Head of Buildings and Estates: Longworth, Carl A. R., BSc *Leic.*, MSc *Strath.*

Sport and recreation. Director of Sport and Recreation: Dodwell, Mark E. J., MA *Birm.*

Staff development and training. Priest, Judy R., BA *Syr.*

Student union. President: Macpherson, Gordon

Student welfare/counselling. Head of Student Services: Cooper, Keith H., BA *Oxf.*

Students from other countries. International Students Adviser: Ames, Mark F., BA *Birm.*

Students with disabilities. Disabled Students Adviser: Collin, Madeleine P., BSc *Brad.*

[*Information supplied by the institution as at 9 April 1998, and edited by the ACU*]

UNIVERSITY OF PAISLEY

University title awarded 1992; originally founded as Paisley Technical College and School of Art

Member of the Association of Commonwealth Universities

Postal Address: Paisley, Renfrewshire, Scotland PA1 2BE
Telephone: (0141) 848 3000 **Fax**: (0141) 887 0812 **Telex**: 778951

PRINCIPAL AND VICE-CHANCELLOR*—Shaw, Prof. Richard W., CBE, BA *Camb.*, MA *Camb.*
VICE-PRINCIPAL—McDaid, Prof. Seamus, MBA *Strath.*
ASSISTANT PRINCIPAL—Wilson, Prof. Gordon M., MA *Glas.*, PhD *Glas.*
SECRETARY TO THE UNIVERSITY‡—Fraser, James M., MA *Edin.*, MEd *Stir.*
REGISTRAR AND DEPUTE SECRETARY—Rigg, David, MA *Dund.*
LIBRARIAN—James, Stuart, BA *Birm.*

GENERAL INFORMATION

History. The university was originally founded in 1897 and gained university status in 1992. It has two campuses, in Paisley and Ayr.

Admission to first degree courses (see also United Kingdom Introduction). Through Universities and Colleges Admissions Service (UCAS).

First Degrees (see also United Kingdom Directory to Subjects of Study). BA, BEng, BSc, MEng.

Higher Degrees (see also United Kingdom Directory to Subjects of Study). MSc.

Libraries. 200,000 volumes; 1200 periodicals subscribed to.

Academic Year. Two semesters.

Income (1995–96). Total, £35,519,000.

Statistics. Staff: 1275 (444 academic, 831 support). Students: 9686.

FACULTIES/SCHOOLS

Business
Dean: Struthers, John J., MA *Glas.*, MPhil *Glas.*

Education
Dean: Lowrie, Patricia, BSc *Nott.*

Engineering
Dean: Marshall, Prof. Ian H., BSc *Strath.*, PhD *Strath.*, FIMechE

Health and Social Sciences
Dean: Clarke, Tony P., BSc *S'ton.*, PhD *S'ton.*

Science and Technology
Dean: McLean, Roger O., BSc *Wales*, PhD *Wales*

ACADEMIC UNITS

Accounting, Economics and Languages
Tel: (0141) 848 3351 Fax: (0141) 848 3395
Cochrane, Stuart, BA *Leic.*, PhD *Qld.* Sr. Lectr.
Coleshill, Paul, MSc *Wales* Sr. Lectr.
Danson, Michael, MA *Aberd.* Personal Prof.
Deakins, David, BSc *Staffs.*, BA *Sheff.Hallam*, MA *Essex* Renfrewshire Enterprise Prof., Enterprise Development
El-Ashker, Ahmed, MSc *Birm.*, PhD *Hull* Sr. Lectr.
Fleming, A. Iain M., BA *H.-W.* Sr. Lectr.
McKinstry, Samuel, BA *Open(UK)*, PhD *St And.* Reader
Morrison, Alana, BA *Paisley*
Myant, Martin, BA *Camb.*, PhD *Glas.* Reader
Pyper, Douglas, BA *Strath.*, MSc *Strath.* Sr. Lectr.
Reeves, Alan F., MPhil *York(UK)*, BA PhD Sr. Lectr.
Struthers, John J., MA *Glas.*, MPhil *Glas.* Sr. Lectr.

Young, Alistair, MA *Glas.*, PhD *Reading* Prof.; Head*

Applied Social Studies
Tel: (0141) 848 3766 Fax: (0141) 848 3891
Brady, John, MA *Edin.*, MPhil *York(UK)* Sr. Lectr.
Fabb, Janet E., BA *N.Y.State* Sr. Lectr.
Faulds, Morag C., OBE Visiting Prof.
Foster, John O., MA *Camb.*, PhD *Camb.* Prof.; Head*
Gilhooly, Mary, BSc *Leeds*, BSc *Oregon*, MEd *Aberd.*, PhD *Aberd.* Prof., Health Studies
Hobbs, Alexander, MA *Aberd.* Sr. Lectr.
Jay, C. D. Visiting Prof.
Madigan, Christopher W., BA *Leeds* Sr. Lectr.
McKechnie, James, BA *G.Caledonian*, PhD *Stir.* Sr. Lectr.
Mooney, Gerald, PhD *Glas.*, BA Sr. Lectr.
Slocock, Brian, BA *S.Fraser*, MA *Lond.*
Turner, Michael, MA *N.Y.*, PhD *N.Y.* Sr. Lectr.

Biological Sciences
Tel: (0141) 848 3101 Fax: (0141) 848 3116
Anderson, Thomas A. Visiting Prof.
Bickerstaff, Gordon F., BSc *H.-W.*, PhD *Stir.* Sr. Lectr.
Cook, John P., MSc *H.-W.* Sr. Lectr.
Curtis, David J., BSc *Liv.*, PhD *Liv.* Prof.
Hammerton, Desmond Visiting Prof.
MacDonald, Caroline M., BSc *Glas.*, PhD *Glas.* Prof.; Head*
Nicholl, Desmond, BSc *Belf.*, PhD *Belf.* Sr. Lectr.
Tatner, P., BSc PhD

Chemistry and Chemical Engineering
Tel: (0141) 848 3201 Fax: (0141) 848 3204
Carpenter, Keith J. Visiting Prof.
Hursthouse, Andrew, BSc *Reading*, PhD *Glas.* Sr. Lectr.
MacPherson, Ian A. Visiting Prof.
Nicoll, Alistair J. S., BSc *Glas.*, PhD *Strath.* Sr. Lectr.
Rendall, Henry M., BSc *Edin.*, PhD *Edin.* Sr. Lectr.
Roach, Alan C., BSc *Glas.*, PhD *Glas.* Prof.; Head*
Smith, Francis J., BSc *Strath.*, PhD *Strath.* Sr. Lectr.
Stewart, Brian, BSc *Dund.*, PhD *Lond.* Reader
Tucker, Peter, BA *Oxf.*, PhD *Newcastle(UK)* Prof.
Vaughan, D. Huw, BSc *Lond.*, PhD *Lond.* Sr. Lectr.
Watson, Arthur, BSc *Belf.*, PhD *Belf.* Reader

Computing and Information Systems
Tel: (0141) 848 3301 Fax: (0141) 848 3542
Balint, Susan, BSc *Durh.*, MBA *Glas.*
Beeby, Richard, BSc *Edin.*, PhD *Edin.* Sr. Lectr.
Branki, C., BSc MSc PhD
Connolly, Thomas M., BSc *Strath.* Sr. Lectr.
Crowe, Malcolm K., BA *Trinity(Dub.)*, DPhil *Oxf.* Prof.; Head*
Frew, Russell W., BSc *Staffs.* Sr. Lectr.
Fyfe, George, BSc *Glas.*, MEd *Glas.*, MSc *Strath.* Sr. Lectr.

Girolami, M., BSc *Glas.*, BA *Open(UK)*, MSc *Open(UK)*, PhD *Paisley*
Howell, James G., MSc *Glas.* Sr. Lectr.
Lees, Brian, BSc *Manc.*, MSc *H.-W.* Sr. Lectr.
Norris, Peter R., BSc *W.Aust.*, PhD *W.Aust.* Sr. Lectr.
West, Daune, BSc MA PhD Sr. Lectr.
Williamson, Adrian, BSc *Lough.* Sr. Lectr.

Curricular Studies
Fax: (01292) 611705
Finnigan, Thomas, BSc *Glas.*, MEd *Glas.*, MA *Open(UK)* Sr. Lectr.
Hall, Iain N. S., MA *Glas.* Sr. Lectr.
Hamilton, Thomas H., BEd *Strath.*, BA *Open(UK)* Sr. Lectr.
Hartsthorn, Bryce J., MA *Glas.*, BD *Aberd.* Sr. Lectr.
Livingston, P. Kay, BEd Sr. Lectr.
McCreath, Jean K. Sr. Lectr.
Merrick, Harry, BSc *Glas.*, BA *Open(UK)* Sr. Lectr.
Robertson, John W., BA *Stir.* Head*
Stefani, Robert A. J., BA *Open(UK)* Sr. Lectr.

Economics, see Acctg., Econ. and Langs.

Education, see In-Service Educn., and Professl. Studies (Educn.)

Electronic Engineering and Physics
Tel: (0141) 848 3601 Fax: (0141) 848 3616
No staff at present

Engineering, Chemical, see Chem. and Chem. Engin.

Engineering, Civil, Structural and Environmental
Tel: (0141) 848 3251 Fax: (0141) 848 3275
Bartos, Peter, MSc *T.U.Prague*, PhD *S'ton.* Prof.
Hardy, Robert, BSc *Glas.*, MEng Sr. Lectr.
Little, John A., MSc *Durh.*, PhD *City(UK)*, FGS Prof.; Head*
McKenzie, Alastair J., BSc *Aberd.*, FGS Sr. Lectr.
Provan, Thomas F., BSc *Lond.* Sr. Lectr.
Smith, Paul, BSc *Birm.*, MSc *Birm.*, PhD *Strath.* Prof.
Stark, Walter G., BSc *Glas.*, MEng Sr. Lectr.
Younger, James D., BSc Sr. Lectr.

Engineering, Electronic, and Physics
Tel: (0141) 848 3601 Fax: (0141) 848 3616
Anderson, A. J., BSc *Glas.*
Campbell, Douglas R., BSc *Strath.*, PhD *Strath.* Reader
Chapman, Robert, BSc *Glas.*, PhD *Glas.* Prof.; Head*
Forrest, Allister M., BSc *St And.*, MA *Tor.*, PhD *Tor.* Sr. Lectr.
Galbraith, Farquar S., MSc *Birm.* Sr. Lectr.
Howie, I., MSc *Aberd.*, PhD *Aberd.* Sr. Lectr.
Moir, Thomas J., BSc *Sheff.*, PhD *Sheff.* Sr. Lectr.
Placido, Francis, BSc *Edin.*, PhD *Edin.* Reader
Robertson, Donald G., BSc *Glas.* Sr. Lectr.

Shackleford, Robert A., BSc *Strath.*, MBA *Strath.* Sr. Lectr.
Watt, Alan S. M., MSc Sr. Lectr.

Engineering, Mechanical and Manufacturing, and Quality Centre

Tel: (0141) 848 3561 Fax: (0141) 848 3555
Drummond, Siobhan, BA *Strath.*, MPhil *Strath.* Sr. Lectr.
Findlay, George E., PhD *Lond.*, BSc Prof.
Gibson, Francis, BSc *Strath.*, PhD *Strath.* Sr. Lectr.
Little, William, BA *Strath.*, MSc *Lond.* Sr. Lectr.
Marshall, Ian H., BSc *Strath.*, PhD *Strath.*, FIMechE Prof.; Head*
Smyth, David S., BSc *Strath.*, PhD *Strath.* Sr. Lectr.
Wood, James, BSc PhD Sr. Lectr.

Health Studies, see Appl. Soc. Studies

In-Service Education

Forbes, David, MA *Aberd.*, MA *Lond.* Head*

Land Economics

Tel: (0141) 848 3451 Fax: (0141) 887 9799
Fraser, William D., MSc *Strath.*, PhD *City(UK)*, FRICS Prof.; Head*
Jones, Colin A., MA *Manc.* Reader
McConan, A. C., LLB *Glas.*
McMaster, Ray, BSc *H.-W.* Sr. Lectr.
Mowbray, Richard, BA *Lond.*, MSc *Lond.* Sr. Lectr.

Languages, see Acctg., Econ. and Langs.

Marketing and Management

Tel: (0141) 848 3863 Fax: (0141) 848 3395
Brough, Ian, BSc *Lond.*, PhD *Strath.* Sr. Lectr.
Connor, Sandra, BA Sr. Lectr.
Drummond, Siobhan, BA *Strath.*, MPhil *Strath.*
Galloway, Alasdair M., MA *Glas.*, PhD *Glas.* Sr. Lectr.
Gudim, Mairi, BA *Strath.* Sr. Lectr.
Krawczyk, W., BA MBA
McLean, Alexis J., MSc *Strath.* Sr. Lectr.
Turner, W. John, BSc *Brist.*, MBA *Lond.* Sr. Lectr.
Von Zugbach, Reginald, BA *Open(UK)*, PhD *Lond.* Prof.; Head*

Mathematics and Statistics

Tel: (0141) 848 3501
Burnside, Robert R., BSc *Strath.*, PhD *St And.*, FIMA Prof.; Head*
MacArthur, Ewan W., MSc *Strath.*, PhD *Edin.* Sr. Lectr.
MacDivitt, Arthur R. G., MA *Glas.*, MSc *Glas.* Sr. Lectr.
MacLeod, Allan, BSc *Edin.*, PhD *Edin.* Sr. Lectr.
Russell, Robert J., MSc *Wales* Sr. Lectr.
Smith, Edward A., BSc *St And.*, PhD *St And.* Sr. Lectr.

Physics, see Engin., Electronic, and Phys.

Professional Studies (Education)

Fax: (01292) 611705
Errington, Malcolm P. M., BA *Open(UK)*, MEd *Edin.* Sr. Lectr.
Smith, Ian K., MA *Glas.*, MEd *Glas.* Sr. Lectr.

Quality Centre, see Engin., Mech. and Manufacturing, and Quality Centre

Social Studies, see Appl. Soc. Studies

Statistics, see Maths. and Stats.

SPECIAL CENTRES, ETC

Alcohol and Drug Studies, Centre for

Tel: (0141) 848 3141 Fax: (0141) 848 3904
Barrie, Kenneth, BA *Strath.* Dir.*

Educational Development Unit

Tel: (0141) 848 3821 Fax: (0141) 848 3822
Rowatt, Robert W., BSc *Strath.* Dir.*
Telfer, William S. Sr. Lectr.

Electromagnetic Compatibility Centre

Tel: (0141) 848 3430
Galbraith, Farquar S., MSc *Birm.* Dir.*

Environmental and Waste Management, Centre for

Tel: (0141) 848 3146 Fax: (0141) 848 3142
No staff at present

Land Value Information Unit

Tel: (0141) 848 3473 Fax: (0141) 887 9799
Martin, David, MSc, FRICS Dir.*
Pitticas, Nondas, MSc Manager

Management Information Services

Tel: (0141) 848 3644 Fax: (0141) 848 3911
Shaw, R. Anthony, BSc *St And.* Dir.*

Materials and Components Development and Testing Association (MACDATA)

Tel: (0141) 848 3259 Fax: (0141) 848 3257
Arthur, M. Dir.*

Technology and Business Centre

Tel: (0141) 848 0178 Fax: (0141) 848 3739
Cross, Brian G. Manager*

CONTACT OFFICERS

Academic affairs. Vice-Principal: McDaid, Prof. Seamus, MBA *Strath.*
Accommodation. Accommodation Officer: Dryburgh, Alec
Admissions (first degree). Assistant Registrar: Copland, Alison M., BA *Open(UK)*
Admissions (higher degree). Assistant Registrar: Copland, Alison M., BA *Open(UK)*
Adult/continuing education. Director, Department of Continuing Education: Knox, Hazel, BA *Open(UK)*, BSc *Belf.*, MSc *Stir.*
Careers. Director, Student Advisory Service: Nisbet, Jennifer, MA *Edin.*, MBA *Open*, PhD *Lanc.*
Computing services. James, Stuart, BA *Birm.*
Credit transfer. Director, Department of Continuing Education: Knox, Hazel, BA *Open(UK)*, BSc *Belf.*, MSc *Stir.*
Distance education. Director of International Office and Distance Learning Unit: Ramsay, Kirk, BSc *Strath.*

Equal opportunities. Personnel Officer: Russell, Jackie, MA *Glas.*
Estates and buildings/works and services. Director of Estates and Buildings: Lynch, Adam Ls
Examinations. Registrar and Depute Secretary: Rigg, David, MA *Dund.*
Finance. Director of Finance: McKechnie, Andrew
General enquiries. Director, Corporate Communications: MacLennan, Prof. Alexander, BSc PhD
Health services. Secretary to the University: Fraser, James M., MA *Edin.*, MEd *Stir.*
International office. Director of International Office and Distance Learning Unit: Ramsay, Kirk, BSc *Strath.*
Library (chief librarian). Librarian: James, Stuart, BA *Birm.*
Personnel/human resources. Personnel Officer: Paton, Susan, MA *Glas.*
Personnel/human resources. Personnel Officer: Russell, Jackie, MA *Glas.*
Public relations, information and marketing. Public Relations and Marketing Manager: Ross, Marcus, BA *R.Gordon*
Public relations, information and marketing. Director, Corporate Communications: MacLennan, Prof. Alexander, BSc PhD
Publications. Assistant Manager Public Relations and Marketing: Kyle, David, MA *Glas.*
Purchasing. Secretary to the University: Fraser, James M., MA *Edin.*, MEd *Stir.*
Quality assurance and accreditation. Registrar and Depute Secretary: Rigg, David, MA *Dund.*
Research. Assistant Registrar: Shearer, Jen, MA *Glas.*
Safety. Safety Officer: ......
Scholarships, awards, loans. Registrar and Depute Secretary: Rigg, David, MA *Dund.*
Schools liaison. Education Liaison Manager: Alexander, Muriel, MA *Edin.*, MSc *Sheff.*
Security. Director of Estates and Buildings: Lynch, Adam Ls
Sport and recreation. Director of Estates and Buildings: Lynch, Adam Ls
Staff development and training. Assistant Principal: Wilson, Gordon M., MA *Glas.*, PhD *Glas.*
Student union. Manager: Mulholland, Gordon, BA *G.Caledonian*
Student welfare/counselling. Director, Student Advisory Service: Nisbet, Jennifer, MA *Edin.*, MBA *Open*, PhD *Lanc.*
Students from other countries. Director, Student Advisory Service: Nisbet, Jennifer, MA *Edin.*, MBA *Open*, PhD *Lanc.*
Students with disabilities. Director, Student Advisory Service: Nisbet, Jennifer, MA *Edin.*, MBA *Open*, PhD *Lanc.*
University Press. Public Relations and Marketing Manager: Ross, Marcus, BA *R.Gordon*

[Information supplied by the institution as at 2 March 1998, and edited by the ACU]

UNIVERSITY OF PLYMOUTH

Founded 1992; previously Polytechnic South West 1989

Member of the Association of Commonwealth Universities

Postal Address: Drake Circus, Plymouth, Devon, England PL4 8AA
Telephone: (01752) 600600 Fax: (01752) 232293 E-mail: postmaster@plymouth.ac.uk
WWW: http://www.plym.ac.uk

CHANCELLOR—......
CHAIRMAN OF THE BOARD OF GOVERNORS—Parsons, V.
VICE-CHANCELLOR*—Bull, Prof. R. John, BSc(Econ)
DEPUTY VICE-CHANCELLOR—Ebdon, Prof. L., BSc PhD, FRSChem
DEPUTY VICE-CHANCELLOR—Reid, N., BSc MSc DPhil
REGISTRAR—Hopkinson, J., LLB
DEAN OF ACADEMIC SERVICES—Sidgreaves, I. D., BA
UNIVERSITY DEAN OF RESEARCH—Hart, M.

GENERAL INFORMATION

History. The university was created by the merger of Plymouth Polytechnic, Rolle College in Exmouth, Exeter College of Art and Design and Seale-Hayne Agricultural College.

Admission to first degree courses (see also United Kingdom Introduction). Through Universities and Colleges Admissions Service (UCAS) or, for nursing and midwifery applications, through NMAS. Normal minimum requirements are passes in 3 General Certificate of Secondary Education (GCSE) subjects, and 2 General Certificate of Education (GCE) A levels or 2 Advanced General National Vocational Qualifications (GNVQs). Alternatively, a good Business and Technology Edcuation Council (BTEC) National Certificate or National Diploma may be accepted. Technology and science candidates offering a BTEC National Certificate or Diploma should have merit passes in 3 level III units in subjects relevant to the programme to be undertaken.

First Degrees (see also United Kingdom Directory to Subjects of Study). BA, BEd, BEng, BSc, LLB, MChem, MEng, MMath.
Programmes usually last 3 years full-time or 4 years on a sandwich basis.

Higher Degrees (see also United Kingdom Directory to Subjects of Study). MA, MBA, MEd, MS, MSc, MPhil, PhD, DClinPsy, DLitt, DM, DSc, DTech, LLD.
Applicants for admission to higher degrees must normally hold a degree or equivalent qualification from an approved UK or overseas university.

Language of Instruction. English. Pre-sessional courses available for one or two months in the summer.

Libraries. 410,000 volumes; 2973 periodicals subscribed to. Special collection: maritime history.

Fees. Undergraduate: £1000. Postgraduate: UK/EU students £2610; non-EU students £5760 (low band programmes), £6720 (high band programmes). Fees are dependent upon course type.

Academic Awards (1997). 6967 awards.

Academic Year (1998–99). Two semesters: 21 September–7 February; 8 February–18 June.

Statistics (1996–97) (figures relate to the university and its partner colleges). Staff (full-time): 2458 (983 academic, 1475 administrative). Students: full-time 15,934; part-time 6283; international 1233 (701 men, 532 women); total 22,217 (10,224 men, 11,993 women).

FACULTIES/SCHOOLS

Agriculture, Food and Land Use
Tel: (01626) 325601 Fax: (01626) 325605
Dean: Broom, C., BSc MSc, FRSA FRGS
Secretary: Tiley, L.

Arts and Education
Tel: (01395) 255301 Fax: (01395) 255303
Dean: Newby, Prof. M. J. B., MA
Secretary: ......

Human Sciences
Tel: (01752) 233190 Fax: (01752) 233194
Dean: Beveridge, M. C., BA PhD
Secretary: Darch, M. C.

Plymouth Business School
Tel: (01752) 232805 Fax: (01752) 232498
Dean: Jones, Prof. P., BSc MSc PhD
Secretary: Hills, Heather

Plymouth Postgraduate Medical School
Tel: (01752) 792711 Fax: (01752) 763531
Dean: Rogers, Prof. K., MB ChB MSc MD
Secretary: Wallace, P.

Science
Tel: (01752) 233093 Fax: (01752) 233095
Dean: O'Neill, P., BSc MSc PhD, FGS
Secretary: Higman, L.

Technology
Dean: Cope, Prof. R. J., DSc, FICE, FIStructE
Secretary: ......

ACADEMIC UNITS

Agriculture and Food Studies
Tel: (01626) 325686 Fax: (01626) 325605
Blackshaw, R. P., BSc PhD Prof.; Head*
Brennan, C., BSc PhD, FLS Sr. Lectr.
Brockman, J., BSc PhD Principal Lectr.
Brooks, P., BSc PhD Prof., Research
Campbell, A. C., BSc PhD Sr. Lectr.
Cleverdon, Julia M., BA MApplSci Sr. Lectr.
Clowes, G. F., MSc Sr. Lectr.; Food Technol. Manager
Coates, D., BSc Sr. Lectr.
Cooper, R. A., MSc PhD Principal Lectr.
Eddison, J., BSc PhD Sr. Lectr.
Fuller, M. P., BSc PhD Reader
James, C. S., BSc PhD Sr. Lectr.; Manager, Food Sci.
Jellings, Anita J., BSc PhD Sr. Lectr.; Manager, Agric. Degree
Julyan, B. K. Sr. Lectr.; Manager, Hospitality Degree
Kirk, J. A., BSc PhD Principal Lectr.
Kuri, V., BSc PhD Sr. Lectr.
Margerison, J., BSc PhD Sr. Lectr.
Morgan, D. T., MSc Principal Lectr.
Moule, G. M., MSc Sr. Lectr.
Orr, R. M., BSc PhD Sr. Lectr.
Parkinson, R. J., MSc PhD Principal Lectr.

Randle, H., BSc PhD Sr. Lectr.; Manager, Agric. Degree
Other Staff: 3 Lectrs.; 3 Res. Fellows
Research: behaviour and welfare of domestic livestock; dairy cow nutrition and milk production systems; fermented liquid feeding of pigs; frost tolerance in vegetable plants; waste management through on-farm composting

Architecture
Tel: (01752) 233600 Fax: (01752) 233634
Elkadi, H. A., PhD
Griffiths, R., BSc PhD Sr. Lectr.
Harris, P. H. Sr. Lectr.
Lyons, F. A., MPhil Sr. Lectr.
Mackie, Mhairi M., MPhil Sr. Lectr.
Pearson, M. D., BA Sr. Lectr.
Phillipou, S., PhD
Voyatzaki, M., BA Sr. Lectr.
Watson, Linda L., BSc BArch Sr. Lectr.
Wigginton, M. J., MA Camb., FRSA Prof.; Head*
Willey, D. S., BArch PhD Principal Lectr.
Research: sustainable building (earthen architecture, humane architecture, sustainable buildings and intelligence architecture, sustainable settlement design)

Arts and Design, Exeter School of
Tel: (01392) 475022 Fax: (01392) 475012
Adams, B. C., MDes RCA, BA Sr. Lectr.
Beament, J. G. Sr. Lectr.
Beardon, C., BA NSW, MA NSW, MSc NSW, PhD Res. Prof.
Bennett, Sarah, BA Sr. Lectr.
Berry, S. K. Sr. Lectr.
Buss, D. R., BA Assoc. Dean*
Butler, J. H., BA MA Principal Lectr.
Clucas, G., BA Sr. Lectr.
Coslett, D. L., BA MA(Ed) Principal Lectr.
Danvers, T. J., BA Principal Lectr.; Postgrad. Programme Dir.
Diggle, J., MA RCA, BA MEd Sr. Lectr.
Enright, T., BA MA Sr. Lectr.
Friend, Marion, BA MA Sr. Lectr.
Garton, M. Sr. Lectr.
Griffith, Joanne, BA Sr. Lectr.
Hall, Christine M., BEd MEd Sr. Lectr.
Hawkins, D. J., BSc PhD Sr. Lectr.
Hull, P. J., BSc Sr. Lectr.
Jeremiah, D. Visiting Prof.
Klunder, A., BA Lond. Sr. Lectr.
Okagbue, Osi, PhD Sr. Lectr.
Pay, P. R. Sr. Lectr.
Smith, A. J. Principal Lectr.
Southam, J. V., BA Sr. Lectr.
Southwell, Edith R. Sr. Lectr.
Standing, S. P., BA Sr. Lectr.
Stevenson, M. L. Principal Lectr.
Thorpe, S., BA Sr. Lectr.
Woolner, M. P., MDes RCA, BA Sr. Lectr.
Other Staff: 1 Reader†; 3 Sr. Lectrs. †
Research: history of art, architecture and design

Arts and Education, School of Graduate Studies in

Tel: (01395) 255322 Fax: (01395) 255303
Taylor, G. T., PhD   Assoc. Dean*

Biological Sciences

Tel: (01752) 232900 Fax: (01752) 232970
Albrecht, A. S., PhD   Sr. Lectr.
Attrill, M. J., BSc PhD   Sr. Lectr.
Bilton, D. T., BSc PhD   Sr. Lectr.
Bradley, G., PhD   Sr. Lectr.
Brown, M. T., BSc PhD   Sr. Lectr.
Dale, M. Pamela, BSc PhD   Sr. Lectr.
Davies, S. J., MSc PhD   Sr. Lectr.
Depledge, M. H.   Prof.
Donkin, Maria E., BSc PhD   Sr. Lectr.
Evenden, A., BSc PhD   Sr. Lectr.
Foggo, A., BSc PhD   Sr. Lectr.
Galloway, T. S., BSc PhD   Sr. Lectr.
Gaudie, D., BSc PhD   Sr. Lectr.
Gilpin, M. L., BSc PhD   Sr. Lectr.
Glynn, P. J., BSc PhD   Sr. Lectr.
Gresty, K.   Sr. Lectr.
Handy, R. D., BSc PhD   Sr. Lectr.
Harris, J. E., BSc PhD   Principal Lectr.
Jervis, L., BSc PhD   Principal Lectr.
Jha, A.   Sr. Lectr.
Jones, M. B., BSc PhD, FIBiol   Reader
King, Christine A., BSc PhD   Principal Lectr.
Lane, C. S., BSc PhD   Sr. Lectr.
Matthews, R. A., BSc PhD   Principal Lectr.;
   Dir., Postgrad. Programmes
Moody, A. J., BSc PhD   Sr. Lectr.
Morgan, Miriam, BSc PhD, FLS   Principal
   Lectr.; Dir., Undergrad. Programmes
Munn, C. B., BSc PhD   Head*
Price, D. J., MSc PhD   Sr. Lectr.
Price, D. N., BSc PhD   Principal Lectr.; Dir.,
   Teaching and Learning Policy
Ramsay, P. M., BSc PhD   Sr. Lectr.
Rowden, A. A., BSc PhD   Sr. Lectr.
Rundle, S. D., BSc PhD   Sr. Lectr.
Uttley, M. G., BA DPhil   Principal Lectr.
Wigham, G. D., BSc PhD   Principal Lectr.
Research: comparative physiology
   (ecophysiology, neuroscience, toxicology);
   ecology (phylogeography, quatic and
   terrestrial communities); fish health
   (control, diagnosis, nutrition); marine
   biology and ecotoxicology (biomarkers,
   genotoxicology)

Business, see Plymouth Bus. Sch.

Computing

Tel: (01752) 232541 Fax: (01752) 232540
Barlow, G. N. D., BSc MSc PhD   Sr. Lectr.
Blackwell, G. K., BTech PhD   Sr. Lectr.
Cady, M. J.   Sr. Lectr.
Cangelosi, A.   Sr. Lectr.
Denham, M. J., BSc PhD   Prof.
Hawley, R. J., BA   Sr. Lectr.
Hindle, C. M., MA PhD   Principal Lectr.
Jagodzinski, A. P., BA MSc DPhil   Reader
Livingstone, D., BA MA   Sr. Lectr.
Maull, R. S., BA MSc PhD   Sr. Lectr.
Mayne, F., BSc   Sr. Lectr.
McAtackney, P.   Sr. Lectr.
McCabe, Sue, BSc PhD   Sr. Lectr.
Melhuish, P. W., MSc   Sr. Lectr.
Merritt, R. J., BSc   Sr. Lectr.
Mushens, B. G., BSc MSc   Programmes Dir.
Oldfield, S. J., MA MSc MTech   Principal
   Lectr.
Parmee, I. C., BSc PhD   Reader; Sr. Lectr.
Pearce, Patricia D., BSc MSc PhD   Prof.; Head*
Phillips, M. L., BA   Sr. Lectr.
Rowe, D. M., MA   Sr. Lectr.
Rowley, K. J., BA MSc   Sr. Lectr.
Singh, S.   Sr. Lectr.
Speed, C.   Sr. Lectr.
Squire, Mary L.   Sr. Lectr.
Sturley, C. R., BSc   Sr. Lectr.
Research: computer networks and security;
   engineering design; human-centred design
   and interactive media; manufacturing and
   business systems; neural and adaptive
   systems

Education, Rolle School of

Tel: (01395) 255319 Fax: (01395) 255303
Bromfield, W. C.   Sr. Lectr.
Burnett, J., BA   Sr. Lectr.; Programme Dir.,
   Steiner
Burns, Christina M., BEd MEd   Sr. Lectr.
Connett, R., BEd   Sr. Lectr.
Davies, J. W., MA   Sr. Lectr.; Programme Dir.
Dibbo, J., BA BEd MSc   Sr. Lectr.
Douglas, Maureen E., BA   Sr. Lectr.
Dyer, A. J., BSc MPhil   Sr. Lectr.
Fallows, M. D., MSc   Principal Lectr.
Firth, R., BSc MSc   Sr. Lectr.
Fisher, Rosalind J., BA MEd PhD   Principal
   Lectr.
Gatrell, M., BEd MPhil   Sr. Lectr.
Graham, J. D., MSc   Sr. Lectr.
Hannan, A. W., MA PhD   Reader; Dir., Res.
Hayes, D., BSc MEd PhD   Sr. Lectr.
Holt, D. A., BEd PhD   Sr. Lectr.
Housego, Elizabeth, BA MEd   Sr. Lectr.
Howarth, S., MA   Principal Lectr.
Lawson, K. T., BA MEd   Principal Lectr.
Lee, C. G., BEd MEd   Sr. Lectr.
Lewis, J. P., MEd   Principal Lectr.
Lewis, M., BA   Sr. Lectr. (on secondment)
Mackenzie, R. N., MPhil PhD   Principal Lectr.
Mackintosh, Margaret A. P., BSc PhD   Sr.
   Lectr.
McBurnie, W., MA   Principal Lectr.;
   Programme Dir., PGCE Primary
McLean, A. L., BSc MEd   Sr. Lectr.;
   Programme Dir., PGCE Secondary
Medwell, J. A.   Sr. Lectr.
Nias, J., Rolle Visiting Prof.†
Noon, P., BSc MEd   Sr. Lectr.
Ovens, A. R., MSc   Principal Lectr.
Pagett, L. M., BSc   Sr. Lectr.
Palmer, J.   Sr. Lectr.
Palmer, K. G., MEd   Principal Lectr.
Parker, D. H., BEd MPhil PhD   Principal
   Lectr.; Postgrad. Programme Dir.
Parker-Rees, R., MA MPhil   Sr. Lectr.
Payne, Gill, MEd   Assoc. Dean*
Pratt, N., BSc   Sr. Lectr.
Richards, W. F., BEd   Sr. Lectr.
Rodd, J., BPsych PhD   Sr. Lectr.; Reader, Early
   Childhood Educn.
Savage, J. E., BEd   Sr. Lectr.
Silver, H., Visiting Prof.†
Tyrer, R., BA MA   Sr. Lectr.
Waters-Adams, S. L., BSc   Sr. Lectr.
Zaman, F.   Sr. Lectr.
Other Staff: 2 Visiting Profs.; 1 Sr. Lectr.†

Electron Microscopy

Tel: (01752) 233096 Fax: (01752) 233095
Moate, R., BSc MSc PhD   Head*
Research: biomedical environmental sciences;
   geology (micropalaentology); materials
   (metallurgy, semi-conductors)

Electronic Communication and Electrical Engineering

Akhter, M. A., MSc PhD   Sr. Lectr.
Ali Aburgheff, M., BSc PhD
Barlow, I. M., BA MSc   Sr. Lectr.
Burn-Thornton, K., BSc MSc PhD
Clegg, W., BSc MSc PhD   Prof.
Culverhouse, P. F., BA PhD   Sr. Lectr.
Donnelly, T., MSc PhD   Sr. Lectr.
Filmore, P. R., BSc PhD   Sr. Lectr.
Furnell, S., BSc PhD
Hamer, C. F., BSc   Sr. Lectr.
Hanley, G. A., MSc PhD   Principal Lectr.
Ifeachor, E. C., MSc PhD   Prof.; Head*
Jackson, J. K., BSc   Sr. Lectr.
Kennedy, R. T., MSc, FIEE   Sr. Lectr.
Lines, B. M., MSc PhD   Sr. Lectr.
Linford, R. S., MSc   Sr. Lectr.
Mapps, D. J., BEng PhD, FIEE, FIP   Prof.
Neal, R.   Sr. Lectr.
Rees, R. A.   Sr. Lectr.
Reeve, C. D., BSc PhD   Sr. Lectr.
Robinson, P., BSc   Sr. Lectr.
Shortman, B. H., BSc   Sr. Lectr.
Simpson, A. J., MA   Sr. Lectr.
Stamp, A. C., MSc   Sr. Lectr.

Wade, J. G., MSc PhD   Principal Lectr.
White, P. J., BSc PhD   Sr. Lectr.
Wilson, G., BSc PhD   Reader
Research: biomedical electronics; digital signal
   processing; electronic variable speed drives;
   information storage technology; neural
   networks

Engineering, Civil and Structural

Tel: (01752) 233664 Fax: (01752) 233658
Azizi, F., PhD   Sr. Lectr.
Borthwick, M. F., BEng   Sr. Lectr.
Chadwick, A. J., BSc MSc PhD   Reader
Dawe, R., BSc MSc
Easterbrook, D. J., BSc   Sr. Lectr.
Foulkes, M. D., BSc PhD   Sr. Lectr.
Goodhew, S. M. R., BSc MSc   Sr. Lectr.
Hamill, L., BSc PhD   Sr. Lectr.
Kennedy, C. K., BSc MSc PhD   Visiting Prof.
Murphy, P., BSc   Sr. Lectr.
Murray, P. E., BSc   Head, Bldg. Programmes
Paterson, I. G.   Sr. Lectr.
Rafiq, M. Y., MSc PhD   Sr. Lectr.
Saxton, R. H., BSc   Sr. Lectr.
Southcombe, C., MSc   Head*
Wilkinson, D., FRICS
Williams, C., BSc PhD   Principal Lectr.
Research: coastal engineering; geotechnical
   engineering; hydraulic and environmental
   engineering; structural engineering

Engineering, Mechanical, see

   Manufacturing, Materials and Mech. Engin.

Environmental Sciences

Tel: (01752) 233000 Fax: (01752) 233035
Achterberg, E., BSc PhD   Sr. Lectr.
Andrew, K., BSc PhD   Sr. Lectr.
Belt, S. T., BSc PhD   Sr. Lectr.
Braven, J., BSc PhD, FRSChem   Principal Lectr.
Bull, J. N., BSc   Principal Lectr.
Evans, E. H., BSc PhD   Sr. Lectr.
Foulkes, M. E., PhD   Sr. Lectr.
Gledhil, M., BSc PhD   Sr. Lectr.
Harwood, D. J., BSc PhD   Sr. Lectr.
Hill, S. J., BSc PhD   Head*
Howard, D. E., MSc   Sr. Lectr.
Jones, P., MSc PhD   Principal Lectr.
Lowry, R. B., BSc PhD   Sr. Lectr.
Matthews, G. P., MA DPhil,
   FRSChem   Principal Lectr.
Millward, G., MSc PhD, FRSChem   Prof.
Nimmo, M., BSc PhD   Sr. Lectr.
O'Sullivan, P. E., BSc DPhil   Sr. Lectr.
Rowland, S. J., BSc PhD, FGS, FRSChem   Prof.
Saha, J. K., MSc MS PhD   Sr. Lectr.
Trier, C. J., BSc PhD   Sr. Lectr.
Turner, A., BSc PhD   Sr. Lectr.
Worsfold, P. J., MSc PhD, FRSChem   Prof.
Research: environmental biology; environmental
   chemistry; geo-environmental sciences;
   marine physical sciences (coastal and
   estuarine processes)

Geographical Sciences

Tel: (01752) 233053 Fax: (01752) 233054
Blacksell, A. M. Y., MA DPhil   Prof.; Head*
Brayshay, W. M., BA PhD   Principal Lectr.
Chalkley, B. S., BA PhD   Principal Lectr.
Charlton, C. A., BA   Sr. Lectr.
Charman, D. J., BSc PhD   Sr. Lectr.
Cleary, M. C., BA PhD   Sr. Lectr.
Croot, D. G., BA PhD   Sr. Lectr.
Essex, S. J., BA PhD   Sr. Lectr.
Gibb, R. A., BSc DPhil   Sr. Lectr.
Jones, A. R., MA PhD   Sr. Lectr.
Kent, M., BA MSc PhD   Principal Lectr.
Mather, Anne E., BSc PhD   Sr. Lectr.
Matthews, Judith A., BA PhD   Principal Lectr.
Newnham, R. N., MSc PhD   Sr. Lectr.
Pinder, D. A., BA PhD   Reader
Saiko, T.   Sr. Lectr.
Sallnow, J. A., BA   Sr. Lectr.
Sims, P. C., MSc, FGS   Principal Lectr.
Stainfield, J., BSc BSc(Econ) MA   Sr. Lectr.
Ternan, J. L., BA PhD   Principal Lectr.
Tonts, M. A.   Sr. Lectr.
Weaver, Ruth E., BA PhD   Sr. Lectr.

Williams, A. G., MSc PhD Reader
Wise, M., MA DPhil Principal Lectr.
Research: developing areas; educational issues; European economic and social change; quaternary environments; soils and hydrology

Geological Sciences

Tel: (01752) 233100 Fax: (01752) 233117

Anderson, M. W., BSc PhD Sr. Lectr.
Diver, W. L., MSc, FGS Principal Lectr.
Griffiths, J. S., BSc PhD, FGS Acting Head*
Harries, W. J. R., MSc PhD Sr. Lectr.
Hart, M. B., BSc PhD DSc, FGS Prof.
Scott, S. C., BA PhD, FGS Principal Lectr.
Tarling, D. H., PhD DSc, FGS Prof.
Taylor, G. K., BSc PhD Sr. Lectr.
Vines, K. J., BSc PhD, FGS Sr. Lectr.
Watkinson, M. P., BSc PhD Sr. Lectr.
Williams, C. L., BSc MSc PhD, FGS Principal Lectr.
Research: basin analysis (Brazil, India, South America, UK); magnetostratigraphy (dating, milnakovich cycles, sedimentation); micropalaeontology (cretaceous stratigraphy, global bioevents); palaeomagnetism (crustal rotation, plate motion); tectonics (geometry, shearzone, subduction complexes)

Health Studies, Institute of

Tel: (01752) 233198 Fax: (01752) 233194

Ball, D. Lectr./Sr. Lectr.
Billing, A. M. Dir., Post Registration Programme
Borlase, J. Lectr./Sr. Lectr.
Bradbury, M. Lectr./Sr. Lectr.
Brewer, J. Lectr./Sr. Lectr.
Burt, S. Lectr./Sr. Lectr.
Bush, T. Lectr./Sr. Lectr.
Cadman, C. Lectr./Sr. Lectr.
Carberry, A. Lectr./Sr. Lectr.
Carson, S. Lectr./Sr. Lectr.
Carter, R. Lectr./Sr. Lectr.
Clack, E. Lectr./Sr. Lectr.
Clancy, E. Assoc. Lectr./Sr. Lectr.
Coleman, C. Lectr./Sr. Lectr.
Deakin, H. Lectr./Sr. Lectr.
Doman, M. Lectr./Sr. Lectr.
Dominey, M. Lectr./Sr. Lectr.
Earl, D. Lectr./Sr. Lectr.
Fisher, T. Lectr./Sr. Lectr.
Friend, M. R. Lectr./Sr. Lectr.
Green, G. Assoc. Lectr./Sr. Lectr.
Grigg, E. M. Academic Co-ordinator
Hagley, A. Lectr./Sr. Lectr.
Haigh, D. Assoc. Lectr./Sr. Lectr.
Hamber, J. Lectr./Sr. Lectr.
Harding, V. Lectr./Sr. Lectr.
Harris, W. Assoc. Lectr./Sr. Lectr.
Haydon, J. Lectr./Sr. Lectr.
Humphreys, A. J. Academic Co-ordinator
Hyde, V. Principal Lectr./Subject Adviser
Janitsch, P. Lectr./Sr. Lectr.
Jeffery, K. Assoc. Lectr./Sr. Lectr.
Jenkinson, T. Lectr./Sr. Lectr.
Jowett, R. M. Dir., Pre Registration Programmes
Keen, T. Lectr./Sr. Lectr.
Kerslake, D. Lectr./Sr. Lectr.
Kevern, J. Lectr./Sr. Lectr.
King, J. Lectr./Sr. Lectr.
Kwakwa, J. Assoc. Lectr./Sr. Lectr.
Lander, J. Lectr./Sr. Lectr.
Lee-Smith, J. Lectr./Sr. Lectr.
Lethbridge, Z. Lectr./Sr. Lectr.
Llywelyn, D. Lectr./Sr. Lectr.
McConnon, A. Lectr./Sr. Lectr.
McEvansoneya, S. Lectr./Sr. Lectr.
McEwing, G. Lectr./Sr. Lectr.
Millward, J. Lectr./Sr. Lectr.
Mitchell, C. Lectr./Sr. Lectr.
Murray, T. Lectr./Sr. Lectr.
Nicholls, L. Lectr./Sr. Lectr.
O'Sullivan, G. Lectr./Sr. Lectr.
Pankhurst, K. Lectr./Sr. Lectr.
Peacham, C. Lectr./Sr. Lectr.
Perry, L. Lectr./Sr. Lectr.
Pope, S. Lectr./Sr. Lectr.

Pufahl, E. Lectr./Sr. Lectr.
Rea, P. Lectr./Sr. Lectr.
Reeve, J. Lectr./Sr. Lectr.
Ringer, I. Lectr./Sr. Lectr.
Rossiter, M. Lectr./Sr. Lectr.
Rowe, T. Assoc. Lectr./Sr. Lectr.
Slade, D. Lectr./Sr. Lectr.
Southorn, E. Lectr./Sr. Lectr.
Stanley, C. Academic Co-ordinator
Swain, J. Assoc. Lectr./Sr. Lectr.
Twose, S. Lectr./Sr. Lectr.
Watkins, M. Head*
Watts, A. Lectr./Sr. Lectr.
Wheeler, C. Lectr./Sr. Lectr.
White, D. Lectr./Sr. Lectr.
White, S. Assoc. Lectr./Sr. Lectr.
Wiggins, R. Assoc. Lectr./Sr. Lectr.
Wilkinson, J. Lectr./Sr. Lectr.
Williamson, G. M. Lectr./Sr. Lectr.
Williamson, G. R. Lectr./Sr. Lectr.

Humanities and Cultural Interpretation, School of

Tel: (01395) 255410 Fax: (01395) 255303

Bartlett, M. G. Principal Lectr.
Collins, J. M., MA Sr. Lectr.
Ellis, Christine M., BA MA Principal Lectr.; Postgrad. Programme Dir.
Gee, G. R., BA MA PhD Assoc. Dean; Head*
Gill, Jeanette, BA MEd Sr. Lectr.
Halstead, J. M., BEd MA MPhil PhD Principal Lectr.; Reader, Moral and Spiritual Educn.
Hilton, D. E., BA MA PhD Principal Lectr.
Hole, R. J., BA MA PhD Principal Lectr.
Honeywill, P. W. N., BA Sr. Lectr.
Howard, P. J., BA PhD Principal Lectr.
Jefferys, K., BA PhD Principal Lectr.; Reader, Contemporary Hist.
Lawley, P. A., BA PhD Sr. Lectr.
Leathlean, H., BA MA PhD Sr. Lectr.
Lopez, A. C., BA MA PhD Principal Lectr.; Reader, Poetry
Macleod, Katherine A., BA MEd Sr. Lectr.
Nicol, Elizabeth, BA Sr. Lectr.
O'Brien, D. M., BA Sr. Lectr.
Peel, R. W., BEd MA PhD Sr. Lectr.
Pidgley, M. R., BA PhD Sr. Lectr.
Reeves, Mary E., BA MA Principal Lectr.; Undergrad. Programme Dir.
Searls, C. B., BA Lond. Sr. Lectr.
Smart, N., BA PhD Sr. Lectr.
Smiles, S. A., BA MA PhD Principal Lectr.
Williams, R. J., BA PhD Sr. Lectr.
Other Staff: 3 Sr. Lectrs.†

Land Use and Rural Management

Tel: (01626) 325661 Fax: (01626) 325657

Blackburn, Susan P., BSc Sr. Lectr.; Manager, Rural Resource Management Programme
Brassley, P. W., BSc BLitt Sr. Lectr.
Brunt, P. R., BSc PhD Principal Lectr.
Cullinane, S. L., BA PhD Sr. Lectr.
Ellsworth, D. S., BA Sr. Lectr.
Errington, A. J., BA MSc PhD Prof.
Felton, T. J. F., DFM, LLB Sr. Lectr.
Fisher, S. J., BSc Sr. Lectr.
Holgate, P. R., FRICS Sr. Lectr.; Manager, Rural Estates Programme
Shepherd, D. B., MSc Sr. Lectr.
Soffe, R. J., MPhil Sr. Lectr.
Stone, M. A. H., BA MSc Sr. Lectr.
Usher, J. W., BSc Principal Lectr.
Warren, M. F., MSc Head*
Whitehead, I. R. G., MA Oxf., MSc, FRICS Sr. Lectr.
Williams, Eirene N. D., BA PhD Principal Lectr.; Manager, Rural Resource Programme
Williams, R. J., BSc Sr. Lectr.
Other Staff: 1 Lectr.
Research: farm and estate management (farming entry and exit, land tenure systems); rural economy (economic restructuring, role of small towns); rural transport (livestock marketing, traffic management); tourism and management (tourism and crime, tourism management skills)

Manufacturing, Materials and Mechanical Engineering

Tel: (01752) 232637 Fax: (01752) 232638

Barlow, J. W., BSc Sr. Lectr.
Bell, M. A., BEng MSc PhD, FIMechE Principal Lectr.
Davies, T. F., MSc Sr. Lectr.
Gates, B. P., MSc Sr. Lectr.
Grieve, D. J., BSc PhD Sr. Lectr.
Grove, S. M., BSc PhD MPhil Sr. Lectr.
James, M. N., PhD Camb., BSc, FIM Prof.
Miles, M. E., BSc MPhil Sr. Lectr.
Mingo, E. R., BSc MSc Sr. Lectr.
Nurse, P. Sr. Lectr.
Paterson, T., BSc Sr. Lectr.
Plane, D. C., BSc PhD Sr. Lectr.
Summerscales, John, BSc MSc PhD, FIM Sr. Lectr.
Research: advanced composites manufacturing; automatic guidance and control of marine vehicles; intelligent system controls; optimal filtering and control; system identification

Marine Studies, Institute of

Tel: (01752) 232400 Fax: (01752) 232406

Abbott, V. J., MSc Sr. Lectr.
Atkinson, Helen L., BSc Sr. Lectr.
Chudley, J., BSc PhD Head*
Cullinane, K. P. B., BA BSc MSc PhD Principal Lectr.
Dai, Y. M., BSc PhD Sr. Lectr.
Dinwoodie, J., MA Camb., MA(Econ) MEd Sr. Lectr.
Dyer, K. R., MSc PhD Prof. Res. Fellow
Findlay, M. M., BSc MSc Sr. Lectr.
George, K. J., BSc Lond., PhD Lond., MSc S'ton., Dr3rdCy Brest Principal Lectr.
Glegg, G. A., BSc PhD Sr. Lectr.
Gray, R., BA MSc PhD Principal Lectr.
Heijveld, H., MSc Sr. Lectr.
Hooper, J. B., MSc Sr. Lectr.
Huntley, D. A., MA Camb., PhD Prof.
Jarvis, S., BSc Sr. Lectr.
Jones, G. E., BSc Sr. Lectr.
Kennerley, A., BA MA PhD Principal Lectr.
Kitching, J. A., BSc Sr. Lectr.
Manhire, B. J., MSc PhD Sr. Lectr.
Menachof, D. A., MBA MSc PhD Sr. Lectr.
Miller, K. M., BSc PhD Sr. Lectr.
Moreby, D. H., PhD Prof.†
Motte, R., MSc PhD Prof.†
Munson, M. Sr. Lectr.
O'Hare, T. J., BA MSc PhD Sr. Lectr.; Dir., Undergrad. Programmes
Panayides, P., BSc Sr. Lectr.
Pilgrim, D. A., BSc MSc PhD Principal Lectr.
Roe, M. S., BA MSc PhD Prof.
Rubin, J. A., MSc PhD Sr. Lectr.
Russell, P. E., BSc PhD Sr. Lectr.
Seymour, P. A. H., MSc PhD Principal Lectr.
Sutton, R., BEng MEng PhD Reader
Usher, J. G., MSc Sr. Lectr.
Willerton, P. F., BSc MSc Sr. Lectr.
Witt, N., BSc PhD Sr. Lectr.
Wood, N. L. H., MSc PhD Sr. Lectr.
Wright, P. G., MSc Sr. Lectr.
Research: logistics; maritime business; maritime technology

Mathematics and Statistics

Tel: (01752) 232700, 232720 Fax: (01752) 232780

Aron, M., MSc PhD Reader
Berry, J. S., BSc PhD, FIMA Prof.
Clinton, N. C., MSc Sr. Lectr.
Crocker, G. R., BSc PhD Sr. Lectr.
Davies, J. M., BSc PhD Sr. Lectr.
Dyke, P. P. G., BSc PhD, FIMA, FRMetS Prof.; Assoc. Dean; Head*
Eales, J. D., MSc PhD Sr. Lectr.
Graham, E., BSc PhD Sr. Lectr.
Horan, R. E., BSc MPhil PhD Sr. Lectr.
Huggett, S. A., MSc DPhil Reader
Ingram, Shirley V., BSc Sr. Lectr.
James, P. W., BSc PhD, FIMA Principal Lectr.
Jones, T. E. R., BSc PhD Prof.
Jozsa, R. O., BSc MSc DPhil Sr. Lectr.

McMullan, D., BSc PhD   Sr. Lectr.
Moyeed, R. A., BSc MSc PhD   Sr. Lectr.
Ricketts, C., BSc PhD   Principal Lectr.
Sanders, Hilary P., BSc   Sr. Lectr.
Shalliker, J. A., MSc   Sr. Lectr.
Shaw, S. R., MSc PhD   Sr. Lectr.
Smith, Caroline, BSc PhD   Sr. Lectr.
Stander, J., MA PhD   Sr. Lectr.
Undy, M. B., MSc   Sr. Lectr.
Watkins, A. J. P., BSc   Sr. Lectr.
Wilton, D. T., BA DPhil   Principal Lectr.
Winsor, P. J. S., BSc   Sr. Lectr.
Wright, D. E., BSc MSc PhD   Principal Lectr.
Research: constrained dynamics; quantisation of
   gauge theories; quantum algorithms and
   error correction (quantum field theory);
   quantum computation and quantum
   information theory; twistor theory
   (conformal field)

Medicine, see Plymouth Postgrad. Med. Sch.

Modern Languages, Centre for, see under
   Plymouth Bus. Sch.

Plymouth Business School

Tel: (01752) 232800 Fax: (01752) 232853
Atrill, Peter F., MPhil MA PhD, FCA   Dir.,
   Acctg. Group
Badger, Beryl A., BSc   Dir., Human Resource
   Studies Group
Bishop, Paul R., BA MA DPhil   Principal
   Lectr., Economics
Biss, Tom H., MSc   Sr. Lectr., Business
   Operations and Policy
Boston, John, BA   Sr. Lectr., Accounting
Brooks, N. R., BSc   Sr. Lectr., Economics
Butel, Lynne H., BA MA   Sr. Lectr., Corporate
   Strategy
Cappi, Paul A., LLB LLM   Sr. Lectr., Law
Chaston, Ian, BSc MBA PhD   Reader,
   Marketing
Churchill, Harry, BA MSc   Sr. Lectr.,
   Economics
Clayton, Graham, BSc   Sr. Lectr., Accounting
Cole, Bill J., MA LLB   Prof.
Collins, Mary, LLB LLM   Sr. Lectr., Law
Cook, Peter, BA MD PhD   Sr. Lectr.
Dalton, Fiona K., BSc   Sr. Lectr., Accounting
Dyke, Eric G. L., BSc MSc   Sr. Lectr.,
   Economics
Farrar, S., BA PhD   Sr. Lectr., Accounting
Garland, N., BA MSc   Sr. Lectr., Economics
Gripaios, Peter A., BA MSc   Prof.; Dir., Econ.
   Group
Harris, C., BSc LLB   Sr. Lectr., Law
Holden, J., BEd MSc   Sr. Lectr., Law
Homan, Russell, BSc MSc   Sr. Lectr.,
   Marketing
Jones, P., BSc MSc PhD   Prof.; Head*
Kaler, John H., BA MA   Sr. Lectr., Humanities
Lace, Jonathan M., BA MBA   Sr. Lectr.,
   Marketing
Lean, J., BA PhD   Sr. Lectr., Business
   Operations
Leat, Michael J., BScEcon MScEcon   Sr. Lectr.,
   Human Resource Studies
Lindley, Lindsey M., BSc   Principal Lectr.,
   Accounting and Finance
Mangles, Terry H., MSc   Principal Lectr., Data
   Interpretation
McIntyre, Jacquiline, BSc   Sr. Lectr., Human
   Resource Studies
McLaney, Edward, MA, FCA   Principal Lectr.,
   Accounting
McLeish, Gordon D., BA   Sr. Lectr., Law
McVittie, E., BA PhD   Sr. Lectr., Economics
Megicks, Philip R., BCom MBA   Sr. Lectr.,
   Marketing
Morgan, Elaine A., LLB   Sr. Lectr., Law
Nettleton, Malcolm L., BSc(Econ) MSc, FCA,
   FCIS   Sr. Lectr., Accountancy
Nicholas, Paul, BSc BPhil MSc   Sr. Lectr.,
   Economics
O'Mahoney, Kevin P., BSc(Econ), FCA   Sr.
   Lectr., Accounting and Finance
Payne, Simon, LLB   Sr. Lectr., Law

Pearce, Jim F., BTech MSc   Principal Lectr.,
   Business Operations and Policy
Pearson, Elizabeth M., BSc   Sr. Lectr., Human
   Resource Studies
Pointon, J., BSc PhD, FCA   Reader
Sadler-Smith, Eugene, BSc PhD   Sr. Lectr.,
   Human Resource Studies
Shears, Peter G., BA LLB LLM   Dir., Law
   Group
Smith, G., BSc MBA   Sr. Lectr., Business
   Operations
Spencer, Jill, LLB PhD   Sr. Lectr., Law
Spratley, Derek J., MA, FCA   Sr. Lectr.,
   Accountancy
Stapleton, Jeanette E., BA MA   Sr. Lectr., Law
Toovey, Ronald J., BSc MSc, FCA   Sr. Lectr.,
   Accounting
Ward, Allan, BSc MA   Sr. Lectr., Economics
Whisker, Pamela M., BSc PhD   Sr. Lectr.,
   Economics
White, J., BA   Sr. Lectr., Marketing
Williams, Jasmine E. M., BA   Sr. Lectr.,
   Marketing
Winch, G., BSc PhD   Prof.
Research: corporate investment; organisational
   learning; regional economic performance;
   retail marketing and advertising;
   technologies and change management

Modern Languages, Centre for

Tel: (01752) 232877 Fax: (01752) 232885
Andres, C., Lic Madrid   Sr. Lectr.
Beverly, Eric A., MA   Sr. Lectr.
Beverly, J., BA MA   Sr. Lectr.
Bickerton, David M., BA PhD   Prof.; Dir.*
Bishop, D., BA PhD   Sr. Lectr.
Bower, Lucette A., LèsL   Sr. Lectr.
Cornell, Alan, BA MA DPhil   Principal Lectr.
Coutts, Joseph W., BA LèsL MA MSc   Principal
   Lectr.
Edwards, P., BA   Sr. Lectr.
Hope, Jacqueline, BA DPhil   Sr. Lectr.
Kent, H., BA MPhil   Sr. Lectr.
Proud, Judith, BA PhD   Principal Lectr.,
   French
Stacey, Susan G., BA MA   Sr. Lectr.

Plymouth Postgraduate Medical School

Tel: (01752) 792711 Fax: (01752) 763531
Bakheit, A. M. O., MSc MB PhD MD   Prof.
Deardon, D. J., FRCSEd, FRCS   Sr. Lectr.
Demaine, A. G., BSc PhD   Sr. Lectr.
Dobbs, F. F., MD, FRCGP   Sr. Lectr.
Kingsnorth, A. N., BSc MB BS MS, FRCS   Prof.
Millward, B. A. M., BA MB BChir MA MD   Sr.
   Lectr.
Rogers, Prof. K., MB ChB MSc MD   Dir.*
Sewell, G. J., BPharm PhD   Reader
Sneyd, J. R., MA MB BChir MD,
   FRCA   Reader
Wilkin, T. J., MD, FRCP   Prof.

Politics

Tel: (01752) 233275 Fax: (01752) 233206
Cooper, R. N., MA PhD   Sr. Lectr.
Cordell, K., BSc PhD   Sr. Lectr.
Cunliffe, S. A., BA PhD   Principal Lectr.
Dogan, P. M. J., MA   Sr. Lectr.
Lee, A. N., MSc   Head*
Pugh, M. C., BA MA PhD   Reader
Rallings, C. S., BA MSc PhD   Prof.
Tant, A. P., BA PhD   Sr. Lectr.
Thrasher, M. A. M., BA PhD   Prof.
Wilton, J. F., BA MSc PhD   Sr. Lectr.
Woods, B., BSc   Sr. Lectr.
Research: comparative study of the 1989 East
   European revolutions; enhancing turnout in
   local elections; politics of the German
   minority in post-war Poland

Psychology

Tel: (01752) 233157 Fax: (01752) 233176
Auburn, T., MSc PhD   Sr. Lectr.
Carr, A. T., BSc PhD   Principal Lectr.
Clibbens, J. S., BA BSc PhD   Sr. Lectr.
Coventry, K. R., BSc PhD   Sr. Lectr.
Dennis, I., MA PhD   Head*
Edworthy, Judy, BA PhD   Reader

Evans, J. S. B. T., BSc PhD   Prof.
Franklyn-Stokes, A., BA BSc PhD   Sr. Lectr.
Hyland, M. E., BSc PhD   Prof.
Jacobs, Pamela A., MSc   Sr. Lectr.
Kenyon, C. A. P., BSc PhD   Sr. Lectr.
Lea, S. J., BSc BA MA PhD   Sr. Lectr.
Morris, R. C., BA PhD   Sr. Lectr.
Newstead, S. E., BA PhD, FBPsS   Prof.
Reid, F. J. M., BTech PhD   Principal Lectr.
Rickwood, Ludmilla V., MA PhD   Sr. Lectr.
Rose, D. H., BSc PhD   Sr. Lectr.
Russell, G. C., BSc MPhil   Sr. Lectr.
Stephenson, D., BSc PhD   Principal Lectr.

Rural Management, see Land Use and Rural
   Management

Social Policy and Social Work

Tel: (01752) 233235 Fax: (01752) 233209
Asthana, Sheena   Sr. Lectr., Social Policy
Brodribb, Carolyn A.   Sr. Lectr., Social Work
   (Palliative Care)
Butler, Avril   Sr. Lectr., Social Work
Dixon, J., BEcon MEcon PhD   Sr. Lectr., Social
   Policy
Giarchi, George G., MA   Emer. Prof., Social
   Care Studies
Gilling, Daniel J.   Sr. Lectr., Social Policy
Gray, P., MA PhD   Sr. Lectr., Social Policy and
   the Criminal Justice System (CJS)
Green, Alison J., BA PhD   Sr. Lectr., Research
   Methods
Hay, Will T., BA MPhil   Sr. Lectr., Social
   Work
Iganski, Paul S., MA PhD   Sr. Lectr., Social
   Policy
Jacobs, Sid, BA PhD   Sr. Lectr., Social Policy
Jefferies, S. Ann   Head*
Mawby, Rob I., BA MSc PhD   Prof.,
   Criminology and Criminal Justice
Popple, Keith J., MA   Sr. Lectr., Community
   Work
Sheppard, Michael G., BSc MA   Prof., Social
   Work
Smith, J., BSc MA   Sr. Lectr., Social Work
Williams, Stuart   Sr. Lectr., Social Work
Woodward, V., BA MLitt   Sr. Lectr.,
   Community Work

Sociology

Tel: (01752) 233217 Fax: (01752) 233201
Anderson, Alison G., BA PhD   Sr. Lectr.
Benson, D. W., MA PhD   Principal Lectr.
Bryant, Lynette C., BA   Principal Lectr.
Chandler, Joan, BA PhD   Head*
Ettorre, Elizabeth, BA PhD   Reader
Harrison, E. K., BA MSc   Sr. Lectr.
Mason, D. J.   Prof.
Meethan, K., BA PhD   Sr. Lectr.
Sheaff, M., BA MA PhD   Sr. Lectr.
Sutton, Carole D., BSc   Sr. Lectr.
Williams, M., BA MSc   Sr. Lectr.

Statistics, see Maths. and Stats.

SPECIAL CENTRES, ETC

Advanced Composite Manufacturing, Centre for Research in

Grove, S. M., BSc MPhil PhD   Sr. Lectr.

Analytical Chemistry, Centre for Research in

Ebdon, Prof. L. C., BSc PhD, FRSChem   Dir.*

Business Taxation, Centre for Research in

Pointon, J., BSc PhD, FCA   Dir.*

Engineering Design, Centre for Research in

Parmee, I., BSc PhD   Reader; Dir.*

Environmental Studies, Centre for Research in

Worsfold, Prof. P., MSc PhD, FRSChem   Dir.*

Human Assessment, Centre for Research in

Irvine, Prof. S. H., MA MEd PhD, FBPsS   Dir.*

Information Storage, Centre for Research in

Mapps, Prof. D. J., BEng PhD, FIEE   Dir.*

Local Government Chronicle Elections, Centre for Research in

Rallings, M., BA MSc PhD   Dir.*
Thrasher, M. A. M., BA PhD   Dir.*

Marine Studies, Centre for Research in

Dyer, Prof. K., MSc PhD, FGS   Dir.*

Moral, Spiritual and Cultural Understanding and Education, Centre for Research into (RIMSCUE)

Tel: (01392) 255373
Halstead, J. M., PhD

Satellite Communications, Centre for Research in

Tomlinson, Prof. M., BSc PhD   Manager

Science and Geography in Education (SAGE)

Tel: (01392) 255365
Waters-Adams, S. L., MPhil

South West Economics, Centre for Research in

Gripaios, Prof. P. A., BA MSc   Dir.*

Study of the Arts in Primary Education, Centre for (CENSAPE)

Tel: (01392) 255326
Jones, H. F.

Teaching Mathematics, Centre for Research in

Berry, Prof. J. S., BSc PhD, FIMA   Dir.*

Visual Computing, Centre for

Tel: (01392) 475028
Beardon, Prof. C. E., BA   Dir.*

World Class Manufacturing, Centre for Research in

No staff at present

CONTACT OFFICERS

Academic affairs. Registrar: Hopkinson, J., LLB
Accommodation. Simpson, M.
Admissions (first degree). Todd, C.
Admissions (higher degree). Todd, C.
Adult/continuing education. Head, Centre for Innovation and External Development: Bell, Christopher D., BSc MEd
Alumni. Horton, M.
Careers. Head of Learning & Research Support Services: Gosling, J., BSc
Computing services. Associate Dean of Academic & Information Services: Marshall, K. J., BSc MSc PhD
Consultancy services. Bell, C.
Credit transfer. Academic Partnerships and Liaison: Tunbridge, I.
Estates and buildings/works and services. Estates Manager: Lane, Rodney K., FRICS
Examinations. Chapman, J. M., BA
Finance. Director of Finance: Clarke, R.
General enquiries. Registrar: Hopkinson, J., LLB
Health services. Head of Student Support Services: Coles, W., MA
International office. Director of International Office: Roden, Carol
Library (chief librarian). Associate Dean of Academic and Information Services: Priestley, John, BA
Library (enquiries). Head of Public Services: Holland, P. C., BA
Personnel/human resources. Buckley, Roland D., FCIS
Public relations, information and marketing. Communications Manager: Bradbury, S.
Publications. Communications Manager: Bradbury, S.
Quality assurance and accreditation. Head, Quality Evaluation and Enhancement Unit: Jennett, S.
Safety. Thompson, P.
Scholarships, awards, loans. Morgan, G. R., BA
Schools liaison. Linnen, P.
Security. Administrative Services Manager: White, John A.
Sport and recreation. Head of Student Support Services: Coles, W., MA
Staff development and training (academic staff). Head of Educational Development Services: Fullerton, H., BA
Staff development and training (administrative/technical staff). Johns, A.

Student welfare/counselling. Head of Student Support Services: Coles, W., MA
Students from other countries. Director of International Office: Roden, Carol
Students with disabilities. Manager and Advisor for Special Learning Needs: Wakefield, J. H.

CAMPUS/COLLEGE HEADS

Bicton College of Agriculture. (Tel: (01395) 562300; Fax: (01395) 567502.) Principal: Florey, M., MA
Cornwall College. (Tel: (01209) 712911; Fax: (01209) 718802.) Principal: Stanhope, A., BSc MSc PhD
Dartington College of Arts. (Tel: (01803) 862224; Fax: (01803) 863569.) Principal: Thomson, Prof. K., MA MPhil
East Devon College. (Tel: (01884) 235200; Fax: (01884) 259262.) Acting Principal: Morris, S., BA MEd
Exeter College. (Tel: (01392) 205222; Fax: (01392) 210282.) Principal: Smith, T., MEd
Falmouth College of Art. (Tel: (01326) 211077; Fax: (01326) 211205.) Principal: Livingston, Prof. A. G., BA
Highlands College. (Tel: (01534) 608608; Fax: (01534) 608600.) Principal: Sallis, E., BSc(Econ) MA(Soc) MA PhD
North Devon College. (Tel: (01271) 45291; Fax: (01271) 388121.) Principal: Trueman, D., BSc
Plymouth College of Art and Design. (Tel: (01752) 203434; Fax: (01752) 385977.) Principal: Kennedy, A.
Plymouth College of Further Education. (Tel: (01752) 385300; Fax: (01752) 385098.) Principal: Rospigliosi, G., BA
Somerset College of Arts and Technology. (Tel: (01823) 366366; Fax: (01823) 366418.) Principal: Scott, A., BA, FRSA
South Devon College. (Tel: (01803) 291212; Fax: (01803) 386403.) Principal and Chief Executive: Bentley, I., BA PhD
St Austell College. (Tel: (01726) 67911; Fax: (01726) 659262.) Principal: Hill, W., BA
Truro College. (Tel: (01872) 264251; Fax: (01872) 222360.) Principal: Burnett, J.
Yeovil College. (Tel: (01935) 423921; Fax: (01935) 29962.) Principal: Atkins, R.

[Information supplied by the institution as at 28 April 1998, and edited by the ACU]

UNIVERSITY OF PORTSMOUTH

Inaugurated 1992; originally established as Portsmouth and Gosport School of Science and Art (1869)

Member of the Association of Commonwealth Universities

Postal Address: University House, Winston Churchill Avenue, Portsmouth, England PO1 2UP
Telephone: (01705) 876543 **Fax**: (01705) 843082 **E-mail**: admissions@reg.port.ac.uk
WWW: http://www.port.ac.uk
E-mail formula: staff e-mail addresses available on World Wide Web via http://www.port.ac.uk/phonebook.html

CHANCELLOR—Palumbo of Walbrook, The Lord, MA Oxf., Hon. DLitt, Hon. FRIBA
CHAIRMAN OF GOVERNORS—Williams, Caroline A., LLB S'ton.
VICE-CHANCELLOR*—Craven, Prof. John A. G., BA Camb., MA Camb.
PRO-VICE-CHANCELLOR—Bateman, Michael, BA Leeds, PhD Leeds
PRO-VICE-CHANCELLOR—McVicar, Malcolm T., MA Exe., PhD Lond.
PRO-VICE-CHANCELLOR—Monk, Colin T., BSc Lond., MBA Stan.
SECRETARY AND CLERK TO THE BOARD OF GOVERNORS—Moore, R. J., BA Lond.

FACULTIES/SCHOOLS

Business School
Dean: Dunn, M., BSc S'ton.

Environment
Dean: Shurmer-Smith, J. L., BA Lond.

Humanities and Social Science
Dean: Mitchell, M., BA Leeds, MSc

Science
Dean: Rogers, Prof. D. J., BA Open(UK), MPhil CNAA, PhD CNAA

Technology
Dean: Arrell, D. J., MSc Oxf.

ACADEMIC UNITS

Accounting and Management Science
Tel: (01705) 844095 Fax: (01705) 844037
Abraham, Roy J., MSc CNAA Sr. Lectr.
Acheampong, Nana O., MSc S'ton. Sr. Lectr.
Arnold, Michael E., BSc CNAA, MSc S'ton. Principal Lectr.; Programme Area Dir.
Baden-Powell, Imogen, MA Oxf., LLM Lond. Sr. Lectr.
Botten, Neil J., MA Oxf., MSc Sus. Principal Lectr.
Bowhill, Bruce N., BSc Bath Sr. Lectr.
Cahill, Philip, MSc CNAA Sr. Lectr.
Callaghan, Clare, BCom N.U.I. Sr. Lectr.
Capon, Nicholas C., BSc Nott., MBA CNAA Sr. Lectr.
Daynes, Arief, BA Auck., MSc Auck., PhD Well. Sr. Lectr.
Fargher, E. Keith, BSc Liv. Sr. Lectr.
Fearnley, Stella, BA Leeds Principal Lectr.
Gladstone-Millar, Charlotte, BA Kent Sr. Lectr.
Hey, Sam O., BCom Liv., MA CNAA Sr. Lectr.
Hicks, James R., MSc Calif., DPhil Oxf. Sr. Lectr.
Hines, Anthony C., BSc Bath, MSc Wales Principal Lectr.
Jepson, Barry, BSc CNAA, MSc S'ton. Sr. Lectr.
Kay, M., BSc Brad., MSc S'ton. Prof.
Major, R., BSc Sheff. Sr. Lectr.
McBride, K., BA Portsmouth Sr. Lectr.
McGranaghan, M., BSc Wales Sr. Lectr.
Moulton, Michael, BSc CNAA, MBA CNAA Sr. Lectr.
Page, Michael J., MA Camb., PhD S'ton. Halpern and Woolf Prof., Accounting
Parker, David, MSc S'ton. Principal Lectr.
Read, Martin J., BA CNAA, MSc Birm. Sr. Lectr.
Ridley, Ann, BA Witw., LLB Lond. Principal Lectr.; Head*
Roberts, Martyn, BA CNAA, MSc Leic. Sr. Lectr.
Sinclair, Adele, LLB Brist. Sr. Lectr.
Tonge, Richard C., MA CNAA Sr. Lectr.
Walton, John A., BA Leeds, MBA Sheff. Sr. Lectr.
Willett, Caroline, BA Sus. Sr. Lectr.

Wood, Michael J., MSc Sus., DPhil Oxf. Principal Lectr.
Other Staff: 4 Sr. Lectrs.†

Architecture, School of
Tel: (01705) 842083 Fax: (01705) 842087
Blott, Dan Sr. Lectr.
Bunt, Richard E., PhD Lond. Sr. Lectr.
Day, Roger, MSc CNAA, PhD CNAA Sr. Lectr.
Hodson, Peter, BA Virginia, MA Virginia Sr. Lectr.
McCartney, Kevin, PhD RCA Principal Lectr.
Mills, Nigel K., BArch Wales, MArch Harv. Sr. Lectr.
Pardey, John, BA Sr. Lectr.
Pearce, Martin L., BA CNAA Sr. Lectr.
Potts, James M. Sr. Lectr.
Potts, Wendy S. Sr. Lectr.; Head*
Stansfield-Smith, Sir Colin, CBE, MA Camb. Prof., Architecture Design
Wakefield, Tod Sr. Lectr.
Youle, Anthony, BA Camb., MA Camb., PhD Camb. Principal Lectr.
Other Staff: 2 Principal Lectrs.†; 6 Sr. Lectrs.†

Area Studies, see Langs. and Area Studies, Sch. of

Art, Design and Media, School of
Tel: (01705) 843803 Fax: (01705) 843808
Bridge, David Sr. Lectr.
Bromwich, Hans Sr. Lectr.
Clarke, Simon, BA Newcastle(UK) Principal Lectr.
Cooper, Paul, BA Portsmouth Sr. Lectr.
Craven, Michael, MA CNAA Principal Lectr.
Dauppe, Michèle-Anne, BA Sheff.Hallam, MA Leeds Sr. Lectr.
Dennis, C. Maurice, BA Wales Head*
Devine, Ken, BA Portsmouth, MA Brighton Sr. Lectr.
Harvey, Edward Principal Lectr.
Hayworth, Roger Sr. Lectr.
Jain, Sadhna, BA Portsmouth Sr. Lectr.
Jenkins, David, BA NE, MA Manc.Met. Principal Lectr.
Jones, David Principal Lectr.
Kochberg, Searle, BSc Lond., MA CNAA Sr. Lectr.
Lamburn, Louise Sr. Lectr.
Lunn, Brian Sr. Lectr.
Molyneux, John, PhD S'ton. Sr. Lectr.
Mussell, Nigel Sr. Lectr.
Nicholls, Greg, MA Brighton Sr. Lectr.
O'Neill, Maureen, BA CNAA Sr. Lectr.
Ridley-Ellis, Terry Principal Lectr.
Sparshott, Ingrid, BA CNAA Sr. Lectr.
Steele, Glenda, BA Lond. Sr. Lectr.
Stickley, Paul, BA CNAA Sr. Lectr.
Swales, Valerie, BA Brist., MA CNAA Principal Lectr.; Programme Area Dir.
Tidbury, Roger Sr. Lectr.
Walden, Jenny, BA Essex Sr. Lectr.
Warden, David, MA Manc.Met. Sr. Lectr.
Way, Mark Sr. Lectr.
Williams, Claire Sr. Lectr.

Williams, P., MA RCA Sr. Lectr.
Wright, Robert Sr. Lectr.
Young, Jane, BA Brist. Sr. Lectr.
Other Staff: 1 Principal Lectr.†; 23 Sr. Lectrs.†

Biological Sciences, School of
Tel: (01705) 842036 Fax: (01705) 842070
Cragg, Simon M., BSc Wales, PhD Wales Principal Lectr.
Crane-Robinson, C., MA Oxf., DPhil Oxf. Prof., Microbiology
Eaton, R. A., BSc Sheff., PhD CNAA Reader
Farnham, W. F., MSc Wales, PhD CNAA, FLS Sr. Lectr.
Firman, K., BSc Hull, PhD Newcastle(UK) Principal Lectr.
Fletcher, Robert L., BSc Hull, PhD Lond. Reader
Ford, M. G., BTech Brun., PhD Lond. Prof., Applied Biology
Greenwood, R., BSc Birm., PhD CNAA Principal Lectr.; Head*
Jenkins, T., BSc Wales, PhD Wales Principal Lectr.
Kneale, G. G., BSc Leeds, PhD Leeds Prof., Biomolecular Science
May, E., BSc Dund., PhD Dund. Principal Lectr.
McClellan, J. A., BSc Wales, PhD Wales Sr. Lectr.
McNair, D. J., BSc Edin., PhD Edin. Principal Lectr.
Mitchell, J. I., BSc Liv., PhD Liv. Sr. Lectr.
Morgan-Huws, D. I., BSc Leic., PhD Leic., FLS Sr. Lectr.
Moss, S. T., MSc Lond., PhD Reading Reader
Peterkin, J. H., BSc Sheff., PhD Sheff. Sr. Lectr.
Powling, A. H., MSc PhD Sr. Lectr.
Strophair, B. A., BSc Newcastle(UK), PhD Newcastle(UK) Sr. Lectr.
Taylor, D. C., BSc Hudd., PhD Edin. Sr. Lectr.
Thorne, Alan, BSc CNAA Sr. Lectr.
Other Staff: 1 Reader†; 1 Principal Lectr.†; 2 Sr. Lectrs.†

Biomedical Sciences, see Pharm., Biomed. and Phys. Scis., Sch. of

Business and Management Studies, see also Acctg. and Management Sci., and Portsmouth Management Centre

Tel: (01705) 844060 Fax: (01705) 844319
Adam-Smith, Derek W., BTech Brun., MA Warw. Principal Lectr.
Akehurst, Gary, BSc Wales, MSc Wales Prof., Marketing
Appia-Adu, Kwaku, BSc Kumasi, MA Wales Sr. Lectr.
Banks, Gerry, MPhil CNAA Principal Lectr.
Brewis, Joanna, BSc Manc. Sr. Lectr.
Brown, Jill, BA S'ton. Sr. Lectr.
Christy, Richard H., MA Camb., MBA City(UK) Sr. Lectr.
Clarke, Kenneth J., BSc Lond., MSc Lond. Sr. Lectr.
Conway, Clifford, BA Kingston(UK), MBA Brun. Sr. Lectr.

Corbridge, Marjorie J., BA CNAA   Principal Lectr.

Dace, Roger W., BA CNAA, MBA Aston   Sr. Lectr.

Farnham, David A., BA Lond., MSc Lond.   Prof., Employment Relations

Fill, Christopher Y., BA CNAA, MSc Warw.   Principal Lectr.

French, Raymond D., BA Essex, PhD CNAA   Principal Lectr.

Gilbert, Alan, BSc S'ton.   Principal Lectr.

Goss, David M., BA Kent, PhD Kent   Prof., Organisational Behaviour

Halliday, Susan, MA Camb., MBA Lond.   Sr. Lectr.

Hankinson, Alan, BSc S'ton., MPhil S'ton., PhD Bath   Principal Lectr.

Hicks, Linda, BA Sur., PhD Sur.   Principal Lectr.; Programme Area Dir.

Hoecht, Andreas H., MA Hamburg, MSc Reading   Sr. Lectr.

McCormack, Brian A., BSc Sheff., MA CNAA   Sr. Lectr.

Meudell, Karen A., MBA CNAA   Sr. Lectr.

Norris, Gillian, MA Camb.   Sr. Lectr.

Oliver, Gordon, BSc Lond., MPhil Reading   Principal Lectr.; Head*

Penn, Joe M., MBA Aston   Principal Lectr.

Pilbeam, Stephen P.   Sr. Lectr.

Preece, David A., BA Manc., MPhil Brad.   Sr. Lectr.

Rees, Raymond G., BSc Wales, MBA City(UK)   Sr. Lectr.

Rodgers, Cheryl, BA Leeds, MSc Cran.IT   Sr. Lectr.

Rutter, Kenneth A., BA Leeds   Sr. Lectr.

Smith, David M., BSc Lond., MBA Wales   Sr. Lectr.

Thorp, Heather M., BA Syd., MA Syd.   Sr. Lectr.

Trott, Paul, BSc CNAA, PhD Cran.   Sr. Lectr.

Other Staff: 1 Principal Lectr.†; 1 Bus. Devel. Consultant†

Chemistry, see under Pharm., Biomed. and Phys. Scis., Sch. of

Computer Science and Mathematics, School of

Tel: (01705) 843109 Fax: (01705) 843106

Addis, T. R., BSc Aston, PhD Brun.   Prof., Computer Science

Anderson, D., BA Belf., PhD Belf.   Principal Lectr.

Baker, Mark   Sr. Lectr.

Barrett, J. D., BSc(Tech) Wales, MPhil   Sr. Lectr.

Bavan, Arugugam, BSc CNAA, PhD CNAA   Principal Lectr.

Bramer, M. A., BSc S'ton., PhD Open(UK)   Digital Prof.

Briggs, J. S., BA York(UK), DPhil York(UK)   Sr. Lectr.

Britt, J. P., BA Warw., MSc Warw., PhD S'ton.   Principal Lectr.

Charlton, P. J., BTech Brun., MSc Kent   Sr. Lectr.

Davies, H. B., BSc Wales, MSc Oxf.   Sr. Lectr.

Elliott, G. H., PhD Lond.   Sr. Lectr.

Evans, C. W., PhD S'ton., FIMA   Sr. Lectr.

Heal, Ann, BSc CNAA   Sr. Lectr.

Heal, B. W., BSc CNAA, MPhil CNAA   Sr. Lectr.

Higgins, B. R., BSc CNAA   Sr. Lectr.

Jerrams-Smith, Jennifer, MSc Birm., PhD Birm.   Principal Lectr.

Kalus, A., BSc Lond., MSc CNAA   Sr. Lectr.

Leonard, G. L., BSc CNAA, MSc Birm.   Sr. Lectr.

Lester, C., BSc Hull, MSc Essex, PhD Lond.   Principal Lectr.

Maartens, Roy, PhD Cape Town   Reader

Makgrolou, Athena, PhD Manc.   Sr. Lectr.

Manns, Tom, BSc Portsmouth   Sr. Lectr.

Matravers, D., BSc Natal, MSc S.Af., PhD Rhodes, FRAS, FIMA   Prof., Applied Mathematics; Head*

McCabe, E. M., BA Calif., BSc Sus., DPhil Sus.   Principal Lectr.

Mew, Jacqueline, MPhil S'ton.   Sr. Lectr.

Nesterux, Alexei, PhD St.Petersburg   Sr. Lectr.

Pearson, C. M., MSc S'ton.   Sr. Lectr.

Pevy, Lynn, PhD Durh.   Sr. Lectr.

Salt, D. W., PhD Lond.   Principal Lectr.

Sharkey, Angela J., MSc Lond.   Sr. Lectr.

Sharkey, W. P. P., MPhil Sur., MSc N.U.I., FIMA   Sr. Lectr.

Tamiz, M., BSc Lond., PhD Brun.   Principal Lectr.

Topp, R. G., BSc S'ton.   Sr. Lectr.

Vernon, N. S., MSc Lond.   Principal Lectr.

Other Staff: 2 Principal Lectrs.†; 1 Sr. Lectr.†

Construction Management, see Land and Construcn. Management

Design, see Art, Des. and Media, Sch. of

Economics

Tel: (01705) 844098 Fax: (01705) 844037

Andrew, Barry P., BA CNAA   Sr. Lectr.

Collins, Alan O. M., BSc Brad., MSc Salf.   Principal Lectr.

Cooper, P. J., BA Keele, MA Leic.   Sr. Lectr.

Cunningham, Stephen, BA CNAA, PhD CNAA   Principal Lectr.; Dir., Market Res.

Dunn, Anthony, MA Lond.   Sr. Lectr.

Fysh, David, BA CNAA, MSc Lond.   Sr. Lectr.

Gillard, Linda, BSc Reading, MA Open(UK)   Sr. Lectr.

Grainger, Jeff S., BA CNAA, MA Essex   Principal Lectr.

Hallett, Mary E., BSc Lond., MPhil CNAA   Sr. Lectr.

Hampton, Mark, BA E.Anglia, PhD E.Anglia   Sr. Lectr.

Harris, Richard, BA Kent, MA Lanc., PhD Belf.   Prof., Local Economy Studies

Heather, Ken F., BSc S'ton.   Sr. Lectr.

Hunt, Lester, BSc Lough., MA Essex   Prof., Business Economics; Head*

Jaffry, Shabbar, BA Islamia, Bahawal., MSc Quaid-i-Azam, MAppSc Karachi   Sr. Lectr.

Judge, Guy, BA Warw., MA Warw.   Principal Lectr.

Murphy, F. P. (Barry), BCom Trinity(Dub.), MEconSc Trinity(Dub.), MSc Lond.   Sr. Lectr.

Price, Bronwen, BA Wales, PhD Wales   Sr. Lectr.

Reid, Chris, BA CNAA, PhD Portsmouth   Sr. Lectr.

Rooth, Tim J. T., BSc Hull, PhD Hull   Principal Lectr.

Scott, Peter, BA York(UK), MSc Lond., DPhil Oxf.   Sr. Lectr.

Slaymaker, John C., BA CNAA, MA CNAA, PhD CNAA   Sr. Lectr.

Smith, G. A. E. (Sandy), BA CNAA, MPhil Glas.   Sr. Lectr.

Snell, Martin C., MA Edin., DPhil York(UK)   Sr. Lectr.

Thomas, Rob F. M., BA Warw., MA Warw.   Principal Lectr.

Thorpe, Andy T., BSc CNAA, MA Sus.   Principal Lectr.

Walker, Paul, BSc Bath, MSocSci Birm., PhD Reading   Sr. Lectr.

Whitmarsh, David T., BA Exe., MA Exe.   Principal Lectr.

Wright Lovett, Verena, BA CNAA, MA Sus.   Sr. Lectr.

Yao, Shujie, BSc S.China Coll.Trop.Crops, MA Manc., PhD Manc.   Reader

Other Staff: 1 Sr. Lectr.†

Education and English, School of

Tel: (01705) 844502 Fax: (01705) 844517

Allen, D., MPhil CNAA, PhD S'ton.   Principal Lectr.

Birch, R., PhD S'ton.   Principal Lectr.; Head*

Brook, J., BA Open(UK), MEd Exe.   Principal Lectr.

Coeshott, M., BA Warw.   Sr. Lectr.

Edwards, F., BA Wales, MSc Oxf.   Sr. Lectr.

Haslehurst, Dorothy, BSc Nott.   Sr. Lectr.

Holloway, D., BA Sheff., MA E.Anglia   Principal Lectr.

Jeffcote, R., MSc Sus.   Principal Lectr.

Lawrence, Brenda, PhD Wales   Sr. Lectr.

Martin, J., BA Open(UK), MEd Brun.   Sr. Lectr.

Murray, L., BEd Lond., MEd W.Aust., PhD Qld.   Principal Lectr.

Race, Angela, MPhil S'ton.   Priincipal Lectr.

Rea, Priscilla, BA Open(UK)   Sr. Lectr.

Scriven, A., BA Open(UK)   Sr. Lectr.

Stallard, Patricia, MA(Ed) S'ton.   Sr. Lectr.

Stinton, M., BA Open(UK)   Sr. Lectr.; Quality Assurance Co-ordinator

Ward, Terence, BSc Lond.   Sr. Lectr.

Other Staff: 5 Sr. Lectrs.†

Engineering, Civil

Tel: (01705) 842523 Fax: (01705) 842521

Alani, Morteza, BSc E.Lond., PhD   Sr. Lectr.

Begg, David W., BSc CNAA, PhD   Principal Lectr.

Butler, John E., BSc Sur., PhD Lond.   Reader

Cross, Ian G., MSc Leeds   Principal Lectr.

Fox, Dominic, BSc CNAA, PhD Portsmouth   Sr. Lectr.

Langdon, Nicholas J., BSc Liv., MSc Lond., FGS   Sr. Lectr.

Lee, Brian E., PhD Leic., FICE   Balfour Beatty Prof.; Head*

Nassif, Ayman, PhD Lond.   Sr. Lectr.

Otter, Robert A., BSc Birm.   Sr. Lectr.

Petersen, Andrew K., BSc Wales   Sr. Lectr.

Reynolds, John H., BSc CNAA   Principal Lectr.

Sangha, Chander M., BSc St And., PhD Dund., FGS   Principal Lectr.

Walden, Philip J., BSc CNAA   Sr. Lectr.

Wharf, Douglas, BSc Leic., MSc Lond.   Sr. Lectr.

Williams, John, BEng CNAA, PhD Portsmouth   Sr. Lectr.

Other Staff: 3 Principal Lectrs.†; 8 Sr. Lectrs.†

Engineering, Electrical and Electronic

Tel: (01705) 842609 Fax: (01705) 842561

Alkadhimi, K. I., BSc Sheff., MEng Sheff., PhD Sheff.   Sr. Lectr.

Austin, J., BSc CNAA, PhD CNAA   Principal Lectr.

Ayoubi, Masoud, PhD Strath.   Sr. Lectr.

Chen, S., BSc City(UK), PhD City(UK)   Reader

Cowan, F. J., MSc CNAA   Sr. Lectr.

Cox, B. R., MSc S'ton.   Sr. Lectr.

Cripps, Martin D., BSc(Eng) S'ton., PhD Lond.   Prof., Information Engineering; Head*

Dadd, R. H., BSc Lond.   Principal Lectr.

Dunn, V., MSc S'ton.   Sr. Lectr.

Dyer, B., MSc Reading   Sr. Lectr.

Filip, M., BEng Belgrade, PhD Portsmouth   Principal Lectr.

Geddes, E. J., BA Oxf.   Sr. Lectr.

Haynes, B. P., MSc CNAA   Sr. Lectr.

Hewitt, A., BA CNAA, MSc CNAA, PhD CNAA   Sr. Lectr.

Hosking, M. W., MSc Sur.   Principal Lectr.

Hunter, R. D. M., BSc H.-W.   Principal Lectr.

Istepanian, Robert S., BSc Baghdad, MSc Baghdad, PhD Lough.   Sr. Lectr.

Liu, Ying, PhD Strath.   Sr. Lectr.

Lovett, C. B., BA Open(UK)   Sr. Lectr.

Luk, Bing, BEng CNAA, MSc Brun., PhD Portsmouth   Sr. Lectr.

Papademetriou, R. C., MSc Patras   Sr. Lectr.

Parchizadeh, G., MSc Wales   Sr. Lectr.

Tawfik, A. N., PhD Portsmouth   Principal Lectr.

Villar, E., PhysLic Barcelona, DrCien Barcelona, DrenElect Paris, PhD Lond., FIEE   Prof., Telecommunications Systems

Virk, Gurvinder, PhD Lond.   Prof., Control Engineering

Other Staff: 4 Principal Lectrs.†; 3 Sr. Lectrs.†

Engineering, Mechanical and Manufacturing

Tel: (01705) 842338 Fax: (01705) 842351

Baker, J., MSc Birm.   Sr. Lectr.

Bedford, G. M., BSc Manc., PhD Manc., FIM   Principal Lectr.; Acting Head*

Bement, J. M., BEng(Tech) CNAA, MSc CNAA, PhD C.N.A.A.   Sr. Lectr.

Bennett, N. G., BSc Bath, MBA   Principal Lectr.

Bishop, J., BEng CNAA   Sr. Lectr.

Black, R., BSc S'ton. Principal Lectr.;
Programme Area Dir.
Bryne, J., MSc CNAA, PhD CNAA Prof.,
Materials Engineering
Cawte, H., BSc CNAA, PhD CNAA Principal
Lectr.
Claridge, S. P., BSc CNAA, PhD CNAA Sr.
Lectr.
Foster, J. V., BSc Lond. Principal Lectr.
George, P. A., BSc Lond. Principal Lectr.
Hicks, P. J., MA Oxf. Principal Lectr.
Hogan, V., BSc CNAA Sr. Lectr.
Hughes, V., MSc CNAA Principal Lectr.
Little, A. F. P., BSc City(UK) Sr. Lectr.
Mason, Simonne, BSc PhD Principal Lectr.
Oliver, Terry, BSc CNAA Principal Lectr.
Powell, B. E., PhD Lond. Reader
Prichard, B. L., MSc Cran., PhD S'ton. Sr. Lectr.
Purvis, M. I., MSc Leeds, PhD Leeds Prof.,
Energy Engineering
Ross, Carlisle, BSc Durh., PhD Manc. Prof.,
Structural Dynamics
Saidpour, S., MSc Cran. Sr. Lectr.
Sanders, D. A., BA CNAA, BSc CNAA, PhD
CNAA Principal Lectr.
Shen, Wei Qin, PhD Shanghai Sr. Lectr.
Taylor, R. W., BSc Lond., MPhil Lond. Sr. Lectr.
Vitanov, V., MSc St.Petersburg, PhD
St.Petersburg Sr. Lectr.
Waite, M. L., BSc CNAA, MPhil CNAA Sr.
Lectr.
Other Staff: 1 Reader†; 4 Sr. Lectrs.†

English, see Educn. and Engl., Sch. of

Exercise Science, see Sports and Exercise
Sci.

French Studies, see Langs. and Area Studies,
Sch. of

Geography
Tel: (01705) 842507 Fax: (01705) 842512
Bradbeer, J., BA Oxf., MPhil CNAA Principal
Lectr.
Burtenshaw, D., MA Lond. Principal Lectr.
Chapman, J., MA Lond., PhD Lond. Principal
Lectr.
Collier, P., BSc Newcastle(UK), PhD
Aston Principal Lectr.
Cubitt, Tessa, MA Edin., PhD Edin. Sr. Lectr.
Farres, P., BSc Reading, PhD Reading Principal
Lectr.
Healey, R. G., MA Camb., PhD Camb. Prof.
Hooke, Janet, BSc Brist., PhD S'ton. Prof.,
Physical Geography
Inkpen, R., BA Oxf., PhD Lond. Sr. Lectr.
Jones, K., BSc S'ton., PhD S'ton. Prof.; Head*
Leonard, S., BA CNAA, MSc Lond. Sr. Lectr.
Mason, H., MA Camb., PhD Wales Principal
Lectr.
Mohan, J. F., BA Durh., PhD Durh. Reader
Nowell, D., BA CNAA, MSc Aberd. Sr. Lectr.
Pearson, A., BA Leeds Sr. Lectr.
Ryder, A., BA Conn., DPhil Oxf. Sr. Lectr.
Shurmer-Smith, Pamela, BSc Rhodesia, MPhil
Lond. Principal Lectr.
Taylor, Michael, BSc Lond., PhD Lond. Prof.
White, I., BSc Lond. Principal Lectr.;
Programme Area Dir.
Other Staff: 1 Principal Lectr.†; 3 Sr. Lectrs.†

Geology
Tel: (01705) 842259 Fax: (01705) 842244
Barker, Michael J., BSc Manc., PhD Keele,
FGS Principal Lectr.
Chaplin, E. Michael, BSc Wales, FGS Sr. Lectr.
Daley, Brian F., BSc Reading, MA(Ed) S'ton., PhD
Reading, FGS Principal Lectr.
Giles, David P., BSc, FGS Principal Lectr.
Hall, R. Peter, BSc Lond., MPhil PhD,
FGS Reader
Hughes, David J., BSc Leic., PhD Manc.,
FGS Principal Lectr.
Jones, Mervyn E., BSc Lond., PhD Lond.,
FGS Prof.; Head*
Jones, Peter C., MSc Lond. Sr. Lectr.

Murphy, William, BSc Strath., PhD Lond.,
FGS Sr. Lectr.
Petley, David N., BSc Lond., PhD Lond. Sr.
Lectr.
Poulsom, Andrew J., BSc Portsmouth, MSc
Lond. Sr. Lectr.
Power, Gregory M., BSc Liv., MSc Keele, PhD
Keele, FGS Sr. Lectr.
Ryan, Michael J., BSc Nott., PhD Nott., FGS Sr.
Lectr.
Walton, Nicholas R. G., BSc Leeds, MSc Oxf.,
FGS Sr. Lectr.
Whalley, John S., BSc Leic., MSc Lond.,
FGS Principal Lectr.
Other Staff: 1 Principal Lectr.†

Health Studies, School of
Tel: (01705) 266823 Fax: (01705) 377904
Alexander, Joanne, PhD S'ton. Reader
Antoniou, Vasos, BEd CNAA Programme
Leader
Astor, Roberta, MA CNAA Sr. Lectr.
Barnett, Karen Sr. Lectr.
Billington, Enid, MA S'ton. Sr. Lectr.
Boyle, Patricia, MA S'ton. Sr. Lectr.
Campbell, Gill, BEd S.Bank Sr. Lectr.
Carpenter, Diane, BA CNAA Sr. Lectr.
Carter, Sidney, BA CNAA Sr. Lectr.
Chislett, Lesley, BSc Portsmouth Sr. Lectr.
Coney, Timothy, BA CNAA Principal Lectr.
Critchell, Margaret, MSc Wolv. Sr. Lectr.
Davies, James, MA CNAA Sr. Lectr.
Davies, Peter, MA Oxf., PhD Wales Prof.,
Health Sociology
Douglas, Ian, BA Portsmouth Sr. Lectr.
Flahey, Hazel, BSc Portsmouth Sr. Lectr.
Fulbrook, Paul, BSc Bourne., MSc Manc. Sr.
Lectr.
Gardner, Lyn, MSc Sr. Lectr.
Garrett, Bernard, BSc CNAA Sr. Lectr.
Green, Anita, BA Portsmouth Sr. Lectr.
Greig, Maria, BA CNAA Sr. Lectr.
Harper, Lesley, BSc Hull, MSc Manc. Principal
Lectr.
Haves, Richard, BSc Portsmouth Sr. Lectr.
Howarth, Amanda Sr. Lectr.
Humphrys, Kevin, MSc Portsmouth Sr. Lectr.
Jackson, Patricia, BA Leeds Sr. Lectr.
Jasper, Melanie, BA Open(UK), MSc
Manc. Principal Lectr.
Jefferson, Harriett, BA Sheff., MSc S'ton. Sr.
Lectr.
Joly, Iris, BA Open(UK) Sr. Lectr.
Knol, Heni Sr. Lectr.
Lim, Shirley, BSc Liv. Sr. Lectr.
Lindfield, Neil, MSc Sur. Head*
Lloyd-Williams, Glenys Sr. Lectr.
Marjoram, Barbara, TD, MA Portsmouth Sr.
Lectr.
Mathews, Vivienne Sr. Lectr.
McHale, Carol, MSc Wolv. Principal Lectr.
McRay, Janet, BSc Principal Lectr.
McSwiggan, Sue Sr. Lectr.
Moore, Susan, BA Newcastle(UK), MSc
Birm. Principal Lectr.
Morris, Patricia, MA Portsmouth Sr. Lectr.
O'Kell, Stephen, BSc MBA Principal Lectr.
Okubadejo, Tinuade, BSc Lond. Sr. Lectr.
Paice, Sandie, MSc S'ton. Principal Lectr.;
Programme Area Dir.
Parboteeah, Somduth, MSc Portsmouth Sr. Lectr.
Parfitt, Michael Sr. Lectr.
Peck, Simon Sr. Lectr.
Porter, Nigel, BEd Sund. Principal Lectr.
Rolfe, Gary, BSc Sur., MA S'ton., PhD
S'ton. Principal Lectr.
Ryder, Isobel, MSc Portsmouth Sr. Lectr.
Sadik, Ruth, BA Portsmouth Sr. Lectr.
Sallam, Sumeyah, MSc Sur. Sr. Lectr.
Sander, Ruth, BA Open(UK) Sr. Lectr.
Simpson, Penelope, MSc Sur. Principal Lectr.
Skinner, Anne Principal Lectr.
Spencer, Anne, MA Principal Lectr.
Stosiek, Jan, MSc Sur. Sr. Lectr.
Thrower, Catherine, BSc CNAA Sr. Lectr.
Watkinson, Graham Sr. Lectr.
Williams, James, BA CNAA, MA Portsmouth Sr.
Lectr.

Wilson, Michael, BA Lond., MA Lond. Sr. Lectr.
Wise, Joyce Sr. Lectr.
Other Staff: 1 Principal Lectr.†; 12 Sr. Lectrs.†

Historical Studies, see Soc. and Hist.
Studies, Sch. of

Iberian and Latin American Studies, see
Langs. and Area Studies, Sch. of

Information Systems
Tel: (01705) 844005 Fax: (01705) 844006
Allan, G. W., BSc Reading Sr. Lectr.
Beresford, R. A., BSc Lond., PhD
S'ton. Principal Lectr.
Billinge, D. J., BA Lond., MSc CNAA Sr. Lectr.
Burt, Janet Sr. Lectr.
Callear, D. H., BSc Birm., MEd Lond., PhD
Lough. Sr. Lectr.
Chandler, Jane M., BSc Brun., MSc
CNAA Principal Lectr.
Crellin, Jonathon, BA Open(UK), PhD
Open(UK) Sr. Lectr.
Dore, Linda A., BSc CNAA Sr. Lectr.
Early, G. H., BSc CNAA Sr. Lectr.
Garlick, F. G., BA Open(UK), MSc City(UK) Sr.
Lectr.; Programme Area Dir.
Hand, S. C., BSc S'ton., PhD S'ton. Principal
Lectr.; Acting Head*
Hills, Jennifer, BA Open(UK) Sr. Lectr.
Hills, R. C., LLB Sheff. Principal Lectr.
King, T., BSc Manc., MSc Brad. Sr. Lectr.
Lightfoot, I. R., BA Birm., MSc CNAA Principal
Lectr.
Norris, Tony, MSc Hull, PhD Lond. Principal
Lectr.
Paterson, Pat, BA Lond., MSc CNAA Sr. Lectr.
Raine-Evans, B., BSc City(UK), MSc Lond. Sr.
Lectr.; Schs. and Colls. Programmes Officer
Rosbottom, J., BEd Manc., MEd Liv., MSc
Lond. Sr. Lectr.
Snook, Jean, BA CNAA, MSc CNAA, PhD
Herts. Sr. Lectr.
Tyrell, Roger, BA CNAA Sr. Lectr.
Wilson, Annette C., BSc Lond. Principal Lectr.
Wilson, S. T., BSc CNAA Principal Lectr.
Zwiggelarm, Reyer, PhD Lond. Sr. Lectr.
Other Staff: 1 Sr. Lectr.†

Land and Construction Management
Tel: (01705) 842918 Fax: (01705) 842913
Belcher, Robert G., BSc CNAA, MSc Lond.,
FRICS Principal Lectr.; Acting Head*
Blackledge, Michael J., FRICS Sr. Lectr.
Chapman, G. Keith, BSc Aston Sr. Lectr.
Edwards, Victoria, BSc Reading, MSc Cant., PhD
Reading Principal Lectr.
Ellison, Louise, BSc CNAA Sr. Lectr.
Gibson, Graham C., BSc CNAA Sr. Lectr.
Goodhead, Timothy, BA Nott., MSc Reading,
MPhil Reading Principal Lectr.; Programme
Area Dir.
Lee, Rosalind M., LLB Sheff., MA Sheff. Sr.
Lectr.
Osborn, Sylvia J., BSc CNAA Sr. Lectr.
Packer, Andrew D., BSc CNAA Sr. Lectr.
Pitchforth, Steven J., BA CNAA, MSc Sur. Sr.
Lectr.
Seabrooke, William, PhD Reading, FRICS Prof.,
Land Economy
Tate, Brian, MSc Sur., MSc Lond. Sr. Lectr.
Upson, Alan Sr. Lectr.
Walker, Nigel, MSc Reading Dir.
Waterson, Geoffrey, LLB Lond., LLM S'ton., MA
Wales Principal Lectr.
Webster, Bernard, BA Manc. Principal Lectr.;
Head of Quality Assurance
Other Staff: 2 Principal Lectrs.†; 1 Sr. Lectr.†

Languages and Area Studies, School of
Tel: (01705) 846100 Fax: (01705) 846040
Aldridge, Eve-Marie, MA Grenoble Sr. Lectr.
Arrebola-Sanchez, Miguel Sr. Lectr.
Brierley, William, BA Wales, MA
Lond. Principal Lectr.; Programme Area Dir.
Bryant, Janet, MA Reading Sr. Lectr.
Callen, A., MA S'ton., DPhil Sus. Principal
Lectr.

Chafer, A., BA Nott., MA Reading, MA Lond., LèsL Nantes, PhD Lond.   Principal Lectr.

Cleminson, R., MA Oxf., DPhil Oxf.   Reader, Slavonic Studies

Coleman, J., MA Exe.   Prof., Foreign Language Learning

Dore, Elizabeth, BA Vassar, MPhil Col., PhD Col.   Sr. Lectr.

Evans, M., BA Sus., DPhil Sus.   Sr. Lectr.

Flenley, P., MA St And., PhD Birm.   Principal Lectr.

Freeland, Jane, BA Camb., MA Lond.   Sr. Lectr.

Gillespie, R., BA Liv., PhD Liv.   Prof., Iberian and Latin American Studies

Gould, R., BA CNAA, MA Sus.   Sr. Lectr.

Hand, Penelope, MA Lond.   Sr. Lectr.

Humphreys, P., BA CNAA, MA Lond.   Sr. Lectr.

Hutchinson, D., BA Leeds   Sr. Lectr.

Jenkins, B., BA Camb., MSc Lond., PhD Lond.   Prof.†, French Area Studies

Kemble, I., BSc Sur.   Principal Lectr.; Head*

Kenny, Naomi, BA CNAA, MA CNAA   Sr. Lectr.

Knischewski, G., MA CNAA   Sr. Lectr.

Landsman, N., BA Manc., PhD Lond.   Principal Lectr.

Mitchell, Samia, LES Oran, MES Rouen   Sr. Lectr.

Moore-Blunt, Jennifer, MA Camb., PhD Lond.   Sr. Lectr.

Oughton, Sabrea, MA Toulouse   Sr. Lectr.

Palmer, David, BA Exe., MPhil Lond.   Sr. Lectr.; Dir., Lang. Centre

Parkes, Genevieve, MèsL Nancy   Sr. Lectr.

Pickett-Rose, Lorraine, BA CNAA, MA   Sr. Lectr.

Poole, B., BA Nott., MA Lanc.   Sr. Lectr.

Rawlings, Helen, BA CNAA, MPhil Liv.   Sr. Lectr.

Shaw, Deborah, BA CNAA, MA Leeds   Sr. Lectr.

Smyth, T., BA Liv., BLitt Oxf.   Sr. Lectr.

Syngellakis, Anna, LLB Athens, LLM Lond., MA Rutgers   Sr. Lectr.

Williams, P., BA Nott., PhD Lond.   Sr. Lectr.

Other Staff: 2 Principal Lectrs.†; 1 Sr. Lectr.†

Management, see Acctg. and Management Sci., Bus. and Management Studies, and Portsmouth Management Centre

Mathematics, see Computer Sci. and Maths., Sch. of

Media, see Art, Des. and Media, Sch. of

Pharmacy, Biomedical and Physical Sciences, School of

Tel: (01705) 843576 Fax: (01705) 843565

Arkle, S., BSc Newcastle(UK), PhD Newcastle(UK)   Principal Lectr.

Barwell, C. J., BSc Bath, PhD Bath   Sr. Lectr.

Blunden, G., MPharm Nott., PhD CNAA   Prof., Pharmacology

Brown, D. T., BPharm Bath, PhD Penn.   Sr. Lectr.

Bunker, Valda W., MSc S'ton., PhD S'ton.   Sr. Lectr.; Programme Area Dir.

Cook, D. J., BSc Aston, MPhil Aston   Sr. Lectr.

Dacke, C. G., BTech Reading, PhD Reading   Reader

Ebenezer, I. S., BSc Newcastle(UK), PhD Newcastle(UK)   Sr. Lectr.

Gibbs, R., BSc Portsmouth, PhD Portsmouth   Sr. Lectr.

Green, K. L., PhD Lond.   Sr. Lectr.

Hone, R. E., BPharm   Principal Lectr.

Hunt, A. J., BSc CNAA   Sr. Lectr.

Jones, E. B. G., PhD Leeds, DSc Wales   Prof.

Jones, I. F., MSc Leeds, PhD CNAA   Prof., Pharmacy Practice

Jones, R. W., BSc Leic., PhD Dund.   Sr. Lectr.

Keysell, G. R., BPharm Lond., MSc Lond., PhD Lond.   Sr. Lectr.

Mason, T. G., MSc Warw., PhD Warw.   Sr. Lectr.

McLellan, D. S., MSc Brun., PhD Brun.   Principal Lectr.

Norris, M., MSc Wales, PhD Wales   Sr. Lectr.

Oliver, G. W. O., BSc S'ton., PhD S'ton.   Principal Lectr.

Patel, A. V., BSc CNAA, PhD CNAA   Sr. Lectr.

Rogers, D. J., BA Open(UK), MPhil CNAA, PhD CNAA   Prof.

Sautreau, Asmita, BSc CNAA, MSc Liv., PhD Lond.   Sr. Lectr.

Smart, J. D., BSc CNAA, PhD Wales   Sr. Lectr.

Thomas, G., BSc Nott., PhD Nott.   Sr. Lectr.

Thurston, D. E., BSc CNAA, PhD CNAA   Prof., Medicinal Chemistry

Walsh, Frank, BSc CNAA, PhD Lough.   Prof., Electrochemical Technology

White, G. L., BSc Birm., PhD Birm.   Sr. Lectr.

Wong, J. C. L., BSc Monash, MPhil Monash, PhD Monash   Principal Lectr.

Other Staff: 1 Reader†; 1 Sr. Lectr.†

Chemistry, Division of

Tel: (01705) 843596 Fax: (01705) 843592

Banting, B. D., BSc Reading, PhD CNAA   Sr. Lectr.

Barker, D., MSc(Eng) Lond., PhD Lond.   Principal Lectr.

Beech, Iwona, MSc Lond., PhD CNAA   Reader

Campbell, Sheelagh, BSc Lond., PhD CNAA   Principal Lectr.

Cox, P. A., BSc Lond., PhD Keele   Sr. Lectr.

Hardman, J. S., BSc Leeds, PhD Leeds, FRSChem, FIP   Principal Lectr.

Mills, G. A., BA Portsmouth, PhD S'ton.   Sr. Lectr.

Nevell, T. G., BSc Lond., PhD Lond.   Principal Lectr.

Ottewill, Geraldine, BSc Nott., PhD Nott.   Sr. Lectr.

Tsibouklis, John, MSc Lond., PhD CNAA   Sr. Lectr.

Other Staff: 1 Principal Lectr.†

Physics, Division of

Tel: (01705) 842150 Fax: (01705) 842157

Dewdney, C., BSc Lond., PhD Lond.   Reader

Franklin, D., BSc Portsmouth, PhD Portsmouth   Sr. Lectr.

Gardiner, M. K., BSc Leic., PhD Leic.   Sr. Lectr.

Griffiths, A., BSc Wales, PhD Wales   Principal Lectr.

Horton, G. M., BSc Lond.   Sr. Lectr.

Nixon, D. E., BSc Lond., PhD Lond.   Principal Lectr.

Schmidt, M., PhD Bremen   Sr. Lectr.

Staynov, Yana, MSc Moscow, PhD Moscow   Sr. Lectr.

Timms, D. N., BSc Warw., PhD Warw.   Sr. Lectr.

Turner, C. E., BSc Sheff., PhD Sheff.   Principal Lectr.

White, C., MSc CNAA   Sr. Lectr.

Radiography Education, Centre for

Tel: (01705) 863596 Fax: (01705) 863592

Adrian-Harris, Derek, TD, BA Open(UK), MPhil Open(UK)   Principal Lectr.; Head*

Anderson, Dorothy   Sr. Lectr.

Castle, Alan, BEd S'ton., MA S'ton., PhD S'ton.   Principal Lectr.

Clarke, Harold   Sr. Lectr.

Evered, Helen, MSc Sur.   Sr. Lectr.

Haines, Penny, BSc Portsmouth, MSc Portsmouth   Sr. Lectr.

Heath, Madge, BA Open(UK), MSc Lond.   Sr. Lectr.

Hussain, Pervez   Sr. Lectr.

Physics, see under Pharm., Biomed. and Phys. Scis., Sch. of

Portsmouth Management Centre, see also Acctg. and Management Sci., and Bus. and Management Studies

Tel: (01705) 815605 Fax: (01705) 830434

Davis, Michael, BSc Lond., MA Kingston(UK)   Sr. Lectr.

Doodson, Graham   Sr. Lectr.

Edwards, Noel, BA Oxf., MA Lond.   Principal Lectr.

Hobbs, Roger, BA Open(UK)   Principal Lectr.; Head*

Lockyer, Lynne C.   Sr. Lectr.

McMenamin, Jim   Sr. Lectr.

Reavill, Barry, FIEE   Principal Lectr.

Salter, Dennis J., BSc CNAA   Sr. Lectr.

Wright, Norman, BSc Sheff., MSc Lond.   Sr. Lectr.

Other Staff: 3 Sr. Lectrs.†

Psychology

Tel: (01705) 876312 Fax: (01705) 846300

Bachman, Talis, PhD Moscow   Sr. Lectr.

Brandon, Douglas, BA Keele   Sr. Lectr.

Buckley, Sue J., BA Reading   Prof.†, Developmental Disability

Bull, Raymond H. C., BSc Exe., MSc Exe., DSc Portsmouth, FBPsS   Prof.

Costall, Alan, BSc Wales, PhD Birm.   Reader

Fluck, Michael J., BSc Wales, PhD Nott.   Principal Lectr.

Foxcroft, David R., BSc Hull, PhD Hull   Sr. Lectr.; Dir., Res. and Devel. Support Unit

Gale, Anthony, BA Exe., PhD Exe., FBPsS   Prof.†

MacDonald, John, BSc Glas., MSc Stir., PhD Sur.   Principal Lectr.; Head*

Morris, Paul H., BSc S'ton., PhD S'ton.   Sr. Lectr.

Nunkoosing, Karl K., BA Open(UK)   Sr. Lectr.

Palmén, Hilary K., BSc Aston, PhD Lough.   Sr. Lectr.

Read, Ann M., BSc Wales, MSc Birm.   Sr. Lectr.; Head of Quality Assurance

Reddy, Vasudevi, BA Osm., MA Osm., PhD Edin.   Sr. Lectr.

Smith, Marica, BSc Tulane, MA Missouri, PhD Missouri   Sr. Lectr.

Van Laar, Darren L., BSc CNAA, MSc York(UK), PhD Lond.   Principal Lectr.

Vrij, Aldert, BA Amst., PhD Amst.   Reader

Other Staff: 3 Sr. Lectrs.†

Radiography Education, see under Pharm., Biomed. and Phys. Scis., Sch. of

Slavonic Studies, see Langs. and Area Studies, Sch. of

Social and Historical Studies, School of

Tel: (01705) 842173 Fax: (01705) 842174

Ackerley, Beryl, MA Kent   Sr. Lectr.

Atkinson, Robert, BSc Essex, MA Essex, PhD Kent   Principal Lectr.

Bruley, Susan, MSc Lond., PhD Lond.   Sr. Lectr.

Carpenter, David, BA   Principal Lectr.

Carr, Fergus, BSc Hull, MSc Lond.   Head*

Cope, Stephen, BA CNAA, MSc Lond., PhD Lond.   Principal Lectr.

Davis, John R., BA Sus., MA PhD   Sr. Lectr.

Evans, Neil T., BA Wales, MA Kent   Principal Lectr.; Programme Dir.

Germann, Otto, MSc Sur.   Sr. Lectr.

Giddey, Martin N., MA CNAA   Sr. Lectr.

Gillespie, Rosemary, BA Sheff., MA Portsmouth   Sr. Lectr.

Gray, Robbie, BA Edin., PhD Edin.   Prof., Social History

Harper-Ditmar, Susan, BA MPhil PhD   Reader

Hatton, Kieron, BA Portsmouth, MSc Brist.   Sr. Lectr.

Johnson, Norman, BSc(Econ) Lond., MA Keele, MSc(Econ) Lond.   Prof., Public Policy

Kendall, Ian, BSc Lond.   Prof., Social Policy

Kenny, Brendan, BA Lond., MA Leic.   Sr. Lectr.

Lunn, Kenneth, MA Glas., PhD Sheff.   Reader

Massey, Andrew, BA CNAA, MSc Lond., PhD Lond.   Reader

Moon, Graham, BA Exe., PhD CNAA   Prof., Health Services Research

Nash, Mike R., BA CNAA, MPhil S'ton.   Principal Lectr.

North, Nancy, BA Leic., MA CNAA   Principal Lectr.

Nugent, Christine, BA Sus.   Sr. Lectr.

Prior, Robin, BSc Lond., MSc CNAA   Principal Lectr.

Purvis, June, BA Leeds, MEd Manc., PhD Open(UK)   Prof., Sociology

Russell, David, BA *Manc.*, MSc *Lond.* Principal Lectr.; Programme Dir.
Sears, Maureen, BA *Open(UK)*, MSc *Wales* Principal Lectr.
Shepherd, Peter, BSc *CNAA*, MSc *S'ton.* Sr. Lectr.
Smart, Barry, BSc *Lond.*, PhD *Sheff.* Prof., Sociology
Starie, Peter, BA *CNAA* Sr. Lectr.
Tester, Keith, BSc *CNAA*, PhD *Leeds* Prof., Social Theory
Thomas, James H., BA *Lond.*, PhD, FRHistS Principal Lectr.
Thomas, Roger, BA *Nott.* Sr. Lectr.
Toussaint, Pamella, BA *Leic.* Sr. Lectr.
Walinski-Kiehl, Robert, BA *CNAA*, MPhil *CNAA* Sr. Lectr.
Wilson, Charles R. M., BSc *Lond.*, MA *Kent* Sr. Lectr.
Other Staff: 1 Principal Lectr.†; 4 Sr. Lectrs.†

Sociology, see Soc. and Hist. Studies, Sch. of

Sports and Exercise Science

Tel: (01705) 843544 Fax: (01705) 843609
Boyle, Paul, BSc *Belf.*, MSc *Belf.* Sr. Lectr.
Farrington, Tracie, BA Sr. Lectr.
Hall, Kim, MSc *S'ton.* Sr. Lectr.
Iredale, Fiona, BA *Strath.*, MSc *Lough.* Sr. Lectr.
Rees, Alun, BSc *Nott.Trent* Sr. Lectr.
Reid, Graham, BSc *Lond.*, MPhil *Sur.* Head*
Strickland, Paul, BEng *Portsmouth*, PhD *Portsmouth* Sr. Lectr.

SPECIAL CENTRES, ETC

Care, Independent and Public Sector Management, Centre for

Tel: (01705) 895565 Fax: (01705) 845555
Betts, Penny, BA *Portsmouth* Sr. Lectr.
Gray, Ivan L., BA *Durh.*, MA *Nott.*, MBA *Portsmouth* Principal Lectr.; Dir.*
MacKenzie, Robert J., MA *Edin.* Sr. Lectr.
Other Staff: 1 Sr. Lectr.†

Continuing and Community Education, Centre for

Darbyshire, Lewis Head*

Economics and Management of Aquatic Resources, Centre for the (CEMARE)

Tel: (01705) 844082 Fax: (01705) 844037
Cunningham, Stephen, BA *CNAA*, PhD *CNAA* Principal Lectr.

Slaymaker, John C., BA *CNAA*, MA *CNAA*, PhD *CNAA* Sr. Lectr.
Whitmarsh, David T., BA *Exe.*, MA *Exe.* Principal Lectr.

Police and Criminological Studies, Institute of

Brearley, Nigel, BA *Essex*, MA *Sheff.* Sr. Lectr.
Loveday, Barry, BA *Lanc.*, MPhil *Glas.* Principal Lectr.
McKenzie, Ian, BA *Exe.*, MPhil *Exe.*, PhD *Bath* Principal Lectr.; Dir.*
Savage, Stephen, BA *Liv.*, PhD *Liv.* Prof., Criminology
Wright, Alan, BA *S'ton.*, PhD *S'ton.* Sr. Lectr.

Project and Quality Management, Centre for

Balthazor, Lee, BTech *Lough.*, MSc *Cran.IT*, FRAeS Principal Lectr.
Daly, John, MSc *Cran.* Sr. Lectr.
Hathorn, David, BA *Open(UK)* Sr. Lectr.
Moody, Tony, BSc *Birm.*, PhD *Birm.* Principal Lectr.

Utilization of the Built Environment, Centre for the (CUBE)

Tel: (01705) 843201 Fax: (01705) 843384
Youle, Antony, MA *Camb.*, PhD *Camb.* Dir.*

CONTACT OFFICERS

Academic affairs. Academic Registrar: Rees, Andrew, BA *CNAA*
Accommodation. Director of Accommodation and Hospitality Services: Webster, Michelle
Admissions (first degree). Assistant Academic Registrar (Admissions): Jordan, David, BSc *CNAA*
Admissions (higher degree). Assistant Academic Registrar (Admissions): Jenkins, Margaret
Adult/continuing education. Head of Centre for Continuing and Community Education: Darbyshire, Lewis
Alumni. Marketing Projects Manager: Spurgeon, David
Archives. Humanities Librarian: Francis, D., BA *Exe.*
Careers. Head of Careers: Martin, Carole, BA *Exe.*
Computing services. Director of Information Services: McQuistan, Allan
Credit transfer. Head, Academic Development: Findlay, Peter, MA *Camb.*
Development/fund-raising. Marketing Projects Manager: Spurgeon, David

Estates and buildings/works and services. Director of Physical Resources: Finch, Patrick
Examinations. Assistant Academic Registrar (Admissions): Jordan, David, BSc *CNAA*
Finance. Finance Director/Head of Purchasing and Supplies: Hunt, David
General enquiries. Academic Registrar: Rees, Andrew, BA *CNAA*
International office. International Director: Asteris, Michael, BSc *Lond.*, MSocSc *Birm.*, PhD *Brun.*
Library (chief librarian). Acting Librarian: Bonar, Ian
Ombudsperson. Secretary and Clerk to the Board of Governors: Moore, R. J., BA *Lond.*
Personnel/human resources. Head of Personnel: Boam, John
Public relations, information and marketing. Head of Marketing: Harris-Burland, John, MSc *S'ton.*
Publications. Acting Librarian: Bonar, Ian
Purchasing. Finance Director/Head of Purchasing and Supplies: Hunt, David
Quality assurance and accreditation. Head, Academic Development: Findlay, Peter, MA *Camb.*
Research. Director of Research: Butler, Prof. John, BSc *Sur.*, PhD *Lond.*
Safety. Health and Safety Officer: Denholm, Ian
Scholarships, awards, loans. Assistant Academic Registrar (Awards, Loans): Smith, Malcolm
Schools liaison. Information Officer: Henderson, Barry
Security. Estates Officer: Cardy, Andrew
Staff development and training. Staff Development Manager: Collins, Jeannette, BA *Kent*, MA *Portsmouth*
Student welfare/counselling. Student Counsellor: Barden, Nicola
Students from other countries. International Director: Asteris, Michael, BSc *Lond.*, MSocSc *Birm.*, PhD *Brun.*
Students with disabilities. Disability Co-ordinator: Hine, Gail
University press. Central Production Manager: Stait, Bryan

[Information supplied by the institution as at March 1998, and edited by the ACU]

QUEEN MARGARET COLLEGE, EDINBURGH

Founded 1971; originally established as Edinburgh School of Cookery (1875); later Edinburgh College of Domestic Science (1930)

Additional Member of the Association of Commonwealth Universities

Postal Address: Corstorphine Campus, Edinburgh, Scotland EH12 8TS
Telephone: (0131) 317 3000 **Fax**: (0131) 317 3256

PATRON—Alice, H.R.H. Princess, Duchess of Gloucester
PRO-PATRON—Elgin and Kincardine, The Rt. Hon. the Countess of
PRINCIPAL AND VICE-PATRON*—Stringer, Joan K., BA Keele, PhD Keele
VICE PRINCIPAL (ACADEMIC DEVELOPMENT)—Reid, Austin, PhD Belf.
VICE PRINCIPAL (STRATEGIC PLANNING AND DEVELOPMENT)‡—Marshall, Rosalyn, BSc Dund.
VICE PRINCIPAL (RESOURCE PLANNING AND DEVELOPMENT)—King, Geoffrey, PhD

GENERAL INFORMATION

History. Originally established as Edinburgh School of Cookery in 1875, the college was founded under its present name in 1871. It has three campuses: Corstorphine, 6km from Edinburgh city centre; Leith, at the city's port; and at Gateway Theatre, near the city centre.

Admission to first degree courses (see also United Kingdom Introduction). Through Universities and Colleges Admissions Service (UCAS).

First Degrees (see also United Kingdom Directory to Subjects of Study). BA, BSc (also available with honours): 3–4 years.

Higher Degrees (see also United Kingdom Directory to Subjects of Study). MSc, MPhil, PhD.

MSc: 1 year full-time or 2–3 years part-time.

Libraries. 100,000 books; 1500 audio-visual items; 1000 periodicals subscribed to.

Academic Year (1998–99). 21 September–12 December; 4 January–26 March; 12 April–28 May.

Income. £17,000,000.

Statistics. Staff (academic): 175. Students: about 3000.

ACADEMIC UNITS

Applied Consumer Studies

Brennan, Carol, BA MA DCA   Sr. Lectr.
Hughes, A. H., BTech Lough., MSc Newcastle(UK), MBA H.-W., PhD Newcastle(UK)   Sr. Lectr.
Kirk, D., BSc MPhil   Acting Head*
Woods, Margaret, BSc Durh., MBA Edin.   Sr. Lectr.
Other Staff: 13 Lectrs.; 1 Res. Fellow
Research: consumer research: housing, local government, retail; food: sensory appraisal; nutrition and food choice

Communication and Information Studies

Davenport, E., MA Edin., MSc Strath., PhD Strath.   Sr. Lectr.
Herring, J. E., MA Edin., MA(Lib)   Sr. Lectr.; Acting Head*
Tolson, A. V., BA Birm., MA Open(UK), PhD Birm.   Sr. Lectr.
Research: household informatics; media consumption; networked learning; politics and the media

Consumer Studies, see Appl. Consumer Studies

Dietetics and Nutrition

de Looy, Anne, BSc Lond., PhD Lond.   Prof.; Head*
McDermott, J. C., BSc Salf., PhD Liv.   Sr. Lectr.

Pender, F. T., BSc R.Gordon, PhD CNAA   Sr. Lectr.
Turnbull, W., MSc PhD   Sr. Lectr.

Drama

Bains, Lynn, MA Northwestern   Sr. Lectr.
Bell, B., BA MA MFA PhD   Sr. Lectr.
Bracewell, H.   Visiting Prof.
Brown, Ian, MA MLitt PhD   Head*
Perry, C., MA Camb.   Prof., Theatre
Stone, J., BA Open(UK)   Dir.*
Other Staff: 14 Lectrs.; 2 Res. Fellows; 1 Hon. Prof.; 1 Hon. Res. Fellow
Research: contemporary, especially Scottish theatre; theatre and cultural identity (cultural policies and management; playwriting and design; theories of theatre, directing and acting)

Health and Nursing

Dobson, Carol, BA Open(UK), BA   Sr. Lectr.
Munro, Kathy, BA Open(UK)   Sr. Lectr.
Runciman, Phyllis, MSc Edin., MPhil Edin.   Sr. Lectr.
Sydie, Linda, BA Open(UK), BA   Head*

Hospitality and Tourism Management

Buick, J. W., MBA Edin.   Sr. Lectr.
Ingram, A., BSc Lough., MA Warw., MLitt Glas.   Sr. Lectr.
Kirk, D., BSc Reading, MPhil Sur.   Prof.; Head*
Prentice, R., BA Liv., PhD Reading   Sr. Lectr.

Information Studies, see Communicn. and Information Studies

Management and Social Sciences

Buchan, J., MA PhD   Reader
Gilloran, A., MA PhD   Head*
McWhannel, D., MSc Aston   Sr. Lectr.
Turnbull, Jane, MA PhD   Sr. Lectr.

Nursing, see Health and Nursing

Nutrition, see Dietetics and Nutr.

Occupational Therapy and Art Therapy

Blair, Sheena E. E., MEd Edin.   Sr. Lectr.
Nicol, Margaret M., MPhil Strath., PhD Strath.   Sr. Lectr.
Stewart, Averil M., BA Open(UK)   Prof.; Head*
Other Staff: 10 Lectrs.; 5 Lectrs.†; 1 Temp. Lectr.†
Research: evaluating existing measurements of functional ability; evaluating occupational therapy interventions; pain management in rehabilitation of amputees; predicting functional ability with stroke patients

Physiotherapy

Durward, B., MSc Strath., PhD   Sr. Lectr.
Nicholas, Katherine J., BA Open(UK), MPhil   Sr. Lectr.
Payne, A. C., BSc Lond., PhD Edin.   Sr. Lectr.
Salter, P. M., MSc Strath., PhD Strath.   Prof; Head*
Research: analysis of force applied in vertebral manipulation; effect of vertebral manipulation on movement; effects of

exercise on problem drinkers; stroke rehabilitation; use of interferential and TENS

Podiatry and Radiography

Conway, Anne-Marie   Sr. Lectr.
Ellis, B. M., BA Open(UK)   Sr. Lectr.
Shenton, P. A.   Head*

Social Sciences, see Management and Soc. Scis.

Speech and Language Sciences

Dean, E. C., BA Open(UK), MEd Edin., PhD Open(UK)   Reader
Hardcastle, W., MA Qld., PhD Edin.   Prof.; Head*
Stansfield, Jois, MSc Lond.   Sr. Lectr.
Other Staff: 6 Lectrs.; 3 Res. Fellows; 2 Clin. Tutors
Research: normal speech and language functioning and aquistion; speech pathology

SPECIAL CENTRES, ETC

Educational Resource Centre

Bain, J.   Supervisor

Information Technology Centre

McLeish, J., BA Open(UK)   Computer Manager
Mortimer, T., BSc Stir.   Head*

International Health Studies, Centre for

Ager, Alistair, BA Keele, MSc Birm., PhD Wales   Prof.; Dir.*
Robson, Patricia, MBE, BSc Lond., MEd Manc.   Sr. Lectr.
Other Staff: 3 Lectrs.; 1 Hon. Prof.; 6 Hon. Lectrs.; 3 Temp. Lectrs.
Research: developing educational provision in professional health care; disability and technology; health economics and developing health systems; NGOs, innovation and development; refugees, displacement and psychosocial assistance

CONTACT OFFICERS

Academic affairs. Vice Principal (Academic Development): Reid, Austin, PhD Belf.
Accommodation. Sampson, Keith, BSc
Admissions (first degree). Easson, Alexis, MA PhD
Admissions (higher degree). Easson, Alexis, MA PhD
Adult/continuing education. Easson, Alexis, MA PhD
Alumni. Duncan, Gordon, BSc BA MEd PhD
Careers. Cook, Christine, BA
Computing services. Mortimer, Tom, BSc
Development/fund-raising. Vice Principal (Strategic Planning and Development): Marshall, Rosalyn, BSc Dund.
Distance education. Easson, Alexis, MA PhD
Equal opportunities. Pithie, Alison, BA
Estates and buildings/works and services. Graham, William
Examinations. Easson, Alexis, MA PhD

Finance. Cutt, Malcolm, LLB
General enquiries. Vice Principal (Strategic Planning and Development): Marshall, Rosalyn, BSc *Dund.*
Industrial liaison. Pithie, Alison, BA
International office. Duncan, Gordon, BSc BA MEd PhD
Library (chief librarian/enquiries). Aitken, Penny, BA
Personnel/human resources. Pithie, Alison, BA
Public relations, information and marketing. Duncan, Gordon, BSc BA MEd PhD

Publications. Duncan, Gordon, BSc BA MEd PhD
Purchasing. Cutt, Malcolm, LLB
Research. Vice Principal (Academic Development): Reid, Austin, PhD *Belf.*
Safety. Bendall, Douglas
Security. Marshall, George
Sport and recreation. Wighton, Charlotte
Staff development and training. Pithie, Alison, BA
Student union. Sim, Juliette

Student welfare/counselling. Vice Principal (Academic Development): Reid, Austin, PhD *Belf.*
Students from other countries. Duncan, Gordon, BSc BA MEd PhD
Students with disabilities. Gillies-Denning, Philip, BA MSc
University press. Duncan, Gordon, BSc BA MEd PhD

[Information supplied by the institution as at 13 April 1998, and edited by the ACU]

QUEEN'S UNIVERSITY OF BELFAST

Founded 1908; previously established as Queen's College, Belfast 1845

Member of the Association of Commonwealth Universities

Postal Address: Belfast, Northern Ireland BT7 1NN
Telephone: (01232) 245133 **Fax**: (01232) 247895 **Cables**: University, Belfast, Northern Ireland
Telex: 74487 QUBADM G **WWW**: http://www.qub.ac.uk

VISITOR—Elizabeth, H.M. The Queen
CHANCELLOR—Orr, Sir David, LLB *Trinity(Dub.)*, Hon. LLD *Trinity(Dub.)*, Hon. LLD *Liv.*, Hon. LLD *N.U.I.*, Hon. LLD *Belf.*, Hon. DUniv *Sur.*
PRO-CHANCELLOR—McGuckian, J. B., BSc(Econ) *Belf.*
PRO-CHANCELLOR—Macmahon, Clare, OBE, BSc *Belf.*
PRESIDENT AND VICE-CHANCELLOR*—Bain, Prof. George S., BA *Manit.*, MA *Manit.*, DPhil *Oxf.*, Hon. DBA *De Mont.*
SENIOR PRO-VICE-CHANCELLOR—Shanks, Prof. Robin G., MD DSc, FRCP, FRCPEd, FRCPI
PRO-VICE-CHANCELLOR—Cormack, Prof. R. J., MA *Aberd.*
PRO-VICE-CHANCELLOR—Clarkson, Prof. L. A., PhD *Nott.*
SECRETARY TO THE ACADEMIC COUNCIL—......
HONORARY TREASURER—Stewart, N., OBE, FCA
ACADEMIC ASSESSOR—Bridges, Prof. J. M., CBE, MD *Belf.*, FRCPEd, FRCP, FRCPath
LIBRARIAN—Russell, Norman J., BA *Belf.*, MPhil *CNAA*
BURSAR—O'Kane, James P. J., BA *CNAA*
ADMINISTRATIVE SECRETARY—Wilson, D. H., JP, BSc *Belf.*
CHAIRMAN OF CONVOCATION—McDowell, J. W., BSc(Econ)

GENERAL INFORMATION

History. The university, founded in 1908, was previously established as Queen's College, Belfast (1845). The main university site is situated within 1km of the centre of Belfast.

Admission to first degree courses (see also United Kingdom Introduction). Through Universities and Colleges Admissions Service (UCAS). Applicants must satisfy the general entrance requirement and specific course requirements, and must have reached the age of 17 on 15 October of year of entry. General requirement may be satisfied in one of a number of ways. 1) General Certificate of Secondary Education (GCSE), General Certificate of Education (GCE) A and AS level, and Scottish Certificate of Education (SCE) ordinary grade and higher grade, with passes in 5 subjects including English language, of which 2 should be at A level (or, for SCE, 3 at higher grade); or 4 subjects including English language, of which 3 should be at A level (or, for SCE, all 4 at higher grade). 2) Business and Technology Education Council (BTEC) National or Higher National Certificate or Diploma at an approved standard. 3) Advanced General National Vocational Qualification (GNVQ) is considered equivalent to 2 A levels, and 6 additional units to a third A level. 4) International Baccalaureate, Diploma. 5) Irish Leaving Certificate, with passes in 5 subjects,

including English, 4 of which should be at higher level (Grade C or better).
An approved test in English may be offered in place of English language.

First Degrees (see also United Kingdom Directory to Subjects of Study). BA, BAgr, BD, BDS, BEd, BEng, BMedSc, BMus, BSc, BSSc, BTh, LLB, MB BCh BAO, MEng.

Higher Degrees (see also United Kingdom Directory to Subjects of Study). LLM, MA, MAcc, MAgr, MArch, MBA, MD, MEd, MMedSc, MSc, MSSc, MSW, MTh, MPhil, PhD, DLitt, DSc, EdD, LLD.

Fees (1998–99). Postgraduate (international students): £6720 (classroom, laboratory, pre-clinical); £10,610 (clinical).

Academic Awards (1997–98). Approximately 20 awards ranging in value from £2000 to £17,500.

Academic Year (1998–99). Two semesters: 28 September–5 February; 8 February–18 June.

Income (1996–97). Total, £124,474,000.

Statistics (1996–97). Staff: 2899 (1454 academic and academic-related). Students: 14,425.

FACULTIES/SCHOOLS

Agriculture and Food Science
Tel: (01232) 255450 Fax: (01232) 668251
Dean: Gilmour, Prof. A., BSc *Strath.*, PhD *Strath.*

Arts
Tel: (01232) 335347 Fax: (01232) 249864
Dean: Lewis, Prof. J. M., BA *Lond.*, PhD *Lond.*

Economics and Social Sciences
Tel: (01232) 273282 Fax: (01232) 232571
Dean: Lyttle, E. G., BA MSSc

Education
Tel: (01232) 337141 Fax: (01232) 248045
Dean: McEwen, A., BA *CNAA*, PhD

Engineering
Tel: (01232) 274002 Fax: (01232) 660831
Dean: Hogg, Prof. B. W., BE *N.U.I.*, PhD *Liv.*, DSc *N.U.I.*, FIEE

Law
Tel: (01232) 273472 Fax: (01232) 325590
Dean: Jackson, Prof. J. D., BA *Durh.*, LLM *Wales*

Medicine
Tel: (01232) 273477 Fax: (01232) 330571
Dean: Stout, Prof. Robert W., MD *Belf.*, DSc *Belf.*, FRCP, FRCPEd, FRCPI, FRCPSGlas

Science

Tel: (01232) 335344 Fax: (01232) 328995
Dean: Brown, Prof. K., MA Aberd., FBPsS

Theology

Tel: (01232) 335108 Fax: (01232) 314058
Dean: Hibbert, Prof. A., MA Oxf., DPhil Oxf.

ACADEMIC UNITS

Accounting, see under Management

Adult Education, School of

Fax: (01232) 236909
Craig, D., BA Belf. Sr. Lectr., Languages
Mezey, Nicole J. A., BA Sus., MA York(UK) Sr. Lectr., Art History
Patten, M. Patricia, OBE, BA Liv. Sr. Lectr.; Head*

Agricultural and Food Science, School of

Tel: (01232) 250666 Fax: (01232) 668384
Blakeman, J. P., BSc Wales, MSc Nott., PhD Nott. Prof., Mycology and Plant Pathology
Collins, M. A., BSc Liv., PhD Edin. Sr. Lectr., Food Microbiology
Cooper, J. E., BA York(UK), DPhil York(UK) Reader, Food Microbiology
Davis, J., BAgr Belf., MSc Newcastle(UK), PhD Belf. Sr. Lectr., Agriculture and Food Economics
Ellis, W. A., PhD Glas., FRCVS Hon. Prof., Veterinary Science
Gibson, C., PhD Wales, DSc Wales Hon. Prof., Aquatic Sciences
Gilmour, A., BSc Strath., PhD Strath. Prof., Food Microbiology; Head*
Goodall, E. A., BA Belf., MSc Belf., PhD Belf. Sr. Lectr., Biometrics
Gordon, Frederick J., BAgr Belf., PhD Belf. Prof., Crop and Animal Production
Harper, D. B., BSc Brist., PhD Lond., FRSChem Prof., Microbial and Fungal Biochemistry
Johnston, D. E., BSc Belf., PhD Belf., FRSChem Sr. Lectr., Food Chemistry
Kilpatrick, D. J., BSc Belf., MSc Edin., PhD Belf. Sr. Lectr., Biometrics
Laidlaw, A. S., BSc Glas., PhD Glas. Sr. Lectr., Agricultural Botany
Marks, R. J., BSc Belf., MSc Lond., PhD Lond. Prof., Applied Plant Science
McAdam, J. H., BSc Belf., MAgr Belf., PhD Belf. Reader, Agricultural Botany
McCaughey, W. J., MA Trinity(Dub.), MVB Trinity(Dub.), MSc Ohio, PhD Trinity(Dub.) Sr. Lectr., Veterinary Science
McCracken, A. R., BSc Strath., PhD Belf. Sr. Lectr., Mycology and Plant Pathology
McCracken, K. J., BSc Belf., BAgr Belf., PhD Camb., FRSChem Reader, Nutrition
McNulty, M. S., PhD Trinity(Dub.) Prof., Veterinary Science
Moss, B. W., BSc Leeds, MSc Lond., PhD Brist. Sr. Lectr., Food Chemistry
Moss, J. E., BSc Ulster, PhD E.Anglia Sr. Lectr., Agricultural and Food Economics
Mowat, D. J., BSc St And., MSc Birm., PhD Belf. Sr. Lectr., Agricultural Zoology
Pearce, J., BSc Liv., PhD Liv., FRSChem Prof., Food Science
Steen, R. W. J., BAgr Belf., PhD Belf. Reader, Crop and Animal Production
Other Staff: 1 Hon. Reader

Archaeology, see under Geoscis.

Architecture, see under Built Environment

Biology and Biochemistry, School of

Davies, R. J. H., MA Camb., PhD Camb. Prof., Biochemistry
Elwood, R. W., BSc Reading, PhD Reading Prof., Animal Behaviour
Ferguson, A., BSc Belf., PhD Belf. Prof., Biology

Halton, D. W., PhD Leeds, DSc Leeds, FIBiol Prof., Parasitology
Martin, S. J., MSc Belf., PhD Belf. Prof., Gene Biochemistry
Rima, B. K., MSc T.H.Delft, PhD McM. Prof., Biology

Biochemistry

Fax: (01232) 236505
Lewis, M. H. R., BSc Wales, PhD Trinity(Dub.) Sr. Lectr.
Wisdom, G. B., BA Trinity(Dub.), PhD Trinity(Dub.) Sr. Lectr.

Biology

Boaden, P. J. S., BSc Belf., PhD Wales Sr. Lectr.
Brown, Fred, PhD Manc., Hon. DSc Belf., FRS Prof. Fellow, Molecular Virology
Cosby, S. L., BSc Belf., PhD Belf. Sr. Lectr.
Dring, M. J., BSc Brist., PhD Lond. Reader, Biology
Elwood, R. W., BSc Reading, PhD Reading Prof., Animal Behaviour
Fairweather, I., BSc Lond., MSc Liv., PhD Lond. Reader
Hickey, G. I., BSc Belf., PhD Glas. Sr. Lectr.
Laming, P. R., BSc Reading, PhD Lond. Reader
Larkin, M. J., BSc CNAA, PhD Wales Sr. Lectr.
Montgomery, W. I., BSc Manc., PhD Manc. Prof.; Head*
Roberts, D., BSc Liv., PhD Liv. Sr. Lectr.
Savidge, G. J., BSc Belf., PhD Wales Reader

Biomedical Science, see Medicine

Built Environment, School of the

Cleland, D. J., BSc Belf., PhD Belf. Prof., Civil Engineering
Doran, I. G., OBE, MSc PhD, FICE, FIStructE, FGS Hon. Prof.
Hendry, J., BArch Liv., MCD Liv., PhD Prof., Environmental Planning
Jennings, A., DSc Manc., FIMA, FIStructE Prof., Civil Engineering
Long, A. E., PhD Belf., DSc Belf., FEng, FICE, FIStructE Prof., Civil Engineering; Head*
Whittaker, T. J. T., BSc Belf., PhD Belf. Prof., Civil Engineering
Woolley, T. A., BArch Edin., PhD Belf. Prof., Architecture

Architecture

Fax: (01232) 682475
Gilfillan, J. R., BSc Belf., PhD Belf. Sr. Lectr.
Johnston, L. J. G., MSc Belf. Sr. Lectr.
Larmour, P. F., MSc Belf., PhD Belf. Reader
Ó Cathain, C. S., BArch N.U.I., MSc Trinity(Dub.) Sr. Lectr.
Wylie, R. J., PhD Belf. Sr. Lectr.

Civil Engineering

Fax: (01232) 663754
Basheer, P. A. Mohammed, BSc(Eng) Kerala, MSc(Eng) Calicut, PhD Sr. Lectr.
Farouki, O. T., MA Oxf., MSE Prin., PhD Prin. Sr. Lectr.
Ferguson, J. D., MSc Leeds Sr. Lectr.
Gilbert, S. G., BSc Belf., PhD Belf. Sr. Lectr.
Johnston, H. T., BSc Belf., PhD Belf. Sr. Lectr.
Kalin, R. M., BSc N.Y., MSc Arizona, PhD Arizona Sr. Lectr.
McKeown, J. J., BSc Belf., BSc Lond., PhD Lond. Sr. Lectr.
Montgomery, F. R., BSc Belf., PhD Belf. Sr. Lectr.
Sloan, T. D., BSc Belf. Sr. Lectr.

Environmental Planning

Fax: (01232) 687652
Caldwell, J. H., MA Belf., PhD Belf. Sr. Lectr.
Greer, J. V., BA Belf., MSc Belf. Sr. Lectr.
McEldowney, J. M., BSc Belf., MCD Liv. Sr. Lectr.
Neill, W. J. V., BSc(Econ) Belf., MSc Belf., MUP Mich., PhD Nott. Sr. Lectr.

Celtic, see under Mod. Langs., Sch. of

Chemistry, School of

Fax: (01232) 382117
Adams, C. J., MA Oxf., DPhil Oxf., FRSChem Hon. Prof.
Boyd, D. R., PhD Belf., DSc Belf., FRSChem Prof.
Burnett, M. G., MA Camb., PhD Camb. Sr. Lectr.
Burns, D. T., BSc Leeds, PhD Leeds, DSc Lough., FRSChem, FRSEd Prof., Analytical Chemistry
De Silva, A. P., BSc Ceyl., PhD Belf. Reader
Fawcett, A. H., BSc Leeds, PhD Belf. Reader
Green, M. J., BSc Lond., PhD UMIST Hon. Prof.
Holmes, R. G. G., PhD UMIST, Hon. DSc De Mont. Hon. Prof.
Malone, J. F., BSc N.U.I., PhD Leeds Sr. Lectr.; Head*
McGarvey, J. J., BSc Belf., PhD Belf., FRSChem Prof.
McKee, E. Vickie, BSc Belf., PhD Belf., FNZIC Reader
McKervey, M. A., PhD Belf., DSc Belf., FRSChem Prof., Organic Chemistry
Nelson, J., MSc Belf., PhD Belf., FRSChem Hon. Prof.
Rooney, J. J., BSc Belf., PhD Belf. Prof., Catalytic Chemistry
Seddon, K. R., BSc Liv., MA Oxf., PhD Liv. Prof., Inorganic Chemistry
Walker, B. J., BSc Leic., PhD Leic., FRSChem Reader

Classics, see Greek, Roman and Semitic Studies, Sch. of

Computer Science, see under Engin., Electr., and Computer Sci.

Continuing Education, Institute of, see Special Centres, etc

Dentistry, see Medicine (Clin. Dent.)

Economic and Social History, see under Soc. Scis., Sch. of

Economics, see under Soc. Scis., Sch. of

Education, Graduate School of

Fax: (01232) 239263
Gallagher, A. M., MSc Belf., PhD Belf. Reader
Gardner, J. R., MSc Belf., PhD Belf. Reader; Head*
Leitch, M. R., MA Dund., MSc Belf. Sr. Lectr.
McBride, F. V., MSc Belf., PhD Belf. Hon. Prof.
McEwen, A., BA CNAA, PhD Belf. Prof.
McMillen, A. R., BSc Belf. Sr. Lectr.
Wallace, I. H., BSc Belf. Hon. Prof.

Engineering, Aeronautical, see under Engin., Mech. and Process

Engineering, Chemical, see under Engin., Mech. and Process

Engineering, Civil, see under Built Environment

Engineering, Control, see under Engin., Electr., and Computer Sci.

Engineering, Electrical, and Computer Science

Fax: (01232) 331332
Clint, M., MSc Belf., PhD Belf. Prof., Computer Science
Cowan, C. F. N., BSc Edin., PhD Edin. Royal Academy of Engineering/Northern Telecom Res. Prof., Telecommunications Systems Engineering
Crookes, D., BSc Belf., PhD Belf. Prof., Computer Engineering
Gamble, H. S., BSc Belf., PhD Belf. Prof., Microelectronic Engineering

Hogg, Brian W., BE N.U.I., PhD Liv., DSc
N.U.I., FIEE   Prof., Electrical Engineering
Irwin, G. W., BSc Belf., PhD Belf.   Prof.,
Control Engineering
McCanny, J. V., BSc Manc., DPhil Ulster, FEng,
FIEE   Prof., Microelectronic Engineering
Perrott, R. H., BSc Belf., PhD Belf.   Prof.,
Software Engineering
Smith, F. J., BSc Belf., MA C.U.A., PhD Belf.,
FIMA   Prof., Computer Science; Head*
Stewart, J. A. C., BSc Belf., PhD Belf.,
FIEE   Prof., Communications Engineering

Computer Science
Fax: (01232) 331332
Fay, D. Q. M., BTech Lough.   Sr. Lectr.
McKeag, R. M., MSc Lond.   Sr. Lectr.
Milligan, P., BSc Belf., PhD Belf.   Sr. Lectr.
Scott, N. S., BSc Belf., PhD Belf.   Reader

Control Engineering
No staff at present

Digital Signal Processing
Marshall, A. J., BSc Ulster, PhD Aberd.   Sr.
Lectr., Digital Communications
Vaseghi, S. V., BSc Newcastle(UK), PhD
Camb.   Reader
Woods, R. F., BSc Belf., PhD Belf.   Sr. Lectr.

Electrical and Electronic Engineering
Fax: (01232) 667023
Armstrong, B. M., BSc Belf., PhD Belf.   Reader
Armstrong, G. A., BSc Belf., PhD Belf.   Reader
Beattie, W. C., BSc Belf., PhD Brist., FIEE   Sr.
Lectr.
Doherty, J. G., MSc Belf., PhD Belf.   Sr. Lectr.
Fox, B., BScBelf., PhD Belf.   Reader
Fusco, V. F., BSc Belf., PhD Belf.   Prof., High
Frequency Electronic Engineering
Hossain, S. Q. A. M. A., BSc Bihar, MScTech
Manc.   Sr. Lectr.
McCaughan, D. V., BSc Belf., PhD Belf., DSc
Belf., FIP   Prof. Fellow of the Univ.
Swidenbank, E., BSc Belf., PhD Belf.   Sr. Lectr.
Tindall, C. E., BSc Durh., PhD Newcastle(UK)   Sr.
Lectr.
Wilkinson, A. J., BSc Belf., PhD Belf., FIEE   Sr.
Lectr.

Engineering, Manufacturing, see under
Engin., Mech. and Process

Engineering, Mechanical and Process
Fax: (01232) 661729
Armstrong, C. G., BSc Belf., PhD Belf.   Prof.
Beatty, E. K., MBE, BSc Belf., PhD Belf.,
FIMechE   Hon. Prof.
Crawford, R. J., PhD Belf., DSc Belf., FIMechE,
FIM   Prof., Mechanical and Manufacturing
Engineering; Head*
Fleck, R., BSc Belf., PhD Belf.   Prof.
McKie, P., BSc Belf.   Hon. Prof.
Murphy, W. R., BSc Belf., FIChemE,
FRSChem   Prof., Chemical Engineering
Storrar, A. M., MA Camb., PhD Camb.   Prof.,
Manufacturing Systems Engineering
Weatherley, L. R., BSc Belf., PhD Belf.,
FIChemE   Prof., Process Engineering

Aeronautical Engineering
Fax: (01232) 382701
Cooper, R. K., BEng Syd., PhD Syd.   Sr. Lectr.
Raghunathan, S. R., BE Mys., MTech IIT Bombay,
MSc Belf., PhD IIT Bombay, DSc Belf.,
FRAeS   Prof.
Sterling, S. G., BSc(Eng) Lond., MSc Cran.IT   Sr.
Lectr.

Chemical Engineering
Fax: (01232) 381753
Allen, S. J., BSc Belf., PhD Belf.   Sr. Lectr.
Cooper, T. J. R., BSc Belf., PhD Belf.,
FIMechE   Sr. Lectr.
Holland, C. R., BSc(Tech) Sheff., PhD Sheff.   Sr.
Lectr.
Magee, T. R. A., BSc Belf., PhD Belf.   Sr. Lectr.
McNally, G. M. P., MSc Belf.   Sr. Lectr.

Mechanical and Manufacturing Engineering
Fax: (01232) 661729
Armstrong, P. J., BSc Belf., PhD Belf.   Sr. Lectr.
Artt, D. W., BSc Belf., PhD Belf.   Reader
Austin, B. A., BSc Belf., PhD Belf.   Sr. Lectr.
Douglas, R., BSc Belf., PhD Belf.   Sr. Lectr.
Gallagher, A. P., MSc N.U.I., PhD Belf.   Sr.
Lectr., Engineering Mathematics
Hinds, B. K., BSc Belf., PhD Belf.   Sr. Lectr.
Kenny, R. G., BSc Belf., PhD Belf.   Sr. Lectr.
McCartney, J., BSc Belf., PhD Belf.   Sr. Lectr.
Orr, J. F., BSc Belf., PhD Belf.   Reader
Skelton, W. J., BSc Belf., PhD Belf.   Sr. Lectr.
Thompson, S., BSc Salf., MSc City(UK),
PhD   Reader
Williams, J. D., BSc Manc., MScTech Manc., PhD
Manc., FIM   Sr. Lectr.
Wright, E. J., BSc Belf., PhD Belf.   Reader

English, School of
Fax: (01232) 314615
Allen, M. L., MA Leeds, PhD Birm.   Sr. Lectr.
Andrew, Malcolm R., MA Camb., MA S.Fraser,
DPhil York(UK)   Prof., English Language &
Literature
Caraher, B. G., MA N.Y.State, PhD
N.Y.State   Prof.
Douglas-Cowie, Ellen E., BA Ulster, DPhil
Ulster   Sr. Lectr.; Head*
Fitzgerald, Jennifer M. P., MA N.U.I., PhD
Camb.   Sr. Lectr.
Longley, Edna, BA Trinity(Dub.)   Prof., English
Literature
Magennis, H., MA Belf., PhD Belf.   Sr. Lectr.
Prior, R., MA Camb., MA Sus.   Sr. Lectr.
Simpson, P. W., BA Ulster, PhD Ulster   Reader
Thompson, J. J., MA Belf., DPhil York(UK)   Sr.
Lectr.

Food Science, see Agric. and Food Sci., Sch.
of

French, see under Mod. Langs., Sch. of

Geosciences, School of
Fax: (01232) 321280
Baillie, M. G. L., BSc Belf., PhD Belf.   Prof.,
Archaeology and Palaeoecology
Hitzman, M. W., BA Dartmouth, MS Wash., PhD
Stan.   Hon. Prof., Earth Resources
Livingstone, D. N., BA Belf., PhD Belf.,
FBA   Prof., Geography and Intellectual
History
Orford, J. D., BA Keele, MSc Salf., PhD
Reading   Prof., Physical Geography
Pilcher, J. R., BSc Lond., PhD Belf.   Prof.,
Archaeology and Palaeoecology
Simpson, D. D. A., MA Edin., FSA   Prof.,
Archaeology and Palaeoecology
Whalley, W. B., BSc Leic., PhD Camb.   Prof.,
Physical Geography; Head*
Wright, A. D., BSc Nott., PhD, FGS   Prof.†,
Geology

Archaeology and Palaeoecology
Avery, M., MA Oxf., DPhil Oxf.   Sr. Lectr.
Mallory, J. P., AB Calif., PhD Calif.   Reader
McNeill, T. E., MA Oxf., PhD Belf., FSA   Sr.
Lectr.

Environmental Monitoring
McCormac, F. G., BSc Ulster, PhD CNAA   Sr.
Lectr.

Geography
Douglas, J. N. H., BA Belf., PhD Wales   Sr.
Lectr.
Proudfoot, L. J., BA Belf., MA Birm., PhD
Belf.   Reader
Smith, B. J., BSc Reading, PhD Reading   Reader
Tomlinson, R. W., BSc Hull, PhD Hull   Sr.
Lectr.

Geology
Anderson, T. B., BSc Belf., PhD Liv., FGS   Sr.
Lectr.
Jones, K. A., BSc Wales, PhD Wales, FGS   Sr.
Lectr.

Leslie, A. G., BSc Aberd., PhD Aberd.   Sr. Lectr.
Meighan, I. G., BSc Edin., PhD Belf., FGS   Sr.
Lectr., Geochemistry
Parnell, J., BA Camb., PhD Lond.   Reader

Greek, Roman and Semitic Studies, School of
Fax: (01232) 315325
Beattie, D. R. G., MA Trinity(Dub.), PhD St
And.   Sr. Lectr., Semitic Studies
Campbell, J. B., BA Belf., DPhil Oxf.   Reader,
Ancient History
Mullet, Margaret E., BA Birm., PhD Birm.,
FSA   Sr. Lectr., Byzantine Studies
Whitehead, D., MA Camb., PhD Camb.   Prof.;
Head*
Williams, F. J., MA Oxf., PhD Lond.   Prof.,
Greek

History, Ancient, see Greek, Roman and
Semitic Studies, Sch. of

History and Philosophy of Science, see
under Philos. and Anthropol. Studies, Sch. of

History, Modern, School of, see also under
Soc. Scis., Sch. of (Econ. and Soc. Hist.)
Fax: (01232) 314611
Connolly, S. J., BA Trinity(Dub.), DPhil
Ulster   Prof., Irish History
Flanagan, Marie T., MA N.U.I., DPhil Oxf.   Sr.
Lectr.
Green, I. M., MA Oxf., DPhil Oxf.,
FRHistS   Prof.
Green, Judith A., BA Lond., DPhil Oxf.,
FRHistS   Reader
Hempton, D. N., PhD St And., BA,
FRHistS   Prof.; Head*
Jackson, T. A., BA Oxf., MA Oxf., DPhil Oxf.,
FRHistS   Reader
Jupp, P. J., BA Reading, PhD Reading,
FRHistS   Prof.
Lynn, M. R. S., MA Lond., PhD Lond.,
FRHistS   Sr. Lectr.
Middleton, C. R., BA Exe., PhD Exe.   Reader,
American History
O'Dowd, Mary, BA N.U.I., PhD N.U.I.   Sr.
Lectr.
Wichert, S.   Sr. Lectr.

Information Management, see under
Management, Sch. of

Irish Studies, see Hist., Mod., and Special
Centres, etc

Law, School of, see also Special Centres, etc
(Professl. Legal Studies, Inst. of)
Fax: (01232) 325590
Boyd, D., LLB Belf.   Sr. Lectr., Commercial and
Property Law
Capper, D. J. S., LLB Belf., LLM Camb.   Sr.
Lectr., Private Law
Childs, B. A., LLB Hull   Sr. Lectr., Private Law
Dawson, Norma M., LLB Belf.   Prof.,
Commercial and Property Law
Doran, S., LLB Belf., MPhil Camb.   Reader,
Public Law
Dowling, J. A., LLB Belf., PhD Belf.   Sr. Lectr.,
Private Law
Geary, R. V., LLB Strath., LLM Glas.   Sr. Lectr.,
Jurisprudence
Greer, D. S., BCL Oxf., LLD   Prof., Common
Law
Hadden, T. B., BA Camb., LLB Camb., PhD
Camb.   Prof.†
Hadfield, Brigid V. A. M. M., LLB Edin.,
LLM   Prof., Public Law
Harkness, E. E., LLM Belf.   Sr. Lectr., Private
Law
Ingram, P. G., MA McG., LLM Edin., PhD
Edin.   Sr. Lectr., Jurisprudence
Jackson, J. D., BA Durh., LLM Wales   Reader,
Public Law; Head*
Lavery, C. R., BCL Oxf., LLB Belf.   Sr. Lectr.,
Public Law

Leith, P., BSc Edin., PhD Open(UK) Reader, Jurisprudence
McMahon, J. A., LLB Edin., PhD Edin. Reader, Public Law
Morison, J. W. E., LLB Wales, PhD Wales Prof., Jurisprudence
Sartor, G., PhD European Univ.Inst. Prof., Jurisprudence
Stannard, J. E., BA Oxf., BCL Oxf., PhD Belf. Sr. Lectr., Public Law
Steele, R. E. A., LLB Belf., MBA Belf. Sr. Lectr., Commercial and Property Law

Management, School of

Fax: (01232) 328649, 248372

Barrett, T. F., BCom N.U.I., MA Lanc., PhD Cran.IT Prof.
Jeffcut, P., BSc Lond., MEd Manc., PhD Manc. Prof., Management Knowledge
Kitchen, P., BA CNAA, MSc Manc., MBSc Manc., PhD Keele Martin Naughton Prof., Business Strategy
Moore, M. J., BA Trinity(Dub.), MSc S'ton., PhD N.U.I. Prof., Finance; Head*

Accounting

Fax: (01232) 328649

Forker, J. J., BSc(Econ) Lond., MSc Lond. Prof., Accounting and Finance
McKillop, D. G., BSc Ulster, MSc(Econ) Ulster Prof., Accounting and Finance
Nesbitt, D. W. G., BSc(Econ) Belf. Sr. Lectr.
Radcliffe, G. W., MA Oxf., FCA Sr. Lectr., Accounting and Finance
Sangster, A. J. A., BA CNAA, MSc Strath. Prof., Accounting

Information Management

Davies, C. A., BA Belf. Sr. Lectr., Management and Information Systems
Hill, Frances M., BA Belf., MBA Belf., PhD Belf. Sr. Lectr.
MacLaran, E. P., MA Ulster Sr. Lectr., Marketing
Philip, G., BSc Kerala, MSc Agra, MSc Sheff., PhD Bom. Prof.
Titterington, A. J., BSc Liv., MBA Sr. Lectr.

Mathematics and Physics, School of

Armitage, D. H., BSc Liv., PhD Liv. Prof., Pure Mathematics
Bailey, M. E., MA Camb., MSc Sus., PhD Edin. Hon. Prof.
Bates, B., MSc Nott., PhD Lond. Prof., Physics
Burke, P. G., CBE, BSc Lond., PhD Lond., Hon. DSc Exe., FIP, FAPS, FRS Prof., Mathematical Physics
Crothers, D. S. F., MA Oxf., PhD Belf., FIP, FIMA, FIEE, FAPS Prof., Theoretical Physics
Dufton, P. L., MA Camb., PhD Camb. Prof., Physics
Dunwoody, J., BSc Belf., PhD Belf., FIMA Prof., Theoretical Mechanics
Earnshaw, J. C., BSc Durh., PhD Durh., FIP Prof., Physics
Finnis, M. W., MA Camb., PhD Camb. Prof., Physics
Hibbert, A., MA Oxf., DPhil Oxf. Prof., Applied Mathematics
Keenan, F. P., BSc Belf., PhD Belf. Prof., Physics
Kingston, Arthur E., BSc Lond., PhD Lond., FIP Prof., Theoretical Atomic Physics
Lewis, C. L. S., BSc Belf., PhD Belf. Prof., Experimental Physics
Lynden-Bell, Ruth M., MA Camb., PhD Camb., ScD Camb., FIP, FRSChem Prof., Condensed Matter Simulation
Menon, A. K., BTech Tennessee, MSc Tennessee, DEng Stan. Hon. Prof.
Patterson, T. N. L., BSc Belf., PhD Belf., FIMA Prof., Numerical Analysis
Peacock, N. Hon. Prof., Mathematical Physics
Phillips, K. J. H., BSc Lond., PhD Lond. Hon. Prof.
Taylor, K. T. A., BSc Belf., PhD Belf. Prof.
Walmsley, D. G., MSc McM., PhD McM., DSc Belf., FIP Prof., Physics; Head*

Wickstead, A. W., MA Camb., PhD Lond. Prof., Pure Mathematics

Applied Mathematics and Theoretical Physics

Fax: (01232) 239182

Bell, K. L., BSc Belf., MA Calif., PhD Belf., FIP, FAPS Prof., Theoretical Physics
Berrington, K. A., BSc Birm., PhD Durh. Reader
Fitzsimmons, A., BSc Sus., PhD Leic. Reader, Observational Astrophysics
Reid, R. H. G., BSc Belf., PhD Belf. Sr. Lectr.
Rudge, M. R. H., BSc Lond., PhD Lond. Reader
Swain, S., BA Camb., PhD Nott. Prof., Quantum Optics
Walters, H. R. J., BA Camb., PhD Camb. Reader

Engineering Mathematics

Sprevak, D., MSc Lond., MSc Cuyo, PhD Cuyo Sr. Lectr.

Operational Research

Davison, W. D., MSc Belf., PhD Camb. Sr. Lectr.
Hudson, P. D., BA Camb., PhD Manc. Sr. Lectr.

Pure and Applied Physics

Fax: (01232) 438918

Atkinson, R., BSc Salf., PhD Salf., FIP Reader
Coulter, J. R. M., BSc Belf., PhD Belf. Sr. Lectr.
Dawson, P., BSc Ulster, DPhil Ulster Sr. Lectr.
Duncan, I., BSc St And., PhD Reading Sr. Lectr.
Findlay, D., BSc Aberd., PhD Aberd. Sr. Lectr.
Geddes, J., BSc Belf., PhD Belf., FIP Prof.
Graham, W. G., BSc Belf., PhD Belf., FIP, FAPS Prof., Physics
Greer, R. G. H., BSc Belf., PhD Belf. Sr. Lectr.
Lamb, M. J., BSc Belf., PhD Belf. Sr. Lectr.
Latimer, C. J., BSc Belf., PhD Belf., FIP Prof.
McCullough, R. W., BSc Belf., PhD Belf. Reader
Mee, C. H. B., MA Camb., MSc Birm., PhD Birm., FIP Sr. Lectr.
Morrow, T., BSc Belf., PhD Belf. Reader
Simpson, F. Rosemary, BSc Belf., PhD Belf. Sr. Lectr. (on secondment to Academic Council)
Whitaker, M. A. B., MA Oxf., PhD Nott., FIP, FIMA Reader
Williams, I. D., BSc Belf., PhD Belf. Reader

Pure Mathematics

Glass, K. W. H., BSc Belf., PhD Indiana Sr. Lectr.
McCartan, S. D., MSc Belf., PhD Belf. Sr. Lectr.
McMaster, T. B. M., MSc Belf., PhD Belf. Sr. Lectr.

Statistics

Cran, G. W., BSc Aberd., PhD Belf. Sr. Lectr.

Medicine, see below

Microbiology, see Medicine (Clin. Med.), below

Modern Languages, School of

Fax: (01232) 324549

Bales, R. M., BA Exe., MA Kansas, PhD Lond. Prof., French
Broome, P., BA Nott., PhD Nott. Prof., French
Johnston, D. W., PhD Ulster, BA Prof., Hispanic Studies

Celtic

Andrews, R. M., BA Wales, MPhil N.U.I. Sr. Lectr.
O'Muraile, E. N., MA N.U.I., PhD N.U.I. Sr. Lectr.

French

Davies, S. F., MA Exe., PhD Exe. Reader
Lewis, J. M., BA Lond., PhD Lond. Sr. Lectr.; Head*
Shorley, C. M. J., BA Oxf., DPhil Oxf. Sr. Lectr.
Tame, P. D., BA Lond., PhD Lond. Sr. Lectr.

Music, School of

Fax: (01232) 238484

Alcorn, M. P., BA Ulster, MMus Durh., PhD Durh. Sr. Lectr.
Carver, A. F., BMus Birm., PhD Birm. Sr. Lectr.
Marsden, A. A., BA S'ton., PhD Camb. Sr. Lectr.
Smaczny, J. A., MA Oxf., DPhil Oxf. Prof.; Head*
Woodfield, I. D., BMus Nott., MMus Lond., PhD Lond. Reader

Palaeoecology, see under Geoscis., Sch. of (Archaeol. and Palaeoecol.)

Pharmacy, School of

Fax: (01232) 247794

Collier, P. S., BPharm Lond., PhD Belf. Sr. Lectr.
Gorman, S. P., BSc Belf., PhD Belf. Reader
Jones, D. S., BSc Belf., PhD Belf. Sr. Lectr.
McCafferty, D. F., BSc Belf., PhD Belf. Reader
McElnay, J. C., BSc Belf., PhD Belf. Reader; Head*
Scott, Eileen M., BSc Belf., PhD Belf. Sr. Lectr.
Swanton, J. G., BSc Edin., PhD Edin. Sr. Lectr.
Woolfson, A. D., BSc Belf., PhD Belf., FRSChem Reader

Philosophical and Anthropological Studies, School of

Donnan, H. S. C., BA Sus., DPhil Sus. Prof.
Evans, J. D. G., MA Camb., PhD Camb. Prof., Logic and Metaphysics
Tonkin, J. Elizabeth, MA Oxf., DPhil Oxf. Prof., Social Anthropology; Head*

History and Philosophy of Science

Bowler, P. J., BA Camb., MSc Sus., PhD Tor. Prof.

Philosophy

Cullen, Bernard A., BA Belf., BSc(Econ) Belf., MA Mich., PhD Mich. Prof.
Gorman, J. L., MA Edin., PhD Camb. Prof., Moral Philosophy

Scholastic Philosophy

Bredin, H. T., BA N.U.I., MA Belf., PhD Belf. Sr. Lectr.
Daly, J. P., BA N.U.I., LPh Maynooth Sr. Lectr.

Social Anthropology

McFarlane, W. G., BA Belf., PhD Belf. Sr. Lectr.
Milton, K., BA Durh., PhD Belf. Reader
Quigley, D., BSc Lond., MPhil Camb., PhD Lond. Reader

Physics, Pure and Applied, see under Maths. and Phys.

Physics, Theoretical, see under Maths. and Phys. (Appl. Maths. and Theoret. Phys.)

Political Science, see under Soc. Scis., Sch. of

Psychology, School of

Fax: (01232) 664144

Brown, K., MA Aberd., FPsSI, FBPsS Prof.; Head*
Byth, W., MA Aberd., PhD Aberd. Sr. Lectr.
Cowie, R. I. D., BA Stir., DPhil Sus. Sr. Lectr.
Greer, G. B., BA Camb., MSc Belf., PhD Belf. Reader
Hale, D. J., MSc Manc. Sr. Lectr.
Hepper, P. G., BSc Exe., PhD Durh., FBPsS Prof.
Kremer, J. M. B., BSc Lough., PhD Lough. Reader
McGuinness, Carol M., MA N.U.I., PhD Belf. Sr. Lectr.
Moriarty, Ann, BA Sheff., MPhil Glas., PhD Lond. Sr. Lectr.
Mulhern, G. A., BSc Liv., PhD Belf. Sr. Lectr.
Reilly, J., BSSc Belf., PhD Belf. Sr. Lectr.
Sheehy, N. P., MA N.U.I., PhD Wales, FBPsS Prof., Psychology

Sneddon, I. A., BSc *St And.*, PhD *St And.* Sr. Lectr.

Sykes, D. H., BA *Liv.*, MA *Qu.*, PhD *McG.* Sr. Lectr.

Trew, Karen J., BA PhD Sr. Lectr.

Roman Studies, see Greek, Roman and Semitic Studies

Semitic Studies, see Greek, Roman and Semitic Studies

Social Anthropology, see under Philos. and Anthropol. Studies, Sch. of

Social Sciences, School of

Fax: (01232) 242136

Bew, P. A. E., MA *Camb.*, PhD *Camb.* Prof., Irish Politics

Breen, R. J., MA *Camb.*, PhD *Camb.* Prof., Sociology

Brewer, J. D., BA *Nott.*, MSocSc *Birm.* Prof., Sociology

Brown, K. D., BA *Reading*, MA *McM.*, PhD *Kent*, FRHistS Prof., Economics and Social History

Canning, D. J. H., BA *Camb.*, PhD *Camb.* Prof., Economics

Clarkson, L. A., BA *Nott.*, PhD *Nott.* Prof., Social History

Cormack, R. J., MA *Aberd.* Prof., Sociology

Eccleshall, R. R., BA *Hull*, PhD *Hull* Prof., Politics

Guelke, A. B., MA *Cape Town*, PhD *Lond.* Prof., Politics

Iwaniec, Stanislawa D., MA *Cracow*, PhD *Leic.* Prof., Social Work

Meehan, Elizabeth M., BA *Sus.*, DPhil *Oxf.* Prof., Politics

Spencer, J. E., BSc(Econ) Prof., Economics; Head*

Velupillai, K., BE *Kyoto*, MSocSci *Lund*, PhD *Camb.* Prof., Economics

Economic and Social History

Fax: (01232) 314768

Campbell, B. M. S., BA *Liv.*, PhD *Camb.* Prof.

Davies, A. C., MA *Wales*, AM *Prin.*, PhD *Belf.* Reader

Johnson, D. S., BA *Oxf.*, BPhil *Oxf.* Sr. Lectr.

Kennedy, L., MSc *N.U.I.*, DPhil *York(UK)* Reader

Economics

Fax: (01232) 242136

Black, J. B. H., BA *Oxf.*, MBA *Col.*, MIA *Col.*, PhD *Belf.* Sr. Lectr.

Bradley, J. F., BComm *N.U.I.*, BA *N.U.I.*, MEconSc *N.U.I.* Sr. Lectr.

Hitchens, D. M. W. N., BScEcon *Wales*, PhD *Aston* Prof.

Jefferson, C. W., BSc(Econ) *Belf.*, PhD *Belf.* Sr. Lectr.

McGurnaghan, M. A., BSc(Econ) Sr. Lectr.

Prendergast, Catherine C., BE *N.U.I.*, MEconSc *N.U.I.*, PhD *Belf.* Sr. Lectr.

Trewsdale, Janet M., BA *York(UK)* Sr. Lectr.

Political Science

Fax: (01232) 235373

Elliott, S., BA *Belf.*, PhD *Belf.* Sr. Lectr.

English, R. L., BA *Oxf.*, PhD *Keele*, FRHistS Reader

Geoghegan, V., BA *Newcastle(UK)*, PhD *Newcastle(UK)*, FRHistS Prof., Politics

Jay, R., MA *Oxf.*, MPhil *Oxf.* Sr. Lectr.

Larres, K. W., MA *Cologne*, DrPhil *Cologne*, FRHistS Reader

Walker, G. S. W., MA *Glas.*, MA *McM.*, PhD *Manc.* Reader

Wilford, R. A., BSc *Lond.*, MSc *Bath*, PhD *Wales* Sr. Lectr.

Social Studies

Fax: (01232) 320668

Hayes, B. C., BSocSc *N.U.I.*, MA *Duquesne*, PhD *Calg.* Reader

McLaughlin, Eithne, BA *Belf.*, MPhil *Camb.*, PhD *Belf.* Prof.

Miller, R. L., BA *Duke*, MA *Flor.*, PhD *Belf.* Sr. Lectr.

O'Dowd, L. G., MA *N.U.I.*, PhD *S.Illinois* Prof., Sociology and Social Policy

O'Hearn, D. A., BA *New Mexico*, AM *Mich.*, PhD *Mich.* Reader

Social Work

Fax: (01232) 239907

Kelly, G. M., BSc(Econ) *Belf.*, MSSc *Belf.* Sr. Lectr.

O'Hagan, K. P., BA *N.U.I.*, MPhil *York(UK)* Reader

Pinkerton, J. R., MSc *Lond.*, MSSc *Belf.*, PhD *Belf.* Sr. Lectr.

Statistics, see under Maths. and Phys.

Theology, see Edgehill Theological College, Irish Baptist College, St Mary's College (Religious Studies) and Union Theological College, below

MEDICINE

Biomedical Science, School of

Fax: (01232) 248052, 331838

Anatomy

Fax: (01232) 235483

Carr, Katharine E., BSc *Glas.*, PhD *Glas.* Prof.; Head*

Meban, C., BSc *Belf.*, MD *Belf.*, PhD *Belf.* Prof.

Owens, P. D. A., BSc *Belf.*, BDS *Belf.*, PhD *Belf.* Reader

Wilson, David J., BSc *Wales*, PhD *Wales* Sr. Lectr.

Physiology

Allen, J. D., MD *Belf.* Reader

Allen, Judith A., BSc *Belf.*, MD *Belf.* Sr. Lectr.

McGeown, J. G., BSc MB *Belf.* Sr. Lectr.

McHale, N. G., BSc *Belf.*, PhD *Belf.* Prof.

Scholfield, C. N., BSc *Lond.*, PhD *Lond.* Sr. Lectr.

Thornbury, K. D., BSc *Belf.*, MB *Belf.*, PhD *Belf.* Sr. Lectr.

Wallace, W. F. M., BSc *Belf.*, MD *Belf.*, FRCA, FRCP Prof., Applied Physiology

Clinical Dentistry, School of

Fax: (01232) 438861

Douglas, W. H., BDS *Lond.*, MSc *Belf.*, PhD *Belf.* Hon. Prof.

Lamey, P. J., BSc *Edin.*, BDS *Edin.*, MB ChB *Glas.*, DDS *Edin.*, FDSRCPSGlas, FFDRCSI Prof., Oral Medicine

Mulally, B. H., MDS *Glas.*, FDSRCPSGlas Sr. Lectr.

Dental Radiology

No staff at present

Dental Surgery

Cowan, G. C., BDS, FDSRCS, FFDRCSI Sr. Lectr.

McGimpsey, J. G., BSc MDS, FDSRCPSGlas, FFDRCSI Prof.

Dentistry: Orthodontics

Burden, D., BDS *Belf.*, PhD *Belf.*, FDSRCPSGlas, FFDRCSI Sr. Lectr.

Richardson, A., BDS *St And.*, MSc, FFDRCSI Prof.

Dentistry, Paediatric and Preventive

Freeman, Ruth E., BDS *Belf.*, MMedSc *Belf.*, MSc *Lond.*, PhD *Belf.* Sr. Lectr.

Kinirons, M. J., BDS *N.U.I.*, PhD *Belf.*, FDSRCS, FFDRCSI Sr. Lectr.

Dentistry, Restorative

Benington, I. C., OBE, BDS *Belf.*, FDSRCS, FFDRCSI, FDSRCPSGlas Prof., Dental Prosthetics and Materials; Head*

Clifford, T. J., BDS, FDSRCPSGlas Sr. Lectr.

Hussey, D. L., BDS, FDSRCPSGlas Sr. Lectr.

Kennedy, J. G., BSc *Belf.*, MDS *Belf.*, PhD *Belf.*, FDSRCPSGlas Sr. Lectr.

Linden, G. J., BSc *Belf.*, BDS *N.U.I.*, FDSRCS Sr. Lectr.

Russell, M. D., BDS *Lond.*, MSc *Manc.*, FDSRCS Sr. Lectr.

Vacant Posts: 1 Prof. (Periodontics)

Clinical Medicine, School of

Fax: (01232) 324543

Anaesthetics

Fax: (01232) 329605

Fee, J. P. H., MD *Belf.*, PhD *Belf.*, FFARCSI Prof.

Mirakhur, R., MD *Delhi*, PhD, FFARCS, FFARCSI Prof.

Biochemistry, Clinical

Fax: (01232) 236143

Ennis, M., BSc *Lond.*, PhD *Lond.* Sr. Lectr.

Trimble, Elisabeth R., MD *Belf.*, FRCP, FRCPath Prof.

Young, I. S., BSc *Belf.*, MD *Belf.* Sr. Lectr.

Child Health

Fax: (01232) 236455

Carson, D. J., MB *Belf.*, FRCP Sr. Lectr.

Glasgow, J. F. T., BSc *Belf.*, MD *Belf.*, FRCP, FRCPI Reader

Halliday, H., MD *Belf.*, FRCP, FRCPEd Hon. Prof.

McClure, B. G., MB *Belf.*, FRCPEd Prof., Neonatal Medicine

Savage, J. M., MB *Belf.*, FRCP Sr. Lectr.

Shields, M. D., MB *Brist.*, MD *Belf.* Sr. Lectr.

Epidemiology and Public Health

Fax: (01232) 236298

Evans, A. E., MD *Belf.*, FRCP Prof., Epidemiology

Gavin, Anna T., MSc *Belf.*, MB *Belf.* Sr. Lectr.

Kee, F., BSc *Belf.*, MSc *Edin.*, MD *Belf.* Sr. Lectr.

Patterson, C. C., BSc *Belf.*, MSc *Lond.*, PhD *Belf.* Sr. Lectr.

Stewart, Moira C., MD *Belf.*, FRCP Sr. Lectr.

Yarnell, J. W. G., MD *Manc.* Sr. Lectr.

Vacant Posts: 1 Prof.

General Practice

Fax: (01232) 310202

Cupples, Margaret E., BSc *Belf.*, MD *Belf.* Sr. Lectr.

Gilliland, A. E. W., MD *Belf.* Sr. Lectr.

McGlade, K. J., MD *Belf.*, MSc *Belf.* Sr. Lectr.

McKnight, Agnes, MD *Belf.*, FRCGP Sr. Lectr.

Reilly, P. M., MD *Belf.*, FRCGP Prof.

Steele, W. K., MD *Belf.*, FRCGP Sr. Lectr.

Geriatric Medicine

Fax: (01232) 325839

Passmore, A. P., BSc *Belf.*, MD *Belf.*, FRCP, FRCSGlas Sr. Lectr.

Rea, I. M., BSc *Belf.*, MB *Belf.*, FRCP, FRCPEd Sr. Lectr.

Stout, Robert W., MD *Belf.*, DSc *Belf.*, FRCP, FRCPEd, FRCPI, FRCPSGlas Prof.

Haematology

Fax: (01232) 325272

Lappin, T. R. J., MSc *Belf.*, PhD *Belf.*, FRCPath Prof.

McMullin, M. F., MD *Belf.*, FRCP, FRCPI Sr. Lectr.

Other Staff: 1 Hon. Reader

History of Medicine

No staff at present

Medical Genetics

Fax: (01232) 236911

Hughes, A. E., BSc *Belf.*, PhD *Belf.* Reader

Nevin, N. C., BSc *Belf.*, MD *Belf.*, FRCP, FRCPath, FRCPEd Prof.

Medicine

Fax: (01232) 329899

Adgey, A. A. J., MD *Belf.*, FRCP Hon. Prof.

Atkinson, A. B., MD Belf., DSc Belf., FRCP   Hon. Prof.
Bell, A. L., MD Belf.   Sr. Lectr.
Buchanan, K. D., MD Glas., PhD Belf., FRCP, FRCPEd, FRCPGlas, FRCPI   Prof., Metabolic Medicine
Corbett, J. R., BSc Belf., MB Belf., FRCP   Sr. Lectr.
Hadden, D. R., MD Belf., FRCPEd, FRCP   Hon. Prof., Endocrinology
Hawkins, S. A., BSc Belf., MB Belf., FRCP   Reader
Hayes, J. R., BSc Belf., MD Belf., FRCP, FRCPI   Prof.
Johnston, C. F., BSc Belf., PhD Belf.   Reader
Love, Andrew H. G., CBE, BSc Belf., MD Belf., FRCPI, FRCP   Prof.
Maxwell, A. P., MD Belf., PhD Belf.   Sr. Lectr.
McCluskey, D. R., MD Belf., FRCPEd, FRCPI   Sr. Lectr.
McGeown, Mary G., CBE, MD PhD, FRCPEd, FRCP, FRCPI   Prof. Fellow of the Univ., Nephrology
Porter, K. G., BSc Belf., MD Belf., FRCP   Sr. Lectr.
Shaw, C., BSc Ulster, PhD Belf.   Prof.
Watson, R. G. P., BSc Belf., MD Belf., FRCP   Sr. Lectr.

Mental Health

Fax: (01232) 324543

Adams, C. E. A., MB Belf.   Sr. Lectr.
Cooper, S. J., MD Belf., FRCPsych   Sr. Lectr.
King, D. J., MD Belf., FRCPsych   Prof., Clinical Psychopharmacology
McClelland, R. J., PhD Lond., MD, FRCPsych   Prof.; Head*
O'Gorman, E. C., MD N.U.I., FRCPsych   Sr. Lectr.

Metabolism and Endocrinology

No staff at present

Microbiology and Immunobiology

Fax: (01232) 439181

Simpson, D. I. H., MD, FRCPath, FIBiol   Prof., Microbiology

Molecular Medicine and Nephrology

No staff at present

Neuropathology

No staff at present

Obstetrics and Gynaecology

Fax: (01232) 328247

Harper, Margaret A., MD Belf., FRCOG   Sr. Lectr.
McClure, N., MD Belf.   Sr. Lectr.
Thompson, W., BSc Belf., MD Belf., FRCOG   Prof.

Oncology

Fax: (01232) 314055

Atkinson, R. J., MD, FRCSGlas, FRCOG   Sr. Lectr.
Johnston, P. G., MD N.U.I., PhD N.U.I.   Prof.
McAleer, J. J. A., MD Belf., FRCPEd, FRCR   Sr. Lectr.

Ophthalmology

Fax: (01232) 330744

Archer, D. B., MB Belf., FRCS, FRCSEd   Blackmore Prof.
Chakravarthy, U., PhD Belf., FRCS, FRCSEd   Sr. Lectr.
Silvestri, Giviliana, MD, FRCS   Sr. Lectr.

Oral Medicine

No staff at present

Orthopaedic Surgery

Fax: (01232) 661112

Brown, J. G., MD Belf., FRCSEd   Sr. Lectr.
Marsh, D. R., MD Belf., FRCS   Prof.

Otorhinolaryngology

Fax: (01232) 315528

Adams, D. A., BSc Belf., MB Belf., MSc Manc., FRCSEd   Sr. Lectr.

Pathology

Fax: (01232) 233643

Bamford, Kathleen B., MB   Sr. Lectr.
Bharucha, H., MB BS Madr., MD Madr., FRCPath   Sr. Lectr.
Cosby, S. L., BSc Belf., PhD Belf.   Sr. Lectr.
Crane, J., MB Belf., FRCP   Hon. Prof.
Hamilton, P. W., BSc Ulster, PhD Belf.   Sr. Lectr., Quantitative Pathology
Hill, Claire M., MD, FRCPath, FRCPI   Sr. Lectr.
McCormick, D. F. W., BSc PhD   Sr. Lectr., Neuro-Pathology
O'Hara, M. D., BSc MB, FRCPath   Sr. Lectr.
Sloan, J. M., MD, FRCPath   Reader
Toner, P. G., MB ChB Glas., DSc Glas., FRCP, FRCPath, FRCPEd, FRCPGlas   Musgrave Prof.

Radiology

No staff at present

Surgery

Fax: (01232) 321811

Gardiner, K. R., MD Belf., MCh Belf., FRCS   Sr. Lectr.
Odling-Smee, G. W., MB BS Durh., FRCS   Sr. Lectr.
Parks, T. G., MB MCh, FRCSEd, FRCSI   Prof., Surgical Science

Therapeutics and Pharmacology

Fax: (01232) 438346

Johnston, G. D., MD PhD, FRCPEd, FRCP   Prof.
McDermott, B. J., BSc PhD   Sr. Lectr.
Riddell, J. G., BSc MD, FRCP   Reader
Shanks, R. G., CBE, DSc MD, FRCP, FRCPEd, FRCPI   Whitla Prof.
Silke, B., MD N.U.I., FRCPI   Reader
Van den Berg, H. W., BSc Leeds, PhD Leeds   Reader

Nursing and Midwifery, School of

Fax: (01232) 681950

Orr, Jean A., BA CNAA, MSc Manc.   Prof.; Head*

Pharmacology, see Clin. Med., Sch. of (Therap. and Pharmacol.)

Physiology, see under Biomed. Sci., Sch. of

Radiology, see under Clin. Med., Sch. of

SPECIAL CENTRES, ETC

Canadian Studies, Centre of

Tel: (01232) 273794

Othick, J. R., BA Belf.   Dir.*

Computer Based Learning, Institute of

Tel: (01232) 335051 Fax: (01232) 335051

McBride, F. V., MSc Belf., PhD Belf.   Prof.; Dir.*

Continuing Education, Institute of

Fax: (01232) 236909

Patten, M. Patricia, OBE, BA Liv.   Sr. Lectr., Social Studies; Acting Dir.*

Criminology and Criminal Justice, Institute of

Tel: (01232) 335458 Fax: (01232) 664816

Brogden, M. E., BSc(Soc) Lond., MPhil Leeds   Prof.; Dir.*
Bryett, K., BA Q'ld., PhD Aberd.   Sr. Lectr.
McEvoy, K., LLB Belf., MSc Edin.   Sr. Lectr.

Drug Utilisation Unit

Tel: (01232) 272182

McGavock, H., BSc Belf., MD, FRCGP   Dir.*

European Studies, Institute of

Tel: (01232) 335544 Fax: (01232) 683543

Dixon, C. S., MA St And., PhD Camb.   Sr. Lectr.
Smith, M. L., MA Camb.   Dir.*

Health and Health Care Research Unit

Jamison, J.Q., BSc Belf., PhD Belf.   Dir.*

Irish Studies, Institute of

King, S. M. H., MA Belf., PhD Belf.   Sr. Lectr.
Walker, B. M., MA Trinity(Dub.), PhD Trinity(Dub.)   Prof.; Dir.*

Marine Resources and Mariculture, Centre for

Roberts, D., BSc Liv., PhD Liv., FIBiol   Dir.*

Northern Ireland Cancer Registry

Gavin, A. T., MSc Aberd., MB Belf.   Dir.*

Northern Ireland Semi-Conductor Research Centre

Gamble, H. S., BSc Belf., PhD Belf.   Dir.*

Northern Ireland Technology Centre

Fax: (01232) 663715

Beatty, Prof. E. K., MBE, BSc Belf., PhD Belf.   Dir., Automation*
Edgar, J., BSc Belf.   Manager, Design
Fleck, R., BSc Belf., PhD Belf.   Head of Div., Manufacturing
Gilmour, G., BEng Napier   Manager, Automatic Design
Long, A. E., PhD Belf., DSc Belf., FEng, FICE, FIStructE   Head of Div., Construction
Stewart, J. A., BSc Belf., PhD Belf.   Head of Div., Electronics

Pharmaceutical Education and Training, Northern Ireland Centre for

Maguire, T. A., MSc Belf., PhD Belf.   Dir.*

Physical Education Centre

Fax: (01232) 681129

Cusdin, M., BSc Leic.   Dir.*

Professional Legal Studies, Institute of

Craig, H. Ruth, LLB Belf.   Sr. Lectr.
Fenton, I. A., LLB Belf.   Sr. Lectr.

Queen's University Environmental Science and Technology Centre (Questor)

Larkin, M. J., BSc CNAA, PhD Wales   Res. Cttee. Chairman
McGarel, W., BSc Belf., PhD Belf.   TDP and IFI Project Manager
Swindall, W. J., MSc, FRSChem   Dir.*

Rural Studies, Centre for

Tel: (01232) 683538

Davis, J., BAgr Belf., MSc Newcastle(UK), PhD Belf.   Dir.*

Social Research, Centre for

Breen, R. J., MA Camb., PhD Camb.   Dir.*

Women's Studies, Centre for

Tel: (01232) 273142 Fax: (01232) 325651

Hill, M., BA Belf., PhD Belf.   Dir.*

EDGEHILL THEOLOGICAL COLLEGE

Independent College—Recognised Staff

Cooke, Rev. W. Dennis, BA Belf., BD Belf., MTh Lexington, PhD Belf.   Principal, Church History

IRISH BAPTIST COLLEGE

Independent College—Recognised Staff

Moore, Rev. H., BD *Belf.*, MTh *Belf.*, PhD *Belf.* Principal, New Testament Studies

LOUGHRY COLLEGE OF AGRICULTURE AND FOOD TECHNOLOGY

Independent College—Recognised Staff

Communication

Stevenson, R. C., BAgr *Belf.*, MSc *Mich.State*, PhD *Belf.* Principal

Food Processing Technology

No staff at present

ST MARY'S COLLEGE

Independent College—Recognised Staff

Art and Design
No staff at present

Biological Science
No staff at present

Business Studies
No staff at present

Celtic
No staff at present

Chemistry
No staff at present

Craft, Design and Technology
No staff at present

Dramatic Art
No staff at present

Education
No staff at present

English
No staff at present

Geography
No staff at present

Information Technology
No staff at present

Mathematics, Pure and Applied
No staff at present

Modern History
No staff at present

Music
No staff at present

Physical Education
No staff at present

Physical Science
No staff at present

Religious Studies

O'Callaghan, M., BA *Belf.*, BD *N.U.I.*, LSS *Pontif.Bibl.Inst.* Recog. Teacher, Old Testament, New Testament, Greek; Principal

STRANMILLIS COLLEGE

Independent College—Recognised Staff

Art and Design
No staff at present

Biological Science
No staff at present

Business Studies
No staff at present

Dramatic Art
No staff at present

Education
No staff at present

English
No staff at present

Geography
No staff at present

History
No staff at present

Information Technology
No staff at present

Language Studies
No staff at present

Mathematics
No staff at present

Music
No staff at present

Physical Education
No staff at present

Physical Science
No staff at present

Religious Studies
No staff at present

UNION THEOLOGICAL COLLEGE

Independent College—Recognised Staff

Reid, Rev. Prof. Thomas S., BA *Belf.*, BD *Belf.*, MTh *Belf.* Principal, Comparative Ecclesiology, Pastoral Studies

CONTACT OFFICERS

Academic affairs. Secretary to the Academic Council: ......
Accommodation. Accommodation Manager: Browne, T. Connor, BSc(Econ) *Belf.*
Admissions (first degree). Admissions Office: Wisener, Stirling M., BSc *Belf.*
Admissions (higher degree). Admissions Office: Wisener, Stirling M., BSc *Belf.*
Alumni. Alumni Officer: Power, Gerry, LLB *Belf.*
Careers. Careers Adviser: Adrain, J. Jill, BSc *Belf.*
Computing services. Director of Computer Centre: McBride, Prof. F. V., MSc *Belf.*, PhD *Belf.*
Estates and buildings/works and services. Buildings Officer: Martin, J. Hubert, BSc *Belf.*, FICE
Examinations. Head of Student Records: Doherty, James, BSc *Belf.*
Finance. Bursar: O'Kane, James P. J., BA *CNAA*

General enquiries. Administrative Secretary: Wilson, D. H., JP, BSc *Belf.*
Health services. Senior Medical Officer: Todd, Denis O., MB *Belf.*, FRCSEd
Industrial liaison. Director of QUBIS (Queen's University Business and Industrial Services): Shanks, R. G., MD *Belf.*, DSc *Belf.*, FRCP, FRCPEd, FRCPI
International office. International Liaison Officer: Eve, Judith, LLB *Belf.*
Library (chief librarian). Librarian: Russell, Norman J., BA *Belf.*, MPhil *CNAA*
Personnel/human resources. Director of Human Resources: ......
Public relations, information and marketing. Information Director: ......
Publications. Publications Officer: Boyd, Lynn, BA *Belf.*, MBA *Belf.*
Purchasing. Purchasing Officer: Gregg, F. I., BSc *Belf.*, MSc *Ulster*
Safety. Safety Officer: Bradley, Brian, MSc *Belf.*
Scholarships, awards, loans. Administrative Officer: Murphy, Angela T., BA *Belf.*
Schools liaison. Student Admissions Officer: Cleary, P. Gerald, BA *Belf.*, PhD *Belf.*
Security. Security Supervisor: Haddon, Michael R.
Sport and recreation. Director of Physical Education Centre: Cusdin, M., MSc *Leic.*
Staff development and training. Staff Training and Development Officer: Baillie, Patricia M.
Student welfare/counselling. Student Counsellor: Grant, Heather, BA *Belf.*
Students from other countries. Student Admissions Officer: Cleary, P. Gerald, BA *Belf.*, PhD *Belf.*
Students with disabilities. Admissions Office: Wisener, Stirling M., BSc *Belf.*

CAMPUS/COLLEGE HEADS

Edgehill Theological College, Lennoxvale, Belfast, Northern Ireland BT9 5BY. (*Tel*: (0232) 665870.) Principal: Cooke, Rev. W. Dennis, BA *Belf.*, BD *Belf.*, MTh *Lexington*, PhD *Belf.*

Irish Baptist College, 67 Sandown Road, Belfast, Northern Ireland BT5 6GU. (*Tel*: (0232) 471908.) Principal: Moore, Rev. H., BD *Belf.*, MTh *Belf.*, PhD *Belf.*

Loughry College of Agriculture and Food Technology, Cookstown, County Tyrone, Northern Ireland BT80 9AA. (*Tel*: (06487) 62491.) Principal: Stevenson, R. C., BAgr *Belf.*, MSc *Mich.State*, PhD *Belf.*

St Mary's College, 191 Falls Road, Belfast, Northern Ireland BT12 6FE. (*Tel*: (0232) 327678.) Principal: O'Callaghan, Rev. Martin, BD *Belf.*, BA *Belf.*

Stranmillis College, Stranmillis Road, Belfast, Northern Ireland BT9 5DY. (*Tel*: (0232) 381271.) Principal: McMinn, John R. B., BA *Belf.*, PhD *Belf.*

Union Theological College, Botanic Avenue, Belfast, Northern Ireland BT7 1JT. (*Tel*: (0232) 325374.) Principal: Reid, Rev. Prof. Thomas S., BA *Belf.*, BD *Belf.*, MTh *Belf.*

[*Information supplied by the institution as at 5 March 1998, and edited by the ACU*]

UNIVERSITY OF READING

Founded 1926; previously established as University Extension College (1892), Reading College (1898) and University College, Reading (1902)

Member of the Association of Commonwealth Universities

Postal Address: Whiteknights, PO Box 217, Reading, Berkshire, England RG6 6AH
Telephone: (0118) 987 5123 **Fax**: (0118) 931 4404 **Telex**: 847813 **WWW**: http://www.rdg.ac.uk/
E-mail formula: 1stinitial.2ndinitial.surname@reading.ac.uk

VISITOR—Elizabeth, H.M. The Queen
CHANCELLOR—Carrington, The Rt. Hon. Lord , KG, GCMG, CH, MC
VICE-CHANCELLOR*—Williams, Prof. Roger, MA Oxf., MA(Econ) Manc.
DEPUTY VICE-CHANCELLOR—Mead, Prof. Roger, BA Camb.
PRO-VICE-CHANCELLOR—Fulford, Prof. Michael G., BA S'ton., PhD S'ton., FBA, FSA
PRO-VICE-CHANCELLOR—Gregory, Prof. Peter J., BSc Reading, PhD Nott.
PRESIDENT OF THE COUNCIL—Orchard-Lisle, Paul, CBE, TD, MA, FRICS
TREASURER—Barclay, William, MA
REGISTRAR—Frampton, David C. R., MA St And.
LIBRARIAN—Corrall, Sheila, MA Camb., MBA Sus., FLA
BURSAR—Ascott, Robert H. C., MA Camb.
DIRECTOR OF INFORMATION SERVICES—Haworth, Annette E., MA Oxf.

GENERAL INFORMATION

History. The university was originally established in 1892 as an extension college of the University of Oxford. It gained independent status in 1926.

The main campus is located about $2\frac{1}{2}$km from Reading town centre, and about 64km west of London.

Admission to first degree courses (see also United Kingdom Introduction). Through Universities and Colleges Admissions Service (UCAS).

First Degrees (see also United Kingdom Directory to Subjects of Study). BA, BA(Ed), BEng, BSc, LLB, MChem, MEng, MMath, MPhys.

Most full-time courses last 3 years, others last 4 years. BA also available part-time.

Higher Degrees (see also United Kingdom Directory to Subjects of Study). LLM, MA, MAgrSc, MBA, MEd, MFA, MMus, MRes, MSc, MSW, MPhil, PhD, DLitt, DSc, LLD.

Applicants for admission to master's degrees must normally hold a good first degree in appropiate subject. Postgraduate applications are made directly to the faculty concerned.

Most master's courses last 1 year full-time or 2 years part-time. MBA: part-time by distance learning.

Libraries. 1,000,445 volumes; 3591 periodicals; 71 databases on CD-ROM.

Fees (1998–99, annual). Undergraduate UK students: £1000. Postgraduate: UK students £2610; international students £8370 (science-based courses), £6462 (other courses).

Academic Awards (1997–98). 42.

Academic Year (1998–99). Three terms: 5 October–11 December; 11 January–19 March; 26 April–1 July.

Income (1996–97). Total, £104,909,000.

Statistics. Staff: 3586 (1563 academic, 641 clerical, 1382 technical and manual). Students: total 12,928.

FACULTIES/SCHOOLS

Agriculture and Food

Tel: (0118) 931 8370 Fax: (0118) 935 2063
Dean: Summerfield, Prof. Rod J., BSc Nott., PhD Nott., DSc Reading
Sub Dean: Moss, P., BA Syd.

Education and Community Studies

Tel: (0118) 931 8812 Fax: (0118) 935 2080
Dean: Pope, Prof. Maureen L., BTech Brun., PhD Brun.
Sub Dean: Trethewy, N. G., MA Dund.

Letters and Social Sciences

Tel: (0118) 931 8061 Fax: (0118) 931 0748
Dean: Downes, Prof. T. A. (Tony), BA Oxf., BCL Oxf.
Sub Dean: Must, P. J., BA Reading

Science

Tel: (0118) 931 8342 Fax: (0118) 975 5509
Dean: Baker, Prof. Keith D., BSc Sus., DPhil Sus., FIEE
Sub Dean: Kishore, L. J., BA Reading

Urban and Regional Studies

Tel: (0118) 931 8183 Fax: (0118) 931 6658
Dean: Goodall, Prof. Brian, BSc(Econ) Lond.
Sub Dean: Samman, N., BA Wales, PhD Wales

ACADEMIC UNITS

Agricultural and Food Economics

Tel: (0118) 931 8370 Fax: (0118) 935 2063
Collins, E. J. T., BA Birm., PhD Nott. Prof.
Hallam, D., MSc Oxf., BA PhD Sr. Lectr.
Stansfield, J. M., BSc Leeds Sr. Lectr.
Swinbank, A., MA McM., PhD Lond., BSc Prof.; Head*
Thirtle, C. G., BSc Lond., MS S.Illinois, MPhil Col., PhD Col. Reader
Traill, W. B., BSc Glas., PhD Cornell Prof.
Upton, M., MSc Prof.
Other Staff: 8 Lectrs.; 1 Hon. Res. Fellow
Research: agricultural and food marketing; environmental economics; farm management and production economics; trade and policy

Agricultural Botany, see also Bot.

Tel: (0118) 931 8092 Fax: (0118) 931 6577
Caligari, P. D. S., BSc Birm., PhD Birm. Prof.
Dennett, M. D., BSc Lond., MSc PhD Reader
Elston, J., BSc PhD Visiting Prof.
John, Prof. P., BSc Lond., PhD Lond.
Shaw, M. W., BA Camb., MSc Newcastle(UK), PhD E.Anglia Reader; Head*
Other Staff: 4 Lectrs.; 5 Res. Fellows; 2 Hon. Sr. Lectrs.
Research: crop ecology and climatology; crop physiology and biochemistry; genetics, plant breeding and crop evolution; plant pathology

Agricultural Extension and Rural Development

Tel: (0118) 931 8119 Fax: (0118) 926 1244
Farrington, J., BA Reading, MA Reading, MPhil Reading, PhD Reading Visiting Prof.
Garforth, C. J., MA Camb., PhD Camb. Prof.; Head*
Jones, G. E., BA Manc., MLitt Oxf. Sr. Lectr.
Other Staff: 13 Lectrs.; 2 Visiting Fellows; 4 Res. Fellows; 4 Academic Fellows
Research: agricultural education and training; rural social development

Agriculture

Tel: (0118) 931 8471 Fax: (0118) 935 2421
Beever, D. E., BSc Durh., PhD Newcastle(UK) Prof., Animal Production
Bryant, M. J., BSc(Agric) Nott., PhD Liv. Sr. Lectr.
Ellis, R. H., BSc Wales, PhD Prof.
Esslemont, R. J., BSc Wales, PhD Sr. Lectr.
James, A. D., BA Oxf., PhD Sr. Lectr.
Keating, E. J. D. H., BSc Brist., MSc Manit., PhD Belf. Prof.
Owen, E., BSc Wales, PhD Wales Prof.
Rehman, T., MSc W.Pak.Ag., PhD Sr. Lectr.
Stansfield, J. M., BSc Leeds Sr. Lectr.
Summerfield, Ron J., BSc Nott., PhD Nott., DSc Reading, FIBiol Prof.; Head*
Wilkins, R. J., PhD NE, BSc Visiting Prof.
Other Staff: 12 Lectrs.; 2 Principal Res. Fellows; 3 Sr. Res. Fellows; 9 Res. Fellows; 7 Hon. Principal Res. Fellows; 2 Hon Sr. Res. Fellows; 4 Hon. Res. Fellows
Research: animal production; crop physiology and growth; crop protection; dairy research; seed science

Animal and Microbial Sciences, School of

Tel: (0118) 931 8011 Fax: (0118) 931 0180
Almond, J. W., BSc Leeds, PhD Camb. Prof.
Andrews, S. C., BSc Sheff., PhD Sheff. Reader
Crabbe, M. J. C., BSc Hull, MA Oxf., PhD Manc., DSc Manc., FRSChem Prof.
Cunningham, F. J., BSc Liv., MSc Birm., PhD Birm., DSc Prof., Reproductive Physiology
Gladwell, R. T., BSc Durh., PhD Durh. Sr. Lectr.
Grainger, J. M., BSc Birm., PhD Sr. Lectr.
Hilton, J. E., BSc Liv. Visiting Prof.
Holland, P., MA Oxf., PhD Lond. Prof.
Hopkin, S. P., BSc Wales, PhD Wales Sr. Lectr.
Jones, A. R., BSc Brist., PhD Brist. Sr. Lectr.
Knight, P. G., BSc Wales, MSc Birm., PhD Prof.
Leake, D. S., BSc Birm., PhD Camb. Reader
Lowry, P. J., PhD Leeds, DSc Leeds, FIBiol Prof.; Head*

McCaffery, A. R., BSc *Sheff.*, PhD *Sheff.* Sr. Lectr.

McKeating, J. A., BSc *Warw.*, PhD *Lond.* Reader

Robson, R., BA *York(UK)*, PhD *Wales* Prof.; Head of Res.

Sibly, R. M., MA *Oxf.*, DPhil *Oxf.* Prof.

Simkiss, K., DSc *Lond.*, PhD Prof.

Skidmore, C. J., MA *Oxf.*, DPhil *Oxf.* Sr. Lectr.; Head of Teaching

Strange, P. G., BA *Camb.*, MA *Camb*, PhD *Camb.* Prof.

Vincent, J. F. V., BA *Camb.*, PhD *Sheff.* Sr. Lectr.

Williams, D. L., MA *Camb.*, MB BChir *Camb.*, PhD *Reading*, FRCPath, FRSChem Visiting Prof.

Other Staff: 19 Lectrs.; 3 Sr. Res. Fellows; 28 Res. Fellows; 3 Hon. Lectrs.; 7 Hon. Fellows

Research: bacteriology; biomimetics; molecular and cell biology; molecular endocrinology; pest management

Applied Language Studies, Centre for,
see Special Centres, etc

Applied Statistics
Tel: (0118) 931 8022 *Fax*: (0118) 975 3169

Balding, D. J., BMath *Newcastle(NSW)*, DPhil *Oxf.* Prof.

Collett, D., BSc *Leic.*, MSc *Newcastle(UK)*, PhD *Hull* Sr. Lectr.; Head*

Mead, Roger, BA *Camb.* Prof.

Whitehead, J. R., BSc *Oxf.*, MSc *Sheff.*, PhD *Sheff.* Prof.

Wilson, I. M., BSc *St And.*, MSc *Wales* Sr. Lectr.

Woodward, M., BSc *Birm.*, MSc PhD Sr. Lectr.

Other Staff: 6 Lectrs.; 2 Sr. Res. Fellows; 3 Res. Fellows; 2 Res. Officers

Research: experimental design and data analysis; interpretation of DNA evidence; quantitative genetics; sequential methods

Archaeology
Tel: (0118) 931 8132 *Fax*: (0118) 931 6718

Astill, G. G., BA *Birm.*, PhD *Birm.* Reader

Bell, M. G., BSc *Lond.*, PhD *Lond.*, FSA Sr. Lectr.

Bradley, R. J., MA *Oxf.* Prof.

Chapman, R. W., MA *Camb.*, PhD *Camb.* Reader

Fulford, Michael G., BA *S'ton.*, PhD *S'ton.*, FSA Prof.

Gilchrist, Roberta, BA *York(UK)*, DPhil *York(UK)* Prof.; Head*

Härke, H., MA *Gött.*, DrPhil *Gött.* Reader

Leech,, MA *Camb.*, PhD *Brist.*, FSA Visiting Prof.

Meirion-Jones, BSc *Lond.*, MPhil *Lond.*, PhD *Lond.*, FSA Visiting Prof.

Mithen, S. J., BA *Sheff.*, MSc *York*, PhD *Camb.* Sr. Lectr.

Other Staff: 5 Lectrs.; 6 Res. Fellows; 2 Hon. Lectrs.;

Research: computers and quantitative methods; geoarchaeology; mediaeval monasticism; prehistoric hunters and gatherers; prehistoric rock art

Art, see Fine Art, and Hist. of Art

Botany, see also Agric. Bot.
Tel: (0118) 931 8160 *Fax*: (0118) 975 3676

Barnett, J. R., BSc *Manc.*, PhD *Leeds* Reader; Head*

Bennett, M. D., BSc *Wales*, PhD *Wales*, FLS Visiting Prof.

Bisby, F. A, BA *Oxf.*, DPhil *Oxf.*, FLS

Blackmore, S., BSc *Reading*, PhD *Reading*, FLS Visiting Prof.

Dick, M. W., PhD *Lond.*, DSc *Lond.* Prof.†

Hawksworth, D. L., PhD *Leic.*, DSc *Leic.*, FLS, FIBiol Visiting Prof.

Humphries, C. J., BSc *Reading*, PhD *Reading*, FLS Visiting Prof.

Longton, R. E., PhD *Birm.*, DSc *Birm.*, DSc Sr. Lectr.

Prance, Sir Ghillean T., MA *Oxf.*, DPhil *Oxf.* Visiting Prof.

Other Staff: 5 Lectrs.; 1 Res. Phytochemist; 1 Herbarium Curator; 1 Principal Res. Fellow; 2 Advanced Res. Fellows; 3 Res. Fellows

Research: physiology and ecology; plant diversity; structure and development; systematics

Chemistry
Tel: (0118) 931 8447 *Fax*: (0118) 931 1610

Bowker, Michael, BSc *E.Anglia*, PhD *Liv.* Prof., Physical Chemistry

Burch, R., PhD *Belf.*, DSc *Belf.* Prof., Catalytic Chemistry

Cardin, D. J., BSc *Sus.*, DPhil *Sus.* Prof.

Drew, M. G. B., BSc *Lond.*, PhD *Lond.* Reader

Gilbert, A., PhD DSc Prof.

Hardman, Thelma M., MA *Oxf.*, DPhil *Oxf.* Reader

Harwood, L. M., BSc *Manc.*, MSc *Manc.*, MA *Oxf.*, PhD *Manc.*, FRSChem Prof., Organic Chemistry

Hollins, P., MA *Camb.*, PhD *Lond.* Reader

Isaacs, N. S., BSc *S'ton.*, PhD *S'ton.* Sr. Lectr.

Mann, J., PhD *Lond.*, DSc *Lond.* Prof., Organic Chemistry

Mitchell, P. C. H., MA *Oxf.*, DPhil *Oxf.* Reader

Pethybridge, A. D., BSc PhD Sr. Lectr.

Rice, D. A., BSc *Hull*, PhD *Exe.*, DSc *Exe.* Prof.; Head*

Rodger, P. M., BSc *Syd.*, PhD *Syd.* Sr. Lectr.

Sweeney, J. B., BSc *Lond.*, DPhil *Oxf.*

Tadros, T. F., BSc *Alexandria*, MSc *Alexandria*, PhD *Alexandria* Visiting Prof.

Walsh, R., BA *Camb.*, PhD *Camb.* Prof.

Other Staff: 9 Lectrs.; 1 Sr. Res. Chemist; 1 Sr. Res. Fellow; 1 Visiting Fellow; 1 Sr. Sci. Officer

Research: catalysis and surface science; kinetics; organic synthesis; solution chemistry; spectroscopy

Classics
Tel: (0118) 931 8420 *Fax*: (0118) 931 6661

Gardner, Jane F., MA *Glas.*, MA *Oxf.* Prof.

Rajak, Tessa, MA *Oxf.*, DPhil *Oxf.* Reader

Rutherford, I. C., MA *Oxf.*, DPhil *Oxf.*

Wallace-Hadrill, A. F., MA *Oxf.*, DPhil *Oxf.* Prof. (on leave)

Wyke, Maria del C., MA *Oxf.*, PhD *Camb.* Sr. Lectr.

Other Staff: 5 Lectrs.; 1 Visiting Fellow; 4 Hon. Fellows; 4 Hon. Res. Fellows

Research: gender and the classical tradition; Greek lyric poetry; Hellenistic Judaism; papyrology and philology; Roman social history

Community Studies
Tel: (0118) 931 8853 *Fax*: (0118) 935 2080

Denicolo, Pam, BA *Open(UK)*, PhD *Sur.* Reader

Gothard, W. P., BSocSc *Birm.*, PhD Sr. Lectr.

Howkins, Liz J., BA *Open(UK)*, MSc *Sur.* Sr. Lectr.; Head*

Lathlean, J., BSc *Wales*, MA *Brun.*, DPhil *Oxf.* Visiting Prof.

Nursten, Jean P., MASocW *Smith* Visiting Prof.

Pope, Maureen L., BTech *Brun.*, PhD *Brun.* Prof., Community Studies and Education

Ward, A., BA *Oxf.*, MSW *Sus.* Sr. Lectr.

Other Staff: 14 Lectrs.; 11 Lectrs†

Research: bereavement and palliative care; crisis intervention; mental health social work; school refusal; therapeutic child care

Computer Science
Tel: (0118) 931 8611 *Fax*: (0118) 975 1994

Baker, Keith D., BSc *Sus.*, DPhil *Sus.*, FIEE Prof.

Loader, R. J., BSc PhD Sr. Lectr.

Megson, G. M., BSc *Leeds*, PhD *Lough.* Prof.

Ogden, J. A., BSc *S'ton.*, PhD *Glas.* Sr. Lectr.

Williams, Shirley A., BSc *Lough.*, PhD *Lough.* Sr. Lectr.; Head*

Other Staff: 11 Lectrs.; 1 Sr. Res. Fellow; 1 Res. Fellow; 1 Sr. Sci. Officer; 5 Hon. Fellows

Research: active robots; computational vision group; formal methods and software engineering; parallel emergent and distributed architectures

Construction Management and Engineering
Tel: (0118) 931 8201 *Fax*: (0118) 931 3856

Atkin, B. L., BSc *Aston*, MPhil *CNAA*, PhD Visiting Prof.

Awbi, H. B., MSc *Manc.*, PhD *CNAA* Sr. Lectr.

Bennett, J., DSc Prof., Quantity Surveying

Bon, R., MA PhD Prof.; Head*

Bright, K. T., MSc Sr. Lectr.

Clements-Croome, T. D. J., MSc *Lond.*, PhD *Lough.* Prof., Construction Engineering

Cook, G. K., BSc *Aston*, PhD *Sur.* Sr. Lectr.

Fisher, G. N., MSc *Aston* Prof.

Flanagan, R., MSc *Aston*, PhD *Aston* Prof.

Gray, C., MPhil Sr. Lectr.

Green, S. D., BSc *Birm.*, MSc *H-W*, PhD *Reading* Sr. Lectr.

Hollis, M. R., BSc, FRICS Prof.†

Ingram, J. F. G., PhD *Brun.* Visiting Indust. Prof.

Lansley, Peter R., BSc *Leic.*, MSc *Newcastle(UK)*, PhD *Reading* Prof., Management Studies

Other Staff: 10 Lectrs.; 2 Visiting Lectrs.; 3 Visiting Res. Fellows; 12 Res. Staff; 1 Adjunct Prof.

Research: building services and environmental engineering; professional practice in the construction process; project management

Cybernetics
Tel: (0118) 931 8219 *Fax*: (0118) 931 8220

Andrews, B., BSc *Reading*, MSc *Sheff.*, PhD *Strath.* Visiting Indust. Prof.

MacQueen, J., BSc *St And.*, PhD *Dund.*, FIMA Visiting Indust. Prof.

Mitchell, R. J., BSc Sr. Lectr.; Head*

Sharkey, P. M., PhD *Strath.*, BSc(Eng) MA Reader

Warwick, K., BSc *Aston*, PhD *Lond.*, DSc *Lond.* Prof.

Winter, C., BA *Oxf.*, PhD *Lanc.* Visiting Indust. Prof.

Other Staff: 8 Lectrs.; 5 Sr. Res. Fellows; 7 Res. Fellows; 1 Visiting Res. Fellow; 3 Res. Officers; 1 Sr. Sci. Officer; 3 Hon. Res. Fellows

Research: artificial neural networks; control; intelligent systems; robotics; virtual reality

Drama, see Film and Drama

Economics
Tel: (0118) 931 8226 *Fax*: (0118) 975 0236

Barron, M. J. B., BSc *S'ton.*, PhD *S'ton.* Visiting Prof.

Booth, S. A., BA *Leeds*, PhD *Reading* Sr. Lectr.

Buckley, P. J., BA *York(UK)*, MA *E.Anglia*, PhD *Lanc.* Visiting Prof.

Cantwell, John, BA *Oxf.*, MSc *Lond.*, PhD *Reading* Prof., International Economics

Casson, M. C., BA *Brist.* Prof.

Clare, A., BA *CNAA*, MSc *S'ton.*, PhD *S'ton.* Visiting Prof.

Dale, R. S., BSc *Lond.*, PhD *Kent* Visiting Prof.

Eltis, W., BA *Camb.*, MA *Oxf.*, DLitt *Oxf.* Visiting Prof.

Evans, A. W., BA *Lond.*, PhD *Lond.*, FCA Prof., Environmental Economics

Jones, E., BA *Nott.*, MA *Oxf.*, DPhil *Oxf.*, DLitt *Oxf.*, FASSA Visiting Prof.

Kipping, M., BA *Munich*, MA *Paris IV*, PhD *Munich* Reader

McQueen, M., BScEcon *Wales*, MA *Sus.* Sr. Lectr.

Meen, G. P., BA *Reading*, MSc *Lond.*, PhD *Lond.* Reader

Mosley, P., BA *Essex*, PhD *Camb.*, PhD *Essex* Prof.

Nobes, C. W., BA *Exe.*, PhD *Exe.* Deloitte Prof., Accounting

Oulton, N., BA Oxf., MSc Lond. Visiting Prof.
Patterson, K. P., BA Essex, BPhil Oxf. Prof.
Pearce, R. D., BA Reader
Pemberton, James, BA Camb., PhD
 Camb. Prof.; Head*
Purdy, D. E., MSc Hull, PhD CNAA Reader
Rugman, A., MSc Lond., PhD S.Fraser Visiting
 Prof.
Scott-Quinn, B. S., BA CNAA, MAcc Glas. Prof.
Skinner, F., BCom Nfld., MBA Tor., PhD
 Tor. Sr. Lectr.
Storey, D. J., BSc Hull, PhD
 Newcastle(UK) Visiting Prof.
Taylor, M., BA Oxf., DPhil Oxf.
Thomas, S. H., BSc Lond., MSc S'ton., PhD
 S'ton. Visiting Prof.
Utton, M. A., BA Nott., PhD Prof.
Other Staff: 19 Lectrs.; 2 Res. Fellows; 12
 Visiting Res. Fellows
Research: comparative international accounting;
 econometrics; international business;
 international securities markets; urban and
 regional economics

Education, School of

Boorman, Julia, BA PhD Sr. Lectr.
Brehony, K., BA Open(UK), PhD Open(UK) Sr.
 Lectr.
Copeland, I. C., BA Manc., MSc CNAA, MA Sr.
 Lectr.
Croll, Paul, BA York(UK), MSc Strath. Prof.;
 Head*
Dillon, P. J., BEd Brist. Sr. Lectr.
Edwards, Vivien, BA Reading, PhD Reading Prof.
Fidler, F. B., BSc Lond., MSc Sheff., MA Lanc.,
 PhD Sheff. Sr. Lectr.
Gayford, C. G., BSc Lond., MEd Lond., PhD
 Lond. Reader
Gellert, C. E., MA Munich, PhD Camb., DrHabil
 Humboldt Prof.
Gilbert, J. K., BSc Leic., DPhil Sus. Prof.
Hegarty, S., PhD Lond., BSc Visiting Indust.
 Prof.
James, H. C. L., BA Lond. Sr. Lectr.
Kemp, A. E., MA Sus., DPhil Sus., FTCL Prof.
Malvern, D. D., MA Oxf. Sr. Lectr.
Redfern, Angela, BA Sr. Lectr.
Richards, B. J., BA Wales, MEd Brist., PhD
 Brist. Sr. Lectr.
Smith, I. F. Sr. Lectr.
Southworth, G. W., BEd Lanc., MEd Liv., MA
 Camb., PhD E.Anglia Prof.
Straughan, R. R., MA Camb., MA Lond., PhD
 Lond. Reader
Watson, J. K. P., MA Edin., PhD Prof.
Wells, C., MSc CNAA Sr. Lectr.
Wheldall, K., BA PhD, FBPsS Visiting Prof.
Other Staff: 35 Lectrs.; 1 Sr. Visiting Fellow; 4
 Visiting Fellows; 1 Res. Officer; 6 Lectrs.
Research: educational research methods; higher
 education; international and comparative
 education; science and environmental
 education; special educational needs

Engineering

Tel: (0118) 931 8567 Fax: (0118) 931 3327
Atkins, A. G., BSc Wales, MA Oxf., PhD Camb.,
 ScD Camb., FIM Prof., Mechanical
 Engineering
Burton, J. D., BSc(Eng) Lond., PhD S'ton. Sr.
 Lectr.
Chaplin, C. R., MA Camb., PhD Camb. Prof.;
 Head*
Jeronimidis, G., DottChim Rome Prof.
Pretlove, A. J., BSc(Eng) S'ton., PhD S'ton. Sr.
 Lectr.; Dep. Dir., Engin. Labs.
Stansfield, E. V., BA Open(UK), BSc(Eng) Lond.,
 PhD Lond. Visiting Indust. Prof.
Other Staff: 5 Lectrs.; 2 Visiting Sr. Res.
 Fellows; 2 Visiting Res. Fellows; 15 Res.
 Staff
Research: biomimetics; materials and structures;
 renewable energy

English

Tel: (0118) 931 8361 Fax: (0118) 931 6561
Brown, C. C., BA PhD Prof.; Head*
Bullen, J. B., MA Camb., MA Oxf., PhD
 Camb. Prof.
Gurr, A. J., MA Auck., PhD Camb. Prof.
Hardman, C. B., MA Oxf., BLitt Oxf. Sr. Lectr.
Harvey, G., BA Hull, PhD Hull Sr. Lectr.
Howells, Coral A., MA Qld., PhD Lond. Prof.
Kelly, L., BA Sr. Lectr.
Knowles, R. G., BA Wales Sr. Lectr.
Parrinder, J. P., MA Camb., PhD Camb. Prof.
Pilling, J., BA Lond., PhD Lond. Prof.
Salvesen, C. G., BA Oxf., BLitt Oxf. Prof.†
Woodman, T. M., MA Oxf., MPhil Oxf., PhD
 Yale Sr. Lectr.
Other Staff: 13 Lectrs.
Research: children's literature; contemporary
 literature; mediaeval and Renaissance
 literature; romantic poetry and prose;
 Victorian literature

Film and Drama

Tel: (0118) 931 8878 Fax: (0118) 931 8873
Bull, J. S., BA Wales Prof.
Hillier, J. M., BA Oxf. Sr. Lectr.; Head*
Pye, D., BA Reading Sr. Lectr.
Other Staff: 6 Lectrs.
Research: critical and theatrical studies of film,
 television and twentieth-century theatre

Fine Art, see also Hist. of Art

Tel: (0118) 931 8051 Fax: (0118) 926 2667
Buckley, Stephen, BA Newcastle(UK),
 MFA Prof.; Head*
Edmond, T. A., BA CNAA Sr. Lectr.
Other Staff: 3 Lectrs.; 9 Lectrs.†; 1 Hon.
 Fellow
Research: contemporary art

Food Science and Technology

Tel: (0118) 931 8700 Fax: (0118) 931 0080
Ames, Jennifer M., PhD Lond., BSc Reader
Asenjo, J. A., MSc Leeds, PhD Lond. Reader
Birch, G. G., BSc Lond., PhD Lond. Prof.
Birch, J., BSc Lond., PhD Lond. Visiting Prof.
Brennan, J. G., MSc N.U.I. Sr. Lectr.
Bright, S. W. J., MA Camb., PhD
 Camb. Visiting Indust. Prof.
Davies, R., SM M.I.T., PhD M.I.T., BSc Sr.
 Lectr.
Frazier, P. J., BSc Leeds, PhD Leeds Visiting
 Prof.
Gordon, M. H., MA Oxf., DPhil Oxf. Sr. Lectr.
Gutteridge, C. S., BSc Sur., PhD Visiting Prof.
Jarvis, B., BSc PhD Visiting Prof.
Ledward, D. A., MSc Leeds, PhD Leeds Prof.
Lewis, M. J., MSc Birm., PhD Birm. Sr. Lectr.
MacFie, H. J. H., BSc Bath, PhD Bath Visiting
 Prof.
Mottram, D. S., BSc Leeds, PhD Leeds Reader
Niranjan, K., BChemEng Bom., MChemEng
 Bom., PhD Bom. Sr. Lectr.
Owens, J. D., BSc Brist., PhD Sr. Lectr.
Pyle, D. L., BSc(Tech) Manc., PhD Camb. Prof.,
 Biotechnology; Head*
Righelato, R. C., BSc Brist., PhD Lond. Visiting
 Prof.
Schofield, J. D., BSc Wales, PhD Manc. Prof.
Selman, J. D., BSc Reading, PhD Reading Visiting
 Prof.
Traill, W. B., BSc Glas., PhD Cornell Prof.
Vallance, P. J., LLB Brist. Sr. Lectr.
Walker, Ann F., BSc Brist., MSc WI, MSc
 Reading, PhD Sr. Lectr.
Williams, Christine M., BSc Lond., PhD
 Lond. Prof.
Other Staff: 12 Lectrs.; 1 Visiting Lectr.; 2 Sr.
 Res. Fellows; 20 Res. Fellows
Research: biotechnology and biochemical
 engineering; economic and food policy
 issues; food processing sciences; food quality

French Studies

Tel: (0118) 931 8121 Fax: (0118) 931 8122
Bryden, K. M., BA Reading, MA Salf., PhD
 Reading Sr. Lectr.

Kerr, Anne P., BA PhD Sr. Lectr.
Knapp, A. F., BA Oxf., DPhil Oxf. Sr. Lectr.
Lee, D. C. J., MA Oxf., DPhil Oxf. Sr. Lectr.
Noble, P. S., MA Camb., PhD Lond. Prof.;
 Head*
Redfern, W. D., MA Camb., PhD Camb. Prof.
Segal, Naomi D., BA Camb., PhD Camb. Prof.
Tucker, G. H., MA Camb., PhD Camb. Prof.
Waites, N. H., BA Sheff., PhD Lond. Sr. Lectr.
Other Staff: 6 Lectrs.; 1 Visiting Res. Fellow
Research: contemporary and mediaeval French
 history; film studies; literature; politics

Geography

Tel: (0118) 931 8733 Fax: (0118) 975 5865
Bowlby, Sophia R., BA Camb., MSc Northwestern,
 PhD Northwestern Sr. Lectr.
Breheny, M. J., MSc Prof.; Head*
Chapra, S. C., BE Manhattan Coll., ME Manhattan
 Coll., PhD Mich. Visiting Prof.
Cox, K. R., BA Camb., MA Ill., PhD
 Ill. Visiting Prof.
Fenwick, I. M., MSc Sr. Lectr.
Foot, D. H. S., BSc Wales Sr. Lectr.
Goodall, Brian, BSc(Econ) Lond. Prof.
Gordon, I. R., BA Oxf. Prof.
Gurney, R. J., BSc Lond., PhD Brist. Prof.
Hanson, S. E., BA Middlebury, PhD
 Northwestern Visiting Prof.
Hornberger, G. M., BScE Drexel, MScE Drexel,
 PhD Stan. Visiting Prof.
Johnes, P. J., BSc CNAA, DPhil Oxf. Reader
Mannion, Antoinette M., BSc Liv., PhD
 Brist. Sr. Lectr.
Reynolds, C. S., BSc Lond., PhD Lond., DSc
 Lond. Visiting Prof.
Thompson, R. D., MSc Wales, PhD Sr. Lectr.
Whitehead, P. G., BSc Lough., MSc Manc., PhD
 Camb. Prof.
Other Staff: 12 Lectrs.; 4 Res. Officers; 1 Hon.
 Res. Fellow
Research: aquatic environments; GIS and remote
 sensing; resource evaluation and appraisal;
 tourism; urban and regional systems

German Studies

Tel: (0118) 931 8331 Fax: (0118) 931 8333
Roe, I. F., BA Durh., PhD Durh. Sr. Lectr.
Sandford, J. E., MA Camb., PhD Lond. Prof.;
 Head*
Other Staff: 5 Lectrs.
Research: German literature; German mass
 media; mediaeval German history and
 culture; political issues in Germany since
 1945

History

Tel: (0118) 931 8147
Arnold, B. C. B., BA Oxf., DPhil Oxf. Prof.
Barber, M. C., BA Nott., PhD Nott. Prof.
Biddiss, M. D., MA Camb., PhD Camb.,
 FRHistS Prof.
Curry, Anne E., MA Manc., PhD CNAA Sr.
 Lectr.; Head*
Houlbrooke, R. A., MA Oxf., DPhil
 Oxf. Reader
James, E. F., MA Oxf., DPhil Oxf., FRHistS,
 FSA Prof.
Kemp, B. R., BA PhD, FRHistS Prof.
Tallett, F., JP, BA PhD Sr. Lectr.
Whitney, E., BA San Francisco, PhD
 N.Y. Visiting Prof. Other Staff: 15 Lectrs.; 1
 Hon. Visiting Fellow
Research: agrarian history; religious organisation
 from the middle ages to the nineteenth
 century; twentieth-century history of Britain,
 France, Germany and the US

History of Art, see also Fine Art

Tel: (0118) 931 8890 Fax: (0118) 931 8918
Lee, S., BA PhD Lectr.; Head*
Potts, A., BA Tor., PhD Lond. Prof.
Robertson, E. Clare, MA Oxf., MPhil Lond., PhD
 Lond. Reader
Other Staff: 4 Lectrs.
Research: British artists and the First World War;
 European and American hospital

architecture; Michele Sanmichele; Walter Sickert; Paolo Veronese

Horticulture and Landscape

Tel: (0118) 931 8071 Fax: (0118) 975 0630

Battey, N. H., BSc Wales, PhD Edin. Reader
Bisgrove, R. J., MLA Mich., BSc Sr. Lectr.
Hadley, P., BSc Wales, PhD Wales Prof.
van Emden, H. F., BSc Lond., PhD Lond. Prof., Applied Entomology; Head*
Other Staff: 5 Lectrs.; 2 Res. Fellows; 1 Hon. Res. Fellow

Research: amenity horticulture; crop protection; plant physiology

Italian Studies

Tel: (0118) 931 8400

Barański, Z. G., BA Hull Prof.; Head*
Duggan, C. J. H., BA Oxf., DPhil Oxf. Reader
Jones, Verina R., DottFil Turin, BLitt Oxf. Sr. Lectr.
Lepschy, G. C., DottLett Pisa Prof.
Martines, L., PhD Harv. Visiting Prof.
Robey, D. J. B., MA Oxf. Prof.
Vinall, Shirley W., MA Oxf., MA Reading, PhD Sr. Lectr.
Wagstaff, C. G., BA Oxf. Sr. Lectr.
Other Staff: 4 Lectrs.

Research: dialectology and linguistics; film studies; Italian history and politics; Italian women's studies; literature

Land Management and Development

Tel: (0118) 931 8175 Fax: (0118) 931 8172

Barras, R., BA Camb., MSc Lond., PhD Camb. Visiting Prof.
Baum, Andrew, BSc(EstMan) MPhil PhD, FRICS Prof., Land Management
Byrne, P. J., BA Manc. Sr. Lectr.; Head*
Crosby, N., PhD Reading Prof.
Geltner, D., BGS Mich., MS Carnegie-Mellon, PhD M.I.T. Visiting Prof.
Gibson, Virginia A., BA W.Ont., MSc Sr. Lectr.
Hart, D. A., BA Colorado, MA Exe., PhD Lond. Reader
Lizieri, C. M., BA Oxf., PhD Lond. Sr. Lectr.
Ward, C. W. R., MA Camb., MA Exe., PhD Prof.
Other Staff: 9 Lectrs.; 5 Visiting Fellows

Research: housing; IT in real estate; property investment and evaluation; rural property; town and country planning

Landscape, see Hort. and Landscape

Law

Tel: (0118) 931 6568 Fax: (0118) 975 3280

Buckley, R. A., MA Oxf., DPhil Oxf. Prof.
Downes, T. A. (Tony), BA Oxf., BCL Oxf. Prof.
Ghandhi, P. R., MA Oxf., LLM Lond. Sr. Lectr.
Jackson, P., BCL Oxf., MA Trinity(Dub.), LLD Liv. Prof.
James, Jennifer A., LLB Exe., BCL Oxf. Sr. Lectr.; Head*
Leopold, Patricia M., LLB Belf., LLM Exe. Sr. Lectr.
Murdoch, J. R., LLB Lond. Prof.
Murdoch, Sandra E., LLM Birm. Sr. Lectr.
Newdick, C., BA CNAA, LLM Lond. Reader
Niemi, M. I., LLD Visiting Res. Prof.
Smith, P. F., MA Oxf., BCL Oxf. Reader
Stychin, C. F., BA Alta., LLB Tor., LLM Col. Prof.
Other Staff: 7 Lectrs.

Research: European Community law; human rights; medical law; property law; public law

Linguistic Science

Tel: (0118) 931 8140 Fax: (0118) 975 3365

Brasington, R. W. P., MA Oxf. Sr. Lectr.
Cook, G. W. D., MA Camb., PhD Leeds Prof.
Edwards, Susan I., MSc Lond. Sr. Lectr.
Fletcher, P. J., BA Oxf., PhD Alta., MPhil Prof.
Fudge, E. C., MA Camb., PhD Camb. Prof.
Garman, M. A. G., BA Oxf., PhD Edin. Prof.

Huang, Y., BA Nanking, MA Nanking, PhD Camb. Reader
Hughes, G. A., BA Montr. Sr. Lectr.
Kerswill, P. E., BA Camb., MPhil Camb., PhD Camb. Sr. Lectr.
Roach, Peter, MA Oxf., PhD Prof.; Head*
Warburton, Irene P., BA Athens, PhD Indiana Prof.
Wilkins, D. A., BA Manc. Prof.†
Other Staff: 5 Lectrs.; 7 Visiting Lectrs.; 3 Res. Fellows; 2 Clin. Tutors; 2 Hon. Res. Fellows

Research: accents and dialects; acquisition of language; phonetics; speech therapy and language pathology; theoretical linguistics

Mathematics, see also Appl. Stats.

Tel: (0118) 931 8996 Fax: (0118) 931 3423

Baines, M. J., BSc Lond., PhD Lond., FIMA Prof.
Bunce, L. J., BSc Wales, BSc Reading, MSc Oxf., PhD Reading Reader
Hilton, A. J. W., BSc PhD Prof.
Needham, David, BSc Leeds, PhD Leeds Prof.
Nichols, Nancy K., BA Harv., DPhil Oxf. Prof.
Porter, D., BSc Wales, PhD Leic. Sr. Lectr.; Head*
Sewell, M. J., BSc Nott., PhD Nott., FIMA Prof., Applied Mathematics
Stirling, D. S. G., BSc Glas., PhD Edin. Sr. Lectr.
Sweby, P. K., BSc Brist., PhD Sr. Lectr.
Wright, J. D. M., MA Aberd., DPhil Oxf. Prof., Pure Mathematics
Other Staff: 8 Lectrs.; 2 Visiting Lectrs.; 2 Res. Officers; 2 Hon. Fellows

Research: combinatorics; control theory; fluid mechanics; functional analysis; numerical analysis

Meteorology

Tel: (0118) 931 8954 Fax: (0118) 935 2604

Browning, K. A., BSc Lond., PhD Lond., FRS Prof.
Craig, G. C., BSc Tor., MSc Tor., PhD Tor. Reader
Hoskins, Brian J., CBE, CBE Camb., MA Camb., PhD Camb., FRMetS, FRS Prof.
Illingworth, A. J., BA Camb., PhD Camb., DSc Manc. Reader
James, I. N., BSc Leeds, PhD Manc. Sr. Lectr.
O'Neill, A., MA Oxf., PhD Prof.
Pedder, M. A., BSc Wales, PhD Camb. Sr. Lectr.
Shine, K. P., BSc Lond., PhD Edin. Prof.
Thorpe, A. J., BSc Warw., PhD Lond., FRMetS Prof.; Head*
Valdes, P. J., BSc Lond., DPhil Oxf. Reader
Other Staff: 6 Lectrs.; 2 Teaching Fellows; 1 Principal Res. Fellow; 51 Res. Fellows

Research: atmospheric chemistry; climate change; computational fluid dynamics; urban and boundary layer meteorology; weather systems

Music

Tel: (0118) 931 8411 Fax: (0118) 931 8412

Burton, N. M., MA Camb., MusB Camb., MA Trinity(Dub.), MusB Trinity(Dub.), FRCO Sr. Lectr.
Dunsby, J. M., MA Oxf., PhD Leeds Prof.; Head*
Kent, C. J., MusB Manc., MMus Lond., PhD Lond. Sr. Lectr.
Whittall, A. M., MA Camb., PhD Camb. Visiting Prof.
Other Staff: 2 Lectrs.

Research: historical musicology and musical composition; music theory; organ historiography; performance studies

Philosophy

Tel: (0118) 931 8325 Fax: (0118) 931 8295

Andrews, J. N., MEd Edin., MA Edin., MA Lond. Sr. Lectr.
Cottingham, J. G., MA Oxf., DPhil Oxf. Prof.
Dancy, J. P., BPhil Oxf., MA Oxf. Prof.
Glock, H.-J., MA F.U.Berlin, DPhil Oxf. Reader (on leave)
Hooker, B., BA Prin., DPhil Oxf. Sr. Lectr.

Proudfoot, M. A., MA Camb., MLitt Camb. Sr. Lectr. (on leave)
Other Staff: 4 Lectrs.; 3 Tutors†

Research: environmental and applied ethics; history of philosophy; metaphysics; moral philosophy; philosophy of mind

Physics

Tel: (0118) 931 8543 Fax: (0118) 975 0203

Bassett, D. C., MA Camb., ScD Camb., PhD Brist. Prof.
Blackman, J. A., BA Oxf., DPhil Oxf. Reader
Codling, K., PhD Lond., DSc Lond. Prof., Atomic and Molecular Physics; Head*
Frasinski, L. J., PhD Cracow Reader
Jennings, B. R., BSc S'ton., PhD S'ton., DSc S'ton., FRSChem Prof.
Lettington, A. H., BSc Sheff., PhD Exe. Prof.
Lidiard, A. B., PhD Lond., DSc Lond., FIP Visiting Prof.
Macdonald, J., MSc Lond., PhD Sr. Lectr.
Mitchell, G. R., MSc CNAA, PhD CNAA Prof.
Newman, R. C., BSc Lond., PhD Lond. Visiting Prof.
Sangster, M. J. L., BSc Aberd., PhD Reader
Sinclair, R. N., BSc Sheff., PhD Sheff. Visiting Prof.
Stewart, R. J., BSc Reading, PhD Reading Reader; Dep. Dir., J. J. Thompson Phys. Lab.
Tinker, M. H., MA Oxf., DPhil Oxf Sr. Lectr.
Wright, A. C., PhD Brist. Prof.
Other Staff: 8 Lectrs.; 1 Sr. Res. Fellow; 3 Sr. Sci. Officers; 11 Res. Officers; 4 Hon. Visiting Fellows

Research: applied optics; atomic and molecular physics; condensed matter physics; polymer physics

Politics

Tel: (0118) 931 8501 Fax: (0118) 975 3833

Bellamy, R. P., MA Camb., PhD Camb. Prof.; Head*
Bluth, C., BA Trinity(Dub.), MPhil Trinity(Dub.), PhD Lond. Prof.
Giddings, P. J., MA Oxf., DPhil Oxf. Sr. Lectr.
Gregory, R. G., MA Oxf., DPhil Oxf. Prof.
Holden, B. B., BA Keele Sr. Lectr.
Jones, R. J. B., BA Sheff., DPhil Sus. Sr. Lectr.; Head*
Silverman, L., BSc(Econ) Lond., PhD Lond. Sr. Lectr.
Woodward, P. R., BA S'ton., MA Essex, PhD Prof.
Other Staff: 10 Lectrs.; 9 Visiting Res. Fellows; 3 Hon. Sr. Res. Fellows; 1 Hon. Res. Fellow

Research: comparative government/area studies; international relations; political theory

Psychology

Tel: (0118) 931 8523 Fax: (0118) 931 6604

Berry, Dianne C., BSc CNAA, DPhil Oxf. Prof.; Head*
Box, Hilary O., BA Brist., PhD Sheff. Sr. Lectr.
Cooper, P. J., BA Cape Town, DPhil Oxf. Prof.
Gaffan, Elizabeth A., MA Oxf., DPhil Oxf. Sr. Lectr.
Harris, J. P., BA Camb., BA Reading, PhD CNAA Reader
McKenna, F. P., BSc Glas., PhD Lond. Prof.
Murray, Lynne, MA Edin., PhD Edin. Prof.
Smith, P. T., BA Camb., DPhil Oxf. Prof.
Wann, John, BA Leeds, MPE W.Aust., PhD Camb. Reader
Warburton, D. M., BSc Lond., AM Indiana, PhD Indiana Prof.
Other Staff: 8 Lectrs.; 3 Visiting Fellows; 1 Sci. Officer; 29 Res. Staff

Research: cognitive psychology; developmental psychology; human skills and information processing; neurochemistry of behaviour; visual psychophysics

Sociology

Tel: (0118) 931 8519 Fax: (0118) 931 8922

Davies, J. C. H., MA Camb., PhD Camb. Prof.
Hamilton, M. B., BScEcon Wales, MPhil PhD Sr. Lectr.; Head*
Robertson, K. G., MA Aberd., PhD Sr. Lectr.

Waddington, P. A. J., BSc(Soc) Lond., MA Leeds, PhD Leeds   Prof.

Walter, J. A., BA Durh., PhD Aberd.   Reader
Other Staff: 7 Lectrs.
Research: death and society; jokes and humour; moral controversies; public order and policing; sociology of food, diet and health

Soil Science

Tel: (0118) 931 6557 Fax: (0118) 931 6660

Alloway, B. J., BSc Lond., PhD Wales   Prof.; Head*

Catt, J. A., BSc Hull, PhD Hull, DSc Hull   Visiting Prof.

Greenland, D. J., MA Oxf., DPhilOxf., FRS   Visiting Prof.

Gregory, Peter J., BSc Reading, PhD Nott.   Prof.

Jenkinson, D. S., BA Trinity(Dub.), BSc Trinity(Dub.), PhD Trinity(Dub.)   Visiting Prof.

Nortcliff, S., BA Brist., PhD E.Anglia   Reader

Powlson, D. S., BSc E.Anglia, PhD Reading   Visiting Prof.

Rowell, D. L., BSc Nott., DPhil Oxf.   Sr. Lectr.

Simmonds, L. P., BSc Leeds, PhD Nott.   Sr. Lectr.

Swift, R. S., BSc Birm., PhD Birm., FRSChem   Visiting Prof.

Webster, R., BSc Sheff., DPhil Oxf., DSc Sheff.   Visiting Prof.

Wood, M., BA Oxf., PhD Belf.   Reader
Other Staff: 3 Lectrs.; 1 Visiting Lectr.; 1 Advanced Res. Fellow; 5 Res. Fellows; 1 Sr. Visiting Res. Fellow; 2 Sessl. Lectrs.
Research: agriculture; agricultural development; environmental management

Statistics, Applied, see Appl. Stats.

Typography and Graphic Communication

Tel: (0118) 931 8081 Fax: (0118) 935 1680

Stiff, P., BA   Reader

Twyman, M. L., BA PhD   Prof.

Unger, Gerard   Prof.†
Other Staff: 8 Lectrs.
Research: historical research; information design; theoretical issues in typography

SPECIAL CENTRES, ETC

Agricultural Strategy, Centre for

Tel: (0118) 931 8152 Fax: (0118) 935 3423

Hallam, D., BA Reading, MSc Oxf., PhD Reading   Dir.*

Sharkey, P. H., MA Oxf., MSc Reading   Visiting Indust. Prof.
Other Staff: 2 Sr. Res. Fellows; 3 Res. Fellows; 1 Res. Assoc.; 2 Hon. Res. Fellows

Applied Language Studies, Centre for

Tel: (0118) 931 8511 Fax: (0118) 975 6506

Porter, D., BA Leic.   Sr. Lectr.

White, R. V., MA Auck., MA Essex   Sr. Lectr.; Dir.*
Other Staff: 10 Lectrs.

Continuing Education, Centre for

Tel: (0118) 931 8347 Fax: (0118) 975 3507

Petyt, K. M., MA Camb., MA Reading, PhD   Dir. of Extramural and Continuing Educn.; Head*
Other Staff: 4 Lectrs.

Environmental Systems Science Centre (NERC)

Gurney, Prof. R. J., BSc Lond., PhD Brist.   Dir.*

Mason, D. C., BSc Lond., PhD Lond.   Reader

Monteith, J. L., BSc Edin., PhD Lond., FRS   Visiting Prof.

Morris, E. M., BSc Brist., PhD Brist.   Visiting Prof.

Wadge, G., BSc Lond., PhD Lond.   Prof. Res. Fellow

Wallace, J. S., BSc Belf., PhD Nott.   Prof.
Other Staff: 1 Principal Res. Fellow; 1 Sr. Res. Fellow; 1 Sr. Sci. Officer; 1 Higher Sci. Officer; 6 Res. Fellows

European and International Studies, Graduate School of

Tel: (0118) 931 8378 Fax: (0118) 975 5442

Barker, J. C., LLB Glas., PhD Glas.   Dir., Diplomacy

Bluth, C., BA Trinity(Dub.), MPhil Trinity(Dub.), PhD Lond.   Dir.*

Kipping, M., BA Munich, MA Paris IV, PhD Munich   Dir., European Studies

Peters, J., BSc(Econ) Lond., MLitt Oxf., DPhil Oxf.   Dir., Internat. Relns.

Waites, N. H., BA Sheff., PhD Lond.   Dir., Euro-Med. Studies

Medieval Studies, Graduate Centre for

Tel: (0118) 931 8148

James, E. F., MA Oxf., DPhil Oxf., FSA, FRHistS   Prof.; Dir.*

Music Education, International Centre for Research in

Tel: (0118) 931 8821

Kemp, A. E., MA Sus., DPhil Sus., FTCL   Dir.*

Reading and Language Information Centre

Tel: (0118) 931 8820

Edwards, Vivien, BA PhD   Prof.; Dir.*
Other Staff: 1 Lectr.; 1 Res. Officer

Rural History Centre

Tel: (0118) 931 8660 Fax: (0118) 975 1264

Brigden, R. D., BA Durh.   Keeper of the Museum of Engl. Rural Life

Collins, Prof. E. J. T., BA Birm., PhD Nott.   Dir.*

Sedimentology, Postgraduate Research Institute for

Tel: (0118) 931 6713 Fax: (0118) 931 0279

Allen, John, BSc Sheff., DSc Sheff., Hon. LLD Sheff., FSA, FRS   Prof.†

Coleman, M. L., BSc Lond., PhD Leeds   Prof.

Ivanovich,, BSc Tas., PhD ANU   Visiting Prof.

Jones, G. P., BSc Wales, MSc Wales   Visiting Prof.

McCann, C., BSc Lond., PhD Wales   Prof.

Parker, A., BA Keele, PhD Reading   Sr. Lectr.; Head*

Price, M., BSc Birm., MSc Lond.   Sr. Lectr.

Pye, K., MA Camb., PhD Camb.   Prof.

Rae, J. E., BSc Durh., PhD Lanc.   Reader

Sellwood, B. W., DPhil Oxf., BSc   Prof.

Worsley, P., BA Keele, PhD Manc.   Prof.
Other Staff: 2 Sr. Res. Fellows; 8 Res. Fellows; 9 Visiting Res. Fellows; 1 Sci. Officer; 3 Res. Officers

CONTACT OFFICERS

. Vice-Chancellor: Williams, Prof. Roger, MA Oxf., MA(Econ) Manc.

Academic affairs. Registrar: Frampton, David C. R., MA St And.

Accommodation. Senior Assistant Registrar: Goddard, Susan M., BA Open(UK), MA Reading, PhD Reading

Admissions (first degree). Academic Registrar: Clark, Roger M. G., BA Lond.

Admissions (higher degree). Academic Registrar: Clark, Roger M. G., BA Lond.

Adult/continuing education. Director of Extramural and Continuing Education: Petyt, Malcolm, MA Camb., MA Reading, PhD Reading

Alumni. Alumni Relations Officer: Armson, Marion A., BA York(U.K.)

Archives. Archivist: Bott, G. Mike C., MA Oxf.

Careers. Director of Careers Advisory Service: Bottomley, Andrew, BSc Liv., PhD Leeds

Computing services. Director of IT Services: Roch, D. Michael, BA Open(UK)

Consultancy services. Senior Assistant Bursar: Ansell, Alison, BSc Reading

Credit transfer. Academic Registrar: Clark, Roger M. G., BA Lond.

Development/fund-raising. Bursar: Ascott, Robert H. C., MA Camb.

Estates and buildings/works and services. Director of Estates and Buildings: Davies, Gordon E., MA Edin., MA York(UK)

Examinations. Assistant Registrar: Messer, Richard J., BA Oxf., PhD Birm.

Finance. Finance Officer: Sutton, Graham J., MA Oxf.

General enquiries. Registrar: Frampton, David C. R., MA St And.

Health services. Director of Health Service: Johnson, Peter P., OBE, MB BS Lond.

Industrial liaison. Senior Assistant Bursar: Ansell, Alison, BSc Reading

International office. Director of International Office: Betts, David, BSc(Agric) Reading

Library (chief librarian/enquiries). Librarian: Corrall, Sheila, MA Camb., MBA Sus., FLA

Personnel/human resources. Director of Personnel: Price, Roger C., BSc Nott.

Public relations, information and marketing (public relations and information). Press and Information Officer: Dickinson, Kay, BSc Brist.

Public relations, information and marketing (marketing). Director of Student Recruitment and Schools Liaison: Buss, Dorothy, BA Reading

Publications. Senior Administrative Assistant: Nyirenda, Joanna M., BA Brist.

Purchasing. Purchasing Officer: Coombs, Gillian

Quality assurance and accreditation. Senior Assistant Registrar: Hodgson, Keith N., BA Leic.

Research. Pro-Vice-Chancellor: Gregory, Prof. Peter J., BSc Reading, PhD Nott.

Safety. Safety Officer: Kibblewhite, John F. J., BSc City(UK), FRSChem

Scholarships, awards, loans. Academic Registrar: Clark, Roger M. G., BA Lond.

Schools liaison. Director of Student Recruitment and Schools Liaison: Buss, Dorothy, BA Reading

Security. Security Officer: Millership, Alan

Sport and recreation. Director of Sport and Recreation: Atwell, Philip, BSc Sus., MSc Sheff.

Staff development and training. Pryse, Janet, E., BSc Lond.

Student welfare/counselling. Counsellor: Ross, Peter J., BA Trinity(Dub.), MA Trinity(Dub.), MSc Belf., MSc Warw.

Students from other countries. Director of International Office: Betts, David, BSc(Agric) Reading

Students with disabilities. Senior Administrative Assistant: Dixon, Rachel, BA Strath.

[Information supplied by the institution as at 17 June 1998, and edited by the ACU]

ROBERT GORDON UNIVERSITY

Founded 1992; orginally established as Robert Gordon's Hospital 1750

Member of the Association of Commonwealth Universities

Postal Address: Schoolhill, Aberdeen, Scotland AB10 1FR
Telephone: (01224) 262000 **Fax**: (01224) 263000 **E-mail**: i.centre@rgu.ac.uk **WWW**: http://www.rgu.ac.uk/
E-mail formula: initial.surname@rgu.ac.uk

CHANCELLOR—Reid, Sir Bob
PRINCIPAL AND VICE-CHANCELLOR*—Stevely, Prof. William S., BSc *Glas.*, DPhil *Oxf.*,
    FIBiol
VICE-PRINCIPAL—Ross, Gavin T. N., MArch *Penn.*
UNIVERSITY SECRETARY‡—Caldwell, David C., MA BPhil
DIRECTOR OF FINANCE—Briggs, Patricia, MA, FCA

GENERAL INFORMATION

History. The university, founded in 1992, has been a teaching institution since 1881. It is situated in Aberdeen, on the north east coast of Scotland.

Admission to first degree courses (see also United Kingdom Introduction). Through Universities and Colleges Admissions Services (UCAS).

First Degrees (see also United Kingdom Directory to Subjects of Study) (* = also available with honours). BA*, BEng*, BSc*, MPharm.
    All courses last 3 years with an additional year for honours.

Higher Degrees (see also United Kingdom Directory to Subjects of Study). MA, MBA, MSc, MPhil, DPhil.

FACULTIES/SCHOOLS

Design
Dean: Spiller, Prof. Eric, MA RCA

Health and Food
Dean: Harper, Prof. John, BSc PhD, FRSChem

Management
Dean: McIntosh, P. William, BA

Science and Technology
Dean: McIntosh, Prof. Frank G., BSc(Eng) MSc

ACADEMIC UNITS

Arranged by Schools The university has 520 full-and part-time academic staff.

Applied Sciences
Tel: (01224) 262801 Fax: (01224) 262828
Bradley, Robert, BSc PhD, FRSChem   Head*

Applied Social Studies
Tel: (01224) 263201 Fax: (01224) 263222
Lishman, Joyce, MA Oxf., PhD   Prof.; Head*

Architecture, Scott Sutherland School of
Tel: (01224) 263501 Fax: (01224) 263535
Webster, Robin G. M., MA Camb., MA(Arch), FRIAS   Prof.; Head*

Art, Gray's School of
Tel: (01224) 263601 Fax: (01224) 263636
Milligan, Barbara, BA   Head*

Business
Tel: (01224) 283806 Fax: (01224) 283809
Vacant Posts: Head*

Computer and Mathematical Sciences
Tel: (01224) 262701 Fax: (01224) 262727
Harper, David J., BSc PhD   Prof.; Head*

Educational Development Unit
Tel: (01224) 263341 Fax: (01224) 263344
Ellington, Henry I., BSc PhD, FIEE, FIP   Prof.; Dir.*

Engineering, Electronic and Electrical
Tel: (01224) 262401 Fax: (01224) 262444
Deans, Norman D., BSc(Eng) PhD, FIEE   Prof.; Head*

Engineering, Mechanical and Offshore
Tel: (01224) 262301 Fax: (01224) 262333
Power, Laurie, BMet MMet   Actg. Head*

Food and Consumer Studies
Tel: (01224) 263002 Fax: (01224) 263333
Houston, Veronica M., BA PhD   Head*

Health Sciences
Tel: (01224) 627146 Fax: (01224) 404025
Maehle, Valerie A., MEd PhD   Head*

Occupational Therapy
Tel: (01224) 627146 Fax: (01224) 404029
Paterson, Catherine F., MEd   Dir. of Dept.*

Physiotherapy
Tel: (01224) 627146 Fax: (01224) 404025
Maehle, Valerie A., MEd PhD   Dir. of Dept.*

Radiography Education
Tel: (01224) 627146 Fax: (01224) 404025
Graham, Donald T., MEd   Dir. of Dept.*

Information and Media
Tel: (01224) 262950
Johnson, Ian M., BA, FLA   Head*

Law, see Public Admin. and Law

Mathematics, see Computer and Mathl. Scis.

Media, see Information and Media

Nursing, Midwifery and Community Studies
Tel: (01224) 263360 Fax: (01224) 263363
Lowis, Ann, MEd   Prof.; Dir.*

Pharmacy
Tel: (01224) 262501 Fax: (01224) 626559
Richards, Robert M. E., OBE, BPharm PhD DSc, FRPharmS   Prof.; Head*

Public Administration and Law
Tel: (01224) 262901 Fax: (01224) 262929
Levy, Roger P., BA MPhil PhD   Prof.; Head*

Surveying
Tel: (01224) 263701 Fax: (01224) 263777
Pollock, Robert, BSc MSc, FRICS   Head*

SPECIAL CENTRES, ETC

Environmental Studies, Centre for
Tel: (01224) 263703 Fax: (01224) 263737
Baxter, Prof. Seaton, FRICS   Dir.*

Heritage Unit
Tel: (01224) 263705 Fax: (01224) 263535
Fladmark, Prof. J. Magnus, FSA   Dir.*

Hyperbaric Research Unit
Tel: (01224) 262242
Shields, Thomas, BSc MB ChB PhD, FRCP   Dir.*

Offshore Management Centre (Consultancy)
Tel: (01224) 263124 Fax: (01224) 263100
McCarten, Sharon, BComm MBA   Bus. Manager*

Univation (Industrial Unit)
Training consultancy
Tel: (01224) 263321 Fax: (01224) 263323
Mackinlay, Vivien, BSc MBA   Managing Dir.*

CONTACT OFFICERS

Academic affairs. Academic Registrar: Douglas, Hilary J., BSc
Accommodation. Senior Accommodation Services Officer: Webster, Ian C., BSc
Admissions (first degree). Admissions Officer: Youngson, Jenny
Alumni. Alumni Officer: Stronach, Alison
Careers. Senior Careers Adviser: Buchanan, Christine A., MA
Computing services. Director, Computer Services Unit: Murton, Barry, BSc MSc
Consultancy services. Business Manager, Offshore Management Centre: McCarten, Sharon, BComm MBA
Credit transfer. Admissions Officer: Youngson, Jenny
Development/fund-raising. Development Officer: Wright, Benjamin P. M., BA
Estates and buildings/works and services. Manager, Physical Resources: Wilson, David
Examinations. Registration Officer: Bryan, David C., MA
Finance. Director of Finance: Briggs, Patricia, MA, FCA
General enquiries. University Secretary: Caldwell, David C., MA BPhil
Health services. Customer Services Manager: Cumming, Brian D., BSc
Industrial liaison. Managing Director, Univation Ltd: Mackinlay, Vivien, BSc MBA
International office. International Officer: Barry, Phillippa
Library. Chief Librarian: Dunphy, Elaine A., MA
Personnel/human resources. Personnel Manager: Kennedy, Iain
Public relations, information and marketing. Marketing Officer: Payne, Enid

Purchasing. General Services Officer: Keith, Stephen, MA

Research. Depute Registrar: Murray, Anne, MA MBA

Safety. Safety Officer: McCracken, Brian, BEng

Scholarships, awards, loans. Customer Services Manager: Cumming, Brian D., BSc

Schools liaison. Schools Liaison Officer: Mackay, Alan, BA

Security. Ancillary Services Officer: Kaye, Ian A.

Sport and recreation. Student Association Administrator: Bainbridge, Audrey

Staff development and training. Senior Training Officer: Armstrong, Melanie, BA

Student union. Business Operations Administrator: Levack, David

Student welfare/counselling. Senior Student Counsellor: Lough, Mark, BA

Students from other countries (Europe). European Officer: Forsyth, Marlene

Students with disabilities. Officer with Responsibility for Disabled Students: Ryan, Aiveen

University press. Press Officer: Pacitti, Katherine, MA

[Information supplied by the institution as at 7 February 1998, and edited by the ACU]

ROYAL COLLEGE OF ART

Royal Charter 1967; originally established as the School of Design 1837, present name adopted 1896

Postal Address: Kensington Gore, London, England SW7 2EU
Telephone: (0171) 590 4444 **Fax**: (0171) 590 4500 **E-mail**: admissions@rca.ac.uk **WWW**: http://www.rca.ac.uk
E-mail formula: initial.surname@rca.ac.uk

RECTOR AND VICE-PROVOST*—Frayling, Prof. Christopher J., MA *Camb.*, PhD *Camb.*

DIRECTOR OF ADMINISTRATION‡—Philpott, Garry S., BA *Open(UK)*

UNIVERSITY OF ST ANDREWS

Founded 1411

Member of the Association of Commonwealth Universities

Postal Address: St Andrews, Fife, Scotland KY16 9AJ
Telephone: (01334) 476161 **Fax**: (01334) 462570 **WWW**: http://www.st-and.ac.uk

CHANCELLOR AND PRESIDENT OF THE GENERAL COUNCIL—Dover, Sir Kenneth, MA *Oxf.*, DLitt *Oxf.*, Hon. LLD, FBA, FRSEd

RECTOR AND PRESIDENT OF THE UNIVERSITY COURT—Findlay, D. R., QC, LLB MPhil

PRINCIPAL AND VICE-CHANCELLOR*—Arnott, Prof. Struther, CBE, BSc *Glas.*, PhD *Glas.*, DSc *Purdue*, Hon. ScD *St.And.(Laurinburg)*, FRSEd, FRS, FKC

MASTER OF UNITED COLLEGE AND VICE-PRINCIPAL—Vincent, C. A., BSc *Glas.*, PhD *Glas.*, DSc *Glas.*, FRSChem, FRSEd

PRINCIPAL OF ST MARY'S COLLEGE—Piper, R. A., BA *Calif.*, BD *Lond.*, PhD *Lond.*

HEBDOMADAR/DIRECTOR OF ACADEMIC AUDIT—Quinault, F. C., BSc *Brist.*, PhD *Brist.*

PROCTOR—Sanderson, J. J., BSc *Birm.*, PhD *Manc.*

SECRETARY OF THE UNIVERSITY‡—Corner, D. J., BA *Oxf.*, FRHistS

CONTROLLER AND FACTOR—Menzies, A. M., BSc *CNAA*

LIBRARIAN—Dumbleton, N. F., MA *Camb.*, MA *Sheff.*

FACULTIES/SCHOOLS

Arts
Dean: Kettle, Ann J., MA *Oxf.*, FSA

Divinity
Dean: Esler, Prof. P. F., BA *Syd.*, LLM *Syd.*, DPhil *Oxf.*

Science
Dean: Slater, Prof. P. J. B., PhD *Edin.*, DSc *Edin.*, FRSEd

ACADEMIC UNITS
Arranged by Schools

Anatomy, see Biomed. Scis.

Anthropology, see Philos. and Anthropol. Studies

Arabic Studies, see under Hist.

Art History
Tel: (01334) 462400 Fax: (01334) 462401
Brown, C., BA *Oxf.*, PhD *Lond.* Hon. Prof.
Carradice, I. A., BA *Liv.*, PhD *St And.* Sr. Lectr.
Cassidy, Brendan F., MA *Edin.*, PhD *Camb.* Reader
Frew, J. M., MA *Glas.*, DPhil *Oxf.* Sr. Lectr.
Humfrey, P. B., BA *Trinity(Dub).*, MA *Lond.*, PhD *Lond.* Prof.
Lodder, Christina A., BA *York(UK)*, MA *Sus.*, DPhil *Sus.* Prof.
Muir Wright, R. E., MA *St And.* Sr. Lectr.
Normand, T. A., BA *CNAA*, PhD *Durh.* Sr. Lectr.
Smith, G., PhD *Prin.*, MA Prof.; Head*
Spencer, R. A., BA *Manc.*, MA *Lond.* Sr. Lectr.
Walker, D. M., OBE, LLD *Dund.*, FSA, FRSEd, Hon. FRIAS Prof.
Other Staff: 4 Lectrs.

Astronomy, see Phys. and Astron.

Biology, Environmental and Evolutionary
Tel: (01334) 463441 Fax: (01334) 463400
Abbott, R. J., BSc *Wales*, DPhil *Oxf.* Sr. Lectr.
Blaxter, John H. S., BSc *Oxf.*, DPhil *Oxf.* Hon. Prof.

Clarke, Andrew, BA Camb., PhD Camb. Hon. Prof.
Crawford, R. M. M., BSc Glas., DrNatSci Liège, FRSEd Prof., Plant Ecology
Fedak, M. A., BA New Br., MA Duke, PhD Duke Prof.
Gibbs, P. E., BSc Liv., PhD Liv. Sr. Lectr.
Hammond, P. S., BA York(UK), DPhil York(UK) Reader
Harwood, J., BSc Lond., PhD W.Ont. Prof.
Hazon, N., BSc Manc., PhD Sheff. Reader
Johnston, I. A., BSc Hull, PhD Hull, FRSEd Prof.; Head*
Kinghorn, J. R., BSc Strath., PhD Glas. Sr. Lectr.
Magurran, A. E., BSc Glas., PhD Bath Reader
Slater, P. J. B., PhD Edin., DSc Edin., FRSEd Kennedy Prof., Natural History
Smith, V. J., BSc Wales, PhD Wales Reader
Todd, C. D., BSc Leeds, PhD Leeds Sr. Lectr.
Willmer, P. G., MA Camb., PhD Camb. Reader
Wray, J. L., BSc Birm., PhD Birm. Sr. Lectr.
Other Staff: 2 Lectrs.

Biomedical Sciences

Tel: (01334) 463501 Fax: (01334) 463600

Aiton, J. F., BSc St And., PhD St And. Sr. Lectr.
Bryant, P. E., BSc Exe., MSc Lond., PhD Lond. Reader
Brynmor Thomas, D., MB BS Lond., BSc Lond., DSc Birm., FRCPath, FIBiol, FRSEd Bute Hon. Prof., Anatomy and Experimental Pathology
Burchell, Brian, BSc St And., PhD Dund. Hon. Prof.
Cobb, J. L. S., BSc PhD Sr. Lectr.
Cottrell, G. A., PhD S'ton., DSc S'ton., FRSEd Prof., Neuropharmacology
Cramb, G., BSc Edin., PhD Edin. Sr. Lectr.
Dale, N. E., BA Camb., PhD Brist. Reader
Davies, A. M., MB ChB Liv., BSc Liv., PhD Liv. Prof., Medical Science
Flitney, F. W., BSc Leic., PhD Lond., FIBiol Sr. Lectr.
Griffiths, R., BSc Wales, PhD Wales Sr. Lectr.
Harrison, Bryan D., CBE, BSc Reading, PhD Lond., FRS, FRSEd Hon. Prof.
Hay, R. T., BSc H-W, PhD Glas. Prof.
Heitler, W. J., BA Oxf., DPhil Oxf. Reader
Homans, S. W., BA Oxf., DPhil Oxf. Prof.; Head*
Ingledew, W. J., BA York(UK), PhD Brist. Sr. Lectr.
Kemp, G. D., BSc St And., PhD St And. Sr. Lectr.
Lamb, Joseph F., BSc Edin., MB ChB Edin., PhD Edin., FRSEd Hon. Res. Prof.
McLachlan, J. C., BSc Glas., PhD Lond. Sr. Lectr.
McPhate, G. F., MB ChB Aberd., MA Camb., MD Camb., MSc Sur., MTh Edin. Sr. Lectr.
Pitman, R. M., BSc S'ton., PhD S'ton. Sr. Lectr.
Ramsay, Rona R., BSc Edin., MA Edin., PhD Camb. Reader
Randall, R. E., BSc Leeds, PhD Leeds Reader
Riches, A. C., BSc Birm., MSc Birm., PhD Birm. Sr. Lectr.
Russell, William C., BSc Glas., PhD Glas., FRSEd Hon. Res. Prof.
Sinclair, D. W., MB ChB, FRCSEd Sr. Lectr.
Sommerville, J., BSc Edin., PhD Edin. Reader
Steel, C. M., MB ChB Edin., PhD Edin., DSc Edin., FRCPEd, FRCPath, FIBiol, FRSEd Prof.
Thirkell, D., BSc PhD Sr. Lectr.
Tucker, J. B., MA Camb., PhD Camb. Prof.
Other Staff: 10 Lectrs.

Physical Education

Tel: (01334) 462180 Fax: (01334) 464322

Farrally, M. R., MEd Leeds, MA Leeds, PhD Leeds Sr. Lectr.

Chemistry

Tel: (01334) 463800 Fax: (01334) 463808

Aitken, R. A., BSc Edin., PhD Edin. Sr. Lectr.
Bruce, P. G., BSc Aberd., PhD Aberd. Prof.; Head*
Butler, A. R., BSc Lond., PhD Lond., DSc Reader

Cole-Hamilton, D. J., BSc Edin., PhD Edin., FRSChem, FRSEd Irvine Prof.
Gani, D., BSc Sus., DPhil Sus. Prof., Organic Chemistry
Glidewell, C., MA Camb., PhD Camb., ScD Camb., FRSEd Reader
Green, M. J., BSc Manc., PhD UMIST Hon. Prof.
Hay, R. W., PhD Glas., DSc Glas., FRSChem, FRSEd Prof.
Ingold, K. U., BSc Lond., DPhil Oxf. Hon. Prof.
Iqbal, A., MSc Dhaka, DrRerNat Aachen Hon. Prof.
Irvine, John T. S., BSc Edin., DPhil Ulster Reader
Ley, S. V., BSc Lough., PhD Lough., DSc Lond., FRS, FRSChem Hon. Prof.
MacCallum, J. R., PhD Glas., DSc Glas., FRSChem, FRSEd Prof., Polymer Chemistry
Mackie, R. K., BSc PhD, FRSChem Sr. Lectr.
Mackroot, William C., BSc Birm., PhD Birm., FRCS, FIP Reader
Macpherson, I. A., PhD Glas., PhD Glas. Hon. Prof.
Rees, D. C., BSc S'ton., PhD Camb. Hon. Prof.
Riddell, F. G., BSc Liv., PhD Liv. Reader
Smith, D. M., BSc Glas., PhD Glas. Sr. Lectr.
Vincent, C. A., PhD Glas., DSc Glas., FRSChem, FRSEd Prof., Electrochemistry
Walton, J. C., DSc Sheff., PhD Prof.
Ward, W. H. J., BSc Birm., PhD Edin. Hon. Prof.
Other Staff: 1 Hon. Reader; 6 Lectrs.

Classics, see Greek, Latin and Anc. Hist.

Computational Science, see Mathl. and Computational Scis.

Continuing Education, see Special Centres, etc

Divinity

Tel: (01334) 462850 Fax: (01334) 462852

Bauckham, R. J., MA Camb., PhD Camb. Prof., New Testament
Esler, P. F., BA Syd., LLM Syd., DPhil Oxf. Prof.
Gorringe, Timothy J., MA Oxf., MPhil Leeds Reader
Hall, G. B., BA Buffalo, BD Roch., PhD Hon. Prof.
Hampson, M. Daphne, BA Keele, DPhil Oxf., ThD Harv. Sr. Lectr.
Hart, Trevor A., BA Durh., PhD Aberd. Prof.
Piper, R. A., BA Calif., BD Lond., PhD Lond. Prof., New Testament Language and Literature; Head*
Salters, R. B., MA Trinity(Dub.), BD Knox(Tor.), PhD Sr. Lectr., Hebrew and Old Testament
Other Staff: 5 Lectrs.

Economics, see under Soc. Scis.

English

Tel: (01334) 462666 Fax: (01334) 462655

Alexander, M. J., MA Oxf. Prof.
Ashe, A. H., BLitt Oxf., MA Sr. Lectr.
Corcoran, C. D., BA Oxf., MA Oxf., MLitt Oxf. Prof.
Crawford, R., MA Glas., DPhil Oxf. Prof.
Duncan, T. G., MA Glas., BLitt Oxf. Sr. Lectr.
Dunn, D. E., BA Hull, LLD Dund., FRSL Prof.; Head*
Graham, E. F., MA St And., PhD Durh. Sr. Lectr.
Jamison, K. R., BA Calif., MA Calif., CPhil Calif., PhD Calif. Hon. Prof.
Mallett, P. V., MA Camb. Sr. Lectr.
Prave, A. R., BS Indiana, MS Penn.State, PhD Penn.State Sr. Lectr.
Rhodes, N. P. P., BA Oxf., DPhil Oxf. Reader
Roe, N. H., MA Oxf., DPhil Oxf. Prof.
Sellers, Susan C., BA Kent, MA Lond., PhD Lond. Reader
Smith, C. J., BSc Lond., MA Mich., PhD Mich. Prof.
Other Staff: 6 Lectrs.

French, see under Mod. Langs.

Geography and Geosciences

Tel: (01334) 463940 Fax: (01334) 463949

Ballantyne, C. K., MA Glas., MSc McM., PhD Edin. Prof.
Bowden, P., BSc Durh., PhD Lond. Sr. Lectr.
Brown, Peter E., BSc Manc., PhD Manc., FRSEd Prof. Emer.
Dalziel, I., BSc Edin., PhD Edin., FRSEd Hon. Prof.
Dawson, A. H., BA Lond., PhD Lond. Sr. Lectr.
Doherty, J. M., BA Trinity(Dub.), MSc Penn., PhD Lond. Sr. Lectr.
Donaldson, C. H., BSc PhD, FRSEd Reader
McManus, J., BSc Lond., PhD Lond., DSc Dund., FRSEd Prof.; Head*
Oliver, G. J. H., BSc Sheff., PhD Otago Sr. Lectr.
Runnegar, B. N., BSc Qld., PhD Qld., DSc Qld. Hon. Prof.
Soulsby, J. A., MA Aberd., MA Trinity(Dub.), PhD Trinity(Dub.) Sr. Lectr.
Stephens, W. E., BSc Wales, PhD Wales Sr. Lectr.
Tooley, Michael J., BA Birm., PhD Lanc. Prof.
Whittington, G. W., BA Reading, PhD Reading Prof. Emer.
Other Staff: 8 Lectrs.

German, see under Mod. Langs.

Greek, Latin and Ancient History

Ancient History

Tel: (01334) 462600 Fax: (01334) 462602

Austin, M. M., MA Camb., PhD Camb. Sr. Lectr.
Harries, Jill D., MA Oxf., DPhil Oxf. Sr. Lectr.
Other Staff: 1 Lectr.

Greek

Tel: (01334) 462600 Fax: (01334) 462602

Campbell, M., MA Edin., PhD Reader
Dover, Sir Kenneth, MA Oxf., DLitt Oxf., Hon. LLD, FBA, FRSEd Prof. Emer.
Halliwell, Francis S., MA Oxf., DPhil Oxf. Prof.
Henry, A. S., MA St And., PhD St And. Hon. Prof.
Kidd, I. G., BA Oxf., MA St And., FBA Prof. Emer.
Other Staff: 1 Lectr.; 1 Hon. Sr. Lectr.

Latin (Humanity)

Tel: (01334) 462600 Fax: (01334) 462602

Gratwick, A. S., MA Camb., DPhil Oxf. Prof.
Hine, H. M., MA Oxf., DPhil Oxf. Scotstarvit Prof.; Head*
Other Staff: 3 Lectrs.

Hebrew, see Div.

History

Arabic Studies

Tel: (01334) 463632 Fax: (01334) 462914

Bray, J. M. A., BA Oxf., DPhil Oxf. Sr. Lectr.
Other Staff: 2 Lectrs.

History, Mediaeval

Tel: (01334) 463308 Fax: (01334) 463334

Adam, R. J., OBE, MA Oxf., FRHistS Prof. Emer.
Bartlett, R. J., MA Camb., DPhil Oxf., FRHistS Prof.
Bullough, Donald A., MA Oxf., FSA Prof. Emer., German History
Given-Wilson, C. J., MA PhD Sr. Lectr.
Hudson, J. G. H., MA Tor., MA Oxf., DPhil Oxf. Reader
Kennedy, H. N., BA Camb., PhD Camb. Prof.
Kettle, Ann J., MA Oxf., FSA Sr. Lectr.; Chair*
Magdalino, P., BA Oxf., DPhil Oxf. Reader
Maxwell, G., MA, FSA Hon. Prof.
Smith, Julia M. H., BA Camb., MA Camb., DPhil Oxf. Reader
Watt, D. E. R., MA Aberd., DPhil Oxf., FRHistS, FRSEd Prof. Emer.

Other Staff: 4 Lectrs.

History, Modern

Tel: (01334) 462923 Fax: (01334) 462927

Bentley, Michael J., BA Sheff., PhD Camb., FRHistS Prof.

De Groot, G. J., BA Whitman, PhD Edin., FRHistS Hon. Prof.

Guy, J. A., MA Camb., PhD Camb., FRHistS Prof.

Houston, R. A., PhD Camb., MA, FRHistS Prof.

Lenman, B. P., MA Aberd., LittD Camb., FRHistS Prof.

Pettegree, A. D. M., MA Oxf., DPhil Oxf., FRHistS Prof.

Scott, H. M., MA Edin., PhD Lond., FRHistS Sr. Lectr.

Upton, Anthony F., MA Oxf., AM Duke, FRHistS Hon. Prof., Nordic History

Other Staff: 6 Lectrs.

History, Scottish

Tel: (01334) 462890 Fax: (01334) 462927

Brown, Keith M., MA Glas., PhD Glas., FRHistS Prof.; Head*

Macdougall, N. A. T., MA Glas., PhD Glas. Sr. Lectr.

Martin, C. J. M., PhD Reader

Mason, R. A., MA Edin., PhD Edin. Reader

Smout, Christopher T., CBE, MA Camb., PhD Camb., FRSEd, FBA Hon. Prof.

Stevenson, D., BA Trinity(Dub.), PhD Trinity(Dub.), DLitt Glas., FRHistS, FRSEd Prof. Emer.

Other Staff: 1 Lectr.

History, Ancient, see Greek, Latin and Anc. Hist.

International Relations, see under Soc. Scis.

Italian, see under Mod. Langs.

Latin, see Greek, Latin and Anc. Hist.

Management, see under Soc. Scis.

Mathematical and Computational Sciences

Tel: (01334) 463744 Fax: (01334) 463748

Atkinson, M. D., BA Oxf., DPhil Oxf. Prof., Computational Science

Bell, G. E., BTech Brun., PhD Brun. Sr. Lectr.

Blyth, T. S., DèsSc Paris, DSc, FRSEd, FIMA Prof., Pure Mathematics

Buckland, S. T., BSc S'ton., MSc Edin., PhD Aberd. Prof., Statistics

Cairns, R. A., BSc Glas., PhD Glas. Prof.

Campbell, C. M., MA Edin., MSc McG., PhD Sr. Lectr.

Cormack, R. M., BSc Lond., MA Camb., PhD Aberd. Prof. Emer.

Craik, A. D. D., PhD Camb., BSc, FRSEd Prof.

Falconer, K. J., MA Camb., PhD Camb. Prof., Pure Mathematics

Gordon, A. D., BSc Lond., MA Oxf., PhD Camb. Reader

Grundy, R. E., BSc Lond., PhD Lond. Sr. Lectr.

Hood, A. W., BSc PhD Reader

Howie, J. M., CBE, MA Aberd., DSc Aberd., DPhil Oxf., FRSEd Regius Prof., Pure Mathematics

Jupp, P. E., BA Camb., PhD Camb. Reader

Kemp, Cecil D., BSc Brist., PhD Brad. Hon. Prof.

Martin, U. H. M., MA Camb., MSc Warw., PhD Warw. Prof., Computational Science

Morrison, R., BSc Strath., MSc Glas., PhD Prof.

O'Connor, J. J., BA Oxf., DPhil Oxf. Sr. Lectr.

Phillips, G. M., MA Aberd., MSc Aberd., PhD Reader, Numerical Analysis

Priest, E. R., BSc Nott., MSc Leeds, PhD Leeds, FRSEd Prof., Theoretical Solar Physics

Roberts, B., BSc Hull, PhD Sheff. Prof.

Robertson, E. F., MSc Warw., PhD Warw., BSc Prof.; Head*

Sanderson, J. J., BSc Birm., PhD Manc. Hon. Prof., Theoretical Plasma Physics

Other Staff: 16 Lectrs.

Modern Languages

French

Tel: (01334) 463647 Fax: (01334) 463677

Culpin, D. J., BA Brist., MA Brist., MèsL Bordeaux III, PhD Brist. Sr. Lectr.

Gascoigne, D. J., MA Camb., PhD Camb. Sr. Lectr.

Gifford, P. P.-D., MA Camb., Dr3rdCy Toulouse, DèsL Toulouse Buchanan Prof.

Higgins, I. R. W., BA Oxf., BLitt Oxf. Sr. Lectr.

Lodge, Raymond A., BA Manc., PhD Manc. Prof.

Read, P. F., BA Hull, PhD Hull Sr. Lectr.

Scott, M., BA Hull, DPhil Oxf. Prof.; Head*

Other Staff: 3 Lectrs.

German

Tel: (01334) 463655

Ashcroft, J. R., MA Camb., PhD Camb. Sr. Lectr.

Furness, R. S., MA Wales, PhD Manc. Prof.

Jackson, W. H., BA Camb., PhD Camb. Sr. Lectr.

Mullan, W. N. B., BA Trinity(Dub.), BA Oxf., MLitt Oxf. Sr. Lectr.

Other Staff: 4 Lectrs.

Italian

Tel: (01334) 463678

Ferguson, R. G., MA Glas., BPhil St And. Sr. Lectr.

Other Staff: 1 Lectr.

Russian

Tel: (01334) 462949 Fax: (01334) 462959

Drage, C. L., MA Oxf., MA Lond., PhD Lond. Hon. Prof.

Press, Jeffrey I., BA Lond., PhD Lond. Prof.

Pugh, Stefan M., BA Duke, MA Yale, PhD N.Carolina Reader

Sullivan, J., MA Manc. Sr. Lectr.

Other Staff: 1 Lectr.

Spanish

Tel: (01334) 462961 Fax: (01334) 462959

Dennis, Nigel R., BA Camb., MA Camb., PhD Camb. Prof.

Paterson, A. K. G., MA Aberd., PhD Camb. Prof.

Other Staff: 3 Lectrs.

Philosophical and Anthropological Studies

Logic and Metaphysics

Tel: (01334) 462486 Fax: (01334) 462485

Clark, P. J., BSc Manc., MSc Lond., PhD Lond. Sr. Lectr.

Read, S. L., BA Keele, MSc Brist., DPhil Oxf. Sr. Lectr.

Squires, J. E. R., BA Oxf., BPhil Oxf. Sr. Lectr.

Wright, C. J. G., MA Camb., MA Oxf., PhD Camb., BPhil Oxf., DLitt Oxf. Prof.

Philosophy, Moral

Tel: (01334) 462486 Fax: (01334) 462485

Archard, David W., BA Oxf., PhD Lond. Reader

Broome, John, MA Lond., PhD M.I.T. Prof.

Haldane, J. J., BA CNAA, BA Lond., PhD Lond. Prof.; Head*

Skorupski, J. M., MA Camb., PhD Camb., FRSEd Prof.

Other Staff: 3 Lectrs.

Social Anthropology

Tel: (01334) 462977 Fax: (01334) 462985

Dilley, R. M., BSc CNAA, DPhil Oxf. Sr. Lectr.

Hervey, S. G. J., MA Oxf., DPhil Oxf. Reader

Overing, Joanna, BA Conn., MA Conn., PhD Brandeis Prof.

Rapport, N. J., BA Camb., MA Camb., PhD Manc. Prof.

Riches, D. J., MA Camb., PhD Lond. Sr. Lectr.

Other Staff: 1 Lectr.

Physical Education, see under Biomed. Scis.

Physics and Astronomy

Tel: (01334) 463103 Fax: (01334) 463104

Allen, J. F., BA Manit., MA Tor., PhD Tor., FRS, FRSEd Prof. Emer.

Allen, John W., MA Camb., FRSEd Prof. Emer.

Allen, Leslie, BSc Lond., PhD Lond., DSc Lond. Hon. Prof.

Cameron, Andrew C., BA Camb., PhD Camb. Reader

Cornwell, J. F., BSc Lond., PhD Lond., FRSEd Prof., Theoretical Physics

Cywinski, Robert, BSc Manc., PhD Salf. Prof.

David, William I. F., BA Oxf., MA Oxf., DPhil Oxf. Hon. Prof.

Dunn, M. H., BA Camb., PhD St And., FRSEd Prof.

Hilditch, R. W., BSc St And., PhD St And. Reader

Hill, P. W., MA Oxf., PhD Camb. Sr. Lectr.

Horne, Keith D., BA Cal.Tech., PhD Cal.Tech. Prof.

Lawrence, J. L., BSc St And., MSc Dund., PhD St And. Sr. Lectr.

Lesurf, J. C. G., BSc Lond., PhD Lond. Reader

Little, C. E., BSc Macq., PhD Macq. Reader

McGill, N. C., BSc St And., PhD St And. Sr. Lectr.

Menown, Hugh, MBE, BSc Belf., MSc Belf. Hon. Prof.

Miller, A., BSc Edin., PhD Bath Prof.; Head*

Parkes, David Hon. Prof.

Riedi, P. C., MSc Lond., PhD S'ton. Prof.

Sibbett, W., BSc Belf., PhD Belf. Prof.

Sinclair, B. D., BSc St And., PhD St And. Sr. Lectr.

Tunstall, D. P., BSc Wales, PhD Wales, FIP, FRSEd Reader

Van Stryland, Eric W., BS Arizona, PhD Arizona Hon. Prof.

Wan, K. K., BSc St And., PhD St And. Reader

Other Staff: 1 Lectr.; 1 Hon. Reader

Psychology

Tel: (01334) 462027 Fax: (01334) 463042

Byrne, R. W., BA Camb., PhD Camb. Prof.

Heeley, D. W., BSc Sus., PhD Camb. Reader

Jeeves, Malcolm A., MA Camb., PhD Camb., Hon. DSc Edin., FBPsS, FRSEd Hon. Res. Prof.

Johnston, D. W., MA Hull, PhD Hull Head*

Johnston, Marie, BSc Aberd., PhD Hull, FBPsS Prof.

Lee, Terrance R., MA Camb., PhD Camb. Hon. Prof.

Macrae, C. N., BSc Aberd., PhD Aberd. Reader

Milner, A. D., MA Oxf., PhD Lond., FRSEd Prof.

Perrett, D. I., DPhil Oxf., BSc Reader

Reicher, S. D., BSc Brist., PhD Brist. Reader

Rugg, M. D., BSc Leic., PhD Leic. Prof.

Whiten, D. A., BSc Sheff., PhD Brist. Prof.

Winn, P., BA Hull, PhD Hull Reader

Other Staff: 8 Lectrs.

Russian, see under Mod. Langs.

Social Sciences

Economics

Tel: (01334) 462420 Fax: (01334) 462444

Beath, J. A., MA Penn., MA Camb., MA St And., MPhil Lond. Prof.

Bhaskar, Venkataraman, BA Madr., MSc J.Nehru U., DPhil Oxf. Reader

Cobham, D. P., MA Manc., PhD Manc. Sr. Lectr.

Fitzroy, F. R., BSc Lond., MSc Aberd., PhD Heidel. Prof.

Jensen-Butler, Christopher, BA Durh., PhD Durh. Prof.

La Manna, Manfredi M. A., DottScEc Siena, MSc Lond., PhD Lond. Reader

Ploberger, Werner, DrTechHabil T.U.Vienna Prof.

Reid, G. C., MA *Aberd.*, MSc *S'ton.*, PhD
Edin. Prof.
Robson, Peter, MA *Camb.*, MSc *Lond.* Prof.
Emer.
Shea, Gary S., BA *Indiana*, PhD *Wash.* Reader
Other Staff: 7 Lectrs.

International Relations

Tel: (01334) 462938 Fax: (01334) 462937
Beloff, Lord, MA *Oxf.*, DLitt *Oxf.*, FBA,
FRHistS Hon. Prof.
Hinnebusch, R., BA *Duquesne*, MA *Pitt.*, PhD
Pitt. Prof.
Hoffman, Bruce R., DPhil *Oxf.* Reader
Imber, M. F., BSc *Lond.*, PhD *S'ton.* Sr. Lectr.
Mackintosh, M., CMG, MA *St And.* Hon. Prof.
Platzgraff, Robert, BA *Swarthmore*, MA *Penn.*, PhD
Penn. Hon. Prof.
Rengger, N. J., BA *Durh.*, PhD *Durh.* Reader
Schultz, R., PhD *Miami* Hon. Prof.
Walker, W. B., BSc *Edin.*, MSc *Essex* Prof.
Wilkinson, P., MA *Wales* Prof.
Other Staff: 3 Lectrs.

Management

Tel: (01334) 462800 Fax: (01334) 462812
Grinyer, P. H., MA *Oxf.*, PhD *Lond.* Prof.
Hadji-Malek, M. M., BSc *Teheran*, MSc *Lond.*,
PhD *Lond.* Prof.; Head*
McKiernan, P., BA *CNAA*, MA *Lanc.*, PhD
Sur. Prof.
Smith, P. C., BA *Oxf.*, MSc *Lond.* Hon. Prof.
Starkey, K., BA *Sheff.*, BSc *Lond.*, PhD
Aston Hon. Prof.
Other Staff: 5 Lectrs.

Spanish, see under Mod. Langs.

Statistics, see Mathl. and Computational Scis.

Theology, see Div.

SPECIAL CENTRES, ETC

Advanced Historical Research, St John's House Centre for

Tel: (01334) 463300 Fax: (01334) 462914
Smout, T. C., CBE, MA *Camb.*, PhD *Camb.*,
FRSEd, FBA Dir.*

Advanced Materials, St Andrew's Centre for

Tel: (01334) 463825 Fax: (01334) 463808
Bruce, P. G., BSc *Aberd.*, PhD *Aberd.*,
FRSEd Dir.*

Biomolecular Sciences, Centre for

Tel: (01334) 463861 Fax: (01334) 463808
Gani, D., BSc *Sus.*, DPhil *Sus.*, FRSChem,
FRSEd Dir.*

Continuing Education, Centre for

Tel: (01334) 462211 Fax: (01334) 462208
Rougvie, A., BSc *H-W* Dir.*

Environmental History, Institute for

Tel: (01334) 463300 Fax: (01334) 462914
Smout, T. C., CBE, MA *Camb.*, PhD *Camb.*,
FRSEd, FBA Dir.*

Gatty Marine Laboratory

Tel: (01334) 463441 Fax: (01334) 463443
Johnston, I. A., BSc *Hull*, PhD *Hull*,
FRSEd Dir.*

Housing Research, Joint Centre for Scottish

Tel: (01334) 463940 Fax: (01334) 463949
Doherty, J. M., BA *N.U.I.*, MS *Penn.State*, PhD
Lond. Dir.*

Industry Enterprise Finance and the Firm, Centre for Research into

Tel: (01334) 462420 Fax: (01334) 462812
Reid, G. C., MA *Aberd.*, MSc *S'ton.*, PhD
Edin. Dir.*

Maritime Studies, Scottish Institute of

Tel: (01334) 462916 Fax: (01334) 462921
Prescott, R. G. W., MA *Camb.*, PhD
Camb. Dir.*

Middle East Studies, Institute for

Tel: (01334) 463308 Fax: (01334) 463677
Kennedy, H., MA *Camb.*, PhD *Camb.* Dir.*

Pharmacoeconomics Research Centre

Tel: (01334) 462420 Fax: (01334) 462812
Malek, M. M. H., BSc *Teheran*, MSc *Lond.*, PhD
Lond. Dir.*

Philosophy and Public Affairs, Centre for

Tel: (01334) 462486 Fax: (01334) 462485
Haldane, J. J., BA *CNAA*, PhD *Lond.* Dir.*

Reformation Studies Institute, St Andrews

Tel: (01334) 462903 Fax: (01334) 462914
Pettegree, A. D. M., BA *Oxf.*, MA *Oxf.*, DPhil
Oxf. Dir.*

Russian, Soviet and East European Studies, Centre for

Tel: (01334) 462949 Fax: (01334) 463677
Hippisley, A. R., MA *Oxf.*, DPhil *Oxf.* Dir.*

Scottish Studies Institute, St Andrews

Tel: (01334) 462666 Fax: (01334) 462655
Dunn, D., BA *Hull*, LLD *Dund.*, FRSL Dir.*

Social Sciences, St Andrews Centre for the

Tel: (01334) 463908 Fax: (01334) 463949
Graham, E. F., MA *St And.*, PhD *Durh.* Dir.*

Terrorism and Political Violence, Centre for the Study of

Tel: (01334) 462938 Fax: (01334) 462937
Hoffman, B. R., AB *Conn.*, BPhil *Oxf.*, DPhil
Oxf. Dir.*

CONTACT OFFICERS

Academic affairs. Proctor: Sanderson, J. J., BSc
Birm., PhD *Manc.*
Accommodation. Director, Residential and
Business Services: Smith, R. G., MBA
Admissions (first degree). Director,
Admissions: Magee, S. R., MA *St And.*, MSc
Edin.
Admissions (higher degree). Director,
Admissions: Magee, S. R., MA *St And.*, MSc
Edin.
Adult/continuing education. Director, Centre
for Continuing Education: Rougvie, A., BSc
H-W
Alumni. Alumnus Relations Officer: Hodge, J.,
MA *St And.*, LLM *Nott.*
Archives. Keeper of University Collections:
Carradice, I. A., BA *Liv.*, PhD *St And.*, FSA
Careers. Secretary, Careers Advisory Service:
Daniels, T. H., BA *Trinity(Dub.)*
Computing services. Director of Information
Technology Services: Bain, M., BSc *Sus.*, MSc
Liv., PhD *Liv.*
Consultancy services. Director of Sponsored
Programmes: Sillar, L. M., BSc *Glas.*
Consultancy services. Director of Sponsored
Programmes: Ferrari, B. J. F., BA *Lond.*, PhD
St And.

Credit transfer. Proctor: Sanderson, J. J., BSc
Birm., PhD *Manc.*
Development/fund-raising. Acting Director of
External Relations: Cunningham, S., BA
Middx.
Distance education. Proctor: Sanderson, J. J.,
BSc *Birm.*, PhD *Manc.*
Equal opportunities. Director of Personnel
Services: Beaton, D. D., BA *Manc.*, MBA *Dund.*
Estates and buildings/works and services.
Director, Estates and Buildings: Louden, D.
W., MA *Strath.*
Examinations. Examinations Officer: Taylor, S.
M., MA *St And.*
Finance. Controller and Factor: Menzies, A.
M., BSc *CNAA*
General enquiries. Secretary of the University:
Corner, D. J., BA *Oxf.*, FRHistS
Health services. Occupational Health Adviser:
Mackinnon, J.
Industrial liaison. Director of Sponsored
Programmes: Sillar, L. M., BSc *Glas.*
Industrial liaison. Director of Sponsored
Programmes: Ferrari, B. J. F., BA *Lond.*, PhD
St And.
International office. Director, Admissions:
Magee, S. R., MA *St And.*, MSc *Edin.*
Library. Librarian: Dumbleton, N. F., MA
Camb., MA *Sheff.*
Minorities/disadvantaged groups.
Hebdomadar/Director of Academic Audit:
Quinault, F. C., BSc *Brist.*, PhD *Brist.*
Personnel/human resources. Director of
Personnel Services: Beaton, D. D., BA *Manc.*,
MBA *Dund.*
Public relations, information and marketing.
Public Relations Officer: Lind, L., BA
Newcastle(UK)
Publications. Head of Reprographic Services:
Bremner, C. B.
Purchasing. Director, Residential and Business
Services: Smith, R. G., MBA
Quality assurance and accreditation.
Hebdomadar/Director of Academic Audit:
Quinault, F. C., BSc *Brist.*, PhD *Brist.*
Research. Provost: ......
Safety. Safety Adviser: Armitt, C. S.
Scholarships, awards, loans. Hebdomadar/
Director of Academic Audit: Quinault, F. C.,
BSc *Brist.*, PhD *Brist.*
Schools liaison. Director, Admissions: Magee,
S. R., MA *St And.*, MSc *Edin.*
Security. Director, Estates and Buildings:
Louden, D. W., MA *Strath.*
Sport and recreation. Director of Physical
Education: Farally, M. R., BEd *Leeds*, MA *Leeds*,
PhD *Leeds*
Staff development and training. Director of
Personnel Services: Beaton, D. D., BA *Manc.*,
MBA *Dund.*
Student union. Proctor: Sanderson, J. J., BSc
Birm., PhD *Manc.*
Student welfare/counselling. Counselling
Services: ......
Students from other countries. Director,
Admissions: Magee, S. R., MA *St And.*, MSc
Edin.
Students with disabilities. Hebdomadar/
Director of Academic Audit: Quinault, F. C.,
BSc *Brist.*, PhD *Brist.*
University press. Head of Reprographic
Services: Bremner, C. B.
Women. Director of Personnel Services:
Beaton, D. D., BA *Manc.*, MBA *Dund.*

[Information supplied by the institution as at 20 June
1998, and edited by the ACU]

UNIVERSITY OF SALFORD

Founded by Royal Charter 1967; previously established as the Royal Technical Institute 1896

Member of the Association of Commonwealth Universities

Postal Address: Salford, England M5 4WT
Telephone: (0161) 295 5000 **Fax**: (0161) 295 5999 **Telex**: 668680 **WWW**: http://www.salford.ac.uk/

CHANCELLOR—Bodmer, Sir Walter, PhD, FRCPath, FRS
PRO-CHANCELLOR—Goldberg, J., BCL MA Hon. DLitt
PRO-CHANCELLOR—Shields, R. M. C., BSc
VICE-CHANCELLOR*—Harloe, Prof. Michael H., BA Oxf., MA Oxf., PhD Essex
PRO-VICE-CHANCELLOR—Brandon, Prof. Peter S., MSc Brist., DSc Brist., FRICS
PRO-VICE-CHANCELLOR—Emmott, Colin, BSc Aston, PhD Aston, FRICS
PRO-VICE-CHANCELLOR—Sanger, Prof. D. John, MSc Wales, PhD, FIMechE
PRO-VICE-CHANCELLOR—Wheeler, Prof. Peter, BSc Lond., MSc Lond., PhD S'ton., FIEE
REGISTRAR—Winton, Malcolm D., BA Camb., MSc Manc., PhD Manc.

GENERAL INFORMATION

History. The university was established in 1967. It was previously founded as the Royal Technical Institute in 1896.
It is located near the centre of Manchester.

Admission to first degree courses (see also United Kingdom Introduction). UK students apply through: Universities and Colleges Admissions Service (UCAS); Social Work Admissions System (SWAS); Nurses and Midwives Admissions System (NMAS). International students should contact the university's International Office.

First Degrees (see also United Kingdom Directory to Subjects of Study). BA, BEng, BSc, MChem, MEng, MPhys.
Courses are full-time and normally last 3 or 4 years, with additional optional placement years. Some courses are available part-time.

Higher Degrees (see also United Kingdom Directory to Subjects of Study). MA, MBA, MRes, MSc, MPhil, PhD.
Applicants for admission to master's degrees must normally hold a good honours degree, or equivalent qualification.
MA, MBA, MSc: 1 year full-time or 2 years part-time.

Language of Instruction. English. English summer school and preliminary-year English courses are available.

Libraries. 397,233 volumes; 2277 current subscriptions.

Fees (annual). Undergraduate international: £6400 (arts, health, humanities); £8250 (engineering, science).

Academic Year (1998–99). Two semesters: 21 September–31 January; 1 February–11 June.

Income (1996–97). Total, £109,926,000.

Statistics. Staff: 2285 (955 academic/research, 1330 support). Students: full-time 12,539; part-time 4356.

FACULTIES/SCHOOLS

Art and Design Technology
Tel: (0161) 295 6153 Fax: (0161) 835 2453
Dean: Gunner, Alan
Secretary: Whittaker, D.

Business, Management and Consumer Studies
Tel: (0161) 295 2218 Fax: (0161) 295 2130
Dean: Hall, Nigel R., BSc(Econ) Lond., MEd Manc.
Secretary: Weekes, J.

Engineering
Tel: (0161) 295 4512 Fax: (0161) 295 5479
Dean: Pardoe, Bev H., BSc Hull, MSc Essex, PhD Essex, FIEE
Secretary: Johnson, A.

Environment
Tel: (0161) 295 2351 Fax: (0161) 295 2353
Dean: March, C. G., BSc Manc.
Secretary: Ford, D.

Health Care and Social Work Studies
Tel: (0161) 295 2363 Fax: (0161) 295 2368
Dean: Bowker, Prof. Peter, BSc Salf., PhD Salf.
Secretary: Evans, Andrea

Media, Music and Performance
Tel: (0161) 295 6207 Fax: (0161) 834 0699
Dean: Wilson, Keith, MA Camb.
Secretary: Jones, Jane

Science
Tel: (0161) 295 5230 Fax: (0161) 295 4382
Dean: Richards, John T., BSc Durh., PhD Newcastle(UK)
Secretary: Colbeck, C.

Social Sciences and Arts
Tel: (0161) 295 2349 Fax: (0161) 295 2348
Dean: Harrison, Colin, BSc Wales, MSc Manc.
Secretary: Macmillan, M.

ACADEMIC UNITS

Acoustics and Audio Engineering
Tel: (0161) 295 5282 Fax: (0161) 295 5585, 5427
Darlington, P., BSc S'ton., PhD S'ton. Sr. Lectr.
Ford, Roy D., BSc(Eng) S'ton., PhD S'ton. Reader
Hempstock, Thomas I., BSc Lond., PhD Liv. Sr. Lectr.
Lam, Yiu Wai, BSc HK, PhD Birm. Sr. Lectr.
Lord, Peter, MScTech Manc., PhD Manc., FIP Prof.†
O'Connor, E. O., MSc Manc. Sr. Lectr.
Saunders, David J., BSc Nott., PhD St And. Sr. Lectr.; Head*
West, Martin, BScTech Manc., MSc Manc., PhD Salf. Sr. Lectr.
Wheeler, Peter D., BSc Lond., MSc Lond., PhD S'ton., FIEE Prof.

Arabic, see Mod. Langs.

Biological Sciences
Tel: (0161) 295 4475, 3283 Fax: (0161) 295 5210
Alexander, John B., BSc Exe., MSc Lond., PhD Salf. Sr. Lectr.
Bisby, Roger H., BSc Nott., PhD Nott. Sr. Lectr.
Bradley, Janette E., BSc Hull, PhD Lond. Sr. Lectr.
Craig, Philip S., BSc Leeds, MSc Liv., PhD Melb. Prof.; Head*
Davies, David H., BSc Aston, MSc Lond., PhD Sr. Lectr.
Foster, Howard A., BSc Leeds, PhD Leeds Sr. Lectr.
Heath, Stephen, BSc Manc., MSc Liv., PhD Liv. Sr. Lectr.
Lawson, Ronald, BSc Durh., PhD Durh., FLS Prof.
Moore, John S., BSc Wales, PhD Wales Sr. Lectr.
Morgan, Christopher G., MA Oxf., DPhil Oxf. Prof.
Pentreath, Victor W., MSc St And., PhD St And. Reader
Richards, John T., BSc Durh., PhD Newcastle(UK) Sr. Lectr.
Rogan, Michael T., BSc Belf., PhD Keele Sr. Lectr.
Storey, David M., MSc Salf., PhD Salf., FIBiol Prof.
Thomas, Emrys W., BSc Wales, DPhil Oxf. Sr. Lectr.
Villiers, Trevor A., BSc Lond., PhD Lond. Res. Prof., Biology
Washington, John R., MSc Edin., PhD Salf., FRSChem

Business Studies
Fax: (0161) 295 5556
Cleary, Richard, BEd Hull, MSc Salf. Sr. Lectr.
Dangerfield, Brian C., BScEcon Wales, PhD Sr. Lectr.
Dobson, John R., BA Liv., MA Warw. Sr. Lectr.
Edwards, Mike, BA Open(UK), MSc Aston Sr. Lectr.
Gee, Kenneth P., BSc Brist., PhD Manc. Prof., Accounting; Head*
Kennedy, Alison J., BA Lanc. Sr. Lectr.
Mason, Roger S., BA(Econ) Manc., MSc Salf., PhD Salf. Prof., Marketing
Neal, Frank, BSc(Econ) Lond., MA Liv., PhD Prof.
Roberts, Carole A., BSc S'ton., MSc Birm. Sr. Lectr.
Schofield, Peter, BA Manc., MA York(UK) Sr. Lectr.
Southan, John M., BTech Lough. Sr. Lectr.
Sugden, Keith F., BA Sheff., FCA Sr. Lectr.
Whitelock, Jeryl M., MSc Salf. Sr. Lectr.
Wieteska, Paul, BSc Lond., MSc Lond. Sr. Lectr.
Wood, Graham, BSc Wales Sr. Lectr.
Wood, Laurie, BA CNAA, PhD Sr. Lectr.

Chemistry and Applied Chemistry
Fax: (0161) 295 5111
Barnes, Austin J., MA Camb., PhD Wales, DSc Wales Head*
Baugh, Peter J., BSc Wales, PhD Wales Sr. Lectr.
Blackburn, Robert, BSc Durh., PhD Durh. Sr. Lectr.
Boag, Neil, BSc Lond., PhD Brist. Sr. Lectr.

Colquhoun, Howard M., MA Camb., PhD Lond., FRSChem Prof.
Davies, Leslie, BSc Lond., PhD Salf., FRSChem Sr. Lectr.
Dyer, Alan, BSc Sheff., PhD Lond., DSc Salf., FRSChem Reader
Hill, John, BSc lond., PhD Lond. Sr. Lectr.
Jones, Simon A., PhD Liv.J.Moores Sr. Lectr.
Leonard, John, BSc E.Anglia, PhD Manc. Sr. Lectr.
McClelland, Bernard J., BSc Leeds, BSc Lond., PhD Manc., FRSChem Reader
Pemble, Martyn E., BSc S'ton., PhD S'ton., FRSChem Prof., Physical Chemistry
Price, Dennis, BSc Wales, PhD Wales, FRSChem Sr. Lectr.
Procter, Garry, BA Oxf., DPhil Oxf. George Ramage Prof.
Redhouse, Alan D., BSc Brist., PhD Brist. Sr. Lectr.
Rice, Colin L., MA Camb. Sr. Lectr.
Simpson, Stephen J., BSc Lond., DPhil Oxf. Sr. Lectr.
Tiddy, Gordon J. T., BSc Leic., MSc E.Anglia, PhD E.Anglia Prof.
Vernon, Fred, PhD Manc., DSc Salf., FRSChem Sr. Lectr.
Wallace, Timothy W., BSc Lond., PhD Lond. Sr. Lectr.
Wyn-Jones, Evan, PhD Wales, DSc Wales, DPhil Oxf. Res. Prof.†

Computer and Mathematical Sciences
Tel: (0161) 295 3393 Fax: (0161) 295 5559
Addyman, A. M., MSc Manc., FBCS Sr. Lectr.
Amini, S., MSc Manc., PhD Manc. Reader
Ashworth, J., BSc Sheff. Sr. Lectr.
Christer, A. H., MSc Lond., DSc Lond., PhD Strath., FIMA Prof., Operational Research
Fletcher, L. R., BSc Manc., DPhil Oxf. Prof.; Head*
Hill, Arthur E., BSc Manc., PhD Manc., FIEE Sr. Lectr.
Hill, R., BSc Manc., MSc Manc., PhD Warw. Reader
Kobbacy, K. H., MSc Strath., PhD Bath Sr. Lectr.
Lynn, N., BSc Belf., PhD Belf., FIMA Sr. Lectr.
Paulson, R. W., BSc Lond. Sr. Lectr.
Wadsworth, M., BSc Manc., PhD Manc. Sr. Lectr.
Walkden, F., BSc Manc., PhD Manc., FIMA Res. Prof., Applied Mathematics and Computing
Wood-Harper, A. T., MA Lanc., PhD E.Anglia Prof., Computer Science
Wood, J. R. G., BA CNAA, MPhil CNAA Gemisis Prof., Information and Educational and Materials Development
Wragg, Alan, MA Camb., PhD Camb. Reader

Construction and Building Services
Tel: (0161) 295 3268 Fax: (0161) 295 3475
Ward, P. A., MSc Aston Sr. Lectr.; Head*

Design and Creative Technology
Fax: (0161) 295 2451
Bolton, Simon, BA CNAA, MDes RCA Sr. Lectr.
Rivlin, Christopher, BA CNAA, PhD CNAA Head*

Design Practice
Fax: (0161) 295 6180
Nuttall, John, BA Sheff., MA RCA ; Head*
Thomas-Shaw, Geoffrey, BA CNAA, MA CNAA Sr. Lectr.
Williams, A., BA CNAA Sr. Lectr.

Economics
Tel: (0161) 295 5570 Fax: (0161) 295 5992
Anderson, G. L., BA York(UK), MA Lanc., PhD Lanc. Head*
Aylen, J. M., BA Sus. Sr. Lectr.
Cain, Michael, BSc Sheff., MSc Sheff., PhD Wales, FIMA Reader
Ingham, B. M., BA(Econ) Manc., MSc(Econ) Lond., PhD Manc. Reader
Lucas, John, BA Lanc., MSc Lond., MBA Open(UK) Sr. Lectr.

Sampson, A. A., BA Oxf. Prof., Applied Economics
Simmons, C. P., BSc Hull, MA Lond., DPhil Oxf. Reader
Topham, N., BSc(Econ) Hull Prof.

Engineering, Aeronautical, Mechanical and Manufacturing
Tel: (0161) 295 3914, 5586 Fax: (0161) 295 5575
Arnell, R. D., BSc Manc., PhD Salf., FIP Prof., Surface Engineering
Chisholm, A. W. J., BSc(Eng) Lond., FIMechE Prof. Fellow
Crossley, Roger T., BSc Lond., PhD Salf., FRAeS, FIEE Res. Prof.
Ekere, N. N., BEng Nigeria, MSc Lough., PhD Manc. Sr. Lectr.
Green, William L., MSc Manc. Sr. Lectr.
Howard, David, BSc Brun., PhD Bath Sr. Lectr.
Jolley, Graham, BSc Aston, PhD Aston Sr. Lectr.
Jones, A. H., PhD Sr. Lectr.
Jouri, Walid, BSc Liv. Sr. Lectr.
Kerr, D. R., MA Camb., PhD Salf. Reader
Laws, Elizabeth M., BSc Lond., PhD Salf. Sr. Lectr.
Livesey, J. L., BSc Manc., PhD Manc. Res. Prof.
Mynett, John A., MSc Brist. Sr. Lectr.
Myring, D. F., BSc Lond., PhD Lond. Sr. Lectr.
Petty, D., BSc Manc., MSc Manc., PhD Manc. Sr. Lectr.
Redford, Alan H., PhD CNAA Reader
Sanger, D. J., MSc Wales, PhD Salf. Prof., Mechanism Dynamics
Sharp, J. M., BEng Brad., PhD Brad. Sr. Lectr.
Tate, Derek, MSc Leeds, PhD Leeds Sr. Lectr.
Tatnall, M. L., BSc Durh., PhD Newcastle(UK) Sr. Lectr.
Thomason, Peter F., PhD Salf., DSc Salf. Reader
White, Anthony J., BSc Manc., MSc Salf. Sr. Lectr.
Whomes, Terence L., BSc Leeds, PhD Leeds Sr. Lectr.
Woodhead, M. A., BSc Salf., PhD Salf. Head*
Zdravkovic, M. M., MSc Belgrade, PhD Belgrade, DSc Belgrade Reader

Engineering, Audio, see Acoustics and Audio Engin.

Engineering, Civil and Environmental
Tel: (0161) 295 4042 Fax: (0161) 295 5060
Baker, Raymond, BSc Salf., MSc Leeds, PhD Salf. Sr. Lectr.
Berry, P. L., BSc Salf., MSc Manc., PhD Manc. Sr. Lectr.
Cluckie, I. D., BSc Sur., MSc Birm., PhD Birm. Prof., Water Resources
Collier, C. G., BSc Lond., FRMetS Prof., Environmental Remote Sensing
Eastaff, D. J., BSc Manc., FICE, FGS Sr. Lectr.
Henson, Ralph R., BA Warw., MSc Salf., Sr. Lectr.
McNicholas, John B., MSc Wales, PhD Salf., FGS Sr. Lectr.
Melbourne, C., BEng Sheff., PhD Sheff., FICE, FIStructE Prof., Civil Engineering
Nalinkumar, Dave J., MEng Baroda, PhD Leeds, Sr. Lectr.
O'Leary, D. C., MSc Wales, FICE, FIStructE Head*
Webster, P. J., BSc Lond., PhD Sheff. Prof., Materials Engineering

Engineering, Electronic and Electrical
Tel: (0161) 295 3018 Fax: (0161) 295 5145
Ball, E., MSc Salf., PhD Salf., FIEE Sr. Lectr.
Barnes, David P., BTech Brad., MSc Lond., PhD Wales Sr. Lectr.
Boothroyd, Michael B., MSc Birm. Sr. Lectr.
Colligon, John S., BEng Liv., PhD Liv., FIEE, FIP Res. Prof.
Finn, Alan E., BSc Lond., PhD Lond., FIEE Sr. Lectr.
Gray, J. O., MSc Belf., PhD Manc., DSc Manc., FIEE Prof., Control and Systems Engineering; Head*

Linge, Nigel, BSc Salf., PhD Salf. Gemisis Prof.
Mansell, A. D., MSc Salf., PhD Salf. Sr. Lectr.
Martin, David J., BSc Durh., DPhil Oxf. Sr. Lectr.
Pardoe, Bev H., BSc Hull, MSc Essex, PhD Essex, FIEE Sr. Lectr.
Rabbitt, L. J., BSc Salf., PhD Salf. Sr. Lectr.
Smith, Cyril W., BSc Lond., PhD Lond., FIEE Sr. Lectr.
Staniforth, Alan J., BEng Sheff., PhD Sheff., FIEE Sr. Lectr.
Tomlinson, Gerald H., MSc Manc., PhD Manc. Sr. Lectr.
Tomlinson, Robert D., BSc Liv., PhD Liv. Sr. Lectr.

Engineering, Manufacturing, see Engin., Aeron., Mech. and Manufacturing

Engineering, Mechanical, see Engin., Aeron., Mech. and Manufacturing

English
Tel: (0161) 295 5133 Fax: (0161) 295 5511
Callick, P., BA CNAA, MA Kent Sr. Lectr.
Easson, A. W., BA Nott., DPhil Oxf. Prof.; Head*
Horner, A., BA Sus., MA Salf., PhD Manc. Sr. Lectr.

Environmental Management
Tel: (0161) 295 3394 Fax: (0161) 295 5141
Ford, Norman J., BSc Salf. Sr. Lectr.
Miller, Christopher E., BSc Lond., PhD Lond. Sr. Lectr.
Rennie, Denise M., BSc Strath., MSc Manc. Sr. Lectr.; Head*
Todd, Stephen, BSc Manc., MSc Leeds, PhD Salf. Sr. Lectr.

Environmental Resources
Tel: (0161) 295 5636
Frost, S., BSc Wales, MSc Liv., PhD Liv. Sr. Lectr.
Lippiatt, J. H., BSc Wales, PhD Wales Sr. Lectr.; Head*
Pugh-Thomas, M., BSc Liv., PhD Liv. Sr. Lectr.

French, see Mod. Langs.

Geography
Tel: (0161) 295 5478 Fax: (0161) 295 5015
Gleave, Michael B., MA Hull, PhD Hull Res. Prof.
Hindle, B. Paul, BA Manc., MSc Salf., PhD Salf. Sr. Lectr.
Knowles, Richard D., BA Newcastle(UK), PhD Newcastle(UK) Sr. Lectr.
Law, Christopher M., MSc Nott. Head*

German, see Mod. Langs.

Health Sciences
Tel: (0161) 295 3406 Fax: (0161) 295 3406
Clarke, Davina M., BSc Sus., MSc Manc. Sr. Lectr.; Head*
Eachus, Peter, BSc Wales, MSc Manc., PhD Manc. Sr. Lectr.

History, see Pol. and Contemp. Hist.

Housing
Fax: (0161) 295 8386
Hale, Janet, BA CNAA Head*

Information Technology Institute
Tel: (0161) 295 5182 Fax: (0161) 295 8169
Avis, Nicholas, BSc Reading, PhD Sheff. Reader
Baric, Lorraine F., BA Syd., PhD Lond., FRAI, FIEE, FIMA Prof. Fellow†
Basden, Andrew, BSc S'ton., PhD S'ton. Sr. Lectr.
Chadwick, David W., BSc Salf., PhD Salf. Sr. Lectr.
Cooper, Graham S., BSc Liv., MSc Salf., PhD Salf. Head*
Kirkham, John A., BScTech Wales, MSc Warw. Sr. Lectr.

Larmouth, John, TD, MA Camb., PhD Camb., FBCS Prof.

N-Nagy, Francis, MSc Bud., PhD Salf., FIEE, FIMA Prof.†

Powell, James A., OBE, BSc Manc., MSc Manc., PhD Salf. Prof.

Rae, John, BSc Salf., MA Newcastle(UK), DPhil York(UK) Sr. Lectr.

Yau, Yip J., BSc Manc., PhD Manc. Sr. Lectr.

International Institute

Tel: (0161) 295 5751 Fax: (0161) 295 5135

Hanstock, H. Jane, BA Leeds, MésL Paris XII Head*

Leisure and Hospitality Studies

Tel: (0161) 295 2021-3 Fax: (0161) 295 2020

Gurney, Tessa A., MSc Manc. Sr. Lectr.
Messenger, R. Sr. Lectr.
Moran, Timothy, BA Hudd. Sr. Lectr.
Mulkeen, James, BSc Manc. Sr. Lectr.
Rudder, H. G. E. Sr. Lectr.
Wilson, M. Sr. Lectr.; Head*

Linguistics, see Mod. Langs.

Management School

Tel: (0161) 295 5530 Fax: (0161) 295 5022

Adkins, R. W., BSc Reading, MSc S'ton., MPhil S'ton., MBA City(UK) Head*

Doran, Edward J., BA Open(UK), MSc Salf., PhD Salf. Sr. Lectr.

Jenkins, H. M., BA Wales British Rail Prof.

Varey, R. J., BSc Newcastle(UK), MSc Manc. Dir., Corporate Communicns. Unit

Mathematical Sciences, see Computer and Mathl. Scis.

Media and Performance

Tel: (0161) 295 6027 Fax: (0161) 295 6023

Cook, Ronald P., BA Manc., MA Manc. Sr. Lectr.; Head*

Dixon, Stephen R., BA Manc., MA Middx. Sr. Lectr.

Palmer, Gareth E., BA Sund., PhD Stir. Sr. Lectr.

Plowright, D. Visiting Prof.†

Midwifery

Tel: (0161) 959 3350 Fax: (0161) 959 3371

Butler, Marie, MA Salf. Sr. Lectr.
Moore, Lynne, MEd York(UK) Sr. Lectr.
Ward, Susan, MA Manc. Sr. Lectr.; Head*

Modern Languages

Tel: (0161) 295 5990 Fax: (0161) 295 5335

Carr, Myriam S., Lic Lyons, Maitrise Paris, PhD Paris Sr. Lectr.

Fiorato, Barbara, BA Durh., LèsL Nancy, Maitrise Nancy Sr. Lectr.

Harris, G., MA Manc., PhD Manc. Prof.,

Hickey, L. D., LLB N.U.I., LicFil Madrid, MA N.U.I., DrFil&Let Madrid Prof., Spanish

Hoffmann, Charlotte, MA Reading Sr. Lectr., German

Hollis, A. A., BA Newcastle(UK), MLitt Newcastle(UK) Sr. Lectr., German

Keiger, J. F. V., PhD Camb. Prof., International History

Lang, M., MA Glas., MSc Salf., PhD Salf. Reader

Mailhac, Jean-Pierre, LèsL Pau, PhD Salf. Sr. Lectr.

Mustapha, H., BA Alexandria, MA Essex, PhD Essex Sr. Lectr.

Thomas, Noel L., BA Manc., MA Liv., PhD Salf. Res Prof., German

Tomlinson, P., BA Liv., PhD Liv. Sr. Lectr., French

Towell, R. J., MA Aberd., PhD Salf. Prof., French and Applied Linguistics; Head*

Zemke, U. J., BA Hull, PhD Camb. Sr. Lectr., German

Music

Tel: (0161) 834 6633 Fax: (0161) 834 3327

Scott, Derek B., BA Hull, MMus Hull, PhD Hull Sr. Lectr.; Head*

Whiteley, Sheila, BA Open(UK), PhD Open(UK) Sr. Lectr.

Nursing, see also Midwifery

Tel: (0161) 295 2741-3 Fax: (0161) 295 2963

Chadwick, R. H., BA Manc., MSc Manc. Sr. Lectr.

Garrity, M., BEd Manc., MSc Brist., MA Manc. Sr. Lectr.; Head*

Grant, J. M., BSc Manc.Met., MSc Salf. Sr. Lectr.

Holland, Catherine, BSc Manc.Met., MSc Salf. Sr. Lectr.

Holliday, W., BSc CNAA Sr. Lectr.

Horrocks, S., BA Manc., MPhil Manc. Sr. Lectr.

Howard, B., MSc Manc. Sr. Lectr.

Howe, Paula D., BA Manc., MSc Salf. Sr. Lectr.

Jenkins, Jane, BA Manc., MSc Manc. Sr. Lectr.

Leyden, M. M., BEd Manc., MEd Manc. Sr. Lectr.

Lindley, E., BA Open(UK), BEd Manc., MEd Manc. Sr. Lectr.

Mitchell, D. C., BA Kent., MA C.Lancs. Sr. Lectr.

Murphy, P. R., BSc Manc. Sr. Lectr.

Murray, C. J., BA Manc., MSc Salf. Sr. Lectr.

Noyes, Jane, MSc Manc. Sr. Lectr.

Ryan, J. M., BA Manc., MA Keele Sr. Lectr.

Thomas, M., BSc Manc., MA Liv.J.Moores Sr. Lectr.

Tyrer, S. W., BEd Manc., MA Manc. Sr. Lectr.

Wild, J., MBA C.Lancs. Sr. Lectr.

Wild, K., MA Manc. Sr. Lectr.

Physics

Tel: (0161) 295 5054, 295 5117 Fax: (0161) 295 5903

Armour, David G., BEng Liv., PhD Liv., FIEE Prof., Ion Beam Technology

Barnard, Ronald D., BSc Birm., PhD Nott., FIP Sr. Lectr.

Boardman, Allan D., BSc Durh., MSc Durh., DSc Durh., PhD Salf., FIMA, FIP Prof., Applied Physics; Head*

Booth, John G., BSc Sheff., PhD Sheff., DSc Sheff., FIP Prof. Fellow

Carter, George, BSc Lond., PhD Liv., FIP Res. Prof., Electronic Materials and Devices

Darby, Martin I., BSc Sheff., PhD Sheff., FIP Reader

Donnelly, Stephen E., BSc Liv., MSc Sus., PhD Salf. Prof., Experimental Physics

Gerber, Richard, CSc Prague, RNDr Prague, DSc Salf., FIP, FIEE Prof.

Grundy, Philip J., BSc Sheff., PhD Sheff., DSc Sheff., FIP, FIEE Prof., Materials Physics

Hill, Arthur E., BSc Manc., PhD Manc., FIEE, FIMA Sr. Lectr.

James, Brian W., MSc St And., PhD Sr. Lectr.

Jones, Grenville A., BSc Sheff., PhD Sheff., DSc Sheff., FIP Sr. Lectr.

Keeler, Graham J., BSc Lond., PhD Lond. Sr. Lectr.

Lord, Donald G., BSc Lond., PhD Lond. Reader

Ross, Keith, MA Camb., MSc Birm., PhD Birm., DSc Birm. Prof.

Van den Berg, Jacob, BSc Salf., PhD Salf. Sr. Lectr.

Whitehead, Colin, BA Oxf., DPhil Oxf. British Nuclear Fuels Prof.

Podiatry

Tel: (0161) 295 2207 Fax: (0161) 295 2202

Braid, S. J., MSc Manc. Sr. Lectr.
Fraser, D. J., MSc Manc. Sr. Lectr.; Head*

Politics and Contemporary History

Tel: (0161) 295 5996, 295 5540 Fax: (0161) 295 5077

Alexander, Martin, BA Oxf., MA Oxf., DPhil Oxf. Prof.; Head*

Blunt, Michael E., BSc Lond., PhD Lond. Sr. Lectr.

Bull, Martin J., BA Nott., MA Oxf., PhD Florence Prof.

Garrard, John A., BA Keele, MA Manc. Sr. Lectr.

Goldsmith, Michael J. F., BA Reading, MA(Econ) Manc. Prof., Government and Politics

White, Ralph T., MA Camb., PhD Salf. Sr. Lectr.

Professional Studies

Tel: (0161) 295 2221 Fax: (0161) 295 2130

Conway, T., BA CNAA, MSc Manc. Sr. Lectr.
Harding, M., BA CNAA, MSc Salf. Sr. Lectr.
Hemmings, Martin, MA Oxf. Head*
Lord, Reg, MSc CNAA Sr. Lectr.

Quality Management

Tel: (0161) 295 2098 Fax: (0161) 295 2094

Peart, M. Geoff, BSc CNAA, BEd CNAA Sr. Lectr.; Head*

Radiography

Tel: (0161) 295 2154 Fax: (0161) 736 9989

Fisher, Judith M., BA Open(UK), MSc Salf. Sr. Lectr.

Williams, Patricia L., BSc CNAA, MSc Manc. Sr. Lectr.; Head*

Rehabilitation

Bowker, Peter, BSc Salf., PhD Salf. Prof., Prosthetics and Orthotics

Christie, S. Sr. Lectr.

Edwards, Jack, BSc Lond., MSc Lond., PhD Lond. Res. Prof., Orthopaedic Mechanics

Howard, R., MEd Sr. Lectr.

Melia, Jacqueline, BSc Salf., MSc Salf. Sr. Lectr.; Head*

Simpson, G. H., BSc Open(UK) Sr. Lectr.

Wilkinson, Joseph J. Sr. Lectr.

Social Work

Tel: (0161) 295 2374 Fax: (0161) 295 2378

Billingsley, R., BA Liv., MA Manc. Sr. Lectr.

Hearn, D. M., BA Manc., MA Manc. Sr. Lectr.; Head*

Sociology

Tel: (0161) 295 3268 Fax: (0161) 295 5424

Bryant, C. G. A., BA Leic., MA Leic., PhD S'ton. Prof.

Duke, V. W., BA Lond., MSc Strath. Sr. Lectr.

Edgell, S. R., BSc Lond., PhD Salf. Prof.

Flynn, R., BA Sus., MA Kent Sr. Lectr.; Head*

Longhurst, B. J., BA Lanc., PhD Lanc. Sr. Lectr.

Taylor, I. R., BA Durh., PhD Sheff. Prof.

Walters, Patricia A., BSc Manc. Sr. Lectr.

Spanish, see Mod. Langs.

Surveying

Tel: (0161) 295 4600 Fax: (0161) 295 5011

Al-Shawi, M., BSc Basrah, MSc Ohio, PhD Leeds Prof., Management and Information Technology in Construction

Aouad, Ghassan, BSc Beirut, MSc Lough., PhD Lough. Sr. Lectr.

Baggott, R., BSc Durh., PhD Leeds Sr. Lectr.; Head*

Barrett, P. S., MSc Brun., PhD CNAA, FRICS Prof., Management Systems in Property and Construction

Betts, M., BSc Reading, PhD CNAA Prof.

Brandon, Peter S., MSc Brist., FRICS Prof., Quantity and Building Surveying

Brown, G. R., BArch Liv., MA Liv., PhD Reading Prof., Construction Information Technology

Curwell, S., BSc Belf., MSc Belf. Sr. Lectr.

Eaton, David, BSc Salf., MSc H.-W. Sr. Lectr.

Lees, Melvyn, BSc Salf. Sr. Lectr.

March, C. G., BSc Manc. Sr. Lectr.

Watson, Ian, BSc Essex, MSc Essex, PhD Liv. Sr. Lectr.

Wright, F. B., LLB Leeds, LLM Leic., PhD Leic. Prof.

Visual Culture

Tel: (0161) 295 2601 Fax: (0161) 736 2799

Dunbar, T. D., BA Brist., MA Reading Sr. Lectr.

Pelik, R. A., BA CNAA, MA RCA Sr. Lectr.; Head*

SPECIAL CENTRES, ETC

Computational Fluid Dynamics and Turbulence, Centre for
Tel: (0161) 295 3531 Fax: (0161) 295 5559
Sajjadi, S. G., BSc CNAA, PhD CNAA, FIMA Dir.*

Computers in Education and Training, Centre for
Tel: (0161) 295 5047 Fax: (0161) 295 5145
Flinn, E. Alan, BSc Lond., PhD Lond., FIEE Dir.*

Development Studies, Centre for
Tel: (0161) 295 5385 Fax: (0161) 295 5992
Ingham, Barbara M., BA(Econ) Manc., MSc(Econ) Lond., PhD Manc. Dir.*

Digital Communications, Centre for
Tel: (0161) 295 5305 Fax: (0161) 295 5145
Ball, E., MSc Salf., PhD Salf. Dir.*

Education in Science, Design and Technology, Centre for
Tel: (0161) 295 5047 Fax: (0161) 295 5145
Flinn, E. Alan, BSc Lond., PhD Lond., FIEE Dir.*

European Marketing, Northwest Centre for
Tel: (0161) 295 5987 Fax: (0161) 295 5556
Whitelock, Jeryl M., MSc Salf. Dir.*

European Occupational Health and Safety Law Unit
Tel: (0161) 295 4957 Fax: (0161) 295 5011
Wright, F. B., LLB Leeds, LLM Leic. Prof.; Dir.*

European Studies Research Institute
Tel: (0161) 295 5614 Fax: (0161) 295 5335
Garside, Patricia L., BA Birm., PhD Birm. Res. Prof., Contemporary Social History
Harris, Geoffrey, MA Manc., PhD Manc. Prof.; Dir.*
Neal, Frank, BSc(Econ) Lond., MA(Econ) Liv., PhD Salf.

Graduate School
Tel: (0161) 295 5382 Fax: (0161) 295 5553
Powell, Prof. James A., OBE, BSc MSc PhD Dir.*

Health Service Management, Centre for
Tel: (0161) 295 5363 Fax: (0161) 295 5022
Hall, G. I., BSc Manc., MA Lanc. Dir.*

Instrumentation and Automation, Centre for
Tel: (0161) 295 5952, 295 5579 Fax: (0161) 295 5145
Gray, Prof. J. O., MSc Belf., PhD Manc., FIEE Dir.*

International Media Centre
Tel: (0161) 295 6207 Fax: (0161) 834 0699
Wilson, Keith Dir.*

Marine Technology, Centre for
Tel: (0161) 295 5081 Fax: (0161) 295 5111
Hughes, R., PhD Manc., DSc Leeds, FIChemE Dir.*

National Gas Engineering, Centre for
Tel: (0161) 295 5422
Bowler, A. L., BSc Salf., MSc Lond. Dir.*

North West Public Sector Research Centre
Tel: (0161) 295 5602 Fax: (0161) 295 5077
Goldsmith, M. J. F., BA Reading, MA(Econ) Manc. Dir.*

Operational Research and Applied Statistics, Centre for
Tel: (0161) 295 4022 Fax: (0161) 295 5559
Christer, A. H., MSc Lond., PhD Strath., DSc Lond., FIMA Dir.*

Problem Solving Skills, Centre for
Tel: (0161) 295 5277
Allison, B., BA Sheff. Dir.*

Public Health Research and Resource Centre
Tel: (0161) 295 2809 Fax: (0161) 295 2818
Popay, Jennie, BA Massey, MA Essex Dir.*

Quality Management, Centre for
Tel: (0161) 295 5557 Fax: (0161) 295 5022
Doran, E. J., BA Open(UK), MSc Salf. Dir.*

Research and Graduate College
Tel: (0161) 295 5164 Fax: (0161) 295 5553
Brandon, Prof. Peter S., MSc DSc, FRICS Dir.*

Science Research Institute
Tel: (0161) 295 5881, 295 4633 Fax: (0161) 295 5903
Ross, Prof. D. Keith, MA Camb., MSc Birm., PhD Birm., DSc Birm. Dir.*

Services for Export and Language
Tel: (0161) 295 4227 Fax: (0161) 295 5110
McLeish, Graeme, BA Salf. Manager*
Murphy, Patrick M., BA Salf., MA Brad. Translations Manager

Social Research, Institute for
Tel: (0161) 295 3366 Fax: (0161) 295 5424
Bryant, Prof. Christopher G. A., MA Leic., PhD S'ton. Dir.*

Telford Research Institute
Tel: (0161) 295 5465, 295 4042 Fax: (0161) 295 5060
Collier, Christopher G., BSc Lond. Prof.

Thin Film and Surface Research, Centre for
Tel: (0161) 295 5247, 295 4670 Fax: (0161) 295 5145
Colligon, John S., BEng Liv., PhD Liv., FIEE, FIP Dir.*

TIME Research Institute
Technology, Information, Management and Economics
Tel: (0161) 295 5588 Fax: (0161) 295 5011
Barrett, Prof. Peter S., MSc Brun., PhD CNAA, FRICS Dir.*

CONTACT OFFICERS

Accommodation. Accommodation Officer: Kirby, S. G., BSc Nott., PhD Nott.
Admissions (first degree). Admissions Officer: Keane, P. M., MA Manc.Met.
Admissions (higher degree). Admissions Officer: Houlgrave, Brian, BA Exe.
Adult/continuing education. Director of Continuing Education: Smith, E., BSc CNAA, PhD Nott.
Careers. Director, Careers and Appointments Service: Farr, Kim, BSc E.Anglia
Computing services. Director of Academic Information Services: Clark, Prof. Mark, MSc Birm., PhD CNAA
Development/fund-raising. Bentley, Jane, BA CNAA
Estates and buildings/works and services. Director of Estates and Buildings: Ledger, C., BSc Durh.
Finance. Director of Finance: Corner, Raymond A.
General enquiries. Registrar: Winton, Malcolm D., BA Camb., MSc Manc., PhD Manc.
Industrial liaison. CAMPUS Contact: Parker, Prof. Edward, MSc Manc., Hon. DSc Salf.
Library (chief librarian). Director of Academic Information Services: Clark, Prof. Mark, MSc Birm., PhD CNAA
Personnel/human resources. Personnel Director: Willis, Malcolm, BA Hull
Public relations, information and marketing. Wright, Gary
Purchasing. Brewer, Peter, BA E.Anglia
Safety. Craig, Alan G., BSc Lond., PhD Lond.
Schools liaison. Schools and Colleges Liaison Officer: Uden, J., BA Lond.
Security. Chief Security Officer: Cannon, M., BA Manc.
Student union. President: Bragg, G.
Student welfare/counselling. Prusmann, Anna
Students from other countries. International Student Officer: Evans, B., BA Wales, BLitt Oxf.
Students with disabilities. Learning Support Officer: Wilson, Carol, BSc Newcastle(UK)

[Information supplied by the institution as at February 1998, and edited by the ACU]

UNIVERSITY OF SHEFFIELD

Founded 1905; previously University College, Sheffield, established 1897 by amalgamation of Firth College (1879), Sheffield School of Medicine (1828), and Sheffield Technical School (1884)

Member of the Association of Commonwealth Universities

Postal Address: Sheffield, England S10 2TN
Telephone: (0114) 222 2000 **Fax**: (0114) 273 9826 **Cables**: University Sheffield **WWW**: http://www.shef.ac.uk
E-mail formula: initial.surname@sheffield.ac.uk

VISITOR—Elizabeth, H.M. The Queen
CHANCELLOR—......
PRO-CHANCELLOR—Douglas, R. A., MC, TD
PRO-CHANCELLOR—Lee, P. W., CBE
VICE-CHANCELLOR*—Roberts, Prof. Sir Gareth, BSc Wales, MA Oxf., PhD Wales, DSc Wales, Hon. LLD Wales, Hon.
    DSc W.England, FIP, FIEE, FRS
PRO-VICE-CHANCELLOR—Gow, Prof. I. T. M., MA Edin., PhD
PRO-VICE-CHANCELLOR—Gamble, Prof. Andrew M., BA Camb., MA Durh., PhD Camb.
PRO-VICE-CHANCELLOR—Lewis, Prof. D. H., MA Oxf., DPhil Oxf., FIBiol
PRO-VICE-CHANCELLOR—Waldron, Prof. P., BSc Nott., PhD Lond.
TREASURER—Johnson, H. S.
REGISTRAR AND SECRETARY‡—Fletcher, David E., BA Sheff., PhD Sheff.
LIBRARIAN—Hannon, Michael S.-M., MA Trinity(Dub.)

GENERAL INFORMATION

History. The university's origins can be traced back to the foundation of Sheffield School of Medicine in 1828. In 1897 the University College of Sheffield was created by the amalgamation of the school of medicine with Firth College (founded 1879) and Sheffield Technical School (1884). The university was granted its charter in 1905.

Admission to first degree courses (see also United Kingdom Introduction). Through Universities and Colleges Admissions Service (UCAS). International applicants: certificates/diplomas satisfying matriculation requirements in country of origin will be considered on an individual basis, provided they reach the level of attainment required by the university.

First Degrees (see also United Kingdom Directory to Subjects of Study). BA, BDS, BEng, BMS, BMus, BSc, BScTech, LLB, MB ChB.
   The university operates a modular structure for most of its degree programmes. Most courses take 3 years to complete. MB ChB: 5 years.

Higher Degrees (see also United Kingdom Directory to Subjects of Study). LLM, MA, MArch, MArchStudies, MClinPsy, MD, MDS, MEd, MMedSci, MMet, MMus, MSc, MPhil, PhD, DClinPsy, EdD.
   Applicants for admission to master's degree courses must normally hold an appropriate first degree with at least second class honours. PhD: at least upper second class honours.

Language of Instruction. English. Preparatory courses and English language support classes available for international students.

Libraries. Over 1,300,000 books, periodicals and other items.

Fees (1997–98, annual). Undergraduate: £750–8550 (arts, sciences, social sciences); £750–6450 (law); £1600–6450 (architectural studies); £1600–15,708 (medicine). Postgraduate: £2540–8550.

Academic Year (1998–99). Two semesters: 28 September–6 February; 8 February–12 June.

Income (1996–97). Total, £183,100,000.

Statistics. Staff: 5380 (1781 academic, 3599 administrative and other). Students: full-time 16,683; part-time 3872; international 2693.

FACULTIES/SCHOOLS

Architectural Studies
Tel: (0114) 222 0301 Fax: (0114) 279 8276
Dean: Tregenza, Prof. Peter R., BArch Durh., MBdgSc Syd., PhD Nott.
Secretary: Hall, H.

Arts
Tel: (0114) 222 7404 Fax: (0114) 222 7416
Dean: Leatherbarrow, Prof. W. J., MA Exe.
Secretary: Speight, C.

Educational Studies
Tel: (0114) 222 7061 Fax: (0114) 222 7001
Dean: Wright, Philip W., MA Camb., Drs Amst.

Engineering
Tel: (0114) 222 5511 Fax: (0114) 275 4325
Dean: Sellars, Prof. C. M., BMet Sheff., PhD Sheff., DMet Sheff., Hon. CMechD Navarra, FEng, FIM

Law
Tel: (0114) 222 6769 Fax: (0114) 272 1319
Dean: Jones, P. A., LLB Lond., LLM Lond., MA Essex

Medicine
Dean: Woods, Prof. H. Frank, BSc Leeds, BM BCh Oxf., DPhil Oxf., FRCP
Secretary: Price, B.

Pure Science
Tel: (0114) 222 4270 Fax: (0114) 272 8079
Dean: Combley, Prof. Frederick H., BSc Leic., PhD Leic., DSc Leic., FIP

Social Sciences
Tel: (0114) 222 3405 Fax: (0114) 222 3348
Dean: Else, P. K., BSc(Econ) Lond., MCom Birm.

ACADEMIC UNITS

Adult Continuing Education
Tel: (0114) 222 7000 Fax: (0114) 222 7001
Cameron, Robert A. D., BA Oxf., PhD Manc., FIBiol Prof.; Dir.*
Chivers, G. E., BSc Birm., PhD Birm. Prof., Continuing Education
Crossley, D. W., BA Oxf. Reader, Archaeology
Hey, David G., BA Keele, MA Leic., PhD Leic., FRHistS Prof., Local History
McConnell, David, BA Stir., PhD Sur. Prof.
Wright, Philip W., MA Camb., Drs Amst. Reader, Economics and Industrial Studies

Other Staff: 16 Lectrs.; 3 Res. Assocs.; 5 Hon. Lectrs.
Research: adult education; energy studies; field archaeology; geology; local history

Animal and Plant Sciences
Tel: (0114) 222 0123 Fax: (0114) 276 0159
Baker, A. J. M., BSc Lond., PhD Lond., FIBiol, FLS Reader
Bayne, B. L., BSc Wales, PhD Wales, FIBiol Hon. Prof. Fellow
Birkhead, T. R., DSc Newcastle(UK), DPhil Oxf. Prof., Zoology
Callaghan, T. V., PhD Birm., FilDr Lund, DSc Manc. Prof.; Dir., Sheffield Centre for Arctic Ecol.
Calow, P., PhD Leeds, DSc Leeds, FIBiol, FLS Prof., Zoology; Hon. Curator, Alfred Denny Museum
Grime, J. P., BSc PhD Prof., Plant Ecology
Henderson, I. W., DSc PhD, FIBiol Prof., Vertebrate Endocrinology
Hill, L., BSc PhD, FIBiol Sr. Lectr.
Jarvis, B. C., BSc Wales, PhD Wales Sr. Lectr.
Lee, J. A., BSc PhD Prof., Environmental Biology; Chairman*
Leegood, R. C., MA Camb., PhD Camb. Prof., Plant Biochemistry
Lewis, D. H., MA Oxf., DPhil Oxf., FIBiol Prof., Plant Sciences
Maltby, L. L., BSc Newcastle(UK), PhD Glas. Sr. Lectr.
Messenger, J. B., MA Camb., PhD Lond. Reader
Press, M. C., BSc Lond., PhD Manc. Reader
Quick, W. P., BSc Essex, PhD Sr. Lectr.
Read, D. J., BSc Hull, PhD Hull, FRS Prof., Plant Sciences
Wheeler, B. D., BSc Durh., PhD Durh. Reader
Woodward, F. I., BA Oxf., MA Camb., PhD Lanc., FLS Prof., Plant Ecology
Other Staff: 10 Lectrs.; 1 Lectr.†; 3 Hon. Sr. Lectrs.
Research: aquatic ecology; behavioural ecology; metabolic and molecular biology; plant and fungal ecophysiology

Archaeology and Prehistory
Tel: (0114) 222 2900 Fax: (0114) 272 2563
Barrett, J. C., BSc Wales Reader
Branigan, K., BA Birm., PhD Birm., FSA Prof.
Buckland, P. C., BSc Birm., PhD Birm., FGS Sr. Lectr.
Chamberlain, A. T., BSc Liv., PhD Liv., MSc S'ton. Sr. Lectr.
Collis, J. R., MA Camb., PhD Camb., FSA Prof.
Dennell, R. W., MA Camb., PhD Camb. Prof.
Edmonds, M. P., PhD Camb., BA Sr. Lectr.
Edwards, Kevin J., MA St And., PhD Aberd. Prof., Palaeoecology; Head*

Halstead, P. L. J., MA Camb., PhD Camb. Sr. Lectr.

Jones, G., BSc Wales, MPhil Camb. Sr. Lectr.

Ottaway, Barbara S., MA Edin., PhD Edin. Reader; Dir. of Res. Sch.

Parker Pearson, M. G., BA S'ton., PhD Camb. Sr. Lectr.

Zvelebil, M., MPhil Camb., BA, FSA Sr. Lectr.

Other Staff: 5 Lectrs.; 1 Res. Fellow; 1 Res. Assoc.; 1 Lectr.†; 7 Hon. Lectrs.; 2 Hon. Res. Assocs.

Research: archaeology and prehistory; archaeomaterials; environmental archaeology and palaeoeconomy; landscape archaeology; osteology, palaeopathology and funerary archaeology

Architecture

Tel: (0114) 222 0399 Fax: (0114) 279 8276

Blundell Jones, Peter, MA Camb. Prof.

Craven, A. M., BA Manc., PhD Sr. Lectr.

Cruickshank, D., BA Lond.Inst., Hon. FRIBA Visiting Prof.

Harper, R. H., PhD Reader

Hunt, Antony, FIStructE Visiting Prof.

Jefferson, J. B., CB, CBE, Hon. DEng Brad., Hon. LittD, PPRIBA Visiting Prof.

Lawson, B. R., MSc Aston, PhD Aston Prof.; Head of Sch.

Light, R. D., BA CNAA Sr. Lectr.

Plank, R. J., BSc Birm., PhD Birm. Prof.

Sharples, S., BSc Nott., PhD Sr. Lectr.

Smith, K. T. Sr. Lectr.

Tregenza, Peter R., BArch Durh., MBdgSc Syd., PhD Nott. Prof.

Ward, I. C., BSc Strath. Reader

Worthington, J. Visiting Prof.

Yeang, Ken, PhD Visiting Prof.

Other Staff: 8 Lectrs.; 2 Lectrs.†

Research: architectural humanities; architectural processes; architectural science and technology

Biblical Studies

Tel: (0114) 222 0508 Fax: (0114) 222 0500

Alexander, L. C. A., MA Oxf., DPhil Oxf. Sr. Lectr.

Clines, D. J. A., BA Syd., MA Camb. Prof.; Head*

Davies, M., BA Birm., PhD Birm. Sr. Lectr.

Davies, P. R., MA Oxf., PhD St And. Prof.

Exum, J. C., BA Wake Forest, MA Col., MPhil Col., PhD Col. Prof.

Moore, S., BA Trinity(Dub.), PhD Trinity(Dub.) Sr. Lectr.

Other Staff: 3 Lectrs.; 1 Res. Fellow; 1 Res. Assoc.; 1 Stephenson Fellow; 1 Teaching Fellow; 3 Hon. Lectrs.

Research: biblical ethics; biblical interpretation; feminist biblical criticism; interpretation of the Dead Sea scrolls; social world of the New Testament

Catalan, see Hispanic Studies

Chemistry

Tel: (0114) 222 9300 Fax: (0114) 273 8673

Aggarwal, V. K., BA Camb., PhD Camb. Prof.

Blackburn, G. M., MA Camb., PhD Nott., FRSChem Prof.

Cook, D. B., BSc PhD Sr. Lectr.

Devonshire, R., BSc Durh., PhD Newcastle(UK), FRSChem Sr. Lectr.

Dunmur, D. A., MA Oxf., DPhil Oxf., FRSChem Emer. Prof.

Fenton, D. E., PhD Lond., DSc Lond., FRSChem Prof., Inorganic Chemistry

Hunter, C. A., BA Camb., PhD Camb. Reader

Jackson, G., BSc Lond., DPhil Oxf. Reader

Ledwith, A., CBE, BSc Lond., PhD Liv., DSc Liv., Hon. DSc City(UK) Prof.; Head*

Maczek, A. O. S., MA Oxf., DPhil Oxf., FRSChem Sr. Lectr.

Maitlis, P. M., BSc Birm., DSc Lond., PhD Lond., FRSChem, FRS Res. Prof., Inorganic Chemistry

Mann, B. E., MA Oxf., DPhil Oxf., DSc Oxf. Prof.

McLure, I. A., BSc Glas., PhD Glas., FRSChem Reader

Pickup, B. T., BSc Manc., PhD Manc. Reader

Raynes, W. T., PhD Lond., DSc Lond., FRSChem Reader

Ryan, A. J., BSc Manc., PhD Manc. Prof., Physical Chemistry

Stirling, C. J. M., BSc St And., PhD Lond., DSc Lond., FRSChem, FRS Prof., Organic Chemistry

White, C., BSc Leeds, DPhil York(UK), FRSChem Sr. Lectr.

Winter, M. J., BSc Brist., PhD Brist. Sr. Lectr.

Young, R. N., BSc Aberd., PhD Aberd., FRSChem Reader

Other Staff: 7 Lectrs.; 1 BP Lectr.; 3 Royal Soc. Univ. Res. Fellows

Research: biologically-active compounds; catalysis by metal complexes; new materials; reaction mechanisms; the search for selectivity and new methodologies

Computer Science

Tel: (0114) 222 1800 Fax: (0114) 222 1810

Cooke, M. P., BSc Manc., PhD Reader

Croll, P. R., BSc CNAA, PhD Sr. Lectr.

Cvetkovic, S. R., BSc City(UK), PhD Lond. Sr. Lectr.

Green, P. D., BSc Reading, PhD Keele Reader

Holcombe, W. M. L., MSc Leeds, PhD Leeds Prof.

Manson, G. A., BSc Strath., PhD Strath., MSc Manc. Sr. Lectr.

Renals, S. J., BSc Sheff., MSc Edin., PhD Edin. Sr. Lectr.

Sharkey, Noel, BA Exe., PhD Exe. Prof.

Smythe, C., BSc Durh., PhD Durh. Prof.; Head*

Wilks, Y., MA Camb., PhD Camb. Prof.

Other Staff: 12 Lectrs.

Research: CASE tools for parallel systems; computer speech and hearing; natural language processing; neural networks; object-oriented programming

Criminology, see Law

Dental School, see below

Earth Sciences

Tel: (0114) 222 3600 Fax: (0114) 222 3650

Carswell, D. A., PhD Edin., DSc Edin., FGS Reader

Chapman, N., BSc Durh., PhD Edin., FGS Prof.

Cripps, J. C., BSc Aston, MSc Durh., PhD Durh., FGS Sr. Lectr.

Gibb, F. G. F., BSc St And., PhD St And., FGS Reader

Ineson, P. R., DSc Leic., PhD Durh., FGS Sr. Lectr.

McLeod, C. W. M., BSc Edin., PhD Lond. Prof.; Head*

Owens, B., BSc PhD DSc Prof.

Romano, M., BSc Liv., PhD Liv., FGS Sr. Lectr.

Spears, D. A., BSc PhD, FGS Sorby Prof.

Other Staff: 5 Lectrs.; 3 Res. Fellows; 7 Hon. Lectrs.

Research: environmental geochemistry; hydrogeology; igneous and metamorphic geochemistry, petrology, tectonics; macropalaeontology, bio-stratigraphy

East Asian Studies

Tel: (0114) 222 8400 Fax: (0114) 272 9479

Gow, I. T. M., MA Edin., PhD Prof.; Chairman*

Grayson, J. H., BA Rutgers, MA Col., MDiv Duke, PhD Edin. Reader

Healey, G. H., MA Oxf. Sr. Lectr.

Hook, G. D., MA Br.Col. Prof.

Kinmonth, E. H., MA Wis., PhD Wis. Reader

Taylor, Robert I. D., MSc Lond., MBA Warw., PhD Lond. Sr. Lectr.

Weiner, M. A., BA Sophia, PhD Sr. Lectr.

Other Staff: 10 Lectrs.; 1 Sr. Res. Fellow; 1 Res. Fellow; 1 Hon. Lectr.

Research: international relations; language; literature; politics; society

Economics

Tel: (0114) 222 3346 Fax: (0114) 222 3348

Baxter, J. L., MA Glas., PhD Sr. Lectr.

Bowden, S., BA PhD Sr. Lectr.

Chappell, D., BA Liv., PhD Liv., FIMA Prof., Mathematical Economics

Dowd, K., MA W.Ont., PhD W.Ont. Prof.; Head*

Else, P. K., BSc(Econ) Lond., MCom Birm. Sr. Lectr.

Tylecote, A. B., BA Oxf., BPhil Oxf., MA Sus., PhD Prof., Strategic Management

Wilkinson, R. K., BA Leeds Prof.

Other Staff: 9 Lectrs.; 1 Baring Res. Fellow

Research: applied economics and econometrics; economic theory; industrial organisation and public sector economics; international and development economics; political economy

Education, Division of, see also Adult Continuing Educn.

Tel: (0114) 222 8086 Fax: (0114) 279 6236

Barton, L. F., BA Liv., MEd Manc. Prof.

Bayliss, V., CH, BA Wales, MA Wales Prof. Assoc.

Carr, W., MA Warw. Prof.; Head*

Gilroy, D. P., MA Lond., PhD Lond. Sr. Lectr.

Hannon, P. W., BSc Liv., BA Liv., PhD Manc. Reader

Inglis, F., MA Camb., MPhil S'ton., PhD Brist. Prof.

Mac an Ghaill, M., BEd Liv., MSc Aston, PhD Aston Prof.

McCulloch, Gary J., MA Camb., PhD Camb. Prof.

Poppleton, Pamela K., BA PhD Hon. Prof. Fellow

Quicke, J. C., BA Leeds, PhD Prof.

Roberts, M. G., BA Camb. Sr. Lectr.

Rowland, S., MA Camb., MEd Leic. Sr. Lectr.

Thompson, D. A., BSc Edin., MA Belf., PhD Sheff. Sr. Lectr.

Trafford, A. J., BA Oxf. Sr. Lectr.

Unwin, Lorna, BA Manc., MPhil Sheff. Sr. Lectr.

Wellington, J. J., Bsc Brist., MA Lond., PhD Reader

Wilcox, B., BSc Lond., MEd Leeds Hon. Prof. Fellow

Other Staff: 23 Lectrs.; 1 Sr. Assoc. Fellow; 1 Lectr.†; 4 Hon. Lectrs.

Research: educational policy; literacy; post-compulsory education and training; professional development; special/inclusive education

Engineering, Automatic Control and Systems

Tel: (0114) 222 5250 Fax: (0114) 273 1729

Alleyne, H. S. K., BSc Lond., MSc WI, PhD WI Sr. Lectr.

Banks, S. P., MSc PhD Prof.

Bennett, S., PhD Reader

Billings, S. A., BEng Liv., PhD, FIEE Prof.

Edwards, J. B., BSc(Eng) Nott., MSc Birm. Emer. Prof.

Fleming, P. J., BSc Belf., PhD Belf., FIEE Prof.; Head*

Harrison, R. F., BSc S'ton., PhD S'ton. Sr. Lectr.

Holliday, Prof. K. H., OBE, BSc Manc., FRAeS Royal Academy of Engin. Prof.

Linkens, Derek A., BSc(Eng) Lond., MSc Sur., PhD Sheff., DSc(Eng) Lond., FIEE Prof.

Morris, A. S., BEng PhD Sr. Lectr.

Mort, N., BSc Leic., MSc Manc., PhD Sheff. Sr. Lectr.

Tokhi, M. O., BSc Kabul, PhD H.-W. Sr. Lectr.

Other Staff: 5 Lectrs.; 4 Hon. Lectrs.

Research: automation and systems architectures; intelligent and adaptive sytems; non-linear systems and signal processing

Engineering, Chemical and Process

Tel: (0114) 222 7500 Fax: (0114) 278 0611

Allen, R. W. K., MSc Manc., PhD McG., FEng, FIChemE Prof.; Head*

Bull, D. C., BSc *Wales*, PhD *Wales*   Visiting Prof.
Cliffe, K. R., BSc *Birm.*, PhD *Aston*   Sr. Lectr.
Edyvean, R. G. J., BSc *Wales*, MSc *Portsmouth*, PhD *Newcastle(UK)*, FIM, FIBiol   Reader
Foster, P. J., BScTech PhD   Reader
Pitt, M. J., MPhil *Aston*, PhD *Lough.*   Sr. Lectr.
Priestman, G. H., BScTech PhD, FEng   Sr. Lectr.
Swithenbank, J., BSc *Birm.*, PhD, FEng   Prof.
Other Staff: 6 Lectrs.; 1 Sr. Res. Fellow; 2 Hon. Lectrs.
Research: environmental engineering; incineration and combustion; process innovation and intensification; process safety and loss prevention

Engineering, Civil and Structural

Tel: (0114) 222 5053 Fax: (0114) 272 8910
Allsop, N. W. H., BSc *Reading*   Prof. Assoc.
Anderson, W. F., BSc *Belf.*, MSc *Strath.*, PhD *Strath.*, FGS   Prof.; Head*
Burgess, I. W., BA *Camb.*, PhD *Lond.*   Sr. Lectr.
Crouch, R. S., BSc *CNAA*, MSc *Lond.*, PhD *Manc.*   Sr. Lectr.
Hird, C. C., MA *Camb.*, PhD *Manc.*   Sr. Lectr.
Hyde, A. F. L., BSc *Nott.*, PhD *Nott.*   Sr. Lectr.
Kirby, P. A., BEng *Liv.*, PhD *Liv.*   Sr. Lectr.
Pilakoutas, K., BSc *Lond.*, PhD *Lond.*   Reader
Saul, A. J., BEng *Liv.*, PhD *H.-W.*   Prof.
Waldron, P., BSc *Nott.*, PhD *Lond.*   Prof.
Watson, A. J., BEng *Liv.*, MEng *McG.*, PhD *Birm.*   Reader
Other Staff: 10 Lectrs.
Research: civil engineering dynamics; concrete engineering; geotechnical engineering; numerical modelling; steel and composite structures

Engineering, Electronic and Electrical

Tel: (0114) 222 5355 Fax: (0114) 272 6391
Bennett, J. C., BEng PhD   Reader
Birch, T. S., BEng PhD   Sr. Lectr.
Chambers, B., BEng PhD   Reader
Cullis, A. G., MA *Oxf.*, DPhil *Oxf.*, DSc *Oxf.*, FIP   Prof.
Freeston, I. L., BSc *Leeds*, MSc *Lond.*, PhD *Lond.*, FIEE   Prof.
Houston, P. A., BSc *Strath.*, PhD *Strath.*   Reader
Howe, D., BTech *Brad.*, MSc *Brad.*, PhD *S'ton.*   Lucas Prof.
Ivey, P. A., BSc *Brist.*, PhD *Brist.*   Prof.
Kingsley, S. P., BSc *Nott.*, MSc *Manc.*, PhD, FRAS   Reader
Mellor, P. H., BEng *Liv.*, PhD *Liv.*   Sr. Lectr.
Rees, G. J., BA *Oxf.*, PhD *Brist.*   Reader
Whitehouse, C. R., BSc *Lond.*, MSc *Birm.*, PhD *CNAA*   Prof.; Head*
Woodhead, J., BSc *Lond.*, PhD *Reading*   Sr. Lectr.
Woods, R. C., MA *Oxf.*, DPhil *Oxf.*   Sr. Lectr.
Other Staff: 11 Lectrs.; 3 Sr. Res. Scientists; 5 Sr. Experimental Officers
Research: communications and radar; electrical machines and drives; electronic systems; medical electronics; micro-electromechanical systems

Engineering Materials

Tel: (0114) 222 5467 Fax: (0114) 275 4325
Argent, B. B., PhD DMet, FIM   Emer. Prof.
Atkinson, Helen V., MA *Camb.*, PhD *Lond.*   Sr. Lectr.
Bailey, J. E., BSc *Brist.*, PhD *Camb.*, FIP, FIM   Emer. Prof.
Buckley, R. A., MSc *Manc.*, DPhil *Oxf.*   Sr. Lectr.
Cable, M., PhD DScTech   Emer. Prof.
Davies, H. A., BSc(Eng) *Lond.*, PhD *Lond.*, FIM   Prof.
Greenwood, G. W., BSc PhD DMet, FIM, FIP, FEng, FRS   Emer. Prof.
James, P. F., BSc *Reading*, PhD *Reading*   Prof.
Jones, F. R., PhD *Keele*, FRSChem   Prof.
Jones, H., BSc *Manc.*, PhD *Manc.*, FIM   Prof.
Lee, W. E., BSc *Aston*, DPhil *Oxf.*   Reader
Messer, P. F., BSc *S'ton.*, PhD *S'ton.*   Sr. Lectr.
Parker, J. M., MA *Camb.*, PhD *Camb.*   Reader
Rainforth, W. M., PhD *Leeds*, BMet   Sr. Lectr.

Seddon, Angela B., BSc *Nott.*, MPhil *CNAA*, PhD *CNAA*, FRSChem   Sr. Lectr.
Sellars, C. M., BMet *Sheff.*, PhD *Sheff.*, DMet *Sheff.*, Hon. CMechD *Navarra*, FEng, FIM   Prof., Iron and Steel Technology
Sharp, J. H., BSc *Nott.*, PhD *Nott.*, FIM   Prof.; Head*
Short, R. D., BSc *Durh.*, PhD *Durh.*   Sr. Lectr.
Whiteman, J. A., BSc *Birm.*, MMet PhD, FIM   Sr. Lectr.
Wright, P. V., MScTech *Manc.*, DPhil *York(UK)*   Sr. Lectr.
Other Staff: 6 Visiting Profs.; 5 Lectrs.; 2 Sr. Experimental Officers; 4 Hon. Sr. Lectrs.; 4 Hon. Lectrs.
Research: ceramics and glasses; metallic and magnetic materials; polymers and polymer matrix composites

Engineering, Mechanical

Tel: (0114) 222 7700 Fax: (0114) 275 3671
Beynon, J. H., BMet PhD   Prof.
Bilby, B. A., BA *Camb.*, PhD *Birm.*, FRS   Emer. Prof.
Brown, G. T., MSc *Birm.*   Visiting Prof.
Brown, M. W., MA *Camb.*, PhD *Camb.*   Prof.
Bullough, W. A., BSc *Strath.*, MSc *Birm.*   Reader
Dugdale, D. Steven, BSc *Brist.*, FIEE   Hon. Prof. Fellow
Gostling, R. J., MA *Camb.*, FIMechE   Visiting Prof.
Holliday, K. H., OBE, BSc *Manc.*   Visiting Prof.
Howard, I. C., BSc *Manc.*, PhD *Manc.*   Reader
Johnson, Andrew R., BEng *Sheff.*, PhD *Hull*   Sr. Lectr.
Liversidge, P., BSc *Aston*, FIMechE   Visiting Prof.
McKittrick, Robert A., BSc *Glas.*, FICE, FIStructE   Visiting Prof.
McQuaid, J., BEng *Trinity(Dub.)*, PhD *Camb.*, DSc *Trinity(Dub.)*, FIMechE, FEng   Visiting Prof.
Miller, K. J., BSc *Lond.*, PhD *Lond.*, MA *Camb.*, ScD *Camb.*, FIM, FIMechE   Prof.
Murakami, Yukitaka, BA *Kyushu*, MA *Kyushu*, PhD *Kyushu*   Hon. Prof.
Parsons, D.   Visiting Prof.
Patterson, E. A., BEng PhD   Prof.
Ridgway, Keith, BSc *Manc.*, MSc *Salf.*, PhD *Manc.*   Prof.
Schmid, F., PhD *Brun.*   Sr. Lectr.
Smith, R. A., MA *Oxf.*, PhD *Camb.*   Prof.
Smyth, R., BSc *Belf.*, PhD *Belf.*   Sr. Lectr.
Stanway, R., MSc *Sus.*, DPhil *Sus.*   Reader
Stone, P. G., BA *CNAA*, BMet   Visiting Prof., Engineering Design
Swamy, R. N., BE *Annam.*, MEng PhD   Emer. Prof.
Tomlinson, G. R., BSc *Aston*, MSc *Aston*, PhD *Salf.*   Prof., Engineering Dynamics; Head*
Walters, D. G., BSc *Lond.*   Visiting Prof., Engineering Design
Wearing, J. L., BSc *Strath.*, PhD *Edin.*   Sr. Lectr.
Yates, J. R., MA *Camb.*, MSc *Cran.IT*, PhD   Reader
Other Staff: 16 Lectrs.; 3 Sr. Res. Fellows; 1 Res. Fellow; 2 Hon. Lectrs.
Research: computer-aided-design and computer-aided manufacturing; computer analysis using numerical methods; engineering dynamics; experimental stress analysis; materials and tribology

English Language and Linguistics

Tel: (0114) 222 0210 Fax: (0114) 276 8251
Blake, N. F., MA *Oxf.*, BLitt *Oxf.*   Prof., Res.
Burnley, John D., MA *Durh.*, PhD *Durh.*   Prof.; Head*
Lester, G. A., MA PhD   Reader
Widdowson, J. D. A., MA *Oxf.*, MA *Leeds*, PhD *Nfld.*   Prof.
Other Staff: 3 Visiting Profs.; 6 Lectrs.; 2 Erasmus Tutors
Research: cultural tradition, sociolinguistics; dialect study; history of English; history of linguistics; mediaeval language and literature

English Literature

Tel: (0114) 222 8480 Fax: (0114) 222 8481
Foster, Shirley, BA *Lond.*, MA *Mich.*, PhD *Liv.*   Sr. Lectr.
Gray, F. B., MA *Hull*   Sr. Lectr.
Haffenden, J. C. R., MA *Trinity(Dub.)*, DPhil *Oxf.*   Prof.
Hattaway, M., BA *NZ*, MA *Well.*, PhD *Camb.*   Prof.
MacKillop, I. D., MA *Camb.*, PhD *Leic.*   Reader
Roberts, N. J., MA *Camb.*, PhD *Camb.*   Sr. Lectr.
Roberts, P. E., MA *Oxf.*, PhD *Edin.*   Prof.
Shuttleworth, Sally A., BA *York(UK)*, PhD *Camb.*   Prof.; Head*
Other Staff: 1 Visiting Prof.; 11 Lectrs.; 1 Hon. Tutor (Drama)
Research: American studies; early modern period; literary biography; modern and contemporary literature; nineteenth-century literature and culture

Exercise Science, see Sports Med. and Exercise Sci., Sheffield Inst. of, under Medical School

French

Tel: (0114) 222 4385 Fax: (0114) 275 1198
Cross, M. F., MA *Reading*, PhD *Northumbria*   Sr. Lectr.
Duffy, Jean H., MA *Glas.*, DPhil *Oxf.*   Prof.
Eley, Penelope A., MA *Oxf.*, PhD *Wales*, MEd   Sr. Lectr.
Gauna, S. M., BA *Lond.*, PhD *Lond.*   Reader
Pratt, T. M., MA *Wales*, PhD *Leeds*   Sr. Lectr.
Rouxeville, Annie, LèsL *Rennes*, MA   Sr. Lectr.
Walker, David H., BA *Liv.*, PhD *Liv.*   Prof.; Head*
Williams, David, BA *Birm.*, PhD *Birm.*, Hon. DU *Maine(USA)*   Prof.
Windebank, J. E., BSc *Aston*, PhD *Bath*   Lectr.
Other Staff: 3 Lectrs.; 5 Lecteurs; 1 Hon. Res. Prof.
Research: the contemporary novel; the Enlightenment; mediaeval and Renaissance studies; nineteenth-century poetry; surrealism

Geography

Tel: (0114) 222 7900 Fax: (0114) 279 7912
Armstrong, H. W., MA *Lond.*   Prof.
Ferguson, R. I., MA *Camb.*, PhD *Camb.*   Prof., Physical Geography
Gregson, N. A., BA *Durh.*, PhD *Durh.*   Sr. Lectr.
Haining, R. P., MA *Camb.*, DPhil *Northwestern*   Prof.
Heathwaite, A. L., BSc *E.Anglia*, PhD *Brist.*   Sr. Lectr.
Jackson, P. A., BA *Oxf.*, DPhil *Oxf.*   Prof., Human Geography
Knighton, A. D., MA *Camb.*, PhD *Manc.*   Reader
Pattie, Charles J., BSc *Glas.*, PhD *Sheff.*   Sr. Lectr.
Rowley, G., BA *Wales*, PhD *Wales*   Reader
Smithson, P. A., BSc *Liv.*, PhD *Liv.*   Sr. Lectr.
Thomas, D. S. G., BA *Oxf.*, DPhil *Oxf.*   Prof.; Chairman*
Watts, H. D., BA *Leic.*, MA *Hull*, PhD *Hull*   Reader
White, P. E., BA *Oxf.*, DPhil *Oxf.*   Prof.
Other Staff: 12 Lectrs.; 6 Res. Contract Staff; 1 Hon. Res. Fellow
Research: economic and political geography; environmental change and drylands; environmental hydrology and fluvial geomorphology; geographic information systems in human geography; social geography

Germanic Studies

Tel: (0114) 222 4396
McGowan, N. M., MA *Newcastle(UK)*, DrPhil *Hamburg*   Prof.; Head*
Newton, G., BA *Liv.*, PhD *Liv.*   Sr. Lectr.
Other Staff: 3 Lektorinnen (German); 1 Lektorin (Dutch); 1 Lektor (Swedish)

Research: German Romanticism; Heine and Nietzsche; Ernst Jünger; political extremist literature in the Weimar Republic; the Thingspiel

Health and Related Research, School of,
see below

Hispanic Studies
Tel: (0114) 222 4398
England, J. P., BA Durh., PhD   Sr. Lectr.
Round, Nicholas G., MA Oxf., DPhil Oxf.   Hughes Prof.; Head*
Yates, A., MA Camb., PhD Camb.   Prof., Catalan
Other Staff: 6 Lectrs.; 1 Res. Fellow; 1 Hon. Res. Fellow
Research: Catalan; early modern literature; eighteenth-century studies; Peruvian and Uruguayan studies; translation studies

History, see also Archaeol. and Prehist.
Tel: (0114) 222 2555 Fax: (0114) 278 8304
Binfield, J. C. G., MA Camb., PhD Camb., FRHistS, FSA   Reader
Carwardine, R. J., MA Oxf., DPhil Oxf.   Prof.
Daniels, G., BSc(Econ) Lond., DPhil Oxf.   Reader
Greengrass, M., BA Oxf., DPhil Oxf., FRHistS, FSA   Prof.
Holmes, C., MA Nott.   Prof.
Kershaw, I., BA Liv., DPhil Oxf., FBA   Prof., Modern History; Head*
King, E. J., MA Camb., PhD Camb., FRHistS, FSA   Prof.
Kirk, L. M., MA Camb., PhD Lond., FRHistS   Sr. Lectr.
Luscombe, D. E., MA Camb., PhD Camb., LittD Camb., FRHistS, FSA, FBA   Leverhulme Personal Res. Prof., Mediaeval History
Thurlow, R. C., BA York(UK), MA Sus.   Sr. Lectr.
Walker, S. K., MA Oxf., DPhil Oxf.   Reader
Woodward, J. H., BA York(UK), DPhil York(UK)   Sr. Lectr.
Other Staff: 11 Lectrs.; 2 Sr. Res. Fellows; 1 Res. Fellow; 1 Postdoctoral Fellow; 1 Temp. Lectr.
Research: American history; early modern studies; European history; mediaeval studies; modern British history

Information Studies
Tel: (0114) 222 2630 Fax: (0114) 278 0300
Correia, A. M. R., PhD Liv., FIInfSc   Prof. Assoc.
Ellis, D., BA Durh., MA PhD   Sr. Lectr.
Ford, N. J., BA Leeds, MA   Sr. Lectr.
Line, M. B., MA H.-W., FLA   Prof. Assoc.
Lynch, M. F., BSc N.U.I., PhD N.U.I.   Emer. Prof.
Saunders, W. L., CBE, MA Camb., Hon. LittD, FLA, FIInfSc   Emer. Prof.
Usherwood, R. C., BA Open(UK), PhD, Hon. FLA   Reader
Willett, P., MA Oxf., MSc PhD   Prof.; Head*
Wilson, T. D., BSc(Econ) Lond., PhD, FIInfSc, FLA   Prof.
Wood, Frances E., BSc Lond.   Sr. Lectr.
Other Staff: 9 Lectrs.; 13 Res. Contract Staff; 4 Hon. Lectrs.; 1 Hon. Res. Fellow
Research: information management; librarianship; networked work and learning; public library services

Journalism Studies
Tel: (0114) 222 2500 Fax: (0114) 266 8918
Foster, J. D., BA   Sr. Lectr.
Gunter, B., BSc Wales, MSc Lond., PhD CNAA   Prof.; Dir. of Res.
Stephens, E., MA Oxf.   Sr. Lectr.
Trelford, D. G., MA Camb., Hon. LittD   Prof.; Head*
Other Staff: 4 Lectrs.; 1 Professl. Skills Manager
Research: journalism, law and ethics; media coverage and understanding of science; media violence; sport and the media

Landscape
Tel: (0114) 222 0600 Fax: (0114) 275 4176
Hitchmough, J. D., BSc Bath, PhD Bath   Reader
Swanwick, C. A., BA York(UK), MSc Lond.   Prof.; Head*
Other Staff: 5 Lectrs.; 3 Tutors†
Research: landscape design; landscape management

Law
Tel: (0114) 222 6771 Fax: (0114) 272 1319
Adams, John N., LLB Durh.   Prof., Intellectual Property
Battersby, G., JP, BA Oxf.   Prof.
Beyleveld, D., BSc Witw., MA Camb., PhD E.Anglia   Prof.
Birds, J. R., LLM Lond.   Prof., Commercial Law; Head*
Bradgate, J. R., MA Camb.   Reader, Commercial Law
Brownsword, R., LLB Lond.   Prof.
Dignan, J., LLB Manc., MA   Sr. Lectr.
Ditton, J., BA Durh., PhD Durh.   Prof., Criminology
Harden, I. J., MA Camb., LLB   Prof.
Hayes, Mary, JP, BA S'ton.   Prof.
Howells, G. G., LLB Brun.   Reader
Jones, P. A., LLB Lond., LLM Lond., MA Essex   Dir., Legal Practice
Lewis, N., LLB Brist.   Prof.
Longley, D., LLB MA   Sr. Lectr.
Luxton, P., LLB Leic., LLM Lond., PhD Lond.   Sr. Lectr.
McClean, J. D., CBE, QC, DCL Oxf.   Prof.
Merrills, J. G., MA Oxf., BCL Oxf.   Prof., International Law
Mesher, J., BA Oxf., BCL Oxf., LLM Yale   Prof. Assoc.
Shapland, Joanna M., MA Oxf., DPhil Oxf.   Prof., Criminal Justice
Steiner, Josephine M., BA Lond., LLB Sheff.   Prof. Assoc.
Wiles, Paul N. P., BSc(Econ) Lond.   Prof., Criminology
Wood, Sir John, CBE, LLM Manc., Hon. LLD CNAA, Hon. LLD Sheff.   Emer. Prof.
Other Staff: 25 Lectrs.; 1 Sr. Lectr.†; 2 Lectrs.†
Research: biotechnological law and ethics; commercial law studies; criminological and legal research; international, comparative and European law; socio-legal studies

Leisure Management
Tel: (0114) 222 2181 Fax: (0114) 275 1216
Taylor, P. D., BA Warw., MA Leeds   Prof.; Dir.*
Other Staff: 4 Lectrs.
Research: innovation in leisure industries; internationalisation in leisure industries; leisure and urban regeneration; sustainable development in leisure industries; understanding the leisure consumer

Linguistics, see Engl. Lang. and Linguistics

Management School
Tel: (0114) 222 3346 Fax: (0114) 222 3348
Armstrong, P. J., BSc(Eng) Brist., MSc Bath, PhD Brist.   Prof., Accounting
Boden, R., BA Manc., PhD Manc.   Sr. Lectr.
Clegg, C. W., BA Newcastle(UK), MSc Brad., FBPsS   Prof., Organisational Psychology
Coutts, J. A., BA CNAA, MSc CNAA   Sr. Lectr.
Currie, W. L., BSc Kingston(UK), PhD Brun.   Prof.
Demirag, I. S., BSc Birm., MSc Glas., PhD Glas.   Reader
Gow, I. T. M., MA Edin., PhD   Prof.; Chairman*
Humphrey, C. G., BCom Liv., MA(Econ) Manc., PhD Manc.   Prof., Accounting
Jacobs, E. M., BA Col., MSc(Econ) Lond., MBA Lond., PhD Lond.   Sr. Lectr.
Lewis, L. A., BA CNAA, MPhil CNAA   Sr. Lectr.
Macdonald, S., MA Camb., PhD Newcastle(UK)   Prof., Information and Organisation
Meidan, A., BSc(Econ) Jerusalem, MBA Jerusalem, PhD Brad.   Prof., Marketing

Norman, J. M., BA Oxf., MSc Birm., PhD Manc.   Prof., Management Studies
Owen, D. L., BA Kent   Prof., Accounting
Sparrow, P. R., BSc Manc., MSc Aston, PhD Aston   Prof.
West, M. A., BSc Wales, PhD Wales   Prof., Organisational Psychology
Other Staff: 16 Lectrs.; 1 Assoc. Lectr.; 4 Res. Fellows; 2 Lectrs.†
Research: accounting and finance; human resource management and organisational behaviour; information management; marketing; operations management and operational research

Materials, see Engin. Materials

Mathematics and Statistics
Tel: (0114) 222 3800 Fax: (0114) 222 3759
Anderson, C. W., MA Camb., MSc Lond., PhD Lond.   Prof.
Atkin, R. J., PhD E.Anglia, BSc   Reader
Bailey, G. J., BSc PhD   Prof.
Baker, J. W., MSc Reading, PhD Wales   Sr. Lectr.
Biggins, J. D., MA Camb., MSc Oxf., DPhil Oxf.   Prof.
Cannings, C., BSc Lond., PhD Lond.   Prof.
Chatwin, P. C., MA Camb., PhD Camb., FIMA   Prof., Applied Mathematics
Cook, R. J., PhD Lond., DSc Lond.   Prof.
Dixon, P. G., MA Camb., PhD Camb., ScD Camb.   Reader
Dunsmore, I. R., BSc Liv., PhD Liv.   Prof.; Head*
Fieller, N. R. J., MA Camb., MSc Birm., PhD Hull   Sr. Lectr.
Greenlees, J. P. C., MA Camb., PhD Camb.   Prof.; Head of Res.
Holland, M. P., BSc Leeds, PhD Leeds   Reader
Hutson, V. C. L., BA Camb., PhD Camb.   Prof.
Jordan, D. A., BSc Belf., PhD Leeds   Reader
Loynes, R. M., BA Camb., PhD Camb., ScD Camb.   Prof.
Moffett, R. J., BSc Belf., PhD Belf., FRAS   Prof.
Outhwaite, C. W., BSc Manc., PhD Manc.   Prof.; Head of Teaching
Pickering, W. M., BSc Manc., MSc Leeds, PhD, FIMA   Reader
Pym, J. S., BSc Birm., PhD Camb.   Town Trust Prof.
Quegan, Shaun, BA Warw., MSc Warw., PhD Sheff.   Prof.
Shanbhag, D. N., MSc Karn., PhD Karn.   Reader
Sharp, R. Y., MA Oxf., DPhil Oxf.   Prof.
Sozou, C., BA Lond., PhD Lond.   Prof.
Wyatt, Lucy R., BSc Manc., MSc Brist., PhD S'ton.   Reader
Zinober, A. S. I., MSc(Eng) Cape Town, PhD Camb.   Prof.
Other Staff: 15 Lectrs.; 9 Res. Contract Staff; 3 Computing Officers
Research: algebraic topology; analysis of remotely sensed data; applications of mathematics to engineering, physics, biology and control; environmental statistics; human genetics and medical statistics

Medicine, see Medical School, below

Midwifery, see Nursing and Midwifery, School of, below

Music
Tel: (0114) 222 0470 Fax: (0114) 266 8053
Brown, A. M., MA Camb., MusB Camb., PhD Camb., FRCO   Reader
Clarke, E. F., MA Sus., PhD Exe.   James Rossiter Hoyle Prof.; Head*
Hill, P. H. A. W., MA Oxf.   Prof., Musical Performance
Lawson, C. J., MA Oxf., MA Birm., PhD Aberd.   Reader
Nicholson, G., BA York(UK), DPhil York(UK)   Sr. Lectr.
Other Staff: 3 Lectrs.
Research: opera; popular music of the eighteenth and nineteenth centuries; psychology of music; sixteenth-and seventeenth-century

English music; twentieth-century piano music

Nursing, see Nursing and Midwifery, School of, below

Philosophy

Tel: (0114) 222 0570 Fax: (0114) 279 8760

Bell, D. A., BA Trinity(Dub.), MA McM., PhD McM.   Prof.

Carruthers, P., BA Leeds, MPhil Leeds, DPhil Oxf.   Prof.; Head*

Hookway, C. J., BPhil E.Anglia, MA Oxf., PhD Camb.   Prof.

Makin, S. A. R., MA Edin., PhD Camb.   Sr. Lectr.

Smith, P. J., MA Camb.   Sr. Lectr.

Other Staff: 6 Lectrs.

Research: aesthetics; ancient philosophy; ethics and political philosophy; metaphysics and epistemology; philososphy of mind and language

Physics

Tel: (0114) 222 4278 Fax: (0114) 272 8079

Blythe, H. J., BSc Lond., PhD Leeds   Reader

Booth, C. N., BA Camb., PhD Camb.   Sr. Lectr.

Bradley, D. D. C., BSc Lond., PhD Camb.   Prof.

Cartwright, Susan L., BSc Glas., PhD Glas.   Sr. Lectr.

Combley, Frederick H., BSc Leic., PhD Leic., DSc Leic., FIP   Prof.

Cowlam, N., BSc PhD   Reader

Gehring, Gillian A., BSc Manc., MA Oxf., DPhil Oxf., Hon. DSc Salf.   Prof., Solid State Physics; Head*

Gibbs, M. R. J., PhD Camb., BSc   Reader

Hughes, D. W., BSc Birm., DPhil Oxf., FRAS   Reader

Richardson, T., BSc Durh., DPhil Oxf.   Sr. Lectr.

Searle, T. M., BSc Lond., PhD Lond.   Reader

Skolnick, M. S., BA Oxf., DPhil Oxf.   Prof., Experimental Condensed Matter

Tadhunter, C. N., BSc Sus., DPhil Sus.   Sr. Lectr.

Titman, J. M., BSc Durh., PhD Durh.   Sr. Lectr.

Tucker, J. W., PhD Nott., DSc Nott., FIP, FIMA   Reader, Theoretical Physics

Williams, J. M., PhD Manc., DSc Manc., FIP   Reader

Other Staff: 6 Lectrs.; 2 Advanced Fellows; 11 Res. Fellows; 12 Res. Contract Staff; 2 Hon. Lectrs.

Research: high energy particle physics; magnetism and magnetic materials; opto-electronic properties of semiconductor low dimensional structures; space physics; theoretical condensed matter physics

Plant Sciences, see Animal and Plant Scis.

Politics

Tel: (0114) 222 1700 Fax: (0114) 273 9769

Arblaster, A. E., BA Oxf.   Reader

Gamble, A. M., BA Camb., PhD Camb., MA Durh.   Prof.

George, S. A., BA Leic., MPhil Leic.   Jean Monnet Prof.

Meadowcroft, J. R., BA McG., DPhil Oxf.   Sr. Lectr.

Payne, A. J., MA Camb., PhD Manc.   Prof.

Seyd, P., BSc(Econ) S'ton., MPhil S'ton., PhD   Prof.; Chairman*

Smith, M. J., MA Essex, PhD Essex   Sr. Lectr.

Whitely, Paul F., BA Sheff., MA Essex, PhD Essex   Prof.

Williams, G. L., MA Wales   Sr. Lectr.

Other Staff: 6 Lectrs.; 1 Hon. Res. Fellow; 1 Temp. Lectr.

Research: democratisation; international political economy; political parties; political theory, political thought; public policy

Psychology

Tel: (0114) 222 9272 Fax: (0114) 276 6515

Blades, M., MA Camb., BA PhD   Sr. Lectr.

Connolly, K. J., BSc Hull, PhD Lond., FBPsS   Prof.

Dean, P., MA Camb., DPhil Oxf.   Reader

Frisby, J. P., BA Camb., PhD   Prof.; Head*

Jackson, P. R., MSc CNAA, BA PhD   Sr. Lectr.

Mayhew, J. E. W., BSc Brist., PhD Brist.   Prof.

Nicolson, R. I., BA Camb., PhD Camb., MSc Sus.   Prof.

Redgrave, P., BA Hull, MSc Hull, PhD Hull   Reader

Siegal, M., BA McG., MEd Harv., DPhil Oxf., DSc Oxf.   Prof.

Slade, Pauline, BSc Nott., MSc Leeds, PhD Sheff.   Sr. Lectr.

Spencer, C. P., MA Oxf., DPhil Oxf.   Reader

Turpin, G., BSc Lond., MPhil Lond., PhD S'ton.   Reader

Wall, T. D., BA Nott., PhD Nott., FBPsS   Prof.

Warr, P. B., MA Camb., PhD, FBPsS   Prof.

Westby, G. W. M., BSc Reading, PhD Reading   Sr. Lectr.

Other Staff: 16 Lectrs. (4 in Clin. Psychol.); 1 Consultant Clin. Psychologist; 1 Royal Soc. Fellow; 2 Sr. Experimental Officesr; 1 Res. Contract Staff Member; 1 Hon. Prof. Assoc.; 7 Hon. Lectrs.; 43 Hon. Teachers in Clin. Psychol.

Research: clinical psychology; developmental psychology; occupational psychology; social and health psychology

Russian and Slavonic Studies

Tel: (0114) 222 7400 Fax: (0114) 222 7416

Gotteri, N. J. C., MA Oxf.   Sr. Lectr.

Leatherbarrow, W. J., MA Exe.   Prof.

Russell, R., MA Edin., PhD Edin.   Prof.

Shepherd, David G., MA Oxf., PhD Manc.   Prof.; Head*

Other Staff: 1 Lectr.; 1 Lektor (Russian); 3 Visiting Lectrs. (2 in Russian, 1 in Bulgarian); 1 Res. Fellow

Research: Bakhtin studies; Dostoevsky studies; nineteenth- and twentieth-century Russian literature; Russian language; Slavonic languages and linguistics

Sociological Studies

Tel: (0114) 222 6400 Fax: (0114) 276 8125

Booth, T. A., BA Essex, PhD   Prof., Social Policy; Chair*

Franklin, R., BA Hull, PhD Hull   Reader

Holdaway, S. D., BA Lanc., PhD   Prof., Sociology

Hoogvelt, Johanna M. M., Drs Ley.   Sr. Lectr.

Jenkins, R., BA Belf., PhD Camb.   Prof., Sociology

Marsh, P., BSc S'ton., MPhil S'ton.   Reader

Noble, T., BA Nott.   Sr. Lectr.

Phillips, D. R., BA E.Anglia, MPhil York(UK)   Sr. Lectr.

Richardson, L. Diane, BA Camb., MA Nott.   Reader

Roche, M. C., BSc(Econ) Lond., PhD Lond.   Sr. Lectr.

Shardlow, S. M., MSc Oxf.   Sr. Lectr.

Walker, A. C., BA Essex, DLitt Essex   Prof., Social Policy

Other Staff: 8 Lectrs.; 1 Res. Assoc.; 3 Lectrs.†; 10 Hon. Assocs.; 1 Temp. Lectr.

Research: changes in society; citizenship and social integration; participation and power in health, social service and criminal justice services

Statistics, see Maths. and Stats.

Town and Regional Planning

Tel: (0114) 222 6180 Fax: (0114) 272 2199

Booth, P. A., MA Camb., MA Sheff., PhD   Sr. Lectr.

Campbell, H. J., BA Durh., MA PhD   Sr. Lectr.

Crook, A. D. H., BA Brist., MPhil Lond., PhD   Prof.; Head*

Friend, J., MA Camb.   Prof. Assoc.

Henneberry, John M., MA Camb., MA Sheff.   Reader

Marshall, R. J., MA Camb.   Sr. Lectr.

Masser, F. Ian, BA Liv., MCD Liv., PhD Liv., LittD Liv.   Res. Prof.†

Other Staff: 6 Lectrs.

Research: information management; local economic development and housing; planning systems (theory and practice)

Zoology, see Animal and Plant Scis.

DENTAL SCHOOL

Child Dental Health

Tel: (0114) 271 7885

Brook, A. H., BDS Lond., MDS Lond., FDSRCS   Prof.; Head*

Minors, C. J., MDS, FDSRCS   Sr. Lectr.

Other Staff: 2 Lectrs.; 1 Non-Clin. Lectr.; 2 Lectrs.†; 5 Hon. Clin. Lectrs.; 5 Hon. Clin. Teachers; 1 Hon. Teacher

Research: study of normal and abnormal dental growth and development

Dental Services

Tel: (0114) 275 6410 Fax: (0114) 278 7406

Rothwell, P. S., DDS Manc.   Prof.; Head*

Other Staff: 1 Lectr.; 3 Hon. Clin. Lectrs.; 17 Hon. Clin. Teachers; 1 Hon. Lectr.

Research: behavioural sciences; cross-infection control; disorders of the temporomandibular joint; epidemiological studies; postgraduate education

Oral and Maxillofacial Surgery

Tel: (0114) 271 7849 Fax: (0114) 271 7863

Brook, I. M., BDS Liv., PhD Sheff., FDSRCS   Prof.; Head*

Robinson, P. P., BDS Brist., PhD Brist., FDSRCS   Prof.

Smith, K. G., BDS Newcastle(UK), FDSRCS   Sr. Lectr.

Other Staff: 5 Lectrs.; 4 Res. Contract Staff; 1 Lectr.†; 5 Hon. Clin. Lectrs.; 11 Hon. Clin. Teachers; 2 Hon. Teachers; 1 Hon. Res. Fellow

Oral Pathology

Tel: (0114) 271 7951 Fax: (0114) 271 7894

Craig, G. T., BDS PhD, FDSRCS, FRCPath   Reader

Douglas, C. W. I., BSc Birm., PhD Birm.   Reader

Franklin, C. D., BDS Newcastle(UK), PhD, FDSRCS   Sr. Lectr.

Smith, C. J., BDS Lond., PhD Lond., FRCPath   Prof.; Head*

Other Staff: 1 Lectr.

Research: diagnostic oral histopathology; electron microscopy; histochemistry; immunocytochemistry; stereology

Restorative Dentistry

(including Mechanics, Materials and Prosthetics)

Tel: (0114) 271 7930 Fax: (0114) 266 5326

Barros, V. M. R., MA Sao Paulo, PhD Sao Paulo   Visiting Prof.

Lamb, D. J., BDS Durh., MDS, FDSRCS   Sr. Lectr.

Rawlinson, A., BChD Leeds, FDSRCSEd   Sr. Lectr.

Van Noort, R., BSc Sus., DPhil Sus.   Prof.

Walsh, T. F., BDS Lond., MSc Lond., DDS Birm.   Prof.; Head*

White, G. E., MMedSci PhD   Sr. Lectr.

Winstanley, R. B., MDS, FDSRCSEd   Sr. Lectr.

Other Staff: 6 Lectrs.; 2 Lectrs.; †; 2 Hon. Clin. Lectrs.; 23 Hon. Clin. Teachers

Research: clinical services and standards; dental biomaterials, dental materials and dental technology; dental education science

HEALTH AND RELATED RESEARCH, SCHOOL OF

Ageing and Rehabilitation Studies, Centre for

Tel: (0114) 271 5772 Fax: (0114) 271 5771

Enderby, P. E., MSc Brist., PhD Brist.   Prof., Community Rehabilitation

Jennings, Michael, BMedSci Nott., BM BS Nott.   Sr. Lectr.

Morgan, Kevin, BSc *Ulster*, PhD *Edin.* Sr. Lectr.; Dir.*

Philp, Ian, MB ChB *Edin.*, MD *Edin.*, MD *Lond.* Marjorie Coote Prof., Health Care for Elderly People

Warnes, Anthony M., BA *Hull*, PhD *Salf.* Prof., Social Gerontology

Wilson, K., BSc *Lond.*, MMedSci Prof. Assoc., Primary and Community Care

Other Staff: 2 Lectrs.; 1 Res. Fellow; 1 Hon. Clin. Lectr.

Research: factors influencing health and well-being in old age; health care of older people; methods and approaches to rehabilitation

Forensic Psychiatry

Cordess, C., BA *Trinity(Dub.)*, MA *Trinity(Dub.)*, MPhil *Lond.*, MB ChB, FRCPsych Prof.; Dir.*

General Practice and Primary Care

Tel: (0114) 271 4302

Campbell, M. J., BA *York(UK)*, MSc *Edin.*, PhD *Edin.* Prof., Medical Physics with an interest in Primary Care Res.

Fox, N. J., BSc *Brist.*, MSc(Econ) *Lond.* Sr. Lectr.

Howe, A., MD Sr. Lectr.

Mathers, N. J., BSc MB ChB MD Prof.; Head*

Other Staff: 1 Lectr. 4 Res. Fellows; 5 Res. Assocs.; 8 Lectrs.†; 5 Hon. Lectrs.; 127 Hon. Clin. Teachers; 1 Hon. Res. Fellow

Research: educational innovations; mental health; organisation of primary health care team; use of IT

Health Economics

Brazier, J. E., BA *Exe.*, MScYork(UK) Sr. Lectr.; Dir.*

Other Staff: 4 Lectrs.; 1 Res. Fellow; 4 Res. Assocs.; 2 Statisticians

Research: economic evaluations of purchasing health care; health service outcomes

Health Policy and Management

Martin, D. N., BA *Manc.*, PhD *Manc.* Dir.*

Nicolson, P., BSc *Wales*, MSc *Sur.*, PhD *Lond.* Sr. Lectr.

Whitney, D. J., BA *Exe.*, MA *Lond.* Prof. Assoc.

Other Staff: 1 Consultant; 3 Sr. Res. Fellows; 1 Res. Fellow

Research: general practice; primary care

Information Resources

Booth, A., BA *Wales* Sr. Information Officer; Dir.*

Other Staff: 1 Information Officer

Medical Care Research Unit

Nicholl, J. P., BA *Brist.*, MSc *CNAA* Prof.; Dir.*

Other Staff: 1 Res. Fellow; 12 Res. Assocs.; 1 Statistician; 1 Clin. Lectr.

Research: aspects of primary care; services for acute illness

Nursing Research

Read, S. M., PhD *Sheff.* Sr. Lectr., Acute and Critical Care

Other Staff: 2 Lectrs. (1 Lectr./Practitioner); 3 Res. Fellows; 3 Res. Assocs.; 1 Res. Midwife

Research: health service research

Operational Research

Brennan, A., BSc *Lond.*, MSc *Lond.* Dir.*

Other Staff: Sr. OR Analysts; 1 Analyst

Research: efficiency studies; operational contract planning; performance management and monitoring; strategic planning of services and investment; what-if modelling

Psychiatry

Tel: (0114) 271 5218 Fax: (0114) 271 6352

Hale, A. S., BSc *Lond.*, MB BS *Lond.*, PhD *Lond.* Prof.; Head*

Kendall, T. J. G., BMedSci *Sheff.*, MB ChB *Sheff.* Dir., Centre for Psychotherapeutic Studies

Nicolson, Paula, BSc *Wales*, MSc *Sur.*, PhD *Lond.* Sr. Lectr., Health Psychology

O'Dwyer, J., MB BCh *N.U.I.* Sr. Lectr., Learning Disabilities

Peet, M., BSc *Leeds*, MB ChB *Leeds*, FRCPsych Reader

Peters, S., BA *Stir.*, MB BS *Lond.* Sr. Lectr.

Tantam, D. J. H., BM BCh *Oxf.*, BA *Open(UK)*, MPh *Harv.*, PhD *Lond.*, FRCPsych Prof., Psychotherapy

Young, R. M., BA *Yale*, MA *Camb.*, PhD *Camb.* Prof., Psychotherapy and Psychoanalytic Studies

Other Staff: 9 Lectrs.; 2 Lectrs.†; 26 Hon. Clin. Lectrs.; 1 Hon. Clin. Lectr.†

Research: biological psychiatry and psychopharmacology; psychotherapy

Psychotherapeutic Studies, Centre for

Kendall, T. J. G., BMedSci *Sheff.*, MB ChB *Sheff.* Dir.*

Tantam, D. J. H., BA *Open(UK)*, BM BCh *Oxf.*, MPH *Harv.*, PhD *Lond.*, FRCPsych Clin. Prof., Psychotherapy

Young, R. M., BA *Yale*, MA *Camb.*, PhD *Camb.* Prof., Psychotherapy and Psychoanalytic Studies

Other Staff: 15 Lectrs.; 3 Clin. Trainers

Research: health care's impact on identity, subjectivity and intersubjectivity; psychiatry; psychoanalysis; psychotherapy

Public Health Medicine

Tel: (0114) 222 0719

Dixon, R. A., BSc PhD Sr. Lectr.

Hutchinson, A., MB BS *Newcastle(UK)*, FRCGP Prof.; Dir.*

Shickle, D. A., MB BCh *Wales*, MPH *Wales* Sr. Lectr.

Other Staff: 2 Res. Fellows; 1 Clin. Sr. Lectr.; 3 Hon. Clin. Sr. Lectrs.; 7 Hon. Clin. Lectrs.; 1 Hon. Res. Fellow

Research: promoting public health at local, national and international levels

MEDICAL SCHOOL

Anaesthetics, see Surg. and Anaesth. Scis.

Biochemistry, Clinical, see Human Metabolism and Clin. Biochem.

Biomedical Science

Tel: (0114) 222 2320 Fax: (0114) 276 5413

Andrews, P. W., BSc *Leeds*, DPhil *Oxf.* Arthur Jackson Prof.; Head*

Angel, A., BSc *Lond.*, PhD *Lond.* Prof., Physiology

Atkinson, M. E., BSc *Birm.*, PhD Sr. Lectr., Oral Anatomy

Chess-Williams, R., BSc *Wales*, PhD *Wales* Sr. Lectr.

Cope, G. H., BSc *Leic.*, PhD Sr. Lectr.

Dunne, M. J., BSc *Warw.*, PhD *Liv.* Reader

Grundy, D., BSc *Lond.*, PhD *Dund.* Sr. Lectr.

Hardcastle, Jacqueline, BSc PhD Sr. Lectr.

Hardcastle, P. T., BSc PhD Sr. Lectr.

Ingham, P. W., MA *Camb.*, DPhil *Sus.* Prof.

Jacob, S., MB MS *Madr.* Sr. Lectr., Oral Anatomy

James, N. T., MA *Camb.*, MA *Oxf.*, MB BChir *Camb.*, BM MSc *Oxf.* Sr. Lectr.

Levin, R. J., MSc *Liv.*, PhD Reader

Pearson, R. C. A., BM BCh *Oxf.*, DPhil *Oxf.*, MA *Oxf.* Prof., Neuroscience

Reynolds, G. P., BA *York*, PhD *Lond.* Prof.

Rumsey, R. D. E., MSc *Edin.*, PhD *Edin.* Sr. Lectr.

Warren, M. A., BSc *Aston*, PhD *Aberd.* Sr. Lectr.

Other Staff: 6 Lectrs.; 1 Hon. Reader; 4 Hon. Lectrs.

Research: anatomy; cell biology; developmental biology; neurobiology; physiology

Cancer Studies

Coleman, R. E., MB BS *Lond.*, MD *Lond.*, FRCP, FRCPEd Reader

Dobson, P. R. M., BSc *Strath.*, PhD *Lond.* Sr. Lectr.

Hancock, B. W., MD, FRCP, FRCPEd, FRCR YCRC Prof., Clinical Oncology; Co-Dir.

Lorigan, P., BA *Trinity(Dub.)*, MB BCh BAO *Trinity(Dub.)* Sr. Lectr.

Potter, C. W., BSc *Reading*, PhD *Sheff.*, FRCPath Sir George Martin Prof., Virology; Dir.*

Robinson, M. H., MB BChir *Camb.*, MA *Camb.*, FRCP, FRCR Sr. Lectr.

Other Staff: 1 Lectr.; 2 Non-Clin. Lectrs.; 1 Sr. Res. Scientist; 1 Hon. Lectr.

Research: cell cycle control in malignant disease; cellular oncology; molecular genetics, cytogenetics of lymphomas; ocular melanoma; receptor biology and molecular signalling

Clinical Neurology

Tel: (0114) 271 3579 Fax: (0114) 276 0095

Mayes, Andrew R., BA *Oxf.*, DPhil *Oxf.* Prof., Cognitive Neuroscience

Sagar, H. J., MA *Oxf.*, DM *Oxf.*, FRCP Frank Moody Prof.; Head*

Other Staff: 1 Clin. Lectr.; 1 Non-Clin. Lectr.; 9 Hon. Clin. Lectrs.

Research: cognitive neuroscience, particularly amnesiac syndromes; neurodegenerative disease, particularly Parkinson's disease

Clinical Oncology

Tel: (0114) 267 9589 Fax: (0114) 267 8140

Coleman, R. E., MB BS *Lond.*, MD Reader

Hancock, B. W., MD, FRCP, FRCR YCRC Prof.; Head*

Lorigan, P., BA *Trinity(Dub.)*, MB BCh BAO *Trinity(Dub.)* Sr. Lectr.

Robinson, M. H., MD *Camb.*, FRCR Sr. Lectr.

Other Staff: 2 Lectrs.; 2 Clin. Res. Fellows; 8 Hon. Clin. Lectrs.; 1 Hon. Lectr.

Research: biological therapy of cancer; evaluation of new radiotherapy technology; high-dose chemotherapy; management of lymphomas; multidisciplinary management of bone and soft tissue sarcomas

Forensic Pathology

Tel: (0114) 273 8721 Fax: (0114) 279 8942

Carter, N., BSc *Liv.*, MB ChB *Liv.* Sr. Lectr.

Clark, J. C., MB ChB *Aberd.* Sr. Lectr.

Green, M. A., MB ChB *Leeds* Prof.; Head*

Milroy, C. M., MB ChB *Liv.* Sr. Lectr.

Rutty, G. N., MB BS *Lond.* Sr. Lectr.

Other Staff: 4 Hon. Lectrs.

Research: ageing and dating skeletal remains; changing trends in murder-suicide; estimation in the time of death; forensic aspects of drug abuse; ocular and lung pathological aspects of childhood NAI

General Practice, see under Health and Related Research, School of

Human Communication Sciences

Tel: (0114) 222 2400 Fax: (0114) 222 2414

Boucher, Jill M., BA *Oxf.*, PhD *Birm.* Prof. Assoc.

Locke, A., BA *Newcastle(UK)* Sr. Lectr.

Locke, J. L., BA *Ripon*, MA *Ohio*, PhD *Ohio* Prof.; Head*

Perkins, M. R., BA *Leeds*, MA *Leeds*, PhD *Wales* Sr. Lectr.

Other Staff: 8 Lectrs.; 1 Sr. Experimental Res. Officer; 1 Clin. Tutor

Research: clinical communication studies; language and communication impairment in children

Human Metabolism and Clinical Biochemistry

Tel: (0114) 271 3037 Fax: (0114) 272 6938

Brown, B. L., BSc *Lond.*, PhD *Lond.* Prof.

Buttle, David J., BSc *E.Anglia*, PhD *Camb.* Sr. Lectr.

Eastell, Richard, BSc *Edin.*, MB ChB *Edin.*, MD *Edin.* Prof.

Kanis, J. A., BSc *Edin.*, MB ChB *Edin.*, MA *Oxf.*, FRCP Prof.

Russell, R. G. G., MA Camb., MB BChir Camb., PhD Leeds, DM Oxf., FRCP, FRCPath Prof.; Head*
Other Staff: 2 Lectrs.; 4 Res. Fellows; 3 Res. Contract Staff; 4 Clin. Res. Fellows; 9 Hon. Lectrs.; 3 Hon. Clin. Teachers
Research: basic and clinical aspects of calcium and phosphate metabolism; cytokines and proteolytic enzymes in connective tissues; intracellular signalling systems and neuroendocrinology; pathogenic mechanisms in bone disease, arthritis and cancer

Medical Physics and Clinical Engineering

Tel: (0114) 271 2688 Fax: (0114) 271 3403
Barber, David C., BA Camb., MSc Lond., PhD Aberd. Prof. Assoc.
Black, M. M., BSc Strath., MSc Durh., PhD Glas., FIP Emer. Prof.
Brown, B. H., BSc Lond., PhD, FIP, FIEE Prof. Assoc.
Smallwood, R. H., BSc Lond., MSc Lanc., PhD, FIEE, FIP Prof., Medical Engineering; Head*
Other Staff: 3 Lectrs.; 6 Contract Res. Staff; 22 Hon. Lectrs.
Research: audiology; clinical instrumentation; feature extraction from medical images; physiological measurement; prosthetic heart valves

Medicine

Tel: (0114) 271 4160 Fax: (0114) 256 0458
Crossman, D. C., BSc Lond., MB BS Lond., MD Lond. Prof., Cardiology
Cumberland, D. C., MB ChB Edin., FRCR, FRCPEd, FRCS Prof., Interventional Cardiology
El-Nahas, A. M., PhD Wales Prof., Nephrology
Haylor, J., BPharm Wales, PhD Birm. Sr. Lectr.
Mac Neil, Sheila, BSc Aberd., PhD Reader
Morice, A. H., MA Camb., MD Camb. Reader
Munro, D. S., MB ChB Aberd., MD Aberd., Hon. LLD, FRCP Emer. Prof.
Newman, C. H., MA Camb., MB BS PhD Sr. Lectr.
Read, N. W., MA Camb., MD BChir Camb., FRCP Prof., Gastrointestinal Physiology and Nutrition
Ross, R. J. M., MD Lond. Sr. Lectr.
Ward, A. M., MA Camb., MB BChir Camb., FRCPath Reader, Immunology
Weetman, A. P., BMedSc Newcastle(UK), MD Newcastle(UK), DSc Newcastle(UK), FRCP Sir Arthur Hall Prof.; Head*
Other Staff: 8 Lectrs.; 5 Res. Fellows; 22 Res. Contract Staff; 20 Hon. Clin. Lectrs.; 1 Hon. Res. Fellow; 2 Temp. Lectrs.
Research: human nutrition; immunology; medicine and endocrinology

Medicine and Pharmacology

Tel: (0114) 271 2475 Fax: (0114) 273 7623
Collins, G. G. S., BPharm Lond., MSc Lond., PhD Lond. Reader
Cork, Michael, BSc St And., MB BChir Camb., PhD St And. Sr. Lectr.
Di Giovine, F. S., MD Florence, PhD Edin. Sr. Lectr.
Dower, S. K., MA Oxf., DPhil Oxf. Prof., Molecular Immunology
Duff, G. W., MA Oxf., BM BCh Oxf., PhD Lond., FRCP Lord Florey Prof., Molecular Medicine
Hampton, K. K., BSc Leeds, MD Leeds Sr. Lectr.
Higenbottam, T. W., BSc Lond. Prof., Respiratory Medicine
Jackson, P. R., MA Oxf., MB ChB Reader
Lennard, M. S., MSc Birm., PhD Reader
Makris, M., MA Oxf., MB BS Lond. Sr. Lectr.
Morice, A. H., MA Camb., MD BChir Camb. Sr. Lectr.
Peake, I. R., BSc Liv., PhD Liv. Sir Edward Mellanby Prof., Molecular Medicine
Preston, F. E., MD Liv., FRCP, FRCPath Prof. Assoc., Haematology
Qwarnstrom, E. E., PhD Lund Sr. Lectr.

Ramsay, L. E., MB ChB Glas. Prof., Clinical Pharmacology and Therapeutics
Sayers, J., BSc Birm., PhD Birm. Sr. Lectr.
Snaith, M. L., MB BS Newcastle(UK), MD Newcastle(UK), FRCP Sr. Lectr.
Tucker, G. T., BPharm Lond., PhD Lond. Prof., Pharmacology and Therapeutics
Ward, J. D., BSc Lond., MB BS Lond., MD Lond. Prof., Medicine
Whyte, M. K., BSc Lond., MB BS Lond., PhD Lond. Prof., Respiratory Medicine
Wilson, R. M., MB ChB Dund., DM Nott. Sr. Lectr.
Woods, H. Frank, BSc Leeds, BM BCh Oxf., DPhil Oxf., FRCP Sir George Franklin Prof., Medicine; Head*
Yeo, W. W., BMedSci MB ChB Sr. Lectr.
Other Staff: 10 Lectrs.; 7 Res. Fellows; 23 Res. Contract Staff; 4 Hon. Lectrs.; 19 Hon. Clin. Lectrs.; 2 Hon. Teachers
Research: clinical pharmacology and therapeutics; molecular medicine; molecular pharmacology and pharmacogenetics; respiratory medicine; rheumatology

Microbiology, Medical

Tel: (0114) 272 4072 Fax: (0114) 273 9926
Eley, A. R., MSc Sheff.Hallam, PhD Nott. Sr. Lectr.
Jennings, R., BSc Birm., PhD WI Prof.; Head*
Other Staff: 3 Lectrs.; 3 Res. Assocs.; 1 Sr. Clin. Lectr.; 8 Hon. Clin. Lectrs.
Research: application of modern molecular biological and immunological techniques to problems concerned with the pathogenesis and control of micro-organisms

Molecular Biology and Biotechnology

Tel: (0114) 222 2722 Fax: (0114) 272 8697
Artymiuk, P. J., BA Oxf., DPhil Oxf. Reader
Attwood, Margaret M., BSc Nott., PhD Nott. Sr. Lectr.
Bailey, E., BSc Leeds, PhD Leeds Prof.
Carey, E. M., BSc Nott., PhD Birm. Sr. Lectr.
Ford, G. C., BA Oxf., DPhil Oxf. Reader
Grindle, M., BSc Durh., MSc Qu., PhD Birm. Sr. Lectr.
Guest, J. R., BSc Leeds, DPhil Oxf., FRS Prof.
Higgins, Joan A., BSc Liv., PhD Liv. Reader
Hornby, D. P., BSc PhD Sr. Lectr.
Horton, P., BA York(UK), DPhil York(UK), DSc York(UK) Prof.
Hunter, C. N., BSc Leic., PhD Brist. Prof.
Ingham, P. W., MA Camb., DPhil Sus. Prof.
Kelly, D. J., BSc Bath, PhD Warw. Sr. Lectr.
Kelly, S., BSc Wales, PhD Wales Sr. Lectr.
Kinderlerer, J., BSc CapeT., PhD Camb. Sr. Lectr.
Moir, Anne, BSc Aberd., PhD Edin. Sr. Lectr.
Moore, H. D. M., BSc Reading, PhD Reading Prof.
Poole, R. K., BSc Wales, PhD Lond. Prof.
Rice, D. W., MA Oxf., DPhil Oxf. Prof.; Chairman*
Sudbery, P. E., BSc Leic., PhD Leic. Sr. Lectr.
Turner, G., BSc Wales, PhD Wales Prof.
Wainwright, M., BSc Nott., PhD Nott. Sr. Lectr.
Waltho, J. P., BSc Durh., PhD Camb. Sr. Lectr.
Williamson, M. P., BA Camb., PhD Camb. Reader
Other Staff: 13 Lectrs.; 3 Sr. Experimental Officers; 55 Res. Contract Staff; 2 Hon. Lectrs.; 1 Hon. Assoc.
Research: biomolecular research; biotechnology and cell culture; molecular cell biology and development; photosynthesis

Obstetrics and Gynaecology

Jessop Hospital

Tel: (0114) 276 6333 Fax: (0114) 275 2153
Cooke, I. D., MB BS Syd., FRCOG Prof.; Head*
Lenton, Elizabeth A., BSc PhD Sr. Lectr.
Moore, H. D. M., BSc Reading, PhD Reading Non-Clin. Prof.

Other Staff: 1 Lectr.; 1 Res. Contract Staff Member; 5 Hon. Clin. Lectrs.
Research: investigation and treatment of infertility

Northern General Hospital

Tel: (0114) 243 7988 Fax: (0114) 244 1728
Fraser, R. B., MD Sr. Lectr.; Head*
Patel, D., MB ChB Sr. Lectr.
Sharp, F., MD Glas., FRCOG Prof.
Tidy, J. A., MD Lond. Sr. Lectr.
Other Staff: 2 Lectrs.; 5 Hon. Clin. Lectrs.
Research: gynaecological cancer

Ophthalmology and Orthoptics

Tel: (0114) 271 2902 Fax: (0114) 276 6381
Davis, H., MSc Manc. Sr. Lectr., Orthoptics
Rennie, I. G., MB ChB, FRCSEd Prof.; Head*
Other Staff: 7 Lectrs.; 5 Hon. Clin. Lectrs.
Research: ophthalmic pathology

Paediatrics

Tel: (0114) 271 7303 Fax: (0114) 275 5364
Finn, A. H. R., MA Camb., BM BCh Oxf., PhD Lond. Sr. Lectr.
Hall, D. M. B., BSc Lond, MB BS Lond, FRCP Prof., Community Paediatrics
Powers, Hilary J., BSc Leic., PhD Lond. Sr. Lectr.
Primhak, R. A., MD, FRCP Sr. Lectr.
Rigby, A. S., MSc Lanc. Sr. Lectr.
Tanner, M. S., MB BS Lond., MSc Lond., FRCP Prof.; Head*
Taylor, C. J., MB ChB Liv., FRCP Prof., Paediatric Gastroenterology
Wales, J. K. H., MA Oxf., DM Oxf., FRCP Sr. Lectr.
Other Staff: 3 Lectrs.; 10 Res. Contract Staff; 3 Clin. Res. Fellows; 67 Hon. Clin. Lectrs.; 6 Hon. Teachers
Research: antioxidant activity of micronutrients; control of intestinal epithelial cell function; mechanisms of hepatoxicity; role of adhesion molecules in the inflammatory response; the aetiology of tissue damage in respiratory disease

Pathology

Tel: (0114) 271 2683 Fax: (0114) 278 0059
Angel, C. A., MB ChB Leic. Sr. Lectr.
Cross, Simon S., BSc Lond., MB BS Lond. Sr. Lectr.
Goepel, J. R., MB ChB Sr. Lectr.
Lee, J. A., BSc Lond., MB BS Lond., PhD Lond. Sr. Lectr.
Lewis, C. E., BSc Reading, DPhil Oxf. Sr. Lectr.
Parsons, M. A., MB ChB, FRCPath Sr. Lectr.
Underwood, J. C. E., MD Lond., FRCPath Joseph Hunter Prof.; Head*
Wells, M., BSc Manc., MD Manc., FRCPath Prof., Gynaecological Pathology
Other Staff: 3 Lectrs.; 14 Hon. Clin. Lectrs.
Research: clinical pathology; histopathology; pathological sciences

Pharmacology, see Med. and Pharmacol.

Public Health Medicine, see under Health and Related Research, School of

Radiodiagnosis

Tel: (0114) 271 2587 Fax: (0114) 272 4760
Cleveland, T. J., BMedSci Nott., BM BS Nott., FRCS, FRCR Sr. Lectr., Vascular Radiology
Griffiths, P. D., MB ChB Manc., PhD Manc. Prof., Radiology; Head*
Other Staff: 15 Hon. Clin. Lectrs.

Sports Medicine and Exercise Science, Sheffield Institute of

Tel: (0114) 271 1900 Fax: (0114) 271 2522
Bickerstaff, D. R., MB ChB, FRCS Clin. Co-ordinator
Bownes, E. C. Physiother. Manager
Cochrane, T., BSc Belf., PhD Belf. Academic Dir.
Duckworth, T., BSc Manc., MB ChB Manc., FRCS Prof.; Chairman*

Saleh, M., MB ChB *Sheff.*. MSc *Dund.*, FRCS,
    FRCSEd   Prof., Orthopaedics
Other Staff: 2 Lectrs.; 2 Res. Assocs.; 1
    Orthopaedic Physician
Research: contribution of sport and exercise to
    public health; enhancement of human
    performance; prevention or rehabilitation of
    injury and disease

Surgical and Anaesthetic Sciences

Tel: (0114) 271 2510 Fax: (0114) 271 3771

Ahmedzai, S., BSc *Manc.*, MB ChB *Manc.*,
    FRCP   Prof., Palliative Medicine
Clark, D., BA *Newcastle(UK)*, MA *Newcastle(UK)*,
    PhD *Aberd.*   Prof., Medical Sociology
Duckworth, T., BSc *Sheff.*, MD *Sheff.*,
    FRCS   Prof., Orthopaedic Surgery
Edwards, Neil D., MB BS *Lond.*, FRCA   Sr.
    Lectr., Anaesthesia
Forster, D. M. C., MB *Camb.*, MA *Camb.*   Sr.
    Lectr., Neurosurgery
Johnson, A. G., MA *Camb.*, MChir *Camb.*,
    FRCS   Prof., Surgery
Mills, G. H., MB chB, FRCA   Sr. Lectr.,
    Anaesthesia
Noble, W., MB ChB MD   Sr. Lectr., Palliative
    Medicine
Reilly, C. S., MD *Glas.*, FRCA   Prof.,
    Anaesthesia; Head*
Other Staff: 7 Clin. Lectrs.; 2 Non-Clin. Lectrs.;
    62 Hon. Clin. Lectrs.; 1 Hon. Clin. Teacher
Research: anaesthetics; ENT; palliative medicine;
    surgery; urology

Surgical Sciences

Tel: (0114) 271 4648 Fax: (0114) 261 9246

Chan, P., MA *Camb.*, MChir *Camb.*, FRCS   Sr.
    Lectr.
El Shazly, M., BSc *Alexandria*, MB BCh
    MChOrth   Sr. Lectr.
Hosie, K. B., BSc MB ChB MD, FRCS   Sr.
    Lectr.
Pockley, A. G., BSc *CNAA*, PhD *CNAA*   Reader
Saleh, M., MB ChB *Dund.*, MSc *Dund.*,
    FRCS   Prof., Orthopaedic and Traumatic
    Surgery
Wood, R. F. M., MB ChB *Glas.*, MA *Oxf.*, MD
    Glas., FRCS   Prof., Surgery; Head*
Other Staff: 5 Lectrs.; 1 Clin. Lectr.; 25 Hon.
    Clin. Lectrs.
Research: general surgery; orthopaedic surgery;
    vascular surgery, transplantation

NURSING AND MIDWIFERY, SCHOOL OF

Tel: (0114) 271 3349 Fax: (0114) 271 3960

Research: delivery and management of health
    care; education of health care professionals;
    the practice of nursing, midwifery and
    health visiting

Acute and Critical Care Nursing

Brown, R., BA *Open(UK)*, MA *Lough.*   Sr.
    Nursing Lectr.
Calpin-Davis, P., BEd *Wales*, MBA *Keele*   Sr.
    Nursing Lectr.
Fairbrother, P., BA *CNAA*, MSc *CNAA*   Sr.
    Nursing Lectr.
Platt, J., BSc *CNAA*   Sr. Nursing Lectr.
Read, S., PhD   Sr. Lectr.
Rowland, T., BEd *CNAA*, MSc *Brad.*   Sr.
    Nursing Lectr.
Ruffle, H., BEd *CNAA*, MEd *CNAA*   Sr. Nursing
    Lectr.
Venables, A., BSc *CNAA*, MA *Leeds*   Sr. Lectr.;
    Head*
Other Staff: 7 Lectrs.; 41 Nursing Lectrs.

Community, Primary Care and Public Health Nursing

Basford, L., BA *CNAA*, MA *Sheff.Hallam*   Head*
Day, M., BEd *CNAA*, MEd *Wales*   Sr. Nursing
    Lectr.
Glossop, D., BA *Open(UK)*, MSc *Leeds Met.*   Sr.
    Nursing Lectr.
Marvell, G., BA *CNAA*   Sr. Nursing Lectr.
Pearson, S., BSc *Liv.*, MMedSci *Sheff.*   Sr.
    Nursing Lectr.
Saverimoutou, J., BA *CNAA*   Sr. Nursing Lectr.

Other Staff: 5 Lectrs.; 18 Nursing Lectrs.

Gerontological and Continuing Care Nursing

Harrison, J., BA *Open(UK)*, MMedSci *Sheff.*   Sr.
    Nursing Lectr.
James, J., MA *CNAA*   Sr. Lectr.
Jones, D., OBE, BEd *Wales*   Prof.
Marr, A., MA *CNAA*   Head*
Nolan, M. R., BEd *Wales*, BSc *Wales*, MSc *Wales*,
    PhD *Wales*   Prof.
Norcliffe, P., BEd *CNAA*, MA *Lough.*   Sr.
    Nursing Lectr.
Procter, P., MSc *Brun.*   Sr. Nursing Lectr.
Roberts-Davis, M., BA *CNAA*, MA *Lough.*   Sr.
    Nursing Lectr.
Sykes, P., BSc *CNAA*   Sr. Nursing Lectr.
Other Staff: 5 Lectrs.; 18 Nursing Lectrs.

Mental Health and Learning Disability

Blackburn, J., BSc *Leeds Met.*   Sr. Nursing Lectr.
Bush, J., BA *CNAA*, MA *York(UK)*   Sr. Nursing
    Lectr.
Dowd, C., MSc *CNAA*   Sr. Lectr.
Goward, P., MSc *CNAA*   Sr. Nursing Lectr.
Grant, G. W. B., BSc *Manc.*, MSc *Manc.*, PhD
    UMIST   Prof., Cognitive Disability
Kellett, J., BEd *CNAA*, MSc *Sheff.Hallam*   Head*
Matanga, R., BSc *CNAA*, MA *Leeds*   Sr. Nursing
    Lectr.
Richardson, M., BEd *CNAA*, MSc *CNAA*   Sr.
    Nursing Lectr.
Other Staff: 5 Lectrs.; 23 Nursing Lectrs.,

Midwifery and Child Health Nursing

Drew, J., MA *Sheff.Hallam*   Sr. Nursing Lectr.
Guest, C., BSc *CNAA*, MMedSci   Sr. Nursing
    Lectr.
Peat, A., BEd *CNAA*, MEd *CNAA*   Head*
Walker, A., BEd *CNAA*   Sr. Nursing Lectr.
Other Staff: 26 Nursing Lectrs.

SPECIAL CENTRES, ETC

Advanced Magnetic Materials and Devices, Sheffield Centre for

Tel: (0114) 270 1277 Fax: (0114) 270 1277

Davies, H. A., BSc(Eng) *Lond.*, PhD *Lond.*,
    FIM   Dir.*
Research: novel and improved magnetic
    materials

Advanced Railway Research Centre

Tel: (0114) 222 0151 Fax: (0114) 275 5625

Smith, R. A., MA *Oxf.*, PhD *Camb.*,
    FIM   Chair*
Other Staff: 5 Res. Assocs.
Research: affordable rail vehicles; composite
    material structures; low-cost rail
    infrastructure; technological challenges;
    telematics and train control

Aegean Archaeology, Centre for

Tel: (0114) 222 2900 Fax: (0114) 272 2563

Branigan, Prof. K., BA *Birm.*, PhD *Birm.*,
    FSA   Dir.*

AIVRU Ltd

Tel: (0114) 222 1511 Fax: (0114) 222 1500
Frisby, Prof. J. P., BA *Camb.*, PhD *Sheff.*   Chair*

Anaesthetic Mechanisms, Centre for Research into

Tel: (0114) 222 4658 Fax: (0114) 276 5413
Angel, Prof. Tony, BSc *Lond.*, PhD *Lond.*   Dir.*
Research: fundamental and applied mechanisms
    involved in anaesthesia

Analytical Sciences, Centre for

Tel: (0114) 222 3602 Fax: (0114) 222 3650

McLeod, Prof. C. W., BSc *Edin.*, PhD
    Lond.   Dir.*

Research: trace analysis, particularly the water
    sector

Analytical Services Unit

Tel: (0114) 222 0090 Fax: (0114) 222 4773
Croft, Terry B., MBE, BA *Open(UK)*   Dir.*

Archaeological Research and Consultancy Service

Tel: (0114) 279 7158 Fax: (0114) 279 7158

Symonds, Jim, BA *Sheff.*   Exec. Dir.*
Other Staff: 3 Advisory Staff
Research: dendochronology; environmental
    science; field services; human remains;
    materials science

Arctic Ecology, Sheffield Centre for

Tel: (0114) 222 0099 Fax: (0114) 268 2521

Callaghan, Prof. T. V., BSc *Manc.*, PhD *Birm.*,
    FilDr *Lund*, DSc *Manc.*   Dir.*
Research: Fennoscandian sub-Arctic and high
    Arctic Svalbard

Artificial Intelligence Vision Research Unit

Tel: (0114) 222 6554 Fax: (0114) 276 6515

Mayhew, Prof. J. E. W., BSc *Brist.*, PhD
    Brist.   Sci. Dir.*

Bakhtin Centre

Tel: (0114) 222 7415 Fax: (0114) 222 7416

Shepherd, Prof. D. G., MA *Oxf.*, PhD
    Manc.   Dir.*
Other Staff: 1 Res. Fellow; 1 Hon. Res. Fellow

Biomaterials and Tissue Engineering, Centre for

Van Noort, Prof. R., BSc *Sus.*, DPhil *Sus.*   Co-
    ordinator*
Research: elucidating materials-tissue
    interactions; new materials and coatings

Biomolecular Research, Krebs Institute for

Tel: (0114) 222 4242 Fax: (0114) 272 8697

Rice, Prof. David W., BA *Oxf.*, DPhil
    Oxf.   Dir.*
Research: activity of biological enzymes,
    antibodies, gene repressors, hormones

Biotechnological Law and Ethics, Sheffield Institute of

Tel: (0114) 222 6734 Fax: (0114) 272 1319

Beyleveld, Prof. Derek, BSc *Witw.*, MA *Camb.*,
    PhD *E.Anglia*   Dir.*
Research: ethical and legal issues raised by
    developments in biotechnology

Bone and Joint Medicine, Institute of

Tel: (0114) 271 3780 Fax: (0114) 271 3781

Snaith, Michael L., MB BS *Newcastle(UK)*, MD
    Newcastle(UK), FRCP   Co-ordinator*
Research: basic and applied research in bone,
    collagen and cartilage structure

Cement and Concrete, Centre for

Tel: (0114) 222 5065 Fax: (0114) 272 8910

Waldron, Prof. Peter, BSc *Nott.*, PhD
    Lond.   Dir.*
Research: durability problems; introduction of
    new materials; performance of concrete and
    concrete structures

Ceregen Ltd

Pearson, Prof. R. C. A., BA *Oxf.*, BM BCh *Oxf.*,
    MA *Oxf.*, DPhil *Oxf.*   Dir.*
Research: human molecular neurobiology

Chemical Instrumental Analysis and Services

Fax: (0114) 273 8673
White, J. Derek   Dir.*

Cities and Regions Research Centre

Tel: (0114) 222 6180 Fax: (0114) 272 2199

Crook, Prof. A. D. H., BA Brist., MPhil Lond., PhD Sheff. Dir.*

Research: economic geography; environmental sustainability; housing; landscape planning and management; local economic development

Claremont Systems Ltd

Tel: (0114) 222 2631 Fax: (0114) 278 0300

Wilson, Prof. T. D., BSc(Econ) Lond., PhD, FLA Dir.*

Cognitive Studies, Hang Seng Centre for

Tel: (0114) 222 0570 Fax: (0114) 279 8760

Carruthers, Prof. P., BA Leeds, MPhil Leeds, DPhil Oxf. Dir.*

Commercial Law Studies, Institute for

Tel: (0114) 222 6759 Fax: (0114) 272 1319

Bradgate, J. R., MA Camb. Co-ordinator*

Comparative Plant Ecology, Unit of

Tel: (0114) 222 4315 Fax: (0114) 222 0013

Grime, Prof. J. Philip, BSc Sheff., PhD Sheff. Dir.*

Research: fundamental studies of the mechanisms controlling plant distribution and the structure and dynamics of vegetation in the UK and abroad

Conteque Ltd

Waldron, Prof. P., BSc Nott., PhD Lond. Dir.*
Pilakoutas, K., BSc Lond., PhD Lond. Dir.*

Control Technology Transfer Network

Mort, N., BSc Leic., MSc Manc., PhD Sheff. Dir.*

Corrosion Technology, Centre for

Akid, R., BSc Lond., PhD Sheff. Dir.*

Research: risk assessment, investigation and remedy of corrosion-related problems

Criminological and Legal Research, Centre for

Tel: (0114) 222 6734 Fax: (0114) 272 1319

Crow, I. D., BA Keele, MSc Lond. Dir.*

Research: criminal justice; operation of the legal system; the social nature of law

Dental Advice Research and Technology Service

Tel: (0114) 271 7931 Fax: (0114) 266 5326

Johnson, A., MMedSci Sheff., PhD Sheff. Dir.*
Research: dental technology; problem solving; product development; testing and analysis

Early Modern Studies, Centre for

Tel: (0114) 222 2574 Fax: (0114) 278 8304

Hattaway, Prof. M., BA NZ, MA Well., PhD Camb. Dir.*
Milton, A., BA Camb., MA Camb., PhD Camb., FRHistS Dir.*
Research: research across the humanities, 1500-1800

Earth Observation Science, Sheffield Centre for

Tel: (0114) 222 3803 Fax: (0114) 222 3759

Quegan, Prof. Shaun, BA Warw., MSc Warw., PhD Sheff. Dir.*
Research: theory, methodology, application of remote sensing

East Asia Business Services

Tel: (0114) 222 8070 Fax: (0114) 272 8028

Bland, John L., MA Oxf., DPhil Oxf. Dir.*

East Asia Research Centre

Tel: (0114) 222 8421 Fax: (0114) 272 9479

Weiner, M. A., BA Sophia, PhD Sheff. Dir.*
Research: migration systems; regional security; technology transfer

Electron Microscopy and Microanalysis, Sorby Centre for

Tel: (0114) 222 5474 Fax: (0114) 275 4325

Lee, W. E., BSc Aston, DPhil Oxf., FIM Manager*
Research: microstructures

Endocrinology, Institute of

Tel: (0114) 271 3416 Fax: (0114) 273 9976

Brown, Prof. Barry L., BSc Lond., PhD Lond., FIBiol Co-Dir.*
Henderson, Prof. I. W., PhD DSc, FIBiol Co-Dir.*
Research: molecular to clinical diagnostic studies

Energy Design Advice Scheme

Tel: (0114) 272 1140 Fax: (0114) 272 0676

Ward, Ian C., BSc Strath. Dir.*

Energy, Pollution and Waste Management, Centre for

Tel: (0114) 222 7502 Fax: (0114) 278 0611

Swithenbank, Prof. J., BSc Birm., PhD Sheff., FEng Dir.*
Research: environmentally sustainable development

English Cultural Tradition, National Centre for

Tel: (0114) 222 6296

Widdowson, Prof. John D. A., MA Oxf., MA Leeds, PhD Nfld. Dir.*
Research: the study of modern English usage

Environet

Calow, Prof. P., PhD Leeds, DSc Leeds, FIBiol, FLS Dir.*

Environmental and Engineering Geosciences, Centre for

Tel: (0114) 222 3600 Fax: (0114) 222 3650

Chapman, Prof. N., BSc Durh., PhD Edin., FGS Dir.*
Research: geological, surface and groundwater environment

Environmental Consultancy (ECUS)

Tel: (0114) 266 9292 Fax: (0114) 266 7707

Routh, Christopher J. S., BSc Leic. Manager*
Research: ecological survey; environmental assessment and audit; environmental management and planning; landscape design

Folklore Studies in Britain and Canada, Institute for

Tel: (0114) 222 0193

Smith, Paul S., BA Sheff., PhD Sheff. Co-Dir.*
Widdowson, Prof. John D. A., MA Oxf., MA Leeds, PhD Nfld. Co-Dir.*

Geographic Information and Spatial Analysis, Centre for

Tel: (0114) 222 7905 Fax: (0114) 279 7912

Haining, Prof. R. P., MA Camb., BSc PhD Dir.*
Research: use of geographic information systems technology

Glass Research, Centre for

Tel: (0114) 222 5467 Fax: (0114) 275 4325

Seddon, A. B., BSc Nott., MPhil CNAA, PhD CNAA, FRSChem Dir.*

Health Information Management Research, Centre for

Tel: (0114) 222 2642 Fax: (0114) 278 0300

Wilson, Prof. Tom D., BSc(Econ) Lond., PhD Sheff., FLA Dir.*

History of Medicine, Sheffield Centre for the

Woodward, J. H., BA York(UK), DPhil York(UK) Co-Dir.*
Worboys, M. Co-Dir.*

Research: role of hospitals and other health-related institutions

Holocaust Studies, Centre for

Tel: (0114) 222 2555 Fax: (0114) 278 8304

Burns, P. B., MA Durh., PhD Lond. Co-Dir.*
Holmes, Prof. C., MA Nott. Co-Dir.*
Vice, S., MA Camb., DPhil Oxf. Co-Dir.*
Research: cultural representations; historical interpretations

Human Nutrition, Centre for

Tel: (0114) 271 5380 Fax: (0114) 261 0112

Read, Prof. Nicholas W., MA Camb., MB BChir Camb., MD Camb., FRCP Dir.*
Research: effects of food on behaviour; relevance of nutrition in disease

Humanities Research Institute

Tel: (0114) 222 0217

Blake, Prof. N. F., MA Oxf., BLitt Oxf. Dir. for Res.*
Luscombe, Prof. D. E., MA Camb., PhD Camb., LittD Camb. Chair*
Research: application of new technology to text- and image-based research

III-V Semiconductors, EPSRC Central Facility for

Tel: (0114) 222 5143 Fax: (0114) 272 6391

Whitehouse, Prof. Colin R., BSc Lond., MSc Birm., PhD CNAA, FIP Dir.*
Research: next-generation III-V semiconductor materials and devices

International Drylands Research, Sheffield Centre for

Tel: (0114) 222 7909 Fax: (0114) 279 7912

Thomas, Prof. David S. G., BA Oxf., DPhil Oxf. Dir.*
Research: past, present and future environmental changes in drylands

Invector Ltd

Tel: (0114) 222 4232 Fax: (0114) 272 8697

Hornby, D. P., BSc Sheff., PhD Sheff. Dir.*
Research: the development of novel reagents in technology for molecular biology

Language, Speech and Hearing, Institute of

Tel: (0114) 222 1804

Wilks, Prof. Yorick, BA Camb., MA Camb., PhD Camb. Dir.*

Legal Profession, Institute for the Study of the

Tel: (0114) 222 6768 Fax: (0114) 272 1319

Shapland, Prof. Joanna M., MA Oxf., DPhil Oxf. Dir.*
Research: legal system

Leisure Industries Research Centre

Tel: (0114) 222 2181 Fax: (0114) 275 1216

Gratton, Prof. C. Co-Dir.*
Taylor, Prof. P., BA Warw., MA Leeds Co-Dir.*
Research: nature of competitive advantage in leisure industries

Lincoln Theological Institute

Percy, Rev. Canon M., BA Brist., PhD Lond. Dir.*
Research: religion and society

Luxembourg Studies, Centre for

Tel: (0114) 222 4396

Newton, G., BA Liv., PhD Liv. Dir.*

Magnetic Systems Technology Ltd

Tel: (0114) 244 8416 Fax: (0114) 244 8417

Eardley, J. E., JP, Hon. LLD Sheff. Dir.*
Howe, Prof. David, BTech Brad., MSc Brad., PhD S'ton. Dir.*
Jenkins, M. K., BEng Sheff., MPhil Sheff. Dir.*
Research: electrical drive systems; magnetic devices; power electronics

Manufacturing Systems Management Unit

Fax: (0114) 275 3671

Ridgway, Prof. Keith, BSc *Manc.*, MSc *Salf.*, PhD *Manc.* Dir.*

Research: technology transfer

Materials Advice and Research Centre

Tel: (0114) 222 5500 Fax: (0114) 275 4325

Sharp, Prof. J. H., BSc *Nott.*, PhD *Nott.*, FIM Dir.*

Mediaeval Studies, Centre for

Tel: (0114) 222 2577 Fax: (0114) 278 8304

Blake, Prof. N. F., MA *Oxf.*, BLitt *Oxf.* Dir.*

Membrane Protein Function, Sheffield Laboratory of

Tel: (0114) 222 4636 Fax: (0114) 276 5413

Dunne, M. J., BSc *Warw.*, PhD *Liv.* Dir.*

Research: cell membrane processes, their structure and role in health and disease

Metals Advisory Centre

Tel: (0114) 222 5511 Fax: (0114) 275 4325

Sellars, Prof. C. Michael, BMet *Sheff.*, PhD *Sheff.*, DMet *Sheff.*, Hon. CMechD *Navarra*, FIM Dir.*

Research: metal component failure; special alloy manufacture and development

Micro-Electromechanical Systems Unit

Tel: (0114) 222 5146 Fax: (0114) 272 6391

Yates, R. B., BSc *Lond.*, MSc *Manc.* Head*

Research: circuit design; mechanical modelling; semiconductor processing

Microstructural and Mechanical Process Engineering, Institute for (IMMPETUS)

Sellars, Prof. C. M., BMet *Sheff.*, PhD *Sheff.*, DMet *Sheff.*, Hon. CMechD *Navarra*, FEng, FIM Dir.*

Research: process planning and control; steels, aluminium and nickel-based alloys

Migration and Ethnicity Research Centre

Tel: (0114) 222 7908 Fax: (0114) 279 7912

Holdaway, S., BA *Lanc.*, PhD *Sheff.* Co-Dir.*
Holme, Prof. C., MA *Nott.* Co-Dir.*
Jackson, Prof. P. A., MA *Oxf.*, DPhil *Oxf.* Co-Dir.*

Research: ethnic minority aspects of identity formation and social policy; history of human migration

Molecular Materials, Centre for

Tel: (0114) 222 9497 Fax: (0114) 272 0182

Bradley, Prof. D. D. C., BSc *Lond.*, PhD *Camb.* Dir.*

Research: design and synthesis of compounds; property measurement; structural and phase characterisation

Music Performance and Perception, Centre for Research in

Tel: (0114) 222 0470 Fax: (0114) 266 8053

Clarke, Prof. E. F., BA *Sus.*, MA *Sus.*, PhD *Exe.* Dir.*

Research: free improvisation and creativity; historical performance practices; performance of contemporary music; performance skills in children; psychology of performance

Nineteenth Century Studies, Centre for

Tel: (0114) 222 8480 Fax: (0114) 222 8481

Shuttleworth, Prof. S. A., BA *York(UK)*, PhD *Camb.* Dir.*

Research: Europe and America, 1789-1914

Ophthalmic Sciences Unit

Tel: (0114) 271 2644 Fax: (0114) 276 6381

Parsons, Malcolm A., MB ChB *Sheff.*, FRCPath Dir.*

Research: biomedical, molecular sciences into the causes and treatment of eye diseases; ophthalmic pathology; ophthalmology

Palynological Studies, Centre for

Tel: (0114) 222 3682 Fax: (0114) 222 3677

Owens, Prof. B. Dir.*

Political Economy Research Centre

Tel: (0114) 222 0660 Fax: (0114) 275 5921

Payne, Prof. A. J., BA *Camb.*, MA *Camb.*, PhD *Manc.* Dir.*

Research: current transformation of the world economy

Research, Education and Development On-Line, Centre for

Tel: (0114) 276 8740 Fax: (0114) 272 7563

Cvetkovic, S., BSc *City(UK)*, PhD *Lond.* Dir.*

Research: virtual environments

Robert Hill Institute

Photosynthesis

Tel: (0114) 222 4189 Fax: (0114) 272 8697

Horton, Prof. Peter, BA *York(UK)*, DPhil *York(UK)*, DSc *York(UK)* Dir.*

Research: photosynthesis in plants and micro-organisms

Rolls Royce University Technology Centre

Tel: (0114) 272 2768 Fax: (0114) 273 1729

Fleming, Prof. Peter J., BSc *Belf.*, PhD *Belf.*, FIEE Dir.*

Research: control systems and embedded software

Sensor Technology and Research, Centre for

Tel: (0114) 222 5254 Fax: (0114) 272 6391

Whitehouse, Prof. C. R., BSc *Lond.*, MSc *Birm.*, PhD *CNAA* Dir.*

Research: automobile, aerospace and chemical processing industries; next-generation medical sensors

Sheffield Hybridomas

Tel: (0114) 222 7480 Fax: (0114) 279 6682

Howard, Bryan R., BVMS *Glas.*, MSc *Lond.*, PhD *Edin.* Tech. Dir.*
Partridge, Linda J., BSc *Birm.*, MSc *Lond.*, PhD *Birm.* Tech. Dir.*

Research: production of monoclonal antibodies by biotechnological means

Sheffield Kidney Institute

Tel: (0114) 243 4343

El Nahas, A. Maguid, BSc *Lond.*, FRCP Co-ordinator*

Research: different heomodialysis and CAPD modalities; glomerulonephritis

Sheffield University Waste Incineration Centre

Tel: (0114) 222 7502

Swithenbank, Prof. J., BSc *Birm.*, PhD *Sheff.*, FEng Dir.*

Research: new techniques for controlling pollutant from incinerators

Signalbox Ltd

Tel: (0114) 222 5232 Fax: (0114) 273 1729

Billings, Prof. S. A., BEng *Liv.*, PhD *Sheff.*, DEng *Liv.*, FIMA Dir.*

Research: neural network software

Socio-Legal Studies, Centre for

Tel: (0114) 222 6770 Fax: (0114) 272 1319

Lewis, Prof. N., LLB *Brist.* Dir.*

Research: sociological, philosophical, political and moral dimensions of the law

Statistical Services Unit

Tel: (0114) 222 3900 Fax: (0114) 222 3759

Ashman, Chris J., BSc *CNAA*, MSc *Sheff.* Dir.*

Steel Construction, Academy for

Tel: (0114) 222 0303 Fax: (0114) 279 8276

Plank, Prof. R. J., BSc *Birm.*, PhD *Birm.* Dir.*

Research: connections; environmental issues; fire engineering

Structural Integrity Research Institute

Tel: (0114) 222 7707 Fax: (0114) 275 3671

Beynon, Prof. J. H., BMet PhD, FIM Dir.*

Research: assessment of failure mechanisms; lifetime predictions; safety evaluations

SupaPlants Ltd

Tel: (0114) 222 0003 Fax: (0114) 276 0159

Jarvis, Bernard C., BSc *Wales*, PhD *Wales* Tech. Dir.*

Research: enhancing root formation and growth; plant propagation

Telerise

Knowledge and Technology Transfer
Cvetkovic, S. R., BSc *City(UK)*, PhD *Lond.* Dir.*

Training Policy Studies, Centre for

Tel: (0114) 222 1370 Fax: (0114) 222 1377

Marquand, Prof. Judith M., MA *Oxf.*, MSc *Open(UK)* Dir.*

Research: analysis of training policies; training systems

Unisheff Properties Ltd

Tel: (0114) 222 1511 Fax: (0114) 222 1500

Cotton, B. E., CBE, Hon. LLD *Sheff.* Dir.*

Unisheff Ventures Ltd

Tel: (0114) 222 1511

Birtles, Richard M. Company Sec.*

Vaccine Studies, Sheffield Institute for

Tel: (0114) 271 7419

Finn, A. H. R., BM BCh *Oxf.*, MA *Camb.*, PhD *Lond.* Co-Dir.*
Jennings, Prof. J., BSc *Birm.*, PhD *WI* Co-Dir.*

Research: development and testing of vaccines

Waste Management and Technology Centre

Coggins, P. C., BSc *Wales*, PhD *Wales* Dir.*

Wetlands Research Centre

Baird, A. J., BSc *Hull*, PhD *Brist.* Co-ordinator*

Research: construction and use of artificial wetlands; hydrological processes in wetlands; wetland ecology and restoration

Work Psychology, Institute of

Tel: (0114) 222 3266 Fax: (0114) 272 7206

Wall, Prof. Toby D., BA *Nott.*, PhD *Nott.*, FBPsS Dir.*

Research: psychological causes of effectiveness and mental health at work

CONTACT OFFICERS

Academic affairs. Academic Secretary: O'Donovan, John B., BSc *Lond.*, MSc *Newcastle(UK)*, PhD *Newcastle(UK)*

Accommodation. Director of Housing Services: Flower, Geoffrey A.

Admissions (first degree). Admissions Officer (Undergraduate): Hindmarsh, Andrew M., MA *Oxf.*, DPhil *Oxf.*

Admissions (higher degree). Admissions Officer (Graduate): Howells, A., BSc *Wales*, PhD *Wales*

Adult/continuing education. Assistant Registrar: Smith, T. A., BA *Sheff.*, MA *Sheff.Hallam*

Careers. Director of Careers Advisory Service: Pethen, R. W., BSc *Birm.*, PhD *Camb.*

Computing services. Deputy Director of Corporate Information and Computing Services: Cartledge, Christopher J., BSc *Lond.*

Computing services. Head of Corporate Information: Sexton, Christine E., BSc *Sheff.*, PhD *Sheff.*

Consultancy services. Director, Research and Consultancy Unit: Lilley, Prof. Terry H., BSc Durh., PhD Newcastle(UK), FRSChem

Equal opportunities. Director of Human Resource Management: Valerio, Rosie A., BA Sheff.

Estates and buildings/works and services. Director of Estates: MacDonald, John

Examinations. Senior Assistant Registrar: Morrison, Julia E., MA Glas.

Finance. Director of Finance: Bearpark, David R., BSc Hull

General enquiries. Registrar and Secretary: Fletcher, David E., BA Sheff., PhD Sheff.

Health services. Director of University Health Service: Burton, James A., MB ChB Sheff.

Industrial liaison. Director of Business Link: Handscombe, Robert D., BSc Lond., PhD Lond.

International office. Director of International Office: ......

Library (chief librarian). Librarian: Hannon, Michael S.-M., MA Trinity(Dub.)

Minorities/disadvantaged groups. Assistant Registrar: Green, Debora G. M., BEd Lond., MEd Wales

Personnel/human resources. Director of Human Resource Management: Valerio, Rosie A., BA Sheff.

Public relations, information and marketing. Director of Public Relations: Allum, Roger C., BSc Nott., PhD Nott.

Publications. Director of Public Relations: Allum, Roger C., BSc Nott., PhD Nott.

Purchasing. Director of Procurement: South, S. L.

Research. Director, Research and Consultancy Unit: Lilley, Prof. Terry H., BSc Durh., PhD Newcastle(UK), FRSChem

Safety. Director of Safety Services: Hellings, Robert O., BSc Lond.

Schools liaison. Director of Schools and Colleges Liaison Service: Johnson, F. Allan, BSc Leeds, PhD Leeds

Security. Head of Security: Mole, Brian L.

Sport and recreation. Director of Sport and Recreation Services: Bracewell, Michael B., MSc Oregon

Staff development and training. Director of Staff Development Unit: Killingley, Patricia A., BA Hull, MSc CNAA

Student union. Manager: Windle, John C.

Student welfare/counselling. Director of University Counselling Service: Lago, Colin O., MEd Leic.

Student welfare/counselling. Head of Student Services: Holding, Mary H., BA Sheff., MPhil Sheff.

Students from other countries. Assistant Registrar: Green, Debora G. M., BEd Lond., MEd Wales

Students with disabilities. Disability Officer: Norris, M., BSc Lond.

University press. Director of Sheffield Academic Press: Clines, Prof. David J. A., BA Syd., MA Camb.

University press. Director of Sheffield Academic Press: Davies, Prof. Philip R., MA Oxf., PhD St And.

Women. Director of Human Resource Management: Valerio, Rosie A., BA Sheff.

[Information supplied by the institution as at 12 March 1998, and edited by the ACU]

SHEFFIELD HALLAM UNIVERSITY

Designated 1992; established as Sheffield College of Technology 1950

Member of the Association of Commonwealth Universities

Postal Address: City Campus, Howard Street, Sheffield, England S1 1WB
Telephone: (0114) 225 5555 **Fax**: (0114) 225 3398 **Telex**: 54680 **WWW**: http://www.shu.ac.uk
E-mail formula: name@shu.ac.uk

CHANCELLOR—Nicholson, Sir Bryan
CHAIR OF THE BOARD OF GOVERNORS—Adsetts, W. Norman, OBE, MA Oxf.
PRINCIPAL AND VICE-CHANCELLOR*—Green, Prof. Diana M., BA Reading, BSc(Econ) Lond., PhD Lond.
DEPUTY PRINCIPAL—Johnston, Ian A., BSc Birm., PhD Birm.
ASSISTANT PRINCIPAL (DEVELOPMENT AND MARKETING)—Hobbs, Jack M., PhD Newcastle(UK), BSc, FIMA
ASSISTANT PRINCIPAL (STAFF STRATEGY AND STUDENT SUPPORT)—Willcocks, Prof. Dianne M., BA Sur.
UNIVERSITY SECRETARY‡—Neocosmos, Sally, BA Lough.
DIRECTOR OF FINANCE AND RESOURCES—Lane, Ronald J. B., BA Newcastle(UK), BA Durh.
LIBRARIAN—Bulpitt, Graham, BA Open(UK), MA Lond.

GENERAL INFORMATION

History. The oldest constituent part of the university, the College of Art, was founded in 1843. The university was designated in 1992, having previously been a polytechnic (1969).

Admission to first degree courses (see also United Kingdom Introduction). Through Universities and Colleges Admissions Service (UCAS). International students must possess good English language skills and acceptable qualifications.

First Degrees (* = also available with honours). BA*, BEng*, BSc*, BTP (town planning), LLB*.

Higher Degrees. MA, MEng, MSci.

Libraries. 500,000 volumes; 2000 periodicals subscribed to.

Fees. UK students: £750 (band 1); £1000 (band 2). International students: £6100 (band 1); £8100 (band 2).

Academic Year. Two semesters: 21 September–22 January; 25 January–28 May.

Income (1997–98). Total, £100,000,000.

Statistics. Students: full-time 15,939; part-time 5168; international 1075; total 22,182.

FACULTIES/SCHOOLS

Business and Management, School of
Tel: (0114) 225 5330 Fax: (0114) 225 5036
Director: Worsdale, Graham, BA Lanc., MSc Manc., PhD Lanc.
Secretary: Cadd, Ann

Computing and Management Sciences, School of
Tel: (0114) 225 3160 Fax: (0114) 225 3161
Director: Draffan, Rev. Prof. Ian W., BSc Aston, MSc Aston
Secretary: Harrison, Linda

Construction, School of
Tel: (0114) 225 4267 Fax: (0114) 225 3179
Director: Balmforth, Prof. David J., BSc Sheff., PhD Sheff.
Secretary: Clayton, B.

Cultural Studies, School of
Tel: (0114) 225 2607 Fax: (0114) 225 2603
Director: Thomas, Prof. Elaine
Secretary: Threlfall, J.

Education, School of
Tel: (0114) 225 2306 Fax: (0114) 225 2324
Director: Bentley, Prof. Diana, BSc Manc., MSc Manc.
Secretary: Cuthbertson, J.

Engineering, School of
Tel: (0114) 225 2306 Fax: (0114) 225 3433
Director: Eaton, David E., MSc Manc.
Secretary: Richardson, S.

Financial Studies and Law, School of
Tel: (0114) 225 5120 Fax: (0114) 225 5036
Director: Harrison, Keith, BA Lanc.
Secretary: Hill, L.

Health and Community Studies, School of
Tel: (0114) 225 2543 Fax: (0114) 225 2430
Director (Acting): King, Martin E., BSc Lond., MSc Lond.
Secretary: Hammond, G.

Leisure and Food Management, School of
Tel: (0114) 225 3325 Fax: (0114) 225 2881
Director: Rick, Valerie E., BA Liv., MSc S'ton.
Secretary: Dyer, V.

Science and Mathematics, School of

Tel: (0114) 225 3072 Fax: (0114) 225 3085
Director: Parkinson, Prof. John J.
Secretary: Shepherd, A.

Sheffield Business School

Tel: (0114) 225 5107 Fax: (0114) 225 5036
Acting Director: Croney, Paul, BA CNAA, MA Warw.
Secretary: Montgomery, L.

Urban and Regional Studies, School of

Tel: (0114) 225 4267 Fax: (0114) 225 4546
Acting Director: Mackmin, Prof. David, BSc Lond., MSc Reading
Secretary: Adderley, A.

ACADEMIC UNITS

Arranged by Schools

Business and Management, see also Sheffield Bus. Sch.

Tel: (0114) 225 5330 Fax: (0114) 225 5036
Gilligan, Prof. Colin T.   Sr. Academic
Goacher, David J.   Sr. Academic
Owen, Glyn W., BA Sheff.   Sr. Academic
Worsdale, Graham, BA Lanc., MSc Manc., PhD Lanc.   Acting Dir.*

Computing and Management Sciences

Tel: (0114) 225 3160 Fax: (0114) 225 3161
Al-Khayatt, Samir S., BSc Baghdad, MPhil Lond., PhD Lough.   Sr. Lectr.
Bacsich, Prof. Paul   Sr. Academic
Band, Graham   Sr. Lectr.
Bell, Douglas, BSc Lond., DPhil Sus.   Principal Lectr.
Bertram, Richard G., BSc Liv.   Principal Lectr.
Bissett, Andrew K., BSc Kent, MSc CNAA   Sr. Lectr.
Bouhadef, Mouloud   Sr. Lectr.
Bowler, Elizabeth   Sr. Lectr.
Brunsdon, Teresa M., BSc Lough., MSc S'ton., PhD S'ton.   Sr. Lectr.
Butcher, Roy, BSc Hull   Principal Lectr.
Carter, Christopher E., BSc Newcastle(UK), PhD Sheff.   Sr. Lectr.
Chenery, Lynne, MSc Sheff.Hallam   Sr. Lectr.
Clothier, Heather   Sr. Lectr.
Coates, Elizabeth, BA Oxf., MSc CNAA   Sr. Lectr.
Collingwood, Peter C., BSc Warw., MSc CNAA, PhD Warw.   Sr. Lectr.
Conheeney, Kevin, BSc Sheff., MSc CNAA, PhD Sheff.   Sr. Lectr.
Cooper, David, BA Oxf., MSc Oxf., MSc Sheff., DPhil Oxf.   Sr. Lectr.
Cooper, Ian, BSc Liv., MSc Liv., PhD Keele   Sr. Lectr.
Curtis, Susan, BSc Leeds   Sr. Lectr.
Cutts, Geoffrey, BSc Leic., MSc CNAA, PhD CNAA   Sr. Academic Postholder; Head, Postgrad. Programmes
Davies, Glyn, MSc Sheff.Hallam   Sr. Lectr.
Doole, Gordon, BA Keele, MSc CNAA   Sr. Lectr.
Draffan, Rev. Ian W., BSc Aston, MSc Aston   Prof.; Dir.*
Drew, David, BSc S'ton., MSc Birm., PhD Sheff.   Sr. Lectr.
Elliott, Charles   Sr. Lectr.
Furminger, Michael F., BSc Lond., MSc Leic.   Principal Lectr.
Gadsden, Richard J., MSc Hull, PhD Leeds   Sr. Academic Postholder; Head, Undergrad. Programmes
Gibson, Michael D., BA CNAA, MSc CNAA, PhD Manc.   Sr. Lectr.
Goldsmith, Geraldine R., BSc Sheff., MSc Manc.   Sr. Lectr.
Grimsley, Michael F., BSc Lond., MSc Lond.   Principal Lectr.
Hall, Christopher J., BA E.Anglia, MSc Manc.   Sr. Lectr.
Heath, Andrew K., MSc CNAA   Sr. Lectr.
Houghton, David S., BA Nott., MSc Oxf., PhD Nott.   Principal Lectr.
Houldcroft, Alan, BSc Manc.   Sr. Lectr.

Howell, Barbara, BSc Leeds Met.   Sr. Lectr.
Hughes, William I., BSc Leeds   Sr. Lectr.
Jacobi, Mark J., BEng Sheff.   Sr. Lectr.
Jayaratne, Prof. Nimal A.   Sr. Academic
Johns, Stuart L.   Sr. Lectr.
Johnston, Susan M., BA Open(UK), MBA Aston   Sr. Lectr.
Jones, Keith F., BSc Sus., MSc Sus., PhD Stir.   Sr. Lectr.
Kanji, Prof. Gopal K., BSc Patna, MSc Patna, MSc Sheff., PhD   Sr. Academic
Khazaei, Babek, BSc MSc PhD   Sr. Lectr.
Leigh, Peggy A., BA Open(UK), MSc CNAA   Sr. Lectr.
Love, Matthew, BSc CNAA   Sr. Lectr.
MacMillan, Ross, BSc CNAA   Sr. Lectr.
Mardell, Jane, BSc Lond., MSc Lond.   Sr. Lectr.
Matthews, Deborah, BSc MSc   Sr. Lectr.
McEwan, Andrew, BA Sheff., MSc CNAA   Sr. Lectr.
McLaughlin, Raymond, BTech Brad., PhD   Sr. Lectr.
Meehan, Anthony, BSc CNAA   Sr. Lectr.
Millington, Clare, BSc CNAA, MSc Warw.   Sr. Lectr.
Mir-Ghasemi, Mehdi, MSc CNAA   Sr. Lectr.
Morrey, Ian C., BA Lanc., MPhil City(UK)   Principal Lectr.
Morton, Susan A., BSc S'ton., MSc CNAA, MA Sheff.Hallam   Principal Lectr.
Moullin, Max, BSc S'ton., MSc Warw.   Sr. Lectr.
Norcliffe, Prof. Allan   Sr. Academic
Okell, Eric G., BA Oxf., MSc Oxf., MSc Leeds   Sr. Lectr.
Osborn, Richard J. W., MA Leeds, MSc CNAA   Sr. Lectr.
Ozcan, Mehmet B., BSc Ankara, MSc Manc., PhD Manc.   Sr. Lectr.
Pain, Dennis E., BSc Reading   Sr. Lectr.
Parr, Michael, BSc Lond.   Sr. Lectr.
Poole, Prof. Frank, BSc PhD, FBCS   Sr. Academic
Quinn, Michael, BSc Lond., PhD   Sr. Lectr.
Rangecroft, Margaret, BEd Sheff., MSc CNAA   Sr. Lectr.
Roast, Christopher R., BSc Leeds, MA York(UK), DPhil York(UK)   Sr. Lectr.
Rotherham, D.   Sr. Lectr.
Saeedi, Mohammed H., MSc Lond., PhD Sheff.   Sr. Lectr.
Salter, Stephen J., BA Oxf., MSc Sus.   Sr. Lectr.
Scott, Peter   Sr. Lectr.
Siddiqi, Jawed I., BSc Lond., MSc Aston, PhD Aston   Principal Lectr.
Steele, Robert A., MPhil CNAA   Principal Lectr.
Stone, John, BSc Lond., PhD Brist.   Principal Lectr.
Straker, Christine, BA MSc   Sr. Lectr.
Topp, Sonia G., BSc Leic.   Sr. Lectr.
Tricker, Anthony R., BSc Wales, MSc Wales, PhD CNAA   Principal Lectr.
Vacher, Pascale   Sr. Lectr.
Wallace, William, BSc Leeds, MSc Leeds, MPhil CNAA   Sr. Lectr.
Walton, John R., BSc Warw., MSc CNAA   Sr. Lectr.
Ward, Roy, MSc Manc.   Sr. Lectr.
Wheway, Paul   Sr. Lectr.
Wilkinson, Julie, BA Leeds, MSc Hudd.   Sr. Lectr.
Williams, Philip   Sr. Lectr.

Construction

Tel: (0114) 225 3181 Fax: (0114) 225 3179
Al-Shawi, Fathi, BEng Sheff., PhD Sheff.   Sr. Lectr.
Balmforth, Prof. David J., BSc Sheff., PhD Sheff.   Dir.*
Bettridge, John E., BSc Aston   Sr. Lectr.
Birkett, Geoffrey   Sr. Lectr.
Blanksby, John, BSc Aston   Sr. Lectr.
Bougdah, Hocine N. D.   Sr. Lectr.
Brayshaw, Jeremy D., MSc H-W   Sr. Lectr.
Cole, Nicholas   Sr. Lectr.
Cook, Sarah, BSc Greenwich   Sr. Lectr.
Croft, Philip   Sr. Lectr.
Davis, Richard   Sr. Lectr.
Ellis, Clifford, BSc CNAA, MPhil CNAA   Sr. Lectr.

Goodwin, Andrew K., BSc Sur., PhD Sheff.   Sr. Lectr.
Griffith, Prof. Alan   Sr. Academic
Hill, Christopher, MSc Birm.   Sr. Lectr.
Jones, Phillip A., BSc CNAA   Sr. Lectr.
Mangat, Prof. Pritpal   Sr. Academic
McNamara, Terry E., MSc Sheff.   Sr. Lectr.
Parnham, Phillip, BSc De Mont.   Sr. Lectr.
Read, Allan   Sr. Lectr.
Ridal, John, MSc Manc.   Sr. Lectr.
Simpson, Derek S., BEng Liv.   Sr. Lectr.
Smith, Martyn J., MA Sheff.   Sr. Lectr.
Smith, Peter F., MA Camb., PhD Manc.   Prof.
Stephenson, Paul, MSc Aston, PhD Sheff.   Principal Lectr.
Stoneman, Graham R. W., MSc Brad.   Sr. Lectr.
Tebbutt, Prof. Thomas H. Y., BSc PhD   Sr. Academic
Tipple, Christopher, MSc Manc., PhD Manc.   Sr. Lectr.
Turrell, Patricia, BSc Aston   Sr. Lectr.
Watson, Paul A., MSc PhD   Sr. Lectr.
Westland, Peter, BSc Manc.   Sr. Lectr.

Cultural Studies

Tel: (0114) 225 2689 Fax: (0114) 225 2603
Baggott, Jeffrey   Principal Lectr.
Bairstow, John, BA Lough., MA Buckingham   Sr. Lectr.
Baker, Ian P., BA Sheff., MA Birm.   Sr. Lectr.
Barber, Bob, MA Buckingham   Sr. Lectr.
Baxendale, John, MA Oxf., DPhil Oxf.   Principal Lectr.
Betterton, Rosemary S., BA Manc., MA Essex   Principal Lectr.
Bort, Stephen A., BA Lough., MA RCA   Sr. Lectr.
Cain, Prof. Peter J., BA Oxf., BLitt Oxf.   Sr. Academic
Carder, Jan, BEd S'ton., MPhil Sheff.   Sr. Lectr.
Cere, Rinella, BA Sus., MA Sus.   Sr. Lectr.
Chamberlain, Paul, BA Brist., MDes RCA   Sr. Lectr.
Chapman, Gill M., BA Tees., MSc Tees., MA Oxf.   Sr. Lectr.
Cooper, Rosemary, BA Leic., MA Lond.   Sr. Lectr.
Copper, Susan   Sr. Lectr.
Coubro, Gerry T. C., BA Camb., MA Camb.   Principal Lectr.
Counsell, Alison G., BA Lond., MA RCA   Sr. Lectr.
Cowdell, Theo, BA Lond., MBA Sheff., PhD Lond.   Principal Lectr.
Cox, Philip T., BA York(UK), DPhil York(UK)   Principal Lectr.
Critcher, Prof. Chas, BA Birm.   Reader
Cunliffe-Charlesworth, Hilary, BA CNAA, MA RCA, PhD CNAA   Sr. Lectr.
Dann, Frances M., BPhil Oxf., MA Oxf.   Sr. Lectr.
Dryden, Caroline, BSc Brist., PhD Brist.   Sr. Lectr.
Dujardin, Anne-Florence, Lic Paris IV, MA Paris IV   Sr. Lectr.
Dutton, Stephen, BA Sheff.Hallam, MA RCA   Sr. Lectr.
Eagleton, David J., MDes RCA   Principal Lectr.
Evans, Prof. Francis T., MA Camb.   Principal Lectr.
Fisher, Tom, BA Leeds   Sr. Lectr.
Goldie, Christopher   Sr. Lectr.
Gore, Van J., BA MA   Sr. Academic
Grainger, Karen, BA Reading, MA San Jose, PhD Wales   Sr. Lectr.
Greaves, J., BA Nott., MA Sheff.   Sr. Lectr.
Green, Keith M., BA Exe., MA Exe., PhD Sheff.   Sr. Lectr.
Grover, Peter, BSc Brun., MDes RCA   Sr. Lectr.
Harriman, Stephen A., BA CNAA   Sr. Lectr.
Hartley, Peter, BA Sheff., MSc Lond.   Sr. Academic Postholder; Head, Academic Devel.
Harvey, Sylvia, BA S'ton., MA Calif., PhD Calif.   Reader
Hawley, Glyn   Sr. Lectr.
Hawley, Stephen, BA Brighton   Sr. Lectr.
Haywood, Paul, BA Reading, MPhil CNAA   Sr. Lectr.
Heath, Virginia   Sr. Lectr.

Hegarty, Frances, BA *Leeds*, MA *Manc.* Principal Lectr.

Hermitt, Mandy, BA *Sheff.Hallam* Sr. Lectr.

Hilyer, Roger G., BA *Oxf.*, MA *Kansas State* Sr. Academic Postholder; Head, Resources

Hodges, Patricia A., BA *Birm.*, MA *CNAA* Principal Lectr.

Hopkins, Catherine L. M. Sr. Lectr.

Hurry, David J., BA *Wales*, PhD *Wales* Sr. Lectr.

Jones, Peter E., BA *York(UK)*, PhD *Camb.* Sr. Lectr.

Jordan, Melanie, BA *Leic.*, MA *Birm.* Sr. Lectr.

Jordin, Martin, BA *Sheff.*, MA *Essex* Sr. Lectr.

Kaye, Peter, BA *Sheff.Hallam*, BA *Sus.* Sr. Lectr.

Kenny, Marilyn J., BA *CNAA* Sr. Lectr.

Kinsey, Anne-Marie, BA *Lond.* Sr. Lectr.

Kivland, Sharon Sr. Lectr.

LeBihan, Jill, BA *Leeds*, MA *Leeds*, MA *Sheff.*, PhD *Leeds* Principal Lectr.

Lee, John, BEd *CNAA* Sr. Lectr.

Lewis, John T., MPhil *CNAA* Principal Lectr.

Lewis, Merr J., BSc *Wales*, MSc *Wales*, PhD *Sheff.Hallam* Sr. Lectr.

Lloyd-Jones, Roger, BA *York(UK)*, MSc *Lough.* Principal Lectr.

Lovering, Tim Principal Lectr.

Markham, Edward, BA *Wales* Sr. Lectr.

Marris, Paul, BA *Oxf.* Sr. Lectr.

Martin, Angela, MA *Lanc.* Sr. Lectr.

Maxfield, Cameron Sr. Lectr.

Mayall, David, BA *Sheff.*, MA *Warw.*, PhD *Sheff.* Sr. Lectr.

McDermott, Kevin, BA *Leeds*, PhD *Leeds* Sr. Lectr.

McKenna, Gillian, BA *Sheff.* Sr. Lectr.

Miles, Robert, BA *Lond.*, MPhil *Lond.*, PhD *Sheff.* Reader

Mills, Prof. Sara Sr. Academic

Mitchell, Andrew, BEd *Lough.*, MA *Open(UK)* Sr. Lectr.

Moss, Linda, MA *Edin.*, PhD *Camb.* Sr. Lectr.

Murphy, Robert, BA *Lond.*, MA *CNAA*, MSc *Lond.*, PhD *Kent* Sr. Lectr.

Neale, Stephen, BA *Exe.* Sr. Lectr.

Norman, Elizabeth H., BA *Oberlin*, MA *Harv.* Sr. Lectr.

Peacock, Percy, BA *Brist.*, MA *RCA* Sr. Lectr.

Perkins, Tessa, BA *Essex*, MA *Reading* Sr. Lectr.

Perks, Jeff Sr. Lectr.

Piette, Breched, BA *Wales*, PhD *CNAA* Sr. Lectr.

Pittard, Vanessa, BA *Sheff.*, MSc *Sheff.Hallam* Sr. Lectr.

Press, Prof. Michael P. O. Sr. Academic

Pritchard, Martin E. Sr. Lectr.

Quinn, Lulu, BA *Lond.Inst.* Sr. Lectr.

Rigby, Elizabeth J. Sr. Lectr.

Roddis, Jim N. Prof.; Sr. Academic Postholder; Head, Res. Devel.

Rust, Chris, BA *CNAA* Sr. Lectr.

Ryall, Tom, BA *Hull*, MPhil *Sheff.* Principal Lectr.

Sanderson, Lesley V. Sr. Lectr.

Sellars, Derek Principal Lectr.

Silverman, Lynn H. Sr. Lectr.

Slater, Peter, MPhil *Leeds*, MDes *RCA* Sr. Academic Postholder; Head, Information Technol. Devel.

Stewart, Nicholas, BA *Ulster* Sr. Lectr.

Thomas, Prof. Elaine Dir.*

Todd, Rowan, BTech *Brun.* Sr. Lectr.

Turner, John Sr. Lectr.

Waddington, David P., BA *York(UK)*, PhD *Aston* Sr. Lectr.

Ward, Michael Sr. Lectr.

Westerman, Julie Sr. Lectr.

Williams, Noel R., MA *Camb.*, PhD *Sheff.* Principal Lectr.

Worboys, Michael R., BSc *Sus.*, MSc *Manc.*, DPhil *Sus.* Sr. Academic

Worth, Jan Sr. Lectr.

Zellweger, Christopher, MA *RCA* Sr. Lectr.

Education

Tel: (0114) 225 2308 Fax: (0114) 225 2330

Aspinwall, Kathleen, MEd *Sheff.* Sr. Lectr.

Bamford, Susan J. Sr. Lectr.

Bentley, Prof. Diana, BSc *Manc.*, MSc *Manc.* Dir*

Boulton, Pamela, BEd *Lond.*, MEd *Leic.* Sr. Lectr.

Catterall, Rona Sr. Lectr.

Chatterton, John L., BSc *Sheff.*, MSc *Sheff.*, PhD *CNAA* Sr. Lectr.

Coldron, John H., BA *Sheff.*, MPhil *Sheff.* Sr. Lectr.

Dall, Ian, BEd *Sheff.*, MEd *Sheff.* Sr. Lectr.

Daniels, Jaqueline Sr. Lectr.

Dickinson, Paul, BA MEd Sr. Lectr.

Dixon, Jacqueline, BSc *Wales*, MSc *Nott.* Sr. Lectr.

Eliott, Susan Sr. Lectr.

Feltham, Colin, MTheol *St And.*, MSc *CNAA* Sr. Lectr.

Garland, Paul, BA *E.Anglia*, MEd *Brist.* Sr. Lectr.

Garrett, Vivienne, MSc *CNAA* Sr. Lectr.

Gray, Herbert A., BA *CNAA*, MEd *Sheff.* Sr. Lectr.

Haigh, Alan D., BSc *Durh.*, MSc *CNAA* Sr. Lectr.

Holland, Michael R., BSc *Exe.*, MEd *Reading*, PhD *Leeds* Principal Lectr.

Hudson, Brian G. Principal Lectr.

Hutchison, Stephanie A., BA *Manc.*, MA *York(UK)* Principal Lectr.

Johnson, Sylvia M., BSc *Warw.*, MA *Warw.* Sr. Academic

Jones, Joan L. Sr. Lectr.

Kirkby, David R., BSc *CNAA* Sr. Lectr.

Lingard, David Sr. Lectr.

McDonagh, James, BA *Essex*, MA *Sheff.*, MPhil *CNAA* Sr. Lectr.

Merchant, Guy H., BEd *Nott.*, MEd *Nott.* Sr. Lectr.

Monteith, Moira, BA *Sheff.*, MA *Montr.* Principal Lectr.

Nott, Michael, BSc *Sus.* Sr. Lectr.

O'Hara, Mark P., MSc *CNAA* Sr. Lectr.

Overall, Lynda S., BA *Open(UK)*, MEd *Manc.*, MSc *CNAA* Sr. Lectr.

Owen, David H., BSc *Wales* Sr. Lectr.

Peacock, Graham A., BSc *Hull*, MEd *Sheff.* Sr. Lectr.

Povey, Hilary A., BA *Lond.*, PhD *Birm.* Sr. Lectr.

Rees, Angela M., BEd MA Sr. Academic

Routledge, John L., BSc MEd Principal Lectr.

Ryan, Alison, BA *Reading* Sr. Lectr.

Sangster, Margaret, BEd *Westminster* Sr. Lectr.

Shelton, Keith, BEd *Lanc.*, MEd *CNAA* Sr. Lectr.

Simkins, Timothy J., BSocSc *Birm.*, MA *Sus.* Principal Lectr.

Smith, David N. Sr. Lectr.

Smith, Janice, BA *Hull*, MEd *Manc.* Sr. Lectr.

Smith, Peter J. Sr. Lectr.

Smith, Robin G., BSc *Lond.*, PhD *Leeds* Principal Lectr.

Spode, Frank, BSc *Sheff.*, PhD *Sheff.* Sr. Lectr.

Stirton, John, BA *York(UK)*, MA *McM.* Sr. Lectr.

Thomas, Pamela M., BA *Wales*, MA Sr. Lectr.

Tooth, Reginald J., BSc *Wales* Sr. Lectr.

Trickey, David S., BSc *Leeds*, MEd *Manc.*, PhD *Leeds* Principal Lectr.

Wileman, Kathleen M. Sr. Lectr.

Wilkinson, Jeffrey, BA *Liv.*, MA *Birm.* Sr. Lectr.

Willan, Christopher E., BA *Exe.* Sr. Lectr.

Williams, John, BEd *Sus.*, MA *Lanc.* Sr. Lectr.

Woodfield, Lynda Sr. Lectr.

Young, Patricia, BSc *Nott.* Sr. Lectr.

Engineering

Tel: (0114) 225 3389 Fax: (0114) 225 3434

Acheson, Robin, BSc *CNAA*, PhD *CNAA* Sr. Lectr.

Ali, Mohammed S., BSc *Punjab*, MMet *Sheff.*, PhD *Manc.* Sr. Lectr.

Atkinson, John D., BSc *Aston*, MSc *Brist.*, PhD *Camb.* Prof.

Barraclough, William A., MA *Oxf.*, PhD *Leeds* Sr. Lectr.

Basareb-Howath, Ivan, BSc *Brad.*, MSc *Birm.*, PhD *Manc.* Sr. Lectr.

Bell, Brian T., BEng *Brad.*, MEng *Alta.* Sr. Lectr.

Birchall, Stuart, BSc *CNAA*, MSc *Nott.* Sr. Lectr.

Blakey, Stephen C., BTech *Lough.*, PhD *Sheff.* Sr. Lectr.

Bond, Kay Sr. Lectr.

Bramhall, Michael D., BSc *Sheff.*, PhD *Sheff.* Sr. Lectr.

Bucknell, Roger J., BSc *CNAA*, PhD Sr. Lectr.

Campbell, Terence D., BSc *Lond.*, PhD *Nott.* Sr. Lectr.

Cockerham, Graham, BEng *Brad.*, MPhil *CNAA* Head of Div.

Colan, John, BSc *Lanc.* Sr. Lectr.

Collington, Rachel A., BSc Sr. Lectr.

Crampton, Richard, BSc *CNAA*, PhD *CNAA* Sr. Lectr.

Davies, Paul J., BSc *CNAA* Sr. Lectr.

Denman, Malcolm J., BSc *CNAA*, PhD *CNAA* Sr. Lectr.

Dutton, Kenneth, BSc *Sheff.Hallam*, PhD Principal Lectr.

Eaton, David E., MSc *Manc.* Dir.*

Evans, Karl, BEng *Sheff.*, MSc *Manc.* Principal Lectr.

Fernando, Upul S. Sr. Lectr.

Foss, Peter W., BSc *Lond.*, MSc *Cran.*, PhD *S'ton.* Sr. Lectr.

Garbett, Eric Sr. Lectr.

Ghassemlooy, Zabih, BSc *CNAA*, MSc *Manc.*, PhD Reader

Gillibrand, Derek, BSc *Salf.*, PhD *Nott.* Sr. Lectr.

Goude, Alan, BSc *CNAA*, MSc *CNAA* Sr. Lectr.

Hafeez, Khalid, BSc *Wales*, MSc *Wales*, PhD *Wales* Sr. Lectr.

Hague, Christopher, BTech *Brad.* Sr. Lectr.

Hales, William M., BSc *CNAA*, PhD *CNAA* Sr. Lectr.

Harris, Robert G., BEng *Sheff.*, MSc *Nott.* Sr. Lectr.

Hasan, Syed Sr. Lectr.

Heng, Raymond, BEng *Sheff.*, DPhil *CNAA* Sr. Lectr.

Holding, John M., BSc *Lond.*, PhD Principal Lectr.

Hubbard, Michael, MSc *CNAA* Sr. Lectr.

Islam, M. N., PhD *Leeds*, BSc Sr. Lectr.

Jennings, Joanna, BA *Oxf.* Sr. Lectr.

Jeremiah, Brian P. Sr. Academic Postholder; Head, Comml. Activities

Jervis, Barrie W., BA *Camb.*, MA *Sheff.*, PhD *Sheff.* Reader

Jones, Timothy M., BA *CNAA* Sr. Lectr.

Leggett, Peter, BSc *Birm.*, MMet *Sheff.*, MA *Sheff.* Sr. Lectr.

Lo, Edmond K., MSc *Strath.*, PhD *Salf.* Prof.

Madin, Richard L., BSc *Nott.*, MSc *Nott.* Sr. Lectr.

Marsh, Tony, BMet *Sheff.* Principal Lectr.

McQuillin, Brian, MSc *Nott.* Sr. Lectr.

Mullins, John T. Sr. Lectr.

Mulroy, Timothy J., BSc *Salf.*, MEng Sr. Lectr.

Naylor, Brett D., BSc *Wales* Sr. Lectr.

Perera, Dehiwalage T. S., BSc *Moratuwa*, PhD *Strath.* Principal Lectr.

Pickford, Charles L., MSc *Manc.* Sr. Lectr.

Ray, Prof. Asim K., BSc MSc PhD Sr. Academic

Richardson, Gordon J., PhD IGDS Programme Dir.

Rippon, Francis, BSc *CNAA* Sr. Lectr.

Robinson, Ian M. Sr. Academic

Rodgers, John M., BSc *Sheff.*, PhD Sr. Lectr.

Rowe, John W. K., MSc *CNAA* Sr. Lectr.

Saatchi, Reza, MSc *S'ton.*, PhD Sr. Lectr.

Short, Chris, BSc *CNAA*, MSc *CNAA* Sr. Lectr.

Simmonds, Andrew J., BSc *Aston*, MSc *Aston*, PhD Sr. Lectr.

Slater, John A. Sr. Lectr.

Smith, Alan J., PhD *Sheff.* Sr. Lectr.

Smith, David N. Sr. Lectr.

Smith, Janice Sr. Lectr.

Smith, Peter J. Sr. Lectr.

Sutton, Herbert C., BSc *Strath.*, MMet *Sheff.*, PhD *Sheff.* Sr. Lectr.

Taylor, Ian, BA *Camb.*, MSc *Nott.*, MA Sr. Lectr.

Tipple, Roger Sr. Lectr.

Tranter, Ian, BA *Oxf.*, MA *Oxf.* Sr. Lectr.

Travis, Jonathan R., BEng *Sheff.*, MEng
Sheff. Principal Lecturer
Wardman, David, BTech *Lough.* Sr. Lectr.
Williams, Peter D., PhD *Exe.* Sr. Lectr.
Wynn, Prof. Richard J., BSc PhD Sr.
Academic
Yazdanpanah, Amir Sr. Lectr.
Other Staff: 2 Sr. Devel. Officers

Financial Studies and Law

Tel: (0114) 225 5045 Fax: (0114) 225 3726
Ahmed, Mirghani, BSc *Khart.*, MA *Manc.*, PhD
Manc. Sr. Lectr.
Apps, Rod J., BA *CNAA*, MA *Manc.*, PhD
Manc. Principal Lectr.
Axelby, Graham L. A., MA *Sheff.* Sr. Lectr.
Blank-Klaff, Lesley D., BA *CNAA*, MA *Sheff.* Sr.
Lectr.
Blore, Christopher, BSc *Lond.*, MBA
City(UK) Sr. Lectr.
Brownlee, Ian D. Principal Lectr.
Burns, James L. E. Sr. Lectr.
Campbell, Prof. David, BSc *Wales*, LLM *Mich.*,
PhD *Edin.* Subject Leader
Chatterton, Martin, LLB *Sheff.* Sr. Lectr.
Coad, Alan F., MBA *Aston* Principal Lectr.
Connally, Joan E. Sr. Lectr.
Cowdell, Jane Sr. Lectr.
Cowdell, Paul F. Principal Lectr.
Cracknell, Sarah, LLB *Newcastle(UK)*, MA
Sheff. Sr. Lectr.
Croft, Elizabeth A., BA *Lanc.*, MBA *Brad.* Sr.
Lectr.
Cullen, John Principal Lectr.
Ducker, Jayne E., BA *CNAA* Sr. Lectr.
Dunlop, Alex J., MBA *Nott.* Sr. Lectr.
Evans, Jonathan G. Sr. Lectr.
Grimes, Richard H., LLB *Birm.*, MA *Sheff.* Sr.
Lectr.
Harris, Donald R. Sr. Academic
Harris, Philip J. Sr. Academic
Harrison, Keith, BA *Lanc.* Dir.*
Hasan, Mohammad S. Sr. Lectr.
Hassall, Trevor, BA *Trent* Principal Lectr.
Head, Antony M., BSc Sr. Lectr.
Helme, Lisabeth A., BSc *Brad.* Sr. Lectr.
Henderson, Michael J., BA *Hull*, MA
E.Anglia Sr. Lectr.
Hill, Deborah K., BA *Open(UK)*, BA *Sheff.* Sr.
Lectr.
Hill, Gillian Y., BA *CNAA* Sr. Lectr.
Holmes, David E. A. Sr. Lectr.
Hunter, Jayne A. Sr. Lectr.
Hyde, Derek E. Sr. Lectr.
Johnson, Nigel C., LLB *Warw.*, MSc *Lond.* Sr.
Lectr.
Jones, Christopher J., BA *Sheff.*, MA
Lanc. Principal Lectr.
Joyce, John Sr. Lectr.
Kyle, David G., BA *CNAA* Sr. Lectr.
Lomax, Lesley, BJur *Sheff.* Sr. Lectr.
May, Marilyn, BA *CNAA*, MSc *Warw.* Sr. Lectr.
McGregor, Peter C. Sr. Lectr.
Moss, Finola M. H., LLB *Liv.* Sr. Lectr.
Mulvihill, Peter J., BA *CNAA* Sr. Lectr.
Nollent, Andrea C., LLB *Dund.* Sr. Lectr.
Norton, Ann, BA *CNAA* Sr. Lectr.
O'Brien, Rona M., BA Sr. Lectr.
Payne, Nicholas J., BA *CNAA*, MBA *CNAA* Sr.
Lectr.
Richardson, Judith E., BA *Calif.*, MA *Nott.*, PhD
Calif. Sr. Lectr.
Richardson, Susan Sr. Lectr.
Ryan, Jim, BA *N.U.I.*, MBA *Strath.* Sr. Lectr.
Savas, Diane Sr. Lectr.
Seal, William B., BA *Reading*, BPhil *York(UK)*,
PhD *CNAA* Principal Lectr.
Sedgwick, Robert, BSc *Hull* Principal Lectr.
Seneviratne, Mary W., LLB *Leeds*, MA *Sheff.*, PhD
Sheff. Principal Lectr.
Sharpe, Ian, MBA *Durh.* Sr. Lectr.
Smith, Colleen T., LLB *Manc.* Sr. Lectr.
Smith, Douglas, BA *Exe.*, MA *CNAA*, MA
Brun. Sr. Lectr.
Taylor, Dennis Sr. Lectr.
Vincent-Jones, Peter C., BA *Camb.*, MA *Sheff.*,
PhD *Sheff.* Principal Lectr.

Watson, Hugh D., BA *Sheff.*, MA *Sheff.* Sr.
Lectr.
Webb, Brian J., BA *Sheff.* Principal Lectr.
Williams, Kevin M., LLB *Exe.*, LLM
Warw. Principal Lectr.

Food Management, see Leisure and Food
Management

Health and Community Studies

Tel: (0114) 225 2508 Fax: (0114) 225 2430
Alcock, Prof. Peter, BA *Oxf.*, MPhil
CNAA Principal Lectr.
Amos, Mary, BA *S'ton.*, BA *Portsmouth* Sr. Lectr.
Beckwith, Lynda, BSc *CNAA* Sr. Lectr.
Best, Helen, BSc *CNAA* Sr. Lectr.
Birkett, Marian M., BSc *Lough.*, MMedSci
Sheff. Sr. Lectr.
Booth, Karen, MEd *Sheff.* Sr. Lectr.
Brook, Norma, BSc *Brad.* Principal Lectr.
Brookes, Elaine, MBA *Sheff.Hallam* Sr. Lectr.
Bryer, Melanie J. Sr. Lectr.
Bufton, Serena A. Sr. Lectr.
Burton, Rita M. Sr. Lectr.
Carter, Peter H., BEd *CNAA*, MA
Open(UK) Principal Lectr.
Channer, Yvonne M., BA *Sheff.*, MPhil
Sheff. Sr. Lectr.
Cleak, John, BSc *Lond.* Sr. Lectr.
Cooke, Kathryn, BSc *S.Bank* Sr. Lectr.
Dawe, Catherine, BSc Sr. Lectr.
Dean, Anne, MPhil *CNAA* Principal Lectr.
Dunn, Karen, BA *Sus.*, PhD *Sheff.* Sr. Lectr.
Duxbury, Angela Principal Lectr.
Eales, Carole A. Sr. Lectr.
Eddy, David, MEd *Sheff.* Sr. Lectr.
Elkington, Marcus Sr. Lectr.
Empson, Janet M., BSc *Sheff.*, PhD *Sheff.* Sr.
Lectr.
Ferris, Christine Sr. Lectr.
Fine, Kay Sr. Lectr.
Firth, Margaret Sr. Lectr.
Franklin, Anita Sr. Lectr.
Gajos, Martin Sr. Lectr.
Gee, Magdalen T., BSc *St And.*, BSc *Salf.* Sr.
Lectr.
Grant, Linda M. Sr. Lectr.
Greeff, Roger J., LLB *Brist.* Sr. Lectr.
Hampshire, Gillian M., BA *CNAA*, BA
Manc. Sr. Lectr.
Hargreaves, Janet, BA *Open(UK)*, MA *Leeds* Sr.
Lectr.
Hartley-Vimpany, Nesta R., MSc *Liv.* Sr. Lectr.
Harvey-Jordan, Stephanie, BA Sr. Lectr.
Hirst, Julia, BSc *Hull* Sr. Lectr.
Hyatt, Andrew, BA *Open(UK)* Sr. Lectr.
Jones, Rhiannon Sr. Lectr.
Keating, Valerie, BSc *Leeds*, MEd *CNAA* Sr.
Lectr.
Kenyon, Joan, MEd Sr. Lectr.
King, Martin E., BSc *Lond.*, MSc *Lond.* Head of
Resource Devel.; Acting Dir.*
Larkin, Prof. Gerald V. Sr. Academic
Lawrence, Elizabeth H., BA *Kent*, MPhil *CNAA*,
PhD *CNAA* Sr. Lectr.
Macaskill, Ann, MA *Aberd.*, PhD
Aberd. Principal Lectr.
MacKay, Elizabeth, BEd MSc Sr. Lectr.
Mason, Allen H., BA *Open(UK)*, MSc *Manc.* Sr.
Lectr.
Mawson, Susan Sr. Lectr.
McCamley, Alison M. Sr. Lectr.
McGauley, James A., BA *Liv.*, MA *Birm.* Sr.
Lectr.
McHale, Susan, BSc *Plym.*, PhD *Plym.* Sr. Lectr.
McInnes, Elaine Sr. Lectr.
McManus, Michael, BA *Liv.* Sr. Lectr.
Mitchell, John C. C., BA *S.Af.*, MSc
Lond. Principal Lectr.
Moore, Aileen M. Sr. Lectr.
Moore, Michele P., BSc *Newcastle(UK)*, MSc *Lond.*,
PhD *Greenwich* Principal Lectr.
Morgan-Jones, Edward J. Sr. Lectr.
Munir, Sajjad Sr. Lectr.
Nicholls, David A., MA Sr. Lectr.
Nicholson, Pamela, MSc *Keele* Sr. Lectr.
Parker, Audrey, BSc *Manc.*, BA *Sheff.Hallam* Sr.
Lectr.

Parry, Anne W., PhD *CNAA* Reader
Pearson, Robert A., BA *Sheff.* Sr. Lectr.
Pengelly, Hilary, MSc *Oxf.*, BEd Sr. Lectr.
Pirrie, John Sr. Lectr.
Plowright, Phillip R. Sr. Lectr.
Raban, Colin, BA *Manc.*, MPhil *E.Anglia* Sr.
Academic Postholder; Head, Academic
Affairs
Reeve, Julie Sr. Lectr.
Rosie, Anthony J., BA *Lond.*, MA *Lond.*, PhD
Lond. Principal Lectr.
Senior, Paul, BA *York(UK)*, MA *CNAA* Principal
Lectr.
Spashett, Elaine M., BSc *Sheff.* Principal Lectr.
Steyne, David P., BSc *Leic.*, MA *Leeds* Sr. Lectr.
Sykes, Robert H., BA *York*, MSc *Lond.* Sr. Lectr.
Turner, Gillian Sr. Lectr.
Twomey, Peter, MSc *Manc.* Sr. Academic
Postholder; Head, Student Services
Vitler, Karen Sr. Lectr.
Walker, Carol, BA *Essex*, MA *Manc.* Sr. Lectr.
Walsh, Susan, MA *Warw.* Sr. Lectr.
Whyte, Lawrence, BA *Kent*, MA *Leeds* Sr. Lectr.
Williams, Janet, BA *Lond.* Sr. Lectr.
Woodhill, David, BA *York* Principal Lectr.
Woodhill, Susan R. Sr. Lectr.
Yeandle, Susan, BA *Brad.*, PhD *Kent* Principal
Lectr.

Law, see Financial Studies and Law

Leisure and Food Management

Tel: (0114) 225 3349 Fax: (0114) 225 3343
Aagawal, Sheela Sr. Lectr.
Alderson, George J., BEd *Leeds*, MA *Leeds*, PhD
Leeds Sr. Academic Postholder; Head,
Academic Quality
Beard, Colin Sr. Lectr.
Bell, Alison, BSc *Sur.* Sr. Lectr.
Bramwell, William, BA *Camb.*, MA *Camb.*, PhD
Lond. Principal Lectr.
Burkinshaw, Diane J., BA MA Sr. Lectr.
Cartwright, Geoffrey A., BA *CNAA* Sr. Lectr.
Chambers, Helene, BA *Belf.* Sr. Lectr.
Chapman, Janet H., BSc *Sheff.*, MSc *Salf.*, PhD
Sheff. Sr. Lectr.
Clark, John, BA *CNAA*, MPhil *Sheff.Hallam* Sr.
Lectr.
Cockill, Jennifer Sr. Lectr.
Cooper, Timothy, BSc *Bath* Sr. Lectr.
Crowe, Lynne, BSc *Durh.*, MSc *Lond.* Sr. Lectr.
Crutchley, David, MSc *Lough.* Principal Lectr.
Daly, Lorna, BSc *Lond.*, MSc *Leeds* Principal
Lectr.
Davies, Jan, BA *Open(UK)*, MSc *CNAA* Sr. Lectr.
Dick, Malcolm Sr. Lectr.
Dickson, Malcolm J., MSc *Aston*, PhD *CNAA*,
BSc Sr. Lectr.
Eastham, Jane Sr. Lectr.
Egan, David J., BA *Wales*, MPhil *CNAA* Sr.
Lectr.
Enzenbacher, Debra Sr. Lectr.
Fysh, Mary L., BSc *S'ton.*, PhD *S'ton.* Sr. Lectr.
Gainsley, Keith, BA *CNAA*, MSc *CNAA* Sr.
Lectr.
Gratton, Prof. Christopher Sr. Academic
Green, Suzan, BSc *Manc.*, MSc *Manc.*, PhD
Manc. Sr. Lectr.
Greenhoff, Karen, BSc *Aston*, MSc *Lough.* Sr.
Lectr.
Handley, John, BSc *Oregon*, MA Sr. Lectr.
Harvey, Barbara, BEd *Brist.*, MSc
CNAA Principal Lectr.
Harvey, David, BSc *Salf.* Sr. Lectr.
Hespe, George, BSc *Lond.* Sr. Lectr.
Horner, Susan, BSc *CNAA*, MBA *CNAA* Sr.
Lectr.
Kay, John, BSc *CNAA* Sr. Lectr.
Kinderlerer, Judy, BSc *Lond.*, MSc *Lond.* Reader
Laws, Dianne, BSc *CNAA*, MSc *Strath.* Sr. Lectr.
Le Grys, Prof. Geoffrey, MA *Oxf.* Sr.
Academic Postholder; Head of Div.
Leckie, Suzanne, BA *CNAA* Sr. Lectr.
Lewis, Richard, BSc *Wales*, MA *Sheff.* Sr. Lectr.
Long, Philip E., BA *CNAA*, DPhil *Sus.* Sr. Lectr.
Lyons, Howard, BSc *CNAA*, MSc
Durh. Principal Lectr.
Monk, Michael F. Sr. Lectr.

Murphy, Chris, BEd Manc., MEd Manc.   Sr. Lectr.

Nicholson, John W.   Sr. Lectr.

Nield, Kevin, BA CNAA, MSc CNAA   Principal Lectr.

Owen, Elizabeth, BA Birm., MA City(UK)   Sr. Lectr.

Power, Anthony, BA York   Sr. Lectr.

Pugh, Janet, BEd Sus., MA Warw.   Sr. Lectr.

Rick, Valerie E., BA Liv., MSc S'ton.   Dir.*

Rimmington, Michael, BSc CNAA, MSc Durh.   Principal Lectr.

Rose, John C.   Sr. Lectr.

Rotherham, Ian, BSc Sheff., PhD Sheff.   Sr. Lectr.

Sharples, Ann E.   Sr. Lectr.

Spencer, Peter, BEd Bolton IHE   Sr. Lectr.

Swarbrooke, John, BA Birm., MA Liv.   Sr. Lectr.

Wade, Jennifer, BSc Durh.   Sr. Lectr.

Walder, Peter, BEd Lough., MA Leeds   Sr. Lectr.

Westbury, Anthony J., BSc Lond., PhD Brighton   Sr. Lectr.

Whittaker, Vivien, BSc CNAA, MSc Sheff.Hallam   Sr. Lectr.

Wigmore, Sheila, BA Open(UK), MA CNAA   Sr. Lectr.

Wood, Lisa M. C.   Sr. Lectr.

Management, see Business and Management, and Computing and Management Scis.

Science and Mathematics

Tel: (0114) 225 3072 Fax: (0114) 225 3066

Allen, Prof. David W., PhD Keele, DSc Keele   Reader

Battye, Andrew, BSc Nott.   Sr. Lectr.

Bell, Norman A., BSc Durh., PhD Durh., DSc Durh.   Sr. Lectr.

Biggin, Haydn C., BSc Birm., MSc Birm., PhD Birm.   Sr. Lectr.

Blair, Maria E., MSc Warsaw, PhD Warsaw   Reader

Blakemore, Alexandra I. F., BSc Sheff., PhD Sheff.   Sr. Lectr.

Boyle, Michael H., BSc Leic., MPhil Lond., PhD CNAA   Sr. Lectr.

Breen, Christopher, BSc Wales, PhD Wales   Sr. Lectr.

Brodie, Marilyn, BSc Lond., MSc Sheff.Hallam   Sr. Lectr.

Brown, Simon J. S., BSc St And., MSc Reading, PhD Reading   Sr. Lectr.

Bunning, John D., BSc Lond., PhD Leeds   Sr. Lectr.

Bunning, Rowena A. D., BSc Lond., PhD Sheff.   Sr. Lectr.

Care, Prof. Christopher M., BA Camb., MA Camb., PhD Sheff.   Reader

Challis, Neil, BSc Brist., PhD Sheff.   Sr. Lectr.

Clark, Simon A., BSc Reading, PhD Wales   Sr. Lectr.

Cleaver, Douglas J., BSc PhD   Sr. Lectr.

Clench, Malcolm R., BSc CNAA, PhD Sheff.   Sr. Lectr.

Crowther, David, BSc Brist., PhD Brist.   Sr. Lectr.

Davis, Barry, BSc Lond., PhD Brad.   Principal Lectr.

Dharmadasa, Imyhamy M., BSc Ceyl., PhD Durh.   Sr. Lectr.

Douglass, Maureen, PhD CNAA   Sr. Lectr.

Drew, Peter K., BSc Lond., PhD Lond.   Sr. Lectr.

Evans, David H., BA Oxf., MA Oxf., PhD Nott.   Sr. Lectr.

Forder, Susan D., BSc Sheff., PhD Sheff.   Sr. Lectr.

Fuller, Leonard S. D., BSc Sheff., MSc Sheff.   Sr. Lectr.

Gardiner, Philip H. E., BSc Ife, MSc Strath, PhD Strath.   Sr. Lectr.

Gilbert, Daphne, BSc Hull, PhD   Sr. Lectr.

Gretton, Harry, BSc Sheff., PhD   Principal Lectr.

Gurman, Jane   Sr. Lectr.

Haigh, John, MA Oxf., DPhil Oxf.   Sr. Lectr.

Halliday, Ian, BSc Sheff., PhD Sheff.   Sr. Lectr.

Harrison, Prof. William   Sr. Academic

Hewson, Alan T., MA Camb., PhD Camb.   Sr. Lectr.

Holden, Graham J., BSc Salf., MSc Manc., PhD Sheff.   Sr. Lectr.

Hudson, Brian, BSc Manc., PhD Sheff.   Principal Lectr.

Hudson, Terence A., BSc Newcastle(UK), MSc CNAA   Sr. Lectr.

Jackson, Roger, BSc Manc., PhD   Sr. Lectr.

Khan, Muhammad, BSc Sheff., MSc Sheff., PhD Sheff.   Sr. Lectr.

Laird, Susan M., BSc Edin., PhD Lond.   Sr. Lectr.

Lawson, Kim, PhD CNAA   Sr. Lectr.

Little, John H., BSc Nott., PhD Nott.   Sr. Lectr.

Mannion, Kenneth, BSc Sheff.   Sr. Lectr.

Mills, John, BSc Aston, PhD Aston   Sr. Lectr.

New, Roger, BSc Birm., PhD Birm.   Principal Lectr.

Page, Andrew, BSc Sheff., MBA Sheff.Hallam, PhD Wales   Sr. Lectr.

Parkinson, David, BSc Bath, PhD Camb.   Sr. Lectr.

Parkinson, Prof. John J.   Dir.*

Peck, Hazel, MSc Leeds   Sr. Lectr.

Penny, Gerald G., BTech Brun., PhD Leeds   Sr. Lectr.

Pitt, Richard, BSc Lond., MSc Lond., PhD Leic.   Sr. Lectr.

Porteous, Hugh, MA Edin., PhD Warw.   Sr. Lectr.

Rainsford, Prof. Kim D., BSc Lond., PhD Lond.   Prof.; Sr. Academic

Rodgers, Glinn, BSc Hull, MSc Hull, PhD   Principal Lectr.

Routledge, John, BSc Leeds, MEd   Principal Lectr.

Samson, Andrew, BA Leic., MSc Leic., PhD Kent   Sr. Lectr.

Sant, David, BSc Sheff., MSc Sheff., PhD Sheff.   Sr. Lectr.

Shelton, Jennifer B., BSc Sheff., PhD Sheff.Hallam   Sr. Lectr.

Sherborne, Antony J., BA Camb.   Sr. Lectr.

Simmonds, Derek J., BSc Nott., PhD Nott.   Sr. Lectr.

Smith, Robert F., MSc Brun.   Sr. Lectr.

Spells, Stephen J., BSc Manc., PhD Manc.   Sr. Lectr.

Spencer, Ian M., BSc Reading, PhD Birm.   Sr. Lectr.

Tetler, Lee   Sr. Lectr.

Thomlinson, Michael, BSc Sheff., PhD   Principal Lectr.

Waldock, Jeffery, BSc PhD   Sr. Lectr.

Walton, Richard J., BSc Manc., MEd Sheff.   Sr. Lectr.

Wardlaw, Rodney S., BSc Nott., PhD Nott.   Sr. Lectr.

Wardle, John L., BA Lanc.   Sr. Lectr.

Wilson, Peter A., MSc CNAA   Sr. Lectr.

Windale, Mark, BSc Lond.   Sr. Lectr.

Woodroofe, Nicola, BSc Lond., PhD Lond.   Sr. Lectr.

Young, John, BTech PhD   Sr. Academic

Sheffield Business School

Tel: (0114) 225 3072 Fax: (0114) 225 3628

Al-Shaghana, Kadhim M., BSc Basrah, MPhil Nott., PhD Lond.   Sr. Lectr.

Baker, Jeannette   Sr. Lectr.

Banfield, Paul, BA Strath., MA Warw.   Principal Lectr.

Barclay, Jean, BA CNAA, MSc Lond.   Sr. Lectr.

Berry, Prof. Anthony J., BSc Bath, MPhil Lond., PhD Manc.   Sr. Academic

Boraston, Ian, BEc Monash, MEc Monash, MSc Aston   Principal Lectr.

Bowden, John C., BA Sheff., MA McM., PhD Sheff.   Sr. Lectr.

Bryant, Prof. Jim W., BA Open(UK), BSc Durh., MA Lanc., PhD Lanc.   Principal Lectr.

Capon, Claire H., BSc H.-W.   Sr. Lectr.

Cavan, Sean P., BSc CNAA, MSc CNAA   Sr. Lectr.

Chandler, James, BA Keele, MA Keele, PhD Manc.   Sr. Lectr.

Chapman, David, MSc CNAA   Principal Lectr.

Cose, Francoise   Sr. Lectr.

Croney, Paul, BA CNAA, MA Warw.   Sr. Lectr.; Acting Dir.*

Darwin, John, BSc Lond., MSc Lond., MBA CNAA   Principal Lectr.

Das, Ranjit, BSc Liv., MBA Cran.   Sr. Lectr.

Dawes, Brian, BA Nott., MBA Brad., MPhil Brad.   Sr. Lectr.

Disbury, Andrew, BA Leeds   Sr. Lectr.

Dotchin, John A., BSc Leic., MBA Brad.   Sr. Lectr.

Drew, Fiona, MA Edin., MA Leeds   Principal Lectr.

Duberley, Joanne P., BA Lanc., PhD Lough.   Sr. Lectr.

Duggan, Christine M.   Sr. Lectr.

Eddowes, Muriel, BSc Birm., MSc Birm.   Sr. Lectr.

El Kahal, Sonia J., BA N.Y.State, MA Sus.   Principal Lectr.

Gardiner, Katherine, BSc Ghana, MSc Durh., PhD Strath.   Sr. Lectr.

Gladstone, Bryan, BA Liv., MSc Stir.   Sr. Lectr.

Graham, Timothy, BA Sheff.   Sr. Lectr.

Gregory, Anthea, BA Sheff.   Sr. Lectr.

Haigh, Prof. Robert H.   Sr. Academic

Halsall, David N.   Sr. Lectr.

Hawkins, Roger, MBA CNAA   Sr. Lectr.

Hawley, David, MSc CNAA   Sr. Lectr.

Hills, Steven, MA Oxf., MBA S'ton.   Sr. Lectr.

Hristov, Latchezar L.   Sr. Lectr.

Imrie, Gary, BSc H.-W., MSc CNAA   Sr. Lectr.

Ivanov, Dimitri M., BSc Fin.& Bus.Affairs, Svishtov, PhD Sofia Econ.Inst.   Sr. Lectr.

Johnson, Philip, BA Sheff., MSc CNAA, MSc Open(UK), PhD CNAA   Principal Lectr.

Jones, Peter, BA Camb., MA Stan., MA Camb.   Principal Lectr.

Jones, Robert, BA Lond., MSc Lond.   Sr. Lectr.

Joy-Matthews, Jennifer, BA NE, MSc CNAA   Sr. Lectr.

Kawalek, John P., BA CNAA, MSc Manc.   Sr. Lectr.

Kingdom, John, BSc Wales   Reader

Kirkham, Janet, BA Sheff., PhD Sheff.   Sr. Lectr.

Laffin, Janet, BA Belf.   Sr. Lectr.

Lancaster, Peter, MA Lanc.   Sr. Lectr.

Latham, Jim T., BSc Wales, MSc Nott.   Sr. Lectr.

Laughton, David, BA Leic., MA Leeds   Sr. Lectr.

Lawless, Peter N.   Sr. Lectr.

Lawson, Stephen, BA Sheff., MBA Sheff.   Sr. Lectr.

Leeson, Susan, MSc Sheff.Hallam   Sr. Lectr.

Long, Peter D., BA Oxf., DPhil Sus.   Principal Lectr.

McAuley, Michael J., MA Manc. BA PhD   Sr. Academic

McCarthy, Angela, MA Edin.   Sr. Lectr.

Megginson, David, BSc Brist., MSc Manc.   Sr. Lectr.

Montanheiro, Luiz, BA Lond., MSc Lond., MPhil Bath   Sr. Lectr.

Morgan, Gareth, BA Brist., MA Camb., PhD CNAA   Sr. Lectr.

Morris, David, BSc Lond., MSc Strath.   Reader

Moullin, Laurence J.   Sr. Lectr.

Murray, Peter J.   Sr. Lectr.

Musson, Gillian, BA CNAA, PhD Sheff.   Sr. Lectr.

Myers, Gudrun, BA Sheff.   Sr. Lectr.

Myers, Peter, BA Lond., MA Lond.   Sr. Lectr.

Newey, Yvonne, MSc Sheff.Hallam   Sr. Lectr.

Nwankwo, Azubrike, BSc Nigeria, MBA Nigeria, PhD Lond.   Sr. Lectr.

O'Leary, Christine, BA Sheff., MA Sheff.   Sr. Lectr.

Oldham, Roger B., BTech Lough., MA Lanc.   Sr. Lectr.

Ottewill, Roger, BSc Lond.   Principal Lectr.

Owen, Barry, BPhil Liv.   Sr. Lectr.

Oxholm, Alice M., BSc Manc.   Sr. Lectr.

Parker, Raymond J., MA Edin., BPhil(Ed) Birm.   Sr. Lectr.

Prowse, Peter, BA Camb., MSc Leeds, MPhil Leeds   Sr. Lectr.

Quincey, Roger W., BSc Sheff., MSc Sheff.   Principal Lectr.

Rahtz, Nicholas, BA Hull, MA Leic.   Sr. Lectr.

Rossiter, Judith, BEd Sheff., MA Sheff.   Sr. Lectr.

Rotherham, David, BSc CNAA   Sr. Lectr.

Rushton, Diane, BA *Leic.*, MBA *Warw.* Sr. Lectr.
Scheule, Maria   Sr. Lectr.
Scott, Barbara, BEd *Sheff.*   Principal Lectr.
Shipton, John, BSc *Lond.*, MSc *Salf.*   Principal Lectr.
Smith, Kenneth, BA *Stir.*, MA *Manc.*   Sr. Lectr.
Spence, Ralph, BA *Leeds*, MA *Kent*   Sr. Lectr.
Stansfield, Robin D., MA *Camb.*, MSc *Lond.*   Sr. Lectr.
Sutton, Yvonne M.   Sr. Lectr.
Taylor, Nicholas   Sr. Lectr.
Terry, Malcolm S., MBA *Aston*   Sr. Lectr.
Thomas, Jane, BA *Wales*, MPhil *Sheff.*   Sr. Lectr.
Thompson, John   Sr. Lectr.
Tietze, Susanne, MA *Heidel.*, MBA *Sheff.Hallam*   Sr. Lectr.
Transfield, Prof. David R., PhD *CNAA*   Sr. Academic
Turner, Royce, BA *Sheff.*, MA *Manc.*, PhD *Liv.*   Sr. Lectr.
Underhill, Nicholas, BA *Sus.*, MA *Reading*   Head, TESOL
Wall, Ann, BA *Nott.*   Sr. Lectr.
White, Colette   Sr. Lectr.
White, Donald, BA *Birm.*, MA *Sheff.*, PhD *Sheff.*   Sr. Lectr.
Whitmarsh, Harry, BA *CNAA*, MA *City(UK)*   Sr. Lectr.
Williams, Helen M., BA *S'ton.*, MA *Birm.*   Sr. Lectr.
Williams, Timothy, BSc *Sheff.*, MSc *Warw.*   Sr. Lectr.
Woodman, Clive L., BA MA   Sr. Academic
Woodward, Robert, BA *Sheff.*, MA *Warw.*   Principal Lectr.
Worsdale, Graham, BA *Lanc.*, MSc *Manc.*, PhD *Lanc.*   Sr. Academic
Yates, Jacqueline, BA *CNAA*, MPhil *CNAA*   Sr. Lectr.

Urban and Regional Studies

Tel: (0114) 225 3525 Fax: (0114) 225 3553
Askham, Philip, BA *Open(UK)*, MA *Leic.*   Sr. Lectr.
Blandy, Sarah, LLB *Warw.*   Sr. Lectr.
Booth, Christine, BSc *Lond.*   Sr. Lectr.
Brown, Frank, BA *Camb.*   Principal Lectr.
Chamberlain, Oliver R., BSc *S'ton.*   Sr. Lectr.
Close, Roger, LLB *Leeds*   Sr. Lectr.
Cole, Prof. Ian D., BA *Reading*, MPhil *York(UK)*   Head of Div.
Conway, Jean   Sr. Lectr.
Crocker, Stephen A., BSc *Lond.*, MA *Sheff.*, MBA *Brad.*   Sr. Lectr.
Crosby, David, BA(Arch) *Lond.*, BA *Open(UK)*, MA *Newcastle(UK)*   Sr. Lectr.
Cumming, Robert R., BA *Leic.*   Sr. Lectr.
Dabinett, Gordon E., BSc *H-W*, MSc *Camb.*   Sr. Lectr.
Dawson, Monica G., LLB *Leic.*   Sr. Lectr.
Dehesh, Alireza, MPhil *Edin.*, PhD *Manc.*, BSc   Sr. Lectr.
Fortune, Jennifer   Sr. Lectr.
Foster, Colin, BA *Leeds*   Sr. Lectr.
Furbey, Robert A., BA *Sheff.*, MA *E.Anglia*   Principal Lectr.
Gardiner, Christopher, BA *Lanc.*, MA *Lanc.*   Sr. Lectr.
Gidley, Glen, BA *Brad.*   Sr. Lectr.
Goodchild, Barry, BA *Keele*, MPhil *Glas.*   Reader
Green, Michael W., BSc *Lond.*   Head, Surveying Div.
Hamilton, John M.   Sr. Lectr.
Haynes, Barry, BSc *CNAA*, MSc *Sheff.*   Sr. Lectr.
Haywood, Russell, BA *Liv.*, MA *Nott.*   Sr. Lectr.

Hinxman, Lynda, BSc *Sheff.*   Sr. Lectr.
Horne, Ralph E., BSc MSc   Sr. Lectr.
Jones, Ian G., BSc *Sheff.*   Sr. Lectr.
Jowsey, Ernest, BA *Sheff.*, MA *Nott.*   Sr. Lectr.
Kellett, Jonathan, BA *Sheff.*, PhD *Sheff.*   Sr. Lectr.
Kennie, Tom   Principal Lectr.
Kirkwood, John, BSc *Lond.*   Sr. Lectr.
Kitchen, Prof. John E.   Principal Lectr.
Lawless, Paul, BPhil *Oxf.*, MA *Camb.*   Prof.
Mackmin, Prof. David, BSc *Lond.*, MSc *Reading*   Sr. Academic; Acting Dir.*
McHardy, Jolian P.   Sr. Lectr.
Midgley-Hunt, Janine, BA *Hull*, MA *Lond.*   Sr. Lectr.
Mortimer, Nigel, BSc *Manc.*, PhD *Open(UK)*   Principal Lectr.
Nixon, Judith   Sr. Lectr.
Nunnington, Nicholas, BSc *CNAA*   Sr. Lectr.
Parsons, David E.   Sr. Lectr.
Pritchard, Neil   Sr. Lectr.
Pugh, Cedric, BA *Wales*, MSc *Wales*, PhD *Adel.*   Reader
Reid, Barbara, BSc *Edin.*, MSc *Reading*, PhD   Principal Lectr.
Smith, Richard E., LLB *Newcastle(UK)*   Principal Lectr.
Storr, David, MSc *Salf.*   Sr. Lectr.
Syms, Paul M.   Principal Lectr.
Truscott, Roger, BSc *Lond.*   Principal Lectr.
Walker, David   Sr. Lectr.
Wood, Linda, MA   Sr. Lectr.

SPECIAL CENTRES, ETC

Cultural Research Institute

Tel: (0114) 225 2686 Fax: (0114) 225 2603
Worboys, Michael R., DPhil *Sus.*   Dir.*

Learning and Teaching Institute

Tel: (0114) 225 2558 Fax: (0114) 225 2446
Mowthorpe, David   Dir.*

Management Research Institute

Tel: (0114) 225 2804 Fax: (0114) 225 2801
Transfield, Prof. David R., PhD *CNAA*   Dir.*

Materials Research Institute

Tel: (0114) 225 3890 Fax: (0114) 225 3501
Yarwood, Prof. Jack, PhD *Wales*   Dir.*

Regional Economic and Social Research, Centre for

Tel: (0114) 225 3073 Fax: (0114) 225 3553
Lawless, Prof. Paul, BPhil *Oxf.*, MA *Camb.*   Dir.*

CONTACT OFFICERS

Academic affairs. Academic Registrar: Tory, Jane H., BA *Sheff.*
Academic affairs. Assistant Principal (Academic Operations and Quality): ......
Accommodation. Head of Residential Services: May, Marie
Admissions (first degree). Academic Registrar: Tory, Jane H., BA *Sheff.*
Admissions (first degree). Student Systems and Operations: Blakemore, Shirley
Alumni. Alumni Officer: Oates, Kathryn
Careers. Head of Careers: Quinn, Patricia, BA *Sheff.*
Computing services. Director of Corporate Information Systems: Reynolds, Eddie, BSc *Lond.*, PhD *Lond.*

Credit transfer. Academic Credit Manager: Booth, Jackie, BSc *Salf.*
Development/fund-raising. Sutcliffe, Moyra, BA *York(UK)*, MA *Sheff.*
Equal opportunities. Development Officer, Equal Opportunities: Merriman, Jenny
Estates and buildings/works and services (services). Facilities Director: Pettifer, Alex, BA *CNAA*
Estates and buildings/works and services (buildings). Head of Projects: Cameron, Neil
Examinations. Academic Registrar: Tory, Jane H., BA *Sheff.*
Examinations. Principal Officer, Examinations and Awards: Sidorowicz, Joan
Finance. Director of Finance and Resources: Lane, Ronald J. B., BA *Newcastle(UK)*, BA *Durh.*
General enquiries. University Secretary: Neocosmos, Sally, BA *Lough.*
Health Services. Nursing Sister: Winter, Marilyn
Health services. Nursing Sister: Taylor, Helen
International office. International Development Manager: Kirk, John, BA *Sheff.*, MBA *Cran.*
Library (chief librarian). Librarian: Bulpitt, Graham, BA *Open(UK)*, MA *Lond.*
Minorities/disadvantaged groups. Assistant Principal (Staff Strategy and Student Support): Willcocks, Prof. Dianne M., BA *Sur.*
Personnel/human resources. Human Resources Director: Orton, Miriam, BA *Birm.*, MSocSci
Public relations, information and marketing. Assistant Principal (Development and Marketing): Hobbs, Jack M., PhD *Newcastle(UK)*, BSc, FIMA
Publications. Head of Marketing Communications: Horner, Jennifer, BA *Nott.*
Purchasing. Purchasing Controller: Wordsworth, Peter
Quality assurance and accreditation. Head of Quality Division: Arnold, Gwyn, BA *Sheff.*
Quality assurance and accreditation. Assistant Principal (Academic Operations and Quality): ......
Research. Wainman, Mark, BA *Brist.*
Safety. Safety Officer: Fleming, Tom
Scholarships, awards, loans. Head of Student Financial Support: Hill, Keith
Security. Head of Security: Salmen, Paul P.
Sport and recreation. Head of Recreation Services (Acting): Ridge, Patricia
Staff development and training. Training and Development Manager: Merriman, Jenny.
Student union. (Contact the President of the Union)
Student welfare/counselling. Director of Student Guidance: Toomey, Patrick J., BA *Leeds*, MA *Leeds*
Student welfare/counselling. Head of Counselling: Seddon, Vicky, BSc *Sheff.*
Students from other countries. International Development Manager: Kirk, John, BA *Sheff.*, MBA *Cran.*
Students with disabilities. Head of Access and Guidance: Layer, Geoffrey, LLB *Newcastle(UK)*
Women. Development Officer, Equal Opportunities: Merriman, Jenny

[*Information supplied by the institution as at March 1998, and edited by the ACU*]

SOUTH BANK UNIVERSITY

Founded 1992; previously established as Polytechnic of the South Bank 1970 and the Borough Polytechnic Institute 1892

Member of the Association of Commonwealth Universities

Postal Address: Borough Road, London, England SE1 0AA
Telephone: (0171) 928 8989 **Fax**: (0171) 815 8155 **WWW**: http://www.sbu.ac.uk

CHANCELLOR—McLaren, Christopher
VICE-CHANCELLOR AND CHIEF EXECUTIVE*—Bernbaum, Prof. Gerald, BSc(Econ) *Lond.*, PhD
DEPUTY VICE-CHANCELLOR (RESOURCES)—Watkins, Prof. Trevor, BA MSc PhD
DEPUTY VICE-CHANCELLOR AND REGISTRAR—Phillips, A. R., BSc(Econ) MBA
UNIVERSITY SECRETARY—Gander, L.

FACULTIES/SCHOOLS

Built Environment
Dean: Wood, Prof. L. A., BSc *Brist.*, PhD *Brist.*

Business School
Dean: Rowe, Prof. N., BSc MSc, FIMA

Engineering, Science and Technology
Dean: Clare, Prof. C., MBA MSc

Health and Social Science
Dean: Goldstone, Prof. L. A., BA(Econ) MSc

ACADEMIC UNITS
Arranged by Schools

Accounting, see under Business

Applied Science
Fax: (0171) 815 7999

Amuna, P., MB ChB MMedS   Sr. Lectr.
Barrass, A. S., BSc MSc   Sr. Lectr.
Bartlett, I., BSc MSc   Sr. Lectr.
Basi, D. S., BSc MSc MBA   Sr. Lectr.
Beeby, A. N., BSc *Salf.*, PhD *Leic.*   Principal Lectr.
Best, R. J., BSc *Lond.*, PhD *Lond.*   Principal Lectr.
Brennan, A. M., BSc MSc PhD, FLS   Sr. Lectr.
Burns, P. A., BSc PhD   Principal Lectr.
Cadbury, R. G., BA MEng   Principal Lectr.
Cameron, A., BSc   Sr. Lectr.
Chaplin, M. F., BSc PhD, FRSChem   Prof.
Clark, A. D., MA *Camb.*, PhD *Camb.*   Principal Lectr.
Coultate, T. P., PhD   Principal Lectr.
Davis, J., BSc PhD   Prof.
Dunne, L., BSc MSc PhD   Prof.
Evans, T. G., BSc   Head*
Hammond, M. P., BSc PhD   Sr. Lectr.
Henderson, J. P., BSc PhD   Sr. Lectr.
Hibbs, M., BSc *Manc.*, PhD *Reading*   Sr. Lectr.
Higton, G., BSc PhD   Sr. Lectr.
Hulm, S., BSc *Stir.*, PhD *Aberd.*   Sr. Lectr.
Kassim, H., BSc PhD   Sr. Lectr.
Larkai, S., BSc PhD   Sr. Lectr.
Laurenson, N., BSc MSc   Sr. Lectr.
Lis-Balchin, M., BSc *Lond.*, PhD *Lond.*   Sr. Lectr.
Maidment, M., BSC PhD   Sr. Lectr.
Man, D., BSc MSc   Sr. Lectr.
Manos, G., BSc PhD   Sr. Lectr.
Mitra, A., BSc MSc   Sr. Lectr.
Morgan, N., BSc *Wales*, PhD *Brist.*   Sr. Lectr.
Murray, S., MSc
Nolan, P. F., BSc PhD   Prof.
Ojinnaka, C., BSc MSc PhD
Orrin, J. E., BSc PhD   Sr. Lectr.
Pawsey, R. K., BSc *Newcastle(UK)*, MSc *Reading*, PhD *Reading*   Principal Lectr.
Price, A. L., BSc   Sr. Lectr.
Price, A. T., BSc *Wales*, PhD *Lond.*   Sr. Lectr.
Roberts, A. M., BSc PhD   Principal Lectr.
Rockey, J. S., BSc MSc PhD   Sr. Lectr.
Roller, S., BSc PhD   Prof.
Shukla, H., BSc PhD   Sr. Lectr.
Spear, K., BSc MSc   Principal Lectr.
Steele, C., BSc MSc PhD   Sr. Lectr.
Sumar, S., BSc PhD   Reader

Waites, M. J., BSc PhD   Sr. Lectr.
Walters, D., BSc PhD   Principal Lectr.
Wang, W., BSc PhD   Sr. Lectr.
Ward, S. A., BSc BA MA DPhil   Prof.

Business
Fax: (0171) 815 7865

Begg, I., PhD   Prof., International Economics
Bosco, A.   Jean Monnet Prof., European Integration
Green, D., MA *Camb.*   Head, Postgrad. Programmes
Guerrier, Y., BA MA PhD   Prof., Hotel Management
Hearne, W. E., BSc(Econ) MSc(Econ)   Prof., Management
Ietto-Gillies, I., BSc   Prof., Applied Economics
Koch, K., PhD   Prof., Modern Languages
Richards, N. R., BSc MSc   Head, Undergrad. Programmes
Ridley, J., FIA   Prof., Auditing

Accounting, Division of
Fax: (0171) 815 7793

Alakeson, H., BSc   Principal Lectr.
Balachandran, K., BA LLB MBA MA   Sr. Lectr.
Batchelor, D., BA MA   Sr. Lectr.
Benedict, A. T., BA, FCA   Sr. Lectr.
Bingham, M., MSc   Sr. Lectr.
Blowes, P., BSc   Sr. Lectr.
Boatman, I., BSc MCA   Sr. Lectr.
Clark, C. V. B., BEcon, FCPA   Sr. Lectr.
D'Silva, K. E. J., BCom MSc PhD, FCA   Sr. Lectr.
Harvey, Prof. M., BSc MSc   Principal Lectr.
Knight, M. G., BA MSc, FCA   Principal Lectr.; Head of Div.*
Lawrence, M. J., BSc   Sr. Lectr.
Lee, V., BA MA MBA   Principal Lectr.
Munyangiri, M., MSc   Sr. Lectr.
O'Connor, S., BA   Sr. Lectr.
O'Meara, M., BA   Principal Lectr.
Ratnam, I.   Sr. Lectr.
Severn, J. M., BA, FCA   Sr. Lectr.
White, P.   Sr. Lectr.
Williams, S., BA *Liv.*, MPhil *Liv.*   Sr. Lectr.

Corporate Strategy and Marketing, Division of
Fax: (0171) 815 7793

Aston, H., BSc   Sr. Lectr.
Barnes, M. C., BA MA   Sr. Lectr.
Bennett, D., BA MBA   Sr. Lectr.
Boukersi, L., BSc MBA PhD   Principal Lectr.
Crummie, J. M., BA   Sr. Lectr.
Donnithorne, E. G.   Sr. Lectr.
Emuh, C., BA MBA   Sr. Lectr.
Evans, K., MA MBA   Sr. Lectr.
Fenech, C., BA(Econ) MSc(Econ)   Principal Lectr.
Godfrey, M., MBA   Sr. Lectr.
Gountas, J. Y., MSc   Sr. Lectr.
Gregory, T. C., MBA   Principal Lectr.
Harrow, J., BA *Exe.*, MSc *Lond.*, PhD *Lond.*   Principal Lectr.
Hill, N. C. M., BA   Sr. Lectr.
John, R. A., BSc(Econ) MA MBA   Principal Lectr.; Head*
Lloyd, B. D., BScEng MSc MBA   Principal Lectr.

Millar, C. J., BA MSc   Sr. Lectr.
Monye, S., MBA MCom PhD   Sr. Lectr.
Murdock, A. J. M., BSc MA MSc MBA   Principal Lectr.
Owusu-Frimpong, N., MBA PhD   Sr. Lectr.
Randall, J., BSc MBA   Sr. Lectr.

Economics, Division of
Fax: (0171) 815 7793

Cox, H., BA MSc PhD   Principal Lectr.
Freeman, S., BA MSc   Sr. Lectr.
Grimwade, N. S., BA MA   Principal Lectr.; Head*
Lintott, J., BA *Camb.*, MSc *Lond.*, PhD *Lond.*   Sr. Lectr.
Lloyd, J. H., MA *Leeds*, MTech *Brun.*   Principal Lectr.
Prevezer, M., BA MA MSc(Econ) PhD
Sayfoo, R., BA MA   Sr. Lectr.
Thomas, P., BA BSocSc   Sr. Lectr.
Wood, M. L., BA MA(Econ)   Sr. Lectr.

Finance, Quantitative and Information Studies, Division of
Fax: (0171) 815 7793

Abram, M. R., BSc   Sr. Lectr.
Biggs, C., BSc MBA   Sr. Lectr.
Dwek, R., BA   Sr. Lectr.
Eaton, M., BCom   Sr. Lectr.
Fleming, J. A., BSc MSc   Sr. Lectr.
Gharibi, R. R., BSc   Sr. Lectr.
Giles, R. L., BSc MA PhD   Sr. Lectr.
Griffiths, H. R., BSc MSc PhD   Sr. Lectr.
Juric, R., BSc *Zagreb*   Sr. Lectr.
Kelly, J., BA MBA   Sr. Lectr.
Kilmister, J., BA MA   Sr. Lectr.
Lane, V., BEng MEng PhD   Sr. Lectr.
Mandal, A., BA MA   Sr. Lectr.
Moorthy, U. T., BSc *Colombo*, MSc *Lond.*   Principal Lectr.
O'Broin, S., BSc MSc PhD   Principal Lectr.; Head of Div.*
O'Hagan, G., BSc *N.U.I.*   Sr. Lectr.
Olanrewaju, E. A. A., BSc *Ib.*, MEd *Ib.*   Sr. Lectr.
Penney, D. B., BCom   Principal Lectr.
Rossiter, R. F., BA PhD   Sr. Lectr.
Snaith, J., BA MSc   Sr. Lectr.
Tallent, G., BSc MSc   Sr. Lectr.
Tanner, J., BA   Sr. Lectr.
Wise, D. E., FCA   Sr. Lectr.

Human Resources, Division of
Fax: (0171) 815 7793

Bell, G., BA BSc MSc   Sr. Lectr.
Bravette, G.   Sr. Lectr.
Chandler, C., BA MSc   Sr. Lectr.
Davi, H. J., BA MSc(Econ)   Sr. Lectr.
Gamble, R., MA *Edin.*   Sr. Lectr.
Garner, S., BA MBA   Sr. Lectr.
George, H.   Sr. Lectr.
Giannopoulou, K., MSc   Sr. Lectr.; Head of Div.*
Kellner, K., BSc MA   Sr. Lectr.
Knapp, C., BSc MA   Sr. Lectr.
Macnamara, T. E.   Sr. Lectr.
McCallum, C. J., BA MSc   Sr. Lectr.
Newton, D. J., BA MA   Sr. Lectr.
Oldfield, C., BA *CNAA*, MA *Warw.*   Sr. Lectr.

Redman, G., BA Sr. Lectr.
Rigby, M. A., BA(Econ) MA(Econ) Principal Lectr.
Saunders, M. B., MSc City(UK), MA Lond., MPhil CNAA, BA Sr. Lectr.
Smith, R. F., BSc MSc Sr. Lectr.
Stein, M., BA MSc MPhil PhD Sr. Lectr.

Law, Division of

Fax: (0171) 815 7793

Andronicou, L., BA MA Sr. Lectr.
Aquino, T., LLB Sr. Lectr.
Bellis, J., LLB LLM Sr. Lectr.
De Freitas, J., LLB LLM MA Sr. Lectr.
Deveci, H., MA LLM Sr. Lectr.
Hurst, K., LLB MA Sr. Lectr.
Jeeves, M. C., LLB Principal Lectr.
Lever, J. H., BA MA Sr. Lectr.
Molan, M., BA LLM Principal Lectr.; Head*
Moran, G., LLB
Newns, M., BA MA Sr. Lectr.
Rodney, M., BPharm MA Sr. Lectr.
Shepherd, C. P., LLB MA Sr. Lectr.
Stylianou, K., BA LLM Sr. Lectr.
Thatcher, C., LLB MPhil Sr. Lectr.
Tiagi, N., BA LLM Sr. Lectr.
Unger, R. A. D., LLB Sr. Lectr.
Wakefield, J., BA LLM
Wilson, A. B., LLB Sr. Lectr.

Leisure and Tourism Industries, Division of

Fax: (0171) 815 7793

Askew, A. Sr. Lectr.
Ciaravaglia, R. Sr. Lectr.
Guerrier, Y. R., BA MA PhD Principal Lectr.; Head of Div.*
Lillis, R., BSc Sr. Lectr.
Thomas, M., BA Sr. Lectr.
Tyler, D., BSc MSocSci Sr. Lectr.
Want, P., MA Sr. Lectr.

Modern Languages, Division of

Fax: (0171) 815 7793

Cleeve, D. F., BA MSc Principal Lectr.
Gaitte, C., BA MA PhD Sr. Lectr.
Gallardo, M., BA MA Sr. Lectr.
Gervais-le Garff, M. M., Maîtrise MA PhD Sr. Lectr.
Kahl, J. Principal Lectr.
King, I., MA PhD Reader
Kite, U. R., MA Lond. Sr. Lectr.
Koch, K., PhD Head*
Landor, J., MA PhD Sr. Lectr.
Langley, G., BA MA Sr. Lectr.
Lecanuet, J. A., LèsL Principal Lectr.
Nichols, E. C., BA MA PhD Principal Lectr.
Plyman, A. M., BA MA PhD Sr. Lectr.
Robbins, S., BA MA Sr. Lectr.
Tombs, I., Maîtrise Paris I, PhD Camb. Sr. Lectr.
Wengler, B. Sr. Lectr.
White, L. M., BA Sr. Lectr.

Computing, Information Systems and Mathematics

Fax: (0171) 815 7499

Banissi, E. K., BSc MSc PhD Sr. Lectr.
Blair, A. P. P., BA Sr. Lectr.
Bradley, M., BA MSc Sr. Lectr.
Burrell, P. R., BSc Leeds, MSc Lond. Principal Lectr.
Bush, M. F., BSc PhD Sr. Lectr.
Carter, G. D., BA MSc Sr. Lectr.
Chalk, B., BSc Sr. Lectr.
Chalk, P., BSc S'ton., MSc Essex Sr. Lectr.
Culwin, F., BSc PhD Sr. Lectr.
Curnock, A., BSc MPhil PhD Sr. Lectr.
Dalcher, D., MSc Sr. Lectr.
Darlington, K. W., BSc Sr. Lectr.
Elliott, G. D., BSc MSc Sr. Lectr.
Faulkner, C., BA MSc Sr. Lectr.
Flower, A., BA MSc Sr. Lectr.
Flynn, V., BA MSc Sr. Lectr.
Hashim, A., BSc(Eng) MSc PhD, FIEE Head*
Hayes, A. M., BA MSc Sr. Lectr.
Hepworth, N., BSc Lond. Sr. Lectr.
Inman, D., BTech MSc Sr. Lectr.

Jennings, Sylvia M., BSc Lond., MSc Oxf., PhD Lond. Sr. Lectr.
Kemp, R. M., BSc MSc Sr. Lectr.
Kennedy, M., BA MBA Principal Lectr.
Linecar, P., BSc MSc Sr. Lectr.
Parker, M. J., BSc MSc Principal Lectr.
Patel, D., MSc Open(UK), PhD Principal Lectr.
Pollard, A. J., BA MSc Sr. Lectr.
Rourke, G. D., BA MBA Sr. Lectr.
Shingleton-Smith, D., BSc MSc Sr. Lectr.
Siviter, D. W., BSc Sr. Lectr.
Starkings, Susan A., BSc MSc Sr. Lectr.
Thomas, D., MSc Lond., PhD Lond. Sr. Lectr.
Warwick, J. P., BSc PhD, FIMA Principal Lectr.

Construction

Fax: (0171) 815 7399

Adriaanse, J. S., LLB Sr. Lectr.
Atkinson, A. K., MSc, FRICS Sr. Lectr.
Bailey, G., Lic MSc Principal Lectr.
Bevan, D. J. Sr. Lectr.
Burkinshaw, R. F., BSc MA, FRICS Sr. Lectr.
Cavilla, J. L., BSc Manc. Sr. Lectr.
Charles, C., BA Sr. Lectr.
Datoo, M. H., BSc Leeds, PhD Leeds Sr. Lectr.
Davies, K. G., BA Sr. Lectr.
Douglas, J. T., BSc MSc Sr. Lectr.
Dunkeld, M., BSc MSc Sr. Lectr.
Edgecombe, N., BA MA Sr. Lectr.
Fielding, S. J., BSc Sr. Lectr.
Fisher, D., BSc PhD Sr. Lectr.
Fong, D., BEng MSc Sr. Lectr.
Gruneberg, S., BSc MSc Sr. Lectr.
Haddar, F., MA PhD Sr. Lectr.
Haywood, P. G., BSc MSc Sr. Lectr.
Howell, J., BSc MA Sr. Lectr.
Howes, Prof. R., MPhil MBA PhD Head*
Jones, J. N. V., FICE Sr. Lectr.
Kelly, M. W., BSc Sr. Lectr.
Khosrowshahi, F., BSc MSc PhD Sr. Lectr.
Knowles, J. B., BSc Principal Lectr.
Kumar, S., BA MH Sr. Lectr.
Kusimo, A. W., BSc MSc Sr. Lectr.
Leetch, C. S., FRICS Sr. Lectr.
Luu, P. N., MSc Cran.IT, PhD Belf., BSc Sr. Lectr.
McCrea, A. M., MEng MSc PhD Sr. Lectr.
Mellow, P., BSc Sr. Lectr.
Moore, T. G., BEng MSc Sr. Lectr.
Moran, J. A., BSc MSc Sr. Lectr.
Naoum, S. G., BSc MSc PhD Sr. Lectr.
Nardini, P. D., BSc MSc Sr. Lectr.
Novis, D. M., BSc Sr. Lectr.
Page, M. W., BA MA PhD Sr. Lectr.
Parine, N. I., BSc MSc(Arch) PhD Sr. Lectr.
Pearson, S. H., BSc MSc, FRICS Principal Lectr.
Pithia, K., BSc PhD Sr. Lectr.
Powell, C. J., BArch BSc Principal Lectr.
Pryke, S. D., MSc, FRICS Sr. Lectr.
Schaffer, T. Sr. Lectr.
Symonds, B. C., MSc Lond., FRICS Principal Lectr.
Townsend, M., FRICS Sr. Lectr.
Trodden, G., BSc MSc Sr. Lectr.
Tweedy, K. Sr. Lectr.
Viaravamoorthy, K., BSc MSc PhD Sr. Lectr.
Wall, D. M., MSc Witw., BSc MPhil Sr. Lectr.
White, D. A., BSc MSc(Eng), FGS Sr. Lectr.
Wright, P. J., BSc MSc Sr. Lectr.

Education, Politics and Social Sciences

Fax: (0171) 815 5799

Allsop, Prof. J. M., BSc MSc Principal Lectr.
Athill, C. Sr. Lectr.
Atkinson, H. P., BA MSc Principal Lectr.
Bailey, W. J., BA MA Sr. Lectr.
Baldry, M., BEd Sr. Lectr.
Bosco, A., MA Prof.
Buchan, M., BA MSc PhD Sr. Lectr.
Budd, A. M., BA MA Sr. Lectr.
Calder, P. A., MA MSc Sr. Lectr.
Cowling, S., BA Sr. Lectr.
Daniels, T., BSc Sr. Lectr.
De Zoysa, R., MSc Lond., MA Lond., BSc Sr. Lectr.
Fitzgerald, R., BSc MSc(Econ) Sr. Lectr.

Freeman, R., BA PhD Sr. Lectr.
Gold, L. M., BSc PhD Sr. Lectr.
Grier, T., BSc Sr. Lectr.
Hastings, S., BSc(Econ) Lond. Sr. Lectr.
Hebden, P. A., BSc MA Sr. Lectr.
Hickox, M. S. H., BA PhD Sr. Lectr.
Hind, D., BA MA
Hudson, K. J., BA MA PhD Sr. Lectr.
Hughes, S., BA MA Sr. Lectr.
Jeffs, H., BEd BA Sr. Lectr.
Katz, H., BA PhD
King, R. J., MA PhD Principal Lectr.
Kinsman, M., BA MA Sr. Lectr.
Ladly, P., BA MSc(Econ) Principal Lectr.
Laungani, P., MA PhD Sr. Lectr.
Lovell, A., BSc MSc Sr. Lectr.
Lyon, E. S., BA Brandeis, FilKand Lund, MSc Lund Principal Lectr.
Mace, J., BA PhD
Marlow, L. A., BSc Lond., MA Warw., PhD Warw. Principal Lectr.
Martin, C. J., BA MPhil PhD Sr. Lectr.
McCarney, H. J., BA MA DPhil Sr. Lectr.
McGonagle, R., BEd MEd Sr. Lectr.
Meadows, J., BSc MA Sr. Lectr.
Mirza, H. F., BA PhD Reader
Oppenheim, C. Sr. Lectr.
Owen, J., BA PhD Sr. Lectr.
Parkinson, A., BEd Belf., MA Lond., PhD Sr. Lectr.
Reading, A., BA PhD Sr. Lectr.
Rojas, R., BSc MPhil PhD Sr. Lectr.
Rooke, R., BA PhD Sr. Lectr.
Scafe, S. Sr. Lectr.
Stokes, J. Sr. Lectr.
Takhar, S., BEd MSc Sr. Lectr.
Taylor, Prof. J. G., BA Sus., MA City(UK), PhD City(UK) Principal Lectr.
Thatcher, C., LLB MPhil Sr. Lectr.
Tucker, C., BSc Sr. Lectr.
Van Dyke, R., BA PhD Sr. Lectr.
Walter, M., MA Sr. Lectr.
Weeks, Prof. J., BA MPhil PhD Head*
Weiner, Prof. G., BEd Lond., MA Lond., PhD Open(UK) Principal Lectr.

Engineering, Electrical, Electronic and Information

Fax: (0171) 815 7599

Alford, N. McN., BSc PhD Prof., Physical Electronics
Bridge, Prof. B., BSc DSc, FIP, FIEE Head*
Edwards-Shea, L., BSc MSc Sr. Lectr.
Evans, F., BSc PhD DSc(Eng), FIEE, FIMA Emer. Prof., Electrical and Electronic Engineering
Fradkin, L. Ju, MSc PhD Sr. Lectr.
Hayton, C., BA Essex, MSc Principal Lectr.
Hogarth, C. A., BSc PhD DSc, FIEE, FIP Visiting Prof., Physical Electronics
Howson, A., BSc Sr. Lectr.
Imhof, R. E., BSc PhD, FIEE, FIP Prof., Electrical Engineering
Jennings, B. R., BSc PhD DSc Visiting Prof., Optoelectronics
Kaye, R., BSc PhD Principal Lectr.
Klimo, P., MSc PhD Sr. Lectr.
Ljepojevic, N., PhD DSc Reader, Computer and Mathematical Modelling
Lunn, C., MSc Sr. Lectr.
Mukherjee, D., BSc MTech PhD Sr. Lectr.
Nyerges, G., BSc MSc Sr. Lectr.
Pekris, J., BSc MSc Sr. Lectr.
Pervez, A., BSc Pesh., BSc Salf., MSc Essex, PhD Lond. Sr. Lectr.
Pettitt, R., BSc PhD Sr. Lectr.
Protheroe, D. W., BSc PhD Sr. Lectr.
Reehal, H. S., BSc PhD Reader, Thin Film Technology
Ridler, P., BSc Wales, MSc Lond., PhD Brun. Sr. Lectr.
Sattar, T., BSc PhD Principal Lectr.
Selig, J., BSc York(UK), PhD Liv. Sr. Lectr.
Shirkoohi, G. H., MSc PhD Sr. Lectr.
Tavsanoglu, V., PhD Prof., Circuits and Signal Processing
Viscard, K., BA
Webster, N., BSc PhD Sr. Lectr.

Yates, J., BSc MSc PhD   Principal Lectr.

Engineering, Systems and Design

Fax: (0171) 815 7699

Ajmal, A., MSc Manc., PhD Manc., BSc   Sr. Lectr.
Andrews, S. D., MA RCA   Sr. Lectr.
Atherton, M. A., BSc Aston, MSc Lond.   Principal Lectr.
Benjamin, E. L., BSc MSc MPhil   Sr. Lectr.
Bradley, J., BA   Sr. Lectr.
Brickle, B. V., BTech MSc PhD, FIMechE   Prof.
Brown, D., MA RCA   Sr. Lectr.
Burgess, N. J., MPhil   Sr. Lectr.
Cavanagh, J., BSc   Sr. Lectr.
Collins, K., MSc   Principal Lectr.
Cook, D., BEd   Sr. Lectr.
Dalke, H., BA   Sr. Lectr.
Day, A. R., BEng   Sr. Lectr.
Dickenson, R. P., BSc MSc PhD   Sr. Lectr.
Dowlen, C. M. C., BTech   Sr. Lectr.
Duke, M. D., BEng   Sr. Lectr.
Dwyer, T. C., BSc   Sr. Lectr.
Ezugwu, E. O., MSc PhD   Reader
Forsyth, E. M., BSc MSc   Sr. Lectr.
Fuad, A. H., BEng MEng   Sr. Lectr.
Gabbitas, B. L., BSc MSc PhD   Principal Lectr.
Gawne, D. T., BSc PhD, FIM   Prof.
Grieves, B. R., BA MTech   Sr. Lectr.
Hardy, D. J., MPhil PhD   Sr. Lectr.
Hunt, D. G., BSc MSc PhD   Prof.
James, R., BSc MEng PhD, FIMechE   Prof.
Karayiannis, T. G., BSc PhD   Reader, Heat Transfer
Matthews, Prof. R. D., BSc PhD, FIMechE   Head*
Missenden, J. F., BSc PhD   Sr. Lectr.
Newton, A. M., BSc Manc., PhD Lond., MSc   Sr. Lectr.
Norman, L. D., BSc   Principal Lectr.
Özturk, A., MPhil   Sr. Lectr.
Pain, C., BSc MSc   Sr. Lectr.
Ratcliffe, M. S., BSc   Sr. Lectr.
Rose, L., BSc MSc MBA   Principal Lectr.
Rotter, K. R., BA MA MSc, FIMarE   Sr. Lectr.
Shacklock A., BSc PhD   Sr. Lectr.
Shield, Bridget M., BSc MSc PhD   Reader
Terry, A. V., MSc Cran.IT   Principal Lectr.
Welch, T. C., MPhil   Sr. Lectr.
Wen, J., BEng BSc MSc PhD   Sr. Lectr.
Yiakoumetti, K., BSc MSc   Sr. Lectr.

Health and Social Care, see also Redwood College of Health Studies

Adams, K., BN MSc
Aird, T., BA
Alsop, A., BA MPhil
Anderson, C.
Appleby, F. M., BEd MA
Barry, D., BSc
Beckwith, S.
Bond, B. M., BA MA
Bradding, A., BSA MA
Brett, M., MA
Brown, S. A., BSc
Burke, L., BA MA
Carr, G., BSc MSc
Castleton, L. V., BSc
Charles-Edwards, I., MA
Chudleigh, P. M., BSc
Clarridge, A., BSc MSc
Conroy, D., MSc
Cooper, K., MA PhD
Cootes, L.
Corlett, S., BSc
Couchman, Prof. W., BA MSc   Head*
Cumpper, J., BA
Davis, C., BA MSc
Davis, P., BEd MA
Dean, K., BA
Dhillon, H., BA MSc
Dransfield, G., BA MSc
Farmer, A., BSc
Fowler, P. S., BSc
Gannon, E., MSc
Gibson, F., MSc
Hall, T., BSc
Harper, M., BA

Harris, D. F., MSc
Henderson, I., MSc
Horstman, M., MA
Hughes, J., BSc MSc
Jenkins, M., MA
Joannu, M., MA
Jupp, S., BSc MSc
Katz, A., BA MA PhD
Keane, P. A., MA
Kelly, J.
Knox, M. A., MA
Lawrence, C., BSc MSc
Leathard, A., BA PhD
Leiba, P. A., BA MSc MPhil PhD
Leitao, P., BEd
Leonard, K., BA MA
Lewis, J.
Littlewood, J., BSc PhD
Lovegrove, M., MSc
Lund, W., MSc
Luthra, M., BSc MSc
MacDonald, G., MSc
Markowe, L. A., BSc MSc PhD
McFerran, T.
McIver, M. P., BA
McNabb, M. T., BSc BA
Meek, L., BEd MA
Miller, T.
Mobbs, S., BSc
Mobbs, S., BSc
Moore, M., BA MA
Mukherjee, A., BSc MSc
Murcott, A., MA PhD
Norris, D., BSc MSc
O'Brian, O.
Parsons, P., MSc
Payling, J., MA
Payne, S., BSc
Raymond, A. E., BEd MSc
Rendell, P., BA MA
Richardson, G., BScEng MS PhD
Robertshaw, D., BSc
Rogers, D., MSc
Roth, C., BA MSc
Ryan, P. M.
Saunders, K.
Saunders, M., BA
Schickler, P. D., BSc MSc
Scotter, J.
Seaman, S.
Shaw, S. L., BSc MA
Simpson, S., BA MSc
Sims, D., BA MA
Sinclair, N., BSc MA
Slavin, H., BA MSc
Smith, M.
Sooboodoo, E., BEd
Spires, K., BA
Stocks, M. A., MSc
Stocksley, M. I., MSc
Taket, A., BA MSc PhD
Tatlow, M., MSc
Tomlinson, D. R., BA PhD
Trew, W., BA MSc
Usher, C., MA
Waddington, K. E., BSc MSc
Webley-Brown, C., BSc
Weinstein, J. A., BA BPhil MSc MA
Whiting, M., BN MSc
Wills, J., BA MA MSc
Wright, A., BSc MSc
Zur, J., BSc

Information Engineering, see Engin., Electr., Electronic and Information

Information Systems, see Computing, Information Systems and Maths.

Languages, Modern, see under Business

Law, see under Business

Leisure and Tourism Industries, see under Business

Mathematics, see Computing, Information Systems and Maths.

Politics, see Educn., Pol. and Soc. Scis.

Science, see Appl. Sci.

Social Care, see Health and Social Care

Social Sciences, see Educn., Pol. and Soc. Scis.

Trade Union Studies

No staff at present

Urban Development and Policy

Fax: (0171) 815 7330

Adams, M.   Sr. Lectr.
Allison, P.   Sr. Lectr.
Attree, J., BA BSc MA   Sr. Lectr.
Bayldon, N.   Sr. Lectr.
Bowkett, S., BA MA   Sr. Lectr.
Brown, J. P., LLB   Sr. Lectr.
Bruegel, I., BA MSc(Econ)   Sr. Lectr.
Buckley, M., BA MSc(Econ) MPhil   Sr. Lectr.
Chaker, W., BSc BSA MSc   Sr. Lectr.
Davies, P., BA   Sr. Lectr.
Evans, R., BA(Econ) Sheff., MSc Lond., DPhil Sus., PhD   Principal Lectr.
Francis, S., BA MA   Sr. Lectr.
Fraser, C. F., MA MPhil   Principal Lectr.
Ghanbari-Parsa, A. R., MPhil PhD   Sr. Lectr.
Hollins, K. M., LLB LLM   Sr. Lectr.
Homes, W.   Sr. Lectr.
James, R., BA MSc   Sr. Lectr.
Jarvis, R. K., BA MPhil PhD   Sr. Lectr.
Jones, T. M., MA RCA   Sr. Lectr.
Kane, M., BA   Sr. Lectr.
King, S., BSc   Sr. Lectr.
Kudic, L.   Sr. Lectr.
Lake, M. G., BSc   Sr. Lectr.
Landers, H., BSc   Sr. Lectr.
Leary, M., BSc MSc   Sr. Lectr.
Lewers, T. H., BSc MSc   Sr. Lectr.
Lyons, M., MSc   Sr. Lectr.
MacKenzie, J. L., BA   Sr. Lectr.
Melvin, J. P., BSc MSc   Sr. Lectr.
Paice, D. L., BA MA   Sr. Lectr.
Percy, S., BSc MA   Sr. Lectr.
Pinch, P. L., BA PhD   Sr. Lectr.
Pople, N.   Sr. Lectr.
Rapley, N. M., BA, FCIS   Sr. Lectr.
Redding, Prof. B., BSc MBA, FRICS   Head*
Richards, R., BSc   Sr. Lectr.
Robbins, M. W., MA RCA   Sr. Lectr.
Rooney, M. J., BSc   Sr. Lectr.
Scott, N. A., BSc MSc   Sr. Lectr.
Shonfield, K. P., BA BSc   Sr. Lectr.
Spier, S., BA MArch   Sr. Lectr.
Sullivan, K., BSc MSc   Sr. Lectr.
Threipland, C.   Sr. Lectr.
Tomkins, J., BA MSc PhD   Sr. Lectr.
Winter, A. J., BA MA   Sr. Lectr.
Woodroffe, E. N., BSc MSc   Principal Lectr.

REDWOOD COLLEGE OF HEALTH STUDIES

Agbolegbe, K., BA MSc   Head of Sch./ Principal*

Midwifery and Women's Health Division

Tel: (0171) 815 5906 Fax: (0171) 815 4732

Asiedu, J., BSc MA   Sr. Lectr.
Cook, P.   Sr. Lectr.
Ejindu, A., MA   Sr. Lectr.
Ellender, M., BEd   Sr. Lectr.
Emery, S. F., MA   Head*
Foolchand, V., BA MSc   Sr. Lectr.
Graham, L., BA
Hicks, A., BEd MSc   Sr. Lectr.
King, L.   Sr. Lectr.
McEwen, B., BA   Sr. Lectr.
Nicholson, K., BSc MSc   Sr. Lectr.
Nnaemeka, B., BSc   Sr. Lectr.
Sanni-Thomas, P.   Sr. Lectr.
Sutton, T., BA   Sr. Lectr.
Too, S.-K., BEd MSc   Sr. Lectr.

Willis, B., BA   Sr. Lectr.

Post-Registration and Continuing Education Division
Tel: (0171) 815 5906 Fax: (0171) 815 4732
Allen, S.   Sr. Lectr.
Asiedu-Addo, E., BEd   Sr. Lectr.
Collison, E.   Sr. Lectr.
Davis, L., BA   Sr. Lectr.
Francis, H., MA   Sr. Lectr.
Gopal, A., BA MA   Sr. Lectr.
Gunnoo, V., BA MSc   Sr. Lectr.
Johnson, V.   Sr. Lectr.
MacDonald, N., MA   Sr. Lectr.
Mawoyo, B., MSc   Sr. Lectr.
Ramnaulth, A., BSc   Sr. Lectr.
Teh, B., BSc   Head*
Ward, M., BA MSc   Sr. Lectr.
Williams, L., BSc   Sr. Lectr.

Pre-Registration Education Division
Barker, E., MSc   Sr. Lectr.
Campbell, A., BA   Sr. Lectr.
Cock, M., BA   Sr. Lectr.
Crangle, J., BSc   Sr. Lectr.
Edwards, L.   Sr. Lectr.
Farrow, J.   Sr. Lectr.
Gordon, P., BSc   Sr. Lectr.
Heckman, C., BEd BSc   Sr. Lectr.
Henderson, N., BSc   Sr. Lectr.
Lee, R., BSc   Sr. Lectr.
Licorish, E., MEd   Head*
Maidwell, A., BA MSc   Sr. Lectr.
Richards, A., BA MSc   Sr. Lectr.
Somers, J. T. D., BA   Sr. Lectr.
Williams, S., BA MSc   Sr. Lectr.

Training (Health Care) Division
Tel: (0171) 815 5906 Fax: (0171) 815 4732
Baker, J., BSc MBA   Sr. Lectr.
Bauckham, D.   Sr. Lectr.
Broughton, G., BA   Sr. Lectr.

Carpenter, K.   Sr. Lectr.
Carroll, J.   Sr. Lectr.
Cullotty, M., BA   Sr. Lectr.
Driscoll, J. D., BSc
Fisher, R.   Sr. Lectr.
Garnham, E.   Sr. Lectr.
Goodman, N.   Sr. Lectr.
Harris, C.   Sr. Lectr.
Kirby, S., BA MA   Sr. Lectr.
Kok, J., BSc   Sr. Lectr.
Lattimer, S., BA   Sr. Lectr.
Mahoney, C.   Sr. Lectr.
Mills, P., MSc   Sr. Lectr.
Morten, E., BA MA   Sr. Lectr.
Rai, V., BA   Sr. Lectr.
Robinson, J., BA   Sr. Lectr.
Snell, H., BA   Sr. Lectr.
Tandoh, J., BA MA MSc   Acting Head*
Terrell, A., MSc   Sr. Lectr.

CONTACT OFFICERS
Academic affairs. Deputy Vice-Chancellor (Resources): Watkins, Prof. Trevor, BA MSc PhD
Accommodation. Head of Residential and Catering Services: Kay, Stephen
Admissions (first degree). Deputy Registrar (Admissions): Morrison, N., BA PhD
Adult/continuing education. Head: Storan, J., BEd MSc
Archives. Llewellyn-Jones, R., BA PhD
Careers. Head of Careers Service: Edmonds, S., BA
Computing services. Head of Computer Services Department: Payne, Carl, BSc MTech
Estates and buildings/works and services. Head, Department of Property Services: Dryborough, John, FRICS
Examinations. Deputy Registrar (Student Affairs): Benson, J., BSc
Finance. Acting Head of Finance: Findlay, D., BA

General enquiries. Deputy Vice-Chancellor and Registrar: Phillips, A. R., BSc(Econ) MBA
International office. Head of Recruitment: Roden, C., BA
Library (chief librarian). Head of Library and Learning Resources: Akeroyd, John, BSc Birm., MPhil
Personnel/human resources. Head, Department of Human Resources: Boyce, K., MA
Public relations, information and marketing (publications). Dix, C., BA
Public relations, information and marketing (marketing). Head, Department of External Relations: Masheter, A., BA
Purchasing. Purchasing Manager: Becker, Ron, MBA
Quality assurance and accreditation. Deputy Registrar (Course Administration): Hooper, G., BA
Research. Head of Research Office: Tinley, E., BSc PhD
Safety. Health and Safety Officer: Tyler, P.
Sport and recreation. Dean of Student Services: ......
Student welfare/counselling (international). Student Counsellor with responsibility for International Students: Barty, A., MA Oxf.

CAMPUS/COLLEGE HEADS
Redwood College of Health Studies, Harold Wood Education Centre, Harold Wood Hospital, Gubbins Lane, Harold Wood, Romford RM3 0BE. (Tel: (0171) 815 5959; Fax: (0171) 815 5906.) Head of School/Principal: Agbolegbe, K., BA MSc

[Information supplied by the institution as at 4 March 1998, and edited by the ACU]

UNIVERSITY OF SOUTHAMPTON

Founded 1952; previously established as Hartley University College, Southampton 1902

Member of the Association of Commonwealth Universities

Postal Address: Highfield, Southampton, England SO17 1BJ
Telephone: (01703) 595000 Fax: (01703) 593939 Telex: 86626 WWW: http://www.soton.ac.uk
E-mail formula: initials.surname@soton.ac.uk

VISITOR—Elizabeth, H.M. The Queen
CHANCELLOR—Selborne, The Earl , KBE, FRS
PRO-CHANCELLOR—Swire, Sir Adrian, MA
PRO-CHANCELLOR—Williams, K., MA Camb., LLB Camb.
PRO-CHANCELLOR—Plant of Highfield, Baron, PhD DLitt
VICE-CHANCELLOR*—Newby, Prof. Howard J., CBE, BA Essex, PhD Essex, Hon. DLitt CNAA, Hon. DLitt Portsmouth, Hon. DLitt S.Bank, Hon. DUniv Sur., Hon. DLitt Ulster.
TREASURER—Whitehead, G., FCA
DEPUTY VICE-CHANCELLOR—Farrar, Prof. R. A., BSc(Eng) Lond., PhD Lond.
DEPUTY VICE-CHANCELLOR—Ulph, Prof. A. M., BPhil Oxf., MA Glas.
DEPUTY VICE-CHANCELLOR—Lanchester, P. C., BSc Monash, PhD Monash
SECRETARY AND REGISTRAR‡—Lauwerys, J. F. D., BEd Lond., MA Lond.
LIBRARIAN—Naylor, B., MA Oxf.

GENERAL INFORMATION

History. The university's origins date from 1862 when the Hartley Institution was founded in central Southampton, the result of a benefaction by local philanthropist Henry

Robinson Hartley. Renamed Hartley University College, it moved to the present Highfield Campus in 1919, and was granted its charter in 1952. The university merged with Winchester School of Art in 1996.

Admission to first degree courses (see also United Kingdom Introduction). Through Universities and Colleges Admissions Services (UCAS). Applicants must be at least 17 years of age on 1 October of the year of admission. Candidates with current UK qualifications must satisfy the relevant faculty and specific course requirements. Certain non-UK qualifications are acceptable, including: Irish Leaving Certificate, with a score of 260 points or above in 5 subjects, of which 4 must be at Higher (or Honours) level obtained at one sitting; International Baccalaureate; European Baccalaureate; 2 subjects at grade 4 or 5 in USA Advanced Placement (AP) exams; qualifications such as school leaving certificates from member states of the European Community which allow admission to University in a candidate's home country (candidates from Greece: 2 General Certificate of Education (GCE) A level passes in addition to Apolytirion); overseas GCE and school certificate exams comparable to UK equivalents; Australian Year 12 Certificate; Canadian Senior Matriculation Certificate; Norwegian Certificate of Upper Secondary Education; Sijil Tinggi Persekolahan Malaysia (STPM/Advanced Certificate of Education); other qualifications deemed equivalent to UK entry requirements by the British Council's National Academic Recognition Information Centre (NARIC). UK qualifications no longer offered may be accepted, subject to approval by board of faculty concerned, such as Ordinary or Higher National Certificate or Diploma (HNC/HND), pre-GCE school-leaving examinations and AO levels. Candidates over the age of 21 not possessing any of the above qualifications may be admitted to a first degree course provided they can submit evidence of previous serious study and demonstrate the capacity and attainments to pursue the proposed course: eligibility for admission is subject to approval of board of faculty concerned.

Candidates whose first language is not English must reach a satisfactory standard in an approved test in English.

First Degrees (see also United Kingdom Directory to Subjects of Study). BA, BEng, BM, BMid, BN, BSc, LLB, MEng, MMath, MPhys.

Most courses last 3 or 4 years. BM, BMid, MEng: 5 years.

Higher Degrees (see also United Kingdom Directory to Subjects of Study). LLM, MA, MA(Ed), MBA, MMaths, MMus, MRes, MS, MSc, MSc(Ed), MS, MSW, MTh, MPhil, PhD, DBA, DCP, DEd, DL, DLitt, DM, DMus, DSc, LLD, PhD.

Applicants for admission to master's degrees must normally hold an appropriate first degree with at least second class honours. PhD: appropriate master's degree.

Master's degree courses: normally not less than 1 year full-time or 2 years part-time; doctoral degrees: normally not less than 2 years full-time or 3 years part-time.

Language of Instruction. English. Intensive remedial courses available prior to the beginning of each academic year.

Libraries. About 1,150,000 volumes; about 6000 periodicals subscribed to. Special collections: Ford (official publications); Hartley (military, political, official and diplomatic papers, including those of the first Duke of Wellington, third Viscount Palmerston and Earl Mountbatten of Burma); National Oceanographic Library (marine science); Parkes (material relating to Jewish communities, Anglo-Jewish archive collections).

Fees (1998–99, annual, subject to confirmation). Undergraduate (UK/EU students): £1000. Postgraduate: UK/EU students £2540; international students £6500 (classroom-based courses); £7100–9610 (laboratory/workshop-based courses); £17,320 (clinical courses).

Academic Year (1998–99). Two semesters: 24 September–30 January; 1 February–19 June.

Income (year ended 31 July 1997). Total, £160,500,000.

Statistics. Staff: 4454 (1765 academic and research, 2689 administrative and other).

FACULTIES/SCHOOLS

Arts
Tel: (01703) 593380 Fax: (01703) 593868
Dean: Cook, Prof. N. J., MA Camb., PhD Camb.

Educational Studies
Tel: (01703) 593475 Fax: (01703) 593556
Dean: Brumfit, Prof. C. J., BA Oxf., MA Essex, PhD Lond.
Secretary: Paul, H.

Engineering and Applied Science
Tel: (01703) 592705 Fax: (01703) 592225
Dean: Rice, Prof. C. G., MSc Lond., Hon. MD

Law
Tel: (01703) 593550 Fax: (01703) 593857
Dean: Wikeley, Prof. N. J., MA Camb.
Secretary: Worwood, T.

Mathematical Studies
Tel: (01703) 393700 Fax: (01703) 592225
Dean: King, Prof. R. C., BSc Lond., PhD Lond.

Medicine, Health and Biological Sciences
Tel: (01703) 594263 Fax: (01703) 594159
Dean: George, Prof. C. F., BSc MD, FRCP

New College
Tel: (01703) 216200 Fax: (01703) 230944
Director: Clark, Prof. J. W., BA Birm., DrPhil Bremen

Science
Tel: (01703) 593307 Fax: (01703) 593781
Dean: Evans, Prof. J., BSc Lond., PhD Camb.

Social Sciences
Tel: (01703) 592518 Fax: (01703) 593846
Dean: Diamond, Prof. I., BSc Lond., PhD St And.
Secretary: Oddie, L.

ACADEMIC UNITS

Aeronautics and Astronautics
Tel: (01703) 592315 Fax: (01703) 593058
East, R. A., BSc S'ton., PhD S'ton., FRAeS Prof.†, Aeronautics
Gabriel, S. B., BSc Strath., PhD Strath. Sr. Lectr.
Goodyer, M. J., MSc Cran.IT, PhD S'ton., FIMechE, FRAeS Prof.†, Experimental Aerodynamics
Hodson, K. G., MBE, FRAeS Visiting Prof.
Holdaway, R., BSc S'ton., PhD S'ton. Visiting Prof.
McLean, D., PhD Lough. Prof., Flight Control
Roberts, G. T., BSc S'ton., PhD S'ton. Sr. Lectr.
Swinerd, G. G., BSc Kent, PhD Kent, FRAS Sr. Lectr.
Tutty, O. R., MSc Otago, PhD Otago Reader, Fluid Mechanics
White, R. G., PhD S'ton., DSc, FEng Prof., Vibration Studies; Head*
Other Staff: 5 Lectrs.; 3 Res. Fellows; 2 Teaching Fellows; 1 Sr. Lectr.†; 3 Hon. Visiting Lectrs.
Vacant Posts: Cobham Lectr.; 1 Lectr.
Research: aerodynamics, rotorcraft and vertical/short takeoff and landing; aerospace materials; aerospace structures (control); astronautics; computational fluid dynamics and theoretical dynamics

Engineering Materials
Tel: (01703) 595090 Fax: (01703) 593016
Gregson, P. J., BSc(Eng) Lond., PhD Lond. Prof., Aerospace Materials
Trethewey, K. R., BSc Leic., PhD Leic. Sr. Lectr.
Willoughby, A. F. W., BSc(Eng) Lond., PhD Lond. Prof., Electronics Materials

Archaeology
Tel: (01703) 592247, 594194 Fax: (01703) 593032
Champion, Timothy C., MA Oxf., DPhil Oxf., FSA Prof.
Gamble, Clive S., MA Camb., PhD Camb., FSA Prof.; Head*
Hinton, David A., MA Oxf., FSA Reader
Keay, Simon J., BA Lond., PhD Lond. Prof.
McGrail, Sean, BA Brist., MA Oxf., PhD Lond., DSc Oxf., FSA Visiting Prof.
Peacock, David P. S., BSc St And., PhD St And., FSA Prof.
Sparkes, Brian A., BA Lond., PhD Lond. Emer. Prof.
Thomas, Julian S., MA Sheff., PhD Sheff. Sr. Lectr.
Wainwright, Geoffrey J., MBE, BA Wales, PhD Lond., FSA Visiting Prof.

Art, Winchester School of, see below

Biochemistry, see Medicine, Health and Biological Sciences

Biological Sciences, see Medicine, Health and Biological Sciences

Chemistry
Tel: (01703) 593333 Fax: (01703) 593781
Attard, George S., BSc Warw., PhD S'ton. Sr. Lectr.
Bartlett, Philip N., BA Oxf., PhD Lond. Prof.
Bradley, Mark, BA Oxf., DPhil Oxf. Prof.
Brown, Tom, BTech Brad., PhD Brad. Prof.
Carrington, Alan, BSc S'ton., MA Camb., PhD S'ton., FRS Royal Society Res. Prof.
Dominic, J., BSc S'ton., DPhil Oxf. Prof.
Dunmur, David A., MA Oxf., DPhil Oxf. Prof.†
Dyke, John M., BSc Wales, PhD Brist. Prof.; Chairman*
Emsley, James W., BSc Leeds, PhD Leeds Prof.
Evans, John, BSc Lond., PhD Camb. Prof.
Frey, Jeremy G., MA Oxf., DPhil Oxf. Sr. Lectr.
Grossel, Martin C., BSc Lond., MA Oxf., PhD Lond. Sr. Lectr.
Hayden, Brian E., BSc Brist., PhD Brist. Prof.
Howard, Alan G., BSc Brist., PhD Brist. Sr. Lectr.
Kilburn, Jeremy D., MA Camb., PhD Camb. Reader
Levason, William, BSc Manc., PhD Manc. Reader
Luckhurst, Geoffrey R., BSc Hull, PhD Camb. Prof.
Mellor, John M., MA Oxf., DPhil Oxf. Prof.
Moss, Richard E., MA Camb., PhD Camb. Sr. Lectr.
Ogden, J. Steven, MA Camb., PhD Camb. Sr. Lectr.
Owen, John R., BSc Lond., PhD Lond. Sr. Lectr.
Parsons, Roger, BSc Lond., PhD Lond., DSc Brist., FRS Res. Prof.†
Pletcher, Derek, BSc Sheff., PhD Sheff. Prof.†
Rest, Anthony J., BSc Brist., PhD Brist. Sr. Lectr.
Rogers, David E., BSc Brist., PhD Brist. Sr. Lectr.
Turner, David L., MA Oxf., DPhil Oxf. Sr. Lectr.
Weller, Mark T., MA Oxf., DPhil Oxf. Prof.
Whitby, Richard J., BA Camb., PhD Leeds Reader
Vacant Posts: 1 Prof.; 3 Lectrs.

Computer Science, see Electronics and Computer Sci.

Earth Science, see Ocean and Earth Sci., Sch. of

Economics
Tel: (01703) 592537 Fax: (01703) 593858
Canova, F., MA Brown, PhD Minn. Prof.†
Cremer, J., MSc Mass., PhD Mass. Prof.†
Driffill, E. J., MA Camb., PhD Prin. Prof.; Head*

Hamlin, A. P., BSc(Tech) *Wales*, DPhil
York(UK) Prof.
Hillier, G. H., BEc *Penn.*, PhD *Penn.* Prof.,
Econometrics
Karp, L., BA *Calif.*, PhD *Calif.* Prof.†
Malcomson, J. M., MA *Camb.*, PhD *Harv.* Prof.
McCormick, B., MA *Manc.*, PhD *M.I.T.* Prof.
Mizon, G. E., MA *Oxf.*, MSc(Econ) *Lond.*, PhD
Lond. Leverhulme Prof., Econometrics (on
leave)
O'Brien, R. J., BSc(Econ) *Lond.* Sr. Lectr.
Piccione, M., MSc *Lond.*, PhD *N.Y.* Prof.
Smith, P., BA *Warw.*, PhD *Birm.* Sr. Lectr.
Ulph, A. M., MA *Glas.*, BPhil *Oxf.* Prof.

Education

Tel: (01703) 593475 Fax: (01703) 593556
Benton, M. G., BA *Leeds*, MA *Tor.*, PhD Prof.
Brumfit, C. J., BA *Oxf.*, MA *Essex*, PhD
Lond. Prof.; Head*
Davis, G. E., BSc *Monash*, PhD *Monash* Prof.
Figueroa, P. M. E., LicPhilos *Pontif.Urb.*, PhD
Lond. Reader
Foskett, N. H., MA *Oxf.*, PhD, FRMetS Sr.
Lectr.
Hart, A. P., MA *Oxf.*, DPhil *Oxf.* Sr. Lectr.
Kelly, P. J., BSc *Lond.*, MA *Lond.*, PhD *Lond.*,
FIBiol Emer. Prof.†
Mitchell, Rosamond F., BA *Trinity(Dub.)*, MSc
Edin., PhD *Stir.* Reader
Simons, Helen, BA *Melb.*, PhD *E.Anglia* Prof.
Usher, R. S., MA *Oxf.*, PhD Reader
Weare, Katherine, BA *Kent*, MA *Lond.* Sr. Lectr.
Other Staff: 13 Lectrs.; 5 Teaching Fellows
Research: education and social science; health
education; language in education; science,
technology and mathematics education

Electronics and Computer Science

Tel: (01703) 593649 Fax: (01703) 593045
Ashburn, P., BSc *Leeds*, PhD *Leeds* Prof.,
Microelectronics
Barron, D. W., MA *Camb.*, PhD *Camb.* Prof.,
Computer Science
Brignell, J. E., BSc(Eng) *Lond.*, PhD *Lond.*, FIEE,
FIP Prof., Industrial Instrumentation
Brown, A. D., BSc PhD, FIEE Reader
Brunnschweiler, A., BA *Camb.*, MS *Penn. State*,
PhD *Manc.* Sr. Lectr.
Chapman, B., BSc *NZ*, MSc *NZ* Sr. Lectr.
Dakin, J. P., BSc *S'ton.*, DPhil *S'ton.* Reader
Damper, R. I., BSc *Salf.*, MSc *Lond.*, PhD *Lond.*,
FIEE Sr. Lectr.
DeRoure, D. C., BSc *S'ton.*, PhD *S'ton.* Sr. Lectr.
Evans, A. G. R., BSc *Liv.*, DPhil *Oxf.* Reader
Glaser, H. W., BSc *Lond.* Reader
Hall, W., MSc PhD, FBCS Prof., Computer
Science
Hanzo, L., MSc *Bud.*, PhD *Bud.* Reader
Harnard, S. R., BA *McG.*, MA *Prin.*, PhD
Prin. Prof.
Harris, C. J., BSc *Leic.*, MA *Oxf.*, PhD, FIEE,
FEng Prof., Aerospace Systems Engineering
Harrison, R., BA *Oxf.*, MSc *Lond.*, MA *Oxf.*,
PhD Sr. Lectr.
Hartel, P. H., MSc *V.U.Amst.*, PhD *Amst.* Sr.
Lectr.
Henderson, P., BSc *Manc.*, MSc *Newcastle(UK)*,
PhD *Newcastle(UK)* Prof., Computer Science
Hey, A. J. G., MA *Oxf.*, DPhil *Oxf.*, FIEE,
FBCS Prof., Computation; Head*
Kemhadjian, H. A., BSc(Eng) MSc(Eng),
FIEE Prof., Microelectronics
Lewis, P. H., BSc *Lond.*, PhD *Lond.* Sr. Lectr.
Nicole, D. A., MA *Camb.*, PhD Reader
Nixon, M. S., BSc *Reading*, PhD *Reading* Sr.
Lectr.
Parker, G. J., BSc *Sus.*, PhD *Sur.*, FIP Sr. Lectr.
Payne, D. N., BSc PhD, FRS Pirelli Prof.,
Photonics
Redman-White, W., BSc *Exe.*, MSc
PhD Reader
Reeve, J. S., BSc *NZ*, MSc *NZ*, PhD Sr. Lectr.
Rogers, E., BSc *Belf.*, MEng *Sheff.*, PhD
Sheff. Reader
Rutt, H. N., BSc PhD, FIP Rank Prof.,
Infrared Science and Technology

Steele, R., BSc *Durh.*, PhD *Lough.*, DSc *Lough.*,
FIEE, FEng Prof., Communications
Wilkinson, J. S., BSc *Lond.*, PhD *Lond.* Reader
Zaluska, E. J., BSc, FIEE Sr. Lectr.

Engineering, Civil and Environmental

Tel: (01703) 594651 Fax: (01703) 594986
Ahm, P., MSc, FEng, FICE, FIStructE Royal
Academy of Engin. Visiting Prof.†,
Engineering Design
Allen, H. G., BEng *Liv.*, PhD *Liv.*,
FIStructE Res. Prof.†, Structural Engineering
Banks, C. J., BSc *Salf.*, DPhil *York(UK)* Reader
Barton, M. E., BSc *Lond.*, MSc *Birm.*, PhD *Birm.*,
FGS Sr. Lectr.
Butterfield, R., BSc(Eng) *Lond.*, DSc Res.
Prof.†
Clarke, J. L., MA PhD Sir William Halcrow &
Partners Visiting Prof.
Haq, N., BSc *Rajsh.*, MSc *Rajsh.*, PhD *S'ton.* Sr.
Lectr.
Holloway, L. C., MSc(Eng) *Lond.*, PhD *Lond.*,
FICE Visiting Prof.†, Composite Structures
Jolly, C. K., MSc *S'ton.*, PhD *S'ton.*,
FIStructE Sr. Lectr.
McDonald, M., BSc *Newcastle(UK)*, PhD Prof.,
Transportation Engineering; Head*
Morice, P. B., PhD DSc, FEng, FICE,
FISructE Res. Prof.†
Moy, S. S. J., BSc *Nott.*, PhD *Nott.* Sr. Lectr.;
Dir. of Teaching
Powrie, W., MA *Camb.*, MSc *Lond.*, PhD
Lond. Prof.; Dir. of Res.
Rycroft, D. W., PhD *Dund.* Sr. Lectr.
Stoner, R. F., BSc *Durh.*, FICE Res. Prof.†
Tanton, T. W., BSc *Hull*, PhD *S'ton.* British Gas
Prof., Environmental Technology
Williams, T. E. H., CBE, MSc PhD, FICE Res.
Prof.†
Wootton, J., BSc(Eng) *Lond.*, MEng *Calif.* Res.
Prof.†
Other Staff: 14 Lectrs.; 3 Res. Fellows
Research: coastal engineering; geotechnics;
irrigation engineering; transportation; waste
management

Engineering, Electrical

Tel: (01703) 595164 Fax: (01703) 593709
Bailey, A. G., BEng *Sheff.*, PhD *Sheff.*, FIP Prof.,
Applied Electrostatics
Barnes, S. R., BSc *Lond.*, PhD *Lond.* Visiting
Indust. Prof.
Crowder, R. M., BSc *Leic.*, PhD *Leic.* Sr. Lectr.
Davies, A. E., BEng(Tech) *Wales*, PhD
Wales Prof., Electrical Power Engineering
Hammond, P., MA *Camb.*, ScD *Camb.*, FIEE,
FEng Hon. Res. Prof.
Harris, M. R., BSc(Eng) *Lond.*, FIEE Res. Prof.
Hughes, J. F., BSc *Wales*, PhD *Wales*, FIEE,
FIP Prof., New Technologies
Knowles, J. B., MSc *Manc.*, PhD *Manc.* Visiting
Indust. Prof.
McBride, J. W., BSc *CNAA*, PhD *CNAA* Sr.
Lectr.
Stoll, R. L., PhD *Camb.*, FIEE Reader, Electrical
Machines; Head*
Swingler, S. G., BA *Lanc.*, PhD *Lanc.* Visiting
Indust. Prof.
Sykulski, J. K., MSc *Lodz*, PhD *Lodz* Prof.,
Distribution Engineering

Engineering, Environmental, see Engin.,
Civil and Environmental

Engineering Materials, see under Aeron.
and Astronautics

Engineering, Mechanical

Tel: (01703) 593582 Fax: (01703) 593230
Allen, R., BSc *Leeds*, PhD *Leeds*, FIEE,
FIMechE Sr. Lectr.
Atkinson, J. K., BSc *Essex* Sr. Lectr.
Beduz, C., MSc *Buenos Aires*, PhD
T.H.Delft Reader
Bowen, R. J., BSc(Eng) *Lond.*, DPhil *Oxf.* Sr.
Lectr.
Calvert, J. R., BA *Camb.*, PhD *Camb.* Sr. Lectr.
Crowder, R. M., BSc *Leic.*, PhD *Leic.* Sr. Lectr.

Farrar, R. A., BSc(Eng) *Lond.*, PhD *Lond.* Prof.
Keane, A. J., MSc *Lond.*, MA *Oxf.*, PhD
Brun. Prof.; Head*
McBride, J. W., BSc *S'ton.*, PhD *CNAA* Sr.
Lectr.
Mucci, P. E. R., FIMechE Sr. Lectr.
Richardson, R. N., BSc(Eng) *Lond.*, DPhil
Oxf. Sr. Lectr.
Stephen, N. G., BTech *Lough.*, PhD *Exe.* Sr.
Lectr.
Syngellakis, S., MSE *Prin.*, MA *Prin.*, PhD
Prin. Sr. Lectr.
Turner, J. D., BSc *Reading*, PhD *Reading* Royal
Academy of Engin. Res. Prof., Automotive
Telematics; Ford Motor Prof., Automotive
Electronics
Westbrook, M. H., BSc(Eng), FIEE, FIMechE,
FIP Visiting Prof.
Whatley, D. R. Chief Exper. Officer
Vacant Posts: 1 Lectr.
Research: computational mechanics (bio-
mechanics, design, design optimisation,
structural mechanics); electro-mechanical
engineering (instrumentation, metrology,
robotics, sensors (thick film)); thermo-fluid
engineering (biomedical fluid mechanics,
computational fluid dynamics (CFD), pipe
freezing, tribology)

English

Tel: (01703) 593410 Fax: (01703) 592859
Bygrave, Stephen, BA *Camb.*, PhD *Camb.* Sr.
Lectr.
Kaplan, Cora, BA *Smith*, MA *Brandeis* Prof.;
Head*
McGavin, John, MA *Edin.*, PhD *Edin.* Sr. Lectr.
McLuskie, Kathleen, MA *Glas.*, PhD *Glas.* Prof.
Middleton, Peter L., BA *Oxf.*, PhD *Sheff.* Sr.
Lectr.
Millett, Bella, MA *Oxf.*, DPhil *Oxf.* Reader
Peacock, John, BA *Syd.*, BLitt *Oxf.* Sr. Lectr.
Sawday, J., BA *Lond.*, PhD *Lond.* Sr. Lectr.
Williams, Linda, BA *Sus.*, DPhil *Sus.* Sr. Lectr.

Film and Media, see under Mod. Langs.,
Sch. of

French, see under Mod. Langs., Sch. of

Geography

Tel: (01703) 592215 Fax: (01703) 593295
Arnell, Nigel W., BSc *S'ton.*, PhD *S'ton.* Reader
Barber, Keith E., BSc *Brist.*, PhD *S'ton.* Reader
Clark, Mike J., BA *S'ton.*, PhD *S'ton.* Prof.
Curran, Paul J., BSc *Sheff.*, PhD *Brist.*, DSc
Brist. Prof.; Head*
Foody, G. M., BSc *Sheff.*, PhD *Sheff.* Prof.
Hart, J. K., BSc *Reading*, PhD *E.Anglia* Sr. Lectr.
Hoyle, Brian S., MA *Nott.*, PhD *Lond.* Reader
Lowe, M. S., BA *Birm.*, PhD *Camb.* Sr. Lectr.
Martin, David J., BSc *Brist.*, PhD *Wales* Reader
Mason, Colin M., MA *Edin.*, PhD *Manc.* Reader
Milton, Edward J., BSc *Exe.*, PhD *Reading* Sr.
Lectr.
Pinch, Steven P., BA *Sus.*, MSc(Econ) *Lond.*, PhD
Lond. Reader
Wagstaff, J. Malcolm, BA *Liv.*, PhD *S'ton.* Prof.
Wrigley, Neil, BA *Wales*, PhD *Camb.*, DSc
Brist. Prof.

German, see under Mod. Langs., Sch. of

Health Policy Studies, Institute for

Tel: (01703) 593394 Fax: (01703) 593177
Robinson, R., BA *E.Anglia*, MSc *Lond.* Prof.;
Dir.*

History

Tel: (01703) 592211 Fax: (01703) 593458
Bernard, G. W., MA *Oxf.*, DPhil *Oxf.*,
FRHistS Reader
Cesarani, D., MA *Oxf.*, DPhil *Oxf.* Parkes-
Wiener Prof., Modern Jewish History and
Culture
Colson, R. F., BSc(Econ) *Lond.*, MA *Prin.*, PhD
Prin. Sr. Lectr.
Duke, A. C., MA *Camb.*, LittD *Ley.*,
FRHistS Reader

Golding, B. J., MA Oxf., DPhil Oxf.,
FRHistS   Reader
Kushner, A. R. W., BA Sheff., MA Conn., PhD
Sheff.   Reader
Oldfield, J. R., MA Camb., PhD Camb.   Sr.
Lectr.
Platt, C. P. S., MA Oxf., PhD Leeds, FSA,
FRHistS   Prof.
Reuter, T., MA Oxf., DPhil Oxf., FRHistS   Prof.,
Medieval History
Rule, J. G., MA Camb., PhD Warw.,
FRHistS   Prof.
Sharpe, K. M., MA Oxf., DPhil Oxf.,
FRHistS   Prof.
Vinson, A. J., BA Camb.   Lectr.; Head*

Language Centre, see under Mod. Langs.,
Sch. of

Latin American Studies, see Spanish,
Portuguese and Latin American Studies
under Mod. Langs., Sch. of

Law

Tel: (01703) 593632 Fax: (01703) 593024
Beddard, F. R., LLB Sheff., PhD Sheff.   Sr. Lectr.
Carson, D. C. C., LLB Belf.   Reader,
Behavioural Sciences and Law
Debattista, C., LLD Malta, MA Oxf.   Reader,
Commercial Law
Ganz, Gabriele, LLM Lond.   Emer. Prof.
Gaskell, N. J. J., LLB Hull   Prof., Maritime and
Commercial Law
Green, Penelope J., BA ANU, MPhil Camb., PhD
Camb.   Sr. Lectr.
Grime, R. P., BA Oxf., BCL Oxf.   Prof.,
Maritime Law
Hannigan, Brenda M., MA Trinity(Dub.), LLM
Harv.   Reader, Corporate Law
Jackson, D. C., MA Oxf., BCL Oxf., LLD
S'ton.   Visiting Prof.†
Lewis, R. M., LLB Lond., MSc(Econ)
Lond.   Visiting Prof.
Lustgarten, L., BA Amherst, MSc Lond., JD
Yale   Prof.
Meredith, A. P. K., LLB Edin., PhD Camb.   Sr.
Lectr.
Montgomery, J., BA Camb., LLM Camb.   Sr.
Lectr.
Poulter, S. M., MA Oxf., DPhil Oxf.   Reader
Rutherford, A. F., BA Durh.   Prof.
Saxby, S. J., BA Kent, PhD S'ton.   Sr. Lectr.
Tridimas, T., LLB Athens, LLM Camb.   Prof.,
European Community Law
Wikeley, N. J., MA Camb.   Prof.; Head*
Other Staff: 2 Sr. Res. Fellows; 14 Lectrs.; 1
Temp. Lectr.
Research: behavioural sciences and law; criminal
justice; environmental law; maritime law

Management

Tel: (01703) 592562 Fax: (01703) 593844
Avison, D. E., BA(Econ) Leic., MSc Lond., PhD
Aston, FBCS   Prof., Information Systems
Bourn, A. M., BSc(Econ) Lond., FCA   Prof.†,
Accounting
Chapman, C. B., BASc Tor., MSc Birm.,
PhD   Prof., Management Science; Dir.,
Management Sch.*
Connell, N. A. D., BSc Lond., MSc Aston,
PhD   Sr. Lectr.
Dale, R. S., BSc(Econ) Lond., PhD Kent   Prof.,
International Banking and Financial
Institutions
Davies, Ruth M., BSc Warw., MSc Birm.,
PhD   Sr. Lectr.
Goddard, A. R., BSc Manc.   Sr. Lectr.
Johnson, J. E. V., BSc Manc., PhD   Sr. Lectr.
Klein, J. H., MSc Sus., PhD Lond.   Sr. Lectr.
Mar-Molinero, C., MSc PhD   Reader,
Operational Research
McKenzie, G. W., BA Wesleyan, MA Tufts, PhD
Calif.   Prof., Finance; Head*
Napier, Christopher J., MA Oxf., MSc Lond.,
FCA   Prof., Accounting
Sutcliffe, C. M. S., BA Reading   Prof.,
Accounting and Finance

Thomas, Steve H., BSc(Econ) Lond., MSc
PhD   Prof., Financial Markets
Ward, S. C., BSc Nott., MSc Lond., PhD   Sr.
Lectr.
Wilkinson, C., BSc Lough., MA Lanc., PhD
Lanc.   Dir., MBA Programme
Other Staff: 11 Lectrs.; 2 Res. Fellows
Vacant Posts: 3 Lectrs.

Mathematics

Tel: (01703) 593612 Fax: (01703) 595147
Baston, Victor J. D., BSc Birm., PhD Lond.   Sr.
Lectr.
Bowditch, Brian H., BA Camb., PhD
Warw.   Reader
Chillingworth, David R. J., BA Camb., PhD
Camb.   Sr. Lectr.
Clarke, Christopher J. S., MA Camb., PhD
Camb.   Prof.†, Applied Mathematics
Craine, Robert E., BSc Manc., PhD Manc.,
FIMA   Sr. Lectr.
d'Inverno, Raymon A., MA Oxf., MSc Lond.,
PhD Lond.   Reader
Dunwoody, Martin J., BSc Manc., PhD
ANU   Prof., Pure Mathematics
Fitt, Alistair D., MA Oxf., MSc Oxf., DPhil
Oxf.   Sr. Lectr.
Hirst, Keith E., BSc Lond., PhD Lond.   Sr. Lectr.
Jones, Gareth A., MA Oxf., DPhil Oxf.   Reader
King, Ronald C., BSc Lond., PhD Lond.,
FIP   Prof.; Head*
Landsberg, Peter T., PhD Lond., DSc Wat.,
FRSEd   Emer. Prof.; Res. Fellow
Lewis, Susan M., MSc Lond., PhD S'ton.   Reader
Lloyd, E. Keith, BSc Birm., PhD Birm.,
FIMA   Sr. Lectr.
Please, Colin P., BSc S'ton., MSc Oxf., DPhil
Oxf.   Sr. Lectr.
Potts, Christopher N., BSc Manc., MSc Hull, PhD
Birm.   Sr. Lectr.
Prescott, Philip, BSc Lond., PhD Lond.   Reader
Singerman, David, BSc Birm., PhD
Birm.   Reader
Sluckin, Timothy J., BA Camb., PhD
Nott.   Prof., Applied Mathematical Physics
Snaith, Victor P., MSc Warw., MA Camb., PhD
Warw., ScD Camb.   Prof., Pure Mathematics
Vickers, James A. G., BA Oxf., DPhil
York(UK)   Sr. Lectr.
Wheeler, Adam A., BSc E.Anglia, PhD
E.Anglia   Prof., Industrial Applied
Mathematics
Williams, H. Paul, MA Camb., PhD Leic.   Prof.,
Operational Research
Other Staff: 16 Lectrs.; 3 Res. Fellows; 1
Lectr.†
Vacant Posts: 2 Profs.
Research: applied mathematics (industrial general
relativity, theoretical physics); operational
research (discrete optimisation, game theory,
health modelling); pure mathematics
(combinatorics, dynamics, geometric group
theory, topology); statistics (crossover
designs, sample surveys, simultaneous
inference)

Medicine, see Medicine, Health and
Biological Sciences, below

Modern Languages, School of

Tel: (01703) 593974 Fax: (01703) 593288

Film and Media

Tel: (01703) 592256 Fax: (01703) 593288
Cook, Pam, BA Birm.   Prof., European Film
and Media
Research: American cinema; British cinema;
European cinema; television; transnational
cinemas

French

Tel: (01703) 592256 Fax: (01703) 593288
Brooks, W. G. A., MA Exe, PhD Exe   Sr. Lectr.
Cogman, P. W., MA Camb., PhD Camb.   Sr.
Lectr.
Kelly, M. H., BA Warw., MBA S'ton., PhD
Warw.   Prof.; Head*
Marshall, W. J., BA Lond., DPhil Oxf.   Sr. Lectr.

Research: cultural studies (French and Quebecois
cinema, Liberation period); language studies
(French language and linguistics); literary
studies (nineteenth- and twentieth-century
literature and thought); social, political and
historical studies (French foreign policy,
West Africa)

German

Tel: (01703) 592256 Fax: (01703) 593288
Bance, A. F., BA Lond., PhD Camb.   Prof.
Livingstone, R. S., MA Camb.   Prof.
Stevenson, P. R. A., BA Oxf., MA Reading   Sr.
Lectr.
Research: cultural studies (German cinema and
German/Turkish literature); language studies
(sociolinguistics of German); literary studies
(nineteenth- and twentieth-century German
and Austrian literature)

Language Centre

Tel: (01703) 592224 Fax: (01703) 593849
Piper, Alison, BA Sus., MSc Edin.   Sr. Lectr.,
English
Research: applied linguistics; language and
politics; multi-media language learning;
writing in a foreign language

**Spanish, Portuguese and Latin American
Studies**

Tel: (01703) 592256 Fax: (01703) 593288
Ettinghausen, H. M., MA Oxf., DPhil
Oxf.   Prof.
Freeland, D. A. McK., MA Camb., PhD
Camb.   Sr. Lectr.
Research: cultural studies (film and gender
studies); language studies (language and
nationalism, language policy,
sociolinguistics); Latin America and the
Caribbean (literature and popular culture,
modern history); literary studies (modern
Portuguese fiction, seventeenth-century
Spanish prose); social and political studies
(modern Spanish and Catalan history)

Music

Tel: (01703) 593425 Fax: (01703) 593197
Cook, N. J., MA Camb., PhD Camb.   Prof.
Drabkin, W. M., BA Cornell, MFA Prin., PhD
Prin.   Sr. Lectr.
Everist, Mark E., MMus Lond., DPhil Oxf.   Prof.;
Head*
Pople, Anthony J. L., MA Oxf., DPhil
Oxf.   Prof.

Nursing, see Medicine, Health and Biological
Sciences, below

Nutrition, see Medicine, Health and
Biological Sciences (Biol. Scis., Sch. of),
below

Ocean and Earth Science, School of, see
also Southampton Oceanog. Centre

Tel: (01703) 592011 Fax: (01703) 593052
Beattie, Ian R., MA Oxf., PhD Lond., DSc
Lond.   Res. Prof.†, Geochemistry
Collins, M. B., BSc CNAA, DPhil Sus., DSc,
FGS   Prof., Sediment Dynamics
Foster, Robert P., BSc Durh., PhD Manc.,
FGS   Reader
Hamilton, Norman, BSc Brist., PhD Birm.,
FGS   Prof.
Holligan, Patrick M., MA Camb., PhD
Leeds   Prof., Oceanography; Head*
House, Michael R., MA Camb., MA Oxf., PhD
Durh., DSc Oxf., FGS   Prof.†
Jenkins, William   Chemical Oceanography
Kemp, Alan E. S., BA Cant.CCC, PhD
Edin.   Reader, Marine Geology
Marshall, John E. A., BA Camb., PhD Brist.,
FGS   Sr. Lectr.
Murray, John W., BSc Lond., PhD Lond., DSc
Lond., FGS   Prof.
Nesbitt, Robert W., BSc Durh., PhD Durh., FGS,
FGSA   Prof.; Head*

Richards, K. J., MSc Exe., PhD   Sr. Lectr.,
    Physical Oceanography
Roberts, Stephen, BSc Wales, PhD Open(UK),
    FGS   Sr. Lectr.
Robinson, I. S., MA Camb., PhD
    Warw.   Reader, Satellite Oceanography
Sanderson, David J., BSc Newcastle(UK), PhD
    Newcastle(UK)   Prof., Geophysics
Sheader, Martin, BSc Newcastle(UK), PhD
    Newcastle(UK)   Sr. Lectr., Marine Biology
Statham, Peter J., BSc Nott., PhD S'ton.   Sr.
    Lectr., Chemical Oceanography
Stow, Dorrik A. V., MA Camb., PhD Dal.,
    FGS   Reader
Thorpe, S. A., BSc Lond., BA Camb., PhD Camb.,
    FRS   Prof., Oceanography
Tyler, P. A., BSc Wales, PhD Wales, DSc   Prof.,
    Marine Ecology

Philosophy

Tel: (01703) 593400 Fax: (01703) 593344

Collier, Andrew S., BA Lond., MPhil
    Lond.   Reader
Monk, Ray, BA York(UK), BLitt Oxf.   Sr. Lectr.
Palmer, Anthony, BA Hull, BPhil Oxf.   Prof.;
    Head*

Physics and Astronomy

Tel: (01703) 592093 Fax: (01703) 593910

Barnes, K. J., BSc Lond., PhD Lond., FIP   Prof.
Blott, B. H., BSc Lond., PhD S'ton.   Sr. Lectr.
Coe, M. J., BSc Lond., PhD Lond.   Sr. Lectr.
Coles, H. J., BSc Lond., PhD Brun., DSc Manc.,
    FIP   Prof.
Daniell, G. J., MA Camb., PhD Camb.   Sr. Lectr.
de Groot, P. A. J., MSc T.H.Delft, PhD
    Leuven   Reader
Dean, A. J., BSc S'ton., PhD S'ton.   Prof.
del Moral, A., PhD Saragossa   Visiting Prof.
Eason, R. W., BSc Lond., DPhil York(UK)   Sr.
    Lectr.
Ellwood, D. C., BSc PhD   Prof.†
Hanna, D. C., BA Camb., PhD, FIP   Prof.
Harley, R. T., MA Oxf., DPhil Oxf.   Reader
King, S. F., BSc Leeds, PhD Manc.   Sr. Lectr.
Lanchester, P. C., BSc Monash, PhD Monash   Sr.
    Lectr.
Lockwood, M., BSc Exe., PhD Exe.   Visiting
    Prof.
McHardy, I. H., BSc Lond., PhD Camb.   Sr.
    Lectr.
Newman, D. J., BSc Lond., PhD Lond., FIP   Res.
    Prof.†
Rainford, B. D., MA Oxf., DPhil Oxf.   Prof.
Ramsden, D., BSc Birm., PhD Birm.   Sr. Lectr.
Rees, M. H., BSc Colorado, PhD
    Colorado   Visiting Prof.
Ross, D. A., BA Oxf., DPhil Oxf., FIP   Prof.
Ross, K. J., BSc S'ton., PhD S'ton.   Reader
Sachrajda, C. T. C., BSc Sus., PhD Lond., FIP,
    FRS   Prof.; Head*
Tropper, A. C., MA Oxf., DPhil Oxf.   Reader
Watson, J. H. P., BSc Liv., PhD Tor.   Prof.
Zheludev, N. I., BSc Moscow, PhD Moscow, DSc
    Moscow   Reader

Politics

Tel: (01703) 592511 Fax: (01703) 593276

Brown, Chris, BSc(Econ) Lond., PhD Kent   Prof.
Calvert, Peter A. R., MA Camb., AM Mich., PhD
    Camb., FRHistS   Prof.
Gregory, Frank E. C., BA Brist.,
    MSc(SocialSciences)   Sr. Lectr.
Hill, Dilys M., BA Leeds, PhD Leeds   Prof.
Lovenduski, Joni, BA Manc., MA Manc., PhD
    Lough.   Prof.; Head*
Plant, Raymond, BA Lond., MA Oxf., PhD Hull,
    DLit Lond., DLitt Hull   Prof.†
Simpson, John, MSc(Econ) Lond., PhD   Prof.
Thomas, Caroline, BSc(Econ) Lond., PhD
    Lond.   Prof.
Other Staff: 7 Lectrs.; 2 Res. Fellows; 2 Temp.
    Lectrs.
Research: comparative politics and public policy;
    international relations; political theory;
    security studies

Portuguese, see Spanish, Portuguese and
    Latin American Studies under Mod. Langs.,
    Sch. of

Psychology

Tel: (01703) 592619 Fax: (01703) 594597

Gale, M. A., BA Exe., PhD Exe., FBPsS   Emer.
    Prof.
Harnad, Stevan, BA McG., MA McG., MA Prin.,
    PhD Prin.   Prof.
Ingham, R., BSc Lond., DPhil Oxf.   Reader
Remington, Bob, BSc Exe., PhD Exe.,
    FBPsS   Prof.
Sonuga-Barke, E., BSc Wales, PhD Exe.   Prof.;
    Head*
Stevenson, J., BA Oxf., MSc Sus., PhD Sur.   Prof.
Stratford, R. J., BA Sheff., PhD, FBPsS   Sr. Lectr.
Trasler, G. B., MA Exe., BSc(Econ) Lond., PhD
    Lond., FBPsS   Emer. Prof.

Ship Science

Tel: (01703) 592316 Fax: (01703) 593299

Goodrich, G. J., BSc Durh.   Emer. Prof.
Molland, A. F., BSc Durh., MSc Newcastle(UK),
    PhD   Sr. Lectr.
Price, W. G., BSc Wales, PhD Wales, DSc Lond.,
    FEng, FRS   Prof.; Head*
Shenoi, R. A., BTech Kharagpur, PhD
    Strath.   Reader
Temarel, P., MSc Lond., PhD Lond.   Vosper
    Thornycroft Sr. Lectr.
Wellicome, J. F., BSc Durh., PhD
    Newcastle(UK)   Sr. Lectr.
Wilson, P. A., BSc Leic.   Sr. Lectr.
Xing, J. T., MEngSc Tsing Hua,
    DEngSc   Visiting Res. Prof.

Social Statistics

Tel: (01703) 592527 Fax: (01703) 593846

Chambers, R., BSc W.Aust., MSc ANU, PhD Johns
    H.   Prof.
Cooper, P. J., BSocSc Birm., MSc Reading   Sr.
    Lectr.
Diamond, I. D., BSc(Econ) Lond., MSc Lond.,
    PhD St And.   Prof.
Hinde, P. R. A., MA Camb., PhD Sheff.   Sr.
    Lectr.
McDonald, J. W., MA Calif., PhD Seattle   Sr.
    Lectr.
Ní Bhrolcháin, Máire, BA Trinity(Dub.), MSc
    Trinity(Dub.), PhD Lond.   Sr. Lectr.
Skinner, C. J., BA Camb., MSc Lond., PhD
    S'ton.   Prof.; Head*

Social Work Studies

Tel: (01703) 592575 Fax: (01703) 581156

Bagley, Chris, MA Oxf., MEd Lond., DPhil
    Sus.   Prof.
Dominelli, Lena, MA Sus., DPhil Sus.,
    BA   Prof.
Glastonbury, Bryan, MA Oxf.   Res. Prof.
Orme, Joan, BA Sheff.   Reader
Powell, Jackie, MA Oxf.   Sr. Lectr.; Head*
Pritchard, Colin, MA Brad., PhD S'ton.   Prof.
Vacant Posts: 1 Sr. Lectr.

Sociology and Social Policy

Tel: (01703) 592558 Fax: (01703) 593859

Allan, G. A., BA Essex, PhD Essex, MA
    McM.   Reader
Lawson, R. J., MA Oxf.   Sr. Lectr.; Head*
Rees, A. M., BA Camb.   Sr. Lectr.
Solomos, J., BA Sus., DPhil Sus.   Prof.
Ungerson, C., BA Oxf., MSc Lond., PhD
    Kent   Prof.
Other Staff: 6 Lectrs.; 3 Res. Fellows

Sound and Vibration Research, Institute of

Tel: (01703) 592294 Fax: (01703) 593190

Davies, Peter O. A. L., BE Syd., PhD
    Cant.   Emer. Prof.
Elliott, Stephen J., BSc Sur., PhD Sur.   Prof.,
    Adaptive Systems
Fahy, Francis J., BSc Lond., PhD   Emer. Prof.,
    Engineering Acoustics

Fisher, Michael J., BSc Reading, PhD
    Reading   Rolls Royce Reader
Griffin, Michael J., BSc PhD   Prof., Human
    Factors
Hammond, Joseph K., BSc PhD   Prof., Signal
    Analysis; Dir.*
Leighton, Timothy G., MA PhD   Reader
Lutman, Mark E., BSc S'ton., PhD S'ton.   Prof.,
    Audiology
Morfey, Christopher L., BA Camb., MSc
    PhD   Prof., Biomechanics
Nelson, Philip A., BSc PhD   Prof., Acoustics
Petyt, Maurice, MSc Hull, PhD   Prof.,
    Structural Dynamics
Pinnington, Roger J., MSc PhD   Sr. Lectr.
Rice, Christopher G., MSc Lond., Hon.
    MD   Prof., Subjective Acoustics
Robinson, Douglas W., BSc Lond., BSc(Eng)
    Hon. DSc   Res. Prof.†
Walker, John G., BSc Lond., PhD   Sr. Lectr.

Southampton Oceanography Centre

Tel: (01703) 595106 Fax: (01703) 595107

Shepherd, J. G., BA PhD   Prof., Marine
    Sciences; Dir.*

Challenger Division for Seafloor Processes

Tel: (01703) 596555 Fax: (01703) 596554

Weaver, P. P. E., BSc PhD, FGS   Sr. Principal
    Scientist; Head of Div.*

George Deacon Division for Ocean Processes

Tel: (01703) 596015 Fax: (01703) 596382

Roe, H. S. J., BSc   Sr. Principal Scientist; Head
    of Div.*

James Rennel Division

Tel: (01703) 596434 Fax: (01703) 596204

Guymer, T. H., BSc MSc   Sr. Principal
    Scientist; Head of Div.*

Ocean Technology Division

Tel: (01703) 596097 Fax: (01703) 596149

Griffiths, G., BA MSc   Sr. Principal Scientist;
    Head of Div.*

Research Vessel Services

Tel: (01703) 596012 Fax: (01703) 596295

Fay, C. W., BA MSc PhD   Superintendent,
    RVS; Head of Div.*

Spanish, see under Mod. Langs., Sch. of

Teaching Support and Media Services

Tel: (01703) 593785 Fax: (01703) 593005

Mathias, Haydn S., BSc Sus., DPhil Sus.   Dir.*

Textiles, see Winchester School of Art

Theology and Religion, School of

Tel: (01703) 228761 Fax: (01703) 230944

No staff at present

Winchester School of Art, see below

MEDICINE, HEALTH AND BIOLOGICAL SCIENCES

Biological Sciences, School of

Tel: (01703) 594338 Fax: (01703) 594338

Biochemistry and Molecular Biology

Fax: (01703) 594459

Akhtar, M., MSc Punjab, PhD Lond., FRS   Prof.
Anthony, C., PhD Reading, DSc Reading   Prof.
East, J. M., BSc CNAA, PhD Open(UK)   Sr. Lectr.
Fox, K. R., MA Camb., PhD Camb.   Reader
Giles, I. G., BSc S'ton., PhD S'ton.   Sr. Lectr.
Gore, M. G., BSc Wales, PhD E.Anglia   Sr. Lectr.
Lee, A. G., MA Camb., PhD Camb.   Prof.;
    Head*
O'Connor, D., MSc Lond., PhD Liv.   Sr. Lectr.
Sale, G. J., BSc S'ton., PhD S'ton.   Sr. Lectr.
Shoolingin-Jordan, P. M., PhD S'ton.,
    FRSChem   Prof.; Head of Sch.
Wilton, D. C., BSc S'ton., PhD S'ton.   Sr. Lectr.
Wood, S. P., BSc Wales, DPhil Sus.   Reader
Other Staff: 1 Sr. Lectr.†

Biodiversity and Ecology

Tel: (01703) 594397 Fax: (01703) 594269

Allen, J. A., BSc Edin., PhD Edin. Sr. Lectr.
Hawkins, Stephen J., BSc Liv., PhD Liv. Prof., Environmental Biology; Head*
Howse, P. E., PhD Lond., DSc Lond. Reader
Maclean, N., BSc Edin., PhD Edin., FIBiol Prof.†
Sleigh, M. A., PhD Brist., DSc Brist., FIBiol Prof.†

Cell Sciences

Tel: (01703) 594431 Fax: (01703) 594319

Chad, J. E., BSc S'ton., PhD S'ton. Sr. Lectr.
Chapman, B. J., BSc S'ton., PhD S'ton. Sr. Lectr.
Fleming, T. P., BSc Wales, PhD CNAA Sr. Lectr.; Head*
Hall, J. L., BSc Lond., DPhil Oxf. Prof.
Holden-Dye, L. M., BSc Wales, PhD S'ton. Sr. Lectr.
Maclean, N., BSc Edin., PhD Edin. Prof.
Morris, D. A., BSc Reading, PhD Nott., DSc Nott. Reader
Noble, A. R., BSc S'ton., PhD S'ton. Sr. Lectr.
Perry, V. H., BA Oxf., MA Oxf., DPhil Oxf. Prof.
Walker, R. J., PhD S'ton., DSc, FIBiol Prof.
Warner, Jane A., BSc Lond., PhD Lond. Sr. Lectr.
Wheal, H. V., BSc S'ton., PhD S'ton. Prof.
Wild, A. E., BSc Manc., PhD Wales Sr. Lectr.
Other Staff: 9 Lectrs.; 16 Res. Fellows

Human Nutrition, Institute of

Tel: (01703) 594302 Fax: (01703) 594383

Forrester, T., MSc Lond. Visiting Prof.
Grimble, R. F., BSc Wales, PhD Wales Prof.
Jackson, A. A., BA Camb., MB BChir Camb., MD Camb., FRCP Prof.; Head*
Wiseman, M. J., MB BS Lond. Visiting Prof.
Other Staff: 2 Lectrs.; 4 Res. Fellows
Research: dietary lipids and immunity; energy and substrate metabolism; nutrition and inflammation; programming metabolic capacity in fetal life

Medicine, School of

Tel: (01703) 796581 Fax: (01703) 786933

Anaesthetics

Tel: (01703) 796137 Fax: (01703) 794348

Norman, J., MB ChB Leeds, PhD Leeds, FRCA Prof.
Smith, D., BM BS Nott., MD Nott., FRCA Sr. Lectr.

Child Health

Tel: (01703) 796160 Fax: (01703) 796378

Clough, J. B. Sr. Lectr., Paediatric Respiratory Medicine
Kohler, Janice A., MB ChB Brist. Sr. Lectr., Paediatric Oncology
Radford, M., MD Lond., FRCP Sr. Lectr.
Warner, J. A. Sr. Lectr., Allergy and Immunology
Warner, J. O., MD Sheff., FRCP Prof.; Head*

Clinical Neurological Sciences

Tel: (01703) 796617 Fax: (01703) 704236

Desai, Parul, PhD Lond., FRCS Sr. Lectr.
Elkington, Andrew R., CBE, MA Camb., MB BChir Camb., FRCS Prof.
Gray, William P., MD N.U.I., FRCSEd Sr. Lectr.
Iannotti, Fausto, MD Naples, FRCSEd Prof.; Head*
Lees, Peter D., MB ChB Manc., MS S'ton., FRCS Sr. Lectr.
Sedgwick, E. Michael, BSc Brist., MB ChB Brist., MD Brist., FRCP Prof.
Sundstrom, Lars E., BA Oxf., DPhil Oxf. Sr. Lectr.
Other Staff: 1 Lectr.; 3 Postdoctoral Res. Fellows; 3 Res. Fellows; 1 Hon. Reader; 3 Hon. Lectrs.; 1 Hon. Visiting Clin. Sr. Lectr.
Research: aetiological and applied epidemiological research on ageing, cataract, glaucoma and diabetic eye disease, maculopathy; audiology (otoacoustic emissions, MLS, Volterra kernels); cognitive mechanisms; mechanisms of brain damage and brain protection; neurophysiology of human spinal cord and somatosensory system

Geriatric Medicine

Tel: (01703) 796134 Fax: (01703) 796134

Anderson, Frazer H., MB ChB Edin. Sr. Lectr.
Briggs, R. S. J., MB BS Lond., MSc Lond., FRCP Prof.; Head*
Coleman, P. G., MA Oxf., PhD Lond., FBPsS Prof., Psychogerontology
Steiner, Andrea C., AB Brown, MSc S.Calif., PhD RAND Policy Stud. Sr. Lectr.

Human Genetics, Wessex Institute of

Tel: (01703) 796421 Fax: (01703) 794264

Day, I. M. H., MB BChir MA PhD Prof.
Dennis, Nick R., MB BChir Camb., FRCP Sr. Lectr.
Jacobs, Patricia A., DSc St And. Hon. Prof.; Head*
Morton, Newton E., PhD Wis. Hon. Prof. Res. Fellow
Thompson, R. J., MA Camb., MB BChir Camb., PhD Camb., FRCPath Prof.
Other Staff: 2 Lectrs.; 3 Res. Fellows; 12 Hon. Res. Fellows

Human Morphology

Tel: (01703) 594231 Fax: (01703) 594433

Collins, Patricia, BSc Sur., PhD Camb. Sr. Lectr.
Mitchell, John, DPhil Sus. Sr. Lectr.; Head*
Peel, Sandra, BSc Manc., PhD Leeds, DSc Leeds Reader
Other Staff: 3 Lectrs.; 1 Res. Fellow
Research: neuroscience: peptitudes in epilepsy; reproductive biology: metrial gland cells

Immunochemistry

Tel: (01703) 796590 Fax: (01703) 704061

Glennie, M. J., BSc PhD Reader
Hamblin, T. J., MB ChB Brist. Prof., Immunohaematology
Smith, J. L., PhD, FRCPath Visiting Sr. Lectr.
Stevenson, F. K., MSc DPhil, FRCPath Reader
Stevenson, G. T., MD Syd., DPhil Oxf., FRCPath Prof.; Dir., Tenovus Res. Lab.; Head*

Medical Education Development Unit

Tel: (01703) 594557 Fax: (01703) 594159

Millard, Lesley, BSc S'ton., MBA Open(UK)

Medical Oncology

Tel: (01703) 796184 Fax: (01703) 783839

Johnson, P. W. M., MA Camb., MD Camb. Prof.; Head*
Simmonds, P. D., MB BS, FRACP Sr. Lectr.
Sweetenham, J. W., BSc Lond., DM, FRCP Leukaemia Res. Fund Sr. Lectr.

Medical Statistics and Computing

Tel: (01703) 796566 Fax: (01703) 794460

Bryant, T. N., BSc Brist., PhD Brist. Sr. Lectr.; Head*
Other Staff: 1 Sr. Res. Fellow

Medicine

Tel: (01703) 796886 Fax: (01703) 794154

Arthur, Michael J. P., DM S'ton., FRCP Prof.; Head*
Djukanovic, Ratko, MSc Belgrade, MD Belgrade Sr. Lectr.
Frew, Anthony, MA Camb., MD Camb. Sr. Lectr.
Friedmann, Peter S., MD Camb., FRCP Prof., Dermatology
Holgate, Stephen T., BSc Lond., MD Lond., DSc Lond., FRCP Prof., Immunopharmacology
Howarth, Peter H., BSc Lond., MB BS Lond., DM, FRCP Sr. Lectr.
Johnston, Sebastian, MB Lond. Sr. Lectr.
Patel, Rajul, MB ChB Sheff. Sr. Lectr., Venereology

Roberts, Kevan, BSc Manc., PhD Manc. Sr. Lectr.
Rosenberg, William M. C., MB BS Lond., MA Camb., DPhil Oxf. Sr. Lectr.
Sheron, Nicholas, MD Sheff., FRCP Sr. Lectr.
Smith, Colin L., BSc Leeds, MB ChB Leeds, MD Leeds, FRCP Sr. Lectr.
Walls, Andrew F., BSc Aberd., PhD Lond. Sr. Lectr.
Other Staff: 1 Sr. Fellow

Microbiology

Tel: (01703) 796995 Fax: (01703) 774316

Clarke, I. N., BSc Leeds, PhD Warw. Reader
Heckels, J. E., BSc Newcastle(UK), PhD Newcastle(UK) Prof.
Ward, M. E., BSc Lond., PhD Lond. Prof.
Watt, P. J., MB BS Lond., MD Lond. Prof.; Head*

Obstetrics and Gynaecology

Tel: (01703) 796033 Fax: (01703) 786933

Stones, R. William, MB BS Lond., MD Lond. Sr. Lectr.
Thomas, Eric J., MB BS Newcastle(UK), MD Newcastle(UK) Prof.; Head; Head of Sch.*
Wheeler, Timothy, MA Oxf., BM BCh Oxf., DM Oxf., FRCOG Reader
Other Staff: 1 Lectr.
Research: determinants of fetal growth; endometrial proliferation and differentiation; the follicle and corpus luteum; gynaecological cancer

Orthopaedics

Tel: (01703) 796140

Clarke, Nicholas M. P., MB ChB Brist., ChM Brist., FRCS, FRCSEd Sr. Lectr.; Head*
Other Staff: 1 Hon. Sr. Lectr.†
Research: biology of skeletal cells: chonrocyte differentiation and apoptosis; development dysplasia of the hip: diagnosis, treatment and basic science; leg and foot pathology: gait and biomechanics; talipes (club foot): treatment, development of

Pathology

Tel: (01703) 796663 Fax: (01703) 796603

Du Boulay, Claire E. H., DM, FRCPath Sr. Lectr.
Ellison, D. W., MB BChir Camb., MD Camb., MA Oxf., MSc Lond., PhD S'ton. Sr. Lectr.
Flavell, D., BSc Liv., PhD Sheff. Sr. Lectr.
Gallagher, P. J., MB BS Lond., MD Lond., PhD, FRCPath Reader
Jones, D. B., BSc Durh., PhD Birm. Reader
Provan, A. B., BSc Leic., MB ChB Leic., DM S'ton. Sr. Lectr., Haematology
Roche, W. R., MB ChB BAO N.U.I., BSc N.U.I., MD N.U.I., FRCPath Prof.; Head*
Weller, R. O., BSc Lond., MB BS Lond., MD Lond., PhD Lond., FRCPath Prof., Neuropathology
Wilkins, Bridget S., BM BCh DM Sr. Lectr.

Pharmacology/Clinical Pharmacology

Tel: (01703) 594261 Fax: (01703) 594262

Church, M. K., MPharm Wales, PhD CNAA, DSc S'ton. Prof.
George, C. F., BSc Birm., MD Birm., FRCP Prof.
Hillier, K., BSc Lond., PhD Lond., DSc Lond. Sr. Lectr.
Renwick, A. G., BSc Lond., PhD Lond., DSc Lond. Prof.; Head*
Waller, D. G., BSc S'ton., DM S'ton., FRCP Sr. Lectr.
Research: cardiovascular therapeutics; dermal pharmacology (action and absorption); gastrointestinal pharmacology in humans; immunopharmacology; pharacokinetics/toxicokinetics

Primary Medical Care

Tel: (01703) 797700 Fax: (01703) 701125

Kendrick, Anthony, MB BS Lond., MD Lond., BSc, FRCGP Chair*
Mant, David, MA Camb., MSc Lond. Prof., Primary Care Epidemiology (on leave)

Smith, Helen E., BMedSci Nott., BM BS Nott., MSc Lond., DM Nott. Sr. Lectr.
Williamson, Ian G., MB ChB Edin., MD Edin., FRCSEd Sr. Lectr.
Other Staff: 2 Res. Fellows; 2 Sr. Lectrs.†; 1 Clin. Sci. Fellow (MRC)

Psychiatry

Tel: (01703) 825533 Fax: (01703) 234243

Baldwin, D., MB BS Lond. Sr. Lectr.
Peveler, R., BA Oxf., DPhil Oxf. Sr. Lectr.
Thompson, C., MB BS Lond., BSc Lond., MD Lond., MPhil Lond., FRCPsych, FRCP Prof.; Head*

Public Health Medicine

Tel: (01962) 863511 Fax: (01962) 877425

Gabbay, J., BSc Manc., MB ChB Manc., MSc Lond. Prof.; Head*
George, S. L., MB BS Lond., MSc Lond. Sr. Lectr.
Law, Catherine M., MB BS Lond. Sr. Lectr.
Margetts, B. M., BSc W.Aust., MSc Lond., PhD W.Aust. Sr. Lectr.
Milne, R., BA Oxf., MB BS Lond., MSc Lond. Sr. Lectr. ((seconded from Oxford Health Authority))
Roderick, P. J., BSc Camb., MB BS Lond., MSc Lond. Sr. Lectr.
Speller, V., BSc Manc., PhD Manc. Sr. Lectr.
Stein, K. W. T., MB ChB Brist., MSc Lond. Sr. Lectr.
Waters, W. E., MB BS Lond. Emer. Prof.
Research: health promotion; health sevices research; health technology assessments

Rehabilitation

Tel: (01703) 796466 Fax: (01703) 794943

Ashburn, A., MPhil PhD Sr. Lectr., Rehabilitation and Research; Co-ordinator, MSc
McLellan, D. L., MA Camb., MB BChir Camb., PhD Glas., FRCP Europe Prof., Rehabilitation; Head*
Smith, D., MB ChB Birm., FRCP, FRACP Prof.†
Wilson, B. A., OBE, PhD, FBPsS Visiting Prof.†
Other Staff: 1 Lectr.
Research: acquisition of motor skills and balance; assessment, prediction of outcome and treatment of severe acquired brain injury; rehabilitiation needs of disabled people living at home

Renal Medicine

Tel: (01705) 866130 Fax: (01705) 866108

Millar, J. G. B., BA Camb., MB BChir Camb., MSc Lond. Sr. Lectr., Endocrinology; Head*
Venkat Raman, G., MB BS Poona, MD Delhi Sr. Lectr., Nephrology

Surgery

Tel: (01703) 796145 Fax: (01703) 794020

Griffiths, M., MS, FRCS Sr. Lectr., Paediatric Surgery
Johnson, C. D., MChir Camb., FRCS Sr. Lectr.
Karran, S. J., MA Camb., MB BChir Camb., MChir Camb., FRCS, FRCSEd Reader
Primrose, J. N., MD Glas., MB ChB, FRCS Prof.; Head*
von Haake, N., MB BS Lond., FRCS Sr. Lectr., New Testament

Nursing and Midwifery, School of

Tel: (01703) 796549 Fax: (01703) 796922

Brooking, Julia I., BSc CNAA, PhD Lond. Dir., Res.
Glasper, E. Alan, BA CNAA, PhD Prof.
Hulbert, Patricia, MAEd Teaching Fellow; Dir., Academic Affairs
Kennerley, Dorothy, MA Dir., Post-Registration Studies
Long, Garth, BEd MAEd Lectr.; Dir., Mental Health and Learning Disability Studies
Smith, Barbara M., MSc Head*
Wright, Stephen G., MBE, MSc Manc. Visiting Prof.

Occupational Therapy and Physiotherapy, School of

Tel: (01703) 595260 Fax: (01703) 595301

Barnitt, Rosemary, MSc Lond., PhD Lond. Reader, Occupational Therapy
Kitsell, Fleur, MSc S'ton. Sr. Lectr., Physiotherapy; Head*

Other Appointments

Faculty Appointments

Tel: (01703) 796583 Fax: (01703) 794760

Hillier, E. R., MB BS Lond., MD Lond. Sr. Lectr., Palliative Medicine
Platt, H. S., BSc Lond., MD, FRCPath Regional Postgrad. Dean of Med. Studies
Reed, R., FDSRCS Dent. Dean

NEW COLLEGE

Tel: (01703) 216200 Fax: (01703) 230944

Clark, J. W., BA Birm., DrPhil Bremen Prof.; Dir.*

Culture and Language, School of

Dunn, D., BA Keele, PhD Lond. Principal Lectr.
Jones, W. R., BA S'ton., PhD S'ton. Sr. Lectr.
Smith, A., BA Kent, PhD Kent Principal Lectr.

Science, Health and Technology, School of

Potter, M., BA Open(UK), MSc Principal Lectr.
Shephard, K., BSc Reading, PhD Reading Principal Lectr.

Social and Policy Studies, School of

Graham, D., BA Leic., MA Hull Principal Lectr.
Ogles, M., BA Sus., PhD S'ton. Principal Lectr.

WINCHESTER SCHOOL OF ART

Constituent Institution

Tel: (01962) 842500 Fax: (01962) 842496

Crouan, Katharine, BA Reading Prof.; Head of Sch.

Design

Pilgrim, Peter, MDes RCA Prof.; Head*

Fine Art

Fax: (01703) 869968

Cooper, Stephen, BA CNAA, MA RCA
Ferry, David, BA CNAA Sr. Lectr.; Head*
Gibbons, John, BA CNAA Prof.
Other Staff: 1 Lectr.

Foundation Studies

Naylor, Roy, BA CNAA Head*

History of Art and Design

Burman, Barbara, BA Essex, MA Lond., MA Sus. Head*
Taylor, Brandon, BA Brist., MLitt Edin., PhD Lond. Prof.

History of Textiles and Dress, Centre for the

Burman, Barbara, BA Essex, MA Lond., MA Sus. Dir.*

Textile Design, Centre for Research in

Pilgrim, Prof. Peter, MDes RCA Dir.*
Research: developing hand-woven products for the Western market in Assam, India

CONTACT OFFICERS

Academic affairs. Academic Registrar: Knight, R., MA Camb.
Accommodation. Accommodation Officer: Cliburn, M., BA Lampeter, MA Lampeter
Admissions (first degree). Senior Assistant Registrar: Rogers, C. J., BA Sus.

Admissions (higher degree). Senior Assistant Registrar: Rogers, C. J., BA Sus.
Adult/continuing education. Director, New College: Clark, Prof. J. W., BA Birm., DrPhil Bremen
Alumni. Alumni Officer: Impey, N., BSc S'ton.
Archives. Archivist and Head of Special Collections: Woolgar, C., BA S'ton., PhD Durh.
Careers. Director, Careers Advisory Service: Jones, G. R., BSc Lond.
Computing services. Director, Computing Services: Heard, K. S., MA Oxf., DPhil Oxf.
Conferences/corporate hospitality. Conference Manager: McGloin, Sue
Consultancy services. Director, Innovation and Research Support: Fox, D. P., BSc Durh., PhD Birm., DSc
Credit transfer. Assistant Registrar: Sweetman, M., BA Lond., MA CNAA
Development/fund-raising. Development Officer: Barker, P.., BSc(Eng) Lond.
Distance education. Director, New College: Clark, Prof. J. W., BA Birm., DrPhil Bremen
Equal opportunities. Equal Opportunities Officer: ......
Estates and buildings/works and services. Director, Estates and Buildings: Reynolds, P. C., BSc Manc., MSc
Examinations. Assistant Registrar: Mears, E. G., BA Lanc.
Finance. Director, Finance: Showell, C. R., BCom Birm.
General enquiries. Secretary and Registrar: Lauwerys, J. F. D., BEd Lond., MA Lond.
Health services. Partner, University Health Service: Wilson, Heather N., MB BS Lond., FFARCS
Industrial liaison. Director, Innovation and Research Support: Fox, D. P., BSc Durh., PhD Birm., DSc
International office. Administrative Officer: Nesbitt, J. L., BA Kent
Language training for international students. Director of Language Centre: Piper, A., BA Sus., MSc Edin.
Library (chief librarian). Librarian: Naylor, B., MA Oxf.
Library (enquiries). Assistant Librarian, Enquiry Service: Boagey, P. W., MSc Brist.
Minorities/disadvantaged groups. Equal Opportunities Officer: ......
Personnel/human resources. Director, Personnel Services: Strike, A. J., MSc Portsmouth
Public relations, information and marketing. Head, Public Affairs: Reader, P., BA Leeds
Publications. Head, Public Affairs: Reader, P., BA Leeds
Purchasing. Supplies Officer: White, I.
Quality assurance and accreditation. Assistant Registrar: Sweetman, M., BA Lond., MA CNAA
Research. Director, Innovation and Research Support: Fox, D. P., BSc Durh., PhD Birm., DSc
Safety. Safety Adviser: Booker, M. D., BSc Birm., MSc Lond.
Schools liaison. Assistant Registrar: Milln, A. S., BA Leeds
Security. Chief Security Officer: Owen, D. R., BA Open(UK)
Sport and recreation. Director, Physical Education: ......
Staff development and training. Training and Development Manager: Cooper, A., BSc CNAA
Student union. Permanent Secretary: Clegg, G. R.
Student welfare/counselling. Co-ordinator, Student Services: Green, R. J., BA S'ton., MA Leeds, PhD Warw.
Students from other countries. Adviser to International Students: Cooke, E. C., MSc Lond.
Students from other countries. Adviser to International Students: Trost, R. S., LLB Brist., DrenDroit Nancy

Students with disabilities. Adviser to Disabled Students: Price, G. A., BA *Newcastle(UK)*, MEd *CNAA*

Women. Equal Opportunities Officer: ......

[Information supplied by the institution as at 27 March 1998, and edited by the ACU]

STAFFORDSHIRE UNIVERSITY

Founded 1992; previously established as Staffordshire Polytechnic 1970

Member of the Association of Commonwealth Universities

Postal Address: College Road, Stoke-on-Trent, England ST4 2DE
Telephone: (01782) 294000 **Fax**: (01782) 744035 **E-mail**: postmaster@staffs.ac.uk
WWW: http://www.staffs.ac.uk **E-mail formula**: initial.surname@staffs.ac.uk

VICE-CHANCELLOR*—King, Prof. Christine E., BA *Birm.*, MA *Birm.*, PhD *CNAA*, FIM, FRHistS
UNIVERSITY SECRETARY‡—Sproston, Kenneth B. G.

UNIVERSITY OF STIRLING

Founded 1967

Member of the Association of Commonwealth Universities

Postal Address: Stirling, Scotland FK9 4LA
Telephone: (01786) 473171 **Fax**: (01786) 463000 **WWW**: http://www.stir.ac.uk
E-mail formula: forename.surname@stirling.ac.uk
(where only one forename) or initial.initial.initial.surname@stirling.ac.uk

CHANCELLOR—Rigg, Dame Diana
PRINCIPAL AND VICE-CHANCELLOR*—Miller, Prof. Andrew, BSc *Edin.*, MA *Oxf.*, PhD *Edin.*, FRSEd
SENIOR DEPUTY PRINCIPAL—Jackson, Prof. M. P., JP, MA *Hull*
DEPUTY PRINCIPAL—Brown, Prof. S. A., BSc *Lond.*, MA *Smith*, PhD *Stir.*
DEPUTY PRINCIPAL—Bruce, Prof. V. G., OBE, MA *Camb.*, PhD *Camb.*, FBPsS
SECRETARY—Clarke, Kevin J., BA *Stir.*
DEPUTY SECRETARY—Farrington, Dennis J., BSc *Kent*, LLB *Lond.*, LLM *Hull*, DPhil *Ulster*
ACADEMIC REGISTRAR—Wood, Douglas G., BSc *Edin.*
DIRECTOR OF INFORMATION SERVICES AND LIBRARIAN—Kemp, P., MA *Camb.*, PhD *Camb.*

FACULTIES/SCHOOLS

Arts
Tel: (01786) 467490 Fax: (01786) 451335
Head: Izod, John K., BA *Leeds*, PhD *Leeds*
Secretary: Fairbrother, J.

Human Sciences
Tel: (01786) 467595 Fax: (01786) 467641
Head: Watt, Prof. Roger J., BA *Camb.*, PhD *Keele*, FRSEd
Secretary: Campbell, P. S.

Management
Tel: (01786) 467278 Fax: (01786) 467279
Head: Sparks, Prof. Leigh, MA *Camb.*, PhD *Wales*
Secretary: Bruce, M.

Natural Sciences
Tel: (01786) 467750 Fax: (01786) 466896
Head: Ross, Lindsay G., BSc *CNAA*, PhD *Stir.*

Secretary: Burnett, M. A.

ACADEMIC UNITS

Academic Innovation and Continuing Education, Division of
Tel: (01786) 467940 Fax: (01786) 463398
Osborne, M. J., BSc *Reading*, PhD *Lond.* Sr. Lectr.; Acting Head*
Other Staff: 5 Lectrs.; 1 Hon. Prof.

Accountancy and Finance
Tel: (01786) 467280, 467282 Fax: (01786) 467308
Beattie, V. A., MA *St And.*, PhD *S'ton* Prof.
Goodacre, A., PhD *Exe.* Sr. Lectr.
Limmack, R. J., MBA *Liv.*, FCA Prof.
Little, G., LLB *Edin.*, PhD *Edin.* Sr. Lectr.
McInnes, W. M., MS *Durh.*, PhD *Glas.* Prof.; Head*
Morris, P. E., LLB *C.Lancs.*, LLM *Camb.*, MPhil *Camb.* Sr. Lectr.
Pratt, K. C., BCom *Edin.*, MBA *Calif.* Sr. Lectr.

Stopforth, D. P., PhD *Glas.* Prof.
Other Staff: 10 Lectrs.
Research: auditing; business law; financial reporting and finance; taxation

Applied Social Science
Tel: (01786) 467691 Fax: (01786) 467689
Bowes, A. M., BA *Durh.*, PhD *Durh.*, FRAI Sr. Lectr.
Clasen, J., PhD *Edin.* Sr. Lectr.
Erskine, A., MA *Edin.*, PhD *Edin.* Sr. Lectr.
Hallett, C. M., MA *Camb.*, PhD *Lough.* Prof.; Head*
Robertson, D. S., MA *Aberd.*, PhD *Glas.* Sr. Lectr.
Rowlings, C., BA *York(UK)* Prof.; Dir., Soc. Work Educn.
Scott, S. J., BSc *CNAA*, MA *Manc.* Prof.
Sim, D. F., BA *Sheff.*, PhD *Glas.* Sr. Lectr.
Tester, S., BA *Leic.*, MSc *Sur.* Sr. Lectr.
Timms, D. W. G., BA *Camb.*, PhD *Camb.* Prof.
Turner, C., BA *Durh.*, PhD *Durh.* Prof.
Other Staff: 12 Lectrs.

Research: care and protection (children, young people); social care and health; social exclusion and marginalisation

Aquaculture, Institute of

Tel: (01786) 467878 *Fax*: (01786) 472133

Beveridge, M. C. M., BSc *Glas.*, PhD *Glas.* Sr. Lectr. (Res.)

Bromage, N. R., BSc *Leic.*, PhD *Leic.* Prof.

Inglis, V. B. M., BSc *Edin.*, PhD *Edin.* Sr. Lectr. (Res.)

McAndrew, B. J., BSc *Wales*, PhD *Wales* Sr. Lectr.

Muir, J. F., BSc *Edin.*, PhD *Strath.* Sr. Lectr.

Richards, R. H., MA *Camb.*, VetMB *Camb.*, PhD *Stir.* Prof.; Dir.*

Ross, Lindsay G., BSc *CNAA*, PhD *Stir.* Reader

Sommerville, C., BA PhD Reader

Wootten, R., BSc *Lond.*, BA *Open(UK)*, PhD *Lond.* Sr. Lectr.; Asst. Dir.

Other Staff: 4 Lectrs.; 11 Res. Fellows; 4 Res. Lectrs.; 2 Hon. Profs.; 3 Hon. Lectrs.

Research: aquaculture sytems; disease; environment; genetics and reproduction; nutrition

Biological and Molecular Sciences

Tel: (01786) 467755-6 *Fax*: (01786) 464994

Berry, A. J., BSc *Lond.*, PhD *Lond.* Sr. Lectr.

Bryant, D. M., BSc *Lond.*, PhD *Lond.* Prof.

Duncan, A. J., BSc *St And.*, MS *Stan.*, PhD *Stan.*, FRSEd Reader

Hudson, P. J., BSc *Leeds*, DPhil *Oxf.* Reader

McLusky, D. S., BSc *Aberd.*, PhD Sr. Lectr.; Head*

Newbery, D. M., BSc *Lond.*, PhD *Brist.* Sr. Lectr.

Price, N. C., MA *Oxf.*, DPhil *Oxf.* Prof.

Proctor, J., MA *Oxf.*, DPhil *Oxf.*, DSc *Oxf.* Prof.

Reid, J. S. G., BSc *Aberd.*, PhD *Aberd.* Prof.

Sargent, J. R., BSc *Aberd.*, PhD *Aberd.*, FIBiol, FRSEd Prof.

Sexton, R., BSc *Lond.*, DPhil *Sus.* Sr. Lectr.

Stevens, L., MA *Oxf.*, DPhil *Oxf.* Sr. Lectr.

Tytler, P., BSc *Aberd.*, PhD *Aberd.* Sr. Lectr.

Willmer, C. M., BSc *Lond.*, PhD *Lanc.* Sr. Lectr.

Woolsey, J. M., BSc *Belf.*, PhD *Belf.* Sr. Lectr.

Other Staff: 14 Lectrs.; 14 Res. Fellows; 3 Hon. Profs.; 3 Hon. Lectrs.; 2 Hon. Res. Fellows

Research: ecology and wildlife epidemiology; molecular life sciences

Computing Science and Mathematics

Tel: (01786) 467420 *Fax*: (01786) 464551

Bland, R., BA *Open(UK)*, MA *Edin.* Sr. Lectr.

Clark, R. G., BSc *St And.*, PhD *Dund.* Sr. Lectr.

Dearle, A., BSc *St And.*, PhD *St And.* Prof.

Greenman, J. V., BA *Camb.*, PhD *Camb.* Prof., Mathematics and its Applications

Rattray, C. M. I., BSc *Adel.*, MSc *Manc.*, FIMA Reader; Head*

Rowlinson, P., MA *Oxf.*, DPhil *Oxf.* Prof.

Smith, L. S., BSc *Glas.*, PhD *Glas.* Sr. Lectr.

Turner, K. J., BSc *Glas.*, PhD *Edin.* Prof.

Wilson, I. R., BA *Lond.*, MSc *Strath.* Sr. Lectr., Logic

Other Staff: 9 Lectrs.; 1 Teaching Fellow

Research: algebraic graph theory; applied artifical intelligence; mathematical ecology; neural computing; persistent systems

Economics

Tel: (01786) 467470 *Fax*: (01786) 467469

Bell, D. N. F., MA *Aberd.*, MSc *Lond.*, PhD *Strath.* Prof.

Dow, S. C., MA *St And.*, MA *Manit.*, PhD *Glas.* Prof.

Ghosh, D., MA *Calc.*, MSocSc *Birm.*, PhD Sr. Lectr.

Hanley, N. D., PhD *Newcastle(UK)*, BA Reader

Hart, Robert A., BA *Liv.*, MA *Liv.* Prof., Applied Economics

King, D. N., MA *Oxf.*, DPhil *York(UK)* Sr. Lectr.

Ma, Y., BSc *Xiamen*, PhD *Manc.* Reader

Ruffell, R. J., MA *Camb.*, PhD *Brist.* Sr. Lectr.; Head*

Shone, R., BSc *Hull*, MA *Essex* Sr. Lectr.

Wright, R. E., BA *W.Ont.*, MA *W.Ont.*, PhD *W.Ont.* Prof.

Other Staff: 2 Lectrs.; 1 Hon. Prof.; 1 Hon. Lectr.

Research: economic thought; finance; labour economics

Education

Tel: (01786) 467600 *Fax*: (01786) 467633

Brown, S. A., BSc *Lond.*, MA *Smith*, PhD Prof.

Cope, P. A., BSc *Aberd.*, PhD *Belf.* Sr. Lectr.

Inglis, W. F. J., BSc(Econ) *Lond.*, BA *Oxf.*, PhD *Stir.* Sr. Lectr.

Johnstone, R. M., BA *Lond.*, MA *Edin.* Prof.; Head*

Nixon, J., MA *Oxf.*, MA *Lond.*, PhD *E.Anglia* Prof.

Other Staff: 14 Lectrs.; 4 Res. Fellows

Research: curriculum, teaching and learning; policy into practice; practitioner thinking and development

English Language Teaching, Centre for

Tel: (01786) 467934 *Fax*: (01786) 463398

Vacant Posts: Dir.*; 1 Lectr.

English Studies

Tel: (01786) 467495 *Fax*: (01786) 466210

Butler, L. St. J., MA *Camb.*, PhD *Stir.* Sr. Lectr.

Drakakis, J., MA *Wales*, PhD *Leeds* Prof.

Karolyi, O. J., BMus *Lond.* Sr. Lectr.

Keeble, N. H., BA *Lampeter*, PhD *Oxf.*, DLitt *Stir.*, FRHistS Prof.; Head*

Mack, D. S., MA *Glas.*, PhD Reader

Macrae, A. D. F., MA *Edin.* Sr. Lectr.

McGowan, I. D., MA *Oxf.*, PhD *Stir.* Sr. Lectr.

Punter, D. G., MA *Camb.*, PhD *Camb.* Prof.

Royle, N. W. O., MA *Oxf.*, DPhil *Oxf.* Reader

Smith, A. M., MA *Birm.*, MLitt *Camb.* Sr. Lectr.

Smith, G. F., MA *Aberd.*, PhD *Camb.* Prof.

Sowerby, R. E., MA *Camb.*, PhD *Camb.* Sr. Lectr.

Watson, R. B., MA *Aberd.*, PhD *Camb.*, FRSEd Prof.

Other Staff: 8 Lectrs.; 3 Hon. Profs.

Research: computational and descriptive linguistics; early modern studies; modern writing; Scottish literature

Entrepreneurship

Tel: (01786) 467348 *Fax*: (01786) 450201

Westhead, P., BA *Wales*, PhD *Wales* Prof.; Head*

Other Staff: 1 Sr. Lectr.; 1 Sr. Teaching Fellow; 4 Teaching Fellows; 1 Hon. Prof.

Environmental Science

Tel: (01786) 467840 *Fax*: (01786) 467843

Davidson, D. A., BSc *Aberd.*, PhD *Sheff.*, FRSEd Prof.; Head*

Gilvear, D. J., BSc *S'ton.*, PhD *Lough.* Sr. Lectr.

Grieve, I. C., BSc *Glas.*, PhD *Brist.* Sr. Lectr.

Harrison, S. J., BSc *Wales*, PhD *Wales* Sr. Lectr.

Moffatt, I., BSc *CNAA*, MSc *Newcastle(UK)*, PhD *Newcastle(UK)* Sr. Lectr.

Smith, Keith, BA *Hull*, PhD *Hull*, FRSEd, FRMetS Prof.

Thomas, M. F., MA *Reading*, PhD *Lond.*, FGS, FRSEd Prof.

Tipping, R. M., BSc *Hull*, PhD *CNAA* Sr. Lectr.

Other Staff: 8 Lectrs.; 2 Res. Fellows; 3 Hon. Profs.; 2 Hon. Lectrs.; 5 Hon. Res. Fellows

Research: climatic and hydrological variability; land resources; landscape change

Film and Media Studies

Tel: (01786) 467520 *Fax*: (01786) 466855

Cormack, M. J., MA *Aberd.*, PhD *Stir.* Sr. Lectr.; Head*

Izod, John K., BA *Leeds*, PhD *Leeds* Sr. Lectr.

Kilborn, R. W., BA *Nott.*, MA *Lond.*, MPhil *Nott.* Sr. Lectr.

McNair, B., MA *Glas.*, MPhil *Glas.*, PhD *Glas.* Sr. Lectr.

Meech, P. H., BA *Wales*, MA *Manc.*, MA *Leic.* Sr. Lectr.

Schlesinger, P. R., BA *Oxf.*, PhD *Lond.* Prof.

Other Staff: 9 Lectrs.; 1 Sr. Teaching Fellow; 5 Teaching Fellows; 7 Hon. Profs.; 5 Hon. Lectrs.

Research: cultural policy; media and national identity; media systems; screen interpretation; sociology of journalism

Finance, see Accty. and Finance

French

Tel: (01786) 467530 *Fax*: (01786) 451335

Duncan, A. B., MA *Aberd.*, PhD *Aberd.* Sr. Lectr.; Head*

Kidd, W., MA *Glas.*, PhD *Stir.* Sr. Lectr.

Reynolds, S., BA *Oxf.*, MA *Sus.*, PhD *Paris* Prof.

Swift, B. C., MA *Manc.*, PhD *Aberd.* Sr. Lectr.

Other Staff: 5 Lectrs.

Research: twentieth-century France: culture, history, literature

German

Tel: (01786) 467547

Murdoch, B. O., BA *Exe.*, PhD *Camb.*, LittD Prof.

Thompson, B., BA *Lond.*, MA *McM.*, PhD *Lond.* Sr. Lectr.; Head*

Other Staff: 2 Lectrs.

Research: literary translations; mediaeval and modern literature and society

History

Tel: (01786) 467580 *Fax*: (01786) 467581

Bebbington, D. W., MA *Camb.*, PhD *Camb.*, FRHistS Reader

Hutchison, I. G. C., MA *Aberd.*, PhD *Edin.* Sr. Lectr.

Law, R. C. C., BA *Oxf.*, PhD *Birm.* Prof.

McCracken, K. John, MA *Camb.*, PhD *Camb.* Sr. Lectr.

McKean, R. B., MA *Glas.*, PhD *E.Anglia* Sr. Lectr.

Peden, G. C., MA *Dund.*, DPhil *Oxf.*, FRHistS Prof.; Head*

Stachura, P. D., MA *Glas.*, PhD *E.Anglia*, FRHistS Reader

Tranter, N. L., BA *Nott.*, PhD *Nott.* Sr. Lectr.

Other Staff: 8 Lectrs.; 1 Hon. Prof.; 2 Hon. Res. Fellows

Research: African history; British history; continental European history; Scottish history; social history

Japanese

Tel: (01786) 466080 *Fax*: (01786) 466088

Crump, J. D., BA *Sheff.*, BDS *Lond.*, PhD *Sheff.* Prof.; Head*

Reader, I., BA *Reading*, MA *Brist.*, PhD *Leeds* Reader

Other Staff: 4 Lectrs.

Research: culture and society; international relations; religion

Management and Organisation

Tel: (01786) 467311 *Fax*: (01786) 467329

Ball, R., MA *Oxf.*, MSc *Birm.*, PhD *Stir.* Sr. Lectr.; Acting Head*

Dalrymple, J. F., BA *Stir.*, PhD *Strath.* Sr. Lectr.

Edgar, D. L., BA *Stir.*, MSc *Stir.* Programme Dir.

Fincham, R., BSc *Exe.*, MA *Exe.*, PhD *Lond.* Sr. Lectr.

Hughes, M. D., BTech *Brun.* Prof., Management

Jackson, M. P., BA *Hull*, MA *Hull* Prof., Human Resources Management

Other Staff: 14 Lectrs.; 3 Teaching Fellows; 2 Hon. Profs.; 1 Hon. Lectr.

Research: human resource management; organisational management and change; public sector management

Marketing

Tel: (01786) 467380 *Fax*: (01786) 467745

Brownlie, D. B. T., BA *Strath.* Reader

Burt, S. L., BA *Oxf.*, PhD *Stir.* Sr. Lectr.

Hart, S. J., BA *Strath.*, PhD *Strath.* Prof.

Kent, R. A., BSc *S'ton.*, MA *Essex*, MSc *Strath.* Sr. Lectr.

Saren, M. A. J., BA H-W, PhD Bath Prof.
Sparks, Leigh, MA Camb., PhD Wales Prof.
Young, J. A., BSc Aberd., PhD CNAA Sr. Lectr.;
  Head*
Other Staff: 7 Lectrs.; 1 Teaching Fellow; 1
  Res. Fellow
Research: consumer, social and macromarketing;
  innovation; internationalisation

Retail Studies, Institute for

Tel: (01786) 467386 Fax: (01786) 465290

Fernie, J., MA Dund., MBA Brad., PhD
  Edin. Dir.*
Freathy, J. P., MA Warw. Sr. Lectr.
Other Staff: 2 Lectrs.

Mathematics, see Computing Sci. and Maths.

Media Studies, see Film and Media Studies

Nursing and Midwifery

Farmer, E. S., PhD Edin. Sr. Lectr.
Murphy-Black, T., MSc Manc., PhD Manc. Prof.
Niven, C. A., BSc Stir., PhD Stir. Prof.; Head*
Reynolds, W. J., MPhil CNAA Sr. Lectr.
Scott, P. A., BA Edin., MSc Edin., PhD Glas. Sr.
  Lectr.
Other Staff: 6 Lectrs.; 6 Sr. Teaching Fellows;
  54 Teaching Fellows; 1 Hon. Prof.
Research: health care ethics; pain

Philosophy

Tel: (01786) 467555

Duff, R. A., BA Oxf. Prof.
Marshall, S. E., BA Wales Lectr.; Head*
Millar, A., MA Edin., PhD Camb. Prof.
Travis, C., MA Calif., PhD Calif. Prof.
Other Staff: 5 Lectrs.
Research: history of philosophy; legal, moral and
  social philosophy; philosophy of language;
  philosophy of mind

Politics

Tel: (01786) 467568 Fax: (01786) 466266

Ingle, S. J., MA Sheff., PhD Well. Prof.; Head*
Kleinberg, S. S., MA St And., BPhil Glas. Sr.
  Lectr.
Shaw, E. D., BA Sheff., MPhil Leeds, PhD
  Manc. Sr. Lectr.
Other Staff: 5 Lectrs.
Research: citizenship and the liberal state;
  democracy; political parties and strategies;
  politics of war and peace; territorial politics

Psychology

Tel: (01786) 467640 Fax: (01786) 467641

Anderson, J. R., BSc Stir., PhD Stir. Sr. Lectr.
Bruce, V. G., OBE, MA Camb., PhD Camb.,
  FBPsS, FRSEd Prof.
Fryer, D. M., MA Lond., PhD Edin. Reader
Markova, I., CSc Prague, MA Prague, PhD Prague,
  FRSEd Prof.
Phillips, W. A., BSc Manc., PhD ANU Prof.
Power, K. G., MA Edin., MAppSci Glas., PhD
  Stir. Prof.
Watt, Roger J., BA Camb., PhD Keele,
  FRSEd Prof.
Wilson, J. T. L., BA Stir., PhD Stir. Sr. Lectr.;
  Head*
Other Staff: 13 Lectrs.; 1 Sr. Tutor; 1 Sr. Res.
  Fellow; 6 Res. Fellows; 2 Hon. Profs.; 1
  Hon. Reader; 1 Hon. Sr. Lectr.; 3 Hon. Res.
  Fellows; 4 Hon. Tutors
Research: clinical and health psychology;
  comparative and developmental
  psychology; neural computation and
  neuroscience; neuropsychology; perception

Religious Studies

Tel: (01786) 467565

Whitelam, K. W., BD Manc., PhD Manc. Prof.;
  Head*

Other Staff: 8 Lectrs.
Research: world religious traditions

Retail Studies, Institute for, see under
  Marketing

Spanish

Tel: (01786) 467530 Fax: (01786) 451335

Bruton, K. J., MA Lond., PhD Lond. Prof.
Pertaub, W. I., BA Leeds, PhD Leeds Lectr.;
  Head*
Other Staff: 2 Lectrs.

Sports Studies

Jarvie, G., BEd Exe., MA Belf., PhD Leic. Prof.
Other Staff: 1 Lectr.; 1 Teaching Fellow; 1
  Hon. Prof.

SPECIAL CENTRES, ETC

Aquatic Biochemistry, NERC Research Unit of

Tel: (01786) 467824

Sargent, J. R., BSc Aberd., PhD Aberd., FIBiol,
  FRSEd Dir.*
Other Staff: 6 Res. Fellows; 1 Hon. Reader; 3
  Hon. Lectrs.

Christianity and Contemporary Society, Centre for the Study of

Bebbington, D. W., MA Camb., PhD
  Camb. Reader
Drane, J. W., MA Aberd., PhD Manc. Dir.*
Harrison, S. J., BSc Wales, PhD Wales Sr. Lectr.
Keeble, N. H., BA Lampeter, DPhil Oxf., DLitt
  Stir. Prof.

Commonwealth Studies, Centre of

Law, R. C. C., BA Oxf., PhD Birm. Prof.
McCracken, K. John, MA Camb., PhD
  Camb. Sr. Lectr.
Smith, A. M., MA Birm., MLitt Camb. Dir.*
Other Staff: 2 Lectrs.
Research: Commonwealth literature and culture

Dementia Services Development Centre

Tel: (01786) 467740-1

Downs, M. G., MA Vermont, PhD Vermont Res.
  Manager
Marshall, M. T., OBE, MA Edin. Prof.; Dir.*
Other Staff: 1 Lectr.; 1 Res. Fellow
Research: social research into dementia

Drugs Training Project

Fax: (01786) 467979

Yates, P. R., MBE Dir.*

MacRobert Arts Centre

Fax: (01786) 451369

Moran, Liz, BA Strath. Dir.*

Publishing Studies, Centre for

Tel: (01786) 467495

McGowan, I. D., MA Oxf., PhD Stir. Course
  Dir.*

Scot's Law Research Unit

Tel: (01786) 467285

Marshall, E. A., MA St And., LLB St And., PhD St
  And. Reader

Social Work Research Centre

Tel: (01786) 467691 Fax: (01786) 467689

Hallett, C. M., MA Camb., PhD Lough. Prof.;
  Dir.*
McIvor, C. G., BA Strath., PhD Stir. Reader
Other Staff: 2 Sr. Res. Fellows; 4 Res. Fellows;
  1 Hon. Prof.
Research: social work policy and practice

CONTACT OFFICERS

Academic affairs. Academic Registrar: Wood,
  Douglas G., BSc Edin.
Accommodation. Accommodation Officer:
  Broadfoot, C. W.
Admissions (first degree). Admissions Officer:
  Davidson, Kate, MAEd
Admissions (higher degree). (Contact the
  Faculty Officer of the relevant faculty)
Adult/continuing education. Director,
  Division of Academic Innovation and
  Continuing Education: Osborne, M. J., BSc
  Reading, PhD Lond.
Careers. Chief Careers Adviser: Nicholson,
  Graham, BA H-W
Computing services. Associate Director:
  Annan, Angus
Credit transfer. Admissions Officer: Davidson,
  Kate, MAEd
Distance education. (Contact the Faculty
  Officer of the relevant faculty)
Equal opportunities. Deputy Secretary:
  Farrington, Dennis J., BSc Kent, LLB Lond.,
  LLM Hull, DPhil Ulster
Estates and buildings/works and services.
  Director of Estates and Buildings: Weir, G.
  McDonald, FRICS
Examinations. Assistant Registrar: Halliday,
  Ronald, MA Edin., MLitt Stir.
Finance. Director of Finance: Gordon, John
General enquiries. Secretary: Clarke, Kevin J.,
  BA Stir.
Health services. Occupational Health Adviser:
  Sinclair, A. M. R.
International office. Assistant Registrar (Head
  of Recruitment and Admissions): Cockbain,
  Ian
Library (enquiries). Associate Librarian:
  Davis, Robin, BA Reading
Personnel/human resources. Director of
  Personnel: Desmond, Brian
Public relations, information and marketing.
  Director of Public Relations: Dove, G., MA St
  And., MPhil St And.
Publications. Assistant Registrar: Halliday,
  Ronald, MA Edin., MLitt Stir.
Publications (prospectuses). Assistant
  Registrar (Head of Recruitment and
  Admissions): Cockbain, Ian
Quality assurance and accreditation. Assistant
  Registrar: Barron, Thelma, MA Glas.
Research. Assistant Secretary: McFadzean,
  Gillian, MA Aberd.
Safety. Safety Adviser: Barrett, J. A., BSc Stir.
Scholarships, awards, loans. Assistant
  Registrar (Head of Recruitment and
  Admissions): Cockbain, Ian
Scholarships, awards, loans. Admissions
  Officer: Eliot, Paula, MA Aberd.
Schools liaison. Assistant Registrar (Head of
  Recruitment and Admissions): Cockbain, Ian
Security. Director of Estates and Buildings:
  Weir, G. McDonald, FRICS
Sport and recreation. Director of Physical
  Recreation: Nichols, Alan, MEd Manc.
Staff development and training. Director of
  Personnel: Desmond, Brian
Student union. (Contact the President, Stirling
  University Students' Association)
Students from other countries. Study Abroad
  Officer: Love, Gordon, BA Stir.
Students with disabilities. Deputy Secretary:
  Farrington, Dennis J., BSc Kent, LLB Lond.,
  LLM Hull, DPhil Ulster

[Information supplied by the institution as at 6 April
1998, and edited by the ACU]

UNIVERSITY OF STRATHCLYDE

Founded by Royal Charter 1964; originally established 1796 as Anderson's Institution (later Anderson's University)

Member of the Association of Commonwealth Universities

Postal Address: McCance Building, 16 Richmond Street, Glasgow, Scotland G1 1XQ
Telephone: (0141) 552 4400 **Fax**: (0141) 552 0775 **Telex**: 77472 **WWW**: http://www.strath.ac.uk

CHANCELLOR—Hope of Craighead, Lord, QC, BA LLB MA Hon. LLD
PRINCIPAL AND VICE-CHANCELLOR*—Arbuthnott, Prof. Sir John, CBE, BSc *Glas.*, PhD *Glas.*, ScD Trinity(Dub.), FIBiol, FRSEd, FRCPath
VICE-PRINCIPAL—Sherwood, Prof. John N., PhD *Durh.*, DSc *Durh.*, FRSChem, FRSEd
PRO VICE-PRINCIPAL—Spence, Prof. John, MEng *Sheff.*, BSc PhD DSc, FIMechE, FEng, FRSEd
DEPUTY PRINCIPAL—Farish, Prof. Owen, BSc PhD, FEng, FRSEd, FIEE
DEPUTY PRINCIPAL—Shaw, Prof. Susan, MA *Camb.*
DEPUTY PRINCIPAL—Suckling, Prof. Colin J., PhD DSc, FRSChem, FRSEd
SECRETARY TO THE UNIVERSITY—West, Peter W. A., MA *St And.*
LIBRARIAN—Law, Derek, MA, FLA

FACULTIES/SCHOOLS

Arts and Social Sciences
Dean: Midwinter, Prof. Arthur F., MA *Dund.*, MSc *Strath.*, PhD *Aberd.*

Education
Dean: Weir, Prof. Douglas, MA MEd

Engineering
Dean: Hendry, Prof. Alan H., BSc PhD, FIM

Science
Dean: Bramley, J. Stuart, BSc *Leeds*, PhD *Leeds*, FIMA

Strathclyde Business School
Dean: Pitt, Prof. Douglas C., MA *Exe.*, PhD *Manc.*

ACADEMIC UNITS

Accounting and Finance
Fax: (0141) 552 3547
Arrington, C. Edward, BA MA DBA   Prof.
Ciancanelli, Penelope   Sr. Lectr.
Davies, John R., BSc *Lond.*, MBA *Mich.*   Sr. Lectr.
Draper, Paul R., BA *Exe.*, MA *Reading*, PhD *Stir.*   Prof.
Hiemstra, Craig, BA *Calvin*, PhD *Maryland*   Sr. Lectr.
Yadav, Pradeep K., MSc *Delhi*, PhD   Prof.; Head*
Other Staff: 12 Lectrs.

Applied Arts Education
Tel: (0141) 950 3476 Fax: (0141) 950 3314
Coutts, R. Glen, BA   Sr. Lectr.
Dougall, Paul K., BA PhD   Head*
Lavender, Tony M., BSc MA MLitt   Head of Section
McLellan, Marion, BA   Head of Section
Sheridan, Mark, BMus   Head of Section
Watson, Ronald
Other Staff: 9 Lectrs.

Architecture and Building Science
Tel: (0141) 548 3023 Fax: (0141) 552 3997
Bridges, H. Alan, MSc PhD   Reader
Corcoran, Michael, MSc *Lond.*   Prof.; Head*
Ferguson, Robert   Sr. Lectr.
Frey, Hildebrand W.   Sr. Lectr.
Kartvedt, Per, MA   Prof., Architecture
Laing, W. Lamond, BA MSc PhD   Sr. Lectr.
Maver, Thomas, BSc *Glas.*, PhD *Glas.*   Prof., Computer Aided Design
Reed, Peter A., BA *Manc.*, FRIAS   Prof.
Walker, Frank A., BArch PhD   Prof.
Yaneske, Paul P., BSc *Leeds*, PhD *Leeds*   Sr. Lectr.
Other Staff: 12 Lectrs.

Biochemistry, see Biosci. and Biotechnol.

Bioengineering Unit
Barbenel, Joseph C., BDS *Lond.*, MSc PhD, FIBiol, FIP, FRSEd   Prof.
Courtney, James M., BSc *Glas.*, PhD, FRSChem, FIM   Prof.; Head*
Gaylor, John D. S., BSc PhD   Sr. Lectr.
Granat, Malcolm, BSc PhD   Sr. Lectr.
Grant, M. Helen, BSc *Aberd.*, PhD *Aberd.*   Sr. Lectr.
Nicol, Alexander C., BSc PhD   Sr. Lectr.
Paul, John, BSc *Glas.*, PhD, FIMechE, FEng, FRSEd   Emer. Prof.
Solomonidis, Stephanos E., BSc *Lond.*   Sr. Lectr.
Other Staff: 1 Lectr.; 3 Res. Fellows; 9 Hon. Lectrs.

Bioscience and Biotechnology
Anderson, John G., BSc PhD   Reader
Burge, Michael N., BSc *Wales*, PhD *Cant.*   Sr. Lectr.
Gardner, Isobel C., BSc PhD   Sr. Lectr.
Hunter, Iain S., BSc PhD   Prof.
Kirkwood, Ralph C., BSc PhD, FRSEd   Reader
McNeil, Brian, BSc PhD   Sr. Lectr.
Paterson, Alistair, BSc *Edin.*, PhD *Lond.*   Sr. Lectr.
Piggott, John R., BA *Camb.*, MSc *Leeds*, PhD *Reading*   Sr. Lectr.
Robb, Donald, BSc PhD
Scott, Alexander, BSc PhD   Sr. Lectr.
Smith, John E., BSc PhD DSc, FIBiol, FRSEd   Prof.
Watson, John, BSc *Glas.*, PhD DSc   Prof., Biochemistry; Head*
Watson-Craik, Irene A., BSc *Glas.*, PhD   Sr. Lectr.
Wood, Brian J. B., BSc PhD   Reader
Other Staff: 5 Lectrs.; 2 Res. Fellows

Building Science, see Archit. and Bldg. Sci.

Business, see Strathclyde Grad. Bus. Sch., and Technol. and Bus. Studies

Business and Computer Education
Finlayson, Barry   Sr. Lectr.
Hawthorn, Jack, BSc   Sr. Lectr.
Hoey, W. Ross, BSc MEd   Course Dir.
Kirkwood, Margaret J., BSc MEd   Sr. Lectr.
Muir, David D., BSc   Course Dir.
Munro, Robert K., MA   Sr. Lectr.
Ramsay, Anne C., MA MEd   Sr. Lectr.
Shaw, David F. B., BSc   Sr. Lectr.
Winch, John R., BSc   Head*
Other Staff: 8 Lectrs.

Chemistry, Pure and Applied
Tel: (0141) 548 2282 Fax: (0141) 552 5664
Affrossman, Stanley, BSc *Glas.*, PhD *Glas.*   Sr. Lectr.
Armstrong, David R., DSc *Newcastle(UK)*, PhD *Newcastle(UK)*   Sr. Lectr.

Bailey, Raymond T., BSc *Wales*, PhD *Wales*   Reader
Caddy, Brian, BSc *Sheff.*, PhD *Sheff.*   Prof.†
Cole, Michael D., BA PhD   Sr. Lectr.
Cruickshank, Francis R., BSc *Aberd.*, PhD *Aberd.*   Reader
Dunkin, Ian R., BSc *Birm.*, PhD *Birm.*, FRSChem   Sr. Lectr.
Ferguson, James, PhD *Glas.*, DSc *Glas.*, FRSChem   Prof.†
Gibson, Colin L., BSc PhD
Graham, Neil B., BSc PhD, FRSChem, FRSEd   Prof.
Hall, Peter J., BSc *Durh.*, MLitt *Newcastle(UK)*, PhD *Newcastle(UK)*   Sr. Lectr.
Halling, Peter J., BA PhD   Prof.
Hitchman, Michael L., BSc *Lond.*, DPhil *Oxf.*, FRSChem   Young Prof.
Kerr, William J., BSc PhD   Sr. Lectr.
Knox, Graham R.
Littlejohn, David, BSc PhD, FRSChem   Philips Prof.
Moore, Barry D., BSc PhD   Sr. Lectr.
Morris, John H., BSc PhD   Reader
Mulvey, Robert E., BSc PhD   Prof.
Murphy, John, BSc PhD   Prof.
Nonhebel, Derek C., BSc DSc, FRSChem, FRSEd   Reader
Pethrick, Richard A., BSc *Lond.*, PhD *Salf.*, DSc *Salf.*, FRSChem, FRSEd   Prof.
Pugh, David, MA *Oxf.*, PhD *Wales*   Reader
Reglinski, John, BSc *Dund.*, PhD *St And.*   Sr. Lectr.
Sherrington, David C., BSc *Liv.*, PhD *Liv.*, FRSChem, FRSEd   Prof.
Sherwood, John N., PhD *Durh.*, DSc *Durh.*, FRSChem, FRSEd   Burmah Prof.
Smith, W. Ewen, BSc *Glas.*, PhD *Lond.*   Prof.; Head*
Suckling, Colin J., PhD DSc, FRSChem, FRSEd   Freeland Prof.
Thorpe, James W., BSc *Glas.*, PhD *Glas.*   Sr. Lectr.
Whewell, Richard J., BSc *Oxf.*, MA *Oxf.*, DPhil *Oxf.*   Sr. Lectr.
White, Peter, PhD   Sr. Lectr.
Other Staff: 10 Lectrs.; 5 Res. Officers

Community Education
Tel: (0141) 950 3378 Fax: (0141) 950 3374
Curran, Margaret, MA   Course Dir.
Hough, Michael T., MA   Sr. Lectr.
Milburn, R. E., BA MSc   Sr. Lectr.
Rowlands, Clive J., BA MEd   Head*
Seddon, James, BA MA(Ed)   Programme Co-ordinator
Smith, Duncan P., BA   Sr. Lectr.
Other Staff: 7 Lectrs.

Computer Science, see also Bus. and Computer Educn.
Fax: (0141) 552 5330
Buchanan, John T., BSc *Glas.*, MSc PhD   Prof.; Head*

Cockshott, W. Paul, BA Manc., MSc H.-W., PhD Edin. Sr. Lectr.
Fryer, Richard J., BSc Lond., PhD Lanc. Sr. Lectr.
Gent, Ian P., MA MSc PhD Sr. Lectr.
Goldfinch, Paul, MA Oxf., MSc Essex Sr. Lectr.
Hunter, Robin B., BSc Glas., PhD Glas., FRAS Sr. Lectr.
Kingslake, Richard, MA Oxf., PhD Lond. Sr. Lectr.
McGettrick, Andrew D., BSc Glas., PhD Camb. Prof.
McGregor, Douglas R., BSc Aberd., PhD Glas. Prof.
McInnes, John A., BSc Lond., PhD Lond. Sr. Lectr.
Other Staff: 14 Lectrs.

Design, Manufacture and Engineering Management

Balendra, Raj, PhD, FIM Sr. Lectr.
Banerjee, Sisir K., BE Calc., MSc PhD Sr. Lectr.
Bitici, Umit S., MSc PhD Sr. Lectr.
Callander, T. M. S., MSc Sr. Lectr.
Carrie, Allan S., BSc Lond., MSc Birm., PhD, FIEE Prof.
Duffy, Alexander H. B., BSc PhD Sr. Lectr.
Ion, William J., BSc Sr. Lectr.
Juster, Neil Prof.; Head*
Mair, Gordon M., BSc Sr. Lectr.
Patrick, James K., BSc Glas., PhD Glas. Sr. Lectr.
Other Staff: 10 Lectrs.; 2 Visiting Profs.

Dynamics and Control

Fax: (0141) 552 2086
Barron, Ronald, PhD Sr. Lectr.
Fleming, John S., BSc PhD Sr. Lectr.; Head*

Economics

Fax: (0141) 552 5589
Alpine, Robert L. W., MA Glas. Sr. Lectr.
Brooks, Richard G., BA Sheff., MSc Sr. Lectr.
Cross, Rodney B., BSc Lond., BPhil York(UK) Sr. Lectr.
Holden, Darryl R., BSc MA Sr. Lectr.
Hughes Hallett, Andrew, BA Warw., MSc Lond., DPhil Oxf. Prof., Macroeconomics
Huq, Mozammel M., MA Rajsh., MLitt Glas., PhD Glas. Sr. Lectr.
Kay, Neil M., BA Stir., PhD Stir. Prof., Business Economics
Love, James, BA MSc PhD Prof.; Head*
Love, James H., BA PhD Sr. Lectr.
MacDonald, Ronald, BA H.-W., MA Manc., PhD Manc. Prof.
McNicoll, Iain H., BA PhD Prof.
Sandilands, Roger J., MA S.Fraser, BA PhD Sr. Lectr.
Scouller, John, BA Sr. Lectr.
Stephen, Frank H., BA PhD Prof.
Stewart, William J., BSc(Econ) Lond., BA Sr. Lectr.
Other Staff: 7 Lectrs.; 1 Sr. Res. Fellow; 2 Visiting Sr. Res. Fellows

Scottish Economy, Fraser of Allander Institute for Research on the

Fax: (0141) 552 8347
Ashcroft, Brian K., MA Lanc. Dir.*
McGregor, Peter G., BA Stir., MSc Stir. Reader
Swales, John K., BA Camb. Reader
Other Staff: 1 Lectr.

Education, see Appl. Arts Educn.; Bus. and Computer Educn.; Community Educn.; Educnl. Studies; Further Educn., Scottish Sch. of; Inservice Educn.; Lang. Educn.; Maths., Sci. and Technol. Educn.; Phys. Educn., Sport and Outdoor Educn.; Primary Educn.; Special Educnl. Needs

Educational Studies

Tel: (0141) 950 3367-8 Fax: (0141) 950 3367
Ainsworth, Stuart, BA Sr. Lectr.
Bryce, Thomas G. K., BSc MEd PhD Prof.

Christie, Donald F. M., BA Sr. Lectr.; Programme Co-ordinator
Clarke, Peter T., MEd MPhil Sr. Lectr.
Cornwell, David G., MA Sr. Lectr.
Cumming, Mary M., BA Sr. Lectr.
Finn, Gerard P. T., BSc PhD Reader
Johnson, Andrew, BPhil Sr. Lectr.
Macbeath, John, OBE, MA MEd Prof.; Dir., Quality in Educn. Unit
MacLellan, Euphemia M., BA PhD Sr. Lectr.
Mangan, J. Tony, BA PhD, FRHistS, FRAI Prof.
Martin, Peter J., BSc MEd PhD Sr. Lectr.; Head*
McCall, James, BSc MEd PhD Prof.
McLaren, David, MA MEd PhD Sr. Lectr.
Mearns, David J., BSc Reader; Dir., Counselling Unit
Menmuir, Joan G., BSc MEd Sr. Lectr.
Peck, Bryan T., MA MA(Ed) MPhil Sr. Lectr.
Ramsay, William, BSc MEd Sr. Lectr.
Stark, Rae E., BSc BA MSc MA(Ed) Sr. Lectr.
Thomson, William P., MA MEd Sr. Lectr.
Other Staff: 5 Lectrs.; 1 Res. Fellow

Energy Systems

Fax: (0141) 552 8513
Barrowman, E. M. Sr. Lectr.
Clarke, Joseph A., BSc PhD Prof.
Fraser, Simon M., BSc Glas., PhD Prof.; Head*
Gilchrist, Alistair, MSc Birm., PhD Sr. Lectr.
Hensen, Jan L., BSc MSc PhD Sr. Lectr.
Lee, Chee Kong, BSc PhD Sr. Lectr.
Waddell, Peter, MSc Birm., PhD Sr. Lectr.

Engineering, Chemical and Process

Fax: (0141) 552 2302
Bell, George, BSc PhD Sr. Lectr.
Crawley, Francis K., BSc Sr. Lectr.
Grant, Colin D., BSc PhD, FIChemE Roche Prof.; Head*
Larsen, Vidar F., BSc PhD Sr. Lectr.
Muir, David M., BSc Glas., PhD Sr. Lectr.
Postlethwaite, Bruce E., BSc PhD Sr. Lectr.
Other Staff: 7 Lectrs.; 1 Visiting Prof.

Engineering, Civil

Fax: (0141) 553 2066
Andrawes, Kamal Z., BSc(Eng) Cairo, MSc Manc., PhD S'ton. Prof.
Bache, David H., BSc St And., PhD Strath., DSc St And. Reader
Barr, David I. H., BSc Glas., PhD Glas., DSc Glas., FICE Emer. Prof.
Copeland, Graham J. M., MA Camb., MSc Wales, PhD Liv. Sr. Lectr.
Fleming, George, BSc Strath., PhD Strath., FICE, FEng, FRSEd Prof.
Jackson, Michael H., BA Open(UK), PhD Strath. Prof.
Langford, David A., MSc Aston, MPhil Aston Barr Prof., Construction
MacLeod, Iain A., BSc Glas., PhD Glas., FICE, FIStructE Prof., Structural Engineering
McGown, Alan, CBE, BSc Strath., PhD Strath., DSc Strath., FGS, FICE Prof.
Milne, Peter H., BSc Glas., PhD Strath., FICE Sr. Lectr.
Retik, Arkady, BSc MSc PhD DSc Sr. Lectr.
Riddell, John F., BSc Glas., PhD Strath. Reader
Wright, Howard D., BEng Sheff., PhD Wales, FIStructE, FICE Prof., Structural Engineering; Head*
Other Staff: 12 Lectrs.; 1 Res. Officer; 2 Res. Fellows

Engineering, Electronic and Electrical

Fax: (0141) 552 2487
Andonvic, Ivan, BSc PhD Sr. Lectr.
Campbell, Leslie C., MSc PhD Reader
Chalmers, Ian D., BSc PhD, FIEE Prof.
Chapman, Roy, MSc Newcastle(UK) Sr. Lectr.
Crichton, Bruce H., BSc Edin., PhD Sr. Lectr.
Culshaw, Brian, BSc Lond., PhD Lond. Prof., Opto-Electronics
Dunlop, John, MSc Wales, PhD Wales Prof., Electronic Systems

Durrani, Tariq S., BSc Karachi, BSc Dacca, MSc S'ton., PhD S'ton., FIEE, FRSEd, FEng Prof., Signal Processing
Farish, Owen, BSc Glas., PhD Glas., FIEE, FRSEd, FEng Prof., Power Engineering
Fouracre, Richard A., BSc Birm., MSc Aston, PhD Sr. Lectr.
Grant, Douglas M., BSc Glas., MSc Sr. Lectr.
Grimble, Michael J., BA Open(UK), DSc CNAA, MSc Birm., PhD Birm., FIEE Prof., Control
Hayward, Gordon, BSc Glas., MSc PhD Prof., Ultrasonics
Johnson, Michael A., BSc CNAA, MSc(Eng) Lond., PhD Lond. Reader
Johnstone, Walter, BSc PhD Reader
Katebi, Mohammed R., BSc Shiraz, MSc Manc., PhD Manc. Sr. Lectr.
Leithead, William E., BSc Edin., PhD Edin. Reader
Lo, Kwok Lun, MSc Manc., PhD Manc. Prof., Power Systems
MacGregor, Scott J., BSc PhD Sr. Lectr.
Marshall, Stephen, BSc Nott., PhD Sr. Lectr.
McDonald, James R., BSc MSc PhD Rolls-Royce Prof., Power Systems
McGhee, Joseph, BSc Sr. Lectr.
McNab, Alistair, BSc Glas., PhD Glas. Sr. Lectr.
Nandi, Asoke, BSc CNAA, PhD Camb. Sr. Lectr.
Sandham, William A., BSc Glas., PhD Birm. Sr. Lectr.
Simpson, Ronald R. S., BSc PhD Sr. Lectr.
Smith, D. Geoffrey, BEng Sheff., PhD Sheff., FIEE, FRSEd Prof., Communications Engineering; Head*
Smith, John R., MSc PhD Prof.†
Soraghan, John J., MEng Trinity(Dub.), PhD Sr. Lectr.
Stewart, George S., BSc Glas., PhD Glas. Sr. Lectr.
Stewart, Robert W., BSc PhD Sr. Lectr.
Stimpson, Brian P., BEng Lond., PhD Liv. Sr. Lectr.
Tedford, David J., OBE, BSc Glas., PhD Glas., FIEE, FIP, FRSEd Prof., Electrical Engineering
Uttamchandani, Deepak G., BEng A.Bello, MSc Lond., PhD Lond. Reader
Other Staff: 11 Lectrs.; 3 Sr. Res. Fellows

Engineering, Process, see Engin., Chem. and Process

English Studies

Fax: (0141) 552 3493
Bath, Michael E., MA Oxf., PhD Strath. Reader
Cameron, Deborah J., BA Newcastle(UK), MLitt Oxf. Prof.
Fabb, Nigel, BA Camb., PhD M.I.T. Sr. Lectr.
Frith, Simon W., BA Oxf., MA Calif., PhD Calif. Prof.
Furniss, Thomas E., MA S'ton., PhD Sr. Lectr.
Jago, David M., MA Camb., PhD Leic. Sr. Lectr.
Montgomery, Martin, BA Birm., MA Birm., PhD Strath. Sr. Lectr.
Noble, Andrew A. J., MA Aberd., DPhil Sus. Sr. Lectr.
Pittock, Murray, MA Glas., DPhil Oxf., FRHistS Prof.; Head*
Ross, Ian S. Visiting Prof.
Simpson, Kenneth G., MA Glas., PhD Strath. Sr. Lectr.
Other Staff: 7 Lectrs.

Environmental Planning

Tel: (0141) 548 3906 Fax: (0141) 552 2511
Brand, Janet M. V., BA Exe. Sr. Lectr.
Coon, Anthony, BSc Manc., MSc Northwestern Sr. Lectr.
Forbes, Jean, BA MSc MEd Sr. Lectr.
Green, Peter, BA MA PhD Sr. Lectr.
Hayton, Keith, BA Lond., BPhil Newcastle(UK) Prof.; Head*
Lamb, Robert, BSc Sr. Lectr.
Parnell, Brian K., BSc Visiting Prof.
Rich, Daniel, BA PhD Visiting Prof.
Wannop, Urlan A., MA Edin., MCD Liv. Emer. Prof.†
Other Staff: 4 Lectrs.

European Policies Research Centre

Fax: (0141) 552 1757

Klemmer, Paul   Visiting Prof.
Yuill, Douglas, MA MPhil   Prof.; Head*
Other Staff: 2 Sr. Res. Fellows

Finance, see Acctg. and Finance

French, see Mod. Langs.

Further Education, Scottish School of

Fax: (0141) 950 3539

Gordon, Andrew T., BA MBA   Sr. Lectr.
McQueeney, Elizabeth A., MN   Course Coordinator
Nicolson, Anne E., MBA   Course Dir.
Niven, Stuart M., BSc   Dir.*
Payne, George R., BA MSc   Sr. Lectr.
Ross, Magnus M. B., BA MEd   Course Dir.
Soden, Rebecca, BA MEd PhD   Sr. Lectr.
Taylor, David, MEd   Sr. Lectr.
Thomson, Alexander F., MA MEd   Course Dir.

Geography

Fax: (0141) 552 7857

Jones, Gareth E., BSc *Wales*, PhD *Wales*   Sr. Lectr.; Head*
Martin, Tony, BA *Liv.*   Sr. Lectr.
Pacione, Michael, MA *Dund.*, PhD *Dund.*   Prof.
Rogerson, Robert J., BSc *Glas.*, PhD *Lond.*   Sr. Lectr.

German, see Mod. Langs.

Government

Fax: (0141) 552 5677

Brand, Jack A., MA *Aberd.*, PhD *Lond.*   Reader
Chapman, Jennifer P., MA *Edin.*, PhD *Strath.*   Sr. Lectr.
Cox, Terence M., BA *Durh.*, PhD *Glas.*   Sr. Lectr.
Croall, Hazel, BA *Strath.*, MA *Keele*, PhD *Lond.*   Sr. Lectr.
Curtice, John, MA *Oxf.*   Sr. Lectr.
Diani, Mario, BA *Milan*, PhD *Turin*   Prof.
Hogwood, Brian W., BA *Keele*, PhD *Keele*   Prof.
Jackson, Stephanie, BA *Kent*, BPhil *York(UK)*   Sr. Lectr.
Judge, David, BA *Exe.*, PhD *Sheff.*   Prof; Head*
Mackie, Thomas T., BA *Lond.*, MSc(Econ) *Lond.*, MSc *Strath.*   Sr. Lectr.
Midwinter, Arthur F., MA *Dund.*, MSc *Strath.*, PhD *Aberd.*   Prof.
Mitchell, James, MA *Aberd.*, DPhil *Oxf.*   Sr. Lectr.
Pierre, Jon, BA *Lund*, PhD *Lund*   Prof.
Preston, Peter W., BA *Leeds*, PhD *Leeds*   Sr. Lectr.
Rudig, Wolfgang, DP *F.U.Berlin*, PhD *Manc.*   Sr. Lectr.
Stoker, Gerry, BA *Manc.*, PhD *Manc.*   Prof.
Witz, Anne, BA *Exe.*, PhD *Lanc.*   Sr. Lectr.

History

Tel: (0141) 548 2206 Fax: (0141) 552 8509

Adams, Simon L., BA *Haverford*, MA *Harv.*, DPhil *Oxf.*, FRHistS   Sr. Lectr.
Brown, Callum, MA *St And.*, PhD *Glas.*   Sr. Lectr.
Fischer, Conan J., BA *E.Anglia*, MA *Sus.*, DPhil *Sus.*   Reader
Fraser, W. Hamish, MA *Aberd.*, DPhil *Sus.*   Prof.
Jackson, Gordon, BA *Lond.*, PhD *Hull*, FRHistS   Reader
McMillan, James F., MA *Glas.*, DPhil *Oxf.*   Prof.
Tomlinson, Brian R., MA *Camb.*, PhD *Camb.*   Prof.; Head*

Scottish History, Research Centre in

Devine, Tom M., BA PhD DLitt, FRHistS, FRSEd, FBA   Prof.; Dir.*
Smout, T. Christopher, FBA   Visiting Prof.

Hotel School, see Scottish Hotel Sch.

Human Resource Management

Alexander, Alan, MA *Glas.*   Prof.
Baldry, Christopher J., BSc *S'ton.*, MSc *Lond.*, PhD *Durh.*   Prof.
Gennard, John, BA(Econ) *Sheff.*, MA(Econ) *Manc.*   Prof.; Head*
Hyman, Jeffrey D., MA *Warw.*   Sr. Lectr.
Kelly, James, PhD *Warw.*, BA   Sr. Lectr.
Livingstone, Hugh, MA *Glas.*   Sr. Lectr.
Lockyer, Clifford J., BA   Sr. Lectr.
Moore, Christopher B., BA *Leeds*   Sr. Lectr.
Pitt, Douglas C., MA *Exe.*, PhD *Manc.*   Prof.
Ramsay, Harvey E., MA *Camb.*, PhD *Durh.*   Reader
Snape, Edward J., BA MSc PhD   Sr. Lectr.
Towers, Brian, BA *Manc.*, BSc *Lond.*   IPM Prof.
Other Staff: 11 Lectrs.

Immunology

Fax: (0141) 552 6674

Alexander, James, BSc *Glas.*, PhD *Glas.*   Prof.
Harnett, William, BSc *Glas.*, PhD *Glas.*   Sr. Lectr.
Stimson, William H., BSc *St And.*, PhD *St And.*, FIBiol, FRSEd   Prof.; Head*
Other Staff: 7 Lectrs.

Information Science

Fax: (0141) 553 1393

Burton, Paul F., MA *Sheff.*, BA   Sr. Lectr.
Gibb, Forbes, BA *Edin.*   Sr. Lectr.; Head*
MacMorrow, Noreen, BBS *Trinity(Dub.)*, MPhil   Sr. Lectr.
Revie, Crawford, DPhil *Sus.*, BSc   Sr. Lectr.
Other Staff: 5 Lectrs.
Vacant Posts: 1 Prof.

Inservice Education

Fax: (0141) 950 3268

Cumming, Molly M., BA   Programme Coordinator
Mortimer, Gerald, MA   Programme Coordinator
Rand, James, MA   Head*
Robertson, Alistair H., MA MEd   Programme Co-ordinator
Smith, Iain R. M., BSc MEd   Sr. Lectr.
Watterson, Patricia R., BA   Sr. Lectr.

Italian, see Mod. Langs.

Language Education

Fax: (0141) 950 3268

De Cecco, G. R. John, BA   Sr. Lectr.
Hughes, Sheila, MA   Sr. Lectr.
Robertson, A. G. Boyd, MA   Sr. Lectr.
Tierney, Daniel, BA   Sr. Lectr.
Williams, W. Tony, MA MLitt   Head*
Other Staff: 10 Lectrs.

Latin American Studies, see Mod. Langs.

Law School

Fax: (0141) 553 1546

Bates, T. St. John, MA LLM   Visiting Prof.
Blackie, John W. G., BA *Camb.*, LLB *Edin.*   Prof., Scots Law
Burgess, Robert A., LLB *Lond.*, PhD *Edin.*   Prof., Business Law and Practice
Evans, Martyn, BA MA   Visiting Prof.
Huntley, John A. K., LLM *Birm.*   Sr. Lectr.
Lloyd, Ian J., LLM *Exe.*, LLB PhD   Prof., Information Technology Law
MacLeod, Norman, QC, LLB MA   Visiting Prof.
Maher, Gerard, LLB *Glas.*, BLitt *Oxf.*   Prof., Private Law
McFall, John F., BSc BA MBA   Visiting Prof.
Miller, Kenneth, LLM *Qu.*, LLB PhD   Prof., Employment Law
Norrie, Kenneth M., LLB *Dund.*, PhD *Aberd.*   Sr. Lectr.
Paterson, Alan A., LLB *Edin.*, DPhil *Oxf.*   Prof.; Head*
Pritchard, Kenneth, OBE   Visiting Prof.
Robson, Peter W., LLB *St And.*, PhD   Prof.

Susskind, Richard, LLB DPhil   Visiting Prof.
Toth, Akos, DrJur&RerPol *Szeged*, PhD   Exe. Prof., European Law
Other Staff: 10 Lectrs.
Vacant Posts: 1 Sr. Lectr.

Local Authorities Management Centre, see Scottish Local Authorities Management Centre

Management Science, see also Human Resource Management

Fax: (0141) 552 6686

Ackermann, Frances, BA *W.Aust.*, PhD   Sr. Lectr.
Belton, Valerie, BSc *Durh.*, MA *Lanc.*, PhD *Camb.*   Sr. Lectr.; Head*
Bennett, Peter G., BSc *S'ton.*, MSc *Sus.*, DPhil *Sus.*   Reader (on leave)
Eden, Colin, BSc *Leic.*, PhD *S'ton.*   Prof.
Van der Heijden, K.   Prof.
Williams, Howard, BEd *Exe.*, MSc *Newcastle(UK)*   Prof.
Williams, Terence M., MA *Oxf.*, MSc *Birm.*   Sr. Lectr.
Other Staff: 7 Lectrs.

Manufacturing Sciences and Engineering Course

No staff at present

Marine Technology, see Ship and Marine Technol.

Marketing

Fax: (0141) 552 2802

Baker, Michael J., BA *Durh.*, BSc(Econ) *Lond.*, DBA *Harv.*   Prof.
Crosier, Keith, BSc MSc   Sr. Lectr.
Donaldson, William G., BA *Strath.*, PhD *Strath.*   Sr. Lectr.
Hamill, James, BSc PhD   Reader
Hastings, Gerard, BSc PhD   Prof.; Dir., Centre for Soc. Marketing; Head*
Hood, Neil, MA *Glas.*, MLitt *Glas.*, FRSEd   Prof., Business Policy
Kitchen, Philip J., BA *CNAA*, MSc *Manc.*, MBSc *Manc.*, PhD *Keele*   Sr. Lectr.
McDermott, Michael C., MA *Glas.*, PhD *Glas.*   Sr. Lectr.
Shaw, Susan A., MA *Camb.*   Prof.
Taggart, James H., MBA PhD   Sr. Lectr.
Thomas, Michael J., BSc *Lond.*, MBA *Indiana*   Prof.
Wheeler, Colin N., BA *Newcastle(UK)*, MA *Lanc.*   Sr. Lectr.
Young, Stephen, BCom *Liv.*, MSc *Newcastle(UK)*   Prof.

Mathematics

Fax: (0141) 552 8657

Barratt, P. J., BSc *Manc.*, PhD   Sr. Lectr.
Bramley, J. Stuart, BSc *Leeds*, PhD *Leeds*, FIMA   Sr. Lectr.
Constanda, Christian, MSc *Jassy*, PhD *Roumanian Acad. Sci.*   Reader
Hunt, Roland L., BSc *Manc.*, PhD *Camb.*, FRAS   Sr. Lectr.
Leslie, Frank M., JP, BSc *Dund.*, PhD *Manc.*, DSc *St And.*, FIMA, FIP, FRSEd, FRS   Prof.
McBride, Adam C., BSc *Edin.*, PhD *Edin.*, DSc *Edin.*   Reader
McGhee, Desmond, BSc PhD
McKee, J. C. St. C. Sean, BSc *St And.*, MA *Oxf.*, PhD *Dund.*, DSc, FIMA, FRSEd   Prof.
Murdoch, I. Alan, MA *Oxf.*, MS *Pitt.*, PhD *Pitt.*   Reader
Parkes, John, MA PhD   Sr. Lectr.
Sloan, David McP., BSc *Glas.*, MSc *Keele*, PhD DSc, FRSEd   Prof.; Head*
Stewart, Ian W., MA *Glas.*, PhD *H.-W.*   Sr. Lectr.
Tweddle, Ian, BSc *Glas.*, PhD *Glas.*   Sr. Lectr.
Wallace, David A. R., BSc *St And.*, PhD *Manc.*, FRSEd   Emer. Prof.
Wilson, Stephen K., BA MSc DPhil   Sr. Lectr.
Other Staff: 11 Lectrs.

Mathematics, Science and Technological Education

Bell, James C., BSc   Lectr.; Head, Phys.
Clarke, David, MA   Sr. Lectr.
Lindsay, William G., BSc   Sr. Lectr.; Head, Technol.
MacFarlane, Dugald, BSc MEd   Sr. Lectr.
MacGregor, John A., BSc   Sr. Lectr.; Head, Chem.
Meechan, Robert C., BSc
Moffat, Jennifer, MA   Sr. Lectr.
Robertson, George, MA   Head, Maths.
Weston, Roy, MA   Head*
Other Staff: 13 Lectrs.

Mechanics of Materials

Tel: (0141) 548 2315 Fax: (0141) 552 5105

Baker, T. Neville, BMet Sheff., PhD Sheff., DMet Sheff., FIM, FIP   Prof.
Boyle, James T., BSc PhD   Prof.
Burdett, Cedric F., BSc Leeds, PhD Leeds   Sr. Lectr.
Gray, Thomas G. F., BSc Glas., PhD   Prof.; Head*
Hendry, Alan H., BSc PhD, FIM   Prof.
Hossack, John D. W., BSc Glas., PhD Glas.   Sr. Lectr.
Mackenzie, Donald, BSc PhD   Sr. Lectr.
McKelvie, James, BSc Glas., PhD   Reader
Pomfret, Roger J., BMet Sheff., PhD Sheff.   Sr. Lectr.
Rhodes, James, BSc PhD   Prof.
Spence, John, MEng Sheff., BSc PhD DSc, FIMechE, FEng, FRSEd   Trades House of Glasgow Prof.
Tooth, Alwyn S., MSc PhD, FIMechE   Emer. Prof.†
Walker, Colin A., BSc Glas., PhD Glas.   Sr. Lectr.
Watson, Lewis M., BSc Glas., PhD Glas.   Sr. Lectr.

Modern Languages

Fax: (0141) 552 4979

Dickson, Michèle   Sr. Lectr., French
Farrell, Joseph, MA Glas.   Sr. Lectr., Italian
Foley, Keith B., BA Leeds, PhD Leeds   Sr. Lectr., French
Harper, Anthony J., MA Brist., PhD Edin.   Prof.†, German Studies
Kinloch, David P., MA DPhil   Sr. Lectr., French
Martin, Graham D. C., MA Camb., MLitt Trinity(Dub.), PhD   Sr. Lectr., German
McAllester Jones, E. Mary, BA Reading, PhD Reading   Sr. Lectr., French
Millan, C. Gordon, MA Edin., PhD Edin.   Prof., French; Head*
Morris, Alan I., MA St And., PhD St.And.   Sr. Lectr., French
Pender, Malcolm J., MA Camb., PhD   Reader, German
Rodgers, Eamonn J., BA Belf., PhD Belf., MA Trinity(Dub.)   Prof., Spanish and Latin American Studies
Stewart, Miranda M., BA PhD   Sr. Lectr., Spanish
Supple, James J., BA Sus., DPhil Sus.   Prof., French
Walters, Barrie, MA Birm.   Sr. Lectr., French
Wilkin, Andrew, BA Manc.   Sr. Lectr., Italian
Wood, Sharon L., BA Brist., PhD Brist.   Reader, Italian
Other Staff: 16 Lectrs.

Pharmaceutical Sciences

Tel: (0141) 548 2863 Fax: (0141) 552 6443

Baillie, Alan J., BSc PhD   Sr. Lectr.
Coggans, Niall, BA   Sr. Lectr.
Converse, Carolyn A., ScB Brown, PhD Harv.   Sr. Lectr.
Eccleston, Gillian M., BSc Leeds, PhD CNAA   Sr. Lectr.
Gray, Alexander I., BSc Trinity(Dub.), MA Trinity(Dub.), PhD   Sr. Lectr.
Healey, Terence, BSc H.-W., PhD H.-W.   Sr. Lectr.

Hudson, Steve, BPharm Nott., MPharm Brad.   Prof.
Hunter, Iain S., BSc PhD   Prof.
Midgley, John M., MSc Manc., PhD Lond., FRPharmS   Prof.†
Skellern, Graham G., BSc CNAA, PhD   Sr. Lectr.
Sneader, Walter E., BSc Glas., PhD Glas.   Sr. Lectr.
Stenlake, John B., CBE, PhD DSc, FRPharmS   Hon. Prof.
Uchegbu, Ujeoma F., BPharm MSc PhD   Sr. Lectr.
Waigh, Roger D., BPharm Lond., PhD Bath, FRSChem, FRPharmS   Prof.; Head*
Waterman, Peter G., BPharm Lond., PhD, FLS, FRSEd   Prof.
Watson, David G., BSc Leic., PhD Lond.   Sr. Lectr.
Whateley, Tony L., MA Oxf., MSc NSW, PhD Camb., FRSChem   Reader
Wilson, Clive G., BSc CNAA, PhD Sur.   James P. Todd Prof.
Other Staff: 7 Lectrs.

Pharmacology, see Physiol. and Pharmacol.

Physical Education, Sport and Outdoor Education

Scottish School of Sports Studies

Fax: (0141) 950 3132

Cosgrove, Ian N.   Programme Co-ordinator
Green, Brian N., BEd MSc   Programme Co-ordinator; Head*
Mortimer, Gerald, MA   Sr. Lectr.
Nimmo, Myra, BSc PhD   Prof.
Renfrew, Thomas P., BA MSc   Course Dir.
Watkins, James, BEd MA PhD   Sr. Lectr.
Other Staff: 7 Lectrs.

Physics and Applied Physics

Tel: (0141) 548 3363 Fax: (0141) 552 2891

Barnett, Stephen M., BSc Lond., PhD Lond., FRSEd   Prof.
Birch, David J. S., BSc Manc., PhD Manc., FIP   Prof., Photophysics
Cunningham, Alexander, BSc Edin., PhD, FRMetS   Sr. Lectr.
Donaldson, Gordon B., MA Camb., PhD Camb., FIP, FRSEd   Prof.; Chair, Appl. Phys.
Duxbury, Geoffrey, BSc Sheff., PhD Sheff., FIP   Prof., Chemical Physics
Ferguson, Allister I., BSc St And., MA Oxf., PhD St And., FRSEd, FIP   Prof.; Chair, Photonics
Firth, William J., BSc Edin., PhD H.-W., FRSEd   Prof.; Chair, Exper. Phys.
Henderson, Brian, BSc Birm., PhD Birm., ScD Trinity(Dub.), FIP, FAIP, FRSEd   Freeland Prof., Natural Philosophy
Illingworth, Robert, BSc St And., PhD Birm.   Sr. Lectr.
Kidd, Donald E., BSc Birm., PhD Birm.   Sr. Lectr.
Lockerbie, Nicholas A., BSc Nott., PhD Nott.   Sr. Lectr.
Maas, Peter, SB M.I.T., MS Stan., PhD Colorado, FIP   Sr. Lectr.
O'Donnell, Kevin P., BSc Glas., PhD Trinity(Dub.)   Reader
Oppo, Gian-Luca, PhD Florence   Reader
Pegrum, Colin M., MA Camb., MSc Lanc., PhD Lanc.   Sr. Lectr.
Phelps, Alan D. R., MA Camb., DPhil Oxf., FIP   Prof., Plasma Physics; Head*
Riis, Erling, MSc Aarhus, PhD Aarhus   Sr. Lectr.
Ruddock, Ivan S., BSc Belf., PhD Lond.   Sr. Lectr.
Stewart, Robert S., BSc Belf., PhD Belf.   Sr. Lectr.
Summers, Hugh P., BSc Edin., PhD Camb., FRAS   Prof., Theoretical Atom Physics
Wilkinson, Michael, BSc Leeds, PhD Brist.   Sr. Lectr.
Other Staff: 10 Lectrs.

Physiology and Pharmacology

Fax: (0141) 552 2562

Bowman, W. C., BPharm Lond., PhD Lond., DSc Lond., FIBiol, FPS, FRSEd   Emer. Prof.
Furman, Brian L., BPharm Lond., PhD   Sr. Lectr.; Head*
Gurney, Alison, BSc PhD   Prof.
Harvey, Alan L., BSc PhD   Prof.; Dir., Strath. Inst. for Drug Res.
Kane, Kathleen A., BSc Edin., PhD Edin.   Reader
Marshall, Ian G., BSc Glas., PhD   Prof.†
Parratt, James R., BPharm Lond., MSc Lond., PhD Lond., DSc, FPS, FIBiol, FRSEd   Prof., Cardiovascular Pharmacology
Pratt, Judith, BSc Reading, PhD Lond.   Sr. Lectr.
Pyne, Nigel J., BSc Birm., PhD Manc.   Sr. Lectr.
Sneddon, Peter, BSc Glas., DPhil Oxf.   Sr. Lectr.
Wadsworth, Roger M., BPharm Lond., PhD   Reader
Wainwright, Cherry, BSc Aberd., PhD   Sr. Lectr.
Zeitlin, Isaac J., BSc Edin., PhD Edin.   Prof.

Primary Education

Fax: (0141) 950 3151

Allan, James G., BA   Sr. Lectr.
Dundas, Kenneth, BSc MEd   Sr. Lectr.
Ellis, Susan, BA Essex, MSc Lond.   Sr. Lectr.
Hughes, Anne, MPhil   Sr. Lectr.
Keith, Lynda, MA Glas.   Programme Co-ordinator
Kleinberg, Susan M., BSc Lond., MSc Stir.   Sr. Lectr.; Programme Co-ordinator
Laing, Moira F., MA MEd   Programme Co-ordinator
Livingstone, MA MEd   Sr. Lectr.
Mackay, Ronald, MA   Head*
McGregor, Anne S., BEd BA MEd   Programme Co-ordinator
Pearson, Myra A., MBA Strath.   Dir., Professl. Devel.
Robertson, Alistair H., MA MEd   Sr. Lectr.
Twiddle, Brian L., BSc Hull   Course Dir.
White, Graham R., BEd   Course Dir.
Other Staff: 15 Lectrs.

Prosthetics and Orthotics, National Centre for Training and Education in

Fax: (0141) 552 1283

Govan, Norman A.   Sr. Lectr.
Hughes, John, BSc Strath., FIMechE   Prof.; Dir.*
Jacobs, Norman A., MSc Manc.   Sr. Lectr.; Dep. Dir.
Jones, Derek, BSc Salf., PhD Strath.   Sr. Lectr.
Mackie, Hamish J. C., BSc Strath., PhD Strath.   Sr. Lectr.
Other Staff: 12 Lectrs.

Psychology

Fax: (0141) 552 6307

Boyle, James M. E., BSc Glas.   Sr. Lectr.
Cheyne, William M., MA Aberd., PhD Aberd.   Sr. Lectr.
Davies, John B., BA PhD   Prof.
Foot, Hugh, BA Durh., PhD St And.   Prof.
Howe, Christine J., BA Sus., PhD Camb.   Sr. Lectr.; Head*
Thomson, James A., MA Edin., PhD Edin.   Sr. Lectr.
Warden, David A., BA Belf., PhD Lond.   Sr. Lectr.
Other Staff: 6 Lectrs.

Public Policy, Centre for the Study of

Fax: (0141) 552 4711

Rose, Richard, BA Johns H., DPhil Oxf., FBA   Prof.; Dir.*

Scottish Hotel School

Fax: (0141) 552 2870

Baum, Thomas G., BA Wales, MA CNAA, MPhil CNAA, PhD Strath.   Prof., International Hospitality Management; Head*
Carter, Roger, PhD   Visiting Prof.
Dieke, Peter U. C., BA Nigeria, MSc Mass., PhD Strath.   Sr. Lectr.

Forte, Hon. Sir Rocco, MA *Oxf.* Visiting Prof.
Jeffrey, Graham Visiting Prof.
Jenkins, Carson L., BSc(Econ) *Hull*, PhD *Strath.* Prof., International Tourism
Levin, David Visiting Prof.
O'Connor, John, BSc *Birm.* Visiting Prof.
Schlentrich, Udo A., BS *Cornell* Visiting Prof.
Seaton, Anthony V., BA *Open(UK)*, MA *Oxf.* Reader
Wood, Roy C., BA *York(UK)*, MPhil *Bath*, PhD *Strath.* Prof., Hospitality Management
Other Staff: 9 Lectrs.

Scottish Local Authorities Management Centre

Fax: (0141) 552 6587

Donnelly, Mike, BA MSc PhD Sr. Lectr.
Mair, Colin, BA Dir.*
Other Staff: 2 Lectrs.

Ship and Marine Technology

Fax: (0141) 552 2879

Kuo, Chengi, BSc *Glas.*, PhD *Glas.* Prof.; Head*
Lee, Byung S., BSc *Seoul*, MSc PhD Sr. Lectr.
MacFarlane, Colin J., BSc Lloyd's Register Prof.
Sayer, Philip G., BSc *Manc.*, PhD *Manc.*, FIMA Sr. Lectr.
Vassalos, Dracos, BSc PhD Prof.
Other Staff: 3 Lectrs.

Social Studies

Forrest, Joan
Gray, Iain, MA Head of Section
Hillis, Peter L. M., MA PhD Head*
MacDonald, Donald, MA MEd Head of Section
Martles, BSc MPhil Head of Section
McKellar, Ian B., MA Programme Co-ordinator
Robinson, Alastair, MA Head of Section
Weir, Douglas, MA MEd Prof.
Other Staff: 3 Lectrs.

Social Work

Campbell, John, MA Course Dir.
Chakrabarti, Mono R., MA MSc Prof.
McCullough, Dennis R., MSc Sr. Lectr.; Head*
McMaster, Andrew Sr. Lectr.
Other Staff: 8 Lectrs.

Spanish, see Mod. Langs.

Special Educational Needs

Tel: (0141) 950 3330 Fax: (0141) 950 3129

Clark, Kathleen A., MSc Course Dir.
Hamill, Paul, BA MEd Head*
Hewitt, Carol M., MA MEd Sr. Lectr.
MacKay, Gilbert F., MA PhD Sr. Lectr.; Res. Co-ordinator
Semple, Sheila, MA MPhil Sr. Lectr.; Dir., Centre for Careers Educn.
Other Staff: 4 Lectrs.

Speech and Language Therapy

Boyle, Bernadette E., MPhil Sr. Lectr.
Lees, Roberta M., MSc Sr. Lectr.
Mackenzie, Catherine, MEd Sr. Lectr.
McCartney, Elspeth, BSc MEd Sr. Lectr.; Head*
Other Staff: 4 Lectrs.

Statistics and Modelling Science

Ahmad, Rashid, MA *Punjab*, PhD *Case W. Reserve* Sr. Lectr.
Blythe, Stephen P., BSc *Ulster*, PhD Sr. Lectr.

Gettinby, George C., BSc *Belf.*, DPhil *Ulster* Prof.; Head*
Greenhalgh, David, MA PhD
Gurney, William S. C., BSc *Brist.*, PhD *Brist.* Prof.
Henery, Robert J., MSc *Glas.*, PhD *Glas.* Sr. Lectr.
Mao, Xeurong, MSc PhD Sr. Lectr.
McKenzie, Edward, MSc *Glas.*, PhD Sr. Lectr.
Renshaw, Eric, BSc *Lond.*, MPhil *Sus.*, PhD *Edin.* Prof.
Other Staff: 5 Lectrs.

Strathclyde Graduate Business School

Alexander, Keith, BSc BArch Sr. Lectr.
Bothams, John, BSc MA Sr. Lectr.
Greensted, Christopher S., BSc *Lond.*, MSc Prof.; Dir.*
Huxham, Christine S., BSc MSc DPhil Dir., MBA
Shea, Michael S. M., MA PhD Visiting Prof.
Other Staff: 10 Lectrs.

Technology and Business Studies

Interface Studies Unit

Fax: (0141) 552 3607

Gerrard, William, BSc *Strath.*, MSc *Cran.IT*, PhD *Strath.* Sr. Lectr.
Macrosson, W. D. Keith, BSc *Glas.*, MBA *Strath.*, PhD *Glas.* Prof., Management of Technology; Head*
Sheen, Margaret R., MSc *Lond.*, PhD *Leeds* Sr. Lectr.
Vacant Posts: 1 Lectr.

SPECIAL CENTRES, ETC

Academic Practice, Centre for

Fax: (0141) 553 2053

Brown, Rosemary M., BA MSc Co-ordinator
Gordon, Prof. George, MA *Edin.*, PhD Dir.*
Johnston, W. R., BA Co-ordinator
Murray, Rowena, MA *Glas.*, PhD *Penn.* Sr. Lectr.
Nicol, D. J., BA PhD Sr. Lectr.
Other Staff: 2 Lectrs.

Continuing Education Centre

Fleming, Archibald M., MA *Edin.*, BCom *Edin.*, PhD *Strath.* Dir.*
Hart, Lesley A., MA *Glas.* Head of Sr. Studies Inst.

Scottish Universities Research and Reactor Centre, see under University of Glasgow

Strathclyde Science and Technology Forum

Nuttall, R. H., BSc *Lond.*, PhD *Lond.* Dir.†*

Television, Film and Music, John Logie Baird Centre for Research in

Frith, Prof. S. W., BA *Oxf.*, MA *Camb.*, PhD *Camb.* Res. Dir.*

CONTACT OFFICERS

Academic affairs. Academic Registrar: Mellows, Sue M., BSc *Edin.*, PhD *Lond.*
Accommodation. Director of Residence and Catering: Cook, Robert J.
Admissions (first degree). Senior Assistant Registrar: Kilgariff, Joe
Admissions (higher degree). Senior Assistant Registrar: Kilgariff, Joe

Adult/continuing education. Director, Continuing Education Centre: Fleming, Archibald M., MA *Edin.*, BCom *Edin.*, PhD
Alumni. Alumni Relations Officer: Nicholson, Sally, LLB
Archives. Senior Assistant Registrar and Archivist: McGrath, James S., MA *Glas.*, PhD *Glas.*
Careers. Director: Graham, Barbara, MA *Glas.*, MLitt *Glas.*
Computing services. Director: Kay, Nigel, BSc
Consultancy services. Director of Research and Consultancy Services: Thomson, Hugh G., BSc(Eng) *Lond.*
Credit transfer. Academic Registrar: Mellows, Sue M., BSc *Edin.*, PhD *Lond.*
Development/fund-raising. Director of External Affairs and Development: ......
Estates and buildings/works and services. Director of Estates Management: Herbert, Peter
Examinations. Senior Assistant Registrar: Kilgariff, Joe
Finance. Director: Coyle, David, MA *Glas.*
General enquiries. Secretary to the University: West, Peter W. A., MA *St And.*
Health services. Medical Adviser to the University: Boyle, Iain T., BSc MB ChB, FRCP, FRCPGlas
Industrial liaison. Director of Research and Consultancy Services: Thomson, Hugh G., BSc(Eng) *Lond.*
International office. Manager of International Office: Brownlee, Janice E., MA *Edin.*
Library (chief librarian). Librarian: Law, Derek, MA, FLA
Personnel/human resources. Director of Personnel: Sutherland, William M., LLB *Glas.*
Public relations, information and marketing. Director of External Affairs and Development: ......
Publications. Publications Officer: Watson, Sally, MA *Edin.*
Purchasing. Procurements Officer: McSheaffrey, James
Quality assurance and accreditation. Academic Registrar: Mellows, Sue M., BSc *Edin.*, PhD *Lond.*
Research. Director of Research and Consultancy Services: Thomson, Hugh G., BSc(Eng) *Lond.*
Safety. Safety Officer: Blue, Donald
Scholarships, awards, loans. Student Advisory and Counselling Officer/Student Adviser: McLean, Lin
Schools liaison. Head of Schools and Colleges Liaison: Foulds, Jennifer, MA *Aberd.*
Security. Security Services Manager: Sneddon, Richard
Sport and recreation. Director of Physical Education: Manzie, Andrew, BEd
Staff development and training. Director, Centre for Academic Practice: Gordon, Prof. George, MA *Edin.*, PhD
Student welfare/counselling. Student Advisory and Counselling Officer/Student Adviser: McLean, Lin
Students from other countries. Manager of International Office: Brownlee, Janice E., MA *Edin.*
Students with disabilities. Adviser for Students with Special Needs: Simpson, Anne

[Information supplied by the institution as at 22 July 1998, and edited by the ACU]

UNIVERSITY OF SUNDERLAND

Founded 1992; previously established as Sunderland Polytechnic

Member of the Association of Commonwealth Universities

Postal Address: Langham Tower, Ryhope Road, Sunderland, England SR2 7EE
Telephone: (0191) 515 2000 **Fax**: (0191) 515 2044 **E-mail**: postmaster@sunderland.ac.uk
WWW: http://orac.sund.ac.uk

VICE-CHANCELLOR*—Wright, Anne M., CBE, BA Lond., PhD Lond.
PRO-VICE-CHANCELLOR (DEPUTY CHIEF EXECUTIVE)—Brown, Prof. Jeff R., BSc MSc PhD, FRPharmS, FRSChem, FIBiol
PRO-VICE-CHANCELLOR—......
PRO-VICE-CHANCELLOR—Thorne, Prof. Mike, BSc PhD, FIMA
PRO-VICE-CHANCELLOR—Burns, Ian
SECRETARY—Pacey, John D., LLB

ACADEMIC UNITS

Arranged by Schools

Arts, Design and Communications

Tel: (0191) 515 2000

Archer, G. C. Sr. Lectr.
Ayisi, F. I. Sr. Lectr.
Bodman, V. M. Sr. Lectr.
Bowen, E. M. Sr. Lectr.
Burton, R. W. Sr. Lectr.
Cemmick, D. Sr. Lectr.
Clarke, D. Principal Lectr.
Crisell, A. P. Sr. Lectr.
Crozier, R. Sr. Lectr.
Davies, K. Sr. Lectr.
Davis, M. R. Sr. Lectr.
Dawson, J. Sr. Lectr.
Dempsey, P. W. Sr. Lectr.
Forsyth, A. Sr. Lectr.
Fulcher, R. A. Reader
Holmes, C. Sr. Lectr.
Kirk, C. H. Sr. Lectr.
Lewis, B. Sr. Lectr.
Madge, S. L. Sr. Lectr.
Masters, R. J. Reader
McAvoy, J. Sr. Lectr.
McNulty, S. P. Sr. Lectr.
Millington, A. R. Principal Lectr.
Mitchell, C. A. Sr. Lectr.
Norten, G. H. Reader
Nutter, H. B. Sr. Lectr.
Rainer, R. W. Sr. Lectr.
Revell, K. Lectr./Sr. Lectr., Media Studies
Robertson, A. E. Sr. Lectr.
Robinson, S. C. Sr. Lectr.
Saul, J. Sr. Lectr.
Sefton, B. Principal Lectr.
Sim, S. D. Prof.
Singh, G. Sr. Lectr.
Southall, T. H. Sr. Lectr.
Storey, J. C. Reader
Strachan, J. R. Principal Lectr.
Swann, Prof. Flavia, BA Dir.*
Tate, M. E. Sr. Lectr.
Terry, R. G. Sr. Lectr.
Thomas, D. R. Reader
Thompson, B. Reader
Thornham, S. Team Leader: Media
Tillotson, E. Sr. Lectr.
Trodd, C. B. Sr. Lectr.
Wakeley, J. H. Sr. Lectr.
Ward, R. Sr. Lectr.
Wheatley, J. Sr. Lectr.
Whitley, J. S. W. Principal Lectr.
Williams, S. Sr. Lectr.
Younger, L. Sr. Lectr.

Business

Tel: (0191) 515 2000

Adamson, I. Sr. Lectr.
Altshul, R. C. Sr. Lectr.
Ang'awa, E. W. Sr. Lectr.
Armstrong, S. J. Sr. Lectr.
Aylott, R. P. Sr. Lectr.
Barker, M. G.W. Sr. Lectr.
Broach, A. J. Sr. Lectr.

Brookes, W. L. Sr. Lectr.
Callaghan, J. B. Principal Lectr.
Carr, L. E. Acting Dir.*
Clarke, M. L. Sr. Lectr.
Corcoran, J. G. Sr. Lectr.
Davison, H. Sr. Lectr.
Dixon Dawson, J. Sr. Lectr.
Falade, J. A. Sr. Lectr.
Forster, R. E. Reader
Gallagher, J. K. Sr. Lectr.
Harle, A. Sr. Lectr.
Hind, J. L. Sr. Lectr.
Hunter, W. N. Sr. Lectr.
Lawler, K. A. Principal Lectr.
Lennox, J. A. Sr. Lectr.
Liddle, J. Sr. Lectr.
Maguire, J. A. Sr. Lectr.
Marrington, P. S. Sr. Lectr.
Marshall, C. D. Principal Lectr.
McBain, N. Sr. Lectr.
McCall, M. S. Sr. Lectr.
McCormick, W. A. Sr. Lectr.
McDonnell, M. C. Sr. Lectr.
Mohon, W. R. Sr. Lectr.
Morrison, J. B. Sr. Lectr.
Moss, C. D. Principal Lectr.
Neilson, J. R. Sr. Lectr.
Nuttall, M. W. Sr. Lectr.
Owen, E. Sr. Lectr.
Paterson, J. P. Sr. Lectr.
Paton, K. F. Sr. Lectr.
Porrelli, A. N. Sr. Lectr.
Proud, S. Sr. Lectr.
Ramm, K. Sr. Lectr.
Ridley, A. Sr. Lectr.
Ripley, P. J. Sr. Lectr.
Rowe, J. Sr. Lectr.
Seddighi, H. R. Sr. Lectr.
Spowart-Taylor, A. Principal Lectr.
Storey, S. Sr. Lectr.
Tabatabai, B. O. Sr. Lectr.
Teale, M. Sr. Lectr.
Thompson, G. Sr. Lectr.
Vinton, J. W. Sr. Lectr.
Watson, G. E. Sr. Lectr.
Weston, C. Reader
Wilson, M. Sr. Lectr.
Winter, M. G. Sr. Lectr.
Woodfield, W. R. E. Sr. Lectr.
Woodward, R. G. Principal Lectr.

Computing and Information Systems

Tel: (0191) 515 2000

Ahmad, J. N. Sr. Lectr.
Arthington, D. R. Sr. Lectr.
Bloor, C. Principal Lectr.
Bowerman, G. D. C. Sr. Lectr.
Cliffe, W. A. Sr. Lectr.
Comer, P. G. Sr. Lectr.
Curran, D. A. S. Sr. Lectr.
Deeks, D. A. Sr. Lectr.
Dunne, P. C. Sr. Lectr.
Edwards, H. H. Sr. Lectr.
Farrow, M. Reader
Fellows, P. Sr. Lectr.
Fletcher, E. J. Prof.
Foster, R. A. Sr. Lectr.

Fowler, J. R. Sr. Lectr.
Golightly, B. I. Sr. Lectr.
Holmes, M. C. Sr. Lectr.
Hunter, A. Sr. Lectr.
Irving, P. Sr. Lectr.
Kendal, S. L. Sr. Lectr.
Lejk, M. D. Sr. Lectr.
Mansi, M. M. Sr. Lectr.
Middleton, W. Reader
Milburn, C. W. M. Sr. Lectr.
Moscardini, A. O. A. Prof.
Moses, J. Sr. Lectr.
Newton, N. D. Sr. Lectr.
Parrington, W. F. Principal Lectr.
Patience, F. E. Sr. Lectr.
Pearson, N. Sr. Lectr.
Potts, I. W. Principal Lectr.
Prior, D. E. Sr. Lectr.
Ramshaw, N. Principal Lectr.; Project Co-ordinator
Reed, P. Principal Lectr.
Silk, R. N. Principal Lectr.
Smith, P. Prof.
Spencer, L. M. Sr. Lectr.
Steward, A. P. Principal Lectr.
Stirk, S. Sr. Lectr.
Sutcliffe, S. J. Sr. Lectr.
Tait, J. I. Reader
Tan, T. C. Sr. Lectr.
Temke, A. G. Sr. Lectr.
Thompson, J. B. Prof.
Veitch, C. R. Sr. Lectr.
Walton, P. G. Sr. Lectr.
White, L. N. Sr. Lectr.
Wyvill, N. Principal Lectr.

Design, see Arts, Des. and Communicns.

Education

Tel: (0191) 515 2000

Andrew, C. H. Sr. Lectr.
Arthurs, J. Sr. Lectr.
Ashfield, M. J. Sr. Lectr.
Atkinson, E. A. Sr. Lectr.
Atkinson, E. S. Sr. Lectr.
Bell, N. Sr. Lectr.
Birbeck, W. C. Sr. Lectr.
Bowles, C. H. Sr. Lectr.
Bremner, I. R. Sr. Lectr.
Chalkley, C. M. Sr. Lectr.
Clark, A. C. Sr. Lectr.
Constable, H. Prof.
Cooke, S. R. Sr. Lectr.
Coulthard, A. Sr. Lectr.
Cumming, J. B. Sr. Lectr.
Dockerty, A. Sr. Lectr.
Ecclestone, K. Sr. Lectr.
Elliott, J. G. C. Principal Lectr.
Evans, B. A. Principal Lectr.
Farnsworth, C. A. Sr. Lectr.
Fleetham, D. E. Sr. Lectr.
Hills, J. I. Sr. Lectr.
Holdon, E. H. Sr. Lectr., Primary Education
Hufton, N. R. Principal Lectr.
Hunter, L. D. Sr. Lectr.
Hutton, N. A. Sr. Lectr.
Iddon, D. A. Sr. Lectr.

Jones, A. C.   Sr. Lectr.
Kennard, R. A.   Principal Lectr.
Lewis, E. N.   Sr. Lectr.
Mahoney, R. H.   Sr. Lectr.
Mercer, D.   Sr. Lectr.
Neal, I. G.   Principal Lectr.
Norton, J. G.   Sr. Lectr.
Prescott, B.   Sr. Lectr.
Reay, G. N.   Principal Lectr.
Seabourne, M. J.   Sr. Lectr.
Shield, G.   Principal Lectr.
Singh, B. R.   Reader
Stafford, I. V.   Sr. Lectr.
Stewart-Smith, Prof. Yvonne C., BA Open(UK),
   MBA Newcastle(UK)   Dir.*
Stokoe, R.   Sr. Lectr.
Taylor, C. M.   Sr. Lectr.
Wass, R. W.   Sr. Lectr.
Whiston, P. J.   Principal Lectr.
Wilson, L.   Sr. Lectr.
Wood, P. O.   Sr. Lectr.
Wright-Stephenson, M. E.   Sr. Lectr.

Engineering and Advanced Technology

Tel: (0191) 515 2000
Amin, M. B.   Sr. Lectr.
Arden, W. J.B.   Principal Lectr.
Ashworth, H. J.   Sr. Lectr.
Attewell, B.   Principal Lectr.
Bishop, H. W.   Principal Lectr.
Bradford, P.   Sr. Lectr.
Brown, K. B.   Sr. Lectr.
Brown, L.   Sr. Lectr.
Cox, C. S.   Prof.
Dovaston, N. G.   Sr. Lectr.
Duffy, H. C.   Sr. Lectr.
Fell, A.   Sr. Lectr.
Fletcher, I.   Sr. Lectr.
French, I. G.   Sr. Lectr.
Gill, C.   Sr. Lectr.
Happian-Smith, J.   Sr. Lectr.
Hargrave, J. G.   Principal Lectr.
Harrington, H. H.   Sr. Lectr.
Hillam, C. E.   Sr. Lectr.
Hilton, G.   Sr. Lectr.
Hogg, R. A.   Sr. Lectr.
Holmes, J. H.   Sr. Lectr.
Hutchinson, R. J.   Principal Lectr.
Iley, L. J.   Sr. Lectr.
Jones, F. L.   Sr. Lectr.
Morris, H.   Sr. Lectr.
Morrison, G. E.   Sr. Lectr.
Murphy, B. J.   Sr. Lectr.
Nesbit, T.   Sr. Lectr.
Newton, M. J.   Reader
Oliver, S.   Sr. Lectr.
Otway, D.   Sr. Lectr.
Prickett, P. J.   Principal Lectr.
Roberts, J.   Sr. Lectr.
Ryan, Prof. H. M.   Dir.
Saadat, M.   Sr. Lectr.
Sheldrake, T. H.   Sr. Lectr.
Taylor, D. E.   Principal Lectr.
Tindle, J.   Sr. Lectr.
Trimble, R.   Sr. Lectr.
Venus, A. D.   Sr. Lectr.
Wadsworth, A. P.   Sr. Lectr.
Webb, A. I. C.   Principal Lectr.
Wheatley, A. R.   Sr. Lectr.
Wheeler, J. D.   Sr. Lectr.
Wilcock, Prof. Dennis, BSc CNAA, MSc Birm.,
   PhD Coventry   Dir.*
Young, R. G.   Sr. Lectr.

Environment

Tel: (0191) 515 2000
Abel, P. D.   Reader
Alabaster, T.   Reader
Andrews, M.   Sr. Lectr.
Arthur, W. W.   Prof.
Barrass, R.   Principal Lectr.
Blair, D. J.   Reader
Bromley, R. R.   Sr. Lectr.
Chandler, C.   Sr. Lectr.
Cherrill, A. J.   Sr. Lectr.
Clear Hill, E. R. R.   Sr. Lectr.
Davies, N. S.   Sr. Lectr.
Eady, P. E.   Sr. Lectr.

Giusti, L.   Sr. Lectr.
Hall, D. R.   Reader
Harrison, R.   Prof.; Acting Dir.*
Hill, A. J.   Principal Lectr.
Hodgson, S.   Sr. Lectr.
Humphries, L. P.   Sr. Lectr.
Jamnejad, G.   Sr. Lectr.
Judd, A. G.   Reader
Kinnaird, V. H.   Sr. Lectr.
Lane, A. N.   Sr. Lectr.
Leddra, M. J.   Sr. Lectr.
Matthews, D.   Sr. Lectr.
Murphy, J. R.   Sr. Lectr.
Nicholson, R.   Sr. Lectr.
Percival, S. N.   Sr. Lectr.
Petley, D. N.   Lectr./Sr. Lectr.
Robertson, G. W.   Principal Lectr.
Rotheroe, N. C.   Lectr./Sr. Lectr.
Salam, T. F.   Sr. Lectr.
Schlesinger, A. P.   Sr. Lectr.
Scott, W. B.   Principal Lectr.
Stone, C. J.   Sr. Lectr.
Turner, D. D.   Sr. Lectr.
Wheeler, D. A.   Reader
Wose, A   Sr. Lectr.
Yeomans, I. G.   Principal Lectr.

Health Sciences

Tel: (0191) 515 2000
Adams, D. B.   Sr. Lectr.
Anderson, R. J.   Sr. Lectr.
Ashton, N.   Sr. Lectr.
Beveridge, E. G.   Principal Lectr.
Blackwell, D.   Sr. Lectr.
Boachie-Ansah, G.   Sr. Lectr.
Bowen, D. H.   Principal Lectr.
Brown, J. A.   Sr. Lectr.
Buchanan, J.   Sr. Lectr.
Cairns, D.   Sr. Lectr.
Charnock, A.   Sr. Lectr.
Clark, B. P.   Sr. Lectr.
Colby, J.   Prof.
Crawley, R. A.   Sr. Lectr.
Deshmukh, A. A.   Prof., Pharmacy
Donnelly, W. C. J.   Sr. Lectr.
Duggan, J. P.   Sr. Lectr.
Eagle, L. A.   Lectr./Sr. Lectr., Cell/Human
   Biology
Emes, A. V.   Principal Lectr.
Etherington, R.   Sr. Lectr.
Ewart, B. W.   Sr. Lectr.
Freeman, L. C.   Sr. Lectr.
Fulton, J. A.   Principal Lectr.
Garbutt, G.   Sr. Lectr.
Griffin, B. L.   Sr. Lectr.
Halliwell, R. F.   Sr. Lectr.
Hambleton, P. A.   Sr. Lectr.
Hawkins, P. J.   Principal Lectr.
Holden, K.   Sr. Lectr.
Hood, A. J. C.   Sr. Lectr.
Kendall, H. E.   Principal Lectr.; Dir., Pharm.
Kilcoyne, J. P.   Principal Lectr.
Kingston, W. P.   Sr. Lectr.
Lewis, C.   Sr. Lectr.
Lough, W. J.   Sr. Lectr.
Mair, A. R.   Sr. Lectr.
Markham, A.   Reader
Marshall, K. M.   Sr. Lectr.
Marshall, T.   Reader
McInnes, A.   Lectr./Sr. Lectr., Applied
   Psychology
McLaren, I.   Principal Lectr.
Meth-Cohn, O.   Prof.
Morgan, R. M.   Reader
Munby, J.   Sr. Lectr.
Nieland, M. N. S.   Sr. Lectr.
Noble, L.   Sr. Lectr.
Pook, P. C.   Reader
Potts, A. D.   Lectr./Sr. Lectr.
Pullen, R. G. L.   Principal Lectr.
Quinn, H. R. M. A.   Sr. Lectr.
Reeve, R. H.   Sr. Lectr.
Rowell, F. J.   Prof.
Rowley, G.   Principal Lectr.
Sanders, D. C.   Principal Lectr.
Seheult, C. L.   Sr. Lectr.
Shamssain, M. H.   Sr. Lectr.
Shattock, P. E. G.   Sr. Lectr.

Sheldon, W. L.   Sr. Lectr.
Smith, J. L.   Sr. Lectr.
Sneddon, John H., BSc PhD   Dir.*
Taylor, G. W.   Sr. Lectr.
Terry, J.   Sr. Lectr.
Thomas, K. R.   Sr. Lectr.
Thornton, H. M.   Sr. Lectr.
Vaughan, D. P.   Sr. Lectr.
Walters, P. A.   Sr. Lectr.
Wilkie, K. M.   Principal Lectr.
Wood, P. R.   Principal Lectr.
Wyn-Jones, A. P.   Principal Lectr.

Information Systems, see Computing and
   Information Systems

Social and International Studies

Tel: (0191) 515 2000
Adamson, K.   Sr. Lectr.
Adshead, D. H.   Sr. Lectr.
Ali, S.   Sr. Lectr.
Anderson, P. S.   Sr. Lectr.
Atkinson, D. J.   Sr. Lectr.
Banim, M.   Sr. Lectr.
Beardow, F.   Reader
Brown, N.   Sr. Lectr.
Bruch, A. S.   Sr. Lectr.
Cannon, S. M.   Sr. Lectr.
Charles, Prof. Tony F., BSc(SocSc) S'ton., PhD
   S'ton.   Dir.*
Durrans, P. J.   Principal Lectr.
Flockhart, T. B.   Sr. Lectr.
Francis, Rev. J. H. M.   Sr. Lectr.
Gritzan, H. H.   Principal Lectr.
Hargrave, J. H.   Principal Lectr.
Harvey, B. P.   Reader
Hepburn, A. C.   Prof., Modern Irish
Hill, I.   Sr. Lectr.
Howard, W. S.   Sr. Lectr.
Kearney, J.   Principal Lectr.
Kurian, A.   Sr. Lectr.
Land, J. G.   Sr. Lectr.
MacQueen, H. J. D.   Reader
Maunders, A. R.   Sr. Lectr.
Meyer, E. C.   Sr. Lectr.
Morgan, G.   Reader
Morris, K. A.   Sr. Lectr.
Okumura, K.   Sr. Lectr.
Over, D. E.   Prof.
Parkes, K. S.   Reader
Parkin, C.   Sr. Lectr.
Potts, G. R.   Principal Lectr.
Presdee, M.   Reader
Pringle, K. R.   Sr. Lectr.
Rowell, P. J.   Principal Lectr.
Rushton, P.   Reader
Spence, J.   Sr. Lectr.
Stubbs, C. E.   Principal Lectr.
Taras, M.   Sr. Lectr.
Waldron, P. R.   Reader
Wallace, P. J.   Sr. Lectr.
Watson, M. J.   Principal Lectr.
Wefelmeyer, F. H.   Reader

Technology, see Engin. and Advanced
   Technol.

SPECIAL CENTRES, ETC

Continuing Education Unit

Tel: (0191) 515 2000
Lenston, Martyn   Dir.*

Industry Centre

Tel: (0191) 515 2000
Haywood, N. B.   Dir.*

International Development

Tel: (0191) 515 2680 Fax: (0191) 515 2960
Robson, G.   Dir.*

Learning Developing Services

Tel: (0191) 515 2000
Robertson, S.   Dir.*

Micro Technology Centre

Tel: (0191) 515 2000

Wood, D. G.   Acting Dir.*

Research Development

Tel: (0191) 515 2000

Slade, A.   Dir.*

CONTACT OFFICERS

Academic affairs. Vice-Chancellor: Wright, Anne M., CBE, BA Lond., PhD Lond.

Development/fund-raising. Director of Corporate Affairs: Wilson, Kevin, BA MA

Finance. Director of Finance: Burns, Ian

General enquiries. Secretary: Pacey, John D., LLB

Library (chief librarian). Director of Information Services: McDonald, A. C.

Personnel/human resources. Director of Personnel Services: Higgins, Michael, BSc MBA

Student welfare/counselling. Director of Student Services: Settle, Anthony J., BEd MBA MPhil

[Information supplied by the institution as at December 1996, and edited by the ACU]

UNIVERSITY OF SURREY

Incorporated by Royal Charter 1966; previously designated Battersea College of Advanced Technology; originally established as Battersea Polytechnic Institute 1891

Member of the Association of Commonwealth Universities

Postal Address: Guildford, Surrey, England GU2 5XH
Telephone: (01483) 300800 **Fax**: (01483) 300803 **Telex**: 859331 **WWW**: http://www.surrey.ac.uk
E-mail formula: firstinitial.surname@surrey.ac.uk

CHANCELLOR—Kent, H.R.H. The Duke of , KG, GCMG, GCVO

PRO-CHANCELLOR EMERITUS—Edwards, Sir George, OM, CBE, FRS

PRO-CHANCELLOR EMERITUS—Pearce, Sir Austin, CBE, BSc Birm., PhD Birm., Hon. DSc Birm., FEng

PRO-CHANCELLOR—Pearce, Sir Idris, CBE, TD, FRICS, FEng

PRO-CHANCELLOR—Ash, Sir Eric, CBE, FEng, FRS

VICE-CHANCELLOR AND CHIEF EXECUTIVE*—Dowling, Prof. Patrick J., BE N.U.I., PhD Lond., Hon. LLD N.U.I., Hon. DSc Vilnius T.U., Hon. DSc Ulster, FRS, FEng, FICE, FIStructE

SENIOR PRO-VICE-CHANCELLOR—Butterworth, Prof. Peter H. W., BSc Liv., PhD Liv.

PRO-VICE-CHANCELLOR (RESEARCH)—Breakwell, Prof. Glynis M., BA Leic., MA Oxf., MSc Strath., PhD Brist., DSc Oxf., FBPsS

PRO-VICE-CHANCELLOR (TEACHING AND LEARNING)—Harding, Prof. John E., BSc(Eng) Lond., MSc Lond., PhD Lond., FIStructE, FICE

PRO-VICE-CHANCELLOR (STAFF DEVELOPMENT)—Gilbert, Prof. Nigel, MA Camb., PhD Camb.

SECRETARY AND REGISTRAR—Davies, H. Wyn B., BSc(Econ) Lond.

LIBRARIAN/DEAN OF INFORMATION SERVICES—Crawshaw, Tom J. A., BEng Sheff.

GENERAL INFORMATION

History. The university was originally established as Battersea Polytechnic Institute in 1891, subsequently designated Battersea College of Advanced Technology, and was incorporated by royal charter in 1966.

Admission to first degree courses (see also United Kingdom Introduction). Through Universities and Colleges Admissions Service (UCAS). The university's general entrance requirement must be satisfied, as well as particular requirements for the chosen course. The university accepts a range of educational qualifications as satisfying the minimum general entrance requirement.

First Degrees (see also United Kingdom Directory to Subjects of Study). BA, BEng, BMus, BSc, LLB, MChem, MEng, MMath, MPhys.

Courses normally last 3 years full-time, or 4 years including 1-year professional/research-based placement. BEng/BSc: either 4 years including integrated foundation year or 5 years including integrated foundation year and 1-year professional placement; MMath: 4 years full-time; MEng: 4, $4\frac{1}{2}$ or 5 years according to pattern of professional placement; BSc in public and environmental health: 1 year part-time for appropriately qualified candidates; BA/BSc in combined studies: part-time self-paced courses.

Higher Degrees (see also United Kingdom Directory to Subjects of Study). LLM, MA, MBA, MMus, MSc, MPhil, PhD, DLitt, DSc, EdD, EngD, PsychD.

Applicants for admission to master's degrees must normally hold an appropriate first degree with at least second class honours, or an equivalent overseas qualification; non-graduates with appropriate professional or other qualifications may also be admitted. PhD: appropriate master's degree; EdD: master's degree and minimum 4 years' relevant experience; PsychD: first degree in psychology with at least upper second class honours and relevant experience.

Master's degree courses normally last 1 year full-time or up to 6 years part-time. MPhil: 21 months full-time or 33 months part-time; PhD, EdD: 33 months full-time or 45 months part-time; PsychD: 33 months full-time or up to 60 months part-time; EngD: 45 months full-time. DLitt, DSc: awarded on published work to graduates of this university of minimum 10 years' standing.

Fees (1998–99, annual). Undergraduate: £1000 (UK/EU students); £ 6560–7590 (international students, arts); £8700–9590 (international students, science and engineering). Postgraduate: minimum £2610 (UK/EU students); £6560–7230 (international students, arts); £8700–10,070 (international students, science and engineering).

Academic Year (1998–99). Two semesters: 7 September–18 December; 18 January–26 March and 26 April–28 May.

Income (1996–97). Total, £92,669,000.

Statistics. Staff: 2647 (1225 academic/research, 1422 administrative). Students: full-time 6547 (3023 men, 3524 women); part-time 7402 (2503 men, 4899 women); international 3124 (1707 men, 1417 women); total 13,949.

FACULTIES/SCHOOLS

Biological Sciences, School of

Head: Lynch, Prof. James M., BTech Lough., PhD Lond., DSc Lond., FIBiol, FRSChem
Administrator: Wakile, Lawrence A.

Chemical, Civil and Environmental Engineering, School of

Head: Müller-Steinhagen, Prof. Hans, DEng DrIng, FIChemE
Administrator: Jacob, John G. E.

Educational Studies, School of

Head: Oglesby, Prof. Katherine L., BA Wales, MA Leic.
Administrator: ......

Electronic Engineering, Information Technology and Mathematics, School of

Head: Kelly, Prof. Michael J., MSc Well., MA Camb., PhD Camb., ScD Camb., FIP, FIEE, FRS

Manager: Clapham, Mike J.

Human Sciences, School of

Head: Breakwell, Prof. Glynis M., BA *Leic.*, MSc *Strath.*, MA *Oxf.*, PhD *Brist.*, DSc *Oxf.*, FBPsS
Administrator: Carruthers, H. Graham

Language and International Studies, School of

Head: Flockton, Prof. Christopher H., BA *Sus.*, MPhil *Sus.*, MSc(Econ) *Lond.*
Administrator: Stonefield, Diane F. M.

Management Studies for the Service Sector, School of

Head: Kipps, Prof. Michael, BSc *Lond.*, MSc *Sur.*, PhD *Sur.*
Administrator: Kolsaker, Ailsa M.

Mechanical and Materials Engineering, School of

Head: Goringe, Prof. Mike
Administrator: Millington, Tony H.

Performing Arts, School of

Head: Lansdale, Prof. Janet, MA *Leeds*, PhD *Leeds*
Administrator: ......

Physical Sciences, School of

Head: Gelletly, Prof. William, OBE, BSc *Edin.*, PhD *Edin.*, FIP
Administrator: Emsley, Alan M.

ACADEMIC UNITS

Biological Sciences, School of

¶= joint appointment with S.-W. Thames Regional Health Authority
Tel: (01483) 259721 Fax: (01483) 259728
Adams, Martin R., BSc *Warw.*, PhD *Manc.*, MSc   Sr. Lectr.
Aggett, Peter J. A., MSc *Lond.*, MB ChB, FRCP   Visiting Prof.
Arendt, Josephine, BSc *Lond.*, PhD *Lond.*   Prof.†, Endocrinology
Bridges, Jim W., BSc *Lond.*, PhD *Lond.*, FRSChem, FIBiol   Prof., Toxicology
Bushell, Michael E., BSc *Lond.*, PhD *Kent*   Prof., Microbiology
Butterworth, Peter H. W., BSc *Liv.*, PhD *Liv.*   Prof., Molecular Biology
Carter, Michael J., BA *Oxf.*, PhD *Camb.*   Reader
Carter, Richard L., CBE, MA DM DSc, FRCPath   Visiting Prof.
Cartwright, R. Y., MB ChB *Birm.*, FRCPath   Visiting Prof., Clinical Microbiology
Chakraborty, Jagadish, MSc *Dacca*, PhD *Lond.*   Sr. Lectr., Biochemistry
Chamberlain, Anthony H. L., BSc *Leeds*, PhD *Leeds*   Sr. Lectr., Microbiology
Clifford, Michael N., BSc *Reading*, PhD *Strath.*   Reader, Food Science
Dale, Jeremy W., BSc *Lond.*, PhD *Lond.*   Prof., Microbiology
Ferns, Gordon A. A., BSc *Lond.*, MB BS *Lond.*, MSc *Lond.*, MD *Lond.*   Prof., Molecular and Metabolic Medicine
Firth, J. B., BSc *Sheff.*, PhD *Sheff.*, FRSChem   Visiting Prof., Occupational Hygiene
Forsyth, Isabel A., MA DPhil, FIBiol   Visiting Prof.
Gibson, Gordon G., BSc *Glas.*, PhD *Lond.*   Prof., Molecular Toxicology
Goldfarb, Peter S. G., BSc *Aberd.*, PhD *Lond.*   Prof., Molecular Biology
Gould, Barry J., MSc *Lond.*, PhD *Lond.*   Sr. Lectr., Biochemistry
Grasso, Paul, BSc MD   Visiting Prof.
Hill, Raymond G., BPharm PhD   Visiting Prof.
Hinton, Richard H., BA *Camb.*, PhD *Sur.*, FIBiol, FRSChem   Reader, Cell Pathology
Howell, Nazlin K., BSc *Nott.*, PhD *Nott.*, FRSChem   Reader, Food Science
Howland, Roger J., BSc *Hull*, PhD *Hull*   Sr. Lectr., Physiology

Jarvis, Basil, BSc *Reading*, PhD *Reading*, FIBiol   Visiting Prof.
Jones, Robin S., BSc *Wales*, PhD *Wales*, FRSChem   Dir., Postgrad. Studies
King, Laurence J., BA *Oxf.*, BSc *Oxf.*, PhD *Lond.*   Prof., Biochemistry
King, Roger, BSc MSc PhD DSc   Visiting Prof.
Kitchen, Ian, BSc *CNAA*, PhD *Lond.*   Prof., Neuropharmacology
Lynch, James M., BTech *Lough.*, PhD *Lond.*, DSc *Lond.*, FIBiol, FRSChem   Prof., Biotechnology; Head*
McFadden, Johnjoe J., BSc *Lond.*, PhD *Lond.*   Reader, Molecular Microbiology
Millward, D. Joe, PhD *WI*, DSc *Wales*   Prof., Nutrition
Morgan, Jane B., MSc *Lond.*, PhD *Lond.*   Sr. Lectr.
Morgan, Linda M., BSc *Brist.*, MSc *Sur.*, PhD *Lond.*   Reader
Parke, Dennis V. W., PhD *Lond.*, DSc *Lond.*, FIBiol, FRSChem, FRCPath   Emer. Prof.
Salway, Jack G., BSc *Manc.*, MSc *Birm.*, PhD *Birm.*   Sr. Lectr., Biochemistry
Smith, Lewis L., BSc PhD   Visiting Prof.
Spier, Raymond E., MA *Oxf.*, DPhil *Oxf.*, FIBiol, FIChemE   Prof., Science and Engineering Ethics
Symons, Andrew M., BSc *Bath*, PhD *Bath*, FIBiol   Sr. Lectr.; Dir. of Studies
Walker, David, BVSc *Liv.*, FRCVS   Visiting Prof., Animal Pathology and Toxicology
Walker, Ron, BSc *Reading*, PhD *Reading*, FRSChem   Prof., Food Science
Wiseman, Alan, BSc *Lond.*, PhD *Lond.*, FRSChem   Sr. Lectr.
Wright, John W., MB BS *Lond.*, MSc *Sur.*   Reader, Metabolic Medicine¶
Other Staff: 14 Lectrs.; 1 Tutor; 3 Res. Fellows
Research: endocrinology and molecular medicine (atherosclerosis, chronobiology, cytokines, diagnostics, shiftwork, sleep); microbial physiology and ecology (antibiotics, bioremediation, biosensors, environmental biotechnology, process control); molecular microbiology (diagnostics, meningitis, mycobacteria, tuberculosis, vaccines, virology); nutrition and food science (bone, coronary heart disease, diabetes, food safety, food spoilage, lipids, phenols, phyto-oestrogens, proteins); pharmacology and toxicology (cytochrome P450, drug metabolism, in-vitro toxicology, neuroscience, opioids, purinoceptors, receptors)

Chemistry

Tel: (01483) 259584 Fax: (01483) 259514
Bolton, Roger, BSc *ANU*, PhD *Hull*, FRSChem   Reader
Catlow, C. Richard A., MA *Oxf.*, DPhil *Oxf.*   Visiting Prof.
de Namor, Angela D., BSc *Natnl.Santiago*, PhD *Sur.*   Reader
Feeney, James, PhD *Liv.*, DSc *Liv.*   Visiting Prof.
Gillies, Duncan G., BSc *Lond.*, PhD *Lond.*, FRSChem   Sr. Lectr.
Hammerton, Ian, BSc *Sur.*, PhD *Sur.*   Sr. Lectr.
Hay, John N., BSc *Edin.*, PhD *Edin.*, FRSChem   Reader
Heyes, David M., PhD *Manc.*, DSc *Brist.*, FRSChem   Reader
Howlin, Brendan J., BSc *Essex*, PhD *Essex*   Sr. Lectr.
Jones, John R., PhD *Wales*, DSc *Wales*, FRSChem   Prof., Radiochemistry
Lu, Jian R., PhD *Hull*, BSc   Reader
Povey, David C., MSc *Lond.*, PhD *Sur.*   Sr. Lectr.
Sammes, Peter G., BSc *Lond.*, PhD *Lond.*, FRSChem   Prof., Organic Chemistry
Sermon, Paul A., BSc *Wales*, PhD *Brist.*, DSc *Brist.*   Prof., Physical Chemistry
Shaw, S. J., MSc *Lough.*, PhD *City(UK)*   Visiting Prof.
Slade, Robert C. T., BA *Oxf.*, MA *Oxf.*, DPhil *Oxf.*, FRSChem, FIM   Prof.; Head*

Sutcliffe, Les H., BSc *Lond.*, PhD *Leeds*   Visiting Prof.
Ward, Neil I., MSc *NZ*, PhD *NZ*   Sr. Lectr.
Webb, Graham A., PhD *Lond.*, DSc *Bath*, FIP, FRSChem   Prof.
Other Staff: 5 Lectrs.; 2 Res. Fellows
Research: kinetics and mechanisms (carbon acids, metallo-porphyrin and other catalysts); polymer chemistry (epoxy resins, high-performance polymers, interfaces); structure and computational chemistry (molecular dynamics and modelling, NMR and ESR spectroscopy); supramolecular and analytical chemistry (inductively coupled plasma source mass spectrometry, radiochemistry, thermochemistry); synthetic organic chemistry (asymmetric synthesis, immunoassays)

Computing Sciences, see Mathl. and Computing Scis.

Dance

Tel: (01483) 259326 Fax: (01483) 259392
Buckland, Theresa, BA *Leeds*, PhD *Leeds*   Sr. Lectr.; MA Course Dir.
Jasper, Linda M., MA *Sus.*   Sr. Lectr./Tutor
Johnson-Jones, Jean, BA *Ill.*, MA *Ill.*   Staff Tutor; Dir., Labanotation Inst.
Lansdale, Janet, MA *Leeds*, PhD *Leeds*   Prof.; Head*
White, Joan, BA *Open(UK)*, MA *Leeds*   Sr. Lectr.; BA Course Dir.
Other Staff: 5 Lectrs./Tutors

Economics

Tel: (01483) 259380 Fax: (01483) 303775
Bird, Graham R., MA *Camb.*, PhD   Prof.; Head*
El-Mokadem, Ahmed, BAEcon *Cairo*, PhD *Manc.*   Visiting Reader
Hawdon, David, MSc(Econ) *Lond.*   Sr. Lectr.
Hunt, Lester C., BSc *Lough.*, MA *Essex*   Visiting Prof.
Katrak, Homi, BA *Manc.*, MSc(Econ) *Lond.*   Reader
Killick, Tony J., BA *Oxf.*   Visiting Prof.
Levine, Paul, BSc *Manc.*, MSc(Econ) *Lond.*, PhD *Manc.*   Foundation Fund Prof.
Nankervis, John C., MA *Auck.*   Reader
Pearson, Peter J. G., BA *Keele*, MSc *Lond.*, PhD *Sur.*   Visiting Reader
Pierse, Richard, BA *Oxf.*, MSc(Econ) *Lond.*   Reader
Reisman, David A., MSc *Lond.*, PhD   Prof.
Robinson, Colin, BA(Econ) *Manc.*   Prof.†
Robinson, J. Nick, BA *Brist.*, MSc *Brist.*   Visiting Prof.
Smee, Clive, OBE, BSc(Econ) MBA   Visiting Prof.
Witt, Robert J., BSc *CNAA*, MSc *Wales*, MA *Essex*, PhD *Essex*   Sr. Lectr.
Other Staff: 6 Lectrs.; 1 Sr. Tutor
Research: energy economics (energy demand modelling and policy analysis); health and other interdisciplinary research (crime and unemployment, health economics and health services, political economy); international economics (arms trade, developing and emerging countries, European integration, IFIs, technology transfer); macroeconomics, mathematical economics and econometrics (dynamic optimisation, finite sampling properties of estimators, theory of growth)

Educational Studies, School of

Fax: (01483) 259519
Brown, Alan J., BSc *Liv.*, MSc(Econ) *Lond.*, PhD *Sur.*   Sr. Lectr.
Brownhill, Robert J., BA(Admin) *Manc.*, MA(Econ) *Manc.*, PhD   Sr. Lectr.
Chadwick, Alan F., PhD *Manc.*   Sr. Lectr.
Christodoulou, Anastasios, MA *Oxf.*, Hon. DUniv *Open(UK)*, Hon. DUniv *Athab.*   Visiting Prof.
Evans, Karen, BSc *Brist.*, PhD   Prof., Post Compulsory Education; Dir., Postgrad. Centre for Professl. and Adult Educn.

Jarvis, Peter, BA(Econ) Sheff., BA Lond., MSocSc Birm., PhD Aston   Prof.; Head, Continuing Educn.

Lathlean, Judith, BScEcon Wales, MA Brun.   Visiting Prof.

Loewenthal, Derek E., BSc Brad., MA Sus., DPhil Sus.   Sr. Lectr.

Nicholls, Gill, BEd Lond., MA Kent, PhD Lond.   Sr. Lectr.

Oglesby, Katherine L., BA Wales, MA Leic.   Prof., Education; Head*

Parry, Gareth, BA CNAA, PhD City(UK)   Reader, Education

Ragg, Nicholas M., MA Camb., PhD Belf.   Sr. Lectr.

Other Staff: 9 Lectrs.; 1 Sr. Tutor; 7 Tutors

Research: adult learning and curriculum development; change management and therapeutic education; policy and change in higher education; post-sixteen education, training and employment; professional development and education

Engineering, Chemical and Process

Tel: (01483) 259473 Fax: (01483) 259510

Clift, Roland, OBE, MA Camb., PhD McG., FIChemE, FEng   Prof.; Dir., Environmental Policy Centre

Ghadiri, Mojtaba, BSc Teheran, MSc Lond., PhD Camb.   Prof., Particle Technology

Guidoboni, Giovanni E., BTech, FIMechE   Visiting Prof.

Jamialahmadi, Mohammad, MSc Aston, PhD Aston, BIndChem   Visiting Prof.

Kirkby, Norman F., BSc Nott., PhD Camb.   Sr. Lectr.

Müller-Steinhagen, Hans, DEng DrIng, FIChemE   Prof.; Head*

Perriman, Rodney J., BSc   Visiting Prof.

Schulz, Ronald A., MBE, TD, BSc Qld., MSc NSW, PhD Lond.   Sr. Lectr.

Smith, John M., BSc(Tech) Manc., DSc Manc., FIChemE   Prof., Process Engineering; Dir. of Process Biotechnol.

Taylor, Keith H., BSc Birm., PhD Birm.   Visiting Prof.

Taylor, Kenneth, PhD, FIChemE   Visiting Prof.

Tüzün, Ugur, BSc Leeds, PhD Camb.   Prof., Process Engineering

Other Staff: 8 Lectrs.; 2 Experimental Officers; 1 Univ. Dir. of Studies; 5 Res. Fellows

Research: bioreactor engineering (fundamental dynamics of microbiological systems); environmental technology (application of life cycle assessment to manufacturing process); multiphase flow (experimental and theoretical studies of interaction of gases, liquids and solids during co-and counter-current flow); particle technology (study of particulate matter at fundamental level for development of new and improved processes); process heat and mass transfer (heat transfer, energy efficiency and heat exchanger fouling investigations at interface between fundamental research and industrial application)

Engineering, Civil

Tel: (01483) 259537 Fax: (01483) 450984

Bailey, John E., BSc Brist., PhD Camb., FIP, FIM   Visiting Prof.

Basu, Amiya K., BE PhD   Visiting Prof.

Clayton, Christopher R. I., BSc CNAA, MSc(Eng) Lond., PhD, FGS, FICE   Prof., Geotechnical Engineering

Colbourne, Jennifer S., BSc PhD   Visiting Prof.

Elnashai, Amr S., BSc Cairo, MSc Lond., PhD Lond.   Visiting Prof.

Farrar, Neil S., MSc(Eng) Lond., PhD Lond., FGS   Sr. Lectr., Geology

Griffiths, David R., BSc Newcastle(UK), PhD   Sr. Lectr.

Hannant, David J., BSc(Eng) Nott., PhD Nott., DSc   Prof., Construction Materials

Harding, John E., BSc(Eng) Lond., MSc Lond., PhD Lond., FIStructE, FICE   Prof., Structural Engineering; Head*

Helmer, Richard, MPH N.Carolina, DrIng Stuttgart   Visiting Prof.

Huxley, Michael A., BSc   Univ. Dir.*

Lloyd, Barry J., BSc Leeds, MPhil Reading, PhD Sur.   Prof.

Nooshin, Hoshyar, BSc Teheran, PhD Lond., FIStructE   Prof., Space Structures

Onoufriou, Toula, BSc(Eng) PhD   Reader, Structural Engineering

Parke, Gerard A. R., BSc CNAA, MSc City(UK), PhD, FIStructE   Reader

Toy, Norman, BSc City(UK), PhD City(UK)   Prof., Fluid Mechanics

Other Staff: 14 Lectrs.; 1 Experimental Officer; 6 Res. Fellows; 7 Res. Officers

Research: construction materials (new materials for construction, repair and remediation of stone and concrete); environmental health engineering (air, water and ground pollution, water quality, water treatment and distribution systems (especially for the developing world)); geotechnical engineering (behaviour of geomaterials, environmental geotechnics, numerical modelling, site characterisation); structural engineering (space structures, steel structures, structural composites, timber structures); wind engineering (flow measurement and visualisation, wind loading on buildings and transmission towers)

Engineering, Materials, see Materials Sci. and Engin.

Engineering, Mechanical

Fax: (01483) 306039

Allison, Brian G., BSc(Econ) Lond.   Visiting Prof.

Branemark, Per-Ingver, MD PhD   Visiting Prof.

Cartwright, Anthony G., BSc Wales, PhD Sur.   Sr. Lectr.

Castro, Ian P., MA Camb., MSc Lond., PhD Lond., FRAeS   Prof., Fluid Dynamics

Crocombe, Andrew D., BSc Brist., PhD Brist., FIMechE   Sr. Lectr.

Driscoll, John, BSc Aston, PhD Aston, FIMechE   Sr. Lectr.

Foster, Keith, MA PhD, FIMechE   Visiting Prof.

Hughes, Stephen, BSc Glas.   Sr. Lectr.

Lohr, Ray D., BSc CNAA, PhD Brist.   Visiting Prof.

Mason, Paul J., BSc Nott., PhD Reading, FRS   Visiting Prof.

Mottram, Robert C., BSc(Eng) S'ton., PhD   Sr. Lectr.

Parker, Graham A., BSc Birm., PhD Birm., FIMechE   Prof.; Head*

Pollard, David J., BSc CNAA, PhD, FIMechE   Sr. Lectr.

Robins, Alan G., BSc Lond., PhD Lond., FRMetS   Res. Prof., Environmental Fluid Mechanics

Voke, Peter R., MSc PhD   Reader

Williams, Brian R., BSc S'ton., PhD Reading   Visiting Prof.

Other Staff: 10 Lectrs.; 12 Res. Fellows

Research: biomedical engineering (biomechanics, electrical stimulation, gait, microengineering, osseointegration); fluid dynamics (dispersion, environmental flows, numeric modelling, turbulence); mechatronic systems and robotics (image processing, telepresence, ultrasonic/radioscopic NDT, virtual reality); solid mechanics and design (adhesives, CAE, concept design, durability, material modelling, solid diffusion)

French, see Linguistic and Internat. Studies

German, see Linguistic and Internat. Studies

Health and Medical Sciences, European Institute of

School of Education and Professional Training Postgraduate Research School

Tel: (01483) 302239 Fax: (01483) 440821

Allen, Peter T., BSc S'ton., PhD S'ton.   Sr. Res. Fellow; Head, Appl. Psychol.

Atkinson, Christopher, BA Open(UK), MA Open(UK), PhD Lanc.   Sr. Lectr.

Bridges, James W., BSc Lond., PhD Lond., DSc, FIBiol, FRSChem   Head, Postgrad. Res. Sch.; Dir.*

Buckle, Peter, BSc Leic., MSc Lond., PhD Cran.IT   Prof., Ergonomics and Epidemiology; Head, Ergonomics

Chan, Pam, MA Keele   Sr. Lectr./Sr. Tutor

Clarke, Margaret, BSc Nott., MPhil Sur.   Prof.†, Nursing Studies

Crow, Rosemary A., MA Edin., PhD Edin.   Prof., Nursing Sciences; Dir., Centre for the Advancement of Clin. Practice

Cullingford, Sarah, BEd Sus.   Sr. Lectr./Sr. Tutor

Elliott, D. H., OBE, MB BS Lond., DPhil Oxf., FRCPEd   Visiting Prof.†, Occupational Health

Getliffe, Kathryn, BSc Sur., MSc Qld., PhD Sur.   Sr. Lectr./Sr. Tutor

Hart, Sue, BA Kingston(UK)   Sr. Lectr./Sr. Tutor

Hawkins, Leslie H., BSc Sur., PhD Sur.   Sr. Lectr., Physiology; Head, Occupnl. Health

Helmer, Richard, MPH N.Carolina, DrIng Stuttgart   Visiting Prof., Water Quality

Macleod, Christina, BEd CNAA, MSc Sur.   Co-ordinator of MSc Course

Marks, Vincent, BA Oxf., BM BCh Oxf., MA Oxf., DM Oxf., FRCP, FRCPEd, FRCPath   Dean of Med.

Moore, Claire, BEd Sus., MSc Sur.   Sr. Lectr./Sr. Tutor

Morley, Joseph, BA Youngstown, BSc Sur., PhD Sur.   Co-ordinator of MSc Course

Nelson Cole, Jan, BSc   Sr. Lectr./Sr. Tutor

Rush, Denise, BSc Sur., MBA Brighton   Sr. Lectr./Sr. Tutor

Smith, Lynn, BEd S.Bank, MSc S.Bank   Sr. Lectr./Sr. Tutor

Sque, Margaret, BSc Sur., PhD S'ton.   Co-ordinator of MSc Course

Stevenson, Derek, PhD Sur.   Sr. Lectr., Analytical Science; Head, Analyt. Centre

Stubbs, David A., BEd Lough., PhD Sur.   Prof., Ergonomics

Vlachonikolis, Ioannis, BSc Athens, MSc Lough., DPhil Oxf.   Reader, Clinical Medical Statistics

Waterhouse, P., BSc Leeds, PhD Leeds   Visiting Prof., Occupational Safety

Wright, Graham, MPhil CNAA   Dir., Education and Professional Training

Other Staff: 7 Lectrs./Tutors; 8 Lectrs./Practitioners; 9 Res. Fellows; 1 Sr. Experimental Officer; 2 Clin. Teachers

Industrial Health and Safety, Robens Centre for

Tel: (01483) 259211 Fax: (01483) 503517

Pedley, Stephen, BSc Manc., PhD Manc.   Sr. Res. Fellow; Head, Environmental Health; Head*

Other Staff: 6 Res. Fellows

Linguistic and International Studies

Tel: (01483) 259950 Fax: (01483) 302605

Anderman, Gunilla M., FilMag Stockholm, PhD Lond.   Sr. Lectr., Linguistics and Swedish Language; Dir., Centre for Translation Studies

Corbett, Greville G., MA Birm., PhD Birm.   Prof., Linguistics and Russian Languages

Flockton, Christopher H., BA Sus., MPhil Sus., MSc(Econ) Lond.   Prof., Economics; Head*

Flood, Christopher G., MA Edin., MA Reading, DPhil Oxf.   Sr. Lectr., French

Judge, Anne, LèsL Bordeaux, PhD Lond.   Prof., French

Lutzeier, Peter, MLitt *Oxf.*, DPhil *Stuttgart*, DrHabil *Berlin*   Prof., German
Malcolm, Rosalind, LLB *Lond.*   Sr. Lectr.
Riordan, James W., BSocSc *Birm.*, PhD *Birm.*   Prof., Russian Studies
Rogers, Margaret A., BA *Birm.*, MA *Kent*, PhD   Sr. Lectr., German
Sanders, Carol, MA *Camb.*, DU *Paris*   Prof., French
Other Staff: 1 Hon. Sr. Fellow
Research: area studies (cultural studies, European borders, European legal studies); language (applied linguistics, colour and categorisation, French sociolinguistics and stylistics, morphology, translation and terminology)

Management Studies

Tel: (01483) 259653 *Fax:* (01483) 259387
Airey, David, BA MSc   Prof., Tourism Management
Archer, B. H., BSc(Econ) *Lond.*, MA *Camb.*, PhD *Wales*   Emer. Prof.†, Tourism Management
Archer, G. Simon H., MA *Oxf.*, FCA   Prof., Financial Management
Butler, Richard, BA PhD   Prof., Tourism
Dawes, P., MSc *Bath*, PhD *NSW*   Reader, Marketing
Gilbert, David C., BA *Lond.*, MA *CNAA*, PhD   Sr. Lectr.
Hales, Colin P., MA *Camb.*, PhD *Kent*   Sr. Lectr.
Jones, P. L. M., BA *Open(UK)*, MBA *Lond.*   Reader
Karim, Rifaat A. A., BSc *Birm.*, MSocSc *Birm.*, PhD *Bath*   Visiting Prof.
Kipps, Michael, BSc *Lond.*, MSc *Sur.*, PhD *Sur.*   Prof.
Lockwood, Andrew J., BSc   Sr. Lectr.
Medlik, S. Rick, BCom MA   Visiting Prof.
Parlett, Graham R., BSc *Lond.*, PhD *Lond.*   Dir., Management Studies; Head*
Ravenscroft, N., BSc *Reading*, MSc *Reading*   Reader
Riley, Michael J., MA *Sus.*, PhD *Essex*   Prof.
Sussman, Silvia, MSc *Essex*   Sr. Lectr.
Wilt, S., BA *Warw.*, MSc *Leeds*, MA *Warw.*, PhD *Brad.*   Prof.†
Other Staff: 18 Lectrs.; 1 Sr. Tutor; 5 Tutors; 1 Res. Fellow
Research: finance and law (accounting practices, competition law, Islamic banking, venture capital); food and health care (clinical outcome, food choice, health in the workplace); hospitality and management (business format, international development, organisational issues); retail and marketing (business-to-business marketing, internationalisation of retailing, new product development); tourism (development, education, impacts, leisure, policy, sustainability)

Materials Science and Engineering

Tel: (01483) 259619 *Fax:* (01483) 259508
Bader, Michael G., BSc(Eng) *Lond.*, FIM   Emer. Prof.
Castle, James E., PhD *Exe.*, DSc *Exe.*, FRSChem   Prof., Materials Science; Head*
McCartney, L. Neil, BSc MSc PhD, FIMA   Visiting Prof.
Miodownik, A. Peter, BSc(Eng) *Lond.*, PhD *Lond.*, FIM   Emer. Prof.
Phillips, D. Clive, BSc *Brist.*, MSc *Birm.*, PhD *Lond.*   Visiting Prof.
Saunders, Derek A., BSc *Nott.*   Manager, Continuing Educn.
Smith, Paul A., MA *Camb.*, PhD *Camb.*   Prof., Composite Materials
Towner, Jeremy M., BSc(Eng) *Lond.*   Sr. Lectr.
Tsakiropoulos, Panos, MMet *Sheff.*, PhD *Sheff.*   Prof., Metallurgy
Walker, Robert, BSc *Sheff.*, MSc(Eng) *Lond.*, PhD, FIM   Sr. Lectr.
Watts, John F., BSc PhD, FIM   Reader, Adhesion Science
Other Staff: 3 Lectrs.; 11 Res. Fellows
Research: ceramic materials (ceramic-matrix composites, ceramics, functional materials); composites (fibre reinforced materials for engineering structures); physical and process metallurgy (microstructures, modelling, phase equilibria, processing, transformations); surface and interface reactions (surface characterisation and reaction kinetics in technology)

Mathematical and Computing Sciences

Ahmad, Khurshid, BSc *Karachi*, MSc *Karachi*, PhD *Sur.*   Reader
Bowers, David S., MA *Camb.*, PhD *Camb.*   Sr. Lectr.
Bridges, Thomas J., BSc *Rhode I.*, MSc *Texas*, MA *Penn.*, PhD *Penn.*   Reader
Crowder, Martin J., BSc *Manc.*, PhD *Sur.*   Prof., Statistics
Hinton, Terry, BSc *Brist.*, PhD *Lond.*   Sr. Lectr.
Kimber, Alan C., BSc *Hull*, MSc *Sheff.*, PhD *Hull*   Sr. Lectr.
Schuman, Stephen A., BSc *M.I.T.*   Prof., Computing Science
Shail, Ronald, BSc *Lond.*, PhD *Lond.*, DSc *Lond.*, FIMA   Prof., Mathematics
Sweeting, Trevor J., BA *Sheff.*, MSc *Sheff.*, PhD *Sheff.*   Prof., Statistics; Head*
Tawn, Jonathan A., BSc PhD   Visiting Prof.
Williams, W. Elwyn, PhD *Manc.*, DSc *Manc.*, FIMA   Emer. Prof.
Work, L. Brent, BSc *Oklahoma*   Sr. Lectr.
Other Staff: 13 Lectrs.; 3 Res. Fellows
Research: computing (artificial intelligence, theoretical computer science); mathematics and statistics (nonlinear problems from iterated maps to integro-differential equations)

Music

Tel: (01483) 259317 *Fax:* (01483) 259386
Demidenko, Nickolai   Visiting Prof.
Fisher, David M., MA *Camb.*   Sr. Lectr., Recording Techniques
Forbes, Sebastian, MA *Camb.*, MusD *Camb.*   Prof.
Messenger, Thomas, BMus *Glas.*, PhD *Wales*   Univ. Dir.; Head*
Rumsey, Francis, MMus PhD   Sr. Lectr., Acoustics and Recording
Other Staff: 4 Lectrs.; 1 Sr. Res. Fellow; Artists in Residence (Medici String Quartet)

Nursing, see Health and Med. Scis., European Inst. of

Physics

Tel: (01483) 259400 *Fax:* (01483) 259501
Adams, Alfred R., PhD *Leic.*, DSc *Leic.*, FIP, FRS   Prof.
Bacon, Richard A., MSc *Lond.*, PhD *Sur.*   Sr. Lectr.
Bailey, John E., BSc *Brist.*, PhD *Camb.*, FIP, FIM   Visiting Prof.
Barrett, Roger C., MSc *Cape Town*, DPhil *Oxf.*, FIP   Reader
Clarke, Roger H., BSc *Birm.*, MSc *Birm.*, PhD *CNAA*   Visiting Prof.
Clough, Anthony S., BSc *Lond.*, PhD *Lond.*, FIP   Sr. Lectr.
Crocker, Alan G., PhD *Sheff.*, DSc *Lond.*, FIP   Prof., Solid State Physics
Faux, David A., BSc *Nott.*, MSc *Birm.*, PhD *Birm.*   Sr. Lectr.
Flewitt, Peter E. J., PhD *Lond.*, DSc *Lond.*, FIP, FIM   Visiting Prof.
Gelletly, William, OBE, BSc *Edin.*, PhD *Edin.*, FIP   Prof.
Gilboy, Walter B., BSc *Leeds*, PhD *Leeds*, FIP   Sr. Lectr.
Horton, Patrick W., BSc *Lond.*, PhD *Manc.*, FIP, FIEE   Hon. Prof., Medical Physics
Johnson, Ronald C., PhD *Manc.*, DSc *Manc.*, FIP   Prof., Nuclear Physics
McDonald, Peter J., PhD *Nott.*   Sr. Lectr.
O'Reilly, Eoin, BA *Trinity(Dub.)*, PhD *Camb.*   Prof.; Head*
Puttick, Keith E., PhD *Brist.*   Emer. Prof.
Spyrou, Nicholas M., MPhil *Lond.*   Reader

Taylor, David G., BSc *Nott.*, PhD *Nott.*   Sr. Lectr.
Thompson, Ian J., MSc *Massey*, PhD *Auck.*   Reader
Tostevin, Jeffrey A., PhD   Sr. Lectr.
Walker, Philip M., MA *Camb.*, PhD *ANU*   Prof.
Warner, David D., BSc *E.Anglia*, DPhil *Sus.*   Visiting Prof.
Other Staff: 11 Lectrs.; 2 Sr. Res. Fellows; 2 Experimental Officers
Research: materials physics (ellipsometry, ion-beam analysis, polymers, semiconductors); medical physics (imaging, MRI, semiconductor x-ray sensors, tomography); nuclear physics (halo nuclei, nuclear structures, radioactive beams); optoelectronic devices; radiation physics

Psychology

Tel: (01483) 259175 *Fax:* (01483) 32813
Barrett, Martyn D., MA *Camb.*, DPhil *Sus.*   Prof.
Breakwell, Glynis M., BA *Leic.*, MSc *Strath.*, MA *Oxf.*, PhD *Brist.*, DSc *Oxf.*, FBPsS   Prof.
Brown, Jennifer M., BA *Reading*, PhD *Sur.*   Sr. Lectr.
Davies, Ian R., BSc *Brist.*   Prof.; Head*
Dowdney, Linda R., BA *York*, MA *Col.*, PhD *Lond.*, MPhil, FBPsS   Sr. Lectr.
Farmer, Eric W., BSc *Glas.*, PhD *Glas.*   Visiting Prof.
Fife-Shaw, Christopher R., BSc *Newcastle(UK)*, MSc *Strath.*, PhD *Sheff.*   Sr. Lectr.
Foulds, J., MA *Aberd.*, MSc *Glas.*, PhD *Lond.*   Sr. Lectr., Clinical Psychology
Groeger, John A., BA *N.U.I.*, MA *N.U.I.*, PhD *Belf.*   Prof., Cognitive Psychology
Hampson, Sarah E., BA *Exe.*, PhD *Exe.*   Prof., Psychology and Health
Herriot, Peter, BA *Oxf.*, MEd *Belf.*, PhD *Manc.*, FBPsS   Visiting Prof.
Kemp, Ray, BA *York(UK)*, MSc *Wales*, PhD *Wales*   Visiting Prof.
McMillan, Thomas M., BSc *Aberd.*, MAppSci *Glas.*, PhD *Lond.*   Prof., Clinical Psychology
Moray, Neville P., BA *Oxf.*, MA *Oxf.*, DPhil *Oxf.*   Prof., Applied Cognitive Psychology
Perkins, Derek, BSc *Lond.*, MSc *Birm.*, PhD *Birm.*   Visiting Prof.
Raw, Gary J., BA *Oxf.*, DPhil *Oxf.*   Visiting Prof.
Rogers, Brian J., BSc *Brist.*, MA *Oxf.*, PhD *Brist.*   Visiting Prof.
Uzzell, David L., BA *Liv.*, MSc *Lond.*, PhD   Sr. Lectr.
Wilkinson, Jill D., MSc *Sur.*, PhD *Sur.*   Sr. Lectr.
Other Staff: 2 Visiting Readers; 1 Visiting Fellow; 18 Lectrs.; 2 Sr. Tutors; 5 Tutors; 1 Sr. Res. Fellow; 7 Res. Fellows

Russian, see Linguistic and Internat. Studies

Sociology

Tel: (01483) 259365 *Fax:* (01483) 306290
Arber, Sara L., MSc *Lond.*, PhD   Prof.; Head*
Bulmer, Martin I. B., BSc *lond.*, PhD *Lond.*   Prof.
Fielding, Nigel G., BA *Sus.*, MA *Kent*, PhD *Lond.*   Prof.
Gilbert, G. Nigel, MA *Camb.*, PhD *Camb.*   Prof.
Hornsby-Smith, Michael P., PhD *Sheff.*   Reader
Tarling, Roger, PhD *Lond.*   Prof.
Tunstill, Jane, BSc *Brun.*, MSc *Brun.*   Visiting Prof.
Other Staff: 12 Lectrs.; 8 Res. Fellows

Swedish, see Linguistic and Internat. Studies

Tourism, see Management Studies

Other Appointments

School Appointments

Boulter, P. S., MB BS *Lond.*, FRCSEd, FRCS, FRACS   Hon. Prof.
Jesshope, Christopher R., BSc *S'ton.*, MSc *S'ton.*, PhD *S'ton.*   Visiting Prof. (Sch. of Electronic Engin., Information Technol. and Maths.)
Negishi, H.   Hon. Fellow

Rugaard, Peer, MSc Visiting Prof. (Sch. of Electronic Engin., Information Technol. and Maths.)

Saito, K. Hon. Fellow

Street, Brian F., BSc Birm., DUniv Sur., FIChemE, FEng Hon. Univ. Prof.

SPECIAL CENTRES, ETC

Applied Electronics Research Group

Bateson, Keith N., BA Oxf., DPhil Sus. Sr. Lectr.

Hamill, David C., BSc(Eng) S'ton., MSc S'ton., PhD Sur. Sr. Lectr.

Jefferies, David J., MA Oxf., MS Stan., PhD Stan. Sr. Lectr.

Mulhall, Brian E., MA Camb., PhD Camb. Sr. Lectr.

Seebold, Roger J. A., BSc Lond., PhD Warw. Sr. Lectr.

Underhill, Michael J., MA Oxf., PhD Sur., FIEE, FEng Prof.; Head*

Research: circuits and subsystems from dc through radio frequency to microwave frequency

Communication Systems Research, Centre for

Barclay, Leslie W., OBE, BSc, FIEE Visiting Prof.

Coakley, Francis P., MSc Manc. Sr. Lectr.

Evans, Barry G., BSc Leeds, PhD Leeds, FEng, FIEE Prof., Information Systems Engineering; Dir.*

Jeans, Tony G., MA Camb., MSc S'ton. Sr. Lectr.

Kondoz, Ahmet M., BSc Birm., MSc Essex, PhD Sur. Prof.

Maral, Gerard Visiting Prof.

Ramsdale, Peter A., PhD Birm., FIEE Visiting Prof.

Sweeney, Peter, MA Oxf., PhD Camb. Sr. Lectr.

Tafazolli, Rahim, BSc Bath, MSc Lond., PhD Sur. Reader

Other Staff: 2 Lectrs.; 1 Sr. Res. Fellow; 15 Res. Fellows

Research: global, multimedia, personal and universal communication systems

Computer Systems Research Group

Sapaty, Peter, PhD Kiev Reader

Shafarenko, Sasha A. V., MSc Novosibirsk, PhD Novosibirsk Sr. Lectr.

English Language Institute

Tel: (01483) 259910 Fax: (01483) 259507

Fulcher, N. Glenn, BD Lond., MTh Lond., MA Birm., PhD Lanc. Dir.*

Olearnik, Irene, MA Cracow, MA Leeds Tutor; In-Sessl. Programme Co-ordinator

Environmental Strategy, Centre for

Fax: (01483) 259394

Clift, Roland, OBE, BA Camb., MA Camb., PhD McG., FEng Foundation Fund Prof., Environmental Technology; Dir.*

France, C., BSc Salf., MSc Manc., PhD UMIST Sr. Lectr.

Jackson, Tim, MA Camb., MA W.Ont., PhD St And. Reader

Other Staff: 4 Lectrs.; 1 Sr. Res. Fellow; 1 Res. Fellow

Research: ecological economics and ethics; life cycle and systems analysis (tools for reporting company environmental performance); management of risks by public and private sector organisations

Epidemiology, National Institute of

Balarajan, Rasaratnam Prof.; Head*

Research: development of health outcome indicators; health inequalities in England (Acheson Report); health of ethnic minorities in UK; profile of health in London

Human Psychopharmacology Research Unit

Tel: (01483) 418208 Fax: (01483) 418453

Beaumont, George, JP, MB ChB Manc., FRCPsych, FIBiol Visiting Prof., Pharmacopsychiatry

Hindmarch, Ian, BSc Leeds, PhD Leeds, FBPsS Prof.; Dir.*

Lobo, A. A., BSc Lond., MB BChir Camb., MSc Lond. Med. Dir.†

Stonier, Peter D., BA Open(UK), BSc Birm., MB ChB Manc., PhD Sheff., FRCPEd Visiting Prof., Pharmaceutical Medicine

Waterhouse, Peter, BSc Leeds, PhD Leeds Visiting Prof.

Other Staff: 1 Res. Fellow; 7 Res. Officers

Ion Beam Applications, Surrey Centre for Research in

Forbes, Richard G., PhD Camb., DSc Aston, FIEE, FIP Reader

Hemment, Peter L. F., BSc City(UK), PhD Reading, DSc City(UK), FIP, FIEE Prof.; Res. Fellow

Homewood, Kevin P., BSc Newcastle(UK), PhD Manc. Reader

Kelly, Michael J., MSc Well., MA Camb., PhD Camb., ScD Camb., FIP, FIEE, FRS Prof.

Reeson, Karen J., BSc Leic., PhD CNAA Sr. Lectr.

Sealy, Brian J., BSc Sur., PhD Sur., DSc Sur., FIP, FIEE Prof., Solid State Devices; Dir., Surrey Ion Beam Facility for Microelectronics; Dir.*

Shannon, John M., BTech Brun., PhD Sur., DSc Brun., FIP Prof. Res. Fellow†

Webb, Roger P., BSc Salf., PhD Salf. Sr. Lectr.

Weiss, Bernard L., BSc Newcastle(UK), PhD Newcastle(UK), FIEE, FIP Prof., Microelectronics

Other Staff: 3 Lectrs.; 1 Sr. Res. Fellow; 10 Res. Fellows

Research: ion implantation aspects of silicon; III-V semiconductor and amorphous semiconductor technologies

Satellite Engineering Research, Centre for

Dyer, Clive S., BA Camb., PhD Lond. Visiting Prof.

Fan, Changxin Visiting Prof.

Sweeting, Martin N., OBE, BSc Sur., PhD Sur., FEng, FIEE, FRAeS Prof.; Dir.*

Ward, Jeff W., BEng Mich., PhD Sur. Tech. Dir.

Other Staff: 3 Lectrs.; 2 Experimental Officers; 15 Res. Fellows

Research: low-cost spacecraft engineering

Surrey European Management School

Tel: (01483) 259347 Fax: (01483) 259511

Baker, Michael J., TD, BA Durh., BSc Lond. Visiting Prof.

Gamble, Paul R., BSc Sur., MPhil Sur., PhD Sur. Prof., European Management Studies; Dir.*

Ryan, Robert J., BSc Stir., MSc Stir., FCA Visiting Prof.

Other Staff: 2 Dep. Dirs.; 7 Lectrs.

Research: corporate strategy (advantage, alignment, best practice, decision-making); direct marketing (customer, relationship, retention, surveys); financial services (marketing, quality, risk, strategy); human resources management (change, communications, culture, stress); information services (professional, satisfaction, SME, strategy)

Vision, Speech and Signal Processing, Centre for

Illingworth, John, BSc Birm., DPhil Oxf. Reader

Kittler, Josef V., MA Camb., PhD Camb., ScD Camb. Prof., Machine Intelligence; Dir.*

Petrou, Maria, BSc Salonika, PhD Camb. Prof.

Szajnowski, George W. J., MSc Warsaw, PhD Warsaw Sr. Lectr.

Other Staff: 5 Lectrs.; 10 Res. Fellows

Research: developing methodology; software implementation of algorithms, including image processing and computer vision

CONTACT OFFICERS

Academic affairs. Academic Registrar: Beardsley, Peter W., BA Lond.

Accommodation. Accommodation and Conference Manager: Paxton, Richard

Admissions (first degree). Undergraduate Admissions Officer: Joel, Cynthia I., BA Open(UK)

Admissions (higher degree). Postgraduate Officer: Morrison, Diana

Adult/continuing education. Continuing Education Officer: Butt, Faith, BA Durh.

Alumni. Alumni Officer: Cohen, Jane

Archives. University Archivist: Chandler, Arthur R.

Careers. Head of Service and Senior Careers Adviser: Clark, Russ M., BSc Brist., MSc S'ton., PhD Lond.

Computing services. Director of University Computing Services: Harman, Valerie A., FBCS

Conferences/corporate hospitality. Barker-Benfield, Jane E.

Credit transfer. Senior Assistant Registrar: Watson, Anthony C., BSc Lond.

Development/fund-raising. Director, Academic Investment Campaign: Manning-Prior, Christine, BA N.U.I.

Estates and buildings/works and services. Director of Estates and Buildings: Caleb, Derry A., BSc

Examinations. University Examinations Officer: Chrystall, R. Stuart B., MA Camb., PhD Camb.

Finance. Director of Finance: Knapp, Anthony J.

General enquiries. Secretary and Registrar: Davies, H. Wyn B., BSc(Econ) Lond.

Health services. Student Medical Officer: Carr-Bains, Stephen, MB BChir

International office. Director of International Office and Dean of Overseas Students: Brown, Gwyn, BSc S'ton., PhD S'ton.

Language training for international students. Wright, Cleo N., BA San Francisco State, MA San Francisco State

Library (chief librarian). Librarian/Dean of Information Services: Crawshaw, Tom J. A., BEng Sheff.

Ombudsperson. Academic Director, Educational Liaison/Dean of Students: Hobrough, John E., MSc Manc., PhD Salf.†

Personnel/human resources. Director of Human Resources: Behagg, Alan, MA Oxf., MBA

Public relations, information and marketing. Director of Communications: Ashford, Katherine, BA Brist., MA CNAA

Publications. Director of Communications: Ashford, Katherine, BA Brist., MA CNAA

Purchasing. Purchasing Officer: Swinerd, Dave L.

Quality assurance and accreditation. Senior Assistant Registrar: Watson, Anthony C., BSc Lond.

Research (research higher degrees). Postgraduate Officer: Morrison, Diana

Research (research services). Research Services Officer: Brooks, Peter G., BA E.Anglia, MA Reading

Research (strategic academic planning and resource allocation). Butterworth, Peter H. W., BSc Liv., PhD Liv.

Safety. Safety and Radiation Protection Officer: Harris, Stephen J., MSc Lond., PhD Sur.

Scholarships, awards, loans. Senior Assistant Registrar: Barter, Laraine, BA Leeds

Schools liaison. Academic Director, Educational Liaison/Dean of Students: Hobrough, John E., MSc Manc., PhD Salf.†

Security. Chief Security Officer: Watling, Anthony

Sport and recreation. Director, University Centre for Sport and Recreation: Hitchcock, Barry G.

Staff development and training. Staff Development Manager and Personnel Officer: Grant, Jennifer

Student welfare/counselling. Welfare Officer: Thompson, Elizabeth A., BA

Students from other countries. Director of International Office and Dean of Overseas Students: Brown, Gwyn, BSc *S'ton.*, PhD *S'ton.*

Students with disabilities. Welfare Officer: Thompson, Elizabeth A., BA

University press. Bookshop Manager: Micel, M., BSc *Lough.*

[Information supplied by the institution as at 11 March 1998, and edited by the ACU]

SURREY INSTITUTE OF ART AND DESIGN

Founded 1994; previously established as West Surrey College of Art and Design and Epsom School of Art and Design

Postal Address: Falkner Road, The Hart, Farnham, England GU9 7DS
Telephone: (01252) 722441 **Fax**: (01252) 733869 **E-mail**: registry@surrart.ac.uk
WWW: http://www.surrart.ac.uk **E-mail formula**: name@surrart.ac.uk

DIRECTOR*—Taylor, N. J.
ACADEMIC REGISTRAR‡—Kupferman-Hall, Andrea, BA *Union(N.Y.)*, MA *Union(N.Y.)*

UNIVERSITY OF SUSSEX

Founded 1961

Member of the Association of Commonwealth Universities

Postal Address: Sussex House, Falmer, Brighton, England BN1 9RH
Telephone: (01273) 606755 **Fax**: (01273) 678335 **Cables**: University, Brighton **Telex**: UNISEX 877159
WWW: http://www.sussex.ac.uk **E-mail formula**: initial(s)surname@sussex.ac.uk

VISITOR—Elizabeth, H.M. The Queen
CHANCELLOR—Attenborough of Richmond upon Thames, Lord, CBE, Hon. DLitt, Hon. DCL
CHAIRMAN OF THE COUNCIL AND SENIOR PRO-CHANCELLOR—Manley, B. W., CBE, BSc *Lond.*, Hon. DSc *Lough.*, FEng, FIEE
PRO-CHANCELLOR—Davies, Sir David, CBE, PhD *Birm.*, DSc *Birm.*, Hon. DSc, FRS, FEng, FIEE
TREASURER—Toynbee, M. R., JP
VICE-CHANCELLOR*—Smith, Prof. M. Alasdair M., MA *Glas.*, MSc *Lond.*, DPhil *Oxf.*
PRO-VICE-CHANCELLOR—Brooks, Colin, MA *Camb.*, BPhil *Oxf.*, PhD *Camb.*
PRO-VICE-CHANCELLOR—McCaffery, Prof. A. J., BSc *Exe.*, PhD *Exe.*, FRSChem
PRO-VICE-CHANCELLOR—Roberts, Prof. J. B., BSc *Exe.*, PhD *Exe.*, FRSChem
REGISTRAR AND SECRETARY‡—Gooch, Barry, BA *Hull*
FINANCE OFFICER—Pavey, Stephen, BSc *Brist.*
LIBRARIAN—Peasgood, Adrian N., BA *Camb.*

GENERAL INFORMATION

History. The university was founded in 1961. Its campus is located on the outskirts of Brighton, on the Sussex coast.

Admission to first degree courses (see also United Kingdom Introduction). Through Universities and Colleges Admissions Service (UCAS). Applicants under 21: evidence of a broad general education, including competence in the use of English. General Certificate of Education (GCE) A level passes in 2 subjects, or 1 subject at A level and 2 at AS level, or 4 at AS level.

First Degrees (see also United Kingdom Directory to Subjects of Study). BA, BEng, BSc, LLB, MChem, MEng, MMath, MPhys.

Higher Degrees (see also United Kingdom Directory to Subjects of Study). LLM, MA, MSc, DPhil.

Libraries. 750,000 volumes; 3500 periodicals. Special collections: British Library for Development Studies; European Documentation Centre; Kipling; mass observation; New Statesman; Woolf.

Fees (1998–99). Undergraduate: home students £1000 (all courses); international students £6675 (arts), £8850 (sciences). Postgraduate: home students £2610 (all

courses); international students £6675 (arts), £8850 (sciences).

Academic Year (1998–99). Three terms: 5 October–11 December; 4 January–12 March; 19 April–25 June.

Income (1996–97). £74,300,000.

Statistics. Staff: 2143 (823 academic, 1320 support). Students: full-time 8265; part-time 820; international 2236; total 9085 (4170 men, 4915 women).

FACULTIES/SCHOOLS

African and Asian Studies, School of
Tel: (01273) 678024 Fax: (01273) 673572
Dean: Robinson, David A., BSc Lond., PhD Lond.
Secretary: Emberton, Sue

Biological Sciences, School of
Tel: (01273) 678057 Fax: (01273) 678433
Dean: Moore, Prof. Anthony L., BSc CNAA,
PhD Aberd.
Secretary: Glazebrook, Esme

Chemistry, Physics and Environmental Sciences, School of
Tel: (01273) 678068 Fax: (01273) 678097
Dean: Murrell, Prof. John N., BSc Lond.,
PhDCamb., FRS, FRSChem
Secretary: Fowey, Lorraine

Cognitive and Computing Sciences, School of
Tel: (01273) 678030 Fax: (01273) 671320
Dean: du Boulay, Prof. J. Benedict H., BSc
Lond., PhD Edin.
Secretary: Gains, Jackie

Cultural and Community Studies, School of
Tel: (01273) 678021 Fax: (01273) 678644
Dean: Short, Brian M., BA Lond., PhD Lond.
Secretary: Woodbridge, Anne

Engineering, School of
Tel: (01273) 678915 Fax: (01273) 678399
Dean: Powner, Prof. Ed T., BSc Durh., MSc
Manc., PhD Manc.
Secretary: Nutley, Linda

English and American Studies, School of
Tel: (01273) 678013 Fax: (01273) 625972
Dean: Crozier, Andrew T. K., MA Camb., PhD
Essex
Secretary: Astill, Joan

European Studies, School of
Tel: (01273) 678004 Fax: (01273) 623246
Dean: Llewellyn, Nigel G., BA E.Anglia, MPhil
Camb., PhD Lond.
Secretary: McCabe, Patricia

Mathematical Sciences, School of
Tel: (01273) 678105 Fax: (01273) 678097
Dean: Bushell, Peter J., BSc Aberd., MA Oxf.,
DPhil Oxf.
Secretary: Collier, Sheila

Social Sciences, School of
Tel: (01273) 678033 Fax: (01273) 673563
Dean: Dearlove, John N., BSc(Econ) Hull, MA
DPhil
Secretary: Harrison, Beatrice

ACADEMIC UNITS

Note—There are no departments in the
university. Members of the teaching staff are
listed according to their main subject
interest(s). Many members, however, teach
·in more than one school and several in
more than one subject.

American Studies
Fax: (01273) 625972
Brooks, Colin, MA Camb., PhD Camb. Sr.
Lectr., History
Burman, Stephen F., BA Camb., DPhil Oxf. Sr.
Lectr., Social Studies (on leave)
Dunne, Michael, BA Oxf., MA Calif., DPhil Sr.
Lectr., History
Fender, Stephen A., BA Stan., MA Wales, PhD
Manc. Prof.
Hart, Vivien M., BA Lond., AM Harv., PhD
Harv. Reader, Social Studies
Nicholls, Peter A., MA Camb., PhD
Camb. Prof., Literature

Tapper, Edward R., BA Exe., MA Oregon, PhD
Manc. Reader, Social Studies
Way, Peter, BA Trent, MA W.Ont., PhD
Maryland Prof.
Whitley, John S., MA Sheff. Reader, Literature
Wilkinson, Rupert H., BA Harv., PhD
Stan. Prof., American Studies and History

Art, History of
Fax: (01273) 623246
Cherry, Deborah, BA Edin., PhD Lond. Prof.
Clunas, Craig, BA Camb., PhD Lond. Prof.
Crow, Thomas E., BA Pomona, MA Calif., PhD
Calif. Prof.
Howard, Maurice, BA Camb., MA Lond., PhD
Lond. Sr. Lectr.
Llewellyn, Nigel G., BA E.Anglia, MPhil Camb.,
PhD Lond. Sr. Lectr.
Mellor, David A., BA DPhil Sr. Lectr.

Astronomy
Fax: (01273) 678097
Barrow, John D., BSc Durh., DPhil Oxf. Prof.
Smith, Robert C., BSc Glas., PhD Glas. Sr.
Lectr.

Biological Sciences
Fax: (01273) 678433
Andrew, Richard J., MA Camb., PhD
Camb. Prof., Animal Behaviour
Bacon, Jonathon P., MA Camb., MSc Manc., PhD
Manc. Sr. Lectr.
Beebee, Trevor J. C., BSc E.Anglia, DPhil Sr.
Lectr.
Benjamin, Paul R., BSc Liv., BSc(Econ) Lond.,
PhD Durh. Prof.
Burke, Julian F., BSc Leic., PhD Aberd. Reader
Collett, Thomas S., BA Lond., PhD Lond. Prof.
Davies, Jane, BSc Manc., MSc Lond., PhD
Lond. Sr. Lectr.
Flowers, Timothy J., BSc Lond., MSc Nott., PhD
Nott. Prof.
Ford, Christopher, BA Oxf., DPhil Oxf. Sr.
Lectr.
Hutchings, Michael J., BSc Lond., PhD
E.Anglia Reader
Kay, John E., MA Camb., PhD Camb. Reader
Land, Michael F., BA Camb., PhD Lond.,
FRS Prof., Neurobiology
Moore, Anthony L., BSc CNAA, PhD
Aberd. Prof.
O'Shea, Michael R., BSc Leic., PhD S'ton. Prof.
Pain, Virginia, BSc Lond., PhD Lond. Sr. Lectr.
Roper, Timothy J., PhD Camb. Reader
Russell, Ian J., BSc Lond., MSc Br.Col., PhD
Camb., FRS Prof., Neurobiology
Spratt, Brian G., BSc Lond., PhD Lond. Prof.
Streeter, David T., BSc Lond. Reader
Taylor, Gail, BSc Lanc., PhD Lanc. Sr. Lectr.
Titheradge, Michael A., BSc Birm., PhD
Birm. Sr. Lectr.
Tribe, Michael A., BSc Durh., PhD Durh. Sr.
Lectr.
Wallis, Michael, MA Camb., PhD Camb. Prof.
Watts, Felicity, BSc Lond., PhD Lond. Sr. Lectr.
Wheeler, Kenneth P., MA Oxf., DPhil Oxf. Sr.
Lectr.
Whittle, J. Robert S., BA Camb., PhD Camb. Sr.
Lectr.

Chemistry
Fax: (01273) 677196
Armes, Steven, BSc Brist., PhD Brist. Sr. Lectr.
Billingham, Norman C., BSc Birm., PhD
Birm. Reader
Caddick, Stephen, PhD S'ton. Sr. Lectr.
Chaloner, Penelope A., MA Camb., PhD
Camb. Sr. Lectr.
Cloke, Francis G. N., DPhil Oxf. Reader
Hanson, James R., MA Oxf., PhD Lond., DSc
Oxf., FRSChem Reader
Hudson, Andrew, BA Camb., PhD Camb. Sr.
Lectr.
Jackson, Richard A., MA Oxf., DPhil
Oxf. Reader
Kroto, Sir Harold, BSc Sheff., PhD Sheff.,
FRS Prof.

Lappert, Michael F., PhD Lond., DSc Lond.,
FRSChem, FRS Prof.
Lawless, Gerry, BSc PhD Sr. Lectr.
Leigh, Geoffrey J., OBE, BSc Lond., PhD Lond.,
DSc Lond. Hon. Prof.
McCaffery, Anthony J., BSc Exe., PhD Exe.,
FRSChem Prof.
Murrell, John N., BSc Lond., PhD Camb., FRS,
FRSChem Prof.
Nixon, John F., BSc Manc., PhD Manc., DSc
Manc. Prof.
Parsons, Philip J., BSc CNAA, MPhil Aston, PhD
S'ton. Prof.
Prassides, Kosmas, DPhil Oxf. Prof.
Smith, J. David, MA Camb., PhD Camb. Reader
Stace, Anthony J., PhD Essex Prof.
Taylor, Roger, PhD Lond., DSc Lond. Reader
Topping, R. Malcolm, BScTech Manc., PhD
Manc. Sr. Lectr.
Walton, David R. M., MSc Leic., PhD Leic., DSc
Lond., FRSChem Reader
Young, Douglas W., BSc Glas., PhD Glas. Prof.

Computer Science and Artificial Intelligence
Fax: (01273) 671320
Boden, Margaret A., MA Camb., AM Harv., PhD
Harv., FBA Prof.
Buxton, Hilary, BSc Brist., PhD Camb. Prof.
du Boulay, J. Benedict H., BSc Lond., PhD
Edin. Prof., Artificial Intelligence
Edelman, Shimon, BSc MSc PhD Sr. Lectr.
Gazdar, Gerard J. M., BA E.Anglia, MA Reading,
PhD Reading Prof., Linguistics and Cognitive
Science
Hennessy, Matthew C. B., BSc N.U.I., MA
Trinity(Dub.), PhD Wat. Prof.
Sampson, Geoffrey R., BA Camb., MA Yale, PhD
Camb. Reader
Sharples, Michael, BSc St And., PhD Edin. Sr.
Lectr.
Watson, Des, MA Camb., PhD Camb. Sr. Lectr.

Economics
Fax: (01273) 678466
Dyker, David A., MA Glas., DPhil Reader
Holmes, Peter M., MA Camb., PhD Camb. Sr.
Lectr.
Reilly, Barry, MA Warw., PhD Warw., MA Sr.
Lectr.
Smith, M. Alasdair M., MA Glas., MSc Lond.,
DPhil Oxf. Prof.
Sumner, Michael T., BA(Econ) Manc. Prof.
Wagstaff, Adam, BA Wales, DPhil
York(UK) Prof.
Wall, David G., BSc(Econ) Lond. Reader
Winch, Donald N., BSc(Econ) Lond., PhD Prin.,
FBA Prof.

Education, Continuing and Professional
Fax: (01273) 678568
Abbs, Peter F., BA Brist. Sr. Lectr.
Bliss, Joan, PhD Lond.
Cooper, Barry, BA Camb., MA Sr. Lectr.
Eraut, Michael R., BA Camb., PhD Camb. Prof.
Gray, Fred G., BA Hull, PhD Camb. Sr. Lectr.
Lewin, Keith M., MSc Manc., DPhil Prof.
Lowerson, John R., MA Leeds Reader
Pateman, Trevor J., BA Oxf., DPhil Reader
Torrance, Harry, BSc Brist., PhD E.Anglia Sr.
Lectr.

Engineering, Biomedical
Denbigh, Philip N., BSc Edin., MA Camb., PhD
Camb. Reader
English, Michael J., BSc Wales, PhD Wales,
DPhil Sr. Lectr.
Lister, Paul F., MSc Aston, PhD Aston Prof.
Ripley, Lionel G., BSc Wales, PhD
Wales Reader
Williams, Graham, BSc Brist., PhD Belf. Sr.
Lectr.

Engineering, Civil, see Engin., Mech., Struct. and Civil

Engineering, Electrical, Electronic and Control

Atherton, Derek P., BEng Sheff., PhD Manc., DSc Manc., FIEE   Prof.

Clark, Terry D., BSc Lond., PhD Lond.   Prof.

Denbigh, Philip N., BSc Edin., MA Camb., PhD Camb.   Reader

English, Michael J., BSc Wales, DPhil   Sr. Lectr.

Gough, M. Paul, MSc Leic., PhD S'ton.   Prof.

Jayawant, Balchandra V., BE Bom., PhD Brist., DSc, FIEE   Prof.

Lister, Paul F., MSc Aston, PhD Aston   Prof.

Powner, Ed T., BSc Durh., MSc Manc., PhD Manc.   Prof.

Ripley, Lionel G., BSc Wales, PhD Wales   Reader

Unsworth, Peter J., MA Camb., PhD Camb.   Sr. Lectr.

Williams, Graham, BSc Brist., PhD Belf.   Sr. Lectr.

Engineering, Mechanical, Structural and Civil

Fax: (01273) 678399

Chatwin, Chris R., BSc Aston, MSc Birm., PhD Birm.   Prof.

Neller, Philip H., BSc(Eng) Lond.   Sr. Lectr.

Riddington, John R., BSc S'ton., PhD S'ton.   Sr. Lectr.

Roberts, J. Brian, BSc(Eng) Lond., PhD Lond., DSc Lond.   Prof.

Turner, Alan B., BSc Newcastle, DPhil   Prof.

English

Fax: (01273) 678466

Crozier, Andrew T. K., MA Camb., PhD Essex   Sr. Lectr.

Hemstedt, Geoffrey, BA Oxf., PhD Prin.   Sr. Lectr.

Inglis, Anthony A. H., BA Camb.   Sr. Lectr.

Josipovici, Gabriel D., BA Oxf.   Prof.†

Littlewood, Ian, MA Oxf., MPhil Oxf., DPhil   Sr. Lectr.

Medcalf, Stephen E., BLitt Oxf., MA Oxf.   Reader

Sinfield, Alan J., MA Lond.   Prof.

Smith, Lindsay, BA Wales, PhD S'ton.   Sr. Lectr.

Taylor, Jenny, BA York(UK), MA Warw., PhD Warw.   Sr. Lectr.

Vance, R. Norman C., DPhil Oxf.   Prof.

Watts, Cedric T., MA Camb., PhD Camb.   Prof.

French

Fax: (01273) 673246

Bennington, Geoffrey P., MA Oxf., DPhil Oxf.   Prof.

Burton, Richard D. E., MA Oxf., DPhil Oxf.   Prof.

Duchen, Clare F., PhD N.Y., BA   Sr. Lectr.

Geography

Fax: (01273) 678466

Binns, J. Anthony, BA Sheff., MA Birm., PhD Birm.   Sr. Lectr.

Dunford, M. F., MSc Brist.   Prof.

Fielding, Anthony J., BA Lond., PhD Lond.   Prof.

King, Russell, BA Lond., MSc Lond., MA Trinity(Dub.), MLitt Trinity(Dub.), PhD Lond.   Prof.

Rendell, Helen M., BSc Nott., PhD Lond.   Prof.

Robinson, David A., BSc Lond., PhD Lond.   Sr. Lectr.

Short, Brian M., BA Lond., PhD Lond.   Sr. Lectr.

Williams, Rendell B. G., MA Camb., PhD Camb.   Reader

German

Fax: (01273) 673246

Löb, Ladislaus, DrPhil Zür.   Prof.

Timms, Edward F., MA Camb., PhD Camb.   Prof.

History

Fax: (01273) 678466

Brooks, Colin, MA Camb., PhD Camb.   Sr. Lectr.

Dubow, Saul H., BA Cape Town, DPhil Oxf.   Sr. Lectr.

Dyhouse, Carol, BA Reading, MA Lanc.   Sr. Lectr.

Hawkins, Michael J., MA Oxf.   Reader

Howkins, Alun J., BA Oxf.   Prof.

Kedward, H. Rod, BPhil Oxf., MA Oxf.   Prof.

Kitch, Malcolm J., MA Oxf.   Reader

Lamont, William M., BA Lond., PhD Lond.   Prof.

Lowerson, John R., MA Leeds   Reader

Mazower, Mark, BA Oxf., MA Johns H., DPhil Oxf.   Sr. Lectr.

Röhl, John C. G., MA Camb., PhD Camb.   Prof.

Thane, Patricia, MA Oxf., PhD Lond.   Prof.

Thomson, James K. J., MA Camb., PhD Reading   Reader, Economic History

van Gelderen, Mark, PhD European Univ.Inst.   Prof.

Wilkinson, Rupert H., BA Harv., PhD Stan.   Prof., American Studies and History

Williams, Beryl J., BA Lond.   Reader

Winch, Donald, BSc(Econ) Lond., PhD Prin.   Prof.

Worden, Blair, MA Oxf., DPhil Oxf.   Prof.

International Relations and Politics

Fax: (01273) 673563

Benewick, Robert J., BS Cornell, MA Ohio, PhD Manc.   Prof.

Cawson, Alan, DPhil Oxf., BA   Prof.

Dearlove, John N., BSc(Econ) Hull, MA DPhil   Reader

Duncan, R. Ian, BA York(UK), BPhil Hull, DPhil   Sr. Lectr.

Graham, Bruce D., MA NZ, PhD ANU   Prof.

MacLean, John S., BA Lanc., MSc(Econ) Lond.   Sr. Lectr.

Mazower, Mark, BA Oxf., MA Johns H., DPhil Oxf.   Sr. Lectr.

Nicholson, Michael, PhD Camb.   Prof.

Scholte, Jan-Aart, BA Pomona, MA DPhil   Sr. Lectr.

Shaw, Martin, BA Lond., PhD Hull   Prof.

Tapper, Ted R., BA Exe., MA Oregon, PhD Manc.   Reader

Williams, Marc, BSc Lond., PhD Lond.   Sr. Lectr.

Italian

Fax: (01273) 673246

Ryan, Christopher J., PhL Rome, STL Rome, MA Glas., PhD Camb.   Prof.

Law

Fax: (02173) 673563

Dean, Meryll, JP, BA CNAA, LLM Camb.   Sr. Lectr.

Keating, Heather M., LLB Leic., LLM Lond.   Sr. Lectr.

Koffman, Laurence, BA Keele   Reader

Rayak, Harry, BA S.Af., LLB S.Af., LLM Lond.   Prof.

Temkin, Jennifer, LLM Lond.   Prof.

Vogler, Richard K., BA Warw., MPhil Camb., PhD Camb.   Sr. Lectr.

Linguistics

Fax: (01273) 671320

Coates, Richard A., MA Camb., PhD Camb.   Prof.

Gazdar, Gerald J. M., BA E.Anglia, MA Reading, PhD Reading   Prof.

Wheeler, Max W., MA Oxf., DPhil Oxf.   Reader

Mathematics

(including Statistics)

Fax: (01273) 678097

Bather, John A., BA Camb., PhD Camb.   Prof., Statistics

Bushell, Peter J., BSc Aberd., MA Oxf., DPhil Oxf.   Reader

Cooper, Graeme J., BSc W.Aust., PhD Leeds   Reader

History (continued)

Edmunds, David E., BSc Wales, PhD Wales   Prof.

Elliot, Charles M., BSc Birm., MSc Oxf., DPhil Oxf.   Prof.

Fenn, Roger A., MA Camb., PhD Lond.   Reader

Foster, James, MA Oxf., PhD Lond.   Sr. Lectr.

Goldie, Charles, BSc Lond., PhD Lond.   Prof.

Haigh, John, MA Oxf., PhD Camb.   Sr. Lectr., Statistics

Hennessy, Matthew C. B., BSc N.U.I., MA Trinity(Dub.), PhD Wat.   Prof., Computer Science

Hirschfeld, James W. P., MSc Syd., PhD Edin.   Reader

Mulvey, Christopher J., MA Camb., MSc Sheff., DPhil   Sr. Lectr.

Vassiliev, Dimitri, PhD Moscow, DSc Moscow   Prof.

Wraith, Gavin C., MA Camb., PhD Camb.   Reader

Media Studies

Fax: (01273) 678644

Donald, James, MA Oxf., MSc Lond., PhD Open(UK)   Reader

Silverstone, Roger, MA Oxf., PhD Lond.   Prof.

Music

Fax: (01273) 678644

Butler, Martin C., MusB Manc., MFA Prin.   Sr. Lectr.

Osmond-Smith, David, MA Camb.   Prof.

Philosophy

Fax: (01273) 678466

Boden, Margaret A., MA Camb., AM Harv., PhD Harv., ScD Camb., FBA   Prof., Philosophy and Psychology

Clark, Andrew J., BA Stir., PhD Stir.   Prof.

Diffey, Terry J., BA Brist., PhD Brist.   Reader

Gaskin, Richard, BA Oxf., BPhil Oxf., DPhil Oxf.   Sr. Lectr.

Morris, Michael R., BPhil Oxf.   Sr. Lectr.

Physics, Experimental

Fax: (01273) 678097

Boshier, Malcolm, BA Oxf., DPhil Oxf.   Sr. Lectr.

Byrne, James, MSc N.U.I., PhD Edin., FIP   Reader

Dawber, Peter G., MA Oxf., DPhil Oxf.   Sr. Lectr.

Hinds, Ed A., BA Oxf., DPhil Oxf.   Prof.

Palmer, Derek W., MA Camb., PhD Reading   Sr. Lectr.

Pendlebury, James M., PhD Camb.   Prof.

Thomson, A. Low, BSc St And., PhD Duke   Sr. Lectr.

Townsend, Peter D., BSc Reading, PhD Reading, FIP   Prof.

Physics, Theoretical

Fax: (01273) 678097

Bailin, David, MA Camb., PhD Camb.   Prof.

Barton, Gabriel, MA Oxf., DPhil Oxf., FIP   Reader

Blin-Stoyle, Roger J., MA Oxf., DPhil Oxf.   Hon. Prof.

Copeland, Ed, BSc Newcastle(UK), PhD Newcastle(UK)   Sr. Lectr.

Dombey, Norman D., BA Oxf., PhD Cal.Tech.   Prof.

Waxman, David, BSc Lond., DPhil   Sr. Lectr.

Politics, see Internat. Relns. and Pol.

Psychology

Fax: (01273) 673563

Abraham, Charles, BA DPhil   Sr. Lectr.

Bates, Brian C., BA Calif., MA Oregon, PhD Oregon   Sr. Lectr.

Boden, Margaret A., MA Camb., AM Harv., PhD Harv., ScD Camb., FBA   Prof., Philosophy and Psychology

Butterworth, George E., BSc Lond., MSc Birm., DPhil Oxf.   Prof.

Davey, Graham, BA Wales, PhD Wales   Prof.

Griffin, Dale, BA Br.Col., AM Stan., PhD Stan.

Smith, Peter B., BA Camb., PhD Camb.   Reader

Psychology, Experimental

Fax: (01273) 678611

Darwin, Christopher J., MA Camb., PhD
    Camb.   Prof.
Garnham, Alan, BA Oxf., DPhil
Mather, George W., BA Sheff., PhD Reading   Sr.
    Lectr.
McComb, Karen, BSc Edin., PhD Camb.
Oakhill, Jane, BE DPhil
Parkin, Alan J., BSc Reading, MSc DPhil   Prof.
Rusted, Jennifer, BSc CNAA, PhD Lond.
Stephens, David, PhD Lond., BSc   Prof.

Russian and East European Studies

Fax: (01273) 673246

Dyker, David A., MA Glas., DPhil   Sr. Lectr.
Milner-Gulland, Robin R., MA Oxf.   Prof.
Williams, Beryl J., BA Lond.   Reader

Social Anthropology

Fax: (01273) 623572

Pratt, Jeffrey C., BA DPhil   Sr. Lectr.
Stirrat, Jock, MA Camb., PhD Camb.   Sr. Lectr.

Social Policy and Social Work

Fax: (01273) 678644

Ambrose, Peter J., BA Lond., MA McG.,
    DPhil   Sr. Lectr.
Cannan, Crescy, BA York(UK), MSc Sur., PhD
    Lond.
England, Hugh, BA MSW   Sr. Lectr.
Harwin, Judith, BA Oxf.   Prof.
Jacobs, John, BA Camb.   Sr. Lectr.

Sociology

Fax: (01273) 678644

Dickens, Peter M. S., PhD Camb.   Reader
Outhwaite, R. William, BA Oxf., MA
    DPhil   Prof.
Platt, Jennifer A., MA Camb., MA Chic.   Prof.
Saunders, Peter R., BA Kent, PhD Lond.   Prof.
Shaw, Jennifer M., BSc Lond.   Sr. Lectr.

Statistics, see Maths.

SPECIAL CENTRES, ETC

Language Centre

Tel: (01273) 678006 Fax: (01273) 678476
Evans, Michael J., BA Wales, PhD Edin.   Dir.*

Medical Research, Trafford Centre for

Tel: (01273) 678331 Fax: (01273) 623714

Vincent, R., BSc Lond., MB BS Lond., MD
    Lond.   Prof.; Dir.*

Neuroscience, Sussex Centre for

Fax: (01273) 678433

O'Shea, M. R., BSc Leic., PhD S'ton.   Prof.;
    Dir.*

Science Policy Research Unit

Tel: (01273) 686758 Fax: (01273) 685865

Chesshire, John, BA Durh., MA   Prof. Fellow
Freeman, Christopher, BSc Lond.   Prof. Fellow
Gann, David, BSc Reading, MSc   Prof. Fellow
Hicks, Diana M., BA Grinnell, MSc DPhil   Sr.
    Lectr.
Mansell, Robin E., BA Manit., MSc Lond., MA
    S.Fraser, PhD S.Fraser   Prof.
Martin, Ben, MA Camb., MSc Manc.   Prof.;
    Dir.*
Millstone, Erik P., BSc Kent, MA Kent, MPhil
    Lond., PhD Lond.   Sr. Lectr.
Pavitt, Keith L. R., MA Camb.   R. M. Phillips
    Prof.
Surrey, John, BSc(Econ) Lond.   Prof. Fellow
Von Tunzelmann, Nicholas, MA Camb., MA
    Cant., DPhil Oxf.   Reader

CONTACT OFFICERS

Academic affairs. Registrar and Secretary:
    Gooch, Barry, BA Hull
Accommodation. Business Manager: Dudley,
    Charles, BA Warw.
Admissions (first degree). Senior Assistant
    Registrar: Stewart, Elizabeth
Admissions (higher degree). Assistant
    Registrar: Gee, Linda
Adult/continuing education. Director of
    Continuing Education: Gray, Fred, BA PhD
Alumni. Alumni Officer: Dyer, Sara, BA
Careers. Director of Career Development Unit:
    Morris, Carolyn, BA Belf.
Computing services. Librarian: Peasgood,
    Adrian N., BA Camb.
Development/fund-raising. Development
    Officer: Street, Robin
Estates and buildings/works and services.
    Registrar and Secretary: Gooch, Barry, BA
    Hull
Examinations. Senior Assistant Registrar:
    Stewart, Elizabeth

Finance. Finance Officer: Pavey, Stephen, BSc
    Brist.
General enquiries. Information Officer: Yates,
    Sue, BA
Health services. Medical Officer: McConnell,
    Rosemary, MB ChB Birm.
International office. International Officer:
    Baker, Phillip, BA Lond., PhD Lond.
Library (chief librarian). Librarian: Peasgood,
    Adrian N., BA Camb.
Minorities/disadvantaged groups. Pro-Vice-
    Chancellor: ......
Personnel/human resources. Personnel
    Officer: McCallister, Adrian, BA Birm.
Public relations, information and marketing.
    Information Officer: Yates, Sue, BA
Publications. Publications Officer: Proctor,
    Andrew, BSc Brad.
Purchasing. Purchasing Officer: Harmer,
    Michael
Quality assurance and accreditation. Senior
    Pro-Vice-Chancellor: ......
Quality assurance and accreditation. Pro-
    Vice-Chancellor: Brooks, Colin, MA Camb.,
    BPhil Oxf., PhD Camb.
Research. Senior Pro-Vice-Chancellor: ......
Safety. Safety Officer: Ballance, Peter, BSc PhD
Scholarships, awards, loans. Pro-Vice-
    Chancellor: ......
Schools liaison. Senior Assistant Registrar:
    Stewart, Elizabeth, BA Liv.
Security. Operations Manager: Feast, Paul, BSc
Sport and recreation. Director of Sport: ......
Staff development and training. Staff
    Development Officer: Hood, Andrew, BSc
    Lond., MSc CNAA
Student union. General Manager: ......
Students from other countries. International
    Officer: Baker, Phillip, BA Lond., PhD Lond.

CAMPUS/COLLEGE HEADS

Cell Mutation Unit. Dir.: Bridges, Prof. B. A.,
    BSc Reading, PhD Reading, FIBiol
Institute of Development Studies. (Tel:
    (01273) 606261.) Dir.: Bezanson, Keith, BA
    Car., PhD Stan.
Institute of Employment Studies. Dir.:
    Pearson, Richard, BSc PhD

[Information supplied by the institution as at 9 April
1998, and edited by the ACU]

UNIVERSITY OF TEESSIDE

Founded 1992; previously established as Constantine College 1930, and Teesside Polytechnic 1970

Member of the Association of Commonwealth Universities

Postal Address: Middlesbrough, Cleveland, England TS1 3BA
Telephone: (01642) 218121 Fax: (01642) 342067 Telex: 587537 WWW: http://www.tees.ac.uk

CHANCELLOR—Brittan, Rt. Hon. Sir Leon, QC, MA Camb.
VICE-CHANCELLOR*—Fraser, Prof. Derek, BA Leeds, MA Leeds, PhD Leeds, FRHistS
SECRETARY AND REGISTRAR—McClintock, J. M., BA Trinity(Dub.), LLB Trinity(Dub.), MA Trinity(Dub.), LLM
    Penn.

THAMES VALLEY UNIVERSITY

Founded 1992; previously established as Polytechnic of West London 1991

Member of the Association of Commonwealth Universities

Postal Address: St Mary's Road, Ealing, London, England W5 5RF
Telephone: (0181) 579 5000 **Fax**: (0181) 566 1353

CHANCELLOR—Hamlyn, Paul
ACTING VICE-CHANCELLOR*—Taylor, Prof. Sir William, CBE, BSc(Econ) Lond., PhD Lond., Hon. DSc Aston, Hon. DLitt Leeds, Hon. DLitt Lough., Hon. DCL Kent, Hon. DUniv Open(UK), Hon. LLD Hull, Hon. DEd Plym., Hon. DEd W.Eng., Hon. DEd, Hon. FCCEA
DIRECTOR OF FINANCE—Eley, Richard
PRO-VICE-CHANCELLOR (ACADEMIC)—Hazelgrove, Susanne
DIRECTOR OF HUMAN RESOURCES—Thomas, Charlotte
PRO-VICE-CHANCELLOR (DEVELOPMENT)—Wolfe, Andy
DIRECTOR OF COMPLEMENTARY LEARNING—Irving, Ann
CLERK TO THE BOARD OF GOVERNORS—Denton, Stephen
DIRECTOR OF REGISTRY SERVICES‡—Head, Paul

ACADEMIC UNITS
Arranged by Schools

Accountancy
Pratt, Nick   Head*

Business
Owen, Monica   Head*

Creative, Cultural and Social Studies
Grant, David   Head*

English Language Teaching
Thomas, Helen   Head*

European and International Studies
Ross, Andy   Head*

Health Sciences, Wolfson School of
Crooke, Lois   Head*

Hospitality Studies
Hambleton, Paul   Head*

Information Studies, see Technol. and Information Studies

Law
Webster, George   Head*

Management
Hankinson, Graham   Head*

Social Studies, see Creative, Cultural and Soc. Studies

Technology and Information Studies
Kayes, Peter   Head*

CONTACT OFFICERS

Academic affairs. Pro-Vice-Chancellor (Academic): Hazelgrove, Susanne
Accommodation. Accommodation Officer: Smith, Linda
Admissions (first degree). Recruitment Manager: Marchant, Christine
Admissions (higher degree). Recruitment Manager: Marchant, Christine
Adult/continuing education. Director of Further and Continuing Education: Thurston, Sue
Alumni. (Contact the Development Office)
Careers. Guidance Services Manager: Shacklady, David
Computing services. Head of ISD: De Witt, Bob
Consultancy services. Head of Business Development: Chisnall, Nick
Development/fund-raising. Head of Corporate Relations: Ward, Andrew
Estates and buildings/works and services. Head of Campus Services: Verrall, Richard
Examinations. Assessments Manager: Spinoza, Anne
Finance. Director of Finance: Eley, Richard
General enquiries. Press and Public Relations Manager: Marsh, Sue
Health services. Health and Safety Officer: Maxwell-Smith, Nigel
Industrial liaison. McNicholas, Stuart
International office. Head of International Development: Barr, Pauline
Library (chief librarian). Director of Complementary Learning: Irving, Ann
Library (enquiries). (Contact the enquiry desk, Learning Resources Centre)

Minorities/disadvantaged groups. Recruitment Manager: Marchant, Christine
Ombudsperson. Director of Registry Services: Head, Paul
Personnel/human resources. Director of Human Resources: Thomas, Charlotte
Public relations, information and marketing. Press and Public Relations Manager: Marsh, Sue
Publications. Publications and Advertising Manager: Lambert, Trevor
Purchasing. Purchasing Manager: Bunyan, Sandie
Quality assurance and accreditation. Director of Quality Management and Enhancement: Walker, Lawrie
Research. Quality Manager: Sundle, Stephanie
Safety. Health and Safety Officer: Maxwell-Smith, Nigel
Scholarships, awards, loans. Student Financial Advisor: Aldridge, Jayne
Schools liaison. Access/Community Links Leader: Asher, Shirley
Security. Security Manager: Sasson, Yosi
Staff development and training. Director of Staff Development: Larden, Fiona
Student union. General Manager: Savage, Les
Student welfare/counselling. Student Services Manager: Richards, Nancy
Students from other countries. Head of International Office: Makin, Dan
Students with disabilities. Student Advisor: Jacobs, Estelle
Women. Recruitment Manager: Marchant, Christine

[Information supplied by the institution as at 9 May 1997, and edited by the ACU]

UNIVERSITY OF ULSTER

Founded 1984 by merger of the New University of Ulster (1965, 1970) and the Ulster Polytechnic

Member of the Association of Commonwealth Universities

Postal Address: University House, Cromore Road, Coleraine, County Londonderry, Northern Ireland BT52 1SA
Telephone: (01265) 44141 **Fax**: (01265) 324927 **Telex**: 747597 **WWW**: http://www.ulst.ac.uk

CHANCELLOR—Neuberger, Rabbi Julia
PRO-CHANCELLOR—Hanna, R. J., CBE, JP
PRO-CHANCELLOR—Keegan, G. M., OBE, MEd Belf.
VICE-CHANCELLOR*—Smith of Clifton, Prof. Lord, BSc Lond., Hon. LLD Trinity(Dub.), Hon. LLD Hull, Hon. LLD Belf., FRHistS
TREASURER—Carson, W. M., CBE, FCA
PRO-VICE-CHANCELLOR (PLANNING), AND PROVOST, MAGEE COLLEGE—Monds, F. C., BSc Belf., PhD Belf.
PRO-VICE-CHANCELLOR (EXTERNAL AFFAIRS), AND PROVOST, JORDANSTOWN—Tate, A., BSc MSc
PRO-VICE-CHANCELLOR (ACADEMIC AFFAIRS), AND PROVOST, COLERAINE—Roebuck, P. R., BA Hull, PhD Hull, FRHistS
PRO-VICE-CHANCELLOR (RESEARCH)—McKenna, P. G., BSc Ulster, PhD Belf., FIBiol

GENERAL INFORMATION

History. The university was founded in 1984 by the merger of New University of Ulster and Ulster Polytechnic. It has four campuses: at Coleraine, Jordanstown, Belfast and Magee College (Londonderry).

Admission to first degree courses (see also United Kingdom Introduction). Through Universities and Colleges Admissions Service (UCAS).

First Degrees (see also United Kingdom Directory to Subjects of Study). BA, BEng, BMus, BSc, BTech, MEng.
   Courses last 3 years full-time; sandwich courses last 4 years.

Higher Degrees (see also United Kingdom Directory to Subjects of Study). MA, MBA, MFA, MMedSc, MRes, MSc, MPhil, DPhil, DEng, DEnvSc, DMan, DMedSc, DMidSc (midwifery science), DNSc (nursing science), DTech.
   Applicants for admission to master's degree courses should hold a first degree with at least second class honours or relevant postgraduate qualifications. MRes, MPhil: honours degree with at least second class honours in a relevant subject; MMedSc: honours degree, professional health or social services qualification and 2 years post-qualification work experience; DPhil: MPhil; other doctorates: relevant master's degree. For DPhil by published work, applicants must have been active in research for at least 5 years and have produced a significant contribution to knowledge.
   MA, MFA, MSc: 1 year full-time or 2 years part-time; MBA: 2 years full-time or 3 years part-time; MMedSc: 2 years part-time; MPhil: 2 years full-time or 4 years part-time; doctorates: 3 years full-time or 5 years part-time: DPhil by published work: 6–12 months.

Academic Year (1998–99). Two semesters: 28 September–29 January; 1 February–4 June. Some modules are also available in a third semester: 19 July– 10 September.

FACULTIES/SCHOOLS

Art and Design
Tel: (01232) 324517 Fax: (01232) 324925
Acting Dean: O'Keeffe, Prof. T. M., BA BD LPh
Secretary: Platt, P.

Business and Management
Tel: (01232) 366350 Fax: (01232) 366834
Dean: Barnett, Prof. R. R., BSc PhD
Secretary: Webb, G. E.

Engineering
Tel: (01232) 366285 Fax: (01232) 366855
Dean: Norton, Prof. B., BSc MSc PhD DSc

Secretary: Saberton, L. E.

Humanities
Tel: (01265) 324517 Fax: (01265) 324925
Dean: O'Keeffe, Prof. T. M., BA BD LPh
Secretary: Platt, P.

Informatics
Tel: (01232) 366125 Fax: (01232) 366803
Dean: Hughes, Prof. J. G., BSc PhD, FBCS
Secretary: Hunter, B.

Science
Tel: (01265) 324424 Fax: (01265) 324596
Dean: Watts, Prof. W. E., BSc PhD DSc, FRSChem, FRSEd
Secretary: Shortt, P.

Social and Health Sciences, and Education
Tel: (01232) 326157 Fax: (01232) 368266
Dean: Allen, Prof. J. M., BSc PhD, FIBiol
Secretary: Barr, V.

Ulster Business School
Tel: (01232) 368087 Fax: (01232) 366843
Dean: Parkinson, Prof. S. T., BA MSc PhD
Secretary: Cameron, H.

ACADEMIC UNITS
Arranged by Schools

Applied Biology and Chemical Studies
Adams, K. R.   Sr. Lectr.
Bishop, R. H.   Sr. Lectr.
Brown, N. M. D.   Prof.
Eggins, B. R.   Reader
Flinn, A. M.   Sr. Lectr.
Irwin, S. W. B.   Sr. Lectr.
Jones, J. G.   Sr. Lectr.
Knipe, A. C.   Prof.
Logan, S. R.   Reader
Marchant, R.   Prof.; Head*
McClean, W. S.   Sr. Lectr.
McHale, A. P.   Reader
McKerr, G.   Sr. Lectr.
Rushton, B. S.   Reader
Smyth, W. F.   Sr. Lectr.
Wyness, J.   Sr. Lectr.
Research: biotechnology; natural resources; surface science

Behavioural and Communication Sciences
Ball, M. J.   Prof.
Cairns, S. E.   Prof.
Commins, B. G.   Sr. Lectr.
Dickson, D. A.   Sr. Lectr.
Dusoir, A. E.   Sr. Lectr.
Ekins, R. J.   Sr. Lectr.
Hargie, O. D. W.   Prof.
James, D. T. D.   Sr. Lectr.
Leslie, J. C.   Prof.

Liddell, C.   Sr. Lectr.
Patterson, A. M.   Sr. Lectr.
Rae, G.   Prof.
Saunders, C. Y. M.   Sr. Lectr.
Shephard, R. A.   Sr. Lectr.
Stringer, M.   Sr. Lectr.
Weinreich, P.   Prof.
Wilson, J.   Prof.; Head*
Wilson, R.   Sr. Lectr.
Woodward, R. J.   Sr. Lectr.
Research: interpersonal communication; language and communication; psychology (behavioural analysis, behavioural biology, health psychology, social behaviour)

Biology, see Appl. Biol. and Chem. Studies

Biomedical Sciences
Anderson, R. S.   Sr. Lectr.
Barnett, C. R.   Sr. Lectr.
Barnett, Y. A.   Sr. Lectr.
Best, G. T.   Prof.
Downes, C. S.   Prof.
Eaton-Evans, M. J.   Sr. Lectr.
Flatt, P. R.   Prof.
Gilmore, W. S.   Sr. Lectr.
Hannigan, B. M.   Prof.; Head*
Hirst, D. G.   Prof.
Livingstone, M. B. E.   Sr. Lectr.
McIntyre, I. A.   Sr. Lectr.
McKelvey-Martin, V. J.   Sr. Lectr.
McKeown, S. R.   Sr. Lectr.
McNulty, H. M.   Sr. Lectr.
Nevin, G. B.   Reader
O'Neill, C.   Sr. Lectr.
Rowland, I. R.   Prof.
Strain, J. J.   Prof.
Thurnham, D. I.   Prof.
Welch, R. W.   Sr. Lectr.
Research: cancer and ageing; diabetes; diet and health; radiation science; vision science

Built Environment
Adair, A. S.   Prof.; Head*
Berry, J. N.   Sr. Lectr.
Birnie, J. W.   Sr. Lectr.
Deddis, W. G.   Sr. Lectr.
Eames, P. C.   Reader
Gunning, J. G.   Sr. Lectr.
Harvey, H. D.   Sr. Lectr.
Lyness, J. F.   Reader
McCluskey, W. J.   Sr. Lectr.
McGreal, W. S.   Prof.
Meban, A. G.   Sr. Lectr.
Myers, W. R. C.   Sr. Lectr.
O'Connor, D. J.   Sr. Lectr.
Schmidt, F. A.   Sr. Lectr.
Shields, T. J.   Prof.
Silcock, G. W. H.   Sr. Lectr.
Smyth, A. W.   Prof.
Woodside, A. R.   Prof.
Yohanis, Y. G.   Sr. Lectr.

Research: fire safety engineering; performance research on the built environment; property, planning and logistics

Business, see Ulster Bus. Sch.

Chemistry, see Appl. Biol. and Chem. Studies

Commerce and International Business Studies

Brown, S.   Prof.
Cradden, T. G.   Sr. Lectr.; Head*
Glass, J. C.   Prof.
Hutchinson, R. W.   Prof.
Johnson, W.   Sr. Lectr.
Johnston, A. J.   Sr. Lectr.
Kinsella, R. P.   Prof.
Scharf, W. F.   Sr. Lectr.
Stark, T.   Sr. Lectr.
Ward, J. D.   Prof.
Research: accounting; banking; finance; retailing and marketing

Communication, see Behavioural and Communicn. Scis., and Des. and Communicn.

Computing and Mathematics

Anderson, T. J.   Prof.
Bell, W. C.   Sr. Lectr.
Copeland, C. J.   Sr. Lectr.
Donegan, H. A.   Sr. Lectr.
Gillespie, E. S.   Sr. Lectr.
Houston, S. K.   Prof.
Hull, M. E. C.   Prof.
McAlpin, D. A.   Sr. Lectr.
McClinton, S. I.   Sr. Lectr.
McMillan, W. T.   Sr. Lectr.
Millar, R. J.   Sr. Lectr.
Murphy, C. J. V.   Sr. Lectr.
Neill, N. T.   Sr. Lectr.
O'Dubhchair, K. M.   Sr. Lectr.
Scott, T. M.   Sr. Lectr.; Head*
Sweeney, P. J.   Sr. Lectr.
Woods, D.   Sr. Lectr.
Research: artificial intelligence and data engineering; computer vision and image processing; knowledge and information engineering; mathematics; software engineering

Design and Communication

Aston, T. G.   Sr. Lectr.
Burns, A.   Sr. Lectr.
Catto, M. A.   Sr. Lectr.
Hill, B. J.   Reader
Kelly, W.   Sr. Lectr.
Lawrence, C. N.   Sr. Lectr.
McClelland, B.   Prof.; Head*
McKeag, D.   Prof.
McLaughlin, P. B.   Sr. Lectr.
Montgomery, M. A.   Sr. Lectr.
Research: engineering components; history and theory of art, design, film, visual culture; visual communication and multi-media

Economics, see Public Policy, Econ. and Law

Education

Bleakley, E. W.   Sr. Lectr.
Collins, J. J.   Sr. Lectr.
Crouch, C. W. J.   Sr. Lectr.
Dallat, J. P.   Sr. Lectr.
Farren, S. N.   Sr. Lectr.
Hutchinson, B. W.   Sr. Lectr.
Marriott, S.   Sr. Lectr.
McAleavy, G. J.   Sr. Lectr.
McAleer, J. A.   Sr. Lectr.
McMahon, H. F.   Prof.; Head*
Moran, A.   Sr. Lectr.
North, R. F. J.   Sr. Lectr.
O'Hara, M. B.   Sr. Lectr.
O'Neill, W. G.   Sr. Lectr.
Pritchard, R. M. O.   Sr. Lectr.
Strain, D. M.   Sr. Lectr.
Whitehouse, P. G.   Sr. Lectr.
Wilkinson, C. W.   Sr. Lectr.
Research: education and contemporary society; educational organisation and management;

further and higher education and lifelong learning; information and communications technology; social, civic and political education

Engineering, Electrical and Mechanical

Akay, M.   Sr. Lectr.
Anderson, J. M. C. C.   Prof.; Head*
Bell, J. M. C. C.   Sr. Lectr.
Black, N. D.   Prof.
Brown, D.   Sr. Lectr.
Cross, G.   Sr. Lectr.
Evans, N. E.   Sr. Lectr.
Hepburn, C.   Prof.
Katzen, S. J.   Sr. Lectr.
Laverty, S. J.   Sr. Lectr.
Maguire, P. D.   Reader
McAdams, E. T.   Reader
McGinnity, T. M.   Sr. Lectr.
McIlhagger, R.   Prof.
McLaughlin, J. A.   Reader
Mitchell, R. H.   Prof.
Owens, F. J.   Sr. Lectr.
Webb, J. A.   Sr. Lectr.
Research: advanced forming; bioengineering; engineering composites; thin film devices

Engineering, Information and Software

Adamson, K.   Sr. Lectr.
Bell, D. A.   Prof.; Head*
Bustard, D. W.   Prof.
Duntsch, I.   Prof.
Farahmand, K.   Reader
Glass, D.   Sr. Lectr.
Lundy, P. J.   Sr. Lectr.
McAllister, H. G.   Sr. Lectr.
McClean, S. I.   Prof.
McSherry, D. M.   Sr. Lectr.
McTear, M. F.   Prof.
Murtagh, F.   Prof.
Parr, G. P.   Sr. Lectr.
Smith, M. W. A.   Reader
Weston, J. S. C.   Sr. Lectr.
Research: artificial intelligence and data engineering; computer vision and image processing; knowledge and information engineering; mathematics; software engineering

Engineering, Mechanical, see Engin., Electr. and Mech.

Environmental Studies

Cooper, A.   Sr. Lectr.
Cooper, J. A. G.   Reader
Day, K. R.   Reader
Eastwood, D. A.   Prof.; Head*
Graham, B. J.   Prof.
Jewson, D.   Reader
McCabe, A. M.   Reader
McCloskey, J.   Sr. Lectr.
McMullan, J. T.   Prof.
Pollard, H. J.   Sr. Lectr.
Poole, M.   Sr. Lectr.
Roberts, J. C.   Sr. Lectr.
Thomas, C.   Reader
Wilcock, D. N.   Prof.
Williams, B. C.   Reader
Wilson, P.   Sr. Lectr.
Research: coastal studies (coastal management, estuaries, geophysics, palaeoenvironments, sedimentology, seismicity); energy (energy conversion systems, heat pump systems, industrial refrigeration, techno-economic analysis); human environment (air transport policies, cultural geography, geotelematics, integrated regional development); natural resources (ecotoxicology, fisheries, forestry, hydrology, lakes and rivers, landscape ecology)

Fine and Applied Arts

Aiken, S. M.   Sr. Lectr.
Barker, D. S.   Sr. Lectr.
Crone, D.   Reader; Head*
Duffield, D. B.   Reader
Ledsham, D. S.   Sr. Lectr.
MacLennan, A. M.   Prof.
Meanley, P.   Sr. Lectr.

Yasuda, T.   Prof.
Research: history and theory of fine and applied arts

Health Sciences

Baxter, G. D.   Prof.
Boore, J. R. P.   Prof.
Chambers, M. G. A.   Sr. Lectr.
Eakin, P. A.   Prof.
Kernohan, W. G.   Prof.
Long, M. A.   Sr. Lectr.
McConkey, R. A.   Prof.
McCoy, M. P.   Prof.
McKenna, H. P.   Prof.
Parahoo, A. K.   Sr. Lectr.
Sines, D. T.   Prof.; Head*
Whittington, D. A.   Sr. Lectr.
Research: nursing (chronic illness, learning disability, mental health, primary care, telematics); rehabilitation sciences (electrotherapy, low back pain, muscle damage, neurological investigation)

History, Philosophy and Politics

Arthur, P. J.   Prof.
Aughey, A. H.   Sr. Lectr.
Brown, J. M.   Sr. Lectr.
Dunn, J. A.   Prof.
Emmerson, W. A.   Sr. Lectr.
Fitzpatrick, B. J.   Sr. Lectr.
Fraser, T. G.   Prof.; Head*
Hainsworth, P. A.   Sr. Lectr.
Jeffery, K. J.   Prof.
Jones, G. J.   Prof.
Lindley, K. J.   Sr. Lectr.
Loughlin, J. P.   Sr. Lectr.
Morgan, V.   Prof.
O'Brien, M. G. R.   Sr. Lectr.
O'Connor, P. E. J.   Sr. Lectr.
Patterson, H. H.   Prof.
Pearson, R.   Prof.
Riches, W. T. M.   Sr. Lectr.
Roulston, M. C. M.   Sr. Lectr.
Ryan, S.   Sr. Lectr.
Sharp, A. J.   Prof.
Smith, D. B.   Sr. Lectr.
Springhall, J. O.   Reader
Sturdy, D. J.   Sr. Lectr.
Ward, K. E.   Sr. Lectr.
Research: history (American history, ethnic conflict, Irish history, social history of science and medicine); politics and international studies (Conservative political thought, European politics, UK politics)

International Business Studies, see
Comm. and Internat. Bus. Studies

Languages and Literature

Alcock, A. E.   Prof.
Andrews, W. D. E.   Sr. Lectr.
Bareham, T.   Prof.
Bradford, R. W.   Prof.
Connor, I. D.   Sr. Lectr.
Gargett, G.   Sr. Lectr.
Gillespie, J. H.   Sr. Lectr.
Hendrick, P. J.   Sr. Lectr.
Jones, M. R.   Sr. Lectr.
Lillie, E. M.   Sr. Lectr.
Longstaffe, M. R. A.   Sr. Lectr.
Macklin, G. M.   Sr. Lectr.
MacMathuna, S.   Prof.
McBride, R.   Prof.
McMinn, J. M.   Prof.
McVeagh, J.   Sr. Lectr.
O'Doibhlin, D.   Sr. Lectr.
Welch, R. A.   Prof.
York, R. A.   Prof.; Head*
Research: English (including Irish literature and bibliography, and literary history and theory)); French thought and literature; German language, literature and history; Irish and Celtic studies; Spanish literature and history

Law, see Public Policy, Econ. and Law

Leisure and Tourism

Blair, I. S.   Sr. Lectr.
Boreham, C. A.   Prof.
Fawcett, S. L.   Sr. Lectr.
McDowell, D. A.   Prof.; Head*
McKenna Black, M. A.   Sr. Lectr.
Murray, A. E.   Sr. Lectr.
Palmer, A. J.   Prof.
Saunders, E. D.   Prof.
Research: food and consumer studies; hospitality
   and tourism; sports-related subjects

Management

Bell, J. D.   Sr. Lectr.
Boyle, E. J.   Sr. Lectr.
Carey, M.   Prof.
Carson, D. J.   Prof.
Clarke, W. M.   Prof.; Head*
Dickson, G.   Sr. Lectr.
Gilmore, A. J.   Sr. Lectr.
Green, J. P.   Sr. Lectr.
Harrison, R.   Prof.
Hyndman, N. S.   Reader
Kirk, R. J.   Prof.
Kirk-Smith, M. D.   Sr. Lectr.
Lundy, M. O.   Sr. Lectr.
Mapstone, R. H.   Sr. Lectr.
McAleer, W. E.   Prof.
McClung, R.   Sr. Lectr.
McHugh, M. L.   Sr. Lectr.
McKeown, E.   Sr. Lectr.
McNamee, P. B.   Prof.
Morgan, J. B.   Sr. Lectr.
Mulvenna, J. A.   Sr. Lectr.
Pyper, I. F.   Sr. Lectr.
Rankin, D. C.   Sr. Lectr.
Turner, J. A.   Sr. Lectr.
Research: accounting and finance; marketing;
   operational research/operations
   management; strategy, organisational
   behaviour and human resource management

Mathematics, see Computing and Maths.

Media and Performing Arts

Bracefield, H. M.   Sr. Lectr.
Cranston, D.   Sr. Lectr.
Fleming, D. R.   Sr. Lectr.
Hadfield, P. J. A.   Sr. Lectr.
Hill, W. J.   Sr. Lectr.
Hunter, D. M.   Sr. Lectr.
McCarthy, G. F.   Prof.
McLoone, J. M.   Sr. Lectr.; Head*
Russ, M.   Sr. Lectr.
Research: media studies; music (analysis,
   composition, contemporary music,
   performance practice); theatre studies

Philosophy, see Hist., Philos. and Pol.

Politics, see Hist., Philos. and Pol.

Public Policy, Economics and Law

Bell, J. K.   Sr. Lectr.
Borooah, V. K.   Prof.
Carmichael, P.   Sr. Lectr.
Carswell, L. A.   Sr. Lectr.
Collins, C. A.   Prof.
Dickson, S. B.   Prof.
Erridge, A. F.   Sr. Lectr.
Fitzpatrick, T. M.   Prof.
Geary, F.   Sr. Lectr.
Hart, M.   Reader
Harvey, S. P.   Sr. Lectr.

Knox, C. G.   Prof.
Kula, E. I.   Sr. Lectr.
McAlister, D. A.   Sr. Lectr.; Head*
McGregor, P. P. L.   Sr. Lectr.
Mullan, K.   Sr. Lectr.
Murray, M. R.   Sr. Lectr.
O'Loan, N. P.   Sr. Lectr.
Osborne, R. D.   Prof.
Osmani, S. R.   Prof.
Smyth, M. F.   Sr. Lectr.
Teague, P.   Prof.
Thain, C.   Prof.
Topping, J. W.   Sr. Lectr.
Research: community relations; higher education

Social and Community Sciences

Bamford, D. R.   Prof.
Birrell, W. D.   Prof.; Head*
Evason, E. M. T.   Prof.
Gaffikin, F. J.   Sr. Lectr.
Gray, P. F.   Sr. Lectr.
Griffiths, S. E.   Sr. Lectr.
Griffiths, W. H.   Sr. Lectr.
Harrison, S. J.   Reader
MacGabhann, R.   Sr. Lectr.
McCormack, P. J.   Sr. Lectr.
McCullough, A. E.   Sr. Lectr.
McCullough, W.   Sr. Lectr.
McWilliams, M. M.   Sr. Lectr.
Morrissey, M. J.   Sr. Lectr.
Murphy, P.   Sr. Lectr.
Offer, J. W.   Sr. Lectr.
Paris, C. T.   Prof.
Robinson, A.   Sr. Lectr.
Rolston, W. J.   Sr. Lectr.
Sanders, A. D.   Sr. Lectr.
Shanahan, P. O.   Sr. Lectr.
Shannon, M.   Sr. Lectr.
Warm, D. D.   Sr. Lectr.
Williamson, A. P.   Sr. Lectr.
Wilson, D.   Sr. Lectr.
Research: social policy; social work; sociology

Tourism, see Leisure and Tourism

Ulster Business School

Adams, J. S.   Sr. Lectr.
Bond, D.   Sr. Lectr.
Cromie, S.   Prof.
Ferguson, C.   Sr. Lectr.
Fox, A. F.   Prof.
McCartan, P. A.   Sr. Lectr.
McIlwaine, C.   Sr. Lectr.
McWhinney, J. G.   Sr. Lectr.
O'Neill, K. E.   Prof.
Parkinson, S. T., BA MSc PhD   Prof.; Dean*
Patterson, G.   Sr. Lectr.
Preston, J. A.   Sr. Lectr.
Stewart, K. M.   Sr. Lectr.
Research: business entrepreneurship; business
   improvement; management development;
   management of change; strategic
   management

CONTACT OFFICERS

Academic affairs. Pro-Vice-Chancellor
   (Academic Affairs), and Provost, Coleraine:
   Roebuck, P. R., BA Hull, PhD Hull, FRHistS
Accommodation. Director of Student Affairs:
   Caul, B. P., BA Belf., PhD Belf.
Admissions (first degree). Academic Registrar:
   Millar, K. I. M., BSc Belf., PhD Belf.
**Admissions (higher degree) (postgraduate
   taught courses)**. Academic Registrar: Millar,
   K. I. M., BSc Belf., PhD Belf.

Admissions (higher degree) (research). Pro-
   Vice-Chancellor (Research): McKenna, P. G.,
   BSc Ulster, PhD Belf., FIBiol
Alumni. Alumni Officer: Rees, S. Y., BA CNAA
Careers. Careers Officer: Linden, B. F.
Computing services. Director of Educational
   Services: Ewart, R. W., OBE, BSc Belf., MSc
   Belf.
Consultancy services. Pro-Vice-Chancellor
   (Research): McKenna, P. G., BSc Ulster, PhD
   Belf., FIBiol
Equal opportunities. Hunter, S. P., MA
Estates and buildings/works and services.
   Director of Physical Resources: Donnelly, P.
   P. G.
Examinations. Academic Registrar: Millar, K. I.
   M., BSc Belf., PhD Belf.
Finance. Director of Corporate Services: Cheal,
   D. G. A.
General enquiries. Director of Corporate
   Services: Cheal, D. G. A.
Health services. Director of Student Affairs:
   Caul, B. P., BA Belf., PhD Belf.
International office. Green, M. A., BA Liv.,
   PhD Liv.
Library (chief librarian). Director of
   Educational Services: Ewart, R. W., OBE, BSc
   Belf., MSc Belf.
Library (enquiries). User Services Librarian:
   Shorley, D. S., BA Durh.
Personnel/human resources. Director of
   Human Resources: Hamilton, B., BSc
Public relations, information and marketing.
   Pro-Vice-Chancellor (External Affairs), and
   Provost, Jordanstown: Tate, A., BSc MSc
Publications (prospectuses). Head of
   Communications Group: Kelleher, B., BA
   Belf.
Purchasing. Purchasing Officer: Barr, J. H.
Quality assurance and accreditation.
   Academic Registrar: Millar, K. I. M., BSc
   Belf., PhD Belf.
Research. Pro-Vice-Chancellor (Research):
   McKenna, P. G., BSc Ulster, PhD Belf., FIBiol
Safety. Safety Officer: Robinson, J., BSc Sur.,
   MSc Aston
Schools liaison. Schools Liaison Officer:
   Barwick, S. D. A., BSc DPhil
Security. Director of Physical Resources:
   Donnelly, P. P. G.
Sport and recreation. Director of Sport and
   Physical Recreation: Brown, M., BEd Lond.,
   BA Open(UK), MA Leeds
Staff development and training. Director of
   Staff Development: Kemplay, A.
Student welfare/counselling. Director of
   Student Affairs: Caul, B. P., BA Belf., PhD Belf.
Students with disabilities. Director of Student
   Affairs: Caul, B. P., BA Belf., PhD Belf.

CAMPUS/COLLEGE HEADS

Coleraine Campus, University House,
   Cromore Road, Coleraine, County
   Londonderry BT52 1SA, Northern Ireland,
   United Kingdom. (Fax: (01265) 40927.)
   Provost: Roebuck, P. R., BA Hull, PhD Hull,
   FRHistS
Jordanstown Campus. Provost: Tate, A., BSc
   MSc
Magee College. Provost: Monds, F. C., BSc
   Belf., PhD Belf.

[*Information supplied by the institution as at 10 May
1998, and edited by the ACU*]

UNIVERSITY OF WALES

Founded 1893

Member institutions:
University of Wales, Aberystwyth
University of Wales, Bangor
University of Wales, Cardiff
University of Wales Swansea
University of Wales, Lampeter
University of Wales College of Medicine
University of Wales Institute, Cardiff
University of Wales College, Newport

Member of the Association of Commonwealth Universities

Postal Address: University Registry, Cathays Park, Cardiff, Wales CF1 3NS
Telephone: (01222) 382656 **Fax**: (01222) 396040 **E-mail**: registry@wales.ac.uk (JANET)
Cables: University Registry, Cardiff **E-mail formula**: initial.surname@wales.ac.uk

VISITOR—Elizabeth, H.M. The Queen
CHANCELLOR—Wales, H.R.H. The Prince of, KG, KT, GCB, Hon. DMus
PRO-CHANCELLOR—Williams of Mostyn, The Rt. Hon. Lord, QC, LLB *Camb.*, MA *Camb.*
SENIOR VICE-CHANCELLOR*—(until 31 August 2001) Robbins, Prof. Keith G., MA *Oxf.*, DPhil *Oxf.*, DLitt *Glas.*,
   FRSEd, FRHistS
SECRETARY GENERAL‡—Pritchard, Jeffrey D., BA *Wales*, MA *Camb.*

GENERAL INFORMATION

History. The university was founded in 1893, bringing together three existing colleges: University College of Wales, Aberystwyth; University College of South Wales and Monmouthshire; and University College of North Wales in Bangor. It now consists of six constituent institutions, two university colleges, and other associated, affiliated and validated institutions. The registry is located in the centre of Cardiff.

Admission to first degree courses (see also United Kingdom Introduction). All applications for admission should be referred to the individual institutions and colleges.

First Degrees (see also United Kingdom Directory to Subjects of Study). BA, BArch, BD, BDS, BEd, BEng, BLib, BMedSc, BMus, BN, BPharm, BSc, BScEcon, BTh, EMBS, LLB, MB BCh, MChem, MEng, MMath, MPharm, MPhys.
   Most courses are modular and normally last 3 years full-time.

Higher Degrees (see also United Kingdom Directory to Subjects of Study). LLM, MA, MBA, MCh, MD, MEd, MLib, MMus, MPH, MRes, MSc, MScD, MScEcon, MTh, MPhil, PhD, DClinPsy, DD, DDSc, DLitt, DMus, DSc, DScEcon, EdD, EngD, LLD.

Applications for admission to master's degrees must be of graduate equivalence as recognised by the university. DClinPsy, EdD, EngD, PhD: appropriate first or master's degree; DD, DDSc, DLitt, DMus, DSc, DScEcon, LLD: awarded for published work.

Language of Instruction. English and, for some degrees, Welsh.

ACADEMIC UNITS

Advanced Welsh and Celtic Studies, Centre for

At Aberystwyth

Tel: (01970) 626717 Fax: (01970) 627066

Gruffydd, R. G., BA *Wales*, DPhil *Oxf.*, Hon. DLitt *Wales*, FBA   Prof. Emer.; Hon. Sr. Fellow
Jenkins, Geraint H., BA *Wales*, PhD *Wales*, DLitt *Wales*   Prof.; Dir.*
Williams, J. E. C., BD *Wales*, MA *Wales*, DLitt *Wales*, DLittCelt N.U.I., FSA, FBA   Prof. Emer.; Hon. Consulting Editor
Other Staff: 1 Hon. Sr. Fellow; 7 Hon. Fellows; 14 Res. Fellows
Research: language, literature and history of Celtic countries; mediaeval Welsh poetry; modern social history of Welsh language; Welsh place names

CONTACT OFFICERS

Academic affairs. Academic Secretary: Hall, Ashley D., BA *Warw.*
Alumni. Assistant Secretary: Ab Ieuan, Ruth, MPhil
Computing services. Head, Administrative Computing Unit: Parry, Owen D., BSc *Sur.*, PhD *CNAA*
Estates and buildings/works and services. Director of Resources: George, D. Ian, BScEcon *Wales*
Examinations. Administrative Assistant: Goodman, Eleri, BA *Essex*
Finance. Director of Resources: George, D. Ian, BScEcon *Wales*
General enquiries. Secretary General: Pritchard, Jeffrey D., BA *Wales*, MA *Camb.*
Personnel/human resources. Personnel and Training Officer: Mullens, Helen, BA *CNAA*
Quality assurance and accreditation. Assistant Secretary: Bradley, Deborah J., BA *Wales*
Scholarships, awards, loans. Assistant Secretary: Ab Ieuan, Ruth, MPhil
Staff development and training. Personnel and Training Officer: Mullens, Helen, BA *CNAA*
University press. Director: Thomas, Edward M., MA *Oxf.*

[*Information supplied by the institution as at 2 July 1998, and edited by the ACU*]

UNIVERSITY OF WALES, ABERYSTWYTH

Founded1872 as University College of Wales, Aberystwyth; present name adopted 1995

Associate Member of the Association of Commonwealth Universities

Postal Address: PO Box 2, Aberystwyth, Ceredigion, Wales SY23 2AX
Telephone: (01970) 623111 **Fax**: (01970) 611446 **Cables**: University of Wales, Aberystwyth
Telex: 35181 ABY UCW9 **WWW**: http://www.aber.ac.uk

PRESIDENT AND CHAIRMAN OF THE COUNCIL—Rosser, Sir Melvyn, Hon. LLD, FCA
VICE-PRESIDENT—Elystan-Morgan, His Honour Judge Lord, LLB
VICE-PRESIDENT—Gruffydd, Emer. Prof. R. Geraint, BA *Wales*, DPhil Oxf., Hon. DLitt
  Wales, FBA
TREASURER—James, J. M., BA
VICE-CHANCELLOR AND PRINCIPAL*—Morgan, Prof. Derec Ll., BA *Wales*, DPhil Oxf.
PRO-VICE-CHANCELLOR—Llody, Prof. Noel G., MA *Camb.*, PhD *Camb.*
PRO-VICE-CHANCELLOR—Hammond, Prof. Brean S., MA *Edin.*, DPhil Oxf.
REGISTRAR AND SECRETARY—Jones, D. Gruffydd, BA
DIRECTOR OF INFORMATION SERVICES—Hopkins, Mike, BA *Leic.*, PhD *Lough.*

GENERAL INFORMATION

History. Founded in 1872, Aberystwyth was the first university institution to be established in Wales. The institution's new title of the University of Wales, Aberystwyth was formally approved in 1996.

Admission to first degree courses (see also United Kingdom Introduction). Through Universities and Colleges Admissions Service (UCAS).

First Degrees (of University of Wales). BA, BEng, BSc(Econ), LLB, MEng, MMath, MPhys.
  All courses are full-time and normally last 3 years. BEng, MMath, MPhys: 4 years; MEng: 5 years.

Higher Degrees (of University of Wales). MA, MSc, MSc(Econ), LLM, MPhil, PhD.
  Many courses are also available part-time or through distance learning.

Language of Instruction. English and Welsh. The university has a language and learning centre where courses are offered to overseas students whose first language may be other than English.

Libraries. 600,000 volumes; 3500 periodicals subscribed to. Special collections include information and library studies and Celtic studies.

Fees. Full-time students: £7017; full-time students charged overseas fees: £1773; part-time fees: £697.

Academic Year (1998–99) Two semesters: 28 September–30 January; 1 February–5 June. Three terms: 28 September–19 December; 11 January–27 March; 19 April–5 June.

Income (1996–97). Total, £54,500,000.

Statistics. Staff: 1673 (712 academic and related, 961 technical, manual and clerical). Students: 6593 full-time; 740 part-time; 421 international; total 7333.

FACULTIES/SCHOOLS

Arts
Dean: Trotter, Prof. David A., MA Oxf., DPhil Oxf.

Economic and Social Studies
Dean: Williams, John R., LLB *Wales*, LLB *Camb.*

Science
Dean: Jones, Prof. Neil R., PhD DSc

Welsh Medium Studies, School of
Chair: Evans, W. Gareth, BA *Wales*, MEd *Wales*, MA *Wales*, PhD *Wales*

ACADEMIC UNITS

Accounting
Tel: (01970) 622202 Fax: (01970) 622409
Gwilliam, David, MA *Camb.*, FCA Ernst and Young Prof.; Head*
Holland, Kevin, BA *Wales* Sr. Lectr.
Other Staff: 5 Lectrs.; 2 Tutors; 1 Lectr.†
Research: auditing; businesses in Wales; corporate taxation; management accounting and education; personal and financial planning

American Studies, see Engl. Lang. and Lit., and Hist. and Welsh Hist.

Archaeology, see Hist. and Welsh Hist.

Art, School of
Tel: (01970) 622460 Fax: (01970) 622461
Crawford, Alistair, DA Prof.
Harvey, John, BA *CNAA*, MA PhD Prof.; Head*
Meyrick, R. K., BA MA Sr. Lectr.
Other Staff: 4 Lectrs.; 1 Asst. Curator; 3 Tutors†
Research: material culture; visual and religious studies

Biological Sciences, Institute of
Tel: (01970) 622313 Fax: (01970) 622350
Adams, William A., BSc *Nott.*, PhD *Nott.* Reader
Ap Gwynn, Iolo, BSc PhD Sr. Lectr.
Barrett, John, MA *Camb.*, MA Oxf., PhD *Camb.*, DSc Prof., Zoology
Beechey, Ronald B., BSc *Leeds*, PhD *Leeds*, FRSChem Prof.†
Care, Anthony D., BA *Camb.*, PhD *Leeds*, DSc *Leeds*, BVM&S *Edin.* Hon. Prof.
Fish, John D., BSc *Durh.*, PhD *Newcastle(UK)* Sr. Lectr.
Gee, John H. R., BSc *Glas.*, DPhil Oxf. Sr. Lectr.
Hall, Michael A., PhD *Lond.*, DSc *Lond.* Prof., Botany; Dir.*
Hinchliffe, John R., BA Oxf., PhD *Lond.* Prof.
Hopper, David J., BSc *Birm.*, PhD *Hull* Sr. Lectr.
Ireland, Michael P., PhD *Brist.*, BSc Sr. Lectr.
Jones, R. Neil, PhD DSc Prof.
Kaderbhai, Mustak A., BSc *Sheff.*, PhD *Kent* Sr. Lectr.
Kell, Douglas B., MA Oxf., DPhil Oxf. Prof.
Kemp, Richard B., BSc PhD Reader
Landon, John, MB BS *Lond.*, MD *Lond.*, FRCP Hon. Prof.
Morris, John G., CBE, BSc *Leeds*, DPhil Oxf., FIBiol, FRS Prof., Microbiology
Rogers, Lyndon J., BSc *Leeds*, PhD *Leeds*, FRSChem Prof.
Shirazi-Beechey, Soraya, BSc *Mich.*, PhD *Lond.* Sr. Lectr.

Smith, Arnold J., BA Oxf., DPhil Oxf. Sr. Lectr.
Stoddart, John L., PhD *Durh.*, DSc *Durh.*, FIBiol Hon. Prof.
Wathern, Peter, BSc *Lond.*, PhD *Sheff.* Prof.
Wilson, David, BSc PhD Hon. Prof.
Wootton, Robert J., MA *Camb.*, PhD *Br.Col.* Reader
Young, Michael, BSc *Brist.*, PhD *E.Anglia* Reader
Research: analytical biotechnology; environmental biology, ecology and evolution; molecular cell biology and parasitology; molecular microbial physiology and biotechnology; plant molecular biology and biotechnology

Classics, see Engl. Lang. and Lit.

Computer Science
Tel: (01970) 622424 Fax: (01970) 622455
Bott, M. Frank, MA *Camb.* Sr. Lectr.; Head*
Brady, J. Mike, MSc *Manc.*, PhD *ANU* Hon. Prof.
Davey, Peter G., CBE, MA *Camb.*, Hon. DSc *Hull* Hon. Prof.
Lee, Mark H., MSc *Wales*, PhD *Nott.* Prof.
Price, Chris J., BSc *Wales*, PhD *Wales* Sr. Lectr.
Ratcliffe, Mark B., BSc *Wales*, PhD *Wales* Sr. Lectr.
Rowland, Jem J., MSc *Manc.* Sr. Lectr.
Tedd, Michael D., MA *Camb.* Prof.†
Thomas, Martyn C., BSc *Lond.*, Hon. DSc *Hull*, FIEE Hon. Prof.
Other Staff: 12 Lectrs.; 3 Res. Fellows; 15 Res. Assocs.; 1 Hon. Lectr.
Research: advanced reasoning (model based); bio-informatics and biocomputing; intelligent robotics; software engineering

Continuing Education
Tel: (01970) 622677 Fax: (01970) 622686
Arnold, Christopher J., BA *S'ton.*, PhD *S'ton.* Sr. Lectr.; Acting Head*
Other Staff: 4 Lectrs.

Earth Sciences, see Geog. and Earth Scis., Inst. of

Economics
Tel: (01970) 622500 Fax: (01970) 622740
Black, Jane, BPhil Oxf., MA Oxf. Prof.
Cable, John R., BA *Nott.*, MA(Econ) *Manc.*, PhD *Warw.* Prof.; Head*
Cowling, Keith G., BSc *Lond.*, PhD *Ill.* Hon. Prof.
Henley, Andrew, BA *Nott.*, PhD *Warw.* Prof.
McGuinness, Anthony J., BSc *Wales*, MA *Warw.* Sr. Lectr.
Other Staff: 8 Lectrs.
Research: economic theory; industrial and business economics; international macroeconomics; labour markets

Education

Tel: (01970) 622104 Fax: (01970) 622258

Daugherty, Richard A., BA *Oxf.* Prof.; Head*
Edwards, D. Gareth, BA *Wales*, PhD *Wales* Sr. Lectr.
Ghuman, Paul A. S., BA *Punjab*, BEd *Punjab*, MEd *Birm.*, PhD *Birm.*, FBPsS Reader
Martin-Jones, Marilyn Prof.
Other Staff: 12 Lectrs.; 1 Sr. Res. Assoc.; 8 Lectrs.†; 1 Res. Fellow†
Research: assessment; educational policy; language in education; media education; multiculturalism

English Language and Literature

Tel: (01970) 622534 Fax: (01970) 622530

Aaron, Jane, BA *Wales*, DPhil *Oxf.* Sr. Lectr.
Barry, Peter T., MA *Lond.* Sr. Lectr.
Dunker, Patricia, BA *Camb.*, DPhil *Oxf.*
Hammond, Brean S., MA *Edin.*, DPhil *Oxf.* Rendel Prof.
Prichard, R. Telfryn, BA *Lond.*, MA *Wales*, PhD *Wales* Reader, Classics
Pykett, Lyn, BA *Lond.*, PhD *Lond.* Prof.; Head*
Other Staff: 11 Lectrs.; 2 Temp. Lectrs.
Research: eighteenth-century studies; mediaeval women's writing; nineteenth-century literature; Renaissance studies; twentieth-century fiction and poetry

European Languages

Tel: (01970) 622552 Fax: (01970) 622553

Edwards, Gwynne, PhD *Lond.*, BA Prof., Spanish
Havard, Robert G., BA PhD Prof., Spanish
Trotter, David A., MA *Oxf.*, DPhil *Oxf.* Prof., French; Head*
Other Staff: 10 Lectrs.; 3 Lectors; 2 Tutors; 9 Lectrs.†
Research: lingustics and literature

Film, see Theatre, Film and TV Studies

French, see European Langs.

Geography and Earth Sciences, Institute of

Tel: (01970) 622631 Fax: (01970) 622659

Aitchison, John W., MA PhD Gregynog Prof., Human Geography
Bates, Dennis E. B., BSc *Belf.*, PhD *Belf.*, FGS Sr. Lectr.
Batten, David J., BA *Qu.*, BSc *Qu.*, MSc *Lond.*, PhD *Camb.*, FGS Reader
Dobson, Maxwell R., BSc *Lond.*, PhD *Lond.*, FGS Reader
Dodgshon, Robert A., BA *Liv.*, PhD *Liv.* Prof.
Dowdeswell, Julian A., BA *Camb.*, MA *Colorado*, PhD *Camb.* Prof.
Gilbertson, David D., BSc *Lanc.*, PhD *Brist.*, DSc *Brist.*, FGS Prof.; Dir.*
Goodwin, Mark A., BA *Sus.*, PhD *Lond.* Prof.
Haynes, John R., BSc PhD DSc, FGS Emer. Prof.†
Jacobs, John A., MA *Lond.*, PhD *Lond.*, DSc *Lond.* Hon. Prof.
Jones, J. Anthony A., BA *Lond.*, MSc *McG.*, PhD *Camb.* Sr. Lectr.
Lamb, Henry F., BA *Trinity(Dub.)*, MSc *Minn.*, PhD *Camb.* Sr. Lectr.
Lewis, C. Roy, BA PhD Sr. Lectr.
Maltman, Alexander J., BSc *Liv.*, MSc *Ill.*, PhD *Ill.*, FGS Reader
Moyes, Anthony, BA *Manc.*, MA *Keele* Sr. Lectr.
Palmer, Timothy J., MA *Oxf.*, DPhil *Oxf.*, FGS Sr. Lectr.
Perkins, William T., BSc *CNAA*, PhD *CNAA*, FGS Sr. Lectr.
Taylor, James A., BA *Liv.*, MA *Liv.* Emer. Prof.
Whatley, Robin C., BSc *Hull*, PhD *Hull*, FGS Prof.
Whittington, Robert J., MSc *Durh.*, PhD *Wales*, FGS Sr. Lectr.
Wintle, Ann G., BSc *Sus.*, DPhil *Oxf.* Reader
Other Staff: 17 Lectrs.; 1 Res. Assoc.
Research: environmental geochemistry; glaciology; historical geography; hydrology; quaternary sciences

Glaciology, Centre for

Tel: (01970) 622782 Fax: (01970) 622780

Dowdeswell, Julian A., BA *Camb.*, MA *Colorado*, PhD *Camb.* Prof.; Dir.*

Rural Surveys Research Unit and Institute for Protected Landscapes

Tel: (01970) 622617 Fax: (01970) 622619

Aitchison, John W., MA PhD Prof.; Dir.*

History and Welsh History

Tel: (01970) 622662 Fax: (01970) 622676

Davies, Jeffrey L., BA PhD Sr. Lectr., Archaeology
Fitzpatrick, Martin H., BA PhD, FRHistS Sr. Lectr.
Jones, Aled G., BA *York(UK)*, MA *Warw.*, PhD *Warw.*, FRHistS Sir John Williams Prof.; Head*
Price, Roger D., BA *Wales*, PhD *Wales*, LittD *E.Anglia*, FRHistS Prof.
Rubinstein, William D., BA *Swarthmore*, PhD *Johns H.*, FRHistS Prof.
Schlenther, Boyd S., BA *Texas Christian*, MA *San Francisco*, PhD *Edin.* Reader, American History
Smith, Llinos O. W., BA *Lond.*, PhD *Lond.* Sr. Lectr.
Thomas, Peter D. G., MA *Wales*, PhD *Lond.*, FRHistS Prof.
Williams, Gareth W., MA *Oxf.*, MA *Chic.*, MSc(Econ) *Lond.*, FRHistS Sr. Lectr.
Other Staff: 15 Lectrs.
Research: American history; economic and social history; modern history and politics; Welsh history

Information and Library Studies

Tel: (01970) 622155 Fax: (01970) 622190

Huws, Gwilym, BA Sr. Lectr.
Lonsdale, Ray E., BA Sr. Lectr.
Roberts, D. Hywel E., JP, MA Prof.; Head*
Stoker, David A., MPhil *Reading*, FLA Sr. Lectr.
Other Staff: 15 Lectrs./Tutors; 2 Res. Assocs.
Research: archive administration/records management

International Politics

Tel: (01970) 622702 Fax: (01970) 622709

Baylis, John B., BA MScEcon PhD Prof.
Booth, Kenneth, BA PhD Prof.
Clark, Ian, MA *Glas.*, PhD *ANU* Prof.
Cox, Michael, BA *Reading* Prof.
Foley, Michael, BA *Keele* Prof.
Garnett, John C., MSc(Econ) *Lond.* MA PhD Prof.
Maddock, Rowland T., MA Sr. Lectr.
McInnes, Colin, BScEcon PhD Reader
Scott, Len V., BA *Nott.*, MA *Lond.*, DPhil *Oxf.* Sr. Lectr.
Smith, Steven M., BSc *S'ton.*, MSc *S'ton.*, PhD *S'ton.* Prof.; Head*
Tooze, Roger, BSc(Econ) *Lond.*, MSc(Econ) *Lond.* Reader
Watson, Michael M., MA *Oxf.*, PhD Sr. Lectr.
Williams, Howard Ll., BSc(Econ) *Lond.*, PhD *Durh.* Prof.
Other Staff: 17 Lectrs.; 1 Postdoctoral Fellow; 1 Leverhulme Postdoctoral Fellow
Research: international history; international theory; politics/area studies (Europe and the Third World); strategy and security

Law

Tel: (01970) 622712 Fax: (01970) 622729

Andrews, John A., JP, MA *Oxf.*, BCL *Oxf.* Hon. Prof.
Coleman, J. Allison, LLM Sr. Lectr.
Davies, Gillian, LèsL *Grenoble* Hon. Prof.
Harding, Christopher S. P., BA *Oxf.*, LLM *Exe.* Prof.
Hirst, David M., LLB *Manc.*, LLM Reader
Ireland, Richard W., MA *Oxf.*, LLM *Lond.* Sr. Lectr.
Kidner, Richard A. W., MA *Oxf.*, BCL *Oxf.* Prof.; Head*

Macdonald, Elizabeth A., LLB *Brist.*, LLB *Camb.* Sr. Lectr.
Rodgers, Christopher P., LLB *Camb.*, LLB *Wales* Prof.
Warren, Lynda, BSc *Lond.*, MSc *Wales*, PhD *Lond.* Prof.
Williams, John R., LLB *Camb.*, LLB *Wales* Sr. Lectr.
Other Staff: 21 Lectrs.
Research: commercial law; criminal law; criminal justice and the history of crime; environmental law; European law; human rights and legal protection of the individual

Library Studies, see Information and Library Studies

Mathematics

Tel: (01970) 622753 Fax: (01970) 622777

Barnes, Howard A., BSc *Wales*, PhD *Wales* Hon. Prof.
Davies, Arthur R., MSc *Oxf.*, DPhil *Oxf.* Prof.
Lindley, Dennis V., MA *Camb.* Hon. Prof.
Lloyd, Noel G., MA *Camb.*, PhD *Camb.* Prof.
Macdonald, Ian G., MA *Camb.*, FRS Hon. Prof.
Mavron, Vasili C., MA *Camb.*, MSc *Lond.*, PhD *Lond.* Reader
Morris, Alun O., BSc *Wales*, PhD *Wales* Prof.; Head*
Pearson, J. R. Anthony, BA *Camb.*, PhD *Camb.*, ScD *Camb.* Hon. Prof.
Phillips, Timothy N., MSc *Oxf.*, MA *Oxf.*, DPhil *Oxf.* Reader
Swinnerton-Dyer, Sir Peter, Bt., KBE, MA *Camb.*, Hon. LLD *Aberd.*, Hon. DSc *Wales*, FRS Hon. Prof.
Thomas, Kenneth, BSc *Wales* Hon. Prof.
Walters, Kenneth, BSc *Wales*, PhD *Wales*, DSc *Wales*, FRS Prof.
Other Staff: 9 Lectrs.; 1 Res. Assoc.
Research: design theory and permutation groups; nonlinear analysis and differential equations; rheology, numerical analysis and computational applied mathematics

Physical Education

Tel: (01970) 622275 Fax: (01970) 622279

Evans-Worthing, Lesley J., BEd *Lanc.*, PhD *Brad.* Dir.*
Other Staff: 1 Lectr.; 1 Recreation Officer

Physics

Tel: (01970) 622802 Fax: (01970) 622826

Birkinshaw, Keith, BSc *Leeds*, PhD *Leeds* Reader
Greaves, G. Neville, BSc *St And.*, PhD *Camb.*, FIP Prof.; Head*
Jenkins, Tudor E., MA *Oxf.*, DPhil *Oxf.* Sr. Lectr.
Kersley, Leonard, BSc *Edin.*, PhD *Edin.* Prof.
Thomas, Geraint O., BSc PhD Sr. Lectr.
Thomas, Lance, BSc PhD DSc, FIP, FIEE Prof.†
Vaughan, Geraint, MA *Camb.*, DPhil *Oxf.* Reader
Williams, Phillip J. S., MA *Camb.*, PhD *Camb.*, FIP, FRAS Prof.
Other Staff: 7 Lectrs.; 1 Hon. Lectr.; 4 Hon. Fellows; 2 Lectrs.†
Research: combustion; glasses; ozone; semiconductors; space plasma

Politics, see Internat. Pol.

Rural Studies, Welsh Institute of

Tel: (01970) 624471 Fax: (01970) 611264

Haines, Michael, BSc *Leeds*, PhD Prof.; Head*
Haresign, William, BSc *Nott.*, PhD *Nott.* Prof.
Harries, John, BSc *Wales*, PhD *Wales* Sr. Lectr.
Hughes, James T., MA *Glas.* Hon. Prof.
Midmore, Peter, BSc(Econ) *Wales*, PhD *Wales* Prof.
Moore-Colyer, Richard J., BSc *Lond.*, PhD, FRHistS, FSA Prof.
Richards, Brian M. Hon. Prof.
Slater, David H., BSc *Wales*, PhD *Wales*, FRSChem Hon. Prof.
Wilman, David, BSc *Leeds*, MA *Camb.*, PhD *Leeds*, FIBiol Sr. Lectr.

Other Staff: 35 Lectrs.; 5 Res. Assocs.; 1 Farm Manager

Research: animal science and production; crop science and production; rural business; rural and environmental economics; rural systems and agroecology

Spanish, see European Langs.

Theatre, Film and Television Studies

Tel: (01970) 622828

Clos Stephens, E., MA Oxf.   Sr. Lectr.
Davies, Hazel A., BA *Wales*, MPhil *Wales*, PhD *Wales*   Sr. Lectr.
Gough, Richard   Artistic Dir.
Rabey, David I., MA Calif., MA Birm., PhD Birm.   Sr. Lectr.
Williams, Ioan M., MA Oxf., BLitt Oxf., PhD   Prof.; Head*
Other Staff: 6 Lectrs.

Welsh History, see Hist. and Welsh Hist.

Welsh Language and Literature

Tel: (01970) 622137 Fax: (01970) 622976

Haycock, Marged, BA *Camb.*, MA *Camb.*, PhD Camb.   Reader
Hincks, Rhisiart J., MA *Wales*, PhD *Wales*   Sr. Lectr.
Rowlands, John, DPhil Oxf., MA   Prof.
Sims-Williams, Patrick, MA Camb., PhD Birm.   Prof., Celtic Studies
Williams, Gruffydd A., BA *Wales*, PhD *Wales*   Prof.; Head*
Research: Celtic languages and literature; Celtic philosophy

Zoology, see Biol. Scis., Inst. of

CONTACT OFFICERS

Academic affairs. Academic Registrar: Foster, Brian R., BScEcon *Wales*
Accommodation. Director of Residential Services: Matthewman, J. David
Admissions (first degree). Admissions and Recruitment Officer: Davies, Hywel M., MA Oxf., PhD *Wales*

Admissions (higher degree). Administrative Assistant: Preston, Gina, BLib *Wales*
Alumni. Director, Development and External Affairs: Lawrence, Stephen R., MScEcon *Wales*
Archives. Administrative Assistant: Salmon, Ian J., MA Camb., MA Oxf., DPhil Oxf.
Careers. Acting Director of Careers Service: Jalloq, Monica, PhD
Computing services. Deputy Director of Information Services: Matthews, Roger F., BSc Lond.
Consultancy services. Director, Research, Innovation and Business Services: Wood, Stephen, BSc *Wales*
Credit transfer. Academic Secretary: McParlin, David F., BA *Wales*
Development/fund-raising. Director, Development and External Affairs: Lawrence, Stephen R., MScEcon *Wales*
Distance education. Director, Open Learning Unit: Thomas, Clare, BA *Wales*
Equal opportunities. Equal Opportunities Officer: Evans, Nona, BA *Wales*
Estates and buildings/works and services. Director of Estates: Davies, Roy, BEng Sheff.
Examinations. Academic Secretary: McParlin, David F., BA *Wales*
Finance. Director of Finance: Lewis, Keith, BA CNAA
General enquiries. Registrar and Secretary: Jones, D. Gruffydd, BA
Health services. Administrative Secretary: Jones, Hywel W., BA *Wales*
Industrial liaison. Director, Research, Innovation and Business Services: Wood, Stephen, BSc *Wales*
International office. Director, Development and External Affairs: Lawrence, Stephen R., MScEcon *Wales*
Library (chief librarian). Director of Information Services: Hopkins, Mike, BA Leic., PhD Lough.
Minorities/disadvantaged groups. Equal Opportunities Officer: Evans, Nona, BA *Wales*
Personnel/human resources. Director of Personnel: Fletcher, R. Colin T., BScEcon *Wales*, MA Lanc.

Public relations, information and marketing. Dafis, Arthur, BA
Publications. Assistant Registrar: Davies, D. Russell, BA *Wales*, PhD *Wales*
Purchasing. Director of Finance: Lewis, Keith, BA CNAA
Quality assurance and accreditation. Academic Registrar: Foster, Brian R., BScEcon *Wales*
Research. Academic Registrar: Foster, Brian R., BScEcon *Wales*
Safety. Safety Officer: Broadbent, Julian, BSc Manc., PhD Manc.
Scholarships, awards, loans. Senior Assistant Registrar: Daniel, Olwen M., BA *Wales*
Schools liaison. Schools Liaison Officer: Jones, Dewi W., BSc Liv., MEd *Wales*
Security. Director of Estates: Davies, Roy, BEng Sheff.
Sport and recreation. Director, Physical Education: Evans-Worthing, Lesley J., BEd Lanc., PhD Brad.
Staff development and training. Director of Staff Development: Horgan, Jennifer, BSc *Wales*, PhD *Wales*
Student welfare/counselling. Senior Tutor and Welfare Co-ordinator: Jones, Gareth, BA Liv.
Students from other countries. Administrator: Wells, Jeffrey, BA Leeds
Students with disabilities. Senior Tutor and Welfare Co-ordinator: Jones, Gareth, BA Liv.
University press. Dafis, Arthur, BA
Women. Equal Opportunities Officer: Evans, Nona, BA *Wales*

[*Information supplied by the institution as at 13 March 1998, and edited by the ACU*]

UNIVERSITY OF WALES, BANGOR

Founded 1884 as University College of North Wales (Bangor)

Associate Member of the Association of Commonwealth Universities

Postal Address: Bangor, Gwynedd, Wales LL57 2DG
Telephone: (01248) 351151 **Fax**: (01248) 370451 **WWW**: http://www.bangor.ac.uk
E-mail formula: initial.surname@bangor.ac.uk

PRESIDENT—Cledwyn of Penrhos, Lord, CH, Hon. LLD *Wales*
CHAIRMAN OF THE COUNCIL—Roberts, His Hon. Judge Eifion, LLB *Wales*, BCL *Oxf.*
VICE-PRESIDENT—Roberts, Anne L.
VICE-PRESIDENT—Williams, Prof. Emer. J. Gwynn, MA *Wales*
VICE-CHANCELLOR*—Evans, Prof. H. Roy, BSc *Wales*, MSc *Wales*, PhD *Wales*, FEng, FICE, FIStructE
TREASURER—Jones, D. E. Alun, CBE, LLB *Wales*
PRO-VICE-CHANCELLOR—Underhill, Prof. Alan E., BSc *Hull*, PhD *Hull*, DSc *Wales*, FRSChem
PRO-VICE-CHANCELLOR—Roberts, H. Gareth Ff., MA *Oxf.*, MEd *Wales*, PhD *Nott.*
PRO-VICE-CHANCELLOR—Williams, Prof. J. Mark G., MA *Oxf.*, MSc *Oxf.*, DPhil *Oxf.*, FBPsS
PRO-VICE-CHANCELLOR—Jones, Prof. R. Merfyn, BA *Sus.*, MA *Warw.*, PhD *Warw.*, FRHistS
SECRETARY AND REGISTRAR‡—Thomas, Gwyn R., BA *Well.*, MA *Wales*
DIRECTOR OF INFORMATION SERVICES—Brady, Philip R., BSc *Nott.*

GENERAL INFORMATION

History. A constituent of the federal University of Wales, the university was founded in 1884. It is situated on the coast of north Wales.

Admission to first degree courses (see also United Kingdom Introduction). Through Universities and Colleges Admissions Service (UCAS). UK nationals: 2 passes at General Certificate of Education (GCE) A level plus a General Certificate of Secondary Education (GCSE) pass at grade C or above in English language or Welsh language. Vocational and other qualifications are considered. International applicants: qualifications equivalent to those listed above (eg International Baccalaureate), plus a pass in an internationally recognised English language exam.

First Degrees (of University of Wales) (see also United Kingdom Directory to Subjects of Study). BA, BD, BEd, BEng, BMus, BSc, BTh, MChem, MEng, MMath.
  Most courses last 3 years full-time (although some BA courses may be studied part-time). Four years: MChem, MEng, MMath; science degrees requiring industrial or European experience; language degrees that incorporate a year abroad; wide-entry BEng degrees for those who do not have appropriate qualifications.

Higher Degrees (of University of Wales) (see also United Kingdom Directory to Subjects of Study). MA, MBA, MEd, MMus, MSc, MTh, PhD, DClinPsy, DSc.
  Applicants for admission to master's degree courses must normally hold an appropriate first degree with at least second class honours. PhD, DClinPsy: normally a first class or upper second class degree in an appropriate subject.
  MBA may be studied either full-time or by distance learning. DSc: awarded on published work.

Language of Instruction. English, except for courses in the Welsh department, where the language is Welsh. Some degrees may be studied in either Welsh or English; students may write exams in either language. International students may attend remedial English classes.

Libraries. 500,000 volumes. Special collections include: Bangor Diocesan Library; Sir Frank Brangwyn (art); department of archives and manuscripts (includes archives of most major estates in north Wales); Owen Pritchard (modern private press); Welsh library (books in Welsh and books in other languages relating to Wales).

Fees (1997–98, annual). Undergraduate: £750 (arts), £1600 (science). Postgraduate: (UK/EU students) £2540 full-time, £1270 part-time; (international students) £6000 (arts/education), £7900 (science).

Academic Awards (1996–97). 65 awards ranging in value from £15 to £1000.

Academic Year (1998–99). Two semesters: 28 September–31 January; 1 February–4 June.

Income (1996–97). Total, £63,672,000.

Statistics. Staff: 1902 (958 academic/academic-related, 944 secretarial/clerical/technical). Students: full-time 6242 (2675 men, 3567 women); part-time 1492 (954 men, 538 women); international 1148; total 7734.

FACULTIES/SCHOOLS

Arts and Social Sciences
Dean: ......

Education
Tel: (01248) 382934 *Fax:* (01248) 372187
Acting Dean: Jones, Gwilym T., BA *Liv.*

Health Studies
Tel: (01248) 383141 *Fax:* (01248) 383114
Dean: Pye, Philip J., OBE, BEd *Liv.*, MSc *Manc.*

Science and Engineering
Tel: (01248) 382314 *Fax:* (01248) 371644
Dean: Whitbread, Robert, MA *Camb.*, PhD *Camb.*

ACADEMIC UNITS

Accounting, Banking and Economics, School of
Tel: (01248) 382158 *Fax:* (01248) 364760
Burke, Christopher M., MA *Sheff.*, FCA   Sr. Lectr.; Head*
Chakravarty, Shanty P., BS *George Washington*, MS *Roch.*, PhD *Roch.*   Sr. Lectr.
Gardener, Edward P. M., MSc *Wales*, PhD *Wales*, FCIS   Prof.
Henry, Robert H.   Exec. Dir., MBA
Jones, David R., MA *Wales*, PhD *Wales*   Sr. Lectr.
MacKay, Ross R., MA *Aberd.*   Prof.
McLeay, Stuart J., MSc *Brad.*, PhD *Lanc.*, FCA   TSB Prof.
Molyneux, Philip, MA *Wales*   Prof.
Treble, John G., BA *Wales*, MA *Essex*, PhD *Northwestern*   Prof.

Other Staff: 8 Lectrs.; 2 Res. Officers
Research: finance; management studies

Agricultural and Forest Sciences, School of
Tel: (01248) 382441 *Fax:* (01248) 354997
Bolton, A. James, BSc *Wales*, PhD *Aberd.*   Sr. Lectr.
Cooper, Roger J., BSc(Econ) *Lond.*   Sr. Lectr.; Head*
Dinwoodie, John M., BSc *Aberd.*, MTech *Brun.*, PhD *Aberd.*, DSc *Aberd.*   Hon. Prof.
Evans, Julian, BSc *Wales*, PhD *Wales*, DSc *Wales*   Hon. Prof.
Gibson, E. J., CBE, BSc *Lond.*, PhD *Lond.*, FRSChem   Hon. Prof. Fellow
Godbold, Douglas L., BSc PhD   Prof., Forest Sciences
Hall, John B., BSc *Lond.*, PhD *Lond.*   Sr. Lectr.
Mercer, I. D., BA *Birm.*   Hon. Prof.
Owen, John B., BSc *Wales*, MA *Camb.*, PhD *Wales*, FIBiol   Prof., Agriculture
Price, Colin, MA *Oxf.*, DPhil *Oxf.*   Prof.
Roberts, R. C., PhD *Edin.*, DSc *Edin.*   Hon. Prof.
Other Staff: 19 Lectrs.; 7 Sr. Fellows; 1 Res. Fellow; 2 Res. Officers; 3 Hon. Lectrs.
Research: agroforestry; animal science; soil and environmental science; water resources; wood science/forest products

Archaeology, see Hist. and Welsh Hist., Sch. of

Biological Sciences, School of
Tel: (01248) 382314 *Fax:* (01248) 371644
Assinder, Susan J., BSc *Lanc.*, PhD *Lanc.*   Sr. Lectr.
Bell, Adrian D., BSc *Wales*, PhD *Wales*, FLS   Sr. Lectr.
Doenhoff, Michael, BSc *Lond.*, PhD *Lond.*, DSc *Lond.*   Reader
Farrar, John F., MA *Oxf.*, DPhil *Oxf.*   Prof.
Gatehouse, A. Gavin, BA *Oxf.*, PhD *Lond.*   Sr.Lectr.
Gaunt, John K., BSc *Lond.*, BSc *Wales*, PhD *Wales*   Sr. Lectr.
Gliddon, Chris J., BA *Oxf.*, DPhil *Sus.*   Sr. Lectr.
Hughes, Roger N., BSc *Wales*, PhD *Wales*, DSc *Wales*   Prof.
Johnson, D. Barrie, BSc *Wales*, PhD *Wales*   Sr. Lectr.
Lehane, Michael J., BSc *Lond.*, PhD *Leeds*   Reader
Lock, Maurice A., BSc *Newcastle(UK)*, PhD *Wales*, DSc *Durh.*   Reader; Head*
Lockwood, S. J., BSc *Hull*, PhD *E.Anglia*   Hon. Prof.
Marshall, Chris, BSc *Nott.*, PhD *Wales*   Sr. Lectr.
Milner, Cedric, BSc *Wales*, PhD *Edin.*   Hon. Prof.

Payne, John W., PhD *Hull*, DSc *Hull*, FIBiol   Prof.

Shattock, Richard C., MSc *Lond.*, PhD   Sr. Lectr.

Shaw, David S., BSc *Glas.*, PhD *Glas.*   Sr. Lectr.

Smith, A. J. E., MA *Oxf.*, DPhil *Oxf.*, DSc *Oxf.*, FLS   Reader

Thorpe, Roger S., BSc *Lond.*, PhD *CNAA*, DSc *Aberd.*   Prof.

Tomos, A. Deri, MA *Camb.*, PhD *Camb.*   Prof.

Webster, Simon G., BSc *Liv.*, PhD *Liv.*   Sr. Lectr.

Whitbread, Robert, MA *Camb.*, PhD *Camb.*   Sr. Lectr.

Williams, Dudley D., MSc *Wat.*, PhD *Wat.*, DSc *Wales*   Hon. Prof.

Williams, Peter A., BA *Oxf.*, DPhil *Oxf.*, DSc *Oxf.*   Prof.

Wyn Jones, R. Gareth, MSc *Br.Col.*, DPhil *Oxf.*, DSc *Oxf.*, FIBiol, FRSChem   Hon. Prof.

Other Staff: 9 Lectrs.; 1 Royal Soc. Fellow; 1 Wellcome Fellow; 32 Res. Officers; 15 Hon. Lectrs.; 2 Hon. Res. Fellows

Research: biometry and biomechanics; cellular and molecular biology; medical and veterinary entomology; molecular and evolutionary ecology; plant biochemistry and physiology

Chemistry

Tel: (01248) 382375 Fax: (01248) 370528

Baird, Mark S., BSc *Lond.*, PhD *Camb.*, FRSChem   Prof.; Head*

Baker, Paul K., BSc *Brist.*, PhD *Brist.*, FRSChem   Reader

Beckett, Michael A., BSc *E.Anglia*, PhD *E.Anglia*, FRSChem   Sr. Lectr.

Macdonald, John N., BSc *Glas.*, PhD *Glas.*   Sr. Lectr.

Quirke, Nick, BSc *Leic.*, PhD *Leic.*   Prof.

Underhill, Alan E., BSc *Hull*, PhD *Hull*, DSc *Wales*, FRSChem   Prof.

Other Staff: 7 Lectrs.; 2 Lectrs.†

Research: anti-cancer/anti-viral drug synthesis; boron-S, boron-O and boron-N ring systems; chemistry of cyclopropenes; intramolecular reactions of aryl cations; magneto- and electro-rheological fluids

Community, Regional and Communication Studies, School of

Tel: (01248) 383229

Owen, Hywel W., BA *Liv.*, MA *Wales*, PhD *Wales*   Head*

Other Staff: 20 Lectrs.

Computer Systems, see Electronic Engin. and Computer Systems, Sch. of

Economics, see Acctg., Banking and Econ., Sch. of

Education, School of

Tel: (01248) 382940 Fax: (01248) 372187

Baker, Colin R., BA *Wales*, PhD *Wales*   Prof.

Jones, Geraint W., BA *Wales*, PhD *Wales*   Sr. Lectr.

Owen, T. Martin, BSc *Manc.*, MEd *Lond.*   Sr. Lectr.

Roberts, H. Gareth Ff., MA *Oxf.*, MEd *Wales*, PhD *Nott.*   Head*

Other Staff: 45 Lectrs.; 1 Professl. Services Officer; 1 Hon. Res. Fellow

Research: bilingualism; children's literature; information technology; language teaching; telematics

Electronic Engineering and Computer Systems, School of

Tel: (01248) 382681 Fax: (01248) 361429

Bone, Stephen, BSc *Wales*, PhD *Wales*   Sr. Lectr.

Bradley, David A., BTech *Brad.*, PhD *Brad.*   Prof., Computer Systems

Chantrell, Roy W., BSc *Wales*, PhD *Wales*, FIP   Prof., Computational Magnetics

Fish, Peter J., MSc *Lond.*, FIP   Reader

Jones, Dewi I., MSc *Wales*, PhD *Wales*, FIEE   Sr. Lectr.

Last, J. David, BSc *Brist.*, PhD *Sheff.*, FIEE   Prof.

O'Grady, Kevin D., BSc *Wales*, PhD *Wales*, FIP   Reader

Pethig, Ron, BSc(Eng) *S'ton.*, PhD *S'ton.*, PhD *Nott.*, DSc *S'ton.*, FIEE   Prof.

Shore, K. Alan, MA *Oxf.*, PhD *Wales*   Prof., Electrical Engineering

Taylor, D. Martin, BSc *Wales*, PhD *Wales*, FIP   Prof.; Head*

Other Staff: 11 Lectrs.; 10 Res. Officers; 4 Lectrs.†; 4 Hon. Res. Fellows

Research: communications engineering (microwave, optical fibre, radio, telecommunication); control engineering; electronic materials (including molecular electronics, magnetics); medical physics

English and Linguistics, School of

English

Tel: (01248) 382102 Fax: (01248) 382102

Bellringer, Alan W., MA *Glas.*, PhD *Aberd.*   Sr. Lectr.

Brown, Anthony D., BA *Wales*, MA *Leic.*, PhD *Wales*   Sr. Lectr.

Corns, Thomas N., MA *Oxf.*, DPhil *Oxf.*   Prof.; Head*

Field, Peter J. C., BLitt *Oxf.*, MA *Oxf.*   Prof.

Humphreys, Emyr, BA *Wales*   Hon. Prof.

Jones, Christopher B., MA *Birm.*   Sr. Lectr.

Lindsay, David W., MA *Edin.*, PhD *Aberd.*   Sr. Lectr.

Rumbold, Valerie, MA *Oxf.*, PhD *Camb.*   Sr. Lectr.

Other Staff: 8 Lectrs.

Research: Anglo-Welsh literature; Arthurian literature; contemporary British writing; seventeenth- to nineteenth-century literature

Linguistics

Tel: (01248) 382264 Fax: (01248) 382928

Borsley, Robert D., BA *Wales*, PhD *Edin.*   Prof.

Crystal, David, OBE, MA *Lond.*, PhD *Lond.*   Hon. Prof.

Deuchar, Margaret, BA *Camb.*, PhD *Stan.*   Sr. Lectr.

James, Carl, BA *Nott.*, PhD *Wales*   Sr. Lectr.

Thomas, Alan R., MA   Res. Prof.

Thomas, Jennifer A., BA *Brad.*, MA *Lanc.*, PhD *Lanc.*   Prof.

Other Staff: 6 Lectrs.

Research: child language and second language acquisition; computational linguistics; experimental phonetics and pragmatics; psycholinguistics; theoretical and comparative syntax

Forest Sciences, see Agric. and Forest Scis., Sch. of

French, see Mod. Langs., Sch. of

German, see Mod. Langs., Sch. of

History and Welsh History, School of

Tel: (01248) 382144 Fax: (01248) 382759

Brooks, J. Ron, MA *Wales*, PhD *Wales*   Sr. Lectr.

Canning, Joe P., MA *Camb.*, PhD *Camb.*, FRHistS   Sr. Lectr.

Carr, Anthony D., MA *Wales*, PhD *Wales*, FSA, FRHistS   Reader, Welsh History

Dyer, Alan D., BA *Birm.*, PhD *Birm.*   Sr. Lectr.

Edwards, Nancy, BA *Liv.*, PhD *Durh.*, FSA   Sr. Lectr., Archaeology

Jones, R. Merfyn, BA *Sus.*, MA *Warw.*, PhD *Warw.*   Prof.

Pryce, A. Huw, MA *Oxf.*, DPhil *Oxf.*, FRHistS   Sr. Lectr.

Tanner, Duncan M., BA *Lond.*, PhD *Lond.*, FRHistS   Prof.; Head

Other Staff: 6 Lectrs.; 3 Hon. Lectrs.

Research: archaeology (particularly north Wales and Ireland); modern British political/ educational/social history; relationships between secular and ecclesiastical authority; twentieth-century Europe; Welsh history (mediaeval to modern)

Linguistics, see under Engl. and Linguistics, Sch. of

Mathematics, School of

Tel: (01248) 382476 Fax: (01248) 383663

Brown, Ronnie, MA *Oxf.*, DPhil *Oxf.*, FIMA   Prof.

Davies, Bryn L., MA *Oxf.*, DPhil *Oxf.*   Sr. Lectr.

James, Ioan M., MA *Oxf.*, DPhil *Oxf.*, FRS   Hon. Prof.

Lambe, L. A., MS *Ill.*, PhD *Ill.*, Hon. Dr *Stockholm*   Hon. Prof.

Porter, Tim, BSc *Sus.*, DPhil *Sus.*   Prof.

Rymer, Neil W., MA *Oxf.*, DPhil *Oxf.*   Lectr.; Head*

Yates, C. E. Michael, BSc *Manc.*, PhD *Manc.*   Hon. Prof.

Other Staff: 6 Lectrs.; 5 Hon. Res. Fellows

Research: crystallographic group theory; homological algebra; non-Newtonian fluid mechanics; quantum mechanics; topology

Midwifery, see Nursing and Midwifery Studies, Sch. of

Modern Languages, School of

Tel: (01248) 382130 Fax: (01248) 382551

Bushell, Anthony, BA *Ulster*, MA *Warw.*, PhD *Birm.*   Prof., German

Busst, Alan J. L., BA *Reading*, PhD *Reading*   Prof., French

Griffiths, Bruce, MA *Oxf.*, DPhil *Oxf.*   Reader, French

Hilton, Ian, BA *S'ton.*, PhD *S'ton.*   Sr. Lectr., German

Jones, W. Gareth, RD, MA *Camb.*   Prof., Russian

Minto, Marilyn A., MA *Birm.*, AM *Penn.*   Sr. Lectr.; Head*

Other Staff: 6 Lectrs.

Research: European culture; French and German literature; language teaching technology

Music

Tel: (01248) 382181 Fax: (01248) 370297

Harper, John M., MA *Camb.*, MA *Oxf.*, PhD *Birm.*, FRCO   Prof.; Head*

Wood, Bruce, MusB *Camb.*, MA *Camb.*, PhD *Camb.*, FRCO   Sr. Lectr.

Other Staff: 5 Lectrs.; 4 Tutors; 1 Lectr.†

Research: Celtic traditional music; electro-acoustic composition; historical and editorial musicology; music and the Christian church; popular music culture

Nursing and Midwifery Studies, School of

Tel: (01248) 383112 Fax: (01248) 383114

Allsup, David M., BEd *Wales*   Sr. Co-ordinator

Behi, Ruhi H., BSc *Wales*, MSc *Manc.*   Dir., Post-Registration Studies

Godwin, J. Malcolm, BEd *Wales*, MA *Keele*   Sr. Co-ordinator

Owen, Raymond, BA *Open(UK)*, MEd *Wales*   Sr. Co-ordinator

Povey, Myfanwy   Sr. Co-ordinator

Pye, Philip J., OBE, BEd *Liv.*, MSc *Manc.*   Head*

Other Staff: 66 Lectrs.; 3 Res. Assocs.

Research: health care practice; health care professional education; health education; health promotion

Ocean Sciences, School of

Tel: (01248) 382294 Fax: (01248) 716367

Barton, E. Des, BSc *Liv.*, PhD *Liv.*   Sr. Lectr.

Beaumont, Andy, MSc *Wales*   Sr. Lectr.

Buchan, Sinclair, MA *Aberd.*, BSc *Aberd.*   Sr. Lectr.

Dando, Paul R., BSc *Lond.*, PhD *Lond.*   Prof., Marine Biology

Davies, Alan G., BSc *Lond.*, MSc *Wales*, PhD *Lond.*   Reader

Davis, Angela M., BSc *Sheff.*, MSc *Wales*, PhD *Wales*   Sr. Lectr.

Elliott, Alan J., BSc *Sheff.*, PhD *Liv.*   Reader

Grove, David J., BSc *Wales*, PhD *Lond.*, PhD *Gothenburg* Sr. Lectr.

Hill, A. Edward, BSc *Sheff.*, MSc *Wales*, PhD *Wales* Sr. Lectr.

Holland, David L., BSc *Birm.*, PhD *Birm.* Sr. Lectr.

Huthnance, John M., BA *Camb.*, PhD *Camb.* Hon. Prof.

Jago, Colin F., BSc *Lond.*, PhD *Lond.* Sr. Lectr.

Jones, David A., BSc *Lond.*, PhD *Lond.* Reader

Lucas, Ian A. N., BSc *Wales*, PhD *Wales* Sr. Lectr.

Richardson, Christopher A., BSc *Wales*, PhD *Wales* Sr. Lectr.

Seed, Ray, BSc *Leeds*, PhD *Leeds* Prof.

Simpson, John H., BA *Oxf.*, PhD *Liv.*, DSc *Liv.* Prof., Physical Oceanography; Head*

Walker, Graham, PhD *Wales*, DSc *Wales* Reader

Williams, Peter J. leB., BSc *Birm.*, PhD *Birm.*, DSc *Birm.* Prof., Biogeochemistry

Wood, Denis S., BSc *Liv.*, PhD *Leeds* Hon. Prof.

Other Staff: 14 Lectrs.; 30 Res. Staff; 1 Hon. Lectr.

Research: geological oceanography (sediment properties and geotechnics); marine biogeochemistry; marine biology (aquaculture, shellfish biology); optical oceanography and remote sensing; physical oceanography (ocean modelling, shelf-edge processes)

Psychology, School of

Tel: (01248) 382210 Fax: (01248) 382599

Appleton, Peter, BSc *Durh.*, MSc *Glas.*, MSc *Strath.*, PhD *Liv.* Sr. Lectr.

Cox, W. Miles, BA *Georgia S.*, MA *W.Georgia*, PhD *S.Calif.* Prof., Psychology of Addictive Behaviours

Davis, Bryn, BSc *Lond.*, PhD *Lond.* Hon. Prof.

Ellis, Nick C., BA *Oxf.*, PhD *Wales* Reader

Gathercole, Virginia C., BA *St.Louis*, MA *Kansas*, MPhil *Kansas*, PhD *Kansas* Prof.

Jackson, Stephen, BA *Open(UK)*, PhD *Camb.* Sr. Lectr.

Jones, David T., MB ChB *Leeds*, FRCGP Hon. Prof.

Jones, Robert S. P., MA *Trinity(Dub.)*, PhD *Trinity(Dub.)* Sr. Lectr.

Lowe, C. Fergus, BA *Trinity(Dub.)*, PhD *Wales*, FBPsS Prof.; Head*

Miles, Tim R., MA *Oxf.*, PhD *Wales*, FBPsS Emer. Prof.

Pidgeon, Nicholas F., BA *Keele*, PhD *Brist.* Sr. Lectr.

Raymond, Jane, BSc *Dal.*, MSc *Wash.*, PhD *Dal.* Prof.

Shapiro, Kimron, BSc *N.Carolina*, MSc *Wash.*, PhD *Dal.* Reader

Startup, Michael J., BA *Lond.*, PhD *Lond.*, MSc *Sur.* Sr. Lectr.

Tipper, Steven P., BSc *Hudd.*, MSc *Sus.*, DPhil *Oxf.* Prof., Cognitive Science

Vihmann, Marilyn M., BA *Bryn Mawr*, PhD *Calif.* Prof., Developmental Psychology

Williams, J. Mark G., MA *Oxf.*, MSc *Oxf.*, DPhil *Oxf.*, FBPsS Prof., Clinical Psychology

Woods, Robert T., MA *Camb.*, MSc *Newcastle(UK)*, FBPsS Prof., Clinical Psychology of the Elderly

Other Staff: 21 Lectrs.; 3 Teaching Fellows; 3 Sr. Res. Fellows; 5 Res. Fellows; 5 Res. Officers

Research: child development and language; clinical psychology of the elderly; cognitive psychology and neuroscience; experimental consumer psychology; schizophrenia

Radiography

Tel: (01978) 316205 Fax: (01978) 316209

Reeves, Pauline J., MSc *Open(UK)* Sr. Lectr.; Head*

Other Staff: 11 Lectrs.

Research: medical ultrasound

Religious Studies, see Theol. and Religious Studies, Sch. of, and Special Centres, etc

Russian, see Mod. Langs., Sch. of

Sociology and Social Policy, School of

Tel: (01248) 382215 Fax: (01248) 362029

Borland, John A., BA *Keele*, MA *Wales* Sr. Lectr.

Davis, Howard H., BA *Camb.*, PhD *Edin.* Prof.

Day, Graham A. S., MA *Oxf.*, MPhil *Oxf.* Sr. Lectr.; Head*

Hester, Stephen, BA *Kent*, PhD *Kent* Sr. Lectr.

King, Roy D., BA *Leic.*, PhD *Lond.* Prof.

Wenger, G. Clare, MA *Calif.*, PhD *Calif.* Prof.

Other Staff: 8 Lectrs.

Research: childhood and family; crime and criminal justice; ethnomethodology and conversation analysis; gerontology; rural and community sociology

Sport, Health and Physical Education Sciences, School of

Tel: (01248) 382756 Fax: (01248) 371053

Eston, Roger G., BEd *Birm.*, MEd *Mass.* Sr. Lectr.

Hardy, J. P. Lew, MA *Wales*, PhD *Wales* Prof.; Head*

Other Staff: 9 Lectrs.; 1 Lectr.†; 1 Hon. Res. Fellow

Research: exercise psychology and physiology; health psychology; kinanthropometry and kinesiology; motor control and learning; sport psychology

Theology and Religious Studies, School of, see also Special Centres, etc (Religious Educn. Centre)

Tel: (01248) 382079 Fax: (01248) 383759

Allchin, Canon A. M., BLitt *Oxf.*, MA *Oxf.*, Hon. DD *Bucharest*, Hon. DD *Wis.*, Hon. DD *Wales* Hon. Prof.

Davies, Eryl W., BA *Wales*, PhD *Camb.* Sr. Lectr.

Jones, Canon Gareth Ll., BA *Wales*, BD *Trinity(Dub.)*, MA *Camb.*, STM *Yale*, PhD *Lond.*, Hon. DD *Austin* Reader; Head*

Mastin, Rev. Brian A., BD *Camb.*, MA *Camb.* Sr. Lectr.

Morgan, Rev. D. Densil, BA *Wales*, BD *Wales*, DPhil *Oxf.* Sr. Lectr.

Thomas, J. Heywood, STM *N.Y.*, DD *Edin.*, DD *Wales*, Hon. DLitt *Wales* Hon. Prof.

Tudur Jones, Rev. R., BA *Wales*, DD *Wales*, DPhil *Oxf.*, Hon. DLitt *Wales* Hon. Prof.

Other Staff: 3 Lectrs.; 5 Tutors†

Research: Hebrew and Greek biblical texts; interaction between Judaism and Christianity; mediaeval mysticism; religion in literature; twentieth-century Christianity

Welsh

Tel: (01248) 382240 Fax: (01248) 382551

Allchin, Canon A. M., BLitt *Oxf.*, MA *Oxf.*, Hon. DD *Bucharest*, Hon. DD *Wis.*, Hon. DD *Wales* Hon. Prof.

Jarvis, Branwen, MA *Wales* Sr. Lectr.

Jones, Dafydd G., BPhil *Oxf.*, MA *Wales* Reader

Thomas, Gwyn, MA *Wales*, DPhil *Oxf.* Prof.; Head*

Other Staff: 4 Lectrs.; 3 Tutors†; 4 Hon. Lectrs.

Research: the bardic tradition; Celtic studies (history, languages, mythology); literature presented on radio, television and film; Welsh literature from sixth to twentieth centuries

Welsh History, see Hist. and Welsh Hist., Sch. of.

SPECIAL CENTRES, ETC

Applicable Mathematics, Centre for

Tel: (01248) 382480 Fax: (01248) 355881

Roberts, Gareth W., BSc *Lond.*, PhD *Wales* Dir.*

Applied Community Studies, Centre for

Tel: (01248) 382127 Fax: (01248) 383729

Collins, Stewart A., BA *Lanc.*, MA *Brad.* Sr. Lectr.

Other Staff: 4 Lectrs.

Research: adoption and foster care; child protection; health care and the elderly; recording practice in social work

Arid Zone Studies, Centre for

Tel: (01248) 382346 Fax: (01248) 364717

Harris, David, BSc *E.Anglia*, PhD *E.Anglia* ODA Programme Manager

Robinson, W. Ian, BSc *Lond.*, PhD *Wales* Dir.*

Witcombe, J. R., BSc *Wales*, PhD *Nott.* ODA Programme Manager

Other Staff: 5 Sr. Fellows; 4 Res. Fellows

Research: animal nutrition and husbandry; cereal and legume agronomy; participatory fuel wood and forage use studies; plant breeding for arid areas; soil and water engineering and conservation

Biocomposites Centre

Tel: (01248) 382869 Fax: (01248) 370594

Bolton, A. James, BSc *Wales*, PhD *Aberd.* Dir.*

Other Staff: 39 Res. Staff

Research: plant fibres in biocomposites; polysaccharides and polyphenolics; processing non-wood plants; pulp and paper manufacture; wood-based panels

Coastal and Estuarine Studies, Unit for

Tel: (01248) 713808 Fax: (01248) 716367

Elliott, Alan J., BSc *Sheff.*, PhD *Liv.* Dir.*

Other Staff: 9 Res. Staff

Research: applied oceanography (tides, waves, acoustics, advection and diffusion); numerical modelling (simulation of coastal currents and winds); oil and chemical spills (predictions of slick movement and fate); remote sensing (analysis and interpretation of satellite data); water quality (coastal outfalls, plumes, theory and practice)

Comparative Criminology and Criminal Justice, Centre for

Tel: (01248) 382214 Fax: (01248) 362029

King, Prof. Roy D., BA *Leic.*, PhD *Lond.* Dir.*

Other Staff: 8 Res. Staff

Research: ethnomethodology (crime, deviance and social control); police (national and international); prisons (USA, Europe, health); Russian organised crime; space, crime, deviance (urban/rural criminology)

Continuing Education, Centre for

Tel: (01248) 382258 Fax: (01248) 382044

Griffiths, Miriam, MA *Wales* Head*

Other Staff: 2 Sr. Tutors; 10 Tutors

Economic Research, Institute of

Tel: (01248) 382169 Fax: (01248) 364760

MacKay, R. Ross, MA *Aberd.* Dir.*

Other Staff: 2 Sr. Lectrs.; 1 Lectr.

Research: economic impact of decommissioning Trawsfynydd nuclear power station; economics of a Welsh assembly; Keynesian revolution and counter-revolution; measuring labour market slack-work and non-work

European Finance, Institute of

Tel: (01248) 382277 Fax: (01248) 364760

Gardener, Prof. Edward P. M., MSc *Wales*, PhD *Wales*, FCIS Dir.*

Molyneux, Prof. Philip, MA *Wales*, PhD *Wales* Dir.*

Revell, Prof. Jack R. S., BSc(Econ) *Lond.*, MA *Camb.* Consultant Dir.

Other Staff: 3 Res. Staff; 9 Visiting Res. Fellows

Research: development of financial systems; efficiency of financial services firms; financial services regulation; strategies of banks and financial institutions; structure and performance of financial systems

Industrial Development Bangor Ltd

Tel: (01248) 382748 Fax: (01248) 372105

Davies, M. Wyn H., DSc *Wales*, FIEE   Jt. Dir.
Evans, Prof. H. Roy, MSc *Wales*, PhD *Wales*,
 FEng, FICE, FIStructE   Jt. Dir.
Hughes, Dewi W., BScEcon *Wales*   Jt. Dir.
Jones, Emlyn D.   Jt. Dir.
Jones, Tom P., OBE, BSc *Wales*, PhD *Alta.*   Jt.
 Dir.
Thomas, Gwyn R., BA *Well.*, MA *Wales*   Jt. Dir.
Research: contactless transfer of data and power;
 differential GPS coverage predictions; gas
 detection using UV ion collectors;
 instrumentation for nuclear industry;
 precision profile measurements for steel
 industry

Menai Technology Enterprise Centre (MENTEC)

Tel: (01248) 382580 Fax: (01248) 352497

Jones, Dafydd V., BSc   Dir.*

Molecular and Biomolecular Electronics, Institute of

Tel: (01248) 382682 Fax: (01248) 361429

Pethig, Prof. Ron, BSc(Eng) *S'ton.*, PhD *S'ton.*,
 PhD *Nott.*, DSc *S'ton.*, FIEE   Dir.*
Other Staff: 1 Visiting Res. Prof.; 3 Res.
 Fellows; 1 Visiting Res. Fellow
Research: AC electrokinetic properties of cells,
 micro-organisms and sub-cellular
 bioparticles; development of novel sensors
 for application in industry, medicine,
 biotechnology and the environment;
 synthesis and evaluation of molecular
 materials

Religious Education Centre

Tel: (01248) 382956 Fax: (01248) 382952

Thomas, Rheinallt A., JP, BA *Wales*, MEd
 Wales   Dir.*
Other Staff: 1 Lectr.
Research: approaches to introducing world
 religions to key stages 1 and 2; survey of
 religious education and collective worship in
 Clywd schools

Research Centre Wales

Tel: (01248) 382931 Fax: (01248) 370791

Baker, Prof. Colin R., BA *Wales*, PhD *Wales*,
 FBPsS   Dir.*
Jones, Gwilym T., BA *Liv.*   Dir.*
Williams, Glyn, BSc *Wales*, MA *Calif.*, PhD
 Wales   Res. Unit Head
Research: bilingual education; bilingualism and
 multilingualism; information technology in
education; language planning and
translation; telematics

Social Policy Research and Development, Centre for

Tel: (01248) 382225 Fax: (01248) 362029

Wenger, Prof. G. Clare, MA *Calif.*, PhD
 Calif.   Dir.*
Other Staff: 2 Res. Fellows; 4 Res. Officers; 1
 Hon. Prof.
Research: ageing and social networks; case/care
 management; health and social services for
 the elderly; policy and care for mentally
 handicapped people; statistical modelling

CONTACT OFFICERS

Academic affairs. Academic Registrar: Roberts,
 David M., MA *Wales*, PhD *CNAA*
Accommodation. Director of Residential
 Services: Clayton, John M., BScEcon *Wales*
Admissions (first degree). Senior Assistant
 Registrar: Lewis, Ainsley C., BA *Wales*
Admissions (higher degree). Senior Assistant
 Registrar: Lewis, Ainsley C., BA *Wales*
Adult/continuing education. Head of
 Continuing Education: Griffiths, Miriam, MA
 Wales
Alumni. Senior Assistant Registrar: Jones, John
 W., BScEcon *Wales*, MA *Liv.*
Archives. Archivist: Roberts, Tomos, BA *Liv.*
Careers. Head of Career Development Unit:
 Jones, Eluned G., BA *Lond.*
Computing services. Director of Information
 Services: Brady, Philip R., BSc *Nott.*
Consultancy services. Manager of European/
 Industrial Programmes: Peacock, Nigel, BSc
 Brist., MSc *Lanc.*, MBA *Brun.*
Credit transfer. Senior Assistant Registrar:
 Hughes, Catrin, BA *Wales*, PhD *Wales*
Development/fund-raising. Director of
 Development Trust: Jones, John W., BScEcon
 Wales, MA *Liv.*
Distance education. Executive Director, MBA:
 Henry, Robert H.
Equal opportunities. Assistant Personnel
 Officer, Pensions and Equal Opportunities:
 Hughes, Siân P., BA *Wales*
Estates and buildings/works and services.
 Director of Estates: Swann, F. Malcolm, BA
 Manc., BArch *Manc.*
Examinations. Assistant Registrar: Thomas,
 Patricia J., BSc *Wales*, MA *Mich.*, PhD *Wales*
Finance. Director of Financial Services:
 Hughes, Dewi W., BScEcon *Wales*
General enquiries. Secretary and Registrar:
 Thomas, Gwyn R., BA *Well.*, MA *Wales*
Industrial liaison. Manager of European/
 Industrial Programmes: Peacock, Nigel, BSc
 Brist., MSc *Lanc.*, MBA *Brun.*
International office. International Officer:
 Chapman, David J. M., BA *Camb.*, MA *Manc.*
Language training for international students.
 Director, English Language Courses for
 Overseas Students (ELCOS): Pearson, Tony,
 MA *Wales*
Library (chief librarian). Director of
 Information Services: Brady, Philip R., BSc
 Nott.
Library (enquiries). Desk Services Manager:
 Anderson, Gillian, BA *CNAA*
Minorities/disadvantaged groups. Assistant
 Registrar: Tate, Fran
Personnel/human resources. Director of
 Personnel Services: James, Alan P. J.,
 MScEcon *Wales*
Public relations, information and marketing.
 Senior Assistant Registrar: Jones, John W.,
 BScEcon *Wales*, MA *Liv.*
Publications. Publications Officer: Brindley,
 Gwyneth
Purchasing. Director of Financial Services:
 Hughes, Dewi W., BScEcon *Wales*
Quality assurance and accreditation.
 Academic Registrar: Roberts, David M., MA
 Wales, PhD *CNAA*
Research. Assistant Registrar: Perkins, John C.
 T., BSc *Wales*, PhD *Wales*
Research. Deputy Director of Financial Services:
 Hayward, Selwyn G., BA *CNAA*, MSc *Manc.*
Safety. Safety Adviser: Hague, David, MSc
 Wales
Scholarships, awards, loans. Academic
 Registrar: Roberts, David M., MA *Wales*, PhD
 CNAA
Schools liaison. Marketing and Recruitment
 Officer: Roberts, Carys W., BA *Wales*
Sport and recreation. Director of Physical
 Recreation and Amenities: Gray, Anthony J.
Staff development and training. Staff
 Development Officer: Fazey, John A., MSc
 Dal., PhD *Wales*
Student union. President: Drew, Christopher,
 BA *Wales*
Student welfare/counselling. Assistant
 Registrar: Clifford, Susan A., BA *Reading*
Students from other countries. International
 Officer: Chapman, David J. M., BA *Camb.*,
 MA *Manc.*
Students with disabilities. Assistant Registrar:
 Tate, Fran

*[Information supplied by the institution as at 17 March
1998, and edited by the ACU]*

UNIVERSITY OF WALES, CARDIFF

Founded 1988 as successor to University College, Cardiff (founded 1883, incorporated 1884) and University of Wales Institute of Science and Technology (founded 1866, incorporated 1967)

Associate Member of the Association of Commonwealth Universities

Postal Address: PO Box 920, Cardiff, Wales CF1 3XP
Telephone: (01222) 874000 **Fax:** (01222) 371921 **Telex:** 498635 **WWW:** http://www.cf.ac.uk

VISITOR—Griffiths,The Rt. Hon. The Lord, MC, QC, BA Camb., Hon. LLD Wales
PRESIDENT—Crickhowell,The Rt. Hon. The Lord, MA Camb.
VICE PRESIDENT—John, William H., BA Wales, Hon. MA Wales
VICE PRESIDENT—Lloyd Jones, Sir Richard
VICE PRESIDENT—Kane, Vincent, OBE, BA Wales, Hon. MA Wales
VICE PRESIDENT—Powell, His Honour Judge Dewi W., MA Oxf.
VICE PRESIDENT—Walters, Sir Donald, LLB Lond., Hon. LLD Wales
TREASURER—Harries, Stephen S.
VICE-CHANCELLOR*‡—Smith, Prof. E. Brian, BSc Liv., MA Oxf., PhD Liv., DSc Oxf., FRSChem
SENIOR EXECUTIVE AND HEAD OF VICE-CHANCELLOR'S OFFICE—Cunningham, Vanessa, BA Manc.
PRO-VICE-CHANCELLOR—King, Prof. John, BSc(Tech) Wales, MSc Wales, PhD Wales, FRICS
PRO-VICE-CHANCELLOR—Ellis, Prof. Haydn D., BA Reading, PhD Reading, DSc Aberd., FBPsS
PRO-VICE-CHANCELLOR—Mansfield, Prof. Roger, MA Camb., PhD Camb.
PRO-VICE-CHANCELLOR—Spencer, Prof. Paul S. J., OBE, PhD Lond., DSc Wales, FIBiol, FRPharmS
PRO-VICE-CHANCELLOR—Percival, Prof. John, MA Oxf., DPhil Oxf., FSA
DIRECTOR OF FINANCE—Davies, D. Michael, BScEcon Wales
LIBRARIAN—Roberts, John K., MSc Manc.

GENERAL INFORMATION

History. The university was established in 1883. It is located in Cardiff's civic centre in the heart of the city.

Admission to first degree courses (see also United Kingdom Introduction). Through Universities and Colleges Admissions Service (UCAS).

First Degrees (of University of Wales) (see also United Kingdom Directory to Subjects of Study). BA, BArch, BEng, BMus, BSc, BScEcon, BTh, LLB, MChem, MEng, MPharm, MPhys.

BA: 3 years or 4 years integrated, joint honours available; BEng: 3 years or 4 years sandwich, some courses include 1 year in France, Germany or Spain; BSc: 3 years or 4 years sandwich, joint honours available; BScEcon: 3 years or 4 years sandwich; MEng: 4 years extended or 5 years extended, some courses include 1 year in France, Germany or Spain.

Higher Degrees (of University of Wales) (see also United Kingdom Directory to Subjects of Study). LLM, MA, MBA, MMus, MSc, MScEcon, MTh, MPhil, PhD, DClinPsy, EdD, EngD.

LLM (by coursework): 1 year full-time or 2 years part-time; LLM (by research): 1–2 years full-time or 3 years part-time; MA: 1 year full-time or (certain courses) 2 years part-time (education courses 2–5 years modular, social work 2 years full-time); MBA: 1 year full-time or 2 years part-time or 2–5 years modular; MMus: 1 year full-time; MSc: 1 year full-time or (certain courses) 2–3 years part-time (housing courses 2 years full-time or 3 years part-time, international planning practice 2 years full-time); MScEcon: 1 year full-time or 2 years part-time; MTh: 1 year full-time or 2 years part-time; MPhil: 1–2 years full-time or 2–3 years part-time; PhD: 2–3 years full-time or 3–5 years part-time; DClinPsy, EngD: 3 years full-time; EdD: 2–3 years full-time or 5 years part-time.

Language of Instruction. English. The university offers facilities for international students to improve their English.

Libraries. Almost 1,000,000 volumes; 9000 journal titles. Special collections include: European Documentation Centre; Salisbury Library (Welsh language history and culture).

Fees (1998–99). Home undergraduate: (LEA) £1000 at university, £500 on placement/year abroad; (self-financing) new students £1000, continuing students at university £774 (arts) or £885 (science), continuing students on placement/year abroad £387 (arts) or £442 (science). Home postgraduate: £2610. Overseas postgraduate: £6510 (arts); £8550 (science).

Academic Awards (year ending 31 July 1997). Awards totalling £102,450.

Academic Year (1998–99). Two semesters: 23 September–17 January; 18 January–30 May.

Income (1996–97). Total, £120,298,000.

Statistics. Staff: 2766 (1142 full-time academic, 1066 full-time administrative and other). Students: total 14,830.

FACULTIES/SCHOOLS

Business Studies and Law
Dean: Mansfield, Prof. Roger, MA Camb., PhD Camb.

Engineering and Environmental Design
Tel: (01222) 874824
Dean: Hamdi, Essam E. S., MSc Alexandria, PhD Manc.

Health and Life Sciences
Dean: Moxham, Prof. Bernard J., BSc Brist., BDS Brist., PhD Brist.

Humanities and Social Studies
Tel: (01222) 874235
Dean: Skilton, Prof. David J., MA Camb., MLitt Camb.

Physical Sciences
Dean: Hewlins, Michael J. E., MA Camb., PhD Camb.

ACADEMIC UNITS

Accounting, see Bus. Sch.

Archaeology, see Hist. and Archaeol., Sch. of

Architecture, Welsh School of
Tel: (01222) 874430 Fax: (01222) 874926
Birtles, Anthony B., BSc Sheff., PhD Sheff., FIMA Hon. Prof.
Davies, Ceri Prof.†
Fowles, R. A., MScTech Manc. Sr. Lectr.

Hawkes, Dean U., MA Camb., PhD Camb. Prof.
Jones, P. J., BSc Wales, PhD Wales Prof.
Loach, Judi D., PhD Camb. Sr. Lectr.
Parry, C. Malcolm, BArch Wales Sr. Lectr.; Head*
Silverman, H. R., MSc Edin. Prof.
Other Staff: 4 Lectrs.; 2 Des. Tutors/Lectrs.; 3 Sr. Res. Fellows; 1 Sr. Teaching Fellow; 1 Res. Fellow†; 1 Hon. Res. Fellow
Research: architectural science: sustainable development in the built environment; construction and materials: research in building and housing industries; estate strategy research unit: strategic estate management and resource planning; history and theory: historical understanding and theory of architecture; professional methods: contextual changes and the architectural profession

Astronomy, see Phys. and Astron.

Biology, Pure and Applied, School of
Tel: (01222) 874048 Fax: (01222) 874305
Bennett, M. D., BSc Wales, PhD Wales Hon. Prof.
Boddy, L., BSc Exe., PhD Lond., DSc Exe. Prof.
Bowen, I. D., PhD Wales, DSc Wales, FIBiol Prof.
Claridge, M. F., MA Oxf., DPhil Oxf., FIBiol Prof.
Coakley, W. T., MSc N.U.I., DSc N.U.I., PhD Prof.
Dancer, B. N., BSc Sheff., DPhil Oxf. Sr. Lectr.
Davies, M. S., BSc Wales, PhD Reading Sr. Lectr.
Day, M. J., BSc CNAA, PhD Lond. Reader
Dickinson, J. R., BSc Warw., PhD Warw. Sr. Lectr.
Ferns, P. N., BSc Manc., PhD Exe. Sr. Lectr.
Francis, Dennis, BSc Newcastle(UK), PhD Newcastle(UK), DSc Newcastle(UK) Reader
Free, J. B., CMG, MA Camb., ScD Camb., PhD Lond., DSc Lond., FIBiol Hon. Prof.
Fry, J. C., BSc Wales, PhD Wales Prof.; Head*
Hemingway, Janet, BSc Sheff., PhD Lond. Prof.
Hughes, G. M., MA Camb., PhD Camb., ScD Camb. Hon. Prof.
Jervis, M. A., BSc Lond., PhD Wales Sr. Lectr.
Jones, O. T., BSc Wales, PhD Camb. Hon. Prof.
Jones, T., OBE, BSc Lond., FIBiol Hon. Prof.
Kidd, N. A. C., BSc Glas., PhD Glas. Reader
Langley, Peter A., BSc Nott., PhD Nott., DSc Brist., FIBiol Prof. Consultant†
Lloyd, D., PhD Wales, DSc Sheff. Prof.
Mettam, C. J., BSc Reading, PhD Reading Sr. Lectr.

Moore, J. L., BSc *Wales*, PhD *Wales*, FIBiol   Hon. Prof.

Morgan, P. J., BSc *Wales*   Hon. Prof.

Ormerod, Stephen J., BSc *CNAA*, MSc *Wales*, PhD *Wales*   Reader

Pascoe, D., BSc *Wales*, PhD *Wales*   Sr. Lectr.

Slater, J. H., BSc *Lond.*, PhD *Lond.*, DSc *Lond.*, FIBiol   Prof.

Stickler, D. J., BSc *Wales*, MA *Trinity(Dub.)*, DPhil *Oxf.*   Sr. Lectr.

Thomas, Barry A., BSc *Sheff.*, PhD *Reading*, FLS   Hon. Prof.

Thomas, D. H., BSc *Sheff.*, MSc *Aberd.*, PhD *Hull*   Sr. Lectr.

Venables, W. A., BSc *Wales*, PhD *Wales*   Sr. Lectr.

Weightman, A. J., BSc *Kent*, PhD *Warw.*   Sr. Lectr.

Wimpenny, J. W. T., MA *Camb.*, PhD *Lond.*   Prof.

Other Staff: 10 Lectrs.; 3 Res. Fellows; 8 Hon. Lectrs.; 1 Hon. Res. Fellow

Research: aquatic biology; cell and developmental biology; microbiology; molecular ecology; pest management

Business School

Tel: (01222) 874417 Fax: (01222) 874419

Blyton, P. R., BA *Leic.*, PhD *Sheff.*   Prof.

Boyns, Trevor, BSc *Warw.*, PhD *Wales*   Sr. Lectr.

Bridge, J., BScEcon *Wales*, MA *Sheff.*, PhD *Wales*   Sr. Lectr.

Byers, John D., BA *Durh.*, MSc *Lond.*, PhD *Wales*   Sr. Lectr.

Clarke, R., BSc *Wales*, MA *Essex*, PhD *Leic.*   Prof.

Congdon, T., BA *Oxf.*   Hon. Prof.

Copeland, Laurence S., BA *Oxf.*, MA(Econ) *Manc.*, PhD *Manc.*   Prof.

Curry, B., BA(Econ) *Manc.*, MSc *Sus.*   Sr. Lectr.

Davidson, James E. H., BSocSc *Birm.*, MSc *Lond.*   Prof.

Debrah, Y. A., MA *S.Fraser*, PhD *Warw.*   Sr. Lectr.

Edwards, J. R., MScEcon *Wales*, FCA   Prof.

Fosh, Patricia, BA(Econ) *Sheff.*, PhD *Camb.*   Prof.

Foxall, Gordon R., MSc *Salf.*, PhD *Strath.*, PhD *Birm.*, DSocSc *Birm.*   Prof.

Groves, R. E. V., BCom *Birm.*, MSc *Purdue*, PhD *Purdue*, FCA   Sir Julian Hodge Prof., Accountancy

Heery, Edmund J., BA *Camb.*, MA *Essex*   Prof.

Hill, S., MScEcon *Wales*   Sr. Lectr.

Hines, Peter A., MA *Camb.*   Prof.

Jones, D. T., BA *Sus.*   Prof., Lean Enterprise

Jones, M. J., BA *Oxf.*, FCA   Prof., Financial Reporting

Katsikeas, C. S., BSc *Athens*, MA *Lanc.*, PhD *Wales*   Prof., Marketing and International Business

Makepeace, Gerald H., BA *Durh.*, MSocSc *Birm.*   Prof., Labour Economics

Mansfield, Roger, MA *Camb.*, PhD *Camb.*   Prof.; Head*

Matthews, Kent G. P., MSc(Econ) *Lond.*, PhD *Liv.*   Prof., Banking and Finance

Minford, A. Patrick L., CBE, BA *Oxf.*, MSc *Lond.*, PhD *Lond.*   Prof.

Ogbonna, Emmanuel O., MBA *Wales*, PhD *Wales*   Sr. Lectr.

Peattie, K. J., BA *Leeds*   Sr. Lectr.

Peel, David A., BA *Warw.*   Prof.

Pendlebury, M. W., MA *Lanc.*   Prof., Accounting

Piercy, Nigel F., BA *H.-W.*, MA *Durh.*, PhD *Wales*   Prof., Marketing and Strategy

Pitt, Leyland F., BCom *Pret.*, MBA *Pret.*, MCom *Rhodes*, PhD *Pret.*   Prof., Marketing and Strategy

Poole, M. J. F., BA(Econ) *Sheff.*, PhD *Sheff.*   Prof., Human Resource Management

Rhys, D. G., OBE, BA *Wales*, MCom *Birm.*, FIMA   SMMT Prof., Motor Industry Economics

Sadler, P., MSc(Econ) *Lond.*   Hon. Prof.

Shorey, J. C., BA(Econ) *Manc.*, MSc(Econ) *Lond.*, PhD *Lond.*   Sr. Lectr.

Silver, M. S., BA *Leeds*, PhD *Leeds*   Prof., Business Statistics

Smith, I. G., MScEcon *Wales*, PhD *Wales*   Sr. Lectr.

Thomas, D. R., MA *Oxf.*, BPhil *Oxf.*   Sr. Lectr.

Whipp, R. T. H., MA *Camb.*, MA *Warw.*, PhD *Warw.*   Prof., Human Resource Management

Other Staff: 50 Lectrs.; 7 Distinguished Sr. Res. Fellows; 5 Sr. Res. Fellows; 8 Sr. Res. Assocs.; 4 Res. Fellows; 1 Distinguished Sr. Res. Fellow†; 2 Sr. Res. Assocs.†; 1 Hon. Res. Fellow

Research: automotive industry: international economic studies of industry structure; employment; financial economics: theoretical and econometric approaches; lean enterprise: supply chain and operations management; regional economics with particular emphasis on Welsh economy

Chemistry and Applied Chemistry

Tel: (01222) 874023 Fax: (01222) 874030

Attard, G. A., BSc *Liv.*, PhD *Liv.*   Sr. Lectr.

Edwards, Peter G., BSc *Lond.*, PhD *Lond.*   Prof.

Gillard, R. D., BA *Oxf.*, BSc *Oxf.*, PhD *Lond.*   Prof.†

Heller, H. G., BSc *H.-W.*, PhD *Edin.*, FRSChem   Prof.

Hewlins, Michael J. E., MA *Camb.*, PhD *Camb.*   Sr. Lectr.

Hursthouse, M. B., BSc *Lond.*, PhD *Lond.*   Prof.

Hutchings, Graham J., BSc *Lond.*, PhD *Lond.*, FRSChem   Prof.; Head*

Knight, David W., BSc *Nott.*, PhD *Nott.*, FRSChem   Prof.

Maynard, J. C., OBE, BSc *Lond.*, PhD *Lond.*   Hon. Prof.

Owen, E. D., BSc *Wales*, PhD *Wales*   Sr. Lectr.†

Rao, C. N. Ram, MSc *Ban.*, MPhil *Purdue*, DSc *Mys.*, Hon. DSc *Wales*   Hon. Prof.

Roberts, M. W., PhD *Wales*, DSc *Wales*, FRSChem   Prof.

Shannon, P. V. R., BSc *St And.*, DPhil *Oxf.*   Reader†

Spencer, M. S., MA *Camb.*, PhD *Camb.*, FRSChem   Hon. Prof.

Taylor, D. M., PhD *Lond.*, DSc *Liv.*, FRSChem   Hon. Prof.

Williams, D. R., OBE, BSc *Wales*, PhD *Wales*, DSc *St And.*, FRSChem   Prof.

Other Staff: 11 Lectrs.; 2 Sr. Res. Officers; 1 Res. Fellow; 1 Sr. Lectr.†; 1 Hon. Res. Fellow

Research: coordination and speciation chemistry and metal analysis; inorganic chemistry: metal ligand synthesis, liquid crystals, materials; organic chemistry: synthetic methodology, total synthesis, asymmetric ligands; structural and computational chemistry: x-ray defraction, molecular modelling, quantum chemistry; surface science and catalysis: catalyst design, zeolites, surface chemistry

City and Regional Planning

Tel: (01222) 874882 Fax: (01222) 874845

Alden, J. D., JP, BSc *S'ton.*, MLitt *H.-W.*, PhD *Wales*   Prof.; Head*

Aspinwall, Rod, BSc *Wales*, FGS   Hon. Prof.

Bishop, Kevin D., BSc *Reading*, PhD *Reading*   Sr. Lectr.

Clapham, David F., BA *CNAA*, MSc *Lond.*, PhD *Lond.*   Prof.

Crow, H. Stephen, CB, MA *Camb.*   Hon. Prof.

Guy, C. M., BA *Camb.*, MPhil *Lond.*, PhD *Reading*   Reader

Higgs, Gary, BSc *Wales*, PhD *Wales*   Sr. Lectr.

Lovering, John, BA *Wales*   Prof.

Marsden, Terry K., BA *Hull*, PhD *Hull*   Prof.

Morgan, K. J., BA *Leic.*, MA *McM.*, DPhil *Sus.*   Prof.

Murdoch, Jonathan L., BSc Econ *Wales*, PhD *Wales*   Sr. Lectr.

Phillips, A. A. C., BA *Oxf.*   Prof.†

Punter, John V., BA *Newcastle(UK)*, MA *Tor.*, PhD *Tor.*   Prof.

Rakodi, Carole I., BA *Manc.*, PhD *Wales*   Prof.

Romaya, S. M., MA *Manc.*, PhD *Nott.*   Sr. Lectr.

Senior, Martyn L., BA *Leeds*, PhD *Leeds*   Sr. Lectr.

Thomas, A. Huw, BA *Oxf.*, MPhil *Lond.*   Sr. Lectr.

Webster, C. J., MSc *Wales*, PhD *Hull*   Reader

Williams, H. C. W. L., BA *Oxf.*, DPhil *Oxf.*, MA *Lanc.*   Prof.

Other Staff: 11 Lectrs.; 1 Sr. Res. Assoc.; 4 Res. Fellows; 4 Hon. Res. Fellows

Research: environmental planning and sustainability; housing management and development; spatial analysis, urban planning and transport; urban and regional governance

Computer Science

Tel: (01222) 874812 Fax: (01222) 874598

Batchelor, B. G., BSc *S'ton.*, PhD *S'ton.*   Prof.

Brown, B. M., BSc *Wales*, PhD *Wales*   Sr. Lectr.

Eastham, Michael S. P., MA *Oxf.*, DPhil *Oxf.*, DSc *Oxf.*   Hon. Prof.

Fiddian, N. J., MSc *Lond.*, PhD *S'ton.*   Reader; Head*

Gray, W. A., MA *Edin.*, MSc *Newcastle(UK)*   Prof.

Jeffrey, Keith G., BSc *Exe.*, PhD *Exe.*, FGS   Hon. Prof.

Jones, Antonia J., BSc *Reading*, PhD *Camb.*   Prof.

Martin, R. R., MA *Camb.*, PhD *Camb.*   Sr. Lectr.

Waltz, Frederick M., MS *Mich.*, PhD *Mich.*   Hon. Prof.

Walker, David W., MA *Camb.*, MSc *Lond.*, PhD *Lond.*   Prof.

Other Staff: 8 Lectrs.

Research: object and knowledge based sytems: distributed information systems and their interoperability; parallel and scientific computation: high performance, evolutionary and neural computing; vision and geometry: machine vision, geometric modelling, image processing

Continuing Education and Professional Development

Tel: (01222) 874831 Fax: (01222) 668935

Havard, Madeleine S. C., BSc *Wales*, PhD *Wales*   Lectr.; Head*

Pikoulis, J., BA *Cape Town*, MA *Leic.*, PhD *Wales*   Sr. Lectr.

Webster, P. V., BA *Manc.*, MPhil *Lond.*, DLitt *Wales*, FSA   Sr. Lectr.

Other Staff: 3 Lectrs.

Earth Sciences

Tel: (01222) 874830 Fax: (01222) 874326

Amos, Carl L., BSc *Wales*, PhD *Lond.*   Hon. Prof.; Distinguished Visiting Fellow

Annels, A. E., BSc *Lond.*, PhD *Lond.*   Sr. Lectr.

Barnes, H. L., BS *Mass.*, PhD *Col.*   Hon. Prof.; Distinguished Visiting Fellow

Bassett, M. G., BSc *Wales*, PhD *Wales*, DSc *Wales*, FGS   Hon. Prof.

Bowen, David Q., BSc *Lond.*, PhD *Lond.*   Prof.

Cope, J. C. W., BSc *Brist.*, PhD *Brist.*, DSc *Brist.*, FGS   Reader

Edwards, Dianne, MA *Camb.*, PhD *Camb.*, ScD *Camb.*, FGS, FLS   Prof.

Fry, N., BA *Camb.*, PhD *Manc.*, FGS   Sr. Lectr.

Gayer, R. A., BA *Camb.*, PhD *Camb.*, FGS   Reader

Gibbons, F. A., BSc *Lond.*, PhD *CNAA*, FGS   Sr. Lectr.

Harris, C., BSc *Durh.*, PhD *Reading*, FGS   Sr. Lectr.

Liang, Liyuan, BS *Boston*, MS *Cal.Tech.*, PhD *Cal.Tech.*   Sr. Lectr.

Lisle, R. J., BSc *Birm.*, MSc *Lond.*, PhD *Lond.*   Reader

Luther, George W., BA *La Salle(Penn.)*, PhD *Pitt.*   Hon. Prof.; Distinguished Visiting Fellow

O'Hara, Michael J., MA *Camb.*, PhD *Camb.*, FGS   Prof.

Ramsay, A. T. S., BSc *Wales*, PhD *Wales*   Sr. Lectr.

Rickard, D. T., BSc *Lond.*, PhD *Lond.*   Prof.; Head*

Riding, R. E., BSc *Sheff.*, PhD *Sheff.*   Reader

Wright, Victor P., BSc *Wales*, PhD *Wales*, DSc *Wales*   Prof.

Other Staff: 8 Lectrs.; 1 Sr. Visiting Fellow; 1 Res. Fellow; 5 Hon. Lectrs.; 5 Hon. Res. Fellows

Research: geochemistry and petrogenesis: environmental geochemistry, magma evolution, ore geology; palaeobiology: palaeobotany and palaeozoology; quaternary geology: climate processes, periglacial geology, environmental geophysics; sedimentology: petroleum geology, carbonate sedimentology, coastal processes; structural geology: strain analysis, marine geology, coalfield geology

Education, Collegiate Faculty of

Education, School of

Tel: (01222) 874459 Fax: (01222) 874160

Bolam, Raymond, BA *Manc.*, PhD *Brist.*   Prof.; Head*

Crozier, W. R., BA *Belf.*, MSc *Stir.*, PhD *Keele*   Sr. Lectr.

Davies, W. B., BSc(Econ) *Lond.*, MA *Lond.*   Prof.

Fitz, J., BA *Tas.*, MA *Lond.*, PhD *Open(UK)*   Sr. Lectr.

Melhuish, Edward C., BSc *Brist.*, PhD *Lond.*   Prof.

Moss, G. D., BSc *Birm.*, PhD *Birm.*   Sr. Lectr.

Pellegrini, Anthony D., MA *Ohio*, PhD *Ohio*, BA   Hon. Prof.

Rees, Gareth M., BA *Oxf.*, MPhil *Oxf.*   Prof.

Wallace, Allan M., BA *Camb.*, PhD *E.Anglia*   Prof.

Other Staff: 14 Lectrs.; 1 Lectr.†; 1 Sr. Res. Assoc.†; 5 Hon. Res. Fellows

Research: education management and policy: professional learning in educational change and policy processes; post-compulsory education and training: learning work and labour markets; psychology and special education needs: learning and human development

Engineering, School of

Tel: (01222) 874824 Fax: (01222) 874292

Barr, B. I. G., BSc *Wales*, PhD *Wales*   Prof.

Bates, C. J., MSc *Wales*, PhD *Wales*   Reader

Beckley, Phillip, BSc *S'ton.*, PhD *CNAA*, DSc *S'ton.*   Hon. Prof.

Bolton, H. R., BSc(Eng) *Nott.*, PhD *Lond.*   Prof.

Brandon, J. A., BSc *Lond.*, MSc *Manc.*, PhD *Manc.*   Sr. Lectr.

Bridle, R. J., BSc *Brist.*   Hon. Prof.

Davies, A. W., BSc *Wales*   Hon. Prof.

Evans, H. P., BSc *Exe.*, PhD *Exe.*   Sr. Lectr.

Falconer, Roger A., BSc *Lond.*, MSCE *Wash.*, PhD *Lond.*   Prof.

Griffiths, Anthony J., BEng *Wales*, PhD *Wales*   Sr. Lectr.

Horrocks, D. H., BSc *CNAA*, PhD *Newcastle(UK)*   Sr. Lectr.

Hughes, T. G., MSc *Wales*, PhD *Wales*   Sr. Lectr.

Hunt, J. G., BSc *Wales*, PhD *Lond.*   Sr. Lectr.

Isaac, A. K., BSc *Wales*, PhD *Wales*   Reader

Karihaloo, B. L., BSc(Eng) *Ranchi*, MTech *Bom.*, PhD *Moscow*, DEng *Syd.*, FIEAust   Prof.

Khalatov, Artem, MSc *Kazan*, PhD *Kazan*   Hon. Prof.

McWhirter, J. G., BSc *Belf.*, PhD *Belf.*, FEng, FIEE, FIMA   Hon. Prof.

Miles, J. C., BSc *Manc.*, MSc *Birm.*, PhD *Birm.*   Sr. Lectr.

Morgan, D. V., BSc *Wales*, PhD *Camb.*, DSc *Leeds*, FIEE, FEng, FIP   Prof.; Head*

Moses, A. J., BEng(Tech) *Wales*, PhD *Wales*, DSc *Wales*, FIEE   Prof.

Nokes, Leonard D. M., BEng *Wales*, MB BCh *Wales*, MSc *Wales*, PhD *Wales*   Sr. Lectr.

Nussey, I., OBE, MA *Camb.*, PhD *Lond.*, FEng, FIMechE   Hon. Prof.

Pham, D. T., BE *Cant.*, PhD *Cant.*, DEng *Cant.*, FIEE   Prof.

Pooley, F. D., MSc *Wales*, PhD *Wales*   Prof.

Roberts, T. M., BSc *Wales*, PhD *Wales*   Reader

Rowe, D. M., BSc *Wales*, MSc *Brist.*, PhD *Wales*, DSc *Wales*, FIEE   Prof.

Sabir, A. B., BSc *Wales*, PhD *Wales*   Reader

Snidle, R. W., BSc *Leic.*, PhD *Leic.*, DSc *Leic.*   Reader

Syred, N., BEng *Sheff.*, PhD *Sheff.*   Prof.

Tasker, Paul J., BSc *Leeds*, PhD *Leeds*   Prof.

Thomas, H., BSc *Wales*, PhD *Wales*   Reader

Thomas, H. R., BSc *Wales*, MSc *Lond.*, PhD *Wales*, DSc *Wales*   Prof.

Tilley, R. J. D., BSc *Brist.*, PhD *Brist.*, DSc *Brist.*, FRSChem   Prof.

Watton, J., BSc *Wales*, PhD *Wales*, DSc *Wales*   Prof.

Williams, F. W., MA *Camb.*, ScD *Camb.*, PhD *Brist.*, FICE, FIStructE, FRAeS   Prof.

Williams, K. P., MSc *Wales*, PhD *Wales*   Sr. Lectr.

Yong, Raymond N., BA *Wash.*, BSc *Mass.*, MSc *Purdue*, MEng *McG.*, PhD *McG.*, FRSCan   Distinguished Res. Prof.†

Zhong, W., BEng *Shanghai Jiaotong*   Hon. Prof.

Other Staff: 40 Lectrs.; 2 Sr. Res. Fellows; 10 Sr. Res. Assocs.; 1 Hon. Lectr.

Research: civil engineering: geotechnical engineering, performance of lightweight structures, structural testing and analysis, concrete and masonry structures, artificial intelligence, environmental water management; electrical, electronic and systems engineering: electrical power, machines and drives, magnetics technology, microelectronics and thermoelectrics engineering, electronic systems, computer-aided engineering, medical systems; mechanical engineering: renewable energy, combustion thermofluids, emissions/effluent processes, materials control and dynamics, tribology

English, Communication and Philosophy, School of

Tel: (01222) 874501 Fax: (01222) 874502

Attfield, R., MA *Oxf.*, PhD   Prof.

Belsey, Catherine, BA *Oxf.*, MA *Warw.*., PhD *Warw.*   Prof.

Candlin, Christopher N., MA *Oxf.*, MPhil *Yale*   Hon. Prof.

Coupland, Justine, BA *Wales*, PhD *Wales*   Sr. Lectr.

Coupland, N. J., BA *Oxf.*, BLing *Manc.*, MA *Reading*, PhD *Wales*   Prof.

Coyle, M. J., BA *Nott.*, PhD *Nott.*   Sr. Lectr.

Durrant, M., BA *Leeds*, BPhil *Oxf.*   Reader

Elam, Diane M., AB *Kenyon*, MA *Brown*, PhD *Brown*   Prof.

Ellis, R. M., BA *Adel.*, DPhil *Oxf.*   Sr. Lectr.

Fawcett, R. P., MA *Oxf.*, PhD *Lond.*   Reader

Garrett, Peter D., BScEcon *Lond.*   Sr. Lectr.

Garside, P. D., MA *Camb.*, AM *Harv.*, PhD *Camb.*   Reader

Giles, Howard, BA *Wales*, PhD *Brist.*   Hon. Prof.

Hawkes, T. F., MA *Wales*, PhD *Wales*   Prof.†

Hunt, P. L., MA *Wales*, PhD *Wales*   Prof.

Kelsall, M. M., MA *Oxf.*, BLitt *Oxf.*   Prof.

Knight, Stephen T., BLitt *Oxf.*, MA *Oxf.*, PhD *Syd.*   Prof.

Norris, C. C., BA *Lond.*, PhD *Lond.*   Distinguished Res. Prof.

Peck, J., MA *Wales*, PhD *Lond.*   Sr. Lectr.

Sarangi, S. K., MA *Utkal*, MLitt *Lanc.*, PhD *Lanc.*   Sr. Lectr.

Skilton, David J., MA *Camb.*, MLitt *Camb.*   Prof.; Head*

Tench, Paul W., BA *Wales*, PhD *Wales*   Sr. Lectr.

Thomas, D. S., BA *Oxf.*, MA *Lond.*, PhD *Lond.*   Reader

Thomas, P. W., MA *Oxf.*, DPhil *Oxf.*   Sr. Lectr.

Weedon, Christine M., BA *S'ton.*, PhD *Birm.*   Reader

Other Staff: 19 Lectrs.; 2 Lectrs.†; 1 Hon. Sr. Res. Fellow

Research: centre for editorial and intertextual research: editorial methods, bibliography, electronic text; English literature: English from 1500 to the present day; language and

communication: sociolinguistics, discourse, linguistics, human communication; philosophy: continental philosophy, history of philosophy, social philosophy

European Studies, School of

Tel: (01222) 874586 Fax: (01222) 874946

Bettinson, C. D., BA *Reading*, PhD *Reading*   Sr. Lectr.

Hanley, D. L., MA *Oxf.*, PhD *Warw.*   Prof.; Head*

Jackson, D. A., MA *Oxf.*, DPhil *Oxf.*   Sr. Lectr.

Jones, J. B., BA *Wales*, MA *Alta.*   Sr. Lectr.

Loughlin, John P., BA *CNAA*, PhD *Florence*   Prof.

Peitsch, H. E., DrPhilHabil *F.U.Berlin*   Prof.

Vincent, A. W., BA *Exe.*, PhD *Manc.*   Prof.

White, A. D., MA *Oxf.*, DPhil *Oxf.*   Sr. Lectr.

Other Staff: 19 Lectrs.; 2 Hon. Res. Fellows

Research: European history, memory and fiction; European literary and cultural studies; European politics, national and comparative; European public policy and labour movements; nationalism and regionalism: parties and ideologies

History and Archaeology, School of

Tel: (01222) 874259 Fax: (01222) 874929

Aldhouse-Green, S. H. R., BA *Wales*, PhD *Wales*, FSA   Hon. Prof.

Burleigh, Michael C. B., BA *Lond.*, PhD *Lond.*   Distinguished Res. Prof.

Coss, Peter R., BA *Wales*, PhD *Birm.*, FSA   Prof.

Edbury, P. W., MA *St And.*, PhD *St And.*   Reader

Evans, J. G., BSc *Reading*, PhD *Lond.*, FSA   Prof.

Fisher, N. R. E., MA *Oxf.*, DPhil *Oxf.*   Sr. Lectr.

Hines, J. A., MA *Oxf.*, DPhil *Oxf.*   Reader

Hudson, Patricia, BSc(Econ) *Lond.*, DPhil *York(UK)*   Prof.

Jones, J. G., MA *Wales*, PhD *Wales*   Prof.

Loyn, Henry R., MA *Wales*, DLitt *Wales*, FSA   Hon. Prof.

Manning, W. H., BSc *Nott.*, PhD *Lond.*, FSA   Prof.

Newton, Christopher C. S., MA *Camb.*, PhD *Birm.*   Sr. Lectr.

Osmond, Jonathon P., MA *Oxf.*, DPhil *Oxf.*   Prof.; Head*

Percival, J., MA *Oxf.*, DPhil *Oxf.*, FSA   Prof.

Perkin, Harold J., MA *Camb.*   Hon. Prof.

Stradling, R. A., BA *Wales*, PhD *Wales*   Reader

Watkinson, D. E., MSc *Wales*   Sr. Lectr.

Whittle, A. W. R., MA *Oxf.*, DPhil *Oxf.*, FSA   Prof.

Wiliam, E., BA *Wales.*, MA *Manc.*, PhD *Manc.*, FSA   Hon. Prof.

Other Staff: 20 Lectrs.; 5 Hon. Lectrs.; 1 Hon. Res. Fellow

Research: archaeological science and conservation; archaeology and ancient history: Egypt, Greece and Rome; mediaeval and modern history: British Isles, Europe, British Empire; prehistory: British Isles and Europe; Welsh history: all periods

Journalism, Media and Cultural Studies, School of

Tel: (01222) 874041 Fax: (01222) 238832

Bogdanov, M., MA *Trinity(Dub.)*   Hon. Prof.

Davies, Maire J., BA *CNAA*, MPhil *E.Lond.*, PhD *E.Lond.*   Sr. Lectr.

Hartley, John A. E., BA *Wales*, PhD *Murd.*   Prof.; Head*

Jaworski, A., MA *Poznan*, PhD *Poznan*   Sr. Lectr.

Mungham, G., BA *Leic.*, BLitt *Oxf.*   Sr. Lectr.

Pearson, Roberta E., AB *Duke*, MPhil *Yale*, PhD *N.Y.*   Sr. Lectr.

Price, Gareth, BA *Wales*   Hon. Prof.

Traverse-Healey, T., OBE   Hon. Prof.

Williams, Kevin M., BA *Keele*, MSc(Econ) *Lond.*   Sr. Lectr.

Other Staff: 8 Lectrs.; 1 Res. Fellow; 1 Lectr.†; 2 Sr. Res. Fellows†; 1 Hon. Res. Fellow

Research: international media; media and children; media history; media and national/regional identity; visual culture, popular journalism and democracy

Law, School of

Tel: (01222) 874348 *Fax:* (01222) 874097

Alldridge, P. W., LLB *Lond.*, LLM *Wales* Sr. Lectr.
Churchill, R. R., LLM *Lond.*, PhD *Wales* Reader
Doe, C. Norman, LLM *Wales*, MTh *Wales*, PhD *Camb.* Sr. Lectr.
Douglas, Gillian F., LLB *Manc.*, LLM *Lond.* Reader
Felstiner, William L. F., BA *Yale*, JD *Yale* Distinguished Res. Prof.
Fennell, P. W. H., BA *Kent*, MPhil *Kent*, PhD *Wales* Reader
Foster, N. G., BA *Kent*, LLM *Exe.* Sr. Lectr.
Grubb, Andrew, MA *Camb.* Prof.
Harpwood, Vivienne, LLM *Birm.* Sr. Lectr.
Jones, Carol A. G., MA *Camb.*, PhD *Oxf.* Sr. Lectr.
Lee, Robert G., LLB *Brun.* Prof.; Head*
Lewis, R. K., MA *Oxf.* Prof.
Lowe, N. V., LLB *Sheff.* Prof.
Merkin, Robert M., LLB *Wales*, LLM *Lond.* Prof.
Miers, D. R., LLM *Leeds*, DJur *Tor.* Prof.
Morgan, Derek M., BA *Kent* Sr. Lectr.
Murch, M., BA *Oxf.* Prof.
Nelken, David, MA *Camb.*, PhD *Camb.* Distinguished Res. Prof.
Sedley, The Hon. Mr. Justice S., BA *Camb.* Hon. Prof.
Smith, Keith J. M., LLM *Lond.*, DPhil *Oxf.* Prof.
Thomas, P. A., LLB *Wales*, LLM *Mich.*, LLM *Wales* Prof.
Watkin, T. G., BCL *Oxf.*, MA *Oxf.* Sr. Lectr.
Wells, Celia K., LLB *Warw.*, LLM *Lond.* Prof.
Wylie, J. C. W., LLD *Belf.*, LLM *Harv.* Prof.
Wylie, O. P., LLB *Belf.*, FCA Sr. Lectr.
Other Staff: 20 Lectrs.; 1 Res. Fellow; 2 Lectrs.†; 1 Sr. Res. Assoc.†; 1 Hon. Lectr.
Research: civil legal systems; commercial law; criminal law and justice; family law and justice; law, medicine and health care

Maritime Studies and International Transport

Tel: (01222) 874271 *Fax:* (01222) 874301

Barston, Ronald P., MSc Econ *Wales* Prof.
Brown, Edward D., BL *Edin.*, LLM *Lond.*, PhD *Lond.* Prof.
Davies, Anthony J., BA *Open(UK)*, MSc *Wales*, PhD *Wales* Prof.
Gardner, B. M., BA *Lanc.* Sr. Lectr.
King, J., BSc(Tech) *Wales*, MSc *Wales*, PhD *Wales*, FRICS Prof.; Head*
Lane, Anthony D., BA *Liv.* Prof.
Marlow, P. B., MScEcon *Wales*, PhD *Wales* Sr. Lectr.
Naim, Mohamed M., BEng(Tech) *Wales*, PhD *Wales* Sr. Lectr.
Smith, H. D., BSc *Aberd.*, PhD *Aberd.*, FRICS Reader
Thomas, B. J., BSc(Tech) *Wales*, PhD *Wales* Sr. Lectr.
Towill, Denis R., BScEng *Birm.*, DSc *Birm.*, FEng, FIEE Prof.†
Walker, J. M., BSc *Aston*, MSc *Lond.*, FRMetS Sr. Lectr.
Wonham, Jon, BSc *Wales*, PhD *Glas.*, FRSA Prof.
Other Staff: 8 Lectrs.; 3 Sr. Res. Assocs.; 1 Hon. Lectr.
Research: environment: natural, economic and social contexts of operations and trading; operations: movement and control of people and goods; trade (commerce): marketing, trading environment, technical infrastructure and services; trade (law and policy): operations, regulation, trade and environment

Marketing, see Bus. Sch.

Mathematics, School of

Tel: (01222) 874811 *Fax:* (01222) 874199

Cohen, A. M., MSc *Manc.*, PhD *Manc.*, FIMA Sr. Lectr.
Evans, D. E., BA *Oxf.*, MSc *Oxf.*, DPhil *Oxf.* Prof.
Evans, W. D., BSc *Wales*, DPhil *Oxf.* Prof.

Everitt, William N., BSc *Birm.*, MA *Oxf.*, DPhil *Oxf.*, FIMA Hon. Prof.
Greaves, G. R. H., MA *Edin.*, BA *Camb.*, PhD *Brist.* Sr. Lectr.
Griffiths, Jeffrey D., BSc *Wales*, PhD *Wales*, FIMA Prof.; Head*
Harman, G., BSc *Lond.*, PhD *Lond.*, DSc *Wales* Prof.
Hooley, C., MA *Camb.*, PhD *Camb.*, ScD *Camb.*, FRS Distinguished Res. Prof.
Hoyle, Sir Fred, MA *Camb.*, Hon. DSc *Leeds*, Hon. DSc *Brad.*, Hon. DSc *Newcastle(UK)*, Hon. ScD *E.Anglia*, FRS Hon. Prof.
Huxley, M. N., MA *Camb.*, PhD *Camb.* Prof.
John, T. L., BSc *Wales*, PhD *Lond.* Reader
Jones, J. E., MSc *Manc.*, PhD *Manc.* Reader
Khoukhro, Evgueni, PhD *Novosibirsk* Distinguished Res. Prof.
Nandy, Kashinath, MSc *Calc.*, MSc *Edin.*, PhD *Edin.*, FRS Hon. Prof.
Wickramasinghe, N. C., BSc *Ceyl.*, MA *Camb.*, PhD *Camb.*, ScD *Camb.*, FRAS Prof.
Wiegold, J., MSc *Manc.*, PhD *Manc.*, DSc *Wales* Prof.
Zhigljavsky, Antoly A., MS *St.Petersburg*, PhD *St.Petersburg* Prof.
Other Staff: 9 Lectrs.; 1 Sr. Res. Assoc.; 1 Hon. Visiting Lectr.†; 1 Hon. Res. Fellow
Research: applied mathematics; pure mathematics: analytic number theory, differential equations and analysis, operator algebras; statistics/operational research

Media Studies, see Journalism, Media and Cultural Studies, Sch. of

Molecular and Medical Biosciences, School of

Tel: (01222) 874829 *Fax:* (01222) 874116

Archer, C. W., BSc *Wales*, PhD *Wales* Prof.
Benjamin, M., BSc *Wales*, PhD *Wales* Sr. Lectr.
Carter, David A., BSc *Bath*, PhD *Lond.* Reader
Caterson, Bruce, BSc *Monash*, PhD *Monash* Prof.
Chapman, Paul F. J., BA *Wash.*, PhD *Stan.* Sr. Lectr.
Crunelli, V., Laur *Catania* Prof.
Cryer, A., BSc *Sheff.*, PhD *Sheff.* Prof.; Head*
Duance, Victor C., BSc *Bath*, PhD *Brist.* Reader
Foster, G. A., BA *Camb.*, MA *Camb.*, PhD *S'ton.* Reader
Fox, Kevin D., BSc *Bath*, PhD *Lond.* Sr. Lectr.
Harwood, J. L., PhD *Birm.*, DSc *Birm.* Prof.
Jacob, Timothy T. J., BSc *Sus.*, PhD *E.Anglia* Prof.
John, R. A., BSc *Wales*, PhD *Wales* Prof.
Jones, J. G., BPharm *Wales*, PhD *Wales* Sr. Lectr.
Kay, J., BSc *Edin.*, PhD *Edin.* Prof.
Lodge, David, BVSc *Brist.*, PhD *Brist.* Hon. Prof.
Moxham, Bernard J., BSc *Brist.*, BDS *Brist.*, PhD *Brist.* Prof.
Presley, R., MA *Camb.*, MB BChir *Camb.* Sr. Lectr.
Ralphs, J. R., BSc *Lond.*, PhD *CNAA* Sr. Lectr.
Richards, R. J., PhD *Wales*, DSc *Wales* Prof.
Roberts, M. H. T., BSc *Lond.*, PhD *Birm.*, DSc *Birm.* Prof.
Santer, R. M., BSc *St And.*, PhD *St And.* Sr. Lectr.
Wallis, D. I., MA *Camb.*, PhD *Camb.* Prof.
Watson, A. H. D., BSc *Edin.*, PhD *St And.* Sr. Lectr.
White, G. F., BSc *Lond.*, PhD *Lond.* Sr. Lectr.
Other Staff: 10 Lectrs.; 2 Sr. Res. Fellows; 3 Sr. Res. Assocs.; 2 Lectrs.†; 4 Sr. Prof. Tutors; 2 Res. Fellows; 1 Hon. Lectr.; 1 Hon. Res. Fellow
Research: connective tissue biology; gene regulation and cellular physiology; neuroscience; protein processing and design; regulatory mechanisms and enzymology

Music

Tel: (01222) 874816 *Fax:* (01222) 874379

Jones, D. W., BMus *Wales*, MA *Wales*, PhD *Wales* Sr. Lectr.

Jones, R. E., BA *Wales*, MMus *Wales*, PhD *Wales*, FRCO Sr. Lectr.
Robbins Landon, H. C., BMus *Boston*, Hon. DMus *Boston*, Hon. DMus *Belf.*, Hon. DMus *Brist.* Hon. Prof.
Stowell, R., MA *Camb.*, PhD *Camb.* Prof.
Thomas, Adrian T., BMus *Nott.*, MA *Wales* Prof.; Head*
Walsh, S., MA *Camb.* Reader
Williams, P. F., MusB *Camb.*, MA *Camb.*, PhD *Camb.*, LittD *Camb.* John Bird Prof.
Other Staff: 4 Lectrs.; 1 Res. Fellow; 1 Hon. Lectr.
Research: aesthetics, popular culture, music and politics; composer studies: Bach, Haydn, Beethoven, Stravinsky; composition; eighteenth-century studies including organology, performance practice; twentieth-century British, French and Polish music

Optometry and Vision Sciences

Tel: (01222) 874374 *Fax:* (01222) 874859

Erichsen, Jonathon T., BA *Harv.*, DPhil *Oxf.* Sr. Lectr.
Hodson, S. A., BSc *Brist.*, PhD *E.Anglia* Prof.
McNaughton, P. A., BSc *Auck.*, DPhil *Oxf.* Hon. Prof.
Rovamo, Jyrki M., MB *Helsinki*, MD *Helsinki* Prof.
Wigham, C. G., BSc *Aston*, PhD *Aston* Sr. Lectr.; Head*
Woodhouse, J. Margaret, BSc *Aston*, PhD *Camb.* Sr. Lectr.
Other Staff: 5 Lectrs.; 1 Sr. Res. Assoc.; 1 Distinguished Res. Fellow†
Research: ocular biophysics: cornea, transparency, ion transport, retinal pigment epithelium, tears, visual evoked potentials; ocular and refractive development: ocular growth, regulation, myopia, visual development, children, pathologies; visual psychophysics: computational modelling, foveal and peripheral spatial vision, colour vision, quantal noise, visual performance in pathology

Pharmacy, Welsh School of

Tel: (01222) 874782 *Fax:* (01222) 874149

Armstrong, N. A., BPharm *Lond.*, PhD *Lond.* Sr. Lectr.
Brain, K. R., BPharm *Nott.*, PhD *Bath* Sr. Lectr.
Broadley, K. J., BPharm *Lond.*, PhD *Lond.*, DSc *Lond.*, FRPharmS Prof.
Cox, B., PhD *Manc.*, DSc *Manc.*, FRPharmS Hon. Prof.
Daniels, Stephen, MA *Oxf.*, DPhil *Oxf.* Sr. Lectr.
Guy, R. H., MA *Oxf.*, PhD *Lond.* Hon. Prof.
Hadgraft, J., MA *Oxf.*, DPhil *Oxf.*, DSc *Oxf.*, FRSChem Prof.
Kellaway, I. W., BPharm *Lond.*, PhD *Lond.*, DSc *Lond.*, FRPharmS Prof.
Luscombe, D. K., BPharm *Lond.*, PhD *Lond.*, FIBiol, FRPharmS Prof.; Head*
Machin, P. J., BSc *Lond.*, PhD *Lond.*, FRSChem Hon. Prof.
McGuigan, Christopher, BSc *Birm.*, PhD *Birm.* Prof.
Nicholls, P. J., BSc *Birm.*, PhD *Wales*, FRSChem, FIBiol Prof.
Russell, A. D., BPharm *Wales*, PhD *Nott.*, DSc *Wales*, FPS, FRCPath Prof.
Sewell, R. D. E., BPharm *Brad.*, PhD *Wales* Sr. Lectr.
Shayegan-Salek, Mir-Saeed, BSc *Oklahoma*, PhD *Wales* Sr. Lectr.
Spencer, P. S. J., OBE, BPharm *Lond.*, PhD *Lond.*, DSc *Wales*, Hon. DSc *De Mont.*, FIBiol, FRPharmS Prof.
Taylor, G., BSc *Aston*, PhD *Manc.* Sr. Lectr.
Walker, R. D., BPharm *Brad.*, PhD *Aston* Prof.
Walker, S. R., BSc *Lond.*, PhD *Lond.*, FRSChem, FIBiol Hon. Prof.
Other Staff: 10 Lectrs.; 2 Sr. Res. Assocs.; 1 Sr. Res. Fellow; 1 Sr. Teaching Fellow†; 4 Sr. Res. Assocs.†; 1 Sr. Res. Fellow†; 5 Hon. Lectrs.

Research: design and synthesis of drugs; drug delivery; drug usage; molecular and cellular basis of drug action

Philosophy, see Engl., Communicn. and Philos., Sch. of

Physics and Astronomy

Tel: (01222) 874458 Fax: (01222) 874056

Blood, P., BSc *Leeds*, PhD *Leeds*, FIP Prof.; Head*
Disney, M. J., BSc *Manc.*, PhD *Lond.*, FRAS Prof.
Edmunds, M. G., MA *Camb.*, PhD *Camb.*, FRAS Prof.
Grishchuk, Leonid P., PhD *Moscow*, DSc *Moscow*, FRAS Prof.
Heckingbottom, R., MA *Oxf.*, DPhil *Oxf.*, FRSChem Hon. Prof.
Inglesfield, John E., MA *Camb.*, PhD *Camb.* Prof.
Matthai, C. C., BSc *Lond.*, DPhil *Oxf.* Reader
Nelson, A. H., BSc *Glas.*, PhD *Lond.*, FRAS Sr. Lectr.
Schutz, B. F., BSc *Clarkson*, PhD *Cal. Tech.*, FRAS Prof.
Whitworth, A. P., MA *Oxf.*, PhD *Manc.*, FRAS Reader
Other Staff: 12 Lectrs.; 1 Sr. Res. Fellow; 6 Hon. Lectrs.; 1 Hon. Res. Fellow
Research: astrophysics: galaxy formation, gravitation waves, quasars, star-clusters; condensed matter physics: semiconductor surfaces and theory; optoelectronics: guided wave optics and semiconductor lasers

Planning, see City and Regional Planning

Psychology, School of

Tel: (01222) 874007 Fax: (01222) 874858

Aggleton, John P., MA *Camb.*, DPhil *Oxf.* Prof.
Barry, Christopher, BSc *Lond.*, PhD *StAnd.* Sr. Lectr.
Blackman, D. E., BA *Exe.*, PhD *Belf.*, FBPsS Prof.
Carroll, Howard C. M., BSc *Brist.*, PhD *Wales*, FBPsS Sr. Lectr.
Ellis, H. D., BA *Reading*, PhD *Reading*, DSc *Aberd.*, FBPsS Prof.; Head*
Fincham, F. D., BA *Natal*, MA *Witw.*, MS *N.Y.State*, DPhil *Oxf.*, FBPsS Prof.
Frude, N., BA *Newcastle(UK)*, MPhil *Lond.*, PhD *Wales*, FBPsS Sr. Lectr.
Gaffan, D., BA *Oxf.*, PhD *Lond.* Hon. Prof.
Giles, Howard, BA *Wales*, PhD *Brist.*, FBPsS Hon. Prof.
Griffiths, Robert D. P., BA *Manc.*, MA *Lond.*, PhD *Lond.*, FRCS, FBPsS Hon. Prof.
Hewstone, M. R. C., BSc *Brist.*, DPhil *Oxf.*, FBPsS Prof.
Jones, D. M., BSc(Tech) *Wales*, PhD *Wales*, DSc *Wales*, FBPsS Prof.
Martin, Robin P., BA *CNAA*, PhD *Open(UK)* Sr. Lectr.
Oaksford, Michael R., BA *Durh.*, PhD *Edin.* Prof.
Patrick, J., BA *Hull*, PhD *Hull*, FBPsS Sr. Lectr.
Payne, S. J., BSc *Lough.*, PhD *Sheff.* Prof.
Pearce, J. M., BSc *Leeds*, DPhil *Sus.* Prof.
Seligman, Martin E.P., AB *Prin.*, PhD *Penn.*, Hon. PhD *Uppsala* Hon. Prof.
Snowden, R. J., BSc *York(UK)*, PhD *Camb.* Reader
Tattersall, Andrew J., BSc(Tech) *Wales*, DPhil *Oxf.* Sr. Lectr.
White, P. A., BA *Nott.*, DPhil *Oxf.* Sr. Lectr.
Young, A. W., BSc *Warw.*, DSc *Lond.*, FBPsS Hon. Prof.
Other Staff: 13 Lectrs.; 1 Sr. Distinguished Fellow; 3 Res. Fellows; 2 Sr. Lectrs.†; 2 Lectrs.†; 14 Hon. Lectrs.; 5 Hon. Res. Fellows
Research: behavioural neuroscience; cognitive ergonomics; cognitive neuropsychology; personal relationships; social cognition

Religious Studies

Tel: (01222) 874240 Fax: (01222) 874500

Ballard, Rev. P. H., MA *Camb.*, BD *Lond.* Sr. Lectr.; Head*
Johnson, William J., BA *Sus.*, DPhil *Oxf.* Sr. Lectr.
Palmer, N. H., MA *Oxf.*, PhD *Wales* Prof.†
Trevett, Christine, MA *Sheff.*, PhD *Sheff.* Sr. Lectr.
Trombley, F. R., BA *San Diego*, MA *Calif.*, PhD *Calif.* Sr. Lectr.
Watt, J. W., MA *Camb.*, PhD *St And.* Sr. Lectr.
Williams, Rt. Rev. Rowan D., MA *Camb.*, DPhil *Oxf.*, FBA Hon. Prof.
Other Staff: 1 Sr. Distinguished Res. Fellow; 1 Res. Fellow; 1 Hon. Lectr.; 2 Hon. Res. Fellows
Research: Indian/Asian religion especially Jainism, Buddhism, Shintoism; practical theology especially church; mission and society; religion in late antiquity including Syriac, patristics, Byzantium

Social and Administrative Studies, School of

Tel: (01222) 874803 Fax: (01222) 874436

Adam, Barbara E., BScEcon *Wales*, PhD *Wales* Reader
Atkinson, P. A., MA *Camb.*, PhD *Edin.*, FRAI Prof.
Baker, Susan C., MA *N.U.I.*, PhD *Florence* Sr. Lectr.
Beck, Ulrich, PhD *Munich* Distinguished Res. Prof.†
Bloor, M. J., BA *Camb.*, MLitt *Aberd.*, PhD *Aberd.* Prof.
Brown, Phillip, BEd *CNAA*, PhD *Wales* Prof.
Butler, I. G., BA *S'ton.*. MPhil *Wales* Sr. Lectr.
Collins, Harold M., BSc(Econ) *Lond.*, MA *Essex*, PhD *Bath* Distinguished Res. Prof.
Delamont, K. Sara, MA *Camb.*, PhD *Edin.* Reader; Head*
Fevre, Ralph W., BA *Durh.*, PhD *Aberd.* Prof.
Levi, M., BA *Oxf.*, PhD *S'ton.* Prof.
Maguire, E. M. W., BA *Oxf.*, BLitt *Oxf.* Prof.
Pithouse, A. J., BScEcon *Wales*, PhD *Wales* Sr. Lectr.
Prior, Lindsay F., BSc *Open(UK)*, BSc *Lond.*, MA *Reading*, PhD *Aberd.* Sr. Lectr.
Shaw, I., BA(Econ) *Sheff.*, MA *Sheff.*, PhD *Wales* Sr. Lectr.
Other Staff: 13 Lectrs.; 1 Res. Fellow; 2 Lectrs.†; 1 Sr. Res. Assoc.†; 1 Hon. Lectr.; 3 Hon. Res. Fellows
Research: criminology and criminal justice; education and work time; environment and risk; social welfare systems; sociology of science and medicine

Welsh, see also Special Centres, etc

Tel: (01222) 874843 Fax: (01222) 874604

Davies, Sioned M., BA *Wales*, DPhil *Oxf.* Prof.; Head*
Jones, G. E., MA *Wales*, PhD *Wales* Res. Prof.†
Owen, T. M., MA *Wales*, FSA Hon. Prof.
Thomas, P. W., BA *Wales*, PhD *Wales* Reader
Williams, Colin H., BScEcon *Wales*, PhD *Wales* Prof.
Other Staff: 2 Lectrs.; 1 Hon. Lectr.; 1 Hon. Res. Fellow
Research: applied Welsh: education, language planning and policy, comparative multiculturalism; mediaeval narrative studies: orality/literacy/performance; Welsh linguistic studies: linguistic analysis, sociolinguistics, geolinguistics; Welsh literary studies: the bardic tradition, textual criticism and cultural interpretation

SPECIAL CENTRES, ETC

Common Cold and Nasal Research Centre

Tel: (01222) 874099 Fax: (01222) 874093

Eccles, Ronald, PhD *Liv.*, DSc *Liv.* Prof.; Dir.*

Other Staff: 2 Sr. Res. Assocs.

Computing Centre

Tel: (01222) 874876 Fax: (01222) 874285

Martin, John W., BSc *Leeds*, PhD *Brist.* Dir.*
Other Staff: 1 Sr. Lectr.†

English Language Service for International Students

No staff at present

European Language Centre

Tel: (01222) 875836

No staff at present

Japanese Studies Centre

Tel: (01222) 874959

Anthony, Douglas W., BA *Wales*, MSc *Wales* Prof.; Dir.*
Other Staff: 2 Lectrs.

Population Centre, Sir David Owen

Tel: (01222) 874794 Fax: (01222) 874372

Gabriel, Thomas M. G., BA *Durh.*, MLitt *Camb.*, PhD *Col.* Dir.†*
Other Staff: 1 Lectr.; 2 Lectrs.†

Professional Legal Studies, Centre for

Tel: (01222) 874964 Fax: (01222) 874984

Miers, D. R., LLM *Leeds*, DJur *Tor.* Prof.; Dir.*
Other Staff: 13 Lectrs.; 1 Sr. Professl. Tutor

Social Sciences, Centre for Advanced Studies in the

Tel: (01222) 874945 Fax: (01222) 874994

Cooke, Philip N., BA *Liv.* Prof.; Dir.*

Welsh Language Teaching Centre

Tel: (01222) 874710 Fax: (01222) 874708

Jones, Robert O., BA *Wales*, MA *Wales*, PhD *Wales* Dir. of Studies
Prosser, Helen, BA *Wales* Dir. of Teaching

CONTACT OFFICERS

Academic affairs. Director of Registry: Burdon, Christopher F., BA *Lond.*
Accommodation. Allocations Officer: Keelan, Jan
Admissions (first degree). Admissions Officer: Hoose, Kathryn, BA *Wales*
Admissions (higher degree). Assistant Registrar: Devine, Brenda, BScEcon *Wales*, MEd *Wales*
Adult/continuing education. Head of Continuing Education and Professional Development Department: Havard, Madeleine S. C., BSc *Wales*, PhD *Wales*
Archives. Clerical Assistant: Parry, Barbara J.
Careers. Director of Careers Service: Mutlow, Derek M. F., BA *Exe.*
Computing services. Assistant Director, Computing Centre: Williams, Roger A. S., BSc *Hull*
Consultancy services. Research Grants Manager: Edwards, Graham J.
Equal opportunities. Personnel Administration Officer: Bevan, David J., BScEcon *Wales*
Estates and buildings/works and services. Director of Estates: Morton, Andy L., BSc *CNAA*, FRICS
Examinations. Assistant Registrar: Evans, Rhodri P., BEng *Wales*, MBA *Wales*
Finance. Director of Finance: Davies, D. Michael, BScEcon *Wales*
General enquiries. Senior Executive and Head of Vice-Chancellor's Office: Cunningham, Vanessa, BA *Manc.*
Health services. Medical Officer: Jones, Sandra, MB BCh *Wales*
International office. Head of International Office: Westlake, Timothy J., MSc *Wales*, PhD *Wales*
Library (chief librarian). Librarian: Roberts, John K., MSc *Manc.*
Personnel/human resources. Deputy Director of Personnel: Williams, Eirwen G., BA *Wales*

Public relations, information and marketing.
Director of External Relations: Richardson,
Brian J., BA *Liv.*

Purchasing. Purchasing Manager: Coulbeck,
Norman B.

Quality assurance and accreditation. Director
of Registry: Burdon, Christopher F., BA *Lond.*

Research. Director of Research and
Consultancy: Jones, Geraint W., BSc *Wales*

Safety. Director of Safety Services: Mallows,
Bernard, MBE

Schools liaison. Student Recruitment Manager:
Owen, Dylan R., BA *CNAA*

Security. Security Manager: Lacey, William

Sport and recreation. Manager of Sports and
Recreation: Coveney, Jayne L., BA *CNAA*,
MSc *Lough.*

Staff development and training. Personnel
Development Manager: Midha, Susan M., BA
Wales

Student welfare/counselling. Dean of
Students: Owens, David J., BScEcon *Wales*,
MA *New Hampshire*, PhD *Wales*

Students from other countries. Head of
International Office: Westlake, Timothy J.,
MSc *Wales*, PhD *Wales*

Students with disabilities. Dean of Students:
Owens, David J., BScEcon *Wales*, MA *New
Hampshire*, PhD *Wales*

*[Information supplied by the institution as at 4 March
1998, and edited by the ACU]*

UNIVERSITY OF WALES SWANSEA
Prifysgol Cymru Abertawe

Founded 1920 as University College of Swansea

Associate Member of the Association of Commonwealth Universities

Postal Address: Singleton Park, Swansea, Wales SA2 8PP
Telephone: (01792) 205678 **Fax**: (01792) 295618 **E-mail**: registrar@swansea.ac.uk
Cables: Swansea University College **WWW**: http://www.swansea.ac.uk
E-mail formula: initial.surname@swansea.ac.uk

PRESIDENT—Prys-Davies, Lord, LLD *Wales*
CHAIRMAN OF THE COUNCIL—Davies, D. P. L., FCA
TREASURER—Walters, A. J., BA *Lond.*, FCA
VICE-CHANCELLOR*—Williams, Prof. Robin H., BSc *Wales*, PhD *Wales*, DSc *Wales*, FIP, FRS
PRO-VICE-CHANCELLOR—Griffiths, Prof. R. A. G., PhD *Brist.*, DLitt *Brist.*, FRHistS
PRO-VICE-CHANCELLOR—Herbert, Prof. David T., BA *Wales*, PhD *Birm.*, DLitt *Wales*
PRO-VICE-CHANCELLOR—Williams, Prof. R. W., MA *Oxf.*, DPhil *Oxf.*
PRO-VICE-CHANCELLOR—Wilshire, Prof. Brian, OBE, BSc *Wales*, PhD *Wales*, DSc *Wales*,
FEng, FIM
REGISTRAR‡—Townsend, Prof. Peter, BSc *Wales*, PhD *Wales*
LIBRARIAN—Green, Andrew M. W., MA *Camb.*

GENERAL INFORMATION

History. The university was established in
1920 as University College of Swansea, a
constituent college of the University of Wales.
It is located on the south coast of Wales.

Admission to first degree courses (see also
United Kingdom Introduction). Through
Universities and Colleges Admissions Service
(UCAS). General Certificate of Education (GCE)
or General Certificate of Secondary Education
(GSCE) pass in English language or Welsh
language and at least 2 passes at GCE A level
or 1 pass at A level and 2 at AS level.
Equivalent qualifications (such as International
or European Baccalaureate, Business and
Technology Education Council (BTEC) exams)
are acceptable.

First Degrees (of University of Wales) (see
also United Kingdom Directory to Subjects of
Study). BA, BEng, BSc, BScEcon, LLB, MEng,
MMath, MPhys.
    All courses are full-time and normally last 3
years. Meng, MMath, MPhys: 4 years.

Higher Degrees (of University of Wales)
(see also United Kingdom Directory to
Subjects of Study). MA, MEd, MBA, MSc,
MScEcon, MRes, MPhil, PhD, EngD.
    Applicants for admission to master's degree
courses should hold a first degree with at least
second class honours. International candidates
should also meet English language
requirements (eg IELTS score of 7.0 or TOEFL
score of 590).

Language of Instruction. English. Students
may sit exams in Welsh.

Libraries. Over 700,000 books and
periodicals. Special collection: South Wales
coalfields.

Fees (1997–98, annual). Undergraduate: UK/
EU students £750 (arts), £1600 (sciences);
international students £6100–8100.
Postgraduate: UK/EU students £2610;
international students £6280 (arts), £8340
(sciences and engineering).

Academic Year (1998–99). Three terms: 23
September–11 December; 11 January–9 March;
19 April–23 June.

Income (1997–98). Total, £74,163,000.

Statistics. Staff: 1000 (784 academic, 216
administrative). Students: full-time 8938
(4108 men, 4830 women); part-time 1520
(501 men, 1019 women); international 998
(523 men, 475 women).

FACULTIES/SCHOOLS

Arts and Social Studies
Dean: Eastwood, Prof. David S., MA *Oxf.*, DPhil
Oxf., FRHistS

Business, Economics and Law
Dean: Jacobs, Gabriel C., BA *Lond.*, PhD *Wales*

Education and Health Studies
Dean: Sanders, Susan, BA *Open(UK)*, MEd *Birm.*

Engineering
Dean: Morgan, Prof. Kenneth, PhD *Brist.*, DSc
Brist., FIMA, FICE

Graduate School
Dean: Meara, Paul M., BA *Camb.*, MSc *Sus.*,
DPhil *York(UK)*

Science
Dean: Rowley, Prof. Andrew F., BSc *Wales*, PhD
Wales, DSc *Wales*

ACADEMIC UNITS

American Studies
Fax: (01792) 295719

French, Warren G., BA *Penn.*, MA *Texas*, PhD
Texas   Hon. Prof.
Melling, P. H., BA *Manc.*, PhD *Manc.*   Sr. Lectr.
Roper, J. R., BA *Oxf.*, PhD *Kent*   Sr. Lectr.;
Head*
Other Staff: 3 Lectrs.; 2 Tutors
Research: Americanisation of culture; literature,
history and politics

Ancient History, see Classics and Anc. Hist.

Anthropology, see Sociol. and Anthropol.

Biological Sciences, School of
Tel: (01792) 295361 Fax: (01792) 295447
Ashby, J., BSc *Lond.*, PhD *Lond.*, FRCS   Hon.
Prof.
Bayne, B. L., BSc *Wales*, PhD *Wales*,
FIBiol   Hon. Prof.
Beardmore, J. A., BSc *Sheff.*, PhD *Sheff.*,
FIBiol   Prof.

Berry, M. S., MSc Birm., PhD Brist., BSc   Sr. Lectr.

Brain, P. F., BSc Hull, PhD Hull, FIBiol   Prof.; Head*

Dyson, P. J., BSc E.Anglia, PhD Glas.   Sr. Lectr.

England, P. J., PhD Brist., DSc Brist.   Hon. Prof.

Flynn, K. J., BSc Wales, PhD Wales   Sr. Lectr.

Gallon, J. R., MA Oxf., DPhil Oxf., DSc Oxf.   Prof.

Hayward, P. J., BSc Reading, PhD Wales, DSc Wales   Sr. Lectr.

Hipkin, C. R., BSc Wales, PhD Wales   Sr. Lectr.

James, B. L., PhD Wales, DSc Wales, FIP, FIBiol   Sr. Lectr.

Merrett, M. J., PhD Exe., DSc Brad., FIBiol   Prof. Fellow

Newton, R. P., BSc Liv., PhD Liv., FRSChem   Reader, Biochemistry

Parry, J. M., BSc Lond., PhD Liv., DSc Liv.   Prof.

Ratcliffe, N. A., PhD Wales, DSc Wales, FIBiol   Prof.

Rowley, Andrew F., BSc Wales, PhD Wales, DSc Wales   Prof., Immunology

Ryland, J. S., MA Camb., PhD DSc, FIBiol   Res. Prof.

Shackley, Susan E., BSc PhD   Sr. Lectr.

Skibinski, D. O. F., BSc Lond., PhD Camb., FIBiol   Prof., Evolutionary Biology

Smith, C. J., BSc PhD   Sr. Lectr.

Stirton, C., MSc Natal, PhD Cape Town, FLS

Walton, T. J., BSc Liv., PhD Liv.   Sr. Lectr.

Waters, R., BSc Wales, PhD Wales, DSc Wales   Prof.

Other Staff: 5 Lectrs.; 1 Res. Fellow; 1 Sr. Lectr.†; 1 Hon. Sr. Res. Fellow; 4 Hon. Lectrs.

Research: biochemistry; biomedical and physiological research; genetics; marine and environmental biology; molecular biology

Business Management, see European Bus. Management, Sch. of

Chemistry

Tel: (01792) 295506 Fax: (01792) 295747

Bentley, T. W., BSc Lond., PhD Liv., DSc Wales   Reader

Betteridge, D., PhD Birm., DSc Birm., FRSChem   Hon. Prof.

Cadogan, Sir John, CBE, PhD Lond., FRSChem, FRS   Hon. Prof. Fellow

Davies, J. S., BSc PhD, FRSChem   Sr. Lectr.

Evans, David, MSc Manc., PhD Manc.   Hon. Prof.

Games, D. E., BSc Lond., PhD Lond., DSc Wales, FRSChem   Prof.; Head*

Mason, R. S., BSc Birm., PhD Birm.   Sr. Lectr.

Mills, A., BSc Lond., PhD Lond.   Prof.

Morley, J. O., PhD Manc., DSc Manc., FRSChem   Prof.

Parry, D. E., MA Oxf., DPhil Oxf.   Sr. Lectr.

Pelter, A., PhD Brist., DSc Brist., FRSChem   Prof., Organic Chemistry

Smith, K., MSc Manc., PhD Manc., FRSChem   Prof.

Ward, R. S., MA Camb., PhD Camb., FRSChem   Reader

Williams, G., PhD DSc, FRSChem   Res. Prof.

Other Staff: 4 Lectrs.; 2 Sr. Lectrs.†; 1 Hon. Reader; 2 Hon. Lectrs.

Research: chromatographic analysis; gas phase ion chemistry; heterocyclic chemistry; natural products; synthetic reactions and reagents

Mass Spectrometry Research Unit

Tel: (01792) 295297 Fax: (01792) 295717

Brenton, A. G., BSc PhD   Prof.

Games, Prof. D. E., BSc Lond., PhD Lond., DSc Wales, FRSChem   Dir.*

Harris, F. M., PhD DSc, FIP   Prof.

Research: combined chromatography -MS; instrumentation and analytical techniques

Classics and Ancient History

Tel: (01792) 295187 Fax: (01792) 295739

Booth, Joan, BA Lond., PhD Lond.   Sr. Lectr.

Davies, C., MPhil Oxf., DLitt Wales, BA   Sr. Lectr.

Gill, D. W. J., BA Newcastle(UK), DPhil Oxf.   Sr. Lectr.

Lloyd, A. B., BA Wales, MA Oxf., DPhil Oxf., FSA   Prof.; Head*

Mitchell, S., BA Oxf., DPhil Oxf., FSA   Prof.

Morgan, J. R., BA Oxf., DPhil Oxf.   Sr. Lectr.

Other Staff: 3 Lectrs.; 1 Hon. Res. Fellow

Research: ancient novel; Egyptology; Greek, Roman history; historiography

Computer Science

Tel: (01792) 295393 Fax: (01792) 295708

Bergstra, Jan   Hon. Prof.

Grant, P. W., BSc Manc., DPhil Oxf.   Sr. Lectr.

Tucker, J. V., BA Warw., MSc Brist., PhD Brist.   Prof.; Head*

Webster, M. F., MSc Manc., PhD Wales   Reader

Other Staff: 8 Lectrs.; 1 Hon. Res. Fellow

Research: algorithims for non-Newtonian fluid mechanics; computer-aided engineering; computer graphics; fluid mechanics; theory of computation

Development Studies, Centre for

Tel: (01792) 295333 Fax: (01792) 295682

Booth, David K., BA Essex, PhD Sur.   Prof.

Rew, Alan W., MA(Econ) Manc., PhD ANU   Prof.; Dir.*

Saha, S. K., MA Patna, PhD   Sr. Lectr.

Other Staff: 16 Lectrs.; 2 Res. Fellows; 4 Lectrs.†; 1 Hon. Res. Fellow

Research: economic migration; famine; health planning and development; regional development policy and planning

Economics

Tel: (01792) 295168 Fax: (01792) 295872

Bennett, J. S., MA Sus., DPhil Sus.   Prof.

Blackaby, D. H., MA Manc., BA   Reader

Choudry, T., BS Iowa, MA Clemson, PhD Clemson

George, K. D., MA Wales, MA Camb.   Prof.

Hopkin, Sir Brian   Hon. Prof. Fellow

Mainwaring, Lynn, BSc Wales, MA(Econ) Manc., PhD Manc.   Prof.; Head*

Manning, D. N., MScEcon   Sr. Lectr.

Murphy, P. D., BSc(Econ) Hull, MA Sheff.   Reader

Speight, Alan E. H., BA Essex, MSc Lond., PhD Lond.   Sr. Lectr.

Other Staff: 8 Lectrs.; 1 Hon. Res. Fellow

Research: industrial organisation; labour economics; macro-economic theory and policy

Education

Fax: (01792) 290219

Carroll, H. C. M., BSc Brist., PhD Wales, FBPsS   Sr. Lectr.

Jenkins, S., BSc CNAA, DPhil Oxf.   Sr. Lectr.

Lowe, Roy A., MA Keele, PhD Birm.   Prof.; Head*

Parkinson, J., BSc Exe., PhD Exe.

Other Staff: 13 Lectrs.; 1 Sr. Lectr.†; 18 Tutors†; 2 Hon. Res. Fellows

Research: history and policy studies; mathematical education

Engineering, Chemical

Tel: (01792) 295196 Fax: (01792) 295701

Atkinson, B., BSc Birm., PhD Manc.   Hon. Prof.

Bowen, J. H., TD, MA Camb., PhD Lond., FRSChem, FIMechE, FIChemE   Sr. Lectr.

Bowen, W. R., MA Oxf., DPhil Oxf.   Prof.

Conder, J. R., MA Camb., PhD Camb., FRSChem   Reader

Padley, Peter J., BSc Lond., PhD Camb., ScD Camb., FRSChem   Reader

Pittman, J. F. T., BSc Wales, PhD Lond., FIChemE, FIMA, FIM   Reader

Preece, P. E., BSc Aston, PhD Aston, FIChemE   Prof.; Head*

Wardle, A. P., BSc PhD   Sr. Lectr.

Other Staff: 5 Lectrs.; 1 EPSRC Advanced Fellow; 2 Hon. Lectrs.

Research: biochemical engineering; colloids and interfaces; computer-aided process engineering

Engineering, Civil

Tel: (01792) 295866 Fax: (01792) 295676

Bonet, J., PhD Wales   Sr. Lectr.

Clarkson, Brian L., PhD Leeds, Hon. DSc Leeds, Hon. DSc S'ton., Hon. DSc Sci.U.Malaysia, FRAeS, FEng   Res. Prof.

Hinton, E., PhD Wales, DSc Wales   Prof.

Lee, M.-K., BSc Birm., PhD Birm.   Sr. Lectr.

Luxmoore, A. R., MSc Leeds   Sr. Lectr.

Middleton, J., MSc Wales   Reader

Morgan, Kenneth, PhD Brist., DSc Brist., FIMA, FICE   Prof.

Murphy, John A., BSc Sheff., PhD Sheff., FIMA   Hon. Prof.

Owen, D. R. J., PhD Northwestern, DSc Wales, FICE   Prof.

Pande, G. N., BTech Kharagpur, PhD Wales   Prof.

Peric, Djordje, PhD Wales   Reader

Weatherill, N. P., BSc S'ton., PhD S'ton., FIMA   Prof.; Head*

Wood, R. D., MSc PhD   Sr. Lectr.

Other Staff: 4 Lectrs.; 2 Hon. Res. Fellows

Research: finite element analysis; numerical methods; structural mechanics

Engineering, Electrical and Electronic

Tel: (01792) 295587 Fax: (01792) 295686

Barker, H. A., TD, BSc Nott., PhD Camb., FIEE   Prof.

Board, K., PhD Wales, DSc Wales   Prof.; Head*

Coles, G. S. V., BSc Wales, PhD Wales   Sr. Lectr.

Halsall, F., MSc Manc., DPhil Sus., FIEE   Newbridge Prof.

Mason, J. S. D., BSc CNAA, MSc Sur., PhD Sur.   Sr. Lectr.

Mawby, P. A., BSc Leeds, PhD Leeds   Sr. Lectr.

McCowen, A., BSc Lond., PhD Leeds   Sr. Lectr.

Rodd, M. G., MSc(Eng) Cape Town, PhD Cape Town, FIEE   Prof.

Watson, J., BSc Nott., PhD Nott., SM M.I.T., FIEE   Reader

Other Staff: 10 Lectrs.; 1 Reader†; 3 Hon. Lectrs.

Research: communications; real-time artificial intelligence; speech and image processing

Engineering, Materials

Tel: (01792) 295699 Fax: (01792) 295244

Alberry, Peter J., BSc Sheff., PhD Sheff., FIM   Hon. Prof.

Brown, S. G. R., BSc Wales, PhD Wales   Sr. Lectr.

Elliot, D., BSc Sheff., PhD Sheff.   Hon. Prof.

Evans, R. W., BSc Wales, PhD Wales   Prof.

Evans, W. J., BSc PhD   Prof.

Hurst, Roger C., MSc Manc., PhD Manc.   Hon. Prof.

Isaac, D. H., BSc Brist., PhD Brist.   Reader

Jack, Kenneth H., MSc Durh., PhD Camb., ScD Camb., FRSChem, FRS   Hon. Prof.

King, Julia E., MA Camb., PhD Camb., FIM   Hon. Prof.

Marshall, J. M., BSc Sheff., PhD Edin., FIP   Prof.

Parker, J. D., BSc Wales, PhD Wales   Prof.

Randle, Valerie, BSc Wales, PhD Wales   Reader

Spittle, J. A., BSc Birm., PhD Birm.   Reader

Wilshire, B., OBE, DSc PhD, FEng, FIM   Prof.; Head*

Other Staff: 6 Lectrs.; 3 Hon. Lectrs.

Research: materials for high-performance applications; polymers and composites; steel products

Engineering, Mechanical

Tel: (01792) 295534 Fax: (01792) 295676

Gethin, D. T., BSc Wales, PhD Wales   Reader

Griffiths, R. T., BSc Brist., MSc Wales   Sr. Lectr.

Hardy, S. J., BSc CNAA, PhD Nott.   Sr. Lectr.

Jones, M. H., BSc   Sr. Lectr.

Jost, P., CBE, DSc Manc., FIMechE   Hon. Prof.

Lees, Arthur W., BSc Manc., PhD Manc.   Hon. Prof.

Lewis, R. W., PhD *Wales*, DSc *Wales*,
FICE Prof.; Head*
Morris, W. D., BSc *Lond.*, PhD *Wales*, DSc(Eng)
Lond., FIMechE, FIEE Prof.
Roylance, B. J., BSc *Wales*, PhD *Wales* Sr.
Lectr.
Other Staff: 1 EPSRC Advanced Fellow; 1 Sr.
Lectr.†
Research: condition monitoring; manufacturing
processes; printing and coating

English Language and Literature

Tel: (01792) 295926 Fax: (01792) 295761

Bell, Ian A., MA *Glas.*, DPhil *Oxf.* Prof.; Head*
Davies, J. A., BA PhD Sr. Lectr.
Hardy, Barbara, MA *Lond.* Hon. Prof.
Pursglove, G., BA *Oxf.*, BLitt *Oxf.* Sr. Lectr.
Stephens, J. R., BA *Wales*, PhD *Wales* Sr. Lectr.
Thomas, M. W. T., BA, FBA Prof.
Turner, J. F., BA *Camb.*, PhD *Camb.* Sr. Lectr.
Other Staff: 8 Lectrs.; 1 Hon. Lectr.; 1 Hon.
Res. Fellow
Research: linguistics and sociolinguistics; Scottish
and Irish literature; Welsh writing in English

European Business Management, School of

Tel: (01792) 295601 Fax: (01792) 295626

Betteridge, David, BSc *Birm.*, PhD *Birm.*, DSc
Birm., FRSChem Hon. Prof.
Bischoff, E., MSc PhD Sr. Lectr.
Bissell, A. F., PhD *Bath* Hon. Prof.
Dowsland, Kathryn, MSc PhD Sr. Lectr.
Dowsland, W. B., BSc PhD Sr. Lectr.
Gravenor, R. B., MSc PhD Res. Prof.
Hawkes, A. G., BSc *Lond.*, PhD *Lond.* Prof.;
Head*
Jacobs, Gabriel C., BA *Lond.*, PhD *Wales* Sr.
Lectr.
Sykes, A. M., BSc *Sus.*, DPhil *Sus.* Sr. Lectr.
Witt, S. F., MA *Warw.*, MSc *Leeds*, PhD
Brad. Lewis Prof., Tourism Studies
Other Staff: 19 Lectrs; 1 Hon. Res. Fellow
Research: discrete optimisation; forecasting and
planning; statistical computing; tourism

French

Tel: (01792) 205968 Fax: (01792) 295710

Cardy, M. J., BA *Oxf.*, BLitt *Oxf.* Prof.
Connon, D. F., BA *Liv.*, PhD *Liv.* Sr. Lectr.;
Head*
Other Staff: 9 Lectrs.; 2 Tutors; 1 Sr. Lectr.†
Research: French politics and literature;
seventeenth- and eighteenth-century drama

Geography

Tel: (01792) 295228 Fax: (01792) 205955

Barnsley, Michael J., BA *Reading*, PhD
Reading Prof.
Herbert, D. T., PhD *Birm.*, BA DLitt Prof.;
Head*
Matthews, John A., BSc *Lond.*, PhD *Lond.* Prof.
McCarroll, D., BA *Sheff.*, PhD *Wales*
Perry, A. H., BA *S'ton.*, PhD *S'ton.* Sr. Lectr.
Robinson, V., MA *Oxf.*, DPhil *Oxf.* Reader
Shakesby, R. A., BA *CNAA*, PhD *Birm.* Sr.
Lectr.
Street-Perrott, F. Alayne, MA *Colorado*, MA *Oxf.*,
MA *Camb.*, PhD *Camb.* Prof.
Walsh, R. P. D., BA *Camb.*, PhD *Camb.* Reader
Other Staff: 9 Lectrs.; 1 Sr. Lectr.†; 2 Hon.
Res. Fellows
Research: environmental change; geographical
information systems; migration; retail
geography

German

Tel: (01792) 295170 Fax: (01792) 295710

Riordan, C., BA *Manc.*, PhD *Manc.* Sr. Lectr.
Williams, R. W., MA *Oxf.*, DPhil *Oxf.* Prof.;
Head*
Other Staff: 8 Lectrs.
Research: nineteenth- and twentieth-century
literature

Government, see Pol. Theory and Govt.

Health Care Studies, Institute of, see also

Philos. and Health Care, Centre for the Study
of

Tel: (01792) 295498 Fax: (01792) 295643

McGann, O., BScEcon *Wales*, MBA *Wales* Dir.*
Other Staff: 5 Lectrs.; 2 Hon. Sr. Lectrs.; 1
Hon. Lectr.; 1 Hon. Res. Fellow
Research: epidemiology; health care planning

Health Science, School of, see also Philos.

and Health Care, Centre for the Study of

Fax: (01792) 295487

Clark, Prof. Dame June, DBE, BA *Lond.*, MPhil
Reading, PhD *CNAA* Prof.
Coleman, M. R. Programme Manager
Earles, H. Carwen M. Programme Manager
Green, Barbara F., BA *Open(UK)*, MA
Warw. Dir.*
Hastings, Faye E., MScEcon Nursing Res.
Manager
Hughes, D. J., BA *Kent*, MA *Essex*, PhD Reader
Jenkins, D. W., MN Learning Resource/
Quality Assurance Manager
Jenkins, E. R., BEd *Wales*, MA
Wales Programme Manager
Jones, S. P., BA *Open(UK)* Information
Technol. and Comm. Manager
Lloyd, Valerie, MEd Programme Manager
Mort, Diane Academic Support Manager
Pearson, Nerys A., BN Contracts Manager
Phillips, C., MSc *Wales*, PhD *Wales* Sr. Lectr.
Pointon, D. J. Human Resources Manager
Rafferty, M. A., MN Clin. Devel. Manager
Torrance, C., BSc *Lond.*, PhD *Edin.* Sr. Lectr.
Wainwright, P. J., MSc *Manc.* Sr. Lectr.
White, Jean C., BN *Wales* Sr. Lectr.
Williams, B., BEd Programme Manager
Other Staff: 57 Lectrs.; 1 Lectr.†; 6 Hon.
Lectrs.
Research: health economics; primary health
education in the community; social policy
and nursing

Hispanic Studies

Fax: (01792) 295710

Gagen, D. H., BA *Manc.* Prof.; Head*
George, D. J., BA PhD Sr. Lectr.
Hall, J. B., TD, MA *Oxf.*, BPhil *Oxf.* Sr. Lectr.
Other Staff: 2 Lectrs.
Research: Latin-American literature; twentieth-
century drama

History, see also Classics and Anc. Hist.

Fax: (01792) 295746

Anglo, S., BA *Lond.*, PhD *Lond.*, FSA,
FRHistS Res. Prof.
Clark, D. S. T., PhD *Camb.*, BA, FRHistS Sr.
Lectr.
Eastwood, David S., MA *Oxf.*, DPhil *Oxf.*,
FRHistS Prof.; Head*
France, J., BA *Nott.*, PhD *Nott.*, FRHistS Sr.
Lectr.
Griffiths, R. A., BA *Brist.*, PhD *Brist.*, DLitt *Brist.*,
FRHistS Prof., Medieval History
Howell, D. W., PhD *Lond.*, MA Reader
Jackson, J. T., MA *Camb.*, PhD *Camb.* Reader
Latham, A. J. H., BA *Birm.*, PhD *Birm.* Sr.
Lectr.
Law, J. E., MA *St And.*, DPhil *Oxf.*, FRHistS Sr.
Lectr.
Morgan, Kenneth O., MA *Oxf.*, DPhil *Oxf.*, DLitt
Oxf., FRHistS, FBA Hon. Prof.
Morgan, P. T. J., BA *Oxf.*, DPhil *Oxf.*,
FRHistS Reader
Shannon, R. T., MA *NZ*, PhD *Camb.*,
FRHistS Prof., Modern History
Simpson, M. A., MA *Camb.*, MLitt *Glas.*,
FRHistS Reader
Spurr, J., BA *Oxf.*, DPhil *Oxf.*, FRHistS
Thompson, N. W., MA *St And.*, MSc *Belf.*, PhD
Camb. Reader
Waller, B., AB *Flor.*, PhD *Lond.* Sr. Lectr.
Other Staff: 5 Lectrs.; 1 Reader†; 1 Sr. Lectr.†;
4 Hon. Res. Fellows
Research: mediaeval history; modern British
history; modern economic and social history

Italian

Fax: (01792) 295710

Bedani, Gino L. C., BA *Wales*, PhD
Wales Prof.; Head*
Other Staff: 4 Lectrs.
Research: grammatical and lexical change;
modern fiction; post-war politics

Law

Tel: (01792) 295831 Fax: (01792) 295855

Davies, Iwan R., LLM *Wales*, LLM *Camb.*, PhD
Wales Reader
Kaye, Peter, LLM *Lond.*, PhD *Lond.* Prof.
Levin, Jennifer, LLB *Lond.*, LLM *Lond.* Prof.;
Head*
Townshend-Smith, R. J., BA *Oxf.* Sr. Lectr.
Other Staff: 6 Lectrs.; 2 Hon. Lectrs.
Research: European and commercial law; family
law; medical law

Management, see European Bus.

Management, Sch. of

Mathematics

Tel: (01792) 295457 Fax: (01792) 295843

Clarke, F. W., BSc *Birm.*, MSc *Warw.*, PhD
Warw. Sr. Lectr.
Davies, I. M., BSc *H-W*, PhD *H-W* Sr. Lectr.
Dorlas, T. C., PhD *Gron.* Reader
Elliott, George A., MSc *Qu.*, PhD *Tor.* Hon.
Prof.
Evans, D. E., BA *Oxf.*, MSc *Oxf.*, DPhil
Oxf. Prof.
Jones, J. R., MSc PhD Sr. Lectr.
Lewis, J. T., PhD *Belf.* Hon. Prof.
Thomas, D. K., BSc *Lond.*, PhD *Lond.*, PhD
Wales Sr. Lectr.
Truman, A., MA *Oxf.*, DPhil *Oxf.*, FRSEd Prof.;
Head*
Wood, G. V., MA *Camb.*, PhD *Newcastle(UK)* Sr.
Lectr.
Other Staff: 5 Lectrs.; 1 Reader†; 1 Hon.
Lectr.; 1 Hon. Res. Fellow
Research: mathematical computing; number
theory; operator algebras; quantum physics

Philosophy

Tel: (01792) 295190 Fax: (01792) 295893

Beardsmore, R. W., MA Sr. Lectr.
Osborne, Catherine J., BA *Camb.*, PhD
Camb. Sr. Lectr.
Phillips, D. Z., BLitt *Oxf.*, MA Rush Rhees
Res. Prof.
Williams, I. J. H., BA *Wales*, PhD *Stir.* Lectr.;
Head*
Other Staff: 5 Lectrs.; 1 Reader†; 1 Hon.
Lectr.; 1 Hon. Res. Fellow
Research: moral philosophy; philosophy of logic
and language; philosophy of religion

Philosophy and Health Care, Centre for the Study of

Tel: (01792) 295611 Fax: (01792) 295769

Evans, H. M., BA PhD Sr. Lectr.; Dir.*
Other Staff: 4 Lectrs.; 1 Teaching Fellow
Research: ethics of health care; ethical review of
clinical research; philosophy of medicine
and nursing

Physics

Tel: (01792) 295849 Fax: (01792) 295324

Davies, A. J., BSc PhD, FIEE, FIP Prof.; Head*
Evans, C. J., BSc PhD, FIP Sr. Lectr.
Halliday, Ian G., MA *Edin.*, MSc *Edin.*, PhD
Camb., FIP Prof.
Olive, David I., BA *Camb.*, MA *Edin.*, PhD *Camb.*,
FRS Res. Prof.
Shore, G. M., BSc *Edin.*, PhD *Camb.* Reader
Telle, H. H., MSc *Cologne*, PhD *Cologne* Res.
Prof.
Other Staff: 8 Lectrs.; 1 Hon. Sr. Res. Fellow;
2 Hon. Res. Fellows
Research: biomagnetism; laser physics;
theoretical particle physics

Political Theory and Government

Tel: (01792) 295303 Fax: (01792) 295716
Bideleux, R. J., MA Edin., MA Sus.   Sr. Lectr.
Boucher, D. E. G., MSc Lond., PhD Lond.,
  BA   Reader
Boyce, D. G., BA Belf., PhD Belf., FRHistS   Prof.
Dobson, A. P., BA Durh., MSc S'ton., PhD
  Durh.   Reader
Evans, G., MA   Sr. Lectr.
Haddock, B. A., BA Leic., DPhil Oxf.,
  FRHistS   Sr. Lectr.
Harding, G. N., MSc(Econ) Lond., MA   Prof.;
  Head*
Martin, Rex, BA Rice, MA Col., PhD Col.   Prof.
Pethybridge, R. W., MA Oxf., DèsScPol
  Geneva   Res. Prof.
Ponting, Clive, BA Reading   Sr. Lectr.
Taylor, R., MA Camb., PhD Lond.,
  FRHistS   Prof., Politics and Russian Studies
Vali, A., BA Teheran, MA Keele, PhD Lond.   Sr.
  Lectr.
Other Staff: 5 Lectrs.; 5 Hon. Res. Fellows
Research: history of political thought;
  international politics

Psychology

Tel: (01792) 295280 Fax: (01792) 295679
Benton, D., BSc Aston, PhD Birm.   Prof.
Clark, D. R., BSc CNAA, PhD Reading   Wellcome
  Trust Sr. Lectr.
Folkard, Simon, BSc Lond., PhD Lond., DSc
  Lond.   Prof.
Gruneberg, M. M., MA Edin., MSc Edin., PhD
  Edin.   Sr. Lectr.
Oborne, D. J., MSc PhD, FBPsS   Prof.
Sykes, R. N., BSc Lond.   Sr. Lectr.; Head*
Willner, P. J., MA Oxf., DPhil Oxf.   Prof.
Other Staff: 11 Lectrs.; 2 Hon. Lectrs.; 4 Hon.
  Res. Fellows
Research: biological psychology; body rhythms
  and shiftwork; substance abuse

Russian

Tel: (01792) 295170 Fax: (01792) 295710
Martin, D. W., MA Oxf., BLitt Oxf.   Lectr.;
  Head*
Woodward, J. B., MA Oxf., DPhil Oxf.   Res.
  Prof.
Other Staff: 1 Lectr.†
Research: language and history of Russia

Russian and East European Studies, Centre of

Fax: (01792) 295716
Bideleux, R. J., MA Edin., MA Sus.   Dir.,
  Russian Economic History
Harding, G. N., MSc(Econ) Lond., MA   Prof.,
  International Communism
Taylor, R., MA Camb., PhD Lond.,
  FRHistS   Prof., Politics and Russian Studies
Other Staff: 1 Sr. Lectr.†
Research: East-West relations; Soviet cinema;
  transition to democracy since 1989

Social Policy and Applied Social Studies

Tel: (01792) 295318 Fax: (01792) 295856
Colton, M. J., BA Keele, DPhil Oxf.   Reader
Jackson, Sonia, BA Camb.   Prof.; Head*
Raynor, P. C., MA Oxf., BPhil Exe., PhD   Prof.
Sullivan, M. J., MA Oxf., PhD   Reader
Other Staff: 10 Lectrs.; 1 Hon. Lectr.
Research: child welfare; criminal justice system;
  social policy formulation

Sociology and Anthropology

Fax: (01792) 295750
Byron, R. F., BA S.Calif., PhD Lond.   Prof.;
  Head*
Charles, Nicola, BA Keele, PhD Keele   Reader,
  Sociology
Harris, C. C., BA Oxf., PhD Wales   Prof.†
Startup, R., MA Oxf., PhD   Sr. Lectr.,
  Sociology
Other Staff: 11 Lectrs.; 1 Hon. Res. Fellow
Research: anthropology of the media; women
  escaping domestic violence; youth
  homelessness

Spanish, see Hispanic Studies

Tourism Studies, see European Bus.
  Management, Sch. of

Welsh
(Cymraeg)

Tel: (01792) 295193 Fax: (01792) 295710
Edwards, Hywel T., MA Wales   Res. Prof.
Ellis Evans, D., DPhil Oxf., MA, FBA   Hon.
  Prof.
Johnston, David R., BA Camb., PhD
  Wales   Prof.; Head*
Other Staff: 3 Lectrs.
Research: literature of the Welsh valleys; popular
  eighteenth- and nineteenth-century
  literature; sociolinguistics and dialectology

SPECIAL CENTRES, ETC

Adult Continuing Education
University Department

Tel: (01792) 295786 Fax: (01792) 295751
Francis, D. Hywel, BA Wales, PhD Wales   Prof.;
  Head*
Roderick, Gordon, BSc Wales, MA Liv., PhD
  Lond.   Res. Prof.
Smith, D. B., MA Oxf., PhD Wales   Hon. Prof.
Walters, P. J., BSc Durh., PhD Durh.   Sr. Lectr.
Williams, Michael, BSc(Econ) Lond., MA
  Reading   Res. Prof.
Other Staff: 8 Lectrs.
Research: community-based adult education;
  women and continuing education

Applied Language Studies, Centre for
Tel: (01792) 295391 Fax: (01792) 295641
Milton, J. M., BA Liv., PhD   Dir.*
Ryan, Ann M. G., MA StAnd., PhD Wales   Sr.
  Lectr.
Other Staff: 3 Lectrs.; 8 Tutors
Research: lexical acquisition in a foreign
  language

CONTACT OFFICERS

Academic affairs. Academic Registrar: Barnes,
  Robert V., BA Wales, MSc CNAA
Accommodation. Accommodation Officer:
  Barney, Helen, BA Wales
Admissions (first degree/higher degree).
  Admissions Officer: Lewis, M. P., BA Wales,
  PhD Wales
Adult/continuing education. Professor of
  Adult Continuing Education: Francis, Prof.
  D. Hywel, BA Wales, PhD Wales
Alumni. Alumni Officer: Bennett, Judith, BA
  Wales
Archives. Librarian: Green, Andrew M. W.,
  MA Camb.

Careers. Careers Director: Slater, Frank W., BSc
  Aberd., BA Open(UK)
Computing services. Librarian: Green, Andrew
  M. W., MA Camb.
Conferences/corporate hospitality.
  Conference Manager: Belcher, Peter
Credit transfer. Academic Registrar: Barnes,
  Robert V., BA Wales, MSc CNAA
Equal opportunities. Personnel Secretary:
  Ganz, Judith, BA Lond.
Estates and buildings/works and services.
  Director of Estates: Watkin, John, BA
  Open(UK)
Examinations. Academic Registrar: Barnes,
  Robert V., BA Wales, MSc CNAA
Finance. Director of Finance: Gough, Phillip R.
  C., BSc Brist.
General enquiries. Registrar: Townsend, Prof.
  Peter, BSc Wales, PhD Wales
Health services. Director of Occupational
  Health and Emergency Unit: Tudor-Jones,
  T., MB ChB Birm.
Industrial liaison. Business Services Manager:
  Griffiths, W. Eifion
International office. Dean of International
  Affairs: McGann, Orian, BScEcon Wales, MBA
  Wales
Language training for international students.
  Director, Centre for Applied Language
  Studies: Ryan, Ann M. G., MA StAnd., PhD
  Wales
Library (chief librarian). Librarian: Green,
  Andrew M. W., MA Camb.
Library (enquiries). Sub-Librarian (Public
  Services): Marsh, Sara, BA Camb., MA Sheff.
Minorities/disadvantaged groups. Guidance
  Worker: Pudner, Heather, MSc Wales
Personnel/human resources. Personnel
  Secretary: Ganz, Judith, BA Lond.
Public relations, information and marketing.
  Director of Planning and Marketing:
  Thomas, Roger, BA Wales, PhD Wales
Publications. Assistant Registrar: Bullingham,
  Joan, BA Sheff.
Purchasing. Purchasing Officer: Morgan, J. R.
Quality assurance and accreditation.
  Academic Registrar: Barnes, Robert V., BA
  Wales, MSc CNAA
Research. Pro-Vice-Chancellor: Wilshire, Prof.
  Brian, OBE, BSc Wales, PhD Wales, DSc Wales,
  FEng, FIM
Safety. Safety Officer: Jones, Ann
Scholarships, awards, loans. Academic
  Registrar: Barnes, Robert V., BA Wales, MSc
  CNAA
Schools liaison. Schools Liaison Officer: Clark,
  Barrie M., BScEcon Wales
Security. Director of Estates: Watkin, John, BA
  Open(UK)
Sport and recreation. Director of Physical
  Recreation: Addicott, W. Stanley, BA Wales,
  MEd Liv.
Staff development and training. Staff
  Development Officer: Sykes, Robert N., BSc
  Lond.
Student welfare/counselling. Senior Student
  Counsellor: Lowe, Ruth, MSc Wales
Students from other countries. Dean of
  International Affairs: McGann, Orian,
  BScEcon Wales, MBA Wales
Students Union. Union Manager: Tregoning,
  Nicholas

[Information supplied by the institution as at 31 March
1998, and edited by the ACU]

UNIVERSITY OF WALES, LAMPETER

Founded 1822 as Saint David's University College, Lampeter

Associate Member of the Association of Commonwealth Universities

Postal Address: Lampeter, Ceredigion, Wales SA48 7ED
Telephone: (01570) 422351 **Fax**: (01570) 423423 **E-mail**: tdr@admin.lamp.ac.uk **Telex**: (Library) 48475
WWW: http://www.lamp.ac.uk

VISITOR—St Davids, The Lord Bishop of (*ex officio*)
PRESIDENT—Sunderland, Prof. Eric, MA *Wales*, PhD *Lond.*, Hon. LLD *Wales*, FIBiol
VICE-CHANCELLOR*‡—Robbins, Prof. Keith G., BA *Oxf.*, MA *Oxf.*, DPhil *Oxf.*, DLitt *Glas.*, FRSEd, FRHistS
PRO VICE-CHANCELLOR—Davies, Prof. D. P., MA *Camb.*, BD *Oxf.*

GENERAL INFORMATION

History. The university was founded in 1822 as St David's College, and joined the University of Wales in 1971 as St David's University College. It gained its current name in 1996.

Admission to first degree courses (see also United Kingdom Introduction). Through Universities and Colleges Admissions Service (UCAS).

First Degrees (of University of Wales) (see also United Kingdom Directory to Subjects of Study). BA, BD, BTh.
    Degree courses last 3 or 4 years.

Higher Degrees (of University of Wales) (see also United Kingdom Directory to Subjects of Study). MA, MTh, MPhil, PhD.
    MA, MTh: 1 year full-time or 2 years part-time; MPhil, PhD: 2–3 years full-time or 3–5 years part-time.

Language of Instruction. English, except in department of Welsh, where Welsh is the main language. Students may write exams in Welsh.

Libraries. 215,000 volumes; 1000 periodicals.

Fees (1998–99, annual). International students £5000 (full-time undergraduate and postgraduate); £2000 (part-time postgraduate).

Academic Year (1998–99). Three terms: 2 October–18 December; 8 January–26 March; 16 April–11 June.

Income (1996–97). Total, £10,350,000.

Statistics. Staff: 250 (100 academic, 150 other). Students: full-time 1700; part-time 220; international 200; total 1920.

FACULTIES/SCHOOLS

Arts
Dean: Sutherland, E., BSc *Glas.*, MSc *Strath.*

Theology
Dean: Davies, Prof. D. P., MA *Camb.*, BD *Oxf.*
Secretary: Ablett, Marlene

ACADEMIC UNITS

Anthropology
Bowie, F., BA *Durh.*, DPhil *Oxf.*   Head*
Research: social and environmental archaeology

Archaeology
Fax: (01570) 423669
Austin, D., BA *S'ton.*, FSA   Prof.
Burnham, B. C., MA *Camb.*, PhD *Camb.*, FSA   Sr. Lectr.
Fleming, A., MA *Oxf.*, FSA   Reader
Shanks, M., BA *Camb.*, PhD *Camb.*   Reader; Head*
Research: archaeological theory; prehistoric, historic and mediaeval archaeology

Classics
Fax: (01570) 423877
Brothers, A. J., MA *Oxf.*, MPhil *Oxf.*   Sr. Lectr.
Eatough, G., MA *Lond.*   Sr. Lectr.
Wright, M. R., BLitt *Oxf.*, MA *Lond.*   Prof.; Head*
Research: ancient history; classical art and architecture; classical philosophy and mythology; Renaissance Latin of the Americas

English
Fax: (01570) 423634
Blamires, A. G., BA *Oxf.*, BPhil *Oxf.*   Sr. Lectr.
Dennis, Barbara L., BA *Lond.*, BLitt *Oxf.*   Sr. Lectr.
Humfrey, Belinda, BLitt *Oxf.*, MA *Oxf.*   Sr. Lectr.
Manning, J., MA *Syd.*, PhD *Edin.*   Prof.; Head*
Marx, C. W., MA *Tor.*, DPhil *York(UK)*   Sr. Lectr.
Williams, G. I., BA *Wales*, PhD *Wales*   Reader
Research: American literature; Australian literature; English literature from mediaeval period to twentieth century

French, see Hist.

Geography
Fax: (01570) 424714
Beaumont, P., MA *Durh.*, PhD *Durh.*   Prof.
Crowther, J., MA *Camb.*, PhD *Hull*   Sr. Lectr.
Walker, M. J. C., BA *Oxf.*, MSc *Calg.*, PhD *Edin.*   Prof.; Head*
Research: human and physical geography

History
Fax: (01570) 423885
Borsay, P. N., BA *Lanc.*, PhD *Lanc.*   Sr. Lectr.; Head*
Eldridge, C. C., BA *Nott.*, PhD *Nott.*, FRHistS   Reader
Peach, T., BA *Liv.*, PhD *Liv.*   Prof., French
Smith, M. S., BA *Lanc.*, PhD *Lanc.*   Sr. Lectr.
Research: history of seventeenth century; mediaeval history; nineteenth- and twentieth-century history, British and European

Information Systems, see Management and Information Systems

Management and Information Systems
Owen, L., BSc *Wales*, PhD *Wales*   Head*
Venus, J., BSc *Wales*, PhD *Wales*   Sr. Lectr.

Philosophy
Cockburn, D. A., MA *St And.*, DPhil *Oxf.*   Reader
Rockingham Gill, R. R., MA *St And.*   Lectr.; Head*

Theology and Religious Studies
Fax: (01570) 423641
Arthur, C., MA *Edin.*, PhD *Edin.*   Sr. Lectr.
Badham, P. B. L., MA *Oxf.*, MA *Camb.*, PhD *Birm.*   Prof.; Head*
Cohn-Sherbok, Rabbi D., MLitt *Camb.*, PhD *Camb.*   Prof.
Davies, D. P., MA *Camb.*, BD *Oxf.*   Prof.

Davies, O., BA *Oxf.*, DPhil *Oxf.*   Reader
Flood, G. D., MA *Lanc.*, PhD *Lanc.*   Sr. Lectr.
Francis, L., MA *Oxf.*, BD *Oxf.*, MSc *Lond.*, MTh *Nott.*, PhD *Camb.*, FBPsS   Prof.
Selwyn, Rev. D. G., MA *Camb.*, MA *Oxf.*   Reader
Yao, X., MA *Peking*, PhD *Peking*   Sr. Lectr.
Research: Islamic studies; major world religions; Old Testament and Jewish studies

Welsh
Fax: (01570) 423874
Thorne, D. A., BA *Wales*, MA *Wales*, PhD *Wales*   Reader; Head*
Research: modern Welsh literature; Welsh hymns; Welsh linguistics and dialectology

CONTACT OFFICERS

Academic affairs. Academic Registrar: Roderick, T. D., BA *Lond.*, PhD *Lond.*
Accommodation. Accommodation Officer: James, T.
Admissions (first degree). Recruitment Manager: ......
Admissions (higher degree). Assistant Registrar: Thornton, G. A., BA *Lond.*
Alumni. Administrative Assistant: Jones, C.
Archives. Archivist: Price, Rev. Canon D. T. W., MA *Oxf.*
Careers. Careers Officer: Owen, H. L., BSc *Wales*, PhD *Wales*
Computing services. Director of Academic Computing Service: Rogers, A. J., BSc *CNAA*
Computing services. Management and Administration Computing Officer: Thomas, J.
Credit transfer. Academic Registrar: Roderick, T. D., BA *Lond.*, PhD *Lond.*
Estates and buildings/works and services. Estates Manager: Rollason, A.
Examinations. Academic Registrar: Roderick, T. D., BA *Lond.*, PhD *Lond.*
Finance. Bursar: Jones, G. O., FCIS
International office. Recruitment Manager: ......
Library (chief librarian). Acting Librarian: Perrett, M. A., BA *Camb.*
Minorities/disadvantaged groups. Academic Registrar: Roderick, T. D., BA *Lond.*, PhD *Lond.*
Public relations, information and marketing. Recruitment Manager: ......
Publications. Recruitment Manager: ......
Purchasing. Bursar: Jones, G. O., FCIS
Quality assurance and accreditation. Academic Registrar: Roderick, T. D., BA *Lond.*, PhD *Lond.*
Research. Academic Registrar: Roderick, T. D., BA *Lond.*, PhD *Lond.*
Safety. Estates Manager: Rollason, A.
Scholarships, awards, loans. Academic Registrar: Roderick, T. D., BA *Lond.*, PhD *Lond.*
Schools liaison. Recruitment Manager: ......
Security. Estates Manager: Rollason, A.
Sport and recreation. Estates Manager: Rollason, A.
Student union. President of Students' Union: ......

Students from other countries. Academic Registrar: Roderick, T. D., BA Lond., PhD Lond.

Students with disabilities. Academic Registrar: Roderick, T. D., BA Lond., PhD Lond.

[Information supplied by the institution as at 19 March 1998, and edited by the ACU]

UNIVERSITY OF WALES COLLEGE OF MEDICINE

Incorporated by Royal Charter 1931 as Welsh National School of Medicine

Associate Member of the Association of Commonwealth Universities

Postal Address: Heath Park, Cardiff, Wales CF4 4XN
Telephone: (01222) 747747 **Fax**: (01222) 742914

PRESIDENT—Roberts Conwy, The Rt. Hon. the Lord, MA *Oxf.*
CHAIRMAN OF COUNCIL—Griffith, E. M., CBE
HONORARY TREASURER—Walshe, Grant
PROVOST AND VICE-CHANCELLOR*—Cameron, Prof. Ian R., BA *Oxf.*, MA *Oxf.*, BM BCh *Oxf.*, DM *Oxf.*, FRCP
VICE-PROVOST AND DEAN OF DENTAL SCHOOL—Whitehouse, Prof. Norman H., BChD *Leeds*
REGISTRAR—Rees, Leslie F. J., BA *Wales*
SECRETARY—Turner, Christopher B., BA *Wales*, PhD *Wales*
DIRECTOR OF INFORMATION SERVICES—Lancaster, John M., MPhil *Salf.*

GENERAL INFORMATION

History. The college was originally established in 1931 as the Welsh National School of Medicine and adopted its present name in 1984. The college was granted full college status within the university in 1988. It shares a 53-acre site with the University Hospital of Wales Healthcare NHS Trust at Heath Park, some 5km north of the centre of Cardiff.

Admission to first degree courses (see also United Kingdom Introduction). Through Universities and Colleges Admissions Service (UCAS). Acceptable qualifications include: 3 General Certificate of Education (GCE) A level subjects (subject and grade requirements vary for each course), International or European Baccalaureate Diplomas, or equivalent. A pass in English language (or Welsh) at GCE/General Certificate of Secondary Education (GCSE) level, or equivalent, is also required.

First Degrees (of University of Wales) (see also United Kingdom Directory to Subjects of Study). BDS, BN, BSc, MB BCh.
BSc: 3 years; BN: 4 years; BDS, MB BCh: 5 years or (if lacking appropriate science qualifications) 6 years.

Higher Degrees (of University of Wales) (see also United Kingdom Directory to Subjects of Study). MCh, MD, MPH, MSc, MScD, MPhil, PhD.
Applicants for admission to master's degree courses must normally hold an appropriate first degree or have relevant long-standing experience. MCh, MD: open only to medical graduates of this college; PhD: first degree with at least upper second class.
MCh, MD: 1 year; MPH, MSc, MPhil: 1 year full-time or 2 years part-time; PhD: 3 years full-time or 5 years part-time.

Libraries. 150,000 volumes; over 1350 journals subscribed to.

Academic Year (1998–99). Two semesters: 21 September–17 January; 18 January–28 May.

Statistics. Staff: 1376 (797 academic, 579 non-teaching). Students: full-time 2098; part-time 593; international 136; total 2727.

FACULTIES/SCHOOLS

Dental School
Tel: (01222) 742470 Fax: (01222) 766343
Dean: Whitehouse, Prof. Norman H., BChD *Leeds*
Secretary: Graham, Susan

Healthcare Studies
Tel: (01222) 744185 Fax: (01222) 747763
Dean: Palastanga, Nigel P., BA *Open(UK)*, MA *Lond.*
Secretary: Price, Irene

Medicine
Tel: (01222) 742020 Fax: (01222) 743199
Dean: Roberts, Prof. Geraint M., CBE, MD *Lond.*, FRCP, FRCR, FRACR
Secretary: Short, Amber

Nursing Studies
Tel: (01222) 744160 Fax: (01222) 744160
Dean: Davis, Prof. Bryn D., BSc *Lond.*, PhD *Lond.*
Secretary: Moss, Ross

Postgraduate Studies
Tel: (01222) 743927 Fax: (01222) 754966
Dean and Director: Hayes, Prof. Tom M., MB ChB *Liv.*, FRCP
Secretary: Phillips, Suzanne

ACADEMIC UNITS

For subjects of first 3 years—Anatomy, etc.—see under University of Wales, Cardiff

Adult Dental Health
Tel: (01222) 744356 Fax: (01222) 743120
Dummer, P. M. H., BDS *Wales*, MScD *Wales*, PhD *Wales* Prof.
Edmunds, D. H., BDS *Brist.*, PhD *Wales*, FDSRCS Sr. Lectr.
Gilmour, A. S. M., BDS PhD, FDSRCSEd Sr. Lectr.
Glantz, P. O. J., DrOdont *Lund*, Hon. FDSRCSEd Hon. Prof.
Jacobsen, P. H., BDS *Lond.*, MDS *Lond.*, FDSRCS Reader
Jagger, R. G., BDS *Wales*, MScD *Wales*, FDSRCSEd Sr. Lectr.
Murphy, W. M., BDS *N.U.I.*, MDS *Newcastle(UK)*, FDSRCS Sr. Lectr.

Rees, J. S., BDS *Wales*, MScD *Wales*, PhD *Wales*, FDSRCSEd Sr. Lectr.
Wilton, J. M. A., BDS *Lond.*, PhD *Lond.*, FRCPath Prof.; Head*
Other Staff: 4 Lectrs.; 9 Lectrs.†

Anaesthetics and Intensive Care Medicine
Tel: (01222) 743110 Fax: (01222) 747203
Harmer, M., MB BS *Lond.*, FRCA Prof.; Head*
Jenkins, B. J., MB BS *Lond.*, FRCA Sr. Lectr.
Mecklenburgh, J. S., MSc *Lond.*, PhD *Wales* Sr. Lectr.
Other Staff: 1 Lectr.
Research: anaesthetic equipment; inhaled volatile anaesthetics; perioperative pain management

Basic Dental Science
Tel: (01222) 742544 Fax: (01222) 744509
Embery, G., BSc PhD Prof.; Head*
Whittaker, D. K., BDS *Manc.*, PhD *Wales*, FDSRCS Reader
Williams, K. R., BSc PhD Reader
Other Staff: 2 Lectrs.

Cancer Research Centre, see Special Centres, etc (Tenovus Cancer Res. Centre)

Cardiology
Tel: (01222) 744430 Fax: (01222) 761442
Cockcroft, J. R., BSc *Leic.*, MB ChB *Leic.*, FRCP Sr. Lectr.
Fraser, A. G., BSc *Edin.*, MB ChB *Edin.* Sr. Lectr.
Frenneaux, Michael P., MB BS *Lond.*, MD *Lond.*, FRACP Sir Thomas Lewis Prof.; Head*
Shah, A. M., MB BCh Sr. Lectr.; MRC Sr. Clin. Fellow
West, Robert R., MA *Oxf.*, PhD *Leeds* Reader
Other Staff: 3 Lectrs.
Research: cardiological aspects of Morfan's syndrome; post-operative intensive care after congenital heart disease surgery

Child Health
Tel: (01222) 743374 Fax: (01222) 744283
Cartlidge, P. H. T., MB ChB *Sheff.*, DM *Nott.*, FRCP Sr. Lectr.
Davies, D. P., BSc *Wales*, MD, FRCP Prof.; Head*
Gregory, J. W., MD *Dund.* Sr. Lectr.

Payne, Elizabeth H., MB BS Lond.   Sr. Lectr.
Sibert, J. R., MA Camb., MB BChir Camb., MD Camb., FRCP   Prof.
Verrier Jones, Kate, MB BCh Wales, FRCP   Sr. Lectr.
Other Staff: 3 Lectrs.; 2 Sr. Lectrs.†; 1 Hon. Teacher
Research: community and population (making the environment safer for children)

Dental Health and Development

Tel: (01222) 742447 Fax: (01222) 742447
Chadwick, Barbara L., BDS Lond., MScD Wales
Hunter, B., BDS Edin.   Sr. Lectr.
Jones, M. L., BDS Wales, MSc Lond., PhD Wales, FDSRCS   Prof.; Head*
Oliver, R. G., BDS Wales, MScD Wales, PhD Wales, FDSRCSEd   Sr. Lectr.
Richmond, S., BDS Sheff., MScD Wales, PhD Manc., FDSRCS   Prof.
Treasure, Elizabeth T., BDS Birm., PhD Birm., FRACDS   Sr. Lectr.
Whitehouse, Norman H., BChD Leeds   Prof.
Other Staff: 3 Lectrs.; 3 Lectrs.†

Dermatology

Tel: (01222) 742885 Fax: (01222) 762314
Marks, R., BSc Lond., MB BS Lond., FRCP, FRCPath   Prof.; Head*
Other Staff: 2 Lectrs.; 1 Sr. Lectr.†; 3 Lectrs.†
Research: photocarcinogenesis and skin bioengineering; screening for keratin gene defects

Emergency Medicine

Tel: (01222) 492233
1 Hon. Clin. Teacher

Epidemiology and Public Health

Tel: (01222) 742321 Fax: (01222) 742898
Matthews, I. P., BSc Liv., MSc Sur., PhD Sur.   Reader
Vetter, N. J., MB ChB Edin., MD Edin.   Reader
Other Staff: 1 Sr. Lectr.†
Research: national survey of purchasing practice; resource and capacity analysis of clinical services provided by trusts and clinical directorates in England and Wales

Forensic Medicine

Tel: (01222) 484358 Fax: (01222) 484358
James, D. S., MB ChB Sheff.
Leadbeatter, S., MB ChB Brist.   Sr. Lectr.
Vacant Posts: 1 Prof.

General Practice

Tel: (01222) 541133 Fax: (01222) 540129
Finlay, Ilora G., MB BS Lond., FRCGP   Hon. Prof.
Kinnersley, P., MB ChB Brist.   Sr. Lectr.
Pill, Roisin, MA Camb., MScEcon Wales, PhD Wales   Prof.
Stott, N. C. H., BSc Edin., MB ChB Edin., FRCPEd, FRCGP   Prof.; Head*
Other Staff: 1 Sr. Lectr.†
Research: clinical guidelines to breast disorders; patient-centred and negotiated self-management plans in asthma; smoking cessation; substitution of nurse practitioners for disorders in primary care; upper respiratory infection interventions

Genito-Urinary Medicine

Tel: (01222) 492233 Fax: (01222) 487096
No staff at present

Geriatric Medicine

Tel: (01222) 716986 Fax: (01222) 711267
Hasan, M., MB BS Patna, MD Patna   Sr. Lectr.
Meara, R. J., MA Camb., MB BChir Camb., MD Camb.   Sr. Lectr.
O'Mahony, Sinead, BSc N.U.I., MB N.U.I.   Sr. Lectr.
Woodhouse, K. W., BM S'ton., MD Newcastle(UK), FRCP   Prof.; Head*
Other Staff: 1 Lectr.
Research: biomedical gerontology and biology of ageing

Haematology

Tel: (01222) 742375 Fax: (01222) 744655
Burnett, A. K., MD Glas., FRCPGlas, FRCPEd, FRCPath   Prof.; Head*
Cavill, I. A. J., BSc Wales, PhD Wales, FRCPath   Sr. Lectr.
Giddings, J. C., PhD CNAA   Sr. Lectr.
Lim, S. H., MB ChB Aberd., MD Aberd.   Sr. Lectr.
Mills, K. I., BSc S'ton., PhD S'ton.   Sr. Lectr., Molecular Haemato-Oncology
Padua, R. A., BSc Edin., PhD Edin.   Reader
Poynton, C. H., MA Oxf., BM BCh Oxf.   Sr. Lectr.
Wardrop, C. A. J., MB ChB St And., FRCPEd, FRCPath   Sr. Lectr.
Whittaker, J. A., MB ChB Liv., MD Liv., FRCP   Reader
Worwood, M., BSc Exe., PhD Lond.   Reader
Other Staff: 5 Lectrs.; 1 Leukaemia Res. Fund Fellow; 1 MRC Fellow
Research: molecular basis and treatment of disorders of coagulation; molecular and cellular biology of haemopoiesis and its disorders, particularly leukaemia and preleukaemia

Healthcare Studies, School of

Tel: (01222) 744185 Fax: (01222) 747763

Occupational Therapy

Tel: (01222) 742257 Fax: (01222) 747763
Booy, M. J., BA Open(UK), MA Lanc.   Sr. Lectr.
Other Staff: 9 Lectrs.

Operating Department Practice

Tel: (01222) 745067 Fax: (01222) 747763
Morgan, A., BSc Wales   Lectr.; Centre Manager*
Other Staff: 2 Lectrs.

Physiotherapy

Tel: (01222) 744185 Fax: (01222) 747763
Palastanga, Nigel P., BA Open(UK), MA Lond.   Sr. Lectr.
Other Staff: 13 Lectrs.

Radiography

Tel: (01222) 744605 Fax: (01222) 747763
Newton, J., MSc Wales, MEd Wales   Sr. Lectr.; Head*
West, M. K., MPhil   Sr. Lectr.
Other Staff: 13 Lectrs.

Media Resources Centre

Tel: (01222) 743306 Fax: (01222) 742120
Morton, R. A., MSc Aberd.   Prof.; Dir.*
Thompson, I., BA CNAA   Learning Resource Centre Manager
Other Staff: 1 Lectr.

Medical Biochemistry

Tel: (01222) 742799 Fax: (01222) 766276
Campbell, A. K., MA Camb., PhD Camb.   Prof.
Dormer, R. L., BSc Leeds, PhD Brist.   Sr. Lectr.
Elder, G. H., BA Camb., MB BChir Camb., MD Camb., FRCP, FRCPath   Prof.; Head*
Evans, M. H., PhD Lond., DSc Liv., FIBiol   Hon. Prof., Res. Council External Sci. Staff
McDowell, I. F. W., BA Oxf., MSc Oxf., BM BCh Oxf.   Sr. Lectr.
McPherson, M. A., BSc Brist., PhD Brist.   Sr. Lectr., Cystic Fibrosis
Morgan, B. P., BSc Wales, MB BCh Wales, PhD Wales   Prof.; Wellcome Trust Sr. Clin. Fellow
Woodhead, J. S., BSc Newcastle(UK), PhD Manc.   Reader
Other Staff: 1 Lectr.
Research: biochemical immunology; cell signalling and communication

Medical Computing and Statistics

Tel: (01222) 742311 Fax: (01222) 743664
Coles, E. C., MB BS Lond., MTech Brun.   Sr. Lectr.; Dir., Med. Computing; Head*

Lewis, P. A., BTech Lough., PhD Birm.   Sr. Lectr.
Newcombe, R. G., MA Camb., PhD Wales   Sr. Lectr.
Other Staff: 1 Lectr.; 5 Hon. Lectrs.

Medical Genetics

Tel: (01222) 74058 Fax: (01222) 747603
Clarke, A., MA Oxf., DM Oxf.   Reader
Cooper, D. N., BSc Edin., PhD Edin.   Prof., Human Molecular Genetics
Harper, P. S., CBE, BA Oxf., DM Oxf., FRCP   Prof.; Head*
Owen, M. J., BSc Birm., MB ChB Birm., PhD Birm.   Prof., Neuropsychiatric Genetics
Other Staff: 3 Lectrs.; 2 Hon. Sr. Lectrs.; 1 Hon. Lectr.
Research: thrombosis and vascular biology (causative mechanisms underlying gene mutation and their consequences)

Medical Microbiology and Public Health Laboratory

Tel: (01222) 742168 Fax: (01222) 744123
Barnes, Rosemary A., MA Camb., MB BS MD   Sr. Lectr.
Duerden, B. I., BSc Edin., MD Edin., FRCPath   Prof.; Head*
Jackson, S. K., BSc Wales, PhD Wales   Sr. Lectr.
Other Staff: 3 Lectrs.; 1 Hon. Lectr.
Research: microbial pathogenesis (bacterial, fungal and viral infections)

Medical Physics and Bioengineering

Tel: (01222) 742204 Fax: (01222) 742012
Woodcock, J. P., BSc Durh., MPhil Lond., PhD Lond., FIP   Prof.

Medicine

Tel: (01222) 742307 Fax: (01222) 744091
Borysiewicz, L. K., BSc Wales, MB BCh Wales, PhD Lond., FRCP   Prof.; Head*
Chawla, J. C., MB BS Brist., MD Brist., FRCS   Sr. Lectr.; Dir., Spinal and Neurol. Rehabilitation
Coles, G. A., MD Lond., FRCP   Hon. Prof.
Davies, M., BPharm Wales, PhD Wales   Reader, Nephrology
Freedman, A. R., MA Camb., MB BChir Camb., MD Camb.   Sr. Lectr., Infectious Diseases
Griffiths, T. L., BSc Wales, MB BCh Wales, PhD S'ton.   Sr. Lectr., Respiratory Medicine
Harvey, J. N., MB ChB Leeds, MD Leeds   Sr. Lectr., Diabetes, Endocrine Metabolism, Academic Sub-Dept. of Med., N. Wales
Labeta, M. O., PhD   Sr. Lectr.
Lazarus, J. H., MA Camb., MD Camb., MD Glas., FRCP   Sr. Lectr.
Mason, M., MB BS Lond., MD Lond., FRCR   Prof., Clinical Oncology
Mir, M. A., MB BS Vikram, FRCP   Sr. Lectr.
Rhodes, J., MD Manc., FRCP   Hon. Prof.
Rowe, M., BSc Lond., PhD Lond.   Prof., Cell Biology
Rutherford, BMedSci Newcastle(UK), MB ChB Newcastle(UK), PhD Newcastle(UK)   Sr. Lectr.
Scanlon, M. F., BSc Newcastle(UK), MB BS Newcastle(UK), MD Newcastle(UK), FRCP   Prof., Endocrinology
Shale, D. J., BSc Newcastle(UK), MB BS Newcastle(UK), MD Newcastle(UK), FRCP   Prof., Respiratory and Communicable Disease
Steadman, R., BSc Wales, PhD Wales   Sr. Lectr., Nephrology
Topley, N., BSc Wales, PhD Wales   Sr. Lectr., Nephrology
Wiles, C. M., BSc Lond., MB BS Lond., PhD Lond., FRCP   Prof., Neurology
Wilkinson, G. W. G., BSc Edin., MSc Warw., PhD Warw.   Sr. Lectr., Molecular Biology
Williams, B. D., MSc Birm., MB BCh Wales, FRCP, FRCPath   Prof., Rheumatology
Williams, J. D., BSc Wales, MB BCh Wales, MD Wales, FRCP   Prof.; Dir., Inst. of Nephrol.
Other Staff: 5 Lectrs.; 1 Royal Soc. Fellow; 2 Wellcome Trust Fellows; 1 Arthritis and Rheumatism Council Trg. Fellow; 2 Hon. Sr. Lectrs.; 3 Hon. Lectrs.

Research: infectious diseases; kidney research and renal disease

Neurology

Tel: (01222) 743660 Fax: (01222) 744166
No staff at present

Nursing Studies, School of

Tel: (01222) 744160 Fax: (01222) 744160
Burnard, P., MSc *Sur.*, PhD *Wales* Reader
Davis, Bryn D., BSc *Lond.*, PhD *Lond.* Prof., Nursing Education; Head*
Lloyd, Llynos M., LLM *Wales*, BEd Dir., Educn. Support; Dir., South East Wales Inst. of Nursing and Midwifery Educn.
Lyne, Patricia A., BSc *Leeds*, PhD *Leeds* Prof., Nursing Research; Dir., Nursing Res. Unit
Parsons, Evelyn, BSc *Lond.*, PhD *Wales* Sr. Lectr., Sociology and Social Policy
Other Staff: 104 Lectrs.

Obstetrics and Gynaecology

Tel: (01222) 743235 Fax: (01222) 743722
Pearson, J. F., MB BS *Lond.*, MD *Lond.*, FRCOG Reader
Shaw, R. W., MB ChB *Birm.*, MD *Birm.*, FRCSEd, FRCOG Prof.; Head*
Walker, Sheila M., MB ChB *Sheff.*, FRCOG Sr. Lectr.
Other Staff: 2 Lectrs.
Research: reproductive medicine and infertility

Occupational Therapy, see under
Healthcare Studies, Sch. of

Oncology

Tel: (01222) 615888 Fax: (01222) 522694
No staff at present

Ophthalmology

Tel: (01222) 743862 Fax: (01222) 743222
Morgan, J. E., BA MB BCh DPhil Sr. Lectr.

Oral Surgery, Medicine and Pathology

Tel: (01222) 744215 Fax: (01222) 742442
Absi, E. G., DDS *Damascus*, MSc *Wales*, MScD *Wales*, PhD *Wales* Sr. Lectr.
Lewis, M. A. O., BDS *Glas.*, PhD *Glas.*, FDSRCS Reader
Potts, A. J. C., BSc *Manc.*, BDS *Manc.* Sr. Lectr.
Shepherd, J. P., BDS *Lond.*, MSc *Oxf.*, PhD *Brist.*, FDSRCS, FDSRCSEd Prof.; Head*
Thomas, D. W., BDS *Wales*, MScD *Wales*, PhD *Brist.*, FDSRCSEd Sr. Lectr., Oral and Maxillofacial Surgery
Other Staff: 2 Lectrs.

Oto-Rhino-Laryngology

Tel: (01222) 743345
No staff at present

Pathology

Tel: (01222) 742700 Fax: (01222) 744276
Attanoos, R. L., MB BS *Lond.*, MSc *Lond.* Sr. Lectr., Histopathology
Douglas-Jones, A. G., MA *Camb.*, MB BChir *Camb.*, PhD, FRCPA Sr. Lectr.
Griffiths, D. F. R., BA *Camb.*, MB BCh Sr. Lectr.
Ismail, S. M., MB ChB *Brist.* Sr. Lectr.
Jasani, B., BSc *Glas.*, MB ChB *Birm.*, PhD *Birm.* Sr. Lectr.
Laidler, P., MA *Oxf.*, BM BCh *Oxf.*, DM *Oxf.* Sr. Lectr.
Lazda, E. J., MB BS *Lond.*, BA MA Sr. Lectr., Paediatric Pathology
Leadbeater, S., MB ChB *Brist.* Forensic Pathology
Neal, J. W., BSc *Brist.*, MB ChB *Brist.*, FRCS Sr. Lectr., Neuropathology
Newman, G. R., BSc *S'ton.*, PhD *S'ton.* Sr. Lectr.; Electron Microscopy Unit
Smith, P. J., BSc *Brist.*, PhD *Manc.* Prof., Cancer Biology
Vujanic, G. M., DM *Belgrade*, DS *Belgrade*, PhD *Belgrade* Sr. Lectr.

Williams, G. T., BSc MB BCh MD, FRCP, FRCPath Prof.
Wynford Thomas, D., MB BCh PhD Prof.; Head*
Other Staff: 1 Lectr.

Pharmacology, Therapeutics and Toxicology

Tel: (01222) 742052 Fax: (01222) 747484
Davies, J. A., BSc *Bath*, PhD *Bath* Sr. Lectr.
Lewis, M. J., MB BCh PhD Prof., Cardiovascular Pharmacology; Head*
Rees, Huw G., MB BCh *Wales* Sr. Lectr., Toxicology, Occupational and Environmental Medicine
Routledge, P. A., MB BS *Newcastle(UK)*, MD *Newcastle(UK)*, FRCP Prof., Clinical Pharmacology
Wilson, J. F., BSc *Leeds*, PhD *Wales* Sr. Lectr.
Other Staff: 2 Lectrs.; 1 Hon. Lectr.

Physical Medicine

Tel: (01222) 742626 Fax: (01222) 744388
No staff at present

Physiotherapy, see Healthcare Studies, Sch. of

Postgraduate Medical and Dental Education

Tel: (01222) 743977 Fax: (01222) 754966
Allery, Lynne A., BA *Warw.*, MA *Sheff.* Sr. Lectr., Medical Education
Hayes, Prof. Tom M., MB ChB *Liv.*, FRCP Dir.; Dean*
Jones, Elwyn G., BA *Wales*, MB BCh *Wales*
Nash, E. S., BDS *Wales*, MSc *Wales*, FDSRCS Dir., Postgrad. Dent. Educn.
Parry-Jones, G., MB ChB *Liv.*, FRCGP Sr. Lectr.; Assoc. Adviser in Gen. Practice for N. Wales
Other Staff: 3 Lectrs.; 1 Hon. Sr. Lectr.

Psychological Medicine

Tel: (01222) 743241 Fax: (01222) 747839
Buckland, P., BSc *Leeds*, PhD *Leeds* Sr. Lectr.
Deb, S., MB BS *Calc.*, MD *Leic.* Sr. Lectr., Learning Disabilities/Mental Handicap
Farmer, Anne E., MB ChB MD, FRCPsych Prof.
Felce, D., BSc *S'ton.*, MSc *Oxf.*, PhD *S'ton.* Prof.; Dir., Welsh Centre for Learning Disabilities Appl. Res. Unit
Fraser, W. I., MB ChB *Glas.*, MD *Glas.*, FRCPsych Prof., Mental Handicap
Harris, B. B., BSc *Lond.*, MB BS *Lond.*, FRCPsych Sr. Lectr.
Healy, D. T., MD *Trinity(Dub.)*, FRCPsych Reader; Dep. Dir., Academic Sub-Dept. of Psychol. Med., N. Wales
Kerr, M. P., MB ChB *Brist.* Sr. Lectr., Mental Handicap
Lewis, G. H., BA *Lond.*, MSc *Lond.*, MB BS *Lond.*, PhD *Lond.* Prof., Community and Epidemiology Psychiatry
MacCulloch, M. J., MB ChB *Manc.*, MD *Manc.*, FRCPsych Prof., Forensic Psychiatry
McGuffin, P., MB ChB *Leeds*, PhD *Lond.*, FRCP, FRCPsych Prof.; Head*
O'Donovan, M. C., BSc *Glas.*, MB ChB *Glas.*, PhD *Wales* Sr. Lectr.
Owen, M. J., BSc *Birm.*, MB ChB *Birm.*, PhD *Birm.* Prof., Neuropsychiatric Genetics
Thomas, P. F., MB ChB *Manc.*, MPhil *Edin.* Sr. Lectr.
Williams, Julie, BSc *Wales*, PhD *Wales* Sr. Lectr., Behavioural Sciences
Other Staff: 1 Lectr.; 1 Wellcome Trust Sr. Res. Fellow; 1 Hon. Lectr.
Research: genetics in Alzheimer's disease

Radiography, see under Healthcare Studies, Sch. of

Radiology, Diagnostic

Tel: (01222) 743070 Fax: (01222) 744726
Griffith, T. M., MB BCh *Wales*, MA *Camb.*, PhD *Wales*, FRCR Prof.
Roberts, Geraint M., CBE, MD *Lond.*, FRCP, FRCR, FRACR Prof.

Radiotherapy

Tel: (01222) 615888 Fax: (01222) 522694
No staff at present

Renal Medicine

Tel: (01222) 735213 Fax: (01222) 453643
Davies, M., BPharm *Wales*, PhD *Wales* Reader
Rutherford, P. A., BMedSci *Newcastle(UK)*, MB BS *Newcastle(UK)*, PhD *Newcastle(UK)* Sr. Lectr.
Williams, J. D., BSc *Wales*, MB BCh *Wales*, MD *Wales*, FRCP Prof.; Dir., Inst. of Nephrol.
Other Staff: 2 Lectrs.; 1 Hon. Lectr.

Respiratory Medicine

Tel: (01222) 711711 Fax: (01222) 708973
No staff at present

Rheumatology

Tel: (01222) 743184 Fax: (01222) 744388
No staff at present

Surgery

Tel: (01222) 742749 Fax: (01222) 741623
Carey, P. D., MB BCh BAO *Trinity(Dub.)*, MCh *Trinity(Dub.)*, FRCSI Sr. Lectr.
Hallett, M., BSc *Lond.*, PhD *Lond.* Sr. Lectr., Surgical Immunology
Mansel, R. E., MB BS *Lond.*, MS *Lond.*, FRCS Prof.; Head*
Mills, R. G. S., BA *Camb.*, MB BChir *Camb.*, FRCS Sr. Lectr., Otolaryngology
Peeling, W. B., MB BChir *Camb.*, MA *Camb.*, FRCS Hon. Prof.
Puntis, M. C. A., PhD *Camb.*, MB BCh, FRCS Sr. Lectr.
Sweetland, Helen M., MB ChB *Sheff.*, MD *Sheff.*, FRCS Sr. Lectr.
Webster, David J. T., MB ChB *Brist.*, MD *Brist.*, FRCS Sr. Lectr.
Wheeler, M. H., MB BCh *Wales*, MD *Wales*, FRCS Hon. Prof.
Other Staff: 1 Lectr.
Research: breast cancer

Cardiothoracic Surgery

No staff at present

Neurological Surgery

No staff at present

Paediatric Surgery

No staff at present

Traumatic and Orthopaedic Surgery

Tel: (01222) 492233 Fax: (01222) 494855
Dent, C., MB BS *Lond.*, FRCS Sr. Lectr.

Urological Surgery

Tel: (01222) 492233
No staff at present

Vascular Surgery

No staff at present

Wound Healing Research Unit

Tel: (01222) 743270 Fax: (01222) 745299
Bale, S. E., BA *Open(UK)* Dir., Nursing Res.
Harding, K. G., MB ChB *Birm.* Prof., Rehabilitation; Dir.*
Jones, Vanessa, MScEcon *Wales* Educn. Dir.
Moore, K., BSc *Manc.*, PhD *Manc.* Res. and Devel. Dir.
Other Staff: 2 Sr. Res. Officers

SPECIAL CENTRES, ETC

Applied Public Health Medicine, Centre for

Tel: (01222) 231021 Fax: (01222) 371104

Bainton, D., BA Camb., MB BChir Camb., MSc Lond.   Sr. Lectr.
Burr, M. L., MB BS Lond., MD Lond.   Sr. Lectr.
Chamberlain, D. A., CBE, MA Camb., MD Camb., Hon DSc, FRCP, FRCA   Hon. Prof.
Elwood, P. C., MD Belf., FRCP
Pickett, George, BA Harv., MD McG.   Sr. Lectr.
Robbe, I. J., BSc Lond., MB BS Lond., MSc   Sr. Lectr.
Other Staff: 3 Lectrs.; 1 Hon. Sr. Lectr.
Research: aspirin and cognitive function

Breast Screening in Wales, Development, Evaluation and Research Unit for

Tel: (01222) 787836 Fax: (01222) 787800

No staff at present
Vacant Posts: Dir.*

Diabetes Research Unit

Tel: (01222) 716069 Fax: (01222) 350147

Owens, D. R., MB BCh Wales, MD Wales, FIBiol   Sr. Lectr.

Health and Social Care, Wales Office of Research and Development for

Tel: (01222) 460015 Fax: (01222) 492046

Edwards, Richard H. T., BSc Lond., MB BS Lond., PhD Lond., FRCP   Prof.; Dir.*

Public Health, Welsh Combined Centres for

Tel: (01222) 521997 Fax: (01222) 521987

Palmer, S. R., MA Camb., MB BChir Camb.   Dir.*
Other Staff: 2 Lectrs.

Tenovus Cancer Research Centre

Tel: (01222) 742579 Fax: (01222) 747618

Griffiths, K., BSc Edin., PhD Edin., DSc   Tenovus Prof., Steroid Biochemistry
Nicholson, R. I., BSc Reading, PhD Wales   Reader

CONTACT OFFICERS

Academic affairs. Registrar: Rees, Leslie F. J., BA Wales
Accommodation. Warden and Accommodation Officer: Parsons, A. J., BA MEd
Admissions (first degree). Registrar: Rees, Leslie F. J., BA Wales
Admissions (higher degree). Secretary: Turner, Christopher B., BA Wales, PhD Wales
Adult/continuing education. Dean of Postgraduate Studies: Hayes, Prof. Tom M., MB ChB Liv., FRCP
Alumni. Registrar: Rees, L. F. J., BA
Archives. Senior Assistant Registrar: Sims, M. W. F., BScEcon
Careers. Secretary: Turner, Christopher B., BA Wales, PhD Wales
Computing services. Director of Computing: Coles, E. C., MB BS Lond., MTech Brun.
Consultancy services. Research Support Officer: Pittard Davies, Kathy J., BSc Wales, PhD Wales
Development/fund-raising. Director of Finance: Grant, Michael, BA Oxf., MA Oxf.
Distance education. Secretary: Turner, Christopher B., BA Wales, PhD Wales
Equal opportunities. Deputy Director of Personnel: Powley, Sharron, BA
Estates and buildings/works and services. Planning and Projects Officer: Duddridge, Stephen C., BSc Wales, BArch Wales
Estates and buildings/works and services. Estates Officer: Cawley, P. J.
Examinations. Senior Assistant Registrar: Sims, M. W. F., BScEcon
Examinations (Dental School). Assistant Registrar: Richards, D. H., BA Wales, MSt Oxf.
Finance. Director of Finance: Grant, Michael, BA Oxf., MA Oxf.

General enquiries. Secretary: Turner, Christopher B., BA Wales, PhD Wales
Health services. Occupational Health Service: Bell, D. C., MB BS
International office. International Officer: Davies, R. A., LLB Wales
Library (chief librarian). Director of Information Services: Lancaster, John M., MPhil Salf.
Minorities/disadvantaged groups. Deputy Director of Personnel: Powley, Sharron, BA
Personnel/human resources. Director of Personnel: Newman, Amanda E., BA Wales, MSc Brist.
Public relations, information and marketing. Deputy Director of Personnel: Powley, Sharron, BA
Publications. Secretary: Turner, Christopher B., BA Wales, PhD Wales
Purchasing. Purchasing Officer: Mackay, D. M.
Research. Secretary: Turner, Christopher B., BA Wales, PhD Wales
Safety. Health and Safety: Davies, R. Ll., MSc PhD
Scholarships, awards, loans. Assistant Registrar: ......
Schools liaison. Admissions Officer: Clarke, Pamela
Security. Security Officer: Vincent, M.
Sport and recreation. Recreation Organiser: Lang, N.
Staff development and training. Deputy Director of Personnel: Powley, Sharron, BA
Student union. Student President: Haynes, Mark
Student welfare/counselling. Student Counsellor: Green, A., BA MPhil
Student welfare/counselling. Elective Period Adviser/Student Counsellor: Mudge, M., MB ChB
Students with disabilities. Senior Assistant Registrar: Sims, M. W. F., BScEcon
University Press. Secretary: Turner, Christopher B., BA Wales, PhD Wales

[Information supplied by the institution as at 5 March 1998, and edited by the ACU]

UNIVERSITY OF WALES INSTITUTE, CARDIFF

Founded 1996; previously established as Cardiff Institute 1976

Associate Member of the Association of Commonwealth Universities

Postal Address: Central Administration, Llandaff Campus, Western Avenue, Cardiff, Wales CF5 2SG
Telephone: (01222) 506070 **Fax**: (01222) 506911 **E-mail**: uwicinfo@uwic.ac.uk **WWW**: http://www.uwic.ac.uk

PRINCIPAL AND CHIEF EXECUTIVE*—Chapman, Prof. Antony J., BSc Leic., PhD Leic.
DIRECTOR OF ACADEMIC AFFAIRS—Birchenough, Prof. Allan, BSc CNAA, PhD CNAA, FIMechE
DIRECTOR OF CORPORATE SERVICES—Martin, A. David, BA CNAA
DIRECTOR OF FINANCE—Warren, Martin J., BSc Hull, FCA
ACADEMIC REGISTRAR—Cockroft, Bea, BA CNAA
HEAD OF INFORMATION SERVICES—James, Mike, BSc

GENERAL INFORMATION

History. The institute was established in 1976 as a result of the merger of Cardiff College of Education, Llandaff Technical College, Cardiff College of Food and Technology and Cardiff College of Art.

Admission to first degree courses (see also United Kingdom Introduction). Through

Universities and Colleges Admissions Service (UCAS).

First Degrees (of University of Wales) (see also United Kingdom Directory to Subjects of Study). BA, BSc.
   Courses last 3 years full-time or 4 years sandwich.

Higher Degrees (of University of Wales) (see also United Kingdom Directory to Subjects of Study). MA, MBA, MSc.

Libraries. 255,000 volumes; 1064 periodicals.

FACULTIES/SCHOOLS

Art, Design and Engineering
Tel: (01222) 506600 Fax: (01222) 506644, 506690
Dean: Brown, Prof. Robert, BA Staffs., MDes RCA

Dean of Academic Affairs: Lewis, Alan, BSc *Wales*
Dean of Resources: Gorst, Geoffrey, BSc *Wales*

Business, Leisure and Food
Tel: (01222) 506400 Fax: (01222) 506930
Dean: ......
Dean of Academic Affairs: Griffith, Christopher, BSc *Liv.*, PhD *Liv.*
Dean of Resources: Jones, Eleri, BSc *Wales*, MSc *Lond.*, PhD *Wales*

Community Health Sciences
Tel: (01222) 506800 Fax: (01222) 506980
Dean: Hazell, Prof. Anthony J., BA *Brist.*, MA *Brun.*
Dean of Academic Affairs: Parry, Prof. Thelma, MSc *Wales*

Education and Sport
Tel: (01222) 506500 Fax: (01222) 506589
Dean: Pugh, John M., BEd *Wales*, MPhil *Glam.*, PhD *Wales*
Dean of Resources: Power, Sean, MA *W.Kentucky*
Dean of Academic Affairs: Hare, Jacqueline, MA *Lanc.*

ACADEMIC UNITS
Arranged by Schools

Biomedical Sciences
Tel: (01222) 506830 Fax: (01222) 506982
Ashmead, Bryan V., BSc *Wales*, PhD *Wales*   Sr. Lectr.
Bond, Geoffrey, BSc *St And.*, PhD *Edin.*   Sr. Lectr.
Bowen, S. Maureen, BSc *Wales*, PhD *Wales*   Head*
Burton, Neil, BSc *Wales*, PhD *Wales*   Sr. Lectr.
Cooper, Rosemary A., BSc *Wales*, PhD *Wales*   Principal Lectr.
Eccles, Khwala S., MB ChB *Baghdad*, MSc *Baghdad*, PhD *Wales*   Sr. Lectr.
Edwards, Malcolm, BSc *Wales*, PhD *Wales*   Sr. Lectr.
Jones, Alan H., BSc *Wales*   Sr. Lectr.
Jones, Karin E., BSc *Wales*   Sr. Lectr.
Jones, Ken P., MPhil *Wales*, PhD *Wales*   Sr. Lectr.
Morgan, Hubert D. R., BSc *Wales*, PhD *Wales*   Sr. Lectr.
Morgan, Julia G.   Sr. Lectr.
Morris, R. H. Keith, BSc *Wales*, BA *Open(UK)*, MSc *CNAA*   Sr. Lectr.
Mulligan, Leslie A., BSc *Wales*, PhD *Wales*   Sr. Lectr.
Mumford, Cedric, PhD *Alta.*   Sr. Lectr.
Munro, Robert I., BA *Open(UK)*   Sr. Lectr.
Watkins, Peter J., BSc *CNAA*, PhD *Lond.*   Sr. Lectr.
Williams, Robert G., MEd *Wales*   Sr. Lectr.

Business
Tel: (01222) 506375 Fax: (01222) 506932
Arthur, Leonard, BA *Durh.*   Sr. Lectr.
Avery, Ian A., BA *Wales*   Sr. Lectr.
Breverton, Terence, BA *Manc.*, MA *Lanc.*   Sr. Lectr.
Choo, Kok L., MBA *Wales*   Sr. Lectr.
Clarke, Denis, BSc *Lond.*, MBA *Wales*   Sr. Lectr.
Cockburn, Thomas S., BA *Leic.*, MBA *Wales*   Head*
Elliot, Tracey S.   Sr. Lectr.
Gaunt, John N., BA *Wales*, MEd *Wales*   Head*
Gilhooly, Eileen, MBA *Glam.*   Sr. Lectr.
Holden, Russell, BSc *Wales*, MA *Sus.*   Sr. Lectr.
James, Malcolm D., BA *Brist.*   Sr. Lectr.
Jones, Gareth R., BSc *Wales*, LLB *Wales*, MSc *Brist.*   Sr. Lectr.
Jones, Lawrence J., BSc *Wales*, MBA *Wales*   Sr. Lectr.
Kemp, Raymond E., MBA *Open(UK)*   Sr. Lectr.
Lewis, Trevor G., BA *Calif.*, MSc *Arizona*, MPhil *Wales*   Sr. Lectr.
Lowell, Jonathan, BA *Wales*, MBA *Wales*   Sr. Lectr.
Luther, Angela P., BA *Wales*   Sr. Lectr.

Macdonald, Janine, LêsL *Haute-Bretagne*   Sr. Lectr.
McNamara, Ross, BSc *Warw.*   Sr. Lectr.
Parry, Christopher T., BSc *CNAA*   Sr. Lectr.
Screen, Allan D., BA *Wales*   Sr. Lectr.
Smith, Russell, BA *CNAA*, MA *Reading*   Sr. Lectr.
Walters, Christopher, BA *Open(UK)*   Sr. Lectr.
Weiss, Reinhild, BA *F.U.Berlin*, MA *F.U.Berlin*, MEd *F.U.Berlin*   Sr. Lectr.
Williams, Alan, MBA *Wales*   Sr. Lectr.

Community Studies, see Health and Community Studies

Computer Information Systems
Tel: (01222) 506395 Fax: (01222) 506933
Bacon, Frances R., BA *Open(UK)*   Sr. Lectr.
Ball, David, BSc *Lond.*, MSc *Aston*, PhD *Aston*   Sr. Lectr.
Barlow, Ann, BSc *Sus.*   Sr. Lectr.
Carnduff, Thomas W., BSc *Wales*, MSc *Wales*, PhD *Wales*   Sr. Lectr.
Corner, Anthony D., BSc *Wales*   Sr. Lectr.
Dakin, Terence A., MSc *Wales*   Sr. Lectr.
Hopkin, Graham D., BSc *Wales*, MSc *CNAA*   Sr. Lectr.
Joice, P. Ann, BSc *CNAA*   Sr. Lectr.
Jones, Caroline, BSc *Wales*   Sr. Lectr.
Koukouravas, Theodoros, BSc *Herts.*, MSc *Wales*   Sr. Lectr.
Lloyd-Williams, David   Sr. Lectr.
Marsh, Stephen J., BA *Open(UK)*   Sr. Lectr.
Newth, Michael, BSc *Aberd.*, MSc *CNAA*   Sr. Lectr.
Stocking, Susan, BSc *CNAA*   Sr. Lectr.

Cultural Studies, see Sport and Cultural Studies

Design, see also Engin., Product, and Des.
Tel: (01222) 506647 Fax: (01222) 506944
Barker, Terry, BSc *Wales*, BArch *Wales*   Sr. Lectr.; Course Dir.
Castle, Peter, BA *CNAA*   Sr. Lectr.
Cousins, Simon E., BSc *S.Bank*   Sr. Lectr.; Course Dir.
Coward, Timothy, MDes *RCA*   Head*
Evans, Nicholas   Sr. Lectr.
Fleetwood, Michael E.   Principal Lectr.
Hann, Anne E., BSc *Wales*   Sr. Lectr.; Course Dir.
Hannay, Patrick J. S., MA   Sr. Lectr.; Course Dir.
Hose, Michael A., MDes *RCA*   Principal Lectr.; Course Dir.
Starkey, Peter   Sr. Lectr.; Course Dir.
Swindell, Geoffrey H., MA *RCA*   Sr. Lectr.

Design, Two-Dimensional
Fax: (01222) 506640
Cusack, Patricia, BA *Open(UK)*, PhD *Edin.*   Sr. Lectr.
Dineen, Ruth V., BEd *Wales*, BA *Reading*, MSc *Wales*   Sr. Lectr.
Gould, David P., MA *RCA*   Sr. Lectr.
Owen, Graham C., BA *Middx.*, MA *Manc.Met.*   Sr. Lectr.
Sheilds, Susan S.   Sr. Lectr.
Taylor, Alison   Sr. Lectr.
Thornton, David, BSc *Wales*, PhD *Wales*   Sr. Lectr.
Watkins, Helen, BA *CNAA*, MA *RCA*   Sr. Lectr.
Weir, Ian P., BA *Wolv.*   Sr. Lectr.
Young, Stephen   Head*

Education
Fax: (01222) 506589
Baird, Adela, BA *Open(UK)*, PhD *Wales*   Sr. Lectr.
Ball, George, BSc *Wales*, MSc *Wales*, PhD *Wales*   Sr. Lectr.
Bartlett, Peter R., BSc *Leic.*   Sr. Lectr.
Bassett, Phillip J., BEd *Wales*, MEd   Head*
Betts, L. Eleri, BA *Wales*   Sr. Lectr.
Cook, Martin J., BEd *Wales*   Sr. Lectr.
Cooke, Alan R., BSc *Wales*, PhD *Wales*   Sr. Lectr.
Davies, Jayne E.   Sr. Lectr.

Dodd, Graham, BSc *Tor.*, MEd *Sheff.*   Sr. Lectr.
Egan, David W., BA *Wales*, MA *Wales*   Head*
Evans, Hadyn, BSc *Wales*, MSc *Wales*, PhD *Wales*   Sr. Lectr.
Griffiths, Rev. David W., BD *Wales*, MEd *Wales*   Sr. Lectr.
Haines, Graham A., BEd *Wales*, MEd *Wales*   Principal Lectr.
Hanney, Margaret E., BEd *Wales*   Sr. Lectr.
Hare, David B., BSc *Wales*, DPhil *York(UK)*   Principal Lectr.
Hughes, Ann, BEd *Wales*, MEd *Wales*   Sr. Lectr.
James, Marilyn, BA *Lond.*   Sr. Lectr.
Jones, Helen J., BEd *Wales*, MEd   Sr. Lectr.
Jones, Heulwen, BA *Wales*   Sr. Lectr.
Jones, Jeffrey R., MEd *Wales*, BEd   Sr. Lectr.
Laugharne, Janet G., MA *Oxf.*, MPhil *Oxf.*   Sr. Lectr.
Morgan, Susan, BEd *Glam.*, MEd *Wales*   Sr. Lectr.
Pickin, Michael G., BSc *Lond.*, MSc *Lond.*   Sr. Lectr.
Rawle, D. M., BA *Birm.*, MPhil *Wales*   Sr. Lectr.
Roese, Caryl B., BEd MEd   Sr. Lectr.
Rowlands, Clive, MA   Sr. Lectr.
Rowlands, Meilyr, MA *Oxf.*   Sr. Lectr.
Stevens, Joan E., BEd *Wales*   Sr. Lectr.
Strange, Keith, BSc *Wales*, PhD *Wales*   Sr. Lectr.
Thomas, D. Meurig, BMus *Sheff.*   Sr. Lectr.
Thomas, Paul, BMus *Wales*, MEd *Wales*   Sr. Lectr.
Williams, David T., BSc *Wales*, MEd *Wales*   Sr. Lectr.
Williams, Sian R., BA *Wales*, PhD *Wales*   Sr.. Lectr.

Education, Graduate and Continuing
Tel: (01222) 506570 Fax: (01222) 506589
Carter, Peter G., MEd *Wales*   Sr. Lectr.
Cooper, Stephen M., BEd *Wales*, MA *Birm.*   Sr. Lectr.
Davies, Helen J., MEd *Wales*   Sr. Lectr.
Evans, Patricia, BEd *Wales*   Sr. Lectr.
Geen, Arthur, BA *Wales*, MEd *Wales*, PhD *Wales*   Sr. Lectr.
Hadley, Eric A., BA *Camb.*   Principal Lectr.
Harris, Charles J., BA *Wales*, MEd *Nott.*, MPhil *Nott.*   Sr. Lectr.
Henshall, Julie   Sr. Lectr.
Herrington, Paul, BA *CNAA*   Sr. Lectr.
Howard-Jones, Paul, BSc *Manc.*   Sr. Lectr.
Hughes, Michael D., BSc *Manc.Met.*, PhD *Manc.Met.*   Principal Lectr.
Jackson, Ceinwen B., BEd *Wales*   Sr. Lectr.
Longville, Julia H., BEd *Glam.*   Sr. Lectr.
Lyons, Keith, BA *York(UK)*, MSc *Lond.*, PhD *Sur.*   Sr. Lectr.
Peters, Susan   Sr. Lectr.
Rathkey, Michael, BSc *Wales*   Sr. Lectr.
Rivett, Sarah E., BA *Staffs.*, MA *Wales*   Sr. Lectr.
Treadwell, Peter J., BEd *Lough.*, MEd *Exe.*   Head*
Webb, Clive B., BEd *Wales*, MEd *Wales*   Sr. Lectr.

Engineering, Product, and Design
Fax: (01222) 506944
Bichard, Simon H., BSc *CNAA*   Sr. Lectr.
Holifield, David M., BSc *Wales*   Sr. Lectr.
Jacklin, David A., BA *Open(UK)*   Sr. Lectr.
O'Connell, Michael, BSc *Lond.*   Sr. Lectr.
Pole, Glyn, BSc *Wales*, MEng *Wales*   Sr. Lectr.
Powell, Howell, BSc *Wales*   Sr. Lectr.
Rafik, Tahseen A.   Sr. Lectr.
Roberts, Keith, BA *Open(UK)*   Head*
Shepherd, Alan J., BEng *Wales*, MEng *Wales*   Sr. Lectr.
Sihra, Tarsem S.   Sr. Lectr.
Wilgeroth, Paul M.   Sr. Lectr.

Environmental and Human Sciences
Tel: (01222) 506820 Fax: (01222) 506983
Belcher, Paul C., BA *Open(UK)*, MSc *Brist.*   Sr. Lectr.
Coleman, Gary, LLB *Lond.*, MBA *Wales*   Dir., WHO Centre
Collins, Jeffrey G.   Sr. Lectr.
Curnin, Andrew D., MPH *Wales*   Sr. Lectr.

Harries, Clive   Sr. Lectr.
Harris, Pamela J., BSc Brist., MA Nott., PhD
   Nott.   Head*
Harris, Philip E., BSc Brist., MPhil CNAA   Sr.
   Lectr.
Karani, George, MSc Nair., PhD Leeds   Sr. Lectr.
Lewis, Jeffrey   Sr. Lectr.
Murray, Alison C., BSc Lond., MPhil Camb.,
   PhD   Sr. Lectr.
Noble, Teresa E., BSc Strath., MSc H-W   Sr.
   Lectr.
Powell, Colin, BSc(Tech) Wales   Sr. Lectr.
Redding, Peter, BSc Rice, MSc Vanderbilt   Sr.
   Lectr.
Sander, Paul, BSc Lond., MSc Brun.   Sr. Lectr.
Sanders, Lalage, BScEcon Wales, PhD Wales   Sr.
   Lectr.
Smalley, Terrence, BSc(Econ) Lond., BA Oxf.,
   MA Oxf., PhD Aston   Sr. Lectr.
Smith, Derek J., BSc Lond.   Sr. Lectr.
Stephens, Janig, BEd S'ton., PhD Lond.   Sr. Lectr.
Upton, Dominic, BSc Leic., MSc Middx., PhD
   Lond.   Sr. Lectr.
Wildsmith, John D., BSc Wolv.   Sr. Lectr.
Williams, Robert J., BA Keele, PhD Keele   Sr.
   Lectr.

Fine Art

Tel: (01222) 506669 Fax: (01222) 506943

Beauchamp, Paul M.   Sr. Lectr.
Butler, Susan   Sr. Lectr.
Cazeaux, Clive J., BA CNAA, MA Wales, PhD
   Wales   Sr. Lectr.
Crowther, Michael J.   Sr. Lectr.
Davies, John   Sr. Lectr.; Res. Fellow
Gaughan, Martin I., BA Trinity(Dub.), BA
   E.Anglia, PhD E.Anglia   Sr. Lectr.
Gingell, John A.   Principal Lectr.
Hiscock, Karen A., BA Bath, MA C.England   Sr.
   Lectr.
Hood, Harvey, MA RCA   Sr. Lectr.
Howell, Anthony   Sr. Lectr.
Jones, Glyn   Prof.; Head*
Long, Helen, BA Lond., MA E.Anglia, PhD
   Brighton   Sr. Lectr.
Marchant, Alison   Sr. Lectr.
Mitchell, Robert   Principal Lectr.
Pickles, Cherry   Sr. Lectr.
Piper, Tom D., BFA S.Dakota, MFA Mich.   Sr.
   Lectr.
Setch, Terry   Sr. Lectr.
Shepherd, David J.   Sr. Lectr.
Worton, Trefor   Sr. Lectr.

Food and Consumer Science

Tel: (01222) 506445 Fax: (01222) 506941

Andrews, Antony T., MA Oxf., DPhil Oxf., DSc
   Reading, FRSChem   Prof., Food Chemistry
Brownsell, Vivian L., BSc Wales, PhD Wales   Sr.
   Lectr.
Crabtree, Joan, BSc Durh., MSc Leeds   Head*
Evans, Lynne   Sr. Lectr.
Fairchild, Ruth, BSc Wales, PhD Wales   Sr.
   Lectr.
Gilhooly, Gerard   Sr. Lectr.
Jones, Sarah H., BSc Wales   Sr. Lectr.
Kangkanian, Ava, BSc Baghdad, MSc Reading, PhD
   Reading   Sr. Lectr.
Ladd, Mariea   Sr. Lectr.
Peters, Adrian, BSc Wales, PhD Wales   Sr. Lectr.
Williams, Ronald J. H., BSc Wales, MSc Wales,
   PhD Wales   Sr. Lectr.

Health and Community Studies

Tel: (01222) 506810 Fax: (01222) 506983

Bailey, Jean M., BA Birm., MSc Lond.   Sr. Lectr.
Barasi, Mary E., BSc Lond., BA Open(UK), MSc
   Lond.   Principal Lectr.
Brown, Glynis, MEd Wales   Sr. Lectr.
Bryan, Ann, BEd Wales   Sr. Lectr.
Cleverly, Anne, BA Manc., MBA Bath   Head*
Connor, Colleen, BScEcon Wales, MSc
   Wales   Sr. Lectr.
Cooper, Francesca J., BSc Wales   Sr. Lectr.
Delaney, Calum, BA Witw.   Sr. Lectr.
Evans, Jeffrey, BA Open(UK), MScEcon
   Wales   Sr. Lectr.

Finch, Susan E., BA York(UK), MSc Wales   Sr.
   Lectr.
Fowler, Peter, BA Keele, MScEcon Wales   Sr.
   Lectr.
Frowen, Paul, MPhil Wales   Sr. Lectr.
Hayward, Vanessa   Sr. Lectr.
Isaac, Bryan, BA Wales, MSc Manc.   Sr. Lectr.
Jenkins, Elaine, BA Open(UK), MEd Wales   Sr.
   Lectr.
Jessett, Donald, MEd Brist.   Principal Lectr.
Johnson, Sheila, MPhil Leic.   Sr. Lectr.
Jones, Aled, BScEcon Wales   Sr. Lectr.
Lewis, Brynda, BA Open(UK), MScEcon
   Wales   Sr. Lectr.
Lock, David, BA Leic., MSc Lough., MA Brun.   Sr.
   Lectr.
Munro, Siân, MSc PhD   Principal Lectr.
Nicholls, Alison, BSc Lond., MPhil Wales   Sr.
   Lectr.
Protheroe, Amanda, BA CNAA, MSc Aston   Sr.
   Lectr.
Rees, Nigel, BA CNAA, MSc Aston   Sr. Lectr.
Spargo, Jeffrey, BEd Wales   Sr. Lectr.
Statham, Gwyneth, BSc Brist.   Principal Lectr.
Tyrrell, Wendy, MEd Wales   Sr. Lectr.
Wilkins, Judi, BTech Brun.   Sr. Lectr.

Hospitality, Leisure and Tourism Management

Tel: (01222) 506425 Fax: (01222) 506940

Avery, Patricia M.   Sr. Lectr.
Bennett, Noreen W., BScEcon Wales, MScEcon
   Wales   Sr. Lectr.
Botterill, T. David, BSc Sur., MSc Lough., PhD
   Texas A.& M.   Head*
Bradshaw, Philip E.   Sr. Lectr.
Coleman, Philip D., BA Open(UK)   Sr. Lectr.
Fallon, Julia M., BA Brad., MBA Wales   Sr.
   Lectr.
Flynn, Michael J., BSc Wales, MBA Wales   Sr.
   Lectr.
Honey, Martin D., BA Sur.   Sr. Lectr.
Hunter-Powell, Patricia A., BA Open(UK)   Sr.
   Lectr.
Jones, Julian, BA York(UK), MA Open(UK), MBA
   Wales   Sr. Lectr.
Joseph, Angela, BA MA   Sr. Lectr., Law
Liu, Zhen Hua, BAEcon Beijing, MBA Beijing,
   PhD Strath.   Sr. Lectr.
Llewelyn, J. Lawrence, BSc Wales, MSc
   Wales   Sr. Lectr.
Moore, Stephen P.   Sr. Lectr.
Morgan, N., BA Exe., PhD Exe.   Sr. Lectr.
Norris, Lynne S., LLB Glam.   Sr. Lectr.
Pepper, S. Alice, BA Wales   Sr. Lectr.
Ritchie, Caroline, BSc Lond.   Sr. Lectr.
Roberts, Andrew   Sr. Lectr.
Savage, Timothy J., BSc CNAA, MSc Lough.   Sr.
   Lectr.
Sedgley, Diane Z., BA CNAA, MSocSci
   Birm.   Sr. Lectr.
Silk, T. Michael   Sr. Lectr.
Tresidder, F. Kenneth, BA Lond.   Sr. Lectr.

Human Sciences, see Environmental and Human Scis.

Sport and Cultural Studies

Fax: (01222) 506589

Butterworth, Malcolm   Sr. Lectr.
Cobner, David E., BEd Wales, MA Leeds   Head*
Davies, Gwilym, BA Wales, MEd Wales, PhD
   Wales   Sr. Lectr.
Davies, Lynn, MBE, MA Open(UK)   Sr. Lectr.
Davies, Paul, MPhil Glas., PhD Edin.   Sr. Lectr.
Fenner, Anthony J.   Sr. Lectr.
Hanton, Sheldon   Sr. Lectr.
Jennings, Christopher W., BA Wales   Sr. Lectr.
John, Geraint W., BA Wales   Sr. Lectr.
Lancey, Keith W., BEd Wales, MA Birm.   Sr.
   Lectr.
Paradiss, Giorgios   Sr. Lectr.
Tong, Richard J., BA Wales, MSc Lough.   Sr.
   Lectr.
Wiltshire, Huw D., BA Wales   Sr. Lectr.

Tourism Management, see Hospitality, Leisure and Tourism Management

CONTACT OFFICERS

Academic affairs. Director of Academic Affairs:
   Birchenough, Prof. Allan, BSc CNAA, PhD
   CNAA, FIMechE
Accommodation. Accommodation Officer:
   Edwards, Alan, BA Wales
Admissions (first degree). Academic Registrar:
   Cockroft, Bea, BA CNAA
Admissions (higher degree). Academic
   Registrar: Cockroft, Bea, BA CNAA
Alumni. Head of External Affairs: Taylor, R.
   Christopher
Archives. Academic Registrar: Cockroft, Bea,
   BA CNAA
Careers. Careers Officer: Twyman, Alison, BA
   Lanc.
Computing services. Head of IT Services:
   Harrison, David I., BSc Wales, MSc Brad.
Consultancy services. Industrial Liaison Officer:
   ......
Credit transfer. Director of Academic Affairs:
   Birchenough, Prof. Allan, BSc CNAA, PhD
   CNAA, FIMechE
Development/fund-raising. Director of
   Finance: Warren, Martin J., BSc Hull, FCA
Distance education. Director of Academic
   Affairs: Birchenough, Prof. Allan, BSc CNAA,
   PhD CNAA, FIMechE
Equal opportunities. Equality Development
   and Training Officer: ......
Estates and buildings/works and services.
   Director of Corporate Services: Martin, A.
   David, BA CNAA
Examinations. Academic Registrar: Cockroft,
   Bea, BA CNAA
Finance. Director of Finance: Warren, Martin
   J., BSc Hull, FCA
General enquiries. Head of External Affairs:
   Taylor, R. Christopher
Health services. Director of Academic Affairs:
   Birchenough, Prof. Allan, BSc CNAA, PhD
   CNAA, FIMechE
International office. Head of International
   Marketing: Phillips, John, BEd
Ombudsperson. Chairman, Board of
   Governors: Harrhy, Gordon
Personnel/human resources. Personnel
   Manager: Hall, Howard, MMS
Public relations, information and marketing.
   Head of External Affairs: Taylor, R.
   Christopher
Publications. Head of External Affairs: Taylor,
   R. Christopher
Purchasing. Standfast, Peter
Quality assurance and accreditation. Head of
   Academic Unit: ......
Research. Director of Academic Affairs:
   Birchenough, Prof. Allan, BSc CNAA, PhD
   CNAA, FIMechE
Safety. Stuart, Anthony B.
Scholarships, awards, loans. Academic
   Registrar: Cockroft, Bea, BA CNAA
Schools liaison. Schools and Colleges Liaison
   Officer: Evans, Clifford
Security. Director of Corporate Services:
   Martin, A. David, BA CNAA
Sport and recreation. Director of Finance:
   Warren, Martin J., BSc Hull, FCA
Student union. President: Grundy, Jamie
Student welfare/counselling. Head of Student
   Services: Gunston, Sheila, BEd Wales, MSc
   Wales
Students from other countries. Head of
   International Marketing: Phillips, John, BEd
Students with disabilities. Director of
   Academic Affairs: Birchenough, Prof. Allan,
   BSc CNAA, PhD CNAA, FIMechE

[Information supplied by the institution as at 17 June
1998, and edited by the ACU]

UNIVERSITY OF WALES COLLEGE, NEWPORT

Founded 1975, incorporated 1996

Postal Address: Caerleon Campus, PO Box 179, Newport, Wales NP6 1YG
Telephone: (01633) 430088 **Fax**: (01633) 432006 **E-mail**: initial.surname@newport.ac.uk
WWW: http://www.newport.ac.uk

CHAIRMAN—Tudno Jones, Elwyn, FRICS
VICE-CHAIRMAN—Peachey, Roger, FCA
PRINCIPAL AND CHIEF EXECUTIVE*—Overshott, Prof. K. J., MSc Birm., PhD *Wales*, DEng Birm., FIEE, FIP
VICE-PRINCIPAL—Tatum, Susan, BA *Manc.*, PhD *Salf.*
ACADEMIC REGISTRAR—Sexton, John
ASSISTANT PRINCIPAL (DEPARTMENTS)—Noyes, Peter, BSc Lough., PhD Lond.
ASSISTANT PRINCIPAL (SERVICES)—Edge, Geoffrey, BEng Liv., MEng Sheff.
DIRECTOR OF FINANCE—Kutner, Bernard, FCA

GENERAL INFORMATION

History. The university college was founded in 1975 as Gwent College of Higher Education, with the merger of several specialist institutions. It became University of Wales College, Newport in 1996.

Admission to first degree courses (see also United Kingdom Introduction). Through Universities and Colleges Admissions Service (UCAS). Passes in 2 subjects at General Certificate of Education (GCE) A Level or equivalent qualifications (including qualifications from overseas institutions) or experience.

First Degrees (of University of Wales) (see also United Kingdom Directory to Subjects of Study). BA, BEd, BEng, BSc, BSc(Econ).

All courses are available full-time and normally last 3 years. Special BEd: 2 years (at least 1 year of higher education study required for entry). Some programmes are also available part-time (normally 6 years).

Higher Degrees (of University of Wales) (see also United Kingdom Directory to Subjects of Study). MA, MBA, MSc, MSc(Econ), MPhil, PhD.

Applicants for admission to master's degrees must normally hold an appropriate first degree awarded by a recognised institution. For applicants over 25, relevant experience may be accepted in place of a first degree. PhD: good honours degree.

Taught masters' courses: normally 1 year full-time or 3 years part-time; MPhil: 1–3 years full-time or 3–5 years part-time; PhD: 3–5 years full-time or 5–9 years part-time.

Language of Instruction. English. Classes available for students needing help.

Libraries. 130,000 volumes; 650 periodicals subscribed to; 30,000 art slides. Special collections include: Primrose Hockey (local history); David Hurn (documentary photography).

Fees (1998–99, annual). Undergraduate and postgraduate courses (except initial teacher training), £1000; international students, £6345.

Academic Year (1998–99). Three terms: 4 October–17 December; 10 January–7 April; 2 May–7 July. Two semesters: 11 October–11 February; 28 February–30 June.

Income (1996–97). Total, £25,190,000.

Statistics. Staff (full-time equivalents): 379 (159 academic, 140 administrative, 80 technical/manual). Students: full-time 3163; part-time 4970.

ACADEMIC UNITS

Art and Design

Tel: (01633) 432643 Fax: (01633) 432610

Adams, L., BA *CNAA*, MA Lond.   Sr. Lectr.
Appleton, P. J., BA Newcastle(UK), MFA Newcastle(UK)   Sr. Lectr.
Carlisle, A., BA Ulster, MA Lond.   Head*
Evans, G., MA Lond.   Sr. Lectr.
Hall, R. G. B., MA *CNAA*   Sr. Lectr.
Lyons, K., MFA Yale   Sr. Lectr.
Mason, R., BA *CNAA*   Sr. Lectr.
McCormick, R. H.   Principal Lectr.
Morris, P. J., MA Lond.   Sr. Lectr.
Newman, E. A., BA *CNAA*   Sr. Lectr.
Punt, M. J., BA *CNAA*, MA E.Anglia   Sr. Lectr.
Quarmby, A. S.   Sr. Lectr.
Rees, S. L., BA *CNAA*   Sr. Lectr.
Shields, S. S.   Sr. Lectr.
Smith, D., BSc Lond., MSc Lanc.   Sr. Lectr.
Taylor, A., BA *CNAA*   Sr. Lectr.
Thompson, S. J., BA *CNAA*, MA Lond.   Sr. Lectr.
Topping, D., BA *Wales*, MA Brighton   Sr. Lectr.
Walmsley, J. E., MA *CNAA*   Acting Head*
Other Staff: 1 Lectr.; 1 Teaching Fellow

Business and Management

Tel: (01633) 432365 Fax: (01633) 432307

Brown, N. P., BA *Kent*, FCA   Sr. Lectr.
Brown, V. M., LLB Durh.   Sr. Lectr.
Cole, S. M., BA Open(UK), MBA Open(UK)   Sr. Lectr.
Davidson, M. J., BEng *Wales*, MBA *Wales*   Sr. Lectr.
Evans, A. T., BSc(Econ) Lond., FCA   Sr. Lectr.
Fehler, E. A., LLB Hull   Sr. Lectr.
Floyd, C. T., BSc Lough.   Sr. Lectr.
Griffiths, L. G., FCA   Principal Lectr.
Hamer-Jones, B., MSc Bath CHE   Sr. Lectr.
Jones, E. B., BSc *Wales*, MBA *Wales*   Sr. Lectr.
Lawson, R., MBA *Wales*   Sr. Lectr.
Mills, G. J., LLB *Wales*, LLM Brist.   Sr. Lectr.
Orford, D., BScEcon *Wales*, MEd *Wales*   Sr. Lectr.
Ringwald, K., MBA Glam.   Sr. Lectr.
Roberts, D., BSc *Wales*   Sr. Lectr.
Robins, P. A., BSc Lond., FCA   Principal Lectr.
Royle, A., BA Leic.   Sr. Lectr.
Stephens, B. J., BSc Salf., MA Melb.   Principal Lectr.
Talbot, L. N., BA Open(UK), MBA *Wales*   Sr. Lectr.
Travis, M. A., MA Oxf.   Principal Lectr.
Wellard, N., BSc Kent, PhD Manc.   Sr. Lectr.
Williams, T. H., MScEcon *Wales*   Acting Head*

Education and Training

Tel: (01633) 432160 Fax: (01633) 432640

Adams, K. A., BEd Lanc.   Sr. Lectr.
Davies, A. G., BScEcon *Wales*, MA Open(UK)   Sr. Lectr.
Davies, V. P., BA *Kent*, MScEcon *Wales*   Head*
Griffiths, R. D., BSc Bath   Sr. Lectr.
Hamilton, I. F., BA York(UK)   Sr. Lectr.
Roberts, J. S., BSc Brad., MA Wolv.   Sr. Lectr.

Rowlands, A.
Waddington, D., BScEcon *Wales*   Sr. Lectr.
Other Staff: 2 Lectrs.

Engineering

Tel: (01633) 432427 Fax: (01633) 432530

Baicher, G. S., BSc Jab., BEng A.Bello, MSc Leeds   Sr. Lectr.
Breeze, E. W., BSc *Wales*, PhD Sheff.   Sr. Lectr.
Cousins, D., BSc *Wales*, MEd *Wales*   Sr. Lectr.
Edwards, K. P., BSc *Wales*, PhD *Wales*   Sr. Lectr.
Evans, D. S., BSc Bath   Sr. Lectr.
Harwood, D. J., BSc *CNAA*, PhD *CNAA*   Principal Lectr.
Hayes, A., BA *Essex*, MSc Brun.   Principal Lectr.
James, J. L., MSc *Wales*, PhD *Wales*   Sr. Lectr.
Jones, A., BSc *CNAA*, MSc *Wales*   Sr. Lectr.
Jones, C., BSc Dund., MBEng   Sr. Lectr.
Jones, R. I., BSc *Wales*   Sr. Lectr.
Oelmann, Lyndon A., MSc *Wales*   Head*
Robins, G. W., BSc *Wales*, MSc *Wales*   Sr. Lectr.
Rowlands, Hefin, BSc *Wales*, MEng *Wales*, PhD *Wales*   Head of Res.
Russell, G. K., BSc Cant., MSc Syd., PhD Syd.   Sr. Lectr.
Sansom, J. W., BSc *CNAA*   Sr. Lectr.
Timothy, P. J., BA MA   Sr. Lectr.
Waldron, R., BSc *CNAA*   Sr. Lectr.
Watkins, P. J.   Sr. Lectr.
Waythe, M. A., MSc Lough.   Sr. Lectr.
Other Staff: 5 Lectrs.

Health and Social Care

Tel: (01633) 432389 Fax: (01633) 432530

Davies, I., BA *CNAA*, MScEcon *Wales*, MBA *Wales*   Sr. Lectr.
Lewis, L.
Lyons, A., BSc Lanc., MSc Sur.   Head*
Morgans, D., BA MPhil   Sr. Lectr.
Simmons, M.   Sr. Lectr.
Spencer, L., BA *CNAA*   Sr. Lectr.
Wills, F. R., BA(Econ) Manc., MA York(UK)   Sr. Lectr.

Humanities and Science

Tel: (01633) 432093 Fax: (01633) 432150

Aldhouse-Green, M. J., BA *Wales*, MLitt Oxf., PhD Open(UK), FSA   Reader; Head of Res.
Aldhouse-Green, S., BA *Wales*, PhD *Wales*, FSA   Sr. Lectr.
Davies, G. B., BA *CNAA*   Sr. Lectr.
Egley, S. A., BA Durh., MEd Birm.   Sr. Lectr.
Fisher, I. C., MA Leic., PhD Leic.   Head*
Fowler, M. D., BEd *Wales*, PhD Liv.   Sr. Lectr.
Goldsworthy, G. T., BSc *Wales*   Sr. Lectr.
Harris, A., BSc Hull, MSc Salf.   Sr. Lectr.
Hawthorn, D. T., BA Open(UK), MEd   Sr. Lectr.
Howell, R. C., MA Lond., PhD Lond.   Sr. Lectr.
James, L. W., MA Lond.   Sr. Lectr.
Matheson, H., BEd Warw., MSc Iowa   Principal Lectr.
McElhone, M. J., BSc Newcastle(UK), PhD *Wales*   Sr. Lectr.
Morgan Thomas, I., BA *Wales*   Sr. Lectr.
Norcliffe, D. J., BA *Wales*, PhD Leeds

Peters, C. W., BSc *Wales*, PhD *Aston*   Sr. Lectr.
Ruhemann, L., MA *Manc.*, MA *Lond.*   Sr. Lectr.
Stephens, D. V., BSc(Econ) *Belf.*, MEd
  Wales   Sr. Lectr.
Taylor, P. J., MEd *Wales*   Sr. Lectr.
Thomas, H. S. C., BA *Birm.*, PhD *Wales*   Sr.
  Lectr.
Other Staff: 3 Lectrs.

Media Arts

Tel: (01633) 432180 Fax: (01633) 432606

Crews, A. B., BA *New Mexico*, MA *San
  Francisco*   Sr. Lectr.
Davies, P.   Sr. Lectr.
Dewdney, A., BA *CNAA*, MFA *CNAA*, MA
  Lond.   Head*
Furlong, R., BA *Anglia PU*, MA *Lond.*   Sr. Lectr.
Grove-White, A. B., BA *Reading*   Sr. Lectr.
Heatley, R., BA *Camb.*, MA *CNAA*   Principal
  Lectr.
Landen, C.   Sr. Lectr.
Little, E. P., BA *Colorado*, MFA *Colorado*   Sr.
  Lectr.
Moore, S., BA *Exe.*   Sr. Lectr.
Niblo, A.
Seawright, P. H., BA *CNAA*   Sr. Lectr.
Walker, I. C., BA *Manc.*, MA *Lond.*, DPhil
  Sus.   Sr. Lectr.
Waterhouse, M. J., BA *Reading*, MSc *Aston*, MPhil
  Reading   Sr. Lectr.
Williams, A. B.   Sr. Lectr.

Teacher Education

Tel: (01633) 432277 Fax: (01633) 432074

Adams, M. S., MEd *Wales*, PhD *Wales*   Head*
Edmunds, J. A., MEd *Wales*   Sr. Lectr.
Edwards, N. J., MEd *Wales*   Sr. Lectr.
Fear, A. D., BSc *Lond.*, MEd *Wales*   Sr. Lectr.
Feather, D., MA   Sr. Lectr.
George, S., BEd *Wales*   Sr. Lectr.
Green, K. F., BSc *Kent*, PhD *Kent*   Sr. Lectr.
Harries, L., MEd *Wales*   Principal Lectr.
Heard, C. D., BEd *CNAA*   Sr. Lectr.
Kuraiki, R. B., MEd *Wales*   Sr. Lectr.
Lawton, J. L., MEd *Wales*   Sr. Lectr.
Morris, K. P., BEd *Wales*, MPhil *Wales*   Sr.
  Lectr.
Newcomb, J. W., MA *Open(UK)*   Sr. Lectr.
Pagan, A. J., MEd *Wales*   Sr. Lectr.
Palmer, H. R., BA *Open(UK)*   Sr. Lectr.
Petrie, L. G., BA *Open(UK)*, MA *Lond.*   Sr. Lectr.
Powell, E. R., MEd *Wales*   Principal Lectr.
Sobol, K., MEd *Wales*   Sr. Lectr.
Sparks, J. M., BEd *Wales*   Principal Lectr.
Steer, S., MEd *Wales*   Sr. Lectr.
Watson, J. K., BEd *Manc.*, MEd *Wales*   Sr. Lectr.
Young, W., MEd *Wales*   Sr. Lectr.
Other Staff: 1 Lectr.

SPECIAL CENTRES, ETC

Advanced Inquiry in the Interactive Arts, Centre for

Tel: (01633) 432174 Fax: (01633) 432174
Ascott, R., BA *Durh.*   Reader

Culture, Archaeology, Religions and Biogeography, Centre for the Study of (SCARAB)

Tel: (01633) 432240 Fax: (01633) 432240
Aldhouse-Green, M. J., BA *Wales*, MLitt *Oxf.*,
  PhD *Open(UK)*   Head*

Mechatronics Research Centre

Welsh Development Agency Centre of
Expertise

Tel: (01633) 432424 Fax: (01633) 432430
Roberts, Geoff N., MSc *CNAA*, PhD *Wales*,
  FIEE   Head*
Rowlands, Hefin, BSc *Wales*, MEng *Wales*, PhD
  Wales   Head of Res.

CONTACT OFFICERS

Academic affairs. Academic Registrar: Sexton,
  John
Accommodation. Student Accommodation
  Officer: Pope, James, BA *Glam.*
Admissions (first degree). Head of University
  Information Centre: Fishlock, Karen, BA
  Glam.
Admissions (higher degree). Research
  Administrator: Jeans, Richard, BSc(Econ)
  Wales
Adult/continuing education. Associate Dean:
  Rowlands, Arwyn, BA *Wales*, MEd *Wales*
Alumni. Alumni Officer: Gurner, Helen, BA
  Wales
Archives. Alumni Officer: Gurner, Helen, BA
  Wales
Careers. Head of Careers: Stewart, William J.,
  MA
Computing services. Head of Information
  Technology Centre: Storey, Robert, BSc *Tor.*
Consultancy services. Commercial Manager:
  Turnbull, Karen, BSc *Wales*
Credit transfer. Deputy Assistant Principal
  (Departments): Blaney, David, BA *CNAA*,
  MBA *CNAA*
Development/fund-raising. Head of External
  Affairs: Mullin, Catherine, BSc *Wales*
Distance education. Deputy Assistant Principal
  (Departments): Blaney, David, BA *CNAA*,
  MBA *CNAA*
Equal opportunities. Assistant Personnel
  Officer: Townsend-Daly, Anna, BA *Aberd.*,
  MA
Estates and buildings/works and services.
  Director of Estates: Hawkins, J. Nicholas,
  MA *Camb.*
Examinations. Assistant Academic Secretary:
  Steer, Peter

Finance. Director of Finance: Kutner, Bernard
  M., FCA
General enquiries. Head of University
  Information Centre: Fishlock, Karen, BA
  Glam.
Health services. Head of Student Support
  Services: Jamison, Stephanie M., BSc *Lond.*
Industrial liaison. Commercial Manager:
  Turnbull, Karen, BSc *Wales*
International office. Dean: Day, Clive C. B.,
  MSc *Wales*, PhD *Bath*
Library (chief librarian). Head: Peters, Janet,
  MA *Oxf.*, MLS *Lough.*
Library (enquiries). Library Supervisor:
  McDougall, Elizabeth, BA *Wales*
Minorities/disadvantaged groups. Assistant
  Personnel Officer: Townsend-Daly, Anna, BA
  Aberd., MA
Personnel/human resources. Assistant
  Personnel Officer: Townsend-Daly, Anna, BA
  Aberd., MA
Public relations, information and marketing.
  Head of External Affairs: Mullin, Catherine,
  BSc *Wales*
Publications. Research Administrator: Jeans,
  Richard, BSc(Econ) *Wales*
Purchasing. Director of Finance: Kutner,
  Bernard M., FCA
Quality assurance and accreditation.
  Academic Registrar: Folan, Paul, BA *Liv.*
Research. Research Administrator: Jeans,
  Richard, BSc(Econ) *Wales*
Safety. Health and Safety Officer: Wilson,
  Alexander
Scholarships, awards, loans. Research
  Administrator: Jeans, Richard, BSc(Econ)
  Wales
Schools liaison. Schools and Colleges Liaison
  Officer: Worrell, Amanda, BA *Humb.*
Security. Director of Estates: Hawkins, J.
  Nicholas, MA *Camb.*
Sport and recreation. Executive Officer:
  Phipps, Keith H., BA *CNAA*
Staff development and training. Assistant
  Personnel Officer: Townsend-Daly, Anna, BA
  Aberd., MA
Student union. Senior Administration Officer
  of the Union: McKimmie, Leanne, BA *CNAA*
Student welfare/counselling. Head of Student
  Support Services: Jamison, Stephanie M., BSc
  Lond.
Students from other countries. Assistant
  Dean/International Officer: Arnold, Bill
Students with disabilities. Head of Student
  Support Services: Jamison, Stephanie M., BSc
  Lond.
University press. Press and Communications
  Officer: Weltch, Andrew, BA *Kent*
Women. Assistant Personnel Officer:
  Townsend-Daly, Anna, BA *Aberd.*, MA

[*Information supplied by the institution as at 4 March
1998, and edited by the ACU*]

UNIVERSITY OF WARWICK

Incorporated by Royal Charter 1965

Member of the Association of Commonwealth Universities

Postal Address: Coventry, England CV4 7AL
Telephone: (01203) 523523 **Fax**: (01203) 461606 **Telex**: 317472 UNIREG **WWW**: http://www.warwick.ac.uk/
E-mail formula: initials.surname@warwick.ac.uk

CHANCELLOR—Ramphal, The Hon. Sir Shridath, GCMG, OE, OM(J), AC, QC, LLM *Lond.*, Hon. LLD *Panjab*, Hon. LLD *S'ton.*, Hon. LLD *St FX*, Hon. LLD *WI*, Hon. LLD *Benin*, Hon. LLD *Hull*, Hon. LLD *Aberd.*, Hon. LLD *Cape Coast*, Hon. LLD *Lond.*, Hon. LLD *Yale*, Hon. LLD *Camb.*, Hon. LLD *Warw.*, Hon. DUniv *Sur.*, Hon. DU *Essex*, Hon. DHL *Simmons*, Hon. DHL *Duke*, Hon. DCL *Oxf.*, Hon. DCL *E.Anglia*, Hon. DCL *Durh.*, Hon. DLitt *Brad.*, Hon. DSc *Cran.IT*, Hon. LLD *York(UK)*, Hon. LLD *Malta*, Hon. LLD *Otago*, Hon. LLD *Nigeria*, Hon. DLitt *I.Gandhi Nat.Open*, FKC

PRO-CHANCELLOR—Williams, R. J., BSc *Lond.*

VICE-CHANCELLOR*—Follett, Prof. Sir Brian, BSc *Brist.*, PhD *Brist.*, DSc *Wales*, Hon. LLD *Wales*, FRS, Hon. FLA

PRO-VICE-CHANCELLOR—Burgess, Prof. Robert G., BA *Durh.*, PhD *Warw.*

PRO-VICE-CHANCELLOR—Bassnett, Prof. Susan E., BA *Manc.*, PhD *Lanc.*

PRO-VICE-CHANCELLOR—Palmer, Prof. Stuart B., BSc *Sheff.*, PhD *Sheff.*, DSc *Sheff.*, FIP, FIEE

TREASURER—Hearth, J. D. M., CBE, MA *Oxf.*

REGISTRAR‡—Shattock, Michael L., OBE, MA *Oxf.*, Hon. LLD *Reading*

LIBRARIAN—Henshall, John A., BA *Manc.*, MA *Manc.*, PhD *Manc.*

GENERAL INFORMATION

History. The university was established in 1965. It is located about 5km from the centre of Coventry.

Admission to first degree courses (see also United Kingdom Introduction). Through Universities and Colleges Admissions Service (UCAS). Applicants must satisfy the general entrance requirement. Equivalent overseas qualifications are accepted. Applicants whose first language is not English must demonstrate competence in the English language.

First Degrees (see also United Kingdom Directory to Subjects of Study). BA, BA(QTS), BEd, BEng, BPhil(Ed), BSc, LLB, MChem, MEng, MMORSE, MPhys, MMath, MMathStat.

Courses last 3–4 years full-time and may also be taken part-time.

Higher Degrees (see also United Kingdom Directory to Subjects of Study). LLM, MA, MBA, MD, MHist, MMedSci, MRes, MS, MSc, MPhil, PhD, DLitt, DSc, EdD, EngD, LLD.

Applicants for admission to master's degree courses should normally hold an appropriate first degree with at least second class honours. DLitt, DSc, LLD: awarded on published work.

Libraries. 900,000 volumes; 5600 periodicals subscribed to. Special collections include: British Petroleum Company archives; Modern Records Centre; political groups and figures (including Frank Cowins, Richard Crossman, Sir Victor Gollancz); trades union, employers' and trade associations' records.

Fees (1997–98, annual, full-time). Undergraduate: £750 (arts, education, mathematics, social sciences, statistics); £1600 (sciences). Postgraduate: home/EU students £2090–3445; international students £6162–8300; MBA (all students) £13,000.

Academic Year (1998–99). Three terms: 5 October–12 December; 11 January–20 March; 26 April–3 July.

Income (1996–97). Total, £134,812,000.

Statistics. Staff: 3317 (1293 academic, 2024 adminsitrative and other). Students: full-time 10,004; part-time 3913; international 2474.

FACULTIES/SCHOOLS

Arts
Tel: (01203) 524159
Chairman: Mack, P. W. D., MA *Oxf.*, MPhil *Lond.*, PhD *Lond.*
Secretary: Hall, D. E., BA *Reading*

Science
Tel: (01203) 523760 *Fax*: (01203) 524170
Chairman: Carpenter, Prof. Peter W., BSc *Lond.*, MSc *Cinc.*, PhD *Cinc.*
Secretary: Robinson, L., BSc *Sheff*, MA *Warw.*

Social Studies
Tel: (01203) 522065 *Fax*: (01203) 524752
Chairman: Wensley, Prof. J. Robin C., BA *Camb.*, MSc *Lond.*, PhD *Lond.*
Secretary: ......

ACADEMIC UNITS

Applied Social Studies
Tel: (01203) 523508 *Fax*: (01203) 524415
Carpenter, Mick J., BSc *Lond.*, MA *Warw.*, PhD *Warw.*   Reader; Chairman*
Harris, John, BA *CNAA*, MA *Warw.*, PhD *Warw.*   Sr. Lectr.
McLeod, Eileen, BA *Camb.*   Sr. Lectr.
Mullender, Audrey E., BA *Sheff.*, MA *Nott.*   Prof., Social Work
Spencer, Nick J., MPhil *Oxf.*, MPhil *Nott.*, FRCPEd   Prof., Community Child Health
Other Staff: 7 Lectrs.; 1 Sr. Res Fellow; 1 Teaching Fellow
Research: community care; health-related behaviour; welfare of children and young people

Biological Sciences
Tel: (01203) 523508 *Fax*: (01203) 523701
Atkinson, Anthony, BSc *Manc.*, PhD *Manc.*   Hon. Prof.
Ayers, John G., BSc *Lond.*, MBBS *Lond.*, MD, FRCP   Hon. Prof.
Boseley, Paul G., BSc PhD   Hon. Prof.
Brown, Michael R. W., MSc *Lond.*, PhD *Lond.*, DSc *Manc.*, FIBiol, FRPharmS   Hon. Prof.
Casson, Alan, MB ChB *Manc.*, MS *Mun.*   Prof., Thoracic Surgery
Dalton, Howard, BSc *Lond.*, DPhil *Sus.*, FRS   Prof.
Dimmock, Nigel J., BSc *Liv.*, PhD *Lond.*   Prof.
Dow, Crawford S., BSc *Edin.*, PhD *Warw.*   Reader
Dowson, Christopher G., BSc *Bath*, PhD *Bath*   Reader
Easton, Andrew J., BSc *Aberd.*, PhD *Glas.*   Sr. Lectr.
Fulop, Vilmos, BSc *Bud.*, PhD *Bud.*   Reader
Hillhouse, Edward W., BSc *Lond.*, MB BS *Lond.*, PhD *Lond.*   Prof., Medicine
Hodgson, David A., BSc *Warw.*, PhD *E.Anglia*   Sr. Lectr.
Hulten, M. A., Mag *Stockholm*, PhD *Stockholm*, MD, FRCPath
Jones, Elizabeth A., BSc *Manc.*, DPhil *Oxf.*   Sr. Lectr.

Lilford, Richard J., PhD *Lond.*   Hon. Prof.
Lord, J. Michael, BSc *Salf.*, PhD *Brad.*   Prof.
Mann, Nicolas H., BSc *Liv.*, PhD *Liv.*   Reader
McCrae, M. A., BSc *Edin.*, PhD *Glas.*   Prof.
Morris, Alan G., BA *Oxf.*, DPhil *Oxf.*   Reader
Murrell, J. Colin, BSc *S'ton.*, PhD *Warw.*   Prof.
Norris, Paul R., BSc *CNAA*, PhD *Lond.*   Sr. Lectr.
Old, Robert W., BA *Camb.*, PhD *Edin.*   Reader
Payne, Christopher, MA *Oxf.*, DPhil *Oxf.*   Hon. Prof.
Price, Andrew R. G., BSc *Wales*, PhD *Wales*   Sr. Lectr.
Primrose, Sandy B., BSc *Strath.*, PhD *Calif.*   Hon. Prof.
Roberts, Lynne M., BTech *Brad.*, PhD *Brad.*   Reader
Robinson, Colin, BSc *Edin.*, PhD *Warw.*   Prof.
Rowlands, David J., BSc *Lond.*, PhD *S'ton.*   Hon. Prof.
Whittenbury, Roger, CBE, BSc *Leeds*, MSc *Edin.*, PhD *Edin.*   Prof.; Chairman*
Woodland, Hugh R., MA *Oxf.*, DPhil *Oxf.*   Prof.
Other Staff: 9 Lectrs.; 14 Res. Fellows; 3 Hon. Lectrs.
Research: cell and molecular development; ecosystems analysis and management; microbiology; molecular cell biology; molecular medicine

British and Comparative Cultural Studies, Centre for
Tel: (01203) 523655 *Fax*: (01203) 524468
Bassnett, Susan E., BA *Manc.*, PhD *Lanc.*   Prof.
Dabydeen, David, MA *Camb.*, PhD *Lond.*   Prof.
Kuhiwczak, Piotr, MA *Warsaw*, PhD *Warsaw*   Lectr.; Dir.*
Snell-Hornby, M., MA *St And.*, DPhil *Zür.*   Hon. Prof.
Tymoczko, Maria, BA *Harv.*, MA *Harv.*, PhD *Harv.*   Hon. Prof.
Yamanouchi, Hisaaki, BA *Tokyo*, MA *Tokyo*, PhD *Camb.*   Hon. Prof.
Other Staff: 2 Lectrs.; 2 Res. Fellows
Research: Caribbean studies; literary criticism; literature; translation in theory and practice

Business, see Warwick Bus. Sch.

Chemistry
Tel: (01203) 523678 *Fax*: (01203) 524112
Alcock, Nathaniel W., BA *Camb.*, PhD *Camb.*, FSA   Reader
Crout, David H. G., MA *Camb.*, PhD *Wales*, FRSChem   Prof., Organic Chemistry
Derrick, Peter J., BSc *Lond.*, PhD *Lond.*, FIP, FRACI, FRSChem   Prof.; Chairman*
Elson, Stephen W., BSc *Liv.*   Hon. Prof.

Haddleton, D. M., BSc York(UK), PhD York(UK) Sr. Lectr.

Hirst, David M., BSc Oxf., MA Oxf., DPhil Oxf. Reader

Howarth, Oliver W., MA Oxf., DPhil Oxf. Sr. Lectr.

Jenkins, Donald B., BScTech Manc., DPhil Sus. Reader

Jennings, Keith R., MA Oxf., DPhil Oxf., FRSChem Prof., Physical Chemistry

Kemp, Terry J., MA Oxf., DPhil Oxf., DSc Oxf., FRSChem Prof.

Matlin, Stephen A., BSc Lond., PhD Lond., DSc City(UK), FRSChem Hon. Prof.

Moore, Peter, BSc Sheff., PhD Sheff. Prof., Co-ordination Chemistry

Scrivens, James H., BSc Manc., MSc Manc., PhD Manc. Hon. Prof.

Unwin, Patrick R., BSc Liv., DPhil Oxf. Sr. Lectr.

Wallbridge, Malcolm G. H., BSc Lond., PhD Exe., FRSChem Prof., Inorganic Chemistry

Willey, Gerald R., BSc Brist., PhD Brist., FRSChem Sr. Lectr.

Wills, Martin, BSc Lond., DPhil Oxf. Reader

Other Staff: 11 Lectrs.; 1 Sr. Res. Fellow; 19 Res. Fellows

Research: analytical, biological, inorganic, organic, physical and theoretical chemistry

Classics

Tel: (01203) 523023 Fax: (01203) 524973

Whitby, L. Michael, MA Oxf., DPhil Oxf. Prof.; Chairman*

Other Staff: 5 Lectrs.; 2 Res. Fellows

Research: archaeology of the Black Sea coast; east Roman studies; Greek and Roman poetry and drama

Computer Science

Tel: (01203) 523668 Fax: (01203) 525714

Beynon, W. Meurig, BSc Lond., PhD Lond. Sr. Lectr.

Campbell-Kelly, Martin, BSc Manc., PhD CNAA Reader

Larcombe, Madeline H. E., MA Camb., PhD Newcastle(UK) Reader

Martin, Graham R., BSc Lond., PhD Lond. Sr. Lectr.

Nudd, Graham R., BSc S'ton., PhD S'ton. Prof.; Chairman*

Paterson, Michael S., MA Camb., PhD Camb. Prof.

Wilson, Roland G., BSc Glas., PhD Glas. Reader

Research: applications; software; systems; theory

Continuing Education

Tel: (01203) 523827 Fax: (01203) 524223

Bown, Lalage, OBE, MA Oxf., Hon. DUniv Stir., Hon. DLitt Hon. Prof.

Burgess, Robert, BA Durh., PhD Warw. Prof.

Field, John, BA CNAA, PhD Warw., FRSA Prof.; Chairman*

Fordham, P., BA Leeds Hon. Prof.

Leicester, Mal, BA Wales, MEd Manc., PhD Manc. Sr. Lectr.

Lowe, J., BA Liv., PhD Lond. Hon. Prof.

Preston, Rosemary, BA Leeds, MA Leeds, PhD Leeds Sr. Lectr.

Stubbs, Sir; William, BSc Glas., PhD Glas. Hon. Prof.

Tight, Malcolm, BSc Lond., PhD Lond. Reader

Other Staff: 4 Lectrs.; 1 Sr. Res. Fellow

Research: gender; human resource development and adult learning; institutional change; multicultural education and equal opportunities; philosophy of education

Economics

Tel: (01203) 523055 Fax: (01203) 523032

Arulampalam, S. Wiji, BSc(Econ) Lond., MSc Lond., PhD Lond. Reader

Broadberry, Stephen N., BA Warw., DPhil Oxf. Prof.

Cowling, Keith G., BSc(Agric) Lond., PhD Ill. Clarkson Prof., Industrial Economics

Crafts, Nicholas F. R., BA Camb., FBA Hon. Prof.

Cripps, Martin W., MSc(Econ) Lond., PhD Lond. Prof.

Harrison, R. Mark, BA Camb., DPhil Oxf. Reader

Ireland, Norman J., BSocSci Birm., MSocSc Birm., PhD Prof.; Chairman*

Knight, Ben, BA Manc., MA(Econ) Manc. Sr. Lectr.

Leech, Dennis, BA Manc., MA(Econ) Manc., PhD Warw. Sr. Lectr.

Miller, Marcus H., BA Oxf., MA Yale, PhD Yale Prof.

Naylor, Robin A., BSc(Econ) Lond., MPhil Oxf., PhD Warw. Sr. Lectr.

Oswald, Andrew, BA Stir., MSc Strath., DPhil Oxf. Prof.

Rankin, Neil, MA Oxf., DPhil Oxf. Sr. Lectr.

Roe, Alan R., MA Wales, BComm Sr. Lectr.

Round, Jeffrey I., BSc Nott., PhD Wales Reader

Skidelsky, Lord, MA Oxf., DPhil Oxf., FRHistS, FRSL, FBA Prof., Political Economy

Stewart, Mark B., MSc(Econ) Lond., BA Warw. Prof.

Thomas, Jonathan P., MA Camb., MPhil Oxf., DPhil Oxf. Prof.

Wallis, Kenneth F., BSc Manc., MScTech Manc., PhD Stan., FBA Prof., Econometrics

Waterson, Michael J., BSc Lond., BA Warw., PhD Warw. Prof.

Whalley, John, BA Essex, MA Essex, PhD Yale Prof., Development Economics

Other Staff: 17 Lectrs.; 6 Sr. Res. Fellows; 1 Sr. Lectr.†

Research: econometrics; economic history; economic theory; industrial and labour economics; macroeconomics

Education, Institute of

Tel: (01203) 523220 Fax: (01203) 524177

Alexander, Robin J., MA Camb., MEd Manc., PhD Camb. Prof., Primary Education

Campbell, R. James, BA Hull, MSc Brad. Prof.; Chairman*

Ellis, Philip, MA York(UK), PhD Warw. Sr. Lectr.

Gray, E. M., BA Open(UK), MSc Lough., PhD Warw. Sr. Lectr.

Heward, Christine M., MA Edin., MSocSc Birm., PhD Birm. Sr. Lectr.

Husbands, Christopher R., MA Camb., PhD Camb. Reader

Jackson, Robert M. D., BA Wales, MA Warw., PhD Warw. Prof.

Kelly, Donald O., BSc Lond., PhD Lond., DSc Lond., FIBiol Prof.

Lang, Peter L. F., MA Camb., MA Warw. Sr. Lectr.

Lewis, Ann, BEd Warw., BPhil(Ed) Birm., MEd Birm., PhD Warw. Reader

Lindsay, Geoffrey A., BSc Durh., MEd Birm., PhD Birm., FBPsS Prof., Special Educational Needs

Luddy, Mona, BA N.U.I., PhD N.U.I. Sr. Lectr.

Moore, George E., BA Nott., MA Nott. Sr. Lectr.

Neill, Sean R. St. J., BA Oxf., DPhil Oxf. Sr. Lectr.

Richards, C. Hon. Prof.

Robinson, Kenneth, BEd Leeds, PhD Lond. Prof.

Tall, David O., MA Oxf., DPhil Oxf., PhD Warw. Prof.†

Other Staff: 2 Sr. Lectrs. †

Research: arts education; industry collaboration; mathematics education; primary education; special needs

Engineering

Fax: (01203) 418922

Anderson, David, BSc Manc., PhD Manc., FIStructE, FICE Prof.

Arunachalam, V. S., BSc Mys., MSc Saug., PhD Wales, Hon. DSc Indore, Hon. DLitt Annam., Hon. DEngg Roor. Hon. Prof.

Bass, J. C., CBE, MSc Lond., PhD Sheff., FEng Hon. Prof.

Bhattacharya, Ashak K., MSc I.I.T., PhD Camb. Dir., Catalysis and Emissions Res. Unit

Bhattacharyya, Kumar, CBE, BTech Kharagpur, MSc Birm., PhD Birm., FEng Prof., Manufacturing Systems Engineering

Boldy, Adrian P., BSc Leic., PhD Leic. Sr. Lectr.

Bowen, D. Keith, MA Oxf., DPhil Oxf., FIM Prof.

Bryanston-Cross, Peter J., BSc Aston, PhD Aston Prof.

Carpenter, Peter W., BSc Lond., MSc Cinc., PhD Cinc. Prof., Mechanical Engineering

Chetwynd, Derek G., BA Oxf., PhD Leic. Reader

Clark, J. L. C., BSc Durh., PhD Durh., FIP Hon. Prof.

Cullyer, William J., BSc Brist., PhD Brist., FRAeS, FIEE Prof.†, Electronics

Cumming, A., Hon. DSc, FEng, FRAeS Indust. Prof.

Dowd, Amanda L., BSc Leic., PhD Leic. Lectr.; Academic Dir., Grad. Studies

Duncomb, P., MA Camb., PhD Camb., FRS FIP Hon. Prof.

Ferrie, J. Indust. Prof.

Flower, John O., BSc Lond., PhD Lond., DSc Lond., FIEE FIMarE Prof.; Chairman*

Franks, A., DSc Lond., FIP Hon. Prof.

Gardner, Julian W., BSc Birm., PhD Camb. Reader

Godfrey, Keith R., BSc(Eng) Lond., PhD Lond., DSc Warw., FIEE Prof.

Harris, J., FIEE Hon. Prof.

Hart, M., BSc Brist., PhD Brist., DSc Brist., FRS Hon. Prof.

Hill, John F., MSc Birm. Sr. Lectr.

Hines, Evor L., BSc CNAA, PhD Brad. Sr. Lectr.

Horlock, J., MA Camb., PhD Camb., DSc Camb. Hon. Prof.

Hutchins, David A., BSc Aston, PhD Aston Prof.

Johnson, R. P., MA Camb., FEng, FICE, FIStructE Prof., Civil Engineering

Jones, R. P., BSc Sheff., MScTech Sheff., PhD Sheff., FIMA Sr. Lectr.

Lau, W. S., MSc Manc., PhD Manc. Hon. Prof.

Lawson, Stuart S., BSc CNAA, PhD Lond. Reader

Lewis, W. J., BSc Opole, MSc Birm., PhD CNAA Sr. Lectr.

McNulty, R., CBE, BA Trinity(Dub.), BComm Trinity(Dub.) Indust. Prof.

Menzies, J. B., BSc Durh., FEng, FIStructE Hon. Prof.

Mottram, J. Toby, BSc Durh., PhD Durh. Sr. Lectr.

Pashby, Ian R., BMet Sheff., PhD Warw. Sr. Lectr.

Pollock, Charles, BSc Lond., PhD H.-W. Sr. Lectr.

Price, A. M., BSc Newcastle(UK), PhD Newcastle(UK) Dir., Undergrad. Studies

Roy, Rajat, BSc Calc., MSc Birm. Sr. Lectr.

Ruffles, P. C., BSc Brist., FEng, FIMechE, FRAeS Hon. Prof.

Shaw, Christopher T., MA Camb., PhD Cran.IT Sr. Lectr.

Simpson, G., FCCA Indust. Prof.

Swinden, Kenneth H., BSc Sheff., PhD Sheff. Lectr.

Thomas, Terry H., BA Camb., PhD Warw. Sr. Lectr.

Towers, J., CBE, FEng Indust. Prof.

Turner, F. Indust. Prof.

Veshagh, Ali, BSc Teheran, PhD Bath Sr. Lectr.

Wallbank, James, BSc Wales, MSc Strath., PhD Birm. Sr. Lectr.

Warry, P. T. Indust. Prof.

Whitehouse, David J., BSc Brist., PhD Leic., DSc Warw., FIEE Prof., Mechanical Engineering

Other Staff: 26 Lectrs.; 4 Principal Teaching Fellows; 55 Sr. Teaching Fellows; 10 Teaching Fellows; 7 Principal Fellows; 9 Sr. Fellows; 5 Principal Res. Fellows; 39 Sr. Res. Fellows; 35 Res. Fellows

Research: advanced materials assessment and characterisation; control engineering;

development studies; electronics; fluid mechanics and aerodynamics

English and Comparative Literary Studies

Tel: (01203) 523665 Fax: (01203) 524750

Beaver, Harold L., MA Oxf., MA Harv. Hon. Prof.
Bell, Michael, BA Lond., PhD Lond. Prof.
Davidson, MA Camb., MA York(UK), PhD Camb. Sr. Lectr.
Edwards, Michael, MA Camb., PhD Camb. Prof.
Hardman, Malcolm, MA Camb., PhD Camb. Sr. Lectr.
Hughes, Derek W., MA Oxf., PhD Liv. Reader
Hunter, George K., MA Glas., DPhil Oxf. Hon. Prof.
Janowitz, Anne F., BA Reed, BA Oxf., PhD Stan. Reader
Mack, Peter W. D., MA Oxf., MPhil Lond., PhD Lond. Reader
Mulryne, J. Ronald, MA Camb., PhD Camb. Prof.
Nash, Christopher W., BA Calif., MA N.Y., PhD N.Y. Sr. Lectr.
Rawson, Claude J., MA Oxf., BLitt Oxf. Hon. Prof.
Rignall, John M., MA Camb., DPhil Sus. Sr. Lectr.
Taylor, Helen R., BA Lond., MA Louisiana, DPhil Sus. Reader
Treglown, Jeremy, MA Oxf., BLitt Oxf., PhD Lond., FRSL Prof.; Chairman*
Winnifrith, Thomas J., MA Oxf., BPhil Oxf., PhD Liv. Sr. Lectr.
Other Staff: 14 Lectrs.; 2 Winter Fellows; 2 Res. Fellows; 1 Sr. Lectr.†
Research: literature in the English language from the Middle Ages to the present

English Language Teacher Education, Centre for

Tel: (01203) 523200 Fax: (01203) 524318

Henderson, Thelma, BA Lond., MA Essex Sr. Lectr.; Jt. Dir.*
Khan, Julia P., MA Manc., MEd Leic. Lectr.; Jt. Dir.*
Spencer, John, MA Oxf. Hon. Prof.
Other Staff: 8 Lectrs.; 1 Sr. Teaching Fellow; 2 Res. Fellows
Research: English language teacher education; language education policy; planning, grammar and discourse; testing and evaluation

Film and Television Studies

Tel: (01203) 523511 Fax: (01203) 524757

Brunsdon, Charlotte M., BA Lond. Sr. Lectr.
Dyer, R. W., MA St And., PhD Birm Prof.
Perkins, V. F., BA Oxf. Sr. Lectr.
Vincendeau, Ginette, LèsL Paris, PhD E.Anglia Prof.; Chairman*
Other Staff: 3 Lectrs.
Research: European cinema and television; gender and ethnicity

French Studies

Tel: (01203) 523013 Fax: (01203) 524679

Hill, Leslie J., MA Camb., PhD Camb. Reader
Howarth, William D., MA Oxf., DLitt Brist., Hon. DUniv Bordeaux Hon. Prof.
Paterson, Linda M., MA Camb., PhD Camb. Reader
Shields, James G., MA Glas., PhD Glas. Sr. Lectr.
Thompson, Christopher W., MA Camb., PhD Camb. Prof.; Chairman*
Other Staff: 5 Lectrs.; 1 Sr. Lectr. †
Research: cinema, politics and culture; francophone Caribbean writing; French literature; philosophy and critical theory

German Studies

Tel: (01203) 524419 Fax: (01203) 524419

Burns, Robert A., BA Birm., MA Warw., PhD Warw. Reader
Carr, Godfrey R., BA Manc., PhD Birm. Sr. Lectr.

Lamb, S. J., BA Birm., MA Warw.
Osborne, John, BA Wales, PhD Camb., DLitt Wales Prof.
Phelan, Anthony, MA Camb., PhD Camb. Sr. Lectr.; Chairman*
Other Staff: 2 Lectrs.; 2 Res. Fellows
Research: German culture from 1870 to the present day

History

Tel: (01203) 522080 Fax: (01203) 523437

Berg, Maxine L., BA S.Fraser, MA Sus., DPhil Oxf. Reader
Butters, Humfrey C., BA Oxf., DPhil Oxf. Sr. Lectr.
Capp, Bernard S., MA Oxf., DPhil Oxf., FRHistS Prof.
Clark, C., BA Warw., MA Harv., PhD Harv. Prof.
Clifton, Robin, MA Well., DPhil Oxf., FRHistS Sr. Lectr.
Cohn, Henry J., MA Oxf., DPhil Oxf., FRHistS Reader
Darnton, Robert, BA Oxf., DPhil Oxf. Hon. Prof.
Heuman, Gad J., AB Columbia Coll., MA Yale, MPhil Yale, PhD Yale Reader
Hinton, James S., BA Camb., PhD Lond., FRHistS Reader; Chairman*
Jones, Colin D. H., BA Oxf., DPhil Oxf., FRHistS Prof.
King, John P., MA Edin., DPhil Oxf. Prof.
Lenman, Robin J. V., MA Oxf., BPhil Oxf., DPhil Oxf. Sr. Lectr.
Lowry, Martin J. C., MA Oxf., PhD, FRHistS Reader
Magraw, Roger W., BA Oxf., BPhil Oxf. Sr. Lectr.
Mallett, Michael E., MA Oxf., DPhil Oxf., FRHistS Prof.
McFarlane, Anthony J., BSc(Econ) Lond., PhD Lond. Reader
Okey, Robin F. C., MA Oxf., DPhil Oxf., FRHistS Sr. Lectr.
Read, Christopher J., BA Keele, MPhil Glas., PhD Lond. Reader
Smith, Iain R., MA Edin., MA Wis., DPhil Oxf., FRHistS Sr. Lectr.
Thomson, G. P. C., BSc Lond., DPhil Oxf. Sr. Lectr.
Other Staff: 8 Lectrs.; 3 Res. Fellows
Research: British, European and comparative American history, including social history and the history of medicine

History of Art

Tel: (01203) 523005 Fax: (01203) 523006

Gardner, Julian, MA Oxf., PhD Lond., FSA Prof.
Hills, J. G. Paul, BA Camb., MA Lond., PhD Lond. Sr. Lectr.
Morris, Richard K., BA Camb., PhD Lond., FSA Reader
Rosenthal, Michael J., BA Lond., MA Camb., PhD Lond. Sr. Lectr.
Other Staff: 1 Lectr.; 2 Res. Fellows
Research: art and architecture of Western Europe; mediaeval art in the East and West; Venice

International Studies, see Pol. and Internat. Studies

Italian

Tel: (01203) 524126 Fax: (01203) 524126

Rawson, Judith A., MA Oxf. Sr. Lectr.; Chairman*
Other Staff: 1 Lectr.; 2 Sr. Teaching Fellows; 1 Sr. Lectr.†
Research: narrative and theatre from the Middle Ages to the present day

Law

Tel: (01203) 523075 Fax: (01203) 524105

Baxi, Upendra, BA Gujar., LLB Bom., LLM Bom., LLM Calif., JSD Calif. Prof., Law and Development
Beale, Hugh G., BA Oxf. Prof.
Bridges, L. T., BA Dartmouth Prof.

Burridge, Roger H. M., LLB Birm. Sr. Lectr.
Cooper, Davina, LLB Lond., PhD Warw. Reader
Faundez, Julio, LCJ Santiago(Chile), LLM Harv., SJD Harv. Prof.
Ghai, Y. P., CBE, BA Oxf., LLM Harv. Hon. Prof.
Leng, Roger, LLB Nott. Reader
Luckhaus, L., LLB Warw., MA Sheff. Sr. Lectr.
Masson, Judith M., MA Camb., PhD Leic. Prof.
McConville, Michael J., LLB Lond., PhD Nott. Prof.; Chairman*
McEldowney, John F., LLB Belf., PhD Camb. Reader
Moffat, Graham J., LLB Warw., MA Warw. Sr. Lectr.
Paliwala, Abdul H., LLB Lond., PhD Lond. Prof.
Pogany, Istvan, LLB Edin., LLM Edin., PhD Exe. Reader
Rogowski, Ralf, DrJur Florence, LLM Wis. Sr. Lectr.
Sedley, Sir Stephen, QC, MA Camb. Hon. Prof.
Stewart, Ann, LLB Leic., MJur Birm. Sr. Lectr.
Whelan, Christopher J., LLB Lond., MA Oxf., PhD Lond. Sr. Lectr.
Willett, Christopher, LLB Strath., PhD Brun. Sr. Lectr.
Willey, D. Hon. Prof.
Other Staff: 17 Lectrs.; 5 Res. Fellows
Research: social and theoretical contexts of the operation of legal rules and institutions; UK, European and international law

Mathematics

Tel: (01203) 524683 Fax: (01203) 524182

Carter, Roger W., MA Camb., PhD Camb. Prof.†
Dritschel, David G., BSc Texas, PhD Prin. Reader
Elworthy, K. David, MA Oxf., DPhil Oxf. Prof.
Epstein, David B. A., BSc Witw., BA Camb., PhD Camb. Prof.
Hajarnavis, Charu R., BA Camb., MSc Leeds, PhD Leeds Reader
Hawkes, Trevor O., MA Camb., PhD Camb. Reader
Holt, Derek F., BA Oxf., MSc Oxf., DPhil Oxf. Reader
Jones, John D. S., BSc Manc., MSc Oxf., DPhil Oxf. Prof.
Macbeath, A. M. Hon. Prof.
Manning, Anthony K., MA Camb., PhD Warw. Reader
Markus, Lawrence, BS Chic., MS Chic., PhD Harv. Hon. Prof.
Micallef, Mario J., BSc Sus., MS N.Y., PhD N.Y. Reader
Mond, David M. Q., BA Oxf., MA Col., PhD Liv. Sr. Lectr.
Newell, Alan C., PhD M.I.T., BA Trinity(Dub.) Prof.; Chairman*
Parry, William, BSc Lond., PhD Lond., MSc Liv., FRS Prof.
Pritchard, Anthony J., BSc Lond., PhD Warw., FIMA Prof.
Rand, David A., BSc S'ton., PhD S'ton. Prof.
Rawnsley, John H., BA Oxf., DPhil Oxf. Reader
Reid, Miles A., BA Camb., PhD Camb. Prof.
Robinson, C. Alan, BA Camb., MSc PhD Sr. Lectr.
Rourke, Colin P., MA Camb., PhD Camb. Reader
Salamon, Dietmar A., PhD Bremen Prof.
Series, Caroline M., MA Oxf., AM Harv., PhD Harv. Prof.
Stewart, Ian N., BA Camb., PhD Warw. Prof.
Stonehewer, Stewart E., MA Oxf., PhD Camb. Reader
Swinnerton-Dyer, Sir Peter, KBE, Hon. DSc, FRS Hon. Prof.
van Strien, Sebastien J., MSc Gron., PhD Utrecht, PhD Warw. Reader
Walters, Peter, BSc Birm., DPhil Sus. Prof.
Zeeman, Sir Christopher, MA Camb., PhD Camb., Hon. Dr Stras., Hon. DSc Hull, Hon. DSc Warw., FRS Hon. Prof.
Other Staff: 10 Lectrs.; 1 Sr. Res. Fellow; 12 Res. Fellows; 1 Reader†

Research: pure and applied mathematics

Medical Education, Postgraduate School of

Tel: (01203) 523745 Fax: (01203) 524311

Booth, L. J., MB ChB *Liv.*, FRCP Dir., Postgrad. Med. Educn.

Dale, J., BA *Camb.*, MBBS *Lond.* Prof., Primary Care

Fulford, K. W. M., MD *Camb.*, MA *Camb.*, PhD *Lond.*, DPhil *Oxf.*, FRCP, FRCPhys Prof.†, Philosophy of Mental Health

Hillhouse, Edward, BSc *Lond.* MBBS *Lond.*, PhD *Lond.*, FRCP Prof., Medicine; Chairman*

Spencer, N. J., MPhil *Nott.*, FRCPEd, FRCPH Prof., Community Child Health

Other Staff: 5 Res. Fellows; 6 Hon. Sr. Clin. Lectrs.

Research: child health; health sciences; medicine; obstetrics and gynaecology; primary health care

Philosophy

Tel: (01203) 523421 Fax: (01203) 523019

Ansell-Pearson, Keith, BA *Hull*, MA *Sus.*, DPhil *Sus.* Sr. Lectr.

Battersby, Christine, BA *York(UK)*, DPhil *Sus.* Sr. Lectr.

Benjamin, Andrew E., BA *ANU*, MA *ANU*, PhD *Warw.* Prof.

Fulford, K. William M., MD *Camb.*, MA *Camb.*, PhD *Lond.*, DPhil *Oxf.*, FRCPhys, FRCP Prof.†, Philosophy and mental health

Houlgate, Stephen, BA *Camb.*, MA *Camb.*, PhD *Camb.* Prof.

Hunt, Greg M. K., BSc *Melb.*, MA *Melb.* Sr. Lectr.; Chairman*

Luntley, Michael, BA *Warw.*, BPhil *Oxf.*, DPhil *Oxf.* Sr. Lectr.

Miller, David W., MA *Camb.*, MSc(Econ) *Lond.* Reader

Trigg, Roger H., JP, MA *Oxf.*, DPhil *Oxf.* Prof.

Warner, Martin M., MA *Oxf.*, BPhil *Oxf.* Sr. Lectr.

Wood, David C., BA *Manc.*, PhD *Warw.* Hon. Prof.

Other Staff: 5 Lectrs.; 6 Res. Fellows

Research: European philosophy; philosophy in literature; philosophy of consciousness and self-consciousness; philosophy of psychiatry; political and social theory

Physics

Tel: (01203) 523353 Fax: (01203) 692016

Chapman, Sandra C., BSc *Lond.*, PhD *Lond.*, FIP, FRAS Reader

Cooper, Malcolm J., MA *Camb.*, PhD *Camb.*, FIP Prof.

d'Ambrumenil, Nicholas H., MA *Camb.*, DrRerNat *T.H.Darmstadt* Sr. Lectr.

Dendy, R. O., BA *Oxf.*, DPhil *Oxf.* Hon. Prof.

Dixon, John M., BSc *Nott.*, PhD *Nott.*, DSc *Nott.*, FIP, FIMA Reader

Dowsett, Mark G., BSc *Lond.*, PhD *CNAA* Reader

Dupree, Raymond, BSc *Exe.*, PhD *Exe.*, FIP Prof.

Forsyth, J. Bruce, MA *Camb.*, PhD *Camb.*, FIP Hon. Prof.

Holland, Diane, MA *Oxf.*, DPhil *Oxf.* Sr. Lectr.

Hyland, Gerard J., BSc *Liv.*, PhD *Liv.* Sr. Lectr.

Kearney, Michael J., BA *Oxf.*, MA *Oxf.*, PhD *Warw.* Hon. Prof.

Lewis, Michael H., BSc *Wales*, DPhil *Oxf.* Prof.; Dir., Electron Optical Lab.

McConville, C. F., BSc *Lanc.*, PhD *Warw.* Sr. Lectr.

Melville, D., BSc *Sheff.*, PhD *Sheff.*, FIP, FRSA Hon. Prof.

Palmer, Stuart B., BSc *Sheff.*, PhD *Sheff.*, DSc *Sheff.*, FIP, FIEE Prof., Experimental Physics; Chairman*

Parker, Evan H. C., BSc *Lond.*, DPhil *Sus.* Prof., Semiconductor Physics

Paul, Donald McK., BSc *St And.*, DPhil *Sus.* Prof.

Pettifer, Robert F., BSc *Leic.*, MSc *CNAA*, PhD *Warw.* Sr. Lectr.

Robinson, James, BSc *S'ton.*, PhD *S'ton.* Sr. Lectr.

Rowlands, George, BSc *Leeds*, PhD *Leeds*, FIP Prof.

Smith, M., BA *Camb.*, PhD *Warw.* Reader

Staunton, Jane B., BSc *Brist.*, PhD *Brist.* Reader

Thomas, Pamela A., BA *Oxf.*, DPhil *Oxf.* Sr. Lectr.

Whall, Terry E., BSc *Lond.*, DPhil *Sus.* Prof.

Woodruff, Philip, BSc *Brist.*, PhD *Warw.*, DSc *Warw.* Prof.

Other Staff: 4 Lectrs.; 43 Res. Fellows

Research: astronomy; experimental solid state physics; physics of materials; theoretical condensed matter physics

Politics and International Studies

Tel: (01203) 524141 Fax: (01203) 524221

Allison, Lincoln R. P., MA *Oxf.* Reader

Bulpitt, James G., BA *Exe.*, MA *Manc.* Prof.; Chairman*

Burnell, Peter J., BA *Brist.*, MA *Warw.*, PhD *Warw.* Sr. Lectr.

Ferdinand, C. I. Peter, BA *Oxf.*, MSc(Econ) *Lond.*, DPhil *Oxf.* Reader

Grant, Wyn P., BA *Leic.*, MSc *Strath.*, PhD *Exe.* Prof.

Halliday, R. John, BA *Manc.* Sr. Lectr.

Higgott, Richard A., BA *CNAA*, MSc *Lond.*, PhD *Birm.* Prof.

Hurley, Susan, BA *Prin.*, BPhil *Harv.*, MA *Harv.*, DPhil *Harv.*, JD *Harv.* Prof.

Layton-Henry, Zig A., BSocSc *Birm.*, PhD *Birm.* Prof.

Lockwood, B., BA *Sus.*, PhD *Warw.* Prof.

Mervin, David, BA *Exe.*, PhD *Cornell* Reader

Mortimer, Edward, MA *Oxf.* Hon. Prof.

Rai, Shirin M., MA *Delhi*, PhD *Camb.* Sr. Lectr.

Reeve, Andrew W., BA *Oxf.*, DPhil *Oxf.* Reader

Other Staff: 17 Lectrs.; 2 Res. Fellows

Research: democratisation; international business history; international political economy; political theory; politics of environmental policy and sport

Psychology

Tel: (01203) 523189 Fax: (01203) 524225

Annett, John, MA *Oxf.*, DPhil *Oxf.* Emer. Prof.

Brown, Gordon D. A., MA *Oxf.*, DPhil *Sus.* Prof.

Chater, Nicholas, MA *Camb.*, PhD *Edin.* Prof.

Jones, Gregory V., MA *Oxf.*, MA *Camb.*, PhD *Camb.*, DPhil *Oxf.* Prof.

Morley, Ian E., BA *Keele*, PhD *Nott.* Sr. Lectr.; Chairman*

Van-Toller, Steve, BSc *Lond.*, PhD *Durh.*, FBPsS Reader

Other Staff: 6 Lectrs.; 7 Res. Fellows; 1 Hon. Clin. Sr. Lectr.

Research: cognitive, developmental and chemosensory psychology; philosophy of psychology; relationships support and health

Social Studies, see Appl. Soc. Studies

Sociology

Tel: (01203) 523150 Fax: (01203) 523497

Archer, Margaret S., BSc(Soc) *Lond.*, PhD *Lond.* Prof.

Beckford, James A., BA *Reading*, PhD *Reading*, DLitt *Reading* Prof.

Burgess, Robert G., BA *Durh.*, PhD *Warw.* Prof.

Clarke, Simon R. C., BA *Camb.*, PhD *Essex* Prof.

Cohen, Robin, BA *Witw.*, MSc *Lond.*, PhD *Birm.* Prof.

Elger, Anthony J., BA *Hull*, PhD *Durh.* Sr. Lectr.

Fairbrother, Peter D., BA *Monash*, DPhil *Oxf.* Reader

Fine, Robert D., BA *Oxf.*, PhD *Warw.* Reader

Procter, I., BA *Durh.*, PhD *Durh.* Sr. Lectr.; Chairman*

Ratcliffe, Peter B., BSc *Lond.*, MSc *Lond.* Lectr.

Wagner, P., PhD *Berl.* Prof.

Other Staff: 15 Lectrs.; 8 Res. Fellows

Research: labour studies; political sociology; social and political thought; social theory and philosophy; sociologies of crime, education, gender, health, migration, race and racism, and religion

Statistics

Tel: (01203) 523066 Fax: (01203) 524532

Copas, John B., BSc *Lond.*, PhD *Lond.* Prof.

Harrison, P. Jeffrey, BSc *Nott.* Prof.

Jacka, Saul D., MA *Camb.*, PhD *Camb.* Reader

Kendall, Wilfred S., MA *Oxf.*, MSc *Oxf.*, DPhil *Oxf.* Prof.

Smith, James Q., BSc *Nott.*, PhD *Warw.* Prof.; Chairman*

Wynn, Henry P., MA *Oxf.*, PhD *Lond.* Prof., Industrial Statistics

Other Staff: 3 Lectrs.; 8 Res. Fellows

Research: Bayesian statistics; image analysis; numerical methods; probability theory and applications; socio-medical statistics

Television Studies, see Film and TV Studies

Theatre Studies

Tel: (01203) 523020 Fax: (01203) 524446

Beacham, Richard C., MFA *Yale*, DFA *Yale* Prof.

Bennett, Oliver, BA *York(UK)* Sr. Lectr.

Cousin, Geraldine, BA *Exe.*, PhD *Exe.* Sr. Lectr.

Kaye, Nick J., BA *Birm.*, PhD *Manc.* Sr. Lectr.

Shewring, Margaret E., BA *Birm.*, PhD *Birm.* Sr. Lectr.

Thomas, David B., MA *Camb.*, PhD *Camb.* Prof.; Chairman*

Other Staff: 2 Lectrs.; 1 Res. Fellow

Research: European cultural policy and administration; history of theatre; Third World theatre; twentieth-century performance theory and analysis

Warwick Business School

Tel: (01203) 524534 Fax: (01203) 523719

Benington, John, MA *Camb.* Prof.

Boothroyd, BSc *Lond.* Emer. Reader

Bryer, Robert A., BA *CNAA*, MSc *Warw.*, PhD *Warw.* Reader

Burrell, Gideon, BA *Leic.*, MPhil *Leic.*, PhD *Manc.* Prof., Organisational Behaviour

Carr, G. R., BA *Manc.*, PhD *Birm.* Sr. Lectr.

Collinson, David, BSc *Manc.*, MSc *Manc.*, PhD *Manc.* Sr. Lectr.

Corbett, Martin J., BA *Leeds*, MA *Lanc.*, PhD *Warw.* Sr. Lectr.

Davidson, Ian, MA *Oxf.*, PhD *Brist.*, FCA Prof., Accounting and Finance

Dibb, C. Sally, BSc *Manc.*, MSc *Manc.*, PhD *Warw.* Sr. Lectr.

Dickens, Linda J., BA *Kent*, MA *Warw.* Prof.

Doyle, Peter, BA *Manc.*, MA(Econ) *Manc.*, MSc *Carnegie-Mellon*, PhD *Carnegie-Mellon* Prof., Marketing/Strategic Management

Dyson, Robert G., BSc *Liv.*, PhD *Lanc.* Prof.

Edwards, Paul K., BA *Camb.*, BPhil *Oxf.*, DPhil *Oxf.* Prof.

Galliers, Robert D., BA *Harv.*, MA *Lanc.*, PhD *Lond.*, Hon. DSc(Econ) *Turku*, FBCS Lucas Prof., Business Systems Engineering; Chairman*

Hall, Mark, BA *York(UK)*, MA *Warw.* Sr. Lectr.

Hodges, Stuart, MSc *S'ton.*, PhD *Lond.*, FIMA Esmée Fairbairn Prof., Financial Management

Hurrion, Robert D., BSc *Hull*, MSc *Lond.*, PhD *Lond.* Reader

Hyman, Richard, BA *Oxf.*, DPhil *Oxf.* Prof.

Johnston, Robert, BSc *Aston* Reader

Langlands, A., BSc *Glas.*, FRCP Hon. Prof.

Legge, K., MA *Oxf.* Prof.

Leighfield, J., MA *Oxf.*, FBCS, FIDPM, FIOM Hon. Prof.

Lilford, R. J., PhD *Lond.* Hon. Prof.

Lowry, Sir Pat Hon. Prof.

Luff, S. T., BA *Manc.*, MSc *Manc.*, PhD *Manc.* Sr. Lectr.

McGee, John, BA *Manc.*, PhD *Stan.* Prof., Strategic Management

Mingers, John, BSc *Warw.*, MA *Lanc.*, PhD *Warw.* Sr. Lectr.

Ormerod, Richard S., BSc *Lond.*, MSc *Warw.* Prof., Operational Research and Systems

Pettigrew, Andrew M., BA *Liv.*, PhD *Manc.*, Hon. PhD *Linköping* Prof., Strategy and Organisation

Powell, Phillip, BSc *S'ton.*, PhD *S'ton.* Sr. Lectr.

Scarborough, Harold, BA *Durh.*, MBA *Brad.*, PhD *Aston* Sr. Lectr.

Sisson, Keith F., MA *Oxf.* Prof.

Slack, Nigel D. C., BTech *Brad.*, MSc *Brad.*, PhD *Brun.* A. E. Higgs Prof., Manufacturing Strategy and Policy

Steele, Anthony J., MA *Camb.*, MA *Lanc.*, FCA Ernst and Young Prof., Accounting

Stoneman, Paul L., BA *Warw.*, MSc(Econ) *Lond.*, PhD *Camb.* Prof.

Storey, David J., BSc *Hull*, PhD *Newcastle(UK)* Prof.

Swan, BSc *Sus.*, PhD *Wales* Sr. Lectr.

Terry, Michael A., BSc *Sus.*, MA *Warw.*, PhD *Warw.* Prof.

Thanassoulis, Emanuel, BSc *Sus.*, MSc *Warw.*, PhD *Warw.* Sr. Lectr.

Thomas, H., BSc *Lond.*, MSc *Lond.*, MBA *Chic.*, PhD *Edin.* Hon. Prof.

Tricker, R., MA *Oxf.*, PhD *CNAA*, FICA, FCIMA Hon. Prof.

Tristem, C. E. R., BSc *Nott.*, PhD *Warw.* Hon. Prof.

Waddams, Catherine A., BSc *Nott.*, PhD *Nott.* Prof.

Waddington, Jeremy D., BA *Lanc.*, MSc *Wales*, PhD *Warw.* Sr. Lectr.

Wensley, J. Robin C., BA *Camb.*, MSc *Lond.*, PhD *Lond.* Prof., Marketing/Strategic Management

Wilson, D. C., BA *Leeds*, MA *Leeds*, PhD *Brad.* Prof., Strategic Management

Wong, Veronica W. Y., BSc *Brad.*, MBA *Brad.*, PhD *CNAA* Sr. Lectr.

Other Staff: 48 Lectrs.; 7 Res. Fellows; 4 Sr. Lectrs.†

Research: accounting and finance; industrial relations and organisational behaviour; marketing and strategic management; operational research and systems; operations management

SPECIAL CENTRES, ETC

Advanced Materials, Centre for
Lewis, Prof. M. H., BSc *Wales*, DPhil *Oxf.* Dir.*
Research: development of novel ceramics and glasses

Advanced Technology, Centre for
Tel: (01203) 523102 Fax: (01203) 523387
Bhattacharyya, S. K., CBE, BTech *Kharagpur*, MSc *Birm.*, PhD *Birm.*, FEng Prof.; Dir.*
Research: design analysis and modelling; knowledge-based systems; materials; recycling; vehicle systems

Caribbean Studies, Centre for
Tel: (01203) 523443 Fax: (01203) 523443
Dabydeen, David, MA *Camb.*, PhD *Lond.* Reader
Heuman, Gad, BA *Col.*, MA *Yale*, MPhil *Yale*, PhD *Yale* Sr. Lectr.; Dir.*
Research: Caribbean history and literary culture

Comparative Labour Studies, Centre for
Tel: (01203) 524675
Fairbrother, Peter D., BA *Monash*, DPhil *Oxf.* Dir.*

Corporate Strategy and Change, Centre for
Tel: (01203) 523918 Fax: (01203) 524393
McGee, Prof. John, BA *Manc.*, PhD *Stan.* Dir.*
Other Staff: 11 Res. Fellows

Research: corporate strategy and change in the public and private sectors

Democratisation, Centre for the Study of
Ferdinand, C. Peter I., BA *Oxf.*, MSc(Econ) *Lond.*, DPhil *Oxf.* Dir.*
Research: economic, historical, legal, political and social dimensions of democratisation

Development Technology Unit
Thomas, T. H., BA *Camb.*, PhD *Warw.* Dir.*
Research: new technologies for application in developing countries; role of technology in rural economic development

East Roman Studies, Centre for Research in
Whitby, Prof. L. Michael, MA *Oxf.*, DPhil *Oxf.* Dir.*
Research: archaeology; economy; history; literature; religion

Education and Industry, Centre for
Tel: (01203) 523948 Fax: (01203) 523617
Huddleston, P., BA *Lond.*, MEd *Warw.* Dir.*
Other Staff: 2 Sr. Res. Fellows

Education in Development, International Centre for
Preston, Rosemary, BA *Leeds*, PhD *Leeds* Dir.*
Research: education and training in economic, political and social development, especially in developing countries

Educational Development, Appraisal and Research, Centre for (CEDAR)
Tel: (01203) 523638 Fax: (01203) 524472
Burgess, Prof. Robert G., BA *Durh.*, PhD Dir.*
Research: education and training

Elementary and Primary Education, Centre for Research in
Alexander, Prof. Robin J., MA *Camb.*, MEd *Manc.*, PhD *Camb.* Dir.*
Other Staff: 2 Lectrs., 4 Res. Fellows

Employment Research, Institute for
Tel: (01203) 523514 Fax: (01203) 524241
Elias, D. P. B., BSc *Manc.*, MA *Sheff.*, PhD *Calif.* Prof.
Lindley, Prof. Robert M., BSc *Lond.*, MSc *Lond.*, PhD *Warw.* Dir.*
Other Staff: 12 Res. Fellows
Research: developments in education, household, population and training behaviour; employment; labour market

ESRC Macroeconomic Modelling Bureau
Wallis, Prof. K. F., BSc *Manc.*, MScTech *Manc.*, PhD *Stan.* Dir.*
Other Staff: 3 Res. Fellows
Research: comparative assessment of macroeconomic models

Ethnic Relations, Centre for Research in
Tel: (01203) 522980 Fax: (01203) 524324
Anwar, Prof. M., MA *Punjab*, MA(Econ) *Manc.*, PhD *Brad.* Prof.
Layton-Henry, Prof. Zig, BSocSc *Birm.*, PhD *Birm.* Dir.*
Other Staff: 1 Lectr., 9 Res. Fellows
Research: economic change and racial discrimination; ethnic mobilisation and nationalism; migration and citizenship

Financial Options Research Centre
Tel: (01203) 524118 Fax: (01203) 524167
Hodges, Prof. Stuart D., MSc *S'ton.*, PhD *Lond.*, FIMA Dir.*
Other Staff: 6 Res. Fellows
Research: derivative instruments and risk management

Globalisation and Regionalisation, Centre for the Study of
Tel: (01203) 572533 Fax: (01203) 572548
Cohen, R., BA *Witw.*, MSc *Lond.*, PhD *Birm.* Prof.
Higgott, R., BA *CNAA*, Msc *Lond.*, PhD *Birm.* Prof.; Dir.*
Lockwood, B., BA *Sus.*, PhD *Warw.* Prof.

Health Services Studies, Centre for
Szczepura, A., MA *Oxf.*, DPhil *Oxf.* Dir.*
Other Staff: 12 Res. Fellows
Research: effectiveness and cost-effectiveness of health care interventions and services

Humanities Research Centre
Tel: (01203) 523401
Janowitz, Anne F., BA *Reed*, BA *Oxf.*, MA *Stan.*, PhD *Stan.* Dir.*
Other Staff: 1 Res. Fellow

Industrial Relations Research Unit
Tel: (01203) 524265 Fax: (01203) 524184
Edwards, P. K., BA *Camb.*, DPhil *Oxf.* Prof.
Sisson, Prof. Keith F., MA *Oxf.* Dir.*
Other Staff: 8 Res. Fellows
Research: employment relationships in Britain in the context of the internationalisation of the world economy

Legal Research Institute
Bridges, L. T. Prof.; Dir.*

Local Government Centre
Tel: (01203) 524505 Fax: (01203) 524410
Benington, Prof. J., MA *Camb.* Prof.; Dir.*
Other Staff: 3 Res. Fellows
Research: local government economic, social and organisational strategies

Mass Spectrometry, Institute of
Derrick, Prof. Peter J., BSc *Lond.*, PhD *Lond.*, FIP, FRACI, FRSChem Dir.*

Mathematics Education Research Centre
Gray, E. M., BA *Open(UK)*, MSc *Lough.*, PhD *Warw.* Dir.*
Research: forms and acquisition of mathematical knowledge

Nanotechnology and Microengineering, Centre for
Gardner, Julian W., BSc *Birm.*, PhD *Camb.* Dir.*
Research: nanotechnology and ultra-precision engineering

Non-Linear Systems Laboratory
Tel: (01203) 523584
Rand, Prof. David A., BSc *S'ton.*, PhD *S'ton.* Dir.*
Research: non-linear mathematics and non-linear phenomena in the other sciences

Philosophy and Literature, Centre for Research in
Tel: (01203) 522582
Benjamin, Andrew E., MA *ANU* Dir.*

Renaissance, Centre for the Study of
Mulryne, Prof. J. Ronnie, MA *Camb.*, PhD *Camb.* Dir.*
Trapp, J. B., CBE, FBA, FSA Hon. Prof.
Research: history, literature and theatre and art of Renaissance Europe, especially England, France and Italy

Small and Medium-Sized Enterprises, Centre for
Tel: (01203) 522818 Fax: (01203) 523747
Storey, Prof. David T., BSc *Hull*, PhD *Newcastle(UK)* Dir.*
Other Staff: 1 Lectr., 4 Res. Fellows

Social History, Centre for the Study of

Tel: (01203) 523292 Fax: (01203) 524451

Mason, Anthony, BA *Hull*, PhD *Hull* Reader; Dir. of Studies

Steedman, Caroline K., BA *Sus.*, MLitt *Camb.*, PhD *Camb.* Prof.; Chairman*

Yeo, S., BA *Oxf.*, PhD *Sus.* Hon. Prof.

Other Staff: 5 Res. Fellows

Research: early modern and modern social history; histories of childhood

Sport in Society, Centre for the Study of

Allison, Lincoln R. P., MA *Oxf.* Dir.*

Research: history and politics of sport; legal intervention in sport; social and political theory; sports structures and organisation

Warwick Business School Research Bureau

Tel: (01203) 522993 Fax: (01203) 524965

Stoneman, P., BA *Warw.*, MSc(Econ) *Lond.*, PhD *Camb.* Prof.

Waddams, Catherine A., BSc *Nott.*, PhD *Nott.* Res. Prof.; Dir.*

Other Staff: 7 Res. Fellows

Research: problems and methods of business, industrial and public administration and management

Warwick Risk Initiative

Fax: (01203) 692368

Wynn, Prof. Henry P., MA *Oxf.*, PhD *Lond.* Dir.*

Women and Gender, Centre for the Study of

Tel: (01203) 523600

Lovell, Terry, BA *Leeds* Dir.*

Other Staff: 3 Lectrs.

Research: feminism; gender and development; science communication; sociology of literature and culture

CONTACT OFFICERS

Academic affairs. Academic Registrar: Nicholls, J. W., BA *Brist.*, PhD *Camb.*

Accommodation. Accommodation Officer: Stannage, Robert, MA *Edin.*

Admissions (first degree). Admissions Officer: Robinson, Lynn, BSc *Sheff.*, MA *Warw.*

Admissions (higher degree). Senior Assistant Registrar: Nutkins, Jennifer G., MA *Camb.*, PhD *Camb.*

Adult/continuing education. Assistant Registrar: Moseley, Russell, BSc *Edin.*, MSc *Sus.*, DPhil *Sus.*

Alumni. Administrator: Cole, Joan M., BA *Warw.*

Archives. Acting Archivist: Woodland, C., MA *Oxf.*T

Careers. Director of Careers Advisory Service: Wallis, Margaret S., BA *Lond.*

Computing services. Director of Computing Services: Halstead, Keith S. H., MSc *City(UK)*

Credit transfer. Admissions Officer: Robinson, Lynn, BSc *Sheff.*, MA *Warw.*

Development/fund-raising. Development Officer: Watson, Peter, BA *Oxf.*, MBA *Europ.Inst.Bus.Admin.*

Distance education. Administrative Director for MBA (Distance Learning): ......

Equal opportunities. Personnel Officer: Bell, Diane, BA *Liv.*

Estates and buildings/works and services. Estates Officer: Barker, Ian G., BSc

Examinations. Assistant Registrar: Taylor, Joseph A., MA *Leeds*, DPhil *Oxf.*

Finance. Finance Officer: Hunt, H. James, MA *Oxf.*, MBA *Warw.*

General enquiries. Registrar: Shattock, Michael L., OBE, MA *Oxf.*, Hon. LLD *Reading*

Health services. Medical Officer: Ballantine, Richard J., MB MS

Industrial liaison. Director of Industrial Development: Davies, John A., MSc *Birm.*, PhD *Birm.*

International office. Director of International Office: Gribbon, Anthony St. G., MA *Oxf.*

Library (chief librarian). Librarian: Henshall, John A., BA *Manc.*, MA *Manc.*, PhD *Manc.*

Ombudsperson. Academic Registrar: Nicholls, J. W., BA *Brist.*, PhD *Camb.*

Personnel/human resources. Director of Personnel Services: Brant, James W., MA *Camb.*

Public relations, information and marketing. Director of Public Affairs: Read, John, BA *Warw.*

Publications. Publicity Services Officer: Warman, Roberta M., BA *Oxf.*, PhD *Lond.*

Purchasing. Purchasing Manager: Lightbown, Martin J.

Quality assurance and accreditation. Senior Assistant Registrar: Duddridge, Dawn E., BA *Oxf.*, MA *Warw.*

Research. Senior Assistant Registrar (Research): Sanders, Lee, BA *Manc.*

Safety. Safety Officer: Veale, David R., BSc *Birm.*, MSc *Birm.*, PhD *Birm.*

Scholarships, awards, loans. Fees and Grants Officer: Lindsay, Chris, MA *Sus.*

Schools liaison. Director of Schools and Colleges Liaison Service: Stamp, Rosemary, BA *Birm.*, MA *York(UK)*, MSc *Nott.Trent*

Security. Security Manager: Farr, L. R.

Sport and recreation. Director of Sports Facilities: Monnington, Terence, MA *Birm.*

Sport and recreation. Director, Arts Centre: Hall, Stella, BA *Exe.*

Staff development and training. Academic Staff Development Officer: Blackmore, Paul, BA *E.Anglia*, MEd *Bath*

Student union. Permanent Secretary: Simpson, J.

Student welfare/counselling. Senior Tutor: Stone, Thomas J., JP, MA *Oxf.*, DPhil *Oxf.*

Students from other countries. Director of International Office: Gribbon, Anthony St. G., MA *Oxf.*

Students with disabilities. Senior Tutor: Stone, Thomas J., JP, MA *Oxf.*, DPhil *Oxf.*

[*Information supplied by the institution as at 5 March 1998, and edited by the ACU*]

UNIVERSITY OF THE WEST OF ENGLAND, BRISTOL

Present designation 1992; Bristol Polytechnic 1969

Member of the Association of Commonwealth Universities

Postal Address: Frenchay Campus, Coldharbour Lane, Bristol, England BS16 1QY
Telephone: (0117) 965 6261 **Fax**: (0117) 976 3804 **WWW**: http://www.uwe.ac.uk
E-mail formula: initial-surname@uwe.ac.uk

CHANCELLOR—Butler-Sloss, Dame Elizabeth, DBE
VICE-CHANCELLOR*—Morris, Alfred C., MA *Lanc.*, Hon. LLD *Brist.*, FCA
DEPUTY VICE-CHANCELLOR—Wookey, P. E., BSc PhD
PRO-VICE CHANCELLOR AND ASSISTANT VICE-CHANCELLOR (PROGRAMMES)—Bone, Jennifer M., MBE, MA
ASSISTANT VICE-CHANCELLOR (PLANNING AND RESOURCES)—Cuthbert, R. E., MA MSc MBA
ASSISTANT VICE-CHANCELLOR—Rees, Prof. J. M., BSc(Eng) MSc

GENERAL INFORMATION

History. The university was founded as Bristol Polytechnic in 1969 and gained university status in 1992.

Admission to first degree courses (see also United Kingdom Introduction). Through Universities and Colleges Admissions Service (UCAS). Minimum international language qualifications: IELTS (6) or TOEFL (570).

First Degrees (see also United Kingdom Directory to Subjects of Study). BA, BEng, BSc, LLB, MEng.

Higher Degrees (see also United Kingdom Directory to Subjects of Study). LLM, MA, MBA, MPhil, PhD.

Libraries. 500,000 volumes.

Fees (1997–98). Home/EU students (undergraduate): £750 (classroom-based courses); £1600 (laboratory-based courses). International students (undergraduate and postgraduate): £6150 (classroom-based courses); £6500 laboratory-based courses).

Academic Year (1998–99). Three terms: 21 September–18 December; 11 January–26 March; 19 April–25 June.

Income (1995–96). Total, £93,550,000.

Statistics. Staff: 2398 (914 academic, 85 research, 1010 administrative/technical, 389 manual). Students: full-time 16,103; part-time 7332; total 23,435.

FACULTIES/SCHOOLS

Applied Sciences
Fax: (0117) 976 3871
Dean: Hawkes, Prof. C., BSc PhD
Faculty Administrator: Williams, Tina

Art, Media and Design
Tel: (0117) 966 0222 Fax: (0117) 976 3946
Dean: van der Lem, Paul, BA BSc PhD
Faculty Administrator: Hughes, Jane

Bristol Business School
Fax: (0117) 976 3851
Dean: ......
Faculty Administrator: Inglis, Jessica

Built Environment
Fax: (0117) 976 3895
Dean: Fudge, Prof. C., BArch MA
Faculty Administrator: McDouall, Janet

Computer Studies and Mathematics
Fax: (0117) 976 3860
Dean: Jukes, Prof. K. A., BSc PhD
Faculty Administrator: Needles, Margaret

Economics and Social Science
Fax: (0117) 976 3870
Dean (Acting): Lawrence, Prof. Philip, FRAeS
Faculty Administrator: Briers, Ena

Education
Tel: (0117) 974 1251 Fax: (0117) 976 2146
Dean: Ashcroft, Prof. Kate, BEd MEd
Faculty Administrator: Maxwell, Susan

Engineering
Fax: (0117) 976 3873
Dean: Hoddell, Prof. S. E. J., BA MA MSc, FIEE
Faculty Administrator: Holbrook, Susie

Health and Social Care
Tel: (0117) 958 5655 Fax: (0117) 975 8481
Dean: West, Steven, BSc
Business Manager: Longmire, S.

Humanities
Tel: (0117) 965 5384 Fax: (0117) 975 0402
Dean: Channon, Geoff, BSc PhD, FRHistS
Faculty Administrator: Huggins, Christine

Languages and European Studies
Fax: (0117) 976 3843
Dean: Scriven, Prof. Michael, BA MA PhD
Faculty Administrator (Acting): Wheeler, Michèle

Law
Fax: (0117) 976 3841
Dean: Benstead, Prof. A. R., BA LLM
Faculty Administrator: Frost, S.

ACADEMIC UNITS
Arranged by Faculties

Applied Sciences
Tel: (0117) 976 2170 Fax: (0117) 976 3871
Alcock, D., BA MSc Sr. Lectr.
Alford, C. A., BSc MSc PhD Sr. Lectr.
Bird, D. J., BSc MSc PhD Sr. Lectr.
Blackmore, Susan J., MSc PhD Sr. Lectr.
Corke, Josephine M., MSc Sr. Lectr.
Costello, J., BSc PhD Sr. Lectr.
Cowell, D. C., PhD Principal Lectr.
Currell, G., BSc DPhil PhD Principal Lectr.
Dearnaley, D. P., MA PhD Principal Lectr.
Dowman, A. A., BA PhD Sr. Lectr.
Drew, Susan, MEd Sr. Lectr.
Easton, A., MSc Sr. Lectr.

Emerson, Mick Sr. Lectr.
English, S. L., BSc PhD Sr. Lectr.
Gardner, Wayne Sr. Lectr.
Gavin, H., BSc MSc PhD Sr. Lectr.
Gleeson, Kathryn, BA PhD Sr. Lectr.
Gomez, S., BSc PhD Sr. Lectr.
Greenman, J., BSc PhD Sr. Lectr.
Grey, M. R., BSc Sr. Lectr.
Griffin, R. L., MPhil Sr. Lectr.
Grimsell, David Sr. Lectr.
Hampson, P. J., BSc PhD Prof.; Head of Dept.
Hancock, J. T., BSc PhD Sr. Lectr.
Hapeshi, K., PhD Sr. Lectr.
Harker, D. W., BSc PhD Sr. Lectr.
Hart, J. P., BTech MSc PhD Sr. Lectr.
Haslum, Mary N., BSc PhD Reader
Hawkes, C., BSc PhD Prof.; Dean*
Hawkins, P., BSc PhD Sr. Lectr.
Heard, Priscilla, BSc PhD Sr. Lectr.
Hodson, Annabelle G. W., BSc PhD Sr. Lectr.
Holland, Prof. P. R. H., BSc PhD Principal Lectr.
Hunter, C. S., BSc PhD Head of Dept.
Iwugo, K., BSc MSc PhD Sr. Lectr.
Johnstone, Lucy C., MA Sr. Lectr.
Knapper, J. Sr. Lectr., Research Methods
Lamont, R., BA Sr. Lectr.
Lewis, R. J., MSc Sr. Lectr.
Longhurst, J. W. S., BSc MSc PhD Prof.; Head of Dept.
Lown, D., BSc Sr. Lectr.
Lush, D. J., BSc PhD Sr. Lectr.
Luxton, R. W., MSc PhD Sr. Lectr.
McCalley, D. V., MSc PhD Principal Lectr.
Morris, Marianne, BSc MSc PhD Sr. Lectr.
Morton, C. E. M., PhD Sr. Lectr.
Murphy, S. M., BA MSc Sr. Lectr.
Neill, S. J., BSc PhD Principal Lectr.
Newton, L. N., BSc MSc PhD Sr. Lectr.
Osborne, R. H., MSc PhD Principal Lectr.
Pallister, C. J., MSc Sr. Lectr.
Paradice, Katherine R., BSc PhD Sr. Lectr.
Parry, W. H., MSc PhD Principal Lectr.
Philippidis, C., BSc PhD Principal Lectr.
Phillpotts, C. J., BA PhD Principal Lectr.
Pill, M., BSc MSc Sr. Lectr.
Pollock, Jane, PhD Sr. Lectr.
Pope, R., BSc PhD Sr. Lectr.
Potter, G. W. H., BA MSc Sr. Lectr.
Praulitis, E. R., BSc PhD Principal Lectr.
Purcell, Wendy, BSc PhD Prof.; Head of Dept.
Ratcliffe, N. M., BSc PhD Sr. Lectr.
Redshaw, M., BA PhD Sr. Lectr.
Rumsey, Nichola J., BA MSc PhD Principal Lectr.
Salisbury, Vyvyan C., BSc PhD Sr. Lectr.
Schaffer, A. G., MSc PhD Principal Lectr.
Schwieso, J., PhD Sr. Lectr.
Scragg, A. H., BSc PhD Sr. Lectr.
Scull, P. S., BSc MSc Sr. Lectr.
Shales, S. W., BSc PhD Sr. Lectr.
Shaw, D. G., BSc PhD Principal Lectr.
Smith, A. J., BSc MEd PhD Sr. Lectr.
Spencer-Phillips, P. T. N., BSc PhD Sr. Lectr.
Stygall, T. C., BSc PhD Sr. Lectr.
Sutton, K. J., MSc PhD Sr. Lectr.
Thompson, J. F. A., MSc Principal Lectr.
Thornton, Dilys M., BSc PhD Principal Lectr.
Troup, Lucy, PhD Sr. Lectr., Psychology
Tubb, A. L. T., MSc PhD Sr. Lectr.
Veal, D., BSc PhD Sr. Lectr.
Vivian, A., BSc PhD Principal Lectr.
Waite, J. H., BA MSc Principal Lectr.
Watson, M. S., MSc Sr. Lectr.
Webb, A. J., MSc Sr. Lectr.
Whitwell, I., BSc PhD Sr. Lectr.

Art, Media and Design
Tel: (0117) 966 0222 Fax: (0117) 976 3946
Aitken, Ian W., BA MA PhD Sr. Lectr.
Anderton, Richard, MA RCA, BA Sr. Lectr.
Aston, Judith, MA Sr. Lectr.
Biggs, I. A., MA RCA Principal Lectr.
Clamp, Stuart, BA Sr. Lectr.
Clements, Christine, BA Principal Lectr.
Crickmay, C. L., BArch Sr. Lectr.
Depledge, Julie A., BA Sr. Lectr.

Dunhill, M. T., MA Sr. Lectr.
Elsey, Eileen, BA MA Sr. Lectr.
Grandon, Adrian Sr. Lectr.
Hales, C., BSc MA Sr. Lectr.
Hill, Christine J., BA Sr. Lectr.
Homoky, N., MA Sr. Lectr.
Hughes, Brian, MA Sr. Lectr.
Jupp, M. V., MA Sr. Lectr.
Keeler, Prof. W. C. J. Sr. Lectr.
Kneebone, Valerie A. Sr. Lectr.
McCullough, I., BA Sr. Lectr.
McLaren, I. Visiting Prof.
Merrit, D., MA Visiting Prof.
Morgan, Sally J., BA Principal Lectr.
Ng, Mian Har, MA Sr. Lectr.
Peters, Gary, BSc MA PhD Sr. Lectr.
Reiser, Martin, MA Sr. Lectr.
Sandford, Gillian R., MA Principal Lectr.
Singer, A., DPhil Visiting Prof.
Truran, Christine J., MA Sr. Lectr.
Turrell, Roger Principal Lectr.
van der Lem, Paul, BA BSc PhD Dean*
Other Staff: 1 Sr. Res. Fellow; 2 Lectrs.

Bristol Business School
Fax: (0117) 976 3851
Adnum, D. M., BSc Sr. Lectr.
Apostolides, N., BA MBA Sr. Lectr.
Beckett, A. G., BA Sr. Lectr.
Beeby, J. M., MA Principal Lectr.
Behennah, M. J., BA Sr. Lectr.
Bence, D. J., BA Sr. Lectr.
Bendrey, M. L., MSc Principal Lectr.
Binks, S. G., BA, FCA Principal Lectr.
Booth, C. E., BA MA Sr. Lectr.
Bowie, S. A., MA MSc Principal Lectr.
Bradley-Jones, A. R., LLB MSc, FCA Principal Lectr.
Broussine, M. P., BSc MSc MPhil Principal Lectr.
Bruce, D. M., MA MPhil Principal Lectr.
Canning, L. E., BA MBA Sr. Lectr.
Castle, J. A., MA Sr. Lectr.
Cicmil, Svetlana, BSc(Eng) MBA Sr. Lectr.
Clark, M. G., BA Sr. Lectr.
Cope, Beulah, BA Sr. Lectr.
Cox, P. S., BSc MA MBA PhD Principal Lectr.
Danford, Andrew, BSc PhD Sr. Lectr.
Davies, Janette, BSc MA Sr. Lectr.
Donnelly, M., BA MSc PhD Head., Sch. of Operations Management
Dugdale, D., BSc MSc PhD Principal Lectr.
Ells, G. A., MA MBA Sr. Lectr.
Evans, Iris, BSc Sr. Lectr.
Evans, Jane M., BA MA MSc Principal Lectr.
Evans, Prof. M. J., BA MA Principal Lectr.
French, R., BA MEd Sr. Lectr.
Grisoni, Louise, MSc MA Sr. Lectr.
Haddrell, J. E. Sr. Lectr.
Hansford, Ann, BA Sr. Lectr.
Harrington, Jane, BA MPhil PhD Sr. Lectr.
Heaven, G. W., BSc MA Sr. Lectr.
Henricksen, H. D. Sr. Lectr.
Hill, Beverley Sr. Lectr.
Hill, Paula Sr. Lectr.
Hilton, Rosalind T., LLB MA Sr. Lectr.
Holden, I. C., BA MBA Sr. Lectr.
Hollinshead, G., BA MSc Sr. Lectr.
Howe, Sally G., BA Sr. Lectr.
Hussey, R. D., MA MSc PhD Reader
Jones, Penelope H., BA MA MSc MPhil Sr. Lectr.
Jordan, Judith R., BA MA Head, Sch. of Strategic Management
Kelly, Sarah E., BA Sr. Lectr.
Kirk, P. L., BA MSc Principal Lectr.
Lathwood, Elizabeth A., BA Sr. Lectr.
Laurent, Sandra, MSc Sr. Lectr.; Head, Sch. of Acctg. and Finance
Lowe, Prof. J. F., MA Principal Lectr.
Lucas, Ursula C., BA, FCA Principal Lectr.
Mackie, Sarah E., BA Sr. Lectr.
Maltby, Alice H. J., BA MA Sr. Lectr.
May, J. P., MA Principal Lectr.
McCloskey, BSc MBA Head., Sch. of Marketing
McDowell, Raymond Principal Lectr.
Milford, P. H., BSc Sr. Lectr.

Nancarrow, C., BA MSc   Principal Lectr.
Nicholls, P. J., BA MA   Principal Lectr.
Nicol, D. P., MA   Sr. Lectr.
Nutman, Dorian   Principal Lectr.
O'Brien, Lisa, BA   Sr. Lectr.
Paul, Salima, BA MSc MPhil   Sr. Lectr.
Pillinger, R. J., MSc   Sr. Lectr.
Ramsay, J. E.   Sr. Lectr.
Reed, M. H., MSc, FCA   Principal Lectr.
Richards, M. P.   Sr. Lectr.
Riley, Helen, BSc   Sr. Lectr.
Robson, N., BA   Sr. Lectr.
Russell, K. D., BSc MBA PhD   Sr. Lectr.; Dir.,
  MBA Programmes
Sampson, Nicola A., BA MBA   Sr. Lectr.; Dir.,
  Marketing Communicns.
Shankar, Avi   Principal Lectr.
Simpson, P. F., BA PhD   Principal Lectr.
Smart, R. B., FCA   Sr. Lectr.
Stone, L. G., BSc   Sr. Lectr.
Sturge, Deborah T., BA   Sr. Lectr.
Tailby, Stephanie A., MA PhD   Principal
  Lectr.; Head, Sch. of Human Resource
  Management
Tan Phaik, L., BA MA PhD   Sr. Lectr.
Taylor, P. J., BA MSc   Sr. Lectr.
Thorne, Marie, BA MEd PhD   Principal Lectr.;
  Head, Sch. of Orgnl. Behaviour
Upchurch, Martin, BSc(Econ) MSc   Sr. Lectr.
Vince, R. G., BA PhD   Principal Lectr.
White, P. D., MA MPhil   Sr. Lectr.
Whiteley, P., BA MPhil   Sr. Lectr.
Wilkins, Gill   Sr. Lectr.
Woolley, Jill, BA   Sr. Lectr.
Wornham, D. R., BA MSc MBA   Sr. Lectr.
Wozniak, D., BSc   Sr. Lectr.
Other Staff: 1 Lectr.

Built Environment

Fax: (0117) 976 3895

Allday, Leonie A., BA   Sr. Lectr.
Allinson, J. S., BA MPhil   Sr. Lectr.
Askew, Janet M., BSc   Sr. Lectr.
Bailey, J. A., BSc   Principal Lectr.
Baker, J. S., MA   Sr. Lectr.
Barton, H. J. M., MPhil   Sr. Lectr.
Baxendale, A. T., BSc PhD   Principal Lectr.
Bignell, W. H., MA   Sr. Lectr.
Birch, C. A., BSc   Sr. Lectr.
Bolan, P. J., MA   Principal Lectr.
Boyden, B. P., BA MSc   Principal Lectr.
Bryan, A. J., MSc   Principal Lectr.
Burnside, K. C. D., BSc   Sr. Lectr.
Burton, Rosemary C. J., BA MPhil   Sr. Lectr.
Carlton, Nancy, BA   Sr. Lectr.
Cartwright, E., BSc   Sr. Lectr.
Case, D. J., BSc PhD   Principal Lectr.
Chick, M., MSc   Principal Lectr.
Claydon, P. J., MSc   Principal Lectr.
Cook, M. A., BSc   Sr. Lectr.
Cooke, N. J.   Sr. Lectr.
Costello, V. F., BA PhD   Sr. Lectr.
Dann, N., BSc   Sr. Lectr.
Davies, D. G., BA   Sr. Lectr.
Davies, Linda   Sr. Lectr.
Davison, L. R., BA MEng PhD   Sr. Lectr.
Donovan, D. W.   Sr. Lectr.
Drewer, S. P., BA PhD   Principal Lectr.
Dulaimi, M. F., MSc   Sr. Lectr.
Dury, B. L., BA PhD   Sr. Lectr.
Edge, W. J.   Sr. Lectr.
Farthing, S. M., MA PhD   Principal Lectr.
Fudge, Prof. C., BArch MA   Dean*
Galliford, S. J., BSc   Principal Lectr.
Galloway, Jane, BSc   Sr. Lectr. (on leave)
Garnett, D. J., MA PhD   Principal Lectr.
Greed, Clara H., BSc PhD   Sr. Lectr.
Greed, J. A., LLB   Sr. Lectr.
Griffiths, R. R., BSc MPhil   Sr. Lectr.
Grimshaw, R., BA   Reader/Principal Lectr.
Guise, R.   Sr. Lectr.
Harrison, A. R., BA MSc   Principal Lectr.
Hathway, A. G., BSc MA   Principal Lectr.
Heath, R. M.   Sr. Lectr.
Hoddell, J. Alison, BA MSc   Principal Lectr.
Hodge, Margaret F., BSc   Sr. Lectr.
Hucker, M., MSc   Sr. Lectr.
Hudson, Rachel M., BA   Sr. Lectr.

Innocent, P. J., BSc   Sr. Lectr.
Johnson, C.   Sr. Lectr.
Jones, J. M., BSc   Principal Lectr.
Lambert, Christine, MSc   Sr. Lectr.
Lawes, G. N.   Sr. Lectr.
Malpass, Prof. P. N., MA PhD   Principal Lectr.
Manley, J. J., MA   Sr. Lectr.
Manley, Sandra   Sr. Lectr.
Marshall, D. J., BSc   Sr. Lectr.
Martin, A. F.   Sr. Lectr.
May, A., BA   Sr. Lectr.
McElwee, A. J., MA   Sr. Lectr.
Mitchell, D. G., BSc   Sr. Lectr.
Mooring, M. J.   Sr. Lectr.
Moynihan, Patricia A., BA   Sr. Lectr.
Myers, D., BA MSc   Sr. Lectr.
Nadin, V., BA   Reader/Principal Lectr.
Nounu, G. F. E., BSc PhD   Sr. Lectr.
O'Donoghue, S., BA LLB   Sr. Lectr.
Oatley, N. A., MA   Sr. Lectr.
Pannell, Jennifer A., BA   Sr. Lectr.
Parnaby, R., BA MA   Sr. Lectr.
Pay, Vivienne, BA   Sr. Lectr.
Pitman, G. C., MPhil   Sr. Lectr.
Pitt, T. J., MSc   Sr. Lectr.
Rowe, Janet, BSc PhD   Sr. Lectr.
Scrase, A. J., MA   Principal Lectr.
Selman, A. J., BSc   Sr. Lectr.
Simpson, S., MSc   Sr. Lectr.
Stanton, G. R. T., MSc   Sr. Lectr.
Stewart, M., MA   Reader/Principal Lectr.
Stokes, I. R.   Sr. Lectr.
Tanner, R. B., BSc   Sr. Lectr.
Taylor, N. M., MA PhD   Sr. Lectr.
Vernon, Milica A., BA   Sr. Lectr.
Walker, A. R., BA PhD   Sr. Lectr.
Walker, R. G., BA PhD   Principal Lectr.
Wellman, Jennifer C.   Sr. Lectr.
Westcott, A. J., MSc, FRICS   Sr. Lectr.
Winn, R. G., BSc   Sr. Lectr.
Wood, Teresa Y., BEd   Sr. Lectr.
Worthing, D. J., BSc   Principal Lectr.
Wrigley, M., BA   Sr. Lectr.

Computer Studies and Mathematics

Fax: (0117) 976 3860

Arnold, Caroline E., MSc   Sr. Lectr.
Bakehouse, G. J.   Sr. Lectr.
Baker, N. L., BSc MSc   Sr. Lectr.
Barry, A. M., BSc   Sr. Lectr.
Beeson, I. A., MA MSc   Principal Lectr.
Berry, C. J.   Sr. Lectr.
Betts, J., BEng MSc   Principal Lectr.
Cawthorne, B. V., BA   Principal Lectr.
Clements, Margaret, BA   Principal Lectr.
Cobby, J. M., BSc PhD   Principal Lectr.
Counsell, J. L., MSc   Sr. Lectr.
Coward, P. D., BSc PhD   Principal Lectr.
Davis, C. J.   Sr. Lectr.
Devitt, A. M.   Sr. Lectr.
Doyle, K. G., MPhil   Sr. Lectr.
Drewry, A. J., BA   Sr. Lectr.
Duffy, C., BA MA   Principal Lectr.
Forsyth, R. S., BA MSc   Sr. Lectr.
Gillies, A. D., MSc   Sr. Lectr.
Gilligan, J.   Sr. Lectr.
Goodwin, P., BA MSc   Principal Lectr.
Green, S. J. M., BSc MSc   Sr. Lectr.
Henderson, Karen   Sr. Lectr.
Johnson, Ian   Sr. Lectr.
Kamm, Richard   Sr. Lectr.
Kellard, Robert   Sr. Lectr.
Lang, L. R., BSc   Sr. Lectr.
Langley, S., MSc   Principal Lectr.
Lawton, R. B., BSc MSc   Sr. Lectr.
Lewis, A. J., MSc   Sr. Lectr.
Lynch, M., BSc MSc   Sr. Lectr.
Maddix, F. J., BSc   Sr. Lectr.
Maines, P. W., MSc   Principal Lectr.
Martin, P. C. S., BSc PhD   Sr. Lectr.
May, Margaret, MA   Sr. Lectr.
McClatchey, R. H., BSc PhD   Sr. Lectr.
Miller, C. R., BSc MEd   Sr. Lectr.
Moggridge, E. Anne, BA   Sr. Lectr.
Moore, Paul   Sr. Lectr.
Oakshott, L. A., BSc MSc   Sr. Lectr.
Perry, Christine E., BA MA   Sr. Lectr.
Petheram, B. L., BA PhD   Sr. Lectr.

Plant, N. J., BSc   Sr. Lectr.
Pollard, Pauline A., BA MSc   Sr. Lectr.
Rackley, Lesley, BSc   Sr. Lectr.
Raynor, P. D., BSc PhD   Principal Lectr.
Roberts, R. G., BSc   Sr. Lectr.
Sa, J.   Sr. Lectr.
Sarkar, P. A., MA PhD   Sr. Lectr.
Sharpe, Peter   Principal Lectr.
Solomonides, A. E., MSc   Head, Computing
Storey-Day, Bob   Sr. Lectr.
Storey-Day, R. C., BA   Sr. Lectr.
Street, Deborah   Sr. Lectr.
Thomas, Peter   Principal Lectr.
Vince, A. J., MSc   Sr. Lectr.
Wakefield, A. J., MA MSc   Sr. Lectr.
Wakefield, Tony   Sr. Lectr.
Wallace, C. J., BSc   Principal Lectr.
Waters, Prof. S., BSc MSc PhD   Principal Lectr.
Watkins, G., BA MSc   Sr. Lectr.
Webb, J. T., BSc   Sr. Lectr.
Webber, C. D., BA   Principal Lectr.
Weir, Ian   Principal Lectr.
Welton, Nicola   Sr. Lectr.
Williams, R., BA PhD   Principal Lectr.
Williams, R. M., MSc   Sr. Lectr.
Yearworth, M., BSc PhD   Principal Lectr.
Other Staff: 1 Assoc. Sr. Lectr.; 2 Principal
  Lectrs.†; 5 Sr. Lectrs.†

Economics and Social Science

Fax: (0117) 976 3870

Baxter, A., BSc MA   Principal Lectr.
Bird, J. F., BSc MA   Principal Lectr.
Braddon, D. L., MA PhD   Principal Lectr.
Bradley, N. J., BA   Sr. Lectr.
Britton, Carolyn J., BSc MA   Sr. Lectr.
Brookes, J. S., MA MSc   Sr. Lectr.
Buttle, N. J., MA PhD   Sr. Lectr.
Cullen, P. J., BSc MPhil   Sr. Lectr.
Cummins, Anne M., BSc   Sr. Lectr.
Dowdall, P. G., BSc   Sr. Lectr.
Duff, Madeline L., BSc PhD   Sr. Lectr.
Flegg, A. T., MA MPhil   Principal Lectr.
Foster, Deborah J., BA PhD   Sr. Lectr.
Garrod, B., BA MSc PhD   Sr. Lectr.
Hatt, J. G., BA MSc   Principal Lectr.
Hatt, Susan, BA   Sr. Lectr.
Hill, W. T., BA   Sr. Lectr.
Hoggett, Prof. P., BA   Principal Lectr.
Jackson, Marion J., MA MPhil   Principal Lectr.
Jones, T. C., BSc MA PhD   Principal Lectr.
Jowers, P. T., MA   Sr. Lectr.
Lawrence, Philip, FRAeS   Prof.; Dean
  (Acting)*
Mahony, G., BCom MEc   Sr. Lectr.
McSweeney, D. L., MA PhD   Principal Lectr.
Mulvey, Gail   Sr. Lectr.
O'Doherty, R. K., BA MSc   Sr. Lectr.
Palmer, Anna J., BA PhD   Sr. Lectr.
Plumridge, A. E. C., BA BSc   Sr. Lectr.
Rothman, H., BSc PhD   Reader
Sloman, J., BA MSc   Principal Lectr.
Stein, S. D., MSc PhD   Sr. Lectr.
Sutcliffe, Mark   Sr. Lectr.
Tempest, C. G., MA   Principal Lectr.
Thomas, J. J. R., MA   Principal Lectr.
Thompson, Simon   Sr. Lectr.
Thurlow, T. W., BSc   Sr. Lectr.
Wood, C. A., MSc   Principal Lectr.

Education

Tel: (0117) 974 1251 Fax: (0117) 973 2251

Ashcroft, Prof. Kate, BEd MEd   Dean*
Attwood, Gaynor M., BA   Principal Lectr.
Bassett, Sally E.   Sr. Lectr.
Billington, Eileen M., MPhil   Sr. Lectr.
Brockington, D. P., BA   Head, Accredited Trg.
  Centre
Butcher, H., BA   Sr. Lectr.
Callaway, Gloria J., MEd   Sr. Lectr.
Chidgey, Angela M., BA   Sr. Lectr.
Clough, N. N., BA MEd   Sr. Lectr.
Davies, J. D., MEd   Principal Lectr.
Dempsey, Mary C., MA   Sr. Lectr.
Dickson, D. D., BA   Principal Lectr.
Dudman, Sara, MA   Sr. Lectr.
Eke, R. J., BEd MA   Principal Lectr.
Fitzgerald, Bernadette   Sr. Lectr.

Forrest, M. S. J., BA MEd PhD Principal Lectr.
Foster, Victoria J., BA MSc Sr. Lectr.
Fowler, P. B., BSc Sr. Lectr.
Frawley, P. A., BA Principal Lectr.
Guest, A. G. Sr. Lectr.
Harnett, Penelope A. M., BA MEd Sr. Lectr.
Homewood, J. R., BA MEd MPhil Sr. Lectr.
Ingram, N. R., BSc Sr. Lectr.
James, D. R., BSc Sr. Lectr.
Jones, G. W., MSc Sr. Lectr.
Kay, Norma, BA Sr. Lectr.
Kear, Mary B., MEd Sr. Lectr.
Kumar, L., BA Sr. Lectr.
Lang, G. D., BA MEd Principal Lectr.
Lee, J. T., BA Principal Lectr.
Martyres, A. S., BA MEd Principal Lectr.
Maughan, Sylvia C., BSc MEd Principal Lectr.
McInally, B. J., MA Sr. Lectr.
Mitton, P., BA Sr. Lectr.
Newman, Elizabeth C., BA MEd Sr. Lectr.
Nicholson, M. B., MEd Sr. Lectr.
Postlewaite, Keith Head, Res. and Staff Devel.
Reed, Lynn E. R., BA MSc Sr. Lectr.
Ryan, J. N., MA Sr. Lectr.
Sharpe, Mary R., BSc Sr. Lectr.
Slocombe, Susan J. Principal Lectr.
Smith, Margaret Sr. Lectr.
Tarr, Jane M., BEd Sr. Lectr.
Taylor, Alison Sr. Lectr.
Thomas, Gary, BA MEd PhD Reader
White, R., BA MEd Sr. Lectr.
Woodward, Elizabeth A. Sr. Lectr.

Engineering

Fax: (0117) 976 3873

Atcliffe, P. A., BEng Sr. Lectr.
Calvert, P. C., MSc Sr. Lectr.
Carse, B., BA MA Sr. Lectr.
Carter, I. J. Sr. Lectr.
Coveney, V., BA PhD Sr. Lectr.
Dailami, F., MSc Sr. Lectr.
Daniell, J. R., BSc Sr. Lectr.
Davies, T. S., BSc PhD Principal Lectr.
Dragffy, G., MSc Sr. Lectr.
Fagan, A. N., MSc Sr. Lectr.
Gibson, R. K., MSc Sr. Lectr.
Head, P. A. Sr. Lectr.
Hill, T. M., MSc Sr. Lectr.
Hoddell, Prof. S. E. J., BSc MA MSc,
    FIEE Dean*
Holland, O. E., BSc Sr. Lectr.
Jefferson, C. M., BSc MSc MPhil PhD Sr.
    Lectr.
Kamalu, J. N., BSc PhD Sr. Lectr.
Lanham, J. D., BSc Sr. Lectr.
Larsen, N., BSc MPhil Sr. Lectr.
Long, Jacqueline L., BSc PhD Principal Lectr.
Longden, A. R. K., BSc Sr. Lectr.
Lowe, G. A., MSc Sr. Lectr.
May, A. P. H., BSc PhD Principal Lectr.
Melhuish, C. R., BSc MSc Sr. Lectr.
Midha, P. S., BSc PhD Principal Lectr.
Pipe, A. G., BSc Sr. Lectr.
Savage, Barbara, MSc PhD Sr. Lectr.
Scanlan, J. P., BSc MSc PhD Sr. Lectr.
Smith, G., BA MSc PhD Principal Lectr.
Stamp, R. J., BSc MSc PhD Sr. Lectr.
Trmal, G. J., PhD Principal Lectr.
Tyler, M. J., BSc Sr. Lectr.
Vinney, J. E., BEng Sr. Lectr.
Way, J. L., BSc PhD Principal Lectr.
Williams, D. J., MSc Sr. Lectr.
Withers, J. W., BSc Sr. Lectr.

Health and Social Care

Tel: (0117) 958 5655 Fax: (0117) 975 0403

Abbott, G. Sr. Lectr.
Ahmad, Y. I., MSc Sr. Lectr.
Albarran, J., BSc MSc Sr. Lectr.
Allen, M. A., MA Sr. Lectr.
Andrew, J. L. Sr. Lectr.
Ashmore, Catherine, BEd Principal Lectr.;
    Head, Sch. of Community Nursing
Augousti, C. A. Sr. Lectr.
Aust, R. Sr. Lectr.
Badlan, K. S. Sr. Lectr.
Bampfylde, R. Sr. Lectr.
Barrett, D. L. E., BSc Sr. Lectr.

Barrett, G. A. Sr. Lectr.
Bashforth, H., BSc Sr. Lectr.
Bedford, D. F., BEd Sr. Lectr.
Ben-Ali, Y. Sr. Lectr.
Benjamin, Catherine M., BSc MSc Sr. Lectr.
Bennett, J. E., BSc Sr. Lectr.
Bheenuck, S., BA MS Principal Lectr.
Blunden, Gill, MA PhD Head, Res.
Boddy, G. M., BSc Sr. Lectr.
Brice, P. H. Sr. Lectr.
Broadberry, M. E., MA Sr. Lectr.
Brooks, S. L., BSc Sr. Lectr.
Broussine, E., BSc Sr. Lectr.
Burdett, P., BEd Sr. Lectr.
Callister, A. A., BSc Sr. Lectr.
Channon, B. T., MSc Sr. Lectr.
Chianese, J., MSc Sr. Lectr.
Clark, C. D., MSc Sr. Lectr.
Clarke, B. A., MN Sr. Lectr.
Collins, M. T., MN Sr. Lectr.
Cook, D. J., MSc Sr. Lectr.
Cooper, S. A., MEd Sr. Lectr.
Crumpton, E. J., BSc MSc Sr. Lectr.
Dando, M. C., BEd Sr. Lectr.
Davies, S. Sr. Lectr.
Davis, S. M., BA Sr. Lectr.
Daykin, Norma, BA MSc PhD Sr. Lectr.
Desbottes, Z. E., MN Sr. Lectr.
Dewer, A. M. S., BSc MA Principal Lectr.
Donovan, Lesley C., BSc Principal Lectr.;
    Head, Adult Nursing
Downing, A. M. Sr. Lectr.
Doyle, M., BEd Sr. Lectr.
Dyer, J. L. Sr. Lectr.
Edgar, D. A., BSc Sr. Lectr.
Edmunds-Jones, J., MSc Sr. Lectr.
Emerson, M. P. Sr. Lectr.
Esling, G. A. Sr. Lectr.
Fear, C. E., MA Sr. Lectr.
Fenn, V. M. Sr. Lectr.
Ferguson, J. Sr. Lectr.
Fitzpatrick, J., BSc MSc Sr. Lectr.
Fletcher, I. P., MA Sr. Lectr.
Foxwell, D. M. Sr. Lectr.
Fraher, M. A., MSc Sr. Lectr.
Frost, Elizabeth A., BA MSc Sr. Lectr.
George, M. M., MA Sr. Lectr.
Gilchrist, Alison, BA Sr. Lectr.
Gilchrist, M., BA MA Sr. Lectr.
Godfrey, Helen, BSc PhD Sr. Lectr.
Godsell, M. J., BA MEd Sr. Lectr.
Goodman, J. C., MPhil Sr. Lectr.
Gray, C., BA Sr. Lectr.
Greenwood, R. L. A., MSc Sr. Lectr.
Gregory, J. P., BA Sr. Lectr.
Griffiths, G. J., BEd Sr. Lectr.
Grindrod, E. M., MA Sr. Lectr.
Gurr, A. G., BA Sr. Lectr.
Hadwin, P. B., BA MSc Sr. Lectr.
Halliday, A. R. Sr. Lectr.
Harding, R. V., BSc Sr. Lectr.
Harrison, J. R., MA Sr. Lectr.
Hathaway, V. J., BEd Sr. Lectr.
Havard, Cathryn P., BSc Sr. Lectr.
Hawes, D. L., MEd Sr. Lectr.
Hawking, S. J., BEd Sr. Lectr.
Hayward, M. E., BEd Sr. Lectr.
Hek, G. A., MA Sr. Lectr.
Hill, P. F., MA(Ed) MSc Sr. Lectr.
Hobbs, J. A., BA BEd Sr. Lectr.
Hollingsbee, I. M., MA Sr. Lectr.
Holmes, K. G., MSc Sr. Lectr.
Hook, G., MSc Sr. Lectr.
Hopkinson, C. M., BA Sr. Lectr.
Hughes, A. E. Sr. Lectr.
Hughes, M., BA Sr. Lectr.
Hunter, D. G., MSc Sr. Lectr.
Ingram, R., BA Sr. Lectr.
James, J., MSc Sr. Lectr.
James, J. E., MSc Sr. Lectr.
Jones, K., LLB Principal Lectr.; Head, Sch. of
    Radiography
Jones, L. E., BA Principal Lectr.; Head, Sch.
    of Physiotherapy/Occupnl. Therapy
Judd, M. L., BA Sr. Lectr.
Kandiah, R. S., BEd MA Sr. Lectr.
Keeble, Stephanie, BA Sr. Lectr.
Knight, C. M., MSc Sr. Lectr.

Knowles, G. A., BA Sr. Lectr.
Langton, H. E., BA MSc Sr. Lectr.; Head, Sch.
    of Child Nursing
Lavender, V. B., BA Sr. Lectr.
Leigh, Sarah, MSc Sr. Lectr.
Limpinnian, M. G., MSc Sr. Lectr.
Lismore, M. A. Head, Sch. of Mental Health/
    Learning Disabilities Nursing
Lloyd-Cape, R. E., BSc PhD Sr. Lectr.
Lloyd-Jones, G., BEd Sr. Lectr.
Madden, R. I., MA Sr. Lectr.
Mall, M. J., BEd Sr. Lectr.
Manook, I., BSc Sr. Lectr.
Martin, C. A., MA Sr. Lectr.
McKendry, Catherine A., BEd MEd Sr. Lectr.
Mead, J. M. Sr. Lectr.
Michael, Maria, MSc Sr. Lectr.
Miers, Margaret E., BA MSc PhD Sr. Lectr.
Miller, C. J., BA Ma PhD Principal Lectr.
Miller, L. C., BA MA Sr. Lectr.
Mitchell, M. C., MEd Sr. Lectr.
Mitchell, T., BEd Sr. Lectr.
Moody, H. S., BSc Sr. Lectr.
Moore, L. J., MA Sr. Lectr.
Moule, P., BSc Sr. Lectr.
Mowforth, G. M., BEd MSc Sr. Lectr.
Naidoo, Jennie S., BSc MSc Sr. Lectr.
Orme, Judith, BSc MSc Sr. Lectr.
Pardoe, R. W., BSc Sr. Lectr.
Parry, S. R., BSocSci Sr. Lectr.
Payne, S. M., MEd Sr. Lectr.
Pearson, B. E., MEd Sr. Lectr.
Philippa-Walsh, G. M. Sr. Lectr.
Phillips, E. S., MSc Sr. Lectr.
Price, T. E., BSc Sr. Lectr.
Pringle, D. W., MSc Sr. Lectr.
Rees, D. P., BEd Sr. Lectr.
Robbins, S. J., BEd Sr. Lectr.
Rosser, E. A., MN Sr. Lectr.
Ryder, M. J., BSc Sr. Lectr.
Senior, B., BA MA Principal Lectr.
Shackell, J. M. A., BA Sr. Lectr.
Sherratt, D., BEd MA Sr. Lectr.
Singer, L. Sr. Lectr.
Smith, C. R. Sr. Lectr.
Smith, R. J., BA MSc Sr. Lectr.
Snelson, L. B., MEd Sr. Lectr.
Springett, G., MSc Sr. Lectr.
Squires, S. A., BSc Sr. Lectr.
Stevens, C. D., BA Sr. Lectr.
Summers, N., BA MSc Sr. Lectr.
Sutcliffe, B. P., MSc MA Sr. Lectr.
Swinkels, A., MSc Sr. Lectr.
Tanner, M. P. L., BA Sr. Lectr.
Taylor, Patricia A., BSc MSc Sr. Lectr.
Thomas, A. R., BA Sr. Lectr.
Thomas, J. A. Sr. Lectr.
Thomas, R. S. Sr. Lectr.
Thomas, S., MEd Sr. Lectr.
Tonks, J. S., MSc Sr. Lectr.
Townley, M. D., MA Sr. Lectr.
Townley, S. E., MSc Sr. Lectr.
Tucker, C., BEd MEd Head, Sch. of
    Midwifery
Turner, B. E., BA Sr. Lectr.
Turner, J. H. Sr. Lectr.
Upton, P. A. Principal Lectr.
Ventura, S. E., BA Sr. Lectr.
Waddington, S. P., BSc MSc Sr. Lectr.
Walker, G. P. Sr. Lectr.
Walters, E. J. Sr. Lectr.
Weeks, N. P., MA Sr. Lectr.
West, Steven, BSc Dean*
Wharton, J. P., BA Sr. Lectr.
White, P. J. Sr. Lectr.
Whittle, M. E. Sr. Lectr.
Wiles, M. E., MSc Sr. Lectr.
Wilkinson, G. M., MSc Sr. Lectr.
Williams, J. A., BA Sr. Lectr.
Wilton, Tamsin E., BA MSc Sr. Lectr.
Witt-Way, J. R. M., BA Sr. Lectr.
Wrigley, K. M., MSc Sr. Lectr.
Yates, S. A. Sr. Lectr.
Young, P. M., MSc Sr. Lectr.
Zarrabi, T., MEd Sr. Lectr.

Humanities

Tel: (0117) 975 5384 Fax: (0117) 975 0402

Arthurs, J., BA   Sr. Lectr.
Barker, M. J., BA DPhil   Principal Lectr.
Beezer, P. Anne, BSc MSc MPhil   Sr. Lectr.
Butler, C. C., BA MSc DPhil   Sr. Lectr.
Channon, Geoff, BSc PhD, FRHistS   Dean*
Dresser, Madge J., BA MSc   Principal Lectr.
Fleming, P. W., BA PhD   Sr. Lectr.
Greenslade, W. P., BA MA PhD   Sr. Lectr.
Grimshaw, M. Jean, BA   Principal Lectr.
Habeshaw, Susan B., BA MA   Sr. Lectr.
Hancock, Ann E., BA PhD   Principal Lectr.
Hannam, June B., BA MA PhD,
   FRHistS   Principal Lectr.
Jarvis, R. J., BA PhD   Principal Lectr.; Head,
   Sch. of Literary Studies
Lister, M. D., MA   Principal Lectr.; Head, Sch.
   of Cultural and Media Studies
Mulvey-Roberts, Marie, BA MA PhD   Sr. Lectr.
Ollerenshaw, P. G., BA MSc PhD   Principal
   Lectr.
Otty, N. T., BA MA   Sr. Lectr.
Reid, J. M., BA PhD   Sr. Lectr.
Slater, M. Renee, BA MA   Sr. Lectr.
Swain, G. R., BA PhD   Principal Lectr.; Head,
   Sch. of Hist.
Wardley, P., BSc PhD   Sr. Lectr.
Woodiwiss, M., BA MPhil   Sr. Lectr.

Languages and European Studies

Fax: (0117) 976 3843

Beeching, Katherine, MA   Sr. Lectr.
Cannon, Jackie, MA   Sr. Lectr.
Chebli-Saadi, M., LèsL PhD   Sr. Lectr.
Claus, H., MA PhD   Principal Lectr.
Cousquer, J-Y., MA   Sr. Lectr.
Dennis, Marisol, MA   Sr. Lectr.
Fletcher, Catherine, BA   Sr. Lectr.
Gallery, R. C., MEd   Principal Lectr.
Gold, P. J., MA MLitt DPhil   Principal Lectr.
Hodgkin, G. C., BA   Principal Lectr.
Hollyman, J. L., MA MPhil   Principal Lectr.
Jackel, Anne A., MA   Sr. Lectr.
Kennard, Ann, MA   Sr. Lectr.
Lewis, Annie L. E., LèsL   Sr. Lectr.
Mander, Gretel M., BA   Sr. Lectr.
Mann, S. G., MA   Sr. Lectr.
Middleditch, Anne M., MSc   Sr. Lectr.
Neilson, Nora, MA   Sr. Lectr.
Pattison, Janice L., BA   Sr. Lectr.
Pepiol, R. M., MA PhD   Sr. Lectr.
Picard, Jeanine, BA MBA   Sr. Lectr.
Pruetzel-Thomas, Monika H. U., MSc   Sr.
   Lectr.
Ruhlmann, Felicitas, MA   Sr. Lectr.
Saad, M., MSc PhD   Principal Lectr.
Shaw, Gisela K., BA MPhil PhD   Principal
   Lectr.
Tidball, Marie-Francoise   Sr. Lectr.
Wilkie, Irene S., BA   Sr. Lectr.

Law

Tel: (0117) 976 3976 Fax: (0117) 976 3841

Aspinall, D. G., BA   Sr. Lectr.
Beckerlegge, Grace E.   Sr. Lectr.
Bell, Bernadette C., LLB   Sr. Lectr.
Bensted, Prof. A. R., BA LLM   Dean*
Berkan, B. H., LLB   Sr. Lectr.
Brady, Ann C., LLB   Sr. Lectr.
Briody, J., LLB MA   Sr. Lectr.
Brown, I., LLB   Sr. Lectr.
Clare, Vivien   Sr. Lectr.
Clarke, A. D., LLB   Sr. Lectr.
Clements, R. J., LLM   Sr. Lectr.
Connor, T. C., LLB MPhil   Sr. Lectr.
Crowdy, Carol A., LLB   Principal Lectr.
Cummings, B. M., BSc LLB   Principal Lectr.
Cunningham, Fiona, LLB MA   Sr. Lectr.
Denyer, Pauline S., LLM   Sr. Lectr.

Dinning, S., LLB   Sr. Lectr.
Doble, P., BA   Sr. Lectr.
Douglas, G. R., LLM   Sr. Lectr.
Edworthy, Julie, LLB   Sr. Lectr.
Farran, Susan E., BA LLM   Principal Lectr.
Francis, J.   Sr. Lectr.
Geal, Alexandra M., LLM   Principal Lectr.
Geddes, Fiona R., LLB MA   Sr. Lectr.
Higgins, S. R., BA   Sr. Lectr.
Holden, J. N., LLM   Sr. Lectr.
Horrocks, J. L., LLB   Sr. Lectr.
James, D. R. M., LLB   Sr. Lectr.
Jenkins, M., LLB   Sr. Lectr.
Kaye, Jane, LLM MA   Sr. Lectr.
Keppel-Palmer, M. C., BA   Sr. Lectr.
Light, R. A., LLM MPhil PhD   Principal Lectr.
Lloyd-Cape, E. F. P., BT LLM   Principal Lectr.
Maughan, Caroline R., MA   Sr. Lectr.
Opstad, C. T., MA MPhil   Principal Lectr.
Parry, H. B., BLaw BA   Sr. Lectr.
Reed, Jenifer S., LLB   Principal Lectr.
Southworth, F., BA   Principal Lectr.
Thacker, S. G., BSc LLM   Sr. Lectr.
Theunissen, A. E., MA   Sr. Lectr.
Trevis, R. G.   Sr. Lectr.
Webb, J. S., BA LLM   Principal Lectr.
Whiting, R. J., LLB   Sr. Lectr.
Williams, P. L., LLB   Sr. Lectr.
Winch, Frances M., LLM   Sr. Lectr.
Wood, G. C., LLB MA   Sr. Lectr.

SPECIAL CENTRES, ETC

Applied Research in Science, Centre for

Fax: (0117) 976 3871

Cowell, D. C., PhD   Dir.*

Comparative International and European Law Unit

Fax: (0117) 976 3841

Farran, Susan E., BA LLM   Head*

Criminal Justice, Centre for

Fax: (0117) 976 3841

Light, Prof. R. A., LLM MPhil PhD   Head*

Industrial Law Unit

Fax: (0117) 976 3841

Chandler, P. A., LLM PhD   Jt. Head*
Holland, J. A., LLB PhD   Jt. Head*

Intelligent Computer Systems Centre

Tel: (0117) 976 3857 Fax: (0117) 975 0416

Yearworth, M.   Dir.*

Personal Information Management, Centre for

Tel: (0117) 976 3973 Fax: (0117) 976 2613

Thomas, Prof. P., BA MPhil PhD   Dir.*

Regional History Centre

Tel: (0117) 975 5384 Fax: (0117) 975 0402

Wardley, P., BSc PhD   Sr. Lectr.

Social and Economic Research, Centre for

including Science and Technology Policy Unit

Fax: (0117) 976 3870

Hoggett, Prof. Paul, BA   Dir.*

CONTACT OFFICERS

Academic affairs. Registrar (Academic):
   Carter, Margaret J., BA
Accommodation. Residences (Student Halls):
   Thomas, Pam
Accommodation. Sapsworth, Neil

Admissions (first degree). Recruitment and
   Information (Admissions): Francombe,
   Dianne
Admissions (higher degree). Recruitment and
   Information (Admissions): Francombe,
   Dianne
Careers. Widdows, Janet, BA
Computing services. IT Services: Saville, J.
Conferences/corporate hospitality. Bailey,
   Joanne
Credit transfer. Programme Approval and
   Credit Unit: Yilmaz, Sue
Distance education. External Awards and
   Research Administration: Bennett, David
Estates and buildings/works and services.
   Fell, J. D., BA MBA
Examinations. Registrar (Academic): Carter,
   Margaret J., BA
Finance. Financial Services: Marshall, W., BA
General enquiries. Assistant Vice-Chancellor
   (Planning and Resources): Cuthbert, R. E.,
   MA MSc MBA
Industrial liaison. Executive Director, Centre
   for Research, Innovation and Industry:
   Skinner, Linda A., BSc
International office. Overseas Students'
   Welfare: Makepeace, Eira
Language training for international students.
   Mann, George
Library (chief librarian). Heery, M., BA MA
Personnel/human resources. Gregory, G., BA
Public relations, information and marketing.
   Media Officer: Kelly, Jane
Public relations, information and marketing.
   Events Officer: Fox, Sue
Public relations, information and marketing.
   Media Officer: Price, Mary, BA BSc
Public relations, information and marketing.
   Marketing and Communications Manager:
   Hicks, Keith
Publications. Publications Officer: Paker,
   Josephine, BA
Purchasing. Baker, Helen
Quality assurance and accreditation.
   Programme Approval and Credit Unit:
   Yilmaz, Sue
Research. Centre for Research, Innovation and
   Industry: Bond, R., MSc
Safety. Champion, R.
Scholarships, awards, loans (loans). Shields,
   Sue, BA
**Scholarships, awards, loans (student
   records)**. Porter, Sue
Schools liaison. Recruitment and Information
   (Admissions): Simmons, Tony
Security. Site Services: Dunne, J.
Sport and recreation. Physical Recreation:
   Hibbert, M.
Staff development and training. Gregory, G.,
   BA
Student union. Manager: Cadogan, Peter
Student welfare/counselling (counselling).
   Topham, Phil
Student welfare/counselling (welfare).
   Shearn, Clare, BSc
Students from other countries. Overseas
   Students' Welfare: Makepeace, Eira
Students with disabilities. Disability Officer:
   Wray, M.
University press. Printing and Stationery
   Manager: Ambrose, J. C. C.

[Information supplied by the institution as at 6 April
1998, and edited by the ACU]

UNIVERSITY OF WESTMINSTER

Founded 1992; previously Polytechnic of Central London (1970); originally established as Royal Polytechnic Institution (1838-39)

Member of the Association of Commonwealth Universities

Postal Address: 309 Regent Street, London, England W1R 8AL
Telephone: (0171) 911 5115 **Fax**: (0171) 911 5103 **WWW**: http://www.wmin.ac.uk
E-mail formula: initial.initial.surname@wmin.ac.uk

CHAIRMAN OF THE COURT OF GOVERNORS—Peach, Sir Leonard, MA Oxf.
VICE-CHANCELLOR AND RECTOR*—Copland, Geoffrey M., MA Oxf., DPhil Oxf.
DIRECTOR OF RESOURCES—Mainstone, C., MBA Brun.
ACADEMIC REGISTRAR‡—Green, Evelyne, BA Manc.
COMPANY SECRETARY AND FINANCIAL CONTROLLER—Strang, Alan T., MA Edin., MSc Bath
PROVOST (CAVENDISH) AND DEPUTY VICE-CHANCELLOR—Trevan, Prof. Michael D., BSc Lond., PhD Lond.
PROVOST (HARROW)—Tyler, Maud, BA Lond., PhD Camb.
PROVOST (MARYLEBONE)—Romans, Prof. Michael, BSc Aston, PhD Brun.
PROVOST (REGENT)—Blunden, Prof. Margaret, BA Exe., MA Exe., DPhil Oxf.

GENERAL INFORMATION

History. The university was originally founded as Royal Polytechnic Institution in 1838 and became known as Regent Street Polytechnic after the Second World War. It was subsequently renamed Polytechnic of Central London (1970) and became a university under its present name in 1992. It has two campuses in the West End of London and one suburban campus.

Admission to first degree courses (see also United Kingdom Introduction). Through Universities and Colleges Admissions Service (UCAS). International candidates: certificates and diplomas corresponding to UK matriculation requirements are usually accepted.

First Degrees. BA, BEng, BMus, BSc, LLB.
Courses may be taken full-or part-time.

Higher Degrees. LLM, MA, MBA, MMus, MSc, MPhil, PhD.
Applicants for admission to master's degree courses must normally hold at least a second class honours degree or equivalent qualification. PhD: appropriate master's degree, or appropriate publications.

Language of Instruction. English. Polylang scheme, available to all undergraduates, provides classes in English for academic purposes.

Fees (1998–99, annual). Undergraduate: home students £1000 (arts), £1600 (science); international students £6500. Postgraduate £6500-8500.

Academic Year (1998–99). Three terms: 28 September–18 December; 11 January–26 March; 19 April–16 July.

Income. £85,000,000.

Statistics. Staff: 698 academic/research, 458 administrative. Students: full-time 10,515 (5402 men, 5113 women); part-time 10,973; international 1583 (773 men, 810 women).

ACADEMIC UNITS

Arranged by Schools

Behavioural Sciences, see Soc. and Behav. Scis.

Biosciences

Tel: (0171) 911 5086 Fax: (0171) 911 5087
Adlard, Maxwell W., BSc S'ton., MSc Lond., PhD Sur. Principal Lectr.
Bedford, Colin T., BSc Manc., MSc Manc., PhD Glas. Sr. Lectr.
Blackburn, John Sr. Lectr.

Bond, Andrew N., PhD Sr. Lectr.
Bucke, Christopher, BSc Wales, PhD Liv. Prof.
Clow, Angela J., BSc Leic., PhD Lond. Sr. Lectr.
Davies, Peter L., BSc Wales, MSc Sur., MSc York(UK) Sr. Lectr.
Elliott, Robert J., MSc Lond. Sr. Lectr.
Evans, Christine S., BSc Sheff., MSc Sheff., PhD Lond. Prof.
George, Jennifer J., MSc S'ton., FIBiol Prof.; Head*
Greenwell, Pamela, BSc CNAA, PhD CNAA Sr. Lectr.
Hester, Norman G., BSc Lond., PhD Lond. Sr. Lectr.
Hucklebridge, Frank H., BSc Hull, PhD Hull Sr. Lectr.
Hudson, Janet G., BSc Oxf., MSc Lond. Sr. Lectr.
Keshavarz, Taj, MSc Lond., PhD Lond. Sr. Lectr.
Knights, Brian, BSc Brist., MSc Brist. Principal Lectr.
Lewis, Jane M., BSc Wales, PhD Lond. Sr. Lectr.
Luck, Carol A., BSc CNAA, MSc Lond. Sr. Lectr.
Mackenzie, Jennifer R., MSc Lond. Sr. Lectr.
McEldowney, Sharron, BSc Wales, PhD Warw. Sr. Lectr.
Mellerio, John, BSc Lond., PhD Lond. Prof.
Miles, Elizabeth A., BSc Lond., PhD Lond. Sr. Lectr.
Milne, Ian D., BSc S'ton., MSc Lond. Sr. Lectr.
Mobey, Nigel A. Sr. Lectr.
Parry, Martin W., BSc S'ton., MSc Lond., PhD Lond. Sr. Lectr.
Perry, David, BSc Birm., PhD Birm. Sr. Lectr.
Redway, Keith F., BSc Sus., MSc CNAA Sr. Lectr.
Reed, Stephen C., MSc Lond. Sr. Lectr.
Saunders, Gunter, BSc Lond., PhD CNAA Reader
Scott, Robert I., BSc Lond., PhD Lond. Principal Lectr.
Stubbs, Geoffrey, PhD CNAA Sr. Lectr.
Trickey, Roderick J. Sr. Lectr.
Warren, Jeff J., BSc Lond. Principal Lectr.
Whitlock, Will, BSc CNAA, MSc Lond. Sr. Lectr.
Willcocks, Teresa C., BA Trinity(Dub.), DPhil Oxf. Sr. Lectr.

Business, see Harrow Bus. Sch., and Westminster Bus. Sch.

Communication, Design and Media

Tel: (0171) 911 5940 Fax: (0171) 911 5939
Ang, Tom Sr. Lectr.
Attridge, Geoffrey G., PhD Principal Lectr.
Axford, Norman R., BSc CNAA Sr. Lectr.
Barbrook, Richard, BA Essex, MA Essex, PhD Kent Sr. Lectr.
Barnett, Steven, BA Camb., MSc Lond. Sr. Lectr.
Bezencenet, Stephanie, MA Sus. Principal Lectr.
Bickers, Patricia E. Sr. Lectr.
Boysen, Ole Sr. Lectr.

Buj, Roman S. Sr. Lectr.
Eacott, John, BA Sus. Sr. Lectr.
Garnham, Nicholas R., BA Camb. Prof.
Gleeson, Edward J., MA Lond. Sr. Lectr.
Golding, Andrew J., BA CNAA Principal Lectr.
Green, Ian M., BSc Lond., BA CNAA, MA RCA Sr. Lectr.
Hampshire, David, BA CNAA, BA Reading Sr. Lectr.
Hiscock, Alan E., BA Exe., MA Exe. Sr. Lectr.
Houston, John A. Reader
Howell, Geraldine A., BA Reading, MA Reading Sr. Lectr.
Hunningher, Joost G., BA CNAA Principal Lectr.
Jacobson, Ralph E., MSc Lond., PhD Lond. Prof.; Reader
Jones, Anthony Sr. Lectr.
Kavanagh, Peter Sr. Lectr.
Killick, Danny J. Principal Lectr.
King, S. Carolyn Sr. Lectr.
Litherland, Michael, BA CNAA, MA RCA Sr. Lectr.
Luck, Nigel J., MA RCA Sr. Lectr.
Lynch-Yates, Gaye Sr. Lectr.
Mandelson, Ilana, MA RCA Sr. Lectr.
Matlow, Erica G., MA Lond. Sr. Lectr.
Morrison, Alex Sr. Lectr.
Mulvey, Jeremy F. Principal Lectr.
Peck, Robert E., BA Calif., MSc Lond., PhD Berlin Sr. Lectr.
Porter, Vincent J., BA Oxf. Prof.
Ray, Sidney F., BSc Lond., MSc City(UK) Sr. Lectr.
Scannell, G. Patrick, BA Oxf., MA Oxf. Reader
Seaton, Jeannette A., BSc Brist., MSc CNAA, PhD CNAA Reader
Sparks, Colin S., BA Sus., PhD Birm. Principal Lectr.
Tabrizian, Mitra, BA CNAA, MPhil CNAA Sr. Lectr.
Tulloch, John D., BA York(UK) Principal Lectr.
Welch, Edward A., BA Lond. Sr. Lectr.
Whaley, Stephen P. Principal Lectr.
Williams, Christopher D., BA CNAA Reader
Winston, Brian N., BA Oxf., MA Oxf. Head*
York, Norton O., BA Sus., MA Sus., MPhil Sus. Sr. Lectr.

Community Care and Primary Health, Centre for

Tel: (0171) 580 7989 Fax: (0171) 580 8168
Avis, Angela R. Sr. Lectr.
Bartels-Ellis, Fiona, MPhil Sr. Lectr.
Chaitow, Leon K., BSc Sr. Lectr.
Cohen, John, MD Dir.*
Davies, Peter R., MA Camb., PhD McG. Principal Lectr.
Isbell, Brian, BSc Lond., PhD Lond. Principal Lectr.
Kane, Mark, MA Exe. Sr. Lectr.
Peters, David, MD Sr. Lectr.
Wykurz, Geoff P. Sr. Lectr.

Computer Science

Harrow

Tel: (0171) 911 5000

Alston, David A., BSc Brist., MSc CNAA, PhD CNAA   Principal Lectr.
Baldwin, Mark, BSc CNAA   Sr. Lectr.
Brown, Dennis J., BSc CNAA, MSc Westminster   Principal Lectr.
Brown, Jerry S., BSc CNAA, MSc CNAA   Sr. Lectr.
Carroll, Denis, BSc CNAA, MSc CNAA   Sr. Lectr.
Carroll, Terence W.   Sr. Lectr.
Conlon, Michael   Sr. Lectr.
Evans, J. Philip, BSc Lond., MSc Lond., PhD Lond.   Sr. Lectr.
Finely, Philip I., BSc Wales, MSc Wales, MSc CNAA   Sr. Lectr.
Getov, Vladimir S., PhD Bulgarian Acad.Sc.   Sr. Lectr.
Ghurbhurun, Kesswarsing, MSc Wales   Sr. Lectr.
Hargreave, Martin, BSc Lond., PhD Lond.   Sr. Lectr.
Hearnshaw, David P., BSc Essex, MSc City(UK)   Sr. Lectr.
Higginbotham, Michael   Sr. Lectr.
Jayaram, Narayanaswamy D.   Sr. Lectr.
Knibbs, Robert W., BSc City(UK), MSc CNAA   Sr. Lectr.
Konstantinou, Vassilis, BSc CNAA, MSc Lond.   Head*
O'Reilly, Peter, BSc CNAA, MSc Lond.   Sr. Lectr.
Poslad, Stefan, BSc S'ton., MSc Aberd., PhD Newcastle(UK)   Sr. Lectr.
Psarrou, Alexandra, BSc Lond., MSc Lond.   Sr. Lectr.
Seaman, Graham, BA Camb., MSc CNAA   Sr. Lectr.
Sharp, David S., BSc Lond., MSc CNAA   Sr. Lectr.
Singh, Sirjit, MSc CNAA, MPhil CNAA   Sr. Lectr.
Taylor, Michael W., BSc Lond.   Sr. Lectr.
Theodorides, Andreas, BSc CNAA, MSc Lond.   Sr. Lectr.
Thorpe, Christopher, BSc CNAA   Sr. Lectr.
Winkworth, David J., BA Open(UK)   Sr. Lectr.

Design, see Communicn., Des. and Media

Engineering, Computing, Mathematics and Electronic

Tel: (0171) 911 5825 Fax: (0171) 911 5089

Barker, Steven G., BA Camb., BSc Open(UK), MSc Lond.   Sr. Lectr.
Bartlett, Vivian A., BSc Lond.   Sr. Lectr.
Bean, Keith L.   Sr. Lectr.
Bhattacharya, Pijushkanti, BSc Calc., MSc Calc., PhD City(UK)   Sr. Lectr.
Cain, Gerald D., BSc Auburn, MSc New Mexico, PhD Flor., FIEE   Prof.
Carsley, Roger, BSc Lond., MSc Lond.   Sr. Lectr.
Carter, Alison J., BSc Lond.   Sr. Lectr.
Charrington, Keith L., BSc City(UK)   Sr. Lectr.
Cohen, Stanley S., BSc Lond., PhD Lond.   Sr. Lectr.
Douglas, Paul, BA Keele, MSc Lond.   Sr. Lectr.
El-Darzi, Elia G., BSc Beirut, MSc S'ton., PhD Brun.   Sr. Lectr.
Ellis, Rod, BA Brist.   Principal Lectr.
Ettinger, Jean P., BSc Nott., MSc Lond.   Principal Lectr.
Finch, David J., BSc Manc., MSc Lond.   Sr. Lectr.
Gillies, Duncan F., BMus Lond., MSc Lond., PhD Lond.   Prof.
Greenwood, Ken L., BSc CNAA   Principal Lectr.
Hall, Tracy, BA CNAA, MSc CNAA   Sr. Lectr.
Harrison, Malcolm A., BSc Leeds, MSc CNAA, PhD Leeds   Sr. Lectr.
Howells, Paul, BSc Lond., MSc Lond.   Sr. Lectr.
Kale, Izzet, BSc CNA, MSc Edin., PhD Westminster   Principal Lectr.
Karran, Tereska L., BSc Exe., MA Lond., MSc City(UK)   Sr. Lectr.
Lambrou, Nicholas, PhD   Principal Lectr.

Lees, Patrick F., BSc Lond.   Principal Lectr.
Leigh, Richard A., BSc Birm., MSc CNAA   Sr. Lectr.
Lyon, Susan, BSc Lond.   Sr. Lectr.
Madani, Kambiz, BSc Lond., PhD   Principal Lectr.
McCarthy, John, BSc Lond., MSc Lond.   Principal Lectr.
Moazzam, Mohammad R., MSc Teheran, PhD Lond.   Sr. Lectr.
Morling, Richard C., BSc CNAA, PhD Lond.   Principal Lectr.
Murphy, N. Paul, BSc CNAA   Sr. Lectr.
Myers, Colin A., BA Sus., MSc Lond.   Principal Lectr.
Naughton, Michael F., MSc CNAA   Sr. Lectr.
Neale, Douglas F., BSc Birm., PhD Nott.   Principal Lectr.
Pattinson, Stuart D., BSc S'ton.   Sr. Lectr.
Phillips, A. Paul, BSc Leic., MSc City(UK), PhD Lond.   Sr. Lectr.
Poulter, Charles G., BSc Lond., MSc Lond.   Sr. Lectr.
Priestley, P. Mark, BA Oxf., MSc Lond.   Principal Lectr.
Rees, Michael W., BA Essex, MSc Newcastle(UK)   Sr. Lectr.
Ruparelia, Seema J., BA CNAA, MSc City(UK)   Sr. Lectr.
Simmons, Jack A., BSc Lond., MSc Lond., PhD Lond.   Prof.
Sivagurunathan, Kamalini, BSc City(UK), MSc CNAA   Sr. Lectr.
Solanki, Kamlesh   Sr. Lectr.
Thompson, David M., BSc Lond.   Principal Lectr.
Tohill, Shaun   Sr. Lectr.
Turner, Christopher R.   Sr. Lectr.
Turner, John G., BSc Wales, MSc City(UK), PhD Wales   Sr. Lectr.
Uttamchandani, Lal, BSc Pune, PhD CNAA, MBA   Sr. Lectr.
Winter, Stephen C., BSc Lough., MSc Lond., PhD Westminster   Head*
Xanthis, Leo   Reader
Yardim, Anush, BSc CNAA   Sr. Lectr.

Engineering, Design and Manufacturing, Department of

Tel: (0171) 911 5081 Fax: (0171) 580 4319

Afoke, Ng Y., BSc CNAA, PhD CNAA   Principal Lectr.
Allen, Michael, BSc Kingston(UK), MSc Lond.   Sr. Lectr.
Bailey, A. Lloyd   Sr. Lectr.
Bailey, Christopher N.   Sr. Lectr.
Bilinskis, Ivars   Prof.; Researcher
Bird, Kenneth E.   Principal Lectr.; Chair*
Eastwood, Mark, BEng CNAA, BSc Open(UK)   Sr. Lectr.
Fraser, Ian   Sr. Lectr.
Lee, Wah Cheng, BSc Lond., PhD Lond.   Principal Lectr.
Marquand, Christopher J., BSc CNAA, BSc E.Anglia, PhD Leeds   Principal Lectr.
Ormiston, Peter L., BSc Birm., PhD S'ton.   Principal Lectr.
Patterson, Alistair C., BSc Lond., MSc City(UK)   Principal Lectr.
Stride, Frederick, BSc Sur., MSc Lond.   Sr. Lectr.

Built Environment

Tel: (0171) 911 5196 Fax: (0171) 911 5190

Al-Hussaini, Abbas, BSc CNAA, MSc Sur., PhD Lond.   Principal Lectr.
Allen, Judith A.   Principal Lectr.
Armishaw, James W., BSc CNAA, MSc CNAA   Principal Lectr.
Armitage, David J., BSc Salf.   Sr. Lectr.
Bailey, Nicholas J., MSc Birm.   Principal Lectr.
Barlow, James, BA Lond., PhD Lond.   Reader
Berzins, Andris, BArch Auck.   Principal Lectr.
Bignell, Leonard, MSc CNAA   Sr. Lectr.
Booth, Anthony I., BSc Wales, PhD Lond.   Sr. Lectr.
Brown, Peter C., BSc Lond., MPhil Lond.   Sr. Lectr.

Browne, Michael, BA Lond., MSc CNAA   Prof.; Principal Lectr.
Camp, Sheila, MA CNAA   Sr. Lectr.
Castle, David M.   Principal Lectr.
Coupland, Andrew C., BA Lanc.   Sr. Lectr.
Cox, David W., BSc CNAA, MSc CNAA, PhD CNAA   Sr. Lectr.
Crompton, Robin N., BSc Ulster, MSc Aberd., MPhil CNAA   Sr. Lectr.
Diston, Eric W., BSc Aston   Sr. Lectr.
Edmundson, Timothy, BA Manc., BPlan CNAA, MA CNAA   Sr. Lectr.
Gilby, Anthony R.   Principal Lectr.
Gould, Nicholas, BSc CNAA   Sr. Lectr.
Greene, David J.   Sr. Lectr.
Grinfeld, Monica L., BSc CNAA   Sr. Lectr.
Harvie, Peter J., BA CNAA   Sr. Lectr.
Haworth, Anna, BSc Lond., MSc Lond.   Sr. Lectr.
Hinchcliffe, Tanis F., BA Vic.(Tor.), MA Tor., MA Lond., PhD Lond.   Sr. Lectr.
Hoare, John C., BSc CNAA, PhD CNAA   Principal Lectr.
Ireland, John V., BSc Nott., PhD Lond.   Sr. Lectr.
Jacobs, Keith A., BA Manc., MSc CNAA   Sr. Lectr.
Jago, Alan, BA S'ton., MPhil Lond.   Prof.; Head*
Jashapara, Ashok, BSc City(UK), MBA City(UK)   Sr. Lectr.
Jones, Brian N.   Principal Lectr.
Jones, Peter M., BSc Brist., PhD Lond.   Prof.; Dir., Transport Studies
Littler, John G., BA Oxf., PhD Nott.   Prof.; Reader
Lockyer, Kenneth A., BSc Lanc., BA CNAA   Sr. Lectr.
Madge, James W., BA Camb.   Principal Lectr.
Maitland, Robert A., BA Camb., MA Nott., MA Camb., MBA CNAA   Principal Lectr.
Manzi, Tony F., BA Wales   Sr. Lectr.
Marsh, Christopher, BSc CNAA   Principal Lectr.
McEvoy, Michael, BA Camb., MA Camb.   Sr. Lectr.
Moossavi Nejad, Edin, BSc Teheran, PhD Lond.   Sr. Lectr.
Murphy, Ian H., BArch Newcastle(UK), PhD Newcastle(UK)   Sr. Lectr.
Neale, Stephen, BSc CNAA   Sr. Lectr.
Newman, Peter, BSc Leic., MSc CNAA, PhD Birm.   Sr. Lectr.
Peckham, Andrew O., BA Camb.   Sr. Lectr.
Roberts, Marion E., BSc Lond., PhD Wales   Sr. Lectr.
Rose, Michael P.   Sr. Lectr.
Seex, David H., BA CNAA, MSc CNAA   Sr. Lectr.
Simpson, Yvonne M., BSc CNAA, MSc Lond.   Sr. Lectr.
Smith-Bowers, William J., BSc Lond., MA Essex   Principal Lectr.; Enterprise Dir.
Talbot, Peter J., BSc CNAA, MA Lond.   Sr. Lectr.
Walker, Helen J., BA Sus., MA Sus., DPhil Sus.   Principal Lectr.
Watson, Gordon N.   Sr. Lectr.
Whibley, David F., BSc CNAA, MPhil CNAA   Sr. Lectr.
White, Peter R., BSc Salf.   Prof.
Winters, Ed J., BA Lond., MPhil Lond.   Sr. Lectr.
Wright, Jane A., BSc CNAA   Sr. Lectr.
Youens, Andrew   Sr. Lectr.

Harrow Business School, see also

Westminster Bus. Sch.

Tel: (0171) 911 5932 Fax: (0171) 911 5931

Allen, Anthony J., BSc Hull, MA Lond., MSc Brun.   Sr. Lectr.
Armfield, Jill D., BSc Open(UK), MA Camb., MA Leic.   Sr. Lectr.
Batley, Helen M., BSc Lond.   Sr. Lectr.
Beaman, Michael W., BA Birm.   Sr. Lectr.
Bradley, Nigel, BA CNAA   Sr. Lectr.
Butcher, Kathleen, MSc CNAA   Sr. Lectr.
Byrom, Marie   Sr. Lectr.
Chelms, Debra, BA Manc., MBA CNAA   Sr. Lectr.
Clarke, Elaine L., BA Leeds, MBA CNAA   Sr. Lectr.

Crosby, David R., BSc Edin., MA Edin., MSc Brun. Non-Sch. Head

Evans, Leonard R., BA Open(UK), MEd Birm., MBA Wales Sr. Lectr.

Faulkner, Guy F., MA De Mont. Sr. Lectr.

Foard, David S. Sr. Lectr.

Gardner, Neville J., MSc Brun. Sr. Lectr.

Gordon, Alexander G., MA Glas., MSc Lond. Sr. Lectr.

Harding, Richard H., BA Leic., PhD Lond. Principal Lectr.

Hesni, Bijan, BA CNAA, MBA CNAA Sr. Lectr.

Hitchcock, David H., BSc Liv., PhD Liv. Principal Lectr.

Inns, Dawn E., BA S'ton., MA Lanc. Sr. Lectr.

Jones, Philip J., BA Lond. Sr. Lectr.

Kellock, Anne D., BA CNAA Sr. Lectr.

Maling, John, BSc Newcastle(UK), MBA CNAA Principal Lectr.

Mcloughlin, Peter J., BA Leeds, MSc Lond. Sr. Lectr.

Mehta, Usha S. Sr. Lectr.

O'Neil, Sue, MBA Thames V. Sr. Lectr.

Pritchard, Helene S. Sr. Lectr.

Radia, Jagdish L. Sr. Lectr.

Rieple, P. Alison, BMus MBA Sr. Lectr.

Stein, Peter D., MSc Brun. Head*

Thompson, Michael W., BA Lond. Sr. Lectr.

Tucker, Benita Sr. Lectr.

Tyler, Kathy C., MA Camb. Principal Lectr.

Vassell, Clive Sr. Lectr.

Widdis, Diane E., BEd Camb. Sr. Lectr.

Wright, Donald G., BSc CNAA Sr. Lectr.

Languages

Tel: (0171) 911 5004 Fax: (0171) 911 5001

Aldwinkle, Linda, BA Oxf., MSc Lond., PhD Lond. Sr. Lectr.

Alpert, Michael, BA Camb., MA Lond., PhD Reading Reader

Ashby, Patricia D., BA Lanc., MA Lond. Principal Lectr.

Avsey, Ignat Sr. Lectr.

Bostock, Peter E., BA Leeds, PhD CNAA Principal Lectr.

Bray, Maryse, MA Rennes, MA Lond. Sr. Lectr.

Brooke, Gerald Principal Lectr.

Brookeman, Christopher E. Principal Lectr.

Cairns, Christopher S., BA Leeds, MA Tor., PhD Reading Prof.; Principal Lectr.

Collard-Abbas, Lucy, BA CNAA, MA Lond. Sr. Lectr.

Cook, Aline J., BA Montpellier, MA Montpellier Sr. Lectr.

Czech, Adolf, BA Duquesne, DrIur Vienna Sr. Lectr.

de Otaola, Ana, BA MA Principal Lectr.

Di Napoli, Roberto, BA Lond., MA Lond. Sr. Lectr.

El-Ghobashy, Mohamad S., BA Cairo Principal Lectr.

Elshayyal, Muhammad F., BA Alexandria, MA Tor., PhD Edin. Sr. Lectr.

Evans, Harriet, PhD Sr. Lectr.

Footitt, Hilary A., BA Brist., MSc Lond., MPhil Reading Head*

Fraser, Janet E., BA H.-W., MA CNAA Sr. Lectr.

Garran, Madrid, BA Lond., MA Lond. Sr. Lectr.

Gill, Helen J. Sr. Lectr.

Godfrey, Jeanne M., BA Sus., MA Reading Sr. Lectr.

Hilton, Mark, BA Camb. Sr. Lectr.

Huss, Marie-Monique, MA Lond. Principal Lectr.

Kelly, Debra J., BA Lond., MA Lond., PhD Lond. Sr. Lectr.

Laufer, Michelle, MA Lond. Sr. Lectr.

Lonergan, John P., BA Durh., MEd Manc. Prof.

Lynch, Frances M., PhD Reader

Martin, Christine Sr. Lectr.

Masoliver, Juan A., BA Reader

Morrison, Alan G., BA Belf. Principal Lectr.

Paterson, Ken, BA Sr. Lectr.

Peck, Havila, BA Nott. Sr. Lectr.

Scurfield, Elizabeth C., BA Lond. Principal Lectr.

Smallwood, Ingeborg Sr. Lectr.

Sponza, Lucio, MA Lond., PhD Lond. Reader

Steiner, Riccardo, MA Milan, PhD Milan Sr. Lectr.

Syea, Anand, BA Wales, MA Wales, PhD Essex Sr. Lectr.

Szusterman, Julia C., MA Essex, DPhil Oxf. Sr. Lectr.

Thorold, Dinny, MA Edin., MA Lond. Sr. Lectr.

Tolansky, Ethel Principal Lectr.

Verrinder, Jeremy H., BA Brist. Sr. Lectr.

Law

Tel: (0171) 911 5153 Fax: (0171) 911 5152

Abbey, Robert M., BA Keele Principal Lectr.

Aber, S. Paul Sr. Lectr.

Auchmuty, Rosemary K., BA ANU, LLB CNAA, LLM Lond., PhD ANU Principal Lectr.

Bearcroft, Patricia T., LLB Brist., LLM Lond., MA Lond. Principal Lectr.

Boon, Andrew, LLB Leic., MEd Lond. Head*

Boulby, Caroline A., LLB Lond. Sr. Lectr.

Darcy, Leo Sr. Lectr.

Denny, Ralph, LLB Birm. Sr. Lectr.

Duff, Elizabeth M., LLB Hudd. Sr. Lectr.

Dunford, Fiona, BCL Oxf. Sr. Lectr.

Earle, Richard F. Sr. Lectr.

Ellins, Christopher J. Sr. Lectr.

Flood, John A., LLB Lond., LLM Warw., LLM Yale, PhD Northwestern Prof.; Vizard Reader

Galas, Helen, LLB Lond., BA Oxf. Principal Lectr.

Greenfield, Steven, MSc Lond. Sr. Lectr.

Hodgkinson, F. Peter, BSc Lond. Sr. Lectr.

Juss, Satvinder S., BA CNAA, PhD Camb. Sr. Lectr.

Miller, Jonathan M. Sr. Lectr.

Nash, Susan J., BEd Sus., LLM Lond., PhD Aberd. Sr. Lectr.

O'Brien, Derek A., BA CNAA, MA CNAA Sr. Lectr.

Osborn, Guy, BA CNAA, LLB De Mont. Sr. Lectr.

Payne, J. Sebastian Sr. Lectr.

Purcell, John T., LLB CNAA Sr. Lectr.

Quane, Helen A., BA Sr. Lectr.

Richards, Mark B., LLB CNAA Sr. Lectr.

Saka-Siriboe, Georgina Sr. Lectr.

Walker-Bannon, S. Sr. Lectr.

Media, see Communicn., Des. and Media

Social and Behavioural Sciences

Tel: (0171) 911 5025 Fax: (0171) 911 5106

Adam, Stephen J., BSc Hull, MA Durh. Principal Lectr.

Ayad, M. Nabil, BA Ain Shams, MA Ain Shams, PhD Ain Shams Dir., Diplomatic Studies

Barnard, Rachel, BA CNAA, MA Essex Principal Lectr.

Benton, Stephen Sr. Lectr.

Blair, Alasdair M., BSc Lond., PhD Lond. Sr. Lectr.

Brennan, Irene Jean Monnet Prof.

Buzan, Barry, BA Br.Col., PhD Lond. Prof.

Cohen, Judith R., BSc CNAA, MSc Lond., MA Lond. Sr. Lectr.

Colwill, Jeremy G., LLB Manc., MA Brun., PhD Lond. Principal Lectr.

Davidson, Laurence M., BSc CNAA, MSc Lond. Sr. Lectr.

Dewart, Margaret H., BA Belf., PhD Lond. Sr. Lectr.

Evans, Philip D., BA Camb., MA Camb., PhD Wales Prof.

Fishman, Nina, BA Sus., BA Lond., PhD Lond. Sr. Lectr.

Gorst, Anthony, BA Lanc., MA Lond. Sr. Lectr.

Griffiths, Penri J., BSc Lond. Principal Lectr.

Groome, David H., BSc Reading, PhD CNAA Sr. Lectr.

Hepworth, Catherine M., BSc Leic., MPhil Camb. Sr. Lectr.

Hixenbaugh, Paula, BA Col., MEd Col., PhD Col. Principal Lectr.

Jenkins, Celia M., BSocSc Birm., MSc Lond., PhD Lond. Sr. Lectr.

Keane, John C., BA Adel., MA Tor., PhD Tor. Prof.; Reader

Kemp, Richard I., BSc Durh. Sr. Lectr.

Lewis, Dai B. Sr. Lectr.

McNally, Roger Sr. Lectr.

Milner, David L., BA Brist., PhD Brist. Prof.; Principal Lectr.

Nourallah, M. R., PhD Sr. Lectr.

Owens, John E., BA Reading, PhD Essex Sr. Lectr.

Phillips, Keith C., BSc Camb., MA Camb., PhD Hull Prof.; Head*

Snelgar, Rosemary S., BA Keele, PhD Keele Sr. Lectr.

Swirsky, Ruth M., BA Lond., MA Essex Principal Lectr.

Taylor, Keith, BA Kent, MA CNAA Principal Lectr.

Towell, Anthony D., BSc CNAA, PhD CNAA Sr. Lectr.

Towell, Nicola A., BSc CNAA Sr. Lectr.

Whitehouse, Patrick D. Sr. Lectr.

Williams, Alan P., BA E.Anglia, MA Sr. Lectr.

Williams, Trevor L., BA Lond., MSc Lond. Sr. Lectr.

Westminster Business School, see also Harrow Bus. Sch.

Tel: (0171) 911 5024 Fax: (0171) 911 5832

Adcock, Christopher J., BSc S'ton., PhD S'ton. Reader

Al-Karaghouli, Wafi Y. R., BA Al-Mustansiriyah, MPhil Lond. Sr. Lectr.

Allison, Kevin G., BA Kent, MSc S'ton. Sr. Lectr.

Amoa-Kumi, Sophia K., MA CNAA Sr. Lectr.

Ashcroft, Michael J., BSc Lond., MSc Lond. Sr. Lectr.

Bailey, George N. A., OBE, BSc Edin., MSc Exe., MBA Brun., PhD Exe. Sr. Lectr.

Barker, Anne K., BSc CNAA, MA Aston Sr. Lectr.

Barkman, Kerstin M., BA Stockholm, MSc Lond. Principal Lectr.

Blackman, Carol A., BA S'ton., MSc Brad. Principal Lectr.

Booker, Pauline, MSc Lond. Principal Lectr.

Botten, Neil Principal Lectr.

Bowden, John M., BA Sheff. Principal Lectr.

Boyt, Anthony F., BEd Sheff., LLB Lond., LLM CNAA Sr. Lectr.

Brady, Kathleen, BA Belf. Sr. Lectr.

Burke, Terence F., BA CNAA, MSc Lond. Principal Lectr.

Coakes, Elayne W. Sr. Lectr.

Croft, George, BSc E.Anglia, MSc Kent Sr. Lectr.

Croissant, Peter G., BA Oxf., MA Oxf. Sr. Lectr.

Cudlip, Irene J., BEd Lond. Sr. Lectr.

David, Alan H., MBA Liv. Principal Lectr.

El-Murad, Jaffar, BA City(UK) Sr. Lectr.

Fasey, Antonia, MA CNAA, MSc Lond. Principal Lectr.

Foley, Michael Sr. Lectr.

Freedman, J. Robert, PhD Principal Lectr.

Girson, Ilya, MSc Lond. Sr. Lectr.

Gough, Orla C., MPhil Lond. Sr. Lectr.

Graham, Anne, BSc CNAA, MSc Sur. Sr. Lectr.

Guedalla, Martin, BA CNAA, MA Westminster Principal Lectr.

Gurevitz, Simon, BSc Glas. Sr. Lectr.

Haberberg, Adrian B., BA Camb., MSc Lond. Sr. Lectr.

Haines, Brian C., BSc Lond., MSc Lond. Sr. Lectr.

Heagney, Brian, BA CNAA, MSc Middx. Sr. Lectr.

Healeas, Simon, MA Aberd. Sr. Lectr.

Hill, E. Peter, BA Lond., MBA Lond. Principal Lectr.

Hodd, Michael R., BA Camb., MSc Lond. Sr. Lectr.

Hollins, William J., BSc Sus., PhD Strath. Sr. Lectr.

Hooton, John, MA Camb. Principal Lectr.

Iles, Jennifer, BA CNAA, MA Lond. Principal Lectr.

John, Brian W., BA CNAA, MSc Lond. Principal Lectr.

Jones, Jill T. Sr. Lectr.

Kadhim, Talal A., MSc City(UK), PhD City(UK) Sr. Lectr.
Kemp, Michael F., MBA Lond. Sr. Lectr.
Khan, Shanaj, BA CNAA Sr. Lectr.
Killick, Geoffrey, BA Lond., MSc Lond. Principal Lectr.
King, Anthony J., BA Exe. Sr. Lectr.
Kolb, Bonita M., BA Alaska Pacific, PhD Golden Gate Enterprise Dir.
Lambert, Patricia L., BA CNAA, MA CNAA, MSc CNAA Sr. Lectr.
Leiwy, Daniel H. A., BA Open(UK), MA Lanc. Sr. Lectr.
Maddock, Sheila, BSc Lond., MSc Lond. Sr. Lectr.
Madhaven, Shobhana, BA Calc., MA Calc., MSc Lond., PhD Lond. Principal Lectr.
Melnikoff, Anthony, BSc Lond., MSc Lond. Sr. Lectr.
Moorjani, Bhagwan, BA Kent Sr. Lectr.
Morgan, F. Dorothy, BSc Brist., MSc Lond. Sr. Lectr.
Motamen-Samadian, Sima, BA Teheran, MA Essex, PhD Essex Sr. Lectr.
Mulreany, Philip V., BSc Wales, MSc Lond., MPhil Aston Sr. Lectr.
Pascalis, Bernadette, BA Oxf. Principal Lectr.
Perera, Ridivitaga D. Sr. Lectr.
Pilkington, Mark R., MSc Brun. Sr. Lectr.
Porter, Christine M., BSc CNAA, MSc Lond. Principal Lectr.
Powell-Williams, Karen H., BSc S'ton., MSc Lond. Sr. Lectr.
Price, Patricia, BA CNAA, MSc Lond. Sr. Lectr.
Reid, Allan, MBA Sr. Lectr.
Rich, Vincent G., BA E.Anglia, MSc Reading Sr. Lectr.
Richards, Haik, BSc Lond., MSc CNAA Sr. Lectr.
Rizvi, Syed M. Sr. Lectr.
Romer, Stephen, BSc Manc., MSc Lond., PhD Brun. Sr. Lectr.
Rose, Amanda M., BSc Lond., MSc Lond. Principal Lectr.
Rossano, Valerie N. Sr. Lectr.
Shackleton, John R., BA Lond., MSc Lond. Prof.; Head*
Skinner, Ronald P., BA CNAA, MSc Lond. Sr. Lectr.
Stanworth, M. John K., BSc Aston, MSc Lough., PhD Kent Prof.; Reader
Sturt, Alan R., BSc Lond., PhD Lond. Principal Lectr.
Sugden, Gillian F., BA Open(UK), MSc Brun., MSc S.Bank Principal Lectr.
Sunnassee, A. Vivek, BA CNAA, MSc Lond. Sr. Lectr.
Theobald, Robin C., BSc Lond., MA Lond., PhD Lond. Principal Lectr.
Weich, Alexander F. L., BSc Lond., MA E.Anglia, PhD Lond. Sr. Lectr.
Whitford, Anthony, BA CNAA, MSc Lond. Sr. Lectr.
Williams, Philip J., LLB Exe. Sr. Lectr.
Wong Chee, Harold K., MSc Lond., MA Lond. Sr. Lectr.
Zinkin, Jacqueline M., BA CNAA, MA CNAA Sr. Lectr.

SPECIAL CENTRES, ETC

American Studies Resources Centre
Tel: (0171) 911 5000 Fax: (0171) 911 5001
Brookeman, Christopher Dir.*

Applied Ecology Research Group
Tel: (0171) 911 5086 Fax: (0171) 911 5087
George, Prof. Jennifer, MSc S'ton., FIBiol Dir.*

Applied Psychology Research Group
Tel: (0171) 911 5000 Fax: (0171) 911 5174
Milner, Prof. David L., BA Brist., PhD Brist. Dir.*

Biotechnology Research Group
Tel: (0171) 911 5000 Fax: (0171) 911 5087
Bucke, Prof. Christopher, BSc Wales, PhD Liv. Dir.*

Building Research Group
Tel: (0171) 911 5000
Littler, Prof. John G. F., MA Oxf., PhD Nott. Dir.*

Communication and Information Studies, Centre for
Tel: (0171) 911 5941 Fax: (0171) 911 5942
Garnham, Prof. Nicholas, BA Camb. Dir.*

Computer Centre for People with Disabilities
Tel: (0171) 911 5000
Laycock, David W., BSc Liv., MSc Liv. Dir.*

Democracy, Centre for the Study of
Tel: (0171) 911 5138 Fax: (0171) 911 5164
Keane, Prof. John C., BA Adel., MA Tor., PhD Tor. Dir.*

Diplomatic Academy of London
Tel: (0171) 911 5701 Fax: (0171) 911 5105
Ayad, Nabil, MA Cairo, PhD Cairo Dir.*

Educational Initiative Centre
Tel: (0171) 911 5097
Rumpus, Ann E., BSc Exe., PhD Exe. Principal Lectr.; Dir.*

English Language Testing Service
Tel: (0171) 911 5000
Paterson, K. Dir.*

Future of Work Research Group
Tel: (0171) 911 5000
Stanworth, Prof. M. John K., BSc Aston, MSc Lough., PhD Kent Dir.*

Housing Education Centre
Tel: (0171) 911 5000
Smith-Bowers, William Dir.*

Imaging Technology Research Group
Tel: (0171) 911 5000
Jacobson, Prof. Ralph E., MSc Lond., PhD Lond. Dir.*

Industrial Control Centre
Tel: (0171) 911 5826 Fax: (0171) 911 5150
Leigh, Prof. J. Ron, MSc Lond., PhD Camb., FIMA, FIMechE Dir.*

Micro Electronics Systems Applications
Tel: (0171) 911 5081 Fax: (0171) 580 4139
Cain, Gerald D., PhD Flor. Prof.

Psychophysiology and Stress Research Group
Tel: (0171) 911 5000
Evans, Prof. Philip D., BA Camb., MA Camb., PhD Wales Dir.*

Self Access Language Centre
Tel: (0171) 911 5000
Press, Marie-Christine Dir.*

Signal Processing Research Group
Tel: (0171) 911 5081 Fax: (0171) 911 4319
Cain, Prof. Gerald D., PhD Flor. Dir.*

Sir George Cayley Institute
Computer science
Tel: (0171) 911 5000
Xanthis, Leo Dir.*

Structures and Geotechnics Research Group
Tel: (0171) 911 5000
Regan, Prof. P., BSc Lond., PhD Lond. Dir.*

Systems Engineering
Tel: (0171) 911 5000
Winter, Stephen C., BSc Lough., MSc Lough., PhD Westminster Dir.*

Translation Service
Tel: (0171) 911 5000
Burke, Jacqueline, MA Dir.*

Transport Studies Group
Tel: (0171) 911 5021 Fax: (0171) 911 5057
Browne, Michael, BA Lond., MSc CNAA BRS Prof., Transport
Jones, Peter M., BSc Brist., PhD Lond. Dir.*

Water Services
Tel: (0171) 911 5000
No staff at present

CONTACT OFFICERS

Academic affairs. Academic Registrar: Green, Evelyne, BA Manc.
Accommodation. Director of Estates and Facilities: Jackson, Peter
Admissions (first degree). Deputy Registrar (Student Administration): Neil, Lindsay
Admissions (higher degree). Research Degrees Administrator: Fisher, Michael
Adult/continuing education. Head of Educational Initiative Centre: Rumpus, Ann E., BSc Exe., PhD Exe.
Alumni. Alumni and Friends Officer: Stillman, Ruth
Archives. Archivist: Weeden, Brenda
Careers. Head of Careers Service: Pearce, Patricia
Computing services. Deputy Director of Information Resource Services: Enright, S.
Consultancy services. Director of Research Liaison: Trevan, Prof. Michael D., BSc Lond., PhD Lond.
Credit transfer. Director of Academic Credit: Rumpus, Ann E., BSc Exe., PhD Exe.
Development/fund-raising. Director of Development and Alumni Relations: Hornden, Carol, PhD
Distance education. Open and Flexible Learning Co-ordinator: Adam, Stephen
Equal opportunities. Multi-Ethnic Education and Equal Opportunities Officer: Amoa-Kumi, Sophie, MA CNAA
Estates and buildings/works and services. Director of Estates and Facilities: Jackson, Peter
Examinations. Conferments Officer: Banks, Shirley
Finance. Company Secretary and Financial Controller: Strang, Alan T., MA Edin., MSc Bath
General enquiries. Academic Registrar: Green, Evelyne, BA Manc.
Health services. University Health Service: ......
Industrial liaison. Director of Research Liaison: Trevan, Prof. Michael D., BSc Lond., PhD Lond.
International office. Director, International Education Office: van Rooijen, Maurits
Library (enquiries). Deputy Director, Information Resource Services: Enright, Suzanne
Minorities/disadvantaged groups. Multi-Ethnic Education and Equal Opportunities Officer: Amoa-Kumi, Sophie, MA CNAA
Ombudsperson. Vice-Chancellor's Executive Assistant: Pattison, Kate
Personnel/human resources. Director of Personnel Services: Bunt, Larry
Public relations, information and marketing. Director of Corporate Communications: Homden, Carol, PhD
Publications. Director of Corporate Communications: Homden, Carol, PhD
Purchasing. Company Secretary and Financial Controller: Strang, Alan T., MA Edin., MSc Bath
Quality assurance and accreditation. Deputy Registrar: Morrison, Melanie

Research. Director of Research Liaison: Trevan,
Prof. Michael D., BSc Lond., PhD Lond.
Safety. Health and Safety Officer: Tibbert,
Peter
Schools liaison. Schools and Colleges Liaison
Officer: Hewlett, Katherine
Security. Director of Estates and Facilities:
Jackson, Peter
Sport and recreation. Head of Recreation: ......
Staff development and training. Head of
Educational Initiative Centre: Rumpus, Ann
E., BSc Exe., PhD Exe.
Student union. General Manager: Humphries,
Martin
Student welfare/counselling. Head of
Counselling and Advisory Services: Heyno,
Ann

Students from other countries. International
Student Officer: ......
Students with disabilities. Director, Computer
Centre for People with Disabilities: Laycock,
David W., BSc Liv., MSc Liv.
University press. Director of Corporate
Communications: Homden, Carol, PhD
Women. Multi-Ethnic Education and Equal
Opportunities Officer: Amoa-Kumi, Sophie,
MA CNAA

CAMPUS/COLLEGE HEADS

Cavendish Campus, 115 New Cavendish
Street, London, England W1M 8JS. Provost:
Trevan, Prof. Michael D., BSc Lond., PhD Lond.
Harrow Campus, Watford Road, Northwick
Park, Harrow, England HA1 3TP. Provost:
Tyler, Maud, BA Lond., PhD Camb.
Marylebone Campus, 35 Marylebone Road,
London, England NW1 5LS. Provost:
Romans, Prof. Michael, BSc Aston, PhD Brun.
Regent Campus. Provost: Blunden, Prof.
Margaret, BA Exe., MA Exe., DPhil Oxf.

[Information supplied by the institution as at June 1998,
and edited by the ACU]

UNIVERSITY OF WOLVERHAMPTON

Founded 1992; previously established as Wolverhampton Polytechnic 1969

Member of the Association of Commonwealth Universities

Postal Address: Wolverhampton, England WV1 1SB
Telephone: (01902) 321000 **Fax**: (01902) 322680 **WWW**: http://www.wlv.ac.uk

CHANCELLOR—Shrewsbury and Talbot, The Rt. Hon. the Earl of, Hon. LLD Wolv.
PRO-CHANCELLOR AND CHAIRMAN OF THE BOARD OF GOVERNORS—Smith, A. J., FCIS
VICE-CHANCELLOR*—Brooks, Prof. John S., BSc Sheff., PhD Sheff., FIP
DEPUTY VICE-CHANCELLOR—White, J. E. G., MA Camb., LèsL Lille
PRO-VICE-CHANCELLOR (MARKETING AND DEVELOPMENT)—Bennett, Prof. G. F., BSc Birm., MBA Manc., PhD Manc.
PRO-VICE-CHANCELLOR (ACADEMIC PLANNING)—Wylie, N. V., MA Oxf., DPhil Oxf.

GENERAL INFORMATION

History. The university, established in 1992,
was originally founded as Wolverhampton
Polytechnic (1969).

Admission to first degree courses (see also
United Kingdom Introduction). Through
Universities and Colleges Admissions Service
(UCAS). The university accepts a wide range
of entry qualifications.

First Degrees (see also United Kingdom
Directory to Subjects of Study). BA, BEng, BSc,
LLB.
Most courses last 3 years full-time.
Sandwich courses and courses including a year
abroad: 4 years. All courses may be taken part-
time.

Higher Degrees (see also United Kingdom
Directory to Subjects of Study). LLM, MA,
MBA, MEd, MMedSc, MSc, MPhil, PhD.
Applicants for admission to taught master's
degree courses must normally hold a first
degree with at least second class honours, or
equivalent qualification.
LLM, MA, MBA, MMedSc, MSc: 1 year full-
time or equivalent part-time; MPhil: 2 years
full-time or equivalent part-time; PhD: 3 years
full-time or equivalent part-time.

Libraries. 494,896 volumes; 13,636 serials.

Fees (1998–99, annual). Home students:
(undergraduate) up to £1000; (postgraduate)
£2540–6700. International students:
(undergraduate and postgraduate) £5550;
(MBA) 5700.

Academic Year. October–June (most
courses).

Income (1996–97). Total, £77,891,000.

Statistics. Staff: 828 academic, 927
administrative. Students: 23,497 (10,161 men,
13,336 women).

ACADEMIC UNITS
Arranged by Schools

Applied Sciences
Tel: (01902) 322139
Addison, Kenneth, BA Oxf., DPhil Oxf. Sr.
Lectr.
Anderson, Richard G., BSc Brist., PhD
Brist. Principal Lectr.
Bennett, Janet, BSc Birm., PhD Birm. Principal
Lectr.
Boden, Graham F., BSc Manc., MSc Manc., PhD
Aston, FRSChem Sr. Lectr.
Burns, Alan T., BSc Newcastle(UK), PhD Edin. Sr.
Lectr.
Codling, Alan N., BSc Sheff. Sr. Lectr.
Connock, Martin J., BSc Wales, MSc Birm., PhD
Birm. Sr. Lectr.
Cox, Jeffrey J., BA Oxf., MA Oxf., DPhil
Oxf. Sr. Lectr.
Dackcombe, Roger V., BSc Liv., PhD Liv. Sr.
Lectr.
Farr, Katherine M., BA Oxf., MA Oxf., PhD
Aberd. Sr. Lectr.
Fincham, Daron A., BSc Nott., MPhil Chinese HK,
PhD Chinese HK Sr. Lectr.
Fullen, Michael A., BSc Hull, PhD CNAA Sr.
Lectr.
Hailes, Norman S., BSc Nott., PhD
Reading Principal Lectr.
Hill, David J., BSc Wales, PhD Wales Principal
Lectr.
Hitchen, Edward T., BSc Manc., PhD Manc. Sr.
Lectr.
Hooley, Paul, BSc Liv., PhD Wales Sr. Lectr.

Jarvis, Peter J., BA Lond. Principal Lectr.
Kenward, Melvin A., BSc Herts., PhD Aston Sr.
Lectr.
Mitchell, David J., BSc Lond., MSc Birm., PhD
Birm., FRMetS Sr. Lectr.
Mole, Edward J., BSc CNAA Sr. Lectr.
Morgan, Edward, BSc Wales, PhD Wales Dean*
Nallaiah, Charah, BSc Ceyl.(Colombo), PhD CNAA,
FRSChem Sr. Lectr.
Necklen, David K., BSc Wales, PhD Wales Sr.
Lectr.
Norton, Kenneth, BSc Leeds, PhD
Leeds Principal Lectr.
Perry, Christopher J., BSc Lanc., FRSChem Sr.
Lectr.
Protheroe, Roy G., BSc Wales, PhD Brist. Sr.
Lectr.
Reynolds, Stephen B., BSc Durh., PhD
Durh. Principal Lectr.
Ridgway, David J., BSc Liv., PhD Liv.,
FRSChem Sr. Lectr.
Roberts
Stuttard, Robin A., BA Oxf., MA Oxf., PhD
CNAA Principal Lectr.
Sunderland, Duncan W., BSc Lond., MSc Lond.,
PhD Brad. Sr. Lectr.
Sutton, Raul, BSc E.Anglia, PhD Edin. Sr. Lectr.
Tobin, Caterine M., BSc Trinity(Dub.), DPhil
Ulster Sr. Lectr.
Trueman, Ian C., BSc Reading, MSc Liv., PhD
Liv. Principal Lectr.
Ward, Richard D., BSc Newcastle(UK) Sr. Lectr.
Whitehead, Michael P., BSc H-W, PhD St
And. Sr. Lectr.
Other Staff: 8 Lectrs.; 2 Res. Fellows; 2 Temp.
Lectrs.
Vacant Posts: 1 Assoc. Head; 1 Lectr./Sr. Lectr.

Art and Design

Tel: (01902) 321905 Fax: (01902) 321944

Bainbridge, David, MA C.England Principal Lectr.

Bird, Edward, BA CNAA, MA Leic. Principal Lectr.

Brettell, Edwin, MA C.England Sr. Lectr.

Brewerton, Andrew J., BA Camb., MA Camb. Dean*

Brierley, John E., BA CNAA Principal Lectr.

Brown, Irene S., BA Nott.Trent, MA Reading Sr. Lectr.

Calow, Jane M., BA CNAA, MA Leeds Sr. Lectr.

Emberton, David, BA CNAA Sr. Lectr.

Farrell, Dennis C. Sr. Lectr.

Garfoot, Stuart, BA Staffs., MA RCA Sr. Lectr.

Hedges, Nick Sr. Lectr.

Henley, David W., BA CNAA Sr. Lectr.

Holland, Brian J., BA CNAA Sr. Lectr.

Hosking, Knighton S. Sr. Lectr.

Lloyd, Nicholas D., BA Newcastle(UK), MA Newcastle(UK) Sr. Lectr.

Loveless, Veronica M. Principal Lectr.

Madeley, Ian J. Principal Lectr.

Marks, George Z., BA CNAA Sr. Lectr.

Meacham, Lester, BA CNAA, MA Lond. Sr. Lectr.

Myers, John R., BA Newcastle(UK), MA C.England Sr. Lectr.

Olley, Peter J. Sr. Lectr.

Rowles, Kenneth M. Principal Lectr.

Sampson, Gill M., BA RCA, MA RCA Sr. Lectr.

Winning, Ross A., BA E.Anglia, MFA Newcastle(UK), MA Bourne. Sr. Lectr.

Wooldridge, Richard, BA CNAA Sr. Lectr.

Research: educational history (theory of art, design); specialist design projects, including medical equipment

Built Environment, see Engin. and the Built Environment

Business, see Wolverhampton Bus. Sch.

Computing and Information Technology

Tel: (01902) 321450 Fax: (01902) 321491

Ashdown, Helen J., BSc Lanc. Sr. Lectr.

Atherden, Anthony J., BA Open(UK), MSc Oxf. Sr. Lectr.

Bates, Peter E., BSc Brist., MSc Aston Principal Lectr.

Beardsmore, Derek I., BSc CNAA, MSc Birm. Sr. Lectr.

Binns, Ray, BSc Lond., PhD Lond. Principal Lectr.

Blakeley, William T., BSc Lond., PhD Warw. Principal Lectr.

Bradfield, Philip, BA Camb., MSc Aston Sr. Lectr.

Burden, John P., MA Camb. Sr. Lectr.

Byrne, Bernadette M., BSc Hull, MSc Aston Sr. Lectr.

Chester, Myrvin F., BSc Birm., MSc Nott. Sr. Lectr.

Coulson, Ian M., BSc CNAA, PhD CNAA Sr. Lectr.

Davies, Jennifer, BSc Newcastle(UK), PhD CNAA Sr. Lectr.

Davies, Wendy M., BA Birm. Sr. Lectr.

Garvey, Mary A., BSc CNAA, MSc CNAA Sr. Lectr.

Goda, David F., BA Oxf., MA Oxf. Sr. Lectr.

Gough, Norman E. Reader

Grealish, Helena M., BA Keele Principal Lectr.

Grimer, Anthony D., BTech CNAA Sr. Lectr.

Handley, Ivan M., MSc CNAA Sr. Lectr.

Harries, Gareth, MA Oxf., MSc Aston, PhD Birm. Sr. Lectr.

Harris, Arthur J., BSc Lond., MSc Lough., MSc CNAA Sr. Lectr.

Homer, Garry R., PhD Aston Principal Lectr.

Jackson, Mike S., BSc CNAA, MSc Manc. Reader

Jenner, Malcolm S., BA Oxf., MA Oxf., MSc CNAA Sr. Lectr.

Latham, Ann, BSc CNAA, MSc Aston Principal Lectr.

Lawrence, David R., BSc CNAA Sr. Lectr.

McKenna, Richard, BSc CNAA, MSc C.England Sr. Lectr.

Mehdi, Qassim H., BSc Baghdad, MSc Wales, PhD Wales Sr. Lectr.

Mooney, Robert J., BSc Sheff., PhD Sheff. Sr. Lectr.

Moore, Gary M., BSc Nott., MSc CNAA Sr. Lectr.

Musgrove, Peter B., BSc CNAA, MSc Lond., PhD CNAA Reader

Pearl, Laurence, BSc Birm., DPhil York(UK) Principal Lectr.

Penfold, Brian R., BSc CNAA Principal Lectr. (on leave)

Reeve, Robert C., BSc Durh., MSc Brad. Dean*

Roche, John, BSc Nott., MSc Wolv. Sr. Lectr.

Seedhouse, David E., BSc Wales, MSc Birm., PhD Birm. Sr. Lectr.

Singh, Jasbir

Simon, Errol S., BSc Birm. Principal Lectr.

Sloane, Andrew, BSc Wales, PhD Wales Sr. Lectr.

Thompson, Diana M., BSc Lond. Principal Lectr.

Traxler, John M., BSc S'ton., BSc Open(UK), MSc Brighton, MSc Sus. Sr. Lectr.

Wade, Keith, BSc CNAA Sr. Lectr.

Wallis, Jonathan P., BA CNAA, MSc CNAA Sr. Lectr.

Wilkinson, David F., BA York(UK), MSc Warw. Sr. Lectr.

Williams, John R., BSc CNAA, MSc Birm. Sr. Lectr.

Wilson, Peter I., MSc Aston Sr. Lectr.

Winwood, Graham, BA Wales, MSc Aston Principal Lectr.

Wrighton, Naomi, BSc S'ton., MSc Aston Sr. Lectr.

Other Staff: 11 Lectrs.; 4 Temp. Lectrs./Sr. Lectrs.

Vacant Posts: 3 Lectrs./Sr. Lectrs.; 2 Principal Lectrs.

Design, see Art and Des.

Education

Tel: (01902) 323255 Fax: (01902) 323180

Allan, Joanna L., BEd Birm., MEd Birm., PhD Wolv. Principal Lectr.

Allman, Geoffrey T., BA Wales, MA Keele, MEd Manc., PhD Birm. Sr. Lectr.

Atkins, Justyn N., BEd CNAA, MA C.England Sr. Lectr.

Avis, R. James, BSc Manc., MA Kent, PhD Birm. Principal Lectr.

Bartlett, Stephen J., BA CNAA, MA Keele, PhD Wolv. Sr. Lectr.

Bicknell, Simon, BEd Wolv. Sr. Lectr.

Bill, Karen E., BEd CNAA, MEd Lough. Sr. Lectr.

Biscomb, Kay, BEd CNAA, MA Warw. Sr. Lectr.

Booth, Robert J., BA Open(UK), MA C.England Principal Lectr.

Brown, Christine, BA Lond., MEd Birm., PhD Principal Lectr.

Buckley, Diane C., BEd Birm. Sr. Lectr.

Burke, Diedrie M., BA Lanc., MA Lanc. Sr. Lectr.

Buxton, Christopher T., BEd Open(UK) Sr. Lectr.

Canning, Barbara Sr. Lectr.

Carpanini, David L., BA CNAA, MA RCA Sr. Lectr.

Chorley, John E., BEd CNAA, MEd CNAA Sr. Lectr.

Chryssides, George D., BD Glas., DPhil Oxf. Sr. Lectr.

Crotty, Margaret, BSc Wolv. Sr. Lectr.

Dearden, Philip N., BSc E.Anglia, MSc Aberd. Principal Lectr.

Dhillon, Jaswinder K., BEd CNAA, MEd MSc Sr. Lectr.

Doggart, L. Sr. Lectr.

Draper, N., BEd Exe., MA Lond., PhD Principal Lectr.

Dudley, Jonathan H., BA Camb., MA Leeds Principal Lectr.

Dunning, Lesley A., BEd Birm., MEd Wolv. Sr. Lectr.

Dye, Vanessa L., BEd CNAA, MA Leic. Sr. Lectr.

Florida-James, Geraint Sr. Lectr.

Floyd, David C., BA CNAA Sr. Lectr.

Geaves, Ronald A., BA Open(UK), MA Leeds, PhD Sr. Lectr.

Jackson, Philip E., BEd Leic. Sr. Lectr.

Jarrett, Haydn, BEd CNAA, MSc Ill. Sr. Lectr.

Jones, Jeffrey L., BEd Brist., MEd Leic., MBA Leic., PhD Exe. Principal Lectr.

Jones, Malcolm, BEd Open(UK), MEd CNAA Sr. Lectr.

Jones, Philip S., BSc Stir., PhD Stir. Sr. Lectr.

Kowalski, Robert, BSc Lond., DPhil Oxf. Sr. Lectr.

Lanaway, Anthony D., BA Exe., BEd Exe., MEd Wash. Principal Lectr.

Ledgard, Dorothy R., BPhil Nott. Sr. Lectr.

Mahony, Desmond W., BSc CNAA, MSc CNAA Sr. Lectr.

Mars, Mel, BA CNAA, MA Wolv. Principal Lectr.

Marshall, Carole A., BA CNAA Sr. Lectr.

McKay, Jean M., BA Birm., MEd Warw. Dean*

Miller, Joyce Sr. Lectr.

Mortiboys, Alan F., BSc(Soc) Lond., MPhil Wolv. Sr. Lectr.

Parsons, John K., BSc Sheff., MEd Sheff. Principal Lectr.

Pavey, Elizabeth, BA Sur. Lectr./Sr. Lectr.

Preston, John R., BSc Aston, PhD Aston Principal Lectr.

Proctor, Malcolm D., BMus Durh. Sr. Lectr.

Prudham, Brian, BA Liv., MEd Warw. Sr. Lectr.

Richards, Gill, BEd BPhil MPhil Sr. Lectr.

Robbins, Vincent, BA Nott., MEd Birm. Sr. Lectr.

Roland, Rachel J., MA CNAA, MSc Cran. Sr. Lectr.

Serf, Jeffrey M., BA Lond., MEd Birm. Sr. Lectr.

Somervell, J. Hugh, BEd Birm., MPhil Wolv. Principal Lectr.

Sporton, Gregory, BA Victorian Coll.Arts, MA Warw. Principal Lectr.

Stoker, David, BEd CNAA Sr. Lectr.

Surridge, Mary E., MEd Manc. Sr. Lectr.

Taylor, Paul E., BEd CNAA Sr. Lectr.

Thomas, Adam Sr. Lectr.

Warburton, Keith, BA Lanc., MEd CNAA Principal Lectr.

Wareing, Paul, BEng Lough. Sr. Lectr.

Whyte, Greg Sr. Lectr.

Winter, Christopher, BA Open(UK) Sr. Lectr.

Wright, Alexis D., MA Nott.Trent Sr. Lectr.

Vacant Posts: 12 Lectrs./Sr. Lectrs.

Engineering and the Built Environment

Tel: (01902) 323255 Fax: (01902) 323180

Ambrose, Brian Principal Lectr.

Billingham, John, BSc Aston Sr. Lectr.

Brettell, Barry T., BSc Aston, FICE Principal Lectr.

Collie, Donald N. Sr. Lectr.

Cooper, Patricia A., BA CNAA, FRIBA Principal Lectr.

Corbett, Pauline, MSc Lough. Sr. Lectr.

Dews, Stanley J., BSc Wales, MSc Brist., PhD Wolv., FRSChem Principal Lectr.

Felce, Alison, BSc Lectr.; Course Leader, ADI

Felton, Anthony J., BEng CNAA, FIMechE Sr. Lectr.

Garner, Kevin B., BSc CNAA Principal Lectr.

Goodwin, Michael G., BSc CNAA Sr. Lectr.

Hall, F. Richard, BEng PhD Head, Engin. Div.

Harris, Phillip T. Sr. Lectr.

Havell, Paul R., BEng Lond. Sr. Lectr.

Holt, Gary D., BSc PhD Reader

Hudson, Graham R., MSc CNAA Sr. Lectr.

Kibble, Kevin A., MPhil CNAA, PhD Wolv. Sr. Lectr.

Kite, B. J., BSc Wales, MSc Lough. Sr. Lectr.

Lewis, Geoffrey, BSc Leic., PhD CNAA, FIM, FRSChem Principal Lectr.

Lister, Paul M., BEng CNAA, PhD Manc. Sr. Lectr.

Mihsein, Musa, BSc *Lond.*, MBA *CNAA*, PhD
 Lond. Dean*
Morgan, Colin, BSc *Wales* Sr. Lectr.
Ndekugri, Issaka E., BSc *Ghana*, MSc *Lough.*, PhD
 Lough. Principal Lectr.
Oakes, Graham L., BSc *CNAA* Sr. Lectr.
Potts, Keith F., MSc *Lough.*, FRICS Principal
 Lectr.
Reynolds, Philip, FRICS Sr. Lectr.
Roberts, Neil, BTech *Lough.*, MSc *Warw.* Sr.
 Lectr.
Rowley, William A., BSc *CNAA*, MPhil
 CNAA Principal Lectr.
Sagoo, Amritpal S., BSc MSc Sr. Lectr.,
 Building Surveying
Shaw, Tony, BEng *Salf.*, MSc *Lough.* Sr. Lectr.
Stanford, Mark, BEng *CNAA* Sr. Lectr.
Zakeri, Ahmad, BSc *Arya-Mehr*, MSc *Aston*, PhD
 Aston Sr. Lectr.
Other Staff: 4 Lectrs.

European Studies, see Langs. and European
Studies

Health Sciences

Tel: (01902) 321107 Fax: (01902) 321161
Adamson-Macedo, Elvidina N., MSc *Lond.*, PhD
 Lond. Sr. Lectr.
Bailey, Carol A., MSc *Lond.* Principal Lectr.
Bergin, John P., BA *CNAA*, MA *Lanc.* Sr. Lectr.
Brown, Colin A., BSc *Manc.Met.*, PhD *Keele* Sr.
 Lectr.
Carson, Ray J., BSc *Lond.*, PhD *Lond.* Sr. Lectr.
Coleman, Iain P., BSc *CNAA*, PhD
 Aston Principal Lectr.
Collins, Jacqueline, MSc *Aston* Principal Lectr.
Crome, Ilana B., MA *Camb.*, MB ChB *Birm.*,
 MPhil *Lond.*, MD *Birm.* Reader
Crossfield, Timothy M., BSc *CNAA*, BSc
 Keele Sr. Lectr.
Dunmore, Simon J., BSc *Dund.*, PhD *Lond.* Sr.
 Lectr.
Dyer, Valerie A., MA *Keele*, MEd *Birm.*, MSc
 Wolv., PhD *Birm.* Sr. Lectr.
El Ansari, Walid, MB ChB *Alexandria*, MSc
 Lond. Sr. Lectr.
Grace, Richard H., MB BS *Lond.*, FRCS Hon.
 Prof.
Griffiths, Peter J., BSc *Wales*, PhD *Wales* Sr.
 Lectr.
Hart, Nicola M., BSc *Manc.* Sr. Lectr.
Hassan, Hassan T., MB ChB *Alexandria*, MSc
 Lond., PhD *Camb.*, MD *Berlin* Sr. Lectr.
Henshaw, Ann, BA *Keele* Principal Lectr.
Hogan, Kevin M., BSc *Aston*, PhD
 Aston Principal Lectr.
Jolley, David, MB BS *Lond.*, MSc *Manc.*,
 FRCPsych Hon. Prof.
Khokher, Mohammed A., BSc *Lond.*, MSc *Warw.*,
 PhD *Lond.* Sr. Lectr.
Koutedakis, Yiannis, BSc *Salonika*, MA *Birm.*,
 PhD *Birm.* Sr. Lectr.
Logan, James G., BSc *St And.*, MSc *N.U.I.*, PhD
 N.U.I. Dean*
Lowe, David, BSc *Hull*, MSc *Lond.* Sr. Lectr.
Luft, Sarah A. Sr. Lectr.
Manktelow, Kenneth I., BA *CNAA*, PhD
 CNAA Reader
Martin, Ashley, BSc *Leeds*, PhD *Nott.* Sr. Lectr.
Maslin, David J., BSc *Newcastle(UK)*, PhD
 Newcastle(UK) Sr. Lectr.
McDonald, Maureen F., BA *CNAA*, PhD
 C.Lancs. Sr. Lectr.
Miles, David M., BSc *Lond.*, MSc *Keele* Sr. Lectr.
Morris, Neil G., BSc *CNAA*, BA *Open(UK)*, PhD
 Durh. Sr. Lectr.
Murray, Paul G., MSc *Nott.* Sr. Lectr.
Nelson, Paul N., BSc *Lond.*, PhD *Birm.* Sr.
 Lectr.
Nune, Petula A., BSc *Aston*, PhD *Aston* Sr.
 Lectr.
Padgham, Cheryl, MSc *Lond.*, PhD *Lond.* Sr.
 Lectr.
Perera, Shantha A., BSc *Lond.*, MSc *Aberd.*, PhD
 Lond. Sr. Lectr.
Phillips, Jonathan D., BSc *CNAA*, PhD
 CNAA Principal Lectr.
Richardson, Deborah R., MSc *Birm.* Sr. Lectr.

Robotham, Elizabeth A., BA *Open(UK)*, MEd
 Wolv. Principal Lectr.
Thomas, Robert, BSc *Birm.*, MSc *Birm.*, PhD
 Birm. Principal Lectr.
Toms, Margaret K., BSc *Wales*, PhD *Wales* Sr.
 Lectr.
Walh, Ruth
Young, David, BA *Hull*, MSc *Lough.*, PhD
 Lough. Sr. Lectr.
Other Staff: 11 Lectrs.; 8 Res. Fellows; 13
 Hon. Clin. Sr. Lectrs.; 2 Hon. Clin. Lectrs.; 3
 Hon. Readers
Vacant Posts: 1 Prof.; 1 Principal Lectr.; 2
 Lectrs.

Humanities and Social Sciences

Tel: (01902) 323408 Fax: (01902) 323379
Almond, Thomas A., MA *Camb.*, MA *Keele* Sr.
 Lectr.
Apted, Edwin P., BA *Aston*, MA *Warw.* Sr.
 Lectr.
Barker, Christopher J., BA *Birm.*, MA *Sheff.*, PhD
 Leeds Sr. Lectr.
Barrett, Gillian F., PhD *Belf.* Sr. Lectr.
Bartley, Paula A., BA *Lond.*, MA *Lond.*, MA
 CNAA, PhD *Wolv.* Sr. Lectr.
Benson, John, BA *Leic.*, MA *Manit.*, PhD
 Leeds Reader
Bernardes, Jon, BA *Hull*, MSc *Aston*, PhD
 Hull Principal Lectr.
Boutonnet, Josiane, BA *Wolv.*, MA *Birm.* Sr.
 Lectr.
Callaghan, John T., MA *Essex*, PhD
 Manc. Reader
Cameron, Andrew A., BA *Lond.*, MA *Lough.* Sr.
 Lectr.
Clark, Urszula I., BA *York(UK)* Principal Lectr.
Colbert, Benjamin, BA *Oxf.*, MPhil *Oxf.*, PhD
Cook, Dee
Cooper, Andrew J., BA *S'ton.*, PhD
 S'ton. Principal Lectr.
Crowther, Barbara, BA *York(UK)*, MPhil *Liv.*
Cunningham, Michael, BA *Leeds*, MA *Leeds*, PhD
 Manc.
Denham, David J., BA *Brad.*, MA *Birm.*, PhD
 Birm. Sr. Lectr.
Dennis, John M., BA *Liv.*, PhD *Liv.* Principal
 Lectr.
Durham, Martin, BA *Birm.*, PhD *Birm.* Sr. Lectr.
Fowler, Julia, BA *Leeds*
Free, Marcus, BA *Trinity(Dub.)*, PhD
 Trinity(Dub.)
Green, Marci R., BSc *Arizona State*, MA *Birm.* Sr.
 Lectr.
Gwinnett, Barbara, BA *C.England*, PhD *Aston* Sr.
 Lectr.
Henderson, Paul, BA *E.Anglia*, PhD *E.Anglia*
Housee, Shirin, BA *Essex*, MEd *Birm.*
Hurd, Geoffrey W., BA *S'ton.*, MSc *S'ton.*, MA
 Birm. Dean*
Johnson, Maxwell H., BA *Birm.*, MA *Keele*, PhD
 Birm. Sr. Lectr.
Jones, Maria, BA *Wolv.*, MA *Birm.*
Leese, Roger, BA *Manc.*, PhD *Manc.* Principal
 Lectr.
Levinson, Margot, BSc MSc
Lintonbon, Roger M., PhD *Nott.* Principal
 Lectr.
Magill, Kevin B., BA *Kent*, MA *Kent*, PhD
 Lond. Sr. Lectr.
McLeay, Peter, MA *Birm.* Sr. Lectr.
Michelson, Joan, BA MFA MA Sr. Lectr.
Morgan-Daley, Claudette
Norton, Christopher, BA *Ulster*, MA *Leeds*, PhD
 Ulster
Page, Kenneth, BA *Warw.*, MPhil *Birm.*
Rees, Graham C., BA *Birm.*, MA *Birm.*, PhD
 Birm. Sr. Lectr.
Saywood, Barrie C., BA *Leic.*, MA *Leic.*, PhD
 Warw. Principal Lectr.
Scholes, Marc C., BA *CNAA*, MA
 CNAA Principal Lectr.
Shade, Ruth E., MA *Essex* Sr. Lectr.
Stredder, James E., BA *Camb.*, MA *Birm.*, PhD
 CNAA Principal Lectr.
Taylor, Eric, BA *Keele*, MA *Yale*, PhD *Keele* Sr.
 Lectr.
Terry Chandler, Fiona, BA *Birm.*, PhD

Walker, Alistair G., BSc *Hull*, MA
 Lanc. Principal Lectr.
Wanklyn, Malcolm D., MA *Manc.*, PhD
 Manc. Principal Lectr.
Watkin, David G., BA *Wales*, PhD
 Wales Principal Lectr.
Watson, Peter, BA *Oxf.*, MA *Lond.*, MSocSc
 Birm., MA *Oxf.* Sr. Lectr.
Williams, Jenny, BA *Lond.*, MSc *Aston*
Williams, Jill E., BA *Lond.*, MA *Aston* Principal
 Lectr.
Willis, Paul, MA MSc PhD
Young, Bruce, BPhil *Oxf.*, MA *Aberd.* Principal
 Lectr.
Other Staff: 1 Lectr.
Vacant Posts: 1 Principal Lectr.

Information Technology, see Computing
and Information Technol.

Languages and European Studies

Tel: (01902) 322481 Fax: (01902) 322739
Andrews, Eleanor V., BA *Leeds*, MPhil
 CNAA Sr. Lectr.
Bateman, Milford J., BA *CNAA*, PhD *Wolv.* Sr.
 Lectr.
Berryman, John F., BA *Birm.* Principal Lectr.
Blake, Susan, BA *Wolv.*, MA *Birm.* Sr. Lectr.
Brett, Paul A., BSc *Aston*, MA *Birm.* Sr. Lectr.
Capitanio, Sarah J., BA *Manc.Met.*, MA *Montpellier*,
 PhD *Manc.Met.* Principal Lectr.
Carel, Magali G., BA *Montpellier* Sr. Lectr.
Dangerfield, Martin V., BA *Wolv.*, MSc
 Wolv. Sr. Lectr.
Davies, Megan J., BA *Wolv.* Principal Lectr.
Dickins, Thomas, BA *Leeds*, MA *Leeds* Sr. Lectr.
Goodison, Terence A., BA *Birm.*, PhD
 Birm. Principal Lectr.
Gorman, Michael P., BA *S'ton.*, MA *Liv.*, PhD
 S'ton. Sr. Lectr.
Green, Jean, MA *Durh.* Sr. Lectr.
Hagen, Stephen G., BA *Durh.*, MA *Durh.*, MA
 Newcastle(UK) Dean*
Hambrook, Glyn M., BA *Nott.*, PhD *Nott.* Sr.
 Lectr.
Haughey, James R., BA *Belf.* Sr. Lectr.
Hawkesworth, Richard I., BA *Sheff.*, MSc
 Nott. Principal Lectr.
Hawkins, Richard A., BA *Portsmouth*, MSc *Lond.*,
 PhD *Lond.* Sr. Lectr.
Haynes, Michael J., BA *Lond.*, MA *Lond.* Sr.
 Lectr.
Higgins-Cezza, Josephine M., BA *Reading* Sr.
 Lectr.
Kapcia, Antoni M., BA *Lond.*, PhD
 Lond. Principal Lectr.
Lawrance, Elizabeth A., BA *Coventry*, MA
 Sus. Principal Lectr.
Milhavy, Patricia, BA *Liv.* Sr. Lectr.
Mitkov, Ruslan, MA *Humboldt*, PhD
 T.H.Dresden Sr. Lectr.
Moore, Irina, BA *Vilnius* Sr. Lectr.
Nield, Ronald F., BA *Brad.*, MA *Birm.* Sr. Lectr.
Niven, Gordon W., BA *Stir.*, MSc *CNAA* Sr.
 Lectr.
Norton-Uhl, Hildegard, MagPhil *Vienna* Sr.
 Lectr.
Power, Patrick, MA *RCA* Sr. Lectr.
Richards, Jonathon, BA *Wales* Sr. Lectr.
Rooney, Peter J., BA *Sus.*, MSc *Birm.* Principal
 Lectr.
Shannon-Little, Paul A., BA *Liv.*, MA
 Reading Sr. Lectr.
Steiner, Ben, BA *Lond.*, MA *Durh.* Sr. Lectr.
Squires, Joy, BA *CNAA*, MA *Sus.* Sr. Lectr.
Steinke, Gabriela M., BA *Bielefeld* Sr. Lectr.
Tomlinson, Paul, BA *Wolv.*, MBA *Wolv.* Sr.
 Lectr.
Wadia, Khursheed, BSc *Aston*, PhD *Aston* Sr.
 Lectr.
Welch, Penny, BA *Keele* Principal Lectr.
Vacant Posts: 1 Principal Lectr.; 1 Lectr./Sr.
 Lectr.

Legal Studies

Tel: (01902) 321512 Fax: (01902) 321567
Cartwright, Martin J., BA *CNAA*, BPhil
 Hull Principal Lectr.

Clark, Robert A., LLB S'ton. Dean*
Clevenger, J., BA Mississippi, LLB CNAA, MSc Mississippi, LLM Leic.
Crug, H. D., LLB Wolv. Sr. Lectr.
Davies, Alan H., BA S'ton. Sr. Lectr.
Evans, Judith M., LLB Wales Sr. Lectr.
Finucane, Tony H., BA CNAA, MPhil CNAA Sr. Lectr.
Fletcher-Tomenius, Paul H., LLB Lond., LLM Lond. Sr. Lectr.
Handley, P., BSc Sheff., LLB CNAA Sr. Lectr.
Haynes, Andrew, BA CNAA, LLB C.England Principal Lectr.
Higgott, Rosemary A., LLB Birm. Sr. Lectr.
Hughes, John R., LLB Lond. Principal Lectr.
Hussain, Mumtaz J., LLB CNAA Sr. Lectr.
Keay, A., LLB Adel., LLM Qld., PhD Qld. Reader
Law, Richard T., LLB Brist. Sr. Lectr.
Leighton-Johnstone, Lynn, LLB CNAA, MA Keele Principal Lectr.
McCartly, F., LLB Belf. Sr. Lectr.
Migdal, Stephen D., LLB Kingston(UK) Sr. Lectr.
Miles, Louise M., LLB Birm. Sr. Lectr.
Newcombe, Gillian L. Sr. Lectr.
Perks, Linda, LLB CNAA Sr. Lectr.
Senior, K., BA Birm. Sr. Lectr.
Shardlow, Janice B., LLB Lond. Sr. Lectr.
Vallely, Christine, LLB Nott. Principal Lectr.
Walker, Andrew D., LLB Brist., LLM Warw. Sr. Lectr.
Walsh, Margaret I., BA Keele Sr. Lectr.
Wells, Ian G., LLB Birm. Sr. Lectr.
Woollard, Suzanne C., LLB Leic. Sr. Lectr.
Other Staff: 2 Lectrs.
Vacant Posts: 2 Sr. Lectrs.

Nursing and Midwifery

Tel: (01902) 323047 Fax: (01902) 322886
Bagnall, Louise Sr. Lectr.
Ballard, Elaine C., MA Coventry Sr. Lectr.
Barnfather, Anne Sr. Lectr.
Bartram, Isobel H., MA Wolv. Dean*
Bartter, Karen E., MA Sr. Lectr.
Batson, Anthony A. Sr. Lectr.
Bayley, Rita F., BA Open(UK) Sr. Lectr.
Bolton, Janet M. Sr. Lectr.
Bond, Patricia A. Sr. Lectr.
Boyle, Maggie Sr. Lectr.
Boynton, Elsie A. Sr. Lectr.
Brewer, Eileen A., BSc Wolv. Sr. Lectr.
Bryan, Karen, BSc CNAA Sr. Lectr.
Butler, Robert D. Sr. Lectr.
Byrne, Roger J., BSc Coventry Sr. Lectr.
Callow, Sue Sr. Lectr.
Callwood, Ingrid J. Sr. Lectr.
Carnwell, Ros, BA MA Principal Lectr.
Cawley, Timothy A. Sr. Lectr.
Chellembrun, Michael F., BEd CNAA, MA CNAA Principal Lectr.
Chinyanganya, Kingsley Sr. Lectr.
Clayton, Loretta J. Sr. Lectr.
Clinch, Christine A., BSc CNAA Sr. Lectr.
Confedra-Levine, Elaine L., MA Warw. Sr. Lectr.
Cox, Mavis, BSc MSc Sr. Lectr.
Crofts, Robert S. Principal Lectr.
Cushing, Sylvia M. Sr. Lectr.
Cysewski, Ann T. Sr. Lectr.
Daly, William M., BA Sr. Lectr.
Davies, Albert J., BA Open(UK), MSc Aston Principal Lectr.
Davies, Barbara E., MSc Keele Sr. Lectr.
Drew, Denise, MSc C.England Sr. Lectr.
Dudley, Lesley A. Principal Lectr.
Edwards, Lynn Sr. Lectr.
Edwards, Marcia A. Sr. Lectr.
Edwards, Margaret A., BSc Wolv. Sr. Lectr.
Eggison, Peter D., BSc Leic., MA Leic. Principal Lectr.
Evans, Deborah S. J., BSc CNAA Sr. Lectr.
Fisher, David J. Sr. Lectr.
Flavell, Patricia L. Sr. Lectr.
Fogarty, Michael D. Sr. Lectr.
Foolchand, Madhun K., MPhil Sr. Lectr.
Foxall, Fiona D. Sr. Lectr.
Francis, Linda E., BSc CNAA Sr. Lectr.
Fuchs, Janet, BSc Sr. Lectr.
Gallagher, Luke J. Principal Lectr.

Glaze, Jane E., BSc CNAA Sr. Lectr.
Gray, Alastair D. Sr. Lectr.
Grizzell, Jose H., BSc CNAA Sr. Lectr.
Gunga, Yuswant C., MSc Sr. Lectr.
Hammon-Turner, Denise J., BA Open(UK), MA Keele Sr. Lectr.
Hargraves, Julie, BA Warw. Sr. Lectr.
Harrison, Lilian E. Sr. Lectr.
Holmes, John W. Sr. Lectr.
Iles, Ian K., MA Sr. Lectr.
Ingleston, Lorraine H., BSc CNAA, MA Keele, MBA Keele Head(2)
Jijita, Tunai F., BSc CNAA Sr. Lectr.
Joshi, Nirmala K. Sr. Lectr.
Killingworth, Leslie G. Sr. Lectr.
Lewis, Linda M., BSc CNAA Sr. Lectr.
Lim, Pauline, BSc Sr. Lectr.
Lumsden, Hilary, BSc Wolv. Sr. Lectr.
Lyle, Dorothy, MBA Sr. Lectr.
McCoy, Mary, BSc Manc., MA Keele Sr. Lectr.
Miles, Sheila Sr. Lectr.
Moran, B. A. Sr. Lectr.
Moran, Patricia Sr. Lectr.
Moran, Wendy A. Sr. Lectr.
Murray, Roy J. Sr. Lectr.
Norcott, Lyn Sr. Lectr.
Norman, Claire Sr. Lectr.
O'Grady, Dympna P., MA Sr. Lectr.
Okonedo, Josephine A. Sr. Lectr.
Owen, Patricia A., BSc Sr. Lectr.
Paniagua, Hilary Sr. Lectr.
Parkes, Margaret A. Sr. Lectr.
Parsons, Colette M., BEd Wales, MSc Principal Lectr.
Pemberton, Jean, BSc Wolv. Principal Lectr.
Phillips, Patricia A., BSc CNAA Sr. Lectr.
Philp, Ann M. Sr. Lectr.
Pitt, Lindsay D. Sr. Lectr.
Preen, Carol A., BA Open(UK) Sr. Lectr.
Ramsorrun, Oman D. Sr. Lectr.
Raynor, Mary A., BA Open(UK) Sr. Lectr.
Reynolds, Angela J., BA Open(UK) Principal Lectr.
Richards, Hew Sr. Lectr.
Rutty, Evelyn, BEd MA Principal Lectr.
Rushton, Stuart Sr. Lectr.
Saddler-Moore, Della, BA Open(UK) Sr. Lectr.
Sandbrook, Sandra P. Sr. Lectr.
Sarson, Lynda A., BSc Wolv. Sr. Lectr.
Saul, Siva Y., BA Open(UK) Sr. Lectr.
Sherratt, Wendy, BSc Derby Sr. Lectr.
Smith, Haley C. Sr. Lectr.
Smith, Maureen Sr. Lectr.
Smith, Milly Principal Lectr.
Smith, Pamela Y., BSc CNAA Sr. Lectr.
Southall, Susan, BSc Sr. Lectr.
Speight, Susan M. Sr. Lectr.
Speight, William A., BEd Sr. Lectr.
Stephens, Nicola J., BA Open(UK) Principal Lectr.
Stevenson, Elizabeth A. Sr. Lectr.
Sutton, Diane Principal Lectr.
Swift, Lorraine Sr. Lectr.
Swindlehurst, Lyn, BSc Coventry Sr. Lectr.
Swindlehurst, Mathew C., MA Warw. Principal Lectr.
Taylor, Louise M. Sr. Lectr.
Thain, John D., BSc Sr. Lectr.
Thompson, Christine A. Sr. Lectr.
Tonks, Edna B. Principal Lectr.
Van Der Woning, Melanie, BSc Wolv. Sr. Lectr.
Veeramah, Enkanah Sr. Lectr.
Vials, Joyce M., BSc Sr. Lectr.
Wakefield, Pamela M. Sr. Lectr.
Walsh, Pauline N. Principal Lectr.
Westcott, Lorraine I. Sr. Lectr.
Westwood, Lynn R. Sr. Lectr.
Whitfield, Tracie S. Sr. Lectr.
Wildsmith, Peter A., BSc Wales, MA Sr. Lectr.
Williams, Marilyn, BSc Wolv. Sr. Lectr.
Wood, Georgina, BSc Wolv. Sr. Lectr.
Woodward, Val J. Sr. Lectr.
Wright, David F., BA Sheff. Sr. Lectr.
Vacant Posts: 1 Principal Lectr.; 2 Lectrs./Sr. Lectrs.

Social Sciences, see Humanities and Soc. Scis.

Wolverhampton Business School

Tel: (01902) 323874 Fax: (01902) 323955
Alken, John M., BSc Manc., MBA Aston Sr. Lectr.
Arrowsmith, David A., MBA Liv. Sr. Lectr.
Bate, Anthony J., MBA CNAA Sr. Lectr.
Bennett, Martin D., BA Nott., MA Sheff. Sr. Lectr.
Black, John, BSc Birm., MA Warw. Principal Lectr.
Bloom, Sydney, BA CNAA, MSc Manc. Sr. Lectr.
Booth, Jennifer, MBA CNAA Sr. Lectr.
Bunch, Graham J., BSc Open(UK) Sr. Lectr.
Buszard, Paul M., BSc Durh., MBA Sr. Lectr.
Chambers, Christopher A., MSc Sheff.Hallam Sr. Lectr.
Chryssides, John C., MA Glas., PhD Birm. Sr. Lectr.
Conway, Bryony M., BA Car., MA Dean*
Cooper, Christopher S., BA Wolv., MBA Wolv. Principal Lectr.
Copus, Colin M., MA CNAA Sr. Lectr.
Dale, John, BA Wolv., MA Liv. Sr. Lectr.
Dandy, Colin T., LLB Birm. Principal Lectr.
Davies, Goronwy F., BSc Lond., MSc Lond., MA N.Carolina, PhD Bath Principal Lectr.
Evans, Angela M., BA CNAA Sr. Lectr.
Fisher, Virginia C., BA Birm. Sr. Lectr.
Gibney, Susan R., BA Coventry, MA Trinity(Dub.) Sr. Lectr.
Gilbert, Kathryn M., BA Wales, MA Wales Sr. Lectr.
Gittens, Josephine A., BSc Aston Sr. Lectr.
Glenn, Ian, BSc Hull Sr. Lectr.
Gollins, Gillian E., BSc Sheff. Principal Lectr.
Goulding, Christina C., BA CNAA Sr. Lectr.
Grady, Stephen W., BA CNAA, MA E.Anglia Sr. Lectr.
Grainger, Clive N., MSocSc Birm., FCA Sr. Lectr.
Groves, Andrew J., BA Lond., MA Aston Sr. Lectr.
Hallett, David J., BSc CNAA, MBA Aston Sr. Lectr.
Hamlin, Robert G., BSc Sheff., MPhil CNAA Principal Lectr.
Harris, Robert J., BA CNAA Sr. Lectr.
Hassall, John C., BSc Manc., MBA Aston Sr. Lectr.
Hockings, Christine S., BA CNAA Sr. Lectr.
Homer, Philip, BA Essex Sr. Lectr.
Jagus, Antony B., BSc Reading, MBA CNAA, MSc Brist. Principal Lectr.
Jones, Christopher R., BA Wolv. Sr. Lectr.
Kemp, Brian, BA Open(UK), MBA Aston Sr. Lectr.
Law, David A., BA Nott., MA Manc. Sr. Lectr.
Lowbridge, Robin, BA Camb., MA Camb., MBA Wolv. Sr. Lectr.
Lyons, Gillian A., BA CNAA Sr. Lectr.
Macefield, Ritchie C., BA Lough. Sr. Lectr.
Mahdi, Mohammad S., BA Baghdad, PhD Wales Sr. Lectr.
Marsh, John, BSc Aston, MSc Aston Principal Lectr.
McPhee, Ian A., BA CNAA Sr. Lectr.
Mills, Paul, BA CNAA, PhD CNAA Sr. Lectr.
Mott, William J., MBA Aston Sr. Lectr.
O'Donoghue, John R., BEd Sus., MSc Lond. Sr. Lectr.
Oakley, Anthony J., BSc Liv., MBA Aston Sr. Lectr.
Oxtoby, David, MBA Wolv. Sr. Lectr.
Parkes, Carole, MSc Wolv. Sr. Lectr.
Perry, Robert W., MBA Wolv. Principal Lectr.
Pinkney, Roger J., MBA Aston Sr. Lectr.
Price, Mark A., BSc Birm., MBA Wolv. Principal Lectr.
Priddey, Lynette P., BA Open(UK), MSc CNAA Sr. Lectr.
Richards, Peter, FCA Sr. Lectr.
Richer, Glenn J., BA CNAA Sr. Lectr.
Scarff, William J., BA Lanc. Sr. Lectr.

Singh, Gurmak, BSc *Wales*, MSc *Aston*,
MPhil   Sr. Lectr.
Songhurst, David J., MA *Aston*   Sr. Lectr.
Stone, Robert F., MPhil *Birm.*   Principal Lectr.
Sullivan, Vivienne L., BEd *CNAA*, MSc
CNAA   Sr. Lectr.
Tsamenyi, Matthew, BA *Ghana*, MA *ANU*, PhD
Wolv.   Sr. Lectr.
Underwood, Richard L.   Sr. Lectr.
Vallely, Chris J., BA *Exe.*, MA *Manc.*   Sr. Lectr.
Walker, Graham F., MBA *Aston*   Sr. Lectr.
West, Terence, BA *Open(UK)*, MBA *Aston*   Sr.
Lectr.
Westwood, Geoffrey, MBA *Aston*   Sr. Lectr.
Williams, Julie A., BA *Wales*   Sr. Lectr.
Williams, Peter, MBA   Principal Lectr.
Williams, Susan C., BSc *Aston*, MSc *Sheff.*   Sr.
Lectr.
Woollam, John L., FCA   Sr. Lectr.
Worrall, Leslie, BA *Hull*, MCD *Liv.*, PhD
Liv.   Principal Lectr.
Wright, Colin D., BBS *Trinity(Dub.)*, MBA
Aston   Principal Lectr.
Other Staff: 5 Lectrs./Sr. Lectrs.; 4 Lectrs.; 1
Temp. Sr. Lectr.
Vacant Posts: 3 Principal Lectrs.

SPECIAL CENTRES, ETC

Corporate and Academic Development, Centre for

Tel: (01902) 323407 Fax: (01902) 323316
Gilbert, Jennifer F., BSc *Durh.*, MSc
Warw.   Teaching and Learning Coordinator

CONTACT OFFICERS

Academic affairs. Registrar: Baldwin, Jon F., BA *CNAA*, MBA *Open(UK)*, FCIS
Accommodation. Services Manager: Warrender, Susan J.
Admissions (first degree). Registrar: Baldwin, Jon F., BA *CNAA*, MBA *Open(UK)*, FCIS
Adult/continuing education. Registrar: Baldwin, Jon F., BA *CNAA*, MBA *Open(UK)*, FCIS
Alumni. Events and Alumni Officer: Hinton, Helen E., BA *Nott.Trent*
Careers. Director, Corporate Enterprise Centre: Mabey, Mark, BSc *CNAA*, PhD *CNAA*
Computing services. Head, Computing Centre: Hayward, Keith N.
Conferences/corporate hospitality. Conference Development Officer: Davis, Sue M., BA *Wales*
Consultancy services. Director, Corporate Enterprise Centre: Mabey, Mark, BSc *CNAA*, PhD *CNAA*
Credit transfer. Registrar: Baldwin, Jon F., BA *CNAA*, MBA *Open(UK)*, FCIS
Development/fund-raising. Director, Corporate Enterprise Centre: Mabey, Mark, BSc *CNAA*, PhD *CNAA*
Distance education. Academic Development Advisor, Centre for Corporate and Academic Development: Vaughan, Michael G., BA *Camb.*, MA *Camb.*
Estates and buildings/works and services. Estates Manager: Bailey, George D.
Examinations. Registrar: Baldwin, Jon F., BA *CNAA*, MBA *Open(UK)*, FCIS
Finance. Director of Finance: Sproston, Garry
General enquiries. Clerk to the Board of Governors: Lee, Antony W., LLB *CNAA*, FCIS
Industrial liaison. Director, Corporate Enterprise Centre: Mabey, Mark, BSc *CNAA*, PhD *CNAA*
International office. Director: Malcolm, Neil R., BA *Oxf.*, MSocSc *Birm.*, DPhil *Oxf.*

Library (enquiries). Director of Learning Centres: Heaney, Mary E., BA *N.U.I.*
Ombudsperson. Clerk to the Board of Governors: Lee, Antony W., LLB *CNAA*, FCIS
Personnel/human resources. Director of Personnel: Snowden, Andrew C., BA *Sheff.*
Public relations, information and marketing. Head, Media and Publicity Services Office: Whyatt, Melanie J., BA *Warw.*
Publications. Head, Media and Publicity Services Office: Whyatt, Melanie J., BA *Warw.*
Purchasing. Purchasing Officer: Porter, Gordon G.
Quality assurance and accreditation. Head, Department for Total Quality Management: Sen, Arko, BSc *Wales*, MSc *Aston*, MA *Wolv.*
Research. Dean of Research: Gilkison, Prof. Jean E., BA *Wis.*, MA *Wis.*, PhD *Wis.*
Safety. Health and Safety Adviser: Collins, Franklyn A.
Schools liaison. Education Guidance Officer: Blunt, Arthur G., BA *Oxf.*, MA *Oxf.*, MPhil *Wolv.*
Sport and recreation. Sports and Recreation Services Manager: Cooper, Phillip E., BA *CNAA*
Staff development and training. Director of Personnel: Snowden, Andrew C., BA *Sheff.*
Student welfare/counselling. Director, University of Wolverhampton Counselling and Guidance Service; Registrar: Haynes, Robert J., BSc *Lond.*, MA *Warw.*
Students from Other Countries. Head, Office for International Education: Milhavy, Yves G. L., MSc *Aston*
Students with disabilities. Registrar: Baldwin, Jon F., BA *CNAA*, MBA *Open(UK)*, FCIS

[Information supplied by the institution as at June 1998, and edited by the ACU]

UNIVERSITY OF YORK

Founded 1963

Member of the Association of Commonwealth Universities

Postal Address: Heslington, York, England Y010 5DD
Telephone: (01904) 430000 **Fax**: (01904) 433433 **Telex**: 57933 YORKUL **Cables**: University, York, England
WWW: http://www.york.ac.uk
E-mail formula: username@york.ac.uk (searchable directory available on university's WWW home page);
(department of health studies) firstinitial.surname@pulse.york.ac.uk

CHANCELLOR—Baker, Dame Janet, CH, DBE, DMus Lond., Hon. DMus Birm., Hon. DMus Hull, Hon. DMus Lanc., Hon. DMus Leeds, Hon. DMus Leic., Hon. DMus Oxf., Hon. MusD Camb., Hon. LLD Aberd., Hon. DLitt Brad., Hon. DUniv

PRO-CHANCELLOR—Wheway, Richard C., MA Oxf., FCA

PRO-CHANCELLOR—Carlisle, Sir Michael, BEng Sheff., Hon. LLD Sheff., Hon. LLD Nott., FIMechE

PRO-CHANCELLOR AND CHAIRMAN OF COUNCIL—Dixon, Kenneth H. M., CBE, BA(Econ) Manc., Hon. DUniv

VICE-CHANCELLOR*—Cooke, Prof. Ronald U., BSc Lond., MSc Lond., PhD Lond., DSc Lond.

DEPUTY VICE-CHANCELLOR—Fidler, Prof. J. Kelvin, BSc Durh., PhD Newcastle(UK)

PRO-VICE-CHANCELLOR—Forrest, Prof. Alan I., MA Aberd., DPhil Oxf.

PRO-VICE-CHANCELLOR—Wand, Prof. Ian C., BSc Leic., PhD Leic.

PRO-VICE-CHANCELLOR—Robards, Prof. Anthony W., PhD Lond., DSc Lond.

TREASURER—Horsfield, Gordon, BA Nott.

REGISTRAR‡—Foster, David J., BA Durh.

ACTING LIBRARIAN—Heaps, A. Elizabeth M., BA Hull, MA Leeds

DIRECTOR OF FINANCE—Gilbert, Graham C., BSc Brist.

DIRECTOR OF FACILITIES MANAGEMENT—MacDonald, Andrew, BSc Edin., MBA Cran., PhD E.Anglia

GENERAL INFORMATION

History. The university was founded in 1963. In 1996 the North Yorkshire College of Health was incorporated into the university, forming the department of health studies.

The main campus is situated at Heslington, just outside York; a second smaller campus is situated at Kings Manor in the city itself. The department of health studies has centres in the cities of York and Ripon, and in the towns of Harrogate, Scarborough and Northallerton.

Admission to first degrees (see also United Kingdom Introduction). Applicants should offer 5 subject passes at General Certificate of Secondary Education (GCSE) and General Certificate of Education (GCE) A level, or recognised UK or overseas equivalents. Specific advice on acceptability of qualifications and admissions requirements can be obtained from the Undergraduate Admissions Office or from departmental admissions tutor for course concerned. Students whose mother tongue is not English are normally required to provide evidence of English Language ability prior to admission. Applications are welcomed from mature students (over 21 on entry) who may not possess qualifications usually required for entry.

Part-time degrees in social policy: written applications to departmental admissions tutor; health sciences: contact Undergraduate Admissions Office; health studies, pre-registration courses: through Nursing and Midwifery Admissions Service, post-registration applicants: contact the department. Visiting students (who study at York for a full year or 1–2 terms): contact Undergraduate Admissions Office.

First Degrees (see also United Kingdom Directory to Subjects of Study). BA, BEng, BSc, MChem, MEng, MMath, MPhys.

Bachelor's degrees normally last 3 years full-time; sandwich courses include 1 additional year industrial placement. Undergraduate master's degrees: 4 years full-time.

Higher Degrees (see also United Kingdom Directory to Subjects of Study). MA, MRes, MSc, MSW, MPhil, DPhil, DLitt, DMus, DSc. Applicants for admission must usually hold a first degree with at least second class honours, or an approved equivalent qualification. Full- and part-time MA/MSc candidates must normally be resident within 30 miles of York

for the whole of their course. Part-time MPhil/DPhil candidates must normally be resident within 60 miles of York, or must attend the university for at least 2 terms (MPhil) or 3 terms (DPhil). DLitt, DMus, DSc: awarded on the basis of published work to graduates of the university of 10 years' standing. Applications are welcomed from postgraduate UK and overseas students who wish to spend 1–3 terms in York as visiting students. Further details available from Graduate Schools Office.

Libraries. 600,000 volumes; 2800 periodicals subscribed to. Special collections: Dyson (seventeenth-, eighteenth- and early nineteenth-century English literature); Mirfield (pre-1800 printed books); Poetry Society. King's Manor Library (architectural conservation and mediaeval studies): Wormald, Newbold and Newton collections (art history, mediaeval history, stained glass).

Fees (1998–99, annual). Undergraduate: up to £1000 (UK/EC students); £6390 (overseas students, lower cost subjects); £8820 (overseas students, higher cost subjects). Postgraduate: £2610 (UK/EC students); £6615 (overseas students, lower cost subjects); £8820 (overseas students, higher cost subjects).

Academic Awards (1997–98). 88 awards ranging in value from £1200 to £8500.

Academic Year (1998–99). Three terms: 5 October–11 December; 4 January–12 March; 19 April–25 June.

Income (1996-7). Total, £79,700,000.

Statistics. Staff: 2254 (842 academic/research, 1412 administrative and other). Students: full-time 5786 (2877 men, 2909 women); part-time 1118 (367 men, 751 women); international 441 (202 men, 239 women); total 7345.

ACADEMIC UNITS

Archaeology

Tel: (01904) 433901 Fax: (01904) 433902

Brothwell, Donald R., BSc Lond., MA Camb., Hon. PhD Stockholm Prof.†; Dir., Palaeo-ecol. Studies

Burman, P. A., OBE, MA Camb., FSA Sr. Lectr.

Butler, L. A. S., MA Camb., PhD Nott., FSA Sr. Lectr.

Carver, Martin O. H., BSc Lond., FSA Prof.

Mytum, Harold C., MA Camb., FSA Lectr.; Head*

Richards, Julian D., MA Camb., PhD CNAA, FSA Sr. Lectr.

Other Staff: 8 Lectrs.; 1 Sr. Lectr.†

Research: archaeological heritage studies; early mediaeval Anglo-Saxon/Anglo-Scandinavian archaeology; late mediaeval archaeology; palaeoecology; post-mediaeval and colonial burial

Biology

Tel: (01904) 432837 Fax: (01904) 432860

Bowles, Diana J., BSc Newcastle(UK), PhD Camb. Prof., Biochemistry

Bronk, J. Ramsey, AB Prin., DPhil Oxf. Emer. Prof., Biochemistry

Chadwick, M. J., BSc Wales, MA Camb., PhD Wales Hon. Prof.

Currey, John D., MA Oxf., DPhil Oxf. Prof.

Digby, John, BSc Leic., PhD Wales Sr. Lectr.

Douglas, Angela, MA Oxf., PhD Aberd. Sr. Lectr.

Firn, Richard D., BAgricSci Edin., MAgSc Adel., PhD Lond. Sr. Lectr.

Fitter, Alistair H., BA Oxf., PhD Liv. Prof.; Head*

Garner, R. Colin, BPharm Lond., PhD Lond. Prof.†

Hardy, Simon J. S., BA Camb., PhD Wis. Sr. Lectr.

Hoggett, J. G., BSc Exe., PhD Exe. Sr. Lectr.

Kellett, George L., BSc Birm., PhD Birm. Sr. Lectr.

Law, Richard, PhD Liv., BA Reader

Leech, Rachel M., MA Oxf., DPhil Oxf. Prof.

Leese, Henry J., BSc Reading, PhD Lond. Reader

Maitland, Norman J., BSc Glas., PhD Birm. Prof., Molecular Biology

Milner, Jo, BSc Lond., PhD Camb. Prof., Cell Biology

Ormond, Rupert F. G., MA Camb., PhD Camb. Sr. Lectr.

Robards, Anthony W., PhD Lond., DSc Lond. Prof.

Rumsby, Martin G., BSc Birm., PhD Birm. Sr. Lectr.

Sanders, Dale, PhD Camb., ScD Camb., BA Prof.

Searle, Jeremy B., MA Oxf., PhD Aberd. Sr. Lectr.

Skerry, Timothy, BVetMed Lond., PhD Lond., Prof.

Sparrow, John C., BSc Sus., DPhil Sus. Reader

Warr, J. Roger, BSc Sheff., PhD Sheff. Sr. Lectr.

Williamson, Mark H., MA Oxf., DPhil
Oxf. Emer. Prof.
Wilson, R. Alan, BSc Lond., PhD Lond. Prof.
Young, J. Peter W., MA Camb., PhD
Camb. Prof., Molecular Ecology
Other Staff: 12 Lectrs.; 6 Res. Fellows
Research: applied biology and biochemistry; biomedical research (cancer, infection/
immunity, reproduction); ecology
(population, marine, physiological and
community); neurobiology and musculoskeletal systems; plant cell and molecular
biology

Chemistry

Tel: (01904) 432511 Fax: (01904) 432605
Anastasi, Christopher, MSc Lond., PhD
Camb. Sr. Lectr.
Clark, James H., BSc Lond., PhD Lond. Prof.,
Industrial and Applied Chemistry
Dodson, Guy G., MSc Auck., PhD Auck.,
FRSChem Prof.†
Gilbert, Bruce C., MA Oxf., DPhil Oxf.,
FRSChem Prof.; Head*
Goodall, David M., BA Oxf., DPhil Oxf. Reader
Halstead, Tom K., BA Oxf., DPhil Oxf. Sr.
Lectr.
Hanson, Peter, BSc St And., PhD St And.,
FRSChem Sr. Lectr.
Hester, Ronald E., PhD Cornell, DSc Lond.,
FRSChem Prof.
Hubbard, Roderick E., BA DPhil Prof.,
Chemistry and Computing
Lindsay Smith, John R., BA Oxf., DPhil Oxf.,
FRSChem Reader
Mawby, Roger J., MA Oxf., DPhil Oxf. Reader
McCash, Elaine M., BSc E.Anglia, PhD E.Anglia,
FRSChem Sr. Lectr.
Müller-Dethlefs, Klaus, PhD Lond. Prof.,
Physical Chemistry
Perutz, Robin N., MA Camb., PhD Camb. Prof.
Taylor, Richard J. K., BSc Sheff., PhD
Sheff. Prof., Organic Chemistry
Thomas, C. Barry, BA Oxf., DPhil Sr. Lectr.
Waddington, David J., BSc Lond., PhD
Lond. Prof.†
Walton, P. H., BSc Nott., PhD Nott. Sr. Lectr.
Wilkinson, Anthony J., BSc Lond., PhD
Lond. Sr. Lectr.
Wilson, Keith S., BA Oxf., DPhil Oxf. Prof.;
Dir., Crystallog. Res.
Other Staff: 2 Sr. Lectrs.; 13 Lectrs.; 80 Res.
Fellows; 1 Sr. Lectr.†; 1 Lectr.†
Research: chemical education and public
understanding of science; inorganic
chemistry (organometallic photochemistry,
mechanistics); organic chemistry (synthetic,
physical); physical chemistry (spectroscopy,
theoretical chemistry); structural and
biological chemistry

Computer Science

Tel: (01904) 432722 Fax: (01904) 432767
Austin, J., BSc Sus., PhD Brun. British
Aerospace Sr. Lectr.
Bennett, Philip, DPhil, FEng, FIEE Visiting
Prof., Safety Critical Systems
Burns, Alan, BSc Sheff., DPhil Prof.
Freeman, William, BSc Leeds Sr. Lectr.
Frisch, Alan M., BSc Carnegie-Mellon, MSc Roch.,
PhD Roch. Reader
Hancock, Edwin R., BSc Durh., PhD Durh. Sr.
Lectr.
Harrison, Michael D., BA York(UK), DPhil
Oxf. Prof., Human Computer Interaction
Mander, Keith C., BSc Nott., PhD Nott. Sr.
Lectr.; Head*
McDermid, John A., MA Camb., PhD Birm.,
FIEE, FRAeS Prof., Software Engineering
Muggleton, Stephen H., BSc Edin., MA Oxf.,
PhD Edin. Prof., Machine Learning
Runciman, Colin, BA DPhil Reader
Stepney, Susan, MA Camb., PhD Camb. Visiting
Prof.
Wand, Ian C., BSc Leic., PhD Leic., FIEE Prof.
Wellings, Andy J., BA DPhil Prof., Real-time
Systems

Other Staff: 1 Sr. Lectr.; 18 Lectrs.; 3 Res.
Fellows; 43 Res. Assocs.
Research: advanced computer architectures; high-
integrity systems engineering; human-
computer interaction; intelligent systems and
real-time systems; programming languages
and systems

Economics and Related Studies

Tel: (01904) 433788 Fax: (01904) 433759
Abadir, Karim, MA Cairo, DPhil Oxf. Prof.
Aronson, R., AB Clark, MSc Stan., PhD
Clark Hon. Visiting Prof.
Bös, Dieter, PhD Vienna, LLD Vienna Hon.
Visiting Prof.
Burrows, H. Paul, BSc(Econ) Lond.,
DPhil Reader
Culyer, Anthony J., BA Exe. Prof.; Head*
Cuthbertson, Keith, BSc Sus., PhD Manc. Hon.
Visiting Prof.
De Fraja, Gianni, BA Pisa, PhD Siena, DPhil
Oxf. Reader
Dixon, Huw D., MA Oxf., MPhil Oxf., DPhil
Oxf. Prof., Macroeconomics
Drummond, Michael F., BSc Birm., MCom
Birm., DPhil York(UK) Prof.
Godfrey, Leslie G., BA Exe., MSc Lond. Prof.,
Econometrics
Gravelle, Hugh, BCom Leeds, PhD Lond. Prof.
Han, Seung-Soo, DPhil Hon. Visiting Prof.
Hartley, Keith, BSc(Econ) Hull, PhD Hull Prof.
Hey, John D., MA Camb., MSc Edin. Prof.†,
Economics and Statistics
Hitiris, Theodore, BA Athens, DPhil Sr. Lectr.
Hutton, John P., MA Edin. Prof., Economics
and Econometrics
Jones, Andrew M., BA York(UK), MSc York(UK),
DPhil York(UK) Sr. Lectr.
Lambert, Peter J., BSc Manc., DPhil Oxf.,
MSc Prof.
Loomes, Graham, BA Essex, MSc Lond. Hon.
Visiting Prof.
Maynard, Alan K., BA Newcastle(UK),
BPhil Hon. Prof.
Mayston, David J., MA Camb., MSc Lond., PhD
Camb. Prof., Public Sector Economics,
Finance and Accountancy
Orme, Christopher, BSc York(UK), MSc Lond.,
DPhil York(UK) Hon. Visiting Prof.
Peacock, Sir Alan, MA St And., DSc St And.,
FBA Hon. Visiting Prof.
Rees, R., BSc Lond., MSc Lond. Hon. Visiting
Prof.
Sheils, William J., BA York(UK), PhD Lond. Sr.
Lectr.
Simmons, Peter J., BA Exe., MSc(Econ) Lond.,
PhD S'ton. Prof.
Smith, Peter C., BA Oxf., MSc Lond. Prof.
Smith, Peter N., BSc S'ton., MA Warw., PhD
S'ton. Sr. Lectr.
Stafford, G. Bernard, BA Strath., DPhil
York(UK) Lectr.; Dir., York Res. Partnership
Sutherland, Alan J., BA E.Anglia, MA
Warw. Prof.
Tremayne, A. Hon. Visiting Prof.
Weir, Ronald B., MA Edin., PhD Edin. Sr.
Lectr., Economic and Social History
Wickens, Michael R., MSc Lond. Prof.
Williams, Alan H., BCom Birm., Hon. DPhil
Lund Prof.
Other Staff: 14 Lectrs.; 18 Res. Fellows; 1 Sr
Lectr.†
Research: health economics (particularly
microeconomics of health); macroeconomics
(particularly monetary economics); modern
industrial and economic history; public
sector economics and public finance

Educational Studies

Tel: (01904) 433788 Fax: (01904) 433759
Campbell, Robert M., MSc St And., PhD St
And. Sr. Lectr.; Head*
Kyriacou, Christopher, BSc Reading, PhD
Camb. Sr. Lectr.
Lister, Ian, MA Camb. Prof.
Millar, Robin H., BA Camb., MPhil Edin., PhD
Edin. Prof.

Vulliamy, J. Graham, MA Camb., MSc Lond.,
DPhil Sr. Lectr.
Other Staff: 7 Lectrs.; 1 Sr Lectr.†; 2 Teaching
Fellows†
Research: global and international education;
humanities education; primary education;
science education; teachers, teaching and
classroom interaction

Global and International Education, Centre for

Tel: (01904) 433461
Lister, Ian, MA Camb. Prof.; Dir.*
Research: development and human rights;
education for international understanding;
multicultural education; teaching and
learning about the future

Language Teaching Centre

Tel: (01904) 432493 Fax: (01904) 434683
Low, Graham D., BA Birm., MA Manc., DPhil
York(UK) Sr. Lectr.; Dir.*

Modern Language Services, Centre for

Tel: (01904) 432493 Fax: (01904) 434683
Ferguson, Margaret, MA St And., PhD
Aston Lectr.; Co-Dir.*
Low, Graham D., BA Birm., MA Manc., DPhil
York(UK) Lectr.; Co-Dir.*

Electronics

Tel: (01904) 432370 Fax: (01904) 432335
Angus, James A. S., BSc Kent, PhD Kent British
Telecom Sr. Lectr.
Bloodworth, Greville G., MA Oxf., PhD
S'ton. Emer. Prof.
Burr, Alister G., BSc S'ton., PhD Brist. Sr. Lectr.
Clarke, Timothy, MSc CNAA, BA Sr. Lectr.
El Gomati, Mohamed, BSc Al-Fateh, MSc
Calif.State, DPhil Reader
Everard, Jeremy K. A., BSc Lond., PhD
Camb. Prof.
Fidler, J. Kelvin, BSc Durh., PhD
Newcastle(UK) Prof.; Dir., Electronics Service
Howard, David M., BSc Lond., PhD Lond. Prof.;
Head*
Kirk, P. Ross, BSc Leeds Sr. Lectr.
Marvin, Andrew C., MEng Sheff., PhD
Sheff. Prof., Applied Electro-Magnetics
Szymanski, John E., BSc DPhil Sr. Lectr.
Tozer, Timothy C., MA Camb. Sr. Lectr.
Tyrrell, Andrew M., BSc CNAA, PhD Aston Sr.
Lectr.
Watson, A. Peter, BSc Durh., PhD Durh. Prof.;
Head of Res.
Other Staff: 14 Lectrs.
Research: applied electromagnetics;
communication systems; electronic devices
and circuits; sensors, remote sensing and
imaging; speech-processing, acoustics and
real-time systems

English and Related Literature

Tel: (01904) 433369 Fax: (01904) 433372
Barrell, John C., MA Camb., PhD Essex Prof.
Berthoud, Jacques A., BA Witw. Prof.; Head*
Binns, James W., MA Birm., PhD Birm., DLitt
Birm. Reader, Latin Literature
Bradley, S. A. J., MA Oxf., FSA Sr. Lectr.
Cordner, Michael, MA Camb. Reader
Donovan, John P., BA Boston, MA Kansas, PhD
Birm. Sr. Lectr.
Guest, Harriet, MA Camb., PhD Camb. Sr.
Lectr.
Haughton, Hugh B., BA Camb., MA Oxf. Sr.
Lectr.
Havely, Nicholas R., MA Oxf., BPhil Oxf. Sr.
Lectr.
Hollindale, Peter, MA Camb. Sr. Lectr.
Lillie, Amanda R., BA Auck., MA Lond., PhD
Lond. Sr. Lectr.
Marks, Richard, BA Lond., PhD Lond. Prof.,
Medieval Stained Glass; Dir., Hist. of Art
Minnis, A. J., BA Belf., PhD Belf. Prof.,
Medieval Literature; Acting Head*
Minta, Stephen M. J., BA Oxf., DPhil Sus. Sr.
Lectr.
Moody, A. D., MA NZ, MA Oxf. Prof.

Parry, Graham, MA Camb., PhD Col. Prof.
Pearsall, D. A., MA Birm. Hon. Prof.
Riddy, Felicity J., MA Auck., BPhil Oxf. Prof.
Ward-Jouve, Nicole A.-M. F., LèsL Paris Prof.†
Other Staff: 12 Lectrs.; 1 Lectr.†
Research: eighteenth-century literature
  (Romantics, colonialism, Enlightenment);
  literature in women's studies (bisexual/
  lesbian, post-colonial); mediaeval literature
  and thought; modern literature (post-
  modernist, contemporary, post-colonial);
  Renaissance literature

Environment

Tel: (01904) 432999 Fax: (01904) 432998
Barbier, Edward, BA Yale, MSc Lond., PhD
  Lond. Reader
Chadwick, M. Hon. Visiting Prof.
Common, Michael, BA Liv., BPhil Liv. Hon.
  Visiting Prof.
Perrings, Charles, BA Lond., PhD Lond. Prof.;
  Head*
Smith, Sir David, FRS, FRSEd Hon. Visiting
  Prof.
Other Staff: 6 Lectrs.; 2 Res. Assocs.
Research: biodiversity and habitat fragmentation;
  ecosystem management (wetlands, drylands,
  forests, coasts); environmental economics
  (pollution, resource depletion,
  development); environmental valuation,
  ecological-economic modelling and
  sustainability

Health Sciences and Clinical Evaluation

Tel: (01904) 434501
Godfrey, Christine, BA Exe. Reader
Russell, Ian T., BA Camb., MA Camb., MSc Birm.,
  PhD Essex Prof.; Head*
Wood, John, BSc Lond., MSc Oxf. Sr. Lectr.
Other Staff: 2 Lectrs.; 8 Res. Fellows
Vacant Posts: 1 Lectr.; 1 Lectr.†
Research: assessment of health technology;
  economic and psychological evaluation of
  health care; evidence-based health care;
  multivariate statistical methods; non-
  pharmaceutical clinical trials

Health Studies

Tel: (01904) 435222 Fax: (01904) 435225
Allen, Linda, MEd Programme Co-ordinator,
  Midwifery
Cullum, Nicky, PhD Reader, Health Care
  Studies
Dean, John, BA Open(UK) Sr. Lectr.
Duree, Daphne, BSc Programmes Leader
Egan, Gerard, PhD Hon. Visiting Prof.
Fritchie, Dame Rennie, DBE, Hon. PhD Hon.
  Visiting Prof.
Jacques, Elizabeth, BSc Open(UK) Programme
  Leader, Open and Distance Learning
James, C. Louise, BScN Sr. Lectr.
Jarrold, Ken, CBE, MA Hon. Visiting Prof.
Lankshear, Annette, BSc Edin., MA
  York(UK) Dir., Nursing, Midwifery and
  Child Health Studies
Lewin, Robert, MA MPhil Prof.,
  Rehabilitation
Nicholson, Nicholas, BA Sr. Lectr.
Nicklin, Peter, MEd Nott., MBA Leeds Dir.,
  Management and Continuing Education
  Studies; Academic Dir., Centre for Dental
  Services Studies
Parish, Richard, BSc Lond., MEd Hudd. Prof.;
  Head*
Pearson, Maggie A., MA PhD Prof.†, Health
  and Community Care
Rowden, Raymond Hon. Visiting Prof.
Thompson, David, BSc MA PhD Prof.,
  Nursing
Watt, Ian S., MB ChB MSc MPH Prof.,
  Primary and Community Care
Other Staff: 55 Lectrs.; 8 Practitioner/Lectrs.; 4
  Res. Fellows; 27 Hon. Visiting Res. Fellows

Health and Social Care Management, Centre for

Tel: (01904) 435106
Nicolson, Nicholas, BA Sr. Lectr.

Other Staff: 2 Lectrs.

Leadership Development, Centre for

Tel: (01423) 507771
Jones, Helen, BA Dir.*

History, see also Econ. and Related Studies

Tel: (01904) 432981 Fax: (01904) 432986
Biller, Peter P. A., MA Oxf., DPhil Oxf.,
  FRHistS Sr. Lectr.
Bossy, John A., MA Camb., PhD Camb.,
  FRHistS Prof.
Cross, M. Claire, MA Camb., PhD Camb.,
  FRHistS Prof.†
Divall, Colin, BSc Brist., MSc Manc., PhD
  Manc. Prof., Railway Studies
Fletcher, Richard A., MA Oxf., FRHistS Reader
Forrest, Alan I., MA Aberd., DPhil Oxf. Prof.
Marks, Richard, BA Lond., PhD Lond.,
  FSA Prof., Medieval Stained Glass; Dir.,
  Hist. of Art
Norton, E. Christopher, MA Camb., PhD Camb.,
  FSA Sr. Lectr., Medieval Architecture
  History
Ormrod, W. Mark, BA Lond., DPhil Oxf.,
  FRHistS Prof., Medieval History
Rendall, Jane, BA Lond., PhD Lond. Sr. Lectr.
Royle, Edward, MA Camb., PhD Camb.,
  FRHistS Reader
Sharpe, James A., BA Oxf., DPhil Oxf.,
  FRHistS Prof.
Walvin, James, BA Keele, MA McM.,
  DPhil Prof.
Warren, Allen J., MA Oxf., DPhil Oxf.,
  FRHistS Lectr.; Head*
Other Staff: 11 Lectrs.; 2 Sr. Lectrs.†; 1 Lectr.†
Research: history of art; local history; mediaeval
  history (political, social, religious); railway
  history and railway studies; women's history

History of Art, see Engl. and Related Lit., and Hist.

Language and Linguistic Science

Tel: (01904) 432650 Fax: (01904) 432652
Harlow, Stephen J., BA Lond. Sr. Lectr.
Local, John K., BA Newcastle(UK), PhD
  Newcastle(UK) Prof.; Head*
Russ, Charles V. J., BA Newcastle(UK), MLitt
  Newcastle(UK), MA Reading, PhD S'ton. Reader
Warner, Anthony R., BA Oxf., PhD Edin. Prof.
Other Staff: 10 Lectrs.; 2 Res. Assocs.
Research: linguistic variation and change
  (empirical methods, history); morphology
  and phonology; non-segmental declarative
  phonology and phonetics; syntax and
  semantics (minimalism, principles,
  discourse)

Mathematics

Tel: (01904) 433070 Fax: (01904) 433071
Abadir, Karim, BA Cairo, MA Cairo, DPhil
  Oxf. Prof.
Anderson, Norman, BSc Durh., PhD
  Durh. Reader
Arthurs, Arnold M., MA Oxf., DSc Oxf. Prof.
Clunie, James G., BSc St And., PhD Aberd. Hon.
  Prof.
Cornish, Fred H. J., MA Oxf., DPhil
  Oxf. Emer. Prof.†
Dodson, Maurice M., MSc Auck., MA Camb.,
  PhD Camb. Sr. Lectr.
Fountain, John B., BSc Leeds, PhD Leeds Reader
Hall, Richard R., BA Camb., PhD Nott., ScD
  Camb. Prof.
Sheil-Small, Terry B., BSc Lond., PhD
  Lond. Prof.
Smith, Michael J., BSc Birm. Reader
Sudbery, Anthony, MA Camb., PhD
  Camb. Prof.; Head*
Waugh, William A. O., MA Oxf., DPhil
  Oxf. Hon. Prof.
Other Staff: 9 Lectrs.; 2 Res. Fellows
Research: algebra; analysis and number theory;
  geometry; mathematical physics; traffic
  equilibrium theory

Medieval Studies, see Engl. and Related Lit., and Hist.

Music

Tel: (01904) 432446 Fax: (01904) 432450
Blake, David L., MA Camb. Prof.
Khan, Ustad A. A. Hon. Visiting Prof.
Lefanu, Nicola, MA Oxf., DMus Oxf. Prof.;
  Head*
Lumsdaine, David, DMus Hon. Visiting Prof.
Marsh, Roger, BA DPhil Sr. Lectr.
Mellers, Wilfrid, OBE, MA DMus Emer. Prof.
Mitchell, Donald, MA York(UK), PhD York(UK),
  DUniv York(UK) Hon. Visiting Prof.
Seymour, Peter G., BA, FRCO Sr. Lectr.
Sorrell, Neil F. I., MA Camb., MA Lond., PhD
  Wesleyan Sr. Lectr.
Other Staff: 1 Reader Emer.; 5 Lectrs.
Research: analysis; composition; contemporary
  and historical music studies;
  ethnomusicology; music technology

Philosophy

Tel: (01904) 433251 Fax: (01904) 433251
Baldwin, Tom R., MA Camb., PhD
  Camb. Prof.; Head*
McGinn, Marie, BSc Manc., DPhil Oxf. Sr.
  Lectr.
Woolhouse, Roger S., BA Lond., PhD
  Camb. Prof.
Other Staff: 5 Lectrs.; 2 Teaching Fellows
Research: aesthetics (Adorno, Derrida, ancient
  aesthetics); early modern philosophy
  (Descartes to Hume); German idealism
  (Kant and Hegel); political philosophy;
  twentieth-century philosophy (Russell,
  Moore, Wittgenstein)

Physics

Tel: (01904) 432201 Fax: (01904) 432214
Chambers, Austin, BSc Leeds, PhD Leeds, FIP Sr.
  Lectr.
Gallon, Tom E., BSc Lond., PhD Lond. Sr. Lectr.
Godby, Rex, MA Camb., PhD Camb. Prof.,
  Theoretical Physics
Greenhow, Rodney C., MA Oxf., DPhil Oxf.,
  FIP Sr. Lectr.
Main, Peter, BSc Manc., PhD Manc., FIP Reader
Matthew, James A. D., BSc Aberd., PhD Aberd.,
  FIP Prof.
Pert, Geoffrey J., BSc Lond., PhD Lond., FIP,
  FRS Prof., Computational Physics; Head*
Prutton, Martin, BSc Birm., PhD Lond.,
  FIP Prof.
Wadsworth, Robert, BSc Liv., PhD Liv. Sr.
  Lectr.
Watson, Douglas L., BSc Birm., PhD Birm.,
  FIP Sr. Lectr.
Whiting, Jeremy S. S., MA Oxf., DPhil Oxf. Sr.
  Lectr.
Woolfson, Michael M., MA Oxf., PhD Manc.,
  DSc Manc., FRAS, FIP, FRS Emer. Prof.
Other Staff: 6 Lectrs.; 1 EPSRC Advanced
  Fellow; 18 Res. Fellows; 1 Hon. Fellow
Vacant Posts: 1 Lectr.
Research: condensed matter physics (surface,
  thin film); magnetospheric physics; nuclear
  physics; theoretical astrophysics; X-rays
  (crystallography, lasers, plasma physics)

Politics

Tel: (01904) 433561 Fax: (01904) 433563
Afshar, Haleh, PhD Camb., BA Reader
Alderman, R. K., BSc(Econ) Lond., PhD
  Lond. Sr. Lectr.
Callinicos, Alex T., BA Oxf., DPhil Oxf. Prof.
Howell, David, MA Oxf., PhD Manc. Prof.;
  Head*
Leftwich, Adrian, BA Cape Town, DPhil Sr.
  Lectr.
Mendus, Susan L., BA Wales, BPhil Oxf. Prof.
Nicholson, Peter P., BA Exe. Reader
Other Staff: 11 Lectrs.
Vacant Posts: 1 Staff Member
Research: British politics, policy and public
  administration; comparative international
  politics; development studies and politics;

labour movements; political theory and
political philosophy

Psychology

Tel: (01904) 433189 Fax: (01904) 433181

Altmann, Gerald T. M., BSc Sus., PhD Edin. Sr.
Lectr.

Bailey, Peter J., BA Sus., PhD Camb. Sr. Lectr.

Bull, Peter E., MA Oxf., MA Exe., PhD Exe.,
FBPsS Sr. Lectr.

Christie, Margaret, BA Lond., PhD Lond.,
FBPsS Hon. Prof.

Cox, Maureen V., BA Hull, PhD Hull,
FBPsS Reader

Ellis, Andrew W., MA Camb., PhD Edin.,
FBPsS Prof.

Hall, Geoffrey, MA Camb., PhD Camb. Prof.;
Head*

Hammond, Nicholas V., BSc Birm., PhD
Lond. Reader

Hulme, Charles, MA Oxf., DPhil Oxf. Prof.

MacPhail, Euan M., MA Oxf., DPhil
Oxf. Reader

Monk, Andrew F., BSc Brist., PhD Brist. Reader

Roger, Derek B., MA P.Elizabeth, PhD Exe. Sr.
Lectr.

Snowling, Margaret J., BSc Brist., PhD Lond.,
FBPsS Prof.

Thompson, Peter G., BSc Reading, PhD
Camb. Sr. Lectr.

Venables, Peter, BA Lond., PhD Lond., DSc Brad.,
FBPsS Hon. Prof.

Whiting, John, MA Leeds, PhD Leeds,
FBPsS Hon. Prof.

Young, Andy, BSc Camb., PhD Camb. Prof.

Other Staff: 3 Lectrs.; 16 Res. Fellows

Research: behavioural neuroscience (learning
mechanisms and memory); cognitive
neuropsychology; developmental studies
(cognition, perception, language);
perceptual and sensory motor processes;
personality, social and communication
studies

Railway Studies, see Hist.

Social Policy and Social Work

Tel: (01904) 433481 Fax: (01904) 433475

Baldwin, Sally M., MA Edin., DPhil Prof.;
Head*

Bradshaw, Jonathan R., BSS Trinity(Dub.), MA
Trinity(Dub.), DPhil Prof., Social Policy

Brown, John, BSc Bath, MPhil Sr. Lectr.,
Social Policy

Coles, Robert W., BA Sr. Lectr., Social Policy

Ditch, John, BA York(UK), BPhil York(UK), DPhil
Ulster Prof.

Ford, Janet, BA Manc., MSc Lough. Joseph
Rowntree Prof., Housing Policy

Huby, Meg, BSc E.Anglia, BA Open(UK),
DPhil Sr. Lectr., Social Policy

Maynard, Mary A., BA BPhil Sr. Lectr.

Sinclair, Ian A. C., BA Oxf., PhD Lond. Prof.†,
Social Work

Stein, Michael, BA Brad., MPhil Leeds Prof.,
Social Work

Wilson, A. Kate, BA Oxf. Sr. Lectr.

Other Staff: 8 Lectrs.; 1 Visiting Lectr.; 1 Sr.
Teaching Fellow; 1 Teaching Fellow; 1
Lectr.†

Research: child welfare and child care; health
and social care; housing policy; social
security and personal social services; social
work practice

Sociology

Tel: (01904) 433041 Fax: (01904) 433043

Campbell, Colin B., BSc(Econ) Lond., PhD
Lond. Sr. Lectr.; Head*

Drew, W. Paul, BA Exe., PhD Lanc. Sr. Lectr.

Mulkay, Michael J., BA Lond., MA S.Fraser, PhD
Aberd. Prof.

Tudor, Andrew F., BA Leeds Reader

Yearley, Steven, MA Camb., DPhil
York(UK) Prof.

Other Staff: 3 Lectrs.

Vacant Posts: 1 Staff Member

Research: consumption, cultural change and
cultural theory; language and conversational
analysis, communication and discourse;
sociology of science and technology,
environmental sociology; qualitative
sociology and qualitative methods; women's
studies

SPECIAL CENTRES, ETC

Applied Biology, Institute for

Tel: (01904) 432940 Fax: (01904) 433029

Robards, Anthony W., PhD Lond., DSc
Lond. Prof.; Dir.*

Cell and Tissue Research, Centre for

Tel: (01904) 432936 Fax: (01904) 432936

Wilson, Ashley J., BSc Lond., DPhil
York(UK) Dir.*

Research: low temperature electron microscopy;
microscope design

Medical Cyrobiology Unit

Tel: (01904) 434083 Fax: (01904) 434090

Pegg, David E., MB BS Lond., MD Lond. Dir.*

Other Staff: 1 Res. Fellow

Research: cryopreservation of cornea, organs and
tissue

Bone and Joint Biology and Repair, Smith and Nephew Unit for

Tel: (01904) 434384 Fax: (01904) 434396

Skerry, Timothy, BVetMed Lond., PhD
Lond. Prof.; Dir.*

Other Staff: 6 Res. Fellows

Research: excitatory amino acids in bone
stimulus; nitric oxide in inflammatory
diseases; syndecans in bone

Computing Service

Tel: (01904) 433838 Fax: (01904) 433740

Atkin, David L., BA Head, Systems
Programming

Hubbard, Roderick E., BA DPhil Prof.,
Chemistry and Computing

Jinks, K. Michael, MA Oxf., DPhil Oxf. Dir.*

Souter, Brian Operations Manager

Conservation Studies, Centre for

Tel: (01904) 434962

Burman, P. A., OBE, MA Camb., FSA Sr.
Lectr.; Dir.*

Research: arts and crafts movement in
architecture; conservation in Buddhist
architecture and art; conservation,
management and preservation of historic
buildings; conservation philosophy and
ethics; traditional building materials

Continuing Education, Centre for

Tel: (01904) 434620 Fax: (01904) 434621

Booth, Lesley C., BA York(UK) Co-ordinator*

Eighteenth-Century Studies, Centre for

Tel: (01904) 434980 Fax: (01904) 433996

Barrel, John C., MA Camb., PhD Essex Prof.;
Co-Dir.*

Rendall, Jane, BA Lond., PhD Lond. Sr. Lectr.;
Co-Dir.*

Research: Britain and France in the 'long'
eighteenth century (1650-1848)

Environmental Archaeology Unit

Tel: (01904) 433846 Fax: (01904) 433850

Kenward, Harold K., BSc Lond. Dir.*

Other Staff: 9 Res. Fellows

Research: invertebrate fossils; palaeocology; plant
macrofossils; soil and sediments; vertebrate
fossils

Environmental Carcinogenesis, Jack Birch Unit for

Tel: (01904) 432900 Fax: (01904) 423954

Garner, R. Colin, BPharm Lond., PhD
Lond. Prof.†; Dir.*

Research: human bio-monitoring

Evidence-Based Nursing, Centre for

Tel: (01904) 435137

Cullum, Nicky, PhD Reader; Dir.*

Research: effectiveness of guidelines for nurses,
and PAMs; nurses use of research findings in
decision-making; wound care literature

Historical Research, Borthwick Institute of

Tel: (01904) 437223

Smith, David M., MA Oxf., PhD Nott.,
FSA Prof.; Dir.*

Research: local history; religious and
ecclesiastical history of northern England;
social, economic and cultural history of the
North; social, economic and cultural history
of York

Management, Centre for

Tel: (01904) 433432 Fax: (01904) 433431

Milborrow, Graham C., MSc Northwestern, PhD
Brun. Prof.; Dir.*

Other Staff: 2 Lectrs.

Research: human resource management practice;
logistics and operational research; long-
range forecasting and scenario planning;
public sector management

Medieval Studies, Centre for

Tel: (01904) 433910 Fax: (01904) 433918

Riddy, Felicity J., MA Auck., BPhil Oxf. Prof.;
Dir.*

Other Staff: 1 Lectr.; 3 Teaching Fellows

Research: cultural studies; literature, religion and
politics in the mediaeval period; urban
studies; women's studies

Microbiology Research Unit

Tel: (01904) 432810 Fax: (01904) 432923

Betts, W. Bernard, BA Open(UK), MSc Lough.,
PhD Lough. Lectr.; Dir.*

Research: bioremediation of wasters and
pollutants; dielectrophoretic analytical
systems for identifying micro-organisms

Reviews and Dissemination, NHS Centre for

Tel: (01904) 433634 Fax: (01904) 433661

Vacant Posts: Dir.*

Research: research-and evidence-based practice;
systematic reviews of health care, provision,
delivery etc.

Performance Evaluation and Resource Management, Centre for

Tel: (01904) 433761

Mayston, David J., MA Camb., MSc Lond., PhD
Camb. Prof., Public Sector Economics,
Finance and Accountancy; Dir.*

Research: performance outputs in the public
sector; resource allocation in health and
education

Post-War Reconstruction and Development Unit

Tel: (01904) 433959 Fax: (01904) 433949

Barakat, Sultan, BSc York(UK), MA York(UK),
DPhil York(UK) Lectr.; Dir.*

Research: Islamic conservation; post-war
reconstruction in the Middle East and the
former Yugoslavia; reconstruction and
development issues

Railway Studies, Institute of

Tel: (01904) 432990 Fax: (01904) 432986

Divall, Colin, BSc Brist., MSc Manc., PhD
Manc. Prof.; Dir.*

Research: archiving and conservation of railway
history and heritage; geographical
development of railways; social, political,
economic history of railways

Social Sciences, Institute for Research in the

Tel: (01904) 433523 *Fax:* (01904) 433524

Bradshaw, Jonathan R., MA *Trinity(Dub.)*, DPhil *York(UK)* Prof., Social Policy; Dir.*

Defence Economics, Centre for

Tel: (01904) 433684 *Fax:* (01904) 432300

Hartley, Keith, BSc(Econ) *Hull*, PhD *Hull* Prof.; Dir.*
Research: defence procurement (UK and EU); disarmament and peace; economics of the UK arms trade; retraining services personnel for civilian occupations

Experimental Economics, Centre for

Tel: (01904) 437777 *Fax:* (01904) 437777

Hey, John D., MA *Camb.*, MSc *Edin.* Prof.†; Dir.*
Other Staff: 1 Lectr.; 2 Res. Fellows
Research: experimental methods in economics; group decision-making; oligopoly; risk

Health Economics, Centre for

Tel: (10904) 433657 *Fax:* (01904) 433644

Drummond, Michael F., BSc *Birm.*, MCom *Birm.*, DPhil *York(UK)* Prof.; Dir.*
Gravelle, Hugh, BCom *Leeds*, PhD *Lond.* Prof.
Research: community care; economics of preventative medicine and addiction; health technology assessment; measurement and valuation of health outcomes; resource allocation and deployment

Housing Policy, Centre for

Tel: (01904) 433691 *Fax:* (01904) 432318

Ford, Janet, BA *Manc.*, MSc *Lough.* Joseph Rowntree Prof., Housing Policy; Dir.*
Other Staff: 1 Sr. Res. Fellow; 7 Res. Fellows
Research: homelessness and access to housing; home ownership; housing and community care; housing management; rented housing, particularly in the private sector

Social Policy Research Unit

Tel: (01904) 433608 *Fax:* (01904) 433618

Baldwin, Sally M., MA *Edin.*, DPhil Prof.; Dir.*
Other Staff: 2 Sr. Res. Fellows; 20 Res. Fellows; 1 Visiting Res. Fellow
Research: analysis of living standards; comparative analysis of social welfare systems; delivery and impact of social security benefits; disability and chronic illness; policy and practice in health and social care

Social Work Research and Development Unit

Tel: (01904) 433523 *Fax:* (01904) 433524

Sinclair, Ian A. C., BA *Oxf.*, PhD *Lond.* Prof.†; Co-Dir.*
Stein, Michael, BA *Brad.*, MPhil *Leeds* Prof.; Co-Dir.*
Other Staff: 6 Res. Fellows
Research: analysis, description and evaluation of services; measures for monitoring, inspecting and developing; quality of residential care for the elderly; quality of residential child care

Women's Studies, Centre for

Tel: (01904) 433671

Broughton, Treva, BA DPhil Lectr.; Dir.*
Jackson, Stevie F., BA *Kent*, BPhil *York(UK)* Prof.
Other Staff: 1 Teaching Fellow†
Research: feminist theory and methodology; study of women in archaeology, English, history, history of art, language, mediaeval studies, politics, social policy and sociology

York Health Economics Consortium

Tel: (01904) 433620 *Fax:* (01904) 433628

Posnett, John W., BA *York(UK)*, DPhil *York(UK)* Dir.*
Other Staff: 6 Sr. Res. Fellows; 5 Res. Fellows

Stockholm Environment Institute at York

Tel: (01904) 432897 *Fax:* (01904) 432898

Kuylenstierna, Johan, BSc *Lond.*, DPhil *York(UK)* Dir.*
Other Staff: 8 Res. Assocs.
Research: acid rain; ozone depletion; pollution studies; sustainability teaching

Tropical Marine Research Unit

Tel: (01904) 432945

Ormond, Rupert F. G., MA *Camb.*, PhD *Camb.* Sr. Lectr.; Dir.*
Research: management and conservation of tropical marine environments

York Cancer Research Unit

Tel: (01904) 432931 *Fax:* (01904) 432615

Maitland, Norman J., BSc *Glas.*, PhD *Birm.* Prof., Molecular Biology; Dir.*
Other Staff: 1 Res. Fellow
Research: human papillomaviruses; prostrate and cervical cancers

York Electronics Centre

Tel: (01904) 432323 *Fax:* (01904) 432333

No staff at present
Research: applied electromagnetics; electronic devices and circuits; parallel times and systems

CONTACT OFFICERS

Academic affairs. Senior Assistant Registrar: Hardman, Sue J., BA *Warw.*
Accommodation. Accommodation Officer: Maughan, David J., BA *Wales*
Admissions (first degree). Admissions Officer and International Officer: Willis, Simon J. M., BA *E.Anglia*
Admissions (higher degree). Assistant Registrar: Simison, Philip, MA *Oxf.*
Adult/continuing education. Co-ordinator of Continuing Education: Booth, Lesley C., BA *York(UK)*
Alumni. Press and Public Relations Officer: Layton, Hilary R., BA *Hull*
Careers. Director, Careers Service: ......
Computing services. Director, Computing Service: Jinks, K. Michael, MA *Oxf.*, DPhil *Oxf.*
Conferences/corporate hospitality. Director, Conference Office: Hainsworth, Richard
Consultancy services. Director, Industrial Development Office: Robards, Prof. Anthony W., PhD *Lond.*, DSc *Lond.*
Credit transfer. Senior Assistant Registrar: Hardman, Sue J., BA *Warw.*
Development/fund-raising. Director of Development: Pennant, John, BA *Br.Col.*
Equal opportunities. Equal Opportunities Advisor: Holder, Yvie E., BA *York(UK)*†
Estates and buildings/works and services. Director of Facilities Management: MacDonald, Andrew, BSc *Edin.*, MBA *Cran.*, PhD *Edin.*
Finance. Director of Finance: Gilbert, Graham C., BSc *Brist.*
General enquiries. Registrar: Foster, David J., BA *Durh.*
Health services. Senior Medical Adviser: Price, Keith G., MB ChB *Liv.*
Industrial Development Office. Director: Robards, Anthony W., PhD *Lond.*, DSc *Lond.*

Industrial liaison. Director, Industrial Development Office: Robards, Prof. Anthony W., PhD *Lond.*, DSc *Lond.*
International office. Admissions Officer and International Officer: Willis, Simon J. M., BA *E.Anglia*
Language training for international students. Director, Language Training Centre: Low, Graham D., BA *Birm.*, MA *Manc.*, DPhil *York(UK)*
Library (chief librarian). Acting Librarian: Heaps, A. Elizabeth M., BA *Hull*, MA *Leeds*
Personnel/human resources. Equal Opportunities Advisor: Holder, Yvie E., BA *York(UK)*†
Personnel/human resources. Director of Personnel: Murray, Ged A., BA *Leic.*
Public relations, information and marketing. Press and Public Relations Officer: Layton, Hilary R., BA *Hull*
Publications. Press and Public Relations Officer: Layton, Hilary R., BA *Hull*
Purchasing. Supplies Officer: ......
Quality assurance and accreditation. Assistant Registrar: ......
Research. Planning Officer: Muckersie, David A., MA *Oxf.*, MBA *Warw.*
Safety. Safety Adviser: Reay, Francis C.
Scholarships, awards, loans. Senior Assistant Registrar: Hardman, Sue J., BA *Warw.*
Schools liaison. University Senior Admissions Tutor: Cullen, Constance J., BA *PEI*, MA *Lond.*
Security. Security Services Manager: Batten, Kenneth M.
Sport and recreation. Director, Physical Recreation: Smith, Colin C., BA *Open(UK)*, MA *York(UK)*
Staff development and training. Director of Staff Development: Marshall, Stephanie J., BA *Open(UK)*, MA *York(UK)*, DPhil *York(UK)*
Student union. Senior Assistant Registrar: Hardman, Sue J., BA *Warw.*
Student welfare/counselling. Senior Assistant Registrar: Hardman, Sue J., BA *Warw.*
Students from other countries. Admissions Officer and International Officer: Willis, Simon J. M., BA *E.Anglia*
Students with disabilities. Adviser on Disability: Edwards, Alistair, BSc *Warw.*, MSc *Penn.State*, PhD *Open(UK)*
University press. Press and Public Relations Officer: Layton, Hilary R., BA *Hull*

CAMPUS/COLLEGE HEADS

Alcuin College. (*Tel:* (01904) 433313; *Fax:* (01904) 433319.) Provost: Fidler, J. Kelvin, BSc *Durh.*, PhD *Newcastle(UK)*
Derwent College. (*Tel:* (01904) 433513; *Fax:* (01904) 433519.) Provost: Weir, Ronald B., MA *Edin.*, PhD *Edin.*
Goodricke College. (*Tel:* (01904) 433113; *Fax:* (01904) 433119.) Provost: Marshall, Stephanie J., BA *Open(UK)*, MA *York(UK)*, DPhil *York(UK)*
James College. (*Tel:* (01904) 433013.) Provost: Todd, Kenneth, BSc *Lond.*, MSc *St And.*, MA *Lanc.*
Langwith College. (*Tel:* (01904) 433413; *Fax:* (01904) 433419.) Provost:......
Vanbrugh College. (*Tel:* (01904) 433213; *Fax:* (01904) 433216.) Provost: Warren, Allen J., MA *Oxf.*, DPhil *Oxf.*
Wentworth College. (*Tel:* (01904) 433013; *Fax:* (01904) 433019.) Provost: Lee, Peter M., BSc *Liv.*, MA *Camb.*, PhD *Camb.*

[*Information supplied by the institution as at 28 April 1998, and edited by the ACU*]

United Kingdom Directory to Subjects of Study follows on p. 1804

UNITED KINGDOM : DIRECTORY

The table below shows which of the institutions indicated provide facilities for study and/or research in the subjects named. the table covers *broad subjects areas* only: ie the individual subjects of specialisation in certain professional fields such as education, law, medicine or veterinary science, are not included. In the case of related subject areas which have been grouped together (eg Botany/Plant Science), it should be borne in mind that one or more of the subjects may be offered by the institution concerned.

	Abertay Dundee	Aston	Bath	Birmingham	Bolton Institute	Bournemouth	Bradford	Bristol	Brunel	Cambridge	Central England in Birmingham	City	Coventry	Cranfield	De Montfort	Dundee	Durham	East Anglia	East London	Edinburgh	Essex	Exeter	Glamorgan	Glasgow Caledonian	Greenwich	Hertfordshire	Huddersfield	Hull
Accountancy/Accounting	X	UM	M	X	U	UM		X	U		U	X	U	MD		X	MD	X	X	MD	X	X	UD	X	UM	U	UD	X
Agriculture/Agricultural Science			M			U		MD		X			X	X						X		X				M	U	
American Studies				X					UD	D						U		X		X	X		UD			U		UD
Animal Science				X				X		X				X		U				X								
Anthropology									X	X							X	UM	UD	MD								X
Arabic										X										X		X						
Archaeology				X	X		X	X		X										X	X	X	MD					
Architecture			X							X	U		X	X	X	MD							U				X	
Art, History of				X	UD			UD		X					X	MD	X	X	X	X			UD					U
Asian Studies						UD				D							X	MD		X								X
Astronomy				X				X		X										X		UD		D		X		
Behavioural Sciences	UM			X		U							X		X		MD							D			X	UD
Biochemistry		D	X	X				X	X	X	X	U		MD	D	X	X	X	X	X	X	X	X	D	X	UM	X	UD
Biology	X	U	X	X	UD			X	X	X			UD	MD	UD	UD	X	X	X	UD	X	X	UD		UM	X	UD	X
Botany/Plant Science	X		UD	X	D			X		X					D	UD	X	X		X						X		
Building/Built Environment/Construction	X		X		UD	U			M	X	U	X	X	MD	UD	X	MD		X	D			X	X	X	U	UD	
Business/Commerce	X	X	X	X	X	X	X	X	MD	U		X	X	X	MD	X	X	X	X	MD	X	X	X	X	UM	X	UD	X
Celtic Studies/Welsh										X										U			D					
Chemistry	X	UD	UD	X				X	X	MD			UD			X	X	X	X	UD	X	X	X	X	X	X	X	X
Chinese			M							X										X		X						
Classics/Greek/Latin/Ancient History				X				X		X										X		U	X					
Computer Science	X	UD	X	X	U	X	X	X	X	X	X	X	X	X	X	X	X	X	X	MD	X	X	X	X	X	X	X	X
Dentistry				X				X								X				M								
Design					UD	X		X	U			X		X	X					X			X			U	X	UD
Development Studies		X	MD				X	MD		X			UD	D	M		X	UM		M			M					X
Drama/Theatre/Dance				X	UD			X	UD			U		X		X	U			MD	X	UD				U	UD	X
Economics	U	X	UD	X	U	M	X	X	X	X	X	U	X	UD	X	X	X	X	X	MD	X	X	D	X	UM	X	UD	X
Education			MD	MD	X			MD	X	X	X	MD			X	MD	X	MD	X	M		X	MD		X	X	X	X
Engineering	X	X	X	X	X	X	X		X	X	X	X	X	X	X	X	X		X	UD			X	X	X			X
aeronautical/aerospace		X						X	U	X		X	UD	X												X	D	
chemical/process		X	UD	X				X	D	X										M		X	UD		X			D
civil/environmental/structural	X	X	X	X	X			X	UD	UM		X	X	X	X	X			X	UD			X	X	X	X	UD	
computer		UD	X		UD			X		X	X	X		X	X	X				X	X					X	X	
electrical/electronic	X	X	X	X	X	X	X	X	X	X	U	X	X	X	X	X		UD	X	UD			X	X	X		UD	X
manufacturing				X	X	UD	UM	X	X	X	X	X	U	X	X	X	X			X		X	UD	X	UM	X	UD	X
mechanical	X	X	X	X	UD	UM	X	X	X	X	U	X	X	X	X					UD		X	UD	X	X		UD	X
English				X	D			X	UD	X	X					X	X	X	X	X	X	X	X	UD	U	X	UD	X
Environmental Science/Studies	X	UD	MD	X	UD	X	X	X	UM	MD		U	X	X	X	X	X	X	X	M			X		UM	X	UD	X

TO SUBJECTS OF STUDY

For further information about the individual subjects taught at each institution, please refer to the *Index to Department Names* at the end of the Yearbook, but for full details about subjects/courses offered at universities in the Commonwealth each institution's own official publications must be consulted. U = may be studied for first degree course; M = may be studied for master's degree course; D = research facilities to doctoral level; X = all three levels (UMD). **Note**— The table only includes information provided by institutions currently in membership of the Association of Commonwealth Universities, submitted for this edition of the Yearbook. (*The University of London's subject directory is shown on page 1586.*)

Keele	Kent at Canterbury	Kingston	Lancaster	Leeds	Leeds Metropolitan	Leicester	Lincolnshire and Humberside	Liverpool John Moores	Loughborough	Luton	UMIST	Manchester Metropolitan	Napier	Newcastle upon Tyne	Northumbria at Newcastle	Nottingham	Open	Oxford	Oxford Brookes	Paisley	Plymouth	Queen Margaret Coll. Edinburgh	Queen's U. of Belfast	Reading	Robert Gordon	St Andrews	Salford	Sheffield	South Bank	Southampton	Strathclyde	Surrey	Sussex	Ulster	Wales: U. of Wales Bangor	Wales: U. of Wales Cardiff	Wales: U. of Wales Swansea	Wales: U. of Wales Lampeter	Wales: U. of Wales Coll. of Med.	Wales: U. of Wales Inst. Cardiff	Wales: U. of Wales Coll. Newport	Warwick	West of England Bristol	Wolverhampton	York
	X	X	X	X	X		U	X	U	U	MD	UD	X	U	U	X	MD		U	U	X		X	X	U		UM	X	UM	X	X			UM	X	UD						U	X	X	U
		M			U								X		X								UD	X	X						X														D
X	X		U	DM		UD		X				X				X							U	U		MD		X				X	U			X	U					X	U	UD
		U	X		UD									U		X							U	X		X		X						MD								U		U
X	X		U													X	X		UD				X		X					X			X	X										
			UM													X							X	U										U										
UM			D		X							X		UD		X							X	X		X		X		X			X	X		X			X	X				X
	X			X		UM	UM		U		X	U	X	U	X			X	U	X		X		X		U	X	X		X			U		X						U		MD
X	X	UM	U	MD	UD		X	U			X			UD	X	UD	MD	X			U	X		X			X			X			U		X						X		X
			X																					X				X			U													
			DM		X		UM				U		UD			UD						X		X		MD		UD						D					
MD	U	X					U		M		UD	X	UD		U			U		X		X			X	X	MD		X		X		D		X
UD	X	X	X	UM	X		X		U	X		X	UD	X	X	U	UD	UD	UD	UD	X	U	X	X	X	X	UM	X	X	UD	X	D	X	U	UD
UD	X	X	X	X	X	X	UM	U	U	X	X	UD	U	X	UD	X	X	U	UD	UD	X	X	X	X	X	X	X	X	X	X	X	X	X	X
		X	U	X	X	U		U	X	UD	X	UD		X	U	X	X	X	UM	UD	X	X	X	U	UD
	X	DM	X	X	X	U	X	X	X	X	X	UM	U	X	X	UD	X	X	X	X	MD	X	X	X	X
X	X	X	X	X	X	X	X	X	X	X	UM	X	X	UM	X	X	X	X	UM	X	UM	X	X	UM	X	X	X	X	X	UM	UM	X	X	X
												MD				X	UD	X	X	X	X
UD	X	X	X	X	UD	X	X	X	X	U	X	X	UD	UD	X	U	UD	X	X	X	X	X	X	X	X	X	X	UD	X	X	U	X	X
	U	X	X	X	U
UD	X	U	X	UD	X	X	UD	X	X	X	U	X	X	X	X	X	X	X	X
X	X	X	X	X	X	UD	U	X	X	U	X	X	X	X	X	X	X	X	X	U	X	X	X	UM	X	X	X	X	X	X	D	U	X	X	X	X	X
			X	UD	X	X	X	X	X	X
	X	X	U	X	U	X	X	UD	X	X	UD	X	UM	UM	X	X	UM	X	U	X
	U	X	M	X	MD	UD	MD	M	MD	MD	MD
	X	X	X	X	X	UD	U	X	X	X	U	X	UD	X	U	X	X	U	X	X	X
X	X	X	X	X	UD	X	U	X	X	U	UD	X	X	UD	X	UD	X	U	U	X	X	X	X	X	X	U	X	X	X	X	UD	X	X	X	UD	X
X	X	X	X	X	MD	D	X	X	M	X	X	UD	X	X	MD	X	U	X	X	X	X	MD	MD	MD	X	X	MD	UM	X	X	X
X	X	X	X	X	U	U	X	X	UD	X	UD	UD	X	X	X	X	X	U	X	X	X	X
X	X	MD	X	UD	UD	UM	X	X	X
X	X	X	X	X	X	U	UD	X	X	X
X	X	U	X	X	X	X	X	X	U	UD	X	X	X	X	X	X	X	X	X	U	UD
U	X	X	U	U	X	X	UM	UD	MD	X	U	X	X	X	X	U	X	X	U
X	X	X	UD	UD	U	X	X	X	U	X	X	X	U	X	X	X	X	UM	UD	X	X	X
X	DM	X	UM	X	X	X	U	M	X	U	X	M	MD	U	X	X	UM	UD	U	X	X	X	X	UD
X	X	X	UD	U	UM	X	X	X	U	X	U	X	UD	UD	X	U	X	U	UD	X	X	UM	X	X	X	X	X	X	U	UD	X	X	X
X	X	X	X	X	X	X	U	X	X	U	X	X	X	U	X	X	X	X	X	X	UM	X	U	X	X	X	X	U	X	X	X	X	X
UD	X	X	X	X	M	U	X	X	U	MD	X	X	MD	U	X	UD	MD	X	X	X	UM	X	X	X	UD	U	UM	X	X	X

	Abertay Dundee	Aston	Bath	Birmingham	Bolton Institute	Bournemouth	Bradford	Bristol	Brunel	Cambridge	Central England in Birmingham	City	Coventry	Cranfield	De Montfort	Dundee	Durham	East Anglia	East London	Edinburgh	Essex	Exeter	Glamorgan	Glasgow Caledonian	Greenwich	Hertfordshire	Huddersfield	Hull
European Studies		X	X	X	U	X				M			X		X	U	UM	X		U	X		UD		UM	X	UD	X
Fashion/Textiles				X	U							X				U	X			UM						U	X	
Finance/Banking	UM	UM	MD	X		UM		U	M			X	X			UD	X		M	X	X	U	X	UM	X		UD	M
Film Studies/Television				M	U	X	U	X	UD			X				X		X	X	M							U	D
Fine Art								X	X			X			X	X					X	X					UD	
Food Science/Nutrition						UM			U			U	X			UD	MD				U	X	U			X		
French		X	X	X	U	X	X			X	U	UD				X	U	X	X	UM	X	X	X				UD	UD
Geography			X			U	U	X	X	X			X				X	X		X		X	X		U	U	UD	X
Geology/Earth Sciences			X			UM		X	X	X				MD			X	X		UD		X	UD		X	UM		D
German		X	X	X	U		X	X		X	U	UD				X	U	X	X	UM	X	X					UD	UD
Health Sciences/Studies		MD	X	U	UM	X	MD	X				U	X	X		UD	X	MD	X		UM	MD	X	X	UM		UD	X
Hebrew/Semitic Studies										X										X								
History				X			X			X	X	UD	X			UD	X	X	X	X	X	X	X		UD	U	X	X
Horticulture														X												U	U	
Industrial Relations/Human Resource Management	M	X	X	MD	UM	X	D			MD	X	X	MD	UM	MD		MD	X				X	X	M	X		MD	
Information Science/Systems/Technology	X	X	X	X	UM	X	X			X	X	X	X	MD	X	X	X	X	X	X	X	MD	X	X	X	UM	X	UD
International Relations/Studies		MD	X		UM	X	MD		X				D	X	D		MD	X		MD	MD	D		U	X		UD	X
Islamic/Middle Eastern Studies		D								X							X				X	X						
Italian		X	X				UD			X		U				U				U	X	U	X					UD
Japanese		MD								X										X	X							
Journalism/Communication/Media Studies						X		X				U	X	X					X	X	M		UM	X		UM	UD	
Law/Legal Studies	U	U		X	U	UM	U	X	X	X	U	X	X		X	X	X	X	X	X	X	X	X	X	X	UM	X	X
Library/Information Science								M				U	MD														D	
Linguistics		MD	MD	U						X							X	X	UM	X	X		D			X	D	X
Management	X	X	X	MD	X	X	MD		X	X	X	X	X	X	X	X	X	X	X	X	MD	X	MD	X	X	UM	UD	X
Marketing	UM	X	MD		U	X	D						X	MD	X	X	X	U	MD		X	D	X	X	UM	X	X	
Materials Science		D	UD	X	D				X	X					D	MD	X	MD				D			X		D	
Mathematics	U	U	UD	X	UD		D	X	X	X		UD	X	MD	X	X	X	X	X	X	X	X	X		X		UD	UD
Medicine/Surgery		D		X				X	X							UD				X								D
Microbiology	X	D	D	X			X	X						MD		UD	MD	X	X			X				X	D	
Music				X							X	UD	X	U	X	U	X	X	X	X	U	X				UM	X	X
Nursing/Midwifery	UM			X	UD	UM	UM						X	UD	X	X				X	UM	UM	UD	X	U	X	UD	X
Optometry		UD				X	MD						X											X				
Pharmacology	UD	UD	X			UD		X		X		U		D	UD	MD		X	X							UM	X	
Pharmacy		X	UD				X									X												
Philosophy				X				X	UM	X	U	X					X	X		X	U	X	D		U		D	X
Physical Education/Sports Science		U	X			MD	X							MD	U					U		U	UM	X	UD	U	U	U
Physics			UD	X				X	MD	X				D		UD	X	X	MD	UD	MD	X	D	U	U	X	D	UD

Keele	Kent at Canterbury	Kingston	Lancaster	Leeds	Leeds Metropolitan	Leicester	Lincolnshire and Humberside	Liverpool John Moores	Loughborough	Luton	UMIST	Manchester Metropolitan	Napier	Newcastle upon Tyne	Northumbria at Newcastle	Nottingham	Open	Oxford	Oxford Brookes	Paisley	Plymouth	Queen Margaret Coll. Edinburgh	Queen's U. of Belfast	Reading	Robert Gordon	St Andrews	Salford	Sheffield	South Bank	Southampton	Strathclyde	Surrey	Sussex	Ulster	Wales: U. of Wales Bangor	Wales: U. of Wales Cardiff	Wales: U. of Wales Swansea	Wales: U. of Wales Lampeter	Wales: U. of Wales Coll. of Med.	Wales: U. of Wales Inst. Cardiff	Wales: U. of Wales Coll. Newport	Warwick	West of England Bristol	Wolverhampton	York
X	X	X	X	X	X		U		X	X	U		U		UM	U	X		UM	U	U		X	X		X	UD		UM	X	X	X	U	X	UM		X		U		U	UM	U	U	X
		U		X				U	U		X	U				UD											U			X			X										UM		U	
U	X	X	X	X	U	MD	UM	U	X			U	X	D	U	X	M		U				X	X		U			X	X	M		X	X	X							UM		X	
	X	M	X	DM	M			U		U		X	M	U	MD								X			U	M		X			X	U	UD					X	X	M	U
	X		X	X		UM	U	U			X		UM	X			U	X		X		X	U	X	X	X		U			X					UM			UM	X
	X		X	X		X	U		U		X		U	U	X			X	UD	X	X	X	X		U	MD	X	X	X	X		X					UM			X
UD	X	X	X	X	U	UD	U	X	U	U		UD		X	UM	X	U	X	X		U		X	X		X	U	X	UM	X	X	U	X	X	UD	X	U			X	X	UD	U
UD		X	X	X	U	X		X	X	U		X		X	UD	X	UD	X	U		UD		UD	X		X	UM	X		X	X	X	U		U	X	X		UM		U	UD
X		X	X	X		X		U		U				UD	X	UD		UD	UD	X		X		X		X			X	X			X	X						U
X	X	U	X	X	U	UD	U	X	U	U		UD		X	U	X	U	X	U	X	U		U		X	X		X	U	X	UM	X	X	U	U	X	X	X	UD	X	U		X	X	U	U
MD	MD	U	X	DM	X	M	U	X		U		X	U	X	U	MD	UD	MD	X		X	U	MD	MD		MD	X	X	X	X	X	X		X	X	X	U	MD		U	UM	MD	X	X	X
			DM												X							UD		U	X							X									
X	X	X	X	X	UD	X		X		UM		X		X	UD	X	X	X	X		X		UD		X	X		X	U		X	X	X	X	X	X					X	X	X	X
				U	U									X				D		X				U				U											
X	X	UM	X	DM	M	MD	UM	MD		UM	MD	M	UM	M	U	X	M		UM	U	X					UM	X	X		X	M		MD		UD					UM	MD	MD	X
MD		X	X	X	X		UM	UM	X	U	X	X	X		X	X	X		UM	UM	X	X	X	X	X	X	X	X		X	MD		X	MD	UD	U	D		U		UM			X	X	X
X	X		X	X		MD	U	U	U		U			M	U		MD						X		X	U	X	U	X		X	UM		UD	X					X	M	MD
			X					MD				X					X						X							X									X		U
	X		X	X	U	UD		U			UD					X	U		U		UD	X		U	U			X		U		U	UD	X				X		U
			U					U		U						X										X				U	U							U
	X	X	X	X	UM	X	U	U		X	UM			M				U	M	X		U		UM	X			X		X	UM	UM	X					UM		X	X
X	X	UM	X	X	X	X	UM	X		U		X	UM	X	X	X	U	X	UM		X		X	X	U		X	U	X	X	M	X	UM		X	X			X	X	X
				X			MD	X		X	UM		X					UM	X		X			X			X						X							
	X		X	X	X			X	UM			X				MD						X	MD	M		X	X	UD	X	U	X	UD					MD	UM	UD	X
X	X	X	X	X	X	MD	X	M	X	UM	X	X	X	X	X	X	X	X	U	X	U	X	X	X	X	UM	X	X	X		X	X	UD	UD	U		UM	X	X	X	MD
	X	X	X	X	MD	UM	UM		UM	MD	MD	U		UD		MD		U	UM	X	U		U	MD		UM		X		X	MD	X		UD	D			UM	X	X	X
	D		X			X		X	UD		U	UM	X	UD	X			X	MD				X	X	MD	MD		X	X		MD	MD	X				X	UD
UD	X	X	X		UD		UD	U	X	X	X	X	UD	D	X	X	UD		X	X		X	X	U	X	X	U	X	UD	U			X	U	U	X
MD		X		X	MD		X	X	X		X	U	X	X	M			X		X		MD	M
	X	X	X	X	U		D	U	U	X	UD	MD	D	U	UD	UD	X	X	X	X	UD		MD	X	U	X
X		X	X	X		UD	U	X	X	UD	X	X	U	X	X	UM	X	U	X	X	X	X	UD	X	MD	X
D	X	UM	X	X	UM	U	UM	U	X	X	UM	M	X	X	X	U	X	X	X	X	U
	U	X	U	D	D	X	MD	UD	X	X	U	UD	U	UD
MD	X	U	U	X	X	X	X	UD
UD	X	X	X	X	UD	UD	X	X	X	X	X	X	U	UD	X	X
U	X	X	MD	X	X	U	UM	D	X	D	MD	UM	MD	UM	X	X	X	X	U	UM	U	X
UD	X	X	X	X	X	X	U	MD	UD	U	X	U	UD	UD	X	U	UD	X	X	X	X	UD	X	X

For University of London, see p. 1586.

	Abertay Dundee	Aston	Bath	Birmingham	Bolton Institute	Bournemouth	Bradford	Bristol	Brunel	Cambridge	Central England in Birmingham	City	Coventry	Cranfield	De Montfort	Dundee	Durham	East Anglia	East London	Edinburgh	Essex	Exeter	Glamorgan	Glasgow Caledonian	Greenwich	Hertfordshire	Huddersfield	Hull
Physiology				D				X		X						UD	MD	X		X				X			UM	
Physiotherapy				U			U		X			UM						X	X					X	U		X	U
Planning, Urban/Regional				X			X	MD		X		X	UM		D	X							D	UM			D	
Politics/Political Science/Government		U		X			X	X	X	X	X	UD	X	X	X	X		MD	X			UD		M		UM	UD	X
Portuguese				U			MD			X										U	U							
Psychology	X	UD	X	X	X	UM	UD	X	X	X	U	X	U		MD	X	X		X	X	X	X	X	X	U	X	UD	X
Religion/Theology				X				X		X							X			X	X	UD						X
Russian			X	X			X	X		X			U				X			UD	X	X						
Sanskrit										X										X								
Scandinavian Studies										X							UD			U								UD
Slavonic Languages/Studies				X						X							U											
Social Work/Policy/Studies		U	X	X		UM	X	X	X			U	MD	UD	UD	X	MD		X	MD	X	MD	X	U	X		UD	X
Sociology	UM	U	U	X	UD		UD	X	X	X	U	X	UD				X	X	X	MD	X	UD	X	UM	X		UD	X
Spanish/Hispanic/Latin American Studies				X			X	X		X		U	X	U	X					U	UD	X	X				UD	UD
Statistics		UD	X	U				X	X				X	U	X	X	MD	MD	X	X	X	X	D	U	UM	X	D	UD
Surveying	U		U									U	X		UD			X					UD	U	U	U		
Teacher Training			M	M				X			UM					X	MD				X			U	X		UD	X
Tourism/Hospitality/Leisure	U				U	X		U		U			U	U									D	UD	X	U	U	X
Veterinary Science								X		X										X								
Zoology								X		X					UD	U	UD			UD								

Keele	Kent at Canterbury	Kingston	Lancaster	Leeds	Leeds Metropolitan	Leicester	Lincolnshire and Humberside	Liverpool John Moores	Loughborough	Luton	UMIST	Manchester Metropolitan	Napier	Newcastle upon Tyne	Northumbria at Newcastle	Nottingham	Open	Oxford	Oxford Brookes	Paisley	Plymouth	Queen Margaret Coll. Edinburgh	Queen's U. of Belfast	Reading	Robert Gordon	St Andrews	Salford	Sheffield	South Bank	Southampton	Strathclyde	Surrey	Sussex	Ulster	Wales: U. of Wales Bangor	Wales: U. of Wales Cardiff	Wales: U. of Wales Swansea	Wales: U. of Wales Lampeter	Wales: U. of Wales Coll. of Med.	Wales: U. of Wales Inst. Cardiff	Wales: U. of Wales Coll. Newport	Warwick	West of England Bristol	Wolverhampton	York
		U		X		MD						D		X					X				X	UD		X		X		X						UD								U	
UD		U		X							U	U				U		X			X			U		U				X				U						X				U	
		U		DM	X			X		U					U	X		X	M	U		M	X			U	X	X		X			X	U		X	MD							X	
X	X	X	X	X	UD	X	UD	X	U	U		X		X	UD	X	UD	X	X	U	X		X	X		MD	UM	X	UM	X	X		X	U		UD	X					X	X	UD	X
				X											X		X									U		X					U												
X	X	U	X	X	X	X	X	X	X	U		X		X	U	X	X	X	U		X	U	X	X		X		X	U	X	X	X	X	UM	X	X	X			U		X	X	X	X
	X		X	X								U		X		X	UD	X				X		X		X		X		X			X	X		X		X			UM			U	D
UD			X				U							X		X					X		X	UM	U			UD																U	
																X																													
			X											X		X												M	X																
X	X	UM	X	X	X	MD	U	X	U	U		X		X	X	X	UD	MD	X	U	X	U	MD	MD	X		UM	X	X	X		X	X	X	X	X			U	UM	X	X	U	X
X	X	X	X	X	X	UD		X	U	U		X		UM	X	X	U	X	U	X	U	UD	X			UM	X	X	X		X	UD	X	X				X	X	UD	X
	X	U		X	U	UD	U	X	U			UD		X	U	X	U	X			U		X		X	U	X		X			X	U	X				X	UD
UD	X	X	X	X			X		U	MD		X	X	X	UD	UD	MD	U		UD			X	X	MD	X		X	X	U	U	UD	UD				X	UM	U
	X		DM	U		U					U	X	UD			U	U	U			U	UD	UM	UM			X						U
M	X		DM	X	MD		UM	UM		X			U	MD	U	MD	X	X	X	X		X	X	M	M	UM			U	UM	X	UM	U
		UM		X		U	U	UM	X	X	U		X	U	UD	X	U	MD	U	X	X	X	UM	UM	U	U	U	U
												MD	
		U		UD	U			U	X	UD	X	UD	X	X	U	UD	U

For University of London, see p. 1586.

WEST INDIES

University of the West Indies (p.1811)

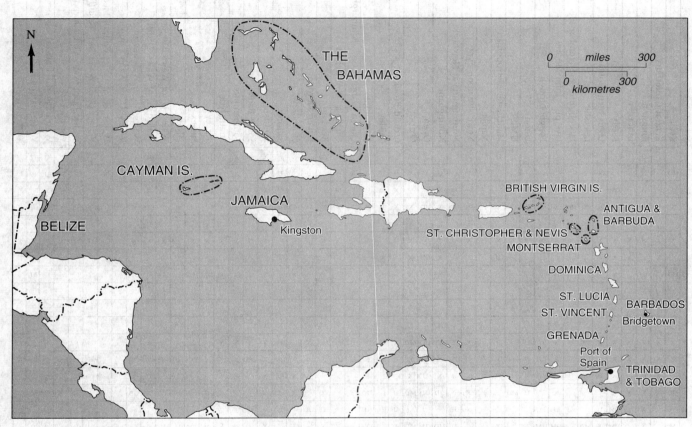

The seats of the university of the West Indies are shown in upper/lower case letters. States and Territories supporting the university are shown in capital letters

UNIVERSITY OF THE WEST INDIES

Founded 1948; incorporated by Royal Charter 1962

Member of the Association of Commonwealth Universities

Postal Address: Mona, Kingston 7, Jamaica, West Indies
Telephone: 927 1660-9 **Fax**: 927 2765, 927 4869 **E-mail**: gsobers@uwimona.edu.jm **Cables**: Univers Jamaica
Telex: 2123 UNIVERS JA **WWW**: http://www.uwimona.edu.jm

VISITOR—Elizabeth, H.M. The Queen
CHANCELLOR—Ramphal, The Hon. Sir Shridath, OE, GCMG, OM(J), AC, QC, LLM *Lond.*, Hon. LLD *Panjab*, Hon.
   LLD *S'ton.*, Hon. LLD *St FX*, Hon. LLD *Aberd.*, Hon. LLD *Cape Coast*, Hon. LLD *Lond.*, Hon. LLD *Benin*, Hon. LLD *Hull*,
   Hon. LLD *Yale*, Hon. LLD *Camb.*, Hon. LLD *Warw.*, Hon. LLD *WI*, Hon. DUniv *Sur.*, Hon. DU *Essex*, Hon. DHL
   Simmons, Hon. DHL *Duke*, Hon. DCL *Oxf.*, Hon. DCL *E.Anglia*, Hon. DCL *Durh.*, Hon. DLitt *Brad.*, Hon. DSc *Cran.IT*,
   FKC
VICE-CHANCELLOR*—(resident in Jamaica) Nettleford, Prof. The Hon. Rex M., OM(J), BA *Lond.*, BPhil *Oxf.*, Hon.
   DLitt *St.John's*
DEPUTY VICE-CHANCELLOR—......
PRO-VICE-CHANCELLOR (BOARD FOR UNDERGRADUATE STUDIES)—(resident in Jamaica) Hamilton, Marlene, BSc
   WI, MAEd *WI*, PhD *WI*
PRO-VICE-CHANCELLOR (BOARD FOR GRADUATE STUDIES AND RESEARCH)—Robotham, Donald, BSc *WI*, MA *Chic.*,
   PhD *Chic.*
PRO-VICE-CHANCELLOR—......
PRO-VICE-CHANCELLOR (STUDENT AND ALUMNI RELATIONS)—(resident in Jamaica) Hall, Kenneth O., BA *WI*, MA
   Qu., PhD *Qu.*
PRO-VICE-CHANCELLOR (BOARD FOR NON-CAMPUS COUNTRIES AND DISTANCE EDUCATION)—(resident in
   Barbados) Marshall, Prof. W. K., BA *Lond.*, PhD *McG.*
DIRECTOR OF ADMINISTRATION/UNIVERSITY REGISTRAR—Barrett-Sobers, Gloria P., BA *Lond.*, MAEd *Col.*, MBA
   Miami(Fla.)
UNIVERSITY LIBRARIAN—(resident in Jamaica) Ferguson, Stephney, BA *WI*, MLS *Indiana*
DIRECTOR OF FINANCE/UNIVERSITY BURSAR—(resident in Jamaica) Bayley, W. H., BSc *Lond.*

GENERAL INFORMATION

History. The university was first established at Mona, Jamaica in 1948, as a college in special relationship with the University of London to serve the British territories in the Caribbean area. Campuses were later created at St Augustine, Trinidad (1960) and Cave Hill, Barbados (1963). In 1962 the university was granted its charter and became empowered to grant its own degrees.

Admission to first degree courses. General requirement: passes in 5 subjects at CXC General Proficiency/General Certificate of Education (GCE) O level and GCE A level (including English language), of which at least 2 must be at A level grade A, B or C. For medical sciences, at least 3 subjects must be at A level in physical and biological sciences. Other qualifications accepted as equivalent to those above include: Ontario Secondary School Diploma with 60% marks; French or International Baccalaureate; German Abitur; certain other qualifications from tertiary institutions. Evidence of proficiency in English is required for those whose first language is not English.

First Degrees. BA, BEd, BPharm, BSc, DDS, DVM, LLB, MB BS.
   Courses normally last 3 years full-time or 6 years part-time. Medical sciences: 6 years full-time.

Higher Degrees. DM, MA, MBA, MD, MEd, MSc, MPhil, PhD.
   Applicants for admission to higher degree courses must hold at least a second class honours degree from an approved university or possess appropriate professional qualifications and experience. PhD: master's degree by research (applicants without this qualification must first register for MPhil).

Libraries. 495,272 volumes; 833,760 periodicals. Special collections include: Institute of Social and Economic Research; West Indiana.

Academic Year (1998–99). Two semesters: August–December; January–May.

Statistics. Staff: 968 academic, 282 administrative. Students: full-time 11,210; part-time 6263.

ACADEMIC UNITS

(C) = Cave Hill Campus; (M) = Mona Campus; (S) = St Augustine Campus Note: The Centre comprises the Vice-Chancellory, the School of Continuing Studies, Centre for Environment and Development, Institute of Social and Economic Research (ISER), Institute of Education, Tropical Metabolism Research Unit (TMRU) and the Distance Education Experiment (UWIDITE); also the Consortium Graduate School of Social Sciences.
The vice-chancellor heads a management team of pro-vice-chancellors, university registrar and university bursar, operating across campuses, with offices as follows: Board for Undergraduate Studies, Graduate Studies and Research, Non-Campus Countries and Distance Education, science education and gender and development studies, administration (university registrar), finance (university bursar).

Continuing Studies, School of
Tel: 448 3482 Fax: 448 8706

Antrobus, Peggy, BA *Brist.*   Tutor; Regional
   Co-ordinator, Women's Programme (C)
Brown, Janet, BA *Indiana*, MSW *Col.*   Tutor;
   Co-ordinator, Caribbean Child Devel. Centre
   (M)

Education, Institute of (TEDD)

Evans, Hyacinth, MEd *Ott.*, PhD *Calif.*, BA   Sr.
   Lectr.
King, Ruby, MA *Lond.*, PhD *Mich.State*   Sr. Lectr.
   (M)
Miller, E. L., CD, BSc *Lond.*, MA PhD   Prof.;
   Head*
Wilson, D. G., MA *Lond.*, PhD *Mich.State*   Sr.
   Lectr.

Environment and Development, Centre for
Tel: 977 1659 Fax: 977 1658

Binger, A., BS *Calif.*, PhD *Georgia*   Prof.; Dir.*
Clayton, A., MA *Edin.*, PhD *Edin.*   Prof.

Social and Economic Research, Institute of (ISER)

Tel: (Cave Hill) (246) 417 4484; (Mona) 927
   1020; (St. Augustine) 662 1334
Downes, Andrew S., BSc *WI*, MSc *WI*, PhD
   Manc.   Dir.* (C)
LeFranc, Elsie, BA(Econ) *Manc.*, MPhil *Yale*, PhD
   Yale   Dir.* (M)
Ryan, S. V. D., BA *Tor.*, PhD *Cornell*   Prof.;
   Univ. Dir. (S)

Social Sciences, Consortium Graduate School of

Girvan, N., PhD *Lond.*, BScEcon   Hon. Prof.;
   Dir.* (M)
Riviere, B., BA *WI*, PhD *Glas.*
Tindigarukayo, Jimmy, PhD *Dal.*   Sr. Lectr.

Tropical Metabolism Research Unit (TMRU)

Forrester, T., MSc *Marquette*, MB MS PhD
   DM   Dir.* (M)
McFarlane Anderson, Norma, BSc *WI*, PhD
   Lond.   Sr. Lectr. (M)
McGregor, Sally, MB BS *Lond.*, MD *Lond.*   Prof.
   (M)

CONTACT OFFICERS

Academic affairs. Campus Registrar: (resident in Trinidad) Ali, Zaffar, MA *Aberd.*
Accommodation. Assistant Estate Manager: (resident in Jamaica) Heron, A., BA *WI*, MSc *WI*
Accommodation. Senior Assistant Registrar (Appointments): (resident in Trinidad) Fraser, Marian E., BA *Lond.*
Admissions (first degree). Senior Assistant Registrar: (resident in Jamaica) Davis, BA *Lond.*, MA *N.Y.State*
Admissions (first degree). Assistant Registrar: (resident in Trinidad) Bacon, Tyra, BSc *WI*, MSc *WI*
Admissions (first degree). Senior Assistant Registrar: (resident in Barbados) Crichlow, Desmond R., BSc *WI*
Admissions (higher degree). Assistant Registrar: (resident in Trinidad) Bacon, Tyra, BSc *WI*, MSc *WI*

Admissions (higher degree). Senior Assistant Registrar: (resident in Barbados) Crichlow, Desmond R., BSc *WI*

Admissions (higher degree). Assistant Registrar: (resident in Jamaica) Miller, Barbara S., BA *WI*

Adult/continuing education. Resident Tutor: (resident in Trinidad) Bernard, Lennox, BA *WI*, MEd *Tor.*

Adult/continuing education. Professor and Director: (resident in Jamaica) Carrington, Prof. L. D., BA *Lond.*, PhD *WI*

Alumni. Senior Assistant Registrar: (resident in Trinidad) Cowan, Victor, BA *Lond.*

Archives. University Archivist: (resident in Jamaica) Lemieux, V., BA *Tor.*, MA *Br.Col.*

Archives. Records Manager: (resident at Trinidad) Georges, Jo-Ann, BA *WI*, MLS *Col.*

Careers. Director: (resident in Jamaica) Henry, Merrit, BSc *WI*

Computing services. Manager: (resident in Barbados) Williams, R. N., BSc *Lond.*

Computing services. Planning Officer: (resident in Jamaica) Manison, K. I.

Computing services. Manager, Computer Centre: (resident in Trinidad) Cazabon, Kenneth A., BSc *Nott.*, BSc(Eng) *Nott.*

Distance education. Pro-Vice-Chancellor (Board for Non-Campus Countries and Distance Education): (resident in Barbados) Marshall, Prof. W. K., BA *Lond.*, PhD *McG.*

Estates and buildings/works and services. Estate Manager: (resident in Trinidad) Nobbee, Kenrick A. W., BSc *Strath.*, MSc *Strath.*

Estates and buildings/works and services. Estate Manager: (resident in Jamaica) Scott, W., BSc *Qu.*, MSc(Eng) *Qu.*

Examinations. Senior Assistant Registrar: (resident in Barbados) Crichlow, Desmond R., BSc *WI*

Examinations. Campus Registrar: (resident in Jamaica) Robinson, E., BSc(Econ) *WI*

Examinations. Assistant Registrar: (resident in Jamaica) Nelson, C., BA *WI*

Finance. Director of Finance/University Bursar: (resident in Jamaica) Bayley, W. H., BSc *Lond.*

Finance. Campus Bursar: (resident in Trinidad) Lackhan, Sooknath B., BSc(Econ) *WI*

Finance. Campus Bursar: (resident in Barbados) Maharaj, Mervyn, MBA *Lond.*

Finance. Campus Bursar: (resident in Jamaica) Beman, John

General enquiries. Director of Administration/University Registrar: Barrett-Sobers, Gloria P., BA *Lond.*, MAEd *Col.*, MBA *Miami(Fla.)*

Health services. Director: (resident in Jamaica) Anglin Brown, Blossom, MB BS *WI*, DM *WI*

Health services. Campus Registrar: (resident in Trinidad) Ali, Zaffar, MA *Aberd.*

Industrial liaison. Senior Assistant Registrar: (resident in Jamaica) Eytle, R., BSc *Cornell*

Library (chief librarian). University Librarian: (resident in Jamaica) Ferguson, Stephney, BA *WI*, MLS *Indiana*

Library. Law Librarian: (resident in Barbados) Newton, Velma E., BA *WI*, LLB *WI*, MA *WI*, FLA

Library (Cave Hill Campus). Campus Librarian: (resident in Barbados) Gill, M. E., BSc *Lond.*

Library (St Augustine Campus). Campus Librarian: (resident in Trinidad)

Personnel/human resources. Senior Assistant Registrar: (resident in Barbados) Wade, Jacqueline E., JP, BA *WI*

Personnel/human resources. Senior Assistant Registrar (Appointments): (resident in Trinidad) Fraser, Marian E., BA *Lond.*

Personnel/human resources. Assistant Registrar (Centre): (resident in Jamaica) Young, Pansy, BA *WI*

Personnel/human resources. Senior Assistant Registrar (Appointments): (resident in Jamaica) Smythe, D., BA *WI*, MSc *Lond.*

Public relations, information and marketing. Assistant Registrar: (resident in Barbados) Atherley, Patricia, BA *WI*, MSc *Sheff.*

Public relations, information and marketing. Public Relations Officer: (resident in Jamaica) Edwards, Carroll, BA *WI*, MJ *Car.*

Public relations, information and marketing. Public Relations Co-ordinator: (resident in Trinidad) Henry, Robert, BSc *WI*

Publications. Pro-Vice-Chancellor (Board for Graduate Studies and Research): Robotham, Donald, BSc *WI*, MA *Chic.*, PhD *Chic.*

Purchasing. Campus Registrar: (resident in Jamaica) Robinson, E., BSc(Econ) *WI*

Purchasing. Campus Bursar: (resident in Trinidad) Lackhan, Sooknath B., BSc(Econ) *WI*

Purchasing (Cave Hill Campus). Campus Bursar: (resident in Barbados) Maharaj, Mervyn, MBA *Lond.*

Quality assurance and accreditation. Pro-Vice-Chancellor (Board for Undergraduate Studies): (resident in Jamaica) Hamilton, Marlene, BSc *WI*, MAEd *WI*, PhD *WI*

Safety (Cave Hill Campus). Campus Registrar: (resident in Barbados) Lewis, A. G., JP, BA *WI*, MA *Tor.*

Safety (Mona Campus). Campus Registrar: (resident in Jamaica) Falloon, G. E. A., BA *WI*, MA *Oxf.*

Safety (St Augustine Campus). Campus Registrar: (resident in Trinidad) Ali, Zaffar, MA *Aberd.*

Scholarships, awards, loans. Campus Registrar: (resident in Trinidad) Ali, Zaffar, MA *Aberd.*

Scholarships, awards, loans. Senior Assistant Registrar: (resident in Jamaica) Daley, R., BA *WI*, MA *Antioch*

Security (Cave Hill Campus). Campus Registrar: (resident in Barbados) Lewis, A. G., JP, BA *WI*, MA *Tor.*

Security (Mona Campus). Campus Registrar: (resident in Jamaica) Falloon, G. E. A., BA *WI*, MA *Oxf.*

Security (St Augustine Campus). (resident in Trinidad) Farrell, Steve

Sport and recreation. Director of Student Services: (resident in Barbados) Jebodhsingh, Jailal, BA *Manit.*, MA *Manit.*

Sport and recreation. Director of Sports: (resident in Jamaica) Dolphin, Horton, BA *WI*

Sport and recreation. Co-ordinator, Sports and Physical Education: (resident at Trinidad) Gloudon, Iva, BSc *Ill.*, MSc *Ill.*

Student welfare/counselling. Director of Student Services: (resident in Barbados) Jebodhsingh, Jailal, BA *Manit.*, MA *Manit.*

Student welfare/counselling. Director of Student Services: (resident in Jamaica) Reynolds, Theolora, JP, BA *WI*, MA *WI*

Student welfare/counselling. Senior Assistant Registrar: (resident in Trinidad) Cowan, Victor, BA *Lond.*

Students with disabilities. Deputy Principal: (resident in Jamaica) Leo-Rhynie, Prof. Elsa, BSc PhD

University press. Acting Director: (resident in Jamaica) Benn, Pansy

Women. (resident in Trinidad) Sirju-Charran, Grace, BSc *WI*, PhD *WI*

Women. (resident in Jamaica) Bailey, Barbara, BSc *WI*, PhD *WI*

[Information supplied by the institution as at May 1998, and edited by the ACU]

UNIVERSITY OF THE WEST INDIES, CAVE HILL CAMPUS

Postal Address: PO Box 64, Bridgetown, Barbados, West Indies
Telephone: 417 4000 **Fax**: 425 1327 **Cables**: UNIVADOS Barbados **Telex**: UNIVADOS WB 2257

CHAIRMAN OF CAMPUS COUNCIL—Nicholls, Sir Neville, KA, BA *Camb.*, Hon LLD *WI*
PRINCIPAL AND PRO-VICE-CHANCELLOR*—Hunte, Sir Keith, KA, BA *Lond.*, MA *McG.*, PhD *McG.*
DEPUTY PRINCIPAL—Carnegie, Prof. A. Ralph, BA *Lond.*, MA *Oxf.*
PRO-VICE-CHANCELLOR—Marshall, Prof. Woodville K., BA *Lond.*, PhD *Camb.*
CAMPUS REGISTRAR‡—Lewis, Andrew G., JP, BA *WI*, MA *Tor.*
ACTING CAMPUS BURSAR—Webster, M. A. T., MSc *Sheff.*
CAMPUS LIBRARIAN—Gill, Michael E., BSc *Lond.*
PUBLIC ORATOR—Fraser, Prof. Henry, BSc *Lond.*, PhD *Lond.*, MB BS, FRACP, FACP

GENERAL INFORMATION

History. The campus was established in 1963. It is located in Barbados.

Admission to first degree courses. See under University of the West Indies, above.

ACADEMIC UNITS

Biological and Chemical Sciences

Carrington, C. M. Sean, BSc *Edin.*, DPhil *York(UK)* Sr. Lectr.; Head* (on leave)
Chinnery, Louis E., BSc *Ulster*, DPhil *Ulster* Sr. Lectr.
Delauney, Ashton J., BSc *Sur.*, PhD *Durh.* Sr. Lectr.
Hunte, Wayne, BSc PhD Prof.
Mathison, George E., BSc *Brist.*, PhD *Nott.* Prof.
O'Garro, Leonard W., BSc PhD Sr. Lectr.
Rogers, George K., BS *Mich.*, MS *Mich.*, PhD *Mich.* Dir., Tropical Horticulture
Sutrina, Sarah, BA *Colorado*, PhD *Johns H.* Sr. Lectr.
Other Staff: 1 Lectr.; 2 Temp. Lectrs.

Chemistry

Kulikov, Sergei M., MS *Novosibirsk*, PhD *Russian Acad.Sc.* Sr. Lectr.
Newton, Anthony, PhD *Calg.*, MSc Sr. Lectr.
Tinto, Winston, BSc PhD Reader
Other Staff: 2 Lectrs.; 2 Temp. Lectrs.

Computer Science, Mathematics and Physics

Cadogan, Charles C., BSc *Lond.*, PhD Prof.; Head*
Other Staff: 8 Lectrs.
Vacant Posts: 1 Prof.

Economics

Alleyne, Frank W., BA MSc PhD Sr. Lectr.
Howard, Michael, BA MSc PhD Sr. Lectr.; Head*
McClean, A. Wendell A., MSc Sr. Lectr.
Whitehead, Judy A., MA *Wat.*, PhD *Edin.*, BA Sr. Lectr.
Other Staff: 3 Lectrs.
Vacant Posts: 1 Prof.; 1 Lectr.

Education, School of

Clarke, Desmond C., BA *Lond.*, MA *Lanc.*, MEd *Manc.*, PhD *Penn.State* Sr. Lectr.
King, Winston K., BSc *Mt.All.*, MEd *Lond.*, PhD *S'ton.* Sr. Lectr.
Layne, Anthony, BEd *Calg.*, MA *Calg.*, PhD *Calg.*, BA Sr. Lectr. (on leave)
Newton, Earle H., BA *Lond.*, MA *Essex*, PhD *Manit.* Prof.; Head*
Richardson, Arthur G., BEd PhD Sr. Lectr.
Other Staff: 1 Lectr.; 1 Res. Fellow
Vacant Posts: 2 Lectrs.

Environmental Studies, see Resource Management and Environmental Studies, Centre for

French and Spanish

Hollingsworth, Charles, MA *Lond.*, PhD *Calif.* Sr. Lectr., Spanish
Other Staff: 4 Lectrs.
Vacant Posts: 3 Lectrs.

Government, Sociology and Social Work

Barrow, Christine E., BA *Sus.*, DPhil *Sus.* Sr. Lectr., Sociology; Head*
Belle, G. A., PhD *Manc.*, MSc Sr. Lectr., Political Science
Brathwaite, Farley S., BSc *Lond.*, MA *Essex*, PhD *Pitt.* Sr. Lectr., Sociology
Duncan, Neville C., PhD *Manc.*, MSc Sr. Lectr., Government
Other Staff: 2 Lectrs.
Vacant Posts: 1 Lectr.

History

Beckles, Hilary McD., BA *Hull*, MPhil *Hull*, PhD *Hull* Prof.
Cobley, Alan G., BA *Manc.*, MA *York(UK)*, PhD *Lond.* Sr. Lectr.; Head*
Marshall, Woodville K., BA *Lond.*, PhD *Camb.* Prof.
Mayo, John, BA *Adel.*, MA *P&NG*, DPhil *Oxf.* Sr. Lectr.
Phillips, Anthony DeV., MA *Lond.*, PhD Sr. Lectr.
Thompson, Alvin O., MPhil *Lond.*, BA Sr. Lectr.
Other Staff: 1 Lectr.

Language, Linguistics and Literature

Gibson, Kean A., BA *Guy.*, DPhil *York(UK)* Sr. Lectr.
McWatt, Mark, MA *Tor.*, PhD *Leeds* Reader
O'Callaghan, Evelyn, BA *N.U.I.*, MLitt *Oxf.* Sr. Lectr.
Roberts, Peter A., MA PhD Reader
Simmons-McDonald, Hazel C., PhD *Stan.*, BA Sr. Lectr.; Head*
Other Staff: 4 Lectrs.
Vacant Posts: 1 Lectr.

Law

Fax: 424 1788
Burgess, Andrew D., LLM *York(Can.)*, LLB Sr. Lectr.; Head*
Carnegie, A. Ralph, BA *Lond.*, MA *Oxf.* Prof.
Cumberbatch, Jefferson O'B., LLB Sr. Lectr.
DeMerieux, Margaret K., LLB *Manc.*, LLM *Lond.* Sr. Lectr.
Fiadjoe, Albert, LLB *Ghana*, LLM *Lond.*, PhD *Lond.* Reader
Kodilinye, A. Gilbert, MA *Oxf.*, LLM *Lond.* Reader
McIntosh, Simeon C., BA *York(Can.)*, LLM *Col.*, JD Prof.
Other Staff: 10 Lectrs.; 1 Res. Fellow
Vacant Posts: 2 Profs.; 1 Lectr.

Linguistics, see Lang., Linguistics and Lit.

Management Studies

Chaderton, Robertine, BCom *Windsor*, PhD *Manc.*, BSc Sr. Lectr.
Khan, Jamal, MA *Dacca*, MPA *Cinc.*, PhD *Cinc.* Sr. Lectr.
Nurse, Lawrence, MS *Mass.*, DPhil *Mass.*, BA Sr. Lectr.; Head*
Smith, Ann M., BSc *Manc.*, MSc *Manc.*, PhD *Manc.* Sr. Lectr.
Hendry, Malcolm D., BSc *Lond.*, PhD Sr. Lectr.
Other Staff: 5 Lectrs.
Vacant Posts: 1 Prof.; 2 Lectrs.

Medicine, see Clin. Med. and Res., Sch. of, below

Physics

Moseley, Leo L., PhD *Wales*, MSc Sr. Lectr.
Other Staff: 4 Lectrs.

Political Science, see Govt., Sociol. and Soc. Work

Resource Management and Environmental Studies, Centre for

Headley, Oliver St. C., BSc *Lond.*, PhD *Lond.* Prof.; Dir.*
Vacant Posts: 1 Sr. Lectr.; 1 Lectr.

Social Work, see Govt., Sociol. and Soc. Work.

Sociology, see Govt., Sociol. and Soc. Work

Spanish, see French and Spanish

CLINICAL MEDICINE AND RESEARCH, SCHOOL OF

Fax: 429 6738

Attapattu, J., MB BS *Ceyl.*, MS(O&G) *Ceyl.(Colombo)*, FRCOG Sr. Lectr., Obstetrics and Gynaecology
Fraser, Henry, BSc *Lond.*, PhD *Lond.*, MB BS, FRCP Prof., Medicine
Hoyos, M. D., MB BS Sr. Lectr., Community Medicine
Levett, Paul N., BSc *Sur.*, PhD *CNAA* Sr. Lectr., Microbiology
Moseley, Harley S. L., FFARCS Sr. Lectr., Anaesthesia and Intensive Care
Naidu, Raana P., MD *Gött.*, MSc DM Sr. Lectr., Family Medicine
Nicholson, George D., BA *Oxf.*, BM BCh *Oxf.*, FRCP, FACP Prof., Medicine
Prussia, Patsy R., MB BS DM Sr. Lectr., Pathology
Walrond, Errol R., CH(B), BSc *Lond.*, MB BS *Lond.*, FRCS, FACS Prof., Surgery; Head*
Other Staff: 6 Lectrs.; 2 Temp. Lectrs.

SPECIAL CENTRES, ETC

Caribbean Law Institute Centre

Carnegie, A. Ralph, BA Lond., MA Oxf.   Prof.; Exec. Dir.*

Gender and Development Studies, Centre for

1 Lectr.

IDB/CDB UWI Development Programme—Campus Project Execution Unit (CPEU)

Burke, Walter A.   Project Manager

Management Development, Centre for

Comma, Jeannine L., MA George Washington, PhD George Washington, BA   Dir.*

CONTACT OFFICERS

Accomodation. Campus Registrar: Lewis, Andrew G., JP, BA WI, MA Tor.
Admissions (first degree). Assistant Registrar: Crichlow, Desmond R., BSc WI
Adult/continuing education. Resident Tutor/ Organisor: Niles, Bradley E., BA Andrews, MA W.Mich., PhD Mich.State
Computing services. Manager: Williams, Robert N., BSc Lond.
Distance education. Director: Koul, Badri N., MA Reading, PhD CIE&F Langs.
Examinations. Assistant Registrar: Brewster, Henri O., BA
Finance. Acting Campus Bursar: Webster, M. A. T., MSc Sheff.
General enquiries. Campus Registrar: Lewis, Andrew G., JP, BA WI, MA Tor.
Health services. Director, Student Services: Jebodhsingh, Jailal, BA Manit., MA Manit.
Library (chief librarian). Campus Librarian: Gill, Michael E., BSc Lond.

Library (enquiries). Campus Librarian: Gill, Michael E., BSc Lond.
Personnel/human resources. Campus Registrar: Lewis, Andrew G., JP, BA WI, MA Tor.
Public relations, information and marketing. Assistant Registrar: Atherley, Patricia, BA WI, MSc Sheff.
Purchasing. Acting Campus Bursar: Webster, M. A. T., MSc Sheff.
Security. Campus Registrar: Lewis, Andrew G., JP, BA WI, MA Tor.
Sport and recreation. Director, Student Services: Jebodhsingh, Jailal, BA Manit., MA Manit.
Student welfare/counselling. Director, Student Services: Jebodhsingh, Jailal, BA Manit., MA Manit.

[Information supplied by the institution as at 23 March 1998, and edited by the ACU]

UNIVERSITY OF THE WEST INDIES, MONA CAMPUS

Postal Address: Mona, St Andrew, Jamaica, West Indies
Telephone: 927 1660 **Fax**: 927 2765 **Cables**: Univers Jamaica **Telex**: 2123 UNIVERS JA
WWW: http://www.uwimona.edu.jm

CHAIRMAN OF CAMPUS COUNCIL—Brice, The Hon. Don, OJ, CD, BA Lond.
PRINCIPAL AND PRO-VICE-CHANCELLOR*—Hall, Kenneth O., BA WI, MA Qu., PhD Qu.
DEPUTY PRINCIPAL AND PRO-VICE-CHANCELLOR—Leo-Rhynie, Prof. Elsa, BSc Lond., PhD WI
CAMPUS REGISTRAR—Falloon, G. E. A., BA WI, MA Oxf.
CAMPUS BURSAR—Robinson, Elaine, BSc(Econ) WI
CAMPUS LIBRARIAN—Ferguson, Stephney, BA WI, MLS Indiana
PUBLIC ORATOR—Baugh, Prof. E. A. C., BA Lond., MA Qu., PhD Manc.

GENERAL INFORMATION

History. The campus was established in 1948. It is located in Mona, Jamaica.

Admission to first degree courses. See under University of the West Indies, above.

First Degrees. BA, BEd, BSc, MB BS. See also under University of the West Indies, above.

Higher Degrees. DM, MA, MSc, MPhil, PhD. See also under University of the West Indies, above.

Academic Year. 1 August–31 July.

Fees (annual, undergraduate, full-time). Jamaican students: J$65,182 (arts and education); J$ 62,005 (law); J$101,971–119,318 (medical sciences); J$82,041 (pure and applied science); J$52,315 (social sciences). Government-sponsored Caribbean students (contributing countries): J$76,685 (arts and education); J$72, 947 (law); J$119,966–138,021 (medical sciences); J$96,519 (pure and applied science); J$61,547 (social sciences). Non-sponsored Caribbean students (contributing countries): J$127,796 (arts and education); J$121,567 (law); J$599,828–1,162,576 (medical sciences); J$160, 848 (pure and applied science); J$102,569 (social scienes). International students: J$383,425 (arts and education); J$ 364,737 (law); J$599,838–1,162,576 (medical sciences); J$482,593 (pure and applied science); J$307,737 (social sciences).

Income. Total, J$5,065,697.

ACADEMIC UNITS

Chemistry

Tel: 977 1834 Fax: 977 1835

Dasgupta, T. P., BSc Calc., PhD Calc., MSc Bihar   Prof.; Head*
Ellis, H. A., BSc Leeds, PhD Leeds   Sr. Lectr.
Greenaway, A. M., BSc Cant., PhD Cant.   Sr. Lectr.
Kahwa, I., BSc(Ed) Dar., MSc Dar., PhD Louisiana State   Sr. Lectr.
Lancashire, R., BSc Monash, PhD Monash   Sr. Lectr.
Szentpaly, L. V., MA Basle, DPhil Basle, DSc Stuttgart   Sr. Lectr.

Computer Science and Mathematics

Tel: 977 1810 Fax: 977 1810

Henry, L., BSc WI, PhD Manc.   Sr. Lectr.
Reichgelt, J., MA Nijmegen, PhD Edin.   Prof.; Head*
Robinson, Leslie R. B., OJ, BA WI, MA Lond.   Prof.

Early Childhood Education, Centre for

Tel: 927 2456 Fax: 927 1920

Gaynor-Daley, Myrtle, BA St.John's, MA Col., MEd Col.   Dir.*

Economics

Tel: 977 1188 Fax: 977 1483

Francis, A., BSc S'ton., PhD M.I.T.   Prof.; Head*

Witter, M., BSc Ill., MSc Wis., PhD Wis.   Sr. Lectr.
Vacant Posts: 1 Prof.; 1 Sr. Lectr.

Education, Institute of, see Academic Staff (The Centre), above

Educational Studies, see also Early Childhood Educn., Centre for

Tel: 927 2130 Fax: 927 7581

James-Reid, Olga, BScEcon WI, MA Col., MEd Col., EdD Col.   Lectr.; Head* (on leave)
Morrissey, M. P., BA Wales, MSc MAEd   Sr. Lectr.
Pollard, Velma, MA McG., MA Col., BA PhD   Sr. Lectr.
Soyibo, Kolawole, BSc Lagos, MA Leeds, PhD Leeds   Sr. Lectr.
Vacant Posts: 2 Profs.

English, see Lits. in English

Geography and Geology

Tel: 927 2728, 927 2129 Fax: 927 1566, 927 1640

Bailey, Wilma, BA Newcastle(UK), MA Leic., PhD WI   Sr. Lectr.
Barker, D., BSc Wales, PhD Brist.   Sr. Lectr.
Donovan, S. K., BSc Manc., PhD Liv.   Prof.
Jackson, T., MSc WI, PhD WI   Sr. Lectr.; Head*
Mulchansingh, V. C., BA Belf., PhD Belf.   Sr. Lectr.
Robinson, E., BSc Birm., PhD Lond.   Prof.
Vacant Posts: 1 Prof.

Government

Tel: 927 8864 Fax: 977 1809

Jones, E. S., BScEcon *WI*, MSc *WI*, PhD *Manc.* Prof., Public Administration (on leave)

Lewis, R., BScEcon *WI*, MSc *WI* Reader; Head*

Mills, G. E. M., OJ, CD, BSc(Econ) *Lond.*, MPA *Harv.* Emer. Prof., Public Administration

Munroe, T. St. G., MSc *WI*, DPhil *Oxf.* Reader

Vascianne, S., BSc *WI*, BA *Oxf.*, LLM *Camb.*, DPhil *Oxf.* Sr. Lectr.

History

Tel: 927 1922 Fax: 927 1640

Augier, Sir Roy, MA *St.And.*, PhD *St.And.* Emer. Prof.

Bryan, P., MA *WI*, PhD *WI* Reader, Caribbean History

Campbell, C. C., MA *Lond.*, PhD *WI* Prof.

Dalby, J. R., MA *St And.*, PhD *Manc.* Sr. Lectr.

Moore, B. L., BA *WI*, PhD *WI* Sr. Lectr.; Head*

Hotel and Tourism Management, UWI Centre for

Nassau, Bahamas

Tel: 323 5714 Fax: 325 3246

O'Reilly, A., BA *WI*, MSc *Sur.* Sr. Lectr.; Head*

Vacant Posts: 1 Prof.

Language, Linguistics and Philosophy

Tel: 927 2743 Fax: 927 3540

Alleyne, M. C., BA *Lond.*, DU *Stras.* Prof., Socio-Linguistics; Head*

Bewaji, John, BA *Ife*, MA *Ife*, PhD Sr. Lectr.

Christie, Pauline G., MA *Edin.*, DPhil *York(UK)* Sr. Lectr.

Devonish, H., BA *Guy.*, DPhil *York(UK)* Reader

Law

Tel: 927 1855

No staff at present

Library and Information Studies

Tel: 927 2944

Ferguson, Stephaney, BA *WI*, MLS *Indiana* Sr. Lectr.; Head*

Mohammedali, O. N., BA *Mak.*, MS(LS) *C.U.A.*, MA *Sheff.* Sr. Lectr.

Life Sciences

Tel: 927 2753, 927 1202 Fax: 977 2937, 977 1075

Coates-Beckford, Phyllis, BSc *WI*, MSc *Lond.*, PhD *Ill.* Sr. Lectr.; Head*

Freeman, Brian E., BTech *Brun.*, PhD *Lond.* Reader, Animal Ecology

Mansingh, Ajai, BSc *Agra*, MSc *Agra*, PhD *Alta.* Prof., Entomology

Prasad, P. V. Devi, BSc *And.*, MSc *Bhopal*, PhD *Ban.* Sr. Lectr.

Steele, Russell D., BSc *Lond.*, PhD *Lond.* Sr. Lectr.; Head*

Vacant Posts: 1 Prof.

Literatures in English

Tel: 927 2217 Fax: 977 0622

Baugh, E. A. C., BA *Lond.*, MA *Qu.*, PhD *Manc.* Prof.

Chang, V., BA *WI*, MA *Alta.*, PhD *Qu.* Sr. Lectr.; Head*

Cooper, Carolyn, BA *WI*, MA *Tor.*, PhD *Tor.* Sr. Lectr.

Lewis, Maureen P., BA *WI*, MPhil *York(UK)*, PhD *WI* Reader

Morris, M., BA *Lond.*, MA *Oxf.* Prof.

Management Studies

Tel: 977 3775 Fax: 977 1605

Shirley, G. V., MBA *Harv.*, PhD *Harv.*, BSc Carlton Alexander Prof.; Head*

Wint, Alvin, BSc *WI*, MA *Northeastern*, MA *Harv.* Prof.

Marine Sciences, Centre for

Tel: 927 1609 Fax: 977 1033

Goodbody, I. M., CD, MA *Trinity(Dub.)*, PhD *Aberd.* Emer. Prof.

Woodley, Jeremy D., MA *Oxf.*, DPhil *Oxf.* Sr. Lectr.; Dir.*

Mass Communication, Caribbean Institute of

Tel: 977 0591 Fax: 977 1597

Brown, A., BA *Hamline*, MA *Prin.*, PhD *Prin.* Prof.; Dir.*

De Bruin, Marjan, Drs *Amst.* Sr. Lectr.

Medical Sciences, see below

Modern Languages and Literatures

Tel: 927 2293 Fax: (876) 977 0622

Dash, Jean M., BA *WI*, PhD *WI* Prof., Francophone Literature; Head*

Pereira, Joseph, BA *WI*, MA *Qu.* Sr. Lectr.

Williams, Claudette, BA *WI*, MA *WI*, PhD *Stan.* Sr. Lectr.

Wilson, Elizabeth, BA *Newton Coll.(Mass.)*, MA *Mich.State*, PhD *WI* Sr. Lectr.

Vacant Posts: 1 Prof.

Physics

Tel: 927 2480 Fax: 977 1595

Chen, A., BSc *Boston Coll.*, MA *Harv.*, MSc *Maryland*, PhD *WI* Sr. Lectr.

Chin, P. N., BSc *Lond.*, PhD *WI* Sr. Lectr.; Head*

Lodenquai, J., BSc *WI*, MA *Col.*, PhD *Col.* Reader

McMorris, M. N., BSc *Lond.*, PhD *Camb.* Sr. Lectr.

Ponnambalam, M. J., BSc *Madr.*, MSc *IIT Madras*, PhD *Illinois Tech.Inst.* Sr. Lectr.

Vacant Posts: 2 Profs.

Sociology and Social Work

Tel: 977 0315 Fax: 927 2163

Anderson, Patricia, BSc *WI*, MA *Chic.*, PhD *Chic.* Sr. Lectr.

Maxwell, J., MSW *McG.*, PhD *Cornell* Sr. Lectr.; Head*

McKenzie, H. I., BSc(Soc) *Lond.* Sr. Lectr.

McKenzie, Hermione C. E., BSc(Soc) *Lond.*, MS *Brandeis* Sr. Lectr.

Vacant Posts: 2 Profs.

MEDICAL SCIENCES

Anaesthetics, see Surg., Radiol., Anaesth. and Intensive Care

Basic Medical Sciences

Tel: 927 0586 Fax: 927 0586

Fletcher, C., MB BS *WI*, FRCSEd Sr. Lectr.

Mills, J., MD *Düsseldorf*, PhD *WI* Sr. Lectr.

Parshad, O., BVSc&AH *Haryana Ag.*, MSc *Punj.Ag.*, PhD *Punj.Ag.* Sr. Lectr.

Poddar, S., MB MS *Patna*, MSc *Patna* Sr. Lectr.

Reid, H. L., BSc *Lond.*, PhD *Lond.* Reader, Clinical Haemorheology

Simon, O. R., MSc *Lond.*, PhD *Howard* Sr. Lectr.

Young, R. E., PhD *St And.*, MSc Prof.; Head*

Vacant Posts: 1 Prof.; 3 Lectrs.

Biochemistry

Tel: 977 1749 Fax: 927 2290

Ahmad, M. H., BSc *Bhagal.*, MSc *IARI*, PhD *IARI* Reader, Applied Microbiology; Head, Biotechnol. Unit

Morrison, E. Y. St. A., MD *Malta*, MSc *Lond.*, PhD, FRCPGlas, FACP Prof.

Wais, A., BS *Cornell*, PhD *Tufts* Sr. Lectr.

Community Health and Psychiatry

Tel: 927 2492 Fax: 927 2116

Bain, B. C., MB BS *WI*, DM *WI*, BSc Sr. Lectr.

Desai, Patricia, BA *Keele*, MPH *WI* Sr. Lectr.

Segree, Winsome, MB BS *WI* Sr. Lectr.

Thesiger, C., MB BS *Lond.* Sr. Lectr.

Vacant Posts: 1 Prof.

Medicine

Tel: 927 1707 Fax: 977 0691

Barrow, K. Orin, MB BS *Lond.*, FRCP, FACP Sr. Lectr.

Barton, Everard, BSc *WI*, MB BS *Ib.*, DM *WI* Sr. Lectr.

Denbow, C. E., BSc *WI*, MB BS *WI*, DM *WI*, FACP Sr. Lectr.

La Grenade, Lois, MB BS *WI* Sr. Lectr., Dermatology

Lee, M., MB BS *WI*, DM *WI*, FRCPCan, FACP Sr. Lectr.

Morgan, O., MA *Trinity(Dub.)*, MB BCh BAO *Trinity(Dub.)*, MD *Trinity(Dub.)*, FRCP, FRCPI, FACP Prof.; Head*

Rogers-Johnson, Pamela, MB BS *Lond.*, FRCPEd Prof.

Serjeant, G. R., MB BChir *Camb.*, MA *Camb.*, MD *Camb.*, FRCP Hon. Prof.

Williams, W., MB BS *WI*, DM *WI* Sr. Lectr.

Microbiology

Tel: 977 1265 Fax: 977 1265

Bodonaik, N. C., MB BS *Madr.*, MD *Madr.* Sr. Lectr.

Chen, W. N., MB BS *Lond.* Sr. Lectr.

King, S. Dorothy, MB BS *Lond.*, MD *Lond.*, FRCPath Prof.; Head*

Moosdeen, Faridah, MSc *Indonesia*, DPhil *Lond.* Prof.

Vacant Posts: 1 Prof.; 3 Lectrs.

Nursing Education, Advanced

Tel: 927 1640 Fax: 927 2472

Marshall-Burnett, Syringa, CD, BScN *Tor.*, MA *N.Y.* Sr. Lectr.; Head*

Obstetrics, Gynaecology and Child Health

Tel: 927 1466

Fletcher, H. M., BSc *WI*, MB BS *WI*, DM *WI* Sr. Lectr.

Frederick, J., MB BS *WI*, DM *WI* Sr. Lectr.

Gray, R., MB ChB *Edin.*, FRCPEd Prof.; Head*

Lee, Amy, BSc *WI* Res. Co-ordinator

Matadial, L., BSc *McG.*, MB BS MS, FRCOG Sr. Lectr.

Munroe, Merle J., BA *WI*, MSc *WI* Dir.*

Pate, E., BSc *WI*, MB BS *WI*, DM *WI* Sr. Lectr. (on leave)

Wynter, H. H., OJ, CD, MB BS *Lond.*, MD *Lond.*, FRCOG, FACS Prof.

Pathology

Tel: 927 1410 Fax: 977 1811

Bennett, F. I., BSc *WI*, MSc *McG.*, PhD *WI* Sr. Lectr., Chemical Pathology

Chan, H., BSc *Lond.*, MB BS *Lond.*, MD *Lond.* Sr. Lectr., Chemical Pathology

Char, Gurendra, MB BS *B'lore.*, MD *B'lore.* Sr. Lectr., Anatomical Pathology

Choo-Kang, E., MB BS *WI*, FRCPCan Sr. Lectr., Chemical Pathology

Coard, Kathleen, MSc *Brist.*, MB BS DM Sr. Lectr., Anatomical Pathology

Escoffrey, C. T., BSc *WI*, MB BS *WI*, DM *WI* Sr. Lectr.

Gibbs, Nigel, MB BS *WI*, DM *WI*, FRCPath, FRCPGlas, FACP Prof.

Hanchard, B., MB BS *Lond.*, FRCPCan Reader, Anatomical Physiology; Head*

Persaud, V., MB BS *Lond.*, MD *Lond.*, FRCPath Prof., Anatomical Pathology

Shah, D., MB BS *Baroda*, DM *WI* Sr. Lectr., Anatomical Pathology

Surgery, Radiology, Anaesthetics and Intensive Care

Tel: 927 1270 Fax: 927 1270

Branday, J. M., MB BS *WI*, MS *WI*, FRCSEd, FACS Sr. Lectr.

Carpenter, R., MB BChir *Camb.*, MA *Camb.*, FRCS, FRCSEd Prof. Emer.

Chutkan, W., MB BS *Lond.*, FRCS, FACS Sr. Lectr.

Fletcher, P., MB BS *Lond.*, FACS, FRCSEd Prof.; Head*

Hanna, W., MB BS *WI*, DM *WI*, FFARCSI   Sr. Lectr.; Head*

Moule, N., MB ChB *Edin.*, FRCR, FRCSEd   Sr. Lectr.; Head*

Raje, D., MB BS *Jiw.*, FRCS   Sr. Lectr.

Spencer, H., MB BS *WI*, MPH *WI*, FRCSEd, FACS   Sr. Lectr., Cardio-Thoracic Surgery

Vacant Posts: 3 Profs.

Tropical Metabolism Research Unit, see

Academic Staff (The Centre), above

SPECIAL CENTRES, ETC

Business, Institute of

Tel: 927 2775 Fax: 977 1605

Sampson, C., MA *Lanc.*   Dir.*

Nuclear Sciences, Centre for

Tel: 927 1777

Lalor, The Hon. G. C., OJ, CD, MSc *WI*, PhD *Lond.*   Dir. Gen.*

Vacant Posts: 1 Res. Fellow

CONTACT OFFICERS

General enquiries. Campus Registrar: Falloon, G. E. A., BA *WI*, MA *Oxf.*

[Information supplied by the institution as at May 1998, and edited by the ACU]

UNIVERSITY OF THE WEST INDIES, ST AUGUSTINE CAMPUS

Postal Address: St Augustine, Trinidad, West Indies
Telephone: 663 1359 **Fax**: 663 9684 **Cables**: Stomata, Port of Spain, Trinidad **Telex**: 24520 UWIWG

CHAIRMAN OF CAMPUS COUNCIL—Mansoor, Michael
PRINCIPAL AND PRO-VICE-CHANCELLOR*—Bourne, Prof. C., BSc *Lond.*, MSc *Birm.*, PhD *WI*
CAMPUS REGISTRAR—Ali, Zaffar, MA *Aberd.*
CAMPUS BURSAR—Lackhan, Sooknath B., BSc(Econ) *WI*
CAMPUS LIBRARIAN—Rouse-Jones, Margaret, BA *WI*, MA *Johns H.*, PhD *Johns H.*
PUBLIC ORATOR—Ramchand, Prof. K., MA *Edin.*, PhD *Edin.*

GENERAL INFORMATION

History. The campus was established in 1960.

Admission to first degree courses. See under University of the West Indies, above.

First Degrees. BA, BEd, BPharm, BSc, DDS, DVM, LLB, MB BS. See also under University of the West Indies, above.

Higher Degrees. DM, MA, MBA, MD, MEd, MSc, MPhil, PhD. See also under University of the West Indies, above.

Libraries. 355,000 monographs; 44,000 bound volumes of serials; over 6700 serials subscribed to. Medical sciences library: 19,000 volumes; 500 journal titles.

Fees (annual). Home students, undergraduate (full-time): TT$6367 (social sciences); TT$7743 (humanities and education); TT$10,611 (law); TT$11,976 (engineering); TT$12,617 (agriculture and natural sciences); TT$66,770 (medical sciences, students not subsidised by government). International students (full-time): US$12,000. Postgraduate (full-time): US$5102 (social sciences); US$6204 (humanities and education); US$9589 (engineering); US$10,110 (agriculture and natural sciences). All part-time students pay half full-time fees.

Academic Year. Two semesters: August–December; January–May.

Statistics. Staff: 1632 (582 academic, 1050 non-academic). Students: full-time 4198 (1940 men, 2258 women); part-time 2120; international 251 (160 men, 91 women); total 6318.

FACULTIES/SCHOOLS

Agriculture and Natural Sciences

Tel: 663 1334 Fax: (Agriculture) 663 9686; (Natural Sciences) 645 7132

Dean: McDavid, C. R., BSc *Wales*, PhD *Wales*
Administrative Assistant (Agriculture): Ramlakhan, Ivan
Administrative Assistant (Natural Sciences): Sobers, M., BA *WI*

Engineering

Tel: 663 1334 Fax: 662 4414

Dean: Kochhar, G. S., BE *Baroda*, MS *Wis.*, PhD *WI*
Administrative Assistant: Campbell, A., BA *WI*

Humanities and Education

Tel: 663 1334 Fax: (Humanities) 645 5601; (Education) 662 6615

Dean: Singh, V., BA *WI*
Administrative Assistant (Humanities): Akong, J., BA *H-W*
Administrative Assistant (Education): Adams-Stowe, M., BSc *WI*

Medical Sciences

Tel: 645 2640 Fax: 663 9836

Dean: Roopnarinesingh, S., MB BS *Durh.*, MD *Newcastle(UK)*, FRCOG, FACS
Administrative Officer: Garcia, A., BSc *WI*

Social Sciences

Tel: 663 1334 Fax: 662 6295

Dean: Watson, P., BCom *Leeds*, LèsEcon *Paris*, MèsEcon *Paris*, PhD *Paris*
Administrative Assistant: Steele, Linda, BSc *WI*

ACADEMIC UNITS

Agricultural Economics and Extension

Birla, S. C., MSc *Agra*, MS *Ill.*, PhD *Ill.*   Sr. Lectr.
Pemberton, C. A., MSc *WI*, PhD *Manit.*   Sr. Lectr.; Head*

Rankine, L. B., BSc *N.Carolina*, MS *Hawaii*, PhD *Hawaii*   Sr. Lectr.
Singh, R. H., MSc *Manit.*, PhD *Manit.*   Sr. Lectr.
Other Staff: 1 Temp. Lectr.
Vacant Posts: 1 Prof.
Research: food (human ecology)

Agricultural Extension

Seepersad, J., BSc *WI*, MSc *WI*, PhD *Ill.*   Sr. Lectr.
Other Staff: 3 Lectrs.
Vacant Posts: Dir.*
Research: extension analysis

Behavioural Sciences

Deosaran, R., MA *Tor.*, PhD *Tor.*   Prof.; Head*

Political Sciences

LaGuerre, J. G., BSc *WI*, MSc *WI*, PhD *Manc.*   Reader
Parris, W. C., BA *WI*, MSc *WI*   Sr. Lectr. (on leave)
Premdas, R., MA *Ill.*, PhD *Ill.*   Prof.
Other Staff: 2 Lectrs.; 1 Temp. Lectr.
Research: Caribbean politics; comparative/ international politics; political theory/ sociology; public policy/administration

Psychology/Sociology

5 Lectrs.
Research: criminology; gender studies; industrial sociology; social psychology; sociology of education/health

Social Work

3 Lectrs.

Biochemistry, see also Basic Health Sciences, School of (Pre-Clin. Scis.), below

No staff at present
Research: inflammatory response (plasma factors affecting RNA/synthesis in bone marrow cells); ornithine decarboxylase in RES cells; polyamine metabolism

Botany, see Plant Sci. under Life Scis.

Chemistry

Chang-Yen, I., BSc Guy., PhD Brist.   Sr. Lectr.
Hall, L., BSc WI, MSc Tor., PhD WI   Sr. Lectr.
Maharajh, D., BSc Mt.All., PhD S.Fraser   Sr. Lectr.
Maxwell, A., MSc WI, PhD Br.Col.   Sr. Lectr.
Mootoo, B. S., MSc Lond., PhD WI   Prof.
Narinesingh, D., BSc WI, PhD WI   Sr. Lectr.; Head*
Seaforth, C. E., BSc Lond., PhD Wales   Sr. Lectr.
Stephenson, D., BA York(UK), MPhil Sheff., PhD Lond.   Sr. Lectr.
Other Staff: 4 Lectrs.; 1 Temp. Lectr.
Research: biocensors; environmental monitoring; materials science; natural products

Computer Science, see Maths. and Computer Sci.

Creative Arts, see under Liberal Arts

Crop Science, see under Food Prodn.

Dentistry, School of, see below

Economics

Farrell, T., BA McG., MA Cornell, PhD Cornell   Sr. Lectr.
Pantin, D., BSc WI, MPhil Sus.   Sr. Lectr.; Head*
Theodore, K., BA Lond., MSc Lond., PhD Boston   Sr. Lectr.
Watson, P. K., BCom Leeds, PhD Paris I   Sr. Lectr.
Other Staff: 3 Lectrs.; 1 Temp. Lectr.
Vacant Posts: 1 Prof.

Education, School of

Research: curriculum theory, development and supervision; educational administration, planning and management; measurement and evaluation; teacher education

Educational Foundations and Teacher Education

Durojaiye, M. O. A., MA Manc., MSc Manc., PhD Manc.   Prof.
Keller, C., BA WI, MA Stan.   Lectr.; Head*
Other Staff: 11 Lectrs.; 5 Temp. Lectrs.
Vacant Posts: 1 Lectr.

Educational Research and Development

2 Res. Fellows

Engineering, Agricultural, see Engin., Mech.

Engineering, Chemical

Commissiong, E., BSc WI, MSc Mass., PhD Mass.   Sr. Lectr.
Farabi, H., BSc Arya-Mehr, MSc Aston, PhD Aston   Sr. Lectr.
McGaw, D. R., BSc Wales, MSc Wales, PhD WI   Prof.; Head*
Mellowes, W. A., MSc WI, PhD WI   Reader
Pilgrim, A., BSc WI, BSc(Eng) WI, PhD WI   Sr. Lectr.
Thomas, S., MSc New Br., BSc   Sr. Lectr. (on leave)
Young Hoon, A., BSc Birm., PhD Birm.   Sr. Lectr.
Other Staff: 5 Lectrs.
Vacant Posts: 2 Profs.; 1 Lectr.
Research: enhanced oil recovery; food sciences and technology; mineral processing; sugar technology; utilisation of biomass

Engineering, Civil

Charles, R. F., BSc WI, MPhil WI   Sr. Lectr.
Chin, M. W. S., BSc Lough., PhD Manc., FICE   Sr. Lectr.
Lewis, T. M., BSc Liv., MEng Liv., MSc Stir.   Sr. Lectr.
Osborne, R. W. A., BSc WI, PhD WI   Sr. Lectr.
Ramamurthy, K. N., BE Madr., MTech IIT Madras, PhD IIT Madras   Sr. Lectr.

Sharma, A. K., BSc Ban., ME Roor., PhD Raj.   Prof.; Head*
Suite, W., MSc WI, PhD WI   Prof.
Venkatarama, K., BE IIT Madras, MTech IIT Madras, PhD IIT Madras   Sr. Lectr.
Venkobacher, C., BTech IIT Madras, MTech IIT Kanpur, PhD IIT Kanpur, BSc
Other Staff: 6 Lectrs.
Research: analysis and design of hydraulic systems; analysis and design of structures; construction management and administration; environmental engineering; transport engineering

Engineering, Electrical and Computer

Copeland, Brian R., BSc WI, MSc Tor., PhD S.Calif.   Sr. Lectr.; Head*
Gift, S., BSc WI, PhD WI   Prof.
King, St. C. A., BSc Glas., MSc M.I.T., PhD Glas.   Prof., Electronics and Instrumentation
Sharma, C., MSc WI   Sr. Lectr.
Tripathi, J. N., BSc Agra, ME IISc., PhD Aston   Sr. Lectr.
Other Staff: 7 Lectrs.
Vacant Posts: 2 Sr. Lectrs.; 1 Lectr.
Research: data communications; energy systems; real time systems (transputers and industrial communications networks)

Engineering, Mechanical

Anantharaman, N., BE Annam., ME Annam., PhD Bom.   Sr. Lectr.
Bhattacharya, A. P., BSc Ban., ME Calc., DrIng T.U.Trondheim   Sr. Lectr.
Dumas, McD., BSc(Eng) WI, MS N.Y.State, MBA N.Y.State, PhD N.Y.State, FIMechE   Sr. Lectr.
Keshavan, S. Y., BE B'lore., ME IISc., PhD IISc.   Sr. Lectr.
Kochhar, G. S., BE Baroda, MS Wis., PhD WI   Prof.
Lau, S. M. J., BSc(Eng) WI, MEng Cornell, MSc WI   Sr. Lectr.
Narayan, C. V., BSA Guelph, MSc Guelph, PhD Mich.   Prof., Agricultural Engineering
Persad, P., BSc WI, BSc(Eng) WI, PhD WI   Sr. Lectr.; Head*
Sankat, C., PhD Guelph, MSc   Reader
Other Staff: 5 Lectrs.
Vacant Posts: 1 Prof.
Research: mechanical, industrial and agricultural engineering; production engineering and management

Food Production

Research: animals (ruminant and forage production); crops (production systems/ post-harvest physiology); soils

Crop Science

Brathwaite, R., BSc Poona, PhD   Sr. Lectr.
Wickham, Lynda, BSc WI, PhD WI   Sr. Lectr.
Wilson, L. A., MSc Lond., PhD Brist.   Prof.
Other Staff: 5 Lectrs.

Livestock Science

Rastogi, R. K., BVSc&AH UP Ag., MVSc UP Ag., PhD Minn.   Sr. Lectr.
Youssef, F. G., BSc Ain Shams, PhD Reading   Sr. Lectr.
Other Staff: 2 Lectrs.
Vacant Posts: 1 Prof.; 1 Lectr.

Soil Science

Gumbs, F. A., BSc Reading, PhD McG.   Reader, Soil Physics*
Other Staff: 1 Temp. Lectr.
Vacant Posts: 1 Prof.; 2 Lectrs.

French, see under Liberal Arts

History

Baptiste, F. A., BA Lond., MA Manc., PhD WI   Sr. Lectr.
Brereton, Bridget, MA Tor., PhD   Prof.
Haraksingh, K., BA WI, PhD Lond.   Sr. Lectr.
Samaroo, B., MA Delhi, PhD Lond.   Sr. Lectr.
Singh, K., BA WI, PhD WI   Sr. Lectr.; Head*
Other Staff: 3 Lectrs.
Vacant Posts: 1 Sr. Lectr.

Research: African history; American history; Asian history; Caribbean/West Indian history; European history

Law

1 Lectr.; 1 Temp. Lectr.

Liberal Arts

Research: French and Spanish language and literature; structure of the English language

Creative Arts

4 Lectrs.; 2 Asst. Lectrs.

French and Spanish

3 Lectrs.; 1 Temp. Lectr.

Language and Linguistics

Cowle, L., BA WI, PhD WI   Sr. Lectr.
Lalla, Barbara, BA WI, PhD WI   Sr. Lectr., English
Robertson, Ian, BA WI, PhD WI   Sr. Lectr.
Other Staff: 5 Lectrs.

Literatures in English

Ismond, Patricia, BA WI, PhD Kent   Sr. Lectr.
Ramchand, K., MA Edin., PhD Edin.   Prof., West Indies Literature
Rohlehr, D. F. G., BA Lond., PhD Birm.   Prof., West Indies Literature
Salick, R., BA Sir G.Wms., MA McG., PhD Manit.   Sr. Lectr.
Singh, V., BA WI   Sr. Lectr.
Other Staff: 1 Temp. Lectr.

Life Sciences

Plant Science

Comeau, Yasmin, BSc WI   Curator, National Herbarium
Duncan, E. J., BSc Lond., PhD St And.   Prof., Botany; Head*
McDavid, C. R., BSc Wales, PhD Wales   Sr. Lectr., Botany
Sirju-Charran, G., BSc WI, PhD WI   Sr. Lectr.
Other Staff: 5 Lectrs.; 1 Temp. Lectr.
Research: entomology and plant pathology; general botany and ecology; plant biotechnology; plant breeding; plant and crop physiology

Zoology

Bacon, P. R., BSc Lond., PhD WI   Prof.
Starr, C. K., BA Car., MA Kansas, PhD Georgia   Sr. Lectr.
Other Staff: 5 Lectrs.
Research: aquatic sciences/fisheries biology; parasitology; physiology and reproductive biology; terrestrial ecology/entomology

Livestock Science, see under Food Prodn.

Management Studies

Baptiste, R., BA Howard, MA Howard, MSc Manc.   Sr. Lectr.
Simms, E., MBA Ohio, MSc WI   Lectr.; Head*
Other Staff: 7 Lectrs.
Vacant Posts: 1 Prof.; 2 Lectrs.
Research: accounting (environmental accounting, reporting requirements); ethical considerations in business decision-making; human resource management (cross-cultural management, organisational behavioural issues); international marketing; management information systems

Mathematics and Computer Science

Crichlow, J. McL., BA Guy., MSc WI, PhD WI   Sr. Lectr., Computer Science
Farrell, E. J., BSc WI, MSc Wat., PhD Wat.   Prof.
Owen, D. R., BSc Lond., PhD Birm.   Sr. Lectr.
Posthoff, Christian, BSc Leip., PhD Leip., DrIng   Prof.; Head*
Ramkissoon, H., BSc WI, MSc Tor., PhD Calg.   Reader
Other Staff: 10 Lectrs.; 1 Temp. Lectr.
Vacant Posts: 1 Prof.
Research: coding theory and transportation planning; distributed computing; electro

(magnets) statics; fluid dynamics; graph theory and combinations

Medicine, School of, see below

Physics

Knight, J. C., BSc *WI*, PhD *Camb.*   Sr. Lectr.

McDoom, I. A., BSc *Lond.*, MSc *WI*, PhD *WI*   Sr. Lectr.

Saunders, R. McD., BSc *WI*, PhD *Lond.*   Prof.; Head*

Tang Kai, A., MSc *WI*, PhD *Uppsala*   Sr. Lectr.

Whiting, R., BSc *Brist.*, MSc *Sur.*, PhD *Lond.*   Sr. Lectr.

Other Staff: 3 Lectrs.

Vacant Posts: 2 Lectrs.

Research: earth materials; extragalactic astronomy; medical physics and bioengineering; physics and technology of materials; solar energy

Seismic Research

5 Res. Fellows

Plant Science, see under Life Scis.

Political Sciences, see under Behavioural Scis.

Psychology, see under Behavioural Scis.

Social Work, see under Behavioural Scis.

Sociology, see under Behavioural Scis.

Soil Science, see under Food Prodn.

Spanish, see French and Spanish under Liberal Arts

Surveying and Land Information

Opadeyi, J., MSc *Lagos*, MEng *New Br.*, PhD *New Br.*   Lectr.; Head*

Other Staff: 5 Lectrs.; 1 Temp. Lectr.

Vacant Posts: 1 Prof.

Research: cadastral studies; engineering geodetic surveying; land economy; photogrammetry; remote sensing

Veterinary Medicine, School of, see below

Zoology, see under Life Scis.

BASIC HEALTH SCIENCES, SCHOOL OF

Para-Clinical Sciences

Tel: 645 2640

Adesiyun, A. A., DVM *A.Bello*, MPH *Minn.*, PhD *Minn.*   Reader

Daisley, H., BSc *WI*, MB BS *WI*, DM *WI*   Sr. Lectr.

Georgiev, G. D., MD *Bulgarian Acad.Med.*   Prof., Community Health

Jones-Lecointe, Altheia, BSc *Lond.*, MB BS *WI*   Sr. Lectr.

Kaminjolo, J. S., BVetSc *E.Af.*, DMVJ *Leip.*   Prof.

Monteil, Michele A., BSc *Lond.*, MB BS *WI*, MSc *WI*   Sr. Lectr.

Telang, B. V., MB BS *Mys.*, MD *Bom.*   Prof.; Head*

Other Staff: 17 Lectrs.; 4 Temp. Lectrs.

Vacant Posts: 3 Profs.; 2 Lectrs.

Research: community and public health, including dental health; microbiology; pathology; pharmacology

Pre-Clinical Sciences

Tel: 645 2640

Addae, J. I., MB ChB *Ghana*, PhD *Lond.*   Sr. Lectr., Physiology; Head*

Barnes, J., BSc *Lond.*, MSc *Lough.*, PhD *Birm.*   Sr. Lectr., Biochemistry

Feytmans, E., MSc *Louvain*, PhD *Louvain*   Prof.

Isitor, G. N., MS *Kansas*, DVM *A.Bello*, PhD *A.Bello*   Sr. Lectr.

McRae, Amanda, BSc *Alabama*, PhD *Lyons I*   Prof., Anatomy

Melville, G. N., BSc *Manit.*, MSc *Dal.*, MD *Bochum*, PhD   Prof., Physiology

Molokwu, Eliezer C., BS *Tuskegee*, MS *Iowa*, DVM *Tuskegee*, PhD *A.Bello*   Sr. Lectr.

Ovchinnikov, N. A., MD *Perm State Inst.Med.*, PhD *Perm State Inst.Med.*   Sr. Lectr., Anatomy

Other Staff: 9 Lectrs.

Vacant Posts: 1 Sr. Lectr.; 1 Lectr.

Research: biochemistry (chronic disasters, including malnutrition); human anatomy (morphological and functional investigations of the brain: normal/pathological conditions); human physiology (normal biological macro-and microsystems)

DENTISTRY, SCHOOL OF

Clinical Dental Sciences

Tel: 645 2640 Fax: 645 3823

Thomson, E. R. E., BDS *Brist.*, MB ChB *Brist.*, FFDRCSI, FDSRCS   Prof.; Head*

Other Staff: 8 Lectrs.; 1 Asst. Lectr.

Vacant Posts: 5 Profs.

MEDICINE, SCHOOL OF

Clinical Medical Sciences

Tel: 645 2640 Fax: 663 9836

Ali, Zulaika, MB BS *WI*, DM *WI*   Sr. Lectr., Neonatology; Head*

Bartholomew, C. F., MB BCh BAO *Trinity(Dub.)*, MD *N.U.I.*, FRCPEd, FRCPI   Prof.

Khan, O., MB BS *Newcastle(UK)*, MSc *Lond.*, PhD *Lond.*   Sr. Lectr., Nuclear Medicine

Neehall, J. E., MB ChB *St And.*   Sr. Lectr., Psychiatry

Other Staff: 9 Lectrs.

Vacant Posts: 4 Profs.; 2 Sr. Lectrs.; 2 Lectrs.

Research: adult medicine; paediatric medicine; psychiatry; radiology and nuclear medicine

Clinical Surgical Sciences

Tel: 645 2640 Fax: 663 9836

Kumar, Kush, MB BS *Lucknow*, MS *Ban.*, PhD *Los Angeles*   Sr. Lectr., Orthopaedic Surgery

Naraynsingh, V., BSc *Lond.*, MB BS *WI*, FRCSEd   Reader

Pitt-Miller, Phyllis, MB ChB *Edin.*, FFARCS   Sr. Lectr., Anaesthesia and Intensive Care; Head*

Other Staff: 7 Lectrs.

Vacant Posts: 1 Prof.; 2 Lectrs.

Research: anaesthetic and intensive care; general orthopaedic and paediatric surgery; obstetrics and gynaecology; otorhinolaryngology

Obstetrics and Gynaecology

Tel: 663 6796 Fax: 663 9836

Gopeesingh, T. D., MB BS *WI*   Sr. Lectr.

Ramsewak, S., MB BS *WI*   Sr. Lectr.

Roopnarinesingh, S., MB BS *Durh.*, MD *Newcastle(UK)*, FRCOG, FACS   Prof.

Other Staff: 2 Lectrs.

VETERINARY MEDICINE, SCHOOL OF

Vacant Posts: Dir.*; 1 Lectr.

Clinical Veterinary Sciences

Tel: 645 2640 Fax: 663 9836

Ezeokoli, Chukwudozie O., BS *Cornell*, DVM *Cornell*, MS *Kansas State*, PhD *Yale*   Prof.; Acting Dir. of Sch.*

Other Staff: 7 Lectrs.; 1 Asst. Lectr.

Research: parasitology; pharmacology; physiology; public health; veterinary anatomy

SPECIAL CENTRES, ETC

Business, Institute of (IOB)

Tel: 645 7363

Tewarie, B., BA *Northwestern*, MA *Chic.*, PhD *Penn.*   Dir.*

Cocoa Research Unit

Butler, D., BSc *Durh.*, PhD *Wales*   Prof.; Head*

Other Staff: 1 Res. Fellow

Vacant Posts: 1 Res. Fellow; 1 Botanist/ Collector

Continuing Studies, School of (SOCS)

No staff at present

Distance Education, Centre for

Kuboni, O., BA *WI*, MA *C'dia.*, PhD *Open(UK)*   Acting Dir.*

Vacant Posts: 1 Editor

Gender and Development Studies, Centre for

Reddock, R., BSc *WI*, MSc *Inst.Soc.Stud.(The Hague)*, PhD *Amst.*   Sr. Lectr.

Research: feminist theory and epistemology; gender in Caribbean history; gender sciences and technology; manhood and masculinity; women and development

International Relations, Institute of (IIR)

Francis, A., LLB *Lond.*, LLM *Lond.*   Sr. Lectr.

Gonzales, P. A., BA *WI*, PhD *Geneva*   Sr. Lectr.

Parris, C., BA *WI*, MSc *WI*   Dir.*

Ramsaran, R., BSc *WI*, MSc *WI*, PhD *WI*   Reader

Wedderburn, C. M., PhD *Paris*   Sr. Lectr.

Other Staff: 1 Lectr.

Research: international relations of developing countries (Latin America/the Caribbean)

Language Learning, Centre for

Moodie-Kublalsingh, Sylvia, BA *N.U.I.*, LicFil&Let *Madrid*, DrFil&Let *Madrid*   Sr. Lectr.; Dir.*

Other Staff: 1 Lectr.

Medical Education, Centre for, and Skills Laboratory

Tel: 654 2640

Uchegbu, B. O., BA *Nigeria*, MA *N.Y.*, PhD *N.Y.*   Sr. Lectr.

Other Staff: 1 Lectr.

Vacant Posts: 3 Lectrs.

Monetary Studies, Caribbean Centre for (CCMS)

Clarke, L., BSc *Guy.*, MBA *Windsor*, PhD *WI*   Consultant; Dir.*

Other Staff: 1 Res. Fellow

Research: financial innovations in the Caribbean; micro-operations of Caribbean commercial banks; monetary transmissions mechanisms; private pension funds in the Caribbean; role of the US dollar in the Caribbean Community (Caricom)

Social and Economic Research, Institute of (ISER)

Ryan, Prof. S., BA *Tor.*, PhD *Cornell*   Dir.*

Research: privatisation; race relations; sociology of enterprise; voting behaviour

CONTACT OFFICERS

Academic affairs. Campus Registrar: Ali, Zaffar, MA *Aberd.*

Accommodation. Assistant Registrar (Appointments): ......

Admissions (first degree). Assistant Registrar: Bacon, Tyra, BSc *WI*, MSc *WI*

Admissions (higher degree). Assistant Registrar: Bacon, Tyra, BSc *WI*, MSc *WI*

Adult/continuing education. Resident Tutor: Bernard, Lennox, BA *WI*, MEd *Tor.*

Alumni. Senior Assistant Registrar (Student Affairs): Cowan, Victor, BA *Lond.*

Archives. Record Manager: Georges, Jo-Ann, BA *WI*, MLS *Col.*

Careers. Senior Assistant Registrar (Student Affairs): Cowan, Victor, BA *Lond.*

Development/fund-raising. Principal and Pro-Vice-Chancellor: Bourne, Prof. C., BSc *Lond.*, MSc *Birm.*, PhD *WI*

Distance education. Curriculum Specialist (Distance Education): Harvey, Claudia, BA *WI*, PhD *Tor.*

Estates and buildings/works and services.
Estate Manager: Nobbee, Kenrick, BSc *Strath.*,
MSc *Strath.*

Examinations. Assistant Registrar: George,
Jessie-Ann, BA *Howard*, MEd *Howard*

Finance. Campus Bursar: Lackhan, Sooknath
B., BSc(Econ) *WI*

General enquiries. Campus Registrar: Ali,
Zaffar, MA *Aberd.*

Health services. Campus Registrar: Ali, Zaffar,
MA *Aberd.*

Library (chief librarian/enquiries). Campus
Librarian: Rouse-Jones, Margaret, BA *WI*,
MA *Johns H.*, PhD *Johns H.*

Personnel/human resources. Assistant
Registrar (Appointments): ......

Public relations, information and marketing.
Public Relations Co-ordinator: Henry,
Robert, BSc *WI*

Purchasing. Campus Bursar: Lackhan,
Sooknath B., BSc(Econ) *WI*

Scholarships, awards, loans. Campus Registrar:
Ali, Zaffar, MA *Aberd.*

Security. Farrell, Steve

Sport and recreation. Co-ordinator, Sports
and Physical Education: Gloudon, Iva, BSc
Ill., MSc *Ill.*, EdD *Mass.*

Student welfare/counselling. Senior Assistant
Registrar (Student Affairs): Cowan, Victor,
BA *Lond.*

Students from other countries. Assistant
Registrar: Bacon, Tyra, BSc *WI*, MSc *WI*

University press. Public Relations Co-
ordinator: Henry, Robert, BSc *WI*

Women. Reddock, Rhoda, BSc *WI*, MSc
Inst.Soc.Stud.(The Hague), PhD *Amst.*

*[Information supplied by the institution as at 20 March
1998, and edited by the ACU]*

ZAMBIA

Copperbelt University (p. 1820)　　　　University of Zambia (p. 1821)

COPPERBELT UNIVERSITY

Established 1987; previously University of Zambia at Ndola

Member of the Association of Commonwealth Universities

Postal Address: PO Box 21692, Kitwe, Zambia
Telephone: (02) 222066, 223015, 225155 **Fax**: (02) 222469, 222881, 223972 **E-mail**: cbu@zamnet.zm
Cables: CBU Kitwe **Telex**: CBU ZA 53270 KITWE

CHANCELLOR—Mulikita, F., BA *Rhodes*, MA *Stan.*, Hon. LLD *Fort Hare*
CHAIRMAN OF COUNCIL—Chali, Isaac C. T., LLB *Zambia*
VICE-CHANCELLOR*—Simwinga, George K., BA *Zambia*, MA *Wis.*, PhD
　Pitt.
DEPUTY VICE-CHANCELLOR—Lungu, J.
ACTING REGISTRAR‡—Kapika, K. K., BA *Zambia*, MA *Lond.*
BURSAR—Samakayi, F. K., FCIS
LIBRARIAN—Lundu, M. C., BA *Zambia*, MSLS *Case W.Reserve*, PhD *Sheff.*

GENERAL INFORMATION

History. The university was established in 1987. It is located 8km from Kitwe.

Admission. General entrance requirements: minimum 5 passes in General Certificate of Education (GCE) exam, or credit passes in at least 5 subjects at Cambridge Overseas School Certificate level, or equivalent.

First Degrees. BAc, BArch, BBA, BEng, BSc.
　BAc, BBA: 4 years; BArch, BEng: 5 Years;
BSc: 4 or 5 years depending on subject studied.

Higher Degrees. MBA: 18 months.

Libraries. 25,000 volumes; 148 periodicals subscribed to.

Fees. Undergraduate: K1,500,000 (Zambian); US$3500 (international). Postgraduate: US$2500 (Zambian); US$3750 (international).

Academic Year. March–November.

Income. (1995–96). Total, K370,000,000.

FACULTIES/SCHOOLS

Built Environment, School of
Tel: (02) 225086
Dean: Silengo, M.
Secretary: Soko, E. Z.

Business, School of
Tel: (02) 227946, 228006 *Fax*: (02) 229354
Dean: Gillings, T., PhD
Secretary: Nkoma, J. M.

Consultancy, Applied Research and Extension Studies, Institute of
Director: Taylor, T. K., MS *Haifa(Technion)*, DSc
　Haifa(Technion), BSc
Secretary: Mugala, C.

Forestry and Wood Sciences, School of
Tel: (02) 225761
Dean: Moonga, P. C.
Secretary: Mubiana, I. T.

Technology, School of
Tel: (02) 228212
Dean: Kanungwe, Capt. F., MSc *Ulyanovsk*
Secretary: Daka, M. P.

ACADEMIC UNITS

Accounting and Finance
Tel: (02) 228006 *Fax*: (02) 229354
Gillings, T., PhD　Sr. Lectr.
Ronan, N., MBA *N.U.I.*, MEd *Sheff.*　Head*

Architecture and Building Science
Tel: (02) 225086
Hill, W. F., BArch *Brist.*, MA
　Newcastle(UK)　Assoc. Prof.; Head, Archit.
Ngoma, G. C., BEng *Belf.*, MSc *Belf.*　Lectr.;
　Head*
Shakantu, W. M., BSc *Copperbelt*, MSc
　Reading　Head, Bldg. Sci.
Topham, P. M.　Sr. Lectr.
Wetter, M., DrIngArch *T.U.Berlin*　Sr. Lectr.

Business Administration
Tel: (02) 228006 *Fax*: (02) 229354
Chilipamushi, D., BA *Zambia*, MSc *Brad.*
Kapika, K. K., BA *Zambia*, MA *Lond.*　Lectr.;
　Head*
Mumba, K., BA *Zambia*, PhD *Lond.*　Sr. Lectr.
Tembo, J. M., BA *Zambia*, MBA *McM.*, PhD
　N.U.I.　Sr. Lectr.
Research: consultancy in public and private sector

Computer Science
Tel: (02) 228212
Chikowa, P. C., BSc *Car.*, MSc
　Kaiserslautern　Lectr.; Head*

Engineering, Chemical
Tel: (02) 228212
Mwale, Alex H., BEng *Wales*, MSc
　Wales　Lectr.; Head*
Research: water hycinth: Kafue river and
　Konkola deep

Engineering, Electrical
Tel: (02) 228212
Mwangana, G. M.　Head*

Research: pollution in Kafue river
　(environmental impact assessment for new
　companies)

Forestry
Tel: (02) 225761
5 Lectrs.
Research: forestry inventory and environmental assessments

Mining
Tel: (02) 228212
Lesho, M. B., BEng *CNAA*　Lectr.; Head*

Planning and Land Economy
Tel: (02) 225086 *Fax*: (02) 225086
Boakye, E., MSc *Aston*　Acting Head*
Other Staff: 1 Lectr.

Postgraduate Studies
Tel: (02) 228006 *Fax*: (02) 229354
Mumba, K., BA *Zambia*, PhD *Lond.*　Sr. Lectr.
Nyirenda, J. C., BSc *Newcastle(UK)*, PhD
　Kent　Acting Head*

Production Management
Tel: (02) 228006 *Fax*: (02) 229354
Mukula, E. B., BEng *Liv.*, MSc *Limerick*　Lectr.;
　Head*
Mwila, Col. L., BSc *Zambia*, MSc *Zambia*　Sr.
　Lectr.

CONTACT OFFICERS

Academic affairs. Senior Assistant Registrar:
　Kalima, G.
Accommodation. Accommodation Officer:
　Moyo, G.
Admissions (first degree). Senior Assistant
　Registrar: Kalima, G.
Admissions (higher degree). Senior Assistant
　Registrar: Kalima, G.
Adult/continuing education. Co-ordinator:
　Chunda, E.
Careers. Placement Officer: Mkunsha, Brown
Computing Services. Co-ordinator: Taylor, T.
　K., MS *Haifa(Technion)*, DSc *Haifa(Technion)*, BSc
Consultancy services. Director: Taylor, T. K.,
　MS *Haifa(Technion)*, DSc *Haifa(Technion)*, BSc

Estates and buildings/works and services.
   Director of Works: Sepiso, L., BSc *Zambia*
Examinations. Senior Assistant Registrar:
   Kalima, G.
Finance. Bursar: Samakayi, F. K., FCIS
General enquiries. Acting Registrar: Kapika,
   K. K., BA *Zambia*, MA *Lond*.
Health services. Medical Officer: Simooya, O.
   O., BSc *Zambia*, MB ChB *Zambia*, MSc *Ib*.
International office. Dean of Students: Beele,
   E. M., LLB *Zambia*, MA *Warw*., LLM *Wis*., PhD
   Warw.
Library (chief librarian). Librarian: Lundu,
   M. C., BA *Zambia*, MSLS *Case W.Reserve*, PhD
   Sheff.

Personnel/human resources. Senior Assistant
   Registrar: Chiyanika, R. M., BA *Zambia*
Public relations, information and marketing.
   Planning/Public Relations Officer:
   Munyemba, A. S., BA *Zambia*
Publications. Planning/Public Relations Officer:
   Munyemba, A. S., BA *Zambia*
Purchasing. Purchasing Officer: Chishimba, J.
Research. Director: Taylor, T. K., MS
   Haifa(Technion), DSc *Haifa(Technion)*, BSc
Safety. Director of Works: Sepiso, L., BSc
   Zambia
Security. Chief Security Officer: Chilala, Lt.-
   Col. (Retd.) L. T.

Sport and recreation. Sports Officer: Ng'ambi,
   A.
Staff development and training. Staff
   Development Officer: Lungu, C.
Student welfare/counselling. Head,
   Counselling Unit: Silavwe, G. W., MSc *Wales*
Students from other countries. Dean of
   Students: Beele, E. M., LLB *Zambia*, MA
   Warw., LLM *Wis*., PhD *Warw*.

[Information supplied by the institution as at 9 March 1998, and edited by the ACU]

UNIVERSITY OF ZAMBIA

Founded 1965

Member of the Association of Commonwealth Universities

Postal Address: PO Box 32379, Lusaka, Zambia
Telephone: (01) 293058, 293580, 291777 **Fax**: (01) 253952 **E-mail**: registrar@unza.gn.ape.org
Cables: UNZA, Lusaka **Telex**: UNZALU ZA 44370

CHANCELLOR—......
CHAIRMAN OF COUNCIL—Nalumango, N., MB ChB *Natal*
ACTING VICE-CHANCELLOR*—Chanda, Prof. Mutale W., MSc *Qu*., PhD *Wales*
DEPUTY VICE-CHANCELLOR (ACTING)—Mumba, E. C., BA(Educn) *Zambia*, MSc *Indiana*, PhD
   Br.Col.
REGISTRAR—Tandeo, M., BAEd *Zambia*, MEd *Leeds*
UNIVERSITY LIBRARIAN—Mwacalimba, H. C., MSLS *Syr*., PhD *Syr*., BLS
BURSAR—......

GENERAL INFORMATION

History. The university was established in 1965.

First Degrees. The following subjects may be studied at first degree level: agriculture, education, engineering, humanities and social sciences, law, medicine, mines, veterinary medicine.

Higher Degrees. A number of postgraduate courses are offered depending on availability of supervisors.

Fees (1996–97, annual). Arts: K66,700 (full-time), K167,000 (part-time); science: K59,900 (full-time), K225,000 (part-time); medicine, including veterinary medicine: K1,668,000 (full-time), K417,000 (part-time).

Academic Year. Two semesters.

Income. Total, K7,532,996.

Statistics. Students: 3464 (2667 men, 797 women).

FACULTIES/SCHOOLS

Agricultural Sciences
Dean: Mwape, F. A., BAgrSc *Zambia*, MAgrEc MSc PhD

Education
Acting Dean: Chikalanga, I. W., BA(Educn) *Zambia*, MA *Leeds*, PhD *Reading*

Engineering
Dean: Kanyanga, S. B., BEng *Zambia*, MSc *Lond*., PhD *Sheff*.

Humanities and Social Sciences
Dean: Chileshe, J. D., MA *Sus*., DPhil *Sus*., BAEd

Law
Dean: Simbyakula, N. R., LLB *Zambia*, LLM *Zambia*, SJD *Wis*.

Medicine
Dean: Munkonge, Prof. L., MB BS MD, FRCS

Mines
Dean: Kamona, F. A., BSc MSc PhD

Natural Sciences
Dean: Theo, D., BSc *Zambia*, MSc *Wales*, PhD *Wales*

Veterinary Medicine
Dean: Samui, K. L., DVM *Kiev*, MSc *Louisiana State*, PhD *Louisiana State*

ACADEMIC UNITS

Administrative Studies, see Pol. and Admin. Studies

Agricultural Economics and Extension Education
Tel: (01) 295419 Fax: (01) 295448
Maimbo, F., BA *Zambia*, MSc *Guelph*, MPhil *Reading* Sr. Lectr.
Musaba, E. C., BScAgric *Zambia*, MSc PhD Head*

Animal Science
Tel: (01) 295422 Fax: (01) 295448
Lungu, J. C., MSc *Mass*., PhD *Manit*. Sr. Lectr.
Yambayamba, E. S. K., BAgricSc *Zambia*, MSc *Alta*., PhD *Alta*. Lectr.; Head*

Biochemistry, see Chem. and Biochem.

Biology
Tel: (01) 254406
Chidumayo, E. N., BSc *Zambia*, MSc *Zambia* Prof.
Kapooria, R. G., BSc *Agra*, MSc *Agra*, PhD *Agra* Assoc. Prof.
Mumba, L. E., BSc *Zambia*, MSc *Wales*, PhD *Camb*. Head*
Mwauluka, K., BSc *Lond*., PhD *Cant*. Prof.
Shinondo, C., MSc *Cant*., MPH *Tulane*, PhD *Cant*., DSc *Tulane* Sr. Lectr.
Zulu, J. N., BSc *Zambia*, PhD *Lond*. Assoc. Prof.

Business and Economic Studies
Tel: (01) 253827
Ndulo, M., MA *Ohio*, PhD *Mich*., BA Sr. Lectr.; Head*
Seshamani, V., MA *Bom*., MA *Stan*. Prof.

Chemistry and Biochemistry
Tel: (01) 254406
Anekwe, G., MSc *Tuskegee*, PhD *N.Y*. Prof.
Banda, S. F., BSc MSc PhD Head*
Belenavicious, K. K., MSc *U.S.S.R.Acad.Sc*., PhD *U.S.S.R.Acad.Sc*.
Cernak, J., PhD *Purkyne*, MSc Prof.
Kumar, G., BSc *Alld*., MSc *Kanpur*, PhD *Alld*. Sr. Lectr.
Obidoa, O., BSc *Nigeria*, PhD *Ib*., MSc Prof.
Phiri, S. J., MA *Boston*, PhD *Boston*, BSc Sr. Lectr.
Prakash, S., BSc *Lucknow*, MSc *Lucknow*, PhD *Lucknow* Sr. Lectr.
Siamwiza, M., BSc *Bowdoin*, MS *Mass*., PhD *Mass*.

Crop Science

Tel: (01) 295655 Fax: (01) 295655

Deedat, Y., MSc Guelph, PhD Manit., BSc Sr. Lectr.

Mwala, M. S., BAgrSc Zambia, PhD Columbia, MSc Lectr.; Head*

Development Studies

Tel: (01) 253827

Akuffo, F. W. B., BA Ghana, DPhil Oxf. Sr. Lectr.

Mutesa, F., BA Zambia, MA Constance, DrRerSoc Constance Lectr.; Head*

Economics, see Agric. Econ. and Extension Educn., and Business and Econ. Studies

Education

Adult Education and Extension Studies

Tel: (01) 253974

Kamwengo, M. M., BA Zambia, MSc Flor., PhD Ill. Sr. Lectr.

Mwansa, D. M., BA Zambia, MEd Tor. Sr. Lectr.

Sibalwa, D. M., BA Marian, MA Ball, PhD Mich. Head*

Other Staff: 1 Lectr.

Education Administration and Policy Studies

Tel: (01) 253974

Adeyinka, A. A., BA Ib., MEd Ib., PhD Wales Prof.

Kelly, Fr. M. J., MA N.U.I., LPh St.Joseph(Dublin), STL St.Joseph(Dublin), PhD Birm. Prof.

Lungwangwa, G., MEd Ill., PhD Ill., BA Sr. Lectr.

Sikwibele, A. L., BA Zambia, MA Stan., PhD Ill. Sr. Lectr.; Head*

Education Psychology, Sociology and Special Education

Tel: (01) 290675

Chakulimba, O. C., BA(Educn) Zambia, MEd Harv., PhD Tor. Head*

In-Service Education and Advisory Services

Tel: (01) 292701

Chishimba, C. P., MA Col., PhD Col., BA(Educn) MEd Sr. Lectr.

Tambulukani, G., BA(Educn) Zambia, MSc Aston Head*

Language and Social Science Education

Tel: (01) 253974

Carmody, Rev. B. P., BPhil Trinity(Dub.), MA Grad.Theol.Union, PhD Grad.Theol.Union Sr. Lectr.

Namafe, C. M., BSc(Educn) Zambia, MEd McG., PhD Lond. Acting Head*

Mathematics and Science Education

Kostyuk, V. S., PhD Kiev Prof.

Nkhata, B., BA(Educn) Zambia, MA Lond. Head.*

Education, Extension, see Agric. Econ. and Extension Educn.

Engineering, Agricultural

Tel: (01) 253194

Kwendakwema, N. J., BEng Zambia, MSc McG., PhD Utah Head*

Engineering, Civil

Tel: (01) 253194

Kang, L. Q., MSc Hohai, PhD Texas, BEng Prof.

Mukherje, P. R., MSc W.Virginia, PhD W.Virginia, BEng Sr. Lectr.

Mulenga, M. N., MSc Rutgers, PhD Alta., BEng Lectr.; Head*

Zhang, F., BCEng MEng PhD Sr. Lectr.

Engineering, Electrical and Electronic

Tel: (01) 253194

Lo-A-Njoe, L. H., MSc T.U.Eindhoven, BSc Sr. Lectr.; Head*

Engineering, Mechanical

Tel: (01) 253194

Kanyanga, S. B., BEng Zambia, MSc Lond., PhD Sheff. Sr. Lectr.

Ngandu, A. N., BEng Zambia, MSc Cran., PhD Nott. Head*

Vasilijev, V. A., MSc Moscow, PhD Moscow Sr. Lectr.

Yamba, F. D., MSc Moscow, PhD Leeds Prof.

Engineering, Mining

Tel: (01) 251672

Chanda, Mutale W., MSc Qu., PhD Wales Assoc. Prof.

Krishna, R., MPhil Nott., PhD Leeds Prof.; Head*

Sinkala, T., BMinSc Zambia, MSc Luleå, PhD Luleå Sr. Lectr.

Engineering, Survey

Bujakiewick, A., MSc Warsaw, PhD Warsaw, DSc Warsaw Prof.†; Head*

Lahtinen, R. Sr. Lectr.

Extension Studies and Conferences

No staff at present

Gender Studies

Milimo, M. C., BA(Educn) Zambia, MA Lond., DPhil Oxf. Sr. Lectr.; Head*

Sinyangwe, M. I., BA Zambia, MA Chic., PhD Calif.

Geography

Tel: (01) 254406 Fax: (01) 253552

Kajoba, G. M., MA Arizona, MPhil Sus., BA(Educn) Sr. Lectr.

Mulenga, C. M., MA Zambia, PhD Lond., BA Lectr.; Head*

Geology

Tel: (01) 251672

Nyambe, I. A., MSc Windsor, PhD Ott., BSc Lectr.; Head*

History

Tel: (01) 253827

Mulenga, F. E., BA Zambia, MA Zambia Lectr.; Head*

Law

Tel: (01) 290739 Fax: (01) 290733

Anyangwe, C., LLB Yaounde, LLM N.Y., PhD Lond. Assoc. Prof.

Kamuwanga, B. M., LLB Zambia, LLM Wis., SJD Wis. Sr. Lectr.

Ngandu, F., LLB Zambia, LLM N.Y., PhD Lond. Sr. Lectr.

Simbyakula, N. R., LLB Zambia, LLM Zambia, SJD Wis. Sr. Lectr.

Library Studies

Tel: (01) 253974

Kularatne, E. D. T., BA Lond., PhD Lond. Lectr.; Head*

Literature and Languages

Tel: (01) 253827

Chanda, V. M., PhD Zaire Sr. Lectr.

Chileshe, J. D., MA Sus., DPhil Sus., BAEd Sr. Lectr.

Hirst, S. B., MA Oxf., MA Essex, BA Sr. Lectr.; Head*

Musonda, M. M., MA Kent State, PhD Bryn Mawr Assoc. Prof.

Mass Communication

Tel: (01) 253827

Kasoma, F., BA Zambia, MA Oregon, PhD Prof.; Head*

Nkunika Billy, S., MFA Sr. Lectr.

Mathematics

Tel: (01) 254406

Chikunji, J. C., BSc Zambia, MSc Zambia, PhD Lectr.; Head*

Choudhary, B., MSc Lond., PhD Lond., MSc Prof.

Jain, S., BA Delhi, MA Delhi, MPhil Delhi Sr. Lectr.

Ngwengwe, A., BSc Zambia, MSc Wales, MSc Mass., PhD Wales, PhD Cornell Lectr.; Head*

Theo, D., BSc Zambia, MSc Wales, PhD Wales Assoc. Prof.

Medicine, see below

Metallurgy and Mineral Processing

Tel: (01) 251672

Chama, C. C., BMinSc Zambia, MSc Penn., PhD Penn. Sr. Lectr.

Jere, E. H., BSc Rutgers, MSc Lehigh, PhD Lehigh Sr. Lectr.

Mwalula, J. B., PhD Ljubljana, BSc MSc MPhil Sr. Lectr.

Nkonde, G. K., MSc Helsinki, DrTech Helsinki Sr. Lectr.

Simukanga, S., BMinSc Zambia, MMinSc Zambia, PhD Strath. Sr. Lectr.; Head*

Philosophy

Tel: (01) 253827

Dillon-Mallone, C., PhD N.Y. Assoc. Prof.; Head*

Physics

Tel: (01) 254406

Husain, M. M., BSc Karachi, MSc Karachi, PhD Louvain Sr. Lectr.

Jain, P. C., BSc Delhi, MSc Delhi, PhD Delhi Prof.

Mweene, V. H., BSc Zambia, MSc Zambia, PhD Sur. Lectr.; Head*

Sheth, C. V., BSc Karn., MSc Karn., PhD Karn. Prof.

Singh, S., BSc Meerut, MSc Meerut, PhD Indore Sr. Lectr.

Political and Administrative Studies

Tel: (01) 253827

Mulikita, N. M., BA Zambia, DrRerSoc Constance, MA Lectr.; Head*

Psychology

Tel: (01) 253827

Kathuria, R., BA Delhi, PhD Lond. Sr. Lectr.

Menon, A., BA Madr., MA Delhi, PhD Sr. Lectr.

Mwape, G., BA Zambia, MPhil Camb., MEd Zambia Lectr.; Head*

Social Development Studies

Tel: (01) 253827

Kapungwe, A., BA Zambia, MA Ghana, MA Zambia, PhD Penn. Head*

Siamwiza, R., BA Tulsa, MA Boston Sr. Lectr.

Soil Sciences

Tel: (01) 250587 Fax: (01) 295448

Chinene, V. R. N., BAgrSc Zambia, MSc Wageningen, PhD Hawaii Assoc. Prof.

Chipeleme, A. C., BSc Zambia, MSc CNAA Head*

Lungu, O. I. M., BAgrSc Zambia, MSc Newcastle, PhD California Sr. Lectr.

Surveying

Tel: (01) 253194

Bujakiewicz, A., MSc Warsaw, PhD Warsaw, DSc Warsaw Prof.; Head*

Veterinary Medicine, see below

MEDICINE

Tel: (01) 252641

Anatomy

Karashani, J. T., MB ChB Mak., PhD Qu. Prof.; Head*

Community Health

Baboo, K. S., MD All India IMS, MB BS Lectr.; Head*

Chiwele, L., MD Ljubljana, MPH Boston Acting Head*

Sims, P., BDS Lond., MB BS Lond., MSc
Liv. Assoc. Prof.

Medicine

Matondo, P. M., MB ChB Zambia Head*
Tshibwabwa-Tumba, E., MD Kinshasa, PhD
Louvain Assoc. Prof.
Wolff, M. M., MPH Johns H., BDN MMed
PhD Sr. Lectr.

Nursing (Post Basic)

Lambwe, L.
Ndulo, J. C. C., BSc Madr., MSc Boston Lectr.;
Head*

Obstetrics and Gynaecology

Agboola, A., BM BS MD, FRCOG Prof.
Ahmed, Y., BSc Manc., BM S'ton. Lectr.; Head*

Paediatrics and Child Health

Bhat, G. J., MB BS Karn., MD Bom. Assoc.
Prof.; Head*
Chintu, C., MD Tor., FRCPCan Prof.
Chomba, E. M. N., BSc Zambia, MB ChB
Zambia Sr. Lectr.
Shakankale, BSc Zambia, MB ChB Zambia Acting
Head*

Pathology and Microbiology

Shinondo, C. J., BSc Tulane, MSc Camb., MPH
Tulane, PhD Tulane, ScD Tulane, BSc PhD

Physiological Sciences

Khare, A. K., MB BS Kanpur, MD Kanpur Sr.
Lectr.
Manakov, A. K., BSc Mys., PhD Moscow,
MSc Prof.
Prasanna, C. V., MSc Baroda, BSc PhD Sr.
Lectr.; Head*

Psychiatry

Haworth, A., MB BChir Camb., MA Camb., BA,
FRCPsych Prof.

Surgery

Desai, G., MB BS, FRCS Sr. Lectr.
Erzingatsian, K., FRCSI Assoc. Prof.; Head*
Jellis, J. E., MB BS Lond., FRCS Assoc. Prof.
Munkonge, L., MB BS MD, FRCS Prof.

VETERINARY MEDICINE

Tel: (01) 291512, 291508

Biomedical Sciences

Lovelace, C. E. A., BSc Birm., PhD Lond. Prof.
Siulapwa, N. J., BSc Zambia, MSc Newcastle(UK),
PhD Wales Nutritional Physiology; Head*

Clinical Studies

Lutz, W. W., DVM Munich Sr. Lectr.
Omamegbe, O. J., DVM Ib., MVM Glas. Assoc.
Prof.
Phiri, I. K., MVSc Leip., MEd F.U.Berlin, PhD
Edin. Acting Head*
Sayer, D. A. D., BVMS Glas., FRCVS Assoc.
Prof.; Head*

Disease Control

Fujikura, T., DVM Hokkaido, PhD
Hokkaido Visiting Assoc. Prof.
Mlangwa, J. E. D., BVM Nair., MSc Lond., PhD
Copenhagen Sr. Lectr.
Nambota, A., DVM Leip., MSc
Leip. Parasitology/Protozology; Head*
Pandey, S. G., BSc BVSc MVSc Assoc. Prof.
Takatori, I., DVM Tokyo, PhD Tokyo Visiting
Prof.

Paraclinical Studies

Chitambo, H., BScAgric Zambia, MSc Wales, PhD
Osaka Head, Parasitology/protozology*
Makumyaviri, A. M., DVM Lubumbashi,
DSc Prof.
Musonda, M. M., BVM Nair., PhD Sr. Lectr.
Mwase, T. E., BSc Zambia, MSc Lond. Lectr.;
Head*
Nagabayashi, T., DVM Hokkaido, PhD
Hokkaido Visiting Prof.
Sharma Nath, R., BVSc&AH Agra, MVSc Agra,
PhD Agra Prof.

SPECIAL CENTRES, ETC

Creative Arts, Centre for

Mapopa, M., BA Zambia, MA Ghana, PhD Sr.
Lectr.; Dir.*
Ngandu, J., BMusE Bard Arts Manager

Distance Education, Directorate of

Tel: (01) 290719

Siaciwena, R. C. M., BA Zambia, MA Lond., PhD
Wales Assoc. Prof.; Dir.*

Economic and Social Research, Institute of

Tel: (01) 294131

Kashoki, M. E., BA C.U.A., MA Baroda, MA
Mich. Res. Prof.
Saasa, O., BA Zambia, MSc S'ton., PhD
S'ton. Assoc. Prof.; Dir.*

Research and Postgraduate Studies, Directorate of

Tel: (01) 290258

Lungwangwa, G., BA(Educn) Zambia, MEd
Zambia, PhD Ill.

CONTACT OFFICERS

Academic affairs. Deputy Registrar (Academic
Affairs): Mwansa, M., BA Zambia, MSocSci
Accommodation. Dean of Students' Affairs:
Banda, D. A., BA Zambia, LLM Zambia
Admissions (first degree). Deputy Registrar
(Academic Affairs): Mwansa, M., BA Zambia,
MSocSci
Admissions (higher degree). Director,
Directorate of Research and Graduate Studies:
Lungwangwa, G., BA(Educn) Zambia, MEd
Zambia, PhD Ill.
Alumni. Acting Deputy Dean, Student Affairs:
Ngwenya, M., BA(Eucn) Zambia

Careers. Student Counsellor: Mseteka, N., BA
Zambia
Computing services. Director: Munsaka, J.,
BCompSci Zambia
Consultancy services. Deputy Vice-Chancellor
(Acting): Mumba, E. C., BA(Educn) Zambia,
MSc Indiana, PhD Br.Col.
Credit transfer. Bursar: ......
Development/fund-raising. Bursar: ......
Distance education. Director, Directorate of
Distance Education: Lungwangwa, G.,
BA(Educn) Zambia, MEd Zambia, PhD Ill.
Estates and buildings/works and services.
Resident Architect: Baxi, J. B.
Examinations. Deputy Registrar (Academic
Affairs): Mwansa, M., BA Zambia, MSocSci
Finance. Bursar: ......
General enquiries. Registrar: Tandeo, M.,
BAEd Zambia, MEd Leeds
Health services. Medical Officer:
Mulasikwanda, T., BSc Zambia, BSc(HB)
Zambia
Industrial liaison. Deputy Vice-Chancellor
(Acting): Mumba, E. C., BA(Educn) Zambia,
MSc Indiana, PhD Br.Col.
Library (chief librarian). University Librarian:
Mwacalimba, H. C., MSLS Syr., PhD Syr., BLS
Personnel/human resources. Staff
Development Officer: Mponda, K., BA
Public relations, information and marketing.
Community Relations: Kamanga, B. H.
Publications. Acting Publisher: Kasankha, S.,
BA (Educn) Zambia
Purchasing. Purchasing Officer: Sami, C. S.
Research. Director, Directorate of Research and
Graduate Studies: Lungwangwa, G.,
BA(Educn) Zambia, M(Educn) Zambia, PhD Ill.
Scholarships, awards, loans. Staff
Development Officer: Mponda, K., BA
Security. Chief Security Officer: Chimoka, J. C.
Sport and recreation. Dean of Students'
Affairs: Banda, D. A., BA Zambia, LLM Zambia
Staff development and training. Staff
Development Officer: Mponda, K., BA
Student union. President: Yuyi, Brian
Student welfare/counselling. Senior Cousel
Chiboola, H., MA Reading
Students with disabilities. Student Counsellor:
Kalapula, E. P., BSW Zambia
University press. Acting Publisher: Kasankha,
S., BA (Educn) Zambia

CAMPUS/COLLEGE HEADS

Copperbelt Secondary Teachers' College,
Kitwe, Zambia. Principal: Sikazwe, A. K.,
BA(Educn) Zambia, MSc N.Y.State
George Benson Christian College,
Namwianga, Zambia. Principal: Chona, F.
Nkrumah Secondary Teachers' College,
Kabwe, Zambia. Principal: Mpundu, S. B.
Technical and Vocational Teachers' College,
Luanshya, Zambia. Principal: Zulu, G. D.

[Information supplied by the institution as at 17 July
1998, and edited by the ACU]

ZIMBABWE

Africa University (p. 1824)
Solusi University (p. 1825)

National University of Science and Technology, Bulawayo (p. 1824)
University of Zimbabwe (p. 1826)

AFRICA UNIVERSITY

Established 1992

Postal Address: PO Box 1320, Mutare, Zimbabwe
Telephone: (020) 61611, 61618, 60026, 60075 **Fax**: (020) 61785 **E-mail**: africa@africau.uz.zw

VICE-CHANCELLOR*—Murapa, Prof. Rukudzo
REGISTRAR‡—Mafarachisi, Constance M., BSc *Mass.*, MA
W.Mich.

NATIONAL UNIVERSITY OF SCIENCE AND TECHNOLOGY, BULAWAYO

Incorporated 1990

Member of the Association of Commonwealth Universities

Postal Address: PO Box 346, Bulawayo, Zimbabwe
Telephone: (09) 76833, 74626-7 **Fax**: (09) 76804

CHANCELLOR—Mugabe, Cde R. G.H.E. the President of the Republic of Zimbabwe (*ex officio*)
CHAIRMAN OF COUNCIL—Mubako, Justice S. V., BA *Rome*, LLB *Trinity(Dub.)*, BCL *Trinity(Dub.)*, LLM *Lond.*, LLM *Harv.*,
MPhil *Lond.*
VICE-CHANCELLOR*—Makhurane, Prof. Phinias M., BSc *Lond.*, MSc *Sheff.*, PhD *Sheff.*
PRO-VICE-CHANCELLOR—Nyathi, Prof. Clever B., BSc *Zambia*, PhD *Sask.*
REGISTRAR‡—Kariwo, Michael T., BA *Rhodesia*, MA *Lond.*
BURSAR—Sithole, Lameck, BAdmin *Z'bwe.*, MBA *Brun.*
LIBRARIAN—Matsika, Katherine, BA *Rhodesia*

GENERAL INFORMATION

History. The university was established in 1990 and opened in 1991. It is located in the city of Bulawayo, south-west of Zimbabwe.

Admission to first degree courses. Applicants should normally hold the Cambridge School Certificate exam or equivalent, with 5 O level passes at grade C or above including English language and mathematics, and either 2 relevant subjects at A level (for commerce, applied sciences, architecture and quantity surveying), or 3 relevant subjects at A level (for engineering).

First Degrees BArch, BCom, BEng, BQSurv, BSc.

Higher Degrees MBA, MSc.

Academic Year. August–July.

FACULTIES/SCHOOLS

Applied Sciences
Tel: (09) 72077, 66391 Fax: (09) 66983
Dean: Dlodlo, Themba S., MSc(Eng) *Delft*, PhD *Helsinki*

Commerce
Tel: (09) 77402, 77439 Fax: (09) 76804
Dean: Razemba, Elton G., BA *Hampton*, MA(Econ) *C.U.A.*

Industrial Technology
Tel: (09) 72077, 66391 Fax: (09) 66983
Dean: Sihwa, Lawrence, BSc *Edin.*, PhD *Edin.*

ACADEMIC UNITS

Accounting
Tel: (09) 77402, 77439
Moyo, A. T. C., MBA *Hull*, MCom *Punjab* Chairman*

Banking
Tel: (09) 77402, 77439
Mhlope, C. M., BSc(Econ) *Z'bwe.* Chairman*
Razemba, Elton G., BA *Hampton*, MA *C.U.A.* Sr. Lectr.

Biology, Applied
Tel: (09) 66391, 72077 Fax: (09) 66983
Djarova, Trayana G., MSc *Sofia Acad.Med.*, PhD *Sofia Acad. Med.*, MD *Sofia Acad. Med.* Assoc. Prof.; Chairman*
Iklov, A. T., MSc *Sofia Acad.Med.*, MD *Sofia Acad.Med.* Visiting Prof.
Mladenovski, L. N., MSc *Belgrade*, PhD *Belgrade* Sr. Lectr.
Okagbue, Richard N., BSc *Nigeria*, MSc *Edin.*, PhD *Calif.* Prof.

Business Management
Tel: (09) 75952
Mlilo, S. B., BBS *Z'bwe.*, MBA *Z'bwe.* Chairman*

Chemistry, Applied

Tel: (09) 66391, 72077 Fax: (09) 66983

Bantcheva, PhD *Bulgarian Acad.Sc.* Sr. Lectr.
Ogunniyi, D. S., BSc *Lagos*, MSc *Lough.*, PhD *Lough.* Sr. Lectr.
Parekh, Champaklal T., BSc *Gujar.*, MSc *Gujar.*, MSc *Manc.*, PhD *Manc.* Chairman*

Computer Science

Tel: (09) 71736-7

Dzidonu, C., BSc *Sur.*, PhD *Trinity(Dub.)*, FIA Sr. Lectr.
Mangena, S. Bayeza, MSc *Belgrade* Chairman*
Reddy, P. G., MSc *Kharagpur*, PhD *IIT Delhi* Sr. Lectr.
Sarukesi, Karunakaran, BE *Annam.*, MSc *Madr.*, PhD *Warw.* Assoc. Prof.

Engineering, Chemical

Tel: (09) 64304 Fax: (09) 64363

Ikhu-Omoregbe, D. I. O., BEng *Benin*, MSc *Birm.*, PhD *Birm.* Sr. Lectr.
Kuipa, P. K., MSc(Eng) *Ivanovo*, PhD *Brad.* Acting Chairman*

Engineering, Civil and Water

Tel: (09) 66391, 72077 Fax: (09) 66983

Diarra, S., MSc *Sofia*, PhD *Sofia* Chairman*
Taigbenu, A. E., BSc(Eng) MSc PhD Prof.

Engineering, Electronic

Tel: (09) 64304 Fax: (09) 64363

Dlodlo, M. E., BSEE *Geneva*, MSEE *Kansas State* Chairman*

Engineering, Industrial

Tel: (09) 79686, 79679 Fax: (09) 66983

Onwubolu, Godfrey C., BEng *Benin*, MSc *Aston*, PhD *Aston* Chairman*

Finance

Tel: (09) 77402, 77439 Fax: (09) 75953

Mutungwazi, Rassam, BSc *Punjab*, MSc *Punjabi* Chairman*

Insurance and Actuarial Science

Tel: (09) 77402, 77439

Mutiti, A. B., PhD *Prague*, LLM DSc Assoc. Prof.
Tshuma, Henry, BSc *Lagos*, MSc *Lough.* Chairman*

Mathematics, Applied

Tel: (09) 71736-7

Ewer, J. P. G., BSc *Cape Town*, MSc *Cape Town*, MSc *Sus.* Sr. Lectr.
Jones, B. C., MA *Camb.*, DPhil *Sus.* Assoc. Prof.
Kumar, Santosh, BSc *Raj.*, MSc *Vikram*, PhD *Delhi*, FIMA Prof.; Chairman*

Physics, Applied

Tel: (09) 42880 Fax: (09) 66983

Dlodlo, Themba S., MSc(Eng) *Delft*, PhD *Helsinki* Sr. Lectr.
Gholap, A. V., MSc *Vikram*, PhD *Indore* Assoc. Prof.
Joshua, Soney J., BSc *Raj.*, MSc *Raj.*, MSc *Keele*, PhD *Essex* Prof.; Chairman*
Makhurane, Phinias M., BSc *Lond.*, MSc *Sheff.*, PhD *Sheff.* Prof.

CONTACT OFFICERS

Academic affairs. Deputy Registrar: Phiri, Richmond, BA *Lond.*
Admissions. Senior Assistant Registrar: Mhlanga, F., BEd *Z'bwe.*, MSc *Z'bwe.*
Careers. Director of Information and Public Relations: Matshe, S. Priscillah, BSW *Z'bwe.*
Development/fund-raising. Industrial Liaison Officer: Moyo, Felix F., BA *S.Af.*
Estates and buildings/works and services. Director of Works: Mafico, Christopher J., BAdmin *Rhodesia*, MSc *Z'bwe.*, PhD *Liv.*
Finance. Bursar: Sithole, Lameck, BAdmin *Z'bwe.*, MBA *Brun.*
General enquiries. Registrar: Kariwo, Michael T., BA *Rhodesia*, MA *Lond.*
Health services. Director of Student Health Services: Mthamo, Nkosilomusa

Industrial liaison. Industrial Liaison Officer: Moyo, Felix F., BA *S.Af.*
Library (Chief librarian). Librarian: Matsika, Katherine, BA *Rhodesia*
Personnel/human resources. Senior Assistant Registrar: Bidi, Mavis, BAdmin *Z'bwe.*, MBA *Wales*
Public Relations, Information and Marketing. Director of Information and Public Relations: Matshe, S. Priscillah, BSW *Z'bwe.*
Publications. Kumar, Prof. Santosh, BSc *Raj.*, MSc *Vikram*, PhD *Delhi*, FIMA
Purchasing. Bursar: Sithole, Lameck, BAdmin *Z'bwe.*, MBA *Brun.*
Research. Chairman, Research Board: Kumar, Prof. Santosh, BSc *Raj.*, MSc *Vikram*, PhD *Delhi*, FIMA
Safety. Registrar: Kariwo, Michael T., BA *Rhodesia*, MA *Lond.*
Scholarships, awards, loans. Deputy Registrar: Phiri, Richmond, BA *Lond.*
Schools Liaison. Director of Information and Public Relations: Matshe, S. Priscillah, BSW *Z'bwe.*
Security. Registrar: Kariwo, Michael T., BA *Rhodesia*, MA *Lond.*
Sport and recreation. Director of Sports: Muller, Berenice, LLB *Z'bwe.*
Staff development and training. Senior Assistant Registrar: Bidi, Mavis, BAdmin *Z'bwe.*, MBA *Wales*
Student union. President, Student Representative Council: Hopewell Gumbo
Student welfare/counselling. Dean of Students: Sifobela, Lobi, BA *Birm.*, MA *Birm.*, PhD *Lond.*
Students from other countries. Dean of Students: Sifobela, Lobi, BA *Birm.*, MA *Birm.*, PhD *Lond.*
Students with disabilities. Dean of Students: Sifobela, Lobi, BA *Birm.*, MA *Birm.*, PhD *Lond.*

[Information supplied by the institution as at 3 June 1998, and edited by the ACU]

SOLUSI UNIVERSITY

Postal Address: PO Solusi, Bulawayo, Zimbabwe
Telephone: (09) 83226-8 **Fax**: (09) 83229 **E-mail**: solusi@esanet.zw

VICE-CHANCELLOR*—Maphosa, Norman, BA *Lond.*, MEd *Z'bwe.*
REGISTRAR‡—Sithole, Richard, BA *Andrews*, MA *Andrews*, MA *Z'bwe.*

UNIVERSITY OF ZIMBABWE

Originally incorporated 1955 as the University College of Rhodesia and Nyasaland

Member of the Association of Commonwealth Universities

Postal Address: PO Box MP 167, Mount Pleasant, Harare, Zimbabwe
Telephone: (04) 303211 **Fax**: (04) 333407, 335249 **E-mail**: postmaster@mango.apc.org
Cables: University, Harare **Telex**: 26580 UNIVZ ZW **WWW**: http://www.uz.ac.zw

CHANCELLOR—H.E. the President of the Republic of Zimbabwe (*ex officio*)
CHAIRMAN OF COUNCIL—Gono, G., MBA *Z'bwe.*
VICE-CHANCELLOR*—Hill, Prof. F. W. Graham, BVetMed *Lond.*, PhD *Brist.*, DSc *Z'bwe.*
PRO-VICE-CHANCELLOR—Nyagura, L. M., BSc *Lond.*, BSc *Rhodesia*, MSc *S.Af.*, PhD *S.Illinois*
REGISTRAR—Mukondiwa, W. M., BA *Rhodesia*
LIBRARIAN—Made, S. M., BA *S.Af.*, MA *Lond.*, FLA
BURSAR—Mapani, W., BAcc *Botswana*
SENIOR PROCTOR—Ncube, W., BL *Z'bwe.*, LLB *Z'bwe.*, MPhil *Z'bwe.*

FACULTIES/SCHOOLS

Agriculture
Dean: Ndlovu, L. R., BSc *S.Leone*, MSc *Wales*, PhD *Guelph*

Arts
Dean: Chimhundu, H., BA *Z'bwe.*, DPhil *Z'bwe.*

Commerce
Dean: Mukwenha, H. O., MCom *Strath.*

Education
Dean: Peresuh, M. P. N., MEd *Manc.*, PhD *Manc.*

Engineering
Dean: Zingoni, A., BSc(Eng) *Z'bwe.*, MSc *Lond.*, PhD *Lond.*

Law
Dean: Zowa, J., BL *Z'bwe.*, LLB *Z'bwe.*

Medicine
Dean: Mufunda, J., MB ChB *Z'bwe.*, PhD *Mich.State*

Science
Dean: Dzinotyiwei, Prof. H. A. M., BSc *Rhodesia*, MSc *Aberd.*, PhD *Aberd.*

Social Studies
Dean: Mukonoweshuro, Prof. E. G., BA *Birm.*, MA *Birm.*, PhD *Birm.*

Veterinary Science
Dean: Obwolo, M. J., BVM *Nair.*, PhD *Brist.*

ACADEMIC UNITS

Accountancy
Chikondo, J. T. M., MAcc *Glas.* Lectr.; Chairman*
Other Staff: 6 Lectrs.

Administrative Studies, see Pol. and Admin. Studies

Adult Education
Vacant Posts: 1 Lectr. and Head*

African Languages and Literature
Chimhundu, H., BA *Z'bwe.*, DPhil *Z'bwe.* Sr. Lectr.
Chiwome, E. M., BA *Z'bwe.*, MPhil *Z'bwe.*, DPhil *Z'bwe.* Sr. Lectr. (on leave)
Dube, K., BA *Z'bwe.*
Hachipola, J. S., BA(Educn) *Zambia*, MA *Indiana*, PhD *Lond.*
Khumalo, L., BA *Z'bwe.*, MA *Z'bwe.*
Maraire, D., MA *Wash.*, PhD *Wash.* Lectr.; Chairman*
Matambirofa, F., BA *Z'bwe.*, MA *Z'bwe.*
Matshakayile-Ndlovu, T., BA *Lond.*, MPhil *Z'bwe.* Sr. Lectr.

Mutswairo, S. M., BA *S.Af.*, BSc *Rhodes*, MA *Ott.*, PhD *Howard* Assoc. Prof.
Other Staff: 6 Lectrs.; 4 Res. Fellows; 2 Temp. Lectrs.

Afrikaans, see Mod. Langs.

Agricultural Economics and Extension
Chimedza, Ruvimbo, BA *Clark*, MA *Clark*, MSc *Oxf.*, DPhil *Z'bwe.* Lectr.; Chairman*
Muchena, Olivia, BA *Lond.*, MS *Cornell*, PhD *Iowa State* Sr. Lectr. (on leave)
Mudimu, Godfrey D., MSc *Mich.State*, BScAgric BSc(Econ) Sr. Lectr.
Muir-Leresche, Kay, BA *S.Af.*, DPhil *Z'bwe.* Sr. Lectr.
Oni, S. A., BSc *Calif.*, MSc *Calif.*, PhD *Ib.* Prof.
Rukuni, Mandivamba, BSc(Agric) *Z'bwe.*, MSc(Agric) *Reading*, DPhil *Z'bwe.* Prof.
Stack, Jayne L., MA *Camb.*, MSc *Reading*, DPhil *Z'bwe.*, PhD *Iowa State* Sr. Lectr. (on leave)

Animal Science
Gandiya, F., BScAgric *Rhodesia*, MSc *Mich.State* Sr. Lectr.
Mutisi, C., BSc *Reading*, PhD *Reading* Lectr.; Chairman*
Ndlovu, L. R., BSc *S.Leone*, MSc *Wales*, PhD *Guelph* Sr. Lectr.
Ngongoni, N. T., BScAgric *Rhodesia*, MSc *Aberd.*, PhD *Aberd.* Sr. Lectr.

Arts Education, see Curric. and Arts Educn.

Biochemistry
Cadman, Hilary, BSc *Leeds*, DPhil *Sus.* Sr. Lectr.
Chetsanga, C. J., BSc *Calif.*, MSc *Tor.*, PhD *Tor.* Prof.
Gooch, J. A. A., BSc *Lond.*, PhD *Lond.* Sr. Lectr.
Hasler, Julie A., BSc *Cape Town*, PhD *Cape Town* Assoc. Prof.
Masola, B., BSc *CNAA*, PhD *Lond.* Lectr.; Chairman*
Ogunleye, A. J., MSc PhD Sr. Lectr.
Read, J. S., BScAgric *Natal*, PhD *Cape Town* Sr. Lectr.

Biological Sciences
Fax: (04) 333407
du Toit, J. T., BSc *Cape Town*, PhD *Witw.* Sr. Lectr.
Dube, B. N., BSc *S.Leone*, MSc *Flor.*, DPhil *Z'bwe.* Lectr.; Chairman*
Feresu, Sarah, BSc *CNAA*, PhD *Leic.* Assoc. Prof.
Loveridge, J. P., BSc *Lond.*, PhD *Lond.* Prof.
Marshall, B. E., BSc *Lond.*, MPhil *Lond.*, PhD *Rhodes* Assoc. Prof.

Business Studies
Muranda, Z., BBS *Z'bwe.*, MPhil *Z'bwe.* Lectr.; Chairman*
Muzamani, J., BBA *Oregon*, MB *Z'bwe.*
Other Staff: 10 Lectrs.

Chemistry
Gurira, R. C., BS *Central State(Ohio)*, PhD *Penn.State* Sr. Lectr.
Hove, E. G., BSc *S.Leone*, PhD *Penn.State* Lectr.; Chairman*
Key, D. L., BSc *Lond.*, PhD *Sur.* Sr. Lectr.
Mebe, P. P., BSc *Texas Luth.*, MSc *Southwest Texas State*, PhD *New Br.* Sr. Lectr.
Sibanda, S., BSc *CNAA*, PhD *Lond.* Sr. Lectr.
Simoyi, R. H., BSc *Ife*, MSc *Brandeis*, PhD *Brandeis* Prof.
Zaranyika, M. F., BSc *Lond.*, PhD *Boston* Sr. Lectr.

Classics, see Religious Studies, Classics and Philos.

Computer Science
Chikohora, S., BSc *Z'bwe.*, MSc *Manc.*, PhD *Lough.* Lectr.; Chairman*
Velinov, Y. P., MSc *Sofia*, PhD *Sofia* Sr. Lectr.

Crop Science
Canhao, Sr. Jane, BSc *Lond.*, BSc *S.Af.*, MA *San Jose State* Sr. Lectr.
Chivinge, O. A., BSc *Ib.*, MSc *Ib.*, DPhil *Z'bwe.* Sr. Lectr.
Giga, D. P., MSc *Reading*, PhD *Reading*, BScAgric Prof.
Mariga, I. K., BScAgric *Zambia*, MSc *Nair.*, PhD *Mich.State* Sr. Lectr.; Chairman*
Schweppenhauser, M. A., BScAgric *Stell.*, MSc *Stell.*, DSc *Stell.* Prof.
Tongoona, P., BScAgric MPhil DPhil Sr. Lectr.

Curriculum and Arts Education
Maravanyika, O. E., MEd *Manc.*, DPhil *Z'bwe.* Sr. Lectr.
Nondo, S. J., BA *S.Af.*, MA *Lond.*, MPhil *Rhodesia* Lectr.; Chairman*

Economic History
Majonga, M., BA *Z'bwe.*, MA *Z'bwe.*
Mlambo, A. S., BA *Cant.*, MA *Lond.*, MA *Wesleyan*, PhD *Duke* Sr. Lectr.; Chairman*
Other Staff: 8 Lectrs.

Economics
Davies, R. J., BComm *Cape Town*, BA *Cape Town*, MLitt *St And.* Assoc. Prof.
Godana, T., MSc(Econ) *Leningrad*, PhD *Stockholm* Lectr.; Chairman*
Moyo, T., BSc(Econ) *Z'bwe.*, MA *Dal.*, MPhil *Z'bwe.*, PhD *Dal.* Chairman*
Mumbengegwi, C., BEc *Monash*, MEc *Monash*, PhD *W.Syd.* Sr. Lectr.
Other Staff: 13 Lectrs.

Education: Science and Mathematics, see Sci. and Maths. Educn.

Education, Teacher
Ademiran, S. A., BSc(Ed) *A.Bello*, MSc *Kansas*, PhD *Kansas* Sr. Lectr.

Bhila, Q. M., BA *Wales*, MA *Lond.*
Bourdillon, T. J. E., BA *Rhodes*, MEd *Rhodesia* Sr. Lectr.; Chairman*
Chivore, B. R. S., BA *Sus.*, MA *Lond.*, PhD *Lond.* Assoc. Prof.
Shumba, O., BEd *Z'bwe.*, MSc *Iowa State*, PhD *Iowa State* Sr. Lectr.
Siyakwazi, P. D., BA *Rutgers*, MEd *Rutgers* Sr. Lectr.
Other Staff: 9 Lectrs.

Education, Technical

No staff at present

Educational Administration

Chikombah, C. E. M., BA *Lincoln(Pa.)*, MEd *Qu.*, MEd *Alta.*, PhD *Alta.* Prof.
Chitekuteku, S. R., BEd *Z'bwe.*, MEd *Z'bwe.* Lectr.; Chairman*
Other Staff: 2 Lectrs.

Educational Foundations

Atkinson, N. D., BA *Trinity(Dub.)*, MLitt *Trinity(Dub.)*, PhD *Trinity(Dub.)*, PhD *Lond.* Sr. Lectr.
Zindi, F., BEd *Lond.*, MA *Lond.*, PhD *Lond.* Lectr.; Chairman*
Other Staff: 9 Lectrs.

Educational Technology, Centre for

Hungwe, K. N., BSc*Z'bwe.*, MSc *Wis.*, PhD *Mich.State* Chairman*
Other Staff: 1 Lectr.

Engineering, Agricultural, see Soil Sci. and Agric. Engin.

Engineering, Civil

Djivarova-Vassileva, L., MArch *Sofia*, PhD *Sofia* Assoc. Prof.
Grant, M. P., BSc(Eng) *Cape Town*, MSc *Birm.* Sr. Lectr.
Hranova, R., MSc *Sofia*, PhD *Sofia* Sr. Lectr.
Mawiri, K., BSc(Eng) *Z'bwe.*, MSc *Lond.* Lectr.; Chairman*
Owoade, I. A., BSc *Nigeria*, MSc *Lough.*, PhD *Lough.* Sr. Lectr.
Zingoni, A., BSc(Eng) *Z'bwe.*, MSc *Lond.*, PhD *Lond.* Sr. Lectr.

Engineering, Electrical

Fax: (04) 303280
Collier, M., BA *Camb.*, MA *Camb.*, PhD *HK*, FIEE Sr. Lectr.
El Mahdy, G., BSc *Alexandria*, PhD Sr. Lectr.
El-Missiry, M. M., BSc *Alexandria*, MSc *Manc.*, PhD *Manc.*, FIEE Assoc. Prof.
Gotchev, B., PhD *T.U.Sofia* Sr. Lectr.; Co-ordinator
Harlen, R. M., MA *Camb.*, PhD *Brist.*, FIEE Prof.
Kapuya, E. T., BSc(Eng) *Z'bwe.*, MSc *Manc.*, PhD *Manc.* Lectr.; Chair*
Nedev, N. N., MSc *Sofia*, PhD *Sofia* Sr. Lectr.

Engineering, Mechanical

Elsarnagawy, B. A. F., BSc *Cairo*, MSc *Brno*, PhD *Brno* Sr. Lectr.
Sheikh, M. S., BSc(Eng) *Lond.*, MSc(Eng) *Lond.* Sr. Lectr.; Chairman*

Engineering, Metallurgical

Chinyamakobvu, O. S., BSc *Manc.*, PhD *Lond.* Sr. Lectr.
Navara, E., BSc(Eng) *Ostrava*, MSc *T.U.Kosice*, PhD *Chalmers U.T.* Prof.
Simbi, D. J., BSc *CNAA*, PhD *Leeds* Lectr.; Acting Chairman*
Varbanov, R., MScEng *Sofia*, MScMinProc *Sofia*, PhD *Sofia* Assoc. Prof.

Engineering, Mining

Voss, J. G., MSc *T.H. Aachen* Assoc. Prof.; Chairman*
Wright, E. A., BSc *Zambia*, DrIng *T.U.Clausthal* Assoc. Prof.
Other Staff: 2 Lectrs.

English, see also Theatre Arts

Brown, G. R., MA *Nott.* Sr. Lectr.
Chennells, A. J., BA *Natal*, DPhil *Rhodesia* Assoc. Prof.
Gecau, K., BA *E.Af.*, MA *McM.*, PhD *N.Y.State* Sr. Lectr.
Louw, W. E., BA *Rhodes*, MA *Reading* Sr. Lectr.
Malaba, M. Z., BA *Rhodesia*, DPhil *York(UK)* Sr. Lectr.
McLoughlin, T. O., BA *Trinity(Dub.)*, MA *Sheff.*, PhD *Lond.* Prof.
Zhuwarara, R., BA *Wales*, MA *Sheff.*, PhD *New Br.* Lectr.; Chairman*
Zimunya, M. B., BA *Kent*, MA *Kent* Sr. Lectr.
Other Staff: 1 Lectr.

French, see Mod. Langs.

Geography

Heath, Robin A., BA *Cape Town*, MPhil *Z'bwe.* Sr. Lectr.
Mutambirwa, C. C., MA *Penn.*, PhD *W.Ont.* Chairman*
Tevera, D. S., BA *S.Leone*, MA *Qu.*, MPA *Cinc.*, PhD *Cinc.* Sr. Lectr.; Chairman*
Zinyama, L. M., BA *Lond.*, MPhil *Rhodesia*, PhD *Z'bwe.* Prof.
Other Staff: 6 Lectrs.

Geology

Blenkinsop, T. G., MA *Oxf.*, MSc *Lond.*, PhD *Keele* Assoc. Prof.; Chairman*
Lister, Linley A., MSc *Natal*, DPhil *Rhodesia* Sr. Lectr.
Okujeni, C., PhD *Berl.* Sr. Lectr.
Wilson, J. F., BSc *Edin.*, PhD *Witw.*, DSc *Edin.*, FGS Prof.

History, see also Econ. Hist.

Beach, D. N., BA *Cape Town*, PhD *Lond.* Prof.
Bhebe, N., BA *UBLS*, PhD *Lond.* Prof.
Pikirayi, I., BA *Z'bwe.*, MA *Z'bwe.*, PhD *Uppsala* Chairman*
Zvobgo, C. J., BA *Calif.*, PhD *Edin.* Assoc. Prof.
Other Staff: 9 Lectrs.

Law, Private

Fax: (04) 304008
Gumbo, A., BL *Z'bwe.*, LLM *Lond.*
Maboreke, F. Mary, BL *Z'bwe.*, MPhil *Z'bwe.*, PhD *Warw.*
Manase, A. J., BL *Z'bwe.*, LLB *Z'bwe.*, LLM *Camb.* Lectr.; Chairman*
Mandudzo, D. T., LLB *Z'bwe.*, LLM *Tor.*
Ncube, W., BL *Z'bwe.*, LLB *Z'bwe.*, MPhil *Z'bwe.* Assoc. Prof.
Stewart, Julie E., LLB *Lond.* Assoc Prof.
Tsanga, F. A., BL *Z'bwe.*, LLB *Z'bwe.*

Law, Procedural

Nyapadi, T. J., LLM *Lond.*, BA Sr. Lectr.; Chairman*

Law, Public

Feltoe, G., BA *Rhodes*, LLB *Lond.*, MPhil *Kent* Assoc. Prof.
Hlatshwayo, B., BL *Z'bwe.*, LLB *Z'bwe.*, LLM *Harv.* Sr. Lectr.; Chairman*
Makamure, K. M., LLM *Lond.*, LLB Sr. Lectr.
Other Staff: 3 Lectrs.

Linguistics

Love, A., BA *Brist.*, MA *Z'bwe.*, MLitt *Brist.* Sr. Lectr.
Mkanganwi, K. G., BA *Lond.*, MPhil *Lond.* Sr. Lectr.
Thondhlama, J., BA *Z'bwe.*, MA *Flor.*, MA *Lanc.*, DPhil *Z'bwe.* Chairperson*
Other Staff: 8 Lectrs.

Management

No staff at present

Mathematics, see also Sci. and Maths. Educn.

Belinsky, E. S., PhD Assoc. Prof.
Bye, B. H., MSc DPhil Sr. Lectr.
Dzinotyiweyi, H. A. M., BSc *Rhodesia*, MSc *Aberd.*, PhD *Aberd.* Prof.

Henwood, D., BA *Camb.*, MTech *Brun.*, PhD *Brun.* Sr. Lectr.
Hitchcock, A. G., BA *Oxf.*, PhD *Keele* Sr. Lectr.
Hristov, V. H., MSc *Sofia*, PhD *Sofia* Sr. Lectr.
Lampitt, G. A., BSc *Lond.*, MSc *Newcastle(UK)* Sr. Lectr.
Petrov, M. B., BSc *Leningrad*, MSc *Leningrad*, PhD *Leningrad* Sr. Lectr.
Stewart, A. G. R., BSc *Rhodes*, MSc *ANU*, PhD *ANU* Prof.
Vuma, D., MSc *Leeds*, BSc Lectr.; Chairman*

Medical Microbiology

Chihota, V., BSc *Z'bwe.*, MSc *Lond.*
Hazlett, D. G., BSc PhD Prof.
Moyo, S. R., MMedSci
Mutetwa, S. M., MB BCh *Z'bwe.*, BA *York(UK)*, MSc *Lond.*, PhD *Lond.*
Nziramasanga, P., BSc *Wash.*, MSc *Nevada*, PhD *Fran.*
Obi, C. L., BSc *P.Harcourt*, MSc *Lagos*, PhD *Lagos*
Robertson, Valerie J., BSc *Lond.*, MSc *Lond.*, PhD *Lond.* Sr. Lectr.
Tswana, S. A., BA *N.Carolina*, MSc *W.Kentucky*, PhD *Vanderbilt* Assoc. Prof.; Chairman*

Medicine, see below

Modern Languages

Amonoo, Prof. R. F., BA *Lond.*, MA *Manc.*, PhD *Paris IV* Prof.
O'Flaherty, Patricia S. E., BA *Belf.*, MA *Witw.*, PhD *Witw.* Lectr., French; Chairman*
Other Staff: 5 Lectrs. (Afrikaans 1, French 3, Portuguese 1)

Pharmacy, see Medicine, below

Philosophy, see Religious Studies, Classics and Philos.

Physics

Carelse, X. F., BSc *Rhodes*, MSc *Witw.*, PhD *Brun.* Sr. Lectr.
Jones, D. L., BSc *Lond.*, PhD *Exe.* Prof.
Milford, J. R., BA *Oxf.*, DPhil *Oxf.* Assoc. Prof.
Mujaji, M., BSc *Z'bwe.*, PhD *Cant.*
Mushayandebvu, M. F., BSc *Z'bwe.*, MSc *Leeds*, PhD *Z'bwe.* Sr. Lectr.; Chairman*
Olumekor, L., MTech *Brun.*, PhD *Brun.* Sr. Lectr.
Podmore, F., MA *Camb.*, PhD *Lond.* Sr. Lectr.
Selden, A. C., MA *Oxf.*, PhD *Stan.* Assoc. Prof.
Zengeni, T. G., BSc *Lond.*, MS *Stan.*, PhD *Stan.* Sr. Lectr.
Other Staff: 6 Lectrs.

Political and Administrative Studies

Chipangura, T., BScPolAdmin *Z'bwe.*, MPA *Z'bwe.*
Kambudzi, A. M., BScPolAdmin *Z'bwe.*, MSc *Z'bwe.*, PhD *Paris*
Linington, G., LLB *Z'bwe.*, MSc *Z'bwe.*
Makumbe, J., BA *UBS*, BAdmin *Z'bwe.*, PhD *Tas.*
Masumungure, E., BAdmin *Z'bwe.*, MPA *Dal.*, MPhil *Z'bwe.*
Mavima, P., BScPolAdmin *Z'bwe.*, MPA *Z'bwe.* (on leave)
Mukonoweshuro, E. G., BA *Birm.*, MA *Birm.*, PhD *Birm.* Prof.
Nhema, A. G., BAdmin *Z'bwe.*, MPA *Indiana*, PhD *Dal.* Chairman*
Nkiwane, S. M., BA *Colorado*, MA *Mak.*, PhD *McG.* Sr. Lectr. (on leave)
Nsingo, S., BScPolAdmin *Z'bwe.*, MPA *Z'bwe.*
Patel, H. H., BSc *Lond.*, MA *Calif.*, PhD *Calif.* Prof. (on leave)
Sithole, M., BA *Muskingum*, MA *Cinc.*, PhD *Cinc.* Assoc. Prof.
Sithole, M. S., BScPolAdmin *Z'bwe.*, MPA *Z'bwe.* (on leave)

Portuguese, see Mod. Langs.

Psychology

Bundy, R. P., BSc *Brist.*, PhD Sr. Lectr.
Chiroro, P. M., BSc(Psych) *Z'bwe.*, MSc *Manc.*, PhD *Durh.* Lectr.; Chairman*
McMaster, J. M., MSocSci *Natal* Sr. Lectr.

Mundy-Castle, A. C., MA Camb., PhD Witw., FBPsS Prof.
Myambo, K. A., BA Penn.State, MA Penn.State, PhD Syr. Sr. Lectr.
Other Staff: 2 Lectrs.

Religious Studies, Classics and Philosophy

Mandivenga, E. C., BA Lond., MPhil Rhodesia, PhD Aberd. Sr. Lectr., Theology; Chairman*
Moyo, Rev. A., BA S.Af., ThM Harv., MA Harv., PhD Harv. Sr. Lectr., Theology
Verstraelen, F. J., Lic Leuven, MA Ghana, ThD Greg. Prof.

Rural and Urban Planning

Brand, C. M., MA Stell. Sr. Lectr.
Mbiba, B., BSc Z'bwe., MSc Z'bwe. Sr. Lectr. (on leave)
Mubvami, T., BA MSc Lectr.; Chairman*
Vuckovic, BSc Belgrade, MSc Belgrade, PhD Belgrade Sr. Lectr.
Wekwete, K. H., BA Leeds, MA Nott., PhD Lond. Assoc. Prof.

Science and Mathematics Education

Chagwedera, S. M., BScEd S.Leone, MS Penn. State, DEd Penn. State Sr. Lectr.
Chinhanhu, C., BEd Z'bwe., BSc Z'bwe., MSc Z'bwe., MSc Iowa State
Gancheva, V. P. F., MSc Sofia
Gwekwerere, Y., BSc Z'bwe., MSc Z'bwe.
Gwimbi, E. M., BEd Z'bwe., MSc S'ton.
Manokore, V., BSc Z'bwe., MSc Z'bwe.
Mashava, P. M., BSc S.Leone, MSc Stevens, PhD Stevens Sr. Lectr.
Mtetwa, K. J., BSc NUL, MSc Car., MEd Virginia, PhD Virginia
Mukono, T. T., BSc Z'bwe., MSc Z'bwe.
Munowenyu, E. M., BA Lond., BA S.Af., MEd
Mushaikwa, E., BEd Z'bwe., MPhil Camb.
Namasasu, O., BA(Ed) NUL, MA Qu.
Ncube, K., BEd Z'bwe., MAT New Mexico
Ngwazikazana, P. S., BA Rhodesia, MA Alabama
Nyagura, L. M., BSc Lond., BSc Rhodesia, MSc S.Af., PhD Prof.
Tambo, T., LicEd BEd MEd

Sociology

Bourdillon, M. F. C., LicPhil Heythrop, MPhil Oxf., DPhil Oxf. Assoc. Prof.; Chairman*
Gaidzanwa, Rudo B., BSc Rhodesia, MA Inst.Soc.Stud.(The Hague) Asst. Prof.
Patel, Diana H., BA Reading, MPhil Rhodesia Sr. Lectr.

Soil Science and Agricultural Engineering

Hussein, J., BSc Newcastle(UK), MSc Newcastle(UK), PhD Newcastle(UK) Sr. Lectr.
McGowan, M., BSc Camb., MA Camb., PhD Camb. Prof.
Piha, M. I., BSc Exe., MSc Calif., PhD Calif. Sr. Lectr.

Statistics

Keogh, E. C., BSc Z'bwe., MSc Z'bwe. Lectr.; Chairman*
Nikolov, H. M., MSc Minsk, PhD Moscow Sr. Lectr.

Surveying

Davies, J., BSc Portsmouth, MSc Lond. Lectr.; Chairman*
Naraja, H. N., PhD Ohio Asst. Prof.

Technical Education, see Educn., Tech.

Theatre Arts

McLaren, R., BA Cape Town, MPhil Oxf., PhD Leeds Sr. Lectr., Drama
Zimunya, M. B., BA Kent, MA Kent Sr. Lectr., English; Chairman*
Other Staff: 2 Lectrs.; 1 Teach. Asst.

Theology, see Religious Studies, Classics and Philos.

Urban Planning, see Rural and Urban Planning

Veterinary Science, see below

MEDICINE

Anaesthetics

Chinyanga, H. M., MSc Jerusalem, MD Jerusalem, FRCPCan Prof.
Chironga, M., MB ChB Z'bwe., MMed Z'bwe. Chairman*
Clark, N. J., BS Atlantic Union, MD Loma Linda Sr. Lectr.
Kunzekweguta, BTech
Other Staff: 4 Lectrs.

Anatomy

Asala, S. A., PhD Sheff., MB BS Sr. Lectr.
Chaudhary, S. C., BSc Agra, MB BS Raj., MSc Raj. Sr. Lectr.
Katzarski, M., MD Sofia Sr. Lectr.
Mawera, G., MB ChB Lectr.; Chairman*
Petropoulos, P. G., DDS Sr. Lectr.
Rao, P. V. V. P., BSc And., MSc Madr., PhD Ib. Sr. Lectr.
Other Staff: 2 Lectrs.

Chemical Pathology

Gomo, Z. A. R., BSc Sur., PhD Birm. Sr. Lectr.
Mujaji, W. B., BSc Kent, MSc Leeds, PhD Leeds Lectr.; Chair*
Other Staff: 1 Lectr.

Clinical Pharmacology

Gewoe, J. A. O. Prof.
Neil, P., MB ChB Z'bwe. Assoc. Prof.
Nhachi, C. F. B., BSc Aberd., MSc Lough., PhD Lond. Assoc. Prof.; Chairman*
Nyazema, N. Z., BSc Liv., PhD Liv. Assoc. Prof.

Community Medicine

Tel: (04) 791631
Bassett, M. T., MD Col., MPH Wash. Sr. Lectr.
Matchaba, R. B., MB ChB Z'bwe., MSc Lond. Lectr.; Chairman*
Siziya, S. I., BA(Educn) Zambia, MSc Lond., PhD Zmabia Sr. Lectr.
Woelk, G. B., BSc(Soc) Z'bwe., MCommH Liv., PhD Wash. Sr. Lectr.
Other Staff: 5 Lectrs.; 1 Hon. Lectr.

Haematology

Tel: (04) 793185
Adewuyi, M. J. O., MB BS Lagos Assoc. Prof.
Coutts, Alison M., MB ChB Edin., FRCPath Lectr.; Chairman*
Singh, M. Amarendra K., MB BS Patna, PhD Lond. Assoc. Prof.
Other Staff: 1 Lectr.

Histopathology

Gwavava, N. J. T., BSc Ib., MD Zaire Sr. Lectr.; Chairman*

Medical Laboratory Technology

Mandisodza, A. R., BSc MSc Chairman*
Mason, D., BA PhD Prof.
Other Staff: 5 Lectrs.

Medical Microbiology, see above

Medicine

Latif, A. S., MB ChB Birm., FCP(SA) Assoc. Prof.
Levy, Lorraine M., MB ChB Birm., MD Birm., FRCP Assoc. Prof.
Matenga, J. A., MB ChB Birm., FRCP Lectr.; Chairman*
Palmer, D. L., MA MD, FACP Visiting Prof.

Nursing Science

Mapanga, K. G., PhD Chairman*
Ndlovu, Rose J., BSc Syr., MSc Syr., PhD Syr. Sr. Lectr.
Other Staff: 9 Lectrs.

Obstetrics and Gynaecology

Chipato, Tsungai, MB ChB Brist. Lectr.; Chairman*
Kassim, M. M., MB ChB Birm. Asst. Prof.
Kasule, J., MB ChB Mak., MSc Lond., FRCOG, FRCSEd Asst. Prof.
Mahomed, Kassim, MB ChB Birm. Assoc. Prof.
Mbizvo, M. T., MPhil Z'bwe., DPhil Z'bwe. Sr. Lectr.

Paediatrics and Child Health

Chidede, O. S., MB ChB Birm. Sr. Lectr.
Glyn-Jones, R., MB ChB Cape Town Sr. Lectr.
Nathoo, Kusum J., MB ChB Birm. Sr. Lectr.; Chairman*

Pharmacy

Ball, D., BSc(Pharm) Natal, MSc Newcastle, PhD Newcastle Sr. Lectr.
Chagonda, L. S., BSc S.Leone, MSc Lough., PhD Lough. Sr. Lectr.
Chagwedera, T. E., BSc S.Leone, MSc McG., PhD Laval Assoc. Prof.
Chigwanda, R. J. J., BPharm Z'bwe., PhD Bath
Dzeka, T. N., BPharm Z'bwe., MSc V.U.Brussels
Gundidza, M. G., BSc Salf., MSc Strath., PhD Nott. Assoc. Prof.
Kasilo, Ossy, PharmD Pavia, PhD Milan, FIP Assoc. Prof.
Maponga, C. C., BPharm Z'bwe., PharmD N.Y.State
Munjeri, O. B., BPharm Sur., PhD Manc. Lectr.; Chairman*
Musana, G. B., BPharm Z'bwe., MSc Lond.
Other Staff: 1 Lectr.

Physiology

Mufunda, J., MB ChB Z'bwe., PhD Mich.State Sr. Lectr.
Musabayane, C. T., BSc CNAA, DPhil Z'bwe. Assoc. Prof.; Chairman*
Osim, E. E., BSc Ib., MSc Lond., PhD Lond. Sr. Lectr.
Parry, O., BSc Wales, PhD Wales Sr. Lectr.
Umapathy, E., MSc Madr., PhD Madr. Asst. Prof.
Vengesa, P. M., BSc UBLS, DPhil York(UK) Sr. Lectr.
Watt, A. J., BSc Aberd., PhD Aberd. Sr. Lectr.
Other Staff: 3 Lectrs.

Psychiatry

Acuda, S. W., MB ChB E.Af., FRCPsych Prof.; Chairman*

Radiology

Harid, A. C., MD, FACS Sr. Lectr.

Rehabilitation

Jelsma, J., BSc Stell., MPhil Z'bwe.
Madzivire, Dorcas M., BSc N.Y., MA N.Y. Lectr.; Chairman*
Marks, G., BSc Cape Town, MSc
Moyo, A., MSc S'ton.
Muderedzi, J., MSc Kent

Surgery

Faranisi, C. T., MB ChB Rhodesia, FRCSEd Sr. Lectr., General Surgery
Harid, A. C., MD Jerusalem, FACS Sr. Lectr.; Chairman*
Iliya, A. A., MD Sr. Lectr.
Levy, L. F., MB BS Lond., MSc N.Y., FRCS, FRCSEd, FACS Prof., Neurosurgery

VETERINARY SCIENCE

Clinical Veterinary Studies

Adeyanju, DVM MSc PhD Assoc. Prof.
Agumbah, G. J. O., BVM Nair., MSc Nair., PhD Glas. Assoc. Prof.; Chairman*
Bobade, P. A., DVM Ib., PhD Ib., MVM Glas. Assoc. Prof.
Hill, Graham F. W., BVetMed Lond., MA Melb., PhD Brist. Lectr.
Kelly, P. J., BVSc Pret., MSc Witw., DPhil Z'bwe. Assoc. Prof.
Ogaa, J. S., BVSc E.Af., DVM Giessen Assoc. Prof.

Paraclinical Veterinary Studies

Hove, T., MSc Edin., DVM   Lectr.; Chairman*
Kock, Nancy, BS Calif., MS Calif., DVM Calif.,
    PhD Z'bwe.   Assoc. Prof.
Lander, K. P., BVMS Edin., PhD Lond.   Sr. Lectr.
Mohan, K., PhD Mag., BVSc&AH   Prof.
Obwolo, M. J., BVM Nair., PhD Brist.   Assoc.
    Prof.
Other Staff: 6 Lectrs.

Preclinical Veterinary Studies

Baggot, J. D, BSc Trinity(Dub.), MVB
    Trinity(Dub.), MVM Trinity(Dub.), PhD Ohio,
    DSc Trinity(Dub.)   Prof.
Chamunorwa, J. P., BSc Z'bwe., BVSc Z'bwe.,
    PhD Liv.   Lectr.; Chairman*
Gupta, S. K., BSc BVSc&AH MVSc   Sr. Lectr.
Morton, D. J., BPharm Z'bwe., PhD
    Z'bwe.   Assoc. Prof.
Other Staff: 9 Lectrs.

SPECIAL CENTRES, ETC

Applied Social Sciences, Centre for

Murphree, M. W., BA Asbury, BD Asbury, MA
    Northwestern, PhD Lond.   Prof.
Nhira, C., BSc Z'bwe., MA York, DPhil
    Z'bwe.   Lectr.; Dir.*

Computer Centre

Sheppard, J. G., BSc Rhodes, MSc Natal, PhD
    Lond.   Prof.; Dir.*

Continuing Health Education, Institute of

Tel: (04) 791631 Fax: (04) 724912, 704867
Samkange, C. A., MA Birm., MB BChir Camb.,
    FRCSEd   Dir.*
Other Staff: 1 Lectr.

Development Studies, Institute of

Chimanikire, D. P., MA Kiev, MPhil PhD   Res.
    Fellow; Chair*
Moyo, S., BA S.Leone, MA PhD   Assoc. Prof.
Sachikonye, L. M., BA Abuja, MSc Abuja, PhD
    Leeds   Res. Fellow; Chairman*
Wekwete, N. N., BScEcon Z'bwe., MSc
    Z'bwe.   Res. Fellow; Chairman*

Development Technology Centre

Ascough, W. J., BSc(Agric) Reading   Dir.*

Distance Education, Centre for

Hill, Graham F. W., BVetMed Lond., MA Melb.,
    PhD Brist.   Prof.

Electron Microscope Unit

Mufunda, J., MB ChB Z'bwe., PhD
    Mich.State   Acting Chairman*

Human Resources Research Centre

Tel: (04) 303271 Fax: (04) 302182
Nherera, C. M., BEd Exe., MA Linköping, PhD
    Lond.   Dir.*

Mining Research, Institute of

Ansari, H., BSc MSc   Chief Chemist
Roberts, A., BSc Natal, PhD Natal   Sr. Econ.
    Geologist*

University Lake Kariba Research Station

Magadza, C. H. D., BSc Lond., MPhil Lond., PhD
    Auck.   Assoc. Prof.; Sci. Dir.*

University Teaching and Learning Centre

Nziramasanga, C. T., DPhil   Dir.*

Water and Sanitation, Training Centre for

Taylor, P., BSc Leic., DPhil Rhodesia   Dir.*

CONTACT OFFICERS

Academic affairs. Acting Deputy Registrar
    (Academic): Takawira, N.
Accommodation. Director: Kasese, F. J.
Admissions (first degree). Senior Assistant
    Registrar: Silamba, Sindiso, BSc(Soc) Z'bwe.
Admissions (higher degree). Assistant
    Registrar: Takawira, N.
Adult/continuing education. Chairperson:
    Nondo, Clara S., BAdEd Z'bwe., MAdEd Z'bwe.
Alumni. Director, Public and International
    Relations: Murandu, Margaret S., BA Rhodesia,
    MBA Z'bwe.
Archives. Librarian: Made, S. M., BA S.Af., MA
    Lond., FLA
Careers. Dean of Students: Madzima, G., BSc
    Z'bwe., DPhil Z'bwe.
Computing services. Deputy Bursar, Data
    Processing: Murahwi, Z. B., BSc Z'bwe.
Consultancy services. Vice-Chancellor: Hill,
    Prof. F. W. Graham, BVetMed Lond., PhD
    Brist., DSc Z'bwe.
Credit transfer. Acting Deputy Registrar
    (Academic): Takawira, N.
Distance education. Vice-Chancellor: Hill,
    Prof. F. W. Graham, BVetMed Lond., PhD
    Brist., DSc Z'bwe.
Equal opportunities. Registrar: Mukondiwa,
    W. M., BA Rhodesia
Estates and buildings/works and services.
    Director: Chinhengo, C. M., BScEcon Z'bwe.,
    MScEcon Z'bwe.

Examinations. Assistant Registrar: Sikwila, S.,
    BA S.Af.
Finance. Bursar: Mapani, W., BAcc Botswana
General enquiries. Registrar: Mukondiwa, W.
    M., BA Rhodesia
Health services. Sister-in-Charge: Mupunga,
    Florence
International office. Director, Public and
    International Relations: Murandu, Margaret
    S., BA Rhodesia, MBA Z'bwe.
Library. Librarian: Made, S. M., BA S.Af., MA
    Lond., FLA
Minorities/disadvantaged groups. Registrar:
    Mukondiwa, W. M., BA Rhodesia
Ombudsperson. Legal Advisor: Mugugu,
    Sheila
Personnel/human resources. Acting Deputy
    Registrar (Administration): Mupawaenda, A.
Public relations, information and marketing.
    Assistant to the Vice-Chancellor: Kuimba,
    Giles
Publications. Publications Officer: Mutetwa, D.
Purchasing. Buyer: Chivinge, F. B., BBS Z'bwe.
Quality assurance and accreditation. Acting
    Deputy Registrar (Academic): Takawira, N.
Research. Senior Assistant Bursar, Research:
    Kaseke, P. R.
Safety. Vice-Chancellor: Hill, Prof. F. W.
    Graham, BVetMed Lond., PhD Brist., DSc Z'bwe.
Scholarships, awards, loans. Senior Assistant
    Registrar: Silamba, Sindiso, BSc(Soc) Z'bwe.
Schools liaison. Dean of Students: Madzima,
    G., BSc Z'bwe., DPhil Z'bwe.
Security. Chief Security Officer: Shoko, D., BA
    Z'bwe.
Sport and recreation. Acting Sports Director:
    Zvomuya, I. T.
Staff development and training. Senior
    Assistant Registrar: Sasa, W. M., BA(Educn)
    Zambia
Student union. Dean of Students: Madzima,
    G., BSc Z'bwe., DPhil Z'bwe.
Student welfare/counselling. Dean of
    Students: Madzima, G., BSc Z'bwe., DPhil
    Z'bwe.
Students from other countries. Acting Deputy
    Registrar (Academic): Takawira, N.
Students with disabilities. Co-ordinator,
    Disabled Students: ......
University press. Director of Information and
    Media: Mutamba, Webster F., BA Missouri,
    BJourn&Comm Missouri, MA Z'bwe.
Women. Registrar: Mukondiwa, W. M., BA
    Rhodesia

[Information supplied by the institution as at 9 March
1998, and edited by the ACU]

APPENDIX 1

ACU Members of Former Commonwealth Countries (People's Republic of China/Hong Kong)

THE UNIVERSITIES OF HONG KONG

Information compiled by the University Grants Committee, Hong Kong as at 23 October 1998

The University System

The University Grants Committee (UGC) is appointed by the Chief Executive of the Hong Kong Special Administrative Region (HKSAR) as the principal advisory committee on the development of tertiary education in the HKSAR and on the financing of eight publicly funded higher education institutions. The Committee comprises eminent local and overseas academics and prominent lay members from the Hong Kong community. The Open University of Hong Kong and the Hong Kong Academy for the Performing Arts are the only degree-awarding institutions not within the ambit of the UGC.

All of the universities in Hong Kong are autonomous institutions, with the authority to grant their own degrees, and with their own ordinances and governing councils. Each institution determines its own establishment, governance, structure and operation. As most of the universities are mainly supported by public funds, the UGC takes on the role of an intermediary, to ensure both academic freedom and autonomy for the institutions as well as public accountability and value for money. The UGC has also broad oversight responsibility in respect of the institutions' development, quality assurance and their general academic and administrative operations.

In 1988, the UGC assumed responsibility for administering research project funding provided separately by the Government. In 1991, a Research Grants Council was established, under the aegis of the UGC, to administer this funding and to advise on the development of research in Hong Kong universities.

Academic Year

The academic year in Hong Kong begins in September/October and ends in May/June.

Language of Instruction

English and Chinese.

Pre-University Education

Primary and secondary education in Hong Kong is provided by government schools, aided schools (largely funded by government but managed by voluntary bodies) and private schools. The curriculum is divided into grammar, technical and pre-vocational. Grammar and technical schools offer a five-year course leading to the Hong Kong Certificate of Education Examination (HKCEE) and often run the two-year sixth form courses leading to the Hong Kong Advanced Level Examination (HKALE).

Admission to First Degree Courses

Each university sets its own entry regulations. For school leavers, admission is based mainly on the results of the HKALE. Students with qualifications gained overseas are considered individually, though entry to university courses requires the equivalent of matriculation.

Method of application. The admissions system is managed by the Joint University Programmes Admission System (JUPAS). Applicants decide on up to 20 study programmes which must be listed in order of preference. Each programme will then give the student a rating based on: HKALE and HKCEE results; information contained on the application form; performance at interviews and during tests. Through matching preferences and ratings applicants are then offered the highest priority for which they have the required rating. Applications should be made by early December, for entrance in the following academic year. Results are announced in mid-August, followed two weeks later by the clearing round.

Finance

The UGC is the primary source of advice to the government on all funding needs of the tertiary institutions. Assessment of the institution's funding requirements and allocations of public funds are made according to discipline, programme levels (undergraduate, postgraduate, sub-degree), nature of studies/tuition (eg coursework, postgraduate, research postgraduate), student numbers by categories and active research workers in each field.

Recurrent operating grants are allocated to universities on a triennial basis. For 1998–2001, the government has imposed a funding reduction aimed at achieving a reduction of 3% in per student unit costs for each of those three years.

Student finance. Students in Hong Kong universities are required to pay tuition fees. The fees are the same across all UGC-funded institutions and across all disciplines so that students' course choices are not affected by financial considerations. The Hong Kong Academy for the Performing Arts follows the UGC in setting its tuition fee levels. The Open University of Hong Kong has, until recently, charged considerably higher fees for its courses but the differential has disappeared due to recent sharp increases in UGC-funded fee levels.

The increase in fees was a result of the government established target of an 18% recovery rate of total student unit costs across the university system. The fees are projected to rise to HK$47,300 in 1999–2000. Government grants and loans to means-tested students have risen accordingly, in support of the promise that no student would be denied a place in higher education for want of financial resources.

Staff and Student Numbers

In 1997–98 there were 69,723 students enrolled in Hong Kong universities, constituting a marginal increase from the previous year. In 1997–98 the number of full-time equivalent teaching staff at the universities was 5725.

Bibliography

University Grants Commission (UGC). *Higher education in Hong Kong -a report by the University Grants Committee.* Hong Kong, 1996.

Hong Kong Special Administrative Region Government. *Annual Report of the Hong Kong Special Administrative Region Government.* (Chapter 10: Education). Hong Kong, 1998.

CHINESE UNIVERSITY OF HONG KONG

Founded 1963

Member of the Association of Commonwealth Universities

Postal Address: Shatin, New Territories, Hong Kong
Telephone: 2609 6000, 2609 7000 **Fax**: 2603 5544 **Cables**: Sinoversity, Hong Kong **Telex**: 50301 CUHK HX
WWW: http://www.cuhk.edu.hk **E-mail formula**: userid@cuhk.edu.hk

CHANCELLOR—The Chief Executive of the Hong Kong Special Administrative Region (*ex officio*)
CHAIRMAN OF COUNCIL—Lee, Hon-chiu, JP, BS MS DBA LLD
VICE-CHANCELLOR*‡—Li, Prof. Arthur K. C., MA *Camb.*, MB BChir *Camb.*, MD *Camb.*, FRCS, FRCSEd, FRACS, FACS, Hon. FRCSGlas, Hon. FRCSI
PRO-VICE-CHANCELLOR—King, Ambrose Y. C., JP, BA *Natnl.Taiwan*, MA *Natnl.Chengchi*, MA *Pitt.*, PhD *Pitt.*
PRO-VICE-CHANCELLOR—Liu, P. W., BA *Prin.*, MA *Stan.*, MA(Ed) *Stan.*, PhD *Stan.*
PRO-VICE-CHANCELLOR—Young, Kenneth, BS *Cal.Tech.*, PhD *Cal.Tech.*
TREASURER—Kwok, Raymond P. L., MA *Camb.*, MBA *Harv.*
SECRETARY—Leung, Jacob S. K., BSocSc *HK*, MDiv *S.Baptist Theol.Sem.*
REGISTRAR—Ho, Richard M. W., JP, BA *HK*, MPhil *HK*, PhD *Lond.*
LIBRARIAN—Lee, Michael M., BA *Natnl.Taiwan*, MA *W.Mich.*, PhD *Loyola(Ill.)*
BURSAR—Chan, Terence C. W., BSocSc *HK*, FCA, FCA(Aust)
UNIVERSITY DEAN OF STUDENTS—Kwok, S. T., BA *Chinese HK*, MA *Calif.*, PhD *Calif.*

GENERAL INFORMATION

History. Established in 1963, the university had its origin in three post-secondary colleges: New Asia College, Chung Chi College and United College of Hong Kong. Its fourth constituent, Shaw College, became operational in 1988.

It is located in the north of Shatin new town in the New Territories.

Admission to first degree courses (see also Hong Kong Introduction). Hong Kong applicants: through the Joint University Programmes Admissions System (JUPAS). Hong Kong Certificate of Education Exam (HKCEE) with 7 subjects (taken in one sitting) at grade E, including 2 language subjects (Chinese, English, French or German), and the Hong Kong Advanced Level Exam (HKALE) with (taken in one sitting) grade E in advanced supplementary level (AS) Chinese language and culture and use of English, and at least 2 A level subjects, or 1 A and 2 AS level subjects.

International applicants: apply direct to the university. General Certificate of Education (GCE) Exam with (taken in one sitting) pass grades in 3 A level subjects or 2 A and 2 AS level subjects; or International Baccalaureate Diploma; or other equivalent qualifications.

First Degrees (see also Hong Kong Directory to Subjects of Study). BA, BBA, BEd, BEng, BMedSc, BNurs, BPharm, BSc, BSSc, MB ChB.

Most courses are full-time and last 3–4 years. BMedSc: 1 year for appropriately qualified candidates; BNurs (post-registration programme): 2 years full-time or 4 years part-time; BEd (in primary education): 2 years full-time (for appropriately qualified candidates) or 5–6 years part-time; MB ChB: 5 years full-time.

Higher Degrees (see also Hong Kong Directory to Subjects of Study). MA, MArch, MBA, MClinPharm, MDiv, MEd, MFA, MMus, MNurs, MPH, MSc, MSSc, MSW, MPhil, PhD, DEd, DMus, DSc, MD.

Applicants for admission to master's degrees must normally hold an appropriate first degree with at least second class honours. DEd, DMus, PhD: appropriate master's degree; MD: MB ChB, or equivalent, plus specified qualifications and experience; DSc: awarded on published work.

Master's degrees normally last 1–2 years full-time or 2–3 years part-time. Doctoral programmes: 36–84 months full-time or 48–96 months part-time.

Language of Instruction. Mainly Chinese, but English is also widely used. All students in their first year of study are required to complete an intensive programme in Putonghua, Cantonese and English. Elective Chinese and English language courses are also offered to help students enhance their language proficiency.

Libraries. 1,365,441 volumes and bound journals; 9652 current journals. Special collections include: Hong Kong; modern drama; William Faulkner.

Fees (1997–98, annual). Undergraduate: HK$42,100 (full-time); HK$28,066 (part-time). Postgraduate: HK$42,100 (full-time); HK$21,050–89,550 (part-time).

Academic Awards (1996–97). 1275 awards ranging in value from HK$400 to HK$40,000.

Academic Year (1997–98). Full-time undergraduate programmes (two terms): 8 September–23 December; 5 January–9 May; 18 May–7 July (summer session).

Part-time undergraduate programmes (three terms): 1 September–9 December; 10 December–2 April; 7 April–23 June.

Postgraduate programmes (two terms): 8 September–20 December; 5 January–25 April.

Income (1996–97). HK$2,840,229,000.

Statistics (1997). Staff: 4284 (1007 teaching, 246 professional, 379 research, 2652 administrative and support). Students: undergraduate 9639 (9152 full-time, 487 part-time); postgraduate 3474; international 106.

FACULTIES/SCHOOLS

Arts

Tel: 2609 7107 Fax: 2603 5621
Dean: Ho, Prof. H. H., BA *Natnl.Taiwan*, MA *Natnl.Taiwan*, PhD *Mich.*
Secretary: Chan, M. K., BSocSc *HK*

Business Administration

Tel: 2609 7785 Fax: 2603 5917
Dean: Lee, Prof. K. H., BCom *Chinese HK*, MCom *Chinese HK*, PhD *Northwestern*
Secretary: Young, L. D. L. K. Woo, BA *HK*

Education

Tel: 2609 6937 Fax: 2603 6129
Dean: Chung, Prof. S. Y. P., BA *Oregon*, MA *Mich. State*, MA *Stan.*, PhD *Stan.*

Administrative Assistant: Tang, P. K. P. Lau, BBA *Chinese HK*

Engineering

Tel: 2609 8446 Fax: 2603 5701

Dean: Ching, P. C., BEng *Liv.*, PhD *Liv.*, FIEE
Secretary: Law, D. S. L. Chu, BA *HK*, MSocSc *HK*

Medicine

Tel: 2609 6891 Fax: 2603 5821

Dean: Lee, Prof. J. C. K., MB BS *HK*, PhD *Roch.*, FRCPCan, FRCPA
Secretary: Lee, A. S. M. Siu, MSc *Edin.*, MEd *Edin.*

Science

Tel: 2609 6327 Fax: 2603 5315

Dean: Lau, Prof. Oi Wah, BSc *HK*, MSc *Lond.*, PhD *HK*, FRSChem
Secretary: Yang, A., BA *Alta.*

Social Science

Tel: 2609 6239 Fax: 2603 6774

Dean: Chau, Prof. K. K. L., MSW *McG.*, PhD *S.Calif.*
Secretary: Law, J. K. H., BSocSc *HK*, MSocSc *HK*, MA *Chinese HK*

ACADEMIC UNITS

Kao, Charles K., CBE, BSc *Lond.*, PhD *Lond.*, DSc *Sus.*, DEng *Glas.*, DSc *Durh.*, DUniv *Griff.*, DSc *Chinese HK*, FEng, FIEE Hon. Prof., Engineering
Yang, C. N., BSc *Natnl.S.W.*, PhD *Chic.*, DSc *Drexel*, Hon. DSc *Chinese HK* Distinguished Prof.-at-Large

Accountancy

Tel: 2609 7838 Fax: 2603 5114

Chan, K. H., BCom *Chinese HK*, MAccSc *Ill.*, PhD *Penn.State* Prof.
Cheng, P. S. T., BA *Mich.State*, PhD *Mich. State* Assoc. Prof.
Ho, S. S. M., BBA *Wash.*, MSc *Lond.*, PhD *Brad.* Prof.; Dir.*
Lee, Dominica S. Y., BSocSc *HK*, MSc *Edin.* Assoc. Prof.
Other Staff: 1 Visiting Prof.; 16 Lectrs.; 1 Visiting Scholar

Anthropology

Tel: 2609 7670 Fax: 2603 5218

Tan, C. B., BSocSc *Sci.U.Malaysia*, MA *Cornell*, PhD *Cornell* Prof.; Acting Chairman*
Wu, D. Y. H., BA *Natnl.Taiwan*, MA *Hawaii*, PhD *ANU* Prof.
Other Staff: 6 Lectrs.; 2 Visiting Profs.; 1 Res Assoc.; 2 Hon. Res. Assocs.

Architecture

Tel: 2609 6517 Fax: 2603 5267

Ho, P. P., MA *Edin.*, PhD *Lond.* Assoc. Prof.
Lee, C. N., MMus *Manhattan Sch.*, MArch *Yale* Prof.
Lee, T. F., BArch *Mich.* Prof.; Chairman*
Ochshorn, J., BArch *Cornell*, MS *M.I.T.*, MUrbDes *C.U.N.Y.* Assoc. Prof.
Sidener, J. T., BArch *Calif.*, PhD *Calif.*, MArch *Penn.*, MCP *Penn.* Assoc. Prof.
Other Staff: 16 Lectrs.; 4 Res. Assocs.

Biochemistry

Tel: 2609 6359 Fax: 2603 5123

Cheng, H. K., BSc *Chinese HK*, PhD *Lond.* Prof.
Choy, Y. M., BSc *HK*, MSc *S.Fraser*, PhD *Br.Col.* Prof.
Fung, K. P., BSc *Chinese HK*, MPhil *Chinese HK*, PhD *HK* Prof.
Ho, W. K. K., AB *Calif.*, PhD *Calif.* Prof.
Kong, Y. C., BSc *Natnl.Sun Yat Sen*, PhD *Brussels* Prof.
Lee, C. Y., MSc *Br.Col.*, PhD *Br.Col.* Prof.; Chairman*
Leung, K. N., BSc *Chinese HK*, PhD *ANU* Prof.
Liew, C. C., BSc *Nan.*, MA *Tor.*, PhD *Tor.* Visiting Prof.

Ng, T. B., BSc *HK*, MPhil *HK*, PhD *Nfld.* Prof.
Shaw, P. C., PhD *Lond.*, BSc MPhil Sr. Lectr.
Tsang, D. S. C., BSc *McG.*, PhD *McG.* Prof.
Tso, W. W., MSc *Miami(Fla.)*, PhD *Wis.* Sr. Lectr.
Waye, M. Y., BSc *W.Ont.*, PhD *Tor.* Assoc. Prof.
Other Staff: 13 Lectrs.; 4 Res. Assocs.

Biology

Tel: 2609 6348 Fax: 2603 5745

Buswell, J. A., BSc *Birm.*, PhD *Birm.* Prof.
But, P. P. H., BSc *Chinese HK*, MBA *Chinese HK*, MA *Calif.*, PhD *Calif.* Prof.
Chu, K. H., BA *Calif.*, PhD *M.I.T.* Assoc. Prof.
Kwan, H. S., BSc *Chinese HK*, MPhil *Chinese HK*, PhD *Calif.* Assoc. Prof.
Ooi, V. E. C., BS *Natnl.Taiwan*, MSc *Sask.*, PhD *Tor.* Prof.
Sun, S. S. M., BSc *Chinese HK*, MSc *HK*, PhD *Wis.* Prof.; Chairman*
Wong, C. K., BSc *Tor.*, PhD *Tor.*, MSc *Ott.* Assoc. Prof.
Wong, P. K., BSc *Chinese HK*, MPhil *Chinese HK*, PhD *Calif.* Prof.
Woo, N. Y. S., BSc *HK*, PhD *HK* Prof.
Other Staff: 10 Lectrs.; 1 Res. Assoc.; 1 Hon.Sr. Res. Fellow

Business, International, see Internat. Business

Chemistry

Tel: 2609 6344 Fax: 2603 5057

Au Yeung, S. C. F., BSc *S.Fraser*, PhD *McM.* Assoc. Prof.; Acting Chairman*
Chan, K. S., BSc *HK*, PhD *Chic.* Assoc. Prof.
Chan, T. L., BSc *St FX*, MSc *Missouri*, PhD *Tulane* Sr. Lectr.
Lau, Oi Wah, BSc *HK*, MSc *Lond.*, PhD *HK*, FRSChem
Leung, K. W. P., BSc *Kent*, MSc *Sus.*, PhD *W.Aust.* Assoc. Prof.
Li, W. K., BS *Ill.*, MS *Mich.*, PhD *Mich.* Prof.
Mak, T. C. W., BSc *Br.Col.*, PhD *Br.Col.* Prof.
Shing, T. K. M., BSc *HK*, MSc *Lond.*, PhD *Lond.* Prof.
So, S. P., BSc *HK*, PhD *McM.*, FRSChem Prof.
Wong, N. C., PhD *Lond.*, DSc *Lond.*, FRSChem
Wu, C., BSc *China U.S.T.*, PhD *N.Y.* Prof.
Other Staff: 9 Lectrs.

Chinese Language and Literature, see also Special Centres, etc., and Chinese Studies, Institute of

Tel: 2609 7074 Fax: 2603 6048

Chan, S. C., MA *Harv.*, MA Prof.
Chang, S. H., MA Prof.
Cheung, A. K. Y., MA *Natnl.Taiwan*, PhD *Natnl.Taiwan* Prof.
Chiang, Y. H., BA *Chinese HK*, MPhil *Chinese HK*, PhD *Calif.* Prof.
Dang, S. L., MA Prof.; Chairman*
Lo, Wai Luen, BA *Chinese HK*, MPhil *HK* Prof.
Tay, L. S., MA *Natnl.Taiwan*, LittD *Natnl.Taiwan* Prof.
Wong, K. C., MA *HK* Prof.
Wong, W. L., BA *Chinese HK*, MS *Oklahoma State*, PhD *Ohio State* Prof.
Wu, H. I., MA *Natnl.Taiwan*, PhD *Natnl.Taiwan* Prof.
Yeung, C. K., BA *Chinese HK*, MA *Kyoto* Prof.
Other Staff: 10 Lectrs.; 1 Res. Assoc.

Communication, see Journalism and Communicn.

Computer Science and Engineering

Tel: 2609 8440 Fax: 2603 5024

Hung, H. S., BS *Stan.*, MS *Ill.*, MS *Wis.*, PhD *Wis.* Prof.
Leung, K. S., BSc *Lond.*, PhD *Lond.* Prof.
Lyu, M. R. T., BS *Natnl. Taiwan*, MS *Calif.*, PhD *Calif.* Assoc. Prof.
Moon, Y. S., BSc *Manit.*, MSc *Tor.*, PhD *Tor.* Sr. Lectr.

Ng, K. W., MSc *Brad.*, PhD *Brad.* Prof.; Chairman*
Wong, C. K., BA *HK*, MA *Col.*, PhD *Col.* Prof., Computer Science
Xu, L., BEng *Harbin*, DEng *Tsing Hua* Prof.
Other Staff: 19 Lectrs.; 4 Res. Fellows; 11 Res. Assocs.

Curriculum and Instruction

Tel: 2609 6905 Fax: 2603 6724

Chung, C. M., BSc MA(Ed) Prof.; Chairman*
Mak, S. Y., MSc *Brown*, PhD *Brown*, BSc Prof.
Wong, H. W., BSSc *Chinese HK*, MA(Ed) *Chinese HK*, EdD *Calif.* Assoc. Prof.
Other Staff: 14 Lectrs.; 3 Asst. Lectrs.; 1 Res. Assoc.

Decision Sciences and Managerial Economics

Tel: 2609 7813 Fax: 2603 5104

Chan, C. I., BBA *Chinese HK*, MBA *Br.Col.* Assoc. Prof.
Devereux, M. B., MA *Trinity(Dub.)*, PhD *Qu.* Prof.
Fung, K. Y., BSSc *Chinese HK*, MA *W.Ont.*, PhD *W.Ont* Assoc. Prof.
Law, J. S., BA *Texas*, PhD *Texas* Prof.
Lee, T. S., MS *Natnl.Chiao Tung*, MBA *Missouri*, PhD *Missouri* Prof.
Leung, L. C. K., BSIE *Northwestern*, MS *Virginia Polytech.*, PhD *Virginia Polytech.* Prof.
Mok, H. M. K., MA *Tor.*, MSW *Hawaii*, MURP *Hawaii*, PhD *Hawaii* Assoc. Prof.
Ng, L. F. Y., BS *Northwestern(Oklahoma)*, MS *Oklahoma State*, PhD *Oklahoma State* Prof.
Tuan, C., BS *Chung Hsing*, MSc *Ohio State*, PhD *Ohio State* Prof.
Yu, E. S. H., MS *S.Illinois*, PhD *Wash.*, BSSc Prof., Operations and Systems Management; Chairman*
Other Staff: 12 Lectrs.; 2 Res. Assocs.

Economics

Tel: 2609 7035 Fax: 2603 5805

Chao, C. C., BC *Natnl.Chengchi*, MA *Natnl.Taiwan*, PhD *S.Illinois* Assoc. Prof.
Chou, Win Lin, BA *Fujen*, MS *Ill.*, PhD *Ill.* Prof.
Hsueh, T. T., MA *Natnl.Taiwan*, PhD *Colorado* Prof.
Liu, P. W., BA *Prin.*, MA *Stan.*, MA(Ed) *Stan.*, PhD *Stan.* Prof.
Stark, O., BA *Jerusalem*, DPhil *Sus.* Visiting Prof.
Sung, Y. W., BSocSc *HK*, PhD *Minn.* Prof.; Chairman*
Tsui, K. Y., MA *Tor.*, PhD *Tor.* Assoc. Prof.
Yip, C. K., BSSc *Chinese HK*, MA(Econ) *Penn.State*, MA(Stat) *Penn.State*, PhD *Penn.State* Assoc. Prof.
Zhang, J., BSc *Zhejiang*, MA *McM.*, PhD *McM.* Assoc. Prof.
Other Staff: 12 Lectrs.; 1 Hon. Res. Fellow

Educational Administration and Policy

Tel: 2609 6953 Fax: 2603 6761

Chung, S. Y. P., BA *Oregon*, MA *Mich.State*, MA *Stan.*, PhD *Stan.* Prof.
Dimmock, C. A. J., BSc *Lond.*, MEd *Reading*, PhD *Lond.* Assoc. Prof.
Lo, L. N. K., BA *Oregon*, MIA *Col.*, EdD *Col.* Prof.; Acting Chairman*
Tsang, W. K., BSSc PhD Assoc. Prof.
Other Staff: 1 Visiting Prof.; 10 Lectrs.; 2 Res. Assocs.

Educational Psychology

Tel: 2609 6904 Fax: 2603 6921

Chan, D. W. O., BA *Brock*, MA *W.Ont.*, PhD *W.Ont.* Prof.
Hau, K. T., BSc *Chinese HK*, MA(Ed) *Chinese HK*, PhD *HK* Assoc. Prof.; Chairman*
Lam, M. P., MS *Wagner*, PhD *Ill.* Prof.
Lo, L. F., BSc *Wash.*, MSc *Seattle Pacific*, MEd *Nevada*, EdD *Pitt.* Assoc. Prof.
Other Staff: 11 Lectrs.; 1 Res. Assoc.

Engineering, Electronic

Tel: 2609 8274 Fax: 2603 5558

Cham, W. K., BSc Chinese HK, MSc Lough., PhD Lough.   Assoc. Prof.
Chan, K. T., BSc HK, MSc Cornell, PhD Cornell   Assoc. Prof.
Ching, P. C., BEng Liv., PhD Liv., FIEE   Prof.; Chairman*
Leung, H. C., BS C.U.N.Y., MS M.I.T., PhD M.I.T.   Assoc. Prof.
Tsui, H. T., BSc(Eng) HK, MSc Manc., PhD Birm.   Prof.
Wilson, I. H., BSc Reading, PhD Reading   Prof.
Wong, J. S. P., BSc MPhil PhD   Prof.
Wong, M. K., PhD Lond., DSc(Eng) Lond., FIEE, FIP   Visiting Prof.
Other Staff: 1 Visiting Prof.; 11 Lectrs.; 1 Res. Fellow; 7 Res. Assocs.

Engineering, Information

Tel: 2609 8385 Fax: 2603 5032

Cheung, K. W., BSc(Eng) HK, MS Yale, PhD Cal.Tech.   Prof.
Hui, Y. N., MS M.I.T., PhD M.I.T.   Prof.
Lee, T. T., BS Natnl.Cheng Kung, MS Cleveland, MS N.Y.Polytech., PhD N.Y.Polytech.   Prof.
Li, R. S. Y., BS Natnl.Taiwan, PhD Calif.   Prof.
Liew, S. C., SM M.I.T., PhD M.I.T.   Prof.
Tong, F. F. K., MA Calif., PhD Col.   Assoc. Prof.
Wei, V. K., BS Natnl.Taiwan, PhD Hawaii   Prof.
Wing, Omar, BS Tennessee, MS M.I.T., EngScD Col.   Prof.
Wong, W. S., MA Yale, MS Harv., PhD Harv.   Prof.; Chairman*
Yeung, W. H., BS Cornell, MEng Cornell, PhD Cornell   Assoc. Prof.
Yum, P. T. S., MS Col., PhD Col.   Prof.
Other Staff: 9 Lectrs.; 1 Visiting Lectr.; 1 Res. Fellow; 1 Res Assoc.

Engineering Management, see Engin., Systems, and Engin. Management

Engineering, Mechanical and Automation

Tel: 2609 8337 Fax: 2603 6002

Kwong, C. P., MSc Lough., PhD   Prof.
Xu, Y., MEng Zhejiang, PhD Penn.   Assoc. Prof.; Chairman*
Other Staff: 1 Visiting Prof.; 9 Lectrs.; 2 Res. Assocs.

Engineering, Systems, and Engineering Management

Tel: 2609 8313 Fax: 2603 5505

Cai, X., BEng Harbin Shipbldg.Engin., DEng Tsing Hua   Assoc. Prof.; Chairman*
He, J., BS Heilongjiang, MS Shanghai Jiaotong, PhD Penn.   Assoc. Prof.
Lam, K. P., BSc HK, MPhil Chinese HK, DPhil Oxf.   Sr. Lectr.
Li, D., MEng Shanghai Jiaotong, PhD Case W.Reserve   Assoc. Prof.
Other Staff: 9 Lectrs.; 1 Visiting Lectr.; 1 Asst. Lectr.; 1 Res. Fellow

English

Tel: 2609 7005 Fax: 2603 5270

Boyle, J., BD Lond., MA Oxf., PhD HK, LPhil Heythrop   Prof.
Lee, T. H. T., BA Swarthmore, MA HK, PhD Calif.   Sr. Lectr.
Luk, T. Y. T., BA Chinese HK, MA York(Can.), PhD Mich.   Sr. Lectr.
Parkin, A. T. L., BA Camb., MA Camb., PhD Brist.   Prof.; Chairman*
Tam, J. K. K., BA Chinese HK, MA Ill., PhD Ill.   Prof.
Wong, K. Y., MA Redlands, PhD Calif.   Prof.
Other Staff: 11 Lectrs.; 1 Res. Assoc.

English Language Teaching Unit

Tel: 2609 7465 Fax: 2603 5157

Fu, Gail S., BA Wellesley, MA Mich., PhD Mich.   Prof.

Gong, G., MA Mississippi, PhD Purdue   Prof.; Acting Dir.*
Other Staff: 5 Lectrs.; 1 Asst. Lectr.

Finance

Tel: 2609 7805 Fax: 2603 6586

Chiang, R., BBA C.U.N.Y., PhD Penn.   Prof.
Lang, L. H. P., BA Tunghai, MA Natnl.Taiwan, MA Penn., PhD Penn.   Prof.
McGuinness, P. B., BA Newcastle(UK), MPhil Camb., PhD Leeds   Assoc. Prof.
Shih, E. Y. C., BA Taiwan Normal, MA Ohio State, PhD S.Illinois   Prof.; Chairman*
Wang, K., LLB Chinese Culture, MS Texas, MBA Texas, PhD Texas   Prof.
Young, L., MSc Well., DPhil Oxf.   Prof.
Other Staff: 10 Lectrs.; 1 Sr. Res. Fellow

Fine Arts

Tel: 2609 7615 Fax: 2603 5755

Jao, T. I., Hon. DLitt HK, Dr(HumSc) École Pratique des Hautes Études   Hon. Prof.
Kao, Mayching, BA Chinese HK, MA New Mexico, PhD Stan.   Prof.
Other Staff: 6 Lectrs.; 1 Asst. Lectr.

French Studies

Tel: 2609 7724 Fax: 2603 5089

2 Lectrs.

Geography

Tel: 2609 6532 Fax: 2603 5006

Chu, D. K. Y., BA HK, MPhil HK, PhD Lond.   Prof.
Lam, K. C., BA HK, MPhil HK, PhD NE   Prof.; Chairman*
Leung, Y., BSSc Chinese HK, MA Colorado, MS Colorado, PhD Colorado   Prof.
Wong, K. Y., BA HK, MA Melb., PhD Melb.   Prof.
Yeung, Y. M., OBE, JP, BA HK, MA W.Ont., PhD Chic.   Prof.
Other Staff: 7 Lectrs.; 1 Asst. Lectr.; 5 Res. Assocs.

German Studies

Tel: 2609 7659 Fax: 2603 7224

3 Lectrs.

Government and Public Administration

Tel: 2609 7530 Fax: 2603 5229

Chang, C. Y., BA Nan., MA W.Ont., PhD N.Y.State   Sr. Lectr.
Davis, M. C., BA Ohio State, LLM Yale, JD Calif.   Prof.
Kuan, H. C., LLB Natnl.Chengchi, MA F.U.Berlin, PhD Munich   Prof.
Lee, P. N. S., BA Natnl.Taiwan, MA Indiana, PhD Chic.   Prof.
Weng, B. S. J., LLB Natnl.Taiwan, MS Wis., PhD Wis.   Prof.; Chairman*
Other Staff: 10 Lectrs.; 1 Res. Assoc.

History

Tel: 2609 7117 Fax: 2603 5685

Chan, H. L., BA HK, MA HK, MA Prin., PhD Prin.   Prof.; Chairman*
Chu, H. L., BA Taiwan, MA Taiwan, PhD Prin.   Prof.
Hsu, C. Y., MA Natnl.Taiwan, PhD Chic.   Prof.
Kwok, S. T., BA Chinese HK, MA Calif., PhD Calif.   Prof.
Leung, P. Y. S., BA Chinese HK, MPhil Chinese HK, PhD Calif.   Prof.
Ng, Ngai Ha Lun, MA HK, PhD Minn.   Prof.
So, B. K. L., BA Chinese HK, MPhil Chinese HK, PhD ANU   Assoc. Prof.
Other Staff: 9 Lectrs.; 1 Res. Assoc.

International Business

Tel: 2609 7824 Fax: 2603 5473

Fukuda, K. J., BS Iowa State, MBA Col., PhD HK   Prof.
Lau, H. F., MBA Col., PhD N.U.I., BCom MCom   Prof.; Chairman*
Lo, T. W. C., BBA Chinese HK, MBA Calif., PhD City(UK)   Prof.

Mun, K. C., MA Freib., PhD Freib.   Prof., Marketing
Young, K. Y. H., BA Whittier, MBA Chinese HK, PhD Chinese HK   Assoc. Prof.
Other Staff: 7 Lectrs.; 1 Visiting Scholar

Italian Studies

Tel: 2609 7736 Fax: 2603 7736

No staff at present

Japanese Studies

Tel: 2609 6563 Fax: 2603 5118

Fong, Ming-choo C., MA Hitotsubashi   Assoc. Prof.
Yue, K. C., BA Tokyo Foreign, MA   Sr. Lectr.
Other Staff: 1 Visiting Prof.; 1 Lectr. (Chairman*); 1 Visiting Lectr.; 1 Asst. Lectr.

Journalism and Communication

Tel: 2609 7680 Fax: 2603 5007

Chan, J. M., BS Minn., PhD Minn., MPhil Chinese HK   Prof.; Chairman*
Lee, C. C., BA Natnl.Chengchi, MA Hawaii, PhD Mich.   Prof.
Lee, P. S. N., BSSc Chinese HK, MPhil Chinese HK, PhD Mich.   Assoc. Prof.
Leung, K. W. Y., MA Minn., PhD Minn.   Sr. Lectr.
Other Staff: 10 Lectrs.; 1 Res. Assoc.

Management, see also Decision Scis. and Managerial Econ.

Tel: 2609 7898 Fax: 2063 6840

Chow, I. H. S., BBA Chinese HK, MBA Georgia State, PhD Georgia State   Prof.
Kane, J. S., BS Boston, MA Minn., PhD Mich.   Assoc. Prof.
Lau, C. M., BSSc Chinese HK, MBA Chinese HK, PhD Texas A. & M.   Assoc. Prof.; Chairman*
Poon, W. K., BA Tor., MEd Tor., PhD Tor.   Assoc. Prof.
Other Staff: 13 Lectrs.

Marketing

Tel: 2609 7809 Fax: 2603 5473

Chan, A. C. F., MBA Calif., BBA Chinese HK, PhD Chinese HK   Prof.
Hui, M. K. M., BBA Chinese HK, PhD Lond.   Assoc. Prof.
Ingene, C. A., AB Wash., AM Brown, PhD Brown   Prof.
Lee, K. H., BCom Chinese HK, MCom Chinese HK, PhD Northwestern   Prof.
Steilen, C. F., BS Bradley, MBA Calif.State, PhD Oregon   Sr. Lectr.
Tung, Suk-Ching H., BBA Chinese HK, MBA Indiana   Prof.; Chairman*
Other Staff: 10 Lectrs.

Mathematics

Tel: 2609 7988 Fax: 2603 5154

Chan, H. F., MSc N.Y., PhD N.Y., BSc   Prof.
Chou, K. S., MSc Chinese HK, PhD N.Y.   Prof.
Lau, K. S., BSc Chinese HK, PhD Wash.   Prof.; Chairman*
Ng, K. F., PhD Wales, DSc Wales   Prof.
Shum, K. P., MSc Leeds, PhD Alta.   Prof.
Tam, L. F., BSc Stan., PhD Stan.   Prof.
Yau, S. T., PhD Calif.   Prof.
Other Staff: 11 Lectrs.; 2 Visiting Scholars; 1 Res. Fellow

Medicine, see below

Music

Tel: 2609 6510 Fax: 2603 5273

Chan, S. Y., BA Chinese HK, MA Pitt., PhD Pitt.   Assoc. Prof.
Chan, W. W., MusDoc Tor., BA, FTCL   Prof.; Chairman*
Law, D. P. L., BA Chinese HK, MMus Northwestern, PhD Northwestern   Prof.
Olson, Greta J., MA S.Calif., PhD S.Calif.   Assoc. Prof.
Ryker, H. C., BA Calif., MM Wash., PhD Wash.   Prof.
Tsao, B. P. Y., MMus Br.Col., PhD Pitt.   Prof.

Witzleben, J. L., BA *Calif.*, MA *Hawaii*, PhD
Pitt. Assoc. Prof.
Other Staff: 4 Lectrs.; 1 Res. Assoc.

Nursing, see Medicine, below

Philosophy

Tel: 2609 7135 Fax: 2603 5323

Allinson, R. E., AB *S.Illinois*, PhD *Texas* Prof.
Chen, T., PhD *S.Illinois* Prof.
Ho, H. H., BA *Natnl.Taiwan*, MA *Natnl.Taiwan*,
PhD *Mich.* Prof.
Kwan, T. W., BA *Bochum*, MPhil *Bochum*, DrPhil
Bochum Prof.
Liu, C. Y., BA *Natnl.Taiwan*, MA *S.Illinois*, PhD
S.Illinois Prof.
Liu, S. H., MA *Natnl.Taiwan*, PhD *S.Illinois* Prof.
Shih, Y. K., MA *Natnl.Taiwan*, PhD *Ott.* Prof.;
Chairman*
Other Staff: 8 Lectrs.; 1 Asst. Lectr.

Physical Education Unit, see also Sports
Sci. and Phys. Educn.

Tel: 2609 6092 Fax: 2603 5275
1 Lectr. (Dir*)

Physics

Tel: 2609 6339 Fax: 2603 5204

Hui, P. M., BSc *HK*, MS *Ohio*, PhD *Ohio* Assoc.
Prof.
Kui, H. W., BS *Cal.Tech.*, PhD *Harv.* Assoc.
Prof.
Lai, H. M., BSc *Chinese HK*, PhD
Dartmouth Prof.; Chairman*
Lau, L. W. M., PhD *Br.Col.*, BSc Prof.,
Materials Science
Leung, P. T., BSc *Chinese HK*, MS *Cal.Tech.*, PhD
Chinese HK Assoc. Prof.
Liu, K. L., BSc *Chinese HK*, MSc *Tor.*, PhD
Tor. Sr. Lectr.
Wong, H. K., BSc *Chinese HK*, MPhil *Chinese HK*,
PhD *Northwestern* Assoc. Prof.
Yang, C. N., BSc *Natnl.S.W.*, PhD *Chic.*, DSc
Drexel, Hon. DSc *Chinese HK* Hon. Prof.
Young, K., BS *Cal.Tech.*, PhD *Cal.Tech.* Prof.
Yu, K. W., BSc *Chinese HK*, MSc *Calif.*, PhD
Calif. Prof.
Other Staff: 11 Lectrs.; 1 Res. Fellow; 5 Res.
Assocs.; 4 Hon. Res. Assocs.

Psychology

Tel: 2609 6578 Fax: 2603 5019

Bond, M., BA *Tor.*, PhD *Stan.* Prof.
Chen, H. C., BA *Fujen*, MA *Calif.State Coll.(San
Bernardino)*, PhD *Kansas* Prof.
Cheung, Fanny M. C., JP, BA *Calif.*, PhD
Minn. Prof.
Leung, J. J. P., BA *Massey*, PhD *Massey* Assoc.
Prof.
Leung, K., BSc *Chinese HK*, MA *Ill.*, PhD
Ill. Prof.; Chairman*
Tang, C. S. K., BA *N.Texas*, MS *N.Texas*, PhD
N.Texas Assoc. Prof.
Other Staff: 13 Lectrs.; 1 Res. Assoc.

Public Administration, see Govt. and
Public Admin.

Religion

Tel: 2609 6477 Fax: 2603 5280

Lee, Rev./ A. C. C., PhD *Edin.*, BA MDiv Prof.
Overmyer, D. L., BA *Westmar*, BD
Evangel.Theol.Sem., MA *Chic.*, PhD *Chic.* Prof.;
Acting Chairman*
Yu, A. C., BA *Houghton*, STB *Fuller*, PhD
Chic. Prof.
Other Staff: 7 Lectrs.; 1 Asst. Lectr.; 1 Res.
Assoc.; 1 Hon. Sr. Res. Fellow; 5 Hon. Res.
Assocs.

Social Work

Tel: 2609 7507 Fax: 2603 5018

Chau, K. K. L., MSW *McG.*, PhD *S.Calif.* Prof.
Lam, Mong Chow, BSSc *Chinese HK*, MSW *Minn.*,
PhD *S.Calif.* Prof.; Chairman*
Ma, L. C., MSocSc *HK*, PhD *HK* Assoc. Prof.

Mok, B. H., BSSc *Chinese HK*, MSW *Hawaii*, PhD
S.Calif. Prof.
Shek, D. T. L., BSocSc *HK*, PhD *HK* Prof.
Other Staff: 8 Lectrs.; 1 Res. Assoc.

Sociology

Tel: 2609 6604 Fax: 2603 5213

Chan, Y. K., BSSc *Chinese HK*, DU *Bordeaux* Prof.
Cheung, T. S., BSSc *Chinese HK*, MA *N.Y.State*,
PhD *N.Y.State* Prof.
Cheung, Y. W., BSSc *Chinese HK*, MA *McM.*, PhD
Tor. Prof.
King, A. Y. C., JP, BA *Natnl.Taiwan*, MA
Natnl.Chengchi, MA *Pitt.*, PhD *Pitt.* Prof.
Lau, C. C., BSSc *Chinese HK*, MA *Pitt.*, PhD
Pitt. Prof.
Lau, S. K., BSocSc *HK*, PhD *Minn.* Prof.;
Chairman*
Lee, R. P. L., OBE, JP, BSSc *Chinese HK*, PhD
Pitt. Prof.
Lui, T. L., BA *HK*, MPhil *HK*, DPhil *Oxf.* Assoc.
Prof.
Other Staff: 10 Lectrs.; 1 Res. Assoc.

Sports Science and Physical Education,
see also Phys. Educn. Unit

Tel: 2609 6096 Fax: 2603 5781

Johns, D. P., BPE *Alta.*, MA *Alta..* PhD
Alta. Assoc. Prof.
Other Staff: 5 Lectrs.

Statistics

Tel: 2609 7931 Fax: 2603 5188

Chan, N. N., BSc *Peking*, PhD *Liv.* Prof.
Lam, Y., BSc *Peking*, MSc *Lond.*, PhD
Manc. Prof.; Chairman*
Lee, S. Y., BSc *Chinese HK*, MA *Calif.*, MSc *Calif.*,
PhD *Calif.* Prof.
Li, K. H., MSc *Chic.*, PhD *Chic.*, BSc MPhil Sr.
Lectr.
Poon, Wai Yin, BSc *Chinese HK*, MPhil *Chinese
HK*, PhD *Calif.* Sr. Lectr.
Other Staff: 6 Lectrs.; 2 Adjunct Profs.

Translation

Tel: 2609 7700 Fax: 2603 5173

Almberg, E. S. P. Ng, BA *HK*, PhD
Stockholm Assoc. Prof.
Chan, S. W., BA *Chinese HK*, PhD *Lond.* Prof.
Fong, G. C. F., BA *Chinese HK*, MA *York(Can.)*,
MA *Tor.*, PhD *Tor.* Assoc. Prof.
Jin, Serena, MA *Wash.*, Dr3rdCy *Paris* Prof.;
Chairman*
Other Staff: 6 Lectrs.

MEDICINE

Anaesthesia and Intensive Care

Tel: 2632 2735 Fax: 2637 2422

Aun, Cindy S. T., MB BS *Rangoon*, MD,
FRCA Prof.
Chung, D. C. W., MD *Br.Col.*, FRCA,
FRCPCan Prof.
Critchley, L. A. H., BMedSci *Sheff.*, MB ChB
Sheff., FFARCSI Assoc. Prof.
Low, J. M., BA *Oxf.*, BM BCh *Oxf.*, FRCA Prof.
Ngan Kee, W. D., BHB *Auck.*, MB ChB *Auck.*,
FANZCA Assoc. Prof.
Other Staff: 6 Lectrs.; 1 Visiting Lectr.

Anatomical and Cellular Pathology

Tel: 2632 3334 Fax: 2637 6274

Allen, P. W., MB BS *Adel.*, FRCPA Prof.
Chang, A. R., MD *Otago*, FRCPA Prof.
Huang, Wai Sin P., BSc *Calif.*, PhD *HK* Prof.
Lee, J. C. K., MB BS *HK*, PhD *Roch.*, FRCPCan,
FRCPA Prof., Morbid Anatomy; Chairman*
Leong, A. S. Y., MB BS *Malaya*, MD *Adel.*,
FRCPath Prof., Anatomical and Cellular
Pathology
Mac-Moune Lai, F., MD *Lyons*, FRCPA Assoc.
Prof.
Ng, H. K., MB ChB *Edin.*, MD, FRCPA,
FRCPath Prof.
Other Staff: 5 Clin. Lectrs.; 1 Res. Assoc.

Anatomy

Tel: 2609 6853 Fax: 2603 5031

Chew, E. C., BSc *Nan.*, MSc *W.Ont.*, PhD
W.Ont. Prof.
Chow, P. P. H., BSc *HK*, PhD *HK* Prof.
Dixon, J. S., BSc *Manc.*, PhD *Manc.* Prof.
Gosling, J. A., MD *Manc.*, FRCSEd Prof.;
Chairman*
Liu, W. K., BSc *Chinese HK*, MPhil *Chinese HK*,
DrRerNat *Düsseldorf* Prof.
Yew, D. T. W., BSc *Chinese HK*, PhD *Wayne State*,
DrScMed *Rostock* Prof.
Other Staff: 1 Visiting Prof.; 8 Lectrs.

Chemical Pathology

Tel: 2632 3367 Fax: 2636 5090

Hjelm, N. M., LicMed *Uppsala*, MD *Uppsala*, Dr
Uppsala, FRCPath Prof.; Chairman*
Lam, C. W. K., BSc *HK*, BSc *Chinese HK*, MSc
Warw., PhD *S'ton.*, FRSChem Prof.
Lo, D. Y. M., BM BCh *Oxf.*, MA *Camb.*, DPhil
Oxf. Assoc. Prof.
Pang, C. P., BSc *Lond.*, DPhil *Oxf.* Prof.
Other Staff: 2 Lectrs.; 2 Clin. Lectrs.; 1 Hon.
Res. Assoc.

Clinical Immunology Unit

Tel: 2632 2709

Lim, P. L., PhD *Adel.* Prof.
Other Staff: 1 Lectr.

Clinical Oncology

Tel: 2632 2118 Fax: 2649 7426

Johnson, P. J., MB ChB *Manc.*, MD *Manc.*,
FRCP Prof.; Chairman*
Leung, W. T., MB BS *HK*, MD *Chinese
HK* Assoc. Prof.
Other Staff: 1 Lectr.; 2 Res. Assocs.; 4 Clin.
Lectrs.

Community and Family Medicine

Tel: 2692 8784 Fax: 2606 3500

Dickinson, J. A., MB BS *Q'ld.*, PhD
Newcastle(NSW), FRACGP Prof., Family
Medicine
Ho, Suzanne S. Y., BA *Calif.*, MSc *Brown*, MPH
Col., PhD *Sing.* Prof.
Lau, E. M. C., MB BS *HK*, MSc *Lond.*, MD *Chinese
HK* Assoc. Prof.
Lee, S. H., MB BS *HK*, MD *HK* Prof.,
Community Medicine; Chairman*
To, C. Y., MA *Wash.*, PhD *S.Illinois* Prof.,
Education
Wong, T. W., MB BS *HK*, MSc NU
Singapore Prof.
Other Staff: 1 Lectr.; 3 Res. Assocs.; 4 Clin.
Lectrs.

**Diagnostic Radiology and Organ
Imaging**

Tel: 2632 2290 Fax: 2636 0012

Ahuja, A. T., MB BS *Bom.*, MD *Bom.*,
FRCR Assoc. Prof.
Chan, Y. L., MB BS *HK*, FRCR Assoc. Prof.
Lam, W. W. M., MB BS *HK*, FRCR Assoc.
Prof.
Metreweli, C., MB BChir *Camb.*, MA *Camb.*,
FRCP, FRCR Prof.; Chairman*
Yang, W. T., MB BS NU *Singapore*,
FRCR Assoc. Prof.
Other Staff: 5 Clin. Lectrs.

Medicine and Therapeutics

Tel: 2632 3126 Fax: 2637 3852

Chan, J. C. N., MB ChB *Liv.*, MD *Liv.*, FRCPEd,
FRCP Assoc. Prof.
Chan, T. Y. K., MB ChB *Glas.*, FRCPEd,
FRCP Assoc. Prof.
Cheng, G., MD *Tor.*, PhD *Tor.*,
FRCPCan Assoc. Prof.
Cockram, C. S., BSc *Lond.*, MB BS *Lond.*, MD
Lond., FRCP, FRCPEd Prof.
Critchley, J. A. J. H., BSc *Edin.*, MB ChB *Edin.*,
PhD *Edin.*, FRCPEd Prof., Clinical
Pharmacology
Kay, R. L. C., MA *Camb.*, MB BChir MD *Camb.*,
FRCP Prof.

Li, K. M. E., BS Loma Linda, MD East(Manila),
FRCPCan   Assoc. Prof.
Sanderson, J. E., MB BChir Camb., MA Camb.,
MD Camb., FRCP   Prof.
Sung, J. Y., MB BS HK, PhD Calg.   Prof.
Tomlinson, B., BSc Lond., MD Lond., FRCP,
FRCPEd, FACP   Prof.
Woo, Jean, MB BChir Camb., MA Camb., MD
Camb., FRCP   Prof.; Chairman*
Woo, K. S., MB BS HK, MD HK, MMed Sing.,
FRACP   Prof.
Other Staff: 2 Res. Assocs.; 7 Clin. Lectrs.

Microbiology

Tel: 2632 3333 Fax: 2647 3227
Chan, R. C. Y., BSc Calg., PhD Calg.   Sr. Lectr.
Chan, T. S. Houang, MB ChB Brist.,
FRCPath   Prof.
Cheng, A. F. B., MSc Manit., MD Manit., PhD
Manit., FRCPath, FRCPA   Prof.; Chairman*
Tam, S. L. J., MSc Tor., PhD HK   Prof.
Other Staff: 1 Lectr.; 4 Clin. Lectrs.

Nursing

Tel: 2609 7475 Fax: 2603 5935
Callaghan, P., BSc Lond., MSc Middx.   Assoc.
Prof.
Chang, A. M., MEd Qld.   Assoc. Prof.
Levy, V. A., MPhil Exe.   Assoc. Prof.
Mackenzie, A. E., MA Lond., PhD Sur.   Prof.,
Clinical Nursing; Chairman*
Twinn, S. F., BA CNAA, PhD Lond.   Sr. Lectr.
Other Staff: 17 Lectrs.; 1 Asst. Lectr.

Obstetrics and Gynaecology

Tel: 2632 2810 Fax: 2636 0008
Chang, A. M. Z., MB BS Syd., PhD Monash,
FRACOG, FRCOG   Prof.; Chairman*
Chung, T. K. H., MB BS Syd., FRACOG   Assoc.
Prof.
Haines, C. J., MB BS Adel., MD Chinese HK,
FRACOG   Prof.
Loong, P. L., BSc Edin., MB ChB Edin.,
FRCOG   Prof.
Rogers, M. S., MB ChB Birm., FRCOG,
FRCS   Prof.
Other Staff: 2 Lectrs.; 5 Clin. Lectrs.

Ophthalmology and Visual Sciences

Tel: 2632 2878 Fax: 2648 2943
Lam, D. S. C., MB BS HK, FRCSEd   Assoc.
Prof.
Lam, K. W., BS E.Texas Baptist, PhD Pitt.   Prof.
Tso, M. O. M., MB BS HK   Prof.; Chairman*
Other Staff: 1 Lectr.; 1 Visiting Scholar; 1 Res.
Assoc.; 3 Clin. Lectrs.

Orthopaedics and Traumatology

Tel: 2632 2722 Fax: 2637 7889
Chan, K. M., OBE, MB BS HK, MCh Liv.,
FRCSEd, FRCSGlas   Prof.
Cheng, J. C. Y., MB BS HK, FRCSEd,
FRCSGlas   Prof.; Chairman*
Hung, L. K., MB BS HK, MChOrth Liv., FRCSEd,
FRCSGlas   Assoc. Prof.
Leung, K. S., MB BS HK, MD, FRCSEd   Prof.
Leung, P. C., OBE, MB BS HK, MS HK, DSc,
FRACS, FRCSEd   Prof.
Other Staff: 1 Visiting Prof.; 1 Lectr.; 3 Clin.
Lectrs.; 1 Hon. Res. Assoc.

Paediatrics

Tel: 2632 2851 Fax: 2636 0020
Fok, T. F., MB BS HK, MD Chinese HK,
FRCPEd   Prof.; Chairman*
Leung, Suk-fong S., MB BS HK, MD   Prof.
Ng, P. C., MB ChB Dund.   Assoc. Prof.
Sung, Rita Y. T., MB Natnl.Taiwan, MSc Wales,
MD Wales, FRCP   Prof.
Yuen, M. P. P., MD Sask., FRCPCan   Prof.
Other Staff: 1 Lectr.; 5 Clin. Lectrs.; 1 Hon.
Res. Assoc.

Pharmacology

Tel: 2609 6885 Fax: 2603 5139
Jones, R. L., BPharm Lond., PhD Lond., DSc
Lond.   Prof.; Chairman*
Yeung, J. H. K., BSc Liv., PhD Liv.   Prof.

Other Staff: 6 Lectrs.

Pharmacy

Tel: 2609 7960 Fax: 2603 5295
Raymond, K., MPharm Lond., PhD Lond.   Prof.;
Acting Chairman*
Other Staff: 7 Lectrs.

Physiology

Tel: 2609 6882 Fax: 2603 5022
Chew, Siew-Boon C., BA W.Ont., PhD
HK   Prof.
Fiscus, R. R., BS Iowa State, MS Iowa State, PhD
Iowa State   Prof.
Tam, M. S. C., MSc Tor., PhD Tor.   Prof.;
Acting Chairman*
Wong, C. C., BSc Natnl.Taiwan Normal, MPhil
Chinese HK, DrRerNat Hanover   Sr. Lectr.
Wong, P. Y. D., MA Camb., PhD Camb., DSc
Lond., FIBiol   Prof.; Chairman*
Other Staff: 8 Lectrs.; 1 Hon. Res. Fellow

Psychiatry

Tel: 2632 3637 Fax: 2637 7884
Chen, C. N., MB Natnl.Taiwan, MSc Lond.,
FRCPsych, FRANZCP   Prof.
Chiu, Fung Kam H., MB BS HK   Assoc. Prof.;
Chairman*
Lee, S., MB BS HK   Assoc. Prof.
Ungvari, G. S., MD Semmelweis, PhD Hungarian
Acad.Sc., FRANZCP   Assoc. Prof.
Other Staff: 6 Clin. Lectrs.

Surgery

Tel: 2632 2789 Fax: 2637 7974
Chan, P. S. F., MB ChB Leeds, FRCS   Sr. Lectr.
Chung, S. S. C., MB BCh BAO N.U.I., MD,
FRCSEd, FRCSGlas   Prof.
Cocks, R. A., MB BS Lond., MD Lond.,
FRCSEd   Prof.
King, W. W. K., BA Wis., MD Vanderbilt, FACS,
FRCSEd, FRCSCan   Prof., Head, Neck and
Reconstructive Surgery
Lau, J. W. Y., MB BS HK, MD, FRCSEd, FRACS,
FACS   Prof.; Chairman*
Leow, C. K., MB ChB Brist., MD Brist.,
FRCS   Assoc. Prof.
Li, Arthur K. C., MA Camb., MB BChir Camb,
MD Camb., FRCS, FRCSEd, FRACS, FACS,
Hon. FRCSGlas, Hon. FRCSI   Prof.
Poon, W. S., MB ChB Glas., FRCSGlas   Prof.
Van Hasselt, C. A., MB BCh Witw., MMed
Witw., FCS(SA), FRCSEd   Prof.,
Otorhinolaryngology
Yeung, C. K., MB BS HK, MD, FRCSEd,
FRCSGlas, FRACS   Assoc. Prof.
Yim, A. P. C., MA Camb., BM BCh Oxf., MA
Oxf., FRCSGlas   Assoc. Prof.
Other Staff: 1 Lectr.; 1 Visiting Scholar; 3 Res.
Assocs.; 10 Clin. Lectrs.

SPECIAL CENTRES, ETC

Art Museum

Tel: 2609 7416 Fax: 2603 5366
Kao, M. C., BA Chinese HK, MA New Mexico, PhD
Stan.   Dir.*
Other Staff: 2 Res. Fellows

Asia–Pacific Studies, Hong Kong Institute of

Tel: 2609 8780 Fax: 2603 5215
Yeung, Y. M., OBE, JP, BA HK, MA W.Ont.,
PhD Chic.   Dir.*
Other Staff: 1 Assoc. Dir.; 1 Sr. Res. Fellow†; 3
Res. Officers; 2 Hon. Sr. Res. Fellows; 5
Hon. Res. Fellows

Biotechnology, Hong Kong Institute of

Tel: 2609 6007 Fax: 2603 5012
Chang, A. Y., BS Natnl.Taiwan, MS Calif., PhD
Ill.   Dir.*
Other Staff: 1 Assoc. Dir.; 1 Res. Scientist

Business, Asia–Pacific Institute of

Tel: 2609 7428 Fax: 2603 5136
Chiang, R., BBA C.U.N.Y., PhD Penn.   Dir., Res.
Devel.
Ingene, C. A., AB Wash., AM Brown, PhD
Brown   Dir., Business Devel.
Young, L., BSc Well., MSc Well., DPhil
Oxf.   Exec. Dir.*

Continuing Studies, School of

Tel: 2723 7996 Fax: 2739 2797
Wan, C. C., BSc Seattle Pacific, PhD
W.Ont.   Dir.*
Other Staff: 1 Assoc. Dir.

Educational Research, Hong Kong Institute of

Tel: 2609 6999 Fax: 2603 6850
Lo, Prof. L. N. K., BA Oregon, MIA Col., EdD
Col.   Dir.*
Other Staff: 3 Assoc. Dirs.

Humanities, Research Institute for the

Tel: 2609 7167 Fax: 2603 5298
Leung, P. Y. S., BA Chinese HK, MPhil Chinese HK,
PhD Calif.   Dir.*
Other Staff: 1 Assoc. Dir.; 1 Sr. Res. Fellow

Mathematical Sciences, Institute of

Tel: 2609 7988 Fax: 2603 5154
Yang, C. N., BSc Natnl.S.W., PhD Chic., DSc
Drexel   Dir.*
Yau, S. T., PhD Calif.   Dir.*
Other Staff: 2 Assoc. Dirs.

New Asia–Yale-in-China Chinese Language Centre

Tel: 2609 6727 Fax: 2603 5004
Jamieson, J. C., AB Calif., MA Calif., PhD
Calif.   Dir.*
Other Staff: 1 Asst. Dir.; 1 Visiting Prof.

Sports Medicine and Sports Science, Hong Kong Centre of

Tel: 2646 3020
Chan, K. M., OBE, MB BS HK, MChOrth Liv.,
FRCSEd, FRCSGlas   Dir.*

CHINESE STUDIES, INSTITUTE OF

Tel: 2609 7394 Fax: 2603 5149
Chen, F. C., BA Harv., MA Brandeis, PhD
Brandeis   Dir.*
Jao, T. I., DrHumSc École Pratique des Hautes Études,
Hon. DLitt HK   Hon. Prof.
Lau, D. C., BA HK, MA Glas., DLitt HK, Hon.
LLD Chinese HK   Hon. Prof.; Adviser
Other Staff: 1 Res. Assoc.; 1 Hon. Sr. Res.
Fellow; 1 Hon. Res. Fellow

Chinese Archaeology and Art, Centre for

Tel: 2609 7417 Fax: 2603 7539
Tang, C., BA Chinese HK, MA Chinese HK, DLet
Tokyo   Archaeologist; Dir.*
Other Staff: 1 Hon. Visiting Prof.; 1 Hon Res.
Fellow

Chinese Language Research Centre

Tel: 2609 7392 Fax: 2603 5149
Lau, D. C., BA HK, MA Glas., DLitt HK, Hon.
LLD Chinese HK   Dir.*
Other Staff: 1 Dep. Dir.

Contemporary Chinese Culture, Research Centre for

Tel: 2609 7394 Fax: 2603 5149
Jin, G. T.   Sr Res. Fellow; Dir.*
Other Staff: 3 Hon. Res. Fellows

Thermoluminescence, Yeung Shui Sang Laboratory of

Tel: 2609 6323
Chik, K. P., BSc HK, DrRerNat
T.H.Stuttgart   Hon. Dir.*
Other Staff: 1 Asst. Dir.

Translation, Research Centre for

Tel: 2609 7399 Fax: 2603 5110

Hung, Eva W. Y., BA HK, MPhil HK, PhD Lond.
Editor of Renditions; Dir.*
Other Staff: 1 Res. Assoc.

SCIENCE AND TECHNOLOGY, INSTITUTE OF

Tel: 2609 6279

Mak, T. C. W., BSc Br.Col., PhD Br.Col. Dir.*

Chinese Medicinal Material Research Centre

Tel: 2609 6140 Fax: 2603 5248

But, P. P. H., BSc Chinese HK, MBA Chinese HK, MA Calif., PhD Calif. Dir.*
Other Staff: 2 Assoc. Dirs.; 1 Hon. Sr. Res. Fellow

Environmental Studies, Centre for

Tel: 2609 6643 Fax: 2603 5174

Leung, Y., BSSc Chinese HK, MA Colorado, MS Colorado, PhD Colorado Dir.*
Other Staff: 1 Assoc. Dir.

Materials Technology Research Centre

Tel: 2609 8276 Fax: 2603 5558

Wilson, I. H., BSc Reading, PhD Reading, FIP Dir.*
Other Staff: 1 Assoc. Dir.; 2 Postdoctoral Fellows

CONTACT OFFICERS

Academic affairs. Deputy Registrar: Lee, S. W., BSc MPhil
Admissions (first degree). Senior Assistant Registrar: Yeung, E. Y. F., BSc
Admissions (higher degree). Senior Assistant Registrar: Lai, J., BA HK
Alumni. Director of Administrative Services: Yui, A., BSSc
Careers. Director of Student Affairs: Lee, C. K. W. Chan, BA MPhil
Computing services. Director, Computer Services Centre: Hu, S., BScE Ohio, MBA Ohio, PhD Ohio
Development/fund-raising. Secretary: Leung, Jacob S. K., BSocSc HK, MDiv S.Baptist Theol.Sem.
Examinations. Deputy Registrar: Lee, S. W., BSc MPhil
Finance. Bursar: Chan, Terence C. W., BSocSc HK, FCA, FCA(Aust)
General enquiries. Secretary: Leung, Jacob S. K., BSocSc HK, MDiv S.Baptist Theol.Sem.
Health services. Director, Health Service: Pang, K. K. H., MB BS HK, MSc NU Singapore
International office. Director, Office of International Studies Programmes: Leung, K. W. Y., MA Minn., PhD Minn.
Library (chief librarian). Librarian: Lee, Michael M., BA Natnl.Taiwan, MA W.Mich., PhD Loyola(Ill.)
Personnel/human resources. Director of Personnel: Lau, S., BSocSc HK
Public relations, information and marketing. Director, Information and Public Relations Office: Hui, E. W. H., MA Reading
Publications. Publication Officer: Leung, A. K. Y., BA HK

Purchasing. Senior Assistant Bursar, Business Section: Yiu, P. K. C., BA HK
Scholarships, awards, loans. Director of Student Affairs: Lee, C. K. W. Chan, BA MPhil
Security. Security Officer: Ma, R. K. S., BA
Sport and recreation. Director, Physical Education Unit: Hon, K. Y., MA N.Y.
Staff development and training. Administrative Assistant, Personnel Office: Lo, B. Y. P. To, BA HK, MBA City Poly.HK
Student welfare/counselling. Director of Student Affairs: Lee, C. K. W. Chan, BA MPhil
Students from other countries. Director, Office of International Studies Programmes: Leung, K. W. Y., MA Minn., PhD Minn.
University press. Director: Wong, S. L. P., BA HK, MBA Stan.

CAMPUS/COLLEGE HEADS

Chung Chi College (Tel: 2609 6441; Fax: 2603 5440.) Head of College: Lee, Rance P. L., OBE, JP, BSSc Chinese HK, PhD Pitt.
New Asia College (Tel: 2609 7609; Fax: 2603 5418.) Head of College: Leung, P. C., OBE, MB BS HK, MS HK, DSc Chinese HK, FRCSEd, FRACS
Shaw College (Tel: 2609 7363; Fax: 2603 5427.) Head of College: Yeung, Y. M., OBE, JP, BA HK, MA W.Ont., PhD Chic.
United College (Tel: 2609 7579; Fax: 2603 5412.) Head of College: Lee, C. Y., BSc Br.Col., MSc Br.Col., PhD Br.Col.

[Information supplied by the institution as at 4 March 1998, and edited by the ACU]

UNIVERSITY OF HONG KONG

Founded 1910

Member of the Association of Commonwealth Universities

Postal Address: Pokfulam Road, Hong Kong
Telephone: 2859 2111 **Fax**: 2858 2549, 2559 9459 **Cables**: University, Hong Kong **WWW**: http://www.hku.hk
E-mail formula: user@node.hku.hk

CHANCELLOR—The Chief Executive of the Hong Kong Special Administrative Region (ex officio)
PRO-CHANCELLOR—Yang, Ti-liang, LLB Lond., Hon. LLD Chinese HK, Hon. DLitt
VICE-CHANCELLOR*—Cheng, Prof. Yiu-Chung, CBE, JP, BSc HK, PhD Br.Col., FIEE
ACTING DEPUTY VICE-CHANCELLOR—Cheung, Prof. Y. K., OBE, BSc(Eng) S.China Tech., PhD Wales, DSc Wales, DE Adel., FICE, FIEAust, FIStructE
PRO-VICE-CHANCELLOR—Cheng, Prof. K. M., JP, BSc HK, MEd HK, PhD Lond.
PRO-VICE-CHANCELLOR—Cheung, Prof. Y. K., OBE, BSc(Eng) S.China Tech., PhD Wales, DSc Wales, DE Adel., FICE, FIEAust, FIStructE
PRO-VICE-CHANCELLOR—Davies, Prof. W. I. R., JP, BDS Lond., MSc Penn., FDSRCS
PRO-VICE-CHANCELLOR—Wong, Prof. S. L., BSocSc HK, MPhil Chinese HK, BLitt Oxf., DPhil Oxf.
PRO-VICE-CHANCELLOR—Wu, Felix F., BS Natnl.Taiwan, MS Pitt., PhD Calif.
TREASURER—Li, David K. P., OBE, JP, MA Camb., Hon. LLD Camb., Hon. LLD Warw., Hon. LLD HK, FCA
ACTING REGISTRAR—Cheung, Prof. Y. K., OBE, BSc(Eng) S.China Tech., PhD Wales, DSc Wales, DE Adel., FICE, FIEAust, FIStructE
DIRECTOR OF FINANCE—Lam, Philip B. L.
LIBRARIAN—Kan, Lai-Bing, BSc HK, MA Calif., MLS Calif., PhD HK, Hon. DLitt C.Sturt

GENERAL INFORMATION

History. The university was founded in 1910 and opened in 1912. Its history dates from the establishment of the College of Medicine in 1887.

Admission to first degree courses (see also Hong Kong Introduction). Hong Kong Certificate of Education Examination (HKCEE) grade E or above in 7 subjects, which must include English language(syllabus B), Chinese language (or other language) and mathematics; and Hong Kong A level exam (HKALE)with

grade D or above in AS level use of English, and grade E or above in AS Chinese language and culture (or other language), and either grade E or above in 2 A level subjects or grade E or above in 1 A level subject and 2 AS subjects (other than use of English and Chinese language and culture).

First Degrees (see also Hong Kong Directory to Subjects of Study). BA, BA(ArchStud), BBA, BBA(Acc&Fin), BCogSc, BDS, BEcon, BEd, BEd(LangEd), BEng, BFin, BNurs, BSc, BSc(ActuarSc), BSc(BiomedSc), BSc(CSIS), BSc(Sp&HearSc), BSc(Surv), BSocSc, BSW, LLB, MB BS.

Courses normally last 3 years. BEd, BEd(LangEd), BNurs, BSc(Sp&HearSc): 4 years; BDS, MB BS: 5 years.

Higher Degrees (see also Hong Kong Directory to Subjects of Study). LLM, MA, MA(AppliedLinguistics), MArch, MBA, MD, MDS, MEcon, MEd, MHousMan, MLA, MMedSc, MOrth, MPA, MS, MSc, MSc(Audiology), MSc(CompSc), MSc(ConstProjectMan), MSc(Eng), MSc(EnvMan), MSc(RealEst), MSc(UrbanPlanning), MSocSc, MStat, MSW, MUrbanDesign, MPhil, PhD, DLitt, DSc, DSocSc, LLD.

Master's degrees by coursework: 1–3 years (available full-or part-time). MPhil: 24–36 months full-time or 36–48 months part-time; PhD: 36–60 months full-time or, 54–72 months part-time; MD, MS: maximum 60 months.

Language of Instruction. English, except for courses in Chinese and other languages.

Libraries. 1,300,000 printed volumes; 16,500 periodical titles received.

Fees (1998–99, annual). Undergraduate: HK$47,150. Postgraduate: full-time courses, MPhil, PhD HK$44,500; part-time courses HK$22,500–29,670 (except MA in transport policy and planning HK$68,500; MBA HK$57,150).

Academic Awards (1997-98). Undergraduate: 417 awards ranging in value from HK$1000 to HK$40,000. Postgraduate: 187 awards ranging in value from HK$2500 to HK$100,000.

Academic Year. Two semesters (except for of dentistry and medicine programmes): September–December; January–April (or, for certain courses, January–June).

Income (1998-99). Total, approximately HK$3,000,000,000.

Statistics. Full-time staff 3663 (832 academic, 69 administrative, 2762 other). Students: 14,113.

FACULTIES/SCHOOLS

Architecture
Tel: 2859 2125 Fax: 2857 2852
Dean: Will, Barry F., BArch Qld., MUS Qld.
Secretary: Lai, C. K., BSSc Chinese HK

Arts
Tel: 2859 2730 Fax: 2548 5231
Dean: Martin, Michael R., AB Prin., MA Harv., PhD Harv.

Dentistry
Tel: 2859 0342 Fax: 2517 0544, 2547 6257
Dean: Smales, Prof. Frederick C., BSc Durh., BDS Newcastle(UK), PhD Lond., FDSRCS
Secretary: Chiu, Mable M. P., BA HK, MPA HK

Education
Tel: 2859 2355 Fax: 2517 0075
Dean: Leung, Frederick K. S., BSc HK, MEd HK, PhD Lond.
Secretary: Lin, Wendy Y. L., BSocSc HK, MBA Chinese HK

Engineering
Tel: 2859 2700 Fax: 2546 9142
Dean: Cheung Ying Sheung, BSc Lond., PhD Lond.
Secretary: Tsang, Angela O. M., BSocSc HK

Law
Tel: 2859 2943 Fax: 2559 5690
Dean: Chen, Prof. Albert H. Y., LLB HK, LLM Harv.
Secretary: Wong, Vivian T. V., BA HK, MPA HK

Medicine
Tel: 2819 9210 Fax: 2855 9742
Dean: Tang, Prof. Grace W. K., MB BS HK, FRCOG
Secretary: Tsang, Amy W. C., BSc Aston, MSc Manc.

Science
Tel: 2859 2682 Fax: 2858 4620
Dean: Cheng Kin Fai, Prof., BSc HK, PhD Br.Col., FRSChem
Secretary: Brodie, Kaye E., BA NE

Social Sciences
Tel: 2859 2982 Fax: 2517 0806
Dean: Shen, Shir Ming, BA HK, MSc Lond., PhD HK
Secretary: Tsang, Renee K. L., BSocSc HK, MSc Lond.

ACADEMIC UNITS

Anatomy, see Medicine

Architecture
Tel: 2859 2133 Fax: 2559 6484
Bradford, J. W., MArch Virginia Polytech. Assoc. Prof.
Ganesan, S., BSc(Eng) S.Lanka, MEng Tokyo, PhD Lond. Prof.
Hui, D. C. K., BArch Cornell, PhD Camb. Assoc. Prof.
Kvan, Thomas, MA Camb., MArch Calif. Assoc. Prof.
Lau, P. S. S., BArch Manit., MBA E. Asia Prof.; Head*
Lau, S. S. Y., BArch HK, MSc Lond. Assoc. Prof.
Lo, S. C., BArch Cooper Union Assoc. Prof.
Lu, L. L., BArch Houston, MArch Yale Assoc. Prof.
Lung, D., MBE, MArch Oregon, MA Oregon Prof.
Lye, K. C., OBE, BArch Miami(Ohio), MFA Prin., FRAIC Prof.
Matsuda, N., BFA Tokyo, MA RCA Assoc. Prof.
Tracy, Eve P. H., BA Wellesley, MArch Harv. Assoc. Prof.
Will, Barry F., BArch Qld., MUS Qld. Sr. Lectr.
Wong, C. K., BArch HK, MLA Penn. Assoc. Prof.
Wong, W. S., BArch HK Assoc. Prof.
Other Staff: 12 Asst. Profs./Lectrs.; 26 Hon. Lectrs.
Research: art, design and professional practice; computer-aided architectural design (CAAD): multimedia and visual reality; history and theory of architecture; housing, urban design and development; technology and environmental studies

Biochemistry, see Medicine

Botany
Tel: 2859 2820 Fax: 2858 3477
Chye, Mee Len, BSc Malaya, PhD Melb. Assoc. Prof.
Corke, Harold, BSc Rhodesia, MSc Guelph, PhD Weizmann Assoc. Prof.
Ma, C. Y., MSc HK, MSc Br.Col., PhD Br.Col. Prof.
Zee, S. S. Y., BSc Melb., PhD Melb. Prof.; Head*
Other Staff: 3 Asst. Profs./Lectrs.; 3 Hon. Profs.; 1 Hon. Assoc. Prof.; 5 Hon. Asst. Profs.
Research: fermentation technology; food starch, polysaccharide and protein technology; molecular microbiology; plant molecular biology and biotechnology; rice sexual reproduction and biotechnology

Business, School of
Tel: 2857 1000 Fax: 2858 5614
Chan, S. H., BScEd Malaya, MBA Louisiana Tech, PhD Texas Sr. Lectr.
Chang, Eric C., BS Natnl.Cheng Kung, MBA Wright, PhD Purdue Prof.
Child, John, MA Camb., PhD Camb., ScD Camb. Prof.
Farhoomand, A. F., BEng C'dia., MBA C'dia., PhD McG. Assoc. Prof.
Helsen, K., MBA Cornell, PhD Penn. Assoc. Prof.
Lam, Simon S. K., MSc Essex, PhD ANU Assoc. Prof.
Leung, W. K., BSSc Chinese HK, MA Fudan, PhD Texas Assoc. Prof.
Lin, Z., BA Jimei Finance & Econ., MSc Xiamen, MSc Sask., PhD Xiamen Assoc. Prof.
Ng, S. H., BSocSc HK, MSocSc HK, MSc Lond., PhD Lond. Reader
Tse, David K. C., BBA Chinese HK, MBA Calif., PhD Calif. Prof.
Tung, Samuel S. L., BComm Natnl.Chengchi, PhD Hawaii, PhD Wis. Prof.
Ure, John C., BSc Hull, MSc(Econ) Lond., PhD CNAA Assoc. Prof.
Wong, G. Y. Y., BSc HK, MBA Manc., PhD Brad. Assoc. Prof.
Wong, Richard Y. C., AB Chic., AM Chic., PhD Chic. Prof.; Dir.*
Other Staff: 12 Asst. Profs./Lectrs.; 7 Hon. Profs,; 2 Hon. Asst. Profs.; 3 Hon. Lectrs.
Research: Asian financial markets (derivative securities markets and international finance); Asia-Pacific economic co-operation (APEC) (finance and forecasting, human resources, regulation); Chinese management (management development and internationalisation of Chinese business; competitiveness and economic development in Hong Kong; international marketing (customer satisfaction, marketing in China, services)

Poon Kam Kai Institute of Management
Tel: 2857 8222 Fax: 2858 5614
Wong, G. Y. Y., BSc HK, MBA Manc., PhD Brad. Exec. Dir.*

Chemistry
Tel: 2859 7919 Fax: 2857 1586
Chan, G. K. Y., BSc Alta., MS Cornell, PhD Cornell Sr. Lectr.
Che, C. M., BSc HK, PhD HK Prof.
Cheng Kin Fai, BSc HK, PhD Br.Col., FRSChem Prof.
Cheung, A. S. C., BSc Wat., PhD Br.Col. Sr. Lectr.; Head*
Fung, Y. S., BSc HK, MPhil HK, PhD Lond. Assoc. Prof.
Lie Ken Jie, M. S. F., BSc HK, PhD St And., DSc St And., DSc HK, FRSChem Prof.
Miskowski, Vincent M., BS Case W.Reserve, PhD Calif. Assoc. Prof.
Phillips, D. L., BS Iowa, PhD Calif. Assoc. Prof.
Wong, W. T., BSc HK, MPhil HK, PhD Camb. Assoc. Prof.
Yam, Vivian W. W., BSc HK, PhD HK, FRSChem Prof.
Other Staff: 6 Asst. Profs./Lectrs.; 1 Hon. Prof.; 3 Hon Asst. Profs.
Research: analytical chemistry; inorganic chemistry; organic chemistry; physcial chemistry; polymer chemistry and synthesis

Chinese
Tel: 2859 2426 Fax: 2858 1334
Chan, M. S., BA HK, MPhil HK, PhD ANU Prof.
Chiu, L. Y., MA HK, PhD Syd. Prof.; Head*
Fung, K. W., BA HK, MLitt Kyoto Assoc. Prof.
Ho, K. P., BA HK, MPhil HK, PhD HK Sr. Lectr.
Ho, K. P. H., MA HK, DPhil Oxf. Prof.
Hui, C. H., BA HK, MPhil HK, PhD HK Assoc. Prof.
Lai, W. Y., BA Chinese HK, MA Kyoto, PhD HK Assoc. Prof.

Lee, K. S., BA HK, MPhil HK, PhD HK   Prof.

Liu, M. W., BA HK, MPhil HK, PhD
Calif.   Prof.

Sin, C. Y., BA HK, MPhil HK, PhD HK   Prof.

Wong, S. K., MA HK, DPhil Oxf.   Prof.

Other Staff: 8 Asst. Profs./Lectrs.; 1 Lectr./Asst.
Lectr.; 3 Hon. Profs.; 1 Hon. Reader; 1 Hon.
Asst. Prof.; 3 Hon. Lectrs.

Research: Chinese literature (classics, literary
criticisim, poetry, prose); language
(etymology, lexicology, philology,
phonology, semantics); history (cultural,
dynastic, institutional, scientific); philosophy
(Buddhism, classical and intellectual
scholarship, Confucianism,.Daoism);
translation (bilingualism, literary studies,
simultaneous interpretation)

Comparative Literature

Tel: 2859 2769 Fax: 2857 7955

Abbas, M. A., MA HK   Sr. Lectr.

Erens, Patricia B., BA George Washington, MA
Chic., PhD Northwestern   Assoc. Prof.

Lee, G. B., BA Lond., PhD Lond.   Assoc. Prof.

Sabine, Maureen A., BA Fordham, MA Penn., PhD
Penn.   Assoc. Prof.

Tambling, J. C. R., BA York(UK), MPhil Nott.,
PhD Essex   Prof.

Wong, T. W., BA Natnl.Taiwan, MA Wash., PhD
Wash.   Sr. Lectr.; Head*

Other Staff: 4 Asst. Profs./Lectrs.; 1 Lectr./Asst.
Lectr.; 1 Hon. Assoc. Prof.

Research: East-West comparative literature/
cultural relations; film and media studies;
gender studies, women's studies and
feminist theories; Hong Kong/China cultural
studies; literary and cultural theories

Computer Science

Tel: 2859 2178 Fax: 2559 8447

Chan, C., BSc Natnl.Taiwan, MSc Manit., PhD
Br.Col.   Prof.

Chan, K. P., BSc(Eng) HK, PhD HK   Assoc.
Prof.

Cheung, D. W. L., BSc Chinese HK, MSc S.Fraser,
PhD S.Fraser   Assoc. Prof.

Chin, F. Y. L., BASc Tor., MSc Prin., MA Prin.,
PhD Prin.   Prof.; Head*

Choi, A. K. O., BS San Francisco, MS Calif., PhD
Calif.   Assoc. Prof.

Chow, K. P., MA Calif., PhD Calif.   Assoc. Prof.

Hwang, K., BS Natnl.Taiwan, MS Hawaii, PhD
Calif.   Prof.

Lam, T. W., BSc Chinese HK, MS Wash., PhD
Wash.   Assoc. Prof.

Lau, F. C. M., BSc Acad., MMath Wat., PhD
Wat.   Assoc. Prof.

Pun, K. H., BSc HK, LLM Lond., MS Ill., PhD
Ill.   Assoc. Prof.

Tsang, W. W., BSc Chinese HK, MS Wash.State,
PhD Wash.State   Assoc. Prof.

Tse, T. H., MBE, BSc HK, MSc Lond., PhD Lond.,
FIMA   Assoc. Prof.

Yen, J. C. H., PhD Arizona   Assoc. Prof.

Other Staff: 9 Asst. Profs./Lectrs.; 1 Lectr./Asst.
Lectr.; 1 Hon. Prof.; 2 Hon. Asst. Profs.; 1
Hon. Sr. Lectr.; 1 Hon. Lectr.

Research: database, computer graphics and
software engineering; design and anaylsis of
algorithms (circuit routing, graph
algorithms, on-line scheduling); information
systems (digital library, electronic
commerce, financial computing); parallel
and distributed systems (designing high-
performance systems using multi-processing
techniques); speech processing and pattern
recognition (human-computer
communication in speech and optical
character recognition (OCR))

Construction, see Real Estate and
Construction

Curriculum Studies, see also Educn.

Tel: 2859 2542 Fax: 2858 5649

Andrews, S. J., MA Camb., MA Essex   Assoc.
Prof.

Falvey, P., BA Durh., MA Essex, PhD Birm.   Sr.
Lectr.; Head*

Ki, W. W., BSc HK, MEd HK   Assoc. Prof.

Kwo, O. W. Y., BA Hull, MA Lond., PhD
HK   Assoc. Prof.

Lai, Winnie Y. W., BA Chinese HK, MEd HK,
PhD HK   Assoc. Prof.

Law, Nancy W. Y., BSc HK, MPhil HK, PhD
Lond.   Sr. Lectr.

Leung, Frederick K. S., BSc HK, MEd HK, PhD
Lond.   Assoc. Prof.

Lopez-Real, Francis J., BSc S'ton, MA Lond.,
MPhil Camb.   Assoc. Prof.

Morris, P. J. T. F., BEd Leeds, MSc CNAA, DPhil
Sus.   Prof.

Stimpson, P. G., BSc Brist., MSc Sheff., PhD
Sheff.   Sr. Lectr.

Tao, L. P. K., BSc Chinese HK, MA Leeds, PhD
Monash   Assoc. Prof.

Tse, S. K., BA HK, MA(Ed) Chinese HK, MPhil
HK, PhD Nott.   Assoc. Prof.

Tsui, Amy B. M., MA HK, PhD Birm.   Prof.;
Head*

Other Staff: 18 Asst.Profs./Lectrs.; 1 Hon. Asst.
Prof.; 1 Hon. Lectr.

Research: curriculum areas (teaching and
learning of science, maths and humanities);
curriculum development (evaluation,
implementation); information technology in
education (use of IT in English and Chinese
language teaching and learning, and in
science education); language education
(learning and teaching of Chinese and
English language); teacher education
(knowledge, professional development,
supervision)

Dentistry, see below

Earth Sciences

Tel: 2859 1084 Fax: 2517 6912

Aitchison, Jonathan C., BSc Otago, MSc Otago,
PhD NE   Assoc. Prof.

Chan, L. S., BSSc Chinese HK, MA Calif., PhD
Calif.   Assoc. Prof.

Malpas, John G., MA Oxf., MSc Nfld., PhD
Nfld.   Prof.; Head*

Yim, W. W. S., BSc Lond., MPhil Lond., PhD
Tas., DSc Lond., FGS   Assoc. Prof.

Other Staff: 3 Asst. Profs./Lectrs.; 1 Hon. Prof.;
4 Hon. Assoc. Profs.; 1 Hon. Lectr.

Research: analytical techniques (ground
penetrating radar, laser ablation microprobe-
inductively coupled plasma mass
spectrometer (LAM-ICPMS)); engineering
and applied geology (applied geophysics,
hydrogeology, rock mechanics,
sedimentology, soil mechanics); evolution of
oceanic lithosphere (age constraints,
geochemistry, mineralogy, palaeontology,
petrology, tectonics); palaeoclimate and
quaternary geology (environmental
reconstruction, micro palaeontology, sea-
level change, tephra chronology); tectonic
evolution of the Asia/Pacific region
(palaeomagnetics, petrology, sedimentology,
stratigraphy)

Ecology and Biodiversity

Tel: 2517 1010 Fax: 2517 6082

Corlett, R. T., BA Camb., PhD ANU, FLS   Assoc.
Prof.

Dickman, M. D., BA Calif., MSc Oregon, PhD
Br.Col.   Prof.

Dudgeon, A. D. M., BSc Newcastle(UK), PhD
HK   Prof.

Hodgkiss, I. J., JP, BSc Wales, PhD Wales, FLS,
FIBiol   Prof.; Head*

Hyde, K. D., BSc Wales, MSc CNAA, PhD
CNAA   Assoc. Prof.

Morton, B. S., JP, BSc Lond., PhD Lond.,
FLS   Prof.

Sadovy, Yvonne J., BSc Manc., PhD
Manc.   Assoc. Prof.

Other Staff: 3 Asst. Profs./Lectrs.; 5 Hon.
Profs.; 3 Hon. Assoc. Profs.; 3 Hon. Asst.
Profs.; 11 Hon. Lectrs.

Research: biodiversity, conservation and
managment; freshwater and marine ecology
(including fisheries); human environmental
impacts (monitoring and control);
microfungal diversity and fungal product
studies; vascular plant taxonomy and
biosystematics

Economics and Finance, School of

Tel: 2859 2912 Fax: 2548 1152

Cheung, M. T., BScoSc HK, MSc(Econ) Lond.,
PhD Lond.   Assoc. Prof.

Cheung, S. N. S., MA Calif., PhD Calif.   Prof.;
Head*

Hau, T. D. K., BA Stan., MA Calif., PhD
Calif.   Assoc. Prof.

Ho, H. C. Y., BA HK, MSc Lond., PhD Lond.   Sr.
Lectr.

Shea, K. L., BSocSc HK, MA Wash., PhD
Wash.   Assoc. Prof.

Song, F. M., BS Zhejiang, MS Huazhong U.S.T., MA
Ohio State, PhD Ohio State   Assoc. Prof.

Suen, W. C., BSocSc HK, PhD Wash.   Sr. Lectr.

Walls, W. D., BA Calif.State, MA Calif.State, PhD
Calif.   Assoc. Prof.

Wong, R. Y. C., AB Chic., AM Chic., PhD
Chic.   Prof.

Yeung, D. W. K., BSocSc HK, MA York(Can.),
PhD York(Can.)   Assoc. Prof.

Yuen, C. W., BSocSc HK, PhD Chic.   Assoc.
Prof.

Other Staff: 11 Asst. Profs./Lectrs.; 1 Hon.
Assoc. Prof.; 1 Hon. Asst. Prof.; 2 Hon.
Lectrs.

Research: Chinese economy (economic
development and reform); finance (asset
pricing, corporate finance, investments);
industrial organisation (business strategies,
market structure); labour economics
(employment, human capital, wages); neo-
institutional economics (property rights,
transaction costs)

Education, see also Curric. Studies

Tel: 2859 2544 Fax: 2858 5649

Bray, M., BA Newcastle(UK), MSc Edin., PhD
Edin.   Prof.

Cheng Kai Ming, JP, BSc HK, MEd HK, PhD
Lond.   Prof.

Constas, M. A., BS Northeastern, MS Cornell, PhD
Cornell   Assoc. Prof.

Evers, Colin W., BA Syd., BLitt NE, PhD
Syd.   Assoc. Prof.

Hui, E. K. P., BSocSc HK, MSc Lond., PhD
Lond.   Assoc. Prof.

Johnson, R. K., BA Camb., MA Essex, PhD
Essex   Sr. Lectr.

Lee, W. O., BA HK, PhD Durh.   Assoc. Prof.

Postiglione, G. A., BS N.Y.State, PhD
N.Y.   Assoc. Prof.

Rao, Nirmala, BA B'lore., MS Tulane, PhD
Tulane   Assoc. Prof.

Watkins, Prof. D. A., BSc Syd., MSc Melb., PhD
ANU   Prof.

Winter, S. J., BSc S'ton, MEd Exe., PhD
HK   Assoc. Prof.

Wong, A. K. C., BA Chinese HK, PhD
Lond.   Assoc. Prof.; Head*

Other Staff: 11 Asst. Profs./Lectrs.; 2 Hon.
Assoc. Profs.; 3 Hon. Asst. Profs; 2 Hon.
Lectrs.

Research: civic education; comparative
education; cross-cultural studies on learning;
higher education; research in minority areas
in China

Engineering, Civil and Structural

Tel: 2859 2668 Fax: 2559 5337

Chan, H. C., BSc(Eng) HK, PhD Lond.,
FICE   Prof.; Head*

Chau, J. K. W., MSc(Eng) HK, PhD HK,
FIStructE   Assoc. Prof.

Cheung, Y. K., OBE, BSc(Eng) S.China Tech.,
PhD Wales, DSc Wales, DE Adel., FICE, FIEAust,
FIStructE   Prof.

Fang, H. H. P., BS Natnl.Taiwan, MS Roch., PhD
Roch.   Prof.

Jayawardena, A. W., BSc(Eng) *S.Lanka*, MEng *Tokyo*, MS *Calif.*, PhD *Lond.*   Assoc. Prof.

Kay, J. N., BE *NSW*, MS *Northwestern*, PhD *Northwestern*, FIEAust   Assoc. Prof.

Koeng, A., BSAE *Philippines*, MS *Cornell*, PhD *Cornell*   Assoc. Prof.

Kumaraswamy, M. M., BSc(Eng) *S.Lanka*, MSc *Lough.*, PhD *Lough.*, FICE, FIE(SL)   Assoc. Prof.

Kwan, A. K. H., BSc(Eng) *HK*, PhD *HK*   Sr. Lectr.

Lee Chack Fan, BSc(Eng) *HK*, MSc(Eng) *HK*, PhD *W.Ont.*   Prof.

Lee, J. H. W., BSc(Eng) *M.I.T.*, MSc *M.I.T.*, PhD *M.I.T.*   Prof.

Lee, P. K. K., MSc(Eng) *Sur.*, FIStructE, FICE   Sr. Lectr.

Lo, S. H., BSc(Eng) *HK*, MPhil *HK*, DrIng *E.N.Ponts & Chaussées, Paris*   Sr. Lectr.

Pam, Hoat Joen, ME *Cant.*, PhD *Cant.*   Assoc. Prof.

Pan, A. D. E., BS *Texas*, MS *Calif.*, PhD *Calif.*   Assoc. Prof.

Tham, L. G., BSc(Eng) *HK*, PhD *HK*   Sr. Lectr.

Tong, C. O., BSc(Eng) *HK*, MSc *Leeds*, PhD *Monash*   Assoc. Prof.

Tsui, Y., BSc(Eng) *HK*, PhD *Duke*   Sr. Lectr.

Other Staff: 6 Asst. Profs./Lectrs.; 3 Hon. Profs.; 3 Hon. Assoc. Profs.; 7 Hon. Asst. Profs.

Research: construction management; environmental hydraulics (waste treatment, waste water); geotechnical engineering (rock mechanics, slope stability); structural engineering and computational mechanics; traffic flow modelling and control

Engineering, Electrical and Electronic

Tel: 2859 7093 Fax: 2559 8738

Chan, C. C., BSc *Peking Coll.Mining Engin.*, MSc *Tsing Hua*, PhD *HK*, Hon. DSc *Odessa*, FIEE, FEng   Prof.; Head*

Chan, F. H. Y., PhD *Brist.*, FIEE   Prof.

Chan, S. C., BSc(Eng) *HK*, PhD *HK*   Assoc. Prof.

Chau, K. T., BSc(Eng) *HK*, PhD *HK*   Assoc. Prof.

Cheung, S. W., BSc *CNAA*, PhD *Lough.*   Assoc. Prof.

Cheung Ying Sheung, BSc *Lond.*, PhD *Lond.*   Assoc. Prof.

Ho, K. L., BSc(Eng) *HK*, MPhil *HK*, PhD *Lond.*   Assoc. Prof.

Hong, M. K. M., BSc *HK*, MSc *Tor.*, PhD *Tor.*   Sr. Lectr.

Hung, Y. S., BSc(Eng) *HK*, BSc *HK*, MPhil *Camb.*, PhD *Camb.*   Assoc. Prof.

Hwang, K., BS *Natnl.Taiwan*, MS *Hawaii*, PhD *Calif.*   Prof.

Kwok, P. C. K., BSc *Essex*, PhD *Camb.*   Assoc. Prof.

Lam, F. K., BSc(Eng) *HK*, MSc *Lough.*, PhD *Lough.*   Assoc. Prof.

Leung, C. H., BSc(Eng) *HK*, MEng *McG*, PhD *HK*   Assoc. Prof.

Li, E. H., BS *W.Wash.*, MSc *Wash.*, MPhil *HK*, PhD *Sur.*   Assoc. Prof.

Li, Victor O. K., MS *M.I.T.*, ScD *M.I.T.*   Prof.

Ma, Q., BS *Anhui*, PhD *Col.*   Assoc. Prof.

Ng, T. S., BSc(Eng) *HK*, MEngSc *Newcastle(NSW)*, PhD *Newcastle(NSW)*, Hon. DEng *Newcastle(NSW)*, FIEAust, FIEE   Prof.

Ni, Yixin, DEng *Tsing Hua*   Assoc. Prof.

Pang, G. K. H., BSc *City(UK)*, PhD *Camb.*   Assoc. Prof.

Pong, M. H., BSc *Birm.*, PhD *Camb.*   Assoc. Prof.

Shen, C. M., MSc(Eng) *HK*, PhD *Lond.*   Assoc. Prof.

Wang, J., BS *Xidian*, PhD *Ghent*   Assoc. Prof.

Wu, F. F., BS *Natnl.Taiwan*, MS *Pitt.*, PhD *Calif.*   Prof.

Yang, Edward S., BS *Cheng Kung*, MS *Oklahoma State*, PhD *Yale*   Prof.

Yung, N. H. C., BSc *Newcastle(UK)*, PhD *Newcastle(UK)*   Assoc. Prof.

Other Staff: 13 Asst. Profs./Lectrs.; 6 Hon. Profs.; 2 Hon. Assoc. Profs.; 6 Hon. Asst. Profs.; 6 Hon. Lectrs.

Research: automation, control and biomedical engineering; computer systems; energy systems and electric vehicles; microelectronics, optoelectonics and very large scale integration (VLSI); telecommunications

Engineering, Industrial and Manufacturing Systems

Tel: 2859 2583 Fax: 2858 6535

Chan, P. L. Y., BSc *HK*, PhD *HK*   Assoc. Prof.

Choi, S. H., BSc *Birm.*, PhD *Birm.*   Assoc. Prof.

Courtney, A. J., BTech *Brun.*, MSc *Birm.*   Sr. Lectr.

Lau, T. L., MSc *Manc.*, PhD *Manc.*   Assoc. Prof.

Mak, K. L., MSc *Salf.*, PhD *Salf.*   Prof.; Head*

Porter, B., MA *Camb.*, PhD *Durh.*, DSc *Durh.*   Prof.

Sculli, D., MSc *Birm.*, FIMA   Sr. Lectr.

Wong, A. C. Y., BTech *Brad.*, PhD *Brad.*   Assoc. Prof.

Wong, T. N., MSc *Aston*, PhD *Aston*   Assoc. Prof.

Other Staff: 7 Asst. Profs./Lectrs.; 1 Hon. Prof.; 5 Hon. Lectrs.

Research: artificial intelligence (AI) applications (evolutionary optimisation, fuzzy-logic automation, knowledge based systems, simulation); engineering management (manufacturing strategies, production and operations management); ergonomics (anthropometry, display-control configuration, occupational biomechanics); manufacturing systems design (automated assembly, computer in integrated manufacturing (CIM), forms management system (FMS), virtual reality); manufacturing technology (CAD/CAM), product development, robotics/computer vision)

Engineering, Mechanical

Tel: 2859 2635 Fax: 2858 5415

Chan, K. W., BSc *CNAA*, MSc *Lough.*, PhD *Lough.*   Assoc. Prof.

Cheung, K. C., BSc *Birm.*, PhD *Wales*   Assoc. Prof.

Chwang, A. T., MSc *Sask.*, PhD *Cal.Tech.*   Prof.; Head*

Duggan, B. J., BSc *Aston*, PhD *Birm.*, DEng *Birm.*, FIM   Prof.

Gibson, I., BSc *Hull*, PhD *Hull*   Assoc. Prof.

Ko, N. W. M., BSc(Eng) *HK*, PhD *S'ton.*, DSc *HK*, FIMechE   Prof.

Lam, J., BSc *Manc.*, PhD *Camb.*   Assoc. Prof.

Leung, Y. C., BSc(Eng) *HK*, PhD *HK*   Assoc. Prof.

Soh, A. K., BEng *Sing.*, PhD *Sur.*   Assoc. Prof.

Sze, W. S., MSc *Aston*   Assoc. Prof.

Tan, S. T., BSc *Leeds*, PhD *Leeds*   Prof.

Other Staff: 14 Asst. Profs./Lectrs.; 7 Hon. Profs.; 1 Hon. Asst. Prof.

Research: building services (energy/ environmental engineering); CAD/CAM; dynamics and control (robotics); material science and mechanics of solids; thermofluid mechanics (marine and offshore engineering)

English, see also Compar. Lit.

Tel: 2859 8950 Fax: 2559 7139

Bolton, K. R., BA *Kent*, MSc *Edin.*   Assoc. Prof.

Browne, Nicholas K., BA *Williams*, MA *Chic.*, EdD *Harv.*   Prof.

Ho, Elaine Y. L., BA *HK*, MPhil *HK*, PhD *Lond.*   Assoc. Prof.

Hutton, C. M., MA *Col.*, MA *Oxf.*, DPhil *Oxf.*   Assoc. Prof.

Kerr, D. W. F., MA *Camb.*, PhD *Warw.*   Assoc. Prof.; Head*

Ooi, Vicki C. H., BA *HK*, PhD *Brist.*   Sr. Lectr.

Slethaug, G. E., BA *Pacific Lutheran*, MA *Nebraska*, PhD *Nebraska*   Assoc. Prof.

Other Staff: 6 Asst. Profs./Lectrs.; 2 Hon. Profs.; 2 Hon. Asst. Profs.

Research: political, historical and social aspects of literary and linguistic phenomena

Finance, see Econ. and Finance, Sch. of

Fine Arts

Tel: 2859 7040 Fax: 2548 0987

Clarke, D. J., BA *Lond.*, PhD *Lond.*   Assoc. Prof.

Muir, Carolyn D., BA *Wellesley*, MA *Penn.*   Lectr.; Head*

Wan, Q., BA *Beijing*, MFA *Beijing*, MA *Kansas*, PhD *Kansas*   Assoc. Prof.

Other Staff: 2 Asst. Profs./Lectrs.; 1 Lectr./Asst. Lectr.; 1 Hon. Prof.; 1 Hon. Asst. Prof.; 1 Hon. Lectr.

Research: Chinese archaeology; Hindu-Buddhist sacred art; Japanese ink painting and mediaeval gardens; mediaeval and Renaissance sacred art; modern Chinese and Hong Kong art

Geography and Geology

Tel: 2859 2836 Fax: 2559 8994

Jim, C. Y., BA *HK*, PhD *Reading*, FLS   Prof.; Head*

Kyle, W. J., BSc *Nott.*, MSc *McM.*, PhD *McM.*, FRMetS   Assoc. Prof.

Lai, Poh Chin, BES *Wat.*, MA *Wat.*, PhD *Wat.*   Sr. Lectr.

Sit, V. F. S., BA *HK*, MA *HK*, PhD *Lond.*   Prof.

Other Staff: 6 Asst. Profs./Lectrs.; 1 Lectr.; 1 Asst. Lectr.; 5 Hon. Lectrs.

Research: China and the Pacific Rim (central-local relationships, development policies, Hong Kong-Guangdong integration, urban environmental management); environment and resources (geomorphology, hazards, hydrology, soil science, tropical climatology, urban ecology); methodology (computer cartography, geographical information systems, spatial analysis); urban and transport (industrial geography, regional development, transport geography and modelling, urban planning, urbanisation)

Hearing Sciences, see Speech and Hearing Scis.

History

Tel: 2859 2861 Fax: 2858 9755

Chan, Kit Ching, BA *Lond.*, BA *HK*, PhD *Lond.*   Prof.

Lin, A. H. Y., BA *HK*, MPhil *HK*, PhD *Lond.*   Assoc. Prof.

Lui, A. Y. C., BA *HK*, MA *HK*, PhD *Lond.*   Prof.

MacPherson, Kerrie L., BA *N.Y.State*, MA *N.Y.State*, PhD *N.Y.State*   Assoc. Prof.

Owen, N. G., BA *Lond.*, MA *Mich.*, PhD *Mich.*   Prof.

Stanley, T. A., BA *Antioch*, MA *Arizona*, PhD *Arizona*   Lectr.; Head*

Other Staff: 6 Asst. Profs./Lectrs.; 1 Lectr./Asst. Lectr.; 1 Hon. Prof.; 1 Hon. Asst. Prof.; 3 Hon. Lectrs.

Vacant Posts: 1 Prof.

Research: Chinese and Hong Kong history; early modern and modern European history; modern Japanese history; Southeast Asian history; US and diplomatic history

Japanese Studies

Tel: 2859 2879 Fax: 2548 7399

Murakami, F., BEd *Hokkaido*, MLitt *Hokkaido*   Assoc. Prof.

Refsing, K., BA *Copenhagen*, MA *Copenhagen*, PhD *Copenhagen*   Prof.; Head*

Other Staff: 5 Asst. Profs./Lectrs.

Research: gender in Japan; Japanese linguistics and Ainu; Japanese literature; Sino-Japanese relations; tourism and popular culture

Law, see also Professl. Legal Educn.

Tel: 2859 2951 Fax: 2559 3543

Byrnes, A. C., BA *ANU*, LLB *ANU*, LLM *Harv.*, LLM *Col.*   Assoc. Prof.

Chan, J. M. M., LLB *HK*, LLM *Lond.*   Assoc. Prof.

Chen, Albert H. Y., LLB *HK*, LLM *Harv.*   Prof.

Cottrell, Jill, LLM *Lond.*, LLM *Yale*   Sr. Lectr.

Feng, X., BA *Kumming Teachers*, MA *Beijing*, PhD *Harv.*, JD *Yale*   Assoc. Prof.

Ghai, Y. P., CBE, MA *Oxf.*, DCL *Oxf.*, LLM *Harv.*   Prof.

Glofcheski, R. A., BA *W.Laur.*, LLB *Windsor*, LLM *Camb.*   Assoc. Prof.; Head*

Ho, Betty M. F., BA *Immaculate Heart*, MA *Calif.*, LLB *Tor.*, LLM *Camb.*   Assoc. Prof.

Lewis, D. J., AB *S.Calif.*, JE *Emory*, LLM *Lond.*   Assoc. Prof.

Liu, Athena N. C., BA *CNAA*, PhD *Glas.*   Assoc. Prof.

Mushkat, Roda, LLB *Jerusalem*, LLM *Well.*, LLD *S.Af.*   Prof.

Rwezaura, B. A., LLB *Mak.*, LLM *Harv.*, PhD *Warw.*   Sr. Lectr.

Sihombing, Judith E., LLB *Melb.*, LLM *Malaya*   Sr. Lectr.

Smart, P. St. J., LLM *Lond.*   Assoc. Prof.

Wacks, R. I., BA *Witw.*, LLB *Witw.*, LLM *Lond.*, PhD *Lond.*, MLitt *Oxf.*, LLD *Lond.*   Prof.

Wesley-Smith, Peter, BA *Adel.*, LLB *Adel.*, PhD *HK*   Prof.

Other Staff: 13 Asst. Profs./Lectrs.

Research: corporate and commercial law, especially tax, insolvency and intellectual property; law of the People's Republic of China; legal theory and social issues (family law, medico-legal, privacy); public law, especially comparative constitutions and human rights; real property, conveyancing, construction and environment

Linguistics

Tel: 2859 2758 Fax: 2546 4943

Luke, K. K., BA *HK*, MPhil *York(UK)*, DPhil *York(UK)*   Sr. Lectr.; Head*

Other Staff: 5 Asst. Profs./Lectrs.; 1 Hon. Assoc. Prof.

Research: bilingualism; Chinese linguistics; conversation analysis; corpus linguistics; reference grammars and dictionaries

Management, see under Business, Sch. of

Mathematics

Tel: 2859 2250 Fax: 2559 2225

Chan, K. Y., BSc *HK*, PhD *Birm.*   Assoc. Prof.; Head*

Cheung, W. S., BSc *Chinese HK*, AM *Harv.*, MPhil *Chinese HK*, PhD *Harv.*   Assoc. Prof.

Chu, S. C. K., MS *Cornell*, MS *Col.*, EngScD *Col.*   Sr. Lectr.

Liu, M. C., BSc *Chinese HK*, BSc *HK*, MSc *HK*, PhD *HK*   Prof.

Mok Ngaiming, MA *Yale*, PhD *Stan.*   Prof.

Siu, M. K., BSc *HK*, MA *Col.*, PhD *Col.*   Prof.

Tsang, K. M., BA *HK*, MA *Prin.*, MPhil *HK*, PhD *Prin.*   Sr. Lectr.

Other Staff: 10 Asst. Profs./Lectrs.; 1 Hon. Asst. Prof.; 1 Hon. Lectr.

Research: analytical number theory; differential equations and control theory; linear and commutative algebra; scientific computation and operations research; several complex variables and differential geometry

Medicine, see below

Microbiology, see Medicine, below

Music

Tel: 2859 2893 Fax: 2858 4933

Mora, M., BMus *N.S.W.Conservatorium*, PhD *Monash*   Lectr.; Head*

Noone, M. J., BA *Syd.*, MA *Syd.*, PhD *Camb.*   Assoc. Prof.

Yung, Bell, BSc *Calif.*, PhD *M.I.T.*, PhD *Harv.*   Prof.

Other Staff: 3 Asst. Profs./Lectrs.; 1 Hon. Prof.; 1 Hon. Asst. Prof.

Research: Chinese music (Cantonese narrative songs, Cantonese opera, history, seven-string zither); music aesthetics (Southeast Asian music, western modernist and postmodern); music composition (contemporary and traditional methods, electro-acoustic music,

orchestration); musicological theory and method, including ethnography (particularly Southeast Asia); western music history (Spanish and Portuguese Renaissance vocal music, twentieth-century music)

Philosophy

Tel: 2859 2796 Fax: 2559 8452

Goldstein, L., BA *Liv.*, PhD *St And.*   Prof.

Hansen, C., BA *Utah*, PhD *Mich.*   Prof.

Martin, Michael R., AB *Prin.*, MA *Harv.*, PhD *Harv.*   Assoc. Prof.

Moore, F. C. T., MA *Oxf.*, DPhil *Oxf.*   Prof.; Head*

Other Staff: 4 Asst. Profs./Lectrs.; 1 Hon. Asst. Prof.

Research: Chinese philosophy, comparative philosophy; computer-assisted learning; contemporary Anglo-American political philosophy; philosophy of logic and language; philosophy of mind and cognitive science

Physics

Tel: 2859 2359 Fax: 2559 9152

Cheng, K. S., BSc *Chinese HK*, MPhil *Col.*, PhD *Col.*, FRAS   Prof.

Fung, P. C. W., BSc *Tas.*, PhD *Tas.*   Prof.

Gao, Ju, BSc *Beijing*, MSc *Chinese Acad.Sc.*, PhD *T.H.Twente*   Assoc. Prof.

MacKeown, P. K., BSc *N.U.I.*, PhD *Durh.*   Prof.

Tong, David S. Y., BSc *HK*, MS *Calif.*, PhD *Calif.*   Prof.; Head*

Wang, Jian, BSc *Beijing*, PhD *Penn.*   Assoc. Prof.

Wang, Z. D., BS *China U.S.T.*, MS *Nanjing*, PhD *Nanjing*   Assoc. Prof.

Other Staff: 7 Asst. Profs./Lectrs.; 1 Hon. Assoc. Prof.; 1 Hon. Asst. Prof.

Research: semi-conductor and positron physics (material and devices); surface physics (electron holography, photoelectron diffraction); theoretical astrophysics (gamma-ray bursts, neutron stars, pulsars); theoretical condensed matter (ab initio calculation, mesoscopic systems, superconductivity); thin film (technology, devices)

Physiology, see Medicine, below

Politics and Public Administration

Tel: 2859 2393 Fax: 2858 3550

Burns, J. P., BA *St.Olaf*, MA *Oxf.*, MA *Col.*, MPhil *Col.*, PhD *Col.*   Prof.; Head*

Chan, J. C. W., BSSc *Chinese HK*, MSc *Lond.*, DPhil *Oxf.*   Assoc. Prof.

Cheung, P. T. Y., BSSc *Chinese HK*, MA *Indiana*, PhD *Wash.*   Assoc. Prof.

Hu, R. W., BA *Beijing*, MA *Johns H.*, PhD *Maryland*   Assoc. Prof.

Lo, S. H., BA *York(Can.)*, MA *Wat.*, PhD *Tor.*   Assoc. Prof.

Tang, J. T. H., BA *HK*, MPhil *Camb.*, PhD *Lond.*   Assoc. Prof.

Other Staff: 4 Asst. Profs./Lectrs.; 1 Hon. Asst. Prof.; 1 Hon. Lectr.

Research: China and Hong Kong politics; Chinese foreign policy; human rights in Asia; public administration (alternative public service delivery systems, institutional change, inter-governmental relations, public personnel administration); security issues in East Asia

Poon Kam Kai Institute of Management, see under Business, Sch. of

Professional Legal Education, see also Law

Tel: 2859 2951 Fax: 2559 3543

Booth, C. D., BA *Yale*, JD *Harv.*   Assoc. Prof.

Carver, Anne R., MA *Camb.*   Sr. Lectr.

Halkyard, A. J., LLB *ANU*, LLM *Virginia*   Assoc. Prof.

McInnis, J. A., BA *Regina*, LLB *Sask.*, BCL *McG.*, LLM *McG.*   Assoc. Prof.

Nathanson, S. B., BCom *McG.*, LLB *Br.Col.*   Assoc. Prof.

Sherrin, C. H., LLB *Lond.*, LLM *Lond.*, PhD *Lond.*   Prof.

Wilkinson, R. M., LLB *Camb.*, MA *Camb.*   Prof.; Head*

Other Staff: 8 Asst. Profs./Lectrs.; 43 Hon. Lectrs.

Psychology

Tel: 2859 2375 Fax: 2858 3518

Blowers, G. H., BSc *Sheff.*, MPhil *Sus.*, PhD *HK*   Sr. Lectr.

Chiu, C. Y., BSocSc *HK*, MA *Col.*, MPhil *HK*, PhD *Col.*   Assoc. Prof.

Ho, D. Y. F., BSc *Acad.*, MA *Roosevelt*, PhD *Illinois Tech.Inst.*   Prof.

Hoosain, R., MA *HK*, PhD *Ill.*, FBPsS   Prof.

Hui, H. C., BSocSc *HK*, MA *Ill.*, PhD *Ill.*   Sr. Lectr.

Kao, H. S. R., BA *Natnl.Taiwan*, MS *W.Virginia*, PhD *Wis.*   Prof.

Salili, Farideh, MA *Teheran*, PhD *Ill.*   Assoc. Prof.

Spinks, J. A., BSc *Newcastle(UK)*, PhD *S'ton.*   Prof.; Head*

Vera, A. H., BS *McG.*, PhD *Cornell*   Assoc. Prof.

Yang, Chung-fang, BS *Natnl.Taiwan*, MA *Chic.*, PhD *Chic.*   Sr. Lectr.

Other Staff: 7 Asst. Profs./Lectrs.; 9 Hon. Asst. Profs.; 22 Hon. Lectrs.

Research: applied psychology (clinical, educational cognitive science); Chinese language (attentional studies, brain mapping, calligraphy); cross-cultural psychology; indigenous Chinese psychology; social and personality psychology (Chinese self, social cognition)

Public Administration, see Pol. and Public Admin.

Real Estate and Construction, see also Archit.

Tel: 2859 2128 Fax: 2559 9457

Chau, K. W., BBuilding *HK*, PhD *HK*   Assoc. Prof.

Hamer, Andrew M., BA *Amherst*, MA *Harv.*, PhD *Harv.*   Assoc. Prof.

Ho, Daniel C. W., BSc *CNAA*, MBA *Chinese HK*   Assoc. Prof.

Hsu, Berry F. C., BSc *Alta.*, LLM *Alta.*, MA *Oregon*, PhD *Lond.*   Assoc. Prof.

Lai, Lawrence W. C., LLB *Lond.*, MSocSc *HK*, MTCP *Syd.*, PhD *HK*   Assoc. Prof.

McKinnell, K. G., BSc *CNAA*, MSc *Edin.*, MPhil *Aston*   Sr. Lectr.; Head*

Rowlinson, S. M., BSc *Nott.*, MSc *Lond.*, PhD *Brun.*   Sr. Lectr.

Walker, A., MSc *Brad.*, PhD *CNAA*, FRICS   Prof.

Other Staff: 9 Asst. Profs./Lectrs.; 5 Hon. Asst. Profs.; 2 Hon. Lectrs.

Research: construction and land economics; construction and project management; legal principles in real estate and construction (land law, landlord and tenant's implication, town planning and related legislation); safety, productivity and labour provision in construction; urban land and housing reform in China and other transitional economies

Social Work and Social Administration

Tel: 2859 2288 Fax: 2858 7604

Boey, K. W., BSc *Natnl.Taiwan*, MSc *Natnl.Taiwan*, PhD *HK*   Sr. Lectr.

Chan, Cecilia L. W., BSocSc *HK*, MSocSc *HK*, PhD *HK*   Prof.; Head*

Chi, Iris, BSSc *Chinese HK*, MSW *San Diego State*, DSW *Calif.*   Assoc. Prof.

Chow, N. W. S., MBE, JP, BA *HK*, MA(Econ) *Manc.*, PhD *HK*   Prof.

Law, C. K., BSocSc *HK*, MBA *Chinese HK*, MSW *HK*, DSW *Calif.*   Assoc. Prof.

Pearson, Veronica J., BScEcon *Wales*, MSc *Brist.*, DPhil *York(UK)*   Assoc. Prof.

Tsang, Sandra K. M., MSocSc *HK*, PhD *HK*   Assoc. Prof.

Other Staff: 5 Asst. Profs./Lectrs.; 1 Hon. Assoc. Prof.; 13 Hon. Asst. Profs.; 6 Hon. Lectrs.

Research: community care; gerontology; health and mental health; social policy; social work intervention

Sociology

Tel: 2859 2299 Fax: 2559 8044

Broadhurst, R. G., BA W.Aust., BEd W.Aust., MPhil Camb., PhD W.Aust. Assoc. Prof.

Evans, G. R., BA La Trobe, MA La Trobe, PhD La Trobe Reader

Laidler, Joe, MA Calif., PhD Calif. Assoc. Prof.

Leung, B. K. P., BSocSc HK, MPhil HK, PhD York(Can.) Assoc. Prof.; Head*

Levin, D. A., BA(Econ) Wis., MA Ill. Sr. Lectr.

Traver, H. H., BA Calif.State, MA Calif.State, PhD Calif. Assoc. Prof.

Wong, S. L., BSocSc HK, MPhil Chinese HK, BLitt Oxf., DPhil Oxf. Prof.

Other Staff: 5 Asst. Profs./Lectrs.; 1 Hon. Asst. Prof.

Research: crime and deviance; cultural studies, especially popular culture; gender studies; Hong Kong studies; studies of Southeast Asian societies

Speech and Hearing Sciences

Tel: 2859 0599 Fax: 2559 0060

Fletcher, P., BA Oxf., MPhil Reading, PhD Alta. Prof.; Head*

So, Lydia K. H., MA Macq., PhD Macq. Assoc. Prof.

Stokes, Stephanie, BAppSc W.Aust.I.T., PhD Curtin Assoc. Prof.

Whitehill, Tara L., BA Oberlin, MS Col. Assoc. Prof.

Other Staff: 6 Asst. Profs./Lectrs.; 45 Hon. Asst. Profs.

Research: hearing impairment; normal and non-normal child language development; speech and language disorders in adults; speech perception; the voice and its disorders

Statistics

Tel: 2859 2466 Fax: 2858 9041

Chiu, W. K., BA HK, BSc HK, MA HK, MSc Lond., PhD Bath Assoc. Prof.

Fung, T. W. K., BSocSc HK, MSc Lond., PhD HK Assoc. Prof.

Lauder, I. J., BSc Edin., MSc Kent, PhD HK Assoc. Prof.

Li, W. K., BSc York(Can.), MA York(Can.), PhD W.Ont. Prof.; Head*

Lloyd, C. J., BSc Melb., PhD Melb. Assoc. Prof.

Ng, K. W., BSc Chinese HK, MSc Alta., PhD Tor. Sr. Lectr.

Shen, Shir Ming, BA HK, MSc Lond., PhD HK Assoc. Prof.

Tong, H., MSc Manc., PhD Manc. Prof.

Yip, P. S. F., BSc Melb., PhD La Trobe Sr. Lectr.

Other Staff: 7 Asst. Profs./Lectrs.; 3 Lectrs./ Asst. Lectrs.; 1 Hon. Prof.

Research: clinical trials in mathematical finance and actuarial science; linear and nonlinear time series analysis; multivariate statistics

Zoology

Tel: 2859 2846 Fax: 2559 9114

Chan, Daniel K. O., JP, MSc HK, PhD Sheff. Prof.; Head*

Chan, S. T. H., BSc HK, PhD HK, FIBiol Prof.

Ko, R. C. C., BSc Manit., MSc Br.Col., PhD Guelph Prof.

Lee, W. W. M., BSc Wis., MPhil Chinese HK, PhD HK Assoc. Prof.

Leung, Frederick C., BA Calif., PhD Calif. Assoc. Prof.

Li, E. T. S., BSc Tor., MSc Tor., PhD Tor. Assoc. Prof.

Sun, M., BSc Nanjing, PhD Br.Col. Assoc. Prof.

Xu, R. J., BAgrSc Nanjing, MAgr Syd., PhD La Trobe Assoc. Prof.

Other Staff: 7 Asst. Profs./Lectrs.; 1 Hon. Lectr.

Research: aquaculture biotechnology induced reproduction-growth; comparative

endocrinology-transmembrane signalling; immunodiagnosis (parasitology, livestock-poultry-shrimp viruses); molecular biology (site directed mutagenesis); reproduction (gonadotropin releasing hormone (GnRH) analogues, male contraceptine implantation)

DENTISTRY

Tel: 2859 0342 Fax: 2517 0544, 2547 6257

Cheung, G. S. P., BDS HK, MDS HK MSc Lond., FRACDS Assoc. Prof.

Cheung, L. K., BDS Glas., PhD HK, FFDRCSI, FDSRCPSGlas, FRACDS Assoc. Prof.

Chow, T. W., BDS Lond., MSc Lond., PhD Lond., FRACDS Sr. Lectr.

Comfort, Margaret B., BDS Manc., MSc Manc., FDSRCS Assoc. Prof.

Cooke, M. S., BChD Leeds, LDS Leeds, PhD HK, FDSRCSEd, FFDRCSI Prof.

Corbet, E. F., BDS N.U.I., FDSRCS, FFDRCSI Assoc. Prof.

Darvell, B. W., MSc Wales, PhD Birm., FRSChem Sr. Lectr.

Davies, W. I. R., JP, BDS Lond., MSc Penn., FDSRCS Prof.

Hagg, E. U. O., DDS Lund, DrOdont Lund Prof.

King, N. M., BDS Lond., MSc Lond., PhD HK Prof.

Lo, E. C. M., BDS HK, MDS HK, PhD HK Assoc. Prof.

Newsome, P. R. H., BChD Leeds, MBA Warw., FDSRCSEd Sr. Lectr.

Nordberg, L. G., MD Gothenburg, PhD Gothenburg Assoc. Prof.

Rodrigo, M. R. C., MB BS S.Lanka, FFARCSI, FFARCS Assoc. Prof.

Samaranayake, L. P., BDS S.Lanka, DDS Glas., FRCPath Prof.

Samman, N., BDS Syd., FDSRCS Assoc. Prof.

Smales, Frederick C., BSc Durh., BDS Newcastle(UK), PhD Lond., FDSRCS Prof.

Smales, Roger J., BDS Otago, MDS Otago, DDSc Otago, FDSRCSEd Prof.

Tideman, H., DDS Utrecht, MD Nijmegen, PhD Amst., FRACDS Prof.

Other Staff: 15 Asst. Profs./Lectrs.; 1 Hon. Prof.; 4 Hon. Assoc. Profs.; 10 Hon. Asst. Profs.; 5 Hon. Lectrs.

Research: clinical and laboratory studies of dental materials; clinical and laboratory studies of maxillofacial surgical procedures; dental and skeletal changes during growth and orthodontic treatment; oral microbiology and periodontology; provision of dental health care services

MEDICINE

Anaesthesiology

Tel: 2855 3303 Fax: 2855 1654

Irwin, M. G., MB ChB Glas., FRCA Assoc. Prof.

Yang, Joseph C. S., MD Düsseldorf, FFARCSI Prof.; Head*

Other Staff: 1 Asst. Prof.; 5 Hon. Assoc. Profs.; 12 Hon. Asst. Profs.

Research: chronic pain management in the Chinese population; effect of traditional Chinese medicine on cancer pain; effects of anaesthesia and surgery on blood coagulation; patient-maintained target: controlled drug delivery systems in anaesthesia; transoesophageal echocardiographic patient monitoring in non-cardiac surgery

Anatomy

Tel: 2819 9259 Fax: 2817 0857

Lucas, P. W., BSc Lond., PhD Lond. Prof.

O, Wai-Sum, BSc HK, MPhil HK, PhD Edin. Assoc. Prof.

So, K. F., BA Northeastern, PhD M.I.T. Prof.

Tay, D. K. C., BSc Flin., PhD Flin. Assoc. Prof.

Tipoe, G. L., BA East(Manila), MD East(Manila), PhD HK Assoc. Prof.

Tsao, G. S. W., BSc Chinese HK, PhD Lond. Assoc. Prof.

Wong, Y. C., BSc Nan., MSc W.Ont., PhD W.Ont. Prof.; Head*

Wu, W., MMed Sun Yat Sen, PhD Old Dominion Assoc. Prof.

Other Staff: 3 Asst. Profs./Lectrs.; 2 Hon. Profs.; 1 Hon. Asst. Prof.; 4 Hon. Lectrs.

Research: cell and cancer biology; functional morphology and biomechanics; neurobiology; reproductive biology

Biochemistry

Tel: 2819 9241 Fax: 2855 1254

Cheah, Kathryn S. E., BSc Lond., PhD Camb. Prof.; Head*

Lam, Veronica M. S., BSc Lond., PhD Lond. Sr. Lectr.

Opstelten, Davina, PhD Gron. Assoc. Prof.

Shum, Daisy K. Y., BSc HK, PhD HK Assoc. Prof.

Tam, J. W. O., BSc Chinese HK, PhD Calif. Assoc. Prof.

Other Staff: 5 Asst. Profs./Lectrs.; 1 Hon. Prof.; 1 Hon. Reader; 5 Hon. Lectrs.

Research: developmental genetics and immunology transgenic research; molecular genetics; molecular signalling; neurobiology, glycobiology, neurochemistry; protein structure and function (traditional Chinese medicinal herbs)

Community Medicine

Tel: 2819 9280 Fax: 2855 9528

Hedley, A. J., MB ChB Aberd., MD Aberd., Hon. MD Khon Kaen, FRCP, FRCPEd, FRCPGlas, FACE Prof.; Head*

Lam, T. H., MD HK, MSc Lond., FRCPEd Prof.

Other Staff: 3 Asst. Profs./Lectrs.; 3 Hon. Profs.; 7 Hon. Assoc. Profs.; 9 Hon. Asst. Profs.; 11 Hon. Lectrs.

Research: chronic disease and cancer epidemiology; environmental health and air pollution; health behaviour, communication in medicine, psycho-oncology; health services research, medical informatics, micro-health economics; tobacco control and smoking prevention

Behavioural Sciences Unit

Tel: 2819 9280 Fax: 2855 9528

Fielding, R., BA Lond., PhD Sheff. Sr. Lectr.; Head*

Stewart, Sunita M., BA Reed, MS Mass., PhD Mass. Assoc. Prof.

Other Staff: 1 Asst. Prof.

Diagnostic Radiology

Tel: 2855 3307 Fax: 2855 1652

Ngan, Henry, MB BS Lond., FRCP, FRCPEd, FRCR Prof.; Head*

Ooi, Clara G. C., MB BCh BAO Belf. Assoc. Prof.

Peh, W. C. G., MB BS Sing., FRCR Prof.

Other Staff: 2 Hon. Asst. Profs.; 2 Hon. Sr. Lectrs.; 2 Hon Lectrs.

Research: chemoembolisation in inoperable hepatocellular carcinoma; high-resolution computed tomography in respiratory diseases; laboratory and clinical study of intussusception; radiology in musculoskeletal diseases; regional chemotheraphy in gastric cancer

Medicine

Tel: 2855 4604 Fax: 2855 1143

Chan, D. T. M., MD HK Assoc. Prof.

Chan, Moira M. W., MB BS HK, FRCPCan, FRCPEd, FACP Prof.

Chan, Vivian N. Y., MSc Lond., PhD Lond., FRCPath Prof.

Ho, D. S. W., MB BS Syd., PhD Syd., FRACP Assoc. Prof.

Ho, S. L., MD Wales Assoc. Prof.

Ip, Mary S. M., MD HK, FRCPEd Prof.

Kumana, C. R., BSc Lond., MB BS Lond., FRCP, FRCPCan Prof.

Kung, Annie W. C., MD HK, FRCPEd Prof.

Kwong, Y. L., MD HK Assoc. Prof.

Lai, C. L., MD *HK*, FRCPEd, FRCP, FRACP   Prof.

Lai, K. N., MD *HK*, DSc *HK*, FRCPEd, FRCP, FRCPGlas, FRACP   Prof.

Lam, Karen S. L., MD *HK*, FRCPEd, FRCP, FRACP   Prof.

Lam, S. K., OBE, MD *HK*, FRCPEd, FRCP, FRCPGlas, FRACP   Prof.; Head*

Lam, W. K., MD *HK*, FRCPEd, FRCP, FRCPGlas, FRACP   Prof.

Lau, C. P., MD *HK*, FRCP, FRCPEd, FRCPGlas   Prof.

Lau, W. C. S., MD *Dund.*   Assoc. Prof.

Liang, R. H. S., MD *HK*, FRCP, FRCPEd, FRCPGlas, FRACP   Prof.

Tan, Kathryn C. B., MD *Wales*   Assoc. Prof.

Tsang, K. W. T., MD *Glas.*   Assoc. Prof.

Young, Rosie T. T., CBE, JP, MD *HK*, Hon. DSc *HK*, FRCP, FRCPEd, FRACP, FRCPGlas   Prof.

Other Staff: 6 Asst. Profs./Lectrs.; 2 Hon. Profs.; 39 Hon. Assoc. Profs.; 24 Hon. Asst. Profs.

Research: bio/cellular/immuno-pathogenesis of disease (bronchiectasis, hepatitis B, IgA nephropathy, lupus nephritis, peptic ulcer); innovative therapy (cancers, cardiovascular angioplasty/stenting, diabetes, hepatitis B, marrow and stem cell transplant, osteoporosis, pace-makers, peptic ulcer); molecular diagnostics (haemic malignancies, thalassaemia); molecular pathogenesis of disease (atherosclerosis, cancers, hypertension, lupus erythematosis, Parkinsonism)

General Practice Unit

Tel: 2552 6021 Fax: 2814 7475

Dixon, Anthony S., MB ChB *Leeds*   Prof.; Head*

Lam, Cindy L. K., MB BS *HK*, FRCGP   Assoc. Prof.

Lam, T. P., MB BS *W.Aust.*, MFM *Monash*   Assoc. Prof.

Other Staff: 77 Hon. Asst. Profs.; 2 Hon. Tutors

Research: health beliefs including qualitative measures; health status (evaluation of instruments measuring health); medical education (evaluation of problem-based learning); mental illness and community impact

Microbiology

Tel: 2855 4897 Fax: 2855 1241

Im, S. W. K., BSc *Melb.*, PhD *Melb.*   Asst. Prof.; Head*

Ng, M. H., BSc *Melb.*, PhD *N.Y.*   Prof.

Peiris, J. S. M., MB BS *Ceyl.*, DPhil *Oxf.*, FRCPath   Assoc. Prof.

Shortridge, K. F., BSc *Qld.*, PhD *Lond.*, FIBiol   Prof.

Yuen, K. Y., MB BS *HK*, FRCSGlas   Prof.

Other Staff: 5 Asst. Profs./Lectrs.; 1 Lectr./Asst. Lectr.; 2 Hon. Profs.; 2 Hon. Assoc. Profs.; 4 Hon. Asst. Profs.; 1 Hon. Reader; 1 Hon. Sr. Lectr.; 1 Hon. Lectr.

Research: antibiotics and antibiotics resistance; ecology of influenza; emerging and re-emerging pathogens; immunotherapy for diseases relating to chronic viral infections; virus associated cancers

Nursing Studies

Tel: 2819 2622 Fax: 2872 6079

Sullivan, Patricia L., BSc *Mt.St.Vin.(N.Y.)*, MSc *Boston*, PhD *Alta.*   Prof.; Head*

Other Staff: 9 Asst. Profs./Lectrs.

Research: lifelong primary care of girls and women; nursing education; patient education

Obstetrics and Gynaecology

Tel: 2855 2622 Fax: 2855 0947

Ho, P. C., MB BS *HK*, MD *HK*, FRCOG   Prof.; Head*

Lam, Y. H., MB BS *HK*   Assoc. Prof.

Lao, Terence T. H., MB BS *HK*   Assoc. Prof.

Ngan, Hextan Y. S., MD *HK*, FRCOG   Prof.

Tang, Grace W. K., MB BS *HK*, FRCOG   Prof.

Wong, Rosamond L. C., MB BS *HK*, FRCOG   Prof.

Yeung, W. S. B., BSc *HK*, PhD *HK*   Assoc. Prof.

Other Staff: 7 Asst. Profs./Lectrs.; 1 Hon. Prof.; 12 Hon. Assoc. Profs.; 8 Hon. Asst. Profs.

Vacant Posts: 1 Prof.

Research: assisted reproduction (co-cultures, intra-interine insemination); fertility regulation (mifepristone and misoprostol); gynaecological oncology (oncogenes and virus, tumour markers); perinatology (diabetes mellitus, placenta size and foetal growth); prenatal diagnosis (thalassaemia and foetal anenploidy)

Orthopaedic Surgery

Tel: 2855 4254 Fax: 2817 4392

Cheung, K. M. C., MB BS *Lond.*, FRCS   Assoc. Prof.

Chiu, P. K. Y., MB BS *HK*, FRCSEd   Assoc. Prof.

Chow, S. P., JP, MB MS *HK*, MS *HK*, FRCSEd, FACS   Prof.

Leong, John C. Y., OBE, JP, MB BS *HK*, FRCSEd, FRCS, FRACS   Prof.; Head*

Luk, K. D. K., MB BS *HK*, MChOrth *Liv.*, FRCSEd, FRCSGlas, FRACS   Prof.

Other Staff: 4 Asst. Profs/Lectrs.; 2 Hon. Profs.; 9 Assoc. Profs.; 7 Hon. Asst. Profs.

Research: hand surgery (digital nerve repair, finger biomechanics, finger fractures); joints (Asian femoral stem design, cartilage growth, knee pain); microsurgery (plexus injuries, toe-to-hand transplant, venous flap); scoliosis (muscle functions, respiratory biomechanics, surgical treatment); spine (biomechanics, fixation implant, fusion)

Paediatrics

Tel: 2855 4482 Fax: 2855 1523

Cheung, P. T., MB BS *HK*, FRCPEd   Assoc. Prof.

Karlberg, J. P. E., BSc *Gothenburg*, MD *Gothenburg*, PhD *Gothenburg*   Prof.

Lau, Y. L., MB ChB *Glas.*, MD *Glas.*, FRCPEd   Prof.

Leung, M. P., MB BS *HK*, MD *HK*, FRCPEd   Prof.

Low, L. C. K., BSc *Glas.*, MB ChB *Glas.*, FRCPEd, FRCPGlas   Prof.

Wong, Virginia C. N., MB BS, FRCPEd   Prof.

Yeung, C. Y., MB BS *HK*, FRCP, FRCPI, FRCPGlas, FRCPEd, FRCPCan   Prof.; Head*

Other Staff: 4 Asst. Profs./Lectrs.; 19 Hon. Assoc. Profs.; 8 Hon. Asst. Profs.

Research: clinical studies on local paediatric problems; molecular genetic studies on endocrine disorders; neonatal bilirubin metabolism

Pathology

Tel: 2855 4872 Fax: 2872 5197

Chan, K. W., MB BS *HK*   Sr. Lectr.

Chan, L. C., BA *Camb.*, MB BChir *Camb.*, PhD *Lond.*   Prof.

Cheung, Annie N. Y., MB BS *HK*   Assoc. Prof.

Dickens, P., MB BS *Newcastle(UK)*, FRCPath, FRCPCan   Sr. Lectr.; Head*

Higgins, D. A., BVSc *Liv.*, PhD *Cornell*, DVSc *Liv.*, FRCPath, FRCVS   Reader

Lawton, J. W. M., MB BS *Adel.*, MD *Adel.*, FRCPA   Prof.

Leung, Suet Yi, MB BS *HK*, FRCPA   Assoc. Prof.

Ng, Irene O. L., MD *HK*, FRCPath   Assoc. Prof.

Nicholls, J. M., MB BS *Adel.*, FRCPA   Assoc. Prof.

Srivastava, G., BSc *Punj.Ag.*, MSc *Punj.Ag.*, PhD *Adel.*   Assoc. Prof.

Wong, Maria P., MB BS *HK*, FRCPA   Assoc. Prof.

Other Staff: 2 Asst. Profs./Lectrs.; 3 Hon. Assoc. Profs.; 20 Hon. Asst. Profs.; 2 Hon. Lectrs.; 4 Hon. Tutors

Research: chemical pathology (lipids and vascular disease); forensic pathology (fatal

industrial/traffic accidents); haematology (epidemiological cytogenetics, molecular studies of haemato-malignancies); histopathology (clinical, molecular and genetic studies of tumours); immunology (autoimmunity, duck immunobiology, immunodeficiencies)

Pharmacology

Tel: 2819 9250 Fax: 2817 0859

Cho, C. H., BPharm *Natnl.U.Defence Technol.(China)*, PhD *HK*   Prof.

Man, R. Y. K., BSc *Manit.*, PhD *Manit.*   Prof.; Head*

Other Staff: 3 Asst. Profs./Lectrs.; 1 Hon. Assoc. Prof.

Research: cardiovascular pharmacology; Chinese medicine; drug metabolism and toxicology; gastrointestinal pharmacology

Physiology

Tel: 2819 9162 Fax: 2855 9730

Ballard, H. J., BSc *Leeds*, PhD *Leeds*   Assoc. Prof.

Bourreau, J. P., MS *Poitiers*, PhD *Poitiers*   Assoc. Prof.

Bruce, I. C., BSc *Aberd.*, PhD *Calg.*   Assoc. Prof.

Chan, Y. S., BSc *HK*, PhD *HK*   Prof.

Kwan, D. C. Y., MSc *Wilkes*, PhD *Penn.*   Prof.

Loh, T. T., MSc *W. Aust.*, PhD *W.Aust.*   Prof.

Lung, Mary A. K. Y., BSc *HK*, PhD *HK*   Assoc. Prof.

Pang, S. F., BSc *Chinese HK*, MA *Calif.*, PhD *Pitt.*   Prof.; Head*

Poon, Angela M. S., MB BS *HK*, PhD *HK*   Assoc. Prof.

Sheng, H. P., BSc *Sing.*, PhD *Baylor*   Assoc. Prof.

Shiu, S. Y. W., MB BS *HK* DPhil *Oxf.*   Assoc. Prof.

Tang, F., BSc *HK*, MSc *HK*, PhD *Hull*   Prof.

Wong, T. M., BSc *Chinese HK*, MSc *HK*, PhD *HK*   Prof.

Other Staff: 1 Asst. Prof.; 3 Hon. Profs.

Research: cardiovascular science (arrhythmia, muscle, nasal and salivary circulation); cell physiology (apotosis, CA+ homeostasis, excitation-contraction coupling); molecular physiology (flaviviruses, receptor gene regulation, signal transduction); neuroendocrinology (Alzheimer's disease, biorhythms, melatonin, neuroimmunomodulation, neuropeptides); neurophysiology (circulation control, respiration control, vestibular system)

Psychiatry

Tel: 2855 4486 Fax: 2855 1345

Chen, E. Y. H., MB ChB *Edin.*, MA *Oxf.*   Assoc. Prof.

Lee, P. W. H., MSocSc *HK*, PhD *HK*   Sr. Lectr.

Mak-Lieh, Felice, OBE, JP, MD *Santo Tomas*, FRCPsych   Prof.; Head*

Ng, M. L., MB BS *HK*, MD *HK*, FRCPsych   Prof.

Other Staff: 4 Asst. Profs./Lectrs.; 8 Hon. Assoc. Profs.; 10 Hon. Asst. Profs.; 3 Hon. Lectrs.

Research: community psychiatry; health psychology; human sexuality: sexual behaviour and attitude in the Chinese; sleep disorders; schizophrenia (cognitive processes and neuroimaging, genetics, neuropsychology)

Radiation Oncology

Tel: 2855 4351 Fax: 2872 6426

Sham, J. S. T., JP, MB MS *HK*, MD *HK*, FRCR   Prof.; Head*

Other Staff: 2 Asst. Profs./Lectrs.; 1 Hon. Reader; 1 Hon. Assoc. Prof.

Research: adoptive immunotherapy and tumour vaccine; colorectal cancers; nasopharyngeal carcinoma; oesophageal carcinoma; stereotactic radiosurgery and radiotherapy

Surgery

Tel: 2855 4589 Fax: 2855 1897

Branicki, Frank J., MB BS Lond., MD Nott.,
FRCS, FRACS Prof.
Cheng, S. W. K., MB BS HK, MS HK,
FRCSEd Assoc. Prof.
Cheung, D. L. C., MB BS Lond., MA Camb.,
MChir Camb., FRCS Assoc. Prof.
Chow, L. W. C., MB BS HK, FRCSGlas Assoc.
Prof.
Fan, S. T., MB BS HK, MS HK, FRCSGlas, FACS,
FRCSEd Prof.
He, G. W., MD Anhui, MMedSc Chinese
Acad.Med.Scis., PhD Monash Prof.
Lo, Chung Mau, MB BS HK, FRCSEd,
FRACS Assoc. Prof.
Luk, J. M. C., BSc HK, MPhil HK, DrMedSc
Karolinska Assoc. Prof.
Nandi, P., MB BS Calc., FRCS, FRCSEd,
FACS Assoc. Prof.
Saing, H., MB BS Rangoon, FRCSEd, FACS Prof.
Tam, Paul K. H., MB BS HK, ChM Liv., MA
Oxf., FRCSEd, FRCSGlas, FRCSI Prof.
Wei, W. I., MB BS HK, MS HK, FRCSEd,
FACS Prof.
Wong, J., BSc(Med) Syd., MB BS Syd., MS HK,
PhD Syd., Hon. MD Syd., FRACS, FRCSEd,
FACS Prof.; Head*
Yuen, P. W., MB BS HK, MS HK, FRCSEd,
FRCSGlas Assoc. Prof.
Other Staff: 6 Asst. Profs./Lectrs.; 40 Hon.
Assoc. Profs.; 3 Hon. Asst. Profs.; 31 Hon.
Lectrs.
Research: cardiothoracic and vascular surgery,
endothelial biology; head and neck oncology
and surgery; liver disease, oncology and
transplantation; oesophageal and
gastroduodenal oncology and surgery;
paediatric surgery, molecular genetics and
development

SPECIAL CENTRES, ETC

Asian Studies, Centre of

Tel: 2859 2465 Fax: 2559 5884

Wong, S. L., BSocSc HK, MPhil Chinese HK,
DPhil Oxf. Dir.*
Other Staff: 1 Hon. Prof.; 1 Hon. Assoc. Prof.;
1 Hon. Asst. Prof.; 4 Hon. Lectrs.
Research: China and Asian countries (changes in
China and effects on Asia); China-ASEAN
project (bridging China and Southeast Asia);
Chinese music (history of new music in
China); Hong Kong studies (history of Hong
Kong stock market); industry-related
telecommunications and information
technology studies

Clinical Biochemistry Unit

Tel: 2855 3202 Fax: 2855 9915

Dickens, P., MB BS Newcastle(UK), FRCPath,
FRCPCan Acting Head*
Research: biochemical epidemiology, particularly
diabetes mellitus; coronary risk factors in
Hong Kong; molecular genetics of
apolipoproteins

Comparative and Public Law, Centre
for

Byrnes, A. C., BA ANU, LLB ANU, LLM Harv.,
LLM Col. Dir.*
Research: equality and the law in Hong Kong;
Hong Kong bill of rights; human rights
protection under basic law and international
human rights law; immigration law and
practice; international law: implications of
the resumption of Chinese sovereignty in
1997

Computer Centre

Tel: 2859 2491 Fax: 2559 7904

Ng Nam, MSc(Eng) HK, MASc Br.Col., PhD
Alta. Dir.*
Ying, W. C., BSc(Eng) HK, LLB Lond., MSc
Lond. Chief Programmer

Other Staff: 1 Systems Analyst; 8 Sr. Computer
Officers; 16 Computer Officers

English Centre

Tel: 2859 2009 Fax: 2547 3409

Lam, Agnes S. L., MA Sing., PhD Pitt. Assoc.
Prof.
Lewkowicz, J. A., BA Reading, MA Lanc., PhD
Lanc. Assoc. Prof.
Nunan, David C., BA NSW, MEd Exe., PhD
Flin. Prof.; Dir.*
Smith, G. P. S., BSc Brist., MPhil PNG
Tech. Assoc. Prof.
Other Staff: 4 Asst. Profs./Lectrs.; 2 Principal
Lang. Instrs.; 7 Sr. Lang. Instrs.; 17 Lang.
Instrs.
Research: computers and language learning and
research; facilitating language learning;
language assessment and programme
evaluation; nature of academic and
professional discourse; self-access learning

Kadoorie Agricultural Research Centre

Tel: 2488 5060 Fax: 2488 5285

Chan, Daniel K. O., JP, MSc HK, PhD
Sheff. Prof.; Dir.*
Other Staff: 1 Hon. Prof.
Research: gene bank for native Chinese chickens;
recycled water-polyculture system fish
hatchery; soy sauce flavour and fermentation
technology; sustainable agriculture and
ecology of eroded lands; vaccines for pigs
and poultry

Laboratory Animal Unit

Tel: 2819 9110 Fax: 2817 9970

Lo, K. S., BSc HK, BVSc Qld. Head*

Language Centre

Tel: 2859 2007 Fax: 2548 0487

Martin, Michael R., AB Prin., MA Harv., PhD
Harv. Acting Dir.*
Other Staff: 2 Sr. Lang. Instrs.; 4 Lang. Instrs.;
1 Hon. Assoc. Prof.

Marine Science, Swire Institute of

Tel: 2809 2551 Fax: 2809 2197

Morton, B. S., JP, BSc Lond., PhD Lond.,
FLS Prof.; Dir.*
Other Staff: 3 Asst. Profs./Lectrs.
Research: ecology of Hong Kong corals; ecology
of Hong Kong's resident dolphins; effects of
trace metal pollution; grazing on rocky
shores; reproductive biology of fishes

Molecular Biology, Institute of

Tel: 2816 8405 Fax: 2817 1006

Chan, Vivian N. Y., MSc Lond., PhD Lond.,
FRCPath Prof.; Dep. Dir.
Other Staff: 1 Principal Investigator; 1
Investigator
Research: aldose reductase in kidney function;
endothelin-1 in vascular diseases; nitric
oxide synthase in vascular diseases; polyol
pathway in diabetic complications;
regulation of aldose reductase gene
expression

Physical Education and Sports Science
Unit

Tel: 2817 9576 Fax: 2818 8042

Lindner, K. J., MEd Toledo(Ohio), PhD
Toledo(Ohio) Assoc. Prof.; Head*
Other Staff: 2 Asst. Profs.; 1 Hon. Assoc. Prof.;
9 Hon. Asst. Profs.
Research: habitual physical activity in children;
health-related fitness in children; sport and
physical activity participation

Postgraduate Medical Education and
Training, School of

Tel: 2819 9212 Fax: 2816 2293

Leong, John C. Y., JP, MB BS HK, FRCSEd,
FRCS, FRACS Prof.; Dir.*
Research: continuing medical education;
internship training in Hong Kong: defining
qualities needed for today's doctors

Professional and Continuing Education,
School of

Tel: 2975 5751 Fax: 2559 7528

Chan, F. T., BSc HK, MBA HK, MPhil
HK Assoc. Prof.
Hui, Sarah S. C., BTech Brad., PhD Brad. Prof.
Ng, W. S., MSc Strath., PhD HK Assoc. Prof.
Peterson, Carole J., BA Chic., JD Harv. Assoc.
Prof.
Wong, O. H. H., MA HK, PhD Camb. Sr.
Lectr.
Young, Enoch C. M., BSc HK, PhD Brist.,
FRAS Prof.; Dir*
Other Staff: 18 Asst. Profs./Lectrs.; 2 Hon.
Profs.; 2 Hon. Assoc. Profs.; 5 Hon. Sr.
Lectrs.; 1 Hon. Asst. Prof.; 15 Hon. Lectrs.
Research: adult and continuing education
(effective media for adult learning,
training); meeting needs in the knowledge
economy; knowledge industry (twenty-first
century, self-funding adult learners);
learning society (human capital formation,
personal development); life long learning
(access, delivery, international collaboration,
quality assurance)

Radioisotope Unit

Tel: 2859 1068 Fax: 2559 5557

Tso Wong, Man-Yin, BSc Chinese HK, MSc
Miami(Fla.), PhD Wis., FRSChem Dir.*
Other Staff: 3 Asst. Profs./Lectrs.
Research: environmental radioactivity (hazards of
indoor radon and mitigation methods,
radiological impact of nuclear power
plants); food irradiation (identification of
irradiated food by TL and OSL); non-
ionising radiation (sources and health
hazard); optically stimulated luminescence
(dating archaeological objects)

Research Studies, School of

Tel: 2559 3306 Fax: 2857 3543

Wu, Felix F., BS Natnl.Taiwan, MS Pitt., PhD
Calif. Prof.; Dir*

Social Sciences Research Centre

Tel: 2859 2412 Fax: 2858 4327

Bacon-Shone, John H., BSc Durh., MSc Lond.,
PhD Birm. Dir.*
Other Staff: 1 Res. Officer
Research: computerised surveys; drug addiction
research; public opinion program; social
sciences data archive; student evaluation

Teachers of English Language Education
Centre

Tel: 2859 2395 Fax: 2517 2100

Tsui, A. B. M., BA HK, MA HK, PhD
Birm. Dir.*
Research: computer networks and teacher
education; design and structure of computer
networks; hypermedia and teacher
knowledge construction; language awareness
and corpus linguistics; socio-psychological
aspects of computer-mediated
communications

University Industrial Centre

Tel: 2859 2352 Fax: 2858 4152

Lee, T. Y., MSc(Eng) HK, PhD Qld. Dir.*
Other Staff: 1 Workshop Engineer
Research: quality management (ISO 9000,
quality awards and QCC, re-engineering,
TQM (total quality management))

University Teaching, Centre for the
Advancement of

Tel: 2859 8953 Fax: 2540 9941

Chan, Rita Y. P., BEd Nott., MA City(UK), PhD
Nott. Assoc. Prof.
Cheng, K. M., JP, BSc HK, MEd HK, PhD
Lond. Prof.; Acting Dir.*
MacKinnon, Marjorie M., BA PEI, BEd New Br.,
MEd McG., PhD McG. Assoc. Prof.
Marsh, J. P., MA C'dia. Assoc. Prof.
Research: appraisal of classroom teaching;
cognitive technology; information

technology in higher education; on-line support for evaluation of teaching; problem-based learning

Urban Planning and Environmental Management, Centre of

Tel: 2859 2720 Fax: 2559 0468

Barron, W. F., BA La Salle(Penn.), MA S.Ill., MEd S.Carolina State, PhD Johns H.   Assoc. Prof.

Chan, R. C. K., BSSc Chinese HK, MSc Lond., DPhil Oxf.   Assoc. Prof.

Chiu, Rebecca L. H., BA NSW, PhD ANU   Assoc. Prof.

Hills, P. R., BA Lond., MA York(Can.), PhD Aston   Prof.; Dir.*

Ng, Mee Kam, BA HK, MSc(Urban Planning) HK, PhD Calif.   Assoc. Prof.

Yeh, Anthony G. O., BA HK, MSc Asian I.T., Bangkok, MRP Syr., PhD Syr.   Prof.

Other Staff: 1 Asst. Prof.

Research: comparative analysis of Asian planning systems; geographical information systems (GIS): methodology and development; housing policy analysis (Hong Kong/China); sustainability studies (Hong Kong/Pearl River Delta region); urban transport/accident analysis)

CONTACT OFFICERS

Academic affairs. Deputy Registrar (Academic): Wai, Henry W. K., MA HK, FCIS

Accommodation. Director of Estates: McGraw, Malcolm, FRICS

Admissions (first degree). Deputy Registrar (Academic): Wai, Henry W. K., MA HK, FCIS

Admissions (higher degree). Deputy Registrar (Academic): Wai, Henry W. K., MA HK, FCIS

Adult/continuing education. Director, School of Professional and Continuing Education: Young, Prof. Enoch C. M., BSc HK, PhD Brist., FRAS

Alumni. Director of External Relations: Chan, Rupert K. Y., BA HK, MBA Chinese HK

Archives. Assistant Registrar: Yue, Dora K. M., BA HK, MA York(UK)

Careers. Director, Careers Education and Placement Centre: Li, Louisa W. T., BSocSc HK

Computing services. Director, Computer Centre: Ng Nam, MSc HK, MASc Br.Col., PhD Alta.

Consultancy services. Acting Deputy Vice-Chancellor: Cheung, Prof. Y. K., OBE, BSc(Eng) S.China Tech., PhD Wales, DSc Wales, DE Adel., FICE, FIEAust, FIStructE

Credit transfer. Deputy Registrar (Academic): Wai, Henry W. K., MA HK, FCIS

Development/fund-raising. Programme Director: Tsui, B. W. S., BA HK, MPhil HK

Distance education. Director, School of Professional and Continuing Education: Young, Prof. Enoch C. M., BSc HK, PhD Brist., FRAS

Equal opportunities. Acting Dean of Student Affairs: Young, Prof. Rosie T. T., CBE, JP, MD HK, Hon. DSc HK, FRCP, FRCPEd, FRCPGlas, FRACP

Estates and buildings/works and services. Director of Estates: McGraw, Malcolm, FRICS

Examinations. Deputy Registrar (Academic): Wai, Henry W. K., MA HK, FCIS

Finance. Director of Finance: Lam, Philip B. L.

General enquiries. Acting Registrar: Cheung, Prof. Y. K., OBE, BSc(Eng) S.China Tech., PhD Wales, DSc Wales, DE Adel., FICE, FIEAust, FIStructE

Health services. Acting Director, University Health Service: Chan, Kitty K. C., MB BS HK, MHP NSW

International office. Deputy Registrar (Academic): Wai, Henry W. K., MA HK, FCIS

Library (chief librarian). Librarian: Kan, Lai-Bing, BSc HK, MA Calif., MLS Calif., PhD HK, Hon. DLitt C.Sturt

Minorities/disadvantaged groups. Acting Dean of Student Affairs: Young, Prof. Rosie T. T., CBE, JP, MD HK, Hon. DSc HK, FRCP, FRCPEd, FRCPGlas, FRACP

Personnel/human resources. Acting Deputy Registrar (Staffing): Koo, Yvonne Y. F., BA HK

Public relations, information and marketing. Director of External Relations: Chan, Rupert K. Y., BA HK, MBA Chinese HK

Publications. Director of External Relations: Chan, Rupert K. Y., BA HK, MBA Chinese HK

Purchasing. Director of Finance: Lam, Philip B. L.

Research. Director, School of Research Studies: Wu, Prof. Felix F., BS Natnl.Taiwan, MS Pitt., PhD Calif.

Safety. Safety Officer: Mabbott, Derek J., BSc Sheff., PhD Sheff.

Scholarships, awards, loans. Deputy Registrar (Research): ......

Schools liaison. Deputy Registrar (Academic): Wai, Henry W. K., MA HK, FCIS

Security. Director of Estates: McGraw, Malcolm, FRICS

Sport and recreation. Director, Centre for Physical Education and Sport: ......

Staff development and training. Acting Deputy Registrar (Staffing): Koo, Yvonne Y. F., BA HK

Student union. President, HKU Students' Union: ......

Student welfare/counselling. Director, Personal Development and Counselling Centre: Wong, Ada M. P., BSc NSW, MSocSc HK

Student welfare/counselling. Acting Dean of Student Affairs: Young, Prof. Rosie T. T., CBE, JP, MD HK, Hon. DSc HK, FRCP, FRCPEd, FRCPGlas, FRACP

Students from other countries. Acting Dean of Student Affairs: Young, Prof. Rosie T. T., CBE, JP, MD HK, Hon. DSc HK, FRCP, FRCPEd, FRCPGlas, FRACP

Students with disabilities. Acting Dean of Student Affairs: Young, Prof. Rosie T. T., CBE, JP, MD HK, Hon. DSc HK, FRCP, FRCPEd, FRCPGlas, FRACP

University press. Publisher: Clarke, Barbara E., BA Lond., MA Essex

Women. Publisher: Clarke, Barbara E., BA Lond., MA Essex

[Information supplied by the institution as at 31 March 1998, and edited by the ACU]

HONG KONG POLYTECHNIC UNIVERSITY

Founded 1994; previously established as Hong Kong Polytechnic 1972

Member of the Association of Commonwealth Universities

Postal Address: Yuk Choi Road, Hung Hom, Kowloon, Hong Kong
Telephone: 2766 5111 **Fax**: 2764 3374 **E-mail**: polyu@polyu.edu.hk **Telex**: 38964 Polyx Hx
WWW: http://www.polyu.edu.hk

CHANCELLOR—The Chief Executive of the Hong Kong Special Administrative Region of the People's Republic of China (*ex officio*)
CHAIRMAN OF COUNCIL—Wu, Sir Gordon Y. S., KCMG, BSE *Prin.*, DBA *Strath.*, DEng *HKPU*, Hon. Dr *Edin.*
DEPUTY CHAIRMAN OF COUNCIL—Fung Yuk-bun, P., BEng *Tor.*, MBA *Tor.*
PRESIDENT*—Poon Chung-kwong, Prof., JP, BSc *HK*, PhD *Lond.*, DSc *Lond.*, FRSChem
TREASURER—Lam Yiu-kin, K., FCIS
VICE-PRESIDENT (INDUSTRIAL DEVELOPMENT AND CORPORATE COMMUNICATION)—Tzang, Alexander H. C., BPharm *Natnl.Def.Med.Coll.*, Taiwan
VICE-PRESIDENT (QUALITY ASSURANCE)—Wong, Prof. Joshua S. L., BSc(Eng) *HK*, PhD *Leeds*, FIEE
VICE-PRESIDENT (RESEARCH AND POSTGRADUATE STUDIES)—Cheng, Prof. Edwin T. C., BSc(Eng) *HK*, MSc *Birm.*, PhD *Camb.*, FIMA
VICE-PRESIDENT (STAFF DEVELOPMENT)—Leung Tin-pui, Prof., JP, BSc(Eng) *HK*, MPhil *HK*, DEng *Tsing Hua*, PhD *City(UK)*, FIEE, FIMechE
ACADEMIC SECRETARY—Tong, Nancy Y. L., BA *Chinese HK*
DIRECTOR OF PERSONNEL—Li, Alan Y. S., MBA *E.Asia*, FCIS
DIRECTOR OF FINANCE—Mong, Chris C., BSc *Chinese HK*, MPhil *HK*
UNIVERSITY LIBRARIAN—Burton, Barry L., BA *Keele*

GENERAL INFORMATION

History. The University, formerly known as Hong Kong Polytechnic (established in 1972), achieved full university status in 1994. It is located in Hung Hom.

Admission to first degree courses (see also Hong Kong Introduction). Applicants holding Hong Kong Advanced Level Examination (HKALE): through Joint University Programmes Admissions System (JUPAS); other applicants: direct to the university. Minimum requirements: grade E or above in either 2 HKALE subjects or 1 HKALE subject and 2 Hong Kong Advanced Supplementary Level Examination (HKASLE) subjects, and grade E or above in HKASLE use of English, and grade E or above in either HKASLE (Chinese language and culture) or HKALE (Chinese literature or Chinese language and literature) or grade D in a language other than English or Chinese in Hong Kong Certificate of Education Examination (HKCEE), and grade E or above in 5 HKCEE subjects. General Certificate of Education (GCE), General Certificate of Secondary Education (GCSE) and International GCSE are considered equivalent to HKALE/HKCEE.

For those applying on the basis of other qualifications: an appropriate diploma from this university or from a technical institute with credit or pass at merit level in at least 3 Level III subjects; or an appropriate Higher Certificate. For applicants with non-Hong Kong qualifications: International Baccalaureate (IB) or equivalent qualifications may be considered. Applicants should normally have good results in appropriate examinations preparing them for university entrance or have completed the first year of a recognised degree programme in their own country.

First Degrees (see also Hong Kong Directory to Subjects of Study) (* = also available with honours; † = honours only). BA*, BEng†, BSc*, BSW†.

Programmes may be taken full-time (3 years or 4 years (including 1 placement year)), or part-time (3–4 years), except for: BA (accountancy), 2 years part-time; BSW, 2 years full-time; BSc (nursing), 2 years part-time or 4 years full-time; BSc (optometry), 4 years full-time.

Higher Degrees (see also Hong Kong Directory to Subjects of Study). MA, MBA, MEd, MEng, MSc, MPhil, PhD, DBA.

Applicants for admission to master's degrees must normally hold a first degree. MPhil: first or second class honours degree or equivalent professional or academic qualifications; PhD: relevant master's degree or relevant first class honours degree or equivalent; DBA: master's degree.

Master's degrees normally last 1 year full-time or up to 6 years part-time. MPhil: 2 years full-time or 3 years part-time; PhD: 3 years full-time or 5 years part-time; MA (Chinese linguistics, design, English language teaching): 2 years part-time; MBA, MSc (information systems): 27 months part-time; MEd (teaching in higher education), MSc (facility management, nursing, project management): 3 years part-time; DBA: normally 3–4 years part-time.

Libraries. About 640,000 volumes; 12,000 serial titles; almost 320,000 audio-visual items including 270,000 single slides. Special collections include: China studies; industrial standards; textiles and design.

Fees (1998–99). Undergraduate (part-time): HK$44,500 (annual), HK$1485 (per credit). Taught master's degrees: HK$44,500 (annual, full-time), HK$1485 (per credit, part-time).

Academic Year (1998–99). Two semesters: 14 September–6 February; 8 February–3 July. Summer term: 5 July–11 September.

Income (1996–97). Total, HK$2,204,000,000.

Statistics. Staff: 3402 (1016 academic, 287 administrative, 2099 executive, technical, clerical and ancillary). Students (1997–98): full-time 11,543 (6095 men, 5448 women); part-time 9644 (5472 men, 4172 women).

FACULTIES/SCHOOLS

Applied Science and Textiles
Tel: 2766 5057 Fax: 2362 2578

Dean: Yeung, Prof. Philip K. W., PhD *Belf.*, FTI
Secretary: Lau, Lydia W. Y., BA *HK*

Business and Information Systems
Tel: 2766 5082 Fax: 2362 5773

Dean: Cheung, Prof. Joseph K. L., BBA *Houston*, MS *Houston*, PhD *Mich.*

Secretary: Lee, Desmond Y. T., BA *Chinese HK*, MA *Chinese HK*

Communication
Tel: 2766 5062 Fax: 2363 8955

Acting Dean: Cheng, Prof. Edwin T. C., BSc(Eng) *HK*, MSc *Birm.*, PhD *Camb.*, FIMA
Secretary: Cheng, Vivian W. W., MEd *Missouri*

Construction and Land Use
Tel: 2766 5038 Fax: 2362 2574

Dean: Anson, Michael, BA *Oxf.*, PhD *Lond.*, FICE
Secretary: Lee, Carmen S., BA *HK*, MLitt *Oxf.*, MA(PSA) *City HK*

Engineering
Tel: 2766 5048 Fax: 2362 4741

Dean: Demokan, Prof. Muhtesem S., BSc *Middle East Tech.*, MSc *Lond.*, PhD *Lond.*, FIEE
Secretary: Wan, Monica B. Y., BA *HK*

Health and Social Studies
Tel: 2766 5077 Fax: 2363 0146

Dean: Woo, Prof. George, MS *Indiana*, PhD *Indiana*, OD *Wat.*
Secretary: Mak, Winnie S. H., BSocSc *HK*

ACADEMIC UNITS

Accountancy
Tel: 2766 7038 Fax: 2330 9845

Cheung, Daniel K. C., BBA *Chinese HK*, MBA *Warw.* Assoc. Prof.
Cheung, Joseph K. L., BBA *Houston*, MS *Houston*, PhD *Mich.* Chair Prof.; Head*
Chow, M. Y., BA *Natnl.Taiwan*, MBA *Chinese HK*, PhD *HKPU* Assoc. Prof.
Firth, Michael A., BS *Metropol.State*, MA *Colorado*, MBS *Colorado*, MSc *Brad.*, MPhil *Warw.*, PhD *Brad.*, FCA Chair Prof.
Kim, J. B., BBA *Seoul*, MBA *Seoul*, PhD *Temple* Assoc. Prof.
Other Staff: 26 Asst. Profs.; 6 Lectrs.; 1 Temp. Lectr.; 1 Temp. Asst. Lectr.
Research: accounting issues in China; financial reporting practices; firm valuation and related accounting issues; management accounting issues; taxes and ethical issues

Applied Biology and Chemical Technology
Tel: 2766 5610 Fax: 2364 9932

Chan, Albert S. C., BA *Internat.Christian(Tokyo)*, MSc *Chic.*, PhD *Chic.* Chair Prof.; Head*

Chau, F. T., BSc Chinese HK, MSc Chinese HK, PhD Br.Col., FRSChem   Prof.

Tang, P. L., BSc HK, PhD HK   Prof.

Tsang, C. W., BSc HK, MSc Tor., PhD Tor., FRSChem   Assoc. Prof.

Wong, K. Y., BSc HK, PhD HK, FRSChem   Prof.

Other Staff: 13 Asst. Profs.; 3 Sr. Lectrs.; 7 Lectrs.; 1 Assoc. Lectr.; 3 Temp. Lectrs.

Research: chemical technology and biotechnology; development of advanced analytical techniques; environmental engineering and biotechnology; molecular biology application and biopharmaceutical production; synthesis and characterisation of new materials and polymers

Bilingual Studies, see Chinese and Bilingual Studies

Biology, see Appl. Biol. and Chem. Technol.

Building and Real Estate

Tel: 2766 5807 Fax: 2764 5131

Davies, Hilary A., BSc Lond., PhD Lond., FRICS   Assoc. Prof.

Drew, D. S., BSc CNAA, PhD Salf., FRICS   Assoc. Prof.

Fan, Linda C. N., BSc CNAA, MSc Brun.   Assoc. Prof.

Li, Heng, BEng Tongji, MEng Tongji, PhD Syd.   Assoc. Prof.

Raftery, John J., BSc CNAA, PhD CNAA, FRICS   Prof.

Scott, David, BSc(Eng) Nott., PhD Nott., FIEAust   Chair Prof.; Head*

Wong, Francis K. W., BSc Brighton, MSc Lond.   Assoc. Prof.

Other Staff: 18 Asst. Profs.; 2 Sr. Lectrs.; 4 Lectrs.; 3 Temp. Lectrs.

Research: construction economics and finance; construction information technology; construction management; property and housing

Business Studies, see also Management

Tel: 2766 7113 Fax: 2765 0611

Davies, Howard A., BA Lanc., MSc Lanc.   Prof.

Lau, P. K., BSSc Chinese HK, MA Calif.State   Assoc. Prof.

Stott, Vanessa, LLB Wales, LLM Lond.   Assoc. Prof.

Walters, Peter G. P., BSc Lond., MBA Liv., PhD Georgia State   Chair Prof.; Head*

Yip, Leslie S. C., BA Leeds, MA Lanc.   Assoc. Prof.

Other Staff: 28 Asst. Profs.; 1 Sr. Lectr.; 1 Lectr.; 2 Temp. Lectrs.

Research: China–Hong Kong business; economic development in China; Hong Kong's commercial and service industries

Chemical Technology, see Appl. Biol. and Chem. Technol.

Chinese and Bilingual Studies

Tel: 2766 7454 Fax: 2334 0185

Cheung, K. H., BA Chinese HK, MA Chinese HK, PhD Lond.   Assoc. Prof.; Head*

Lee, H. M., BA Chinese HK, MA Chinese HK, PhD HK   Assoc. Prof.

Minford, John M., BA Oxf., PhD ANU   Prof.

So, Daniel W. C., BA HK, MA HK, EdD Hawaii   Assoc. Prof.

Other Staff: 15 Asst. Profs.; 1 Sr. Lectr.; 6 Lectrs.; 7 Instrs.; 8 Lang. Instrs.

Research: bilingualism; corpus linguistics, sociolinguistics and language education; cultural and inter-cultural studies; studies in Cantonese and Yue dialects; translation

Clothing, see Textile and Clothing, Inst. of

Computing

Tel: 2766 7295 Fax: 2774 0842

Lee, John W. T., BSc HK, MBA NSW   Assoc. Prof.

Yeung, Daniel S., MA Missouri, MBA Rochester I.T., MSc Rochester I.T., MSc Case W.Reserve, PhD Case W.Reserve   Chair Prof.; Head*

Other Staff: 25 Asst. Profs.; 3 Sr. Lectrs.; 5 Temp. Lectrs.

Research: Chinese computing and software engineering; computer communications and networks; information systems and database management; intelligent computing; multimedia and computer graphics

Design, School of

Tel: 2766 5436 Fax: 2774 5067

Clark, Hazel, PhD CNAA   Assoc. Prof.

Cooke, Sheila E., BA CNAA, MSc Manc.Met.   Assoc. Prof.

Dilnot, Clive S., BA CNAA, MA Leeds   Assoc. Prof.

Frazer, John H., MA Camb.   Chair Prof.; Head*

Fung, Alexander S. Y.   Assoc. Prof.

Lam, Yanta H. T.   Assoc. Prof.

Other Staff: 23 Asst. Profs.; 1 Sr. Lectr.; 9 Lectrs.; 1 Assoc. Lectr.; 1 Instr.; 2 Visiting Fellows

Research: computer-based design technology and systems; design education; design theories and history; urban culture (urban design)

Engineering, Building Services

Tel: 2766 5847 Fax: 2774 6146

Burnett, John, BEng(Tech) Wales, PhD Wales, FIEE   Chair Prof.; Head*

Chan, W. T., BSc(Eng) HK, MPhil HK   Assoc. Prof.

Chow, W. K., MST Portland State, BSc HK, PhD HK   Prof.

Gilleard, John D., BSc Manc., MEng Liv., PhD Salf.   Assoc. Prof.

Yik, Francis W. H., BSc(Eng) HK, MSc HK, PhD Northumbria   Assoc. Prof.

Other Staff: 12 Asst. Profs.; 2 Sr. Lectrs.; 3 Lectrs.; 1 Instr.

Research: building and system energy use; building environmental performance; fire engineering (emphasis on fire safety design); indoor environmental quality (indoor air pollution); safe electricity utilisation in tall buildings

Engineering, Civil and Structural

Tel: 2766 6022 Fax: 2334 6389

Anson, Michael, BA Oxf., PhD Lond., FICE   Chair Prof.

Chan, L. Y., BSc Chinese HK, BSc Lond., MSc Akron, PhD N.Y.State   Assoc. Prof.

Chan, S. L., MSc Wales, PhD Qld.   Prof.

Chau, K. T., MEng Asian I.T., Bangkok, PhD Northwestern   Assoc. Prof.

Ko, J. M., BSc(Eng) HK, PhD HK, FIStructE   Chair Prof.; Head*

Lam, William H. K., BSc Calg., MSc Calg., PhD Newcastle(UK)   Assoc. Prof.

Li, C. W., BSc(Eng) HK, PhD HK   Assoc. Prof.

Li, Y. S., BSc(Eng) HK, PhD HK   Prof.

Poon, C. S., BSc Newcastle(UK), PhD Lond.   Assoc. Prof.

Other Staff: 25 Asst. Profs.; 1 Sr. Lectr.; 2 Lectrs.; 1 Assoc. Lectr.

Research: construction and transportation (construction management); environmental engineering (air, noise, impact assessment); geotechnical (rock and soil mechanics); hydraulics (coastal, environmental and computational hydraulics); structural (dynamics, stability, nonlinear analysis)

Engineering, Electrical

Tel: 2766 6172 Fax: 2330 1544

Chung, T. S., BSc(Eng) HK, MSc Lond., PhD Strath.   Assoc. Prof.

David, Asvini K., BSc(Eng) Ceyl., PhD Lond., FIEE   Prof.; Head*

Demokan, Muhtesem S., BSc Middle East Tech., MSc Lond., PhD Lond., FIEE   Chair Prof.

Ho, S. L., BSc Warw., PhD Warw.   Assoc. Prof.

MacAlpine, John M. K., BA Camb., MA Camb., PhD Lond.   Assoc. Prof.

Oldfield, Keith A.   Principal Lectr.

Soetanto, Darmawan, BEng W.Aust., PhD W.Aust.   Prof.

Other Staff: 15 Asst. Profs.; 3 Lectrs.

Research: control and computing (system identification); fibre-optics and materials (fibre-optic sensors); power systems (power systems economics); utilization (power electronics)

Engineering, Electronic

Tel: 2766 6211 Fax: 2362 8439

Feng, Dagan D., ME Shanghai Jiaotong, MSc Calif., PhD Calif.   Prof.

Kwok, Daniel P. S., BE NSW, MEngSc NSW   Assoc. Prof.

Lee, Y. S., MSc S'ton., PhD HK, FIEE   Prof.

Li, C. K., BSc(Eng) CNAA, MSc Lond., PhD CNAA   Assoc. Prof.

Sheikh, Asrar U. H., BSc W.Pak.Eng., MSc Birm., PhD Birm., FIEE   Prof.

Siu, W. C., MPhil Chinese HK, PhD Lond., FIEE   Chair; Head*

Tam, Peter K. S., BE Newcastle(NSW), ME Newcastle(NSW), PhD Newcastle(NSW)   Assoc. Prof.

Tong, K. Y., BSc(Eng) HK, MSc Chinese HK   Assoc. Prof.

Tse, C. K., BE Melb., PhD Melb.   Assoc. Prof.

Other Staff: 25 Asst. Profs.; 3 Sr. Lectrs.; 4 Lectrs.; 1 Temp. Lectr.

Research: digital signal processing for multimedia applications; power electronics; thin film optoelectronics; wireless information systems

Engineering, Manufacturing

Tel: 2766 6626 Fax: 2362 5267

Frankland, Stephen, MSc Birm.   Assoc. Prof.

Lee, Edmund T. C., MTech Brun., PhD Aston   Assoc. Prof.

Lee, W. B., MTech Brun., PhD HK   Chair Prof.; Head*

Tsang, Albert H. C., BSc(Eng) HK, MSc(Eng) HK, MASc Tor.   Principal Lectr.

Other Staff: 20 Asst. Profs.; 1 Sr. Lectr.; 6 Lectrs.

Research: concurrent engineering and design for manufacture; control, automation and computer integrated manufacturing (CIM); laser technology for manufacturing; manufacturing management and information systems; ultra-precision and non-conventional machining

Engineering, Mechanical

Tel: 2766 6657 Fax: 2365 4703

Fung, K. Y., BS Natnl.Taiwan, PhD Cornell   Prof.

Ho, Y. S., BSc(Eng) HK, MPhil HK, PhD City(UK)   Assoc. Prof.

Leung, C. W., BSc CNAA, MSc Cran.IT, PhD CNAA, FIMarE   Assoc. Prof.

So, Ronald M. C., BSc HK, MEng McG., MA Prin., PhD Prin., DSc HK, FIMechE   Chair Prof.; Head*

Woo, C. H., BSc HK, MSc Calg., PhD Wat.   Prof.

Other Staff: 15 Asst. Profs.; 3 Sr. Lectrs.; 6 Lectrs.; 1 Assoc. Lectr.

Research: dynamics and control; heat transfer and combustion; mechanics and materials; teaching innovation; thermofluid mechanics

Engineering, Rehabilitation, see also Rehabilitation Scis.

Jockey Club Rehabilitation Engineering Centre

Tel: 2766 7683 Fax: 2362 4365

Mak, Arthur F. T., BS Ill., MA Westminster Theol.Sem., MSc Northwestern, PhD Northwestern   Chair Prof.; Head*

Other Staff: 4 Asst. Profs.

Research: clinical electrophysiology; human movement analysis; musculoskeletal biomechanics; prosthetics and orthotics; rehabilitation engineering

English

Tel: 2766 7546 Fax: 2333 6569

Bilbow, Grahame T., BEd Sus., MA Reading, MEd Birm., PhD City HK   Assoc. Prof.

Farmer, Richard J., BA Lond., MA Essex   Principal Lectr.

Hamp-Lyons, Liz, MEd Exe., PhD Edin.   Chair Prof.; Head*

Hood, Susan E., BA Flin., MA Syd.   Principal Lectr.

Littlewood, William T., BA Camb., MA Essex   Assoc. Prof.

Smith, Pamela, MA Edin.   Assoc. Prof.

Spratt, Mary E., BA Birm., MA Lanc.   Principal Lectr.

Warren, Martin J., BA CNAA, MA Birm., PhD Birm.   Principal Lectr.

Other Staff: 23 Asst. Profs.; 2 Sr. Lectrs.; 12 Lectrs.; 48 Lang. Instrs.; 1 Temp. Lectr.

Research: academic writing; language performance assessment and programme evaluation; languages for specific purposes; learner autonomy

Geo-Informatics, see Land Surv. and Geo-Informatics

Health Sciences, see Nursing and Health Scis.

Hotel and Tourism Management

Tel: 2766 6375 Fax: 2362 9362

Hsu, William S. F., BA Brigham Young, MPS Cornell   Principal Lectr.

Pine, Ray. J., BSc CNAA, MPhil CNAA, PhD Brad.   Assoc. Prof.; Acting Head*

Other Staff: 14 Asst. Profs.; 2 Sr. Lectrs.; 12 Lectrs.; 1 Sr. Instr.; 1 Instr.; 3 Temp. Lectrs.; 1 Temp. Asst. Lectr.

Research: education training and employment; executive performance; hospitality/tourism and accounting; strategic service management; tourism management

Jockey Club Rehabilitation Engineering Centre, see Engin., Rehabilitation

Land Surveying and Geo-Informatics

Tel: 2766 5968 Fax: 2330 2994

Chen, Y. Q., PhD New Br., FRICS   Chair Prof.; Head*

Lee, Y. C., BSc S.Fraser, PhD New Br.   Prof.

Other Staff: 9 Asst. Profs.; 4 Lectrs.; 2 Instrs.

Research: cadastre models/systems; engineering surveying (deformation monitoring, hydrographic surveys); geodesy/geodetic surveying (crust movement); geographical information systems (GIS) (data model, virtual reality, uncertainty); photogrammetry and remote sensing (image processing)

Management

Tel: 2766 7370 Fax: 2774 3679

Chan, K. F., BSSc Chinese HK, MBM Adel.   Assoc. Prof.

Cheng, Edwin T. C., BSc HK, BSc Birm., PhD Camb., FIMA   Chair Prof.

Lo, Carlos W. H., BSSc Chinese HK, MPhil Chinese HK, PhD Flin.   Assoc. Prof.

So, Rick K. C., BS Roosevelt, MS Stan., PhD Stan.   Chair Prof.; Head*

Thompson, David J. C., BA Lond., PhD Birm.   Assoc. Prof.

Wan, C. K., PhD N.Y.   Assoc. Prof.

Yuen, Peter P. M., BA N.Y.State, MBA N.Y.State, PhD Birm.   Prof.

Other Staff: 18 Asst. Profs.; 1 Lectr.; 1 Temp. Lectr.

Research: health services management; human resources management/organisational behaviour; operations management/operations research; public sector management; strategic management

Maritime Studies

Tel: 2766 7409 Fax: 2330 2704

Cullinane, Kevin P. B.   Prof.

Ng, C. K., MSc HK   Principal Lectr.; Head*

Other Staff: 5 Asst. Profs.; 1 Sr. Lectr.; 5 Lectrs.; 1 Temp. Lectr.; 2 Temp. Asst. Lectrs.

Research: environmental aspects of port planning; maritime accident analysis and prevention; maritime law; operational aspects of marine simulation; transportation sector financing

Mathematics, Applied

Tel: 2766 6946 Fax: 2362 9045

Hou, S. H., BSEE Mich., MSc Mich., PhD Mich.   Assoc. Prof.; Head*

Other Staff: 17 Asst. Profs.; 4 Sr. Lectrs.; 5 Lectrs.

Research: bootstrap (econometrics); scientific computation (numerical integration, combustion); submanifold geometry of minimal surfaces; survival analysis

Nursing and Health Sciences

Tel: 2766 6405 Fax: 2364 9663

Arthur, David G., BAppSci Lincoln Inst., BEdSt Monash, MEdStud Newcastle(NSW), PhD Newcastle(NSW)   Assoc. Prof.

Boost, Maureen V., MSc Liv.   Principal Lectr.

Martinson, Ida M., BS Minn., MNA Minn., PhD Ill.   Chair Prof.; Head*

Wong, Francis K. Y., BSc St.Olaf, MA Chinese HK, PhD Chinese HK   Assoc. Prof.

Wong, Thomas K. S., BEd S.Aust.C.A.E., MSc Lough., PhD G.Caledonian   Assoc. Prof.

Other Staff: 25 Asst.Profs.; 1 Sr. Lectr.; 13 Lectrs.

Research: children with special needs; chronic disease risk assessment and modulation; nursing care and nursing education improvement; promotion of health molecular epidemiology

Optometry and Radiography

Tel: 2766 6112 Fax: 2764 6051

Edwards, Marion H., MPhil Brad., PhD Brad.   Prof.

Mckay, Janice C., PhD HKPU   Assoc. Prof.

Woo, George, MS Indiana, PhD Indiana, OD Wat.   Chair Prof.; Head*

Other Staff: 18 Asst. Profs.; 1 Lectr.

Research: applications in diagnostic ultrasound; contact lenses; epidemiology of human myopia; human tear physiology/characteristics; physiology of myopia

Physics, Applied

Tel: 2766 5674 Fax: 2333 7629

Chan, Helen L. W., BSc Chinese HK, MPhil Chinese HK, PhD Macq.   Prof.

Chan, P. W., BSc HK, MSc Br.Col., PhD Br.Col.   Prof.

Choy, C. L., BSc HK, PhD Rensselaer   Chair; Head*

Shin, Franklin G., MSc Florida I.T., PhD Texas A.&M.   Prof.

Other Staff: 10 Asst. Profs.; 3 Sr. Lectrs.; 3 Lectrs.

Research: computational physics; ferroelectric materials, polymers and composites; laser materials processing and thin films

Radiography, see Optom. and Radiog.

Real Estate, see Bldg. and Real Estate

Rehabilitation Sciences, see also Engin., Rehabilitation

Tel: 2766 5398 Fax: 2330 8656

Dasari, B. D., MSc S'ton.   Assoc. Prof.

Gardner, Agnes K. K., BSc Wis., MPhil Chinese HK   Assoc. Prof.

Hui-Chan, Christina W. Y., BPhysThy McG., MSc McG., PhD McG.   Chair Prof.; Head*

Webb, Cecilia Y. Y., BA Open(UK), MPhil Chinese HK, PhD Lond.   Assoc. Prof.

Other Staff: 33 Asst. Profs.; 1 Lectr.; 1 Temp. Asst. Prof.

Research: biomechanics and orthopaedics; ergonomics and work rehabilitation; exercise science and sports physiotherapy;

neurosciences and neuro-rehabilitation; rehabilitation technology

Social Studies, Applied

Tel: 2766 5773 Fax: 2773 6558

Lee, Carrie H. Y., BSocSc HK, MSW Mich.   Principal Lectr.

Lee, M. K., BSocSc HK, MPhil ChineseHK, MPhil Col.   Prof.

Li Chui, Dorothea L. S., BA HK, MSW Mich.   Principal Lectr.

Lui, P. K., BA HK, MSc Lond.   Principal Lectr.

Mak, Diana P. S., BA HK, MA(Ed) Chinese HK, MSocSc Wales, MSW Mich.   Head*

Yuen, Angelina W. K., BSocSc HK, MSW Tor., MEd Manc., PhD HK   Assoc. Prof.

Other Staff: 25 Asst. Profs.; 7 Sr. Lectrs.; 13 Lectrs.; 1 Visiting Fellow; 9 Temp. Instrs.

Research: critical social theory and social work; politics and political development; social issues and social work practices; social service administration and evaluation; social work education

Textile and Clothing, Institute of

Tel: 2766 6499 Fax: 2773 1432

Chong, Patrick T. F., MSc Brad., PhD Rensselaer   Assoc. Prof.; Head*

Liew, K. L., MDes RCA   Principal Lectr.

Tao, X. M., PhD NSW, BEng, FTI   Assoc. Prof.

Taylor, Gail, BA Leeds, FTI   Assoc. Prof.

Wong, Alan K. S., MSc(Eng) HK   Principal Lectr.

Yeung, Philip K. W., PhD Belf., FTI   Chair Prof.

Other Staff: 29 Asst. Profs.; 9 Sr. Lectrs.; 19 Lectrs.; 5 Assoc. Lectrs.; 1 Asst. Lectr.; 4 Instrs.

Research: design (historic costume, computer-aided design); fabric objective measurement (optimal processing parameters); marketing and management (quick response); textile and colour chemistry (dyeing behaviour); textiles and clothing technology (rotor spinning)

Tourism Management, see Hotel and Tourism Management

SPECIAL CENTRES, ETC

Business Technology Centre

Tel: 2766 6985 Fax: 2765 6323

Wong, Sidney S. Y., BSSc Chinese HK, MSSc Chinese HK   Co-ordinator*

China Business Centre

Tel: 2766 7769 Fax: 2765 6323

Chan, Thomas M. H., BSocSc HK, MPhil Chinese HK, PhD Flin.   Head*

Industrial Centre

Tel: 2766 7579 Fax: 2334 4634

Wong, Chris H. C., MSc(Eng) HK, FIEE   Dir.*

Professional and Business English, Centre for

Tel: 2766 5584 Fax: 2362 8954

Johns, Bruce R., BA Exe., PhD Exe.   Head*

Other Staff: 1 Sr. Lectr.; 1 Lectr.; 4 Lang. Instrs.; 4 Instrs.

Professional and Continuing Education, Centre for

Tel: 2766 5388 Fax: 2363 0540

Tam, Anthony C. W., BSc Alta., MBA Alta., PhD Bath   Dir.*

CONTACT OFFICERS

Academic affairs. Academic Secretary: Tong, Nancy Y. L., BA Chinese HK

Accommodation. Assistant Director of Personnel: Ng, David P. Y., BSc HK, MA City HK

Admissions (first degree). Senior Assistant Academic Secretary: Chan, Ada W. C., MA *Lanc.*

Admissions (higher degree). Head, Research and Postgraduate Studies Office: Ho, Aster C. S., BSc *HK*

Adult/continuing education. Director, Centre for Professional and Continuing Education: Tam, Anthony C. W., BSc(Pharm) *Alta.*, MBA *Alta.*, PhD *Bath*

Alumni. Communications and Public Affairs Officer: Sit, Cora L. K., BA *City Poly.HK*

Archives. Assistant Director of Personnel: Hung, Dorothy S. C., BSSc *Chinese HK*, MSocSc *HK*

Careers. Acting Assistant Director of Student Affairs (counselling services): Fung, Dorinda M. C., BSocSc *HK*, MSc *Lond.*

Computing services. Acting Chief Computing Officer, Office of Information Technology Services: Tang, Michael M. K., BSc(Eng) *HK*, MSc(Eng) *HK*, MBA *Chinese HK*

Conferences/corporate hospitality. Administrative Officer, Office of Academic and Professional Collaboration: Lam, Annie S. Y., BA *HK*

Consultancy services. Head, Office of Industrial Development (Technology Resources): Wong, Alwin L., BSc *Qu.*, MSc *Qu.*, MBA *Strath.*

Credit transfer. Senior Assistant Academic Secretary: Chan, Ada W. C., MA *Lanc.*

Development/fund-raising. Vice-President (Industrial Development and Corporate Communication): Tzang, Alexander H. C., BPharm *Natnl.Def.Med.Coll.*, *Taiwan*

Development/fund-raising. Executive Manager, Resources Development Office: Li, Irene H. L., BBA

Distance education. Director, Centre for Professional and Continuing Education: Tam, Anthony C. W., BSc(Pharm) *Alta.*, MBA *Alta.*, PhD *Bath*

Estates and buildings/works and services. Director of Estates: Chiu, Ernest T. C., BSc *Wis.*, MEng *McM.*

Examinations. Senior Assistant Academic Secretary: Chan, Ada W. C., MA *Lanc.*

Finance. Director of Finance: Mong, Chris C., BSc *Chinese HK*, MPhil *HK*

General enquiries. Academic Secretary: Tong, Nancy Y. L., BA *Chinese HK*

Health services. Head, University Health Services: Ho, Steven Y. K., BSc *W.Aust.*, MB BS *W.Aust.*, FRACGP

Industrial liaison. Head, Office of Industrial Development (Technology Resources): Wong, Alwin L., BSc *Qu.*, MSc *Qu.*, MBA *Strath.*

Industrial liaison. Head, Office of Industrial Development (Human Resources): Wong, Sidney S. Y., BSSc *Chinese HK*, MSSc *Chinese HK*

Library (chief librarian). University Librarian: Burton, Barry L., BA *Keele*

Library (enquiries). Senior Assistant Librarian (Information): Chim, Winnie Y. M., BSc *Br.Col.*, MLS *W.Ont.*

Personnel/human resources. Director of Personnel: Li, Alan Y. S., MBA *E.Asia*, FCIS

Public relations, information and marketing. Head, Office of Communication and Public Affairs: Poon, David J. T., BSSc *Chinese HK.*, MJ *Calif.*

Publications. Head, Office of Communication and Public Affairs: Poon, David J. T., BSSc *Chinese HK.*, MJ *Calif.*

Purchasing. Assistant Director of Finance: Tau, H. L., BChemEng *Minn.*, MSc *Clarkson*

Quality assurance and accreditation. Vice-President (Quality Assurance): Wong, Prof. Joshua S. L., BSc(Eng) *HK*, PhD *Leeds*, FIEE

Research. Vice-President (Research and Postgraduate Studies): Cheng, Prof. Edwin T. C., BSc(Eng) *HK*, MSc *Birm.*, PhD *Camb.*, FIMA

Safety. Head, Health and Safety Office: Kam, Y. K., BPharm *China Med.Coll.*, MPhil *Chinese HK*

Scholarships, awards, loans. Assistant Director of Student Affairs: Wong, Christine K. M., BSSc *Chinese HK*

Security. Senior Estates Officer (Security and Fire Protection): Cheung, W. M., BEng *C.Lancs/City HK*

Sport and recreation. Assistant Director of Student Affairs (Physical Education): Chan, Patrick P. C., MEd *Springfield*

Staff development and training. Assistant Director of Personnel: Hung, Dorothy S. C., BSSc *Chinese HK*, MSocSc *HK*

Student Union. Assistant Director of Student Affairs (Administration): Tang, Rita P. C., BA *HK*

Student welfare/counselling. Acting Assistant Director of Student Affairs: Fung, Dorinda M. C., BSocSc *HK*, MSc *Lond.*

Students with disabilities. Acting Assistant Director of Student Affairs: Fung, Dorinda M. C., BSocSc *HK*, MSc *Lond.*

[Information supplied by the institution as at 11 March 1998, and edited by the ACU]

OPEN UNIVERSITY OF HONG KONG

Founded 1989 as Open Learning Institute of Hong Kong; renamed 1997

Member of the Association of Commonwealth Universities

Postal Address: 30 Good Shepherd Street, Ho Man Tin, Kowloon, Hong Kong
Telephone: 2768 6000 **Fax**: 2789 2725 **E-mail**: dwong@ouhk.edu.hk **WWW**: http://www.ouhk.edu.hk
E-mail formula: name@ouhk.edu.hk

CHANCELLOR—The Chief Executive of the Hong Kong Special Administrative Region (*ex officio*)
CHAIRMAN OF COUNCIL—Wong, The Hon. Peter H. Y., JP
DEPUTY CHAIRMAN OF COUNCIL—Wu, Philip P. H., JP, MBA *Calif.*, PhD *Oklahoma*
TREASURER—Sun, David T. K., BSc *Kansas State*, MAccounting *Ill.*
PRESIDENT*—Tam, Prof. Sheung-wai, JP, BSc *HK*, MSc *HK*, PhD *Nott.*, FRSChem
VICE PRESIDENT (ACADEMIC)—Wong, Prof. Danny S. N., BSc *Calif.State*, MSc *Penn.*, PhD *Penn.*
VICE PRESIDENT (ADMINISTRATION)—......
REGISTRAR—Armour, Richard, MA *Glas.*, MSc *Open(UK)*
LIBRARIAN—Mok, W. M., BSc *Chinese HK*

GENERAL INFORMATION

History. The university, formerly the Open Learning Institute of Hong Kong, was established in June 1989. It was officially retitled the Open University of Hong Kong in May 1997.

Admission to first degree courses (see also Hong Kong Introduction). There are normally no academic requirements. Applicants should be 17 years or above.

First Degrees (see also Hong Kong Directory to Subjects of Study). BA, BBA, BEd, BGS (general studies), BNursing, BSc, BSocSc.

Higher Degrees (see also Hong Kong Directory to Subjects of Study). MBA, MEd, MPhil.

Applicants for admission to master's degrees must normally hold an appropriate first degree.

Language of Instruction. English. Chinese is used for some courses in Chinese

humanities, language and translation, and education.

Libraries. 43,000 volumes; 2200 periodicals subscribed to; electronic library (collection equivalent to nearly 300,000 volumes).

Fees (as at October 1998, per course). Undergraduate: HK$4675–20,600 (arts); HK$4675–10,870 (business, education); HK$5150–30,640 (science). Postgraduate: HK$13,250–26,500 (MBA); HK$21,500 (MEd).

Academic Awards (1997–98). 62 awards ranging in value from HK$2000 to $34,000.

Academic Year. Two semesters: April–September; October–March.

Income (1997–98). Total, HK$391,000,000.

Statistics. Staff: 400 (88 academic, 104 administrative, 208 general support). Students: 22,904 (11,654 men, 11,250 women).

FACULTIES/SCHOOLS

Arts and Social Sciences, School of

Tel: 2768 5717 Fax: 2391 3184

Dean: Ip, Prof. P. K., BA *Chinese HK*, MPhil *Chinese HK*, PhD *W.Ont.*
Secretary: Mak, Daise W. Y.

Business and Administration, School of

Tel: 2768 6931 Fax: 2391 9095

Acting Dean: Ip, Y. K., BSc *N.Y.State*, MBA *Indiana*, PhD *S.Carolina*
Secretary: Au, Estella Y. L.

Education, School of

Tel: 2768 5807 Fax: 2395 4235

Dean: Carr, Prof. R., MA *Glas.*, MEd *Glas.*, PhD *Glas.*
Secretary: Wong, Anissa F. S.

Science and Technology, School of

Tel: 2768 6823 Fax: 2789 1170

Dean: Wong, Prof. T. M., BSc *Otago*, PhD *Otago*
Secretary: Wong, Winnie M. C.

ACADEMIC UNITS

Arranged by Schools

Arts and Social Sciences

Tel: 2768 5717 Fax: 2391 3184

Cheuk, W. H., BSc *Texas A.& M.*, MSc *Texas A.& I.*, PhD *Georgia*   Assoc. Prof.
Crewe, W. J., BA *Camb.*, MA *Reading*, MSc *Edin.*   Assoc. Prof.
Lo, W. C., MA *Georgia*, PhD *Georgia*   Assoc. Prof.
So, W. C., BA *HK*, MPhil *HK*, PhD *ANU*   Assoc. Prof.
Yeung, C. K., BA *Chinese HK*, MPhil *Chinese HK*, PhD *ANU*   Assoc. Prof.
Other Staff: 7 Asst. Profs.; 5 Lectrs.
Research: Chinese families; Nanjing collaboration government

Business and Administration

Tel: 2768 6931 Fax: 2391 9095

Chen, Theodore T. Y., BCom *McG.*, MBA *Br.Col.*   Assoc. Prof.
Chui, Alice P. L., BA *Liv.*, MA *Manc.*, PhD *Manc.*   Assoc. Prof.
Chung, S. L., BSc *HK*, MS *Ill.*, PhD *Ill.*   Assoc. Prof.
Hole, T., BSc *Wales*, LLB *Dal.*, MBA *Dal.*   Assoc. Prof.
Lee, V. S. K., BSc *Indiana(Penn.)*, MSc *Indiana(Penn.)*, MBA *Strath.*   Assoc. Prof.

Other Staff: 14 Asst. Profs.; 7 Lectrs.; 2 Lectrs.†
Research: business information systems; corporatisation; language awareness and performance

Education

Fung, Yvonne S. Y. H., BSc *HK*, MEd *HK*   Assoc. Prof.
Tang, T. K. W., BSc *Lond.*, MEd *HK*   Assoc. Prof.
Other Staff: 5 Asst. Profs.; 1 Lectr.
Research: adult learning and distance education

Science and Technology

Tel: 2768 6823 Fax: 2789 1170

Diu, C. K., BSc *N.Y.State*, MSc *N.Y.State*, PhD *N.Y.State*   Assoc. Prof.
Ho, K. C., BSc *Chinese HK*, MSc *Salf.*, PhD *HK*   Assoc. Prof.
Mirza, J. S., BSc *Panjab*, MSc *Panjab*, MSc *Salf.*, PhD *Salf.*   Assoc. Prof.
Robertshaw, M., BSc *Manc.*, PhD *Manc.*   Assoc. Prof.
Swearse, B., BAppSc *La Trobe*   Assoc. Prof.
Other Staff: 12 Asst. Profs.; 3 Lectrs.; 2 Lectrs.†
Research: nursing; use of World Wide Web in teaching; water pollution

SPECIAL CENTRES, ETC

Continuing and Community Education, Centre for

Tel: 2768 5910 Fax: 2381 8456

Butcher, R. E., BSc *Lond.*, PhD *E.Anglia*   Sr. Academic Manager
Ha, Susan L. Y. Y., BEd *La Trobe*   Project Manager
Lui, Y. H., BBA *Chinese HK*, MA *Lanc.*, PhD *Lanc.*   Dir.*
Other Staff: 1 Asst. Prof.; 8 Lectrs.
Research: banking

Distance and Adult Learning, Centre for

Tel: 2768 6702 Fax: 2715 9042

Jegede, Prof. O. J., BSc(Ed) *A.Bello*, MEd *A.Bello*, PhD *Wales*   Dir.*
Other Staff: 2 Res. Fellows; 1 Res. Co-ordinator

Information Technology Unit

Tel: 2768 6522 Fax: 2396 5009

Wong, C. Y., BE *C.C.N.Y.*, MSc *Syr.*   Computer Centre Manager
Wong, E. K. K., BSc *Chinese HK*   Head*

CONTACT OFFICERS

Academic affairs. Vice President (Academic): Wong, Prof. Danny S. N., BSc *Calif.State*, MSc *Penn.*, PhD *Penn.*
Accommodation. Senior Estates Officer: Lam, Cybill M. L. Y.

Admissions (first degree). Senior Assistant Registrar: Watt, Wendy Y. H., BA *HK*, MA *City(HK)*
Adult/continuing education. Director, Centre for Continuing and Community Education: Lui, Y. H., BBA *Chinese HK*, MA *Lanc.*, PhD *Lanc.*
Archives. Senior Assistant Librarian: Wong, M. T., BA *Oregon*, MBus *RMIT*
Computing services. Head, Information Technology: Wong, E. K. K., BSc *Chinese HK*
Consultancy services. Senior Executive Officer: Tsui, Gwenny M. K., BA *Chinese HK*, MBA *City(HK)*
Credit Transfer. Senior Assistant Registrar: Watt, Wendy Y. H., BA *HK*, MA *City(HK)*
Development/fund-raising. Senior Development Officer: Lip, Belinda L. K., BSocSc *HK*
Estates and buildings/works and services. Senior Estates Officer: Lam, Cybill M. L. Y.
Examinations. Deputy Registrar: Hui, Syliva W. L., BSocSc *HK*
Finance. Head (Finance): Sun, Christopher K. C.
General enquiries. Vice President (Administration): ......
Library (chief librarian). Librarian: Mok, W. M., BSc *Chinese HK*
Library (enquiries). Senior Assistant Librarian: Wong, M. T., BA *Oregon*, MBus *RMIT*
Personnel/human resources. Head (Human Resources): Fan, Jack, BA *HK*
Public relations, information and marketing. Head (Public Affairs): Wong, Alex J. W., BA *ChineseHK*
Publications. Publishing Manager: Chow, Linda K. B. I., BSc *NSW*
Purchasing. Deputy Head (Finance): Tsui, Stephen H. M., BSSc
Quality assurance and accreditation. Vice President (Academic): Wong, Danny S. N., BSc *Calif. State*, MSc *Penn.*, PhD *Penn.*
Research. Director, Research Centre: Jegede, Prof. O. J., BSc(Ed) *A.Bello*, MEd *A.Bello*, PhD *Wales*
Scholarships, awards, loans. Senior Assistant Registrar: Watt, Wendy Y. H., BA *HK*, MA *City(HK)*
Staff development and training. Senior Executive Officer: Shek, Vincent K. C., BA *HK*
Student welfare/counselling. Senior Assistant Registrar: Watt, Wendy Y. H., BA *HK*, MA *City(HK)*
Students' union. Senior Assistant Registrar: Watt, Wendy Y. H., BA *HK*, MA *City(HK)*
Students with disabilities. Senior Assistant Registrar: Watt, Wendy Y. H., BA *HK*, MA *City(HK)*
University press. Publishing Manager: Chow, Linda K. B. I., BSc *NSW*

[Information supplied by the institution as at 11 March 1998, and edited by the ACU]

HONG KONG : DIRECTORY TO SUBJECTS OF STUDY

The table below shows which of the institutions indicated provide facilities for study and/or research in the subjects named. The table covers *broad subject areas* only: ie the individual subjects of specialisation in certain professional fields such as education, law, medicine or veterinary science, are not included. In the case of related subject areas which have been grouped together (eg Botany/Plant Science), it should be borne in mind that one or more of the subjects may be offered by the institution concerned.

For further information about the individual subjects taught at each institution, please refer to the *Index to Department Names* at the end of the Yearbook, but for full details about subjects/courses offered by the universities in this directory each institution's own official publications must be consulted. U = may be studied for first degree course; M = may be studied for master's degree course; D = research facilities to doctoral level; X = all three levels (UMD). **Note**— The table only includes information provided by institutions currently in membership of the Association of Commonwealth Universities, submitted for this edition of the Yearbook.

	Chinese U. of Hong Kong	Hong Kong	Hong Kong Polytechnic U.	Open U. of Hong Kong
Accountancy/Accounting	X	X	X	U
Anthropology	X			
Architecture	X	X		
Behavioural Sciences		X		
Biochemistry	X	X	D	
Biology	X	X	D	
Botany/Plant Science		X		
Building/Construction		X	X	
Business/Commerce	X	X	X	M
Chemistry	X	X	UD	
Chinese	X	X	D	
Computer Science	U	X	X	U
Dentistry		X		
Design		X	X	
Economics	X	X	D	U
Education	X	X	UM	M
Engineering		X		
Chemical			D	
Civil		X	X	
Computer	X	X	D	U
Electrical/Electronic	X	X	X	U
Manufacturing/Materials	U	X	X	U
Mechanical	X	X	X	
English	X	X	UD	
Environmental Science/Studies	X	X	D	U
Finance/Banking	X	X	UD	U
Fine Art	X	X		
French		X		
Geography	X	X		
Geology/Earth Sciences		X	D	
German		X		

	Chinese U. of Hong Kong	Hong Kong	Hong Kong Polytechnic U.	Open U. of Hong Kong
Health Sciences/Studies	U	X	X	
History	X	X		
Hospitality/Leisure/Tourism			X	
Information Science/Systems/Technology	X	X	X	U
International Studies	MD			U
Japanese	U	X		
Journalism/Communication	X			
Law/Legal Studies		X		
Linguistics/Translation	X	X	X	U
Management	X	X	X	M
Marketing	X	X	X	U
Mathematics	X	X	D	U
Medicine/Surgery	X	X		
Music	X	X		
Nursing	X	X	X	U
Optometry			UD	
Pharmacy	X			
Philosophy	X	X	D	
Physical Education/Sports Science	UM	X		
Physics	X	X	D	
Politics/Political Science	X	X	D	
Psychology	X	X	D	
Public Administration	X	X	X	
Religion/Theology	X			
Social Work/Studies	X	X	X	
Sociology	X	X	D	
Statistics	X	X	D	
Surveying		X	X	
Teacher Training	U	X		
Textiles/Fibre Science/Technology			D	
Zoology		X		

APPENDIX 2

INTER-UNIVERSITY BODIES

This section is divided into two parts. The first describes, for each of the Commonwealth countries that has one, the vice-chancellors' committee or corresponding body. The regional body for East Africa, and five provincial or inter-provincial bodies in Canada are included here. The second section describes certain international inter-university organisations whose constituents may include Commonwealth universities.

Commonwealth

Australia Australian Vice-Chancellors' Committee (Council of Australian University Presidents) (p. 1852)

Bangladesh Association of Universities of Bangladesh (p. 1852)

Canada Association of Universities and Colleges of Canada (p. 1853)

Association of Atlantic Universities (p. 1853)

Conference of Rectors and Principals of Quebec Universities (p. 1854)

Council of Nova Scotia University Presidents (p. 1854)

Council of Ontario Universities (p. 1854)

Council of Western Canadian University Presidents (p. 1855)

East Africa Inter-University Council for East Africa (p. 1855)

Ghana Committee of Vice-Chancellors and Principals (Ghana) (p. 1855)

India Association of Indian Universities (p. 1856)

New Zealand New Zealand Vice-Chancellors' Committee (p. 1856)

Nigeria Committee of Vice-Chancellors of Nigerian Federal Universities (p. 1857)

Pakistan Vice-Chancellors' Committee of Pakistan (p. 1857)

South Africa South African Universities' Vice-Chancellors' Association (p. 1858)

Sri Lanka Committee of Vice-Chancellors and Directors (Sri Lanka) (p. 1858)

United Kingdom Committee of Vice-Chancellors and Principals of the Universities of the United Kingdom (p. 1859)

Part-Commonwealth

Agence Universitaire de la Francophonie (p. 1859)

Asian Association of Agricultural Colleges and Universities (p. 1860)

Association of African Universities (p. 1860)

Association of American Universities (p. 1860)

Association of Caribbean Tertiary Institutions (p. 1860)

Association of Caribbean Universities and Research Institutes (p. 1861)

Association of Eastern and Southern African Universities (p. 1861)

Association of European Universities (p. 1861)

Association of South-East Asian Institutions of Higher Learning (p. 1862)

Association of Universities of Asia and the Pacific (p. 1862)

Community of Mediterranean Universities (p. 1862)

Inter-American Organization for Higher Education (p. 1863)

International Association of Universities (p. 1863)

International Federation of Catholic Universities (p. 1863)

Union of Latin American Universities (p. 1864)

AUSTRALIA

Australian Vice-Chancellors' Committee (Council of Australian University Presidents)

GPO Box 1142, Canberra, ACT, Australia 2601
(Australian Universities Centre, 1 Geils Court, Deakin, Canberra, ACT, Australia 2600)

Telephone: (06) 285 8200 **Fax**: (06) 285 8211 **E-mail**: enquiries@avcc.edu.au **Cables**: Vicom Canberra
WWW: http://www.avcc.edu.au **E-mail formula**: firstname.surname@avcc.edu.au

President—Niland, Prof. John R., AO, BCom *NSW*, MCom *NSW*, PhD Ill., FASSA, Vice-Chancellor and President, University of New South Wales.
Vice-President—Chubb, Prof. Ian W., MSc *Oxf.*, DPhil *Oxf.*, Vice-Chancellor, Flinders University of South Australia
Executive Director*—Hamilton, Stuart A., AO, BA *Tas.*, BEc *ANU*
Deputy Executive Director—Mullarvey, T. John

Mission
The aims of the Committee are (a) to assist vice-chancellors in the performance of their university responsibilities; (b) to provide a forum within which to discuss higher education issues, including teaching and learning, scholarship, research and research training; (c) to develop policy positions and guidelines on various higher education matters; (d) to promote the needs, interests and purposes of Australian universities and their communities to government, industry and other groups; (e) to encourage international co-operation; (f) to act as a source of information on Australian universities; and (g) to administer programmes and services for Australian universities.

Membership
The vice-chancellors of 37 Australian universities are members of the AVCC.

[Information supplied by the institution as at 28 October 1998, and edited by the ACU]

BANGLADESH

Association of Universities of Bangladesh

House No 6/A, Road No 9, Dhanmondi R/A, Dhaka 1207, Bangladesh

Telephone: (02) 325233, 861666 **Fax**: (02) 863046, 865583 **E-mail**: vc-cu@spnetctg.com, vc-cu@global.net

Chairman—Mannan, Prof. Abdul, MCom *Dhaka*, MBA *Hawaii*, Vice-Chancellor, University of Chittagong
Secretary*—Saifuddin, Prof. Sheikh Muhammad, MA *Dhaka*

Mission
The aims of the Association are to foster and promote the cause of higher education in Bangladesh, and to this end the Association performs such things as are deemed fit to promote the interests and well-being of the universities of the country.

Membership
The AUB is composed of the following universities: University of Dhaka; University of Rajshahi; Bangladesh Agricultural University; Bangladesh University of Engineering and Technology; University of Chittagong; Jahangirnagar University; the Islamic University of Bangladesh; Shahjalal University of Science and Technology; Khulna University; National University; and Bangladesh Open University.

Membership of the Association is at present limited to the universities above. A university is admitted to membership by a resolution adopted by the Association.

Each university is represented by its vice-chancellor and two other persons (usually deans of faculties and senior professors), each to be nominated by the academic council of the university for a period of two years. The terms of the representatives expire with the calendar year.

[Information supplied by the institution as at 12 November 1998, and edited by the ACU]

CANADA

Association of Universities and Colleges of Canada

350 Albert Street, Suite 600, Ottawa, Ontario, Canada K1R 1B1

Telephone: (613) 563 1236 **Fax**: (613) 563 9745 **WWW**: http://www.aucc.ca
E-mail formula: initialoffirstnamelastname@aucc.ca (initial and last name: total of 8 characters)

Chair—Davenport, Paul, BA *Stan.*, MA *Tor.*, PhD *Tor.*, President and Vice-Chancellor, University of Western Ontario
President*—Giroux, Robert J. Y., OC, BCom *Ott.*, MSc *Ott.*

Mission

The Association represents Canadian universities, at home and abroad. Its mandate is to foster and promote the interests of higher education. AUCC believes strong universities are vital to Canada's prosperity and well-being: they function as major forces for renewal and innovation in society, by developing and transferring new knowledge through research, teaching and other scholarly activities, as well as through community leadership and international co-operation.

Membership

Membership of the Association is made up of universities from every province. Members are represented within the membership and on the Association's governing bodies by their presidents. There are three categories of membership: institutional, associate and regional/provincial. Institutions qualify for membership in the Association by meeting standards as outlined in the by-laws of the Association, accepting inspection by a visiting committee, and obtaining support of the board of directors and of the majority of delegates to the Association's annual meeting. Several national organisations representing major academic or administrative divisions or interests within Canadian universities hold associate membership in AUCC. The Association of Atlantic Universities, the Conference of Rectors and Principals of Quebec Universities, the Council of Ontario Universities and the Council of Western Canadian University Presidents are provincial/regional members of the Association. The federal research granting councils and a small number of other national agencies whose objectives are in keeping with those of the Association are honorary associates.

[Information supplied by the institution as at October 1998, and edited by the ACU]

Association of Atlantic Universities

Suite 403, 5657 Spring Garden Road, Halifax, Nova Scotia, Canada B3J 3R4

Telephone: (902) 425 4230 **Fax**: (902) 425 4233 **E-mail**: ammack@hfx.andara.com
WWW: http://www.dal.ca/aau/

Chair—(1998-2000) Robichaud, Jean-Bernard, BA *Sacred Heart*(N.B.), MA *Montr.*, PhD *Chic.*, President, Université de Moncton
Executive Director*—MacKinnon, Anne Marie, BSA *St FX*

Mission

Established in 1964, the Association is a voluntary association of the universities and colleges in the Atlantic region and in the West Indies, which offer a programme leading to a degree or have degree-granting status. It provides a forum where university executive heads reflect, consult and collaborate on all aspects of the whole university; define common objectives and positions; develop strategies to promote, collectively and co-operatively, the highest ideals of post-secondary education; and exercise leadership to promote the objectives of the collective.

Membership

The following 17 Atlantic universities and colleges, plus the University of the West Indies, are currently members of the Association: Acadia University, Atlantic School of Theology, University College of Cape Breton, Dalhousie University, Memorial University of Newfoundland, Mount Allison University, Mount Saint Vincent University, Nova Scotia Agricultural College, Nova Scotia College of Art and Design, Saint Mary's University, St Francis Xavier University, St Thomas University, Université de Moncton, Université Sainte-Anne, University of King's College, University of New Brunswick, and University of Prince Edward Island. Each institution is represented by its executive head.

[Information supplied by the institution as at 5 November 1998, and edited by the ACU]

Conference of Rectors and Principals of Quebec Universities

CP 952, Place du Parc, Montréal, Québec, Canada H2W 2N1
(300 rue Léo Pariseau, Suite 1200, Montréal, Québec, Canada)

Telephone: (514) 288 8524 **Fax**: (514) 288 0554 **E-mail**: jacques.bordeleau@crepuq.qc.ca
WWW: http://www.crepuq.qc.ca

President—Shapiro, Bernard J., BA McG., MAT Harv., EdD Harv., Hon. LLD McG., Hon. LLD Tor., Hon. LLD Ott.,
Principal and Vice-Chancellor, McGill University
Director-General*—Bordeleau, Jacques, MScAdm Laval

Mission

The Conference's main objective is to provide a forum where university administrators can reflect, consult and collaborate on all aspects of university life, define common objectives and positions and develop strategies to preserve university autonomy and academic freedom and to enhance performance and quality. To support this effort, the CREPUQ staff carries out research and administers services for the benefit of its members.

Membership

All of Quebec's universities.

[Information supplied by the institution as at 3 November 1998, and edited by the ACU]

Council of Nova Scotia University Presidents

Suite 403, 5657 Spring Garden Road, Halifax, Nova Scotia, Canada B3J 3R4

Telephone: (902) 425 4230 **Fax**: (902) 425 4233

Chair*—d'Entremont, Harley, BA St Mary's(Can.), MPA Dal.,
PhD W.Ont.

Mission

The objectives of the Council are: to work for the improvement of higher education in Nova Scotia; to exercise leadership in matters concerning post-secondary education; to promote co-operation and inter-university planning among those institutions listed in the membership; to be the channel of collective communication between the universities and the government, as well as between the universities and the Nova Scotia Council on Higher Education and other bodies or individuals. The Council will make or recommend appointments to national, regional and provincial bodies as required.

Membership

The presidents of the 11 degree-granting institutions in Nova Scotia: Acadia University, Atlantic School of Theology, University College of Cape Breton, Dalhousie University, University of King's College, Mount Saint Vincent University, Nova Scotia Agricultural College, Nova Scotia College of Art and Design, Université Sainte-Anne, St Francis Xavier University and Saint Mary's University.

[Information supplied by the institution as at 5 November 1998, and edited by the ACU]

Council of Ontario Universities

180 Dundas Street West, 11th Floor, Toronto, Ontario, Canada M5G 1Z8

Telephone: (416) 979 2165 **Fax**: (416) 979 8635 **E-mail**: acadieux@coupo.cou.on.ca
WWW: http://www.cou.on.ca **E-mail formula**: firstinitiallastname@coupo.cou.on.ca

Chair—(until 30 June 1999) Prichard, Prof. J. Robert S., LLB Tor., MBA Chic., LLM Yale, Hon. PhD Montr., Hon. LLD
Law Soc.Upper Canada, President, University of Toronto
President*—Clark, Ian, BSc Br.Col., MA Harv., DPhil Oxf.

Mission

The Council is an advocacy, communications and research organisation representing the collective interests of its 17 member institutions and 2 associate members. It is the mandate of the Council to provide leadership on issues facing Ontario's provincially assisted universities, to promote the contribution of higher education to the province of Ontario, and to foster co-operation and understanding among member universities, the government, interest groups and the general public.

Membership

17 universities and 2 associate members.

[Information supplied by the institution as at 5 November 1998, and edited by the ACU]

Council of Western Canadian University Presidents

Brandon University, 270-18th St., Brandon, Manitoba, Canada R7A 6A9

Telephone: (204) 727 7427 **Fax**: (204) 729 9016

Chair*—Anderson, C. Dennis, BSc *Bran.*, MBA *McM.*, PhD *W.Ont.*, President and Vice-Chancellor, Brandon University

Mission
The Council provides a forum for communication among university presidents on common problems and to address issues in higher education that are unique to Western Canada.

Membership
The chief executive officers of university institutions in Western Canada: University of Alberta, Athabasca University (Alberta), Augustana University College (Alberta), Brandon University (Manitoba), University of British Columbia, University of Calgary (Alberta), Concordia University College of Alberta, King's University College (Alberta), University of Lethbridge (Alberta), University of Manitoba, University of Northern British Columbia, Open Learning Agency (British Columbia), University of Regina (Saskatchewan), Royal Roads University (British Columbia), University of Saskatchewan, Saskatchewan Indian Federated College, Simon Fraser University (British Columbia), Trinity Western University (British Columbia), University of Victoria (British Columbia), University of Winnipeg (Manitoba).

[Information supplied by the institution as at 6 November 1998, and edited by the ACU]

EAST AFRICA

Inter-University Council for East Africa

East African Development Bank Building, Plot 4, Nile Avenue, Kampala, Uganda, East Africa
(PO Box 7110, Kampala, Uganda)

Telephone: (041) 256251-2 **Fax**: (041) 242007 **Cables**: Intervarsity **Telex**: 62179 IUC

Chairman—(1997-98) Ssebuwufu, Prof. John P. M., BSc *Mak.*, PhD *Belf.*, Vice-Chancellor, Makerere University
Executive Secretary*—Kigozi, Eric K., BA *Lond.*

Mission
The Inter-University Council for East Africa aims to facilitate contact and co-operation among the universities of East Africa.

Membership
University of Dar es Salaam, Egerton University, Kenyatta University, Makerere University, Mbarara University of Science and Technology, Moi University, University of Nairobi, Open University of Tanzania, Sokoine University of Agriculture.

[Information supplied by the institution as at 25 June 1998, and edited by the ACU]

GHANA

Committee of Vice-Chancellors and Principals (Ghana)

PO Box 25, Legon, Ghana, West Africa

Telephone: (021) 501967 **Fax**: (021) 502701 **Telex**: 2556 UGL GH

Chairman—Addae-Mensah, Prof. Ivan, BSc *Ghana*, MSc *Ghana*, PhD *Camb.*, Vice-Chancellor, University of Ghana
Secretary*—Yeboah, Frank K., BA *Ghana*, MPA *Ghana*

Mission
The aim of the Committee, which came into being in 1965, is to provide a consultative forum for the heads of university institutions in Ghana to discuss problems of common interest to their institutions. The Committee is a non-statutory body and has no power to take decisions on any issue on behalf of any university. Decisions of the

Committee are in the form of recommendations to the governing bodies of the universities.

Membership

The vice-chancellors of the four universities and the principal of the university college in Ghana.

[Information supplied by the institution as at 15 November 1998, and edited by the ACU]

INDIA

Association of Indian Universities

AIU House, 16 Kotla Marg, New Delhi, India 110 002

Telephone: (011) 323 6105 **Fax**: (011) 323 6105 **E-mail**: aiu@de12.vsnl.net.in **Cables**: Asindu
Telex: 31 66180 AIU IN

President—(1998) Rinpoche, Prof. Samdhong, Director, Central Institute of Higher Tibetan Studies
Secretary General*—Powar, Prof. Krishnapratap B., BSc *Nag.*, MSc *Nag.*, PhD *Ban.*

Mission

The Association provides liaison between the universities and central and state governments and co-operates with other universities and bodies (national and international) in matters of common interest in the field of higher education. It also acts as the representative of Indian universities at various forums in India and abroad.

Membership

Indian universities, institutions 'deemed to be universities', and institutions of national importance; also universities from neighbouring countries as associate members. The present membership numbers 223.

[Information supplied by the institution as at 12 June 1997, and edited by the ACU]

NEW ZEALAND

New Zealand Vice-Chancellors' Committee

PO Box 11–915, Manners Street, Wellington, New Zealand

Telephone: (04) 801 5086 **Fax**: (04) 801 5089 **E-mail**: marlene@nzvcc.ac.nz
E-mail formula: firstname@nzvcc.ac.nz

Chairperson—Fogelberg, Graeme, BCom NZ, MCom *Well.*, MBA *W.Ont.*, PhD *W.Ont.*, FCA(NZ), Vice-Chancellor, University of Otago
Executive Director*—Taiaroa, Lindsay S., BA *Cant.*, MPP *Well.*

Mission

The Committee provides administrative machinery for the formulation and implementation of policies on any matters where collective action is considered to be to the advantage of the university institutions, both internally among themselves, and externally when a collective viewpoint is needed. The Committee is also a useful and important forum for the exchange of views on all aspects of university development.

Membership

The vice-chancellors of the seven universities in New Zealand.

[Information supplied by the institution as at 9 November 1998, and edited by the ACU]

NIGERIA

Committee of Vice-Chancellors of Nigerian Federal Universities

3 Idowu Taylor Street, Victoria Island, Lagos, Nigeria
(PMB 12022, Lagos, Nigeria)

Telephone: (01) 611554, 612465 **Fax**: (01) 612425 **Cables**: Nivicom, Lagos **Telex**: 23555 COMVIC NG

Chairman—Obah, Prof. Chuka O. G., BSc(Eng) *Lond.*, MSc *Lond.*, PhD *Qu.*, Vice-Chancellor, Federal University of Technology, Owerri.
Secretary-General*—Aboaba, Prof. Folagbade O., BSc *Lond.*, MSc *Durh.*, PhD *Wis.*

Mission

The objectives of the Committee are: (a) to provide a focus of academic leadership through bold initiatives in higher education in Nigeria with particular reference to the roles of universities; (b) to act as a channel through which the joint opinion of Nigerian universities on any matter affecting higher education in Nigeria is expressed; (c) to study, comment and make recommendations on proposals, legislation, regulations or rules affecting universities in Nigeria; (d) to act as a bureau of information and to facilitate communication and mutual consultation among the universities; (e) to co-operate with organisations that have similar aims and objectives and to protect the interests of Nigerian universities; (f) to organise, sponsor or promote conferences, seminars, workshops, lectures, colloquia and symposia on higher education, particularly in Nigeria; (g) to provide a platform for discussing common problems such as inter-university co-operation, administrative and academic practices, maintenance of academic standards, staff recruitment, physical exchange and student affairs; (h) to serve as a forum for collaboration with the National Universities Commission (NUC) and federal government on matters concerning university education; (i) to do all such other lawful things as are necessary for the attainment and furtherance of these objectives.

Membership

The vice-chancellors of all 24 federal universities in Nigeria.

[Information supplied by the institution as at 30 May 1997, and edited by the ACU]

PAKISTAN

Vice-Chancellors' Committee of Pakistan

Sector H-9, Islamabad, Pakistan

Telephone: (051) 434798, 9290131-9 **Fax**: (051) 434823, 9290128 **E-mail**: ugc@paknet2.ptc.pk
Cables: Unigrant

Chairman—Khan, Yar M., BSc, Vice-Chancellor, North-West Frontier Province Agricultural University
Secretary (ex officio)*—Virk, Dr. Mohammad Latif, Secretary, University Grants Commission

Mission

The Committee is an advisory body for the promotion of higher education in Pakistan.

Membership

The vice-chancellors of all the 26 state-funded and 9 privately chartered universities of Pakistan are the members of the Committee.

[Information supplied by the institution as at 30 October 1998, and edited by the ACU]

SOUTH AFRICA

South African Universities' Vice-Chancellors' Association

PO Box 27392, Pretoria, Sunnyside, South Africa 0132

Telephone: (012) 429 3015, 429 3161 **Fax**: (012) 429 3071 **E-mail**: sauvca1@alpha.unisa.ac.za

Chairperson—Ramphele, Mamphela A., MB ChB *Natal*, BCom *S.Af.*, PhD *Cape Town*, Hon. MD *Natal*, Hon. DHL *Hunter*, Hon. DSocSc *Tufts*, Hon. DSc *Lond.*, Hon. LLD *Prin.*, Hon. Dr *Inst.Soc.Stud.*(*The Hague*), Vice-Chancellor, University of Cape Town
Chief Executive*—Kotecha, Piyushi, BA *Sus.*, MEd *Witw.*

Mission

The South African Universities' Vice-Chancellor's Association seeks to play an authentic and reputable leadership role in the educational life of South Africa through: successfully promoting innovative scholarship, educational quality and equity amongst higher education institutions; developing leadership within the higher education sector; becoming a credible resource for policy and decision makers, and other actors in the education sector; establishing a successful relationship with key national sectors with a vital interest in higher education; building and maintaining active linkages with the international higher education sector; enhancing the organisational quality of SAUVCA; fostering values of mutual trust, collegiality and innovation in support of SAUVCA's strategic objectives.

Membership

The previous (and still statutory name) of SAUVCA is the Committee of University Principals (CUP). It consists of the Vice-Chancellors of all 21 universities within the borders of South Africa. The Vice-Chancellor of the University of Namibia has observer status. In practice this means he/she has no voting rights, but otherwise participates fully in all the activities of SAUVCA. In terms of a recent decision other universities in neighbouring countries are also invited to join SAUVCA with observer status.

[Information supplied by the institution as at 9 November 1998, and edited by the ACU]

SRI LANKA

Committee of Vice-Chancellors and Directors (Sri Lanka)

University of Peradeniya, Peradeniya, Sri Lanka

Telephone: (08) 388151, 388055 **Fax**: (08) 388151, 388104 **Cables**: University, Peradeniya

Chairman—(1999) Gunawardana, Prof. R. A. Leslie H., BA *Ceyl.*, PhD *Lond.*, Vice-Chancellor, University of Peradeniya, Sri Lanka
Secretary*—Warakaulle, H. M. Nissanka, BA *Ceyl.*

Mission

The principal aims of the Committee are: (a) to serve as an inter-university organisation; (b) to make recommendations to the University Grants Commission (UGC), in an advisory capacity, regarding the formulation and adoption of schemes of recruitment and promotion for all categories of staff and any other matters relating to the internal management of the universities; (c) to act as a bureau of information and to facilitate communication, co-ordination and consultation among universities; (d) to act as an intermediary between the universities and international universities and institutions in furtherance of common interests; (e) to act as the representative of the university system in Sri Lanka in international organisations; (f) to promote and safeguard the principle of university autonomy; (g) to promote, facilitate and monitor the maintenance of quality education in the university system in Sri Lanka; (h) to promote activities relating to staff development; (i) to advise the UGC on matters such as recruitment schemes, staff welfare, salaries and emoluments; (j) to co-ordinate and process applications for fellowships and scholarships referred to the committee by national and international agencies and donors, and to represent the universities' interests in the UGC committee on scholarships, fellowships and other awards; (k) to advise and assist universities on matters relating to student counselling, student participation in university governance, student welfare, careers guidance, bursaries, loans and other financial assistance to students; (l) to advise the UGC on matters of academic administration such as the rationalisation of university faculties, departments and courses; (m) to assist in securing the recognition in Sri Lanka and abroad of degrees, diplomas and other academic distinctions awarded by the universities and other higher education institutions; (n) to assist in the obtaining of information relating to degrees, diplomas, etc awarded by universities and other higher education institutions in Sri Lanka.

Membership

The vice-chancellors of the universities of Sri Lanka: Buddhist and Pali University (associate member); University of Colombo; Eastern University; University of Jaffna; University of Kelaniya; University of Moratuwa; Open University of Sri Lanka; University of Peradeniya; Rajarata University of Sri Lanka; University of Ruhuna; Sabaragamuwa University of Sri Lanka; South Eastern University of Sri Lanka; and University of Sri Jayewardenepura.

[Information supplied by the institution as at 4 November 1998, and edited by the ACU]

UNITED KINGDOM

Committee of Vice-Chancellors and Principals of the Universities of the United Kingdom

Woburn House, 20 Tavistock Square, London, England WC1H 9HQ

Telephone: (0171) 419 4111 **Fax**: (0171) 388 8649 **E-mail**: info@cvcp.ac.uk **WWW**: http://www.cvcp.ac.uk
E-mail formula: name.surname@cvcp.ac.uk

Chairman—Harris, Prof. Martin B., CBE, BA *Camb.*, MA *Camb.*, PhD *Lond.*, Hon. LLD *Belf.*, Hon. DU *Essex*, Hon. DLitt *Salf.*, Vice-Chancellor, University of Manchester
Chief Executive*—Warwick, Diana, BA *Lond.*, Hon. DLitt *Brad.*, Hon. Dr *Open(UK)*

Mission

The Committee of Vice-Chancellors and Principals (CVCP) exists to represent the university sector of higher education in the United Kingdom, and to promote, encourage and develop it. The Committee's aims are: to improve the funding, regulatory and marketing environment within which United Kingdom universities pursue their diverse missions; to promote public understanding of the roles, achievements, needs and objectives of UK universities; to assist in developing good practice in all spheres of university activity by sharing ideas and experience.

Membership

All vice-chancellors or principals of the universities in the United Kingdom are eligible for membership, together with the principals of the constituent institutions of the University of Wales. The University of London may nominate as additional members a number agreed with the council of the CVCP from among the heads of colleges or schools of that university. The University of Wales may nominate as additional members a number agreed with the council of the CVCP from among the heads of university colleges of that university.

[Information supplied by the institution as at 3 June 1997, and edited by the ACU]

PART-COMMONWEALTH

Agence Universitaire de la Francophonie

BP 400, succursale Côte des Neiges, Montréal, Québec, Canada H3S 2S7

Telephone: (514) 343 6630 **Fax**: (514) 343 2107 **E-mail**: refer@refer.qc.ca **WWW**: http://www.aupelf-uref.org

Rector*—Guillou, Michel
Hon. President—Bodson, Arthur, former Rector, State University of Liège
(Belgium)

Mission

The *Agence Universitaire de la Francophonie* (university agency for the French speaking world) has as its main aim the development of international co-operation to maintain both a permanent dialogue between cultures and an exchange of people, ideas and experience between university institutions, in the interest of education and scientific progress within the French-speaking world. General assemblies are held every four years.

Membership

Approximately 400 member institutions in 42 countries.

[Information supplied by the institution as at 4 December 1998, and edited by the ACU]

Asian Association of Agricultural Colleges and Universities

c/o Searca, College, Laguna 4031, Phillipines

President—Koh, Hak-Kyun
Executive Secretary*—Sajise, Percy E.

Mission

The aims of the Association are: to help enhance the effectiveness of programmes that will enable member institutions to achieve their objectives in research, extension and academic programmes; and to contribute to the improvement of the human condition through co-operation in higher education.

Membership

48 members; 4 affiliate members.

[Information supplied by the institution as at 15 August 1997, and edited by the ACU]

Association of African Universities

PO Box 5744, Accra-North, Ghana

Telephone: (021) 774495, 761588 **Fax**: (021) 774821 **E-mail**: secgen@aau.org **Cables**: Afuniv

Secretary-General*—Matos, Prof. Narciso

Mission

The objectives of the Association are: to collect, classify and disseminate information on higher education and research in Africa; to promote co-operation among African institutions in training, research, community services and higher education policy, as well as in curriculum development and in the determination of equivalence in academic degrees; to encourage increased contacts between members and the international academic world; to encourage the development and wide use of African languages and support exchange of university teachers and administrators to deal with problems in African education in general.

Membership

148 members in 43 African countries.

[Information supplied by the institution as at 22 October 1998, and edited by the ACU]

Association of American Universities

1 Dupont Circle, NW, Suite 730, Washington DC 20036, USA

Telephone: (202) 466 5030 **Fax**: (202) 296 4438 **E-mail**: beth_matlick@aau.nche.edu

Association of Caribbean Tertiary Institutions

c/o University of Technology, Jamaica, 237 Old Hope Road, Kingston 6, Jamaica

Telephone: 927 1680–8 **Fax**: 977 4388

President*—McIntyre, The Hon. Sir Alister, OM, DC, CCH, BSc(Econ) Lond., BLitt Oxf., Hon. LLD WI, Hon. LLD Sheff.
Vice-President—Holder, Norma
Vice-President—Hunte, Sir Keith, KA, BA Lond., MA McG., PhD McG., Principal and Pro-Vice-Chancellor, Cave Hill Campus, University of the West Indies
Honorary Secretary/Treasurer—Stills, Helen
Executive Officer—Higgins, Dottie

Mission

The broad objectives of the Association as stated in its constitution are: to facilitate co-operation and collaboration between institutions in a wide range of academic, administrative and other areas; to facilitate more effective utilisation of scarce resources in seeking to enhance access, mobility and quality in tertiary education; to facilitate articulation among its member institutions; to facilitate the development and delivery of particular programmes and services; to assist in identifying and meeting the ongoing tertiary education needs of the region and of individual territories; to provide a professional forum for discussion and problem-solving.

Membership

There are three categories of membership of the Association: full, associate and honorary. Full membership is open to tertiary institutions that provide post-secondary education and/or training leading to a certificate, diploma or degree. Associate membership is open to organisations and other institutions which have responsibilities relating to tertiary education at the regional, territorial or extra-regional levels.

Honorary membership is conferred on an organisation, institution, or individual deemed by the Association to have given outstanding service to education, particularly at the tertiary level.

[Information supplied by the institution as at 24 May 1996, and edited by the ACU]

Association of Caribbean Universities and Research Institutes

PO Box 11532, Caparra Heights Station, San Juan, Puerto Rico 00922

Telephone: 720 4381 **Fax**: 567 9219

Association of Eastern and Southern African Universities

East African Development Bank Building, Plot 4, Nile Avenue, Kampala, Uganda, East Africa
(PO Box 7110, Kampala, Uganda)

Telephone: (041) 256251-2 **Fax**: (041) 242007 **Cables**: Intervarsity **Telex**: 62179 IUC

Executive Secretary*—Kigozi, Eric K., BA Lond.

Mission

The Association aims to promote co-operation among universities of eastern and southern Africa; to provide a forum for discussion on a wide range of academic and other matters relating to higher education; to help maintain high comparable standards; and to strengthen the work of the Association of African Universities, especially on a regional basis.

Membership

The executive heads of universities in Botswana, Eritrea, Ethiopia, Kenya, Lesotho, Madagascar, Malawi, Mauritius, Mozambique, Somalia, South Africa, Sudan, Swaziland, Tanzania, Uganda, Zambia and Zimbabwe.

[Information supplied by the institution as at 19 January 1995, and edited by the ACU]

Association of European Universities

10 rue du Conseil-Général, 1211 Geneva 4, Switzerland

Telephone: (22) 329 2644, 329 2251 **Fax**: (22) 329 2821 **E-mail**: cre@uni2a.unige.ch
WWW: http://www.unige.ch/cre/ **E-mail formula**: lastname@uni2a.unige.ch (lastname up to 8 letters)

President—Edwards, Kenneth J. R., BSc *Reading*, MA *Camb.*, PhD *Wales*, Hon. LLD *Belf.*, Hon. DSc *Reading*, Hon. DSc *Lough.*, Hon. MA *Leic.*, Vice-Chancellor, University of Leicester
Vice-President—Blasi, Prof. Paolo, Rector, University of Florence
Vice-President—Smith, Prof. Lucy, Rector, University of Oslo
Treasurer—Lamicq, Prof. Hélène, President, University of Paris Val-de-Marne (Paris XII)
Secretary General*—Barblan, Dr. Andris

Mission

CRE's main objective is to promote inter-university co-operation throughout the whole of Europe.

Membership

527 universities and institutions of higher education, including 6 associate members, in 40 European countries.

[Information supplied by the institution as at 22 October 1998, and edited by the ACU]

Association of Southeast Asian Institutions of Higher Learning

Ratasastra Building 2, Chulalongkorn University, Bangkok, Thailand 10330

Telephone: (02) 251 6966 **Fax**: (02) 255 4441

Membership

Membership is drawn from 120 institutions in Australia, Brunei, Canada, Hong Kong, Indonesia, Japan, Malaysia, New Zealand, Philippines, Singapore, Sweden, Thailand and the United States. It also has associate members outside the region.

Association of Universities of Asia and the Pacific

c/o Centre for International Affairs, Suranaree University of Technology, 111 University Avenue, Muang District, Nakhon Ratchasima 30000 Thailand

Telephone: (44) 224141-5 **Fax**: (44) 224140 **E-mail**: cenintaf@ccs.sut.ac.th

President—McNicol, Prof. Donald, BA *Adel.*, PhD *Camb.*, FAPsS, Vice-Chancellor and Principal, University of Tasmania
Secretary-General*—Umaly, Prof. Ruben C., PhD Birm.

Mission

The Association's main objectives are: to discharge more effectively the responsibility for providing higher education and training, to extend the frontiers of knowledge and contribute actively to the well-being of the community, to develop human resources, to preserve and enhance the cultural heritage thereby serving the cause of socio-economic development and peace; to promote wider understanding of the value and importance of these basic goals; to strengthen the institutional capacity for serving society; to co-operate with university bodies at the international, national, regional and sub-regional levels, as well as with inter-governmental, governmental and private bodies concerned with higher education; to implement programmes which will assist in the development of the Association's member institutions, whether financed by the members themselves or by other funding agencies.

Membership

84 member institutions (including associate members) in Australia, Bangladesh, Cambodia, China, Fiji, India, Indonesia, Iran, Japan, Korea, Macau, Malaysia, Kazakhstan, New Zealand, Pakistan, Philippines, Thailand, United States of America and Vietnam.

[Information supplied by the institution as at 4 November 1998, and edited by the ACU]

Community of Mediterranean Universities

Università degli Studi, Piazza Umberto, 70121 Bari, Italy

Telephone: (080) 556 0786, 547 8336-7 **Fax**: (080) 547 8203 **E-mail**: cum@cimedoc.uniba.it
Telex: 810598 UNIVBA I

President*—Ambrosi, Prof. Luigi

Mission

The Community of Mediterranean Universities (CMU) is a non-governmental and non-profit organisation whose main objectives are: to reaffirm the role and function of culture and of technological and scientific research in the countries of the Mediterranean Basin; to promote scientific co-operation among Mediterranean universities; and to set up permanent links between its members through the reciprocal exchange of scientific and cultural experience, information, teaching staff and students.

Membership

161 universities of the Mediterranean Basin.

[Information supplied by the institution as at 26 October 1998, and edited by the ACU]

Inter-American Organization for Higher Education

Place Iberville IV, 2954 boulevard Laurier, Sainte-Foy, Quebec, Canada G1V 4T2

Telephone: (418) 650 1515 **Fax**: (418) 650 1519 **E-mail**: secretariat@oui-iohe.qc.ca
WWW: http://www.oui-iohe.qc.ca

President—Romero Hicks, Juan C., BA *Guanajuato*, MPsychol *S.Oregon State*, MBA
S.Oregon State
Executive Director*—Van Der Donckt, Pierre

Mission
The Organization's mission is to promote co-operation among universities in the Americas in order to improve the quality of higher education.

Membership
The IOHE has 380 members in 24 countries of the Americas and the Caribbean. They are universities, university associations, higher education institutes and research centres.

[Information supplied by the institution as at 22 October 1998, and edited by the ACU]

International Association of Universities

UNESCO House, 1 rue Miollis, 75732 Paris Cedex 15, France

Telephone: (01) 45 68 25 45 **Fax**: (01) 47 34 76 05 **E-mail**: iau@unesco.org **WWW**: http://www.unesco.org/iau
E-mail formula: surname.iau@unesco.org

President—Mori, Wataru, former President, University of Tokyo
Vice-President—Fava de Moraes, Flavio, former Rector, University of
São Paulo
Vice-President—van Ginkel, Hans, Rector, United Nations University
Secretary-General*—Eberhard, Franz

Mission
The Association provides a global forum for the universities of the world working together to implement the following objectives: to exchange experience and learn from each other; to restate and defend the values that underlie and determine the proper functioning of universities; to develop a long-term vision of the universities' role and responsibilities in society; to represent the universities' interests with regard to the policies of international bodies such as UNESCO and the World Bank, and at the same time respond to international requirements in regional settings; to contribute to a better understanding of current trends and developments through analysis, research and debate; to foster university co-operation and academic exhange through linkages and networks and to provide authoritative information on systems and institutions of higher education world-wide. IAU provides world wide information on higher education systems and institutions. The Association regularly publishes research on higher education.

Membership
About 600 member institutions in over 150 countries.

[Information supplied by the institution as at 6 November 1998, and edited by the ACU]

International Federation of Catholic Universities

21 rue d'Assas, 75270 Paris Cedex 06, France

Telephone: (01) 44 39 52 26 **Fax**: (01) 44 39 52 28 **E-mail**: sgfiuc@club_internet.fr **WWW**: http://www.fiuc.org

President—Gonzalez, Br. Andrew
Secretary General*—Hanssens, Prof.
Vincent

Mission
The main objectives of the Federation are: to promote communication and co-operation between its members and increase their openness to the outside world; and to represent the interests of its members to international organisations, especially in the fields of education, teaching and research.

Membership
About 200 Catholic universities and institutions of higher education.

[Information supplied by the institution as at 4 October 1998, and edited by the ACU]

Union of Latin American Universities

Costada Norponiente del Estadio Olímpico, Ciudad Universitaria, Deleg Coyoacán 04510, Mexico DF
(Apartado Postal 70-232, 04510 Coyoacán, Mexico DF)

Telephone: (05) 622 0091-3 **Fax**: (05) 616 1414, 616 2383 **E-mail**: johannes@servidor.unam.mxs

President—Pinto, Faverio L., Rector, Technological Metropolitan
University of Chile
General Secretary*—Sanchez, Sosa J. J.

Mission

The main objectives of the Union are: to promote, strengthen and improve relationships between Latin American universities, cultural organisations and other institutions; to co-ordinate the academic and administrative structures of its member institutions; to promote the academic exchange of staff and students in order to improve communication and mutual understanding among its members; and to develop the role played by the universities in the areas of economic, social and cultural development—both in their own environment and in the context of full cultural integration throughout Latin America.

Membership

166 universities in 19 Latin American countries. Institutions may become ordinary or associate members.

[Information supplied by the institution as at 12 November 1998, and edited by the ACU]

APPENDIX 3

COMMONWEALTH OF LEARNING

Postal Address: 1285 West Broadway, Suite 600, Vancouver, British Columbia, V6H 3X8 Canada
Telephone: (604) 775 8200 **Telex**: 0450 7508 COMLEARN **Fax**: (604) 775 8210 **E-mail**: info@col.org
WWW: http://www.col.org **E-mail formula**: initialsurname@col.org

Chairman of the Board of Governors—Macdonald, H. Ian, OC, BCom *Tor.*, BPhil *Oxf.*, MA *Oxf.*, Hon. LLD *Tor.*
President and Chief Executive Officer*—Dhanarajan, Dato' Prof. Gajaraj (Raj), MSc *Madr.*, MSc *Lond.*, PhD *Aston*,
Hon. DHumLett *Maryland*, Hon. DUniv *Open(UK)*, Hon. DLett *Kota*, Hon. DEd *Abertay*, Hon. DUniv *C.Sturt*,

Senior staff

Irvine, D. H., CCH, BSc *Leeds*, PhD *Camb.*, Hon. DSc *Leeds*   Regional
Advisor to the President, Caribbean

Mmari, Prof. Geoffrey R. V., MA *N.Iowa*, PhD *Dar.*   Regional Advisor to
the President, Eastern Africa

Pecku, Prof. N. K., BA *Lond.*, MEd *New Hampshire*, EdD *Indiana*   Regional
Advisor to the President, Western Africa

Perinbam, L., OC, Hon. Dr *Queb.*, Hon. LLD *Calg.*, Hon. LLD
York(Can.)   Adviser to the President

Sharom, Dato' Ahmat, BA *Sing.*, MA *Brown*, PhD *Lond.*, Hon. LittD
Sheff.   Regional Advisor to the President, Southeast Asia

Swartland, Jakes, MEd *Newcastle(UK)*   Regional Advisor to the President,
Southern Africa

Takwale, Prof. Ram, BSc *Poona*, MSc *Poona*, PhD *Moscow*   Regional
Advisor to the President, South Asia

Williams, Peter R. C., BA *Camb.*, Hon. LLD *Abia State*   Regional Advisor
to the President, United Kingdom and Europe

Woolley, Madeleine   Regional Advisor to the President, Australia and
New Zealand

Profile

The Commonwealth of Learning (COL) was set up by Commonwealth
governments in September 1988, to promote collaboration in distance
education. In proposing the creation of this new institution, heads of
government stated that its objects would be to widen access to
education, share resources, raise educational quality, and support the
mobility of ideas, of teaching, of relevant research and of people. "Our
long-term aim is that any learner, anywhere in the Commonwealth,
shall be able to study any distance teaching programme available from
any *bona fide* college or university in the Commonwealth.'

The purpose of COL, as defined under its 'memorandum of
understanding', is to create and widen access to opportunities for
learning, by promoting co-operation between universities, colleges and
other educational institutions throughout the Commonwealth, making
use of the potential offered by distance education and by the
application of communication technologies to education. The agency's
activities aim to strengthen member countries' capacities to develop the
human resources required for their economic and social development,
and give priority to those developmental needs to which
Commonwealth co-operation can apply.

The organisation has provided a wide range of services to many
Commonwealth countries especially those that are less well endowed,
small and in great need of increasing educational access to their
people. These services have made a significant impact in the orientation
and thinking of policy-makers in the area of educational provision.
Through demonstrations, advice, training and the exchange of materials
and information, COL has been able to sensitise educational planners to
the advantageous ways in which both tested and emerging
communication technologies can be applied to enhance learning
opportunities.

Background

Proposals for COL grew out of the work of the Commonwealth
Standing Committee on Student Mobility. The committee realised that
the rapid developments in communications technology offered the
potential for Commonwealth universities and colleges to share their
resources, and thus to complement the established programmes of staff
and student mobility. In the light of the committee's reports,
Commonwealth heads of government in 1985 asked the
Commonwealth secretary-general to 'explore the scope for new

Commonwealth initiatives in open learning'. He, in turn, brought
together a group of eminent educators and others from across the
Commonwealth under the chairmanship of Lord Briggs of Lewes. Their
proposals for a Commonwealth institution to promote co-operation in
distance education were endorsed by heads of government in 1987.
Work on the detailed structure of the new institution by a group
chaired by Dr. J. S. Daniel, led to the formal establishment of COL as
an independent international organisation by means of a
'memorandum of understanding' between governments in September
1988.

COL is governed by a board of governors which is representative of
all parts of the Commonwealth. The Commonwealth secretary-general
and the president of COL sit on the board as *ex-officio* members. The
first chairman was the Rt. Hon. Lord Briggs of Lewes. Professor James
A. Maraj was appointed in January 1989 as the founding president. In
January 1994, former president of York University (Canada), Dr. H.
Ian Macdonald, was appointed chairman, and in September 1995 the
former director of the Open Learning Institute of Hong Kong, took up
duties as president and chief executive officer.

COL was launched with pledged funds from Commonwealth
governments amounting to some £15 million for its first five years. In
addition, the institution seeks funds from donor agencies of all kinds
in order to finance individual projects and programmes. Canada, the
province of British Columbia, India, Britain and Australia continue to
provide sustaining financial support.

Activities

The fundamental mission of the COL is to promote the development of
human resources through the application of distance teaching
techniques and technologies, in response to the developmental needs of
member countries. The focus of COL's work is in developing
Commonwealth countries. The organisation supports the development
and use of the entire spectrum of communication technologies, from
print materials to satellite transmission, in order to expand learning
opportunities. Activities are principally in three areas.

First, COL encourages and arranges the sharing of distance-teaching
materials and supports the development of new materials to meet
identified educational needs. In these ways it assists institutions in
extending the range of their courses, raising quality, and making more
economic use of their resources.

Second, it helps to support institutions through staff training,
improved communications, an information service about distance
education, and programmes of evaluation and research.

Third, it plans to assist institutions to provide better services to
students, improve study support systems, facilitate the transfer of
course credits between Commonwealth institutions and develop
telecommunications networks.

> The Commonwealth of Learning does not enrol
> individual students. It works with colleges and
> universities that can enrol students, and so enables these
> to tap into each other's resources. It does not teach
> students directly.

In seeking to achieve these goals, COL works closely with a range of
institutions and organisations. It contracts out services as required,
encouraging regional programmes, and seeks to pool and share

techniques and distance-teaching experiences of benefit to all participating member countries.

Model-building is also an important aspect of COL's work. The Commonwealth Educational Media Centre for Asia (CEMCA), located in New Delhi, was established by COL in 1994 to promote co-operation and collaboration in technical applications among educational institutions and media organisations. It also serves as a regional resource centre, facilitating the exchange of audio/video productions. Work is progressing on the establishment of a similar centre for Africa.

Responding to other expressed needs, COL is developing distance education curriculum material in fields such as environmental engineering, technical/vocational education and training and teacher education —where existing materials are not available or not particularly suitable—and is developing copyright protocols for the transfer, use and adaptation of materials that do exist.

Headquarters

COL's headquarters are in Vancouver, Canada. Much of the institution's work is, however, decentralised. Thus, the development of materials is carried out largely by the staff of Commonwealth universities and colleges under contract. Its information services network draws on the strengths available from other institutions and databases.

COL also works regionally where it can, both through existing regional institutions and by itself promoting the development of regional activity where appropriate.

Further information

Information about the current activities of COL is available from the public affairs officer at the Vancouver address.

[Information supplied by the institution as at July 1998, and edited by the ACU]

APPENDIX 4

COMMONWEALTH SCHOLARSHIP AND FELLOWSHIP PLAN

Origin

On the opening day of the Eighth Quinquennial Congress of Commonwealth Universities at Montreal in early September 1958, Sidney Smith, former president of the University of Toronto and then Canadian minister for external affairs, delivered a speech stressing the importance of developing educational links between Commonwealth countries. Later that month the Commonwealth Trade and Economic Conference met in the same city, and it was from that conference that there emerged the proposal to establish a new scheme of Commonwealth scholarships and fellowships. The purpose and operation of the scheme were elaborated at the First Commonwealth Education Conference, held at Oxford in July 1959, and the first Commonwealth Scholars took up their awards in 1960.

Aims

The Commonwealth Scholarship and Fellowship Plan was created to enable Commonwealth students of high intellectual promise to pursue studies in Commonwealth countries other than their own so that on their return home they could make a distinctive contribution to life in their own countries and to mutual understanding in the Commonwealth.

Operation

Any Commonwealth country that wishes to do so may institute awards under the Plan. In the 1995–96 academic year, the most recent year for which data is available, invitations to nominate were made by Australia, Canada, India, Jamaica, New Zealand, Nigeria and the United Kingdom*. No data was received from Brunei, Malaysia, Malta, Sierra Leone, Sri Lanka, Swaziland, Tanzania or Uganda. Nigeria was subsequently suspended from the Commonwealth.

Between Commonwealth Education Conferences (at which the Plan is usually a major topic of discussion) there is no single authority exercising central control over the Plan's operation. Each member country of the Commonwealth and each dependency or state associated with such a member has designated an agency (the 'Commonwealth Scholarship agency') which draws up the list of recommended candidates from its country and nominates them direct to the agency in the awarding country.

The agencies in each of the fourteen countries named above have of course the dual function of nominating candidates to other awarding countries on the one hand; and of receiving nominations from other countries and selecting and placing candidates for its own awards.

The addresses of the Commonwealth Scholarship agencies are given below.

There are two types of award: *Commonwealth Scholarships* and *Commonwealth Fellowships*.

Commonwealth Senior Awards

Professorships and Fellowships have so far been instituted by Australia, Canada, New Zealand and the United Kingdom; and awards for senior educational administrators by India. These awards are intended for a few scholars of established reputation and achievement—or occasionally for people outside the academic world who play an important part in the life of their country. They are made by invitation and are not open to direct application from candidates. (The United Kingdom no longer offers Visiting Professorships, but *see* 'Special categories of award', *below*.)

Commonwealth Scholarships

These are intended mainly for *postgraduate* study by course work or research at university and not for the purpose of acquiring technical training or professional qualifications. In addition, awards for *undergraduate* study can be made to students from countries in which there are no universities or whose universities do not offer the course desired.

Each awarding country determines the value of its own awards and gives details in a prospectus which it circulates to the Commonwealth Scholarship agency in the countries which are invited to nominate candidates. The following allowances are regarded as basic: fares to and from the awarding country for the Scholar (but not usually for spouse or dependants); approved fees; personal maintenance allowances; contributions towards the cost of books, apparatus and (if necessary) special clothing; contributions towards approved travel expenses within the awarding country. In some countries a marriage and child allowance may be paid.

An individual candidate must apply to the Commonwealth Scholarship agency in his/her own country (*see* list, *below*); awarding countries do not accept applications direct from candidates.

Only rarely are Scholarships awarded to men or women who have completed a first degree more than ten years prior to the proposed start of an award.

Scholarships may be held in any academic discipline, subject to such restrictions as the awarding or nominating countries may impose.

Special categories of award

Alone of the countries participating in the Plan, the United Kingdom makes available the following academic staff awards, created to enhance the experience and training of locally-born members of staff in universities of developing Commonwealth countries (nomination of candidates should be initiated by the head of the *employing* university): *Academic Staff Scholarships*, like the Commonwealth Scholarships offered by the United Kingdom, awarded for postgraduate study or research, normally leading to a degree; *Commonwealth Fellowships* given in all subjects to established and already fully qualified members of staff for special programmes of study (*ie* not for study leading to a higher degree) for either six or twelve months.

What the Plan has achieved

The annual reports for the first thirty-five years record that 28,118 scholarships, fellowships or professorships were held under the Commonwealth Scholarship and Fellowship Plan, including 5373 by women. Almost all have returned to play an active and sometimes prominent part in the life of their countries. Many hundreds, for example, have returned to academic posts in their own countries; and up to the time of writing nearly 30 vice-chancellors or other heads of university institutions in different parts of the Commonwealth have been former Commonwealth Scholars. The Plan has also played a significant part in meeting the manpower needs of the developing countries of the Commonwealth, and has come to occupy an important role in the educational life of the Commonwealth.

Further sources of information

(a) Reports of the Commonwealth Education Conferences, the first of which was held in 1959 and thereafter at three-yearly intervals. (b) Reports on the Commonwealth Scholarship and Fellowship Plan issued by the Commonwealth Secretariat (frequency varies—annually until 1976 and since 1980). (c) Annual Reports, where issued, of countries participating in the Plan, *eg* of the Commonwealth Scholarship Commission in the United Kingdom.

Commonwealth Scholarship Agencies

Candidates must apply to the agency in their own country and not to the agency in the awarding country. Agency addresses are listed below.

Anguilla: Department of Public Administration, Secretariat, The Valley, Anguilla, West Indies (Permanent Secretary)

*At the Ninth Conference of Commonwealth Ministers (Cyprus 1984) the Bahamas, Guyana, Kenya, Papua New Guinea and Zimbabwe declared their intention of becoming awarding countries under the Plan.

COMMONWEALTH SCHOLARSHIPS

The Table below shows the number of Scholars holding awards in each country in the year April 1, 1995 to March 31, 1996 (the count was taken in the first term of the academic year beginning in that year).

		AWARDING COUNTRIES (i.e. Countries where Awards Held)							
		Australia	Canada	India	New Zealand	Nigeria	Trinidad	United Kingdom	Total
1	Anguilla		1					2	3	1
2	Antigua and Barbuda		3					2	5	2
3	Australia		17		2			52	71	3
4	Bahamas		3		2			1	6	4
5	Bangladesh	27	24	4	3		1	56	115	5
6	Barbados		3		3			6	12	6
7	Belize		0		2			1	3	7
8	Bermuda		2					3	5	8
9	Botswana		2		1			2	5	9
10	British Virgin Islands		3					0	3	10
11	Brunei Darussalam		0					0	0	11
12	Canada	5	n/a	3	9			90	107	12
13	Cayman Islands		0					0	0	13
14	Cook Islands	3	0					0	3	14
15	Cyprus		4	1	2			14	21	15
16	Dominica		1					0	1	16
17	Falkland Islands		0					1	1	17
18	Gambia		3					7	10	18
19	Ghana	5	14	5	3	1		14	42	19
20	Gibraltar		0					1	1	20
21	Grenada		2		1			1	4	21
22	Guyana		5	1				13	19	22
23	Hong Kong		8		1			7	16	23
24	India	83	56		6			129	274	24
25	Jamaica		8		3			8	19	25
26	Kenya	52	14	8	1		1	15	91	26
27	Kiribati		0					0	3	27
28	Lesotho	2	4					2	8	28
29	Malawi	2	5		1			5	13	29
30	Malaysia		0	2				17	19	30
31	Maldives		2		1			3	6	31
32	Malta	1	5	3	2			6	17	32
33	Mauritius	5	4	24	2			6	41	33
34	Monserrat		0					0	0	34
35	Namibia		0	1				2	3	35
36	Nauru	1	0					0	1	36
37	New Zealand	7	9	1				19	36	37
38	Nigeria	15	26	3			1	72	117	38
39	Pakistan	55	12					36	103	39
40	Papua New Guinea	45	2					4	51	40
41	St Helena		0					1	1	41
42	St Kitts and Nevis		2					2	4	42
43	St Lucia		1		2			1	4	43
44	St Vincent		2		2			1	5	44
45	Seychelles		2					4	6	45
46	Sierra Leone	2	5			1		3	11	46
47	Singapore		0					8	8	47
48	Solomon Islands		1					2	3	48
49	South Africa		0		1			1	2	49
50	Sri Lanka	6	18	8				25	57	50
51	Swaziland		2				1	2	5	51
52	Tanzania		19	3	2			16	40	52
53	Tonga	7	0					1	8	53
54	Trinidad and Tobago		4	2		1		11	18	54
55	Turks and Caicos		1					0	1	55
56	Tuvalu		0		1			0	1	56
57	Uganda	32	11	9				8	60	57
58	United Kingdom	11	26	5	10			n/a	52	58
59	Vanuatu	2	0					1	3	59
60	Western Samoa	6	0		1	1		0	7	60
61	Zambia		4	4				13	21	61
62	Zimbabwe	2	15	3	1			9	30	62
	Total	379	365	90	65	3	4	706	1612	

There was no data received from the following awarding countries: Brunei, Hong Kong, Malaysia, Malta, Sierra Leone, Sri Lanka, Swaziland, Tanzania or Uganda. The origin of Canada's new awardees was not specified. Nigeria was suspended from the Commonwealth in the year under review.
Source: Commonwealth Scholarship and Fellowship Plan Report (1993–94, 1994–95, 1995–96), Commonwealth Secretariat.

Antigua and Barbuda: Ministry of Education, Youth, Sports and Community Development, Church Street, St John's, Antigua, West Indies (Permanent Secretary)

Australia: (in respect of developing countries) Australian International Development Assistance Bureau, GPO Box 887, Canberra, ACT, Australia 2601 (Secretary)

(In respect of developed countries) Scholarships Unit, I.D.P. Education Australia, GPO Box 2006, Canberra, ACT, Australia 2601 (Manager)

Bahamas: Ministry of Education and Culture, PO Box N-3913, Shirley Street, Nassau, Bahamas (Permanent Secretary)

Bangladesh: Ministry of Education, Building No 6, 17th & 18th Floor, Bangladesh Secretariat, Dhaka, Bangladesh (Secretary)

Barbados: Ministry of Education, Youth Affairs and Culture, Jemmotts Lane, St Michael, Barbados (Permanent Secretary)

Belize: Ministry of the Public Service, Belmopan, Belize (Permanent Secretary)

Bermuda: Ministry of Education, PO Box HM1185, Hamilton HM EX, Bermuda (Chief Education Officer)

Botswana: Department of Student Placement and Welfare, Ministry of Education, Private Bag 005, Gaborone, Botswana (Bursaries Secretary)

British Virgin Islands: Ministry of Education and Culture, Government of the British Virgin Islands, Road Town, Tortola, British Virgin Islands (Permanent Secretary)

Brunei Darussalam: Ministry of Education, Bandar Seri Bagawan 1170, Negara Brunei Darussalam (Permanent Secretary)

Cameroon: Ministry of Higher Education, Department of Student Assistance, Academic and Professional Guidance, PO Box 1457, Yaoundé, Cameroon (Secretary)

Canada: International Council for Canadian Studies, Commonwealth Scholarships Section, 325 Dalhousie Street, Suite 800, Ottawa, Ontario, Canada K1N 7G2 (Program Officer)

Cayman Islands: Department of Education, PO Box 910, George Town, Grand Cayman (Chief Education Officer)

Cyprus: Ministry of Foreign Affairs, Nicosia, Cyprus (Permanent Secretary)

Dominica: Establishment, Personnel and Training Department, Office of the Prime Minister, Government Headquarters, Kennedy Avenue, Roseau, Dominica (Chief Personnel Officer)

Falkland Islands: Education Department, Falkland Islands Government, Stanley, Falkland Islands, South Atlantic (Director of Education)

Fiji: Education, Science and Technology, Fiji (Permanent Secretary)

Gambia: Ministry of Education, No 1 Bedford Place Building, Banjul, The Gambia (Permanent Secretary)

Ghana: Scholarships Secretariat, PO Box M75, Ministry Branch Post Office, Accra, Ghana (Registrar of Scholarships)

Gibraltar: Department of Education, 40 Town Range, Gibraltar (Director of Education)

Grenada: Department of Personnel and Management Services, Prime Minister's Office, Botanical Gardens, Tanteen, St George's, Grenada (Permanent Secretary)

Guyana: Office of the President, Public Service Management, Scholarships Administration Division, Vlissengen Road and Durban Street, Georgetown, Guyana (Permanent Secretary)

India: (in respect of offers to Indians) Ministry of Human Resource Development (Department of Education), External Scholarships Division, A1, W3, Curzon Road Barracks, Kasturba Gandhi Marg, New Delhi, India 110 001 (Deputy Educational Adviser)

(In respect of awards held in India) Indian Council for Cultural Relations, Azad Bhavan, Indraprastha Estates, New Delhi, India 110 002 (Director-General)

Jamaica: (in respect of awards made to Jamaican nationals) Management Development Division, Human Resource Management and Development Branch, (Office of the Cabinet), Citibank Building, 8th Floor, 63–67 Knutsford Boulevard, Kingston 5, Jamaica (Principal Director)

(In respect of awards held in Jamaica) Ministry of Education and Culture, 2 National Heroes Circle, PO Box 498, Kingston, Jamaica (Permanent Secretary)

Kenya: Ministry of Education, Jogoo House, Harambee Avenue, PO Box 30040, Nairobi, Kenya (Permanent Secretary)

Kiribati: Ministry of Education, Training and Technology, PO Box 263, Bikenibeu, Tarawa, Kiribati, Central Pacific (Secretary)

Lesotho: National Manpower Development Secretariat, PO Box 517, Maseru 100, Lesotho (Director)

Malawi: Department of Human Resource Management and Development, PO Box 30227, Lilongwe 3, Malawi (Secretary)

Malaysia: Public Services Department, Training Division, Level 2, Block B, Complex JPA, Tun Ismail Road, 50510 Kuala Lumpur, Malaysia (Director-General)

Maldives: Department of External Resources, Ministry of Foreign Affairs, Malé, The Maldives (Director of External Resources)

Malta: Ministry of Education and Human Resources, Floriana, Malta (Assistant Director of Education)

Mauritius: Ministry of Education and Human Resource Development, Edith Cavell Street, Port Louis, Mauritius (Permanent Secretary)

Montserrat: Department of Administration, Government Headquarters, PO Box 292, Plymouth, Montserrat, West Indies (Permanent Secretary)

Mozambique: Ministry of Education, 167–24 Julho Avenue, Maputo, Mozambique (Minister of Education)

Namibia: Ministry of Higher Education, Vocational Training, Science and Technology, Bursaries and Qualifications Division, Private Bag 13391, Windhoek, Namibia (Permanent Secretary)

Nauru: Department of Education, Aiwo District, Republic of Nauru (Secretary)

New Zealand: New Zealand Vice-Chancellors' Committee, PO Box 11–915, Manners Street, Wellington, New Zealand (Scholarships Officer)

Nigeria: Federal Scholarship Board, Federal Ministry of Education, Block 353, Wuse, Zone 6, PMB 134, Abuja, Nigeria (Secretary, Scholarship Board)

Pakistan: (International Co-operation Wing), Ministry of Education, Islamabad, Pakistan (Deputy Educational Adviser (Scholarships))

Papua New Guinea: Department of Personnel Management, PO, Wards Strip, Waigani, National Capital District, Papua New Guinea (Secretary)

St Helena: Education Department, Government of St Helena, Jamestown, St Helena (Chief Education Officer)

St Kitts Nevis: Establishment Division, Government Headquarters, PO Box 186, Church Street, Basse terre, St Kitts, West Indies (Permanent Secretary)

St Lucia: Ministry of Education, Human Resource Development, Youth and Sports, Castries, St Lucia, West Indies (Permanent Secretary)

St Vincent and the Grenadines: Service Commissions Department, Kingstown, St Vincent and the Grenadines , West Indies (Chief Personnel Officer)

Seychelles: Ministry of Education, PO Box 48, Mont Fleuri, Victoria, Mahe, Republic of Seychelles (Principal Secretary)

Sierra Leone: Ministry of Education, New England, Freetown, Sierra Leone (Chief Education Officer)

Singapore: Prime Minister's Office, Public Service Division, 100 High Street, No. 07–01, The Treasury, Singapore 179 434 (Permanent Secretary)

Solomon Islands: National Training Unit, Ministry of Education and Human Resources Development, PO Box G28, Honiara, Solomon Islands (Permanent Secretary)

South Africa: International Relations, Department of Education, 123 Schoeman Street, Pretoria, 0002 South Africa (Director)

Sri Lanka: Office of the Minister of Higher Education, 18 Ward Place, Colombo 7, Sri Lanka (Secretary)

Swaziland: Ministry of Labour and Public Service, PO Box 170, Mbabane, Swaziland (Principal Secretary)

Tanzania: Ministry of Science, Technology and Higher Education, PO Box 2645, Dar es Salaam, Tanzania (Principal Secretary)

Tonga: Ministry of Education, PO Box 61, Nuku'alofa, Tonga (Minister)

Trinidad & Tobago: Personnel Department, Scholarships and Advanced Training Section, AMBA Building, 55–57 St Vincent Street, Port of Spain, Trinidad (Chief Personnel Officer)

Turks & Caicos Islands: Staff Training Unit, South Base, Grand Turk, Turks and Caicos Islands, West Indies (Training Manager)

Tuvalu: Personnel and Training Division, Office of the Prime Minster, Private Mail Bag, Funafuti, Tuvalu (Deputy Secretary)

Uganda: The Central Scholarships Committee (CSC), Ministry of Education and Sports, PO Box 7063, Kampala, Uganda (Permanent Secretary)

United Kingdom: Commonwealth Scholarship Commission in the United Kingdom, John Foster House, 36 Gordon Square, London, England WC1H 0PF (Executive Secretary)

Vanuatu: Training and Scholarships Co-ordination Unit, Ministry of Education, PMB 059, Port Vila, Vanuatu (Principal Scholarships Officer)

Western Samoa: Staff Training and Scholarships Committee, Ministry of Foreign Affairs, PO Box L1861, Apia, Western Samoa (Secretary)

Zambia: Bursaries Committee, Ministry of Higher Education, PO Box 50093, Lusaka, Zambia (Secretary)

Zimbabwe: Ministry of Higher Education, PO Box UA275, Union Avenue, Harare, Zimbabwe (Secretary)

[Information compiled by the secretariat of the Commonwealth Scholarship Commission in the United Kingdom as at July 1998 and edited by the ACU]

INDEXES

INDEX TO INSTITUTIONS

The contents of the Yearbook are listed at the beginning of each volume.

This is a selective index to institutions and organisations named in the Yearbook. Where appropriate, the letters a, b and c are used to indicate the first, second and third columns of each page, and the abbreviated name of the university in whose chapter a particular institution appears is included.

The index does not attempt to include all the references that there may be to every institution or organisation mentioned in the book. For example, references in 'national introductions' are not indexed.

Centres, institutes, etc., which form an integral part of a university are individually indexed only if they have a distinctive name. For example, there are index entries for the John Deutsch Institute for the Study of Economic Policy at Queen's University at Kingston (but not for its Centre for International Relations) and for the Scottish Hotel School at the University of Strathclyde (but not for the Strathclyde Graduate

Business School). However all colleges, centres, institutes, etc, which have an independent existence but are also constituents of, or associated with, the universities are entered by name in this index, whether or not they have a distinctive title. Institutions affiliated to universities in Bangladesh, India, Pakistan and Sri Lanka are indexed only by locality, under 'Bangladesh colleges located at', 'Indian colleges located at', etc.

INDEX TO WORLD WIDE WEB ADDRESSES

The following index lists the World Wide Web addresses, or uniform resource locators (urls), supplied for publication in the Yearbook by universities, inter-university bodies and other institutions with entries in the book. In most cases, the url for the institution's home page is given here. The non-inclusion of an institution's web address does not imply that it does not have one, only that it has not been supplied. Other contact details are provided in the body of the book under the relevant institution's heading.

Aberdeen, University of — http://www.abdn.ac.uk
Abertay Dundee, University of — http://www.tay.ac.uk
Abitibi-Témiscamingue, Université du
  Québec en — http://www.uqat.uquebec.ca
Acadia University — http://www.acadiau.ca
Adelaide, University of — http://www.adelaide.edu.au
Advanced Study, School of (*Lond.*) — http://www.sas.ac.uk
Aga Khan University — http://www.aku.edu
Agence Universitaire de la Francophonie — http://www.aupelf-uref.org
Alberta, University of — http://www.ualberta.ca
Anglia Polytechnic University — http://www.anglia.ac.uk
Anna University — http://www.annauniv.org
Armand-Frappier, Institut (*Queb.*) — http://www.iaf.uquebec.ca
Association of Atlantic Universities — http://www.dal.ca/aau/
Association of Commonwealth Universities — http://www.acu.ac.uk
Association of European Universities — http://www.unige.ch/cre/
Association of Universities and Colleges of Canada — http://www.aucc.ca
Aston University — http://www.aston.ac.uk
Athabasca University — http://www.athabascau.ca
Atlantic Universities, Association of — http://www.dal.ca/aau/
Auckland, University of — http://www.auckland.ac.nz
Augustana University College — http://www.augustana.ab.ca
Australian Catholic University — http://www.acu.edu.au
Australian National University — http://www.anu.edu.au
Australian Vice-Chancellors' Committee (Council of
  Australian University Presidents) — http://www.avcc.edu.au

Ballarat, University of — http://www.ballarat.edu.au
Bath, University of — http://www.bath.ac.uk
Belfast, Queen's University of — http://www.qub.ac.uk
Bharathiar University — http://www.bharathi.ernet.in
Birkbeck College (*Lond.*) — http://www.bbk.ac.uk
Birmingham, University of — http://www.bham.ac.uk
Bishop's University — http://www.ubishops.ca
Bolton Institute — http://www.bolton.ac.uk
Bond University — http://www.bond.edu.au
Botswana, University of — http://www.ub.bw
Bournemouth University — http://www.bournemouth.ac.uk
Bradford, University of — http://www.brad.ac.uk
Brandon University — http://www.brandonu.ca
Brighton, University of — http://www.brighton.ac.uk
Bristol, University of — http://www.bris.ac.uk
British Columbia, University of — http://www.ubc.ca
British Columbia Institute of Technology — http://www.bcit.bc.ca
Brock University — http://www.brocku.ca
Brunei Darussalam, University of — http://www.ubd.edu.bn
Brunel University — http://www.brunel.ac.uk/
Business Agriculture and Technology,
  International University of — http://www.bangla.net/iubat

Calgary, University of — http://www.ucalgary.ca
Cambridge, University of — http://www.cam.ac.uk
Canada, Association of Universities and Colleges of — http://www.aucc.ca
Canberra, University of — http://www.canberra.edu.au
Canterbury, University of — http://www.regy.canterbury.ac.nz
Cape Breton, University College of — http://www.uccb.ns.ca
Cape Town, University of — http://www.uct.ac.za
Cariboo, University College of the — http://www.cariboo.bc.ca
Carleton University — http://www.carleton.ca
Catholic Universities, International Federation of — http://www.fiuc.org
Central England in Birmingham, University of — http://www.uce.ac.uk
Central Lancashire, University of — http://www.uclan.ac.uk
Central Queensland University — http://www.cqu.edu.au
Charles Sturt University — http://www.csu.edu.au
Cheltenham and Gloucester College
  of Higher Education — http://www.chelt.ac.uk
Chinese University of Hong Kong — http://www.cuhk.edu.hk
Chittagong, University of — http://www.spctnet.com/cu.html
City University (UK) — http://www.city.ac.uk
Cochin University of Science and Technology — http://cusat.edu/home.htm
Committee of Vice-Chancellors and Principals
  of the Universities of the United Kingdom — http://www.cvcp.ac.uk
Commonwealth Universities, Association of — http://www.acu.ac.uk
Concordia University — http://www.concordia.ca
Concordia University College of Alberta — http://www.concordia.ab.ca
Conference of Rectors and Principals
  of Quebec Universities — http://www.crepuq.qc.ca

Council of Ontario Universities — http://www.cou.on.ca
Cranfield University — http://www.cranfield.ac.uk
Curtin University of Technology — http://www.curtin.edu.au
Cyprus, University of — http://www.ucy.ac.cy

Dalhousie University — http://www.dal.ca
De Montfort University — http://www.dmu.ac.uk
Deakin University — http://www.deakin.edu.au
Delhi, University of — http://www.du.ac.in
Derby, University of — http://www.derby.ac.uk
Dundee, University of — http://www.dundee.ac.uk
Durham, University of — http://www.dur.ac.uk

East Anglia, University of — http://www.uea.ac.uk
East London, University of — http://www.uel.ac.uk
École de Technologie Supérieure (*Queb.*) — http://www.etsmtl.ca
École nationale d'administration
  publique (*Queb.*) — http://www.enap.uquebec.ca
Edinburgh, University of — http://www.ed.ac.uk
Edith Cowan University — http://www.cowan.edu.au/
Eduardo Mondlane University — http://www.uem.mz
Education, Institute of (*Lond.*) — http://www.ioe.ac.uk/
Emily Carr Institute of Art and Design — http://www.eciad.bc.ca
Essex, University of — http://www.essex.ac.uk
European Universities, Association of — http://www.unige.ch/cre/
Exeter, University of — http://www.ex.ac.uk

Flinders University of South Australia — http://www.flinders.edu.au
Fraser Valley, University College of the — http://www.ucfv.bc.ca

Ghana, University of — http://www.ug.edu.gh
Ghulam Ishaq Khan Institute of Engineering
  Sciences and Technology — http://giki.edu.pk
Glamorgan, University of — http://www.glam.ac.uk
Glasgow, University of — http://www.gla.ac.uk
Goldsmiths College, University of London — http://www.gold.ac.uk
Greenwich, University of — http://www.gre.ac.uk
Griffith University — http://www.gu.edu.au/
Guelph, University of — http://www.uoguelph.ca

Hawkesbury, University of
  Western Sydney — http://www.hawkesbury.uws.edu.au
Heriot-Watt University — http://www.hw.ac.uk
Hertfordshire, University of — http://www.herts.ac.uk
Higher Education, Inter-American
  Organization for — http://www.oui-iohe.qc.ca
Historical Research, Institute of (*Lond.*) — http://ihr.sas.ac.uk
Hong Kong, Chinese University of — http://www.cuhk.edu.hk
Hong Kong, University of — http://www.hku.hk
Hong Kong Polytechnic University — http://www.polyu.edu.hk
Huddersfield, University of — http://www.hud.ac.uk
Hull, Université du Québec à — http://www.uqah.uquebec.ca
Hull, University of — http://www.hull.ac.uk
Hyderabad, University of — http://www.uohyd.ernet.in

Imperial College of Science, Technology
  and Medicine (*Lond.*) — http://www.ic.ac.uk
Independent University, Bangladesh — http://www.iub-bd.edu
Indian Institute of Technology, Bombay — http://www.iitb.ernet.in
Indian Institute of Technology, Kanpur — http://www.iitk.ernet.in
Indian Institute of Technology, Madras — http://www.iitm.ernet.in
Indira Gandhi Institute of Development Research — http://www.igidr.ac.in
Indira Gandhi National Open University — http://www.ignou.edu
Indira Kala Sangit Vishwavidyalaya — http://www.mp.nic.in/kghuniv.html
Institut Armand-Frappier (*Queb.*) — http://www.iaf.uquebec.ca
Institut national de la recherche
  scientifique (*Queb.*) — http://www.inrs.uquebec.ca
Institute of Education (*Lond.*) — http://www.ioe.ac.uk/
Institute of Historical Research (*Lond.*) — http://ihr.sas.ac.uk
Inter-American Organization for
  Higher Education — http://www.oui-iohe.qc.ca
International Association of Universities — http://www.unesco.org/iau
International Federation of Catholic Universities — http://www.fiuc.org
International Islamic University, Malaysia — http://www.iiu.edu.my
International University of Business
  Agriculture and Technology — http://www.bangla.net/iubat
Isra University — http://www.isra.edu.pk

INDEX TO DEPARTMENT NAMES

This index includes a reference to the names of all academic departments, sub-departments and special centres which appear under the heading 'Academic Units' in the university chapters. The letters a, b and c are used to indicate the first, second and third columns of each page, and the abbreviated name of the university in whose chapter a particular department appears is included (*example*: Geography, *Adel.* 7a, *Dar.* 1293a, *Waik.* 993a).

Since names are shown exactly as they appear in the university chapters, this means that a department called, for example, Agricultural Engineering, may, depending on the institution, appear under either 'Agricultural Engineering' or 'Engineering, Agricultural'. Cross-references from/to departments in the university chapters have also been included in order to make the index as full a 'subject index' as possible. Multi-departmental faculty names (eg Medicine) and campus names are not indexed, but their departments are included. Acronyms have not been indexed.

Aboriginal and Islander Support Unit, *S.Aust.* 156b
Aboriginal and Multicultural Studies, Centre for Research in, *NE* 105b
Aboriginal and Torres Strait Islanders Program Unit, *Macq.* 72b
Aboriginal Economic Policy Research, Centre for, *ANU* 17c
Aboriginal Education Centre, *W'gong.* 215b, *Windsor* 540b
Aboriginal Environments Research Centre, *Qld.* 139b
Aboriginal Management and Human Services, *N.Territory* 126c
Aboriginal Programmes, Centre for, *W.Aust.* 205b
Aboriginal Research and Resource Centre, *NSW* 118b
Aboriginal Research Institute, *S.Aust.* 159a
Aboriginal Studies, *Macq.* 71b
Aboriginal Studies, Centre for, *Curtin* 38a
Aboriginal Studies in Music, Centre for, *Adel.* 5a
Aboriginal Teacher Education, *Qu.* 457c
Academic Development, *De Mont.* 1390a
Academic Development Centre, *N-W(S.Af.)* 1190c, *Witw.* 1247a
Academic Development, Centre for, *Durban-W.* 1172b
Academic Development Programme, *Cape Town* 1168b
Academic Development Programmes, Division for (DADP), *Stell.* 1231a
Academic Development Unit, *La Trobe* 68c
Academic Innovation and Continuing Education, Division of, *Stir.* 1730b
Academic Pharmacy Practice, Division of, *Leeds* 1489c
Academic Planning and Course Production, Bureau of, *A.Iqbal Open* 1087b
Academic Practice, Centre for, *Strath.* 1737b
Academic Staff College, *And.* 590a, *B'thiar.* 626c, *Calicut* 638a, *DAV* 651b, *Gauh.* 667c, *GND* 681b, *Gujar.* 670b, *HP* 685a, *Hyd.* 689c, *Kashmir* 728a, *Mys.* 778c, *Pondicherry* 806c, *Saur.* 838c, *S.Venkat.* 855a
Academic Surgical Unit, *Hull* 1467b
Academic Virology Section, *Lond.* 1555c
Academic Writing, *Winn.* 541a
Access and Advice, *E.Lond.* 1412a
Access and Community Studies, *N.Territory* 126c
Access China Centre, *Macq.* 75b
Accident and Emergency, *Lond.* 1538c, 1561b, 1576c
Accident Research and Road Safety, Centre for, *Qld.UT* 148a
Accident Service (Johannesburg Hospital), *Witw.* 1246c
Accountancy, *Aberd.* 1313b, *Abuja* 1003b, *Baroda* 749a, *C'dia.* 321a, *C.England* 1398a, *Chinese HK* 1832a, *Durban-W.* 1170a, *Enugu SUST* 1024b, *Exe.* 1426b, *HKPU* 1845c, *Hudd.* 1459a, *H-W* 1449c, *L&H* 1504b, *Maid.* 1047b, *Malawi* 907c, *Malta* 946b, *Maur.* 952b, *Natal* 1183c, *N.Azikiwe* 1056c, *Nigeria* 1050b, *Otago* 980a, *Pret.* 1202b, *Qld.UT* 145c, *RMIT* 150a, *Stell.* 1224a, *Thames V.* 1749a, *Utara, Malaysia* 943c, *Z'bwe.* 1826a
Accountancy and Audit, *Potchef.* 1201a
Accountancy and Auditing, *Stell.* 1230c
Accountancy and Business, *Nan.Tech.* 1136a
Accountancy and Business Finance, *Dund.* 1396b
Accountancy and Business Law, *Massey* 974a
Accountancy and Commercial Law, School of, *Well.* 986b
Accountancy and Finance, *Hudd.* 1461a, *H-W* 1451a, *L&H* 1505a, *Sab.* 1281b, *S.Leone* 1131b, *Stir.* 1730b
Accountancy and Financial Management, *Sri Jay.* 1283b
Accountancy and Human Resource Management, *Kelaniya* 1267c
Accountancy and Law, *Abertay* 1318b
Accountancy and Statistics, *M.Sukh.* 772a
Accountancy, Applied, *S.Af.* 1216c
Accountancy, Finance and Information Systems, *Cant.* 968c
Accountancy Group, *Massey* 974a
Accountancy, School of, *Pret.* 1202b, *Wat.* 511c
Accountancy, Statistics and Mathematics, School of, *Potchef.* 1199c
Accountant Training, Chartered, *Potchef.* 1199c
Accountant Training, Financial, *Potchef.* 1199c
Accountant Training, Management, *Potchef.* 1199c

Accounting, *A.Bello* 1008b, *Alta.* 280a, *Athab.* 290b, *Belf.* 1684a, 1686a, *Benin* 1014c, *Bhutto IST* 1118a, *Bond* 23b, *Brad.* 1341a, *Br.Col.* 295c, 297a, *Brist.* 1345a, *Cape Town* 1159c, *Chitt.* 234a, *Cran.* 1387b, *Curtin* 34c, *Dar.* 1291c, *Dhaka* 237b, *E.Cowan* 44a, *E.Lond.* 1410a, 1410b, *G.Caledonian* 1444b, *IIU Malaysia* 912b, *Islamic(B'desh.)* 246a, *JN Vyas* 703a, *Kent* 1472c, *Kenyatta* 890a, *Laval* 350b, *Liv.* 1507c, *Lond.Bus.* 1544a, *Mak.* 1302a, *Montr.* 419a, *Nair.* 900c, *Namibia* 955a, *N.Lond.* 1627a, *Nott.* 1633a, *Nott.Trent* 1639a, *NSW* 108a, *NU Malaysia* 923b, *NU Singapore* 1145c, *NUST Bulawayo* 1824b, *N-W(S.Af.)* 1189a, *O.Awolowo* 1059a, *OFS* 1192a, *Ogon State* 1064a, *Ondo State* 1066a, *Oxf.* 1648c, *P.Elizabeth* 1195b, *P.Harcourt* 1067b, *Queb.* 449a, *Rajsh.* 254b, *Rand Afrikaans* 1210b, *Rhodes* 1213c, *S.Af.* 1217a, *St Mary's(Can.)* 471a, *S.Aust.* 156b, *S.Bank* 1720a, *S.Leone* 1133a, *Swazi.* 1288b, *Syd.* 170b, *Uyo* 1072b, *Waik.* 991b, *Wales* 1754b, 1761b, *W.Cape* 1235c, *Witw.* 1240a, *W.Syd.* 210a, *York(Can.)* 545a
Accounting and Auditing, *North(S.Af.)* 1187c, *Venda* 1233b
Accounting and Business Management, *La Trobe* 69c
Accounting and Business Method, *Edin.* 1413c
Accounting and Finance, *Auck.* 959b, *Birm.* 1327a, 1327c, *Bourne.* 1339a, *Brock* 311b, *City(UK)* 1380a, *Copperbelt* 1820b, *De Mont.* 1390a, *Deakin* 39c, *Edo State* 1022a, *Glas.* 1436c, *Griff.* 54b, *Hull* 1467c, *James Cook* 61b, *Kingston(UK)* 1476b, *Lanc.* 1479c, *Leeds Met.* 1495c, *Lond.* 1546a, *Luton* 1593a, *Macq.* 72c, *Manc.* 1596c, *Manc.Met.* 1610b, *Manit.* 390a, *Melb.* 78a, *Monash* 88b, *Napier* 1617a, *Natal* 1178b, *Newcastle(NSW)* 122b, *Newcastle(UK)* 1620a, *Putra* 928b, *Rajarata* 1279a, *Strath.* 1733a, *Tas.* 183a, 186b, *Uganda Martyrs* 1307b, *Victoria UT* 195b, *W.Aust.* 200a, *W'gong.* 212c
Accounting and Finance, Centre for Research in, *Monash* 95c
Accounting and Financial Management, *NE* 102b, *S.Pac.* 1252c
Accounting and Management Sciences, *Jos* 1040b, *Portsmouth* 1677a
Accounting and Management Studies, *Botswana* 262a
Accounting and Mathematics, School of, *Glam.* 1432b
Accounting, Banking and Economics, School of, *Wales* 1757b
Accounting, Banking and Finance, *Griff.* 54c
Accounting, Banking and Finance, School of, *Canberra* 25b
Accounting, Business and Finance, *Hull* 1464b
Accounting, Centre for, *OFS* 1194b
Accounting, Division of, *S.Bank* 1720b
Accounting, Economics and Languages, *Paisley* 1670a
Accounting, Finance and Business Law, *N.Territory* 126c
Accounting, Finance and Management, *Essex* 1423b
Accounting, Finance and Property Studies, *Lincoln(NZ)* 973a
Accounting, International Centre for Research in, *Lanc.* 1482b
Accounting Research and Education, Centre for, *Wat.* 519b
Accounting Research Centre, *Syd.* 180a
Accounting, School of, *P.Elizabeth* 1198a, *Technol.Syd.* 188c
Accounting Science, School for, *Potchef.* 1199c
Accounting Studies, *Ghana* 567a
Acoustics and Audio Engineering, *Salf.* 1700b
Action Research in Professional Practice, Centre for, *Bath* 1324c
Activity and Ageing, Centre for, *W.Ont.* 530c
Actuarial Mathematics and Statistics, *H-W* 1449c
Actuarial Research Centre, *City(UK)* 1382b
Actuarial Science, *Kent* 1474a, *Lond.* 1546a, *NU Malaysia* 925b, *Pret.* 1202c, *Stell.* 1224a, *Wat.* 511c, *Witw.* 1240a
Actuarial Science and Insurance, *Nan.Tech.* 1136a
Actuarial Science and Statistics, *City(UK)* 1380a
Actuarial Sciences, *W.Ont.* 521c
Actuarial Sciences, School of, *Laval* 350b
Actuarial Studies and Demography, *Macq.* 72c

Actuarial Studies and Research, Warren Centre for, *Manit.* 399c
Acute and Critical Care, *Luton* 1593b, 1594b
Acute and Critical Care Nursing, *Sheff.* 1711a
Addictive Behaviour and Psychological Medicine, *Lond.* 1562c
Adhunik Bhasha and Bhasha Vigyan, *Samp.Sanskrit* 834b
Administration, *A.Bello* 1008b, *Laur.* 346a, *Laval* 350c, *Maid.* 1047b, *Malaya* 916b, *New Br.* 427c, *Ott.* 438b, *Queb.* 449a, *Regina* 461b, *Sci.U.Malaysia* 932a, *Tas.* 183a
Administration and Educational Services, *Bran.* 292c
Administration and Information Management, School of,, *Ryerson* 467a
Administration and Management, *S.Leone* 1131b
Administration and Training, *NE* 102b
Administration, Institute of, *A.Bello* 1011a, *NSW* 118b
Administration, School of, *Ghana* 567a
Administrative and Information Studies, *W.Ont.* 521c
Administrative Science, *Baloch.* 1093a, *Punjab* 1112b
Administrative Sciences, *Quaid-i-Azam* 1115a
Administrative Studies, *Botswana* 262a, *Malawi* 906b, *NUL* 903a, *P.Harcourt* 1067b, *PNG* 1127a, *Swazi.* 1288b, *York(Can.)* 552a, *Zambia* 1821b, *Z'bwe.* 1826a
Administrative Studies Programme, *Trent* 509b
Administrative Studies, School of, *Canberra* 25b
Administrative Studies/Business Computing, *Winn.* 541a
Adult and Communications Studies, *Mak.* 1305b
Adult and Community Education, *Aust.Cath.* 13b, *Natal* 1178c
Adult and Continuing Education, *And.* 590c, *B'thiar.* 626a, *B'tullah.V.* 623b, *Calabar* 1019b, *De Mont.* 1390a, *Glas.* 1436c, *Madr.* 743b
Adult and Continuing Education and Extension, *Dr RML Awadh* 662b, *GRI* 664a, *JMI* 709a, *Kakatiya* 719b, *Mumbai* 776b, *SSJ Maharaj* 846c
Adult and Continuing Education, Centre for, *NE Hill* 791c, *W.Cape* 1238b
Adult and Continuing Education Programme, *Malta* 946c
Adult and Vocational Education, *New Br.* 428a
Adult, Continuing and Extension Education, *M.Gandhi* 757a
Adult Continuing Education, *Kashmir* 728a, *Sheff.* 1704b, *Wales* 1769b
Adult Continuing Education and Extension, *Burd.* 634a, 635b, *Delhi* 647a, *Gauh.* 667c, *Panjab* 803c
Adult Dental Health, *Wales* 1771b
Adult Education, *Botswana* 262a, *Exe.* 1426b, *HNB Garh.* 683a, *Ib.* 1034b, *Leic.* 1502a, *Nagar.* 782c, *Nigeria* 1051c, *NUL* 904b, *St FX* 469b, *S.Venkat.* 855a, *Z'bwe.* 1826a
Adult Education and Community Services, *Bayero* 1012b
Adult Education and Extension, *Dar.* 1291c
Adult Education and Extension Services, Centre for, *A.Bello* 1011a
Adult Education and Extension Studies, *Zambia* 1822a
Adult Education and Extra Mural Studies, *Cape Town* 1159c
Adult Education and Extra-Mural Studies, *Benin* 1017c, *S.Leone* 1133c
Adult Education, Centre for, *Natal* 1183c
Adult Education, Centre of, *Jammu* 712a
Adult Education, Continuing Education and Extension, *Guj.Vid.* 673a
Adult Education, Division of, *Witw.* 1241c
Adult Education, Institute of, *Ghana* 569c
Adult Education, School of, *Belf.* 1684a
Adult Learning, Centre for, *Ryerson* 486b
Adult Nursing, *City(UK)* 1382b
Adult Physical Health, *Napier* 1618b
Advaita Vedanta, *Rashtriya SV* 827b
Advanced Analytical Centre, *James Cook* 63a
Advanced Biblical Studies, Centre for, *Lond.* 1542b
Advanced Biomedical Studies, Centre for, *S.Aust.* 159a
Advanced Business Programme, *Otago* 980a
Advanced Catalysts and Adsorbents Research Group, *S.Aust.* 159a
Advanced Composite Manufacturing, Centre for Research in, *Plym.* 1675c

Advanced Composite Structures, Co-operative Research Centre for, Monash 95c
Advanced Computational Modelling Centre, Qld. 139b
Advanced Computing Research Centre, S.Aust. 159a
Advanced Construction Studies, Centre for, Nan.Tech. 1138a
Advanced Empirical Software Research, Centre for, NSW 118b
Advanced Engineering Centre for Manufacturing, RMIT 154b
Advanced Engineering, Warren Centre for, Syd. 180a
Advanced Historical Research, St John's House Centre for, St And. 1699a, Zululand 1248a
Advanced Inquiry in the Interactive Arts, Centre for, Wales 1778b
Advanced Magnetic Materials and Devices, Sheffield Centre for, Sheff. 1711b
Advanced Manufacturing Research, Centre for, S.Aust. 159a
Advanced Manufacturing Technology, School of, C.England 1376a
Advanced Manufacturing, Unit for (SENROB), Stell. 1231a
Advanced Materials Centre, Napier 1618b
Advanced Materials, Centre for, Warw. 1783a
Advanced Materials Research Centre, Nan.Tech. 1137b
Advanced Materials, St Andrew's Centre for, St And. 1699a
Advanced Materials Technology, Centre for, Monash 95c
Advanced Molecular Biology Centre, Punjab 1114a
Advanced Musical Studies, Institute of, Lond. 1542b
Advanced Numerical Computation in Engineering and Science, Centre for, NSW 118b
Advanced Nursing and Midwifery Studies, Napier 1618b
Advanced Performance Studies, Centre for, Lond. 1542b
Advanced Railway Research Centre, Sheff. 1711b
Advanced Research, Institute of, Aust.Cath. 11b
Advanced Social Research, Institute for, Witw. 1247b
Advanced Software, Laboratory for, Tech.U.Malaysia 941b
Advanced Studies, Centre for, NU Singapore 1154a
Advanced Studies, Directorate of, Faisalabad 1085b
Advanced Studies, Institute of, Brist. 1350b, Malaya 920b, Syd. 180a
Advanced Studies, School for, P.Elizabeth 1198a
Advanced Study, Centre of, Panjab 802c
Advanced Systems Engineering, CSIRO–Macquarie University Joint Research Centre for, Macq. 75b
Advanced Technologies and Processes, C.Qld. 28b
Advanced Technology Centre, Napier 1618c
Advanced Technology, Centre for, Warw. 1783a
Advanced Technology Education, Centre for, Ryerson 468b
Advanced Technology in Microelectronics, Centre for, Br.Col. 309a
Advanced Technology in Telecommunications, Centre for, RMIT 154b
Advanced Wastewater Management Centre, Qld. 139b
Advanced Welsh and Celtic Studies, Centre for, Wales 1753b
Advancement of Medicine, Centre for the, Manit. 399c
Advancement of Thinking, Centre for, Lond. 1542b
Advertising, MCN Journ. 759a
Advertising Management, G.Jamb. 678a
Aegean Archaeology, Centre for, Sheff. 1711b
Aerial Photography, Committee for, Camb. 1365b
Aeronautical Engineering, Anna 597a, Belf. 1685a, Kingston(UK) 1476b
Aeronautics, City(UK) 1380b, Lond. 1527a
Aeronautics and Astronautics, S'ton. 1724b
Aeronautics, College of, Cran. 1387b
Aerospace Design Technology, Sir Lawrence Wackett Centre for, RMIT 154b
Aerospace Engineering, NSW 111b
Aerospace Engineering Division, Manc. 1599b
Aerospace Medical Research Unit, McG. 376b
Aerospace Structures, Co-operative Research Centre for, RMIT 154b
Aerospace Studies, Institute for, Tor. 491c
Aesthetic Studies, Institute of, Kelaniya 1269c
Africa, Languages and Cultures of, Lond. 1563b
African and General Studies, Cape Coast 562a
African Languages, A.Bello 1008b, Kenyatta 890b, Nair. 901a, Namibia 955b, O.Awolowo 1059a, OFS 1192a, P.Elizabeth 1195c, Potchef. 1199c, Pret. 1202c, Rand Afrikaans 1210b, Rhodes 1213c, 1214c, S.Af. 1217a, Stell. 1224a, Venda 1233b, Witw. 1240a, Zululand 1248a
African Languages and Linguistics, Malawi 906b
African Languages and Literature, Botswana 262a, Cape Town 1159c, Lagos State 1045b, NUL 903a, Swazi. 1288b, Z'bwe. 1826a
African Law, North(S.Af.) 1187c
African Literature, Uyo 1072b, Witw. 1240a
African Ornithology, Percy Fitzpatrick Institute of, Cape Town 1168b
African Research and Documentation Centre, Uganda Martyrs 1307c
African Research Institute, La Trobe 69a
African Studies, Benin 1015a, Delhi 647a, Devel.Studies(Ghana) 564b, Dschang 269b, Ib. 1034b, J.Nehru U. 712a, Kumasi 571a, Nigeria 1051c, P.Harcourt 1067b, Uganda Martyrs 1307b
African Studies, Centre for, Cape Town 1160a, Dal. 334a, Liv. 1514b, Mumbai 776b
African Studies, Centre of, Camb. 1365b, Edin. 1413c, Lond. 1565b
African Studies, Hansberry Institute of, Nigeria 1055a
African Studies, Institute of, Ghana 569c, Ib. 1038c, Nair. 901a, 901c, S.Leone 1133a, 1133c
African Studies Unit, Leeds 1491a
Afrikaans, Namibia 955b, North(S.Af.) 1187c, N-W(S.Af.) 1189a, Pret. 1202c, Rand Afrikaans 1210b, S.Af. 1217b, Venda 1233b, Z'bwe. 1826b
Afrikaans and Dutch, P.Elizabeth 1195c, Potchef. 1199c, Stell. 1224a
Afrikaans and Nederlandic Studies, Rhodes 1213c, 1214c
Afrikaans and Nederlands, Durban-W. 1170a, OFS 1192a, W.Cape 1235c
Afrikaans and Netherlandic Studies, Cape Town 1160a
Afrikaans Cultural History, Stell. 1224b
Afrikaans, Division of, Stell. 1225a
Afrikaans en Nederlands, Natal 1178c, 1183c, Witw. 1240a
Afrikaanse Taal-en Kultuurvereniging Creative Writing School, Potchef. 1199c
Age and Cognitive Performance Research Centre, Manc. 1605c
Ageing and Health, Centre for Research on, La Trobe 69a
Ageing, Interdisciplinary Group on, W.Ont. 530c
Ageing, McGill Centre for Studies in, McG. 376c
Ageing Studies, Centre for, Flin. 52a
Aging and Health, Educational Centre for, McM. 387b
Aging, Centre on, Manit. 399c
Agnes Etherington Arts Centre, Qu. 460a
Agrarian Development Unit, Lond. 1578b
Agribusiness, Dschang 269b
Agribusiness and Economics Research, Lincoln(NZ) 973a, 973b
Agribusiness and Rural Development, L.Akin.UT 1043b
Agribusiness Management, Sab. 1281c
Agricultural and Biosystems Engineering, McG. 378b
Agricultural and Environmental Science, Newcastle(UK) 1620a
Agricultural and Food Economics, Reading 1690b
Agricultural and Food Science, Maur. 952b
Agricultural and Food Science, School of, Belf. 1684a
Agricultural and Forest Sciences, School of, Wales 1757c
Agricultural and Plantation Engineering, Open S.Lanka 1272a
Agricultural and Resource Economics, NE 102b, W.Aust. 200a
Agricultural and Science Education, Makurdi Ag. 1007a
Agricultural Biology, Jaffna 1265a, Peradeniya 1274b, 1277c, Ruhuna 1279b
Agricultural Botany, Annam. 598a, Reading 1690b
Agricultural Business Research Institute, NE 105b
Agricultural Chemistry, Annam. 598a, Ban. 614c, B'desh.Ag. 226b, Jaffna 1265a, McG. 378c, Ruhuna 1279c
Agricultural Chemistry and Biochemistry, Assam Ag. 605c
Agricultural Chemistry and Soil Science, Syd. 175c
Agricultural Economics, Annam. 598a, Assam Ag. 605b, Ban. 614c, B'desh.Ag. 226b, Br.Col. 295c, Eastern(S.Lanka) 1262b, Faisalabad 1083b, HPKV 686b, Ib. 1034b, Jaffna 1265a, McG. 378c, Mak. 1302a, Makurdi Ag. 1007a, Manc. 1596c, Nair. 896c, Natal 1183c, NDRI 786a, Nigeria 1051c, North(S.Af.) 1187c, O.Awolowo 1059a, OFS 1192a, Oxf. 1648c, Peradeniya 1274b, 1277c, Putra 928b, Rajendra Ag. 824c, Ruhuna 1279c, Stell. 1224b, Syd. 175c
Agricultural Economics and Agribusiness, Sokoine Ag. 1297a
Agricultural Economics and Business Management, Egerton 888a, Guelph 339b, Lond. 1578b
Agricultural Economics and Consumer Sciences, Laval 350c
Agricultural Economics and Extension, Akure 1028b, AT Balewa 1002a, Benin 1015a, Calabar 1019b, Cape Coast 562a, Edo State 1022a, Enugu SUST 1025c, Guy. 576b, Maid. 1047b, N-W(S.Af.) 1189b, Owerri 1031b, S.Leone 1134a, U.Danfodiyo 1070b, Uyo 1072b, Venda 1233c, WI 1816b, Yola 1033a, Zambia 1821b, Z'bwe. 1826b
Agricultural Economics and Farm Management, Abeokuta Ag. 1005b, Assam Ag. 605c, Kumasi 571a, Manit. 390b, Ogun State 1064a
Agricultural Economics and Food Marketing, Newcastle(UK) 1620a
Agricultural Economics and Management, Swazi. 1288c
Agricultural Economics and Rural Sociology, A.Bello 1010a, NUL 903b
Agricultural Economics, Extension and Rural Development, Pret. 1202c
Agricultural Economics, Rural Sociology and Extension, Umudike 1027b
Agricultural Economics Unit, Exe. 1426b, 1427a
Agricultural Economy and Farm Management, Ghana 567b
Agricultural Education, Faisalabad 1083b, S.Leone 1134a, Winneba 565b
Agricultural Education and Extension, Egerton 888b, Sokoine Ag. 1297b, Swazi. 1288c
Agricultural Engineering, A.Bello 1010a, Assam Ag. 605c, Cape Coast 562a, Dschang 269b, Egerton 888b, HPKV 686b, Ib. 1034c, Jaffna 1265a, Laval 350c, Lincoln(NZ) 973a, Maid. 1047b, Mak. 1302a, Makurdi Ag. 1007a, Malawi 906a, Nair. 897a, Natal 1183c, Nigeria 1051c, O.Awolowo 1059b, OFS 1192a, Owerri 1031b, Peradeniya 1274c, 1277c, Rajarata 1279a, Ruhuna 1280a, S.Leone 1134b, VB 873b
Agricultural Engineering and Land Planning, Sokoine Ag. 1297b
Agricultural Engineering and Mechanisation, Akure 1028b
Agricultural Engineering (Mechanisation) Division, Ghana 567b
Agricultural Entomology, Faisalabad 1083b
Agricultural Extension, Faisalabad 1083b, Ghana 567b, Ib. 1034c, NDRI 786a, Nigeria 1051c, North(S.Af.) 1187c, Peradeniya 1274c, 1278a, WI 1816c
Agricultural Extension and Communication, Makurdi Ag. 1007a
Agricultural Extension and Rural Development, Abeokuta Ag. 1005b, Reading 1690c, O.Awolowo 1059b, Ogun State 1064a
Agricultural Extension, Economics and Statistics, VB 873b
Agricultural Extension Education, B'desh.Ag. 226b, HPKV 686b, Mak. 1302a
Agricultural Extension, South African Institute for, Pret. 1208c
Agricultural Finance, B'desh.Ag. 226c
Agricultural, Food and Nutritional Science, Alta. 280a
Agricultural Journalism, Language and Culture, Punj.Ag. 816c
Agricultural Machinery Research and Design Centre, S.Aust. 159a
Agricultural Marketing, Faisalabad 1083b
Agricultural Mechanisation and Irrigation Technology, Devel.Studies(Ghana) 564b
Agricultural Media Resources and Extension Centre, Abeokuta Ag. 1006a
Agricultural Meteorology, Assam Ag. 605b, Faisalabad 1083b, Punj.Ag. 814c
Agricultural Meteorology and Water Management, Abeokuta Ag. 1005b
Agricultural Policy Unit, Lond. 1578c
Agricultural Production and Systems, Maur. 952b
Agricultural Research and Development, Institute of, P.Harcourt 1067b, 1069b
Agricultural Research, Directorate of, Assam Ag. 604b
Agricultural Science, Tas. 183a
Agricultural Sciences, Brist. 1345a, IUBAT 244b
Agricultural Sciences, Institute of, Ban. 612b
Agricultural Statistics, B'desh.Ag. 226c, NDRI 786a
Agricultural Strategy, Centre for, Reading 1694a
Agricultural Structure and Process Engineering, NDRI 786a
Agricultural Zoology, Ban. 614c
Agriculture, A.Bello 1008b, Aberd. 1313b, Azad J&K 1089a, B.Zak. 1091a, E.Af.Baraton 887a, Glas. 1436c, Guelph 336a, La Trobe 64c, 66a, McG. 363a, Newcastle(UK) 1620a, Nott. 1633a, Peradeniya 1274c, PNG Tech. 1129b, Reading 1690c, Syd. 170b, W.Aust. 200a, W.Syd. 207a, Zululand 1248a
Agriculture and Animal Husbandry, GRI 664a
Agriculture and Biochemistry, Assam Ag. 605b
Agriculture and Food Studies, Plym. 1672b
Agriculture and Horticulture, De Mont. 1390a, Lond. 1579a
Agriculture and Horticulture, Division of, Nott. 1633a
Agriculture and Rural Development, B'desh.Open 233a
Agriculture and Veterinary Medicine, Abia State 1000b
Agriculture Diploma Program, Manit. 390b
Agriculture Economics and Extension, Devel.Studies(Ghana) 564b
Agriculture, Food and Environment, School of, Cran. 1389a
Agriculture, Institute of, Malta 949c
Agriculture Management, Centre for, OFS 1194b
Agriculture Marketing and Co-operatives, Moi 893a
Agriculture, Muresk Institute of, Curtin 34c, 38a
Agriculture Policy Research Unit, Malawi 905c
Agriculture School, YCM Open 876a
Agriculture, School of, S.Pac. 1252c
Agriculture Sciences, A.Iqbal Open 1086a
Agro-Economic Research Centre, SP 837a, VB 875c
Agro-Forestry, B'desh.Ag. 226c, Kumasi 574a
Agro-Forestry and Environment, HPKV 686b
Agrometeorology, Guelph 339b, 340b, OFS 1192a
Agronomy, A.Bello 1010a, Annam. 598b, Assam Ag. 605b, 606a, Ban. 614c, B'desh.Ag. 226c, Devel.Studies(Ghana) 564b, Eastern(S.Lanka) 1262b, Edo State 1022b, Egerton 888c, Faisalabad 1083b, HPKV 686b, Ib. 1034c, Jaffna 1265a, L.Akin.UT

Arch...Aust INDEX TO DEPARTMENT NAMES 1896

Architecture, Centre for Advanced Studies in (CASA), *Bath* 1324c, *SPA Delhi* 840b
Architecture, Construction and Planning, *Curtin* 34c
Architecture (Housing and Planning Research), *Kumasi* 571b
Architecture, Hull School of, *L&H* 1504c
Architecture, Interior and Industrial Design, Charles Fulton School of, *Qld.UT* 145c
Architecture, Landscape and Three Dimensional Design, *Manc.Met.* 1611a
Architecture, Mackintosh School of, *Glas.* 1437a
Architecture, Manchester School of, *Manc.* 1597a
Architecture, Planning and Allied Arts, *Syd.* 170c
Architecture Research Centre, *Moratuwa* 1271c
Architecture Research Unit, *N.Lond.* 1630a
Architecture, School of, *Br.Col.* 296b, *Car.* 315c, *C.England* 1376c, *H-W* 1450a, 1451c, *Laval* 351a, *McG.* 363b, *Montr.* 410b, *NU Singapore* 1145c, *Portsmouth* 1677b, *Wat.* 512a, *Well.* 986b
Architecture, Scott Sutherland School of, *R.Gordon* 1695a
Architecture, Sir J. J. College of, *Mumbai* 774c
Architecture, Welsh School of, *Wales* 1761b
Archival Studies, *Ghana* 567b, *Ib.* 1035a
Archival Studies, Centre for, *Pondicherry* 806b
Archive Studies, Centre for, *Liv.* 1514b
Archives, *Lond.* 1569b
Archives and Records Management, *Moi* 893a
Arctic Ecology, Sheffield Centre for, *Sheff.* 1711c
Area Studies, *Portsmouth* 1677b
Arid Zone Studies, Centre for, *Maid.* 1049b, *Wales* 1759c
Armenian Studies, *Oxf.* 1649b
Art, *Aberd.* 1313c, *Acad.* 277b, *Ban.Vid.* 618b, *Brist.* 1345a, *C'dia.* 321b, *C.England* 1376b, *Curtin* 35a, *E.Anglia* 1407b, *Glas.* 1437a, *JMI* 709a, *Kingston(UK)* 1476c, *Lanc.* 1480a, *Leeds* 1484a, *Leth.* 360a, *Lond.* 1522a, 1569b, *Mak.* 1302b, *Malta* 946c, *Manc.Met.* 1611a, *Melb.* 78b, *Mt.All.* 423a, *Nott.Trent* 1639b, *NSW* 108b, *N.Territory* 126c, *OFS* 1192a, *Oxf.* 1649b, *Qu.* 452c, *Reading* 1691a, *RMIT* 150c, *S.Af.* 1217c, *St FX* 469b, *Stell.* 1224c, *Tor.* 483b, *VB* 874a
Art and Archaeology, *Lond.* 1564a
Art and Art History, *McM.* 380b
Art and Arts Therapies, *Herts.* 1453b
Art and Culture, School for Studies in, *Car.* 315c
Art and Design, *Alta.* 280b, *Belf.* 1689a, 1689b, *E.Lond.* 1410b, *Monash* 89a, *Wales* 1777b, *Wolv.* 1794a
Art and Design, Coventry School of, *Coventry* 1384a
Art and Design Education, *Lond.* 1534a
Art and Design, Gippsland Centre for, *Monash* 95c
Art and Design History, *Kingston(UK)* 1476c
Art and Design, Hull School of, *L&H* 1504c
Art and Design, School of, *Lough.* 1589a
Art and Painting, *SNDT* 843b, 844a, 844b
Art, Architecture and Design: History and Theory Research Group, *S.Aust.* 159a
Art, Architecture and Design, School of, *Leeds Met.* 1494b
Art Centre, *New Br.* 431a
Art, Design and Media, School of, *Portsmouth* 1677b
Art, Design and Performing Arts, *Middx.* 1616a
Art, Drama and Music, School of, *McM.* 380b
Art, Edinburgh College of, *H-W* 1450a
Art Education, *Kumasi* 571b, *NSW* 108b, *Winneba* 565b
Art Education and Art Therapy, *C'dia.* 321b
Art Education Research Group, *S.Aust.* 159a
Art (Fine Art), *Edin.* 1414a
Art Gallery, *Acad.* 278c
Art, Gray's School of, *R.Gordon* 1695a
Art History, *ANU* 18a, *Auck.* 960a, *Car.* 316a, *C'dia.* 321c, *La Trobe* 65a, *McG.* 363b, *Mak.* 1302b, *Nott.* 1633a, *Open(UK)* 1644c, *Otago* 980a, *Qld.* 131c, *St And.* 1696b, *Waik.* 991c, *Well.* 986c
Art History, Aesthetics and Fine Arts, *Madurai-K.* 745c
Art History and Aesthetics, *Baroda* 749a
Art History and Archaeology, *Manc.* 1597a
Art History and Theory, *Essex* 1423b, *NSW* 108b
Art, History and Theory of, *Kent* 1472c
Art, History of, *Ban.* 612b, *Cape Town* 1160b, *Lond.* 1569b, 1580a, *Montr.* 410b, *Sus.* 1746b
Art, Media and Design, *W.England* 1785b
Art Museum, *Chinese HK* 1835b
Art, Publishing and Music, *Oxf.Brookes* 1665c
Art, Queensland College of, *Griff.* 54c
Art School, *Melb.* 83b
Art, School of, *ANU* 20b, *Manit.* 390c, *Wales* 1754b
Art, South Australian School of, *S.Aust.* 156b
Art, Tasmanian School of, *Tas.* 183a, 186c
Art Theory Workshop, *ANU* 20b
Art, Winchester School of, *S'ton.* 1724c
Arthritic Diseases, Centre for, *McM.* 387b
Artificial Cells and Organs Research Centre, *McG.* 376c
Artificial Intelligence, *Edin.* 1416a, *Leeds* 1485a
Artificial Intelligence and Robotics, Centre of (CAIRO), *Tech.U.Malaysia* 941b
Artificial Intelligence Applications Institute (AIAI), *Edin.* 1422a
Artificial Intelligence Vision Research Unit, *Sheff.* 1711c
Artificial Internal Organs, *SC Tirunal* 848a
Artificial Neural Networks and Their Applications, Centre for, *Qld.* 139c
Arts, *Ballarat* 21b, *Brun.* 1351c, *C.Sturt* 31b, *Griff.* 55a, *La Trobe* 69b, *Nan.Tech.* 1142a, *N.Azikiwe* 1056c, *N.Guj.* 789a, *Sci.U.Malaysia* 932b, *S.Qld.* 163b, *Syd.* 171a
Arts, Academy of the, *Qld.UT* 145c
Arts and Associated Studies, *De Mont.* 1390b
Arts and Culture, Oceania Centre for, *S.Pac.* 1254a
Arts and Design, Exeter School of, *Plym.* 1672c
Arts and Education, *La Trobe* 69b
Arts and Education, School of Graduate Studies in, *Plym.* 1673a
Arts and Humanities, *De Mont.* 1390b
Arts and Humanities Education, *E.Cowan* 44a, *Manc.Met.* 1611a
Arts and Image Studies, School of, *Kent* 1472c
Arts and Languages in Education, *Malta* 946c
Arts and Media, *La Trobe* 65a
Arts and Sciences, *IUBAT* 244b, *Notre Dame Aust.* 129b
Arts and Social Science, *Islamic Uganda* 1301b
Arts and Social Science Education, *Jos* 1040b
Arts and Social Sciences, *Open HK* 1849a, *Open Tanz.* 1296b, *W.Syd.* 208b
Arts and Social Sciences Education, *Brunei* 264b, *Cape Coast* 562a
Arts and Technology, Australian Centre for the, *ANU* 20b
Arts, Brock Centre for the, *Brock* 314a
Arts Centre, *Sci.U.Malaysia* 937c
Arts, Centre for Research and Education in the, *Technol.Syd.* 192c
Arts, Centre for the, *NU Singapore* 1154a
Arts, Community Development and International Studies, *S.Aust.* 156b
Arts, Design and Communications, *Sund.* 1738a
Arts, Design and Performance, *Manc.Met.* 1611b
Arts, Division of, *Nfld.* 408a
Arts Education, *Nigeria* 1052b, *Z'bwe.* 1826b
Arts, Faculty of, *Potchef.* 1201a, *Sunshine Coast* 166b
Arts of Africa, Oceania and the Americas, Sainsbury Research Unit for the, *E.Anglia* 1409a
Arts Policy and Management, *City(UK)* 1380b
Arts, Sciences and Education, *Bolton Inst.* 1337a
Ashmolean Museum of Art and Archaeology, *Oxf.* 1661a
Asia and the Pacific, Research Institute for, *Syd.* 180a
Asia Australia Institute, *NSW* 118c
Asia Centre, *Tas.* 185c
Asia Pacific Arts, Centre for, *N.Territory* 128a
Asia Pacific Intellectual Property Law Institute, *Murd.* 100c
Asia Pacific Studies, Centre for, *Victoria UT* 197c
Asia Pacific Studies, Joint Centre for, *York(Can.)* 550c
Asia Pacific Studies, University of Toronto-York University Joint Centre for, *Tor.* 501c
Asia Research Centre, *Lond.* 1547c
Asia Research Centre on Social, Political and Economic Change, *Murd.* 100c
Asia-Canada Program, *S.Fraser* 476b
Asia–Pacific Studies, Hong Kong Institute of, *Chinese HK* 1835b
Asian and International Studies and Languages, *Victoria UT* 195c
Asian and Pacific Law, Centre for, *Syd.* 180a
Asian Business and Language Studies, *NSW* 108b
Asian Business Centre, *Melb.* 87a
Asian Business History Centre, *Qld.* 139c
Asian Business Research Unit, *Monash* 95c
Asian Communication and Media Studies, Centre for, *E.Cowan* 45c
Asian History Centre, *ANU* 18a
Asian Languages, *Cant.* 968c, *Curtin* 35a, *La Trobe* 65a, 66c, *Otago* 980a, *Well.* 986c
Asian Languages and European Languages, *Malaya* 918b
Asian Languages and Literatures, *Auck.* 960a
Asian Languages and Societies, Institute of, *Melb.* 78b
Asian Languages and Studies, *Monash* 89a, *Qld.* 131c, *Tas.* 183b
Asian Law Centre, *Melb.* 87a
Asian Pacific Studies, *Brock* 311c
Asian Research, Institute of, *Br.Col.* 309b
Asian Societies, *NE* 102c
Asian Spatial Information and Analytic Network, Australian Centre of the, *Griff.* 58a
Asian Studies, *Br.Col.* 296b, *Hull* 1464c, *Manit.* 390c, *Murd.* 99a, *St Mary's(Can.)* 471b, *W.Aust.* 200b, *W.Syd.* 210a
Asian Studies and Languages, *Flin.* 48b
Asian Studies Centre, *Manit.* 399c, *Qld.* 139c
Asian Studies, Centre for, *Adel.* 5b, *Waik.* 994b
Asian Studies, Centre of, *HK* 1843a
Asian Studies Institute, *Well.* 989c
Asian Studies, Institute of, *La Trobe* 69a
Asian Studies, Modern, *Griff.* 55a
Asian Studies, School of, *Syd.* 171a
Asia-Pacific Research Institute, *Macq.* 75b
ASPECT, *Cape Town* 1168b
Assamese, *Delhi* 647a, *Dib.* 652a, *Gauh.* 665c
Assessment and Evaluation Research Unit, *Qld.* 139c
Assessment, Guidance and Effective Learning, *Lond.* 1534a
Aston Business School, *Aston* 1320b
Astronomy, *Birm.* 1327a, *Bran.* 292c, *Br.Col.* 296b, *Cant.* 969a, *Cape Town* 1160b, *Durh.* 1402b, *Edin.* 1414a, *Glas.* 1437a, *Laur.* 346b, *Leeds* 1484a, *Leic.* 1497c, *Lond.* 1569b, *Lucknow* 738a, *McM.* 380c, *Manc.* 1597a, *Manit.* 390c, *Nigeria* 1052a, *Osm.* 798c, *S.Af.* 1217c, *St And.* 1696c, *Sci.U.Malaysia* 932b, *Sus.* 1746b, *Tor.* 483b, 503c, *Wales* 1761c, *W.Ont.* 521c, *York(Can.)* 544c
Astronomy and Atmospheric Research, Centre for, *S.Qld.* 164c
Astronomy and Atmospheric Science Research Unit, *Sci.U.Malaysia* 937c
Astronomy and Physics, *St Mary's(Can.)* 471b
Astronomy and Space Science, *Punjabi* 819b
Astronomy, Centre for, *W.Syd.* 211b
Astronomy, Institute of, *Camb.* 1355c
Astronomy Unit, *Lond.* 1551c
Astrophysical Theory Centre, *ANU* 17c
Astrophysics, *Camb.* 1356a, *Delhi* 647a, *Oxf.* 1649c
Astrophysics and Optics, *NSW* 114c
Astrophysics, Theoretical, Canadian Institute for, *Tor.* 483b
Athletics and Recreational Services, *Windsor* 537a
Atlantic Canada Studies, *St Mary's(Can.)* 471b
Atlantic Canada Studies, Gorsebrook Research Institute for, *St Mary's(Can.)* 473b
Atlantic Health Promotion Centre for Productive Living, *Dal.* 334a
Atlantic Region Magnetic Resonance Centre, *Dal.* 334a
Atlantic Research Centre, *Dal.* 334a
Atlantic Salmon, Inter-University Centre for Research on (CIRSA), *Montr.* 417c
Atmospheric and Marine Sciences, Flinders Institute for, *Flin.* 52a
Atmospheric and Oceanic Sciences, Centre for, *IISc.* 692a, *Kuruk.* 733a, *McG.* 363b
Atmospheric Chemistry, Centre for, *York(Can.)* 550c
Atmospheric Science, *York(Can.)* 545a
Atomic and Molecular Physics Laboratories, *ANU* 17a
Atomic, Molecular and Surface Physics, Centre for, *Murd.* 100c
Audio Visual Centre, *E.Anglia* 1409a, *Newcastle(UK)* 1626c
Audiology, *Manc.* 1597a, 1603b, *Montr.* 415b, *NU Malaysia* 926a
Audiology and Speech Sciences, School of, *Br.Col.* 305a
Audiology/Speech Therapy Programme, *Ott.* 438c
Audio-Visual Centre, *YCM Open* 876a
Audio-Visual Production and Research Centre, *Dr BRA Open* 654b
Audio-Visual Research Centre, *DAV* 651b, *Punjabi* 820c, *Roor.* 831b
Auditing, *S.Af.* 1217c
Auditing and Income Tax, *Namibia* 955b
Auditing and Taxation, *Nan.Tech.* 1136b
Augmentative and Alternative Communication, Centre for, *Pret.* 1209a
Austin Repatriation Medical Centre, *Melb.* 84c, 86c
Australasian Cochrane Centre, *Flin.* 52b
Australasian Human Resource Management, Centre for, *Macq.* 75b
Australasian Legal Information Institute, *Technol.Syd.* 192c
Australasian Pig Institute, *Qld.* 139c
Australia–Asia Relations, Centre for the Study of, *Griff.* 58a
Australia-Japan Research Centre, *ANU* 16b
Australian and International Studies, *Deakin* 40a
Australian Banking Research Unit, *Monash* 96a
Australian Centre, *Melb.* 87a
Australian Community Organisations and Management, Centre for, *Technol.Syd.* 192c
Australian Computer Abuse Research Bureau (ACARB), *RMIT* 154b
Australian Crustal Research Centre, *Monash* 96a
Australian Defence Studies Centre, *NSW* 118c
Australian Dictionary of Biography, *ANU* 17b
Australian Drama Studies Centre, *Qld.* 139c
Australian Electrical Test Centre, *S.Aust.* 159a
Australian Equine Blood Typing Laboratory, *Qld.* 139c
Australian Financial Institutions, Centre for, *S.Qld.* 164c
Australian Food Marketing Centre, *Victoria UT* 197c
Australian Geodynamics Co-operative Research Centre, *Monash* 96a
Australian Graduate School of Management, *NSW* 108b
Australian Housing and Urban Research Institute, *Qld.* 140a, *RMIT* 154b
Australian Indigenous Studies, *James Cook* 61a
Australian Indigenous Studies, Education and Research, Jumbunna Centre for, *Technol.Syd.* 192c
Australian Irrigation Technology Centre, *S.Aust.* 159a
Australian Language and Literature Studies, Centre for, *NE* 105c
Australian Maritime Engineering Co-operative Research Centre, *Monash* 96a
Australian Mineral Exploration Technologies, Co-operative Research Centre for, *Macq.* 75b

Business Administration, Institute of, *Dhaka* 238a, *Punjab* 1112b, *Rajsh.* 254c, 257c
Business Administration Programme, *S.Pac.* 1253a
Business Administration, School of, *Acad.* 277b, *Dal.* 328a
Business Advanced Technology Centre (BATC), *Tech.U.Malaysia* 941b
Business and Accounting, *Malaya* 916c
Business and Administration, *Open HK* 1849a
Business and Commerce, *GND* 679c
Business and Computer Education, *Strath.* 1733b
Business and Economic Studies, *Zambia* 1821c
Business and Economics, School of, *Exe.* 1426c, *Nipissing* 433a
Business and Finance, *Herts.* 1454a
Business and Government Management, Graduate School of, *Well.* 987a, 989c
Business and Innovation Studies, Institute for, *S.Fraser* 480c
Business and Law, *Deakin* 40b
Business and Management, *Sheff.Hallam* 1715a, *Wales* 1777b
Business and Management Development, *NUL* 904b, *N-W(S.Af.)* 1190c
Business and Management Effectiveness, *R.Roads* 465c
Business and Management Studies, *Guy.* 576b, *Manc.Met.* 1611c, *Portsmouth* 1677c
Business and Personnel Management, *Potchef.* 1200a, 1201a
Business and Professional Ethics, Centre for, *Leeds* 1491a
Business and Public Management, School of, *Well.* 987a
Business and Technical Communication, *Ryerson* 467b
Business and Technology, *W.Syd.* 208c
Business, Asia–Pacific Institute of, *Chinese HK* 1835c
Business Central, *Leeds Met.* 1495c
Business Communications, *C'dia.* 322a
Business Computing, *RMIT* 150c, *Winn.* 541b
Business Development and Corporate History, *Melb.* 78c
Business Economics, *APSV* 609c, *Baroda* 749b, *Delhi* 647b, *Durban-W.* 1170b, *G.Jamb.* 678a, *Jiw.* 718a, *Witw.* 1241a, *Zululand* 1248a
Business Education, *Uyo* 1072c, *Winneba* 565b
Business Education and Development, Centre for, *Griff.* 58b
Business, Faculty of, *Sunshine Coast* 166b
Business Finance and Economics, *JN Vyas* 703b
Business, Graduate School of, *Curtin* 35a, *Durban-W.* 1170b, *N.Territory* 126c, *Stell.* 1224c, *Syd.* 171b, *Technol.Syd.* 189b
Business History, Centre for, *Leeds* 1491a
Business History Unit, *Lond.* 1547c
Business Information Systems, *E.Lond.* 1410b, *Nott.Trent* 1639b
Business Information Technology, *Manc.Met.* 1611c
Business, Institute of, *WI* 1816b
Business, Institute of (IOB), *WI* 1818b
Business, International, *Chinese HK* 1832b, *Luton* 1593b, *Qld.UT* 145c
Business Law, *Curtin* 35a, *E.Cowan* 44b, *Macq.* 72c, *Massey* 974c, *Nan.Tech.* 1136c, *RMIT* 150c, *Uganda Martyrs* 1307b
Business Law and Practice, Centre for the Study of, *Leeds* 1491a
Business Law and Taxation, *NSW* 109a
Business Law Group, *Massey* 974b
Business Law, Research Centre for, *Auck.* 967a
Business Leadership, Graduate School of, *S.Af.* 1222b
Business Management, *Dr BRA Open* 654a, *Dr HGV* 660a, *Egerton* 889a, *G.Jamb.* 678a, *HNB Garh.* 683a, *L&H* 1505b, *Maid.* 1047c, *North(S.Af.)* 1188a, *NUST Bulawayo* 1824c, *OFS* 1192b, *Osm.* 798a, *P.Elizabeth* 1196a, *Potchef.* 1200a, 1201a, *Pret.* 1203b, *Punjabi* 819c, *Punj.Ag.* 817a, *Rajarata* 1279a, *Rand Afrikaans* 1210c, *S.Af.* 1217c, *SPMV* 851b, *SSJ Maharaj* 846b, *Stell.* 1224c, *S.Venkat.* 855b, *Uyo* 1072c, *Venda* 1233c, *Wales* 1767a
Business Management and Commerce, *Mys.* 779a
Business Management and Entrepreneurship, *Dr RML Awadh* 662a
Business Management (MBA Course), *Rohil.* 828b
Business Management, School of, *Ryerson* 467b
Business Mathematics and Informatics, *Potchef.* 1200a
Business Operations Management, *Napier* 1617a
Business Organisation, *H-W* 1450a, 1451a
Business Policy, *E.Lond.* 1410c, *L&H* 1505c, *NU Singapore* 1146b
Business Research, Bureau of, *Dhaka* 242c
Business Research, Centre for, *Manc.* 1605c
Business Research, ESRC Centre for, *Camb.* 1365b
Business, Richard Ivey School of, *W.Ont.* 521c
Business School, *C.England* 1376c, *Glam.* 1433b, *Glas.* 1437c, *Lough.* 1589a, *Middx.* 1616a, *Wales* 1762a, *W'gong.* 215b
Business, School of, *Aust.Cath.* 12b, *Car.* 316a, *E.Af.Baraton* 887a, *HK* 1837c, *Qu.* 453a
Business, Schulich School of, *York(Can.)* 545a
Business Statistics, *Monash* 89b
Business Strategy, *Leeds Met.* 1495c
Business Strategy and Development, *Kingston(UK)* 1476c
Business Studies, *Belf.* 1689a, 1689b, *Brun.* 1352a, *Cape Coast* 562b, *Edin.* 1414b, *E.Lond.* 1410b, *HKPU* 1846a, *JMI* 709a, *Kenyatta* 890c, *Manc.Met.* 1611c, *P.Harcourt* 1067c, *PNG Tech.* 1129c, *Salf.* 1700c, *SP* 836b, *S.Pac.* 1253a, *Z'bwe.* 1826b
Business Studies and Economics, *Nair.* 899a
Business Studies and Entrepreneurial Development, *S.Leone* 1131b
Business Studies, Institute of, *Sindh* 1119a
Business Systems, *W'gong.* 213a
Business Systems, School of, *Monash* 89b
Business Taxation, Centre for Research in, *Plym.* 1675c
Business Technology Centre, *HKPU* 1847c
Byzantine and Modern Greek Studies, *Cyprus* 558b, *Lond.* 1536b
Byzantine, Ottoman and Modern Greek Studies, Centre for, *Birm.* 1327c, 1329c
Byzantine Studies, *Oxf.* 1650a

CAD Research Group, *Montr.* 417c
Cadet Training Wing, *Kotelawala DA* 1264a
CADMI Microelectronics, Inc., *New Br.* 431a
CAE/CAD/CAM Centre, *NU Singapore* 1147c
Camborne School of Mines, *Exe.* 1427a
Campbell Collections, *Natal* 1183b
Campus Law Centre, *Delhi* 648b
Campus Law Clinic, *Natal* 1180b
Canada, Institute for the Study of, *McG.* 376c
Canadian Bacterial Diseases Network (CBDN), *Guelph* 341b
Canadian Church History, Research Centre in, *St Paul(Ott.)* 447c
Canadian Circumpolar Institute, *Alta.* 288b
Canadian Co-operative Wildlife Health Centre (CCWHC), *Guelph* 341b
Canadian Native Languages, Centre for Research and Teaching in, *W.Ont.* 531a
Canadian Network of Toxicology Centres (CNTC), *Guelph* 341b
Canadian Plains Research Centre, *Regina* 463c
Canadian Studies, *Birm.* 1327c, *Brock* 311c, *Mt.St.Vin.* 425a, *Nott.* 1633c, *Wat.* 512b, *W.Laur.* 534b
Canadian Studies, Centre for, *Leeds* 1491a, *Lond.* 1523c, *Mt.All.* 423a, *S.Fraser* 477a, *SNDT* 843c
Canadian Studies, Centre of, *Belf.* 1688b, *Edin.* 1414b
Canadian Studies, Institute of, *Ott.* 446a
Canadian Studies Programme, *Ott.* 439a, *Trent* 509b
Canadian Studies, Robarts Centre for, *York(Can.)* 550c
Canadian Studies, School of, *Car.* 316b
Canadian Urban Research Studies, Institute for, *S.Fraser* 480c
Canadian–American Research Centre, *Windsor* 540b
Cancer and Developmental Biology, Wellcome Trust and Cancer Research Campaign Institute of, *Camb.* 1365b
Cancer Campaign Research Laboratory, *Nott.* 1638a
Cancer Medicine and Cell Biology, Centenary Institute of, *Syd.* 180a
Cancer Research Centre, *Laval* 358a, *Wales* 1771c
Cancer Studies, *Sheff.* 1709b
Cancer Studies, Institute of, *Birm.* 1333c
Cancer Tissue Bank, *Liv.* 1514b
Canon Law, *CUE Af.* 886a, *Ott.* 439a, *St Paul(Ott.)* 447a
Canterbury Business School, *Kent* 1473a
Capricornia Aboriginal and Islander Tertiary Education Centre, *C.Qld.* 29c
Carbon Dating Unit, *Waik.* 994c
Cardiac Anaesthesia, *All India IMS* 585c
Cardiac Pathology, *All India IMS* 585c
Cardiac Prevention Research Centre, *Dal.* 334a
Cardiac Radiology, *All India IMS* 585c
Cardiac Surgery, *Glas.* 1442a
Cardiac Technology, Co-operative Research Centre for, *Technol.Syd.* 193a
Cardiology, *Aberd.* 1316a, *All India IMS* 585c, *Br.Col.* 305b, 306a, *Lond.* 1538c, 1541a, 1554c, 1562a, 1576c, *Lucknow* 739c, *Manipal AHE* 765b, *Natal* 1181c, 1182b, *Newcastle(UK)* 1623c, 1624a, *OFS* 1193c, *Pg.IMER* 807c, *P.Harcourt* 1069a, *Pret.* 1207b, *S.Af.Med.* 1174a, *SC Tirunal* 848c, *S.Ramachandra Med.* 853a, *Wales* 1771c, *Witw.* 1241a
Cardiothoracic and Vascular Surgery, *All India IMS* 586a
Cardiothoracic Centre, *All India IMS* 585c
Cardiothoracic Surgery, *Cape Town* 1165b, *Lond.* 1561c, *Manipal AHE* 765b, *Manit.* 399b, *Natal* 1181c, *OFS* 1193c, *Pret.* 1207b, *S.Af.Med.* 1174a, *S.Ramachandra Med.* 853a, *Stell.* 1229b, *Wales* 1773c
Cardio-Thoracic Surgery (Johannesburg Hospital), *Witw.* 1246c
Cardiovascular and Thoracic Surgery, *Pg.IMER* 807c, *W.Ont.* 530c
Cardiovascular Biochemistry, *Lond.* 1554c
Cardiovascular Epidemiology Unit, *Dund.* 1399b
Cardiovascular Medicine, *Birm.* 1333c, *Oxf.* 1660a
Cardiovascular Research, Centre for, *Tor.* 502a
Cardiovascular Research Group, *Alta.* 288b
Cardiovascular Research, Rotary District 9600 Centre for, *Griff.* 58b
Cardiovascular Research Unit, *Edin.* 1420a
Cardiovascular Thoracic Surgery, *SC Tirunal* 848c
Care, Independent and Public Sector Management, Centre for, *Portsmouth* 1681a
Career Education and Development, Garware Institute of, *Mumbai* 776b
Careers Guidance, *Hudd.* 1462a
Caribbean Law Institute Centre, *WI* 1814a
Caribbean Studies, *N.Lond.* 1627b
Caribbean Studies, Centre for, *Warw.* 1783a
Caribbean Studies, Division of, *Guy.* 576b
Cartoons and Caricature, Centre for the Study of, *Kent* 1475a
Case Method Development Group, *Montr.* 420a
Catalan, *Liv.* 1508b, *Sheff.* 1705a
Catchment and In-Stream Research, Centre for, *Griff.* 58b
Catchment Hydrology, Co-operative Research Centre for, *Monash* 96a
Cathie Marsh Centre for Census and Survey Research, *Manc.* 1599a
Cattle and Beef Industry (Meat Quality), Co-operative Research Centre for, *NE* 105c
Cell and Molecular Biology, Institute of (ICMB), *Edin.* 1414b
Cell and Tissue Research, Centre for, *York(UK)* 1801b
Cell, Animal and Population Biology, Institute of (ICAPB), *Edin.* 1414c
Cell Biology, *IISc.* 690b
Cell Biology and Anatomy, *Alta.* 286b
Cell Biology, Manitoba Institute of, *Manit.* 399c
Cell Physiology and Pharmacology, *Leic.* 1500b
Cell Sciences, *S'ton.* 1728a
Cells, Immunology and Development, Research Division of, *Manc.* 1597b
Cellular and Molecular Cardiology, *SC Tirunal* 849a
Cellular and Molecular Medicine, *Ott.* 443b
Cellular Science, *Oxf.* 1660a
Celtic, *Aberd.* 1314a, 1315a, *Belf.* 1684c, 1686b, 1689a, *Camb.* 1356b, *Edin.* 1414c, *Glas.* 1437c, *Oxf.* 1650a
Celtic Studies, *St FX* 469c
Cement and Concrete, Centre for, *Sheff.* 1711c
Central and Eastern European Studies, Centre for, *Liv.* 1514b
Central Animal Facility, *IISc.* 692a
Central Asia Research Forum, *Lond.* 1565b
Central Asian Studies, *J.Nehru U.* 712c, *Kashmir* 727a, *Panjab* 802a
Central Biomedical Services, *Camb.* 1365a
Central Cryogenic Facility, *IISc.* 692a
Central Eurasian Studies, Centre of, *Mumbai* 776b
Central European Studies, Centre for, *Lond.* 1581c
Central Instrumentation and Service Laboratory, *Madr.* 743b
Central Instrumentation Service Laboratory, *Mys.* 780c
Central Nervous System, Research Group on the, *Montr.* 417c
Central University Laboratory, *TN Vet.* 861b
Central Workshop, *Anna* 597b, *IISc.* 692a
Central/East European and Russian Area Studies, Institute of, *Car.* 316b
Centralised Clinical Laboratory, *TN Vet.* 862b
Centre for Educational Studies, *Hull* 1466b
Centre for Lifelong Learning, *Hull* 1466b
Centre for Magnetic Resonance Investigations, *Hull* 1467b
Centre for Metabolic Bone Disease, *Hull* 1467b
Centre for Policy Modelling, *Manc.Met.* 1615b
Centre for Professional Development and Training in Education, *Hull* 1466b
Ceramic Engineering, *Ban.* 616a
Ceramics, *Leeds* 1484b, 1487c
Ceramics Workshop, *ANU* 20b
Cereal Improvement Programme, *O.Awolowo* 1063a
Cerebral and Sensory Functions Unit, *Qld.* 140a
Ceregen Ltd, *Sheff.* 1711c
Certificate Training Centre, *S.Leone* 1134c
Certified General Accountants–Accounting Research Centre, *Ott.* 446a
Certified General Accountants–Taxation Research Centre, *Ott.* 446a
Challenger Division for Seafloor Processes, *S'ton.* 1727c
Challenging Needs and Learning Research Group, *Montr.* 417c
Change Management, Centre for, *Deakin* 42b
Chembiomed, *Alta.* 288b
Chemical Analysis, Centre for, *NSW* 118c
Chemical and Biochemical Engineering, *W.Ont.* 523b
Chemical and Biological Sciences, *Hudd.* 1459a
Chemical and Biomedical Sciences, *C.Qld.* 28c
Chemical and Environmental Toxicology, Collaborative Programme of, *Ott.* 446a
Chemical and Life Sciences, *Greenwich* 1447a, *Northumbria* 1631b
Chemical and Physical Sciences, Applied, *Napier* 1617b
Chemical and Physical Sciences, School of, *Well.* 987a
Chemical and Process Engineering, *NU Malaysia* 923c
Chemical Ecology Research Group, *S.Fraser* 480c
Chemical Endocrinology, *Lond.* 1554c
Chemical Engineering, *And.* 591c, *Anna* 595b, *Belf.* 1685a, *BITS* 631a, *Dal.* 328c, *Dr BAT* 658b, *Edin.*

Comm...Comp INDEX TO DEPARTMENT NAMES 1902

Communications Research Laboratory, McM. 387b
Communications Studies, Institute of, Leeds 1491a
Communicative and Cognitive Disabilities, Centre for, W.Ont. 531a
Community and Cross-Cultural Studies, Centre for, Qld.UT 148a
Community and Family Medicine, Chinese HK 1834c, Kelaniya 1269b
Community and Health Nutrition, O.Awolowo 1062a
Community and Health Studies, School of, Hull 1467a
Community and Mental Health, Malawi 907b
Community and Primary Health Care, City(UK) 1382b
Community and Regional Planning, Br.Col. 297c
Community and Rural Health, Tas. 186c
Community and Rural Health, Division of, Tas. 185b
Community and Youth Work, Durh. 1402c
Community Care and Primary Health, Centre for, Westminster 1789c
Community Care Studies Unit, Nuffield, Leic. 1502a
Community Child Health, Lond. 1577a
Community Dental Health, Peradeniya 1276c
Community Dentistry, Malaya 919a, Manipal AHE 762b, 763a, Pret. 1206c, S.Af.Med. 1176a, Stell. 1229a, Witw. 1241b, W.Ont. 527b
Community Development, S.Aust. 156c
Community Directed Health Research, Hans Snyckers Institute for, Pret. 1209a
Community Economic Development Centre, S.Fraser 480c
Community Education, Strath. 1733c, Victoria UT 197c
Community Education and Extra-Mural Studies, Mak. 1305b
Community Education, Centre for, Pret. 1209a
Community Health, Auck. 965b, Benin 1017a, Calabar 1020c, Cape Town 1165c, Dar. 1295c, G.Caledonian 1444b, Ghana 569b, J.Nehru U. 712c, Jos 1041c, Kumasi 573a, Malawi 907a, Nair. 899c, Natal 1181c, NU Malaysia 926b, OFS 1193c, Pret. 1207b, Putra 929a, S.Af.Med. 1174a, Stell. 1229b, U.Danfodiyo 1071b, Witw. 1241b, Zambia 1822c
Community Health and Epidemiology, Dal. 332a, Qu. 458b
Community Health and Psychiatry, WI 1815b
Community Health Care, S.Leone 1132b
Community Health Nursing Science, Namibia 956b
Community Health, School of, Syd. 176c
Community Health Sciences, Aga Khan 1081b, Manit. 396c, N.Br.Col. 435a
Community Health Sciences, School of, Nott. 1637a
Community History, Centre for, NSW 118c
Community Law and Research Centre, Technol.Syd. 193a
Community Law Centre, W.Cape 1238c
Community Law, Centre for, Potchef. 1200c
Community Medicine, A.Bello 1010b, Annam. 600b, Colombo 1261b, Enugu SUST 1024a, HK 1841c, Jaffna 1266a, Maid. 1049a, Manipal AHE 763c, 765b, Melb. 84b, N.Azikiwe 1057c, Nfld. 406c, 407a, Nigeria 1051a, NSW 116a, Ott. 443c, Peradeniya 1277a, Pg.IMER 807c, PNG 1128c, Ruhuna 1280c, Sci.U.Malaysia 936c, S.Ramachandra Med. 853a, Syd. 177b, Z'bwe. 1828b
Community Medicine and Family Medicine, Sri Jay. 1285a
Community Medicine and General Practice, Monash 94b
Community Medicine and Primary Care, Ogun State 1065b
Community Medicine and Primary Health Care, Bayero 1013c
Community Medicine, Centre for, All India IMS 586a
Community, Occupational and Family Medicine, NU Singapore 1152c
Community Oncology, Manipal AHE 765b
Community Paediatrics, Lond. 1539a
Community Practice, Mak. 1304b
Community, Primary Care and Public Health Nursing, Sheff. 1711a
Community, Regional and Communication Studies, School of, Wales 1758a
Community Services, Punjabi 819c
Community Services, MEDUNSA Institute for, S.Af.Med. 1177a
Community Studies, E.Cowan 44b, Manc.Met. 1612b, Reading 1691b, Wales 1775b, W.Syd. 210a
Companion Animal Medicine and Surgery, S.Af.Med. 1176c
Comparative and Applied Social Sciences, Hull 1465a
Comparative and Public Law, Centre for, HK 1843a
Comparative Criminology and Criminal Justice, Centre for, Wales 1759c
Comparative Criminology, International Centre for, Montr. 417c
Comparative Development Studies Programme, Trent 509b
Comparative Education, North(S.Af.) 1188a, Qu. 457c
Comparative Education and Educational Management, OFS 1192b
Comparative Genocide Studies, Centre for, Macq. 75c
Comparative Infectious Diseases, Centre for, Liv. 1514c
Comparative International and European Law Unit, W.England 1788b
Comparative Labour Studies, Centre for, Warw. 1783a
Comparative Language and Culture, DAV 650c
Comparative Law, Zululand 1248a
Comparative Languages and Culture, B'tullah.V. 623a
Comparative Literary Studies, Car. 316c, 318b
Comparative Literature, HK 1838a, Hyd. 688b, McM. 381c, Montr. 411a, Mumbai 775b, Oxf. 1650c, Witw. 1241b
Comparative Literature and Civilization, W.Ont. 525b
Comparative Literature and Cultural Studies, Centre for, Monash 96a
Comparative Literature, Centre for, Tor. 502a
Comparative Literature, Research Institute for, Alta. 288b
Comparative Management, Centre for, Open(UK) 1646a
Comparative Medicine, Centre for, Tor. 502a
Comparative Plant Ecology, Unit of, Sheff. 1712a
Comparative Religion, Dal. 328b, Eastern(S.Lanka) 1263a
Comparative Religion and Islamic Culture, Sindh 1119b
Comparative Religion, Faith (Aqidah), Human Thought and Dawah, IIU(P'stan.) 1099a
Comparative Studies, Potti ST 809b, W.Ont. 532b
Complementary Health, Exe. 1430a
Complementary Health Studies, Centre for, Exe. 1430b
Complexity and Change, Centre for, Open(UK) 1645a
Composite Structures and Materials, Centre for, C'dia. 326a
Composition, ANU 20b
Composition Unit, Syd. 181b
Computation, UMIST 1607b
Computation and its Applications, Centre for Research on (CERCA), Montr. 418a
Computational and Applied Mechanics, FRD/UCT Centre for Research in (CERECAM), Cape Town 1168b
Computational Fluid Dynamics and Turbulence, Centre for, Salf. 1703a
Computational Fluid Dynamics, Centre for, Leeds 1491b
Computational Mathematics, Brunel Institute of, Brun. 1353b
Computational Mathematics, Centre for, Monash 96b
Computational Mathematics Unit, Technol.Syd. 192a
Computational Science, NU Singapore 1147a, St And. 1697b
Computer Aided Art Studio, ANU 20b
Computer Aided Design Centre, IIT Bombay 695c
Computer Aided Design Laboratory, Manit. 400a
Computer Aided Engineering Centre, Napier 1618c
Computer Aided Learning Centre, Victoria UT 197c
Computer Aided Process Engineering Centre, Qld. 140b
Computer Analysis of Language and Speech, Centre for, Leeds 1491b
Computer and Control, Division for, Stell. 1225c
Computer and Information Sciences, De Mont. 1391a, Hyd. 688b, S.Aust. 156c
Computer and Information Technology Institute, Jahang. 247c
Computer and Mathematical Sciences, R.Gordon 1695a, Salf. 1701a
Computer and Systems Sciences, School of, J.Nehru U. 712c
Computer Animation, Bourne. 1339b
Computer Application, Samb. 832a
Computer Applications, DAV 650c, G.Jamb. 678a, MCN Journ. 759a, MDSU 755a, Rajendra Ag. 825a, S.Venkat. 856b
Computer Applications, Training Centre for, Kakatiya 719b
Computer Architecture and VLSI, Inter-University Centre in (GRIAO), Montr. 418a
Computer Based Learning, Institute of, Belf. 1688b
Computer Centre, Abuja 1004c, A.Iqbal Open 1087b, Alagappa 584a, Anna 597b, Annam. 599c, AT Balewa 1002c, Azad J&K 1089b, Baroda 752a, Brad. 1343b, Burd. 635b, DAV 651b, Dhaka 242c, GRI 665a, HK 1843a, IIT Bombay 695c, I.Sch.Mines 698b, Jammu 712b, J.Hamdard 708b, Kashmir 728a, Kerala 729a, Monash 96b, M.Sund. 770b, Mys. 778c, Putra 929a, Roor. 831b, Saur. 838c, S.Krishna. 851a, Sokoine Ag. 1298c, SSJ Maharaj 847a, Swazi. 1289b, Utara, Malaysia 944b, YCM Open 876a, Z'bwe. 1829a
Computer Centre for People with Disabilities, Westminster 1792b
Computer Communications Network, Wat. 520a
Computer Engineering, Ban. 616b, Curtin 35b, Dr BAT 658b, Open S.Lanka 1272b, W.Ont. 522b
Computer Graphics Laboratory, Wat. 520a
Computer, Information and Mathematical Sciences, E.Cowan 44b
Computer Information Systems, Malta 947b, Stell. 1230c, Wales 1775b
Computer Laboratory, Camb. 1356c
Computer Research Institute of Montréal (CRIM), Montr. 418a
Computer Science, Abuja 1004a, Adel. 5c, Amravati 588c, ANU 18b, APSV 609c, Assam 603b, Auck. 960c, 964a, Avina.Home Sci. 608a, Baloch. 1093b, Ban. 613a, Belf. 1684c, 1685a, Benin 1015b, Berh. 624a, Bhutto IST 1118a, Birm. 1328a, BIT(Ranchi) 629a, Botswana 262b, Bran. 293a, Br.Col. 297c, Brist. 1345c, Brock 312a, B'thiar. 626a, B'tullah.V. 623a, Buea 267c, Burd. 634b, B.Zak. 1091b, Cant. 969a, Cape Town 1160c, C'dia. 322b, Cochin 643c, Colombo 1259c, Copperbelt 1820b, Cyprus 558c, Dal. 328b, DAV 650c, De Mont. 1391a, Delhi 647c, Dhaka 238c, Dr BA Marath. 655c, Durban-W. 1170b, Durh. 1402c, Edin. 1416b, Egerton 889a, Essex 1424a, Exe. 1427b, 1427c, Flin. 48c, Gauh. 666b, G.Ghasidas 677a, Ghana 567c, GKV 682a, Herts. 1454a, HK 1838a, HNB Garh. 683a, HP 684b, Hull 1465a, Ib. 1035b, I.Gandhi Nat.Open 701a, IIU(P'stan.) 1099a, Islamia, Bahawal. 1100b, Islamic(B'desh.) 246b, Jaffna 1265b, Jain VB 706b, James Cook 61b, Jammu 711b, JMI 709a, JN Vyas 704a, Karachi 1102c, Keele 1469c, Kerala 729a, Kota Open 731a, Kotelawala DA 1264a, Lahore UET 1095b, L.Akin.UT 1043b, Laur. 346c, Laval 351b, Leeds 1485a, Leic. 1498a, Leth. 360b, Liv. 1508c, Lond. 1522a, 1536c, 1552b, 1558a, 1570a, Lucknow 739c, Madr. 742b, Madurai-K. 746a, Makurdi Ag. 1007b, Malawi 906b, 906c, Manc. 1598a, Manip. 768a, Manit. 391b, Melb. 79a, Minna 1030b, M'lore. 760c, Monash 89c, M.Sukh. 772b, M.Sund. 770a, Mt.All. 423b, M.Teresa Women's 774a, Mumbai 775b, Mys. 779c, Nair. 898b, Namibia 955b, Natal 1179a, Nehru Tech. 715b, 716a, 716b, New Br. 428b, 431b, Newcastle(NSW) 122c, Nfld. 403a, Nigeria 1052b, Nipissing 433c, North(S.Af.) 1188a, Nott. 1633c, NSW 119c, NU Malaysia 923c, NU Singapore 1147a, NUL 903b, NUST Bulawayo 1825a, O.Awolowo 1059c, Otago 980b, Owerri 1031c, P.Harcourt 1067c, PNG Tech. 1129c, Pondicherry 806a, Pret. 1203b, Pune 811a, Putra 929a, Queb. 449b, Rajsh. 255a, Rand Afrikaans 1210c, Reading 1691b, Regina 462a, Rhodes 1214a, Roor. 829b, Ryerson 467b, Sci.U.Malaysia 933b, Sheff. 1705b, Shiv. 842a, Sindh 1119b, SP 836b, SPMV 851c, Stell. 1225a, S'ton. 1724c, Strath. 1733c, Swazi. 1289a, Tamil 858b, Tas. 183b, Tezpur 866b, Tor. 484b, 503c, Uganda Martyrs 1307b, Uyo 1073a, Waik. 992a, Wales 1754c, 1762c, 1767b, Warw. 1780a, Wat. 513a, W.Aust. 200c, W.Cape 1236b, Well. 987b, 988c, Westminster 1790a, W'gong. 213a, WI 1817a, Witw. 1241b, W.Ont. 522b, York(Can.) 545c, 551a, York(UK) 1799a, Z'bwe. 1826c
Computer Science and Applications, Alagappa 584a, GRI 664b, Kuruk. 733a, MDU 753b, Panjab 803c, Utkal 869c
Computer Science and Artificial Intelligence, Malta 947b, Sus. 1746c
Computer Science and Automation, IISc. 690c
Computer Science and Business Administration, St Mary's(Can.) 471c
Computer Science and Computer Centre, SNDT 843c
Computer Science and Computer Engineering, La Trobe 65c
Computer Science and Electrical Engineering, Punj.Ag. 814b
Computer Science and Electronic Systems, Kingston(UK) 1477a
Computer Science and Electronics, Ban.Vid. 618b
Computer Science and Engineering, School of, Anna 596a, B'desh.Engin. 230a, Chinese HK 1832b, Enugu SUST 1024c, G.Jamb. 678b, GND 680a, IIT Bombay 693b, I.Sch.Mines 697b, Khulna 250a, Maur. 952c, Moratuwa 1270b, Nagar. 783a, NSW 109c, Osm. 798b, Punjabi 819c, Thapar IET 867a
Computer Science and Informatics, OFS 1192b
Computer Science and Information Systems, BITS 631b, J.Hamdard 707b, Malaya 917a, Natal 1184b, P.Elizabeth 1196a, Potchef. 1200a, 1201a, S.Af. 1218a, Tech.U.Malaysia 940a
Computer Science and Mathematics, School of, Portsmouth 1678a, WI 1814b, York(Can.) 552a
Computer Science and Software Engineering, School of, Monash 89b, Swinburne UT 168a
Computer Science and Systems Engineering, And. 592a
Computer Science and Technology, S.Venkat. 856b
Computer Science, Basser Department of, Syd. 171c
Computer Science (Bundoora Campus), RMIT 151a
Computer Science Centre, Kumasi 571c
Computer Science, Centre for, NE Hill 792a
Computer Science (City Campus), RMIT 151a
Computer Science, Institute of, Mak. 1302c, 1305a, Nair. 899a
Computer Science, Mathematics and Physics, James Cook 61b, WI 1813a
Computer Science, Ottawa–Carleton Institute for, Ott. 446a
Computer Science Research Centre of Montreal Continuing Education, Centre for, C'dia. 326a
Computer Science School, YCM Open 876a
Computer Science, School of, Acad. 277c, Car. 316c, C.England 1377a, McG. 364a, M.Gandhi 757a, Nehru Tech. 717a, Windsor 538a
Computer Sciences, A.Iqbal Open 1086b, Dschang 269c, NE 103b, N.Maharashtra 790a, Peradeniya 1275a, Quaid-i-Azam 1115c
Computer Sciences Laboratory, ANU 15c
Computer Security Research Centre, Lond. 1548a

Criminal Law Reform and Criminal Justice Policy, International Centre for, *S.Fraser* 480c
Criminological and Legal Research, Centre for, *Sheff.* 1712a
Criminology, *Bond* 23c, *Durban-W.* 1170b, *Edin.* 1415a, *Keele* 1469c, *Madr.* 742b, *Melb.* 79a, *Montr.* 411b, *Mys.* 779a, *North(S.Af.)* 1188a, *OFS* 1192b, *Ott.* 439b, *Pret.* 1203b, *S.Af.* 1218b, *Sheff.* 1705b, *Wat.* 513b, *Zululand* 1248a
Criminology and Correctional Administration, *Tata Inst.Soc.Scis.* 864b
Criminology and Criminal Justice, Institute of, *Belf.* 1688b, *Lond.* 1548a
Criminology and Forensic Sciences, *Dr HGV* 660b, *Karn.* 724a, 725b
Criminology, Atlantic Institute of, *Dal.* 334a
Criminology, Centre of, *Tor.* 502a
Criminology, Institute for, *S.Af.* 1222b
Criminology, Institute of, *Camb.* 1357a, *Cape Town* 1160c, *Syd.* 180a, *Well.* 989c
Criminology Research Centre, *Manit.* 400a, *S.Fraser* 480c
Criminology Research, Centre for, *Alta.* 288b
Criminology, School of, *S.Fraser* 477c
Criminology/Social Justice, *St Thomas(NB)* 474a
Critical and Cultural Studies, Institute for, *Monash* 96b
Critical Care, *OFS* 1193c
Critical Theory, Postgraduate School of, *Nott.* 1633c
Critical Thinking, *Brunei* 264c
Crop and Soil Sciences, *Umudike* 1027b
Crop Botany, *B'desh.Ag.* 227b
Crop Improvement, Horticulture and Agricultural Botany, *VB* 874a
Crop Physiology, *Assam Ag.* 605b, 606a, *Faisalabad* 1084a
Crop Production, *Akure* 1028c, *AT Balewa* 1002b, *Makurdi Ag.* 1007b, *Melb.* 83c, *Minna* 1030b, *Ogun State* 1064b, *Owerri* 1031c, *Swazi.* 1289a, *Yola* 1033b
Crop Production and Crop Protection, *Abeokuta Ag.* 1005c
Crop Production and Seed Technology, *Moi* 893a
Crop Production Unit, *O.Awolowo* 1063a
Crop Protection, *A.Bello* 1010b, *Adel.* 5c, *S.Leone* 1134b
Crop Science, *Benin* 1015b, *Calabar* 1019c, *Cape Coast* 562b, *Ghana* 567c, *Guelph* 336b, 339c, *Guy.* 576c, *Kumasi* 571c, *Maid.* 1047c, *Mak.* 1302c, *Malawi* 906a, *Nair.* 897a, *Namibia* 955b, *Nigeria* 1052b, *NUL* 903b, *Peradeniya* 1275a, 1278a, *Ruhuna* 1280a, *S.Leone* 1134b, *U.Danfodiyo* 1071a, *WI* 1817a, 1817b, *Zambia* 1822a, *Z'bwe.* 1826c
Crop Science and Crop Production, *Enugu SUST* 1026a
Crop Science and Production, *Sokoine Ag.* 1298a
Crop Sciences, *Syd.* 175c
Crops Protection and Environmental Biology, *Ib.* 1035b
Cross Cancer Institute, *Alta.* 288b
Crystal Growth, *Alagappa* 584a
Crystal Growth, Centre for, *Anna* 595c
Crystallography, *Lond.* 1522b, *Madr.* 742b, *Sci.U.Malaysia* 933b
Crystallography Centre, *W.Aust.* 205b
Cultural and Education Central, *Leeds Met.* 1493b
Cultural and Education Studies, *Leeds Met.* 1493b
Cultural and Media Policy, Key Centre for, *Griff.* 58b
Cultural and Media Studies, Centre for, *Natal* 1179a
Cultural and Policy Studies, *Qld.UT* 146a
Cultural and Sporting Activities, *Buea* 267c
Cultural Centre, *Malaya* 920b
Cultural Heritage, *SNDT* 844c
Cultural Heritage Research Centre, *Canberra* 27a
Cultural Heritage Science Studies, *Canberra* 25c
Cultural Histories and Futures, *W.Syd.* 210a
Cultural History Group, *Aberd.* 1317b
Cultural Management, Centre for, *Wat.* 519b
Cultural Research Institute, *Sheff.Hallam* 1719b
Cultural Research, Institute for, *Lanc.* 1482b
Cultural Studies, *Birm.* 1328a, *E.Lond.* 1410b, *Leeds Met.* 1493b, *Lond.* 1524c, *RMIT* 151a, *Sheff.Hallam* 1715c, *Sri Jay.* 1284a, *Victoria UT* 196b, *Wales* 1775b
Cultural Studies and Sociology, *Birm.* 1332c
Cultural Studies, Centre for, *Guelph* 341b, *Kumasi* 573b, *Leeds* 1491b, *Tech.U.Malaysia* 941b
Cultural Studies, Institute of, *O.Awolowo* 1062c
Cultural Studies Programme, *Trent* 509c
Cultural Tourism, *Flin.* 48c
Culture and Arts, Cell for, *GRI* 665a
Culture and Communication, Centre for Research in, *Murd.* 100c
Culture and Language, School of, *S'ton.* 1729b
Culture and Technology, McLuhan Programme in, *Tor.* 502a
Culture, Archaeology, Religions and Biogeography, Centre for the Study of (SCARAB), *Wales* 1778b
Culture, Communication and Societies, *Lond.* 1534a
Cumberland Health and Research Centre, *Syd.* 180a
Curricular Studies, *Paisley* 1670c
Curriculum, *Qu.* 457c
Curriculum and Arts Education, *Z'bwe.* 1826c
Curriculum and Instruction, *Chinese HK* 1832c, *Edo State* 1022c, *Egerton* 889a, *Montr.* 411b, *New Br.* 428b, *Uyo* 1073a
Curriculum and Instruction: Humanities, *Bran.* 293a
Curriculum and Instruction: Mathematics/Science, *Bran.* 293a
Curriculum and Teaching, *Calabar* 1019c, *Dar.* 1292a, *Swazi.* 1289a
Curriculum and Teaching Studies, *Aust.Cath.* 13c, *Malawi* 906b
Curriculum and Teaching/Educational Foundations, *E.Af.Baraton* 887b
Curriculum Development and Evaluation Unit, *Jamaica UT* 883a
Curriculum Development and Instructional Materials Centre, *Nigeria* 1055a
Curriculum Development Centre, *Anna* 597a
Curriculum: Humanities and Social Sciences, *Manit.* 391b
Curriculum: Mathematics and Natural Sciences, *Manit.* 391c
Curriculum Research and Development Centre, *Syd.* 180a, *Victoria UT* 197c
Curriculum Studies, *Br.Col.* 304b, *Durban-W.* 1170b, *HK* 1838a, *Lagos State* 1045b, *Lond.* 1534b, *NE* 103b, *O.Awolowo* 1059c, *Ondo State* 1066a, *Rand Afrikaans* 1211a, *W.Ont.* 523a
Curriculum Studies and Educational Technology, *P.Harcourt* 1067c
Curriculum Studies and Instructional Technology, *Ogun State* 1064b
Curriculum Studies and Teacher Education, *Venda* 1234a
Curriculum Studies (Arts and Humanities), *Edin.* 1415a
Curriculum Studies in Africa, Centre for, *Kenyatta* 892a
Curriculum Studies, Information and Assessment, *Namibia* 955b
Curriculum Studies (Science, Technology, Mathematics and Computing), *Edin.* 1415a
Curriculum, Teaching and Learning, *Griff.* 55b
Curriculum, Teaching and Media, *Mak.* 1302c
Cybernetics, *Reading* 1691c
Cytology and Gynaecological Pathology, *Pg.IMER* 807c
Czech, *Glas.* 1438a, *Oxf.* 1651b

Dairy and Food Science Technology, *Egerton* 889b
Dairy Bacteriology, *NDRI* 786c
Dairy Cattle Nutrition, *NDRI* 786c
Dairy Cattle Physiology, *NDRI* 786c
Dairy Chemistry, *NDRI* 787a
Dairy Engineering, *NDRI* 787a
Dairy Extension, *NDRI* 787b
Dairy Microbiology, *NDRI* 787b
Dairy Process Engineering Centre, *Monash* 96b
Dairy Research Group, *McG.* 377a
Dairy Science, *B'desh.Ag.* 227b, *Glas.* 1438a, *TN Vet.* 863a, 863c
Dairy Sciences and Technology Research Centre, *Laval* 358b
Dairy Technology, *NDRI* 787b
Dairy/Beef Cattle Research Station, *Kumasi* 571b
Dakwah and Leadership Studies, *NU Malaysia* 923c
Dance, *Adel.* 6a, *Ban.* 617a, *Baroda* 749c, *Ghana* 567c, *Jaffna* 1266b, *Kuruk.* 733b, *Melb.* 79a, *NSW* 109c, *Potti ST* 809b, *R.Bhar.* 822b, *Sur.* 1741c, *VB* 874a, *Wat.* 513b, *York(Can.)* 546a
Dance and Drama, *Mak.* 1302c
Dance and Dramatics, *Ban.Vid.* 618b
Dance, Contemporary, *C'dia.* 322c
Dance School, *Melb.* 83b
Dance, School of, *Cape Town* 1161a
Dance Studies, *ANU* 20b
Danish, *Lond.* 1570a
Data Acquisition, Control and Simulation Centre, *Alta.* 288b
Data and Knowledge Engineering, Centre for, *Lond.* 1542c
Data Archive, *Essex* 1425b
Data Communications, *Qld.UT* 146a
Data Encryption, *Wat.* 520a
Data Processing Unit, *Faisalabad* 1084a
Data Storage Institute, *NU Singapore* 1154b
Data Structuring, *Wat.* 520a
David Dunlap Observatory, *Tor.* 502a
David Syme Taxation Research Unit, *Monash* 96b
David Syme Treasury Dealing Centre, *Monash* 96b
Dawah Academy, *IIU(P'stan.)* 1099b
Dawah Study Centre, *IIU(P'stan.)* 1099b
De Lissa Research Centre, *S.Aust.* 159b
De-Addiction Centre, *All India IMS* 586a
Deaf Studies and Sign Language Research, National Institute for, *La Trobe* 69a
Deaf Studies, Centre for, *Brist.* 1350b
Deafness Studies and Research, Centre for, *Griff.* 58b
Deafness, Western Canada Centre of Specialization in, *Alta.* 288b
Decision Analysis, Group for Research on, *Montr.* 420a
Decision Research, Centre for, *Leeds* 1491b
Decision Sciences, *Lond.Bus.* 1544b, *NU Singapore* 1147a
Decision Sciences and Management Information Systems (DS&MIS), *C'dia.* 322c
Decision Sciences and Managerial Economics, *Chinese HK* 1832c
Decision Theory, *Manc.* 1598b
Deer Research Unit, *Syd.* 180a
Defence and Security Studies, Centre for, *Manit.* 400a
Defence and Strategic Studies, *MDU* 753b, *Punjabi* 820a, *Quaid-i-Azam* 1115c
Defence Economics, Centre for, *York(UK)* 1802a
Defence Research and Development Organisation, *Cochin* 644c
Defence Studies, *Aberd.* 1314a, *Madr.* 742b, *Pune* 811a
Defence Studies, Centre for, *Aberd.* 1317b, *Lond.* 1542c
Defence Technology, College of, *Cran.* 1388c
Delinquency, Institute for the Study and Treatment of, *Lond.* 1542c
Deltaic Research Centre, *Dhaka* 242c
Dementia Services Development Centre, *Stir.* 1732b
Democracy, Centre for, *Qld.* 140b
Democracy, Centre for the Study of, *Westminster* 1792b
Democratisation, Centre for the Study of, *Warw.* 1783b
Democratization Studies, Centre for, *Leeds* 1491b
Demographic Research, Centre for, *Nigeria* 1055a
Demographic Unit, *Malawi* 906c
Demography, *Botswana* 262b, *Colombo* 1259c, *Macq.* 72a, *Montr.* 411b, *Swazi.* 1289a
Demography and Population Studies, *Kerala* 729b, *Waik.* 992a
Demography and Social Statistics, *O.Awolowo* 1059c
Demography and Sociology Division, *ANU* 17a
Demography Program, *ANU* 17a
Demography Unit, *NUL* 904b
Dental Advice Research and Technology Service, *Sheff.* 1712a
Dental Auxiliary School, *Lond.* 1554b
Dental Auxiliary Sciences, *PNG* 1128b
Dental Biophysics, *Lond.* 1554b
Dental Clinical Sciences, *Dal.* 331c
Dental Diagnostic and Surgical Sciences, *Manit.* 396b
Dental Education, *Edin.* 1419c
Dental Health, *Moi* 894c
Dental Health and Development, *Wales* 1772a
Dental Hygiene, School of, *Dal.* 331c, *Manit.* 396b
Dental Materials, *Manipal AHE* 762b, 763a
Dental Medicine, *Montr.* 411b
Dental Prosthetics, *Stell.* 1229a
Dental Public Health, *Lond.* 1554c
Dental Public Health and Community Dentistry, *Lond.* 1538c
Dental Public Health, Unit of, *Manc.* 1603a
Dental Radiology, *Belf.* 1687b, *Lond.* 1538c, *Newcastle(UK)* 1624c
Dental School, *Dund.* 1399a, *Sheff.* 1705b
Dental Science, *Melb.* 79a
Dental Science, School of, *Melb.* 84b
Dental Sciences, *Lucknow* 739c
Dental Sciences, Basic, *Ghana* 567c, 569b
Dental Sciences/Oral Medicine and Pathology, *Lond.* 1538c
Dental Services, *Sheff.* 1708c
Dental Statistics and Research Unit, Health and Welfare, Australian Institute of, *Adel.* 9c
Dental Studies, School of, *Syd.* 176a
Dental Surgery, *Aberd.* 1316a, *All India IMS* 586a, *Ban.* 615b, *Belf.* 1687b, *Leeds* 1489b, *Lond.* 1577a, *Malta* 947b, *Nair.* 899c, *Peradeniya* 1275b
Dental Therapy, *Curtin* 35c
Dentistry, *A.Bello* 1008c, 1010b, *Adel.* 6a, *Aga Khan* 1081b, *Alta.* 281a, *Annam.* 598c, *Belf.* 1684c, *Benin* 1015b, *Birm.* 1328b, *Br.Col.* 297c, *Brist.* 1346a, *Dal.* 328c, *Dar.* 1292a, *Dund.* 1397b, *Durban-W.* 1170b, *Glas.* 1438a, *HK* 1838b, *Ib.* 1035b, *Laval* 351c, *Leeds* 1485a, *Lond.* 1536c, 1540c, 1552b, *McG.* 364b, *Mak.* 1304b, *Malaya* 917a, *Manc.* 1598b, *Manit.* 391c, *Newcastle(UK)* 1620c, *NU Singapore* 1147b, *O.Awolowo* 1059c, *Otago* 980c, *Pg.IMER* 808a, *Pret.* 1203b, *S.Af.Med.* 1174a, *S.Leone* 1132b, *Stell.* 1225a, *Syd.* 171c, *Tor.* 484c, *W.Aust.* 201a, *W.Cape* 1236b, *W.Ont.* 522c
Dentistry, Community, *W.Cape* 1236b
Dentistry, Conservative, *W.Cape* 1236b
Dentistry: Orthodontics, *Belf.* 1687b
Dentistry, Paediatric and Preventive, *Belf.* 1687b
Dentistry, Prosthetic, *W.Cape* 1236b
Dentistry, Restorative, *Belf.* 1687b
Dentistry, School of, *Liv.* 1508c, *Newcastle(UK)* 1624b, *Qld.* 132b, *WI* 1817a
Department of Elementary Education Child Centre, *Alta.* 288b
Department of Hugh Devine Professor, St Vincent's Hospital, *Melb.* 86c
Department of James Stewart Professor, Royal Melbourne and Western Hospitals, *Melb.* 84c, 86c
Dermatology, *Aberd.* 1316a, *Br.Col.* 305b, 306a, *Cape Town* 1165c, *Dund.* 1399b, *Edin.* 1419c, *Glas.* 1442a, *Liv.* 1511c, *Lond.* 1539a, 1540c, 1555a, 1562a, 1577a, *Natal* 1181c, 1182b, *Newcastle(UK)* 1624c, *Nigeria* 1051a, *OFS* 1193c, *S.Af.Med.* 1174b, *S.Ramachandra Med.* 853a, *Stell.* 1229c, *Wales* 1772a
Dermatology and S.T.D., *Annam.* 600b
Dermatology and Venereology, *All India IMS* 586a, *Ban.* 615b, *NU Singapore* 1152c, *O.Awolowo* 1062b

Interface Analysis Centre, *Brist.* 1350b
Interface Properties and Catalysis, Centre for Research on, *Laval* 358b
Interface Science Western, *W.Ont.* 531a
Interfaith Marriage and Family Institute, *Winn.* 543a
Intergovernmental Relations, Institute of, *Qu.* 460b
Interior Architecture, *NSW* 112b
Interior Design, *Manit.* 393c, *N.Lond.* 1628c, *Qld.UT* 146c, *SNDT* 844a
Interior Design, School of, *Ryerson* 468a
Interlanguage Studies, Centre for, *Lond.* 1523c
Internal Medicine, *Mbarara* 1306b, *OFS* 1194a, *Pg.IMER* 808a, *Pret.* 1207b, *S.Af.Med.* 1174c, *Stell.* 1229c
International Accounting Research, Centre for, *Hull* 1467c
International Affairs, Office of, *McM.* 387c
International Affairs, School of, *Car.* 318a
International and Commercial Law Centre, *Technol.Syd.* 193b
International and Comparative Politics, Centre for, *Stell.* 1231c
International and Comparative Studies, *W.Ont.* 532b
International and Political Studies, *Swinburne UT* 168b
International and Public Law, Centre for, *ANU* 19a
International and Security Studies, Centre for, *York(Can.)* 551a
International and Tropical Health and Nutrition, Australian Centre for, *Qld.* 141b
International Antioxidant Research Centre, *Lond.* 1542c
International Business, *Auck.* 963a, *Chinese HK* 1833b, *Griff.* 56c, *Massey* 976b
International Business, Centre for, *Stell.* 1231c
International Business, Graduate School of, *Brist.* 1350b
International Business Management, *G.Jamb.* 678b
International Business, School of, *S.Aust.* 157c
International Business Studies, *Ulster* 1751c
International Business Studies, Centre for, *Br.Col.* 309b, *Dal.* 334b, *Manit.* 400b, *Montr.* 420b, *W.Ont.* 531b
International Business Unit, *Manc.Met.* 1614a
International Communication, *Bourne.* 1340a
International Communication, David Lam Centre for, *S.Fraser* 481a
International Competitiveness and the Engineering of Networked Enterprises, Research Centre on (SORCIIER), *Laval* 358b
International Development, *Sund.* 1739c
International Development Studies, *St Mary's(Can.)* 472b
International Development Technology Centre, *Melb.* 87a
International Drylands Research, Sheffield Centre for, *Sheff.* 1712c
International Economic Relations, Centre for the Study of, *W.Ont.* 531b
International Economic Studies, Centre for, *Adel.* 9c
International Education and Development, Centre for, *Alta.* 288c
International Education, Flinders University Institute of, *Flin.* 52b
International Education in Economics, Centre for, *Lond.* 1565c
International Education Office, *Manit.* 400b
International Educational Leadership and Management Centre, *L&H* 1505c
International English, Centre for, *Curtin* 38a
International Global Change Institute, *Waik.* 994c
International Health and Development, Centre for, *Ott.* 446b
International Health Studies, Centre for, *QM Edin.* 1682c
International Institute, *Salf.* 1702a
International Institute of Islamic Thought Malaysia, *IIU Malaysia* 914c
International Journalism, Centre for, *Qld.* 141c
International Labour Resource and Information Group (ILRIG), *Cape Town* 1168c
International Management Centre, *Hull* 1467c
International Management Studies, Centre for, *McG.* 377b
International Marketing, *L&H* 1505b
International Marketing and Entrepreneurship, Centre for, *New Br.* 431a
International Media Centre, *Salf.* 1703b
International Ombudsman Institute, *Alta.* 289a
International Politics, *Wales* 1755b
International Politics, Organisation and Disarmament, Centre for, *J.Nehru U.* 713b
International Programs, Centre for, *Guelph* 341c
International Relations, *Aberd.* 1315a, *ANU* 16b, *Baloch.* 1094a, *Bond* 23c, *Dhaka* 239c, *Karachi* 1103b, *Keele* 1470b, *Kent* 1474a, *Lanc.* 1481b, *Lond.* 1547a, *O.Awolowo* 1060c, *Quaid-i-Azam* 1116a, *SA Latif* 1117b, *St And.* 1698a, 1699a, *Sindh* 1120a, *Witw.* 1243a
International Relations and Asian Politics Research Unit, *Qld.* 141c
International Relations and Politics, *Sus.* 1747b
International Relations, Centre for, *Qu.* 460b
International Relations, Institute of, *Br.Col.* 309b, *WI* 1818c
International Relations, School of, *M.Gandhi* 757a
International Research, Office of, *McG.* 377b
International Security, Research Group in, *Montr.* 418b
International Studies, *Brock* 313a, *De Mont.* 1393a, *Deakin* 41b, *Nair.* 901b, *N.Br.Col.* 435b, *Nott.Trent* 1642a, *S.Aust.* 157c, *Warw.* 1781b, *Wat.* 516a
International Studies and Law, *Coventry* 1385c
International Studies, Centre for, *Lond.* 1548b, *Tor.* 502b
International Studies, Centre of, *Camb.* 1365c
International Studies, Institute for, *Leeds* 1491b, *Technol.Syd.* 193b
International Studies, School of, *Pondicherry* 806b
International Telugu Studies, *Potti ST* 810a
International Water Engineering Centre, *Ott.* 446b
Interoperable Systems Research Centre, *City(UK)* 1382c
Interpreting and Translating, Centre for Research and Development in, *Deakin* 42c
Invector Ltd, *Sheff.* 1712c
Investigative Science, *Lond.* 1530c
Investment, Risk Management and Insurance, *City(UK)* 1381b
Ion Beam Applications, Surrey Centre for Research in, *Sur.* 1744b
Iqbal Institute, *Kashmir* 728a
Iqbaliyat, *A.Iqbal Open* 1087a, *Islamia, Bahawal.* 1100c, *Punjab* 1114a
Irish Studies, *Belf.* 1685c, *St Mary's(Can.)* 472b
Irish Studies Centre, *N.Lond.* 1630a
Irish Studies, Institute of, *Belf.* 1688c, *Liv.* 1510b
Ironbridge Institute, *Birm.* 1335c
Irrigation and Drainage, *Faisalabad* 1084b
Irrigation and Drainage Engineering, Institute of, *Mehran* 1107c
Irrigation and Water Management, *B'desh.Ag.* 228a
Islam, Urdu Encyclopaedia of, *Punjab* 1114b
Islamiat, *N-WFP Eng.* 1111b
Islamic and Middle Eastern Law, Centre of, *Lond.* 1565c
Islamic and Middle Eastern Studies, *Edin.* 1417c
Islamic and Pakistan Studies, *Aga Khan* 1081b
Islamic Centre, *Putra* 930c
Islamic Civilization, *NU Malaysia* 925a, *Sci.U.Malaysia* 935a
Islamic Culture, *Peradeniya* 1276a, *SA Latif* 1117b, *Sindh* 1120a
Islamic Economics, International Institute of, *IIU(P'stan.)* 1099b
Islamic History and Culture, *Chitt.* 235a, *Dhaka* 239c, *Islamic(B'desh.)* 246b, *Rajsh.* 255c
Islamic Law, *Malaya* 918a, *NU Malaysia* 925a
Islamic Learning, *Karachi* 1103b
Islamic Legal Studies, Centre for, *A.Bello* 1011b
Islamic Research Institute, *IIU(P'stan.)* 1099c
Islamic Studies, *A.Iqbal Open* 1087a, *Azad J&K* 1089c, *Baloch.* 1094a, *Bayero* 1013a, *Brunei* 265a, *B.Zak.* 1091c, *Camb.* 1360b, *Colombo* 1260b, *Dhaka* 240a, *Durban-W.* 1171b, *Durh.* 1403c, *Eastern(S.Lanka)* 1263a, *Faisalabad* 1084b, *Glas.* 1439c, *Ib.* 1036a, *Islamia, Bahawal.* 1100c, *Jaffna* 1265c, *J.Hamdard* 707c, *JMI* 709c, *Kashmir* 727b, *Kerala* 729b, *Lahore UET* 1096b, *Maid.* 1048b, *Malaya* 918b, *Osm.* 797b, *Oxf.* 1655a, *Punjab* 1113b, *Rajsh.* 256a, *Sci.U.Malaysia* 935a, *Tech.U.Malaysia* 941a, *Tor.* 487a, *U.Danfodiyo* 1071a, *VB* 874c
Islamic Studies, Academy of, *Malaya* 920b
Islamic Studies and Sharia, *Islamic Uganda* 1301b
Islamic Studies and Social Development, Centre of, *Tech.U.Malaysia* 941c
Islamic Studies, Centre for, *Rand Afrikaans* 1212b, *U.Danfodiyo* 1071c
Islamic Studies, Centre of, *Lond.* 1565c
Islamic Studies, Institute of, *Azad J&K* 1090b, *McG.* 367a
Islamic Studies, Oxford Centre for, *Oxf.* 1661a
Italian, *Alta.* 283b, *Auck.* 962b, 963a, *Bath* 1323c, *Br.Col.* 301a, *Brist.* 1347b, *Brock* 313a, *Camb.* 1360b, *Car.* 318b, 318c, *C'dia.* 324a, *Delhi* 648b, *Durh.* 1403c, *Edin.* 1417c, *Exe.* 1428c, 1429b, *Flin.* 49c, *Glas.* 1439c, *Guelph* 337c, *Hull* 1466a, *Kent* 1473c, 1474a, *Lanc.* 1481b, *Leeds* 1487a, *Lond.* 1553a, 1558c, 1571b, *McG.* 367a, *McM.* 383a, *Macq.* 74a, 75a, *Malta* 948a, *Manc.* 1600b, *Manit.* 393a, 393c, *Melb.* 81b, *Ott.* 441a, *Oxf.* 1655a, *Qu.* 455c, *Rhodes* 1214c, *S.Af.* 1219c, *St And.* 1698a, 1698b, *Strath.* 1735b, *Sus.* 1747b, *Syd.* 173c, *Tas.* 184b, *Tor.* 503a, *VB* 874c, *Wales* 1768c, *Warw.* 1781b, *Wat.* 516a, *W.Aust.* 202b, *Well.* 988b, *Windsor* 538c, *York(Can.)* 548a
Italian and Spanish, *Well.* 988b
Italian Studies, *Birm.* 1330c, 1331a, *Cape Town* 1163a, *Chinese HK* 1833c, *Guelph* 337c, *La Trobe* 66c, *Reading* 1693a, *Tor.* 487a

J. Stewart Marshall Radar Observatory, *McG.* 377b
Jain Baudh Darshan, *Ban.* 613b
Jain Darshan, *Samp.Sanskrit* 834b
Jainology, *Madr.* 742c
Jainology and Comparative Religion and Philosophy, *Jain VB* 706b
Jainology and Prakrit, *M.Sukh.* 773a, *Mys.* 780a
James Rennel Division, *S'ton.* 1727c
Japan Centre, *ANU* 18c, *Birm.* 1335c
Japan Research Centre, *Lond.* 1565c
Japanese, *Auck.* 963a, *Camb.* 1360b, *Cant.* 970c, *CIE&F Langs.* 639c, *Dhaka* 240a, *James Cook* 62b, *Macq.* 75a, *Massey* 976b, *Melb.* 81b, *Newcastle(NSW)* 123c, 124a, *Otago* 981b, *Oxf.* 1655a, *Stir.* 1731c, *VB* 874c, *Waik.* 992b, 993a, *Well.* 988b
Japanese and Chinese, *Melb.* 78b
Japanese and Korean Studies, *Syd.* 171a
Japanese and North East Asian Languages, Centre for, *J.Nehru U.* 713c
Japanese Language, *Bond* 23c
Japanese Language Proficiency Unit, *Qld.* 141c
Japanese New Religions Project, *Lond.* 1542c
Japanese Studies, *Chinese HK* 1833c, *Delhi* 648b, *HK* 1839c, *Monash* 92b, *Newcastle(UK)* 1622a, *NU Singapore* 1150a, *Syd.* 173c
Japanese Studies Centre, *Monash* 97a, *Wales* 1765c
Japanese Studies Centre for Teaching Development, *Macq.* 76a
Jazz, *ANU* 20b
Jazz and Popular Music, Centre for, *Natal* 1183b
Jazz Studies Unit, *Syd.* 181b
Jessop Hospital, *Sheff.* 1710b
Jesuit Centre at St Paul's College Faith Development and Values Project, *Manit.* 400b
Jewellery, School of, *C.England* 1376b
Jewish Civilisation, Australian Centre for, *Monash* 97a
Jewish Studies, *Lond.* 1571b, *McG.* 367b, *Oxf.* 1655a
Jewish Studies and Research, The Isaac and Jessie Kaplan Centre for, *Cape Town* 1168c
Jewish Studies, Centre for, *Leeds* 1491b, *Lond.* 1565c, *York(Can.)* 551a
Jockey Club Rehabilitation Engineering Centre, *HKPU* 1847a
Johannesburg, Helen Joseph and Hillbrow Hospitals (Neurology), *Witw.* 1242c
Johannesburg Hospital, *Witw.* 1240b, 1241a, 1244a, 1244b, 1244c, 1245a, 1245c, 1246b
Johannesburg Hospital (Dermatology), *Witw.* 1242c
John P. Robarts Research Institute, *W.Ont.* 531b
Joint Clinical Sciences Program, *Qld.* 141c
Joint Experimental Haematology Program, *Qld.* 141c
Joint Experimental Oncology Program, *Qld.* 141c
Joint Facilities Bioethics Project, *Alta.* 289a
Joint Program in Transplantation Biology, *Qld.* 141c
Journalism, *Cant.* 970c, *C'dia.* 324a, *Chitt.* 235b, *City(UK)* 1381b, *Dhaka* 240a, *Dr BA Marath.* 656a, *Gauh.* 667a, *Gujar.* 671a, *HNB Garh.* 683c, *Karn.* 724b, *Kerala* 729b, *Kuruk.* 733b, *MCN Journ.* 759a, *Monash* 92a, *Mys.* 779a, *Osm.* 797b, *Potti ST* 810a, *Pune* 811b, *Punj.Ag.* 817b, *Qld.* 135a, *Qld.UT* 146c, *Saur.* 838b, *SPMV* 852a, *Stell.* 1227a, *Technol.Syd.* 191b, *Wat.* 516a
Journalism and Communication, *Baroda* 750c, *Chinese HK* 1833c
Journalism and Communication, School of, *Car.* 318b
Journalism and Communication Science, *Shiv.* 842a
Journalism and Communications, School of, *Regina* 463a
Journalism and Mass Communication, *And.* 591b, *Ban.* 613b, *Berh.* 624b, *Buea* 268a, *DAV* 651a, *G.Ghasidas* 677b, *GND* 681a, *HP* 684c, *Kota Open* 731c, *MDU* 753b, *Mys.* 780a, *Punjabi* 820a
Journalism and Media Studies, *Rhodes* 1214c
Journalism and Publishing, *Nan.Tech.* 1139a
Journalism and Science Communication, *Madurai-K.* 746b
Journalism, Graduate School of, *W'gong.* 214b
Journalism, Media and Cultural Studies, School of, *Wales* 1763c
Journalism, School of, *Nair.* 901b, 902a, *Ryerson* 468a
Journalism, Sing Tao School of, *Br.Col.* 301a
Journalism Studies, *Sheff.* 1707a
Journalism Unit, *Colombo* 1260b
Journalism/Communication, *Madr.* 742c
Julius Kruttschnitt Mineral Research Centre, *Qld.* 141c
Jurisprudence, *North(S.Af.)* 1188b, *S.Af.* 1219c, *Syd.* 173c
Jurisprudence and International Law, *Benin* 1016b
Jurisprudence and Private Law, *O.Awolowo* 1060c
Jurisprudence, Legal History and Comparative Law, *Venda* 1234b
Justice Administration, *Griff.* 56c
Justice and Applied Legal Studies, Institute of, *S.Pac.* 1254a
Justice and Law Enforcement, Studies in, *Winn.* 542b
Justice and Youth Studies, *RMIT* 152c
Justice Studies, School of, *Ryerson* 468a
Justice Training Centre, *Namibia* 956c
Jyothisha, *Potti ST* 810a
Jyotish, *Ban.* 613b, *Samp.Sanskrit* 834b
Jyotisha, *Rashtriya SV* 827b

Kadoorie Agricultural Research Centre, *HK* 1843b
Kakatiya Adhyayana Kendram, *Kakatiya* 719b
Kannada, *B'lore.* 620b, *Delhi* 648b, *Gulb.* 675a, 675b, 675c, *Karn.* 725b, *Kuvempu* 735c, *Madr.* 744a, *Madurai-K.* 746b, *M'lore.* 760c, *Mumbai* 775c, *Mys.* 779a, 781a, *Osm.* 797a, 797b
Kannada Research Institute, *Karn.* 725a
Kannada Studies, Institute of, *Karn.* 724b
Kannada Studies, Kuvempu Institute of, *Mys.* 780a
Kanuri, *Maid.* 1048b

INDEX TO PERSONAL NAMES

Names, in 3-column setting, in university chapters are indexed by page number and column reference (a, b or c) plus abbreviation for the chapter in which they appear (*example*: Gagnon, Alain, *Laval.*, 355a). Names in page-wide setting are column-referenced 'a' and names in Volume 1 preliminary pages are indicated by roman numerals with no column reference. Impersonal titles of post (*example*: President of India) are not indexed.

Finding names. All personal names are indexed under the first letter of the main/surname element as set out first in entries throughout the book.

Example: Abdul Haq, M., *Calicut.*, 637c
Chan Lai Wah, *NU Singapore*, 1151b
Jackson, Richard A., *Sus.*, 1746b
Onwuka, E.C., *Edo State*, 1022c
Van Rhyn, W.J.C., *OFS*, 1193a
Zvekic, U., *Hull*, 1465a

Identical names. Names that are identical are indexed in the following ways *irrespective of whether or not they relate to the same person*. If within the same chapter: as a single name entry. *Example:* Sharma, D. C., *Jiw.*, 717a, 717b, 718a. If in *different* chapters, as two or more name entries in

alphabetical order of universities preceded by non-university entries.
Example: Smith, A.J., xl
A.J., *Edin.*, 1421c
A.J., *Wolv..*, 1793a

One element names. Names which consist of one element only (*example*: Mohiuddin) come before people with the same main element.

Alphabetical order. Names are listed alphabetically in word-by-word order by main/surname element(s). Hyphenated and run-together elements are treated as single words.
Example: El Ansari, Wahid
El Toukhy, M.M.

Elaigwu, J.J.
Elam, Diane M.
El-Ashker, Ahmed

Notes (i) Names beginning Mac or Mc are listed together under Mac, the next letter of each name determining its position with the sequence.

(ii) Same name variant forms are grouped together.
Example:
Côté   MacDonald
Côte   Macdonald
Coté   McDonald

(iii) Names beginning Saint, St. or St- are listed together under Saint.

A Aziz Martunus, *Brunei*, 265b
A Hamid bin A Hadi, *Malaya*, 916c
A K M Jalaludin Khan, *IIU Malaysia*, 913b
A K M Mostafa Kamal, *IIU Malaysia*, 913b
A Rahman A Jamal, *NU Malaysia*, 926c
Aagawal, Sheela, *Sheff.Hallam*, 1717c
Aalandong, O., *Devel.Studies(Ghana)*, 564c
Aalbers, Johannes, *W.Cape*, 1236a
Aalbersberg, W. G. L., *S.Pac.*, 1253a
Aalto, S. K., *St FX*, 470a
Aamir, Ijaz, *Punjab*, 1112c
Aaron, Jane, *Wales*, 1755a
P., *Coventry*, 1384c
S. L., *Alta.*, 286c
Aarons, Debra L., *Stell.*, 1227b
L. J., *Manc.*, 1601b
Aaronson, Philip I., *Lond.*, 1541c
Aarssen, L. W., *Qu.*, 453a
Aarts, Bas, *Lond.*, 1570c
Aasen, Clarence, *Well.*, 986b
Aashikpelokhai, U. S. U., *Edo State*, 1023b
Aaskov, J. G., *Qld.UT*, 147a
Ab Baqoi, *Kashmir*, 727c
Ab Ieuan, Ruth, *Wales*, 1753c
Ab Rahim Hj Ismail, *NU Malaysia*, 923b
Ab Rahman Mustafa, *Utara, Malaysia*, 944b
Ab Rasid b Mat Zin, *Sci.U.Malaysia*, 937c
Abaa, S. I., *A.Bello*, 1009b
Abachi, H. R., *Monash*, 91a
Abad, P., *McM.*, 381b
Abadi, R. V., *UMIST*, 1609a
Abadir, Karim, *York(UK)*, 1799b, 1800b
Abah, J. O., *Maid.*, 1048a
Abaidoo, R. C., *Kumasi*, 571b
Abaitey, A. K., *Kumasi*, 572c
Abakah, E. N., *Winneba*, 565b
Abalaka, J. A., *Minna*, 1030a
Abali ibn Muhammadu, H.R.H. Alhaji Emir of Fika, *Calabar*, 1019a
Abam, D. P. S., *P.Harcourt*, 1068a
Abama, E. A., *Jos*, 1042b
Abane, A. M., *Cape Coast*, 562b
Abang, Sr. A. T., *Jos*, 1041b
Moses O., *Calabar*, 1021c
Sylvanus O. M., *Calabar*, 1019b
T. B., *Jos*, 1041b
Abang Abdullah bin Abang Ali, *Putra*, 928a, 929b
Abanime, E. P., *Nigeria*, 1053b
Abanobi, S. E., *Abia State*, 1000c
Abanteriba, Sylvester, *RMIT*, 151b
Abas bin Abdul Wahab, *Tech.U.Malaysia*, 940b
Abas Salleh, *Putra*, 930c
Abashar, Mohamed E. E., *Durban-W.*, 1170c
Abasi, Rev. A. H. K., *Devel.Studies(Ghana)*, 564b, 564c
Abasiattai, M. B., *Uyo*, 1073b

Abasiekong, E. M., *Uyo*, 1073c
Solomon F., *Umudike*, 1027b
Abass, Z. A., *NED Eng.*, 1108c
Abatan, A. O., *A.Bello*, 1009a
M. O., *Ib.*, 1038c
Abayakoon, S. B. S., *Peradeniya*, 1275b
Abayanansa, K., *Kelaniya*, 1270a
Abayasekara, C. R., *Peradeniya*, 1275b
Abayasundere, A. P. N. de S., *Sri Jay.*, 1284c
Abayawardhana, D. L., *Sri Jay.*, 1284b
Abayeh, O. J., *AT Balewa*, 1002a
Abayomi, I. O., *O.Awolowo*, 1062a
Abba, Isa A., *Bayero*, 1013a
Abbai, J., *And.*, 592b
Abbaiah, R., *S.Venkat.*, 856a
Abbas, A., *Lahore UET*, 1096a
F., *Aga Khan*, 1082a
G., *Islamia, Bahawal.*, 1100c
G., *Lahore UET*, 1095b
Hasan, *Quaid-i-Azam*, 1116c
M. A., *HK*, 1838a
Naheed, *Faisalabad*, 1084c
Shemeem, *A.Iqbal Open*, 1087a
Syed P., *Karachi*, 1102c
Tahir, *B.Zak.*, 1091a, 1091c, 1092c
Abbas Ali, *Osm.*, 798a
Abbas b Hassan, *IIU Malaysia*, 914c
Abbasayulu, Y. B., *Osm.*, 797c
Abbasi, Abdul R., *Sindh*, 1119c
Aitbar A., *Mehran*, 1107a
Atiya, *Karachi*, 1104c
Faizullah, *Mehran*, 1107b
G. A., *Azad J&K*, 1090a
G. Q., *Islamia, Bahawal.*, 1101a
Hafeez, *Bhutto IST*, 1118a
Haji K., *Sindh*, 1120a
Hina Q., *Islamia, Bahawal.*, 1101b
Khursheed A., *Mehran*, 1107b
Khurshid, *Karachi*, 1104b
M. K., *Azad J&K*, 1089a
M. Sarwar, *Azad J&K*, 1089a
Pervez, *Karachi*, 1103a
Rahim Y., *Islamia, Bahawal.*, 1101c
S. A., *Mehran*, 1107a
S. A., *Osm.*, 797b
S. A., *Pondicherry*, 806a, 806c
Saifullah, *Sindh*, 1120b
Shabbir A., *Azad J&K*, 1090b
Shehla, *Sindh*, 1119c
Ubedullah, *Sindh*, 1119a
Abbasy, Hafsa, *Bhutto IST*, 1118c
Abberton, Evelyn R. M., *Lond.*, 1572a
Abbey, Bene W., *P.Harcourt*, 1067b
Robert M., *Westminster*, 1791b
W., *Lond.*, 1582b
Abbi, Anvita, *J.Nehru U.*, 713c
Abbiss, J. C., *Nott.Trent*, 1640b
Abbo, Abdul A., *Cape Town*, 1166b
Abbot, N. J., *Lond.*, 1536b
Abbott, Carmeta A., *Wat.*, 515a
Elizabeth, *Trin.Coll.(Tor.)*, 506b
F. J., *Nott.Trent*, 1643b
F. S., *Br.Col.*, 295c, 302a
Frances, *McG.*, 375b
G., *W.England*, 1787a
George D., *Otago*, 984a

John, *Cape Town*, 1161b
John G., *N-W(S.Af.)*, 1189c
Lynette K., *W.Aust.*, 200a
M. G., *Qu.*, 453c
Malcolm J., *Flin.*, 49a
Marian C., *Nfld.*, 408c
P. R., *Manc.Met.*, 1613c
R. J., *St And.*, 1696c
Tim J., *De Mont.*, 1393a
V. J., *Plym.*, 1674c
W. R., *Wat.*, 517b
Abbott-Chapman, Joan, *Tas.*, 186a, 186b, 186c
Abboud, Raja T., *Br.Col.*, 306b
Abbs, Peter F., *Sus.*, 1746c
Abd Azim Abd Ghani, *Putra*, 930c
Abd Aziz b Muti, *Tech.U.Malaysia*, 940a
Abd Aziz bin Hj Shuaib, *Tech.U.Malaysia*, 939b
Abd Aziz Jemain, *NU Malaysia*, 923a, 925c
Abd Aziz Tajuddin, *Sci.U.Malaysia*, 932c
Abd Aziz Yahya, *NU Malaysia*, 926c
Abd Fatah bin Hassan, Hj , *Tech.U.Malaysia*, 941c
Abd Ghafar Ismail, *NU Malaysia*, 923c
Abd Ghani bin Jalil, *Tech.U.Malaysia*, 941c
Abd Ghani bin Khalid, *Tech.U.Malaysia*, 941a
Abd Ghani Mohd Rafek, *NU Malaysia*, 924c
Abd Halim b Mohd Yatim, *Tech.U.Malaysia*, 940b
Abd Halim Mohamad, *NU Malaysia*, 925a
Abd Halim Shamsuddin, *NU Malaysia*, 923a, 924b
Abd Hamid bin Mohd Tahir, Hj , *Tech.U.Malaysia*, 940c
Abd Hamid bin Othman, *NU Malaysia*, 923c
Abd Khabeer M Ata, *IIU Malaysia*, 914b
Abd Majid bin A Kadir, *Tech.U.Malaysia*, 940c
Abd Rahim bin Abd Rashid, *Malaya*, 917b
Abd Rahni Mt Piah, *Sci.U.Malaysia*, 935b
Abd Razak Habib, *NU Malaysia*, 924a
Abd Razak Hussin, *NU Malaysia*, 927b
Abd Saman bin Abd Kader, *Tech.U.Malaysia*, 940c
Abd Wahab Md Salleh, *NU Malaysia*, 925c
Abd Wahid bin Idris, Hj , *Tech.U.Malaysia*, 940c
Abdalla, H., *De Mont.*, 1392a
Saad H., *Lond.*, 1530c
Abdas, Saleem, *Panjab*, 802b
Abdel Haleem, Muhammad A. S., *Lond.*, 1565c
Abdel Magid, Moustafa F., *S.Fraser*, 476c

Abd-el-Aziz, Alaa, *Winn.*, 541b
Abdel-Gayed, R., *Coventry*, 1384c
Abdel-Haleem, Muhammad A. S., *Lond.*, 1564c
Abdel-Mawgoud, Mohamed, *Lond.*, 1541c
Abdelmessih, A. H., *Tor.*, 492c
Abdelmoty, A. I., *Glam.*, 1433c
Abdelrahman, T., *Tor.*, 484b, 492b
Abdel-Sayed, G., *Windsor*, 538b
Abderrahmane Azzi, *IIU Malaysia*, 913a
Abdo, Nahla, *Car.*, 320a
Abdoh, A. A., *Manit.*, 399b
Abdollah, H., *Qu.*, 458c
Abdool-Karim, Salim S., *Natal*, 1183b
Abdu, P. A., *A.Bello*, 1010c
Abdu-Aguye, I., *A.Bello*, 1009c
Abdul, Ghafoor, *A.Iqbal Open*, 1086b
Hafeez, *A.Iqbal Open*, 1087a
Jabbar, *Punjab*, 1114b
Jalil, *A.Iqbal Open*, 1087b, 1087c
Noor B., *Nagar.*, 783a
Abdul Amir Hassan Kadhum, *NU Malaysia*, 924a
Abdul Azeez, M. Kamal, *IIU(P'stan.)*, 1099a
Abdul Azis, P. K., *Kerala*, 729a
Abdul Aziz, M. Kamal, *IIU(P'stan.)*, 1099a
Abdul Aziz Abu Bakar, *NU Malaysia*, 927c
Abdul Aziz b Ibrahim, *Tech.U.Malaysia*, 940a
Abdul Aziz b Tajuddin, *Sci.U.Malaysia*, 932a
Abdul Aziz Baba, *Sci.U.Malaysia*, 937a
Abdul Aziz Bari, *IIU Malaysia*, 913c
Abdul Aziz Berghout, *IIU Malaysia*, 914c
Abdul Aziz Bidin, *NU Malaysia*, 923b
Abdul Aziz bin Abdul Rahman, *Putra*, 929b
Abdul Aziz bin Abdul Razak, *Malaya*, 919a
Abdul Aziz bin Buang, *Tech.U.Malaysia*, 941a
Abdul Aziz bin Hitam, *Tech.U.Malaysia*, 940c
Abdul Aziz bin Hussin, *Tech.U.Malaysia*, 940c
Abdul Aziz bin Mohd Zin, *Malaya*, 919a
Abdul Aziz Haron, *IIU Malaysia*, 914b
Abdul Aziz Idris, *NU Malaysia*, 925a
Abdul Aziz Othman, *NU Malaysia*, 923a
Abdul Basith, *TN Vet.*, 863c
Abdul Ghaffar bin Abdul Rahman, *Malaya*, 917c
Abdul Ghani b Shafie, *Sci.U.Malaysia*, 935a
Abdul Ghani bin Ibrahim, *Putra*, 930b
Abdul Ghani bin Kamaruddin, *Malaya*, 917c
Abdul Ghani bin Mohammad, *Tech.U.Malaysia*, 940b

Abdul Ghani Yaakob, *IIU Malaysia*, 913c
Abdul Hadi b Endut, *Sci.U.Malaysia*, 932b
Abdul Hadi bin Zakaria, *Malaya*, 916b
Abdul Hakim, *Dhaka*, 243b
Abdul Halim Ahmad, *Utara, Malaysia*, 943c
Abdul Halim bin Abdul Rashid, *Malaya*, 918b
Abdul Halim bin Haji Mat Diah, *Malaya*, 919a
Abdul Halim bin Shaari, *Putra*, 930b
Abdul Halim bin Sulaiman, *Malaya*, 916c
Abdul Halim Mu'adzam Shah ibni Almarhum Sultan Badlishah, H.R.H. Tuanku Alhaj , *Utara, Malaysia*, 943a
Abdul Halim bin Hamid, *Putra*, 930b
Abdul Hameed, Hakim, *J.Hamdard*, 707a
Abdul Hamid Abdullah, *NU Malaysia*, 924c
Abdul Hamid b Hamidon, *Tech.U.Malaysia*, 940b
Abdul Hamid bin Mohd Tahir, Hj , *Tech.U.Malaysia*, 940c
Abdul Hamid Jaafar, *NU Malaysia*, 924a
Abdul Hamid Omar, Tun Dato' Seri , *Utara, Malaysia*, 943a
Abdul Hamid Pawanteh, Tan Sri Dato' Seri , *Utara, Malaysia*, 943a
Abdul Haq, M., *Calicut.*, 637c
Abdul Haseeb Ansari, *IIU Malaysia*, 913c
Abdul Hayei bin Abdul Shukor, *Malaya*, 919a
Abdul Jabbar, *Islamia, Bahawal.*, 1100b
Abdul Jalil bin Abd Kader, *NU Malaysia*, 925b
Abdul Kadir Hj Din, *NU Malaysia*, 924c, 927b
Abdul Kahar D Abdullah Alany, *IIU Malaysia*, 914b
Abdul Kareem, A., *TN Ag.*, 859a
Abdul Kariem bin Hj Mohd Arof, *Malaya*, 920b
Abdul Karim Abdul Ghani, *NU Malaysia*, 923b
Abdul Karim bin Mirasa, *Tech.U.Malaysia*, 940c
Abdul Khader, A. M., *M'lore.*, 760b
M., *Kerala*, 729c
Abdul Khaliq Kazi, *IIU Malaysia*, 914c
Abdul Khayyum, S., *S.Krishna.*, 850b
Abdul Latif, *NU(B'desh.)*, 251b
Abdul Latif bin Haji Ibrahim, Haji , *Brunei*, 264a
Abdul Latiff bin Abu Bakar, Datuk , *Malaya*, 916b
Abdul Latif Mohamad, *NU Malaysia*, 927b
Abdul Latiff Mohamed, *NU Malaysia*, 923b

Achinivu, Kanu A., *Nigeria*, 1054a
Achola, C., *Nair.*, 898c
J. K., *Nair.*, 900b
Mical L. A., *Nair.*, 901b
P. P. W., *Kenyatta*, 892a
Achour, D., *Curtin*, 35c
Dominique, *Laval*, 350c
Achterberg, E., *Plym.*, 1673c
Achufusi, Ifeyinwa G., *Nigeria*, 1053b
Achuta Rau, *Nehru Tech.*, 716b
Achutan, M., *IIT Bombay*, 694c
Achuthan, A., *Calicut*, 637b
K., *Annam.*, 599c
Narasimaha R., *Curtin*, 36c
Achuthan Unni, C. P., *Calicut*, 636a, 637a, 637c, 638a
Achuyutau, Sarla, *Gujar.*, 670c
Achwanya, O. S., *Egerton*, 889a
Achyuta Menon, A., *Cochin*, 644a
Achyutha, R. N., *Mys.*, 779c
Achyutha Rao, H. R., *Mys.*, 778a, 781a
Ackam, R. T., *Kumasi*, 572c
Ackbarally, Rafik, *De Mont.*, 1393b
Ackello-Ogutu, A. C., *Nair.*, 896c
Acker, Mona L., *Regina*, 463b
Sandra, *Tor.*, 493c
Ackerley, Beryl, *Portsmouth*, 1680c
Christopher J., *Otago*, 980c
Ackermann, Denise M., *W.Cape*, 1236b
Frances, *Strath.*, 1735c
Hans-Wolfgang, *Laval*, 357a
Petrus L. S., *S.Af.*, 1222b
Pieter C., *S.Af.Med.*, 1173c
U., *Tor.*, 500a
Ackers, H. Louise, *Leeds*, 1487a
J. P., *Lond.*, 1550a
Janet D., *Manc.Met.*, 1612c
William J., *Newcastle(UK)*, 1621a
Ackland, John W., *Exe.*, 1427b
Michael P., *Monash*, 91b
Timothy R., *W.Aust.*, 202b
Ackom, Paul E., *Winneba*, 566b
Ackroyd, A., *Greenwich*, 1447b
Pam M., *C.Lancs.*, 1379a
Stephen C., *Lanc.*, 1480a
Ackummey, Mary, *Winneba*, 566b
Acland, C. D., *C'dia.*, 321a
Acon, J., *Mak.*, 1305a
Acorn, Annalise E., *Alta.*, 283b
Sonia, *Br.Col.*, 302a
Acosta, Fernando, *Ott.*, 439b
Acquaye, Kpakpo J., *Ghana*, 569b
Actobino, Biko, *Liv.J.Moores*, 1516c
Acton, E. D. J., *E.Anglia*, 1408b
Elizabeth, *Camb.*, 1370b
T. A., *Greenwich*, 1448c
Acuda, S. W., *Z'bwe.*, 1828c
Stanley W., *Keele*, 1471b
Acutt, Bruce, *C.Qld.*, 29b
Acworth, R. Ian, *NSW*, 110c
Aczel, J. D., *Wat.*, 516c
P. H. G., *Manc.*, 1598a, 1601a
Ada, Louise M., *Syd.*, 176c
Adachi, J. D., *McM.*, 385b, 387b
Adadevoh, S. W. K., *Kumasi*, 573b
Adaikan, P. Ganesan, *NU Singapore*, 1153a
Adair, A. S., *Ulster*, 1750c
J. G., *Manit.*, 395b
John, *Exe.*, 1426c, 1431a
Kristin, *S.Pac.*, 1254c
V. A., *Auck.*, 961a
Adakayi, P. E., *Abuja*, 1004a
Adala, H. S., *Nair.*, 900a
Adalakha, S. K., *Kuruk.*, 734b
Adali, Sarp, *Natal*, 1179c
Adam, A., *Bayero*, 1013b
A. A., *Witw.*, 1243b
A. M., *Nair.*, 900a
Albert, *Montr.*, 413c
Allan G., *New Br.*, 428b
Andreas, *Lond.*, 1542a
B. D., *Windsor*, 540a
Barbara E., *Wales*, 1765b
C. S., *Oxf.*, 1661b
Chris M., *Syd.*, 171b
Dyane, *York(Can.)*, 551c, 553c
G. Stuart, *Car.*, 315a, 318b, 320b
Heribert, *S.Fraser*, 480b
Jill, *Leeds Met.*, 1493c
John E., *Ott.*, 443c
K. S., *McM.*, 386c
Kenneth, *Tor.*, 500c
Paul, *NSW*, 108c
R. J., *St And.*, 1697c
S., *Maid.*, 1048c
Stephen, *Westminster*, 1792c
Stephen J., *Westminster*, 1791b
Stewart, *RMIT*, 153b
Adama, David J. B., *Kumasi*, 573a
Hamadau, *Ngaoundéré*, 270a
T. Z., *Minna*, 1030a
Adama-Acquah, R. W., *De Mont.*, 1390c, 1394b
Adamczuk, Henryk, *C.England*, 1376c
Adamec, R. E., *Nfld.*, 405c
Adamiak, K., *W.Ont.*, 523b
Adaminda, I. I., *AT Balewa*, 1002c
Adam-Moodley, Kogila, *Br.Col.*, 304c
Adamowicz, W. L., *Alta.*, 285c
Adamowski, Kazimierz, *Ott.*, 440a
T. H., *Tor.*, 485b
Adams, A. E., *Manc.*, 1598c
A. E., *Newcastle(UK)*, 1621b
A. J., *Manc.Met.*, 1613b
Alfred R., *Sur.*, 1743b
Andrew T., *Edin.*, 1414b
Anne P., *Technol.Syd.*, 192a
Annmarie, *McG.*, 363b
Anthony, *Macq.*, 76c
Anthony, *S.Pac.*, 1253c
Anthony L. E., *Camb.*, 1358a
Anthony P., *Lond.*, 1540b
Austin S., *NSW*, 115a
B. C., *Plym.*, 1672c
B. G., *Laur.*, 348a
B. J., *Tor.*, 492a
Barbara, *Nfld.*, 408c
Bev, *Lake.*, 345b
C. D., *Aberd.*, 1315a
C. E. A., *Belf.*, 1688a
C. J., *Belf.*, 1684a
C. K., *Lincoln(NZ)*, 974a
Carol A. H., *Glas.*, 1436c
D. A., *Belf.*, 1688b
D. B., *Sund.*, 1739b
D. G., *Leeds*, 1490a
D. H., *Birm.*, 1334b
D. J., *Manc.*, 1599c
D. W., *McM.*, 386c
Danny, *W.Cape*, 1238a
David J., *Leeds*, 1490a
David J., *Qld.*, 137b
David M., *ANU*, 19c
David P., *NSW*, 119a
Debra, *Bourne.*, 1339c
Denis C., *Liv.J.Moores*, 1517a
Derek, *Liv.*, 1511b
Donald H., *Macq.*, 73a
F., *Coventry*, 1385b
F. A., *Manc.Met.*, 1613c
Frank R., *Edin.*, 1416a
G. B., *Nfld.*, 407a
G. C., *Acad.*, 278a
G. E., *Manc.*, 1601b
G. R., *Guelph*, 337a
Glenda, *Technol.Syd.*, 192b
Gordon, *Leeds Met.*, 1493b
Gwyneth, *Oxf.Brookes*, 1667c
Hamish, *Nott.*, 1638b
Harvey B., *Natal*, 1184c
Ismail, *W.Cape*, 1236c
J., *City(UK)*, 1381b
J., *Napier*, 1617b
J. A., *Lincoln(NZ)*, 973c
J. C., *Herts.*, 1454b
J. E., *Lond.*, 1553a
J. R. J., *Brist.*, 1346a
J. S., *Ulster*, 1752b
Jerry M., *Melb.*, 84b
John G. U., *Lond.*, 1571a
John N., *Sheff.*, 1707b
Judith E., *Manc.*, 1603c
Julie, *N.Lond.*, 1629c
Julie J., *Monash*, 95c
K., *S.Bank*, 1722a
K. A., *Wales*, 1777c
K. R., *Ulster*, 1750b
Kenneth J., *E.Lond.*, 1411b
Kent, *James Cook*, 63b
Kevin, *RMIT*, 150a
L., *Brock*, 313b
L., *Guelph*, 337b
L., *Lond.*, 1531c
L., *Wales*, 1777c
Laurence P., *Cape Town*, 1165b
Lesley, *S.Aust.*, 156a
Liselyn, *C'dia.*, 324c
M., *S.Bank*, 1722c
M. A., *Qu.*, 459b
M. S., *Wales*, 1778a
Mark A., *W.Aust.*, 200c
Martin R., *Sur.*, 1741a
Michael, *Technol.Syd.*, 191b
Michael J., *Essex*, 1425a
Neryl, *Newcastle(NSW)*, 122b
Nicholas S., *Camb.*, 1374a
Norman, *NE*, 106a
O. A., *De Mont.*, 1390c
P. C., *W.Ont.*, 529a
Parveen, *Brun.*, 1352c
Patricia, *Newcastle(NSW)*, 123b
Paul H., *Exe.*, 1432a
Peter, *Bath*, 1326b
Peter F., *Alta.*, 289a
R., *Coventry*, 1386a
R. D., *Brist.*, 1346c
R. G., *Herts.*, 1454a
R. J., *McM.*, 381b
R. J., *Nfld.*, 405c
R. N., *Lond.*, 1552c
R. S., *Witw.*, 1244b
Robert, *Br.Col.*, 301b
Robert, *Deakin*, 40c
Robert, *L&H*, 1506b
Robert S., *NE*, 106c
Roger D., *Syd.*, 176c
Roger L. P., *Glas.*, 1437a
Ron W., *Victoria UT*, 198a
Roy J., *De Mont.*, 1395b
Russell, *Montr.*, 422b, 422c
S. R., *Herts.*, 1453b
Simon L., *Strath.*, 1735a
Stephen J., *W.Ont.*, 523c
Susan J., *Greenwich*, 1449a, 1449c
Terry A., *Liv.J.Moores*, 1518a
Trevor, *Cape Town*, 1169b
W. M., *Camb.*, 1359b
W. P., *Trent*, 508b
William, *Syd.*, 169a
William A., *Wales*, 1754c
Adam-Smith, Derek W., *Portsmouth*, 1677c
Adamson, A. C. L., *Acad.*, 278c
A. J., *Birm.*, 1330b
Barbara J., *Syd.*, 176b
David L., *Glam.*, 1434a
David M., *Brist.*, 1350c
I., *Abeokuta Ag.*, 1005a, 1005c
I., *Sund.*, 1738a
I. Y. R., *Manit.*, 398c
J., *McM.*, 382b, 383c
J. P. I., *Windsor*, 539b
K., *Sund.*, 1739c
K., *Ulster*, 1751b
Lynne, *C.Sturt*, 32b
Mark, *Bolton Inst.*, 1337c
Martin, *Br.Col.*, 303c
Melitta, *W.Ont.*, 525b
Nancy, *Car.*, 320c
Peter A., *Tor.*, 499a
Robin, *Dund.*, 1400c
Sylvia M., *Camb.*, 1359a
Thomas M., *Monash*, 95a
Adamson-Macedo, Elvidina N., *Wolv.*, 1795a
Adams-Stowe, M., *WI*, 1816b
Adams-Webber, J. R., *Brock*, 313c
Adamu, A. U., *Bayero*, 1012c
Mahdi, *Islamic Uganda*, 1301a, 1301c
U., *Maid.*, 1049c
Adanu, K. G., *Ghana*, 568c
Ada-Okungbowa, Christopher I., *Akure*, 1029b
Adappa, K. Karunakara, *Manipal AHE*, 763b
Adaramola, F., *Lagos State*, 1046a
Adarkwa, Kwasi K., *Kumasi*, 573a
Adatia, A., *Regina*, 463a
Trusha, *N.Lond.*, 1627c
Adaudi, A. O., *A.Bello*, 1010c
Adcock, B. S., *Swinburne UT*, 167b
Christopher J., *Westminster*, 1791c
D., *Coventry*, 1384b
William, *Flin.*, 48c
Addae, J. I., *WI*, 1818a
S. K., *Ghana*, 569c
Addae-Dapaah, Kwame, *NU Singapore*, 1146b
Addae-Kagya, K. A., *Winneba*, 565b
Addae-Mensah, Ivan, 1855c
Ivan, *Ghana*, 566a, 567c
Lawrence, *Kumasi*, 573b
Addai, F. K., *Ghana*, 569a
Addai-Sundiata, J., *Cape Coast*, 563c
J. H., *Cape Coast*, 563a
Addenan Abd Rahman, *NU Malaysia*, 927c
Addepalli, V., *BITS*, 632a
Adderley, A., *Sheff.Hallam*, 1715a
Addicott, J. F., *Alta.*, 280c
W. Stanley, *Wales*, 1769c
Addie, Ronald G., *S.Qld.*, 164b
Addington-Hall, J., *Lond.*, 1539b
Addis, T. R., *Portsmouth*, 1678a
Addison, David J., *Ott.*, 444c
J. P., *Birm.*, 1336b
Kenneth, *Wolv.*, 1793b
Pat A., *Curtin*, 34c
Addlesee, A. J., *H-W*, 1450c
Addley, Pamela J., *Liv.J.Moores*, 1517a
Addo, Adenike A., *Abeokuta Ag.*, 1005c
G. W., *Winneba*, 565c
Geoffrey E., *Kumasi*, 570a, 574c
H. A., *Ghana*, 569b
S. T., *Ghana*, 568a
Addo-Fening, R., *Ghana*, 568a
Addo-Quaye, A. A., *Cape Coast*, 562b
Adds, Peter, *Well.*, 988c
Addy, Ernestine, *Kumasi*, 573a
M., *Brist.*, 1350b
Marian E., *Ghana*, 567b
Addy-Itugu, E., *Maid.*, 1048c
Addyman, A. M., *Salf.*, 1701a
Ade, P. A. R., *Lond.*, 1553c
Adeagbo-Sheikh, A. G., *O.Awolowo*, 1061a
Adebajo, Sola O., *Ogun State*, 1064a, 1065a
Adebambo, O. A., *Abeokuta Ag.*, 1005b
Adebamowo, C. A., *Ib.*, 1038b
Adebanjo, A., *Ogun State*, 1064b, 1065c
A. O., *O.Awolowo*, 1061b
Adebar, P. E., *Br.Col.*, 298b
Adebayo, Chief A., *Ondo State*, 1066a
A. A., *O.Awolowo*, 1061c
Aduke G., *Ib.*, 1036b
Ambrose A., *Natal*, 1178c, 1183b
Babatunde A., *Akure*, 1028a, 1029c
Oluyemisi A., *Akure*, 1029c
Adebisi, A. A., *Ib.*, 1037b
O., *A.Bello*, 1009a
O., *Ib.*, 1035c
R., *A.Bello*, 1009b
Adebitan, S. A., *AT Balewa*, 1002b
Adebo, O. A., *Ib.*, 1038b
Adebona, A. C., *O.Awolowo*, 1059b
Adebowale, E. A., *O.Awolowo*, 1063a
O., *Ondo State*, 1066c
Adeboye, K. R., *Minna*, 1030b
Adedeji, B. O., *O.Awolowo*, 1061a
J. A., *Ib.*, 1036c
Adedibu, A. A., *L.Akin.UT*, 1043a, 1043c
Adedipe, N. O., *Ib.*, 1035b
V. O., *Ogun State*, 1064c
Adediran, A. A., *O.Awolowo*, 1060c
J. A., *O.Awolowo*, 1063a
M. O., *O.Awolowo*, 1059a, 1061a
S. A., *O.Awolowo*, 1060c
S. A., *Ondo State*, 1066b
Y. A., *Minna*, 1030b
Adedire, Chris O., *Akure*, 1028b
Adedoja, Taoheed, *Bayero*, 1013b
Adedokun, J. A., *O.Awolowo*, 1061b
O. O., *Lagos State*, 1046b
Olasupo, *Calabar*, 1020b
T. A., *Bayero*, 1012c
Adedoyin, J. A., *Botswana*, 263b
S. F., *Ogun State*, 1064a
Adedzwa, D. K., *Makurdi Ag.*, 1007b, 1007c
Adeeb, M. A., *Islamia, Bahawal.*, 1100b
S., *Osm.*, 797c
Adeeyinwo, Christina E., *Akure*, 1028b
Adefila, S. S., *A.Bello*, 1009a
Adefolalu, D. O., *Minna*, 1030a, 1030b
Adefule, A. K., *Ogun State*, 1065a
Adefulu, R. A., *Ogun State*, 1065a
Adegbenro, Omololu, *Akure*, 1029c
Adegbite, A. M., *O.Awolowo*, 1061a
Adegbola, M. D., *AT Balewa*, 1003c
T. A., *AT Balewa*, 1002a
Adegboye, R. O., *Ib.*, 1034b
Rachael O., *Ib.*, 1039b
V. O., *Ib.*, 1038b
Adegboyega, G. A., *O.Awolowo*, 1060a
Adegbule-Adesida, Kayode E., *Akure*, 1028a, 1029b, 1029c
Adegbulugbe, A. O., *O.Awolowo*, 1062c
Adegbuyi, P. A. O., *Lagos State*, 1045c
Adegeye, A. J., *Ib.*, 1034b
Adebola O., *Ib.*, 1035c
Adegoke, Cyril O., *Akure*, 1028c
Emmanuel A., *Benin*, 1015a
G. O., *Ib.*, 1035c
J. A., *O.Awolowo*, 1062a
Adegun, J. A., *Ondo State*, 1066a
Adegunleye, Victor O., *Akure*, 1029c
Adeigbo, F. A., *Ib.*, 1036c
Adejare, O., *Lagos State*, 1045c
Adejir, T., *Jos*, 1041a
Adejoh, S. E., *Jos*, 1040b
Adejumo, A. B., *Jos*, 1041a
D. O., *Ib.*, 1035a
Adejuwon, C. A., *Ib.*, 1037c
Adejuyigbe, O., *O.Awolowo*, 1062a, 1062c
Adekanye, J. A., *Ib.*, 1036c
Tomilayo O., *Ib.*, 1034b
Adekeye, E. A., *A.Bello*, 1010b
J. O., *A.Bello*, 1010c
Adekoya, John A., *Akure*, 1029a
L. O., *O.Awolowo*, 1060a
Oluite O., *Ogun State*, 1065b
S. O. A., *Lagos State*, 1045b
Adekoye, E. O., *A.Bello*, 1010c
Adekunle, A. O., *Ib.*, 1038a, 1039c
H. M., *A.Bello*, 1010c
O. O., *Ib.*, 1038b
Adekunmisi, A. A., *Ogun State*, 1064b
Adel Yaseen, *Utara, Malaysia*, 944a
Adelaar, Karl A., *Melb.*, 78b
Adelabu, G. B., *Makurdi Ag.*, 1006a, 1007c
M. A., *O.Awolowo*, 1058a, 1059c, 1063b
S. A., *Abuja*, 1004b
Adelakun, A. O., *Jos*, 1041b
Adelana, B. O., *O.Awolowo*, 1063a
Adele-Jinadu, L., *Lagos State*, 1045a, 1046b
Adelekan, D. A., *O.Awolowo*, 1062a
Adeleke, B. B., *Ib.*, 1035a
R. A., *Jos*, 1040b
Adeleye, G. A., *U.Danfodiyo*, 1071c
I. O. A., *Ib.*, 1035a
Adeli, K., *Windsor*, 537c
Adell, B. L., *Qu.*, 455c
Adelman, Allan G., *Tor.*, 497a
H., *York(Can.)*, 552c
Adeloju, S., *W.Syd.*, 210b
Adelola, I. O. A., *Ondo State*, 1066c
Adelowo, A. A., *Ondo State*, 1066c
O. O., *Ogun State*, 1065b
Adeloye, A., *Malawi*, 907b
Adelugba, D., *Ib.*, 1037b
Adelusi, A. A., *O.Awolowo*, 1059b
Sunday A., *Benin*, 1017b, 1017c
Adelusola, K. A., *O.Awolowo*, 1062b
Ademiluyi, Joel O., *Nigeria*, 1053a
Ademiran, S. A., *Z'bwe.*, 1826c
Ademola, A., *O.Awolowo*, 1061c
Ademoroti, Christopher M. A., *Benin*, 1015a
Ademosun, Cornelius O., *Akure*, 1028a, 1028b
Aden, A. A., *Witw.*, 1244c
Adendorff, Ralph D., *Natal*, 1180b
Susan A., *S.Af.*, 1222b
Adene, D. F., *Ib.*, 1038b
Adenekan, O. O., *Ogun State*, 1065b
Adeneye, J. A., *Ib.*, 1035a
Adeniji, F. A., *Maid.*, 1047b
Adeniran, A., *Abeokuta Ag.*, 1006b
A., *Ib.*, 1036b
B. O., *Ib.*, 1036c
T. M., *Moi*, 894a
Adeniyi, F., *O.Awolowo*, 1062a
F. A., *Ib.*, 1037c
J. D., *Ib.*, 1038a
J. O., *Minna*, 1030c
Adeodu, O., *O.Awolowo*, 1062a
Adeogun, Joshua, *E.Af.Baraton*, 887a, 887c
Margaret O., *E.Af.Baraton*, 888b
Adeola, A. O., *Abeokuta Ag.*, 1005c
O. A., *NUL*, 903c
Adeolola, I. O. A., *Edo State*, 1023c
Adeosun, I. O., *O.Awolowo*, 1062c
Adeoti, S. T., *Ib.*, 1039c
Adeoye, G. O., *Ib.*, 1034c
K. B., *A.Bello*, 1010b
Adepegba, C. O., *Ib.*, 1038c
Adepetu, A. A., *Jos*, 1040c
J. A., *O.Awolowo*, 1061c
Adepoju, Adeleye B., *Bayero*, 1013b
Samuel O., *Akure*, 1028c
Aderibigbe, A. O., *O.Awolowo*, 1059b
E. Y., *Ondo State*, 1066b
F. M., *Ondo State*, 1066b
I. S., *Lagos State*, 1046b
Aderinokun, Gbemisola A., *Ib.*, 1037b
Aderinola, Esan A., *Akure*, 1028b
Aderiye, J. B. I., *Ondo State*, 1066c
Aderoba, Adeyemi A., *Akure*, 1028c
Aderyn, Diane, *Bath*, 1322a, 1325c
Ades, Anthony E., *Lond.*, 1573b
J. Dawn, *Essex*, 1423b
Lesley C., *Syd.*, 178b
Y., *Greenwich*, 1447b
Adesanoye, F. A., *Ib.*, 1035b, 1039c
H.R.H. Oba F. I., *Ondo State*, 1066a
Adesanya, D. A., *O.Awolowo*, 1059b
S. A., *O.Awolowo*, 1061b
Adesemowo, P. O., *Ogun State*, 1064c
Ade-Serrano, M. A., *Lagos State*, 1046c
Adeshina, G. O. O., *Minna*, 1030a
Adesilu, Christianah I., *Ib.*, 1034b
Adesimi, A. A., *O.Awolowo*, 1059a
Adesina, Adesoji A., *NSW*, 109b
F. A., *O.Awolowo*, 1060b
J. O., *Ib.*, 1037a
L. A., *Ondo State*, 1066c
S. K., *O.Awolowo*, 1061b
S. O. A., *Edo State*, 1022b
Adesiyan, S. O., *Ib.*, 1035b
Adesiyun, A. A., *WI*, 1818a
Adesogan, E. K., *Ib.*, 1035a
Adesokan, Elizabeth O., *Ib.*, 1037a
Adesomoju, A. A., *Ib.*, 1035a
Adesulu, Esther, *O.Awolowo*, 1062a
Adesunkanmi, A. R. K., *O.Awolowo*, 1062c
Adesuyi, Samuel A., *Akure*, 1028c
Adetiloye, P. O., *Abeokuta Ag.*, 1006a
V. A., *O.Awolowo*, 1062c
Adetona, H.R.H. Oba Alaiyeluwa S. K., Awujale of Ijebuland, *Yola*, 1033a
Adetoro, Olalekan O., *Ogun State*, 1064a, 1065b
S. A., *Abeokuta Ag.*, 1005c
Adetosoye, A. I., *Ib.*, 1038b
Adetula, Olufeyisayo F., *Akure*, 1029c
Adetunji, A., *Ib.*, 1038c
I. A., *L.Akin.UT*, 1043b
J., *A.Bello*, 1009c
M. T., *Abeokuta Ag.*, 1006a, 1006c
Adetuyi, Fatusa C., *Akure*, 1028b
Adeuja, A. O. G., *Ib.*, 1037c
Adewale, M. O., *Abuja*, 1003b, 1004b, 1004c
Rev. S. A., *Ogun State*, 1065a
Adewole, I. F., *Ib.*, 1038a
M. A., *Jos*, 1040a, 1040b, 1042c
Adewolu, M. A., *Lagos State*, 1045c
Adewoye, D., *A.Bello*, 1008c
O., *Ib.*, 1036a
O. O., *O.Awolowo*, 1060a
Omoniyi, *Ib.*, 1034a
Adewunmi, C. O., *O.Awolowo*, 1061b
Adewusi, S. R. A., *O.Awolowo*, 1059c
Adewuya, S. A., *Ondo State*, 1066c
Adewuyi, A. A., *O.Awolowo*, 1059c
M. J. O., *Z'bwe.*, 1828b
Adey, Kym L., *S.Aust.*, 156a
Michael A., *Newcastle(UK)*, 1620a
P., *Lond.*, 1542b
Philip, *Lond.*, 1536c
Adeyanju, *Z'bwe.*, 1828c
J. B., *A.Bello*, 1010c
S. A., *O.Awolowo*, 1061b
Adeye, Adekunle O., *Camb.*, 1373b
Adeyefa, C. A. O., *Ib.*, 1038b
Zachariah D., *Akure*, 1029a
Adeyemi, Adeyinka E., *Akure*, 1028a, 1028b
F. A., *Ogun State*, 1064b
G., *Ogun State*, 1064b
I. A., *L.Akin.UT*, 1043c
Adeyemo, A. O., *O.Awolowo*, 1062a, 1062c
M. O., *Makurdi Ag.*, 1007b
R., *O.Awolowo*, 1059a
Adeyeri, J. B., *Ondo State*, 1066a, 1066b

Paul I., *Nigeria*, 1054a
Akubugwu, E. I., *Abia State*, 1000c
Akubuilo, Cletus J. C., *Enugu SUST*, 1024a, 1025c
Akubuo, Clement O., *Nigeria*, 1052c
Akueshi, C. O., *Jos*, 1040c
Akuezuilo, E. O., *N.Azikiwe*, 1057a
Akuffo, Emanuel, *Lond.*, 1556b
F. O., *Kumasi*, 572a
F. W. B., *Zambia*, 1822a
Felix O., *Kumasi*, 574c
Akujobi, A., *Nigeria*, 1050b
Akukwe, Francis N., *Nigeria*, 1054b
Akulega, Margret, *Makurdi Ag.*, 1007c
Akundabweni, S., *Nair.*, 897a
Akunyili, Dora N., *Nigeria*, 1051b
Akunyiri, Dorothy N., *Nigeria*, 1054a
Akusoba, E. U., *N.Azikiwe*, 1057a
Akussah, H., *Ghana*, 568b
Akusu, M. O., *Ib.*, 1038c
Akute, O. O., *Ib.*, 1038b
Akwabi, G. O., *Moi*, 894a
Akwesi, C. K., *Cape Coast*, 563b
Akyeampong, D. A., *Ghana*, 568b
Akyel, Cevdet, *Montr.*, 420b
Al Aasam, I. S., *Windsor*, 538a
Al Bakri, Dhia, *Syd.*, 181a
Al Heialy, Hamid, *McG.*, 371b
Al Naib, Shafik K., *E.Lond.*, 1411a
Al Taweel, A. M., *Dal.*, 328c
Al Yasiri, Adil, *Liv.J.Moores*, 1519a
Alaba, I. O., *Lagos State*, 1045c
Alabaster, P. S., *Swinburne UT*, 167b
T., *Sund.*, 1739a
Alabi, B., *Ib.*, 1035c
D. A., *Ogun State*, 1064b
G. A., *Ib.*, 1036b
S. O., *A.Bello*, 1010b
Alade, C. A., *Lagos State*, 1046a
Eunice B., *Ib.*, 1037a
G. A., *Ib.*, 1035c
Aladejana, A. I., *O.Awolowo*, 1060a
Aladekomo, F. O., *O.Awolowo*, 1058a, 1063b
J. B., *O.Awolowo*, 1061b
Aladesanmi, J. A., *O.Awolowo*, 1061b
Alafiatayo, R., *A.Bello*, 1010c
Alagappan, A. R., *Annam.*, 599c
N., *Annam.*, 599a
V., *Madurai-K.*, 746a
Alagar, V. S., *C'dia.*, 322b
Alaghband-Zadeh, J., *Lond.*, 1530c
Alagoa, Chief Hon. Justice A., *Owerri*, 1031a
E. J., *P.Harcourt*, 1069c
Alahakoon, A. M. P. K., *Peradeniya*, 1274c
R., *Moratuwa*, 1270a
Alain, Claude, *Montr.*, 413c
Jean-Marc, *Queb.*, 451a
Al-Akaidi, M., *De Mont.*, 1392a
Alakeson, H., *S.Bank*, 1720b
Alakh, P. P. Singh, *Delhi*, 648b
Alaku, Mary, *Enugu SUST*, 1024a
Stephen O., *Enugu SUST*, 1024a, 1026a
Alalade, F. O., *O.Awolowo*, 1061c
Alalasundaram, S. M., *Jaffna*, 1265a, 1266c
Alali, J., *Manc.Met.*, 1610b
Al-Alousi, Louay M., *Glas.*, 1442a
Alam, A. F., *Dhaka*, 240b
A. H. M. M., *Dhaka*, 238c
A. H. M. Z., *B'desh.Engin.*, 230c
A. K. M. F., *Dhaka*, 243a
A. K. M. N., *B'desh.Ag.*, 227c
A. K. M. S., *Rajsh.*, 254b
A. M. S., *Dhaka*, 238b
A. Q. M. S., *Chitt.*, 235b
Afshar, *J.Hamdard*, 708b
B., *Dhaka*, 241b
F., *B'desh.Engin.*, 230c
F., *Dhaka*, 239a
Faisal, *Bhutto IST*, 1118b
Husne A., *Dhaka*, 241a
J., *Chitt.*, 234c
Javed, *HP*, 685a
K. C. A., *B'desh.Engin.*, 231c
K. F., *Massey*, 974a
K. S., *Dhaka*, 240b
Khursed, *Gauh.*, 666b
Khurshid, *Faisalabad*, 1083a, 1084b
M., *Dhaka*, 240c
M., *J.Nehru U.*, 713b, 713c
M., *Rajendra Ag.*, 825c
M. A., *Brist.*, 1347c
M. A., *Punjab*, 1113c
M. A. U., *Shahjalal*, 259b
M. B., *Chitt.*, 235b
M. D., *Dhaka*, 242a
M. F., *Chitt.*, 234a, 235b
M. G. S., *B'desh.Ag.*, 228c
M. J., *B'desh.Engin.*, 230c
M. J., *Jahang.*, 248a
M. J. B., *B'desh.Engin.*, 230b
M. J. B., *Shahjalal*, 258c
M. K., *B'desh.Engin.*, 231b
M. K., *Dhaka*, 242a
M. M., *B'desh.Engin.*, 231a, 231c
M. M., *Dhaka*, 238c, 239b
M. Monzurul, *B'desh.Ag.*, 227c
M. Morshed, *B'desh.Ag.*, 227c
M. N., *Islamic(B'desh.)*, 246a, 246b, 246c
M. N., *Jahang.*, 248c
M. R., *Chitt.*, 236c
M. R., *Dhaka*, 239a
M. R., *Rajsh.*, 256b
M. S., *B'desh.Ag.*, 227b, 227c, 228a
M. S., *B'desh.Engin.*, 230a
M. S., *Chitt.*, 233a, 234a, 234b, 235a, 235b, 236b, 236c
M. S., *Jahang.*, 248a
M. S., *Rajsh.*, 254b, 254c, 255b
M. Shafiqul, *Rajsh.*, 255c
M. Shafiul, *Rajsh.*, 255c
M. Shamsul, *IUBAT*, 244b
M. Taufiq, *Rajsh.*, 255a
M. U., *Chitt.*, 234c
Mahboob, *Punjab*, 1113c
Manzural, *Waik.*, 991b
Masood, *JMI*, 710c
Md. Ashraful, *Khulna*, 250b
Md. F., *B'desh.Ag.*, 226c
Md. R., *B'desh.Ag.*, 227a
Md. Shafiqul, *B'desh.Open*, 233c
Mehtab, *JMI*, 709b
Mohd S., *J.Nehru U.*, 713b
Mumtaz, *Karachi*, 1103c
N., *Jahang.*, 248b
Nisar, *Sir Syed UET*, 1122a, 1122b
S., *Assam Ag.*, 604b
S., *JMI*, 709b
S. A., *Chitt.*, 235b
S. M. M., *Rajsh.*, 255a
S. M. N., *Jahang.*, 247a
S. S., *Dhaka*, 238a
S. S., *Shahjalal*, 258c, 259c
Seemeen, *Punjab*, 1113c
Shamsul, *Leth.*, 359a
Shamsul K., *Leth.*, 360c
Tariqul, *IUBAT*, 244b
Zafar, *Faisalabad*, 1083c
Alam Khan, Khursheed, *Sir Syed UET*, 1122a
Alam Masood, *JMI*, 709b
Alama, S., *McM.*, 383b
Alamdari, F., *Cran.*, 1387b
Alamgir, A. K. M., *B'desh.Open*, 233c
A. N. M., *Chitt.*, 234b
Group Capt. (Retd.) Haz M., *IUBAT*, 244b
M., *Shahjalal*, 258b
Muhammad, *N-WFP Eng.*, 1110b
Al-Amin Mohammad, *Jahang.*, 248a
Alanana, O. O., *Abuja*, 1004c
Alani, Morteza, *Portsmouth*, 1678c
Alant, Erna, *Pret.*, 1203b, 1209a
Jaco, *W.Cape*, 1236c
Alao, A. O. A., *Ilorin*, 1039a
Christianah, *Ib.*, 1034a
D. A., *Ib.*, 1037a
J. A., *O.Awolowo*, 1059b
Joel O., *Ib.*, 1034a, 1039b
Alaouze, Christian M., *NSW*, 110a
Alarie, Y., *Laur.*, 346b
Al-Arif, A. K. M. M. R., *Rajsh.*, 256a
Alary, Michel, *Laval*, 357c
Al-Assal, A., *IIU(P'stan.)*, 1098a, 1099c
Alaszewski, A. M., *Hull*, 1467a
Alatas, Syed F., *NU Singapore*, 1152a
Alauddin, M., *B'desh.Engin.*, 230b
M., *Chitt.*, 234b
M., *Islamic(B'desh.)*, 245c, 246a
Mohammad, *Qld.*, 132c, 143a
Alausa, O. K., *Ogun State*, 1065b
Alavi, Christine, *Griff.*, 57b
Alawa, J. P., *A.Bello*, 1010a
Al-Azzawi, Farook, *Leic.*, 1501b
Alban, Luis, *RMIT*, 151c
Albanese, C., *Tor.*, 488a
Albani, Alberto, *NSW*, 111c
Albarran, J., *W.England*, 1787a
Albas, D. C., *Manit.*, 395c
Albasu, S. A., *U.Danfodiyo*, 1071a
Al-Bermani, Faris G. A., *Qld.*, 133a
Alberry, Peter J., *Wales*, 1767c
Albert, A., *TN Vet.*, 862a
Alain, *Queb.*, 449b
Gérald, *Montr.*, 415b
P., *C'dia.*, 322a
Sandra, *Manipal AHE*, 767a
Alberti, Kurt G. M. M., *Newcastle(UK)*, 1624a
P. W. R., *Tor.*, 499a
Peter W. R., *Tor.*, 499a
Albert-Osaghae, Victor K., *Benin*, 1015c
Alberts, H. L., *Rand Afrikaans*, 1212a
Hendrik W., *Pret.*, 1206a
Nicolaas F., *Pret.*, 1205b
R. W., *OFS*, 1192c
Ursula U., *S.Af.*, 1220c
V., *Rand Afrikaans*, 1212a
Albertyn, Dawid S., *W.Cape*, 1235c
Erik, *P.Elizabeth*, 1197a
J., *OFS*, 1194a
Albinson, J. G., *Qu.*, 456b
Albo, G., *York(Can.)*, 549a
Alboim, Elly, *Car.*, 318b
Albon, Robert P., *ANU*, 18b
Alboussiere, Thierry, *Camb.*, 1370a
Albrecht, A. S., *Plym.*, 1673a
Andreas, *Lond.*, 1530a
Albright, Lawrence J., *S.Fraser*, 476b
Albrighton, F. C., *Birm.*, 1336c
Albritton, R. R., *York(Can.)*, 549b
Albury, Rebecca M., *W'gong.*, 215a
William R., *NSW*, 115a
Alcidi, Florent, *N.Territory*, 126b
Alcock, A. E., *Ulster*, 1751c
C., *Coventry*, 1385b
C. B., *Tor.*, 493a
D., *W.England*, 1785a
Denise S., *Ott.*, 438b, 442a
J. E., *York(Can.)*, 551c
J. W., *Brist.*, 1347c
Laura, *Natal*, 1178b
Nathaniel W., *Warw.*, 1779c
Peter, *Sheff.Hallam*, 1717b
Robert J., *Exe.*, 1431c
Robyn, *C.Qld.*, 28c
S. R., *Glas.*, 1442a
Alcorn, D. P., *Auck.*, 964a
Daine G., *Melb.*, 78a
M. P., *Belf.*, 1686c
Noeline, *Waik.*, 991b
Al-Dabass, D., *Nott.Trent*, 1639c
Al-Dabbagh, M., *PNG Tech.*, 1130a
Al-Daffaee, H., *Coventry*, 1386b
Al-Daiani, A., *Coventry*, 1384c
Al-Damluji, S., *Lond.*, 1577a
Aldcroft, D. H., *Manc.Met.*, 1613b
Aldeen, M., *Melb.*, 80a
Alden, J. C., *Witw.*, 1243a
J. D., *Wales*, 1762b
Lynn, *Br.Col.*, 303a
R. T. H., *McM.*, 382a
Alder, Chris, *Brad.*, 1342a
Christine M., *Melb.*, 79a
Elizabeth M., *Dund.*, 1399c
George M., *Edin.*, 1416c
H., *Bourne.*, 1339c
J. F., *UMIST*, 1608b
John E., *Newcastle(UK)*, 1622b
R. W., *Brist.*, 1345b
Alderdice, C., *Nfld.*, 407a
David S., *NSW*, 109c
Alderman, Belle Y., *Canberra*, 26a
Geoffrey, *Middx.*, 1615a, 1616c
J., *Open(UK)*, 1645c
R. K., *York(UK)*, 1800c
Alderson, D., *Brist.*, 1349c
Evan W., *S.Fraser*, 477c
George J., *Sheff.Hallam*, 1717c
Grace, *Brad.*, 1341a
J. Charles, *Lanc.*, 1481b
N., *St FX*, 470c
Sue A., *Br.Col.*, 303c
Alderton, Ian W., *S.Af.*, 1220b
Aldgate, A., *Open(UK)*, 1645c
P. Jane, *Leic.*, 1500a
Aldhouse-Green, M. J., *Wales*, 1777a, 1778b
S., *Wales*, 1777a
S. H. R., *Wales*, 1763c
Aldis, Geoffrey K., *NSW*, 120c
Aldous, David E., *Melb.*, 84a
Joan M., *Open(UK)*, 1646b
Stephen, *Tas.*, 184b
Wayne, *N.Territory*, 128c
Aldred, Anthony, *Hudd.*, 1461c
Jonathan S., *Camb.*, 1367c
Keith, *Lond.*, 1551a, 1556c
Michael J., *Melb.*, 84b
Robert E. L., *Otago*, 981c
Steve, *C.England*, 1378b
Aldrich, C. G., *OFS*, 1194a
Chris, *Stell.*, 1225c
R. E., *Lond.*, 1534b
R. J., *Nott.*, 1636a
Ralph F., *W.Ont.*, 525b
Robert, *Syd.*, 171c
W. M., *Nott.Trent*, 1641b
Aldridge, A. E., *Nott.*, 1636a
Barrie J., *Glam.*, 1435c
David C., *Camb.*, 1372b
Eve-Marie, *Portsmouth*, 1679c
Harold E., *Tor.*, 497a
Jan, *Leeds*, 1490c
Jayne, *Thames V.*, 1749c
Jeffrey P., *Edin.*, 1415a
K. D., *York(Can.)*, 546a
Meryl E., *Nott.*, 1636a
R., *E.Anglia*, 1408b
Richard J., *Leic.*, 1498c
Aldwinkle, Linda, *Westminster*, 1791a
Ale, S. O., *AT Balewa*, 1002a, 1002c
Aleem, Khalil A., *Faisalabad*, 1084b
M., *Islamia, Bahawal.*, 1101b
M. A., *Rajsh.*, 255a
Alegbeleye, G. O., *Ib.*, 1036b
Aleksander, Igor, *Lond.*, 1526a, 1528c
Alemika, E. E. O., *Jos*, 1041b
T. E., *Jos*, 1042a
Alemna, A. A., *Ghana*, 568b, 570b
Alesso-Waywell, Lucia M., *Leeds Met.*, 1495c
Aletor, Valentine A., *Akure*, 1028b
Alex, I. U., *U.Danfodiyo*, 1071c
Jack F., *Guelph*, 339c
Alexa, Garry, *Acad.*, 279c
Alexander, A. F., *Manc.Met.*, 1614b
A. M., *Massey*, 978b
Alan, *Strath.*, 1735b
Bruce K., *S.Fraser*, 480a
C., *H-W*, 1451c
Cherry, xl
Christine A., *NSW*, 111c
Christopher G., *James Cook*, 61a
D. A., *Aberd.*, 1316b
D. J., *Manc.Met.*, 1612a
David A., *Liv.J.Moores*, 1516b
David I., *Dal.*, 333c
Donald E., *Qld.*, 132c
E. R., *Tor.*, 487a
Flora M., *Aberd.*, 1314b
Freda E., *Edin.*, 1421b
G., *Herts.*, 1455b
G. J. M., *Camb.*, 1364b
G. R., *Open(UK)*, 1647a
Gavin R., *Camb.*, 1368c
Graham I., *Liv.J.Moores*, 1519a
I. J., *Aberd.*, 1315b
Ian C., *W.Aust.*, 202a
J., *Car.*, 319b
J., *C.England*, 1376c
J., *E.Anglia*, 1408a
J. A., *Camb.*, 1372c
J. H., *Aberd.*, 1314b
J. Lindsay, *Massey*, 976b
James, *Strath.*, 1735b
Jennifer J., *Witw.*, 1240c
Joanne, *Portsmouth*, 1679b
John A., *NSW*, 114a
John B., *Brun.*, 1353c
John B., *Salf.*, 1700b
Keith, *Strath.*, 1737b
Kenneth R., *E.Cowan*, 44a, 46b
L. C. A., *Sheff.*, 1705a
The Hon. Lincoln M., *Guelph*, 335a
Lisa, *Northumbria*, 1631a
M. J., *St And.*, 1697b
M. L., *Griff.*, 56b
Marie, *Malta*, 950b
Marion J. L., *Manit.*, 394c
Mark G., *Cape Town*, 1161b
Martin, *Salf.*, 1702b
Michael D., *Leeds Met.*, 1494c
Minerva, *Guy.*, 576b
Muriel, *Paisley*, 1671c
P., *Camb.*, 1362c
P., *Windsor*, 538b
P. B., *Lincoln(NZ)*, 973a
P. O., *Dr HGV*, 660b
P. S., *Manc.*, 1602a
Patricia M., *S.Af.*, 1218a
Peter F., *NSW*, 111c
Peter W., *Tas.*, 186b
Phyllis, *RMIT*, 155a, 155b
R. D., *W.Syd.*, 208a, 208c
R. McN., *Leeds*, 1484b
R. Paul, *Syd.*, 170b
R. R., *Massey*, 975a
Robert, *Curtin*, 35b
Robin J., *Warw.*, 1780b, 1783b
Sally, *Lond.*, 1525a
Sally A., *E.Lond.*, 1410b
Shirley, *Technol.Syd.*, 193b
Vincent, *Guy.*, 576a
W., *Birm.*, 1330b
W. E., *Tor.*, 493c
W. Robert J., *Otago*, 980c
Alexander John, *Manipal AHE*, 766c
Alexandra, H.R.H. Princess The Hon. Lady Ogilvy, *Lanc.*, 1479a
Alexandre, X., *Avina.Home Sci.*, 608c
Alexandrou, C., *Cyprus*, 559a
Nick, *N.Lond.*, 1629a
Alexandrov, Alexandre, *Lough.*, 1592a
Alexandrowicz, G. A., *Qu.*, 455c
Alexopoulos, Christos C., *Ryerson*, 468a
Alexopoulou, I., *McM.*, 386b
Aleyassine, Hassan, *McG.*, 371b
Alfa, Attahiru, *Manit.*, 392b
M., *Manit.*, 397b
Alfano, D., *Regina*, 463b
Alfazuddin, M., *Rajsh.*, 256c
Alfirevic, Zarko, *Liv.*, 1512c
Alford, B. W. E., *Brist.*, 1347b
C. A., *W.England*, 1785a
G., *Monash*, 92c
J. L., *Melb.*, 82b
N. M., *Aberd.*, 1314a
N. McN., *S.Bank*, 1721c
Philip, *Luton*, 1595a
Ross A., *James Cook*, 61a
Stephen A., *Camb.*, 1368a
Al-Forkan, M., *Chitt.*, 234b
Alfrad Jayaprasad, I., *TN Vet.*, 861a
Alfred, M., *Peradeniya*, 1275b
Alfredson, R. J., *Monash*, 91a
Alfrey, N., *Nott.*, 1633a
Alger, Mark S. M., *N.Lond.*, 1629c
Alghali, A. M., *S.Leone*, 1134b, 1134c
S. T. O., *S.Leone*, 1132c
Algie, J., *City(UK)*, 1382a
Algoo-Baksh, S., *Nfld.*, 404a
Alguacil-Garcia, A., *Manit.*, 398c
Al-Hassan, B. S. Y., *A.Bello*, 1011b
Ramatu, *Ghana*, 567b
Alhassan, A. B., *A.Bello*, 1008c
M. H., *Bayero*, 1013a
Al-Hassani, S. T. S., *UMIST*, 1608b
Alheit, Karin, *S.Af.*, 1219c
Al-Hussaini, A. N., *Alta.*, 283c
Abbas, *Westminster*, 1790b
T. M., *B'desh.Engin.*, 230b
Ali, A., *Assam Ag.*, 606b
A., *B'desh.Ag.*, 227a
A., *Lahore UET*, 1096b
A. F. I., *Chitt.*, 236b
A. F. M. A., *Chitt.*, 235b
A. K. M. I., *Dhaka*, 239c
A. K. M. Y., *Rajsh.*, 254a, 255c
A. M., *Dhaka*, 240b
A. M., *Jahang.*, 247c
A. R. M., *B'desh.Engin.*, 231a
A. S. M. N., *Rajsh.*, 254a, 256a
Aashish, *Syd.*, 181c, 182a
Afirah H., *Punjab*, 1113b
Ali S., *Punjab*, 1114a
Amjad, *Faisalabad*, 1084a
Amjad, *N-WFP Eng.*, 1110c
Anisa M., *Karachi*, 1103c
Anjum, *Lahore MS*, 1105b
Anthony, *Nigeria*, 1052c
Anthony N., *Nigeria*, 1055a
Anuwar, *NU Malaysia*, 922a
Anwar, *JMI*, 709a
Arif, *JMI*, 709a
Asghar, *B.Zak.*, 1092b, 1092c
Asghar, *Faisalabad*, 1083c
Azam, *Aga Khan*, 1082a
Badar S., *Aga Khan*, 1081b
Barkat, *Baloch.*, 1093a
Barkat, *GND*, 680a, 681a
C. Y., *Azad J&K*, 1089a
D. M., *Rajsh.*, 256b
E. H. M. M., *Dhaka*, 239a
Ferzand, *Faisalabad*, 1085c
Firdausia A., *Punjab*, 1114a
H., *Lahore UET*, 1096a
Haider, *Punjab*, 1113c
Hamid, *A.Iqbal Open*, 1088a
I. A., *O.Awolowo*, 1060a
Imam, *S.Pac.*, 1253b
Imran, *Lahore MS*, 1105b
Ismat Ara, *Rajsh.*, 257b
J., *Tor.*, 501a
K., *Manipal AHE*, 764a
K. A., *Quaid-i-Azam*, 1115c
Kamil H. M., *Liv.*, 1509b
Karamat, *B.Zak.*, 1091b
Kazim, *Karachi*, 1102b
Keramat, *Leth.*, 361b
Kh. M., *B'desh.Ag.*, 228a
Khadija, *Azad J&K*, 1089b
L. A., *Quaid-i-Azam*, 1116a
Liaqat, *Punjab*, 1114b
Liaqat, *Baloch.*, 1093c
M., *Chitt.*, 235a, 236c
M., *Lahore UET*, 1095c, 1096b
M., *Quaid-i-Azam*, 1115c
M. A., *A.Bello*, 1010c
M. A., *B'desh.Ag.*, 228c
M. A., *Chitt.*, 235b, 235c
M. A., *Dhaka*, 237c, 238b
M. A., *Islamic(B'desh.)*, 246b
M. A., *Jahang.*, 249a
M. A., *Rajsh.*, 255a, 255b
M. A. M., *McM.*, 386b
M. A. T., *B'desh.Engin.*, 231a
M. Abbas, *Rajsh.*, 256b
M. Ahmed, *Aga Khan*, 1082b
M. Ashraf, *B'desh.Engin.*, 230b
M. Ashraf, *Dhaka*, 238c
M. Ather, *Montr.*, 410c
M. Azhar, *Dhaka*, 238c
M. E., *Islamic(B'desh.)*, 246b
M. E., *Rajsh.*, 255c
M. Emran, *Rajsh.*, 256a
M. H., *B'desh.Engin.*, 230b
M. H., *Dhaka*, 241b
M. H., *Rajsh.*, 256b
M. H., *Shahjalal*, 258c
M. I., *Chitt.*, 235c
M. I., *Jahang.*, 247b
M. Idris, *B'desh.Ag.*, 226a, 229b
M. J., *Rajsh.*, 254b
M. L., *Chitt.*, 236b
M. M., *B'desh.Ag.*, 228a
M. M., *B'desh.Engin.*, 229c, 230a
M. M., *C'dia.*, 323a
M. M., *Lahore UET*, 1095c
M. M., *NED Eng.*, 1108b
M. M., *Rajsh.*, 255a
M. Mahtab, *Rajsh.*, 257b
M. Mehmood, *A.Iqbal Open*, 1087b
M. Omar, *Rajsh.*, 256a
M. R., *B'desh.Ag.*, 228b
M. R., *Chitt.*, 235a
M. Rustom, *Rajsh.*, 255a
M. S., *B'desh.Ag.*, 226b
M. S., *B'desh.Engin.*, 230a, 232c
M. S., *Dhaka*, 237b, 240b, 241b, 242a, 242b
M. S., *Islamic(B'desh.)*, 246a
M. S., *Jahang.*, 247c
M. S., *NED Eng.*, 1108b
M. S. N., *Rajsh.*, 256a
M. Shamsher, *Rajsh.*, 255c
M. Sohrab, *Rajsh.*, 257b
M. U., *Rajsh.*, 255a
M. U., *Shahjalal*, 259a
M. W., *Rajsh.*, 255c
M. Y., *Chitt.*, 236c
M. Yusuff, *Rajsh.*, 255a
M. Z., *Rajsh.*, 256b
Mansoor, *Roor.*, 830c
Masood A., *Karachi*, 1103a
Md., *Osm.*, 797a
Md. Ameer, *Khulna*, 250c
Md H., *B'desh.Ag.*, 227b
Md. H., *B'desh.Ag.*, 229a
Md. M., *B'desh.Ag.*, 227a, 229a
Md. Raihan, *Khulna*, 250a
Md. Rawshon, *B'desh.Open*, 233c
Md. Yasin, *Khulna*, 249c
Mehrunnisa, *Karachi*, 1104a
Mine E., xl
Mohammad, *Jahang.*, 247a, 249b, 249c
Mohammad, *UST Chitt.*, 258a
Mohammed, *Chitt.*, 234c
Mohammed S., *Sheff.Hallam*, 1716b
Muhammad, *Punjab*, 1112c, 1114a
Muhammad, *Rajsh.*, 255a
Muhammad R., *Gauh.*, 665b

Bahemuka, Judith, Nair., 901c
Bahga, C. S., Punj.Ag., 814c
Bahl, Daman K., E.Lond., 1411a
G. S., Punj.Ag., 816b
Rasik, SPA Delhi, 840a
V. K., All India IMS, 585c
Bahlman, G. W., Massey, 978c
Bahr, John L., Otago, 982a
Bahri, M. L., SPA Delhi, 840a
Randhir, Punjabi, 820b
Bahrom bin Sanugi, Tech.U.Malaysia, 941c
Bahry, Romana M., York(Can.), 548a
Bahtiar Kasbi, NU Malaysia, 927c
Bahuguna, A., HNB Garh., 683a
P. P., I.Sch.Mines, 698a
R. P., HNB Garh., 683a
Bai, B. Laxmi, Osm., 795a, 797c
David H., Alta., 280b
L., Nott.Trent, 1639c
Nancy S., M.Teresa Women's, 774a
Tony, Br.Col., 306b
Baicher, G. S., Wales, 1777a
Baid, M. R., JN Vyas, 704b
Baig, A. A., Osm., 796c
M. A., J.Hamdard, 707b
M. A., Quaid-i-Azam, 1116b
M. Atique A., Sindh, 1119c
M. S., Azad J&K, 1089c, 1090a
M. Y. A., S.Venkat., 856b
Md., Osm., 797c
Mirza A., Faisalabad, 1083b, 1085a
S., Aga Khan, 1081b
Baig Salmani, M. N., Osm., 796a
Baigrie, Brian S., Tor., 487a
Ronald S., Tor., 497a
Baijal, J. S., Delhi, 649a
Baijnath, Himansu, Durban-W., 1170a
Baikie, L. D., Dal., 328c
Baildam, A. D., Manc., 1605c
Bailer-Jones, Coryn, Camb., 1372c
Bailes, Paul A., Qld., 133b, 143b
Paul A. C., Qld., 135a
Phil J., Brad., 1341c
Bailet, Dietlinde S., Acad., 278a
Bailetti, A. J., Car., 316a, 317b
Bailey, A. G., S'ton., 1725b
A. Lloyd, Westminster, 1790b
Adrian D., Lough., 1591b
Alan, Cran., 1388c
Anita J., Lond., 1527b
B., Bran., 293a
Barbara, Wl, 1812c
C. J., Greenwich, 1447b
Carol A., Wolv., 1795a
Christopher, Northumbria, 1631c
Christopher J., Keele, 1469b
Christopher N., Westminster, 1790b
Clifford J., Aston, 1321b
D., Herts., 1453c
D. C., Tor., 489b
D. E., Birm., 1332c
D. K., Brist., 1347a
D. M., Glam., 1432c
David, Coventry, 1384c
David, NE, 106c
Donald A., Winn., 542a
E., Sheff., 1710b
G., S.Bank, 1721b
G. J., Sheff., 1707c
Geoffrey N., Newcastle(UK), 1620b
George D., Wolv., 1797b
George N. A., Westminster, 1791c
Graham S., Essex, 1423c
Greg, La Trobe, 69a
Gregory M., La Trobe, 66c
Ian H., Curtin, 37a
J., W.Syd., 211a
J. A., Manit., 394c
J. A., W.England, 1786a
J. D., Oxf., 1662a
J. D., Tor., 499b
J. E., Sheff., 1706a
J. O., Brist., 1347a
J. P., Kingston(UK), 1478b
Jan, Luton, 1594b
Jean M., Wales, 1776a
Joanne, W.England, 1788c
Joe, Bolton Inst., 1337a
John E., Sur., 1742a, 1743b
John M., Murd., 99c
Kirk L., Ryerson, 467b
Kirsty, G.Caledonian, 1446a
Lorna, Open(UK), 1647a
M. E., Belf., 1686a
Margaret J., Keele, 1471a
Mark D., Camb., 1367a
N. L., Swinburne UT, 168a
Nicholas G., Melb., 84a
Nicholas J., Westminster, 1790b
P. C., Manit., 393b
P. D., H-W, 1450a
P. J., Edin., 1417b
Patricia, Laur., 348a
Paul, Monash, 89a
Peter C., Liv.J.Moores, 1517a
Peter J., York(UK), 1801a
R., Lond., 1550a
R. A., Lond., 1553b
R. C., Tor., 486b, 489b
R. C., W.Ont., 527b
R. G., Lond., 1537b
R. N., Newcastle(UK), 1621c
Raymond T., Strath., 1733c
Roger, Lond., 1527c
Roy E., Essex, 1424a
S. E. R., Manc., 1597c
S. H., Nott., 1632a
S. S. C., Manc.Met., 1612b
Stan B., NE, 103b
Stephen, G.Caledonian, 1444c
Steven H., Nott., 1632c, 1635a
Stuart, Curtin, 35b
Sue, Middx., 1616c
Susan E. K., N.Lond., 1629a
T., W.Ont., 525c
T. D., W.Syd., 208c
T. H., Herts., 1456c
Toby, Edin., 1418a
Trevor, Leeds Met., 1495b
Trevor C., Exe., 1428c
W., Greenwich, 1448c
W. G., S.Fraser, 478c
W. H., W.Ont., 530c
W. J., S.Bank, 1721b
W. N., E.Lond., 1411a
William C., Massey, 975b
Wilma, Wl, 1814c
Winston J., W.Aust., 203c
Bailey Metcalfe, Alison, Herts., 1456c
Bailey-Harris, Rebecca J., Brist., 1345a, 1347b
Bailie, Peter E., Flin., 47a, 53b
Bailiff, Ian K., Durh., 1402a
Bailin, David, Sus., 1747c
Sharon, S.Fraser, 478a
Baillargeon, Madeleine, Laval, 351c
Baille, Lesley, Luton, 1594b
Baillie, Alan J., Strath., 1736a
D. L., S.Fraser, 476b
F. G. H., McM., 387b
Gary, Waik., 992b
J., H-W, 1451a
Jean, Herts., 1454a
Lucia, City(UK), 1380a
M. G. L., Belf., 1685b
Patricia M., Belf., 1689c
R. T., Lond., 1552b
T. W. T., Lond., 1558c
Baillon, Jean-Paul, Montr., 420c
Baily, John S., Lond., 1525a
R., Open(UK), 1647c
Baimbridge, Kenneth G., Br.Col., 308b
Bain, A. D., Glas., 1438a
A. D., McM., 381a
B. C., Alta., 282a
B. C., Wl, 1815b
Barbara J., Lond., 1530c
C. D., Oxf., 1650b
D. M., Manc., 1600b
Douglas J. G., Dund., 1399c
George S., Belf., 1683a
H. W., Tor., 499b
J., Griff., 58a
J., QM Edin., 1682c
J. A., W.Ont., 528b
Jerald, Tor., 497a
John F., Leth., 360a
Kathleen, Trent, 510a
Keith, E.Lond., 1410c
M., St And., 1699b
Murray D., Lond., 1561c
S., Birm., 1334b
V. G., Alta., 286c
Bainbridge, Audrey, R.Gordon, 1696b
B. W., Lond., 1537b
David, Wolv., 1794a
David I., Aston, 1320b
Joyce M., Alta., 281c
Lister D., James Cook, 62c
Richard, Oxf.Brookes, 1667a
Roger, Liv.J.Moores, 1517c
S. F., Manc.Met., 1611c
Baines, Andrew D., Tor., 495c
Anthony J., Kent, 1473a
B., Qu., 455c
Charles G. S., Durban-W., 1171c
Cornelia, Tor., 500b
Cornelia J., Tor., 497a
D. E., Lond., 1546c
D. L., Birm., 1332b
J. C., Rhodes, 1214b
J. R., Oxf., 1652a
Jenny, W.Syd., 208c
Jill, Exe., 1431c
K., Adel., 6b
K. M., W.Ont., 522b
M. J., Reading, 1693b
Malcolm G., McG., 372c
Mitchell I., Liv.J.Moores, 1517a
Peter J., Glam., 1434c
Timothy S., Cran., 1387c
W. D., Tor., 492c
Bainham, Andrew W. E., Camb., 1360c
Bains, D. R., SPA Delhi, 839a, 840c
G. S., Punj.Ag., 814c
J. S., Punj.Ag., 816c
Lynn, QM Edin., 1682b
M. S., Panjab, 802c
Sandeep, Punj.Ag., 817c
Bainton, D., Wales, 1774a
Bairagi, N. K., IIT Bombay, 694a
Bairam, Erkin I., Otago, 980c
Baird, A. J., Sheff., 1713c
A. W. S., Cant., 970b
Adela, Wales, 1775b
Daniel, P.Elizabeth, 1198a
David T., Edin., 1420c
George, Well., 986a, 986b
Graham R., Curtin, 38b
J. D., Guelph, 340c
J. D., Tor., 485b
James, G.Caledonian, 1444c
Jeanette, Swinburne UT, 169b
John P., NSW, 120a
John R., Melb., 81c
Louise, Flin., 48b, 49b
M. C., Qu., 453b
M. H. I., McM., 381c
Mark S., Wales, 1758a
Michael G., Ott., 444a
N. C., W.Ont., 522b
Patricia A., Br.Col., 305c
R. J., Tor., 501a
Stephen W., Otago, 980a
Stuart A., G.Caledonian, 1445b
Bairstow, John, Sheff.Hallam, 1715c
Bairy Indira, Manipal AHE, 765c
Bais, H. S. S., Dr HGV, 660b
S. S., JN Vyas, 704c
V. S., Dr HGV, 661a
Baishya, B., Dib., 652c
G., Assam Ag., 607b
N., Assam Ag., 607a
Nalini K., Gauh., 666a
S., Assam Ag., 605b
Baisnab, A. P., Burd., 634c
Baithun, Suhail I., Lond., 1556a
Baiyeroju, Aderonke M., Ib., 1038a
Baiyewu, O., Ib., 1038b
Bajah, S. T., Ib., 1038c
Bajaj, A. V., DAV, 650c
Anil, Pg.IMER, 807a
C. P., Delhi, 649a
K. K., HP, 685b
K. L., Punj.Ag., 816c
Kum K., Punjabi, 820c
M. S., All India IMS, 586c
Madan M., Delhi, 649a
R. K., Punj.Ag., 815c
S. K., Punjabi, 820a
Y. P., Punjabi, 820a
Bajic, V., Windsor, 538a
Bajnok, I., McM., 386a
Bajoria, K. M., IIT Bombay, 694a
Rekha, Manc., 1604c
Bajpai, A. K., Lucknow, 738b
B. L., Lucknow, 738a
Geeta, Baroda, 750c
K. P., J.Nehru U., 713b
Minu, All India IMS, 587a
P. K., G.Ghasidas, 677b
P. K., Thapar IET, 867a
R. B., All India IMS, 586c
R. P., NE Hill, 792a
S. K., Lucknow, 739c
S. P., Dr HGV, 660a
Sunil, Roor., 829b
Vishwa N., Delhi, 648a
Bajwa, E. U., Lahore UET, 1095b
G. S., Punj.Ag., 815c
H. S., Punj.Ag., 814a
M. S., Punj.Ag., 814a, 818c
Muhammad A., Faisalabad, 1084a
Munir A., Faisalabad, 1084c
R. S., GND, 681a
Rukhsana, Punjab, 1112b
S. A., Lahore UET, 1096b
Bajzak, D., Nfld., 403c
Bak, Nelleke, W.Cape, 1236c
Baka, R. S., Victoria UT, 196c
Bakalis, S., Victoria UT, 195c
Bakan, Abagail, Qu., 456c
Joel C., Br.Col., 301a
Bakar, S. M. Abu, Rajsh., 256b
Bakar b Ismail, Tech.U.Malaysia, 941a
Bakare, C. A., Ib., 1037a
Patricia O., Ib., 1037c
S., Lagos State, 1045b
Bakari, M., Nair., 901c
Bakary, Tessilimi, Laval, 355c
Bakehouse, G. J., W.England, 1786b
Baker, A. Barry, Syd., 177a
A. J., Tor., 491a
A. J. M., Sheff., 1704c
Alan, Camb., 1361c
Alan J., Leic., 1498a
Alan R. H., Camb., 1359b
Amanda, Newcastle(NSW), 124c
Andrew G., McG., 369b
Andrew J., Glas., 1440a
Anne M. E., Camb., 1374a
Anthony, Notre Dame Aust., 129b
Astrid T., Massey, 976c
B., Coventry, 1386a
C. D., Adel., 7b
C. G., Alta., 287b
C. J., Nott., 1634a
C. Scott, Auck., 960a
Carolyn D., Qld., 132c
Carolyn M., Durban-W., 1172a
Cathy, Mt.All., 423c
Christopher T. H., Manc., 1601a
Clifford, Liv.J.Moores, 1518b
Colin R., Wales, 1758a, 1760a
Curtis L., Jr., McG., 374a
D., Nott.Trent, 1640a
D. M., E.Anglia, 1406a, 1409a
David, Leeds, 1492b, 1492c
Dennis A., Lond., 1579a
Don, McG., 364b
Donald N., W.Laur., 534c
Duncan C., Pret., 1204a
E., Hull, 1468c
Edward J., Lond., 1541c
Edward N., Auck., 960a, 960b
Felicity R., Lond., 1570c
G., Manc.Met., 1615c
G. A., Liv., 1512c
G. B., Alta., 287c
G. Blaine, McG., 367b, 367c
G. P., Oxf., 1656c
Graham, Qld., 133a
H. J., H-W, 1451b
Helen, Newcastle(NSW), 124a
Helen, W.England, 1788c
Hugh D. R., Lond., 1564a
Ian P., Sheff.Hallam, 1715c
J., Portsmouth, 1678c
J., S.Bank, 1723a
J. A., Wat., 516a
J. G., Manc., 1601c
J. S., W.England, 1786a
J. W., Sheff., 1707c
Jacqueline, Technol.Syd., 192a
James W., Qld., 136b
Janet, St Mary's(Can.), 472a
Dame Janet, York(UK), 1798a
Jeannette, Sheff.Hallam, 1718b
John E., NSW, 111b
John H., Camb., 1360c
Judith, York(Can.), 551c
Keith D., Reading, 1690b, 1691b
Laurie, McG., 377b
Lawrence R., Deakin, 41b
Lin W., Natal, 1182a
Lucy, Nott., 1638b, 1638c
M., City(UK), 1381c
M., NU Singapore, 1145a
M., Tor., 503c
M. A., Rajsh., 255a
M. D., Coventry, 1384c
M. D., Guelph, 336a, 338a, 341a
M. I., C.England, 1378b
M. J., Aberd., 1314b
Marilyn, Manit., 390c
Mark, McG., 367c
Mark, Portsmouth, 1678a
Mark S., W'gong., 212b
Marta, Lond., 1559b
Martyn, Luton, 1595a
Martyn C., E.Lond., 1411c
Maureen, Auck., 965a
Melvin, Nfld., 408c
Michael, Otago, 984c
Michael A., Tor., 497a
Michael J., Strath., 1735c
Michael J., Sur., 1744b
Michelle, Qld., 144c
Mona, UMIST, 1608c
N. L., W.England, 1786b
N. V., Camb., 1355c
Neil R., Essex, 1423c
P. L., Mt.All., 424a
P. N., Nott., 1637b
P. R., Oxf., 1662a
Pat, Mt.All., 423a
Patricia, Mt.St.Vin., 426a, 426b
Paul C., Hudd., 1460a
Paul K., Wales, 1758a
Peter, Tas., 185b
Peter E., Leeds, 1485a
Phillip, Sus., 1748c
R., Glam., 1432c
R. L., Tor., 491a
R. W., Lond., 1520b
Raymond, Salf., 1701b
Richard H., Leic., 1500c
Rob, Curtin, 35c
Robert A., Aga Khan, 1082b
Robert A., S.Cross, 161a
Robert C., Manit., 390a, 396b
Robert G. V., NE, 104a
Robert J., NE, 103a
Robert R., Tor., 497a
Roy R., Tor., 494c
Ruth, Leeds Met., 1493b
S., Manit., 397c
Sandra, NE, 106b
Simon C., Exe., 1432c
Stuart N., Camb., 1366a
Susan C., Wales, 1765b
Susannah M., Camb., 1374c
Suzanne K., W.Aust., 199a
T. C., Nott.Trent, 1640b
T. Neville, Strath., 1736a
Ted, McG., 379c
Terry G., Brad., 1341a
Tony, Technol.Syd., 189b, 193b
W. E., Qu., 453b
William M., Leth., 360c
Baker-Finch, Clem A., Canberra, 25c
Baker-Sennett, J., Br.Col., 304b
Bakheit, A. M. O., Plym., 1675b
Bakhetia, D. R. C., Punj.Ag., 815a
Bakhsh, Rasool, Baloch., 1093a, 1093c
Bakhshi, A. K., Punj.Ag., 815c
Bakht, Nadir, Baloch., 1094b
Bakhtar, F., Birm., 1329a
Bakhurst, D., Qu., 456b
Baki Bakar, Malaya, 916b
Bakibinga, D. J., Mak., 1303b
Bakish, David, Ott., 445b
Bakkappa, B., Kuvempu, 735a
Bakker, Egbert J., Montr., 413c
Isabella, York(Can.), 549b
J. I. H., Guelph, 339a
Karel A., Pret., 1203a
Nigel, Cape Town, 1161a
Peter, C.Qld., 30c
Bakkes, C. Johan, S.Af., 1216c
Piet J., Stell., 1225c
Bakkeshaswamy, K. E., B'lore., 620b
Bako, A., U.Danfodiyo, 1071c
S. A., A.Bello, 1009c
Bakoss, Steve L., Technol.Syd., 190b
Bakre, A. B., Mumbai, 776a
Baksh, I. J., Nfld., 403b
Mohamed, Guy., 577a
Bakshi, A. K., Delhi, 647b
A. K., Panjab, 802b
E. N., Swinburne UT, 167b
Minu, J.Nehru U., 714b
O. P., J.Nehru U., 714c
P. K., Dhaka, 238b
R., CIE&F Langs., 640b
R. A., Azad J&K, 1089c
Rupa, Punj.Ag., 817c
T. S. (Lochan), Athab., 290c
Veena, Delhi, 648b
Bakunzi, Francis R., N-W(S.Af.), 1189b
Bakuwa, Rhoda, Malawi, 907c
Bakvis, H., Dal., 330c, 331a
Bal, A. K., Nfld., 402b
A. S., Punj.Ag., 814b
C. S., All India IMS, 586c
H. K., Punj.Ag., 817a
J. S., Punj.Ag., 815c
R. K., Utkal, 869c
S. S., Punj.Ag., 816c
Sabyasachi, All India IMS, 587c
Bal Krishanan, S., Roor., 829b
Bala, A. L., Rajsh., 254b
B. K., B'desh.Ag., 227c
E. J., A.Bello, 1009a
Indu, Pg.IMER, 807a
Madhu, GND, 680b
N., Qu., 455c
Neelam, Panjab, 802b
Pon, Oxf.Brookes, 1666c
S., Panjab, 803b
S. K., Dhaka, 237b
Uma, Osm., 796c
Bala Gangadhara Rao, Y., Nagar., 783b
Bala Parameswara Rao, M., Nagar., 783b
Bala Ravi, P., Osm., 796c
Bala Swamy, G., Kakatiya, 720b
Balabaskaran, S., Malaya, 919b
Balabyeki, M. A., Witw., 1246c
Balac, Pauline A., Hudd., 1459a
Balachandran, C., Manipal AHE, 767a
C., TN Vet., 862a
E. S., Madr., 742c
G., Delhi, 647c
K., Annam., 598c
K., B'thiar., 626b
K., S.Bank, 1720b
P., Manipal AHE, 767a
R., M.Sund., 770a
S., Jaffna, 1265c
S., SE(S.Lanka), 1282c
S., TN Vet., 862a
Wamedeva, Brun., 1352c
Baladas Ghoshal, NU Malaysia, 926a
Baladhandayutham, S., Annam., 599c
Balagopal, L., CIE&F Langs., 640a
Balagoundar, P. M., B'lore., 620b
Balagurunathan, K., Anna, 596c
Balahura, R. J., Guelph, 336a
Balaji, P. V., IIT Bombay, 693a
U., Osm., 798a
Balaji Prasad, P., S.Venkat., 855b
Balakotaiah, G., Osm., 796a
Balakrishan, Kalpana, S.Ramachandra Med., 853c
Balakrishna, H. K., B'lore., 621a
K. M., M'lore., 761a
R., Manipal AHE, 765b
Balakrishnan, B., Baroda, 751c
C., Madr., 743c
D., Anna, 596b
K., Annam., 598c
K., Calicut, 638b
K. R., S.Ramachandra Med., 853a
M., Anna, 596a, 597a
M., Kerala, 730a
N., IISc., 691a, 692b, 692c
N., Jaffna, 1265b, 1266c
N., McM., 383b
P., Annam., 601b
R., Annam., 598a, 599a
S., Annam., 598b, 600a
S., Manit., 392b
T., Madr., 742b
V., Annam., 598b
V., TN Vet., 863a
Vivian, NU Singapore, 1153b
Balakumar, B., Madr., 742c
Balamani, B., Osm., 797a
Balambal, V. N., Delhi, 647b
Balami, D. H., Maid., 1048a
Balamohan Das, V., And., 593c
Balamohana Das, V., And., 591a
Balamuruganandam, S., Annam., 599c
Balan, N., Kerala, 729c
P., Malaya, 918b
P., S.Aust., 158a
Balanaga Raju, V., And., 592b
Balance, W. D., Windsor, 539c
Balaporia, V. R., Mumbai, 774a
Balarabe, Abubakar, Bayero, 1012b
M., A.Bello, 1009a
Balaraj, B., Kakatiya, 719c
Balarajan, Rasaratnam, Sur., 1744a
Balaram, P., IISc., 691c
Balaram Gupta, G. S., Gulb., 674c

Binns contd.
Colin W., Curtin, 37b, 38c
D., E.Lond., 1410c
J. Anthony, Sus., 1747a
James W., York(UK), 1799c
Ray, Wolv., 1794a
Bin-Sallik, Mary A., S.Aust., 158c
Binski, Paul, Camb., 1360b
Bintliff, John L., Durh., 1402a
Binwal, J. C., NE Hill, 792b
Binyon, T. J., Oxf., 1658c
Biobaku, W. O., Abeokuta Ag., 1005b
Bion, J. F., Birm., 1335c
Bir, S. S., Punjabi, 819b
Bir Bahadur, Kakatiya, 720a, 721b
Bir Hans, Punj.Ag., 817c
Biradar, B. B., Karn., 724b
J. S., Gulb., 674b
Neelamma V., Karn., 725b
V. N., Karn., 723b
Biradara, B. S., Kuvempu, 735c
Birai, U. M., Abuja, 1004b, 1004c
Birbalsingh, F. M., York(Can.), 546b
Birbeck, W. C., Sund., 1738c
Birch, A., Coventry, 1384a
C. A., W.England, 1786a
Colin J., Qld., 135a
D. R., Br.Col., 304c
David, Deakin, 41c
David J. S., Strath., 1736b
Diane J., Nott., 1635a
Dinah L., Oxf., 1652c
E. John, Otago, 980b
Eva, Manc.Met., 1613a
G. G., Reading, 1692b
G. J., Griff., 55b
Gavin F., Syd., 173a
J., Reading, 1692b
Jenny, City(UK), 1381c
Jillian M., Manc., 1603c
Nigel P., Auck., 960b
Paul, Luton, 1593a, 1595c
R., Portsmouth, 1678b
Robert G., Qld., 131c
S., McM., 385a
T. S., Sheff., 1706a
Birchall, J., Manit., 395a
J. P., Nott., 1637c
Martin A., Brist., 1349c
Stuart, Sheff.Hallam, 1716c
Birchby, G., Manc., 1599b
Birchenall, Peter, L&H, 1506a
Birchenhall, C. R., Manc., 1598c
Birchenough, Allan, Wales, 1774a, 1776c
Bircher, David, Laval, 355a
Birchwood, M. J., Birm., 1332a
Bird, A. P., Edin., 1414b
Alan C., Lond., 1575a
C. A., Auck., 959c
C. C., Edin., 1413b, 1421a
Catherine I., Lond., 1535b, 1535c
D. J., W.England, 1785a
David M., Bath, 1324b
David M., McG., 376c, 379a
Delys M., W.Aust., 201c, 206c
Edward, Wolv., 1794a
Elizabeth, Bath, 1322b
Elizabeth, Brist., 1345c
F. B., C'dia., 325a
Graham R., Sur., 1741c
H. A., Leeds, 1489c
H. W., Windsor, 537c
J. F., W.England, 1786c
J. Lise, Well., 988a
J. S., S.Fraser, 478b
James, Kent, 1472a
Juliet F., Melb., 80c
Kenneth E., Westminster, 1790b
Kevin D., NSW, 115a
L., Coventry, 1384b
M., Lond., 1554b
M. G., Nott.Trent, 1643a
M. S., Wat., 515a, 518b
Margaret M., Lond., 1551c, 1554a
Michelle, Newcastle(NSW), 122b
P. H., C'dia., 322a, 326b
R., Car., 318b
R. M., Tor., 484c
R. S., Oxf., 1650c
Ranjana P., Manit., 393a
Richard W., New Br., 430a
Sandra, Br.Col., 295b
Susan, Griff., 59c
Wyndham W., Stell., 1225c
Birds, J. R., Sheff., 1707b
Birdsall, D. L., Brist., 1346b
William, Dal., 334c
Birek, Catelena, Manit., 396b
P., Tor., 493b
Birendra Singh, S., Manip., 768a
Biringer, P. P., Tor., 492b
Biritwum, R. B., Ghana, 569b
Birk, A. M., Qu., 454b
Birkbeck, T. H., Glas., 1437a
Birkeland, Janis L., Canberra, 25b
Birkemoe, P. C., Tor., 492a
Birkenhead, R., De Mont., 1393b
Birkett, Donald J., Flin., 51a
Geoffrey, Sheff.Hallam, 1715b
J., Birm., 1330c
John, L&H, 1504b
Marian M., Sheff.Hallam, 1717b
Nick J., Ott., 443c
Paul E., Bolton Inst., 1338b, 1338c
William P., NSW, 108a, 119a
Birkhead, Roy, C.Sturt, 32c
T. R., Sheff., 1704c
Birkinhead, Patricia A., Herts., 1456b
Birkinshaw, Keith, Wales, 1755c
Mark, Brist., 1348a
P. J., Hull, 1466a, 1468a
Birks, K. Stuart, Massey, 975a
P. B. H., Oxf., 1655a
Renée O., Glas., 1439a
Stuart, Massey, 978c
Birla, G. P., BIT(Ranchi), 629a
K. K., BITS, 630a
S. C., WI, 1816b
Birlasekaran, Sivaswamy, Nan.Tech., 1139a
Birley, Humphrey D. E., Liv., 1512b
Martin H., Liv., 1513c
Sue, Lond., 1529b
Birmingham, A. T., Nott., 1636b
Carl L., Br.Col., 305c
David, Kent, 1473c
Judy M., Syd., 170c
Marion K., McG., 375b
Birnbaum, E., Tor., 488c
Birnboim, H. Chaim, Ott., 443b, 444a
Birnbrauer, Jay S., Murd., 100a
Birnie, J. W., Ulster, 1750c
Patricia, Lond., 1553a
Birnin Yauri, U. A., U.Danfodiyo, 1070c
Biro, George P., Ott., 443b
P. Andrew, Lond., 1555b
Birrell, G. S., UMIST, 1609b
Peter C., NSW, 115a
Robert J., Monash, 88c, 97b
W. D., Ulster, 1752b
Birse, M. C., Manc., 1601c
Birt, B. Derek, Tor., 499a
C. A., Birm., 1335b
Martin, Cape Town, 1163b
Birtchnell, M., W.Syd., 208b
Birtles, A. B., UMIST, 1607c
Ann P., Herts., 1456b
Anthony B., Wales, 1761c
Mervyn J., Massey, 978a
Richard M., Sheff., 1713c
Robert A., James Cook, 61b
Terry G., Canberra, 26c
Birtley, Margaret, Deakin, 40c
N., Coventry, 1384a
Birtwhistle, D., Qld.UT, 146b
Graham M., Leeds, 1485a
R. V., Qu., 458c
Birtwistle, H., Lond., 1537c
Hilary, Bolton Inst., 1337a
Timothy, Leeds Met., 1496a
Biryabarema, M., Mak., 1303b
Bisacre, J., Napier, 1617c
Bisaillon, André, Montr., 417b
Jocelyne, Laval, 354a
Suzanne, Montr., 410a, 413c
Bisaliah, Dr. S., B'lore.Ag.Scis., 583a
Bisallah, H. I., Abuja, 1004b
Bisanda, E. T. N., Dar., 1292c
Bisanz, Gay, Alta., 285b
J. H., Alta., 285b
Bisaria, R., Lucknow, 738b
Bisby, F. A, Reading, 1691a
John A., Melb., 86b
M. A., Qu., 459c
Roger H., Salf., 1700b
Bischak, Diane, Auck., 963c
Bischof, Walter F., Alta., 285c
Bischoff, E., Wales, 1768a
Manfred, Queb., 449c
P. H., Rhodes, 1215b
Peter H., New Br., 429a
Biscoe, Timothy J., Lond., 1568a
Biscomb, Kay, Wolv., 1794b
Bisen, P. S., B'tullah.V., 623b
Biseswar, Ramlall, Durban-W., 1172a
Bisgrove, R. J., Reading, 1693a
Bishnoi, Niraj, All India IMS, 586c
S. R., JN Vyas, 705b
S. R., Punj.Ag., 816b
T. R., Baroda, 749c
Bishop, A. G., McM., 382b
A. Russell, Otago, 980c
Alan J., Monash, 90b
Anne, Dal., 331a
Aubrey, Guy., 577b
Bernard G., Griff., 58a
Brian, Curtin, 37b
C., Manc.Met., 1610b
Christopher D., Liv.J.Moores, 1518c
Christopher M., Camb., 1367b
Christopher M., Edin., 1416a
D., Plym., 1675b
D. Timothy, Leeds, 1491a
David H. L., Qld., 136a
David M., Ott., 439a
Dorothy V. M., Camb., 1366a
Douglas F., La Trobe, 64a, 70b
E. L., Alta., 282c
E. R., Acad., 278b
Elizabeth A., Syd., 179b
George D., NU Singapore, 1151c
H. W., Sund., 1739a
I. D., Melb., 80c
Ian D., Melb., 78b
J., Portsmouth, 1678c
J., Trent, 509b
J. O., Edin., 1422a
James F., Syd., 177b
Jennifer, Notre Dame Aust., 129a, 129c
Jennifer M., P.Elizabeth, 1198b
John C., Auck., 964b
John H., NE, 103a
Judith M., Pret., 1203b
Kevin D., Wales, 1762b
M., Dal., 329b
M., Nfld., 407c
Mark A., Lond., 1554a
N., Nfld., 404b
Nigel T., S.Af., 1220b
P. J., Wat., 516a
P. M., W.Ont., 522a
P. R., S.Aust., 156c
Paul, Glas., 1439a
Paul C., Glas., 1439b
Paul R., Plym., 1675a
Peter, N.Lond., 1628a
R. B., Nfld., 405c
R. F., UMIST, 1609b
R. H., Ulster, 1750b
R. J., Kingston(UK), 1478b
Roger, NSW, 109c
Roy, Nfld., 409a
Ruth F., Melb., 85b
S. J., ANU, 20c
Steven, Lond., 1570b
Terence E., C.Sturt, 32a
Bisht, Krishna, Delhi, 649a
N. S., Forest RI, 663a
N. S., HNB Garh., 683a
R. C., HNB Garh., 684a
S. S., I.Gandhi Nat.Open, 701c
S. S., Lucknow, 738a
Bismarck, J. A. K., Kumasi, 571a
Bismillah, A., JMI, 709c
Bisnauth, R., C.England, 1378a
Bisoi, A. K., Utkal, 869c
Bisong, Joseph O., Calabar, 1021b, 1021c
Biss, Tom H., Plym., 1675a
Bissa, Sudha, JN Vyas, 703a
Bissar, Dounia, N.Lond., 1628c
Bissell, A. F., Wales, 1768a
C., Open(UK), 1647a
Bissett, Andrew K., Sheff.Hallam, 1715a
Bissett-Johnson, Alastair, Dund., 1398a
Bissix, G., Acad., 278c
Bisson, Alain-François, Ott., 441a
André, Montr., 409a
Barry G., New Br., 429a
Michael, McG., 363a
Pierre-Richard, Montr., 410b
Bissonauth-Bedford, Anu, L&H, 1505b
Bissonnette, B., Tor., 494b
Leo A., C'dia., 326c
Bissoondoyal, S., Maur., 952a
Biswajit Sakaravarthy, Annam., 600b
Biswal, Besanti, Samb., 832b
T. K., IIT Bombay, 693c
U. C., Samb., 832b
Biswalo, Paul M., Dar., 1292b
Biswas, A., Burd., 634b, 634c
A., Mumbai, 776b
A., VB, 874b
A. A., Shahjalal, 258b
Arijit, NU Singapore, 1153a
Ashutosh, All India IMS, 586b
B. N., Burd., 635a
D. J., Assam, 603c
G., Pg.IMER, 808c
Goutam, Assam, 603a, 603c
M. A. S., Shahjalal, 258c
M. E. U., Shahjalal, 259a
M. M. H., B'desh.Engin., 232a
M. R., B'desh.Ag., 228a
Marju, Ban., 617b
N., R.Bhar., 823c
N., Windsor, 538b
N. B., Arunachal, 602b
N. B., Assam, 603b
N. C., Dhaka, 242a, 242c
N. G., VB, 874c
N. N., Dhaka, 237c
N. R., Rajsh., 256a
Nihar R., All India IMS, 586c
P. K., VB, 874a
R. K., Assam Ag., 606c, 607b
R. K., Rajsh., 255a
R. N., R.Bhar., 823c
S., IIT Bombay, 693b
S. C., Burd., 634c
S. K., Burd., 634b
S. K., IISc., 691b
S. N., Chitt., 234b
S. P., Dib., 652b
Biswas Ray, P. K., Berh., 624a
Bisztray, G., Tor., 490b
Bithal, P. K., All India IMS, 586c
Bithell, Christine P., E.Lond., 1411a
J. F., Oxf., 1659a, 1663a
Bitici, Umit S., Strath., 1734a
Bitmead, Robert R., ANU, 16a
Bitondo, Dieudonne, Dschang, 270b
Bittegeko, S. B. P., Sokoine Ag., 1298c
Bitter-Suermann, Hinrich, Dal., 333c
Bittles, Alan H., E.Cowan, 44b, 46a
Bittman, Michael P., NSW, 115b
Bittu, Venkateswarlu, Potti ST, 810c
Bixby, Bob, Oxf.Brookes, 1668b
Bixley, Morag D., De Mont., 1392b
Biyani, K. R., Baroda, 751a
Bizley, William H., Natal, 1184c
Bjarnason, Svava, xxxx
Bjerknes, Matthew L., Tor., 494c
Bjork-Billings, Pamela, Deakin, 43b, 43c
Blaauw, Johannes H., Stell., 1226c
Blaber, Jean, G.Caledonian, 1446b
Blache, G., Lond., 1539a
Blachford, Gregg, McG., 379b
Blachut, Jan, Liv., 1509b
Black, A. McL. S., Brist., 1349a
Alan W., E.Cowan, 45c, 46b
Alistair, Leeds Met., 1495b
Andrew, Glas., 1438a
Anthony H., Cape Town, 1161a
Anthony J., Dund., 1398c
Archibald S., C.Sturt, 32c
B., Manit., 399c
Betty, Manit., 400a
C. F., Glas., 1439c
C. R., Nott., 1633b
Carol, Lond., 1577b
Carolyn G., Massey, 975b
Charyln, Manit., 396c
Damien J., Glam., 1434c
David, New Br., 428a
David St. C., NSW, 109c
David W., Curtin, 37b
Deborah, NSW, 116a
E. R., Qu., 456c
E. Taiarahia, Massey, 977a
Earl, Laur., 349c
F. W., Car., 317b
Rev. Frederick A., St M.Coll.Tor., 505c
G. Gordon, Dund., 1400c
Ian D., NSW, 112a
Ian G., Cran., 1388a
J. A., Oxf., 1648c
J. B. H., Belf., 1687a
J. E., Bran., 293a
J. E., Brock, 311c, 313b
J. L., Car., 316b, 318a
J. Michael, Glas., 1436a
J. P., Wat., 511a, 513a
J. R., Nfld., 404b, 405a
Sir James, Lond., 1538c
James A. (Sandy), Ryerson, 468b
Sir James W., Dund., 1396a
Jane, Wales, 1754a
Jean, Ryerson, 468b
Jennifer A., Otago, 979b
Jeremy M., Exe., 1428b
Jerome, McG., 369a
John, Wolv., 1796c
John A., NSW, 110c
Judith L., Syd., 178b
Keith F., Winn., 541a
Kerry P., Waik., 992a
L. D., Lake., 344c
L. G., Oxf., 1648a, 1652c
M. E. A., McM., 386a
M. M., Sheff., 1710a
Margery J. G., P.Elizabeth, 1195b
Maria, Lond., 1572a
Marjorie, Glas., 1442b
Martin J., McG., 374a
Mary E., Qld., 138b
N. A., Lond., 1550b
N. D., Ulster, 1751b
P. A., St FX, 470a
P. N., Auck., 965c
Paul, Acad., 279c
Paul D., N.Territory, 127c
Philippa M., Auck., 962c
R., Portsmouth, 1679a
R. G., Qld.UT, 146b
R. I., Edin., 1414c
Richard M., Tor., 498c
Robert, Edin., 1418a
Robert D., Leeds, 1487a
S. A., S.Fraser, 478c
Sandra E., Tor., 497a
T. Andy, Br.Col., 303b
Terry J., Qld.UT, 145b
V., Dal., 329c
Valerie J., Lough., 1591a
W., Hull, 1464a
W. Bob, W.Aust., 203c
W. D., Guelph, 340c
W. J., UMIST, 1608c
W. S., Auck., 961c
William A., Br.Col., 307c
William W., Br.Col., 301a
William W., Camb., 1366b
Blackaby, D. H., Wales, 1767b
Blackall, Linda L., Qld., 136a
Blackbeard, Marié, S.Af., 1220a
Blackbourn, Anthony, Nipissing, 433c
Blackburn, Alan, Oxf.Brookes, 1666a
Barry J., Winn., 541b
Chris, Oxf.Brookes, 1666a
Don, L&H, 1506b
E. V., Alta., 288a
G. M., Sheff., 1705a
J., Sheff., 1711b
J. M., Camb., 1368a
J. R., Tor., 488c
James, W.Laur., 535b
John, Westminster, 1789a
Keith, Manc., 1598c
Michel, Laval, 356b
N., Manc., 1601a
N., Witw., 1245b
R., Greenwich, 1447a
R. A., Kingston(UK), 1477c, 1478c
R. W., C.England, 1376c
R. W., Lond., 1537b, 1542b
Robert, Salf., 1700c
Robert M., Camb., 1363c
Ronald, Liv., 1511c, 1513b
S., Birm., 1328c
Stuart H., Lond., 1565a, 1566b
Susan, Monash, 93c, 96b
Susan P., Plym., 1674b
Trevor R., NSW, 110c
W. H., Windsor, 538a
Blackett, Heather, Greenwich, 1447a
Val, L&H, 1506c
Blackey, H. E., Glam., 1433b
Blackford, B. L., Dal., 330c
Karen, Laur., 348a
Black-Gutman, Dasia, Aust.Cath., 13c
Blackie, John W. G., Strath., 1735b
Blacklaws, Barbara A., Camb., 1365a
Blackledge, J. M., De Mont., 1393b
Michael J., Portsmouth, 1679c
Blackler, Frank H. M., Lanc., 1480a
Blacklock, R. T., Augustana(Alta.), 291a
Blacklow, W. Marcus, W.Aust., 200a
Blackman, A. Roger, S.Fraser, 480a
Adrian J., Tas., 183b
Carol A., Westminster, 1791c
D. E., Wales, 1765a
D. R., Monash, 91b
J. A., Reading, 1693c
Maurice J., NSW, 114a
Michael M. S., Cape Town, 1163a
Stephen A., Cran., 1387c
Blackmore, Alice, Manc.Met., 1610b
Jill A., Deakin, 41a
Michael, Newcastle(NSW), 125b
Paul, Warw., 1784c
S., Reading, 1691a
Susan J., W.England, 1785a
Timothy, Flin., 51c
Blackorby, C., Br.Col., 298a
Blacksell, A. M. Y., Plym., 1673c
Blackshaw, Judith K., Qld., 139a
R. P., Plym., 1672b
Susanna E., Glas., 1437a
Blackshield, Anthony R., Macq., 74a
Blackstein, Martin E., Tor., 497a
Blackstock, Jim, G.Caledonian, 1444b
Blackstone, Mary, Regina, 463b
Blacktop, Jonathan, Hudd., 1460a
Blackwell, Cecelia C., Edin., 1420a
D., Sund., 1739b
Francis, RMIT, 153b
G., Nott.Trent, 1639a
G. H., Qu., 454c
G. K., Plym., 1673a
J. C., Brock, 313c
Jenefer M., Camb., 1362b
Leonard F., Massey, 975c
Richard J., Nott., 1638c
Roland, Lond., 1574a
Ruth, Leeds Met., 1494a
Blackwood, D. H. R., Edin., 1421a
D. J., Abertay, 1318b, 1319a
D. J., NU Singapore, 1150b
John B., Tas., 184b
Bladen, S., C.England, 1378a
Bladen-Hovell, Robin C., Keele, 1470a
Blades, M., Sheff., 1708a
Michael, Br.Col., 296c
Bladon, Geoffrey L., New Br., 430a
Blagbrough, Ian S., Bath, 1324a
Blagg, Thomas F. C., Kent, 1473c
Blagrave, M., Mt.All., 423c
Blaich, Rhonda, RMIT, 155a
Blaikie, F., Lake., 343c
J., Aberd., 1315a
J., Bran., 293b
J. A. D., Aberd., 1315c
Norman, Sci.U.Malaysia, 932a, 933b
P. M., E.Anglia, 1407c
Blain, Marion, Coventry, 1385c
Neil, G.Caledonian, 1445a
P. G., Newcastle(UK), 1624a
Virginia H., Macq., 73b
Blair, A. P. P., S.Bank, 1721a
Alasdair M., Westminster, 1791b
Celia, Kingston(UK), 1477a
D. J., Sund., 1739a
Daniel E., Winn., 542a
David, James Cook, 61a
David, Macq., 71a, 73b, 76a
David G., W.Aust., 203b
David J., W.Ont., 526b, 532a
Emma, Newcastle(NSW), 122b
G. E., Leeds, 1484a
Geoff O., NE, 106b, 106c
Gordon S., Lanc., 1480a
Graeme J., NE, 102c
Hugh T., Massey, 978b
I. S., Ulster, 1752a
J. A., Windsor, 539b
J. H., OFS, 1194b
Leonie, Technol.Syd., 194b
Lorrie, C'dia., 321b
M. E., Nott., 1637b
Maria E., Sheff.Hallam, 1718a
R. L., Dund., 1400b
Robert, Br.Col., 296a
Roger, Jamaica UT, 883b, 883c
Sheena E. E., QM Edin., 1682b
W., Lond., 1552a
W. J., Oxf., 1654a
Blais, André, Montr., 414a
Christine, Brock, 311c
Diane, Montr., 410b, 417a
Jean-Guy, Montr., 411c

Callow, Geoff, Lough., 1589c
J. A., Birm., 1327b
Sue, Wolv., 1796a
Callus, R., Syd., 180b
Ron, Syd., 173c
Callwood, Ingrid J., Wolv., 1796a
Cally, P. S., Monash, 93a
Calman, K. C., Glas., 1443a
Kenneth, Durh., 1401a
Calnan, M. W., Kent, 1475a
Calne, Donald B., Br.Col., 306b
Sir Roy, Camb., 1374a
Calof, Jonathan L., Ott., 438b
Calon, T. J., Nfld., 403a
Calow, Jane M., Wolv., 1794a
P., Sheff., 1704c, 1712b
Calpin-Davis, P., Sheff., 1711a
Calude, C., Auck., 964a
Calvé, Pierre J., Ott., 439c
Calver, Cheryl D., Leth., 360c
Michael C., Murd., 99a
S., Bourne., 1340a
Calverley, Peter M., Liv., 1512b
Calvert, A. H., Newcastle(UK), 1625c
B., Guelph, 338b
B. D., Auck., 964a
Dennis, W'gong., 215a
George D., NSW, 116b
J. R., S'ton., 1725b
Jane E., Newcastle(UK), 1625b
John R., Lough., 1589a
Mary, Lond., 1554c
Maurice, Leeds Met., 1495a
P. C., W.England, 1787a
P. M., C.England, 1376a
Peter A. R., S'ton., 1727a
Philip J., Well., 987b
Sandra A., Lond., 1561c
Stephen E., Br.Col., 298a
Tom W., S.Fraser, 477b, 479b
Calvet, A. Luis, Ott., 438b
Calway, B. A., Swinburne UT, 168a
Cam, Philip A., NSW, 114b
Camacho-Hubner, Cecilia, Lond., 1555c
Camakaris, J., Melb., 80c
Camara, Cecily J., W.Cape, 1236b
Camarda, Aldo, Montr., 415b
Camarero, Ricardo, Montr., 420c
Camble, E., Maid., 1048b
Cambley, J., Oxf., 1662c
Cambourne, Brian, W'gong., 213b
Cambrell, G. K., Monash, 91a
Cambron, Micheline, Montr., 412a
Cambrosio, Alberto, McG., 369c, 376a
Camerman, Norman, Tor., 494c
Cameron, A., S.Bank, 1720a
A. Barry, New Br., 429b
A. I., Manit., 398b
A. J. R., Wat., 515c, 518a
Alan F., Massey, 976c
Alan M., Well., 986b
Andrew A., Wolv., 1795b
Andrew C., St And., 1698c
Averil M., Oxf., 1662a, 1664a
B. J., Manit., 391c, 400a
B. Jamie, York(Can.), 553a
B. W., Acad., 278a
Barbara, York(Can.), 552c
Barry J., Canberra, 27b
C. Ann, New Br., 430c
Cynthia, Manit., 394c
D. A., S.Aust., 157b
D. J., Nott.Trent, 1640a
D. M., Dal., 330c
D. R., Tor., 489c
D. W., Melb., 78c
D. William, Ott., 443b, 444a
Dave, Waik., 995c
Deborah J., Strath., 1734c
Denis R., NSW, 121c
Donald L., Flin., 51a
Douglas, Leic., 1501c
Dugald, Glas., 1443c
Duncan C., Ott., 442b
E. K., Newcastle(UK), 1622a
E. R., Glas., 1441c
E. W., York(Can.), 547a
Elspeth, Tor., 485b
Euan D., De Mont., 1393a
Eugene C., Br.Col., 306b, 308b
Ewen A., Massey, 977b
G. G., Aberd., 1314a
H., Tor., 501b
H., Ulster, 1750b
I. T., Glas., 1442c
I. T., Qld., 140b
Iain A., Syd., 173b
Ian, Syd., 177b
Ian A., Dal., 332b
Ian D., Dund., 1398b
Ian M., NSW, 112b
Ian R., Wales, 1771a
Ian T., Qld., 133a
J., E.Anglia, 1407c
J., Qu., 454b
J. A., McM., 384a
J. Gary, W.Laur., 535c
J. I., W.Syd., 207a
J. M., York(Can.), 552b
J. R., Aberd., 1315b
James D., La Trobe, 65c
James M. R., N.Territory, 127c
Jan E., Cant., 968b, 971c
Jim, N.Territory, 128a
John M., Technol.Syd., 194b
Judith A., Alta., 282a
K. C., Lincoln(NZ), 973c
Kathleen B., W.Laur., 535a
Keith C., Exe., 1429a
Lachlan E., Ballarat, 22c
M. I., Car., 317c
M. L., Lincoln(NZ), 972a
N. E., Aberd., 1314a
N. E., Manit., 391c
Neil, Sheff.Hallam, 1719c
Neil, Well., 988b
Noel, Lough., 1591b
P. J., Lond., 1553b
Paul M., Ott., 445b
Penny, Canberra, 27b
Peter D., Dund., 1398a
R. A., Lake., 343b
R. C., W.Syd., 207c
Robert, Cape Town, 1164b
Robert A. D., Sheff., 1704b
Robert D., S.Fraser, 477b
Robin K., Tor., 483c
Ross, Tor., 495c
Ruth E., Camb., 1361b
S. A., Oxf., 1650c
S. J., Newcastle(UK), 1623b
Sheila, Open(UK), 1646a
T. Stanley, Dal., 328b
W. Sheila, Windsor, 537a, 539b, 540c
Walter, Tor., 488b
William N., RMIT, 152c
Cameron-Jones, Margot, Edin., 1416a
Cameron-MacDonald, P., Napier, 1617c, 1618c
Cameron-Traub, Elizabeth, Aust.Cath., 11b
Camfield, Carol S., Dal., 333a
Peter R., Dal., 333a
Camiletti, S., W.Ont., 525a
Camilleri, Antoinette, Malta, 947a
Charles J., Malta, 948c
George E., Malta, 947b
Joseph A., La Trobe, 68b
Juanito, Malta, 947b
Marie-Thérèse, Malta, 949b
Patricia, Malta, 950c, 951a
Peter, Aust.Cath., 14b
Rev. René, Malta, 948a
Silvio, Malta, 948b
Camina, A. R., E.Anglia, 1408c
Camiré, Claude, Laval, 352c
Camm, A. John, Lond., 1562a
Cammack, John, Oxf.Brookes, 1666b
P. A., Manc., 1600a
R., Lond., 1537b, 1543a
Cammock, P. A., Cant., 971a
Camous, Roger, Montr., 412b
Camozzi, A., St FX, 469a
Camp, Richard D. R., Leic., 1501a
Sheila, Westminster, 1790c
Campagna, Phil D., Dal., 329b
Campanella, Osvaldo H., Massey, 975b
R. G., Br.Col., 298b
Campanelli, Josephine, York(Can.), 553b
Michael, E.Cowan, 46c
Campbell, A., Birm., 1332b
A., S.Bank, 1723a
A., WI, 1816b
A. C., Lond., 1552a
A. C., Plym., 1672b
A. J., Manc.Met., 1611a
A. John, Otago, 979c, 983a
A. K., Wales, 1772b
A. P., Birm., 1328c
A. S., Lincoln(NZ), 973c
Ailsa M., Glas., 1437a
Alan, Herts., 1454c
Alastair V., Brist., 1349a
Alexandra J., York(Can.), 545b
Angela M., Bourne., 1339b
Anne C., Durh., 1404c
Anne J., Canberra, 26c
Archibald M., Camb., 1358b
B., Alta., 285a
B., C'dia., 323a
B. L., Mt.All., 424a
B. M. S., Belf., 1687a
Most Rev. C., St FX, 469a
C. Bryan, Qld., 136a
C. C., WI, 1815a
C. M., St And., 1698a
Cathy E., Leth., 360b
Claire P., S.Cross, 161b
Colin, G.Caledonian, 1445a
Colin, Nott., 1632a
Colin B., York(UK), 1801a
Craig M., Ott., 444a
D. F., Tor., 490c
D. Murray, Edin., 1418c
D. S., Qu., 457c, 458a
David, Newcastle(UK), 1623a
David, Sheff.Hallam, 1717a
Donald J., NU Singapore, 1151a
Doris M., Aberd., 1316b
Douglas R., Paisley, 1670c
Duncan M., Well., 986c
E. J. M., McM., 385b
E. K., Botswana, 262b
Enid M., Monash, 92b
F., Napier, 1618c
Florence, Qu., 452a, 460c
Frederick C., Newcastle(UK), 1626b
G., Herts., 1455b
G. D., Melb., 83c
G. T., Wat., 517b
Gail, New Br., 429c
Gill, Portsmouth, 1679b
Gillian, G.Caledonian, 1444b
Glen K., Natal, 1178c
Gordon R., Leic., 1498b
Gordon R., Qld., 131b
H., Edin., 1421b
H. E. A., Qu., 455c
H. J., Sheff., 1708b
Harry F., Qld., 132c, 143a
Heather, York(Can.), 546b
I., H-W, 1450a
I., Monash, 89a
I., Victoria UT, 196a
I. C., Cant., 970c
I. C., Lond., 1539c
I. D., Oxf., 1649c, 1663a
I. T., Manc., 1603b
Ian, Edin., 1416c
Ian G., W.Aust., 199c, 202b
Ian R., Tas., 187b
J., Birm., 1331c
J., Glas., 1439a
J., Oxf., 1654a
J., Rhodes, 1214c
J. A., Cant., 971b
J. B., Belf., 1685c
J. B., Tor., 496c
J. D., Car., 317c
J. H., W.Ont., 523c
J. J., Oxf., 1656c
J. K., Cant., 970b
J. L. (Iain), Guelph, 335a, 341c
J. M. R., Tor., 494b
J. P., McM., 383a
James S., Ott., 445a
Jane L., W.Laur., 534c
Janet, Regina, 464c
Jean P., Edin., 1414a
Jennifer, Br.Col., 303a
John, Monash, 98b
John, Strath., 1737a
John A., Lond., 1570a
John B., James Cook, 60c
John L., Lond., 1541c
John R., Waik., 993a
Julie, Qld., 131b
Julie H., Qld., 143c
Juliet J. d'A., Camb., 1368b
K. C., Glas., 1437c
Kathleen M., NU Singapore, 1151a
Kathryn, Trent, 509b
Keith, Syd., 174c
Kenneth B., Ott., 442c
Kenton S. W., ANU, 19c
L. D., Manit., 390b
L. L., Qu., 455c
Lesley, Coventry, 1385c
Lesley, NSW, 119b
Lesley V., NSW, 116b
Leslie C., Strath., 1734b
Lindsay C., Syd., 175c
Lisbeth, ANU, 19a
Lyle, Cant., 970c
M., St And., 1697c
M., W.Syd., 208c
M. A., S.Leone, 1132a
M. C., Wat., 517c
M. J., Sheff., 1709a
M. Karen, W.Ont., 528c
M. M., Oxf., 1658a
Malcolm, G.Caledonian, 1444a
Malcolm M., Bath, 1323a
Margaret, Liv.J.Moores, 1518a
Margaret R., ANU, 18c
Marian L., Manit., 393a
Marion J., Melb., 80b
Marlene, Jamaica UT, 883a
Melanie C., Wat., 517a
Mervyn C. O., S.Af.Med., 1176c
Michael, G.Caledonian, 1445b
Michael I., Cape Town, 1164a
Michael P., Leeds Met., 1496b
Michel-M., Montr., 415a
N., Greenwich, 1448a
N. C. G., Manc., 1602c
Neil, Glas., 1443b
Neil, N.Br.Col., 434a, 436b
O. B., Ib., 1038b
Oona M. R., Lond., 1549c
P. S., Stir., 1730a
Paul, Mt.St.Vin., 426b
R. Colin, Camb., 1366a
R. James, Warw., 1780b
R. L., Car., 318c
R. M., Dal., 330c
R. M., Trent, 509a
R. W. F., Newcastle(UK), 1624a
Richard J., ANU, 15a, 19b
Richard M., Dund., 1400c
Rita, St FX, 469a, 470c
Rob J., Bolton Inst., 1337a
Robert, G.Caledonian, 1445b
Robert M., York(UK), 1799b
Roderick C., New Br., 431a
Russell D., Well., 988a
Ruth, Lond., 1574a
S. J., W.Syd., 209a
Sheelagh, Portsmouth, 1680b
Simon F., Leeds, 1484c
Stewart J., NSW, 120c
Stuart, Lond., 1562b
Susan, RMIT, 151b
Susan L., Monash, 92b
T. I., Qu., 454a
Terence D., Sheff.Hallam, 1716c
Terence J., NSW, 116b, 118a
Thomas, G.Caledonian, 1444c
Tom D., ANU, 18c
Venice, Lond., 1543b
W. H., Manc.Met., 1610c
W. R., Windsor, 538c
William, C.England, 1377a
Campbell-Borland, D., W.Ont., 521b
Campbell-Evans, Glenda H., E.Cowan, 44c
Campbell-Evanson, Patrick, Jamaica UT, 882c
Campbell-Hunt, Colin, Well., 987a
Campbell-Kelly, Martin, Warw., 1780a
Campbell-Lamerton, M. J., Oxf., 1661b
Campenot, R. B., Alta., 286b
Campfens, Hubert L., W.Laur., 535c
Campion, J., Manc.Met., 1611a
Michael, Murd., 100b
P. D., Hull, 1467c
Camplejohn, Richard S., Lond., 1541b
Campling, B., Qu., 459a
John T., James Cook, 61b
Campos, C. L., Lond., 1580a
Campos-Costa, Durval, Lond., 1574c
Canaan, Joyce, C.England, 1378b
Canagaratna, M. C. Pumany, Colombo, 1261a
Canagasabey, E. G. J., Eastern(S.Lanka), 1263c
Canby, J. I., McM., 386b
Candido, E. Peter M., Br.Col., 305a
Candlin, Christopher N., Macq., 73b, 75c, 76a
Christopher N., Wales, 1763b
Julia, Aston, 1320b
Candlish, J. K., NU Singapore, 1152b
M. Stewart, W.Aust., 203b
Candy, D. J., Birm., 1327b
Russell I., W.Aust., 205c
Cane, P. A., Birm., 1334b
Patricia D., Brock, 314b
Canfell, Michael J., NE, 104c
Canfield, J. V., Tor., 489a
Paul J., Syd., 179c
S. Paul, Lond., 1530b
Cangelosi, A., Plym., 1673a
Canham, J. C., Manc.Met., 1613b
P. B., W.Ont., 527b, 529a
Canhao, Sr. Jane, Z'bwe., 1826c
Canitz, Christa, New Br., 429b
Cann, A. B., Acad., 277b
Johnson R., Leeds, 1485a
Ronnie, Edin., 1418a
Cannadine, D. N., Lond., 1582c
Cannan, Crescy, Sus., 1748a
Cannataci, Joseph, Malta, 948a
Cannatella, H. J., Coventry, 1384a
Canne-Hilliker, Judith M., Guelph, 336a
Cannell, Hugh, Lond., 1554c
M., Auck., 966c
Melvin G. R., Edin., 1415b
Canning, B., Coventry, 1385b
Barbara, Wolv., 1794b
D. J. H., Belf., 1687a
Elizabeth U., Lond., 1527b
Joe P., Wales, 1758b
L. E., W.England, 1785c
P., Nfld., 403b
R., Aberd., 1317a
Raymond, Aust.Cath., 14b
Cannings, C., Sheff., 1707c
Canning-Smith, Hazel E., Manc.Met., 1615a
Cannon, A., McM., 380b
C. D., Oxf., 1652c
Colin, Kent, 1473b
Jackie, W.England, 1788a
Jasmine, Griff., 59c
John J., Syd., 174b
M., Lond., 1536a
M., Salf., 1703c
R. D., E.Anglia, 1407c
R. J., E.Lond., 1411c
Robert A., Adel., 10b
S., Aberd., 1313a, 1317c
S. M., Monash, 96a
S. M., Sund., 1739c
T. G., Greenwich, 1448b
W. H., York(Can.), 549a
W. T., Qu., 453a
Cannone, A. J., Witw., 1240c
Canny, Benedict J., Monash, 95b
C. L. B., W.Ont., 530a
G., Tor., 499b
Mary, Luton, 1593a
Canonici, Noverino N., Natal, 1181c
Canonne, Persephone K., Laval, 351b
Canova, F., S'ton., 1724b
Canovan, Margaret E., Keele, 1471a
Cant, A. Gregory, E.Cowan, 47b
Mike C., S.Af., 1217c
Noel W., Macq., 72a
R. J., Nott.Trent, 1639c
R. Stewart, Camb., 1358b
Rosemary V., Syd., 176b
Terry, Notre Dame Aust., 130a, 130b
Cantar, B., Wat., 514c
Cantarovich, Marcelo, McG., 371c
Cantelon, H. A., Qu., 456b
Canter, David V., Liv., 1511a
Canterbury, His Grace The Lord Archbishop of, Kent, 1472a
His Grace The Lord Archbishop of Lond., 1578a
Cantin, Jacques, Montr., 417a
Cantin Cumyn, Madeleine T., McG., 367b
Cantley, W. R. B., H-W, 1450b
Cantlie, Audrey, Lond., 1563c
Cantor, B., Oxf., 1655c
Christopher H., Griff., 57b
G. N., Leeds, 1488b
Geoffrey N., Leeds, 1488a
Cantouris, Andrew, Nott.Trent, 1643b
Cantrell, Leon N., S.Cross, 161b, 162b
M. A., North(S.Af.), 1189a
Cantrill, Judith A., Manc., 1601b
Cantwell, F. F., Alta., 281a
John, Reading, 1691c
Michael A., Liv.J.Moores, 1516b
Wesley J., Liv., 1509a
Canty, Allan J., Tas., 182a, 183b
Canvin, D. T., Qu., 453a
Canzona, L., W.Ont., 527a
Caon, Martin, Flin., 50a
Caouette, Charles, Montr., 414b
Cap, O., Manit., 391c
Capano, Joseph, C'dia., 326c
Caparros, Ernest, Ott., 441b
Cape, Jeremy, S.Aust., 159a
Capek, Radan, McG., 374c
Caperaa, Philippe, Laval, 354c
Capewell, Simon, Glas., 1443b
Capie, Forrest H., City(UK), 1380b
Capitanio, Sarah J., Wolv., 1795c
Capjack, C. E., Alta., 282b
Caplan, A. Patricia, Lond., 1524c, 1582a, 1582b
S., McG., 371c
Caple, Christopher, Durh., 1402a
Ivan W., Melb., 77c, 87a
Caplin, Antony D., Lond., 1530a
William, McG., 368a
Capobianco, J., C'dia., 322a
Capon, Claire H., Sheff.Hallam, 1718b
Nicholas C., Portsmouth, 1677a
P. C., Manc., 1598b
R. J., Melb., 78c
Capone, J. P., McM., 380c
Caporn, S. J. M., Manc.Met., 1614c
Capozzi, R., Tor., 487a
Capp, Bernard S., Warw., 1781b
Cappadocia, Mario, Montr., 410c
Cappeliez, Philippe, Ott., 442c
Cappell, H. D., Tor., 490a
Capper, D. J. S., Belf., 1685c
Wayne L., Cape Town, 1165b
Cappi, Paul A., Plym., 1675a
Cappuccio, Francisco P., Lond., 1562b
Capra, Michael F., Qld.UT, 148a
S., Qld.UT, 148a
Capri, A. Z., Alta., 285a, 289b
Capson, D., McM., 382a
Capstick, Valerie A., Alta., 287a
Caputo, T. C., Car., 320a
Carabine, Deirdre, Uganda Martyrs, 1307b, 1307c
Keith, Kent, 1473b
Michael D., Lond., 1528a
Caracaz, R., Wat., 511b
Caracciolo, Peter L., Lond., 1558a
Carachi, R., Glas., 1443b
Caradoc-Davies, Tudor H., Otago, 983b
Caraher, B. G., Belf., 1685b
Carani, Marie, Laval, 353b
Caras, Lilian, Herts., 1457c
Carasco, Emily F., Windsor, 539a
J. F., Mak., 1302b
Carastathis, A., Lake., 344c
Carati, Colin J., Flin., 52a
Carayanniotis, G., Nfld., 406c, 407a
Carberry, A., Plym., 1674a
Carbery, A., Edin., 1418a
Carbonatto, Charlene L., Pret., 1206b
Carbone, Frank, Monash, 95a
Carbonetto, Salvatore R., McG., 371c, 373a
Carbonneau, Raymond, Montr., 422b
Carbotte, J. P., McM., 384a
R. M., McM., 387a
Carby-Hall, J. R., Hull, 1466a
Card, Howard C., Manit., 392a
Richard I. E., De Mont., 1390a, 1393a
Cardan, B., E.Lond., 1411b
Cardell, Rosemary, Lond., 1525c
Cardella, Carl J., Tor., 497b
Carden, G., Br.Col., 301b
Carder, Jan, Sheff.Hallam, 1715c
Cardew, Richard V. C., Macq., 71a, 73c
Cardew-Hall, M. J., ANU, 18b
Cardia, Emanuela, Montr., 411b
Cardiff, Janet F., Leth., 360a
Cardin, D. J., Reading, 1691b
Martine, Laval, 353b
Cardinal, André, Laval, 350b, 351a
Aurèle, Montr., 415a
Jacques, Montr., 411a
Jean, Montr., 415c
Linda, Ott., 443a
Pierre, Ott., 444a
Pierre, Queb., 449c

Grealish, Helena M., *Wolv.*, 1794a
Gream, George E., *Adel.*, 5c
Greasley, David G., *Edin.*, 1417c
Greason, W. D., *W.Ont.*, 523b
Greatbatch, R. J., *Nfld.*, 405c
Greated, C. A., *Edin.*, 1418c
Greatrex, R., *Leeds*, 1484c
Greatrix, P., *E.Anglia*, 1409c
Greaves, Ben, *C.England*, 1378c
C., *Birm.*, 1328a
David J., *Camb.*, 1357a
G. N., *Manc.*, 1598c
G. Neville, *Keele*, 1469c
G. Neville, *Wales*, 1755c
G. R. H., *Wales*, 1764b
Ian B., *Lond.*, 1533c
J., *Sheff.Hallam*, 1715c
M., *Aberd.*, 1316b
M. F., *Lond.*, 1583b
Malcolm, *Bath*, 1323a
Malcolm W., *Lond.*, 1540c
Monica A., *Nigeria*, 1052c
Robert, *Monash*, 90b
Rosa-Maria, *Durh.*, 1403c
Grebenik, Peter D., *Oxf.Brookes*, 1666a
Grech, Carol M., *S.Aust.*, 158a
Helen, *Malta*, 950b
Joseph L., *Malta*, 950a
Maurice, *Malta*, 947c
Greed, Clara H., *W.England*, 1786a
J. A., *W.England*, 1786a
Greedan, J., *McM.*, 381a
Greeff, M., *Potchef.*, 1200b
Roger J., *Sheff.Hallam*, 1717b
Greeley, Janet D., *James Cook*, 60c
Green, A., *Wales*, 1774c
A., *Wat.*, 515a
A. D., *Lond.*, 1534c
A. G., *Qu.*, 454a
A. T., *Leeds*, 1490b
Alison J., *Plym.*, 1675c
Andrew G., *Camb.*, 1373b
Andrew M. W., *Wales*, 1766a, 1769b, 1769c
Anita, *Portsmouth*, 1679b
Ann, *Coventry*, 1385b
Anna, *Waik.*, 993a
Anne, *Syd.*, 175a
Anthony, *NSW*, 115a
Ashley A., *Oxf.Brookes*, 1667b
B., *C.England*, 1377b
B. D., *Newcastle(UK)*, 1626c
B. S., *York(Can.)*, 550a
Barbara F., *Wales*, 1768b
Barry W., *Stell.*, 1227b
Beverly R., *Br.Col.*, 296b
Brian K., *Stell.*, 1226b
Brian N., *Strath.*, 1736b
Brynmor H., *Lond.*, 1579b
C. D., *York(Can.)*, 549c
C. R., *Auck.*, 965b
C. S., *Manc.Met.*, 1612a
Christine, *Luton*, 1594b
Christopher, *McG.*, 364c
Christopher D., *Liv.*, 1508a
Christopher J., *Lough.*, 1589c
Christopher K., *Lond.*, 1580b
Christopher P., *Lond.*, 1558b
Clarissa P., *Br.Col.*, 302a
Colin J., *Lond.*, 1576a
D., *S.Bank*, 1720b
D. C., *Herts.*, 1455b
D. H., *UMIST*, 1608a
David, *Leeds Met.*, 1493a, 1495c
David, *Technol.Syd.*, 192b
David A., *Camb.*, 1362c
David G., *C.Sturt*, 32c
David H., *ANU*, 15a, 15c, 20c
David L., *C.Sturt*, 31c
David P. L., *Otago*, 983a
David R., *Glas.*, 1436a
David R., *Leeds*, 1490c
David R., *Lough.*, 1591c
David W., *Lond.*, 1572b
Debora G. M., *Oxf.*, 1714a, 1714c
Dennis, *RMIT*, 151c
Dennis H., *Camb.*, 1373b
Diana M., *Sheff.Hallam*, 1714a
E. H. H., *Oxf.*, 1654b
Edward D., *S.Af.Med.*, 1173c, 1176b
Evelyne, *Westminster*, 1789a, 1792c
F. M., *Camb.*, 1367a
Francis, *Leeds*, 1487b
G., *Glas.*, 1438c
G., *Plym.*, 1674a
G. R. G., *Newcastle(UK)*, 1626a
H., *Manc.Met.*, 1612c
H. J., *Wat.*, 516a
Henare, *Massey*, 977a
Herbert S., *Adel.*, 8a
Howard, *Leeds Met.*, 1496c
I. M., *Belf.*, 1685c
Ian M., *Westminster*, 1789c
Ivan R., *W.Cape*, 1236a
J., *Coventry*, 1384b
J., *Lond.*, 1552a
J. K., *Lough.*, 1588a
J. M., *Manc.*, 1605b
J. M., *Nfld.*, 402b
J. Mary-Ann, *Natal*, 1184b
J. P., *Ulster*, 1752a
J. R., *Birm.*, 1327b
J. R., *Windsor*, 537c
J. Richard, *Syd.*, 170c
J. T., *Camb.*, 1371c
Jacqueline, *Leeds Met.*, 1494c
Janet, *Manc.Met.*, 1614c
Jean, *Liv.J.Moores*, 1518a
Jean, *Wolv.*, 1795c
John A., *Liv.*, 1512b
John D., *Waik.*, 991c
John N., *Brad.*, 1341a, 1342c
Judith A., *Belf.*, 1685c
K., *UMIST*, 1608c
K. F., *Wales*, 1778a
K. L., *Nott.Trent*, 1640b
K. L., *Portsmouth*, 1680a
Karen R. H., *Monash*, 93b
Kate M., *E.Lond.*, 1411b
Keith M., *Sheff.Hallam*, 1715c
Kenneth, *Tor.*, 490b
Kimbra, *De Mont.*, 1394b
L. J. M., *York(Can.)*, 549a, 553a
Lance, *NSW*, 112a
Laurence, *McG.*, 372a
Lawrence W., *Br.Col.*, 305b, 309b
Lelia R., *E.Cowan*, 45a
Lena C., *Cape Town*, 1161a
M., *Open(UK)*, 1646a
M. A., *NSW*, 119b
M. A., *Sheff.*, 1709c
M. A., *Ulster*, 1752c
M. B., *Camb.*, 1361b
M. B., *Lond.*, 1554a
M. F., *Qu.*, 454a
M. J., *Belf.*, 1684a
M. J., *St And.*, 1697b
M. L. H., *Oxf.*, 1650a
M. W., *Alta.*, 281a
Marci R., *Wolv.*, 1795b
Margaret D., *Exe.*, 1427c
Martin A., *NSW*, 110c
Martin S., *Ott.*, 444a
Michael, *ANU*, 18b
Michael, *Bath*, 1323a
Michael G., *Lond.*, 1559a
Michael M., *Natal*, 1180a
Michael W., *Sheff.Hallam*, 1719a
Michele A., xl
Milford B., *W.Ont.*, 524b
Mino, *Lond.*, 1528c
Miriam R., *N.Lond.*, 1629b
Murray, *Nipissing*, 432a, 434b
N. J., *Lond.*, 1536b
P. C., *Herts.*, 1454c
P. D., *Sheff.*, 1705b
P. J., *Brist.*, 1347c
P. S., *E.Lond.*, 1411c
Pamela, *RMIT*, 151b
Penelope J., *S'ton.*, 1726a
Peter, *Strath.*, 1734c
Peter, *Victoria UT*, 196c
Peter F., *Qld.UT*, 145b
R., *Herts.*, 1455b
R., *Nfld.*, 406c
R. A., *Camb.*, 1373a
R. C., *Auck.*, 959c
R. H., *W.Ont.*, 527b
R. J., *S'ton.*, 1729a
R. L., *Manc.Met.*, 1612a
R. M., *Glas.*, 1440b
Ralph E. B., *RMIT*, 153b
Richard F., *W.Ont.*, 523c
Richard J., *Camb.*, 1357c
Rodney H., *Bath*, 1323c
Roger, *Manc.*, 1597c
Roger J., *Brad.*, 1342a
Roger P. H., *Glas.*, 1438a
Roy, *Newcastle(NSW)*, 123c, 125a
S., *Brist.*, 1346a
S. D., *Reading*, 1691c
S. H., *Birm.*, 1334c
S. I., *Br.Col.*, 299a
S. J. M., *W.England*, 1786b
Simon E., *Lond.*, 1523c
Simon J. D., *Leeds*, 1487a
Steven, *Lough.*, 1592b
Sulina, *Stell.*, 1228b
Suzan, *Sheff.Hallam*, 1717c
T. G. Allan, *Waik.*, 991c
Thomas M., *Oxf.Brookes*, 1665c
Trevor H., *Macq.*, 72b
Walter B., *Dal.*, 329c
William, *Deakin*, 41a
William L., *Salf.*, 1701b
William S., *Canberra*, 25c
Green-Armytage, Paul, *Curtin*, 35c
Greenaway, A. M., *WI*, 1814b
D., *Nott.*, 1632a, 1633c
H. H., *H-W*, 1451b
Peter, *NSW*, 109a
Greenbaum, Abe, *NSW*, 108c
Geoffrey, *Monash*, 94b
Lesley A., *Natal*, 1180b
Greenberg, A., *Manit.*, 397b
A. H., *Manit.*, 397b, 398c, 399a, 399c
Alan, *McG.*, 379b
B. M., *Wat.*, 512a, 512c
C. R., *Manit.*, 397b
Cheryl, *Manit.*, 398c
David M., *Ott.*, 445b
G. R., *Tor.*, 500a
Gordon R., *Tor.*, 497c
H. M., *Manit.*, 399b
I. D., *Manit.*, 399b
J. S., *Wat.*, 513b
Joseph, *McG.*, 364c
L., *York(Can.)*, 549c
M. L., *Tor.*, 499b
Maurice, *Lond.*, 1577c
Nathan, *Montr.*, 414b
Reesa, *C'dia.*, 321c
Robert, *Ryerson*, 467a
Greenblatt, J. F., *Tor.*, 497a
Greene, Alison, *Lond.*, 1543c
C. M., *Trent*, 508c
D. F., *C'dia.*, 323c
David J., *Westminster*, 1790c
E., *Qu.*, 454c
I., *York(Can.)*, 549b
John R., *Cape Town*, 1161c
Judith M., *Open(UK)*, 1646c
K. T., *Newcastle(UK)*, 1620b
M. Wayne, *Br.Col.*, 310b
Owen J., *Brad.*, 1342c
R., *Lond.*, 1537b
Richard, *ANU*, 19c
Richard L., *Ott.*, 437a, 446c
Roger, *L&H*, 1505c
Greenfield, B., *Dal.*, 329a
Cathy, *Monash*, 92a
H., *Manit.*, 390b
Heather, *NSW*, 109a
L. G., *Cant.*, 971b
Paul F., *Qld.*, 130a, 133a
Peter L., *Natal*, 1184a
Steven, *Westminster*, 1791b
Susan A., *Oxf.*, 1660c
Greenglass, Esther, *York(Can.)*, 549c
Greengrass, M., *Sheff.*, 1707a
P., *Coventry*, 1384b
Greenhaff, P. L., *Nott.*, 1636b
Greenhalgh, Anthony, *Leeds Met.*, 1495c
Charles M. B., *ANU*, 18a
Christine A., *Oxf.*, 1651c
David, *Strath.*, 1737b
Douglas A., *Cran.*, 1388b
John, *Bolton Inst.*, 1338a
R. M., *Lond.*, 1532c
S. A., *Adel.*, 7a
Greenham, Neil C., *Camb.*, 1366c
Greenhill, John G., *Tas.*, 184c
Pauline, *Winn.*, 543a
Greenhoff, Karen, *Sheff.Hallam*, 1717c
Greenhough, Bev, *R.Roads*, 465b
Trevor J., *Keele*, 1471a
Greenhow, Rodney C., *York(UK)*, 1800c
Greeniaus, L. G., *Alta.*, 285b
Greenland, D. J., *Reading*, 1694a
L., *PNG Tech.*, 1129c
Greenleaf, Graham W., *NSW*, 112c
Greenlee, J., *Nfld.*, 404c
J. G. C., *Nfld.*, 408a
Greenlees, J. P. C., *Sheff.*, 1707c
Greenley, Gordon E., *Aston*, 1320b
Greenman, J., *W.England*, 1785b
J. V., *Stir.*, 1731a
Greeno, D. W., *Tor.*, 487c
S., *Herts.*, 1456b
Greenough, A., *Lond.*, 1539a
R. D., *Hull*, 1466c
Greenshaw, A. J., *Alta.*, 287c
Greenshields, Malcolm R., *Leth.*, 360c
Greensides, C. J., *De Mont.*, 1391c
Greenslade, W. P., *W.England*, 1788a
Greensmith, Katherine A., *Herts.*, 1455b
Greenspan, L. I., *McM.*, 384b
Greensted, Christopher S., *Strath.*, 1737b
Greenstreet, Mark R., *Br.Col.*, 297c
Green-Thompson, Ronald W., *Natal*, 1182b
Greenwald, Steve E., *Lond.*, 1556a
Greenway, Anthony P., *Monash*, 90b
Diana E., *Lond.*, 1582c
Margaret, *Griff.*, 56a
S., *E.Lond.*, 1410b
Greenwell, Pamela, *Westminster*, 1789b
Greenwood, Andrew R., *Liv.J.Moores*, 1519b
B., *Tor.*, 486b, 503c
B. D., *Coventry*, 1384b
B. M., *Lond.*, 1550b
Bob P., *Bolton Inst.*, 1337c
C., *E.Anglia*, 1407b
C. J., *Lond.*, 1547a
Carol E., *Tor.*, 498c
D., *Nott.*, 1636c
D. E., *Aberd.*, 1317b
David, *Griff.*, 59b
Donald D., *Br.Col.*, 305a
Duncan J., *Leeds*, 1484b
E. J., *Oxf.*, 1662c
G. W., *Sheff.*, 1706a
Irene, *Luton*, 1594a
J., *Nott.Trent*, 1640c
J., *W.Syd.*, 210c
J. A., *Camb.*, 1358b
J. G., *Qld.*, 142a
J. R., *De Mont.*, 1394b
J. S., *Guelph*, 336a
Jack G., *Qld.*, 139b
John, *De Mont.*, 1391b
John, *Lond.*, 1575a
John, *Well.*, 987b, 989c
Ken L., *Westminster*, 1790a
Ken M., *La Trobe*, 68a
L. Frances, *Tor.*, 493b
Leonard, *N.Territory*, 127a
Priscilla E., *Br.Col.*, 301b
R., *Alta.*, 284c
R., *Portsmouth*, 1677c
R. L. A., *W.England*, 1787b
Rob, *R.Roads*, 466a
Sue, *Oxf.Brookes*, 1666c
Trevor F., *Bolton Inst.*, 1337b
Greer, A. L., *Camb.*, 1361b
Allan R., *Tor.*, 486c
Anthony, *NU Singapore*, 1149b
D. S., *Belf.*, 1685c
David C., *Durh.*, 1404b
G. B., *Belf.*, 1686c
Germaine, *Camb.*, 1370c
I. A., *Glas.*, 1442c
J. V., *Belf.*, 1684c
John W., *Kent*, 1475c
Nancy, *R.Roads*, 466a
R. G. H., *Belf.*, 1686b
S. C., *Brist.*, 1347b
Greer-Wootten, B., *York(Can.)*, 547b
Bryn, *York(Can.)*, 546c
Greeves, Nicholas, *Liv.*, 1508b
Gregg, Bernhard, *Technol.Syd.*, 194b
F. I., *Belf.*, 1689c
P. E. H., *Massey*, 977b
Paul J., *Newcastle(UK)*, 1626c
Peter C., *NE*, 102c
T. R., *Nott.Trent*, 1639b
Vernon H., *Lond.*, 1523c
Grégoire, Jacques C., *Montr.*, 414b
Jean-François, *Montr.*, 422b
Gregoire, Jean-Pierre, *Laval*, 355b
Gregor, A. D., *Manit.*, 391c, 395b, 400a
Anna, *Edin.*, 1420c
Frances, *Dal.*, 330b
K., *H-W*, 1452b
R., *Tor.*, 489c
R. Theo, *Stell.*, 1230a
Shirley, *C.Qld.*, 29a
Gregoriadis, G., *Lond.*, 1567c
Gregoris, Peter, *Glas.*, 1443a
Gregory, A., *Nfld.*, 402b
A. H., *Manc.*, 1602a
A. M., *Oxf.*, 1654b
A. W., *Qu.*, 454a
Alan, *Exe.*, 1426c
Amanda, *L&H*, 1505c
Andrew J., *Monash*, 94a
Anne, *Leeds Met.*, 1495c
Anthea, *Sheff.Hallam*, 1718c
Anthony, *De Mont.*, 1393c
B., *Nfld.*, 402c
Bill, *RMIT*, 149c
C., *Melb.*, 83b
C. D., *Nott.*, 1636b
Christopher A., *ANU*, 17c
D. A., *Qu.*, 456a
D. M., *Manit.*, 394c
David, *Athab.*, 290c
David G., *Aston*, 1321b, 1321c
Derek J., *Br.Col.*, 300b
Evelyn E., *Lond.*, 1524c
Frank E. C., *S'ton.*, 1727a
G., *W.England*, 1788c
Gerald, *Brun.*, 1352a
J. P., *W.England*, 1787b
J. T., *Auck.*, 961b
J. W., *Wales*, 1771c
Janet, *St Mary's(Can.)*, 472a
Jenny, *W.Aust.*, 206c
John, *Lond.*, 1570b
K., *Birm.*, 1329b
Kenneth J., *Lond.*, 1553a
M. R., *Auck.*, 962c
Mark, *RMIT*, 151c
Mark R., *Hudd.*, 1460a
Mary B., *Oxf.*, 1651c
Michael J., *Camb.*, 1358b
N., *Lond.*, 1549b, 1549c
Neville G., *Massey*, 975b
Nuala, *Auck.*, 962b
P. E., *De Mont.*, 1391b
P. J., *Monash*, 91b
Peter J., *Reading*, 1690a, 1694a, 1694c
Philip C., *Br.Col.*, 302b
R., *UMIST*, 1609a
R. D., *Manc.*, 1601a
R. G., *Reading*, 1693c
R. L., *Brist.*, 1348b
Robert G., *ANU*, 17b
Robert J., *Massey*, 977c
Robert J., *Well.*, 987a, 989b
S., *Birm.*, 1328b
Shaun R., *Brad.*, 1342c
Stephen W. G., *NSW*, 114a
Stewart, *Leic.*, 1499c
T. C., *S.Bank*, 1720b
Walter, *McG.*, 372a
Gregory-Smith, David G., *Durh.*, 1403a
Gregson, Edward, *Manc.*, 1601b
K., *Nott.*, 1633b
M. J., *De Mont.*, 1393b
N. A., *Sheff.*, 1706c
Norman A., *Lond.*, 1541b
Olga, *Manc.Met.*, 1611b
P. H., *Dal.*, 329a
P. J., *S'ton.*, 1724a
Greif, Hans-Jurgen, *Laval*, 354b
Greig, D., *Leeds*, 1488b
Donald W., *ANU*, 18c, 19a
Maria, *Portsmouth*, 1679b
P., *Tor.*, 501b
Robert I., *Ballarat*, 22b
Greiner, *Alta.*, 281a
P. C., *Tor.*, 488a
Grek, A. J., *McM.*, 387a
Gren, Elizabeth R., *Hudd.*, 1462a
Grenby, Trevor H., *Lond.*, 1540c
Grencis, R. K., *Manc.*, 1597b
Grendler, Paul F., *Tor.*, 486c
Grenfell, Anasuya, *Lond.*, 1541b
B. T., *Camb.*, 1364a
Ronald I., *RMIT*, 153a
Grenier, Daniel, *Laval*, 351c
Denis, *Laval*, 353b
Dominic, *Laval*, 352b
Gilles, *Ott.*, 439b
Jacques, *Ott.*, 440c
Line, *Montr.*, 411a
Micheline, *Laval*, 359a
Raymond, *Montr.*, 410a, 413b
Y., *St FX*, 470b
Grennan, Wayne, *St Mary's(Can.)*, 472c
Grenon, Aline, *Ott.*, 441b
Grenside, Sara, *Luton*, 1594b
Grenville, J. A. S., *Birm.*, 1330a
Gresset, Jacques, *Montr.*, 413c
Gresson, Marvin, *Nott.Trent*, 1639a
Grest, Christopher J., *Natal*, 1181a
Gresty, K., *Plym.*, 1673a
Gretschel, H. V., *Namibia*, 955c
Gretton, George L., *Edin.*, 1418a
Harry, *Sheff.Hallam*, 1718a
Tom H., *Lond.*, 1569b
Greville-Harris, M. W., *Birm.*, 1332a
Grew, John, *McG.*, 368c
Grewal, A. S., *Punj.Ag.*, 815c, 818b
Bhajan, *Victoria UT*, 198a
G. S., *Punj.Ag.*, 818b
K. S., *Punjabi*, 821a
K. S., *Punj.Ag.*, 815b
Neelam, *Punj.Ag.*, 817c
P. S., *Punj.Ag.*, 814b
R. K., *Panjab*, 802a
R. K., *Punj.Ag.*, 816a
R. S., *Panjab*, 802c, 804c
S. S., *Punjabi*, 820c
S. S., *Punj.Ag.*, 815b
Sukhbir, *Pg.IMER*, 807a
Grewar, D. A. I., *Manit.*, 398c
Grey, Antonia, *Glam.*, 1433b
Jeffrey G., *NSW*, 120b
Julius, *McG.*, 367b
M. R., *W.England*, 1785b
Somarie V., *Pret.*, 1207c
William, *Qld.*, 141a
William L., *Qld.*, 137b
Greybe, Willem G., *Pret.*, 1205b
Greyling, Annemie, *Pret.*, 1202b
Elizabeth J., *Durban-W.*, 1171b
J. P. C., *OFS*, 1192a
Lorraine, *Rand Afrikaans*, 1211a
W. J., *OFS*, 1192b
Greyson, N. David, *Tor.*, 496c
Greyvenstein, G. P., *Potchef.*, 1199b, 1200a
Gribben, J. A., *Auck.*, 965a
R. J., *Brunei*, 265b
Gribbin, Gary, *Deakin*, 39c
Gribble, Alison, *Victoria UT*, 196c
C. D., *Glas.*, 1439b
Jennifer M., *Syd.*, 172c
Gribbon, Anthony St. G., *Warw.*, 1784b, 1784c
Grice, Roger, *Manc.*, 1598a
Grichting, Wolfgang, *Aust.Cath.*, 11a, 14c
Grieder, A., *City(UK)*, 1381c, 1382a
Grief, N., *Bourne.*, 1339a
Griener, G. G., *Alta.*, 287c
Grier, T., *S.Bank*, 1721c
Grierson, D., *Nott.*, 1633b
D. E., *Wat.*, 514a
Douglas, *Cape Town*, 1169c
I. T., *Adel.*, 8c
Ian, *Liv.*, 1512b
Philip, *Camb.*, 1369a
Gries, G. J., *S.Fraser*, 476c
Griesel, Sonja, *Rand Afrikaans*, 1210b
Grieser, F., *Melb.*, 78c
Griessel, Raoul D., *Natal*, 1185c
Grieve, A. I., *E.Anglia*, 1409a
Andrew P., *Keele*, 1470c
Andrew R., *Dund.*, 1399a
Clayton L., *Pret.*, 1207a
D. J., *Plym.*, 1674c
I. C., *Stir.*, 1731b
J. H. K., *Aberd.*, 1316c
James A., *ANU*, 19b
K. M., *C.England*, 1376a
Kate W., *S.Af.*, 1221b
R., *Edin.*, 1419a
Robert J., *Brun.*, 1352c
Grieves, B. R., *S.Bank*, 1722a
K. R., *Kingston(UK)*, 1477a
Griffel, D. H., *Brist.*, 1347c
Griffen, Arlene, *S.Pac.*, 1253b
Griffin, A., *Tor.*, 489b
Anne, *Greenwich*, 1448c
B. L., *Sund.*, 1739b
B. M., *Manc.Met.*, 1612c
Brendan J., *W.Aust.*, 205b
C. E., *Birm.*, 1332a
C. H., *Oxf.*, 1659a
C. P., *Nott.Trent*, 1642a
Dale, *Sus.*, 1747c
Florence J., *PNG*, 1128c
G. A., *Wat.*, 516a, 518a, 520b
G. D., *Monash*, 92c
G. F., *Bourne.*, 1340c

J., *Lahore UET*, 1095c
M. A., *Chitt.*, 235b, 236a
M. A., *Dhaka*, 237b
M. O., *Rajsh.*, 256c
Hakimian, Hassan, *Lond.*, 1564b
Hakim-Larson, J. A., *Windsor*, 539c
Hakin, Andrew W., *Leth.*, 360a
Haksar, V. N., *Edin.*, 1418c
Hakstian, A. Ralph, *Br.Col.*, 303a
Halai, Nilofer, *Aga Khan*, 1082b
Halamandaris, P. G., *Bran.*, 293b
Halborg, A., *Coventry*, 1384b
Halcrow, Kevin, *New Br.*, 431b
Haldane, D., *H-W*, 1450b
J. J., *St And.*, 1698b, 1699b
M. J., *Manc.Met.*, 1612c
Haldar, C., *Ban.*, 614b
M. K., *NU Singapore*, 1148b
Halden, N. M., *Manit.*, 393b
Haldenby, E. R., *Wat.*, 512a
Halder, A. B., *VB*, 874b
A. K., *Dhaka*, 240b
P., *VB*, 875b
P. K., *Tripura*, 869a
Shanti R., *Chitt.*, 235c
Haldon, J. F., *Birm.*, 1329c, 1335c
Hale, A. S., *Sheff.*, 1709a
Beverley, *Guelph*, 340b
C. S., *Alta.*, 284a
Chris, *Kent*, 1473a
D. J., *Belf.*, 1686c
Janet, *Salf.*, 1701c
John K., *Otago*, 980c
Karl J., *Lond.*, 1569c
M., *C'dia.*, 324c
M. J., *Witw.*, 1245a
M. T., *De Mont.*, 1394c
Peter T., *Qld.*, 140b
Robert L. V., *Glas.*, 1440b
Rosemary, *C'dia.*, 325a
Sylvia M., *St Thomas(NB)*, 474c
T., *E.Anglia*, 1408c
William M., *Lond.*, 1565a
Haleem, Abid, *JMI*, 709b
Anwar, *Faisalabad*, 1083a, 1085c
Darakshan J., *Karachi*, 1102b
M. A., *Karachi*, 1102b
Halephota, A. R., *Mehran*, 1106b
Halepota, G. R., *Mehran*, 1107b
Muhammad M. A. A., *Mehran*, 1107a
Hales, Barbara, *McG.*, 374c
C., *W.England*, 1785c
C. N., *Camb.*, 1364b
Colin P., *Sur.*, 1743a
D., *Hudd.*, 1460b
Dinah F., *Macq.*, 71c
William M., *Sheff.Hallam*, 1716c
Halestrap, A. P., *Brist.*, 1345a
Halevi, Joseph, *Syd.*, 172a
Haley, David, *Br.Col.*, 300a
E., *McM.*, 381a, 383a
George T., *New Br.*, 428c
K. B., *Birm.*, 1329a
Michael A., *Keele*, 1470b
Halfani, M. R., *Dar.*, 1292b
M. S., *Dar.*, 1294b
Halford, Graeme S., *Qld.*, 138a
Kim, *Griff.*, 54b
Nigel, *Hull*, 1468b, 1468c
S. E., *Brist.*, 1345a
W. Dean, *Massey*, 975c
Halfpenney, J. Ray, *Bolton Inst.*, 1338a
Halfpenny, J. C., *Nott.Trent*, 1639c
Peter J., *Manc.*, 1602b
Halfyard, C. W., *Nfld.*, 405a
Haliassos, M., *Cyprus*, 558c
Halijah binti Ibrahim, *Malaya*, 916b
Halim, A., *B'desh.Ag.*, 226b
Abd El, *Car.*, 317a
M. A., *B'desh.Engin.*, 231c
M. A., *Dhaka*, 239c
M. A., *Rajsh.*, 257a
R. A., *Assam Ag.*, 605c
Halim Ali, A., *NU Malaysia*, 923c
Halim b Salleh, *Sci.U.Malaysia*, 936b
Halimah Badioze Zaman, *NU Malaysia*, 925a
Halimah bt Hj Ahmad, *Putra*, 928a, 930b
Halimahtun Mohd Khalid, *Malaysia Sarawak*, 921a
Halimaton bte Hamdan, *Tech.U.Malaysia*, 939c
Haliwell, B., *Lond.*, 1536b
Halkyard, A. J., *HK*, 1840b
Hall, A., *S.Fraser*, 481c
A. E., *Br.Col.*, 299a
A. Haulwen, *Manc.Met.*, 1613b
A. J., *Glas.*, 1439b
A. J., *Lond.*, 1550b
A. L., *Lond.*, 1547b
Adrian, *NSW*, 108b
Alan, *Lond.*, 1573a
Alan W., *Waik.*, 994a
Alison, *Leeds Met.*, 1493b
Alistair S., *Leeds*, 1490a
Anne C., *W.Laur.*, 533b, 535a
Anthony J., *Leth.*, 361b
Anthony R., *Liv.J.Moores*, 1517a
Ashley D., *Wales*, 1753c
Avice M., *Herts.*, 1455a
B. A., *Tor.*, 493c
B. K., *Dal.*, 327c
B. M., *C.England*, 1378a
Bert S., *Tor.*, 487a
Bronwyn H., *Oxf.*, 1651c
Bruce M., *NSW*, 116c
C., *UMIST*, 1607c
C. A., *Bourne.*, 1340a
C. D., *Lond.*, 1536b
C. J., *Bourne.*, 1340c
C. Michael, *Otago*, 980a
C. R., *W.Ont.*, 528a
Cedric G. W., *Well.*, 988a
Christine, *Lond.*, 1574b
Christine M., *Plym.*, 1672c
Christopher B., *Macq.*, 74b
Christopher J., *Sheff.Hallam*, 1715a
D., *Cant.*, 972c
D., *Greenwich*, 1448c
D., *Qld.UT*, 148c
D. E., *Warw.*, 1779a
D. J., *Alta.*, 283a
D. M. B., *Sheff.*, 1710c
D. O., *Lond.*, 1537b
D. R., *H-W*, 1451b
D. R., *Sund.*, 1739b
Dave, *Luton*, 1594a
David M., *Hudd.*, 1461a
David R., *Macq.*, 75c
Douglas J., *McG.*, 369c
E., *Nott.*, 1634a
E. A. H., *Camb.*, 1356b
E. R., *Br.Col.*, 298b
Edith M., *Oxf.*, 1650c
Sir Ernest, *Hudd.*, 1458a
F. A., *McM.*, 380c
F. L., *McM.*, 382a, 382c
F. Richard, *Wolv.*, 1794c
G., *De Mont.*, 1394a
G. B., *St And.*, 1697b
G. B., *Wat.*, 515b, 519a
G. I., *Salf.*, 1703a
G. S., *Aberd.*, 1315a
Geoffrey, *York(UK)*, 1801a
Geoffrey G., *Otago*, 981b
George M., *Lond.*, 1561b
George M., *Lough.*, 1590a
Gillian, *Liv.J.Moores*, 1518c
H., *Sheff.*, 1704b
H., *Tor.*, 501b
H. J., *Qld.*, 143c
Howard, *De Mont.*, 1394a
Howard, *Wales*, 1776c
I. P., *Nott.*, 1637c
Iain N. S., *Paisley*, 1670c
Ian, *Liv.*, 1511a
J., *C.England*, 1377a
J., *Coventry*, 1385b
J., *Nfld.*, 403a
J. B., *Wales*, 1768b
J. Barrie, *Lond.*, 1557c
J. C., *Guelph*, 340a
J. L., *S'ton.*, 1728a
James E., *Lond.*, 1573a
James M., *Dal.*, 328c
Jane P., *Syd.*, 178c
Jay J., *Qld.*, 131b
Jerry, *W.Laur.*, 534c
John, *Bolton Inst.*, 1337c
John, *Leeds Met.*, 1495b
John, *McG.*, 369c
John, *Victoria UT*, 196c
John B., *Wales*, 1757a
John C., *W.Aust.*, 205a
John D. McK., *Tas.*, 186c
John T. D., *Durh.*, 1401a, 1406b
Judith G., *Br.Col.*, 305c, 307b
K., *Bourne.*, 1340b
K., *Qu.*, 454a
K. J. F., *Br.Col.*, 298b
Kenneth O., *WI*, 1811a, 1814a
Kevin, *N.Br.Col.*, 435b
Kim, *Portsmouth*, 1681a
L., *Brist.*, 1345a
L., *WI*, 1817a
Laura J., *Deakin*, 40c
Laurance D., *Camb.*, 1364b
Lee Ann, *Technol.Syd.*, 189b
Lesley C., *Deakin*, 42a
Leslie S., *Qld.*, 139a
Leslie W., *Camb.*, 1368c
Lucinda M. C., *Lond.*, 1555c
Lynda, *Greenwich*, 1448c
M. G., *Birm.*, 1331c
Mark, *Warw.*, 1782c
Martin J., *Cape Town*, 1160a
Maximilian J. B., *Lough.*, 1589c
Michael A., *Bolton Inst.*, 1338a
Michael A., *Wales*, 1754c
Michael S., *Exe.*, 1430a
Michael W., *Monash*, 96a
Mike E., *Bolton Inst.*, 1338a
N., *Manc.Met.*, 1612c
Neil, *Liv.J.Moores*, 1517c
Neil, *W'gong.*, 213b
Nicolas D., *Bath*, 1324b
Nigel R., *Salf.*, 1700a
O., *Tor.*, 494c
P. F., *Manit.*, 398a
P. G., *Glam.*, 1433a
P. J., *ANU*, 16a
P. S., *Birm.*, 1329a
P. W., *Manc.Met.*, 1613c
Patricia, *Liv.J.Moores*, 1518a
Patrick A. V., *Open(UK)*, 1645a
Pauline de la M., *Flin.*, 52c
Peter, *NSW*, 120a
Peter A., *Dund.*, 1400a
Peter G., *Lond.*, 1569a
Peter J., *Strath.*, 1733c
Peter R., *P.Elizabeth*, 1197a
Philip, *Lond.*, 1530a
R., *De Mont.*, 1394b
R., *Guelph*, 340a
R., *Nott.Trent*, 1641c
R. D., *W.Ont.*, 524b
R. F., *Rhodes*, 1214b
R. G. B., *Wales*, 1777c
R. L., *C'dia.*, 324b
R. L., *Oxf.*, 1658a
R. Peter, *Portsmouth*, 1679a
R. R., *Cant.*, 971c
Rachel, *Lond.*, 1577c
Ralph, *NSW*, 115b
Ray, *Lond.*, 1553a
Richard, *Durh.*, 1405a
Richard, *New Br.*, 432a
Richard I., *Dal.*, 332a
Richard N., *Hudd.*, 1460b
Richard R., *York(UK)*, 1800b
Robert, *Glam.*, 1433b
Robert, *Lond.*, 1558b
Robert A., *Brun.*, 1354a
Robert A., *NSW*, 118c
Roger J. C., *Lond.*, 1531c
Ross G., *Melb.*, 84a
S. F., *Qu.*, 459b
S. J., *Glas.*, 1440b
S. J., *Herts.*, 1456c
S. J. G., *De Mont.*, 1390b
Sharon J., *Manc.Met.*, 1613a
Stanley R., *C.Sturt*, 32b
Stella, *Warw.*, 1784c
Stephen, *Liv.*, 1509b
Stephen, *Lond.*, 1529c
Stephen J., *Flin.*, 48b, 52c
Stephen J., *NSW*, 112c
Sydney R., *W.Aust.*, 205b
T., *S.Bank*, 1722a
T. E., *Monash*, 93a
T. J., *Lond.*, 1536c
Thomas A., *Essex*, 1425a
Tony D., *Technol.Syd.*, 191a
Tracy, *Westminster*, 1790a
Valerie J., *Brist.*, 1346a
Virginia L., *James Cook*, 62c
Viv B., *Well.*, 987c
W., *S'ton.*, 1725a
Wayne D., *NSW*, 119b
Wendy, *Br.Col.*, 302a
Hallam, A., *Birm.*, 1328b
D., *Reading*, 1690b, 1694a
Ellie, *L&H*, 1504b
I. W., *Manc.Met.*, 1610a, 1615c
J., *Bourne.*, 1340c
John, *Edin.*, 1416a
N. D., *Monash*, 89a
R., *W.Ont.*, 521b
Roger, *N.Lond.*, 1629b
Hallaq, Wael, *McG.*, 367a
Hallard, Anne, *Technol.Syd.*, 194a
Hallbauer, Dieter K., *Stell.*, 1226c
Hallé, Jean-Pierre, *Montr.*, 415c
Michael, *Ryerson*, 468c
Hallebone, Erica, *RMIT*, 154a, 154b
Hallegraeff, Gustaaf M., *Tas.*, 184c, 186a
Hallein, Joseph J., *C.Qld.*, 30c
Hallen, Patricia, *Murd.*, 100b
Hallenbeck, Patrick, *Montr.*, 416a
Haller, Cathy, *Mt.St.Vin.*, 424c
Lorraine T., *New Br.*, 430b
Hallett, Arthur F., *W.Cape*, 1237c
Bonita, *New Br.*, 432c
C. M., *Stir.*, 1730c, 1732b
David J., *Wolv.*, 1796c
F. R., *Guelph*, 338b
M., *Wales*, 1773c
Mary E., *Portsmouth*, 1678b
Michael F., *McG.*, 368a
P. E., *Tor.*, 491b, 500a
William, *Ott.*, 440a
Halley, Robin, *Lond.*, 1556c, 1557a
Halli, M. B., *Gulb.*, 674b
S. S., *Manit.*, 395c
Halliburton, I. W., *Leeds*, 1490a
Halliday, A. R., *W.England*, 1787b
David, *Lond.*, 1532b
Glenda M., *NSW*, 115c
H., *Belf.*, 1687c
Ian, *Sheff.Hallam*, 1718a
Ian G., *Wales*, 1768c
J., *H-W*, 1451a
L., *Bourne.*, 1340b
Michael I., *Macq.*, 74b
R. John, *Warw.*, 1782b
Ronald, *Stir.*, 1732c
S. F. P., *Lond.*, 1547a
Susan, *Portsmouth*, 1678a
Tim R., *Open(UK)*, 1644c
W., *Manit.*, 398c
Halligan, Aiden W. F., *Leic.*, 1501b
John, *Canberra*, 27b
John A., *Canberra*, 25b
Hallikeri, Prema S., *Karn.*, 725a
Hallin, A. L., *Qu.*, 456c
Hallinan, Peter, *C.Qld.*, 29b
T., *Lond.*, 1576c
Halling, Peter J., *Strath.*, 1733c
Hallinon, Chris, *Victoria UT*, 196c
Halliwell, B., *Manc.Met.*, 1612c
B. A., *Lond.*, 1542c, 1543a
D., *Bourne.*, 1340b
Francis S., *St And.*, 1697c
G. L., *Qld.UT*, 146a
J. V., *Lond.*, 1577b
Jonathan J., *Lond.*, 1530a
Neil A., *Lough.*, 1589a, 1590c
R. E. W., *Edin.*, 1421c
R. F., *Sund.*, 1739b
Wayne R., *Montr.*, 413c
Hallman, E. D., *Laur.*, 348a
Hallmayer, Joachim F., *W.Aust.*, 205a
Halloran, P. F., *Alta.*, 286c
Hallpike, C. R., *McM.*, 380b
Halls, Christopher, *Lond.*, 1529a
H. C., *Tor.*, 486b
M., *De Mont.*, 1392a
Michael J., *Victoria UT*, 198b, 198c
Hallworth, Christine, *Herts.*, 1456a
Sarah W., *Oxf.Brookes*, 1667c
Halm, J. M., *Kumasi*, 572b
Halma binti Khatan, *Malaysia Sarawak*, 921b
Halmos, Andrew L., *RMIT*, 152b
Haloi, B., *Assam Ag.*, 605b
Halparin, Lawrence S., *Br.Col.*, 306a
Halpe, K. A. C. G., *Peradeniya*, 1275c
Halperin, I., *Tor.*, 488a
J. S., *Tor.*, 488a
Mitchell L., *Tor.*, 497c
Scott A., *Dal.*, 333a
Halpern, Lisa, *Exe.*, 1432b
Mark, *Br.Col.*, 302b
P. J., *Tor.*, 487b, 487c
Paul J., *Tor.*, 483a
Halpert, H., *Nfld.*, 404b
Halpin, David, *Exe.*, 1429c
David, *Lond.*, 1525a
Joseph, *Durh.*, 1406b
Marjorie, *Br.Col.*, 296a
Nicholas R., *Dund.*, 1401b
Halsall, A., *Car.*, 317c, 318b
David N., *Sheff.Hallam*, 1718c
F., *Wales*, 1767c
R., *Manc.Met.*, 1611a
Halson, D. Roger, *Lond.*, 1571b
Halstead, Alison, *Coventry*, 1386b
David H., *Manit.*, 400c, 401a
Graham, *Hudd.*, 1460b
Ildi, *Luton*, 1594a
J. M., *Plym.*, 1674b, 1676a
Keith S. H., *Warw.*, 1784b
Ken, *Technol.Syd.*, 190b
Michael P., *Camb.*, 1369a
P., *Nott.Trent*, 1639c
P. L. J., *Sheff.*, 1705a
Renata J., *UMIST*, 1609c, 1610a
Tom K., *York(UK)*, 1799a
Halton, Brian, *Well.*, 987a
D. W., *Belf.*, 1684c
Jacqueline, *Ott.*, 445a
Rosalind J., *NE*, 104c
Halverson, Mary L., *Tor.*, 483a
Halvorson, Mary-Claire, *Lond.*, 1525c
Halyal, P. S., *Karn.*, 724c
Ham, C. J., *Birm.*, 1332b
John M., *NSW*, 118b
R., *W.Syd.*, 207c
Hamacher, V. Carl, *Qu.*, 454b
Hamal, I. A., *Jammu*, 711a
Hamalian, Arpi, *C'dia.*, 323a, 325b
Hamann, Conrad C., *Monash*, 94a
Wolfgang C., *Lond.*, 1540b
Hambagda, O. A., *Maid.*, 1047c
Hamber, J., *Plym.*, 1674a
Hambidge, Joan H., *Cape Town*, 1160a
Hamblen, D. L., *Glas.*, 1443a
Hambleton, Bernie, *Well.*, 990c
I., *McM.*, 383b
Ken G., *Lond.*, 1570c
P. A., *Sund.*, 1739b
Paul, *Thames V.*, 1749a
Hamblett, John W., *Leeds Met.*, 1496a
Hambley, Trevor W., *Syd.*, 171b
Hamblin, Ann P., *Adel.*, 10a
Anne S., *Lond.*, 1560c
David, *Luton*, 1595a
John, *Murd.*, 101a
T. J., *S'ton.*, 1728b
Hambly, Arthur D., *ANU*, 18c
Liane, *Nott.Trent*, 1641c
Hambolu, J. O., *A.Bello*, 1010c
Hambraeus, Bengt, *McG.*, 368a
Hambrook, Glyn M., *Wolv.*, 1795c
James P., *Adel.*, 7b
Hamburger, J., *Birm.*, 1333b
Hamby, William, *St Mary's(Can.)*, 471a
Hamdan, Mohammad, *New Br.*, 431c
Hamdan Ariffin, *NU Malaysia*, 925b
Hamdan bin Sheik Tahir, Tuan Yang Terutama Tun Dato' Seri Dr. Haji , *Putra*, 928a
Hamdi, Essam E. S., *Wales*, 1761c
Nabeel K., *Oxf.Brookes*, 1665b
Hamdorf, J. M., *W.Aust.*, 205a
Hamdullahpur, F., *Dal.*, 329a
Hamdy, F. C., *Newcastle(UK)*, 1626b
Hameed, A., *Lahore UET*, 1096a
A., *Quaid-i-Azam*, 1115b
Abdul, *Faisalabad*, 1085c
Allaudeen, *NU Singapore*, 1149b
K., *Aga Khan*, 1081b, 1082b
Saira, *Karachi*, 1102c
Hamel, Edith, *McG.*, 373a
Edna H., *S.Af.*, 1217a
Henri, *Laval*, 359c
Jacques, *Montr.*, 414c
Keith, *Br.Col.*, 301c
Louis-André, *Montr.*, 414a
P. Andre, *S.Af.*, 1216c
Pierre, *Montr.*, 415a
Hamel-Green, Michael, *Victoria UT*, 197c
Hamelin, Marcel, *Ott.*, 437a
Hamer, Andrew M., *HK*, 1840c
C. F., *Plym.*, 1673b
Christopher J., *NSW*, 114c
D. N., *Coventry*, 1386a
David A., *Well.*, 988b
John, *Luton*, 1594a
Kathryn, *Mt.All.*, 422c, 423a
Neil K., *Camb.*, 1373b
R. F. S., *Oxf.*, 1652c
Susan, *Leeds*, 1489c
Hamer-Jones, B., *Wales*, 1777c
Hamerow, Helena F., *Oxf.*, 1654b
Hamers, Josiane, *Laval*, 354a
Hamersma, Teertse, *Pret.*, 1207a
Hamerston, Michael, *Victoria UT*, 195a, 195b, 198c
Hamerton, J. L., *Manit.*, 397b, 398c
Hames, B. D., *Leeds*, 1484a
Hamet, Pavel, *Montr.*, 415c
Hamey, Leonard G. C., *Macq.*, 74c
Hamiadji Tanuseputero, *Sci.U.Malaysia*, 936c
Hamid, A., *Azad J&K*, 1089a
E., *B'desh.Engin.*, 230a
Fazli, *Pesh.*, 1112a
Gulraiz, *Karachi*, 1103a
M. A., *B'desh.Ag.*, 226b, 228c
M. A., *Rajsh.*, 256b
Malka, *Karachi*, 1103a
Naveed, *Punjab*, 1113a
Qutayba A., *McG.*, 374c
S., *Aga Khan*, 1081b
S. A., *Osm.*, 797b
Hamid bin Lazan, *NU Malaysia*, 923b
Hamidah Ismi, *Sci.U.Malaysia*, 938c
Hamid-ul-Qadir, M., *Baloch.*, 1093b
Hamielec, A. E., *McM.*, 382a, 387c
Hamil, Sybile, *Jamaica UT*, 883a
Hamill, David C., *Sur.*, 1744a
J. D., *Monash*, 89a
James, *Strath.*, 1735c
John, *Leeds Met.*, 1495b
K., *Nott.*, 1632a
L., *Plym.*, 1673c
Paul, *Strath.*, 1737a
Hamill-Keays, W. J. P., *Glam.*, 1434a
Hamilton, A. C., *Qu.*, 454c
Annette, *Macq.*, 71b
B., *Ulster*, 1752c
B., *UMIST*, 1609b
Beatrice J., *Aust.Cath.*, 11c
C. I., *Witw.*, 1242c
Carolyn, *Witw.*, 1246b
Carolyn P., *Essex*, 1424c
Charmaine, *Massey*, 976a
Cynthia A., *Manc.Met.*, 1613c
D., *Dal.*, 330a
Darren G., *Camb.*, 1370b
Dave, *Bran.*, 294c
David, *Tas.*, 186c
Emily F., *McG.*, 371a, 373c
F. E. I., *Lond.*, 1546b, 1581b, 1581c
G. J., *Victoria UT*, 197a
Gordon J., *W.Ont.*, 532a
Gordon M., *Glas.*, 1443c
I. F., *Wales*, 1777c
Ian, *W.Laur.*, 534b
Ian R., *Manit.*, 396b
J. R., *McG.*, 374b
J. S., *Lake.*, 343b
J. T., *W.Ont.*, 527c, 530b
Sir James, *Lond.*, 1568a
John D., *Newcastle(NSW)*, 124c
John M., *Sheff.Hallam*, 1719a
Judith, *E.Lond.*, 1410c
L. H., *Qld.UT*, 147b
Leslie, *Leeds Met.*, 1496a
M. B., *Reading*, 1693c
M. P. R., *Aberd.*, 1316b
Margaret A., *Melb.*, 86b
Marlene, *WI*, 1811a, 1812b
Mary G., *Athab.*, 290c
Murray W., *Adel.*, 8a
N., *Nott.Trent*, 1642c
Nigel, *Lond.*, 1558c
Norman, *S'ton.*, 1726c
P. A., *Lond.*, 1552a
P. G., *Alta.*, 286c
P. W., *Belf.*, 1688b
P. W. A., *Lond.*, 1552c
Patricia A., *Lond.*, 1561c
Patricia M., *De Mont.*, 1393c
Paula, *Technol.Syd.*, 192b
Philippa, *Leeds Met.*, 1493c
Phillip, *Deakin*, 39a
R., *Napier*, 1618b
R. A., *Manc.Met.*, 1613b
R. T., *Cant.*, 971a
Richard J., *Liv.J.Moores*, 1519b
Robert, *Glam.*, 1433b
Roberta, *Qu.*, 457b
Ron, *Middx.*, 1615c, 1616b
Rosemary K., *Open(UK)*, 1647c, 1648b
S. M., *Alta.*, 287c
S. W., *Br.Col.*, 297c
Stephen, *Melb.*, 84a
Stuart A., 1852a
Susan, *Alta.*, 282c
Susan E., *Qld.*, 131c, 142c
Thomas H., *Paisley*, 1670c
W. A., *Aberd.*, 1313c
W. D., *Oxf.*, 1659b

2039 INDEX TO PERSONAL NAMES Hill...Ho

G. Paul, Lond., 1578a, 1578c
G. R., McM., 380a, 388b
Gillian Y., Sheff.Hallam, 1717a
Graham F. W., Z'bwe., 1828c, 1829a
Greg J. E., N.Territory, 126b, 126c, 128b
H., C'dia., 323b
H. A. O., Oxf., 1650a
Heather M., De Mont., 1392c
Henry, Greenwich, 1448c
I., Sund., 1739c
Ian A., Leic., 1498c
Ian R., Lond., 1541a
Irène, Oxf.Brookes, 1668b
J., Nott.Trent, 1642a
J., Victoria UT, 197b
J. D., Brist., 1347b
J. D., Dal., 329a
J. D., Malawi, 906c
J. L., C'dia., 324a
J. S., W.Ont., 528a
James M., W'gong., 214c
Janne L. G., Glam., 1434c
Jennifer G., Syd., 174a
John, Salf., 1701a
John F., Newcastle(NSW), 125a
John F., Warw., 1780c
John O., La Trobe, 67b
Jonathan W., Liv., 1513b
Joyce M., Leeds, 1483a, 1486b, 1491c
Kate, L&H, 1505c
Keith, Sheff.Hallam, 1719c
Kenneth A., St Mary's(Can.), 473a
Kevin C., La Trobe, 66b
L., PNG, 1127a
L., Sheff., 1704c
L., Sheff.Hallam, 1714c
Leslie J., Warw., 1781a
M., Belf., 1688c
M. J., Newcastle(UK), 1623b
Malcolm, Glas., 1441a
Malcolm R., Lough., 1589a
Marguerite, Tor., 497c
Martin P., De Mont., 1393a
Mary, Waik., 994a
Michael, RMIT, 152c
Michael, Well., 989b
N., Mt.St.Vin., 425a
N. C., Manit., 399c
N. C. M., S.Bank, 1720b
N. W. F. Berkeley, Lond., 1578c, 1579c
Nicholas A., Leeds, 1487c
Nigel J., Bolton Inst., 1337b
P. F., W.England, 1787b
P. G., Br.Col., 299a
P. H. A. W., Sheff., 1707c
P. M., Coventry, 1385b
P. M. R., Oxf., 1663c
P. W., St And., 1698c
Paula, W.England, 1785c
Peter, Melb., 79c
Peter A., Lond., 1540c
Peter C. J., Cran., 1388c
Peter D., Lond., 1562c
Peter J., Bath, 1325c, 1326a
R., Bourne., 1339c
R., Brist., 1350a
R., Camb., 1369a
R., Nfld., 406b
R., Nott.Trent, 1639c
R., Salf., 1701a
R. A., Glas., 1437c
R. D., Manit., 395a
R. E., McM., 386b
R. G., H-W, 1450c
R. P., Tor., 496b
Railton, La Trobe, 65b
Raymond G., Sur., 1741a
Richard W. F., Liv., 1515a
Rob, Luton, 1595a
Robert M., Lond., 1538a
Robert S., Tas., 184c, 186a
Robin, RMIT, 153b
Roderick O., New Br., 431c
Roger R., Open(UK), 1645a
Roland J., Bath, 1323b
Ross H., S.Fraser, 477a
S., Wales, 1762a
S. A., Oxf., 1658a
S. B., W.Syd., 207a
S. J., Nott., 1636b
S. J., Plym., 1673c
S. R., Lond., 1545a, 1547c, 1548c
Sandra, G.Caledonian, 1445a
Simon, Keele, 1471b
Stephen A., Leeds, 1484b
Susan E., S.Aust., 157a
T. J., Brist., 1350a
T. M., W.England, 1787a
T. R., Brist., 1346a
Terry, Lond.Bus., 1544c
Thomas, Monash, 90b
Thomas A., Lond., 1579c
Valerie, Coventry, 1384a
Vernon, ANU, 20c
W., Plym., 1676c
W. F., Copperbelt, 1820b
W. G., Edin., 1414c
W. J., Ulster, 1752a
W. T., W.England, 1786c
Warren, N.Territory, 127a
Hillam, C. E., Sund., 1739a
Hillan, Edith M., Glas., 1442c
Hillard, Thomas W., Macq., 73c
Hillas, A. M., Leeds, 1488b
John B., Auck., 961a
Hillbrich, Russell E., Melb., 87b
Hille, Jos J., W.Cape, 1237c
Hillel, J., C'dia., 324b
John, Aust.Cath., 12b
Hillenbrand, Carole, Edin., 1417c
R., Edin., 1414a
Hiller, Andrew, Qld., 135b
Claire J., Tas., 186b, 187a
G. G., Monash, 91c
J. K., Nfld., 404c
John B., NSW, 109c
Peter C., Monash, 88c
Roger G., Macq., 71c
Hillery, David, Durh., 1405b
Hillhouse, Edward, Warw., 1782a
Edward W., Warw., 1779b
Hilliard, David L., Flin., 49b
Irwin M., Tor., 497c
John, Lond., 1569b
K. F., Oxf., 1653c
R. I., Tor., 499b
Hilliard-Lomas, Julia L., P.Elizabeth, 1197a
Hillier, A. P., Camb., 1363a
Bill R. G., Lond., 1569b
D., Glam., 1433a
E. P., Nott.Trent, 1641b
E. R., S'ton., 1729b
G. H., S'ton., 1725a
I. H., Manc., 1598a
J. M., Reading, 1692b
Jean S., Curtin, 35a
K., S'ton., 1728c
R. R., Brist., 1348a
Richard, Lond., 1527a
Sheila M., Lond., 1555b
Stephen G., Edin., 1420c
Tim, De Mont., 1393a
V. F., Manc., 1604a
Valerie F., Manc., 1604b
Hilliker, A. J., Guelph, 338b
Hillin, G., C.England, 1377a
Hillis, Peter L. M., Strath., 1737a
R., Adel., 7a
W. S., Glas., 1442c
Hillman, A. Robert, Leic., 1498a
Donald A., Ott., 446b
Elizabeth, Ott., 446b
Gordon C., Lond., 1569a
J., Trent, 509b
J. C., Witw., 1247a
J. R., Edin., 1415b
J. R., Glas., 1437b
John R., Dund., 1397a
Johnathan, Syd., 174b
Kenneth M., NSW, 115c
Richard W., W.Ont., 523c
Roger, ANU, 19b
Hillmer, G. N., Car., 318a
Hillocks, Julie L., S.Qld., 165b
Hills, A. M., W.Syd., 208b
A. P., Qld.UT, 146b
C. C., Nott.Trent, 1639c
Carol, Alta., 289c
Catherine M., Camb., 1355c
D. A., Oxf., 1652b
Debbie, Dal., 334c
G. L. C., Qu., 458a
Heather, Plym., 1672b
J., City(UK), 1382a
J., Lond., 1546b
J. G. Paul, Warw., 1781b
J. I., Sund., 1738c
J. R., Lond., 1547b
Jennifer, Portsmouth, 1679c
Judi D., Bourne., 1340b
Michael D., Waik., 994a
N. M., Bourne., 1340b
P. R., HK, 1844a
P. Robin, Exe., 1428a
Peter J., Newcastle(UK), 1619c, 1621a
R. C., Portsmouth, 1679c
R. N., H-W, 1451b
Ray, De Mont., 1392a
Richard E., Camb., 1362c
Rodney C., PNG, 1127a
Steven, Sheff.Hallam, 1718c
William, Newcastle(UK), 1626c
Hillson, Simon W., Lond., 1569a
Hillyard, P. A. R., Brist., 1348b
Hilmer, Frederick G., NSW, 113a
Hilmi Mahmud, Malaya, 917c
Hilsum, Cyril, Lond., 1572a
Hilton, A. J. Boyd, Camb., 1360a
A. J. W., Reading, 1693b
Alison J., De Mont., 1395b
B. Ann, Br.Col., 302a
Brian J., Cran., 1388c
D., Herts., 1457a
D. E., Plym., 1674b
Elisabeth A., W'gong., 216b
G., Sund., 1739a
Ian, Wales, 1758c
J. E., Reading, 1690c
John L., Natal, 1179a
M. W., Manit., 390a
Mark, Westminster, 1791a
Mary, Cape Town, 1169c
R., Lond., 1536b
Rosalind T., W.England, 1785c
Sean R., Lond., 1562b
Valerie, Leeds, 1492b
Hilts, S. G., Guelph, 339a, 340b, 341c
Hiltz, Edie, Regina, 461a
Hilyer, Ann, R.Roads, 466b
Roger G., Sheff.Hallam, 1716a
Himachalam, D., S.Venkat., 855a
Himal, H. S., Tor., 501b
Himalayanath, M., Osm., 797a
Himbara, D., Witw., 1245c
Himka, J. P., Alta., 283a
Himmelman, John, Laval, 351a
Joy, Lake., 345c
Himmelweit, Susan, Open(UK), 1645b
Himms-Hagen, Jean, Ott., 443b
Himonga, C. N., Cape Town, 1163b
Himsworth, C. M. G., Edin., 1418a
K., Nott.Trent, 1639a
Richard L., Camb., 1364c
Hince, Kevin W., Well., 987a, 990a
Hinch, E. John, Camb., 1361b
Geoffrey N., NE, 102c
John de C., Pret., 1205c
R., Guelph, 339a
T. D., Alta., 285a
Hinchcliffe, P. M., Wat., 514c
Tanis F., Westminster, 1790c
Hinchey, E. John, McG., 376b
M. J., Nfld., 403c
Hinchigeri, S. B., Karn., 724a
Hinchliffe, A., UMIST, 1607b
John R., Wales, 1754c
T. A., Manc., 1598b
Hincke, Maxwell T. C., Ott., 443c
Hincks, Rhisiart J., Wales, 1756a
Hind, D., S.Bank, 1721c
E., C.England, 1376b
J. L., Sund., 1738b
Robert, E.Lond., 1410b
Hinde, Chris J., Lough., 1589b
Joan S., Camb., 1370b
P. R. A., S'ton., 1727b
R. A., Camb., 1373a
Rosalind T., Syd., 171b
Hindi, Khalil, Brun., 1352c
Hindle, B. Paul, Salf., 1701c
C. M., Plym., 1673a
Don, NSW, 116a, 119a
Ian, Manc., 1603a
K., Swinburne UT, 168b, 168c
K. G., Swinburne UT, 168b
Robert D., Cape Town, 1160c
Hindler, Charles G., Lond., 1542a
Hindley, A., Hull, 1465c
B. V., Lond., 1546b
Carol, Liv.J.Moores, 1518a
Peter A., Lond., 1562c
Hindmarch, Ian, Sur., 1744b
Hindmarsh, Andrew M., Sheff., 1713c
J. Thomas, Ott., 443b, 445a
K. Wayne, Manit., 390a, 394c
P. R. C., Lond., 1575a
Peter C., Lond., 1574a
Hindness, Barry, ANU, 17b
Hindocha, H. N., Saur., 838c
Hinds, B. K., Belf., 1685b
Charles J., Lond., 1554c, 1555c
Cora, Ott., 442a
Debbie, G.Caledonian, 1445a
Ed A., Sus., 1747c
Hindsgaul, O., Alta., 281a
Hindsley, W. R., Qld.UT, 146c
Hindson, Douglas C., Durban-W., 1172c
Hinduja, S., UMIST, 1608b
Hine, Christine, Brun., 1353b
D. J., Oxf., 1658a
Gail, Portsmouth, 1681c
H. M., St And., 1697c
John H., Well., 988c
R. C., Nott., 1633c
W. L., York(Can.), 552c
Hinek, Aleksander, Tor., 496a
Hines, Anthony C., Portsmouth, 1677a
Evor L., Warw., 1780c
J. A., Wales, 1763c
Melissa, City(UK), 1382a
Peter A., Wales, 1762a
R. M., Tor., 495b
W. G. S., Guelph, 338a
Hing, Ai Yun, NU Singapore, 1152a
Peter, Nan.Tech., 1137c
Hinings, C. R., Alta., 284c, 288c
Hinkelman, K. W., Alta., 287b
Hinks, A. J., H-W, 1450b
C. E., Edin., 1415b
Hinnebusch, R., St And., 1699a
Hinrichsen, Colin F. L., Tas., 185a
P. Alberto, N.Lond., 1628c
Hinshelwood, Robert L., Essex, 1425b
Hinson, J. P., Lond., 1554b
R. E., W.Ont., 526c
Hinton, C. C., C'dia., 322b
David A., S'ton., 1724b
David H., New Br., 432a
E., Wales, 1767c
G., Tor., 484b, 490a
G. E., Tor., 492b
Geoffrey, Aston, 1321a
Helen E., Wolv., 1797b
James S., Warw., 1781b
M. J., UMIST, 1608b
O. R., Newcastle(UK), 1621b
P., Qld.UT, 148c
Pamela, Herts., 1454a
Penny, Luton, 1594c
Peter D., Syd., 170b
Richard H., Sur., 1741a
Ron, Lough., 1592c
Terry, Sur., 1743b
Hinton-Lever, Justine M. L., UMIST, 1609c
Hintz, Tom, Technol.Syd., 189c
Hintze, Almut, Camb., 1367a
Marie-Anne M. J., Leeds, 1486b
Hinwood, J. B., Monash, 91b
Hinxman, Lynda, Sheff.Hallam, 1719b
Hinz, Evelyn J., Manit., 392c
M. O., Namibia, 956a
Hiol, H. F., Dschang, 270a
Hiorns, R. W., Oxf., 1659a
Hipel, K. W., Wat., 514c, 518c
Hipkin, C. R., Wales, 1767a
I. B., Cape Town, 1163b
Roger G., Edin., 1417a
Hipkiss, A. R., Lond., 1536a
Hippisley, A. R., St And., 1699b
Hippisley-Cox, Charles I., Hudd., 1460b
Hippner, Meciej, Natal, 1179c
Hipwell, G. J., De Mont., 1394b
Hira, C. K., Punj.Ag., 817c
G. S., Punj.Ag., 816b
Hiran, B. L., M.Sukh., 772b
Hirani, M. H., Pune, 811b
Hirantha, S. W., Sri Jay., 1284a
Hirbour, Louise, Montr., 413b
Hird, Brian, Ott., 442b
C. C., Sheff., 1706a
Kathryn, Curtin, 37c
Lew, Aust.Cath., 14a
Hirdes, J. P., Wat., 515c, 518c
John, Tor., 497c
Hiregange, T. K., Karn., 725c
Hiremani Nayak, R., Kuvempu, 735b
Hiremath, A. C., Gulb., 674b
B. R., Karn., 724b
N. S., Karn., 724a
P. S., Gulb., 675a
R. S., Karn., 724b
S. C., Karn., 723c
S. L., Gulb., 675a
Ujwala, Gulb., 675c
Ujwala S., Gulb., 674c
V. A., Karn., 724c
Hirimburegama, S. S. M. Kshanika, Colombo, 1259b
W. K., Colombo, 1259b
Hiriyanna, A., Mys., 780b
Hirj, N. K., UMIST, 1609a
Hirom, Paul C., Lond., 1530b
Hironaka, Robert, Leth., 359a
Hirota, T. T., Windsor, 539c
Hirsch, D. J., Dal., 333b
David J., Dal., 332b
Maureen, Coventry, 1385b
Philip, Syd., 173a
R. S., Adel., 6a
S. R., Lond., 1532a
Hirschberg, Joseph G., Melb., 79b
Hirschbühler, Paul, Ott., 441c
Hirschfeld, James W. P., Sus., 1747c
Michael A., Well., 985a
Hirschhorn, Michael D., NSW, 113b
Hirschorn, R., Qu., 456a
Hirschsohn, P., W.Cape, 1237b
Hirsh, J., McM., 385b
Hirshen, S., Br.Col., 296b
Hirst, B. H., Newcastle(UK), 1626a
C., Glam., 1433a
Catherine, C'dia., 326c
Cherrell, Qld.UT, 144a
D. G., Ulster, 1750c
David J., La Trobe, 65a
David M., Wales, 1755b
David M., Warw., 1780a
G., Tor., 503c
I. R. C., H-W, 1451a
Ian, Hudd., 1462a
John B., La Trobe, 65a
Julia, Sheff.Hallam, 1717b
Keith E., S'ton., 1726b
Lawrence W., Qld., 138c
M. M., W.Ont., 527c, 530b
Mark K., NSW, 113a
Paul, Leeds Met., 1494c
Paul Q., Lond., 1523b
Robert G., James Cook, 61b
S. B., Zambia, 1822b
Stuart L., Leeds Met., 1495b
Timothy R., Brist., 1350a
Hirstle, Ian, Hudd., 1463c
Hirte, H. W., McM., 385b
Hiryati bt Abdullah, Putra, 930b
Hisamuddin, Karachi, 1103b
Hiscock, Alan E., Westminster, 1789c
Karen A., Wales, 1776a
Mary, Bond, 24a
Nigel L., Oxf.Brookes, 1665b
P., Nfld., 407c
Hiscott, J., McG., 372a
John, McG., 372c
Paul S., Liv., 1512b, 1513a
R. D., Wat., 518c
R. N., Nfld., 403a
Hishamuddin bin Jamaluddin, Tech.U.Malaysia, 940b
Hislop, Alison A., Lond., 1573b
Hitch, Graham J., Lanc., 1482a
Hitchcock, A. G., Z'bwe., 1827c
A. P., McM., 381a
Barry G., Sur., 1745a
D. L., McM., 383c
David H., Westminster, 1791a
Michael, N.Lond., 1628c
P., Dal., 328b
Richard, Exe., 1429b
Tim V., N.Lond., 1628b
Hitchen, Edward T., Wolv., 1793b
Judith M., C.England, 1376a
Linda, L&H, 1505c
Hitchens, D. M. W. N., Belf., 1687a
Hitchin, N. J., Oxf., 1656a
Hitchings, Dennis, Lond., 1527a
Hitchins, Geoff, Leeds Met., 1493a
Hitchman, A. M., Manc.Met., 1612c
Michael A., Tas., 183b
Michael L., Strath., 1733c
Hitchmough, J. D., Sheff., 1707b
Hitiris, Theodore, York(UK), 1799b
Hitman, Graham A., Lond., 1555c
Hittalamani, S. V., Karn., 723c
Hitzman, M. W., Belf., 1685b
Hives, Chris, Br.Col., 309c
Hiware, C. J., Dr BA Marath., 656a
Hixenbaugh, Paula, Westminster, 1791b
Hiza, J. R., Dar., 1294c
Hizbullah, A. B. M., Islamic(B'desh.), 246a
Hj Ahmad Bakeri Abu Bakar, IIU Malaysia, 914a
Hj Ali Hj Ahmad, Sci.U.Malaysia, 935a
Hj Mohd Sofian Ahmad, Sci.U.Malaysia, 938c
Hj Wan Salim Md Noor, Sci.U.Malaysia, 935a
Hjartarson, P. I., Alta., 282c
Hjelm, N. M., Chinese HK, 1834c
Hladky, S. B., Camb., 1362b
Hlady, L. Jean, Br.Col., 307b
Hlalele, J. M., NUL, 904c
Hlasa, K., NUL, 903b
Hlatawayo, A., N-W(S.Af.), 1189c
Hlatshwayo, B., Z'bwe., 1827b
N. A., Swazi., 1289b
Hlavac, Richard W., Cant., 968a, 972b
Hlengwa, Msawakhe A., Natal, 1186b
Hluna, J. V., NE Hill, 793b
Hlynka, L. D., Manit., 391c, 400c
M., Windsor, 539b
Hman, Nyi W., James Cook, 62c
Hnatko, G. S., Alta., 287c
Hnizdo, V., Witw., 1245b
Ho, A. K. C., Alta., 287c
Anthony T. S., Nan.Tech., 1140a
Arthur, NSW, 114b
Aster C. S., HKPU, 1848a
Betty M. F., HK, 1840a
Bow, NU Singapore, 1153a
C. C., Malaya, 916c
C. S., Tor., 496c
D. S. W., HK, 1841c
D. Y. F., HK, 1840c
Daniel C. W., HK, 1840c
David, Ryerson, 467a
E. S., Kingston(UK), 1478a
Elaine Y. L., HK, 1839b
Goen E., Murd., 99c, 100c
H. C. Y., HK, 1838c
H. H., Chinese HK, 1831c, 1834a
Helena, Br.Col., 307b
Hua Chew, NU Singapore, 1151b
Hwee Long, Nan.Tech., 1142c
Irene J. W., Nan.Tech., 1144b, 1144c
J. C., NU Singapore, 1148c
K., York(Can.), 552a
K. C., Open HK, 1849b
K. K., NU Singapore, 1146a
K. L., HK, 1839a
K. P., HK, 1837c
K. P. H., HK, 1837c
Kee Hay, NU Singapore, 1152a
Ken K., NSW, 117a
Ken K. Y., NSW, 119b
Khal Leong, NU Singapore, 1151c
Khek Yu, NU Singapore, 1152c
Kim Wai, Nan.Tech., 1136b
King Hee, NU Singapore, 1152c
Kong Chong, NU Singapore, 1152a
Mae Wan, Open(UK), 1644c
P. C., HK, 1842a
P. K. M., S.Fraser, 478b
P. P., Chinese HK, 1832a
Peng Kee, NU Singapore, 1150a
Richard M. W., Chinese HK, 1831a
Robert, C.Qld., 29c
S. C., Sci.U.Malaysia, 932b
S. L., HK, 1841c
S. L., HKPU, 1846b
S. P. S., Br.Col., 298a
S. S. M., Chinese HK, 1832a
Shuit Hung, NU Singapore, 1146a
Siew Y., Lond., 1531c
Stephen C. Y., Curtin, 36a
Steven Y. K., HKPU, 1848b
Suet Y., Leeds Met., 1494c
Suzanne S. Y., Chinese HK, 1834c
Ting Fei, NU Singapore, 1153c
Vincent, Br.Col., 306a
W. K., NU Singapore, 1148b
W. K. K., Chinese HK, 1832a
W. M., Wat., 513c
Y. S., HKPU, 1846c
Y. S., NU Singapore, 1149c
Yeong Khing, Nan.Tech., 1139c
Ho Chi Lui, Paul, NU Singapore, 1151b
Ho Gaik Lui, Malaya, 916a

Mani contd.
N., Monash, 91a
N. D., GRI, 664c
R., Annam., 599a
R. S., Baroda, 749c
T. C., A.Bello, 1009a
Uliyar V., Baroda, 751c
Rev. V., CUE Af., 886a
V., IISc., 691a
V., TN Vet., 863c
V. S., J.Nehru U., 713a
Veena, NDRI, 786b, 786c
Mani Meitei, M., Manip., 768b
Maniam Thambu, NU Malaysia, 927a
Manian, S., B'thiar., 626a
T., Mys., 780b
Maniates, Maria R., Tor., 488b
Manibhushana Rao, K., Madr., 742a
Manickam, M., Annam., 600a
M., B'thiar., 626a
N., Annam., 600b
R., TN Vet., 861a
S., Madurai-K., 746b
S. G., Madr., 742a
Manickavasagam, V., Alagappa, 584a
Manickavasagar, R., Eastern(S.Lanka), 1262c
Manickavasagam, R. M., Roor., 829b
Manicom, A., Mt.St.Vin., 425b
Manihar Sharma, B., Manip., 768b
Manihar Singh, A. K., Manip., 768a
Manik, D. N., IIT Bombay, 694c
R. S., NDRI, 786c
Manikappa, M., Gulb., 675c
Manikas, A., Lond., 1528c
Manikumar, K. A., M.Sund., 770a
Manikyamba, P., Hyd., 689b
P., Kakatiya, 720b
P., Osm., 797b
Manilal, K. S., Calicut, 637a
Manimekalai, A., Annam., 598b
Maninder, Shenhmar, Punj.Ag., 815a
Manion, J., C.England, 1378b
Margaret, Melb., 80b
Manipatro, H. C., And., 590b
Maniruzzaman, M., B'desh.Engin., 231b
M., Chitt., 234b
M., Dhaka, 237b
Manison, K. I., WI, 1812a
Manivachakan, K., Anna, 596b
Manivannan, K., Annam., 601b
Manivasagar, V., Jaffna, 1265b
Manivel, M., Madurai-K., 747a
Manja, B. A., Dar., 1293c
Manjappa, H. D., Karn., 724a
Manjarekar, C. S., Shiv., 842a
Manjeli, Yacouba, Dschang, 269c
Manji, K. P., Dar., 1295a
Manjit, S., Utara, Malaysia, 943c
Manjon, J. E., Glam., 1434b
Manjrekar, J., Baroda, 749b
Manju Bansal, IISc., 691c
Manju Vani, E., SPMV, 852a
Manjula Sridharan, Anna, 595c
Manjunath, R., IISc., 690a
S. M., B'lore., 620c
T. R., Kuvempu, 735b
Manjunatha, N. H., B'lore., 619c
S. M., Kuvempu, 735a, 736a
Manjunatha Pattabi, M'lore., 761a
Manjunathaiah, B. N., Mys., 780a
Mankad, Rahul, Ballarat, 22c
Mankar, R. B., Dr BAT, 658a
Mankhand, T. R., Ban., 616c
Mankodi, P. C., Baroda, 751c
Manktelow, Kenneth I., Wolv., 1795a
R. T., Tor., 501b
Manley, B. W., Sus., 1745a
J. J., W.England, 1786b
Rev. Kenneth R., Melb., 87c
Mary-Elizabeth, York(Can.), 546a
P. L., Windsor, 539b
P. N., Qu., 459b
Peter S., Durh., 1405a
Sandra, W.England, 1786b
Simon W., Qld., 137b
Manley-Casimir, M., S.Fraser, 478b, 480c
Manly, Bryan F. J., Otago, 981c
R., Kingston(UK), 1478a
Manmadha Rao, L., And., 593c
Manmohan Singh, B. K., Osm., 797c
H. K., Punjabi, 820a
Mann, A., Lond., 1577b
A. H., Lond., 1540a
A. J. S., Greenwich, 1447b
A. P. S., Punj.Ag., 816c
Alan J., N.Lond., 1629c
Alan M., McG., 375c
Allan R., Ballarat, 21b
B. E., Sheff., 1705a
Charles, W.Aust., 200b
Christopher G. H., James Cook, 62b
D. M. A., Manc., 1605a
G. E., Lond., 1536b
G. S., Punj.Ag., 815a
George, W.England, 1788c
H. E., Nfld., 402b, 408b
I., De Mont., 1392a
J., Reading, 1691b
J. R., Birm., 1334c
Jill L., Camb., 1359a
Jim I., Otago, 981a
Julia, Leic., 1503c
Karen V., Dal., 332b
Kirk, Leeds, 1488c
L., Melb., 82b
L. A., Car., 317c
M. D., Cape Town, 1167b
N. S., Panjab, 803a
Nicholas, Lond., 1583b, 1583c
Nicolas H., Warw., 1779c
R., UMIST, 1607c
R. B., Wat., 516c, 517c
R. S., Delhi, 647a
R. S., NDRI, 787b
Richard, S.Pac., 1254c, 1255a
S., Tor., 492c
S. B. S., Pg.IMER, 808c
S. G., W.England, 1788a
S. K., Punj.Ag., 816a, 818c
S. R., Herts., 1454b
S. S., Punj.Ag., 815c
Stephen, Bath, 1323a
Susan N., York(Can.), 547b
T., C.England, 1376a
W. Michael, Lond., 1563c
Manna, Rev. G., CUE Af., 886a
P. K., Annam., 600c
P. V. C., Maur., 952b
S. S., IIT Bombay, 695c
Mannan, A. K. M. A., B'desh.Ag., 227b
Abdul, xxxviii, xxxix, 1852a
Abdul, Chitt., 233a
Bashira, Dhaka, 242a
K. A. I. F. M., Dhaka, 241b
M. A., Dhaka, 240a, 243a
M. A., Jahang., 248b
M. A., NU Singapore, 1149a
M. A., Rajsh., 255c, 257b
M. A., Shahjalal, 258a
Md Abdul, Gauh., 667c
Mohammad A., PNG, 1128c
Q. A., Dhaka, 240b
R. Jahan, Dhaka, 238b
S. M., Dhaka, 240a
Mannar Jawahar, P., Anna, 597a
Mannath, J., Madr., 742b
Mannathoko, C., Botswana, 262c
Manne, Robert, La Trobe, 68c
Mannell, R. C., Wat., 518b
Roger C., Wat., 515c
Manners, Ian, Tor., 484a
John M., Leeds Met., 1495c
Mannette, Joy A., York(Can.), 546b
Mann-Feder, V., C'dia., 325b
Mannienen, P., Tor., 494c
Mannikeri, M. S., Karn., 724b
Mannin, Michael L., Liv.J.Moores, 1518c
Manning, A., City(UK), 1382b
A., Coventry, 1385a
A., Lond., 1546b
A. R., Mt.St.Vin., 425b
Alan, Laval, 354a
Anthony K., Warw., 1781c
B., C.England, 1376b
C. E., Cant., 969a
Carl D., Lough., 1590b
D. A. C., Manc., 1598c
D. N., Wales, 1767b
Frank E. C. R., Liv.J.Moores, 1519a
Geoffrey, Lond., 1572a
Gerald F., Guelph, 337a
J., Greenwich, 1448b
J., Wales, 1770c
Janet M., Kingston(UK), 1477a
Joanna M., Auck., 963b
John T., Liv., 1508a
Karen, Victoria UT, 197a
Mark R., Camb., 1372a
N. P., Nott., 1636a
P. A., Adel., 7c
Paul, De Mont., 1390b
Paul L., W'gong., 216b
Peter D., Durh., 1402a, 1404b
Susan L., Camb., 1359a
W. H., Wales, 1763c
Manning-Prior, Christine, Sur., 1744c
Mannings, D. M., Aberd., 1314c
Mannion, Antoinette M., Reading, 1692c
David, Lond., 1558c
J. J., Nfld., 404b
Julie, Qld.UT, 145a
Kenneth, Sheff.Hallam, 1718b
M. A. G., Napier, 1617c
Manns, Tom, Portsmouth, 1678a
Mannsaker, Frances M., Glam., 1434b
Mannur, H. G., PNG, 1127b
Manny, Gilles, Montr., 413b
Manoa, P., S.Pac., 1253b
Pio, S.Pac., 1252a
Manoch, Claire, Liv.J.Moores, 1517b
Manocha, L. M., SP, 836c
M. S., Brock, 311c
S., SP, 836c
Manohanthan, R., Open S.Lanka, 1273a
Manohar, C. S., IISc., 691a
K., Manipal AHE, 763a
P., Anna, 595b
P., Manipal AHE, 765a
Paul, TN Vet., 863b
R., Kenyatta, 890c
S., Moi, 893a
Manohar Chethana, Manipal AHE, 766b
Manohar Rao, D. M., Osm., 799a
G., Osm., 796a
Manohara Murthy, N., S.Krishna., 850c
Manohara Rao, S. P., And., 593b
Manoharachary, C., Osm., 798c, 800a
Manoharan, K., Madurai-K., 745c
Mohan, Nan.Tech., 1137c
P., Anna, 595c
P. T., Madr., 741a, 744b
T., Peradeniya, 1276c
T. R., Annam., 600a
Manoharlal, MDU, 753b, 754b
Manoj, Changat, Kerala, 729b
Manojlovic-Muir, Ljubica, Glas., 1437c
Manokore, V., Z'bwe., 1828a
Manolios, Nicholas, Syd., 177c
Manolopoulos, D. E., Oxf., 1650b
Manong'a, J. S., Malawi, 907c
Manonmoney, N., Madurai-K., 746a
Manonmony, T., Madurai-K., 747a
Manooja, D. C., GND, 681a
Manook, I., W.England, 1787c
Manorama Thinakaran, TN Vet., 863b
Manory, Rafael, RMIT, 151c
Manos, G., S.Bank, 1720a
J., Mt.St.Vin., 425b
Manoukian, John, McG., 374a
Manouzi, Hassan, Laval, 354c
Mans, Koert N., Rand Afrikaans, 1210a, 1212c
Marthinus J., Pret., 1202c
Minette E., Namibia, 956a
Mansaray, Y. K. C., S.Leone, 1132c
Mansard, H. D., Annam., 598c
Mansel, R. E., Wales, 1773c
Mansell, A. D., Salf., 1701c
D. A., Glam., 1435a
D. S., Melb., 80a
Gilbert J., Hudd., 1460a
Jim M., Kent, 1474c
Michael, Manc., 1599b
R. E., Lincoln(NZ), 973b
Robin E., Sus., 1748b
Wade, Kent, 1474a
Mansfield, Averil O., Lond., 1532c
Bruce E., Macq., 73c
John, Nott.Trent, 1643b
John W., Lond., 1579a
Nicholas J., Macq., 73b
Paul, Durh., 1404a
R., Coventry, 1385a
Roger, Wales, 1761a, 1761c, 1762a
Terence A., Lanc., 1480c
Willard R., Durban-W., 1170b
Mansi, M. M., Sund., 1738c
Omaima, McG., 373c
Mansingh, Abai, Delhi, 646a, 650c
Ajai, WI, 1815a
Mansinha, L., W.Ont., 522c
Manson, A. S., Qu., 455c
Andrew H., N-W(S.Af.), 1190a
Andy, N-W(S.Af.), 1191b, 1191c
Doreen E., Manc.Met., 1611a
Elayne P., Napier, 1619a
G. A., Sheff., 1705b
H., Nfld., 407c
J., Wat., 520c
Stuart, Essex, 1423b
Manson-Singer, Sharon, Br.Col., 303b
Mansoor, Michael, WI, 1816a
Mansoori, M. A., Punjab, 1113b
S. A., Punjab, 1113b
Mansoorian, A., York(Can.), 546b
Mansor b Ahmad, Sci.U.Malaysia, 933b
Mansor bin Fadzil, Malaya, 917c
Mansor bin Ibrahim, Tech.U.Malaysia, 941b
Mansor bin Jusoh, NU Malaysia, 924a
Mansor bin Md Isa, Malaya, 916a, 916c
Mansour, S. Y., Lake., 344a
Mansour Hj Ibrahim, IIU Malaysia, 913a
Manstead, A. S. R., Manc., 1602a
Mansur, A., Chitt., 235a
M. A., NU Singapore, 1148a
R. M., Karn., 724a
S. S., W.Ont., 526b
Taslima, Dhaka, 240a
Mansvelt, Erna P. G., Stell., 1230b
Mant, Andrea, NSW, 116a
D., Brist., 1349b
D., Oxf., 1661a
David, S'ton., 1728c
J. W. F., Birm., 1334a
Jenny A., Oxf.Brookes, 1667b
M. J., Alta., 287a
Manteau, Kojo A., Kumasi, 571c
Mantei, M. M., Tor., 484b
Mantel, Gerald D., Pret., 1207c
Mantell, C. D., Auck., 966a
Colin D., Auck., 965c
Sinclair H., Lond., 1579a
Mantha, Robert, Laval, 354c
Manthei, R. J., Cant., 969b
Manthorpe, C., Lond., 1549a
G., Hull, 1467b
Mantle, Hugh I. P., Liv.J.Moores, 1517c
M. Jill, E.Lond., 1411b
Peter G., Lond., 1527b
Manton, Nicholas S., Camb., 1361c
Mantri, A. N., Ban., 613a
Manu, J., Ghana, 568a
Manu Bhaskar, Kerala, 730a
Manuel, Mogamat A., Tor., 498a
P. W., W.Ont., 525b
Stephanie, C'dia., 326b
Manuella, Tulanga, S.Pac., 1252a
Manuja, N. K., HPKV, 687b
Manus, C., O.Awolowo, 1061c
Manuth, V., Qu., 452c
Manuvel, R., S.Venkat., 856a
Manvar, U. V., Saur., 838a
Manvi, M., Osm., 795b
P. K., Hyd., 689a
Manwani, Asandas, SA Latif, 1117b
Manwaring, John A., Ott., 441b
Manyari, D. E., Alta., 287a
Manyatsi, A. M., Swazi., 1289b
S. E., Swazi., 1289a
Manyeh, A. B. J., S.Leone, 1134a
M. K., S.Leone, 1134c
Manyeli, Fr. T. L., NUL, 904b
Manz, Andreas, Lond., 1527c
Manzagol, Claude, Montr., 412a
Manzer, R. A., Tor., 504a
Manzi, Tony F., Westminster, 1790c
Manzie, Andrew, Strath., 1737c
Manzoor, Tasnim, Leeds Met., 1496b
Manzur, Meher, Curtin, 35c
Mao, Jennifer M. H., NU Singapore, 1149b
Xeurong, Strath., 1737b
Yong, Camb., 1373a
Maonga, T. W., Nair., 899a
Mapa, R. B., Peradeniya, 1276c, 1278b
Mapanga, K. G., Z'bwe., 1828b
Mapani, W., Z'bwe., 1826a, 1829c
Mapara, Shakeel, Bhutto IST, 1118b
Mapatuna, M., Ruhuna, 1281b
Mapes, John, Cran., 1388a
Maphai, Vincent, Pret., 1206a
Maphosa, Norman, Solusi, 1825a
Maphumulo, Abednego M., Pret., 1202c
Mapolie, Selwyn F., W.Cape, 1236a
Maponga, C. C., Z'bwe., 1828c
Mapopa, M., Zambia, 1823b
Mappin, D. A., Alta., 288c
Mapps, D. J., Plym., 1673b, 1676a
Mapstone, R. H., Ulster, 1752a
Sally, Oxf., 1653a
Mapunda, A. M., Dar., 1293b
Maqbool, M. A., Karachi, 1105a
M. A., Osm., 795b
Muhammad, Faisalabad, 1084b
Maqbool Ahmed, TN Vet., 862a
Maqbool Uddin Shaikh, IIU Malaysia, 913b
Maqelepo, S. K., NUL, 904a
Maqlid, R., IIU(P'stan.), 1099a
Maqsood, A., Quaid-i-Azam, 1116c
Azra, Bhutto IST, 1118c
Zahida, Karachi, 1102c
Maqsud, Mohammad, N-W(S.Af.), 1190a
Mar, P. Gerhard, Natal, 1181b
Mara, Duncan D., Leeds, 1485c
Maradufu, Asaph, E.Af.Baraton, 887a, 887c
Maraire, D., Z'bwe., 1826a
Marais, Adrian D., Cape Town, 1166b
André de K., S.Af., 1217c
Coenraad W., S.Af., 1218b
D. D., Pret., 1202a, 1209b, 1209c
Estelle, N-W(S.Af.), 1190a
G. Frans, Stell., 1226c
G. van R., Cape Town, 1161b
Hendrik J., S.Af.Med., 1176c
Marinda, S.Af., 1217c
Martin R., S.Af., 1218c
Nicholas J., Cape Town, 1161b
Rene, Pret., 1202c
Maraj, J. A., Bath, 1323c
Maraj Khalid, IIU(P'stan.), 1098a
Marak, C. R., NE Hill, 793c
Marake, M. V., NUL, 904b
Maral, Gerard, Sur., 1744a
Maralabhavi, Y. B., B'lore., 620b
Marambe, B., Peradeniya, 1278a
P. W. M. B. B., Peradeniya, 1275b
Maran, A. G. D., Edin., 1420b, 1421c
Maranda, Laval, 351c
Marandu, E. E., Dar., 1293c
Maranga, E. K., Egerton, 889c
J. S., Moi, 893b
Marangoni, A. G., Guelph, 340a
D. G., St FX, 469c
Marantz, P. J., Br.Col., 303a
Marasinghe, E. W., Sri Jay., 1284b
M. L., Windsor, 539a
S. Charika, Colombo, 1260b
Maraspini, Christiana, Cape Town, 1167a
Marathe, A. G., IIT Bombay, 693c
K. V., Mumbai, 775a
M. P., Pune, 811b
S., Hyd., 688c
S. D., YCM Open, 877b
Maravanyika, O. E., Z'bwe., 1826c
Marazi, Hameed-Ullah, Kashmir, 727b
Marazzani, Micheline, Montr., 417a
Marber, Michael S., Lond., 1541a
Marcau, G., Birm., 1332b
Marceau, François, Laval, 357b
J., W.Syd., 208a
Normand, Laval, 357b
Picard, Laval, 358a
Marcel, Yves L., Ott., 445a
Marcelja, Stephen, ANU, 17a
Marcelle, G., E.Lond., 1411b
Marcellino, Rae, Tas., 184b
Marcenes, Wagner S., Lond., 1573c
March, C. G., Salf., 1700b, 1702c
Lyn, Syd., 177c
Paul, Technol.Syd., 190b
Paul E., NSW, 113c
Peter, St Mary's(Can.), 472c
R. E., Trent, 508a
Marchak, M. Patricia, Br.Col., 296a
Marchand, Denys, Montr., 410b
Louise, Montr., 414c
Mario, Ott., 441a
Pierre D., Laval, 351b
Raymond G., Laval, 357a
Marchant, Alan, L&H, 1505c
Alison, Wales, 1776a
Christine, Thames V., 1749b, 1749c
D. R., Nott.Trent, 1639b
R., Ulster, 1750b
T. R., W'gong., 214c
Marchbank, Jennifer, Coventry, 1385c
Marche, Claude, Montr., 421b
Marchessault, Guy, St Paul(Ott.), 447b
Robert H., McG., 364a
Marchetti-Mercer, Maria C., Pret., 1206b
Marchington, M. P., UMIST, 1607a, 1608c
Marchment, G., Birm., 1333b
Marchon, Maurice N., Montr., 419b
Marcia, James E., S.Fraser, 480a
Marcisz, Leczek T., S.Af.Med., 1175a
Marcon, Norman, Tor., 498a
Marcotte, Denis, Montr., 421b
Gaston, Laval, 355b
Patrice, Montr., 411a
Marcoux, L. W., Alta., 284a
Marcel, Montr., 417b
Sylvie, Laval, 358a
Yves, Laval, 351c
Yves, Montr., 412c
Marcovitz, Sorana, McG., 372a
Marcus, Fitzroy, Guy., 577b
Julie, C.Sturt, 31c
Roxanne, York(Can.), 548b
Tessa S., Natal, 1186a
Marda, Nelly, Greenwich, 1447a
Mardell, Jane, Sheff.Hallam, 1715b
Marden, Adrian, Herts., 1454b
Marder, Todd B., Durh., 1402b
Mardia, K. V., Leeds, 1489a
P., JN Vyas, 703a
Mardiros, Marilyn, Ott., 442a
Mardles, Peter J., Camb., 1374c
Mardon, Helen J., Oxf., 1660b
Maré, Estelle A., S.Af., 1219b
Maria C., S.Af., 1219c
P. Gerard, Natal, 1183b
Maree, D. A., Rhodes, 1215a
H. B., Mehran, 1107a
Hermanus A. P., S.Af.Med., 1177b
Jacobus G., Pret., 1206b
Johannes J., Cape Town, 1164c
K. W., Rhodes, 1213c
Leon, Pret., 1204a
M. Cathy, S.Af., 1221c
Mareels, Iven M. Y., Melb., 80a
Marek, S. A., Napier, 1617b
Marenbon, John A., Camb., 1373c
Mares, Edwin D., Well., 989a
Mareschal, Geneviève, Ott., 443a
Marett, Allan, Syd., 174b
Marfany, Joan-Luis, Liv., 1510a
Marfels, C. T., Dal., 328c
Marfording, Annette, NSW, 112c
Margan, J., C.England, 1376b
Margara, Raul A., Lond., 1532b
Margaritis, A., W.Ont., 523b
Dimitrios, Waik., 992b
Margerison, J., Plym., 1672b
John, Leeds Met., 1494a
Margetts, B. M., S'ton., 1729a
Marggraff, Margaret M., Pret., 1202c
Margham, J. Phil, Liv.J.Moores, 1519c
Sarah, Liv.J.Moores, 1517c
Marginson, Paul, Leeds, 1487b
Simon, Melb., 81a
Margolese, Richard G., McG., 376b
Margolies, David N., Lond., 1525a
Margolin, U., Alta., 284a
Margolis, Hank, Laval, 353a
Harriet, Well., 988a
Kenneth, Qld., 136c
Stephen, Monash, 94b
Margot, Joëlle, Montr., 414a
Marh, B. S., HP, 684c
Mari Ayyah, P., B'thidasan., 628b
Maria Das, M., And., 593a
Mariam bt Ahmad, Sci.U.Malaysia, 936a
Mariam Samariah Mohammad, NU Malaysia, 923a
Mariani, Annajulia, Witw., 1244a
John A., Lanc., 1480a
Marianna, I., Osm., 795c
Mariappa, M. C., B'lore., 620a
Mariappan, A., Delhi, 648c
M., Anna, 595c
Mariati Shakor, Malaya, 920c
Maribei, J. M., Nair., 897b
Marić, Svetislav V., Camb., 1358c
Marie, Phillipe, De Mont., 1393c
Marie Joseph, N. S., Mys., 779c
Mariga, I. K., Z'bwe., 1826c
Marimuthu, G., Madurai-K., 746a
N., TN Vet., 861c
Marin, J. P., Witw., 1244c

George E., *WI*, 1813b
Mathiu, P. M., *Nair.*, 897c
Mathon, J., *City(UK)*, 1382c
Jiri, *City(UK)*, 1381c
R., *Tor.*, 484b
Mathumba, D. I., *S.Af.*, 1217b
Mathunjwa, M. D., *Swazi.*, 1288b, 1290a
Mathur, A. B. L., *JN Vyas*, 703b
A. K., *JN Vyas*, 703c
A. K., *J.Nehru U.*, 714a
A. K., *Roor.*, 829c, 831c
Anand, *JN Vyas*, 705b
Aruna S., *JN Vyas*, 705c
Asha, *Lucknow*, 740a
Atul, *All India IMS*, 585c
B. C., *Roor.*, 830a
B. L., *JN Vyas*, 704a
B. N., *NDRI*, 786a, 787b, 787c
B. S., *Roor.*, 830c
C. N., *M.Sukh.*, 773b
D. K., *NDRI*, 786c
H., *Maur.*, 953b
K., *JN Vyas*, 704c
K. C., *APSV*, 609c, 610b
K. C., *Roor.*, 831a
K. C. K., *JN Vyas*, 703c
K. K., *JN Vyas*, 705c
K. K., *Lucknow*, 738c
Kalpana, *JN Vyas*, 704c
Krishan S., *NU Singapore*, 1146b
Kuldeep, *J.Nehru U.*, 714a
M., *SPA Delhi*, 840a
M. L., *MDSU*, 755a
M. M. S., *JN Vyas*, 705b
M. P., *NDRI*, 787a
Madhu, *Ban.Vid.*, 618c
Mahesh, *JN Vyas*, 704c
Meenakshi, *JN Vyas*, 704c
Meera, *All India IMS*, 587b
Mukesh, *M.Sukh.*, 772a
Naveen, *JN Vyas*, 704c
P., *JN Vyas*, 705a
P. C., *Delhi*, 647c
P. K., *Lucknow*, 738a
P. N., *JN Vyas*, 703c
P. P., *Pondicherry*, 806a
Pavan, *Delhi*, 647b
Pradeep, *IIT Bombay*, 693b
Praveen, *MDSU*, 755b
Pushpa, *Lucknow*, 738b
R., *Jiw.*, 718a
R. K., *Ban.*, 613a
R. M., *Lucknow*, 740a
R. M., *W.Ont.*, 521b, 523c
R. P., *M.Sukh.*, 772b
Rajesh, *JN Vyas*, 704a
Rani, *APSV*, 610a
Rashmi, *All India IMS*, 587b
Ritu, *MDSU*, 755b
S. B., *Ban.Vid.*, 619a
S. C., *JN Vyas*, 704c, 705b
S. M., *JN Vyas*, 704c
S. P., *MDSU*, 755a
S. S., *City(UK)*, 1382b
Sugitha, *Osm.*, 797a
Sushma, *Lucknow*, 738b
T. K., *MDSU*, 755b
T. N. S., *Roor.*, 829c
V. N. S., *Roor.*, 830c
Yogesh K., *Delhi*, 649a
Mathuriya, S. N., *Pg.IMER*, 808b
Mati, J. K. G., *Nair.*, 900a
Maticka-Tyndale, Eleanor, *Windsor*, 540a
Matidza, J. N., *Venda*, 1233a
Matier, Kenneth O., *Durban-W.*, 1170b
Matime, Archibald M., *S.Af.Med.*, 1174b
Matin, A., *B'desh.Engin.*, 231a
A., *Dhaka*, 238a, 241a
A. K. M. A., *Chitt.*, 235b
Abul B. A., *Gauh.*, 665c
C. Z., *Rajsh.*, 254b
C. Zulfiqar, *Rajsh.*, 254a, 257c
Hasina, *Jahang.*, 248b
K. A., *Dhaka*, 242b
M. A., *B'desh.Engin.*, 231c
M. A., *Dhaka*, 240b
M. A., *Jahang.*, 249b
M. A., *Khulna*, 250b
M. M., *Chitt.*, 234b
Md. A., *B'desh.Ag.*, 228c
Matiso, Khaya G., *P.Elizabeth*, 1198c, 1199a
Mativo, John, *E.Af.Baraton*, 887c
Vivian, *E.Af.Baraton*, 887c
Matjila, Maila J., *S.Af.Med.*, 1174a
Matkin, Derek, *Oxf.Brookes*, 1666b
Matlala, D. M., *Venda*, 1234b
Matlani, B., *Mumbai*, 776b
Matlashewski, Gregory J., *McG.*, 379a
Matlin, Stephen A., *Warw.*, 1780a
Matlosa, K., *NUL*, 904a
Matlow, Anne, *Tor.*, 496a, 497a
Erica G., *Westminster*, 1789c
Matolcsy, Zoltan P., *Technol.Syd.*, 188c
Matondo, P. M., *Zambia*, 1823a
Matonhodze, Witw., 1244a
Matos, Narciso, 1860a
Matousek, Jaroslav P., *NSW*, 109b
Matovelo, J. A., *Sokoine Ag.*, 1298b
Matovu, David, *Mak.*, 1302a
K., *Mak.*, 1303b
P. C., *Mak.*, 1305c
Matravers, D., *Portsmouth*, 1678a
Mats'ela, Z. A., *NUL*, 904a
Matshakayile-Ndlovu, T., *Z'bwe.*, 1826a
Matshe, S. Priscillah, *NUST Bulawayo*, 1825b, 1825c
Matsika, Katherine, *NUST Bulawayo*, 1824a, 1825c
Matsinhe, S. F., *S.Af.*, 1217b
Matson, P., *Manc.Met.*, 1611a
R. G., *Br.Col.*, 296a
Matsubara, Joanne A., *Br.Col.*, 307a
Matsuda, N., *HK*, 1837b
Matsui, Sakuko, *Syd.*, 171a
Matsumoto, M., *Br.Col.*, 299c
Matsuoka, Atsuko K., *York(Can.)*, 553a
Matsuuchi, *Br.Col.*, 304a
Matsuura, Takeshi, *Ott.*, 440a, 446b
Matswetu, M., *Namibia*, 956c
Matta, Ali M., *Kashmir*, 727b
N. K., *Kuruk.*, 733a
W. M., *Nair.*, 899c
Mattar, A. G., *W.Ont.*, 528c
Saba M., *New Br.*, 428b
Matte, Ronald, *Montr.*, 415c
Mattee, A. Z., *Sokoine Ag.*, 1297b
Mattei, Rev. L., *CUE Af.*, 886a
Mattessich, R., *Br.Col.*, 297a
Mattey, David P., *Lond.*, 1558b
Matthai, C. C., *Wales*, 1765a
Matthee, Johan A., *Stell.*, 1223c, 1224a
Matthen, M., *Alta.*, 285a
M., *Br.Col.*, 302b
Matthew, C., *Massey*, 977b
H. C. G., *Oxf.*, 1654c
James A. D., *York(UK)*, 1800c
M. I., *Coventry*, 1385a
Philip L., *Qld.*, 135a
Veronica A., *De Mont.*, 1393a
Matthew Jacob, T., *IISc.*, 692b
Matthewman, J. David, *Wales*, 1756a
J. H., *Camb.*, 1373a
Matthews, A., *Hull*, 1465b
Allan, *Hull*, 1468b
B., *Acad.*, 278b
B., *Brist.*, 1348a
B. C., *Wat.*, 515b
Brian E., *Victoria UT*, 198a
C., *Bourne.*, 1340b
C. B., *S.Aust.*, 157a
Claire D., *Massey*, 975b
Colin D., *Adel.*, 9a
D., *Sund.*, 1739b
D. E., *Wat.*, 519a
D. R., *McM.*, 384c
D. R., *Oxf.*, 1659c
David J., *Lond.*, 1565b
Deborah, *Sheff.Hallam*, 1715b
Dewi, *Luton*, 1594b
E. H., *Aberd.*, 1315b
E. K., *Camb.*, 1362b
Frank L., *Lond.*, 1527a
G. P., *Plym.*, 1673c
Geoff, *L&H*, 1504c
Geoffrey, *Brun.*, 1351c
Gerald, *Dund.*, 1398c
Glenda B., *Natal*, 1180c
Graham, *RMIT*, 153a
Graham A., *Lond.*, 1527c
H. R., *Camb.*, 1363a
I. P., *Wales*, 1772a
J. B., *Birm.*, 1333b
J. H., *Qu.*, 459a
J. N. S., *Newcastle(UK)*, 1622c
J. P., *Qu.*, 454c
Janet, *RMIT*, 153c
Jill J., *ANU*, 18c
Joanne, *N.Br.Col.*, 436a
John A., *Wales*, 1768a
John J., *Exe.*, 1428a
John S., *Nan.Tech.*, 1142c
Judith A., *Plym.*, 1673c
K., *Coventry*, 1386a
K. G. P., *Liv.J.Moores*, 1517a
Keith, *Dund.*, 1400b
Keith R., *Qld.*, 135c
Kent G. P., *Wales*, 1762a
Kim L., *Syd.*, 178a
Lindsay R., *Waik.*, 994b
M., *Manit.*, 394b
M. H., *Oxf.*, 1655b
M. K., *Nfld.*, 405b
M. L., *Guelph*, 338c
Madeline, *York(Can.)*, 544b
Margaret R., *Oxf.*, 1660a
Michael R., *NSW*, 110b
Nichole D., *Liv.J.Moores*, 1517b
P. H., *Camb.*, 1361a
P. N. P., *Massey*, 978b
Peter W., *Br.Col.*, 302c
R. A., *Plym.*, 1673a
R. D., *S.Bank*, 1722a
R. D. C., *Kingston(UK)*, 1476c
R. O., *Tor.*, 489c
R. T., *Glam.*, 1433a
R. W., *Brist.*, 1350b
Ralph C., *Br.Col.*, 296a
Ray W., *N.Lond.*, 1627c
Robert C. O., *Camb.*, 1366c
Robin, *Deakin*, 41a
Roger F., *Wales*, 1756b
Ron G., *Cran.*, 1388c
Russell, *Deakin*, 41a
Ruth C., *Manc.*, 1605a
Sara H. M., *Lond.*, 1562c
Steve A., *Bolton Inst.*, 1338a
Steven J., *Oxf.Brookes*, 1668a
T. R., *Trent*, 508a
Timothy, *Lond.*, 1570c
Trevor, *L&H*, 1506b
V. J., *Guelph*, 337c
Matthewson, Maurice B., *Auck.*, 967c
Murray H., *Camb.*, 1369b
Matthias, R. A. J., *Jaffna*, 1265b
Matthiessen, Martin C., *Macq.*, 73b
Matti, Sulochana S., *Karn.*, 724b
Mattick, John S., *Qld.*, 131c, 142b
Richard P., *NSW*, 119b
Mattingley, David J., *Leic.*, 1497c
Mattingly, Michael J., *Lond.*, 1569b
Mattinson, K. G., *Manc.Met.*, 1612c
Mattison, James H. K., *Cape Town*, 1163a
Mattoo, A. M., *Kashmir*, 727a
Amitabh, *J.Nehru U.*, 713c
S. K., *Pg.IMER*, 808c
Mattoo Aijaz Rasool, *Kashmir*, 727c
Mattson, Eric, *Nipissing*, 433c
Matturi, A. S., *S.Leone*, 1134c
Matuja, W. B. M., *Dar.*, 1294c
Matuk, L., *Windsor*, 539b
Matunga, Hirini P., *Auck.*, 964c
Matupa, C. F., *Malawi*, 908a
Matur, B. M., *Abuja*, 1003c
Matus, Jill, *Tor.*, 485c
Matusky, Patricia, *Sci.U.Malaysia*, 935b
Matutes, Estela, *Lond.*, 1584a
Matwin, Stanislaw J., *Ott.*, 441a
Matyas, Thomas A., *La Trobe*, 68a
Matysiak, G. A., *City(UK)*, 1383a
Matzou, A., *Qu.*, 457b
Mau, Rosalind I. P. Y., *Nan.Tech.*, 1142c
Maud, Rodney R., *Natal*, 1180a
Maude, Alaric M., *Flin.*, 49b
Maudsley, Gillian, *Liv.*, 1513b
Mauer, Karl F., *S.Af.*, 1221b
Mauga, E. A. S. K., *Dar.*, 1295c
Mauger, Patricia, *Auck.*, 967c
Maugey, Axel, *McG.*, 366b
Maughan, Barbara, *Lond.*, 1540a
C. C., *De Mont.*, 1394c
Caroline R., *W.England*, 1788b
David J., *York(UK)*, 1802b
R. J., *Aberd.*, 1316a
Sylvia C., *W.England*, 1787a
W., *Bourne.*, 1339a
Maughan Brown, David A., *Natal*, 1177a, 1186c
Mauk, Grant, *Br.Col.*, 305a
J. L., *Auck.*, 962c
Mauldin, I., *Glas.*, 1437b
Maule, A. John, *Leeds*, 1487b
Jeremy F., *Camb.*, 1373c
Maulik, S. K., *All India IMS*, 587b
Maull, D. J., *Camb.*, 1367a
R. S., *Plym.*, 1673a
Maun, M. A., *W.Ont.*, 526b
Maunaguru, S., *Eastern(S.Lanka)*, 1263a
Maund, J. Barry, *W.Aust.*, 203b
Maunder, C. Richard F., *Camb.*, 1366a
Edward A. W., *Exe.*, 1428a
Eleni M. W., *Natal*, 1184b
J. W., *Camb.*, 1374b
W. Peter J., *Lough.*, 1589c
Maunders, A. R., *Sund.*, 1739c
David, *RMIT*, 152c
K. T., *Hull*, 1464b
Maundrell, Richard, *Lake.*, 344c
Maundu, J. N., *Kenyatta*, 891a, 892a
Maung Shein, *Nan.Tech.*, 1136b
Maunmbo, H., *Dar.*, 1291b
Maunsell, Elizabeth, *Laval*, 358a
Maurer, A. A., *Tor.*, 489a
D. McD., *McM.*, 384b
H., *Auck.*, 964a
Oswin, *NE*, 102b, 104c
Maurice, Terry, *Guelph*, 341c
William L., *Br.Col.*, 308b
Maurimootoo, Sam, *De Mont.*, 1393c
Mauro, Arthur V., *Manit.*, 389a
Mauroof, A. L. M., *Peradeniya*, 1275c
Maury, Nicole, *Tor.*, 486a
Maurya, A. K., *Delhi*, 646a, 649b
A. N., *Ban.*, 612a, 615a
Dr. K. R., *Rajendra Ag.*, 826c
M. R., *Roor.*, 829b
Vibha, *Delhi*, 648a
Mauser, Gary A., *S.Fraser*, 477a
Maute, M., *Bran.*, 293a
Mautle, G., *Botswana*, 262b
G. T., *Botswana*, 262a
Mautner, Thomas R., *ANU*, 19b
Mauzy, Diane K., *Br.Col.*, 303a
Mavaddat, F., *Wat.*, 513a
Mavalankar, A. P., *Baroda*, 751b
Mavalwala, J., *Tor.*, 483b
Maver, Thomas, *Strath.*, 1733a
Mavers, D. E., *Manc.Met.*, 1612c
Mavi, G. S., *Punj.Ag.*, 815a
N. S., *Kuruk.*, 733b
Mavima, P., *Z'bwe.*, 1827c
Mavinic, D. S., *Br.Col.*, 298c
Mavituna, Ferda, *UMIST*, 1607c
Mavor, John, *Napier*, 1616a
Mavrikakis, C., *C'dia.*, 323c
Mavromihales, Michael, *Hudd.*, 1461a
Mavron, Vasili C., *Wales*, 1755c
Mavuso, Makana R., *Swazi.*, 1288a, 1289c
Z. M., *Swazi.*, 1290b
Mavuti, K. R. M., *Nair.*, 898c
Mawa, P. N., *PNG*, 1128a
Mawan Nooraini Ismail, *Sci.U.Malaysia*, 938c
Mawan Noraini Ismail, *Sci.U.Malaysia*, 931a
Mawanda, M. M., *NUL*, 904a
Mawardi bin Rahmani, *Putra*, 929a
Mawby, P. A., *Wales*, 1767c
Rob I., *Plym.*, 1675c
Roger J., *York(UK)*, 1799a
Mawdesley, M. J., *Nott.*, 1634a
Mawditt, Richard M., *Bath*, 1325a
Mawdsley, David V., *Liv.J.Moores*, 1517b
E., *Glas.*, 1439c
H. P., *Manc.Met.*, 1615b
Josephine, *Hudd.*, 1462b
Mawela, M. Patience D., *S.Af.Med.*, 1175b
Mawer, E. Barbara, *Manc.*, 1604b
Mawera, G., *Z'bwe.*, 1828b
Mawhiney, Anne-Marie, *Laur.*, 348c, 349a
Mawhinney, Hanne, *Ott.*, 439c
Mawila, P. R., *Venda*, 1233b, 1233c
Mawiri, K., *Z'bwe.*, 1827a
Mawoyo, B., *S.Bank*, 1723a
Mawson, A. John, *Massey*, 975b
John, *Dund.*, 1399a
Ruth, *Macq.*, 72b, 75c
Susan, *Sheff.Hallam*, 1717b
Max, P., *W.Ont.*, 530b
Maxfield, A., *Manc.Met.*, 1611b
Cameron, *Sheff.Hallam*, 1716a
Valerie A., *Exe.*, 1428a
Maxim, Jane E., *Lond.*, 1574a
P. S., *W.Ont.*, 527a
Maxner, Charles E., *Dal.*, 332c
Maxted, William M., *De Mont.*, 1393a
Maxton, J. K., *Glas.*, 1439c
Julie K., *Auck.*, 963b
Maxwell, A., *WI*, 1817a
A. P., *Belf.*, 1688a
Anthony, *Leic.*, 1497c
Christine, *Trent*, 508a
Christopher J., *Durh.*, 1404b
D. J., *Glas.*, 1437b
D. V., *Nfld.*, 405b
David M., *Dal.*, 332b
E. A., *Trent*, 508c, 509c
G., *St And.*, 1697c
George, *Br.Col.*, 301c
Gillian, *G.Caledonian*, 1445a
Graham S., *Qld.*, 132c, 139c
I., *Manit.*, 398a
J., *WI*, 1815b
J. Douglas, *Lond.*, 1562b
J. R., *Brist.*, 1345b
Jonathan, *Lond.*, 1530b
K. J., *Nott.*, 1635c
L., *Auck.*, 966b
Linda, *Auck.*, 965b
Mary P., *Qu.*, 457c
Maureen, *L&H*, 1506b
Michael P., *McG.*, 367a, 377c
Patrick S., *Natal*, 1186a
Philip, *Curtin*, 38b
Robyn, *ANU*, 18a
Simon R. J., *Leic.*, 1501a
Susan, *W.England*, 1785a
T. J., *Aberd.*, 1317a
T. J., *Edin.*, 1415b
Thomas, *NE*, 105b
Tom W., *NE*, 103c
W. H. Chisholm, *Syd.*, 179c
William L., *Glas.*, 1437b
Maxwell Cooper, John, *Tech.U.Malaysia*, 941b
Maxwell-Smith, Nigel, *Thames V.*, 1749b, 1749c
May, A., *W.England*, 1786b
A. D., *Tor.*, 489c
A. P. H., *W.England*, 1787a
Anthony D., *Leeds*, 1483a, 1485c, 1489a, 1492b
Arthur W., xxxviii, xxxix
Arthur W., *Nfld.*, 401a
B., *Birm.*, 1327a
B. K., *Adel.*, 5c
C. A., *Greenwich*, 1447c
Christopher J., *W.Cape*, 1237b
David R., *Dund.*, 1400b
Dawn V., *James Cook*, 62a
E., *Portsmouth*, 1677c
Ester, *S.Aust.*, 158a
Felicity E. B., *Newcastle(UK)*, 1626a
Graham, *Leeds Met.*, 1494c
Helen, *Well.*, 988a, 990a
I. M., *H-W*, 1450b
J., *Lond.*, 1536c
J. D., *Nfld.*, 403b
J. P., *W.England*, 1785c
James, *Syd.*, 179a
James W., *Cape Town*, 1164a
Johanna K., *Lond.*, 1525c
John T., *La Trobe*, 67b
John W., *E.Cowan*, 44b
K. D., *De Mont.*, 1390a
Katharyn A., *Br.Col.*, 302a
L. E., *Car.*, 319a
M. D., *Brist.*, 1345c
Margaret, *W.England*, 1786b
Marie, *Sheff.Hallam*, 1719b
Marilyn, *Sheff.Hallam*, 1717a
P. B., *Melb.*, 84a
Peter M., *Murd.*, 100a
R., *Coventry*, 1386a
Rennie, *Durh.*, 1406a
Sir Robert, *Oxf.*, 1659b
Robert L., *RMIT*, 153b
S. A., *Lond.*, 1560c
S. J., *Nfld.*, 405a
T. C., *Manc.Met.*, 1614b
Therese, *W.Syd.*, 207a
V. J., *Bourne.*, 1339c
Maya, *All India IMS*, 585a
Mayaka, B. T., *Dschang*, 270a
Mayall, David, *Sheff.Hallam*, 1716a
I., *S.Fraser*, 481c
James B. L., *Camb.*, 1372b
James B. L., *Lond.*, 1547a, 1548b
M. Berry, *Lond.*, 1535a
Mayanna, S. M., *B'lore.*, 619c
Mayavansi, B. K., *Baroda*, 750a
Mayberry, Rachel, *McG.*, 370c
Maybery, Murray, *W.Aust.*, 203c
Maybury, Alan, *Leeds Met.*, 1495b
Maycher, B. W., *Manit.*, 399b
Maycock, K., *De Mont.*, 1392a
Maydell, U. M., *Alta.*, 281a
Maydew, Mark, *Coventry*, 1385a
Maye, Brian, *NE*, 103b
Mayee, Charudatta D., *Marath.Ag.*, 771a
Mayegai, H., *Mak.*, 1305c
Mayengo, R. K., *Mak.*, 1302c
Mayer, C. P., *Oxf.*, 1655c
Denis, *Laur.*, 349b, 349c
Geoffrey J., *La Trobe*, 65a
H. L. M., *Tor.*, 486b
Larry, *New Br.*, 429b
P. A., *Glam.*, 1434b
P. B., *Adel.*, 8b
R. G. M., *Lond.*, 1536b
R. J., *Nott.*, 1636b
Raymond, *Montr.*, 421b
Robert, *Montr.*, 414c
Mayers, D. F., *Oxf.*, 1651a
Irvin, *Alta.*, 287a
Patricia, *Cape Town*, 1166c
Mayer-Smith, J., *Br.Col.*, 304b
Mayes, Andrew R., *Sheff.*, 1709c
C., *Coventry*, 1385a
Gillian, *Glas.*, 1440c
Jo, *Greenwich*, 1447c
Terry, *G.Caledonian*, 1446a
Mayet, Z., *Witw.*, 1244c
Mayeza, Mildred N. T., *S.Af.Med.*, 1174c
Mayfield, C. I., *Wat.*, 512a
Wendy, *Leeds Met.*, 1494b
Mayhall, J. T., *Tor.*, 483b, 493b
Mayhew, Ian G., *Edin.*, 1422a
J. E. W., *Sheff.*, 1708b, 1711c
John R., *Liv.J.Moores*, 1516c
K., *Oxf.*, 1651c
Pamela J., *E.Anglia*, 1408b
Robert J., *Camb.*, 1367a
Roger, *Lond.*, 1543c
T. M., *Nott.*, 1636b
Mayla, Lilian, *York(Can.)*, 544c
Maylam, P. R., *Rhodes*, 1214b
Maynard, Alan K., *York(UK)*, 1799b
Clive A., *Curtin*, 36a
Cyril, *Indep.B'desh.*, 243a
Fiona, *Manc.Met.*, 1614a
J. C., *Wales*, 1762b
Jennifer, *Coventry*, 1384c
Margaret, *Qld.*, 131c
Mary A., *York(UK)*, 1801a
P. V., *Nott.*, 1637b
Patrick L., *W.Ont.*, 526a
R. A., *Birm.*, 1336b
Mayne, A. J. C., *Melb.*, 81a
F., *Plym.*, 1673a
Seymour, *Ott.*, 440b
Vincent P., *Newcastle(UK)*, 1626c
Mayner, Lidia, *Flin.*, 50a
Maynes, Elizabeth, *York(Can.)*, 545b
W. G., *Alta.*, 282a
Mayo, A. L., *Rhodes*, 1214a
A. W., *Dar.*, 1292c
H. B., *Car.*, 319b
J. S. M., *Tor.*, 503b
John, *WI*, 1813c
John L., *James Cook*, 61b
Marjorie, *Lond.*, 1525b
Michael, *Ryerson*, 468b
Peter, *Malta*, 946c
Mayon-White, R. T., *Oxf.*, 1659c
Mayoori, Madhu, *Manipal AHE*, 764a
Mayor, Jennifer, *Middx.*, 1616c
R. J., *Greenwich*, 1447a
V., *City(UK)*, 1382b
Mayou, R. A., *Oxf.*, 1660c
May-Parker, I. I., *S.Leone*, 1131a
Mayrand, Denis, *Laval*, 351a, 358c
Mayr-Harting, H. M. R. E., *Oxf.*, 1659b
Mayrhofer, G., *Adel.*, 7c
Mays, Annabelle M., *Winn.*, 541c
Geoff C., *Cran.*, 1387a, 1388c
Herbert J., *Winn.*, 541a, 542a, 543b, 543c
I. D., *Herts.*, 1454c
Janet, *Ryerson*, 468c
M. J., *Camb.*, 1356b
N. B., *Lond.*, 1550c

Van...Venk INDEX TO PERSONAL NAMES 2182